2025 STANDARD POSTAGE STAMP CATALOGUE

ONE HUNDRED AND EIGHTY-FIRST EDITION IN SIX VOLUMES

Volume 5A

N-PHIL

Released August 2024
Includes New Stamp Listings through the June 2024 *Scott Stamp Monthly* Catalogue Update

AMOS MEDIA

1660 Campbell Road, Suite A, Sidney, OH 45365
Publishers of *Linn's Stamp News, Scott Stamp Monthly, Coin World* and *Coin World Monthly.*

Scott catalog editorial team contact information
scottstamp.com | scottcatalogueeditorial@amosmedia.com

Scott catalog customer service contact information
amosadvantage.com | cuserv@amosmedia.com | 800-572-6885 | Monday-Thursday 9 a.m. to 5 p.m.; Friday 9 a.m. to noon, Eastern Standard Time

Table of contents

See the following volumes for other country listings:
Volume 1A: United States, United Nations, Abu Dhabi-Australia; Volume 1B: Austria-B
Volume 2A: C-Cur; Volume 2B: Cyp-F
Volume 3A: G; Volume 3B: H-I
Volume 4A: J-L; Volume 4B: M
Volume 5B: Pit-Sam
Volume 6A: San-Tete; Volume 6B: Thai-Z

Scott Catalogue Mission Statement

The Scott Catalogue Team exists to serve the recreational, educational and commercial hobby needs of stamp collectors and dealers.

We strive to set the industry standard for philatelic information and products by developing and providing goods that help collectors identify, value, organize and present their collections.

Quality customer service is, and will continue to be, our highest priority. We aspire toward achieving total customer satisfaction.

Copyright Notice

Trademark Notice

ISBN 978-0-89487-731-5

Library of Congress Card No. 2-3301

What's new for 2025 Scott Standard Volume 5

Another catalog season is upon us as we continue the journey of the 156-year history of the Scott catalogs.

The 2025 volumes are the 181st edition of the Scott *Standard Postage Stamp Catalogue*. Volume 5A includes listings for the countries of the world Namibia through Philippines.

Listings for Pitcairn Islands through Samoa can be found in Volume 5B.

Because Vol. 5B is a continuation of the first part of the Vol. 5 catalog, the introduction pages are not repeated in each volume.

The covers of this year's catalogs feature a postal theme, a nod to the United States Postal Service's 250th anniversary in 2025 with a photograph of a letter carrier courtesy of the Library of Congress Prints and Photographs Division shown in the background.

The Nicaragua 50¢ Mailman stamp (Scott 1112) from the 1981 Postal Union of Spain and the Americas, 12th Congress, Managua, set of four stamps (1112, C977-C979) is shown on the Vol 5A catalog, and the Pitcairn Islands 35¢ Arrival at Post Office stamp (192d) from the 1980 London International Philatelic Exhibition sheet of four (192) is featured on the Vol. 5B catalog.

Peru was looked at closely for Vol. 5, as part of the Scott editors' ongoing review of Latin America and South America countries for the 2025 Scott Standard catalog. More than 3,100 value changes were made. Many of those changes were slight upward adjustments. For example, the sheet of five 2004 Muscians stamps (Scott 1441) increased from $9.75 to $11 in unused condition and from $7.50 to $9.75 used.

Similarly, El Salvador was reviewed, and more than 3,300 value changes were made. As with Peru, most of the changes were small increases. For example, the 1989 set of two National Fire Brigade 160th Anniversary stamps (Scott 1198-1199) increased from $2 in unused condition to $3, and from 55¢ to 80¢ used.

Approximately 1,400 value changes were made for classic Nicaragua. Slight increases were noted throughout. The set of three 1929 Airplanes Over Mt. Momotombo airmail stamps (Scott C4-C6) increased from $2.25 to $5 in unused condition, and from $2.15 to $5 used.

Paraguay saw approximately 2,000 value changes, most of which were slight increases. One example was the 1970 Easter souvenir sheet (Scott 1253) that went from $10 to $10.50 in unused condition.

However, there was a dramatic increase for the 2001 Year of Dialogue Among Civilizations stamp (2680) that increased from $4.25 to $30 in unused and used condition. The Scott catalog value for that stamp is for an example with two attached labels.

Poland received a methodical review, which yielded more than 4,500 value changes. Increases far surpassed

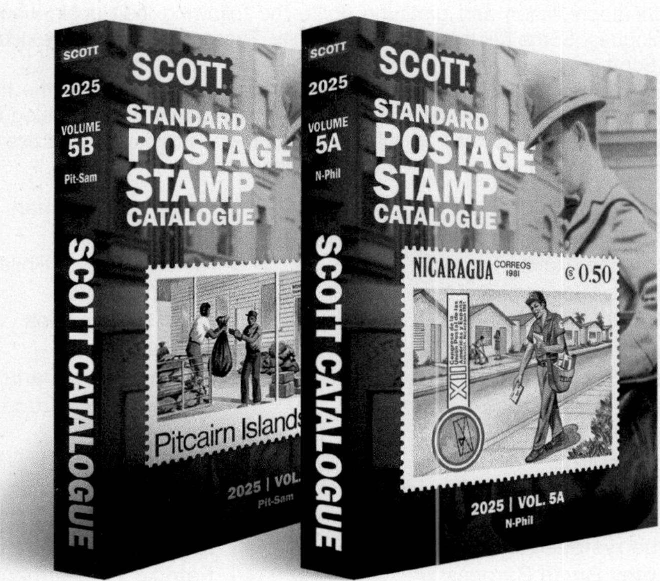

decreases throughout, with approximately 150 changes reflecting a decrease. For post-2020 stamp issues, currency strength played a factor in some of the value increases. One of those issues is the Poland 2021 Czeslaw Slania (1921-2005), Engraver of Postage Stamps souvenir sheet (Scott 4578). This stamp moved from $7.75 in unused and used condition to $13.50 both ways for the 2025 catalog.

The Philippines was reviewed, and more than 2,100 value changes reflecting a mix of increases and decreases were made. In addition, a number of panes were either footnoted or listed as minor numbers. See the Number Additions, Deletions and Changes listing for details.

Other reviewed countries not mentioned in this letter include Panama, Oman and Qatar.

Finally, a number of stamps that were previously valued at the old Scott catalog minimum of 25¢ are now valued at the current 30¢ minimum.

We encourage you to pay special attention to the Number Additions, Deletions and Changes listing in this volume. We also suggest reading the catalog introduction, which includes an abundance of useful information.

A digital subscription is also available for the Scott catalogs, and information about the subscription can be found online at www.amosadvantage.com.

Best wishes in your collecting pursuits!

Jay Bigalke, Scott catalog editor-in-chief

Acknowledgments

Our appreciation and gratitude go to the following individuals who have assisted us in preparing information included in this year's Scott catalogues. Some helpers prefer anonymity. These individuals have generously shared their stamp knowledge with others through the medium of the Scott catalogue.

Those who follow provided information that is in addition to the hundreds of dealer price lists and advertisements and scores of auction catalogues and realizations that were used in producing the catalogue values. It is from those noted here that we have been able to obtain information on items not normally seen in published lists and advertisements. Support from these people goes beyond data leading to catalogue values, for they also are key to editorial changes.

Roland Austin
Michael & Cecilia Ball (A To Z Stamps)
Jim Bardo (Bardo Stamps)
Brian M. Bleckwenn
(The Philatelic Foundation)
Les Bootman
John D. Bowman
(Carriers and Locals Society)
Roger S. Brody
Tom Brougham
(Canal Zone Study Group)
Paul and Josh Buchsbayew
(Cherrystone Auctions, Inc.)
Timothy Bryan Burgess
Tina and John Carlson (JET Stamps)
Jay T. Carrigan
Carlson Chambliss
Bob Coale
Tony L. Crumbley
(Carolina Coin and Stamp, Inc.)
Christopher Dahle
Charles Deaton
Bob and Rita Dumaine
(Sam Houston Duck Co.)
Charles Epting
(Robert A. Siegel Auction Galleries)
Mike Farrell
David Feldman International Auctioneers
Robert A. Fisher
Jeffrey M. Forster
Robert S. Freeman
Henry L. Gitner
(Henry Gitner Philatelists, Inc.)
Stan Goldfarb
Marc E. Gonzales
Daniel E. Grau
Alexander Haimann
Bruce Hecht (Bruce L. Hecht Co.)
Daniel Hill
Eric Jackson
Michael Jaffe (Michael Jaffe Stamps, Inc.)
William A. (Bill) Jones
Allan Katz (Ventura Stamp Co.)
Patricia A. Kaufmann
(Civil War Philatelic Society)
Jon Kawaguchi
(Ryukyu Philatelic Specialist Society)
Han Ki Kim
Ingert Kuzych
Ulf Lindahl (Ethiopian Philatelic Society)
Ignacio Llach (Filatelia Llach, S.L.)
William K. McDaniel
Pat McElroy
Brian Metz
Mark S. Miller (India Study Circle)
Gary Morris (Pacific Midwest Co.)
Bruce M. Moyer
(Moyer Stamps & Collectables)
Scott Murphy
(Professional Stamp Experts)
Dr. Tiong Tak Ngo
Nik and Lisa Oquist
Don Peterson
(International Philippine Philatelic Society)
Todor Drumev Popov
Dr. Charles Posner
Peter W. W. Powell
Ed Reiser (Century Stamp Co.)
Ghassan D. Riachi
Robert G. Rufe
Theodosios D. Sampson Ph.D.
Dennis W. Schmidt
Joyce and Chuck Schmidt
Guy Shaw
(Mexico-Elmhurst Philatelic Society International)
J. Randall Shoemaker
(Philatelic Stamp Authentication and Grading, Inc.)
Jay Smith
Telah Smith
Mark Stelmacovich
Scott R. Trepel
(Robert A. Siegel Auction Galleries)
Dan Undersander
Steven Unkrich
Herbert R. Volin
Val Zabijaka (Zabijaka Auctions)

Addresses, telephone numbers, web sites, email addresses of general and specialized philatelic societies

Collectors can contact the following groups for information about the philately of the areas within the scope of these societies, or inquire about membership in these groups. Aside from the general societies, we limit this list to groups that specialize in particular fields of philately, particular areas covered by the Scott *Standard Postage Stamp Catalogue*, and topical groups. Many more specialized philatelic society exist than those listed below. These addresses are updated yearly, and they are, to the best of our knowledge, correct and current. Groups should inform the editors of address changes whenever they occur. The editors also want to hear from other such specialized groups not listed.

Unless otherwise noted all website addresses begin with http://

General Societies

American Philatelic Society, 100 Match Factory Place, Bellefonte, PA 16823-1367; (814) 933-3803; https://stamps.org; apsinfo@stamps.org

International Society of Worldwide Stamp Collectors, Joanne Murphy, M.D., P.O. Box 19006, Sacramento, CA 95819; www.iswsc.org; executivedirector@iswsc.org

Royal Philatelic Society of Canada, P.O. Box 69080, St. Clair Post Office, Toronto, ON M4T 3A1 Canada; (888) 285-4143; www.rpsc.org; info@rpsc.org

Royal Philatelic Society London, 15 Abchurch Lane, London EX4N 7BW, United Kingdom; +44 (0) 20 7486 1044; www.rpsl.org.uk; secretary@rpsl.org.uk

Libraries, Museums, and Research Groups

American Philatelic Research Library, 100 Match Factory Place, Bellefonte, PA 16823; (814) 933-3803; www.stamplibrary.org; library@stamps.org.

V. G. Greene Philatelic Research Foundation, P.O. Box 69100, St. Clair Post Office, Toronto, ON M4T 3A1, Canada; (416) 921-2073; info@greenefoundation.ca

Aero/Astro Philately

American Air Mail Society, Stephen Reinhard, P.O. Box 110, Mineola, NY 11501; www.americanairmailsociety.org; sreinhard1@optonline.net

Postal History

Auxiliary Markings Club, Jerry Johnson, 6621 W. Victoria Ave., Kennewick, WA 99336; www.postal-markings.org; membership-2010@postal-markings.org

Postage Due Mail Study Group, Bob Medland, Camway Cottage, Nanny Hurn's Lane, Cameley, Bristol BS39 5AJ, United Kingdom; 01761 45959; www.postageduemail.org.uk; secretary.pdmsg@gmail.com

Postal History Society, Yamil Kouri, 405 Waltham St. #347, Lexington, MA 02421; www.postalhistorysociety.org; yhkouri@massmed.org

Post Mark Collectors Club, Bob Milligan, 7014 Woodland Oaks Drive, Magnolia, TX 77354; (281) 259-2735; www.postmarks.org; bob.milligan0@gmail.com

U.S. Cancellation Club, Roger Curran, 18 Tressler Blvd., Lewisburg, PA 17837; rdcnrc@ptd.net

Revenues and Cinderellas

American Revenue Association, Lyman Hensley, 473 E. Elm St., Sycamore, IL 60178-1934; www.revenuer.org; ilrno2@netzero.net

Christmas Seal and Charity Stamp Society, John Denune Jr., 234 E. Broadway, Granville, OH 43023; (740) 814-6031; www.seal-society.org

National Duck Stamp Collectors Society, Anthony J. Monico, P.O. Box 43, Harleysville, PA 19438-0043; www.ndscs.org; ndscs@ndscs.org

State Revenue Society, Kent Gray, P.O. Box 67842, Albuquerque, NM 87193; www.staterevenue.org; srssecretary@comcast.net

Thematic Philately

Americana Unit, Dennis Dengel, 17 Peckham Road, Poughkeepsie, NY 12603-2018; www.americanaunit.org; ddengel@americanaunit.org

American Topical Association, Jennifer Miller, P.O. Box 2143, Greer, SC 29652-2143; (618) 985-5100; americantopical.org; ata@americantopical.org

Astronomy Study Unit, Leonard Zehr, 1411 Chateau Ave., Windsor, ON N8P 1M2, Canada; (416) 833-9317; www.astronomystudyunit.net; lenzehr@gmail.com

Bicycle Stamps Club, Corey Hjalseth, 1102 Broadway, Suite 200, Tacoma, WA 98402; (253) 318-6222; www.bicyclestampsclub.org; coreyh@evergreenhomeloans.com

Biology Unit, Chris Dahle, 1401 Linmar Drive NE, Cedar Rapids, IA 52402-3724; www.biophilately.org; chris-dahle@biophilately.org

Bird Stamp Society, Mr. S. A. H. (Tony) Statham, Ashlyns Lodge, Chesham Road, Berkhamsted, Herts HP4 2ST United Kingdom; www.bird-stamps.org/bss; tony.statham@sky.com

Captain Cook Society, Jerry Yucht, 8427 Leale Ave., Stockton, CA 95212, www.captaincooksociety.com; us@captaincooksociety.com

The CartoPhilatelic Society, Marybeth Sulkowski, 2885 Sanford Ave., SW, #32361, Grandville, MI 49418-1342; www.mapsonstamps.org; secretary@mapsonstamps.org

Casey Jones Railroad Unit, Jeff Lough, 2612 Redbud Land, Apt. C, Lawrence, KS 66046; www.uqp.de/cjr; jeffydplaugh@gmail.com

Cats on Stamps Study Unit, Robert D. Jarvis, 2731 Teton Lane, Fairfield, CA 94533; www.catstamps.info; catmews1@yahoo.com

Chemistry and Physics on Stamps Study Unit, Dr. Roland Hirsch, 13830 Metcalf Ave., Apt. 15218, Overland Park, KS 66223-8017; (301) 792-6296; www.cpossu.org; rfhirsch@cpossu.org

Chess on Stamps Study Unit, Barry Keith, 511 First St. N., Apt. 106; Charlottesville, VA 22902; www.chessonstamps.org; keithfam@embarqmail.com

Cricket Philatelic Society, A. Melville-Brown, 11 Weppons, Ravens Road, Shorham-by-Sea, West Sussex BN43 5AW, United Kingdom; www.cricketstamp.net; mel.cricket.100@googlemail.com

Earth's Physical Features Study Group, Fred Klein, 515 Magdalena Ave., Los Altos, CA 94024; http://epfsu.jeffhayward.com; epfsu@jeffhayward.com

Ebony Society of Philatelic Events and Reflections (ESPER), Don Neal, P.O. Box 5245, Somerset, NJ 08875-5245; www.esperstamps.org; esperdon@verizon.net

Europa Study Unit, Tonny E. Van Loij, 3002 S. Xanthia St.; Denver, CO 80231-4237; (303) 752-0189; www.europastudyunit.org; tvanloij@gmail.com

Fire Service in Philately, John Zaranek, 81 Hillpine Road, Cheektowaga, NY 14227-2259; (716) 668-3352; jczaranek@roadrunner.com

Gastronomy on Stamps Study Unit, David Wolfersburger, 5062 NW 35th Lane Road, Ocala, FL 34482; (314) 494-3795; www.gastronomystamps.org

Gay and Lesbian History on Stamps Club, Joe Petronie, P.O. Box 190842, Dallas, TX 75219-0842; www.glhsonline.org; glhsc@aol.com

Gems, Minerals and Jewelry Study Unit, Fred Haynes, 10 Country Club Drive, Rochester, NY 14618-3720; fredmhaynes55@gmail.com

Graphics Philately Association, Larry Rosenblum. 1030 E. El Camino Real, PMB 107, Sunnyvale, CA 94087-3759; www.graphics-stamps.org; larry@graphics-stamps.org

Journalists, Authors and Poets on Stamps, Christopher D. Cook, 7222 Hollywood Road, Berrien Springs, MI 49103; cdcook2@gmail.com

Lighthouse Stamp Society, www.lighthousestampsociety.org

Lions International Stamp Club, David McKirdy, s-Gravenwetering 248, 3062 SJ Rotterdam, Netherlands; 31(0) 10 212 0313; www.lisc.nl; davidmckirdy@aol.com

Masonic Study Unit, Gene Fricks, 25 Murray Way, Blackwood, NJ 08012-4400; genefricks@comcast.net

Medical Subjects Unit, Dr. Frederick C. Skvara, P.O. Box 6228, Bridgewater, NJ 08807; fcskvara@optonline.net

Napoleonic Age Philatelists, Ken Berry, 4117 NW 146th St., Oklahoma City, OK 73134-1746; (405) 748-8646; www.nap-stamps.org; krb4117@att.net

Old World Archaeological Study Unit, Caroline Scannell, 14 Dawn Drive, Smithtown, NY 11787-176; www.owasu.org; editor@owasu.org

Petroleum Philatelic Society International, Feitze Papa, 922 Meander Drive, Walnut Creek, CA 94598-4239; www.ppsi.org.uk; oildad@astound.net

Rotary on Stamps Fellowship, Gerald L. Fitzsimmons, 105 Calle Ricardo, Victoria, TX 77904; www.rotaryonstamps.org; glfitz@suddenlink.net

Scouts on Stamps Society International, Woodrow (Woody) Brooks, 498 Baldwin Road, Akron, OH 44312; (330) 612-1294; www.sossi.org; secretary@sossi.org

Ships on Stamps Unit, Erik Th. Matzinger, Voorste Havervelden 30, 4822 AL Breda, Netherlands; www.shipsonstamps.org; erikships@gmail.com

Space Topic Study Unit, David Blog, P.O. Box 174, Bergenfield, NJ 07621; www.space-unit.com; davidblognj@gmail.com

Stamps on Stamps Collectors Club, Michael Merritt, 73 Mountainside Road, Mendham, NJ 07945; www.stampsonstamps.org; michael@mischu.me

Windmill Study Unit, Walter J. Hallien, 607 N. Porter St., Watkins Glenn, NY 14891-1345; (607) 229-3541; www.windmillworld.com

Wine On Stamps Study Unit, David Wolfersburger, 5062 NW 35th Lane Road, Ocala, FL 34482; (314) 494-3795; www.wine-on-stamps.org;

United States

American Air Mail Society, Stephen Reinhard, P.O. Box 110, Mineola, NY 11501; www.americanairmailsociety.org; sreinhard1@optonline.net

American First Day Cover Society, P.O. Box 246, Colonial Beach VA 22443-0246; (520) 321-0880; www.afdcs.org; afdcs@afdcs.org

Auxiliary Markings Club, Jerry Johnson, 6621 W. Victoria Ave., Kennewick, WA 99336; www.postal-markings.org; membership-2010@postal-markings.org

American Plate Number Single Society, Rick Burdsall, APNSS Secretary, P.O. BOX 1023, Palatine, IL 60078-1023; www.apnss.org; apnss.sec@gmail.com

American Revenue Association, Lyman Hensley, 473 E. Elm St., Sycamore, IL 60178-1934; www.revenuer.org; ilrno2@netzero.net

American Society for Philatelic Pages and Panels, Ron Walenciak, P.O. Box 1042, Washington Township, NJ 07676; www.asppp.org; ron.walenciak@asppp.org

Canal Zone Study Group, Mike Drabik, P.O. Box 281, Bolton, MA 01740, www.canalzonestudygroup.com; czsgsecretary@gmail.com

Carriers and Locals Society, John Bowman, 14409 Pentridge Drive, Corpus Christi, TX 78410; (361) 933-0757; www.pennypost.org; jbowman@stx.rr.com

Christmas Seal & Charity Stamp Society, John Denune Jr., 234 E. Broadway, Granville, OH 43023; (740) 814-6031; www.seal-society.org; john@christmasseals.net

Civil War Philatelic Society, Patricia A. Kaufmann, 10194 N. Old State Road, Lincoln, DE 19960-3644; (302) 422-2656; www.civilwarphilatelicsociety.org; trishkauf@comcast.net

Error, Freaks, and Oddities Collectors Club, Scott Shaulis, P.O. Box 549, Murrysville, PA 15668-0549; (724) 733-4134; www.efocc.org; scott@shaulisstamps.com

National Duck Stamp Collectors Society, Anthony J. Monico, P.O. Box 43, Harleysville, PA 19438-0043; www.ndscs.org; ndscs@ndscs.org

Plate Number Coil Collectors Club (PNC3), Gene Trinks, 16415 W. Desert Wren Court, Surprise, AZ 85374; (623) 322-4619; www.pnc3.org; gctrinks@cox.net

Post Mark Collectors Club, Bob Milligan, 7014 Woodland Oaks Drive, Magnolia, TX 77354; (281) 259-2735; www.postmarks.org; bob.milligan0@gmail.com

Souvenir Card Collectors Society, William V. Kriebel, www.souvenircards.org; kriebewv@drexel.edu

United Postal Stationery Society, Dave Kandziolka, 404 Sundown Drive, Knoxville, TN 37934; www.upss.org; membership@upss.org

U.S. Cancellation Club, Roger Curran, 18 Tressler Blvd., Lewisburg, PA 17837; rdcnrc@ptd.net

U.S. Philatelic Classics Society, Rob Lund, 2913 Fulton St., Everett, WA 98201-3733; www.uspcs.org; membershipchairman@uspcs.org

US Possessions Philatelic Society, Daniel F. Ring, P.O. Box 113, Woodstock, IL 60098; http://uspps.tripod.com; danielfring@hotmail.com

United States Stamp Society, Rod Juell, P.O. Box 3508, Joliet, IL 60434-3508; www.usstamps.org; execsecretary@usstamps.org

Africa

Bechuanalands and Botswana Society, Otto Peetoom, Roos, East Yorkshire HU12 0LD, United Kingdom; 44(0)1964 670239; www.bechuanalandphilately.com; info@bechuanalandphilately.com

Egypt Study Circle, Mike Murphy, 11 Waterbank Road, Bellingham, London SE6 3DJ United Kingdom; (44) 0203 6737051; www.egyptstudycircle.org.uk; secretary@egyptstudycircle.org.uk

Ethiopian Philatelic Society, Ulf Lindahl, 21 Westview Place, Riverside, CT 06878; (203) 722-0769; https://ethiopianphilatelicsociety.weebly.com; ulindahl@optonline.net

Liberian Philatelic Society, P.O. Box 1570, Parker, CO 80134; www.liberiastamps.org; liberiastamps@comcast.net

Orange Free State Study Circle, J. R. Stroud, RDPSA, 24 Hooper Close, Burnham-on-sea, Somerset TA8 1JQ United Kingdom; 44 1278 782235; www.orangefreestatephilately.org.uk; richard@richardstroud.plus.com

Philatelic Society for Greater Southern Africa, David McNamee, 15 Woodland Drive, Alamo, CA 94507; www.psgsa.org; alan.hanks@sympatico.ca

Rhodesian Study Circle, William R. Wallace, P.O. Box 16381, San Francisco, CA 94116; (415) 564-6069; www.rhodesianstudycircle.org.uk; bwall8rscr@earthlink.net

Society for Moroccan and Tunisian Philately, S.P.L.M., 206, Bld Pereire, 75017 Paris, France; http://splm-philatelie.org; splm206@aol.com

South Sudan Philatelic Society, William Barclay, 1370 Spring Hill Road, South Londonderry, VT 05155; barclayphilatelics@gmail.com

Sudan Study Group, Andy Neal, Bank House, Coedway, Shrewsbury SY5 9AR United Kingdom; www.sudanstamps.org; andywneal@gmail.com

Transvaal Study Circle, c/o 9 Meadow Road, Gravesend, Kent DA11 7LR United Kingdom; www.transvaalstamps.org.uk; transvaalstudycircle@aol.co.uk

West Africa Study Circle, Martin Bratzel, 1233 Virginia Ave., Windsor, ON N8S 2Z1 Canada; www.wasc.org.uk; marty_bratzel@yahoo.ca

Asia

Aden & Somaliland Study Group, Malcom Lacey, 108 Dalestorth Road, Sutton-in-Ashfield, Nottinghamshire NG17 3AA, United Kingdom; www.stampdomain.com/aden; neil53williams@yahoo.co.uk

Burma (Myanmar) Philatelic Study Circle, Michael Whittaker, 1, Ecton Leys, Hillside, Rugby, Warwickshire CV22 5SL United Kingdom; https://burmamyanmarphilately.wordpress.com/burma-myanmar-philatelic-study-circle; manningham8@mypostoffice.co.uk

Ceylon Study Circle, Rodney W. P. Frost, 42 Lonsdale Road, Cannington, Bridgwater, Somerset TA5 2JS United Kingdom; 01278 652592; www.ceylonsc.org; rodney.frost@tiscali.co.uk

China Stamp Society, H. James Maxwell, 1050 W. Blue Ridge Blvd., Kansas City, MO 64145-1216; www.chinastampsociety.org; president@chinastampsociety.org

Hong Kong Philatelic Society, John Tang, G.P.O. Box 446, Hong Kong; www.hkpsociety.com; hkpsociety@outlook.com

Hong Kong Study Circle, Robert Newton, www.hongkongstudycircle.com/index.html; newtons100@gmail.com

India Study Circle, John Warren, P.O. Box 7326, Washington, DC 20044; (202) 488-7443; https://indiastudycircle.org; jw-kbw@earthlink.net

International Philippine Philatelic Society, James R. Larot, Jr., 4990 Bayleaf Court, Martinez, CA 94553; (925) 260-5425; www.theipps.info; jlarot@ccwater.com

International Society for Japanese Philately, P.O. Box 1283, Haddonfield NJ 08033; www.isjp.org; secretary@isjp.org

Iran Philatelic Study Circle, Nigel Gooch, Marchwood, 56, Wickham Ave., Bexhill-on-Sea, East Sussex TN39 3ER United Kingdom; www.iranphilately.org; nigelmgooch@gmail.com

Korea Stamp Society, Peter Corson, 1109 Gunnison Place, Raleigh, NC 27609; (919) 787-7611; koreastampsociety.org; pbcorson@aol.com

Lebanese Association of Philately, P. O. Box 90-1826 Jdeidet El Matn, Beirut, Lebanon; Billy Karam, president, billykaram@billykaram.org; Ghassan Riachi, representative in USA, paraphila2017@gmail.com

Nepal & Tibet Philatelic Study Circle, Colin Hepper, 12 Charnwood Close, Peterborough, Cambs PE2 9BZ United Kingdom; http://fuchs-online.com/ntpsc; ntpsc@fuchs-online.com

Pakistan Philatelic Study Circle, Jeff Siddiqui, P.O. Box 7002, Lynnwood, WA 98046; jeffsiddiqui@msn.com

Society of Indo-China Philatelists, Ron Bentley, 2600 N. 24th St., Arlington, VA 22207; (703) 524-1652; www.sicp-online.org; ron.bentley@verizon.net

Society of Israel Philatelists, Inc., Sarah Berezenko, 100 Match Factory Place, Bellefonte, PA 16823-1367; (814) 933-3803 ext. 212; www.israelstamps.com; israelstamps@gmail.com

Australasia and Oceania

Australian States Study Circle of the Royal Sydney Philatelic Club, Ben Palmer, G.P.O. 1751, Sydney, NSW 2001 Australia; http://club.philas.org.au/states

Fellowship of Samoa Specialists, Trevor Shimell, 18 Aspen Drive, Newton Abbot, Devon TQ12 4TN United Kingdom; www.samoaexpress.org; trevor.shimell@gmail.com

Malaya Study Group, Michael Waugh, 151 Roker Lane, Pudsey, Leeds LS28 9ND United Kingdom; http://malayastudygroup.com; mawpud43@gmail.com

New Zealand Society of Great Britain, Michael Wilkinson, 121 London Road, Sevenoaks, Kent TN13 1BH United Kingdom; 01732 456997; www.nzsgb.org.uk; mwilkin799@aol.com

Pacific Islands Study Circle, John Ray, 24 Woodvale Ave., London SE25 4AE United Kingdom; www.pisc.org.uk; secretary@pisc.org.uk

Papuan Philatelic Society, Steven Zirinsky, P.O. Box 49, Ansonia Station, New York, NY 10023; (718) 706-0616; www.papuanphilatelicsociety.com; szirinsky@cs.com

Pitcairn Islands Study Group, Dr. Everett L. Parker, 207 Corinth Road, Hudson, ME 04449-3057; (207) 573-1686; www.pisg.net; eparker@hughes.net

Ryukyu Philatelic Specialist Society, Laura Edmonds, P.O. Box 240177, Charlotte, NC 28224-0177; (336) 509-3739; www.ryukyustamps.org; secretary@ryukyustamps.org

Society of Australasian Specialists / Oceania, Steve Zirinsky, P.O. Box 230049, New York, NY 10023-0049; www.sasoceania.org; president@sosoceania.org

Sarawak Specialists' Society, Stephen Schumann, 2417 Cabrallo Drive, Hayward, CA 94545; (510) 785-4794; www.britborneostamps.org.uk; vpnam@s-s-s.org.uk

Western Australia Study Group, Brian Pope, P.O. Box 423, Claremont, WA 6910 Australia; (61) 419 843 943; www.wastudygroup.com; wastudygroup@hotmail.com

Europe

American Helvetia Philatelic Society, Richard T. Hall, P.O. Box 15053, Asheville, NC 28813-0053; www.swiss-stamps.org; secretary2@swiss-stamps.org

American Society for Netherlands Philately, Hans Kremer, 50 Rockport Court, Danville, CA 94526; (925) 820-5841; www.asnp1975.com; hkremer@usa.net

Andorran Philatelic Study Circle, David Hope, 17 Hawthorn Drive, Stalybridge, Cheshire SK15 1UE United Kingdom; www.andorranpsc.org.uk; andorranpsc@btinternet.com

Austria Philatelic Society, Ralph Schneider, P.O. Box 978, Iowa Park, TX 76376; (940) 213-5004; www.austriaphilatelicsociety.com; rschneiderstamps@gmail.com

Channel Islands Specialists Society, Richard Flemming, Burbage, 64 Falconers Green, Hinckley, Leicestershire, LE102SX, United Kingdom; www.ciss.uk; secretary@ciss.uk

Cyprus Study Circle, Rob Wheeler, 47 Drayton Ave., London W13 0LE United Kingdom; www.cyprusstudycircle.org; robwheeler47@aol.com

Danish West Indies Study Unit of Scandinavian Collectors Club, Arnold Sorensen, 7666 Edgedale Drive, Newburgh, IN 47630; (812) 480-6532; www.scc-online.org; valbydwi@hotmail.com

Eire Philatelic Association, John B. Sharkey, 1559 Grouse Lane, Mountainside, NJ 07092-1340; www.eirephilatelicassoc.org; jsharkeyepa@me.com

Faroe Islands Study Circle, Norman Hudson, 40 Queen's Road, Vicar's Cross, Chester CH3 5HB United Kingdom; www.faroeislandssc.org; jntropics@hotmail.com

France & Colonies Philatelic Society, Edward Grabowski, 111 Prospect St., 4C, Westfield, NJ 07090; (908) 233-9318; www.franceandcolsps.org; edjjg@alum.mit.edu

Germany Philatelic Society, P.O. Box 6547, Chesterfield, MO 63006-6547; www.germanyphilatelicusa.org; info@germanyphilatelicsocietyusa.org

Gibraltar Study Circle, Susan Dare, 22, Byways Park, Strode Road, Clevedon, North Somerset BS21 6UR United Kingdom; www.gibraltarstudycircle.wordpress.com; smldare@yahoo.co.uk

International Society for Portuguese Philately, Clyde Homen, 1491 Bonnie View Road, Hollister, CA 95023-5117; www.portugalstamps.com; ispp1962@sbcglobal.net

Italy and Colonies Study Circle, Richard Harlow, 7 Duncombe House, 8 Manor Road, Teddington, Middlesex TW118BE United Kingdom; 44 208 977 8737; www.icsc-uk.com; richardharlow@outlook.com

Liechtenstudy USA, Paul Tremaine, 410 SW Ninth St., Dundee, OR 97115-9731; (503) 538-4500; www.liechtenstudy.org; tremaine@liechtenstudy.org

Lithuania Philatelic Society, Audrius Brazdeikis, 9915 Murray Landing, Missouri City, TX 77459; (281) 450-6224; www.lithuanianphilately.com/lps; audrius@lithuanianphilately.com

Luxembourg Collectors Club, Gary B. Little, 7319 Beau Road, Sechelt, BC V0N 3A8 Canada; (604) 885-7241; http://lcc.luxcentral.com; gary@luxcentral.com

Plebiscite-Memel-Saar Study Group of the German Philatelic Society, Clayton Wallace, 100 Lark Court, Alamo, CA 94507; claytonwallace@comcast.net

Polonus Polish Philatelic Society, Daniel Lubelski, P.O. Box 2212, Benicia, CA 94510; (419) 410-9115; www.polonus.org; info@polonus.org

Rossica Society of Russian Philately, Alexander Kolchinsky, 1506 Country Lake Drive, Champaign, IL 61821-6428; www.rossica.org; alexander.kolchinsky@rossica.org

Scandinavian Collectors Club, Alan Warren, Scandinavian Collectors Club, P.O. Box 39, Exton PA 19341-0039; (612) 810-8640; www.scc-online.org; alanwar@att.net

Society for Czechoslovak Philately, Tom Cossaboom, P.O. Box 4124, Prescott, AZ 86302; (928) 771-9097; www.csphilately.org; klfck1@aol.com

Society for Hungarian Philately, Alan Bauer, P.O. Box 4028, Vineyard Haven, MA 02568; (617) 645-4045; www.hungarianphilately.org; alan@hungarianstamps.com

Spanish Study Circle, Edith Knight, www.spaincircle.wixsite.com/spainstudycircle; spaincircle@gmail.com

Ukrainian Philatelic & Numismatic Society, Martin B. Tatuch, 5117 8th Road N., Arlington, VA 22205-1201; www.upns.org; treasurer@upns.org

Vatican Philatelic Society, Dennis Brady, 4897 Ledyard Drive, Manlius NY 13104-1514; www.vaticanphilately.org; dbrady7534@gmail.com

Yugoslavia Study Group, Michael Chant, 1514 N. Third Ave., Wausau, WI 54401; 208-748-9919; www.yugosg.org; membership@yugosg.org

Interregional Societies

American Society of Polar Philatelists, Alan Warren, P.O. Box 39, Exton, PA 19341-0039; (610) 321-0740; www.polarphilatelists.org; alanwar@att.net

First Issues Collector's Club, Kurt Streepy, 3128 E. Mattatha Drive, Bloomington, IN 47401; www.firstissues.org; secretary@firstissues.org

Former French Colonies Specialist Society, Col.fra, BP 628, 75367 Paris, France; www.colfra.org; postmaster@colfra.org

France & Colonies Philatelic Society, Edward Grabowski, 111 Prospect St., 4C, Westfield, NJ 07090; (908) 233-9318, www.franceandcolsps.org; edjjg@alum.mit.edu

Joint Stamp Issues Society, Richard Zimmermann, 29A, Rue Des Eviats, 67220 Lalaye, France; www.philarz.net; richard.zimmermann@club-internet.fr

The King George VI Collectors Society, Brian Livingstone, 21 York Mansions, Prince of Wales Drive, London SW11 4DL United Kingdom; www.kg6.info; livingstone484@btinternet.com

International Society of Reply Coupon Collectors, Peter Robin, P.O. Box 353, Bala Cynwyd, PA 19004; peterrobin@verizon.net

Italy and Colonies Study Circle, Richard Harlow, 7 Duncombe House, 8 Manor Road, Teddington, Middlesex TW118BE United Kingdom; 44 208 977 8737; www.icsc-uk.com; richardharlow@outlook.com

St. Helena, Ascension & Tristan Da Cunha Philatelic Society, Dr. Everett L. Parker, 207 Corinth Road, Hudson, ME 04449-3057; (207) 573-1686; www.shatps.org; eparker@hughes.net

United Nations Philatelists, Blanton Clement, Jr., P.O. Box 146, Morrisville, PA 19067-0146; www.unpi.com; bclemjunior@gmail.com

Latin America

Asociación Filatélica de Panamá, Edward D. Vianna B. ASOFILPA, 0819-03400, El Dorado, Panama; http://asociacionfilatelicadepanama.blogspot.com; asofilpa@gmail.com

Asociacion Mexicana de Filatelia (AMEXFIL), Alejandro Grossmann, Jose Maria Rico, 129, Col. Del Valle, 3100 Mexico City, DF Mexico; www.amexfil.mx; amexfil@gmail.com

Associated Collectors of El Salvador, Pierre Cahen, Vipsal 1342, P.O. Box 02-5364, Miami FL 33102; www.elsalvadorphilately.org; sfes-aces@elsalvadorphilately.org

Association Filatelic de Costa Rica, Giana Wayman (McCarty), #SJO 4935, P.O. Box 025723, Miami, FL 33102-5723; 011-506-2-228-1947; scotland@racsa.co.cr

Brazil Philatelic Association, William V. Kriebel, www.brazilphilatelic.org, info@brazilphilatelic.org

Canal Zone Study Group, Mike Drabik, P.O. Box 281, Bolton, MA 01740; www.canalzonestudygroup.com; czsgsecretary@gmail.com

Colombia-Panama Philatelic Study Group, Allan Harris, 26997 Hemmingway Ct, Hayward CA 94542-2349; www.copaphil.org; copaphilusa@aol.com

Falkland Islands Philatelic Study Groups, Morva White, 42 Colton Road, Shrivenham, Swindon SN6 8AZ United Kingdom; 44(0) 1793 783245; www.fipsg.org.uk; morawhite@supanet.com

Federacion Filatelica de la Republica de Honduras, Mauricio Mejia, Apartado Postal 1465, Tegucigalpa, D.C. Honduras; 504 3399-7227; www.facebook.com/filateliadehonduras; ffrh@hotmail.com

International Cuban Philatelic Society (ICPS), Ernesto Cuesta, P.O. Box 34434, Bethesda, MD 20827; (301) 564-3099; www.cubafil.org; ecuesta@philat.com

International Society of Guatemala Collectors, Jaime Marckwordt, 449 St. Francis Blvd., Daly City, CA 94015-2136; (415) 997-0295; www.guatemalastamps.com; president@guatamalastamps.com

Mexico-Elmhurst Philatelic Society International, Eric Stovner, P.O. Box 10097, Santa Ana, CA 92711-0097; www.mepsi.org; treasurer@mepsi.org

Nicaragua Study Group, Erick Rodriguez, 11817 S. W. 11th St., Miami, FL 33184-2501; nsgsec@yahoo.com

North America (excluding United States)

British Caribbean Philatelic Study Group, Bob Stewart, 7 West Dune Lane, Long Beach Township, NJ 08008; (941) 379-4108; www.bcpsg.com; bcpsg@comcast.net

British North America Philatelic Society, Andy Ellwood, 10 Doris Ave., Gloucester, ON K1T 3W8 Canada; www.bnaps.org; secretary@bnaps.org

British West Indies Study Circle, Steve Jarvis, 5 Redbridge Drive, Andover, Hants SP10 2LF United Kingdom; 01264 358065; www.bwisc.org; info@bwisc.org

Bermuda Collectors Society, John Pare, 405 Perimeter St., Mount Horeb, WI 53572; (608) 852-7358; www.bermudacollectorssociety.com; pare16@mhtc.net

Haiti Philatelic Society, Ubaldo Del Toro, 5709 Marble Archway, Alexandria, VA 22315; www.haitiphilately.org; u007ubi@aol.com

Hawaiian Philatelic Society, Gannon Sugimura, P.O. Box 10115, Honolulu, HI 96816-0115, www.hpshawaii.com; hiphilsoc@gmail.com

Stamp Dealer Associations

American Stamp Dealers Association, Inc., P.O. Box 513, Centre Hall PA 16828; (800) 369-8207; www.americanstampdealer.com; asda@americanstampdealer.com

Midwest Stamp Dealers Association, P.O. Box 411, Salem, WI 53168-0411; (414) 234-9867; www.msdastamp.com; msdastampshow@gmail.com.

National Stamp Dealers Association, Sheldon Ruckens, President, 3643 Private Road 18, Pinckneyville, IL 62274-3426; (618) 357-5497; www.nsdainc.org; nsda@nsdainc.org

Youth Philately

Young Stamp Collectors of America, 100 Match Factory Place, Bellefonte, PA 16823; (814) 933-3803; https://stamps.org/learn/youth-in-philately; ysca@stamps.org

Expertizing services

The following organizations will, for a fee, provide expert opinions about stamps submitted to them. Collectors should contact these organizations to find out about their fees and requirements before submitting philatelic material to them. The listing of these groups here is not intended as an endorsement by Amos Media Co.

General Expertizing Services

American Philatelic Expertizing Service (a service of the American Philatelic Society)
100 Match Factory Place
Bellefonte PA 16823-1367
(814) 237-3803
www.stamps.org/stamp-authentication
apex@stamps.org
Areas of Expertise: Worldwide

BPA Expertising, Ltd.
P.O. Box 1141
Guildford, Surrey, GU5 0WR
United Kingdom
www.bpaexpertising.com
sec@bpaexpertising.org
Areas of Expertise: British Commonwealth, Great Britain, Classics of Europe, South America and the Far East

Philatelic Foundation
353 Lexington Avenue, Suite 804
New York NY 10016
(212) 221-6555
www.philatelicfoundation.org
philatelicfoundation@verizon.net
Areas of Expertise: U.S. & Worldwide

Philatelic Stamp Authentication and Grading, Inc.
P.O. Box 41-0880
Melbourne FL 32941-0880
(305) 345-9864
www.psaginc.com
info@psaginc.com
Areas of Expertise: U.S., Canal Zone, Hawaii, Philippines, Canada & Provinces

Professional Stamp Experts
P.O. Box 539309
Henderson NV 89053-9309
(702) 776-6522
www.gradingmatters.com
www.psestamp.com
info@gradingmatters.com
Areas of Expertise: Stamps and Covers of U.S., U.S. Possessions, British Commonwealth

Royal Philatelic Society London Expert Committee
15 Abchurch Lane
London, EX4N 7BW
United Kingdom
www.rpsl.limited/experts.aspx
experts@rpsl.limited
Areas of Expertise: Worldwide

Expertizing Services Covering Specific Fields or Countries

China Stamp Society Expertizing Service
1050 W. Blue Ridge Blvd.
Kansas City MO 64145
(816) 942-6300
hjmesq@aol.com
Areas of Expertise: China

Civil War Philatelic Society Authentication Service
C/O Stefan T. Jaronski
P.O. Box 232
Sidney, MT 59270-0232
www.civilwarphilatelicsociety.org/authentication/
authentication@civilwarphilatelicsociety.org
Areas of Expertise: Confederate stamps and postal history

Hawaiian Philatelic Society Expertizing Service
P.O. Box 10115
Honolulu HI 96816-0115
www.stampshows.com/hps.html
hiphilsoc@gmail.com
Areas of Expertise: Hawaii

Hong Kong Stamp Society Expertizing Service
P.O. Box 206
Glenside PA 19038
Areas of Expertise: Hong Kong

International Association of Philatelic Experts United States Associate members:

Paul Buchsbayew
300 Frank W. Burr Blvd. - Second Floor
Box 35
Teaneck, NJ 07666.
(212) 977-7734
Areas of Expertise: Russia, Soviet Union

William T. Crowe
P.O. Box 2090
Danbury CT 06813-2090
wtcrowe@aol.com
Areas of Expertise: United States

International Society for Japanese Philately Expertizing Committee
132 North Pine Terrace
Staten Island NY 10312-4052
(718) 227-5229
Areas of Expertise: Japan and related areas, except WWII Japanese Occupation issues

International Society for Portuguese Philately Expertizing Service
P.O. Box 43146
Philadelphia PA 19129-3146
(215) 843-2106
s.s.washburne@worldnet.att.net
Areas of Expertise: Portugal and Colonies

Mexico-Elmhurst Philatelic Society International Expert Committee
Expert Committee Administrator
Marc E. Gonzales
P.O. Box 29040
Denver CO 80229-0040
www.mepsi.org/expert_committeee.htm
expertizations@mepsi.org
Areas of Expertise: Mexico

Ukrainian Philatelic & Numismatic Society Expertizing Service
30552 Dell Lane
Warren MI 48092-1862
Areas of Expertise: Ukraine, Western Ukraine

V. G. Greene Philatelic Research Foundation
P.O. Box 69100
St. Clair Post Office
Toronto, ON M4T 3A1
Canada
(416) 921-2073
www.greenefoundation.ca
info@greenefoundation.ca
Areas of Expertise: British North America

Information on catalogue values, grade and condition

Catalogue value

The Scott Catalogue value is a retail value; that is, an amount you could expect to pay for a stamp in the grade of Very Fine with no faults. Any exceptions to the grade valued will be noted in the text. The general introduction on the following pages and the individual section introductions further explain the type of material that is valued. The value listed for any given stamp is a reference that reflects recent actual dealer selling prices for that item.

Dealer retail price lists, public auction results, published prices in advertising and individual solicitation of retail prices from dealers, collectors and specialty organizations have been used in establishing the values found in this catalogue. Amos Media Co. values stamps, but Amos Media is not a company engaged in the business of buying and selling stamps as a dealer.

Use this catalogue as a guide for buying and selling. The actual price you pay for a stamp may be higher or lower than the catalogue value because of many different factors, including the amount of personal service a dealer offers, or increased or decreased interest in the country or topic represented by a stamp or set. An item may occasionally be offered at a lower price as a "loss leader," or as part of a special sale. You also may obtain an item inexpensively at public auction because of little interest at that time or as part of a large lot.

Stamps that are of a lesser grade than Very Fine, or those with condition problems, generally trade at lower prices than those given in this catalogue. Stamps of exceptional quality in both grade and condition often command higher prices than those listed.

Values for pre-1900 unused issues are for stamps with approximately half or more of their original gum. Stamps with most or all of their original gum may be expected to sell for more, and stamps with less than half of their original gum may be expected to sell for somewhat less than the values listed. On rarer stamps, it may be expected that the original gum will be somewhat more disturbed than it will be on more common issues. Post-1900 unused issues are assumed to have full original gum. From breakpoints in most countries' listings, stamps are valued as never hinged, due to the wide availability of stamps in that condition. These notations are prominently placed in the listings and in the country information preceding the listings. Some countries also feature listings with dual values for hinged and never-hinged stamps.

Grade

A stamp's grade and condition are crucial to its value. The accompanying illustrations show examples of Very Fine stamps from different time periods, along with examples of stamps in Fine to Very Fine and Extremely Fine grades as points of reference. When a stamp seller offers a stamp in any grade from fine to superb without further qualifying statements, that stamp should not only have the centering grade as defined, but it also should be free of faults or other condition problems.

FINE stamps (illustrations not shown) have designs that are quite off center, with the perforations on one or two sides very close to the design but not quite touching it. There is white space between the perforations and the design that is minimal but evident to the unaided eye. Imperforate stamps may have small margins, and earlier issues may show the design just touching one edge of the stamp design. Very early perforated issues normally will have the perforations slightly cutting into the design. Used stamps may have heavier than usual cancellations.

FINE-VERY FINE stamps will be somewhat off center on one side, or slightly off center on two sides. Imperforate stamps will have two margins of at least normal size, and the design will not touch any edge. For perforated stamps, the perfs are well clear of the design, but are still noticeably off center. *However, early issues of a country may be printed in such a way that the design naturally is very close to the edges. In these cases, the perforations may cut into the design very slightly.* Used stamps will not have a cancellation that detracts from the design.

VERY FINE stamps will be just slightly off center on one or two sides, but the design will be well clear of the edge. The stamp will present a nice, balanced appearance. Imperforate stamps will be well centered within normal-sized margins. *However, early issues of many countries may be printed in such a way that the perforations may touch the design on one or more sides. Where this is the case, a boxed note will be found defining the centering and margins of the stamps being valued.* Used stamps will have light or otherwise neat cancellations. This is the grade used to establish Scott Catalogue values.

EXTREMELY FINE stamps are close to being perfectly centered. Imperforate stamps will have even margins that are slightly larger than normal. Even the earliest perforated issues will have perforations clear of the design on all sides.

Amos Media Co. recognizes that there is no formally enforced grading scheme for postage stamps, and that the final price you pay or obtain for a stamp will be determined by individual agreement at the time of transaction.

Condition

Grade addresses only centering and (for used stamps) cancellation. *Condition* refers to factors other than grade that affect a stamp's desirability.

Factors that can increase the value of a stamp include exceptionally wide margins, particularly fresh color, the presence of selvage, and plate or die varieties. Unusual cancels on used stamps (particularly those of the 19th century) can greatly enhance their value as well.

Factors other than faults that decrease the value of a stamp include loss of original gum, regumming, a hinge remnant or foreign object adhering to the gum, natural inclusions, straight edges, and markings or notations applied by collectors or dealers.

Faults include missing pieces, tears, pin or other holes, surface scuffs, thin spots, creases, toning, short or pulled perforations, clipped perforations, oxidation or other forms of color changelings, soiling, stains, and such man-made changes as reperforations or the chemical removal or lightening of a cancellation.

Grading illustrations

On the following two pages are illustrations of various stamps from countries appearing in this volume. These stamps are arranged by country, and they represent early or important issues that are often found in widely different grades in the marketplace. The editors believe the illustrations will prove useful in showing the margin size and centering that will be seen on the various issues.

In addition to the matters of margin size and centering, collectors are reminded that the very fine stamps valued in the Scott catalogues also will possess fresh color and intact perforations, and they will be free from defects.

Examples shown are computer-manipulated images made from single digitized master illustrations.

Stamp illustrations used in the catalogue

It is important to note that the stamp images used for identification purposes in this catalogue may not be indicative of the grade of stamp being valued. Refer to the written discussion of grades on this page and to the grading illustrations on the following two pages for grading information.

Fine-Very Fine →

SCOTT CATALOGUES VALUE STAMPS IN THIS GRADE

Very Fine →

Extremely Fine →

Fine-Very Fine →

SCOTT CATALOGUES VALUE STAMPS IN THIS GRADE

Very Fine →

Extremely Fine →

Fine-Very Fine

SCOTT CATALOGUES VALUE STAMPS IN THIS GRADE

Very Fine

Extremely Fine

Fine-Very Fine

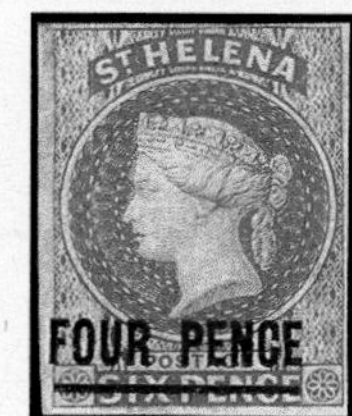

SCOTT CATALOGUES VALUE STAMPS IN THIS GRADE

Very Fine

Extremely Fine

Gum Conditions

For purposes of helping to determine the gum condition and value of an unused stamp, Scott presents the following chart which details different gum conditions and indicates how the conditions correlate with the Scott values for unused stamps. Used together, the Illustrated Grading Chart on the previous pages and this Illustrated Gum Chart should allow catalogue users to better understand the grade and gum condition of stamps valued in the Scott catalogues.

Never Hinged (NH; ★★): A never-hinged stamp will have full original gum that will have no hinge mark or disturbance. The presence of an expertizer's mark does not disqualify a stamp from this designation.

Original Gum (OG; ★): Pre-1900 stamps should have approximately half or more of their original gum. On rarer stamps, it may be expected that the original gum will be somewhat more disturbed than it will be on more common issues. Post-1900 stamps should have full original gum. Original gum will show some disturbance caused by a previous hinge(s) which may be present or entirely removed. The actual value of a post-1900 stamp will be affected by the degree of hinging of the full original gum.

Disturbed Original Gum: Gum showing noticeable effects of humidity, climate or hinging over more than half of the gum. The significance of gum disturbance in valuing a stamp in any of the Original Gum categories depends on the degree of disturbance, the rarity and normal gum condition of the issue and other variables affecting quality.

Regummed (RG; (★)): A regummed stamp is a stamp without gum that has had some type of gum privately applied at a time after it was issued. This normally is done to deceive collectors and/or dealers into thinking that the stamp has original gum and therefore has a higher value. A regummed stamp is considered the same as a stamp with none of its original gum for purposes of grading.

Gum Categories:	**MINT N.H.**	**ORIGINAL GUM (O.G.)**				**NO GUM**
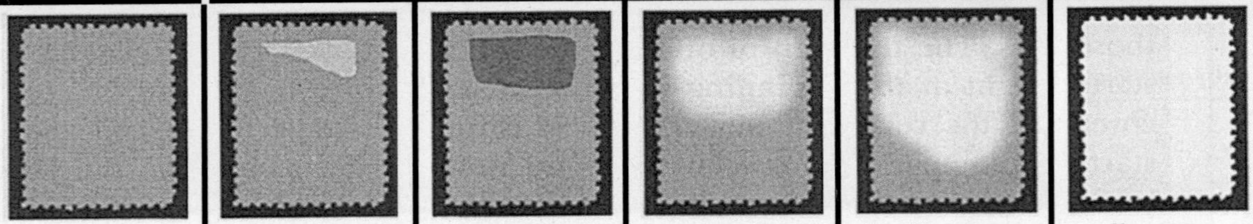	**Mint Never Hinged** *Free from any disturbance*	**Lightly Hinged** *Faint impression of a removed hinge over a small area*	**Hinge Mark or Remnant** *Prominent hinged spot with part or all of the hinge remaining*	**Large part o.g.** *Approximately half or more of the gum intact*	**Small part o.g.** Approximately less than half of the gum intact	**No gum** *Only if issued with gum*
Commonly Used Symbol:	★★	★	★	★	★	(★)
Pre-1900 Issues (Pre-1881 for U.S.)	*Very fine pre-1900 stamps in these categories trade at a premium over Scott value*			Scott Value for "Unused"		Scott "No Gum" listings for selected unused classic stamps
From 1900 to breakpoints for listings of never-hinged stamps	Scott "Never Hinged" listings for selected unused stamps	Scott Value for "Unused" (Actual value will be affected by the degree of hinging of the full o.g.)				
From breakpoints noted for many countries	Scott Value for "Unused"					

Catalogue listing policy

It is the intent of Amos Media Co. to list all postage stamps of the world in the Scott *Standard Postage Stamp Catalogue*. The only strict criteria for listing is that stamps be decreed legal for postage by the issuing country and that the issuing country actually have an operating postal system. Whether the primary intent of issuing a given stamp or set was for sale to postal patrons or to stamp collectors is not part of our listing criteria. Scott's role is to provide basic comprehensive postage stamp information. It is up to each stamp collector to choose which items to include in a collection.

It is Scott's objective to seek reasons why a stamp should be listed, rather than why it should not. Nevertheless, there are certain types of items that will not be listed. These include the following:

1. Unissued items that are not officially distributed or released by the issuing postal authority. If such items are officially issued at a later date by the country, they will be listed. Unissued items consist of those that have been printed and then held from sale for reasons such as change in government, errors found on stamps or something deemed objectionable about a stamp subject or design.

2. Stamps "issued" by non-existent postal entities or fantasy countries, such as Nagaland, Occusi-Ambeno, Staffa, Sedang, Torres Straits and others. Also, stamps "issued" in the names of legitimate, stamp-issuing countries that are not authorized by those countries.

3. Semi-official or unofficial items not required for postage. Examples include items issued by private agencies for their own express services. When such items are required for delivery, or are valid as prepayment of postage, they are listed.

4. Local stamps issued for local use only. Postage stamps issued by governments specifically for "domestic" use, such as Haiti Scott 219-228, or the United States nondenominated stamps, are not considered to be locals, since they are valid for postage throughout the country of origin.

5. Items not valid for postal use. For example, a few countries have issued souvenir sheets that are not valid for postage. This area also includes a number of worldwide charity labels (some denominated) that do not pay postage.

6. Egregiously exploitative issues such as stamps sold for far more than face value, stamps purposefully issued in artificially small quantities or only against advance orders, stamps awarded only to a selected audience such as a philatelic bureau's standing order customers, or stamps sold only in conjunction with other products. All of these kinds of items are usually controlled issues and/or are intended for speculation. These items normally will be included in a footnote.

7. Items distributed by the issuing government only to a limited group, club, philatelic exhibition or a single stamp dealer or other private company. These items normally will be included in a footnote.

8. Stamps not available to collectors. These generally are rare items, all of which are held by public institutions such as museums. The existence of such items often will be cited in footnotes.

The fact that a stamp has been used successfully as postage, even on international mail, is not in itself sufficient proof that it was legitimately issued. Numerous examples of so-called stamps from non-existent countries are known to have been used to post letters that have successfully passed through the international mail system.

There are certain items that are subject to interpretation. When a stamp falls outside our specifications, it may be listed along with a cautionary footnote.

A number of factors are considered in our approach to analyzing how a stamp is listed. The following list of factors is presented to share with you, the catalogue user, the complexity of the listing process.

Additional printings — "Additional printings" of a previously issued stamp may range from an item that is totally different to cases where it is impossible to differentiate from the original. At least a minor number (a small-letter suffix) is assigned if there is a distinct change in stamp shade, noticeably redrawn design, or a significantly different perforation measurement. A major number (numeral or numeral and capital-letter combination) is assigned if the editors feel the "additional printing" is sufficiently different from the original that it constitutes a different issue.

Commemoratives — Where practical, commemoratives with the same theme are placed in a set. For example, the U.S. Civil War Centennial set of 1961-65 and the Constitution Bicentennial series of 1989-90 appear as sets. Countries such as Japan and Korea issue such material on a regular basis, with an announced, or at least predictable, number of stamps known in advance. Occasionally, however, stamp sets that were released over a period of years have been separated. Appropriately placed footnotes will guide you to each set's continuation.

Definitive sets — Blocks of numbers generally have been reserved for definitive sets, based on previous experience with any given country. If a few more stamps were issued in a set than originally expected, they often have been inserted into the original set with a capital-letter suffix, such as U.S. Scott 1059A. If it appears that many more stamps than the originally allotted block will be released before the set is completed, a new block of numbers will be reserved, with the original one being closed off. In some cases, such as the U.S. Transportation and Great Americans series, several blocks of numbers exist. Appropriately placed footnotes will guide you to each set's continuation.

New country — Membership in the Universal Postal Union is not a consideration for listing status or order of placement within the catalogue. The index will tell you in what volume or page number the listings begin.

"No release date" items — The amount of information available for any given stamp issue varies greatly from country to country and even from time to time. Extremely comprehensive information about new stamps is available from some countries well before the stamps are released. By contrast some countries do not provide information about stamps or release dates. Most countries, however, fall between these extremes. A country may provide denominations or subjects of stamps from upcoming issues that are not issued as planned. Sometimes, philatelic agencies, those private firms hired to represent countries, add these later-issued items to sets well after the formal release date. This time period can range from weeks to years. If these items were officially released by the country, they will be added to the appropriate spot in the set. In many cases, the specific release date of a stamp or set of stamps may never be known.

Overprints — The color of an overprint is always noted if it is other than black. Where more than one color of ink has been used on overprints of a single set, the color used is noted. Early overprint and surcharge illustrations were altered to prevent their use by forgers.

Personalized Stamps — Since 1999, the special service of personalizing stamp vignettes, or labels attached to stamps, has been offered to customers by postal administrations of many countries. Sheets of these stamps are sold, singly or in quantity, only through special orders made by mail, in person, or through a sale on a computer website with the postal administrations or their agents for which an extra fee is charged, though some countries offer to collectors at face value personalized stamps having generic images in the vignettes or on the attached labels. It is impossible for any catalogue to know what images have been chosen by customers. Images can be 1) owned or created by the customer, 2) a generic image, or 3) an image pulled from a library of stock images on the stamp creation website. It is also impossible to know the quantity printed for any stamp having a particular image. So from a valuing standpoint, any image is equivalent to any other image for any personalized stamp having the same catalogue number. Illustrations of personalized stamps in the catalogue are not always those of stamps having generic images.

Personalized items are listed with some exceptions. These include:

1. Stamps or sheets that have attached labels that the customer cannot personalize, but which are nonetheless marketed as "personalized," and are sold for far more than the franking value.

2. Stamps or sheets that can be personalized by the customer, but where a portion of the print run must be ceded to the issuing country for sale to other customers.

3. Stamps or sheets that are created exclusively for a particular commercial client, or clients, including stamps that differ from any similar stamp that has been made available to the public.

4. Stamps or sheets that are deliberately conceived by the issuing authority that have been, or are likely to be, created with an excessive number of different face values, sizes, or other features that are changeable.

5. Stamps or sheets that are created by postal administrations using the same system of stamp personalization that has been put in place for use by the public that are printed in limited quantities and sold above face value.

6. Stamps or sheets that are created by licensees not directly affiliated or controlled by a postal administration.

Excluded items may or may not be footnoted.

Se-tenants -- Connected stamps of differing features (se-tenants) will be listed in the format most commonly collected. This includes pairs, blocks or larger multiples. Se-tenant units are not always symmetrical. An example is Australia Scott 508, which is a block of seven stamps. If the stamps are primarily collected as a unit, the major number may be assigned to the multiple, with minors going to each component stamp. In cases where continuous-design or other unit se-tenants will receive significant postal use, each stamp is given a major Scott number listing. This includes issues from the United States, Canada, Germany and Great Britain, for example.

Understanding the listings

On the opposite page is an enlarged "typical" listing from this catalogue. Below are detailed explanations of each of the highlighted parts of the listing.

1 Scott number — Scott catalogue numbers are used to identify specific items when buying, selling or trading stamps. Each listed postage stamp from every country has a unique Scott catalogue number. Therefore, Germany Scott 99, for example, can only refer to a single stamp. Although the Scott catalogue usually lists stamps in chronological order by date of issue, there are exceptions. When a country has issued a set of stamps over a period of time, those stamps within the set are kept together without regard to date of issue. This follows the normal collecting approach of keeping stamps in their natural sets.

When a country issues a set of stamps over a period of time, a group of consecutive catalogue numbers is reserved for the stamps in that set, as issued. If that group of numbers proves to be too few, capital-letter suffixes, such as "A" or "B," may be added to existing numbers to create enough catalogue numbers to cover all items in the set. A capital-letter suffix indicates a major Scott catalogue number listing. Scott generally uses a suffix letter only once. Therefore, a catalogue number listing with a capital-letter suffix will seldom be found with the same letter (lower case) used as a minor-letter listing. If there is a Scott 16A in a set, for example, there will seldom be a Scott 16a. However, a minor-letter "a" listing may be added to a major number containing an "A" suffix (Scott 16Aa, for example).

Suffix letters are cumulative. A minor "b" variety of Scott 16A would be Scott 16Ab, not Scott 16b.

There are times when a reserved block of Scott catalogue numbers is too large for a set, leaving some numbers unused. Such gaps in the numbering sequence also occur when the catalogue editors move an item's listing elsewhere or have removed it entirely from the catalogue. Scott does not attempt to account for every possible number, but rather attempts to assure that each stamp is assigned its own number.

Scott numbers designating regular postage normally are only numerals. Scott numbers for other types of stamps, such as air post, semi-postal, postal tax, postage due, occupation and others have a prefix consisting of one or more capital letters or a combination of numerals and capital letters.

2 Illustration number — Illustration or design-type numbers are used to identify each catalogue illustration. For most sets, the lowest face-value stamp is shown. It then serves as an example of the basic design approach for other stamps not illustrated. Where more than one stamp use the same illustration number, but have differences in design, the design paragraph or the description line clearly indicates the design on each stamp not illustrated. Where there are both vertical and horizontal designs in a set, a single illustration may be used, with the exceptions noted in the design paragraph or description line.

When an illustration is followed by a lower-case letter in parentheses, such as "A2(b)," the trailing letter indicates which overprint or surcharge illustration applies.

Illustrations normally are 70 percent of the original size of the stamp. Oversized stamps, blocks and souvenir sheets are reduced even more. Overprints and surcharges are shown at 100 percent of their original size if shown alone, but are 70 percent of original size if shown on stamps. In some cases, the illustration will be placed above the set, between listings or omitted completely. Overprint and surcharge illustrations are not placed in this catalogue for purposes of expertizing stamps.

3 Paper color — The color of a stamp's paper is noted in italic type when the paper used is not white.

4 Listing styles — There are two principal types of catalogue listings: major and minor.

Major listings are in a larger type style than minor listings. The catalogue number is a numeral that can be found with or without a capital-letter suffix, and with or without a prefix.

Minor listings are in a smaller type style and have a small-letter suffix or (if the listing immediately follows that of the major number) may show only the letter. These listings identify a variety of the major item. Examples include perforation and shade differences, multiples (some souvenir sheets, booklet panes and se-tenant combinations), and singles of multiples.

Examples of major number listings include 16, 28A, B97, C13A, 10N5, and 10N6A. Examples of minor numbers are 16a and C13Ab.

5 Basic information about a stamp or set — Introducing each stamp issue is a small section (usually a line listing) of basic information about a stamp or set. This section normally includes the date of issue, method of printing, perforation, watermark and, sometimes, some additional information of note. *Printing method, perforation and watermark apply to the following sets until a change is noted.* Stamps created by overprinting or surcharging previous issues are assumed to have the same perforation, watermark, printing method and other production characteristics as the original. Dates of issue are as precise as Scott is able to confirm and often reflect the dates on first-day covers, rather than the actual date of release.

6 Denomination — This normally refers to the face value of the stamp; that is, the cost of the unused stamp at the post office at the time of issue. When a denomination is shown in parentheses, it does not appear on the stamp. This includes the nondenominated stamps of the United States, Brazil and Great Britain, for example.

7 Color or other description — This area provides information to solidify identification of a stamp. In many recent cases, a description of the stamp design appears in this space, rather than a listing of colors.

8 Year of issue — In stamp sets that have been released in a period that spans more than a year, the number shown in parentheses is the year that stamp first appeared. Stamps without a date appeared during the first year of the issue. Dates are not always given for minor varieties.

9 Value unused and Value used — The Scott catalogue values are based on stamps that are in a grade of Very Fine unless stated otherwise. Unused values refer to items that have not seen postal, revenue or any other duty for which they were intended. Pre-1900 unused stamps that were issued with gum must have at least most of their original gum. Later issues are assumed to have full original gum. From breakpoints specified in most countries' listings, stamps are valued as never hinged. Stamps issued without gum are noted. Modern issues with PVA or other synthetic adhesives may appear ungummed. Unused self-adhesive stamps are valued as appearing undisturbed on their original backing paper. Values for used self-adhesive stamps are for examples either on piece or off piece. For a more detailed explanation of these values, please see the "Catalogue Value," "Condition" and "Understanding Valuing Notations" sections elsewhere in this introduction.

In some cases, where used stamps are more valuable than unused stamps, the value is for an example with a contemporaneous cancel, rather than a modern cancel or a smudge or other unclear marking. For those stamps that were released for postal and fiscal purposes, the used value represents a postally used stamp. Stamps with revenue cancels generally sell for less.

Stamps separated from a complete se-tenant multiple usually will be worth less than a pro-rated portion of the se-tenant multiple, and stamps lacking the attached labels that are noted in the listings will be worth less than the values shown.

10 Changes in basic set information — Bold type is used to show any changes in the basic data given for a set of stamps. These basic data categories include perforation gauge measurement, paper type, printing method and watermark.

11 Total value of a set — The total value of sets of three or more stamps issued after 1900 are shown. The set line also notes the range of Scott numbers and total number of stamps included in the grouping. The actual value of a set consisting predominantly of stamps having the minimum value of 25 cents may be less than the total value shown. Similarly, the actual value or catalogue value of se-tenant pairs or of blocks consisting of stamps having the minimum value of 25 cents may be less than the catalogue values of the component parts.

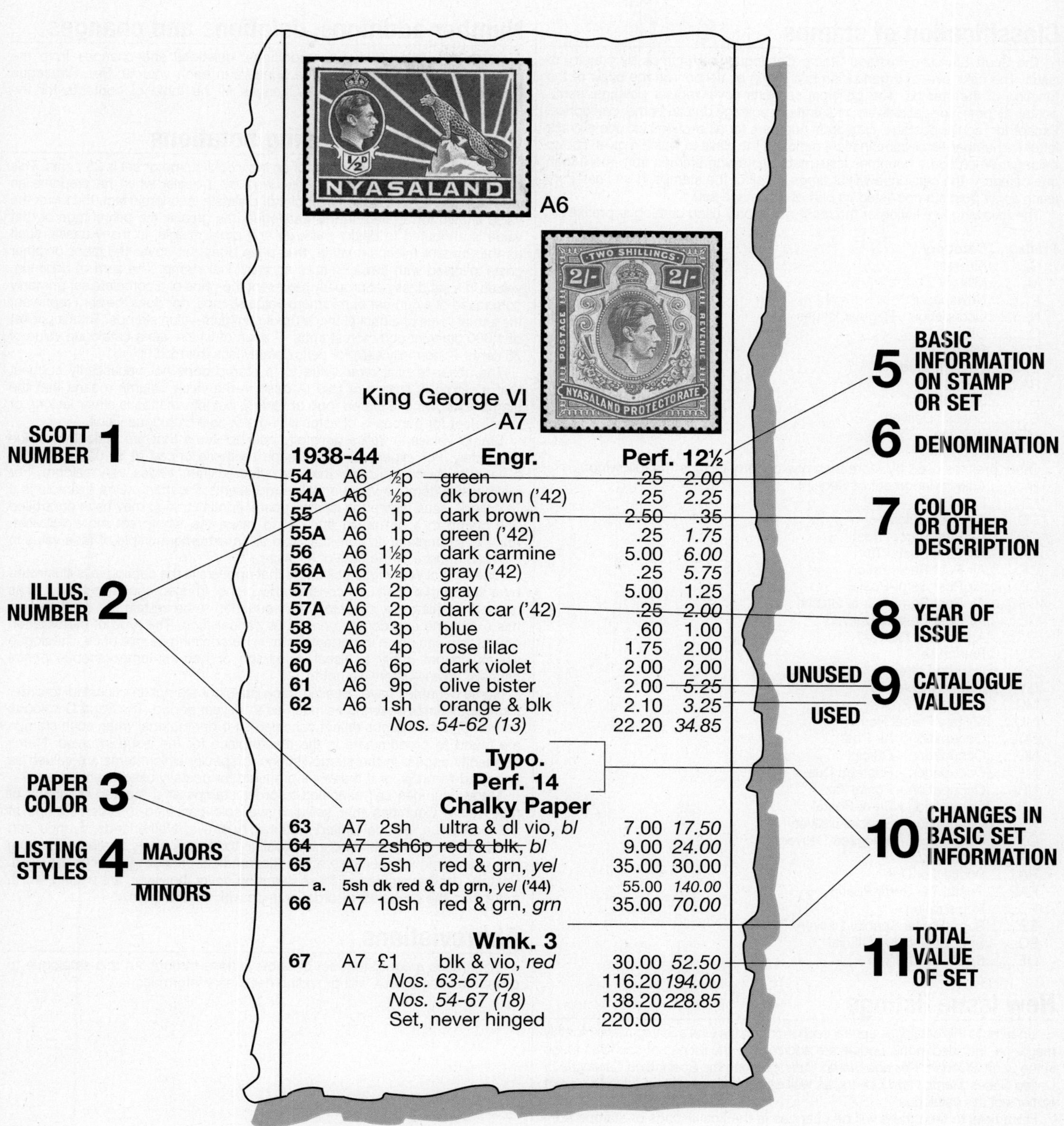
A6
King George VI
A7
SCOTT NUMBER 1
ILLUS. NUMBER 2
PAPER COLOR 3
LISTING STYLES 4 MAJORS MINORS
5 BASIC INFORMATION ON STAMP OR SET
6 DENOMINATION
7 COLOR OR OTHER DESCRIPTION
8 YEAR OF ISSUE
UNUSED 9 CATALOGUE VALUES USED
10 CHANGES IN BASIC SET INFORMATION
11 TOTAL VALUE OF SET
1938-44 Engr. Perf. 12½
54 A6 ½p green .25 2.00
54A A6 ½p dk brown ('42) .25 2.25
55 A6 1p dark brown 2.50 .35
55A A6 1p green ('42) .25 1.75
56 A6 1½p dark carmine 5.00 6.00
56A A6 1½p gray ('42) .25 5.75
57 A6 2p gray 5.00 1.25
57A A6 2p dark car ('42) .25 2.00
58 A6 3p blue .60 1.00
59 A6 4p rose lilac 1.75 2.00
60 A6 6p dark violet 2.00 2.00
61 A6 9p olive bister 2.00 5.25
62 A6 1sh orange & blk 2.10 3.25
Nos. 54-62 (13) 22.20 34.85
Typo.
Perf. 14
Chalky Paper
63 A7 2sh ultra & dl vio, bl 7.00 17.50
64 A7 2sh6p red & blk, bl 9.00 24.00
65 A7 5sh red & grn, yel 35.00 30.00
a. 5sh dk red & dp grn, yel ('44) 55.00 140.00
66 A7 10sh red & grn, grn 35.00 70.00
Wmk. 3
67 A7 £1 blk & vio, red 30.00 52.50
Nos. 63-67 (5) 116.20 194.00
Nos. 54-67 (18) 138.20 228.85
Set, never hinged 220.00

Special notices

Classification of stamps

The Scott Standard Postage Stamp Catalogue lists stamps by country of issue. The next level of organization is a listing by section on the basis of the function of the stamps. The principal sections cover regular postage, semi-postal, air post, special delivery, registration, postage due and other categories. Except for regular postage, catalogue numbers for all sections include a prefix letter (or number-letter combination) denoting the class to which a given stamp belongs. When some countries issue sets containing stamps from more than one category, the catalogue will at times list all of the stamps in one category (such as air post stamps listed as part of a postage set).

The following is a listing of the most commonly used catalogue prefixes.

Prefix.......Category
C..........Air Post
M.........Military
P..........Newspaper
N..........Occupation - Regular Issues
O..........Official
Q..........Parcel Post
J ....Postage Due
RA ....Postal Tax
B..........Semi-Postal
E..........Special Delivery
MR.......War Tax

Other prefixes used by more than one country include the following:
H..........Acknowledgment of Receipt
I ....Late Fee
CO.......Air Post Official
CQ.......Air Post Parcel Post
RAC.....Air Post Postal Tax
CF........Air Post Registration
CB ....Air Post Semi-Postal
CBO ....Air Post Semi-Postal Official
CE ....Air Post Special Delivery
EY........Authorized Delivery
S..........Franchise
G..........Insured Letter
GY ....Marine Insurance
MC.......Military Air Post
MQ ......Military Parcel Post
NC ....Occupation - Air Post
NO.......Occupation - Official
NJ........Occupation - Postage Due
NRA.....Occupation - Postal Tax
NB ......Occupation - Semi-Postal
NE ....Occupation - Special Delivery
QY ....Parcel Post Authorized Delivery
AR ....Postal-fiscal
RAJ......Postal Tax Due
RAB.....Postal Tax Semi-Postal
F ....Registration
EB........Semi-Postal Special Delivery
EO ....Special Delivery Official
QE ....Special Handling

New issue listings

Updates to this catalogue appear each month in the *Linn's Stamp News* monthly magazine. Included in this update are additions to the listings of countries found in the Scott *Standard Postage Stamp Catalogue* and the *Specialized Catalogue of United States Stamps and Covers,* as well as corrections and updates to current editions of this catalogue.

From time to time there will be changes in the final listings of stamps from the *Linn's Stamp News* magazine to the next edition of the catalogue. This occurs as more information about certain stamps or sets becomes available.

The catalogue update section of the *Linn's Stamp News* magazine is the most timely presentation of this material available. Annual subscriptions to *Linn's Stamp News* are available from Linn's Stamp News, Box 4129, Sidney, OH 45365-4129.

Number additions, deletions and changes

A listing of catalogue number additions, deletions and changes from the previous edition of the catalogue appears in each volume. See Catalogue Number Additions, Deletions & Changes in the table of contents for the location of this list.

Understanding valuing notations

The *minimum catalogue value* of an individual stamp or set is 25 cents. This represents a portion of the cost incurred by a dealer when he prepares an individual stamp for resale. As a point of philatelic-economic fact, the lower the value shown for an item in this catalogue, the greater the percentage of that value is attributed to dealer mark up and profit margin. In many cases, such as the 25-cent minimum value, that price does not cover the labor or other costs involved with stocking it as an individual stamp. The sum of minimum values in a set does not properly represent the value of a complete set primarily composed of a number of minimum-value stamps, nor does the sum represent the actual value of a packet made up of minimum-value stamps. Thus a packet of 1,000 different common stamps — each of which has a catalogue value of 25 cents — normally sells for considerably less than $250!

The *absence of a retail value* for a stamp does not necessarily suggest that a stamp is scarce or rare. A dash in the value column means that the stamp is known in a stated form or variety, but information is either lacking or insufficient for purposes of establishing a usable catalogue value.

Stamp values in *italics* generally refer to items that are difficult to value accurately. For expensive items, such as those priced at $1,000 or higher, a value in italics indicates that the affected item trades very seldom. For inexpensive items, a value in italics represents a warning. One example is a "blocked" issue where the issuing postal administration may have controlled one stamp in a set in an attempt to make the whole set more valuable. Another example is an item that sold at an extreme multiple of face value in the marketplace at the time of its issue.

One type of warning to collectors that appears in the catalogue is illustrated by a stamp that is valued considerably higher in used condition than it is as unused. In this case, collectors are cautioned to be certain the used version has a genuine and contemporaneous cancellation. The type of cancellation on a stamp can be an important factor in determining its sale price. Catalogue values do not apply to fiscal, telegraph or non-contemporaneous postal cancels, unless otherwise noted.

Some countries have released back issues of stamps in canceled-to-order form, sometimes covering as much as a 10-year period. The Scott Catalogue values for used stamps reflect canceled-to-order material when such stamps are found to predominate in the marketplace for the issue involved. Notes frequently appear in the stamp listings to specify which items are valued as canceled-to-order, or if there is a premium for postally used examples.

Many countries sell canceled-to-order stamps at a marked reduction of face value. Countries that sell or have sold canceled-to-order stamps at *full* face value include United Nations, Australia, Netherlands, France and Switzerland. It may be almost impossible to identify such stamps if the gum has been removed, because official government canceling devices are used. Postally used examples of these items on cover, however, are usually worth more than the canceled-to-order stamps with original gum.

Abbreviations

Scott uses a consistent set of abbreviations throughout this catalogue to conserve space, while still providing necessary information.

Color Abbreviations

amb.......... amber
anil .... aniline
ap...............apple
aqua..aquamarine
az...............azure
bis............. bister
bl..................blue
bld............. blood
blk..............black
bril...........brilliant
brn .... brown
brnsh ....brownish
brnz.......... bronze
brt .... bright
brnt ....burnt
car..........carmine
cer............cerise
chlky .... chalky
cham......chamois
chnt........chestnut
choc.....chocolate
chr........... chrome
cit............. citron
cl................claret
cob........... cobalt
cop.......... copper
crim.........crimson
cr............. cream
dk............... dark
dl..................dull
dp .... deep
db .... drab
emer...... emerald
gldn......... golden
grysh........grayish
grn .... green
grnsh......greenish
hel....... heliotrope
hn.............henna
ind.............indigo
int............intense
lav ....lavender
lem............lemon
lil .... lilac
lt....................light
mag....... magenta
man..........manila
mar .... maroon
mv..............mauve
multi..multicolored
mlky .... milky
myr............myrtle
ol.................. olive
olvn .... olivine
org .... orange
pck.........peacock
pnksh ...... pinkish
Prus ....Prussian
pur .... purple
redsh........reddish
res............reseda
ros............rosine
ryl................royal
sal ....salmon
saph.......sapphire
scar...........scarlet
sep..............sepia
sien........... sienna
sil .... silver
sl.................slate
stl................steel
turq ...... turquoise
ultra... ultramarine
Ven.........Venetian
ver......... vermilion
vio............... violet
yel .... yellow
yelsh .....yellowish

When no color is given for an overprint or surcharge; black is the color used. Abbreviations for colors used for overprints and surcharges include: "(B)" or "(Blk)," black; "(Bl)," blue; "(R)," red; and "(G)," green.

Additional abbreviations in this catalogue are shown below:

Adm. ....Administration
AFL ....American Federation of Labor
Anniv.............Anniversary
APS..............American Philatelic Society
Assoc............Association
ASSR. ....Autonomous Soviet Socialist Republic
b...................Born
BEP..............Bureau of Engraving and Printing
Bicent. ....Bicentennial
Bklt. ....Booklet
Brit. ....British
btwn.............Between
Bur. ....Bureau
c. or ca. ....Circa
Cat. ....Catalogue
Cent. ....Centennial, century, centenary
CIO ....Congress of Industrial Organizations
Conf. ....Conference
Cong. ....Congress
Cpl. ....Corporal
CTO ....Canceled to order
d...................Died
Dbl. ....Double
EDU ....Earliest documented use
Engr..............Engraved
Exhib............Exhibition
Expo. ....Exposition
Fed...............Federation
GB ....Great Britain
Gen. ....General
GPO.............General post office
Horiz. ....Horizontal
Imperf. ....Imperforate
Impt. ....Imprint
Intl................International
Invtd.............Inverted
L...................Left
Lieut., lt.........Lieutenant
Litho.............Lithographed
LL..................Lower left
LR ....Lower right
mm ....Millimeter
Ms................Manuscript
Natl. ....National
No.................Number
NY................New York
NYC ....New York City
Ovpt.............Overprint
Ovptd...........Overprinted
P ....Plate number
Perf. ....Perforated, perforation
Phil...............Philatelic
Photo. ....Photogravure
PO................Post office
Pr. ....Pair
P.R. ....Puerto Rico
Prec. ....Precancel, precanceled
Pres. ....President
PTT ....Post, Telephone and Telegraph
R ....Right
Rio ....Rio de Janeiro
Sgt. ....Sergeant
Soc. ....Society
Souv.............Souvenir
SSR..............Soviet Socialist Republic, see ASSR
St. ....Saint, street
Surch. ....Surcharge
Typo. ....Typographed
UL ....Upper left
Unwmkd. ....Unwatermarked
UPU ....Universal Postal Union
UR.................Upper Right
US.................United States
USPOD ....United States Post Office Department
USSR............Union of Soviet Socialist Republics
Vert. ....Vertical
VP ....Vice president
Wmk. ....Watermark
Wmkd. ....Watermarked
WWI ....World War I
WWII ....World War II

Examination

Amos Media Co. will not comment upon the genuineness, grade or condition of stamps, because of the time and responsibility involved. Rather, there are several expertizing groups that undertake this work for both collectors and dealers. Neither will Amos Media Co. appraise or identify philatelic material. The company cannot take responsibility for unsolicited stamps or covers sent by individuals.

All letters, emails, etc. are read attentively, but they are not always answered because of time considerations.

How to order from your dealer

When ordering stamps from a dealer, it is not necessary to write the full description of a stamp as listed in this catalogue. All you need is the name of the country, the Scott catalogue number and whether the desired item is unused or used. For example, "Japan Scott 422 unused" is sufficient to identify the unused stamp of Japan listed as "422 A206 5y brown."

Basic stamp information

A stamp collector's knowledge of the combined elements that make a given stamp issue unique determines his or her ability to identify stamps. These elements include paper, watermark, method of separation, printing, design and gum. On the following pages each of these important areas is briefly described.

Paper

Paper is an organic material composed of a compacted weave of cellulose fibers and generally formed into sheets. Paper used to print stamps may be manufactured in sheets, or it may have been part of a large roll (called a web) before being cut to size. The fibers most often used to create paper on which stamps are printed include bark, wood, straw and certain grasses. In many cases, linen or cotton rags have been added for greater strength and durability. Grinding, bleaching, cooking and rinsing these raw fibers reduces them to a slushy pulp, referred to by paper makers as "stuff." Sizing and, sometimes, coloring matter is added to the pulp to make different types of finished paper.

After the stuff is prepared, it is poured onto sieve-like frames that allow the water to run off, while retaining the matted pulp. As fibers fall onto the screen and are held by gravity, they form a natural weave that will later hold the paper together. If the screen has metal bits that are formed into letters or images attached, it leaves slightly thinned areas on the paper. These are called watermarks.

When the stuff is almost dry, it is passed under pressure through smooth or engraved rollers — dandy rolls — or placed between cloth in a press to be flattened and dried.

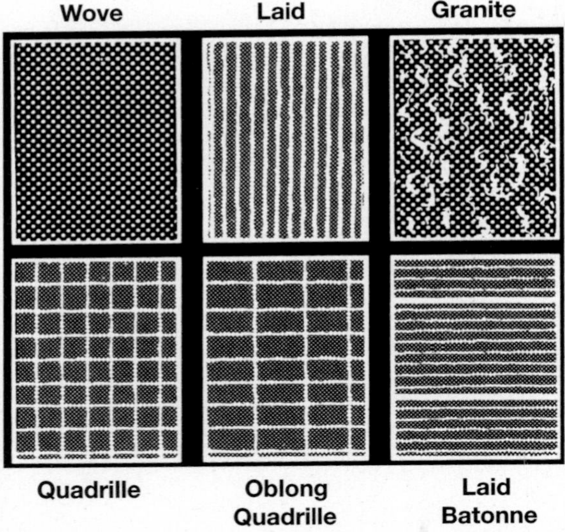

Stamp paper falls broadly into two types: wove and laid. The nature of the surface of the frame onto which the pulp is first deposited causes the differences in appearance between the two. If the surface is smooth and even, the paper will be of fairly uniform texture throughout. This is known as wove paper. Early papermaking machines poured the pulp onto a continuously circulating web of felt, but modern machines feed the pulp onto a cloth-like screen made of closely interwoven fine wires. This paper, when held to a light, will show little dots or points very close together. The proper name for this is "wire wove," but the type is still considered wove. Any U.S. or British stamp printed after 1880 will serve as an example of wire wove paper.

Closely spaced parallel wires, with cross wires at wider intervals, make up the frames used for what is known as laid paper. A greater thickness of the pulp will settle between the wires. The paper, when held to a light, will show alternate light and dark lines. The spacing and the thickness of the lines may vary, but on any one sheet of paper they are all alike. See Russia Scott 31-38 for examples of laid paper.

Batonne, from the French word meaning "a staff," is a term used if the lines in the paper are spaced quite far apart, like the printed ruling on a writing tablet. Batonne paper may be either wove or laid. If laid, fine laid lines can be seen between the batons.

Quadrille is the term used when the lines in the paper form little squares. Oblong quadrille is the term used when rectangles, rather than squares, are formed. Grid patterns vary from distinct to extremely faint. See Mexico-Guadalajara Scott 35-37 for examples of oblong quadrille paper.

Paper also is classified as thick or thin, hard or soft, and by color. Such colors may include yellowish, greenish, bluish and reddish.

Brief explanations of other types of paper used for printing stamps, as well as examples, follow.

Colored — Colored paper is created by the addition of dye in the paper-making process. Such colors may include shades of yellow, green, blue and red. Surface-colored papers, most commonly used for British colonial issues in 1913-14, are created when coloring is added only to the surface during the finishing process. Stamps printed on surface-colored paper have white or uncolored backs, while true colored papers are colored through. See Jamaica Scott 71-73.

Pelure — Pelure paper is a very thin, hard and often brittle paper that is sometimes bluish or grayish in appearance. See Serbia Scott 169-170.

Native — This is a term applied to handmade papers used to produce some of the early stamps of the Indian states. Stamps printed on native paper may be expected to display various natural inclusions that are normal and do not negatively affect value. Japanese paper, originally made of mulberry fibers and rice flour, is part of this group. See Japan Scott 1-18.

Manila — This type of paper is often used to make stamped envelopes and wrappers. It is a coarse-textured stock, usually smooth on one side and rough on the other. A variety of colors of manila paper exist, but the most common range is yellowish-brown.

Silk — Introduced by the British in 1847 as a safeguard against counterfeiting, silk paper contains bits of colored silk thread scattered throughout. The density of these fibers varies greatly and can include as few as one fiber per stamp or hundreds. U.S. revenue Scott R152 is a good example of an easy-to-identify silk paper stamp.

Silk-thread paper has uninterrupted threads of colored silk arranged so that one or more threads run through the stamp or postal stationery. See Great Britain Scott 5-6 and Switzerland Scott 14-19.

Granite — Filled with minute cloth or colored paper fibers of various colors and lengths, granite paper should not be confused with either type of silk paper. Austria Scott 172-175 and a number of Swiss stamps are examples of granite paper.

Chalky — A chalk-like substance coats the surface of chalky paper to discourage the cleaning and reuse of canceled stamps, as well as to provide a smoother, more acceptable printing surface. Because the designs of stamps printed on chalky paper are imprinted on what is often a water-soluble coating, any attempt to remove a cancellation will destroy the stamp. Do not soak these stamps in any fluid. To remove a stamp printed on chalky paper from an envelope, wet the paper from underneath the stamp until the gum dissolves enough to release the stamp from the paper. See St. Kitts-Nevis Scott 89-90 for examples of stamps printed on this type of chalky paper.

India — Another name for this paper, originally introduced from China about 1750, is "China Paper." It is a thin, opaque paper often used for plate and die proofs by many countries.

Double — In philately, the term double paper has two distinct meanings. The first is a two-ply paper, usually a combination of a thick and a thin sheet, joined during manufacture. This type was used experimentally as a means to discourage the reuse of stamps.

The design is printed on the thin paper. Any attempt to remove a cancellation would destroy the design. U.S. Scott 158 and other Banknote-era stamps exist on this form of double paper.

The second type of double paper occurs on a rotary press, when the end of one paper roll, or web, is affixed to the next roll to save time feeding the paper through the press. Stamp designs are printed over the joined paper and, if overlooked by inspectors, may get into post office stocks.

Goldbeater's Skin — This type of paper was used for the 1866 issue of Prussia, and was a tough, translucent paper. The design was printed in reverse on the back of the stamp, and the gum applied over the printing. It is impossible to remove stamps printed on this type of paper from the paper to which they are affixed without destroying the design.

Ribbed — Ribbed paper has an uneven, corrugated surface made by passing the paper through ridged rollers. This type exists on some copies of U.S. Scott 156-165.

Various other substances, or substrates, have been used for stamp manufacture, including wood, aluminum, copper, silver and gold foil, plastic, and silk and cotton fabrics.

Watermarks

Watermarks are an integral part of some papers. They are formed in the process of paper manufacture. Watermarks consist of small designs, formed of wire or cut from metal and soldered to the surface of the mold or, sometimes, on the dandy roll. The designs may be in the form of crowns, stars, anchors, letters or other characters or symbols. These pieces of metal — known in the paper-making industry as "bits" — impress a design into the paper. The design sometimes may be seen by holding the stamp to the light. Some are more easily seen with a watermark detector. This important tool is a small black tray into which a stamp is placed face down and dampened with a fast-evaporating watermark detection fluid that brings up the watermark image in the form of dark lines against a lighter background. These dark lines are the thinner areas of the paper known as the watermark. Some watermarks are extremely difficult to locate, due to either a faint impression, watermark location or the color of the stamp. There also are electric watermark detectors that come with plastic filter disks of various colors. The disks neutralize the color of the stamp, permitting the watermark to be seen more easily.

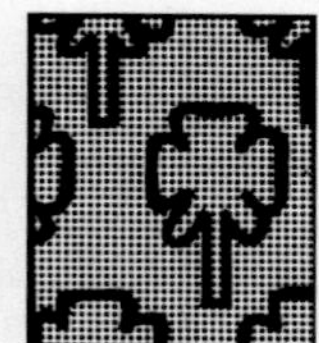

Multiple watermarks of Crown Agents and Burma

Watermarks of Uruguay, Vatican City and Jamaica

WARNING: Some inks used in the photogravure process dissolve in watermark fluids (Please see the section on Soluble Printing Inks). Also, see "chalky paper."

Watermarks may be found normal, reversed, inverted, reversed and inverted, sideways or diagonal, as seen from the back of the stamp. The relationship of watermark to stamp design depends on the position of the printing plates or how paper is fed through the press. On machine-made paper, watermarks normally are read from right to left. The design is repeated closely throughout the sheet in a "multiple-watermark design." In a "sheet watermark," the design appears only once on the sheet, but extends over many stamps. Individual stamps may carry only a small fraction or none of the watermark.

"Marginal watermarks" occur in the margins of sheets or panes of stamps. They occur on the outside border of paper (ostensibly outside the area where stamps are to be printed). A large row of letters may spell the name of the country or the manufacturer of the paper, or a border of lines may appear. Careless press feeding may cause parts of these letters and/or lines to show on stamps of the outer row of a pane.

Soluble printing inks

WARNING: Most stamp colors are permanent; that is, they are not seriously affected by short-term exposure to light or water. Many colors, especially of modern inks, fade from excessive exposure to light. There are stamps printed with inks that dissolve easily in water or in fluids used to detect watermarks. Use of these inks was intentional to prevent the removal of cancellations. Water affects all aniline inks, those on so-called safety paper and some photogravure printings - all such inks are known as fugitive colors. Removal from paper of such stamps requires care and alternatives to traditional soaking.

Separation

"Separation" is the general term used to describe methods used to separate stamps. The three standard forms currently in use are perforating, rouletting and die-cutting. These methods are done during the stamp production process, after printing. Sometimes these methods are done on-press or sometimes as a separate step. The earliest issues, such as the 1840 Penny Black of Great Britain (Scott 1), did not have any means provided for separation. It was expected the stamps would be cut apart with scissors or folded and torn. These are examples of imperforate stamps. Many stamps were first issued in imperforate formats and were later issued with perforations. Therefore, care must be observed in buying single imperforate stamps to be certain they were issued imperforate and are not perforated copies that have been altered by having the perforations trimmed away. Stamps issued imperforate usually are valued as singles. However, imperforate varieties of normally perforated stamps should be collected in pairs or larger pieces as indisputable evidence of their imperforate character.

PERFORATION

The chief style of separation of stamps, and the one that is in almost universal use today, is perforating. By this process, paper between the stamps is cut away in a line of holes, usually round, leaving little bridges of paper between the stamps to hold them together. Some types of perforation, such as hyphen-hole perfs, can be confused with roulettes, but a close visual inspection reveals that paper has been removed. The little perforation bridges, which project from the stamp when it is torn from the pane, are called the teeth of the perforation.

As the size of the perforation is sometimes the only way to differentiate between two otherwise identical stamps, it is necessary to be able to accurately measure and describe them. This is done with a perforation gauge, usually a ruler-like device that has dots or graduated lines to show how many perforations may be counted in the space of two centimeters. Two centimeters is the space universally adopted in which to measure perforations.

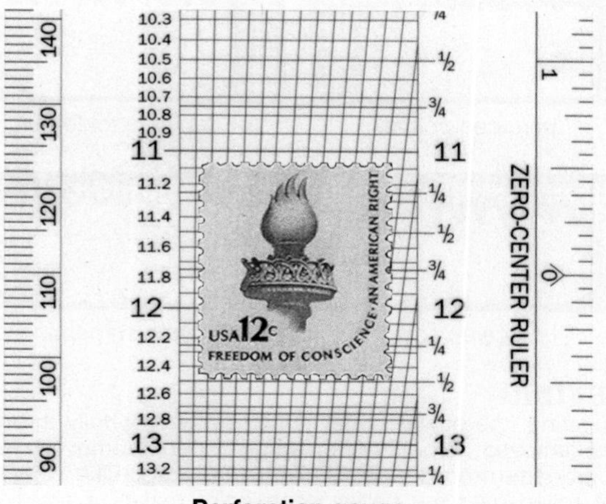

Perforation gauge

To measure a stamp, run it along the gauge until the dots on it fit exactly into the perforations of the stamp. If you are using a graduated-line perforation gauge, simply slide the stamp along the surface until the lines on the gauge perfectly project from the center of the bridges or holes. The number to the side of the line of dots or lines that fit the stamp's perforation is the measurement. For example, an "11" means that 11 perforations fit between two centimeters. The description of the stamp therefore is "perf. 11." If the gauge of the perforations on the top and bottom of a stamp differs from that on the sides, the result is what is known as compound perforations. In measuring compound perforations, the gauge at top and bottom is always given first, then the sides. Thus, a stamp that measures 11 at top and bottom and 10½ at the sides is "perf. 11 x 10½." See U.S. Scott 632-642 for examples of compound perforations.

Stamps also are known with perforations different on three or all four sides. Descriptions of such items are clockwise, beginning with the top of the stamp.

A perforation with small holes and teeth close together is a "fine perforation." One with large holes and teeth far apart is a "coarse perforation." Holes that are jagged, rather than clean-cut, are "rough perforations." *Blind perforations* are the slight impressions left by the perforating pins if they fail to puncture the paper. Multiples of stamps showing blind perforations may command a slight premium over normally perforated stamps.

The term *syncopated perfs* describes intentional irregularities in the perforations. The earliest form was used by the Netherlands from 1925-33, where holes were omitted to create distinctive patterns. Beginning in 1992, Great Britain has used an oval perforation to help prevent counterfeiting. Several other countries have started using the oval perfs or other syncopated perf patterns.

A new type of perforation, still primarily used for postal stationery, is known as microperfs. Microperfs are tiny perforations (in some cases hundreds of holes per two centimeters) that allows items to be intentionally separated very easily, while not accidentally breaking apart as easily as standard perforations. These are not currently measured or differentiated by size, as are standard perforations.

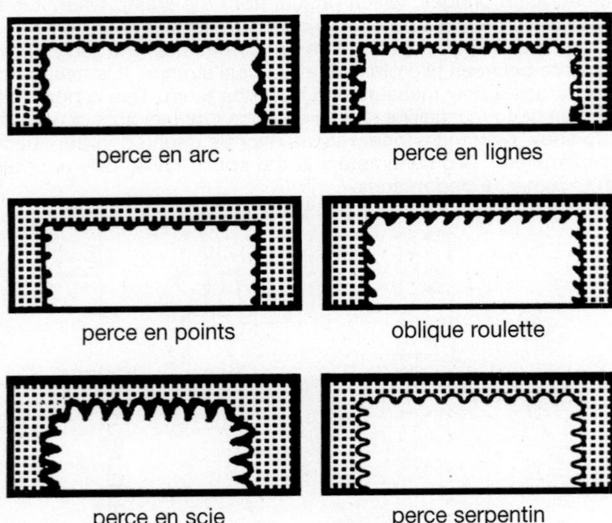

ROULETTING

In rouletting, the stamp paper is cut partly or wholly through, with no paper removed. In perforating, some paper is removed. Rouletting derives its name from the French roulette, a spur-like wheel. As the wheel is rolled over the paper, each point makes a small cut. The number of cuts made in a two-centimeter space determines the gauge of the roulette, just as the number of perforations in two centimeters determines the gauge of the perforation.

The shape and arrangement of the teeth on the wheels varies. Various roulette types generally carry French names:

Perce en lignes — rouletted in lines. The paper receives short, straight cuts in lines. This is the most common type of rouletting. See Mexico Scott 500.

Perce en points — pin-rouletted or pin-perfed. This differs from a small perforation because no paper is removed, although round, equidistant holes are pricked through the paper. See Mexico Scott 242-256.

Perce en arc and perce en scie — pierced in an arc or saw-toothed designs, forming half circles or small triangles. See Hanover (German States) Scott 25-29.

Perce en serpentin — serpentine roulettes. The cuts form a serpentine or wavy line. See Brunswick (German States) Scott 13-18.

Once again, no paper is removed by these processes, leaving the stamps easily separated, but closely attached.

DIE-CUTTING

The third major form of stamp separation is die-cutting. This is a method where a die in the pattern of separation is created that later cuts the stamp paper in a stroke motion. Although some standard stamps bear die-cut perforations, this process is primarily used for self-adhesive postage stamps. Die-cutting can appear in straight lines, such as U.S. Scott 2522, shapes, such as U.S. Scott 1551, or imitating the appearance of perforations, such as New Zealand Scott 935A and 935B.

Printing processes

ENGRAVING (Intaglio, Line-engraving, Etching)

Master die — The initial operation in the process of line engraving is making the master die. The die is a small, flat block of softened steel upon which the stamp design is recess engraved in reverse.

Photographic reduction of the original art is made to the appropriate size. It then serves as a tracing guide for the initial outline of the design. The engraver lightly traces the design on the steel with his graver, then slowly works the design until it is completed. At various points during the engraving process, the engraver hand-inks the die and makes an impression to check his progress. These are known as progressive die proofs. After completion of the engraving, the die is hardened to withstand the stress and pressures of later transfer operations.

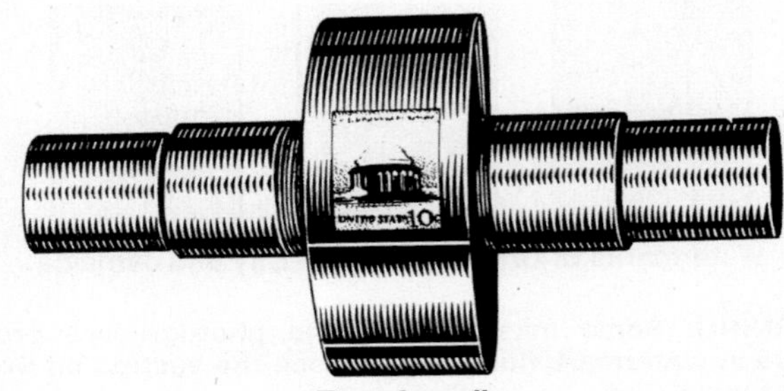

Transfer roll

Transfer roll — Next is production of the transfer roll that, as the name implies, is the medium used to transfer the subject from the master die to the printing plate. A blank roll of soft steel, mounted on a mandrel, is placed under the bearers of the transfer press to allow it to roll freely on its axis. The hardened die is placed on the bed of the press and the face of the transfer roll is applied to the die, under pressure. The bed or the roll is then rocked back and forth under increasing pressure, until the soft steel of the roll is forced into every engraved line of the die. The resulting impression on the roll is known as a "relief" or a "relief transfer." The engraved image is now positive in appearance and stands out from the steel. After the required number of reliefs are "rocked in," the soft steel transfer roll is hardened.

Different flaws may occur during the relief process. A defective relief may occur during the rocking in process because of a minute piece of foreign material lodging on the die, or some other cause. Imperfections in the steel of the transfer roll may result in a breaking away of parts of the design. This is known as a relief break, which will show up on finished stamps as small, unprinted areas. If a damaged relief remains in use, it will transfer a repeating defect to the plate. Deliberate alterations of reliefs sometimes occur. "Altered reliefs" designate these changed conditions.

Plate — The final step in pre-printing production is the making of the printing plate. A flat piece of soft steel replaces the die on the bed of the transfer press. One of the reliefs on the transfer roll is positioned over this soft steel. Position, or layout, dots determine the correct position on the plate. The dots have been lightly marked on the plate in advance. After the correct position of the relief is determined, the design is rocked in by following the same method used in making the transfer roll. The difference is that this time the image is being transferred from the transfer roll, rather than to it. Once the design is entered on the plate, it appears in reverse and is recessed. There are as many transfers entered on the plate as there are subjects printed on the sheet of stamps. It is during this process that double and shifted transfers occur, as well as re-entries. These are the result of improperly entered images that have not been properly burnished out prior to rocking in a new image.

Modern siderography processes, such as those used by the U.S. Bureau of Engraving and Printing, involve an automated form of rocking designs in on preformed cylindrical printing sleeves. The same process also allows for easier removal and re-entry of worn images right on the sleeve.

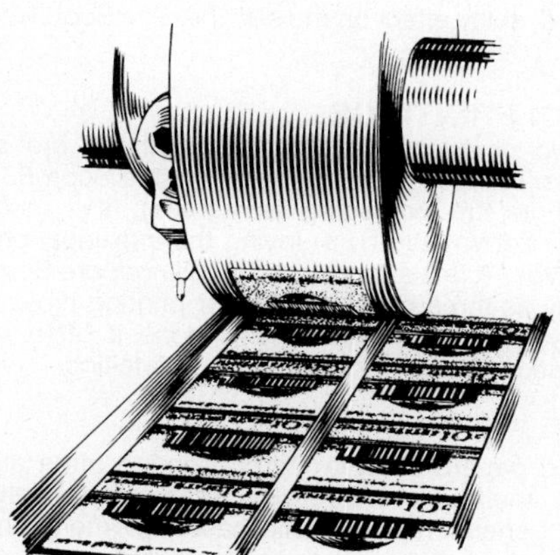

Transferring the design to the plate

Following the entering of the required transfers on the plate, the position dots, layout dots and lines, scratches and other markings generally are burnished out. Added at this time by the siderographer are any required guide lines, plate numbers or other marginal markings. The plate is then hand-inked and a proof impression is taken. This is known as a plate proof. If the impression is approved, the plate is machined for fitting onto the press, is hardened and sent to the plate vault ready for use.

On press, the plate is inked and the surface is automatically wiped clean, leaving ink only in the recessed lines. Paper is then forced under pressure into the engraved recessed lines, thereby receiving the ink. Thus, the ink lines on engraved stamps are slightly raised, and slight depressions (debossing) occur on the back of the stamp. Prior to the advent of modern high-speed presses and more advanced ink formulations, paper had to be dampened before receiving the ink. This sometimes led to uneven shrinkage by the time the stamps were perforated, resulting in improperly perforated stamps, or misperfs. Newer presses use drier paper, thus both *wet and dry printings* exist on some stamps.

Rotary Press — Until 1914, only flat plates were used to print engraved stamps. Rotary press printing was introduced in 1914, and slowly spread. Some countries still use flat-plate printing.

After approval of the plate proof, older rotary press plates require additional machining. They are curved to fit the press cylinder. "Gripper slots" are cut into the back of each plate to receive the "grippers," which hold the plate securely on the press. The plate is then hardened. Stamps printed from these bent rotary press plates are longer or wider than the same stamps printed from flat-plate presses. The stretching of the plate during the curving process is what causes this distortion.

Re-entry — To execute a re-entry on a flat plate, the transfer roll is re-applied to the plate, often at some time after its first use on the press. Worn-out designs can be resharpened by carefully burnishing out the original image and re-entering it from the transfer roll. If the original impression has not been sufficiently removed and the transfer roll is not precisely in line with the remaining impression, the resulting double transfer will make the re-entry obvious. If the registration is true, a re-entry may be difficult or impossible to distinguish. Sometimes a stamp printed from a successful re-entry is identified by having a much sharper and clearer impression than its neighbors. With the advent of rotary presses, post-press re-entries were not possible. After a plate was curved for the rotary press, it was impossible to make a re-entry. This is because the plate had already been bent once (with the design distorted).

However, with the introduction of the previously mentioned modern-style siderography machines, entries are made to the preformed cylindrical printing sleeve. Such sleeves are dechromed and softened. This allows individual images to be burnished out and re-entered on the curved sleeve. The sleeve is then rechromed, resulting in longer press life.

Double Transfer — This is a description of the condition of a transfer on a plate that shows evidence of a duplication of all, or a portion of the design. It usually is the result of the changing of the registration between the transfer roll and the plate during the rocking in of the original entry. Double transfers also occur when only a portion of the design has been rocked in and improper positioning is noted. If the worker elected not to burnish out the partial or completed design, a strong double transfer will occur for part or all of the design.

It sometimes is necessary to remove the original transfer from a plate and repeat the process a second time. If the finished re-worked image shows traces of the original impression, attributable to incomplete burnishing, the result is a partial double transfer.

With the modern automatic machines mentioned previously, double transfers are all but impossible to create. Those partially doubled images on stamps printed from such sleeves are more than likely re-entries, rather than true double transfers.

Re-engraved — Alterations to a stamp design are sometimes necessary after some stamps have been printed. In some cases, either the original die or the actual printing plate may have its "temper" drawn (softened), and the design will be re-cut. The resulting impressions from such a re-engraved die or plate may differ slightly from the original issue, and are known as "re-engraved." If the alteration was made to the master die, all future printings will be consistently different from the original. If alterations were made to the printing plate, each altered stamp on the plate will be slightly different from each other, allowing specialists to reconstruct a complete printing plate.

Dropped Transfers — If an impression from the transfer roll has not been properly placed, a dropped transfer may occur. The final stamp image will appear obviously out of line with its neighbors.

Short Transfer — Sometimes a transfer roll is not rocked its entire length when entering a transfer onto a plate. As a result, the finished transfer on the plate fails to show the complete design, and the finished stamp will have an incomplete design printed. This is known as a "short transfer." U.S. Scott No. 8 is a good example of a short transfer.

TYPOGRAPHY (Letterpress, Surface Printing, Flexography, Dry Offset, High Etch)

Although the word "Typography" is obsolete as a term describing a printing method, it was the accepted term throughout the first century of postage stamps. Therefore, appropriate Scott listings in this catalogue refer to typographed stamps. The current term for this form of printing, however, is "letterpress."

As it relates to the production of postage stamps, letterpress printing is the reverse of engraving. Rather than having recessed areas trap the ink and deposit it on paper, only the raised areas of the design are inked. This is comparable to the type of printing seen by inking and using an ordinary rubber stamp. Letterpress includes all printing where the design is above the surface area, whether it is wood, metal or, in some instances, hardened rubber or polymer plastic.

For most letterpress-printed stamps, the engraved master is made in much the same manner as for engraved stamps. In this instance, however, an additional step is needed. The design is transferred to another surface before being transferred to the transfer roll. In this way, the transfer roll has a recessed stamp design, rather than one done in relief. This makes the printing areas on the final plate raised, or relief areas.

For less-detailed stamps of the 19th century, the area on the die not used as a printing surface was cut away, leaving the surface area raised. The original die was then reproduced by stereotyping or electrotyping. The resulting electrotypes were assembled in the required number and format of the desired sheet of stamps. The plate used in printing the stamps was an electroplate of these assembled electrotypes.

Once the final letterpress plates are created, ink is applied to the raised surface and the pressure of the press transfers the ink impression to the paper. In contrast to engraving, the fine lines of letterpress are impressed on the surface of the stamp, leaving a debossed surface. When viewed from the back (as on a typewritten page), the corresponding line work on the stamp will be raised slightly (embossed) above the surface.

PHOTOGRAVURE (Gravure, Rotogravure, Heliogravure)

In this process, the basic principles of photography are applied to a chemically sensitized metal plate, rather than photographic paper. The design is transferred photographically to the plate through a halftone, or dot-matrix screen, breaking the reproduction into tiny dots. The plate is treated chemically and the dots form depressions, called cells, of varying depths and diameters, depending on the degrees of shade in the design. Then, like engraving, ink is applied to the plate and the surface is wiped clean. This leaves ink in the tiny cells that is lifted out and deposited on the paper when it is pressed against the plate.

Gravure is most often used for multicolored stamps, generally using the three primary colors (red, yellow and blue) and black. By varying the dot matrix pattern and density of these colors, virtually any color can be reproduced. A typical full-color gravure stamp will be created from four printing cylinders (one for each color). The original multicolored image will have been photographically separated into its component colors.

Modern gravure printing may use computer-generated dot-matrix screens, and modern plates may be of various types including metal-coated plastic. The catalogue designation of Photogravure (or "Photo") covers any of these older and more modern gravure methods of printing.

For examples of the first photogravure stamps printed (1914), see Bavaria Scott 94-114.

LITHOGRAPHY (Offset Lithography, Stone Lithography, Dilitho, Planography, Collotype)

The principle that oil and water do not mix is the basis for lithography. The stamp design is drawn by hand or transferred from engraving to the surface of a lithographic stone or metal plate in a greasy (oily) substance. This oily substance holds the ink, which will later be transferred to the paper. The stone (or plate) is wet with an acid fluid, causing it to repel the printing ink in all areas not covered by the greasy substance.

Transfer paper is used to transfer the design from the original stone or plate. A series of duplicate transfers are grouped and, in turn, transferred to the final printing plate.

Photolithography — The application of photographic processes to lithography. This process allows greater flexibility of design, related to use of halftone screens combined with line work. Unlike photogravure or engraving, this process can allow large, solid areas to be printed.

Offset — A refinement of the lithographic process. A rubber-covered blanket cylinder takes the impression from the inked lithographic plate. From the "blanket" the impression is offset or transferred to the paper. Greater flexibility and speed are the principal reasons offset printing has largely displaced lithography. The term "lithography" covers both processes, and results are almost identical.

EMBOSSED (Relief) Printing

Embossing, not considered one of the four main printing types, is a method in which the design first is sunk into the metal of the die. Printing is done against a yielding platen, such as leather or linoleum. The platen is forced into the depression of the die, thus forming the design on the paper in relief. This process is often used for metallic inks.

Embossing may be done without color (see Sardinia Scott 4-6); with color printed around the embossed area (see Great Britain Scott 5 and most U.S. envelopes); and with color in exact registration with the embossed subject (see Canada Scott 656-657).

HOLOGRAMS

For objects to appear as holograms on stamps, a model exactly the same size as it is to appear on the hologram must be created. Rather than using photographic film to capture the image, holography records an image on a photoresist material. In processing, chemicals eat away at certain exposed areas, leaving a pattern of constructive and destructive interference. When the photoresist is developed, the result is a pattern of uneven ridges that acts as a mold. This mold is then coated with metal, and the resulting form is used to press copies in much the same way phonograph records are produced.

A typical reflective hologram used for stamps consists of a reproduction of the uneven patterns on a plastic film that is applied to a reflective background, usually a silver or gold foil. Light is reflected off the background through the film, making the pattern present on the film visible. Because of the uneven pattern of the film, the viewer will perceive the objects in their proper three-dimensional relationships with appropriate brightness. The first hologram on a stamp was produced by Austria in 1988 (Scott 1441).

FOIL APPLICATION

A modern technique of applying color to stamps involves the application of metallic foil to the stamp paper. A pattern of foil is applied to the stamp paper by use of a stamping die. The foil usually is flat, but it may be textured. Canada Scott 1735 has three different foil applications in pearl, bronze and gold. The gold foil was textured using a chemical-etch copper embossing die. The printing of this stamp also involved two-color offset lithography plus embossing.

THERMOGRAPHY

In the 1990s stamps began to be enhanced with thermographic printing. In this process, a powdered polymer is applied over a sheet that has just been printed. The powder adheres to ink that lacks drying or hardening agents and does not adhere to areas where the ink has these agents. The excess powder is removed and the sheet is briefly heated to melt the powder. The melted powder solidifies after cooling, producing a raised, shiny effect on the stamps. See Scott New Caledonia C239-C240.

COMBINATION PRINTINGS

Sometimes two or even three printing methods are combined in producing stamps. In these cases, such as Austria Scott 933 or Canada 1735 (described in the preceding paragraph), the multiple-printing technique can be determined by studying the individual characteristics of each printing type. A few stamps, such as Singapore Scott 684-684A, combine as many as three of the four major printing types (lithography, engraving and typography). When this is done it often indicates the incorporation of security devices against counterfeiting.

INK COLORS

Inks or colored papers used in stamp printing often are of mineral origin, although there are numerous examples of organic-based pigments. As a general rule, organic-based pigments are far more subject to varieties and change than those of mineral-based origin.

The appearance of any given color on a stamp may be affected by many aspects, including printing variations, light, color of paper, aging and chemical alterations.

Numerous printing variations may be observed. Heavier pressure or inking will cause a more intense color, while slight interruptions in the ink feed or lighter impressions will cause a lighter appearance. Stamps printed in the same color by water-based and solvent-based inks can differ significantly in appearance. This affects several stamps in the U.S. Prominent Americans series. Hand-mixed ink formulas (primarily from the 19th century) produced under different conditions (humidity and temperature) account for notable color variations in early printings of the same stamp (see U.S. Scott 248-250, 279B, for example). Different sources of pigment can also result in significant differences in color.

Light exposure and aging are closely related in the way they affect stamp color. Both eventually break down the ink and fade colors, so that a carefully kept stamp may differ significantly in color from an identical copy that has been exposed to light. If stamps are exposed to light either intentionally or accidentally, their colors can be faded or completely changed in some cases.

Papers of different quality and consistency used for the same stamp printing may affect color appearance. Most pelure papers, for example, show a richer color when compared with wove or laid papers. See Russia Scott 181a, for an example of this effect.

The very nature of the printing processes can cause a variety of differences in shades or hues of the same stamp. Some of these shades are scarcer than others, and are of particular interest to the advanced collector.

Luminescence

All forms of tagged stamps fall under the general category of luminescence. Within this broad category is fluorescence, dealing with forms of tagging visible under longwave ultraviolet light, and phosphorescence, which deals with tagging visible only under shortwave light. Phosphorescence leaves an afterglow and fluorescence does not. These treated stamps show up in a range of different colors when exposed to UV light. The differing wavelengths of the light activates the tagging material, making it glow in various colors that usually serve different mail processing purposes.

Intentional tagging is a post-World War II phenomenon, brought about by the increased literacy rate and rapidly growing mail volume. It was one of several answers to the problem of the need for more automated mail processes. Early tagged stamps served the purpose of triggering machines to separate different types of mail. A natural outgrowth was to also use the signal to trigger machines that faced all envelopes the same way and canceled them.

Tagged stamps come in many different forms. Some tagged stamps have luminescent shapes or images imprinted on them as a form of security device. Others have blocks (United States), stripes, frames (South Africa and Canada), overall coatings (United States), bars (Great Britain and Canada) and many other types. Some types of tagging are even mixed in with the pigmented printing ink (Australia Scott 366, Netherlands Scott 478 and U.S. Scott 1359 and 2443).

The means of applying taggant to stamps differs as much as the intended purposes for the stamps. The most common form of tagging is a coating applied to the surface of the printed stamp. Since the taggant ink is frequently invisible except under UV light, it does not interfere with the appearance of the stamp. Another common application is the use of phosphored papers. In this case the paper itself either has a coating of taggant applied before the stamp is printed, has taggant applied during the papermaking process (incorporating it into the fibers), or has the taggant mixed into the coating of the paper. The latter method, among others, is currently in use in the United States.

Many countries now use tagging in various forms to either expedite mail handling or to serve as a printing security device against counterfeiting. Following the introduction of tagged stamps for public use in 1959 by Great Britain, other countries have steadily joined the parade. Among those are Germany (1961); Canada and Denmark (1962); United States, Australia, France and Switzerland (1963); Belgium and Japan (1966); Sweden and Norway (1967); Italy (1968); and Russia (1969). Since then, many other countries have begun using forms of tagging, including Brazil, China, Czechoslovakia, Hong Kong, Guatemala, Indonesia, Israel, Lithuania, Luxembourg, Netherlands, Penrhyn Islands, Portugal, St. Vincent, Singapore, South Africa, Spain and Sweden to name a few.

In some cases, including United States, Canada, Great Britain and Switzerland, stamps were released both with and without tagging. Many of these were released during each country's experimental period. Tagged and untagged versions are listed for the aforementioned countries and are noted in some other countries' listings. For at least a few stamps, the experimentally tagged version is worth far more than its untagged counterpart, such as the 1963 experimental tagged version of France Scott 1024.

In some cases, luminescent varieties of stamps were inadvertently created. Several Russian stamps, for example, sport highly fluorescent ink that was not intended as a form of tagging. Older stamps, such as early U.S. postage dues, can be positively identified by the use of UV light, since the organic ink used has become slightly fluorescent over time. Other stamps, such as Austria Scott 70a-82a (varnish bars) and Obock Scott 46-64 (printed quadrille lines), have become fluorescent over time.

Various fluorescent substances have been added to paper to make it appear brighter. These optical brightners, as they are known, greatly affect the appearance of the stamp under UV light. The brightest of these is known as Hi-Brite paper. These paper varieties are beyond the scope of the Scott Catalogue.

Shortwave UV light also is used extensively in expertizing, since each form of paper has its own fluorescent characteristics that are impossible to perfectly match. It is therefore a simple matter to detect filled thins, added perforation teeth and other alterations that involve the addition of paper. UV light also is used to examine stamps that have had cancels chemically removed and for other purposes as well.

Gum

The Illustrated Gum Chart in the first part of this introduction shows and defines various types of gum condition. Because gum condition has an important impact on the value of unused stamps, we recommend studying this chart and the accompanying text carefully.

The gum on the back of a stamp may be shiny, dull, smooth, rough, dark, white, colored or tinted. Most stamp gumming adhesives use gum arabic or dextrine as a base. Certain polymers such as polyvinyl alcohol (PVA) have been used extensively since World War II.

The *Scott Standard Postage Stamp Catalogue* does not list items by types of gum. The *Scott Specialized Catalogue of United States Stamps and Covers* does differentiate among some types of gum for certain issues.

Reprints of stamps may have gum differing from the original issues. In addition, some countries have used different gum formulas for different seasons. These adhesives have different properties that may become more apparent over time.

Many stamps have been issued without gum, and the catalogue will note this fact. See, for example, United States Scott 40-47. Sometimes, gum may have been removed to preserve the stamp. Germany Scott B68, for example, has a highly acidic gum that eventually destroys the stamps. This item is valued in the catalogue with gum removed.

Reprints and reissues

These are impressions of stamps (usually obsolete) made from the original plates or stones. If they are valid for postage and reproduce obsolete issues (such as U.S. Scott 102-111), the stamps are reissues. If they are from current issues, they are designated as *second, third,* etc., *printing*. If designated for a particular purpose, they are called *special printings*.

When special printings are not valid for postage, but are made from original dies and plates by authorized persons, they are *official reprints*. *Private reprints* are made from the original plates and dies by private hands. An example of a private reprint is that of the 1871-1932 reprints made from the original die of the 1845 New Haven, Conn., postmaster's provisional. *Official reproductions* or imitations are made from new dies and plates by government authorization. Scott will list those reissues that are valid for postage if they differ significantly from the original printing.

The U.S. government made special printings of its first postage stamps in 1875. Produced were official imitations of the first two stamps (listed as Scott 3-4), reprints of the demonetized pre-1861 issues (Scott 40-47) and reissues of the 1861 stamps, the 1869 stamps and the then-current 1875 denominations. Even though the official imitations and the reprints were not valid for postage, Scott lists all of these U.S. special printings.

Most reprints or reissues differ slightly from the original stamp in some characteristic, such as gum, paper, perforation, color or watermark. Sometimes the details are followed so meticulously that only a student of that specific stamp is able to distinguish the reprint or reissue from the original.

Remainders and canceled to order

Some countries sell their stock of old stamps when a new issue replaces them. To avoid postal use, the remainders usually are canceled with a punch hole, a heavy line or bar, or a more-or-less regular-looking cancellation. The most famous merchant of remainders was Nicholas F. Seebeck. In the 1880s and 1890s, he arranged printing contracts between the Hamilton Bank Note Co., of which he was a director, and several Central and South American countries. The contracts provided that the plates and all remainders of the yearly issues became the property of Hamilton. Seebeck saw to it that ample stock remained. The "Seebecks," both remainders and reprints, were standard packet fillers for decades.

Some countries also issue stamps *canceled-to-order (CTO)*, either in sheets with original gum or stuck onto pieces of paper or envelopes and canceled. Such CTO items generally are worth less than postally used stamps. In cases where the CTO material is far more prevalent in the marketplace than postally used examples, the catalogue value relates to the CTO examples, with postally used examples noted as premium items. Most CTOs can be detected by the presence of gum. However, as the CTO practice goes back at least to 1885, the gum inevitably has been soaked off some stamps so they could pass as postally used. The normally applied postmarks usually differ slightly from standard postmarks, and specialists are able to tell the difference. When applied individually to envelopes by philatelically minded persons, CTO material is known as *favor canceled* and generally sells at large discounts.

Cinderellas and facsimiles

Cinderella is a catch-all term used by stamp collectors to describe phantoms, fantasies, bogus items, municipal issues, exhibition seals, local revenues, transportation stamps, labels, poster stamps and many other types of items. Some cinderella collectors include in their collections local postage issues, telegraph stamps, essays and proofs, forgeries and counterfeits.

A *fantasy* is an adhesive created for a nonexistent stamp-issuing authority. Fantasy items range from imaginary countries (Occusi-Ambeno, Kingdom of Sedang, Principality of Trinidad or Torres Straits), to non-existent locals (Winans City Post), or nonexistent transportation lines (McRobish & Co.'s Acapulco-San Francisco Line).

On the other hand, if the entity exists and could have issued stamps (but did not) or was known to have issued other stamps, the items are considered bogus stamps. These would include the Mormon postage stamps of Utah, S. Allan Taylor's Guatemala and Paraguay inventions, the propaganda issues for the South Moluccas and the adhesives of the Page & Keyes local post of Boston.

Phantoms is another term for both fantasy and bogus issues.

Facsimiles are copies or imitations made to represent original stamps, but which do not pretend to be originals. A catalogue illustration is such a facsimile. Illustrations from the Moens catalogue of the last century were occasionally colored and passed off as stamps. Since the beginning of stamp collecting, facsimiles have been made for collectors as space fillers or for reference. They often carry the word "facsimile," "falsch" (German), "sanko" or "mozo" (Japanese), or "faux" (French) overprinted on the face or stamped on the back. Unfortunately, over the years a number of these items have had fake cancels applied over the facsimile notation and have been passed off as genuine.

Forgeries and counterfeits

Forgeries and counterfeits have been with philately virtually from the beginning of stamp production. Over time, the terminology for the two has been used interchangeably. Although both forgeries and counterfeits are reproductions of stamps, the purposes behind their creation differ considerably.

Among specialists there is an increasing movement to more specifically define such items. Although there is no universally accepted terminology, we feel the following definitions most closely mirror the items and their purposes as they are currently defined.

Forgeries (also often referred to as Counterfeits) are reproductions of genuine stamps that have been created to defraud collectors. Such spurious items first appeared on the market around 1860, and most old-time collections contain one or more. Many are crude and easily spotted, but some can deceive experts.

An important supplier of these early philatelic forgeries was the Hamburg printer Gebruder Spiro. Many others with reputations in this craft included S. Allan Taylor, George Hussey, James Chute, George Forune, Benjamin & Sarpy, Julius Goldner, E. Oneglia and L.H. Mercier. Among the noted 20th-century forgers were Francois Fournier, Jean Sperati and the prolific Raoul DeThuin.

Forgeries may be complete replications, or they may be genuine stamps altered to resemble a scarcer (and more valuable) type. Most forgeries, particularly those of rare stamps, are worth only a small fraction of the value of a genuine example, but a few types, created by some of the most notable forgers, such as Sperati, can be worth as much or more than the genuine. Fraudulently produced copies are known of most classic rarities and many medium-priced stamps.

In addition to rare stamps, large numbers of common 19th- and early 20th-century stamps were forged to supply stamps to the early packet trade. Many can still be easily found. Few new philatelic forgeries have appeared in recent decades. Successful imitation of well-engraved work is virtually impossible. It has proven far easier to produce a fake by altering a genuine stamp than to duplicate a stamp completely.

Counterfeit (also often referred to as Postal Counterfeit or Postal Forgery) is the term generally applied to reproductions of stamps that have been created to defraud the government of revenue. Such items usually are created at the time a stamp is current and, in some cases, are hard to detect. Because most counterfeits are seized when the perpetrator is captured, postal counterfeits, particularly used on cover, are usually worth much more than a genuine example to specialists. The first postal counterfeit was of Spain's 4-cuarto carmine of 1854 (the real one is Scott 25). Apparently, the counterfeiters were not satisfied with their first version, which is now very scarce, and they soon created an engraved counterfeit, which is common. Postal counterfeits quickly followed in Austria, Naples, Sardinia and the Roman States. They have since been created in many other countries as well, including the United States.

An infamous counterfeit to defraud the government is the 1-shilling Great Britain "Stock Exchange" forgery of 1872, used on telegraph forms at the exchange that year. The stamp escaped detection until a stamp dealer noticed it in 1898.

Fakes

Fakes are genuine stamps altered in some way to make them more desirable. One student of this part of stamp collecting has estimated that by the 1950s more than 30,000 varieties of fakes were known. That number has grown greatly since then. The widespread existence of fakes makes it important for stamp collectors to study their philatelic holdings and use relevant literature. Likewise, collectors should buy from reputable dealers who guarantee their stamps and make full and prompt refunds should a purchased item be declared faked or altered by some mutually agreed-upon authority. Because fakes always have some genuine characteristics, it is not always possible to obtain unanimous agreement among experts regarding specific items. These students may change their opinions as philatelic knowledge increases. More than 80 percent of all fakes on the philatelic market today are regummed, reperforated (or perforated for the first time), or bear forged overprints, surcharges or cancellations.

Stamps can be chemically treated to alter or eliminate colors. For example, a pale rose stamp can be re-colored to resemble a blue shade of high market value. In other cases, treated stamps can be made to resemble missing color varieties. Designs may be changed by painting, or a stroke or a dot added or bleached out to turn an ordinary variety into a seemingly scarcer stamp. Part of a stamp can be bleached and reprinted in a different version, achieving an inverted center or frame. Margins can be added or repairs done so deceptively that the stamps move from the "repaired" into the "fake" category.

Fakers have not left the backs of the stamps untouched either. They may create false watermarks, add fake grills or press out genuine grills. A thin India paper proof may be glued onto a thicker backing to create the appearance an issued stamp, or a proof printed on cardboard may be shaved down and perforated to resemble a stamp. Silk threads are impressed into paper and stamps have been split so that a rare paper variety is added to an otherwise inexpensive stamp. The most common treatment to the back of a stamp, however, is regumming.

Some in the business of faking stamps have openly advertised fool-proof application of "original gum" to stamps that lack it, although most publications now ban such ads from their pages. It is believed that very few early stamps have survived without being hinged. The large number of never-hinged examples of such earlier material offered for sale thus suggests the widespread extent of regumming activity. Regumming also may be used to hide repairs or thin spots. Dipping the stamp into watermark fluid, or examining it under longwave ultraviolet light often will reveal these flaws.

Fakers also tamper with separations. Ingenious ways to add margins are known. Perforated wide-margin stamps may be falsely represented as imperforate when trimmed. Reperforating is commonly done to create scarce coil or perforation varieties, and to eliminate the naturally occurring straight-edge stamps found in sheet margin positions of many earlier issues. Custom has made straight-edged stamps less desirable. Fakers have obliged by perforating straight-edged stamps so that many are now uncommon, if not rare.

Another fertile field for the faker is that of overprints, surcharges and cancellations. The forging of rare surcharges or overprints began in the 1880s or 1890s. These forgeries are sometimes difficult to detect, but experts have identified almost all. Occasionally, overprints or cancellations are removed to create non-overprinted stamps or seemingly unused items. This is most commonly done by removing a manuscript cancel to make a stamp resemble an unused example. "SPECIMEN" overprints may be removed by scraping and repainting to create non-overprinted varieties. Fakers use inexpensive revenues or pen-canceled stamps to generate unused stamps for further faking by adding other markings. The quartz lamp or UV lamp and a high-powered magnifying glass help to easily detect removed cancellations.

The bigger problem, however, is the addition of overprints, surcharges or cancellations — many with such precision that they are very difficult to ascertain. Plating of the stamps or the overprint can be an important method of detection.

Fake postmarks may range from many spurious fancy cancellations to a host of markings applied to transatlantic covers, to adding normally appearing postmarks to definitives of some countries with stamps that are valued far higher used than unused. With the increased popularity of cover collecting, and the widespread interest in postal history, a fertile new field for fakers has come about. Some have tried to create entire covers. Others specialize in adding stamps, tied by fake cancellations, to genuine stampless covers, or replacing less expensive or damaged stamps with more valuable ones. Detailed study of postal rates in effect at the time a cover in question was mailed, including the analysis of each handstamp used during the period, ink analysis and similar techniques, usually will unmask the fraud.

Restoration and repairs

Scott bases its catalogue values on stamps that are free of defects and otherwise meet the standards set forth earlier in this introduction. Most stamp collectors desire to have the finest copy of an item possible. Even within given grading categories there are variances. This leads to a controversial practice that is not defined in any universal manner: stamp *restoration*.

There are broad differences of opinion about what is permissible when it comes to restoration. Carefully applying a soft eraser to a stamp or cover to remove light soiling is one form of restoration, as is washing a stamp in mild soap and water to clean it. These are fairly accepted forms of restoration. More severe forms of restoration include pressing out creases or removing stains caused by tape. To what degree each of these is acceptable is dependent upon the individual situation. Further along the spectrum is the freshening of a stamp's color by removing oxide build-up or the effects of wax paper left next to stamps shipped to the tropics.

At some point in this spectrum the concept of *repair* replaces that of restoration. Repairs include filling thin spots, mending tears by reweaving or adding a missing perforation tooth. Regumming stamps may have been acceptable as a restoration or repair technique many decades ago, but today it is considered a form of fakery.

Restored stamps may or may not sell at a discount, and it is possible that the value of individual restored items may be enhanced over that of their pre-restoration state. Specific situations dictate the resultant value of such an item. Repaired stamps sell at substantial discounts from the value of sound stamps.

Terminology

Booklets — Many countries have issued stamps in small booklets for the convenience of users. This idea continues to become increasingly popular in many countries. Booklets have been issued in many sizes and forms, often with advertising on the covers, the panes of stamps or on the interleaving.

The panes used in booklets may be printed from special plates or made from regular sheets. All panes from booklets issued by the United States and many from those of other countries contain stamps that are straight edged on the sides, but perforated between. Others are distinguished by orientation of watermark or other identifying features. Any stamp-like unit in the pane, either printed or blank, that is not a postage stamp, is considered to be a *label* in the catalogue listings.

Scott lists and values booklet panes. Modern complete booklets also are listed and valued. Individual booklet panes are listed only when they are not fashioned from existing sheet stamps and, therefore, are identifiable from their sheet stamp counterparts.

Panes usually do not have a used value assigned to them because there is little market activity for used booklet panes, even though many exist used and there is some demand for them.

Cancellations — The marks or obliterations put on stamps by postal authorities to show that they have performed service and to prevent their reuse are known as cancellations. If the marking is made with a pen, it is considered a "pen cancel." When the location of the post office appears in the marking, it is a "town cancellation." A "postmark" is technically any postal marking, but in practice the term generally is applied to a town cancellation with a date. When calling attention to a cause or celebration, the marking is known as a "slogan cancellation." Many other types and styles of cancellations exist, such as duplex, numerals, targets, fancy and others. See also "precancels," below.

Coil Stamps — These are stamps that are issued in rolls for use in dispensers, affixing and vending machines. Those coils of the United States, Canada, Sweden and some other countries are perforated horizontally or vertically only, with the outer edges imperforate. Coil stamps of some countries, such as Great Britain and Germany, are perforated on all four sides and may in some cases be distinguished from their sheet stamp counterparts by watermarks, counting numbers on the reverse or other means.

Covers — Entire envelopes, with or without adhesive postage stamps, that have passed through the mail and bear postal or other markings of philatelic interest are known as covers. Before the introduction of envelopes in about 1840, people folded letters and wrote the address on the outside. Some people covered their letters with an extra sheet of paper on the outside for the address, producing the term "cover." Used airletter sheets, stamped envelopes and other items of postal stationery also are considered covers.

Errors — Stamps that have some major, consistent, unintentional deviation from the normal are considered errors. Errors include, but are not limited to, missing or wrong colors, wrong paper, wrong watermarks, inverted centers or frames on multicolor printing, inverted or missing surcharges or overprints, double impressions, missing perforations, unintentionally omitted tagging and others. Factually wrong or misspelled information, if it appears on all examples of a stamp, are not considered errors in the true sense of the word. They are errors of design. Inconsistent or randomly appearing items, such as misperfs or color shifts, are classified as freaks.

Color-Omitted Errors — This term refers to stamps where a missing color is caused by the complete failure of the printing plate to deliver ink to the stamp paper or any other paper. Generally, this is caused by the printing plate not being engaged on the press or the ink station running dry of ink during printing.

Color-Missing Errors — This term refers to stamps where a color or colors were printed somewhere but do not appear on the finished stamp. There are four different classes of color-missing errors, and the catalog indicates with a two-letter code appended to each such listing what caused the color to be missing. These codes are used only for the United States' color-missing error listings.

FO = A *foldover* of the stamp sheet during printing may block ink from appearing on the face of a stamp. Instead, the color will appear on the back of the foldover (where it might fall on the back of the selvage or perhaps a bit on the back of the stamp or on the back of another stamp. FO also will be used in the case of foldunders, where the paper may fold underneath the other stamp paper and the color will print on the platen.

EP = When the extraneous paper is removed, an unprinted area of stamp paper remains and may show a color or colors to be totally missing on the finished stamp.

CM = A misregistration of the printing plates during printing will result in a *color misregistration*, and such a misregistraion may result in a color not appearing on the finished stamp.

PS = *A perforation shift* after printing may remove a color from the finished stamp. Normally, this will occur on a row of stamps at the edge of the stamp pane.

Measurements – When measurements are given in the Scott catalogues for stamp size, grill size or any other reason, the first measurement given is always for the top and bottom dimension, while the second measurement will be for the sides (just as perforation gauges are measured). Thus, a stamp size of 15mm x 21mm will indicate a vertically oriented stamp 15mm wide at top and bottom, and 21mm tall at the sides. The same principle holds for measuring or counting items such as U.S. grills. A grill count of 22x18 points (B grill) indicates that there are 22 grill points across by 18 grill points down.

Overprints and Surcharges — Overprinting involves applying wording or design elements over an already existing stamp. Overprints can be used to alter the place of use (such as "Canal Zone" on U.S. stamps), to adapt them for a special purpose ("Porto" on Denmark's 1913-20 regular issues for use as postage due stamps, Scott J1-J7) or to commemorate a special occasion (United States Scott 647-648).

A *surcharge* is a form of overprint that changes or restates the face value of a stamp or piece of postal stationery.

Surcharges and overprints may be handstamped, typeset or, occasionally, lithographed or engraved. A few hand-written overprints and surcharges are known.

Personalized Stamps — In 1999, Australia issued stamps with se-tenant labels that could be personalized with pictures of the customer's choice. Other countries quickly followed suit, with some offering to print the selected picture on the stamp itself within a frame that was used exclusively for personalized issues. As the picture used on these stamps or labels vary, listings for such stamps are for any picture within the common frame (or any picture on a se-tenant label), be it a "generic" image or one produced especially for a customer, almost invariably at a premium price.

Precancels — Stamps that are canceled before they are placed in the mail are known as precancels. Precanceling usually is done to expedite the handling of large mailings and generally allow the affected mail pieces to skip certain phases of mail handling.

In the United States, precancellations generally identified the point of origin; that is, the city and state. This information appeared across the face of the stamp, usually centered between parallel lines. More recently, bureau precancels retained the parallel lines, but the city and state designations were dropped. Recent coils have a service inscription that is present on the original printing plate. These show the mail service paid for by the stamp. Since these stamps are not intended to receive further cancellations when used as intended, they are considered precancels. Such items often do not have parallel lines as part of the precancellation.

In France, the abbreviation *Affranchts* in a semicircle together with the word *Postes* is the general form of precancel in use. Belgian precancellations usually appear in a box in which the name of the city appears. Netherlands precancels have the name of the city enclosed between concentric circles, sometimes called a "lifesaver." Precancellations of other countries usually follow these patterns, but may be any arrangement of bars, boxes and city names.

Precancels are listed in the Scott catalogues only if the precancel changes the denomination (Belgium Scott 477-478); if the precanceled stamp is different from the non-precanceled version (such as untagged U.S. precancels); or if the stamp exists only precanceled (France Scott 1096-1099, U.S. Scott 2265).

Proofs and Essays — Proofs are impressions taken from an approved die, plate or stone in which the design and color are the same as the stamp issued to the public. Trial color proofs are impressions taken from approved dies, plates or stones in colors that vary from the final version. An essay is the impression of a design that differs in some way from the issued stamp. "Progressive die proofs" generally are considered to be essays.

Provisionals — These are stamps that are issued on short notice and intended for temporary use pending the arrival of regular issues. They usually are issued to meet such contingencies as changes in government or currency, shortage of necessary postage values or military occupation.

During the 1840s, postmasters in certain American cities issued stamps that were valid only at specific post offices. In 1861, postmasters of the Confederate States also issued stamps with limited validity. Both of these examples are known as "postmaster's provisionals."

Se-tenant — This term refers to an unsevered pair, strip or block of stamps that differ in design, denomination or overprint.

Unless the se-tenant item has a continuous design (see U.S. Scott 1451a, 1694a) the stamps do not have to be in the same order as shown in the catalogue (see U.S. Scott 2158a).

Specimens — The Universal Postal Union required member nations to send samples of all stamps they released into service to the International Bureau in Switzerland. Member nations of the UPU received these specimens as samples of what stamps were valid for postage. Many are overprinted, handstamped or initial-perforated "Specimen," "Canceled" or "Muestra." Some are marked with bars across the denominations (China-Taiwan), punched holes (Czechoslovakia) or back inscriptions (Mongolia).

Stamps distributed to government officials or for publicity purposes, and stamps submitted by private security printers for official approval, also may receive such defacements.

The previously described defacement markings prevent postal use, and all such items generally are known as "specimens."

Tete-Beche — This term describes a pair of stamps in which one is upside down in relation to the other. Some of these are the result of intentional sheet arrangements, such as Morocco Scott B10-B11. Others occurred when one or more electrotypes accidentally were placed upside down on the plate, such as Colombia Scott 57a. Separation of the tete-beche stamps, of course, destroys the tete beche variety.

Pronunciation Symbols

ə .... banana, collide, abut

ˈə, ˌə .... humdrum, abut

ə .... immediately preceding \l\, \n\, \m\, \ŋ\, as in battle, mitten, eaten, and sometimes open \ˈō-p^{ə}m\, lock and key \-^{ə}ŋ-\; immediately following \l\, \m\, \r\, as often in French table, prisme, titre

ər .... further, merger, bird

ˈər-, ˈə-r .... as in two different pronunciations of hurry \ˈhər-ē, ˈhə-rē\

a .... mat, map, mad, gag, snap, patch

ā .... day, fade, date, aorta, drape, cape

ä .... bother, cot, and, with most American speakers, father, cart

ȧ .... father as pronounced by speakers who do not rhyme it with *bother*; French patte

au̇ .... now, loud, out

b .... baby, rib

ch .... chin, nature \ˈnā-chər\

d .... did, adder

e .... bet, bed, peck

ˈē, ˌē .... beat, nosebleed, evenly, easy

ē .... easy, mealy

f .... fifty, cuff

g .... go, big, gift

h .... hat, ahead

hw .... whale as pronounced by those who do not have the same pronunciation for both *whale* and *wail*

i .... tip, banish, active

ī .... site, side, buy, tripe

j .... job, gem, edge, join, judge

k .... kin, cook, ache

k̲ .... German ich, Buch; one pronunciation of loch

l .... lily, pool

m .... murmur, dim, nymph

n .... no, own

^{n} .... indicates that a preceding vowel or diphthong is pronounced with the nasal passages open, as in French *un bon vin blanc* \œ^{n} -bō^{n} -va^{n} -blä^{n}\

ŋ .... sing \ˈsiŋ\, singer \ˈsiŋ-ər\, finger \ˈfiŋ-gər\, ink \ˈiŋk \

ō .... bone, know, beau

ȯ .... saw, all, gnaw, caught

œ .... French boeuf, German Hölle

œ̄ .... French feu, German Höhle

ȯi .... coin, destroy

p .... pepper, lip

r .... red, car, rarity

s .... source, less

sh .... as in shy, mission, machine, special (actually, this is a single sound, not two); with a hyphen between, two sounds as in *grasshopper* \ˈgras-ˌhä-pər\

t .... tie, attack, late, later, latter

th .... as in thin, ether (actually, this is a single sound, not two); with a hyphen between, two sounds as in *knighthood* \ˈnīt-ˌhu̇d\

t̲h̲ .... then, either, this (actually, this is a single sound, not two)

ü .... rule, youth, union \ˈyün-yən\, few \ˈfyü\

u̇ .... pull, wood, book, curable \ˈkyu̇r-ə-bəl\, fury \ˈfyu̇r-ē\

ue .... German füllen, hübsch

ue̅ .... French rue, German fühlen

v .... vivid, give

w .... we, away

y .... yard, young, cue \ˈkyü\, mute \ˈmyüt\, union \ˈyün-yən\

^{y} .... indicates that during the articulation of the sound represented by the preceding character the front of the tongue has substantially the position it has for the articulation of the first sound of *yard*, as in French *digne* \dēn^{y}\

z .... zone, raise

zh .... as in vision, azure \ˈa-zhər\ (actually, this is a single sound, not two); with a hyphen between, two sounds as in *hogshead* \ˈhȯgz-ˌhed, ˈhägz-\

\ .... slant line used in pairs to mark the beginning and end of a transcription: \ˈpen\

ˈ .... mark preceding a syllable with primary (strongest) stress: \ˈpen-mən-ˌship\

ˌ .... mark preceding a syllable with secondary (medium) stress: \ˈpen-mən-ˌship\

\- .... mark of syllable division

( ) .... indicate that what is symbolized between is present in some utterances but not in others: *factory* \ˈfak-t(ə-)rē\

÷ .... indicates that many regard as unacceptable the pronunciation variant immediately following: *cupola* \ˈkyü-pə-lə, ÷-ˌlō\

Currency conversion

Country	Dollar	Pound	S Franc	Yen	HK $	Euro	Cdn $	Aus $
Australia	1.5348	1.9362	1.7019	0.0101	0.1961	1.6553	1.1318	—
Canada	1.3561	1.7107	1.5038	0.0090	0.1733	1.4626	—	0.8836
European Union	0.9272	1.1697	1.0282	0.0061	0.1185	—	0.6837	0.6041
Hong Kong	7.8249	9.8710	8.6770	0.0517	—	8.4393	5.7701	5.0983
Japan	151.48	191.09	167.98	—	19.359	163.37	111.70	98.697
Switzerland	0.9018	1.1376	—	0.0060	0.1152	0.9726	0.6650	0.5876
United Kingdom	0.7927	—	0.8790	0.0052	0.1013	0.8549	0.5845	0.5165
United States	—	1.2615	1.1089	0.0066	0.1278	1.0785	0.7374	0.6516

Country	Currency	U.S. $ Equiv.
Namibia	dollar	.0529
Nauru	Australian dollar	.6516
Nepal	rupee	.0075
Netherlands	euro	1.0785
Nevis	East Caribbean dollar	.3704
New Caledonia	Community of French Pacific (CFP) franc	.0090
New Zealand	dollar	.5975
Nicaragua	cordoba	.0272
Niger	CFA franc	.0016
Nigeria	naira	.0007
Niue	New Zealand dollar	.5975
Norfolk Island	Australian dollar	.6516
Norway	krone	.0917
Oman	rial	2.5974
Pakistan	rupee	.0036
Palau	U.S. dollar	1.0000
Palestinian Authority	Jordanian dinar	1.4104
Panama	balboa	1.0000
Papua New Guinea	kina	.2651
Paraguay	guarani	.0001
Penrhyn Island	New Zealand dollar	.5975
Peru	new sol	.2688
Philippines	peso	.0178

Source: xe.com Apr. 1, 2024. Figures reflect values as of Apr. 1, 2024.

Vols. 5A-5B number additions, deletions and changes

Number in 2024 Catalogue	Number in 2025 Catalogue
New Republic	
reinstated	57C
North Borneo	
136a	136A
137a	137A
139a	138A
140a	140A
141a	141A
142a	142A
143a	143A
144a	144A
145a	145A
146a	146A
148a	148A
149a	149A
152c	152C
153c	153C
Philippines	
new	1238b
new	1678a
new	1679a
new	1755a
new	1862a
new	1973c
2218Cd	deleted
new	2781a
Portuguese Congo	
118	deleted
Russia	
4521	C108A
4600	C108B
Salvador, El	
13a	13b
new	13a
13b	13d
new	13c
13c	13f
new	13e
13d	13g

COMMON DESIGN TYPES

Pictured in this section are issues where one illustration has been used for a number of countries in the Catalogue. Not included in this section are overprinted stamps or those issues which are illustrated in each country. Because the location of Never Hinged breakpoints varies from country to country, some of the values in the listings below will be for unused stamps that were previously hinged.

EUROPA

Europa, 1956

The design symbolizing the cooperation among the six countries comprising the Coal and Steel Community is illustrated in each country.

Belgium	*496-497*
France	*805-806*
Germany	*748-749*
Italy	*715-716*
Luxembourg	*318-320*
Netherlands	*368-369*

Nos. 496-497 (2)	9.00	.50
Nos. 805-806 (2)	5.25	1.00
Nos. 748-749 (2)	7.40	1.10
Nos. 715-716 (2)	9.25	1.25
Nos. 318-320 (3)	65.50	42.00
Nos. 368-369 (2)	25.75	1.50
Set total (13) Stamps	122.15	47.35

Europa, 1958

"E" and Dove — CD1

European Postal Union at the service of European integration.

1958, Sept. 13

Belgium	527-528
France	889-890
Germany	790-791
Italy	750-751
Luxembourg	341-343
Netherlands	375-376
Saar	317-318

Nos. 527-528 (2)	3.75	.60
Nos. 889-890 (2)	1.65	.55
Nos. 790-791 (2)	2.95	.60
Nos. 750-751 (2)	1.05	.60
Nos. 341-343 (3)	1.35	.90
Nos. 375-376 (2)	1.25	.75
Nos. 317-318 (2)	1.05	2.30
Set total (15) Stamps	13.05	6.30

Europa, 1959

6-Link Enless Chain — CD2

1959, Sept. 19

Belgium	536-537
France	929-930
Germany	805-806
Italy	791-792
Luxembourg	354-355
Netherlands	379-380

Nos. 536-537 (2)	1.55	.60
Nos. 929-930 (2)	1.40	.80
Nos. 805-806 (2)	1.35	.60
Nos. 791-792 (2)	.80	.50
Nos. 354-355 (2)	2.65	1.00
Nos. 379-380 (2)	2.10	1.85
Set total (12) Stamps	9.85	5.35

Europa, 1960

19-Spoke Wheel — CD3

First anniverary of the establishment of C.E.P.T. (Conference Europeenne des Administrations des Postes et des Telecommunications.) The spokes symbolize the 19 founding members of the Conference.

1960, Sept.

Belgium	553-554
Denmark	379
Finland	376-377
France	970-971
Germany	818-820
Great Britain	377-378
Greece	688
Iceland	327-328
Ireland	175-176
Italy	809-810
Luxembourg	374-375
Netherlands	385-386
Norway	387
Portugal	866-867
Spain	941-942
Sweden	562-563
Switzerland	400-401
Turkey	1493-1494

Nos. 553-554 (2)	1.25	.55
No. 379 (1)	.55	.50
Nos. 376-377 (2)	1.80	1.40
Nos. 970-971 (2)	.50	.50
Nos. 818-820 (3)	1.90	1.35
Nos. 377-378 (2)	7.00	2.75
No. 688 (1)	4.25	1.75
Nos. 327-328 (2)	1.30	1.85
Nos. 175-176 (2)	*13.25*	*16.00*
Nos. 809-810 (2)	.50	.50
Nos. 374-375 (2)	1.00	.80
Nos. 385-386 (2)	2.00	2.00
No. 387 (1)	1.00	.80
Nos. 866-867 (2)	3.05	1.75
Nos. 941-942 (2)	1.50	.75
Nos. 562-563 (2)	1.05	.55
Nos. 400-401 (2)	1.75	.75
Nos. 1493-1494 (2)	2.10	1.35
Set total (34) Stamps	45.75	35.90

Europa, 1961

19 Doves Flying as One — CD4

The 19 doves represent the 19 members of the Conference of European Postal and Telecommunications Administrations C.E.P.T.

1961-62

Belgium	572-573
Cyprus	201-203
France	1005-1006
Germany	844-845
Great Britain	382-384
Greece	718-719
Iceland	340-341
Italy	845-846
Luxembourg	382-383
Netherlands	387-388
Spain	1010-1011
Switzerland	410-411
Turkey	1518-1520

Nos. 572-573 (2)	.75	.50
Nos. 201-203 (3)	*.90*	*.75*
Nos. 1005-1006 (2)	.50	.50
Nos. 844-845 (2)	.60	.75
Nos. 382-384 (3)	.75	.75
Nos. 718-719 (2)	.80	.50
Nos. 340-341 (2)	1.10	1.60
Nos. 845-846 (2)	.50	.50
Nos. 382-383 (2)	.55	.55
Nos. 387-388 (2)	.50	.50
Nos. 1010-1011 (2)	.60	.50
Nos. 410-411 (2)	1.90	.60
Nos. 1518-1520 (3)	1.55	.90
Set total (29) Stamps	11.00	8.90

Europa, 1962

Young Tree with 19 Leaves — CD5

The 19 leaves represent the 19 original members of C.E.P.T.

1962-63

Belgium	582-583
Cyprus	219-221
France	1045-1046
Germany	852-853
Greece	739-740
Iceland	348-349
Ireland	184-185
Italy	860-861
Luxembourg	386-387
Netherlands	394-395
Norway	414-415
Switzerland	416-417
Turkey	1553-1555

Nos. 582-583 (2)	.65	.65
Nos. 219-221 (3)	*21.35*	*6.75*
Nos. 1045-1046 (2)	.60	.50
Nos. 852-853 (2)	.65	.75
Nos. 739-740 (2)	2.00	1.15
Nos. 348-349 (2)	.85	.85
Nos. 184-185 (2)	1.45	2.75
Nos. 860-861 (2)	1.00	.55
Nos. 386-387 (2)	.75	.55
Nos. 394-395 (2)	1.35	.90
Nos. 414-415 (2)	1.75	1.70
Nos. 416-417 (2)	1.65	1.00
Nos. 1553-1555 (3)	*2.05*	1.10
Set total (28) Stamps	36.10	19.20

Europa, 1963

Stylized Links, Symbolizing Unity — CD6

1963, Sept.

Belgium	598-599
Cyprus	229-231
Finland	419
France	1074-1075
Germany	867-868
Greece	768-769
Iceland	357-358
Ireland	188-189
Italy	880-881
Luxembourg	403-404
Netherlands	416-417
Norway	441-442
Switzerland	429
Turkey	1602-1603

Nos. 598-599 (2)	1.60	.55
Nos. 229-231 (3)	*18.30*	*8.65*
No. 419 (1)	1.25	.55
Nos. 1074-1075 (2)	.60	.50
Nos. 867-868 (2)	.50	.55
Nos. 768-769 (2)	4.65	1.65
Nos. 357-358 (2)	1.20	1.20
Nos. 188-189 (2)	2.75	3.25
Nos. 880-881 (2)	.50	.50
Nos. 403-404 (2)	.75	.55
Nos. 416-417 (2)	1.30	1.00
Nos. 441-442 (2)	2.60	2.40
No. 429 (1)	.90	.60
Nos. 1602-1603 (2)	1.20	.50
Set total (27) Stamps	38.10	22.45

Europa, 1964

Symbolic Daisy — CD7

5th anniversary of the establishment of C.E.P.T. The 22 petals of the flower symbolize the 22 members of the Conference.

1964, Sept.

Austria	738
Belgium	614-615
Cyprus	244-246
France	1109-1110
Germany	897-898
Greece	801-802
Iceland	367-368
Ireland	196-197
Italy	894-895
Luxembourg	411-412
Monaco	590-591
Netherlands	428-429
Norway	458
Portugal	931-933
Spain	1262-1263
Switzerland	438-439
Turkey	1628-1629

No. 738 (1)	1.10	.25
Nos. 614-615 (2)	1.40	.60
Nos. 244-246 (3)	*10.95*	*5.00*
Nos. 1109-1110 (2)	.50	.50
Nos. 897-898 (2)	.50	.50
Nos. 801-802 (2)	4.15	1.55
Nos. 367-368 (2)	1.40	1.15
Nos. 196-197 (2)	4.50	4.25
Nos. 894-895 (2)	.50	.50
Nos. 411-412 (2)	.75	.55
Nos. 590-591 (2)	2.50	.70
Nos. 428-429 (2)	.75	.60
No. 458 (1)	3.50	3.50
Nos. 931-933 (3)	*10.00*	*2.00*
Nos. 1262-1263 (2)	1.15	.80
Nos. 438-439 (2)	1.65	.50
Nos. 1628-1629 (2)	2.00	.80
Set total (34) Stamps	47.30	23.75

Europa, 1965

Leaves and "Fruit" — CD8

1965

Belgium	636-637
Cyprus	262-264
Finland	437
France	1131-1132
Germany	934-935
Greece	833-834
Iceland	375-376
Ireland	204-205
Italy	915-916
Luxembourg	432-433
Monaco	616-617
Netherlands	438-439
Norway	475-476
Portugal	958-960
Switzerland	469
Turkey	1665-1666

Nos. 636-637 (2)	.50	.50
Nos. 262-264 (3)	*10.80*	*7.45*
No. 437 (1)	1.25	.55
Nos. 1131-1132 (2)	.70	.55
Nos. 934-935 (2)	.50	.50
Nos. 833-834 (2)	2.25	1.15
Nos. 375-376 (2)	2.50	1.75
Nos. 204-205 (2)	5.75	4.60
Nos. 915-916 (2)	.50	.50
Nos. 432-433 (2)	.75	.55
Nos. 616-617 (2)	3.25	1.65
Nos. 438-439 (2)	.55	.50
Nos. 475-476 (2)	2.40	1.90
Nos. 958-960 (3)	*16.00*	*2.75*
No. 469 (1)	1.15	.50
Nos. 1665-1666 (2)	2.00	1.25
Set total (32) Stamps	50.85	26.65

Europa, 1966

Symbolic Sailboat — CD9

1966, Sept.

Andorra, French	172
Belgium	675-676
Cyprus	275-277
France	1163-1164
Germany	963-964
Greece	862-863
Iceland	384-385
Ireland	216-217
Italy	942-943
Liechtenstein	415
Luxembourg	440-441
Monaco	639-640
Netherlands	441-442
Norway	496-497
Portugal	980-982
Switzerland	477-478
Turkey	1718-1719

No. 172 (1)	3.00	3.00
Nos. 675-676 (2)	.80	.50
Nos. 275-277 (3)	*3.10*	*3.25*
Nos. 1163-1164 (2)	.55	.50
Nos. 963-964 (2)	.50	.55
Nos. 862-863 (2)	2.10	1.05
Nos. 384-385 (2)	4.50	3.50
Nos. 216-217 (2)	2.35	3.75
Nos. 942-943 (2)	.50	.50
No. 415 (1)	.40	.35
Nos. 440-441 (2)	.70	.55
Nos. 639-640 (2)	2.00	.65
Nos. 441-442 (2)	.85	.50
Nos. 496-497 (2)	2.35	2.15
Nos. 980-982 (3)	*15.90*	2.25
Nos. 477-478 (2)	1.40	.60
Nos. 1718-1719 (2)	3.35	1.75
Set total (34) Stamps	44.35	25.40

Europa, 1967

Cogwheels — CD10

1967

Andorra, French 174-175
Belgium 688-689
Cyprus 297-299
France 1178-1179
Germany 969-970
Greece 891-892
Iceland 389-390
Ireland 232-233
Italy 951-952
Liechtenstein 420
Luxembourg 449-450
Monaco 669-670
Netherlands 444-447
Norway 504-505
Portugal 994-996
Spain 1465-1466
Switzerland 482
Turkey B120-B121

Nos. 174-175 (2)	10.75	6.25
Nos. 688-689 (2)	1.05	.55
Nos. 297-299 (3)	*2.55*	*2.90*
Nos. 1178-1179 (2)	.55	.50
Nos. 969-970 (2)	.55	.55
Nos. 891-892 (2)	3.05	.85
Nos. 389-390 (2)	3.00	2.00
Nos. 232-233 (2)	2.25	2.30
Nos. 951-952 (2)	.60	.50
No. 420 (1)	.45	.40
Nos. 449-450 (2)	1.00	.70
Nos. 669-670 (2)	2.75	.70
Nos. 444-447 (4)	2.70	2.05
Nos. 504-505 (2)	2.00	1.80
Nos. 994-996 (3)	*16.10*	1.85
Nos. 1465-1466 (2)	.50	.50
No. 482 (1)	.60	.30
Nos. B120-B121 (2)	2.50	2.00
Set total (38) Stamps	52.95	26.70

Europa, 1968

Golden Key with C.E.P.T. Emblem — CD11

1968

Andorra, French 182-183
Belgium 705-706
Cyprus 314-316
France 1209-1210
Germany 983-984
Greece 916-917
Iceland 395-396
Ireland 242-243
Italy 979-980
Liechtenstein 442
Luxembourg 466-467
Monaco 689-691
Netherlands 452-453
Portugal 1019-1021
San Marino 687
Spain 1526
Switzerland 488
Turkey 1775-1776

Nos. 182-183 (2)	16.50	10.00
Nos. 705-706 (2)	1.25	.50
Nos. 314-316 (3)	*1.70*	*2.90*
Nos. 1209-1210 (2)	.85	.55
Nos. 983-984 (2)	.50	.55
Nos. 916-917 (2)	3.10	1.45
Nos. 395-396 (2)	3.00	2.20
Nos. 242-243 (2)	2.50	1.70
Nos. 979-980 (2)	.50	.50
No. 442 (1)	.45	.40
Nos. 466-467 (2)	.80	.70
Nos. 689-691 (3)	*5.40*	.95
Nos. 452-453 (2)	1.05	.70
Nos. 1019-1021 (3)	*15.90*	2.10
No. 687 (1)	.55	.35
No. 1526 (1)	.25	.25
No. 488 (1)	.40	.25
Nos. 1775-1776 (2)	2.50	1.25
Set total (35) Stamps	57.20	27.30

Europa, 1969

"EUROPA" and "CEPT" — CD12

Tenth anniversary of C.E.P.T.

1969

Andorra, French 188-189
Austria 837
Belgium 718-719
Cyprus 326-328
Denmark 458
Finland 483
France 1245-1246
Germany 996-997
Great Britain 585
Greece 947-948
Iceland 406-407
Ireland 270-271
Italy 1000-1001
Liechtenstein 453
Luxembourg 475-476
Monaco 722-724
Netherlands 475-476
Norway 533-534
Portugal 1038-1040
San Marino 701-702
Spain 1567
Sweden 814-816
Switzerland 500-501
Turkey 1799-1800
Vatican 470-472
Yugoslavia 1003-1004

Nos. 188-189 (2)	18.50	12.00
No. 837 (1)	.55	.25
Nos. 718-719 (2)	.75	.50
Nos. 326-328 (3)	*1.60*	*2.70*
No. 458 (1)	.75	.75
No. 483 (1)	2.50	.60
Nos. 1245-1246 (2)	.55	.50
Nos. 996-997 (2)	.70	.50
No. 585 (1)	.25	.25
Nos. 947-948 (2)	4.00	1.25
Nos. 406-407 (2)	4.20	2.40
Nos. 270-271 (2)	2.00	2.00
Nos. 1000-1001 (2)	.50	.50
No. 453 (1)	.45	.45
Nos. 475-476 (2)	.95	.50
Nos. 722-724 (3)	*10.50*	2.00
Nos. 475-476 (2)	1.35	1.00
Nos. 533-534 (2)	2.20	1.95
Nos. 1038-1040 (3)	17.75	2.40
Nos. 701-702 (2)	.90	.90
No. 1567 (1)	.25	.25
Nos. 814-816 (3)	4.00	2.85
Nos. 500-501 (2)	1.85	1.00
Nos. 1799-1800 (2)	2.50	1.65
Nos. 470-472 (3)	.75	.75
Nos. 1003-1004 (2)	4.00	4.00
Set total (51) Stamps	84.30	43.90

Europa, 1970

Interwoven Threads — CD13

1970

Andorra, French 196-197
Belgium 741-742
Cyprus 340-342
France 1271-1272
Germany 1018-1019
Greece 985, 987
Iceland 420-421
Ireland 279-281
Italy 1013-1014
Liechtenstein 470
Luxembourg 489-490
Monaco 768-770
Netherlands 483-484
Portugal 1060-1062
San Marino 729-730
Spain 1607
Switzerland 515-516
Turkey 1848-1849
Yugoslavia 1024-1025

Nos. 196-197 (2)	20.00	8.50
Nos. 741-742 (2)	1.10	.55
Nos. 340-342 (3)	*1.70*	*2.75*
Nos. 1271-1272 (2)	.65	.50
Nos. 1018-1019 (2)	.60	.50
Nos. 985,987 (2)	6.35	1.60
Nos. 420-421 (2)	6.00	4.00
Nos. 279-281 (3)	2.55	2.50
Nos. 1013-1014 (2)	.50	.50
No. 470 (1)	.45	.45
Nos. 489-490 (2)	.80	.55
Nos. 768-770 (3)	*6.35*	2.10
Nos. 483-484 (2)	1.30	1.15
Nos. 1060-1062 (3)	*18.95*	2.35
Nos. 729-730 (2)	.90	.55
No. 1607 (1)	.25	.25
Nos. 515-516 (2)	1.85	.70
Nos. 1848-1849 (2)	2.50	1.50
Nos. 1024-1025 (2)	.80	.80
Set total (40) Stamps	73.60	31.80

Europa, 1971

"Fraternity, Cooperation, Common Effort" — CD14

1971

Andorra, French 205-206
Belgium 803-804
Cyprus 365-367
Finland 504
France 1304
Germany 1064-1065
Greece 1029-1030
Iceland 429-430
Ireland 305-306
Italy 1038-1039
Liechtenstein 485
Luxembourg 500-501
Malta 425-427
Monaco 797-799
Netherlands 488-489
Portugal 1094-1096
San Marino 749-750
Spain 1675-1676
Switzerland 531-532
Turkey 1876-1877
Yugoslavia 1052-1053

Nos. 205-206 (2)	20.00	7.75
Nos. 803-804 (2)	1.30	.55
Nos. 365-367 (3)	*1.80*	*2.75*
No. 504 (1)	2.50	.50
No. 1304 (1)	.45	.40
Nos. 1064-1065 (2)	.60	.50
Nos. 1029-1030 (2)	4.00	1.80
Nos. 429-430 (2)	5.00	3.75
Nos. 305-306 (2)	2.45	1.50
Nos. 1038-1039 (2)	.65	.50
No. 485 (1)	.45	.45
Nos. 500-501 (2)	1.00	.65
Nos. 425-427 (3)	*1.25*	*1.70*
Nos. 797-799 (3)	*15.00*	2.80
Nos. 488-489 (2)	1.20	.95
Nos. 1094-1096 (3)	*16.15*	1.75
Nos. 749-750 (2)	.65	.55
Nos. 1675-1676 (2)	.75	.55
Nos. 531-532 (2)	1.85	.65
Nos. 1876-1877 (2)	2.50	1.25
Nos. 1052-1053 (2)	.50	.50
Set total (43) Stamps	80.05	31.80

Europa, 1972

Sparkles, Symbolic of Communications CD15

1972

Andorra, French 210-211
Andorra, Spanish 62
Belgium 825-826
Cyprus 380-382
Finland 512-513
France 1341
Germany 1089-1090
Greece 1049-1050
Iceland 439-440
Ireland 316-317
Italy 1065-1066
Liechtenstein 504
Luxembourg 512-513
Malta 450-453
Monaco 831-832
Netherlands 494-495
Portugal 1141-1143
San Marino 771-772
Spain 1718
Switzerland 544-545
Turkey 1907-1908
Yugoslavia 1100-1101

Nos. 210-211 (2)	21.00	7.00
No. 62 (1)	60.00	60.00
Nos. 825-826 (2)	.95	.55
Nos. 380-382 (3)	*2.45*	*3.25*
Nos. 512-513 (2)	4.00	1.00
No. 1341 (1)	.50	.35
Nos. 1089-1090 (2)	1.10	.50
Nos. 1049-1050 (2)	2.00	1.55
Nos. 439-440 (2)	2.90	2.65
Nos. 316-317 (2)	5.25	3.05
Nos. 1065-1066 (2)	.55	.50
No. 504 (1)	.45	.45
Nos. 512-513 (2)	.95	.65
Nos. 450-453 (4)	1.20	1.70
Nos. 831-832 (2)	5.00	1.40
Nos. 494-495 (2)	1.20	.90
Nos. 1141-1143 (3)	*15.85*	1.50
Nos. 771-772 (2)	.70	.50
No. 1718 (1)	.50	.40
Nos. 544-545 (2)	1.65	.60
Nos. 1907-1908 (2)	4.00	2.00
Nos. 1100-1101 (2)	1.20	1.20
Set total (44) Stamps	133.40	91.70

Europa, 1973

Post Horn and Arrows — CD16

1973

Andorra, French 219-220
Andorra, Spanish 76
Belgium 839-840
Cyprus 396-398
Finland 526
France 1367
Germany 1114-1115
Greece 1090-1092
Iceland 447-448
Ireland 329-330
Italy 1108-1109
Liechtenstein 528-529
Luxembourg 523-524
Malta 469-471
Monaco 866-867
Netherlands 504-505
Norway 604-605
Portugal 1170-1172
San Marino 802-803
Spain 1753
Switzerland 580-581
Turkey 1935-1936
Yugoslavia 1138-1139

Nos. 219-220 (2)	20.00	11.00
No. 76 (1)	1.25	.85
Nos. 839-840 (2)	1.00	.65
Nos. 396-398 (3)	*1.80*	*2.40*
No. 526 (1)	1.25	.55
No. 1367 (1)	1.25	.75
Nos. 1114-1115 (2)	.85	.50
Nos. 1090-1092 (3)	2.10	1.40
Nos. 447-448 (2)	6.65	3.35
Nos. 329-330 (2)	3.95	2.00
Nos. 1108-1109 (2)	.50	.50
Nos. 528-529 (2)	.60	.60
Nos. 523-524 (2)	.90	.75
Nos. 469-471 (3)	.90	1.05
Nos. 866-867 (2)	15.00	2.40
Nos. 504-505 (2)	1.20	.95
Nos. 604-605 (2)	4.00	1.80
Nos. 1170-1172 (3)	*24.95*	2.15
Nos. 802-803 (2)	*1.00*	.60
No. 1753 (1)	.35	.25
Nos. 580-581 (2)	1.55	.60
Nos. 1935-1936 (2)	4.15	2.25
Nos. 1138-1139 (2)	1.15	1.10
Set total (46) Stamps	96.35	38.45

Europa, 2000

CD17

2000

Albania 2621-2622
Andorra, French 522
Andorra, Spanish 262
Armenia 610-611
Austria 1814
Azerbaijan 698-699
Belarus 350
Belgium 1818
Bosnia & Herzegovina (Moslem) 358
Bosnia & Herzegovina (Serb) 111-112
Croatia 428-429
Cyprus 959
Czech Republic 3120
Denmark 1189
Estonia 394
Faroe Islands 376
Finland 1129
Aland Islands 166
France 2771
Georgia 228-229

Germany 2086-2087
Gibraltar 837-840
Great Britain (Jersey) 935-936
Great Britain (Isle of Man) 883
Greece 1959
Greenland 363
Hungary 3699-3700
Iceland 910
Ireland 1230-1231
Italy 2349
Latvia 504
Liechtenstein 1178
Lithuania 668
Luxembourg 1035
Macedonia 187
Malta 1011-1012
Moldova 355
Monaco 2161-2162
Poland 3519
Portugal 2358
Portugal (Azores) 455
Portugal (Madeira) 208
Romania 4370
Russia 6589
San Marino 1480
Slovakia 355
Slovenia 424
Spain 3036
Sweden 2394
Switzerland 1074
Turkey 2762
Turkish Rep. of Northern Cyprus 500
Ukraine 379
Vatican City 1152

Nos. 2621-2622 (2)	9.50	9.50
No. 522 (1)	2.00	1.00
No. 262 (1)	1.75	.80
Nos. 610-611 (2)	4.75	4.75
No. 1814 (1)	1.25	1.25
Nos. 698-699 (2)	6.00	6.00
No. 350 (1)	1.75	1.75
No. 1818 (1)	1.40	.60
No. 358 (1)	4.75	4.75
Nos. 111-112 (2)	110.00	110.00
Nos. 428-429 (2)	6.25	6.25
No. 959 (1)	2.10	1.40
No. 3120 (1)	1.20	.40
No. 1189 (1)	3.50	2.25
No. 394 (1)	1.25	1.25
No. 376 (1)	2.40	2.40
No. 1129 (1)	2.00	.60
No. 166 (1)	1.10	1.20
No. 2771 (1)	1.25	.40
Nos. 228-229 (2)	9.00	9.00
Nos. 2086-2087 (2)	4.35	2.10
Nos. 837-840 (4)	4.20	5.30
Nos. 935-936 (2)	2.40	2.40
No. 883 (1)	1.75	1.75
No. 363 (1)	1.90	1.90
Nos. 3699-3700 (2)	4.50	3.00
No. 910 (1)	1.60	1.60
Nos. 1230-1231 (2)	2.60	2.60
No. 2349 (1)	1.50	.40
No. 504 (1)	5.00	2.40
No. 1178 (1)	2.25	1.75
No. 668 (1)	1.50	1.50
No. 1035 (1)	1.40	.85
No. 187 (1)	3.00	3.00
Nos. 1011-1012 (2)	2.75	4.35
No. 355 (1)	3.50	3.50
Nos. 2161-2162 (2)	2.80	1.40
No. 3519 (1)	1.65	1.50
No. 2358 (1)	1.95	.65
No. 455 (1)	2.00	.50
No. 208 (1)	2.25	.50
No. 4370 (1)	2.50	1.25
No. 6589 (1)	4.00	.85
No. 1480 (1)	1.00	1.00
No. 355 (1)	1.60	.80
No. 424 (1)	3.25	3.25
No. 3036 (1)	1.00	.40
No. 2394 (1)	3.00	1.50
No. 1074 (1)	2.10	1.05
No. 2762 (1)	2.75	2.00
No. 500 (1)	2.50	2.50
No. 379 (1)	4.50	3.00
No. 1152 (1)	1.75	1.75
Set total (68) Stamps	258.00	227.85

The Gibraltar stamps are similar to the stamp illustrated, but none have the design shown above. All other sets listed above include at least one stamp with the design shown, but some include stamps with entirely different designs. Bulgaria Nos. 4131-4132, Guernsey Nos. 802-803 and Yugoslavia Nos. 2485-2486 are Europa stamps with completely different designs.

PORTUGAL & COLONIES

Vasco da Gama

Fleet Departing CD20

Fleet Arriving at Calicut CD21

Embarking at Rastello CD22

Muse of History CD23

San Gabriel, da Gama and Camoens CD24

Archangel Gabriel, the Patron Saint CD25

Flagship San Gabriel CD26

Vasco da Gama CD27

Fourth centenary of Vasco da Gama's discovery of the route to India.

1898

Azores 93-100
Macao 67-74
Madeira 37-44
Portugal 147-154
Port. Africa 1-8
Port. Congo 75-98
Port. India 189-196
St. Thomas & Prince Islands ... 170-193
Timor 45-52

Nos. 93-100 (8)	113.50	73.50
Nos. 67-74 (8)	250.25	170.25
Nos. 37-44 (8)	60.55	37.25
Nos. 147-154 (8)	249.05	84.90
Nos. 1-8 (8)	44.00	29.25
Nos. 75-98 (24)	78.50	64.65
Nos. 189-196 (8)	25.25	15.50
Nos. 170-193 (24)	60.40	44.75
Nos. 45-52 (8)	33.50	23.25
Set total (104) Stamps	915.00	543.30

Pombal
POSTAL TAX
POSTAL TAX DUES

Marquis de Pombal — CD28

Planning Reconstruction of Lisbon, 1755 — CD29

Pombal Monument, Lisbon — CD30

Sebastiao Jose de Carvalho e Mello, Marquis de Pombal (1699-1782), statesman, rebuilt Lisbon after earthquake of 1755. Tax was for the erection of Pombal monument. Obligatory on all mail on certain days throughout the year. Postal Tax Dues are inscribed "Multa."

1925

Angola RA1-RA3, RAJ1-RAJ3
Azores RA9-RA11, RAJ2-RAJ4
Cape Verde RA1-RA3, RAJ1-RAJ3
Macao RA1-RA3, RAJ1-RAJ3
Madeira RA1-RA3, RAJ1-RAJ3
Mozambique RA1-RA3, RAJ1-RAJ3
Nyassa RA1-RA3, RAJ1-RAJ3
Portugal RA11-RA13, RAJ2-RAJ4
Port. Guinea RA1-RA3, RAJ1-RAJ3
Port. India RA1-RA3, RAJ1-RAJ3
St. Thomas & Prince Islands RA1-RA3, RAJ1-RAJ3
Timor RA1-RA3, RAJ1-RAJ3

Nos. RA1-RA3,RAJ1-RAJ3 (6)	6.60	5.40
Nos. RA9-RA11,RAJ2-RAJ4 (6)	6.60	6.60
Nos. RA1-RA3,RAJ1-RAJ3 (6)	7.80	7.65
Nos. RA1-RA3,RAJ1-RAJ3 (6)	36.50	17.25
Nos. RA1-RA3,RAJ1-RAJ3 (6)	7.95	*14.70*
Nos. RA1-RA3,RAJ1-RAJ3 (6)	3.75	3.60
Nos. RA1-RA3,RAJ1-RAJ3 (6)	85.50	76.50
Nos. RA11-RA13,RAJ2-RAJ4 (6)	8.75	8.55
Nos. RA1-RA3,RAJ1-RAJ3 (6)	5.85	5.40
Nos. RA1-RA3,RAJ1-RAJ3 (6)	4.05	4.05
Nos. RA1-RA3,RAJ1-RAJ3 (6)	4.95	3.45
Nos. RA1-RA3,RAJ1-RAJ3 (6)	3.90	3.45
Set total (72) Stamps	182.20	156.60

Vasco da Gama CD34

Mousinho de Albuquerque CD35

Dam CD36

Prince Henry the Navigator CD37

Affonso de Albuquerque CD38

Plane over Globe CD39

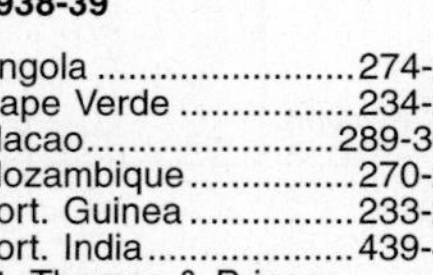

1938-39

Angola 274-291, C1-C9
Cape Verde 234-251, C1-C9
Macao 289-305, C7-C15
Mozambique 270-287, C1-C9
Port. Guinea 233-250. C1-C9
Port. India 439-453, C1-C8
St. Thomas & Prince Islands ... 302-319, 323-340, C1-C18
Timor 223-239, C1-C9

Nos. 274-291,C1-C9 (27)	121.45	20.95
Nos. 234-251,C1-C9 (27)	122.40	38.30
Nos. 289-305,C7-C15 (26)	889.60	338.55
Nos. 270-287,C1-C9 (27)	95.71	15.95
Nos. 233-250,C1-C9 (27)	130.20	49.15
Nos. 439-453,C1-C8 (23)	98.15	34.70
Nos. 302-319,323-340,C1-C18 (54)	468.30	263.80
Nos. 223-239,C1-C9 (26)	213.85	104.90
Set total (237) Stamps	2,140.	866.30

Lady of Fatima

Our Lady of the Rosary, Fatima, Portugal — CD40

1948-49

Angola 315-318
Cape Verde 266
Macao 336
Mozambique 325-328
Port. Guinea 271
Port. India 480
St. Thomas & Prince Islands 351
Timor 254

Nos. 315-318 (4)	68.00	20.60
No. 266 (1)	8.50	9.00
No. 336 (1)	90.00	30.00
Nos. 325-328 (4)	73.25	27.50
No. 271 (1)	6.50	6.00
No. 480 (1)	4.50	4.75
No. 351 (1)	8.50	7.00
No. 254 (1)	6.00	12.50
Set total (14) Stamps	265.25	117.35

A souvenir sheet of 9 stamps was issued in 1951 to mark the extension of the 1950 Holy Year. The sheet contains: Angola No. 316, Cape Verde No. 266, Macao No. 336, Mozambique No. 325, Portuguese Guinea No. 271, Portuguese India Nos. 480, 485, St. Thomas & Prince Islands No. 351, Timor No. 254. The sheet also contains a portrait of Pope Pius XII and is inscribed "Encerramento do Ano Santo, Fatima 1951." It was sold for 11 escudos.

Holy Year

Church Bells and Dove CD41

Angel Holding Candelabra CD42

Holy Year, 1950.

1950-51

Angola 331-332
Cape Verde 268-269
Macao 339-340
Mozambique 330-331
Port. Guinea 273-274
Port. India 490-491, 496-503
St. Thomas & Prince Islands ... 353-354
Timor 258-259

Nos. 331-332 (2)	7.60	1.35
Nos. 268-269 (2)	7.35	4.75
Nos. 339-340 (2)	110.00	34.00
Nos. 330-331 (2)	3.00	1.60
Nos. 273-274 (2)	8.50	5.05
Nos. 490-491,496-503 (10)	14.50	7.30
Nos. 353-354 (2)	10.50	7.25
Nos. 258-259 (2)	8.75	5.00
Set total (24) Stamps	170.20	66.30

A souvenir sheet of 8 stamps was issued in 1951 to mark the extension of the Holy Year. The sheet contains: Angola No. 331, Cape Verde No. 269, Macao No. 340, Mozambique No. 331, Portuguese Guinea No. 275, Portuguese India No. 490, St. Thomas & Prince Islands No. 354, Timor No. 258, some with colors changed. The sheet contains doves and is inscribed 'Encerramento do Ano Santo, Fatima 1951.' It was sold for 17 escudos.

Holy Year Conclusion

Our Lady of Fatima — CD43

Conclusion of Holy Year. Sheets contain alternate vertical rows of stamps and labels bearing quotation from Pope Pius XII, different for each colony.

1951

Angola 357
Cape Verde 270
Macao 352
Mozambique 356
Port. Guinea 275
Port. India 506
St. Thomas & Prince Islands 355
Timor 270

No. 357 (1)	4.50	1.60
No. 270 (1)	1.75	1.25
No. 352 (1)	110.00	23.00
No. 356 (1)	3.25	1.75
No. 275 (1)	2.00	1.00
No. 506 (1)	2.50	1.60
No. 355 (1)	3.50	2.75
No. 270 (1)	3.75	2.75
Set total (8) Stamps	131.25	35.70

Medical Congress

CD44

First National Congress of Tropical Medicine, Lisbon, 1952. Each stamp has a different design.

1952

Angola 358
Cape Verde 287
Macao 364
Mozambique 359
Port. Guinea 276
Port. India 516
St. Thomas & Prince Islands 356
Timor 271

No. 358 (1)	1.35	.45
No. 287 (1)	.95	.75
No. 364 (1)	20.00	7.00
No. 359 (1)	1.90	.90
No. 276 (1)	.75	.65
No. 516 (1)	7.50	3.25
No. 356 (1)	.75	.30
No. 271 (1)	2.00	1.60
Set total (8) Stamps	35.20	14.90

Postage Due Stamps

CD45

1952

Angola J37-J42
Cape Verde J31-J36
Macao J53-J58
Mozambique J51-J56
Port. Guinea J40-J45
Port. India J47-J52
St. Thomas & Prince Islands J52-J57
Timor J31-J36

Nos. J37-J42 (6)	3.15	2.95
Nos. J31-J36 (6)	2.80	2.30
Nos. J53-J58 (6)	27.80	12.05
Nos. J51-J56 (6)	2.40	1.95
Nos. J40-J45 (6)	2.70	2.55
Nos. J47-J52 (6)	6.10	6.10
Nos. J52-J57 (6)	2.85	2.70
Nos. J31-J36 (6)	4.00	2.35
Set total (48) Stamps	51.80	32.95

Sao Paulo

Father Manuel da Nobrega and View of Sao Paulo — CD46

Founding of Sao Paulo, Brazil, 400th anniv.

1954

Angola 385
Cape Verde 297
Macao 382
Mozambique 395
Port. Guinea 291
Port. India 530
St. Thomas & Prince Islands 369
Timor 279

No. 385 (1)	.80	.30
No. 297 (1)	.95	.80
No. 382 (1)	30.00	6.00
No. 395 (1)	.75	.30
No. 291 (1)	.50	.35
No. 530 (1)	1.00	.55
No. 369 (1)	.70	.50
No. 279 (1)	2.00	1.40
Set total (8) Stamps	36.70	10.20

Tropical Medicine Congress

CD47

Sixth International Congress for Tropical Medicine and Malaria, Lisbon, Sept. 1958. Each stamp shows a different plant.

1958

Angola 409
Cape Verde 303
Macao 392
Mozambique 404
Port. Guinea 295
Port. India 569
St. Thomas & Prince Islands 371
Timor 289

No. 409 (1)	3.50	1.00
No. 303 (1)	6.75	3.25
No. 392 (1)	13.00	6.00
No. 404 (1)	3.50	1.50
No. 295 (1)	4.50	2.00
No. 569 (1)	1.75	.75
No. 371 (1)	2.75	2.00
No. 289 (1)	5.50	4.25
Set total (8) Stamps	41.25	20.75

Sports

CD48

Each stamp shows a different sport.

1962

Angola 433-438
Cape Verde 320-325
Macao 394-399
Mozambique 424-429
Port. Guinea 299-304
St. Thomas & Prince Islands 374-379
Timor 313-318

Nos. 433-438 (6)	5.55	3.20
Nos. 320-325 (6)	16.05	7.40
Nos. 394-399 (6)	129.85	28.95
Nos. 424-429 (6)	6.55	2.45
Nos. 299-304 (6)	6.00	3.00
Nos. 374-379 (6)	6.80	3.20
Nos. 313-318 (6)	11.65	5.90
Set total (42) Stamps	182.45	54.10

Anti-Malaria

Anopheles Funestus and Malaria Eradication Symbol — CD49

World Health Organization drive to eradicate malaria.

1962

Angola 439
Cape Verde 326
Macao 400
Mozambique 430
Port. Guinea 305
St. Thomas & Prince Islands 380
Timor 319

No. 439 (1)	2.25	.90
No. 326 (1)	1.90	1.60
No. 400 (1)	12.00	4.00
No. 430 (1)	2.00	.50
No. 305 (1)	1.50	.60
No. 380 (1)	2.25	1.25
No. 319 (1)	2.25	1.40
Set total (7) Stamps	24.15	10.25

Airline Anniversary

Map of Africa, Super Constellation and Jet Liner — CD50

Tenth anniversary of Transportes Aereos Portugueses (TAP).

1963

Angola 490
Cape Verde 327
Mozambique 434
Port. Guinea 318
St. Thomas & Prince Islands 381

No. 490 (1)	1.35	.35
No. 327 (1)	1.50	1.10
No. 434 (1)	.55	.25
No. 318 (1)	1.25	.60
No. 381 (1)	.80	.50
Set total (5) Stamps	5.45	2.80

National Overseas Bank

Antonio Teixeira de Sousa — CD51

Centenary of the National Overseas Bank of Portugal.

1964, May 16

Angola 509
Cape Verde 328
Port. Guinea 319
St. Thomas & Prince Islands 382
Timor 320

No. 509 (1)	.90	.45
No. 328 (1)	1.50	1.30
No. 319 (1)	.95	.60
No. 382 (1)	.95	.50
No. 320 (1)	1.50	1.30
Set total (5) Stamps	5.80	4.15

ITU

ITU Emblem and the Archangel Gabriel — CD52

International Communications Union, Cent.

1965, May 17

Angola 511
Cape Verde 329
Macao 402
Mozambique 464
Port. Guinea 320
St. Thomas & Prince Islands 383
Timor 321

No. 511 (1)	1.25	.65
No. 329 (1)	2.90	2.25
No. 402 (1)	9.00	3.00
No. 464 (1)	.65	.25
No. 320 (1)	2.50	1.00
No. 383 (1)	2.00	1.00
No. 321 (1)	2.20	1.40
Set total (7) Stamps	20.50	9.55

National Revolution

CD53

40th anniv. of the National Revolution. Different buildings on each stamp.

1966, May 28

Angola 525
Cape Verde 338
Macao 403
Mozambique 465
Port. Guinea 329
St. Thomas & Prince Islands 392
Timor 322

No. 525 (1)	.50	.25
No. 338 (1)	.85	.75
No. 403 (1)	9.00	3.75
No. 465 (1)	.65	.30
No. 329 (1)	.85	.65
No. 392 (1)	.80	.50
No. 322 (1)	2.40	1.40
Set total (7) Stamps	15.05	7.60

Navy Club

CD54

Centenary of Portugal's Navy Club. Each stamp has a different design.

1967, Jan. 31

Angola 527-528
Cape Verde 339-340
Macao 412-413
Mozambique 478-479
Port. Guinea 330-331
St. Thomas & Prince Islands 393-394
Timor 323-324

Nos. 527-528 (2)	2.35	1.20
Nos. 339-340 (2)	2.70	2.30
Nos. 412-413 (2)	18.00	4.70
Nos. 478-479 (2)	1.75	.65
Nos. 330-331 (2)	1.65	.90
Nos. 393-394 (2)	3.30	1.30
Nos. 323-324 (2)	4.25	2.40
Set total (14) Stamps	34.00	13.45

Admiral Coutinho

CD55

Centenary of the birth of Admiral Carlos Viegas Gago Coutinho (1869-1959), explorer and aviation pioneer. Each stamp has a different design.

1969, Feb. 17

Angola 547
Cape Verde 355
Macao 417
Mozambique 484
Port. Guinea 335
St. Thomas & Prince Islands 397
Timor 335

No. 547 (1)	.85	.35
No. 355 (1)	.60	.25
No. 417 (1)	7.50	2.25
No. 484 (1)	.30	.25
No. 335 (1)	.50	.25
No. 397 (1)	.70	.35
No. 335 (1)	2.50	1.40
Set total (7) Stamps	12.95	5.10

Administration Reform

Luiz Augusto Rebello da Silva — CD56

Centenary of the administration reforms of the overseas territories.

1969, Sept. 25

Angola 549
Cape Verde 357
Macao 419
Mozambique 491
Port. Guinea 337
St. Thomas & Prince Islands 399
Timor 338

No. 549 (1)	.30	.25
No. 357 (1)	.65	.40
No. 419 (1)	12.50	2.00
No. 491 (1)	.30	.25
No. 337 (1)	.35	.25
No. 399 (1)	.60	.45
No. 338 (1)	1.40	.70
Set total (7) Stamps	16.10	4.30

Marshal Carmona

CD57

Birth centenary of Marshal Antonio Oscar Carmona de Fragoso (1869-1951), President of Portugal. Each stamp has a different design.

1970, Nov. 15

Angola 563
Cape Verde 359
Macao 422
Mozambique 493
Port. Guinea 340
St. Thomas & Prince Islands 403
Timor 341

No. 563 (1)	.45	.25
No. 359 (1)	.70	.50
No. 422 (1)	5.00	1.75
No. 493 (1)	.40	.25
No. 340 (1)	.45	.25

No. 403 (1)	.90	.40
No. 341 (1)	1.00	.50
Set total (7) Stamps	8.90	3.90

Olympic Games

CD59

20th Olympic Games, Munich, Aug. 26-Sept. 11. Each stamp shows a different sport.

1972, June 20

Angola	569
Cape Verde	361
Macao	426
Mozambique	504
Port. Guinea	342
St. Thomas & Prince Islands	408
Timor	343

No. 569 (1)	.65	.25
No. 361 (1)	.85	.40
No. 426 (1)	2.50	1.50
No. 504 (1)	.30	.25
No. 342 (1)	.95	.25
No. 408 (1)	.60	.25
No. 343 (1)	1.60	.80
Set total (7) Stamps	7.45	3.70

Lisbon-Rio de Janeiro Flight

CD60

50th anniversary of the Lisbon to Rio de Janeiro flight by Arturo de Sacadura and Coutinho, March 30-June 5, 1922. Each stamp shows a different stage of the flight.

1972, Sept. 20

Angola	570
Cape Verde	362
Macao	427
Mozambique	505
Port. Guinea	343
St. Thomas & Prince Islands	409
Timor	344

No. 570 (1)	.35	.25
No. 362 (1)	.85	.40
No. 427 (1)	40.00	12.00
No. 505 (1)	.30	.25
No. 343 (1)	.35	.25
No. 409 (1)	.50	.25
No. 344 (1)	1.25	.90
Set total (7) Stamps	43.60	14.30

WMO Centenary

WMO Emblem — CD61

Centenary of international meterological cooperation.

1973, Dec. 15

Angola	571
Cape Verde	363
Macao	429
Mozambique	509
Port. Guinea	344
St. Thomas & Prince Islands	410
Timor	345

No. 571 (1)	.45	.25
No. 363 (1)	.85	.40
No. 429 (1)	15.00	2.50
No. 509 (1)	.40	.25
No. 344 (1)	.55	.40
No. 410 (1)	.80	.50
No. 345 (1)	3.75	2.75
Set total (7) Stamps	21.80	7.05

FRENCH COMMUNITY

Upper Volta can be found under Burkina Faso in Vol. 1

Madagascar can be found under Malagasy in Vol. 3

Colonial Exposition

People of French Empire — CD70

Women's Heads — CD71

France Showing Way to Civilization CD72

"Colonial Commerce" CD73

International Colonial Exposition, Paris.

1931

Cameroun	213-216
Chad	60-63
Dahomey	97-100
Fr. Guiana	152-155
Fr. Guinea	116-119
Fr. India	100-103
Fr. Polynesia	76-79
Fr. Sudan	102-105
Gabon	120-123
Guadeloupe	138-141
Indo-China	140-142
Ivory Coast	92-95
Madagascar	169-172
Martinique	129-132
Mauritania	65-68
Middle Congo	61-64
New Caledonia	176-179
Niger	73-76
Reunion	122-125
St. Pierre & Miquelon	132-135
Senegal	138-141
Somali Coast	135-138
Togo	254-257
Ubangi-Shari	82-85
Upper Volta	66-69
Wallis & Futuna Isls.	85-88

Nos. 213-216 (4)	23.00	18.25
Nos. 60-63 (4)	22.00	22.00
Nos. 97-100 (4)	26.00	26.00
Nos. 152-155 (4)	22.00	22.00
Nos. 116-119 (4)	19.75	19.75
Nos. 100-103 (4)	18.00	*18.00*
Nos. 76-79 (4)	30.00	30.00
Nos. 102-105 (4)	19.00	19.00
Nos. 120-123 (4)	17.50	17.50
Nos. 138-141 (4)	19.00	19.00
Nos. 140-142 (3)	12.00	11.50
Nos. 92-95 (4)	22.50	22.50
Nos. 169-172 (4)	9.25	6.50
Nos. 129-132 (4)	21.00	21.00
Nos. 65-68 (4)	22.00	22.00
Nos. 61-64 (4)	20.00	18.50
Nos. 176-179 (4)	24.00	24.00
Nos. 73-76 (4)	20.50	20.50
Nos. 122-125 (4)	22.00	22.00
Nos. 132-135 (4)	24.00	24.00
Nos. 138-141 (4)	20.00	20.00
Nos. 135-138 (4)	22.00	22.00
Nos. 254-257 (4)	22.00	22.00
Nos. 82-85 (4)	21.00	21.00
Nos. 66-69 (4)	19.00	19.00
Nos. 85-88 (4)	31.00	35.00
Set total (103) Stamps	548.50	543.00

Paris International Exposition Colonial Arts Exposition

"Colonial Resources" CD74 CD77

Overseas Commerce CD75

Exposition Building and Women CD76

"France and the Empire" — CD78

Cultural Treasures of the Colonies — CD79

Souvenir sheets contain one imperf. stamp.

1937

Cameroun	217-222A
Dahomey	101-107
Fr. Equatorial Africa	27-32, 73
Fr. Guiana	162-168
Fr. Guinea	120-126
Fr. India	104-110
Fr. Polynesia	117-123
Fr. Sudan	106-112
Guadeloupe	148-154
Indo-China	193-199
Inini	41
Ivory Coast	152-158
Kwangchowan	132
Madagascar	191-197
Martinique	179-185
Mauritania	69-75
New Caledonia	208-214
Niger	77-83
Reunion	167-173
St. Pierre & Miquelon	165-171
Senegal	172-178
Somali Coast	139-145
Togo	258-264
Wallis & Futuna Isls.	89

Nos. 217-222A (7)	18.80	20.30
Nos. 101-107 (7)	23.60	27.60
Nos. 27-32, 73 (7)	28.10	32.10
Nos. 162-168 (7)	22.50	24.50
Nos. 120-126 (7)	24.00	28.00
Nos. 104-110 (7)	21.15	36.50
Nos. 117-123 (7)	58.50	75.00
Nos. 106-112 (7)	23.60	27.60
Nos. 148-154 (7)	19.55	21.05
Nos. 193-199 (7)	17.70	19.70
No. 41 (1)	21.00	27.50
Nos. 152-158 (7)	22.20	26.20
No. 132 (1)	9.25	11.00
Nos. 191-197 (7)	19.25	21.75
Nos. 179-185 (7)	19.95	21.70
Nos. 69-75 (7)	20.50	24.50
Nos. 208-214 (7)	39.00	50.50
Nos. 73-83 (11)	40.60	45.10
Nos. 167-173 (7)	21.70	23.20
Nos. 165-171 (7)	49.60	64.00
Nos. 172-178 (7)	21.00	23.80
Nos. 139-145 (7)	25.60	32.60
Nos. 258-264 (7)	20.40	20.40
No. 89 (1)	19.00	37.50
Set total (154) Stamps	606.55	742.10

Curie

Pierre and Marie Curie — CD80

40th anniversary of the discovery of radium. The surtax was for the benefit of the Intl. Union for the Control of Cancer.

1938

Cameroun	B1
Cuba	B1-B2
Dahomey	B2
France	B76
Fr. Equatorial Africa	B1
Fr. Guiana	B3
Fr. Guinea	B2
Fr. India	B6
Fr. Polynesia	B5
Fr. Sudan	B1
Guadeloupe	B3
Indo-China	B14
Ivory Coast	B2
Madagascar	B2
Martinique	B2
Mauritania	B3
New Caledonia	B4
Niger	B1
Reunion	B4
St. Pierre & Miquelon	B3
Senegal	B3
Somali Coast	B2
Togo	B1

No. B1 (1)	10.00	10.00
Nos. B1-B2 (2)	12.00	3.35
No. B2 (1)	9.50	9.50
No. B76 (1)	21.00	12.50
No. B1 (1)	24.00	24.00
No. B3 (1)	13.50	13.50
No. B2 (1)	8.75	8.75
No. B6 (1)	10.00	10.00
No. B5 (1)	20.00	20.00
No. B1 (1)	12.50	12.50
No. B3 (1)	11.00	10.50
No. B14 (1)	12.00	12.00
No. B2 (1)	11.00	7.50
No. B2 (1)	11.00	11.00
No. B2 (1)	13.00	13.00
No. B3 (1)	7.75	7.75
No. B4 (1)	16.50	17.50
No. B1 (1)	16.50	16.50
No. B4 (1)	14.00	14.00
No. B3 (1)	21.00	22.50
No. B3 (1)	10.50	10.50
No. B2 (1)	7.75	7.75
No. B1 (1)	20.00	20.00
Set total (24) Stamps	313.25	294.60

Caillie

Rene Caillie and Map of Northwestern Africa — CD81

Death centenary of Rene Caillie (1799-1838), French explorer. All three denominations exist with colony name omitted.

1939

Dahomey	108-110
Fr. Guinea	161-163
Fr. Sudan	113-115
Ivory Coast	160-162
Mauritania	109-111
Niger	84-86
Senegal	188-190
Togo	265-267

Nos. 108-110 (3)	1.20	3.60
Nos. 161-163 (3)	1.20	3.20
Nos. 113-115 (3)	1.20	3.20
Nos. 160-162 (3)	1.05	2.55
Nos. 109-111 (3)	1.05	3.80
Nos. 84-86 (3)	2.35	2.35
Nos. 188-190 (3)	1.05	2.90
Nos. 265-267 (3)	1.05	3.30
Set total (24) Stamps	10.15	24.90

New York World's Fair

Natives and New York Skyline — CD82

1939

Cameroun	223-224
Dahomey	111-112
Fr. Equatorial Africa	78-79
Fr. Guiana	169-170
Fr. Guinea	164-165
Fr. India	111-112
Fr. Polynesia	124-125
Fr. Sudan	116-117
Guadeloupe	155-156
Indo-China	203-204
Inini	42-43
Ivory Coast	163-164
Kwangchowan	133-134
Madagascar	209-210
Martinique	186-187
Mauritania	112-113
New Caledonia	215-216
Niger	87-88
Reunion	174-175
St. Pierre & Miquelon	205-206
Senegal	191-192
Somali Coast	179-180
Togo	268-269
Wallis & Futuna Isls.	90-91

Nos. 223-224 (2)	2.80	2.40
Nos. 111-112 (2)	1.60	3.20
Nos. 78-79 (2)	1.60	3.20
Nos. 169-170 (2)	2.60	2.60
Nos. 164-165 (2)	1.60	3.20
Nos. 111-112 (2)	3.00	*8.00*
Nos. 124-125 (2)	4.80	4.80
Nos. 116-117 (2)	1.60	3.20
Nos. 155-156 (2)	2.50	2.50
Nos. 203-204 (2)	2.05	2.05
Nos. 42-43 (2)	7.50	9.00
Nos. 163-164 (2)	1.50	3.00
Nos. 133-134 (2)	2.50	2.50
Nos. 209-210 (2)	1.50	2.50

Nos. 186-187 (2)	2.35	2.35
Nos. 112-113 (2)	1.40	2.80
Nos. 215-216 (2)	3.35	3.35
Nos. 87-88 (2)	1.60	2.80
Nos. 174-175 (2)	2.80	2.80
Nos. 205-206 (2)	4.80	6.00
Nos. 191-192 (2)	1.40	2.80
Nos. 179-180 (2)	1.40	2.80
Nos. 268-269 (2)	1.40	2.80
Nos. 90-91 (2)	5.00	6.00
Set total (48) Stamps	62.65	86.65

French Revolution

Storming of the Bastille — CD83

French Revolution, 150th anniv. The surtax was for the defense of the colonies.

1939

Cameroun B2-B6
Dahomey B3-B7
Fr. Equatorial Africa B4-B8, CB1
Fr. Guiana B4-B8, CB1
Fr. Guinea B3-B7
Fr. India B7-B11
Fr. Polynesia B6-B10, CB1
Fr. Sudan B2-B6
Guadeloupe B4-B8
Indo-China B15-B19, CB1
Inini B1-B5
Ivory Coast B3-B7
Kwangchowan B1-B5
Madagascar B3-B7, CB1
Martinique B3-B7
Mauritania B4-B8
New Caledonia B5-B9, CB1
Niger B2-B6
Reunion B5-B9, CB1
St. Pierre & Miquelon B4-B8
Senegal B4-B8, CB1
Somali Coast B3-B7
Togo B2-B6
Wallis & Futuna Isls. B1-B5

Nos. B2-B6 (5)	60.00	60.00
Nos. B3-B7 (5)	47.50	47.50
Nos. B4-B8,CB1 (6)	120.00	120.00
Nos. B4-B8,CB1 (6)	79.50	79.50
Nos. B3-B7 (5)	47.50	47.50
Nos. B7-B11 (5)	28.75	*32.50*
Nos. B6-B10,CB1 (6)	122.50	122.50
Nos. B2-B6 (5)	50.00	50.00
Nos. B4-B8 (5)	50.00	50.00
Nos. B15-B19,CB1 (6)	85.00	85.00
Nos. B1-B5 (5)	80.00	100.00
Nos. B3-B7 (5)	43.75	43.75
Nos. B1-B5 (5)	46.25	46.25
Nos. B3-B7,CB1 (6)	65.50	65.50
Nos. B3-B7 (5)	52.50	52.50
Nos. B4-B8 (5)	42.50	42.50
Nos. B5-B9,CB1 (6)	101.50	101.50
Nos. B2-B6 (5)	60.00	60.00
Nos. B5-B9,CB1 (6)	87.50	87.50
Nos. B4-B8 (5)	67.50	72.50
Nos. B4-B8,CB1 (6)	56.50	56.50
Nos. B3-B7 (5)	45.00	45.00
Nos. B2-B6 (5)	42.50	42.50
Nos. B1-B5 (5)	80.00	110.00
Set total (128) Stamps	1,562.	1,621.

Plane over Coastal Area — CD85

All five denominations exist with colony name omitted.

1940

Dahomey C1-C5
Fr. Guinea C1-C5
Fr. Sudan C1-C5
Ivory Coast C1-C5
Mauritania C1-C5
Niger C1-C5
Senegal C12-C16
Togo C1-C5

Nos. C1-C5 (5)	4.00	4.00
Nos. C1-C5 (5)	4.00	4.00
Nos. C1-C5 (5)	4.00	4.00
Nos. C1-C5 (5)	3.80	3.80
Nos. C1-C5 (5)	3.50	3.50
Nos. C1-C5 (5)	3.50	3.50
Nos. C12-C16 (5)	3.50	3.50
Nos. C1-C5 (5)	3.15	3.15
Set total (40) Stamps	29.45	29.45

Defense of the Empire

Colonial Infantryman — CD86

1941

Cameroun B13B
Dahomey B13
Fr. Equatorial Africa B8B
Fr. Guiana B10
Fr. Guinea B13
Fr. India B13
Fr. Polynesia B12
Fr. Sudan B12
Guadeloupe B10
Indo-China B19B
Inini B7
Ivory Coast B13
Kwangchowan B7
Madagascar B9
Martinique B9
Mauritania B14
New Caledonia B11
Niger B12
Reunion B11
St. Pierre & Miquelon B8B
Senegal B14
Somali Coast B9
Togo B10B
Wallis & Futuna Isls. B7

No. B13B (1)	1.60
No. B13 (1)	1.20
No. B8B (1)	3.50
No. B10 (1)	1.40
No. B13 (1)	1.40
No. B13 (1)	1.25
No. B12 (1)	3.50
No. B12 (1)	1.40
No. B10 (1)	1.00
No. B19B (1)	3.00
No. B7 (1)	1.75
No. B13 (1)	1.25
No. B7 (1)	.85
No. B9 (1)	1.50
No. B9 (1)	1.40
No. B14 (1)	.95
No. B12 (1)	1.40
No. B11 (1)	1.60
No. B8B (1)	4.50
No. B14 (1)	1.25
No. B9 (1)	1.60
No. B10B (1)	1.10
No. B7 (1)	1.75
Set total (23) Stamps	40.15

Each of the CD86 stamps listed above is part of a set of three stamps. The designs of the other two stamps in the set vary from country to country. Only the values of the Common Design stamps are listed here.

Colonial Education Fund

CD86a

1942

Cameroun CB3
Dahomey CB4
Fr. Equatorial Africa CB5
Fr. Guiana CB4
Fr. Guinea CB4
Fr. India CB3
Fr. Polynesia CB4
Fr. Sudan CB4
Guadeloupe CB3
Indo-China CB5
Inini CB3
Ivory Coast CB4
Kwangchowan CB4
Malagasy CB5
Martinique CB3
Mauritania CB4
New Caledonia CB4
Niger CB4
Reunion CB4
St. Pierre & Miquelon CB3
Senegal CB5
Somali Coast CB3
Togo CB3
Wallis & Futuna CB3

No. CB3 (1)	1.10	
No. CB4 (1)	.80	5.50
No. CB5 (1)	.80	
No. CB4 (1)	1.10	
No. CB4 (1)	.40	5.50
No. CB3 (1)	.90	
No. CB4 (1)	2.00	
No. CB4 (1)	.40	5.50
No. CB3 (1)	1.10	
No. CB5 (1)	2.00	
No. CB3 (1)	1.25	
No. CB4 (1)	1.00	5.50
No. CB4 (1)	1.00	
No. CB5 (1)	.65	
No. CB3 (1)	1.00	
No. CB4 (1)	.80	
No. CB4 (1)	2.25	
No. CB4 (1)	.35	
No. CB4 (1)	.90	
No. CB3 (1)	7.00	
No. CB5 (1)	.80	6.50
No. CB3 (1)	.70	
No. CB3 (1)	.35	
No. CB3 (1)	2.00	
Set total (24) Stamps	30.65	28.50

Cross of Lorraine & Four-motor Plane — CD87

1941-5

Cameroun C1-C7
Fr. Equatorial Africa C17-C23
Fr. Guiana C9-C10
Fr. India C1-C6
Fr. Polynesia C3-C9
Fr. West Africa C1-C3
Guadeloupe C1-C2
Madagascar C37-C43
Martinique C1-C2
New Caledonia C7-C13
Reunion C18-C24
St. Pierre & Miquelon C1-C7
Somali Coast C1-C7

Nos. C1-C7 (7)	6.30	6.30
Nos. C17-C23 (7)	10.40	6.35
Nos. C9-C10 (2)	3.80	3.10
Nos. C1-C6 (6)	9.30	*15.00*
Nos. C3-C9 (7)	13.75	10.00
Nos. C1-C3 (3)	9.50	3.90
Nos. C1-C2 (2)	3.75	2.50
Nos. C37-C43 (7)	5.60	3.80
Nos. C1-C2 (2)	3.00	1.60
Nos. C7-C13 (7)	8.85	7.30
Nos. C18-C24 (7)	7.05	5.00
Nos. C1-C7 (7)	11.60	9.40
Nos. C1-C7 (7)	13.95	11.10
Set total (71) Stamps	106.85	85.35

Somali Coast stamps are inscribed "Djibouti".

Transport Plane — CD88

Caravan and Plane — CD89

1942

Dahomey C6-C13
Fr. Guinea C6-C13
Fr. Sudan C6-C13
Ivory Coast C6-C13
Mauritania C6-C13
Niger C6-C13
Senegal C17-C25
Togo C6-C13

Nos. C6-C13 (8)	7.15
Nos. C6-C13 (8)	5.75
Nos. C6-C13 (8)	8.00
Nos. C6-C13 (8)	11.15
Nos. C6-C13 (8)	9.75
Nos. C6-C13 (8)	6.20
Nos. C17-C25 (9)	9.45
Nos. C6-C13 (8)	6.75
Set total (65) Stamps	64.20

Red Cross

Marianne CD90

The surtax was for the French Red Cross and national relief.

1944

Cameroun B28
Fr. Equatorial Africa B38
Fr. Guiana B12
Fr. India B14
Fr. Polynesia B13
Fr. West Africa B1
Guadeloupe B12
Madagascar B15
Martinique B11
New Caledonia B13
Reunion B15
St. Pierre & Miquelon B13
Somali Coast B13
Wallis & Futuna Isls. B9

No. B28 (1)	2.00	1.60
No. B38 (1)	1.60	1.20
No. B12 (1)	1.75	1.25
No. B14 (1)	1.50	1.25
No. B13 (1)	2.00	1.60
No. B1 (1)	6.50	4.75
No. B12 (1)	1.40	1.00
No. B15 (1)	.90	.90
No. B11 (1)	1.20	1.20
No. B13 (1)	1.50	1.50
No. B15 (1)	1.60	1.10
No. B13 (1)	2.60	2.60
No. B13 (1)	1.75	2.00
No. B9 (1)	3.00	3.00
Set total (14) Stamps	29.30	24.95

Eboue

CD91

Felix Eboue, first French colonial administrator to proclaim resistance to Germany after French surrender in World War II.

1945

Cameroun 296-297
Fr. Equatorial Africa 156-157
Fr. Guiana 171-172
Fr. India 210-211
Fr. Polynesia 150-151
Fr. West Africa 15-16
Guadeloupe 187-188
Madagascar 259-260
Martinique 196-197
New Caledonia 274-275
Reunion 238-239
St. Pierre & Miquelon 322-323
Somali Coast 238-239

Nos. 296-297 (2)	2.40	1.95
Nos. 156-157 (2)	2.55	2.00
Nos. 171-172 (2)	2.45	2.00
Nos. 210-211 (2)	2.20	1.95
Nos. 150-151 (2)	3.60	2.85
Nos. 15-16 (2)	2.40	2.40
Nos. 187-188 (2)	2.05	1.60
Nos. 259-260 (2)	2.00	1.45
Nos. 196-197 (2)	2.05	1.55
Nos. 274-275 (2)	3.40	3.00
Nos. 238-239 (2)	2.40	2.00
Nos. 322-323 (2)	4.40	3.45
Nos. 238-239 (2)	2.45	2.10
Set total (26) Stamps	34.35	28.30

Victory

Victory CD92

European victory of the Allied Nations in World War II.

1946, May 8

Cameroun C8
Fr. Equatorial Africa C24
Fr. Guiana C11
Fr. India C7

Fr. Polynesia	C10
Fr. West Africa	C4
Guadeloupe	C3
Indo-China	C19
Madagascar	C44
Martinique	C3
New Caledonia	C14
Reunion	C25
St. Pierre & Miquelon	C8
Somali Coast	C8
Wallis & Futuna Isls.	C1

No. C8 (1)	1.60	1.20
No. C24 (1)	1.60	1.25
No. C11 (1)	1.75	1.25
No. C7 (1)	1.00	4.00
No. C10 (1)	2.75	2.00
No. C4 (1)	1.60	1.20
No. C3 (1)	1.25	1.00
No. C19 (1)	1.00	.55
No. C44 (1)	1.00	.35
No. C3 (1)	1.30	1.00
No. C14 (1)	1.50	1.25
No. C25 (1)	1.10	.90
No. C8 (1)	2.10	2.10
No. C8 (1)	1.75	1.40
No. C1 (1)	2.25	1.90
Set total (15) Stamps	23.55	21.35

Chad to Rhine

Leclerc's Departure from Chad CD93

Battle at Cufra Oasis CD94

Tanks in Action, Mareth CD95

Normandy Invasion CD96

Entering Paris CD97

Liberation of Strasbourg CD98

"Chad to the Rhine" march, 1942-44, by Gen. Jacques Leclerc's column, later French 2nd Armored Division.

1946, June 6

Cameroun	C9-C14
Fr. Equatorial Africa	C25-C30
Fr. Guiana	C12-C17
Fr. India	C8-C13
Fr. Polynesia	C11-C16
Fr. West Africa	C5-C10
Guadeloupe	C4-C9
Indo-China	C20-C25
Madagascar	C45-C50
Martinique	C4-C9
New Caledonia	C15-C20
Reunion	C26-C31
St. Pierre & Miquelon	C9-C14
Somali Coast	C9-C14
Wallis & Futuna Isls.	C2-C7

Nos. C9-C14 (6)	12.05	9.70
Nos. C25-C30 (6)	14.70	10.80
Nos. C12-C17 (6)	12.65	10.35
Nos. C8-C13 (6)	12.80	*15.00*
Nos. C11-C16 (6)	17.55	13.40
Nos. C5-C10 (6)	16.05	11.95
Nos. C4-C9 (6)	12.00	9.60
Nos. C20-C25 (6)	6.40	6.40
Nos. C45-C50 (6)	10.30	8.40
Nos. C4-C9 (6)	8.85	7.30
Nos. C15-C20 (6)	13.40	11.90
Nos. C26-C31 (6)	10.25	6.55
Nos. C9-C14 (6)	17.30	14.35
Nos. C9-C14 (6)	18.10	12.65
Nos. C2-C7 (6)	13.75	10.45
Set total (90) Stamps	196.15	158.80

UPU

French Colonials, Globe and Plane CD99

Universal Postal Union, 75th anniv.

1949, July 4

Cameroun	C29
Fr. Equatorial Africa	C34
Fr. India	C17
Fr. Polynesia	C20
Fr. West Africa	C15
Indo-China	C26
Madagascar	C55
New Caledonia	C24
St. Pierre & Miquelon	C18
Somali Coast	C18
Togo	C18
Wallis & Futuna Isls.	C10

No. C29 (1)	8.00	4.75
No. C34 (1)	16.00	12.00
No. C17 (1)	11.50	8.75
No. C20 (1)	20.00	15.00
No. C15 (1)	12.00	8.75
No. C26 (1)	4.75	4.00
No. C55 (1)	4.00	2.75
No. C24 (1)	7.50	5.00
No. C18 (1)	20.00	12.00
No. C18 (1)	14.00	10.50
No. C18 (1)	8.50	7.00
No. C10 (1)	11.00	8.25
Set total (12) Stamps	137.25	98.75

Tropical Medicine

Doctor Treating Infant — CD100

The surtax was for charitable work.

1950

Cameroun	B29
Fr. Equatorial Africa	B39
Fr. India	B15
Fr. Polynesia	B14
Fr. West Africa	B3
Madagascar	B17
New Caledonia	B14
St. Pierre & Miquelon	B14
Somali Coast	B14
Togo	B11

No. B29 (1)	7.25	5.50
No. B39 (1)	7.25	5.50
No. B15 (1)	6.00	4.00
No. B14 (1)	10.50	8.00
No. B3 (1)	9.50	7.25
No. B17 (1)	5.50	5.50
No. B14 (1)	6.75	5.25
No. B14 (1)	16.00	15.00
No. B14 (1)	7.75	6.25
No. B11 (1)	5.00	3.50
Set total (10) Stamps	81.50	65.75

Military Medal

Medal, Early Marine and Colonial Soldier — CD101

Centenary of the creation of the French Military Medal.

1952

Cameroun	322
Comoro Isls.	39
Fr. Equatorial Africa	186
Fr. India	233
Fr. Polynesia	179
Fr. West Africa	57
Madagascar	286
New Caledonia	295
St. Pierre & Miquelon	345
Somali Coast	267
Togo	327
Wallis & Futuna Isls.	149

No. 322 (1)	7.25	3.25
No. 39 (1)	45.00	37.50
No. 186 (1)	8.00	5.50
No. 233 (1)	5.50	7.00
No. 179 (1)	13.50	10.00
No. 57 (1)	8.75	6.50
No. 286 (1)	3.75	2.50
No. 295 (1)	6.50	6.00
No. 345 (1)	16.00	15.00
No. 267 (1)	9.00	8.00
No. 327 (1)	5.50	4.75
No. 149 (1)	7.25	7.25
Set total (12) Stamps	136.00	113.25

Liberation

Allied Landing, Victory Sign and Cross of Lorraine CD102

Liberation of France, 10th anniv.

1954, June 6

Cameroun	C32
Comoro Isls.	C4
Fr. Equatorial Africa	C38
Fr. India	C18
Fr. Polynesia	C22
Fr. West Africa	C17
Madagascar	C57
New Caledonia	C25
St. Pierre & Miquelon	C19
Somali Coast	C19
Togo	C19
Wallis & Futuna Isls.	C11

No. C32 (1)	7.25	4.75
No. C4 (1)	32.50	19.00
No. C38 (1)	12.00	8.00
No. C18 (1)	11.00	8.00
No. C22 (1)	10.00	8.00
No. C17 (1)	12.00	5.50
No. C57 (1)	3.25	2.00
No. C25 (1)	7.50	5.00
No. C19 (1)	19.00	12.00
No. C19 (1)	10.50	8.50
No. C19 (1)	7.00	5.50
No. C11 (1)	11.00	8.25
Set total (12) Stamps	143.00	94.50

FIDES

Plowmen CD103

Efforts of FIDES, the Economic and Social Development Fund for Overseas Possessions (Fonds d' Investissement pour le Developpement Economique et Social). Each stamp has a different design.

1956

Cameroun	326-329
Comoro Isls.	43
Fr. Equatorial Africa	189-192
Fr. Polynesia	181
Fr. West Africa	65-72
Madagascar	292-295
New Caledonia	303
St. Pierre & Miquelon	350
Somali Coast	268-269
Togo	331

Nos. 326-329 (4)	6.90	3.20
No. 43 (1)	2.25	1.60
Nos. 189-192 (4)	3.20	1.65
No. 181 (1)	4.00	2.00
Nos. 65-72 (8)	16.00	6.35
Nos. 292-295 (4)	2.25	1.20
No. 303 (1)	1.90	1.10
No. 350 (1)	6.00	4.00
Nos. 268-269 (2)	5.35	3.15
No. 331 (1)	4.25	2.10
Set total (27) Stamps	52.10	26.35

Flower

CD104

Each stamp shows a different flower.

1958-9

Cameroun	333
Comoro Isls.	45
Fr. Equatorial Africa	200-201
Fr. Polynesia	192
Fr. So. & Antarctic Terr.	11
Fr. West Africa	79-83
Madagascar	301-302
New Caledonia	304-305
St. Pierre & Miquelon	357
Somali Coast	270
Togo	348-349
Wallis & Futuna Isls.	152

No. 333 (1)	1.60	.80
No. 45 (1)	5.25	4.25
Nos. 200-201 (2)	3.60	1.60
No. 192 (1)	6.50	4.00
No. 11 (1)	8.75	7.50
Nos. 79-83 (5)	10.45	5.60
Nos. 301-302 (2)	1.60	.60
Nos. 304-305 (2)	8.00	3.00
No. 357 (1)	4.50	2.25
No. 270 (1)	4.25	1.40
Nos. 348-349 (2)	1.10	.50
No. 152 (1)	3.25	3.25
Set total (20) Stamps	58.85	34.75

Human Rights

Sun, Dove and U.N. Emblem CD105

10th anniversary of the signing of the Universal Declaration of Human Rights.

1958

Comoro Isls.	44
Fr. Equatorial Africa	202
Fr. Polynesia	191
Fr. West Africa	85
Madagascar	300
New Caledonia	306
St. Pierre & Miquelon	356
Somali Coast	274
Wallis & Futuna Isls.	153

No. 44 (1)	9.00	9.00
No. 202 (1)	2.40	1.25
No. 191 (1)	13.00	8.75
No. 85 (1)	2.40	2.00
No. 300 (1)	.80	.40
No. 306 (1)	2.00	1.50
No. 356 (1)	3.50	2.50
No. 274 (1)	3.50	2.10
No. 153 (1)	4.50	4.50
Set total (9) Stamps	41.10	32.00

C.C.T.A.

CD106

Commission for Technical Cooperation in Africa south of the Sahara, 10th anniv.

1960

Cameroun	339
Cent. Africa	3
Chad	66
Congo, P.R.	90
Dahomey	138
Gabon	150
Ivory Coast	180
Madagascar	317
Mali	9
Mauritania	117
Niger	104
Upper Volta	89

No. 339 (1)	1.60	.75
No. 3 (1)	1.60	.75
No. 66 (1)	1.75	.50
No. 90 (1)	1.00	1.00
No. 138 (1)	.50	.25
No. 150 (1)	1.25	1.10
No. 180 (1)	1.10	.50
No. 317 (1)	.60	.30
No. 9 (1)	1.20	.50
No. 117 (1)	.75	.40
No. 104 (1)	.85	.45
No. 89 (1)	.65	.40
Set total (12) Stamps	12.85	6.90

Air Afrique, 1961

Modern and Ancient Africa, Map and Planes CD107

Founding of Air Afrique (African Airlines).

1961-62

Cameroun	C37
Cent. Africa	C5
Chad	C7
Congo, P.R.	C5
Dahomey	C17
Gabon	C5
Ivory Coast	C18
Mauritania	C17
Niger	C22
Senegal	C31
Upper Volta	C4

No. C37 (1)	1.00	.50
No. C5 (1)	1.00	.65
No. C7 (1)	1.00	.25
No. C5 (1)	1.75	.90
No. C17 (1)	.80	.40
No. C5 (1)	11.00	6.00
No. C18 (1)	2.00	1.25
No. C17 (1)	2.40	1.25
No. C22 (1)	1.75	.90
No. C31 (1)	.80	.30
No. C4 (1)	3.50	1.75
Set total (11) Stamps	27.00	14.15

Anti-Malaria

CD108

World Health Organization drive to eradicate malaria.

1962, Apr. 7

Cameroun	B36
Cent. Africa	B1
Chad	B1
Comoro Isls.	B1
Congo, P.R.	B3
Dahomey	B15
Gabon	B4
Ivory Coast	B15
Madagascar	B19
Mali	B1
Mauritania	B16
Niger	B14
Senegal	B16
Somali Coast	B15
Upper Volta	B1

No. B36 (1)	1.00	.45
No. B1 (1)	1.40	1.40
No. B1 (1)	1.00	.50
No. B1 (1)	3.50	3.50
No. B3 (1)	1.40	1.00
No. B15 (1)	.75	.75
No. B4 (1)	1.00	1.00
No. B15 (1)	1.25	1.25
No. B19 (1)	.75	.50
No. B1 (1)	1.25	.60
No. B16 (1)	.50	.50
No. B14 (1)	.75	.75
No. B16 (1)	1.10	.65
No. B15 (1)	7.00	7.00
No. B1 (1)	.75	.70
Set total (15) Stamps	23.40	20.55

Abidjan Games

CD109

Abidjan Games, Ivory Coast, Dec. 24-31, 1961. Each stamp shows a different sport.

1962

Cent. Africa	19-20, C6
Chad	83-84, C8
Congo, P.R.	103-104, C7
Gabon	163-164, C6
Niger	109-111
Upper Volta	103-105

Nos. 19-20,C6 (3)	4.15	2.85
Nos. 83-84,C8 (3)	5.80	1.55
Nos. 103-104,C7 (3)	3.85	1.80
Nos. 163-164,C6 (3)	5.00	3.00
Nos. 109-111 (3)	2.60	1.25
Nos. 103-105 (3)	2.80	1.75
Set total (18) Stamps	24.20	12.20

African and Malagasy Union

Flag of Union — CD110

First anniversary of the Union.

1962, Sept. 8

Cameroun	373
Cent. Africa	21
Chad	85
Congo, P.R.	105
Dahomey	155
Gabon	165
Ivory Coast	198
Madagascar	332
Mauritania	170
Niger	112
Senegal	211
Upper Volta	106

No. 373 (1)	2.00	.75
No. 21 (1)	1.25	.75
No. 85 (1)	1.25	.25
No. 105 (1)	1.50	.50
No. 155 (1)	1.25	.90
No. 165 (1)	1.60	1.25
No. 198 (1)	2.10	.75
No. 332 (1)	.80	.80
No. 170 (1)	.75	.50
No. 112 (1)	.80	.50
No. 211 (1)	.80	.50
No. 106 (1)	1.10	.75
Set total (12) Stamps	15.20	8.20

Telstar

Telstar and Globe Showing Andover and Pleumeur-Bodou — CD111

First television connection of the United States and Europe through the Telstar satellite, July 11-12, 1962.

1962-63

Andorra, French	154
Comoro Isls.	C7
Fr. Polynesia	C29
Fr. So. & Antarctic Terr.	C5
New Caledonia	C33
St. Pierre & Miquelon	C26
Somali Coast	C31
Wallis & Futuna Isls.	C17

No. 154 (1)	2.00	1.60
No. C7 (1)	4.50	2.75
No. C29 (1)	11.50	8.00
No. C5 (1)	29.00	21.00
No. C33 (1)	25.00	18.50
No. C26 (1)	7.25	4.50
No. C31 (1)	1.00	1.00
No. C17 (1)	3.75	3.75
Set total (8) Stamps	84.00	61.10

Freedom From Hunger

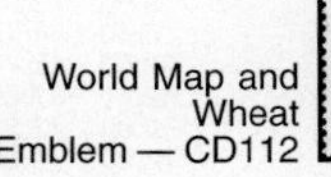

World Map and Wheat Emblem — CD112

U.N. Food and Agriculture Organization's "Freedom from Hunger" campaign.

1963, Mar. 21

Cameroun	B37-B38
Cent. Africa	B2
Chad	B2
Congo, P.R.	B4
Dahomey	B16
Gabon	B5
Ivory Coast	B16
Madagascar	B21
Mauritania	B17
Niger	B15
Senegal	B17
Upper Volta	B2

Nos. B37-B38 (2)	2.25	.75
No. B2 (1)	1.25	1.25
No. B2 (1)	1.10	.50
No. B4 (1)	1.40	1.00
No. B16 (1)	.80	.80
No. B5 (1)	1.00	1.00
No. B16 (1)	1.50	1.50
No. B21 (1)	.60	.45
No. B17 (1)	.60	.60
No. B15 (1)	.75	.75
No. B17 (1)	.80	.50
No. B2 (1)	.75	.70
Set total (13) Stamps	12.80	9.80

Red Cross Centenary

CD113

Centenary of the International Red Cross.

1963, Sept. 2

Comoro Isls.	55
Fr. Polynesia	205
New Caledonia	328
St. Pierre & Miquelon	367
Somali Coast	297
Wallis & Futuna Isls.	165

No. 55 (1)	7.50	6.00
No. 205 (1)	15.00	12.00
No. 328 (1)	8.00	6.75
No. 367 (1)	12.00	5.50
No. 297 (1)	6.25	6.25
No. 165 (1)	4.00	4.00
Set total (6) Stamps	52.75	40.50

African Postal Union, 1963

UAMPT Emblem, Radio Masts, Plane and Mail — CD114

Establishment of the African and Malagasy Posts and Telecommunications Union.

1963, Sept. 8

Cameroun	C47
Cent. Africa	C10
Chad	C9
Congo, P.R.	C13
Dahomey	C19
Gabon	C13
Ivory Coast	C25
Madagascar	C75
Mauritania	C22
Niger	C27
Rwanda	36
Senegal	C32
Upper Volta	C9

No. C47 (1)	2.25	1.00
No. C10 (1)	1.90	.90
No. C9 (1)	1.80	.60
No. C13 (1)	1.40	.75
No. C19 (1)	.75	.25
No. C13 (1)	1.90	.80
No. C25 (1)	2.50	1.50
No. C75 (1)	1.25	.80
No. C22 (1)	1.50	.60
No. C27 (1)	1.25	.60
No. 36 (1)	1.10	.75
No. C32 (1)	1.75	.50
No. C9 (1)	1.50	.75
Set total (13) Stamps	20.85	9.80

Air Afrique, 1963

Symbols of Flight CD115

First anniversary of Air Afrique and inauguration of DC-8 service.

1963, Nov. 19

Cameroun	C48
Chad	C10
Congo, P.R.	C14
Gabon	C18
Ivory Coast	C26
Mauritania	C26
Niger	C35
Senegal	C33

No. C48 (1)	1.25	.40
No. C10 (1)	1.80	.60
No. C14 (1)	1.60	.60
No. C18 (1)	1.25	.65
No. C26 (1)	1.00	.50
No. C26 (1)	.70	.25
No. C35 (1)	1.00	.55
No. C33 (1)	2.00	.65
Set total (8) Stamps	10.60	4.20

Europafrica

Europe and Africa Linked — CD116

Signing of an economic agreement between the European Economic Community and the African and Malagasy Union, Yaounde, Cameroun, July 20, 1963.

1963-64

Cameroun	402
Cent. Africa	C12
Chad	C11
Congo, P.R.	C16
Gabon	C19
Ivory Coast	217
Niger	C43
Upper Volta	C11

No. 402 (1)	2.25	.60
No. C12 (1)	2.50	1.75
No. C11 (1)	1.60	.50
No. C16 (1)	1.60	1.00
No. C19 (1)	1.25	.75
No. 217 (1)	1.10	.35
No. C43 (1)	.85	.50
No. C11 (1)	1.50	.80
Set total (8) Stamps	12.65	6.25

Human Rights

Scales of Justice and Globe — CD117

15th anniversary of the Universal Declaration of Human Rights.

1963, Dec. 10

Comoro Isls.	56
Fr. Polynesia	206
New Caledonia	329
St. Pierre & Miquelon	368
Somali Coast	300
Wallis & Futuna Isls.	166

No. 56 (1)	7.50	6.00
No. 205 (1)	15.00	12.00
No. 329 (1)	7.00	6.00
No. 368 (1)	7.00	3.50
No. 300 (1)	8.50	8.50
No. 166 (1)	7.00	7.00
Set total (6) Stamps	52.00	43.00

PHILATEC

Stamp Album, Champs Elysees Palace and Horses of Marly — CD118

Intl. Philatelic and Postal Techniques Exhibition, Paris, June 5-21, 1964.

1963-64

Comoro Isls.	60
France	1078
Fr. Polynesia	207
New Caledonia	341
St. Pierre & Miquelon	369
Somali Coast	301
Wallis & Futuna Isls.	167

No. 60 (1)	4.00	3.50
No. 1078 (1)	.25	.25
No. 206 (1)	15.00	10.00

No. 341 (1) 6.50 6.50
No. 369 (1) 11.00 8.00
No. 301 (1) 7.75 7.75
No. 167 (1) 3.00 3.00
Set total (7) Stamps 47.50 39.00

Cooperation

CD119

Cooperation between France and the French-speaking countries of Africa and Madagascar.

1964

Cameroun 409-410
Cent. Africa 39
Chad 103
Congo, P.R. 121
Dahomey 193
France 1111
Gabon 175
Ivory Coast 221
Madagascar 360
Mauritania 181
Niger 143
Senegal 236
Togo 495

Nos. 409-410 (2) 2.50 .50
No. 39 (1) .90 .50
No. 103 (1) 1.00 .25
No. 121 (1) .90 .35
No. 193 (1) .80 .35
No. 1111 (1) .25 .25
No. 175 (1) .90 .60
No. 221 (1) 1.10 .35
No. 360 (1) .60 .25
No. 181 (1) .60 .35
No. 143 (1) .80 .40
No. 236 (1) 1.60 .85
No. 495 (1) .70 .25
Set total (14) Stamps 12.65 5.25

ITU

Telegraph, Syncom Satellite and ITU Emblem — CD120

Intl. Telecommunication Union, Cent.

1965, May 17

Comoro Isls. C14
Fr. Polynesia C33
Fr. So. & Antarctic Terr. C8
New Caledonia C40
New Hebrides 124-125
St. Pierre & Miquelon C29
Somali Coast C36
Wallis & Futuna Isls. C20

No. C14 (1) 18.00 9.00
No. C33 (1) 80.00 52.50
No. C8 (1) 200.00 160.00
No. C40 (1) 10.00 8.00
Nos. 124-125 (2) 32.25 27.25
No. C29 (1) 24.00 11.50
No. C36 (1) 15.00 9.00
No. C20 (1) 16.00 16.00
Set total (9) Stamps 395.25 293.25

French Satellite A-1

Diamant Rocket and Launching Installation CD121

Launching of France's first satellite, Nov. 26, 1965.

1965-66

Comoro Isls. C16a
France 1138a
Reunion 359a
Fr. Polynesia C41a
Fr. So. & Antarctic Terr. C10a
New Caledonia C45a
St. Pierre & Miquelon C31a
Somali Coast C40a
Wallis & Futuna Isls. C23a

No. C16a (1) 9.00 9.00
No. 1138a (1) .65 .65
No. 359a (1) 3.50 3.00
No. C41a (1) 14.00 14.00
No. C10a (1) 29.00 24.00
No. C45a (1) 7.00 7.00
No. C31a (1) 14.50 14.50
No. C40a (1) 7.00 7.00
No. C23a (1) 8.50 8.50
Set total (9) Stamps 93.15 87.65

French Satellite D-1

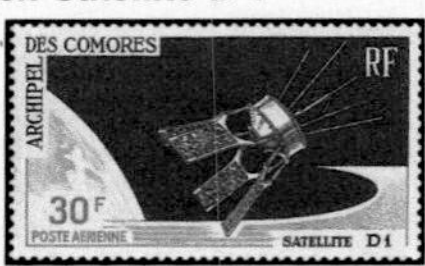

D-1 Satellite in Orbit CD122

Launching of the D-1 satellite at Hammaguir, Algeria, Feb. 17, 1966.

1966

Comoro Isls. C17
France 1148
Fr. Polynesia C42
Fr. So. & Antarctic Terr. C11
New Caledonia C46
St. Pierre & Miquelon C32
Somali Coast C49
Wallis & Futuna Isls. C24

No. C17 (1) 4.00 4.00
No. 1148 (1) .25 .25
No. C42 (1) 7.00 4.75
No. C11 (1) 57.50 40.00
No. C46 (1) 2.25 2.00
No. C32 (1) 9.00 6.00
No. C49 (1) 4.25 2.75
No. C24 (1) 3.50 3.50
Set total (8) Stamps 87.75 63.25

Air Afrique, 1966

Planes and Air Afrique Emblem CD123

Introduction of DC-8F planes by Air Afrique.

1966

Cameroun C79
Cent. Africa C35
Chad C26
Congo, P.R. C42
Dahomey C42
Gabon C47
Ivory Coast C32
Mauritania C57
Niger C63
Senegal C47
Togo C54
Upper Volta C31

No. C79 (1) .80 .25
No. C35 (1) 1.00 .50
No. C26 (1) .85 .25
No. C42 (1) 1.00 .25
No. C42 (1) .75 .25
No. C47 (1) .90 .35
No. C32 (1) 1.00 .60
No. C57 (1) .60 .30
No. C63 (1) .70 .35
No. C47 (1) .80 .30
No. C54 (1) .80 .25
No. C31 (1) .75 .50
Set total (12) Stamps 9.95 4.15

African Postal Union, 1967

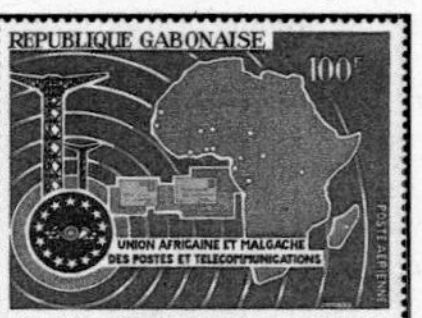

Telecommunications Symbols and Map of Africa — CD124

Fifth anniversary of the establishment of the African and Malagasy Union of Posts and Telecommunications, UAMPT.

1967

Cameroun C90
Cent. Africa C46
Chad C37
Congo, P.R. C57
Dahomey C61
Gabon C58
Ivory Coast C34
Madagascar C85
Mauritania C65
Niger C75
Rwanda C1-C3
Senegal C60
Togo C81
Upper Volta C50

No. C90 (1) 2.40 .65
No. C46 (1) 2.25 .85
No. C37 (1) 2.00 .60
No. C57 (1) 1.60 .60
No. C61 (1) 1.75 .95
No. C58 (1) 2.00 .85
No. C34 (1) 3.50 1.50
No. C85 (1) 1.25 .60
No. C65 (1) 1.25 .60
No. C75 (1) 1.40 .60
Nos. C1-C3 (3) 2.05 1.25
No. C60 (1) 1.75 .50
No. C81 (1) 1.90 .30
No. C50 (1) 1.80 .70
Set total (16) Stamps 26.90 10.55

Monetary Union

Gold Token of the Ashantis, 17-18th Centuries — CD125

West African Monetary Union, 5th anniv.

1967, Nov. 4

Dahomey 244
Ivory Coast 259
Mauritania 238
Niger 204
Senegal 294
Togo 623
Upper Volta 181

No. 244 (1) .65 .65
No. 259 (1) .85 .40
No. 238 (1) .45 .25
No. 204 (1) .55 .25
No. 294 (1) .60 .25
No. 623 (1) .60 .25
No. 181 (1) .65 .35
Set total (7) Stamps 4.35 2.40

WHO Anniversary

Sun, Flowers and WHO Emblem CD126

World Health Organization, 20th anniv.

1968, May 4

Afars & Issas 317
Comoro Isls. 73
Fr. Polynesia 241-242
Fr. So. & Antarctic Terr. 31
New Caledonia 367
St. Pierre & Miquelon 377
Wallis & Futuna Isls. 169

No. 317 (1) 3.00 3.00
No. 73 (1) 2.40 1.75
Nos. 241-242 (2) 22.00 12.75
No. 31 (1) 62.50 47.50
No. 367 (1) 4.00 2.25
No. 377 (1) 12.00 9.00
No. 169 (1) 5.75 5.75
Set total (8) Stamps 111.65 82.00

Human Rights Year

Human Rights Flame — CD127

1968, Aug. 10

Afars & Issas 322-323
Comoro Isls. 76
Fr. Polynesia 243-244
Fr. So. & Antarctic Terr. 32
New Caledonia 369
St. Pierre & Miquelon 382
Wallis & Futuna Isls. 170

Nos. 322-323 (2) 6.75 4.00
No. 76 (1) 3.25 3.25
Nos. 243-244 (2) 24.00 14.00
No. 32 (1) 55.00 47.50
No. 369 (1) 2.75 1.50
No. 382 (1) 8.00 5.50
No. 170 (1) 3.25 3.25
Set total (9) Stamps 103.00 79.00

2nd PHILEXAFRIQUE

CD128

Opening of PHILEXAFRIQUE, Abidjan, Feb. 14. Each stamp shows a local scene and stamp.

1969, Feb. 14

Cameroun C118
Cent. Africa C65
Chad C48
Congo, P.R. C77
Dahomey C94
Gabon C82
Ivory Coast C38-C40
Madagascar C92
Mali C65
Mauritania C80
Niger C104
Senegal C68
Togo C104
Upper Volta C62

No. C118 (1) 3.25 1.25
No. C65 (1) 1.75 1.75
No. C48 (1) 2.40 1.00
No. C77 (1) 2.00 1.75
No. C94 (1) 2.25 2.25
No. C82 (1) 2.00 2.00
Nos. C38-C40 (3) 14.50 14.50
No. C92 (1) 1.75 .85
No. C65 (1) 1.75 1.00
No. C80 (1) 1.90 .75
No. C104 (1) 3.00 1.90
No. C68 (1) 2.00 1.40
No. C104 (1) 2.25 .45
No. C62 (1) 4.00 3.25
Set total (16) Stamps 44.80 34.10

Concorde

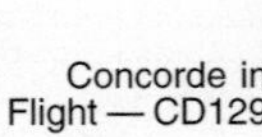

Concorde in Flight — CD129

First flight of the prototype Concorde supersonic plane at Toulouse, Mar. 1, 1969.

1969

Afars & Issas C56
Comoro Isls. C29
France C42
Fr. Polynesia C50
Fr. So. & Antarctic Terr. C18
New Caledonia C63
St. Pierre & Miquelon C40
Wallis & Futuna Isls. C30

No. C56 (1) 26.00 16.00
No. C29 (1) 18.00 12.00
No. C42 (1) .75 .35
No. C50 (1) 55.00 35.00
No. C18 (1) 55.00 37.50
No. C63 (1) 27.50 20.00
No. C40 (1) 32.50 11.00
No. C30 (1) 15.00 10.00
Set total (8) Stamps 229.75 141.85

Development Bank

Bank Emblem — CD130

African Development Bank, fifth anniv.

1969

Cameroun	499
Chad	217
Congo, P.R.	181-182
Ivory Coast	281
Mali	127-128
Mauritania	267
Niger	220
Senegal	317-318
Upper Volta	201

No. 499 (1)	.80	.25
No. 217 (1)	.90	.25
Nos. 181-182 (2)	1.00	.50
No. 281 (1)	.70	.40
Nos. 127-128 (2)	1.00	.50
No. 267 (1)	.60	.25
No. 220 (1)	.70	.30
Nos. 317-318 (2)	1.55	.50
No. 201 (1)	.65	.30
Set total (12) Stamps	7.90	3.25

ILO

ILO Headquarters, Geneva, and Emblem — CD131

Intl. Labor Organization, 50th anniv.

1969-70

Afars & Issas	337
Comoro Isls.	83
Fr. Polynesia	251-252
Fr. So. & Antarctic Terr.	35
New Caledonia	379
St. Pierre & Miquelon	396
Wallis & Futuna Isls.	172

No. 337 (1)	2.75	2.00
No. 83 (1)	1.25	.75
Nos. 251-252 (2)	24.00	12.50
No. 35 (1)	15.00	10.00
No. 379 (1)	2.25	1.10
No. 396 (1)	10.00	5.50
No. 172 (1)	2.75	2.75
Set total (8) Stamps	58.00	34.60

ASECNA

Map of Africa, Plane and Airport — CD132

10th anniversary of the Agency for the Security of Aerial Navigation in Africa and Madagascar (ASECNA, Agence pour la Securite de la Navigation Aerienne en Afrique et a Madagascar).

1969-70

Cameroun	500
Cent. Africa	119
Chad	222
Congo, P.R.	197
Dahomey	269
Gabon	260
Ivory Coast	287
Mali	130
Niger	221
Senegal	321
Upper Volta	204

No. 500 (1)	2.00	.60
No. 119 (1)	2.00	.80
No. 222 (1)	1.00	.25
No. 197 (1)	2.00	.40
No. 269 (1)	.90	.55
No. 260 (1)	1.75	.75
No. 287 (1)	.90	.40
No. 130 (1)	.90	.40
No. 221 (1)	1.40	.70
No. 321 (1)	1.60	.50
No. 204 (1)	1.75	1.00
Set total (11) Stamps	16.20	6.35

U.P.U. Headquarters

CD133

New Universal Postal Union headquarters, Bern, Switzerland.

1970

Afars & Issas	342
Algeria	443
Cameroun	503-504
Cent. Africa	125
Chad	225
Comoro Isls.	84
Congo, P.R.	216
Fr. Polynesia	261-262
Fr. So. & Antarctic Terr.	36
Gabon	258
Ivory Coast	295
Madagascar	444
Mali	134-135
Mauritania	283
New Caledonia	382
Niger	231-232
St. Pierre & Miquelon	397-398
Senegal	328-329
Tunisia	535
Wallis & Futuna Isls.	173

No. 342 (1)	2.50	1.40
No. 443 (1)	1.10	.40
Nos. 503-504 (2)	2.60	.55
No. 125 (1)	1.75	.70
No. 225 (1)	1.20	.25
No. 84 (1)	5.50	2.00
No. 216 (1)	1.00	.25
Nos. 261-262 (2)	20.00	10.00
No. 36 (1)	40.00	27.50
No. 258 (1)	.90	.55
No. 295 (1)	1.10	.50
No. 444 (1)	.55	.25
Nos. 134-135 (2)	1.05	.50
No. 283 (1)	.60	.30
No. 382 (1)	3.00	1.50
Nos. 231-232 (2)	1.50	.60
Nos. 397-398 (2)	34.00	16.25
Nos. 328-329 (2)	1.55	.55
No. 535 (1)	.60	.25
No. 173 (1)	3.25	3.25
Set total (26) Stamps	123.75	67.55

De Gaulle

CD134

First anniversary of the death of Charles de Gaulle, (1890-1970), President of France.

1971-72

Afars & Issas	356-357
Comoro Isls.	104-105
France	1325a
Fr. Polynesia	270-271
Fr. So. & Antarctic Terr.	52-53
New Caledonia	393-394
Reunion	380a
St. Pierre & Miquelon	417-418
Wallis & Futuna Isls.	177-178

Nos. 356-357 (2)	12.50	7.50
Nos. 104-105 (2)	9.00	5.75
No. 1325a (1)	3.00	2.50
Nos. 270-271 (2)	51.50	29.50
Nos. 52-53 (2)	40.00	29.50
Nos. 393-394 (2)	23.00	11.75
No. 380a (1)	9.25	8.00
Nos. 417-418 (2)	56.50	31.00
Nos. 177-178 (2)	20.00	16.25
Set total (16) Stamps	224.75	141.75

African Postal Union, 1971

UAMPT Building, Brazzaville, Congo — CD135

10th anniversary of the establishment of the African and Malagasy Posts and Telecommunications Union, UAMPT. Each stamp has a different native design.

1971, Nov. 13

Cameroun	C177
Cent. Africa	C89
Chad	C94
Congo, P.R.	C136
Dahomey	C146
Gabon	C120
Ivory Coast	C47
Mauritania	C113
Niger	C164
Rwanda	C8
Senegal	C105
Togo	C166
Upper Volta	C97

No. C177 (1)	2.00	.50
No. C89 (1)	2.25	.85
No. C94 (1)	1.50	.50
No. C136 (1)	1.60	.75
No. C146 (1)	1.75	.80
No. C120 (1)	1.75	.70
No. C47 (1)	2.00	1.00
No. C113 (1)	1.10	.65
No. C164 (1)	1.25	.60
No. C8 (1)	2.75	2.50
No. C105 (1)	1.60	.50
No. C166 (1)	1.25	.40
No. C97 (1)	1.50	.70
Set total (13) Stamps	22.30	10.45

West African Monetary Union

African Couple, City, Village and Commemorative Coin — CD136

West African Monetary Union, 10th anniv.

1972, Nov. 2

Dahomey	300
Ivory Coast	331
Mauritania	299
Niger	258
Senegal	374
Togo	825
Upper Volta	280

No. 300 (1)	.65	.25
No. 331 (1)	1.00	.50
No. 299 (1)	.75	.25
No. 258 (1)	.65	.30
No. 374 (1)	.50	.30
No. 825 (1)	.60	.25
No. 280 (1)	.60	.25
Set total (7) Stamps	4.75	2.10

African Postal Union, 1973

Telecommunications Symbols and Map of Africa — CD137

11th anniversary of the African and Malagasy Posts and Telecommunications Union (UAMPT).

1973, Sept. 12

Cameroun	574
Cent. Africa	194
Chad	294
Congo, P.R.	289
Dahomey	311
Gabon	320
Ivory Coast	361
Madagascar	500
Mauritania	304
Niger	287
Rwanda	540
Senegal	393
Togo	849
Upper Volta	297

No. 574 (1)	1.75	.40
No. 194 (1)	1.25	.75
No. 294 (1)	1.75	.40
No. 289 (1)	1.60	.50
No. 311 (1)	1.25	.55
No. 320 (1)	1.40	.75
No. 361 (1)	2.50	1.00
No. 500 (1)	1.10	.35
No. 304 (1)	1.10	.40
No. 287 (1)	.90	.60
No. 540 (1)	3.00	2.00
No. 393 (1)	1.60	.50
No. 849 (1)	1.00	.35
No. 297 (1)	1.25	.70
Set total (14) Stamps	21.45	9.25

Philexafrique II — Essen

CD138

CD139

Designs: Indigenous fauna, local and German stamps. Types CD138-CD139 printed horizontally and vertically se-tenant in sheets of 10 (2x5). Label between horizontal pairs alternately commemoratives Philexafrique II, Libreville, Gabon, June 1978, and 2nd International Stamp Fair, Essen, Germany, Nov. 1-5.

1978-1979

Benin	C286a
Central Africa	C201a
Chad	C239a
Congo Republic	C246a
Djibouti	C122a
Gabon	C216a
Ivory Coast	C65a
Mali	C357a
Mauritania	C186a
Niger	C292a
Rwanda	C13a
Senegal	C147a
Togo	C364a

No. C286a (1)	9.00	8.50
No. C201a (1)	7.50	7.50
No. C239a (1)	7.50	4.00
No. C246a (1)	7.00	7.00
No. C122a (1)	6.50	6.50
No. C216a (1)	6.50	4.00
No. C65a (1)	9.00	9.00
No. C357a (1)	5.00	3.00
No. C186a (1)	5.50	5.00
No. C292a (1)	6.00	6.00
No. C13a (1)	4.00	4.00
No. C147a (1)	10.00	4.00
No. C364a (1)	3.00	1.50
Set total (13) Stamps	86.50	70.00

BRITISH COMMONWEALTH OF NATIONS

The listings follow established trade practices when these issues are offered as units by dealers. The Peace issue, for example, includes only one stamp from the Indian state of Hyderabad. The U.P.U. issue includes the Egypt set. Pairs are included for those varieties issued with bilingual designs se-tenant.

Silver Jubilee

Windsor Castle and King George V — CD301

Reign of King George V, 25th anniv.

1935

Antigua	77-80
Ascension	33-36
Bahamas	92-95
Barbados	186-189
Basutoland	11-14
Bechuanaland Protectorate	117-120
Bermuda	100-103
British Guiana	223-226
British Honduras	108-111
Cayman Islands	81-84
Ceylon	260-263
Cyprus	136-139
Dominica	90-93
Falkland Islands	77-80
Fiji	110-113
Gambia	125-128
Gibraltar	100-103
Gilbert & Ellice Islands	33-36
Gold Coast	108-111
Grenada	124-127
Hong Kong	147-150
Jamaica	109-112
Kenya, Uganda, Tanzania	42-45
Leeward Islands	96-99
Malta	184-187
Mauritius	204-207
Montserrat	85-88
Newfoundland	226-229
Nigeria	34-37
Northern Rhodesia	18-21

Nyasaland Protectorate................47-50
St. Helena 111-114
St. Kitts-Nevis...............................72-75
St. Lucia 91-94
St. Vincent..............................134-137
Seychelles 118-121
Sierra Leone...........................166-169
Solomon Islands............................60-63
Somaliland Protectorate..............77-80
Straits Settlements 213-216
Swaziland 20-23
Trinidad & Tobago 43-46
Turks & Caicos Islands 71-74
Virgin Islands................................69-72

The following have different designs but are included in the omnibus set:

Great Britain 226-229
Offices in Morocco (Sp. Curr.).....67-70
Offices in Morocco (Br. Curr.)........226-229
Offices in Morocco (Fr. Curr.) 422-425
Offices in Morocco (Tangier)....508-510
Australia..................................152-154
Canada....................................211-216
Cook Islands 98-100
India..142-148
Nauru..31-34
New Guinea...................................46-47
New Zealand 199-201
Niue 67-69
Papua 114-117
Samoa 163-165
South Africa.................................68-71
Southern Rhodesia 33-36
South-West Africa 121-124

Nos. 77-80 (4)	20.25	*23.25*
Nos. 33-36 (4)	58.50	*127.50*
Nos. 92-95 (4)	25.00	*46.00*
Nos. 186-189 (4)	30.00	50.30
Nos. 11-14 (4)	11.60	*21.25*
Nos. 117-120 (4)	15.75	*36.00*
Nos. 100-103 (4)	16.80	*58.50*
Nos. 223-226 (4)	22.35	35.50
Nos. 108-111 (4)	15.25	*16.35*
Nos. 81-84 (4)	21.60	*24.50*
Nos. 260-263 (4)	10.40	21.60
Nos. 136-139 (4)	39.75	*38.75*
Nos. 90-93 (4)	18.85	19.85
Nos. 77-80 (4)	55.00	14.75
Nos. 110-113 (4)	20.25	34.00
Nos. 125-128 (4)	13.05	*25.25*
Nos. 100-103 (4)	45.25	61.75
Nos. 33-36 (4)	36.80	*67.00*
Nos. 108-111 (4)	25.75	*78.10*
Nos. 124-127 (4)	16.70	*40.60*
Nos. 147-150 (4)	73.75	20.75
Nos. 109-112 (4)	24.20	*50.50*
Nos. 42-45 (4)	10.25	*11.75*
Nos. 96-99 (4)	35.75	49.60
Nos. 184-187 (4)	22.00	33.70
Nos. 204-207 (4)	44.60	*58.25*
Nos. 85-88 (4)	10.25	*30.25*
Nos. 226-229 (4)	17.50	12.05
Nos. 34-37 (4)	17.50	*73.00*
Nos. 18-21 (4)	17.00	15.00
Nos. 47-50 (4)	43.50	*82.50*
Nos. 111-114 (4)	31.15	*36.50*
Nos. 72-75 (4)	11.80	*18.65*
Nos. 91-94 (4)	16.00	*20.80*
Nos. 134-137 (4)	9.45	*21.25*
Nos. 118-121 (4)	15.75	*40.00*
Nos. 166-169 (4)	23.60	*50.35*
Nos. 60-63 (4)	29.00	38.00
Nos. 77-80 (4)	17.00	*48.25*
Nos. 213-216 (4)	15.00	*25.10*
Nos. 20-23 (4)	6.80	18.25
Nos. 43-46 (4)	18.60	37.50
Nos. 71-74 (4)	9.90	14.50
Nos. 69-72 (4)	25.00	*55.25*
Nos. 226-229 (4)	5.15	*9.90*
Nos. 67-70 (4)	13.60	*30.70*
Nos. 226-229 (4)	16.30	*56.00*
Nos. 422-425 (4)	9.35	3.95
Nos. 508-510 (3)	26.00	*33.50*
Nos. 152-154 (3)	49.50	45.35
Nos. 211-216 (6)	23.85	13.35
Nos. 98-100 (3)	9.65	*12.00*
Nos. 142-148 (7)	28.85	14.00
Nos. 31-34 (4)	12.35	*13.15*
Nos. 46-47 (2)	4.35	1.70
Nos. 199-201 (3)	23.00	*28.50*
Nos. 67-69 (3)	19.25	*31.00*
Nos. 114-117 (4)	9.20	*17.50*
Nos. 163-165 (3)	4.40	6.50
Nos. 68-71 (4)	57.50	*153.00*
Nos. 33-36 (4)	27.75	*45.25*
Nos. 121-124 (4)	13.00	*36.10*
Set total (245) Stamps	1,417.	2,254.

Coronation

Queen Elizabeth and King George VI — CD302

1937

Aden 13-15
Antigua 81-83
Ascension 37-39
Bahamas 97-99
Barbados 190-192
Basutoland......................................15-17
Bechuanaland Protectorate......121-123
Bermuda....................................115-117
British Guiana...........................227-229
British Honduras.......................112-114
Cayman Islands.............................97-99
Ceylon 275-277
Cyprus 140-142
Dominica...94-96
Falkland Islands 81-83
Fiji...114-116
Gambia......................................129-131
Gibraltar....................................104-106
Gilbert & Ellice Islands.................37-39
Gold Coast 112-114
Grenada.....................................128-130
Hong Kong 151-153
Jamaica 113-115
Kenya, Uganda, Tanzania 60-62
Leeward Islands 100-102
Malta..188-190
Mauritius....................................208-210
Montserrat 89-91
Newfoundland...........................230-232
Nigeria 50-52
Northern Rhodesia 22-24
Nyasaland Protectorate................51-53
St. Helena 115-117
St. Kitts-Nevis................................76-78
St. Lucia 107-109
St. Vincent.................................138-140
Seychelles 122-124
Sierra Leone.............................170-172
Solomon Islands............................64-66
Somaliland Protectorate..............81-83
Straits Settlements 235-237
Swaziland 24-26
Trinidad & Tobago 47-49
Turks & Caicos Islands 75-77
Virgin Islands................................73-75

The following have different designs but are included in the omnibus set:

Great Britain 234
Offices in Morocco (Sp. Curr.)..........82
Offices in Morocco (Fr. Curr.) 439
Offices in Morocco (Tangier)...........514
Canada..237
Cook Islands 109-111
Nauru..35-38
Newfoundland...........................233-243
New Guinea...................................48-51
New Zealand 223-225
Niue 70-72
Papua 118-121
South Africa.................................74-78
Southern Rhodesia 38-41
South-West Africa 125-132

Nos. 13-15 (3)	2.70	*5.65*
Nos. 81-83 (3)	1.85	*8.00*
Nos. 37-39 (3)	2.75	*2.75*
Nos. 97-99 (3)	1.05	*3.05*
Nos. 190-192 (3)	1.10	1.95
Nos. 15-17 (3)	1.15	*3.00*
Nos. 121-123 (3)	.95	3.35
Nos. 115-117 (3)	1.25	5.00
Nos. 227-229 (3)	1.50	3.05
Nos. 112-114 (3)	1.20	2.40
Nos. 97-99 (3)	1.10	2.70
Nos. 275-277 (3)	8.25	10.35
Nos. 140-142 (3)	3.75	6.50
Nos. 94-96 (3)	.85	2.40
Nos. 81-83 (3)	2.90	*2.30*
Nos. 114-116 (3)	1.35	*5.75*
Nos. 129-131 (3)	.95	3.95
Nos. 104-106 (3)	2.30	6.45
Nos. 37-39 (3)	.85	*2.15*
Nos. 112-114 (3)	3.10	*10.00*
Nos. 128-130 (3)	1.00	.85
Nos. 151-153 (3)	17.00	17.75
Nos. 113-115 (3)	1.25	1.25
Nos. 60-62 (3)	1.25	2.35
Nos. 100-102 (3)	1.55	4.00
Nos. 188-190 (3)	1.25	1.60
Nos. 208-210 (3)	1.75	*3.50*
Nos. 89-91 (3)	1.00	3.35
Nos. 230-232 (3)	7.00	2.80
Nos. 50-52 (3)	3.25	8.50
Nos. 22-24 (3)	.95	2.25
Nos. 51-53 (3)	1.05	1.30
Nos. 115-117 (3)	1.45	2.05
Nos. 76-78 (3)	.95	2.15
Nos. 107-109 (3)	1.05	2.05
Nos. 138-140 (3)	.80	*4.75*
Nos. 122-124 (3)	1.20	*1.90*
Nos. 170-172 (3)	1.95	5.65
Nos. 64-66 (3)	.90	2.00
Nos. 81-83 (3)	1.10	*3.50*
Nos. 235-237 (3)	3.25	1.60
Nos. 24-26 (3)	.75	2.70
Nos. 47-49 (3)	1.10	3.20
Nos. 75-77 (3)	1.25	.95
Nos. 73-75 (3)	2.20	*6.90*
No. 234 (1)	.30	.25
No. 82 (1)	.80	.60
No. 439 (1)	.50	.25
No. 514 (1)	1.25	.50
No. 237 (1)	.35	.25
Nos. 109-111 (3)	.85	.80
Nos. 35-38 (4)	1.25	*5.50*
Nos. 233-243 (11)	41.90	30.40
Nos. 48-51 (4)	1.40	*7.90*
Nos. 223-225 (3)	1.75	*2.25*
Nos. 70-72 (3)	.90	*2.05*
Nos. 118-121 (4)	1.60	*5.25*
Nos. 74-78 (5)	7.60	9.35
Nos. 38-41 (4)	3.55	15.50
Nos. 125-132 (8)	5.00	8.40
Set total (189) Stamps	166.15	268.90

Peace

King George VI and Parliament Buildings, London — CD303

Return to peace at the close of World War II.

1945-46

Aden 28-29
Antigua 96-97
Ascension 50-51
Bahamas 130-131
Barbados 207-208
Bermuda......................................131-132
British Guiana............................242-243
British Honduras.........................127-128
Cayman Islands..........................112-113
Ceylon 293-294
Cyprus 156-157
Dominica...................................112-113
Falkland Islands 97-98
Falkland Islands Dep.............1L9-1L10
Fiji...137-138
Gambia.......................................144-145
Gibraltar.....................................119-120
Gilbert & Ellice Islands.................52-53
Gold Coast 128-129
Grenada.....................................143-144
Jamaica 136-137
Kenya, Uganda, Tanzania 90-91
Leeward Islands 116-117
Malta..206-207
Mauritius....................................223-224
Montserrat 104-105
Nigeria 71-72
Northern Rhodesia 46-47
Nyasaland Protectorate................82-83
Pitcairn Islands..................................9-10
St. Helena 128-129
St. Kitts-Nevis................................91-92
St. Lucia 127-128
St. Vincent.................................152-153
Seychelles 149-150
Sierra Leone.............................186-187
Solomon Islands............................80-81
Somaliland Protectorate...........108-109
Trinidad & Tobago 62-63
Turks & Caicos Islands 90-91
Virgin Islands................................88-89

The following have different designs but are included in the omnibus set:

Great Britain 264-265
Offices in Morocco (Tangier)....523-524
Aden
  Kathiri State of Seiyun...............12-13
  Qu'aiti State of Shihr and Mukalla 12-13
Australia...................................200-202
Basutoland.....................................29-31
Bechuanaland Protectorate......137-139
Burma..66-69
Cook Islands 127-130
Hong Kong 174-175
India..195-198
  Hyderabad 51-53
New Zealand 247-257
Niue 90-93
Pakistan-Bahawalpur......................O16
Samoa 191-194
South Africa..............................100-102
Southern Rhodesia 67-70
South-West Africa 153-155
Swaziland 38-40
Zanzibar....................................222-223

Nos. 28-29 (2)	.95	2.50
Nos. 96-97 (2)	.50	*.80*
Nos. 50-51 (2)	.80	*2.00*
Nos. 130-131 (2)	.50	1.40
Nos. 207-208 (2)	.50	1.10
Nos. 131-132 (2)	.55	.55
Nos. 242-243 (2)	1.05	*1.40*
Nos. 127-128 (2)	.50	.50
Nos. 112-113 (2)	.80	.80
Nos. 293-294 (2)	.60	*2.10*
Nos. 156-157 (2)	.90	.70
Nos. 112-113 (2)	.50	.50
Nos. 97-98 (2)	.90	1.35
Nos. 1L9-1L10 (2)	1.30	1.00
Nos. 137-138 (2)	.75	*1.75*
Nos. 144-145 (2)	.60	.95
Nos. 119-120 (2)	.75	*3.00*
Nos. 52-53 (2)	.50	*1.10*
Nos. 128-129 (2)	1.85	*3.75*
Nos. 143-144 (2)	.50	*.95*
Nos. 136-137 (2)	2.00	*13.50*
Nos. 90-91 (2)	.65	.85
Nos. 116-117 (2)	.50	1.50
Nos. 206-207 (2)	.65	2.00
Nos. 223-224 (2)	.60	1.05
Nos. 104-105 (2)	.50	.50
Nos. 71-72 (2)	.70	*2.75*
Nos. 46-47 (2)	1.25	*2.00*
Nos. 82-83 (2)	.55	.60
Nos. 9-10 (2)	1.40	.60
Nos. 128-129 (2)	.65	.70
Nos. 91-92 (2)	.50	.50
Nos. 127-128 (2)	.50	.60
Nos. 152-153 (2)	.50	.50
Nos. 149-150 (2)	.55	.50
Nos. 186-187 (2)	.50	.50
Nos. 80-81 (2)	.50	1.50
Nos. 108-109 (2)	.70	.50
Nos. 62-63 (2)	.75	1.85
Nos. 90-91 (2)	.50	.50
Nos. 88-89 (2)	.50	.50
Nos. 264-265 (2)	.50	.50
Nos. 523-524 (2)	2.00	2.55
Nos. 12-13 (2)	.50	.90
Nos. 12-13 (2)	.50	*1.25*
Nos. 200-202 (3)	1.60	*1.25*
Nos. 29-31 (3)	2.10	2.60
Nos. 137-139 (3)	2.05	*4.75*
Nos. 66-69 (4)	1.50	1.25
Nos. 127-130 (4)	2.00	1.85
Nos. 174-175 (2)	6.75	2.75
Nos. 195-198 (4)	5.60	5.50
Nos. 51-53 (3)	1.50	1.70
Nos. 247-257 (11)	3.35	3.65
Nos. 90-93 (4)	1.70	*2.20*
No. O16 (1)	15.00	*10.00*
Nos. 191-194 (4)	2.05	1.00
Nos. 100-102 (3)	1.00	3.25
Nos. 67-70 (4)	1.40	1.75
Nos. 153-155 (3)	1.85	3.25
Nos. 38-40 (3)	2.40	*5.50*
Nos. 222-223 (2)	.65	1.00
Set total (151) Stamps	86.25	120.15

Silver Wedding

King George VI and Queen Elizabeth
CD304 CD305

1948-49

Aden 30-31
  Kathiri State of Seiyun...............14-15
  Qu'aiti State of Shihr and Mukalla 14-15
Antigua 98-99
Ascension 52-53
Bahamas 148-149
Barbados 210-211
Basutoland......................................39-40
Bechuanaland Protectorate......147-148
Bermuda......................................133-134
British Guiana............................244-245
British Honduras.........................129-130
Cayman Islands..........................116-117
Cyprus 158-159
Dominica....................................114-115
Falkland Islands 99-100
Falkland Islands Dep...........1L11-1L12
Fiji...139-140
Gambia.......................................146-147
Gibraltar.....................................121-122
Gilbert & Ellice Islands.................54-55
Gold Coast 142-143
Grenada.....................................145-146
Hong Kong 178-179
Jamaica 138-139
Kenya, Uganda, Tanzania 92-93
Leeward Islands 118-119
Malaya
  Johore 128-129
  Kedah..55-56
  Kelantan..44-45
  Malacca...1-2
  Negri Sembilan 36-37

Pahang....................................44-45
Penang....................................1-2
Perak....................................99-100
Perlis....................................1-2
Selangor....................................74-75
Trengganu....................................47-48
Malta....................................223-224
Mauritius....................................229-230
Montserrat....................................106-107
Nigeria....................................73-74
North Borneo....................................238-239
Northern Rhodesia....................................48-49
Nyasaland Protectorate....................................85-86
Pitcairn Islands....................................11-12
St. Helena....................................130-131
St. Kitts-Nevis....................................93-94
St. Lucia....................................129-130
St. Vincent....................................154-155
Sarawak....................................174-175
Seychelles....................................151-152
Sierra Leone....................................188-189
Singapore....................................21-22
Solomon Islands....................................82-83
Somaliland Protectorate....................................110-111
Swaziland....................................48-49
Trinidad & Tobago....................................64-65
Turks & Caicos Islands....................................92-93
Virgin Islands....................................90-91
Zanzibar....................................224-225

The following have different designs but are included in the omnibus set:

Great Britain....................................267-268
Offices in Morocco (Sp. Curr.)......93-94
Offices in Morocco (Tangier).......525-526
Bahrain....................................62-63
Kuwait....................................82-83
Oman....................................25-26
South Africa....................................106
South-West Africa....................................159

Nos. 30-31 (2)	40.40	56.50
Nos. 14-15 (2)	17.85	16.00
Nos. 14-15 (2)	18.55	12.50
Nos. 98-99 (2)	13.55	15.75
Nos. 52-53 (2)	55.55	50.45
Nos. 148-149 (2)	45.25	40.30
Nos. 210-211 (2)	18.35	13.55
Nos. 39-40 (2)	52.80	55.25
Nos. 147-148 (2)	42.85	47.75
Nos. 133-134 (2)	47.75	55.25
Nos. 244-245 (2)	24.25	28.45
Nos. 129-130 (2)	25.25	53.20
Nos. 116-117 (2)	25.25	33.50
Nos. 158-159 (2)	66.50	83.05
Nos. 114-115 (2)	25.25	32.75
Nos. 99-100 (2)	112.10	76.10
Nos. 1L11-1L12 (2)	4.25	6.00
Nos. 139-140 (2)	18.20	11.50
Nos. 146-147 (2)	21.30	21.25
Nos. 121-122 (2)	66.65	90.50
Nos. 54-55 (2)	14.25	26.25
Nos. 142-143 (2)	35.25	48.20
Nos. 145-146 (2)	21.75	21.75
Nos. 178-179 (2)	329.00	106.75
Nos. 138-139 (2)	30.35	75.25
Nos. 92-93 (2)	51.00	68.00
Nos. 118-119 (2)	7.00	8.25
Nos. 128-129 (2)	29.25	53.25
Nos. 55-56 (2)	35.25	50.25
Nos. 44-45 (2)	35.75	62.75
Nos. 1-2 (2)	35.40	49.75
Nos. 36-37 (2)	28.10	38.20
Nos. 44-45 (2)	28.00	38.05
Nos. 1-2 (2)	40.50	37.80
Nos. 99-100 (2)	27.80	37.75
Nos. 1-2 (2)	33.50	58.00
Nos. 74-75 (2)	30.25	25.30
Nos. 47-48 (2)	32.75	61.75
Nos. 223-224 (2)	40.55	45.25
Nos. 229-230 (2)	19.30	45.25
Nos. 106-107 (2)	8.75	17.25
Nos. 73-74 (2)	17.85	22.80
Nos. 238-239 (2)	35.30	45.75
Nos. 48-49 (2)	100.30	90.25
Nos. 85-86 (2)	18.25	35.25
Nos. 11-12 (2)	44.50	54.00
Nos. 130-131 (2)	32.80	42.80
Nos. 93-94 (2)	13.25	10.50
Nos. 129-130 (2)	22.25	40.25
Nos. 154-155 (2)	27.75	30.25
Nos. 174-175 (2)	52.80	67.80
Nos. 151-152 (2)	16.25	48.25
Nos. 188-189 (2)	25.25	29.75
Nos. 21-22 (2)	116.00	45.40
Nos. 82-83 (2)	13.40	13.40
Nos. 110-111 (2)	8.40	8.75
Nos. 48-49 (2)	40.30	47.75
Nos. 64-65 (2)	31.80	50.25
Nos. 92-93 (2)	16.25	22.75
Nos. 90-91 (2)	16.30	22.25
Nos. 224-225 (2)	29.60	38.00
Nos. 267-268 (2)	30.40	25.25
Nos. 93-94 (2)	17.10	25.75
Nos. 525-526 (2)	22.90	32.75
Nos. 62-63 (2)	38.50	58.00
Nos. 82-83 (2)	69.50	45.50
Nos. 25-26 (2)	41.00	42.50
No. 106 (1)	.80	1.00
No. 159 (1)	1.10	.35
Set total (136) Stamps	2,556.	2,772.

U.P.U.

Mercury and Symbols of Communications CD306

Plane, Ship and Hemispheres CD307

Mercury Scattering Letters over Globe — CD308

U.P.U. Monument, Bern — CD309

Universal Postal Union, 75th anniversary.

1949

Aden....................................32-35
Kathiri State of Seiyun....................................16-19
Qu'aiti State of Shihr and Mukalla....................................16-19
Antigua....................................100-103
Ascension....................................57-60
Bahamas....................................150-153
Barbados....................................212-215
Basutoland....................................41-44
Bechuanaland Protectorate....................................149-152
Bermuda....................................138-141
British Guiana....................................246-249
British Honduras....................................137-140
Brunei....................................79-82
Cayman Islands....................................118-121
Cyprus....................................160-163
Dominica....................................116-119
Falkland Islands....................................103-106
Falkland Islands Dep....................................1L14-1L17
Fiji....................................141-144
Gambia....................................148-151
Gibraltar....................................123-126
Gilbert & Ellice Islands....................................56-59
Gold Coast....................................144-147
Grenada....................................147-150
Hong Kong....................................180-183
Jamaica....................................142-145
Kenya, Uganda, Tanzania....................................94-97
Leeward Islands....................................126-129
Malaya
Johore....................................151-154
Kedah....................................57-60
Kelantan....................................46-49
Malacca....................................18-21
Negri Sembilan....................................59-62
Pahang....................................46-49
Penang....................................23-26
Perak....................................101-104
Perlis....................................3-6
Selangor....................................76-79
Trengganu....................................49-52
Malta....................................225-228
Mauritius....................................231-234
Montserrat....................................108-111
New Hebrides, British....................................62-65
New Hebrides, French....................................79-82
Nigeria....................................75-78
North Borneo....................................240-243
Northern Rhodesia....................................50-53
Nyasaland Protectorate....................................87-90
Pitcairn Islands....................................13-16
St. Helena....................................132-135
St. Kitts-Nevis....................................95-98
St. Lucia....................................131-134
St. Vincent....................................170-173
Sarawak....................................176-179
Seychelles....................................153-156
Sierra Leone....................................190-193
Singapore....................................23-26
Solomon Islands....................................84-87
Somaliland Protectorate....................................112-115
Southern Rhodesia....................................71-72
Swaziland....................................50-53
Tonga....................................87-90
Trinidad & Tobago....................................66-69
Turks & Caicos Islands....................................101-104
Virgin Islands....................................92-95
Zanzibar....................................226-229

The following have different designs but are included in the omnibus set:

Great Britain....................................276-279
Offices in Morocco (Tangier).......546-549
Australia....................................223
Bahrain....................................68-71
Burma....................................116-121
Ceylon....................................304-306
Egypt....................................281-283
India....................................223-226
Kuwait....................................89-92
Oman....................................31-34
Pakistan-Bahawalpur 26-29, O25-O28
South Africa....................................109-111
South-West Africa....................................160-162

Nos. 32-35 (4)	5.85	8.45
Nos. 16-19 (4)	2.75	16.00
Nos. 16-19 (4)	2.60	8.00
Nos. 100-103 (4)	3.60	7.70
Nos. 57-60 (4)	11.10	9.00
Nos. 150-153 (4)	5.35	9.30
Nos. 212-215 (4)	4.40	14.85
Nos. 41-44 (4)	4.75	10.00
Nos. 149-152 (4)	3.35	7.25
Nos. 138-141 (4)	4.75	6.15
Nos. 246-249 (4)	2.75	4.20
Nos. 137-140 (4)	3.30	6.35
Nos. 79-82 (4)	9.50	8.45
Nos. 118-121 (4)	3.60	7.25
Nos. 160-163 (4)	8.10	10.70
Nos. 116-119 (4)	2.30	5.65
Nos. 103-106 (4)	14.00	17.10
Nos. 1L14-1L17 (4)	14.60	14.50
Nos. 141-144 (4)	3.35	15.75
Nos. 148-151 (4)	2.75	7.10
Nos. 123-126 (4)	11.10	11.50
Nos. 56-59 (4)	4.30	13.00
Nos. 144-147 (4)	2.55	10.35
Nos. 147-150 (4)	2.15	3.55
Nos. 180-183 (4)	66.75	19.95
Nos. 142-145 (4)	2.50	2.45
Nos. 94-97 (4)	2.90	4.00
Nos. 126-129 (4)	3.05	9.60
Nos. 151-154 (4)	4.70	8.90
Nos. 57-60 (4)	4.80	12.00
Nos. 46-49 (4)	4.25	12.65
Nos. 18-21 (4)	4.25	17.30
Nos. 59-62 (4)	3.50	10.75
Nos. 46-49 (4)	3.00	7.25
Nos. 23-26 (4)	5.10	11.75
Nos. 101-104 (4)	3.65	10.75
Nos. 3-6 (4)	3.95	14.25
Nos. 76-79 (4)	4.90	12.30
Nos. 49-52 (4)	5.55	12.25
Nos. 225-228 (4)	4.50	4.85
Nos. 231-234 (4)	3.70	7.05
Nos. 108-111 (4)	3.30	4.35
Nos. 62-65 (4)	1.60	4.25
Nos. 79-82 (4)	15.40	22.00
Nos. 75-78 (4)	2.80	9.25
Nos. 240-243 (4)	7.15	6.50
Nos. 50-53 (4)	5.00	6.50
Nos. 87-90 (4)	4.55	6.60
Nos. 13-16 (4)	15.05	14.25
Nos. 132-135 (4)	4.85	7.10
Nos. 95-98 (4)	4.35	5.55
Nos. 131-134 (4)	2.55	3.85
Nos. 170-173 (4)	2.20	5.05
Nos. 176-179 (4)	13.40	13.35
Nos. 153-156 (4)	3.00	5.15
Nos. 190-193 (4)	2.90	9.15
Nos. 23-26 (4)	19.00	13.70
Nos. 84-87 (4)	4.05	4.90
Nos. 112-115 (4)	3.95	9.95
Nos. 71-72 (2)	1.95	2.25
Nos. 50-53 (4)	2.80	4.65
Nos. 87-90 (4)	3.00	5.25
Nos. 66-69 (4)	3.55	6.80
Nos. 101-104 (4)	3.05	8.90
Nos. 92-95 (4)	2.60	5.90
Nos. 226-229 (4)	4.95	13.50
Nos. 276-279 (4)	1.35	1.00
Nos. 546-549 (4)	2.60	16.00
No. 223 (1)	.40	.40
Nos. 68-71 (4)	4.75	16.50
Nos. 116-121 (6)	7.30	5.35
Nos. 304-306 (3)	3.35	4.25
Nos. 281-283 (3)	5.75	2.70
Nos. 223-226 (4)	27.25	10.50
Nos. 89-92 (4)	6.10	10.25
Nos. 31-34 (4)	8.00	17.50
Nos. 26-29,O25-O28 (8)	2.40	44.00
Nos. 109-111 (3)	2.00	2.70
Nos. 160-162 (3)	3.00	5.50
Set total (313) Stamps	475.15	745.55

University

Arms of University College CD310

Alice, Princess of Athlone CD311

1948 opening of University College of the West Indies at Jamaica.

1951

Antigua....................................104-105
Barbados....................................228-229
British Guiana....................................250-251
British Honduras....................................141-142
Dominica....................................120-121
Grenada....................................164-165
Jamaica....................................146-147
Leeward Islands....................................130-131
Montserrat....................................112-113
St. Kitts-Nevis....................................105-106
St. Lucia....................................149-150
St. Vincent....................................174-175
Trinidad & Tobago....................................70-71
Virgin Islands....................................96-97

Nos. 104-105 (2)	1.35	3.75
Nos. 228-229 (2)	1.75	2.65
Nos. 250-251 (2)	1.10	1.25
Nos. 141-142 (2)	1.40	2.20
Nos. 120-121 (2)	1.40	1.75
Nos. 164-165 (2)	1.20	1.60
Nos. 146-147 (2)	1.05	.70
Nos. 130-131 (2)	1.35	4.00
Nos. 112-113 (2)	.85	2.00
Nos. 105-106 (2)	1.40	2.25
Nos. 149-150 (2)	1.40	1.50
Nos. 174-175 (2)	1.00	2.15
Nos. 70-71 (2)	1.00	4.20
Nos. 96-97 (2)	1.50	3.75
Set total (28) Stamps	17.75	33.75

Coronation

Queen Elizabeth II — CD312

1953

Aden....................................47
Kathiri State of Seiyun....................................28
Qu'aiti State of Shihr and Mukalla....................................28
Antigua....................................106
Ascension....................................61
Bahamas....................................157
Barbados....................................234
Basutoland....................................45
Bechuanaland Protectorate....................................153
Bermuda....................................142
British Guiana....................................252
British Honduras....................................143
Cayman Islands....................................150
Cyprus....................................167
Dominica....................................141
Falkland Islands....................................121
Falkland Islands Dependencies....1L18
Fiji....................................145
Gambia....................................152
Gibraltar....................................131
Gilbert & Ellice Islands....................................60
Gold Coast....................................160
Grenada....................................170
Hong Kong....................................184
Jamaica....................................153
Kenya, Uganda, Tanzania....................................101
Leeward Islands....................................132
Malaya
Johore....................................155
Kedah....................................82
Kelantan....................................71
Malacca....................................27
Negri Sembilan....................................63
Pahang....................................71
Penang....................................27
Perak....................................126
Perlis....................................28
Selangor....................................101
Trengganu....................................74
Malta....................................241

Mauritius 250
Montserrat 127
New Hebrides, British 77
Nigeria 79
North Borneo 260
Northern Rhodesia 60
Nyasaland Protectorate 96
Pitcairn Islands 19
St. Helena 139
St. Kitts-Nevis 119
St. Lucia 156
St. Vincent 185
Sarawak 196
Seychelles 172
Sierra Leone 194
Singapore 27
Solomon Islands 88
Somaliland Protectorate 127
Swaziland 54
Trinidad & Tobago 84
Tristan da Cunha 13
Turks & Caicos Islands 118
Virgin Islands 114

The following have different designs but are included in the omnibus set:

Great Britain 313-316
Offices in Morocco (Tangier) 579-582
Australia 259-261
Bahrain 92-95
Canada 330
Ceylon 317
Cook Islands 145-146
Kuwait 113-116
New Zealand 280-284
Niue 104-105
Oman 52-55
Samoa 214-215
South Africa 192
Southern Rhodesia 80
South-West Africa 244-248
Tokelau Islands 4

No. 47 (1)	1.25	1.25
No. 28 (1)	.75	1.50
No. 28 (1)	1.10	.60
No. 106 (1)	.40	.75
No. 61 (1)	1.25	2.75
No. 157 (1)	1.40	.75
No. 234 (1)	1.00	.25
No. 45 (1)	.50	.60
No. 153 (1)	.50	.35
No. 142 (1)	.85	.50
No. 252 (1)	.45	.25
No. 143 (1)	.60	.40
No. 150 (1)	.40	1.75
No. 167 (1)	2.75	.25
No. 141 (1)	.40	.40
No. 121 (1)	.90	1.50
No. 1L18 (1)	1.80	1.40
No. 145 (1)	1.00	.60
No. 152 (1)	.50	.50
No. 131 (1)	.80	2.20
No. 60 (1)	.65	2.25
No. 160 (1)	1.00	.25
No. 170 (1)	.30	.25
No. 184 (1)	3.00	.30
No. 153 (1)	.70	.25
No. 101 (1)	.40	.25
No. 132 (1)	1.00	2.25
No. 155 (1)	1.40	.30
No. 82 (1)	2.25	.60
No. 71 (1)	1.60	1.60
No. 27 (1)	1.10	1.50
No. 63 (1)	1.40	.65
No. 71 (1)	2.25	.25
No. 27 (1)	1.75	.30
No. 126 (1)	1.60	.25
No. 28 (1)	1.75	4.00
No. 101 (1)	1.75	.25
No. 74 (1)	1.50	1.00
No. 241 (1)	.75	.25
No. 250 (1)	1.10	.25
No. 127 (1)	.60	.45
No. 77 (1)	.75	.60
No. 79 (1)	.40	.25
No. 260 (1)	1.75	1.00
No. 60 (1)	.70	.25
No. 96 (1)	.75	.75
No. 19 (1)	2.00	3.50
No. 139 (1)	1.25	1.25
No. 119 (1)	.35	.25
No. 156 (1)	.70	.35
No. 185 (1)	.50	.30
No. 196 (1)	1.75	1.75
No. 172 (1)	.80	.80
No. 194 (1)	.40	.40
No. 27 (1)	2.50	.40
No. 88 (1)	1.00	1.00
No. 127 (1)	.40	.25
No. 54 (1)	.30	.25
No. 84 (1)	.30	.25
No. 13 (1)	1.00	1.75
No. 118 (1)	.40	1.10
No. 114 (1)	.40	1.00
Nos. 313-316 (4)	11.40	4.05
Nos. 579-582 (4)	10.90	5.30
Nos. 259-261 (3)	3.60	2.75
Nos. 92-95 (4)	15.25	12.75
No. 330 (1)	.30	.25
No. 317 (1)	1.40	.25
Nos. 145-146 (2)	2.65	2.65
Nos. 113-116 (4)	16.00	8.50
Nos. 280-284 (5)	3.30	4.55
Nos. 104-105 (2)	2.25	1.50
Nos. 52-55 (4)	14.25	6.50
Nos. 214-215 (2)	2.50	.80
No. 192 (1)	.45	.30
No. 80 (1)	7.25	7.25
Nos. 244-248 (5)	3.00	2.35
No. 4 (1)	2.75	2.75
Set total (106) Stamps	162.10	115.95

Separate designs for each country for the visit of Queen Elizabeth II and the Duke of Edinburgh.

Royal Visit 1953

1953

Aden 62
Australia 267-269
Bermuda 163
Ceylon 318
Fiji 146
Gibraltar 146
Jamaica 154
Kenya, Uganda, Tanzania 102
Malta 242
New Zealand 286-287

No. 62 (1)	.65	4.00
Nos. 267-269 (3)	2.75	2.05
No. 163 (1)	.50	.25
No. 318 (1)	1.00	.25
No. 146 (1)	.65	.35
No. 146 (1)	.75	.25
No. 154 (1)	.50	.25
No. 102 (1)	.50	.25
No. 242 (1)	.30	.25
Nos. 286-287 (2)	.50	.50
Set total (13) Stamps	8.10	8.40

West Indies Federation

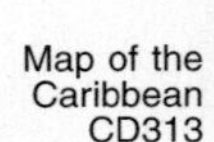

Map of the Caribbean CD313

Federation of the West Indies, April 22, 1958.

1958

Antigua 122-124
Barbados 248-250
Dominica 161-163
Grenada 184-186
Jamaica 175-177
Montserrat 143-145
St. Kitts-Nevis 136-138
St. Lucia 170-172
St. Vincent 198-200
Trinidad & Tobago 86-88

Nos. 122-124 (3)	5.80	3.80
Nos. 248-250 (3)	1.60	2.90
Nos. 161-163 (3)	1.95	1.85
Nos. 184-186 (3)	1.50	1.20
Nos. 175-177 (3)	2.65	3.45
Nos. 143-145 (3)	2.35	1.35
Nos. 136-138 (3)	3.00	3.10
Nos. 170-172 (3)	2.05	2.80
Nos. 198-200 (3)	1.50	1.75
Nos. 86-88 (3)	2.40	2.35
Set total (30) Stamps	24.80	24.55

Freedom from Hunger

Protein Food — CD314

U.N. Food and Agricultural Organization's "Freedom from Hunger" campaign.

1963

Aden 65
Antigua 133
Ascension 89
Bahamas 180
Basutoland 83
Bechuanaland Protectorate 194
Bermuda 192
British Guiana 271
British Honduras 179
Brunei 100
Cayman Islands 168
Dominica 181
Falkland Islands 146
Fiji 198
Gambia 172
Gibraltar 161
Gilbert & Ellice Islands 76
Grenada 190
Hong Kong 218
Malta 291
Mauritius 270
Montserrat 150
New Hebrides, British 93
North Borneo 296
Pitcairn Islands 35
St. Helena 173
St. Lucia 179
St. Vincent 201
Sarawak 212
Seychelles 213
Solomon Islands 109
Swaziland 108
Tonga 127
Tristan da Cunha 68
Turks & Caicos Islands 138
Virgin Islands 140
Zanzibar 280

No. 65 (1)	1.50	1.75
No. 133 (1)	.35	.35
No. 89 (1)	1.00	.50
No. 180 (1)	.65	.65
No. 83 (1)	.50	.25
No. 194 (1)	.50	.50
No. 192 (1)	1.00	.50
No. 271 (1)	.45	.25
No. 179 (1)	.60	.25
No. 100 (1)	3.25	2.25
No. 168 (1)	.55	.30
No. 181 (1)	.30	.30
No. 146 (1)	10.50	2.50
No. 198 (1)	3.50	2.25
No. 172 (1)	.50	.25
No. 161 (1)	4.00	2.25
No. 76 (1)	1.40	.40
No. 190 (1)	.30	.25
No. 218 (1)	37.50	5.00
No. 291 (1)	1.40	2.20
No. 270 (1)	.45	.25
No. 150 (1)	.55	.35
No. 93 (1)	.60	.25
No. 296 (1)	1.90	.75
No. 35 (1)	3.50	1.50
No. 173 (1)	2.25	1.10
No. 179 (1)	.40	.40
No. 201 (1)	.90	.50
No. 212 (1)	1.60	1.00
No. 213 (1)	.85	.35
No. 109 (1)	3.00	.85
No. 108 (1)	.50	.50
No. 127 (1)	.60	.35
No. 68 (1)	.75	.35
No. 138 (1)	.30	.25
No. 140 (1)	.50	.50
No. 280 (1)	1.50	.80
Set total (37) Stamps	89.90	33.00

Red Cross Centenary

Red Cross and Elizabeth II — CD315

1963

Antigua 134-135
Ascension 90-91
Bahamas 183-184
Basutoland 84-85
Bechuanaland Protectorate 195-196
Bermuda 193-194
British Guiana 272-273
British Honduras 180-181
Cayman Islands 169-170
Dominica 182-183
Falkland Islands 147-148
Fiji 203-204
Gambia 173-174
Gibraltar 162-163
Gilbert & Ellice Islands 77-78
Grenada 191-192
Hong Kong 219-220
Jamaica 203-204
Malta 292-293
Mauritius 271-272
Montserrat 151-152
New Hebrides, British 94-95
Pitcairn Islands 36-37
St. Helena 174-175
St. Kitts-Nevis 143-144
St. Lucia 180-181
St. Vincent 202-203
Seychelles 214-215
Solomon Islands 110-111
South Arabia 1-2
Swaziland 109-110
Tonga 134-135
Tristan da Cunha 69-70
Turks & Caicos Islands 139-140
Virgin Islands 141-142

Nos. 134-135 (2)	1.00	2.00
Nos. 90-91 (2)	6.75	3.35
Nos. 183-184 (2)	2.30	2.80
Nos. 84-85 (2)	1.20	.90
Nos. 195-196 (2)	.95	.85
Nos. 193-194 (2)	3.00	2.80
Nos. 272-273 (2)	.85	.60
Nos. 180-181 (2)	1.00	2.50
Nos. 169-170 (2)	1.10	3.00
Nos. 182-183 (2)	.70	1.05
Nos. 147-148 (2)	18.00	5.50
Nos. 203-204 (2)	3.25	2.80
Nos. 173-174 (2)	.80	1.00
Nos. 162-163 (2)	6.25	5.40
Nos. 77-78 (2)	2.00	3.50
Nos. 191-192 (2)	.80	.50
Nos. 219-220 (2)	18.75	7.35
Nos. 203-204 (2)	.75	1.65
Nos. 292-293 (2)	1.95	5.25
Nos. 271-272 (2)	.85	.50
Nos. 151-152 (2)	1.00	.75
Nos. 94-95 (2)	1.00	.50
Nos. 36-37 (2)	2.50	4.00
Nos. 174-175 (2)	1.70	2.30
Nos. 143-144 (2)	.90	.90
Nos. 180-181 (2)	1.25	1.25
Nos. 202-203 (2)	.90	.90
Nos. 214-215 (2)	1.00	1.50
Nos. 110-111 (2)	1.25	1.15
Nos. 1-2 (2)	1.25	1.25
Nos. 109-110 (2)	1.10	1.10
Nos. 134-135 (2)	1.00	1.25
Nos. 69-70 (2)	1.15	.80
Nos. 139-140 (2)	.55	1.00
Nos. 141-142 (2)	.80	1.25
Set total (70) Stamps	89.60	73.20

Shakespeare

Shakespeare Memorial Theatre, Stratford-on-Avon CD316

400th anniversary of the birth of William Shakespeare.

1964

Antigua 151
Bahamas 201
Bechuanaland Protectorate 197
Cayman Islands 171
Dominica 184
Falkland Islands 149
Gambia 192
Gibraltar 164
Montserrat 153
St. Lucia 196
Turks & Caicos Islands 141
Virgin Islands 143

No. 151 (1)	.35	.25
No. 201 (1)	.60	.35
No. 197 (1)	.35	.35
No. 171 (1)	.35	.30
No. 184 (1)	.35	.35
No. 149 (1)	1.60	.50
No. 192 (1)	.35	.25
No. 164 (1)	.55	.25
No. 153 (1)	.35	.25
No. 196 (1)	.45	.25
No. 141 (1)	.30	.25
No. 143 (1)	.45	.45
Set total (12) Stamps	6.05	3.80

ITU

ITU Emblem CD317

Intl. Telecommunication Union, cent.

1965

Antigua 153-154
Ascension 92-93
Bahamas 219-220
Barbados 265-266
Basutoland 101-102
Bechuanaland Protectorate 202-203
Bermuda 196-197
British Guiana 293-294
British Honduras 187-188
Brunei 116-117
Cayman Islands 172-173
Dominica 185-186
Falkland Islands 154-155
Fiji 211-212
Gibraltar 167-168
Gilbert & Ellice Islands 87-88
Grenada 205-206
Hong Kong 221-222
Mauritius 291-292
Montserrat 157-158
New Hebrides, British 108-109

Pitcairn Islands....................52-53
St. Helena....................180-181
St. Kitts-Nevis....................163-164
St. Lucia....................197-198
St. Vincent....................224-225
Seychelles....................218-219
Solomon Islands....................126-127
Swaziland....................115-116
Tristan da Cunha....................85-86
Turks & Caicos Islands....................142-143
Virgin Islands....................159-160

Nos. 153-154 (2)	1.45	1.35
Nos. 92-93 (2)	1.90	1.30
Nos. 219-220 (2)	1.35	1.50
Nos. 265-266 (2)	1.50	1.25
Nos. 101-102 (2)	.85	.65
Nos. 202-203 (2)	1.10	.75
Nos. 196-197 (2)	2.15	*2.25*
Nos. 293-294 (2)	.50	.50
Nos. 187-188 (2)	.75	.75
Nos. 116-117 (2)	1.75	1.75
Nos. 172-173 (2)	1.00	.85
Nos. 185-186 (2)	.55	.55
Nos. 154-155 (2)	6.75	3.15
Nos. 211-212 (2)	2.00	1.05
Nos. 167-168 (2)	6.40	5.95
Nos. 87-88 (2)	.85	.60
Nos. 205-206 (2)	.50	.50
Nos. 221-222 (2)	10.50	4.75
Nos. 291-292 (2)	1.10	.50
Nos. 157-158 (2)	1.05	1.15
Nos. 108-109 (2)	.65	.50
Nos. 52-53 (2)	1.65	1.90
Nos. 180-181 (2)	.80	.60
Nos. 163-164 (2)	.60	.60
Nos. 197-198 (2)	1.25	1.25
Nos. 224-225 (2)	.80	.90
Nos. 218-219 (2)	.75	.60
Nos. 126-127 (2)	.70	.55
Nos. 115-116 (2)	.70	.70
Nos. 85-86 (2)	1.00	.65
Nos. 142-143 (2)	.50	.50
Nos. 159-160 (2)	.85	.85
Set total (64) Stamps	54.25	40.70

Intl. Cooperation Year

ICY Emblem
CD318

1965

Antigua....................155-156
Ascension....................94-95
Bahamas....................222-223
Basutoland....................103-104
Bechuanaland Protectorate....................204-205
Bermuda....................199-200
British Guiana....................295-296
British Honduras....................189-190
Brunei....................118-119
Cayman Islands....................174-175
Dominica....................187-188
Falkland Islands....................156-157
Fiji....................213-214
Gibraltar....................169-170
Gilbert & Ellice Islands....................104-105
Grenada....................207-208
Hong Kong....................223-224
Mauritius....................293-294
Montserrat....................176-177
New Hebrides, British....................110-111
New Hebrides, French....................126-127
Pitcairn Islands....................54-55
St. Helena....................182-183
St. Kitts-Nevis....................165-166
St. Lucia....................199-200
Seychelles....................220-221
Solomon Islands....................143-144
South Arabia....................17-18
Swaziland....................117-118
Tristan da Cunha....................87-88
Turks & Caicos Islands....................144-145
Virgin Islands....................161-162

Nos. 155-156 (2)	.55	.50
Nos. 94-95 (2)	1.30	1.40
Nos. 222-223 (2)	.65	1.90
Nos. 103-104 (2)	.75	.85
Nos. 204-205 (2)	.85	1.00
Nos. 199-200 (2)	2.05	1.25
Nos. 295-296 (2)	.55	.50
Nos. 189-190 (2)	.60	.55
Nos. 118-119 (2)	.85	.85
Nos. 174-175 (2)	1.00	.75
Nos. 187-188 (2)	.55	.55
Nos. 156-157 (2)	6.00	1.65
Nos. 213-214 (2)	1.95	1.25
Nos. 169-170 (2)	1.30	*2.75*
Nos. 104-105 (2)	.85	.60
Nos. 207-208 (2)	.50	.50
Nos. 223-224 (2)	11.00	3.50
Nos. 293-294 (2)	.65	.50
Nos. 176-177 (2)	.80	.65
Nos. 110-111 (2)	.50	.50
Nos. 126-127 (2)	12.00	12.00
Nos. 54-55 (2)	1.60	1.85
Nos. 182-183 (2)	.95	.50
Nos. 165-166 (2)	.80	.60
Nos. 199-200 (2)	.55	.55
Nos. 220-221 (2)	.80	.60
Nos. 143-144 (2)	.70	.60
Nos. 17-18 (2)	1.20	.50
Nos. 117-118 (2)	.75	.75
Nos. 87-88 (2)	1.05	.65
Nos. 144-145 (2)	.50	.50
Nos. 161-162 (2)	.65	.50
Set total (64) Stamps	54.80	41.60

Churchill Memorial

Winston Churchill and St. Paul's, London, During Air Attack — CD319

1966

Antigua....................157-160
Ascension....................96-99
Bahamas....................224-227
Barbados....................281-284
Basutoland....................105-108
Bechuanaland Protectorate....................206-209
Bermuda....................201-204
British Antarctic Territory....................16-19
British Honduras....................191-194
Brunei....................120-123
Cayman Islands....................176-179
Dominica....................189-192
Falkland Islands....................158-161
Fiji....................215-218
Gibraltar....................171-174
Gilbert & Ellice Islands....................106-109
Grenada....................209-212
Hong Kong....................225-228
Mauritius....................295-298
Montserrat....................178-181
New Hebrides, British....................112-115
New Hebrides, French....................128-131
Pitcairn Islands....................56-59
St. Helena....................184-187
St. Kitts-Nevis....................167-170
St. Lucia....................201-204
St. Vincent....................241-244
Seychelles....................222-225
Solomon Islands....................145-148
South Arabia....................19-22
Swaziland....................119-122
Tristan da Cunha....................89-92
Turks & Caicos Islands....................146-149
Virgin Islands....................163-166

Nos. 157-160 (4)	3.05	3.05
Nos. 96-99 (4)	10.00	6.40
Nos. 224-227 (4)	2.30	*3.20*
Nos. 281-284 (4)	3.00	4.95
Nos. 105-108 (4)	2.80	3.25
Nos. 206-209 (4)	2.50	2.50
Nos. 201-204 (4)	4.00	*4.75*
Nos. 16-19 (4)	41.20	18.00
Nos. 191-194 (4)	2.45	1.30
Nos. 120-123 (4)	7.65	6.55
Nos. 176-179 (4)	3.10	3.65
Nos. 189-192 (4)	1.15	1.15
Nos. 158-161 (4)	12.75	9.55
Nos. 215-218 (4)	4.40	3.00
Nos. 171-174 (4)	4.75	5.30
Nos. 106-109 (4)	1.50	1.30
Nos. 209-212 (4)	1.10	1.10
Nos. 225-228 (4)	52.50	11.40
Nos. 295-298 (4)	3.70	3.75
Nos. 178-181 (4)	1.60	1.55
Nos. 112-115 (4)	2.30	1.00
Nos. 128-131 (4)	8.35	8.35
Nos. 56-59 (4)	4.45	6.10
Nos. 184-187 (4)	1.85	1.95
Nos. 167-170 (4)	1.50	1.70
Nos. 201-204 (4)	1.50	1.50
Nos. 241-244 (4)	1.50	1.75
Nos. 222-225 (4)	3.20	4.35
Nos. 145-148 (4)	1.50	1.60
Nos. 19-22 (4)	2.95	2.20
Nos. 119-122 (4)	1.70	2.55
Nos. 89-92 (4)	5.95	2.70
Nos. 146-149 (4)	1.60	1.75
Nos. 163-166 (4)	1.90	1.90
Set total (136) Stamps	205.75	135.10

Royal Visit, 1966

Queen Elizabeth II and Prince Philip — CD320

Caribbean visit, Feb. 4 - Mar. 6, 1966.

1966

Antigua....................161-162
Bahamas....................228-229
Barbados....................285-286
British Guiana....................299-300
Cayman Islands....................180-181
Dominica....................193-194
Grenada....................213-214
Montserrat....................182-183
St. Kitts-Nevis....................171-172
St. Lucia....................205-206
St. Vincent....................245-246
Turks & Caicos Islands....................150-151
Virgin Islands....................167-168

Nos. 161-162 (2)	3.50	2.60
Nos. 228-229 (2)	3.05	3.05
Nos. 285-286 (2)	3.00	2.00
Nos. 299-300 (2)	2.35	.85
Nos. 180-181 (2)	3.45	1.80
Nos. 193-194 (2)	3.00	.60
Nos. 213-214 (2)	.80	.50
Nos. 182-183 (2)	2.00	1.00
Nos. 171-172 (2)	.90	.75
Nos. 205-206 (2)	1.50	1.35
Nos. 245-246 (2)	2.75	1.35
Nos. 150-151 (2)	1.00	.50
Nos. 167-168 (2)	1.75	1.75
Set total (26) Stamps	29.05	18.10

World Cup Soccer

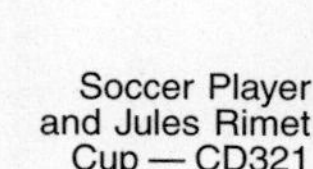

Soccer Player and Jules Rimet Cup — CD321

World Cup Soccer Championship, Wembley, England, July 11-30.

1966

Antigua....................163-164
Ascension....................100-101
Bahamas....................245-246
Bermuda....................205-206
Brunei....................124-125
Cayman Islands....................182-183
Dominica....................195-196
Fiji....................219-220
Gibraltar....................175-176
Gilbert & Ellice Islands....................125-126
Grenada....................230-231
New Hebrides, British....................116-117
New Hebrides, French....................132-133
Pitcairn Islands....................60-61
St. Helena....................188-189
St. Kitts-Nevis....................173-174
St. Lucia....................207-208
Seychelles....................226-227
Solomon Islands....................167-168
South Arabia....................23-24
Tristan da Cunha....................93-94

Nos. 163-164 (2)	.80	.85
Nos. 100-101 (2)	2.50	2.00
Nos. 245-246 (2)	.65	.65
Nos. 205-206 (2)	1.75	1.75
Nos. 124-125 (2)	1.30	1.25
Nos. 182-183 (2)	.75	.65
Nos. 195-196 (2)	1.20	.75
Nos. 219-220 (2)	1.70	.60
Nos. 175-176 (2)	2.00	3.55
Nos. 125-126 (2)	.70	.60
Nos. 230-231 (2)	.65	*.95*
Nos. 116-117 (2)	1.00	1.00
Nos. 132-133 (2)	7.00	7.00
Nos. 60-61 (2)	2.00	2.00
Nos. 188-189 (2)	1.25	.60
Nos. 173-174 (2)	.85	.80
Nos. 207-208 (2)	1.15	.90
Nos. 226-227 (2)	.85	.75
Nos. 167-168 (2)	1.10	1.10
Nos. 23-24 (2)	1.90	.55
Nos. 93-94 (2)	1.25	.80
Set total (42) Stamps	32.35	29.10

WHO Headquarters

World Health Organization Headquarters, Geneva
CD322

1966

Antigua....................165-166
Ascension....................102-103
Bahamas....................247-248
Brunei....................126-127
Cayman Islands....................184-185
Dominica....................197-198
Fiji....................224-225
Gibraltar....................180-181
Gilbert & Ellice Islands....................127-128
Grenada....................232-233
Hong Kong....................229-230
Montserrat....................184-185
New Hebrides, British....................118-119
New Hebrides, French....................134-135
Pitcairn Islands....................62-63
St. Helena....................190-191
St. Kitts-Nevis....................177-178
St. Lucia....................209-210
St. Vincent....................247-248
Seychelles....................228-229
Solomon Islands....................169-170
South Arabia....................25-26
Tristan da Cunha....................99-100

Nos. 165-166 (2)	1.15	.55
Nos. 102-103 (2)	6.60	3.35
Nos. 247-248 (2)	.80	.80
Nos. 126-127 (2)	1.35	1.35
Nos. 184-185 (2)	2.25	1.20
Nos. 197-198 (2)	.75	.75
Nos. 224-225 (2)	4.70	3.30
Nos. 180-181 (2)	6.50	6.75
Nos. 127-128 (2)	.80	.70
Nos. 232-233 (2)	.80	.50
Nos. 229-230 (2)	11.25	2.30
Nos. 184-185 (2)	1.00	1.00
Nos. 118-119 (2)	.75	.50
Nos. 134-135 (2)	8.50	8.50
Nos. 62-63 (2)	5.50	7.00
Nos. 190-191 (2)	3.50	1.50
Nos. 177-178 (2)	.60	.60
Nos. 209-210 (2)	.80	.80
Nos. 247-248 (2)	1.15	1.05
Nos. 228-229 (2)	1.25	.65
Nos. 169-170 (2)	.95	.80
Nos. 25-26 (2)	2.10	.70
Nos. 99-100 (2)	1.90	1.25
Set total (46) Stamps	64.95	45.90

UNESCO Anniversary

"Education"
CD323

"Science" (Wheat ears & flask enclosing globe). "Culture" (lyre & columns). 20th anniversary of the UNESCO.

1966-67

Antigua....................183-185
Ascension....................108-110
Bahamas....................249-251
Barbados....................287-289
Bermuda....................207-209
Brunei....................128-130
Cayman Islands....................186-188
Dominica....................199-201
Gibraltar....................183-185
Gilbert & Ellice Islands....................129-131
Grenada....................234-236
Hong Kong....................231-233
Mauritius....................299-301
Montserrat....................186-188
New Hebrides, British....................120-122
New Hebrides, French....................136-138
Pitcairn Islands....................64-66
St. Helena....................192-194
St. Kitts-Nevis....................179-181
St. Lucia....................211-213
St. Vincent....................249-251
Seychelles....................230-232
Solomon Islands....................171-173
South Arabia....................27-29
Swaziland....................123-125
Tristan da Cunha....................101-103
Turks & Caicos Islands....................155-157
Virgin Islands....................176-178

Nos. 183-185 (3)	1.90	*2.50*
Nos. 108-110 (3)	11.00	5.80
Nos. 249-251 (3)	2.35	2.35
Nos. 287-289 (3)	2.35	2.15
Nos. 207-209 (3)	3.80	*3.90*
Nos. 128-130 (3)	4.65	5.40
Nos. 186-188 (3)	2.50	1.50
Nos. 199-201 (3)	1.60	.75
Nos. 183-185 (3)	6.50	3.25
Nos. 129-131 (3)	2.50	*2.45*
Nos. 234-236 (3)	1.10	1.20
Nos. 231-233 (3)	49.50	24.00
Nos. 299-301 (3)	2.10	1.50
Nos. 186-188 (3)	2.40	2.40
Nos. 120-122 (3)	1.90	1.90
Nos. 136-138 (3)	7.75	7.75
Nos. 64-66 (3)	4.05	4.00
Nos. 192-194 (3)	5.25	3.65
Nos. 179-181 (3)	.90	.90
Nos. 211-213 (3)	1.15	1.15
Nos. 249-251 (3)	2.30	1.35
Nos. 230-232 (3)	2.40	2.40
Nos. 171-173 (3)	2.00	1.50
Nos. 27-29 (3)	5.50	5.50
Nos. 123-125 (3)	1.40	1.40
Nos. 101-103 (3)	2.00	1.40
Nos. 155-157 (3)	1.15	1.20
Nos. 176-178 (3)	1.40	1.30
Set total (84) Stamps	133.40	94.55

Silver Wedding, 1972

Queen Elizabeth II and Prince Philip CD324

Designs: borders differ for each country.

1972

Anguilla	161-162
Antigua	295-296
Ascension	164-165
Bahamas	344-345
Bermuda	296-297
British Antarctic Territory	43-44
British Honduras	306-307
British Indian Ocean Territory	48-49
Brunei	186-187
Cayman Islands	304-305
Dominica	352-353
Falkland Islands	223-224
Fiji	328-329
Gibraltar	292-293
Gilbert & Ellice Islands	206-207
Grenada	466-467
Hong Kong	271-272
Montserrat	286-287
New Hebrides, British	169-170
New Hebrides, French	188-189
Pitcairn Islands	127-128
St. Helena	271-272
St. Kitts-Nevis	257-258
St. Lucia	328-329
St.Vincent	344-345
Seychelles	309-310
Solomon Islands	248-249
South Georgia	35-36
Tristan da Cunha	178-179
Turks & Caicos Islands	257-258
Virgin Islands	241-242

Nos. 161-162 (2)	1.10	*1.50*
Nos. 295-296 (2)	.50	.50
Nos. 164-165 (2)	.70	.70
Nos. 344-345 (2)	.60	.60
Nos. 296-297 (2)	.50	*.65*
Nos. 43-44 (2)	6.50	5.65
Nos. 306-307 (2)	.80	.80
Nos. 48-49 (2)	2.00	1.00
Nos. 186-187 (2)	.70	.70
Nos. 304-305 (2)	.75	.75
Nos. 352-353 (2)	.65	.65
Nos. 223-224 (2)	1.00	1.15
Nos. 328-329 (2)	.70	.70
Nos. 292-293 (2)	.60	.50
Nos. 206-207 (2)	.50	.50
Nos. 466-467 (2)	.70	.70
Nos. 271-272 (2)	1.70	1.50
Nos. 286-287 (2)	.50	.50
Nos. 169-170 (2)	.50	.50
Nos. 188-189 (2)	1.25	1.25
Nos. 127-128 (2)	.90	.85
Nos. 271-272 (2)	.60	1.20
Nos. 257-258 (2)	.65	.50
Nos. 328-329 (2)	.75	.75
Nos. 344-345 (2)	.55	.55
Nos. 309-310 (2)	.90	.90
Nos. 248-249 (2)	.50	.50
Nos. 35-36 (2)	1.40	1.40
Nos. 178-179 (2)	.70	.70
Nos. 257-258 (2)	.50	.50
Nos. 241-242 (2)	.50	.50
Set total (62) Stamps	30.20	29.15

Princess Anne's Wedding

Princess Anne and Mark Phillips — CD325

Wedding of Princess Anne and Mark Phillips, Nov. 14, 1973.

1973

Anguilla	179-180
Ascension	177-178
Belize	325-326
Bermuda	302-303
British Antarctic Territory	60-61
Cayman Islands	320-321
Falkland Islands	225-226
Gibraltar	305-306
Gilbert & Ellice Islands	216-217
Hong Kong	289-290
Montserrat	300-301
Pitcairn Islands	135-136
St. Helena	277-278
St. Kitts-Nevis	274-275
St. Lucia	349-350
St. Vincent	358-359
St. Vincent Grenadines	1-2
Seychelles	311-312
Solomon Islands	259-260
South Georgia	37-38
Tristan da Cunha	189-190
Turks & Caicos Islands	286-287
Virgin Islands	260-261

Nos. 179-180 (2)	.55	.55
Nos. 177-178 (2)	.60	.60
Nos. 325-326 (2)	1.10	.50
Nos. 302-303 (2)	.50	.50
Nos. 60-61 (2)	1.10	1.10
Nos. 320-321 (2)	.50	.50
Nos. 225-226 (2)	.70	.60
Nos. 305-306 (2)	.60	.50
Nos. 216-217 (2)	.50	.50
Nos. 289-290 (2)	2.65	2.00
Nos. 300-301 (2)	.55	.55
Nos. 135-136 (2)	.70	.60
Nos. 277-278 (2)	.50	.50
Nos. 274-275 (2)	.50	.50
Nos. 349-350 (2)	.50	.50
Nos. 358-359 (2)	.50	.50
Nos. 1-2 (2)	.50	.50
Nos. 311-312 (2)	.65	.65
Nos. 259-260 (2)	.70	.70
Nos. 37-38 (2)	.75	.75
Nos. 189-190 (2)	.50	.50
Nos. 286-287 (2)	.50	.50
Nos. 260-261 (2)	.50	.50
Set total (46) Stamps	16.15	14.60

Elizabeth II Coronation Anniv.

CD326

CD327

CD328

Designs: Royal and local beasts in heraldic form and simulated stonework. Portrait of Elizabeth II by Peter Grugeon. 25th anniversary of coronation of Queen Elizabeth II.

1978

Ascension	229
Barbados	474
Belize	397
British Antarctic Territory	71
Cayman Islands	404
Christmas Island	87
Falkland Islands	275
Fiji	384
Gambia	380
Gilbert Islands	312
Mauritius	464
New Hebrides, British	258
New Hebrides, French	278
St. Helena	317
St. Kitts-Nevis	354
Samoa	472
Solomon Islands	368
South Georgia	51
Swaziland	302
Tristan da Cunha	238
Virgin Islands	337

No. 229 (1)	2.00	2.00
No. 474 (1)	1.35	1.35
No. 397 (1)	4.50	5.00
No. 71 (1)	6.00	6.00
No. 404 (1)	2.00	2.00
No. 87 (1)	3.50	*4.00*
No. 275 (1)	4.00	5.50
No. 384 (1)	1.75	1.75
No. 380 (1)	1.50	1.50
No. 312 (1)	1.25	1.25
No. 464 (1)	2.10	2.10
No. 258 (1)	1.75	1.75
No. 278 (1)	3.50	3.50
No. 317 (1)	1.75	1.75
No. 354 (1)	1.00	1.00
No. 472 (1)	2.10	2.10
No. 368 (1)	2.50	2.50
No. 51 (1)	3.00	3.00
No. 302 (1)	1.60	1.60
No. 238 (1)	1.50	1.50
No. 337 (1)	1.80	1.80
Set total (21) Stamps	50.45	52.95

Queen Mother Elizabeth's 80th Birthday

CD330

Designs: Photographs of Queen Mother Elizabeth. Falkland Islands issued in sheets of 50; others in sheets of 9.

1980

Ascension	261
Bermuda	401
Cayman Islands	443
Falkland Islands	305
Gambia	412
Gibraltar	393
Hong Kong	364
Pitcairn Islands	193
St. Helena	341
Samoa	532
Solomon Islands	426
Tristan da Cunha	277

No. 261 (1)	.40	.40
No. 401 (1)	.45	.75
No. 443 (1)	.40	.40
No. 305 (1)	.40	.40
No. 412 (1)	.40	.50
No. 393 (1)	.30	.25
No. 364 (1)	1.10	1.25
No. 193 (1)	.60	.60
No. 341 (1)	.50	.50
No. 532 (1)	.55	.55
No. 426 (1)	.50	.50
No. 277 (1)	.45	.45
Set total (12) Stamps	6.05	6.55

Royal Wedding, 1981

Prince Charles and Lady Diana — CD331

CD331a

Wedding of Charles, Prince of Wales, and Lady Diana Spencer, St. Paul's Cathedral, London, July 29, 1981.

1981

Antigua	623-627
Ascension	294-296
Barbados	547-549
Barbuda	497-501
Bermuda	412-414
Brunei	268-270
Cayman Islands	471-473
Dominica	701-705
Falkland Islands	324-326
Falkland Islands Dep.	1L59-1L61
Fiji	442-444
Gambia	426-428
Ghana	759-764
Grenada	1051-1055
Grenada Grenadines	440-443
Hong Kong	373-375
Jamaica	500-503
Lesotho	335-337
Maldive Islands	906-909
Mauritius	520-522
Norfolk Island	280-282
Pitcairn Islands	206-208
St. Helena	353-355
St. Lucia	543-549
Samoa	558-560
Sierra Leone	509-518
Solomon Islands	450-452
Swaziland	382-384
Tristan da Cunha	294-296
Turks & Caicos Islands	486-489
Caicos Island	8-11
Uganda	314-317
Vanuatu	308-310
Virgin Islands	406-408

Nos. 623-627 (5)	6.55	2.55
Nos. 294-296 (3)	1.00	1.00
Nos. 547-549 (3)	.90	.90
Nos. 497-501 (5)	10.95	10.95
Nos. 412-414 (3)	2.00	2.00
Nos. 268-270 (3)	2.15	*4.50*
Nos. 471-473 (3)	1.20	1.30
Nos. 701-705 (5)	8.35	2.35
Nos. 324-326 (3)	1.65	1.70
Nos. 1L59-1L61 (3)	1.45	1.45
Nos. 442-444 (3)	1.35	1.35
Nos. 426-428 (3)	.90	.80
Nos. 759-764 (9)	6.20	6.20
Nos. 1051-1055 (5)	9.85	1.85
Nos. 440-443 (4)	2.35	2.35
Nos. 373-375 (3)	3.10	2.85
Nos. 500-503 (4)	1.45	1.35
Nos. 335-337 (3)	.90	.90
Nos. 906-909 (4)	1.55	1.55
Nos. 520-522 (3)	2.15	2.15
Nos. 280-282 (3)	1.75	1.75
Nos. 206-208 (3)	1.20	1.10
Nos. 353-355 (3)	.85	.85
Nos. 543-549 (5)	7.00	7.00
Nos. 558-560 (3)	.85	.85
Nos. 509-518 (10)	15.50	15.50
Nos. 450-452 (3)	1.25	1.25
Nos. 382-384 (3)	1.30	1.25
Nos. 294-296 (3)	.90	.90
Nos. 486-489 (4)	2.20	2.20
Nos. 8-11 (4)	5.00	5.00
Nos. 314-317 (4)	3.10	3.00
Nos. 308-310 (3)	1.15	1.15
Nos. 406-408 (3)	1.10	1.10
Set total (131) Stamps	109.15	92.95

Princess Diana

CD332

CD333

Designs: Photographs and portrait of Princess Diana, wedding or honeymoon photographs, royal residences, arms of issuing country. Portrait photograph by Clive Friend. Souvenir sheet margins show family tree, various people related to the princess. 21st birthday of Princess Diana of Wales, July 1.

1982

Antigua	663-666
Ascension	313-316
Bahamas	510-513
Barbados	585-588
Barbuda	544-547
British Antarctic Territory	92-95
Cayman Islands	486-489
Dominica	773-776
Falkland Islands	348-351
Falkland Islands Dep.	1L72-1L75
Fiji	470-473
Gambia	447-450
Grenada	1101A-1105
Grenada Grenadines	485-491
Lesotho	372-375
Maldive Islands	952-955
Mauritius	548-551
Pitcairn Islands	213-216
St. Helena	372-375
St. Lucia	591-594
Sierra Leone	531-534
Solomon Islands	471-474
Swaziland	406-409
Tristan da Cunha	310-313
Turks and Caicos Islands	531-534
Virgin Islands	430-433

Nos. 663-666 (4)	8.25	7.35
Nos. 313-316 (4)	3.50	3.50
Nos. 510-513 (4)	6.00	3.85
Nos. 585-588 (4)	3.40	3.25
Nos. 544-547 (4)	9.75	7.70
Nos. 92-95 (4)	4.25	3.45
Nos. 486-489 (4)	*4.75*	*2.70*
Nos. 773-776 (4)	7.05	7.05
Nos. 348-351 (4)	2.95	2.95
Nos. 1L72-1L75 (4)	2.50	2.60
Nos. 470-473 (4)	3.25	2.95
Nos. 447-450 (4)	2.90	2.85
Nos. 1101A-1105 (7)	16.05	15.55
Nos. 485-491 (7)	17.65	17.65
Nos. 372-375 (4)	4.00	4.00
Nos. 952-955 (4)	5.50	3.90
Nos. 548-551 (4)	5.00	5.00
Nos. 213-216 (4)	1.90	1.85
Nos. 372-375 (4)	2.00	2.00
Nos. 591-594 (4)	8.70	8.70
Nos. 531-534 (4)	7.20	7.20
Nos. 471-474 (4)	2.90	2.90
Nos. 406-409 (4)	3.85	2.25

Nos. 310-313 (4)	3.65	1.45
Nos. 486-489 (4)	2.20	2.20
Nos. 430-433 (4)	3.00	3.00
Set total (110) Stamps	142.15	127.85

250th anniv. of first edition of Lloyd's List (shipping news publication) & of Lloyd's marine insurance.

CD335

Designs: First page of early edition of the list; historical ships, modern transportation or harbor scenes.

1984

Ascension	351-354
Bahamas	555-558
Barbados	627-630
Cayes of Belize	10-13
Cayman Islands	522-526
Falkland Islands	404-407
Fiji	509-512
Gambia	519-522
Mauritius	587-590
Nauru	280-283
St. Helena	412-415
Samoa	624-627
Seychelles	538-541
Solomon Islands	521-524
Vanuatu	368-371
Virgin Islands	466-469

Nos. 351-354 (4)	2.90	2.55
Nos. 555-558 (4)	4.15	2.95
Nos. 627-630 (4)	6.10	5.15
Nos. 10-13 (4)	4.85	4.85
Nos. 522-526 (5)	9.30	8.45
Nos. 404-407 (4)	3.50	3.65
Nos. 509-512 (4)	5.30	4.90
Nos. 519-522 (4)	4.20	4.30
Nos. 587-590 (4)	9.40	9.40
Nos. 280-283 (4)	2.40	2.35
Nos. 412-415 (4)	2.40	2.40
Nos. 624-627 (4)	2.55	2.35
Nos. 538-541 (4)	5.00	5.00
Nos. 521-524 (4)	4.65	3.95
Nos. 368-371 (4)	1.85	1.85
Nos. 466-469 (4)	4.25	4.25
Set total (65) Stamps	72.80	68.35

Queen Mother 85th Birthday

CD336

Designs: Photographs tracing the life of the Queen Mother, Elizabeth. The high value in each set pictures the same photograph taken of the Queen Mother holding the infant Prince Henry.

1985

Ascension	372-376
Bahamas	580-584
Barbados	660-664
Bermuda	469-473
Falkland Islands	420-424
Falkland Islands Dep.	1L92-1L96
Fiji	531-535
Hong Kong	447-450
Jamaica	599-603
Mauritius	604-608
Norfolk Island	364-368
Pitcairn Islands	253-257
St. Helena	428-432
Samoa	649-653
Seychelles	567-571
Zil Elwannyen Sesel	101-105
Solomon Islands	543-547
Swaziland	476-480
Tristan da Cunha	372-376
Vanuatu	392-396

Nos. 372-376 (5)	4.65	4.65
Nos. 580-584 (5)	7.70	6.45
Nos. 660-664 (5)	8.00	6.70
Nos. 469-473 (5)	9.40	9.40
Nos. 420-424 (5)	7.35	6.65
Nos. 1L92-1L96 (5)	8.00	8.00
Nos. 531-535 (5)	6.15	6.15
Nos. 447-450 (4)	9.50	8.50
Nos. 599-603 (5)	6.15	7.00
Nos. 604-608 (5)	11.30	11.30
Nos. 364-368 (5)	5.00	5.00
Nos. 253-257 (5)	5.30	5.95
Nos. 428-432 (5)	5.25	5.25
Nos. 649-653 (5)	8.40	7.55
Nos. 567-571 (5)	8.70	8.70
Nos. 101-105 (5)	6.60	6.60
Nos. 543-547 (5)	3.95	3.95
Nos. 476-480 (5)	7.75	7.25
Nos. 372-376 (5)	5.40	5.40
Nos. 392-396 (5)	5.25	5.25
Set total (99) Stamps	139.80	135.70

Queen Elizabeth II, 60th Birthday

CD337

1986, April 21

Ascension	389-393
Bahamas	592-596
Barbados	675-679
Bermuda	499-503
Cayman Islands	555-559
Falkland Islands	441-445
Fiji	544-548
Hong Kong	465-469
Jamaica	620-624
Kiribati	470-474
Mauritius	629-633
Papua New Guinea	640-644
Pitcairn Islands	270-274
St. Helena	451-455
Samoa	670-674
Seychelles	592-596
Zil Elwannyen Sesel	114-118
Solomon Islands	562-566
South Georgia	101-105
Swaziland	490-494
Tristan da Cunha	388-392
Vanuatu	414-418
Zambia	343-347

Nos. 389-393 (5)	2.80	3.30
Nos. 592-596 (5)	2.75	*3.70*
Nos. 675-679 (5)	3.25	3.10
Nos. 499-503 (5)	4.65	*5.15*
Nos. 555-559 (5)	4.55	5.60
Nos. 441-445 (5)	3.95	*4.95*
Nos. 544-548 (5)	3.00	3.00
Nos. 465-469 (5)	8.75	6.75
Nos. 620-624 (5)	2.75	2.70
Nos. 470-474 (5)	2.25	2.10
Nos. 629-633 (5)	3.50	3.50
Nos. 640-644 (5)	4.10	4.10
Nos. 270-274 (5)	2.80	2.70
Nos. 451-455 (5)	2.50	3.05
Nos. 670-674 (5)	2.55	2.55
Nos. 592-596 (5)	2.70	2.70
Nos. 114-118 (5)	2.15	2.15
Nos. 562-566 (5)	2.90	2.90
Nos. 101-105 (5)	3.30	3.65
Nos. 490-494 (5)	2.15	2.15
Nos. 388-392 (5)	3.00	3.00
Nos. 414-418 (5)	3.10	3.10
Nos. 343-347 (5)	1.65	1.60
Set total (115) Stamps	75.10	77.50

Royal Wedding

Marriage of Prince Andrew and Sarah Ferguson — CD338

1986, July 23

Ascension	399-400
Bahamas	602-603
Barbados	687-688
Cayman Islands	560-561
Jamaica	629-630
Pitcairn Islands	275-276
St. Helena	460-461
St. Kitts	181-182
Seychelles	602-603
Zil Elwannyen Sesel	119-120
Solomon Islands	567-568
Tristan da Cunha	397-398
Zambia	348-349

Nos. 399-400 (2)	1.60	1.60
Nos. 602-603 (2)	2.75	2.75
Nos. 687-688 (2)	2.00	1.25
Nos. 560-561 (2)	1.70	*2.35*
Nos. 629-630 (2)	1.35	1.35
Nos. 275-276 (2)	2.40	2.40
Nos. 460-461 (2)	1.05	1.05
Nos. 181-182 (2)	1.50	2.25
Nos. 602-603 (2)	2.50	2.50
Nos. 119-120 (2)	2.30	2.30
Nos. 567-568 (2)	1.00	1.00
Nos. 397-398 (2)	1.40	1.40
Nos. 348-349 (2)	1.10	1.30
Set total (26) Stamps	22.65	23.50

Queen Elizabeth II, 60th Birthday

Queen Elizabeth II & Prince Philip, 1947 Wedding Portrait — CD339

Designs: Photographs tracing the life of Queen Elizabeth II.

1986

Anguilla	674-677
Antigua	925-928
Barbuda	783-786
Dominica	950-953
Gambia	611-614
Grenada	1371-1374
Grenada Grenadines	749-752
Lesotho	531-534
Maldive Islands	1172-1175
Sierra Leone	760-763
Uganda	495-498

Nos. 674-677 (4)	8.00	8.00
Nos. 925-928 (4)	5.50	6.20
Nos. 783-786 (4)	23.15	23.15
Nos. 950-953 (4)	7.25	7.25
Nos. 611-614 (4)	8.25	7.90
Nos. 1371-1374 (4)	6.80	6.80
Nos. 749-752 (4)	6.75	6.75
Nos. 531-534 (4)	5.25	5.25
Nos. 1172-1175 (4)	6.25	6.25
Nos. 760-763 (4)	5.25	5.25
Nos. 495-498 (4)	8.50	8.50
Set total (44) Stamps	90.95	91.30

Royal Wedding, 1986

CD340

Designs: Photographs of Prince Andrew and Sarah Ferguson during courtship, engagement and marriage.

1986

Antigua	939-942
Barbuda	809-812
Dominica	970-973
Gambia	635-638
Grenada	1385-1388
Grenada Grenadines	758-761
Lesotho	545-548
Maldive Islands	1181-1184
Sierra Leone	769-772
Uganda	510-513

Nos. 939-942 (4)	7.00	*8.75*
Nos. 809-812 (4)	14.55	14.55
Nos. 970-973 (4)	7.25	7.25
Nos. 635-638 (4)	7.80	7.80
Nos. 1385-1388 (4)	8.30	8.30
Nos. 758-761 (4)	9.00	9.00
Nos. 545-548 (4)	7.45	7.45
Nos. 1181-1184 (4)	8.45	8.45
Nos. 769-772 (4)	5.35	5.35
Nos. 510-513 (4)	9.25	10.00
Set total (40) Stamps	84.40	86.90

Lloyds of London, 300th Anniv.

CD341

Designs: 17th century aspects of Lloyds, representations of each country's individual connections with Lloyds and publicized disasters insured by the organization.

1986

Ascension	454-457
Bahamas	655-658
Barbados	731-734
Bermuda	541-544
Falkland Islands	481-484
Liberia	1101-1104
Malawi	534-537
Nevis	571-574
St. Helena	501-504
St. Lucia	923-926
Seychelles	649-652
Zil Elwannyen Sesel	146-149
Solomon Islands	627-630
South Georgia	131-134
Trinidad & Tobago	484-487
Tristan da Cunha	439-442
Vanuatu	485-488

Nos. 454-457 (4)	5.00	5.00
Nos. 655-658 (4)	8.90	4.95
Nos. 731-734 (4)	12.50	8.35
Nos. 541-544 (4)	8.00	*6.60*
Nos. 481-484 (4)	5.45	3.85
Nos. 1101-1104 (4)	4.25	4.25
Nos. 534-537 (4)	11.00	7.85
Nos. 571-574 (4)	8.35	8.35
Nos. 501-504 (4)	8.70	7.15
Nos. 923-926 (4)	8.80	8.80
Nos. 649-652 (4)	12.85	12.85
Nos. 146-149 (4)	11.25	11.25
Nos. 627-630 (4)	7.00	4.45
Nos. 131-134 (4)	6.30	3.70
Nos. 484-487 (4)	10.25	6.35
Nos. 439-442 (4)	7.60	7.60
Nos. 485-488 (4)	4.85	4.85
Set total (68) Stamps	141.05	116.20

Moon Landing, 20th Anniv.

CD342

Designs: Equipment, crew photographs, spacecraft, official emblems and report profiles created for the Apollo Missions. Two stamps in each set are square in format rather than like the stamp shown; see individual country listings for more information.

1989

Ascension	468-472
Bahamas	674-678
Belize	916-920
Kiribati	517-521
Liberia	1125-1129
Nevis	586-590
St. Kitts	248-252
Samoa	760-764
Seychelles	676-680
Zil Elwannyen Sesel	154-158
Solomon Islands	643-647
Vanuatu	507-511

Nos. 468-472 (5)	9.40	8.60
Nos. 674-678 (5)	23.00	19.70
Nos. 916-920 (5)	29.25	21.60
Nos. 517-521 (5)	12.50	12.50
Nos. 1125-1129 (5)	8.50	8.50
Nos. 586-590 (5)	7.50	7.50
Nos. 248-252 (5)	8.00	8.25
Nos. 760-764 (5)	9.85	9.30
Nos. 676-680 (5)	16.05	16.05
Nos. 154-158 (5)	26.85	26.85
Nos. 643-647 (5)	9.00	6.75
Nos. 507-511 (5)	8.60	8.60
Set total (60) Stamps	168.50	154.20

Queen Mother, 90th Birthday

CD343

CD344

Designs: Portraits of Queen Elizabeth, the Queen Mother. See individual country listings for more information.

1990

Ascension	491-492
Bahamas	698-699
Barbados	782-783
British Antarctic Territory	170-171
British Indian Ocean Territory	106-107

Cayman Islands........................622-623
Falkland Islands 524-525
Kenya..527-528
Kiribati 555-556
Liberia..................................1145-1146
Pitcairn Islands..........................336-337
St. Helena 532-533
St. Lucia 969-970
Seychelles 710-711
Zil Elwannyen Sesel 171-172
Solomon Islands.........................671-672
South Georgia 143-144
Swaziland 565-566
Tristan da Cunha........................480-481

Nos. 491-492 (2)	4.75	4.75
Nos. 698-699 (2)	5.25	5.25
Nos. 782-783 (2)	4.00	3.70
Nos. 170-171 (2)	6.00	6.00
Nos. 106-107 (2)	18.00	18.50
Nos. 622-623 (2)	4.00	*5.50*
Nos. 524-525 (2)	4.75	4.75
Nos. 527-528 (2)	6.05	6.05
Nos. 555-556 (2)	4.75	4.75
Nos. 1145-1146 (2)	3.25	3.25
Nos. 336-337 (2)	4.25	4.25
Nos. 532-533 (2)	5.25	5.25
Nos. 969-970 (2)	4.60	4.60
Nos. 710-711 (2)	6.60	6.60
Nos. 171-172 (2)	8.25	8.25
Nos. 671-672 (2)	5.00	*5.30*
Nos. 143-144 (2)	5.50	6.50
Nos. 565-566 (2)	4.10	4.10
Nos. 480-481 (2)	5.60	5.60
Set total (38) Stamps	109.95	112.95

Queen Elizabeth II, 65th Birthday, and Prince Philip, 70th Birthday

CD345

CD346

Designs: Portraits of Queen Elizabeth II and Prince Philip differ for each country. Printed in sheets of 10 + 5 labels (3 different) between. Stamps alternate, producing 5 different triptychs.

1991

Ascension...506a
Bahamas 731a
Belize..970a
Bermuda..618a
Kiribati 572a
Mauritius...734a
Pitcairn Islands.................................349a
St. Helena 555a
St. Kitts..319a
Samoa 791a
Seychelles 724a
Zil Elwannyen Sesel.........................178a
Solomon Islands................................689a
South Georgia 150a
Swaziland 587a
Vanuatu 541a

No. 506a (1)	3.50	3.75
No. 731a (1)	4.00	4.00
No. 970a (1)	4.25	4.25
No. 618a (1)	3.50	*4.00*
No. 572a (1)	4.00	4.00
No. 734a (1)	4.00	4.00
No. 349a (1)	3.25	3.25
No. 555a (1)	2.75	2.75
No. 319a (1)	3.00	3.00
No. 791a (1)	3.75	3.75
No. 724a (1)	5.00	5.00
No. 178a (1)	6.25	6.25
No. 689a (1)	3.75	3.75
No. 150a (1)	4.75	7.00
No. 587a (1)	4.00	4.00
No. 541a (1)	2.50	2.50
Set total (16) Stamps	62.25	65.25

Royal Family Birthday, Anniversary

CD347

Queen Elizabeth II, 65th birthday, Charles and Diana, 10th wedding anniversary: Various photographs of Queen Elizabeth II, Prince Philip, Prince Charles, Princess Diana and their sons William and Henry.

1991

Antigua 1446-1455
Barbuda 1229-1238
Dominica...............................1328-1337
Gambia 1080-1089
Grenada................................2006-2015
Grenada Grenadines............1331-1340
Guyana 2440-2451
Lesotho.....................................871-875
Maldive Islands....................1533-1542
Nevis...666-675
St. Vincent............................1485-1494
St. Vincent Grenadines...........769-778
Sierra Leone.........................1387-1396
Turks & Caicos Islands 913-922
Uganda.....................................918-927

Nos. 1446-1455 (10)	21.70	20.05
Nos. 1229-1238 (10)	125.00	119.50
Nos. 1328-1337 (10)	30.20	30.20
Nos. 1080-1089 (10)	24.65	24.40
Nos. 2006-2015 (10)	25.45	22.10
Nos. 1331-1340 (10)	23.85	23.35
Nos. 2440-2451 (12)	21.40	21.15
Nos. 871-875 (5)	13.55	13.55
Nos. 1533-1542 (10)	28.10	28.10
Nos. 666-675 (10)	23.65	23.65
Nos. 1485-1494 (10)	26.75	25.90
Nos. 769-778 (10)	25.40	25.40
Nos. 1387-1396 (10)	26.35	26.35
Nos. 913-922 (10)	27.50	25.30
Nos. 918-927 (10)	17.65	17.65
Set total (147) Stamps	461.20	446.65

Queen Elizabeth II's Accession to the Throne, 40th Anniv.

CD348

Various photographs of Queen Elizabeth II with local Scenes.

1992

Antigua 1513-1518
Barbuda 1306-1311
Dominica...............................1414-1419
Gambia 1172-1177
Grenada................................2047-2052
Grenada Grenadines............1368-1373
Lesotho.....................................881-885
Maldive Islands....................1637-1642
Nevis...702-707
St. Vincent............................1582-1587
St. Vincent Grenadines...........829-834
Sierra Leone.........................1482-1487
Turks and Caicos Islands.........978-987
Uganda.....................................990-995
Virgin Islands...........................742-746

Nos. 1513-1518 (6)	15.00	*15.10*
Nos. 1306-1311 (6)	125.25	83.65
Nos. 1414-1419 (6)	12.50	12.50
Nos. 1172-1177 (6)	15.00	14.85
Nos. 2047-2052 (6)	15.95	15.95
Nos. 1368-1373 (6)	17.00	15.35
Nos. 881-885 (5)	11.90	11.90
Nos. 1637-1642 (6)	17.55	17.55
Nos. 702-707 (6)	13.55	13.55
Nos. 1582-1587 (6)	14.40	14.40
Nos. 829-834 (6)	19.65	19.65
Nos. 1482-1487 (6)	22.50	22.50
Nos. 913-922 (10)	27.50	25.30
Nos. 990-995 (6)	19.50	19.50
Nos. 742-746 (5)	15.50	15.50
Set total (92) Stamps	362.75	317.25

CD349

1992

Ascension 531-535
Bahamas 744-748
Bermuda...................................623-627
British Indian Ocean Territory 119-123
Cayman Islands........................648-652
Falkland Islands 549-553
Gibraltar...................................605-609
Hong Kong 619-623
Kenya..563-567
Kiribati 582-586
Pitcairn Islands.........................362-366
St. Helena 570-574
St. Kitts.....................................332-336
Samoa 805-809
Seychelles 734-738
Zil Elwannyen Sesel 183-187
Solomon Islands.......................708-712
South Georgia 157-161
Tristan da Cunha......................508-512
Vanuatu 555-559
Zambia......................................561-565

Nos. 531-535 (5)	6.10	6.10
Nos. 744-748 (5)	6.90	4.70
Nos. 623-627 (5)	7.40	*7.55*
Nos. 119-123 (5)	22.75	19.25
Nos. 648-652 (5)	7.60	6.60
Nos. 549-553 (5)	5.95	5.90
Nos. 605-609 (5)	3.55	*3.85*
Nos. 619-623 (5)	5.10	5.25
Nos. 563-567 (5)	7.80	7.75
Nos. 582-586 (5)	3.85	3.85
Nos. 362-366 (5)	5.35	5.35
Nos. 570-574 (5)	5.70	5.70
Nos. 332-336 (5)	6.60	5.50
Nos. 805-809 (5)	7.85	5.90
Nos. 734-738 (5)	10.55	10.55
Nos. 183-187 (5)	9.40	9.40
Nos. 708-712 (5)	5.00	5.30
Nos. 157-161 (5)	5.60	5.90
Nos. 508-512 (5)	8.75	8.30
Nos. 555-559 (5)	3.10	3.10
Nos. 561-565 (5)	5.20	5.15
Set total (105) Stamps	150.10	140.95

Royal Air Force, 75th Anniversary

CD350

1993

Ascension 557-561
Bahamas 771-775
Barbados 842-846
Belize....................................1003-1008
Bermuda...................................648-651
British Indian Ocean Territory 136-140
Falkland Is. 573-577
Fiji...687-691
Montserrat 830-834
St. Kitts.....................................351-355

Nos. 557-561 (5)	15.60	14.60
Nos. 771-775 (5)	24.65	21.45
Nos. 842-846 (5)	14.15	12.85
Nos. 1003-1008 (6)	21.15	16.50
Nos. 648-651 (4)	9.65	*10.45*
Nos. 136-140 (5)	16.10	16.10
Nos. 573-577 (5)	10.85	10.85
Nos. 687-691 (5)	17.75	17.40
Nos. 830-834 (5)	14.10	14.10
Nos. 351-355 (5)	22.80	23.55
Set total (50) Stamps	166.80	157.85

Royal Air Force, 80th Anniv.

Design CD350 Re-inscribed

1998

Ascension 697-701
Bahamas 907-911
British Indian Ocean Terr 198-202
Cayman Islands........................754-758
Fiji...814-818
Gibraltar...................................755-759
Samoa 957-961
Turks & Caicos Islands 1258-1265
Tuvalu 763-767
Virgin Islands.......................... 879-883

Nos. 697-701 (5)	16.10	16.10
Nos. 907-911 (5)	13.60	12.65
Nos. 136-140 (5)	16.10	16.10
Nos. 754-758 (5)	15.25	15.25
Nos. 814-818 (5)	14.00	12.75
Nos. 755-759 (5)	7.85	9.00
Nos. 957-961 (5)	15.70	14.90
Nos. 1258-1265 (2)	27.50	27.50
Nos. 763-767 (5)	7.75	7.75
Nos. 879-883 (5)	15.00	15.00
Set total (47) Stamps	148.85	147.00

End of World War II, 50th Anniv.

CD351

CD352

1995

Ascension 613-617
Bahamas 824-828
Barbados 891-895
Belize....................................1047-1050
British Indian Ocean Territory 163-167
Cayman Islands........................704-708
Falkland Islands 634-638
Fiji...720-724
Kiribati 662-668
Liberia..................................1175-1179
Mauritius..................................803-805
St. Helena 646-654
St. Kitts.....................................389-393
St. Lucia 1018-1022
Samoa 890-894
Solomon Islands.......................799-803
South Georgia 198-200
Tristan da Cunha......................562-566

Nos. 613-617 (5)	21.50	21.50
Nos. 824-828 (5)	22.00	18.70
Nos. 891-895 (5)	14.20	11.90
Nos. 1047-1050 (4)	8.25	5.90
Nos. 163-167 (5)	16.25	16.25
Nos. 704-708 (5)	17.65	13.95
Nos. 634-638 (5)	18.65	17.15
Nos. 720-724 (5)	17.50	14.50
Nos. 662-668 (7)	12.55	12.55
Nos. 1175-1179 (5)	15.25	11.15
Nos. 803-805 (3)	7.50	7.50
Nos. 646-654 (9)	26.10	26.10
Nos. 389-393 (5)	16.40	16.40
Nos. 1018-1022 (5)	12.25	10.15
Nos. 890-894 (5)	15.25	14.50
Nos. 799-803 (5)	14.75	14.75
Nos. 198-200 (3)	14.50	15.50
Nos. 562-566 (5)	20.10	20.10
Set total (91) Stamps	290.65	268.55

UN, 50th Anniv.

CD353

1995

Bahamas 839-842
Barbados 901-904
Belize....................................1055-1058
Jamaica 847-851
Liberia..................................1187-1190
Mauritius..................................813-816
Pitcairn Islands.........................436-439
St. Kitts.....................................398-401
St. Lucia 1023-1026
Samoa 900-903
Tristan da Cunha......................568-571
Virgin Islands...........................807-810

Nos. 839-842 (4)	7.15	6.40
Nos. 901-904 (4)	7.00	5.75
Nos. 1055-1058 (4)	6.80	4.70
Nos. 847-851 (5)	5.40	5.45
Nos. 1187-1190 (4)	10.90	10.90
Nos. 813-816 (4)	4.55	4.55
Nos. 436-439 (4)	8.15	8.15
Nos. 398-401 (4)	6.15	7.15
Nos. 1023-1026 (4)	7.50	7.25
Nos. 900-903 (4)	9.35	8.20
Nos. 568-571 (4)	13.50	13.50
Nos. 807-810 (4)	7.45	7.45
Set total (49) Stamps	93.90	89.45

Queen Elizabeth, 70th Birthday

CD354

1996

Ascension 632-635
British Antarctic Territory 240-243
British Indian Ocean Territory 176-180
Falkland Islands 653-657
Pitcairn Islands 446-449
St. Helena 672-676
Samoa 912-916
Tokelau 223-227
Tristan da Cunha 576-579
Virgin Islands 824-828

Nos. 632-635 (4)	5.30	5.30
Nos. 240-243 (4)	9.45	8.15
Nos. 176-180 (5)	11.50	11.50
Nos. 653-657 (5)	13.55	11.20
Nos. 446-449 (4)	8.60	8.60
Nos. 672-676 (5)	12.45	12.70
Nos. 912-916 (5)	10.50	10.50
Nos. 223-227 (5)	10.50	10.50
Nos. 576-579 (4)	8.35	8.35
Nos. 824-828 (5)	11.30	11.30
Set total (46) Stamps	101.50	98.10

Diana, Princess of Wales (1961-97)

CD355

1998

Ascension 696
Bahamas 901A-902
Barbados 950
Belize 1091
Bermuda 753
Botswana 659-663
British Antarctic Territory 258
British Indian Ocean Terr. 197
Cayman Islands 752A-753
Falkland Islands 694
Fiji 819-820
Gibraltar 754
Kiribati 719A-720
Namibia 909
Niue 706
Norfolk Island 644-645
Papua New Guinea 937
Pitcairn Islands 487
St. Helena 711
St. Kitts 437A-438
Samoa 955A-956
Seycelles 802
Solomon Islands 866-867
South Georgia 220
Tokelau 252B-253
Tonga 980
Niuafo'ou 201
Tristan da Cunha 618
Tuvalu 762
Vanuatu 718A-719
Virgin Islands 878

No. 696 (1)	5.25	5.25
Nos. 901A-902 (2)	5.30	5.30
No. 950 (1)	6.25	6.25
No. 1091 (1)	10.00	10.00
No. 753 (1)	5.00	5.00
Nos. 659-663 (5)	8.25	8.80
No. 258 (1)	5.50	5.50
No. 197 (1)	5.50	5.50
Nos. 752A-753 (3)	7.40	7.40
No. 694 (1)	5.00	5.00
Nos. 819-820 (2)	5.25	5.25
No. 754 (1)	1.10	3.25
Nos. 719A-720 (2)	4.60	4.60
No. 909 (1)	1.75	1.75
No. 706 (1)	5.50	5.50
Nos. 644-645 (2)	5.60	5.60
No. 937 (1)	6.25	6.25
No. 487 (1)	4.75	4.75
No. 711 (1)	4.25	4.25
Nos. 437A-438 (2)	5.15	5.15
Nos. 955A-956 (2)	7.00	7.00
No. 802 (1)	6.25	6.25
Nos. 866-867 (2)	5.40	5.40
No. 220 (1)	4.50	5.00
Nos. 252B-253 (2)	6.00	6.00
No. 980 (1)	4.00	4.00
No. 201 (1)	6.50	6.50
No. 618 (1)	5.00	5.00
No. 762 (1)	3.50	3.50
Nos. 718A-719 (2)	8.00	8.00
No. 878 (1)	4.50	4.50
Set total (46) Stamps	168.30	171.50

Wedding of Prince Edward and Sophie Rhys-Jones

CD356

1999

Ascension 729-730
Cayman Islands 775-776
Falkland Islands 729-730
Pitcairn Islands 505-506
St. Helena 733-734
Samoa 971-972
Tristan da Cunha 636-637
Virgin Islands 908-909

Nos. 729-730 (2)	4.50	4.50
Nos. 775-776 (2)	4.95	4.95
Nos. 729-730 (2)	14.00	14.00
Nos. 505-506 (2)	7.00	7.00
Nos. 733-734 (2)	5.00	5.00
Nos. 971-972 (2)	5.00	5.00
Nos. 636-637 (2)	7.50	7.50
Nos. 908-909 (2)	7.50	7.50
Set total (16) Stamps	55.45	55.45

1st Manned Moon Landing, 30th Anniv.

CD357

1999

Ascension 731-735
Bahamas 942-946
Barbados 967-971
Bermuda 778
Cayman Islands 777-781
Fiji 853-857
Jamaica 889-893
Kirbati 746-750
Nauru 465-469
St. Kitts 460-464
Samoa 973-977
Solomon Islands 875-879
Tuvalu 800-804
Virgin Islands 910-914

Nos. 731-735 (5)	12.80	12.80
Nos. 942-946 (5)	14.10	14.10
Nos. 967-971 (5)	9.45	8.25
No. 778 (1)	9.00	9.00
Nos. 777-781 (5)	9.25	9.25
Nos. 853-857 (5)	9.25	8.45
Nos. 889-893 (5)	8.30	7.18
Nos. 746-750 (5)	8.60	8.60
Nos. 465-469 (5)	7.55	7.10
Nos. 460-464 (5)	11.35	11.65
Nos. 973-977 (5)	12.60	12.45
Nos. 875-879 (5)	7.50	7.50
Nos. 800-804 (5)	6.75	6.75
Nos. 910-914 (5)	11.75	11.75
Set total (66) Stamps	138.25	134.83

Queen Mother's Century

CD358

1999

Ascension 736-740
Bahamas 951-955
Cayman Islands 782-786
Falkland Islands 734-738
Fiji 858-862
Norfolk Island 688-692
St. Helena 740-744
Samoa 978-982
Solomon Islands 880-884
South Georgia 231-235
Tristan da Cunha 638-642
Tuvalu 805-809

Nos. 736-740 (5)	15.50	15.50
Nos. 951-955 (5)	13.75	12.65
Nos. 782-786 (5)	8.35	8.35
Nos. 734-738 (5)	30.00	28.25
Nos. 858-862 (5)	12.80	13.25
Nos. 688-692 (5)	9.50	9.50
Nos. 740-744 (5)	16.15	16.15
Nos. 978-982 (5)	12.50	12.10
Nos. 880-884 (5)	7.50	7.00
Nos. 231-235 (5)	29.75	30.00
Nos. 638-642 (5)	18.00	18.00
Nos. 805-809 (5)	7.00	7.00
Set total (60) Stamps	180.80	177.75

Prince William, 18th Birthday

CD359

2000

Ascension 755-759
Cayman Islands 797-801
Falkland Islands 762-766
Fiji 889-893
South Georgia 257-261
Tristan da Cunha 664-668
Virgin Islands 925-929

Nos. 755-759 (5)	15.50	15.50
Nos. 797-801 (5)	11.15	10.90
Nos. 762-766 (5)	24.60	22.50
Nos. 889-893 (5)	12.90	12.90
Nos. 257-261 (5)	29.00	28.75
Nos. 664-668 (5)	21.50	21.50
Nos. 925-929 (5)	14.50	14.50
Set total (35) Stamps	129.15	126.55

Reign of Queen Elizabeth II, 50th Anniv.

CD360

2002

Ascension 790-794
Bahamas 1033-1037
Barbados 1019-1023
Belize 1152-1156
Bermuda 822-826
British Antarctic Territory 307-311
British Indian Ocean Territory 239-243
Cayman Islands 844-848
Falkland Islands 804-808
Gibraltar 896-900
Jamaica 952-956
Nauru 491-495
Norfolk Island 758-762
Papua New Guinea 1019-1023
Pitcairn Islands 552
St. Helena 788-792
St. Lucia 1146-1150
Solomon Islands 931-935
South Georgia 274-278
Swaziland 706-710
Tokelau 302-306
Tonga 1059
Niuafo'ou 239
Tristan da Cunha 706-710
Virgin Islands 967-971

Nos. 790-794 (5)	14.10	14.10
Nos. 1033-1037 (5)	15.25	15.25
Nos. 1019-1023 (5)	12.90	12.90
Nos. 1152-1156 (5)	17.10	15.10
Nos. 822-826 (5)	18.00	18.00
Nos. 307-311 (5)	23.00	23.00
Nos. 239-243 (5)	19.40	19.40
Nos. 844-848 (5)	13.25	13.25
Nos. 804-808 (5)	23.00	22.00
Nos. 896-900 (5)	4.50	6.50
Nos. 952-956 (5)	16.65	16.65
Nos. 491-495 (5)	17.75	17.75
Nos. 758-762 (5)	15.90	15.90
Nos. 1019-1023 (5)	14.50	14.50
No. 552 (1)	8.50	8.50
Nos. 788-792 (5)	19.75	19.75
Nos. 1146-1150 (5)	12.25	12.25
Nos. 931-935 (5)	12.40	12.40
Nos. 274-278 (5)	28.00	28.50
Nos. 706-710 (5)	12.50	12.50
Nos. 302-306 (5)	14.50	14.50
No. 1059 (1)	8.00	8.00
No. 239 (1)	8.75	8.75
Nos. 706-710 (5)	18.50	18.50
Nos. 967-971 (5)	16.50	16.50
Set total (113) Stamps	384.95	384.45

Queen Mother Elizabeth (1900-2002)

CD361

2002

Ascension 799-801
Bahamas 1044-1046
Bermuda 834-836
British Antarctic Territory 312-314
British Indian Ocean Territory 245-247
Cayman Islands 857-861
Falkland Islands 812-816
Nauru 499-501
Pitcairn Islands 561-565
St. Helena 808-812
St. Lucia 1155-1159
Seychelles 830
Solomon Islands 945-947
South Georgia 281-285
Tokelau 312-314
Tristan da Cunha 715-717
Virgin Islands 979-983

Nos. 799-801 (3)	8.85	8.85
Nos. 1044-1046 (3)	9.10	9.10
Nos. 834-836 (3)	12.25	12.25
Nos. 312-314 (3)	18.75	18.75
Nos. 245-247 (3)	17.35	17.35
Nos. 857-861 (5)	15.00	15.00
Nos. 812-816 (5)	28.50	28.50
Nos. 499-501 (3)	14.00	14.00
Nos. 561-565 (5)	15.25	15.25
Nos. 808-812 (5)	12.00	12.00
Nos. 1155-1159 (5)	12.00	12.00
No. 830 (1)	6.50	6.50
Nos. 945-947 (3)	9.25	9.25
Nos. 281-285 (5)	19.50	19.50
Nos. 312-314 (3)	11.85	11.85
Nos. 715-717 (3)	16.25	16.25
Nos. 979-983 (5)	23.50	23.50
Set total (63) Stamps	249.90	249.90

Head of Queen Elizabeth II

CD362

2003

Ascension 822
Bermuda 865
British Antarctic Territory 322
British Indian Ocean Territory 261
Cayman Islands 878
Falkland Islands 828
St. Helena 820
South Georgia 294
Tristan da Cunha 731
Virgin Islands 1003

No. 822 (1)	12.50	12.50
No. 865 (1)	50.00	50.00
No. 322 (1)	9.50	9.50
No. 261 (1)	11.00	11.00
No. 878 (1)	14.00	14.00
No. 828 (1)	9.00	9.00
No. 820 (1)	9.00	9.00
No. 294 (1)	8.50	8.50
No. 731 (1)	10.00	10.00
No. 1003 (1)	10.00	10.00
Set total (10) Stamps	143.50	143.50

Coronation of Queen Elizabeth II, 50th Anniv.

CD363

2003

Ascension 823-825
Bahamas 1073-1075
Bermuda 866-868
British Antarctic Territory 323-325

British Indian Ocean Territory........262-264
Cayman Islands........................879-881
Jamaica..................................970-972
Kiribati....................................825-827
Pitcairn Islands........................577-581
St. Helena 821-823
St. Lucia 1171-1173
Tokelau 320-322
Tristan da Cunha......................732-734
Virgin Islands.......................1004-1006

Nos. 823-825 (3)	12.50	12.50
Nos. 1073-1075 (3)	13.00	13.00
Nos. 866-868 (2)	14.25	14.25
Nos. 323-325 (3)	23.00	23.00
Nos. 262-264 (3)	28.00	28.00
Nos. 879-881 (3)	19.25	19.25
Nos. 970-972 (3)	10.00	10.00
Nos. 825-827 (3)	13.00	13.00
Nos. 577-581 (5)	14.40	14.40
Nos. 821-823 (3)	7.25	7.25
Nos. 1171-1173 (3)	8.75	8.75
Nos. 320-322 (3)	17.25	17.25
Nos. 732-734 (3)	16.75	16.75
Nos. 1004-1006 (3)	25.00	25.00
Set total (43) Stamps	222.40	222.40

Prince William, 21st Birthday

CD364

2003

Ascension.......................................826
British Indian Ocean Territory.........265
Cayman Islands........................882-884
Falkland Islands 829
South Georgia 295
Tokelau 323
Tristan da Cunha............................735
Virgin Islands.......................1007-1009

No. 826 (1)	7.25	7.25
No. 265 (1)	8.00	8.00
Nos. 882-884 (3)	6.95	6.95
No. 829 (1)	13.50	13.50
No. 295 (1)	8.50	8.50
No. 323 (1)	7.25	7.25
No. 735 (1)	6.00	6.00
Nos. 1007-1009 (3)	10.00	10.00
Set total (12) Stamps	67.45	67.45

Scott Postage Stamp Checklist

- Provides basic information about postage stamps listed with major numbers in the Scott Standard Postage Stamp Catalogue.
- Features the country name, issue date or year, the Scott number, a description and four checkboxes; unused and used. The other two boxes can be used to label other options such as never-hinged or on cover.

$9.99-$19.99 AA*

Item #	Title	Retail	AA
105CK1	US Postal Stationery	19.99	14.99
112CK1	US Possessions	17.99	12.99
115CK1	US Federal and State Ducks	19.99	14.99
129CK1	US Postage semipostals through postal insurance	19.99	14.99
160CK1	US Revenues	19.99	14.99
210CK1	Australia	19.99	14.99
644CK1	Brazil	19.99	14.99
202CK1	British Islands	19.99	14.99
240CK1V2	Canada and Provinces	19.99	14.99
520CK1	China	24.99	19.99
345DMCK1	Denmark	17.99	12.99
345FICK1	Faroe Islands	12.99	9.99
345FNCK1	Finland	19.99	14.99
310CK1	France	19.99	14.99
315CK1	Germany	24.99	19.99
200CK1	Great Britain	19.99	14.99
345GRCK1	Greenland	19.99	14.99
650CK1	Guatemala	17.99	12.99
275HKCK1	Hong Kong	17.99	12.99
345ICK1	Iceland	17.99	12.99
618CK1	India	19.99	14.99
201CK1	Ireland	17.99	12.99
500CK1	Israel/Palestine	17.99	12.99
325CK1	Italy	19.99	14.99
510CK1	Japan	19.99	14.99
515CK1	Korea, South	19.99	14.99
663CK1	Liberia	17.99	12.99
341MCCK1	Macao	17.99	12.99
430CK1	Mexico	19.99	14.99
333CK1	Monaco	19.99	14.99
MMCK1	Mongolia	17.99	12.99
220CK1	New Zealand	19.99	14.99
345NRCK1	Norway	17.99	12.99
360CK1	Russia	24.99	19.99
328CK1	San Marino	19.99	14.99
345SWCK1	Sweden	17.99	12.99
365CK1	Switzerland	17.99	12.99
540CK1	Thailand	19.99	14.99
UNCK1	United Nations	19.99	14.99
375CK1	Vatican City	19.99	14.99

CANADA CHECKLIST 19

DATE	SCOTT NO.	DESCRIPTION	UNUSED	USED		
Canada						
1911-25	**106**	2c carmine	☐	☐	☐	☐
1911-25	**107**	2c yel grn ('22)	☐	☐	☐	☐
1911-25	**108**	3c brown ('18)	☐	☐	☐	☐
1911-25	**109**	3c car (I) ('23)	☐	☐	☐	☐
1911-25	**110**	4c ol bis ('22)	☐	☐	☐	☐
1911-25	**111**	5c dark blue ('12)	☐	☐	☐	☐
1911-25	**112**	5c violet ('22)	☐	☐	☐	☐
1911-25	**113**	7c yel ocher ('12)	☐	☐	☐	☐
1911-25	**114**	7c red brn ('24)	☐	☐	☐	☐
1911-25	**115**	8c blue ('25)	☐	☐	☐	☐
1911-25	**116**	10c plum ('12)	☐	☐	☐	☐

COMING SOON
Austria & Hungary
Available Fall of 2024

AmosAdvantage.com | 1-800-572-6885

ORDERING INFORMATION: *AA prices apply to paid subscribers of Amos Mdia titles, or for orders placed online. Prices, terms and product availability subject to change.
SHIPPING & HANDLING: U.S.: Orders total $0-$20.00 charged $7.49 shipping. U.S. Order total $20.01-$74.99 charged $14.99 shipping. Orders totaling $75+ will ship FREE!
Taxes will apply in CA, OH, & IL. Canada: 20% of order total. Minimum charge $19.99 Maximum charge $200.00. Foreign orders are shipped via FedEx Intl. or USPS and billed actual freight.

British Commonwealth of Nations

Dominions, Colonies, Territories, Offices and Independent Members

Comprising stamps of the British Commonwealth and associated nations.

A strict observance of technicalities would bar some or all of the stamps listed under Burma, Ireland, Kuwait, Nepal, New Republic, Orange Free State, Samoa, South Africa, South-West Africa, Stellaland, Sudan, Swaziland, the two Transvaal Republics and others but these are included for the convenience of collectors.

1. Great Britain

Great Britain: Including England, Scotland, Wales and Northern Ireland.

2. The Dominions, Present and Past

AUSTRALIA

The Commonwealth of Australia was proclaimed on Jan. 1, 1901. It consists of six former colonies as follows:

New South Wales
Queensland
South Australia
Victoria
Tasmania
Western Australia

The following islands and territories are, or have been, administered by Australia: Australian Antarctic Territory, Christmas Island, Cocos (Keeling) Islands, Nauru, New Guinea, Norfolk Island, Papua.

CANADA

The Dominion of Canada was created by the British North America Act in 1867. The following provinces were former separate colonies and issued postage stamps:

British Columbia and Vancouver Island
New Brunswick
Newfoundland
Nova Scotia
Prince Edward Island

FIJI

The colony of Fiji became an independent nation with dominion status on Oct. 10, 1970.

GHANA

This state came into existence March 6, 1957, with dominion status. It consists of the former colony of the Gold Coast and the Trusteeship Territory of Togoland. Ghana became a republic July 1, 1960.

INDIA

The Republic of India was inaugurated on Jan. 26, 1950. It succeeded the Dominion of India which was proclaimed Aug. 15, 1947, when the former Empire of India was divided into Pakistan and the Union of India. The Republic is composed of about 40 predominantly Hindu states of three classes: governor's provinces, chief commissioner's provinces and princely states. India also has various territories, such as the Andaman and Nicobar Islands.

The old Empire of India was a federation of British India and the native states. The more important princely states were autonomous. Of the more than 700 Indian states, these 43 are familiar names to philatelists because of their postage stamps.

CONVENTION STATES

Chamba
Faridkot
Gwalior
Jhind
Nabha
Patiala

FEUDATORY STATES

Alwar
Bahawalpur
Bamra
Barwani
Bhopal
Bhor
Bijawar
Bundi
Bussahir
Charkhari
Cochin
Dhar
Dungarpur
Duttia
Faridkot (1879-85)
Hyderabad
Idar
Indore
Jaipur
Jammu
Jammu and Kashmir
Jasdan
Jhalawar
Jhind (1875-76)
Kashmir
Kishangarh
Kotah
Las Bela
Morvi
Nandgaon
Nowanuggur
Orchha
Poonch
Rajasthan
Rajpeepla
Sirmur
Soruth
Tonk
Travancore
Wadhwan

NEW ZEALAND

Became a dominion on Sept. 26, 1907. The following islands and territories are, or have been, administered by New Zealand:

Aitutaki
Cook Islands (Rarotonga)
Niue
Penrhyn
Ross Dependency
Samoa (Western Samoa)
Tokelau Islands

PAKISTAN

The Republic of Pakistan was proclaimed March 23, 1956. It succeeded the Dominion which was proclaimed Aug. 15, 1947. It is made up of all or part of several Moslem provinces and various districts of the former Empire of India, including Bahawalpur and Las Bela. Pakistan withdrew from the Commonwealth in 1972.

SOUTH AFRICA

Under the terms of the South African Act (1909) the self-governing colonies of Cape of Good Hope, Natal, Orange River Colony and Transvaal united on May 31, 1910, to form the Union of South Africa. It became an independent republic May 3, 1961.

Under the terms of the Treaty of Versailles, South-West Africa, formerly German South-West Africa, was mandated to the Union of South Africa.

SRI LANKA (CEYLON)

The Dominion of Ceylon was proclaimed Feb. 4, 1948. The island had been a Crown Colony from 1802 until then. On May 22, 1972, Ceylon became the Republic of Sri Lanka.

3. Colonies, Past and Present; Controlled Territory and Independent Members of the Commonwealth

Abu Dhabi
Aden
Aitutaki
Alderney
Anguilla
Antigua
Ascension
Australia
Bahamas
Bahrain
Bangladesh
Barbados
Barbuda
Basutoland
Batum
Bechuanaland
Bechuanaland Prot.
Belize
Bermuda
Botswana
British Antarctic Territory
British Central Africa
British Columbia and Vancouver Island

British East Africa
British Guiana
British Honduras
British Indian Ocean Territory
British New Guinea
British Solomon Islands
British Somaliland
Brunei
Burma
Bushire
Cameroons
Canada
Cape of Good Hope
Cayman Islands
Christmas Island
Cocos (Keeling) Islands
Cook Islands
Crete,
British Administration
Cyprus
Dominica
East Africa & Uganda
Protectorates
Egypt
Falkland Islands
Fiji
Gambia
German East Africa
Ghana
Gibraltar
Gilbert Islands
Gilbert & Ellice Islands
Gold Coast
Grenada
Griqualand West
Guernsey
Guyana
Heligoland
Hong Kong
Indian Native States
(see India)
Ionian Islands
Jamaica
Jersey
Jordan
Kenya
Kenya, Uganda & Tanzania
Kiribati
Kuwait
Labuan
Lagos
Leeward Islands
Lesotho
Madagascar
Malawi
Malaya
Federated Malay States
Johore
Kedah
Kelantan
Malacca
Negri Sembilan
Pahang
Penang
Perak
Perlis
Selangor
Singapore
Sungei Ujong
Trengganu
Malaysia
Maldive Islands
Malta
Man, Isle of
Mauritius
Mesopotamia
Montserrat
Mozambique
Muscat
Namibia
Natal
Nauru
Nevis
New Britain
New Brunswick
Newfoundland
New Guinea
New Hebrides
New Republic
New South Wales
New Zealand
Niger Coast Protectorate
Nigeria
Niue
Norfolk Island
North Borneo
Northern Nigeria
Northern Rhodesia
North West Pacific Islands
Nova Scotia
Nyasaland Protectorate
Oman
Orange River Colony
Pakistan
Palestine
Papua New Guinea
Penrhyn Island
Pitcairn Islands
Prince Edward Island
Qatar
Queensland
Rhodesia
Rhodesia & Nyasaland
Ross Dependency
Rwanda
Sabah
St. Christopher
St. Helena
St. Kitts
St. Kitts-Nevis-Anguilla
St. Lucia
St. Vincent
Samoa
Sarawak
Seychelles
Sierra Leone
Singapore
Solomon Islands
Somaliland Protectorate
South Africa
South Arabia
South Australia
South Georgia
Southern Nigeria
Southern Rhodesia
South-West Africa
Sri Lanka
Stellaland
Straits Settlements
Sudan
Swaziland
Tanganyika
Tanzania
Tasmania
Tobago
Togo
Tokelau Islands
Tonga
Transvaal
Trinidad
Trinidad and Tobago
Tristan da Cunha
Trucial States
Turks and Caicos
Turks Islands
Tuvalu
Uganda
United Arab Emirates
Vanuatu
Victoria
Virgin Islands
Western Australia
Zambia
Zanzibar
Zimbabwe
Zululand

POST OFFICES IN FOREIGN COUNTRIES

Africa
East Africa Forces
Middle East Forces
Bangkok
China
Morocco
Turkish Empire

Colonies, former colonies, offices, territories controlled by parent states

Belgium

Belgian Congo
Ruanda-Urundi

Denmark

Danish West Indies
Faroe Islands
Greenland
Iceland

Finland

Aland Islands

France

COLONIES PAST AND PRESENT, CONTROLLED TERRITORIES

Afars & Issas, Territory of
Alaouites
Alexandretta
Algeria
Alsace & Lorraine
Anjouan
Annam & Tonkin
Benin
Cambodia (Khmer)
Cameroun
Castellorizo
Chad
Cilicia
Cochin China
Comoro Islands
Dahomey
Diego Suarez
Djibouti (Somali Coast)
Fezzan
French Colonies (general issues)
French Congo
French Equatorial Africa
French Guiana
French Guinea
French India
French Morocco
French Polynesia (Oceania)
French Southern & Antarctic Territories
French Sudan
French West Africa
Gabon
Germany
Ghadames
Grand Comoro
Guadeloupe
Indo-China
Inini
Ivory Coast
Laos
Latakia
Lebanon
Madagascar
Martinique
Mauritania
Mayotte
Memel
Middle Congo
Moheli
New Caledonia
New Hebrides
Niger Territory
Nossi-Be
Obock
Reunion
Rouad, Ile
Ste.-Marie de Madagascar
St. Pierre & Miquelon
Senegal
Senegambia & Niger
Somali Coast
Syria
Tahiti
Togo
Tunisia
Ubangi-Shari
Upper Senegal & Niger
Upper Volta
Viet Nam
Wallis & Futuna Islands

POST OFFICES IN FOREIGN COUNTRIES

China
Crete
Egypt
Turkish Empire
Zanzibar

Germany

EARLY STATES

Baden
Bavaria
Bergedorf
Bremen
Brunswick
Hamburg
Hanover
Lubeck
Mecklenburg-Schwerin
Mecklenburg-Strelitz
Oldenburg
Prussia
Saxony
Schleswig-Holstein
Wurttemberg

FORMER COLONIES

Cameroun (Kamerun)
Caroline Islands
German East Africa
German New Guinea
German South-West Africa
Kiauchau
Mariana Islands
Marshall Islands
Samoa
Togo

Italy

EARLY STATES

Modena
Parma
Romagna
Roman States
Sardinia
Tuscany
Two Sicilies
  Naples
  Neapolitan Provinces
  Sicily

FORMER COLONIES, CONTROLLED TERRITORIES, OCCUPATION AREAS

Aegean Islands
  Calimno (Calino)
  Caso
  Cos (Coo)
  Karki (Carchi)
  Leros (Lero)
  Lipso
  Nisiros (Nisiro)
  Patmos (Patmo)
  Piscopi
  Rodi (Rhodes)
  Scarpanto
  Simi
  Stampalia
Castellorizo
Corfu
Cyrenaica
Eritrea
Ethiopia (Abyssinia)
Fiume
Ionian Islands
  Cephalonia
  Ithaca
  Paxos
Italian East Africa
Libya
Oltre Giuba
Saseno
Somalia (Italian Somaliland)
Tripolitania

POST OFFICES IN FOREIGN COUNTRIES

"ESTERO"*
Austria
China
  Peking
  Tientsin
Crete
Tripoli
Turkish Empire
  Constantinople
  Durazzo
  Janina
Jerusalem
Salonika
Scutari
Smyrna
Valona

**Stamps overprinted "ESTERO" were used in various parts of the world.*

Netherlands

Aruba
Caribbean Netherlands
Curacao
Netherlands Antilles (Curacao)
Netherlands Indies
Netherlands New Guinea
St. Martin
Surinam (Dutch Guiana)

Portugal

COLONIES PAST AND PRESENT, CONTROLLED TERRITORIES

Angola
Angra
Azores
Cape Verde
Funchal
Horta
Inhambane
Kionga
Lourenco Marques
Macao
Madeira
Mozambique
Mozambique Co.
Nyassa
Ponta Delgada
Portuguese Africa
Portuguese Congo
Portuguese Guinea
Portuguese India
Quelimane
St. Thomas & Prince Islands
Tete
Timor
Zambezia

Russia

ALLIED TERRITORIES AND REPUBLICS, OCCUPATION AREAS

Armenia
Aunus (Olonets)
Azerbaijan
Batum
Estonia
Far Eastern Republic
Georgia
Karelia
Latvia
Lithuania
North Ingermanland
Ostland
Russian Turkestan
Siberia
South Russia
Tannu Tuva
Transcaucasian Fed. Republics
Ukraine
Wenden (Livonia)
Western Ukraine

Spain

COLONIES PAST AND PRESENT, CONTROLLED TERRITORIES

Aguera, La
Cape Juby
Cuba
Elobey, Annobon & Corisco
Fernando Po
Ifni
Mariana Islands
Philippines
Puerto Rico
Rio de Oro
Rio Muni
Spanish Guinea
Spanish Morocco
Spanish Sahara
Spanish West Africa

POST OFFICES IN FOREIGN COUNTRIES

Morocco
Tangier
Tetuan

Dies of British colonial stamps

DIE A:

1. The lines in the groundwork vary in thickness and are not uniformly straight.

2. The seventh and eighth lines from the top, in the groundwork, converge where they meet the head.

3. There is a small dash in the upper part of the second jewel in the band of the crown.

4. The vertical color line in front of the throat stops at the sixth line of shading on the neck.

DIE B:

1. The lines in the groundwork are all thin and straight.

2. All the lines of the background are parallel.

3. There is no dash in the upper part of the second jewel in the band of the crown.

4. The vertical color line in front of the throat stops at the eighth line of shading on the neck.

DIE I:

1. The base of the crown is well below the level of the inner white line around the vignette.

2. The labels inscribed "POSTAGE" and "REVENUE" are cut square at the top.

3. There is a white "bud" on the outer side of the main stem of the curved ornaments in each lower corner.

4. The second (thick) line below the country name has the ends next to the crown cut diagonally.

DIE Ia.
1 as die II.
2 and 3 as die I.

DIE Ib.
1 and 3 as die II.
2 as die I.

DIE II:

1. The base of the crown is aligned with the underside of the white line around the vignette.

2. The labels curve inward at the top inner corners.

3. The "bud" has been removed from the outer curve of the ornaments in each corner.

4. The second line below the country name has the ends next to the crown cut vertically.

Wmk. 1
Crown and C C

Wmk. 2
Crown and C A

Wmk. 3
Multiple Crown and C A

Wmk. 4
Multiple Crown and Script C A

Wmk. 4a

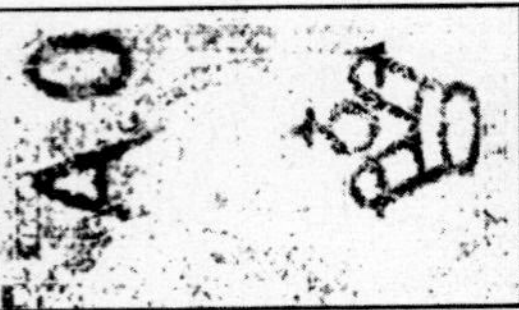
Wmk. 46

Wmk. 314
St. Edward's Crown and C A Multiple

Wmk. 373

Wmk. 384

Wmk. 406

British Colonial and Crown Agents watermarks

Watermarks 1 to 4, 314, 373, 384 and 406, common to many British territories, are illustrated here to avoid duplication.

The letters "CC" of Wmk. 1 identify the paper as having been made for the use of the Crown Colonies, while the letters "CA" of the others stand for "Crown Agents." Both Wmks. 1 and 2 were used on stamps printed by De La Rue & Co.

Wmk. 3 was adopted in 1904; Wmk. 4 in 1921; Wmk. 46 in 1879; Wmk. 314 in 1957; Wmk. 373 in 1974; Wmk. 384 in 1985; Wmk 406 in 2008.

In Wmk. 4a, a non-matching crown of the general St. Edwards type (bulging on both sides at top) was substituted for one of the Wmk. 4 crowns which fell off the dandy roll. The non-matching crown occurs in 1950-52 printings in a horizontal row of crowns on certain regular stamps of Johore and Seychelles, and on various postage due stamps of Barbados, Basutoland, British Guiana, Gold Coast, Grenada, Northern Rhodesia, St. Lucia, Swaziland and Trinidad and Tobago. A variation of Wmk. 4a, with the non-matching crown in a horizontal row of crown-CA-crown, occurs on regular stamps of Bahamas, St. Kitts-Nevis and Singapore.

Wmk. 314 was intentionally used sideways, starting in 1966. When a stamp was issued with Wmk. 314 both upright and sideways, the sideways varieties usually are listed also — with minor numbers. In many of the later issues, Wmk. 314 is slightly visible.

Wmk. 373 is usually only faintly visible.

NAMIBIA

nə-ˈmi-bē-ə

LOCATION — In southwestern Africa between Angola and South Africa, bordering on the Atlantic Ocean
GOVT. — Republic
AREA — 318,261 sq. mi.
POP. — 2,540,000 (2020 est.)
CAPITAL — Windhoek

Formerly South West Africa.

100 Cents = 1 Rand
100 Cents = 1 Dollar (1993)

Catalogue values for unused stamps in this country are for Never Hinged items.

Pres. Sam Nujoma, Map and Natl. Flag — A137

Designs: 45c, Dove, map, hands unchained, vert. 60c, Flag, map.

Perf. 14½x14, 14x14½

1990, Mar. 21	**Litho.**	**Unwmk.**	
659 A137	18c shown	.30	.25
660 A137	45c multicolored	.60	.60
661 A137	60c multicolored	1.40	1.40
	Nos. 659-661 (3)	2.30	2.25

Independence from South Africa.

Sights of Namibia — A138

Designs: 18c, Fish River Canyon. 35c, Quiver-tree Forest. 45c, Tsaris Mountains. 60c, Dolerite Hills.

1990, Apr. 26	***Perf. 14½x14***		
662 A138	18c multicolored	.35	.30
663 A138	35c multicolored	.55	.50
664 A138	45c multicolored	.75	.60
665 A138	60c multicolored	1.00	.90
a.	Souvenir sheet of 1	4.25	4.25
	Nos. 662-665 (4)	2.65	2.30

No. 665a publicizes the 150th anniv. of the Penny Black. Sold for 1.50r.

Architectural Development of Windhoek — A139

Designs: 18c, Early central business area. 35c, Modern central business area. 45c, First municipal building. 60c, Current municipal building.

1990, July 26	***Perf. 14½x14***		
666 A139	18c multicolored	.30	.30
667 A139	35c multicolored	.45	.45
668 A139	45c multicolored	.55	.55
669 A139	60c multicolored	.85	.85
	Nos. 666-669 (4)	2.15	2.15

Farming and Ranching — A140

1990, Oct. 11	***Perf. 14½x14***		
670 A140	20c Cornfields	.25	.25
671 A140	35c Sanga cattle	.40	.40
672 A140	50c Damara sheep	.60	.55
673 A140	65c Irrigation	.90	.95
	Nos. 670-673 (4)	2.15	2.15

Gypsum A141

Oranjemund Alluvial Diamond Mine A142

2c, Fluorite. 5c, Mimetite. 10c, Azurite. 20c, Dioptase. 30c, Tsumeb mine. 35c, Rosh Pinah mine. 40c, Diamond. 50c, Uis mine. 65c, Boltwoodite. 1r, Rossing mine. 1.50r, Wulfenite. 2r, Gold. 5r, Willemite.

1991, Jan. 2	***Perf. 14½x14***		
674 A141	1c shown	.25	.30
675 A141	2c multi	.25	.30
676 A141	5c multi	.30	.30
677 A141	10c multi	.45	.30
679 A141	20c multi	.50	.25
680 A142	25c shown	.50	.30
681 A142	30c multi	.65	.35
682 A142	35c multi	.75	.40
683 A141	40c multi	1.00	.30
684 A142	50c multi	1.00	.35
685 A141	65c multi	.95	.35
686 A142	1r multi	1.20	.50
687 A141	1.50r multi	1.60	.75
688 A141	2r multi	2.25	1.25
689 A141	5r multi	2.50	2.75
	Nos. 674-689 (15)	14.15	8.75

Nos. 676, 677 were reprinted in 1992 on phosphorescent paper.

Namibian Weather Service, Cent. — A143

20c, Weather balloon. 35c, Sunshine recorder. 50c, Measuring equipment. 65c, Gobabeb weather station.

1991, Feb. 2	***Perf. 14½x14***		
690 A143	20c multicolored	.25	.25
691 A143	35c multicolored	.40	.40
692 A143	50c multicolored	.55	.50
693 A143	65c multicolored	.65	.60
	Nos. 690-693 (4)	1.85	1.75

Mountain Zebra — A144

20c, Four zebras. 25c, Mother suckling foal. 45c, Three zebras. 60c, Two zebras.

1991, Apr. 18	***Perf. 14½x14***		
694 A144	20c multi	*1.00*	*.65*
695 A144	25c multi	*1.10*	*.70*
696 A144	45c multi	*1.50*	*1.75*
697 A144	60c multi	*2.10*	*2.50*
	Nos. 694-697 (4)	*5.70*	*5.60*

A souvenir sheet of 1 #696 was sold for 1.50r by the Philatelic Foundation of South Africa. Value $7.

Mountains — A145

1991, July 18	***Perf. 14½x14***		
698 A145	20c Karas	.30	.30
699 A145	25c Gamsberg	.40	.40
700 A145	45c Brukkaros	.55	.55
701 A145	60c Erongo	.70	.70
	Nos. 698-701 (4)	1.95	1.95

Tourist Camps — A146

Designs: 20c, Bernabe De la Bat Tourist Camp, Waterberg. 25c, Von Bach Recreation Resort. 45c, Gross Barmen Hot Springs. 60c, Namutoni Rest Camp.

1991, Oct. 24	***Perf. 14½x14***		
702 A146	20c multicolored	.35	.25
703 A146	25c multicolored	.45	.30
704 A146	45c multicolored	.75	.60
705 A146	60c multicolored	1.15	.95
	Nos. 702-705 (4)	2.70	2.10

Windhoek Conservatoir, 21st Anniv. — A147

Designs: 20c, Artist's palette, brushes. 25c, French horn, neck of violin. 45c, Pan pipes, masks of Comedy and Tragedy, lyre. 60c, Ballet pas de deux.

1992, Jan. 30	***Perf. 14x14½***		
706 A147	20c multicolored	.25	.25
707 A147	25c multicolored	.30	.25
708 A147	45c multicolored	.60	.55
709 A147	60c multicolored	.75	.75
	Nos. 706-709 (4)	1.90	1.80

Freshwater Fish — A148

1992, Apr. 16	***Perf. 14½x14***		
710 A148	20c Blue kurper	.35	.25
711 A148	25c Yellow fish	.50	.25
712 A148	45c Carp	.80	.50
713 A148	60c Catfish	.95	.65
	Nos. 710-713 (4)	2.60	1.65

A souvenir sheet of 1 No. 712 was sold by the Philatelic Foundation of South Africa. Value, $5.75.

Views of Swakopmund A149

20c, Jetty. 25c, Swimming pool. 45c, State House, lighthouse. 60c, Palm beach.

1992, July 2	***Perf. 14½x14***		
714 A149	20c multi	.25	.25
715 A149	25c multi	.35	.25
716 A149	45c multi	.70	.55
717 A149	60c multi	.95	.70
a.	Souvenir sheet of 4, #714-717	3.25	2.50
	Nos. 714-717 (4)	2.25	1.75

1992 Summer Olympics, Barcelona — A150

1992, July 24	***Perf. 14½x14***		
718 A150	20c Runners	.30	.25
719 A150	25c Flag, emblem	.35	.30
720 A150	45c Swimmers	.65	.55
721 A150	60c Olympic stadium	.75	.65
a.	Souvenir sheet of 4, #718-721	2.75	2.75
	Nos. 718-721 (4)	2.05	1.75

No. 721a sold for 2r.

Disabled Workers — A151

Designs: 20c, Wrapping cucumbers. 25c, Finishing a woven mat. 45c, At a spinning wheel. 60c, Cleaning potted plants.

1992, Sept. 10	***Perf. 14x14½***		
722 A151	20c multicolored	.25	.25
723 A151	25c multicolored	.30	.25
724 A151	45c multicolored	.40	.40
725 A151	60c multicolored	.55	.50
	Nos. 722-725 (4)	1.50	1.40

Endangered Animals — A152

Designs: 20c, Loxodonta africana. 25c, Tragelaphus spekei. 45c, Diceros bicornis. 60c, Lycaon pictus.

1993, Feb. 25	***Perf. 14½x14***		
726 A152	20c multicolored	.50	.25
727 A152	25c multicolored	.50	.30
728 A152	45c multicolored	1.00	.50
729 A152	60c multicolored	1.25	.60
a.	Souvenir sheet of 4, #726-729	4.50	4.50
	Nos. 726-729 (4)	3.25	1.65

Namibia Nature Foundation. No. 729a sold for 2.10r.

Arrival of Simmentaler Cattle in Namibia, Cent. — A153

20c, Cows and calves. 25c, Cow and calf. 45c, Head of stud bull. 60c, Arrival on boat, 1893.

1993, Apr. 16	***Perf. 14½x14***		
730 A153	20c multi	.25	.25
731 A153	25c multi	.30	.25
732 A153	45c multi	.50	.40
733 A153	60c multi	.80	.60
	Nos. 730-733 (4)	1.85	1.50

A souvenir sheet of one No. 732 has inscription for National Philatelic Exhibition. Sold for 3r. Value, $3.75.

Namib Desert — A154

1993, June 4	***Perf. 14½x14***		
734 A154	30c Sossusvlei	.25	.25
735 A154	40c Blutkuppe	.35	.30
736 A154	65c Homeb	.60	.60
737 A154	85c Moon landscape	.75	.80
	Nos. 734-737 (4)	1.95	1.95

SOS Children's Village — A155

1993, Aug. 6	**Litho.**	***Perf. 14***	
738 A155	30c Happiness	.25	.25
739 A155	40c A loving family	.30	.25
740 A155	65c Home sweet home	.60	.55
741 A155	85c My village	.75	.75
	Nos. 738-741 (4)	1.90	1.80

A156

Butterflies: 5c, Charaxes jasius saturnus. 10c, Acraea anemosa. 20c, Papilio nireus lyaeus. 30c, Junonia octavia sesamus. (35c), Graphium antheus. 40c, Hypolimnas misippus. 50c, Physcaeneura panda. 65c, Charaxes candiope. 85c, Junonia hierta cebrene. 90c, Colotis celimene pholoe. $1, Cacyreus dicksoni. $2, Charaxes bohemani. $2.50, Stugeta bowkeri tearei. $5, Byblia anvatara acheloia.

1993-94	***Perf. 14x14½***		
742 A156	5c multicolored	.25	.25
743 A156	10c multicolored	.25	.25
744 A156	20c multicolored	.25	.25
745 A156	30c multicolored	.25	.25
745A A156	(35c) multicolored	.55	.25
746 A156	40c multicolored	.25	.25
747 A156	50c multicolored	.30	.30
748 A156	65c multicolored	.40	.35
749 A156	85c multicolored	.50	.40
750 A156	90c multicolored	.50	.40
751 A156	$1 multicolored	.55	.40
752 A156	$2 multicolored	1.00	1.00
753 A156	$2.50 multicolored	1.25	1.25
754 A156	$5 multicolored	1.75	1.75
	Nos. 742-754 (14)	8.05	7.35

No. 745A is inscribed "STANDARDISED MAIL" and sold for 35c when issued.

Issued: No. 745A, 4/8/94; others, 10/1/93.

Perf. 14½x15 Syncopated Type A

1997

742a A156 5c multicolored .35 .35
747a A156 50c multicolored 1.25 1.00

Issued: Nos. 742a, 747a, 3/3/97.

Coastal Angling — A157

1994, Feb. 4 Litho. *Perf. 14*

755 A157 30c Blacktail .25 .25
756 A157 40c Kob .30 .25
757 A157 65c Steenbras .50 .50
758 A157 85c Galjoen .75 .70
a. Souvenir sheet of 4, #755-758 2.75 2.75
Nos. 755-758 (4) 1.80 1.70

Incorporation of Walvis Bay into Namibia — A158

1994, Mar. 1

759 A158 30c Quay .45 .40
760 A158 65c Aerial view .70 .70
761 A158 85c Map of Namibia 1.10 1.10
Nos. 759-761 (3) 2.25 2.20

A159

Flowers: 35c, Adenolobus pechuelii. 40c, Hibiscus elliottiae. 65c, Pelargonium cortusifolium. 85c, Hoodia macrantha.

1994, Apr. 8 Litho. *Perf. 14*

762 A159 35c multicolored .25 .25
763 A159 40c multicolored .30 .25
764 A159 65c multicolored .50 .40
765 A159 85c multicolored .70 .60
Nos. 762-765 (4) 1.75 1.50

Storks of Etosha — A160

1994, June 3 Litho. *Perf. 14*

766 A160 35c Yellowbilled .50 .30
767 A160 40c Abdim's .55 .40
768 A160 80c Openbilled .60 .60
769 A160 $1.10 White .80 .80
Nos. 766-769 (4) 2.45 2.10

Trains — A161

1994, Aug. 5 Litho. *Perf. 13½x14*

770 A161 35c Steam railcar .50 .35
771 A161 70c Class Krauss .70 .50
772 A161 80c Class 24 .75 .55
773 A161 $1.10 Class 7C 1.00 .85
Nos. 770-773 (4) 2.95 2.25

A souvenir sheet of 1 #772 was sold for 3r by the Philatelic Foundation of South Africa. Value $2.25.

Railways in Namibia, Cent. — A162

Locomotives: 35c, Prince Edward, 1st in service. 70c, Ex-German SWA 2-8-0 tank. 80c, Class 8. $1.10, Class 33 400 diesel electric.

1995, Mar. 8 Litho. *Perf. 14*

774 A162 35c multicolored .45 .25
775 A162 70c multicolored .70 .40
776 A162 80c multicolored .75 .55
777 A162 $1.10 multicolored 1.10 .85
a. Souvenir sheet of 4, #774-777 4.00 4.00
Nos. 774-777 (4) 3.00 2.05

No. 777a sold for $3.50.

No. 777a exists inscribed "Reprint November 1996." Value $4.75.

A163

1995, Mar. 21 Litho. *Perf. 14*

778 A163 (35c) multicolored .50 .50

Independence, 5th anniv. No. 778 is inscribed "STANDARDISED MAIL" and sold for 35c on day of issue.

A164

Fossils: 40c, Geochelone stromeri. 80c, Diamantornis wardi. 90c, Prohyrax hendeyi. $1.20, Crocodylus lloydi.

1995, May 24 Litho. *Perf. 14*

779 A164 40c multicolored .55 .30
780 A164 80c multicolored .90 .55
781 A164 90c multicolored 1.00 .60
782 A164 $1.20 multicolored 1.25 1.25
Nos. 779-782 (4) 3.70 2.70

A souvenir sheet of 1 #780 was sold for 3r by the Philatelic Foundation of South Africa. Value $3.

Finnish Mission, 125th Anniv. — A165

Designs: 40c, Mission church, Martti Rautanen (1845-1926). 80c, Albin Savola (1867-1934), Oniipa printing press. 90c, Oxwagon, Karl Emanuel August Weikkolin (1842-91). $1.20, Dr. Selma Raino (1873-1939), Onandjokwe Hospital.

1995, July 10 Litho. *Perf. 14*

783 A165 40c multicolored .35 .25
784 A165 80c multicolored .55 .50
785 A165 90c multicolored .70 .65
786 A165 $1.20 multicolored .85 .75
Nos. 783-786 (4) 2.45 2.15

Traditional Adornments — A166

1995, Aug. 16 Litho. *Perf. 14½x14*

787 A166 40c Ivory buttons .30 .25
788 A166 80c Conus shell .45 .40
789 A166 90c Cowrie shells .55 .50
790 A166 $1.20 Shell button .80 .80
Nos. 787-790 (4) 2.10 1.95

Souvenir Sheet

Singapore '95 — A167

$1.20, Phacochoerus aethiopicus.

1995, Sept. 10 Litho. *Perf. 14*

791 A167 $1.20 multi 1.60 1.60

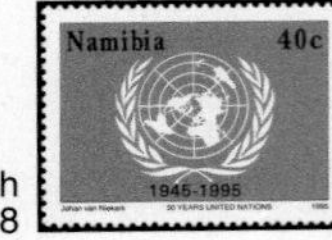

UN, 50th Anniv. — A168

1995, Oct. 24

792 A168 40c blue & black .45 .45

Tourism — A169

1996, Apr. 1 Litho. *Perf. 15x14*

793 A169 (45c) Bogenfels Arch .25 .25
794 A169 90c Ruacana Falls .30 .30
795 A169 $1 Epupa Falls .35 .30
796 A169 $1.30 Wild horses .50 .50
Nos. 793-796 (4) 1.40 1.35

No. 793 is inscribed "Standardised Mail" and sold for 45c on day of issue.

Catholic Missions in Namibia — A170

50c, Döbra Education and Training Centre. 95c, Heirachabis. $1, Windhoek St. Mary's Cathedral. $1.30, Ovamboland Old Church & School.

1996, May 27 Litho. *Perf. 15x14*

797 A170 50c multicolored .25 .25
798 A170 95c multicolored .35 .35
799 A170 $1 multicolored .40 .40
800 A170 $1.30 multicolored .55 .55
Nos. 797-800 (4) 1.55 1.55

Souvenir Sheet

CAPEX 96 A171

1996, June 8 Litho. *Perf. 14½x14*

801 A171 $1.30 African lynx 1.50 1.50

UNICEF, 50th Anniv. — A172

Designs: (45c), Children have rights. $1.30, Educate the girl.

1996, June 14 Litho. *Perf. 15x14*

802 A172 (45c) multicolored .25 .25
803 A172 $1.30 multicolored .60 .60

No. 802 is inscribed "Standard Postage" and sold for 45c on day of issue.

1996 Summer Olympic Games, Atlanta — A173

1996, June 27

804 A173 (45c) Boxing .25 .25
805 A173 90c Cycling .50 .40
806 A173 $1 Swimming .30 .50
807 A173 $1.30 Running .40 .40
Nos. 804-807 (4) 1.45 1.55

No. 804 is inscribed "Standard Postage" and sold for 45c on day of issue.

Constellations A174

Designs: (45c), Scorpio. 90c, Sagittarius. $1, Southern Cross. $1.30, Orion.

1996, Sept. 12 Litho. *Perf. 15x14*

808 A174 (45c) multicolored .25 .25
809 A174 90c multicolored .30 .30
810 A174 $1 multicolored .35 .35
a. Souvenir sheet of 1 2.00 2.00
811 A174 $1.30 multicolored .50 .50
Nos. 808-811 (4) 1.40 1.40

No. 808 is inscribed "Standard Postage" and sold for 45c on day of issue.

No. 810a sold for $3.50. No. 810a exists inscribed "Reprint February 17, 1997. Sold in aid of organized philately N$3.50."

Early Pastoral Pottery — A175

Designs: (45c), Urn-shaped storage vessel. 90c, Bag-shaped cooking vessel. $1, Reconstructed pot. $1.30, Large storage vessel.

1996, Oct. 17 *Perf. 14x15*

812 A175 (45c) multicolored .25 .25
813 A175 90c multicolored .35 .35
814 A175 $1 multicolored .40 .40
815 A175 $1.30 multicolored .45 .45
Nos. 812-815 (4) 1.45 1.45

No. 812 is inscribed "Standard Postage" and sold for 45c on day of issue.

Ancient //Khauxa!nas Ruins, near Karasburg A176

Various views of stone wall.

1997, Feb. 6 Litho. *Perf. 15x14*

816 A176 (50c) multicolored .30 .25
817 A176 $1 multicolored .70 .50
818 A176 $1.10 multicolored .80 .65
819 A176 $1.50 multicolored 1.40 1.25
Nos. 816-819 (4) 3.20 2.65

No. 816 is inscribed "Standard Postage" and sold for 45c on day of issue.

Souvenir Sheet

Hong Kong '97, Intl. Stamp Exhibition — A176a

1997, Feb. 12 Litho. *Perf. 14½x14*

819A A176a $1.30 Sanga bull *1.25 1.25*

No. 819A sold for $3.50. An inscription, "REPRINT 1 APRIL 1997," was added to a later printing of this sheet. Value $2.50.

A177

1997, Apr. 8 Litho. *Perf. 14x14½*

820 A177 $2 multicolored .90 .90

Heinrich von Stephan (1831-97), founder of UPU.

Jackass Penguins — A178

1997, May 15 Litho. *Perf. 14x14½*

821	A178	(50c) shown	.30	.30
822	A178	$1 Nesting	.40	.35
823	A178	$1.10 With young	.50	.40
824	A178	$1.50 Swimming	.60	.60
		Nos. 821-824 (4)	1.80	1.65

Souvenir Sheet

824A	A178	Sheet of 4, #b.-e.	1.75	1.75

World Wildlife Fund. No. 821 is inscribed "Standard Postage" and sold for 45c on day of issue.

Nos. 824Ab-824Ae are like Nos. 821-824 but do not have the WWF emblem. No. 824A sold for $5.

Wild Cats — A179

1997, June 12 Litho. *Perf. 14½x14*

825	A179	(45c) Felis caracal	.25	.25
826	A179	$1 Felis lybica	.40	.40
827	A179	$1.10 Felis serval	.50	.50
828	A179	$1.50 Felis nigripes	.60	.60
		Nos. 825-828 (4)	1.75	1.75

No. 825 is inscribed "Standard Postage" and sold for 45c on day of issue. A souvenir sheet containing a $5 stamp like #828 exists. Value $2.25.

See Nos. 878-881.

Helmeted Guineafowl A180

1997, June 5 *Perf. 14½x14*

829	A180	$1.20 multicolored	1.10	.90

A181

Baskets: 50c, Collecting bag. 90c, Powder basket. $1.20, Fruit basket. $2, Grain basket.

1997, July 8 Litho. *Perf. 14x14½*

830	A181	50c multicolored	.25	.25
831	A181	90c multicolored	.30	.30
832	A181	$1.20 multicolored	.40	.35
833	A181	$2 multicolored	.70	.70
		Nos. 830-833 (4)	1.65	1.60

Cinderella Waxbill — A182

60c, Blackchecked waxbill.

Perf. 14x14½ Syncopated Type A

1997, May 5 Booklet Stamps

834	A182	50c shown	.55	.45
835	A182	60c multicolored	.80	.55
a.		Booklet pane, 5 each #834-835	6.75	
		Complete booklet, #835a	7.00	

A183

Greetings Stamps — A184

Flowers: No. 836, Catophractes alexandri. No. 837, Crinun paludosum. No. 838, Gloriosa superba. No. 839, Tribulus zeyheri. No. 840, Aptosimum pubescens.

Helmeted guineafowl: No. 841, In bed. No. 842, Holding flowers. No. 843, As music conductor. No. 844, Prepared to travel. No. 845, Wearing heart necklace.

1997, July 11 Litho. *Perf. 14x13½*

Booklet Stamps

836	A183	(50c) multicolored	.40	.40
837	A183	(50c) multicolored	.40	.40
838	A183	(50c) multicolored	.40	.40
839	A183	(50c) multicolored	.40	.40
840	A183	(50c) multicolored	.40	.40
a.		Booklet pane, 2 each #836-840 + 10 labels	4.50	
		Complete booklet, #840a	4.50	
841	A184	50c multicolored	.40	.40
842	A184	50c multicolored	.40	.40
843	A184	50c multicolored	.40	.40
844	A184	$1 multicolored	.80	.80
845	A184	$1 multicolored	.80	.80
a.		Booklet pane, 2 each #841-845 + 10 labels	6.25	
		Complete booklet, #845a	6.25	

Nos. 836-840 are inscribed "Standard Postage" and sold for 45c on day of issued.

Namibian Veterinary Assoc., 50th Anniv. — A185

1997, Sept. 12 *Perf. 14*

846	A185	$1.50 multicolored	.60	.60

Souvenir Sheet

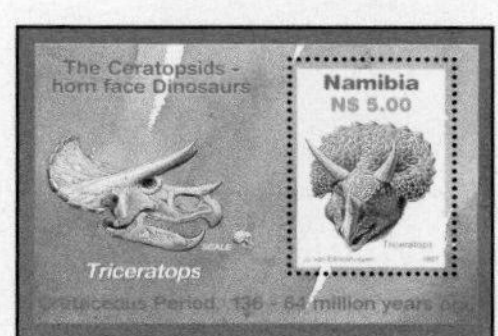

Triceratops — A186

1997, Sept. 27 Litho. *Perf. 13*

847	A186	$5 multicolored	2.00	2.00

World Post Day — A187

1997, Oct. 9 Litho. *Perf. 14x15*

848	A187	(45c) multicolored	.40	.30

No. 848 is inscribed "Standard Postage" and sold for 45c on day of issue.

Trees — A188

Designs: (50c), False mopane. $1, Ana tree. $1.10, Shepherd's tree. $1.50, Kiaat.

1997, Oct. 10

849	A188	(50c) multi	.25	.25
850	A188	$1 multi	.30	.30
851	A188	$1.10 multi	.30	.35
852	A188	$1.50 multi	.50	*.70*
		Nos. 849-852 (4)	1.35	1.60

No. 849 is inscribed "Standard Postage" and sold for 45c on day of issue.

Fauna and Flora — A189

5c, Flame lily. 10c, Bushman poison. 20c, Camel's foot. 30c, Western rhigozum. 40c, Bluecheeked bee-eater. (50c), Rosyfaced lovebird. 50c, Laughing dove. 60c, Lappetfaced vulture. 90c, Yellowbilled hornbill. $1, Lilacbreasted roller. $1.10, Hippopotamus. ($1.20), Leopard. $1.20, Giraffe. $1.50, Elephant. $2, Lion. $4, Buffalo. $5, Black rhinoceros. $10, Cheetah.

1997, Nov. 3 Litho. *Perf. 13½*

853	A189	5c multi	.25	.40
854	A189	10c multi	.25	.40
855	A189	20c multi	.25	.25
856	A189	30c multi	.25	.25
857	A189	40c multi	.25	.25
858	A189	(50c) multi	.25	.25
a.		Booklet pane of 10, perf 14x13½	2.50	
		Complete booklet, #858a	2.50	
859	A189	50c multi	.25	.25
860	A189	60c multi	.30	.25
861	A189	90c multi	.35	.30
862	A189	$1 multi	.40	.35
863	A189	$1.10 multi	.45	.40
864	A189	($1.20) multi	.50	.60
a.		Booklet pane of 10, perf 14x13½	5.50	
		Complete booklet, #864a	5.50	
865	A189	$1.20 multi	.40	.40
866	A189	$1.50 multi	.45	.45
867	A189	$2 multi	.60	.45
868	A189	$4 multi	.90	.80
869	A189	$5 multi	1.25	1.00
870	A189	$10 multi	2.25	2.00
a.		Bklt. pane, 1 ea #853-870, perf 14x13½	10.00	
		Complete booklet, #870a	10.00	
		Nos. 853-870 (18)	9.60	9.05

Self-Adhesive

Die Cut Perf. 12x12½

870B	A189	(45c) like #858	.25	.25
870C	A189	$1 like #862	.40	.30
870D	A189	($1.20) like #864	.50	.40
		Nos. 870B-870D (3)	1.15	.95

No. 858 is inscribed "Standard Postage" and sold for 50c on day issue. No. 864 is inscribed "Postcard Rate" and sold for $1.20 on day of issue. Nos. 853-854, 857, 860, 864, 866-867 and maybe others, exist imperf. Value: $100-$125 each pair.

For surcharges see #959-962, 1060-1063, 1071-1080, 1132-1040.

Christmas — A190

Various pictures of a helmeted guineafowl.

1997, Nov. 3 *Perf. 13x12½*

871	A190	(50c) multicolored	.25	.25
872	A190	$1 multicolored	.35	.25
873	A190	$1.10 multicolored	.40	.30
874	A190	$1.50 multicolored	.50	.50
		Nos. 871-874 (4)	1.50	1.30

Souvenir Sheet

875	A190	$5 multi, vert.	2.25	2.25

No. 871 is inscribed "Standard Postage" and sold for 50c on day of issue.

A191

1997, Nov. 27 *Perf. 14x15*

876	A191	(50c) multicolored	.45	.45

John Muafangejo (1943-87), artist. No. 876 is inscribed "Standard Postage" and sold for 50c on day of issue.

A192

1998, Jan. 15

877	A192	(50c) brown & gray	.35	.35

Gabriel B. Taapopi (1911-85). No. 877 is inscribed "Standard Postage" and sold for 50c on day of issue.

Wild Cats Type of 1997

Designs: $1.20, Panthera pardus. $1.90, Panthera leo, female carrying young. $2, Panthera leo, male. $2.50, Acinonyx jubatus.

1998, Jan. 26 *Perf. 13x12½*

878	A179	$1.20 multicolored	.60	.40
879	A179	$1.90 multicolored	.70	.60
880	A179	$2 multicolored	.75	.75
881	A179	$2.50 multicolored	.90	.90
a.		Souvenir sheet, #878-881	3.50	3.50
		Nos. 878-881 (4)	2.95	2.65

Narra Plant — A194

1998, Feb. 9 *Perf. 12½x13*

882	A194	$2.40 multicolored	.65	.65

Water Awareness — A195

1998, Mar. 23 Litho. *Perf. 14x15*

883	A195	(50c) multicolored	.40	.35

No. 883 is inscribed "Standard Postage" and sold for 50c on date of issue.

Nos. 885-895 were initially not available in Namibia. They were issued Nov. 23, 1997, at a Shanghai, China, stamp exhibition by a Chinese stamp dealer acting for the Namibia Post Office. There is some question whether they were sold in Namibia, but if they were, it was not until early 1998.

A197

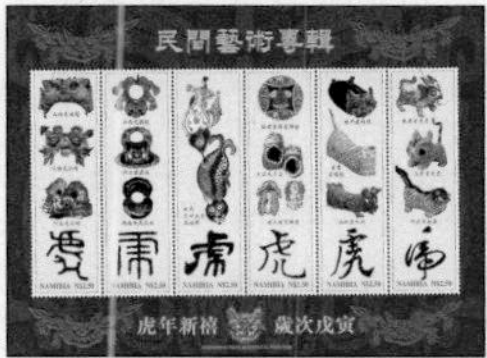

Lunar New Year — A198

Chinese inscriptions, wood cut images of a tiger, stylized drawings of tiger in — #885: a, orange. b, light green. c, yellow. d, blue. e, dark green. f, lilac.

No. 886: Various tiger figures, Chinese inscriptions.

No. 887, Chinese inscriptions, stylized tigers.

Perf. 13½x12½

1997, Nov. 23 **Litho.**

885 A197 $2.50 Sheet of 6, #a.-f. 6.00 6.00

Perf. 14x13½

886 A198 $2.50 Sheet of 6, #a.-f. 6.00 6.00

Souvenir Sheets

Perf. 12½

887 A197 $6 multicolored 2.75 2.75
888 A198 $6 multicolored 2.75 2.75

Nos. 887-888 each contain one 69x38mm stamp.

Macau Returns to China in 1999 — A199

Designs: No. 890, Flag, building. No. 892, Flag, Deng Xiaoping, building.

1997, Nov. 23 *Perf. 13½*

889 A199 $4.50 multicolored 2.50 2.50

Size: 59x27mm

Perf. 13½x13

890 A199 $4.50 multicolored 3.25 3.25

Souvenir Sheets

Perf. 13½x12½

891 A199 $6 multicolored 3.00 3.00

Perf. 12½

892 A199 $6 multicolored 3.00 3.00

Nos. 889-890 issued in sheets of 3. No. 891 contains one 62x33mm stamp, No. 892 one 69x33mm stamp.

Return of Hong Kong to China A200

Chinese landmarks — #892A: b, Beijing, Natl. Capital of China. c, Return of Hong Kong, 1997. d, Return of Macao, 1999. e, The Taiwan Region.

1997, Nov. 17 **Litho.** *Perf. 14x13½*

892A A200 $3.50 Sheet of 4, #b.-e. 7.00 7.00

Souvenir Sheet

Perf. 12½

893 A200 $6 Chinese landmarks 2.50 2.50

No. 893 contains one 72x41mm stamp.

Shanghai Communique, 25th Anniv. — A201

No. 894: a, Pres. Nixon, Mao Zedong, 1972. b, Pres. Carter, Deng Xiaoping, 1979. c, Pres. Reagan, Deng Xiaoping, 1984. d, Pres. Bush, Deng Xiaoping, 1989.
$6, Nixon, Zhou Enlai, 1972.

1997, Nov. 17 *Perf. 13½x12½*

894 A201 $3.50 Sheet of 4, #a.-d. 5.00 5.00

Souvenir Sheet

Perf. 14x13½

895 A201 $6 multicolored 2.75 2.75

No. 895 contains one 67x33mm stamp.

Owls — A204

No. 898, Rat (prey). No. 899, Whitefaced owl. No. 900, Barred owl. No. 901, Spotted eagle owl. No. 902, Barn owl.

1998, Apr. 1 **Litho.** *Perf. 13½x13*

Booklet Stamps

898 A204 55c multi .40 .40

Size: 38x23mm

899 A204 $1.50 multi .70 .70
900 A204 $1.50 multi .70 .70
901 A204 $1.90 multi .90 .90

Size: 61x21mm

902 A204 $1.90 multi .90 .90
a. Booklet pane, #898-902 3.75
Complete booklet, #902a 3.75

See No. 950.

Shells — A205

Designs: (55c), Patella granatina. $1.10, Cymatium cutaceum africanum. $1.50, Conus mozambicus. $6, Venus verrucosa.

1998, May 14 **Litho.** *Perf. 12½*

903 A205 (55c) multicolored .30 .25
904 A205 $1.10 multicolored .45 .30
905 A205 $1.50 multicolored .60 .60
906 A205 $6 multicolored 2.25 2.25
a. Souvenir sheet, #903-906 4.25 4.25
Nos. 903-906 (4) 3.60 3.40

No. 903 inscribed "Standard Postage."

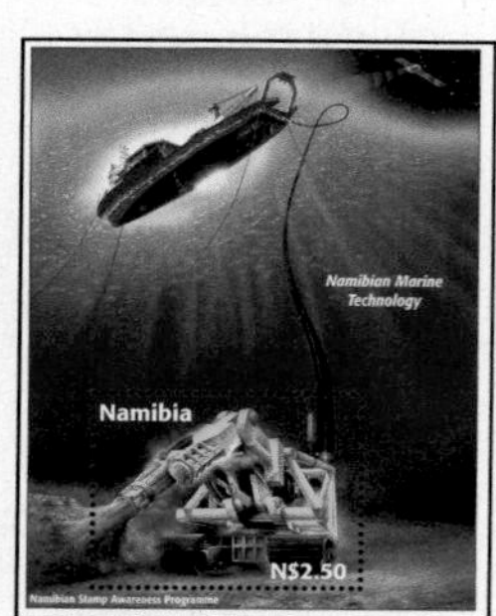

Namibian Marine Technology — A206

1998, May 18 **Litho.** *Perf. 14½x14*

908 A206 $2.50 multicolored 2.00 2.00

Diana, Princess of Wales (1961-97)

Common Design Type

Working for removal of land mines: a, Wearing face shield. b, Wearing Red Cross shirt. c, In white blouse. d, With child.

1998, May 18 **Litho.** *Perf. 14½x14*

909 CD355 $1 Sheet of 4, #a.-d. 1.75 1.75

World Environment Day — A207

(55c), Namibian coast. $1.10, Okavango sunset. $1.50, Sossusvlei. $1.90, African moringo.

1998, June 5 **Litho.** *Perf. 13x13½*

910 A207 (55c) multicolored .30 .25
911 A207 $1.10 multicolored .40 .30
912 A207 $1.50 multicolored .45 .45
913 A207 $1.90 multicolored .60 .55
Nos. 910-913 (4) 1.75 1.55

No. 910 is inscribed "Standard Postage."

Souvenir Sheet

Racing for Survival A208

1998, June 5 *Perf. 13*

914 A208 $5 Acinonyx jubatus 2.00 2.00

Animals and Their Young — A209

a, Chacma baboon. b, Blue wildebeest. c, Suricate. d, Elephant. e, Burchell's zebra.

1998, June 18 *Perf. 13½x13*

915 A209 $1.50 Sheet of 5, #a.-e. 2.50 2.50

Souvenir Sheet

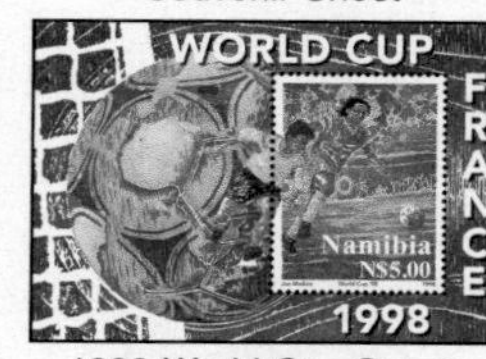

1998 World Cup Soccer Championships, France — A210

1998, July 1 **Litho.** *Perf. 14*

916 A210 $5 multicolored 1.75 1.75

Flora and Fauna of the Caprivi Strip — A211

Designs: a, Carmine bee-eater. b, Sable antelope. c, Lechwe. d, Woodland waterberry. e, Nile monitor. f, African jacana. g, African fish eagle. h, Woodland kingfisher. i, Nile crocodile. j, Black mamba.

1998, Sept. 26 **Litho.** *Perf. 12½*

917 A211 60c Sheet of 10, #a.-j. *7.50* *7.50*

#917b-917c, 917e are 40x40mm, #917i is 54x30mm, #917j is 32x30mm.

Souvenir Sheet

Black Rhinoceros — A212

1998, Oct. 20 **Litho.** *Perf. 13*

918 A212 $5 multicolored 2.00 2.00

Ilsapex '98, Intl. Philatelic Exhibition, Johannesburg.

Souvenir Sheet

Whales A213

1998, Oct. 9 **Litho.** *Perf. 13½x14*

919 A213 $5 multicolored 2.25 2.25

See Norfolk Island No. 665, South Africa No. 1095.

Damara Dik Dik A214

Striped Tree Squirrel A215

1999, Jan. 18 **Litho.** *Perf. 13½*

920 A214 $1.80 multi 2.50 1.50
921 A215 $2.65 multi 4.25 4.25

"Yoka" the Snake A216

"Yoka" the Snake A217

Cartoon pictures of Yoka: No. 922, Turning head. No. 923, Wrapped around tree branch. No. 924, Tail wrapped around branch and female snake. No. 925, With female snake and mouse. No. 926, In love. No. 927, Yoka tied up in knots. No. 928, Smashed with footprint. No. 929, Female snake's tail, Yoka's head. No. 930, Female snake singing to dazed Yoka. No. 931, Lying with tail over nose.

Serpentine Die Cut

1999, Feb. 1 **Self-Adhesive** **Litho.**

Booklet Stamps

922 A216 $1.60 multicolored .50 .50
923 A217 $1.60 multicolored .50 .50
924 A216 $1.60 multicolored .50 .50
925 A217 $1.60 multicolored .50 .50
926 A216 $1.60 multicolored .50 .50
927 A217 $1.60 multicolored .50 .50
928 A216 $1.60 multicolored .50 .50
929 A216 $1.60 multicolored .50 .50
930 A216 $1.60 multicolored .50 .50
931 A217 $1.60 multicolored .50 .50
a. Bklt. pane of 10, #922-931 5.00

The peelable paper backing serves as a booklet cover.

Souvenir Sheet

Passenger Liner "Windhuk" — A218

1999, Mar. 18 *Perf. 14*

932 A218 $5.50 multicolored 1.75 1.75

Gliders — A219

1999, Apr. 13 **Litho.** *Perf. 13*

933 A219 $1.60 Zögling, 1928 .80 .80
934 A219 $1.80 Schleicher, 1998 1.00 1.00

Souvenir Sheet

IBRA '99, Nuremberg, Germany — A220

1999, Apr. 27 Litho. ***Perf. 14x14¼***
935 A220 $5.50 multi 1.75 1.75

Falcons A221

60c, Greater kestrel. $1.60, Rock kestrel. $1.80, Red-necked falcon. $2.65, Lanner falcon.

1999, May 18 Litho. ***Perf. 13¼x13½***
936 A221 60c multicolored .75 .40
937 A221 $1.60 multicolored 1.20 .90
938 A221 $1.80 multicolored 1.20 1.00
939 A221 $2.65 multicolored 1.90 2.00
Nos. 936-939 (4) 5.05 4.30

Souvenir Sheet

Termitomyces Schimperi — A222

1999, June 19 Litho. ***Perf. 13¾***
940 A222 $5.50 multicolored 2.10 2.10

PhilexFrance '99 World Philatelic Exhibition.

Wetland Birds — A223

Designs: $1.60, Wattled crane. $1.80, Burchell's sand grouse. $1.90, Rock pratincole. $2.65, Eastern white pelican.

1999, June 28 ***Perf. 12¾***
941 A223 $1.60 multicolored .75 .60
942 A223 $1.80 multicolored .90 .75
943 A223 $1.90 multicolored 1.20 1.00
944 A223 $2.65 multicolored 1.60 1.60
Nos. 941-944 (4) 4.45 3.95

Orchids A224

Designs: $1.60, Eulophia hereroensis. $1.80, Ansellia africana. $2.65, Eulophia leachii. $3.90, Eulophia speciosa.
$5.50, Eulophia walleri.

Litho. & Embossed

1999, Aug. 21 ***Perf. 12¾***
945 A224 $1.60 multicolored .65 .55
946 A224 $1.80 multicolored .75 .65
947 A224 $2.65 multicolored 1.25 1.25
948 A224 $3.90 multicolored 1.60 1.60
Nos. 945-948 (4) 4.25 4.05

Souvenir Sheet

949 A224 $5.50 multicolored 2.50 2.50

Embossing is found only on the margin of No. 949. China 1999 World Philatelic Exhibition (No. 949).

Owl Type of 1998
Souvenir Sheet

Perf. 13½x12¾

1999, Sept. 30 Litho.
950 A204 $11 Like #902 5.00 5.00

Selection of stamp design as "most beautiful," 5th Stamp World Cup.

Urieta Kazahendike (Johanna Gertze) (1836-1935) — A225

1999, Oct. 1 Litho. ***Perf. 12¾***
951 A225 $20 multicolored 5.00 5.00

Souvenir Sheet

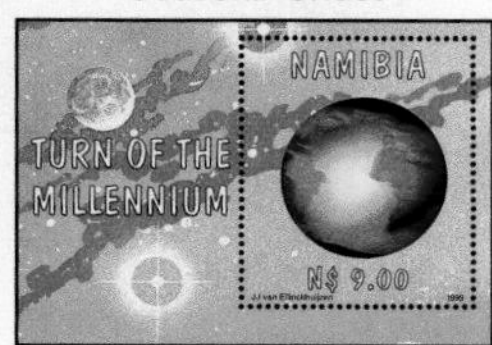

Turn of the Millennium — A226

Perf. 13¾x13¼

1999, Dec. 31 Litho.
952 A226 $9 multi 3.50 3.50

No. 952 has a holographic image. Soaking in water may affect the hologram.

Sunset Over Namibia A227

1999-2000 ***Perf. 13¼x13¾***
953 A227 $2.20 shown 1.25 1.25
954 A227 $2.40 Sunrise 1.40 1.40

Issued: $2.20, 12/31; $2.40, 1/1/00.

Ducks — A228

Designs: $2, South African shelduck. $2.40, Whitefaced duck. $3, Knobbilled duck. $7, Cape shoveller.

2000, Feb. 18 Litho. ***Perf. 13***
955 A228 $2 multi 1.10 1.10
956 A228 $2.40 multi 1.25 1.25
957 A228 $3 multi 1.50 1.50
958 A228 $7 multi 3.25 3.25
Nos. 955-958 (4) 7.10 7.10

Nos. 853-856 Surcharged

2000, Mar. 1 Litho. ***Perf. 13½***
959 A189 (65c) on 5c multi .40 .40
960 A189 $1.80 on 30c multi .90 .90
961 A189 $3 on 10c multi 1.50 1.50
962 A189 $6 on 20c multi 3.00 3.00
Nos. 959-962 (4) 5.80 5.80

See No. 1000.

Independence, 10th Anniv. — A229

2000, Mar. 21 ***Perf. 13¼x13¾***
963 A229 65c Children .75 .40
964 A229 $3 Flag 2.00 2.00

Passion Play — A230

Designs: $2.10, Jesus with crown of thorns. $2.40, Carrying cross.

2000, Apr. 1 ***Perf. 13¾***
965 A230 $2.10 multi .75 .75
966 A230 $2.40 multi .85 .85

Fauna of the Namib Desert A231

Designs: a, $2, Tenebrionid beetle. b, $2 Brown hyena. c, $2, Namib golden mole. d, $2, Shovel-snouted lizard. e, $2, Dune lark. f, $6, Namib side-winding adder.

2000, May 22 ***Perf. 14½***
967 A231 Sheet of 6, #a-f 9.00 9.00

The Stamp Show 2000, London.
Sizes of stamps: Nos. 967a-967c, 30x25mm; No. 967d, 30x50mm; Nos. 967e-967f, 26x37mm. Portions of the design were applied by a thermographic process, producing a shiny raised effect.

Welwitschia Mirabilis — A232

Various views of Welwitschia plants. Denominations: (65c), $2.20, $3, $4.

2000, June 21 Litho. ***Perf. 13¾***
968-971 A232 Set of 4 4.50 4.50

No. 968 is inscribed "Standard inland mail."

Souvenir Sheet

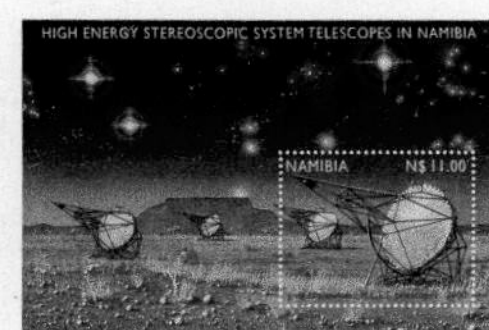

High Energy Stereoscopic Sytem Telescopes — A233

2000, July 7 ***Perf. 13¼x13¾***
972 A233 $11 multi 6.25 6.25

Fruit Trees A234

Designs: (65c), Jackalberry. $2, Sycamore fig. $2.20, Bird plum. $7, Marula.

2000, Aug. 16 Litho. ***Perf. 13¼x14***
973-976 A234 Set of 4 6.25 6.25

No. 973 is inscribed "Standard inland mail."

Souvenir Sheet

Yoka in Etosha A235

2000, Sept. 1 ***Perf. 13¼x13***
977 A235 $11 multi 5.50 5.50

Coelenterates — A236

Designs: ($1), Anthothoe stimpsoni. $2.45, Bundosoma capensis. $3.50, Anthopleura stephensoni. $6.60, Pseudactinia flagellifera.

2001, Apr. 18 Litho. ***Perf. 13¾***
978-981 A236 Set of 4 5.50 5.50

No. 978 is inscribed "Standard inland mail."

Civil Aviation — A237

Designs: ($1), Cessna 210 Turbo. $2.20, Douglas DC-6B. $2.50, Pitts 52A. $13.20, Bell 407 helicopter.

2001, May 9 ***Perf. 13¼x13¾***
982-985 A237 Set of 4 10.00 10.00

No. 982 is inscribed "Standard inland mail."

Renewable Energy Resources — A238

No. 986: a, Wood efficient stove. b, Biogas digester. c, Solar cooker. d, Repair, reuse, recycle. e, Solar water pump. f, Solar home system. g, Solar street light. h, Solar water heater. i, Solar telecommunication. j, Wind water pump.

2001, Aug. 15 ***Perf. 13½x14***
986 A238 Sheet of 10 10.00 10.00
a.-e. ($1) Any single .40 .40
f.-j. $3.50 Any single 1.10 1.10

Nos. 986a-986e are inscribed "Standard Mail."

Central Highlands Flora and Fauna — A239

No. 987: a, ($1.00), Ruppell's parrot (31x29mm). b, $3.50, Camel thorn (54x29mm). c, ($1.00), Flap-necked chameleon (39x29mm). d, ($1.00), Klipspringer (39x29mm). e, $3.50, Berg aloe (39x29mm). f, $3.50, Kudu (39x39mm). g, ($1.00), Rockrunner (39x29mm). h, $3.50, Namibian rock agama (39x39mm). i, ($1.00), Pangolin (39x39mm). j, $3.50, Armored ground cricket (39x29mm).

2001, Sept. 5 ***Perf. 12½x12¾***
987 A239 Sheet of 10, #a-j 12.50 12.50

Nos. 987a, 987c, 987d, 987g, 987i are inscribed "Standard Mail."

Tribal Women A240

No. 988, ($1.30): a, Mbalantu. b, Damara. c, Herero (leather headdress). d, San. e, Mafue. f, Baster.

No. 989, ($1.30): a, Mbukushu. b, Herero (flowered headdress). c, Himba. d, Kwanyama. e, Nama. f, Ngandjera/Kwaluudhi.

2002, Apr. 20 Litho. ***Perf. 13¼x13***

Sheets of 6, #a-f

988-989 A240 Set of 2 9.00 9.00
988g Sheet of 6 with incorrect back inscriptions 10.00 10.00
989g Sheet of 6 with incorrect back inscriptions 15.00 15.00

Stamps are inscribed "Standard Mail."

The back inscriptions on Nos. 988g and 989g are placed incorrectly so that the inscriptions for the stamps on the left side of the sheet have the back inscriptions of the stamps on the right side of the sheet, and vice versa.

The Mbukushu stamp on No. 989g reads "Standard Maiil."

Birds — A241

Designs: ($1.30), African hoopoe. $2.20, Paradise flycatchers. $2.60, Swallowtailed bee-eaters. $2.80, Malachite kingfisher.

2002, May 15 ***Perf. 13¾x13¼***

990-993 A241 Set of 4 7.00 7.00

No. 990 is inscribed "Standard Mail."

Ephemeral Rivers — A242

Designs: ($1.30), Kuiseb River floods halting movement of sand dunes, vert. (36x48mm). $2.20, Bird flying over lake of Tsauchab River flood water. $2.60, Elephants in dry bed of Hoarusib River (86x22mm). $2.80, Birds near Nossob River flood water. $3.50, Birds near Fish River, vert. (55x21mm).

2002, July 1 ***Perf. 13x13¼, 13¼x13***

994-998 A242 Set of 5 8.00 8.00

See No. 1023.

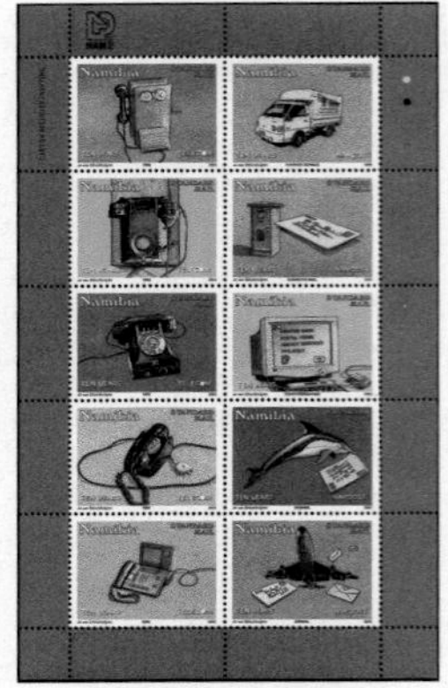
Namibia Post and Telecommunications, 10th Anniv. — A243

No. 999: a, Telephone, blue background. b, Telephone, yellow background. c, Telephone, green background. d, Telephone, lilac background. e, Picturephone, brown background. f, Mail van. g, Pillar box and letter. h, Computer. i, Dolphin with letter. j, Airplane and letters.

2002, Aug. 1 Litho. ***Perf. 13¼x13***

999 A243 ($1.30) Sheet of 10, #a-j 6.00 6.00
k. Sheet of 10, 2 each #a-e 6.00 6.00
l. Sheet of 10, 2 each #f-j 6.00 6.00

Stamps are inscribed "Standard Mail."

Nos. 853-854 Surcharged

2002, Oct. 21 Litho. ***Perf. 13½***

1000 A189 ($1.45) on 5c #853 .75 .75
1001 A189 ($1.45) on 10c #854 .75 .75

Surcharge on No. 1000 has letters that lean more to the right than those on No. 959. The two "d's" have tops that curve to the right on No. 1000, but have serifs that point left on No. 959. The cross line of the "t's" are lower on No. 1000 than on No. 959.

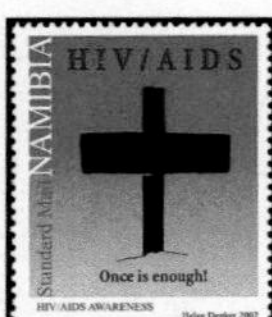

Prevention of AIDS — A244

Designs: ($1.45), Cross. $2.45, Condom. $2.85, Man and hand. $11.50, Test tubes.

2002, Dec. 1 ***Perf. 13½x13***

1002-1005 A244 Set of 4 7.00 7.00

No. 1002 is inscribed "Standard Mail."

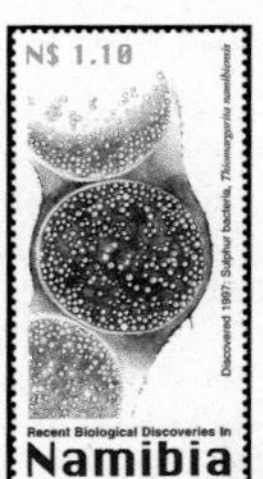

Recent Biological Discoveries — A245

Designs: $1.10, Sulphur bacteria. $2.45, Whiteheadia etesionamibensis. $2.85, Cunene flathead (catfish), horiz. $3.85, Zebra racer, horiz. $20, Gladiator (insect).

Perf. 13¾x13¼, 13¼x13¾

2003, Feb. 24

1006-1010 A245 Set of 5 8.25 8.25

Rural Development — A246

Designs: $1.45, Water and electricity supply. ($2.75), Conservancy formation and land use diversification. $4.40, Education and health services. ($11.50), Communication and road infrastructure.

2003, Apr. 17 Litho. ***Perf. 13¼x13¾***

1011-1014 A246 Set of 4 6.00 6.00

No. 1012 is inscribed "Postcard Rate" and No. 1014 is inscribed "Registered Mail."

Wetlands A247

Designs: $1.10, Women and cattle near oshana. $2.85, Birds at Omadhiya Lakes. ($3.85), Cuvelai Drainage.

2003, June 6

1015-1017 A247 Set of 3 5.75 5.75

No. 1017 is inscribed "Non-Standard Mail."

Heroes Acre Monuments A248

Various monuments with inscriprions: ($1.45), Standard Mail. ($2.75), Postcard Rate. ($3.85), Non-Standard Mail.

2003, Aug. 27 ***Perf. 13¼***

1018-1020 A248 Set of 3 4.25 4.25

Souvenir Sheet

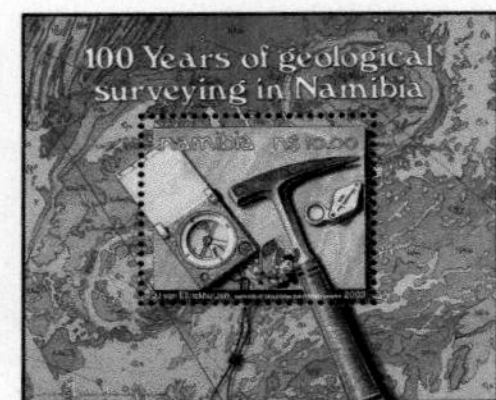

Geological Surveying in Namibia, Cent. — A249

2003, Sept. 10 ***Perf. 13¼x13¾***

1021 A249 $10 multi 8.25 8.25

Souvenir Sheet

Windhoek Philatelic Society, 25th Anniv. — A250

2003, Sept. 10

1022 A250 $10 multi 5.00 5.00

Ephemeral Rivers Type of 2002

Souvenir Sheet

2003, Dec. 8 ***Perf. 13¼x13***

1023 A242 $3.15 Like #996 4.00 4.00

Design voted "most beautiful stamp" at 8th Stamp World Cup, Paris.

Vervet Monkeys — A251

Designs: $1.60, Adult holding fruit. $3.15, Two monkeys on tree branches. $3.40, Adult and young. ($14.25), Adult chewing on twig. $4.85, Like #1024.

2004, Jan. 30 ***Perf. 13***

1024-1027 A251 Set of 4 8.75 8.75

Souvenir Sheet

1028 A251 $4.85 multi 3.00 3.00

No. 1027 is inscribed "Inland Registered Mail Paid." 2004 Hong Kong Stamp Expo (#1028).

Honeybees on Flowers — A252

Honeybees on: ($1.60), Sickle bush. $2.70, Daisy. ($3.05), Aloe. $3.15, Cat's claw. ($14.25), Edging senecio. $4.85, Pretty lady.

2004, Feb. 2 ***Perf. 13x13¼***

1029-1033 A252 Set of 5 7.75 7.75

Souvenir Sheet

1034 A252 $4.85 multi 2.75 2.75

No. 1029 is inscribed "Standard mail;" No. 1031, "Post card rate;" No. 1033, "Inland registered mail paid."

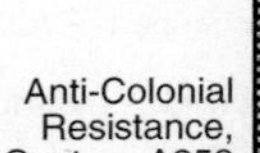

Anti-Colonial Resistance, Cent. — A253

2004, Mar. 23 Litho. ***Perf. 13¼***

1035 A253 ($1.60) multi 1.40 1.40

Souvenir Sheet

1036 A253 $5 multi 2.25 2.25

No. 1035 is inscribed "Standard Mail."

Education in Namibia A254

Designs: $1.60, Pre-school education enhances individual development potential. $2.75, Primary and secondary school education for all lays the foundation for equal opportunity. $4.40, Advanced learning and vocational training provide career options. ($12.65), Lifelong learning encourages personal growth and the capacity for leadership.

2004, Apr. 19 ***Perf. 13¼x13¾***

1037-1040 A254 Set of 4 6.75 6.75

No. 1040 is inscribed "Registered Mail."

Fishing Industry A255

Fish and: $1.60, Ship and dockworkers. $2.75, Ship. $4.85, Workers at processing plant.

Perf. 13¼x13¾

2004, June 22 Litho.

1041-1043 A255 Set of 3 6.00 6.00

Historic Buildings in Bethanie — A256

Designs: ($1.60), Joseph Ferdericks House. ($3.05), Schmelen House. ($4.40), Rhenish Mission Church. ($12.65), Stone Church.

2004, July 7 ***Perf. 14x13½***
1044-1047 A256 Set of 4 8.25 8.25

No. 1044 is inscribed "Standard Mail;" No. 1045, "Postcard rate;" No. 1046, "Non-Standard Mail," No. 1047, "Registered Mail."

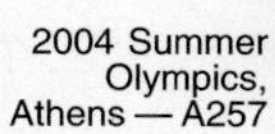

2004 Summer Olympics, Athens — A257

Designs: ($1.60), Wrestling. $2.90, Boxing, vert. $3.40, Pistol shooting. $3.70, Mountain biking, vert.

Perf. 14x13¼, 13¼x14
2004, Aug. 3 **Litho.**
1048-1051 A257 Set of 4 8.75 8.75
1051a Inscribed "XXVIII Olympiad" 5.00 5.00

No. 1048 is inscribed "Standard Mail."
No. 1051 has incorrect inscription "XVIII Olympiad."
No. 1051a issued 9/14.

Miniature Sheet

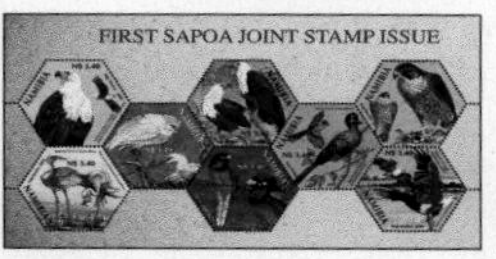

Birds A258

No. 1052: a, African fish eagles, national bird of Namibia. b, African fish eagles, national bird of Zimbabwe. c, Peregrine falcons, national bird of Angola. d, Cattle egrets, national bird of Botswana. e, Purple-crested louries, national bird of Swaziland. f, Blue cranes, national bird of South Africa. g, Bat-tailed trogons. h, African fish eagles, national bird of Zambia.

2004, Oct. 11 **Litho.** ***Perf. 14***
1052 A258 $3.40 Sheet of 8, #a-h 17.00 17.00

See Botswana Nos. 792-793, South Africa No. 1342, Swaziland Nos. 727-735, Zambia No. 1033, and Zimbabwe No. 975.

Rotary International, Cent. — A259

2005, Feb. 23 **Litho.** ***Perf. 13x13¼***
1053 A259 $3.70 multi 2.75 2.75

Pres. Hifikepunye Pohamba — A260

2005, Mar. 21 ***Perf. 13¼x14***
1054 A260 ($1.70) multi 2.25 2.25

Inscribed "Standard Mail."

Sunbirds — A261

Designs: $2.90, Marico sunbird. $3.40, Dusky sunbird. ($4.80), White-bellied sunbird. ($15.40), Scarlet-chested sunbird.
$10, Amethyst sunbird, horiz.

2005, Apr. 14 **Litho.** ***Perf. 13¼x14***
1055-1058 A261 Set of 4 11.50 11.50

Souvenir Sheet

Perf. 14x13¼
1059 A261 $10 multi 5.00 5.00

No. 1057 is inscribed "Non-Standard Mail"; No. 1058, "Registered Inland Postage Paid." Nos. 1055-1058 exists imperf. Value, each pair $40.

Nos. 855, 859, 861 and 868 Surcharged

a

b

c

2005, June 7 **Litho.** ***Perf. 13½***
1060 A189(a) ($1.70) on 50c #859 1.00 1.00
1061 A189(b) $2.90 on 20c #855 5.00 2.00
1062 A189(c) ($4.80) on $4 #868 3.50 1.75
1063 A189(b) $5.20 on 90c #861 2.50 1.75
Nos. 1060-1063 (4) 12.00 6.50

Medicinal Plants — A262

Designs: ($1.70), Nara. $2.90, Devil's claw. ($3.10), Hoodia. ($4.80), Tsamma.

2005, July 22 ***Perf. 14x13¼***
1064-1067 A262 Set of 4 6.00 6.00

No. 1064 is inscribed "Standard Mail"; No. 1066, "Postcard Rate"; No. 1067, "Non-Standard Mail".

Crops — A263

Designs: $2.90, Vegetables. $3.40, Pearl millet. ($13.70), Corn.

2005, Aug. 2 ***Perf. 13¼x13¾***
1068-1070 A263 Set of 3 8.50 8.50

No. 1070 is inscribed "Registered Mail."

Nos. 855, 861, 862, 866, 868-870 Surcharged Type "b" and

d

e

f

g

2005, Aug. 10 **Litho.** ***Perf. 13½***
1070A A189(a) ($1.70) on 10c #854 *200.00 75.00*
1071 A189(d) ($1.70) on 20c #855 1.75 1.50
1071A A189(a) ($1.70) on 20c #855 —
1072 A189(d) ($1.70) on 90c #861 1.90 .75
1073 A189(d) ($1.70) on $1 #862 1.50 1.25
1074 A189(b) $2.90 on 90c #861 2.00 2.00
1075 A189(e) ($4.80) on $1.50 #866 2.00 2.00
1076 A189(b) $5.20 on 20c #855 4.00 4.00
1077 A189(f) ($15.40) on $4 #868 4.75 4.75
1078 A189(g) ($18.50) on $10 #870 8.00 8.00
1079 A189(b) $25 on $5 #869 10.00 10.00
1080 A189(b) $50 on $10 #870 17.50 17.50
Nos. 1070A-1080 (11) 253.40 126.75

Gulls — A264

Designs: $3.10, Cape gulls. $4, Hartlaub's gulls. $5.50, Sabine's gull. ($16.20), Gray-headed gulls.

2006, Feb. 28 **Litho.** ***Perf. 14x13¼***
1081-1084 A264 Set of 4 11.50 11.50

No. 1084 is inscribed "Inland Registered Mail Paid."

Nos. 1003, 1030, 1042 Surcharged

Methods and Perfs As Before

2006, Apr. 13
1085 A244 $3.10 on $2.45 #1003 1.60 1.25
1086 A252 $3.10 on $2.70 #1030 1.60 1.25
1087 A255 $3.10 on $2.75 #1042 1.60 1.25
Nos. 1085-1087 (3) 4.80 3.75

Size, location and fonts of surcharges differ.

Dolphins — A265

Designs: ($1.80), Risso's dolphin. $3.10, Southern right-whale dolphins, vert. $3.70, Benguela dolphin. $4, Common dolphins. $5.50, Bottlenose dolphins, vert.

Perf. 13x13¼, 13¼x13
2006, Apr. 26 **Litho.**
1088-1092 A265 Set of 5 8.25 8.25

No. 1088 is inscribed "Standard Mail."

Miniature Sheets

Traditional Roles of Men — A266

No. 1093, ($1.80): a, Father. b, Musician. c, Carver. d, Shaman. e, Planter. f, Hunter.
No. 1094, ($1.80): a, Leader. b, Blacksmith. c, Protector. d, Pastoralist. e, Trader. f, Storyteller.

2006, May 24 ***Perf. 13x13¼***
Sheets of 6, #a-f
1093-1094 A266 Set of 2 6.75 6.75

Nos. 862, 865 Surcharged

2006, June 20 **Litho.** ***Perf. 13½***
1095 A189 ($3.30) on $1 #862 2.25 1.60
1096 A189 ($3.30) on $1.20 #865 2.25 1.60

Nos. 1095-1096 are inscribed "Postcard Rate." Location of surcharges differs.

Perennial Rivers — A267

Designs: $3.10, Orange River. $5.50, Kumene River, vert. (21x55mm). ($19.90), Zambezi River (87x22mm).

Perf. 14x13¼, 13½ ($5.50)
2006, July 24
1097-1099 A267 Set of 3 11.50 11.50

No. 1099 is inscribed "Registered Non Standard Mail."

A268

Designs: $3.10, Construction of the rail line. $3.70, Henschel Class NG15 locomotive No. 41. $5.50, Narrow gauge Class Jung tank locomotive No. 9.

2006, Aug. 9 ***Perf. 14¾x14***
1100-1102 A268 Set of 3 7.00 7.00

Otavi Mines and Railway Company (OMEG) Rail Line, Cent.

Otjiwarongo, Cent. — A269

2006, Nov. 17 ***Perf. 14***

1103 A269 $1.90 multi		1.40	1.40

Printed in sheets of 10.

Flora and Fauna — A270

Named species: 5c, Bullfrog. 10c, Mesemb. 30c, Solifuge. 40c, Jewel beetle. 60c, Compass jellyfish. ($1.90), Web-footed gecko. $2, Otjikoto tilapia. No. 1111, $6, Milkbush. No. 1112, ($6), African hawk eagle. $10, Black-faced impala. $25, Lichens. $50, Baobab tree.

2007, Feb. 15 **Litho.** ***Perf. 14x13¼***

1104	A270	5c multi	.25	.25
1105	A270	10c multi	.25	.25
1106	A270	30c multi	.25	.25
1107	A270	40c multi	.25	.25
1108	A270	60c multi	.25	.25
1109	A270	($1.90) multi	.65	.35
a.	Perf. 14		.80	.80
1110	A270	$2 multi	.75	.50
1111	A270	$6 multi	2.00	1.00
1112	A270	($6) multi	2.00	1.00
1113	A270	$10 multi	3.25	1.75
1114	A270	$25 multi	7.00	7.00
1115	A270	$50 multi	14.00	14.00
	Nos. 1104-1115 (12)		30.90	26.85

No. 1109 is inscribed "Standard Mail." No. 1112 is inscribed "Non-standard Mail."

See Nos. 1165-1168.

A271

Etosha National Park, Cent. A272

Designs: ($1.90), Otjovasandu Wilderness Area. $3.40, Okaukuejo Waterhole. ($17.20), Scientist conducting anthrax research.

No. 1119: a, Gabar goshawk (30x30mm). b, Umbrella thorn tree (50x30mm). c, Red-billed queleas (40x30mm). d, Burchell's zebras (40x30mm). e, Elephant (40x30mm). f, Blue wildebeest (40x30mm). g, Mustard tree (40x30mm). h, Black emperor dragonfly (40x40mm). i, Springbok (40x40mm). j, Ground agama (40x40mm).

Litho. With Foil Application

2007, Mar. 22 ***Perf. 14x13¼***

1116-1118 A271	Set of 3	11.50	11.50

Miniature Sheet

Litho.

1119 A272 ($2.25)	Sheet of 10, #a-j	12.50	12.50

No. 1116 is inscribed "Standard Mail"; No. 1118, "Inland Registered Mail Paid"; Nos. 1119a-1119j, "Postcard Rate."

Dragonflies A273

Designs: ($1.90), Blue emperor dragonfly. $3.90, Rock dropwing dragonfly. $4.40, Red-veined dropwing dragonfly. ($6), Jaunty dropwing dragonfly.

$6, Blue basker dragonfly.

2007, Apr. 16 **Litho.** ***Perf. 12¾x14***

1120-1123 A273	Set of 4	7.00	7.00

Souvenir Sheet

Perf. 14x13¼

1124 A273 $6 multi	3.25	3.25

No. 1120 is inscribed "Standard Mail"; No. 1123, "Non Standard Mail Paid."

Trees — A274

Designs: ($1.90), Commiphora kraeuseliana. $3.40, Commiphora wildii. $3.90, Commiphora glaucescens. ($6), Commiphora dinteri.

2007, July 20 **Litho.** ***Perf. 13¼x13¾***

1125-1128 A274	Set of 4	6.75	6.75

No. 1125 is inscribed "Standard Mail"; No. 1128, "Non-standard Mail."

Flowers — A275

Designs: ($1.90), Cheiridopsis caroli-schmidtii. ($6), Namibia ponderosa. ($17.20), Fenestraria rhopalophylla.

2007, Aug. 31

1129-1131 A275	Set of 3	10.00	10.00

No. 1129 is inscribed "Standard Mail"; No. 1130, "Non-standard Mail"; No. 1131, "Inland Registered Mail Paid."

Nos. 1129-1131 were each printed in sheets of 10 + 5 labels.

Nos. 861, 865, 866 and 868 Surcharged

h

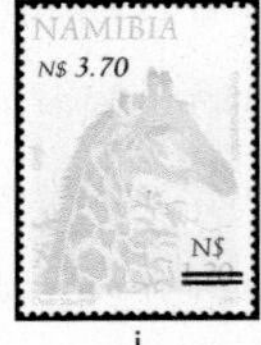

i

j

k

2007, Oct. 1 **Litho.** ***Perf. 13½***

1132 A189(h)	($2) on 90c #861	1.00	.65
1133 A189(h)	($2) on $1.20 #865	1.00	.65
1134 A189(h)	($2) on $1.50 #866	1.00	.65
1135 A189(h)	($2) on $4 #868	1.00	.65
1136 A189(i)	$3.70 on $1.20 #865	1.25	1.10
1137 A189(i)	$4.20 on $1.20 #865	1.40	1.25
1138 A189(i)	$4.85 on $1.20 #865	1.60	1.50
1139 A189(j)	($6.50) on $1.20 #865	2.25	2.00
1140 A189(k)	($16.45) on $1.20 #865	7.00	*8.00*
Nos. 1132-1140 (9)		17.50	16.45

Location of surcharge varies.

Miniature Sheets

National Animals A276

Nos. 1141 and 1142: a, Nyala (Malawi). b, Nyala (Zimbabwe). c, Burchell's zebra (Botswana). d, Oryx (Namibia). e, Buffalo (Zambia).

2007, Oct. 9 **Litho.** ***Perf. 13¾***

Granite Paper (#1141)

Country Name in Black

1141 A276 ($2)	Sheet of 5, #a-e	4.50	4.50

Litho. With Foil Application

Country Name in Silver

1142 A276 ($2)	Sheet of 5, #a-e	5.00	5.00

Nos. 1141a-1141e, 1142a-1142e are inscribed "Standard mail."

See No. 1193A, Botswana No. 838, Malawi No. 752, Zambia Nos. 1097-1101, Zimbabwe Nos. 1064-1068.

Weaver Birds — A277

Designs: ($2), Southern masked weaver. $3.70, Red-headed weaver. ($3.90), White-browed sparrow weaver. $4.20, Sociable weaver. ($18.45), Thick-billed weaver.

2008, Feb. 28 **Litho.** ***Perf. 13½x14***

1143-1147 A277	Set of 5	11.00	11.00

No. 1143 is inscribed "Standard Mail"; No. 1145, "Postcard Rate"; No. 1147, "Inland Registered Mail Paid."

Euphorbia Flowers — A278

Designs: ($3.90), Euphorbia virosa. $6.45, Euphorbia dregeana. ($22.95), Euphorbia damarana.

$6.45 — Type I: "E" over "I" in Latin inscription. Type II: Corrected version, no "I".

2008

1148	A278	($3.90) multi	1.10	.60
1149	A278	$6.45 multi, Type I	1.50	1.50
a.	Type II		2.25	2.25
1150	A278	($22.95) multi	5.75	5.75
	Nos. 1148-1150 (3)		8.35	7.85

Issued: Nos. 1148-1150, 3/3; No. 1149a, 5/27. No. 1148 inscribed "Postcard Rate"; No. 1150, "Registered Non-Standard Mail."

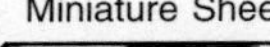

Miniature Sheet

Discovery of Diamonds in Namibia, Cent. — A279

No. 1151: a, Uncut diamonds. b, Land mining. c, Marine mining. d, Diamond jewelry.

Litho. With Foil Application

2008, Apr. 15 ***Perf. 14x13½***

1151 A279 $2	Sheet of 4, #a-d	4.75	4.75

Miniature Sheet

Traditional Houses — A280

No. 1152: a, Herero. b, Kavango. c, Owambo. d, Nama. e, Caprivi. f, San.

2008, May 27 **Litho.**

1152 A280 ($2.20)	Sheet of 6, #a-f	4.00	4.00

Nos. 1152a-1152f are each inscribed "Standard Mail."

Twyfelfontein UNESCO World Heritage Site — A281

Rock drawings: No. 1153, ($7.20), No. 1156a ($2.20), Lion man. No. 1154, ($7.20), No. 1156b ($2.20), Giraffe, Dancing kudu. No. 1155, ($7.20), No. 1156c ($2.20), Elephant.

2008, June 27 ***Perf. 13½x13¾***

1153-1155 A281	Set of 3	6.75	6.75

Souvenir Sheet

1156 A281 ($2.20)	Sheet of 3, #a-c	2.75	2.75

Nos. 1153-1155 are each inscribed "Non-Standard Mail"; Nos. 1156a-1156c, "Standard Mail."

Ediacaran Fossils — A282

Designs: ($2), Rangea. ($3.90), Swartpuntia. ($18.45), Pteridinium. ($22.95), Ernietta.

Litho. & Embossed

2008, Aug. 8 ***Perf. 13¼x14***

1157-1160 A282	Set of 4	12.50	12.50

No. 1157 is inscribed "Standard Mail"; No. 1158, "Postcard Rate"; No. 1159, "Registered Non-standard Mail"; No. 1160, "Registered Inland Mail Paid."

2008 Summer Olympics, Beijing — A283

Designs: $2, Female runner, sun and Earth. $3.70, Athlete with arms raised. $3.90, Athlete at finish line. $4.20, Female runner with arms extended.

2008, Aug. 15 **Litho.** ***Perf. 13¼x13***

1161-1164 A283	Set of 4	3.75	3.75

Flora and Fauna Type of 2007

Designs: $4.10, Thimble grass. $4.60, Bronze whaler shark. $5.30, Deep sea red crab. ($18.20), False ink cap mushroom.

2008, Oct. 1 **Litho.** ***Perf. 14x13¼***

1165	A270	$4.10 multi	1.00	.80
1166	A270	$4.60 multi	1.10	.90
1167	A270	$5.30 multi	1.40	1.25
1168	A270	($18.20) multi	4.75	4.00
	Nos. 1165-1168 (4)		8.25	6.95

No. 1168 is inscribed "Registered Mail."

Eagles A284

Designs: $4.10, Martial eagle. ($4.30), Bataleur eagle. $4.60, Verreaux's eagle. ($25.40), Tawny eagle.

2009, Feb. 2 Litho. ***Perf. 13¼x13¾***
1169-1172 A284 Set of 4 12.00 12.00

No. 1170 is inscribed "Postcard Rate"; No. 1172, "Registered Non-Standard Mail." Nos. 1169-1172 exists imperf. Value, each $90.

New Year 2009 (Year of the Ox) — A285

Litho. With Foil Application

2009, Apr. 10 ***Perf. 14x13¼***
1173 A285 $2.20 multi 1.50 1.50

Miniature Sheet

Flora and Fauna of the Brandberg — A286

No. 1174: a, Augur buzzard (30x30mm). b, Numasfels Peak (50x30mm). c, Quiver tree (40x30mm). d, CMR beetle (40x30mm). e, Leopard (40x30mm). f, Kobas (40x30mm). g, Bokmakiri (40x30mm). h, Jameson's red rock rabbit (40x40mm). i, Brandberg halfmens (40x40mm). j, Jordan's girdled lizard (40x40mm).

2009, Apr. 10 Litho. ***Perf. 14x13¼***
1174 A286 ($4.30) Sheet of 10, #a-j 5.00 5.00

Nos. 1174a-1174j are each inscribed "Post-card Rate."

Souvenir Sheet

First Crossing of Africa by Automobile, Cent. — A287

2009, May 1 ***Perf. 13¾x14¼***
1175 A287 $7.10 multi 2.50 2.50

Wild Horses A288

Designs: $5.30, Two horses. $8, Three horses. ($20.40), Four horses.

2009, July 3 ***Perf. 13¾x14***
1176-1178 A288 Set of 3 9.50 9.50

No. 1178 is inscribed "Inland Registered Mail Paid." See Nos. 1185, 1340-1342.

Souvenir Sheet

German Higher Private School, Cent. A289

2009, Aug. 21 Litho. ***Perf. 13½***
1179 A289 $4.60 multi 2.00 2.00

Geckos — A290

Designs: $4.40, Festive gecko. $5, Koch's barking gecko. $6, Giant ground gecko. $7.70, Velvety thick-toed gecko. ($18.20), Bradfield's Namib day gecko.

2009, Sept. 30 ***Perf. 13¾***
1180-1184 A290 Set of 5 11.00 11.00

No. 1184 is inscribed "Registered Mail."

Horses Type of 2009

Design: Four horses in desert.

2009, Nov. 2 ***Perf. 13¾x14***
1185 A288 ($4.60) multi 6.00 6.00

No. 1185 is inscribed "Postcard Rate."

Miniature Sheet

Endangered Species — A291

No. 1186: a, Wattled crane. b, Gazania thermalis. c, Leatherback turtle. d, Giant quiver tree. e, Cape vulture. f, White Namib toktokkie. g, Cheetah. h, Hook-lipped rhinoceros. i, wild dog. j, Nama-padloper tortoise.

2010, Feb. 8 ***Perf. 13¼x13***
1186 A291 ($4.60) Sheet of 10, #a-j 25.00 25.00

Nos. 1186a-1186j are inscribed "Postcard Rate."

Independence, 20th Anniv. — A292

Perf. 13¼x13¾

2010, Mar. 21 Litho.
1187 A292 ($2.50) multi 1.00 .80

No. 1187 is inscribed "Standard mail."

Miniature Sheet

2010 World Cup Soccer Championships, South Africa — A293

No. 1188 — Soccer players, ball, 2010 World Cup mascot and flag of: a, Namibia. b, South Africa. c, Zimbabwe. d, Malawi. e, Swaziland. f, Botswana. g, Mauritius. h, Lesotho. i, Zambia.

2010, Apr. 9 Litho. ***Perf. 13½***
1188 A293 ($4.60) Sheet of 9, #a-i 14.00 14.00

Nos. 1188a-1188i are inscribed "Postcard rate." A miniature sheet containing No. 1188a and stamps from South Africa, Zimbabwe, Malawi, Swaziland, Botswana, Mauritius, Lesotho and Zambia was sold by Namibia Post for $40. The sheet apparently was not sold by any other country. See Botswana Nos. 896-905, Lesotho No. , Malawi No. 753, Mauritius No. 1086, South Africa No. 1403, Swaziland Nos. 794-803, Zambia Nos. 1115-1118, and Zimbabwe Nos. 1112-1121.

Miniature Sheet

Birds A294

No. 1189: a, Northern black korhaan. b, Red-crested korhaan. c, Black-bellied bustard. d, Rüppell's korhaan. e, Ludwig's bustard. f, Kori bustard.

2010, Apr. 14 ***Perf. 13½x14***
1189 A294 ($4.60) Sheet of 6, #a-f 12.00 12.00

Nos. 1189a-1189f are inscribed "Postcard rate."

Lighthouses — A295

Designs: $4.40, Swakopmund Lighthouse. ($9.50), Diaz Point Lighthouse, Lüderitzbucht. ($18.20), Pelican Point Lighthouse, Walvis Bay.

2010, June 18 ***Perf. 13½x13¾***
1190-1192 A295 Set of 3 10.00 10.00

No. 1191 is inscribed "Non-standard mail." No. 1192 is inscribed "Registered Mail."

Souvenir Sheet

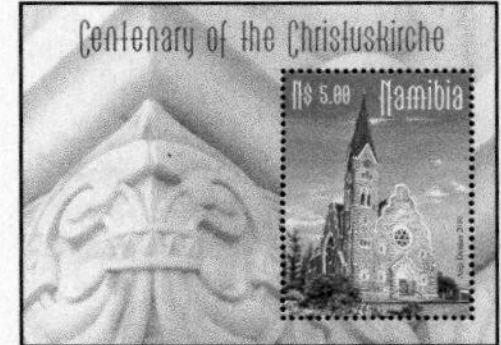

Christuskirche, Windhoek, Cent. — A296

2010, Aug. 6 ***Perf. 14***
1193 A296 $5 multi 1.75 1.75

Oryx — A296a

2010, Sept. 18 ***Perf. 13¾***
1193A A296a ($2.50) multi *4.00 4.00*

No. 1193A was printed in sheets of 5 that sold for $25. The lower half of the stamp, as shown, is a generic image that could be personalized.

See No. 1141d for similarity.

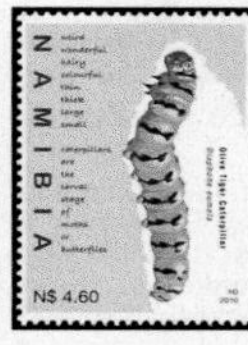

Caterpillars — A297

Designs: $4.60, Olive tiger caterpillar. $5.30, African armyworm. $6.40, Wild silk caterpillar. ($29.40), Mopane caterpillar.

2010, Oct. 1 Litho.
1194-1197 A297 Set of 4 15.00 15.00

Souvenir Sheet

World Standards Day — A298

2010, Oct. 18 ***Perf. 14x13½***
1198 A298 $5.30 multi 1.75 1.75

Wildlife — A299

Designs: $4.60, Leopard. ($5), African elephant, vert. $5.30, Black rhinoceros. $6.40, African buffalo. ($8.50), Lion, vert.

2011, Jan. 28 ***Perf. 14x13¼, 13¼x14***
1199-1203 A299 Set of 5 10.00 10.00

No. 1200 is inscribed "Postcard Rate." No. 1203 is inscribed "Non-standard Mail." Nos. 1199-1203 exists imperf. Value, each $65.

Miniature Sheet

Frogs A300

No. 1204: a, Long reed frog. b, Bubbling kassina. c, Tandy's sand frog. d, Angolan reed frog.

2011, Mar. 23 ***Perf. 13¼x14***
1204 A300 ($5) Sheet of 4, #a-d 7.00 7.00

Nos. 1204a-1204d each were inscribed "Postcard Rate."

Souvenir Sheet

Road Safety Campaign — A301

2011, May 11 *Perf. 13x13¼*
1205 A301 $5.30 multi 8.00 8.00

Miniature Sheet

Endangered Marine Life — A302

No. 1206: a, Cape gannet (30x30mm). b, Atlantic yellow-nosed albatross (50x30mm). c, African penguin (40x30mm). d, Southern right whale (40x30mm). e, Bank cormorant (40x30mm). f, West coast steenbras (40x30mm). g, Split-fan kelp (40x40mm). h, Cape rock lobster (40x40mm).

2011, May 16 *Perf. 14x13¼*
1206 A302 $4.60 Sheet of 8, #a-h 12.00 12.00

Exists imperf. Value, $220.

Personalized Stamps — A303

Designs: No. 1207, Oryx. elephant and leopard, Etosha National Park. No. 1208, Lizard and rock paintings, Twyfelfontein UNESCO World Heritage Site. No. 1209, Bird over Fish River Canyon. No. 1210, Antelope, Sossusvlei Region. No. 1211, Rhinoceros in Community Conservation Area.

2011, June 7 *Perf. 13¼x13*
1207 A303 ($5) multi + label 2.50 2.50
1208 A303 ($5) multi + label 2.50 2.50
1209 A303 ($5) multi + label 2.50 2.50
1210 A303 ($5) multi + label 2.50 2.50
1211 A303 ($5) multi + label 2.50 2.50
a. Sheet of 5, #1207-1211, + 5 labels 12.50 12.50
Nos. 1207-1211 (5) 12.50 12.50

Nos. 1207-1211, each inscribed "Postcard rate," were printed in sheets of 5 stamps + 5 labels that could be personalized. Label shown is a generic image. Sheets of 5, including No. 1211a, each sold for $35.

Aloes — A304

Designs: ($5), Aloe gariepensis. ($8.50), Aloe variegata. ($20.90), Aloe striata ssp. karasbergensis.

2011, June 21 *Perf. 13¼x14*
1212-1214 A304 Set of 3 10.00 10.00

No. 1212 is inscribed "Postcard Rate." No. 1213 is inscribed "Non Standard Mail." No. 1214 is inscribed "Registered Mail."

Grebes — A305

Designs: No. 1215, ($2.70), Little grebe. No. 1216, ($2.70), Great crested grebe. ($23.60), Black-necked grebe, horiz.

2011, July 18 *Perf. 13¼x14, 14x13¼*
1215-1217 A305 Set of 3 8.50 8.50

Nos. 1215-1216 are each inscribed "Standard Mail." No. 1217 is inscribed "Inland Registered Mail." Nos. 1215-1217 exists imperf. Value, each $90.

Grasses A306

Designs: ($2.70), Natal red top. $4.80, Feather-top chloris. $5.40, Urochloa brachyura. $6.50, Nine-awned grass. ($8.50), Foxtail buffalo grass.

2011, Sept. 30 **Litho.** *Perf. 13½x14*
1218-1222 A306 Set of 5 8.00 8.00

No. 1218 is inscribed "Standard mail"; No. 1222, "Non-standard mail."

Birds — A308

Designs: 5c, Carp's tit. 10c, Hartlaub's spurfowl. 20c, Herero chat.30c, Rüppell's parrot. 50c, Rüppell's korhaan. ($2.90), White-tailed shrike. $5, Rockrunner. ($5.30), Dune lark. ($8.90), Damara hornbill. $20, Damara tern. ($21.90), Violet wood hoopoe. $100, Bare-cheeked babbler.

2012, Feb. 15 **Litho.** *Perf. 13¼*
1224 A308 5c multi .25 .25
1225 A308 10c multi .25 .25
1226 A308 20c multi .25 .25
1227 A308 30c multi .25 .25
1228 A308 50c multi .25 .25
1229 A308 ($2.90) multi .80 .80
1230 A308 $5 multi 1.50 1.50
1231 A308 ($5.30) multi 1.75 1.75
1232 A308 ($8.90) multi 3.00 3.00
1233 A308 $20 multi 5.00 5.00
1234 A308 ($21.90) multi 5.75 5.75
1235 A308 $100 multi 25.00 25.00
Nos. 1224-1235 (12) 44.05 44.05

No. 1229 is inscribed "Standard mail"; No. 1231, "Postcard rate"; No. 1232, "Non-standard mail"; No. 1234, "Registered mail." No. 1235 exists imperf. Vlaue, $105.
See Nos. 1254-1258.

Bats — A309

Designs: No. 1236, ($5.30), Straw-colored fruit bats. No. 1237, ($5.30), Egyptian slit-faced bats. No. 1238, ($5.30), Angolan epauletted fruit bats.

2012, Apr. 9 *Perf. 13¼*
Stamps + Labels
1236-1238 A309 Set of 3 6.00 6.00

Nos. 1236-1238 are inscribed "Postcard rate."

2012 Summer Olympics and Paralympics, London — A310

Designs: $2.90, Shooting. $4.80, Running, vert. $5.40, Cycling. $6.50, Wheelchair racer, vert.

2012, Apr. 16 *Perf. 13x13¼, 13¼x13*
1239-1242 A310 Set of 4 6.50 6.50

Scorpions A311

Designs: $4.80, Parabuthus villosus. ($5.30), Parabuthus namibensis. $5.40, Opistophthalmus carinatus. $6.50, Hottentotta arenaceus.

2012, June 11 *Perf. 14x13¾*
1243-1246 A311 Set of 4 8.00 8.00

Souvenir Sheets

Telecom Namibia, 20th Anniv. A312

Nampost, 20th Anniv. — A313

No. 1247: a, Satellite dishes. b, Fiber-optic cable strands.
No. 1248: a, Postman in bush. b, Mail truck.

2012, July 31 *Perf. 12½*
1247 A312 $2.90 Sheet of 2, #a-b 2.00 2.00
1248 A313 $2.90 Sheet of 2, #a-b 2.00 2.00

Souvenir Sheet

Gobabeb Research and Training Center, 50th Anniv. — A314

No. 1249: a, ($3.10), Namaqua chameleon. b, $5.10, Dune grass. c, $5.80, Flying saucer beetle.

2012, Sept. 22 *Perf. 13¼x14*
1249 A314 Sheet of 3, #a-c 5.00 5.00

No. 1249a is inscribed "Standard Mail."

Mongooses — A315

Designs: $5.10, Black mongoose. ($5.60), Yellow mongoose, vert. $5.80, Banded mongoose. $6.90, Dwarf mongoose.

Perf. 14¾x14¼, 14¼x14¾
2012, Oct. 1
1250-1253 A315 Set of 4 8.00 8.00

No. 1251 is inscribed "Postcard Rate."

Birds Type of 2012

Designs: 90c, Benguela long-billed lark. $1, Barlow's lark. $3, Rosy-faced lovebirds. $10, Gray's larks. $12, Monteiro's hornbill.

2013, Mar. 1 *Perf. 13¼*
1254 A308 90c multi .30 .30
1255 A308 $1 multi .30 .30
1256 A308 $3 multi 1.10 1.10
1257 A308 $10 multi 3.50 3.50
1258 A308 $12 multi 4.00 4.00
Nos. 1254-1258 (5) 6.15 6.15

Beetles — A316

Designs: ($3.10), Glittering jewel beetle. $5.10, Red-spotted lily weevil. $5.50, Garden fruit chafer. $6.90, Lunate ladybird. ($26.50), Two-spotted ground beetle.

2013, Apr. 5
1259-1263 A316 Set of 5 14.00 14.00

No. 1259 is inscribed "Standard mail;" No. 1263, "Inland registered mail."

Miniature Sheets

Children A317

No. 1264, ($3.10) — Inscriptions: a, Right to family, shelter & a healthy environment. b, Faith & joy. c, Right to health, nutrition & safety. d, Freedom from neglect, fear, abuse & violence. e, Love & trust. f, Freedom of identity, traditions & beliefs.

No. 1265, ($3.10) — Inscriptions: a, Right to early development support, education & information. b, Aspirations & dreams. c, Right to special care & support. d, Freedom of expression, association & participation. e, Play & creativity. f, Freedom from discrimination & exploitation.

2013, June 17 **Litho.** *Perf. 13x13¼*
Sheets of 6, #a-f
1264-1265 A317 Set of 2 15.00 15.00

Nos. 1264a-1264f and 1265a-1265f are each inscribed "Standard mail."

Souvenir Sheet

Environmental Education — A318

2013, June 20 **Litho.** *Perf. 13¼x13*
1266 A318 $5.10 multi 1.75 1.75

Souvenir Sheet

Man and Woman Riding in Donkey Cart A319

2013, July 12 **Litho.** *Perf. 13x13¼*
1267 A319 $5.80 multi 1.75 1.75

Johanna Benson, Gold Medalist at 2012 Paralympics — A320

2013, Aug. 21 Litho. *Perf. 13¼x13*
1268 A320 ($3.10) multi 1.00 1.00
1269 A320 ($6) multi + label 2.75 2.75

No. 1268 is inscribed "Standard mail" and was printed in sheets of 10.
No. 1269 is inscribed "Postcard rate" and was printed in sheets that sold for $40 containing 5 stamps + 5 labels that could be personalized.

Antelopes A321

Designs: $5.40, Elands. No. 1271, ($6), Greater kudus. No. 1272, ($6), Gemsboks. $6.20, Sables. $7.30, Blue wildebeests.

2013, Sept. 30 Litho. *Perf. 12½*
1270-1274 A321 Set of 5 9.00 9.00

Nos. 1271 and 1272 are both inscribed "Postcard Rate."

Wooden Vessels — A322

Designs: ($3.30), HaMbukushu. $5.40, BaSubiya. ($6), Naman. $6.20, AaWambo. $7.30, OvaHerero.

2014, Feb. 10 Litho. *Perf. 14x13¼*
1275-1279 A322 Set of 5 8.50 8.50

No. 1275 is inscribed "Standard Mail;" No. 1277; "Postcard Rate."

Miniature Sheet

Nocturnal Animals — A323

No. 1280: a, Southern lesser galago. b, Cape porcupine. c, Small-spotted genet. d, Ground pangolin. e, Aardvark. f, Aardwolf.

2014, Mar. 14 Litho. *Perf. 13¼*
1280 A323 ($3.30) Sheet of 6, #a-f, + label 6.00 6.00

Nos. 1280a-1280f are each inscribed "Standard Mail."

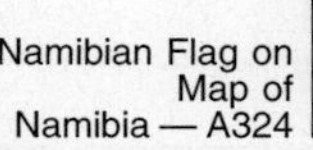

Namibian Flag on Map of Namibia — A324

2014, May 21 Litho. *Perf. 14x13¼*
1281 A324 ($3.30) multi 1.00 1.00

Souvenir Sheet

1282 A324 ($27.20) multi 7.00 7.00

No. 1281 is inscribed "Standard Mail;" No. 1282, "Inland Registered Mail."

Antelopes A325

Designs: No. 1283, ($6), Red lechwes. No. 1284, ($6), Bushbucks. No. 1285, ($6), Red hartebeests. No. 1286, ($6), Springboks.

2014, May 27 Litho. *Perf. 13¼x13½*
1283-1286 A325 Set of 4 7.00 7.00

Nos. 1283-1286 are each inscribed "Postcard Rate."

Snakes — A326

Designs: $5.40, Black mamba. ($6), Boomslang. $6.20, Puff adder. $7.30, Zebra snake.

2014, June 4 Litho. *Perf. 13¾*
1287-1290 A326 Set of 4 7.00 7.00

No. 1288 is inscribed "Postcard Rate."

First Visit of Chinese Navy to Namibia — A327

Designs: No. 1291, $3.30, Taihu. No. 1292, $3.30, Yancheng.

2014, June 11 Litho. *Perf. 13x13¼*
1291-1292 A327 Set of 2 2.00 2.00

A souvenir sheet containing two $3.30 stamps depicting Walvis Bay harbor and the Luoyang sold for $15. Value, $2.50.

Miniature Sheet

Flora and Fauna of the Kalahari Desert A328

No. 1293: a, Peregrine falcon (30x30mm). b, Cape turtle doves (50x30mm). c, Shepherd's tree (40x30mm). d, Giraffe (40x30mm). e, African monarch butterfly (40x30mm). f, Cheetah (40x30mm). g, Gemsbok cucumbers (40x30mm). h, Suricates (40x40mm). i, Trumpet-thorn (40x40mm). j, Spotted sandveld lizard (40x40mm).

2014, July 28 Litho. *Perf. 14x13½*
1293 A328 ($6) Sheet of 10, #a-j 17.50 17.50

Nos. 1293a-1293j are each inscribed "Postcard Rate."

In 2014 and 2015, Namibia postal officials declared as "illegal" souvenir sheets with a $5 denomination depicting various dogs and other wildlife, and a stamp inscribed "Postage Paid" depicting a dog and cat.

Kingfishers A329

Designs: ($5.70), Pied kingfishers. ($6.40), Half-collared kingfishers. ($6.60), Woodland kingfishers. ($7.70), Malachite kingfishers. ($28.30), Giant kingfishers.

2014, Oct. 1 Litho. *Perf. 13¼x14*
1294-1298 A329 Set of 5 15.00 15.00

No. 1294 is inscribed "Zone A;" No. 1295, "Postcard Rate;" No. 1296, "Zone B;" No. 1297, "Zone C;" No. 1298, "Inland Registered Mail." Nos. 1294-1298 exists imperf. Vlaue, each $60.

Souvenir Sheet

Namib Sand Sea UNESCO World Heritage Site — A330

No. 1299: a, Sossusvlei/Deadvlei. b, Comicus spp. c, Sandwich Harbor.

2015, Feb. 6 Litho. *Perf. 13¼*
1299 A330 ($6.40) Sheet of 3, #a-c 2.25 2.25

Nos. 1299a-1299c are each inscribed "Postcard Rate."

Presidents of Namibia — A331

Designs: ($3.50), Pres. Hage Geingob.
$30, Presidents Sam Nujoma, Hifikepunye Pohamba, Hage Geingob, map and flag of Namibia, horiz.

Litho. With Foil Application

2015, Mar. 21 *Perf. 13¼x13¾*
1300 A331 ($3.50) gold & multi .80 .80

Litho., Sheet Margin Litho. With Foil Application

Souvenir Sheet

Perf. 14½x14

1301 A331 $30 sil & multi 4.25 4.25

Inauguration of Pres. Geingob, Independence, 25th anniv. (No. 1301). No. 1301 contains one 75x26mm stamp.

Bee-Eaters — A332

Designs: ($3.50), White-fronted bee-eater. $5.70, Southern carmine bee-eater, horiz. $6.60, Swallow-tailed bee-eater, horiz. $7.70, Little bee-eaters, horiz. ($28.30), European bee-eater.

Perf. 14x14¼, 14¼x14

2015, May 15 Litho.
1302-1306 A332 Set of 5 7.50 7.50

No. 1302 is inscribed "Standard Mail;" No. 1306, "Inland Registered Mail." Nos. 1300-1306 exists imperf. Value, each $65.

Antelopes A333

Designs: No. 1307, ($6.40), Steenbok. No. 1308, ($6.40), Common duiker. No. 1309, ($6.40), Klipspringer. No. 1310, ($6.40), Damara dik-dik.

2015, June 22 Litho. *Perf. 14¼*
1307-1310 A333 Set of 4 4.25 4.25

Nos. 1307-1310 are each inscribed "Postcard Rate."

Juvenile Big Game Animals — A334

Designs: ($3.50), Leopard. $5.70, African elephant. $6.60, Black rhinoceros. $7.70, African buffalo. ($35.50), Lion.

2015, July 6 Litho. *Perf. 14¾x14½*
1311-1315 A334 Set of 5 9.50 9.50

No. 1311 is inscribed "Standard mail;" No. 1315, "Non-standard registered mail."

Sharks A335

Designs: $5.70, Bronze whaler shark. ($6.40), Broadnose sevengill shark. $6.60, Great white shark. $7.70, Smooth hammerhead shark.

2015, Aug. 19 Litho. *Perf. 14½x14*
1316-1319 A335 Set of 4 5.25 5.25

No. 1317 is inscribed "Postcard Rate."

Coursers — A336

Designs: ($6.05), Burchell's courser. ($6.80), Three-banded courser. ($7), Double-banded courser. ($8.20), Bronze-winged courser.

2015, Oct. 1 Litho. *Perf. 13½*
1320-1323 A336 Set of 4 5.00 5.00

No. 1320 is inscribed "Zone A;" No. 1321, "Postcard Rate;" No. 1322, "Zone B;" No. 1323, "Zone C." Nos. 1320-1323 exists imperf. Value, each $60.

Souvenir Sheet

Hong Kong 2015 Intl. Stamp Exhibition — A337

No. 1324: a, Two rhinoceroses. b, Earth. c, Three elephants.

2015, Nov. 22 Litho. *Perf. 13¾*
1324 A337 ($6.80) Sheet of 3, #a-c 3.00 3.00

Nos. 1324a-1324c are each inscribed "Postcard rate."

Namibian postal officials have declared as "illegal" eight sheets dated "2015" having the theme of 2018 World Cup Soccer Championships.

Allgemeine Zeitung Newspaper, Cent. — A338

Newspaper masthead dated: ($3.70), July 22, 2016. ($6.80), Aug. 1, 1919.

2016 Litho. *Perf. 13*
1325-1326 A338 Set of 2 1.40 1.40
1326a Souvenir sheet of 2, #1325-1326 1.50 1.50

Issued: Nos. 1325-1326, 3/4; No. 1326a, 7/22/16.
No. 1325 is inscribed "Standard mail;" No. 1326, "Postcard rate."

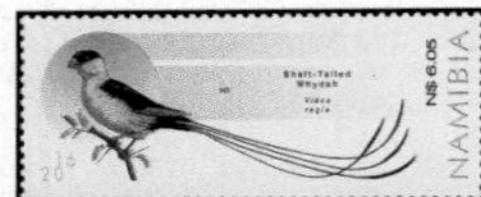

Whydahs — A339

Designs: $6.05, Shaft-tailed whydah. $7, Long-tailed paradise whydah, vert. ($30), Pin-tailed whydah, vert.

2016, Mar. 18 Litho. *Perf. 13¼*
1327-1329 A339 Set of 3 6.50 6.50

No. 1329 is inscribed "Inland registered mail."

Miniature Sheet

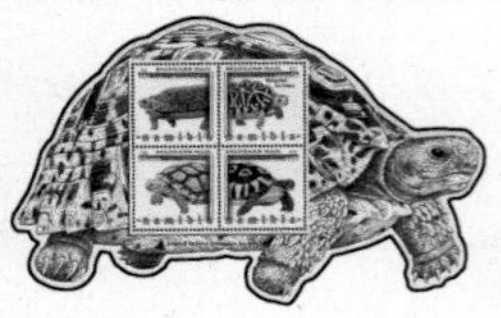

Tortoises A340

No. 1330: a, Speke's hinged tortoise. b, Namaqualand tent tortoise. c, Nama padloper. d, Angulate tortoise.

2016, May 11 Litho. *Perf. 14*
1330 A340 ($3.70) Sheet of 4, #a-d 2.25 2.25

Nos. 1330a-1330d are each inscribed "Standard mail."

Birds — A341

Designs: ($3.70), Cattle egret. $6.05, Green-backed heron, horiz. ($6.80), Goliath heron, horiz. $7, Squacco heron, horiz. $8.20, Black heron, horiz.

Perf. 13¼x12¾, 12¾x13¼
2016, July 7 Litho.
1331-1335 A341 Set of 5 4.75 4.75

No. 1331 is inscribed "Standard mail;" No. 1333, "Post card rate."

Souvenir Sheet

Forestry A342

No. 1336: a, Forestry resources used in commercial buildings and housing, arts and crafts and household utensils. b, Elephant and trees, vert. c, Fruit, soap and oils.

2016, Aug. 11 Litho. *Perf. 14x13¼*
1336 A342 ($6.80) Sheet of 3, #a-c 3.00 3.00

Nos. 1336a-1336c are each inscribed "Postcard rate."

Mammals A343

Designs: ($6.60), African wild dogs. ($7.50), Spotted hyenas. ($8.80), Brown hyena.

2016, Sept. 30 Litho. *Perf. 12½x13*
1337-1339 A343 Set of 3 3.50 3.50

No. 1337 is inscribed "Zone A;" No. 1338, "Zone B;" No. 1339, "Zone C."

Wild Horses Type of 2009

Designs: No. 1340, ($7.30), Two horses (like #1176). No. 1341, ($7.30), Three horses (like #1177). No. 1342, ($7.30), Four horses (like #1178).

2016, Nov. 15 Litho. *Perf. 12½x13*
1340-1342 A288 Set of 3 3.25 3.25

Nos. 1340-1342 are each inscribed "Postcard rate."

Souvenir Sheet

Mandume ya Ndemufayo (1894-1917), Last King of the Oukwanyama and Anti-Colonial Resistance Leader — A344

2017, Feb. 6 Litho. *Perf. 13¼*
1343 A344 ($7.30) multi 1.10 1.10

No. 1343 is inscribed "Post card rate."

Souvenir Sheet

Scouting in Namibia, Cent. A345

2017, Feb. 17 Litho. *Perf. 13¼*
1344 A345 ($4) multi .65 .65

No. 1344 is inscribed "Standard mail."

Barbets — A346

Designs: ($6.60), Black-collared barbets. ($7.50), Crested barbets, horiz. ($8.80), Acacia pied barbets.

Perf. 13¼x13, 13x13¼
2017, Mar. 9 Litho.
1345-1347 A346 Set of 3 3.50 3.50

No. 1345 is inscribed "Zone A;" No. 1346, "Zone B;" No. 1347, "Zone C."

Hares and Rabbits A347

No. 1348: a, Jameson's red rabbit. b, Scrub hare.

2017, Apr. 15 Litho. *Perf. 12½x13*
1348 A347 ($7.30) Horiz. pair, #a-b 2.25 2.25

No. 1348 is inscribed "postcard rate."

Souvenir Sheet

Protestant Reformation, 500th Anniv. — A348

2017, May 12 Litho. *Perf. 13½*
1349 A348 ($7.30) multi 1.10 1.10

No. 1349 is inscribed "Postcard Rate."

Flame Lilies — A349

Designs: ($6.60), Limestone lily. ($7.50), Flame lily. ($8.80), Namib lily, vert.

Perf. 13¼x12¾, 12¾x13¼
2017, June 15 Litho.
1350-1352 A349 Set of 3 3.50 3.50

No. 1350 is inscribed "ZONE A." No. 1351 is inscribed "ZONE B." No. 1352 is inscribed "ZONE C."

Diamond Trains A350

Designs: No. 1353, ($7.30), (1AO) Bo Benzol-electric locomotive. No. 1354, ($7.30), Bo-Bo electric locomotive K.B.G. No. 1355, ($7.30), Bo-Bo Benzol-electric locomotive C.D.M. No. 40. No. 1356, ($7.30), Railcar No. 3 Kolmanskop.

Litho. with Foil Application

2017, July 18 *Perf. 14¼x14*
1353-1356 A350 Set of 4 4.50 4.50

Nos. 1353-1356 are inscribed "Postcard Rate."

Rollers — A351

Designs: No. 1357, ($7.30), Lilac-breasted roller. No. 1358, ($7.30), Purple roller. No. 1359, ($7.30), Racket-tailed roller. No. 1360, ($7.30), Broad-billed roller. No. 1361, ($7.30), European roller.

2017, Aug. 1 Litho. *Perf. 13¼*
1357-1361 A351 Set of 5 5.50 5.50

Nos. 1357-1361 are inscribed "Postcard Rate."

Small Canines A352

Designs: ($4.00), Bat-eared fox. ($6.60), Black-backed jackal. ($7.50), Side-striped jackal. ($8.80), Aardwolf. ($32.10), Cape fox.

2017, Sept. 29 Litho. *Perf. 12½x13*
1362-1366 A352 Set of 5 8.75 8.75

No. 1362 is inscribed "Standard Mail." No. 1363 is inscribed "Zone A." No. 1364 is inscribed "Zone B." No. 1365 is inscribed "Zone C." No. 1366 is inscribed "Inland Registered Mail."

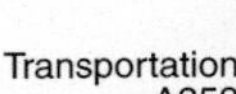

Transportation A353

Designs: ($7.10), Ox-drawn wagon. ($8.10), Cessna 210 airplane. ($34.40), Land Rover.

2018, Mar. 12 Litho. *Perf. 14x13¼*
1367-1369 A353 Set of 3 8.50 8.50

No. 1367 is inscribed "Zone A;" No. 1368, "Zone B;" No. 1369, "Inland Registered Mail."

Birds — A354

Designs: ($4.30), Red-billed spurfowl. ($7.10), Crested francolin. ($7.90), Swainson's spurfowl. ($8.10), Coqui francolin. ($34.40), Orange River francolin.

2018, May 18 Litho. *Perf. 13¼x14*
1370-1374 A354 Set of 5 10.00 10.00

No. 1370 is inscibed "Standard Mail;" No. 1371, "Zone A;" No. 1372, "Postcard Rate;" No. 1373, "Zone B;" No. 1374, "Inland Registered Mail."

Wild Cats — A355

Designs: ($7.10), Serval. ($8.10), Caracal, vert. ($9.50), African wild cat, vert. ($34.40), Small spotted cat.

Perf. 13¼x13½, 13½x13¼
2018, July 18 Litho.
1375-1378 A355 Set of 4 9.00 9.00

No. 1375 is inscribed "Zone A;" No. 1376, "Zone B;" No. 1377, "Zone C;" No. 1378, "Inland Registered Mail."

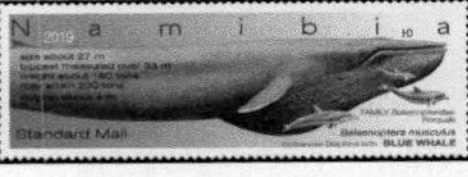

Whales A356

Designs: ($4.60), Blue whale. ($7.60), Southern right whale. ($8.60), Strap-toothed whale. ($10.10), Pygmy right whale. No. 1383, ($32), Pygmy sperm whale. No. 1384, ($36.60), Pygmy killer whale.

2019, Mar. 19 Litho. *Perf. 14¼x14*
1379-1384 A356 Set of 6 14.00 14.00

No. 1379 is inscribed "Standard Mail;" No. 1380, "Zone A;" No. 1381, "Zone B;" No. 1382, "Zone C;" No. 1383, "Registered Mail;" No. 1384, "Inland Registered Mail." See No. 1385.

Whales Type of 2019

Design: No. 1385, Pygmy sperm whale, with added inscriptions of "Reprint" and Kogiidae family information.

2019, Apr. 25 Litho. *Perf. 14¼x14*
1385 A356 ($32) multi 4.50 4.50

No. 1385 is inscribed "Registered Mail."

Cuckoos A357

Designs: ($8.40), African cuckoo. ($8.60), Diderick cuckoo, vert. ($32), Jacobin cuckoo, vert. ($36.60), Great spotted cuckoo.

2019, Apr. 25 Litho. *Perf. 14*
1386-1389 A357 Set of 4 12.00 12.00

No. 1386 is inscribed "Postcard Rate;" No. 1387, "Zone B;" No. 1388, "Registered Mail;" No. 1389, "Inland Registered Mail."

Wild Cats — A358

Designs: No. 1390, ($8.40), Lion. No. 1391, ($8.40), Cheetah. No. 1392, ($8.40), Leopard, vert.

Perf. 14¼x14, 14x14¼

2019, Aug. 1 **Litho.**
1390-1392 A358 Set of 3 3.50 3.50

Nos. 1390-1392 are each inscribed "Postcard Rate."

Miniature Sheet

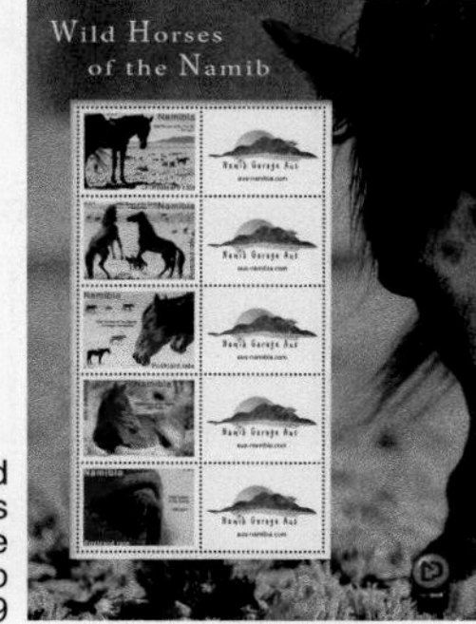

Wild Horses of the Namib A359

No. 1393 — Inscription: a, The herd. b, Living free. c, Amongst the wildlife. d, The future. e, Wild spirit.

2019, Aug. 14 **Litho.** ***Perf. 13x13¼***
1393 A359 ($8.40) Sheet of 5, #a-e, + 5 labels 7.00 7.00

Nos. 1393a-1393e are each inscribed "Postcard rate." No. 1393 sold for $55 and had labels that could be personalized. Generic labels are shown.

Flag of Namibia — A360

2019, Oct. 2 **Litho.** ***Perf. 13¼x13***
1394 A360 ($9) multi + label 1.50 1.50

No. 1394 is inscribed "Postcard Rate" and was printed in sheets of 5 + 5 labels that could be personalized that sold for $55. One of five different generic labels depicting Mohandas K. Gandhi is shown.

Squirrels A361

Designs: ($9.30), Damara ground squirrel. ($34.80), Striped tree squirrel. ($39.90), Tree squirrel, vert.

2020, Feb. 20 **Litho.** ***Perf. 14¼***
1395-1397 A361 Set of 3 11.00 11.00

No. 1395 is inscribed "Postcard Rate"; No. 1396, "Registerd Mail"; No. 1397, "Inland Registered Mail."

Woodpeckers — A362

Designs: ($5.10), Bearded woodpecker. ($9.30), Bennett's woodpecker. ($9.50), Olive woodpecker, horiz. ($34.80), Golden-tailed woodpecker, horiz. ($39.90), Cardinal woodpecker, horiz.

Perf. 13¼x13, 13x13¼

2020, Apr. 2 **Litho.**
1398-1402 A362 Set of 5 10.50 10.50

No. 1398 is inscribed "Standard Mail"; No. 1399, "Postcard Rate"; No. 1400, "Zone B"; No. 1401, "Registered Mail"; No. 1402, "Inland Registered Mail."

Batises — A363

No. 1403 — Male and female: a, ($9.30), Pririt batises. b, ($15.10), Chinspot batises.

2020, June 18 **Litho.** ***Perf. 14***
1403 A363 Vert. pair, #a-b 3.00 3.00

No. 1403a is inscribed "Postcard Rate"; No. 1403b, "Non-standard Mail."

Black-Shouldered Kite — A365

Yellow-Billed Kite — A366

2020, Aug. 20 **Litho.** ***Perf. 14¼***
1405 A365 ($9.50) multi 1.25 1.25
1406 A366 ($49.90) multi 6.00 6.00

No. 1406 is inscribed "Non-Standard Registered Mail."

Greater Painted Snipe — A367

African Snipe — A368

Great Snipe — A369

2021, Mar. 16 **Litho.** ***Perf. 13¼***
1407 A367 ($9.50) multi 1.30 1.30
1408 A368 ($34.80) multi 4.75 4.75
1409 A369 ($39.90) multi 5.50 5.50
Nos. 1407-1409 (3) 11.55 11.55

No. 1408 is inscribed "Registered Mail," and No. 1409 is inscribed "Inland Registered Mail."

Barleria Craveniae A370

Barleria Damarensis A371

Barleria Jubata — A372

Barleria Conacea Subspecies Dinteri — A373

2021, July 14 **Litho.** ***Perf. 13¼***
1410 A370 ($9.50) multi 1.30 1.30
1411 A371 ($9.50) multi 1.30 1.30
1412 A372 ($34.80) multi 5.00 5.00
1413 A373 ($39.90) multi 5.50 5.50
Nos. 1410-1413 (4) 13.10 13.10

No. 1412 is inscribed "Registered Mail," and No. 1413 is inscribed "Inland Registered Mail."

Mustelids — A374

Designs: No. 1414, ($9.90), Striped polecat. No. 1415, ($9.90), African striped weasel. No. 1416, ($36.10), Spotted-necked otter. No. 1417, ($36.10), African clawless otter. No. 1418, ($41.40), Honey badger.

2021, Oct. 12 **Litho.** ***Perf. 13x13¼***
1414-1418 A374 Set of 5 17.50 17.50

Nos. 1414-1415 are each inscribed "Zone B"; Nos. 1416-1417, "Registered Mail"; No. 1418, "Inland Registered Mail".

NATAL

nə-ˈtal

LOCATION — Southern coast of Africa, bordering on the Indian Ocean
GOVT. — British Crown Colony
AREA — 35,284 sq. mi.
POP. — 1,206,386 (1908)
CAPITAL — Pietermaritzburg

Natal united with Cape of Good Hope, Orange Free State and the Transvaal in 1910 to form the Union of South Africa.

12 Pence = 1 Shilling
20 Shillings = 1 Pound

Values for Nos. 1-7 are for examples with complete margins and free from damage. Unused values for No. 8 on are for stamps with original gum as defined in the catalogue introduction. Very fine examples of Nos. 8-49, 61-63 and 79 will have perforations touching the design on one or more sides due to the narrow spacing of the stamps on the plates. Stamps with perfs clear of the design on all four sides are scarce and will command higher prices.

Watermark

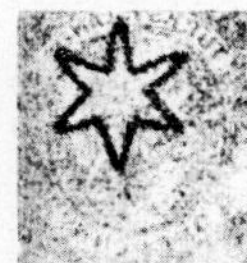

Wmk. 5 — Small Star

Crown and V R (Victoria Regina) A1

Crown and V R (Victoria Regina) A2

Crown and Laurel — A3

A4

A5

Colorless Embossing

1857 **Unwmk.** ***Imperf.***
1 A1 3p *rose* 725.
a. Tete beche pair 55,000.
2 A2 6p *green* 2,000.
a. Diagonal half used as 3p on cover 16,500.
3 A3 9p *blue* 65,000. 13,000.
4 A4 1sh *buff* 10,500.

1858
5 A5 1p *blue* 1,400.
6 A5 1p *rose* 2,200.
a. No. 1 embossed over No. 6 —
7 A5 1p *buff* 1,450.

Reprints: The paper is slightly glazed, the embossing sharper and the colors as follows: 1p pale blue, deep blue, carmine rose or yellow; 3p pale rose or carmine rose; 6p bright green or yellow green; 1sh pale buff or pale yellow. Bogus cancellations are found on the reprints.

The stamps printed on surface-colored paper are revenue stamps with trimmed perforations.

Listings of shades will be found in the *Scott Classic Specialized Catalogue.*

Queen Victoria — A6

1860 **Engr.** ***Perf. 14***
8 A6 1p rose 190.00 95.00
9 A6 3p blue 225.00 60.00
a. Vert. pair, imperf betwn. 13,000.

1863 ***Perf. 13***
10 A6 1p red 130.00 35.00

1861 ***Clean-cut Perf. 14 to 16***
11 A6 3p blue 350.00 82.50

1862 ***Rough Perf. 14 to 16***
12 A6 3p blue 175.00 45.00
a. Imperf., pair 4,500.
b. Horiz. or vert. pair, imperf. between 6,500.
13 A6 6p gray 275.00 75.00

1862 **Wmk. 5**
14 A6 1p rose 180.00 82.50

Imperforate stamps of the 1p and 3p on paper watermarked small star are proofs.

1864 **Wmk. 1** ***Perf. 12½***
15 A6 1p carmine red 140.00 50.00
16 A6 6p violet 90.00 37.50

No. 15 imperf is a proof.

Queen Victoria — A7

1867 Typo. *Perf. 14*
17 A7 1sh green 275.00 52.50

For types A6 and A7 overprinted or surcharged see Nos. 18-50, 61-63, 76, 79.

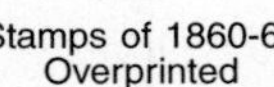

Stamps of 1860-67 Overprinted

1869 Overprint 12¾mm
18 A6 1p carmine red (#15) 525.00 100.00
b. Double overprint — —
19 A6 3p blue (#12) 700.00 110.00
19A A6 3p blue (#9) — 725.00
19B A6 3p blue (#11) 1,050. 325.00
20 A6 6p violet (#16) 650.00 110.00
21 A7 1sh green (#17) *30,000.* 2,100.

Same Overprint 13¾mm
22 A6 1p rose (#15b) 1,200. 325.00
23 A6 3p blue (#12) 2,800. 550.00
a. Inverted overprint
23B A6 3p blue (#9) — —
23C A6 3p blue (#11) — 1,100.
24 A6 6p violet (#16) 2,750. 225.00
25 A7 1sh green (#17) *35,000.* *3,250.*

Same Overprint 14½ to 15½mm
26 A6 1p rose (#15b) 1,050. 250.00
27 A6 3p blue (#12) — 450.00
27A A6 3p blue (#11) — 775.00
27B A6 3p blue (#9) — —
28 A6 6p violet (#16) 2,100. 140.00
29 A7 1sh green (#17) *32,000.* *2,750.*

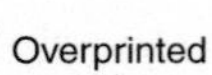

Overprinted

30 A6 1p rose (#15b) 150.00 55.00
b. Inverted overprint
31 A6 3p blue (#12) 250.00 55.00
a. Double overprint *1,800.*
31B A6 3p blue (#11) 225.00 62.50
31C A6 3p blue (#9) 400.00 95.00
32 A6 6p violet (#16) 210.00 77.50
33 A7 1sh green (#17) 350.00 87.50

Overprinted

34 A6 1p rose (#15b) 650.00 120.00
35 A6 3p blue (#12) 825.00 120.00
35A A6 3p blue (#11) 1,200. 375.00
35B A6 3p blue (#9) *4,250.* *925.00*
36 A6 6p violet (#16) 825.00 120.00
b. Inverted overprint
37 A7 1sh green (#17) *37,500.* *2,000.*

Overprinted in Black or Red

1870-73 Wmk. 1 *Perf. 12½*
38 A6 1p red 120.00 16.50
39 A6 3p ultra (R) ('72) 130.00 16.50
40 A6 6p lilac ('73) 250.00 45.00
Nos. 38-40 (3) 500.00 78.00

Overprinted in Red, Black or Green — g

1870 *Perf. 14*
41 A7 1sh green (R) — *9,500.*
42 A7 1sh green (Bk) — *1,750.*
a. Double overprint *3,900.*
43 A7 1sh green (G) 150.00 13.00

See No. 76.

Type of 1867 Overprinted

1873
44 A7 1sh brown lilac 425.00 37.50

No. 44 without overprint is a revenue.

Type of 1864 Overprinted

1874 *Perf. 12½*
45 A6 1p rose red 400.00 95.00
a. Double overprint

Overprinted

1875
46 A6 1p rose red 185.00 70.00
b. Double overprint 1,900. 650.00

Overprinted

1875 Overprint 14½mm *Perf. 12½*
47 A6 1p yellow 100.00 100.00
a. Double overprint, one albino 275.00 —
48 A6 1p rose red 140.00 87.50
a. Inverted overprint 2,250. 575.00
49 A6 6p violet 95.00 10.00
a. Inverted overprint 900.00 190.00
b. Double overprint 1,050.

Perf. 14
50 A7 1sh green 140.00 9.00
a. Double overprint 425.00
Nos. 47-50 (4) 475.00 206.50

The 1p yellow without overprint is a revenue.

A8

A9

A10

A11

Queen Victoria — A12

1874-78 Typo. Wmk. 1 *Perf. 14*
51 A8 1p dull rose 60.00 8.50
52 A9 3p ultramarine 190.00 45.00
a. Perf. 14x12½ 2,500. 1,100.
53 A10 4p brown ('78) 210.00 20.00
54 A11 6p violet 110.00 9.00

Perf. 15½x15
55 A12 5sh claret 525.00 120.00

Perf. 14
56 A12 5sh claret ('78) 450.00 120.00
57 A12 5sh carmine 120.00 42.50

Perf. 12½
58 A10 4p brown ('78) 400.00 82.50

See Nos. 65-71. For types A8-A10 surcharged see Nos. 59-60, 72-73, 77, 80.

Surcharged in Black

n

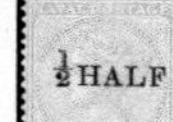

No. 60

o

1877 *Perf. 14*
59 A8(n) ½p on 1p rose 45.00 *82.50*
a. Double surcharge "1/2"
60 A8(n) ½p on 1p rose 110.00 —

Surcharge "n" exists in 3 or more types each of the large "1/2" (No. 59) and the small "1/2" (No. 60).

"HALF" and "½" were overprinted separately; "½" may be above, below or overlapping.

Perf. 12½
61 A6(o) ½p on 1p yel 13.00 *25.00*
a. Double surcharge 400.00 230.00
b. Inverted surcharge 400.00 240.00
c. Pair, one without surcharge 4,750. 3,000.
d. "POTAGE" 350.00 250.00
e. "POSAGE" 350.00 325.00
f. "POSTAGE" omitted 2,500. —
62 A6(o) 1p on 6p vio 82.50 13.00
a. "POSTAGE" omitted
b. "POTAGE" 650.00 190.00
63 A6(o) 1p on 6p rose 150.00 60.00
a. Inverted surcharge 1,750. 600.00
b. Double surcharge — 350.00
c. Dbl. srch., one inverted 400.00 250.00
d. Triple srch., one invtd.
e. Quadruple surcharge 550.00 300.00
f. "POTAGE" 1,000. 390.00
Nos. 61-63 (3) 245.50 98.00

No. 63 without overprint is a revenue.

A14

1880 Typo. *Perf. 14*
64 A14 ½p blue green 30.00 40.00
a. Vertical pair, imperf. between

1882-89 Wmk. Crown and CA (2)
65 A14 ½p blue green ('84) 120.00 22.50
66 A14 ½p gray green ('84) 6.00 1.40
67 A8 1p rose ('84) 8.50 .30
68 A9 3p ultra ('84) 170.00 22.00
69 A9 3p gray ('89) 12.50 5.75
70 A10 4p brown 17.50 1.90
71 A11 6p violet 14.50 2.75
Nos. 65-71 (7) 349.00 56.60

Surcharged in Black

p

q

1885-86
72 A8(p) ½p on 1p rose 24.00 14.00
b. Inverted surcharge *1,000.*
73 A9(q) 2p on 3p gray ('86) 40.00 7.00

A17

1887
74 A17 2p ol grn, die B ('89) 6.00 1.75
a. Die A 60.00 3.00

For explanation of dies A and B see "Dies of British Colonial Stamps" in the catalogue introduction.

Type of 1867 Overprinted Type "g" in Red

1888
76 A7 1sh orange 13.50 2.00
a. Double overprint *3,250.*

Surcharged in Black

1891
77 A10 2½p on 4p brown 17.50 17.50
a. "PENGE" 77.50
b. "PENN" 325.00 275.00
c. Double surcharge 400.00 350.00
d. As "c," in vert. pair with normal stamp 650.00 *750.00*
e. Inverted surcharge 550.00 475.00
f. Vert. pair, surcharge tete-beche 2,250. *3,000.*

A20

1891, June
78 A20 2½p ultramarine 12.50 1.60

Surcharged in Red or Black

No. 79

No. 80

1895, Mar. Wmk. 1 *Perf. 12½*
79 A6 ½p on 6p vio (R) 3.00 *10.00*
a. "Ealf" 27.50 *75.00*
b. "Penny" 27.50 *75.00*
c. Double surcharge, one vertical 350.00
d. Double surcharge 350.00

Stamps with fancy "P," "T" or "A" in surcharge sell for twice as much.

Wmk. 2 *Perf. 14*
80 A8 ½p on 1p rose (Bk) 3.50 2.50
a. Double surcharge 525.00 550.00
b. Pair, one without surcharge and the other with double surcharge —

A23

King Edward VII — A24

1902-03 Typo. Wmk. 2 *Perf. 14*
81 A23 ½p blue green 7.50 .55
82 A23 1p rose 13.00 .25
83 A23 1½p blk & blue grn 4.50 *6.00*
84 A23 2p ol grn & scar 7.00 .45
85 A23 2½p ultramarine 2.25 *6.00*
86 A23 3p gray & red vio 1.60 *2.75*
87 A23 4p brown & scar 14.00 *27.50*
88 A23 5p org & black 5.00 4.00
89 A23 6p mar & bl grn 5.00 5.00
90 A23 1sh pale bl & dp rose 6.50 5.25
91 A23 2sh vio & bl grn 62.50 11.50
92 A23 2sh6p red violet 50.00 15.00
93 A23 4sh yel & dp rose 95.00 95.00

Wmk. 1
94 A24 5sh car lake & dk blue 67.50 14.00
95 A24 10sh brn & dp rose 130.00 45.00
96 A24 £1 ultra & blk 350.00 85.00
97 A24 £1 10sh vio & bl grn 600.00 140.00
Revenue cancel 15.00
98 A24 £5 blk & vio *5,500.* *1,400.*
Revenue cancel 110.00
99 A24 £10 org & grn *14,000.* *6,500.*
Revenue cancel 180.00
100 A24 £20 grn & car *28,000.* *19,000.*
Revenue cancel 325.00
Nos. 81-96 (16) 821.35 323.25

1904-08 Wmk. 3
101 A23 ½p blue green 12.00 .25
102 A23 1p rose 12.00 .25
a. Booklet pane of 6 600.00
b. Booklet pane of 5 + 1 label 500.00
103 A23 2p ol grn & scar 18.50 4.00
104 A23 4p brn & scar 3.50 1.60
105 A23 5p org & blk ('08) 6.50 5.00

106 A23 1sh pale bl & dp rose 90.00 9.00
107 A23 2sh vio & bl grn 75.00 55.00
108 A23 2sh6p red violet 70.00 55.00
109 A24 £1 10sh vio & org brn, chalky paper 1,900. *5,000.*
Revenue cancel *55.00*
Nos. 101-108 (8) 287.50 130.10

A25

A26

1908-09

110 A25 6p red violet 5.75 3.50
111 A25 1sh blk, *grn* 7.75 3.25
112 A25 2sh bl & vio, *bl* 19.00 3.75
113 A25 2sh6p red & blk, *bl* 32.00 5.50
114 A26 5sh red & grn, *yell* 30.00 *52.50*
115 A26 10sh red & grn, *grn* 135.00 135.00
116 A26 £1 blk & vio, *red* 450.00 400.00
Nos. 110-116 (7) 679.50 603.50

OFFICIAL STAMPS

Nos. 101-103, 106 and Type A23 Overprinted

1904 Wmk. 3 *Perf. 14*

O1 A23 ½p blue green 3.75 .45
O2 A23 1p rose 16.00 1.25
O3 A23 2p ol grn & scar 45.00 22.50
O4 A23 3p gray & red vio 27.50 *5.50*
O5 A23 6p mar & bl grn 87.50 82.50
O6 A23 1sh pale bl & dp rose 250.00 *275.00*
Nos. O1-O6 (6) 429.75 *387.20*

Stamps of Natal were replaced by those of the Union of South Africa.

NAURU

nä-'ü-,rü

LOCATION — An island on the Equator in the west central Pacific Ocean, midway between the Marshall and Solomon Islands.
GOVT. — Republic
AREA — 8½ sq. mi.
POP. — 11,000 (2020 est.)
CAPITAL — None. Parliament House is in Yaren District.

The island, a German possession, was captured by Australian forces in 1914 and, following World War I, was mandated to the British Empire. It was administered jointly by Great Britain, Australia and New Zealand.

In 1947 Nauru was placed under United Nations trusteeship, administered by Australia. On January 31, 1968, Nauru became a republic.

See North West Pacific Islands.

12 Pence = 1 Shilling
100 Cents = 1 Dollar (1966)

Catalogue values for unused stamps in this country are for Never Hinged items, beginning with Scott 39.

Watermarks

Wmk. 388 — Multiple "SPM"

Great Britain Stamps of 1912-13 Overprinted at Bottom of Stamp

1916-23 Wmk. 33 *Perf. 15x14*

1 A82 ½p green (#159) 2.75 *12.50*
2 A83 1p scarlet (#160) 2.50 *14.50*
3 A84 1½p red brn (#161) ('23) 65.00 *110.00*
4 A85 2p org (die I) (#162) 1.75 *15.00*
c. 2p deep orange (die II) (#162a) ('23) 80.00 *110.00*
6 A86 2½p ultra (#163) 3.00 *7.50*
7 A87 3p violet (#164a) 2.25 *6.50*
8 A88 4p slate green (#165) 2.25 *9.00*
9 A89 5p yel brown (#166) 2.60 *16.50*
10 A89 6p dull violet (#167a) 8.50 *17.50*
11 A90 9p blk brn (#170) 9.75 *32.50*
12 A90 1sh bister (#172) 8.25 *27.50*
Nos. 1-12 (11) 108.60 *269.00*

Wmk. 34
Overprint Centered

1b A82 ½p green (#159) ('23) 5.75 *62.50*
2c A83 1p scarlet (#160) ('23) 22.50 *50.00*
3a A84 1½p red brn (#161) ('23) 30.00 *60.00*
b. Double ovpt, one albino ('23) 200.00
4d A85 2p dp org (II) (#162a) ('23) 40.00 *87.50*
Nos. 1b-4d (4) 98.25 *260.00*

On Nos. 1-12 "NAURU" is usually 12¾mm wide and at the foot of the stamp. In 1923 four values were overprinted with "NAURU" measuring 13½mm wide and across the middle of the stamp.

Forged overprints exist.

Great Britain Stamps of 1915 Overprinted

Wmk. 34 *Perf. 11x12*

13 A91 2sh6p lt brn 80.00 *125.00*
a. 2sh6p black brown 700.00 *1,900.*
14 A91 5sh carmine 125.00 *175.00*
b. 5sh rose carmine 3,000. 2,750.
15 A91 10sh lt blue (R) 300.00 *450.00*
c. 10sh indigo blue *14,250.* 6,000.

Same Ovpt. on Great Britain No. 179a and 179b

1920

16 A91 2sh6p gray brown 100.00 *200.00*
Nos. 13-16 (4) 605.00 *950.00*
Nos. 1-16 (15) 713.60 *1,219.*

Double and triple overprints, with one overprint albino, exist for most of the 1-16 overprints. Additional color shades exist for No. 13-16, and values given are for the most common varieties. For detailed listings, see *Scott Classic Specialized Catalogue.*

Freighter — A1

1924-48 Unwmk. Engr. *Perf. 11*

17 A1 ½p orange brown 3.75 *3.00*
b. Perf. 14 ('47) 2.50 *14.50*
18a A1 1p green 2.75 *3.50*
19a A1 1½p red 1.10 *1.65*
20a A1 2p orange 7.75 *9.25*
21a A1 2½p blue ('48) 6.00 *4.50*
c. Horiz. pair, imperf between *18,750.* *19,750.*
d. Vert. pair, imperf between *18,750.* *19,750.*
22a A1 3p grnsh gray ('47) 8.75 *24.00*
23a A1 4p olive green 8.75 *16.50*
24 A1 5p dk brown 4.75 *8.75*
25 A1 6p dark violet 5.25 *22.00*
26 A1 9p brown olive 10.50 *21.00*
27a A1 1sh brown red 16.50 3.00
28a A1 2sh6p slate green 35.00 *45.00*
29a A1 5sh claret 42.50 *60.00*
30a A1 10sh yellow 92.50 *133.00*
Nos. 17-30a (14) 245.85 355.15

Two printings were made of Nos. 17-30, the first (1924-34) on unsurfaced, grayish paper (Nos. 17-30), the second (1937-48) on glazed surfaced white paper (Nos. 17a-30a). Values are for the most common type. For detailed listings, see *Scott Classic Specialized Catalogue.*

Stamps of Type A1 Overprinted in Black

1935, July 12 *Perf. 11*
Glazed Paper

31 A1 1½p red .85 *.90*
32 A1 2p orange 1.50 *5.75*
33 A1 2½p blue 1.50 *1.75*
34 A1 1sh brown red 8.50 *4.75*
Nos. 31-34 (4) 12.35 *13.15*
Set, never hinged 385.00

25th anniv. of the reign of George V.

George VI — A2

1937, May 10 Engr.

35 A2 1½p salmon rose .30 *1.00*
36 A2 2p dull orange .30 *2.00*
37 A2 2½p blue .30 *1.25*
38 A2 1sh brown violet .35 *1.25*
Nos. 35-38 (4) 1.25 *5.50*
Set, never hinged 1.75

Coronation of George VI & Elizabeth.

Catalogue values for unused stamps in this section, from this point to the end of the section, are for Never Hinged items.

Casting Throw-net A3

Anibare Bay A4

3½p, Loading phosphate. 4p, Frigate bird. 6p, Nauruan canoe. 9p, Meeting house (domaneab). 1sh, Palms. 2sh6p, Buada lagoon. 5sh, Map.

1954, Feb. 6 *Perf. 14½x14, 14x14½*

39 A3 ½p purple .30 .75
40 A4 1p green .30 .65
41 A3 3½p red 1.75 .75
42 A3 4p deep blue 3.25 2.00
43 A3 6p orange .60 .25
44 A3 9p brown lake .55 .25
45 A4 1sh dk rose violet .30 .30
46 A3 2sh6p dk gray green 3.00 .75
47 A4 5sh lilac rose 8.50 2.40
Nos. 39-47 (9) 18.55 8.10

See Nos. 58-71.

Balsam A5

Black Lizard A6

Capparis A7

Coral Pinnacles A8

White Tern — A9

2p, Micronesian pigeon, vert. 3p, Poison nut flower. 3sh3p, Nightingale reed warbler.

Perf. 13½, Perf. 14½x13½ (10p), Perf. 14½ (2sh3p)
Photo.; Engraved (10p, 2sh3p)

1963-65 Unwmk.

49 A9 2p multi ('65) 1.00 2.25
50 A6 3p red org, sl grn & yel ('64) .40 .30
51 A5 5p gray, bl grn & yellow .40 .70
52 A6 8p green & black 1.75 .75
53 A7 10p black ('64) .40 .30
54 A9 1sh3p ap grn, blk & Prus bl ('65) 2.50 *5.00*
55 A8 2sh3p vio blue ('64) 2.25 .55
56 A6 3sh3p lt yel, bl, brn & blk ('65) 2.50 4.00
Nos. 49-56 (8) 11.20 13.85

Issue dates: 5p, Apr. 22. 8p, July 1. 3p, 10p, 2sh3p, Apr. 16. 2p, 1sh3p, 3sh3p, May 3.

"Simpson and His Donkey" by Wallace Anderson — A9a

Perf. 13½x13

1965, Apr. 14 Photo. Unwmk.

57 A9a 5p brt green, sepia & blk .30 .25

See note after Australia No. 387.

Types of 1954-65
Values in Cents and Dollars

Designs: 1c, Anibare Bay. 2c, Casting throw-net. 3c, Loading phosphate. 4c, Balsam. 5c, Palms. 7c, Black lizard. 8c, Capparis. 10c, Frigate bird. 15c, White tern. 25c, Coral pinnacles. 30c, Poison nut flower. 35c, Reed warbler. 50c, Micronesian pigeon, vert. $1, Map.

Engr.; Photo. (4c, 7c, 15c, 30c-50c)
1966 *Perf. 14½x14, 14x14½*

58 A4 1c dark blue .30 .25
59 A3 2c claret .30 .50
60 A3 3c green .30 *2.50*
61 A5 4c lilac, grn & yel .30 .25
62 A4 5c violet blue .30 .60
63 A6 7c fawn & black .35 .25
64 A7 8c olive green .30 .25
65 A3 10c dark red .40 .25
66 A9 15c ap grn, blk & Prus blue 1.00 *3.00*
67 A3 25c sepia .30 *1.25*
68 A6 30c brick red, sl grn, & yellow .45 .35
69 A6 35c lt yel, bl, brn & black .70 .40
70 A9 50c yel, bluish blk & brown 2.00 .75
71 A4 $1 claret .75 1.00
Nos. 58-71 (14) 7.75 11.60

The engraved stamps are luminescent.

Issued: 2c, 3c, 5c, 15c, 25c, 35c, 5/25; others, 2/14.

Republic

Nos. 58-71 Overprinted in Red, Black or Orange "REPUBLIC / OF / NAURU"

1968

72 A4 1c dark blue (R) .30 .35
73 A3 2c claret .30 .25
74 A3 3c green .30 .25
75 A5 4c lilac, grn & yel .30 .25
76 A4 5c violet blue (O) .30 .25
77 A6 7c fawn & blk (R) .30 .25
78 A7 8c olive green (R) .30 .25
79 A3 10c dark red .60 .25
80 A9 15c ap grn, blk & Prus blue 2.00 *3.00*
81 A3 25c sepia (R) .30 .25
82 A6 30c brick red, sl grn & yellow .55 .25
83 A6 35c multicolored 1.40 .75
84 A9 50c yel, bluish blk & brown 1.50 1.00
85 A4 $1 claret 1.25 1.25
Nos. 72-85 (14) 9.70 8.60

Issued: 4c, 7c, 30c, 35c, 5/15; others, 1/31.

Nauru Woman Watching Rising Sun — A10

Planting Seedling and Map of Nauru — A11

Perf. 13x13½

1968, Sept. 11 Photo. Unwmk.

86	A10	5c multicolored	.30	.25
87	A11	10c brt blue, blk & green	.30	.25

Independence of Nauru.

Flag of Nauru — A12

1969, Jan. 31 Litho. *Perf. 13½*

88	A12	15c dk vio blue, yel & org	.75	.35

For overprint see No. 90.

Commission Emblem and Nauru — A13

1972, Feb. 7 Litho. *Perf. 14½x14*

89	A13	25c blue, yellow & black	.55	.50

South Pacific Commission, 25th anniv.

No. 88 Ovptd. in Gold

1973, Jan. 31 *Perf. 13½*

90	A12	15c multicolored	.35	.35

Fifth anniversary of independence.

Lotus (Ekwenababae) A14

Map of Nauru, Artifacts A15

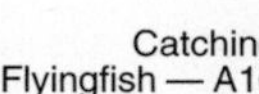

Catching Flyingfish — A16

Designs: 2c, Kauwe iud. 3c, Rimone. 4c, Denea. 5c, Beach morning-glory. 7c, Golden butterflyfish. 10c, Nauruan ball game (itsibweb). 15c, Nauruan wrestling. 20c, Snaring frigate birds. 25c, Nauruan girl with flower garland. 30c, Men catching noddies. 50c, Frigate birds.

1973 Litho. *Perf. 13½x14*

91	A14	1c pale yellow & multi	.30	.25
92	A14	2c pale ocher & multi	.35	.25
93	A14	3c pale violet & multi	.35	.25
94	A14	4c pale green & multi	.35	.35
95	A14	5c pale blue & multi	.35	.35

Perf. 14½x14, 14x14½

96	A16	7c blue & multi	.50	*.90*
97	A16	8c black & multi	.30	.25
98	A16	10c multicolored	.30	.25
99	A15	15c green & multi	.35	.25
100	A15	20c blue & multi	.60	*.90*
101	A15	25c yellow & multi	.45	.45
102	A16	30c multicolored	.55	.50
103	A16	50c multicolored	.80	.75
104	A15	$1 blue & multi	1.00	.75
		Nos. 91-104 (14)	6.55	6.45

Issue dates: Nos. 97-100, May 23; Nos. 96, 101-103, July 25; others Mar. 28, 1973.

Cooperative Store A17

Eigigu, the Girl in the Moon A18

Design: 25c, Timothy Detudamo and cooperative store emblem.

1973, Dec. 20 Litho. *Perf. 14½x14*

105	A17	5c multicolored	.50	.50
106	A17	25c multicolored	.50	.50
107	A18	50c multicolored	1.00	*1.25*
		Nos. 105-107 (3)	2.00	2.25

50th anniversary of Nauru Cooperative Society, founded by Timothy Detudamo.

"Eigamoiya" — A19

10c, Phosphate mining. 15c, "Nauru Chief" plane over Nauru. 25c, Nauru chieftain with frigate-bird headdress. 35c, Capt. J. Fearn, sailing ship "Hunter" & map of Nauru. 50c, "Hunter" off Nauru.

Perf. 13x13½, 13½x13

1974, May 21 Litho.

Sizes: 70x22mm (7c, 35c, 50c); 33x20mm (10c, 15c, 25c)

108	A19	7c multicolored	.70	*.95*
109	A19	10c multicolored	.55	.25
110	A19	15c multicolored	.70	.35
111	A19	25c multicolored	.60	.40
112	A19	35c multicolored	3.50	3.50
113	A19	50c multicolored	2.00	*2.25*
		Nos. 108-113 (6)	8.05	7.70

175th anniversary of Nauru's first contact with the outside world.

Map of Nauru A20

Post Office A21

UPU Emblem and: 20c, Mailman on motorcycle. $1, Flag of Nauru and UPU Building, Bern, vert.

1974, July 23 Litho. *Perf. 14*

114	A20	5c multicolored	.30	.25

Perf. 13½x13, 13x13½

115	A21	8c multicolored	.30	.25
116	A21	20c multicolored	.30	.25
117	A21	$1 multicolored	1.25	1.25
a.		Souv. sheet of 4, #114-117, imperf.	3.00	3.00
		Nos. 114-117 (4)	2.15	2.00

Cent. of the UPU.

Rev. P. A. Delaporte — A22

1974, Dec. 10 Litho. *Perf. 14½*

118	A22	15c brt pink & multi	.30	.30
119	A22	20c blue & multi	.50	.50

Christmas 1974. Delaporte, a German-born American missionary, took Christianity to Nauru and translated the New Testament into Nauruan.

Nauru, Grain, Albert Ellis, Phosphate Rock — A23

Designs: 7c, Phosphate mining and coolie carrying load. 15c, Electric freight train, tugs and ship. 25c, Excavator, cantilever and truck.

1975, July 23 Litho. *Perf. 14½x14*

120	A23	5c multicolored	.30	.30
121	A23	7c multicolored	.40	.40
122	A23	15c multicolored	1.10	1.10
123	A23	25c multicolored	1.40	1.40
		Nos. 120-123 (4)	3.20	3.20

75th anniv. of discovery of phosphate (5c); 70th anniv. of Pacific Phosphate Co. Mining Agreement (7c); 50th anniv. of British Phosphate Commissioners (15c); 5th anniv. of Nauru Phosphate Corp. (25c).

Melanesian Outrigger and Map of SPC's Area — A24

No. 124, Micronesian outrigger. No. 125, Polynesian double hull. No. 127, Polynesian outrigger.

1975, Sept. 1 Litho. *Perf. 14x14½*

124	A24	20c multicolored	.60	.60
125	A24	20c multicolored	.60	.60
126	A24	20c shown	.60	.60
127	A24	20c multicolored	.60	.60
a.		Block of 4, #124-127	3.25	3.25
		Nos. 124-127 (4)	2.40	2.40

South Pacific Commission Conference, Nauru, Sept. 29-Oct. 10.

Nos. 124-127 exist imperf. Value, block of four *$50.*

New Civic Center — A25

Design: 50c, "Domaneab" (meeting house) and flags of participating nations.

1975, Sept. 29 Litho. *Perf. 14½*

128	A25	30c multicolored	.30	.25
129	A25	50c multicolored	.45	.45

South Pacific Commission Conference, Nauru, Sept. 29-Oct. 10.

Nos. 128-129 exist imperf. Value, set $12.

Virgin Mary, Stained-glass Window — A26

Christmas: 7c, 15c, "Suffer little children to come unto me," stained-glass window, Orro Protestant Church. 25c, like 5c, Yaren Catholic Church.

1975, Nov. 7 Litho. *Perf. 14½*

130	A26	5c gray blue & multi	.30	.25
131	A26	7c green & multi	.30	.25
132	A26	15c brown & multi	.30	.50
133	A26	25c lilac & multi	.30	.70
		Nos. 130-133 (4)	1.20	1.70

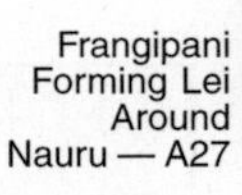

Frangipani Forming Lei Around Nauru — A27

14c, Hand crowning Nauru with lei. 25c, Reed warbler, birds flying from Truk to Nauru. 40c, Reunion of islanders in Boar Harbor.

1976, Jan. 31 Litho. *Perf. 14½*

134	A27	10c green & multi	.30	.25
135	A27	14c violet & multi	.30	.25
136	A27	25c red & multi	.30	.25
137	A27	40c blue & multi	.30	.25
		Nos. 134-137 (4)	1.20	1.00

30th anniversary of the return of the islanders from Japanese internment on Truk.

Nos. 134-137 exist imperf. Value, set $20.

Nauru Nos. 7 and 11 — A28

15c, Nauru Nos. 10, 12. 25c, Nauru No. 13. 50c, Nauru No. 14, "Specimen."

1976, May 6 Litho. *Perf. 13½x14*

138	A28	10c multicolored	.30	.25
139	A28	15c multicolored	.30	.25
140	A28	25c multicolored	.30	.25
141	A28	50c multicolored	.40	.40
		Nos. 138-141 (4)	1.30	1.15

60th anniv. of Nauru's 1st postage stamps.

Nos. 138-141 exist imperf. Value, set $17.50.

Nauru Shipping and Pandanus A29

Designs: 20c, Air Nauru Boeing 737 and Fokker F28, and tournefortia argentea. 30c, Earth satellite station and thespesia populnea. 40c, Area produce and cordia subcordata.

1976, July 26 Litho. *Perf. 13½x14*

142	A29	10c multicolored	.30	.25
143	A29	20c multicolored	.30	.25
144	A29	30c multicolored	.30	.25
145	A29	40c multicolored	.45	.45
		Nos. 142-145 (4)	1.35	1.20

7th South Pacific Forum, Nauru, July 1976.

Nos. 142-145 exist imperf. Value, set $35.

Nauruan Children's Choir — A30

20c, Angels. Nos. 146, 148, denominations at lower right. Nos. 147, 149, denominations at lower left.

1976, Nov. Litho. *Perf. 14x13½*

146		15c multicolored	.30	.25
147		15c multicolored	.30	.25
a.	A30	Pair, #146-147	.55	.55
148		20c multicolored	.30	.25
149		20c multicolored	.30	.25
a.	A30	Pair, #148-149	.55	.55
		Nos. 146-149 (4)	1.20	1.00

Christmas.

Nos. 146-149 exist imperf. Value, set of two se-tenant pairs $65.

Nauru House, Melbourne, and Coral Pinnacles — A32

30c, Nauru House and Melbourne skyline.

1977, Apr. 14 Photo. *Perf. 14½*

150	A32	15c multicolored	.30	.25
151	A32	30c multicolored	.40	.40

Opening of Nauru House in Melbourne, Australia.

For surcharges see Nos. 161-164.

Cable-laying Ship Anglia, 1902 — A33

Designs: 15c, Nauru radar station. 20c, Stern of Anglia. 25c, Radar antenna.

1977, Sept. 7 Photo. *Perf. 14½*

152	A33	7c multicolored	.30	.25
153	A33	15c multicolored	.30	.25
154	A33	20c multicolored	.30	.30
155	A33	25c multicolored	.40	.40
		Nos. 152-155 (4)	1.30	1.20

1st transpacific cable, 75th anniv., and 1st artificial earth satellite, 20th anniv.

Catholic Church, Yaren, and Father Kayser — A34

Designs: 25c, Congregational Church, Orro. 30c, Catholic Church, Arubo.

1977, Oct. Photo. *Perf. 14½*

156	A34	15c multicolored	.30	.25
157	A34	25c multicolored	.30	.25
158	A34	30c multicolored	.30	.25
		Nos. 156-158 (3)	.90	.75

Christmas, and 55th anniversary of first Roman Catholic Church on Nauru.

Coat of Arms of Nauru — A35

1978, Jan. 31 Litho. *Perf. 14½*

159	A35	15c blue & multi	.30	.25
160	A35	60c emerald & multi	.35	.35

10th anniversary of independence. Exists imperf, value $14.

Nos. 150-151 Surcharged with New Value and Two Bars

1978, Apr. Photo. *Perf. 14½*

161	A32	4c on 15c multi	1.25	1.25
162	A32	5c on 15c multi	1.25	1.25
163	A32	8c on 30c multi	1.25	1.25
164	A32	10c on 30c multi	1.25	1.25
		Nos. 161-164 (4)	5.00	5.00

Girls Catching Fish in Buada Lagoon — A36

Designs: 1c, Fisherman and family collecting shellfish. 2c, Pigs foraging near coral reef. 3c, Gnarled tree and birds. 4c, Girl catching fish with hands. 5c, Bird catching fish. 10c, Ijuw Lagoon. 15c, Young girl and coral formation. 20c, Reef pinnacles, Anibare Bay. 25c, Pinnacles, Meneng shore. 30c, Frigate bird. 32c, Coconut palm and noddies. 40c, Iwiyi, wading bird. 50c, Frigate birds. $1, Pinnacles, Topside. $2, Newly uncovered pinnacles, Topside. $5, Old pinnacles, Topside.

1978-79 Photo. *Perf. 14½*

165	A36	1c multicolored	.35	.25
166	A36	2c multicolored	.35	.25
167	A36	3c multicolored	.85	.75
168	A36	4c multicolored	.40	.25
169	A36	5c multicolored	.85	.75
170	A36	7c multicolored	.30	*1.00*
171	A36	10c multicolored	.30	.25
172	A36	15c multicolored	.30	.25
173	A36	20c multicolored	.30	.30
174	A36	25c multicolored	.30	.30
175	A36	30c multicolored	1.00	.45
176	A36	32c multicolored	1.40	1.00
177	A36	40c multicolored	1.00	1.50
178	A36	50c multicolored	1.00	1.10
179	A36	$1 multicolored	.70	.80
180	A36	$2 multicolored	.90	.90
181	A36	$5 multicolored	1.65	1.75
		Nos. 165-181 (17)	11.95	11.85

Issued: #166-169, 6/6/79; others, 5/1978.

Nos. 179-181 exists on an "official black print without franking validity" numbered souvenir sheet of 3. Value, $15.

"APU" — A37

1978, Aug. 28 Litho. *Perf. 13½*

182	A37	15c multicolored	.40	.90
183	A37	20c gold, blk & dk blue	.60	1.10

14th General Assembly of Asian Parliamentary Union, Nauru, Aug. 28-Sept. 1. On sale during conference only.

Mother and Child — A38

Christmas: 15c, 20c, Angel over the Pacific, horiz. 30c, like 7c.

1978, Nov. 1 Litho. *Perf. 14*

184	A38	7c multicolored	.30	.25
185	A38	15c multicolored	.30	.25
186	A38	20c multicolored	.30	.25
187	A38	30c multicolored	.30	.25
		Nos. 184-187 (4)	1.20	1.00

Lord Baden-Powell and Cub Scout — A39

30c, Boy Scout. 50c, Explorer.

1978, Dec. 1 Litho. *Perf. 14*

188	A39	20c multicolored	.30	.25
189	A39	30c multicolored	.30	.25
190	A39	50c multicolored	.35	.35
		Nos. 188-190 (3)	.95	.85

70th anniversary of 1st Scout Troop.

Flyer A over Nauru Airfield — A40

Designs: No. 192, "Southern Cross" and Boeing 727. No. 193, "Southern Cross" and Boeing 737. 30c, Wright Flyer over Nauru.

1979, Jan. *Perf. 14½*

191	A40	10c multicolored	.30	.30
192	A40	15c multicolored	.35	.35
193	A40	15c multicolored	.35	.35
a.		Pair, #192-193	.90	.90
194	A40	30c multicolored	.60	.60
		Nos. 191-194 (4)	1.60	1.60

1st powered flight, 75th anniv. and Kingsford Smith's US-Australia and Australia-New Zealand flights, 50th anniv.

Nos. 192-193 printed checkerwise.

Nos. 191-194 exist imperf. Value, set of two singles (Nos. 191, 194) and pair (193a), $70.

A41

Design: Rowland Hill, Marshall Islands No. 15 with Nauru Cancel.

1979, Feb. 27 Litho. *Perf. 14½*

195	A41	5c shown	.30	.25
196	A41	15c Nauru No. 15	.30	.25
197	A41	60c Nauru No. 160	.40	.60
a.		Souvenir sheet of 3, #195-197	1.00	1.25
		Nos. 195-197 (3)	1.00	1.10

Sir Rowland Hill (1795-1879), originator of penny postage.

Dish Antenna, Earth Station, ITU Emblem A42

ITU Emblem and: 32c, Woman operating Telex machine. 40c, Radio beacon operator.

1979, Aug. Litho. *Perf. 14½*

198	A42	7c multicolored	.30	.25
199	A42	32c multicolored	.30	.30
200	A42	40c multicolored	.35	.35
		Nos. 198-200 (3)	.95	.90

Intl. Radio Consultative Committee (CCIR) of the ITU, 50th anniv.

Nos. 198-200 exist imperf. Value, set $20.

Nauruan Girl — A43

IYC Emblem, Nauruan Children: 15c, Boy. 25c, 32c, 50c, Girls, diff.

1979, Oct. 3 Litho. *Perf. 14½*

201	A43	8c multicolored	.30	.25
202	A43	15c multicolored	.30	.25
203	A43	25c multicolored	.30	.25
204	A43	32c multicolored	.30	.25
205	A43	50c multicolored	.30	.25
a.		Strip of 5, #201-205	1.00	1.00

International Year of the Child.

Star, Scroll, Ekwenababa Flower — A44

Star and Flowers: 15c, Milos. 20c, Denea. 30c, Morning glories.

1979, Nov. 14 Litho. *Perf. 14½*

206	A44	7c multicolored	.30	.25
207	A44	15c multicolored	.30	.25
208	A44	20c multicolored	.30	.25
209	A44	30c multicolored	.30	.25
		Nos. 206-209 (4)	1.20	1.00

Christmas.

Nos. 206-209 exist imperf. Value, set $65.

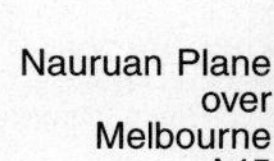

Nauruan Plane over Melbourne A45

Air Nauru, 10th Anniversary (Plane Over): 20c, Tarawa. 25c, Hong Kong. 30c, Auckland.

1980, Feb. 28 Litho. *Perf. 14½*

210	A45	15c multicolored	.35	.25
211	A45	20c multicolored	.35	.25
212	A45	25c multicolored	.45	.30
213	A45	30c multicolored	.55	.40
		Nos. 210-213 (4)	1.70	1.20

Early Steam Locomotive A46

32c, Electric locomotive. 60c, Clyde diesel-hydraulic locomotive.

1980, May 6 Litho. *Perf. 15*

214	A46	8c shown	.30	.25
215	A46	32c multicolored	.30	.30
216	A46	60c multicolored	.45	.45
a.		Souvenir sheet of 3, #214-216	1.50	1.75
		Nos. 214-216 (3)	1.05	1.00

Nauru Phosphate Corp., 10th anniv. No. 216a also for London 1980 Intl. Stamp Exhibition, May 6-14; Penny Black, 140th anniv.

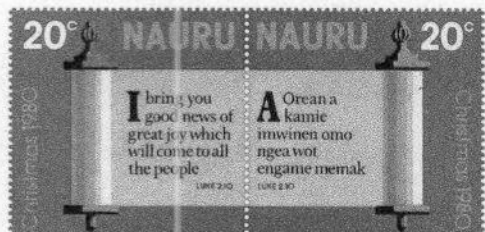

Christmas 1980 — A47

Designs: 30c, "Glory to God in the Highest . . ." in English and Nauruan.

1980, Sept. 24 Litho. *Perf. 15*

217		20c English	.30	.25
218		20c Nauruese	.30	.25
a.	A47	Pair, #217-218	.55	.55
219		30c English	.30	.25
220		30c Nauruese	.30	.25
a.	A47	Pair, #219-220	.55	.55
		Nos. 217-220 (4)	1.20	1.00

See Nos. 236-239.

Flags of Nauru, Australia, Gt. Britain and New Zealand, UN Emblem A49

30c, UN Trusteeship Council. 50c, 1968 independence ceremony.

1980, Dec. 20 Litho. *Perf. 14½*

221	A49	25c shown	.30	.25

Size: 72x22mm

Perf. 14

222	A49	30c multicolored	.30	.30
223	A49	50c multicolored	.40	.40
		Nos. 221-223 (3)	1.00	.95

UN de-colonization declaration, 20th anniv.

No. 222 printed se-tenant with label showing flags of UN and Nauru, issued Feb. 11, 1981.

Timothy Detudamo (Former Head Chief), Domaneab (Meeting House) — A50

1981, Feb. Litho. *Perf. 14½*

224	A50	20c shown	.30	.25
225	A50	30c Raymond Gadabu	.30	.25
226	A50	50c Hammer DeRoburt	.45	.35
		Nos. 224-226 (3)	1.05	.85

Legislative Council, 30th anniversary.

Casting Net by Hand — A51

1981 Litho. *Perf. 12*

227	A51	8c shown	.30	.25
228	A51	20c Ancient canoe	.30	.25
229	A51	32c Powered boat	.30	.25
230	A51	40c Fishing vessel	.30	.25
a.		Souvenir sheet of 4, #230	1.75	1.75
		Nos. 227-230 (4)	1.20	1.00

Bank of Nauru, 5th Anniv. — A52

1981, July 21 Litho. *Perf. 14x14½*

231	A52	$1 multicolored	1.00	1.00

ESCAP Secy. Maramis Delivering Inaugural Speech — A53

20c, Maramis, Pres. de Robert. 25c, Plaque. 30c, Raising UN flag.

1981, Oct. 24 Litho. *Perf. 14½*
232 A53 15c shown .30 .25
233 A53 20c multicolored .30 .25
234 A53 25c multicolored .30 .25
235 A53 30c multicolored .30 .25
Nos. 232-235 (4) 1.20 1.00

UN Day and first anniv. of Economic and Social Commission for Asia and Pacific (ESCAP) liaison office in Nauru.

Christmas Type of 1980

Christmas (Biblical Scriptures in English and Nauruan): 20c, "His Name Shall Be Called Emmanuel." 30c, "To You is Born This Day . . ."

1981, Nov. 14 Litho. *Perf. 14½*
236 A47 20c multicolored .30 .25
237 A48 20c multicolored .30 .25
a. Pair, #236-237 .50 .50
238 A47 30c multicolored .30 .25
239 A48 30c multicolored .30 .25
a. Pair, #238-239 .50 .50
Nos. 236-239 (4) 1.20 1.00

10th Anniv. of South Pacific Forum — A54

1981, Dec. 9 Litho. *Perf. 13½x14*
240 A54 10c Globe, dish antenna .30 .25
241 A54 20c Ship .30 .25
242 A54 30c Jet .35 .35
243 A54 40c Produce .40 .40
Nos. 240-243 (4) 1.35 1.25

Scouting Year — A55

7c, Carrying packages. 8c, Scouts, life preserver, vert. 15c, Pottery making, vert. 20c, Inspection. 25c, Scout, cub. 40c, Troop.

1982, Feb. 23 Litho. *Perf. 14*
244 A55 7c multicolored .30 .25
245 A55 8c multicolored .30 .25
246 A55 15c multicolored .30 .25
247 A55 20c multicolored .30 .25
248 A55 25c multicolored .30 .30
249 A55 40c multicolored .45 .45
a. Souv. sheet of 6, #244-249, imperf. 1.75 1.75
Nos. 244-249 (6) 1.95 1.75

A56

Ocean Thermal Energy Conversion — A57

Designs: No. 250, Plant under construction. No. 251, Completed plant.

1982, June 10 Litho. *Perf. 13½*
250 Pair + 2 labels 1.00 1.00
a.-b. A56 25c any single .45 .45
251 Pair + 2 labels 1.50 1.50
a.-b. A57 40c any single .70 .70

75th Anniv. of Phosphate Industry — A58

5c, Freighter Fido, 1907. 10c, Locomotive Nellie, 1907. 30c, Modern Clyde diesel train, 1982. 60c, Flagship Eigamoiya, 1969. $1, Freighters.

1982, Oct. 11 Litho. *Perf. 14*
252 A58 5c multicolored .30 .25
253 A58 10c multicolored .50 .30
254 A58 30c multicolored .90 .60
255 A58 60c multicolored 1.30 1.10
Nos. 252-255 (4) 3.00 2.25

Souvenir Sheet

256 A58 $1 multicolored 1.75 1.75

ANPEX '82 Natl. Stamp Exhibition, Brisbane, Australia, Nos. 252-255 se-tenant with labels describing stamp. No. 256 contains one 68x27mm stamp.

Visit of Queen Elizabeth II and Prince Philip — A59

1982, Oct. 21 *Perf. 14½*
257 A59 20c Elizabeth, vert. .30 .25
258 A59 50c Philip, vert. .65 .40
259 A59 $1 Couple 1.10 .75
Nos. 257-259 (3) 2.05 1.40

Christmas A60

Clergymen: 20c, Father Bernard Lahn, Catholic Mission Church. 30c, Rev. Itubwa Amram, Orro Central Church. 40c, Pastor James Aingimea, Tsiminita Memorial Church, Denigomodu. 50c, Bishop Paul Mea, Diocese of Tarawa-Nauru-Tuvalu.

1982, Nov. 17
260 A60 20c multicolored .30 .30
261 A60 30c multicolored .30 .40
262 A60 40c multicolored .40 .60
263 A60 50c multicolored .55 .80
Nos. 260-263 (4) 1.55 2.10

15th Anniv. of Independence A61

15c, Speaker of Parliament, vert. 20c, People's Court, vert. 30c, Law Courts. 50c, Parliament.

1983, Mar. 23 Wmk. 373 *Perf. 14½*
264 A61 15c multicolored .30 .25
265 A61 20c multicolored .30 .25
266 A61 30c multicolored .30 .30
267 A61 50c multicolored .50 .50
Nos. 264-267 (4) 1.40 1.30

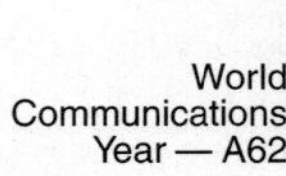

World Communications Year — A62

5c, Earth Satellite Staion NZ. 10c, Omnidirectional Range Installation. 20c, Fixed-station ambulance driver. 25c, Radio Nauru broadcaster. 40c, Air mail service.

1983, May. 11 Litho. *Perf. 14*
268 A62 5c multicolored .30 .25
269 A62 10c multicolored .30 .25
270 A62 20c multicolored .30 .30
271 A62 25c multicolored .40 .40
272 A62 40c multicolored .60 .60
Nos. 268-272 (5) 1.90 1.80

Angam Day (Homecoming) — A63

Perf. 14x13½
1983, Sept. 14 Litho. Wmk. 373
273 A63 15c MV Trinza arriving .30 .25

Size: 25x40mm
Perf. 14
274 A63 20c Elsie Agio in exile .30 .25
275 A63 30c Baby on scale .35 .35
276 A63 40c Children .40 .40
Nos. 273-276 (4) 1.35 1.25

Christmas — A64

Designs: 5c, The Holy Virgin, the Holy Child and St. John, School of Raphael. 15c, The Mystical Betrothal of St. Catherine with Jesus, School of Paolo Veronese. 50c, Madonna on the Throne Surrounded by Angels, School of Seville.

Perf. 14½x14, 14x14½
1983, Nov. 16 Litho. Wmk. 373
277 A64 5c multi, vert. .30 .25
278 A64 15c multi, vert. .30 .25
279 A64 50c multicolored .50 .50
Nos. 277-279 (3) 1.10 1.00

Common Design Types pictured following the introduction.

Lloyd's List Issue
Common Design Type

20c, Ocean Queen. 25c, Enna G. 30c, Baron Minto loading phosphate. 40c, Triadic, 1940.

1984, May 23 Litho. *Perf. 14½x14*
280 CD335 20c multicolored .40 .35
281 CD335 25c multicolored .50 .50
282 CD335 30c multicolored .70 .70
283 CD335 40c multicolored .80 .80
Nos. 280-283 (4) 2.40 2.35

1984 UPU Congress — A65

1984, June 4 Wmk. 373 *Perf. 14*
284 A65 $1 No. 117 1.10 1.40

Coastal Scene — A66

3c, Woman, vert. 5c, Fishing vessel. 10c, Golfer. 15c, Phosphate excavation, vert. 20c, Surveyor, vert. 25c, Air Nauru jet. 30c, Elderly man, vert. 40c, Social service. 50c, Fishing, vert. $1, Tennis, vert. $2, Lagoon Anabar.

Perf. 13½x14, 14x13½
1984, Sept. 21
285 A66 1c shown .30 *.60*
286 A66 3c multi .30 .30
287 A66 5c multi .40 .40
288 A66 10c multi .90 .60
289 A66 15c multi .90 .60
290 A66 20c multi .65 .50
291 A66 25c multi .90 .50
292 A66 30c multi .60 .50
293 A66 40c multi 1.00 1.00
294 A66 50c multi 1.25 1.25
295 A66 $1 multi 2.50 2.50
296 A66 $2 multi 3.25 3.25
Nos. 285-296 (12) 12.95 12.00

For surcharges see Nos. 425-427.

Local Butterflies — A67

25c, Common eggfly (female). 30c, Common eggfly (male). 50c, Wanderer (female).

1984, July 24 *Perf. 14*
297 A67 25c multicolored .50 .50
298 A67 30c multicolored .60 .60
299 A67 50c multicolored .90 .90
Nos. 297-299 (3) 2.00 2.00

Christmas A68

30c, Buada Chapel, vert. 40c, Detudamo Memorial Church, vert. 50c, Candle-light service.

1984, Nov. 14
300 A68 30c multicolored .45 .45
301 A68 40c multicolored .55 .55
302 A68 50c multicolored .75 .75
Nos. 300-302 (3) 1.75 1.75

Air Nauru, 15th Anniv. — A69

20c, Jet. 30c, Crew, vert. 40c, Fokker F28 over Nauru. 50c, Cargo handling, vert.

1985, Feb. 26 Wmk. 373 *Perf. 14*
303 A69 20c multicolored .50 .40
304 A69 30c multicolored .70 .60
305 A69 40c multicolored .90 .90
306 A69 50c multicolored 1.25 1.25
Nos. 303-306 (4) 3.35 3.15

Nauru Phosphate Corp., 15th Anniv. — A70

20c, Open-cut mining. 25c, Rail transport. 30c, Phosphate drying plant. 50c, Early steam engine.

1985, July 31
307 A70 20c multicolored .80 .60
308 A70 25c multicolored 1.65 .90
309 A70 30c multicolored 1.40 .90
310 A70 50c multicolored 2.40 1.50
Nos. 307-310 (4) 6.25 3.90

Christmas — A71

1985, Oct.
311 50c Canoe 1.25 1.25
312 50c Mother and child 1.25 1.25
a. A71 Pair, #311-312 2.50 2.50

No. 312a has a continuous design.

Audubon Birth Bicentenary — A72

Illustrations of the brown noddy by John J. Audubon.

1985, Dec. 31
313 A72 10c Adult and young .40 .40
314 A72 20c Flying .60 .60
315 A72 30c Two adults .75 .75
316 A72 50c Adult 1.10 1.10
Nos. 313-316 (4) 2.85 2.85

Early Transportation A73

15c, Douglas motorcycle. 20c, Truck. 30c, German steam locomotive, 1910. 40c, Baby Austin.

1986, Mar. 5 **Wmk. 384**

317 A73 15c multicolored 1.00 .80
318 A73 20c multicolored 1.25 .90
319 A73 30c multicolored 1.50 1.50
320 A73 40c multicolored 1.90 1.90
Nos. 317-320 (4) 5.65 5.10

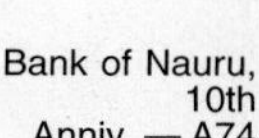

Bank of Nauru, 10th Anniv. — A74

Winning drawings of children's competition.

1986, July 21 **Litho.** ***Perf. 14***

321 A74 20c multicolored .30 .25
322 A74 25c multicolored .30 .30
323 A74 30c multicolored .35 .35
324 A74 40c multicolored .45 .45
Nos. 321-324 (4) 1.40 1.35

Flowers — A75

20c, Plumeria rubra. 25c, Tristellateia australis. 30c, Bougainvillea cultivar. 40c, Delonix regia.

1986, Sept. 30 **Wmk. 384**

325 A75 20c multicolored .40 .40
326 A75 25c multicolored .60 .60
327 A75 30c multicolored .75 .75
328 A75 40c multicolored 1.10 1.10
Nos. 325-328 (4) 2.85 2.85

Christmas A76

1986, Dec. 8 **Wmk. 373**

329 A76 20c Men caroling .60 .50
330 A76 $1 Carolers, invalid 2.25 2.25

Tribal Dances — A77

1987, Jan. 31

331 A77 20c Girls .75 .75
332 A77 30c Men and women 1.00 1.00
333 A77 50c Boy, vert. 2.00 2.00
Nos. 331-333 (3) 3.75 3.75

Artifacts — A78

25c, Hibiscus-fiber skirt. 30c, Headband, necklaces. 45c, Necklaces. 60c, Pandanus-leaf fan.

1987, July 30 ***Perf. 14***

334 A78 25c multicolored .70 .70
335 A78 30c multicolored .80 .80
336 A78 45c multicolored 1.10 1.10
337 A78 60c multicolored 1.65 1.65
Nos. 334-337 (4) 4.25 4.25

World Post Day — A79

40c, UPU emblem, airmail label.

Perf. 14½x14

1987, Oct. 9 **Litho.** **Wmk. 384**

338 A79 40c multicolored 1.75 1.75

Souvenir Sheet

1987, Oct. 20 ***Imperf.***

339 A79 $1 Emblem, vert. 4.00 4.00

Nauru Congregational Church, Cent. — A80

Perf. 13x13½

1987, Nov. 5 **Wmk. 373**

340 A80 40c multicolored 1.50 1.50

Island Christmas Celebration A81

1987, Nov. 27 **Wmk. 384** ***Perf. 14***

341 A81 20c shown .75 .50
342 A81 $1 Sign on building 3.00 3.00

A82

Natl. Independence, 20th Anniv. — A83

Heraldic elements independent of or as part of the natl. arms: 25c, Phosphate mining and shipping. 40c, Tomano flower, vert. 55c, Frigate bird, vert. $1, Natl. arms.

Perf. 13½x14, 14x13½

1988, May 16 **Unwmk.**

343 A82 25c multicolored 1.25 1.25
344 A82 40c multicolored 1.50 1.50
345 A82 55c multicolored 2.25 2.25

Perf. 13

346 A83 $1 multicolored 3.75 3.75
Nos. 343-346 (4) 8.75 8.75

Nauru Post Office, 80th Anniv. — A84

30c, Nauru highlighted on German map of the Marshall Islands, & canceled Marshall Islands #25. 50c, Letter mailed from Nauru to Dresden & post office, 1908. 70c, Post office, 1988, & Nauru #348 canceled on airmail cover.

1988, July 14 **Wmk. 384** ***Perf. 14***

347 A84 30c multicolored .75 .75
348 A84 50c multicolored 1.10 1.10
349 A84 70c multicolored 1.75 1.75
Nos. 347-349 (3) 3.60 3.60

String Games — A85

1988, Aug. 1 **Unwmk.** ***Perf. 13½x14***

350 A85 25c Mat .35 .35
351 A85 40c The Pursuer .55 .55
352 A85 55c Holding Up the Sky .85 .85
353 A85 80c Manujie's Sword 1.25 1.25
Nos. 350-353 (4) 3.00 3.00

UPU, Cent. — A86

1988, Oct. 1 ***Perf. 13½x14***

354 A86 $1 multicolored 1.50 1.50

Hark! The Herald Angels Sing, by Charles Wesley (1703-91) — A87

1988, Nov. 28 ***Perf. 13½***

355 A87 20c "Hark..." .65 .65
356 A87 60c "Glory to..." 1.50 1.50
357 A87 $1 "Peace on Earth" 2.25 2.25
Nos. 355-357 (3) 4.40 4.40

A88

15c, NIC emblem. 50c, APT, ITU emblems. $1, Mounted photograph. $2, UPU emblem, US Capitol.

1989, Nov. 19 ***Perf. 14x15***

358 A88 15c multicolored .50 .50
359 A88 50c multicolored 1.00 1.00
360 A88 $1 multicolored 2.25 2.25
361 A88 $2 multicolored 3.50 3.50
Nos. 358-361 (4) 7.25 7.25

Annivs. and events: Nauru Insurance Corp., 15th Anniv. (15c). World Telecommunications Day and 10th anniv of the Asia-Pacific Telecommunity (50c); Photography 150th anniv. ($1); and 20th UPU Congress, Washington, DC ($2).

Christmas — A89

$1, Children opening gifts.

1989, Dec. 15 **Litho.** ***Perf. 14x15***

362 A89 20c shown .60 .60
363 A89 $1 multicolored 2.50 2.50

A90

Legend of Eigigu, The Girl in the Moon: 25c, Eigigu works while sisters play, rocket lift-off. 30c, Eigigu climbing tree, capsule in lunar orbit. 50c, Eigigu stealing from blind woman, lunar module on moon. $1, Eigigu with husband, Maramen (the moon), astronaut stepping on moon.

1989, Dec. 22 **Litho.** ***Perf. 14x15***

364 A90 25c multicolored *3.25 3.25*
365 A90 30c multicolored *3.50 3.50*
366 A90 50c multicolored *6.50 6.50*
367 A90 $1 multicolored *10.00 8.00*
Nos. 364-367 (4) *23.25 21.25*

Limited supplies of Nos. 364-367 were available through agent.

A91

50c, Mining by hand. $1, Mechanized extraction.

1990, July 3 **Litho.** ***Perf. 14x15***

368 A91 50c multicolored 1.00 1.00
369 A91 $1 multicolored 1.50 1.50

Nauru Phosphate Corp., 20th anniv.

Christmas A92

No. 370, Children. No. 371, Telling Christmas story.

1990, Nov. 26 **Litho.** ***Perf. 14***

370 25c multicolored 1.25 1.25
371 25c multicolored 1.25 1.25
a. A92 Pair, #370-371 2.75 2.75

Legend of Eoiyepiang, Daughter of Thunder and Lightning — A93

1990, Dec. 24 **Litho.** ***Perf. 14x15***

372 A93 25c Woman with baby 1.25 1.00
373 A93 30c Weaving flowers 1.50 1.00
374 A93 50c Listening to storm 2.00 2.25
375 A93 $1 Couple 3.00 3.25
Nos. 372-375 (4) 7.75 7.50

Flowers — A94

1991, July 15 **Litho.** ***Perf. 14½***

380 A94 15c Oleander .30 .25
381 A94 20c Lily .30 .25
382 A94 25c Passion Flower .30 .30
383 A94 30c Lily, diff. .40 .40
384 A94 35c Caesalpinia .45 .45
385 A94 40c Clerodendron .50 .50
387 A94 45c Bauhina pinnata .55 .55
388 A94 50c Hibiscus, vert. .60 .60
389 A94 75c Apocynaceae .85 .85
390 A94 $1 Bindweed, vert. 1.10 1.10
391 A94 $2 Tristellateia, vert. 2.25 2.25
392 A94 $3 Impala lily, vert. 3.00 *4.00*
Nos. 380-392 (12) 10.60 11.50

Souvenir Sheet

Christmas — A95

$2, Stained glass window.

1991, Dec. 12 **Litho.** ***Perf. 14***

395 A95 $2 multicolored 4.50 4.50

Asian Development Bank, 25th Meeting — A96

1992, May 4 **Litho.** ***Perf. 14x14½***

396 A96 $1.50 multicolored 2.75 2.75

Christmas — A97

Children's drawings: 45c, Christmas trees, flags and balloons. 60c, Santa in sleigh, reindeer on flag.

1992, Nov. 23 **Litho.** ***Perf. 14½x14***

397 A97 45c multicolored 1.00 1.00
398 A97 60c multicolored 1.40 1.40

Hammer DeRoburt (1922-1992) — A98

1993, Jan. 31 Litho. *Perf. 14x14½*

399 A98 $1 multicolored 2.50 2.50

Independence, 25th anniv.

Constitution Day, 15th Anniv. — A99

70c, Runners. 80c, Declaration of Republic.

1993, May 17 Litho. *Perf. 14x14½*

400 A99 70c multi 1.20 1.20
401 A99 80c multi 1.30 1.30

24th South Pacific Forum A100

1993, Aug. 9 Litho. *Perf. 14½x14*

402 A100 60c Seabirds 1.60 1.60
403 A100 60c Birds, dolphin 1.60 1.60
404 A100 60c Coral, fish 1.60 1.60
405 A100 60c Fish, coral, diff. 1.60 1.60
a. Block of 4, #402-405 8.00 8.00
b. Souvenir sheet of 4, #402-405 8.00 8.00

No. 405a is a continuous design.

No. 405b exists with SINGPEX '93 overprint, sold at the exhibition. Value, unused or used, $10.

Christmas A101

Designs: 55c, "Peace on earth..." 65c, "Hark the Herald Angels Sing."

1993, Nov. 29 Litho. *Perf. 14½x14*

406 A101 55c multicolored 1.00 1.00
407 A101 65c multicolored 1.25 1.25

Child's Best Friend A102

1994, Feb. 10 Litho. *Perf. 14*

408 $1 Girls, dogs 2.00 2.00
409 $1 Boys, dogs 2.00 2.00
a. A102 Pair, #408-409 4.00 4.00
b. Souvenir sheet of 2, #408-409 4.50 4.50
c. As "b," ovptd. in sheet margin 4.50 4.50
d. As "b," ovptd. in sheet margin 4.50 4.50

No. 409c ovptd. with Hong Kong '94 emblem. No. 409d ovptd. with SINGPEX '94 emblem in gold.

Issued: #409c, 2/18/94; #409d, 8/31/94.

15th Commonwealth Games, Victoria — A103

1994, Sept. 8 Litho. *Perf. 14x14½*

410 A103 $1.50 Weight lifting 2.25 2.25

ICAO, 50th Anniv. — A104

55c, Emblems. 65c, Nauru Intl. Airport. 80c, DVOR navigational aid. $1, Airport fire engines.

1994, Dec. 14

411 A104 55c multicolored .65 .65
412 A104 65c multicolored .75 .75
413 A104 80c multicolored .95 .95
414 A104 $1 multicolored 1.25 1.25
a. Souvenir sheet of 4, #411-414 6.00 6.00
Nos. 411-414 (4) 3.60 3.60

United Nations, 50th Anniv. — A105

No. 415, National flag. No. 416, National coat of arms. No. 417, Canoe, UN emblem. No. 418, Jet, ship, UN emblem.

1995, Jan. 1 *Perf. 14x14½*

415 A105 75c multicolored 1.50 1.50
416 A105 75c multicolored 1.50 1.50
417 A105 75c multicolored 1.50 1.50
418 A105 75c multicolored 1.50 1.50
a. Block of 4, #415-418 6.75 6.75
b. Souvenir sheet of 4, #415-418 7.00 7.00

Nos. 417-418 are a continuous design.

Christmas — A106

75c, Star over Bethlehem.

1994, Nov. 20 Litho. *Perf. 14½x14*

419 A106 65c shown 1.25 1.10
420 A106 75c multicolored 1.40 1.30

Membership in Intl. Olympic Committee — A107

1994, Dec. 27 *Perf. 14x14½*

421 A107 50c multicolored .60 .60

Nauru Phosphate Corporation, 25th Anniv. — A108

Designs: No. 422, Signing of Phosphate Agreement, June 15, 1967. No. 423, Nauru Pres. Bernard Dowiyogo, Australian Prime Minister Paul Keating at signing Nauru-Australia Compact of Settlement. $2, Mining phosphate.

1995, July 1 Litho. *Perf. 14x15*

422 A108 60c multicolored 1.40 1.40
423 A108 60c multicolored 1.40 1.40
a. Pair, #422-423 3.50 3.50

Souvenir Sheet

424 A108 $2 multicolored 4.00 4.00

No. 291 Surcharged & Overprinted

1995, Aug. 19 Litho. *Perf. 13½x14*

425 A66 50c on 25c "at Beijing" 1.35 1.35
426 A66 $1 on 25c "at Singapore" 1.75 1.75
427 A66 $1 on 25c "at Jakarta" 1.75 1.75
a. Strip of 3, #425-427 6.50 6.50

UN, 50th Anniv. — A109

Designs: 75c, Nauru coastline. $1.50, UN headquarters, US, aerial view of Nauru.

1995, Oct. 24 Litho. *Perf. 14*

428 A109 75c multicolored 1.40 1.40
429 A109 $1.50 multicolored 2.75 2.75

Christmas A110

1995, Dec. 7 Litho. *Perf. 14*

430 60c Seeking the Way 1.00 1.00
431 70c Finding the Way 1.10 1.10
a. A110 Pair, #430-431 2.60 2.60

Return From Truk, 50th Anniv. — A111

1996, Jan. 31 *Perf. 12*

432 A111 75c multicolored 1.20 1.20
433 A111 $1.25 multicolored 2.30 2.30
a. Souvenir sheet of 2, #432-433 4.00 4.00

Souvenir Sheet

Nanjing Stone Carving, Keeping off the Evils A112

1996, Mar. 20 Litho. *Perf. 12*

434 A112 45c multicolored 1.25 1.25

CHINA '96, 9th Asian Intl. Philatelic Exhibition.

End of World War II, 50th Anniv. A113

Designs: 75c, Children playing on old cannon. $1.50, Girls making flower leis in front of pillbox.

1995, Sept. 13 Litho. *Perf. 14x13½*

435 A113 75c multicolored 1.75 1.75
436 A113 $1.50 multicolored 3.25 3.25
a. Pair, Nos. 435-436 + label 7.50 *7.50*
b. As "a," ovptd. in gold on label *10.00 10.00*
c. As "a," ovptd. in gold on label *10.00 10.00*

No. 436a exists with two different labels: one showing a war memorial, the other a dove. Gold overprint on memorial label is Hongpex '96 Exhibition emblem (No. 436b); on dove label, a silhouette of a rat (No. 436c). Nos. 436a and 436b-436c may be collected as blocks of four.

Issued: Nos. 436b, 436c, 1996.

1996 Summer Olympic Games, Atlanta — A114

Discobolus and: 40c, Running pictograph, vert. 50c, Weight lifting pictograph, vert. 60c, Weight lifter. $1, Runner.

Perf. 13½x14, 14x13½

1996, July 21 Litho.

437 A114 40c multicolored 1.00 1.00
438 A114 50c multicolored 1.25 1.25
439 A114 60c multicolored 1.50 1.50
440 A114 $1 multicolored 1.75 1.75
Nos. 437-440 (4) 5.50 5.50

Christmas — A115

Designs: 50c, Candles, angel with trumpet, nativity. 70c, Angel, candles, map, fauna.

1996, Dec. 16 Litho. *Perf. 14*

441 A115 50c multicolored 1.00 1.00
442 A115 70c multicolored 1.25 1.25

World Wildlife Fund — A116

Fish: a, 20c, Dolphinfish. b, 30c, Wahoo. c, 40c, Pacific sailfish. d, 50c, Yellowfin tuna.

1997, Feb. 12 Litho. *Perf. 11½*

443 A116 Strip of 4, #a.-d. 4.50 4.50

A117

Giant Buddha (various statues): a, 1c. b, 2c. c, 5c. d, 10c. e, 12c. f, 15c. g, 25c.

1997, Feb. 12 *Perf. 14*

444 A117 Sheet of 7, #a.-g. 3.00 3.00

Hong Kong '97, Hong Kong's return to China. No. 444g is 60x80mm.

A118

Designs: 80c, Engagement portrait. $1.20, 50th Wedding anniversary portrait.

1997, July 15 Litho. *Perf. 13½*

445 A118 80c multicolored 1.40 1.50
446 A118 $1.20 multicolored 2.00 2.25
a. Souvenir sheet, #445-446 4.25 4.25

Queen Elizabeth II and Prince Philip, 50th wedding anniv.

Christmas — A119

1997, Nov. 5 Litho. *Perf. 13½*

447 A119 60c Monument .80 .55
448 A119 80c Church 1.30 1.30

Nauru Congregational Church, 110th anniv.

Souvenir Sheet

Commonwealth, Oceania and South Pacific Weight Lifting Championships — A120

Various contestants lifting weights: a, 40c. b, 60c. c, 80c. d, $1.20.

1998, Mar. 25 Litho. *Perf. 14*
449 A120 Sheet of 4, #a.-d. 4.00 4.00

A121

Design: Visit of Juan Antonio Samaranch, Pres. of Intl. Olympic Committee.

1998, May 4 *Perf. 13½*
450 A121 $2 multicolored 2.75 2.75

Souvenir Sheet

28th Parliamentary Conference — A122

1997, July 24 Litho. *Perf. 14*
451 A122 $2 multicolored 3.25 3.25

A123

Diana, Princess of Wales (1961-97): a, In yellow. b, White blouse. c, Wearing tiara. d, White & black outfit. e, Pink hat. f, White dress.

1998, Aug. 31
452 A123 70c Sheet of 6, #a.-f. 5.25 5.25

A125

1998 Commonwealth Games, Kuala Lumpur: 40c, Gymnast on pommel horse. 60c, Throwing discus. 70c, Runner. 80c, Weight lifter.

1998, Sept. 11 Litho. *Perf. 13½x14*
454 A125 40c multicolored .60 .60
455 A125 60c multicolored .90 .90
456 A125 70c multicolored 1.00 1.00
457 A125 80c multicolored 1.10 1.10
a. Souvenir sheet, #454-457 3.75 3.75
Nos. 454-457 (4) 3.60 3.60

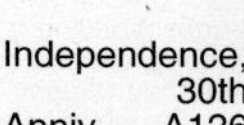

Independence, 30th Anniv. — A126

Squadron Leader L.H. Hicks and: $1, Band. $2, National anthem.

1998, Oct. 26 Litho. *Perf. 14*
458 A126 $1 multicolored .90 .90
459 A126 $2 multicolored 3.00 3.00
a. Souvenir sheet, #458-459 4.25 4.25

Christmas A127

Star, island scene and: 85c, Fish, candle, flowers. 95c, Flowers, fruits, Christmas present.

1998 *Perf. 13½x12½*
460 A127 85c multicolored 1.25 1.25
461 A127 95c multicolored 1.40 1.40

First Contact with Island, Bicent. A128

Designs: No. 462, Sailing ship Snow Hunter. No. 463, Capt. John Fearn.

1998, Dec. 1 *Perf. 12*
462 A128 $1.50 multicolored 2.00 2.00
463 A128 $1.50 multicolored 2.00 2.00
a. Pair, #462-463 4.25 4.25
b. Souvenir sheet, #463a 4.50 4.50

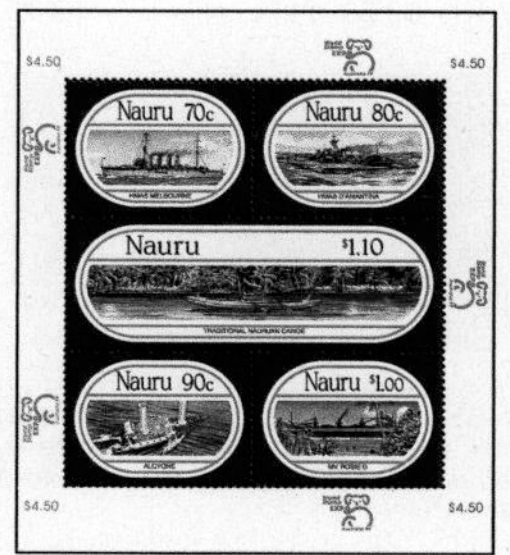

Ships — A129

Designs: a, 70c, HMAS Melbourne. b, 80c, HMAS D'Amantina. c, $1.10, Traditional Nauruan canoe. d, 90c, Alcyone. e, $1, MV Rosie D.

1999, Mar. 19 Litho. *Perf. 12*
464 A129 Sheet of 5, #a.-e. 6.00 6.00

Australia '99, World Stamp Expo. No. 464c is 80x30mm.

1st Manned Moon Landing, 30th Anniv.
Common Design Type

Designs: 70c, Neil Armstrong. 80c, Service module and lunar module fire towards moon. 90c, Aldrin deploying EASEP. $1, Command module enters earth atmosphere.
$2, Earth as seen from moon.

Perf. 14x13¾
1999, July 20 Litho. Wmk. 384
465 CD357 70c multicolored .60 .60
466 CD357 80c multicolored .85 .85
467 CD357 90c multicolored 1.00 1.00
468 CD357 $1 multicolored 2.10 *1.65*
Nos. 465-468 (4) 4.55 4.10

Souvenir Sheet
Perf. 14
469 CD357 $2 multicolored 3.00 3.00

No. 469 contains one circular stamp 40mm in diameter.

China 1999 World Philatelic Exhibition — A130

a, Tursiops truncatus. b, Xiphias gladius.

Perf. 12¾x12½
1999, Aug. 21 Litho. Unwmk.
470 A130 50c Sheet of 2, #a.-b. 3.75 3.75

UPU, 125th Anniv. — A131

1999, Aug. 23 Litho. *Perf. 11¾*
471 A131 $1 multicolored 1.75 1.75

Christmas — A132

Designs: 65c, Native woman. 70c, Christmas tree and candle.

Perf. 13½x13¾
1999, Nov. 10 Litho. Wmk. 388
472 A132 65c multi 1.10 1.10
473 A132 70c multi 1.25 1.25

Millennium A133

70c, Woman in native costume, fishermen on beach. $1.10, Satellite dish, runner, cross, airplane, crane, jeep and boat. $1.20, Man on computer, woman holding globe.

Perf. 11¾x12
2000, Jan. 1 Litho. Wmk. 388
474 A133 70c multi 1.45 2.00
475 A133 $1.10 multi 2.30 3.25
476 A133 $1.20 multi 2.75 3.50
a. Souvenir sheet of 3, #474-476 6.50 6.50
Nos. 474-476 (3) 6.50 8.75

Nauru Phosphate Corp. 30th Anniv. — A134

Designs: $1.20, Power plant. $1.80, Phosphate train. $2, Albert Ellis.

2000, May 27 Litho. *Perf. 12½x12¾*
477-479 A134 Set of 3 6.50 7.75
479a Souv. sheet, #477-479, perf 12 6.25 7.50

No. 479a exists imperf. Value, $12.

Queen Mother, 100th Birthday — A135

Designs: $1, Dark blue hat. $1.10, Lilac hat. $1.20, Waving, light blue hat. $1.40, Blue hat.

2000, Aug. 4 *Perf. 14¼*
480-483 A135 Set of 4 7.00 7.00
483a Souvenir sheet, #480-483, perf. 13¾x13½ 6.50 6.0

2000 Summer Olympics, Sydney — A136

Olympic rings, map of Australia, Sydney Opera House and: 90c, Running. $1, Basketball. $1.10, Weight lifting. $1.20, Olympic torch and runner.

2000 Photo. *Perf. 11¾*
484-487 A136 Set of 4 8.75 8.75

Christmas — A137

Designs: 65c, Flower, girl decorating Christmas tree, star, decorated Christmas tree. 75c, Ornament, child on toy train, palm tree, gift.

2000 Litho. *Perf. 13¾x13½*
488-489 A137 Set of 2 3.00 3.00
489a Souvenir sheet, #488-489 3.25 3.25

Stamps from No. 489a are perf. 14¼x14¼x13¾x14¼.

32nd Pacific Islands Forum A138

No. 490 — Island and: a, 90c, Yellow flowers, bird flying to right. b, $1, Red flowers, bird flying to left. c, $1.10, Yellow flowers, birds facing right. d, $2, Red flowers, bird facing left.

Perf. 14½x14
2001, Aug. 14 Litho. Unwmk.
490 A138 Block of 4, #a-d 11.00 11.00
e. Souvenir sheet, #490 12.00 12.00

Reign Of Queen Elizabeth II, 50th Anniv. Issue
Common Design Type

Designs: Nos. 491, 495a, 70c, Princess Elizabeth in uniform, 1946. Nos. 492, 495b, 80c, Wearing patterned hat. Nos. 493, 495c, 90c, Wearing hat, 1951. Nos. 494, 495d, $1, In 1997. No. 495e, $4, 1955 portrait by Annigoni (38x50mm).

Perf. 14¼x14½, 13¾ (#495e)
2002, Feb. 6 Litho. Wmk. 373
With Gold Frames
491 CD360 70c multicolored 1.50 1.50
492 CD360 80c multicolored 1.75 1.75
493 CD360 90c multicolored 1.85 1.85
494 CD360 $1 multicolored 2.15 2.15
Nos. 491-494 (4) 7.25 7.25

Souvenir Sheet
Without Gold Frames
495 CD360 Sheet of 5, #a-e 10.50 10.50

Miniature Sheet

In Remembrance of Sept. 11, 2001 Terrorist Attacks — A139

No. 496: a, 90c. b, $1. c, $1.10. d, $2.

Wmk. 373
2002, May 17 Litho. *Perf. 13¾*
496 A139 Sheet of 4, #a-d 7.50 7.50

Butterflies — A140

No. 497: a, Parthenos sylvia. b, Delias madetes. c, Danaus philene. d, Arhopala hercules. e, Papilio canopus. f, Danaus schenkii. g, Parthenos figrina. h, Mycalesis phidon. i, Vindula sapor.
$2, Graphium agamemnon.

2002, June 28 *Perf. 13¾x14¼*
497 A140 50c Sheet of 9, #a-i 11.00 11.00

Souvenir Sheet
498 A140 $2 multi 4.50 4.50

Queen Mother Elizabeth (1900-2002)
Common Design Type

Designs: Nos. 499, 501a, $1.50, Wearing hat (black and white photograph). Nos. 500, 501b, $1.50, Wearing light blue hat.

Perf. 13¾x14¼

2002, Aug. 5 Litho. Wmk. 373

With Purple Frames

499 CD361 $1.50 multicolored 3.00 3.00
500 CD361 $1.50 multicolored 3.00 3.00

Souvenir Sheet

Without Purple Frames

Perf. 14½x14¼

501 CD361 Sheet of 2, #a-b 8.00 8.00

Fire Fighting — A141

Designs: 20c, Building fire. 50c, Blaze at sea. 90c, Forest fire. $1, New and old fire helmets. $1.10, Modern ladder truck, old pump engine. $2, Modern and late 19th cent. firefighters.

$5, Modern fire engine and rescue vehicle.

Perf. 14x14¼

2002, Aug. 31 Litho. Wmk. 373

502-507 A141 Set of 6 11.00 11.00

Souvenir Sheet

508 A141 $5 multi 14.00 14.00

Roman Catholic Church in Nauru, Cent. A142

No. 509: a, First church building, Arubo. b, Father Friedrich Gründl, first missionary. c, Sister Stanisla, first sister. d, Second church building, Ibwenape. e, Brother Kalixtus Bader, first lay brother. f, Father Alois Kayser, missionary.

Wmk. 373

2002, Dec. 8 Litho. *Perf. 13¾*

509 A142 $1.50 Sheet of 6, #a-f 16.00 16.00

Christmas — A143

Designs: 15c, The Holy Family with Dancing Angels, by Sir Anthony Van Dyck. $1, The Holy Virgin with the Child, by Luca Cangiasus. $1.20, The Holy Family with the Cat, by Rembrandt. $3, The Holy Family with St. John, by Raphael.

2002, Dec. 8

510-513 A143 Set of 4 10.00 10.00

Worldwide Fund For Nature (WWF) — A144

Designs: 15c, Red-and-black anemone fish, Bubble tentacle sea anemone. $1, Orange-fin anemone fish, Leathery sea anemone. $1.20, Pink anemone fish, Magnificent sea anemone. $3, Clark's anemone fish, Merten's sea anemone.

Wmk. 373

2003, Apr. 29 Litho. *Perf. 14*

514-517 A144 Set of 4 10.00 10.00
517a Miniature sheet, 4 each #514-517 40.00 40.00

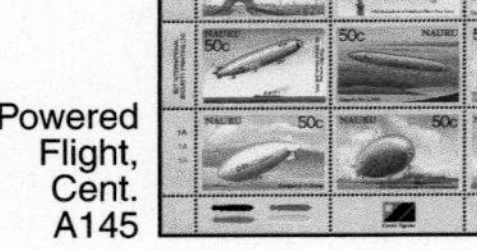

Powered Flight, Cent. A145

No. 518: a, Santos-Dumont wins the Deutsch Prize, Oct. 1901. b, USS Shenandoah at Lakehurst, NJ. c, R101 at Cardington Mast, U.K., Oct. 1929. d, R34 crossing Atlantic, July 1919. e, Zeppelin No. 1, 1900. f, USS Los Angeles moored to the USS Patoka. g, Goodyear C-71 airship. h, LZ-130 Graf Zeppelin II at Friedrichshafen, Germany. i, Zeppelin NT.

No. 519 — LZ-127 Graf Zeppelin: a, Over Mt. Fuji. b, Over San Francisco. c, Exchanging mail with Russian ice breaker, Franz Josef Land.

2003, Oct. 26

518 A145 50c Sheet of 9, #a-i 11.00 11.00
519 A145 $2 Sheet of 3, #a-c 13.00 13.00

Bird Life International — A146

Nauru reed warbler: No. 520, Bird on reed. No. 521, Bird on branch with insect in beak, vert. No. 522a, Close-up of head. No. 522b, Bird with open beak, vert. No. 522c, Nest with chicks.

2003, Nov. 10 *Perf. 14¼x13¾*

520 A146 $1.50 multi 4.75 4.75
a. Perf. 14¼x14½ 4.75 4.75

Perf. 13¾x14¼

521 A146 $1.50 multi 4.75 4.75
a. Perf. 14½x14¼ 4.75 4.75

Souvenir Sheet

Perf. 14¼x14½, 14½x14¼ (#522b)

522 Sheet, #520a, 521a, 522a-522c 15.00 15.00
a.-c. A146 $1.50 Any single 3.50 3.50

Battle of Trafalgar, Bicent. A147

Designs: 25c, Aigle in action against HMS Defiance. 50c, French "Eprouvette." 75c, Santissima Trinidad in action against HMS Africa. $1, Emperor Napoleon Bonaparte, vert. $1.50, HMS Victory. No. 528, $2.50, Vice-Admiral Sir Horatio Nelson, vert.

No. 529, $2.50, vert.: a, Admiral Pierre Villeneuve. b, Formidable.

2005, Mar. 29 Litho. *Perf. 13¼*

523-528 A147 Set of 6 11.50 11.50

Souvenir Sheet

529 A147 $2.50 Sheet of 2, #a-b 10.50 10.50

No. 527 has particles of wood from the HMS Victory embedded in the areas covered by a thermographic process that produces a shiny, raised effect.

End of World War II, 60th Anniv. A148

No. 530: a, German raider Komet shells Nauru, 1940. b, French warship Le Triomphant assists in evacuation of civilians, 1942. c, Japanese forces occupy Nauru, 1942. d, US Air Force B-24 Liberator aircraft bombing missions, 1943. e, USS Paddle stationed off Nauru, 1943. f, B-25G Mitchell "Coral Princess" shot down over Nauru, 1944. g, Spitfires, Battle of Britain, 1940. h, HMAS Diamantine arrives at Nauru, 1945. i, D-Day landings, 1944. j, Union Jack is hoisted again, 1945.

$5, HMAS Manoora sinks Italian MV Romolo, 1940.

2005, Apr. 21 *Perf. 13¾*

530 A148 75c Sheet of 10, #a-j 13.00 13.00

Souvenir Sheet

531 A148 $5 multi 9.00 9.00

Pacific Explorer 2005 World Stamp Expo, Sydney (No. 531).

Pope John Paul II (1920-2005) — A149

2005, Aug. 18 Litho. *Perf. 14x14¼*

532 A149 $1 multi 2.00 2.00

Rotary International, Cent. — A150

2005, Sept. 12 *Perf. 14½x14¼*

533 A150 $2.50 multi 4.75 4.75

BirdLife International — A151

No. 534, 25c: a, Rota bridled white-eye. b, Faichuk white-eye. c, Samoan white-eye. d, Bridled white-eye. e, Long-billed white-eye. f, Golden white-eye.

No. 535, 50c: a, Kuhl's lorikeet. b, Masked shining parrot. c, Crimson shining parrot. d, Blue lorikeet. e, Henderson lorikeet. f, Ultramarine lorikeet.

No. 536, $1: a, Atoll fruit dove. b, Henderson fruit dove. c, Cook Islands fruit dove. d, Rapa fruit dove. e, Whistling dove. f, Mariana fruit dove.

Perf. 14¼x14½

2005, Sept. 12 Litho.

Sheets of 6, #a-f

534-536 A151 Set of 3 28.00 28.00

Christmas — A152

Stories by Hans Christian Andersen (1805-75): 25c, The Little Fir Tree. 50c, The Wild Swans. 75c, The Farmyard Cock and the Weather Cock. $1, The Storks. $2.50, The Toad. $5, The Ice Maiden.

2005, Oct. 10 *Perf. 14*

537-542 A152 Set of 6 16.50 16.50

Battle of Trafalgar, Bicent. — A153

Designs: 50c, HMS Victory. $1, Ships in battle, horiz. $5, Admiral Horatio Nelson.

2005, Oct. 18 *Perf. 13½*

543-545 A153 Set of 3 13.00 13.00

Anniversaries — A154

No. 546, 25c: a, Wolfgang Amadeus Mozart. b, Piano and violin.

No. 547, 50c: a, Isambard Kingdom Brunel. b, Chain and pulley.

No. 548, 75c: a, Edmond Halley. b, Halley's quadrant.

No. 549, $1: a, Charles Darwin. b, Early microscope.

No. 550, $1.25: a, Thomas Alva Edison. b, Light bulb.

No. 551, $1.50: a, Christopher Columbus. b, Astrolabe.

2006, May 27 Litho. *Perf. 13¼x12½*

Horiz. Pairs, #a-b

546-551 A154 Set of 6 22.00 22.00

Birth of Mozart, 250th anniv., Birth of Brunel, bicent., Birth of Halley, 350th anniv., Darwin's voyage on the Beagle, 175th anniv., Death of Edison, 75th anniv., Death of Columbus, 500th anniv.

2006 World Cup Soccer Championships, Germany — A155

Scenes from championship matches won by: $1, Uruguay, 1950. $1.50, Argentina, 1978. $2, Italy, 1982. $3, Brazil, 2002.

2006, June 9 *Perf. 14*

552-555 A155 Set of 4 15.00 15.00

Dinosaurs A156

Designs: 10c, Parasaurolophus. 25c, Quetzalcoatlus. 50c, Spinosaurus. 75c, Triceratops. $1, Tyrannosaurus rex. $1.50, Euoplocephalus. $2, Velociraptor. $2.50, Protoceratops.

2006, Aug. 14 *Perf. 13¼x13½*

556-563 A156 Set of 8 16.00 16.00

Miniature Sheet

Victoria Cross, 150th Anniv. A157

No. 564: a, Lt. Gerald Graham carrying wounded man. b, Pvt. Mac Gregor shooting rifle. c, Pvt. Alexander Wright repelling a sortie. d, Cpl. John Ross viewing evacuation of the Redan. e, Sgt. McWheeney digging with bayonet. f, Brevet Maj. G. L. Goodlake surprising enemy. Descriptions of vignettes are on labels below each stamp.

2006, Sept. 12 *Perf. 13¼x12½*

564 A157 $1.50 Sheet of 6, #a-f, + 6 labels 18.00 18.00

Miniature Sheet

Inaugural Flight of the Concorde, 30th Anniv. — A158

No. 565: a, British Airways Concorde G-BOAF on ground. b, First flight of Concorde 002, 1969. c, Concorde landing. d, Queen's Golden Jubilee flypast, 2002. e, 50th anniv. of Battle of Britain, 1990. f, Concorde at 60,000 feet. g, Extreme condition testing. h, Concorde on runway. i, First commercial flight, 1976. j, Concorde above Earth. k, British Airways Concorde G-BOAF in flight. l, Two Concordes on ground.

2006, Oct. 10 ***Perf. 14¼x13¾***
565 A158 $1 Sheet of 12, #a-l, + 3 labels 26.00 26.00

Miniature Sheet

Year of Three Kings, 70th Anniv. A159

No. 566: a, Queen Elizabeth II. b, King George V and Princess Elizabeth. c, King Edward VIII and Princess Elizabeth. d, King George VI and Princess Elizabeth.

2006, Oct. 17
566 A159 $1.50 Sheet of 4, #a-d 13.00 13.00

Wedding of Queen Elizabeth II and Prince Philip, 60th Anniv. — A160

Designs: $1, Couple. $1.50, Couple in coach. $2, At wedding ceremony. $3, Couple walking.
$5, Queen Elizabeth II in bridal gown.

2007, Jan. 31 **Litho.** ***Perf. 13¾***
567-570 A160 Set of 4 13.00 13.00

Souvenir Sheet

Perf. 14¼

571 A160 $5 multi 10.00 10.00

No. 571 contains one 43x57mm stamp.

A161

Royal Air Force, 90th Anniv. A162

Aviation pioneers: No. 572, 70c, Sir Douglas Bader (1910-82), World War II fighter ace. No. 573, 70c, R. J. Mitchell (1895-1937), designer of Spitfire airplane. No. 574, 70c, Sir Frank Whittle (1907-96), inventor of jet engine. No. 575, 70c, Sir Sydney Camm (1893-1966), designer of Hawker Hurricane airplane. No. 576, 70c, Air Vice Marshal James E. "Johnnie" Johnson (1915-2001), World War II fighter ace.
$3, Avro Vulcan.

Wmk. 373

2008, May 19 **Litho.** ***Perf. 14***
572-576 A161 Set of 5 8.50 8.50

Souvenir Sheet

577 A162 $3 multi 7.00 7.00

Nos. 572-576 were each printed in sheets of 8 + central label.

2008 Summer Olympics, Beijing — A163

Designs: 15c, Bamboo, badminton. 25c, Dragon, archery. 75c, Lanterns, weight lifting. $1, Fish, diving.

Perf. 13¼

2008, Aug. 8 **Litho.** **Unwmk.**
578-581 A163 Set of 4 5.50 5.50

A164

End of World War I, 90th Anniv. A165

World War I recruitment posters inscribed: No. 582, $1, "A Happy New Year to our Gallant Soldiers." No. 583, $1, "The Empire Needs Men." No. 584, $1, "South Australians." No. 585, $1, "Your King and Country Need You." No. 586, $1, "Britons." No. 587, $1, "An Appeal to You."
$2, Queen's Wreath of Remembrance.

Wmk. 406

2008, Sept. 16 **Litho.** ***Perf. 14***
582-587 A164 Set of 6 13.00 13.00

Souvenir Sheet

588 A165 $2 multi 4.50 4.50

Worldwide Fund for Nature (WWF) — A166

Greater frigate bird: 25c, Adult and chick. 75c, Two in flight. $1, Landing. $2, One in flight.

Perf. 13¼x13

2008, Oct. 14 **Unwmk.**
589-592 A166 Set of 4 8.25 8.25
592a Sheet, 4 each #589-592, perf. 13 30.00 30.00

Naval Aviation, Cent. — A167

Designs: No. 593, $1.50, Avro 504C. No. 594, $1.50, Fairey Flycatcher. No. 595, $1.50, Short Folder. No. 596, $1.50, De Havilland Sea Vixen.
$3, Grumman Avenger in Operation Meridian, 1945.

Wmk. 406

2009, Sept. 3 **Litho.** ***Perf. 14***
593-596 A167 Set of 4 12.00 12.00

Souvenir Sheet

597 A167 $3 multi 6.00 6.00

Nos. 593-596 each were printed in sheets of 8 + central label.

Russian Space Program — A168

Flags of Russia and Nauru and: No. 598, 60c, Sputnik satellite, 1957. No. 599, 60c, Yuri Gagarin, first man in space, 1961. $1.20, Nauru Island from space. $2.25, Vostok 1. $3, International Space Station.

Perf. 14½x14

2011, Apr. 12 **Unwmk.**
598-602 A168 Set of 5 14.50 14.50

Souvenir Sheet

Wedding of Prince William and Catherine Middleton — A169

Perf. 14¾x14¼

2011, Apr. 29 **Wmk. 406**
603 A169 $5 multi 11.00 11.00

Port Development Project — A170

Wmk. 406

2018, Jan. 31 **Litho.** ***Perf. 14¼***
604 A170 50c multi .75 .75

Republic of Nauru, 50th anniv.

Independence, 50th Anniv. — A171

Litho. & Embossed With Foil Application

2018, May 17 **Unwmk.** ***Perf. 14¼***
605 A171 $5 gold — —

Constitution Day.

49th Pacific Islands Forum, Nauru — A171a

2018 **Litho.** ***Perf. 14¼***
605A A171a $5 multi — —

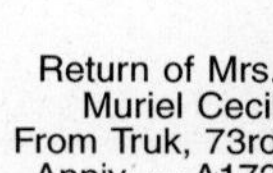

Return of Mrs. Muriel Cecil From Truk, 73rd Anniv. — A172

Perf. 14¼x14

2019, Jan. 31 **Litho.** **Unwmk.**
606 A172 $5 multi — —

Bishar Abdirahman Hussein, Kenyan Diplomat, Director General of Universal Postal Union International Bureau — A173

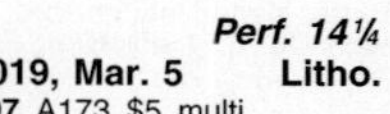

Perf. 14¼

2019, Mar. 5 **Litho.** **Unwmk.**
607 A173 $5 multi — —

Visit of Republic of China Pres. Tsai Ing-wen to Nauru — A174

Perf. 14¼

2019, Mar. 25 **Litho.** **Unwmk.**
608 A174 $5 multi — —

Pres. Baron Waqa — A175

Perf. 14¼

2019, May 17 **Litho.** **Unwmk.**
609 A175 $5 multi — —

Constitution Day.

Christmas A176

2019, Dec. 23 **Litho.** ***Perf. 14¼***
610 A176 $5 multi — —

Deiboe Tribe Mat Design — A177

Perf. 14¼

2020, Aug. 19 **Litho.** **Unwmk.**
611 A177 $5 multi — —

Return of Nauru Islanders From Truk (Chuuk) Island, 75th Anniv. — A178

Perf. 14x14¾

2021, July 10 **Litho.** **Unwmk.**
612 A178 $5 multi — —

Hammer DeRoburt (1922-92), First President of Nauru — A179

Perf. 14¼

2022, Oct. 20 **Litho.** **Unwmk.**
613 A179 $5 multi — —

SEMI-POSTAL STAMP

Miniature Sheet of 4

1996 Summer Olympics, Atlanta — SP1

Designs: a, Birds, denomination UR. b. Birds, denomination UL. c, 4 dolphins. d, 2 dolphins.

1995, Sept. 1 Litho. *Perf. 12*
B1 SP1 60c +15c, #a.-d. 7.00 6.50

Surcharge for sports development in Nauru.

NEPAL

nə-'pol

LOCATION — In the Himalaya Mountains between India and Tibet
GOVT. — Republic
AREA — 56,136 sq. mi.
POP. — 29,140,000 (2020 est.)
CAPITAL — Kathmandu

Nepal stamps were valid only in Nepal and India until April 1959, when they became valid to all parts of the world.

4 Pice = 1 Anna
64 Pice = 16 Annas = 1 Rupee
100 Paisa = 1 Rupee (1958)

Catalogue values for unused stamps in this country are for Never Hinged items, beginning with Scott 103 in the regular postage section, Scott C1 in the air post section and Scott O1 in the officials section.

Nos. 1-24, 29A were issued without gum.

Sripech and Crossed Khukris — A1

1881 Typo. Unwmk. *Pin-perf.*
European Wove Paper

1 A1 1a ultramarine 240.00 *350.00*
2 A1 2a purple 280.00 400.00
a. Tete beche pair — —
3 A1 4a green 325.00 —

Imperf

4 A1 1a blue 160.00 150.00
5 A1 2a purple 125.00 *125.00*
a. Tete beche pair —
6 A1 4a green 240.00 *400.00*

No. 3 postally used is probably unique. Only 2 No. 5a are known unused. No. 5a is only known to exist used in a strip of three.

1886 Native Wove Paper *Imperf.*

7 A1 1a ultramarine 90.00 *120.00*
a. Tete beche pair *400.00* 450.00
8 A1 2a violet 75.00 90.00
a. Tete beche pair *400.00* 525.00
9 A1 4a green 95.00 135.00
a. Tete beche pair *600.00* 700.00
Nos. 7-9 (3) 260.00 345.00

Nos. 7-10 are clear to mostly clear designs on good quality native paper. European wove paper is of substantially higher quality, white, and lacks the wood fibers of the native paper.

Used values for Nos. 10-49 are for telegraph cancels.

Siva's Bow and Two Khukris — A2

1899-1917 *Imperf.*
Native Wove Paper

10 A2 ½a black, clear impression 20.00 13.50
a. Tete beche pair *150.00* 35.00
11 A2 ½a red orange ('17) *1,750.* 500.00
a. Tete beche pair *2,000.*

Pin-perf.

12 A2 ½a black 30.00 17.50
a. Tete beche pair *225.00* 55.00

No. 11 is known postally used on six covers.
No. 11a unused is only known in larger blocks, no unused pairs currently exist.

Type of 1881

1898-1917 *Imperf.*

12B A2 ½a black 35.00 35.00
13 A1 1a pale blue 60.00 60.00
a. 1a bluish green 75.00 75.00
b. Tete beche pair *150.00* *150.00*
c. As "a," tete beche pair *300.00* *300.00*
14 A1 2a gray violet 60.00 60.00
a. Tete beche pair *140.00* *140.00*
15 A1 2a claret ('17) *100.00* 32.50
a. Tete beche pair *225.00* *100.00*
16 A1 2a brown ('17) 25.00 12.00
a. Tete beche pair 55.00 42.50
17 A1 4a dull green 70.00 70.00
a. Tete beche pair 350.00 *350.00*
b. Cliche of 1a in plate of 4a ('04) *500.00* *400.00*
c. As "b," pair — —
Nos. 12B-17 (6) 350.00 269.50

No. 13-17 are blurry impressions on poor quality native paper.
#17b has the recut frame of the 1904 issue. #17b probably was used only on telegraph/telephone forms.

Pin-perf.

18 A1 1a pale blue 17.50 10.00
a. Tete beche pair *325.00* —
19 A1 2a gray violet 90.00 90.00
a. Tete beche pair *300.00* *300.00*
20 A1 2a claret ('17) 90.00 45.00
a. Tete beche pair 250.00 —
21 A1 2a brown ('17) 90.00 45.00
a. Tete beche pair 250.00 —
22 A1 4a dull green 150.00 150.00
a. Tete beche pair *900.00* *900.00*

Frame Recut on All Cliches, Fewer Lines

1903-04 Native Wove Paper *Imperf.*

23 A1 1a bright blue 20.00 13.00
a. Tete beche pair 60.00 42.50

Pin-perf.

24 A1 1a bright blue 30.00
a. Tete beche pair *120.00*

European Wove Paper

23b A1 1a blue 1,500. 1,000.
23c Tete beche pair 2,500.

Pin-perf.

24b A1 1a blue 1,500. 2,000.
24c Tete beche pair 3,500.

No. 23 exists in emerald on native wove paper. All known examples are used with telegraph cancels.

Siva Mahadeva — A3

1907 Engr. *Perf. 13½*
European Wove Paper

26 A3 2p brown 6.00 1.60
27 A3 4p green 6.00 1.60
28 A3 8p carmine 8.00 1.60
29 A3 16p violet 16.00 4.00
Nos. 26-29 (4) 36.00 8.80

Type A3 has five characters in bottom panel, reading "Gurkha Sirkar." Date divided in lower corners is "1964." Outer side panels carry denomination (also on A5).

A4

1917-18 *Imperf.*

29A A4 1a bright blue 12.00 5.00
b. 1a indigo 12.00 6.00
c. Pin-perf. 17.50 15.00

No. 29A may not have been used postally.

In 1917 a telephone and telegraph system was started and remainder stocks and further printings of designs A1 and A2 were used to pay telegrams fees. Design A4 was designed for telegraph use but was valid for postal use. After 1929 design A3 was used for telegrams. The usual telegraph cancellation is crescent-shaped.

Type of 1907 Redrawn

A5

Nine characters in bottom panel reading "Nepal Sirkar"

1930 *Perf. 14, 14½*
Size: 24¾x18¾mm

30 A5 2p dark brown 8.00 .55
31 A5 4p green 8.00 .80
32 A5 8p deep red 30.00 2.00
33 A5 16p dark red vio 20.00 2.00
34 A5 24p orange yellow 16.00 2.50
35 A5 32p dark ultra 20.00 2.50

Size: 26x19½mm

36 A5 1r orange red 24.00 6.00

Size: 28x21mm

37 A5 5r brown & black 27.50 *16.00*
Nos. 30-37 (8) 153.50 *32.35*

On Nos. 30-37 the date divided in lower corners is "1986."

Type of 1929 Redrawn

Date characters in Lower Corners read "1992"

1935 Unwmk. Engr. *Perf. 14*

38 A5 2p dark brown 4.00 .80
39 A5 4p green 4.00 1.20
40 A5 8p bright red 50.00 6.00
41 A5 16p dk red violet 16.00 2.00
42 A5 24p orange yellow 10.00 3.00
43 A5 32p dark ultra 10.00 3.00
Nos. 38-43 (6) 94.00 16.00

Redrawn Type of 1935
Perf. 11, 11x11½, 12x11½

1941-46 Typo.

44 A5 2p black brown .40 .40
a. 2p green (error) 8.00 8.00
45 A5 4p bright green 1.20 .80
46 A5 8p rose red .80 .55
47 A5 16p chocolate ('42) 12.00 3.00
48 A5 24p orange ('46) 12.00 2.00
49 A5 32p deep blue ('46) 16.00 2.50

Size: 29x19½mm

50 A5 1r henna brown ('46) 32.50 20.00
Nos. 44-50 (7) 74.90 29.25
Set, never hinged 160.00

Exist imperf. vert. or horiz. Full imperf. examples were not regularly issued.

Swayambhunath Stupa — A6

Temple of Krishna A7

View of Kathmandu A8

Pashupati (Siva Mahadeva) — A9

Designs: 4p, Temple of Pashupati. 6p, Tri-Chundra College. 8p, Mahabuddha Temple. 24p, Guheswori Temple, Patan. 32p, The 22 Fountains, Balaju.

Perf. 13½x14, 13½, 14

1949, Oct. 1 Litho. Unwmk.

51 A6 2p brown .50 .50
52 A6 4p green .50 .50
53 A6 6p rose pink 1.10 .80
54 A6 8p vermilion 1.20 1.20
55 A7 16p rose lake 1.20 1.20
56 A8 20p blue 1.25 1.10
57 A8 24p carmine 2.50 2.00
58 A8 32p ultramarine 3.50 2.00
59 A9 1r red orange 16.00 20.00
Nos. 51-59 (9) 27.75 29.30
Set, never hinged 60.00

King Tribhuvana Bir Bikram — A10

1954, Apr. 15 Unwmk. *Perf. 14*
Size: 18x22mm

60 A10 2p chocolate 1.10 .50
61 A10 4p green 4.00 1.75
62 A10 6p rose .85 .50
63 A10 8p violet .50 .55
64 A10 12p red orange 9.00 2.75

Size: 25½x29½mm

65 A10 16p red brown .85 .50
66 A10 20p car rose 2.00 1.75
67 A10 24p rose car 1.50 1.75
68 A10 32p ultramarine 2.00 1.75
69 A10 50p rose pink 20.00 7.50
70 A10 1r vermilion 24.00 13.00
71 A10 2r orange 21.00 10.00
Nos. 60-71 (12) 86.80 42.30
Set, never hinged 160.00

Map of Nepal — A11

1954, Apr. 15 Size: 29½x17½mm

72 A11 2p chocolate 1.10 1.10
73 A11 4p green 4.00 1.75
74 A11 6p rose 11.00 2.75
75 A11 8p violet .65 .30
76 A11 12p red orange 17.00 .80

Size: 38x21½mm

77 A11 16p red brown .85 .40
78 A11 20p car rose 1.25 .40
79 A11 24p rose lake 1.25 .40
80 A11 32p ultramarine 1.75 .70
81 A11 50p rose pink 17.50 2.50
82 A11 1r vermilion 21.00 3.00
83 A11 2r orange 15.00 3.00
Nos. 72-83 (12) 92.35 17.10
Set, never hinged 200.00

Planting Rice A12

Throne A13

Hanuman Gate — A14

King Mahendra Bir Bikram and Queen Ratna — A15

Design: 8p, Ceremonial arch and elephant.

Perf. 13½x14, 11½, 13½, 14
Litho., Photo. (6p)

1956 Granite Paper Unwmk.

84 A12 4p green 3.50 *6.75*
85 A13 6p brt scar & yel org 1.60 *3.00*
86 A12 8p dark lilac 1.25 *1.50*
87 A14 24p carmine rose 2.75 *6.00*
88 A15 1r claret 55.00 *82.50*
Nos. 84-88 (5) 64.10 *99.75*
Set, never hinged 135.00

Coronation of King Mahendra Bir Bikram and Queen Ratna Rajya Lakshmi.

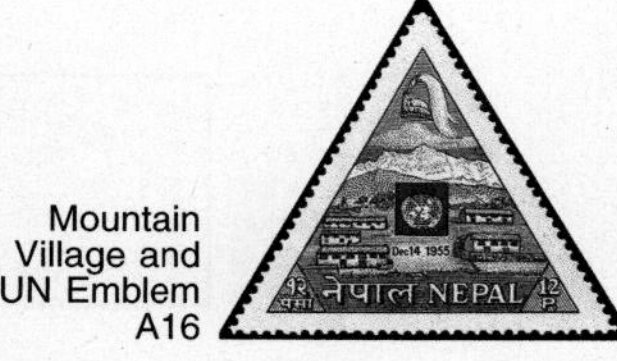
Mountain Village and UN Emblem A16

1956, Dec. 14 Litho. *Perf. 13½*
89 A16 12p ultra & orange 3.75 *6.00*
Never hinged 7.50

1st anniv. of Nepal's admission to the UN.

Crown of Nepal — A17

Perf. 13½x14
1957, June 22 Unwmk.

Size: 18x22mm

90 A17 2p dull brn pur .50 *1.00*
91 A17 4p light green .70 *1.00*
92 A17 6p rose carmine .50 *1.00*
93 A17 8p light violet .50 *1.00*
94 A17 12p orange red 2.75 *1.75*

Size: 25½x30mm

95 A17 16p red brown 4.00 2.75
96 A17 20p rose carmine 6.00 3.75
97 A17 24p rose red 4.00 3.50
98 A17 32p ultramarine 5.50 3.75
99 A17 50p magenta 12.00 8.00
100 A17 1r red orange 15.00 15.00
101 A17 2r orange 10.00 *11.00*
Nos. 90-101 (12) 61.45 *53.50*
Set, never hinged 110.00

Lumbini Temple — A18

1958, Dec. 10 Typo. *Perf. 11*
Without Gum
102 A18 6p yellow 2.00 2.00

10th anniversary of Universal Declaration of Human Rights. Exists imperf.

Catalogue values for unused stamps in this section, from this point to the end of the section, are for Never Hinged items.

Map and Flag — A19

1959, Feb. 18 Engr. *Perf. 14½*
103 A19 6p carmine & light green .85 .50

First general elections in Nepal.

Statue of Vishnu, Changu Narayan A20

Krishna Conquering Black Serpent A21

Designs: 4p, Nepalese glacier. 6p, Golden Gate, Bhaktapur. 8p, Nepalese musk deer. 12p, Rhinoceros. 16p, 20p, 24p, 32p, 50p, Nyatapola Temple, Bhatgaon. 1r, 2r, Himalayan impeyan pheasant. 5r, Satyr tragopan.

Perf. 13½x14, 14x13½
1959-60 Litho. Unwmk.

Size: 18x22mm

104 A20 1p chocolate .25 .25
105 A21 2p gray violet .25 .25
106 A20 4p light ultra .55 .40
107 A20 6p vermilion .55 .25
108 A21 8p sepia .40 .25
109 A21 12p greenish gray .55 .25

Size: 25½x30mm

110 A20 16p brown & lt vio .55 .25
111 A20 20p blue & dull rose 2.00 1.00
112 A20 24p green & pink 2.00 1.00
113 A20 32p brt vio & ultra 1.20 1.00
114 A20 50p rose red & grn 2.00 1.00
115 A20 1r redsh brn & bl 24.00 8.50
116 A20 2r rose lil & ultra 16.00 9.00
117 A20 5r vio & rose red ('60) 100.00 80.00
Nos. 104-117 (14) 150.30 103.40

Nepal's admission to the UPU.

Spinning Wheel — A22

1959, Apr. 10 Typo. *Perf. 11*
118 A22 2p dark red brown .75 .35

Issued to promote development of cottage industries.
Exists imperf. Value $26.

King Mahendra — A23

1959, Apr. 14
119 A23 12p bluish black .65 .50

Nepal's admission to UPU. Exists imperf. and ungummed. Value $200.
No. 119 exists with paper maker's watermark "LOVELY BOND / MADE IN SWEDEN". Value, unused or used, $12.

King Mahendra Opening Parliament A24

1959, July 1 Unwmk. *Perf. 10½*
120 A24 6p deep carmine 3.50 1.20

First session of Parliament. Exists imperf. Value, pair $45.

Sri Pashupati Nath — A25

1959, Nov. 19 *Perf. 11*

Size: 18x24½mm
121 A25 4p dp yellow green .80 .80

Size: 20½x28mm
122 A25 8p carmine 1.60 1.00

Size: 24½x33mm
123 A25 1r light blue 10.00 6.50
Nos. 121-123 (3) 12.40 8.30

Renovation of Sri Pashupati Temple. Nos. 121-123 exist imperf. between.

King Mahendra — A26

1960, June 11 Photo. *Perf. 14*
Size: 25x30mm
124 A26 1r red lilac 1.75 1.25

King Mahendra's 40th birthday. See Nos. 147-151A. For overprint see No. O15.

Children, Temple and Mt. Everest — A27

1960 Typo. *Perf. 11*
125 A27 6p dark blue 17.50 12.00

1st Children's Day, Mar. 1, 1960. Printed in sheets of four. Exists imperf.; value $45 unused.

Mount Everest — A28

Himalaya mountain peaks: 5p, Machha Puchhre. 40p, Mansalu.

1960-61 Photo. *Perf. 14*
126 A28 5p claret & brown ('61) .50 .25
127 A28 10p ultra & rose lilac .70 .25
128 A28 40p vio & red brn ('61) 1.50 .85
Nos. 126-128 (3) 2.70 1.35

King Tribhuvana — A29

1961, Feb. 18 *Perf. 13x13½*
129 A29 10p red brown & orange .75 .25

Tenth Democracy Day.

King Mahendra — A30

1961, June 11 *Perf. 14x14½*
130 A30 6p emerald .40 .40
131 A30 12p ultramarine .55 .55
132 A30 50p carmine rose 1.20 1.20
133 A30 1r brown 2.00 2.00
Nos. 130-133 (4) 4.15 4.15

King Mahendra's 41st birthday.

Prince Gyanendra Canceling Stamps — A31

1961 Typo. *Perf. 11*
134 A31 12p orange *40.00 40.00*

Children's Day, Mar. 1, 1961.
Exists imperf. Value, $75.

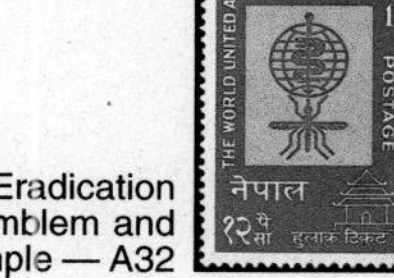
Malaria Eradication Emblem and Temple — A32

Design: 1r, Emblem and Nepalese flag.

1962, Apr. 7 Litho. *Perf. 13x13½*
135 A32 12p blue & lt blue .40 .40
136 A32 1r magenta & orange 1.25 1.25

WHO drive to eradicate malaria.

King Mahendra — A33

1962, June 11 Unwmk. *Perf. 13*
137 A33 10p slate blue .25 .25
138 A33 15p brown .40 .40
139 A33 45p dull red brown .75 .75
140 A33 1r olive gray 1.20 1.20
Nos. 137-140 (4) 2.60 2.60

King Mahendra's 42nd birthday.

Bhanu Bhakta Acharya — A34

10p, Moti Ram Bhatta. 40p, Shambu Prasad.

1962 Photo. *Perf. 14x14½*
141 A34 5p orange brown .40 .40
142 A34 10p deep aqua .40 .40
143 A34 40p olive bister .55 .55
Nos. 141-143 (3) 1.35 1.35

Issued to honor Nepalese poets.

Mahendra Type of 1960 and

King Mahendra — A35

1962-66 *Perf. 14½x14*
144 A35 1p car rose .25 .25
145 A35 2p brt blue .25 .25
145A A35 3p gray ('66) .80 .40
146 A35 5p golden brown .25 .25

Perf. 14x14½
Size: 21½x38mm
147 A26 10p rose claret .25 .25
148 A26 40p brown .40 .40
149 A26 75p blue green 12.00 12.00

Perf. 14
Size: 25x30mm
150 A26 2r red orange 1.50 1.50
151 A26 5r gray green 3.25 3.25
151A A26 10r violet ('66) 11.00 9.50
Nos. 144-151A (10) 29.95 28.05

See No. 199. For overprints see Nos. O12-O14.

Blackboard, Book and UN Emblem — A36

1963, Jan. 6 *Perf. 14½x14*
152 A36 10p dark gray .50 .25
153 A36 15p brown .65 .40
154 A36 50p violet blue 1.20 .75
Nos. 152-154 (3) 2.35 1.40

UNESCO "Education for All" campaign.

Five-pointed Star and Hands Holding Lamps — A37

Unwmk.

1963, Feb. 19 Photo. *Perf. 13*

155 A37 5p blue .30 .25
156 A37 10p reddish brown .30 .25
157 A37 50p rose lilac .90 .55
158 A37 1r blue green 1.75 .80
Nos. 155-158 (4) 3.25 1.85

Panchayat System and National Day.

Man, Tractor and Wheat — A38

1963, Mar. 21 *Perf. 14x14½*

159 A38 10p orange .55 .25
160 A38 15p dark ultra .80 .40
161 A38 50p dp bl grn 1.75 .80
162 A38 1r red brown 2.50 1.40
Nos. 159-162 (4) 5.60 2.85

FAO "Freedom from Hunger" campaign.

Map of Nepal and Hand — A39

1963, Apr. 14 Unwmk. *Perf. 13*

163 A39 10p green .40 .25
164 A39 15p claret .80 .40
165 A39 50p slate 1.75 .55
166 A39 1r violet blue 2.75 .90
Nos. 163-166 (4) 5.70 2.10

Rastriya Panchayat system.

King Mahendra — A40

1963, June 11 *Perf. 13*

167 A40 5p violet .30 .25
168 A40 10p brown orange .50 .25
169 A40 15p dull green .75 .40
Nos. 167-169 (3) 1.55 .90

King Mahendra's 43rd birthday.

East-West Highway on Map of Nepal and King Mahendra — A41

1964, Feb. 19 Photo. *Perf. 13*

170 A41 10p blue & dp orange .40 .25
171 A41 15p dk blue & dp org .60 .25
172 A41 50p dk grn & redsh brn 1.25 .40
Nos. 170-172 (3) 2.25 .90

Issued to publicize the East-West Highway as "The Prosperity of the Country."

King Mahendra Speaking Before Microphone — A42

1964, June 11 *Perf. 14*

173 A42 1p brown olive .30 .25
174 A42 2p gray .40 .25
175 A42 2r golden brown 1.75 1.20
Nos. 173-175 (3) 2.45 1.70

King Mahendra's 44th birthday.

Crown Prince Birendra — A43

Perf. 14x14½

1964, Dec. 28 Photo. Unwmk.

176 A43 10p dark green 1.10 .85
177 A43 15p brown 1.10 .85

19th birthday (coming of age) of Crown Prince Birendra Bir Bikram Shah Deva.

Nepalese Flag and Swords, Olympic Emblem — A44

1964, Dec. 31 Litho. *Perf. 13x13½*

178 A44 10p red & ultra 1.75 .80

18th Olympic Games, Tokyo, Oct. 10-25.

Farmer Plowing A45

Family A46

Designs: 5p, Grain. 10p, Chemical plant.

1965 Photo. *Perf. 13½*

179 A45 2p bl grn & char .40 .40
180 A45 5p dull grn & brn .40 .40
181 A45 10p gray & purple .40 .40
182 A46 15p yellow & brown .55 .55
Nos. 179-182 (4) 1.75 1.75

Issued to publicize land reform.
The 2p also exists on light green paper.
Issue dates: 15p, Feb. 10; others, Dec. 16.

Mail Circling Globe — A47

1965, Apr. 13 *Perf. 14½x14*

183 A47 15p rose lilac .75 .40

Issued for Nepalese New Year.

King Mahendra — A48

Perf. 14x14½

1965, June 11 Photo. Unwmk.

184 A48 50p rose violet 1.00 .75

King Mahendra's 45th birthday.

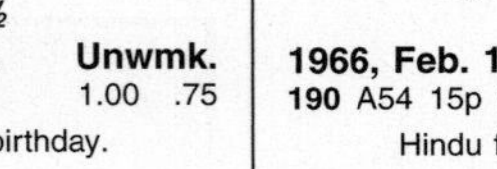

Victims of Revolution, 1939-40 — A49

1965, June 11 *Perf. 13*

185 A49 15p bright green .45 .40

The men executed by the Rana Government 1939-40 were: Shukra Raj Shastri, Dasharath Chand, Dharma Bhakta and Ganga Lal Shresta.

ITU Emblem — A50

1965, Sept. 15 Photo. *Perf. 13*

186 A50 15p deep plum & black .55 .40

Cent. of the ITU.

Devkota — A51

1965, Oct. 14 *Perf. 14x14½*

187 A51 15p red brown .40 .30

Lakshmi Prasad Devkota (1908-1959), poet.

ICY Emblem — A52

Engr. and Litho.

1965, Oct. 24 *Perf. 11½x12*

188 A52 1r multicolored 1.20 .90

International Cooperation Year.

Nepalese Flag and King — A53

1966, Feb. 18 Photo. *Perf. 14½x14*

189 A53 15p blue & red .80 .55

Issued for Democracy Day.

Siva, Parvati and Pashupati Temple — A54

1966, Feb. 18 *Perf. 14*

190 A54 15p violet .50 .40

Hindu festival Maha Sivaratri.

Emblem A55

Perf. 14½x14

1966, June 10 Photo. Unwmk.

191 A55 15p dk green & orange .70 .40

National Philatelic Exhib., June 10-16.

King Mahendra — A56

1966, June 11 *Perf. 13x13½*

192 A56 15p yellow & vio brown .45 .30

Issued for King Mahendra's 46th birthday.

Kanti Rajya Lakshmi — A57

1966, July 5 Photo. *Perf. 14x14½*

193 A57 15p golden brown .40 .40

60th birthday of Queen Mother Kanti Rajya Lakshmi.

Queen Ratna Rajya Lakshmi Devi Shah — A58

1966, Aug. 19 Photo. *Perf. 13*

194 A58 15p yellow & brown .50 .40

Issued for Children's Day.

Krishna with Consort Radha and Flute — A59

1966, Sept. 7

195 A59 15p dk purple & yellow .50 .40

Krishnastami 2023, the birthday of Krishna.

King Mahendra — A60

1966, Oct. 1 Photo. *Perf. 14½x14*

196 A60 50p slate grn & dp car 4.50 1.50

Issued to commemorate the official recognition of the Nepalese Red Cross.

Opening of WHO Headquarters Building, Geneva — A61

1966, Nov. 11 Photo. *Perf. 14*

197 A61 1r purple 2.50 1.50

Lekhnath Paudyal — A62

1966, Dec. 29 Photo. *Perf. 14*

198 A62 15p dull violet blue .60 .50

Lekhnath Paudyal (1884-1966), poet.

King Type of 1962

1967, Feb. 10 Photo. *Perf. 14½x14*

199 A35 75p blue green 1.60 .80

Rama and Sita — A63

1967, Apr. 18 Litho. *Perf. 14*

200 A63 15p brown & yellow .50 .40

Rama Navami 2024, the birthday of Rama.

Buddha — A64

1967, May 23 Photo. *Perf. 13½x13*

201 A64 75p orange & purple 1.00 1.00

2,511th birthday of Buddha.

King Mahendra Addressing Crowd and Himalayas A65

1967, June 11 *Perf. 13*

202 A65 15p dk brown & lt blue .50 .40

King Mahendra's 47th birthday.

Queen Ratna among Children — A66

1967, Aug. 20 Photo. *Perf. 13*

203 A66 15p pale yel & dp brown .50 .40

Issued for Children's Day on the birthday of Queen Ratna Rajya Lakshmi Devi Shah.

Durbar Square, Bhaktapur — A67

5p, Ama Dablam Mountain, ITY emblem.

1967, Oct. 24 *Perf. 13½x14*

Size: 29½x21mm

204 A67 5p violet .40 .40

Perf. 14½x14

Size: 37½x19½mm

205 A67 65p brown .80 .80

Intl. Tourist Year, 1967. See No. C2.

Official Reading Proclamation A68

1967, Dec. 16 Litho. *Perf. 13*

206 A68 15p multicolored .50 .40

"Back to the Villages" campaign.

Crown Prince Birendra, Boy Scouts and Scout Emblem — A69

1967, Dec. 29 Photo. *Perf. 14½x14*

207 A69 15p ultramarine .80 .55

60th anniv. of Boy Scouts.

Prithvi Narayan — A70

1968, Jan. 11 *Perf. 14x14½*

208 A70 15p blue & rose .80 .55

Rajah Prithvi Narayan (1779-1839), founder of modern Nepal.

Arms of Nepal — A71

1968, Feb. 19 Photo. *Perf. 14x14½*

209 A71 15p crimson & dk blue .80 .55

Issued for National Day.

WHO Emblem and Flag of Nepal — A72

1968, Apr. 7 *Perf. 13*

210 A72 1.20r dull yel, red & ultra 3.50 2.50

World Health Day (UN WHO).

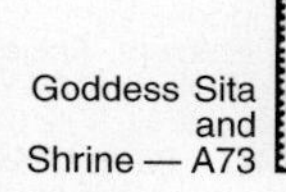

Goddess Sita and Shrine — A73

1968, May 6 Photo. *Perf. 14½x14*

211 A73 15p violet & org brown .80 .40

King Mahendra, Pheasant and Himalayas — A74

1968, June 11 Photo. *Perf. 13½*

212 A74 15p multicolored 4.50 .40

King Mahendra's 48th birthday.

Flag, Children and Queen Ratna — A75

1968, Aug. 19 Litho. *Perf. 13x13½*

213 A75 5p blue grn, yel & ver .50 .30

Fourth National Children's Day.

Buddha and Human Rights Flame — A76

1968, Dec. 10 Photo. *Perf. 14½x14*

214 A76 1r dk green & red 3.00 2.00

International Human Rights Year.

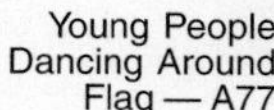

Young People Dancing Around Flag — A77

1968, Dec. 28 Photo. *Perf. 14½x14*

215 A77 25p violet blue .80 .55

23rd birthday of Crown Prince Birendra, which is celebrated as Youth Festival.

UN Building, Nepalese and UN Flags — A78

1969, Jan. 1 *Perf. 13½x13*

216 A78 1r multicolored 1.25 .90

Issued to commemorate Nepal's admission to the UN Security Council for 1969-1970.

Amsu Varma — A79

Portraits: 25p, Ram Shah. 50p, Bhimsen Thapa.

1969, Apr. 13 Photo. *Perf. 14x14½*

217 A79 15p green & purple .55 .55
218 A79 25p blue green .80 .80
219 A79 50p orange brown 1.00 1.00
Nos. 217-219 (3) 2.35 2.35

Amsu Varma, 7th cent. ruler and reformer; Ram Shah, 17th cent. ruler and reformer, and Bhimsen Thapa, 18-19th cent. administrator and reformer.

ILO Emblem — A80

1969, May 1 Photo. *Perf. 14½x14*

220 A80 1r car rose, blk & lt brown 6.00 4.00

50th anniv. of the ILO.

King Mahendra — A81

1969, June 20 *Perf. 13½x13*

221 A81 25p gold & multi .50 .50

King Mahendra's 49th birthday (50th by Oriental count). Issuance delayed from June 11 to 20.

King Tribhuvana and Wives — A82

1969, July 1 *Perf. 14½x14*

222 A82 25p yellow & ol gray .50 .45

64th anniv. of the birth of King Tribhuvana.

Queen Ratna & Child Playing — A83

1969, Aug. 20 Photo. *Perf. 14x14½*

223 A83 25p gray & rose car .50 .50

5th Natl. Children's Day and to for the 41st birthday of Queen Ratna Rajya Lakshmi Devi Shah.

Rhododendron & Himalayas — A84

Flowers: No. 225, Narcissus. No. 226, Marigold. No. 227, Poinsettia.

1969, Sept. 17 Photo. *Perf. 13½*

224 A84 25p lt blue & multi .60 .45
225 A84 25p brown red & multi .60 .45
226 A84 25p black & multi .60 .45
227 A84 25p multicolored .60 .45
a. Block of 4, #224-227 3.50 3.50

Durga, Goddess of Victory — A85

1969, Oct. 17 Photo. *Perf. 14x14½*

228 A85 15p black & orange .50 .40
229 A85 50p black, bis brn & vio 1.10 1.00

Issued to celebrate the Dasain Festival.

Crown Prince Birendra and Princess Aishwarya — A86

1970, Feb. 27 Photo. *Perf. 13½*

230 A86 25p multicolored .70 .40

Wedding of Crown Prince Birendra Bir Bikram Shah Deva and Crown Princess Aishwarya Rajya Lakshmi Devi Rana, Feb. 27-28.

Agricultural Products, Cow, Fish — A87

1970, Mar. 21 Litho. *Perf. 12½*

231 A87 25p multicolored .70 .50

Issued to publicize the Agricultural Year.

Bal Bhadra Kunwar — A88

1970, Apr. 13 Photo. *Perf. 14½x14*

232 A88 1r ol bister & red lilac 1.50 1.00

Bal Bhadra Kunwar, leader in the 1814 battle of Kalanga against British forces.

King Mahendra, Mountain Peak and Crown A89

1970, June 11 Litho. *Perf. 11½*

233 A89 50p gold & multi 1.20 .60

King Mahendra's 50th birthday.

Gosainkund — A90

Lakes: 25p, Phewa Tal. 1r, Rara Daha.

1970, June 11 Photo. *Perf. 13½*

234 A90 5p dull yellow & multi .50 .40
235 A90 25p gray & multi .75 .60
236 A90 1r pink & multi 1.25 1.10
Nos. 234-236 (3) 2.50 2.10

A.P.Y. Emblem — A91

1970, July 1 *Perf. 14½x14*

237 A91 1r dark blue & blue 1.25 .90

Asian Productivity Year 1970.

Bal Mandir Building and Queen Ratna — A92

1970, Aug. 20 Photo. *Perf. 14½x14*

238 A92 25p gray & bister brn .60 .40

Issued for Children's Day. The Bal Mandir Building in Taulihawa is the headquarters of the National Children's Organization.

New UPU Headquarters, Bern — A93

1970, Oct. 9 Photo. *Perf. 14½x14*

239 A93 2.50r ocher & sepia 2.50 1.75

UN Flag — A94

1970, Oct. 24 Photo. *Perf. 14½x14*

240 A94 25p blue & brown .60 .40

25th anniversary of the United Nations.

Royal Palace and Square, Patan — A95

25p, Bodhnath stupa, near Kathmandu, vert. 1r, Gauri Shankar, holy mountain.

Perf. 11x11½, 11½x11

1970, Dec. 28 Litho.

241 A95 15p multicolored .50 .25
242 A95 25p multicolored 1.00 .50
243 A95 1r multicolored 1.75 .80
Nos. 241-243 (3) 3.25 1.55

Crown Prince Birendra's 25th birthday.

Statue of Harihar (Vishnu-Siva) — A96

1971, Jan. 26 Photo. *Perf. 14x14½*

244 A96 25p bister brn & black .60 .40

Torch and Target — A97

1971, Mar. 21 Photo. *Perf. 13½x13*

245 A97 1r bluish gray & dp org 1.50 1.00

Intl. year against racial discrimination.

King Mahendra and Subjects — A98

1971, June 11 Photo. *Perf. 14½x14*

246 A98 25p dull purple & blue .70 .30

King Mahendra's 51st birthday.

Sweta Bhairab (Siva) — A99

Sculptures of Siva: 25p, Manhankal Bhairab. 50p, Kal Bhairab.

1971, July 11 *Perf. 13x13½*

247 A99 15p org brn & blk .50 .40
248 A99 25p lt green & black .60 .50
249 A99 50p blue & black 1.10 .85
Nos. 247-249 (3) 2.20 1.75

Queen Ratna Receiving Garland — A100

1971, Aug. 20 Photo. *Perf. 11½*
Granite Paper

250 A100 25p gray & multi .60 .35

Children's Day, Queen Ratna's birthday.

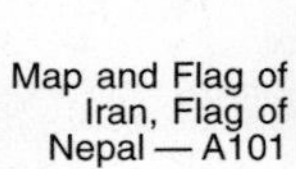

Map and Flag of Iran, Flag of Nepal — A101

1971, Oct. 14 Granite Paper

251 A101 1r pink & multi 1.50 .75

2500th anniversary of the founding of the Persian empire by Cyrus the Great.

UNICEF Emblem, Mother and Child — A102

1971, Dec. 11 *Perf. 14½x14*

252 A102 1r gray blue 1.50 1.00

25th anniversary of UNICEF.

Everest — A103

Himalayan Peaks: 1r, Kangchenjunga. 1.80r, Annapurna I.

1971, Dec. 28 *Perf. 13½x13*

253 A103 25p blue & brown .40 .25
254 A103 1r dp blue & brown .80 .50
255 A103 1.80r blue & yel brown 1.60 1.00
Nos. 253-255 (3) 2.80 1.75

"Visit Nepal."

Royal Standard — A104

1972, Feb. 19 Photo. *Perf. 13*

256 A104 25p dark red & black .75 .30

National Day.

Araniko and White Dagoba, Peking — A105

1972, Apr. 13 Litho. *Perf. 13*

257 A105 15p lt blue & ol gray .30 .25

Araniko, a 14th century Nepalese architect, who built the White Dagoba at the Miaoying Monastery, Peking, 1348.

Book Year Emblem, Ancient Book — A106

1972, Sept. 8 Photo. *Perf. 14½x14*

258 A106 2p ocher & brown .25 .25
259 A106 5p tan & black .30 .25
260 A106 1r blue & black 1.00 .90
Nos. 258-260 (3) 1.55 1.40

International Book Year.

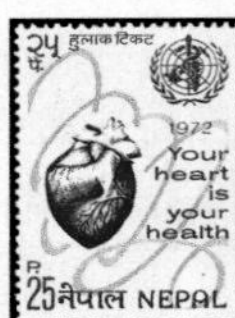
Heart and WHO Emblem — A107

1972, Nov. 6 Photo. *Perf. 13x13½*

261 A107 25p dull grn & claret .50 .40

"Your heart is your health," World Health Month.

King Mahendra (1920-1972) A108

1972, Dec. 15 Photo. *Perf. 13½x13*

262 A108 25p brown & black .50 .30

King Birendra — A109

1972, Dec. 28 Photo. *Perf. 13x13½*

263 A109 50p ocher & purple .60 .50

King Birendra's 27th birthday.

Northern Border Costume — A110

Nepalese Costumes: 50p, Hill dwellers. 75p, Kathmandu Valley couple. 1r, Inner Terai couple.

1973, Feb. 18 Photo. *Perf. 13*

264 A110 25p dull lilac & multi .40 .25
265 A110 50p lemon & multi .50 .40
266 A110 75p multicolored .75 .50
267 A110 1r multicolored 1.00 .70
a. Block of 4, #264-267 3.25 3.25

National Day.

Babu Ram Acharya (1888-1972), Historian — A111

1973, Mar. 12 Photo. *Perf. 13*

268 A111 25p olive gray & car .50 .30

Nepalese Family and Home — A112

1973, Apr. 7 Photo. *Perf. 14½x14*

269 A112 1r Prus blue & ocher 1.25 .85

25th anniv. of the WHO.

Lumbini Garden, Birthplace of Buddha A113

1973, May 17 Photo. *Perf. 13x13½*

270 A113 25p shown .40 .25
271 A113 75p Mt. Makalu .55 .30
272 A113 1r Gorkha Village .80 .80
Nos. 270-272 (3) 1.75 1.35

FAO Emblem, Women Farmers — A114

1973, June 29 Photo. *Perf. 14½x14*

273 A114 10p dark gray & violet .30 .25

World food program, 10th anniversary.

INTERPOL Headquarters and Emblem — A115

1973, Sept. 3

274 A115 25p bister & blue .50 .30

50th anniversary of the International Criminal Police Organization (INTERPOL).

Shom Nath Sigdyal (1884-1972), Scholar — A116

1973, Oct. 5 Photo. *Perf. 13x13½*

275 A116 1.25r violet blue 1.25 .85

Cow — A117

1973, Oct. 25 Photo. *Perf. 13½x13*

276	A117	2p shown	.30	.25
277	A117	3.25r Yak	1.75	1.50

Festival of Lights (Tihar).

King Birendra A118

Perf. 13, 13½x14, 15x14½

1973-74 Photo.

278	A118	5p dark brown	.25	.25
279	A118	15p ol brn & dk brn ('74)	.30	.25
280	A118	1r reddish brn & dk brn ('74)	.80	.55
		Nos. 278-280 (3)	1.35	1.05

King Birendra's 28th birthday.

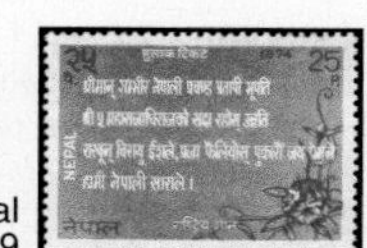

National Anthem — A119

Natl. Day: 1r, Score of national anthem.

1974, Feb. 18 Photo. *Perf. 13½x13*

281	A119	25p rose carmine	.50	.25
282	A119	1r deep green	.80	.65

King Janak on Throne — A120

1974, Apr. 14 Litho. *Perf. 13½*

283	A120	2.50r multicolored	2.00	1.75

Children's Village and SOS Emblem A121

1974, May 20 Litho. *Perf. 13½x13*

284	A121	25p ultra & red	.50	.45

25th anniv. of SOS Children's Village Intl.

Baghchal — A122

1974, July 1 Litho. *Perf. 13*

285	A122	2p Soccer	.25	.25
286	A122	2.75r shown	1.25	.90

Popular Nepalese games.

WPY Emblem — A123

1974, Aug. 19 Litho. *Perf. 13*

287	A123	5p ocher & blue	.30	.25

World Population Year.

UPU Monument, Bern — A124

1974, Oct. 9 Litho. *Perf. 13*

288	A124	1r olive & black	.80	.50

Centenary of Universal Postal Union.

Butterfly — A125

Designs: Nepalese butterflies.

1974, Oct. 16

289	A125	10p lt brown & multi	.25	.25
290	A125	15p lt blue & multi	.65	.30
291	A125	1.25r multicolored	1.25	.75
292	A125	1.75r buff & multi	1.50	1.10
		Nos. 289-292 (4)	3.65	2.40

King Birendra — A126

1974, Dec. 28 Litho. *Perf. 13½x13*

293	A126	25p gray green & black	.30	.25

King Birendra's 29th birthday.

Muktinath A127

Peacock Window A128

1974, Dec. 31 *Perf. 13x13½, 13½x13*

294	A127	25p multicolored	.50	.25
295	A128	1r multicolored	1.00	.55

Tourist publicity.

Guheswari Temple — A129

Rara — A130

Pashupati Temple A131

King Birendra and Queen Aishwarya A132

Designs: 1r, Throne. 1.25r, Royal Palace.

1975, Feb. 24 Litho. *Perf. 13x13½*

296	A129	25p multicolored	.50	.25

Photo.

Perf. 14½x14

297	A130	50p multicolored	.50	.25

Granite Paper

Perf. 11½, 11 (A131)

298	A132	1r olive & multi	.75	.70
299	A132	1.25r multicolored	1.50	.75
300	A131	1.75r multicolored	1.00	.95
301	A132	2.75r gold & multi	1.50	1.25
a.		Souvenir sheet of 3	5.50	5.50
		Nos. 296-301 (6)	5.75	4.15

Coronation of King Birendra, Feb. 24, 1975. No. 301a contains 3 imperf. stamps similar to Nos. 298-299, 301 and label with inscription.

Tourist Year Emblem A133

Swayambhunath Stupa, Kathmandu A134

Perf. 12½x13½, 13½x12½

1975, May 25 Litho.

302	A133	2p yellow & multi	.30	.25
303	A134	25p violet & black	.40	.30

South Asia Tourism Year.

Tiger — A135

1975, July 17 Litho. *Perf. 13*

304	A135	2p shown	.50	.45
305	A135	5p Deer, vert.	.50	.55
306	A135	1r Panda	1.00	1.00
		Nos. 304-306 (3)	2.00	2.00

Wildlife conservation.

Queen Aishwarya and IWY Emblem A136

1975, Nov. 8 Litho. *Perf. 13*

307	A136	1r lt blue & multi	.80	.40

International Women's Year.

Ganesh Peak A137

Rupse Falls A138

Kumari, Living Goddess of Nepal — A139

1975, Dec. 16 Litho. *Perf. 13½*

308	A137	2p multicolored	.25	.25
309	A138	25p multicolored	.35	.30
310	A139	50p multicolored	1.00	.50
		Nos. 308-310 (3)	1.60	1.05

Tourist publicity.

King Birendra — A140

1975, Dec. 28 Photo. *Perf. 13*

311	A140	25p rose lil & red lil	.30	.25

King Birendra's 30th birthday.

Flag and Map of Nepal — A141

1976, Feb. 19 Litho. *Perf. 13*

312	A141	2.50r dark blue & red	1.25	.80

National or Democracy Day.

Rice Cultivation A142

1976, Apr. 11 Litho. *Perf. 13*

313	A142	25p multicolored	.30	.25

Agricultural development.

Flags of Nepal and Colombo Plan — A143

1976, July 1 Photo. *Perf. 13x13½*

314	A143	1r multicolored	.60	.50

Colombo Plan, 25th anniversary.

Runner — A144

1976, July 31 Photo. *Perf. 13x13½*

315	A144	3.25r black & ultra	1.60	1.00

21st Olympic Games, Montreal, Canada, July 17-Aug. 1.

Dove and Map of South East Asia — A145

1976, Aug. 17 Litho. *Perf. 13½*

316	A145	5r bister, black & ultra	2.50	1.50

5th Summit Conference of Non-aligned Countries, Colombo, Sri Lanka, Aug. 9-19.

Folk Dances — A146

1976, Sept. 27 Litho. *Perf. 13½x13*

317	A146	10p Lakha mask	.30	.25
318	A146	15p Maruni	.30	.25
319	A146	30p Jhangad	.50	.25
320	A146	1r Sebru	.75	.40
		Nos. 317-320 (4)	1.85	1.15

Nepalese Lily — A147

Flowers: No. 322, Meconopsis grandis. No. 323, Cardiocrinum giganteum, horiz. No. 324, Megacodon stylophorus, horiz.

1976-77 Litho. *Perf. 13*

321	A147	30p lt ultra & multi	.55	.25
322	A147	30p brown & multi	.55	.25
323	A147	30p violet & multi	.55	.25
324	A147	30p violet & multi	.55	.25
		Nos. 321-324 (4)	2.20	1.00

Issue dates: Nov. 7, 1976, Jan. 24, 1977.

King Birendra — A148

1976, Dec. 28 **Photo.** ***Perf. 14***
325 A148 5p green .30 .25
326 A148 30p multicolored .30 .25

King Birendra's 31st birthday.

Bell and American Bicentennial Emblem — A149

1976, Dec. 31 **Litho.** ***Perf. 13½***
327 A149 10r multicolored 3.00 2.75

American Bicentennial.

Warrior Kazi Amar Singh Thapa, Natl. Hero — A150

1977, Feb. 18 **Photo.** ***Perf. 13x13½***
328 A150 10p multicolored .40 .25

Terracotta Figurine, Kapilavastu Excavations A151

Asoka Pillar, Lumbini — A152

1977, May 3 **Photo.** ***Perf. 14½x14***
329 A151 30p dark violet .30 .25
330 A152 5r green & brown 1.75 1.25

Tourist publicity.

Cheer Pheasant — A153

Birds of Nepal: 5p, Great pied hornbill, vert. 1r, Green magpie. 2.30r, Nepalese laughing thrush, vert.

1977, Sept. 17 **Photo.** ***Perf. 13***
331 A153 5p multicolored .65 .30
332 A153 15p multicolored 1.25 .30
333 A153 1r multicolored 1.75 .65
334 A153 2.30r multicolored 3.50 1.00
Nos. 331-334 (4) 7.15 2.25

Tukuche Peak, Nepalese Police Flag — A154

1977, Oct. 2
335 A154 1.25r multicolored .85 .50

Ascent of Tukuche, Himalaya Mountains, by Nepalese police team, first anniversary.

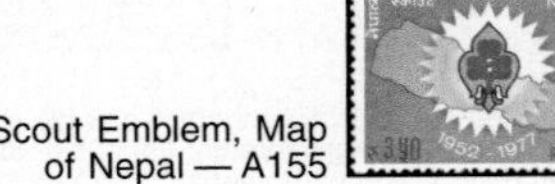
Scout Emblem, Map of Nepal — A155

1977, Nov. 7 **Litho.** ***Perf. 13½***
336 A155 3.50r multicolored 1.25 .85

Boy Scouts of Nepal, 25th anniversary.

Dhanwantari, Health Goddess — A156

1977, Nov. 9 **Photo.** ***Perf. 13***
337 A156 30p bluish green .30 .25

Health Day.

Flags, Map of Nepal — A157

1977, Dec. 5 **Photo.** ***Perf. 13½***
338 A157 1r multicolored .50 .30

Colombo Plan, 26th Consultative Meeting, Kathmandu, Nov. 29-Dec. 7.

King Birendra — A158

1977, Dec. 28
339 A158 5p olive .30 .25
340 A158 1r red brown .55 .50

King Birendra's 32nd birthday.

Post Office Seal, New Post Office — A159

75p, Post Office date stamp & new Post Office.

1978, Apr. 14 **Photo.** ***Perf. 14½x14***
341 A159 25p org brn & blk .25 .25
342 A159 75p bister & black .40 .40

Centenary of Nepalese postal service.

Mt. Everest — A160

Design: 4r, Mt. Everest, different view.

1978, May 29 **Photo.** ***Perf. 13½x13***
343 A160 2.30r red brn & slate 1.25 .75
344 A160 4r grn & vio blue 1.75 1.25

1st ascent of Mt. Everest, 25th anniv.

Mountains, Trees, Environmental Emblem — A161

1978, June 5
345 A161 1r blue green & orange .50 .30

World Environment Day, June 5.

Queen Mother Ratna — A162

1978, Aug. 20 **Photo.** ***Perf. 14***
346 A162 2.30r olive gray .80 .50

Queen Mother Ratna, 50th birthday.

Trisula River Rapids — A163

Tourist Publicity: 50p, Nepalese window. 1r, Dancer, Mahakali dance, vert.

1978, Sept. 15 **Litho.** ***Perf. 14***
347 A163 10p multicolored .30 .25
348 A163 50p multicolored .40 .30
349 A163 1r multicolored .75 .50
Nos. 347-349 (3) 1.45 1.05

Human Rights Emblem — A164

1978, Oct. 10 **Litho.** ***Perf. 13½***
350 A164 25p red brown & red .30 .25
351 A164 1r dark blue & red .50 .30

Universal Declaration of Human Rights, 30th anniversary.

Choerospondias Axillaris — A165

Designs: 1r, Castanopsis indica, vert. 1.25r, Elaeocarpus sphaericus.

1978, Oct. 31 **Photo.** ***Perf. 13***
352 A165 5p multicolored .30 .25
353 A165 1r multicolored .20 .50
354 A165 1.25r multicolored 1.00 .60
Nos. 352-354 (3) 1.50 1.35

King Birendra — A166

1978, Dec. 17 ***Perf. 13½x14***
355 A166 30p brown & indigo .30 .25
356 A166 2r violet & black .80 .65

King Birendra's 33rd birthday.

Kamroop and Patan Temples and Deity A167

Red Machhindra Chariot A168

Perf. 14½x14, 13½
1979 **Photo., Litho.**
357 A167 75p claret & olive .60 .30
358 A168 1.25r multicolored .60 .50

Red Machhindra Nath Festival, Lalitpur (Patan).
Issue dates: 75p, Apr. 27; 1.25r, July 25.

Bas-relief — A169

1979, May 12 **Photo.** ***Perf. 13***
359 A169 1r yellow & brown .60 .30

Lumbini Year.

Tree Planting — A170

1979, June 29 **Photo.** ***Perf. 13x13½***
360 A170 2.30r multicolored 1.25 .75

Afforestation campaign.

Children with Flag, IYC Emblem — A172

1979, Aug. 20 ***Perf. 13½***
362 A172 1r light brown .60 .45

Intl. Year of the Child; Natl. Children's Day.

Mount Pabil — A173

Tourism: 50p, Swargadwari Temple. 1.25r, Altar with statues of Shiva and Parbati.

1979, Sept. 26 **Photo.** ***Perf. 13½x13***
363 A173 30p dk blue green .30 .25
364 A173 50p multicolored .35 .25
365 A173 1.25r multicolored .65 .55
Nos. 363-365 (3) 1.30 1.05

Northern Shrike — A174

Design: 10r, Aethopyga ignicauda.

Perf. 14½x13½
1979, Nov. 22 **Photo.**
366 A174 10p shown .30 .25
367 A174 10r multicolored 7.50 4.75

Intl. World Pheasant Assoc. Symposium, Kathmandu, Nov. 21-23. See No. C7.

Coin, Lichhavi Period, Obverse — A175

Malla Period, Obverse — A175a

Shaw Period, Obverse — A175b

Ancient Coins: No. 369, Lichhavi Period, reverse. No. 371, Malla Period, reverse. No. 373, Shah Period, reverse.

1979, Dec. 16 **Photo.** ***Perf. 15***
368 A175 5p brn & brn org .25 .25
369 A175 5p brn & brn org .25 .25
a. Pair, #368-369 .55 .55
370 A175a 15p dark blue .30 .25
371 A175a 15p dark blue .30 .25
a. Pair, #370-371 .65 .65
372 A175b 1r slate blue .75 .50
373 A175b 1r slate blue .75 .50
a. Pair, #372-373 1.75 1.75
Nos. 368-373 (6) 2.60 2.00

King Birendra A176

Ban-Ganga Dam A177

1979, Dec. 28 Litho. *Perf. 14*

374 A176 25p multicolored .25 .25
375 A177 2.30r multicolored .80 .65

King Birendra's 34th birthday.

Samyak Pooja Festival — A178

1980, Jan. 15 *Perf. 13½*

376 A178 30p vio brn & gray .35 .25

Holy Basil — A179

30p, Himalayan valerian. 1r, Nepalese pepper. 2.30r, Himalayan rhubarb.

1980, Mar. 24 Photo. *Perf. 14x14½*

377 A179 5p shown .25 .25
378 A179 30p multicolored .30 .25
379 A179 1r multicolored .60 .30
380 A179 2.30r multicolored 1.25 .65
Nos. 377-380 (4) 2.40 1.45

Gyandil Das — A180

Nepalese Writers: 30p, Shddhi Das Amatya. 1r, Pahal Man Singh Snwar. 2.30r, Jay Prithibi Bahadur Singh.

1980, Apr. 13 *Perf. 13½x13*

381 A180 5p bister & rose lilac .30 .25
382 A180 30p vio brn & lt red brn .30 .25
383 A180 1r blue & olive gray .40 .30
384 A180 2.30r ol grn & dk blue .80 .60
Nos. 381-384 (4) 1.80 1.40

Jwalaji Dailekh (Temple), Holy Flame — A181

1980, Sept. 14 Litho. *Perf. 14½*

385 A181 10p shown .30 .25
386 A181 1r Godavari Pond .50 .30
387 A181 5r Mt. Dhaulagiri 1.75 1.25
Nos. 385-387 (3) 2.55 1.80

Temple Statue — A182

1980, Oct. 29 *Perf. 14x13½*

388 A182 25r multicolored 7.00 5.00

World Tourism Conf., Manila, Sept. 27.

King Birendra's 35th Birthday — A183

1980, Dec. 28 Litho. *Perf. 14*

389 A183 1r multicolored .60 .25

International Year of the Disabled — A184

1981, Jan. 1

390 A184 5r multicolored 2.00 1.40

Nepal Rastra Bank, 25th Anniv. — A185

1981, Apr. 26 Litho. *Perf. 14*

391 A185 1.75r multicolored .60 .50

Nepalese Stamp Cent. — A186

1981, July 16

392 A186 10p No. 1 .25 .25
393 A186 40p No. 2 .30 .25
394 A186 3.40r No. 3 1.75 1.25
a. Souvenir sheet of 3, #392-394 3.00 3.00
Nos. 392-394 (3) 2.30 1.75

A187

1981, Oct. 30 Litho. *Perf. 14*

395 A187 1.75r multicolored .50 .40

Intl. Hotel Assoc., 70th council meeting, Kathmandu.

Stamp Centenary — A188

1981, Dec. 27 Litho. *Perf. 14*

396 A188 40p multicolored .30 .25

Nepal '81 Stamp Exhibition, Kathmandu, Dec. 27-31.

King Birendra's 36th Birthday — A189

1981, Dec. 28

397 A189 1r multicolored .40 .30

Hrishikesh, Buddhist Stone Carving, Ridi — A190

25p, Tripurasundari Pavilion, Baitadi. 2r, Mt. Langtang Lirung.

1981, Dec. 30

398 A190 5p shown .25 .25
399 A190 25p multicolored .30 .25
400 A190 2r multicolored .75 .50
Nos. 398-400 (3) 1.30 1.00

Royal Nepal Academy, 25th Anniv. — A191

1982, June 23 Litho. *Perf. 14*

401 A191 40p multicolored .35 .25

Balakrishna Sama — A192

1982, July 21 *Perf. 13½*

402 A192 1r multicolored .35 .30

Dish Antenna, Satellite — A193

1982, Nov. 7 Litho. *Perf. 14*

403 A193 5r multicolored 1.40 .80

Mt. Nuptse — A194

Intl. Union of Alpinists Assoc., 50th Anniv. (Himalaya Peaks): b, Mt. Lhotse (31x31mm). c, Mt. Everest (40x31mm). Continuous design.

1982, Nov. 18 *Perf. 13½*

404 A194 Strip of 3 3.50 3.50
a. 25p multicolored .25 .25
b. 2r multicolored .75 .50
c. 3r multicolored 1.75 .90

9th Asian Games — A195

1982, Nov. 19 *Perf. 14*

405 A195 3.40r multicolored 1.25 .80

Kulekhani Hydro-electric Plant — A196

1982, Dec. 2 *Perf. 13½*

406 A196 2r Lake, dam 1.00 .50

King Birendra's 37th Birthday — A197

1982, Dec. 28 *Perf. 12½*

407 A197 5p multicolored .40 .25

A198

1983, June 15 Litho. *Perf. 14*

408 A198 50p multicolored .50 .25

25th anniv. of Nepal Industrial Development Co.

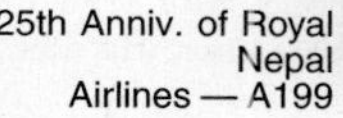

25th Anniv. of Royal Nepal Airlines — A199

1983, Aug. 1 *Perf. 13½*

409 A199 1r multicolored .90 .30

World Communications Year — A200

1983, Oct. 30 Litho. *Perf. 12*

410 A200 10p multicolored .60 .25

Musical Instruments — A201

1983, Nov. 3

411 A201 5p Sarangi .30 .25
412 A201 10p Kwota .50 .25
413 A201 50p Narashinga .60 .25
414 A201 1r Murchunga 1.25 .50
Nos. 411-414 (4) 2.65 1.25

A202

1983, Dec. 20

415 A202 4.50r multicolored 1.75 1.00

Chakrapani Chalise (1883-1957), national anthem composer and poet.

King Birendra's 38th Birthday — A203

1983, Dec. 28 *Perf. 14*

416 A203 5r multicolored 1.50 .80

Temple, Barahkshetra A204

2.20r, Triveni pilgrimage site. 6r, Mt. Cho-oyu.

1983, Dec. 30 *Perf. 14*

417 A204 1r shown .30 .25
418 A204 2.20r multicolored .60 .50
419 A204 6r multicolored 1.75 1.25
Nos. 417-419 (3) 2.65 2.00

Auditor General, 25th Anniv. — A204a

1984, June 28 Litho. *Perf. 14*
419A A204a 25p Open ledger .80 .60

A205

1984, July 1 Litho. *Perf. 14*
420 A205 5r Transmission tower 1.75 1.25

Asia-Pacific Broadcasting Union, 20th anniv.

A206

1984, July 8
421 A206 50p University emblem .45 .25

Tribhuvan University, 25th anniv.

A207

1984, Aug. 5
422 A207 10r Boxing 3.00 2.00

1984 Summer Olympic Games, Los Angeles.

A208

1984, Sept. 18
423 A208 1r multicolored .45 .25

Family Planning Assoc., 25th anniv.

Social Services Day — A209

1984, Sept. 24
424 A209 5p multicolored .40 .25

Wildlife — A210

10p, Gavialis gangeticus. 25p, Panthera uncia. 50p, Antilope cervicapra.

1984, Nov. 30
425 A210 10p multicolored .40 .30
426 A210 25p multicolored .60 .35
427 A210 50p multicolored 1.00 .45
Nos. 425-427 (3) 2.00 1.10

Chhinna Masta Bhagvati Temple and Goddess Sakhandeshwari Devi, Statue — A211

Designs: 10p, Lord Vishu the Giant, Yajna Ceremony on Bali, bas-relief, A. D. 467, vert. 5r, Mt. Api, Himalayas, vert.

1984, Dec. 21
428 A211 10p multicolored .25 .25
429 A211 1r multicolored .30 .30
430 A211 5r multicolored 2.00 1.25
Nos. 428-430 (3) 2.55 1.80

King Birendra, 39th Birthday — A212

1984, Dec. 28
431 A212 1r multicolored .45 .25

Sagarmatha Natl. Park — A213

1985, May 6
432 A213 10r Mt. Everest, wildlife 6.00 2.25

King Mahendra Trust Congress for Nature Conservation, May 6-11.

Illustration from Shiva Dharma Purana, 13th Cent. Book — A214

Design: Maheshware, Lord Shiva, with brahma and vishnu. #433b, left person sitting on wall. #433d, left person on throne.

1985, May 30
433 Strip of 5 3.50 2.50
a.-e. A214 50p any single .40 .25
f. Strip of 5, imperf within 4.50

#433 has a continuous design. Sizes: #433a, 433e, 26x22mm; #433b, 433d, 24x22mm; #433c, 17x22mm.

UN, 40th Anniv. — A215

1985, Oct. 24 Litho. *Perf. 13½x14*
434 A215 5r multicolored 1.50 1.00

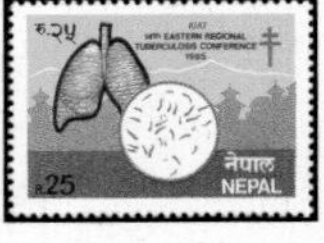
14th Eastern Regional Tuberculosis Conference A216

1985, Nov. 25
435 A216 25r multicolored 6.00 4.00

First South Asian Regional Cooperation Summit — A217

1985, Dec. 8 *Perf. 14*
436 A217 5r Flags 1.50 1.00

Temple of Jaleshwar, Mohottary Underwater Project — A218

1r, Temple of Shaileshwari, Doti. 2r, Lake Phoksundo, Dolpa.

1985, Dec. 15 Litho. *Perf. 14x13½*
437 A218 10p shown .25 .25
438 A218 1r multicolored .55 .30
439 A218 2r multicolored 1.20 .30
Nos. 437-439 (3) 2.00 .85

Intl. Youth Year — A219

1985, Dec. 21 *Perf. 14*
440 A219 1r multicolored .45 .25

Devi Ghat Hydro-electric Dam Project — A220

1985, Dec. 28 Litho. *Perf. 14*
441 A220 2r multicolored .85 .50

King Birendra, 40th Birthday — A221

1985, Dec. 28
442 A221 50p Portrait .45 .25

Panchayat System, 25th Anniv. — A222

1986, Apr. 10 *Perf. 13½*
443 A222 4r multicolored 1.50 1.00

Pharping Hydroelectric Station, 75th Anniv. — A223

1986, Oct. 9 Litho. *Perf. 14x13½*
444 A223 15p multicolored .50 .25

Architecture, Artifacts — A224

5p, Pashupati Temple. 10p, Lumbini Fort. 1r, Crown of Nepal.

1986, Oct. 9 Photo. *Perf. 13x13½*
445 A224 5p multicolored .25 .25
446 A224 10p multicolored .30 .25
446A A224 50p like 5p ('87) .40 .25
447 A224 1r multicolored .50 .25
Nos. 445-447 (4) 1.45 1.00

No. 446A issued Apr. 14.

Asian Productivity Org., 25th Anniv. — A225

1986, Oct. 26 Litho. *Perf. 13½x14*
448 A225 1r multicolored .50 .25

Reclining Buddha, Kathmandu Valley — A226

Mt. Pumori, Khumbu Range — A227

Perf. 14, 13½x13
1986, Oct. 26 Litho.
449 A226 60p multicolored .30 .25
450 A227 8r multicolored 2.75 1.25

King Birendra, 41st Birthday — A228

1986, Dec. 28 Litho. *Perf. 13x13½*
451 A228 1r multicolored .45 .25

Intl. Peace Year — A229

1986, Dec. 28 *Perf. 14*
452 A229 10r multicolored 2.00 1.50

Social Service Natl. Coordination Council, 10th Anniv. — A230

1987, Sept. 22 Litho. *Perf. 13½*
453 A230 1r Natl. flag, emblem .45 .25

Birth of Buddha — A231

Design: Asoka Pillar, enlargement of commemorative text and bas-relief of birth.

1987, Oct. 28 *Perf. 14*
454 A231 4r multicolored 1.25 .75

First Natl. Boy Scout Jamboree, Kathmandu A232

1987, Oct. 28 Litho. *Perf. 14*
455 A232 1r multicolored .85 .40

A233

1987, Nov. 2
456 A233 60p gold & lake .30 .25

3rd SAARC (Southeast Asian Assoc. for Regional Cooperation) Summit Conference, Kathmandu.

A234

1987, Nov. 10
457 A234 4r multicolored 1.10 .75

Rastriya Samachar Samiti (Natl. news agency), 25th anniv.

Intl. Year of Shelter for the Homeless A235

1987, Dec. 21 Litho. *Perf. 14*
458 A235 5r multicolored 1.25 1.00

Kashthamandap Temple, Kathmandu — A236

1987, Dec. 21 Photo. *Perf. 13½x13*
459 A236 25p multicolored .40 .25

Surya Bikram Gyawali (b. 1898), Historian — A237

1987, Dec. 21 *Perf. 13x13½*
460 A237 60p multicolored .50 .25

King Birendra, 42nd Birthday — A238

Perf. 14½x13½
1987, Dec. 28 Litho.
461 A238 25p multicolored .50 .25

Mount Kanjiroba A239

1987, Dec. 30 *Perf. 14*
462 A239 10r multicolored 3.00 1.75

Crown Prince Dipendra's 18th Birthday — A240

1988, Mar. 28 Litho. *Perf. 14*
463 A240 1r multicolored .50 .25

Nepal Bank, Ltd., 50th Anniv. — A241

1988, Apr. 8
464 A241 2r multicolored .50 .25

Kanti Childrens' Hospital, 25th Anniv. — A242

1988, Apr. 8
465 A242 60p multicolored .50 .25

Royal Shuklaphanta Wildlife Reserve — A243

1988, Apr. 8
466 A243 60p Swamp deer 1.00 .25

A244

1988, Aug. 20 Litho. *Perf. 14x13½*
467 A244 5r multicolored 1.25 1.00

Queen Mother Ratna Rajya Laxmi Devi Shah, 60th birthday.

Nepal Red Cross, 25th Anniv. — A245

1988, Sept. 12 Litho. *Perf. 14x13½*
468 A245 1r dull fawn & dark red .50 .25

Bindhyabasini, Pokhara A246

1988, Oct. 16 Litho. *Perf. 14½*
469 A246 15p multicolored .50 .25

King Birendra, 43rd Birthday — A247

1988, Dec. 28 Litho. *Perf. 14*
470 A247 4r multicolored 1.00 .60

A248

1989, Mar. 3 Litho. *Perf. 13½x14*
471 A248 1r Temple .50 .25

Pashupati Area Development Trust.

SAARC Year — A249

1989, Dec. 8 *Perf. 13x13½*
472 A249 60p multicolored *.50* .25

Combating Drug Abuse & Trafficking.

A250

1989, Oct. 5 *Perf. 14*
473 A250 4r vio, brt grn & blk .85 .45

Asia-Pacific Telecommunity, 10th anniv.

King Birendra, 44th Birthday — A251

Perf. 13½x14½
1989, Dec. 28 Litho.
474 A251 2r multicolored .60 .25

Child Survival — A252

Design: Oral rehydration therapy, immunization, breast-feeding and growth monitoring.

1989, Dec. 31 *Perf. 13½*
475 A252 1r multicolored .50 .25

Rara Natl. Park — A253

1989, Dec. 31 *Perf. 14½x15*
476 A253 4r multicolored .60 .30

Mt. Ama Dablam — A254

1989, Dec. 31 *Perf. 14*
477 A254 5r multicolored 1.00 .60

A255

1990, Jan. 3
478 A255 1r multicolored .50 .25

Crown Prince Dipendra investiture, Jan. 3.

Temple of the Goddess Manakamana, Gorkha — A256

1990, Apr. 12 Litho. *Perf. 14½*
479 A256 60p deep blue & black .65 .25

A257

1990, Aug. 20 Litho. *Perf. 14*
480 A257 1r multicolored .50 .25

Nepal Children's Organization, 25th anniv.

Bir Hospital, Cent. — A258

1990, Sept. 13 Litho. *Perf. 14x13½*
481 A258 60p orange, blue & red .50 .25

A259

1990, Oct. 9 *Perf. 14½*
482 A259 4r multicolored .80 .50

Asian-Pacific Postal Training Center, 20th anniv.

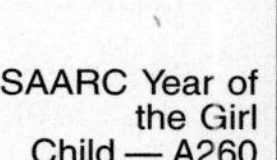

SAARC Year of the Girl Child — A260

1990, Dec. 24 Litho. *Perf. 14½*
483 A260 4.60r multicolored 1.25 .65

Bageshwori Temple, Nepalganj — A261

Mt. Saipal — A262

1990, Dec. 24 *Perf. 13½*
484 A261 1r multicolored .50 .25
485 A262 5r multicolored 1.00 .40

B.P. Koirala (1914-82) — A263

1990, Dec. 31 *Perf. 14*
486 A263 60p red, org brn & blk .50 .25

King Birendra, 45th Birthday — A264

1990, Dec. 28
487 A264 2r multicolored .50 .25

Royal Chitwan Natl. Park — A265

1991, Feb. 10 Litho. *Perf. 14½*
488 A265 4r multicolored 1.25 .65

Restoration of Multiparty Democracy, 1st Anniv. — A266

1991, Apr. 9 Litho. *Perf. 14*
489 A266 1r multicolored .50 .25

Natl. Census — A267

1991, May 3 *Perf. 14x13½*
490 A267 60p multicolored .50 .25

A268

1991, Aug. 15 *Perf. 14½x13½*
491 A268 3r multicolored .50 .25

Federation of Nepalese Chambers of Commerce and Industry, 25th anniv.

A269

1991, Sept. 4 Litho. *Perf. 14*
492 A269 60p gray & red .50 .25

Nepal Junior Red Cross, 25th anniv.

Re-establishment of Parliament, 1st Session — A270

1991, Sept. 10 *Perf. 14½*
493 A270 1r multicolored .50 .25

Constitution Day — A271

1991, Nov. 9 Litho. *Perf. 15x14*
494 A271 50p multicolored .65 .25

Mt. Kumbhakarna A272

1991, Oct. Litho. *Perf. 13½x14*
495 A272 4.60r multicolored .75 .30

Vivaha Mandap — A274

1991, Dec. 11 *Perf. 11½*
497 A274 1r multicolored .50 .25

SAARC Year of Shelter — A275

1991, Dec. 28 *Perf. 13½x14*
498 A275 9r multicolored 1.25 .75

King Birendra, 46th Birthday — A276

1991, Dec. 28 *Perf. 14x13½*
499 A276 8r multicolored 1.25 .60

Nepal Philatelic Society, 25th Anniv. — A277

1992, July 11 Litho. *Perf. 13*
500 A277 4r multicolored .60 .30

Protect the Environment A278

1992, Oct. 24 Litho. *Perf. 12½x13*
501 A278 60p multicolored .65 .25

Rights of the Child — A279

1992, Oct. 24 *Perf. 13½x13*
502 A279 1r multicolored .50 .25

Temples — A280

75p, Thakurdwara. 1r, Namo Buddha. 2r, Narijhowa. 11r, Dantakali.

1992, Nov. 10 *Perf. 14*

503	A280	75p multicolored	.30	.25
504	A280	1r multicolored	.35	.25
505	A280	2r multicolored	.45	.25
506	A280	11r multicolored	2.25	1.00
		Nos. 503-506 (4)	3.35	1.75

No. 506 is airmail.

A281

1992, Dec. 20 Photo. *Perf. 13x13½*
507 A281 40p brown & green .50 .25

Agricultural Development Bank, 25th anniv.

Birds — A282

1r, Pin-tailed green pigeon. 3r, Bohemian waxwing. 25r, Rufous-tailed finch lark.

1992, Dec. 20 Litho. *Perf. 11½*

508	A282	1r multicolored	.30	.25
509	A282	3r multicolored	.60	.30
510	A282	25r multicolored	4.75	2.50
		Nos. 508-510 (3)	5.65	3.05

King Birendra, 47th Birthday — A283

1992, Dec. 28 *Perf. 12½x13*
511 A283 7r multicolored 1.10 .45

Poets — A284

Designs: No. 512, Pandit Kulchandra Gautam. No. 513, Chittadhar Hridaya. No. 514, Vidyapati. No. 515, Teongsi Sirijunga.

1992, Dec. 31 *Perf. 11½*

512	A284	1r blue & multi	*.80*	.25
513	A284	1r brown & multi	*.80*	.25
514	A284	1r tan & multi	*.80*	.25
515	A284	1r gray & multi	*.80*	.25
		Nos. 512-515 (4)	*3.20*	1.00

1992 Summer Olympics, Barcelona — A285

1992, Dec. 31
516 A285 25r multicolored 3.00 2.00

Fish — A286

Designs: 25p, Tor putitora. 1r, Schizothorax plagiostomus. 5r, Anguilla bengalensis, temple of Chhabdi Barahi. 10r, Psilorhynchus pseudecheneis.

1993, Aug. 6 Litho. *Perf. 11½*
Granite Paper

517	A286	25p multicolored	.50	.25
518	A286	1r multicolored	.55	.40
519	A286	5r multicolored	1.25	.90
520	A286	10r multicolored	2.25	1.00
a.		Souvenir sheet of 4, #517-520	7.00	7.00
		Nos. 517-520 (4)	4.55	2.55

World AIDS Day — A287

1993, Dec. 1 Litho. *Perf. 13½x14½*
521 A287 1r multicolored .50 .25

Tanka Prasad Acharya — A288

1r, Sungdare Sherpa. 7r, Siddhi Charan Shrestha. 15r, Falgunand.

1993, Dec. 2 *Perf. 13½*

522	A288	25p shown	.25	.25
523	A288	1r multicolored	.30	.25
524	A288	7r multicolored	.75	.40
525	A288	15r multicolored	1.50	1.00
		Nos. 522-525 (4)	2.80	1.90

Holy Places — A289

1.50r, Halesi Mahadev, Khotang. 5r, Devghat, Tanahun. 8r, Bagh Bhairab, Kirtipur.

Perf. 13½x14½
1993, Dec. 28 Litho.

526	A289	1.50r multicolored	.25	.25
527	A289	5r multicolored	.60	.50
528	A289	8r multicolored	1.00	.80
		Nos. 526-528 (3)	1.85	1.55

Tourism — A290

Designs: 5r, Tushahiti Sundari Chowk, Patan. 8r, White water rafting.

1993, Dec. 28

529	A290	5r multicolored	.60	.30
530	A290	8r multicolored	.90	.50

King Birendra, 48th Birthday — A291

1993, Dec. 28 *Perf. 14*
531 A291 10r multicolored 1.00 .60

Large Building, Courtyard A293

Pagoda, Courtyard A293a

Monument A294

Arms A295

Fort A296

Mt. Everest A299

Pagoda (Nyata Pola) A300

Map of Nepal A301

Design: 50p, Pagoda, vert.

Perf. 14½, 12, (#533A, 538, 540), 14¼x14
Photo., Litho. (#533A, 535A, 538, 540)

1994-96

533	A293	10p green	.45	.25
533A	A293a	10p claret & black	.45	.25
534	A294	20p violet brown	.45	.25

535 A295 25p carmine, 21x23mm .45 .25
535A A295 25p carmine, 21x26mm .75 .25
536 A296 30p slate .45 .25
537 A293 50p dark blue .45 .25
538 A293a 50p black & claret .45 .25
539 A299 1r multicolored 1.00 .25
539A A300 1r blue & claret .75 .25

Perf. 14½x13½

540 A301 5r multicolored .75 .35
Nos. 533-540 (11) 6.40 2.85

Issued: 20p, No. 535, 30p, 5/17/94; No. 539, 7/6/94; 5r, 9/22/94; Nos. 533, 537, 1995; No. 535A, 8/2/96. Nos. 533A, 538, 539A, 10/9/96.

Pasang Lhamu Sherpa (1960-1993) — A304

1994, Sept 2 Litho. *Perf. 14*
544 A304 10r multicolored 1.00 .60

Stop Smoking Campaign — A305

1994, Sept. 26 *Perf. 13½x14*
545 A305 1r multicolored .75 .25

Mail Transport — A306

1994, Oct. 9 *Perf. 13x13½*
546 A306 1.50r multicolored .80 .25

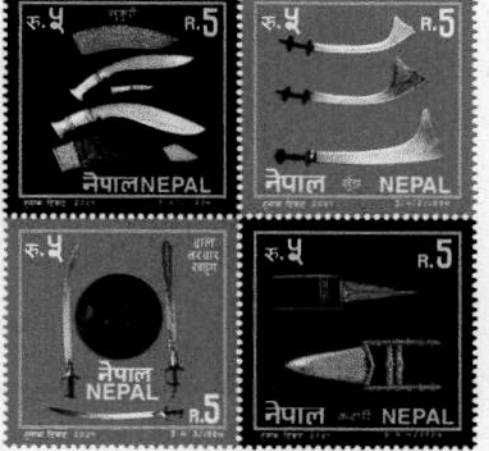

Traditional Weapons — A307

No. 547: a, Daggers, scabbards. b, Yataghans. c, Sabers, shield. d, Carved stone daggers.

1994, Oct. 9 *Perf. 14*
547 A307 5r Block of 4, #a.-d. 3.25 3.25

ILO, 75th Anniv. — A308

1994, Oct. 9 *Perf. 13*
548 A308 15r blue & gold 2.00 1.25

World Food Day A309

1994, Oct. 23 *Perf. 14*
549 A309 25r multicolored 3.00 2.00

Orchids — A310

a, Dendrobium densiflorum. b, Coelogyne flaccida. c, Cymbidium devonianum. d, Coelogyne corymbosa.

1994, Nov. 7 *Perf. 14x13½*
550 A310 10r Block of 4, #a.-d. 4.00 3.00

Intl. Year of the Family — A311

1994, Dec. 5 *Perf. 12½x13*
551 A311 9r green & red 1.00 .60

ICAO, 50th Anniv. — A312

1994, Dec. 7
552 A312 11r blue & gold 1.25 .80

Mushrooms — A313

1994, Dec. 20 *Perf. 14*
553 A313 7r Cordyceps sinensis 1.10 .50
554 A313 7r Morchella conica 1.10 .50
555 A313 7r Amanita caesarea 1.10 .50
556 A313 7r Russula nepalensis 1.10 .50
Nos. 553-556 (4) 4.40 2.00

Famous Men — A314

Designs: 1r, Dharanidhar Koirala, poet. 2r, Narayan Gopal Guruwacharya, singer. 6r, Bahadur Shah, military leader, vert. 7r, Balaguru Shadananda, religious leader.

1994, Dec. 23 *Perf. 13½x14, 14x13½*
557 A314 1r multicolored .35 .25
558 A314 2r multicolored .35 .25
559 A314 6r multicolored .90 .50
560 A314 7r multicolored 1.00 .55
Nos. 557-560 (4) 2.60 1.55

King Birendra, 49th Birthday — A315

1994, Dec. 28 *Perf. 14*
561 A315 9r multicolored 1.00 .70

Tilicho Lake, Manang — A316

11r, Taleju Temple, Katmandou, vert.

1994, Dec. 28 *Perf. 13½x14, 14x13½*
562 A316 9r multicolored 1.10 .70
563 A316 11r multicolored 1.40 .80

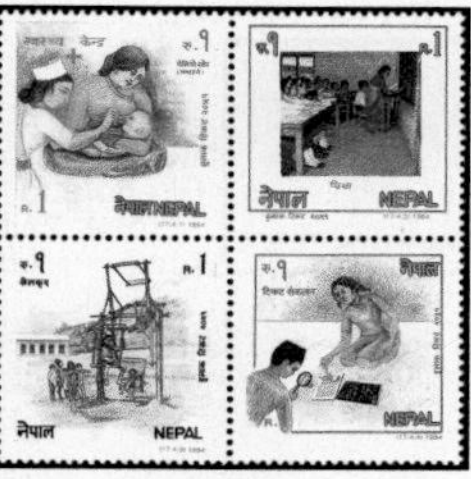

Care of Children — A317

No. 564: a, Vaccination. b, Education. c, Playground activities. d, Stamp collecting.

1994, Dec. 30 *Perf. 14*
564 A317 1r Block of 4, #a.-d. 1.00 .80

Fight Against Cancer — A318

1995, June 23 Litho. *Perf. 14x13½*
565 A318 2r red & black .50 .25

A319

Famous People: a, Bhim Nidhi Tiwari, writer. b, Yuddha Prasad Mishra, writer. c, Chandra Man Singh Maskey, artist. d, Parijat, writer.

1995, July 11 *Perf. 14*
566 A319 3r Block of 4, #a.-d. 2.00 2.00

A320

Famous Men: 15p, Bhakti Thapa, warrior. 1r, Madan Bhandari, politician. 4r, Prakash Raj Kaphley, human rights activist.

1995, Sept. 1 Litho. *Perf. 14x13½*
567 A320 15p multicolored .30 .25
568 A320 1r multicolored .30 .25
569 A320 4r multicolored .50 .30
Nos. 567-569 (3) 1.10 .80

Animals — A321

Designs: a, Bos gaurus. b, Felis lynx. c, Macaca assamensis. d, Hyaena hyaena.

1995, Sept. 1 Litho. *Perf. 12*
570 A321 10p Block of 4, #a.-d. 6.00 6.00

Tourism — A322

1r, Bhimeshwor Temple, Dolakha, vert. 5r, Ugra Tara Temple, Dadeldhura. 7r, Mt. Nampa. 18r, Thanka art, Nrity Aswora, vert.

Perf. 14x13½, 13½x14

1995, Nov. 8 Litho.
574 A322 1r multicolored .25 .25
575 A322 5r multicolored .60 .35
576 A322 7r multicolored 1.00 .50

Size: 26x39mm

577 A322 18r multicolored 2.50 1.25
Nos. 574-577 (4) 4.35 2.35

FAO, 50th Anniv. — A323

1995, Oct. 16 Litho. *Perf. 13½x14*
578 A323 7r multicolored .90 .45

UN, 50th Anniv. — A324

1995, Oct. 22 Litho. *Perf. 11½*
Granite Paper
579 A324 50r multicolored 6.00 3.50

Lumbini, Birth Place of Gautama Buddha — A325

1995, Dec. 23 Litho. *Perf. 14*
580 A325 20r multicolored 3.00 1.50

King Birendra, 50th Birthday
A326 A327

1995, Dec. 28 *Perf. 12*
Granite Paper (No. 581)
581 A326 1r multicolored .50 .25

Perf. 13x13½

582 A327 12r multicolored 1.50 .95

SAARC, 10th Anniv. — A328

1995, Dec. 28 *Perf. 13½*
583 A328 10r multicolored 1.50 .70

Karnali Bridge A329

1996, May 13 Litho. *Perf. 14*
584 A329 7r multicolored 1.00 .50

1996 Summer Olympic Games, Atlanta — A330

1996, Oct. 9 Photo. *Perf. 12*
Granite Paper

585 A330 7r multicolored 1.00 .45

Kaji Kalu Pande A331

Hem Raj Sharma, Grammarian A332

#587, Pushpa Lal Shrestha. #589, Padma Prasad Bhattarai, scholar, philosopher. #590, Suvarna Shamsher Rana. #591, Bhawani Bhikshu, novelist, writer.

Perf. 13½x14, 14x13½
1996, Aug. 6 Litho.

586 A331 75p multicolored .35 .25
587 A331 1r multicolored .35 .25
588 A332 1r multicolored .35 .25
589 A332 3r multicolored .35 .25
590 A331 5r multicolored .60 .30
591 A332 5r multicolored .60 .30
Nos. 586-591 (6) 2.60 1.60

See Nos. 614-615.

Asoka Pillar, Lumbini — A333

1996, Dec. 1 Litho. *Perf. 11½*
592 A333 12r multicolored 2.00 1.00

Tourism — A334

Designs: 1r, Arjun Dhara, Jhapa. 2r, Palace of Nuwakot. 8r, Traditional Gaijatra, Bhaktapur. 10r, Begnash Lake, Kaski.

1996, Nov. 20 Litho. *Perf. 14*
593 A334 1r multicolored .35 .25
594 A334 2r multicolored .35 .25
595 A334 8r multicolored 1.25 .60
596 A334 10r multicolored 1.50 .90
Nos. 593-596 (4) 3.45 2.00

Butterflies and Birds — A335

Designs: a, Krishna pea-cock butterfly. b, Great Himalayan barbet. c, Sarus crane. d, Northern junglequeen butterfly.

1996, Nov. 20 Litho. *Perf. 14*
597 A335 5r Block of 4, #a.-d. 4.25 4.25

Annapurna Mountain Range — A336

Designs: a, Annapurna South, Annapurna I. b, Machhapuchhre, Annapurna III. c, Annapurna IV, Annapurna II.

1996, Dec. 28 Litho. *Perf. 14*
601 A336 18r Strip of 3, #a.-c. 7.00 7.00

King Birendra, 51st Birthday — A337

1996, Dec. 28 Photo. *Perf. 12*
Granite Paper

602 A337 10r multicolored 1.00 .65

Accession of King Birendra to Throne, 25th Anniv. — A338

1997, Feb. 1 Litho. *Perf. 14*
603 A338 2r multicolored 1.00 .25

Nepal Postal Service — A339

1997, Apr. 12 Litho. *Perf. 14*
604 A339 2r brown & red .60 .25

Nepalese-Japanese Diplomatic Relations, 40th Anniv. — A340

1997, Apr. 6 Photo. *Perf. 12*
605 A340 18r multicolored 2.50 1.25

Visit Nepal '98 — A341

2r, Emblem. 10r, Upper Mustang. 18r, Rafting Sunkoshi. 20r, Changunarayan (Bhaktapur), vert.

1997, July 6 Litho. *Perf. 14*
606 A341 2r multicolored .25 .25
607 A341 10r multicolored 1.00 .60
608 A341 18r multicolored 1.75 1.25
609 A341 20r multicolored 2.00 1.40
Nos. 606-609 (4) 5.00 3.50

A342

Traditional costumes.

1997, Sept. 30 Litho. *Perf. 14*
610 A342 5r Rana Tharu .50 .30
611 A342 5r Gurung .50 .30
612 A342 5r Chepang .50 .30
Nos. 610-612 (3) 1.50 .90

A343

1997, Sept. 30 *Perf. 11½*
613 A343 20r multicolored 2.25 1.50

Diplomatic relations between Nepal and US, 50th anniv.

Personality Type of 1996

Designs: No. 614, Riddhi Bahadur Malla, writer. No. 615, Dr. K.I. Singh, political leader.

1997, Nov. 6 Litho. *Perf. 11½*
614 A332 2r multicolored .45 .25
615 A332 2r multicolored .45 .25

A344

Traditional Technology — A345

#616, Janto (grinder), horiz. #617, Dhiki, horiz. #618, Okhal. #619, Kol (oil mill).

1997, Dec. 29 Litho. *Perf. 14*
616 A344 5r multicolored .60 .35
617 A344 5r multicolored .60 .35
618 A344 5r multicolored .60 .35
619 A345 5r multicolored .60 .35
Nos. 616-619 (4) 2.40 1.40

Flowers — A346

40p, Jasminum gracile. 1r, Callistephus chinensis. 2r, Manglietia insignis. 15r, Luculia gratissima.

1997, Dec. 11
620 A346 40p multicolored .25 .25
621 A346 1r multicolored .25 .25
622 A346 2r multicolored .35 .25
623 A346 15r multicolored 2.00 .90
Nos. 620-623 (4) 2.85 1.65

King Birendra, 52nd Birthday — A347

1997, Dec. 29 Photo. *Perf. 11½*
624 A347 10r multicolored 1.00 .75

Visit Nepal '98 — A348

Designs: 2r, Sunrise, Shree Antudanda, Ilam. 10r, Maitidevi Temple, Kathmandu. 18r, Great Reunification Gate, Kapilavastu. 20r, Mt. Cholatse, Solukhumbu, vert.

1998, May 8 Photo. *Perf. 11½*
625 A348 2r multicolored .25 .25
626 A348 10r multicolored 1.10 .65
627 A348 18r multicolored 2.00 1.25
628 A348 20r multicolored 2.25 1.40
Nos. 625-628 (4) 5.60 3.55

Famous People — A349

Designs: 75p, Ram Prasad Rai, freedom fighter. 1r, Imansingh Chemjong, philologist. No. 631, Tulsi Meher Shrestha, social worker. No. 632, Dadhi Ram Marasini, Sanskrit expert. 5.40r, Mahananda Sapkota, linguist.

1998, June 26 Litho. *Perf. 14x13½*
629 A349 75p brown & black .25 .25
630 A349 1r rose lilac & black .25 .25
631 A349 2r blue & black .30 .25
632 A349 2r olive & black .30 .25
633 A349 5.40r red & black .65 .30
Nos. 629-633 (5) 1.75 1.30

1998 World Cup Soccer Championships, France — A350

1998, June 26 *Perf. 14*
634 A350 12r multicolored 1.50 .85

Ganesh Man Singh (1915-97), Senior Democratic Leader — A351

1998, Sept. 18 Photo. *Perf. 11½*
635 A351 5r multicolored .60 .35

A352

1998, Oct. 9 Litho. *Perf. 13½x13*
636 A352 10r multicolored 1.25 .70

Peace Keeping Mission of the Royal Nepalese Army, 40th Anniv.

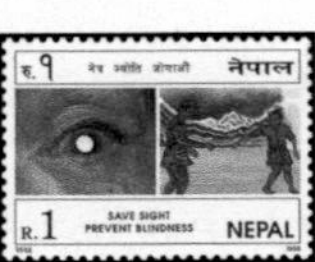
Save Sight, Prevent Blindness — A353

1998, Nov. 29 Photo. *Perf. 12*
Granite Paper

637 A353 1r multicolored .40 .25

Snakes — A354

1.70r, King cobra. 2r, Golden tree snake. 5r, Asiatic rock python. 10r, Karan's pit viper.

1998, Nov. 29 Litho. *Perf. 14*
638 A354 1.70r multicolored .30 .25
639 A354 2r multicolored .35 .25
640 A354 5r multicolored .90 .30
641 A354 10r multicolored 1.75 .75
Nos. 638-641 (4) 3.30 1.55

Universal Declaration of Human Rights, 50th Anniv. — A355

1998, Dec. 10 Litho. *Perf. 14*
642 A355 10r multicolored 1.10 .65

A356

1998, Dec. 27 *Perf. 14x13½*
643 A356 10r multicolored 1.10 .60

Asian and Pacific Decade of Disabled Persons, 1993-2002.

A357

1998, Dec. 29 *Perf. 13x13½*
644 A357 2r multicolored .40 .25

King Birendra, 53rd birthday.

Marsyangdi Dam and Hydro-Electric Power Station — A358

1998, Dec. 29 *Perf. 11½*
Granite Paper
645 A358 12r multicolored 1.35 .85

Nepal Eye Hospital, 25th Anniv. — A359

1999, Apr. 8 **Litho.** *Perf. 14*
646 A359 2r multicolored .50 .40

Tourism — A360

Designs: No. 647, Kalika Bhagawati Temple, Baglung. No. 648, Chandan Nath Temple, vert. 12r, Bajra Yogini Temple, Sankhu, vert. No. 650, Mt. Everest. No. 651, Lumbini Pillar Script translated into English.

1999, June 7 *Perf. 13½x13, 13x13½*
647 A360 2r multicolored .35 .25
648 A360 2r multicolored .35 .25
649 A360 12r multicolored 1.75 1.10
650 A360 15r multicolored 2.00 1.25
651 A360 15r multicolored 2.00 1.25
Nos. 647-651 (5) 6.45 4.10

Tetracerus Quadricornis — A361

No. 653, Ovis ammon hodgsonii.

Granite Paper
1999, June 7 **Photo.** *Perf. 11¾*
652 A361 10r shown 1.40 .85
653 A361 10r multicolored 1.40 .85

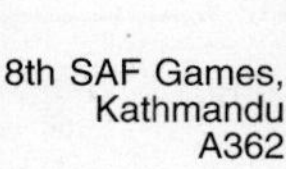

8th SAF Games, Kathmandu A362

Perf. 13½x14¼
1999, Sept. 30 **Litho.**
654 A362 10r multicolored 1.40 .85

UPU, 125th Anniv. — A363

1999, Oct. 9 *Perf. 13½*
655 A363 15r multicolored 1.60 1.60

Famous People — A364

Designs: No. 656, Ram Narayan Mishra (1922-67), freedom fighter. No. 657, Bhupi Sherchan (1935-89), poet. No. 658, Master Mitrasen (1895-1946), writer. No. 659, Rudra Raj Pandey (1901-87), writer. No. 660, Gopal Prasad Rimal (1917-73), writer. No. 661, Mangaladevi Singh (1924-96), politician.

1999, Nov. 20 **Litho.** *Perf. 13¾*
656 A364 1r multicolored .30 .25
657 A364 1r multicolored .30 .25
658 A364 1r multicolored .30 .25
659 A364 2r multicolored .35 .25
660 A364 2r multicolored .35 .25
661 A364 2r multicolored .35 .25
Nos. 656-661 (6) 1.95 1.50

Dances — A365

1999, Dec. 26 **Litho.** *Perf. 11¾x12*
662 A365 5r Sorathi .75 .45
663 A365 5r Bhairav .75 .45
664 A365 5r Jhijhiya .75 .45
Nos. 662-664 (3) 2.25 1.35

Intl. Labor Organization's Campaign Against Child Labor — A366

1999, Dec. 29 *Perf. 13½x14¼*
665 A366 12r multi 1.60 1.00

A367

1999, Dec. 29 *Perf. 14¼x13½*
666 A367 5r multi .70 .50

King Birendra's 54th birthday.

A368

2000, Apr. 2 **Photo.** *Perf. 12x11¾*
Granite Paper
667 A368 15r multi 2.00 1.75

Queen Aishwarya Rajya Laxmi Devi Shah, 50th birthday (in 1999).

Radio Nepal, 50th Anniv. — A369

2000, Apr. 2 **Litho.** *Perf. 13½x14¼*
668 A369 2r multi .45 .25

Gorkhapatra Newspaper, Cent. — A370

2000, May 5 *Perf. 14*
669 A370 10r multi 1.25 1.25

Tourism — A371

Designs: 12r, Tchorolpa Glacial Lake, Dolakha. 15r, Dakshinkali Temple, Kathmandu. 18r, Annapurna.

2000, June 30 **Litho.** *Perf. 13¾x14*
670-672 A371 Set of 3 5.75 5.75

First ascent of Annapurna, 50th anniv. (No. 672).

Rani Pokhari and Temple, Kathmandu — A372

Frame color: 50p, Orange. 1r, Blue. 2r, Brown.

2000, July 7 **Photo.** *Perf. 11½*
673-675 A372 Set of 3 .70 .70

Geneva Conventions, 50th Anniv. — A373

2000, Sept. 7 **Litho.** *Perf. 13½x14¼*
676 A373 5r multi .75 .70

2000 Summer Olympics, Sydney — A374

2000, Sept. 7 **Photo.** *Perf. 11¾x12*
Granite Paper
677 A374 25r multi 3.75 3.25

Famous People — A375

Designs: No. 678, 2r, Hridayachandra Singh Pradhan, writer (olive green frame). No. 679, 2r, Thir Bam Malla, revolutionary (brown frame). No. 680, 5r, Krishna Prasad Koirala, social reformer (indigo frame). No. 681, 5r, Manamohan Adhikari, politician (red frame).

2000, Sept. 7 **Litho.** *Perf. 14*
678-681 A375 Set of 4 1.70 1.70

Worldwide Fund for Nature (WWF) — A376

#682, Bengal florican. #683, Lesser adjutant stork. #684, Female greater one-horned rhinoceros and calf. #685, Male greater one-horned rhinoceros.

2000, Nov. 14 **Photo.** *Perf. 11¾*
Granite Paper
682-685 A376 10r Set of 4 5.75 5.25

King Birendra's 55th Birthday — A377

2000, Dec. 28 **Photo.** *Perf. 12x11¾*
Granite Paper
686 A377 5r multi .80 .65

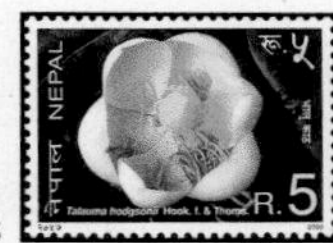
Flowers — A378

Designs: No. 687, Talauma hodgsonii. No. 688, Mahonia napaulensis. No. 689, Dactylorhiza hatagirea, vert.

2000, Dec. 28 *Perf. 11¾x12, 12x11¾*
Granite Paper
687-689 A378 5r Set of 3 2.60 2.10

Establishment of Democracy, 50th Anniv. — A379

Perf. 11¾x11½
2001, Feb. 16 **Photo.**
Granite Paper
690 A379 5r King Tribhuvan .80 .65

2001 Census — A380

2001, Apr. 17 **Photo.** *Perf. 11¾*
Granite Paper
691 A380 2r multi .50 .25

Famous Nepalese — A381

Designs: No. 692, 2r, Khaptad Baba (bright pink background, white Nepalese numeral at UR), ascetic. No. 693, 2r, Bhikkhu Pragyananada Mahathera (red violet background), religious teacher. No. 694, 2r, Guru Prasad Mainali (pink background, red Nepalese numeral at UR), writer. No. 695, 2r, Tulsi Lal Amatya (brown violet background), politician. No. 696, 2r, Madan Lal Agrawal (light blue background), industrialist.

Perf. 14¼x13½
2001, June 29 **Litho.**
692-696 A381 Set of 5 1.25 1.25

Ficus Religiosa — A382

2001, Nov. 2 **Litho.** *Perf. 14¼x13½*
697 A382 10r multi 1.40 1.40

UN High Commissioner for Refugees, 50th Anniv. — A383

2001, Nov. 2 *Perf. 14*
698 A383 20r multi 2.75 2.50

Herbs — A384

Designs: 5r, Water pennywort. 15r, Rockfoil. 30r, Himalayan yew.

2001, Nov. 2 *Perf. 13¾*
699-701 A384 Set of 3 7.50 7.50

Nepalese Flag — A385

2001, Nov. 28 *Perf. 14*
702 A385 10r multi .50 .40

King Birendra (1945-2001) — A386

2001, Dec. 28 *Perf. 14¼x13½*
703 A386 15r multi 2.25 1.75

Year of Dialogue Among Civilizations A387

2001, Dec. 28 *Perf. 14*
704 A387 30r multi 4.00 3.75

Tourism — A388

Designs: 2r, Amargadi Fort. 5r, Hiranyavarna Mahavihar, vert. 15r, Jugal Mountain Range.

Perf. 13½x14¼, 14¼x13½
2001, Dec. 28
705-707 A388 Set of 3 3.50 3.50

Nepal Scouts, 50th Anniv. — A389

2002, Apr. 9 **Litho.** *Perf. 14¼x13½*
708 A389 2r red brn & olive .50 .35

2002 World Cup Soccer Championships, Japan and Korea — A390

2002, May 31 **Litho.** *Perf. 13½x12¾*
709 A390 15r multi 2.10 2.10

King Gyanendra's Accession to Throne, 1st Anniv. — A391

2002, June 5 *Perf. 13¾*
710 A391 5r multi .70 .70

King Birendra (1945-2001) and Queen Aishwarya (1949-2001) — A392

2002, June 5 *Perf. 14*
711 A392 10r multi .80 .80

Paintings A393

Designs: No. 712, 5r, Pearl, by King Birendra. No. 713, 5r, Aryabalokiteshwor, by Siddhimuni Shakya, vert.

Perf. 13½x13¾, 13¾x13½
2002, July 29
712-713 A393 Set of 2 1.40 1.40

Insects — A394

Designs: 3r, Leaf beetle. 5r, Locust.

2002, Sept. 6 *Perf. 14*
714-715 A394 Set of 2 1.25 1.25

Societal Messages — A395

Designs: 1r, Untouchable family behind barbed wire (untouchables should not be discriminated against). 2r, Children and parents waving (female children should not be discriminated against).

2002, Sept. 6 *Perf. 14¼x14*
716-717 A395 Set of 2 .70 .70

Intl. Year of Mountains — A396

2002, Oct. 9 **Litho.** *Perf. 14*
718 A396 5r multi .80 .65

Tourism — A397

Designs: No. 719, 5r, Mt. Nilgiri, Mustang. No. 720, 5r, Pathibhara Devisthan, Taplejung. No. 721, 5r, Ramgram Stupa, Hawalparasi. No. 722, 5r, Galeshwor Mahadevsthan, Myagdi.

2002, Oct. 9
719-722 A397 Set of 4 3.25 2.75

South Asian Association for Regional Cooperation Charter Day — A398

2002, Dec. 8 *Perf. 13½x12¾*
723 A398 15r multi 2.00 1.60

Famous Men — A399

Designs: 2r, Dava Bir Singh Kansakar, social worker. 25r, Rev, Ekai Kawaguchi (1866-1945), Buddhist scholar.

2002, Dec. 8 *Perf. 13x13½*
724-725 A399 Set of 2 3.50 3.50

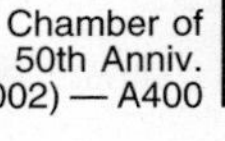

Nepal Chamber of Commerce, 50th Anniv. (in 2002) — A400

2003, Apr. 10 **Litho.** *Perf. 14*
726 A400 5r multi .60 .60

Industry and Commerce Day — A401

2003, Apr. 11 *Perf. 13½x12¾*
727 A401 5r multi .60 .60

First Ascent of Mt. Everest, 50th Anniv. — A402

2003, May 29 **Litho.** *Perf. 13½x14¼*
728 A402 25r multi 3.25 3.25

Babu Chiri Sherpa (1965-2001), Mountaineer A403

2003, June 27 *Perf. 14*
729 A403 5r multi .75 .60

King Gyanendra, 56th Birthday — A404

2003, July 7 *Perf. 13½x14¼*
730 A404 5r multi .75 .65

Tea Garden, Eastern Nepal — A405

2003, July 7 *Perf. 14*
731 A405 25r multi 3.00 3.00

Dr. Dilli Raman Regmi (1913-2001), Politician and Historian — A406

2003, Aug. 31
732 A406 5r brown & blk .60 .60

Gopal Das Shrestha (1930-98), Journalist — A407

2003, Sept. 23 **Litho.** *Perf. 14*
733 A407 5r multi .60 .60

Export Year 2003 — A408

2003, Oct. 9 *Perf. 13½x14*
734 A408 25r multi 3.00 3.00

Sankhadhar Sakhwaa, Initiator of Nepalese Calendar — A409

2003, Oct. 26 *Perf. 13½x12¾*
735 A409 5r multi .60 .60

Flowers A410

No. 736: a, Lotus. b, Picrorhiza. c, Himalayan rhubarb. d, Night jasmine.

Perf. 14¼x13½
2003, Dec. 23 **Litho.**
736 A410 10r Block of 4, #a-d 4.50 4.50

Tourism — A411

Designs: No. 737, 5r, Kali Gandaki "A" hydroelectric dam site. No. 738, 5r, Ganesh idol, Kageshwar, vert. 30r, Buddha icon, Swayambhunath.

2003, Dec. 23 *Perf. 14*
737-739 A411 Set of 3 4.50 4.50

Social Services of United Mission to Nepal, 50th Anniv. — A412

2004, Mar. 5 **Litho.** *Perf. 14*
740 A412 5r multi .60 .60

National Society of Comprehensive Eye Care, 25th Anniv. — A413

2004, Mar. 25
741 A413 5r multi .65 .65

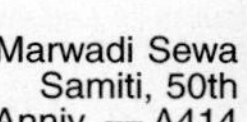
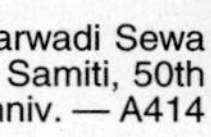

Marwadi Sewa Samiti, 50th Anniv. — A414

2004, Apr. 9
742 A414 5r multi .65 .65

King Gyanendra, 57th Birthday — A415

2004, July 7 **Litho.** ***Perf. 14***
743 A415 5r multi .65 .65

Management Education, 50th Anniv. — A416

2004, Sept. 24 **Litho.** ***Perf. 14***
744 A416 5r multi .60 .60

Asia-Pacific Telecommunity, 25th Anniv. — A417

2004, Sept. 24
745 A417 5r multi .65 .65

FIFA (Fédération Internationale de Football Association), Cent. — A418

2004, Sept. 24
746 A418 20r multi 2.00 2.00

Mountains — A419

No. 747: a, Mt. Everest. b, Mt. Kanchenjunga Main. c, Mt. Lhotse. d, Mt. Makalu I. e, Mt. Cho Oyu. f, Mt. Dhaulagiri. g, Mt. Manasalu. h, Mt. Annapurna I.

2004, Oct. 19 **Litho.** ***Perf. 14***
747 A419 Block of 8 8.00 8.00
a.-h. 10r Any single 1.00 1.00

Famous Men — A420

Designs: No. 748, 5r, Nayaraj Panta (1913-2002), historian. No. 749, 5r, Narahari Nath (1914-2003), yogi.

2004, Nov. 3
748-749 A420 Set of 2 1.20 1.20

Flora and Fauna A421

No. 750: a, Rufous piculet woodpecker. b, Giant atlas moth. c, Serma guru. d, High altitude rice.

2004, Nov. 3
750 A421 10r Block of 4, #a-d 4.00 4.00

Mayadevi Temple, Lumbini — A422

Gadhimai Temples, Bara — A423

2004, Nov. 30 ***Perf. 13½x13***
751 A422 10r multi 1.40 1.00
752 A423 10r multi 1.40 1.00

Madan Puraskar Trust, 50th Anniv. — A424

2004, Dec. 13 ***Perf. 14***
753 A424 5r multi .55 .55

Sculptures — A425

No. 754: a, Jayavarma. b, Umamaheshwar. c, Vishwarupa. d, Banshagopal.

2004, Dec. 27 ***Perf. 13½***
754 A425 10r Block of 4, #a-d 4.00 4.00

Nepal Rastra Bank, 50th Anniv. (in 2006) — A426

2005, Apr. 27 **Litho.** ***Perf. 14***
755 A426 2r multi .60 .60

First Ascent of Mt. Makalu, 50th Anniv. — A427

2005, May 15
756 A427 10r multi 1.00 1.00

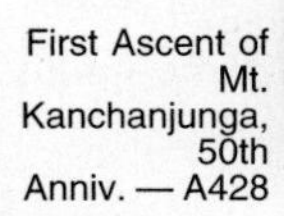

First Ascent of Mt. Kanchanjunga, 50th Anniv. — A428

2005, May 25
757 A428 12r multi 1.25 1.25

King Gyanendra, 58th Birthday — A429

2005, July 7 **Litho.** ***Perf. 14***
758 A429 5r multi .55 .55

Life of Buddha — A430

No. 759: a, Birth at Lumbini. b, Enlightenment at Bodhagaya. c, First Sermon at Sarnath. d, Mahaparinirvana at Kushinagar.

2005, July 21
759 Horiz. strip of 4, any background color 4.00 4.00
a.-d. A430 10r Any single, any background color 1.00 1.00
Sheet of 4 horiz. strips 16.00 —

The sheet has four horizontal strips with background colors of yellow, green, red and purple.

Queen Mother Ratna Rajya Laxmi Devi Shah — A431

2005, Aug. 20
760 A431 20r multi 2.00 2.00

Fruits and Nuts A432

No. 761: a, Indian gooseberry. b, Walnut. c, Wood apple. d, Golden evergreen raspberry.

2005, Aug. 20
761 A432 10r Block of 4, #a-d 4.00 4.00

Mammals A433

No. 762: a, Gangetic dolphin. b, Indian pangolin. c, Asiatic wild elephant. d, Clouded leopard.

2005, Aug. 31 **Litho.** ***Perf. 14***
762 Horiz. strip of 4, any background color 4.00 4.00
a.-d. A433 10r Any single, any background color 1.00 1.00
Sheet of 4 horiz. strips 16.00 —

The sheet has four horizontal strips with background colors of yellow, green, red and purple.

Late Bhupalmansingh Karki, Social Worker — A434

2005, Sept. 24
763 A434 2r multi .60 .60

Tourism A435

No. 764: a, Ghodaghodi Lake, Kailali. b, Budhasubba, Sunasari. c, Kalinchok Bhagawati, Dolakha. d, Panauti City, Kabhrepalanchok.

2005, Oct. 9
764 A435 5r Block of 4, #a-d 2.00 2.00

Diplomatic Relations Between Nepal and People's Republic of China, 50th Anniv. — A436

2005, Dec. 26
765 A436 30r multi 3.25 3.25

Admission to United Nations, 50th Anniv. — A437

2005, Dec. 26
766 A437 50r multi 5.50 5.50

Tribal Ornaments — A438

No. 767 — Ornaments of: a, Limbu tribes. b, Tharu tribes. c, Newar tribes. d, Sherpa tribes.

2005, Dec. 26
767 A438 25r Block of 4, #a-d 11.00 11.00

King Tribhuvan (1906-55) — A439

2006, Feb. 17 **Litho.** ***Perf. 13¼x13***
768 A439 5r multi .55 .55

Democracy Day.

Queen Komal Rayja Laxmi Devi Shah — A440

2006, Mar. 8
769 A440 5r multi .55 .55

Intl. Women's Day.

World Hindu Federation, 25th Anniv. — A441

2006, Apr. 6 ***Perf. 12¾***

770	A441	2r multi	.35	.35

First Ascent of Mt. Lhotse, 50th Anniv. — A442

First Ascent of Mt. Manaslu, 50th Anniv. — A443

2006, May 9 ***Perf. 13x13¼***

771	A442	25r multi	2.50	2.50
772	A443	25r multi	2.50	2.50

Supreme Court, 50th Anniv. — A444

2006, May 21

773	A444	5r multi	.65	.65

Fauna, Flora and Mushrooms — A445

Designs: No. 774, Imperial butterfly. No. 774A, Nepalese primrose. No., 774B, Chaffer beetle. No. 774C, Beautiful stream frog. No. 774D, White pine mushroom.

2006, June 12 ***Perf. 12¾***

774-774D		Set of 5	5.50	5.50
e.		Horiz. strip of 5, #774-774D	7.00	7.00

Nos. 774-774D were printed in sheets of 50 stamps, containing ten of each stamp, but containing only two horizontal strips of the stamps.

Diplomatic Relations Between Nepal and Russia, 50th Anniv. — A446

2006, Aug. 22 ***Perf. 13¼x13***

775	A446	30r multi	1.75	1.75

Diplomatic Relations Between Nepal and Japan, 50th Anniv. — A447

2006, Sept. 1 ***Perf. 13x13¼***

776	A447	30r multi	1.75	1.75

Mt. Everest A448

Stag Beetle A449

2006, Sept. 19 ***Perf. 14¼x14***

777	A448	1r blk & bl grn	.25	.25
778	A449	2r black	.35	.35

Perf. 14x13¾

Size: 29x25mm

779	A448	5r blk, pink & blue	.55	.35
		Nos. 777-779 (3)	1.15	.95

Membership in UPU, 50th Anniv. — A450

2006, Oct. 9 ***Perf. 13x13¼***

780	A450	15r multi	1.00	1.00

Nepalese Postage Stamps, 125th Anniv. — A451

Designs: 5r, #1. 20r, #2. 100r, #3. 125r, #1-3.

2006, Oct. 9 ***Perf. 13¼***

781-783	A451	Set of 3	7.50	7.50

Size: 91x75mm

Imperf

784	A451	125r multi	7.50	7.50

No. 784 contains a perforated label that is not valid for postage showing Nepal #1-3.

Birth of Buddha, 2550th Anniv. — A452

2006, Dec. 20 ***Perf. 13¼x13***

785	A452	30r multi	1.75	1.75

Chhatrapati Free Clinic, 50th Anniv. — A453

2007, Feb. 6 **Litho.** ***Perf. 13x13¼***

786	A453	2r multi	.55	.55

Mt. Everest — A454

2007, Mar. 14

787	A454	5r multi	.80	.80

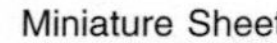

Miniature Sheet

Orchids A455

No. 788: a, Satyrium nepalense. b, Dendrobium heterocarpum. c, Pelantheria insectifera. d, Coelogyne ovalis. e, Coelogyne cristata. f, Dendrobium chrysanthum. g, Phalaenopsis mannii. h, Dendrobium densiflorum. i, Esmeralda clarkei. j, Acampe rigida. k, Bulbophyllum leopardinum. l, Dendrobium fimbriatum. m, Arundina graminifolia. n, Dendrobium moschatum. o, Rhynchostylis retusa. p, Cymbidium devonianum.

2007, Apr. 12

788	A455	10r Sheet of 16, #a-p	10.00	10.00

Sports — A456

Designs: No. 789, 5r, Taekwondo. No. 790, 5r, Cricket.

2007 ***Perf. 13x13¼***

789-790	A456	Set of 2	.90	.90

Issued: No. 789, 4/25; No. 790, 4/28.

Miniature Sheet

Martyrs of the Democratic Movement — A457

No. 791: a, Setu B. K. b, Tulasi Chhetri. c, Anil Lama. d, Umesh Chandra Thapa. e, Chakraraj Joshi. f, Chandra Bayalkoti. g, Devilal Poudel. h, Govindanath Sharma. i, Prof. Hari Raj Adhikari. j, Horilal Rana Tharu. k, Lal Bahadur Bista. l, Mohamad Jahangir. m, Pradhumna Khadka. n, Rajan Giri. o, Suraj Bishwas. p, Sagun Tamrakar. q, Bhimsen Dahal. r, Shivahari Kunwar. s, Basudev Ghimire. t, Bishnu Prasad Panday. u, Yamlal Lamichhane. v, Deepak Kami. w, Darshanial Yadab. x, Tahir Hussain Ansari. y, Hiralal Gautam.

2007, June 4 ***Perf. 12½***

791	A457	2r Sheet of 25, #a-y	15.00	15.00

Diplomatic Relations Between Nepal and Sri Lanka, 50th Anniv. — A458

2007, July 1 ***Perf. 13x13¼***

792	A458	5r multi	.50	.50

Diplomatic Relations Between Nepal and Egypt, 50th Anniv. — A459

2007, July 24

793	A459	5r multi	.50	.50

Scouting, Cent. — A460

2007, Sept. 4

794	A460	2r multi	.55	.55

Nepal Cancer Relief Society, 25th Anniv. — A461

2007, Sept. 17

795	A461	1r multi	.45	.45

Nepalese Parliament Building and Documents — A462

No. 796, 1r: a, Reinstatement of the House of Representatives. b, Proclamation of the House of Representatives.

No. 797, 1r: a, Constitution of Legislature-Parliament. b, Interim Constitution of Nepal.

2007, Dec. 28 **Litho.** ***Perf. 13x13¼***

Horiz. Pairs, #a-b

796-797	A462	Set of 2	.90	.90

Chhaya Devi Parajuli (1918-2006), Politician — A463

2007, Dec. 30

798	A463	2r multi	.50	.50

Famous People A464

No. 799, 5r: a, Shivapuri Baba (1862-1963), religious leader. b, Mahesh Chandra Regmi (1929-2003), writer.

No. 800, 5r: a, Princess Bhrikuti (617-49). b, Pundit Udayananda Arjyal, writer.

No. 801, 5r: a, Ganesh Lal Shrestha, musician. b, Tara Devi (1945-2006), singer.

2007, Dec. 30 **Litho.**

Horiz. Pairs, #a-b

799-801	A464	Set of 3	3.00	3.00

Tourism — A465

No. 802: a, Mt. Abi. b, Shree Bhageshwor Temple, Dadeldhura. c, Shree Shaillya Malikarjun Temple, Darchula. d, Shiddakali Temple, Bhojpur. e, Buddha's Victory over the Mara.

2007, Dec. 30

802		Vert. strip of 5	2.00	2.00
a.-e.		A465 5r Any single	.35	.35

Diplomatic Relations Between Nepal and Germany, 50th Anniv. — A466

2008, Apr. 2 **Litho.** ***Perf. 13x13¼***

803	A466	25r multi	1.50	1.50

Nativity of Buddha — A467

2008, July 18 ***Perf. 13¼x13***

804	A467	2r multi	1.00	1.00

Nepal Coat of Arms — A468

2008, Aug. 21

805	A468	1r multi	.50	.50

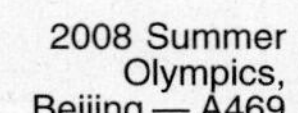

2008 Summer Olympics, Beijing — A469

2008, Aug. 21 ***Perf. 12¾***
806 A469 15r multi 1.00 1.00

National Anthem and Flag of Nepal — A470

2008, Nov. 13 Litho. ***Perf. 13¼x13***
807 A470 1r multi .60 .60

Kaiser Library, Cent. — A471

2008, Nov. 13 ***Perf. 13x13¼***
808 A471 5r multi .50 .50

Dr. Harka Gurung (1935-2006), Minister of Tourism, and Dr. Harka Gurung Peak — A472

2008, Dec. 24 Litho.
Granite Paper
809 A472 5r multi .60 .60

Flora, Fauna and Mushrooms — A473

No. 810: a, Serpentine. b, Long-horned beetle. c, Russula chloroides. d, Golden monitor lizard.

2008, Dec. 24 ***Perf. 13x13¼***
Granite Paper
810 A473 Block or horiz. strip of 4, #a-d 2.25 2.25
a.-d. 5r Any single .50 .50

Tourism — A474

No. 811: a, Mustang village, Mustang District. b, Syarpu Lake, Rukum District. c, Jaljala Hill, Rolpa District. d, Pindeswor Babadham, Dharan. e, Shree Kumair Chariot Festival, Kathmandu.

2008, Dec. 24 Litho.
Granite Paper
811 Vert. strip of 5 3.25 3.25
a.-e. A474 5r Any single .45 .45

Family Planning Association of Nepal, 50th Anniv. — A475

2009, Sept. 14 Litho. ***Perf. 13x13¼***
Granite Paper
812 A475 1r multi .35 .35

Office of Auditor General, 50th Anniv. — A476

2009, Sept. 14 ***Perf. 13x13¼***
Granite Paper
813 A476 5r multi .60 .60

Tribhuvan University, 50th Anniv. — A477

2009, Sept. 14 Litho.
Granite Paper
814 A477 5r multi .60 .60

Birthplace of Buddha UNESCO World Heritage Site, Lumbini — A478

No. 815: a, Nativity sculpture and marker stone. b, Holy Pond. c, Asoka pillar. d, Excavated stupas. e, Mayadevi Temple.

2009, Sept. 14 ***Perf. 13x13¼***
Granite Paper
815 Horiz. strip of 5 4.50 4.50
a.-e. A478 10r Any single .50 .50

Establishment of Federal Democratic Republic — A479

2009, Oct. 8 Granite Paper Litho.
816 A479 2r multi 1.00 1.00

Miniature Sheet

Butterflies — A480

No. 817: a, Common Apollo. b, Striped blue crow. c, Common yellow swallowtail. d, Swinhoe's nawab. e, Great satyr. f, Large cabbage white. g, Common tiger. h, Common brimstone. i, Yellow orange tip. j, Glassy blue bottle. k, Banded Apollo. l, Blue admiral. m, Lime swallowtail. n, Red Helen. o, Spot swordtail. p, Green sapphire.

2009, Oct. 8 ***Perf. 13x13¼***
Granite Paper
817 A480 10p Sheet of 16, #a-p 11.00 11.00

Govinda Biyogi (1929-2006), Journalist — A481

2009, Nov. 2 ***Perf. 13¾x13½***
Granite Paper
818 A481 5r multi .60 .60

Guruji Mangal Das (1896-1985), Religious Leader — A482

2009, Nov. 9 Granite Paper Litho.
819 A482 5r multi .50 .50

Art A483

No. 820: a, Tej Bahadur Chitrakar (1898-1971), painter. b, Tribute to the Forefathers, painting by Chitrakar.

2009, Dec. 5 ***Perf. 13½x13¼***
Granite Paper
820 A483 5r Horiz. pair, #a-b .90 .90

Ramesh Vikal (1928-2008), Writer — A484

2009, Dec. 27 ***Perf. 13¼x13½***
Granite Paper
821 A484 2r multi .60 .60

Krishna Sen Ichhuk (1956-2002), Journalist — A485

2009, Dec. 27 ***Perf. 13½x13¼***
Granite Paper
822 A485 5r multi .50 .50

Laxmi Prasad Devkota (1909-59), Poet — A486

2009, Dec. 31 ***Perf. 13¼x13½***
Granite Paper
823 A486 1r multi .60 .60

Chhath Festival — A487

2009, Dec. 31 Litho.
Granite Paper
824 A487 5r multi .60 .60

Lahurya Folk Dance — A488

2009, Dec. 31 ***Perf. 13¼x13½***
Granite Paper
825 A488 5r multi .65 .65

Kayaking — A489

2009, Dec. 31
826 A489 10r multi .80 .80

Mountain Biking — A490

2009, Dec. 31
827 A490 10r multi .80 .80

Nepal Television, 25th Anniv. — A491

2010, Jan. 31 ***Perf. 13½x13¼***
828 A491 2r multi .50 .50

Worldwide Fund for Nature (WWF) — A492

Perf. 13¼x13½
2010, Sept. 14 Litho.
829 A492 5r multi .75 .75

New Year 2010 (Year of the Tiger).

First Ascent of Mt. Dhaulagiri, 50th Anniv. — A493

2010, Sept. 26
830 A493 25r multi 1.75 1.75

Pemba Doma Sherpa (1970-2007), Mountaineer A494

2010, Sept. 26
831 A494 25r multi 1.75 1.75

Kankalini Mai Temple — A495

2010, Dec. 1 Litho.
832 A495 2r multi .55 .55

Maru Ganesh Temple — A496

2010, Dec. 1
833 A496 2r multi .50 .50

Bhairab Aryal (1936-76), Writer — A497

2010, Dec. 1

834 A497 5r multi .50 .50

Natikaji Shrestha (1925-2003), Musician — A498

2010, Dec. 1 ***Perf. 13½x13¼***

835 A498 5r multi .50 .50

Jibraj Ashrit (1944-93), Politician — A499

2010, Dec. 1 ***Perf. 13¼x13½***

836 A499 5r multi .50 .50

Bhagat Sarbajit Bishwokarma (1893-1955), Social Reformer — A500

2010, Dec. 5 ***Perf. 13½x13¼***

837 A500 5r multi .50 .50

Mahasthabir Bhikshu Amritandanda (1918-90), Religious Leader — A501

2010, Dec. 7 ***Perf. 13¼x13½***

838 A501 5r multi .50 .50

Sadhana Adhikari (1925-2005), Politician A502

2010, Dec. 9 **Litho.**

839 A502 5r multi .50 .50

Mai Pokhari Lake — A503

2010, Dec. 12

840 A503 2r multi .60 .60

Global Handwashing Day — A504

2010, Dec. 30

841 A504 2r multi .50 .50

Nepal Tourism Year (in 2011) — A505

2010, Dec. 30

842 A505 5r multi .55 .55

Stamps and Postmarks A506

Designs: No. 843, 1r, Nepal #1, 1881 Kathmandu postmark. No. 844, 1r, Nepal #27, 1910 Birganj postmark. No. 845, 2r, Nepal #26, 1915 Bethari postmark. No. 846, 2r, Nepal postal stationery indicia, 1934 Kanchanpur postmark. 3r, Nepal #53, 1952 Tamghas / Gulmi postmark.

2011, June 13 ***Perf. 13¼x13½***

843-847 A506 Set of 5 1.00 1.00

Turtles — A507

No. 848: a, Ganges softshell turtle. b, Tricarinate Hill turtle. c, Elongated tortoise. d, Common roofed turtle.

2011, Aug. 28 ***Perf. 13¾x13½***

Granite Paper

848 Horiz. strip or block of 4 2.25 2.25
a.-d. A507 10r Any single .50 .50

Mohan Gopal Khetan (1947-2007), Industrialist A508

2011, Nov. 22 **Litho.**

Granite Paper

849 A508 5r multi .50 .50

Yagyaraj Sharma Aryjal (1903-89), Musician A509

2011, Nov. 23 ***Perf. 13¾x13½***

Granite Paper

850 A509 10r multi .60 .60

Shankar Lamichhane (1928-76), Writer — A510

2011, Nov. 23 ***Perf. 13½x13¾***

Granite Paper

851 A510 10r multi .60 .60

Ekdev Aale (1923-68), Politician — A511

2011, Nov. 23 **Litho.**

Granite Paper

852 A511 10r multi .60 .60

Motidevi Shrestha (1913-97), Politician — A512

2011, Nov. 23 ***Perf. 13½x13¾***

Granite Paper

853 A512 10r multi .60 .60

Rishikesh Shaha (1925-2002), Human Rights Activist — A513

2011, Dec. 9 **Granite Paper**

854 A513 5r multi .60 .60

Religious Sites — A514

Designs: 1r, Badimalika, Bajura. No. 856, 2r, Tansen Bhagawati, Palpa. No. 857, 2r, Siddha Ratannath Temple, Dang. No. 858, 2r, Deuti Bajai, Surkhet. No. 859, 2r, Bhat Bhateni Mai, Kathmandu. No. 860, 5r, Shree Baidhyanath Temple, Achham. No. 861, 5r, Gajurmukhi Dham, Ilam. 25r, Yetser Jangchubling Monastery, Upper Dolpa.

No. 863, 2r, vert.: a, Shree Aryavalokiteswora Seto Machhindranath, Kathmandu. b, Shree Aryavalokiteswora Seto Machhindranath Rath, Kathmandu.

2011, Dec. 30 ***Perf. 13¾x13½***

Granite Paper

855-862 A514 Set of 8 4.00 4.00

Perf. 13½x13¾

863 A514 2r Horiz. pair, #a-b .70 .70

Nepalese Landscapes A515

Designs: No. 864, 10r, Panch Pokhari, Sindhupalchok. No. 865, 10r, Mt. Mera Peak. No. 866, 10r, Badaiya Taal, Bardiya.

2011, Dec. 30 ***Perf. 13¾x13½***

Granite Paper

864-866 A515 Set of 3 1.75 1.75

A516

A517

A518

Cave Murals, Upper Mustang A519

2011, Dec. 30 **Litho.**

Granite Paper

867 Horiz. strip of 4 2.25 2.25
a. A516 10r multi .50 .50
b. A517 10r multi .50 .50
c. A518 10r multi .50 .50
d. A519 10r multi .50 .50

Ramesh Kumar Mahato, Martyr — A520

2012, Jan. 19 ***Perf. 13½x13¾***

Granite Paper

868 A520 10r multi .50 .50

Dated 2011.

Gajendra Narayan Singh (1929-2002), Politician — A521

2012, Jan. 19 **Litho.**

Granite Paper

869 A521 10r multi .50 .50

Dated 2011.

Girija Prasad Koirala (1924-2010), Prime Minister — A522

2012, Feb. 11 ***Perf. 13¾x13½***

Granite Paper

870 A522 10r multi .50 .50

Dated 2011.

Nepalese National News Agency, 50th Anniv. — A523

2012, Feb. 19 ***Perf. 13½x13¾***

Granite Paper

871 A523 10r multi .60 .60

Nepali Shikshya Parishad (Organization Promoting Nepalese Language Education), 60th Anniv. — A524

2012, July 29 **Granite Paper**

872 A524 5r multi .60 .60

Biodiversity — A525

No. 873: a, Delphinium himalayai. b, Dendrobium eriiflorum. c, Podophyllum hexandrum. d, Ganodermna lucidum. e, Prinia burnesii nepalicola. f, Gyps bengalensis. g, Caprolagus hispidus. h, Cyrtopodion markuscombaii.

2012, July 29 Granite Paper
873 A525 10r Block of 8, #a-h 4.50 4.50

Dead Sea, Mt. Everest, Flags of Israel and Nepal — A526

2012, Sept. 4 ***Perf. 13½x13¾***
Granite Paper
874 A526 35r multi 2.25 2.25
Souvenir Sheet
875 A526 50r multi 5.50 5.50

See Israel No. 1944.

B.P. Koirala Museum, Kathmandu, 8th Anniv. — A527

2012, Sept. 10 ***Perf. 13¾x13½***
Granite Paper
876 A527 10r multi .70 .70

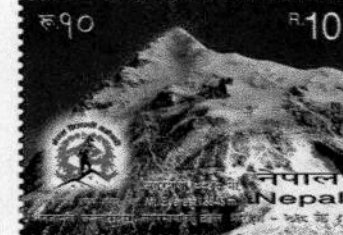

Lions International Blindness Prevention Campaign A528

2012, Sept. 25 Litho.
Granite Paper
877 A528 5r multi .50 .50

World AIDS Day — A529

2012, Dec. 13 ***Perf. 13½x13¾***
Granite Paper
878 A529 5r multi .45 .45

Mt. Everest — A530

2012, Dec. 13 ***Perf. 13¾x13½***
Granite Paper
879 A530 10r multi .75 .75

Asian-Pacific Postal Union, 50th Anniv. — A531

2012, Dec. 13 Granite Paper
880 A531 35r multi 2.00 2.00

Intl. Year of Cooperatives A532

2012, Dec. 24 Litho.
Granite Paper
881 A532 20r multi 1.25 1.25

Sports — A533

Designs: No. 882, 25r, Elephant soccer. No. 883, 25r, Bungee jumping, vert.

Perf. 13¾x13½, 13½x13¾
2012, Dec. 28 Granite Paper
882-883 A533 Set of 2 2.75 2.75

Krishna Prasad Bhattarai (1924-2011), Prime Minister — A534

2012, Dec. 23 ***Perf. 13¾x13½***
884 A534 10r multi .60 .60

Bhikshu Sudarshan (1938-2002), Monk — A535

Perf. 13¾x13½
2012, Dec. 31 Litho.
885 A535 5r multi .50 .50

Basudev Luintel, Writer — A536

Perf. 13¾x13½
2012, Dec. 31 Litho.
886 A536 5r black .50 .50

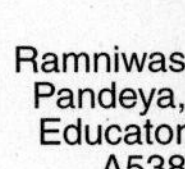

Ali Miyan, Poet — A537

Perf. 13¾x13½
2012, Dec. 31 Litho.
Granite Paper
887 A537 10r multi .50 .50

Ramniwas Pandeya, Educator A538

Perf. 13¾x13½
2012, Dec. 31 Litho.
Granite Paper
888 A538 10r multi .50 .50

Bhuvaneswor Patheya, Writer — A539

Perf. 13¾x13½
2012, Dec. 31 Litho.
Granite Paper
889 A539 10r multi .50 .50

Khagendra Bahadur Basnet, Activist for Rights of the Disabled — A540

Perf. 13¾x13½
2012, Dec. 31 Litho.
Granite Paper
890 A540 10r multi .50 .50

Kishore and Kumar Narsingh Rama, Architects A541

Perf. 13¾x13½
2012, Dec. 31 Litho.
Granite Paper
891 A541 10r multi .50 .50

Karuna (1920-2008) and Lupau Ratna Tuladhar (1918-93), Operators of First Public Bus Service in Nepal — A542

Perf. 13¾x13½
2012, Dec. 31 Litho.
Granite Paper
892 A542 10r multi .50 .50

Visit Lumbini Year — A543

Perf. 13¾x13½
2012, Dec. 31 Litho.
Granite Paper
893 A543 20r multi 1.20 1.20

Rajmansingh Chitrakar (1797-1865), Painter — A544

No. 894 — Chitrakar and his paintings of: a, Tibetan antelopes. b, Birds.

Perf. 13¾x13½
2012, Dec. 31 Litho.
Granite Paper
894 A544 10r Horiz. pair, #a-b 1.20 1.20

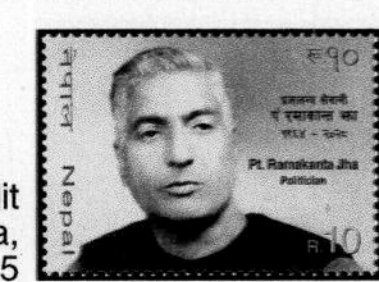

Pandit Ramakanta Jha, Politician — A545

2013, Jan. 18 Litho. ***Perf. 13¾x13½***
895 A545 10r multi .55 .55

Nepalese Partnership With World Bank Group, 50th Anniv. — A546

Perf. 13¾x13½
2013, Mar. 18 Litho.
Granite Paper
896 A546 10r multi .60 .60

Melwa Devi Gurung (1898-1955), Singer — A547

Perf. 13¾x13½
2013, June 10 Litho.
Granite Paper
897 A547 5r multi .50 .50

Lake Salpa — A548

Lomanthang Durbar — A549

Salhes Garden, Lok Nayak Raja Salhes A550

Sahashra Dhara Jatra Festival A551

Perf. 13¾x13½
2013, June 10 Litho.
Granite Paper
898 A548 10r multi .60 .60
899 A549 10r multi .60 .60
900 A550 10r multi .60 .60
Perf. 13½x13¾
901 A551 10r multi .60 .60
Nos. 898-901 (4) 2.40 2.40

Ramraja Prasad Singh (1935-2012), Politician — A552

Moti Kaji Shakya (1913-97), Sculptor — A553

Bhimbahadur Tamang (1933-2012), Politician — A554

Basudev Prasad Dhungana (1933-2012), Advocate for Senior Citizens A555

Harihar Gautam (1901-65), Social Worker A556

Gopal Pande (1913-78), Writer — A557

2013, Oct. 9 Litho. *Perf. 13¾x13½*
Granite Paper

902 A552 10r multi	.55	.55
903 A553 10r multi	.55	.55
904 A554 10r multi	.55	.55
905 A555 10r multi	.55	.55

Perf. 13½x13¾

906 A556 10r multi	.55	.55
907 A557 10r multi	.55	.55
Nos. 902-907 (6)	3.30	3.30

Nepal Red Cross Society, 50th Anniv. — A558

2013, Oct. 9 Litho. *Perf. 13¾x13½*
Granite Paper

908 A558 50r multi 2.75 2.75

Batsaladevi Bhagawali, Dhadhing A559

2013, Oct. 30 Litho. *Perf. 13¾x13½*

909 A559 1r multi .65 .65

Rupchandra Bista (1933-99), Politician — A560

Kewalpure Kisan (1926-2011), Poet — A561

Rupak Raj Sharma (1954-92), Soccer Player — A562

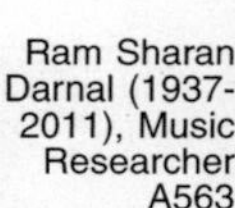

Ram Sharan Darnal (1937-2011), Music Researcher A563

Diamond Shumsher Rana (1919-2011), Writer — A564

2013, Oct. 30 Litho. *Perf. 13¾x13½*

910 A560 5r multi .40 .40

Granite Paper

911 A561 5r multi	.40	.40
912 A562 10r multi	.65	.65
913 A563 10r multi	.65	.65
914 A564 20r multi	1.25	1.25
Nos. 910-914 (5)	3.35	3.35

Bagalamukhi Devi, Lalitpur — A565

Rajdevi Temple, Saptari — A566

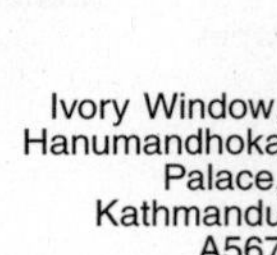

Ivory Window, Hanumandhoka Palace, Kathmandu A567

Kakre Bihar, Surkhet — A568

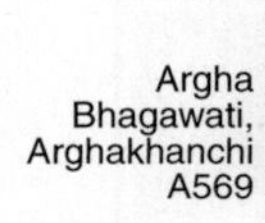

Argha Bhagawati, Arghakhanchi A569

2013, Dec. 31 Litho. *Perf. 13¼*
Granite Paper

915 A565 1r multi	.50	.50
916 A566 1r multi	.50	.50
917 A567 5r multi	.50	.50
918 A568 5r multi	.50	.50
919 A569 5r multi	.50	.50
Nos. 915-919 (5)	2.50	2.50

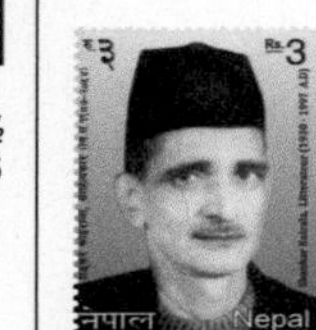

Shankar Koirala (1930-97), Writer A570

Ramhari Sharma (1916-2012), Politician A571

Bhanubhakta Acharya (1814-68), Poet — A572

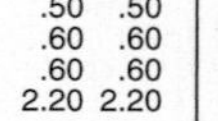
Dr. Dilliraman Regmi (1913-2001), Historian — A573

2013, Dec. 31 Litho. *Perf. 13¼*
Granite Paper

920 A570 3r multi	.50	.50
921 A571 3r multi	.50	.50
922 A572 10r multi	.60	.60
923 A573 10r multi	.60	.60
Nos. 920-923 (4)	2.20	2.20

Museums A574

Designs: No. 924, 20r, National Art Museum, Bhaktapur. No. 925, 20r, International Mountain Museum, Kaski. No. 926, 20r, Patan Museum, Patan. 35r, National Museum, Chhauni.

2013, Dec. 31 Litho. *Perf. 13¼*
Granite Paper

924-927 A574 Set of 4 5.50 5.50

Kathmandu Valley World Heritage Property — A575

Designs: No. 928, 25r, Bhaktapur Durbar Square Monument Zone. No. 929, 25r, Bauddhanath Monument Zone. No. 930, 25r, Changu Narayan Monument Zone. No. 931, 30r, Swayambhu Monument Zone. No. 932, 30r, Hanumandhoka Durbar Square Monument Zone. No. 933, 30r, Pashupati Monument Zone. No. 934, 30r, Patan Durbar Square Monument Zone.

2013, Dec. 31 Litho. *Perf. 13¼*
Granite Paper

928-934 A575 Set of 7 11.00 11.00

Rara Lake, Mugu — A576

2013, Dec. 31 Litho. *Perf. 13¼*
Granite Paper

935 A576 40r multi 2.25 2.25

Flora — A577

Designs: No. 936, 40r, Wild asparagus. No. 937, 40r, Chireta. No. 938, 40r, Long pepper. No. 939, 40r, Fragrant wintergreen.

2013, Dec. 31 Litho. *Perf. 13¼*
Granite Paper

936-939 A577 Set of 4 9.00 9.00

Extinct Animals and Their Fossils — A578

Designs: No. 940, 50r, Giraffa punjabensis and fossil molar teeth. No. 941, 50r, Ramapithecus sivalensis and fossil molar teeth. No. 942, 50r, Hexaprotodon sivalensis and fossil skull. No. 943, 50r, Archidiskidon planifrons and fossil skull.

2013, Dec. 31 Litho. *Perf. 13¼*
Granite Paper

940-943 A578 Set of 4 12.00 12.00

Ascent of Mt. Everest, 60th Anniv, — A579

2013, Dec. 31 Litho. *Perf. 13¼*
Granite Paper

944 A579 100r multi 5.50 5.50

Rishikesh Temple, Ridi — A580

2014, Oct. 9 Litho. *Perf. 13¼*
Granite Paper

945 A580 5r multi .50 .50

Narayanhiti Palace Museum, Kathmandu A581

2014, Oct. 9 Litho. *Perf. 13¼*
Granite Paper

946 A581 20r multi 1.25 1.25

Scouting in Nepal, 60th Anniv. — A582

2014, Oct. 9 Litho. *Perf. 13¼*
Granite Paper

947 A582 30r multi 2.25 1.50

Ascent of Mt. Cho-Oyu, 60th Anniv. — A583

2014, Oct. 9 Litho. *Perf. 13¼*
Granite Paper

948 A583 100r multi 5.50 5.50

Manakamana Cable Car — A584

2014, Oct. 30 Litho. *Perf. 13¼*
Granite Paper

949 A584 50r multi 3.00 3.00

Junior Chamber International of Nepal, 50th Anniv. — A585

2014, Nov. 11 Litho. *Perf. 13¼*
Granite Paper

950 A585 10r multi .50 .50

Kathmandu Buildings — A586

Designs: 1r, Shivaparbati Temple. 2r, Kumari Ghar.

2014, Dec. 9 Litho. *Perf. 13¼*
Granite Paper

951-952 A586 Set of 2 .80 .80

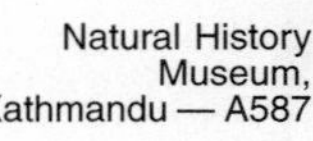
Natural History Museum, Kathmandu — A587

2014, Dec. 9 Litho. *Perf. 13¼*
Granite Paper

953 A587 1r multi .35 .35

Aadeshwor Mahadev, Kathmandu — A588

2014, Dec. 9 Litho. *Perf. 13¼*
Granite Paper

954 A588 1r multi .35 .35

2014 International Cricket Council World Twenty 20 Competition, Bangladesh — A589

2014, Dec. 9 Litho. *Perf. 13¼*
Granite Paper

955 A589 2r multi .35 .35

Female Community Health Volunteers Program, 25th Anniv. (in 2013) — A590

2014, Dec. 9 Litho. *Perf. 13¼*
Granite Paper

956 A590 3r multi .35 .35

Koteshwor Mahadev, Kathmandu — A591

2014, Dec. 9 Litho. *Perf. 13¼*
Granite Paper

957 A591 4r multi .45 .45

Prem Bahadur Kansakar (1917-91), Social Worker — A592

2014, Dec. 9 Litho. *Perf. 13¼*
Granite Paper

958 A592 5r multi .50 .50

Paragliding, Kaski — A593

2014, Dec. 9 Litho. *Perf. 13¼*
Granite Paper

959 A593 10r multi .55 .55

Miniature Sheets

Moths — A594

No. 960, 10r: a, Acherontia lachesis. b, Asota producta. c, Argina argus. d, Biston contectaria.

No. 961, 10r: a, Brahmaea wallichii. b, Campylotes histrionicus. c, Dermaleipa (Lagoptera) juno. d, Episteme adulatrix.

No. 962, 10r: a, Erasmia pulchella. b, Eterusia aedea edocla. c, Eudocima salaminia. d, Gynautocera papilionaria.

2014, Dec. 9 Litho. *Perf. 13¼*
Granite Paper
Sheets of 4, #a-d

960-962 A594 Set of 3 6.75 6.75

Miniature Sheet

Birthplace of Buddha — A595

No. 963: a, Birthplace of Lord Buddha, Lumbini. b, Ashoka Pillar, Lumbini. c, Ramagrama, Nawalparasi. d, Tilaurakot, Kapilavastu.

2014, Dec. 9 Litho. *Perf. 13¼*
Granite Paper

963 A595 20r Sheet of 4, #a-d 4.50 4.50

2014 Winter Olympics, Sochi, Russia — A596

2014, Dec. 10 Litho. *Perf. 13¼*
Granite Paper

964 A596 2r multi .50 .50

Tenzing-Hillary Everest Marathon — A597

2014, Dec. 19 Litho. *Perf. 13¼*
Granite Paper

965 A597 3r multi .40 .40

B. P. Koirala (1914-82), Prime Minister — A598

2014, Dec. 31 Litho. *Perf. 13¼*
Granite Paper

966 A598 10r multi .40 .40

Dwarika Bhakta Mathema (1902-68), Musician — A599

2015, July 1 Litho. *Perf. 13¼*
Granite Paper

967 A599 1r multi .25 .25

Chandeshwori Temple, Banepa — A600

Makwanpur Gadhi, Makwanpur — A601

Lamjung Durbar, Lamjung — A602

Siddha Pokhari, Bhaktapur — A603

Doleshwor Mahadev, Bhaktapur — A604

Sindhuli Gadhi, Sindhuli — A605

Kaliyadaman, Sundari Chowk, Hanumandhoka — A606

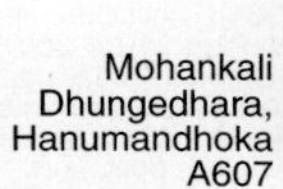

Mohankali Dhungedhara, Hanumandhoka — A607

Taleju Temple, Nuwakot — A608

Bulbule Lake, Surkhet — A609

2015, July 1 Litho. *Perf. 13¼*
Granite Paper

968 A600 1r multi .35 .30
969 A601 1r multi .35 .30
970 A602 2r multi .35 .30
971 A603 2r multi .35 .30
972 A604 5r multi .35 .30
973 A605 5r multi .35 .30
974 A606 5r multi .35 .30
975 A607 8r multi .35 .30
976 A608 10r multi .35 .30
977 A609 10r multi .35 .30
Nos. 968-977 (10) 3.50 3.00

Fewa Lake and Machhapuchchhre, Kaski — A610

Serpentine Die Cut 12¼
2015, July 1 Litho.
Self-Adhesive

978 A610 60r multi 1.40 1.00

A611

A612

A613

B.P. Koirala Highway, Flags of Nepal and Japan — A614

2015, July 1 Litho. *Perf. 13¼*
Granite Paper

979 Strip of 4 2.25 2.25
a. A611 10r multi .50 .30
b. A612 10r multi .50 .30
c. A613 10r multi .50 .30
d. A614 10r multi .50 .30

Nepal-Japan cooperation.

Prehistoric Elephants — A615

Emblem of Tribhuvan University Natural History Museum and: No. 980, 10r, Deinotherium indicum. No. 981, 10r, Elephas hysudricus. No. 982, 10r, Elephas namadicus. No. 983, 10r, Gomphotherium sp. No. 984, 10r, Stegodon bombifrons. No. 985, 10r, Stegodon ganesa.

2015, July 7 Litho. *Perf. 13¼*
Granite Paper

980-985 A615 Set of 6 4.50 4.50

A616

2015, Aug. 1 Litho. *Perf. 13¼*
Granite Paper

986 A616 20r multi .90 .90

Diplomatic Relations Between Nepal and People's Republic of China, 60th Anniv.

Narasimha, Hanumandhoka — A617

Nautale Durbar, Hanumandhoka — A618

Rani Mahal, Palpa — A619

Gaddi Baithak, Hanumandhoka — A620

2015, Aug. 11 Litho. *Perf. 14x13½*
Granite Paper

987 A617 10r multi .40 .40

Perf. 13½x14

988 A618 10r multi .40 .40
989 A619 25r multi .75 .75
990 A620 35r multi 1.10 1.10
Nos. 987-990 (4) 2.65 2.65

Miniature Sheet

Ascent of Mounts Kanchenjunga and Makalu, 60th Anniv. — A621

No. 991: a, Mt. Kanchenjunga. b, Mt. Makalu. c, Airplane over mountains. d, Unnamed mountains. e, Hillary Peak. f, Tenzing Peak.

Perf. 13½x13¼

2015, Aug. 11 **Litho.**
Granite Paper

991 A621 10r Sheet of 6, #a-f 3.25 3.25

Non-Violence, Harmony, Morality and Freedom From Addiction — A622

2015, Aug. 16 **Litho.** ***Perf. 13¼***
Granite Paper

992 A622 25r multi .70 .70

Wildlife Reserves and National Parks — A623

Designs: 1r, Koshi Tappu Wildlife Reserve. No. 994, 2r, Sagarmatha National Park. No. 995, 2r, Chitwan National Park. No. 996, 5r, Shuklaphanta Wildlife Reserve. No. 997, 5r, Lamtang National Park.

2015, Oct. 2 **Litho.** ***Perf. 13¼***
Granite Paper

993-997 A623 Set of 5 1.25 1.25

Flora — A624

Designs: No. 998, 10r, Abies spectabilis. No. 999, 10r, Gentiana robusta. No. 1000, 10r, Lilium nepalense. No. 1001, 10r, Maharanga emodi. No. 1002, 10r, Paris polyphylla. No. 1003, 10r, Saussurea gossipiphora.

2015, Oct. 2 **Litho.** ***Perf. 13¼***
Granite Paper

998-1003 A624 Set of 6 3.25 3.25

Sarbeshwor Mahadev, Lalitpur — A625

2015, Oct. 9 **Litho.** ***Perf. 13¼***
Granite Paper

1004 A625 3r multi .40 .30

Earthquake Survival Techniques A626

2015, Oct. 9 **Litho.** ***Perf. 13¼***
Granite Paper

1005 A626 5r multi .40 .40

18th South Asian Association for Regional Cooperation Summit, Kathmandu, 1st Anniv. — A627

2015, Oct. 9 **Litho.** ***Perf. 13¼***
Granite Paper

1006 A627 10r multi .50 .50

Famous Men — A628

Designs: No. 1007, 8r, Deviprasad Uprety (1912-92), social worker. No. 1008, 8r, Nagendra Prasad Rijal (1927-94), politician. No. 1009, 8r, Yadav Prasad Pant (1915-2007), economist. No. 1010, 8r, Shreeprasad Parajuli (1911-62), martyr. No. 1011, 8r, Ganeshman Singh (1915-97), politician. No. 1012, 8r, Siddhi Charan Shrestha (1912-92), poet, vert.

2015, Dec. 31 **Litho.** ***Perf. 13¼***
Granite Paper

1007-1012 A628 Set of 6 3.25 3.25

Diplomatic Relations Between Nepal and Japan, 60th Anniv. — A630

2016, Nov. 3 **Litho.** ***Perf. 12½***
Granite Paper

1014 A630 10r multi 1.00 1.00

Nepal Philatelic Society, 50th Anniv. — A631

Serpentine Die Cut 11

2016, Nov. 3 **Litho.**
Self-Adhesive
Granite Paper

1015 A631 10r multi .50 .50

Federation of Nepal Chambers of Commerce and Industry, 50th Anniv. — A632

Serpentine Die Cut 11

2016, Nov. 3 **Litho.**
Self-Adhesive
Granite Paper

1016 A632 10r multi .50 .50

Bal Bahadur Rai (1921-2010), Politician A633

Lakhan Thapa Magar (1834-77), Revolutionist and First Martyr of Nepal — A634

Mahendra Narayan Nidhi (1922-99), Politician A635

Yogmaya Neupane (1867-1941), Social Reformer A636

Dev S. J. B. Rana (1862-1914), Social Reformer A637

Ratna Kumar Bantawa (1952-79), Politician and Martyr — A638

2016 **Litho.** ***Perf. 12½***
Granite Paper

1017 A633 10r multi .50 .50
1018 A634 10r multi .50 .50
1019 A635 10r multi .50 .50
1020 A636 10r multi .50 .50
1021 A637 10r multi .50 .50
1022 A638 10r multi .50 .50
Nos. 1017-1022 (6) 3.00 3.00

Aadilinga Kusheshwor Mahadev, Sindhuli — A639

Chandanbharateshwor Mahadev, Kathmandu — A640

Shree Parroha Parmeshwor Shiva Jyotirlinga, Rupandehi A641

Siddhakali Temple, Bhojpur A642

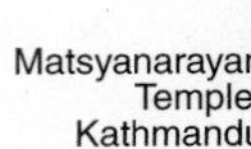

Matsyanarayan Temple, Kathmandu A643

Hatuwaghadi, Capital of Majh Kirat, Bhojpur — A644

2016 **Litho.** ***Perf. 12½***
Granite Paper

1023 A639 1r multi .30 .30
1024 A640 5r multi .30 .30
1025 A641 5r multi .30 .30
1026 A642 10r multi .50 .50
1027 A643 10r multi .50 .50
1028 A644 10r multi .50 .50
Nos. 1023-1028 (6) 2.40 2.40

Bhringareshwor Mahadev, Lalitpur A645

2016 **Litho.** ***Serpentine Die Cut 11***
Self-Adhesive
Granite Paper

1029 A645 2r multi .30 .30

First Issue of Gorkhapatra Daily, 1901 — A646

2016 **Litho.** ***Serpentine Die Cut 11***
Self-Adhesive
Granite Paper

1030 A646 10r multi .50 .50

Relations Between Nepal and Great Britain, 200th Anniv. — A647

2016 **Litho.** ***Serpentine Die Cut 11***
Self-Adhesive
Granite Paper

1031 A647 10r multi 1.00 1.00

Constitution of Nepal — A648

2016 **Litho.** ***Serpentine Die Cut 11***
Self-Adhesive
Granite Paper

1032 A648 10r multi .50 .50

Francolinus Francolinus A649

2016 Litho. ***Serpentine Die Cut 11***
Self-Adhesive
Granite Paper

1033 A649 25r multi 2.25 2.25

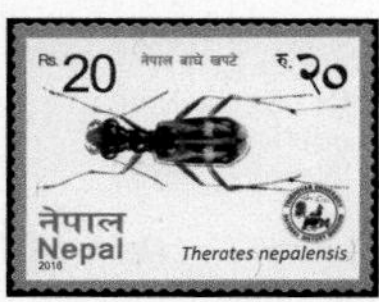

Beetles A650

Designs: No. 1034, 20r, Therates nepalensis. No. 1035, 20r, Mylabris phalerata. No. 1036, 20r, Dorcus nepalensis. No. 1037, 20r, Odontolabis (Calcodes) cuvera.

2016 Litho. ***Serpentine Die Cut 11***
Self-Adhesive
Granite Paper

1034-1037 A650 Set of 4 6.50 6.50

Rhododendrons A651

Designs: No. 1038, 20r, Rhododendron ciliatum. No. 1039, 20r, Rhododendron dalhousiae. No. 1040, 20r, Rhododendron fulgens. No. 1041, 20r, Rhododendron glaucophyllum.

2016 Litho. ***Serpentine Die Cut 11***
Self-Adhesive
Granite Paper

1038-1041 A651 Set of 4 6.50 6.50

Mountains A652

Designs: 35r, Mt. Manaslu. 100r, Mt. Lhotse.

2016 Litho. ***Serpentine Die Cut 11***
Self-Adhesive
Granite Paper

1042-1043 A652 Set of 2 11.00 11.00

Prehistoric Mammals A653

Designs: No. 1044, 10r, Dorcatherium. No. 1045, 10r, Hipparion. No. 1046, 10r, Pachyportax. No. 1047, 10r, Hemibos acuticornis. 100r, Brachypotherium perimense. 200r, Giraffokeryx punjabiensis.

Serpentine Die Cut 11
2017, Sept. 22 Litho.
Self-Adhesive
Granite Paper

1044-1049 A653 Set of 6 16.00 16.00

Mammals A654

Designs: No. 1050, 10r, Marbled cat. No. 1051, 10r, Large Indian civet. No. 1052, 10r, Pygmy hog. No. 1053, 10r, Black giant squirrel. No. 1054, 20r, Crested porcupine. No. 1055, 20r, Roylei's pika.

Serpentine Die Cut 11
2017, Sept. 22 Litho.
Self-Adhesive
Granite Paper

1050-1055 A654 Set of 6 4.50 4.50

Flora — A655

Designs: No. 1056, 1r, Dryopteris cochleata. No. 1057, 1r, Lycopodium japonicum. No. 1058, 2r, Cyathea spinulosa. No. 1059, 2r, Drynaria propinqua. No. 1060, 3r, Nephrolepis cordifolia. No. 1061, 3r, Tectaria coadunate.

2017 Litho. ***Perf. 12½***
Granite Paper

1056-1061 A655 Set of 6 1.75 1.75

Containers — A656

Designs: 3r, Theki Madani. 8r, Karuwa.

2017 Litho. ***Perf. 12½***
Granite Paper

1062-1063 A656 Set of 2 .90 .90

Famous Men — A657

Designs: No. 1064, 10r, Janakabi Keshari Dharmaraj Thapa (1924-2014), folk singer. No. 1065, 10r, Saroj Prasad Koirala (1929-73), politician.

2017 Litho. ***Perf. 12½***
Granite Paper

1064-1065 A657 Set of 2 1.20 1.20

Pokali Waterfall — A658

2017 Litho. ***Perf. 12½***
Granite Paper

1066 A658 1r multi .40 .30

Ugratara Temple, Dadeldhura A659

2017 Litho. ***Perf. 12½***
Granite Paper

1067 A659 1r multi .40 .30

Shreeantu A660

2017 Litho. ***Perf. 12½***
Granite Paper

1068 A660 2r multi .40 .30

Rauta Pokhari — A661

2017 Litho. ***Perf. 12½***
Granite Paper

1069 A661 2r multi .40 .30

Tansen Bhairav, Palpa — A662

2017 Litho. ***Perf. 12½***
Granite Paper

1070 A662 2r multi .40 .30

Junge Mahadev Statue, Banke — A663

2017 Litho. ***Perf. 12½***
Granite Paper

1071 A663 2r multi .40 .30

Flag of Nepal — A664

2017 Litho. ***Perf. 12½***
Granite Paper

1072 A664 5r multi .40 .30

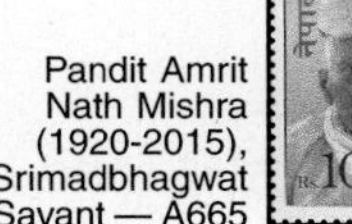

Pandit Amrit Nath Mishra (1920-2015), Srimadbhagwat Savant — A665

2017 Litho. ***Perf. 12½***
Granite Paper

1073 A665 10r multi .90 .90

Nepal Election Commission, 50th Anniv. — A666

2017 Litho. ***Perf. 12½***
Granite Paper

1074 A666 10r multi .90 .90

Foods A667

No. 1075: a, Yomari. b, Sel. c, Anarasa. d, Lakhamari.

2017 Litho. ***Perf. 12½***
Granite Paper

1075 A667 1r Block of 4, #a-d 1.20 1.20

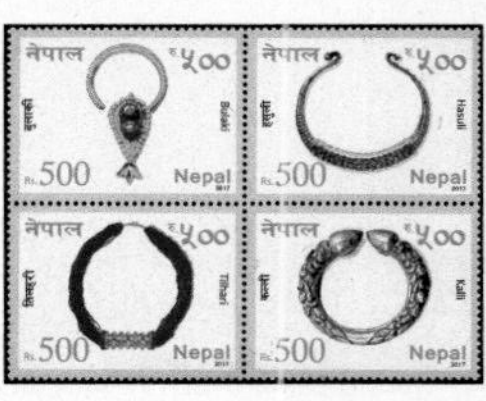

Jewelry A668

No. 1076: a, Bulaki. b, Hasuli. c, Tilhari. d, Kalli.

2017 Litho. ***Perf. 12½***
Granite Paper

1076 A668 500r Block of 4, #a-d 85.00 85.00

Four Martyrs — A669

2017 Litho. ***Perf. 12½***
Granite Paper

1077 A669 10r multi .90 .90

Bel Biwaha — A670

2017 Litho. ***Perf. 12½***
Granite Paper

1078 A670 20r multi 1.75 1.75

Bratabandha A671

2017 Litho. ***Perf. 12½***
Granite Paper

1079 A671 35r multi 2.40 2.40

Wedding Costumes — A672

Costumes of newly-wedded: 10r, Tharu couple. 20r, Limbu couple.

2017 Litho. ***Perf. 12½***
Granite Paper

1080-1081 A672 Set of 2 2.50 2.50

Landscapes A673

Designs: 5r, Gajedi Lake, Rupandehi. 35r, Khangchung (UIAA Peak), Solukhumbu.

2017 Litho. *Perf. 12½*
Granite Paper

1082-1083 A673 Set of 2 3.00 3.00

Temples — A674

Designs: 2r, Sarshwor Mahadev, Siraha. 5r, Mahalaxmi Temple, Lalitpur. 10r, Kshemadevi Temple, Sindhupalchowk.

2017 Litho. *Perf. 12½*
Granite Paper

1084-1086 A674 Set of 3 1.75 1.75

First Paper Banknotes of Nepal — A675

Front and back of: 5r, Five-rupee note. 10r, Ten-rupee note. 100r, One hundred-rupee note.

2017 Litho. *Perf. 12½*
Granite Paper

1087-1089 A675 Set of 3 6.00 6.00

Famous Men — A676

Designs: No. 1090, 5r, Master Ratadnas Prakash (1913-92), musician. No. 1091, 5r, Dronacharya Chhetri (1945-93), politician. No. 1092, 10r, Durga Nanda Jha (1942-64), martyr. No. 1093, 10r, Yagya Bahadur Thapa (1913-78), martyr. No. 1094, 10r, Gaurishankar Khadka (1959-2009), politician. No. 1095, 10r, Gambhir Bahadur Thapa (1924-2009), social worker.

2017 Litho. *Perf. 12½*
Granite Paper

1090-1095 A676 Set of 6 4.50 4.50

Ram Prasad Rai (1909-52), Leader of 1951 Revolution — A677

2018 Litho. *Perf. 12½*
Granite Paper

1096 A677 10r multi .90 .90

Alam Devi Temple, Syangja A678

2019 Litho. *Perf. 12½*
Granite Paper

1097 A678 5r multi .90 .90

Flora — A679

Designs: No. 1098, 5r, Daphne bholua. No. 1099, 5r, Girardinia diversifolia. No. 1100, 5r, Agave americana.

2019 Litho. *Perf. 12½*
Granite Paper

1098-1100 A679 Set of 3 1.60 1.60

Snails A680

No. 1101: a, Rishetia kathmandica. b, Rishetia nagarjunesis. c, Rishetia rishikeshi. d, Rishetia tribhuvana.

2019 Litho. *Perf. 12½*
Granite Paper

1101 A680 5r Block of 4, #a-d 2.25 2.25

Tongue Piercing Ceremony A681

2019 Litho. *Perf. 12½*
Granite Paper

1102 A681 10r multi .90 .90

Yadunath Khanal (1913-2004), Diplomat — A682

2019 Litho. *Perf. 12½*
Granite Paper

1103 A682 10r multi .90 .90

Amber Gurung (1938-2016), Composer and Musician A683

2019 Litho. *Perf. 12½*
Granite Paper

1104 A683 10r multi .90 .90

Nararaj Dhakal (1920-2004), Musician A684

2019 Litho. *Perf. 12½*
Granite Paper

1105 A684 10r multi .90 .90

Toni Hagen (1917-2003), Geologist A685

2019 Litho. *Perf. 12½*
Granite Paper

1106 A685 20r multi 1.60 1.60

Buddha — A686

2019 Litho. *Perf. 12½*
Granite Paper

1107 A686 20r multi 1.60 1.60

Diplomatic Relations Between Nepal and Sri Lanka, 60th Anniv. — A687

2019 Litho. *Perf. 12½*
Granite Paper

1108 A687 25r multi 2.75 2.75

Souvenir Sheet

Temal Jatra, Boudhanath Stupa — A688

2019 Litho. *Perf. 12½*
Granite Paper

1109 A688 50r multi 5.50 5.50

Securities Board of Nepal, 25th Anniv. — A689

Serpentine Die Cut 11
2020, Jan. 1 Litho.
Self-Adhesive

1110 A689 5r multi — —

2021 Census — A690

2020, Jan. 1 Litho. *Perf. 12½*
Granite Paper

1111 A690 10r bl grn & blk — —

100th Birthday of Dr. Satya Mohan Joshi, Writer — A691

2020, Jan. 1 Litho. *Perf. 12½*
Granite Paper

1112 A691 10r multi — —

Ramdhuni Temple, Sunsari A692

Serpentine Die Cut 11
2020, Jan. 1 Litho.
Self-Adhesive

1113 A692 10r multi — —

Lumbini Peace Marathon A693

Serpentine Die Cut 11
2020, Jan. 1 Litho.
Self-Adhesive

1114 A693 20r multi — —

Mount Everest Skydivers A694

2020, Jan. 1 Litho. *Perf. 12½*
Granite Paper

1115 A694 30r multi — —

Flora — A695

Designs: No. 1116, Berberis pendryi. No. 1117, Begonia tribenensis. No. 1118, Begonia leptoptera. No. 1119, Berberis mucrifolia.

2020, Jan. 1 Litho. *Perf. 12½*
Granite Paper

1116-1119 A695 10r Set of 4 — —

Tourism A696

Designs: 5r, Galeshwor Mahadev Temple, Myagdi. No. 1121, 10r, Resunga Yagyashala, Gulmi. No. 1122, 10r, Sirubari, Syangja. No. 1123, 10r, Ghale Gaun, Lamjung.

Serpentine Die Cut 11
2020, Jan. 1 Litho.
Self-Adhesive

1120-1123 A696 Set of 4 — —

Nepal Rastra Bank's First 1-Rupee Banknote A697

No. 1124: a, Front of banknote (with black serial number). b, Back of banknote.

2020, Jan. 1 Litho. *Perf. 12½*
Granite Paper

1124 A697 10r Vert. pair, #a-b — —

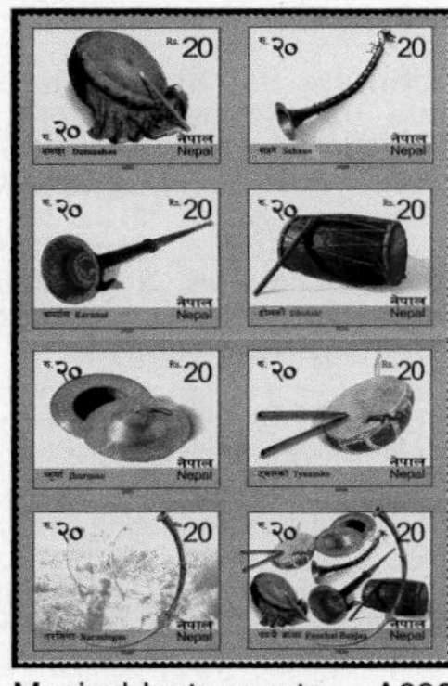

Musical Instruments — A698

No. 1125: a, Damaahaa. b, Sahane. c, Karnaal. d, Dholaki. e, Jhurmaa. f, Tyaamko. g, Narasingaa. h, Panchai baajaa.

Serpentine Die Cut 11
2020, Jan. 1 Litho.
Self-Adhesive

1125 A698 20r Block of 8, #a-h — —

Mahdav Prasad Ghimire (1919-2020), Poet — A698a

2021, Dec. 8 Litho. *Perf. 12½*
Granite Paper

1125I A698a 10r multi — —

Nepal Chamber of Commerce, 70th Anniv. — A699

Serpentine Die Cut 11
2021, Dec. 29 Litho.
Self-Adhesive

1126 A699 5r multi — —

Spiny Babbler — A700

Serpentine Die Cut 11
2021, Dec. 29 Litho.
Self-Adhesive

1127 A700 10r multi — —

Hiking Routes and Bases — A701

Designs: 10r, Ghandruk, Kaski. No. 1129, 20r, Everest Base Camp Route. No. 1130, 20r, Manaslu Circuit Route. No. 1131, 20r, Mardi Himal Trekking Route. No. 1132, 20r, Annapurna Base Camp Route.

Serpentine Die Cut 11
2021, Dec. 29 Litho.
Self-Adhesive

1128-1132 A701 Set of 5 — —

Nos. 1129-1132 have white denominations.

Mountains A702

Designs: No. 1133, 10r, Mt. Everest. No. 1134, 10r, Mt. Cho-Oyu. No. 1135, 10r, Mt. Dhaulagiri. No. 1136, 10r, Mt. Annapurna. No. 1137, 10r, Mt. Kanchenjunga (main peak). No. 1138, 10r, Mt. Lhotse. No. 1139, 10r, Mt. Makalu. No. 1140, 10r, Mt. Manaslu.

Serpentine Die Cut 11
2021, Dec. 29 Litho.
Self-Adhesive

1133-1140 A702 Set of 8 — —

Sustainable Development Goals — A703

Various works of Mithla art and sustainable development goal: No. 1141, Goal 1, No poverty.

No. 1142: a, Goal 2, Zero hunger. b, Goal 3, Good health and well-being. c, Goal 4, Quality education. d, Goal 5, Gender equality.

No. 1143: a, Goal 6, Clean water and sanitation. b, Goal 7, Affordable and clean energy. c, Goal 8, Decent work and economic growth. d, Goal 9, Industry, innovation and infrastructure.

No. 1144: a, Goal 10, Reduced inequalities. b, Goal 11, Sustainable cities and communities. c, Goal 12, Responsible consumption and production. d, Goal 13, Climate action.

No. 1145: a, Goal 14, Life below water. b, Goal 15, Life on land. c, Goal 16, Peace, justice and strong institutions. d, Goal 17, Partnerships for the goals.

Serpentine Die Cut 11
2021, Dec. 29 Litho.
Self-Adhesive

1141 A703 10r multi — —
1142 Horiz. strip of 4 — —
a.-d. A703 10r Any single — —
1143 Horiz. strip of 4 — —
a.-d. A703 10r Any single — —
1144 Horiz. strip of 4 — —
a.-d. A703 10r Any single — —
1145 Horiz. strip of 4 — —
a.-d. A703 10r Any single — —

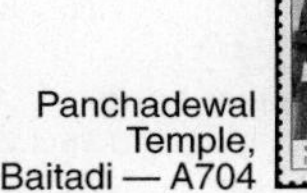

Panchadewal Temple, Baitadi — A704

Mandavya Rishi Temple, Palpa — A705

2022 Litho. *Perf. 12½*
Granite Paper

1146 Vert. pair — —
a. A704 5r multi — —
b. A705 5r multi — —

Sinja Valley, Jumla — A706

2022 Litho. *Perf. 12½*
Granite Paper

1147 A706 10r multi — —

Kaji Kalu Pandey Graveyard, Kathmandu — A707

2022 Litho. *Perf. 12½*
Granite Paper

1148 A707 10r multi — —

Palpa Durbar Museum, Palpa — A708

2022 Litho. *Perf. 12½*
Granite Paper

1149 A708 10r multi — —

Kalinchowk Bhagawati, Dolakha A709

Tanadevi Temple, Kathmandu A710

Saileshwori Bhagawati Temple, Doti — A711

Rambhadevi Temple, Palpa — A712

2022 Litho. *Perf. 12½*
Granite Paper

1150 Vert. strip of 4 — —
a. A709 5r multi — —
b. A710 5r multi — —
c. A711 5r multi — —
d. A712 5r multi — —

Man and Woman Wearing Jirel Costumes and Ornaments A713

Shadar Pidar (Koech) Festival of Sunuwar A714

Man and Woman Wearing Surel Costumes A715

Man and Woman Wearing Tamang Costumes, Damphu Drum A716

Thami Ethnic Culture — A717

2022 Litho. *Serpentine Die Cut 11*
Granite Paper
Self-Adhesive

1151 Vert. strip of 5 — —
a. A713 10r multi — —
b. A714 10r multi — —
c. A715 10r multi — —
d. A716 10r multi — —
e. A717 10r multi — —

Rhododendrons A718

No. 1152: a, Rhododendron thomsonii. b, Rhododendron campanulatum.

No. 1153: a, Pink Rhododendron arboreum. b, Red Rhododendron arboreum. c, Rhododendron lepidoturn. d, White Rhododendron arboreum.

2022 Litho. *Perf. 12½*
Granite Paper

1152 Horiz. pair — —
a.-b. A718 20r Either single — —
1153 Horiz. strip of 4 — —
a.-d. A718 20r Any single — —

A719

A720

A721

Workers of the COVID-19 Pandemic — A722

2022, Dec. 18 Litho. *Perf. 12½*
Granite Paper

1154	Horiz. strip of 4	—	—
a.	A719 10r multi	—	—
b.	A720 10r multi	—	—
c.	A721 10r multi	—	—
d.	A722 10r multi	—	—

Khaptad National Park, Doti — A723

Panini Tapobhumi, Arghakhanchi A724

Statue of Shrawan Kumar and Aandhikhola, Syangja A725

Tribeni Temple, Khaptad National Park, Doti — A726

Taudaha Lake, Kathmandu A727

2022, Oct. 9 Litho. *Perf. 12½*
Granite Paper

1155	Horiz. strip of 5	—	—
a.	A723 5r multi	—	—
b.	A724 5r multi	—	—
c.	A725 5r multi	—	—
d.	A726 5r multi	—	—
e.	A727 5r multi	—	—

Medicinal Plants — A728

No. 1156: a, Didymocarpus nepalensis. b, Tinospora sinensis. c, Justicia adhatoda. d, Acorus calamus.

2022, Oct. 9 Litho. *Perf. 12½*
Granite Paper

1156	Horiz. strip of 4	—	—
a.-d.	A728 10r Any single	—	—

Mountain Peaks — A729

No. 1157: a, Island Peak. b, Abi Peak. c, Lobuche Peak. d, Chulu East Peak. e, Pisang Peak.

Serpentine Die Cut 11
2022, Oct. 9 Litho.
Self-Adhesive
Granite Paper

1157	Horiz. strip of 5	—	
a.-e.	A729 10r Any single	—	—

Padma Ratna Tuladhar (1941-2018), Politician — A730

Angrita Sherpa (1948-2020), Mountaineering Guide — A731

Koili Devi (1929-2007), Singer and Composer A732

Madhav Prasad Devkota (1903-82), Writer A733

Purna Prakash Nepal "Yatri" (1934-2012), Writer — A734

2023, June 20 Litho. *Perf. 12½*
Granite Paper

1158	Vert. strip of 5	—	—
a.	A730 10r multi	—	—
b.	A731 10r multi	—	—
c.	A732 10r multi	—	—
d.	A733 10r multi	—	—
e.	A734 10r multi	—	—

AIR POST STAMPS

Catalogue values for unused stamps in this section are for Never Hinged items.

Bird over Kathmandu — AP1

Rough Perf 11½
1958, Oct. 16 Typo. Unwmk.
Without Gum

C1	AP1	10p dark blue	4.00	2.00

Plane over Kathmandu AP2

1967, Oct. 24 Photo. *Perf. 13½x13*

C2	AP2	1.80r multicolored	2.00	1.50

International Tourist Year.

God Akash Bhairab and Nepal Airlines Emblem — AP3

Map of Nepal with Airlines Network — AP4

Design: 2.50r, Plane over Himalayas.

Perf. 14½x14, 13 (65p)
1968, July 1 Photo.

C3	AP3	15p blue & bis brn	.50	.50
C4	AP4	65p violet blue	1.25	1.00
C5	AP3	2.50r dp blue & scar	3.75	2.75
		Nos. C3-C5 (3)	5.50	4.25

10th anniv. of the Royal Nepal Airlines Corp.

Flyer and Jet — AP5

1978, Dec. 12 Photo. *Perf. 13*

C6	AP5	2.30r blue & ocher	1.25	.80

75th anniversary of 1st powered flight.

Pheasant Type of 1979

3.50r, Impeyan pheasant, horiz.

1979, Nov. 22 Photo. *Perf. 14½x14*

C7	A174	3.50r multicolored	2.25	1.75

OFFICIAL STAMPS

Catalogue values for unused stamps in this section are for Never Hinged items.

Soldiers and Arms of Nepal — O1

Perf. 13½
1959, Nov. 1 Litho. Unwmk.
Size: 29x17½mm

O1	O1	2p reddish brown	.25	.25
O2	O1	4p yel green	.25	.25
O3	O1	6p salmon pink	.25	.25
O4	O1	8p brt violet	.30	.25
O5	O1	12p red orange	.35	.25

Size: 37½x21½mm

O6	O1	16p red brown	.50	.35
O7	O1	24p carmine	.60	.50
O8	O1	32p rose car	1.00	.70
O9	O1	50p ultramarine	1.75	1.25
O10	O1	1r rose red	3.25	2.25
O11	O1	2r orange	6.50	5.00
		Nos. O1-O11 (11)	15.00	11.30

Nos. 144-146 and 124 Overprinted in Black

1960-62 Photo. *Perf. 14½x14*
Overprint 12½mm Long

O12	A35	1p carmine rose ('62)	.25	.25
O13	A35	2p bright blue ('62)	.25	.25
O14	A35	5p golden brown ('62)	.35	.35
		Nos. O12-O14 (3)	.85	.85

Perf. 14
Overprint 14½mm Long

O15	A26	1r red lilac	1.25	1.25

The overprint, "Kaj Sarkari" in Devanagari characters means "Service." Five other denominations, 10p, 40p, 75p, 2r and 5r, were similarly overprinted but not issued. Value, 5 values $3. A few exist on 1960 first day covers.

In 1983 substantial quantities of the set of nine values were sold as remainders by the Post Office at face value (under $1 for the set).

The existence of covers from 1985-86 indicate that some of these may have been used as regular postage stamps.

NETHERLANDS

ˈne-t͟hər-lənˌdz

(Holland)

LOCATION — Northwestern Europe, bordering on the North Sea
GOVT. — Kingdom
AREA — 16,029 sq. mi.
POP. — 17,140,000 (2020 est.)
CAPITAL — Amsterdam

100 Cents = 1 Gulden (Guilder or Florin)
100 Cents = 1 Euro (2002)

Catalogue values for unused stamps in this country are for Never Hinged items, beginning with Scott 216 in the regular postage section, Scott B123 in the semi-postal section, Scott C13 in the airpost section, Scott J80 in the postage due section, and Scott O44 in the official section.

Values for unused stamps are for examples with original gum as defined in the catalogue introduction. Very fine examples of Nos. 4-12 will have perforations touching the frameline on one or more sides due to the narrow spacing of the stamps on the plates. Stamps with perfs clear on all four sides are very scarce and command higher prices.

Watermarks

Wmk. 158

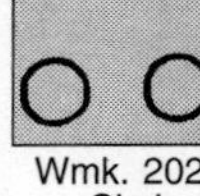

Wmk. 202 — Circles

King William III — A1

Wmk. 158
1852, Jan. 1 Engr. *Imperf.*

1	A1	5c blue	400.00	35.00
a.		5c light blue	450.00	40.00
b.		5c steel blue	750.00	100.00
c.		5c dark blue	450.00	35.00
2	A1	10c carmine	450.00	27.50
3	A1	15c orange	775.00	130.00

In 1895 the 10c was privately reprinted in several colors on unwatermarked paper by Joh. A. Moesman, whose name appears on the back.

King William III — A2

1864 Unwmk. *Perf. 12½x12*

4	A2	5c blue	300.00	16.00
5	A2	10c lake	425.00	8.00
6	A2	15c orange	1,050.	100.00
a.		15c yellow	1,350.	115.00

The paper varies considerably in thickness. It is sometimes slightly bluish, also vertically ribbed.

William III — A3

1867 *Perf. 12¾x11¾*
7 A3 5c ultra 115.00 2.75
8 A3 10c lake 225.00 4.75
9 A3 15c orange brn 640.00 35.00
10 A3 20c dk green 625.00 24.00
11 A3 25c dk violet 2,100. 110.00
12 A3 50c gold 2,500. 160.00

The paper of Nos. 7-22 sometimes has an accidental bluish tinge of varying strength. During its manufacture a chemical whitener (bluing agent) was added in varying quantities. No particular printing was made on bluish paper.

Two varieties of numerals in each value, differing chiefly in the thickness.

Oxidized copies of the 50c are worth much less.

Imperforate varieties of Nos. 7-12 are proofs.

See the *Scott Specialized Catalogue* for listings by perforations.

1869 *Perf. 10½x10*
7c A3 5c ultra 225.00 11.50
8c A3 10c lake 230.00 7.75
9c A3 15c orange brown 2,700. 1,150.
10c A3 20c dark green 1,550. 155.00

Coat of Arms — A4

1869-71 Typo. *Perf. 13¼, 14*
17 A4 ½c red brown ('71) 24.00 3.75
c. Perf. 14 *2,300.* 875.00
18 A4 1c black 210.00 70.00
19 A4 1c green 15.50 2.25
c. Perf. 14 27.50 5.50
20 A4 1½c rose 150.00 77.50
b. Perf. 14 175.00 97.50
21 A4 2c buff 60.00 15.00
c. Perf. 14 55.00 14.00
22 A4 2½c violet ('70) 475.00 70.00
c. Perf. 14 775.00 425.00

Imperforate varieties are proofs.

A5

A6

Perf. 12½, 13, 13½, 13x14, 14, 12½x12 and 11½x12

1872-88
23 A5 5c blue 11.50 .30
a. 5c ultra 14.00 1.25
24 A5 7½c red brn ('88) 35.00 18.00
25 A5 10c rose 57.50 1.60
26 A5 12½c gray ('75) 62.50 2.40
27 A5 15c brn org 350.00 5.25
28 A5 20c green 425.00 5.00
29 A5 22½c dk grn ('88) 77.50 42.50
30 A5 25c dull vio 525.00 4.00
31 A5 50c bister 650.00 11.00
32 A5 1g gray vio ('88) 480.00 40.00
33 A6 2g50c rose & ultra 900.00 105.00

Imperforate varieties are proofs.

Numeral of Value — A7

HALF CENT:
Type I — Fraction bar 8 to 8½mm long.
Type II — Fraction bar 9mm long and thinner.

Perf. 12½, 13½, 14, 12½x12, 11½x12

1876-94
34 A7 ½c rose (II) 11.50 .30
a. ½c rose (I) 15.00 .50
c. Laid paper 60.00
d. Perf. 14 (I) 1,950. 575.00
35 A7 1c emer grn ('94) 2.75 .25
b. As "c," laid paper 70.00 7.25
c. 1c green 8.00 .25
36 A7 2c olive yel ('94) 32.50 2.75
a. 2c yellow 65.00 3.50
37 A7 2½c violet ('94) 14.00 .30
b. 2½c dark violet ('94) 17.50 .45
c. 2½c lilac 100.00 .80
d. Laid paper — —
Nos. 34-37 (4) 60.75 3.60

Imperforate varieties are proofs.

Princess Wilhelmina — A8

1891-94 *Perf. 12½*
40 A8 3c orange ('94) 8.00 2.30
a. 3c orange yellow ('92) 11.50 2.75
41 A8 5c lt ultra ('94) 4.00 .25
a. 5c dull blue 5.00 .25
42 A8 7½c brown ('94) 15.00 6.25
a. 7½c red brown 27.50 6.25
43 A8 10c brt rose ('94) 23.50 1.60
a. 10c brick red 45.00 2.40
44 A8 12½c bluish gray ('94) 23.50 1.60
a. 12½c gray 40.00 1.75
45 A8 15c yel brn ('94) 60.00 5.00
a. 15c orange brown 80.00 5.50
46 A8 20c green ('94) 70.00 3.00
a. 20c yellow green 80.00 3.00
47 A8 22½c dk grn ('94) 32.50 13.50
a. 22½c deep blue green 55.00 13.50
48 A8 25c dl vio ('94) 110.00 6.00
a. 25c dark violet 110.00 6.00
49 A8 50c yel brn ('94) 550.00 20.00
a. 50c bister 575.00 27.50
50 A8 1g gray vio 625.00 77.50

The paper used in 1891-93 was white, rough and somewhat opaque. In 1894, a thinner, smooth and sometimes transparent paper was introduced.

The 5c orange was privately produced.

Princess Wilhelmina — A9

1893-96 *Perf. 11½x11*
51 A9 50c emer & yel brn ('96) 80.00 15.00
a. Perf. 11 *2,500.* 200.00
52 A9 1g brn & ol grn ('96) 200.00 22.50
a. Perf. 11 225.00 60.00
53 A9 2g 50c brt rose & ultra 400.00 130.00
a. 2g 50c lil rose & ultra, perf. 11 475.00 130.00
b. Perf. 11½ 500.00 140.00

Perf. 11
54 A9 5g brnz grn & red brn ('96) 700.00 425.00

A10

Queen Wilhelmina — A11

Perf. 12½ (#70, 73, 75-77, 81-82), 11½, 11½x11, 11x11½

1898-1924
55 A10 ½c violet .45 .25
56 A10 1c red .90 .25
b. Imperf., pair *2,000.* —
57 A10 1½c ultra ('08) 6.00 .85
58 A10 1½c dp blue ('13) 3.00 .35
59 A10 2c yellow brn 3.75 .25
60 A10 2½c deep green 3.25 .25
b. Imperf., pair *6,250.*
61 A11 3c orange 16.50 3.25
62 A11 3c pale ol grn ('01) 1.10 .25
63 A11 4c claret ('21) 1.60 1.10
64 A11 4½c violet ('19) 3.75 3.75
65 A11 5c car rose 1.60 .25
66 A11 7½c brown .75 .25
a. Tête bêche pair ('24) 80.00 72.50
67 A11 10c gray lilac 6.25 .25
68 A11 12½c blue 3.25 .30
69 A11 15c yellow brn 100.00 3.25
70 A11 15c bl & car ('08) 6.25 .25
71 A11 17½c vio ('06) 50.00 12.00
73 A11 17½c ultra & brn ('10) 15.00 .90
74 A11 20c yellow green 150.00 .75
75 A11 20c ol grn & gray ('08) 10.00 .50
76 A11 22½c brn & ol grn 9.25 .60
77 A11 25c rose pink & bl 9.25 .45
78 A11 30c lil & vio brn ('17) 24.00 .50
79 A11 40c grn & org ('20) 34.00 1.10
80 A11 50c brnz grn & red brn 110.00 1.10
81 A11 50c gray & vio ('14) 70.00 1.10
a. Perf 11½x11 70.00 16.50

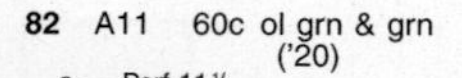

82 A11 60c ol grn & grn ('20) 34.00 1.10
a. Perf 11½ 200.00 20.00
Nos. 55-82 (27) 673.90 35.20
Set, never hinged 3,000.

See Nos. 107-112. For overprints and surcharges see Nos. 102-103, 106, 117-123, 135-136, O1-O8.

A12

I II

Type I — The figure "1" is 3¾mm high and 2¾mm wide.

Type II — The figure "1" is 3½mm high and 2½mm wide, it is also thinner than in type I.

Perf. 11, 11x11½, 11½, 11½x11

1898-1905 **Engr.**
83 A12 1g dk grn, II ('99) 52.50 .75
a. 1g dark green, I ('98) 190.00 110.00
84 A12 2½g brn lil ('99) 100.00 3.25
85 A12 5g claret ('99) 225.00 6.00
86 A12 10g orange ('05) 775.00 675.00
Set, never hinged 2,975.

For surcharge see No. 104.

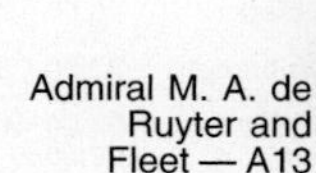

Admiral M. A. de Ruyter and Fleet — A13

1907, Mar. 23 Typo. *Perf. 12x12½*
87 A13 ½c blue 2.00 1.25
88 A13 1c claret 3.50 2.25
89 A13 2½c vermilion 6.00 2.25
Nos. 87-89 (3) 11.50 5.75
Set, never hinged 37.00

De Ruyter (1607-1676), naval hero.
For surcharges see Nos. J29-J41.

King William I — A14

Designs: 2½c, 12½c, 1g, King William I. 3c, 20c, 2½g, King William II. 5c, 25c, 5g, King William III. 10c, 50c, 10g, Queen Wilhelmina.

Perf. 11½x11, 11½ (#97, 100-101)

1913, Nov. 29 **Engr.**
90 A14 2½c green, *grn* .80 .80
91 A14 3c buff, *straw* 1.80 1.50
92 A14 5c rose red, *sal* 1.25 .90
93 A14 10c black brown 4.25 2.40
94 A14 12½c vio blue, *bl* 3.00 1.90
95 A14 20c orange brn 13.00 11.00
96 A14 25c blue 15.00 8.75
97 A14 50c yel grn 32.50 27.50
98 A14 1g claret 47.50 20.00
a. Perf. 11½ 60.00 20.00
99 A14 2½g purple 120.00 50.00
100 A14 5g yel, *straw* 225.00 40.00
101 A14 10g red, *straw* 800.00 725.00
Nos. 90-101 (12) 1,264. 889.75
Set, never hinged 2,285.

Centenary of Dutch independence.
For surcharge see No. 105.

No. 78 Surcharged in Red or Black

a

b

1919, Dec. 1 *Perf. 12½*
102 A11 (a) 40c on 30c (R) 25.00 4.50
103 A11 (b) 60c on 30c (Bk) 25.00 4.50
Set, never hinged 210.00

Nos. 86 and 101 Surcharged in Black

1920, Aug. 17 *Perf. 11, 11½*
104 A12 2.50g on 10g 145.00 80.00
Never hinged 350.00
105 A14 2.50g on 10g 160.00 100.00
Never hinged 400.00
Set, never hinged 750.00

No. 64 Surcharged in Red

1921, Mar. 1 Typo. *Perf. 12½*
106 A11 4c on 4½c vio 3.75 1.40
Never hinged 7.00

A17

1921-22 Typo. *Perf. 12½*
107 A17 5c green ('22) 13.00 .25
108 A17 12½c vermilion ('22) 19.00 1.75
109 A17 20c blue 31.00 .25
Nos. 107-109 (3) 63.00 2.25
Set, never hinged 215.00

Queen Type of 1898-99, 10c Redrawn

1922 *Perf. 12½*
110 A11 10c gray 27.50 .25
Never hinged 85.00

Imperf
111 A11 5c car rose 7.00 7.00
Never hinged 13.00
112 A11 10c gray 7.00 7.00
Never hinged 13.00
Nos. 110-112 (3) 41.50 14.25

In redrawn 10c the horizontal lines behind the Queen's head are wider apart.

Orange Tree and Lion of Brabant A18

Post Horn and Lion A19

Numeral of Value — A20

1923, Mar. 9 *Perf. 12½*

113 A18 1c dark violet .55 .50
Never hinged 2.00
114 A18 2c orange 5.00 .25
Never hinged 10.00
115 A19 2½c bluish green 1.50 .65
Never hinged 4.00
116 A20 4c deep blue 1.25 .60
Never hinged 3.25
Nos. 113-116 (4) 8.30 2.00
Set, never hinged 19.50

See No. 244 and compare to No. 115.

Nos. 56, 58, 62, 65, 68, 73, 76 Surcharged in Various Colors

c

d

1923, July *Perf. 12½*

117 A10(c) 2c on 1c (Bl) .45 .25
Never hinged 1.00
118 A10(c) 2c on 1½c (Bk) .45 .25
Never hinged 1.00
119 A11(d) 10c on 3c (Br) 4.00 .25
Never hinged 13.00
120 A11(d) 10c on 5c (Bk) 8.00 .50
Never hinged 22.50
121 A11(d) 10c on 12½c (R) 6.50 .75
Never hinged 24.00

Perf. 11½x11

122 A11(d) 10c on 17½c (R) 2.75 2.60
Never hinged 8.25
a. Perf. 11½ *1,600. 800.00*
b. Perf. 12½ 4.00 4.00
Never hinged 8.00
123 A11(d) 10c on 22½c (R) 2.75 2.60
Never hinged 8.25
a. Perf. 11½ 3.00 3.50
Never hinged 6.50
b. Perf. 12½ 4.00 4.00
Never hinged 8.00
Nos. 117-123 (7) 24.90 7.20
Set, never hinged 78.00

Queen Wilhelmina A21 A22

Perf. 11½x12½, 11½x12 (5c)

1923, Oct. **Engr.**

124 A22 2c myrtle green .25 .25
Never hinged 1.10
a. Vert. pair, imperf. between *2,400.*
125 A21 5c green .40 .25
Never hinged 1.10
a. Vert. pair, imperf. between *1,800.*
126 A22 7½c carmine .50 .25
Never hinged 2.25
127 A22 10c vermilion .40 .25
Never hinged 1.60
a. Vert. pair, imperf. between *550.00 575.00*
128 A22 20c ultra 3.75 1.00
Never hinged 9.00
129 A22 25c yellow 5.00 1.10
Never hinged 15.00

Perf. 11½

130 A22 35c orange 5.00 3.00
Never hinged 15.00
131 A22 50c black 15.00 1.00
Never hinged 45.00
132 A21 1g red 30.00 7.25
Never hinged 65.00
133 A21 2½g black 190.00 200.00
Never hinged 450.00
134 A21 5g dark blue 175.00 175.00
Never hinged 360.00
Nos. 124-134 (11) 425.30 389.35
Set, never hinged 975.00

25th anniv. of the assumption as monarch of the Netherlands by Queen Wilhelmina at the age of 18.

No. 119 Overprinted in Red

No. 73 With Additional Surcharge in Blue

1923 **Typo.** *Perf. 12½*

135 A11 10c on 3c 1.10 1.00
Never hinged 8.00
136 A11 1g on 17½c 62.50 15.00
Never hinged 190.00
a. Perf. 11½ 95.00 40.00
b. Perf. 11½x11 80.00 30.00

Stamps with red surcharge were prepared for use as Officials but were not issued.

Queen Wilhelmina — A23

1924, Sept. 6 **Photo.** *Perf. 12½*

137 A23 10c slate green 32.50 32.50
Never hinged 65.00
138 A23 15c gray black 40.00 40.00
Never hinged 70.00
139 A23 35c brown orange 32.50 32.50
Never hinged 65.00
Nos. 137-139 (3) 105.00 105.00
Set, never hinged 200.00

These stamps were available solely to visitors to the International Philatelic Exhibition at The Hague and were not obtainable at regular post offices. Set of three on international philatelic exhibition cover dataed Sept. 6-12, 15-17, 1924, value, $110. Set of three on Netherland Philatelic Exhibition cover dated Sept. 13-14, value, $150.

See Nos. 147-160, 172-193. For overprints and surcharge see Nos. 194, O11, O13-O15.

Ship in Distress — A23a

Lifeboat — A23b

1924, Sept. 15 **Litho.** *Perf. 11½*

140 A23a 2c black brn 3.25 2.25
Never hinged 7.25
141 A23b 10c orange brn 5.50 1.75
Never hinged 13.00

Centenary of Royal Dutch Lifeboat Society.

Type A23 and

Gull — A24

1924-26 **Unwmk.** *Perf. 12½*

142 A24 1c deep red .75 .90
Never hinged 1.50
143 A24 2c red orange 2.60 .35
Never hinged 9.00
144 A24 2½c deep green 3.00 1.10
Never hinged 6.00
145 A24 3c yel grn ('25) 16.50 1.50
Never hinged 50.00
146 A24 4c dp ultra 3.25 .95
Never hinged 15.00

Photo.

147 A23 5c dull green 3.50 .75
Never hinged 8.00
148 A23 6c org brn ('25) .75 .50
Never hinged 1.40
149 A23 7½c orange ('25) .35 .25
Never hinged 1.10
150 A23 9c org red & blk ('26) 1.50 1.25
Never hinged 3.00
151 A23 10c red, *shades* 1.50 .25
Never hinged 5.50
152 A23 12½c deep rose 1.60 .35
Never hinged 4.50
153 A23 15c ultra 6.00 .45
Never hinged 15.00
154 A23 20c dp blue ('25) 10.00 .60
Never hinged 22.00
155 A23 25c olive bis ('25) 22.50 .85
Never hinged 40.00
156 A23 30c violet 13.00 .65
Never hinged 40.00
157 A23 35c olive brn ('25) 30.00 6.00
Never hinged 80.00
158 A23 40c dp brown 35.00 .75
Never hinged 200.00
159 A23 50c blue grn ('25) 60.00 .60
Never hinged 275.00
160 A23 60c dk violet ('25) 27.50 .80
Never hinged 100.00
Nos. 142-160 (19) 239.30 18.85
Set, never hinged 725.00

See Nos. 164-171, 243A-243Q. For overprints and surcharges see Nos. 226-243, O9-O10.

Syncopated Perforations

Type A

Type B

Type C

These special "syncopated" or "interrupted" perforations, devised for coil stamps, are found on Nos. 142-156, 158-160, 164-166, 168-185, 187-193 and certain semipostals of 1925-33, between Nos. B9 and B69. There are four types:

A (1st stamp is #142a). On two shorter sides, groups of four holes separated by blank spaces equal in width to two or three holes.

B (1st stamp is #164a). As "A," but on all four sides.

C (1st stamp is #164b). On two shorter sides, end holes are omitted.

D (1st stamp is #174c). Four-hole sequence on horiz. sides, three-hole on vert. sides.

Syncopated, Type A (2 Sides)

1925-26

142a A24 1c deep red .75 .80
Never hinged 1.60
143a A24 2c red orange 2.60 2.60
Never hinged 4.50
144a A24 2½c deep green 2.60 1.60
Never hinged 4.50
145a A24 3c yellow green 17.50 17.50
Never hinged 42.50
146a A24 4c deep ultra 2.25 2.25
Never hinged 7.50
147a A23 5c dull green 5.50 3.00
Never hinged 9.75
148a A23 6c orange brown 110.00 100.00
Never hinged 170.00
149a A23 7½c orange 1.10 1.10
Never hinged 1.60
150a A23 9c org red & blk 1.90 1.60
Never hinged 2.50
151a A23 10c red 9.25 3.00
Never hinged 16.50
152a A23 12½c deep rose 1.75 1.75
Never hinged 3.25
153a A23 15c ultra 90.00 6.25
Never hinged 225.00
154a A23 20c deep blue 11.00 4.75
Never hinged 20.00
155a A23 25c olive bister 40.00 40.00
Never hinged 105.00
156a A23 30c violet 15.00 11.50
Never hinged 30.00
158a A23 40c deep brown 55.00 47.50
Never hinged 210.00
159a A23 50c blue green 60.00 23.00
Never hinged 240.00
160a A23 60c dark violet 30.00 11.50
Never hinged 75.00
Nos. 142a-160a (18) 456.20 279.70
Set, never hinged 1,070.

A25

1925-30 **Engr.** *Perf. 11½*

161 A25 1g ultra 8.00 .65
Never hinged 25.00
162 A25 2½g car ('27) 90.00 3.00
Never hinged 175.00
163 A25 5g gray blk 160.00 2.50
Never hinged 300.00
Nos. 161-163 (3) 258.00 6.15

Types of 1924-26 Issue

Perf. 12½, 13½x12½, 12½x13½

1926-39 **Wmk. 202** **Litho.**

164 A24 ½c gray ('28) .90 1.00
165 A24 1c dp red ('27) .25 .25
166 A24 1½c red vio ('28) 1.10 .25
c. "CEN" for "CENT" 165.00 275.00
d. "GENT" for "CENT" 120.00 115.00
167 A24 1½c dark gray ('35) .25 .25
a. 1½c dark gray .25 .25
168 A24 2c dp org .25 .25
a. 2c red orange .25 .25
169 A24 2½c green ('27) 2.75 .25
170 A24 3c yel grn ('27) .25 .25
171 A24 4c dp ultra ('27) .25 .25

Photo.

172 A23 5c dp green .25 .25
173 A23 6c org brn ('27) .25 .25
174 A23 7½c dk vio ('27) 3.25 .25
175 A23 7½c red ('28) .35 .25
176 A23 9c org red & blk ('28) 11.00 12.00
b. Value omitted *14,500.*
177 A23 10c red 1.30 .25
178 A23 10c dl vio ('29) 2.50 .25
179 A23 12½c dp rose ('27) 42.50 4.50
180 A23 12½c ultra ('28) .25 .25
181 A23 15c ultra 7.25 .25
182 A23 15c orange ('29) 1.30 .25
183 A23 20c dp blue ('28) 7.25 .25
184 A23 21c ol brn ('31) 25.00 .90
185 A23 22½c ol brn ('27) 7.25 3.00
186 A23 22½c dp org ('39) 15.50 16.00
187 A23 25c ol bis ('27) 4.50 .25
188 A23 27½c gray ('28) 4.50 .90
189 A23 30c violet 5.00 .25
190 A23 35c olive brn 62.50 12.50
191 A23 40c dp brown 9.00 .25
192 A23 50c blue grn 5.00 .25
193 A23 60c black ('29) 57.50 .90
Nos. 164-193 (30) 279.20 56.95
Set, never hinged 640.00

Syncopated, Type A (2 Sides), 12½

1926-27

168b A24 2c deep orange .40 .40
170a A24 3c yellow green .60 .60
171a A24 4c deep ultra .60 .60
172a A23 5c deep green .70 .60
173a A23 6c orange brown .40 .45
174a A23 7½c dark violet 4.50 2.00
177a A23 10c red 1.00 .85
181a A23 15c ultra 7.00 3.00
185a A23 22½c olive brown 7.00 2.50
187a A23 25c olive bister 20.00 18.00
189a A23 30c violet 19.00 12.00
190a A23 35c olive brown 77.50 22.50
191a A23 40c deep brown 50.00 40.00
Nos. 168b-191a (13) 188.70 103.50
Set, never hinged 360.00

1928 ***Syncopated, Type B (4 Sides)***

164a A24 ½c gray .50 .50
165a A24 1c deep red .50 .30
166a A24 1½c red violet .50 .30
168c A24 2c deep orange .80 .80
169a A24 2½c green 2.00 .35
170b A24 3c yellow green .75 .75
171b A24 4c deep ultra .75 .75
172b A23 5c deep green 1.00 .75
173b A23 6c orange brown .70 .75
174b A23 7½c dark violet 3.50 2.00
175a A23 7½c red .35 .35
176a A23 9c org red & blk 9.00 10.00
178a A23 10c dull violet 4.50 3.50
179a A23 12½c deep rose 80.00 85.00
180a A23 12½c ultra 1.50 .75
181b A23 15c ultra 7.00 2.00
182a A23 15c orange 1.00 .75
183a A23 20c deep blue 6.50 3.50
187b A23 25c olive bister 17.00 10.00
188a A23 27½c gray 5.00 2.00
189b A23 30c violet 15.00 8.00
191b A23 40c deep brown 34.00 25.00
192a A23 50c blue green 50.00 45.00
193a A23 60c black 36.00 25.00
Nos. 164a-193a (24) 277.85 228.10
Set, never hinged 525.00

Syncopated, Type C (2 Sides, Corners Only)

1930

164b A24 ½c gray 1.00 .70
165b A24 1c deep red 1.00 .40
166b A24 1½c red violet .90 .25
168d A24 2c deep orange .80 .70
169b A24 2½c green 2.75 .25
170c A24 3c yellow green 1.10 .50
171c A24 4c deep ultra .50 .25
172c A23 5c deep green .70 .70
173c A23 6c orange brown .70 .70
178b A23 10c dull violet 8.00 7.00
183b A23 20c deep blue 7.75 3.75
184a A23 21c olive brown 25.00 9.00
189c A23 30c violet 12.00 7.00
192b A23 50c blue green 55.00 45.00
Nos. 164b-192b (14) 107.20 76.20
Set, never hinged 225.00

Syncopated, Type D (3 Holes Vert., 4 Holes Horiz.)

1927

174c A23 7½c dark violet *2,750. 2,100.*
Never hinged *3,750.*

No. 185 Surcharged in Red

1929, Nov. 11 *Perf. 12½*

194 A23 21c on 22½c ol brn 19.00 1.40
Never hinged 47.50

Queen Wilhelmina — A26

1931, Oct. Photo. *Perf. 12½*

195 A26 70c dk bl & red 29.00 .75
Never hinged 110.00
a. Perf. 14½x13½ ('39) 50.00 11.00
Never hinged 190.00

See No. 201.

Arms of the House of Orange A27

William I A28

Designs: 5c, William I, Portrait by Goltzius. 6c, Portrait of William I by Van Key. 12½c, Portrait attributed to Moro.

1933, Apr. 1 Unwmk. Engr.

196 A27 1½c black .55 .40
197 A28 5c dark green 1.75 .40
198 A28 6c dull violet 2.75 .30
199 A28 12½c deep blue 17.00 3.50
Nos. 196-199 (4) 22.05 4.60
Set, never hinged 55.00

400th anniv. of the birth of William I, Count of Nassau and Prince of Orange, frequently referred to as William the Silent.

Star, Dove and Sword — A31

1933, May 18 Photo. Wmk. 202

200 A31 12½c dp ultra 8.00 .75
Never hinged 26.50

For overprint see No. O12.

Queen Wilhelmina Design of 1931

Queen Wilhelmina and ships.

Perf. 14½x13½

1933, July 26 Wmk. 202

201 A26 80c Prus bl & red 100.00 2.90
Never hinged 320.00

Willemstad Harbor — A33

Van Walbeeck's Ship — A34

Perf. 14x12½

1934, July 2 Engr. Unwmk.

202 A33 6c violet blk 3.50 .25
203 A34 12½c dull blue 20.00 3.00
Set, never hinged 70.00

Tercentenary of Curacao.

Minerva A35

Design: 12½c, Gisbertus Voetius.

Wmk. 202

1936, May 15 Photo. *Perf. 12½*

204 A35 6c brown lake 2.50 .25
205 A35 12½c indigo 4.50 4.50
Set, never hinged 16.00

300th anniversary of the founding of the University at Utrecht.

Boy Scout Emblem A37

"Assembly" A38

Mercury — A39

1937, Apr. 1 *Perf. 14½x13½*

206 A37 1½c multicolored .40 .25
207 A38 6c multicolored 1.25 .25
208 A39 12½c multicolored 4.00 1.40
Nos. 206-208 (3) 5.65 1.90
Set, never hinged 12.00

Fifth Boy Scout World Jamboree, Vogelenzang, Netherlands, 7/31-8/13/37.

Wilhelmina — A40

1938, Aug. 27 *Perf. 12½x12*

209 A40 1½c black .25 .25
210 A40 5c red orange .30 .25
211 A40 12½c royal blue 4.00 1.60
Nos. 209-211 (3) 4.55 2.10
Set, never hinged 13.50

Reign of Queen Wilhelmina, 40th anniv.

St. Willibrord — A41

Design: 12½c, St. Willibrord as older man.

Perf. 12½x14

1939, June 15 Engr. Unwmk.

212 A41 5c dk slate grn .75 .25
213 A41 12½c slate blue 5.00 2.75
Set, never hinged 14.00

12th centenary of the death of St. Willibrord.

Woodburning Engine — A43

Design: 12½c, Streamlined electric car.

Perf. 14½x13½

1939, Sept. 1 Photo. Wmk. 202

214 A43 5c dk slate grn .80 .25
215 A43 12½c dark blue 8.00 4.00
Set, never hinged 22.50

Centenary of Dutch Railroads.

Catalogue values for unused stamps in this section, from this point to the end of the section, are for Never Hinged items.

Queen Wilhelmina — A45

1940-47 *Perf. 13½x12½*

216 A45 5c dk green .25 .25
216B A45 6c hn brn ('47) .50 .25
217 A45 7½c brt red .25 .25
218 A45 10c brt red vio .25 .25
219 A45 12½c sapphire .25 .25
220 A45 15c light blue .25 .25
220B A45 17½c slate bl ('46) 1.10 .65
221 A45 20c purple .55 .25
222 A45 22½c olive grn 1.75 1.60
223 A45 25c rose brn .45 .25
224 A45 30c bister .95 .35
225 A45 40c brt green 1.60 .65
225A A45 50c orange ('46) 6.75 .65
225B A45 60c pur brn ('46) 6.75 1.90
Nos. 216-225B (14) 21.65 7.80

Imperf. examples of Nos. 216, 218-220 were released through philatelic channels during the German occupation, but were never issued at any post office. Value, set, $1.

For overprints see Nos. O16-O24.

Type of 1924-26 Surcharged in Black or Blue

Perf. 12½x13½

1940, Oct. Photo. Wmk. 202

226 A24 2½c on 3c ver 4.00 .25
227 A24 5c on 3c lt grn .25 .25
228 A24 7½c on 3c ver .25 .25
a. Pair, #226, 228 5.00 1.50
229 A24 10c on 3c lt grn .25 .25
230 A24 12½c on 3c lt bl (Bl) .35 .35
231 A24 17½c on 3c lt grn 1.00 .55
232 A24 20c on 3c lt grn .70 .25
233 A24 22½c on 3c lt grn 2.75 3.75
234 A24 25c on 3c lt grn 1.25 .35
235 A24 30c on 3c lt grn 1.10 .40
236 A24 40c on 3c lt grn 2.00 1.75
237 A24 50c on 3c lt grn 1.25 .55
238 A24 60c on 3c lt grn 1.35 1.00
239 A24 70c on 3c lt grn 7.25 7.25
240 A24 80c on 3c lt grn 9.25 8.50
241 A24 1g on 3c lt grn 29.00 25.00
242 A24 2.50g on 3c lt grn 32.00 32.00
243 A24 5g on 3c lt grn 32.00 29.00
Nos. 226-243 (18) 126.00 111.70
Set, hinged 80.00

No. 228a is from coils.

Gull Type of 1924-26

1941

243A A24 2½c dk green 1.00 .25
b. Booklet pane of 6 15.00
243C A24 5c brt green .25 .25
s. Booklet pane of 6 15.00
243E A24 7½c henna .25 .25
r. Pair, #243A, 243E 2.50 2.50
t. Booklet pane of 6 15.00
243G A24 10c brt violet .60 .25
243H A24 12½c ultra .35 .25
u. Booklet pane of 6 15.00
243J A24 15c lt blue .60 .30
243K A24 17½c red org .25 .25
243L A24 20c lt violet .85 .25
243M A24 22½c dk ol grn .25 .30
243N A24 25c lake .35 .25
243O A24 30c olive 2.25 .25
243P A24 40c emerald .25 .25
243Q A24 50c orange brn .25 .25
Nos. 243A-243Q (13) 7.50 3.35

No. 243Er is from coils.

Stamps from coils have designs that are 21½mm wide instead of 22¼mm width of the sheet stamps. Stamps are Nos. 496-498, 663-664, 681-682, 705-706, 708-772, 719, 721, 736, 749, 794, 797, 800, 809, 982.

Post Horn and Lion — A46

Gold Surcharge

1943, Jan. 15 Photo. *Perf. 12½x12*

244 A46 10c on 2½c yel .25 .25
a. Surcharge omitted *6,000. 6,500.*

Founding of the European Union of Posts and Telegraphs at Vienna, Oct. 19, 1942.

See No. 115.

Sea Horse — A47

Triple-crown Tree — A48

Admiral M. A. de Ruyter — A54

Designs: 2c, Swans. 2½c, Tree of Life. 3c, Tree with snake roots. 4c, Man on horseback. 5c, Rearing white horses. 10c, Johan Evertsen. 12½c, Martin Tromp. 15c, Piet Hein. 17½c, Willem van Ghent. 20c, Witte de With. 22½c, Cornelis Evertsen. 25c, Tjerk de Vries. 30c, Cornelis Tromp. 40c, Cornelis Evertsen De Jongste.

Perf. 12x12½, 12½x12

1943-44 Photo. Wmk. 202

245 A47 1c black .25 .25
246 A48 1½c rose lake .25 .25
247 A47 2c dk blue .25 .25
248 A48 2½c dk blue grn .25 .25
249 A47 3c copper red .25 .25
250 A48 4c black brown .25 .25
251 A47 5c dull yel grn .25 .25

Unwmk.

252 A54 7½c henna brn .25 .25
a. Thinner numerals and letters ('44) .25 .25
253 A54 10c dk green .25 .25
254 A54 12½c blue .25 .25
255 A54 15c dull lilac .25 .25
256 A54 17½c slate ('44) .25 .25
257 A54 20c dull brown .25 .25
258 A54 22½c org red .25 .25
259 A54 25c vio rose ('44) .35 .55
260 A54 30c cobalt bl ('44) .25 .25

Engr.

261 A54 40c bluish blk .25 .25
Nos. 245-261 (17) 4.35 4.55

In 1944, 200,000 examples of No. 247 were privately punched with a cross and printed on the back with a number and the words "Prijs 15 Cent toeslag ten bate Ned. Roode Kruis." These were sold at an exhibition, the surtax going to the Red Cross. The Dutch post office tolerated these stamps.

Soldier
A64

S. S. "Nieuw Amsterdam"
A65

Pilot
A66

Cruiser "De Ruyter"
A67

Queen Wilhelmina — A68

Perf. 12, 12½

1944-46 Unwmk. Engr.

262 A64 1½c black .25 .25
263 A65 2½c yellow grn .25 .25
264 A66 3c dull red brn .25 .25
265 A67 5c dk blue .25 .25
266 A68 7½c vermilion .25 .25
267 A68 10c yellow org .25 .25
268 A68 12½c ultra .25 .25
269 A68 15c dl red brn ('46) 1.30 1.25
270 A68 17½c gray grn ('46) .75 .85
271 A68 20c violet .35 .25
272 A68 22½c rose red ('46) .90 1.00
273 A68 25c brn org ('46) 1.00 1.10
274 A68 30c blue grn .25 .25
275 A68 40c dk vio brn ('46) 2.00 2.10
276 A68 50c red vio ('46) 1.10 .85
Nos. 262-276 (15) 9.40 9.40

These stamps were used on board Dutch war and merchant ships until Netherlands' liberation.

Lion and Dragon — A69

1945, July 14 ***Perf. 12½x14***
277 A69 7½c red orange .25 .25

Netherlands' liberation or "rising again."

Queen Wilhelmina — A70

1946 Engr. ***Perf. 13½x14***
278 A70 1g dark blue 2.50 .60
279 A70 2½g brick red 125.00 8.00
280 A70 5g dk olive grn 125.00 22.00
281 A70 10g dk purple 125.00 22.00
Nos. 278-281 (4) 377.50 52.60
Set, hinged 200.00

A71

Perf. 12½x13½

1946-47 Wmk. 202 Photo.
282 A71 1c dark red .25 .25
283 A71 2c ultra .25 .25
284 A71 2½c dp orange ('47) 3.50 1.00
285 A71 4c olive green .30 .25
Nos. 282-285 (4) 4.30 1.75

The 1c was reissued in 1969 on phosphorescent paper in booklet pane No. 345b. The 4c was reissued on fluorescent paper in 1962.
The 2c was issued in coils in 1972. Every fifth stamp has black control number on back.
See Nos. 340-343A, 404-406.

Queen Wilhelmina
A72 A73

1947-48 ***Perf. 13½x12½***
286 A72 5c olive grn ('48) 1.00 .25
287 A72 6c brown black .30 .25
288 A72 7½c dp red brn ('48) .40 .25
289 A72 10c brt red vio .75 .25
290 A72 12½c scarlet ('48) .75 .35
291 A72 15c purple 7.00 .25
292 A72 20c deep blue 7.00 .25
293 A72 22½c ol brn ('48) .75 .65
294 A72 25c ultra 14.00 .25
295 A72 30c dp orange 14.00 .25
296 A72 35c dk blue grn 14.00 .45
297 A72 40c henna brown 15.50 .45

Engr.

298 A73 45c dp bl ('48) 16.50 8.50
299 A73 50c brown ('48) 11.50 .35
300 A73 60c red ('48) 14.50 1.90
Nos. 286-300 (15) 117.95 14.65
Set, hinged 60.00

For surcharge see No. 330.

Type of 1947

1948 Photo.
301 A72 6c gray blue .50 .25

Queen Wilhelmina — A74

Perf. 12½x14

1948, Aug. 30 Engr. Unwmk.
302 A74 10c vermilion .25 .25
303 A74 20c deep blue 1.25 1.00

Reign of Queen Wilhelmina, 50th anniv.

Queen Juliana — A75

Perf. 14x13

1948, Sept. 7 Photo. Wmk. 202
304 A75 10c dark brown 1.10 .25
305 A75 20c ultra 1.40 .45

Investiture of Queen Juliana, Sept. 6, 1948.

Queen Juliana — A76

1949 ***Perf. 13½x12½***
306 A76 5c olive green .65 .25
307 A76 6c gray blue .35 .25
308 A76 10c deep orange .35 .25
309 A76 12c orange red 1.90 1.75
310 A76 15c olive brown 3.75 .25
311 A76 20c brt blue 3.25 .25
312 A76 25c orange brn 8.75 .25
313 A76 30c violet 6.25 .25
314 A76 35c gray 21.00 .25
315 A76 40c red violet 35.00 .25
316 A76 45c red orange 1.30 .70
317 A76 50c blue green 8.75 .25
318 A76 60c red brown 12.50 .25
Nos. 306-318 (13) 103.80 5.20

See No. 325-327. For surcharge see No. B248.

Queen Juliana — A77

1949 Unwmk. Engr. ***Perf. 12½x12***
319 A77 1g rose red 3.25 .25
320 A77 2½g black brn 190.00 2.25
321 A77 5g orange brn 340.00 3.50
322 A77 10g dk vio brn 240.00 11.50
Nos. 319-322 (4) 773.25 17.50
Set, hinged 350.00

Two types exist of No. 321.

Post Horns Entwined — A78

Perf. 11½x12½

1949, Oct. 1 Photo. Wmk. 202
323 A78 10c brown red .60 .25
324 A78 20c dull blue 4.50 1.75

75th anniversary of the UPU.

Juliana Type of 1949

1950-51 ***Perf. 13½x12½***
325 A76 12c scarlet ('51) 5.00 1.00
326 A76 45c violet brn 40.00 .45
327 A76 75c car rose ('51) 60.00 1.50
Nos. 325-327 (3) 105.00 2.95

Janus Dousa — A79

Design: 20c, Jan van Hout.

1950, Oct. 3 ***Perf. 11½x13***
328 A79 10c olive brown 2.60 .25
329 A79 20c deep blue 2.60 1.10

375th anniversary of the founding of the University of Leyden.

No. 288 Surcharged in Black

1950, May ***Perf. 13½x12½***
330 A72 6c on 7½c dp red brn 1.10 .25

Miner — A80

Perf. 12x12½

1952, Apr. 16 Engr. Unwmk.
331 A80 10c dark blue 1.30 .25

50th anniversary of the founding of Netherlands' mining and chemical industry.

Telegraph Poles and Train of 1852 — A81

Designs: 6c, Radio towers. 10c, Mail Delivery 1852. 20c, Modern postman.

1952, June 28 ***Perf. 13x14***
332 A81 2c gray violet .40 .25
333 A81 6c vermilion .50 .25
334 A81 10c green .50 .25
335 A81 20c gray blue 4.00 1.60
Nos. 332-335 (4) 5.40 2.35

Centenary of Dutch postage stamps and of the telegraph service.

1952, June 28
336 A81 2c chocolate 14.00 10.00
337 A81 6c dk bluish grn 14.00 10.00
338 A81 10c brown carmine 14.00 10.00
339 A81 20c violet blue 14.00 10.00
Nos. 336-339 (4) 56.00 40.00

Nos. 336 to 339 sold for 1.38g, which included the price of admission to the International Postage Stamp Centenary Exhibition, Utrecht.

Numeral Type of 1946-47

Perf. 12½x13½

1953-57 Wmk. 202 Photo.
340 A71 3c dp org brn .30 .25
341 A71 5c orange .25 .25
342 A71 6c gray ('54) .30 .25
343 A71 7c red org .25 .25
343A A71 8c brt lilac ('57) .25 .25
Nos. 340-343A (5) 1.35 1.25

The 5c and 7c perf. on 3 sides, and with watermark vertical, are from booklet panes Nos. 346a-346b. The 5c perf. on 3 sides, with wmk. horiz., is from No. 349a.
In 1972 the 5c was printed on phosphorescent paper.

A82

1953-71 Wmk. 202 ***Perf. 13½x12½***
344 A82 10c dk red brn .25 .25
a. Bklt. pane of 6 (1 #344 + 5 #346C)('65) 5.00
345 A82 12c dk Prus grn ('54) .25 .25
a. Bklt. pane of 7 + label (5 #345 + 2 #347)('67) 5.50
b. Bklt. pane, 4 #282 + 8 #345 ('69) 12.50
346 A82 15c dp carmine .25 .25
a. Bklt. pane of 8 (2 #341 in vert. pair + 6 #346)('64) 17.00
b. Bklt. pane of 12 (10 #343 + 2 #346)('64) 12.50
e. Bklt. pane of 8 (2 #341 in horiz. pair + 6 #346)('70) 9.00
346C A82 18c dull bl ('65) .25 .25
d. Bklt. pane of 10 (8 #343A + 2 #346C)('65) 4.50
347 A82 20c dk gray .25 .25
b. Bklt. pane of 5 + label ('66) 4.00
347A A82 24c olive ('63) .30 .25
348 A82 25c deep blue .95 .25
349 A82 30c deep orange .35 .25
a. Bklt. pane of 5 + label (2 #341 + 3 #349)('71) 22.50
350 A82 35c dk ol brn ('54) .70 .25
351 A82 37c aqua ('58) .35 .25
352 A82 40c dk slate .35 .25
353 A82 45c scarlet .30 .25
354 A82 50c dk bl grn .55 .25
355 A82 60c brown bister .70 .25
356 A82 62c dl red lil ('58) .80 .80
357 A82 70c blue ('57) .70 .25
358 A82 75c deep plum .70 .25
359 A82 80c brt vio ('58) .70 .25
360 A82 85c brt bl grn ('56) .85 .25
360A A82 95c org brn ('67) .85 .35
Nos. 344-360A (20) 10.40 5.65

Coils of the 12, 15, 20, 25, 30, 40, 45, 50, 60, 70, 75 and 80c were issued in 1972. Black control number on back of every fifth stamp.
Watermark is vertical on some stamps from booklet panes.
Some booklet panes, Nos. 344a, 347b, 349a, etc., have a large selvage the size of four or six stamps, with printed inscription and sometimes illustration.
Phosphorescent paper was introduced in 1967 for the 12, 15, 20 and 45c; in 1969 for the 25c, and in 1971 for the 30, 40, 50, 60, 70, 75 and 80c.
Of the booklet panes, Nos. 345a, 345b, 346d, 346e and 347b were issued on both ordinary and phosphorescent paper, and No. 349a only on phosphorescent paper.
See No. 407. For surcharge see No. 374.

Queen Juliana — A83

Perf. 12½x12

1954-57 Unwmk. Engr.
361 A83 1g vermilion 1.00 .25
362 A83 2½g dk green ('55) 4.25 .25
363 A83 5g black ('55) 2.60 .35
364 A83 10g vio bl ('57) 8.25 1.60
Nos. 361-364 (4) 16.10 2.45

St. Boniface — A84

1954, June 16
365 A84 10c blue 1.25 .25

1200th anniv. of the death of St. Boniface.

Queen Juliana — A84a

Wmk. 202

1954, Dec. 15 Photo. ***Perf. 13½***

366 A84a 10c scarlet .75 .25

Issued to publicize the Charter of the Kingdom, adopted December 15, 1954.

See Netherlands Antilles No. 232, Surinam No. 264.

Flaming Sword — A85

1955, May 4 ***Perf. 12½x12***

367 A85 10c crimson .80 .25

10th anniv. of Netherlands' liberation.

"Rebuilding Europe" — A86

1956, Sept. 15 Unwmk. ***Perf. 13x14***

368 A86 10c rose brn & blk *1.75* .25
369 A86 25c brt bl & blk *24.00 1.25*

Europa. Issued to symbolize the cooperation among the six countries comprising the Coal and Steel Community.

Admiral M. A. de Ruyter — A87

30c, Flagship "De Zeven Provincien."

1957, July 2 Engr. ***Perf. 12½x12***

370 A87 10c orange .35 .25
371 A87 30c dk blue 2.60 1.10

Adm. M. A. de Ruyter (1607-1676).

"United Europe" — A88

1957, Sept. 16 Photo. ***Perf. 13x14***

372 A88 10c blk, gray & ultra *.70* .25
373 A88 30c dull grn & ultra *3.25 1.25*

United Europe for peace and prosperity.

No. 344 Surcharged in Silver with New Value and Bars

Perf. 13½x12½

1958, May 16 Photo. Wmk. 202

374 A82 12c on 10c .80 .25
a. Double surcharge 400.00 400.00
b. Inverted surcharge 400.00 400.00

Common Design Types pictured following the introduction.

Europa Issue, 1958

Common Design Type

Perf. 13x14

1958, Sept. 13 Litho. Unwmk.

Size: 22x33mm

375 CD1 12c org ver & blue *.25* .25
376 CD1 30c blue & red *1.00 .50*

NATO Emblem — A89

1959, Apr. 3 ***Perf. 12½x12***

377 A89 12c yel org & blue .25 .25
378 A89 30c red & blue .50 .40

10th anniversary of NATO.

Europa Issue, 1959.

Common Design Type

1959, Sept. 19 ***Perf. 13x14***

Size: 22x33mm

379 CD2 12c crimson *.50* .25
380 CD2 30c yellow grn *1.60 1.60*

Douglas DC-8 and World Map — A90

Design: 30c, Douglas DC-8 in flight.

1959, Oct. 5 Engr. ***Perf. 14x13***

381 A90 12c carmine & ultra .25 .25
382 A90 30c dp blue & dp grn .90 .90

40th anniversary of the founding of KLM, Royal Dutch Airlines.

J. C. Schroeder van der Kolk — A91

Design: 30c, Johannes Wier.

Perf. 12½x12

1960, July 18 Unwmk.

383 A91 12c red .55 .40
384 A91 30c dark blue 2.75 2.00

Issued to publicize Mental Health Year and to honor Schroeder van der Kolk and Johannes Wier, pioneers of mental health.

Europa Issue, 1960

Common Design Type

1960, Sept. 19 Photo. ***Perf. 12x12½***

Size: 27x21mm

385 CD3 12c car rose & org *.40* .40
386 CD3 30c dk blue & yel *1.60 1.60*

1st anniv. of CEPT. Spokes symbolize 19 founding members of Conference.

Europa Issue, 1961

Common Design Type

1961, Sept. 18 ***Perf. 14x13***

Size: 32½x21½mm

387 CD4 12c golden brown .25 .25
388 CD4 30c Prus blue .25 .25

Queen Juliana and Prince Bernhard — A92

Perf. 14x13

1962, Jan. 5 Unwmk. Photo.

389 A92 12c dk red .25 .25
390 A92 30c dk green 1.00 .65

Silver wedding anniversary of Queen Juliana and Prince Bernhard.

Telephone Dial — A93

Designs: 12c, Map showing telephone network. 30c, Arch and dial, horiz.

1962, May 22 ***Perf. 13x14, 14x13***

391 A93 4c brown red & blk .25 .30
392 A93 12c brown ol & blk .50 .30
393 A93 30c black, bis & Prus bl 1.40 1.40
Nos. 391-393 (3) 2.15 2.00

Completion of the automation of the Netherlands telephone network.

Europa Issue, 1962

Common Design Type

1962, Sept. 17 ***Perf. 14x13***

Size: 33x22mm

394 CD5 12c lemon, yel & blk *.25* .25
395 CD5 30c blue, yel & blk *1.10 .65*

Polder with Canals and Windmills — A94

Design: 4c, Cooling towers, Limburg State Coal Mines. 10c, Dredging in Delta.

Perf. 12½x13½

1962-72 Wmk. 202 Photo.

399 A94 4c dk blue ('63) .25 .25
401 A94 6c grn & dk grn .40 .25
402 A94 10c dp claret ('63) .25 .25
a. Booklet pane of 10 ('66) 3.50

Unwmk.

403 A94 10c dp claret ('72) .25 .25
Nos. 399-403 (4) 1.15 1.00

No. 403 was issued in coils in 1972. Every fifth stamp has black control number on back.

See No. 461Ab.

Types of 1946 and 1953

1962-73 Unwmk.

Phosphorescent Paper

404 A71 4c olive green 1.30 1.30
405 A71 5c orange ('73) 1.30 1.30
406 A71 8c bright lilac 6.00 8.50
407 A82 12c dk Prus green 1.30 1.30
Nos. 404-407 (4) 9.90 12.40

The 5c is from booklets and has the phosphor on the front only.

Issue dates: 5c, Jan. 12; others Aug. 27.

See Nos. 460d, 461c, 461d and 463a.

Wheat Emblem and Globe — A95

1963, Mar. 21 Photo. ***Perf. 14x13***

413 A95 12c dl bl, dk bl & yel .25 .25
414 A95 30c dl car, rose & yel .80 .80

FAO "Freedom from Hunger" campaign.

Inscription in Circle — A96

Perf. 13x14

1963, May 7 Unwmk. Litho.

415 A96 30c brt blue, blk & grn 1.00 1.00

1st Intl. Postal Conf., Paris, cent.

Europa Issue, 1963

Common Design Type

1963, Sept. 16 Photo. ***Perf. 14x13***

Size: 33x22mm

416 CD6 12c red brown & yel *.30* .25
417 CD6 30c Prus green & yel *1.00 .75*

Prince William of Orange Landing at Scheveningen — A97

Designs: 12c, G. K. van Hogendorp, A. F. J. A. Graaf van der Duyn van Maasdam and L. Graaf van Limburg Stirum, Dutch leaders, 1813. 30c, Prince William taking oath of allegiance.

Size: 27½x27½mm

1963, Nov. 18 Photo. ***Perf. 12x12½***

418 A97 4c dull bl, blk & brn .25 .25
419 A97 5c dk grn, blk & red .25 .25
420 A97 12c olive & blk .25 .25
421 A97 30c maroon & blk .50 .50
Nos. 418-421 (4) 1.25 1.25

150th anniversary of the founding of the Kingdom of the Netherlands.

Knights' Hall, The Hague — A98

1964, Jan. 9 ***Perf. 14x13***

422 A98 12c olive & blk .25 .25

500th anniversary of the meeting of the States-General (Parliament).

Arms of Groningen University — A99

Design: 30c, Initials "AG" and crown.

1964, June 16 Engr. ***Perf. 12½x12***

423 A99 12c slate .25 .25
424 A99 30c yellow brown .25 .25

350th anniv. of the University of Groningen.

Railroad Light Signal — A100

Design: 40c, Electric locomotive.

1964, July 28 Photo. ***Perf. 14x13***

425 A100 15c black & brt grn .25 .25
426 A100 40c black & yellow .65 .55

125th anniv. of the Netherlands railroads.

Bible, Chrismon and Dove — A101

1964, Aug. 25 Unwmk.

427 A101 15c brown red .25 .25

150th anniversary of the founding of the Netherlands Bible Society.

Europa Issue, 1964

Common Design Type

1964, Sept. 14 Photo. ***Perf. 13x14***

Size: 22x33mm

428 CD7 15c dp olive grn *.25* .25
429 CD7 20c yellow brown *.50 .35*

Benelux Issue

King Baudouin, Queen Juliana and Grand Duchess Charlotte — A101a

Size: 33x22mm

1964, Oct. 12 ***Perf. 14x13***

430 A101a 15c purple & buff .25 .25

20th anniversary of the signing of the customs union of Belgium, Netherlands and Luxembourg.

Queen Juliana — A102

1964, Dec. 15 Photo. *Perf. 13x14*

431	A102 15c green	.25	.25

10th anniversary of the Charter of the Kingdom of the Netherlands.

"Killed in Action" and "Destroyed Town" — A103

Statues: 15c, "Docker" Amsterdam, and "Killed in Action" Waalwijk. 40c, "Destroyed Town" Rotterdam, and "Docker" Amsterdam.

1965, Apr. 6 Photo. *Perf. 12x12½*

432	A103 7c black & dk red	.25	.25
433	A103 15c black & dk olive	.25	.25
434	A103 40c black & dk red	.70	.60
	Nos. 432-434 (3)	1.20	1.10

Resistance movement of World War II.

Knight Class IV, Order of William — A104

1965, Apr. 29 *Perf. 13x14*

435	A104 1g gray	.75	.50

150th anniversary of the establishment of the Military Order of William.

ITU Emblem — A105

1965, May 17 Litho. *Perf. 14x13*

436	A105 20c dull bl & tan	.25	.25
437	A105 40c tan & dull bl	.30	.30

Centenary of the International Telecommunication Union.

Europa Issue, 1965
Common Design Type

1965, Sept. 27 Photo.
Size: 33x22mm

438	CD8 18c org brn, dk red & blk	.25	.25
439	CD8 20c sapphire, brn & blk	.30	.25

Marines of 1665 and 1965 — A106

1965, Dec. 10 Engr. *Perf. 13x14*

440	A106 18c dk vio bl & car	.25	.25

Netherlands Marine Corps, 300th anniv.

Europa Issue, 1966
Common Design Type

1966, Sept. 26 Photo. *Perf. 13x14*
Size: 22x33mm

441	CD9 20c citron	.25	.25
442	CD9 40c dull blue	.60	.25

Assembly Hall, Delft University — A107

1967, Jan. 5 Litho. *Perf. 14x13*

443	A107 20c dl sage grn & sepia	.25	.25

125th anniversary of the founding of the Delft University of Technology.

Europa Issue, 1967
Common Design Type
Perf. 13x14

1967, May 2 Unwmk. Photo.
Ordinary Paper
Size: 22x32½mm

444	CD10 20c dull blue	*.35*	.25
445	CD10 45c dull vio brn	*.75*	*.60*

Wmk. 202

446	CD10 20c dull blue	*.65*	*.30*
447	CD10 45c dull vio brn	*.95*	*.90*
	Nos. 444-447 (4)	2.70	2.05

Nos. 446-447 are on phosphorescent paper.

Stamp of 1852, #1 — A108

1967, May 8 Engr. Unwmk.

448	A108 20c shown	1.75	1.75
449	A108 25c No. 5	1.75	1.75
450	A108 75c No. 10	1.75	1.75
	Nos. 448-450 (3)	5.25	5.25

AMPHILEX 67, Amsterdam, May 11-21. Sold only in complete sets together with a 2.50g admission ticket to Amsterdam Philatelic Exhibition. Issued in sheets of 10 (5x2).

Coins and Punched Card — A109

1968, Jan. 16 Photo. *Perf. 14x13*

451	A109 20c ver, blk & dl yel	.25	.25

50th anniversary of the postal checking service.

Luminescence

All commemorative issues from No. 451 to No. 511 are printed on phosphorescent paper except No. 478 which is printed with phosphorescent ink, and Nos. 490-492. Some later issues are tagged.

Europa Issue, 1968
Common Design Type

1968, Apr. 29 Photo. *Perf. 14x13*
Size: 32½x22mm

452	CD11 20c deep blue	.30	.25
453	CD11 45c crimson	*.75*	*.45*

National Anthem — A110

1968, Aug. 27 Litho. *Perf. 13x14*

454	A110 20c gray, org, car & dk bl	.25	.25

400th anniversary of the national anthem "Wilhelmus van Nassouwe."

Fokker F.2, 1919, and Friendship F.29 — A111

Planes: 12c, Wright A, 1909, and Cessna sports plane. 45c, De Havilland DH-9, 1919, and Douglas DC-9.

1968, Oct. 1 Photo. *Perf. 14x13*

455	A111 12c crim, pink & blk	.25	.25
456	A111 20c brt grn, bl grn & blk	.25	.25
457	A111 45c brt bl, lt grn & blk	1.00	1.00
	Nos. 455-457 (3)	1.50	1.50

50th anniv. of the founding in 1919 of Royal Dutch Airlines and the Royal Netherlands Aircraft Factories Fokker, and the 60th anniv. in 1967 of the Royal Netherlands Aeronautical Assoc.

"iao" — A112

Design is made up of 28 minute lines, each reading "1919 internationale arbeids-organisatie 1969".

1969, Feb. 25 Engr. *Perf. 14x13*

458	A112 25c brick red & blk	.35	.25
459	A112 45c ultra & blue	.75	.65

International Labor Organization, 50th anniv.

A113

Queen Juliana — A114

Perf. 13½ horiz. x 12½ on one vert. side

1969-75 Photo.

460	A113 25c orange ver	.80	.25
a.	Bklt. pane of 4 + 2 labels	10.00	
460B	A113 25c dull red ('73)	1.00	.25
c.	Booklet pane of 6 (#460B + 5 #461A)	15.00	
d.	Booklet pane of 12 (5 #405 + 7 #460B)	14.00	

Perf. 13x12½

461	A113 30c choc ('72)	.25	.25
d.	Bklt. pane of 10 (4 #405 + 6 #461 + 2 labels)('74)	2.75	
	Complete booklet, #461d	2.75	
461A	A113 35c grnsh bl ('72)	.25	.25
b.	Bklt. pane of 5 (3 #403, 2 #461A + label) ('72)	11.00	
c.	Bklt. pane of 10 (5 #405 + 5 #461A + 2 labels)('75)	3.00	
	Complete booklet, #461c	3.00	
462	A113 40c car rose ('72)	.35	.25
a.	Bklt. pane of 5 + label ('73)	5.50	
463	A113 45c ultra ('72)	.35	.25
a.	Bklt. pane of 8 (4 #405 + 4 #463) ('74)	2.00	
	Complete booklet, #463a	2.00	
464	A113 50c lilac ('72)	.40	.25
a.	Bklt. pane of 4 + 2 labels ('75)	2.00	
	Complete booklet, #464a	2.00	
465	A113 60c slate bl ('72)	.50	.25
a.	Bklt. pane of 5 + label ('80)	3.00	
466	A113 70c bister ('72)	.60	.25
467	A113 75c green ('72)	.60	.25
468	A113 80c red org ('72)	.65	.25
468A	A113 90c gray ('75)	.65	.25

Perf. 13x14

469	A114 1g yel green	.65	.25
470	A114 1.25g maroon	.80	.25
471	A114 1.50g yel bis ('71)	1.00	.25
471A	A114 2g dp rose lil ('72)	1.10	.25
472	A114 2.50g grnsh bl	1.40	.25
473	A114 5g gray ('70)	2.75	.25
474	A114 10g vio bl ('70)	5.50	.85
	Nos. 460-474 (19)	19.60	5.35

Both 25c stamps issued only in booklets.

Printings were both ordinary and phosphorescent paper for Nos. 460, 460a, 469, 471-474.

Coil printings were issued later for Nos. 461, 462-472. Black control number on back of every fifth stamp.

Booklet panes have a large selvage the size of 4 or 6 stamps, with printed inscription.

See No. 542.

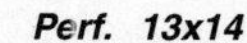

Europa Issue, 1969
Common Design Type

1969, Apr. 28 Photo. *Perf. 14x13*
Size: 33½x22mm

475	CD12 25c dark blue	*.25*	.25
476	CD12 45c red	*1.10*	*.75*

A114a

Möbius strip in Benelux colors.

1969, Sept. 8 Photo. *Perf. 13x14*

477	A114a 25c multicolored	.25	.25

25th anniversary of the signing of the customs union of Belgium, Netherlands and Luxembourg.

A115

Photo. & Engr.

1969, Sept. 30 *Perf. 13x14*

478	A115 25c yellow grn & maroon	.25	.25

Desiderius Erasmus (1469-1536), scholar.

Queen Juliana and Rising Sun — A116

1969, Dec. 15 Photo. *Perf. 14x13*

479	A116 25c blue & multi	.25	.25

15th anniversary of the Charter of the Kingdom of the Netherlands.

Prof. E. M. Meijers — A117

1970, Jan. 13 Photo. *Perf. 14x13*
480 A117 25c blue, vio bl & grn .25 .25

Issued to publicize the new Civil Code and to honor Prof. Meijers, who prepared it.

Dutch Pavilion, EXPO '70 — A118

1970, Mar. 10 Photo. *Perf. 14x13*
481 A118 25c multicolored .25 .25

EXPO '70 International Exposition, Osaka, Japan, Mar. 15-Sept. 13.

"V" for Victory — A119

1970, Apr. 21 Photo. *Perf. 13x14*
482 A119 12c red, ultra, brn ol & lt bl .25 .25

25th anniv. of liberation from the Germans.

Europa Issue, 1970
Common Design Type

1970, May 4 Photo. *Perf. 14x13*
Size: 32½x21½mm
483 CD13 25c carmine *.30* .25
484 CD13 45c dk blue *1.00* .90

Panels A120

Globe A121

1970, June 23 Photo. *Perf. 13x14*
485 A120 25c gray, blk & brt yel grn .30 .25
486 A121 45c ultra, blk & pur .60 .50

#485 publicizes the meeting of the interparliamentary Union; #486 the UN 25th anniv.

Punch Cards — A122

1971, Feb. 16 Photo. *Perf. 14x13*
487 A122 15c dp rose lilac .25 .25

14th national census, 1971.

Europa Issue, 1971
Common Design Type

1971, May 3 Photo. *Perf. 14x13*
Size: 33x22mm
488 CD14 25c lil rose, yel & blk *.40* .25
489 CD14 45c ultra, yel & blk *.80* .70

No. 488 was issued in coils and sheets. In the coils every fifth stamp has a black control number on the back.

Prince Bernhard, Fokker F27, Boeing 747 B — A123

Designs: 15c, Stylized carnation (Prince Bernhard Fund). 20c, Giant Panda (World Wildlife Fund). 15c, 20c horiz.

Photo., Litho. (20c)
1971, June 29 *Perf. 13x14*
490 A123 15c black & yellow .30 .25
491 A123 20c multicolored .75 .30
492 A123 25c multicolored .30 .25
Nos. 490-492,B475 (4) 2.95 2.40

60th birthday of Prince Bernhard. See No. B475.

Map of Delta — A124

1972, Feb. 15 Photo. *Perf. 14x13*
493 A124 20c bl, grn, blk & red .25 .25

Publicity for the Delta plan, a project to shorten the coastline and to build roads.

Europa Issue 1972
Common Design Type

1972, May 5 Photo. *Perf. 13x14*
Size: 22x33mm
494 CD15 30c blue & bis *.40* .25
495 CD15 45c orange & bis *.80* .65

No. 494 was issued in coils and sheets. In the coils every fifth stamp has a black control number on the back.

Thorbecke Quotation — A126

1972, June 2 Photo. *Perf. 14x13*
496 A126 30c lt ultra & blk .40 .25

Jan Rudolf Thorbecke (1798-1872), statesman, who said: "There is more to be done in the world than ever before."

Dutch Flag — A127

1972 *Perf. 13x14*
497 A127 20c blue & multi .30 .25
498 A127 25c blue & multi .60 .25

400th anniversary of the Dutch flag. Issue dates: 20c, July 4; 25c, Nov. 1.

Woman Hurdler — A128

30c, Woman swimmer. 45c, Bicycling.

1972, July 11 *Perf. 14x13*
499 A128 20c multicolored .25 .25
500 A128 30c crimson & multi .30 .25
501 A128 45c violet & multi .60 .60
Nos. 499-501 (3) 1.15 1.10

20th Olympic Games, Munich, 8/26-9/11.

Red Cross — A129

1972, Aug. 15 Photo. *Perf. 13x14*
502 A129 5c red .25 .25
Nos. 502,B485-B488 (5) 2.90 2.75

Netherlands Red Cross.

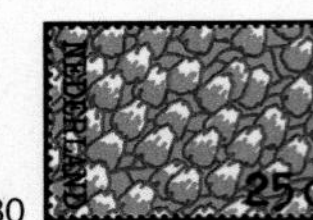

Tulips — A130

1973, Mar. 20 Photo. *Perf. 14x13*
503 A130 25c rose, brt grn & blk .40 .25

Dutch flower and bulb exports.

Europa Issue 1973
Common Design Type

1973, May 1 Photo. *Perf. 14x13*
Size: 32½x22mm
504 CD16 35c bright blue *.40* .25
505 CD16 50c purple *.80* .70

Hockey A132

Woman Gymnast A133

Antenna, Burum A134

Rainbow, Measures A135

Photo. (25c, 35c); Litho. (30c, 50c)
1973, July 31 *Perf. 13x14, 14x13*
506 A132 25c black & green .35 .25
507 A133 30c gray & multi .80 .50
508 A134 35c blue & multi .50 .30
509 A135 50c blue & multi .80 .70
Nos. 506-509 (4) 2.45 1.75

Netherlands Hockey Assoc., 75th anniv. (25c); Rhythmical Gymnastics World Championship, Rotterdam (30c); inauguration of satellite ground station at Burum (35c); cent. of intl. meteorological cooperation (50c).

Queen Juliana, Dutch and House of Orange Colors — A136

Engr. & Photo.
1973, Sept. 4 *Perf. 13x12*
510 A136 40c silver & multi .40 .25

25th anniversary of reign of Queen Juliana.

Chain with Open Link — A137

1973, Oct. 16 Photo. *Perf. 13x14*
511 A137 40c grn, blk, gold & sil .40 .25

Development Corporation.

Nature and Environment — A138

1974, Feb. 19 Photo. *Perf. 13x14*
512 A138 Strip of 3 1.75 1.75
a. 25c Bird of prey .55 .35
b. 25c Tree .55 .35
c. 25c Fisherman in boat and frog .55 .35

75th anniv. of the Netherlands Assoc. for the Protection of Birds and of the State Forestry Service.

Soccer Ball — A139

Tennis Ball — A140

Perf. 14x13, 13x14
1974, June 5 Photo.
513 A139 25c multicolored .40 .25
514 A140 40c multicolored .40 .25

World Cup Soccer Championship, Munich, June 13-July 7 (25c) and 75th anniversary of the Royal Dutch Lawn Tennis Association (40c).

Cattle A141

Pierced Crab under Lens A142

Shipwreck Seen Through Binoculars — A143

1974, July 30 *Perf. 13x14*
515 A141 25c multicolored 1.20 1.20
516 A142 25c sal pink & multi .90 .30
517 A143 40c dk violet & multi .90 .30
Nos. 515-517 (3) 3.00 1.80

Cent. of the Netherlands Cattle Herdbook Soc. (#515); 25th anniv. of Queen Wilhelmina Fund (for cancer research) (#516); sesquicentennial of Royal Dutch Lifeboat Soc. (#517).

BENELUX Issue

"BENELUX" A143a

1974, Sept. 10 Photo. *Perf. 14x13*
518 A143a 30c bl grn, dk grn & lt bl .35 .25

30th anniv. of the signing of the customs union of Belgium, Netherlands and Luxembourg.

Council of Europe Emblem A144

NATO Emblem and Sea Gull A145

1974, Sept. 10 *Perf. 13x14*
519 A144 45c black, bl & yel .40 .25
520 A145 45c dk blue & silver .40 .25

25th anniv. of Council of Europe (No. 519) and of North Atlantic Treaty Organization (No. 520).

Letters and Hands, Papier-maché Sculpture — A146

1974, Oct. 9
521 A146 60c purple & multi .35 .25

Centenary of Universal Postal Union.

People and Map of Dam Square
A147

Brain with Window Symbolizing Free Thought
A148

Design: No. 523, Portuguese Synagogue and map of Mr. Visser Square. 35c, No. 526, like No. 522.

1975 Photo. *Perf. 13x14*

522 A147 30c multicolored .35 .25
523 A147 30c multicolored .35 .25
524 A147 35c multicolored .40 .25
525 A148 45c dp blue & multi .30 .25
Nos. 522-525 (4) 1.40 1.00

Coil Stamps

Perf. 13 Horiz.

526 A147 30c multicolored .35 .25
527 A147 35c multicolored .40 .25

700th anniv. of Amsterdam (No. 522); 300th anniv. of the Portuguese Synagogue in Amsterdam (No. 523) and 400th anniv. of the founding of the University of Leyden and the beginning of higher education in the Netherlands (No. 525).

Issue dates: Nos. 522-523, 525-526, Feb. 26; Nos. 524, 527, Apr. 1.

Eye Looking over Barbed Wire — A149

1975, Apr. 29 Photo. *Perf. 13x14*

528 A149 35c black & carmine .40 .25

Liberation of the Netherlands from Nazi occupation, 30th anniversary.

Company Emblem and "Stad Middelburg" — A150

1975, May 21 Photo. *Perf. 14x13*

529 A150 35c multicolored .50 .25

Zeeland Steamship Company, centenary.

Albert Schweitzer in Boat — A151

1975, May 21

530 A151 50c multicolored .50 .25

Albert Schweitzer (1875-1965), medical missionary.

Symbolic Metric Scale — A152

1975, July 29 Litho. *Perf. 14x13*

531 A152 50c multicolored .50 .25

Cent. of Intl. Meter Convention, Paris, 1875.

Playing Card with Woman, Man, Pigeons, Pens — A153

1975, July 29 *Perf. 13x14*

532 A153 35c multicolored .50 .25

International Women's Year 1975.

Fingers Reading Braille — A154

1975, Oct. 7 Photo. *Perf. 13x14*

533 A154 35c multicolored .50 .25

Sesquicentennial of the invention of Braille system of writing for the blind by Louis Braille (1809-1852).

Rubbings of 25¢ Coins — A155

1975, Oct. 7 *Perf. 14x13*

534 A155 50c green, blk & bl .50 .25

To publicize the importance of saving.

Lottery Ticket, 18th Century — A156

1976, Feb. 3 Photo. *Perf. 14x13*

535 A156 35c multicolored .40 .25

250th anniversary of National Lottery.

Queen Type of 1969 and

A157

1976-86 Photo. *Perf. 12½x13½*

536 A157 5c gray .25 .25
Booklet Panes
a. (3 #536, 2 #537, 3 #542) 3.00
Complete booklet, #536a 3.00
b. (4 #536, 2 #537, 4 #539 + 2 labels) 2.00
Complete booklet, #536b 2.00
c. (#536, 2 #537, 5 #542) 3.00
Complete booklet, #536c 3.00
d. (4 #536, 7 #539 + label) 3.00
Complete booklet, #536d 3.00
e. (2 #536, 2 #540, 4 #541) 3.00
f. (5 #536, 2 #537, 2 #540, 3 #542) + 2 labels 4.00
Complete booklet, #536f 4.00
g. (1 #536, 2 #537, 5 #543) ('86) 3.00
Complete booklet, #536g 3.00
537 A157 10c ultra .25 .25
538 A157 25c violet .25 .25
539 A157 40c sepia .40 .25
540 A157 45c brt blue .40 .25
541 A157 50c lil rose ('80) .40 .25
a. Bklt. pane, 5 each #537, 541 + 2 labels 2.75
Complete booklet, #541a 2.75
542 A113 55c carmine .60 .25
543 A157 55c brt grn ('81) .55 .25
544 A157 60c apple grn ('81) .65 .25
545 A157 65c dk red brn ('86) .95 .25
Nos. 536-545 (10) 4.70 2.50

Compare No. 544 with No. 791. No. 542 also issued in coils with control number on the back of every 5th stamp.

See Nos. 903-905.

Coil Stamps

1976-86 *Perf. 13½ Vert.*

546 A157 5c slate gray .25 .25
547 A157 10c ultra .25 .25
548 A157 25c violet .30 .25
549 A157 40c sepia ('77) .50 .25
550 A157 45c brt blue .50 .25
551 A157 50c brt rose ('79) .75 .25
552 A157 55c brt grn ('81) .75 .25
553 A157 60c apple grn ('81) .85 .25
554 A157 65c dk red brn ('86) .95 .25
Nos. 546-554 (9) 5.10 2.25

See Nos. 772, 774, 786, 788, 791.

De Ruyter Statue, Flushing — A158

1976, Apr. 22 Photo. *Perf. 14x13*

555 A158 55c multicolored .50 .25

Adm. Michiel Adriaenszon de Ruyter (1607-1676), Dutch naval hero, 300th death anniversary.

Van Prinsterer and Page — A159

1976, May 19 Photo. *Perf. 14x13*

556 A159 55c multicolored .40 .25

Guillaume Groen van Prinsterer (1801-1876), statesman and historian.

Women Waving American Flags — A160

Design is from a 220-year old permanent wooden calendar from Ameland Island.

1976, May 25 Litho.

557 A160 75c multicolored .60 .25

American Bicentennial.

Marchers — A161

1976, June 15 Photo. *Perf. 14x13*

558 A161 40c multicolored .50 .25

Nijmegen 4-day march, 60th anniversary.

A number of stamps issued from 1970 on appear to have parts of the designs misregistered, blurry, or look off-center. These stamps are deliberately designed that way. Most prominent examples are Nos. 559, 582, 602, 656, 711-712, 721, B638-B640, B662-B667.

Runners — A162

1976, June 15 Litho. Tagged

559 A162 55c multicolored .55 .25

Royal Dutch Athletic Soc., 75th anniv.

Printing: One Communicating with Many — A163

1976, Sept. 2 Photo. *Perf. 13x14*

560 A163 45c blue & red .50 .25

Netherlands Printers Organization, 75th anniv.

Sailing Ship and City — A164

Design: 75c, Sea gull over coast.

1976, Sept. 2 Litho. *Perf. 14x13*
Tagged

561 A164 40c bister, red & bl .50 .25
562 A164 75c ultra, yel & red .70 .45

Zuider Zee Project, the conversion of water areas into land.

Radiation of Heat and Light
A165

Ballot and Pencil
A166

Perf. 13x14, 14x13

1977, Jan. 25 Photo.

563 A165 40c multicolored .45 .25
564 A166 45c black, red & ocher .45 .25

Coil Stamps

Perf. 13 Horiz.

565 A165 40c multicolored .35 .25

Perf. 13 Vert.

566 A166 45c multicolored .35 .25

Publicity for wise use of energy (40c) and forthcoming elections (45c). Nos. 565-566 have black control number on back of every 5th stamp.

For overprint see No. 569.

Spinoza — A167

1977, Feb. 21 Photo. *Perf. 13x14*

567 A167 75c multicolored .80 .25

Baruch Spinoza (1632-1677), philosopher, 300th death anniversary.

Delft Bible Text, Old Type, Electronic "a" — A168

1977, Mar. 8 *Perf. 14x13*

568 A168 55c ocher & black .50 .25

Delft Bible (Old Testament), oldest book printed in Dutch, 500th anniversary. Printed in sheets of 50 se-tenant with label inscribed with description of stamp design and purpose.

No. 564 Overprinted in Blue

1977, Apr. 15 Photo. *Perf. 14x13*

569 A166 45c multicolored .40 .25

Elections of May 25.

Kaleidoscope of Activities — A169

1977, June 9 Litho. *Perf. 13x14*

570 A169 55c multicolored .45 .25

Netherlands Society for Industry and Commerce, bicentenary.

Man in Wheelchair Looking at Obstacles
A170

Engineer's Diagram of Water Currents
A171

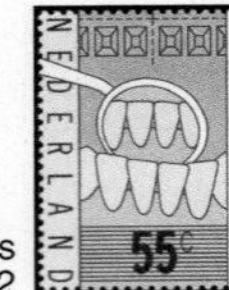

Teeth, Dentist's Mirror — A172

1977, Sept. 6 Photo. ***Perf. 14x13***
571 A170 40c multicolored .45 .25

Litho.
572 A171 45c multicolored .45 .25

Perf. 13x14
573 A172 55c multicolored .45 .25
Nos. 571-573 (3) 1.35 .75

50th anniversaries of AVO (Actio vincit omnia), an organization to help the handicapped (40c), and of Delft Hydraulic Laboratory (45c); centenary of Dentists' Training in the Netherlands (55c).

"Postcode" — A173

1978, Mar. 14 Photo. ***Perf. 14x13***
574 A173 40c dk blue & red .45 .25
575 A173 45c red, dk & lt bl .50 .25

Introduction of new postal code.

European Human Rights Treaty — A174

1978, May 2 Photo. ***Perf. 13x14***
576 A174 45c gray, blue & blk .50 .25

European Treaty of Human Rights, 25th anniv.

Europa Issue

Haarlem City Hall — A175

1978, May 2
577 A175 55c multicolored *.80* .25

Chess Board and Move Diagram A176

Korfball A177

1978, June 1 Photo. ***Perf. 13x14***
578 A176 40c multicolored .40 .25

Litho.
579 A177 45c red & vio bl .50 .25

18th IBM Chess Tournament, Amsterdam, July 12, and 75th anniversary of korfball in the Netherlands.

Man Pointing to his Kidney A178

Heart, Torch, Gauge and Clouds A179

1978, Aug. 22 Photo. ***Perf. 13x13½***
580 A178 40c multicolored .45 .25

Perf. 13x14
581 A179 45c multicolored .45 .25

Importance of kidney transplants and drive against hypertension.

Epaulettes, Military Academy — A180

1978, Sept. 12 Photo. ***Perf. 13x14***
582 A180 55c multicolored .50 .25

Royal Military Academy, sesquicentennial. Printed in continuous design in sheets of 100 (10x10).

Verkade as Hamlet — A181

1978, Oct. 17 Photo. ***Perf. 14x13***
583 A181 45c multicolored .50 .25

Eduard Rutger Verkade (1878-1961), actor and producer.

Clasped Hands and Arrows — A182

1979, Jan. 23 Engr. ***Perf. 13x14***
584 A182 55c blue .60 .25

Union of Utrecht, 400th anniversary.

European Parliament — A183

1979, Feb. 20 Litho. ***Perf. 13½x13***
585 A183 45c blue, blk & red .50 .25

European Parliament, first direct elections, June 7-10.

Queen Juliana — A184

1979, Mar. 13 Photo. ***Perf. 13½x14***
586 A184 55c multicolored .60 .25

70th birthday of Queen Juliana.

A185

Europa: 55c, Dutch Stamps and magnifying glass. 75c, Hand on Morse key, and ship at sea.

1979, May 2 Litho. ***Perf. 13x13½***
587 A185 55c multicolored *.50* .25
588 A185 75c multicolored *1.00* *.30*

A186

Map of Netherlands with chamber locations.

1979, June 5 Litho. ***Perf. 13x14***
589 A186 45c multicolored .50 .25

Netherlands Chambers of Commerce and 175th anniversary of Maastricht Chamber.

Soccer — A187

1979, Aug. 28 Litho. ***Perf. 14x13***
590 A187 45c multicolored .50 .25

Centenary of soccer in the Netherlands.

Suffragettes — A188

1979, Aug. 28 Photo. ***Perf. 13x14***
591 A188 55c multicolored .60 .25

Voting right for women, 60th anniversary.

Inscribed Tympanum and Architrave — A189

1979, Oct. 2 Photo. ***Perf. 14x13***
592 A189 40c multicolored .45 .25

Joost van den Vondel (1587-1679), Dutch poet and dramatist.

"Gay Company," Tile Floor — A190

1979, Oct. 2
593 A190 45c multicolored .50 .25

Jan Steen (1626-1679), Dutch painter.

Alexander de Savornin Lohman (1837-1924) — A191

Politicians: 50c, Pieter Jelles Troelstra (1860-1930), Social Democratic Workmen's Party leader. 60c, Pieter Jacobus Oud (1886-1968), mayor of Rotterdam.

1980, Mar. 4 Photo. ***Perf. 13x13½***
594 A191 45c multicolored .40 .25
595 A191 50c multicolored .45 .25
596 A191 60c multicolored .55 .25
Nos. 594-596 (3) 1.40 .75

British Bomber Dropping Food, Dutch Flag A192

Anne Frank A193

Perf. 13x14, 14x13

1980, Apr. 25 Photo.
597 A192 45c multicolored .55 .25
598 A193 60c multicolored .60 .25

35th anniv. of liberation from the Germans.

Queen Beatrix, Palace — A194

1980, Apr. 30 ***Perf. 13x14, 13x13½***
599 A194 60c multicolored .60 .25
a. Perf. 12¾x13¼ 2.00 1.00

Installation of Queen Beatrix.
See No. 608.

Boy and Girl Inspecting Stamp — A195

1980, May 1 ***Perf. 14x13***
600 A195 50c multicolored .50 .25

Youth philately; NVPH Stamp Show, s'Gravenhagen, May 1-3 and JUPOSTEX Stamp Exhibition, Eindhoven, May 23-27. No. 600 printed se-tenant with label.

Bridge Players, "Netherlands" Hand — A196

1980, June 3 Litho. ***Perf. 13x14***
601 A196 50c multicolored .55 .25

6th Bridge Olympiad, Valkenburg, 9/27-10/11.

Truck Transport — A197

60c, Two-axle railway hopper truck. 80c, Inland navigation barge.

1980, Aug. 26 Photo. ***Perf. 13½x13***
602 A197 50c shown .45 .25
603 A197 60c multicolored .55 .25
604 A197 80c multicolored .75 .25
Nos. 602-604 (3) 1.75 .75

Queen Wilhelmina, Excerpt from Speech, Netherlands Flag — A198

80c, Winston Churchill, British flag.

1980, Sept. 23 Litho. ***Perf. 13½x13***
605 A198 60c shown *.50* .25
606 A198 80c multicolored *1.00* *.30*

Europa.

Abraham Kuyper, University Emblem, "100" — A199

1980, Oct. 14 Litho. ***Perf. 13½x13***
607 A199 50c multicolored .55 .25

Free University centennial (founded by Kuyper).

Queen Beatrix Type of 1980

1981, Jan. 6 Photo. ***Perf. 12¾x13¼***
608 A194 65c multicolored .70 .25
a. Perf. 12¾x14 2.50 1.00

Parcel — A200

Designs: 55c, Dish antenna and telephone. 65c, Bank books.

1981, May 19 Litho. *Perf. 13½x13*
609 A200 45c multicolored .50 .25
610 A200 55c multicolored .50 .25
611 A200 65c multicolored .50 .25
a. Souvenir sheet of 3, #609-611 1.35 1.00

Centenaries: Parcel Post Service (45c); Public telephone service (55c); National Savings Bank (65c).

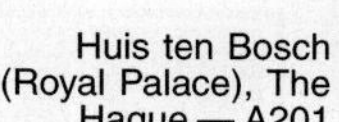

Huis ten Bosch (Royal Palace), The Hague — A201

1981, June 16 Litho. *Perf. 13½x13*
612 A201 55c multicolored .60 .25

Europa Issue

Carillon — A202

1981, Sept. 1 Litho. *Perf. 13½x13*
613 A202 45c shown *.50 .25*
614 A202 65c Barrel organ *.65 .25*

450th Anniv. of Council of State — A203

1981, Oct. 1 Photo. *Perf. 13½x13*
615 A203 65c multi .70 .25

Excavator and Ship's Screw (Exports) — A204

55c, Cast iron component, scale. 60c, Tomato, lettuce. 65c, Egg, cheese.

1981, Oct. 20 Photo. *Perf. 13½x13*
616 A204 45c shown .45 .25
617 A204 55c multi .50 .25
618 A204 60c multi .60 .25
619 A204 65c multi .65 .25
Nos. 616-619 (4) 2.20 1.00

Queen Beatrix — A205

Black Vignette

1981-86 Photo. *Perf. 13½x12½*
620 A205 65c tan .55 .25
621 A205 70c lt vio ('82) .70 .25
a. Bklt. pane, 4 #536, 4 #621 3.00
Complete booklet, #621a 3.00
622 A205 75c pale pink ('82) .70 .25
a. Bklt. pane of 4 ('86) 3.00
623 A205 90c lt grn('82) .70 .25
624 A205 1g lt vio('82) .70 .25
625 A205 1.40g pale grn('82) 1.15 .25
626 A205 2g lem ('82) 1.40 .25
627 A205 3g pale vio ('82) 2.10 .25
628 A205 4g brt yel grn ('82) 2.60 .25
629 A205 5g lt grnsh bl ('82) 3.00 .25
630 A205 6.50g lt lil rose ('82) 3.75 .30
631 A205 7g pale bl ('86) 4.50 .40
Nos. 620-631 (12) 21.85 3.20

Coil Stamps
Perf. 13½ Horiz.
632 A205 70c lt vio ('82) .80 .25
633 A205 75c pale pink ('86) .80 .25
634 A205 1g lt vio ('82) .80 .25
635 A205 2g lem ('82) 1.60 .25
636 A205 6.50g lt lil rose ('82) 5.50 .55
637 A205 7g pale bl ('86) 6.50 .75
Nos. 632-637 (6) 16.00 2.30

See Nos. 685-699.

University of Amsterdam, 350th Anniv. — A206

1982, Jan. 14 Litho. *Perf. 13½x13*
638 A206 65c multi .60 .25

Royal Dutch Skating Assoc. Centenary — A207

1982, Feb. 26 Litho. *Perf. 13x13½*
639 A207 45c multi .50 .25

Bicentenary of US-Netherlands Diplomatic Relations — A208

1982, Apr. 20 Photo. *Perf. 13½x13*
640 A208 50c multi .50 .25
641 A208 65c multi .70 .25

See US No. 2003.

Sandwich Tern and Eider Duck, Waddenzee A209

1982, June 8 Litho. *Perf. 13½x13*
642 A209 50c shown .55 .25
643 A209 70c Barnacle geese .75 .25

Dutch Road Safety Assoc, 50th Anniv. — A210

1982, Aug. 24 Photo. *Perf. 13x14*
644 A210 60c multi .50 .25

Europa 1982 — A211

Fortification Layouts.

1982, Sept. 16 Litho. *Perf. 13x13½*
645 A211 50c Enkhuizen, 1590 *.60 .25*
646 A211 70c Coevorden, 1680 *.75 .25*

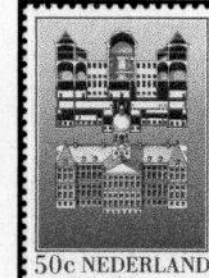
Royal Palace, Dam Square, Amsterdam — A212

50c, Facade, cross-section. 60c, Aerial view.

1982, Oct. 5 Litho. *Perf. 13x13½*
647 A212 50c multi .50 .25
648 A212 60c multi .55 .25

Royal Dutch Touring Club Centenary — A213

1983, Mar. 1 Litho. *Perf. 13½x13*
649 A213 70c multi .70 .25

A214

Europa: 50c, Netherlands Newspaper Publishers Assoc., 75th anniv. 70c, Launching of European Telecommunication Satellite Org. ECS F-1 rocket, June 3.

1983, May 17 Litho. *Perf. 13x13½*
650 A214 50c multi *.50 .25*
651 A214 70c multi *.70 .25*

A215

De Stijl ("The Style") Modern Art Movement, 1917-31: 50c, Composition 1922, by P. Mondriaan. 65c, Maison Particuliere contra Construction, by C. van Eesteren and T. van Doesburg.

1983, June 21 Litho. *Perf. 13x13½*
652 A215 50c multi .50 .25
653 A215 65c multi .65 .25

Symbolic Separation of Church — A216

1983, Oct. 11 Litho. *Perf. 13x13½*
654 A216 70c multi .70 .25

Martin Luther (1483-1546).

2nd European Parliament Election, June 14 — A217

1984, Mar. 13 Litho. *Perf. 13½x13*
655 A217 70c multicolored .70 .25

St. Servatius (d. 384) — A218

1984, May 8 Photo. *Perf. 13x14*
656 A218 60c Statue, 1732 .60 .25

Europa (1959-84) — A219

1984, May 22 *Perf. 13½x13*
657 A219 50c blue *.50 .25*
a. Perf. 14x13 *3.00 2.50*
658 A219 70c yellow green *.70 .30*
a. Perf. 14x13 *3.00 2.50*

Perf. 14x13 stamps are coils. Every fifth stamp has a control number on the back.

William of Orange (1533-84) — A220

1984, July 10 Photo. *Perf. 14x13*
659 A220 70c multicolored .70 .25

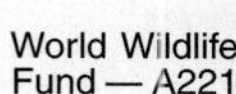

World Wildlife Fund — A221

1984, Sept. 18 Litho. *Perf. 14x13*
660 A221 70c Pandas, globe 1.00 .25

11th Intl. Small Business Congress, Amsterdam, Oct. 24-26 — A222

1984, Oct. 23 Litho. *Perf. 13x13½*
661 A222 60c Graph, leaf .60 .25

Guide Dog Fund — A223

60c, Sunny, first guide dog.

Photogravure and Engraved
1985, Jan. 22 *Perf. 14x13*
662 A223 60c multi .60 .25

A224

Tourism — A224a

1985, Feb. 26 Photo.
663 A224 50c multicolored .50 .25
664 A224a 70c multicolored .70 .25

Cent. of the Tourist office "Geuldal," and 50th anniv. of the Natl. Park "De Hoge Veluwe."

Liberation from German Forces, 40th Anniv. — A225

Designs: 50c, Jewish star, mastheads of underground newspapers, resistance fighter. 60c, Allied supply air drop, masthead of The Flying Dutchman, Polish soldier at Arnhem. 65c, Liberation Day in Amsterdam, masthead, first edition of Het Parool (underground newspaper), American cemetery at Margraten. 70c, Dutch women in Japanese prison camp, Japanese occupation currency, building of the Burma Railway.

1985, May 5 Photo. *Perf. 14x13*
665 A225 50c blk, buff & red .55 .25
666 A225 60c blk, buff & brt bl .65 .25
667 A225 65c blk, buff & org .70 .50
668 A225 70c blk, buff & brt grn .75 .25
Nos. 665-668 (4) 2.65 1.25

WWII resistance effort (1940-1945) and liberation of Europe, 1945.

Europa '85 — A226

50c, Piano keyboard. 70c, Stylized organ pipes.

1985, June 4 Litho. *Perf. 13x13½*
669 A226 50c multi *.85 .25*
670 A226 70c multi *1.15 .30*

Natl. Museum of Fine Arts, Amsterdam, Cent. — A227

Anniversaries and events: 50c, Museum in 1885, 1985. 60c, Nautical College, Amsterdam, bicent.: Students training. 70c, SAIL-85, Amsterdam: Sailboat rigging.

1985, July 2 Photo. *Perf. 13½x13*
671 A227 50c multicolored .50 .25
672 A227 60c multicolored .60 .25

Perf. 14x13
673 A227 70c multicolored .70 .25
Nos. 671-673 (3) 1.80 .75

Wildlife Conservation A228

Designs: 50c, Porpoise, statistical graph. 70c, Seal, molecular structure models.

1985, Sept. 10 Litho. *Perf. 13½x13*
674 A228 50c multicolored .55 .30
675 A228 70c multicolored .75 .30

Penal Code, Cent. — A229
Amsterdam Datum Ordinance, 300th Anniv. — A230

Lithographed, Photogravure (60c)
1986, Jan. 21 *Perf. 14x13*
676 A229 50c Text .55 .30
677 A230 60c Elevation gauge .65 .25

Sexbierum Windmill Test Station Inauguration A231

1986, Mar. 4 Litho. *Perf. 14x13*
678 A231 70c multicolored .75 .25

Het Loo Palace Gardens, Apeldorn — A232

1986, May 13 Litho. *Perf. 13x14*
679 A232 50c shown *.60 .30*

Photo.
680 A232 70c Air and soil pollution *.80 .25*

Europa 1986.

Utrecht Cathedral — A233

60c, German House, c.1350. 70c, Utrecht University charter, horiz.

1986, June 10 Photo. *Perf. 13x14*
681 A233 50c shown .55 .30
682 A233 60c multicolored .65 .30

Perf. 14x13
683 A233 70c multicolored .75 .30
Nos. 681-683 (3) 1.95 .90

Cathedral restoration, 1986. Heemschut Conservation. Soc., 75th anniv. Utrecht University, 350th anniv.

Willem Drees (1886-1988), Statesman — A234

1986, July 1 Litho. *Perf. 13x13½*
684 A234 55c multicolored .60 .25

Queen Type of 1981

1986-90 Photo. *Perf. 13½x12½*
685 A205 1.20g citron & blk .90 .25
686 A205 1.50g lt rose vio & blk .85 .25
688 A205 2.50g tan & blk 1.35 .25
694 A205 7.50g lt grn & blk 5.00 1.00
Nos. 685-694 (4) 8.10 1.75

Coil Stamps
Perf. 13½ Horiz.
697 A205 1.50g lt rose vio & blk 1.25 .25
699 A205 2.50g tan & blk 2.00 .25

Issue dates: Nos. 685, 688, 699, 9/23. Nos. 686, 697, 8/19. 7.50g, 5/29/90.

Billiards — A235

Perf. 14x13, 13x14
1986, Sept. 9 Photo.
705 A235 75c shown .80 .30
706 A235 75c Checkers, vert. .80 .25

Royal Dutch Billiards Assoc., Checkers Association, 75th annivs.

Delta Project Completion — A236

65c, Storm-surge barrier. 75c, Barrier withstanding flood.

1986, Oct. 7 Photo. *Perf. 14x13*
708 A236 65c multicolored .70 .30
709 A236 75c multicolored .80 .25

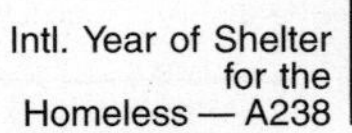
Princess Juliana and Prince Bernhard, 50th Wedding Anniv. — A237

1987, Jan. 6 Photo. *Perf. 13x14*
710 A237 75c multicolored .85 .25

Intl. Year of Shelter for the Homeless — A238

Designs: 75c, Salvation Army, cent.

1987, Feb. 10 Photo. *Perf. 14x13*
711 A238 65c multicolored .95 .30
712 A238 75c multicolored 1.05 .25

Dutch Literature — A239

Authors: 55c, Eduard Douwes Dekker (1820-1887) and De Harmonie Club, Batavia. 75c, Constantijn Huygens (1596-1687) and Scheveningseweg, The Hague.

1987, Mar. 10 Litho. *Perf. 13½x13*
713 A239 55c multicolored .60 .25
714 A239 75c multicolored .80 .25

Europa 1987 — A240

Modern architecture: 55c, Scheveningen Dance Theater, designed by Rem Koolhaas. 75c, Montessori School, Amsterdam, designed by Herman Hertzberger.

1987, May 12 Litho. *Perf. 14x13*
715 A240 55c multicolored *.95* .25
716 A240 75c multicolored *1.05* .25

Produce Auction at Broeck op Langedijk, 1887 — A241

Designs: 65c, Field in Groningen Province, signatures of society founders. 75c, Auction, bidding, price indicator, 1987.

1987, June 16 Photo. *Perf. 14x13*
717 A241 55c shown .55 .25
718 A241 65c multicolored .65 .25
719 A241 75c multicolored .75 .25
Nos. 717-719 (3) 1.95 .75

Sale of produce by auction in the Netherlands, cent., and Groningen Agricultural Society, 150th anniv. (No. 718).

Union of the Netherlands Municipalities, 75th Anniv. — A242

1987, Oct. 6 Litho. *Perf. 13x14*
720 A242 75c multicolored .80 .25

Noordeinde Palace, The Hague — A243

1987, Oct. 27 Photo. *Perf. 14x13*
721 A243 65c multicolored .70 .25

A244

Booklet Stamps
Perf. 13½x13 on 3 Sides
1987, Dec. 1 Photo.
722 A244 50c dk ultra, emer & dk red .50 .25
723 A244 50c dk red, dk ultra & yel .50 .25
724 A244 50c dk ultra, yel & dk red .50 .25
725 A244 50c dk red, emer & yel .50 .25
726 A244 50c emer, dk red & dk ultra .50 .25
a. Bklt. pane, 4 each #722-726 10.00 13.00
Complete booklet #726a 10.00
Nos. 722-726 (5) 2.50 1.25

Netherlands Cancer Institute, 75th Anniv. — A246

1988, Apr. 19 Litho. *Perf. 13½x13*
728 A246 75c multicolored .80 .25

Europa 1988 — A247

Modern transportation meeting ecological requirements: 55c, Cyclist, rural scenery, chemical formulas, vert. 75c, Cyclists seen through car-door mirror.

1988, May 17 Litho. *Perf. 13x13½*
729 A247 55c multicolored *.95 .25*

Perf. 13½x13
730 A247 75c multicolored *1.05* .25

A248

Designs: 65c, Prism splitting light as discovered by Sir Isaac Newton, planet Saturn as observed by Christian Huygens, and pendulum clock, c. 1688. 75c, William of Orange (1650-1702) and Mary II (1662-1694).

1988, June 14 *Perf. 14x13*
731 A248 65c multicolored .70 .25
732 A248 75c multicolored .80 .25

No. 731, Coronation of William III and Mary Stuart, King and Queen of England, 300th anniv. (in 1989). No. 732, Arrival of Dutch William in England, 300th anniv.

Modern Art — A249

Paintings by artists belonging to Cobra: 55c, *Cobra Cat*, 1950, by Appel. 65c, *Stag Beetle*, 1948, by Corneille. 75c, *Fallen Horse*, 1950, by Constant.

1988, July 5 Litho. *Perf. 13½x13*
733 A249 55c multicolored .70 .50
734 A249 65c multicolored .80 .50
735 A249 75c multicolored .90 .30
Nos. 733-735 (3) 2.40 1.30

Each stamp printed se-tenant with label picturing the featured artist's signature.

Cobra, an intl. organization established in 1948 by expressionist artists from Copenhagen, Brussels and Amsterdam.

Australia Bicentennial — A250

1988, Aug. 30 Photo. *Perf. 13x14*
736 A250 75c multicolored .80 .25

A251 A252

1988, Sept. 27 Litho. *Perf. 13x13½*
737 A251 75c dk green & green .80 .25
738 A252 75c bright violet .80 .25

Erasmus University, Rotterdam, 75th anniv. (#737), Amsterdam Concertgebouw & Orchestra, cent. (#738).

Holiday Greetings — A253

1988, Dec. 1 Photo. *Perf. 13½x12½*
739 A253 50c multicolored .55 .25

"Holland," etc.

Stamps inscribed "Holland," "Stadspost," etc., are private issues. In some cases overprints or surcharges on Netherlands stamps may be created.

Privatization of the Netherlands Postal Service
A254

Mailbox, sorting machine, mailbag, mailman, telephone key pad, fiber optics cable, microwave transmitter & telephone handset.

Litho. & Engr.

1989, Jan. 3 *Perf. 13x13½*
740 A254 75c multicolored .85 .25

Dutch Trade Unions — A255

1989, Feb. 7 Litho. *Perf. 13x13½*
741 A255 55c shown .60 .25

Photo.
Perf. 13x14
742 A255 75c Hands, mouths .80 .25

NATO, 40th Anniv. — A256

1989, Mar. 14 Litho. *Perf. 14x13*
743 A256 75c multicolored .80 .25

Europa 1989 — A257

Children's games (string telephone): 55c, Boy. 75c Girl.

1989, May 9 Litho. *Perf. 13½x13*
744 A257 55c multicolored .95 .25
745 A257 75c multicolored 1.05 .25

Dutch Railways, 150th Anniv. — A258

1989, June 20 Litho. *Perf. 13½x13*
746 A258 55c Rails .55 .25
747 A258 65c Trains .65 .25

Perf. 14x13
748 A258 75c Passengers .75 .25
Nos. 746-748 (3) 1.95 .75

Royal Dutch Soccer Assoc., Cent. — A259

1989, Sept. 5 Photo. *Perf. 13x14*
749 A259 75c multicolored .75 .25

Treaty of London, 150th Anniv. — A260

Map of Limburg Provinces

1989, Oct. 2 Litho. *Perf. 13x14*
750 A260 75c multicolored .75 .25

See Belgium No. 1327.

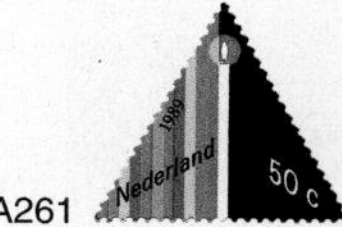

A261

Perf. 13x13x13½
1989, Nov. 30 Photo.
751 A261 50c multicolored .55 .25

Sold only in sheets of 20.

Anniversaries — A262

Designs: 65c, Leiden coat of arms (tulip), and layout of the Hortus Botanicus in 1601. 75c, Assessing work conditions (clock, sky, wooden floor), horiz.

1990, Feb. 6 Litho. *Perf. 13x13½*
752 A262 65c multicolored .70 .25

Perf. 13½x13
753 A262 75c multicolored .80 .25

Hortus Botanicus, Leiden, 400th anniv. (65c); Labor Inspectorate, cent. (75c).

Vincent van Gogh (1853-1890) — A263

Details of works by van Gogh: 55c, *Self-portrait*, pencil sketch, 1886-87. 75c, *The Green Vineyard*, painting, 1888.

1990, Mar. 6 *Perf. 13x13½*
754 A263 55c multicolored .65 .25
755 A263 75c multicolored .85 .25

Rotterdam Reconstruction A264

1990, May 8 Litho. *Perf. 13½x13*
756 A264 55c shown .55 .25
757 A264 65c Diagram .65 .25
758 A264 75c Modern bldgs. .75 .25
Nos. 756-758 (3) 1.95 .75

Europa — A264a

Post offices.

1990, June 12
759 A264a 55c Veere *.95 .25*
760 A264a 75c Groningen *1.05 .25*

Dutch East India Co. Ships A265

Sail '90 A266

1990, July 3 *Perf. 13x13½*
761 A265 65c multicolored .65 .25
762 A266 75c multicolored .75 .25

Queens of the House of Orange — A267

1990, Sept. 5 Litho. *Perf. 13½*
763 A267 150c multicolored 1.50 .90

Century of rule by Queens Emma, Wilhelmina, Juliana and Beatrix.

A268

1990, Oct. 9 Photo. *Perf. 13x14*
764 A268 65c multicolored .70 .30

Natl. emergency phone number.

A269

1990, Nov. 29 Photo. *Perf. 14*
765 A269 50c multicolored .55 .25
a. Tete-beche pair 1.10 .30

All pairs in sheet are tete-beche.

Threats to the Environment A270

1991, Jan. 30 Litho. *Perf. 13½x13*
766 A270 55c Air pollution .55 .25
767 A270 65c Water pollution .65 .25
768 A270 75c Soil pollution .75 .25
Nos. 766-768 (3) 1.95 .75

General Strike, 50th Anniv. — A271

1991, Feb. 25 Photo. *Perf. 14x13*
769 A271 75c multicolored .80 .25

Queen Beatrix and Prince Claus, 25th Wedding Anniv. — A272

1991, Mar. 11 Litho. *Perf. 13½x13*
770 75c shown .80 .30
771 75c Riding horses .80 .30
a. A272 Pair, #770-771 1.60 1.20

Numeral Type of 1976 and

Queen Beatrix — A273

Perf. 12½x13½, 13½x12½
1991-94 Photo.
772 A157 70c gray violet .75 .25
a. Booklet pane, 5 each #537, 772 5.00
773 A273 75c green 1.00 .25
a. Bklt. pane of 4 + 2 labels 4.00 2.00
Complete booklet, #773a 4.00
774 A157 80c red lilac 1.00 .25
774A A273 80c red brown 1.00 .25
b. Booklet pane of 5 + label 4.00 2.00
Complete booklet, #774Ab 4.00
775 A273 90c blue 1.00 1.25
776 A273 1g purple 1.00 .40
777 A273 1.30g gray blue 1.10 .25
778 A273 1.40g gray olive 1.10 .25
779 A273 1.60g magenta 1.40 .25
780 A273 2g yel brown 1.75 .80
781 A273 2.50g red lilac 2.25 1.20
782 A273 3g blue 2.50 1.20
783 A273 5g brown red 4.25 1.15

Perf. 14x13, Syncopated
784 A273 7.50g purple 8.00 2.75
785 A273 10g green 5.00 1.00
Nos. 772-785 (15) 33.10 11.50

Coil Stamps

Perf. 13½ Vert. (A157), Horiz. (A273)
786 A157 70c gray violet .75 .25
787 A273 75c green .95 .50
788 A157 80c red lilac .90 .25
789 A273 80c red brown .90 .25
790 A273 1.60g magenta 1.75 .50
Nos. 786-790 (5) 5.25 1.75

Booklet Stamp

Perf. 12½x13½
791 A157 60c lemon .65 .25
a. Bklt. pane, 2 #791, 4 #772 4.50

Issued: 75c, 3/14/91; 60c, 70c, #774, 1.60g, 6/25/91; #774A, 789, 1.30g, 1.40g, 9/3/91; 1g, 2g, 3g, 5g, 11/11/92; 90c, 2/2/93; 2.50g, 9/7/93; 10g, 11/29/93; 7.50g, 11/28/94.

See #902, 906-913, 1091-1104, 1216, 1218-1221, 1223.

A274

A275

Designs: 55c, Gerard Philips, carbon filament experiments, 1890. 65c, Electrical wiring. 75c, Laser video disk experiment.

Perf. 13x14, 14x13
1991, May 15 Photo.
792 A274 55c multicolored .55 .25
793 A275 65c multicolored .65 .25
794 A274 75c multicolored .75 .25
Nos. 792-794 (3) 1.95 .75

Philips Electronics, cent. (Nos. 792, 794). Netherlands Normalization Institute, 75th anniv. (No. 793).

A276

Europa: 75c, Ladders to another world.

1991, June 11 Litho. *Perf. 13x13½*
795 A276 55c multicolored *.95 .30*
796 A276 75c multicolored *1.05 .25*

Nijmegen Four Days Marches, 75th Anniv. — A277

1991, July 9 Photo. *Perf. 14x13*
797 A277 80c multicolored .90 .25

Dutch Nobel Prize Winners — A278

Designs: 60c, Jacobus H. Van't Hoff, chemistry, 1901. 70c, Pieter Zeeman, physics, 1902. 80c, Tobias M. C. Asser, peace, 1911.

1991, Sept. 3 *Perf. 14x13*
798 A278 60c multicolored .65 .25
799 A278 70c multicolored .70 .25
800 A278 80c multicolored .80 .25
Nos. 798-800 (3) 2.15 .75

Public Libraries, Cent. — A279

1991, Oct. 1 Litho. ***Perf. 13½x13***
801 A279 70c Children reading .75 .25
802 A279 80c Books .85 .25

A280

1991, Nov. 28 Photo. ***Perf. 14***
803 A280 55c multicolored .50 .25

Delft University of Technology, Sesquicent. A281

New Civil Code A282

1992, Jan. 7 Litho. ***Perf. 13½x13***
804 A281 60c multicolored .65 .25
805 A282 80c multicolored .85 .25

Souvenir Sheet

A283

1992 Olympics, Albertville and Barcelona: No. 806a, Volleyball, rowing. b, Shotput, rowing. c, Speedskating, rowing. d, Field hockey.

1992, Feb. 4 Litho. ***Perf. 13x14***
806 A283 80c Sheet of 4, #a.-d. 3.00 3.00

Tulips — A284

Map — A284a

1992, Feb. 25 Litho. ***Perf. 13x12½***
807 A284 70c multicolored .75 .25

Photo.
Perf. 13x14
808 A284a 80c multicolored .85 .25

Expo '92, Seville.

Discovery of New Zealand and Tasmania by Abel Tasman, 350th Anniv. — A285

1992, Mar. 12 Photo. ***Perf. 14x13***
809 A285 70c multicolored .75 .25

A286

A287

1992, Apr. 28 Litho. ***Perf. 13x13½***
810 A286 60c multicolored .65 .25
811 A287 80c multicolored .85 .25

Royal Assoc. of Netherlands Architects, 150th Anniv. (#810). Opening of Building for Lower House of States General (#811).

Discovery of America, 500th Anniv. — A288

Perf. 13½x13, 13x13½
1992, May 12 Litho.
812 A288 60c Globe, Columbus *.60* .30
813 A288 80c Sailing ship, vert. *.75* *.25*

Europa. On normally centered stamps the white border appears at the left side of No. 813.

Royal Netherlands Numismatics Society, Cent. — A289

1992, May 19 Photo. ***Perf. 13x14***
814 A289 70c multicolored .75 .25

Netherlands Pediatrics Society, Cent. — A290

1992, June 16 Litho. ***Perf. 13½x13***
815 A290 80c multicolored .90 .25

First Deportation Train from Westerbork Concentration Camp, 50th Anniv. — A291

1992, Aug. 25 ***Perf. 13x13½***
816 A291 70c multicolored .75 .25

Single European Market — A292

1992, Oct. 6 ***Perf. 13½x13***
817 A292 80c multicolored .80 .25

Queen Beatrix, 12½Years Since Investiture — A293

1992, Oct. 30 ***Perf. 13x13½***
818 A293 80c multicolored .80 .25

Christmas Rose A294

1992, Nov. 30 Photo. ***Perf. 14***
819 55c Red flower .60 .25
820 55c Silver flower .60 .25
a. A294 Pair, #819-820 1.25 .25

Netherlands Cycle and Motor Industry Assoc. (RAI), Cent. — A295

Designs: 70c, Couple riding bicycle. 80c, Early automobile.

1993, Jan. 5 Litho. ***Perf. 13½x13***
821 A295 70c multicolored .80 .25
822 A295 80c black & yellow .90 .25

A296

Greeting Stamps — A296a

Geometric shapes.

1993, Feb. 2 Photo. ***Perf. 14x13½***
823 A296 70c multi .70 .25
824 A296a 70c multi, diff. .70 .25
a. Tete-beche pair, #823-824 1.40 .40

Mouth-to-mouth Resuscitation A297

Royal Horse Artillery Lead Driver, Horses A298

Leaf, Insect Pests — A299

1993, Feb. 16 Litho. ***Perf. 13x13½***
825 A297 70c multicolored .85 .25
826 A298 80c multicolored .85 .25
827 A299 80c multicolored .85 .25
Nos. 825-827 (3) 2.55 .75

Royal Netherlands First Aid Assoc., cent. (#825). Royal Horse Artillery, bicent. (#826). University of Agriculture, 75th anniv. (#827).

On No. 826, normally centered stamps show design extending to top and right sides only.

Royal Dutch Notaries' Assoc., 150th Anniv. A300

Litho. & Engr.
1993, Mar. 2 ***Perf. 14x13***
828 80c Top half of emblem .90 .25
829 80c Bottom half of emblem .90 .25
a. A300 Pair, #828-829 1.80 .40

No. 829a has continuous design.

Butterflies — A301

Designs: 70c, Pearl-bordered fritillary (Zilvervlek). 80c, Large tortoiseshell (Grote vos). 90c, Large white (Koolwitje). 160c, Polyommatus icarus.

1993, Mar. 23 Photo.
830 A301 70c black & multi .80 .50
831 A301 80c yellow & multi .80 .30
832 A301 90c green & multi .80 .80
Nos. 830-832 (3) 2.40 1.60

Souvenir Sheet
833 A301 160c red & multi 2.40 2.40

On normally centered stamps the white border appears at the right side.

Radio Orange A302

Designs: No. 834, Woman broadcasting. No. 835, Man listening.

1993, May 5 Photo. ***Perf. 14x13***
834 80c orange red & purple .85 .25
835 80c purple & orange red .85 .25
a. A302 Pair, #834-835 1.90 .40

European Youth Olympic Days — A303

Symbols of Olympic sports.

1993, June 1 ***Perf. 13x14***
836 A303 70c blue & multi .70 .25
837 A303 80c yellow & multi .80 .25

Europa — A304

Contemporary sculpture by: 70c, Wessel Couzijn. 80c, Per Kirkeby. 160c, Naum Gabo, vert.

Perf. 13½x13, 13x13½
1993, July 6 Litho.
838 A304 70c blk, blue & grn .85 *.40*
839 A304 80c black, red & yel .85 *.30*
840 A304 160c black, blue & pur 1.60 *1.40*
Nos. 838-840 (3) 3.30 2.10

Dutch Nobel Prize Winners — A305

Designs: 70c, J.D. van der Waals, physics, 1910. 80c, Willem Einthoven, medicine, 1924. 90c, Christiaan Eijkman, medicine, 1929.

1993, Sept. 7 Litho. ***Perf. 13x13½***
841 A305 70c multicolored .60 .35
842 A305 80c multicolored .70 .25
843 A305 90c multicolored .80 .80
Nos. 841-843 (3) 2.10 1.40

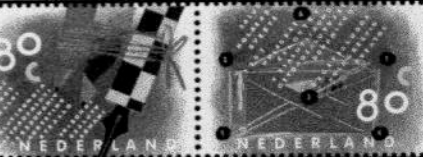
Letter Writing Day A306

1993, Sept. 14 Photo. ***Perf. 14x13***
844 80c Pencils, pen .75 .25
b. Perf. 14x13½ ('94) 2.50 .25
845 80c Envelope, contents .75 .25
a. A306 Pair, #844-845 1.60 .45
b. Perf. 14x13½ ('94) 2.50 .25
c. Pair, #844b-845b ('94) 5.00 1.00

Stamp Day — A307

80c, Dove with envelope.

1993, Oct. 8 Litho. ***Perf. 13½x13***
846 A307 70c shown .70 .30
847 A307 80c multicolored .80 .30

December Stamps A308

Clock hand pointing to "12:" and: No. 848, Star, candle, Christmas tree. No. 849, Fireworks.

1993, Nov. 29 Photo. ***Perf. 12***
848 A308 55c blue & multi .60 .25
849 A308 55c red & multi .60 .25
a. Pair, #848-849 1.25 .25

Issued in sheets of 20, 10 each #848-849 + label. Each stamp contains perforations placed within the design to resemble snowflakes.

Piet Mondrian (1872-1944), Painter — A309

Details from paintings: 70c, The Red Mill. 80c, Rhomboid with Yellow Lines. 90c, Broadway Boogie Woogie.

1994, Feb. 1 Litho. *Perf. 13½x13*
850 A309 70c multicolored .70 .45
851 A309 80c multicolored .75 .40
852 A309 90c multicolored .85 .85
Nos. 850-852 (3) 2.30 1.70

Wild Flowers — A310

70c, Downy rose. 80c, Daisy. 90c, Woods forget-me-not.
160c, Fire lily croceum.

1994, Mar. 15 Photo. *Perf. 14]x13*
853 A310 70c multi .70 .40
854 A310 80c multi .80 .30
855 A310 90c multi .90 .90
Nos. 853-855 (3) 2.40 1.60

Souvenir Sheet
856 A310 160c multi 2.50 2.50

Dutch Aviation, 75th Anniv. — A311

1994, Apr. 6 Litho. *Perf. 13½x13*
857 A311 80c KLM .85 .25
858 A311 80c Fokker .85 .25
859 A311 80c NLR .85 .25
Nos. 857-859 (3) 2.55 .75

Planetarium, Designed by Eise Eisinga — A312

Design: 90c, Television image of moon landing, footprint on moon.

1994, May 5 Photo. *Perf. 13x14*
860 A312 80c multicolored .80 .25
861 A312 90c multicolored 1.00 .80

First manned moon landing, 25th anniv. (#861).

1994 World Cup Soccer Championships, U.S. — A313

1994, June 1
862 A313 80c multicolored .90 .60

No. 862 printed with se-tenant label.

Stock Exchange Floor, Initials KPN — A314

1994, June 13 Litho. *Perf. 13½*
863 A314 80c multicolored .90 .25

Offering of shares in Royal PTT Netherlands NV (KPN).

Bicycle, Car, Road Sign — A315

80c, Silhouettes of horses, riders, carriage.

1994, June 14 Photo. *Perf. 14x13*
864 A315 70c multicolored .75 .25

Litho.
Perf. 13½x13
865 A315 80c multicolored .85 .25

First road signs placed by Dutch motoring assoc. (ANWB), cent. (#864). World Equestrian Games, The Hague (#865).

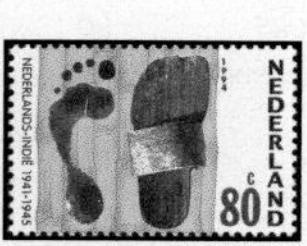
War in Dutch East Indies (1941-45) A316

Operation Market Garden (1944) A316a

Perf. 14x13, 13x14
1994, Aug. 15 Photo.
866 A316 80c multicolored .75 .25
867 A316a 90c multicolored .95 .75

Lighthouses A317

Designs: 70c, Brandaris, Terschelling Island. 80c, Ameland Island, vert. 90c, Vlieland Island, vert.

Perf. 13½x13, 13x13½
1994, Sept. 13 Litho.
868 A317 70c multicolored 1.00 .50
869 A317 80c multicolored 1.00 .25
870 A317 90c multicolored 1.00 .90
Nos. 868-870 (3) 3.00 1.65

December Stamps — A318

1994, Nov. 28 Photo. *Perf. 13½*
871 A318 55c Snowflake, tree .55 .25
872 A318 55c Candle, star .55 .25
a. Pair, #871-872 1.10 .25
b. Min. sheet, 10 #872a + label 11.00 8.00

One stamp in #872a is rotated 90 degrees to the other stamp.

Cow, Dutch Products — A319

1995, Jan 2 Photo. *Perf. 14x13½*
873 A319 100c multicolored 1.25 .30

Hendrik Nicolaas Werkman (1882-1945), Printer A320

Mesdag Museum Restoration A321

Mauritius No. 2 — A322

1995, Jan. 17 Litho. *Perf. 14x13½*
874 A320 80c multicolored 1.00 .35
875 A321 80c multicolored 1.00 .35

Litho. & Engr.
Perf. 13½x14
876 A322 80c multicolored 1.00 .35
Nos. 874-876 (3) 3.00 1.05

Acquisition of Mauritius No. 2 by Netherlands PTT Museum (#876).

Motion Pictures, Cent. — A323

70c, Joris Iven, documentary film maker. 80c, Scene from film, "Turkish Delight," 1972.

1995, Feb. 28 Photo. *Perf. 14x13*
877 A323 70c multicolored .70 .25
878 A323 80c multicolored .80 .25

Mahler Festival — A324

Design: 80c, Gustav Mahler, (1860-1911), composer, 7th Symphony score.

1995, Mar. 21 Litho. *Perf. 13½x13*
879 A324 80c blue & black .90 .25

Institute of Registered Accountants, Cent. — A325

Assoc. of Building Contractors, Cent. — A326

1995, Mar. 28
880 A325 80c multicolored .80 .30
881 A326 80c multicolored .80 .30

50th Anniversaries — A327

Designs: No. 882, End of World War II, "45, 95" No. 883, Liberation of the Netherlands, "40, 45." No. 884, Founding of the UN, "50."

1995, May 3 Litho. *Perf. 13x13½*
882 A327 80c multicolored .80 .30
883 A327 80c multicolored .80 .30
884 A327 80c multicolored .80 .30
Nos. 882-884 (3) 2.40 .90

Signs of the Zodiac, Birthday Cake — A328

1995, May 22 Photo. *Perf. 14x13½*
885 A328 70c multicolored 1.10 .30

18th World Boy Scout Jamboree A329

Sail Amsterdam '95 A330

Perf. 13x13½, 13½x13
1995, June 6 Litho.
886 A329 70c multicolored .70 .35
887 A330 80c multicolored .80 .25

Birds of Prey — A330a

Perf. 13x14, 14x13
1995, Sept. 5 Photo.
888 A330a 70c Kestrel, vert. .80 .25
889 A330a 80c Hen harrier .80 .25
890 A330a 100c Red kite 1.00 1.00
Nos. 888-890 (3) 2.60 1.50

Souvenir Sheet
891 A330a 160c Honey buzzard 2.75 2.75

Nobel Prize Winners — A331

No. 892, F. Zernike, physics, 1953. No. 893, P.J.W. Debye, chemistry, 1936. No. 894, J. Tinbergen, economics, 1969.

1995, Sept. 26 Litho. *Perf. 13½x13*
892 A331 80c green & multi .80 .25
893 A331 80c blue & multi .80 .25
894 A331 80c red & multi .80 .25
Nos. 892-894 (3) 2.40 .75

Dutch Cabaret, Cent. — A332

Designs: 70c, Eduard Jacobs (1868-1914), Jean-Louis Pisuisse (1880-1927). 80c, Wim Kan (1911-83), Freek de Jonge (b. 1944).

1995, Oct. 17 Litho. *Perf. 13½x14*
895 A332 70c multicolored .70 .25
896 A332 80c multicolored .80 .25

Numeral Type of 1976 and Queen Type of 1991

1995-2001 Photo. *Perf. 13½x12½*
902 A273 1.50g green 1.50 .40

Self-Adhesive (Nos. 903-911)
Booklet Stamps
Die Cut Perf. 14¼
903 A157 5c gray .25 .25
a. Double-sided pane of 10 .45
904 A157 10c ultramarine .25 .25
a. Double-sided pane of 10 .85
905 A157 25c violet .30 .25
a. Double sided pane of 10 3.00
906 A273 85c blue green .95 .25
a. Booklet pane of 5 5.00
907 A273 1g purple 1.10 .25
a. Booklet pane of 5 5.50
908 A273 1.10g blue 1.25 .25
a. Booklet pane of 5 6.25
909 A273 1.45g green 1.60 .30
a. Booklet pane of 5 8.00
910 A273 2.50g red lilac 2.75 .55
a. Booklet pane of 5 14.00
911 A273 5g brown red 5.50 1.10
a. Booklet pane of 5 27.50
Nos. 903-911 (9) 13.95 3.45

Coil Stamps
Perf. 13½ Horiz.
912 A273 1g gray violet 1.10 .25
913 A273 1.10g blue 1.25 .25

Issued: No. 912, 10/5; 1.50g, 3/17/98, No. 913, 8/1/00; 5c, 10c, 25c, 6/18/01; 85c, 1.45g, 7/2/01; Nos. 907, 908, 2.50g, 5g, 9/3/01. 85c has added euro denomination.

December Stamps — A333

Serpentine Die Cut 12½x13
1995, Nov. 27 Self-Adhesive
916 A333 55c Children, star .70 .25
917 A333 55c Children, stars .70 .25
a. Pair, Nos. 916-917 1.25

Issued in sheets of 20, checkerboard style.
Nos. 916-917 exist imperf. Value, $62.50 for pair.

Paintings by Johannes Vermeer (1632-75) — A334

Entire paintings or details: 70c, A Lady Writing a Letter, with Her Maid. 80c, The Love Letter. 100c, A Woman in Blue Reading a Letter.

1996, Feb. 27 Litho. *Perf. 13x13½*

918 A334 70c multicolored .85 .45
919 A334 80c multicolored .90 .30
920 A334 100c multicolored 1.10 1.00
a. Souvenir sheet, Nos. 918-920 3.25 3.25
Nos. 918-920 (3) 2.85 1.75

Spring Flowers — A335

Designs: 70c, Daffodil bulb, garden tools. 80c, Closeup of woman, tulip. 100c, Snake's head (fritillaria). 160c, Crocuses.

1996, Mar. 21 Litho. *Perf. 13½x13*

921 A335 70c multicolored .85 .40
922 A335 80c multicolored .90 .30
923 A335 100c multicolored 1.10 1.00
Nos. 921-923 (3) 2.85 1.70

Souvenir Sheet

924 A335 160c multicolored 2.10 1.90

A336

1996, Apr. 1 *Perf. 13x13½*

925 A336 70c Moving stamp .85 .40

No. 925 was sold in sheets of 20. See #951.

Comic Strips, Cent. — A337

Mr. Olivier B. Bommel, by Marten Toonder: a, O.B. Bommel goes on holiday. b, O.B. Bommel receives letter.

1996, May 14 Litho. *Perf. 13½x13*

926 Sheet of 2 + 2 labels 2.60 2.60
a. A337 70c multicolored 1.25 1.00
b. A337 80c multicolored 1.25 1.00

Vacations — A338

Scene, flower: No. 927, Beach, sunflower. No. 928, Cyclists, gerbera. 80c, Gables in Amsterdam, cornflower. 100c, Windmills at "Zaanse Schans"' open air museum, anemone.

1996, May 31

927 A338 70c multicolored .85 .25
928 A338 70c multicolored .85 .45
929 A338 80c multicolored .85 .25
930 A338 100c multicolored .85 .45
Nos. 927-930 (4) 3.40 1.40

Province of North Brabant, Bicent. — A339

1996, June 13 Litho. *Perf. 13½x13*

931 A339 80c multicolored .90 .25

Sporting Events — A340

Designs: 70c, Lighting the Olympic Torch, 1996 Summer Olympic Games, Atlanta. 80c, Tour de France cycling race. 100c, Euro '96 Soccer Championships, Wembley Stadium, England. 160c, Olympic rings, track sports, Atlanta stadium.

1996, June 25

932 A340 70c multicolored .80 .25
933 A340 80c multicolored .80 .25
934 A340 100c multicolored 1.00 .75
935 A340 160c multicolored 1.50 .80
Nos. 932-935 (4) 4.10 2.05

Erasmus Bridge, Rotterdam — A341

Designs: No. 936, Martinus Nijhoff Bridge over Waal River, horiz. No. 938, Wijker Tunnel under North Sea Canal, horiz.

1996, Aug. 6 *Perf. 13½x13, 13x13½*

936 A341 80c multicolored .85 .25
937 A341 80c shown .85 .25
938 A341 80c multicolored .85 .25
Nos. 936-938 (3) 2.55 .75

UNICEF, 50th Anniv. — A342

Designs: 70c, School children from Ghana. 80c, Girl from Ghana with tray on head.

1996, Sept. 3 *Perf. 13x13½*

939 A342 70c multicolored .80 .25
940 A342 80c multicolored .80 .25

Sesame Street in Netherlands, 20th Anniv. — A343

70c, Bert & Ernie. 80c, Pino, Ieiemienie & Tommie.

1996, Sept. 3 *Perf. 13½x13*

941 A343 70c multicolored .80 .25
942 A343 80c multicolored .75 .25

Nos. 941-942 were issued in sheets of 100 and sheets of 10. On Jan. 1, 1997, No. 942 was reprinted reading "Tien voor je post" instead of "Tien voor je brief" in the top selvage.

Voyages of Discovery — A344

Voyages of: 70c, Petrus Plancius (1552-1622), cartographer. #944, Willem Barents (d. 1597). #945, Cornelis de Houtman (1540-99). 100c, Mahu en De Cordes (1598-1600).

1996, Oct. 1

943 A344 70c multicolored .75 .40
944 A344 80c multicolored .75 .30
945 A344 80c multicolored .75 .30
946 A344 100c multicolored 1.15 1.15
Nos. 943-946 (4) 3.40 2.15

December Stamps — A345

Collage of faces, hands: No. 947, Wing, ear, hands. No. 948, Mouth, two faces. No. 949, Woman with eyes closed, hand. No. 950, Eyes, face with mouth open.

Serpentine Die Cut 9 Horiz.

1996, Nov. 26 Self-Adhesive

947 A345 55c multicolored .50 .25
948 A345 55c multicolored .50 .25
949 A345 55c red violet & multi .50 .25
950 A345 55c blue & multi .50 .25
a. Block or strip of 4, #947-950 2.00

Issued in sheets of 20.

Moving Stamp Type of 1996

Die Cut Perf. 13

1997, Jan. 2 Photo.

Self-Adhesive

951 A336 80c like No. 925 .90 .25

No. 951 sold in panes of 20.

Business Stamps — A346

Geometric designs.

Coil Stamps

Sawtooth Die Cut 13½ Horiz., Syncopated (on 1 Side)

1997, Jan. 2 Self-Adhesive

952 A346 80c pink & multi .75 .25
953 A346 160c green & multi 1.40 .25

Cross-Country Skating Championships — A347

1997, Jan. 4 Photo. *Perf. 14x13*

954 A347 80c multicolored .90 .25

Surprise Stamps — A348

Inscriptions beneath scratch-off heart-shaped panels: b, Schrijf me. c, Groetjes. d, Ik hou van je. e, Tot gauw. f, Ik denk aan je. g, XXX-jes. h, Ik mis je. i, Geintje. j, Zomaar. k, Wanneer?

1997, Jan. 21 *Perf. 14x13½*

955 Sheet of 10 7.50 6.50
a. A348 80c Any single, unscratched heart .75 .65
b.-k. A348 80c Any single, scratched heart .25

Unused value for #955a is with attached selvage. Inscriptions are shown in selvage beside each stamp.

Nature and Environment — A349

1997, Feb. 25 Litho. *Perf. 13½x13*

956 A349 80c Pony .90 .30
957 A349 100c Sheep 1.10 1.00

Souvenir Sheet

958 A349 160c Sheep, diff. 2.10 2.10

Suske & Wiske Comic Strip Characters — A350

#959, Suske, Wiske, Tante Sidonia, & Lambik. #960a, Jerome making exclamation.

Perf. 13½x12½

1997, Mar. 18 Litho.

959 A350 80c multicolored .85 .25

Souvenir Sheet

960 Sheet of 2, #959, 960a 2.60 2.10
a. A350 80c violet & red 1.25 .90

A351

Greetings Stamps — A352

#961, Birthday cake. #962, Amaryllis surrounded by cup of coffee, two glasses of wine, hand writing card, candlelight.

1997, May 6 Photo. *Perf. 14x13½*

961 A351 80c multicolored .80 .25
962 A352 80c multicolored .80 .25

See No. 1035.

Marshall Plan, 50th Anniv. A353

Designs: No. 963, Map of Europe. No. 964, Flag, quotation from George C. Marshall.

1997, May 27 Litho. *Perf. 13½x13*

963 80c multicolored .85 .30
964 80c multicolored .85 .30
a. A353 Pair, #963-964 1.75 1.75

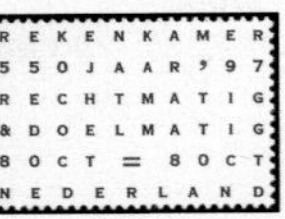

Court of Audit, 550th Anniv. — A354

1997, May 27 *Perf. 13½x13*

965 A354 80c multicolored .85 .30

European Council of Ministers Meeting, Amsterdam A355

1997, June 17 Litho. *Perf. 13½*

966 A355 100c multicolored 1.40 1.10

Water Recreation — A356

80c, Swimming, row boat. 1g, Sailboats.

1997, July 1 *Perf. 13½x13*

967 A356 80c multicolored .85 .25
968 A356 1g multicolored 1.00 .55

Royal Institute of Engineers, 150th Anniv. — A357

1997, Aug. 5

969 A357 80c multicolored .90 .25

Netherlands Asthma Center, Cent. — A358

1997, Aug. 5

970 A358 80c multicolored .90 .25

Horticultural Education at Florens College, Aalsmeer, Cent. — A359

1997, Aug. 5

971 A359 80c multicolored .90 .25

Franz Schubert (1797-1828), Composer — A360

1997, Aug. 5

972 A360 80c multicolored .90 .25

A361

Youth Stamps — A362

1997, Sept. 2

973 A361 80c multicolored .75 .25
a. Bklt. pane of 5 + 2 labels 5.00
Complete booklet, #973a 5.00
974 A362 80c multicolored .75 .25
a. Perf. 14x13 50.00 50.00

Issued: No. 973a, 7/6/99.

Booklet stamps differ from sheet stamps: the year date is closer to the edge.

Birth Announcement Stamp — A363

Die Cut Perf. 13½x13

1997, Oct. 7 Photo.

Self-Adhesive

975 A363 80c multicolored .80 .25
a. Litho. ('99) 1.25 1.25

See Nos. 1033, 1071, 1109, 1260.

A364

December Stamps: Stylized people head to head showing either a star or heart in the center.

Serpentine Die Cut

1997, Nov. 25 Photo.

Self-Adhesive

Background Colors

976 A364 55c yellow .55 .25
977 A364 55c blue .55 .25
978 A364 55c orange .55 .25
979 A364 55c red .55 .25
980 A364 55c yellow green .55 .25
981 A364 55c dark green .55 .25
a. Sheet, 3 ea #976, 978-979, 981, 4 ea #977, 980 11.00 11.00

Death Announcement Stamp — A365

1998, Jan. 2 Litho. *Perf. 13½*

982 A365 80c gray blue .80 .25

See Nos. 1059, 1072, 1110, 1261. Compare with Types A580 and A824.

Delftware — A366

100c, Cow, tiles with pictures of sailing ships. 160c, Tiles, one picturing boy standing on head.

1998, Jan. 2 Photo. *Die Cut*

Self-Adhesive

983 A366 100c multicolored .95 .50
984 A366 160c multicolored 1.50 1.00

Issued in both coil strips and sheets with priority labels.

A368

Growing Fruit in the Four Seasons: No. 986, Orchard in bloom, spring. No. 987, Strawberries, summer. No. 988, Harvesting, autumn. No. 989, Pruning, winter.

1998, Feb. 17 Litho. *Perf. 13x13½*

Booklet Stamps

986 A368 80c multicolored .95 .80
987 A368 80c multicolored .95 .80
988 A368 80c multicolored .95 .80
989 A368 80c multicolored .95 .80
a. Booklet pane, #986-989 4.00
Complete booklet, #989a 4.00

A369

Die Cut Perf. 13½

1998, Mar. 17 Photo.

Self-Adhesive

990 A369 80c multicolored .80 .25
a. Litho. ('99) 4.00 4.00

Marriage and wedding anniversaries. No. 990 was issued in sheets of 10.

See No. 1034.

Anniversaries A370

#991, Men shaking hands, Treaty of Munster, 350th anniv. #992, Statue of John Rudolf Thorbecke, Dutch constitution, 150th anniv. #993, Child on swing, Universal Declaration of Human Rights, 50th anniv.

1998, Mar. 17 Litho. *Perf. 13½x13*

991 A370 80c multicolored .85 .25
992 A370 80c multicolored .85 .25
993 A370 80c multicolored .85 .25
a. Strip of 3, #991-993 2.60 2.60

Letter Writing Day — A371

1998, May 8 Litho. *Perf. 13½*

994 A371 80c multicolored .85 .25

1998 World Cup Soccer Championships, France — A372

1998, May 19 Litho. *Perf. 13½*

995 A372 80c multicolored .90 .25

Rabo Bank, Cent. — A373

1998, May 19 *Perf. 13½x13*

996 A373 80c multicolored .85 .25

Royal Netherlands Field Hockey Federation, Cent. — A374

1998, May 19

997 A374 80c multicolored .85 .25

Central Administration in Friesland, 500th Anniv. — A375

1998, June 9 Litho. *Perf. 13½x13*

998 A375 80c multicolored .85 .25

Water Management A375a

1998, June 9

999 A375a 80c shown .80 .25
1000 A375a 1g Aerial view 1.00 .75

Split of Royal Netherlands PTT — A376

#1001, TNT Post Groep. #1002, KPN NV.

1998, June 29

1001 80c red, black & blue .85 .25
1002 80c blue, blk & grn .85 .25
a. A376 Vert. pair, #1001-1002 1.75 1.75

No. 1002a is a continuous design.

Natl. Library of the Netherlands, Bicent. — A377

1998, July 7

1003 A377 80c multicolored .85 .25

A378

No. 1004, Maurits Cornelis Escher (1898-1972), Graphic Artist. No. 1005, Simon Vestdijk (1898-1971), writer.

1998, July 7 *Perf. 13x13½*

1004 A378 80c multicolored .85 .40
1005 A378 80c multicolored .85 .40
a. Pair, #1004-1005 1.75 1.75

Souvenir Sheet

A379

Inauguration of Queen Wilhelmina, Cent.: a, Queen Wilhelmina. b, Gilded Coach.

1998, Sept. 1 Litho. *Perf. 13x13½*

1006 A379 80c Sheet of 2, #a.-b. 2.60 2.60

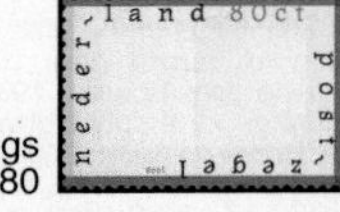

Greetings Stamps — A380

Colors of stamp edges, clockwise from side adjacent to "Neder:" No. 1007: a, yellow, orange, red, red. b, red, orange, pink, yellow orange. c, red, orange, rose, orange. d, orange, red, light orange, yellow orange. e, yellow, orange, pink, red.

Serpentine Die Cut Perf. 13½x13

1998, Sept. 1 Litho.

Self-Adhesive

1007 80c Sheet of 10, 2 each #a.-e. 8.00
a.-e. A380 any single 1.00 .50

Each side of No. 1007 contains a pane of 1 each #1007a-1007e and 10 different self-adhesive labels.

Nos. 1008-1011 are unassigned.

Pets — A381

1998, Sept. 22 *Perf. 13½x13*

1012 A381 80c Dog .80 .30
a. Bklt. pane of 5 + 2 labels 4.75
Complete booklet, #1012a 4.75
1013 A381 80c Kittens .80 .40
1014 A381 80c Rabbits 1.00 .80
Nos. 1012-1014 (3) 2.60 1.50

Issued: No. 1012a, 7/6/99.

Jan, Jans en de Kinderen Comic Strip, by Jan Kruis — A382

Characters: No. 1015, Writing letters. No. 1016, In automobile, mailing letter.

1998, Oct. 6 Litho. *Perf. 13½x13*

1015 A382 80c multicolored .85 .25
a. Booklet pane, 10 #1015 + 20 labels 8.50
Complete booklet, #1015a 8.50
1016 A382 80c multicolored 1.50 .25
a. Sheet of 2, #1015-1016 + 3 labels 2.60 2.50

December Stamps — A383

25c, Stylized tree, house on top of earth.
No. 1018:
Silhouetted against moon: a, Rabbit. b, House. c, Bird. d, Tree. e, Deer.
Silhouetted against horizon: f, Rabbit. g, House. h, Bird. i, Tree. j, Deer.
House with: k, Rabbit. l, Heart. m. Bird. n, Tree. o, Deer.
Tree with: p, Rabbit. q, House. r, Bird. s, Heart. t, Deer.

1998-99 Litho. *Perf. 13*

1017 A383 25c multicolored .30 .25

Self-Adhesive

Die Cut Perf. 9

1018 A383 55c Sheet of 20, #a.-t. 10.00 3.25

Issued: #1018, 11/24; #1017, 1/5/99.

Introduction of the Euro — A384

1999, Jan. 5 Litho. *Perf. 13x12½*

1019 A384 80c multicolored .85 .25

Netherlands Postal Services, Bicent. A385

1999, Jan. 15 Litho. *Perf. 13½x14*

1020 A385 80c multi + label .90 .80

See No. 1039

A386

1999, Feb. 2 Litho. ***Perf. 12¾x13¼***
1021 A386 80c Spoonbill .85 .25
1022 A386 80c Globe, tern .85 .25

Protection of birds and migrating waterfowl. Netherlands Society for Protection of Birds, cent (#1021). African-Eurasian Waterbird Agreement (#1022).

A387

1999, Feb. 2 ***Perf. 12¾x13¼***
Booklet Stamp
1023 A387 80c multicolored .85 .25
a. Booklet pane of 4 3.50
Complete booklet, #1023a 3.50

Royal Dutch Lawn Tennis Assoc., cent.

Views During the Four Seasons — A388

Designs: a, Haarlemmerhout in fall. b, Sonsbeek in winter. c, Weerribben in spring. d, Keukenhof in summer.

1999, Mar. 2 Litho. ***Perf. 13¼x12¾***
1024 A388 Booklet pane of 4, #a.-d. 4.00 4.00
a.-d. 80c Any single .90 .80
Complete booklet, #1024 4.25

I Love Stamps — A389

1999, May 6 Litho. ***Perf. 13¼x12¾***
1025 A389 80c I Love Stamps .80 .40
1026 A389 80c Stamps Love Me 1.00 .75
a. Booklet pane, 3 #1025, 2 #1026 + 2 labels 4.50
Complete booklet, #1026a 4.50

Nos. 1025-1026 each contain a hologram. Soaking may affect the hologram.

Maritime Anniversaries — A390

1999, May 6 Litho. ***Perf. 12¾x13¼***
1027 A390 80c Freighters .80 .25
1028 A390 80c Lifeboats .80 .25

Schuttevaer Ship Masters Assoc., 150th anniv. (#1027). Netherlands Lifeboat Assoc., 175th anniv. (#1028).

Paintings — A391

No. 1029: a, The Goldfinch, by Carel Fabritius. b, Self-portrait, by Rembrandt. c, Self-portrait, by Judith Leyster. d, St. Sebastian, by Hendrick Ter Brugghen. e, Beware of Luxury, by Jan Steen. f, The Sick Child, by Gabriel Metsu. g, Gooseberries, by Adriaen Coorte. h, View of Haarlem, by Jacob van Ruisdael. i, Mariaplaats Utrecht, by Pieter Saenredam. j, Danae, by Rembrandt.

1g, The Jewish Bride, by Rembrandt.

1999, June 8 Litho. ***Perf. 13¼x13¾***
1029 Sheet of 10, #a.-j. 9.00 9.00
a.-j. A391 80c any single .85 .85

Self-Adhesive
Die Cut Syncopated
1030 A391 1g multicolored 1.25 .95

No. 1030 issued in sheets of 5 stamps and blue priority mail etiquettes.

A392

1999, July 6 Litho. ***Perf. 13¼x12¾***
1031 A392 80c multicolored .90 .25

Self-Adhesive
Die Cut 13½ Syncopated Horiz.
1032 A392 80c multicolored .90 .25

Birth Announcement Type of 1997 and Marriage Type of 1998

1999, July 6 Litho. ***Perf. 13¼x12¾***
Booklet Stamps
1033 A363 80c multicolored .90 .25
a. Booklet pane of 5 + 2 labels 4.50
Complete booklet, #1033a 4.50

Perf. 13¼
1034 A369 80c multicolored .90 .25
a. Booklet pane of 5 + 2 labels 4.50
Complete booklet, #1034a 4.50

Greetings Type of 1997
Die Cut 13½ Syncopated Horiz.
1999, July 6 **Litho.**
Self-Adhesive
1035 A352 80c multicolored 1.25 .50

VNO-NCW Employer Organization, Cent. — A392a

1999, Sept. 7 Litho. ***Perf. 13¼x12¾***
1036 A392a 80c multicolored .85 .25

Tintin — A393

No. 1037, Tintin, Snowy in space suits. No. 1038a, Tintin, Snowy, Capt. Haddock in spacecraft.

1999, Oct. 8 ***Perf. 13¼x12¾***
1037 A393 80c multicolored 1.25 .25
a. Booklet pane of 5 + 2 labels 7.75
Complete booklet, #1037a 8.00

Souvenir Sheet
1038 Sheet of 2, #1037, 1038a 3.25 2.75
a. A393 80c multicolored 1.50 1.25

Postal Service Bicentennial Type
Souvenir Sheet

1999, Oct. 15 Litho. ***Perf. 13¼x13¾***
1039 A385 5g multicolored 5.00 5.00

The numeral in the denomination is made up of perforations.

Millennium — A394

Highlights of the 20th Century: a, Construction of barrier dam, 1932. b, Satellite. c, Amsterdam Bourse, 1903, designed by H. P. Berlage. d, Empty highway, 1973-74 oil crisis. e, Prime Minister Willem Drees's social welfare programs, 1947. f, Flood control projects 1953-97. g, European soccer champions, 1988. h, Liberation, 1945. i, Woman suffrage. j, Eleven-city skating race.

1999, Oct. 25 Litho. ***Perf. 13¼x12¾***
1040 Sheet of 10 8.00 8.00
a.-j. A394 80c any single .80 .80

December Stamps — A395

Designs: a, Santa's head. b, Angel, musical notes, vert. c, Ornaments in box. d, Crescent-shaped Santa's head, vert. e, Santa, four trees. f, Clock, vert. g, Skater. h, Tree of people holding candles, vert. i, Man and woman. j, Woman, tree, star, vert. k, Angel, musical score. l, Hand, vert. m, Tree. n, Cat with crown, vert. o, Bird, house. p, Baby as angel, vert. q, Dog with cap. r, Angel with halo, vert. s, Family in house. t, Tree with presents, vert.

Serpentine Die Cut 7
1999, Nov. 30 **Photo.**
Self-Adhesive
1041 A395 Sheet of 20, #a-t 10.00
a.-t. 55c any single .50 .25

A396

2000, Jan. 4 Litho. ***Perf. 13x12¾***
1042 A396 25c multi .30 .25

Souvenir Sheet

Holy Roman Emperor Charles V (1500-58) — A397

Designs: a, Gulden coin, Charles' aunt and guardian, Margaret of Austria, Charles V on Horseback in Bologna, by Juan de la Corte. b, Map of the Netherlands, Charles V on Horseback at the Battle of Mühlberg, by Titian, Charles' daughter, Margaret of Parma.

2000, Jan. 4 ***Perf. 13¼***
1043 A397 Sheet of 2 + label 2.25 2.00
a.-b. 80c Any single 1.00 1.00

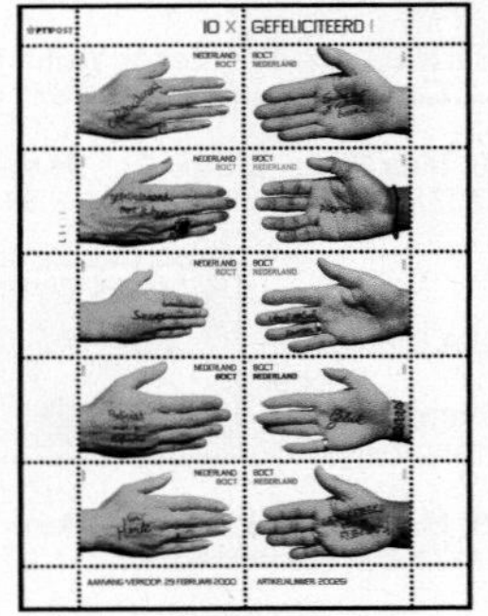
Greetings — A398

Color of denomination or country name and hands (back or palm) with written messages: a, Pink, back. b, Pink, palm. c, Orange, back. d, Orange, palm. e, Green, back. f, Green, palm. g, Blue, back. h, Blue, palm. i, Red, back. j, Red, palm.

Perf. 13¼x13¾
2000, Feb. 29 **Litho.**
1044 A398 Sheet of 10, #a-j 8.00 8.00
a.-j. 80c any single .75 .75

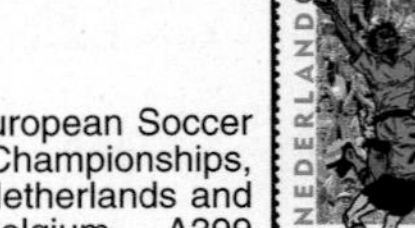
European Soccer Championships, Netherlands and Belgium — A399

2000, Mar. 25 ***Perf. 12¾x13¼***
Booklet Stamps
1045 A399 80c Crowd, players .75 .25
1046 A399 80c Crowd, ball 1.10 .75
a. Booklet pane, 3 #1045, 2 #1046 + 2 labels 4.50
Booklet, #1046a 4.50

See Belgium No. 1796.

Items in Rijksmuseum — A400

a, Feigned Sorrow (woman wiping eye), by Cornelis Troost. b, Harlequin and Colombine, Meissen porcelain piece, by J. J. Kändler. c, Kabuki Actor Ebizo Ichikawa IV, by Sharaku. d, Apsara from India. e, Carved head of St. Vitus. f, Woman in Turkish Costume, by Jean Etienne Liotard. g, J. van Speyk (man with epaulet), by J. Schoemaker Doyer. h, Engraving of King Saul, by Lucas van Leyden. i, Statue, L'Amour Menacant, by E. M. Falconet. j, Photograph of two men, by C. Ariens.

100c, The Night Watch, by Rembrandt.

2000, Apr. 14 ***Perf. 13¼x13¾***
1047 A400 Sheet of 10, #a-j 11.00 11.00
a.-j. 80c any single 1.00 1.00

Die Cut Syncopated
Self-Adhesive
1048 A400 100c multi 1.10 .90

#1048 issued in sheets of 5 + 5 priority mail etiquettes.

See Nos. 1051, 1053.

Doe Maar, Popular Musical Group — A401

2000, May 2 Litho. ***Perf. 13¼x12¾***
1049 A401 80c Song titles 1.00 .75
1050 A401 80c Album cover .75 .35
a. Booklet pane, 2 #1049, 3 #1050, + 2 labels 4.25
Booklet, #1050a 4.25

Rijksmuseum Type of 2000 with Priority Mail Emblem Added and

Dutch Landscape, by Jeroen Krabbé — A402

Designs: Nos. 1051, 1053, The Night Watch, by Rembrandt.

Die cut perf. 4 on right side and right parts of top and bottom sides.

Die Cut Similar to Sync.
2000, Aug. 1 **Litho.**
Self-Adhesive
1051 A400 110c pur & multi 1.25 .60

Die Cut Sync.
1052 A402 110c multi 1.25 .60

Coil Stamp
Die Cut Similar to Sync.
1053 A400 110c blue & multi 3.25 1.60
Nos. 1051-1053 (3) 5.75 2.80

Nos. 1051-1052 issued in sheets of 5. No. 1051 lacks die cut "holes" on left side and at upper left. No. 1053 lacks die cut "holes" on left side, but has only two at upper left.

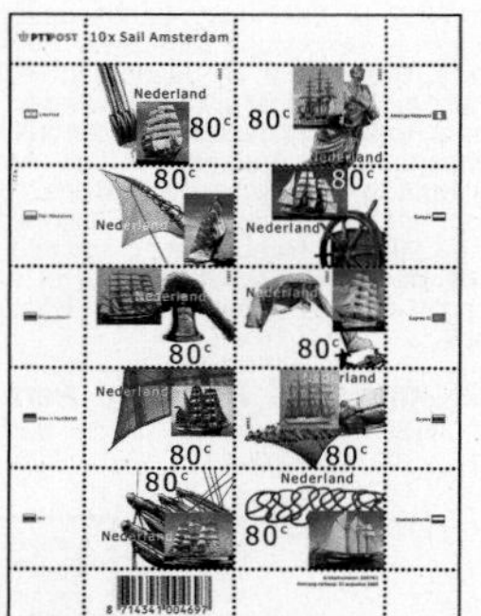

Sail 2000, Amsterdam Harbor — A403

No. 1054: a, Block and Libertad, Argentina. b, Figurehead and Amerigo Vespucci, Italy. c, Unfurled white sail, Dar Mlodziezy, Poland. d, Ship's wheel, Europa, Netherlands. e, Bell, Kruzenshtern, Russia. f, Deckhand adjusting sail, Sagres II, Portugal. g, Green sail, Alexander von Humboldt, Germany. h, Crewmen on bowsprit, Sedov, Russia. i. Spreaders, furled sails and ropes, Mir, Russia. j, Rope, Oosterschelde, Netherlands.

Perf. 13¼x12¾

2000, Aug. 21 **Litho.**

1054 A403 Sheet of 10 9.25 9.25
a.-j. 80c Any single .90 .45

Sjors and Sjimmie — A404

Comic strip characters: No. 1055, Rollerblading. No. 1056, In go-kart. No. 1057, Wearing headphones. No. 1058, Hanging on rope.

2000, Sept. 23

1055 A404 80c multi 1.25 .60
1056 A404 80c multi 1.25 .60
a. Pair, #1055-1056 2.50 1.25
1057 A404 80c multi .90 .45
a. Souvenir sheet, #1056-1057 3.00 3.00

Booklet Stamp

1058 A404 80c multi 1.25 .60
a. Booklet pane, 3 #1057, 2 #1058 + 2 labels 5.25
Booklet, #1058a 5.25
Nos. 1055-1058 (4) 4.65 2.25

Death Announcement Type of 1998

Die Cut Perf. 13¼

2000, Oct. 10 **Photo.**

Self-Adhesive

1059 A365 80c gray blue .90 .50

Endangered Species — A405

Designs: No. 1060, Aeshna viridis (Groene glazenmaker). No. 1061, Misgurnus fossilis (Grote modderkruiper).

2000, Oct. 10 Litho. *Perf. 13¼x12¾*

Booklet Stamps

1060 A405 80c multi .90 .50
1061 A405 80c multi 1.10 .50
a. Booklet pane, 3 #1060, 2 #1061 + 2 labels 5.00
Booklet, #1061a 5.00

Souvenir Sheet

Amphilex 2002 Intl. Stamp Show, Amsterdam — A406

No. 1062: a, Boat. b, Carriage.

2000, Oct. 10

1062 A406 Sheet of 2 2.10 2.10
a.-b. 80c Any single .90 .50

Christmas — A407

No. 1063: a, Woman, man with tree on shoulder. b, Woman, child decorating tree. c, Couple dancing. d, Tuba player. e, Man carrying hat and tree. f, Man with child on shoulder. g, Woman reading. h, Couple kissing. i, Piano player. j, Woman at window. k, Woman in chair. l, Santa by fire. m, Snowman. n, Couple in front of house. o, Violin player. p, Children on sled. q, Man writing letter. r, Woman with food tray. s, Four people. t, Woman asleep.

Serpentine Die Cut 14½x15

2000, Nov. 28 **Photo.**

Self-Adhesive

1063 A407 Sheet of 20 11.00
a.-t. 60c Any single .55 .25

A408

2001, Jan. 2 Litho. *Perf. 12¾x13¼*

1064 A408 20c multi .25 .25

Royal Dutch Nature Society, Cent. — A409

No. 1065: a, Whinchat thrush. b, People in rowboat. c, Fox. d, People with binoculars. e, Scotch rose and June beetles.

2001, Jan. 26 Litho. *Perf. 13½x12¾*

1065 Booklet pane of 5, #a-e, +2 labels 5.25 5.25
a.-e. A409 80c Any single 1.00 .75
Booklet, #1065 6.00

Rotterdam, 2001 European Cultural Capital — A410

Die Cut Similar to Sync.

2001, Mar. 14 **Litho.**

Self- Adhesive

1066 A410 110c multi 1.50 .90

Printed in sheets of 5. Die cutting has no "holes" at left, but has "holes" at top and bottom at the thin vertical line.

Book Week A411

No. 1067: a, Quote by Edgar du Perron. b, Photograph by Ulay. c, Quote by Hafid Bouazza. d, Photograph by Ed van der Elsken. e, Quote by Adriaan van Dis. f, Photograph by Anton Corbijn. g, Quote by Kader Abdolah. h, Photographs by Celine van Balen. i, Quote by Ellen Ombre. j, Photograph by Cas Oorthuys.

2001, Mar. 14 ***Perf. 13¼x13¾***

1067 A411 Sheet of 10 7.25 7.25
a.-j. 80c Any single .90 .25

Souvenir Sheet

Max Euwe (1901-81), Chess Champion — A412

No. 1068: a, Chessboard. b, Euwe, chess pieces.

2001, Apr. 3 ***Perf. 13¼x12¾***

1068 A412 Sheet of 2 2.25 2.25
a.-b. 80c Any single 1.00 .90

Souvenir Sheet

Intl. Volunteers Year — A413

No. 1069: a, Rescue workers. b, People with animal cages.

2001, Apr. 3

1069 A413 Sheet of 2 2.25 2.25
a.-b. 80c Any single 1.00 .75

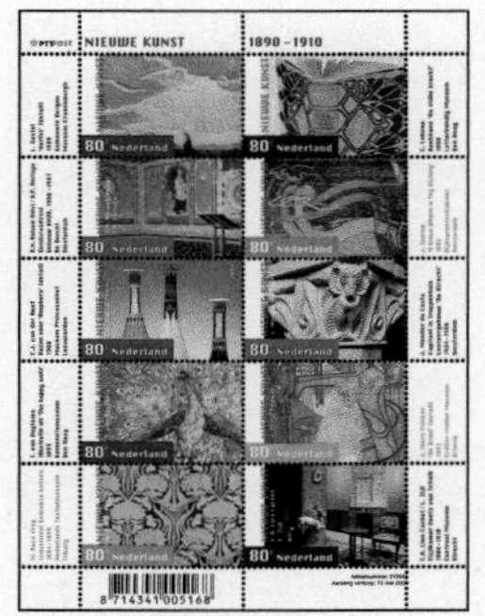

Art of 1892-1910 — A414

Art: a, "Autumn," L. Gestel. b, Book cover for "De Stille Kracht," C. Lebeau. c, Burcht Federal Council Hall, R. N. Roland Holst and H. P. Berlage. d, "O grave, where is thy victory?," J. Toorop. e, Vases from "Amphoras," C. J. van der Hoef. f, De Utrecht office building capital, J. Mendes da Costa. g, Illustration from "The Happy Owls," T. van Hoytema. h, "The Bride," J. Thorn Prikker. i, Printed fabric, M. Duco Crop. j, Dentz van Schaik period room, Central Museum, Utrecht, C. A. Lion Cachet and L. Zijl.

2001, May 15 ***Perf. 14¾***

1070 A414 Sheet of 10 7.25 7.25
a.-j. 80c Any single .70 .50

Birth Announcement Type of 1997 with Added Euro Denomination

Die Cut Perf. 13¼x12¾

2001, July 2 **Litho.**

Booklet Stamp

Self-Adhesive

1071 A363 85c multi 1.10 .80
a. Booklet pane of 5 6.00

Death Announcement Type of 1998 with Added Euro Denomination

Die Cut Perf. 13¼

2001, July 2 **Litho.**

Self-Adhesive

1072 A365 85c gray blue 1.25 1.00

Wedding Stamp — A415

Die Cut Perf. 13¼x12¾

2001, July 2 **Photo.**

Booklet Stamp

Self-Adhesive

1073 A415 85c multi 1.10 .25
a. Booklet pane of 5 5.50

See No. 1111.

A416

2001, July 2 **Booklet Stamp**

Self-Adhesive

1074 A416 85c multi 1.10 .50
a. Booklet pane of 10 11.00

See No. 1112.

Arrows — A417

Serpentine Die Cut 14x13½

2001, July 2 Coil Stamp Photo.

Self-Adhesive

1075 A417 85c pur & silver 1.00 .50

See Nos. 1105-1106.

Change of Address Stamp — A418

Die Cut Perf. 14½x14

2001, July 2 **Photo.**

Self-Adhesive

1076 A418 85c orange & blk 1.25 .80

See No. 1113.

Polder — A419

Coast at Zandvoort A420

Design: 1.65g, Cyclists on Java Island, Amsterdam.

2001, July 2 *Die Cut Perf. 13¼x12¾*

Booklet Stamps

Self-Adhesive

1077 A419 85c multi 1.25 .50
a. Booklet pane of 5 6.25

Serpentine Die Cut 12¾ Syncopated

1078 A420 1.20g multi 1.50 1.10
a. Booklet pane of 5 7.50
1079 A420 1.65g multi 2.00 1.75
a. Booklet pane of 5 10.00

Nos. 1078 and 1079 have rouletting between stamp and etiquette.

See Nos. 1114-1116.

Cartoon Network Cartoons — A421

No. 1080: a, Tom and Jerry. b, The Flintstones. c, Johnny Bravo. d, Dexter's Laboratory. e, The Powerpuff Girls.

Perf. 13½x12¾

2001, Aug. 28 **Litho.**

1080 A421 Booklet pane of 5, #a-e, + 2 labels 5.00 3.75
a.-e. 85c Any single .95 .60
Booklet, #1080 6.00

Greetings — A422

No. 1081: a, Veel Geluk (9 times). b, Gefeliciteerd! (11 times). c, Veel Geluk (4 times), horiz. d, Gefeliciteerd! (5 times), horiz. e, Proficiat (7 times). f, Succes! (7 times). g, Van Harte. . . (9 times). h, Proficiat (3 times), horiz. i, Succes! (3 times), horiz. j, Van Harte. . . (4 times), horiz.

Die Cut Perf. 13x13¼, 13¼x13

2001, Sept. 3 Photo.

Self-Adhesive

1081 Booklet of 10 10.50
a.-j. A422 85c Any single .95 .75

See No. 1117.

Change From Guilder to Euro Currency — A423

Etched on Silver Foil

2001, Sept. 25 ***Die Cut Perf. 12¾***

Self-Adhesive

1082 A423 12.75g Guilder coins *9.50 6.50*

Cancels can be easily removed from these stamps.

Souvenir Sheet

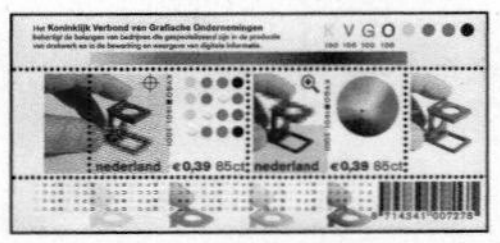

Royal Dutch Association of Printers, Cent. — A424

No. 1083 — Magnifying glass and: a, Color dots. b, Spectrum.

Photo. & Embossed

2001, Oct. 12 ***Perf. 14x13½***

1083 A424 Sheet of 2 2.00 1.75
a.-b. 85c Any single .95 .75

Souvenir Sheet

Dutch Stamps, 150th Anniv. (in 2002) A425

No. 1084: a, Waigaat Canal and ramparts, Williamstad, Curacao. b, Pangka sugar refinery, Java Island, Netherlands Indies.

2001, Oct. 12 Photo. ***Perf. 14x13½***

1084 A425 Sheet of 2 2.00 2.00
a.-b. 85c Any single .95 .25

Amphilex 2002 Intl. Stamp Show, Amsterdam.

December Stamps — A426

No. 1085: a, Clock, grapes. b, Grapes, stars, doughnut balls. c, Doughnut balls, spire of church tower. d, Cherub. e, Champagne bottle. f, Wreath, roof. g, Windows of church tower. h, Ornament on Christmas tree. i, Christmas tree on sign. j, Cake in window. k, Christmas tree with ornaments, church tower. l, Santa Claus. m, Mug of hot chocolate on sign, snowman's head. n, Candles in window. o, Church tower, decorated market stalls. p, Reindeer. q, Snowman. r, Wrapped gift. s, Bonfire. t, Children on sled.

Serpentine Die Cut 13¼x13

2001, Nov. 27 Photo.

Self-Adhesive

1085 Sheet of 20 10.50
a.-t. A426 60c Any single .50 .25

100 Cents = 1 Euro (€)

Queen Type of 1991, Arrows Type of 2001 With Euro Denominations Only and

A427

Die Cut Perf. 14¼, Serpentine Die Cut 14 (#1086, 12c), Serpentine Die Cut 14¼ (55c, 57c 70c, 72c), Perf 14¼x13½ (#1087, 5c, 10c)

Photo, Litho (5c, 12c)

2002-05 Self-Adhesive

1086 A427 2c red .25 .25
a. Booklet pane of 5 .25

Water-Activated Gum

1087 A427 2c red .25 .25
1088 A427 5c red violet .25 .25
1089 A427 10c blue .25 .25

Self-Adhesive Booklet Stamps

1090 A427 12c green .30 .25
a. Booklet pane of 5 1.50
1091 A273 25c brn & dk grn .60 .25
a. Booklet pane of 5 3.00
1092 A273 39c bl grn & red .95 .25
a. Booklet pane of 5 4.75
b. Booklet pane of 10 9.50
1093 A273 40c bl & brn .95 .25
a. Booklet pane of 5 4.75
1094 A273 50c fawn & emer 1.25 .25
a. Booklet pane of 5 6.25
1095 A273 55c lilac & brown 1.40 .25
a. Booklet pane of 5 7.00
1096 A273 57c brn & blue grn 1.50 .30
a. Booklet pane of 5 7.50
1097 A273 61c pur & red brn 1.60 .30
a. Booklet pane of 5 8.00
1098 A273 65c grn & pur 1.60 .30
a. Booklet pane of 5 8.00
1099 A273 70c ol grn & bl grn 1.75 .30
a. Booklet pane of 5 8.75
1100 A273 72c blue & brt vio 1.90 .30
a. Booklet pane of 5 9.50
1101 A273 76c olive & grn 2.00 .30
a. Booklet pane of 5 10.00
1102 A273 78c bl & ol brn 1.90 .30
a. Booklet pane of 5 9.50
1103 A273 €1 grn & blue 2.40 .40
a. Booklet pane of 5 12.00
1104 A273 €3 red vio & grn 7.25 1.25
a. Booklet pane of 5 37.50
Nos. 1086-1104 (19) 28.35 6.25

Coil Stamps

Self-Adhesive

Serpentine Die Cut Perf. 14x13½

1105 A417 39c pur & silver .95 .25
1106 A417 78c blue & gold 1.90 .30

Issued: 12c, 25c, 39c, 40c, 50c, 65c, 78c, €1, €3, 1/2/02; 2c (#1086), 1/28/02; 2c (#1087), 9/2/02; 10c, 11/26/02; 5c, 55c, 70c, 1/2/03; 57c, 72c, 1/2/04; 61c, 76c, 1/3/05.

See No. 1259.

Souvenir Sheet

Wedding of Prince Willem-Alexander and Máxima Zorreguieta — A428

No. 1108: a, Portraits. b, Names.

2002, Jan. 10 Photo. ***Perf. 14***

1108 A428 Sheet of 2 2.00 2.00
a.-b. 39c Either single .95 .50

Types of 1998-2001 With Euro Denominations Only

Die Cut Perf. 13¼x12¾

Photo., Litho. (#1110)

2002, Jan. 28 Self-Adhesive

1109 A363 39c multi .95 .50
a. Booklet pane of 5 4.75

Die Cut Perf. 13¼

1110 A365 39c gray blue .95 .50

Die Cut Perf. 13¼x12¾

1111 A415 39c multi .95 .50
a. Booklet pane of 5 4.75
1112 A416 39c multi .95 .50
a. Booklet pane of 10 9.50

Die Cut Perf. 14½x14

1113 A418 39c orange & blk 1.00 .50

Die Cut Perf. 13¼x12¾

1114 A419 39c multi .95 .50
a. Booklet pane of 5 4.75

Serpentine Die Cut 12¾ Syncopated

1115 A420 54c Like #1078 1.25 .50
a. Booklet pane of 5 6.25
1116 A420 75c Like #1079 1.75 .50
a. Booklet pane of 5 8.75
Nos. 1109-1116 (8) 8.75 4.00

Nos. 1115-1116 have rouletting between stamp and etiquette.

Greetings Type of 2001 with Euro Denominations Only

No. 1117: a, Veel Geluk (9 times). b, Gefeliciteerd! (11 times). c, Veel Geluk (4 times), horiz. d, Gefeliciteerd! (5 times), horiz. e, Proficiat (7 times). f, Succes! (7 times). g, Van Harte. . . (9 times). h, Proficiat (3 times), horiz. i, Succes! (3 times), horiz. j, Van Harte. . . (4 times), horiz.

Die Cut Perf. 13x13¼, 13¼x13

2002, Jan. 28 Photo.

Self-Adhesive

1117 Booklet of 10 10.00
a.-j. A422 39c Any single .95 .70

Provinces — A429

2002 Litho. ***Perf. 14½x14¾***

1118 A429 39c Friesland .95 .95
1119 A429 39c Drenthe .95 .95
1120 A429 39c Noord-Holland .95 .95
1121 A429 39c Gelderland .95 .95
1122 A429 39c Noord-Brabant .95 .95
1123 A429 39c Groningen .95 .95
1124 A429 39c Zuid-Holland .95 .95
1125 A429 39c Utrecht .95 .95
1126 A429 39c Limburg .95 .95
1127 A429 39c Overijssel .95 .95
1128 A429 39c Zeeland .95 .95
1129 A429 39c Flevoland .95 .95
a. Souvenir sheet of 12, #1118-1129 11.40
Nos. 1118-1129 (12) 11.40 11.40

Nos. 1118-1129 each were issued in sheets of 12 + 6 labels.

Issued: No. 1118, 3/12; No. 1119, 3/26; No. 1120, 4/9; No. 1121, 4/23. No. 1122, 5/7; No. 1123, 5/21. No. 1124, 6/4; No. 1125, 6/18; No. 1126, 7/2. No. 1127, 7/16; No. 1128, 7/30; No. 1129, 8/13.

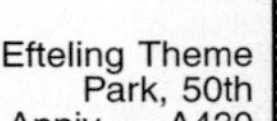

Efteling Theme Park, 50th Anniv. — A430

Characters: a, Bald man. b, Jester. c, Fairy. d, Man with thumb extended. e, Man with mouth open.

Serpentine Die Cut 13¼x12¾

2002, May 14 Photo.

Self-Adhesive

1130 Booklet pane of 5 4.75
a.-e. A430 39c Any single .95 .25

Europa — A431

Designs: No. 1131, Lions and circus tent. No. 1132, Acrobats, juggler, animal acts.

Perf. 14½x14¾

2002, June 11 Litho.

1131 A431 54c multi 1.50 .75
1132 A431 54c multi 1.50 .75
a. Tete-beche pair, #1131-1132 3.50 3.25

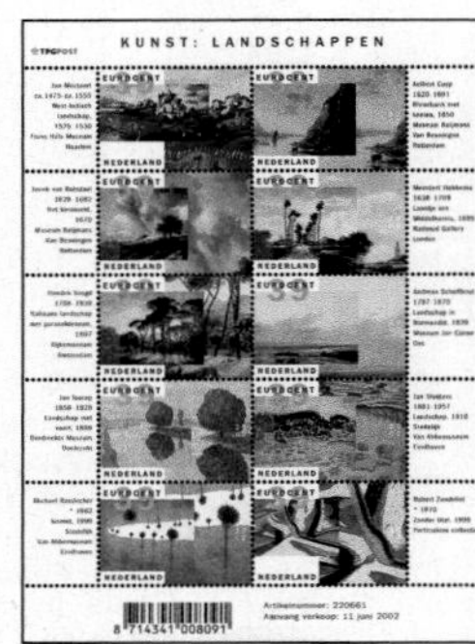

Landscape Paintings — A432

No. 1133: a, West Indian Landscape, by Jan Mostaert. b, Landscape with Cows, by Aelbert Cuyp. c, Grain Field, by Jacob van Ruisdael. d, Path in Middelharnis, by Meindert Hobbema. e, Italian Landscape, by Hendrik Vogel. f, Normandy Landscape, by Andreas Schelfhout. g, Landscape with Canal, by Jan Toorop. h, Landscape, by Jan Sluijters. i, Kismet, by Michael Raedecker. j, Untitled painting, by Robert Zandvliet. Names of artwork and artist are on sheet margins adjacent to stamps.

2002, June 11 Photo. ***Perf. 14½***

1133 A432 Sheet of 10 9.25 6.25
a.-j. 39c Any single .90 .50

A433

Die Cut Perf. 14¼

2002, July Coil Stamps Photo.

1134 A433 39c blue & red .95 .50
1135 A433 78c green & red 1.90 .75

See Nos. 1157, 1173.

Souvenir Sheet

Amphilex 2002 Intl. Stamp Exhibition, Amsterdam — A434

No. 1136: a, One ship. b, Two ships.

2002, Aug. 30 Litho. ***Perf. 14x13½***

1136 A434 Sheet of 2 1.90 1.90
a.-b. 39c Either single .95 .25

Dutch stamps, 150th anniv.; Dutch East India Company, 400th anniv.

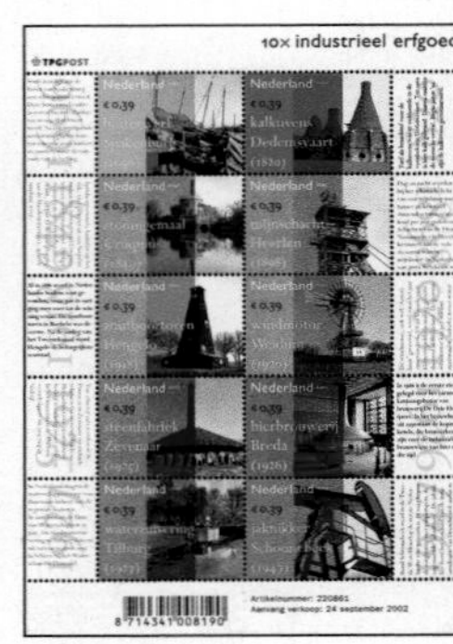

Industrial Heritage A435

No. 1137: a, Spakenberg shipyard, 1696. b, Dedemsvaart lime kilns, 1820. c, Cruquius steam pumping station, 1849. d, Heerlen coal mine shaft, 1898. e, Hengelo salt pumping tower, 1918. f, Weidum windmotor, 1920. g, Zevenaar brick oven, 1925. h, Breda brewery, 1926. i, Water works, Tilburg, 1927. j, Schoonebeck oil well pump, 1947.

2002, Sept. 24 ***Perf. 14½x14¾***

1137 A435 Sheet of 10 9.50 9.50
a.-j. 39c Any single .95 .25

December Stamps — A436

No. 1138: a, Person, child, fence and trees. b, Man seated, trees. c, Head facing left. d, Red tree, person in black. e, Woman with white hair, tree. f, Person standing in grass. g, Man standing with legs crossed. h, Woman, windmill. i, Man on stool. j, Face with black lips. k, Man standing near tree, with bent knee. l, Man standing near trees, both hands in pockets. m, Two people seated. n, Person with black hair. o, Man with child on shoulders. p, Face, with black hair and eye looking right. q, Person with gold lips looking left. r, Head of person near shore. s, Person with sunglasses standing near shore. t, Woman with arms extended.

Serpentine Die Cut 13

2002, Nov. 26 Photo.

Self-Adhesive

1138 A436 Sheet of 20 12.00
a.-t. 29c Any single .60 .25

Paintings by Vincent Van Gogh — A437

Designs: 39c, Self-portrait, 1886. 59c, Sunflowers, 1887. 75c, The Sower, 1888.

Die Cut Perf. 14¼

2003, Jan. 2 Photo.

Booklet Stamps

Self-Adhesive

1139 A437 39c multi .95 .50
a. Booklet pane of 10 9.50

Serpentine Die Cut 13¼ Syncopated

1140 A437 59c multi + etiquette 1.40 1.10
a. Booklet pane of 5+5 etiquettes 7.00
1141 A437 75c multi + etiquette 1.75 1.50
a. Booklet pane of 5+5 etiquettes 8.75

A row of rouletting separates stamps from the etiquettes.

Paintings by Vincent Van Gogh A438

No. 1142: a, Autumn Landscape with Four Trees, 1885. b, The Potato Eaters, 1885. c, Four Cut Sunflowers, 1887. d, Self-portrait with Gray Felt Hat, 1887-88. e, The Zouave, 1888. f, The Cafe Terrace on the Place du Forum, at Night, 1888. g, Pine Trees and Dandelions in the Garden of Saint-Paul Hospital, 1890. h, Blossoming Almond Tree, 1890. i, View of Auvers, 1890. j, Wheat Field with Crows, 1890.

2003, Jan. 2 Litho. *Perf. 14½*

1142 A438 Sheet of 10 10.00 10.00
a.-j. 39c Any single .95 .60

Water Control A439

No. 1143: a, North Pier, Ijmuiden, 1869. b, Hansweert Lock, 1865. c, Damming of the Wieringermeer, 1929. d, Ijsselmeer Dam (no date). e, Water breaching dike at Willemstad, 1953. f, Repairing dike at Stavenisse, 1953. g, Damming of the Zandkreek, 1960. h, Damming of the Grevelingen, 1964. i, Oosterschelde flood barrier, 1995. j, High water in Roermond, 1993.

2003, Feb. 1 Photo.

1143 A439 Sheet of 10 8.75 8.75
a.-j. 39c Any single .85 .60

Johann Enschedé and Sons, Printers, 300th Anniv. — A440

No. 1144: a, Binary code, mathematics symbols. b, Fleischman's musical notation symbols.

Litho. & Embossed

2003, Mar. 4 *Perf. 14x12¾*

1144 A440 Horiz. pair 1.60 1.00
a.-b. 39c Either single .80 .50

No. 1144a has photogravure back printing that can be seen through blank triangle on face of stamp.

Souvenir Sheets

Island Fauna A441

No. 1145: a, Eurasian oyster catcher and pilings. b, Spoonbill, horiz. c, Eider. d, Harbor seal, horiz.

No. 1146: a, Sea gull. b, Stone curlew, horiz. c, Gull and seals. d, Crab, horiz.

2003, May 6 Litho. *Perf. 14½*

1145 A441 Sheet of 4 4.25 4.25
a.-d. 39c Any single .90 .60
1146 A441 Sheet of 4 5.25 5.25
a.-d. 59c Any single 1.25 .80

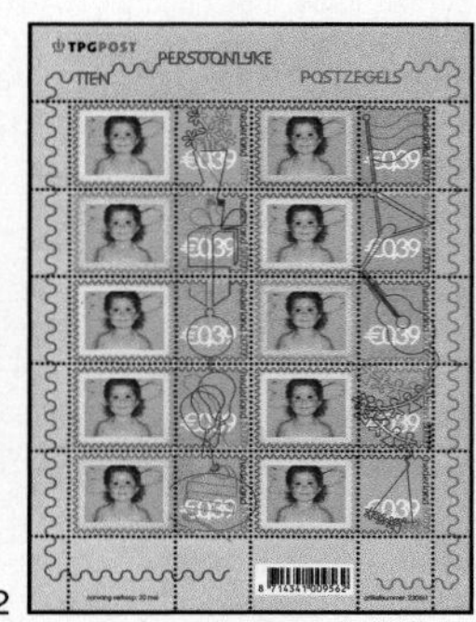

A442

Personalized Stamps — A443

No. 1147: a, Flowers. b, Flag. c, Gift. d, Martini glass. e, Medal. f, Guitar. g, Balloons. h, Paper cut-outs. i, Cake. j, Party hat.

No. 1148 — Numeral color: a, Bright blue. b, Dull green. c, Lilac. d, Red violet. e, Dull orange. f, Yellow green. g, Olive. h, Dull blue. i, Red. j, Orange brown.

Perf. 13½x12¾

2003, May 20 Photo.

1147 A442 Sheet of 10 + 10 labels 9.00 9.00
a.-j. 39c Any single .90 .25
1148 A443 Sheet of 10 + 10 labels 9.00 9.00
a.-j. 39c Any single .90 .25

Labels could be personalized for an additional fee.

Douwe Egberts Co., 250th Anniv. — A444

2003, June 3 Litho. *Perf. 14½x14¾*

1149 39c Spotted cup .95 .45
1150 39c White cup .95 .45
a. A444 Horiz. pair, #1149-1150 1.90 1.60

Land, Air and Water A445

2003, June 24

1151 39c Airplane at UL .95 .45
1152 39c Fish at LR .95 .45
a. A445 Horiz. pair, #1151-1152 1.90 .90

Nelson Mandela, 85th Birthday, and Nelson Mandela Children's Fund — A446

2003, July 18

1153 39c Mandela .95 .45
1154 39c Children's Fund .95 .45
a. A446 Horiz. pair, #1153-1154 1.90 .90

"From Me to You" — A447

Die Cut Perf. 14¼x14½

2003, Sept. 1 Photo.

Booklet Stamp

Self-Adhesive

1155 A447 39c multi .90 .50
a. Booklet pane of 5 4.50

Photographs — A448

No. 1156: a, Children kissing. b, Woman. c, Cat. d, Puppies. e, Girl. f, Bride and groom. g, Automobiles. h, Motorcycle race. i, Butterfly. j, Flowers and sky.

Perf. 14½x14¾

2003, Sept. 23 Litho.

1156 A448 Sheet of 10 9.50 9.50
a.-j. 39c Any single .90 .65

Numeral Type of 2002

Die Cut Perf. 13½

2003, Oct. 2 Photo.

Self-Adhesive

Stamp + Label

1157 A433 39c Prus bl & red 1.15 .75

No. 1157 has "2003" year date and was printed in sheets of 50 stamps + 50 labels. Labels could be personalized for an additional fee.

Stamp Collecting — A449

2003, Oct. 20 Litho. *Perf. 14½x14¾*

1158 A449 39c multi .95 .50

A booklet containing 2 booklet panes of 4 #1158 and three different imperf incomplete progressive proofs of these panes sold for €9.95.

A450

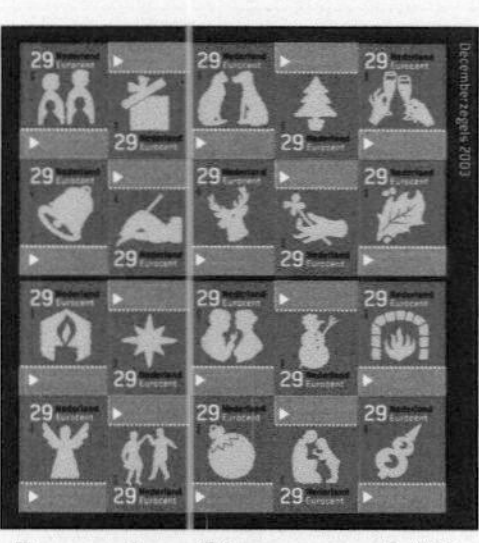

December Stamps — A451

Designs: No. 1159, Five-pointed star.

No. 1160: a, Family. b, Open gift box. c, Cat and dog. d, Christmas tree. e, Toast. f, Bell. g, Hand with pencil. h, Head of reindeer. i, Hand with flower. j, Holly leaf and berries. k, Candle. l, Eight-pointed star. m, Man and woman. n, Snowman. o, Fireplace. p, Angel. q, Man and woman dancing. r, Round Christmas ornament. s, Mother and child. t, Treetop ornament.

Perf. 13½x12¾

2003, Nov. 25 Litho.

1159 A450 29c multi + label .75 .75

Photo.

Self-Adhesive

Serpentine Die Cut 13

1160 A451 Sheet of 20 15.00
a.-t. 29c Any single .60 .25

No. 1159 was printed in sheets of 10 stamps + 10 labels. Labels could be personalized. No. 1160 is printed with panel of thermochromic ink which reveals a message when warmed.

Queen Beatrix and Family A452

No. 1161: a, Princess Beatrix as infant with Queen Juliana and Prince Bernhard, 1938. b, Princess Beatrix playing on swings with Princess Irene, 1943. c, Princess Beatrix with horse, 1951. d, Princess Beatrix reading book, 1964. e, Princess Beatrix talking with Prince Claus, 1965. f, Princess Beatrix, Prince Claus and infant Prince Willem-Alexander, 1967. g, Princess Beatrix, Prince Claus and three young sons, 1975. h, Queen Beatrix and Prince Claus dancing, 1998. i, Royal Family, 1999. j, Queen at art exhibition, 2000.

2003, Dec. 9 Photo. *Perf. 14¼*

1161 A452 Sheet of 10 9.50 9.50
a.-j. 39c Any single .95 .60

A booklet containing five panes each with two horizontally adjacent stamps from Nos. 1161a-1161j, in perf 13½x13¾, sold for €9.95.

Souvenir Sheet

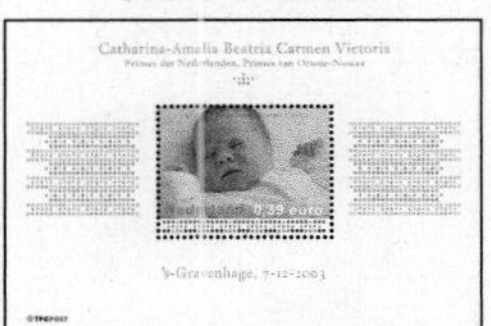

Birth of Princess Catharina-Amalia — A453

2003, Dec. 16 Litho. *Perf. 13¾*

1162 A453 39c multi 1.00 .75

See footnote below No. 1174.

Paintings — A454

Designs: 61c, Woman Reading a Letter, by Gabriel Metsu. 77c, The Letter, by Jan Vermeer.

Serpentine Die Cut 13 Horiz. Syncopated

2004, Jan. 2 Photo.

Booklet Stamps
Stamp + Detachable Etiquette

1163 A454 61c multi 1.20 .50
a. Booklet pane of 5 6.00
1164 A454 77c multi 1.45 .65
a. Booklet pane of 5 7.25

Royal Netherlands Meteorological Institute, 150th Anniv. — A455

Designs: No. 1165, Rain (rainbow at left. No. 1166, Sun (rainbow at right).

2004, Jan. 31 Litho. *Perf. 14½x14¾*
1165 39c multi .80 .60
1166 39c multi .80 .60
a. A455 Horiz. pair, #1165-1166 2.00 .50

Retangles — A456

Die Cut Perf. 14¼

2004, Mar. 2 Photo.

Self-Adhesive

1167 A456 39c red & multi .90 .60
1168 A456 78c green & multi 1.75 1.00

See Nos. 1263-1264.

Spyker Automobiles — A457

Designs: No. 1169, 1922 Spyker. No. 1170, 2003 Spyker C8 Double 12 R.

2004, May 10 Litho. *Perf. 14½*
1169 39c multi .90 .65
1170 39c multi .90 .65
a. A457 Horiz. pair, #1169-1170 1.80 1.80

A booklet containing four panes of perf 13¼x13 stamps (one pane of two No. 1169, one pane of two No. 1170, two panes containing two each of Nos. 1169-1170) sold for €9.95.

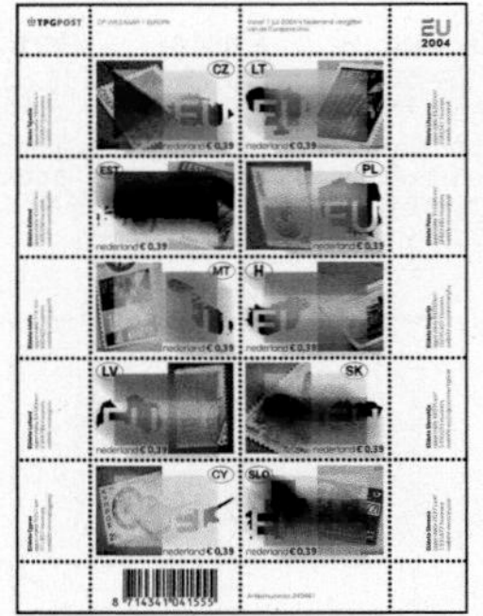
Expansion of European Union — A458

No. 1171 — Map, flag and stamps of new European Union members: a, Czech Republic. b, Lithuania. c, Estonia. d, Poland. e, Malta. f, Hungary. g, Latvia. h, Slovakia. i, Cyprus. j, Slovenia.

2004, May 10 *Perf. 14½*
1171 A458 Sheet of 10 10.00 10.00
a.-j. 39c Any single .95 .75

Numeral A459

Perf. 13½x12¾

2004, June 1 Photo.
1172 A459 39c multi + label .95 .70

Labels could be personalized.

Numeral Type of 2002

2004, June 23 *Die Cut Perf. 13½*

Self-Adhesive

Stamp + Label

1173 A433 39c org red & blue 1.10 1.10

No. 1173 has "2004" year date and has Olympic Torch Relay label.

Miniature Sheet

Prince Willem-Alexander, Princess Máxima and Princess Catharina-Amalia — A460

No. 1174: a, Prince Willem-Alexander and Princess Máxima announcing engagement. b, Princess Máxima showing engagement ring. c, Prince Willem-Alexander (without hat) and Princess Máxima looking at each other at wedding ceremony. d, Prince Willem-Alexander and Princess Máxima looking ahead at wedding ceremony. e, Prince Willem-Alexander and Princess Máxima kissing. f, Prince Willem-Alexander (with hat) looking at Princess Máxima. g, Prince Willem-Alexander and Princess Máxima looking at Princess Catharina-Amalia. h, Prince Willem-Alexander and Princess Máxima looking at book, Princess Máxima holding Princess Catharina-Amalia. i, Baptism of Princess Catharina-Amalia. j, Clergyman holding ceremony notes and touching head of Princess Catharina-Amalia at baptism.

2004, June 23 Litho. *Perf. 13¾*
1174 A460 Sheet of 10 9.50 9.50
a.-j. 39c Any single .90 .65

A booklet containing five panes, each with two horizontally adjacent stamps of Nos. 1174a-1174j, and a booklet pane of No. 1162, sold for €9.95.

Veluwe Nature Park A461

No. 1175: a, Rabbit. b, Bird. c, Doe. d, Boar.
No. 1176: a, Fox. b, Woodpecker. c, Buck. d, Ram.

2004, July 6 Photo. *Perf. 13¼x12¾*
1175 A461 Sheet of 4 4.50 4.50
a.-d. 39c Any single 1.00 .40
1176 A461 Sheet of 4 + 4 etiquettes 5.50 5.50
a.-d. 61c Any single 1.25 .50

Souvenir Sheet

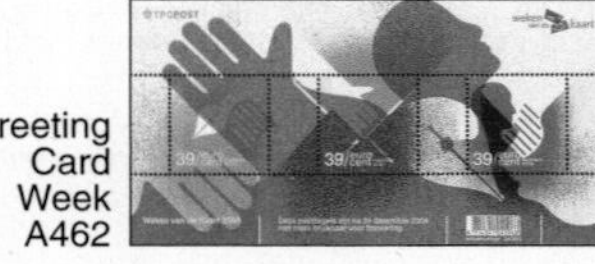
Greeting Card Week A462

No. 1177: a, Pen nib. b, Hand. c, Head.

Perf. 13¼x13¾

2004, Sept. 1 Photo.
1177 A462 Sheet of 3 + 2 labels 2.50 2.50
a.-c. 39c Any single .80 .60

Paintings by Carel Fabritius (1622-54) — A463

No. 1178: a, Mercurius en Argus, c. 1645-47. b, Self-portrait, c. 1645. c, Mercurius en Aglauros, c. 1645-47. d, Abraham de Potter, 1649. e, Hagar en de Engel, c. 1643-45. f, De Schildwacht, c. 1654. g, Hera, c. 1643. h, Self-portrait, 1654. i, Self-portrait, c. 1647-48. j, Het Puttertje, 1654.

2004, Sept. 24 Litho. *Perf. 14½*
1178 A463 Sheet of 10 12.00 12.00
a.-f. 39c Any single .90 .70
g.-j. 78c Any single 1.60 1.25

Snowman A464

December Stamps A465

No. 1180: a, Shadows. b, People with gifts. c, Girl and dog. d, Children. e, Sheep. f, Polar bears. g, Children making snowman. h, People dragging Christmas tree. i, Man and woman in water. j, People around Christmas tree.

Perf. 13½x12¾

2004, Nov. 25 Litho.
1179 A464 29c multi + label .85 .85

Photo.

Self-Adhesive

Serpentine Die Cut 12¾x13¼

1180 Block of 10 8.00
a.-j. A465 29c Any single .80 .25

Hearts — A466

Serpentine Die Cut 14¼

2005, Jan. 3 Photo.

Self-Adhesive

1181 A466 39c multi 1.00 .25
a. Booklet pane of 10 10.00

See No. 1262.

Building Silhouettes — A467

Designs: 39c, Windmill and field. 65c, House and brick wall. 81c, Greenhouse and field.

Serpentine Die Cut 14¼

2005, Jan. 3 Self-Adhesive
1182 A467 39c multi 1.00 .25
a. Booklet pane of 10 10.00

Serpentine Die Cut 13¼ Horiz. Syncopated

1183 A467 65c multi + etiquette 1.75 .45
a. Booklet pane of 5 8.75
1184 A467 81c multi + etiquette 2.10 .50
a. Booklet pane of 5 10.50
Nos. 1182-1184 (3) 4.85 1.20

On Nos. 1183 and 1184 a row of rouletting separates stamp from etiquette.

Netherlands Views — A468

2005 Litho. *Perf. 14¼*
1185 A468 39c shown 1.00 .25
1186 A468 39c Nijmegen 1.00 .25
1187 A468 39c Rotterdam 1.00 .25
1188 A468 39c Weesp 1.00 .25
1189 A468 39c Monnickendam .95 .25
1190 A468 39c Goes .95 .25
1191 A468 39c Boalsert 1.00 .25
1192 A468 39c Amsterdam 1.00 .25
1193 A468 39c Roermond .95 .25
a. Souvenir sheet, #1186, 1187, 1190, 1192, 1193 5.00 5.00
1194 A468 39c Papendrecht .95 .25
a. Souvenir sheet, #1185, 1188, 1189, 1191, 1194 5.00 5.00
Nos. 1185-1194 (10) 9.80 2.50

Issued: Nos. 1185-1186, 2/8; Nos. 1187-1188, 4/12; Nos. 1189-1190, 6/14. Nos. 1191-1192, 8/9; Nos. 1193-1194, 1193a, 1194a, 10/14.

A booklet containing five panes, each with the two stamps issued on the same day with perf. 13½x12¾, sold for €9.95.

Art A469

No. 1195: a, Trying, by Liza May Post. b, Emilie, by Sidi El Karchi. c, ZT, by Koen Vermeule. d, Het Bedrijf, by Lieshout Studio. e, Me Kissing Vinoodh (Passionately), by Inez van Lamsweerde. f, Lena, by Carla van de Puttelaar. g, Nr. 13, by Tom Claasen. h, Untitled, by Pieter Kusters. i, Witte Roos, by Ed van der Kooy. j, Portrait of a Boy (Grand Prix), bu Tiong Ang.

2005, Feb. 25 Litho. *Perf. 14½*
1195 A469 Sheet of 10 10.00 10.00
a.-j. 39c Any single 1.00 .50

Business Symbols — A470

Die Cut Perf. 14¼

2005, Mar. 22 Litho.

Self-Adhesive

1196 A470 39c multi 1.00 .25

Souvenir Sheets

Natuurmonumenten, Cent. — A471

No. 1197: a, Cormorant. b, Dragonfly. c, Water lily. d, Fish.
No. 1198: a, Bird. b, Butterfly. c, Lizard. d, Sheep.

2005, Mar. 22 Photo. *Perf. 13¼x13*
1197 A471 Sheet of 4 4.00 4.00
a.-d. 39c Any single 1.00 .25
1198 A471 Sheet of 4 + 4 etiquettes 6.75 6.75
a.-d. 65c Any single 1.60 .40

A booklet containing four panes, each with two litho., perf 14x13¾ stamps like Nos.

1197a-1197d and 1198a-1198d, sold for €9.95.

Souvenir Sheet

Queen Beatrix, 25th Anniv. of Reign A472

Photos: a, Coronation, 1980. b, Giving speech, 1991. c, With Nelson Mandela, 1999. d, Visiting colonies, 1999. e, At European Parliament, 2004.

2005, Apr. 30 Litho. *Perf. 13¼x13¾*

1199	A472	Sheet of 5	16.00	16.00
a.		39c multi	1.00	.25
b.		78c multi	2.00	.50
c.		117c multi	3.00	.75
d.		156c multi	4.00	1.00
e.		225c multi	6.00	1.50
f.		Booklet pane of 1, #1199a	1.75	—
g.		Booklet pane of 1, #1199b	3.25	—
h.		Booklet pane of 1, #1199c	5.00	—
i.		Booklet pane of 1, #1199d	6.50	—
j.		Booklet pane of 1, #1199e	9.50	—
		Complete booklet, #1199f-1199j	26.00	

Complete booklet sold for €9.95.

Numerals — A473

Die Cut Perf. 14¼

2005, May 24 Photo.

Coil Stamps

Self-Adhesive

1200	A473	39c bronze	.95	.25
1201	A473	78c silver	1.90	.50

Souvenir Sheet

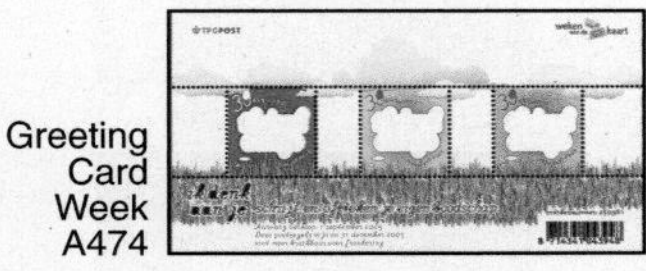

Greeting Card Week A474

No. 1202: a, Red background, denomination in white. b, Yellow background, denomination in red. c, Blue background, denomination in red.

2005, Sept. 1 Litho. *Perf. 13½x13¾*

1202	A474	Sheet of 3 + 2 labels	3.00	3.00
a.-c.		39c Any single	1.00	.25

Farm Technology — A475

Sheep and: No. 1203, Dutch windmills. No. 1204, Chinese water wheel.

2005, Sept. 22 Litho. *Perf. 14½*

1203		81c multi	2.00	.50
1204		81c multi	2.00	.50
a.		A475 Horiz. pair, #1203-1204	4.00	1.00

See People's Republic of China Nos. 3452-3453.

World Press Photo, 50th Anniv. A476

No. 1205 — Silver Camera award-winning news photographs by: a, Douglas Martin, 1957. b, Héctor Rondón Lovera, 1962. c, Co Rentmeester, 1967. d, Hanns-Jörg Anders, 1969. e, Ovie Carter, 1974. f, David Burnett, 1979. g, Anthony Suau, 1987. h, Georges Merillon, 1990. i, Claus Bjorn Larsen, 1999. j, Arko Datta, 2004.

2005, Oct. 8 Litho.

1205	A476	Sheet of 10	9.50	9.50
a.-j.		39c Any single	.95	.25

Trains — A477

Designs: No. 1206, Blue Angel. No. 1207, Locomotive 3737. No. 1208, ICE. No. 1209, Koploper.

2005, Oct. 14 Litho.

1206	A477	39c blue & multi	.95	.25
1207	A477	39c green & multi	.95	.25
1208	A477	39c red & multi	.95	.25
1209	A477	39c yel & multi	.95	.25
a.		Block of 4, #1206-1209	3.80	1.00

A478

December Stamps — A479

No. 1211: a, Flames and hearts. b, Gifts. c, Comets. d, Bells. e, Doves. f, Snowmen. g, Ornaments. h, Ice skates. i, Christmas trees. j, Champagne flutes.

Perf. 13½x12¾

2005, Nov. 24 Litho.

1210	A478	29c multi + label	.70	.25
		Photo.		
1211	A479	Sheet of 10	7.00	7.00
a.-j.		29c Any single	.70	.25

Labels on No. 1210 could be personalized for a fee.

Modern Art — A480

No. 1212: a, Koe in de Optrekkende Avondmist, by Ed van der Elsken. b, Double Dutch, by Berend Strik. c, Hollandse Velden, by Hans van der Meer. d, Tomorrow, by Marijke van Warmerdam. e, A Day in Holland/Holland in a Day, by Barbara Visser. f, Composite mit Rode Ruit, by Daan van Golden. g, Untitled work, by J. C. J. Vanderhayden. h, De Groene Kathedraal, by Mariana Boozem. i, Hollandpan, by John Körmerling. j, Drijfbeeld, by Atelier Van Lieshout.

No. 1213: a, Study for Horizon, by Sigurdur Gudmundsson. b, Lost Luggage Depot, by Jeff Wall. c, 11,000 Tulipes, by Daniel Buren. d, Flets & Stal, by FAT. e, Double Sunset, by Olafur Ellasson.

No. 1214: a, Untitled, by Dustin Larson. b, Working Progress, by Tadashi Kawamata. c, Boerderijgezichten, by Sean Snyder. d, Toc Toc, by Amalia Pica. e, Freude, by Rosemarie Trockel.

Serpentine Die Cut 14¼

2006, Jan. 2 Litho.

Self-Adhesive

1212		Booklet pane of 10	9.50	
a.-j.		A480 39c Any single	.95	.25

Serpentine Die Cut 13 Vert. Syncopated

1213		Booklet pane of 5 + 5 etiquettes	8.50	
a.-e.		A480 69c Any single + etiquette	1.60	.40
1214		Booklet pane of 5 + 5 etiquettes	10.50	
a.-e.		A480 85c Any single + etiquette	2.00	.50

On Nos. 1213 and 1214, a row of microrouletting separates stamps from etiquettes.

Queen Type of 1991

Die Cut Perf. 14¼ Syncopated

2006-09 Photo.

Self-Adhesive

Booklet Stamps

1216	A273	44c rose & ol grn	1.25	.25
a.		Booklet pane of 10	12.50	

Die Cut Perf. 14¼

1218	A273	44c rose & ol grn	1.25	.25
a.		Booklet pane of 10	12.50	
1219	A273	67c bl grn & blue	1.75	.30
a.		Booklet pane of 5	8.75	
1220	A273	74c gray grn & pur	2.10	.50
a.		Booklet pane of 5	10.50	
1221	A273	80c blue & red vio	2.00	.50
a.		Booklet pane of 5	10.00	
1223	A273	88c lilac & gray grn	2.40	.40
a.		Booklet pane of 5	12.00	
		Nos. 1216-1223 (6)	10.75	2.20

Issued: 80c, 1/2; 44c, 67c, 88c, 12/11; 74c, 1/2/09.

Netherlands Tourism Areas — A481

2006 Litho. *Perf. 14½x14¼*

1240	A481	39c Leiden	.95	.25
1241	A481	39c Sittard	.95	.25
1242	A481	39c Vlieland	1.00	.25
1243	A481	39c Woudrichem	1.00	.25
1244	A481	39c Enkhuizen	1.00	.25
a.		Souvenir sheet, #1240-1244	5.00	5.00
1245	A481	39c Schoonhoven	1.00	.25
1246	A481	39c Zutphen	1.00	.25
1247	A481	39c Deventer	1.00	.25
1248	A481	39c Zwolle	1.00	.25
1249	A481	39c Kampen	1.00	.25
a.		Souvenir sheet, #1245-1249	5.00	5.00
		Nos. 1240-1249 (10)	9.90	2.50

Issued: No. 1240, 2/1; No. 1241, 2/3; No. 1242, 4/28; No. 1243, 5/24; Nos. 1244-1245, 6/2; Nos. 1246-1247, 8/4; Nos. 1248-1249, 9/1. Nos. 1244a, 1249a, 10/10.

A booklet containing five panes of one each of Nos. 1240-1241, 1242-1243, 1244-1245, 1246-1247, and 1248-1249 sold for €9.95.

Souvenir Sheet

Dutch Speed Skating Gold Medalists in the Winter Olympics — A482

No. 1250: a, Ard Schenk. b, Yvonne van Gennip.

Litho. With Three-Dimensional Plastic

2006, Feb. 10 *Serpentine Die Cut 9*

Self-Adhesive

1250	A482	Sheet of 2	1.90	
a.-b.		39c Either single	.95	.50

The two stamps and a top and bottom sheet margin are affixed to a sheet of backing paper. A booklet containing five examples of No. 1250 sold for €9.95.

Personalized Stamp — A483

2006, May 1 Litho. *Perf. 13½x14*

1251	A483	39c multi	1.00	.25

No. 1251, showing Dutch soccer player Dirk Kuyt, sold for face value to the public and is the generic image for this stamp. Stamps depicting twenty other Dutch soccer players (Edwin van der Sar, Arjen Robben, Mark van Bommel, Ron Vlaar, Giovanni van Bronckhorst, Khalid Boulahrouz, Romeo Castelen, Jan Vennegoor of Hesselink, Urby Emanuelson, Ruud van Nistelroou, Henk Timmer, Rafael van der Vaart, Hedwiges Maduro, Wesley Sneijder, Robin van Persie, Nigel de Jong, Barry Opdam, Joris Mathijsen, Denny Landzaat, and Phillip Cocu) were produced by postal authorities to sell as a special set for €12.95 per sheet of 10 different players. Examples of No. 1251 with other images are personalized stamps that sold for €12.95 per sheet of 10 stamps.

Miniature Sheet

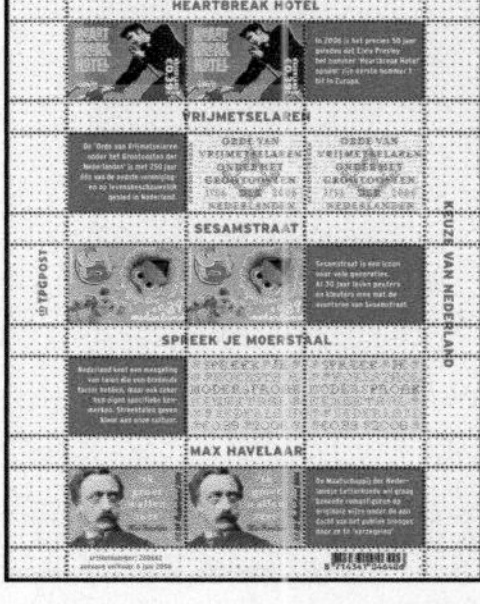

Stamps Chosen By the Public A484

No. 1252: a, Elvis Presley. b, Masonic emblem. c, Muppets Purk and Pino. d, Needlepoint design of sayings in languages used in Twente, Limburg and Friesland. e, Max Havelaar, fictional character.

2006, June 10 *Perf. 14½*

1252	A484	Sheet of 10, 2 each #a-e, + 17 labels	10.00	10.00
a.-e.		39c Any single	1.00	.25

Heartbreak Hotel, by Presley, 50th anniv., Dutch Grand Masonic Lodge, 250th anniv.; Dutch version of Sesame Street. 30th anniv.

Rembrandt (1606-69), Painter — A485

No. 1253: a, Bearded Man in Oriental Cape and Robe. b, Old Woman Seated at a Table. c, Saskia van Uylenburgh. d, Rembrandt's Son, Titus. e, Portrait of a Woman at the Window.

€6.45, Self-portrait with Saskia.

2006, June 15 Litho. *Perf. 13¾*

1253	A485	Block of 5 + label	5.00	5.00
a.-e.		39c Any single	1.00	.25

Souvenir Sheet

Litho. & Engr.

On Thin Card

1254	A485	€6.45 tan & black	17.00	17.00

See Germany No. 2387. A booklet containing two panes, each containing Nos. 1253a, 1253b, and 1253d, one pane of No. 1253c and Germany No. 2387, and one pane containing two No. 1253e, sold for €9.95. The booklet was withdrawn from sale after it was discovered that the German stamp in the booklet was printed with perforations and tagging without the authorization of German postal authorities, but most of the booklets produced had already been distributed. Value, $80.

Drawing by Karel Appel (1921-2006) — A486

2006, Sept. 1 Litho. *Perf. 13¼x14*

1255	A486	39c multi	1.00	.25

A booklet containing five panes of 2 No. 1255 sold for €9.95.

Miniature Sheet

Endangered Animals — A487

No. 1256: a, Giraffe. b, Butterfly. c, Manchurian crane. d, Francois' leaf monkey. e, Blue poison dart frog. f, Red panda. g, Lowland gorilla. h, Sumatran tiger. i, Asian lion. j, Indian rhinoceros. k, Asian elephant. l, Pygmy hippopotamus.

2006, Oct. 4 ***Perf. 13¾***

1256 A487 Sheet of 12 12.00 12.00
a.-l. 39c Any single 1.00 .25

A booklet containing one pane each of Nos. 1256a-1256c, 1256d-1256f, 1256g-1256i, and 1256j-1256l sold for €9.95.

Renaming of Postal Corporation as TNT Post — A488

2006, Oct. 16 **Litho.** ***Perf. 14½***

1257 A488 39c multi 1.00 .25

Snowflakes — A489

No. 1258: a, Small blue green, large dark blue flakes. b, Large pink, small red flakes. c, Small pink, large brown flakes. d, Large blue, small red flakes. e, Small blue green, large brown flakes. f, Small blue, large red flakes. g, Large green, small brown flakes. h, Small blue, large pink flakes. i, Large red, small brown flakes. j, Small pink, large blue green flakes.

Serpentine Die Cut 12¾x13¼

2006, Nov. 23 **Photo.**

Self-Adhesive

1258 Block of 10 7.75
a.-j. A489 29c Any single .75 .25

Numeral and "NL" Type of 2002

Perf. 14¼x13½

2006, Dec. 11 **Photo.**

1259 A427 3c brown .25 .25

Birth Announcement Type of 1997

Serpentine Die Cut 13¼x12¾

2006, Dec. 11 **Photo.**

Self-Adhesive

1260 A363 44c multi 1.25 .30

Death Announcement Type of 1997

Serpentine Die Cut 13¼

2006, Dec. 11 **Photo.**

Self-Adhesive

1261 A365 44c multi 1.25 .30

Hearts Type of 2005

Serpentine Die Cut 14½x14¼

2006, Dec. 11 **Litho.**

Self-Adhesive

1262 A466 44c multi 1.25 .30
a. Booklet pane of 10 12.50

Rectangles Type of 2004

Die Cut Perf. 14¼x14½

2006, Dec. 11 **Photo.**

Self-Adhesive

1263 A456 44c multi 1.25 .30
1264 A456 88c multi 2.40 .40

Dutch Products — A490

No. 1265: a, Glide glass goblet. b, Revolt chair. c, Heineken beer bottle. d, Bugaboo stroller. e, Lapin kettle. f, Milk bottle lamp. g, Carrier bicycle. h, Fluorescent screw-bottom lightbulb. i, Unox smoked sausage. j, Tulip. 72c, Clap skates. 89c, Cheese slicer.

Die Cut Perf. 14¼

2006, Dec. 11 **Photo.**

Self-Adhesive

1265 Booklet pane of 10 12.50
a.-j. A490 44c Any single 1.25 .25

Serpentine Die Cut 11

1266 A490 72c multi + etiquette 1.90 .30
a. Booklet pane of 5 + 5 etiquettes 9.50
1267 A490 89c multi + etiquette 2.40 .40
a. Booklet pane of 5 + 5 etiquettes 12.00

On Nos. 1266-1267, a row of microrouletting separates stamps from etiquettes.

Numerals — A491

2007, Jan. 2 ***Die Cut Perf. 14¼x14½***

Self-Adhesive

1268 A491 44c multi 1.25 .30
a. Serpentine die cut 13½ + label 1.25 .30
1269 A491 88c multi, vert. 2.40 .40

The generic label on No. 1268a depicts a mailbox. These labels could be personalized for an additional fee.

A492

Personalized Stamps — A493

2007 **Litho.** ***Perf. 14x13½***

1270 A492 44c multi 1.25 .30

Self-Adhesive

Serpentine Die Cut 13¼x13

1271 A493 44c multi 1.25 .30

Issued: No. 1270, 1/2; No. 1271, 9/21. The generic vignettes of Nos. 1270 (Royal Dutch Mint), and 1271 (Mathematician L. E. J. Brouwer), which sold for face value, are shown. These stamps, printed in sheets of 10, could be personalized with horizontal or vertical images for an additional fee.

Netherlands Tourism Areas — A494

2007 **Litho.** ***Perf. 14½x14¼***

1272 A494 44c Gouda 1.25 .30
1273 A494 44c Groningen 1.25 .30
1274 A494 44c Vlissingen 1.25 .30
1275 A494 44c Hoorn 1.25 .30
1276 A494 44c Leerdam 1.25 .30
1277 A494 44c Den Helder 1.25 .30
1278 A494 44c Lelystad 1.25 .30
1279 A494 44c Den Haag (The Hague) 1.25 .30
a. Souvenir sheet, #1274-1275, 1277-1279 6.25 6.25
1280 A494 44c Utrecht 1.25 .30
1281 A494 44c Edam 1.25 .30
a. Souvenir sheet, #1272-1273, 1276, 1280-1281 6.25 6.25
Nos. 1272-1281 (10) 12.50 3.00

Issued: Nos. 1272-1273, 2/7; No. 1274, 3/23; No. 1275, 3/26; No. 1276, 4/13; No. 1277, 7/24; No. 1278, 8/8; No. 1279, 8/15. Nos. 1279a, 1281a, 10/17; No. 1280, 10/3; No. 1281, 10/10. A booklet containing five panes of one each of Nos. 1272-1273, 1274-1275, 1276-1277, 1278-1279, and 1280-1281 in perf. 13½x12½ sold for €9.95.

Trees in Spring A495

Trees in Summer A496

Trees in Autumn A497

Trees in Winter A498

Designs: No. 1282, Lime tree. No. 1283, Horse chestnut bud. No. 1284, Bark of plane tree. No. 1285, Oak tree. No. 1286, Maple samaras. No. 1287, Trunk and branches of beech tree. No. 1288, Black alder tree. No. 1289, White willow tree in water.

2007 **Litho.** ***Perf. 14½***

1282 44c multi 1.25 .30
1283 44c multi 1.25 .30
a. A495 Horiz. pair, #1282-1283 2.50 .60
1284 44c multi 1.25 .30
1285 44c multi 1.25 .30
a. A496 Horiz. pair, #1284-1285 2.50 .60
1286 44c multi 1.25 .30
1287 44c multi 1.25 .30
a. A497 Horiz. pair, #1286-1287 2.50 .60
1288 44c multi 1.25 .30
1289 44c multi 1.25 .30
a. A498 Horiz. pair, #1288-1289 2.50 .60
Nos. 1282-1289 (8) 10.00 2.40

Issued: Nos. 1282-1283, 3/23; Nos. 1284-1285, 6/21; Nos. 1286-1287, 9/21; Nos. 1288-1289, 11/12.

Miniature Sheet

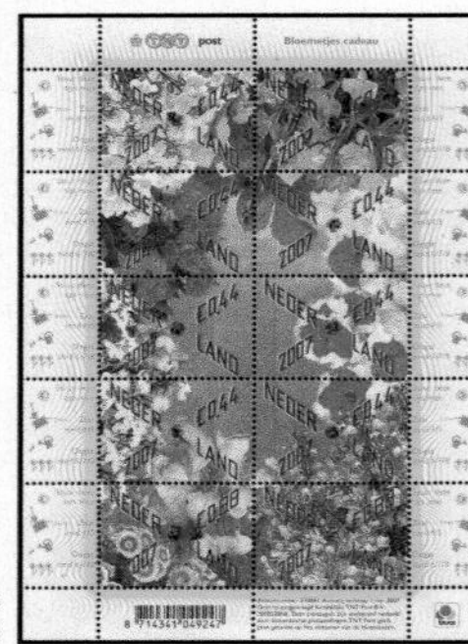

Flowers A499

No. 1290: a, Yellow and white toadflax at L, blue lobelia at R, red pinks at LR. b, Blue lobelias and white petunia. c, Yellow and white toadflax at UL, red pinks at UR and LL, sky at LR. d, Red snapdragon at UL, blue lobelia at top, white petunias at UR, red and white petunias at bottom, sky at LL. e, Red pinks at top, white toadflax at UL and LL, sky at R. f, Red and white petunias at R, sky at left. g, White toadflax at L, pink snapdragons at LR, sky at UR. h, Red and white petunia at top, pink snapdragons at LL, red violet toadflax at LR, sky at UL. i, White toadflax at UL, red and white snapdragons at UR, white and red pinks at LL. j, Red violet toadflax.

Litho & Embossed

2007, May 1 ***Perf. 13½***

1290 A499 Sheet of 10 15.00 15.00
a.-h. 44c Any single 1.25 .30
i.-j. 88c Any single 2.50 .30

Flower seeds are sealed under a round piece of adhesive tape in the embossed circle in the center of the stamps. The left and right sheet selvage contains instructions on planting the stamps and seeds. A booklet containing five panes, each containing one of the five horizontal pairs of stamps from the sheet and the adjacent selvage, sold for €9.95.

Europa A500

2007, July 26 **Litho.** ***Perf. 13½***

1291 72c Moon 2.00 .50
1292 72c Sun 2.00 .50
a. A500 Pair, #1291-1292 4.00 1.00

Scouting, cent. Printed in sheets of 10. Sheet margins inscribed "Priority" serve as etiquettes. A booklet containing three different panes, each containing a horizontal pair and two etiquettes, sold for €9.95.

Greeting Card Weeks — A501

2007, Sept. 3 ***Perf. 13¾***

1293 A501 44c multi 1.25 .30

Printed in sheets of 3.

Kingdom of the Netherlands, Bicent. — A502

Litho. & Embossed

2007, Sept. 11 ***Perf. 13¼***

Booklet Stamp

1294 A502 €6.45 multi 29.00 15.00
Complete booklet 29.00

No. 1294 was sold only in a booklet pane of one stamp in a booklet containing one pane, which sold for €9.95.

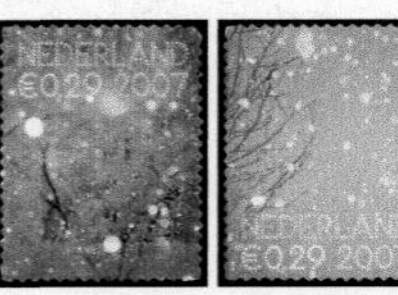

A503 A504

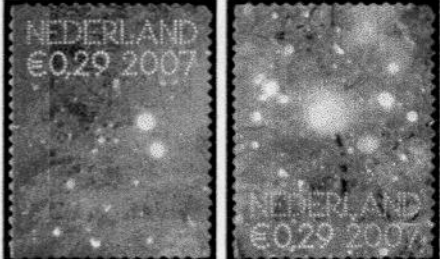

A505 A506

A507 A508

A509 A510

Snowflakes and Trees

A511 A512

A513 A514

A515 A516

A517 A518

A519 A520

Fireworks
A521 A522

Serpentine Die Cut 12¾x13¼

2007, Nov. 22 **Photo.**

Self-Adhesive

1295	Block of 10	8.50	
a.	A503 29c multi	.85	.25
b.	A504 29c multi	.85	.25
c.	A505 29c multi	.85	.25
d.	A506 29c multi	.85	.25
e.	A507 29c multi	.85	.25
f.	A508 29c multi	.85	.25
g.	A509 29c multi	.85	.25
h.	A510 29c multi	.85	.25
i.	A511 29c multi	.85	.25
j.	A512 29c multi	.85	.25

Litho.

Serpentine Die Cut 12¾

1296	Block of 10	13.00	
a.	A513 29c multi, unscratched panel	1.25	.30
b.	A514 29c multi, unscratched panel	1.25	.30
c.	A515 29c multi, unscratched panel	1.25	.30
d.	A516 29c multi, unscratched panel	1.25	.30
e.	A517 29c multi, unscratched panel	1.25	.30
f.	A518 29c multi, unscratched panel	1.25	.30
g.	A519 29c multi, unscratched panel	1.25	.30
h.	A520 29c multi, unscratched panel	1.25	.30
i.	A521 29c multi, unscratched panel	1.25	.30
j.	A522 29c multi, unscratched panel	1.25	.30
k.-t.	As #1296a-1296j, any single, scratched panel		.30

No. 1296 sold for €4.40, with €1.50 of the total going towards lottery prizes awarded to the sender of and mail recipient of stamps with prizes found under the scratch-off panel at the bottom of the stamps. Scratch-off panels are separated from the stamps by a row of rouletting.

Ecology — A523

No. 1297: a, Hybrid vehicle with electric plug. b, House and sun (solar energy). c, Cow with electric plug (biofuels). d, Wind generators. e, Trees. f, Flowers, carpoolers in automobile. g, "Groen" with electric plug. h, Truck (soot filters). i, Birds and envelope (green mail). j, Insulated house.

75c, Bicycle with globe hemispheres as wheels. 92c, Heart-shaped globe.

Die Cut Perf. 14¼

2008, Jan. 2 **Litho.**

Self-Adhesive

1297	Booklet pane of 10	13.00	
a.-j.	A523 44c Any single	1.25	.30

Photo.

Serpentine Die Cut 11

1298	A523 75c multi + etiquette	2.25	.55
1299	A523 92c multi + etiquette	2.75	.70

On Nos. 1298-1299 a row of microrouletting separates stamps from etiquettes.

See Nos. 1324-1325.

A524

A525

A526

A527

A528

A529

Personalized Stamps — A530

2008 **Litho.** ***Perf. 14x13½***

1300	A524 44c multi	1.25	.30

Perf. 13½x14

1301	A525 44c multi	1.25	.30

Perf. 13½x13, 13x13½

1302	Horiz. strip of 5	6.50	3.25
a.	A526 44c multi	1.25	.30
b.	A527 44c multi	1.25	.30
c.	A528 44c multi	1.25	.30
d.	A529 44c multi	1.25	.30
e.	A530 44c multi	1.25	.30

Issued: Nos. 1300-1301, 1/2; No. 1302, 3/18. The generic vignettes of Nos. 1300 (Netherlands Federation of Philatelic Associations, cent.), 1301 (Netherlands Association of Stamp Dealers, 80th anniv.), and 1302 (winning art for personalized stamp design contest), which sold for face value, are shown. These stamps, printed in sheets of 10, could be personalized for an additional fee. A booklet containing 5 panes of Nos. 1300-1301, each with different pane margins, sold for € 9.95. Other booklets containing panes of Nos. 1300 or 1301 with different vignettes exist. These booklets usually sold for €9.95, and may contain fewer than ten stamps.

Netherlands Tourism Areas — A531

2008 **Litho.** ***Perf. 14½x14¼***

1303	A531 44c Sneek	1.40	.35
1304	A531 44c Coevorden	1.40	.35
1305	A531 44c Heusden	1.40	.35
1306	A531 44c Amersfoort	1.40	.35
1307	A531 44c Zoetermeer	1.40	.35
a.	Souvenir sheet of 5, #1303-1307	7.00	3.50
	Nos. 1303-1307 (5)	7.00	1.75

Issued: Nos. 1303-1304, 3/25; Nos. 1305-1306, 4/22; No. 1307, 6/3; No. 1307a, 6/12. A booklet containing five panes, with each pane containing two perf. 13½x12¾ examples of each stamp, sold for €9.95.

Europa — A532

2008, May 20 **Litho.** ***Perf. 13½x12¾***

1308	A532 75c multi	2.40	.60
a.	Tete-beche pair	4.80	1.25

Sheet margins, inscribed "Priority," served as etiquettes.

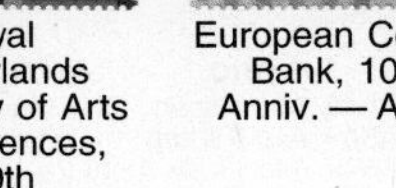

Royal Netherlands Academy of Arts and Sciences, 200th Anniv. — A533

European Central Bank, 10th Anniv. — A534

AEX Stock Index, 25th Anniv. — A535

Bruna Bookshop Chain, 140th Anniv. — A536

Royal Dutch Tourist Board, 125th Anniv. — A537

2008, May 20 ***Perf. 13¼x12¾***

1309	Vert. strip of 5	7.00	3.50
a.	A533 44c multi	1.40	.35
b.	A534 44c multi	1.40	.35
c.	A535 44c multi	1.40	.35
d.	A536 44c multi	1.40	.35
e.	A537 44c multi	1.40	.35

Souvenir Sheet

Rembrandt Association, 125th Anniv. — A538

2008, June 12 ***Perf. 13¾***

1310	A538 €6.65 multi	21.00	10.50

Dutch Food Products — A539

Designs: No. 1311, Container of adobo seasoning mix, Madame Jeannette peppers, Edam cheese. No. 1312, Peas, can of condensed milk, papaya, vert. No. 1313, Ham, plantain, bottle of Ponche Pistachio liqueur, vert.

2008, July 8 ***Perf. 13¾***

1311	A539 92c multi	3.00	.75
1312	A539 92c multi	3.00	.75
1313	A539 92c multi	3.00	.75
a.	Souvenir sheet of 5, #1311-1313, Aruba #330, Netherlands Antilles #1187, + 3 etiquettes, 144x75mm	9.00	4.50
b.	Booklet pane, as "a," 150x102mm	15.50	—
	Complete booklet, 2 #1313b	31.00	
	Nos. 1311-1313 (3)	9.00	2.25

No. 1313a sold for €2.76. Complete booklet sold for €9.95. Nos. 1312-1313 were available only in Nos. 1313a and 1313b. No. 1311 was available in Nos. 1313a, 1313b, Aruba No. 332a, and Netherlands Antilles No. 1189a.

Miniature Sheet

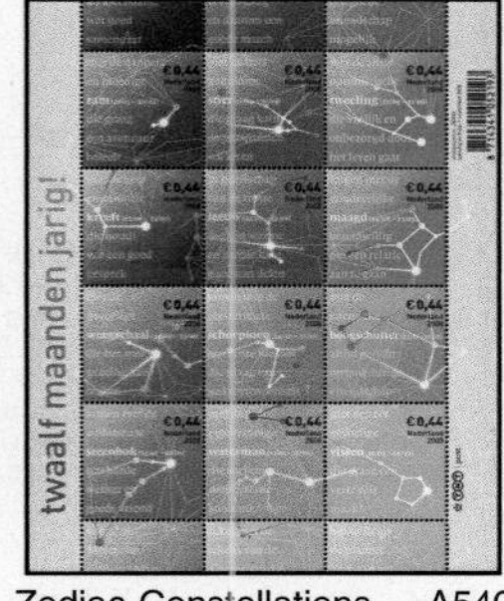

Zodiac Constellations — A540

No. 1314: a, Ram (Aries). b, Stier (Taurus). c, Tweeling (Gemini). d, Kreeft (Cancer). e, Leeuw (Leo). f, Maagd (Virgo). g, Weegschaal (Libra). h, Schorpioen (Scorpio). i, Boogschutter (Sagittarius). j, Steenbok (Capricorn). k, Waterman (Aquarius). l, Vissen (Pisces).

2008, Sept. 1 **Litho.** ***Perf. 13¾***

1314	A540 Sheet of 12	15.00	15.00
a.-l.	44c Any single	1.25	.30

Greeting Card Weeks — A541

2008, Sept. 1 ***Perf. 14½***

1315	A541 44c multi	1.25	.30

Printed in sheets of 3.

Gnomes — A542

Designs: No. 1316, Pinkeltje. No. 1317, Wipneus en Pim. No. 1318, Piggelmee. No. 1319, Paulus de boskabouter. No. 1320, De Kabouter.

2008, Oct. 1 ***Perf. 13½x12¾***

1316	A542 75c multi	2.10	.50
1317	A542 75c multi	2.10	.50
1318	A542 75c multi	2.10	.50
1319	A542 75c multi	2.10	.50
1320	A542 75c multi	2.10	.50
a.	Vert. strip of 5, #1316-1320	10.50	2.50

Nos. 1316-1320 were printed in sheets of 10, containing two of each stamp. The other strip in the sheet is in a different stamp order and the two strips in the sheet are tete-beche.

Miniature Sheet

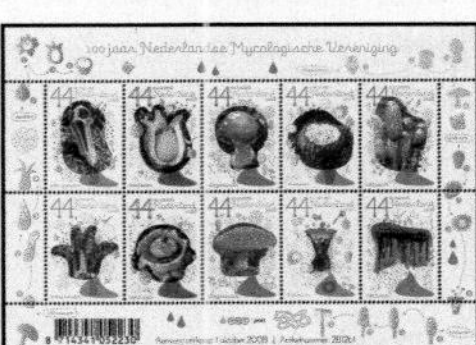

Mushrooms — A543

No. 1321 — Early and late stages of mushroom's life: a, Inktviszwam (early). b, Aardater (early). c, Vliegenzwam (early). d, Nestzwam (early). e, Inktzwam (early). f, Inktviszwam (late). g, Aardater (late). h, Vliegenzwam (late). i, Nestzwam (late). j, Inktzwam (late).

2008, Oct. 1 ***Perf. 14½***

1321	A543 Sheet of 10	12.50	12.50
a.-j.	44c Any single	1.25	.30

A booklet containing 5 panes, each showing a vertical pair from the sheet (same mushroom in different stages), sold for €9.95.

A544

December Stamps — A545

No. 1323: a, Building with large clock face and gift. b, Three dark envelopes, left half of Christmas tree. c, Right half of Christmas tree, top of ladder. d, Bell, Christmas tree. e, Building, gifts. f, Christmas tree, building with people on roof. g, Building, knife, fork and candle. h, House, bottom of ladder. i, Postcard, left side of fireplace. j, Right side of fireplace, fork and spoon.

Serpentine Die Cut 12

2008, Nov. 18 Self-Adhesive

1322 A544 34c multi .90 .25
1323 A545 Block of 10 9.00
a.-j. 34c Any single .90 .25

The vignette of No. 1322 could be personalized for a fee.

Ecology Types of 2008

Designs: 77c, Bicycle with globe hemispheres as wheels. 95c, Heart-shaped globe.

Serpentine Die Cut 11

2009, Jan. 2 Photo.

Booklet Stamps

Self-Adhesive

1324 A523 77c multi + etiquette 2.25 .55
a. Booklet pane of 5 11.50
1325 A523 95c multi + etiquette 2.75 .70
a. Booklet pane of 5 14.00

On Nos. 1324-1325 a row of microrouletting separates stamps from etiquettes.

Miniature Sheet

Braille Alphabet, 180th Anniv. — A546

No. 1326 — Letters (on front and back), and in Braille: a, Hulde roem mythe. b, Adres komst thuis. c, Uniek zelfs dank. d, Super zodra adieu. e, Hevig dwars naief. f, Moed extra kans. g, Begin marge exact. h, Afijn bekaf kus. i, Geluk wens bravo. j, Fabel credo liefs. k, Quasi niets ophef. l, Brief vurig hart.

Litho., Photo & Embossed

2009, Jan. 10 ***Perf. 13¾***

1326 A546 Sheet of 12 14.00 14.00
a.-l. 44c Any single 1.10 .30
m. Booklet pane of 3, #1326a-1326c 6.50 —
n. Booklet pane of 3, #1326d-1326f 6.50 —
o. Booklet pane of 3, #1326g-1326i 6.50 —
p. Booklet pane of 3, #1326j-1326l 6.50 —
Complete booklet, #1326m-13326p 26.00

Louis Braille (1809-52), educator of the blind. Complete booklet sold for €9.95.

A547

Personalized Stamps — A548

Serpentine Die Cut 12

2009, Mar. 10 Litho.

Self-Adhesive

1327 A547 44c multi 1.25 .30
1328 A548 44c multi 1.25 .30

The generic vignettes of Nos. 1327 (Dutch Golf Federation) and 1328 (Dutch Stamp Collectors' Association), which sold at face value, are shown. These stamps, printed in sheets of 10, could be personalized for an additional fee. See Nos. 1300-1301 for perforated stamps having these frames.

Netherlands Tourism Areas — A549

2009 Litho. ***Perf. 14½x14¼***

1329 A549 44c Assen 1.25 .30
1330 A549 44c Tilburg 1.25 .30
1331 A549 44c Oosterhout 1.25 .30
1332 A549 44c Roosendaal 1.25 .30
1333 A549 44c Delfzijl 1.25 .30
a. Souvenir sheet of 5, #1329-1333 6.25 3.25
Nos. 1329-1333 (5) 6.25 1.50

Issued: Nos. 1329-1330, 3/10; Nos. 1331-1332, 4/28; No. 1333, 6/16; No. 1333a, 6/12. A booklet containing five panes, with each pane containing two perf. 13½x12¾ examples of each stamp, sold for €9.95.

Europa A550

Designs: No. 1334, Map of low frequency array radio telescopes superimposed on map of Europe. No. 1335, Sketch of Saturn and Titan, telescope lens of Christiaan Huygens.

2009, Apr. 7 Litho. ***Perf. 13¼x12¾***

1334 77c multi 2.10 .50
1335 77c multi 2.10 .50
a. A550 Horiz. pair, #1334-1335 4.20 1.00

Intl. Year of Astronomy. Sheet margins serve as etiquettes. No. 1335 is upside-down in relation to No. 1334.

Souvenir Sheet

Queens Wilhelmina, Juliana and Beatrix — A551

Litho. & Engr.

2009, Apr. 28 ***Perf. 13¾***

1336 A551 €7 multi 19.00 9.50
a. Booklet pane of 1 27.00 —
Complete booklet, #1336a 27.00

Size of No. 1336a: 145x102mm. Complete booklet sold for €9.95.

Flasks, Artist's Mannequin, Party Streamer A552

Window, Egg, Binoculars A553

Atlas Sheltering Figurines — A554

Coffee Service — A555

Blocks, Pictures of Children — A556

2009, May 12 Photo. ***Perf. 14½***

1337 Vert. strip of 5 6.25 3.25
a. A552 44c multi 1.25 .30
b. A553 44c multi 1.25 .30
c. A554 44c multi 1.25 .30
d. A555 44c multi 1.25 .30
e. A556 44c multi 1.25 .30

Dutch Cancer Society, 60th anniv. (No. 1337a); Netherlands Bird Protection Society, 110th anniv. (No. 1337b); Cordaid Mensen in Nood (Men in Need), 95th anniv. (No. 1337c); National Sunflower Society, 60th anniv. (No. 1337d); SOS Children's Village, 60th anniv. (No. 1337e).

Music A557

No. 1338: a, Tuba, trumpet and saxophone players. b, "When you sing you begin with Do Re Mi." c, Baton twirlers. d, "Jauchzet, frohlocket." e, Sousaphone players. f, "Para bailar la bamba."

2009, July 14 Litho. ***Perf. 13½***

1338 A557 Block of 6 13.50 6.75
a.-f. 77c Any single 2.25 .60

World Music Contest, Kerkrade and Europa Cantat, Utrecht. Printed in sheets of 10 containing Nos. 1338e, 1338f, and 2 each Nos. 1338a-1338d. Sheet margins served as etiquettes. Stamps showing text are upside-down in relation to stamps showing people.

Miniature Sheet

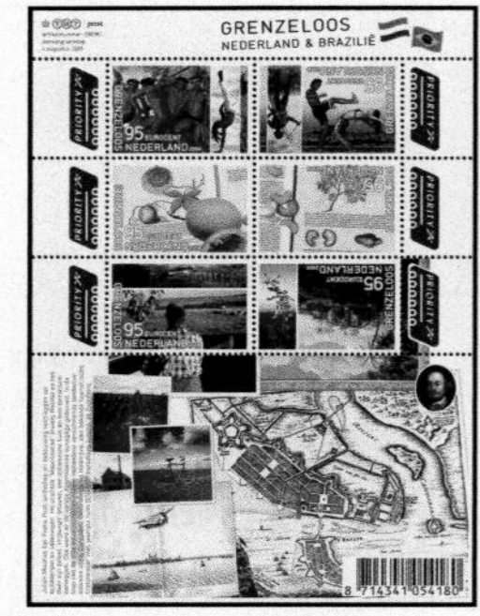

Dutch Connections With Brazil — A558

No. 1339: a, Tarairu Tribe War Dance, painting by Albert Eckhout, man standing on one hand. b, Capoeira performers, Tarairu tribesman. c, Passion fruit, and scientific book picturing passion fruit blossom. d, Cashews and scientific book picturing cashew tree. e, Sugar Plantation, painting by Frans Post; farmer looking at livestock. f, Church, Olinda, painting by Post; rose bush.

2009, Aug. 4 ***Perf. 13½x12¾***

1339 A558 Sheet of 6 16.50 8.25
a.-f. 95c Any single 2.75 .70

No. 1339 was printed with three different illustrations in the bottom sheet margin, with each sheet having a different arrangement of stamps. Sheet margins at left and right served as etiquettes.

Athletes and Their Mentors — A559

No. 1340: a, Anthony van Assche, gymnast, and mentor Jochem Uytdehaage. b, Leon Commandeur, cyclist, and mentor Johan Kenkhuis. c, Mike Marissen, swimmer, and mentor Bas van de Goor. d, Maureen Groefsema, judoist, and mentor Lobke Berkhout. e, Aniek van Koot, wheelchair tennis player, and mentor Marko Koers.

2009, Aug. 25 Photo. ***Perf. 14½***

1340 Vert. strip of 5 6.25 3.25
a.-e. A559 44c Any single 1.25 .30

Stichting Sporttop, Olympic athlete development organization.

Greeting Card Week — A560

2009, Sept. 7 Litho. ***Perf. 14½***

1341 A560 44c multi 1.40 .35

Miniature Sheets

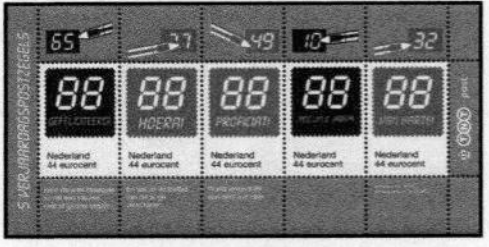

Birthday Greetings — A561

"88" and: Nos. 1342a, 1343e, "Gefeliciteerd!" Nos. 1342b, 1343b, "Hoera!" Nos. 1342c, 1343c, "Proficiat!" Nos. 1342d, 1343d, "Nog Vele Jaren!" Nos. 1342e, 1343a, "Van Harte!"

2009, Sept. 22 Litho. ***Perf. 13½***

1342 A561 Sheet of 5 7.00 3.50
a.-e. 44c Any single 1.40 .35

Self-Adhesive

Serpentine Die Cut 13¼x13

Stamp Size: 20x25mm

1343 A561 Sheet of 5 7.00
a.-e. 44c Any single 1.40 .35

Lines in the "88" on each stamp could be colored in to create all ten digits. Unused values are for stamps without any such alterations. Used values are for stamps with or without alterations.

A562

Personalized Stamps — A563

2009-10 ***Perf. 13¼***

1344 A562 44c multi 1.40 .35

Self-Adhesive

Serpentine Die Cut 12½

1345 A563 44c multi 1.25 .30

Issued: No. 1344, 10/1; No. 1345, 1/12/10. The generic vignettes for Nos. 1344 (Stamp Day) and 1345 (Wadden Sea Society), which sold at face value, are shown. These stamps, printed in sheets of 10, could be personalized for an additional fee. A booklet containing five panes, each with two examples of No. 1344 with the Stamp Day vignette sold for €9.95.

Miniature Sheet

Powered Flight in the Netherlands, Cent. — A564

No. 1346: a, Medical helicopter. b, Boeing 747. c, Apache helicopter. d, Terminal B, Schiphol Airport. e, Fokker F-27. f, Lockheed Super Constellation. g, Fokker F-18 "Pelikaan." h, Douglas DC-2 "Uiver" in Melbourne race. i, Wright Flyer. j, Fokker Spin, piloted by Anthony Fokker.

2009, Oct. 1 ***Perf. 13½***

1346	A564	Sheet of 10	14.00	7.00
a.-j.		44c Any single	1.40	.35

A booklet containing five panes, each with a different horizontal pair from No. 1346, sold for €9.95.

December Stamps — A565

No. 1347: a, Green gift, pink ribbon, red background. b, Candelabra on yellow gift, blue background. c, Christmas tree on light blue gift, bright yellow green background. d, Light pink gift, red ribbon, gray background. e, Woman holding glass on yellow gift, pink background. f, Man holding glass on yellow gift, gray background. g, Christmas tree on blue gift, pink background. h, Red violet gift, red ribbon, carmine background. i, Christmas tree on yellow gift, blue background. j, Christmas tree on blue gift, red background.

Serpentine Die Cut 12¾x13¼

2009, Nov. 19 **Self-Adhesive**

1347		Block of 10	10.00	
a.-j.	A565	34c Any single	1.00	.25

Netherlands Tourism Areas — A566

2010 **Litho.** ***Perf. 14½x14¼***

1348	A566	44c Haarlem	1.25	.35
1349	A566	44c Middelburg	1.25	.35
1350	A566	44c Maastricht	1.25	.35
1351	A566	44c Arnhem	1.25	.35
1352	A566	44c Leeuwarden	1.10	.30
a.		Souvenir sheet of 5, #1348-1352	6.25	3.25

Issued: Nos. 1348-1349, 1/12. Nos. 1350-1351, 3/29; Nos. 1352, 1352a, 6/22. A booklet containing five panes, with each pane containing two perf. 13½x12¾ examples of each stamp, sold for €9.95.

Miniature Sheet

Dutch Patent Act, Cent. A567

No. 1353: a, Submarine invented by Cornelis Drebbel, 1620. b, Light-emitting diode lighting invented by Philips, 2007. c, Artificial kidney invented by Willem Kolff, 1943. d, VacuVin vacuum sealer for wine bottles invented by Bernd Schneider. e, Milking robot invented by Van der Lely, 1987. f, Bicycle chain case invented by Wilhelmine J. van der Woerd. g, Automated handwriting recognition invented by TNT Post, 1980. h, Solar-powered vehicle invented by Solar Team Twente. i, Dyneema fiber invented by DSM, 1979. j, Telescope invented by Hans Lippershey, 1608.

2010, Feb. 9 **Litho.** ***Perf. 13¼x12¾***

1353	A567	Sheet of 10	12.50	6.25
a.-j.		44c Any single	1.25	.35

A booklet containing five panes, with each pane containing a horizontal pair from the sheet, sold for €9.95.

75th Book Week — A568

2010, Mar. 9 **Litho.** ***Imperf.***

1354	A568	€2.20 multi	6.00	3.00

No. 1354 is printed as a miniature book made up of two pieces of paper of different sizes. Both pieces of paper are printed on both sides, and are glued together. The cover of the book is the longer of the two pieces of paper, and is folded into three parts. The stamp, the front cover of the book, is the middle part of this piece of paper. The gum, applied to the left of the stamp, becomes the book's back cover when the longer piece of paper is folded. A photograph of a man holding a book, is to the right of the stamp, and is the book's first page. Text appears on the reverse of this picture and the stamp, and another picture depicting a man reading a book is printed on the back of the gum. The second piece of paper, folded in half to constitute four pages of the book, has text only, and is glued to the back of longer sheet where the fold between the stamp and the photo is found. Values are for the complete item.

VVV, Dutch Tourist Information Office, 125th Anniv. — A569

Royal Tropical Institute, Cent. — A570

Duinrell Amusement Park, Wassenaar, 75th Anniv. — A571

Euromast Tower, Rotterdam, 50th Anniv. — A572

Djoser Travel, 25th Anniv. — A573

2010, Mar. 23 **Photo.** ***Perf. 14½***

1355		Vert. strip of 5	6.25	3.25
a.	A569	44c multi	1.25	.35
b.	A570	44c multi	1.25	.35
c.	A571	44c multi	1.25	.35
d.	A572	44c multi	1.25	.35
e.	A573	44c multi	1.25	.35

Greeting Card Weeks — A574

2010, Mar. 29 **Litho.**

1356	A574	44c multi	1.25	.35

Printed in sheets of 3.

Souvenir Sheet

Breskens Lighthouse — A575

2010, Apr. 27 ***Perf. 13¾***

1357	A575	€7 multi	19.00	9.50

Personalized Stamp — A576

2010, July 1 **Litho.** ***Perf. 13½x14***

1358	A576	1 gray & black	1.10	.30

The generic vignette of No. 1358, which sold for the franking value of 44c, and was printed in sheets of 10, is shown. The vignette part of the stamp could be personalized for an additional fee. Booklets containing stamps showing different vignettes that could not be personalized sold for €9.95.

Rectangles — A577

2010, July 1 ***Die Cut Perf. 14¼***

Self-Adhesive

1359	A577	1 multi	1.10	.30

Sold for 44c on day of issue. Compare with type A456.

Birth Announcement Stamp — A578

2010, July 1 ***Die Cut Perf. 14¼***

Self-Adhesive

1360	A578	1 multi	1.10	.30

Sold for 44c on day of issue.

Hearts — A579

2010, July 1 ***Die Cut Perf. 14¼***

Self-Adhesive

1361	A579	1 multi	1.10	.30
a.		Booklet pane of 10	11.00	

Sold for 44c on day of issue. Compare with type A466.

Death Announcement Stamp — A580

Serpentine Die Cut 11¾

2010, July 1 **Photo.**

Self-Adhesive

1362	A580	1 multi	1.10	.30

Sold for 44c on day of issue. Compare with types A365 and A824.

Numerals
A581 A582

Serpentine Die Cut 13½

2010, July 1 **Litho.**

Self-Adhesive

1363	A581	1 multi + label	1.10	.30

Coil Stamps

Photo.

Die Cut Perf. 14¼

1364	A581	1 multi	1.10	.30
1365	A582	2 multi	2.25	.60

On day of issue Nos. 1363-1364 each sold for 44c, and No. 1365 sold for 88c. Label on No. 1363 could be personalized. Compare with type A491.

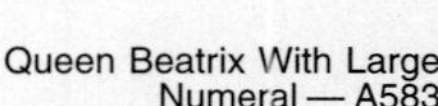

Queen Beatrix With Large Numeral — A583

Die Cut Perf. 14¼ Syncopated

2010, July 1 **Photo.**

Booklet Stamps

Self-Adhesive

1366	A583	1 metallic blue & lil	1.10	.30
a.		Booklet pane of 10	11.00	

Die Cut Perf. 14¼

1367	A583	2 gold & metallic grn	2.25	.60
a.		Booklet pane of 5	11.50	

On day of issue, No. 1366 sold for 44c and No. 1367 sold for 88c. Compare with Type A273.

A584

A585

Ecology — A586

No. 1368: a, Hybrid vehicle with electric plug. b, House and sun (solar energy). c, Cow with electric plug (biofuels). d, Wind generators. e, Trees. f, Flowers, carpoolers in automobile. g, "Groen" with electric plug. h, Truck (soot filters). i, Birds and envelope (green mail). j, Insulated house.

Die Cut Perf. 14¼

2010, July 1 **Litho.**

Booklet Stamps

Self-Adhesive

1368		Booklet pane of 10	11.00	
a.-j.	A584	1 Any single	1.10	.30

Photo.

Serpentine Die Cut 11

1369	A585	1 Europa multi + etiquette	2.00	.50
a.		Booklet pane of 5 + 5 etiquettes	10.00	
1370	A586	1 Wereld multi + etiquette	2.40	.60
a.		Booklet pane of 5 + 5 etiquettes	12.00	

On Nos. 1369-1370 a row of microrouletting separates stamps from etiquettes. On day of issue, Nos. 1368a-1368j each sold for 44c; No. 1369, for 77c; No. 1370, for 95c. Compare with type A523.

Miniature Sheet

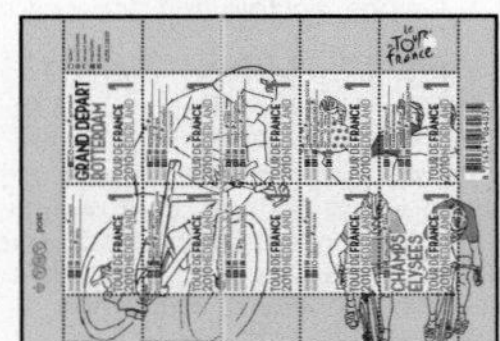
Start of 2010 Tour de France in Rotterdam — A587

No. 1371 — Dates and stages of the Tour de France: a, July 3 (preliminary stage). b, July 4-6 (stages 1-3). c, July 7-9 (stages 4-6). d, July 10-12 (stages 7-8). e, July 13-15 (stages 9-11). f, July 16-17 (stages 12-13). g, July 18-19 (stages 14-15). h, July 20-22 (stages 16-17). i, July 23-24 (stages 18-19). j, July 25 (stage 20).

2010, July 1 **Photo.** ***Perf. 14½***

1371	A587	Sheet of 10	11.00	5.50
a.-j.		1 Any single	1.10	.30

On day of issue, Nos. 1371a-1371j each sold for 44c.

Miniature Sheet

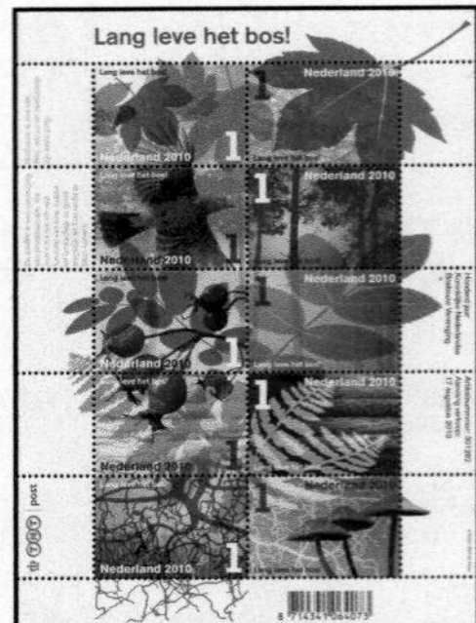

Royal Dutch Forestry Association, Cent. — A588

No. 1372: a, Maple leaves, forest canopy, tip of jay's wing, "1" in white at LR. b, Maple leaves, forest canopy, "1" in brown at UL. c, Jay, forest canopy, "1" in brown at LR. d, Forest canopy, rose leaves, "1" in white at UL. e, Rose hips and leaves, "1" in white at LR. f, Rose leaves, tree trunks, "1" in brown at UL. g, Rose hips, logs, bracken leaves, "1" in brown at LR. h, Bracken leaves, logs, "1" in white at UL. i, Tree roots, moss, "1" in white at LR. j, Tree roots, mushrooms, "1" in brown at UL.

Perf. 13¼x12¾

2010, Aug. 17 **Litho.**

1372 A588 Sheet of 10 12.50 6.25
a.-j. 1 Any single 1.25 .35

On day of issue, Nos. 1372a-1372j each sold for 44c. A booklet containing five panes, each showing a horizontal pair from the sheet, sold for €9.95.

Miniature Sheet

Dutch Connections With Surinam — A589

No. 1373: a, Building with balconies and dormers, lamp. b, Building with stairway, hand rail. c, Women in native dress. d, Two women, one upside-down. e, Wood, feathers, achiote seeds. f, Onions, achiote fruit, tobacco.

2010, Aug. 17 **Litho.** ***Perf. 13½x13***

1373 A589 Sheet of 6 15.00 7.50
a.-f. 1 Wereld Any single 2.50 .65

No. 1373 was printed with three different illustrations in the bottom sheet margin, with each sheet having a different arrangement of stamps. Sheet margins at left and right served as etiquettes. On day of issue Nos. 1373a-1373f each sold for 95c.

Personalized Stamp — A590

2010, Sept. 14 **Litho.** ***Perf. 13½x14***

1374 A590 1 multi 1.25 .35

The generic vignette shown on this stamp, commemorating Stamp Day, sold for 44c on day of issue. This stamp, printed in sheets of 10, could be personalized for an additional fee. A booklet containing five panes, each with two examples of No. 1374 with the generic vignette, sold for €9.95.

Woman and Windmill A591

Litho. With 3-Dimensional Plastic Affixed

Serpentine Die Cut 9x8¾

2010, Sept. 29 **Self-Adhesive**

1375 A591 5 multi 6.25 1.60

Sold for €2.20 on day of issue.

Stop AIDS Campaign — A592

No. 1376: a, African woman with "Stop AIDS Now!" poster on head. b, African woman, ribbon. c, Hand holding pill, ribbon. d, African woman pointing to ribbon. e, Ribbon, heads of African man and woman. f, African woman wearing headdress.

2010, Oct. 12 **Litho.** ***Perf. 14½***

1376 A592 Block of 6 7.50 3.75
a.-f. 1 Any single 1.25 .35

Nos. 1376a-1376f each sold for 44c on day of issue.

Personalized Stamp — A593

2010, Nov. 23 **Litho.** ***Perf. 13½x14***

1377 A593 (34c) multi .95 .25

The generic vignette shown on this stamp depicts Snoopy. This stamp, printed in sheets of 10, could be personalized for an additional fee.

December Stamps — A594

No. 1378: a, Santa Claus carrying tree. b, Bell and ribbon. c, Rocking horse and flowers. d, Embroidered heart. e, Deer, flower and candle on Christmas card. f, Deer and ribbon. g, Santa Claus. h, Handshake and flowers on Christmas card. i, Angel with flowers. j, Gingerbread house.

Serpentine Die Cut 12¾

2010, Nov. 23 **Self-Adhesive**

1378 Block of 10 9.50
a.-j. A594 (34c) Any single .95 .25
k. Booklet pane of 10, #1378a-1378j 13.50
Complete booklet, 2 #1378k 27.00

Complete booklet sold for €9.95.

Personalized Stamp — A595

Die Cut Perf. 13x13¼

2011, Jan. 10 **Litho.**

Self-Adhesive

1379 A595 1 black 1.25 .35

The generic vignette of No. 1379 depicting St. John's Cathedral, 's Hertogenbosch, which sold for the franking value of 46c and printed in sheets of 10, is shown. The vignette part of the stamp could be personalized for an additional fee.

Netherlands Tourism Areas — A596

2011 ***Perf. 14½x14¼***

1380 A596 1 Almere 1.25 .35
1381 A596 1 Eindhoven 1.25 .35
1382 A596 1 Apeldoorn 1.40 .45
1383 A596 1 Breda 1.40 .45
1384 A596 1 Enschede 1.40 .45
a. Souvenir sheet of 5, #1380-1384 6.75 3.50
Nos. 1380-1384 (5) 6.70 2.05

Issued: Nos. 1380-1381, 1/10; Nos. 1382-1383, 4/11; Nos. 1384, 1384a, 5/23. On day of issue, Nos, 1380-1384 each sold for 46c. A booklet containing five panes, with each pane containing two perf. 13½x12¾ examples of each stamp, sold for €9.95.

Personalized Stamp — A597

2011, Jan. 31 ***Perf. 13¾***

1385 A597 1 multi 1.25 .35

The generic vignette of No. 1385 depicting a great tit, which sold for the franking value of 46c and printed in sheets of 10, is shown. The vignette part of the stamp could be personalized for an additional fee. Numerous stamps depicting different birds in the vignette were created after Jan. 31 by postal authorities. An electronic audio pen which sold for €39.95 would play the song of the bird when placed near the stamp. Numerous stamps depicting recording artists in the vignette began appearing in 2012.

Miniature Sheet

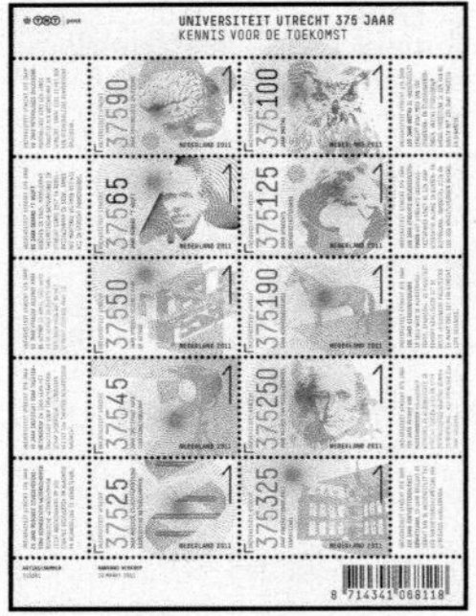

Utrecht University, 375th Anniv. — A598

No. 1386 — Various anniversaries at Utrecht University: a, 90th anniv. of psychology studies (brain). b, 100th anniv. of Unitas Student Society (owl). c, 65th birthday of Gerard t'Hooft. 1999 Nobel Physics laureate (t'Hooft). d, 125th anniv. of Utrecht University Foundation (globe). e, 50th anniv. of Utrecht Science Park de Uithof (aerial view of park). f, 190th anniv. of veterinary medicine program (horse). g, 45th anniv. of Institute of Theater Studies (theater spotlight). h, 250th anniv. of death of Petrus van Musschenbroek, professor of mathematics and philosophy (van Musschenbroek). i, 25th anniv. of Mebiose Student Association for the Biological Sciences (stylized DNA molecule). j, 325th anniv. of Senaatzaal Portrait Gallery (Senaatzaal).

2011, Mar. 28 ***Perf. 13¼x12¾***

1386 A598 Sheet of 10 14.00 7.00
a.-j. 1 Any single 1.40 .45

Nos. 1386a-1386j each sold for 46c on day of issue. A booklet containing 5 panes, each containing a horizontal pair of stamps on the sheet, sold for €9.95.

Miniature Sheet

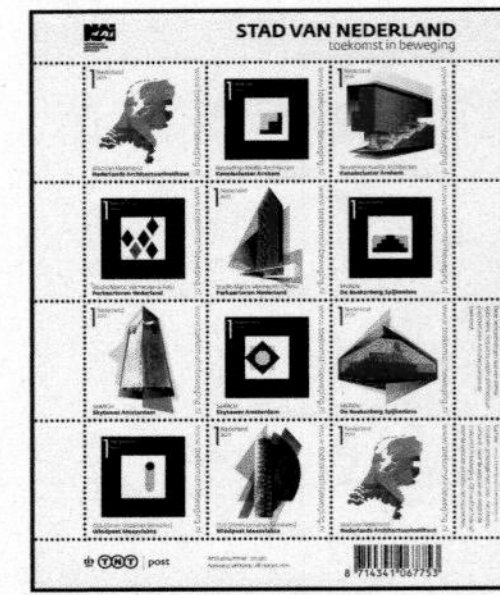

City of the Netherlands — A599

No. 1387 — Inscriptions in bold type: a, Kenniscluster, Arnhem (black-framed code box). b, Kenniscluster, Arnhem (building). c, Parkeertoren Nederland (black-framed code box). d, Parkeertoren Nederland (building). e, De Boekenberg, Spijkenisse (black-framed code box). f, Skytower, Amsterdam (building). g, Skytower, Amsterdam (black-framed code box). h, De Boekenberg, Spijkenisse (building). i, Windpost, Maasvlakte (black-framed code box). j, Windpost, Maasvlakte (building). k, Map of the Netherlands.

2011, Mar. 28 ***Perf. 13¼***

1387 A599 Sheet of 12, #1387a-1387j, 2 #1387k 17.00 8.50

On day of issue, Nos. 1387a-1387k each sold for 46c. The code boxes activate an augmented reality application when scanned by a webcam when visting the www.toekomstinbeweging.nl website.

Greeting Card Week — A600

2011, Apr. 18 ***Perf. 14½***

1388 A600 1 multi 1.40 .45

No. 1388 sold for 46c on day of issue. Printed in sheets of 3.

Organization for Economic Cooperation and Development, 50th Anniv. — A601

Royal Dutch Billiards Federation, Cent. — A602

Royal Dutch Checkers Federation, Cent. — A603

Loevenstein Castle, 650th Anniv. — A604

Association of Dutch Composers, Cent. — A605

2011, May 2 ***Perf. 13¼x12¾***

1389 Vert. strip of 5 7.00 3.50
a. A601 1 multi 1.40 .45
b. A602 1 multi 1.40 .45
c. A603 1 multi 1.40 .45
d. A604 1 multi 1.40 .45
e. A605 1 multi 1.40 .45

Nos. 1389a-1389e each sold for 46c on day of issue.

Miniature Sheet

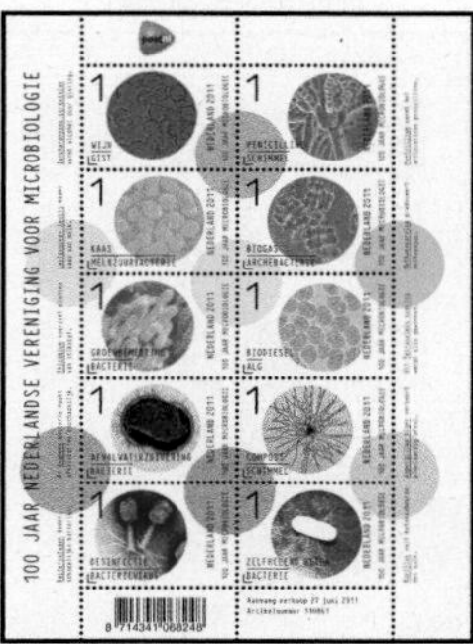

Netherlands Society for Microbiology, Cent. — A606

No. 1390 — Various microorganisms and inscription: a, Wijn / Gist (wine / yeast). b, Penicilline / Schimmel (penicillin / mold). c, Kaas / Melkzuurbacterie (cheese / lactic bacteria). d, Biogas / Archebacterie (biogas / archaea). e, Groenbemesting / Bacterie (green manure / bacteria). f, Biodiesel / Alg. (biodiesel / algae). g, Afvalwaterzuivering / Bacterie (waste water purification / bacteria). h, Compost / Schimmel (compost / mold). i, Desinfectie / Bacterievirus (disinfectant / bacteriophage). j, Zelfhelend beton / bacterie (self-curing concrete / bacteria).

2011, May 27

1390	A606	Sheet of 10	14.00	7.00
a.-j.		1 Any single	1.40	.45

Nos. 1390a-1390j each sold for 46c on day of issue. A booklet containing 5 panes, each containing a horizontal pair of stamps on the sheet, sold for €9.95.

Initial Public Offering of Royal Post NL Stock — A607

2011, May 31 **Litho.**

1391	A607	1 multi	1.40	.45

No. 1391 sold for 46c on day of issue.

Miniature Sheet

Dutch Connections With South Africa — A608

No. 1392: a, Dutch-style South African houses in elephant (olifant). b, Poem by Ingrid Jonker in leopard (luipaard). c, Grapes in buffalo (buffel). d, South African house in rhinoceros (neushoorn). e, Painting of Jan van Riebeeck arriving at Cape of Good Hope in lion (leeuw). f, Dutch East India Company pottery in penguin (pinguin).

2011, July 25 ***Perf. 13¼x12¾***

1392	A608	Sheet of 6	16.50	8.25
a.-f.		1 Wereld Any single	2.75	.85

No. 1392 was printed with three different illustrations in the bottom sheet margin, with each sheet having a different arrangement of stamps. Sheet margins at left and right served as etiquettes. On day of issue Nos. 1392a-1392f each sold for 95c.

De Bond Heemschut Historical Preservation Society, Cent. — A609

No. 1393: a, American Embassy, The Hague. b, Amerongen Castle. c, Tricot factory, Winterswijk. d, Noord-Zuid-Hollands Coffee House, Amsterdam. e, St. Servatius Bridge, Maastricht. f, Synagogue, Groningen.

2011, Aug. 22 ***Perf. 13¼x12¾***

1393	A609	Block of 6	7.50	3.75
a.-f.		1 Any single	1.25	.35

Nos. 1393a-1393f each sold for 46c on day of issue.

A610

A611

Ecology — A612

No. 1394: a, Shirt on clothesline. b, Stylized plant. c, Bird. d, Hen. e, Kites. f, House. g, Laptop computer. h, Suitcase and leaf, horiz. i, Butterfly, horiz. j, Electric vehicle and plug, horiz.

Die Cut Perf. 14¼

2011, Sept. 1 **Litho.**

Booklet Stamps
Self-Adhesive

1394		Booklet pane of 10	12.50	
a.-j.	A610	1 Any single	1.25	.35

Photo.

Serpentine Die Cut 11

1395	A611	1 Europa multi + etiquette	2.25	.60
a.		Booklet pane of 5	11.50	
1396	A612	1 Wereld multi + etiquette	2.60	.80
a.		Booklet pane of 5	13.00	

On Nos. 1395-1396 a row of microrouletting separates stamps from etiquettes. On day of issue, Nos. 1394a-1394j each sold for 46c,; No. 139, for 79c; No. 1396, for 95c.

Miniature Sheet

Herman Renz Circus, Cent. A613

No. 1397: a, Fire eater. b, Snake handler. c, Clown. d, Trained horse. e, Man balancing hat on nose. f, Tumbling act. g, Lion. h, Acrobat lifting another acrobat. i, Elephant. j, Unicyclist on tightrope.

Perf. 12¾x13¼

2011, Sept. 19 **Litho.**

1397	A613	Sheet of 10	12.50	6.25
a.-j.	A613	1 Any single	1.25	.30

On day of issue, Nos. 1397a-1397j each sold for 46c.

Queen Wilhelmina (1880-1962) — A614

2011, Oct. 14 ***Perf. 13¼x13½***

1398	A614	1 multi	1.25	.30

Stamp Day. No. 1398 sold for 46c on day of issue. A booklet containing five panes, each containing two No. 1398, sold for €9.95.

Postcrossing.com — A615

No. 1399 — Postcards depicting: a, Sunset, man and woman kissing under umbrella, donkey and house, puppies, nesting dolls, Eiffel Tower, Asian woman, beach in Rio. b, Baby surrounded by sunflower petals, sheep, beach, bull fight, Sphinx and Pyramid, Cuban car, building in Finland. c, Bridge, fish and coral, building in Antwerp, Belgium, Taj Mahal, Asian woman, soccer players, tower and Arabic text. d, Flamingo in Miami, beach in Rio, Petronas Towers, Kuala Lumpur, Acropolis, buildings in Warsaw, Big Ben and statue, London, woman, and China Central Television Building, Beijing. e, Boat and building in Finland, Prague and Hradcany Castle, tulips, chimpanzee wearing cowboy hat, Hong Kong skyline, Asian woman, bird, comic strip. f, Cat, windmill and tulips, Netherlands, Cliffs of Moher, Ireland, Calgary skyline, churches, St. Petersburg, Russia, Great Wall of China, woman praying, two boys.

2011, Oct. 14 ***Perf. 13¼x12¾***

1399	A615	Block of 6 + 6 etiquettes	15.00	7.50
a.-c.		1 Europa Any single	2.25	.60
d.-f.		1 Wereld Any single	2.60	.80

On day of issue Nos. 1399a-1399c each sold for 79c, and Nos. 1399d-1399f each sold for 95c.

December Stamps — A616

No. 1400: a, Candle. b, Reindeer, bird and fir trees. c, Bird on heart. d, Three Christmas ornaments. e, Church and houses. f, Reindeer with Christmas ornament, birds and candles on antlers. g, Angel with candles. h, Bird, holding Christmas ornament on fir branch. i, Snowman. j, Squirrel and Christmas ornament.

Serpentine Die Cut 12½

2011, Nov. 22 **Litho.**

Self-Adhesive

1400		Block of 10	10.00	
a.-j.	A616	(36c) Any single	1.00	.30

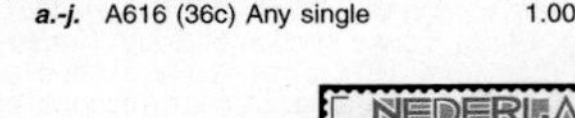

Personalized Stamp — A617

2011, Nov. 22 ***Die Cut Perf. 13x13¼***

Self-Adhesive

1401	A617	(36c) multi	1.00	.30

The generic vignette shown on this stamp depicts two birds under mistletoe. This stamp could be personalized for an additional fee.

A618

Personalized Stamps — A619

2012, Jan. 2 **Litho.** ***Perf. 13½x14***

1402	A618	1 Europa black	2.25	.55
1403	A619	1 Wereld black	2.50	.65

The generic vignettes of Nos. 1402 and 1403, which are shown, sold for the franking value of 85c and 95c, respectively. Nos. 1402 and 1403 each were printed in sheets of 10. The vignette parts of the stamp could be personalized for an additional fee.

Country Houses — A620

Country houses in: No. 1404, Mattemburgh. No. 1405, Amstenrade. No. 1406, Trompenburg. No. 1407, Vollenhoven. No. 1408, Middachten.

2012 ***Perf. 14½x14¼***

1404	A620	1 multi	1.40	.35
a.		Perf. 13½x12¾	2.50	2.50
b.		Booklet pane of 2 #1404a	5.00	5.00
1405	A620	1 multi	1.40	.35
a.		Perf. 13½x12¾	2.50	2.50
b.		Booklet pane of 2 #1405a	5.00	5.00
1406	A620	1 multi	1.40	.35
a.		Perf. 13½x12¾	2.50	2.50
b.		Booklet pane of 2 #1406a	5.00	5.00
1407	A620	1 multi	1.40	.35
a.		Perf. 13½x12¾	2.50	2.50
b.		Booklet pane of 2 #1407a	5.00	5.00
1408	A620	1 multi	1.25	.35
a.		Perf. 13½x12¾	2.50	2.50
b.		Booklet pane of 2 #1408a	5.00	5.00
		Complete booklet, #1404b, 1405b, 1406b, 1407b, 1408b	25.00	
c.		Souvenir sheet of 5, #1404-1408	7.00	3.50
		Nos. 1404-1408 (5)	6.85	1.75

Issued: Nos. 1404-1405, 1/30; Nos. 1406-1407, 2/27; Nos. 1404a, 1404b, 1405a, 1405b, 1406a, 1406b, 1407a, 1407b, 1408, 1408a, 1408b, 1408c, 5/21. Nos. 1404-1408 each sold for 50c on day of issue. Complete booklet sold for €9.95 on day of issue.

Dutch Salvation Army, 125th Anniv. — A621

2012, Feb. 27 ***Perf. 13¼x13½***

1409	A621	1 multi	1.40	.35

No. 1409 sold for 50c on day of issue.

Albert Heijn Grocery Stores, 125th Anniv. — A622

Designs: No. 1410, Original store, employee with first delivery bicycle. No. 1411, Coffee beans, coffee plant workers. No. 1412, Hamster, shoppers in grocery store. No. 1413, Shopper with child in shopping cart, store employees.

Serpentine Die Cut 13¼x13

2012, Feb. 27 **Self-Adhesive**

1410	A622	1 multi	1.40	.35
1411	A622	1 multi	1.40	.35
1412	A622	1 multi	1.40	.35
1413	A622	1 multi	1.40	.35
		Nos. 1410-1413 (4)	5.60	1.40

Nos. 1410-1413 each sold for 50c on day of issue.

Greeting Card Week — A623

2012, Mar. 26 ***Perf. 13¼x13½***

1414	A623 1 multi		1.40	.35

No. 1414 sold for 50c on day of issue. Printed in sheets of 3.

A624

Tourism A625

No. 1415: a, National Maritime Museum, Dutch East Indiaman "The Amsterdam," country name in white. b, Muziekgebouw Concert Hall, cruise ship "MSC Lirica," country name in gold.

No. 1416: a, The Bend in the Herengracht Canal, painting by Gerrit Berckheyde, country name in white. b, Skinny Bridge over Amstel River, country name in gold.

2012, Mar. 26 **Litho.**

1415	A624	Horiz. pair	2.80	1.40
a.-b.		1 Either single	1.40	.35
1416	A625	Pair	4.50	2.25
a.-b.		1 Europa Either single	2.25	.60

Europa (#1416b). On day of issue, Nos. 1415a-1415b each sold for 50c and Nos. 1416a-1416b each sold for 85c.

Netherlands Open Air Museum, Cent. — A626

Historical photographs: Nos. 1417a, 1417k, Women cleaning (green, at left), Marketplace (black, at right). Nos. 1417b, 1417l, Marketplace (black, at left). Woman sewing (purple, at right). Nos. 1417c, 1417m, Children with smartphone (rose, at left), Children crossing street (blue, at right). Nos. 1417d, 1417n, Children crossing street (blue, at left), Children playing (black, at right). Nos. 1417e, 1417o, Cots and worker at migrant worker's lodging (blue, at left), Sod hut (purple at right). Nos. 1417f, 1417p, Sod hut (purple, at left), Children watching television (rose, at right). Nos. 1417g, 1417q, Campers and van (purple, at left), Children with tablet and camp light (green, at right). Nos. 1417h, 1417r, Children with tablet and camp light (green, at left), Hockey players at Netherlands Open Air Museum (blue, at right). Nos. 1417i, 1417s, People boarding airplane at Schiphol Airport (black, at left), Car at gas station (rose, at right). Nos. 1417j, 1417t, Car at gas station (rose, at left), Hay cart (green, at right).

2012, Apr. 23 ***Perf. 13¼x12¾***

1417	A626	Sheet of 10	14.00	7.00
a.-j.		1 Any single	1.40	.35
k.-t.		Any single, perf. 14½	2.60	2.60
u.		Booklet pane of 2, #1417k-1417l	5.25	—
v.		Booklet pane of 2, #1417m-1417n	5.25	—
w.		Booklet pane of 2, #1417o-1417p	5.25	—
x.		Booklet pane of 2, #1417q-1417r	5.25	—
y.		Booklet pane of 2, #1417s-1417t	5.25	—
		Complete booklet, #1417u, 1417v, 1417w, 1417x, 1417y	26.50	

Nos. 1417a-1417t each sold for 50c on day of issue.

Miniature Sheet

Madurodam Miniature Park, 60th Anniv. — A627

No. 1418 — Miniatures of: a, Dutch East India ship. b, Windmills and building. c, Cheese market (crowd in plaza in front of building). d, Port of Rotterdam and tanker ships. e, Field of flowers. f, Rijksmuseum. g, Schiphol Airport. h, Delta Works (people near white conneted pipes). i, Maasvlakte 2 port project (dredger). j, Binnenhof, horses and carriages.

2012, May 21 ***Perf. 13¼x13½***

1418	A627	Sheet of 10	12.50	6.25
a.-j.		1 Any single	1.25	.35

Nos. 1418a-1418j each sold for 50c on day of issue.

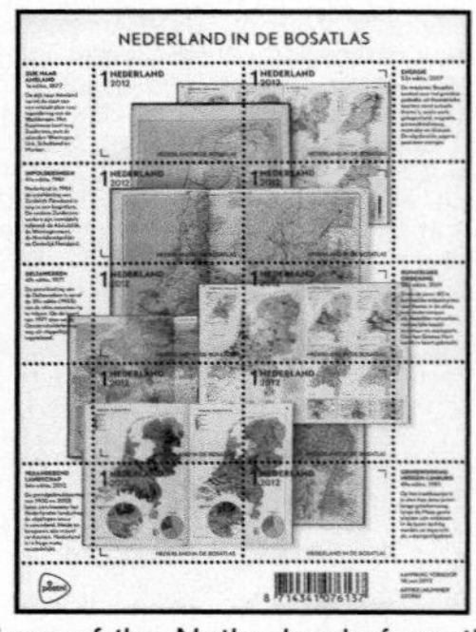

Maps of the Netherlands from the Bosatlas — A628

Designs: Nos. 1419a, 1419k, Upper left section of map from 1877 atlas, upper part of page 62 from 2007 atlas. Nos. 1419b, 1419l, Upper right section of map from 1877 atlas, upper sections of pages 62 and 63 from 2007 atlas. Nos. 1419c, 1419m, Section of map from 1877 atlas, upper left section of page 60 from 1961 atlas. Nos. 1419d, 1419n, Section of map from 1877 atlas, lower section of page 63 from 2007 atlas, upper right section of page 61 from 1961 atlas. Nos. 1419e, 1419o, Section of map from page 60 of 1961 atlas, sections of pages depicting South Netherlands (Zuid-Nederland) from 1971 atlas, upper left section of page 60 from 2001 atlas. Nos. 1419f, 1419p, Section of page 61 from 1961 atlas, upper right section of pages 60 and upper left section of 61 from 2001 atlas. Nos. 1419g, 1419q, Lower section of South Netherlands map from 1971 atlas, lower section of page 60 from 2001 atlas, upper sections of pages 39 from 2012 atlas. Nos. 1419h, 1419r, Lower sections of pages 60 and 61 from 2001 atlas, upper right section of page 39 from 2012 atlas, section of page from 1981 atlas. Nos. 1419i, 1419s, Lower sections of pages 38 and 39 from 2012 atlas. Nos. 1419j, 1419t, Lower right section of page 39 from 2012 atlas, lower right section of page from 1981 atlas.

2012, June 18 ***Perf. 13¼x12¾***

1419	A628	Sheet of 10	12.50	6.25
a.-j.		1 Any single	1.25	.35
k.-t.		Any single, perf. 14½	2.50	2.50
u.		Booklet pane of 2, #1419k-1419l	5.00	—
v.		Booklet pane of 2, #1419m-1419n	5.00	—
w.		Booklet pane of 2, #1419o-1419p	5.00	—
x.		Booklet pane of 2, #1419q-1419r	5.00	—
y.		Booklet pane of 2, #1419s-1419t	5.00	—
		Complete booklet, #1419u, 1419v, 1419w, 1419x, 1419y	25.00	

Nos. 1419a-1419j each sold for 50c on day of issue. Complete booklet sold for €9.95.

Miniature Sheet

Netherlands Olympic Committee and Netherlands Sports Federation, Cent. — A629

No. 1420 — Athletes: a, Sjoukje Dijkstra, figure skater. b, Anton Geesink, judoka. c, Nico Rienks, rower. d, Ellen van Langen, runner. e, Field hockey player. f, Leontien Zijlaard-van Moorsel, cyclist. g, Esther Vergeer, Paralympian tennis player. h, Maarten van der Weijden, swimmer. i, Anky van Grunsven, dressage. j, Nicolien Sauerbreij, snowboarder.

2012, July 4 ***Perf. 13¼x13½***

1420	A629	Sheet of 10	12.50	6.25
a.-j.		1 Any single	1.25	.35

Nos. 1420a-1420j each sold for 50c on day of issue.

Miniature Sheet

Seasons Magazine, 20th Anniv. — A630

No. 1422 — Photography from magazine with inscription at LR: a, Esdoorn (maple leaves). b, IJsbloem (frost flower). c, Peul (snow peas). d, Dahlia. e, Kievitsbloem (fritillaries). f, Lijsterbes (rowanberries). g, Rode zonnehoed (Purple coneflower). h, Rimpelroos, Rozenbottel, Rozengeranium (Rugosa rose, rose hips, rose geranium). i, Tulp (tulips). j, Blauwe bes (blueberries).

2012, July 16 ***Perf. 13½x13¼***

1421	A630	Sheet of 10	12.50	6.25
a.-j.		1 Any single	1.25	.35

Nos. 1421a-1421j each sold for 50c on day of issue.

Cattle Breeds A631

Designs: Nos. 1422a, 1422g, Maas-Rijn-Ijsselvee (Meuse-Rhine-Issel). Nos. 1422b, 1422h, Blaarkop. Nos. 1422c, 1422i, Fries-Hollands (Dutch Friesian). Nos. 1422d, 1422j, Lakenvelder (Dutch Belted). Nos. 1422e, 1422k, Brandrode Rund. Nos. 1422f, 1422l, Witrik.

2012, Aug. 13 ***Perf. 13¼x12¾***

1422	A631	Block of 6	8.50	4.25
a.-f.		1 Any single	1.40	.35
g.-l.		1 Any single, perf. 14½	2.60	2.60
m.		Booklet pane of 2 #1422g	5.25	—
n.		Booklet pane of 2 #1422h	5.25	—
o.		Booklet pane of 2 #1422i	5.25	—
p.		Booklet pane of 2 #1422j	5.25	—
q.		Booklet pane of 2, #1422k, 1422l	5.25	—
		Complete booklet, #1422m, 1422n, 1422o, 1422p, 1422q	26.50	

Nos. 1422a-1422f each sold for 50c on day of issue. Complete booklet sold for €9.95 on day of issue.

Miniature Sheet

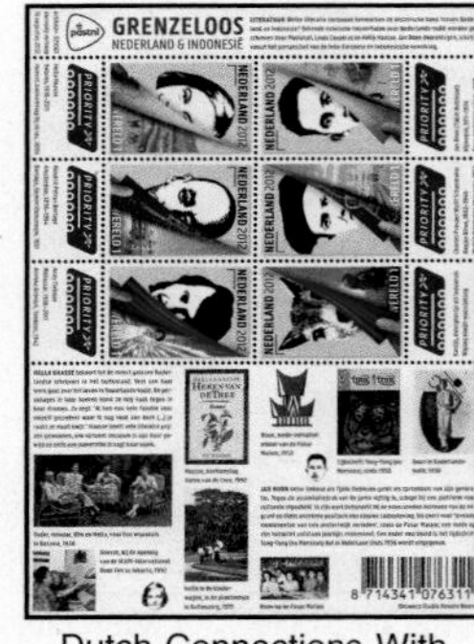

Dutch Connections With Indonesia — A632

No. 1423: a, Hella Haasse (1918-2011), writer, cattle and tea planters. b, Tjalie Robinson (1911-74), writer, dog on chain. c, Hendrik Petrus Berlage (1856-1934), architect, Gemeentemuseum, The Hague. d, Charles Prosper Wolff Schoemaker (1882-1949), architect, (wearing hat), Villa Isola, Bandung, Indonesia. e, Andy Tielman (1936-2011), musician, Anneke Grönloh, singer. f, Chevrotain, Indonesian shadow puppet.

2012, Aug. 13 ***Perf. 13½x13¼***

1423	A632	Sheet of 6	15.00	7.50
a.-f.		1 Wereld Any single	2.50	.65

No. 1423 was printed with three different illustrations in the bottom sheet margin, with each sheet having a different arrangement of stamps. Sheet margins at left and right served as etiquettes. On day of issue, Nos. 1423a-1423f each sold for 95c.

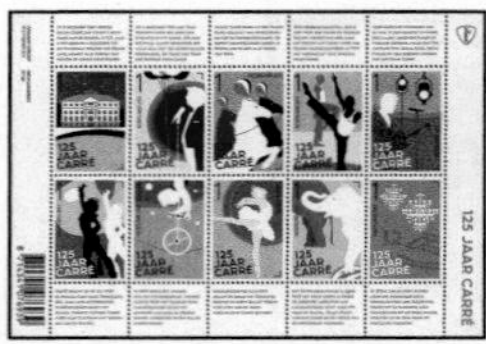

Royal Carré Theater, Amsterdam, 125th Anniv. — A633

No. 1424: a, Theater. b, Toon Hermans, microphone, balloons. c, Oscar Carré's circus horses. d, Two male ballet dancers. e, Guitarist and lights. f, Two dancers from *Cats.* g, Tightrope artist with unicycle. h, Ballerina. i, Circus elephants. j, Chandeliers and "125.".

2012, Sept. 10 ***Perf. 12¾x13¼***

1424	A633	Sheet of 10	14.00	7.00
a.-j.		1 Any single	1.40	.35
k.		Booklet pane of 2, #1424a, 1424c	5.25	—
l.		Booklet pane of 2, #1424b, 1424j	5.25	—
m.		Booklet pane of 2, #1424e, 1424f	5.25	—
n.		Booklet pane of 2, #1424d, 1424h	5.25	—
o.		Booklet pane of 2, #1424g, 1424i	5.25	—
		Complete booklet, #1424k, 1424l, 1424m, 1424n, 1424o	26.50	

On day of issue, Nos. 1424a-1424j each sold for 50c and complete booklet sold for €9.95.

Miniature Sheet

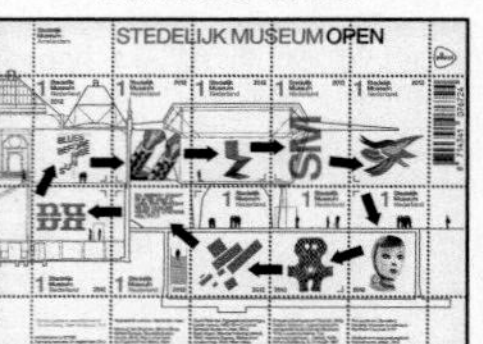

Reopening of Stedelijk Museum, Amsterdam — A634

No. 1425 — Arrows and: a, Blues Before Sunrise poster, by Mevis & Van Deursen. b, As I Opened Fire, by Roy Lichtenstein (cannons). c, Zig-zag chair prototype, by Gerrit Rietveld. d, Musuem logo (SM), by Wim Crouwel. e, Mural, by Karel Appel. f, Now 2, by Willem Sandberg (nu). g, An Object Made. . ., by Lawrence Weiner (text, man on staircase). h, Suprematist Composition (Eight Red Rectangles), by Kazimir Malevich. i, Empathy Displacement 7, by Mike Kelley (polka-dotted object). j, Barbie (With Pearl Necklace), by Marlene Dumas (doll's head).

2012, Sept. 24 *Perf. 13½x13¼*
1425 A634 Sheet of 10 14.00 7.00
a.-j. 1 Any single 1.40 .35

Nos. 1425a-1425j each sold for 50c on day of issue.

Souvenir Sheet

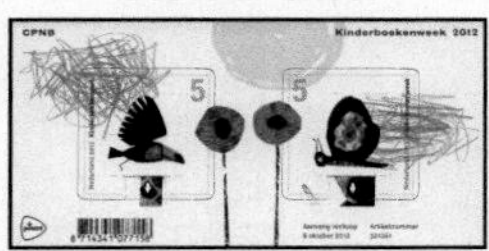

Children's Book Week — A635

No. 1426: a, Bird. b, Butterfly.

2012, Oct. 8 ***Rouletted***
On Cardboard
1426 A635 Sheet of 2 13.00 6.50
a.-b. 5 Either single 6.50 3.25

Nos. 1426a-1426b each sold for €2.50. Parts of the stamps pop up when the cardboard slide on each stamp is pulled out.

Queen Juliana — A636

2012, Oct. 19 *Perf. 13¼x14*
1427 A636 1 multi 1.25 .35
a. Booklet pane of 2 5.00 —
Complete booket, 5 #1427a 25.00

Stamp Day. No. 1427 sold for 50c on day of issue. Complete booklet sold for €9.95 and contains five examples of No. 1427a, each with a different pane margin.

December Stamps A637

No. 1428 — Christmas knitting patterns featuring: a, Christmas trees and red violet hearts. b, Candles. c, Christmas trees and green hearts. d, Reindeer. e, Snowmen. f, Angels with horns. g, Red reindeer and heart. h, Poinsettias. i, Christmas ornaments and poinsettias. j, Angels and musical notes.

Serpentine Die Cut 12¾x12½
2012, Nov. 20 **Self-Adhesive**
1428 A637 Block of 10 11.00
a.-j. (40c) Any single 1.10 .30

A638

Personalized Stamps — A639

2013, Jan. 2 **Litho.** *Perf. 13¼x14*
1429 A638 1 multi 1.50 1.50

Self-Adhesive
1430 A639 1 multi 1.50 1.50

Nos. 1429-1430 each sold for 54c on day of issue. Vignettes shown are the generic images available on the day of issue. Vignettes could be personalized for a fee.

Traditional Women's Head Coverings — A640

Head covering from: No. 1431, Bunschoten-Spakenburg. No. 1432, Staphorst. No. 1433, Marken. No. 1434, Walcheren. No. 1435, Noordwest-Veluwe.

2013 **Litho.** *Perf. 14½x14¼*
1431 A640 1 multi 1.50 1.50
a. Perf. 13½x12½ 2.75 2.75
b. Booklet pane of 2 #1431a 5.50 —
1432 A640 1 multi 1.50 1.50
a. Perf. 13½x12½ 2.75 2.75
b. Booklet pane of 2 #1432a 5.50 —
1433 A640 1 multi 1.40 1.40
a. Perf. 13½x12½ 2.75 2.75
b. Booklet pane of 2 #1433a 5.50 —
1434 A640 1 multi 1.40 1.40
a. Perf. 13½x12½ 2.75 2.75
b. Booklet pane of 2 #1434a 5.50 —
1435 A640 1 multi 1.50 1.50
a. Perf. 13½x12½ 2.75 2.75
b. Booklet pane of 2 #1435a 5.50 —
Complete booklet, #1431b, 1432b, 1433b, 1434b, 1435b 27.50
c. Souvenir sheet of 5, #1431-1435 7.50 7.50
Nos. 1431-1435 (5) 7.30 7.30

Issued: Nos. 1431-1432, 1/2; Nos. 1433-1434, 2/25; Nos. 1431a-1431b, 1432a-1432b, 1433a-1433b, 1434a-1434b, 1435-1435c, 5/21. Nos. 1431-1435 each sold for 54c on day of issue. Complete booklet sold for €9.95.

Miniature Sheet

Netherlands Land Development Society, 125th Anniv. — A641

No. 1436 — Construction projects developed by Arcadis and KNHM: a, Millau Viaduct, France. b, Train under Zanderij Crailoo Wildlife Crossing Bridge. c, Lighthouse, flags and grass-covered dunes. d, Floriade (terraced garden), Venlo. e, Olympic Stadium, London. f, Storm barrier, New Orleans, Louisiana. g, Garden on Meuse River, Rotterdam. h, Water, trees and tower in distance (Kern met Pit Contest). i, Amsterdam Bijlmer ArenA railway station. j, Model constructed for Artcadia children's art and technology contest.

2013, Jan. 28 **Litho.** *Perf. 13¼x13½*
1436 A641 Sheet of 10 15.00 15.00
a.-j. 1 Any single 1.50 1.50

Nos. 1436a-1436j each sold for 54c on day of issue.

Miniature Sheet

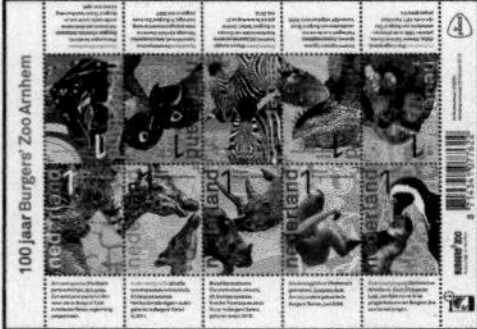

Animals in Burgers' Zoo, Arnhem A642

No. 1437: a, Panthera pardus kotiya (Sri Lankan leopards). b, Pterapogon kauderni (Banggai cardinalfish) witheggs in mouth. c, Giraffa camelopardalis rothschildi (giraffes). d, Anodorhynchus hyacinthinus (hyacinth macaws). e, Ceratotherium simum (white rhinoceroses). f, Equus quagga boehmi (Grant's zebras). g, Nomascus gabriellae (yellow-cheeked gibbons). h, Iguana iguana (green iguanas). i, Spheniscus demersus (jackass penguins). j, Pan troglodytes (chimpanzees).

Perf. 13¼x12¾
2013, Feb. 25 **Litho.**
1437 A642 Sheet of 10 14.00 14.00
a.-j. 1 Any single 1.40 1.40
k. Booklet pane of 2, #1437a-1437b 5.25 —
l. Booklet pane of 2, #1437c-1437d 5.25 —
m. Booklet pane of 2, #1437e-1437f 5.25 —
n. Booklet pane of 2, #1437g-1437h 5.25 —
o. Booklet pane of 2, #1437i-1437j 5.25 —
Complete booklet, #1437k, 1437l, 1437m, 1437n, 1437o 26.50

Nos. 1437a-1437j each sold for 54c on day of issue. Complete booklet sold for €9.95.

Famous Women A643

No. 1438: a, Alexandrine Tinne (1835-69), explorer of Sahara region. b, Belle van Zuylen (1740-1805), writer. c, Trijn van Leemput (c. 1530-1607), heroine in Eighty Years' War. d, Maria van Oosterwijck (1630-93), painter. e, Mary, Duchess of Burgundy (1457-82). f, Anna Zernike (1887-1972), theologian, first female minister in Netherlands.

Perf. 13¼x12¾
2013, Mar. 25 **Litho.**
1438 A643 Block of 6 8.50 8.50
a.-f. 1 Any single 1.40 1.40

Nos. 1438a-1438f each sold for 54c on day of issue.

Miniature Sheet

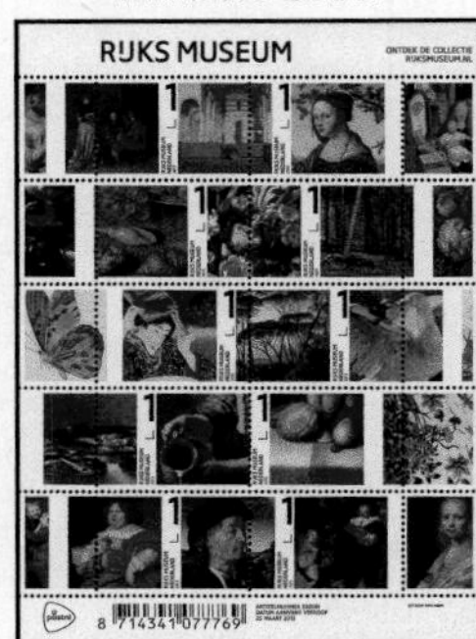

Reopening of Main Building of Rijksmuseum — A644

No. 1439: a, Right part of *The Gallant Conversation,* by Gerard ter Borch, left part of *Interior of the Church of St. Odulphus in Assendelft,* by Pieter Jansz. b, Right part of *Interior of the Church of St. Odolphus in Assendelft, Mary Magdalene,* by Jan van Scorel. c, *Still Life of Fruits and Flowers,* by Balthasar van der Ast, left part of *Still Life with Flowers,* by Hans Bollongier. d, Right part of *Still Life with Flowers,* left part of *Vivi in a Red Dress in a Forest,* by Jacob Olie, Jr. e, Right edge of *Sheet with Five Butterflies a Wasp and Two Flies,* by Pieter Withoos, Bunya no Yasuhide from *Modern Parody on the Six Poets and Six Flowers,* by Kunisada Utagawa, left edge of *Italian Landscape with Stone Pines,* by Hendrik Voogd. f, Right part of *Italian Landcape with Stone Pines,* left part of *The Threatened Swan,* by Jan Asselijn. g, Right part of *Still Life with Gilded Cup,* by Willem Claesz, *The Milkmaid,* by Johannes Vermeer. h, *Still Life with Cheeses,* by Floris Claesz van Dijck, left part of tile from Sommelsdijk Orphanage. i, Right part of *Gerard Andriesz Bicker,* by Bartholomeus van der Helst, left part of *Portrait of Giuliano da Sangallo,* by Piero di Cosomo. j, Right part of *Portrait of Giuliano da Sangallo,* left part of *The Night Watch,* by Rembrandt.

Perf. 13¼x12¾
2013, Mar. 25 **Litho.**
1439 A644 Sheet of 10 14.00 14.00
a.-j. 1 Any single 1.40 1.40

Nos. 1439a-1439j each sold for 54c on day of issue.

Abdication of Queen Beatrix — A645

2013, Mar. 25 **Litho.** *Perf. 14x13½*
1440 A645 1 blue & blk 1.40 1.40

No. 1440 sold for 54c on day of issue.

Europa A646

No. 1441: a and c, Modern mail vans (2013 Renault Kangoo, 1976 Simca 1100 VF, 2010 Fiat Fiorino, 1974 Daf 33). b and d, Old mail vans (1960 Bedford CA, 1936, Opel P4, 1956 Opel Blitz, 1918 GMC).

2013, Apr. 22 **Litho.** *Perf. 13¼x12¾*
1441 A646 Pair 4.80 4.80
a.-b. 1 Europa Either single 2.40 2.40
c.-d. 1 Europa Either single, perf. 14½ 4.25 4.25
e. Booklet pane of 2, #1441c-1441d 8.75 —
Complete booklet, 3 #1441e 26.50

Nos. 1441a-1441b each sold for 90c on day of issue. Complete booklet sold for €9.95, and contains three panes of No. 1441e with different orientations of the stamps.

Ascension to Throne of King Willem-Alexander — A647

Perf. 14¼x14 Syncopated
2013, Apr. 30 **Litho.**
Booklet Stamps
Self-Adhesive
1442 A647 1 blk, red & bl 1.40 1.40
a. Booklet pane of 10 14.00
1443 A647 2 blk, bl & grn 3.00 3.00
a. Booklet pane of 5 15.00

On day of issue, No. 1442 sold for 54c and No. 1443 sold for €1.08.

King Willem-Alexander A648

2013, May 21 **Litho.** *Perf. 14x13½*
1444 A648 1 red & blk 1.50 1.50

No. 1444 sold for 54c on day of issue.

Writers — A649

No. 1445: a, Simon Carmiggelt (1913-87). b, Gerrit Kouwenaar. c, Louis Couperus

(1863-1923). d, Adriaan Roland Holst (1888-1976). e, Godfried Bomans (1913-71).

2013, May 21 Litho. *Perf. 14½*

1445 Horiz. strip of 5 7.50 7.50
a.-e. A649 1 Any single 1.50 1.50

Nos. 1445a-1445e each sold for 54c on day of issue. Printed in sheets containing 2 each of Nos. 1445a-1445e + 5 central labels.

World Blood Donor Day — A650

No. 1446: a, Queen, "1" in red. b, King, "1" in white.

2013, June 17 Litho. *Perf. 14½*

1446 A650 Pair 3.00 3.00
a.-b. 1 Either single 1.50 1.50

On day of issue Nos. 1446a-1446b each sold for 54c.

Miniature Sheet

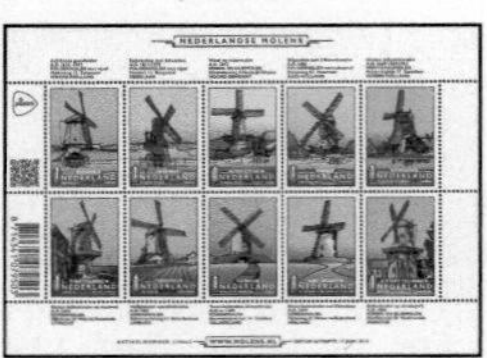

Windmills — A651

No. 1447 — Various windmill types located in: a and k, Schermer. b and l, Burgwerd. c and m, Heeswijk-Dinther. d and n, Hoornaar. e and o, Zaandam. f and p, Wijk bij Duurstede. g and q, Klein Genhout. h and r, Zeddam. i and s, Nieuw- en Sint Joosland. j and t, Roderwolde.

2013, June 17 Litho. *Perf. 14½*

1447 A651 Sheet of 10 15.00 15.00
a.-j. 1 Any single 1.50 1.50
k.-t. 1 Any single, perf. 12¾x13¼ 2.75 2.75
u. Booklet pane of 2, #1447k, 1447p 5.50 —
v. Booklet pane of 2, #1447l, 1447q 5.50 —
w. Booklet pane of 2, #1447m, 1447r 5.50 —
x. Booklet pane of 2, #1447n, 1447s 5.50 —
y. Booklet pane of 2, #1447o, 1447t 5.50 —
Complete booklet, #1447u, 1447v, 1447w, 1447x, 1447y 27.50

Nos. 1447a-1447j each sold for 54c on day of issue. Complete booklet sold for €9.95.

Miniature Sheet

Royal Dutch Swimming Association, 125th Anniv. — A652

No. 1448: a, People standing at edge of pool. b, Two synchronized divers. c, Water polo player. d, Diver about to enter water. e, People standing at edge of pool, people lined up on diving platform. f, Two synchronized swimmers. g, Swimmer and lane barriers. h, Teacher and children learning how to swim. i, Swimmer's head near edge of pool. j, Swimmer bent over ready to start race.

2013, Aug. 12 Litho. *Perf. 14½*

1448 A652 Sheet of 10 16.00 16.00
a.-j. 1 Any single 1.60 1.60

Nos. 1448a-1448j each sold for 60c on day of issue.

Miniature Sheet

Dutch Connections With Belgium — A653

No. 1449: a, Museum aan de Stroom, Antwerp, Belgium, designed by Neutelings Riedijk Architectural Agency. b, Design for Hoenderloo Museum, by Henry van de Velde. c, Twelve books, country name at left. d, Thirteen books, country name at right. e, Après-midi à Amsterdam, by Rik Wouters. f, De Vlakte, by Jakob Smits.

Perf. 13¼x12¾

2013, Aug. 12 Litho.

1449 A653 Sheet of 6 16.50 16.50
a.-f. 1 Wereld Any single 2.75 2.75

Nos. 1449a-1449f each sold for €1 on day of issue. No. 1449 was printed with three different illustrations in the bottom sheet margin, with each sheet having a different arrangement of stamps. Sheet margins at left and right served as etiquettes.

Greeting Card Week — A654

2013, Sept. 9 Litho. *Perf. 14½*

1450 A654 1 multi 1.60 1.60

No. 1450 sold for 60c on day of issue and was printed in sheets of 3.

Miniature Sheet

Peace Palace, The Hague, Cent. A655

No. 1451 — Details of architectural or artistic items of the Peace Palace in circle at left, word at top in inner ring of words in circle at right: a and k, Detail of wall tile, Artes. b and l, Bronze medallion on entrance gates, Amicitia. c and m, Stained-glass window in Central Hall, Iustitia. d and n, Portrait of Hugo de Groot, by Michiel Jansz.van Mierevelt, Mercatura. e and o, Marble floor in Entrance Hall, Scientia. f and p, Relief sculpture by Toon Dupuis, Veritas. g and q, Prestudy for unmade tapestry, Concordia. h and r, Tile panel, Securitas. i and s, Peace Goddess with Child, by Herman Rosse, Prosperitas. j and t, Stained-glass window depicting locomotive, Industria.

2013, Sept. 9 Litho. *Perf. 13¼x12¾*

1451 A655 Sheet of 10 16.00 16.00
a.-j. 1 Any single 1.60 1.60
k.-t. 1 Any single, perf. 14½ 2.75 2.75
u. Booklet pane of 2, #1451k-1451l 5.50 —
v. Booklet pane of 2, #1451m-1451n 5.50 —
w. Booklet pane of 2, #1451o-1451p 5.50 —
x. Booklet pane of 2, #1451q-1451r 5.50 —
y. Booklet pane of 2, #1451s-1451t 5.50 —
Complete booklet, #1451u, 1451v, 1451w, 1451x, 1451y 27.50

Nos. 1451a-1451j each sold for 60c on day of issue. Complete booklet sold for €9.95.

Airplanes and Queen Wilhelmina From Type AP5 — A656

2013, Oct. 18 Litho. *Perf. 14x13½*

1452 A656 1 multi 1.60 1.60
a. Booklet pane of 2 5.50 —
Complete booklet, 5 #1452a 27.50

Stamp Day. No. 1452 sold for 60c on day of issue. Complete booklet sold for €9.95.

Legend of St. Nicholas (Santa Claus) — A657

No. 1453: a, St. Nicholas on horse, Black Peter, and Moon. b, Black Peter with gift. c, Moon, tree and house. d, St. Nicholas with crozier. e, Shoe filled with gifts.

2013, Nov. 4 Litho. *Perf. 13¾x13¼*

1453 Horiz. strip of 5 8.00 8.00
a.-e. A657 1 Any single 1.60 1.60

Nos. 1453a-1453e sold for 60c on day of issue and emit a spice scent when scratched.

Miniature Sheet

December Stamps — A658

No. 1454: a, Buildings at night, comet in sky over Christmas tree. b, Buildings at night, Christmas tree. c, Buildings at night, people viewing fireworks. d, Buildings at night, Christmas tree, large star at left, Moon over top of tower. e, Buildings at night, large star at left, Christmas trees. f, Buildings at night, people viewing large star at right. g, Buildings at night, Christmas tree, man running. h, Buildings at night, clock on tower at right. i, Girl on ice skates looking at bird in tree. j, Boy in sled on ice, man ice skating. k, Two ice skaters, windmill. l, Boy in sled on ice, tower at right. m, Snowman, star and top of Christmas tree. n, Man pulling Christmas tree on cart. o, Dog looking at postman on bicycle. p, Woman holding dog's leash, tower at right. q, Man and woman under mistletoe. r, Birds under bridge, Christmas tree. s, Buildings in day, Christmas tree. t, Buidlings in day, tower at right.

Serpentine Die Cut 12½x12¼

2013, Nov. 19 Litho.

Self-Adhesive

1454 A658 Sheet of 20 30.00
a.-t. (55c) Any single 1.50 1.50

Kingdom of the Netherlands, 200th Anniv. — A659

No. 1455: a, Landing of Willem I, 1813, King Willem I, flag of the Netherlands. b, List of monarchs.

2013, Nov. 30 Litho. *Perf. 14½*

1455 A659 Pair, #a-b 7.00 7.00
a.-b. 2 Either single 3.50 3.50

On day of issue Nos. 1455a-1455b both sold for €1.28.

King Willem-Alexander
A660 A661

Die Cut Perf. 14¼ Syncopated

2013, Nov. 30 Photo.

Booklet Stamps
Self-Adhesive

1456 A660 1 blue & blk 1.75 1.75
a. Booklet pane of 10 17.50
b. Dated "2014" — —
d. Dated "2015" 1.60 1.60
e. Booklet pane of 10 #1456d 16.00
n. Dated "2020" 2.10 2.10
o. Booklet pane of 10 #1456n 21.00
t. Dated "2023" — —
u. Booklet pane of 10 #1456t — —

Issued: No. 1456n, 6/9/20; No. 1458n, 7/15/20.

Serpentine Die Cut 11¼

1457 A661 1 Internationaal gray & blk 3.00 3.00
a. Booklet pane of 5 15.00
b. Dated "2014" — —
d. Dated "2015" 2.60 2.60
e. Booklet pane of 5 #1457d 13.00
h. Dated "2017" — —
i. Booklet pane of 5 #1457h —
j. Dated "2018" — —
k. Booklet pane of 5 #1457j —
n. Dated "2020" — —
o. Booklet pane of 5 #1457n —
t. Dated "2023" — —
u. Booklet pane of 5 #1457t — —

Die Cut Perf. 14¼

1458 A660 2 ver & blk 3.50 3.50
a. Booklet pane of 5 17.50
b. Dated "2014" — —
d. Dated "2015" 3.25 3.25
e. Booklet pane of 5 #1458d 16.50
n. Dated "2020" 4.25 4.25
o. Booklet pane of 5 #1458n 21.50
t. Dated "2023" — —
u. Booklet pane of 5 #1458t — —

Issued: Nos. 1456t, 1456u, 1457t, 1457u, 1458t, 1458u, 5/1/23.

Nos. 1456-1458 (3) 8.25 8.25

On day of issue, No. 1456 sold for 64c; No. 1457, for €1.05; No. 1458, for €1.28.

Issued: Nos. 1456b, 1457b, 1458b, 10/23/14; Nos. 1456d, 1456e, 1457d, 1457e, 1458d, 1458e, 1/5/15; No. 1457h, 6/16/17; No. 1457j, 6/1/18; Nos. 1456n, 1456o, 6/9/20; Nos. 1457n, 1457o, 1458n, 1458o, 7/15/20; Nos. 1456t, 1456u,1457t, 1457u, 1458t, 1458u, 5/1/23.

On day of issues, No. 1456b sold for 64c; No. 1456d, 69c; No. 1457b, €1.05; No. 1457d, €1.15; No. 1458b, €1.28;No. 1458d, €1.38.

Numerals
A662 A663

Die Cut Perf. 13½ Syncopated

2014, Jan. 2 Coil Stamps Litho.

Self-Adhesive

1459 A662 1 multi 1.75 1.75
1460 A663 2 multi 3.50 3.50

On day of issue, No. 1459 sold for 64c; No. 1460, for €1.28.

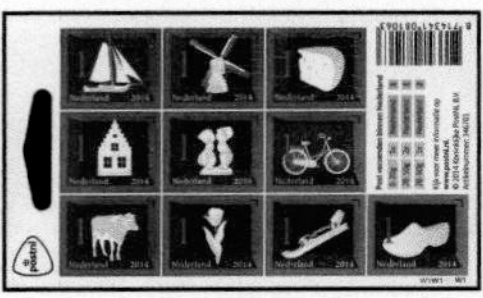

A664

Dutch Items A665

Designs: No. 1461a, Frisian flat-bottomed boat. Nos. 1461b, 1462a, Windmill. No. 1461c, Wedge of Gouda cheese. Nos. 1461d, 1462d, House with step-gable roof. No. 1461e, Boy and girl in Dutch costumes kissing. Nos. 1461f, 1462b, Bicycle. Nos. 1461g, 1462c, Holstein-Frisian cow. Nos. 1461h, 1462e, Tulip. No. 1461i, Ice skate. No. 1461j, Wooden shoe.

Die Cut Perf. 14¼

2014, Jan. 2 **Litho.**

Self-Adhesive

1461 A664 Booklet pane of 10 17.50
a.-j. 1 Any single 1.75 1.75

Serpentine Die Cut 11¼

1462 A665 Booklet pane of 5 15.00
a.-e. 1 Internationaal Any single 3.00 3.00

On day of issue, Nos. 1461a-1461j each sold for 64c; Nos. 1462a-1462 each sold for €1.05.

Miniature Sheet

Automobiles in Louwman Museum Collection — A666

No. 1463: a, 1887 De Dion-Bouton & Trépardoux. b, 1910 Brooke Swan Car. c, 1912 Eysink. d, 1912 Spyker. e, 1932, Bugatti. f, 1935 Duesenberg. g, 1936 Toyota. h, 1960 Porsche race car. i, 1964 Aston Martin. j, 1965 Ferrari.

2014, Jan. 27 Litho. ***Perf. 13¼x13½***

1463 A666 Sheet of 10 17.50 17.50
a.-j. 1 Any single 1.75 1.75
k. Booklet pane of 2, #1463a-1463b 6.75 —
l. Booklet pane of 2, #1463c-1463d 6.75 —
m. Booklet pane of 2, #1463e-1463f 6.75 —
n. Booklet pane of 2, #1463g-1463h 6.75 —
o. Booklet pane of 2, #1463i-1463j 6.75 —
Complete booklet, #1463k-1463o 34.00

On day of issue, Nos. 1463a-1463j each sold for 64c. Complete booklet sold for €12.45.

Ceramics — A667

Ceramics from: No. 1464, Loosdrecht. No. 1465, Tegelen. No. 1466, Harlingen. No. 1467, Makkum. No. 1468, Delft.

2014 **Litho.** ***Perf. 14½x14¼***

1464 A667 1 multi 1.75 1.75
a. Perf. 13½x12½ 3.25 3.25
b. Booklet pane of 2 #1464a 6.75 —
1465 A667 1 multi 1.75 1.75
a. Perf. 13½x12½ 3.25 3.25
b. Booklet pane of 2 #1465a 6.75 —
1466 A667 1 multi 1.75 1.75
a. Perf. 13½x12½ 3.25 3.25
b. Booklet pane of 2 #1466a 6.75 —
1467 A667 1 multi 1.75 1.75
a. Perf. 13½x12½ 3.25 3.25
b. Booklet pane of 2 #1467a 6.75 —
1468 A667 1 multi 1.75 1.75
a. Perf. 13½x12½ 3.25 3.25
b. Booklet pane of 2 #1468a 6.75 —
Complete booklet, #1464b, 1465b, 1466b, 1467b, 1468b 34.00
c. Souvenir sheet of 5, #1464-1468 8.75 8.75

Issued: Nos. 1464, 1465, 1/27; Nos. 1466, 1467, 2/24; Nos. 1464a, 1464b, 1465a, 1465b, 1466a, 1466b, 1467a, 1467b, 1468, 1468a, 1468b, 1468c, 5/19. On day of issue, Nos. 1464-1468 each sold for 64c. Complete booklet sold for €12.45.

Youth Philately Day A668

No. 1469: a, Carrier pigeon (duif). b, Hedgehog (egel).

2014, Mar. 24 **Litho.** ***Die Cut***

Self-Adhesive

1469 A668 Pair, #a-b 3.50
a.-b. 1 Either single 1.75 1.75

Printed in sheets of 10 containing five each Nos. 1469a-1469b, with adjacent stamps at different distances from each other. On day of issue, Nos. 1469a-1469b each sold for 64c.

Constitution of the Kingdom of the Netherlands, 200th Anniv. A669

No. 1470: a, King Willem-Alexander, text from coronation oath, blue panel. b, Statue of King Willem I, text from oath to the Constitution, red panel.

Perf. 13½x13¼

2014, Mar. 29 **Litho.**

1470 A669 Pair, #a-b 7.00 7.00
a.-b. 2 Either single 3.50 3.50

On day of issue, Nos. 1470a-1470b each sold for €1.28.

Europa A670

No. 1471 — Drie Pruiken Barrel Organ: a, Internal machinery. b, Front of organ with figurines and builder's name.

2014, Apr. 22 Litho. ***Perf. 13¼x13½***

1471 A670 Horiz. pair 6.00 6.00
a.-b. 1 Internationaal Either single 3.00 3.00

On day of issue, Nos. 1471a-1471b each sold for €1.05.

Miniature Sheet

Orchids — A671

No. 1472: a, Gymnadenia conopsea. b, Orchis militaris. c, Orchis anthropophora. d, Anacamptis pyramidalis. e, Dactylorhiza maculata. f, Orchis purpurea. g, Platanthera bifolia. h, Orchis mascula. i, Coeloglossum viride. j, Orchis simia.

2014, Apr. 22 Litho. ***Perf. 13½x13¼***

1472 A671 Sheet of 10 17.50 17.50
a.-j. 1 Any single 1.75 1.75
k. Booklet pane of 2, #1472a, 1472f 7.00 —
l. Booklet pane of 2, #1472b, 1472g 7.00 —
m. Booklet pane of 2, #1472c, 1472h 7.00 —
n. Booklet pane of 2, #1472d, 1472i 7.00 —
o. Booklet pane of 2, #1472e, 1472j 7.00 —
Complete booklet, #1472k-1472o 35.00

On day of issue, Nos. 1472a-1472j each sold for 64c. Complete booklet sold for €12.45.

Miniature Sheet

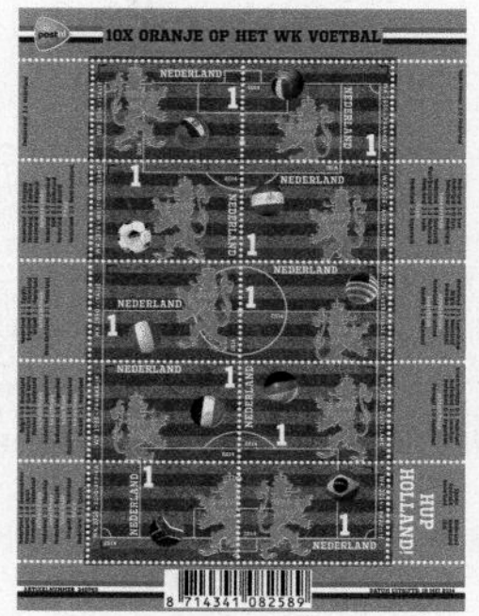

2014 World Cup Soccer Championships, Brazil — A672

No. 1473 — Dutch lion, soccer ball with host county flag and year: a, Italy, 1934. b, France, 1938. c, West Germany, 1974. d, Argentina, 1978. e, Italy, 1990. f, United States, 1994. g, France, 1998. h, Germany, 2006. i, South Africa, 2010, j, Brazil, 2014.

2014, May 19 Litho. ***Perf. 13¼x13½***

1473 A672 Sheet of 10 17.50 17.50
a.-j. 1 Any single 1.75 1.75

On day of issue, Nos. 1473a-1473j each sold for 64c.

Personalized Stamp — A673

2014, July 1 **Litho.** ***Perf. 13½x14***

1474 A673 1 Internationaal multi 3.00 3.00

No. 1474 sold for €1.05 on day of issue. The vignette shown is the generic image available on the day of issue. Vignettes could be personalized for a fee.

Miniature Sheet

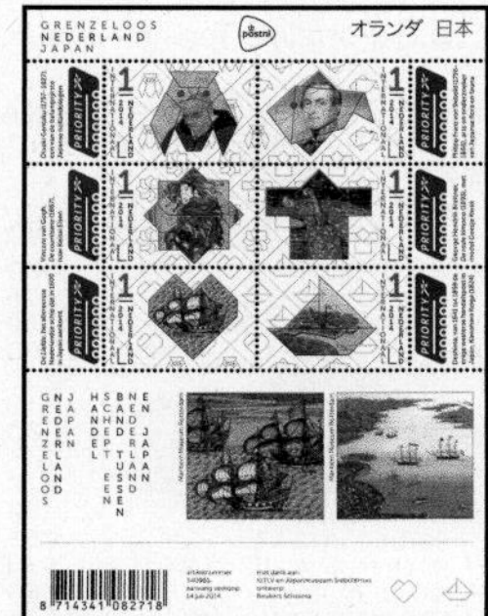

Dutch Connections With Japan — A674

No. 1475: a, Gentaku Otsuki (1757-1827), Japanese expert on the Dutch ("1" at UL). b, Philipp Franz von Siebold (1796-1866), physician in Japan ("1" at UR). c, The Courtesan, by Vincent van Gogh ("1" at UL). d, The Red Kimono, by George Hendrik Breitner ("1" at UR). e, Dutch ship Liefde ("1" at UL). f, Dejima Island, detail of painting by Keiga Kawahara ("1" at UR).

2014, July 14 Litho. ***Perf. 13¼x13½***

1475 A674 Sheet of 6 18.00 18.00
a.-f. 1 Internationaal Any single 3.00 3.00

Nos. 1475a-1475f each sold for €1.05 on day of issue. No. 1475 was printed with three different illustrations in the bottom sheet margin, with each sheet having a different arrangement of stamps. Sheet margins at left and right served as etiquettes.

Royal Family Riding Bicycles — A675

King Willem-Alexander and Queen Máxima at 2014 Winter Olympics — A676

King Willem-Alexander and Queen Máxima — A677

2001 Announcement of Engagement A678

Royal Family in New York City A679

2014, Aug. 2 Litho. ***Perf. 13¼x13½***

1476 Vert. strip of 5 8.75 8.75
a. A675 1 multi 1.75 1.75
b. A676 1 multi 1.75 1.75
c. A677 1 multi 1.75 1.75
d. A678 1 multi 1.75 1.75
e. A679 1 multi 1.75 1.75

12½ year anniv. of marriage of King Willem-Alexander and Queen Máxima. Printed in sheets containing two vertical strips. Nos. 1476a-1476e each sold for 64c on day of sale.

Miniature Sheet

UNESCO World Heritage Sites in the Netherlands — A680

No. 1477: a, Beemster Polder, 1999. b, Wadden Sea, 2009. c, Schokland and Surroundings, 1995. d, Windmill Network at Kinderdijk-Elshout, 1997. e, Rietveld Schröder House, 2000. f, D.F. Wouda Steam Pumping Station, 1998. g, Canal Ring of Amsterdam, 2010. h, Willemstad, Curaçao, 1997. i, Fort near Spijkerboor, Defense Ring of Amsterdam, 1996. j, Pampus Island Fort, Defense Ring of Amsterdam, 1996.

Perf. 13¼x13½

2014, Aug. 11 **Litho.**

1477 A680 Sheet of 10 17.50 17.50
a.-j. 1 Any single 1.75 1.75
k. Booklet pane of 2, #1477a-1477b 6.75 —
l. Booklet pane of 2, #1477c-1477d 6.75 —
m. Booklet pane of 2, #1477e-1477f 6.75 —
n. Booklet pane of 2, #1477g-1477h 6.75 —
o. Booklet pane of 2, #1477i-1477j 6.75 —
Complete booklet, #1477k-1477o 34.00

On day of issue, Nos. 1477a-1477j each sold for 64c. Complete booklet sold for €12.45.

Miniature Sheet

Railways in the Netherlands, 175th Anniv. — A681

No. 1478: a, Locomotives and electric cable towers. b, Locomotive, clock with second hand, Arnhem train station stairway and escalator. c, Tile work and Haarlem station. d, Electric locomotive and map of railway line stations. e, Vertical lift railway bridge, green track signal. f, Emblem for Tienertoer reduced rate program, winged wheel emblem. g, Locomotive and red track signal. h, Clock without second hand, Rotterdam train station. i, New and old symbols for Netherlands Railways, track network. j, Locomotive, Netherlands #215.

2014, Sept. 8 Litho. ***Perf. 13¼x13½***

1478 A681 Sheet of 10 16.00 16.00
a.-j. 1 Any single 1.60 1.60
k. Booklet pane of 2, #1478a-1478b 6.50 —
l. Booklet pane of 2, #1478c-1478d 6.50 —
m. Booklet pane of 2, #1478e-1478f 6.50 —
n. Booklet pane of 2, #1478g-1478h 6.50 —
o. Booklet pane of 2, #1478i-1478j 6.50 —
Complete booklet, #1478k-1478o 32.50

On day of issue, Nos. 1478a-1478j each sold for 64c. Complete booklet sold for €12.45.

Hardwell, Disk Jockey A682

Tiesto, Disk Jockey A683

Afrojack, Disk Jockey A684

Dash Berlin, Disk Jockey A685

Armin Van Buuren, Disk Jockey — A686

2014, Oct. 6 Litho. ***Perf. 13½x13¼***

1479 Horiz. strip of 5 8.00 8.00
a. A682 1 multi 1.60 1.60
b. A683 1 multi 1.60 1.60
c. A684 1 multi 1.60 1.60
d. A685 1 multi 1.60 1.60
e. A686 1 multi 1.60 1.60

Printed in sheets containing two strips. On day of issue, Nos. 1479a-1479e each sold for 64c.

Stamp Day — A687

2014, Oct. 17 Litho. ***Perf. 13x13¼***

1480 A687 1 multi 1.60 1.60
a. Booklet pane of 2 6.25 —
Complete booklet, 5 #1480a 31.50

On day of issue No. 1480 sold for 64c. Complete booklet sold for €12.45. The five examples of No. 1480a in the complete booklet have different margins.

December Stamps — A688

No. 1481: a, Mittens. b, Two round Christmas ornaments. c, Owl, Santa's sleigh in flight. d, People kissing under mistletoe. e, Champagne flutes. f, Plate of Christmas pastries. g, Snowman. h, Christmas tree. i, Hand placing ornament on Christmas tree. j, House, envelope, mailbox. k, Fondue pot and Christmas ornament. l, Bells. m, Candle. n, Candy cane and Christmas ornament. o, Reindeer and sleigh. p, Ice skates. q, Stockings. r, Birds. s, Wrapped gifts. t, Rockets and fireworks.

Serpentine Die Cut 12½

2014, Nov. 17 Photo.

Self-Adhesive

1481 A688 Booklet pane of 20 30.00
a.-t. (59c) Any single 1.50 1.50

Miniature Sheet

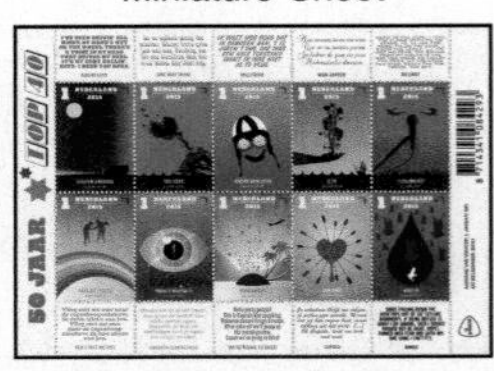

Dutch Top 40 Music Rankings, 50th Anniv. — A689

No. 1482: a, "Radar Love," by Golden Earring. b, "One Way Wind," by The Cats. c, "Willempie," by André van Duin. d, "Mon Amour," by BZN. e, "No Limit," by 2 Unlimited. f, "Vlieg Met Me Mee," by Paul de Leeuw. g, "Dromen Zijn Bedrog," by Marco Borsato. h, "We're Going to Ibiza!" by Vengaboys. i, "Cupido," by Jan Smit. j, "Birds," by Anouk.

2015, Jan. 5 Litho. ***Perf. 13½x13¼***

1482 A689 Sheet of 10 16.00 16.00
a.-j. 1 Any single 1.60 1.60

On day of issue, Nos. 1482a-1482j each sold for 69c.

Fortified Towns — A690

Fortifications of: No. 1483, Bourtange. No. 1484, Elburg. No. 1485, Naarden. No. 1486, Willemstad. No. 1487, Hulst.

2015 Litho. ***Perf. 14½x14¼***

1483 A690 1 multi 1.60 1.60
a. Perf. 13½x12¾ 2.75 2.75
b. Booklet pane of 2 #1483a 5.50 —
1484 A690 1 multi 1.60 1.60
a. Perf. 13½x12¾ 2.75 2.75
b. Booklet pane of 2 #1484a 5.50 —
1485 A690 1 multi 1.60 1.60
a. Perf. 13½x12¾ 2.75 2.75
b. Booklet pane of 2 #1485a 5.50 —
1486 A690 1 multi 1.60 1.60
a. Perf. 13½x12¾ 2.75 2.75
b. Booklet pane of 2 #1486a 5.50 —
1487 A690 1 multi 1.60 1.60
a. Perf. 13½x12¾ 2.75 2.75
b. Booklet pane of 2 #1487a 5.50 —
Complete booklet, #1483b, 1484b, 1485b, 1486b, 1487b 27.50
c. Souvenir sheet of 5, #1483-1487 8.00 8.00
Nos. 1483-1487 (5) 8.00 8.00

Issued: Nos. 1483, 1484, 1485, 2/2/15. Nos. 1483a, 1484a, 1485a, 1486, 1486a, 1487, 1487b, 1487c, 5/26/15. Nos. 1483-1487 each sold for 69c on day of issue. Complete booklet sold for €12.45.

Baby Carriage, Baby Bottle, Rocking Horse and Baby Toys — A691

Die Cut Perf. 14¼x14½

2015, Mar. 2 Photo.

Self-Adhesive

1488 A691 1 multi 1.60 1.60

No. 1488 sold for 69c on day of issue.

Map of Netherlands and Royal Items A692

No. 1489 — Map and: a, Royal arms, inscription "Koning Willem-Alexander / 2013." b, Signature of King William I. inscription "Koning Willem I / 1815."

2015, Mar. 2 Litho. ***Perf. 13½x13¼***

1489 A692 Pair, #a-b 6.50 6.50
a.-b. 2 Either single 3.25 3.25

On day of issue, Nos. 1489a and 1489b each sold for €1.38.

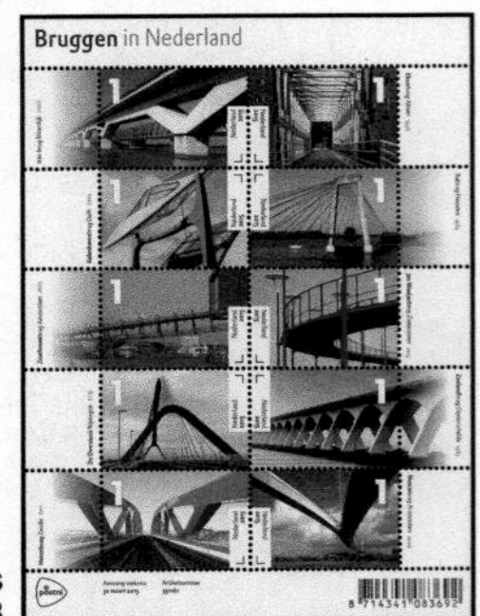

Bridges A693

No. 1490: a and k, High speed railroad Bridge, Moerdijk, 2006. b and l, Ehzer Bridge, Almen, 1946. c and m, Kolenhaven Bridge, Delft, 2004. d and n, Cable-stayed bridge, Heusden, 1989. e and o, Zouthaven Bridge, Amsterdam, 2005. f and p, Jan Waaijer Bridge, Zoetermeer, 2013. g and q, De Oversteek Bridge, Nijmegen, 2013. h and r, Zeeland Bridge, Oosterschelde, 1965. i and s, Hanzeboog Bridge, Zwolle, 2011. j and t, Nescio Bridge, Amsterdam, 2006.

Perf. 13½x12¾

2015, Mar. 30 Litho.

1490 A693 Sheet of 10 16.00 16.00
a.-j. 1 Any single 1.60 1.60
k.-t. 1 Any single, perf. 14½x14¼ 2.75 2.75
u. Booklet pane of 2, #1490k-1490l 5.50 —
v. Booklet pane of 2, #1490m-1490n 5.50 —
w. Booklet pane of 2, #1490o-1490p 5.50 —
x. Booklet pane of 2, #1490q-1490r 5.50 —
y. Booklet pane of 2, #1490s-1490t 5.50 —
Complete booklet, #1490u, 1490v, 1490w, 1490x, 1490y 27.50

On day of issue, Nos. 1490a-1490j each sold for 69c. Complete booklet sold for €12.45. Descriptions of the bridges shown are found on the adjacent sheet selvage.

Hearts and Dots — A694

Die Cut Perf. 14¼x14½

2015, Apr. 28 Photo.

Booklet Stamp
Self-Adhesive

1491 A694 1 multi 1.60 1.60
a. Booklet pane of 10 16.00

No. 1491 sold for 69c on day of issue.

Toys and Games A695

No. 1492: a, Video game equipment. b, Rubik's cube.
No. 1493: a, Robot and wind-up key. b, Board game.

2015, Apr. 28 Litho. ***Perf. 13¼x13½***

1492 A695 Horiz. pair 3.25 3.25
a.-b. 1 Either single 1.60 1.60
1493 A695 Horiz. pair 5.25 5.25
a.-b. 1 Internationaal Either single 2.60 2.60

Europa (No. 1493). On day of issue, Nos. 1492a-1492b each sold for 69c; Nos. 1493a-1493b, €1.15.

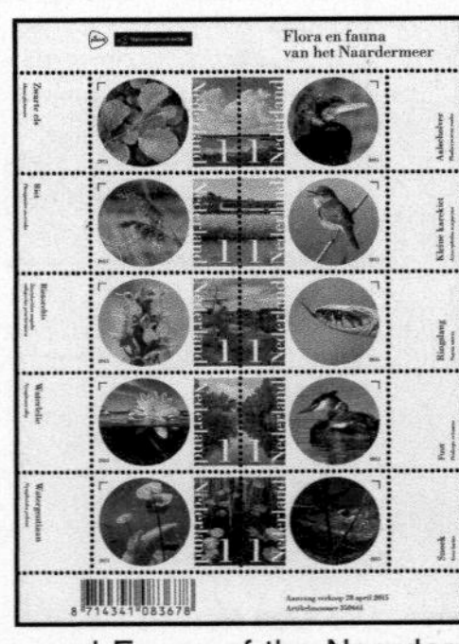

Flora and Fauna of the Naardermeer Nature Reserve — A696

No. 1494: a and k, Alnus glutinosa. b and l, Phalacrocorax carbo. c and m, Phragmites australis. d and n, Acrocephalus scirpaceus. e and o, Dactylorhiza majalis subspecies praetermissa. f and p, Natrix natrix. g and q, Nymphaea alba. h and r, Podiceps cristatus. i and s, Nymphoides peltata. j and t, Esox lucius.

2015, Apr. 28 Litho. ***Perf. 13¼x12¾***

1494 A696 Sheet of 10 16.00 16.00
a.-j. 1 Any single 1.60 1.60
k.-t. 1 Any single, perf. 14½x14¼ 2.75 2.75
u. Booklet pane of 2, #1494s-1494t 5.50 —
v. Booklet pane of 2, #1494q-1494r 5.50 —
w. Booklet pane of 2, #1494o-1494p 5.50 —
x. Booklet pane of 2, #1494m-1494n 5.50 —
y. Booklet pane of 2, #1494k-1494l 5.50 —
Complete booklet, #1494u, 1494v, 1494w, 1494x, 1494y 27.50

On day of issue, Nos. 1494a-1494j each sold for 69c. Complete booklet sold for €12.45.

Volvo Ocean Race A697

No. 1495: a, Three crewmembers on boat. b, Wave crashing against sailboat with Volvo Ocean Race emblem on bow. c, Sailboats in harbor. d, Four crewmembers in protective gear. e, View from mast of crew on deck. f, Boat with sail inscribed "Vestas."

2015, May 26 Litho. ***Perf. 13¼x13¾***

1495 A697 Block of 6 9.75 9.75
a.-f. 1 Any single 1.60 1.60

On day of issue, Nos. 1495a-1495f each sold for 69c.

King William II (1792-1849) — A698

Perf. 13½x13¼

2015, June 22 Litho.

1496 A698 1 Internationaal multi 2.60 2.60

Battle of Waterloo, 200th anniv. No. 1496 sold for €1.15 on day of issue.

Simple Science Experiments — A699

No. 1497: a, Match under egg passing through neck of bottle. b, Water in heated balloon. c, Battery made of lemons. d, Optical illusion of pencil behind glass of water. e, Lightbulb and positively and negatively charged balloons.

2015, July 20 Litho. *Perf. 13½x13¼*

1497 Horiz. strip of 5 7.50 7.50
a.-e. A699 1 Any single 1.50 1.50

On day of issue, Nos. 1497a-1497e each sold for 69c.

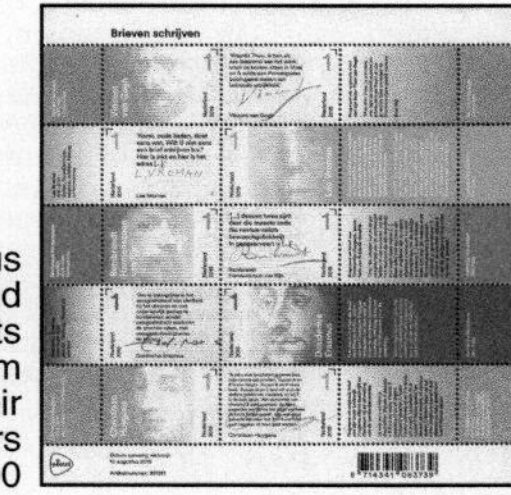

Famous Men and Excerpts From Their Letters A700

No. 1498: a and k, Vincent van Gogh (1853-90), painter. b and l, Signature and excerpt from letter by van Gogh. c and m, Signature and excerpt from letter by Leo Vroman (1915-2014), poet. d and n, Vroman. e and o, Rembrandt van Rijn (1606-69), painter. f and p, Signature and excerpt from letter by Rembrandt. g and q, Signature and excerpt from letter by Desiderius Erasmus (1466-1536), theologian. h and r, Erasmus. i and s, Christiaan Huygens (1629-95), scientist. j and t, Signature and excerpt of letter by Huygens.

Perf. 13½x12¾

2015, Aug. 17 Litho.

1498 A700 Sheet of 10 + 5 labels 16.00 16.00
a.-j. 1 Any single 1.60 1.60
k.-t. 1 Any single, perf. 14½ 2.75 2.75
u. Booklet pane of 2, #1498k-1498l 5.50 —
v. Booklet pane of 2, #1498m-1498n 5.50 —
w. Booklet pane of 2, #1498o-1498p 5.50 —
x. Booklet pane of 2, #1498q-1498r 5.50 —
y. Booklet pane of 2, #1498s-1498t 5.50 —
Complete booklet, #1498u, 1498v, 1498w, 1498x, 1498y 27.50

On day of issue, Nos. 1498a-1498j each sold for 69c. Complete booklet sold for €12.45.

Miniature Sheet

Photographs of Animals by Charlotte Dumas — A701

No. 1499 — Title of photograph: a, Retrieved (retriever named Guinness and trailer in background), 2011. b, Day is Done, 2004 (horse named Isolde, white wall behind horse), 2004. c, Reverie (wolf named Taza sleeping), 2005. d, Tiger Tiger (tiger named Zeus), 2007. e, Heart Shaped Hole (dog named Tom Tom standing next to wall), 2008. f, Retrieved (dog named Moxie sitting on dock), 2011. g, Randagi (street dog laying on step), 2006. h, Anima (horse named Ringo in darkened stall), 2012. i, The Widest Prairies (horse named Rocky Road standing in field), 2013. j, Casa Voyageurs (cat named Kat), 2012.

Perf. 13¼x13½

2015, Sept. 14 Litho.

1499 A701 Sheet of 10 16.00 16.00
a.-j. 1 Any single 1.60 1.60

On day of issue Nos. 1499a-1499j each sold for 69c. Titles of photographs are in sheet selvage adjacent to each stamp.

Miniature Sheet

Dutch Connections With the United States of America — A702

No. 1500: a, "Jan Kees" on pinstriped uniform in script of New York Yankees emblem. b, New York City subway signs using Dutch spellings of Harlem and Brooklyn. c, City Hall, The Hague, designed by Richard Meier. d, High Line Linear Park, New York City. e, Hotdog USA, by Jan Cremer. f, Photograph of breakedancer Kid Freeze holding boom box, by Jamel Shabazz.

Perf. 13¼x13½

2015, Sept. 14 Litho.

1500 A702 Sheet of 6 16.00 16.00
a.-f. 1 Internationaal Any single 2.60 2.60

Nos. 1500a-1500f each sold for €1.15 on day of issue. No. 1500 was printed with three different illustrations in the bottom sheet margin, with each sheet having a different arrangement of stamps. Sheet margins at left and right served as etiquettes.

Miniature Sheet

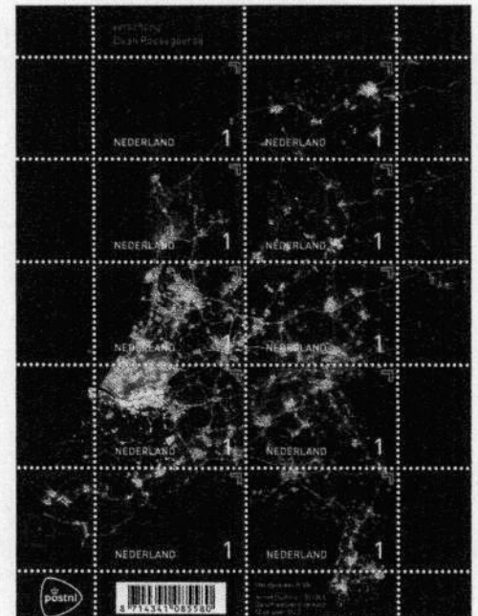

Netherlands at Night as Seen From Space — A703

No. 1501: a, West Frisian Islands. b, Northern Netherlands (area around Groningen and Leeuwarden). c, North Holland Province (area around Alkmaar). d, Drenthe and Overijssel Provinces (area around Hoogeveen and Meppel). e, Area around Amsterdam and Utrecht. f, Flevoland Province (area around Deventer and Apeldoorn). g, Area around Rotterdam. h, Area around Nijmegen and 's Hertogenbosch. i, Zeeland Province and North Brabant Province area north of Belgian border. j, Southeastern Netherlands (area around Eindhoven and Echt).

2015, Oct. 12 Litho. *Perf. 13¼x13½*

1501 A703 Sheet of 10 16.00 16.00
a.-j. 1 Any single 1.60 1.60

On day of issue Nos. 1501a-1501j each sold for 69c.

Ship Models at Rotterdam Maritime Museum — A704

No. 1502: a and k, Aegir. b and l, Bomschuit. c and m, Trio. d and n, Sindoro. e and o, Sultan van Koetei. f and p, Fairmount Expedition. g and q, Mataró. h and r, Assahan. i and s, Nedlloyd Houtman. j and t, Padmos/Blijdorp.

2015, Oct. 12 Litho. *Perf. 13½x12¾*

1502 A704 Sheet of 10 16.00 16.00
a.-j. 1 Any single 1.60 1.60
k.-t. 1 Any single, perf. 14½ 2.75 2.75
u. Booklet pane of 2, #1502q, 1502t 5.50 —
v. Booklet pane of 2, #1502l, 1502m 5.50 —
w. Booklet pane of 2, #1502n, 1502o 5.50 —
x. Booklet pane of 2, #1502r, 1502s 5.50 —
y. Booklet pane of 2, #1502k, 1502p 5.50 —
Complete booklet, #1502u, 1502v, 1502w, 1502x, 1502y 27.50

On day of issue Nos. 1502a-1502j each sold for 69c. Complete booklet sold for €12.45.

Netherlands No. 266 — A705

2015, Oct. 16 Litho. *Perf. 13½x14*

1503 A705 1 multi 1.60 1.60
a. Booklet pane of 2 5.50 —
Complete booklet, 5 #1503a 27.50

No. 1503 sold for 69c on day of issue. Complete booklet sold for €12.45. The five examples of No. 1503a in the complete booklet have different margins.

December Stamps — A706

No. 1504 — Snowflakes and: a, Fox in den, deer and bird. b, Woman and deer. c, Bird on woman's hand. d, Swans. e, Polar bear and bird. f, Rabbits. g, Squirrels. h, Birds in flight. i, Woman and dog. j, Rabbit, bird, fawn, and deer.

Serpentine Die Cut 12½x12¾

2015, Nov. 24 Photo.

Self-Adhesive

1504 A706 Block of 10 14.00
a.-j. (64c) Any single 1.40 1.40

The Hay Wagon, by Hieronymus Bosch (c. 1450-1516) — A707

No. 1505 — Painting details: a and k, Man holding stick, woman holding infant. b and l, Wagon wheel, woman holding stick. c and m, Man in blue with lifted arms at side of wagon. d and n, Man in red looking at wagon wheel from behind. e and o, People with heads of animals. f and p, Man holding stick and carrying infant on back, child. g and q, Bird roasting on a spit. h and r, Man looking in woman's mouth. i and s, Bagpipe player and nun holding hay. j and t, Woman reaching in bag of hay, monk holding glass.

2016, Jan. 4 Litho. *Perf. 13½x13¼*

1505 A707 Sheet of 10 16.00 16.00
a.-j. 1 Any single 1.60 1.60
k. Booklet pane of 2, #1505a, 1505f 5.50 —
l. Booklet pane of 2, #1505b, 1505g 5.50 —
m. Booklet pane of 2, #1505c, 1505h 5.50 —
n. Booklet pane of 2, #1505d, 1505i 5.50 —
o. Booklet pane of 2, #1505e, 1505j 5.50 —
Complete booklet, #1505k, 1505l, 1505m, 1505n, 1505o 27.50

On day of issue, Nos. 1505a-1505j each sold for 73c. Complete booklet sold for €12.45.

Fishing Communities — A708

Designs: No. 1506, Urk. No. 1507, Zoutkamp. No. 1508, Volendam. No. 1509, Arnemuiden. No. 1510, Scheveningen.

2016 Litho. *Perf. 14½x14¼*

1506 A708 1 multi 1.60 1.60
a. Perf. 13½x12¾ 2.75 2.75
b. Booklet pane of 2 #1506a 5.50 —
1507 A708 1 multi 1.60 1.60
a. Perf. 13½x12¾ 2.75 2.75
b. Booklet pane of 2 #1507a 5.50 —
1508 A708 1 multi 1.60 1.60
a. Perf. 13½x12¾ 2.75 2.75
b. Booklet pane of 2 #1508a 5.50 —
1509 A708 1 multi 1.60 1.60
a. Perf. 13½x12¾ 2.75 2.75
b. Booklet pane of 2 #1509a 5.50 —
1510 A708 1 multi 1.60 1.60
a. Perf. 13½x12¾ 2.75 2.75
b. Booklet pane of 2 #1510a 5.50 —
Complete booklet, #1506b, 1507b, 1508b, 1509b, 1510b 27.50
c. Souvenir sheet of 5, #1506-1510 8.00 8.00
Nos. 1506-1510 (5) 8.00 8.00

Issued: Nos. 1506, 1507, 1508, 2/1. Nos. 1506a, 1507a, 1508a, 1509, 1509a, 1510, 1510a, 1510b, 1510c, 5/23. Nos. 1506-1510 each sold for 73c on day of issue. Complete booklet sold for €12.45.

Miniature Sheet

Postcrossing — A709

No. 1511 — Inscriptions: a, Deltawerken (Delta works). b, De Waddeneiland (Wadden Island). c, De Hoge Veluwe (Hoge Veluwe National Park). d, Het Binnenhof (Binnenhof, The Hague) e, Alkmaar Kaasmarkt (Alkmaar Cheese Market). f, Bollenvelden (Flower fields). g, Giethoorn. h, Marken. i, Zaanse Schans. j, Nacht Wacht (Night Watch).

Perf. 13¼x13½

2016, Mar. 29 Litho.

1511 A709 Sheet of 10 30.00 30.00
a.-j. 1 Internationaal Any single 3.00 3.00

On day of issue Nos. 1511a-1511j each sold for €1.25. Sheet margins at left and right served as etiquettes.

Europa A710

No. 1512: a, Painter with roller, buildings, wind generators, bicyclist. b, Bicycle.

2016, Apr. 25 Litho. ***Perf. 13¼x13½***
1512 A710 Pair 6.00 6.00
a.-b. 1 Internationaal Either single 3.00 3.00

Think Green Issue.

On day of issue, Nos. 1512a-1512b each sold for €1.25.

Miniature Sheet

Birds From Griend in the Wadden Islands A711

No. 1513: a, Thalasseus sandvicensis in flight. b, Two Haematopus ostralegus in flight. c, Tadorna tadorna with bill in water. d, Limosa lapponica with beak in water. e, Two Calidris alpina on land. f, Pluvialis squatarola walking. g, Charadrius hiaticula on nest. h, Sterna hirundo on nest. i, Head of Calidris canutus. j, Head of Somateria mollissima.

2016, Apr. 25 Litho. ***Perf. 13¼x13½***
1513 A711 Sheet of 10 17.50 17.50
a.-j. 1 Any single 1.75 1.75
k. Booklet pane of 2, #1513a-1513b 6.00 —
l. Booklet pane of 2, #1513c-1513d 6.00 —
m. Booklet pane of 2, #1513e-1513f 6.00 —
n. Booklet pane of 2, #1513g-1513h 6.00 —
o. Booklet pane of 2, #1513i-1513j 6.00 —
Complete booklet, #1513k, 1513l, 1513m, 1513n, 1513o 30.00

Latin names of birds are on the selvage to left or right of the stamps. On day of issue Nos. 1513a-1513j each sold for 73c. Complete booklet sold for €12.45.

Wolfgang Amadeus Mozart in the Netherlands — A712

No. 1514: a, Musical score at left, Mozart at right. b, Mozart at left, Müller Organ, Church of St. Bavo, Haarlem.

2016, May 23 Litho. ***Perf. 13¼x13½***
1514 A712 Horiz. pair 3.25 3.25
a.-b. 1 Either single 1.60 1.60

On day of issue, Nos. 1514a-1514b each sold for 73c.

Photographs by Ed van der Elsken (1925-90) — A713

No. 1501: a, Women crossing street, women standing on street corner. b, People lying on grass, woman and girls. c, Man lighting cigarette near car, woman and child wearing helmets on bicycle. d, People kissing. e, Women standing near track lanes, men on motorcycles. f, Man with tattoos on cobblestone street, man, woman holding child and cigarette. g, Man and woman holding gardening tools, man, woman pushing baby carriage. h, Man and woman walking past older woman at street corner, woman adjusting shoe near fence. i, Young woman standing in field, man, woman and child standing on vehicle rails. j, Man and woman on crowded street, seated woman.

2016, May 23 Litho. ***Perf. 13¼x13½***
1515 A713 Sheet of 10 16.00 16.00
a.-j. 1 Any single 1.60 1.60

On day of issue Nos. 1515a-1515j each sold for 73c.

Comic Book Characters by Marten Toonder A714

No. 1516: a, Tom Poes. b, Olivier B. Bommel.

2016, June 3 Litho. ***Perf. 13½x13¼***
1516 A714 Pair 3.25 3.25
a.-b. 1 Either single 1.60 1.60

Tom Poes, 75th anniv. On day of issue, Nos. 1516a-1516b each sold for 73c.

Europride Amsterdam 2016 Gay Pride Festival A715

No. 1517: a, Woman, stars at top of circle. b, Man, stars at bottom of circle.

2016, July 18 Litho. ***Perf. 13½x13¼***
1517 A715 Pair 3.25 3.25
a.-b. 1 Either single 1.60 1.60

On day of issue, Nos. 1517a-1517b each sold for 73c.

Souvenir Sheet

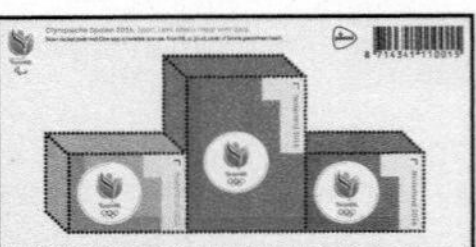

2016 Summer Olympics, Rio de Janeiro — A716

No. 1518 — Netherlands team emblem on winner's platform in: a, Gold (36x50mm). b, Silver (36x25mm). c, Bronze (36x25mm).

2016, July 18 Litho. ***Perf. 14½***
1518 A716 Sheet of 3 5.00 5.00
a.-c. 1 Any single 1.60 1.60

On day of issue, Nos. 1518a-1518c each sold for 73c.

Miniature Sheet

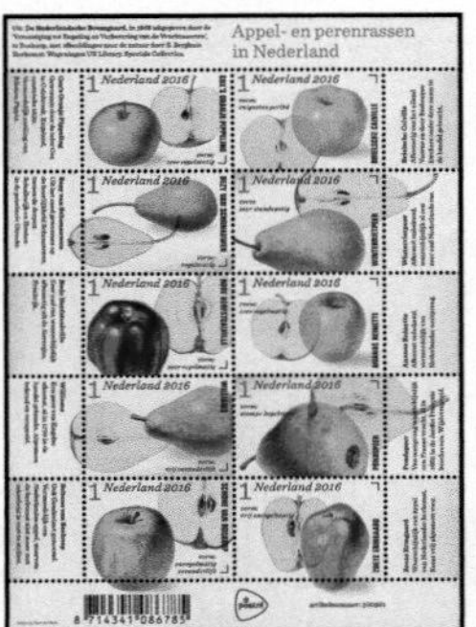

Apple and Pear Varieties A717

No. 1513: a, Cox's orange pippeling apples. b, Brielsche Calville apples. c, Bezy van Schonauwen pears. d, Winterriet pears. e, Rode Herftscalville apples. f, Ananas Reinette apples. g, Williams pears. h, Ponds pears. i, Schone van Boskoop apples. j, Zoete Ermgaard apples.

Perf. 13¼x13½
2016, Aug. 15 Litho.
1519 A717 Sheet of 10 17.50 17.50
a.-j. 1 Any single 1.75 1.75
k. Booklet pane of 2, #1519a-1519b 6.00 —
l. Booklet pane of 2, #1519c-1519d 6.00 —
m. Booklet pane of 2, #1519e-1519f 6.00 —
n. Booklet pane of 2, #1519g-1519h 6.00 —
o. Booklet pane of 2, #1519i-1519j 6.00 —
Complete booklet, #1519k, 1519l, 1519m, 1519n, 1519o 30.00

On day of issue Nos. 1519a-1519j each sold for 73c. Complete booklet sold for €12.45.

Miniature Sheet

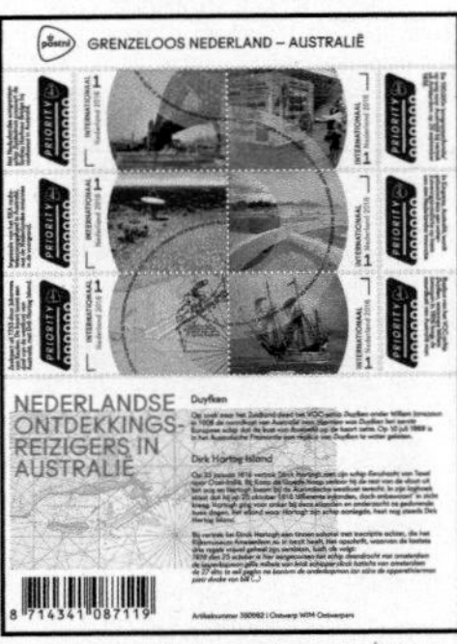

Dutch Connections With Australia — A718

No. 1520: a, Sydney Harbour Bridge. b, Moving crate of 100,000th Dutch emigrant to Australia on dock. c, Radio telescope in Australian desert. d, Water purification plant. e, Nautical chart showing Dirk Hartog's Island. f, Dutch East India Company ship Duyfken.

Perf. 13¼x13½
2016, Aug. 15 Litho.
1520 A718 Sheet of 6 18.00 18.00
a.-f. 1 Internationaal Any single 3.00 3.00

Nos. 1520a-1520f each sold for €1.25 on day of issue. No. 1520 was printed with three different illustrations in the bottom sheet margin, with each sheet having a different arrangement of stamps. Sheet margins at left and right served as etiquettes.

Schiphol Airport, Cent. — A719

No. 1521: a, Airplanes, terminal and control tower. b, Airport check-in area. c, Sign to Gates B21-B33. d, Airplane and portable boarding stairway. e, Old KLM ticket counter and waiting room.

Perf. 13¼x13½
2016, Sept. 12 Litho.
1521 Vert. strip of 5 8.00 8.00
a.-e. A719 1 Any single 1.60 1.60

On day of issue, Nos. 1521a-1521c each sold for 73c.

Photographs of Model Doutzen Kroes by Anton Corbijn — A720

No. 1522 — Kroes: a, With arms raised, no blue violet circle. b, Wearing white panties, blue violet circle over lower back. c, With two blue violet circles over eyes. d, Wearing black swimsuit, blue violet circle at UR. e, Facing left, wearing swimsuit with white straps, large blue violet circle at UR. f, With large blue violet circle over back of ear, jaw and neck. g, Wearing white swimsuit, blue violet circle over legs. h, Topless, with arms crossed, blue violet circle at UR. i, Wearing white swimsuit, looking at hands, small blue violet circle above fingers. j, Wearing black swimsuit, blue violet circle over fingertips.

Perf. 13½x13¼
2016, Sept. 12 Litho.
1522 A720 Sheet of 10 16.00 16.00
a.-j. 1 Any single 1.60 1.60

On day of issue Nos. 1522a-1522j each sold for 73c.

Miniature Sheet

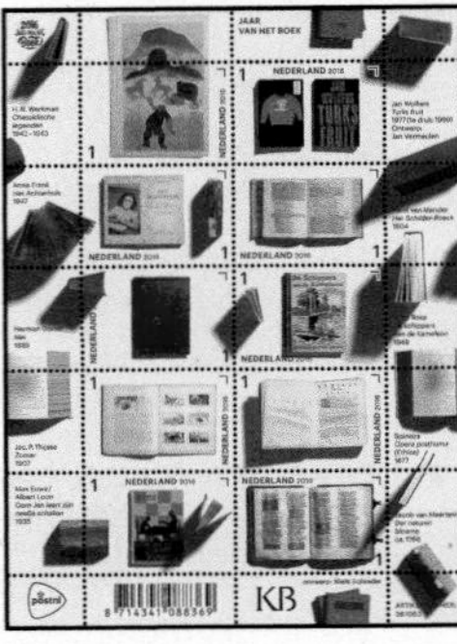

Book Year A721

No. 1523: a, Illustration from *Chassidische Legenden,* by H. N. Werkman. b, Cover of *Turks Fruit,* by Jan Wolkers. c, Photograph and title page of the *Het Achterhuis* (*Diary of Anne Frank*). d, Pages from *Het Schilder-Boeke,* by Karel van Mander. e, *Mei,* by Herman Gorter. f, Cover of *De Schippers van de Kameleon,* by H. de Roos. g, Pages and illustrations of insects from *Zomer,* by Jac. P. Thijsse. h, Title page from *Opera Postuma / Ethica,* by Spinoza. i, Cover of *Oom Jan Leert Zijn Neefje Schaken,* by Max Euwe and Alber Loon. j, Pages with illustrations from *Der Naturen Bloeme,* by Jacob van Maerlant.

Perf. 13¼x13½
2016, Sept. 12 Litho.
1523 A721 Sheet of 10 16.00 16.00
a.-j. 1 Any single 1.60 1.60
k. Booklet pane of 2, #1523a-1523b 5.50 —
l. Booklet pane of 2, #1523c-1523d 5.50 —
m. Booklet pane of 2, #1523e-1523f 5.50 —
n. Booklet pane of 2, #1523g-1523h 5.50 —
o. Booklet pane of 2, #1523i-1523j 5.50 —
Complete booklet, #1523k, 1523l, 1523m, 1523n, 1523o 27.50

Titles and authors are on the selvage to left or right of the stamps. On day of issue Nos. 1523a-1523j each sold for 73c. Complete booklet sold for €12.45.

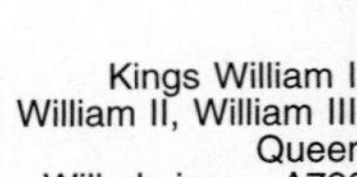

Kings William I, William II, William III, Queen Wilhelmina — A722

2016, Oct. 14 Litho. ***Perf. 13¼x13***
1524 A722 1 multi 1.60 1.60
a. Booklet pane of 2 5.50 —
Complete booklet, 5 #1524a 27.50

No. 1524 sold for 73c on day of issue. Complete booklet sold for €12.45. The five examples of No. 1524a in the complete booklet have different margins.

December Stamps — A723

Designs: No. 1525, Fingers of people making five-pointed star. No. 1526, Gifts on sled. No. 1527, Ice skate. No. 1528, Snow sphere with snowman. No. 1529, Squirrels. No. 1530, Snowflake, Christmas tree and Star of Bethlehem ornaments. No. 1531, Bicycle carrying Christmas tree. No. 1532, Two Christmas ornaments and drink mug. No. 1533, Two champagne glasses. No. 1534, Silhouette of person wearing stocking cap and scarf, Dutch building. No. 1535, Bells, record on turntable.

Serpentine Die Cut 12½
2016, Nov. 14 Litho.
Self-Adhesive
1525 A723 (65c) multi 1.40 1.40
1526 A723 (65c) multi 1.40 1.40
1527 A723 (65c) multi 1.40 1.40
1528 A723 (65c) multi 1.40 1.40

1529 A723 (65c) multi		1.40	1.40
1530 A723 (65c) multi		1.40	1.40
1531 A723 (65c) multi		1.40	1.40
1532 A723 (65c) multi		1.40	1.40
1533 A723 (65c) multi		1.40	1.40
1534 A723 (65c) multi		1.40	1.40
1535 A723 (65c) multi		1.40	1.40
a.	Block of 11, #1525-1535	15.50	
	Nos. 1525-1535 (11)	15.40	15.40

Nos. 1525-1535 are each inscribed "December" at UR, and were printed in sheets of 21, containing No. 1525 and two each Nos. 1526-1535.

Miniature Sheet

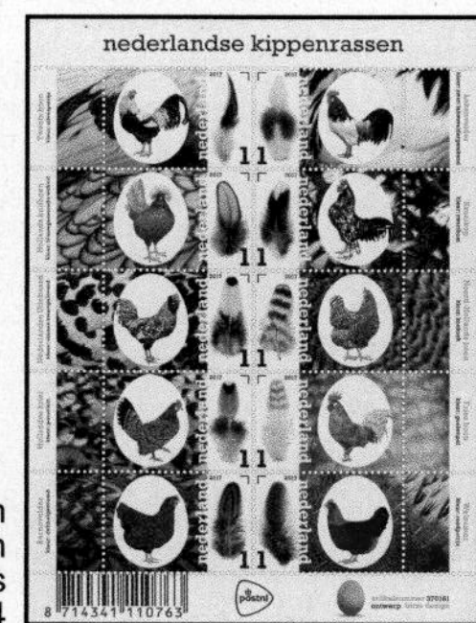

Dutch Chicken Breeds A724

No. 1536: a, Twents hoen. b, Lakenvelder. c, Hollands kuifhoen. d, Kraaikop. e, Nederlandse Uilebaard. f, Noord-Hollands hoen. g, Hollandse kriel. h, Fries hoen. i, Barnevelder. j, Welsumer.

2017, Jan. 2 Litho. *Perf. 13¼x12¾*

1536 A724	Sheet of 10	16.00	16.00
a.-j.	1 Any single	1.60	1.60
k.-t.	1 As #1536a-1536j, any single, perf. 14¼x14½	1.60	1.60
u.	Booklet pane of 2, #1536k-1536l	5.25	—
v.	Booklet pane of 2, #1536m-1536n	5.25	—
w.	Booklet pane of 2, #1536o-1536p	5.25	—
x.	Booklet pane of 2, #1536q-1536r	5.25	—
y.	Booklet pane of 2, #1536s-1536t	5.25	—
	Complete booklet, #1536u, 1536v, 1536w, 1536x, 1536y	26.50	

Breed are on the selvage to left or right of the stamps. On day of issue Nos. 1536a-1536j each sold for 78c. Complete booklet sold for €12.45.

Silver-Studded Blue Butterflies — A725

Tulips A726

Die Cut Perf. 14½

2017, Jan. 30 Litho.

Self-Adhesive Coil Stamps

1537 A725 1 multi		1.75	1.75
1538 A726 1 Internationaal multi		3.00	3.00

On day of issue, No. 1537 sold for 78c; No. 1538, €1.33. Country name, "1," "Internationaal" and codes were printed on the labels by the vending machine at the time of sale. Stamps with other denominations could not be printed.

River Valley Communities — A727

Designs: No. 1539, Church, Oud-Avereest, map of Reest River. No. 1540, Saxon Farm, map of Drentsche Aa River. No. 1541, Fort Asperen, map of Linge River. No. 1542, Vaantje Ferryhouse, map of Dommel River. No. 1543, Wooden house, map of Geul River.

2017 Litho. *Perf. 14¼*

1539 A727 1 multi		1.75	1.75
a.	Perf. 13½x12¾	2.75	2.75
b.	Booklet pane of 2 #1539a	5.50	—
1540 A727 1 multi		1.75	1.75
a.	Perf. 13½x12¾	2.75	2.75
b.	Booklet pane of 2 #1540a	5.50	—
1541 A727 1 multi		1.75	1.75
a.	Perf. 13½x12¾	2.75	2.75
b.	Booklet pane of 2 #1541a	5.50	—
1542 A727 1 multi		1.75	1.75
a.	Perf. 13½x12¾	2.75	2.75
b.	Booklet pane of 2 #1542a	5.50	—
1543 A727 1 multi		1.75	1.75
a.	Perf. 13½x12¾	2.75	2.75
b.	Booklet pane of 2 #1543a	5.50	—
	Complete booklet, #1539b, 1540b, 1541b, 1542b, 1543b	27.50	
c.	Souvenir sheet of 5, #1539-1543	8.75	8.75
	Nos. 1539-1543 (5)	8.75	8.75

Issued: Nos. 1539, 1540, 1541, 1/30. Nos. 1539a, 1540a, 1541a, 1542, 1542a, 1543, 1543a, 1543c, 5/22. Nos. 1539-1543 each sold for 78c on day of issue. Complete booklet sold for €12.45.

Europa A728

No. 1544: a, Doornenburg Castle, three coats of arms at left. b, Ammersoyen Castle, coat of arms at right.

Perf. 13½x12¾

2017, Feb. 20 Litho.

1544 A728	Horiz. pair	5.75	5.75
a.-b.	1 Internationaal Either single	2.75	2.75

On day of issue, Nos. 1544a-1544b each sold for €1.33.

Miniature Sheet

Special Moments A729

No. 1545 — Inscription: a, Gefeliciteerd (31x27mm heart-shaped stamp). b, Liefs (31x27mm heart-shaped stamp). c, Veel geluk (31x27mm heart-shaped stamp). d, Sterkte (28x29mm). e, Succes (28x29mm). f, Hoera (28x29mm). g, Fijne dag (28x29mm). h, Procifiat (31x27mm heart-shaped stamp). i, Voor jou (31x27mm heart-shaped stamp). j, Beterschap (31x27mm heart-shaped stamp).

Die Cut (heart-shaped stamps), Serpentine Die Cut 14¼

2017, Mar. 27 Litho.

Self-Adhesive

1545 A729	Sheet of 10 + 7 stickers	17.50	
a.-j.	1 Any single	1.75	1.75

On day of issue, Nos. 1545a-1545j each sold for 78c.

Miniature Sheet

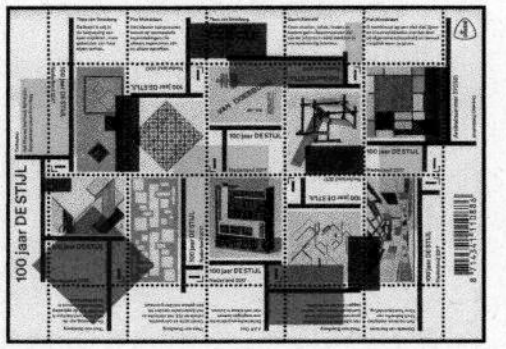

De Stijl Art Movement, Cent. — A730

No. 1546: a, Drawing by Theo van Doesburg (1883-1931), red and blue panels, "1" under red panel. b, Drawing by van Doesburg, yellow and blue panels. c, Drawing by van Doesburg, red and yellow panels. d, Painting of diamond with horizontal and vertical lines by Piet Mondriaan (1872-1944), blue and yellow panels. e, Model of restaurant, by J.J. P. Oud (1890-1963), red and yellow panels, vert. f, De Stijl magazine cover by van Doesburg, yellow and red panels. g, Drawing by van Doesburg, red and blue panels, "1" not under colored panel. h, Chair by Gerrit Rietveld (1888-1964), red and blue panels, vert. i, Architectural drawing by Cornelis van Eesteren (1897-1988), blue and yellow panels. j, Painting of rectangles and squares by Mondrian, yellow and blue panels.

Perf. 13¼x12¾

2017, Mar. 27 Litho.

1546 A730	Sheet of 10	17.50	17.50
a.-j.	1 Any single	1.75	1.75

On day of issue, Nos. 1546a-1546j each sold for 78c.

Miniature Sheet

King Willem-Alexander, 50th Birthday — A731

No. 1547 — Photograph of King Willem-Alexander: a, Reading book as teenager. b, Standing on stairway. c, Standing in boat near bridge. d, Standing in front of building, wearing winter jacket. e, Wearing blue suit and tie. f, With Queen Máxima.

2017, Apr. 24 Litho. *Perf. 14½*

1547 A731	Sheet of 6	10.50	10.50
a.-f.	1 Any single	1.75	1.75

On day of issue, Nos. 1547a-1547f each sold for 78c.

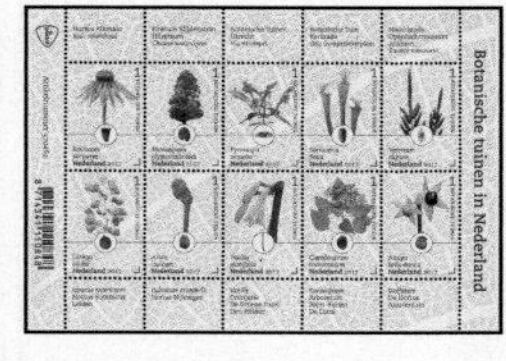

Plants in Dutch Botanical Gardens A732

No. 1548: a, Echinacea purpurea. b, Metasequoia glyptostroboides. c, Pyrostegia venusta. d, Sarracenia flava. e, Veratrum nigrum. f, Ginkgo biloba. g, Arum italicum. h, Vanilla planifolia. i, Clerodendrum trichotomum. j, Atropa belladonna.

2017, Apr. 24 Litho. *Perf. 12¾x13¼*

1548 A732	Sheet of 10	17.50	17.50
a.-j.	1 Any single	1.75	1.75
k.	Booklet pane of 2, #1548a, 1548f	5.50	—
l.	Booklet pane of 2, #1548b, 1548g	5.50	—
m.	Booklet pane of 2, #1548c, 1548h	5.50	—
n.	Booklet pane of 2, #1548d, 1548i	5.50	—
o.	Booklet pane of 2, #1548e, 1548j	5.50	—
	Complete booklet, #1548k, 1548l, 1548m, 1548n, 1548o	27.50	

On day of issue, Nos. 1548a-1548j each sold for 78c. Complete booklet sold for €12.45.

Netherlands Red Cross, 150th Anniv. — A733

No. 1549: a, Red Cross worker comforting elderly woman. b, Child and Red Cross banner. c, Red Cross worker examining woman's arm.

2017, May 22 Litho. *Perf. 14½*

1549	Vert. strip of 3	5.25	5.25
a.-c.	A733 1 Any single	1.75	1.75

On day of issue, Nos. 1549a-1549c each sold for 78c.

Foods A734

Designs: Nos. 1550a, 1550k, Bossche bol. Nos. 1550b, 1550l, Limburgse vlaai. Nos. 1550c, 1550m, Drents kniepertie. Nos. 1550d, 1550n, Fries suikerbrood. Nos. 1550e, 1550o, Zwolse balletjes. Nos. 1550f, 1550p, Goudse stroopwafel. Nos. 1550g, 1550q, Zeeuwse bolus. Nos. 1550h, 1550r, Groningse eierbal. Nos. 1550i, 1550s, Amsterdamse ui. Nos. 1550j, 1550t, Tielse kermiskoek.

2017, June 19 Litho. *Perf. 14½*

1550 A734	Sheet of 10	17.50	17.50
a.-j.	1 Any single	1.75	1.75
k.-t.	1 Any single, perf. 12¾x13¼	3.00	3.00
u.	Booklet pane of 2, #1550k, 1550p	6.00	—
v.	Booklet pane of 2, #1550l, 1550q	6.00	—
w.	Booklet pane of 2, #1550m, 1550r	6.00	—
x.	Booklet pane of 2, #1550n, 1550s	6.00	—
y.	Booklet pane of 2, #1550o, 1550t	6.00	—
	Complete booklet, #1550u, 1550v, 1550w, 1550x, 1550y	30.00	

On day of issue, Nos. 1550a-1550j each sold for 78c. Complete booklet sold for €12.45.

Northern Gannet — A735

Tub Gurnard — A736

Brown Crab — A737

Bladder Wrack and Seaweed — A738

Spotted Ray Egg Case and Shells — A739

2017, July 17 Litho. *Perf. 13¼x12¾*

1551	Vert. strip of 5	9.50	9.50
a.	A735 1 multi	1.90	1.90
b.	A736 1 multi	1.90	1.90
c.	A737 1 multi	1.90	1.90
d.	A738 1 multi	1.90	1.90
e.	A739 1 multi	1.90	1.90
f.	A735 1 multi, perf. 14½	3.00	3.00
g.	A736 1 multi, perf. 14½	3.00	3.00
h.	A737 1 multi, perf. 14½	3.00	3.00
i.	A738 1 multi, perf. 14½	3.00	3.00
j.	A739 1 multi, perf. 14½	3.00	3.00
k.	Booklet pane of 2 #1551f	6.00	—
l.	Booklet pane of 2 #1551g	6.00	—
m.	Booklet pane of 2 #1551h	6.00	—
n.	Booklet pane of 2 #1551i	6.00	—
o.	Booklet pane of 2 #1551j	6.00	—
	Complete booklet, #1551k, 1551l, 1551m, 1551n, 1551o	30.00	

On day of issue, Nos. 1551a-1551j each sold for 78c. Complete booklet sold for €12.45.

Miniature Sheet

Art in Voorlinden Museum — A740

No. 1552: a, Couple Under an Umbrella, by Ron Mueck, and museum visitors. b, R81-4, by Jan Schoonhoeven. c, Flowers and Voorlinden Museum landscaping, by Piet Oudolf. d, Casserole des Moules Noire, by Marcel Broodthaers, and leaf. e, The Performance, by Esther Tielemans. f, Voorlinden Museum and pine cone. g, California #10, by Etel Adnan. h, 2x7x7 by Sol Lewitt, and bird. i, Untitled, by Robert Zandvliet, and flower. j, Larmes de Verre, by Man Ray, and leaf.

2017, July 17 Litho. *Perf. 14½*

1552 A740	Sheet of 10	19.00	19.00
a.-j.	1 Any single	1.90	1.90

On day of issue, Nos. 1552a-1552j each sold for 78c.

Souvenir Sheet

Multilateral Philatelic Exhibition, s'Hertogenbosch — A741

No. 1553: a, Zoete Lieve Gerritje Statue, St. John's Cathedral, s'Hertogenbosch. b, Duke's Palace, Remembrance Monument, Luxembourg Philharmonid, Luxembourg, Church of the Assumption, Ljubljana, Slovenia.

2017, Aug. 25 Litho. *Perf. 14½*

1553 A741 Sheet of 2 5.25 5.25
a. 1 multi 1.90 1.90
b. 1 Internationaal multi 3.25 3.25

On day of issue, No. 1553a sold for 78c, and No. 1553b sold for €1.33. A souvenir sheet containing No. 1553a and Luxembourg No. 1470a was given to standing order customers of Luxembourg Post, and this sheet was sold together with Netherlands No. 1553 and Luxembourg No. 1470 for €15.

Miniature Sheet

Buildings Reconstructed After World War II — A742

No. 1554: a, Velser Tunnel Ventilation Building, Velsen, 1957 (turquoise green panel at center right). b, Purfina gas station, Arnhem, 1957 (turquoise green panel at center left). c, Industriegebouw, Rotterdam, 1953, (yellow green panel at center left). d, Van Leer Drum Factory, Amstelveen, 1958 (yellow green panel at center right). e, Soesterkwartier residential district, Amersfoort, 1957 (pink panel at center right). f, Gemeenteflat (tree in front of building), Maastricht, 1950 (pink panel at center right). g, De Ploeg Weaving Mill, Bergeijk, 1958 (pale dull green panel at center right). h, Blast furnace at steel factory, IJmuiden, 1951 (pale dull green panel at center left). i, Faculty of Geodesy building, Wageningen, 1953 (orange brown panel at center left). j, Second Liberal Christian Lyceum, The Hague, 1954 (orange brown panel at center right).

Perf. 13¼x12¾

2017, Sept. 11 Litho.

1554 A742 Sheet of 10 19.00 19.00
a.-j. 1 Any single 1.90 1.90

On day of issue, Nos. 1554a-1554j each sold for 78c.

Miniature Sheet

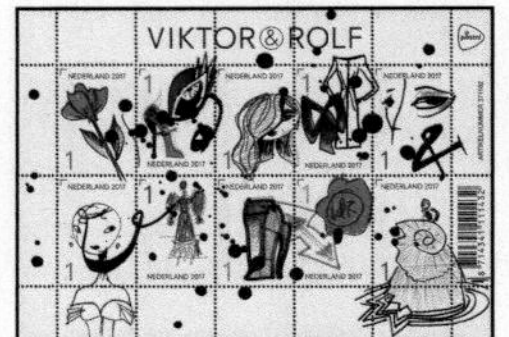

Viktor & Rolf, Fashion Designers, 25th Anniv. — A743

No. 1555 — Ink spots and drawings of: a, Flower. b, Red high-heeled shoe and eye. c, Woman's face covered by long hair. d, Dress and bow. e, Woman's face and ampersand. f, Woman's head and black curved line. g, Faceless woman wearing dress with puffed shoulders. h, Tan high-heeled shoe. i, Arrows and "V&R". j, Woman with yellow green and pink dress.

2017, Sept. 11 Litho. *Perf. 14½*

1555 A743 Sheet of 10 19.00 19.00
a.-j. 1 Any single 1.90 1.90

On day of issue, Nos. 1555a-1555j each sold for 78c.

Wood Engraving and Portrait of Princess Wilhelmina Used on 1891-96 Stamps — A744

2017, Oct. 20 Litho. *Perf. 13¼x14*

1556 A744 1 multi 1.90 1.90
a. Booklet pane of 2 6.00 6.00
Complete booklet, 5 #1556a 30.00

Stamp Day. On day of issue, No. 1556 sold for 78c. Stamps are printed tete-beche on No. 1556a. Complete booklet sold for €12.45 and contains five examples of No. 1556a, each with a different pane margin.

George Michael (1963-2016), Rock Musician A745

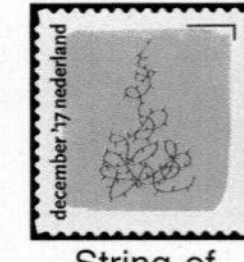

String of Christmas Lights A746

Candle Flame A747

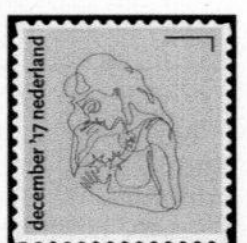

Woman and Stars A748

Fork, G Clef and Musical Notes A749

Christmas Bell and Birds A750

Turkey A751

Stylized Christmas Tree, Hands and Accordion A752

Winter Painting and People Holding Champagne Flutes A753

Christmas Cake A754

Serpentine Die Cut 11

2017, Nov. 20 Photo.

Self-Adhesive

1557 Block of 10 17.50
a. A745 (73c) multi 1.75 1.75
b. A746 (73c) multi 1.75 1.75
c. A747 (73c) multi 1.75 1.75
d. A748 (73c) multi 1.75 1.75
e. A749 (73c) multi 1.75 1.75
f. A750 (73c) multi 1.75 1.75
g. A751 (73c) multi 1.75 1.75
h. A752 (73c) multi 1.75 1.75
i. A753 (73c) multi 1.75 1.75
j. A754 (73c) multi 1.75 1.75

Printed in sheets of 20 containing two each of Nos. 1557a-1557j.

Miniature Sheet

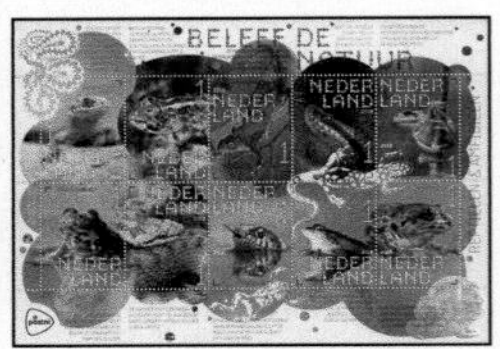

Reptiles and Amphibians — A755

No. 1558 — Inscriptions: a, Levendbarende hagedis. b, Rugstreeppad. c, Kamsalamander. d, Adder. e, Boomkikker. f, Geelbuikvuurpad. g, Gladde slang. h, Ringslang. i, Heikikker. j, Knoflookpad.

2018, Jan. 2 Litho. *Perf. 13½x14*

Self-Adhesive

1558 A755 Sheet of 10 20.00 20.00
a.-j. 1 Any single 2.00 2.00

Nos. 1558a-1558j each sold for 83c on day of issue. Latin names of animals are found in the sheet margin above or below the stamp.

City Gates — A756

City gates in: No. 1559, Hattem. No. 1560, Vianen. No. 1561, Bergen op Zoom. No. 1562, Culemborg. No. 1563, Zierikzee.

2018 Litho. *Perf. 14½x14¼*

1559 A756 1 black 2.10 2.10
a. Perf. 13½x12¾ 3.00 3.00
b. Booklet pane of 2 #1559a 6.00 —
1560 A756 1 black 2.10 2.10
a. Perf. 13½x12¾ 3.00 3.00
b. Booklet pane of 2 #1560a 6.00 —
1561 A756 1 black 2.10 2.10
a. Perf. 13½x12¾ 3.00 3.00
b. Booklet pane of 2 #1561a 6.00 —
1562 A756 1 black 1.90 1.90
a. Perf. 13½x12¾ 3.00 3.00
b. Booklet pane of 2 #1562a 6.00 —
1563 A756 1 black 1.90 1.90
a. Perf. 13½x12¾ 3.00 3.00
b. Booklet pane of 2 #1563a 6.00 —
Complete booklet, #1559b, 1560b, 1561b, 1562b, 1563b 30.00
c. Souvenir sheet of 5, #1559-1563 10.50 10.50
Nos. 1559-1563 (5) 10.10 10.10

Issued: Nos. 1559-1561, 1/29; Nos. 1562-1563, 1559a-1563a, 1563c, 6/4. Nos. 1559-1563 each sold for 83c on day of issue. Complete booklet sold for €12.45.

Miniature Sheet

Children's Birthday Party — A757

No. 1564: a, Child sitting in chair reading book, child opening gift, child holding gift, woman greeting attendees. b, Woman and line of children holding gifts. c, Man giving child gift, girl holding gift, two other children. d, Old woman sitting in chair with hands raised, three children. e, Boy, girl and cat. f, Boy annoying man sitting in chair, boy eating birthday cake.

Perf. 13¼x12¾

2018, Feb. 19 Litho.

1564 A757 Sheet of 6 13.00 13.00
a.-f. 1 Any single 2.10 2.10

Nos. 1564a-1564f each sold for 83c on day of issue.

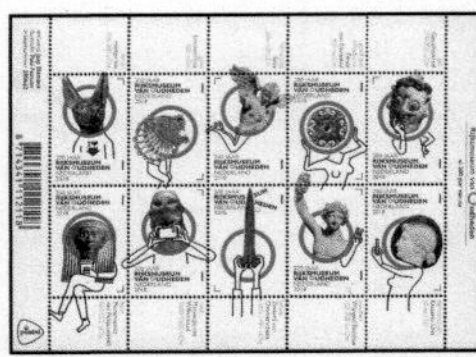

Rijksmuseum van Oudheden (National Museum of Antiquities), Leiden, 200th Anniv. — A758

No. 1565: a and k, Bronze statue of cat, Egypt, 700-300 B.C. b and l, Golden lion's head, Iran, 400 B.C. c and m, Terracotta statue of Eros, Asia Minor, 200-100 B.C. d and n, Gold fibula with precious stones, Wijk bij Duurstede, 800 A.D. e and o, Glass bead depicting face, Egypt, 500-200 B.C. f and p, Wooden case for mummy of Peftjauneith, Egypt, 664-525 B.C. g and q, Wooden figurine of man, Willemstad, Netherlands, 5500-5200 B.C. h and r, Bronze sword, Ommerschans, 1500-1350 B.C. i and s, Marble statue of Bacchus, Italy, 100-200 A.D. j and t, Semi-precious stone sculpture of Empress Livia, Naples area, 10 A.D.

2018, Feb. 19 Litho. *Perf. 14½*

1565 A758 Sheet of 10 21.00 21.00
a.-j. 1 Any single 2.10 2.10
k.-t. 1 Any single, perf. 12¾x13½ 3.00 3.00
u. Booklet pane of 2, #1565k, 1565p 6.00 —
v. Booklet pane of 2, #1565l, 1565q 6.00 —
w. Booklet pane of 2, #1565m, 1565r 6.00 —
x. Booklet pane of 2, #1565n, 1565s 6.00 —
y. Booklet pane of 2, #1565o, 1565t 6.00 —
Complete booklet, #1565u, 1565v, 1565w, 1565x, 1565y 30.00

Nos. 1565a-1565l each sold for 83c on day of issue. Complete booklet sold for €12.45.

Europa A759

No. 1566: a and c, Dedemsvaart Canal swing bridge, Musselkanaal. b and d, Kwakelbrug bascule bridge (with hanging chain), Edam.

2018, Mar. 26 Litho. *Perf. 13½x13*

1566 A759 Horiz. pair 7.00 7.00
a.-b. 1 Internationaal Either single 3.50 3.50
c.-d. 1 Internationaal Perf. 14½x14¼, either single 5.00 5.00
e. Booklet pane of 2, #1566c-1566d 10.00 —
f. Booklet pane of 2 #1566c 10.00 —
g. Booklet pane of 2 #1566d 10.00 —
Complete booklet, #1566e, 1566f, 1566g 30.00

Nos. 1566a-1566b each sold for €1.40 on day of issue. Complete booklet sold for €12.45.

Miniature Sheet

Wild Flowers A760

No. 1567 — Inscriptions: a, Fluitenkruid. b, Hazenpootje. c, Wondklaver. d, Madeliefje. e, Gewone ossentong. f, Pinksterbloem. g, Trilgras. h, Paarse morgenster. i, Paardenbloem. j, Smalle weegbree.

2018, Apr. 9 Litho. *Perf. 13½x14*

Self-Adhesive

1567 A760 Sheet of 10 20.00 20.00
a.-j. 1 Any single 2.00 2.00

Nos. 1567a-1567j each sold for 83c on day of issue. Latin names of flowers are found in the sheet margin above or below the stamp.

A761

Personalized Stamps — A762

2018, Apr. 23 Litho. *Perf. 13½x14*

1568 A761 1 multi 2.00 2.00
1569 A762 1 Internationaal multi 3.50 3.50

Self-Adhesive

1570 A761 1 multi 2.00

On day of issue, Nos. 1568 and 1570 each sold for 83c, and No. 1569 sold for €1.40. The vignettes shown are the generic images available on the day of issue. Vignettes could be personalized for a fee. Used examples of Nos. 1568 and 1570 may be indistinguishable.

In 2019, self-adhesive stamps of type A761, etched on gold foil were produced in limited quantities, packed in an airtight box and sold for €50. In 2022, self-adhesive stamps of type A761, etched on silver foil were produced in limited quantities, packed in a folder and sold for €25.

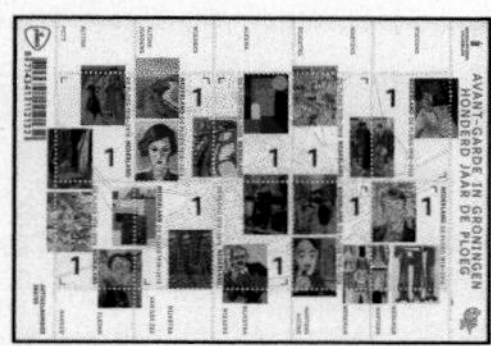

Groninger Museum's Exhibition of Avant-Garde Art by Members of the De Ploeg Artists Collective — A763

No. 1571: a and k, *Blauwborgje, Shadow,* by Alida Pott, and *After the Visit,* by Jan Altink. b and l, *Dike Along the Rietdiep,* by Altink, *Portrait of a Grammar School Student,* by Jan Jordens, and left half of *Groningen Landscape with Canal,* by Jan Wiegers. c and m, Right half of Wiegers painting and *Composition with Diagonal,* by Wobbe Alkema. d and n, *Groningen May Fair,* by Johan Dijkstra, and left half of *Fish Market,* by George Martens. e and o, Right half of Martens painting and *Seated Nude,* by Wiegers. f and p, Lower portion of Pott painting, *Blauwborgje,* by Job Hansen, upper left portion of *Portrait of George Martens,* by Ekke Kleima, and left half of *Landscape Composition,* by Jan van der Zee. g and q, Right half of van der Zee painting, and *Student Path,* by Dijkstra. h and r, *Portrait of Jan Altink,* by Wiegers, and *Courtyard in Winter,* by Dijkstra. i and s, *Kattendiep in the Rain,* by Martens, *Portrait of H. N. Werkman,* by Altink, and upper left portion of *Façade,* by H. N. Werkman. j and t, Upper right portion of Werkmen painting, *Portrait of Alida Pott,* by Martens, and *Composition with the Letter O,* by Werkman.

2018, May 22 Litho. *Perf. 13x13½*

1571 A763 Sheet of 10 20.00 20.00
a.-j. 1 Any single 2.00 2.00
k.-t. 1 Perf. 12¾x13¼, any single 3.00 3.00
u. Booklet pane of 2, #1571k, 1571p 6.00 —
v. Booklet pane of 2, #1571l, 1571q 6.00 —
w. Booklet pane of 2, #1571m, 1571r 6.00 —
x. Booklet pane of 2, #1571n, 1571s 6.00 —
y. Booklet pane of 2, #1571o, 1571t 6.00 —
Complete booklet, #1571u, 1571v, 1571w, 1571x, 1571y 30.00

De Ploeg Artists Collective, cent. On day of issue, Nos. 1571a-1571j each sold for 83c. Complete booklet sold for €12.45. Names of the artists of the painting are found in the upper and lower sheet margins on No. 1571.

Miniature Sheet

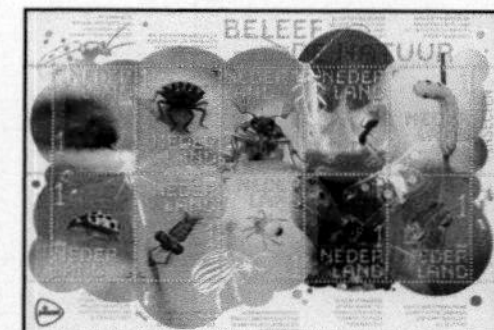

Insects and Spiders A764

No. 1572 — Inscriptions: a, Grote beer. b, Pyjamawants. c, Meikever. d, Zwartbruine wegmier. e, Olifantsrups. f, Citroenlieveheersbeestje. g, Gewone pantserjuffer. h, Kruispin. i, Kleine vuurvlinder. j, Moerassprinkhaan.

2018, June 4 Litho. *Perf. 13½x14*

Self-Adhesive

1572 A764 Sheet of 10 20.00 20.00
a.-j. 1 Any single 2.00 2.00

Nos. 1572a-1572j each sold for 83c on day of issue. Latin names of insects and spider are found in the sheet margin above or below the stamp.

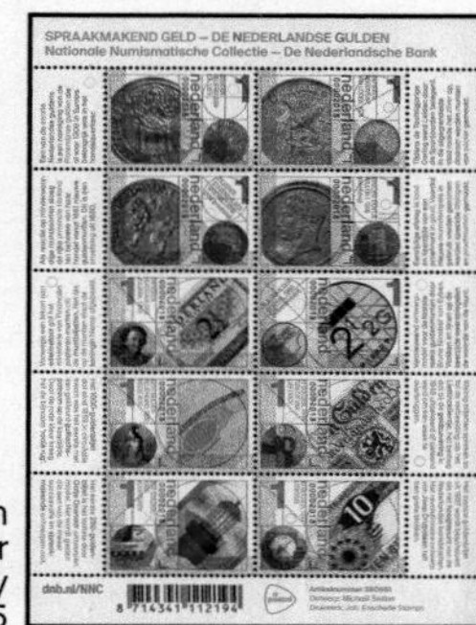

Dutch Guilder Currency A765

No. 1573: a and k, Gold lily guilder, c. 1355. b and l, 1574 paper emergency coin from Leiden. c and m, 1680 proof silver state guilder. d and n, 1818 proof coins from reign of King William I. e and o, 1949 2½-guilder note, Queen Juliana. f and p, Model of 1982 2½-guilder coin for coronation of Queen Beatrix. g and q, 1860 1000-guilder note. h and r, 1945 10-guilder note. i and s, 1986 250-guilder note, j and t, 1997 10-guilder note.

2018, July 23 Litho. *Perf. 13¼x12¾*

1573 A765 Sheet of 10 20.00 20.00
a.-j. 1 Any single 2.00 2.00
k.-t. 1 Perf. 14¼x14½, any single 3.00 3.00
u. Booklet pane of 2, #1573k, 1573l 6.00 —
v. Booklet pane of 2, #1573m, 1573n 6.00 —
w. Booklet pane of 2, #1573o, 1573p 6.00 —
x. Booklet pane of 2, #1573q, 1573r 6.00 —
y. Booklet pane of 2, #1573s, 1573t 6.00 —
Complete booklet, #1573u, 1573v, 1573w, 1573x, 1573y 30.00

On day of issue, Nos. 1573a-1573j each sold for 83c. Complete booklet sold for €12.45.

Van Nelle Factory, Rotterdam, 1931 — A766

Zonnestraal Sanatorium, Hilversum, 1928 — A767

Coöperatie de Volharding Building, The Hague, 1928 — A768

Glaspaleis Department Store, Heerlen, 1935 — A769

House, Utrecht, 1931 — A770

Perf. 13¼x12¾

2018, Sept. 17 Litho.

1574 Vert. strip of 5 10.00 10.00
a. A766 1 multi 2.00 2.00
b. A767 1 multi 2.00 2.00
c. A768 1 multi 2.00 2.00
d. A769 1 multi 2.00 2.00
e. A770 1 multi 2.00 2.00

On day of issue, Nos. 1574a-1574e each sold for 83c.

Miniature Sheet

Mushrooms — A771

No. 1575 — Inscriptions: a, Sparrenveertje. b, Vliegenzwam. c, Takruitertjes. d, Broze russula. e, Knopschimmel op mycena. f, Heideknotszwam. g, Plooivlieswaaiertje. h, Echte kopergroenzwam. i, Grote bloedsteelmycena. j, Grote sponszwam.

2018, Sept. 17 Litho. *Perf. 13½x14*

Self-Adhesive

1575 A771 Sheet of 10 20.00 20.00
a.-j. 1 Any single 2.00 2.00

Nos. 1575a-1575j each sold for 83c on day of issue. Latin names of mushrooms are found in the sheet margin above or below the stamp.

Miniature Sheet

Garden Vegetables — A772

No. 1576: a, Sla (lettuce). b, Aubergine (eggplant). c, Venkel (fennel). d, Radijs (radishes). e, Zoete aardappel (sweet potato). f, Raapstelen (turnip greens).

2018, Oct. 19 Litho. *Perf. 14½*

1576 A772 Sheet of 6 11.50 11.50
a.-f. 1 Any single 1.90 1.90

Nos. 1576a-1576f each sold for 83c on day of issue.

Stamp Day — A773

2018, Oct. 19 Litho. *Perf. 13½x14*

1577 A773 1 multi 1.90 1.90
a. Booklet pane of 2 5.75 —
Complete booklet, 5 #1577a 29.00

No. 1577 sold for 83c on day of issue. Complete booklet sold for €12.45.

December Stamps — A774

No. 1578: a, Dutch buildings. b, Sweater. c, Adult and child ice skating. d, Cat and Christmas tree ornament on tree. e, Holiday foods and table setting. f, Dove carrying letter. g, Snow globe. h, Christmas tree, envelopes and gift. i, Gift boxes. j, Man and woman watching fireworks display.

Serpentine Die Cut 11

2018, Nov. 5 Litho.

Self-Adhesive

1578 Block of 10 17.50
a.-j. A774 (78c) Any single 1.75 1.75

Printed in sheets of 20 containing two each Nos. 1578a-1578j.

Personalized Stamp — A775

2018, Dec. 5 Litho. *Perf. 13½x14*

Self-Adhesive

1579 A775 (78c) multi 1.75 1.75

The vignettes shown is the generic image available on the day of issue. Vignettes could be personalized for a fee.

Miniature Sheet

Mammals — A776

No. 1580 — Inscriptions: a, Wilde kat. b, Ingekorven vleermuis. c, Wolf. d, Grijze zeehond. e, Hermelijn. f, Bunzing. g, Europese otter. h, Vos. i, Das. j, Konijn.

2019, Jan. 2 Litho. *Perf. 13½x14*

Self-Adhesive

1580 A776 Sheet of 10 20.00 20.00
a.-j. 1 Any single 2.00 2.00

Nos. 1580a-1580j each sold for 87c on day of issue. Latin names of mammals are found in the sheet margin above or below the stamp.

Islands — A777

Tourist attractions, landmarks and items from islands and map of: No. 1581, Texel. No. 1582, Vlieland. No. 1583, Terschelling. No. 1584, Ameland. No. 1585, Schiermonnikoog.

2019 Litho. *Perf. 14¼*

1581 A777 1 multi 2.00 2.00
a. Booklet pane of 5 14.00 —
Complete booklet, 2 #1581a 28.00
1582 A777 1 multi 2.00 2.00
a. Booklet pane of 5 14.00 —
Complete booklet, 2 #1582a 28.00
1583 A777 1 multi 2.00 2.00
a. Booklet pane of 5 14.00 —
Complete booklet, 2 #1583a 28.00
1584 A777 1 multi 2.00 2.00
a. Booklet pane of 5 14.00 —
Complete booklet, 2 #1584a 28.00
1585 A777 1 multi 2.00 2.00
a. Booklet pane of 5 14.00 —
Complete booklet, 2 #1585a 28.00
b. Souvenir sheet of 5, #1581-1585 10.00 10.00
Nos. 1581-1585 (5) 10.00 10.00

Issued: No. 1581, 1/2; No. 1582, 2/25; No. 1583, 3/25; No. 1584, 4/23; No. 1585, 5/20. Nos. 1581-1585 each sold for 87c on day of issue. Each complete booklet sold for €12.45.

Souvenir Sheet

Dutch Postal Services, 220th Anniv. A778

No. 1586: a, Six envelopes, three packages. b, Three envelopes, six packages.

2019, Jan. 24 Litho. *Perf. 14¼*

1586 A778 Sheet of 2 4.00 4.00
a.-b. 1 Either single 2.00 2.00

Nos. 1586a-1586b each sold for 87c on day of issue.

Self-portraits of Rembrandt van Rijn (1606-69) — A779

No. 1587: a, Self-portrait in a Soft Cap (c. 1634). b, Self-portrait in a Fur Cap (1630).

2019, Feb. 15 Litho. *Perf. 13¼x14*

1587	A779	Horiz. pair	4.00	4.00
a.-b.		1 Either single	2.00	2.00

Nos. 1587a-1587b each sold for 87c on day of issue. Printed in sheets containing 3 #1578a and 2 #1578b.

Miniature Sheet

Plants A780

No. 1588 — Inscriptions: a, Armbloemig look. b, Gewoon speenkruid. c, Herfsttuloos. d, Bosgeelster. e, Gewoon sneeuwklokje. f, Wilde kievitsbloem. g, Kraailook. h, Gewone vogelmelk. i, Wilde hyacint. j, Winterakoniet.

2019, Feb. 25 Litho. *Perf. 13½x14*
Self-Adhesive

1588	A780	Sheet of 10	20.00	20.00
a.-j.		1 Any single	2.00	2.00

Nos. 1588a-1588j each sold for 87c on day of issue. Latin names of plants are found in the sheet margins above or below the stamps.

Souvenir Sheet

Dutch Aviation Centenaries — A781

No. 1589: a, Fokker F. XXII (tail inscription PH-AJP), fuselage of Douglas DC-2 (tail inscription PH-AJU), tail of Fokker F27 Friendship (tail inscription PH-SAD). b, Fuselage of Fokker F27 Friendship, Fokker 50 (small KLM airplane). c, Cessna 550 Citation II (tail inscription PH-LAB), tail of Fokker 70 (fuselage inscription PH-KZU), wing tip of KLM jet.

2019, Mar. 11 Litho. *Perf. 14x13½*

1589	A781	Sheet of 3	6.00	6.00
a.-c.		1 Any single	2.00	2.00

Centenaries of KLM (Royal Dutch Arilines), Fokker (aircraft manufacturer), and the Netherlands Aersopace Center. Nos. 1589a-1589c each sold for 87c on day of issue.

Europa A782

No. 1590 — Inscriptions: a, Putter (goldfinch). b, Pestvogel (Bohemian waxwing).

2019, Apr. 23 Litho. *Perf. 13¼x12¾*

1590	A782	Horiz. pair	6.50	6.50
a.-b.		1 Internationaal Either single	3.25	3.25

Nos. 1590a-1590b each sold for €1.45 on day of issue.

Miniature Sheet

Birds A783

No. 1591 — Inscriptions: a, Pimpelmees (blue tit). b, Winterkoning (wren). c, Roodborst (robin). d, Huismus (house sparrow). e, Goudhaan (goldcrest). f, Koolmees (great tit).

2019, May 20 Litho. *Perf. 13¼x12¾*

1591	A783	Sheet of 6	12.00	12.00
a.-f.		1 Any single	2.00	2.00

Nos. 1591a-1591f each sold for 87c on day of issue. Latin names of plants are found in the sheet margins to left or right of the stamps.

Miniature Sheet

Butterflies and Moths — A784

No. 1592 — Inscriptions: a, Gentiaan blauwtje. b, Aardbeivlinder. c, Groentje. d, Kleine vos. e, Lieveling. f, Bruine vuurvlinder. g, Icarus blauwtje. h, Sint-Jansvlinder. i, Nachtpauwoog. j, Phegeavlinder.

2019, June 11 Litho. *Perf. 13½x14*
Self-Adhesive

1592	A784	Sheet of 10	20.00	20.00
a.-j.		1 Any single	2.00	2.00

Nos. 1592a-1592j each sold for 87c on day of issue. Latin names of plants are found in the sheet margins above or below the stamps.

Pearls A785

Julius Caesar, Died 44 B.C. A786

Nadia A787

Portrait #5 A788

Portrait of Alex — A789

2019, July 1 Litho. *Perf. 13x13¼*

1593		Horiz. strip of 5	10.00	10.00
a.	A785	1 multi	2.00	2.00
b.	A786	1 multi	2.00	2.00
c.	A787	1 multi	2.00	2.00
d.	A788	1 multi	2.00	2.00
e.	A789	1 multi	2.00	2.00

Photographs by Erwin Olaf. Nos. 1593a-1593e each sold for 87c on day of issue.

Miniature Sheets

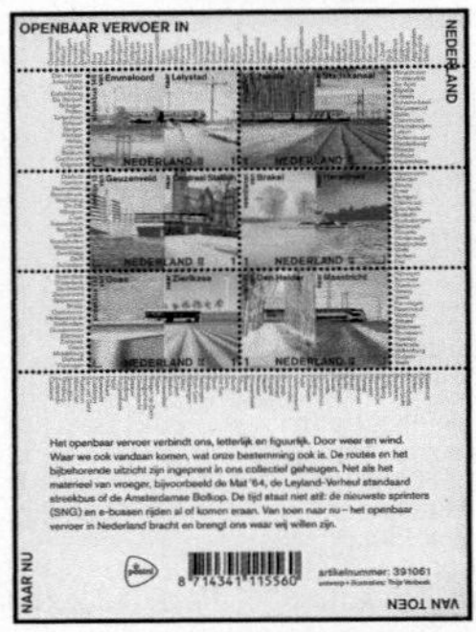

A790

Public Transportation — A791

No. 1594: a, Emmeloord-Lelystad regional bus route 146. b, Zwolle-Stadskanaal local train. c, Geuzenveld District-Amsterdam Central Station tram route 13. d, Brakel-Herwijne ferry service. e, Goes-Zierikzee regional bus route 132. f, Den Helder-Maastricht intercity train.

No. 1595: a, Leeuwarden-Rotterdam intercity train. b, Paddepoel District-De Wijert District city bus route 5. c, Amsterdam Noord-Amsterdam Zuid subway train line 52. d, Amsterdam-Berlin train. e, Den Haag HS Station-Duindorp District tram route 12. f, Arnhem-Winterswijk local train.

Perf. 13¼x12¾
2019, Aug. 19 Litho.

1594	A790	Sheet of 6	11.50	11.50
a.-f.		1 Any single	1.90	1.90
1595	A791	Sheet of 6	19.50	19.50
a.-f.		1 Internationaal Any single	3.25	3.25

On day of issue, Nos. 1594a-1594f each sold for 87c; Nos. 1595a-1595f, €1.45. Sheet margins at left and right served as etiquettes.

Miniature Sheet

Trees A792

No. 1596 — Inscriptions: a, Beuk ("1" at LR). b, Zomerlinde. c, No inscription (leaves, "1" at LL). d, Ratelpopulier. e, Gewone es. f, Mispel. g, No inscription (leaves, "1" at right). h, Linde. i, Beuk ("1" at left). j, Ruwe berk.

2019, Sept. 16 Litho. *Perf. 13½x14*
Self-Adhesive

1596	A792	Sheet of 10	19.00	19.00
a.-j.		1 Any single	1.90	1.90

Nos. 1596a-1596j each sold for 87c on day of issue. Latin names of plants are found in the sheet margins above or below the stamps.

Miniature Sheet

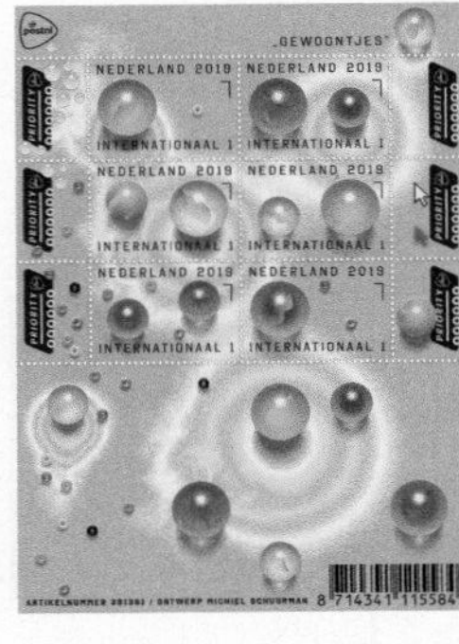

Marbles and Beads A793

No. 1597: a, Large light green and red marble, one bead. b, Large green and red marble, small green marble. c, Small green marble with yellow spiral, large blue and red marble. d, Small blue and yellow marble, large light green marble. e, One small blue and pink marble, One small green and red marble, three beads. f, Large green and yellow marble, two beads.

2019, Oct. 18 Litho. *Perf. 13¼x12¾*

1597	A793	Sheet of 6	19.50	19.50
a.-f.		1 Internationaal Any single	3.25	3.25

On day of issue, Nos. 1597a-1597f each sold for €1.45. Sheet margins at left and right served as etiquettes.

Stamp Day A794

No. 1598 — Seagull in: a, Orange. b, Green.

2019, Nov. 1 Litho. *Perf. 14x13¼*

1598	A794	Horiz. pair	4.00	4.00
a.-b.		1 Either single	2.00	2.00
c.		Booklet pane of 2, #1598a-1598b	5.50	—
		Complete booklet, 5 #1598c	28.00	

Nos. 1598a-1598b each sold for 87c on day of issue. No. 1598 was printed in sheets containing 5 pairs. Complete booklet sold for €12.45, and contains five panes with different pane margins.

Woman With Horn A795

Boy on Reindeer A796

Man Holding String of Lights A797

Raccoon With Gift and Torch A798

Woman With Cake A799

Pig on Sled A800

Woman With Lantern A801

Chickens A802

Man Carrying Christmas Tree A803

Polar Bear Mailing Letters A804

Serpentine Die Cut 11¼

2019, Nov. 4 Litho.

Self-Adhesive

1599	Block of 10	19.00	
a.	A795 (82c) multi	1.90	1.90
b.	A796 (82c) multi	1.90	1.90
c.	A797 (82c) multi	1.90	1.90
d.	A798 (82c) multi	1.90	1.90
e.	A799 (82c) multi	1.90	1.90
f.	A800 (82c) multi	1.90	1.90
g.	A801 (82c) multi	1.90	1.90
h.	A802 (82c) multi	1.90	1.90
i.	A803 (82c) multi	1.90	1.90
j.	A804 (82c) multi	1.90	1.90

Printed in sheets of 20 containing two each of Nos. 1599a-1599j.

Souvenir Sheet

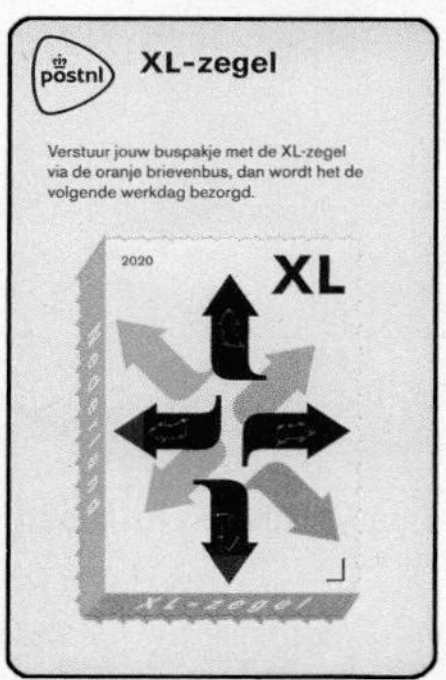

Arrows A805

Zigzag Die Cut 6¾

2020, Jan. 2 Litho.

Self-Adhesive

1600 A805 (€4.40) multi 10.00 10.00

Miniature Sheet

Owls and Birds of Prey A806

No. 1601 — Inscriptions: a, Visarend. b, Wespendief. c, Rode wouw. d, Velduil. e, Grauwe kiekendief. f, Torenvalk. g, Blauwe kiekendief. h, Boomvalk. i, Ransuil. j, Zeearend.

2020, Jan. 2 Litho. *Perf. 13¼x14*

Self-Adhesive

1601	A806 Sheet of 10	21.00	21.00
a.-j.	1 Any single	2.10	2.10

Nos. 1601a-1601j each sold for 91c on day of issue. Latin names of birds are found in the sheet margin above or below the stamp.

Dutch Foods — A807

Designs: No. 1602, Rookworst. No. 1603, Carrots. No. 1604, Hagelslag (chocolate sprinkles) on bread. No. 1605, Tompouce (custard-filled pastry). No. 1606, Bitterballen (meatballs).

2020 Litho. *Perf. 14x13¼*

1602	A807 1 multi	2.10	2.10
a.	Booklet pane of 2	5.50	—
1603	A807 1 multi	2.10	2.10
a.	Booklet pane of 2	5.50	—
1604	A807 1 multi	2.00	2.00
a.	Booklet pane of 2	5.50	—
1605	A807 1 multi	2.00	2.00
a.	Booklet pane of 2	5.50	—
1606	A807 1 multi	2.10	2.10
a.	Booklet pane of 2	5.50	—
	Complete booklet, #1602a, 1603a, 1604a, 1605a, 1606a	27.50	
	Nos. 1602-1606 (5)	10.30	10.30

Issued: No. 1602, 1/2; No. 1603, 2/24; No. 1604, 3/23; No. 1605, 4/6; Nos. 1602a, 1603a, 1604a, 1605a, 1606, 1606a, 6/15. Complete booklet sold for €12.45. On day of issue, Nos. 1602-1606 each sold for 91c.

Miniature Sheet

Farmland Birds A808

No. 1607 — Inscriptions: a, Gele kwikstaart. b, Slobeend. c, Grutto. d, Wulp. e, Zomertortel. f, Patrijs. g, Kievit. h, Steenuil. i, Tureluur. j, Veldleeuwerik.

2020, Feb. 24 Litho. *Perf. 13¼x14*

Self-Adhesive

1607	A808 Sheet of 10	21.00	21.00
a.-j.	1 Any single	2.10	2.10

Nos. 1607a-1607j each sold for 91c on day of issue. Latin names of birds are found in the sheet margin above or below the stamp.

Cartographers and Their Maps of the Low Countries — A809

No. 1608: a, Abraham Ortelius (1527-98), 1571 map in oval. b, Gerard de Jode (1509-91), 1578 map with compass rose at left. c, Gerard Mercator (1512-94), wearing hat, holding compass and globe at left, 1585 map with rectangular legend at upper left. d, Jodocus Hondius (1563-1612), holding compass and globe at right, 1606 map with red and green regions. e, Willem Janszoon Blaeu (1571-1638), 1630 map with large ships at upper right. f, Johannes Janssonius (1588-1664), 1638 map with three small ships at top.

Perf. 13¼x12¾

2020, Mar. 23 Litho.

1608	A809 Sheet of 6	19.50	19.50
a.-f.	1 Internationaal Any single	3.25	3.25
g.	Booklet pane of 2, #1608a-1608b	9.00	—
h.	Booklet pane of 2, #1608c-1608d	9.00	—
i.	Booklet pane of 2, #1608e-1608f	9.00	—
	Complete booklet, #1608g-1608i	27.00	

On day of issue, Nos. 1608a-1608f each sold for €1.50. Cartographer's names are found in the sheet selvage to the left or right of each stamp. The selvage to the left or right of the stamps served as etiquettes. The complete booklet sold for €12.45.

People Born in Freedom A810

No. 1609: a, Yvette Hartman-Mercier, expectant mother due to give birth May 5, 2020. b, Jan van der Linden, born May 5, 1945.

2020, Apr. 16 Litho. *Perf. 14¼x14½*

1609	A810 Pair	4.00	4.00
a.-b.	1 Either single	2.00	2.00
c.	As #1609a, perf. 12¾x13¼	2.25	2.25
d.	As #1609b, perf. 12¾x13¼	2.25	2.25
e.	Booklet pane of 3, #1609d, 2 #1609c	6.75	—
f.	Booklet pane of 3, #1609c, 2 #1609d	6.75	—
	Complete booklet, 2 each #1609e-1609f	27.00	

Restoration of freedom after World War II, 75th anniv. On day of issue, Nos. 1609a-1609b each sold for 91c. The panes in the complete booklet have different pane margins. Complete booklet sold for €12.45.

Miniature Sheet

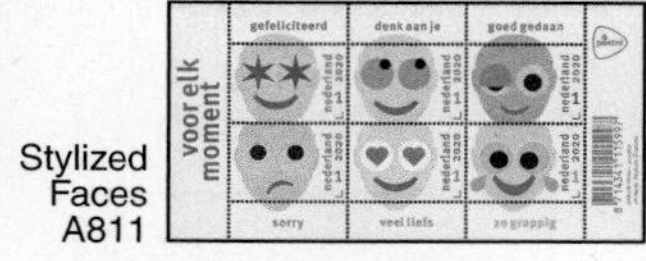

Stylized Faces A811

No. 1610: a, Lilac face with stars for eyes. b, Light blue face with eyes looking upward. c, Brown face with winking eye. d, Light green face with frown. e, Pale orange face with hearts for eyes. f, Yellow face laughing and crying.

2020, May 11 Litho. *Perf. 14½*

1610	A811 Sheet of 6	12.00	12.00
a.-f.	1 Any single	2.00	2.00

On day of issue, Nos. 1610a-1610f each sold for 91c.

Europa A812

No. 1611: a, Postrider on horseback. b, Horse-drawn postal coach.

2020, May 11 Litho. *Perf. 13¼x12¾*

1611	A812 Horiz. pair	7.00	7.00
a.-b.	1 Internationaal Either single	3.50	3.50
c.	Booklet pane of 2, #1611a-1611b + 2 etiquettes.	7.00	—
	Complete booklet, 4 #1611c	28.00	

Ancient Postal Routes.

On day of issue, Nos. 1611a-1611b each sold for €1.50. Sheet selvage to left or right of the stamps served as etiquettes. Each booklet pane has a different pane margin. Complete booklet sold for €12.45.

Miniature Sheet

Coastal Birds A813

No. 1612 — Inscriptions: a, Dwergstern. b, Kleine jager. c, Steenloper. d, Sneeuwgors. e, Drieteenmeeuw. f, Grote mantelmeeuw. g, Strandleeuwerik. h, Kluut. i, Paarse strandloper. j, Strandplevier.

2020, June 15 Litho. *Perf. 13¼x14*

Self-Adhesive

1612	A813 Sheet of 10	21.00	21.00
a.-j.	1 Any single	2.10	2.10

Nos. 1612a-1612j each sold for 91c on day of issue. Latin names of birds are found in the sheet margin above or below the stamp.

Bicycle Parts A814

No. 1613 — Detail of: a, Reflector. b, Fietsframe (bicycle frame). c, Handvat (handlebar grip). d, Fietsbel (bicycle bell). e, Buitenband (tire tread). f, Binnenband (inner tube).

Perf. 13¼x12¾

2020, Aug. 17 Litho.

1613	A814 Sheet of 6	13.50	13.50
a.-f.	1 Any single	2.25	2.25
g.	As #1613a, perf. 14¼	3.00	3.00
h.	As #1613b, perf. 14¼	3.00	3.00
i.	As #1613c, perf. 14¼	3.00	3.00
j.	As #1613d, perf. 14¼	3.00	3.00
k.	As #1613e, perf. 14¼	3.00	3.00
l.	As #1613f, perf. 14¼	3.00	3.00
m.	Booklet pane of 2, #1613g-1613h	6.00	—
n.	Booklet pane of 2, #1613i-1613j	6.00	—
o.	Booklet pane of 2, #1613k-1613l	6.00	—
	Complete booklet, #1313o, 2 each #1613m-1613n	30.00	

On day of issue, Nos. 1613a-1613f each sold for 91c. Each booklet pane has a different pane margin. Complete booklet sold for €12.45.

Miniature Sheet

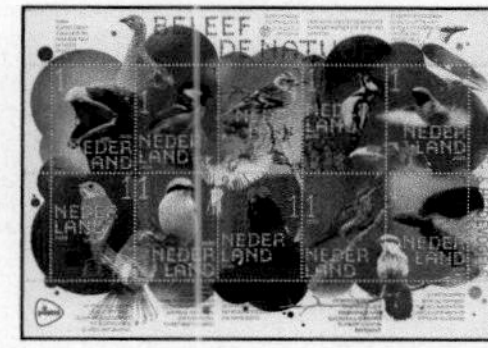

Forest and Heathland Birds — A815

No. 1614 — Inscriptions: a, Raaf. b, Zwarte mees. c, Keep. d, Grote bonte specht. e, Gekraagde roodstaart. f, Grauwe vliegenvanger. g, Klapekster. h, Korhoen. i, Draaihals. j, Matkop.

2020, Sept. 14 Litho. *Perf. 13¼x14*

Self-Adhesive

1614	A815 Sheet of 10	22.50	22.50
a.-j.	1 Any single	2.25	2.25

Nos. 1614a-1614j each sold for 91c on day of issue. Latin names of birds are found in the sheet margin above or below the stamp.

A816

A817

A818

A819

A820

Kaleidoscopic Curves — A821

2020, Sept. 14 Litho. *Perf. 13¼x13*

1615	Miniature sheet of 6	21.00	21.00
a.	A816 1 Internationaal multi	3.50	3.50
b.	A817 1 Internationaal multi	3.50	3.50
c.	A818 1 Internationaal multi	3.50	3.50
d.	A819 1 Internationaal multi	3.50	3.50
e.	A820 1 Internationaal multi	3.50	3.50
f.	A821 1 Internationaal multi	3.50	3.50

On day of issue, Nos. 1615a-1615f each sold for €1.50. The sheet selvage to the left and right of each stamp served as etiquettes.

Stamp Day A822

No. 1616 — Color of large "1": a, White. b, Red.

2020, Oct. 16 Litho. *Perf. 13½x14*

1616	A822 1 Pair	4.25	4.25
a.-b.	1 Either single	2.10	2.10
c.	Booklet pane of 2, #1616a-1616b	5.75	5.75
	Complete booklet, 5 #1616c	29.00	

On day of issue, Nos. 1616a-1616b each sold for 91c. In the complete booklet, each example of No. 1616c has a different booklet pane margin. The complete booklet sold for €12.45.

Martin Garrix, Music Producer and DJ — A823

2020, Oct. 21 Litho. *Perf. 13¼x13¾*

1617 A823 1 multi 2.10 2.10

No. 1617 sold for 91c on day of issue.

Death Announcement Stamp — A824

Serpentine Die Cut 11¾

2020, Nov. 2 Litho.

Self-Adhesive

1618 A824 2 blk & ol sepia 4.25 4.25

No. 1618 sold for €1.82 on day of issue.

Clock, High-heeled Shoe, and Camera Christmas Ornaments A825

Flamingo Christmas Ornament A826

Robot in Box Christmas Ornament A827

Donut, Gingerbread House, and Diamond Christmas Ornaments A828

Dog Wearing Stocking Cap Christmas Ornament A829

Heart and Banner Christmas Ornament A830

Car, House, and Round Starred Christmas Ornaments A831

Nutcracker and Candy Cane Christmas Ornaments A832

Tiger's Head in Box Christmas Ornament A833

Postcard and Hummingbird Christmas Ornaments A834

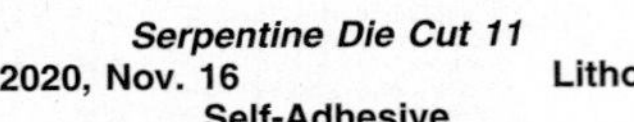

Serpentine Die Cut 11

2020, Nov. 16 Litho.

Self-Adhesive

1619	Block of 10	21.00	
a.	A825 (86c) multi	2.10	2.10
b.	A826 (86c) multi	2.10	2.10
c.	A827 (86c) multi	2.10	2.10
d.	A828 (86c) multi	2.10	2.10
e.	A829 (86c) multi	2.10	2.10
f.	A830 (86c) multi	2.10	2.10
g.	A831 (86c) multi	2.10	2.10
h.	A832 (86c) multi	2.10	2.10
i.	A833 (86c) multi	2.10	2.10
j.	A834 (86c) multi	2.10	2.10

Printed in sheets of 20 containing two each of Nos. 1619a-1619j.

Miniature Sheet

Heathland Flora and Fauna of Dwingelderveld National Park — A835

No. 1620 — Inscriptions: a, Drents heideschaap. b, Geelgors. c, Zandhagedis. d, Hazelworm. e, Bijenwolf. f, Kraanvogel. g, Groveden. h, Veenmos. i, Ringslang. j, Ree.

2021, Jan. 4 Litho. *Perf. 14x13¼*

Self-Adhesive

1620 A835 Sheet of 10 24.00 24.00
a.-j. 1 Any single 2.40 2.40

Nos. 1620a-1620j each sold for 96c on day of issue. Latin names of flora and fauna are found in the sheet margin to left or right of the stamp.

Stolp Farmhouse A836

Wooden Houses — A837

Canal Houses — A838

Houseboats A839

Terraced Houses — A840

2021 Litho. *Perf. 13x13¼*

1621	A836 1 multi	2.40	2.40
a.	Booklet pane of 2	6.00	—
1622	A837 1 multi	2.40	2.40
a.	Booklet pane of 2	6.00	—
1623	A838 1 multi	2.25	2.25
a.	Booklet pane of 2	6.00	—
1624	A839 1 multi	2.40	2.40
a.	Booklet pane of 2	6.00	—
1625	A840 1 multi	2.25	2.25
a.	Booklet pane of 2	6.00	—
	Complete booklet, #1621a, 1622a, 1623a, 1624a, 1625a	30.00	
	Nos. 1621-1625 (5)	11.70	11.70

Issued: No. 1621, 1/4; No. 1622, 2/22; No. 1623, 3/22; No. 1624, 4/6; Nos. 1621a, 1622a, 1623a, 1624a, 1625, 1625a, 6/14. Nos. 1621-1625 each sold for 96c on day of issue. The complete booklet sold for €12.45.

Miniature Sheet

Marshland Flora and Fauna of De Onlanden Nature Reserve — A841

No. 1626 — Inscriptions: a, Kemphaan. b, Grote zilverreiger. c, Smient. d, Groene glazenmaker. e, Grote klaproos. f, Klein hoefblad. g, Gewone margriet. h, Brasem. i, Otter. j, Bruine vuurvlinder.

2021, Feb. 22 Litho. *Perf. 14x13¼*

Self-Adhesive

1626 A841 Sheet of 10 24.00 24.00
a.-j. 1 Any single 2.40 2.40

Nos. 1626a-1626j each sold for 96c on day of issue. Latin names of flora and fauna are found in the sheet margin to left or right of the stamp.

Sustainability — A842

No. 1627 — Arms and: a, Western Europe and Western Africa. b, Eastern Europe, Eastern and Southern Africa and Western Asia.

2021, Mar. 22 Litho. *Perf. 13¼x13*

1627	A842 Horiz. pair	4.50	4.50
a.-b.	1 Either single	2.25	2.25
c.	Vert. tete-beche pair, #1627a-1627b	4.50	4.50
d.	As #1627a, perf. 14½	3.00	3.00
e.	As #1627b, perf. 14½	3.00	3.00
f.	Booklet pane of 2, #1627d-1627e	6.00	—
	Complete booklet, 5 #1627f	30.00	

Nos. 1627a-1627b each sold for 96c on day of issue, and was printed in sheets containing 3 pairs. Complete booklet sold for €12.45.

Endangered Animals — A843

No. 1628 — Bees and hexagons: a, To right of inscriptions. b, To left of inscriptions.

2021, May 10 Litho. *Perf. 13¼x13*

1628	A843 Vert. pair	7.50	7.50
a.-b.	1 Internationaal Either single	3.75	3.75
c.	As #1628a, perf. 14x13¾	5.00	5.00
d.	As #1628b, perf. 14x13¾	5.00	5.00
e.	Booklet pane of 2, #1628c-1628d	10.00	—
	Complete booklet, 3 #1628e	30.00	

Europa. Nos. 1628a-1628b each sold for €1.55 on day of issue, and was printed in sheets containing 3 pairs. The sheet margins to the left and right of the stamps served as etiquettes. The three examples of No. 1628e in the complete booklet have different marginal text. Complete booklet sold for €12.45.

Miniature Sheet

Queen Máxima, 50th Birthday A844

No. 1629 — Queen Máxima: a, Black-and-white photograph, 1999 (36x50mm). b, Wearing crown, 2013 (36x25mm). c, Holding headphones, 2018 (36x25mm). d, With husband, King Willem-Alexander and mother-in-law, Princess Beatrix, 2015 (36x25mm). e, With Indonesians in Jakarta, 2018 (36x25mm).

2021, May 17 Litho. *Perf. 14½*

1629 A844 Sheet of 5 12.00 12.00
a.-e. 1 Any single 2.40 2.40

Nos. 1629a-1629e each sold for 96c on day of issue.

Miniature Sheet

Flora and Fauna of Duin en Kruidberg Dunes — A845

No. 1630 — Inscriptions: a, Duin parelmoervlinder. b, Konin. c, Vos. d, Duindoorn. e, Parnassia. f, Damhert. g, Nachtegaal. h, Duinviooltje. i, Grote tijm. j, Konikpaard.

2021, June 14 Litho. *Perf. 14x13¼*

Self-Adhesive

1630 A845 Sheet of 10 22.50 22.50
a.-j. 1 Any single 2.25 2.25

Nos. 1630a-1630j each sold for 96c on day of issue. Latin names of flora and fauna are found in the sheet margin to left or right of the stamp.

Miniature Sheet

Flora and Fauna of Haarzuilens Country Estate — A846

No. 1631 — Inscriptions: a, Haas. b, Schaatsenrijder. c, Beuk. d, Boomklever. e, Buizerd. f, Gewone esdoorn. g, Bastaardkikker. h, Knotwilg. i, Viervlek. j, Tamme kastanje.

2021, Aug. 16 Litho. *Perf. 14x13¼*

Self-Adhesive

1631 A846 Sheet of 10 22.50 22.50
a.-j. 1 Any single 2.25 2.25

Nos. 1631a-1631j each sold for 96c on day of issue. Latin names of flora and fauna are found in the sheet margin to left or right of the stamp.

Miniature Sheet

Innovation in the Netherlands — A847

No. 1632 — Inscriptions: a, Biobrandstof (biofuel created from elephant dung). b, 4Fold (foldable shipping containers). c, Variable stiffness (printable 3-D structures with flexible stiffness). d, Kitepower (wind energy system). e, Zandmotor (artifical sandbanks). f, Tiler (tile for charging electric bicycles and light vehicles). g, Bluebloqs (system for rainwater treatment, storage and reuse). h, Innozowa (floating solar panels). i, Gaming @ the Dentist (video game for pain distraction). j, Exo-I (3-D printed external ankle ligament).

2021, Aug. 16 Litho. *Perf. 14x13¼*

1632	A847	Sheet of 10	22.50	22.50
a.-j.		1 Any single	2.25	2.25
k.		Booklet pane of 2, #1632a-1632b	6.00	—
l.		Booklet pane of 2, #1632c-1632d	6.00	—
m.		Booklet pane of 2, #1632e-1632f	6.00	—
n.		Booklet pane of 2, #1632g-1632h	6.00	—
o.		Booklet pane of 2, #1632i-1632j	6.00	—
		Complete booklet, #1632k, 1632l, 1632m, 1632n, 1632o	30.00	

Nos. 1632a-1632j each sold for 96c on day of issue. Complete booklet sold for €12.45.

Miniature Sheet

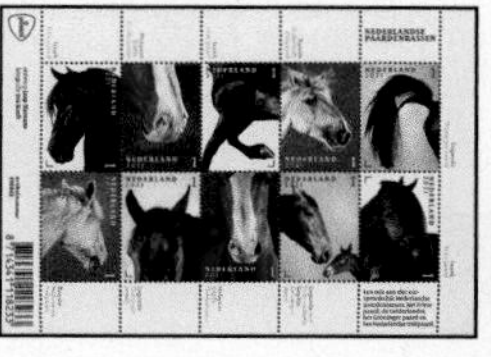

Dutch Horse Breeds A848

No. 1633: a, Head of black Friesian horse facing left. b, Nose of Gelderland horse. c, Chest and front legs of black Friesian horse. d, Head of Dutch draft horse, eye visible. e, Tail of Groningen horse. f, Head of Dutch draft horse, eye hidden. g, Top of head of Groningen horse. h, Eyes and nose of Gelderland horse. i, Heads of Groningen horse and foal. j, Head of black Friesian horse facing right.

Perf. 12¾x13¼

2021, Sept. 13 Litho.

1633	A848	Sheet of 10	22.50	22.50
a.-j.		1 Any single	2.25	2.25
k.		Booklet pane of 2, #1633a,1633f	5.75	—
l.		Booklet pane of 2, #1633b,1633g	5.75	—
m.		Booklet pane of 2, #1633c,1633h	5.75	—
n.		Booklet pane of 2, #1633d,1633i	5.75	—
o.		Booklet pane of 2, #1633e,1633j	5.75	—
		Complete booklet, #1633k, 1633l, 1633m, 1633n, 1633o	29.00	

Nos. 1633a-1633j each sold for 96c on day of issue. Complete booklet sold for €12.45.

Miniature Sheet

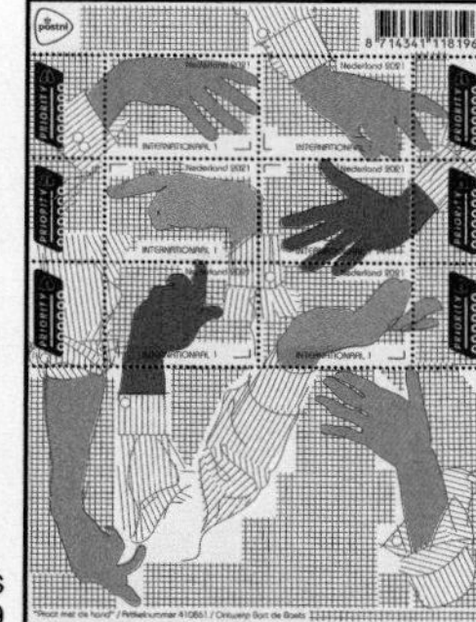

Hands A849

No. 1634: a, Gray hand. b, Orange hand. c, Light blue hand pointing to left. d, Purple hand with fingers outstretched. e, Purple hand with index finger pointing upward. f, Light blue hand with palm up.

Perf. 13¼x12¾

2021, Sept. 13 Litho.

1634	A849	Sheet of 6	22.50	22.50
a.-f.		1 Internationaal Any single	3.75	3.75

Nos. 1634a-1634f each sold for €1.55 on day of issue and sheet margins to left or right of the stamp served as etiquettes,

Stamp Day A850

No. 1653: a, Half of stylized coat of arms with two lions. b, Half of stylized coat of arms with one lion.

2021, Oct. 15 Litho. *Perf. 14x13½*

1635	A850	Pair	4.50	4.50
a.-b.		1 Either single	2.25	2.25
c.		Booklet pane of 2, #1635a-1635b	5.75	—
		Complete booklet, 5 #1635c	29.00	

Nos. 1635a-1635b each sold for 96c on day of issue. The complete booklet sold for €12.45 and contains five examples of No. 1635c, each with different pane margins.

Mole With Candy Cane and Backpack A851

Blue Tits Under Mistletoe A852

Fox Carrying Letter A853

Mouse in Postal Car A854

Badger Decorating Christmas Tree A855

Mice Decorating Peacock A856

Squirrel Pushing Sled A857

Hare, Squirrel and Dog Skating A858

Hare With Poinsettias A859

Deer With Christmas Ornaments A860

Serpentine Die Cut 11¼

2021, Nov. 15 Litho.

Self-Adhesive

1636	Block of 10	21.00	
a.	A851 (91c) multi	2.10	2.10
b.	A852 (91c) multi	2.10	2.10
c.	A853 (91c) multi	2.10	2.10
d.	A854 (91c) multi	2.10	2.10
e.	A855 (91c) multi	2.10	2.10
f.	A856 (91c) multi	2.10	2.10
g.	A857 (91c) multi	2.10	2.10
h.	A858 (91c) multi	2.10	2.10
i.	A859 (91c) multi	2.10	2.10
j.	A860 (91c) multi	2.10	2.10

Printed in sheets of 20 containing two each of Nos. 1636a-1636j.

Dutch Sports — A861

Designs: No. 1637, Skating. No. 1638, Field hockey. No. 1639, Cycling. No. 1640, Sailing. No. 1641, Soccer.

2022 Litho. *Perf. 13½x13*

1637	A861	1 multi	2.25	2.25
a.		Booklet pane of 2	5.00	—
1638	A861	1 multi	2.25	2.25
a.		Booklet pane of 2	5.00	—
1639	A861	1 multi	2.10	2.10
a.		Booklet pane of 2	5.00	—
1640	A861	1 multi	2.10	2.10
a.		Booklet pane of 2	5.00	—
1641	A861	1 multi	2.00	2.00
a.		Booklet pane of 2	5.00	—
		Complete booklet, #1637a, 1638a, 1639a, 1640a, 1641a	25.00	
		Nos. 1637-1641 (5)	10.70	10.70

Issued: No. 1637, 1/3; No. 1638, 3/21; No. 1639, 4/4; No. 1640, 5/9; Nos. 1637a, 1638a, 1639a, 1640a, 1641, 1641a, 8/15. Complete booklet sold for €12.45. On day of issue, Nos. 1637-1641 each sold for 96c.

Miniature Sheets

Flora and Fauna of Fort Ellewoutsdijk — A862

Flora and Fauna of Nieuwkoopse Plassen — A863

No. 1642 — Inscriptions: a, Noordzeekrab. b, Zwartkopmeeuw. c, Rosse grutto. d, Kokkel. e, Kortarige zeekraal. f, Veranderlijke steurgarnaal. g, Gewone mossel. h, Kleine zee-eik. i, Zeehond. j, Gewone zeester.

No. 1643 — Inscriptions: a, Zwarte stern. b, Glassnijder. c, Rietorchis. d, Echte koekoeksbloem. e, Kleine modderkruiper. f, Wateraardbei. g, Kleine lisdodde. h, Krabbenscheer. i, Witte waterlelie. j, Roerdomp.

2022 Litho. *Perf. 13x13¼*

Self-Adhesive

1642	A862	Sheet of 10	22.50	22.50
a.-j.		1 Any single	2.25	2.25
1643	A863	Sheet of 10	22.50	22.50
a.-j.		1 Any single	2.25	2.25

Issued: No. 1642, 1/3; No. 1643, 2/21. Nos. 1642a-1642j, 1643a-1643j each sold for 96c on day of issue. Latin names of flora and fauna are found in the sheet margin to left or right of the stamp.

Mauritshuis Museum, The Hague, 200th Anniv. — A864

No. 1644 — Various flowers from Mauritshuis still-life paintings: a, White and red-striped tulips. b, Iris, lilies and bee. c, Iris and butterfly. d, Yellow iris and tulips. e, Tulip and butterfly. f, Blue irises and tulips.

2022, Feb. 21 Litho. *Perf. 14½*

1644	A864	Sheet of 6	13.50	13.50
a.-f.		1 Any single	2.25	2.25
g.		Booklet pane of 2, #1644a-1644b	5.75	—
h.		Booklet pane of 2, #1644c-1644d	5.75	—
i.		Booklet pane of 2, #1644e-1644f	5.75	—
		Complete booklet, #1644i, 2 each #1644g-1644h	29.00	

Nos. 1644a-1644f each sold for 96c on day of issue. Complete booklet sold for €12.45. The two examples of Nos. 1644g-1644h in the booklet have different pane margins.

Delftware Tulip Vases A865

No. 1645 — Various vases from late 17th-early 18th centuries: a, Vase, pale orange background. b, Four vases. c, Three vases, tall vase at right. d, Vase, gray background. e, Vase, light blue background. f, Three vases, tall vase at left.

2022, Mar. 21 Litho. *Perf. 14½*

1645	A865	Sheet of 6	13.50	13.50
a.-f.		1 Any single	2.25	2.25
g.		Booklet pane of 2, #1645a-1645b	5.50	—
h.		Booklet pane of 2, #1645c-1645d	5.50	—

i. Booklet pane of 2, #1645e-1645f 5.50 —
Complete booklet, #1645i, 2 each #1645g-1645h 27.50

Nos. 1645a-1645f each sold for 96c on day of issue. Complete booklet sold for €12.45. The two examples of Nos. 1645g-1645h in the booklet have different pane margins.

Europa A866

No. 1646 — Folktale of the Lady of Stavoren: a, Ring on hand of the Lady of Stavoren. b, Head of Lady of Stavoren.

2022, May 9 Litho. *Perf. 13½x13*

1646 A866 Horiz. pair 4.25 4.25
a.-b. 1 Either single 2.10 2.10

Nos. 1646a-1646b each sold for 96c on day of issue. Booklets containing three panes, with each pane comprised of a pair of perf. 14x13½ examples of Nos. 1646a-1646b, sold for €12.45.

Miniature Sheet

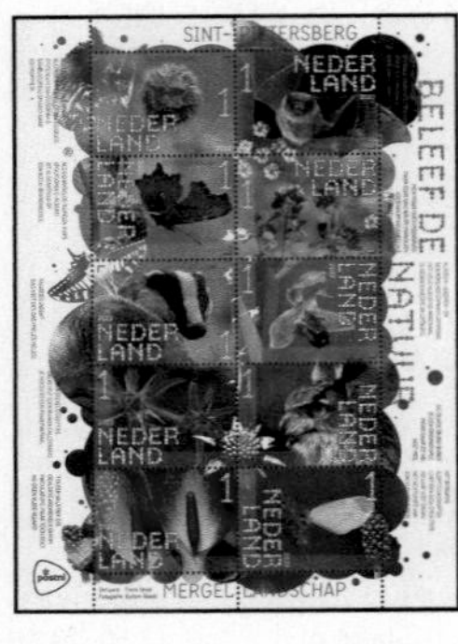

Flora and Fauna of Mount Saint Peter A867

No. 1647 — Inscriptions: a, Kleine pimpernel. b, Baardvleermuis. c, Gehakkelde aurelia. d, Wilde marjolein. e, Das. f, Bijenorchis. g, Kalketrip. h, Oehoe. i, Gevlekte aronskelk. j, Boswitje.

2022, June 13 Litho. *Perf. 13x13¼*
Self-Adhesive

1647 A867 Sheet of 10 20.00 20.00
a.-j. 1 Any single 2.00 2.00

Nos. 1647a-1647j each sold for 96c on day of issue. Latin names of flora and fauna are found in the sheet margin to left or right of the stamp.

King William I (1772-1843) A868

King William I and Queen Wilhelmina of Prussia (1774-1837) A869

Fulda Palace Castle, Germany — A870

2022, June 20 Litho. *Perf. 13½x13*

1648 A868 1 Internationaal multi 3.25 3.25
a. Perf. 14x13½ 4.25 4.25
1649 A869 1 Internationaal multi 3.25 3.25
a. Horiz. pair, #1648-1649 6.50 6.50
b. Perf. 14x13½ 4.25 4.25
c. Booklet pane of 2, #1648a-1649b 8.75 —
1650 A870 1 Internationaal multi 3.25 3.25
a. Perf. 14x13½ 4.25 4.25
b. Booklet pane of 2 #1650a 8.75 —
Complete booklet, #1650b, 2 #1649c 26.50
Nos. 1648-1650 (3) 9.75 9.75

Printed in sheets of 6 containing 2 each Nos. 1648-1650. Sheet margins at left or right of stamps served as etiquettes. Nos. 1648-1650 each sold for €1.55 on day of issue. Complete booklet sold for €12.45. The two examaples of No. 1649c in the booklet have different pane margins.

Miniature Sheet

Flora and Fauna of Leuvenum Woods — A871

No. 1651 — Inscriptions: a, Fluiter. b, Edelhert. c, Porseleinzwam. d, Boommarter. e, Wolf. f, Open rendiermos. g, Gewone eikvaren. h, Wild zwijn. i, Vuurgoudhaan. j, Gewone mestkever.

2022, Aug. 15 Litho. *Perf. 13x13¼*
Self-Adhesive

1651 A871 Sheet of 10 20.00 20.00
a.-j. 1 Any single 2.00 2.00

Nos. 1651a-1651j each sold for 96c on day of issue. Latin names of flora and fauna are found in the sheet margin to left or right of the stamp.

Miniature Sheet

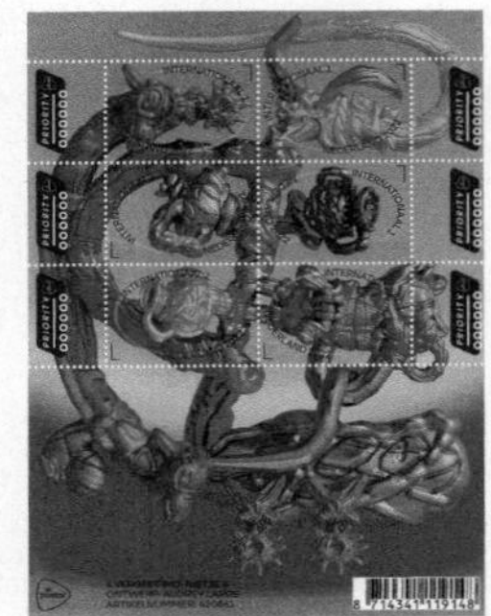
Futuristic Mythological Beast — A872

No. 1652 — Color of beast's appendage: a, Lilac. b, Green. c, Blue. d, Purple. e, Green, diff. f, Olive green.

Perf. 13¼x12¾
2022, Sept. 26 Litho.

1652 A872 Sheet of 6 18.00 18.00
a.-f. 1 Internationaal Any single 3.00 3.00

Nos. 1652a-1652f each sold for €1.55 on day of issue. Sheet margins at left or right of stamps served as etiquettes.

Stamp Day A873

No. 1653: a, Admiral Michiel A. de Ruyter (1607-76). b, Naval battle between Dutch and English ships.

2022, Oct. 17 Litho. *Perf. 13½x14*

1653 A873 Horiz. pair 3.80 3.80
a.-b. 1 Either single 1.90 1.90
c. Booklet pane of 2, #1653a-1653b 5.00 —
Complete booklet, 5 #1653c 25.00

Nos. 1653a-1653b each sold for 96c on day of issue. Complete booklet sold for €12.45. The five examples of No. 1653c in the booklet each have different pane margins.

Miniature Sheet

Flora and Fauna of Marker Wadden Nature Reserve A884

No. 1655 — Inscriptions: a, Knobbelzwaan. b, Grote lisdodde. c, Lepelaar. d, Helmgras. e, Kleine plevier. f, Baardman. g, Visdief. h, Spierling. i, Sprinkhaanzanger. j, Duindoorn.

2023, Jan. 2 Litho. *Perf. 14x13¼*
Self-Adhesive

1655 A884 Sheet of 10 22.50 22.50
a.-j. 1 Any single 2.25 2.25

Nos. 1655a-1655j each sold for €1.01 on day of issue. Latin names of flora and fauna are found in the sheet margin to left or right of the stamp.

Dutch Things — A885

Designs: No. 1656, Museums. No. 1657, Windmills. No. 1658, Flower fields. No. 1659, Cheese markets. No. 1660, Wadden mudflats.

2023 Litho. *Perf. 13½x13*

1656 A885 1 multi 2.25 2.25
a. Booklet pane of 2 6.00 —
1657 A885 1 multi 2.25 2.25
a. Booklet pane of 2 6.00 —
1658 A885 1 multi 2.25 2.25
a. Booklet pane of 2 6.00 —
1659 A885 1 multi 2.25 2.25
a. Booklet pane of 2 6.00 —
1660 A885 1 multi 2.25 2.25
a. Booklet pane of 2 6.00 —
Complete booklet, #1656a, 1657a, 1658a, 1659a, 1660a 30.00
Nos. 1656-1660 (5) 11.25 11.25

Issued: No. 1656, 1/2; No. 1657, 2/13; No. 1658, 3/20; No. 1659, 5/15; Nos. 1656a, 1657a, 1658a, 1659a, 1660, 1660a, 8/14. Complete booklet sold for €13.85. On day of issue, Nos. 1656-1660 each sold for €1.01.

Miniature Sheet

Flora and Fauna of Skrok and Skrins Nature Reserves — A886

No. 1661 — Inscriptions: a, Haas. b, Tureluur. c, Melkkruid. d, Goudplevier. e, Grutto. f, Kluut. g, Kievit. h, Holpijp. i, Goudknopje. j, Kemphaan.

2023, Feb. 13 Litho. *Perf. 14x13¼*
Self-Adhesive

1661 A886 Sheet of 10 22.50 22.50
a.-j. 1 Any single 2.25 2.25

Nos. 1661a-1661j each sold for €1.01 on day of issue. Latin names of flora and fauna are found in the sheet margin to left or right of the stamp.

Journey to the Moon A887

No. 1662: a, Saturn. b, Orion space capsule. c, Astronaut floating in space. d, Satellite with extended solar panels. e, Earth as viewed from the Moon. f, SLS launch vehicle. g, Astronaut's boot. h, Orion capsule and drogue parachutes. i, Astronaut walking on Moon.

2023, Apr. 21 Litho. *Die Cut*
Self-Adhesive

1662 A887 Sheet of 9 20.50
a.-i. 1 Any single 2.25 2.25
j. Booklet pane of 4, #1662a-1662d 13.50
k. Booklet pane of 5, #1662e-1662i 17.00
Complete booklet, #1662j, 1662k 30.50

Nos. 1662a-1662i each sold for €1.01 on day of issue. Complete booklet sold for €13.85.

King Willem-Alexander at King's Games, 2019 — A888

King Willem-Alexander at Netherlands Institute of Ecology, 2022 — A889

King Willem-Alexander and Queen Máxima Visting Indonesia, 2020 — A890

King Willem-Alexander Visting St. Martin, 2013 — A891

King Willem-Alexander Delivering Speech, 2022 — A892

2023, Apr. 28 Litho. *Perf. 13¼x14*

1663 Sheet of 5 11.50 11.50
a. A888 1 org & blk 2.25 2.25
b. A889 1 org & blk 2.25 2.25
c. A890 1 org & blk 2.25 2.25
d. A891 1 org & blk 2.25 2.25
e. A892 1 org & blk 2.25 2.25
f. Booklet pane of 3, #1663a-1663c 9.25 —
g. Booklet pane of 2, #1663d-1663e 6.00 —
h. Booklet pane of 2, #1663a-1663b 6.00 —
i. Booklet pane of 3, #1663c-1663e 9.25 —
Complete booklet, #1663f, 1663g, 1663h, 1663i 30.50

Reign of King Willem-Alexander, 10th anniv. Nos. 1663a-1663e each sold for €1.01 on day of issue. Complete booklet sold for €13.85.

Europa — A893

2023, May 9 Litho. *Perf. 13¼x12¾*

1664	A893 1 Internationaal multi	3.50	3.50
a.	Perf. 14x13½	5.00	5.00
b.	Booklet pane of 2 #1664a	10.00	—
	Complete booklet, 3 #1664b	30.00	

No. 1664 sold for €1.65 on day of issue. Sheet margins at left and right served as etiquettes. Complete booklet sold for €13.85, with the three examples of No. 1664b having different pane margins.

Miniature Sheet

Flora and Fauna of De Wieden Nature Reserve A894

No. 1665 — Inscriptions: a, Bruine kiekendief. b, Zilveren maan. c, Eenstijlige meidoorn. d, Watergentiaan. e, Zomereik. f, Waterral. g, Sleedoorn. h, Kerkuil. i, Purperreiger. j, Kleine zonnedauw.

2023, June 12 Litho. *Perf. 14x13¼*

Self-Adhesive

1665	A894 Sheet of 10	22.50	22.50
a.-j.	1 Any single	2.25	2.25

Nos. 1665a-1665j each sold for €1.01 on day of issue. Latin names of flora and fauna are found in the sheet margin to left or right of the stamp.

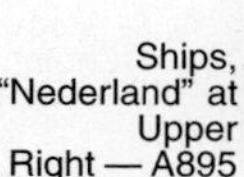

Ships, "Nederland" at Upper Right — A895

Ships, "Nederland" at Lower Left — A896

2023, June 26 Litho. *Perf. 14x13¼*

1666	Pair, #a-b	4.50	4.50
a.	A895 1 multi	2.25	2.25
b.	A896 1 multi	2.25	2.25
c.	Booklet pane of 2, #1666a-1666b	6.00	—
	Complete booklet, 5 #1666c	30.00	

2023 Navy Days and Sail Den Helder Tall Ship Races. No. 1666a-1666b each sold for €1.01 on day of issue. Horizontal pairs are tete-beche in relation to each other, and are from the sheet and booklet pane, while vertical pairs are only found on the sheet. Complete booklet sold for €13.85 and contains 5 examples of No. 1666c with different pane margins.

A897

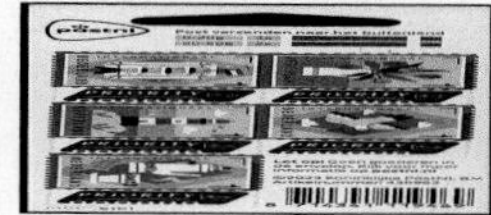

Dutch Things A898

No. 1667 — Stamps with yellow orange frames: a, Tulips in vase. b, Carrier pigeon with letter. c, Cargo bicycle carrying plants. d, Coffee pot, mug and cookie. e, Lighthouse and sailboat. f, Sliced herring with flag of the Netherlands. g, Canal houses. h, Whipped cream cake. i, Travel trailer. j, Cheese wedges and garnished cheese cubes.

No. 1668 — Stamps with gray blue frames and blue "Priority" etiquettes: a, Tulips in vase. b, Carrier pigeon with letter. c, Sliced herring with flag of the Netherlands. d, Lighthouse and sailboat. e, Coffee pot, mug and cookie.

Die Cut Perf. 14¼

2023, July 3 Litho.

1667	A897 Booklet pane of 10	22.50	
a.-j.	1 Any single	2.25	2.25

Serpentine Die Cut 11

1668	A898 Booklet pane of 5	19.00	
a.-e.	1 Internationaal Any single	3.75	3.75

On day of issue, Nos. 1667a-1667j each sold for €1.01, and Nos. 1668a-1668e each sold for €1.65.

Miniature Sheet

Flora and Fauna of Osterwijk Woods and Fens A899

No. 1669 — Inscriptions: a, Koningsvaren. b, Ijsvogel. c, Waterpostelein. d, Kleine Watersalamander. e, Koraaljuffer. f, Zwarte specht. g, Bruine kikker. h, Kuifeend. i, Staartmees. j, Wilde gagel.

2023, Aug. 14 Litho. *Perf. 14x13¼*

Self-Adhesive

1669	A899 Sheet of 10	22.50	22.50
a.-j.	1 Any single	2.25	2.25

Nos. 1669a-1669j each sold for €1.01 on day of issue. Latin names of flora and fauna are found in the sheet margin to left or right of the stamp.

"You Are So Wonderful Yourself" — A900

2023, Oct. 23 Litho. *Perf. 13x13¼*

1670	A900 1 Internationaal multi	3.50	3.50

No. 1670 was printed in sheets of 6. and each stamp sold for €1.65 on day of issue.

Sheet margins at top and bottom served as etiquettes.

Owl, Birds, Gift and Candy Cane A901

Bird, Reindeer and Beaver Carrying Lanterns A902

House and Aurora Borealis A903

Cat and Dog in Window A904

Christmas Foods and Drink A905

Rabbit With Open Letter A906

People and Animals Decorating Christmas Tree — A907

Hedgehog With Gifts — A908

People and Animals Watching Sky A909

Bear and Birds A910

Serpentine Die Cut 11¼

2023, Nov. 13 Litho.

Self-Adhesive

1671	Block of 10	21.00	
a.	A901 (96c) multi	2.10	2.10
b.	A902 (96c) multi	2.10	2.10
c.	A903 (96c) multi	2.10	2.10
d.	A904 (96c) multi	2.10	2.10
e.	A905 (96c) multi	2.10	2.10
f.	A906 (96c) multi	2.10	2.10
g.	A907 (96c) multi	2.10	2.10
h.	A908 (96c) multi	2.10	2.10
i.	A909 (96c) multi	2.10	2.10
j.	A910 (96c) multi	2.10	2.10

Printed in sheets of 20 containing two each of Nos. 1671a-1671j.

SEMI-POSTAL STAMPS

Design Symbolical of the Four Chief Means for Combating Tuberculosis: Light, Water, Air and Food — SP1

Perf. 12½

1906, Dec. 21 Typo. Unwmk.

B1	SP1 1c (+1c) rose red	20.00	*11.00*
B2	SP1 3c (+3c) pale ol grn	30.00	*26.00*
B3	SP1 5c (+5c) gray	30.00	*15.00*
	Nos. B1-B3 (3)	80.00	*52.00*
	Set, never hinged	475.00	

Surtax aided the Society for the Prevention of Tuberculosis.

Nos. B1-B3 canceled-to-order "AMSTERDAM 31.07 10-12 N," sell at $3 a set.

Symbolical of Charity — SP2

SP3

1923, Dec. 15 *Perf. 11½*

B4	SP2 2c (+5c) vio bl	17.00	17.00
B5	SP3 10c (+5c) org red	17.00	17.00
	Set, never hinged	85.00	

The surtax was for the benefit of charity.

Allegory, Charity Protecting Child — SP6

1924, Dec. 15 Photo. *Perf. 12½*

B6	SP6 2c (+2c) emer	1.80	1.80
B7	SP6 7½c (+3½c) dk brn	6.75	8.00
B8	SP6 10c (+2½c) vermilion	4.00	1.80
	Nos. B6-B8 (3)	12.55	11.60
	Set, never hinged	26.00	

These stamps were sold at a premium over face value for the benefit of Child Welfare Societies.

Arms of North Brabant SP7

Arms of Gelderland SP8

Arms of South Holland — SP9

1925, Dec. 17 *Perf. 12½*

B9	SP7 2c (+2c) grn & org	.85	.75
B10	SP8 7½c (+3½c) pur & bl gray	4.25	4.50
B11	SP9 10c (+2½c) red & yel org	3.50	.45
	Nos. B9-B11 (3)	8.60	5.70
	Set, never hinged	19.00	

Surtax went to Child Welfare Societies.

Syncopated Perfs., Type A

B9a	SP7 2c (+2c)	19.00	22.00
B10a	SP8 7½c (+3½c)	37.50	37.50
B11a	SP9 10c (+2½c)	65.00	52.50
	Nos. B9a-B11a (3)	121.50	112.00
	Set, never hinged	300.00	

Arms of Utrecht SP10

Arms of Zeeland SP11

Arms of North Holland SP12

Arms of Friesland SP13

1926, Dec. 1 Wmk. 202 ***Perf. 12½***

B12 SP10 2c (+2c) sil & red .50 .40
B13 SP11 5c (+3c) grn & gray bl 1.40 .75
B14 SP12 10c (+3c) red & gold 2.10 .35
B15 SP13 15c (+3c) ultra & yel 5.50 6.00
Nos. B12-B15 (4) 9.50 7.50
Set, never hinged 30.00

The surtax on these stamps was devoted to Child Welfare Societies.

Syncopated Perfs., Type A

B12a SP10 2c (+2c) 5.25 5.25
B13a SP11 5c (+3c) 8.25 8.25
B14a SP12 10c (+3c) 15.00 8.75
B15a SP13 15c (+3c) 16.50 16.50
Nos. B12a-B15a (4) 45.00 38.75
Set, never hinged 125.00

King William III SP14

Red Cross and Doves SP18

Designs: 3c, Queen Emma. 5c, Prince Consort Henry. 7½c, Queen Wilhelmina.

Perf. 11½, 11½x12 B

1927, June Photo. Unwmk.

B16 SP14 2c (+2c) scar 3.25 2.75

Engr.

B17 SP14 3c (+2c) dp grn 6.75 *7.50*
B18 SP14 5c (+3c) slate bl 1.35 1.25

Photo.

B19 SP14 7½c (+3½c) ultra 4.25 1.60
B20 SP18 15c (+5c) ultra & red 9.25 8.50
Nos. B16-B20 (5) 24.85 21.60
Set, never hinged 65.00

60th anniversary of the Netherlands Red Cross Society. The surtaxes in parentheses were for the benefit of the Society.

Arms of Drenthe SP19

Arms of Groningen SP20

Arms of Limburg SP21

Arms of Overijssel SP22

1927, Dec. 15 Wmk. 202 ***Perf. 12½***

B21 SP19 2c (+2c) dp rose & vio .35 .30
B22 SP20 5c (+3c) ol grn & yel 1.50 1.25
B23 SP21 7½c (+3½c) red & blk 3.25 .35
B24 SP22 15c (+3c) ultra & org brn 4.75 4.25
Nos. B21-B24 (4) 9.85 6.15
Set, never hinged 31.00

The surtax on these stamps was for the benefit of Child Welfare Societies.

Syncopated Perfs., Type A

B21a SP19 2c (+2c) 2.25 2.25
B22a SP20 5c (+3c) 4.00 4.00
B23a SP21 7½c (+3½c) 6.00 6.00
B24a SP22 15c (+3c) 11.00 7.75
Nos. B21a-B24a (4) 23.25 20.00
Set, never hinged 75.00

Rowing SP23

Fencing SP24

Soccer SP25

Yachting SP26

Putting the Shot SP27

Running SP28

Riding SP29

Boxing SP30

Perf. 11½, 12, 11½x12, 12x11½

1928, Mar. 27 Litho.

B25 SP23 1½c (+1c) dk grn 3.00 3.00
B26 SP24 2c (+1c) red vio 3.00 3.75
B27 SP25 3c (+1c) green 4.50 4.50
B28 SP26 5c (+1c) lt bl 3.75 2.25
B29 SP27 7½c (+2½c) org 3.75 2.25
B30 SP28 10c (+2c) scarlet 6.75 5.25
B31 SP29 15c (+2c) dk bl 9.00 5.25
B32 SP30 30c (+3c) dk brn 19.00 19.00
Nos. B25-B32 (8) 52.75 45.25
Set, never hinged 170.00

The surtax on these stamps was used to help defray the expenses of the Olympic Games of 1928.

Jean Pierre Minckelers — SP31

5c, Hermann Boerhaave. 7½c, Hendrik Antoon Lorentz. 12½c, Christiaan Huygens.

1928, Dec. 10 Photo. ***Perf. 12x12½***

B33 SP31 1½c (+1½c) vio .55 .40
B34 SP31 5c (+3c) grn 1.75 .60

Perf. 12

B35 SP31 7½c (+2½c) ver 3.50 .25
a. Perf. 12x12½ 4.75 .50
B36 SP31 12½c (+3½c) ultra 9.75 7.50
a. Perf. 12x12½ 77.50 15.00
Nos. B33-B36 (4) 15.55 8.75
Set, never hinged 45.00

The surtax on these stamps was for the benefit of Child Welfare Societies.

Child on Dolphin — SP35

1929, Dec. 10 Litho. ***Perf. 12½***

B37 SP35 1½c (+1½c) gray 1.75 .40
B38 SP35 5c (+3c) blue grn 2.50 .75
B39 SP35 6c (+4c) scarlet 2.00 .35
B40 SP35 12½c (+3½c) dk bl 14.00 9.75
Nos. B37-B40 (4) 20.25 11.25
Set, never hinged 72.50

Surtax for child welfare.

Syncopated Perfs., Type B

B37a SP35 1½c (+1½c) 3.75 3.00
B38a SP35 5c (+3c) 4.50 4.00
B39a SP35 6c (+4c) 3.75 3.00
B40a SP35 12½c (+3½c) 18.00 14.00
Nos. B37a-B40a (4) 30.00 24.00
Set, never hinged 125.00

Rembrandt and His "Cloth Merchants of Amsterdam" — SP36

Perf. 11½

1930, Feb. 15 Engr. Unwmk.

B41 SP36 5c (+5c) bl grn 6.75 6.00
B42 SP36 6c (+5c) gray blk 5.25 3.50
B43 SP36 12½c (+5c) dp bl 9.00 8.00
Nos. B41-B43 (3) 21.00 17.50
Set, never hinged 62.50

Surtax for the benefit of the Rembrandt Soc.

"Spring" — SP37

5c, Summer. 6c, Autumn. 12½c, Winter.

1930, Dec. 10 ***Perf. 12½***

B44 SP37 1½c (+1½c) lt red 1.75 .45
B45 SP37 5c (+3c) gray grn 2.25 .60
B46 SP37 6c (+4c) claret 1.75 .45
B47 SP37 12½c (+3½c) lt ultra 16.00 8.50
Nos. B44-B47 (4) 21.75 10.00
Set, never hinged 62.50

Surtax was for Child Welfare work.

Syncopated Perfs., Type C

B44a SP37 1½c (+1½c) 4.00 3.75
B45a SP37 5c (+3c) 4.75 4.50
B46a SP37 6c (+4c) 4.00 3.75
B47a SP37 12½c (+3½c) 19.00 14.00
Nos. B44a-B47a (4) 31.75 26.00
Set, never hinged 85.00

Stained Glass Window and Detail of Repair Method — SP41

6c, Gouda Church and repair of window frame.

Wmk. 202

1931, Oct. 1 Photo. ***Perf. 12½***

B48 SP41 1½c (+1½c) bl grn 17.00 15.00
B49 SP41 6c (+4c) car rose 20.00 17.00
Set, never hinged 80.00

Deaf Mute Learning Lip Reading — SP43

Designs: 5c, Mentally retarded child. 6c, Blind girl learning to read Braille. 12½c, Child victim of malnutrition.

1931, Dec. 10 ***Perf. 12½***

B50 SP43 1½c (+1½c) ver & ultra 1.90 1.25
B51 SP43 5c (+3c) Prus bl & vio 5.25 1.25
B52 SP43 6c (+4c) vio & grn 5.25 1.25
B53 SP43 12½c (+3½c) ultra & dp org 29.00 21.00
Nos. B50-B53 (4) 41.40 24.75
Set, never hinged 125.00

The surtax was for Child Welfare work.

Syncopated Perfs., Type C

B50a SP43 1½c (+1½c) 3.75 4.00
B51a SP43 5c (+3c) 7.50 7.75
B52a SP43 6c (+4c) 7.50 7.75
B53a SP43 12½c (+3½c) 27.00 19.50
Nos. B50a-B53a (4) 45.75 39.00
Set, never hinged 150.00

Drawbridge — SP47

Designs: 2½c, Windmill and Dikes. 6c, Council House, Zierikzee. 12½c, Flower fields.

1932, May 23 ***Perf. 12½***

B54 SP47 2½c (+1½c) turq grn & blk 7.00 5.00
B55 SP47 6c (+4c) gray blk & blk 10.50 5.00
B56 SP47 7½c (+3½c) brt red & blk 30.00 12.50
B57 SP47 12½c (+2½c) ultra & blk 32.50 19.00
Nos. B54-B57 (4) 80.00 41.50
Set, never hinged 225.00

The surtax was for the benefit of the National Tourist Association.

Furze and Boy — SP51

Designs (Heads of children and flowers typifying the seasons): 5c, Cornflower. 6c, Sunflower. 12½c, Christmas rose.

1932, Dec. 10 ***Perf. 12½***

B58 SP51 1½c (+1½c) brn & yel 2.10 .45
B59 SP51 5c (+3c) red org & ultra 2.75 .75
B60 SP51 6c (+4c) dk grn & ocher 2.10 .35
B61 SP51 12½c (+3½c) ocher & ultra 27.50 18.00
Nos. B58-B61 (4) 34.45 19.55
Set, never hinged 110.00

The surtax aided Child Welfare Societies.

Syncopated Perfs., Type C

B58a SP51 1½c (+1½c) 3.50 3.50
B59a SP51 5c (+3c) 4.25 4.25
B60a SP51 6c (+4c) 4.25 4.25
B61a SP51 12½c (+3½c) 32.50 20.00
Nos. B58a-B61a (4) 44.50 32.00
Set, never hinged 135.00

Monument at Den Helder SP55

The "Hope," A Church and Hospital Ship SP56

Lifeboat in a Storm SP57

Dutch Sailor and Sailors' Home SP58

1933, June 10 ***Perf. 14½x13½***

B62 SP55 1½c (+1½c) dp red 3.50 2.60
B63 SP56 5c (+3c) bl grn & red org 10.50 4.25
B64 SP57 6c (+4c) dp grn 16.00 3.25
B65 SP58 12½c (+3½c) ultra 24.00 16.00
Nos. B62-B65 (4) 54.00 26.10
Set, never hinged 135.00

The surtax was for the aid of Sailors' Homes.

Child Carrying the Star of Hope, Symbolical of Christmas Cheer — SP59

1933, Dec. 11 ***Perf. 12½***

B66 SP59 1½c (+1½c) sl & org brn 1.50 .55
B67 SP59 5c (+3c) dk brn & ocher 2.00 .65
B68 SP59 6c (+4c) bl grn & gold 2.50 .55

B69 SP59 12½c (+3½c) dk bl & sil 25.00 18.00
Nos. B66-B69 (4) 31.00 19.75
Set, never hinged 100.00

The surtax aided Child Welfare Societies.

Syncopated Perfs., Type C

B66a	SP59	1½c (+1½c)	1.90	.80
B67a	SP59	5c (+3c)	2.60	.90
B68a	SP59	6c (+4c)	3.25	.80
B69a	SP59	12½c (+3½c	27.50	24.50
		Nos. B66a-B69a (4)	35.25	27.00
		Set, never hinged	130.00	

Queen Wilhelmina SP60

Princess Juliana SP61

Perf. 12½

1934, Apr. 28 Engr. Unwmk.

B70 SP60 5c (+4c) dk vio 11.50 3.00
B71 SP61 6c (+5c) blue 10.50 3.75
Set, never hinged 55.00

The surtax was for the benefit of the Anti-Depression Committee.

Dowager Queen Emma — SP62

1934, Oct. 1 ***Perf. 13x14***

B72 SP62 6c (+2c) blue 11.50 1.40
Never hinged 28.00

Surtax for the Fight Tuberculosis Society.

Poor Child — SP63

Perf. 13½x13

1934, Dec. 10 Photo. Wmk. 202

B73 SP63 1½c (+1½c) olive 1.40 .45
B74 SP63 5c (+3c) rose red 2.40 1.00
B75 SP63 6c (+4c) bl grn 2.40 .25
B76 SP63 12½c (+3½c) ultra 22.50 16.00
Nos. B73-B76 (4) 28.70 17.70
Set, never hinged 100.00

The surtax aided child welfare.

Henri D. Guyot SP64

A. J. M. Diepenbrock SP65

F. C. Donders SP66

J. P. Sweelinck SP67

Perf. 12½ x 12, 12

1935, June 17 Engr. Unwmk.

B77 SP64 1½c (+1½c) dk car 1.50 1.50
B78 SP65 5c (+3c) blk brn 4.00 4.00
B79 SP66 6c (+4c) myr grn 4.50 .50
B80 SP67 12½c (+3½c) dp bl 24.00 6.00
Nos. B77-B80 (4) 34.00 12.00
Set, never hinged 100.00

Surtax for social and cultural projects.

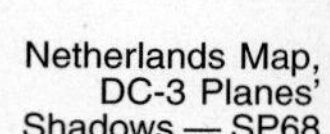

Netherlands Map, DC-3 Planes' Shadows — SP68

Perf. 14x13

1935, Oct. 16 Photo. Wmk. 202

B81 SP68 6c (+4c) brn 24.00 7.50

Surtax for Natl. Aviation.

Girl Picking Apple — SP69

1935, Dec. 4 ***Perf. 14½x13½***

B82 SP69 1½c (+1½c) crim .50 .55
B83 SP69 5c (+3c) dk yel grn 1.40 1.05
B84 SP69 6c (+4c) blk brn 1.25 .55
B85 SP69 12½c (+3½c) ultra 20.00 7.50
Nos. B82-B85 (4) 23.15 9.65
Set, never hinged 110.00

The surtax aided child welfare.

H. Kamerlingh Onnes SP70

Dr. A. S. Talma SP71

Msgr. H. J. A. M. Schaepman SP72

Desiderius Erasmus SP73

Perf. 12½x12

1936, May 1 Engr. Unwmk.

B86 SP70 1½c (+1½c) brn blk .65 .75
B87 SP71 5c (+3c) dl grn 4.00 *3.25*
B88 SP72 6c (+4c) dk red 3.25 .50
B89 SP73 12½c (+3½c) dl bl 11.50 2.50
Nos. B86-B89 (4) 19.40 7.00
Set, never hinged 67.50

Surtax for social and cultural projects.

Cherub — SP74

Perf. 14½x13½

1936, Dec. 1 Photo. Wmk. 202

B90 SP74 1½c (+1½c) lil gray .50 .30
B91 SP74 5c (+3c) turq grn 2.00 .75
B92 SP74 6c (+4c) dp red brn 1.90 .25
B93 SP74 12½c (+3½c) ind 14.00 4.75
Nos. B90-B93 (4) 18.40 6.05
Set, never hinged 52.50

The surtax aided child welfare.

Jacob Maris SP75

Franciscus de la Boe Sylvius SP76

Joost van den Vondel SP77

Antoni van Leeuwenhoek SP78

Perf. 12½x12

1937, June 1 Engr. Unwmk.

B94 SP75 1½c (+1½c) blk brn .50 .40
B95 SP76 5c (+3c) dl grn 4.00 2.75
B96 SP77 6c (+4c) brn vio 1.00 .25
B97 SP78 12½c (+3½c) dl bl 7.00 1.25
Nos. B94-B97 (4) 12.50 4.65
Set, never hinged 40.00

Surtax for social and cultural projects.

"The Laughing Child" after Frans Hals — SP79

Perf. 14½x13½

1937, Dec. 1 Photo. Wmk. 202

B98 SP79 1½c (+1½c) blk .25 .25
B99 SP79 3c (+2c) grn 1.50 1.00
B100 SP79 4c (+2c) hn brn .60 .45
B101 SP79 5c (+3c) bl grn .50 .25
B102 SP79 12½c (+3½c) dk bl 7.25 1.40
Nos. B98-B102 (5) 10.10 3.35
Set, never hinged 35.00

The surtax aided child welfare.

Marnix van Sint Aldegonde SP80

Otto Gerhard Heldring SP81

Maria Tesselschade SP82

Hermann Boerhaave SP84

Harmenszoon Rembrandt van Rijn — SP83

Perf. 12½x12

1938, May 16 Engr. Unwmk.

B103 SP80 1½c (+1½c) sep .30 .35
B104 SP81 3c (+2c) dk grn .55 .35
B105 SP82 4c (+2c) rose lake 1.75 1.75
B106 SP83 5c (+3c) dk sl grn 2.25 .35
B107 SP84 12½c (+3½c) dl bl 7.75 1.00
Nos. B103-B107 (5) 12.60 3.80
Set, never hinged 34.00

The surtax was for the benefit of cultural and social relief.

Child with Flowers, Bird and Fish — SP85

Perf. 14½x13½

1938, Dec. 1 Photo. Wmk. 202

B108 SP85 1½c (+1½c) blk .25 .25
B109 SP85 3c (+2c) mar .30 .25
B110 SP85 4c (+2c) dk bl grn .60 .80
B111 SP85 5c (+3c) hn brn .25 .25
B112 SP85 12½c (+3½c) dp bl 9.00 1.75
Nos. B108-B112 (5) 10.40 3.30
Set, never hinged 35.00

The surtax aided child welfare.

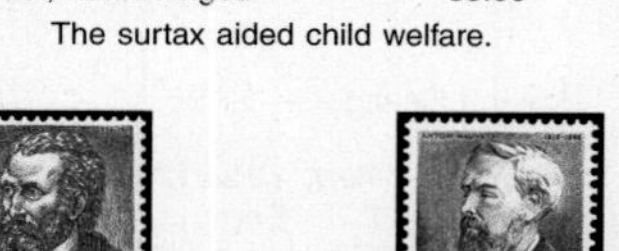

Matthijs Maris SP86

Anton Mauve SP87

Gerard van Swieten SP88

Nikolaas Beets SP89

Peter Stuyvesant — SP90

Perf. 12½x12

1939, May 1 Engr. Unwmk.

B113 SP86 1½c (+1½c) sepia .60 .60
B114 SP87 2½c (+2½c) gray grn 3.00 2.75
B115 SP88 3c (+3c) ver .80 1.00
B116 SP89 5c (+3c) dk sl grn 2.00 .30
B117 SP90 12½c (+3½c) indigo 5.00 .85
Nos. B113-B117 (5) 11.40 5.50
Set, never hinged 40.00

The surtax was for the benefit of cultural and social relief.

Child Carrying Cornucopia — SP91

Perf. 14½x13½

1939, Dec. 1 Photo. Wmk. 202

B118 SP91 1½c (+1½c) blk .25 .25
B119 SP91 2½c (+2½c) dk ol grn 3.75 2.00
B120 SP91 3c (+3c) hn brn .40 .25
B121 SP91 5c (+3c) dk grn .85 .25
B122 SP91 12½c (+3½c) dk bl 4.00 1.00
Nos. B118-B122 (5) 9.25 3.75
Set, never hinged 40.00

The surtax was used for destitute children.

Catalogue values for unused stamps in this section, from this point to the end of the section, are for Never Hinged items.

Vincent van Gogh SP92

E. J. Potgieter SP93

Petrus Camper SP94

Jan Steen SP95

Joseph Scaliger — SP96

Perf. 12½x12

1940, May 11 Engr. Wmk. 202

B123	SP92	1½c +1½c brn blk	4.00	.35
B124	SP93	2½c +2½c dk grn	7.00	.65
B125	SP94	3c +3c car	4.00	.65
B126	SP95	5c +3c dp grn	10.00	.30
a.		Booklet pane of 4	140.00	
B127	SP96	12½c +3½c dp bl	8.00	1.10

Surtax for social and cultural projects.

Type of 1940 Surcharged in Black

1940, Sept. 7

B128	SP95	7½c +2½c on 5c +3c dk red	.80	.30
		Nos. B123-B128 (6)	33.80	3.35

Child with Flowers and Doll — SP97

Perf. 14½x13½

1940, Dec. 2 Photo. Wmk. 202

B129	SP97	1½c +1½c dl bl gray	1.00	.25
B130	SP97	2½c +2½c dp ol	2.75	.55
B131	SP97	4c +3c royal bl	3.00	.60
B132	SP97	5c +3c dk bl grn	3.00	.25
B133	SP97	7½c +3½c hn	1.40	.25
		Nos. B129-B133 (5)	11.15	1.90

The surtax was used for destitute children.

Dr. Antonius Mathijsen SP98

Dr. Jan Ingenhousz SP99

Aagje Deken SP100

Johannes Bosboom SP101

A. C. W. Staring — SP102

Perf. 12½x12

1941, May 29 Engr. Wmk. 202

B134	SP98	1½c +1½c blk brn	.65	.25
B135	SP99	2½c +2½c dk sl grn	.65	.25
B136	SP100	4c +3c red	.65	.25
B137	SP101	5c +3c slate grn	.65	.25
B138	SP102	7½c +3½c rose vio	.65	.25
		Nos. B134-B138 (5)	3.25	1.25

The surtax was for cultural and social relief.

Rembrandt's Painting of Titus, His Son — SP103

Perf. 14½x13½

1941, Dec. 1 Photo. Wmk. 202

B139	SP103	1½c +1½c vio blk	.35	.25
B140	SP103	2½c +2½c dk ol	.35	.25
B141	SP103	4c +3c royal blue	.35	.25
B142	SP103	5c +3c dp grn	.35	.25
B143	SP103	7½c +3½c dp henna brn	.35	.25
		Nos. B139-B143 (5)	1.75	1.25

The surtax aided child welfare.

Legionary
SP104 SP105

1942, Nov. 1 *Perf. 12½x12, 12x12½*

B144	SP104	7½c +2½c dk red	.75	.50
a.		Sheet of 10	100.00	100.00
B145	SP105	12½c +87½c ultra	5.50	6.25
a.		Sheet of 4	75.00	80.00

The surtax aided the Netherlands Legion. #B144a, B145a measure 155x111mm and 94x94mm respectively.

19th Century Mail Cart — SP108

1943, Oct. 9 Unwmk. *Perf. 12x12½*

B148	SP108	7½c +7½c henna brn	.25	.25

Issued to commemorate Stamp Day.

Child and House — SP109

#B150, Mother & Child. #B151, Mother $ Children. #B152, Child Carrying Sheaf of Wheat. #B153, Mother & Children, diff.

Perf. 12½x12

1944, Mar. 6 Wmk. 202

B149	SP109	1½c +3½c dl blk	.25	.25
B150	SP109	4c +3½ rose lake	.25	.25
B151	SP109	5c +5c dk bl grn	.25	.25
B152	SP109	7½c +7½c dp hn brn	.25	.25
B153	SP109	10c +40c royal blue	.25	.25
		Nos. B149-B153 (5)	1.25	1.25

The surtax aided National Social Service and winter relief.

Child — SP114

1945, Dec. 1 Photo. *Perf. 14½x13½*

B154	SP114	1½c +2½c gray	.25	.25
B155	SP114	2½c +3½c dk bl grn	.25	.25
B156	SP114	5c +5c brn red	.25	.25
B157	SP114	7½c +4½c red	.25	.25
B158	SP114	12½c +5½c brt bl	.25	.25
		Nos. B154-B158 (5)	1.25	1.25

The surtax was for Child Welfare.

Fortuna — SP115

Perf. 12½x12

1946, May 1 Engr. Unwmk.

B159	SP115	1½c +3½c brn blk	.40	.30
B160	SP115	2½c +5c dl grn	.45	.45
B161	SP115	5c +10c dk vio	.45	.45
B162	SP115	7½c +15c car lake	.40	.30
B163	SP115	12½c +37½c dk bl	.75	.55
		Nos. B159-B163 (5)	2.45	2.05

The surtax was for victims of World War II.

Princess Irene — SP116

Designs: Nos. B165, B167, Princess Margriet. Nos. B168-B169, Princess Beatrix.

1946, Sept. 16

B164	SP116	1½c +1½c blk brn	.40	.40
B165	SP116	2½c +1½c bl grn	.40	.40
B166	SP116	4c +2c magenta	.50	.40
B167	SP116	5c +2c brown	.50	.40
B168	SP116	7½c +2½c red	.40	.25
B169	SP116	12½c +7½c dk bl	.40	.50
		Nos. B164-B169 (6)	2.60	2.35

The surtax was for child welfare and anti-tuberculosis work.

Child on Merry-go-round — SP119

1946, Dec. 2 Photo. Wmk. 202

B170	SP119	2c +2c lil gray	.35	.30
B171	SP119	4c +2c dk grn	.35	.30
B172	SP119	7½c +2½c brt red	.35	.30
B173	SP119	10c +5c dp plum	.45	.25
B174	SP119	20c +5c dp bl	.50	.45
		Nos. B170-B174 (5)	2.00	1.60

The surtax was for child welfare.

Dr. Hendrik van Deventer SP120

Peter Cornelisz Hooft SP121

Johan de Witt SP122

Jean F. van Royen SP123

Hugo de Groot — SP124

1947, Aug. 1 Engr. Unwmk.

B175	SP120	2c +2c dark red	.55	.30
B176	SP121	4c +2c dk green	.90	.40
B177	SP122	7½c +2½c dk pur brn	1.40	.40
B178	SP123	10c +5c brown	1.40	.25
B179	SP124	20c +5c dk blue	.85	.40
		Nos. B175-B179 (5)	5.10	1.75

The surtax was for social and cultural purposes.

Children SP125

Infant SP126

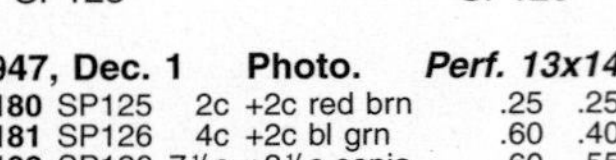

1947, Dec. 1 Photo. *Perf. 13x14*

B180	SP125	2c +2c red brn	.25	.25
B181	SP126	4c +2c bl grn	.60	.40
B182	SP126	7½c +2½c sepia	.60	.55
B183	SP126	10c +5c dk red	.80	.25
B184	SP125	20c +5c blue	.90	.70
		Nos. B180-B184 (5)	3.15	2.15

The surtax was for child welfare.

Hall of Knights, The Hague — SP127

Designs: 6c+4c, Royal Palace, Amsterdam. 10c+5c, Kneuterdyk Palace, The Hague. 20c+5c, New Church, Amsterdam.

1948, June 17 Engr. *Perf. 13½x14*

B185	SP127	2c +2c dk brn	1.15	.50
B186	SP127	6c +4c grn	1.25	.50
B187	SP127	10c +5c brt red	.85	.30
B188	SP127	20c +5c deep blue	1.25	.70
		Nos. B185-B188 (4)	4.50	2.00

The surtax was for cultural and social purposes.

Boy in Kayak — SP128

5c+3c, Swimming. 6c+4c, Sledding. 10c+5c, Swinging. 20c+8c, Figure skating.

1948, Nov. 15 Photo. *Perf. 13x14*

B189	SP128	2c +2c yel grn	.25	.25
B190	SP128	5c +3c dk bl grn	1.50	.50
B191	SP128	6c +4c gray	.80	.25
B192	SP128	10c +5c red	.35	.25
B193	SP128	20c +8c blue	1.50	.75
		Nos. B189-B193 (5)	4.40	2.00

The surtax was for child welfare.

Beach Terrace — SP129

Boy and Girl Hikers — SP130

Campers SP131

Reaping SP132

Sailboats — SP133

1949, May 2 Wmk. 202 *Perf. 14x13*

B194	SP129	2c +2c bl & org yel	1.10	.25
B195	SP130	5c +3c bl & yel	1.75	1.00
B196	SP131	6c +4c dk bl grn	1.60	.35
B197	SP132	10c +5c bl & org yel	1.90	.25
B198	SP133	20c +5c blue	2.40	1.25
		Nos. B194-B198 (5)	8.75	3.10

The surtax was for cultural and social purposes.

Hands Reaching for Sunflower — SP134

Perf. 14½x13½

1949, Aug. 1 Photo. Unwmk.

Flower in Yellow

B199	SP134	2c +3c gray		.95	.25
B200	SP134	6c +4c red brown		1.50	.30
B201	SP134	10c +5c brt blue		2.40	.25
B202	SP134	30c +10c dk brown		5.25	2.40
		Nos. B199-B202 (4)		10.10	3.20

The surtax was for the Red Cross and for Indonesia Relief work.

"Autumn" — SP135

5c+3c, "Summer." 6c+4c, "Spring." 10c+5c, "Winter." 20c+7c, "New Year."

1949, Nov. 14 Engr. *Perf. 13x14*

B203	SP135	2c +3c brown	.25	.25
B204	SP135	5c +3c red	3.50	1.50
B205	SP135	6c +4c dull green	2.50	.30
B206	SP135	10c +5c gray	.25	.25
B207	SP135	20c +7c blue	3.50	1.50
		Nos. B203-B207 (5)	10.00	3.80

The surtax was for child welfare.

Figure from PTT Monument, The Hague SP136

Grain Binder SP137

Designs: 4c+2c, Dike repairs. 5c+3c, Apartment House, Rotterdam. 10c+5c, Bridge section being towed. 20c+5c, Canal freighter.

1950, May 2 *Perf. 12½x12, 12x12½*

B208	SP136	2c +2c brn	2.10	1.10
B209	SP136	4c +2c dk green	6.50	5.75
B210	SP136	5c +3c gray	5.50	4.50
B211	SP137	6c +4c purple	2.75	.75
B212	SP137	10c +5c indigo	3.75	.40
B213	SP137	20c +5c dp bl	7.50	9.50
		Nos. B208-B213 (6)	28.10	22.00

The surtax was for social and cultural works.

Church Ruins and Good Samaritan — SP138

1950, July 17 Photo. *Perf. 12½x12*

B214	SP138	2c +2c ol brn	4.75	2.40
B215	SP138	5c +3c brn red	6.25	*7.25*
B216	SP138	6c +4c dp grn	3.75	3.25
B217	SP138	10c +5c brt lil rose	13.50	.80
B218	SP138	20c +5c ultra	19.00	*24.00*
		Nos. B214-B218 (5)	47.25	*37.70*

The surtax was for the restoration of ruined churches.

Baby and Bees — SP139

Designs: 5c+3c, Boy and rooster. 6c+4c, Girl feeding birds. 10c+5c, Boy and fish. 20c+7c, Girl, butterfly and toad.

1950, Nov. 13 *Perf. 13x12*

B219	SP139	2c +3c car	.30	.25
B220	SP139	5c +3c ol grn	8.25	4.25
B221	SP139	6c +4c dk bl grn	2.40	.65
B222	SP139	10c +5c lilac	.30	.25
B223	SP139	20c +7c blue	8.75	7.50
		Nos. B219-B223 (5)	20.00	12.90

The surtax was to aid needy children.

Hillenraad Castle SP140

Bergh Castle SP141

Castles: 6c+4c, Hernen. 10c+5c, Rechteren. 20c+5c, Moermond.

Perf. 12x12½, 12½x12

1951, May 15 Engr. Unwmk.

B224	SP140	2c +2c purple	1.75	1.00
B225	SP141	5c +3c dk red	5.50	6.00
B226	SP140	6c +4c dk brown	3.50	1.00
B227	SP141	10c +5c dk green	4.00	.25
B228	SP141	20c +5c dp blue	5.50	*6.00*
		Nos. B224-B228 (5)	20.25	*14.25*

The surtax was for cultural, medical and social purposes.

Girl and Windmill — SP142

Designs: 5c+3c, Boy and building construction. 6c+4c, Fisherboy and net. 10c+5c, Boy, chimneys and steelwork. 20c+7c, Girl and apartment house.

1951, Nov. 12 Photo. *Perf. 13x14*

B229	SP142	2c +3c dp green	.60	.25
B230	SP142	5c +3c sl vio	5.25	3.50
B231	SP142	6c +4c dk brown	3.50	.70
B232	SP142	10c +5c red brn	.30	.25
B233	SP142	20c +7c dp bl	5.25	*6.50*
		Nos. B229-B233 (5)	14.90	*11.20*

The surtax was for child welfare.

Jan van Riebeeck — SP143

1952, Mar. *Perf. 12½x12*

B234	SP143	2c +3c dk gray	3.25	2.25
B235	SP143	6c +4c dk bl grn	4.00	3.00
B236	SP143	10c +5c brt red	4.50	2.25
B237	SP143	20c +5c brt blue	3.25	3.00
		Nos. B234-B237 (4)	15.00	10.50

Tercentenary of Van Riebeeck's landing in South Africa. Surtax was for Van Riebeeck monument fund.

Scotch Rose — SP144

Designs: 5c+3c, Marsh marigold. 6c+4c, Tulip. 10c+5c, Ox-eye daisy. 20c+5c, Cornflower.

1952, May 1

B238	SP144	2c +2c cer & dl grn	.60	.50
B239	SP144	5c +3c dp grn & yel	2.40	3.00
B240	SP144	6c +4c red & dl grn	1.60	1.10
B241	SP144	10c +5c org yel & dl grn	1.20	.35
B242	SP144	20c +5c bl & dl grn	6.25	5.25
		Nos. B238-B242 (5)	12.05	10.20

The surtax was for social, cultural and medical purposes.

Girl and Dog — SP145

2c+3c, Boy & goat. 5c+3c, Girl on donkey. 10c+5c, Boy & kitten. 20c+7c, Boy & rabbit.

Design in Black

Perf. 12x12½

1952, Nov. 17 Unwmk.

B243	SP145	2c +3c olive	.25	.25
B244	SP145	5c +3c dp rose	1.90	1.45
B245	SP145	6c +4c aqua	1.35	.40
B246	SP145	10c +5c org yel	.25	.25
B247	SP145	20c +7c blue	4.50	4.25
		Nos. B243-B247 (5)	8.25	6.60

The surtax was for child welfare.

No. 308 Surcharged in Black

Perf. 13½x13

1953, Feb. 10 Wmk. 202

B248	A76	10c +10c org yel	.50	.25

The surtax was for flood relief.

Hyacinth — SP146

Designs: 5c+3c, African Marigold. 6c+4c, Daffodil. 10c+5c, Anemone. 20c+5c, Iris.

1953, May 1 Unwmk. *Perf. 12½x12*

B249	SP146	2c +2c vio & grn	.65	.50
B250	SP146	5c +3c dp org & grn	2.25	3.25
B251	SP146	6c +4c grn & yel	1.30	1.00
B252	SP146	10c +5c dk red & grn	2.90	.50
B253	SP146	20c +5c dp ultra & grn	9.00	9.00
		Nos. B249-B253 (5)	16.10	14.25

The surtax was for social, cultural and medical purposes.

Red Cross on Shield — SP147

Designs: 6c+4c, Man holding lantern. 7c+5c, Worker and ambulance at flood. 10c+5c, Nurse giving blood transfusion. 25c+8c, Red Cross flags.

Cross in Red

1953, Aug. 24 Engr.

B254	SP147	2c +3c dk ol	.60	.45
B255	SP147	6c +4c dk vio brn	3.50	3.25
B256	SP147	7c +5c dk gray grn	.75	.45
B257	SP147	10c +5c red	.60	.25
B258	SP147	25c +8c dp bl	4.50	4.25
		Nos. B254-B258 (5)	9.95	8.65

The surtax was for the Red Cross.

Spade, Flag, Bucket and Girl's Head — SP148

Head of child and: 5c+3c, Apple. 7c+5c, Pigeon. 10c+5c, Sailboat. 25c+8c, Tulip.

1953, Nov. 16 Litho. *Perf. 12x12½*

B259	SP148	2c +3c yel & bl gray	.25	.25
B260	SP148	5c +3c ap grn & brn car	2.25	3.50
B261	SP148	7c +5c lt bl & sep	2.25	1.30
B262	SP148	10c +5c ol bis & lil	.25	.25
B263	SP148	25c +8c pink & bl grn	6.00	8.00
		Nos. B259-B263 (5)	11.00	13.30

The surtax was for child welfare.

Martinus Nijhoff, Poet — SP149

5c+3c, Willem Pijper, composer. 7c+5c, H. P. Berlage, architect. 10c+5c, Johan Huizinga, historian. 25c+8c, Vincent van Gogh, painter.

1954, May 1 Photo. *Perf. 12½x12*

B264	SP149	2c +3c dp bl	1.75	1.50
B265	SP149	5c +3c ol brn	2.00	2.00
B266	SP149	7c +5c dk red	2.60	1.20
B267	SP149	10c +5c dl grn	5.25	.60
B268	SP149	25c +8c plum	6.75	7.75
		Nos. B264-B268 (5)	18.35	13.05

The surtax was for social and cultural purposes.

Boy Flying Model Plane — SP150

Portrait: 10c+4c, Albert E. Plesman.

1954, Aug. 23 *Perf. 12½x12*

B269	SP150	2c +2c ol grn	.75	.65
B270	SP150	10c +4c dk gray bl	2.10	.65

The surtax was for the Netherlands Aviation Foundation.

Children Making Paper Chains SP151

Girl Brushing Teeth SP152

7c+5c, Boy sailing toy boat. 10c+5c, Nurse drying child. 25c+8c, Young convalescent, drawing.

Perf. 12x12½, 12½x12

1954, Nov. 15

B271	SP151	2c +3c brn	.25	.25
B272	SP152	5c +3c ol grn	2.75	2.75
B273	SP152	7c +5c gray bl	1.00	.50
B274	SP152	10c +5c brn red	.25	.25
B275	SP151	25c +8c dp bl	5.75	4.75
		Nos. B271-B275 (5)	10.00	8.50

The surtax was for child welfare.

Factory, Rotterdam SP153

Amsterdam Stock Exchange SP154

5c+3c, Post office, The Hague. 10c+5c, Town hall, Hilversum. 25c+8c, Office building, The Hague.

1955, Apr. 25 Engr.

B276	SP153	2c +3c brnsh bis	1.25	1.00
B277	SP153	5c +3c bl grn	2.25	2.75
B278	SP154	7c +5c rose brn	1.25	1.00
B279	SP153	10c +5c steel bl	1.75	.25
B280	SP153	25c +8c choc	6.75	*7.00*
		Nos. B276-B280 (5)	13.25	*12.00*

The surtax was for social and cultural purposes.

Microscope and Crab — SP155

1955, Aug. 15 Photo. *Perf. 12½x12*

Crab in Red

B281 SP155 2c +3c dk gray .65 .55
B282 SP155 5c +3c dk grn 1.40 1.45
B283 SP155 7c +5c dk vio 1.15 .60
B284 SP155 10c +5c dk bl .95 .25
B285 SP155 25c +8c olive 4.50 3.75
Nos. B281-B285 (5) 8.65 6.60

The surtax was for cancer research.

Willem van Loon by Dirck Santvoort — SP156

Portraits: 5+3c, Boy by Jacob Adriaanszoon Backer. 7+5c, Girl by unknown artist. 10+5c, Philips Huygens by Adriaan Hanneman. 25+8c, Constantijn Huygens by Adriaan Hanneman.

1955, Nov. 14 Unwmk.

B286 SP156 2c +3c dk grn .35 .25
B287 SP156 5c +3c dp car 2.10 1.75
B288 SP156 7c +5c dl red brn 2.10 .65
B289 SP156 10c +5c dp bl .35 .25
B290 SP156 25c +8c purple 5.50 5.00
Nos. B286-B290 (5) 10.40 7.90

The surtax was for child welfare.

Farmer Wearing High Cap — SP157

Rembrandt Etchings: 5c+3c, Young Tobias with Angel. 7c+5c, Persian Wearing Fur Cap. 10c+5c, Old Blind Tobias. 25c+8c, Self-portrait of 1639.

1956, Apr. 23 Engr. *Perf. 13½x14*

B291 SP157 2c +3c dk gray bl 1.25 1.60
B292 SP157 5c +3c ol grn 2.25 2.25
B293 SP157 7c +5c brown 2.50 2.50
B294 SP157 10c +5c dk grn 6.00 .35
B295 SP157 25c +8c redsh brn 9.25 9.25
Nos. B291-B295 (5) 21.25 15.95

350th anniv. of the birth of Rembrandt van Rijn.

Surtax for social and cultural purposes.

Sailboat — SP158

Designs: 5c+3c, Woman runner. 7c+5c, Amphora depicting runners. 10c+5c, Field hockey. 25c+8c, Waterpolo player.

1956, Aug. 27 Litho. *Perf. 12½x12*

B296 SP158 2c +3c brt bl & blk .70 .80
B297 SP158 5c +3c dl yel & blk 1.00 1.15
B298 SP158 7c +5c red brn & blk 1.00 1.15
B299 SP158 10c +5c gray & blk 1.25 .40
B300 SP158 25c +8c brt grn & blk 2.60 *3.50*
Nos. B296-B300 (5) 6.55 *7.00*

16th Olympic Games at Melbourne, Nov. 22-Dec. 8, 1956.

The surtax was for the benefit of the Netherlands Olympic Committee.

Boy by Jan van Scorel — SP159

Children's Portraits: 5c+3c, Boy, 1563. 7c+5c, Girl, 1563. 10c+5c, Girl, 1590. 25c+8c, Eechie Pieters, 1592.

1956, Nov. 12 Photo. Unwmk.

B301 SP159 2c +3c blk vio .35 .25
B302 SP159 5c +3c ol grn 1.60 .65
B303 SP159 7c +5c brn vio 1.75 1.25
B304 SP159 10c +5c dp red .30 .25
B305 SP159 25c +8c dk bl 3.25 2.90
Nos. B301-B305 (5) 7.25 5.30

The surtax was for child welfare.

Motor Freighter — SP160

Ships: 6c+4c, Coaster. 7c+5c, "Willem Barendsz." 10c+8c, Trawler. 30c+8c, S. S. "Nieuw Amsterdam."

1957, May 13 Photo. *Perf. 14x13*

B306 SP160 4c +3c brt bl 1.00 1.00
B307 SP160 6c +4c brt vio 2.00 2.00
B308 SP160 7c +5c dk car rose 1.25 1.10
B309 SP160 10c +8c grn 2.10 .40
B310 SP160 30c +8c choc 3.25 *3.00*
Nos. B306-B310 (5) 9.60 *7.50*

The surtax was for social and cultural purposes.

White Pelican Feeding Young — SP161

Designs: 6c+4c, Vacation ship, "Castle of Staverden." 7c+5c, Cross and dates: 1867-1957. 10c+8c, Cross and laurel wreath. 30c+8c, Globe and Cross.

1957, Aug. 19 Litho. *Perf. 12x12½*

Cross in Red

B311 SP161 4c +3c bl & red .65 .60
B312 SP161 6c +4c dk grn .85 .85
B313 SP161 7c +5c dk grn & pink .85 .85
B314 SP161 10c +8c yel org .75 .25
B315 SP161 30c +8c vio bl 1.90 *1.90*
Nos. B311-B315 (5) 5.00 *4.45*

90th anniversary of the founding of the Netherlands Red Cross.

Girl by B. J. Blommers — SP162

Girls' Portraits by: 6c+4c, William B. Tholen. 8c+4c, Jan Sluyters. 12c+9c, Matthijs Maris. 30c+9c, Cornelis Kruseman.

1957, Nov. 18 Photo. *Perf. 12½x12*

B316 SP162 4c +4c dp car .30 .25
B317 SP162 6c +4c ol grn 1.50 2.00
B318 SP162 8c +4c gray 1.60 1.90
B319 SP162 12c +9c dp claret .25 .25
B320 SP162 30c +9c dk bl 4.50 4.75
Nos. B316-B320 (5) 8.15 9.15

The surtax was for child welfare.

Woman from Walcheren, Zeeland — SP163

Regional Costumes: 6c+4c, Marken. 8c+4c, Scheveningen. 12c+9c, Friesland. 30c+9c, Volendam.

1958, Apr. 28 Photo. Unwmk.

B321 SP163 4c +4c blue .95 .60
B322 SP163 6c +4c bister 1.60 1.60
B323 SP163 8c +4c dk car rose 2.90 1.60
B324 SP163 12c +9c org brn 1.60 .25
B325 SP163 30c +9c vio 5.00 *5.25*
Nos. B321-B325 (5) 12.05 *9.30*

Surtax for social and cultural purposes.

Girl on Stilts and Boy on Tricycle — SP164

Children's Games: 6c+4c, Boy and girl on scooters. 8c+4c, Leapfrog. 12c+9c, Roller skating. 30c+9c, Boy in toy car and girl jumping rope.

1958, Nov. 17 Litho.

B326 SP164 4c +4c lt bl .25 .25
B327 SP164 6c +4c dp red 1.60 1.60
B328 SP164 8c +4c brt bl grn 1.30 .75
B329 SP164 12c +9c red org .25 .25
B330 SP164 30c +9c dk bl 3.25 3.00
Nos. B326-B330 (5) 6.65 5.85

The surtax was for child welfare.

Tugs and Caisson — SP165

Designs: 6c+4c, Dredger. 8c+4c, Laborers making fascine mattresses. 12c+9c, Grab cranes. 30c+9c, Sand spouter.

1959, May 11 *Perf. 14x13*

B331 SP165 4c +4c dk bl, *bl grn* 1.00 1.00
B332 SP165 6c +4c red org, *gray* 1.00 1.30
B333 SP165 8c +4c bl vio, *lt bl* 1.00 1.00
B334 SP165 12c +9c bl grn, *brt yel* 1.75 .25
B335 SP165 30c +9c dk brn, *brick red* 3.25 *4.50*
Nos. B331-B335 (5) 8.00 *8.05*

Issued to publicize the endless struggle to keep the sea out and the land dry.

The surtax was for social and cultural purposes.

Child in Playpen — SP166

Designs: 6c+4c, Playing Indian. 8c+4c, Child feeding geese. 12c+9c, Children crossing street. 30c+9c, Doing homework.

1959, Nov. 16 *Perf. 12½x12*

B336 SP166 4c +4c dp rose & dk bl .25 .25
B337 SP166 6c +4c red brn & emer 1.00 1.00
B338 SP166 8c +4c red & bl 1.75 1.10
B339 SP166 12c +9c grnsh bl, org & gray .25 .25
B340 SP166 30c +9c yel & bl 2.90 2.75
Nos. B336-B340 (5) 6.15 5.35

The surtax was for child welfare.

Refugee Woman — SP167

1960, Apr. 7 Photo. *Perf. 13x14*

B341 SP167 12c +8c dp claret .50 .30
B342 SP167 30c +10c dk ol grn 2.25 2.00

Issued to publicize World Refugee Year, July 1, 1959-June 30, 1960. The surtax was for aid to refugees.

Tulip — SP168

Flowers: 6c+4c, Gorse. 8c+4c, White waterlily, horiz. 12c+8c, Red poppy. 30c+10c, Blue sea holly.

Perf. 12½x12, 12x12½

1960, May 23 Unwmk.

B343 SP168 4c +4c gray, grn & red .95 .75
B344 SP168 6c +4c sal, grn & yel 1.25 1.60
B345 SP168 8c +4c multi 1.75 1.60
B346 SP168 12c +8c dl org, red & grn 1.60 .30
B347 SP168 30c +10c yel, grn & ultra 3.00 4.50
Nos. B343-B347 (5) 8.55 8.75

The surtax was for child welfare.

Girl from Marken — SP169

Regional Costumes: 6c+4c, Volendam. 8c+4c, Bunschoten. 12c+9c, Hindeloopen. 30c+9c, Huizen.

1960, Nov. 14 *Perf. 12½x12*

B348 SP169 4c +4c multi .35 .25
B349 SP169 6c +4c multi 1.60 2.00
B350 SP169 8c +4c multi 3.00 2.00
B351 SP169 12c +9c multi .35 .25
B352 SP169 30c +9c multi 3.75 4.50
Nos. B348-B352 (5) 9.05 9.00

The surtax was for child welfare.

Herring Gull — SP170

Birds: 6c+4c, Oystercatcher, horiz. 8c+4c, Curlew. 12c+8c, Avocet, horiz. 30c+10c, Lapwing.

Perf. 12½x12, 12x12½

1961, Apr. 24 Litho. Unwmk.

B353 SP170 4c +4c yel & grnsh gray .70 .95
B354 SP170 6c +4c fawn & blk 1.40 1.75
B355 SP170 8c +4c ol & red brn .70 1.10
B356 SP170 12c +8c lt bl & gray 1.90 .40
B357 SP170 30c +10c grn & blk 1.90 2.40
Nos. B353-B357 (5) 6.60 6.60

The surtax was for social and cultural purposes.

St. Nicholas on his Horse — SP171

Holiday folklore: 6c+4c, Epiphany. 8c+4c, Palm Sunday. 12c+9c, Whitsun bride, Pentecost. 30c+9c, Martinmas.

1961, Nov. 13 *Perf. 12½x12*

B358 SP171 4c +4c brt red .25 .25
B359 SP171 6c +4c brt bl .90 .75
B360 SP171 8c +4c olive .80 .75
B361 SP171 12c +9c dp grn .25 .25
B362 SP171 30c +9c dp org 2.40 2.40
Nos. B358-B362 (5) 4.60 4.40

The surtax was for child welfare.

SP172

Designs: 4c+4c, Cat, Roman sculpture, horiz. 6c+4c, Fossil Ammonite. 8c+4c, Christian Huygens' Pendulum Clock by van Ceulen. 12c+8c, Figurehead from admiralty ship model. 30c+10c, Guardsmen Hendrick van Berckenrode and Jacob van Lourensz, by Frans Hals, horiz.

Perf. 14x13, 13x14

1962, Apr. 27 Photo.

B363 SP172 4c +4c ol grn .85 .85
B364 SP172 6c +4c gray .70 .85
B365 SP172 8c +4c maroon 1.00 1.25

B366 SP172 12c +8c olive bis 1.00 .35
B367 SP172 30c +10c indigo 1.05 1.25
Nos. B363-B367 (5) 4.60 4.55

The surtax was for social and cultural purposes. Issued to publicize the International Congress of Museum Experts, July 4-11.

Children Cooking — SP173

Children's Activities: 6c+4c, Bicycling. 8c+4c, Watering flowers. 12c+9c, Feeding chickens. 30c+9c, Music making.

1962, Nov. 12 ***Perf. 12½x12***
B368 SP173 4c +4c red .25 .25
B369 SP173 6c +4c yel bis .75 .60
B370 SP173 8c +4c ultra 1.05 1.15
B371 SP173 12c +9c dp grn .25 .25
B372 SP173 30c +9c dk car rose 1.75 1.90
Nos. B368-B372 (5) 4.05 4.15

The surtax was for child welfare.

Gallery Windmill — SP174

Windmills: 6c+4c, North Holland polder mill. 8c+4c, South Holland polder mill, horiz. 12c+8c, Post mill. 30c+10c, Wip mill.

Perf. 13x14, 14x13
1963, Apr. 24 **Litho.** **Unwmk.**
B373 SP174 4c +4c dk bl .85 1.00
B374 SP174 6c +4c dk pur .85 1.00
B375 SP174 8c +4c dk grn 1.05 1.20
B376 SP174 12c +8c blk 1.05 .30
B377 SP174 30c +10c dk car 1.60 1.75
Nos. B373-B377 (5) 5.40 5.25

The surtax was for social and cultural purposes.

Roadside First Aid Station — SP175

Designs: 6c+4c, Book collection box. 8c+4c, Crosses. 12c+9c, International aid to Africans. 30c+9c, First aid team.

1963, Aug. 20 ***Perf. 14x13***
B378 SP175 4c +4c dk bl & red .40 .40
B379 SP175 6c +4c dl pur & red .40 .40
B380 SP175 8c +4c blk & red .75 .55
B381 SP175 12c +9c red brn & red .25 .25
B382 SP175 30c +9c yel grn & red 1.20 1.20
Nos. B378-B382 (5) 3.00 2.80

Centenary of the Intl. Red Cross. The surtax went to the Netherlands Red Cross.

"Aunt Lucy Sat on a Goosey" — SP176

Nursery Rhymes: 6c+4c, "In the Hague there lives a count." 8c+4c, "One day I passed a puppet's fair." 12c+9c, "Storky, storky, Billy Spoon." 30c+9c, "Ride on in a little buggy."

1963, Nov. 12 **Litho.** ***Perf. 13x14***
B383 SP176 4c +4c grnsh bl & dk bl .25 .25
B384 SP176 6c +4c org red & sl grn 1.10 .60
B385 SP176 8c +4c dl grn & dk brn 1.60 .50
B386 SP176 12c +9c yel & dk pur .25 .25
B387 SP176 30c +9c rose & blksh lil 1.60 1.40
Nos. B383-B387 (5) 4.80 3.00

The surtax was for mentally and physically handicapped children.

Seeing-Eye Dog — SP177

8c+5c, Three red deer. 12c+9c, Three kittens. 30c+9c, European bison and young.

1964, Apr. 21 ***Perf. 12x12½***
B388 SP177 5c +5c gray ol, red & blk .35 .35
B389 SP177 8c +5c dk red, pale brn & blk .25 .25
B390 SP177 12c +9c dl yel, blk & gray .35 .25
B391 SP177 30c +9c bl, gray & blk .60 .55
Nos. B388-B391 (4) 1.55 1.40

The surtax was for social and cultural purposes.

Child Painting — SP178

"Artistic and Creative Activities of Children": 10c+5c, Ballet dancing. 15c+10c, Girl playing the flute. 20c+10c, Little Red Riding Hood (masquerading children). 40c+15c, Boy with hammer at work bench.

Perf. 13x14
1964, Nov. 17 **Photo.** **Unwmk.**
B392 SP178 7c +3c lt ol grn & bl .45 .35
B393 SP178 10c +5c red, brt pink & grn .40 .35
B394 SP178 15c +10c yel bis, blk & yel .25 .25
B395 SP178 20c +10c brt pink, brn & red .75 .50
B396 SP178 40c +15c bl & yel grn .95 .70
Nos. B392-B396 (5) 2.80 2.15

The surtax was for child welfare.

View of Veere — SP179

Views: 10c+6c, Thorn. 18c+12c, Dordrecht. 20c+10c, Staveren. 40c+10c, Medemblik.

1965, June 1 **Litho.** ***Perf. 14x13***
B397 SP179 8c +6c yel & blk .25 .30
B398 SP179 10c +6c grnsh bl & blk .40 .35
B399 SP179 18c +12c sal & blk .30 .30
B400 SP179 20c +10c bl & blk .40 .35
B401 SP179 40c +10c ap grn & blk .45 .45
Nos. B397-B401 (5) 1.80 1.75

The surtax was for social and cultural purposes.

Child — SP180

Designs by Children: 10c+6c, Ship. 18c+12c, Woman, vert. 20c+10c, Child, lake and swan. 40c+10c, Tractor.

Perf. 14x13, 13x14
1965, Nov. 16 **Photo.**
B402 SP180 8c +6c multi .25 .25
B403 SP180 10c +6c multi .50 .50
B404 SP180 18c +12c multi .25 .25
a. Min. sheet of 11, 5 #B402, 6 #B404 + label 16.00 *23.50*
B405 SP180 20c +10c multi .75 .60
B406 SP180 40c +10c multi 1.00 .85
Nos. B402-B406 (5) 2.75 2.45

The surtax was for child welfare.

"Help them to a safe haven" — SP181

1966, Jan. 31 **Photo.** ***Perf. 14x13***
B407 SP181 18c +7c blk & org yel .30 .25
B408 SP181 40c +20c blk & red .25 .25
a. Min. sheet of 3, #B407, 2 #B408 1.60 1.20

The surtax was for the Intergovernmental Committee for European Migration (ICEM). The message on the stamps was given and signed by Queen Juliana.

Inkwell, Goose Quill and Book — SP182

Designs: 12c+8c, Fragment of Gysbert Japicx manuscript. 20c+10c, Knight on horseback, miniature from "Roman van Walewein" manuscript, 1350. 25c+10c, Initial "D" from "Ferguut" manuscript, 1350. 40c+20c, Print shop, 16th century woodcut.

1966, May 3 ***Perf. 13x14***
B409 SP182 10c +5c multi .30 .35
B410 SP182 12c +8c multi .30 .35
B411 SP182 20c +10c multi .45 .35
B412 SP182 25c +10c multi .60 .50
B413 SP182 40c +20c multi .45 .50
Nos. B409-B413 (5) 2.10 2.05

Gysbert Japicx (1603-1666), Friesian poet, and the 200th anniversary of the founding of the Netherlands Literary Society.

The surtax was for social and cultural purposes.

Infant — SP183

Designs: 12c+8c, Daughter of the painter S. C. Lixenberg. 20c+10c, Boy swimming. 25c+10c, Dominga Blazer, daughter of Carel Blazer, photographer of this set. 40c+20c, Boy and horse.

1966, Nov. 15 **Photo.** ***Perf. 14x13***
B414 SP183 10c +5c dp org & bl .25 .25
B415 SP183 12c +8c ap grn & red .25 .25
B416 SP183 20c +10c brt bl & red .25 .25
a. Min. sheet of 12, 4 #B414, 5 #B415, 3 #B416 2.00 2.00
B417 SP183 25c +10c brt rose lil & dk bl .65 .65
B418 SP183 40c +20c dp car & dk grn .65 .65
Nos. B414-B418 (5) 2.05 2.05

The surtax was for child welfare.

Whelk Eggs — SP184

15c+10c, Whelk. 20c+10c, Mussel with acorn shells. 25c+10c, Jellyfish. 45c+20c, Crab.

1967, Apr. 11 **Unwmk.** **Litho.**
B419 SP184 12c +8c ol grn & tan .25 .25
B420 SP184 15c +10c lt bl, ultra & blk .25 .25
B421 SP184 20c +10c gray, blk & red .25 .25
B422 SP184 25c +10c brn car, plum & ol brn .50 .50
B423 SP184 45c +20c multi .70 .65
Nos. B419-B423 (5) 1.95 1.90

Red Cross and Dates Forming Cross — SP185

15c+10c, Crosses. 20c+10c, Initials "NRK" forming cross. 25c+10c, Maltese cross and crosses. 45c+20c, "100" forming cross.

1967, Aug. 8 ***Perf. 14x13***
B424 SP185 12c +8c dl bl & red .30 .30
B425 SP185 15c +10c red .35 .35
B426 SP185 20c +10c ol & red .30 .30
B427 SP185 25c +10c ol grn & red .45 .45
B428 SP185 45c +20c gray & red .70 .70
Nos. B424-B428 (5) 2.10 2.10

Centenary of the Dutch Red Cross.

"Lullaby for the Little Porcupine" — SP186

Nursery Rhymes: 15c+10c, "Little Whistling Kettle." 20c+10c, "Dikkertje Dap and the Giraffe." 25c+10c, "The Nicest Flowers." 45c+20c, "Pippeljoentje, the Little Bear."

1967, Nov. 7 **Litho.** ***Perf. 13x14***
B429 SP186 12c +8c multi .25 .25
B430 SP186 15c +10c multi .25 .25
B431 SP186 20c +10c multi .25 .25
a. Min. sheet of 10, 3 #B429, 4 #B430, 3 #B431 4.00 4.00
B432 SP186 25c +10c multi 1.10 .75
B433 SP186 45c +20c multi 1.15 .75
Nos. B429-B433 (5) 3.00 2.25

The surtax was for child welfare.

St. Servatius Bridge, Maastricht SP187

Bridges: 15c+10c, Narrow Bridge, Amsterdam. 20c+10c, Railroad Bridge, Culenborg. 25c+10c, Van Brienenoord Bridge, Rotterdam. 45c+20c, Zeeland Bridge, Schelde Estuary.

1968, Apr. 9 **Photo.** ***Perf. 14x13***
B434 SP187 12c +8c green .35 .35
B435 SP187 15c +10c ol brn .50 .50
B436 SP187 20c +10c rose red .30 .25
B437 SP187 25c +10c gray .35 .35
B438 SP187 45c +20c ultra .60 .60
Nos. B434-B438 (5) 2.10 2.05

Goblin — SP188

Fairy Tale Characters: 15c+10c, Giant. 20c+10c, Witch. 25c+10c, Dragon. 45c+20c, Magician.

1968, Nov. 12 **Photo.** ***Perf. 14x13***
B439 SP188 12c +8c grn, pink & blk .25 .25
B440 SP188 15c +10c bl, pink & blk .25 .25
B441 SP188 20c +10c bl, emer & blk .25 .25
a. Min. sheet of 10, 3 #B439, 4 #B440, 3 #B441 4.00 4.00
B442 SP188 25c +10c org red, org & blk 1.25 1.25
B443 SP188 45c +20c yel, org & blk 1.25 1.25
Nos. B439-B443 (5) 3.25 3.25

The surtax was for child welfare.

Villa Huis ter Heide, 1915 — SP189

Contemporary Architecture: 15c+10c, House, Utrecht, 1924. 20c+10c, First open-air school, Amsterdam, 1960. 25c+10c, Burgweeshuis (orphanage), Amsterdam, 1960. 45c+20c, Netherlands Congress Building, The Hague, 1969.

1969, Apr. 15 **Photo.** ***Perf. 14x13***
B444 SP189 12c +8c lt brn & sl .65 .65
B445 SP189 15c +10c bl, gray & red .65 .65
B446 SP189 20c +10c vio & blk .65 .65
B447 SP189 25c +10c grn & gray .65 .65
B448 SP189 45c +20c gray, bl & yel .65 .65
Nos. B444-B448 (5) 3.25 3.25

Surtax for social and cultural purposes.

Stylized Crab — SP190

1969, Aug. 12 Photo. *Perf. 13x14*

B449 SP190 12c +8c vio .55 .55
B450 SP190 25c +10c org .80 .35
B451 SP190 45c +20c bl grn 1.25 1.25
Nos. B449-B451 (3) 2.60 2.15

20th anniv. of the Queen Wilhelmina Fund. The surtax was for cancer research.

Child with Violin — SP191

12c+8c, Child with flute. 20c+10c, Child with drum. 25c+10c, Three children singing, horiz. 45c+20c, Two girls dancing, horiz.

1969, Nov. 11 *Perf. 13x14, 14x13*

B452 SP191 12c +8c ultra, blk & yel .25 .25
B453 SP191 15c +10c blk & red .25 .25
B454 SP191 20c +10c red, blk & yel 2.00 1.60
B455 SP191 25c +10c yel, blk & red .25 .25
a. Min. sheet of 10, 4 #B452, 4 #B453, 2 #B455 5.00 5.00
B456 SP191 45c +20c grn, blk & red 2.10 1.60
Nos. B452-B456 (5) 4.85 3.95

The surtax was for child welfare.

Isometric Projection from Circle to Square — SP192

Designs made by Computer: 15c+10c, Parallel planes in a cube. 20c+10c, Two overlapping scales. 25c+10c, Transition phases of concentric circles with increasing diameters. 45c+20c, Four spirals.

Lithographed and Engraved

1970, Apr. 7 *Perf. 13x14*

B457 SP192 12c +8c yel & blk .80 .80
B458 SP192 15c +10c sil & blk .80 .80
B459 SP192 20c +10c blk .80 .80
B460 SP192 25c +10c brt bl & blk .80 .80
B461 SP192 45c +20c sil & white .80 .80
Nos. B457-B461 (5) 4.00 4.00

Surtax for social and cultural purposes.

Bleeding Heart — SP193

1970, July 28 Photo. *Perf. 13x14*

B462 SP193 12c +8c org yel, red & blk .60 .60
B463 SP193 25c +10c pink, red & blk .60 .40
B464 SP193 45c +20c brt grn, red & blk .60 .60
Nos. B462-B464 (3) 1.80 1.60

The surtax was for the Netherlands Heart Foundation.

Toy Block — SP194

1970, Nov. 10 Photo. *Perf. 13x14*

B465 SP194 12c +8c bl, vio bl & grn .25 .25
B466 SP194 15c +10c grn, bl & yel 1.15 1.10
B467 SP194 20c +10c lil rose, red & vio bl 1.15 1.10
B468 SP194 25c +10c red, yel & lil rose .25 .25
a. Min. sheet of 11, 9 #B465, 2 #B468 + label 6.00 6.00
B469 SP194 45c +20c gray & blk 1.30 1.30
Nos. B465-B469 (5) 4.10 4.00

The surtax was for child welfare.

St. Paul — SP195

Designs: 15c+10c, "50" and people. 25c+10c, Joachim and Ann. 30c+15c, John the Baptist and the Scribes. 45c+20c, St. Anne. The sculptures are wood, 15th century, and in Dutch museums.

1971, Apr. 20 Litho. *Perf. 13x14*

B470 SP195 15c +10c multi .80 .80

Lithographed and Photogravure

B471 SP195 20c +10c gray, grn & blk .80 .80
B472 SP195 25c +10c buff, org & blk .80 .50
B473 SP195 30c +15c gray, bl & blk .80 .80
B474 SP195 45c +20c pink, ver & blk .80 .80
Nos. B470-B474 (5) 4.00 3.70

50th anniversary of the Federation of Netherlands Universities for Adult Education.

Detail from Borobudur — SP196

1971, June 29 Litho. *Perf. 13x14*

B475 SP196 45c +20c pur, yel & blk 1.60 1.60

60th birthday of Prince Bernhard. Surtax for Save Borobudur Temple Fund.

"Earth" — SP197

Designs: 20c+10c, "Air" (butterfly). 25c+10c, "Sun," horiz. 30c+15c, "Moon," horiz. 45c+20c, "Water" (child looking at reflection).

Perf. 13x14, 14x13

1971, Nov. 9 Photo.

B476 SP197 15c +10c blk, lil & org .25 .30
B477 SP197 20c +10c yel, blk & rose lil .25 .30
B478 SP197 25c +10c multi .25 .30
a. Min. sheet of 9, 6 #B476, #B477, 2 #B478 4.50 *8.75*
B479 SP197 30c +15c bl, blk & pur .95 .75
B480 SP197 45c +20c grn, blk & bl 1.35 1.40
Nos. B476-B480 (5) 3.05 3.05

The surtax was for child welfare.

Luminescence

Some semipostal issues from Nos. B481-B484 onward are on phosphorescent paper.

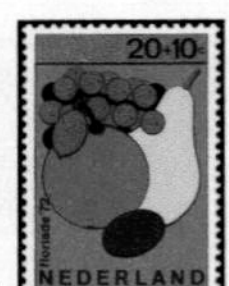

Stylized Fruits — SP198

1972, Apr. 11 Litho. *Perf. 13x14*

B481 SP198 20c +10c shown .75 .75
B482 SP198 25c +10c Flower .75 .75
B483 SP198 30c +15c "Sunlit Landscape" .75 .40
B484 SP198 45c +25c "Music" .75 .75
Nos. B481-B484 (4) 3.00 2.65

Summer festivals: Nos. B481-B482 publicize the Floriade, flower festival; Nos. B483-B484 the Holland Festival of Arts.

Red Cross, First Aid — SP199

Red Cross and: 25c+10c, Blood bank. 30c+15c, Disaster relief. 45c+25c, Child care.

1972, Aug. 15 *Perf. 13x14*

B485 SP199 20c +10c brt pink & red .40 .40
B486 SP199 25c +10c org & red .85 .85
B487 SP199 30c +15c blk & red .55 .40
B488 SP199 45c +25c ultra & red .85 .85
Nos. B485-B488 (4) 2.65 2.50

Surtax for the Netherlands Red Cross.

Prince Willem-Alexander SP200

Photographs of Dutch Princes: 30c+10c, Johan Friso. 35c+15c, Constantijn. 50c+20c, Johan Friso, Constantijn and Willem-Alexander. All are horizontal.

Perf. 13x14, 14x13

1972, Nov. 7 Photo.

B489 SP200 25c +15c multi .25 .25
B490 SP200 30c +10c multi .65 .50
B491 SP200 35c +15c multi .60 .25
a. Min. sheet of 7, 4 #B489, #B490, 2 #B491 + label 4.00 4.00
B492 SP200 50c +20c multi 2.10 2.00
Nos. B489-B492 (4) 3.60 3.00

Surtax was for child welfare.

"W. A. Scholten," 1874 — SP201

Ships: 25c+15c, Flagship "De Seven Provincien," 1673, vert. 35c+15c, "Veendam," 1923. 50c+20c, Zuider Zee fish well boat, 17th century, vert.

1973, Apr. 10 Litho.

B493 SP201 25c +15c multi .80 .80
B494 SP201 30c +10c multi .80 .80
B495 SP201 35c +15c multi .80 .50
B496 SP201 50c +20c multi .80 .80
Nos. B493-B496 (4) 3.20 2.90

Tercentenary of the Battle of Kijkduin and centenary of the Holland-America Line.

Surtax for social and cultural purposes.

Chessboard — SP202

Games: 30c+10c, Tick-tack-toe. 40c+20c, Maze. 50c+20c, Dominoes.

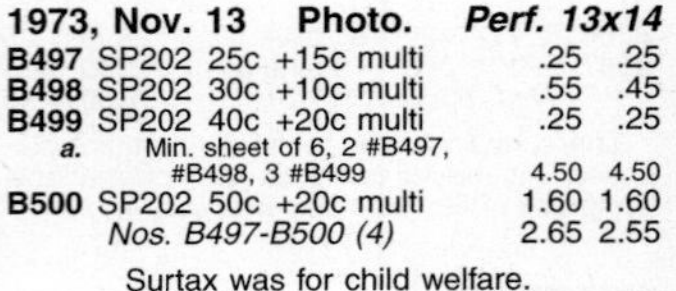

1973, Nov. 13 Photo. *Perf. 13x14*

B497 SP202 25c +15c multi .25 .25
B498 SP202 30c +10c multi .55 .45
B499 SP202 40c +20c multi .25 .25
a. Min. sheet of 6, 2 #B497, #B498, 3 #B499 4.50 4.50
B500 SP202 50c +20c multi 1.60 1.60
Nos. B497-B500 (4) 2.65 2.55

Surtax was for child welfare.

Music Bands SP203

Herman Heijermans SP204

Designs: 30c+10c, Ballet dancers and traffic lights. 50c+20c, Kniertje, the fisher woman, from play by Heijermans.

1974, Apr. 23 Litho. *Perf. 13x14*

B501 SP203 25c +15c multi .75 .75
B502 SP203 30c +10c multi .75 .75

Photo.

B503 SP204 40c +20c multi .75 .40
B504 SP204 50c +20c multi .75 .75
Nos. B501-B504 (4) 3.00 2.65

Surtax was for various social and cultural institutions.

Boy with Hoop — SP205

Designs: 35c+20c, Girl and infant. 45c+20c, Two girls. 60c+20c, Girl sitting on balustrade. Designs are from turn-of-the-century photographs.

1974, Nov. 12 Photo. *Perf. 13x14*

B505 SP205 30c +15c brown .25 .25
B506 SP205 35c +20c maroon .55 .45
B507 SP205 45c +20c black brn .55 .25
a. Min. sheet of 6, 4 #B505, #B506, #B507 3.00 3.00
B508 SP205 60c +20c indigo 1.45 1.25
Nos. B505-B508 (4) 2.80 2.20

Surtax was for child welfare.

Beguinage, Amsterdam SP206

Cooper's Gate, Middelburg SP207

Designs: 35c+20c, St. Hubertus Hunting Lodge, horiz. 60c+20c, Orvelte Village, horiz.

Perf. 14x13, 13x14

1975, Apr. 4 Litho.

B509 SP206 35c +20c multi .55 .50
B510 SP206 40c +15c multi .55 .50
B511 SP207 50c +20c multi .70 .50
B512 SP207 60c +20c multi .90 .90
Nos. B509-B512 (4) 2.70 2.40

European Architectural Heritage Year 1975. Surtax was for various social and cultural institutions.

Orphans, Sculpture, 1785 — SP208

40c+15c, Milkmaid, 17th cent. 50c+25c, Aymon's 4 sons on steed Bayard, 17th cent. 60c+25c, Life at orphanage, 1557. All designs are after ornamental stones from various buildings.

1975, Nov. 11 Photo. *Perf. 14x13*

B513 SP208 35c +15c multi .25 .25
B514 SP208 40c +15c multi .70 .40
B515 SP208 50c +25c multi .35 .25
a. Min. sheet of 5, 3 #B513, 2 #B515 + label 2.00 2.00
B516 SP208 60c +25c multi 1.00 .70
Nos. B513-B516 (4) 2.30 1.60

Surtax was for child welfare.

Hedgehog SP209

Book with "ABC" and Grain; Open Field SP210

Green Frog and Spawn SP212

People and Initials of Social Security Acts SP211

Perf. 14x13, 13x14

1976, Apr. 6 Litho.

B517 SP209 40c +20c multi .65 .50
B518 SP210 45c +20c multi .60 .50

Photo.

B519 SP211 55c +20c multi .60 .25
B520 SP212 75c +25c multi .80 .70
Nos. B517-B520 (4) 2.65 1.95

Surtax for various social and cultural institutions. #B517, B520 for wildlife protection; #B518 cent. of agricultural education and 175th anniv. of elementary education legislation; #B519 75th anniv. of social legislation and the Social Insurance Bank.

Patient Surrounded by Caring Hands — SP213

1976, Sept. 2 Litho. *Perf. 13x14*

B521 SP213 55c +25c multi .55 .45

Dutch Anti-Rheumatism Assoc., 50th anniv.

Netherlands No. 41 — SP214

Designs: No. B523, #64. No. B524, #155. No. B525, #294. No. B526, #220.

1976, Oct. 8 Litho. *Perf. 13x14*

B522 SP214 55c +55c multi .75 .70
B523 SP214 55c +55c multi .75 .70
B524 SP214 55c +55c multi .75 .70
a. Strip of 3, #B522-B524 2.25 2.25

Photo.

B525 SP214 75c +75c multi .75 .70
B526 SP214 75c +75c multi .75 .70
a. Pair, #B525-B526 1.50 1.50
Nos. B522-B526 (5) 3.75 3.50

Amphilex 77 Philatelic Exhibition, Amsterdam, May 26-June 5, 1977. No. B526a printed checkerwise.

See Nos. B535-B538.

Soccer — SP215

Children's Drawings: 45c+20c, Sailboat. 55c+20c, Elephant. 75c+25c, Mobile home.

1976, Nov. 16 Photo. *Perf. 14x13*

B527 SP215 40c +20c multi .25 .25
B528 SP215 45c +20c multi .30 .25
B529 SP215 55c +20c multi .35 .25
a. Min. sheet of 6, 2 each #B527-B529 2.40 2.40
B530 SP215 75c +25c multi 1.10 .80
Nos. B527-B530 (4) 2.00 1.55

Surtax was for child welfare.

Hot Room, Thermal Bath, Heerlen — SP216

45c+20c, Altar of Goddess Nehalennia, 200 A.D., Eastern Scheldt. 55c+20c, Part of oaken ship, Zwammerdam. 75c+25c, Helmet with face, Waal River at Nijmegen.

1977, Apr. 19 Photo. *Perf. 14x13*

B531 SP216 40c +20c multi .45 .30
B532 SP216 45c +20c multi .50 .30
B533 SP216 55c +20c multi .50 .30
B534 SP216 75c +25c multi .65 .50
Nos. B531-B534 (4) 2.10 1.40

Archaeological finds of Roman period. Surtax for various social and cultural institutions.

Type of 1976

Designs: No. B535, Netherlands #83. No. B536, Netherlands #128. No. B537, Netherlands #211. No. B538, Netherlands #302.

1977, May 26 Litho. *Perf. 13x14*

B535 SP214 55c +45c multi .55 .30
B536 SP214 55c +45c multi .55 .30
a. Pair, #B535-B536 1.10 1.10
B537 SP214 55c +45c multi .55 .30
B538 SP214 55c +45c multi .55 .30
a. Souv. sheet of 2, #B535, B538 1.25 1.25
b. Pair, #B537-B538 1.10 1.10
Nos. B535-B538 (4) 2.20 1.20

Amphilex 77 International Philatelic Exhibition, Amsterdam May 26-June 5. No. B538a sold at Exhibition only.

Risk of Drowning — SP217

Childhood Dangers: 45c+20c, Poisoning. 55c+20c, Following ball into street. 75c+25c, Playing with matches.

1977, Nov. 15 Photo. *Perf. 13x14*

B539 SP217 40c +20c multi .40 .25
B540 SP217 45c +20c multi .40 .25
B541 SP217 55c +20c multi .40 .25
a. Min. sheet of 6, 2 each #B539-B541 2.50 2.40
B542 SP217 75c +25c multi .80 .80
Nos. B539-B542 (4) 2.00 1.55

Surtax was for child welfare.

Anna Maria van Schuurman SP218

Delft Plate SP219

Designs: 45c+20c, Part of letter written by author Belle van Zuylen (1740-1805). 75c+25c, Makkum dish with dog.

1978, Apr. 11 Litho. *Perf. 13x14*

B543 SP218 40c +20c multi .40 .30
B544 SP218 45c +20c multi .50 .30

Photo.

B545 SP219 55c +20c multi .55 .30
B546 SP219 75c +25c multi .60 .45
Nos. B543-B546 (4) 2.05 1.35

Dutch authors and pottery products.

Red Cross and World Map — SP220

1978, Aug. 22 Photo. *Perf. 14x13*

B547 SP220 55c +25c multi .50 .40
a. Souvenir sheet of 3 1.50 1.50

Surtax was for Dutch Red Cross.

Boy Ringing Doorbell — SP221

Designs: 45c+20c, Child reading book. 55c+20c, Boy writing "30x Children for Children," vert. 75c+25c, Girl at blackboard, arithmetic lesson.

Perf. 14x13, 13x14

1978, Nov. 14 Photo.

B548 SP221 40c +20c multi .40 .25
B549 SP221 45c +20c multi .40 .25
B550 SP221 55c +20c multi .40 .25
a. Min. sheet of 6, 2 each #B548-B550 2.40 2.25
B551 SP221 75c +25c multi .80 .65
Nos. B548-B551 (4) 2.00 1.40

Surtax was for child welfare.

Psalm Trilogy, by Jurriaan Andriessen SP222

Birth of Christ (detail) Stained-glass Window SP223

Designs: 45c+20c, Amsterdam Toonkunst Choir. 75c+25c, William of Orange, stained-glass window, 1603. Windows from St. John's Church, Gouda.

1979, Apr. 3 Photo. *Perf. 13x14*

B552 SP222 40c +20c multi .40 .30
B553 SP222 45c +20c multi .50 .30
B554 SP223 55c +20c multi .55 .25
B555 SP223 75c +25c multi .60 .45
Nos. B552-B555 (4) 2.05 1.30

Surtax for social and cultural purposes.

Child Sleeping Under Blanket — SP224

Designs: 45c+20c, Infant. 55c+20c, African boy, vert. 75c+25c, Children, vert.

1979, Nov. 13 *Perf. 14x13, 13x14*

B556 SP224 40c +20c blk, red & yel .40 .30
B557 SP224 45c +20c blk & red .40 .30
B558 SP224 55c +20c blk & yel .40 .30
a. Min. sheet, 2 each #B556-B558 2.75 2.75
B559 SP224 75c +25c blk, ultra & red .75 .55
Nos. B556-B559 (4) 1.95 1.45

Surtax was for child welfare (in conjuction with International Year of the Child).

Roads Through Sand Dunes — SP225

50c+20c, Park mansion vert. 60c+25c, Sailing. 80c+35c, Bicycling, moorlands.

Perf. 14x13, 13x14

1980, Apr. 15 Litho.

B560 SP225 45c +20c multi .60 .30
B561 SP225 50c +20c multi .60 .30
B562 SP225 60c +25c multi .60 .30
B563 SP225 80c +35c multi .80 .45
Nos. B560-B563 (4) 2.60 1.35

Society for the Promotion of Nature Preserves, 75th anniv. Surtax for social and cultural purposes.

Wheelchair Basketball — SP226

1980, June 3 Litho. *Perf. 13x14*

B564 SP226 60c +25c multi .80 .40

Olympics for the Disabled, Arnhem and Veenendaal, June 21-July 5. Surtax was for National Sports for the Handicapped Fund.

Harlequin and Girl Standing in Open Book — SP227

Designs: 50c+20c, Boy on flying book, vert. 60c+30c, Boy reading King of Frogs, vert. 80c+30c, Boy "engrossed" in book.

Perf. 14x13, 13x14

1980, Nov. 11 Photo.

B565 SP227 45c +20c multi .45 .25
B566 SP227 50c +20c multi .55 .30
B567 SP227 60c +30c multi .55 .25
a. Min. sheet of 5, 2 #B565, 3 #B567 + label 2.50 2.50
B568 SP227 80c +30c multi .90 .60
Nos. B565-B568 (4) 2.45 1.40

Surtax was for child welfare.

Salt Marsh with Outlet Ditch at Low Tide — SP228

Designs: 55c+25c, Dike. 60c+25c, Land drainage. 65c+30c, Cultivated land.

1981, Apr. 7 Photo. *Perf. 13x14*

B569 SP228 45c +20c multi .50 .30
B570 SP228 55c +25c multi .55 .30
B571 SP228 60c +25c multi .65 .30
B572 SP228 65c +30c multi .75 .30
Nos. B569-B572 (4) 2.45 1.20

Intl. Year of the Disabled — SP229

Various people.

Perf. 14x13, 13x14

1981, Nov. 10 Photo.

B573 SP229 45c +25c multi .45 .25
B574 SP229 55c +20c multi, vert .50 .35
B575 SP229 60c +25c multi, vert. .60 .35
B576 SP229 65c +30c multi .65 .25
a. Min. sheet of 5, 3 #B573, 2 #B576 + label 2.50 2.40
Nos. B573-B576 (4) 2.20 1.20

Surtax was for child welfare.

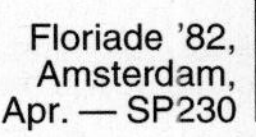

Floriade '82, Amsterdam, Apr. — SP230

No. B578, Anemones. No. B579, Roses. No. B580, African violets.

1982, Apr. 7 Litho. *Perf. 13½x13*

B577 SP230 50c +20c shown .65 .35
B578 SP230 60c +25c multi .65 .35
B579 SP230 65c +25c multi .65 .35
B580 SP230 70c +30c multi .65 .40
Nos. B577-B580 (4) 2.60 1.45

Surtax was for culture and social welfare institutions.

Birds on Child's Head — SP231

Children and Animals: 60c+20c, Boy and cat. 65c+20c, Boy and rabbit. 70c+30c, Boy and bird.

1982, Nov. 16 Photo. *Perf. 13x14*

B581 SP231 50c +30c multi .35 .25
B582 SP231 60c +20c multi .50 .25
a. Min. sheet of 5, 4 #B581, #B582 3.00 2.75
B583 SP231 65c +20c multi .75 .60
B584 SP231 70c +30c multi .85 .60
Nos. B581-B584 (4) 2.45 1.70

Surtax was for child welfare.

Johan van Oldenbarneveldt (1547-1619), Statesman, by J. Houbraken SP232

Portrait of Saskia van Uylenburch, by Rembrandt (1606-1669) — SP232a

Paintings: 60c+25c, Willem Jansz Blaeu (1571-1638), cartographer, by Thomas de Keijser. 65c+25c, Hugo de Groot (1583-1645), statesman, by J. van Ravesteyn.

1983, Apr. 19 Photo. *Perf. 14x13*

B585 SP232 50c +20c multi .75 .35
B586 SP232 60c +25c multi .75 .35
B587 SP232 65c +25c multi .75 .50
B588 SP232a 70c +30c multi .75 .50
Nos. B585-B588 (4) 3.00 1.70

Surtax was for cultural and social welfare institutions.

Red Cross Workers — SP233

Designs: 60c+20c, Principles. 65c+25c, Sociomedical work. 70c+30c, Peace.

1983, Aug. 30 Photo. *Perf. 13x14*

B589 SP233 50c +25c multi .75 .45
B590 SP233 60c +20c multi .75 .50
B591 SP233 65c +25c multi .75 .50
B592 SP233 70c +30c multi .75 .70
a. Bklt. pane, 4 #B589, 2 #B592 4.75 4.75
Complete booklet, #B592a 4.75
Nos. B589-B592 (4) 3.00 2.15

Surtax was for Red Cross.

Children's Christmas — SP235

No. B596, Ox & donkey. No. B597, Snowman. No. B598, Stars. No. B599, Epiphany.

1983, Nov. 16 Photo. *Perf. 14x13*

B596 SP235 50c +10c multi .65 .45
B597 SP235 50c +25c multi .40 .25
B598 SP235 60c +30c multi .75 .60
B599 SP235 70c +30c multi .60 .25
a. Min. sheet, 4 #B597, 2 #B599 3.75 3.25
Nos. B596-B599 (4) 2.40 1.55

Surtax was for Child Welfare.

Eurasian Lapwings — SP236

Birds: 60c+25c, Ruffs. 65c+25c, Redshanks, vert. 70c+30c, Black-tailed godwits, vert.

1984, Apr. 3 *Perf. 14x13, 13x14*

B600 SP236 50c +20c multi .65 .35
B601 SP236 60c +25c multi .65 .35
B602 SP236 65c +25c multi .65 .55
B603 SP236 70c +30c multi .65 .55
a. Bklt. pane, 2 #B600, 2 #B603 3.50 3.50
Complete booklet, #B603a 3.75
Nos. B600-B603 (4) 2.60 1.80

Surtax for cultural and social welfare institutions.

FILACENTO '84 — SP237

Centenary of Organized Philately: 50c+20c, Eye, magnifying glass (36x25mm). 60c+25c, Cover, 1909 (34½x25mm). 70c+30c, Stamp club meeting, 1949 (34½x24mm).

1984, June 13 Litho. *Perf. 14x13*

B604 SP237 50c +20c multi .60 .55
B605 SP237 60c +25c multi .70 .55
B606 SP237 70c +30c multi .80 .55
a. Souv. sheet of 3, #B604-B606 2.50 2.40
Nos. B604-B606 (3) 2.10 1.65

No. B606a issued Sept. 5, 1984.

Comic Strips — SP238

No. B607, Music lesson. No. B608, Dentist. No. B609, Plumber. No. B610, King.

1984, Nov. 14 Litho. *Perf. 13x13½*

B607 SP238 50c +25c multi .40 .30
B608 SP238 60c +20c multi 1.05 .60
B609 SP238 65c +20c multi 1.15 .80
B610 SP238 70c +30c multi .65 .30
a. Min. sheet, 4 #B607, 2 #B610 4.00 3.75
Nos. B607-B610 (4) 3.25 2.00

Surtax was for child welfare.

Winterswijk Synagogue, Holy Arc — SP239

Religious architecture: 50+20c, St. Martin's Church, Zaltbommel, vert. 65+25c, Village Congregational Church, Bolsward, vert. 70+30c, St. John's Cathedral, 'S-Hertogenbosch, detail of buttress.

Perf. 13x14, 14x13

1985, Mar. 26 Photo.

B611 SP239 50c +20c gray & brt bl .80 .50
B612 SP239 60c +25c dk red brn, Prus bl & pck bl .80 .55
B613 SP239 65c +25c sl bl, red brn & gray ol .80 .55
B614 SP239 70c +30c gray, brt bl & bis .80 .40
a. Bklt. pane, 2 #B611, 2 #B614 4.00 4.00
Complete booklet, #B614a 4.00
Nos. B611-B614 (4) 3.20 2.00

Surtax for social and cultural purposes.

Traffic Safety — SP240

No B615, Photograph, lock, key. No. B616, Boy, target. No. B617, Girl, hazard triangle. No. B618, Boy, traffic sign.

1985, Nov. 13 Photo. *Perf. 13x14*

B615 SP240 50c +25c multi .45 .35
B616 SP240 60c +20c multi .75 .65
B617 SP240 65c +20c multi .75 .65
B618 SP240 70c +30c multi .85 .35
a. Souv. sheet, 4 #B615, 2 #B618 3.75 3.25
Nos. B615-B618 (4) 2.80 2.00

Surtax was for child welfare organizations.

Antique Measuring Instruments SP241

No. B619, Balance. No. B620, Clock mechanism. No. B621, Barometer. No. B622, Jacob's staff.

Perf. 13½x13, 13x13½

1986, Apr. 8 Litho.

B619 SP241 50c +20c multi .50 .45
B620 SP241 60c +25c multi .50 .45
B621 SP241 65c +25c multi .50 .45
B622 SP241 70c +30c multi .50 .45
a. Bklt. pane, 2 each #B619, B622 4.00 4.00
Complete booklet, #B622a 4.00
Nos. B619-B622 (4) 2.00 1.80

Nos. B620-B621 vert.

Youth and Culture — SP242

No. B623, Music. No. B624, Visual arts. No. B625, Theater.

1986, Nov. 12 Litho. *Perf. 14x13*

B623 SP242 55c +25c multi .75 .45

Perf. 13½x13

B624 SP242 65c +35c multi .90 .45
B625 SP242 75c +35c multi 1.00 .45
a. Min. sheet of 5, #B623, 2 each #B624-B625, perf. 14x13 4.00 3.75
Nos. B623-B625 (3) 2.65 1.35

Surtax for child welfare organizations.

Traditional Industries — SP243

Designs: 55c+30c, Steam pumping station, Nijkerk. 65c+35c, Water tower, Deventer. 75c+35c, Brass foundry, Joure.

1987, Apr. 7 Photo. *Perf. 14x13*

B626 SP243 55c +30c multi .90 .65
B627 SP243 65c +35c multi 1.05 .65
B628 SP243 75c +35c multi 1.20 .85
a. Bklt. pane, 2 #B626, 2 #B628 4.25 4.25
Complete booklet, #B628a 4.25
Nos. B626-B628 (3) 3.15 2.15

Surtax for social and cultural welfare organizations.

Red Cross — SP244

1987, Sept. 1 Photo. *Perf. 14x13*

B629 SP244 55c +30c multi .90 .75
B630 SP244 65c +35c multi, diff. 1.05 .75
B631 SP244 75c +35c multi, diff. 1.20 .75
a. Bklt. pane, 2 #B629, 2 #B631 4.25 4.25
Complete booklet, #B631a 4.25
Nos. B629-B631 (3) 3.15 2.25

Surtax for nat'l. Red Cross.

Youth and Professions SP245

No. B632, Woodcutter, vert. No. B633, Sailor. No. B634, Pilot.

Perf. 13x14, 14x13

1987, Nov. 11 Photo.

B632 SP245 55c +25c multi .90 .60
B633 SP245 65c +35c multi 1.05 .50
B634 SP245 75c +35c multi 1.20 .25
a. Miniature sheet of 5, #B632, 2 #B633, 2 #B634 4.00 4.00
Nos. B632-B634 (3) 3.15 1.35

Surtax for child welfare organizations.

FILACEPT '88, October 18, The Hague — SP246

Designs: 55c +55c, Narcissus cyclamineus and poem "I call you flowers," by Jan Hanlo. No. B636, Rosa gallica versicolor. No. B637, Eryngium maritimum and map of The Hague from 1270.

1988, Feb. 23 Litho. *Perf. 13½x13*

B635 SP246 55c +55c multi 1.00 .90
B636 SP246 75c +70c multi 1.00 .90
B637 SP246 75c +70c multi 1.00 .90
a. Min. sheet of 3 + 3 labels, #B635-B637 3.25 3.25
Nos. B635-B637 (3) 3.00 2.70

Surtax helped finance exhibition.
No. B637a issued Oct. 18, 1988.

Man and the Zoo — SP247

No B638, Equus quagga quagga. No. B639, Carribean sea cow. No. B640, Sam the orangutan, vert.

Perf. 14x13, 13x14

1988, Mar. 22 Photo.

B638 SP247 55c +30c multi 1.00 .90
B639 SP247 65c +35c multi 1.00 1.00
B640 SP247 75c +35c multi 1.00 .80
a. Bklt. pane, 2 #B638, 2 #B640 4.00 4.00
Complete booklet, #B640a 4.00
Nos. B638-B640 (3) 3.00 2.70

Natural Artis Magistra zoological soc., 150th anniv. Surtax for social and cultural welfare organizations.

Royal Dutch Swimming Federation, Cent. — SP248

Children's drawings on the theme "Children and Water." No. B641, Rain. No. B642, Getting Ready for the Race. No. B643, Swimming Test.

1988, Nov. 16 Photo. *Perf. 14x13*

B641 SP248 55c +25c multi .75 .55
B642 SP248 65c +35c multi .90 .55
B643 SP248 75c +35c multi 1.00 .30
a. Min. sheet of 5, #B641, 2 each #B642-B643 4.75 4.75
Nos. B641-B643 (3) 2.65 1.40

Surtax to benefit child welfare organizations.

Ships — SP249

Designs: No. B644, Pleasure yacht (boyer), vert. No. B645, Zuiderzee fishing boat (smack). No. B646, Clipper.

Perf. 13x14, 14x13

1989, Apr. 11 Photo.

B644 SP249 55c +30c multi 1.00 .80
B645 SP249 65c +35c multi 1.00 .80
B646 SP249 75c +35c multi 1.00 .80
a. Bklt. pane, #B644-B645, 2 #B646 4.00 4.00
Complete booklet, #B646a 4.00
Nos. B644-B646 (3) 3.00 2.40

Surtax for social and cultural organizations.

Children's Rights — SP250

1989, Nov. 8 Litho. ***Perf. 13½x13***

B647	SP250	55c +25c Housing	.75	.55
B648	SP250	65c +35c Food	.90	.45
B649	SP250	75c +35c Education	1.00	.35
a.		Min. sheet of 5, #B647, 2 each #B648-B649	4.00	4.00
		Nos. B647-B649 (3)	2.65	1.35

UN Declaration of Children's Rights, 30th anniv. Surtax for child welfare.

Summer Weather — SP251

No. B650, Girl, flowers. No. B651, Clouds, isobars, vert. No. B652, Weather map, vert.

Perf. 14x13, 13x14

1990, Apr. 3 Photo.

B650	SP251	55c +30c multi	1.00	.75
B651	SP251	65c +35c multi	1.00	.85
B652	SP251	75c +35c multi	1.00	.75
a.		Bklt. pane, #B650-B651, 2 #B652	4.00	4.00
		Complete booklet, #B652a	4.00	
		Nos. B650-B652 (3)	3.00	2.35

Surtax for social & cultual welfare organizations.

Children's Hobbies — SP252

No. B653, Riding. No. B654, Computers. No. B655, Philately.

1990, Nov. 7 Litho. ***Perf. 13½x13***

B653	SP252	55c +25c multi	.75	.75
B654	SP252	65c +35c multi	.85	.45
B655	SP252	75c +35c multi	1.00	.25
a.		Souv. sheet of 5, #B653, 2 each #B654-B655	4.00	4.00
		Nos. B653-B655 (3)	2.60	1.45

Surtax for child welfare.

Dutch Farms — SP253

55c+30c, Frisian farm, Wartena. 65c+35c, Guelders T-style farm, Kesteren. 75c+35c, Closed construction farm, Nuth (Limburg).

1991, Apr. 16 Litho. ***Perf. 13½x13***

B656	SP253	55c +30c multi	1.00	.90
a.		Photo.	.75	.30
B657	SP253	65c +35c multi	1.00	.90
B658	SP253	75c +35c multi	1.00	.90
a.		Photo.	.75	.30
b.		Bklt. pane, 2 #B656a, 3 #B658a	4.00	4.00
		Complete booklet, #B658b	4.00	
		Nos. B656-B658 (3)	3.00	2.70

Surtax for social and cultural welfare organizations.

Children Playing — SP254

No. B659, Doll, robot. No. B660, Cycle race. No. B661, Hide and seek.

1991, Nov. 6 Litho. ***Perf. 13½x13***

B659	SP254	60c +30c multi	.60	.30
a.		Photo., perf. 14x13½	.60	.30
B660	SP254	70c +35c multi	.70	.70
B661	SP254	80c +40c multi	.80	.40
a.		Photo., perf. 14x13½	.80	.40
b.		Min. sheet, 4 #B659a, 2 #B661a	4.00	4.00
		Nos. B659-B661 (3)	2.10	1.40

Floriade 1992, World Horticultural Exhibition — SP255

Various plants and flowers.

1992, Apr. 7 Litho. ***Perf. 13½x13***

B662	SP255	60c +30c multi	1.00	1.00
a.		Photo., perf. 14x13½	.70	.40
B663	SP255	70c +35c multi	1.00	1.00
a.		Photo., perf. 14x13½	.80	.70
B664	SP255	80c +40c multi	1.00	1.00
a.		Photo., perf. 14x13½	3.50	3.00
b.		Booklet pane of 6, 3 #B662a, 2 #B663a, #B664a	7.25	
		Complete booklet, #B664b	7.25	
		Nos. B662-B664 (3)	3.00	3.00

Surtax for social and cultural welfare organizations.

Stamps in No. 664b are tete-beche (1 pair of B662a, 1 pair of B663a, 1 pair of B662a and B664a).

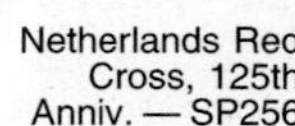

Netherlands Red Cross, 125th Anniv. — SP256

No. B665, Shadow of cross. No B666, Aiding victim. No. B667, Red cross on bandage.

1992, Sept. 8 Litho. ***Perf. 13½x13***

B665	SP256	60c +30c multi	1.00	1.00
a.		Photo., perf. 14 on 3 sides	.70	.40
B666	SP256	70c +35c multi	1.00	1.00
a.		Photo., perf. 14 on 3 sides	.80	.70
B667	SP256	80c +40c multi	1.00	1.00
a.		Photo., perf. 14 on 3 sides	3.50	3.00
b.		Bklt. pane, 3 #B665a, 2 #B666a, 1 #B667a	7.25	
		Complete booklet, #B667b	7.25	
		Nos. B665-B667 (3)	3.00	3.00

On normally centered stamps, the white border appears on the top, bottom and right sides only.

Children Making Music — SP257

No. B668, Saxophone player. No. B669, Piano player. No. B670, Bass player.

1992, Nov. 11 Litho. ***Perf. 13x13½***

B668	SP257	60c +30c multi	.70	.40
a.		Photo., perf. 13½x14	.70	.40
B669	SP257	70c +35c multi	.75	.60
a.		Photo., perf. 13½x14	.75	.60
B670	SP257	80c +40c multi	.85	.85
a.		Photo., perf. 13½x14	.85	.85
b.		Min. sheet, 3 #B668a, 2 #B669a, #B670a	4.50	4.25
		Nos. B668-B670 (3)	2.30	1.85

Senior Citizens — SP258

1993, Apr. 20 Litho. ***Perf. 13x13½***

B671	SP258	70c +35c shown	1.10	1.10
a.		Photo., perf. 13½x14	2.75	2.75
B672	SP258	70c +35c couple	1.10	1.10
a.		Photo., perf. 13½x14	.80	.70
B673	SP258	80c +40c woman	1.10	1.10
a.		Photo., perf. 13½x14	.70	.60
b.		Booklet pane, 1 #B671a, 2 #B672a, 3 #B673a	6.45	6.45
		Complete booklet, #B673b	6.45	
		Nos. B671-B673 (3)	3.30	3.30

Children and the Media — SP259

Designs: No. B674, Child wearing newspaper hat. No. B675, Elephant wearing earphones. 80c + 40c, Television, child's legs.

1993, Nov. 17 Litho. ***Perf. 13½x13***

B674	SP259	70c +35c multi	.90	.90
a.		Photo., perf. 14x13½	.90	.90
B675	SP259	70c +35c multi	.90	.90
a.		Photo., perf. 14x13½	.90	.90
B676	SP259	80c +40c multi	.90	.90
a.		Photo., perf. 14x13½	.90	.90
b.		Min. sheet, 2 each #B674a-B676a	5.50	5.50
		Nos. B674-B676 (3)	2.70	2.70

FEPAPOST '94 — SP260

Birds: 70c+60c, Branta leucopsis. 80c+70c, Luscinia svecica. 90c+80c, Anas querquedula.

1994, Feb. 22 Litho. ***Perf. 14x13***

B677	SP260	70c +60c multi	1.20	1.20
B678	SP260	80c +70c multi	1.20	1.20
B679	SP260	90c +80c multi	1.20	1.20
a.		Min. sheet, #B677-B679 + 3 labels, perf. 13½x13	3.75	3.75
		Nos. B677-B679 (3)	3.60	3.60

Issued: No. B679a, 10/17/94.

Senior Citizens — SP261

Designs: 80c+40c, Man talking on telephone seen from behind. 90c+35c, Man in suit talking on telephone.

1994, Apr. 26 Litho. ***Perf. 13x13½***

B680	SP261	70c +35c shown	1.00	.90
a.		Photo., perf. 13½x14	.80	.70
B681	SP261	80c +40c multi	1.00	.75
a.		Photo., perf. 13½x14	.90	.80
B682	SP261	90c +35c multi	1.00	1.00
a.		Photo., perf. 13½x14	3.50	3.00
b.		Booklet pane, 2 #B680a, 3 #B681a, #B682a	8.00	
		Nos. B680-B682 (3)	3.00	2.65

Child Welfare Stamps — SP262

Designs: 70c+35c, Holding ladder for woman painting. 80c+40c, Helping to balance woman picking cherries, vert. 90c+35c, Supporting boy on top of play house, vert.

Perf. 13½x13, 13x13½

1994, Nov. 9 Litho.

B683	SP262	70c +35c multi	.90	.50
a.		Perf. 14x13	.90	.80
B684	SP262	80c +40c multi	.90	.50
a.		Perf. 13x14	.90	.60
B685	SP262	90c +35c multi	1.35	1.35
a.		SP262 Miniature sheet, 2 #B683a, 3 #B684a, 1 #B685b	5.25	5.25
b.		Perf. 13x14	1.35	1.35
		Nos. B683-B685 (3)	3.15	2.35

Senior Citizens — SP263

Designs: 70c+35c, Indonesia #1422 on postcard. 80c+40c, Couple seen in bus mirror. 100c+45c, Grandparents, child at zoo.

1995, Apr. 11 Litho. ***Perf. 13½x13***

B686	SP263	70c +35c multi	.90	.90
B687	SP263	80c +40c multi	.90	.50
B688	SP263	100c +45c multi	.90	.90
a.		Miniature sheet, 2 #B686, 3 #B687, 1 #B688	6.00	6.00
		Nos. B686-B688 (3)	2.70	2.30

Child Welfare Stamps — SP264

Computer drawings by children: 70c+35c, Dino, by S. Stegeman. 80c+40c, The School Teacher, by L. Ensing, vert. 100c+50c, Children and Colors, by M. Jansen.

Perf. 13½x13, 13x13½

1995, Nov. 15 Litho.

B689	SP264	70c +35c multi	1.10	.75
B690	SP264	80c +40c multi	1.10	.75
B691	SP264	100c +50c multi	1.10	1.10
a.		Min. sheet of 6, 2 #B689, 3 #B690, 1 #B691	6.75	6.75
		Nos. B689-B691 (3)	3.30	2.60

Senior Citizens — SP265

No. B692, Swimming. No. B693, Babysitting. No. B694, Playing piano.

1996, Apr. 23 Litho. ***Perf. 13¼x12¾***

B692	SP265	70c +35c multi	.95	.50
B693	SP265	80c +40c multi	.95	.50
B694	SP265	100c +50c multi	1.75	1.10
a.		Sheet of 6, 2 #B692, 3 #B693, 1 #B694, perf. 13x12½	6.50	6.50
		Nos. B692-B694 (3)	3.65	2.10

Child Welfare Stamps — SP266

Designs: 70c+35c, Baby, books. No. B696, Boy, toys. No. B697, Girl, tools.

Perf. 12¾x13¼

1996, Nov. 6 Litho.

B695	SP266	70c +35 multi	1.00	.50
B696	SP266	80c +40c multi	1.00	.50
B697	SP266	80c +40c multi	1.00	.50
a.		Sheet of 2 each, #B695-B697	6.00	6.00
		Nos. B695-B697 (3)	3.00	1.50

Senior Citizens — SP267

Designs: No. B698, Rose in full bloom. No. B699, Stem of rose. No. B700, Rose bud.

1997, Apr. 15 Litho. ***Perf. 13¼x12¾***

B698	SP267	80c +40c multi	1.10	.80
B699	SP267	80c +40c multi	1.10	.80
B700	SP267	80c +40c multi	1.10	.80
a.		Min. sheet, 2 each #B698-B700	6.75	6.75
		Nos. B698-B700 (3)	3.30	2.40

Netherlands Red Cross — SP268

1997, May 27 Litho. ***Perf. 12¾x13¼***

B701	SP268	80c +40c multi	1.30	1.20

Child Welfare Stamps — SP269

Children's Fairy Tales: No. B702, Hunter with wolf, from "Little Red Riding Hood." No. B703, Dropping loaves of bread, from "Tom Thumb." No. B704, Man opening bottle, from "Genie in the Bottle."

Perf. 13¼x12¾

1997, Nov. 12 Litho.

B702	SP269	80c +40c multi	1.10	.50
B703	SP269	80c +40c multi	1.10	.50
B704	SP269	80c +40c multi	1.10	.50
a.		Min. sheet of 2 each, #B702-B704	6.75	6.75
		Nos. B702-B704 (3)	3.30	1.50

Senior Citizens — SP270

#B705, Sports shoe. #B706, Note on paper. #B707, Wrapped piece of candy.

1998, Apr. 21 Litho. ***Perf. 13¼x12¾***

B705	SP270	80c +40c multi	1.25	1.25
B706	SP270	80c +40c multi	1.25	1.25
B707	SP270	80c +40c multi	1.25	1.25
a.		Sheet, 2 each #B705-B707	7.50	7.50
		Nos. B705-B707 (3)	3.75	3.75

Child Welfare Stamps — SP271

#B708, Elephant riding horse. #B709, Pig, rabbit decorating cake. #B710, Pig, goose, rabbit carrying flower, frog carrying flag.

Perf. 13¼x12¾

1998, Nov. 11 **Litho.**

B708 SP271 80c +40c multi 1.25 .50
B709 SP271 80c +40c multi 1.25 .50
B710 SP271 80c +40c multi 1.25 .50
a. Sheet, 2 each #B708-B710 7.50 7.50
Nos. B708-B710 (3) 3.75 1.50

Intl. Year of Older Persons — SP272

No. B711, Woman. No. B712, Black man. No. B713, Caucasian man.

1999, Apr. 13 Litho. ***Perf. 13¼x12¾***

B711 SP272 80c +40c multi 1.25 1.00
B712 SP272 80c +40c multi 1.25 1.00
B713 SP272 80c +40c multi 1.25 1.00
a. Min. sheet, 2 ea #B711-B713 7.50 7.50
Nos. B711-B713 (3) 3.75 3.00

Child Welfare Stamps — SP273

Designs: No. B714, Boy on tow truck. No. B715, Girl and chef. No. B716, Children stamping envelope.

Perf. 13¼x12¾

1999, Nov. 10 **Litho.**

B714 SP273 80c +40c multi 1.25 .60
B715 SP273 80c +40c multi 1.25 .60
B716 SP273 80c +40c multi 1.25 .60
a. Sheet, 2 each #B714-B716 7.50 7.50
Nos. B714-B716 (3) 3.75 1.80

Senior Citizens — SP274

No. B717, Swimmers. No. B718, Bowlers. No. B719, Fruit picker.

2000, Apr. 4 Litho. ***Perf. 13¼x12¾***

B717 SP274 80c +40c multi 1.40 1.40
B718 SP274 80c +40c multi 1.40 1.40
B719 SP274 80c +40c multi 1.40 1.40
a. Souvenir sheet, 2 each #B717-B719 8.50 8.50
Nos. B717-B719 (3) 4.20 4.20

Souvenir Sheet

Child Welfare — SP275

Designs: Nos. B720a, B721, Children with masks. No. B720b, Child with ghost costume. No. B720c, Child on alligator. Nos. B720d, B722, Child in boat. Nos. B720e, B723, Children cooking. No. B720f, Children in dragon costume.

2000, Nov. 8 Litho. ***Perf. 13¼x12¾***

B720 SP275 Sheet of 6 5.00 5.00
a.-f. 80c +40c Any single .75 .75

Self-Adhesive

Serpentine Die Cut 15

B721 SP275 80c +40c multi 2.25 1.25
B722 SP275 80c +40c multi 2.25 1.25
B723 SP275 80c +40c multi 2.25 1.25
Nos. B721-B723 (3) 6.75 3.75

Flowers — SP276

Designs: No. B724a, Caryopteris. Nos. B724b, B725, Helenium. Nos. B724c, B726, Alcea rugosa. No. B724d, Euphorbia schillingii. No. B724e, B727, Centaurea dealbata. No. B724f, Inula hookeri.

2001, Apr. 24 Litho. ***Perf. 13¼x12¾***

B724 Sheet of 6 6.00 6.00
a.-f. SP276 80c+40c Any single 1.00 1.00

Serpentine Die Cut 14¾x15

Self-Adhesive

B725 SP276 80c +40c multi 1.40 1.40
B726 SP276 80c +40c multi 1.40 1.40
B727 SP276 80c +40c multi 1.40 1.40
a. Booklet, 10 each #B725-727 42.50
Nos. B725-B727 (3) 4.20 4.20

Children and Computers SP277

Black figure: No. B728a, Retrieving letter from printer. No. B728b, Crossing road with letter. No. B728c, Sliding down green vine. No. B728d, Posting letter. Nos. B728e, B729, Crossing river on log. No. B728f, Swinging on rope.

2001, Nov. 6 Photo. ***Perf. 14x13½***

B728 Sheet of 6 6.75 6.75
a.-f. SP277 85c +40c Any single 1.00 .90

Self-Adhesive

Die Cut Perf. 13¼x13

B729 SP277 85c +40c multi 2.50 1.50

Surtax for Dutch Children's Stamp Foundation.

SP278

SP279

SP280

SP281

SP282

Floriade 2002 — SP283

2002, Apr. 2 Litho. ***Perf. 14¾x14½***

B730 SP278 39c +19c multi 1.20 .65
B731 SP279 39c +19c multi 1.20 .65
B732 SP280 39c +19c multi 1.20 .65
B733 SP281 39c +19c multi 1.20 .65
B734 SP282 39c +19c multi 1.20 .65
B735 SP283 39c +19c multi 1.20 .65
a. Block of 6, #B730-B735 7.00 7.00

Nos. B730-B735 are impregnated with a floral scent.

Surtax for National Help the Aged Fund.

Blossom Walk, 10th Anniv. — SP284

2002, Apr. 27 Litho. ***Perf. 14¾x14½***

B736 SP284 39c +19c multi 1.25 .90

Surtax for Red Cross.

Children SP285

No. B737: a, Child with red head, red cat. b, Child with green head, blue father. c, Child with red head, blue ball. d, Child with yellow head, green pet dish. e, Child with brown head, legs of child. f, Child with yellow head, blue dog.

2002, Nov. 5 Photo. ***Perf. 14x13½***

B737 SP285 Sheet of 6 6.75 6.75
a.-f. 39c +19c Any single 1.10 .85

Surtax for Dutch Children's Stamp Foundation.

Flowers — SP286

No. B738: a, Orange yellow lilies of the Incas. b, Lilac sweet peas. c, Pansies. d, Red orange and yellow trumpet creepers. e, Red campions. f, Purple, white and yellow irises.

2003, Apr. 8 Photo. ***Perf. 14½x14¾***

B738 SP286 Block of 6 7.50 7.50
a.-f. 39c +19c Any single 1.25 1.25

Souvenir Sheet

Items in a Child's Life SP287

No. B739: a, Note pad, radio, ballet shoes. b, Theater masks, book. c, Microphone, musical staff, paintbrush. d, Violin, soccer ball, television. e, Television, drum, light bulbs. f, Light bulbs, trombone, hat, headphones.

2003, Nov. 4 ***Perf. 14x13½***

B739 SP287 Sheet of 6 7.25 7.25
a.-f. 39c +19c Any single 1.15 .85

Flowers SP288

No. B740 — Various flowers with background color of: a, Lilac. b, Pink. c, Brownish gray. d, Ocher. e, Blue gray. f, Olive.

2004, Apr. 6 Photo. ***Perf. 14¾x14½***

B740 SP288 Block of 6 7.50 7.50
a.-f. 39c + 19c any single 1.25 .75

Souvenir Sheet

Fruit and Sports SP289

No. B741: a, Watermelon, soccer. b, Lemon, rope jumping. c, Orange, cycling. d, Pear, skateboarding. e, Banana, sit-ups. f, Strawberry, weight lifting.

2004, Nov. 9 Photo. ***Perf. 14½***

B741 SP289 Sheet of 6 7.50 7.50
a.-f. 39c +19c Any single 1.25 .85

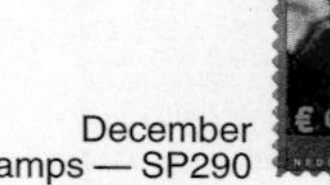

December Stamps — SP290

No. B742 — Inscriptions: a, Novib. b, Stop AIDS Now. c, Natuurmonumenten. d, KWF Kankerbestrijding. e, UNICEF. f, Plan Nederland. g, Tros Helpt. h, Greenpeace. i, Artsen Zonder Grenzen (Doctors Without Borders). j, World Food Program.

Serpentine Die Cut 8¾x9

2004, Nov. 25 **Self-Adhesive**

B742 Block of 10 9.00 9.00
a.-j. SP290 29c +10c Any single .90 .80

The surtax went to the various organizations named on the stamps.

Souvenir Sheets

SP291

Summer Stamps SP292

No. B743 — Illustrations for children's stories and silhouette of: a, Children and barrel. b, Two children. c, Frying pan.

No. B744 — Illustrations for children's stories and silhouette of: a, Monkey. b, Cup, saucer and spoon. c, Cat playing with ball.

2005, Apr. 5 Litho. ***Perf. 13¼x13¾***

B743 SP291 Sheet of 3 + 2 labels 4.00 4.00
a.-c. 39c +19c Any single 1.25 1.25
B744 SP292 Sheet of 3 + 2 labels 4.00 4.00
a.-c. 39c +19c Any single 1.25 1.25

Miniature Sheet

Miffy the Bunny, by Dick Bruna SP293

No. B745: a, Bunny and dog. b, Four bunnies. c, Bunny holding teddy bear. d, Bunny writing letter. e, White and brown bunnies. f, Six bunnies.

2005, Nov. 8 Photo. ***Perf. 14½***

B745 SP293 Sheet of 6 8.50 8.50
a.-f. 39c+19c Any single 1.40 1.40

The surtax went to the Foundation for Children's Welfare Stamps. A booklet containing four panes of two stamps sold for €9.95.

SP294 SP295

SP296 SP297

SP298 SP299

SP300 SP301

Religious Art from Museum Catharijneconvent, Utrecht
SP302 SP303

Serpentine Die Cut 8¾x9

2005, Nov. 24 Litho.

B746 Booklet pane of 10 9.50
a. SP294 29c+10c multi .95 .95
b. SP295 29c+10c multi .95 .95
c. SP296 29c+10c multi .95 .95
d. SP297 29c+10c multi .95 .95
e. SP298 29c+10c multi .95 .95
f. SP299 29c+10c multi .95 .95
g. SP300 29c+10c multi .95 .95
h. SP301 29c+10c multi .95 .95
i. SP302 29c+10c multi .95 .95
j. SP303 29c+10c multi .95 .95

The surtax went to the various organizations named on the margin and backing paper of the booklet pane.

Souvenir Sheets

SP304

Illustrations From Reading Boards — SP305

No. B747: a, Monkey and birds. b, Walnut. c, Cat.

No. B748: a, Boy playing with game. b, Girl holding rattle. c, Girl playing with doll.

2006, Apr. 4 Litho. *Perf. 13½x13¾*

B747 SP304 Sheet of 3 + 2 labels 4.25 4.25
a.-c. 39c +19c Any single 1.40 1.40
B748 SP305 Sheet of 3 + 2 labels 4.25 4.25
a.-c. 39c +19c Any single 1.40 1.40

Surtax for National Fund for Care of the Elderly.

Souvenir Sheet

Children SP306

No. B749: a, Six children, boy in orange shirt with hands up and with foot on ball. b, Eight children, girl in red shirt with hands in air. c, Six children, girl at right standing. d, Six children, boy in orange shirt with hands down and kicking ball. e, Eight children, girl in red shirt with hands at waist. f, Six children, girl at right seated.

2006, Nov. 7 Photo. *Perf. 14½*

B749 SP306 Sheet of 6 9.25 9.25
a.-f. 39c +19c Any single 1.50 1.50

Surtax for Dutch Children's Stamp Foundation.

SP307 SP308

SP309 SP310

SP311 SP312

SP313 SP314

SP315

Children Wearing Angel Costumes — SP316

Serpentine Die Cut 8¾x9

2006, Nov. 23 Litho.

Self-Adhesive

B750 Block of 10 10.50 10.50
a. SP307 29c +10c multi 1.00 1.00
b. SP308 29c +10c multi 1.00 1.00
c. SP309 29c +10c multi 1.00 1.00
d. SP310 29c +10c multi 1.00 1.00
e. SP311 29c +10c multi 1.00 1.00
f. SP312 29c +10c multi 1.00 1.00
g. SP313 29c +10c multi 1.00 1.00
h. SP314 29c +10c multi 1.00 1.00
i. SP315 29c +10c multi 1.00 1.00
j. SP316 29c +10c multi 1.00 1.00

The surtax went to the various organizations named in the sheet selvage.

Souvenir Sheets

Beach Activities SP317

No. B751: a, Woman pulling dress up in surf, boy in water. b, Woman standing in surf, children on ponies on beach. c, Children on ponies on beach, children playing on beach.

No. B752: a, Children playing on beach, family posing for photograph on beach. b, Boy waving, people in large beach chair. c, Boy on sail-powered beach cart, family digging sand at shore.

2007, Apr. 4 Litho. *Perf. 13¼x12¾*

B751 SP317 Sheet of 3 5.50 5.50
a.-c. 44c +22c Any single 1.75 1.75
B752 SP317 Sheet of 3 5.50 5.50
a.-c. 44c +22c Any single 1.75 1.75

Surtax for Natiional Fund for Senior Citizen's Help.

Netherlands Red Cross, 140th Anniv. — SP318

2007, July 19 *Perf. 13¼*

B753 SP318 44c +22c multi 1.90 1.90

Surtax for Netherlands Red Cross. Printed in sheets of 3.

Miniature Sheet

Children and Safety SP319

No. B754 — Child: a, Watching television. b, And building at night. c, In bed. d, And computer. e, And kitten. f, Reading book.

2007, Nov. 6 Litho. *Perf. 14½*

B754 SP319 Sheet of 6 12.00 12.00
a.-f. 44c +22c any single 2.00 2.00

Surtax for Foundation for Children's Welfare Stamps.

SP320

Forget-me-nots — SP321

No. B755: a, Forget-me-not, head-on view. b, Purple crane's bill geranium. c, Pink Japanese anemone.

No. B756: a, Purple larkspur. b, Globe thistle. c, Forget-me-not, side view.

2008, Apr. 1 Litho. *Perf. 14½*

B755 SP320 Sheet of 3 6.25 6.25
a.-c. 44c+22c Any single 2.00 2.00
B756 SP321 Sheet of 3 6.25 6.25
a.-c. 44c+22c Any single 2.00 2.00

Surtax for National Fund for Elderly Assistance.

Miniature Sheet

Children's Education — SP322

No. B757 — Letters of word "Onderwijs" (education): a, "O." b, "ND." c, "ER." d, "W." e, "IJ." f, "S."

2008, Nov. 4 Photo. *Perf. 14½*

B757 SP322 Sheet of 6 10.00 10.00
a.-f. 44c +22c Any single 1.60 1.60

Surtax for Foundation for Children's Welfare Stamps.

Miniature Sheet

Elder Care SP323

No. B758: a, Couple dancing. b, Woman with bag cart. c, Ballet dancer. d, Woman with guide dog. e, Man playing trumpet. f, Woman holding diploma.

2009, Apr. 7 Litho. *Perf. 14½*

B758 SP323 Sheet of 6 10.50 10.50
a.-f. 44c +22c Any single 1.75 1.75

Surtax for National Fund for Elderly Assistance.

Miniature Sheet

Children's Activities — SP324

No. B759 — Stylized children: a, With pencil. b, With magnifying glasses. c, Watching falling star. d, Playing. e, Reading newspaper. f, With stylized Pegasus.

2009, Nov. 3 Photo. *Perf. 14½*

B759 SP324 Sheet of 6 12.00 12.00
a.-f. 44c+22c Any single 2.00 2.00

Surtax for Foundation for Children's Welfare Stamps.

Miniature Sheet

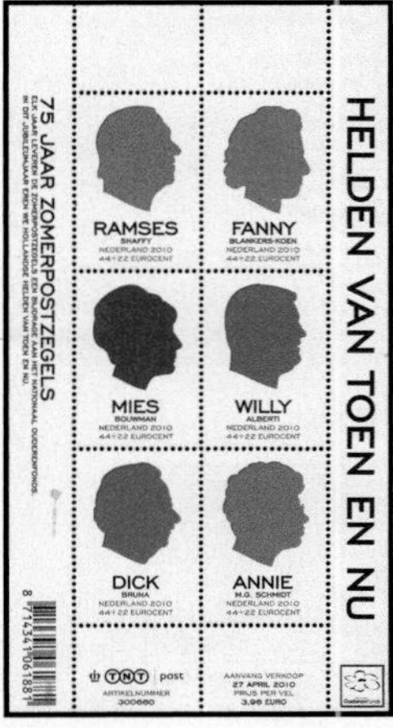

Famous People SP325

No. B760 — Silhouettes of: a, Ramses Shaffy (1933-2009), singer and actor. b, Fanny Blankers-Koen (1918-2004), Olympic gold medalist. c, Mies Bouwman, television personality. d, Willy Alberti (1926-85), singer. e, Dick Bruna, writer and illustrator. f, Annie M. G. Schmidt (1911-95), writer.

2010, Apr. 27 Litho. *Perf. 14½*

B760 SP325 Sheet of 6 10.50 10.50
a.-f. 44c + 22c Any single 1.75 1.75

Surtax for National Fund for Elderly Assistance.

Miniature Sheet

Children and Mathematical Symbols — SP326

No. B761: a, Boy with red shirt. b, Boy with dark gray shirt, hand near head. c, Boy with gray shirt, hand in front of chest. d, Girl with red and orange dress. e, Girl with arms clasped behind head. f, Girl with arm raised.

2010, Nov. 9 *Perf. 14x13¾*

B761 SP326 Sheet of 6 11.00 11.00
a.-f. 1 + 22c Any single 1.75 1.75

Nos. B761a-B761f each had a franking value of 44c, with the 22c surtax going to the Foundation for Children's Welfare Stamps.

Miniature Sheet

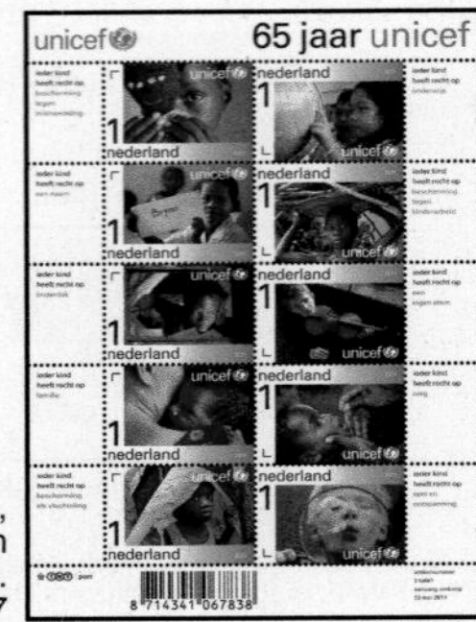

UNICEF, 65th Anniv. SP327

No. B762: a, Child holding doll. b, Children touching globe. c, Boy holding card showing his name. d, Boy carrying branches. e, Boy looking out of broken window. f, Boy playing violin. g, Mother holding child. h, Child receiving medicine. i, Child using dog food bag as hood. j, Child blowing bubbles.

2011, May 23 *Perf. 13¼x12¾*

B762	SP327 Sheet of 10	19.00	19.00
a.-j.	1 + (20c) Any single	1.90	1.90
k.	Booklet pane of 2, #B762a-B762b	5.75	—
l.	Booklet pane of 2, #B762c-B762d	5.75	—
m.	Booklet pane of 2, #B762e-B762f	5.75	—
n.	Booklet pane of 2, #B762g-B762h	5.75	—
o.	Booklet pane of 2, #B762i-B762j	5.75	—
	Complete booklet, #B762k-B762o	29.00	

Nos. B762a-B762j each had a franking value of 46c, with the 20c surtax going to UNICEF. Complete booklet sold for €9.95.

Miniature Sheet

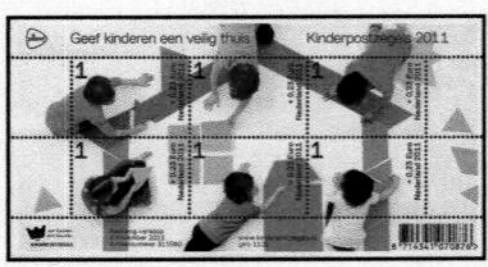

Children at Play SP328

No. B763 — Child wearing: a, Orange shirt. b, Light green shirt. c, Pink shirt. d, Purple shirt. e, Blue green shirt. f, White shirt.

2011, Oct. 29 **Photo.** *Perf. 14½*

B763	SP328 Sheet of 6	11.50	11.50
a.-f.	1 + 23c Any single	1.90	1.90

Nos. B763a-B763f each had a franking value of 46c, with the 23c surtax going to the Foundation for Children's Welfare Stamps.

Red Cross — SP329

No. B764: a, Cross in red, text "Eerste Hulp bij ongellukken." b, Woman in cross, text "Eerste Hulp dóór iedereen." c, Hand and child's head in cross, text "Eerste Hulp vóór iedereen."

2012, Jan. 30 **Litho.** *Perf. 13¼x13½*

B764	SP329 Horiz. strip of 3	6.00	6.00
a.-c.	1 +25c any single	2.00	2.00

Nos. B764a-B764c each had a franking value of 50c, with the 25c surtax going to the Dutch Red Cross. No. B764 was printed in sheets containing two strips.

Miniature Sheet

Princesses — SP330

No. B765: a, Princess Catharina- Amalia. b, Princesses Alexia, Ariane and Catharina-Amalia (five buttons on blouse of Princess Ariane visible). c, Princess Ariane. d, Princesses Catharina-Amalia, Alexia and Ariane (Catharina-Amalia at left). e, Princess Alexia. f, Princesses Alexia, Ariane and Catharina-Amalia (three buttons on blouse of Princess Ariane visible).

2012, Nov. 6 **Photo.** *Perf. 14½*

B765	SP330 Sheet of 6	11.50	11.50
a.-f.	1 + 25c Any single	1.90	1.90

Nos. B765a-B765f each had a franking value of 50c, with the 23c surtax going to the Foundation for Children's Welfare Stamps.

Miniature Sheet

Ethiopian Children SP331

No. B766: a, Boy, multiplication table. b, Boy holding bundle of sticks. c, Girl carrying young boy on her back. d, Girl, letters of Amharic alphabet. e, Boy, poster with pictures and English words. f, Boy carrying goat.

2013, Nov. 4 **Litho.** *Perf. 14½*

B766	SP331 Sheet of 6	14.50	14.50
a.-f.	1+30c Any single	2.40	2.40

Nos. B766a-B766f each had a franking value of 60c on the day of issue, with the 30c surtax going to th Foundation for Children's Welfare Stamps.

Miniature Sheet

Children in Works from the Rijksmuseum — SP332

No. B767: a, Children at the beach (36x25mm). b, Children riding donkey (36x25mm). c, Girl wearing kimono (36x25mm). d, Girl and boys near piano (36x25mm). e, Boy on skateboard (36x50mm).

2014, Nov. 3 **Litho.** *Perf. 14½*

B767	SP332 Sheet of 5	12.00	12.00
a.-e.	1+32c Any single	2.40	2.40

Nos. B767a-B767b had a franking value of 64c on the day of issue, with the 32c surtax going to the Foundation for Children's Welfare Stamps.

Miniature Sheet

Illustrations From Little Golden Books Series of Children's Books — SP333

No. B768: a, Sofa, toys strung together with cart containing dog and cat. b, Bird chasing cat in tree away from nest. c, Child pulling toys strung together. d, Duck, goose and house. e, Cat on mitten. f, Duck, goose, cat and pig.

2015, Nov. 2 **Litho.** *Perf. 13¼*

B768	SP333 Sheet of 6	13.50	13.50
a.-f.	1+34c Any single	2.25	2.25

Nos. B768a-B768f each had a franking value of 69c on the day of issue, with the 34c surcharge going to the Foundation for Children's Welfare Stamps.

Miniature Sheet

Illustrations of Bus and Passengers by Fiep Westendorp (1916-2004) — SP334

No. B769: a, Children with hats and bird cage, child cutting cake. b, Snake, turtles, birds, cat, dog, child. c, Children and chef. d, Bird and musicians. e, Eight children. f, Cats and bus driver.

2016, Nov. 7 **Litho.** *Perf. 13¼x13½*

B769	SP334 Sheet of 6	14.00	14.00
a.-f.	1+36c Any single	2.25	2.25

Nos. B769a-B769f each had a franking value of 73c on the day of issue, with the 36c surcharge going to the Foundation for Children's Welfare Stamps.

Miniature Sheet

Characters From *Jan, Jans, and the Children* Comic Strip, by Jan Kruis — SP335

No. B770: a, Jan and son, Gertje. b, Jans and daughter, Karlijn. c, Grandfather and cat. d, Catootje and dog. e, Jeroen holding letter. f, Cat in basket.

2017, Oct. 9 **Litho.** *Perf. 14½*

B770	SP335 Sheet of 6	16.50	16.50
a.-f.	1+38c Any single	2.75	2.75

Nos. B770a-B770f each had a franking value of 78c on the day of issue, with the 38c surcharge going to the Foundation for Children's Welfare Stamps.

Miniature Sheet

Characters From the Children's Television Series *The Daily Fable* — SP336

No. B771: a, Myra and Martha Hamster and water wheel (36x25mm). b, Mr. Owl (36x50mm). c, Boris the Wolf hammering sign and Miss Stork with picnic basket (36x25mm). d, Crox the Raven and Cunningham the Foxx (36x25mm). e, Fred and Bart Beaver in chairs under umbrella (36x25mm).

2018, Oct. 8 **Litho.** *Perf. 14¼x14½*

B771	SP336 Sheet of 5	15.00	15.00
a.-e.	1 + 41c Any single	3.00	3.00

The Daily Fable, 50th anniv. Nos. B771a-B771e each had a franking value of 83c on day of issue, with the surtax of 41c going to the Foundation for Children's Welfare Stamps.

Nieuwe Avonturen van Pietje Bell, by Chris van Abkoude SP337

De Drieling te Paard, by Trix van Brussel SP338

Uit het Leven van Dik Trom, by Johan Kieviet SP339

Kruimeltje, by Chris van Abkoude SP340

De Schippers van de Kameleon, by Hotze de Roos — SP341

2019, Oct. 3 **Litho.** *Perf. 13¼x13*

B772	Horiz. strip of 5	15.00	15.00
a.	SP337 1+43c multi	3.00	3.00
b.	SP338 1+43c multi	3.00	3.00
c.	SP339 1+43c multi	3.00	3.00
d.	SP340 1+43c multi	3.00	3.00
e.	SP341 1+43c multi	3.00	3.00

Children's books. Nos. B772a-B772e each had a franking value of 87c on day of issue, with the surtax of 43c going to the Foundation for Children's Welfare Stamps. Printed in sheets containing two each Nos. B772a-B772e.

Miniature Sheet

Miffy, the Bunny, by Dick Bruna, 65th Anniv. SP342

No. B773: a, Miffy and parents in car (36x25mm). b, Auntie Alice holding tray of drinks (36x25mm). c, Boris and Barbara with balloon (36x25mm). d, Poppy and Grunty Pig dancing (36x25mm). e, Miffy and birthday cake (36x50mm).

2020, Oct. 5 **Litho.** *Perf. 14¼*

B773	SP342 Sheet of 5	16.50	16.50
a.-e.	1 + 45c Any single	3.25	3.25

On day of issue, Nos. B773a-B773e each had a franking value of 91c, with the 45c surtax going to the Foundation for Children's Welfare Stamps.

Miniature Sheet

Tom Puss, Comic Strip by Martin Toonder (1912-2005), 80th Anniv. — SP343

No. B774: a, Marquis de Canteclaer holding eyeglasses (36x25mm). b, Tom Puss and Mr. Bumble (36x50mm). c, Joost, the butler, and castle (36x25mm). d, Doddeltje and mushrooms (36x25mm). e, Wammes Waggel with accordion (36x25mm).

2021, Oct. 11 **Litho.** *Perf. 14½*

B774	SP343 Sheet of 5	17.50	17.50
a.-e.	1 + 48c Any single	3.50	3.50

On day of issue, Nos. B774a-B774e each had a franking value of 96c, with the 48c surtax going to the Foundation for Children's Welfare Stamps.

Miniature Sheet

Donald Duck Magazine, 70th Anniv. — SP344

No. B775: a, May and Dewey (36x25mm). b, Donald and Huey (36x50mm). c, Louie at computer (36x25mm). d, Scrooge McDuck (36x25mm). e, April on bicycle, and June with skateboard. (36x25mm).

2022, Oct. 10 Litho. *Perf. 14½*

B775	SP344	Sheet of 5	15.00	15.00
a.-e.		1 + 48c Any single	3.00	3.00

On day of issue, Nos. B775a-B775e each had a franking value of 96c, with the 48c surtax going to the Foundation for Children's Welfare Stamps.

Miniature Sheet

Lego Toys, Cent. SP345

No. B776: a, Two Lego "people" riding bicycles (36x25mm). b, Lego "people" ice skating, standing near boom box, sitting in wheelchair, Lego dog (36x50mm). c, Two Lego "people" on skateboards (36x25mm). d, Two Lego "people" on toboggan (36x25mm). e, Two Lego "people" ice skating. (36x25mm).

2023, Oct. 9 Litho. *Perf. 14½*

B776	SP345	Sheet of 5	16.50	16.50
a.-e.		1 + 50c Any single	3.00	3.00

On day of issue, Nos. B776a-B776e each had a franking value of €1.01, with the 50c surtax going to the Foundation for Children's Welfare Stamps.

AIR POST STAMPS

Stylized Seagull — AP1

Perf. 12½

1921, May 1 Unwmk. Typo.

C1	AP1	10c red	1.90	1.25
C2	AP1	15c yellow grn	5.25	2.10
C3	AP1	60c dp blue	23.00	.50
		Nos. C1-C3 (3)	30.15	3.85
		Set, never hinged	260.00	

Nos. C1-C3 were used to pay airmail fee charged by the carrier, KLM.

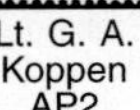

Lt. G. A. Koppen AP2

Capt. Jan van der Hoop AP3

Wmk. Circles (202)

1928, Aug. 20 Litho. *Perf. 12*

C4	AP2	40c orange red	.50	.25
C5	AP3	75c blue green	.50	.25
		Set, never hinged	2.00	

Mercury — AP4

Perf. 11½

1929, July 16 Unwmk. Engr.

C6	AP4	1½g gray	2.25	1.40
C7	AP4	4½g carmine	2.25	4.00
C8	AP4	7½g blue green	26.00	4.00
		Nos. C6-C8 (3)	30.50	9.40
		Set, never hinged	75.00	

Queen Wilhelmina — AP5

Perf. 12½, 14x13

1931, Sept. 24 Photo. Wmk. 202

C9	AP5	36c org red & dk bl	13.00	.75
		Never hinged	70.00	

Fokker Pander — AP6

1933, Oct. 9 *Perf. 12½*

C10	AP6	30c dark green	.75	.75
		Never hinged	1.50	

Nos. C10-C12 were issued for use on special flights.

Crow in Flight — AP7

1938-53 *Perf. 13x14*

C11	AP7	12½c dk blue & gray	.35	.25
C12	AP7	25c dk bl & gray ('53)	2.25	1.60
		Set, never hinged	4.25	

Catalogue values for unused stamps in this section, from this point to the end of the section, are for Never Hinged items.

Seagull — AP8

Perf. 13x14

1951, Nov. 12 Engr. Unwmk.

C13	AP8	15g gray	225.00	80.00
C14	AP8	25g blue gray	225.00	80.00
		Set, hinged	250.00	

Airplane — AP9

1966, Sept. 2 Litho. *Perf. 14x13*

C15	AP9	25c gray, blk & bl	.25	.35

Issued for use on special flights.

AP10

1980, May 13 Photo. *Perf. 13x14*

C16	AP10	1g multicolored	1.00	1.00

REGISTRATION STAMPS

Personalized Stamp — R1

Die Cut Perf. 12¾x12½

Etched on Silver Foil

2011, Oct. 10 Self-Adhesive

F1	R1	(€7) silver	19.00	19.00

The vignette portion of No. F1 could be personalized for €34.95. The image shown, depicting Piet Hein and a warship, is a generic image. Starting in 2013, stamps with different images were produced in limited quantities and sold at prices above face value were sold by Netherlands Post.

Souvenir Sheet

Bull's Head, Tulips and QR Code — R2

Litho. With Foil Application

2022, Sept. 22 *Die Cut Perf. 10x9¾*

Self-Adhesive

F2	R2	R multi	18.00	18.00

Crypto stamp. No. F2 sold for €9.05 on day of issue. See Austria No.

MARINE INSURANCE STAMPS

Floating Safe Attracting Gulls MI1

Floating Safe with Night Flare MI2

Fantasy of Floating Safe — MI3

Perf. 11½

1921, Feb. 2 Unwmk. Engr.

GY1	MI1	15c slate grn	11.00	*75.00*
GY2	MI1	60c car rose	15.00	*75.00*
GY3	MI1	75c gray brn	18.50	*75.00*
GY4	MI2	1.50g dk blue	65.00	*425.00*
GY5	MI2	2.25g org brn	110.00	*550.00*
GY6	MI3	4½g black	165.00	*675.00*
GY7	MI3	7½g red	250.00	*925.00*
		Nos. GY1-GY7 (7)	634.50	*2,800.*
		Set, never hinged	1,500.	

POSTAGE DUE STAMPS

Postage due types of Netherlands were also used for Netherlands Antilles, Netherlands Indies and Surinam in different colors.

D1

Unwmk.

1870, May 15 Typo. *Perf. 13*

J1	D1	5c brown, *org*	72.50	15.00
J2	D1	10c violet, *bl*	150.00	20.00
a.		Perf 12½x12	300.00	32.50

D2

Type I — 34 loops. "T" of "BETALEN" over center of loop; top branch of "E" of "TE" shorter than lower branch.

Type II — 33 loops. "T" of "BETALEN" between two loops.

Type III — 32 loops. "T" of "BETALEN" slightly to the left of loop; top branch of first "E" of "BETALEN" shorter than lower branch.

Type IV — 37 loops. Letters of "PORT" larger than in the other three types.

Imperforate varieties are proofs.

Perf. 11½x12, 12½x12, 12½, 13½

1881-87 Value in Black

J3	D2	1c lt blue (III)	11.00	11.00
a.		Type I	15.00	18.00
b.		Type II	20.00	20.00
c.		Type IV	47.50	52.50
J4	D2	1½c lt blue (III)	15.00	15.00
a.		Type I	18.00	18.00
b.		Type II	24.00	24.00
c.		Type IV	75.00	75.00
J5	D2	2½c lt blue (III)	37.50	5.00
a.		Type I	45.00	5.50
b.		Type II	50.00	6.00
c.		Type IV	210.00	125.00
J6	D2	5c lt blue (III) ('87)	140.00	3.50
a.		Type I	50.00	5.00
b.		Type II	130.00	5.25
c.		Type IV	1,250.	350.00
J7	D2	10c lt blue (III) ('87)	92.50	4.00
a.		Type I	115.00	4.50
b.		Type II	125.00	5.00
c.		Type IV	2,500.	375.00
J8	D2	12½c lt blue (III)	95.00	25.00
a.		Type I	165.00	40.00
b.		Type II	130.00	45.00
c.		Type IV	350.00	100.00
J9	D2	15c lt blue (III)	90.00	4.00
a.		Type I	105.00	4.50
b.		Type II	120.00	5.00
c.		Type IV	130.00	25.00
J10	D2	20c lt blue (III)	35.00	4.00
a.		Type I	47.50	4.25
b.		Type II	50.00	5.50
c.		Type IV	137.50	27.50
J11	D2	25c lt blue (III)	210.00	3.50
a.		Type I	230.00	3.00
b.		Type II	275.00	4.50
c.		Type IV	425.00	170.00

Value in Red

J12	D2	1g lt blue (III)	85.00	30.00
a.		Type I	85.00	37.50
b.		Type II	100.00	40.00
c.		Type IV	175.00	75.00
		Nos. J3-J12 (10)	811.00	105.00

See Nos. J13-J26, J44-J60. For surcharges see Nos. J27-J28, J42-J43, J72-J75.

1896-1910 *Perf. 12½*

Value in Black

J13	D2	½c dk bl (I) ('01)	.40	.35
J14	D2	1c dk blue (I)	1.65	.35
a.		Type III	2.50	3.25
J15	D2	1½c dk blue (I)	.75	.35
a.		Type III	2.50	2.50
J16	D2	2½c dk blue (I)	1.50	.75
a.		Type III	3.25	.55
J17	D2	3c dk bl (I) ('10)	1.65	1.10
J18	D2	4c dk bl (I) ('09)	1.65	2.25
J19	D2	5c dk blue (I)	13.00	.35
a.		Type III	16.00	.55
J20	D2	6½c dk bl (I) ('07)	45.00	45.00
J21	D2	7½c dk bl (I) ('04)	1.75	.55
J22	D2	10c dk blue (I)	35.00	.55
a.		Type III	52.50	1.50
J23	D2	12½c dk blue (I)	30.00	1.10
a.		Type III	45.00	3.50
J24	D2	15c dk blue (I)	35.00	.90
a.		Type III	55.00	1.00
J25	D2	20c dk blue (I)	20.00	8.00
a.		Type III	20.00	8.75
J26	D2	25c dk blue (I)	45.00	.75
a.		Type III	50.00	1.00
		Nos. J13-J26 (14)	232.35	62.35

Surcharged in Black

1906, Jan. 10 *Perf. 12½*

J27	D2	50c on 1g lt bl (III)	125.00	110.00
a.		50c on 1g light blue (I)	165.00	140.00
b.		50c on 1g light blue (II)	175.00	150.00

Surcharged in Red

1906, Oct. 6

J28	D2	6½c on 20c dk bl (I)	5.50	5.00

Nos. 87-89 Surcharged

1907, Nov. 1

No.	Type	Description	Unused	Used
J29	A13	½c on 1c claret	1.25	1.25
J30	A13	1c on 1c claret	.50	.50
J31	A13	1½c on 1c claret	.50	.50
J32	A13	2½c on 1c claret	1.25	1.25
J33	A13	5c on 2½c ver	1.40	.40
J34	A13	6½c on 2½c ver	3.50	3.50
J35	A13	7½c on ½c blue	2.00	1.25
J36	A13	10c on ½c blue	1.75	.75
J37	A13	12½c on ½c blue	5.00	4.75
J38	A13	15c on 2½c ver	6.00	4.00
J39	A13	25c on ½c blue	9.00	8.50
J40	A13	50c on ½c blue	42.50	40.00
J41	A13	1g on ½c blue	60.00	55.00
		Nos. J29-J41 (13)	134.65	121.65

Two printings of the above surcharges were made. Some values show differences in the setting of the fractions; others are practically impossible to distinguish.

No. J20 Surcharged in Red

1909, June

No.	Type	Description	Unused	Used
J42	D2	4c on 6½c dark blue	5.50	5.00
		Never hinged	20.00	

No. J12 Surcharged in Black

1910, July 11

No.	Type	Description	Unused	Used
J43	D2	3c on 1g lt bl, type III	30.00	27.50
		Never hinged	100.00	
a.		Type I	37.50	40.00
		Never hinged	110.00	
b.		Type II	40.00	40.00
		Never hinged	125.00	

Type I

1912-21 ***Perf. 12½, 13½x13***

Value in Color of Stamp

No.	Type	Description	Unused	Used
J44	D2	½c pale ultra	.25	.25
J45	D2	1c pale ultra ('13)	.25	.25
J46	D2	1½c pale ultra ('15)	1.90	1.50
J47	D2	2½c pale ultra	.25	.25
J48	D2	3c pale ultra	.40	.40
J49	D2	4c pale ultra ('13)	.25	.25
J50	D2	4½c pale ultra ('16)	5.25	5.00
J51	D2	5c pale ultra	.25	.25
J52	D2	5½c pale ultra ('16)	5.00	5.00
J53	D2	7c pale ultra ('21)	2.25	2.25
J54	D2	7½c pale ultra ('13)	2.50	1.00
J55	D2	10c pale ultra ('13)	.40	.40
J56	D2	12½c pale ultra ('13)	.40	.40
J57	D2	15c pale ultra ('13)	.40	.40
J58	D2	20c pale ultra ('20)	.40	.25
J59	D2	25c pale ultra ('17)	80.00	.60
J60	D2	50c pale ultra ('20)	.40	.25
		Nos. J44-J60 (17)	100.55	18.70
		Set, never hinged	450.00	

D3

1921-38 Typo. ***Perf. 12½, 13½x12½***

No.	Type	Description	Unused	Used
J61	D3	3c pale ultra ('28)	.25	.25
J62	D3	6c pale ultra ('27)	.25	.25
J63	D3	7c pale ultra ('28)	.45	.45
J64	D3	7½c pale ultra ('26)	.45	.45
J65	D3	8c pale ultra ('38)	.45	.45
J66	D3	9c pale ultra ('30)	.45	.45
J67	D3	11c ultra ('21)	12.50	4.00
J68	D3	12c pale ultra ('28)	.45	.30
J69	D3	25c pale ultra ('25)	.45	.30
J70	D3	30c pale ultra ('35)	.45	.30
J71	D3	1g ver ('21)	.60	.30
		Nos. J61-J71 (11)	16.75	7.50
		Set, never hinged	50.00	

Stamps of 1912-21 Surcharged

1923, Dec. ***Perf. 12½***

No.	Type	Description	Unused	Used
J72	D2	1c on 3c ultra	.75	.65
J73	D2	2½c on 7c ultra	1.20	.65
J74	D2	25c on 1½c ultra	8.00	.65
J75	D2	25c on 7½c ultra	10.00	.65
		Nos. J72-J75 (4)	19.95	2.60
		Set, never hinged	57.50	

Nos. 56, 58, 62, 65 Surcharged

1924, Aug.

No.	Type	Description	Unused	Used
J76	A11	4c on 3c ol grn	1.10	1.10
J77	A10	5c on 1c red	.75	.40
a.		Surcharge reading down	500.00	450.00
J78	A10	10c on 1½c blue	1.10	.60
a.		Tête bêche pair	8.50	10.00
J79	A11	12½c on 5c car	1.50	.60
a.		Tête bêche pair	8.50	10.00
		Nos. J76-J79 (4)	4.45	2.70
		Set, never hinged	14.50	

The 11c on 22½c and 15c on 17½c exist. These were used by the postal service for accounting of parcel post fees.

Catalogue values for unused stamps in this section, from this point to the end of the section, are for Never Hinged items.

D5

Perf. 13½x12½

1947-58 Wmk. 202 Photo.

No.	Type	Description	Unused	Used
J80	D5	1c light blue ('48)	.25	.25
J81	D5	3c light blue ('48)	.40	.30
J82	D5	4c light blue	8.50	.85
J83	D5	5c light blue ('48)	.25	.25
J84	D5	6c light blue ('50)	.35	.35
J85	D5	7c light blue	.25	.30
J86	D5	8c light blue ('48)	.25	.30
J87	D5	10c light blue	.25	.25
J88	D5	11c light blue	.35	.45
J89	D5	12c light blue ('48)	.80	.85
J90	D5	14c light blue ('53)	.80	.65
J91	D5	15c light blue	.35	.25
J92	D5	16c light blue	.70	.80
J93	D5	20c light blue	.35	.30
J94	D5	24c light blue ('57)	.95	1.10
J95	D5	25c light blue ('48)	.35	.30
J96	D5	26c light blue ('58)	1.90	2.10
J97	D5	30c light blue ('48)	.50	.25
J98	D5	35c light blue	.65	.25
J99	D5	40c light blue	.65	.25
J100	D5	50c light blue ('48)	.80	.30
J101	D5	60c light blue ('58)	.85	.45
J102	D5	85c light blue ('50)	13.00	.55
J103	D5	90c light blue ('56)	2.40	.60
J104	D5	95c light blue ('57)	2.40	.60
J105	D5	1g carmine ('48)	1.90	.25
J106	D5	1.75g carmine ('57)	4.50	.35
		Nos. J80-J106 (27)	44.70	13.50

OFFICIAL STAMPS

Regular Issues of 1898-1908 Overprinted

1913 Typo. Unwmk. ***Perf. 12½***

No.	Type	Description	Unused	Used
O1	A10	1c red	4.00	2.75
O2	A10	1½c ultra	1.00	2.25
O3	A10	2c yellow brn	7.00	7.00
O4	A10	2½c dp green	16.00	12.00
O5	A11	3c olive grn	4.00	1.00
O6	A11	5c carmine rose	4.00	4.50
O7	A11	10c gray lilac	35.00	37.50
		Nos. O1-O7 (7)	71.00	67.00

Same Overprint in Red on No. 58

1919

No.	Type	Description	Unused	Used
O8	A10	1½c deep blue (R)	100.00	110.00

Nos. O1 to O8 were used to defray the postage on matter relating to the Poor Laws. Counterfeit overprints exist.

For the International Court of Justice

Regular Issue of 1926-33 Overprinted in Gold

1934 Wmk. 202 ***Perf. 12½***

No.	Type	Description	Unused	Used
O9	A24	1½c red violet	1.50	
O10	A24	2½c deep green	1.50	
O11	A23	7½c red	2.25	
O12	A31	12½c deep ultra	22.50	
O13	A23	15c orange	2.00	
O14	A23	30c violet	2.25	
a.		Perf. 13½x12½	2.25	
		Nos. O9-O14 (6)	32.00	

Same Overprint on No. 180 in Gold

1937 ***Perf. 13½x12½***

No.	Type	Description	Unused	Used
O15	A23	12½c ultra	16.00	

"Mint" Officials

Nos. O9-O15, O20-O43 were sold to the public only canceled. Uncanceled, they were obtainable only by favor of an official or from UPU specimen stamps.

Same on Regular Issue of 1940 Overprinted in Gold

1940 ***Perf. 13½x12½***

No.	Type	Description	Unused	Used
O16	A45	7½c bright red	27.50	7.00
O17	A45	12½c sapphire	27.50	7.00
O18	A45	15c lt blue	27.50	7.00
O19	A45	30c bister	27.50	7.00
		Nos. O16-O19 (4)	110.00	28.00

A second printing with more open letters exists. Value, $750.

Nos. 217 to 219, 221 and 223 Overprinted in Gold

1947

No.	Type	Description	Unused	Used
O20	A45	7½c bright red	1.10	
O21	A45	10c brt red violet	1.10	
O22	A45	12½c sapphire	1.10	
O23	A45	20c purple	1.10	
O24	A45	25c rose brown	1.10	
		Nos. O20-O24 (5)	5.50	

O1

Perf. 14½x13½

1950 Unwmk. Photo.

No.	Type	Description	Unused	Used
O25	O1	2c ultra	8.75	
O26	O1	4c olive green	8.75	

Palace of Peace, The Hague
O2

Queen Juliana
O3

1951-58 ***Perf. 12½x12***

No.	Type	Description	Unused	Used
O27	O2	2c red brown	.40	
O28	O2	3c ultra ('53)	.40	
O29	O2	4c deep green	.40	
O30	O2	5c olive brn ('53)	.40	
O31	O2	6c olive grn ('53)	.80	
O32	O2	7c red ('53)	.60	

Engr.

No.	Type	Description	Unused	Used
O33	O3	6c brown vio	5.50	
O34	O3	10c dull green	.25	
O35	O3	12c rose red	.75	
O36	O3	15c rose brn ('53)	.25	
O37	O3	20c dull blue	.25	
O38	O3	25c violet brn	.25	
O39	O3	30c rose lil ('58)	.35	
O40	O3	1g slate gray	.80	
		Nos. O27-O40 (14)	11.40	

1977, May Photo. ***Perf. 12½x12***

No.	Type	Description	Unused	Used
O41	O2	40c brt grnsh blue	.50	
O42	O2	45c brick red	.50	
O43	O2	50c brt rose lilac	.50	
		Nos. O41-O43 (3)	1.50	

Catalogue values for unused stamps in this section, from this point to the end of the section, are for Never Hinged items.

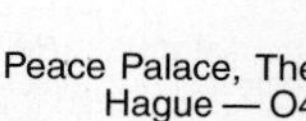

Peace Palace, The Hague — O4

Palm, Sun and Column — O4a

1989-94 Litho.

No.	Type	Description	Unused	Used
O44	O4	5c blk & org yel	.25	.25
O45	O4	10c black & blue	.25	.25
O46	O4	25c black & red	.30	.30
O47	O4	50c black & yel grn	.60	.60
O48	O4	55c black & pink	.55	.55
O49	O4	60c black & bister	.75	.75
O50	O4	65c black & bl grn	.75	.75
O51	O4	70c blk & gray bl	.90	.90
O52	O4	75c black & yellow	.70	.70
O53	O4	80c black & gray grn	1.00	1.00
O54	O4	1g black & orange	1.10	1.10
O55	O4	1.50g blk & blue	1.60	1.60
O56	O4	1.60g blk & rose brn	2.00	2.00

Litho. & Engr.

No.	Type	Description	Unused	Used
O57	O4a	5g multicolored	5.50	5.50
O58	O4a	7g multicolored	6.50	6.50
		Nos. O44-O58 (15)	22.75	22.75

Issued: 55c, 75c, 7g, 10/24/89; 65c, 1g, 1.50g, 5g, 10/23/90; 5c, 10c, 25c, 50c, 60c, 70c, 80c, 10/22/91; 1.60g, 11/28/94.

Intl. Court of Justice — O5

Emblem of Intl. Court of Justice — O6

2004, Jan. 2 Litho. ***Perf. 14¾x14½***

No.	Type	Description	Unused	Used
O59	O5	39c multi	1.00	1.00
O60	O6	61c multi	1.60	1.60

Intl. Court of Justice
O7

Emblem of Intl. Court of Justice
O8

Doves — O9

2011, Apr. 11 ***Perf. 13½x13¼***

No.	Type	Description	Unused	Used
O61	O7	1 multi	1.40	1.40
O62	O8	1 Europa multi	2.40	2.40
O63	O9	1 Wereld multi	2.75	2.75
		Nos. O61-O63 (3)	6.55	6.55

On day of issue, Nos. O61-O63 each sold for 46c, 79c, and 95c, respectively.

Intl. Court of Justice, 70th Anniv. — O10

2016, Apr. 25 Litho. ***Perf. 13½x13¼***

No.	Type	Description	Unused	Used
O64	O10	1 Internationaal multi	3.00	3.00

NETHERLANDS ANTILLES

'ne-<u>th</u>ər-lən,d,z an-'ti-lēz

(Curaçao)

LOCATION — Two groups of islands about 500 miles apart in the West Indies, north of Venezuela
AREA — 383 sq. mi.
POP. — 207,333 (1995)
CAPITAL — Willemstad

Formerly a colony, Curaçao, Netherlands Antilles became an integral part of the Kingdom of the Netherlands under the Constitution of 1954. On Jan. 1, 1986, the island of Aruba achieved a separate status within the Kingdom and began issuing its own stamps.

100 Cents = 1 Gulden

Catalogue values for unused stamps in this country are for Never Hinged items, beginning with Scott 164 in the regular postage section, Scott B1 in the semi-postal section, Scott C18 in the airpost section, Scott CB9 in the airpost semi-postal section, and Scott J41 in the postage due section.

Values for unused examples of Nos. 1-44 are for stamps without gum.

Watermark

Wmk. 202 — Circles

King William III — A1

Regular Perf. 11½, 12½, 11½x12, 12½x12, 13½x13, 14

1873-79 Typo. Unwmk.

No.	Type	Description	Unused	Used
1	A1	2½c green	6.00	9.50
2	A1	3c bister	57.50	*115.00*
3	A1	5c rose	14.00	13.50
4	A1	10c ultra	80.00	19.00
5	A1	25c brown orange	57.50	9.50
6	A1	50c violet	2.00	1.90
7	A1	2.50g bis & pur ('79)	50.00	45.00
		Nos. 1-7 (7)	267.00	*213.40*

See bluish paper note with Netherlands #7-22.

The gulden denominations, Nos. 7 and 12, are of larger size.

See 8-12. For surcharges see #18, 25-26.

Perf. 14, Small Holes

No.	Type	Description	Unused	Used
1b	A1	2½c	18.00	21.00
2b	A1	3c	70.00	*135.00*
3b	A1	5c	20.00	28.00
4b	A1	10c	115.00	97.50
5b	A1	25c	80.00	7.50
6b	A1	50c	40.00	37.50
		Nos. 1b-6b (6)	343.00	*326.50*

"Small hole" varieties have the spaces between the holes wider than the diameter of the holes.

1886-89 *Perf. 11½, 12½, 12½x12*

No.	Type	Description	Unused	Used
8	A1	12½c yellow	130.00	52.50
9	A1	15c olive ('89)	40.00	22.50
10	A1	30c pearl gray ('89)	45.00	52.50
11	A1	60c olive bis ('89)	55.00	19.00
12	A1	1.50g lt & dk bl ('89)	120.00	102.50
		Nos. 8-12 (5)	390.00	249.00

Nos. 1-12 were issued without gum until 1890. Imperfs. are proofs.

Numeral — A2

1889 *Perf. 12½*

No.	Type	Description	Unused	Used
13	A2	1c gray	1.60	1.60
14	A2	2c violet	1.60	2.25
15	A2	2½c green	5.75	5.25
16	A2	3c bister	6.50	6.00
17	A2	5c rose	25.00	1.90
		Nos. 13-17 (5)	40.45	17.00

No. 13 the numeral in the center is in italics, but Nos. 14-17 do not.

Black Handstamped Surcharge

1891 *Perf. 12½x12*

Without Gum

No.	Type	Description	Unused	Used
18	A1	25c on 30c pearl gray	18.00	15.00

No. 18 exists with double surcharge, value $225, and with inverted surcharge, value $275.

Queen Wilhelmina — A4

1892-96 *Perf. 12½*

No.	Type	Description	Unused	Used
19	A4	10c ultra ('95)	1.60	1.60
20	A4	12½c green	18.50	10.50
21	A4	15c rose ('93)	4.00	3.00
22	A4	25c brown orange	145.00	3.75
23	A4	30c gray ('96)	4.00	*7.50*
		Nos. 19-23 (5)	173.10	26.35

No. 4 Handstamped Surcharge in Magenta

No. 10 Handstamped Surcharge in Black

1895 *Perf. 12½, 13½x13*

No.	Type	Description	Unused	Used
25	A1	2½c on 10c ultra	16.00	11.50

Perf. 12½x12

No.	Type	Description	Unused	Used
26	A1	2½c on 30c gray	160.00	7.50

Nos. 25-26 exist with surcharge double or inverted.

No. 26 and No. 25, perf. 13½x13, were issued without gum.

Netherlands No. 77 Surcharged in Black

1902, Jan. 1 *Perf. 12½*

No.	Type	Description	Unused	Used
27	A11	25c on 25c rose pink & bl	2.00	1.90

Netherlands No. 84 Surcharged in Black

1901, May 1 Engr. *Perf. 11½x11*

No.	Type	Description	Unused	Used
28	A12	1.50g on 2.50g brn lil	22.00	26.00

Netherlands No. 68 Surcharged in Black

1902, Mar. 1 Typo. *Perf. 12½*

No.	Type	Description	Unused	Used
29	A11	12½c on 12½c blue	28.00	9.50

A9 A10

1904-08

No.	Type	Description	Unused	Used
30	A9	1c olive green	2.00	1.90
31	A9	2c yellow brown	18.00	3.75
32	A9	2½c blue green	8.00	.75
33	A9	3c orange	10.00	5.75
34	A9	5c rose red	10.00	1.15
35	A9	7½c gray ('08)	32.00	9.50
36	A10	10c slate	24.00	1.90
37	A10	12½c deep blue	2.00	.75
38	A10	15c brown	20.00	13.50
39	A10	22½c brn & ol ('08)	20.00	13.50
40	A10	25c violet	24.00	3.75
41	A10	30c brown orange	50.00	17.00
42	A10	50c red brown	40.00	10.50
		Nos. 30-42 (13)	260.00	83.70

Queen Wilhelmina — A11

1906, Nov. 1 Engr. *Perf. 11½*

Without Gum

No.	Type	Description	Unused	Used
43	A11	1½g red brown	40.00	30.00
44	A11	2½g slate blue	40.00	34.00

A12

Queen Wilhelmina
A13 A14

Perf. 12½, 11, 11½, 11x11½

1915-33 Typo.

No.	Type	Description	Unused	Used
45	A12	½c lilac ('20)	1.60	1.60
46	A12	1c olive green	.40	.25
47	A12	1½c blue ('20)	.40	.25
48	A12	2c yellow brn	1.60	1.35
49	A12	2½c green	1.00	.40
50	A12	3c yellow	3.00	1.90
51	A12	3c green ('26)	3.00	2.60
52	A12	5c rose	2.40	.40
53	A12	5c green ('22)	5.00	2.60
54	A12	5c lilac ('26)	2.40	.25
55	A12	7½c drab	1.45	.25
56	A12	7½c bister ('20)	1.45	.25
57	A12	10c lilac ('22)	5.75	5.75
58	A12	10c rose ('26)	5.00	1.90
59	A13	10c car rose	27.00	3.75
60	A13	12½c blue	3.00	.75
61	A13	12½c red ('22)	2.60	1.90
62	A13	15c olive grn	1.00	1.60
63	A13	15c lt blue ('26)	5.00	3.00
64	A13	20c blue ('22)	8.00	3.00
65	A13	20c olive grn ('26)	3.25	2.25
66	A13	22½c orange	3.25	3.00
67	A13	25c red violet	4.00	1.60
68	A13	30c slate	4.00	1.60
69	A13	35c sl & red ('22)	3.25	6.00

Perf. 11½x11, 11½, 12½, 11

Engr.

No.	Type	Description	Unused	Used
70	A14	50c green	4.00	.40
71	A14	1½g violet	18.00	13.50
72	A14	2½g carmine	26.00	24.00
a.		Perf. 12½ ('33)	160.00	*340.00*
		Nos. 45-72 (28)	146.80	86.10

Some stamps of 1915 were also issued without gum.

For surcharges see #74, 107-108, C1-C3.

A15

Laid Paper
Without Gum

1918, July 16 Typo. *Perf. 12*

No.	Type	Description	Unused	Used
73	A15	1c black, *buff*	6.00	3.75

"HAW" are the initials of Postmaster H. A. Willemsen.

No. 60 Surcharged in Black

1918, Sept. 1 *Perf. 12½*

No.	Type	Description	Unused	Used
74	A13	5c on 12½c blue	4.00	2.60
a.		"5" 2⅛mm wide	72.50	45.00
b.		Double surcharge		1,350.
c.		As "a," double surcharge		*1,800.*

The "5" of No. 74 is 2.75mm wide. Illustration shows No. 74a surcharge.

Queen Wilhelmina — A16

1923 Engr. *Perf. 11½, 11x11½*

No.	Type	Description	Unused	Used
75	A16	5c green	2.00	3.00
76	A16	7½c olive grn	2.00	3.00
77	A16	10c car rose	4.00	4.50
78	A16	20c indigo	4.00	4.50
a.		Perf. 11x11½	4.00	5.75
79	A16	1g brown vio	40.00	37.50
80	A16	2½g gray black	85.00	*180.00*
81	A16	5g brown	105.00	*225.00*
a.		Perf. 11x11½	600.00	475.00
		Nos. 75-81 (7)	242.00	*457.50*

25th anniv. of the assumption of the government of the Netherlands by Queen Wilhelmina, at the age of 18.

Nos. 80-81 with clear cancel between Aug. 1, 1923 and Apr. 30, 1924, sell for considerably more.

Types of Netherlands Marine Insurance Stamps, Inscribed "CURACAO" Surcharged in Black

1927, Oct. 3

No.	Type	Description	Unused	Used
87	MI1	3c on 15c dk green	.80	.75
88	MI1	10c on 60c car rose	.80	.75
89	MI1	12½c on 75c gray brn	.80	.75
90	MI2	15c on 1.50g dk bl	4.00	3.75
a.		Double surcharge	*1,600.*	
91	MI2	25c on 2.25g org brn	9.75	9.00
92	MI3	30c on 4½g black	10.50	9.75
93	MI3	50c on 7½g red	9.75	9.00
		Nos. 87-93 (7)	36.40	33.75

Nos. 90, 91 and 92 have "FRANKEER-ZEGEL" in one line of small capitals. Nos. 90 and 91 have a heavy bar across the top of the stamp.

Queen Wilhelmina — A17

1928-30 Engr. *Perf. 11½, 12½*

No.	Type	Description	Unused	Used
95	A17	6c orange red ('30)	2.40	.40
a.		Booklet pane of 6		
96	A17	7½c orange red	.80	.60
97	A17	10c carmine	1.60	.60
98	A17	12½c red brown	1.60	1.35
a.		Booklet pane of 6		
99	A17	15c dark blue	1.60	.60
a.		Booklet pane of 6		
100	A17	20c blue black	6.00	.95
101	A17	21c yellow grn ('30)	10.00	11.50
102	A17	25c brown vio	4.00	2.10
103	A17	27½c black ('30)	14.50	15.00
104	A17	30c deep green	6.00	1.15
105	A17	35c brnsh black	2.00	3.75
		Nos. 95-105 (11)	50.50	38.00

No. 96 Surcharged in Black with Bars over Original Value

1929, Nov. 1

106 A17 6c on 7½c org red 1.60 1.15
a. Inverted surcharge 280.00 260.00

No. 51 Surcharged in Red

1931, Mar. 1 Typo. *Perf. 12½*

107 A12 2½c on 3c green 1.20 1.15

No. 49 Surcharged in Red

1932, Oct. 29

108 A12 1½c on 2½c grn 4.00 3.75

Prince William I, Portrait by Van Key — A18

1933 Photo. *Perf. 12½*

109 A18 6c deep orange 2.00 1.15

400th birth anniv. of Prince William I, Count of Nassau and Prince of Orange, frequently referred to as William the Silent.

Willem Usselinx A19

Van Walbeeck's Ship A22

Designs: 2½c, 5c, 6c, Frederik Hendrik. 10c, 12½c, 15c, Jacob Binckes. 27½c, 30c, 50c, Cornelis Evertsen the Younger. 1.50g, 2.50g, Louis Brion.

1934, Jan. 1 Engr. *Perf. 12½*

110 A19 1c black 1.40 1.60
111 A19 1½c dull violet 1.00 .40
112 A19 2c orange 1.60 1.90
113 A19 2½c dull green 1.20 1.60
114 A19 5c black brn 1.20 1.60
115 A19 6c violet bl 1.60 .40
116 A19 10c lake 4.00 1.60
117 A19 12½c bister brn 9.00 7.50
118 A19 15c blue 3.00 1.90
119 A22 20c black 4.50 3.75
120 A22 21c brown 20.00 13.50
121 A22 25c dull green 20.00 13.50
122 A19 27½c brown vio 20.00 19.00
123 A19 30c scarlet 14.00 7.50
124 A19 50c orange 14.00 11.50
125 A19 1.50g indigo 60.00 57.50
126 A19 2.50g yellow grn 65.00 65.00
Nos. 110-126 (17) 241.50 209.75

3rd centenary of the founding of the colony.

Numeral A25

Queen Wilhelmina A26

1936, Aug. 1 Litho. *Perf. 13½x13*

Size: 18x22mm

127 A25 1c brown black .25 .25
128 A25 1½c deep ultra .25 .25
129 A25 2c orange .25 .25
130 A25 2½c green .25 .25
131 A25 5c scarlet .25 .25

Engr.

Perf. 12½

Size: 20¼x30½mm

132 A26 6c brown vio .80 .25
133 A26 10c orange red 1.20 .25
134 A26 12½c dk bl grn 1.60 .75
135 A26 15c dark blue 1.60 .75
136 A26 20c orange yel 1.60 .75
137 A26 21c dk gray 3.75 3.75
138 A26 25c brown lake 1.60 1.15
139 A26 27½c violet brn 3.25 3.00
140 A26 30c olive brn .80 .70

Perf. 13x14

Size: 22x33mm

141 A26 50c dull yel grn 4.00 .40
a. Perf. 14 60.00 .40
142 A26 1.50g black brn 18.00 11.50
a. Perf. 14 80.00 37.50
143 A26 2.50g rose lake 18.00 13.50
a. Perf. 14 20.00 19.00
Nos. 127-143 (17) 57.45 38.00

See Nos. 147-151. For surcharges see Nos. B1-B3.

Queen Wilhelmina — A27

Perf. 12½x12

1938, Aug. 27 Photo. Wmk. 202

144 A27 1½c dull purple .40 .40
145 A27 6c red orange .80 .75
146 A27 15c royal blue 1.60 1.15
Nos. 144-146 (3) 2.80 2.30

Reign of Queen Wilhelmina, 40th anniv.

Numeral Type of 1936 and

Queen Wilhelmina — A28

1941-42 Unwmk. Litho. *Perf. 12½*

Thick Paper

Size: 17¾x22mm

147 A25 1c gray brn ('42) 3.00 2.60
148 A25 1½c dull blue ('42) 9.75 .40
149 A25 2c lt orange ('42) 9.75 8.25
150 A25 2½c green ('42) 2.40 1.60
151 A25 5c crimson ('42) 2.00 1.15

Photo.

Perf. 12½, 13

Size: 18½x23mm

152 A28 6c rose violet 3.00 2.25
153 A28 10c red orange 3.00 1.15
154 A28 12½c lt green 3.25 1.15
155 A28 15c brt ultra 8.00 2.60
156 A28 20c orange 3.00 1.90
157 A28 21c gray 12.00 7.50
158 A28 25c brown lake 5.00 2.60
159 A28 27½c deep brown 20.00 16.50
160 A28 30c olive bis 18.00 4.50

Size: 21x26½mm

161 A28 50c olive grn ('42) 24.00 .75
162 A28 1½g gray ol ('42) 30.00 2.25
163 A28 2½g rose lake ('42) 32.00 1.90
Nos. 147-163 (17) 188.15 59.05

Imperfs. are proofs.

See Nos. 174-187.

Catalogue values for unused stamps in this section, from this point to the end of the section, are for Never Hinged items.

Bonaire A29

St. Eustatius A30

Designs: 2c, View of Saba. 2½c, St. Maarten. 5c, Aruba. 6c, Curaçao.

Perf. 13x13½, 13½x13 (No. 165)

1943, Feb. 1 Engr. Unwmk.

164 A29 1c rose vio & org brn .30 .25
165 A30 1½c dp bl & yel grn .30 .25
166 A29 2c sl blk & org brn .60 .35
167 A29 2½c grn & org .35 .25
168 A29 5c red & slate blk 1.15 .25
169 A29 6c rose lil & lt bl .85 .80
Nos. 164-169 (6) 3.55 2.15

Royal Family — A35

1943, Nov. 8 *Perf. 13½x13*

170 A35 1½c deep orange .45 .40
171 A35 2½c red .45 .40
172 A35 6c black 1.30 1.20
173 A35 10c deep blue 1.30 1.20
Nos. 170-173 (4) 3.50 3.20

Princess Margriet Francisca of the Netherlands.

Wilhelmina Type of 1941

1947 Photo. *Perf. 13½x13*

Size: 18x22mm

174 A28 6c brown vio 1.60 *1.90*
175 A28 10c orange red 1.60 *1.90*
176 A28 12½c dk blue grn 1.60 *1.90*
177 A28 15c dark blue 1.60 *2.25*
178 A28 20c orange yel 1.60 *3.25*
179 A28 21c dark gray 2.75 *3.25*
180 A28 25c brown lake .35 .25
181 A28 27½c chocolate 2.25 2.40
182 A28 30c olive bister 1.90 1.30
183 A28 50c dull yel grn 2.00 .25

Perf. 13½x14

Engr.

Size: 25x31¼mm

184 A28 1½g dark brown 6.00 1.90
185 A28 2½g rose lake 60.00 27.00
186 A28 5g olive green 120.00 *170.00*
187 A28 10g red orange 145.00 *275.00*
Nos. 174-187 (14) 348.25 492.55

Used values for Nos. 186-187 are for genuinely canceled copies clearly dated before the end of 1949.

A36

Queen Wilhelmina — A37

1948 Unwmk. Photo. *Perf. 13½x13*

188 A36 6c dk vio brn 1.05 .95
189 A36 10c scarlet 1.05 *1.20*
190 A36 12½c dk blue grn 1.05 .80
191 A36 15c deep blue 1.05 *.95*
192 A36 20c red orange 1.05 *1.90*
193 A36 21c black 1.05 *1.90*
194 A36 25c brt red vio .35 .25
195 A36 27½c henna brn 17.50 16.00
196 A36 30c olive brown 16.50 1.15
197 A36 50c olive green 14.50 .25

Perf. 12½x12

Engr.

198 A37 1.50g chocolate 28.00 6.50
Nos. 188-198 (11) 83.15 31.85

Queen Wilhelmina — A38

1948, Aug. 30 *Perf. 13x14*

199 A38 6c vermilion .70 .55
200 A38 12½c deep blue .70 .55

Reign of Queen Wilhelmina, 50th anniv.

Queen Juliana — A39

Perf. 14x13½

1948, Oct. 18 Photo. Wmk. 202

201 A39 6c red brown .75 .45
202 A39 12½c dark green .75 .45

Investiture of Queen Juliana, Sept. 6, 1948. Nos. 201-202 were issued in Netherlands Sept. 6.

Ship of Ojeda A40

Alonso de Ojeda A41

Perf. 14x13, 13x14

1949, July 26 Photo. Unwmk.

203 A40 6c olive green 4.00 2.25
204 A41 12½c brown red 4.25 3.00
205 A40 15c ultra 4.75 3.25
Nos. 203-205 (3) 13.00 8.50

450th anniversary of the discovery of Curaçao by Alonso de Ojeda, 1499.

Post Horns Entwined — A42

1949, Oct. 3 *Perf. 12x12½*

206 A42 6c brown red 4.75 2.50
207 A42 25c dull blue 4.75 1.30

UPU, 75th anniversary.

A43

A44

Queen Juliana — A45

1950-79 Photo. *Perf. 13x13½*

208 A43 1c red brown .25 .25
209 A43 1½c blue .25 .25
210 A43 2c orange .25 .25
211 A43 2½c green 1.20 .25
212 A43 3c purple .35 .25
212A A43 4c yel grn ('59) .95 .40
213 A43 5c dark red .25 .25

Perf. 13½x13

214 A44 6c deep plum 1.60 .25
215 A44 7½c red brn ('54) 5.50 .25
216 A44 10c red 2.25 .25
a. Redrawn ('79) 1.75 1.60
217 A44 12½c dk green 2.75 .25
218 A44 15c deep blue 2.75 .25
a. Redrawn ('79) .25 .25
219 A44 20c orange 3.25 .25
a. Redrawn ('79) .25 .25
220 A44 21c black 4.00 2.25
221 A44 22½c blue grn ('54) 6.25 .25
222 A44 25c violet 5.25 .25
a. Redrawn ('79) .25 .25
223 A44 27½c henna brn 8.25 1.90
224 A44 30c olive brown 12.50 .25
225 A44 50c olive green 12.50 .25

Perf. 12½x12

Engr.

226 A45 1½g slate grn 40.00 .40
227 A45 2½g black brn 40.00 1.90
228 A45 5g rose red 60.00 17.00
229 A45 10g dk vio brn 190.00 65.00
Nos. 208-229 (23) 400.35 92.85

Nos. 216a, 218a, 219a and 222a are from booklets Nos. 427a and 428a. Background design is sharper and stamps have one or two straight edges.

See Nos. 427-429. For surcharge see No. B20.

Fort Beekenburg — A46

Perf. 13½x12½

1953, June 16 **Photo.**

230 A46 22½c olive brown 6.00 .90

Founding of Fort Beekenburg, 250th anniv.

Beach at Aruba — A47

1954, May 1 *Perf. 11x11½*

231 A47 15c dk bl, sal & dp bl 6.00 3.00

3rd congress of the Caribbean Tourist Assoc., Aruba, May 3-6.

Queen Juliana — A48

1954, Dec. 15 *Perf. 13½*

232 A48 7½c olive green 1.40 1.00

Charter of the Kingdom, adopted Dec. 15, 1954. See Netherlands No. 366, Surinam No. 264.

Beach — A49

Petroleum Refinery, Aruba A50

1955, Dec. 5 **Litho.** *Perf. 12*

233 A49 15c chnt, bl & emer 3.25 2.60
234 A50 25c chnt, bl & emer 4.00 3.25

Caribbean Commission, 21st meeting, Aruba.

St. Annabaai Harbor and Flags — A51

1956, Dec. 6 **Unwmk.** *Perf. 14x13*

235 A51 15c lt bl, blk & red .40 .40

Caribbean Commission, 10th anniversary.

Man Watching Rising Sun — A52

1957, Mar. 14 **Photo.** *Perf. 11x11½*

236 A52 15c black & yellow .40 .40

1st Caribbean Mental Health Conference, Aruba, Mar. 14-19.

Tourism — A53

1957, July 1 **Litho.** *Perf. 14x13*

237 A53 7½c Saba .80 .50
238 A53 15c St. Maarten .80 .50
239 A53 25c St. Eustatius .80 .50
Nos. 237-239 (3) 2.40 1.50

Curaçao Intercontinental Hotel — A54

1957, Oct. 12 *Perf. 14x13*

240 A54 15c lt ultra .40 .40

Intercontinental Hotel, Willemstad, opening.

Map of Curaçao — A55

1957, Dec. 10 *Perf. 14x13½*

241 A55 15c indigo & lt bl .80 .70

International Geophysical Year.

Flamingoes, Bonaire — A56

Designs: 7½c, 8c, 25c, 1½g, Old buildings, Curaçao. 10c, 5g, Extinct volcano and palms, Saba. 15c, 30c, 1g, Fort Willem III, Aruba. 20c, 35c, De Ruyter obelisk, St. Eustatius. 12c, 40c, 2½g, Town Hall, St. Maarten.

1958-59 **Litho.** *Perf. 14x13*

Size: 33x22mm

242 A56 6c lt ol grn & pink 2.25 .25
243 A56 7½c red brn & org .25 .25
244 A56 8c dk bl & org ('59) .25 .25
245 A56 10c gray & org yel .25 .25
246 A56 12c bluish grn & gray ('59) .25 .25
247 A56 15c grn & lt ultra .25 .25
a. 15c green & lilac .25 .25
248 A56 20c crim & gray .25 .25
249 A56 25c Prus bl & yel grn .30 .25
250 A56 30c brn & bl grn .30 .25
251 A56 35c gray & rose ('59) .40 .25
252 A56 40c mag & grn .45 .25
253 A56 50c grysh brn & pink .45 .25
254 A56 1g brt red & gray 1.00 .25
255 A56 1½g rose vio & pale brn 1.35 .25
256 A56 2½g blue & citron 2.60 .30
257 A56 5g lt red brn & rose lil 5.00 .60
Nos. 242-257 (16) 15.60 4.40

See Nos. 340-348, 400-403. For surcharge see No. B58.

Nos. 242, 244-246, and 248-257 were printed on glossy and matte paper. Nos. 243 and 247 were printed on matte paper only. No. 247a was printed on glossy paper only.

Globe — A57

1958, Oct. 16 *Perf. 11x11½*

258 A57 7½c blue & lake .25 .25
259 A57 15c red & ultra .40 .40

50th anniv. of the Netherlands Antilles Radio and Telegraph Administration.

Hotel Aruba Caribbean — A58

1959, July 18 *Perf. 14x13*

260 A58 15c multi .40 .40

Opening of the Hotel Aruba Caribbean, Aruba.

Sea Water Distillation Plant — A59

1959, Oct. 16 **Photo.** *Perf. 14x13*

261 A59 20c bright blue .50 .50

Opening of sea water distillation plant at Balashi, Aruba.

Netherlands Antilles Flag — A60

1959, Dec. 14 **Litho.** *Perf. 13½*

262 A60 10c ultra & red .50 .40
263 A60 20c ultra, yel & red .50 .40
264 A60 25c ultra, grn & red .50 .40
Nos. 262-264 (3) 1.50 1.20

5th anniv. of the new constitution (Charter of the Kingdom).

Fokker "Snip" and Map of Caribbean — A61

Designs: 20c, Globe showing route flown, and plane. 25c, Map of Atlantic ocean and view of Willemstad. 35c, Map of Atlantic ocean and plane on Aruba airfield.

1959, Dec. 22 **Unwmk.** *Perf. 14x13*

265 A61 10c yel, lt & dk bl .80 .40
266 A61 20c yel, lt & dk bl .80 .40
267 A61 25c yel, lt & dk bl .80 .25
268 A61 35c yel, lt & dk bl .80 .55
Nos. 265-268 (4) 3.20 1.60

25th anniv. of Netherlands-Curaçao air service.

Msgr. Martinus J. Niewindt — A62

1960, Jan. 12 **Photo.** *Perf. 13½*

269 A62 10c deep claret .95 .50
270 A62 20c deep violet .95 .55
271 A62 25c olive green .95 .55
Nos. 269-271 (3) 2.85 1.60

Death centenary of Monsignor Niewindt, first apostolic vicar for Curaçao.

Worker, Flag and Factories — A63

1960, Apr. 29 *Perf. 12½x13½*

272 A63 20c multi .50 .50

Issued for Labor Day, May 1, 1960.

US Brig "Andrea Doria" and Gun at Fort Orange, St. Eustatius A64

1961, Nov. 16 **Litho.** *Perf. 14x13½*

273 A64 20c bl, red, grn & blk .80 .65

185th anniv. of 1st salute by a foreign power to the US flag flown by an American ship.

Queen Juliana and Prince Bernhard — A64a

1962, Jan. 31 **Photo.** *Perf. 14x13*

274 A64a 10c deep orange .50 .35
275 A64a 25c deep blue .50 .35

Silver wedding anniversary of Queen Juliana and Prince Bernhard.

Benta Player — A65

6c, Corn masher. 20c, Petji kerchief. 25c, "Jaja" (nurse) with child, sculpture.

Perf. 12½x13½

1962, Mar. 14 **Photo.**

276 A65 6c red brn & yel .40 .25
277 A65 10c shown .40 .25
278 A65 20c crim, ind & brt grn .40 .30
279 A65 25c brt grn, brn & gray .40 .30
a. Souvenir sheet of 4, #276-279 2.00 1.25
Nos. 276-279 (4) 1.60 1.10

Emblem of Family Relationship — A66

25c, Emblem of mental health (cross).

1963, Apr. 17 **Litho.** *Perf. 14x13½*

280 A66 20c dk blue & ocher .40 .40
281 A66 25c blue & red .40 .40

Fourth Caribbean Conference for Mental Health, Curaçao, Apr. 17-23.

Dove with Olive Branch — A67

1963, July 1 **Unwmk.** *Perf. 14x13*

282 A67 25c org yel & dk brn .40 .35

Centenary of emancipation of the slaves.

Hotel Bonaire — A68

1963, Aug. 31 *Perf. 14x13*

283 A68 20c dk red brown .40 .30

Opening of Hotel Bonaire on Bonaire.

Prince William of Orange Taking Oath of Allegiance — A69

1963, Nov. 21 **Photo.** *Perf. 13½x14*

284 A69 25c green, blk & rose .40 .35

150th anniversary of the founding of the Kingdom of the Netherlands.

Chemical Equipment — A70

1963, Dec. 10 **Litho.** *Perf. 14x13½*

285 A70 20c bl grn, brt yel grn & red .50 .50

Opening of chemical factories on Aruba.

Airmail Letter and Wings — A71

Design: 25c, Map of Caribbean, Miami-Curaçao route and planes of 1929 and 1964.

1964, June 22 Photo. *Perf. 11x11½*
286 A71 20c lt bl, red & ultra .40 .40
287 A71 25c lt grn, bl, red & blk .40 .40

35th anniversary of the first regular Curaçao airmail service.

Map of the Caribbean — A72

1964, Nov. 30 Litho. Unwmk.
288 A72 20c ultra, org & dk red .40 .35

5th meeting of the Caribbean Council, Curaçao, Nov. 30-Dec. 4.

Netherlands Antilles Flags, Map of Curaçao and Crest — A73

1964, Dec. 14 Litho. *Perf. 11½x11*
289 A73 25c lt bl & multi .40 .35

10th anniversary of the Charter of the Kingdom of the Netherlands. The flags, shaped like seagulls, represent the six islands comprising the Netherlands Antilles.

Princess Beatrix — A74

1965, Feb. 22 Photo. *Perf. 13½x14*
290 A74 25c brick red .40 .40

Visit of Princess Beatrix of Netherlands.

ITU Emblem, Old and New Communication Equipment A75

1965, May 17 Litho. *Perf. 13½*
291 A75 10c brt bl & dk bl .25 .25

ITU, centenary.

Shell Refinery, Curaçao — A76

10c, Catalytic cracking installation, vert. 25c, Workers operating manifold, primary distillation plant, vert.

Perf. 13½x14, 14x13½
1965, June 22 Photo.
292 A76 10c blk, red & yel .40 .35
293 A76 20c multi .40 .35
294 A76 25c multi .40 .35
Nos. 292-294 (3) 1.20 1.05

50th anniv. of the oil industry in Curaçao.

Floating Market, Curaçao — A77

Designs (flag and): 2c, Divi-divi tree and Haystack Mountain, Aruba. 3c, Lace, Saba. 4c, Flamingoes, Bonaire. 5c, Church ruins, St. Eustatius. 6c, Lobster, St. Maarten.

1965, Aug. 25 Litho. *Perf. 14x13*
295 A77 1c lt grn, ultra & red .25 .25
296 A77 2c yel, ultra & red .25 .25
297 A77 3c chlky bl, ultra & red .25 .25
298 A77 4c org, ultra & red .25 .25
299 A77 5c lt bl, ultra & red .25 .25
300 A77 6c pink, ultra & red .25 .25
Nos. 295-300 (6) 1.50 1.50

Marine Guarding Beach — A78

1965, Dec. 10 Photo. *Perf. 13x10½*
301 A78 25c multi .25 .25

Netherlands Marine Corps, 300th anniv.

Budgerigars, Wedding Rings and Initials — A79

1966, Mar. 10 Photo. *Perf. 13½x14*
302 A79 25c gray & multi .35 .25

Issued to commemorate the marriage of Princess Beatrix and Claus van Amsberg.

M. A. de Ruyter and Map of St. Eustatius A80

1966, June 19 Photo. *Perf. 13½*
303 A80 25c vio, ocher & lt bl .25 .25

Visit of Adm. Michiel Adriaanszoon de Ruyter (1607-1676) to St. Eustatius, 1666.

Liberal Arts and Grammar — A81

10c, Rhetoric and dialectic. 20c, Arithmetic and geometry. 25c, Astronomy and music.

Perf. 13½x12½
1966, Sept. 19 Litho. Unwmk.
304 A81 6c yel, bl & blk .25 .25
305 A81 10c yel grn, red & blk .25 .25
306 A81 20c bl, yel & blk .35 .25
307 A81 25c red, yel grn & blk .35 .25
Nos. 304-307 (4) 1.20 1.00

25th anniversary of secondary education.

Cruiser — A82

Ships: 10c, Sailing ship. 20c, Tanker. 25c, Passenger ship.

Perf. 13½x14
1967, Mar. 29 Litho. Unwmk.
308 A82 6c lt & dk grn .35 .25
309 A82 10c org & brn .35 .25
310 A82 20c sep & brn .35 .25
311 A82 25c chlky bl & dk bl .35 .25
Nos. 308-311 (4) 1.40 1.00

60th anniv. of *Onze Vloot* (Our Fleet), an organization which publicizes the Dutch navy and merchant marine and helps seamen.

Manuel Carlos Piar (1777-1817), Independence Hero — A83

1967, Apr. 26 Photo. *Perf. 14x13*
312 A83 20c red & blk .35 .25

Discobolus after Myron — A84

10c, Hand holding torch, & Olympic rings. 25c, Stadium, doves & Olympic rings.

1968, Feb. 19 Litho. *Perf. 13x14*
313 A84 10c multi .45 .30
314 A84 20c dk brn, ol & yel .45 .30
315 A84 25c bl, dk bl & brt yel grn .45 .30
Nos. 313-315 (3) 1.35 .90

19th Olympic Games, Mexico City, 10/12-27.

Friendship 500 — A84a

Designs: 20c, Beechcraft Queen Air. 25c, Friendship and DC-9.

1968, Dec. 3 Litho. *Perf. 14x13*
315A A84a 10c dl yel, blk & brt bl .45 .30
315B A84a 20c tan, blk & brt bl .45 .30
315C A84a 25c sal pink, blk & brt bl .45 .30
Nos. 315A-315C (3) 1.35 .90

Dutch Antillean Airlines (ALM).

Map of Bonaire, Radio Mast and Waves — A85

1969, Mar. 6 *Perf. 14x13½*
316 A85 25c bl, emer & blk .35 .30

Opening of the relay station of the Dutch World Broadcasting System on Bonaire.

Code of Law — A86

Designs: 25c, Scales of Justice.

Perf. 12½x13½
1969, May 19 Photo.
317 A86 20c dk grn, yel grn & gold .35 .30
318 A86 25c vio bl, bl & gold .35 .30

Court of Justice, centenary.

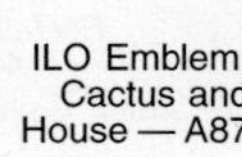

ILO Emblem, Cactus and House — A87

1969, Aug. 25 Litho. *Perf. 14x13*
319 A87 10c bl & blk .35 .25
320 A87 25c dk red & blk .35 .25

ILO, 50th anniversary.

Queen Juliana and Rising Sun — A87a

1969, Dec. 12 Photo. *Perf. 14x13*
321 A87a 25c bl & multi .45 .30

15th anniv. of the Charter of the Kingdom of the Netherlands. Phosphorescent paper.

Radio Bonaire Studio and Transmitter A88

Design: 15c, Radio waves and cross set against land, sea and air.

1970, Feb. 5 Photo. *Perf. 12½x13½*
322 A88 10c multi .25 .25
323 A88 15c multi .25 .25

5th anniv. of the opening of the Trans World Missionary Radio Station, Bonaire.

Altar, St. Anna's Church, Otraband 1752 — A89

20c, Interior, Synagogue at Punda, 1732, horiz. 25c, Pulpit, Fort Church, Fort Amsterdam, 1769.

Perf. 13½x14, 14x13½
1970, May 12 Photo.
324 A89 10c gold & multi .45 .30
325 A89 20c gold & multi .45 .30
326 A89 25c gold & multi .45 .30
Nos. 324-326 (3) 1.35 .90

St. Theresia Church, St. Nicolaas — A90

1971, Feb. 9 Litho. *Perf. 14x13½*
327 A90 20c dl bl, gray & rose .35 .30

40th anniversary of the Parish of St. Theresia at St. Nicolaas, Aruba.

A91

1971, Feb. 24 *Perf. 13½x14*
328 A91 25c Lions emblem .45 .40

Lions Club in the Netherlands Antilles, 25th anniversary.

A91a

Prince Bernhard, Fokker F27, Boeing 747B.

1971, June 29 Photo. *Perf. 13x14*
329 A91a 45c multi .85 .60

60th birthday of Prince Bernhard.

Pedro Luis Brion (1782-1821), Naval Commander in Fight for South American Independence — A92

1971, Sept. 27 Photo. *Perf. 13x12½*

330 A92 40c multi .45 .40

Flamingoes, Bonaire — A93

Designs: 1c, Queen Emma Bridge, Curaçao. 2c, The Bottom, Saba. 4c, Water tower, Aruba. 5c, Fort Amsterdam, St. Maarten. 6c, Fort Orange, St. Eustatius.

1972, Jan. 17 Litho. *Perf. 13½x14*

331 A93 1c yel & multi .30 .25
332 A93 2c yel grn & multi .30 .25
333 A93 3c dp org & multi .30 .25
334 A93 4c brt bl & multi .30 .25
335 A93 5c red org & multi .30 .25
336 A93 6c lil rose & multi .30 .25
Nos. 331-336 (6) 1.80 1.50

Ship in Dry Dock — A94

1972, Apr. 7 *Perf. 14x13½*

337 A94 30c bl gray & multi .45 .40

Inauguration of large dry dock facilities in Willemstad.

Juan Enrique Irausquin — A95

1972, June 20 Photo. *Perf. 13x14*

338 A95 30c deep orange .45 .40

Irausquin (1904-1962), financier and patriot.

Costa Gomez — A96

1972, Oct. 27 Litho.

339 A96 30c yel grn & blk .45 .40

Moises Frumencio da Costa Gomez (1907-1966), lawyer, legislator, patriot.

Island Series Type of 1958-59

Designs: 45c, 85c, Extinct volcano and palms, Saba. 55c, 90c, De Ruyter obelisk, St. Eustatius. 65c, 75c, 10g, Flamingoes, Bonaire. 70c, Fort Willem III, Aruba. 95c, Town Hall, St. Maarten.

1973, Feb. 12 Litho. *Perf. 14x13*
Size: 33x22mm

340 A56 45c vio bl & lt bl .50 .25
341 A56 55c dk car rose & emer .55 .25
342 A56 65c green & pink .80 .30
343 A56 70c gray vio & org 1.30 .50
344 A56 75c brt lilac & salmon .70 .50
345 A56 85c brn ol & apple grn .80 .60
346 A56 90c blue & ocher .95 .75
347 A56 95c orange & yellow 1.10 .80
348 A56 10g brt ultra & sal 8.75 4.25
Nos. 340-348 (9) 15.45 8.20

Mailman — A97

Designs: 15c, King William III from 1873 issue. 30c, Emblem of Netherlands Antilles postal service.

1973, May 23 Photo. *Perf. 13x14*

349 A97 15c lil, gold & vio .40 .35
350 A97 20c dk grn & multi .50 .40
351 A97 30c org & multi .50 .40
Nos. 349-351 (3) 1.40 1.15

Centenary of first stamps of Netherlands Antilles.

Cable Linking Aruba, Curaçao and Bonaire — A98

30c, 6 stars symbolizing the islands, cable. 45c, Saba, St. Maarten and St. Eustatius linked by cable.

1973, June 20 Litho. *Perf. 14x13*

352 A98 15c multi .50 .45
353 A98 30c multi .50 .45
354 A98 45c multi .50 .45
a. Souvenir sheet of 3, #352-354 1.60 1.60
Nos. 352-354 (3) 1.50 1.35

Inauguration of the inter-island submarine cable.

Queen Juliana, Netherlands Antilles and House of Orange Colors — A99a

Engr. & Photo.

1973, Sept. 4 *Perf. 12½x12*

355 A99a 15c silver & multi .55 .55

25th anniversary of reign of Queen Juliana.

Jan Hendrik Albert Eman — A99

1973, Oct. 17 Litho. *Perf. 13x14*

356 A99 30c lt yel grn & blk .40 .40

Eman (1888-1957), founder of the People's Party in Aruba, member of Antillean Parliament.

Lionel Bernard Scott — A100

1974, Jan. 28

357 A100 30c lt bl & multi .40 .40

Scott (1897-1966), architect and statesman.

Family at Supper — A101

Designs: 12c, Parents watching children at play. 15c, Mother and daughter sewing, father and son gardening.

1974, Feb. 18 Litho. *Perf. 13x14*

358 A101 6c bl & multi .30 .30
359 A101 12c bis & multi .35 .30
360 A101 15c grn & multi .35 .30
Nos. 358-360 (3) 1.00 .90

Planned parenthood and World Population Year.

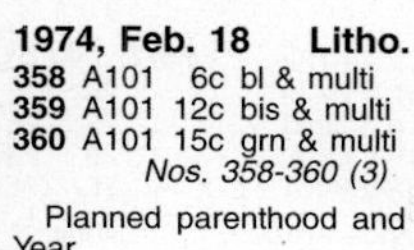

Desulphurization Plant, Lago — A102

Designs: 30c, Distillation plant. 45c, Lago refinery at night.

1974, Aug. 12 Litho. *Perf. 14x13*

361 A102 15c lt bl, blk & yel .35 .30
362 A102 30c lt bl, blk & yel .40 .40
363 A102 45c dk brn & multi .55 .55
Nos. 361-363 (3) 1.30 1.25

Oil industry in Aruba, 50th anniversary.

UPU Emblem — A103

1974, Oct. 9 Litho. *Perf. 13x14*

364 A103 15c yel grn, blk & gold .50 .45
365 A103 30c bl, blk & gold .50 .45

Centenary of Universal Postal Union.

Queen Emma Bridge — A104

Willemstad Bridges: 30c, Queen Juliana Bridge. 40c, Queen Wilhelmina Bridge.

1975, Feb. 5 Litho. *Perf. 14x13*

366 A104 20c ultra & multi .50 .45
367 A104 30c ultra & multi .50 .45
368 A104 40c ultra & multi .60 .55
Nos. 366-368 (3) 1.60 1.45

Dedication of new Queen Juliana Bridge spanning Curaçao Harbor.

Salt Crystals — A105

Designs: 20c, Solar salt pond. 40c, Map of Bonaire and location of solar salt pond, vert.

Perf. 14x13, 13x14

1975, Apr. 24 Litho.

369 A105 15c multi .55 .40
370 A105 20c multi .55 .45
371 A105 40c multi .65 .45
Nos. 369-371 (3) 1.75 1.30

Bonaire's salt industry.

Aruba Airport, 1935 and Fokker F-18 — A106

30c, Aruba Airport, 1950, & Douglas DC-9. 40c, New Princess Beatrix Airport & Boeing 727.

1975, June 19 Litho. *Perf. 14x13*

372 A106 15c vio & multi .45 .35
373 A106 30c blk & multi .45 .35
374 A106 40c yel & multi .45 .45
Nos. 372-374 (3) 1.35 1.15

40th anniversary of Aruba Airport.

International Women's Year Emblem — A107

12c, "Women's role in social development." 20c, Embryos within female & male symbols.

1975, Aug. 1 Photo. *Perf. 14x13*

375 A107 6c multi .35 .25
376 A107 12c multi .40 .30
377 A107 20c multi .50 .40
Nos. 375-377 (3) 1.25 .95

International Women's Year 1975.

Beach, Aruba — A108

Tourist Publicity: No. 379, Beach pavilion and boat, Bonaire. No. 380, Table Mountain and Spanish Water, Curaçao.

1976, June 21 Litho. *Perf. 14x13*

378 A108 40c blue & multi .55 .50
379 A108 40c blue & multi .55 .50
380 A108 40c blue & multi .55 .50
Nos. 378-380 (3) 1.65 1.50

Julio Antonio Abraham — A109

1976, Aug. 10 Photo. *Perf. 13x14*

381 A109 30c tan & claret .65 .45

Julio Antonio Abraham (1909-1960), founder of Democratic Party of Bonaire.

Dike and Produce — A110

1976, Sept. 21 Litho.

382 A110 15c shown .50 .40
383 A110 35c Cattle .55 .45
384 A110 45c Fish .55 .55
Nos. 382-384 (3) 1.60 1.40

Agriculture, husbandry and fishing in Netherlands Antilles.

Plaque, Fort Oranje Memorial — A111

Designs: 40c, Andrea Doria in St. Eustatius harbor receiving salute. 55c, Johannes de Graaff, Governor of St. Eustatius, holding Declaration of Independence.

1976, Nov. 16 Litho. *Perf. 14x13*

385 A111 25c multi .60 .40
386 A111 40c multi .60 .40
387 A111 55c multi .60 .55
Nos. 385-387 (3) 1.80 1.35

First gun salute to US flag, St. Eustatius, Nov. 16, 1776.

See No. 619.

Dancer with Cactus Headdress — A112

Carnival: 35c, Woman in feather costume. 40c, Woman in pompadour costume.

1977, Jan. 20 Litho. *Perf. 13x14*

388 A112 25c multi .60 .45
389 A112 35c multi .60 .45
390 A112 40c multi .60 .45
Nos. 388-390 (3) 1.80 1.35

Bird Petroglyph, Aruba — A113

Indian Petroglyphs: 35c, Loops and spiral, Savonet Plantation, Curaçao. 40c, Tortoise, Onima, Bonaire.

1977, Mar. 29
391 A113 25c red & multi .60 .45
392 A113 35c brn & multi .60 .45
393 A113 40c yel & multi .60 .45
Nos. 391-393 (3) 1.80 1.35

A114

Tropical Trees: 25c, Cordia Sebestena. 40c, East Indian walnut, vert. 55c, Tamarind.

1977, July 20 ***Perf. 14x13, 13x14***
394 A114 25c blk & multi .50 .45
395 A114 40c blk & multi .60 .45
396 A114 55c blk & multi .65 .60
Nos. 394-396 (3) 1.75 1.50

A115

Designs: 20c, Chimes, Spritzer & Fuhrmann Building. 40c, Globe with Western Hemisphere and sun over Curaçao. 55c, Diamond ring and flag of Netherlands Antilles.

1977, Sept. 27 **Litho.** ***Perf. 13x14***
397 A115 20c brt grn & multi .50 .45
398 A115 40c yel & multi .60 .45
399 A115 55c bl & multi .65 .60
Nos. 397-399 (3) 1.75 1.50

Spritzer & Fuhrmann, jewelers of Netherlands Antilles, 50th anniversary.

Island Series Type of 1958-59

Designs: 20c, 35c, 55c, De Ruyter obelisk, St. Eustatius. 40c, Town Hall, St. Maarten.

Perf. 13½ Horiz.

1977, Nov. 30 **Photo.**
Size: 39x22mm
400 A56 20c crim & gray 1.40 1.40
a. Bklt. pane of 6 (2 #400, 4 #402) 5.00
401 A56 35c gray & rose 3.75 3.00
a. Bklt. pane of 4 (1 #401, 3 #403) 6.00
402 A56 40c magenta & grn .50 .50
403 A56 55c dk car rose & emer .70 .70
Nos. 400-403 (4) 6.35 5.60

Nos. 400-403 issued in booklets only. No. 400a has label with red inscription in size of 3 stamps; No. 401a has label with dark carmine rose inscription in size of 2 stamps.

Winding Road, Map of Saba — A116

Tourism: 35c, Ruins of Synagogue, map of St. Eustatius. 40c, Greatbay, Map of St. Maarten.

1977, Nov. 30 **Litho.** ***Perf. 14x13***
404 A116 25c multi .30 .25
405 A116 35c multi .35 .30
406 A116 40c multi .35 .35
Nos. 404-406 (3) 1.00 .90

Tete-beche gutter pairs exist.

Treasure Chest — A117

Designs: 20c, Logo of Netherlands Antilles Bank. 40c, Safe deposit door.

1978, Feb. 7 **Litho.** ***Perf. 14x13***
407 A117 15c brt & dk bl .25 .25
408 A117 20c org & gold .25 .25
409 A117 40c brt & dk grn .25 .25
Nos. 407-409 (3) .75 .75

Bank of Netherlands Antilles, 150th anniv. Tete-beche gutter pairs exist.

Flamboyant — A118

Flowers: 25c, Erythrina velutina. 40c, Guaiacum officinale, horiz. 55c, Gliricidia sepium, horiz.

Perf. 13x14, 14x13

1978, May 31 **Litho.**
410 A118 15c multi .25 .25
411 A118 25c multi .25 .25
412 A118 40c multi .40 .30
413 A118 55c multi .50 .45
Nos. 410-413 (4) 1.40 1.25

Polythysana Rubrescens — A119

Butterflies: 25c, Caligo eurilochus. 35c, Prepona omphale amesis. 40c, Morpho aega.

1978, June 20 ***Perf. 13x14***
414 A119 15c multi .50 .30
415 A119 25c multi .50 .30
416 A119 35c multi .50 .35
417 A119 40c multi .60 .45
Nos. 414-417 (4) 2.10 1.40

"Conserve Energy" — A120

1978, Aug. 31 **Litho.** ***Perf. 13x14***
418 A120 15c org & blk .30 .30
419 A120 20c dp grn & blk .40 .30
420 A120 40c dk red & blk .45 .40
Nos. 418-420 (3) 1.15 1.00

Morse Ship-to-Shore Service — A121

Designs: 40c, Ship-to-shore telex service. 55c, Future radar-satellite service, vert.

Perf. 14x13, 13x14

1978, Oct. 16 **Litho.**
421 A121 20c multi .35 .35
422 A121 40c multi .45 .45
423 A121 55c multi .50 .50
Nos. 421-423 (3) 1.30 1.30

Ship-to-shore communications, 70th anniv.

Villa Maria Waterworks A122

35c, Leonard B. Smith, vert. 40c, Opening of Queen Emma Bridge, Willemstadt, 1888.

1978, Dec. 13
424 A122 25c multi .30 .25
425 A122 35c multi .40 .30
426 A122 40c multi .45 .40
Nos. 424-426 (3) 1.15 .95

L. B. Smith, engineer, 80th death anniv.

Queen Juliana Type of 1950

1979, Jan. 11 **Photo.** ***Perf. 13½x13***
427 A44 5c dp yel .25 .25
a. Bklt. pane of 10 (4 #427, 1 #216a, 2 #222a, 3 #429) 4.00
428 A44 30c brown 1.05 1.05
a. Bklt. pane of 10 (1 #428, 4 #218a, 3 #219a, 2 #222a) 4.00
429 A44 40c brt bl .35 .35
Nos. 427-429 (3) 1.65 1.65

Nos. 427-429 issued in booklets only. Nos. 427a-428a have 2 labels and selvages the size of 6 stamps. Background design of booklet stamps sharper than 1950 issue. All stamps have 1 or 2 straight edges.

Goat and Conference Emblem — A123

75c, Horse & map of Curaçao. 150c, Cattle, Netherlands Antilles flag, UN & Conf. emblems.

1979, Apr. 18 **Litho.** ***Perf. 14x13***
437 A123 50c multi .40 .35
438 A123 75c multi .55 .50
439 A123 150c multi .85 .95
a. Souv. sheet of 3, perf. 13½x13 2.00 2.00
Nos. 437-439 (3) 1.80 1.80

12th Inter-American Meeting at Ministerial Level on Foot and Mouth Disease and Zoonosis Control, Curaçao, Apr. 17-20. No. 439a contains Nos. 437-439 in changed colors.

Dutch Colonial Soldier, Emblem — A124

1979, July 4 **Litho.** ***Perf. 13x14***
440 A124 1g multi .65 .60
Nos. 440,B166-B167 (3) 1.45 1.30

Netherlands Antilles Volunteer Corps, 50th anniv.

A125

Flowering Trees: 25c, Casearia Tremula. 40c, Cordia cylindro-stachya. 1.50g, Melochia tomentosa.

1979, Sept. 3 **Litho.** ***Perf. 13x14***
441 A125 25c multi .40 .30
442 A125 40c multi .50 .45
443 A125 1.50g multi 1.00 1.00
Nos. 441-443 (3) 1.90 1.75

A126

Designs: 65c, Dove and Netherlands flag. 1.50g, Dove and Netherlands Antilles flag.

1979, Dec. 6 **Litho.** ***Perf. 13x14***
444 A126 65c multi .55 .50
445 A126 1.50g multi 1.00 1.05

Constitution, 25th anniversary.

Map of Aruba, Foundation Emblem — A127

1g, Foundation headquarters, Aruba.

1979, Dec. 18 ***Perf. 14x13***
446 A127 95c multi .70 .70
447 A127 1g multi .85 .85

Cultural Foundation Center, Aruba, 30th anniv.

Cupola, 1910, Fort Church — A128

1980, Jan. 9 ***Perf. 13x14***
448 A128 100c multi .85 .70
Nos. 448,B172-B173 (3) 1.65 1.50

Fort Church, Curaçao, 210th anniv. (1979).

Rotary Emblem — A129

Designs: 50c, Globe and cogwheels. 85c, Cogwheel and Rotary emblem.

1980, Feb. 22 **Litho.** ***Perf. 14x13***
449 A129 45c multi .45 .35
450 A129 50c multi .45 .35
451 A129 85c multi .60 .60
a. Souvenir sheet of 3, #449-451, perf. 13½x13 1.75 1.60
b. Strip of 3, #449-451 1.60 1.60

Rotary Intl., 75th anniv. No. 451a has continuous design.

Coin Box, 1905 — A130

Post Office Savings Bank of Netherlands Antilles, 75th Anniv.: 150c, Coin box, 1980.

1980, Apr. 2 **Litho.** ***Perf. 14x13***
452 A130 25c multi .35 .35
453 A130 150c multi 1.10 1.10

Netherlands Antilles No. 200, Arms — A131

60c, No. 290, royal crown.

1980, Apr. 29 **Photo.**
454 A131 25c shown .30 .30
455 A131 60c multicolored .45 .45
a. Bklt. pane of 5 + 3 labels (#428, 2 #454, 2 #455) 3.50

Abdication of Queen Juliana of the Netherlands.
Tete-beche gutter pairs exist.

Sir Rowland Hill (1795-1879), Originator of Penny Postage — A132

60c, London 1980 emblem. 1g, Airmail label.

1980, May 6 **Litho.**
456 A132 45c shown .40 .40
457 A132 60c multicolored .50 .50
458 A132 1g multicolored .80 .80
a. Souv. sheet of 3, perf. 13½x14 1.75 1.40
Nos. 456-458 (3) 1.70 1.70

London 1980 Intl. Stamp Exhibition, May 6-14. No. 458a contains Nos. 456-458 in changed colors.

Leptotila Verreauxi — A133

1980, Sept. 3 Litho. *Perf. 14x13*

459 A133 25c shown .70 .30
460 A133 60c Mockingbird .85 .50
461 A133 85c Coereba flaveola 1.05 .65
Nos. 459-461 (3) 2.60 1.45

Rudolf Theodorus Palm — A134

1g, Score, hand playing piano.

1981, Jan. 27 Litho. *Perf. 13x14*

462 A134 60c shown .60 .60
463 A134 1g multicolored 1.00 .85

Palm, composer, birth centenary.

Alliance Mission Emblem, Map of Aruba — A135

1981, Mar. 24 *Perf. 14x13*

464 A135 30c shown .35 .35
465 A135 50c Curaçao .60 .45
466 A135 1g Bonaire map .95 .85
Nos. 464-466 (3) 1.90 1.65

Evangelical Alliance Mission anniversaries: 35th in Aruba, 50th in Curaçao, 30th in Bonaire.

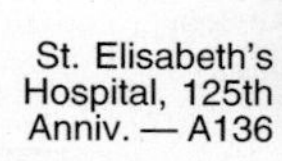

St. Elisabeth's Hospital, 125th Anniv. — A136

1981, June 24 Litho. *Perf. 14x13*

467 A136 60c Gateway .55 .55
468 A136 1.50g shown 1.30 1.30

Oregano Blossom — A137

1981, Nov. 24 Litho. *Perf. 13x14*

469 A137 45c shown .50 .40
470 A137 70c Flaira .80 .65
471 A137 100c Welisali 1.00 .80
Nos. 469-471 (3) 2.30 1.85

Ship Pilot Service Cent. — A138

Designs: Various ships.

1982, Jan. 13 Litho. *Perf. 13x14*

472 A138 70c multi 1.05 .80
473 A138 85c multi 1.15 .85
474 A138 1g multi 1.20 .90
Nos. 472-474 (3) 3.40 2.55

A139

1982, Mar. 15 Litho. *Perf. 13x14*

475 A139 75c Altar 1.05 .65
476 A139 85c Building 1.15 .65
477 A139 150c Pulpit 1.60 1.10
Nos. 475-477 (3) 3.80 2.40

Community Mikve Israel-Emanuel Synagogue, 250th anniv.

Flags, Peter Stuyvesant — A140

1982, Apr. 21 Litho. *Perf. 13x14*

478 A140 75c multicolored 1.15 .90
a. Souvenir sheet 1.25 1.25

US-Netherlands diplomatic relations bicentenary.

See. No. 619b.

A141

1982, May 5

479 A141 35c Radar screen .65 .35
480 A141 75c Control tower 1.05 .65
481 A141 150c Antenna 1.60 1.10
Nos. 479-481 (3) 3.30 2.10

Intl. Air Traffic Controllers' Year.

A142

45c, Emblem. 85c, Mail bag. 150c, Flags of France, Netherland Antilles.

1982, June 9 Litho. *Perf. 13x14*

482 A142 45c multi .65 .45
483 A142 85c multi .90 .70
484 A142 150c multi 1.45 1.10
a. Souvenir sheet of 3, #482-484 3.00 2.50
Nos. 482-484 (3) 3.00 2.25

PHILEXFRANCE '82 Stamp Exhibition, Paris, June 11-21.

Brown Chromis — A143

1982, Sept. 15 Litho. *Perf. 14x13*

485 A143 35c shown .85 .45
486 A143 75c Spotted trunkfish 1.15 .80
487 A143 85c Blue tang 1.30 .90
488 A143 100c French angelfish 1.40 .95
Nos. 485-488 (4) 4.70 3.10

Natural Bridge, Aruba — A144

45c, Lac-Bay, Bonaire. 100c, Willemstad, Curaçao.

1983, Apr. 12 Litho. *Perf. 14x13*

489 A144 35c shown .60 .45
490 A144 45c multi .70 .55
491 A144 100c multi 1.40 1.05
Nos. 489-491 (3) 2.70 2.05

World Communications Year — A145

1983, May 17 Litho. *Perf. 13x14*

492 A145 1g multi 1.40 1.25
a. Souvenir sheet 1.60 1.25

BRASILIANA '83 — A146

45c, Ship, postal building, Waaigat. 55c, Flags, emblem. 100c, Governor's Palace, Sugar Loaf Mt.

1983, June 29 Litho. *Perf. 13x14*

493 A146 45c multi .80 .65
494 A146 55c multi .85 .75
495 A146 100c multi 1.25 1.15
a. Souvenir sheet of 3, #493-495 3.00 2.50
Nos. 493-495 (3) 2.90 2.55

Fruit Tree — A147

45c, Mangifera indica. 55c, Malpighia punicifolia. 100c, Citrus aurantifolia.

1983, Sept. 13 Litho. *Perf. 13x14*

496 A147 45c multicolored 1.00 .65
497 A147 55c multicolored 1.05 .70
498 A147 100c multicolored 1.60 1.15
Nos. 496-498 (3) 3.65 2.50

Local Government Buildings — A148

1983, Dec. 20 Litho. *Perf. 14x13*

499 A148 20c Saba .35 .25
500 A148 25c St. Eustatius .35 .25
501 A148 30c St. Maarten .40 .35
502 A148 35c Aruba *2.40 .40*
503 A148 45c Bonaire .60 .45
a. Perf. 13½ horiz. ('86) 2.40 1.30
504 A148 55c Curaçao .80 .55
a. Perf. 13½ horiz. ('86) 2.40 1.30
b. Bklt. pane of 4 + label (2 #503a, 504a) ('86) 10.00
Nos. 499-504 (6) 4.90 2.25

See Nos. 515-520, 543A-555.

Amigoe di Curaçao Newspaper Centenary — A149

45c, Copy programming. 55c, Printing press. 85c, Man reading newspaper.

1984, Jan. 5 Litho.

505 A149 45c multicolored .75 .60
506 A149 55c multicolored .85 .65
507 A149 85c multicolored 1.30 1.05
Nos. 505-507 (3) 2.90 2.30

40th Anniv. of Intl. Civil Aviation Org. — A150

Various emblems.

1984, Feb. 28 Litho. *Perf. 14x13*

508 A150 25c Winair .65 .35
509 A150 45c ICAO .95 .60
510 A150 55c ALM 1.05 .65
511 A150 100c Plane 1.60 1.05
Nos. 508-511 (4) 4.25 2.65

Chamber of Commerce and Industry Centenary — A151

45c, Bonnet maker. 55c, Emblem. 100c, River, bridge, boat.

1984, May 29 Litho. *Perf. 13½*

512 A151 45c multicolored 1.20 .80
513 A151 55c multicolored 1.25 .80
514 A151 100c multicolored 1.75 1.10
Nos. 512-514 (3) 4.20 2.70

Govt. Building Type of 1983

1984, June 26 Litho. *Perf. 14x13*

515 A148 60c like 20c .65 .55
516 A148 65c like 25c .75 .60
517 A148 75c like 30c 1.00 .80
518 A148 85c like 35c 3.00 .90
519 A148 90c like 45c 1.15 .90
520 A148 95c like 55c 1.20 .95
Nos. 515-520 (6) 7.75 4.70

For surcharges see Nos. B306-B307.

Local Birds — A152

45c, Tiaris bicolor. 55c, Zonotrichia capensis. 150c, Chlorostilbon mellisugus.

1984, Sept. 18 Litho. *Perf. 14x13*

521 A152 45c multi 1.15 .65
522 A152 55c multi 1.30 .85
523 A152 150c multi 2.25 1.60
Nos. 521-523 (3) 4.70 3.10

Eleanor Roosevelt (1884-1962) — A153

45c, At Hyde Park. 85c, Portrait. 100c, Reading to children.

1984, Oct. 11 Litho. *Perf. 13x14*

524 A153 45c multi .80 .55
525 A153 85c multi 1.30 .90
526 A153 100c multi 1.40 .95
Nos. 524-526 (3) 3.50 2.40

Tete-beche gutter pairs exist.

Flamingos — A154

1985, Jan. 9 Litho. *Perf. 14x13*

527 A154 25c Adult pullets .85 .55
528 A154 45c Juveniles 1.25 .65
529 A154 55c Adults wading 1.25 .80
530 A154 100c Adults flying 1.90 1.15
Nos. 527-530 (4) 5.25 3.15

Curaçao Masonic Lodge Bicent. — A155

45c, Compass, sun, moon and stars. 55c, Doorway, columns and 5 steps. 100c, Star, 7 steps.

1985, Feb. 21 Litho. *Perf. 13x14*

531 A155 45c multi 1.75 .65
532 A155 55c multi 1.75 .85
533 A155 100c multi 2.10 1.35
Nos. 531-533 (3) 5.60 2.85

UN, 40th Anniv. — A156

1985, June 5 Litho. *Perf. 14x13*

534 A156 55c multi 1.05 .70
535 A156 1g multi 1.60 1.15

Papiamentu, Language of the Antilles — A157

45c, Pierre Lauffer (1920-1981), author and poem Patria. 55c, Waves of Papiamentu.

1985, Sept. 4 Litho. *Perf. 14x13*

536	A157	45c multi	.70	.55
537	A157	55c multi	.85	.65

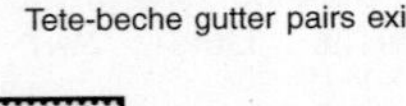

Tete-beche gutter pairs exist.

Flora — A158

5c, Calotropis procera. 10c, Capparis flexuosa. 20c, Mimosa distachya. 45c, Ipomoea nil. 55c, Heliotropium ternatum. 1.50g, Ipomoea incarnata.

1985, Nov. 6 *Perf. 13x14*

538	A158	5c multi	.50	.25
539	A158	10c multi	.50	.25
540	A158	20c multi	.70	.35
541	A158	45c multi	1.05	.55
542	A158	55c multi	1.20	.60
543	A158	1.50g multi	1.90	1.30
		Nos. 538-543 (6)	5.85	3.30

Govt. Building Type of 1983

1985-89 *Perf. 14x13*

543A	A148	70c like 20c ('88)	1.00	.40
543B	A148	85c like 45c ('88)	1.15	.45
544	A148	1g like 20c	1.40	.90
545	A148	1.50g like 25c	1.75	1.15
546	A148	2.50g like 30c ('86)	2.00	1.60
551	A148	5g like 45c ('86)	4.00	3.00
554	A148	10g like 55c ('87)	8.00	4.75
555	A148	15g like 20c ('89)	12.00	7.75
		Nos. 543A-555 (8)	31.30	20.00

Issued: 70c, 85c, 3/16; 1g, 1.50g, 12/4; 2.50g, 1/8; 5g, 12/3; 10g, 5/20; 15g, 2/8.

For surcharge see No. B308.

Curaçao Town Hall, 125th Anniv. — A159

1986, Jan. 8 *Perf. 14x13, 13x14*

561	A159	5c Town Hall	.35	.25
562	A159	15c State room, vert.	.40	.25
563	A159	25c Court room	.60	.35
564	A159	55c Entrance, vert.	1.00	.60
		Nos. 561-564 (4)	2.35	1.45

Amnesty Intl., 25th Anniv. — A160

45c, Prisoner chained. 55c, Peace bird imprisoned. 100c, Prisoner behind bars.

1986, May 28 Litho. *Perf. 14x13*

565	A160	45c multi	.80	.50
566	A160	55c multi	.90	.55
567	A160	100c multi	1.25	.85
		Nos. 565-567 (3)	2.95	1.90

Mailboxes — A161

10c, PO mailbox. 25c, Steel mailbox, vert. 45c, Mailbox on brick wall, vert. 55c, Pillar box, vert.

Perf. 14x13, 13x14

1986, Sept. 3 Litho.

568	A161	10c multi	.30	.25
569	A161	25c multi	.45	.25
570	A161	45c multi	.70	.50
571	A161	55c multi	.85	.60
		Nos. 568-571 (4)	2.30	1.60

Friars of Tilburg in the Antilles, Cent. — A162

10c, Brother Mauritius Vliegendehond, residence, 1886. 45c, Monsignor Ferdinand Kieckens, St. Thomas College, Roodeweg. 55c, Father F.S. de Beer, 1st general-superior, & college courtyard.

1986, Nov. 13 Litho. *Perf. 13x14*

572	A162	10c multi	.35	.25
573	A162	45c multi	.80	.50
574	A162	55c multi	.95	.65
		Nos. 572-574 (3)	2.10	1.40

Princess Juliana & Prince Bernhard, 50th Wedding Anniv. — A163

1987, Jan. 7 Litho. *Perf. 13x14*

575	A163	1.35g multi	2.50	1.25
a.		Souvenir sheet	3.00	2.50

Maduro Holding, Inc., Sesquicent. — A164

70c, Expansion map. 85c, Corporate divisions. 1.55g, S.E.L. Maduro, founder.

1987, Jan. 26

576	A164	70c multi	.85	.55
577	A164	85c multi	1.05	.65
578	A164	1.55g multi	1.75	1.30
		Nos. 576-578 (3)	3.65	2.50

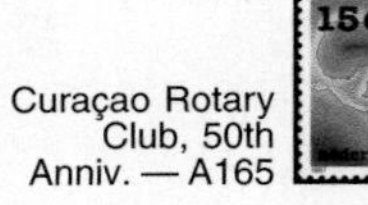

Curaçao Rotary Club, 50th Anniv. — A165

15c, Map of the Antilles. 50c, Rotary headquarters. 65c, Map of Curaçao.

1987, Apr. 2 Litho. *Perf. 14x13*

579	A165	15c multicolored	.40	.25
580	A165	50c multicolored	.75	.55
581	A165	65c multicolored	1.00	.60
		Nos. 579-581 (3)	2.15	1.40

Bolivar-Curaçao Friendship, 175th Anniv. — A166

60c, Octagon, residence of Simon Bolivar in Curaçao. 70c, Bolivarian Soc. Headquarters, 1949, Willemstad. 80c, Octagon interior (bedroom). 90c, Manual Carlos Piar, Simon Bolivar (1783-1830) & Pedro Luis Brion.

1987, July 24 Litho. *Perf. 14x13*

582	A166	60c multi	.75	.55
583	A166	70c multi	.80	.60
584	A166	80c multi	1.05	.80
585	A166	90c multi	1.15	.85
		Nos. 582-585 (4)	3.75	2.80

Bolivarian Society, 50th anniv. (70c, 90c).

Antilles Natl. Parks Foundation, 25th Anniv. — A167

70c, Phaethon lepturus. 85c, Odocoileus virginianus curassavicus. 1.55g, Iguana iguana.

1987, Dec. 1 Litho. *Perf. 14x13*

586	A167	70c multi	.90	.55
587	A167	85c multi	1.05	.65
588	A167	1.55g multi	1.75	1.30
		Nos. 586-588 (3)	3.70	2.50

The Curaçao Courant, 175th Anniv. — A168

Designs: 55c, 19th Cent. printing press, lead type. 70c, Keyboard, modern press.

1987, Dec. 11

589	A168	55c multi	.80	.55
590	A168	70c multi	.85	.60

Mijnmaatschappij Phosphate Mining Co., Curaçao, 75th Anniv. — A169

40c, William Godden, founder. 105c, Processing plant. 155c, Tafelberg.

1988, Jan. 21

591	A169	40c multicolored	.70	.40
592	A169	105c multicolored	1.30	.85
593	A169	155c multicolored	1.75	1.15
		Nos. 591-593 (3)	3.75	2.40

States of the Netherlands Antilles, 50th Anniv. — A170

Designs: 65c, John Horris Sprockel, 1st president, and natl. colors, crest. 70c, Development of state elections, women's suffrage. 155c, Natl. colors, crest, constellation representing the 5 islands and separation of Aruba.

1988, Apr. 5 Litho.

594	A170	65c multi	.85	.60
595	A170	70c multi	1.05	.60
596	A170	155c multi	1.75	1.15
		Nos. 594-596 (3)	3.65	2.35

Abolition of Slavery, 125th Anniv. — A171

190c, Slave Wall, Curaçao.

1988, July 1 Litho. *Perf. 14x13*

597	A171	155c shown	1.60	1.05
598	A171	190c multicolored	1.90	1.20

3rd Conference for Great Cities of the Americas, Curaçao, Aug. 24-27 — A172

1988, Aug. 24 Litho.

599	A172	80c shown	1.05	.60
600	A172	155c Bridge, globe	1.60	1.05

Interamerican Foundation of Cities conference on building bridges between peoples.

Charles Ernst Barend Hellmund (1896-1952) — A173

Men and women who initiated community development: 65c, Atthelo Maud Edwards Jackson (1901-1970). 90c, Nicolaas Debrot (1902-1981). 120c, William Charles De La Try Ellis (1881-1977).

1988, Sept. 20 *Perf. 13x14*

601	A173	55c multi	.70	.40
602	A173	65c multi	.75	.50
603	A173	90c multi	1.20	.75
604	A173	120c multi	1.25	.85
		Nos. 601-604 (4)	3.90	2.50

Tete-beche gutter pairs exist.

Cacti — A174

55c, Cereus hexagonus. 115c, Melocactus. 125c, Opuntia wentiana.

1988, Dec. 13 Litho. *Perf. 13x14*

605	A174	55c multicolored	.85	.55
606	A174	115c multicolored	1.35	.85
607	A174	125c multicolored	1.60	1.05
		Nos. 605-607 (3)	3.80	2.45

A175

1989, Mar. 9 Litho. *Perf. 14x13*

608	A175	65c Crested quail	1.30	.75
609	A175	115c Dogs, cats	1.45	1.10

Wildlife Protection and Curaçao Foundation for the prevention of cruelty to animals.

Cruise Ships at St. Maarten and Curaçao — A176

1989, May 8 Litho.

610	A176	70c Great Bay Harbor	1.05	.75
611	A176	155c St. Annabay	1.75	1.45

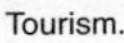

Tourism.

A177

Social and Political Figures: 40c, Paula Clementina Dorner (1901-1969), teacher. 55c, John Aniceto de Jongh (1885-1951), pharmacist, Parliament member. 90c, Jacobo Palm (1887-1982), composer. 120c, Abraham Mendes Chumaceiro (1841-1902), political reformer.

1989, Sept. 20 Litho. *Perf. 13x14*

612	A177	40c multi	.70	.45
613	A177	55c multi	.80	.55
614	A177	90c multi	1.15	.75
615	A177	120c multi	1.40	1.05
		Nos. 612-615 (4)	4.05	2.80

A178

30c, 7 Symptoms of cancer. 60c, Radiation treatment. 80c, Fund emblem, healthy person.

1989, Nov. 7 Litho.

616	A178	30c multi	.60	.45
617	A178	60c multi	.95	.70
618	A178	80c multi	1.15	.70
		Nos. 616-618 (3)	2.70	1.85

Queen Wilhelmina Fund, 40th anniv. Nos. 616-618 printed se-tenant with inscribed labels.

Souvenir Sheet

World Stamp Expo '89 and 20th UPU Congress, Washington, DC — A179

Designs: 70c, Monument, St. Eustatius, where the sovereignty of the US was 1st recognized by a foreign officer, Nov. 16, 1776. 155c, Peter Stuyvesant, flags representing bicent. of US-Antilles diplomatic relations, vert. 250c, 9-Gun salute of the *Andrea Doria*.

1989, Nov. 17 Litho. *Perf. 13*

619 Sheet of 3 5.75 4.50
a. A179 70c multicolored 1.15 .75
b. A179 155c multicolored 1.75 1.30
c. A179 250c multicolored 2.60 2.25

Fireworks — A180

100c, Ornaments on tree.

1989, Dec. 1 *Perf. 13½x14*

620 A180 30c multicolored .60 .40
621 A180 100c multicolored 1.30 .90

Christmas 1989 and New Year 1990. Nos. 620-621 printed se-tenant with labels inscribed "Merry X-mas and Happy New Year" in four languages.

Flowering plants — A181

30c, Tephrosia cinerea. 55c, Erithalis fruticosa. 65c, Evolvulus antillanus. 70c, Jacquinia arborea. 125c, Tournefortia gnaphalodes. 155c, Sesuvium portulacastrum.

1990, Jan. 31 Litho. *Perf. 13x14*

622 A181 30c multi .40 .35
623 A181 55c multi .75 .55
624 A181 65c multi .80 .60
625 A181 70c multi .90 .70
626 A181 125c multi 1.60 1.30
627 A181 155c multi 2.00 1.60
Nos. 622-627 (6) 6.45 5.10

Dominican Nuns in the Netherlands Antilles, Cent. — A182

10c, Nurse, flag, map. 55c, St. Rose Hospital and St. Martin's Home. 60c, St. Joseph School.

1990, May 7 Litho. *Perf. 14x13*

628 A182 10c multicolored .25 .25
629 A182 55c multicolored .75 .50
630 A182 60c multicolored .85 .60
Nos. 628-630 (3) 1.85 1.35

A183

Poets: 40c, Carlos Alberto Nicolaas-Perez (1915-1989). 60c, Evert Stephanus Jordanus Kruythoff (1893-1967). 80c, John De Pool (1873-1947). 150c, Joseph Sickman Corsen (1853-1911).

1990, Aug. 8 Litho. *Perf. 13x14*

631 A183 40c multicolored .55 .35
632 A183 60c multicolored .80 .60
633 A183 80c multicolored 1.00 .75
634 A183 150c multicolored 1.75 1.60
Nos. 631-634 (4) 4.10 3.30

Netherlands Queens — A184

No. 635, Emma. No. 636, Wilhelmina. No. 637, Juliana. No. 638, Beatrix.
250c, Four Queens, horiz.

1990, Sept. 5 *Perf. 13x14*

635 A184 100c multi 1.45 1.05
636 A184 100c multi 1.45 1.05
637 A184 100c multi 1.45 1.05
638 A184 100c multi 1.45 1.05
Nos. 635-638 (4) 5.80 4.20

Souvenir Sheet

Perf. 14x13

639 A184 250c multi 6.25 5.00

Oil Refining in Curaçao, 75th Anniv. — A185

1990, Oct. 1 Litho. *Perf. 14x13*

640 A185 100c multicolored 1.60 1.25

Christmas — A186

1990, Dec. 5 Litho. *Perf. 13½x14*

641 A186 30c Gifts .60 .30
642 A186 100c shown 1.60 .95

25th anniv. of Bon Bisina Project (No. 641). Nos. 641-642 each printed with se-tenant label showing holiday greetings.

Express Mail Service, 5th Anniv. — A187

1991, Jan. 16 Litho. *Perf. 14x13*

643 A187 20g multicolored 15.00 12.50

Fish — A188

Designs: 10c, Scuba diver, French grunt. 40c, Spotted trunkfish. 55c, Coppersweeper. 75c, Skindiver, yellow goatfish. 100c, Blackbar soldierfish.

1991, Mar. 13 *Perf. 13x14*

644 A188 10c multicolored .60 .25
645 A188 40c multicolored .70 .50
646 A188 55c multicolored .85 .75
647 A188 75c multicolored 1.05 1.00
648 A188 100c multicolored 1.60 1.20
Nos. 644-648 (5) 4.80 3.70

Greetings — A189

1991, May 8 *Perf. 14x13*

649 A189 30c Good luck .45 .40
650 A189 30c Thank you .45 .40
651 A189 30c Love you .45 .40
652 A189 30c Happy day .45 .40
653 A189 30c Get well soon .45 .40
654 A189 30c Happy birthday .45 .40
Nos. 649-654 (6) 2.70 2.40

Lighthouses — A190

30c, Westpoint, Curaçao. 70c, Willem's Tower, Bonaire. 115c, Little Curaçao, Curaçao.

1991, June 19 Litho. *Perf. 13x14*

655 A190 30c multicolored 2.50 1.30
656 A190 70c multicolored 2.50 1.30
657 A190 115c multicolored 2.50 1.30
Nos. 655-657 (3) 7.50 3.90

Peter Stuyvesant College, 50th Anniv. — A191

Espamer '91 — A192

1991, July 5 *Perf. 14x13, 13x14*

658 A191 65c multicolored .90 .85
659 A192 125c multicolored 1.75 1.75

Christmas — A193

1991, Dec. 2 Litho. *Perf. 13½x14*

660 A193 30c shown .45 .40
661 A193 100c Angel, shepherds 1.40 1.25

Nos. 660-661 printed with se-tenant labels.

A194

Litho. & Typo.

1991, Dec. 16 *Perf. 13x14*

662 A194 30c J. A. Correa .80 .45
663 A194 70c "75," coat of arms 1.30 .90
664 A194 155c I. H. Capriles 1.90 1.60
a. Strip of 3, #662-664 4.00 3.00

Maduro and Curiel's Bank NV, 75th anniv.

Odocoileus Virginianus — A195

1992, Jan. 29 Litho. *Perf. 14x13*

666 A195 5c Fawn .95 .70
667 A195 10c Two does .95 .70
668 A195 30c Buck .95 .70
669 A195 40c Buck & doe in water .95 .70
670 A195 200c Buck drinking 3.00 2.25
671 A195 355c Buck, diff. 5.00 4.00
Nos. 666-671 (6) 11.80 9.05

World Wildlife Fund. Nos. 670-671 are airmail and do not have the WWF emblem. Nos. 670-671 are airmail.

Souvenir Sheet

Discovery of America, 500th Anniv. — A196

Designs: a, 250c, Alhambra, Granada, Spain. b, 500c, Carthusian Monastery, Seville, Spain.

1992, Apr. 1 Litho. *Perf. 14x13*

672 A196 Sheet of 2, #a.-b. 11.50 9.00

#672a, Granada '92. #672b, Expo '92, Seville.

Discovery of America, 500th Anniv. — A197

250c, Sailing ship. 500c, Map, Columbus.

1992, May 13 Litho. *Perf. 14x13*

673 A197 250c multicolored 3.25 2.60
674 A197 500c multicolored 6.50 5.25

World Columbian Stamp Expo '92, Chicago.

Container Terminal, Curaçao — A198

1992, June 26

675 A198 80c multi 1.15 .90
676 A198 125c multi, diff. 1.60 1.35

Famous People — A199

Designs: 30c, Angela Altagracia de Lannoy-Willems (1913-1983), politician and social activist. 40c, Lodewijk Daniel Gerharts (1901-1983), politician and promoter of tourism for Bonaire. 55c, Cyrus Wilberforce Wathey (1901-1969), businessman and philanthropist. 70c, Christiaan Winkel (1899-1962), deputy governor of Netherlands Antilles. 100c, Franciscan Nuns of Roosendaal, educational and charitable group, 150th anniversary of arrival in Curaçao.

1992, Sept. 1 Litho. *Perf. 13x14*

677 A199 30c grn & blk, *tan* .45 .40
678 A199 40c blue & blk, *tan* .60 .45
679 A199 55c yel org & blk, *tan* .75 .60
680 A199 70c lake & blk, *tan* .85 .70
681 A199 100c blue & blk, *tan* 1.15 1.15
Nos. 677-681 (5) 3.80 3.30

Queen Beatrix's 1992 Visit — A200

Designs: 70c, Queen in white hat, Prince Claus. 100c, Queen signing jubilee register. 175c, Queen in black hat, Prince Claus, native girl.

1992, Nov. 9 Litho. *Perf. 14x13*

682 A200 70c multicolored .95 .80
683 A200 100c multicolored 1.30 1.15
684 A200 175c multicolored 2.10 1.90
Nos. 682-684 (3) 4.35 3.85

Queen Beatrix's accession to the throne, 12½ year anniv. (#683).

Christmas — A201

30c, Nativity scene. 100c, Mary, Joseph, vert.

Perf. 14x13½, 13½x14

1992, Dec. 1 Litho.

685 A201 30c multi .55 .40
686 A201 100c multi 1.45 1.05

No. 686 printed with se-tenant label.

Flowers — A202

75c, Hibiscus. 90c, Helianthus annuus. 175c, Ixora. 195c, Rosea.

1993, Feb. 3 Litho. *Perf. 13x14*

687 A202 75c multi 1.05 .75
688 A202 90c multi 1.25 1.00
689 A202 175c multi 2.10 1.75
690 A202 195c multi 2.40 2.10
Nos. 687-690 (4) 6.80 5.60

Anniversaries A203

Map of islands and: 65c, Airplane, air routes. 75c, Natl. Laboratory, scientist using microscope. 90c, Airplane at Princess Juliana Intl. Airport. 175c, Yellow and white crosses.

1993, Mar. 9 *Perf. 14x13*

691 A203 65c multicolored .85 .65
692 A203 75c multicolored .95 .70
693 A203 90c multicolored 1.15 .95
694 A203 175c multicolored 2.00 1.75
Nos. 691-694 (4) 4.95 4.05

Princess Juliana Intl. Airport, 50th anniv. (#691, 693). Natl. Laboratory, 75th anniv. (#692). Princess Margaret White/Yellow Cross Foundation for District Nursing, 50th anniv. (#694).

Dogs — A204

1993, May 26 Litho. *Perf. 13x14*

695 A204 65c Pekingese .85 .70
696 A204 90c Poodle 1.15 1.00
697 A204 100c Pomeranian 1.40 1.10
698 A204 175c Papillon 2.10 1.75
Nos. 695-698 (4) 5.50 4.55

Entry of Netherlands Antilles into UPAEP — A205

Designs: 150c, Indian cave painting, Bonaire. 200c, Emblem of Brasiliana '93, flag of Netherlands Antilles. 250c, Map of Central and South America, Netherlands Antilles, Spain, and Portugal, document being signed.

1993, July 15 Litho. *Perf. 14x13*

699 A205 150c multicolored 2.60 1.60
700 A205 200c multicolored 3.00 2.10
701 A205 250c multicolored 3.50 2.60
Nos. 699-701 (3) 9.10 6.30

Brasiliana '93 (#700).

Contemporary Art — A206

1993, July 23 Litho. *Perf. 13x14*

702 A206 90c silver & multi 1.15 .95
703 A206 150c gold & multi 1.75 1.50

US Consulate General in Netherlands Antilles, Bicent. — A207

65c, American Consulate. 90c, Coats of Arms. 175c, Eagle in flight.

1993, Nov. 16 Litho. *Perf. 14x13*

704 A207 65c multicolored .80 .70
705 A207 90c multicolored 1.20 1.00
706 A207 175c multicolored 2.00 1.75
Nos. 704-706 (3) 4.00 3.45

Christmas — A208

Designs: 30c, Mosaic of mother and child. 115c, Painting of Mary holding Christ.

1993, Dec. 1 *Perf. 13x14*

707 A208 30c multicolored .55 .35
708 A208 115c multicolored 1.45 1.30

Dogs — A209

1994, Feb. 2 Litho. *Perf. 14x13*

709 A209 65c Basset 1.00 .85
710 A209 75c Pit bull terrier 1.15 .95
711 A209 90c Cocker spaniel 1.35 1.15
712 A209 175c Chow 2.40 2.00
Nos. 709-712 (4) 5.90 4.95

Birds — A210

50c, Polyborus plancus. 95c, Pavo muticus. 100c, Ara macao. 125c, Icterus icterus.

1994, Mar. 2 Litho. *Perf. 13x14*

713 A210 50c multicolored 1.75 .75
714 A210 95c multicolored 1.75 1.35
715 A210 100c multicolored 1.75 1.35
716 A210 125c multicolored 2.25 1.60
Nos. 713-716 (4) 7.50 5.05

A211

Famous People: 65c, Joseph Husurell Lake (1925-76), politician, journalist. 75c, Efrain Jonckheer (1917-87), diplomat. 100c, Michiel Martinus Romer (1865-1937), educator. 175c, Carel Nicolaas Winkel (1882-1973), public official, social worker.

1994, Apr. 8

717 A211 65c olive & blk, *grn* .80 .80
718 A211 75c brn & blk, *lt brn* .95 .95
719 A211 100c grn & blk, *bl* 1.25 1.25
720 A211 175c brn & blk, *tan* 2.25 2.25
Nos. 717-720 (4) 5.25 5.25

A212

1994 World Cup Soccer Championships, US: 90c, Socks, soccer shoes, horiz. 150c, Shoe, ball. 175c, Whistle, horiz.

Perf. 14x13, 13x14

1994, May 4 Litho.

721 A212 90c multicolored 1.20 1.05
722 A212 150c multicolored 1.90 1.75
723 A212 175c multicolored 2.10 2.00
Nos. 721-723 (3) 5.20 4.80

A213

ILO, 75th Anniv.: 90c, Declaration, chair, gavel. 110c, "75" over heart. 200c, Wind-blown tree.

1994, June 1 Litho. *Perf. 13x14*

724 A213 90c multicolored 1.20 1.10
725 A213 110c multicolored 1.35 1.25
726 A213 200c multicolored 2.60 2.50
Nos. 724-726 (3) 5.15 4.85

Wildlife — A214

Designs: 10c, Ware-wara, blenchi, parakeet, dolphin. 35c, Dolphin, pelican, troupial. 50c, Iguana, fish, lobster, sea hedgehog. 125c, Sea hedgehog, sea apple, fish, turtle, flamingos, ducks.

1994, Aug. 4 Litho. *Perf. 14x13*

727 A214 10c multicolored .75 .40
728 A214 35c multicolored .75 .55
729 A214 50c multicolored .80 .75
730 A214 125c multicolored 1.75 1.75
a. Souvenir sheet, #727-730 5.00 4.50
Nos. 727-730 (4) 4.05 3.45

PHILAKOREA '94 (#730a).

FEPAPOST '94 — A215

2.50g, Netherlands #277. 5g, #109.

1994, Oct. 5 Litho. *Perf. 14x13*

731 A215 2.50g multicolored 3.00 3.25
732 A215 5g multicolored 6.00 6.25
a. Souv. sheet of 2, #731-732, perf. 13½x13 10.00 8.25

Christmas — A216

115c, Hands holding earth.

1994, Dec. 1 Litho. *Perf. 14x13*

733 A216 30c shown .85 .45
734 A216 115c multicolored 1.75 1.45

Curaçao Carnivals — A217

Carnival scene and: 125c, Buildings, Willemstad. 175c, Floating market. 250c, House with thatched roof.

1995, Jan. 19 Litho. *Perf. 14x13*

735 A217 125c multicolored 1.60 1.45
736 A217 175c multicolored 2.25 1.90
737 A217 250c multicolored 3.00 2.60
Nos. 735-737 (3) 6.85 5.95

Mgr. Verriet Institute for Physically Handicapped, 50th Anniv. — A218

Design: 90c, Cedric Virginie, handicapped worker at Public Library.

1995, Feb. 2 Litho. *Perf. 13x14*

738 A218 65c multicolored .80 .75
739 A218 90c multicolored 1.15 1.05

Dogs — A219

1995, Mar. 29 Litho. *Perf. 14x13*

740 A219 75c Doberman 1.20 1.00
741 A219 85c Shepherd 1.45 1.20
742 A219 100c Bouvier 1.60 1.30
743 A219 175c St. Bernard 2.60 2.10
Nos. 740-743 (4) 6.85 5.60

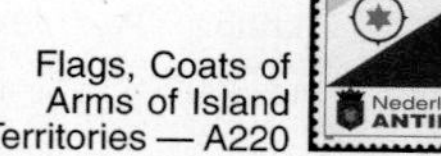

Flags, Coats of Arms of Island Territories — A220

10c, Bonaire. 35c, Curaçao. 50c, St. Maarten. 65c, Saba. 75c, St. Eustatius, natl. flag, coat of arms. 90c, Flags of territories, natl. coat of arms.

1995, June 30 Litho. *Perf. 14x13*

744 A220 10c multicolored .25 .30
745 A220 35c multicolored .60 .45
746 A220 50c multicolored .75 .60
a. St. Maarten flag colors reversed 60.00 —
747 A220 65c multicolored .90 .80
748 A220 75c multicolored 1.05 .85
749 A220 90c multicolored 1.20 1.15
a. St. Maarten flag colors reversed 60.00 —
Nos. 744-749 (6) 4.75 4.15

Nos. 746a and 749a show the colors of the St. Maarten flag reversed: blue on top, red on bottom. Both were quickly withdrawn from sale after the error was discovered. Used examples exist.

Domestic Cats — A221

Designs: 25c, Siamese sealpoint. 60c, Maine coon. 65c, Egyptian silver mau. 90c, Angora. 150c, Persian blue smoke.

1995, Sept. 29 Litho. *Perf. 13x14*

750 A221 25c multicolored .70 .35
751 A221 60c multicolored 1.05 .70
752 A221 65c multicolored 1.15 .80
753 A221 90c multicolored 1.40 1.15
754 A221 150c multicolored 2.10 1.75
Nos. 750-754 (5) 6.40 4.75

Christmas and New Year — A222

Designs: 30c, Three Magi following star. 115c, Fireworks above houses, Handelskade.

1995, Dec. 1 Litho. *Perf. 13½x13*

755 A222 30c multicolored .60 .40
756 A222 115c multicolored 1.60 1.30

Nos. 755-756 each printed with se-tenant label.

A223

Curaçao Lions Club, 50th Anniv.: 75c, List of services to community. 105c, Seal. 250c, Hands clasp.

1996, Feb. 26 Litho. *Perf. 13x14*

757 A223 75c multicolored 1.20 .80
758 A223 105c multicolored 1.45 1.20
759 A223 250c multicolored 3.25 3.00
Nos. 757-759 (3) 5.90 5.00

A224

1996, Apr. 12 Litho. *Perf. 13x14*

760 A224 85c shown .80 .65
761 A224 175c Telegraph key 1.20 .80

Radio, cent.

A225

1996, Apr. 12

762	A225	60c shown	1.15	1.05
763	A225	75c Tornado, sun	2.10	1.90

Dr. David Ricardo Capriles Clinic, 60th anniv.

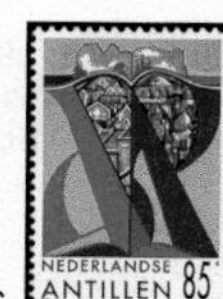

A226

1996, May 8 Litho. *Perf. 13x14*

764	A226	85c shown	1.15	1.15
765	A226	225c Bible	3.00	2.60

Translation of the Bible into Papiamentu.
Nos. 764-765 exist imperf. Value, set $90.

CAPEX '96 — A227

Butterflies: 5c, Agraulis vanillae. 110c, Callithea philotima. 300c, Parthenos sylvia. 750c, Euphaedra francina.

1996, June 5 Litho. *Perf. 14x13*

766	A227	5c multicolored	.90	.25
767	A227	110c multicolored	1.75	1.30
768	A227	300c multicolored	4.50	3.50
a.		Souvenir sheet of 2, #767-768	7.50	5.75
769	A227	750c multicolored	10.50	8.50
		Nos. 766-769 (4)	17.65	13.55

Nos. 766-769 exist imperf. Value, set $120.
No. 768a exists imperf. Value, $110.

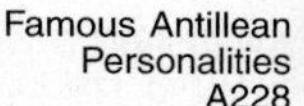

Famous Antillean Personalities A228

Designs: 40c, Mary Gertrude Johnson Hassel (1853-1939), introduced drawn thread (Spanish work) to Saba. 50c, Cornelis Marten (Papa Cornes) (1749-1852), spiritual care giver on Bonaire. 75c, Phelippi Benito Chakutoe (1891-1967), union leader. 85c, Christiaan Josef Hendrikus Engels (1907-80), physician, painter, pianist, poet.

1996, Aug. 21 Litho. *Perf. 14x13*

770	A228	40c orange & black	.65	.50
771	A228	50c green & black	.70	.55
772	A228	75c brown & black	1.05	.80
773	A228	85c blue & black	1.10	1.05
		Nos. 770-773 (4)	3.50	2.90

Horses — A229

1996, Sept. 26 Litho. *Perf. 14x13*

774	A229	110c Shire	1.60	1.25
775	A229	225c Shetland pony	3.25	2.50
776	A229	275c Thoroughbred	3.50	3.25
777	A229	350c Przewalski	4.75	4.00
		Nos. 774-777 (4)	13.10	11.00

Christmas — A230

35c, Money bag, straw hat, candy cane, gifts, poinsettias, star. 150c, Santa Claus.

Serpentine Die Cut 13x13½

1996, Dec. 2 Litho.

Self-Adhesive

778	A230	35c multicolored	.80	.40
779	A230	150c multicolored	2.00	1.60

Mushrooms A231

40c, Galerina autumnalis. 50c, Amanita virosa. 75c, Boletus edulis. 175c, Amanita muscaria.

1997, Feb. 19 Litho. *Perf. 14x13*

780	A231	40c multicolored	1.00	.55
781	A231	50c multicolored	1.20	.65
782	A231	75c multicolored	1.75	.90
783	A231	175c multicolored	3.00	2.25
		Nos. 780-783 (4)	6.95	4.35

Birds — A232

5c, Melopsittacus undulatus. 25c, Cacatua leadbeateri leadbeateri. 50c, Amazona barbadensis. 75c, Ardea purperea. 85c, Chrysolampis mosquitus. 100c, Balearica pavonina. 110c, Pyrocephalus rubinus. 125c, Phoenicopteurus ruber. 200c, Pandion haliaetus. 225c, Ramphastos sulfuratus.

1997, Mar. 26 Litho. *Perf. 13x14*

784	A232	5c multicolored	1.10	.35
785	A232	25c multicolored	1.35	.35
786	A232	50c multicolored	1.60	.60
787	A232	75c multicolored	2.00	.80
788	A232	85c multicolored	2.10	1.00
789	A232	100c multicolored	2.40	1.20
790	A232	110c multicolored	2.40	1.20
791	A232	125c multicolored	2.50	1.45
792	A232	200c multicolored	3.50	2.25
793	A232	225c multicolored	4.00	2.60
		Nos. 784-793 (10)	22.95	11.80

Greetings Stamps — A233

No. 799A, like #794. No. 799B, Correspondence in 3 languages. No. 799C, Positivism, flower, sun. No. 799D, like #795. No. 799E, Success, rising sun. 85c, like #796. 100c, like #797. #799H, like #798. No. 799I, Love, silhouette of couple. 225c, like #799.

1997, Apr. 16

794	A233	40c Love	.55	.50
795	A233	75c Positivism	.90	.80
796	A233	85c Mother's Day	1.05	1.05
797	A233	100c Correspondence	1.15	1.15
798	A233	110c Success	1.30	1.30
799	A233	225c Congratulations	2.60	2.60
		Nos. 794-799 (6)	7.55	7.40

Booklet Stamps

Size: 21x25mm

Perf. 13x14 on 3 Sides

799A	A233	40c multicolored	.75	.75
799B	A233	40c multicolored	.75	.75
799C	A233	75c multicolored	1.15	1.15
799D	A233	75c multicolored	1.15	1.15
799E	A233	75c multicolored	1.15	1.15
799F	A233	85c multicolored	1.15	1.15
799G	A233	100c multicolored	1.60	1.60
799H	A233	110c multicolored	1.60	1.60
799I	A233	110c multicolored	1.60	1.60
799J	A233	225c multicolored	3.00	3.00
k.		Booklet pane of 10, #799A-799J + label	13.50	
		Complete booklet, #799k	13.50	

Stamps arranged in booklet out of Scott order.

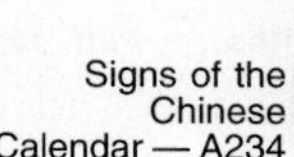

Signs of the Chinese Calendar — A234

Stylized designs.

1997, May 19 Litho. *Perf. 14x13*

800	A234	5c Rat	.25	.25
801	A234	5c Ox	.25	.25
802	A234	5c Tiger	.25	.25
803	A234	40c Rabbit	.65	.45
804	A234	40c Dragon	.65	.45
805	A234	40c Snake	.65	.45
806	A234	75c Horse	1.05	.75
807	A234	75c Goat	1.05	.75
808	A234	75c Monkey	1.05	.75
809	A234	100c Rooster	1.25	1.05
810	A234	100c Dog	1.25	1.05
811	A234	100c Pig	1.25	1.05
a.		Souvenir sheet of 12, #800-811	10.25	9.75
		Nos. 800-811 (12)	9.60	7.50

No. 811a for PACIFIC 97. Issued: 5/19/97.

Coins — A235

85c, Plaka, 2½ cent. 175c, Stuiver, 5 cent. 225c, Fuèrtè, 2½ gulden.

1997, Aug. 6 *Perf. 13x14*

812	A235	85c multi	1.15	1.00
813	A235	175c multi	2.25	1.90
814	A235	225c multi	3.00	2.50
		Nos. 812-814 (3)	6.40	5.40

A236

Shanghai '97, Intl. Stamp Exhibition — A237

15c, Nampu Grand Bridge, Shanghai. 40c, Giant panda, horiz. 75c, Tiger, New Year 1998.
90c, Buildings in downtown Shanghai.

Perf. 14x13, 13x14

1997, Nov. 19 Litho.

815	A236	15c multicolored	.85	.45
816	A237	40c multicolored	1.30	.90
817	A237	75c multicolored	1.75	1.35
		Nos. 815-817 (3)	3.90	2.70

Souvenir Sheet

818	A236	90c multicolored	3.00	2.75

No. 818 exists imperf. Value, $100.

A238

Christmas and New Year: 35c, Left panel of triptych from Roman Catholic Church, Willemstad. 150c, Champagne bottle being opened, calendar.

1997, Dec. 1 *Perf. 13x14*

819	A238	35c multicolored	.80	.40
820	A238	150c multicolored	2.00	1.60

A239

Total Solar Eclipse, Curacao: 85c, Sun partially covered by moon's shadow. 110c, Outer edge of sun showing beyond moon's shadow. 225c, Total solar eclipse.
750c, Hologram of the eclipse.

1998, Feb. 26 Litho. *Perf. 13x14*

821	A239	85c multicolored	1.45	1.20
822	A239	110c multicolored	2.00	1.40
823	A239	225c multicolored	3.50	3.00
		Nos. 821-823 (3)	6.95	5.60

Souvenir Sheet

824	A239	750c multicolored	12.50	11.50

No. 824 contains a hologram which may be damaged by soaking.

ISRAEL '98 World Stamp Exhibition — A240

Designs: 40c, Dead Sea. 75c, Zion Gate, Jerusalem. 110c, Masada.
225c, Mikvé Israel-Emanuel Synagogue, Curacao.

1998, Apr. 29 Litho. *Perf. 13x14*

825	A240	40c multicolored	.90	.70
826	A240	75c multicolored	1.10	.95
827	A240	110c multicolored	1.60	1.45
		Nos. 825-827 (3)	3.60	3.10

Souvenir Sheet

828	A240	225c multicolored	3.75	3.50

Elias Moreno Brandao & Sons, Car Dealership, 75th Anniv. — A241

Chevrolet automobiles: 40c, 1923 Superior, Elias Moreno Brandao. 55c, 1934 Roadster. 75c, 1949 Styleline Deluxe. 110c, 1957 Bel Air Convertible. 225c, 1963 Corvette "Stingray." 500c, 1970 Chevelle SS-454.

1998, May 4 *Perf. 14x13*

829	A241	40c multicolored	1.20	.55
830	A241	55c multicolored	1.30	.90
831	A241	75c multicolored	1.60	.90
832	A241	110c multicolored	2.10	1.35
833	A241	225c multicolored	3.50	3.00
834	A241	500c multicolored	8.00	6.50
		Nos. 829-834 (6)	17.70	13.20

A242

Advisory Council, 50th Anniv.: 75c, Natl. flag, natl. arms. 85c, Gavel, stars, natl. arms.

1998, June 1 Litho. *Perf. 13x14*

835	A242	75c multicolored	1.05	.85
836	A242	85c multicolored	1.20	1.05

A243

Famous People: 40c, Christina Elizabeth Flanders (1908-96). 75c, Abraham Jesurun Dz. (1839-1918). 85c, Gerrit Simeon Newton (1884-1949). 110c, Eduardo Adriana (1925-97).

1998, June 24 *Perf. 13*

837	A243	40c multicolored	.60	.55
838	A243	75c multicolored	1.05	.90
839	A243	85c multicolored	1.15	1.05
840	A243	110c multicolored	1.60	1.35
		Nos. 837-840 (4)	4.40	3.85

Mailboxes — A244

1998, July 29 Litho. *Perf. 13x14*

841	A244	15c Ireland	.35	.30
842	A244	40c Nepal	.70	.55
843	A244	75c Uruguay	1.15	.90
844	A244	85c Curacao	1.20	1.20
		Nos. 841-844 (4)	3.40	2.95

See Nos. 932-935.

A245

Privatization of Natl. Postal Service: 75c, Globe, map of North and South America, horiz. 110c, Numbers and tree on screen. 225c, #207 and #846, horiz.

1998, Aug. 5 *Perf. 13*

845	A245	75c multicolored	1.05	.90
846	A245	110c multicolored	1.60	1.35
847	A245	225c multicolored	3.00	3.00
		Nos. 845-847 (3)	5.65	5.25

A246

Endangered Species: 5c, Black rhinoceros, horiz. 75c, White-tailed hawk. 125c, White-tailed deer, horiz. 250c, Tiger.

1998, Aug. 26 *Perf. 13½*

848	A246	5c multicolored	1.20	.85
849	A246	75c multicolored	1.60	1.30
850	A246	125c multicolored	2.40	1.75
851	A246	250c multicolored	3.75	3.00
		Nos. 848-851 (4)	8.95	6.90

Intl. Year of the Ocean — A247

1998, Sept. 30 **Litho.** *Perf. 13*

852	A247	275c Mako shark	5.25	3.50
853	A247	350c Manta ray	6.25	4.25

1998 Philatelic Exhibition, The Hague, Netherlands A248

1998, Oct. 8 *Perf. 14x13*

854	A248	225c No. 213	3.00	3.00
855	A248	500c No. 218	5.75	5.75

Souvenir Sheet

856	A248	500c Nos. 61, 218	6.75	6.50

Price Waterhouse Coopers in Netherlands Antilles, 60th Anniv. — A249

Emblems, company buildings in Julianaplein, minerals: 75c, Lapis lazuli. 225c, Pyrite.

1998, Nov. 13 *Perf. 13½*

857		75c multicolored	1.60	1.60
858		225c multicolored	3.00	2.25
a.		A249 Pair, #857-858	4.50	3.75

Christmas — A250

Children's drawings: 35c, Christmas tree, vert. 150c, Mail box at Christmas.

Perf. 13x14, 14x13

1998, Dec. 1 **Litho.**

859	A250	35c multicolored	.65	.65
860	A250	150c multicolored	2.10	1.90

Avila Beach Hotel, 50th Anniv. — A251

Designs: 75c, Exterior view of hotel, Dr. Pieter Hendrik Maal. 110c, Beach, delonix regia. 225c, Mesquite tree, porposis juliflora.

1999, Feb. 3 **Litho.** *Perf. 14x13*

861	A251	75c multicolored	1.10	.90
862	A251	110c multicolored	1.60	1.35
863	A251	225c multicolored	3.00	2.75
		Nos. 861-863 (3)	5.70	5.00

A252

Designs: 75c, Rabbit, Great Wall of China. No. 865, Rabbit, Jade Pagoda, Beijing, vert. No. 866, Rabbit, landscape, vert.

Perf. 14x13, 13x14

1999, Mar. 30 **Litho.**

864	A252	75c multicolored	1.60	.90
865	A252	225c multicolored	3.75	2.60

Souvenir Sheet

Perf. 13x13½

866	A252	225c multicolored	4.50	3.50

New Year 1999 (Year of the Rabbit) and China '99, World Stamp Exhibition, Beijing.

Government Correctional Institute (GOG) for Youth, 50th Anniv. — A253

Design, traditional musical instrument: 40c, Couple dancing, wiri. 75c, Building, bamba. 85c, Man using file and vise, triangle.

Perf. 13x14, 14x13

1999, Apr. 28 **Litho.**

867	A253	40c multi, vert.	.75	.55
868	A253	75c multi, vert.	1.20	.90
869	A253	85c multi	1.35	1.10
		Nos. 867-869 (3)	3.30	2.55

Recorded History of Curacao, 500th Anniv. — A254

Curacao 500 emblem and: 75c, Ship launching. 110c, Houses on Rifwater, Otrobanda, Pasa Kontrami Bridge. 175c, #870-871. 225c, Fort Beeckenburg. 500c, #204, sailing ship.

1999, May 19 *Perf. 14x13*

870	A254	75c multicolored	1.35	.85
871	A254	110c multicolored	1.75	1.30
872	A254	175c multicolored	2.60	2.10
873	A254	225c multicolored	3.25	2.60
874	A254	500c multicolored	6.50	6.00
		Nos. 870-874 (5)	15.45	12.85

Nos. 870-874 exist imperf. Value, $120.

Wilson "Papa" Godett (1932-95), Politician — A255

1999, May 28 *Perf. 13x14*

875	A255	75c multicolored	1.25	1.00

No. 875 exists imperf. Value, $57.50.

Millennium A256

Designs: 5c, Indians, map. 10c, Indian, ship, armored horseman. 40c, Flags of islands, Autonomy monument, Curacao, autonomy document. 75c, Telephone, #5. 85c, Airplane. 100c, Oil refinery. 110c, Satellite dish, underwater cable. 125c, Tourist ship, bridge. 225c, Island residents, music box. 350c, Birds, cacti.

1999, Aug. 4 **Litho.** *Perf. 13½*

876	A256	5c multicolored	.45	.45
877	A256	10c multicolored	.45	.45
878	A256	40c multicolored	.90	.75
879	A256	75c multicolored	1.35	1.15
880	A256	85c multicolored	1.35	1.35
881	A256	100c multicolored	1.35	1.35
882	A256	110c multicolored	1.75	1.60
883	A256	125c multicolored	2.25	2.00
884	A256	225c multicolored	3.25	3.25
885	A256	350c multicolored	5.00	5.00

Size: 31x31mm

Self-Adhesive

Serpentine Die Cut 8

886	A256	5c multicolored	.45	.45
887	A256	10c multicolored	.45	.45
888	A256	40c multicolored	.90	.75
889	A256	75c multicolored	1.35	1.15
890	A256	85c multicolored	1.35	1.35
891	A256	100c multicolored	1.35	1.35
892	A256	110c multicolored	1.75	1.60
893	A256	125c multicolored	2.25	2.00
894	A256	225c multicolored	3.25	3.25
895	A256	350c multicolored	5.00	5.00
		Nos. 876-895 (20)	36.20	34.70

A257

Designs: 150c, Church of the Conversion of St. Paul, Saba. 250c, Flamingo, Bonaire. 500c, Courthouse of Philipsburg, St. Martin.

1999, Oct. 1 **Litho.** *Perf. 14x13*

896	A257	150c multicolored	3.00	1.60
897	A257	250c multicolored	3.75	2.75
898	A257	500c multicolored	6.50	5.50
		Nos. 896-898 (3)	13.25	9.85

Flowers A258

Designs: No. 899, Allamanda. No. 900, Bougainvillea. No. 901, Gardenia jasminoides. No. 902, Saintpaulia ionantha. No. 903, Cymbidium. No. 904, Strelitzia. No. 905, Cassia fistula. No. 906, Phalaenopsis. No. 907, Doritaenopsis. No. 908, Guzmania. No. 909, Caralluma hexagona. No. 910, Catharanthus roseus.

1999, Nov. 15 *Perf. 13½*

899	A258	40c multicolored	1.10	1.00
900	A258	40c multicolored	1.10	1.00
a.		Pair, #899-900	2.25	2.25
901	A258	40c multicolored	1.10	1.00
902	A258	40c multicolored	1.10	1.00
a.		Pair, #901-902	2.25	2.25
903	A258	75c multicolored	1.25	1.10
904	A258	75c multicolored	1.25	1.10
a.		Pair, #903-904	2.50	2.50
905	A258	75c multicolored	1.25	1.10
906	A258	75c multicolored	1.25	1.10
a.		Pair, #905-906	2.75	2.75
907	A258	110c multicolored	2.00	1.75
908	A258	110c multicolored	2.00	1.75
a.		Pair, #907-908	4.00	4.00
909	A258	225c multicolored	3.25	3.00
910	A258	225c multicolored	3.25	3.00
a.		Pair, #909-910	6.50	6.50
		Nos. 899-910 (12)	19.90	17.90

Christmas A259

Year 2000 A260

1999, Dec. 1 **Litho.** *Perf. 13x14*

911	A259	35c multi	.90	.40
912	A260	150c multi	2.25	1.60

Greetings Stamps — A261

#913, 40c, #918, 150c, Hearts, roses. #914, 40c, #919, 150c, Mothers, globe. #915, 40c, Father, baby, blocks. #916, 75c, Dog in gift box. #917, 110c, Butterfly, flowers in vase. #920, 225c, Hands, rings.

2000, Jan. 27 **Litho.** *Perf. 13x14*

913-920	A261	Set of 8	12.50	11.50

New Year 2000 (Year of the Dragon) — A262

2000, Feb. 28 *Perf. 14x13*

921	A262	110c shown	2.00	1.90

Souvenir Sheet

922	A262	225c Two dragons	4.50	3.25

Fauna — A263

Designs: 40c, Red eye tree toad. 75c, King penguin, vert. 85c, Killer whale, vert. 100c, African elephant, vert. 110c, Chimpanzee, vert. 225c, Indian tiger.

2000, Mar. 29 *Perf. 14x13, 13x14*

923-928	A263	Set of 6	14.00	11.50

Space — A264

Designs: 75c, Space Shuttle. No. 930, 225c, Astronaut, flag, space station.

2000, June 21 **Litho.** *Perf. 13x14*

929-930	A264	Set of 2	5.00	4.50

Souvenir Sheet

Perf. 13x13¼

931	A264	225c Colonized planet	4.50	4.50

World Stamp Expo 2000, Anaheim.

Mailbox Type of 1998

Mailboxes from: 110c, Mexico. 175c, Dubai. 350c, England. 500c, United States.

2000, Aug. 8 *Perf. 13x14*

932-935	A244	Set of 4	16.50	14.00

Nos. 932-935 exist imperf. Value, set $120.

2000 Summer Olympics, Sydney — A265

75c, Cycling. No. 937, 225c, Running.

2000, Aug. 8 **Litho.** *Perf. 13x14*

936-937	A265	Set of 2	5.25	5.00

Souvenir Sheet

938	A265	225c Swimming	4.50	4.50

Nos. 936-938 exist imperf. Value, set $200.

Social Insurance Bank, 40th Anniv. — A266

Designs: 75c, People, islands, vert. 110c, Hands. 225c, Emblem, vert.

2000, Sept. 1 *Perf. 13x14, 14x13*

939-941	A266	Set of 3	6.25	5.75

Christmas — A267

Songs: 40c, Jingle Bells, vert. 150c, We Wish You a Merry Christmas.

2000, Nov. 15 *Perf. 13x14, 14x13*

942-943	A267	Set of 2	3.25	3.25

New Year 2001 (Year of the Snake) — A268

Designs: 110c, Red milk snake. 225c, Indian cobra, vert.

2001, Jan. 17 Litho. *Perf. 14x13*
944 A268 110c multi 2.40 1.90

Souvenir Sheet
Perf. 13x14
945 A268 225c multi 4.50 4.50

Hong Kong 2001 Stamp Exhibition — A269

Designs: 25c, Birds in forest. 40c, Palm trees and waterfall. 110c, Spinner dolphins.

2001, Feb. 1 *Perf. 13x14*
946-948 A269 Set of 3 4.25 3.75

Cats and Dogs — A270

Designs: 55c, Persian shaded golden. 75c, Burmese bluepoint. 110c, Beagle and American wirehair. 175c, Golden retriever. 225c, German shepherd. 750c, British shorthair black-silver marble.

2001, Mar. 7 Litho. *Perf. 13x14*
949-954 A270 Set of 6 24.00 20.00

Ships — A271

Designs: 110c, Z. M. Mars. 275c, Z. M. Alphen. 350c, Z. M. Curaçao, horiz. 500c, Schooner Pioneer, horiz.

2001, Apr. 26 *Perf. 13x14, 14x13*
955-958 A271 Set of 4 19.00 17.50

Fedjai the Postal Worker — A272

Fedjai: 5c, On bicycle. 40c, With children. 75c, Looking at nest in mailbox. 85c, Talking with woman. 100c, Chased atop mailbox by dog. 110c, Looking at boy's stamp album.

2001, June 5 Litho. *Perf. 13x14*
959-964 A272 Set of 6 8.75 7.50

See No. 1012.

Cave Bats — A273

Designs: 85c, Map of bat species in Kueba Bosá. 110c, Leptonycteris nivalis curasaoe. 225c, Glosophaga elongata.

2001, Aug. 20 Litho. *Perf. 14x13*
965-967 A273 Set of 3 7.50 6.25

Birds A274

No. 968: a, 10c, Trochilus polytmus. b, 85c, Pelecanus onocrotalus. c, 110c, Erythrura gouldiae. d, 175c, Passerina ciris. e, 250c, Fratercula arctica. f, 375c, Anhinga anhinga.

2001, Sept. 28 *Perf. 12¾x13½*
968 A274 Block of 6, #a-f 17.50 16.50

Philipsburg Methodist Church, 150th Anniv. — A275

Map of St. Maarten and: 75c, Church building. 110c, Bibles.

2001, Oct. 19 *Perf. 14x13*
969-970 A275 Set of 2 3.50 3.25

Christmas and New Year's Day — A276

Designs: 40c, Clock, people from 8 countries. 150c, Dove, poinsettias, baby Jesus, and people from 4 countries, vert.

Perf. 13½x12¾, 12¾x13½
2001, Nov. 15 Litho.
971-972 A276 Set of 2 3.50 3.00

Wedding of Prince Willem-Alexander and Máxima Zorreguieta — A277

Designs: 75c, Prince. 110c, Máxima.
No. 975: a, 2.25f, Prince. b, 2.75f, Máxima.

2002, Feb. 2 Litho. *Perf. 12¾x14*
973-974 A277 Set of 2 3.25 3.00

Souvenir Sheet
Perf. 12¾x13½
975 A277 Sheet of 2, #a-b 8.75 7.50

New Year 2002 (Year of the Horse) — A278

Designs: 25c, Horse rearing. 95c, Horse's head.

2002, Mar. 1 *Perf. 12¾x14*
976 A278 25c multi 1.25 1.25

Souvenir Sheet
Perf. 12¾x13½
977 A278 95c multi 3.00 2.50

Flora & Fauna — A279

Designs: 50c, Chlorostilbon mellisugus and Passiflora foetida, vert. 95c, Anolis lineatus and Cordia sebestena. 120c, Odonata. 145c, Coenobita clypeatus. 285c, Polistes versicolor, vert.

Perf. 12¾x13½, 13½x12¾
2002, Mar. 27 Litho.
978-982 A279 Set of 5 11.00 10.00

Butterflies — A280

Designs: 25c, Dryas iulia, vert. 145c, Danaus plexippus. 400c, Mechanitis polymnia. 500c, Pyrhapygopsis socrates.

Perf. 12¾x13½, 13½x12¾
2002, May 22 Litho.
983-986 A280 Set of 4 17.50 16.50

Fedjai the Postal Worker Type of 2001

Fedjai: 10c, Jumping rope with children, horiz. 55c, Scolding dog. 95c, Delivering letter to child. 240c, Helping elderly lady across street.

Perf. 13¾x12¾, 12¾x13¾
2002, July 31
987-990 A272 Set of 4 8.25 8.25

Amphilex 2002 Intl. Stamp Exhibition, Amsterdam — A281

Details from the 1885 version of "The Potato Eaters," by Vincent Van Gogh: 70c, 95c, 145c, 240c.
550c, Entire painting, horiz.

Perf. 12¾x13½
2002, Aug. 26 Litho.
991-994 A281 Set of 4 8.75 8.75

Souvenir Sheet
Perf. 14x12¾
995 A281 550c multi 8.75 8.75

Orchids — A282

Designs: 95c, Wingfieldara casseta. 285c, Cymbidium Magna Charta. 380c, Brassolaeliocattleya. 750c, Miltonia spectabilis.

2002, Sept. 27 *Perf. 12¾x14*
996-999 A282 Set of 4 22.50 21.00

Christmas and New Year — A283

Designs: 95c, Christmas tree decorations. 240c, Lanterns.

2002, Nov. 15 *Perf. 14x12¾*
1000-1001 A283 Set of 2 5.00 4.75

Birds A284

No. 1002: a, 5c, Buteogallus meridionalis. b, 20c, Capito niger. c, 30c, Ara macao. d, 35c, Jacamerops aurea. e, 70c, Florisuga mellivora. f, 85c, Haematoderus militaris. g, 90c, Aratinga aurea. h, 95c, Psarocolius viridis. i, 100c, Sturnella magna, horiz. j, 145c, Aratinga solstitialis, horiz. k, 240c, Trogon viridis. l, 285c, Rhamphastos tucanus.

2002, Dec. 11 Litho. *Perf. 13x14*
1002 A284 Block of 12, #a-l 20.00 20.00

New Year 2003 (Year of the Ram) — A285

Chinese character and: 25c, Ram's head. 95c, Ram.

2003, Feb. 3
1003 A285 25c multi 1.25 1.25

Souvenir Sheet
1004 A285 95c multi 2.40 1.90

Butterflies — A286

No. 1005: a, 5c, Rhetus arcius, vert. b, 10c, Evenus teresina. c, 25c, Bhutanitis thaidina. d, 30c, Semomesia capanea. e, 45c, Papilio machaon. f, 55c, Papilio multicaudata, vert. g, 65c, Graphium weiskei, vert. h, 95c, Ancyluris formosissima venabalis, vert. i, 100c, Euphaedra neophron. j, 145c, Ornithoptera goliath samson. k, 275c, Ancyluris colubra, vert. l, 350c, Papilio lorquinianus, vert.

Perf. 12¾x14 (vert. stamps), 14x12¾
2003, Apr. 23 Litho.
1005 A286 Block of 12, #a-l 21.00 20.00

Printed in sheets of 2 blocks separated by a central gutter.

Miniature Sheet

Musical Instruments — A287

No. 1006: a, 20c, Trumpet. b, 75c, Percussion instruments. c, 145c, Tenor saxophone. d, 285c, Double bass.

2003, May 28 *Perf. 12¾x14*
1006 A287 Sheet of 4, #a-d 7.50 7.50

Johann Enschedé and Sons, Printers, 300th Anniv. — A288

No. 1007: a, 70c, 25-florin bank note, 1827. b, 95c, #4. c, 145c, Revenue stamp. d, 240c, Portion of 1967 bank note.
550c, Enschedé headquarters, Netherlands.

2003, June 3
1007 A288 Sheet of 4, #a-d 8.75 8.75

Souvenir Sheet
1008 A288 550c multi 7.50 7.50

Bank of the Netherlands Antilles, 175th Anniv. — A289

Designs: 95c, Portion of 10-guilder banknote with serial number magnified. 145c, Road map, Bank headquarters. 285c, Early bank document, vert.

Perf. 14x12¾, 12¾x14

2003, June 26

1009-1011 A289 Set of 3 7.00 7.00

Fedjai, the Postal Worker Type of 2001

Miniature Sheet

No. 1012: a, 30c, Fedjai giving gift to Angelina. b, 95c, Fedjai and Angelina at wedding. c, 145c, Fedjai taking pregnant wife on bicycle, horiz. d, 240c, Fedjai shows son to co-workers.

Perf. 12¾x14, 14x12¾ (#1012c)

2003, June 31

1012 A272 Sheet of 4, #a-d 7.50 6.25

Ships A290

No. 1013: a, 5c, Egyptian boat, 15th cent. B.C. b, 5c, Ship of King Tutankhamen. c, 35c, Picture from Greek vase depicting Ulysses and the Sirens. d, 35c, Egyptian river boat. e, 40c, Greek dromond. f, 40c, Illustration from 15th cent. edition of Virgil's Aeneid. g, 60c, Javanese fusta. h, 60c, Greek trade ship. i, 75c, Venetian cog, 16th cent. j, 75c, Mora from Bayeux Tapestry. k, 85c, HMS Pembroke, ship of Capt. James Cook, vert. l, 85c, Savannah, first transatlantic steamship, 1819, vert.

Illustration reduced.

Perf. 14x12¾, 12¾x14 (vert. stamps)

2003, Aug. 7

1013 A290 Block of 12, #a-l 10.00 9.00

Miniature Sheets

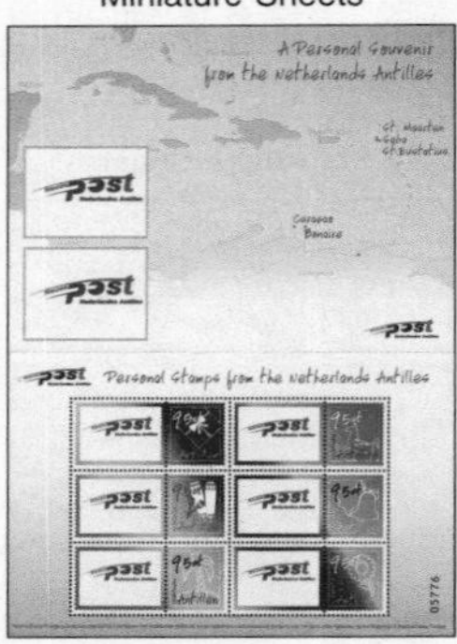

Personalized Stamps — A291

Designs: Nos. 1014a, 1015a, Gift. Nos. 1014b, 1015b, Rocking horse. Nos. 1014c, 1015c, Conga drums. Nos. 1014d, 1015d, Bells. Nos. 1014e, 1015e, Palm tree. Nos. 1014f, 1015f, Flower.

2003, Sept. 17 Litho. ***Perf. 13¼x14***

1014 A291 95c Sheet of 6, #a-f, + 6 labels 10.00 9.00

1015 A291 145c Sheet of 6, #a-f, + 6 labels 15.00 14.00

Labels could be personalized. Nos. 1014-1015 each sold for $6 and $8.50 respectively in US funds.

Cats A292

No. 1016: a, 5c, Bombay. b, 20c, Persian sealpoint. c, 25c, British shorthair blotchy. d, 50c, British blue. e, 65c, Persian chinchilla. f, 75c, Tonkinese red point. g, 85c, Balinese lilac tabbypoint. h, 95c, Persian shaded cameo. i, 100c, Burmilla. j, 145c, Chocolate tortie shaded silver eastern shorthair. k, 150c, Devon Rex silver tabby. l, 285c, Persian black tabby.

2003, Sept. 29 ***Perf. 12¾x14***

1016 A292 Block of 12, #a-l 18.00 17.00

Souvenir Sheet

Christmas and New Year's Day — A293

No. 1017 — Cacti with faces and Christmas lights and: a, 75c, Star. b, 240c, Clock.

2003, Nov. 17 Litho. ***Perf. 13x14***

1017 A293 Sheet of 2, #a-b 3.75 3.75

Airport Code and Local Attraction A294

Curves and Lines A295

Designs: 50c, BON (Bonaire), slave hut. 75c, CUR (Curaçao), Handelskade, Willemstad. 95c, SAB (Saba), Holy Rosary Roman Catholic Church, Hell's Gate, Anglican Church, Valley. 120c, EUX (St. Eustatius), Simon Docker House, Fort Orange. 145c, SXM (St. Maarten), bird at sunset. 240c, CUR, Queen Emma Bridge. 285c, SXM, Simpson Bay.

2003, Nov. 27 ***Perf. 13½x12¾***

1018	A294	50c multi	.65	.65
1019	A294	75c multi	1.00	1.00
1020	A294	95c multi	1.20	1.20
1021	A294	120c multi	1.45	1.45
1022	A294	145c multi	1.60	1.60
1023	A294	240c multi	2.75	2.75
1024	A294	285c multi	3.25	3.25
1025	A295	380c multi	4.25	4.25
		Nos. 1018-1025 (8)	16.15	16.15

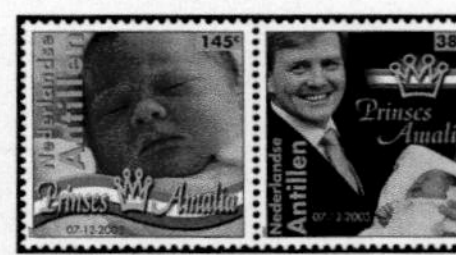

Birth of Princess Catharina-Amalia, Dec. 7, 2003 — A296

No. 1026: a, 145c, Princess Catharina-Amalia. b, 380c, Prince Willem-Alexander and Princess Catharina-Amalia.

2004, Jan. 16 ***Perf. 13½x13¾***

1026 A296 Horiz. pair, #a-b 5.75 5.75

c. Miniature sheet, #1026a, 1026b + central label 5.75 5.75

New Year 2004 (Year of the Monkey) — A297

Designs: 95c, Golden snub-nosed monkey. 145c, Monkey holding peach, on fan.

2004, Jan. 21 ***Perf. 13x13½***

1027 A297 95c multi 2.00 2.00

Souvenir Sheet

1028 A297 145c multi + 2 labels 2.50 2.50

Houses and Mansions — A298

No. 1029: a, 10c, Belvedère, L. B Smithplein 3. b, 25c, Hoogstraat 27. c, 35c, Landhuis Brievengat. d, 65c, Scharlooweg 102. e, 95c, Hoogstraat 21-25. f, 145c, Villa Maria, Van den Brandhofstraat 3 t/m 6. g, 275c, Werfstraat 6. h, 350c, Landhuis Ronde Klip.

2004, Feb. 20 ***Perf. 13½x13***

1029 A298 Block of 8, #a-h 11.50 11.50

See No. 1066.

Wild Animals A299

No. 1030: a, 5c, Loxodonta africana. b, 10c, Loxodonta africana, diff. c, 25c, Loxodonta africana, diff. d, 35c, Pan troglodytes. e, 45c, Pan troglodytes, diff. f, 55c, Pan troglodytes, diff. g, 65c, Ursus maritimus. h, 95c, Ursus maritimus, diff. i, 100c, Ursus maritimus, diff. j, 145c, Panthera leo. k, 275c, Panthera leo, diff. l, 350c, Panthera leo, diff.

2004, Mar. 31

1030 A299 Block of 12, #a-l 16.00 16.00

Transportation — A300

No. 1031: a, 10c, Diesel locomotive, 1977. b, 55c, Water dealer and cart, 1900. c, 75c, 1903 Ford Model A. d, 85c, Oil tanker, 2004. e, 95c, 1903 Wright Flyer. f, 145c Penny Farthing bicycles, 1871.

2004, Apr. 27

1031 A300 Block of 6, #a-f 7.50 7.50

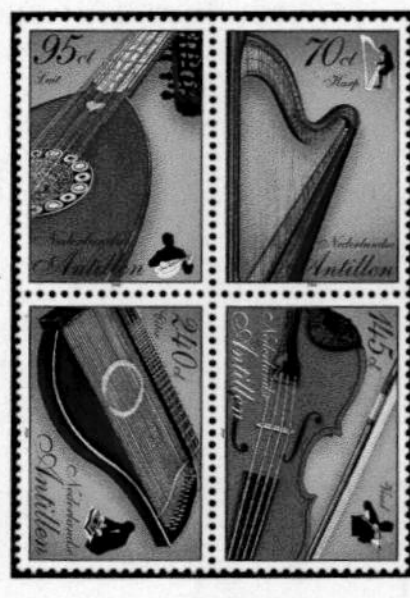

String Instruments A301

No. 1032: a, 70c, Harp. b, 95c, Lute. c, 145c, Violin, horiz. d, 240c, Zither, horiz.

2004, May 26 ***Perf. 13x13½, 13½x13***

1032 A301 Block of 4, #a-d 7.50 7.50

Dogs A302

No. 1033: a, 5c, Miniature pinscher. b, 5c, Pomeranian. c, 35c, Longhaired teckel. d, 35c, Shih tzu. e, 40c, Boxer. f, 40c, Jack Russell terrier. g, 60c, Basset hound. h, 60c, Braque de l'Ariege. i, 75c, Afghan hound. j, 75c, Old English sheepdog (bobtail). k, 85c, Entelbucher Sennen. l, 85c, Mastiff.

2004, June 22 ***Perf. 13x13½***

1033 A302 Block of 12, #a-l 12.50 12.50

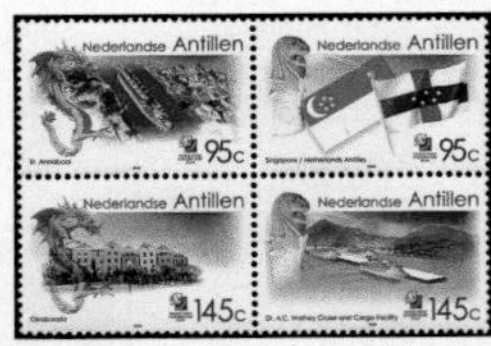

World Stamp Championship 2004, Singapore — A303

No. 1034: a, 95c, Ship in St. Annabay Harbor, Curaçao, dragon. b, 95c, Flags of Singapore and Netherlands Antilles, lion. c, 145c, Brionplein houses, Curaçao, dragon. d, 145c, Ships at Dr. A. C. Wathey Cruise and Cargo Facility, St. Maarten, lion.

500c, Like No. 1034b.

2004, Aug. 23 ***Perf. 13½x13***

1034 A303 Block of 4, #a-d 5.75 5.75

Souvenir Sheet

1035 A303 500c multi 5.75 5.75

Fish and Ducks — A304

No. 1036: a, Pomacanthus paru. b, Epinephelus guttatus. c, Mycteroperca interstitialis. d, Holacanthus isabelita. e, Epinephelus itajara. f, Holacanthus ciliaris. g, Anas americana, Sphyraena barracuda. h, Anas discors. i, Anas bahamensis. j, Aythya affinis.

2004, Sept. 28

1036	Block of 10	15.00	15.00
a.	A304 30c multi	.65	.65
b.	A304 65c multi	.80	.80
c.	A304 70c multi	.90	.90
d.	A304 75c multi	.90	.90
e.	A304 85c multi	1.00	1.00
f.	A304 95c multi	1.05	1.05
g.	A304 100c multi	1.05	1.05
h.	A304 145c multi	1.60	1.60
i.	A304 250c multi	2.60	2.60
j.	A304 285c multi	3.00	3.00

Birds — A305

Designs: 10c, Icterus icterus. 95c, Coereba flaveola. 100c, Zonotrichia capensis. 145c, Sterna hirundo. 250c, Phoenicopterus ruber. 500c, Buteo albicaudatus.

2004, Oct. 8

1037-1042 A305 Set of 6 15.00 15.00

Miniature Sheets

Coats of Arms and Flags A306

Nos. 1043 and 1044 — Arms of: a, Bonaire. b, Curacao. c, Saba. d, St. Eustatius. e, St. Maarten. f, Flags of Islands of Netherlands Antilles.

2004, Oct. Litho. ***Perf. 13½x13¾***

1043 A306 95c Sheet of 6, #a-f, + 6 labels *12.50 12.50*

1044 A306 145c Sheet of 6, #a-f, + 6 labels *20.00 20.00*

Labels on Nos. 1043-1044 could be personalized. The two sheets together sold for €12.42.

Turtles — A307

Designs: 100c, Loggerhead turtle. 145c, Kemp's Ridley turtle. 240c, Green turtle. 285c, Olive Ridley turtle. 380c, Hawksbill turtle. 500c, Leatherback turtle.

2004, Dec. 10 Litho. ***Perf. 13½x13***
1045-1050 A307 Set of 6 22.00 22.00

Buildings A308

Beach Scene A309

Self-Adhesive

2004 Litho. ***Die Cut***
1051 A308 145c multi 3.50 3.50
1052 A309 145c multi 3.50 3.50
a. Horiz. pair, #1051-1052 7.00

Nos. 1051-1052 were printed in sheets of 10 containing five of each stamp at the right of the sheet. At the left of the sheet are three stamp-like vignettes lacking die cutting that were not valid for postage. The spaces at the right of the stamps where the birds are shown in the illustration was intended for personalization by customers on cruise ships that came to St. Maarten or Curacao. The three stamp-like vignettes at the left of the sheet also show the same personalized picture. Four different sheets, each depicting different birds in the space for personalization on each stamp and the three vignettes at the left of the sheet, were created as exemplars. The sheets, depicting birds or a personalized image, sold for $20 in US currency. The stamps were for postage for postcards mailed anywhere in the world.

Flowers — A310

Designs: 65c, Hibiscus rosa sinensis. 76c, Plumbago auriculata. 97c, Tecoma stans. 100c, Ixora coccinea. 122c, Catharanthus roseus. 148c, Lantana camara. 240c, Tradescantia pallida. 270c, Nerium oleander. 285c, Plumeria obtusa. 350c, Bougainvillea spectabilis.

2005, Jan. 3 Litho. ***Perf. 13½x13***
1053 A310 65c multi .80 .80
1054 A310 76c multi .90 .90
1055 A310 97c multi 1.05 1.05
1056 A310 100c multi 1.15 1.15
1057 A310 122c multi 1.30 1.30
1058 A310 148c multi 1.60 1.60
1059 A310 240c multi 2.50 2.50
1060 A310 270c multi 3.00 3.00
1061 A310 285c multi 3.00 3.00
1062 A310 350c multi 3.75 3.75
Nos. 1053-1062 (10) 19.05 19.05

New Year 2005 (Year of the Rooster) — A311

Designs: 145c, Rooster and Chinese character. 500c, Two roosters.

2005, Feb. 9 ***Perf. 13x13½***
1063 A311 145c multi 1.90 1.90

Souvenir Sheet

1064 A311 500c multi 5.75 5.75

Souvenir Sheet

Queen Beatrix, 25th Anniv. of Reign A312

Photos: a, Coronation, 1980. b, Giving speech, 1991. c, With Nelson Mandela, 1999. d, Visiting colonies, 1999. e, At European Parliament, 2004.

2005, Apr. 30 ***Perf. 13¼x13¾***
1065 A312 Sheet of 5 13.50 13.50
a. 50c multi .75 .75
b. 97c multi 1.05 1.05
c. 145c multi 1.50 1.50
d. 285c multi 3.00 3.00
e. 550c multi 5.75 5.75

Houses & Mansions Type of 2004

No. 1066: a, 10c, Scharlooweg 76. b, 21c, Landhuis Zeelandia. c, 25c, Berg Altena. d, 35c, Landhuis Dokterstuin. e, 97c, Landhuis Santa Martha. f, 148c, Landhuis Seri Papaya. g, 270c, Landhuis Rooi Katooje. h, 300c, Plaza Horacio Hoyer 19.

2005, May 31 ***Perf. 13½x13***
1066 A298 Block of 8, #a-h 10.50 10.50

Paintings by Vincent van Gogh A313

No. 1067: a, 10c, Vase with Fourteen Sunflowers, detail. b, 65c, Sunflowers, detail. c, 80c, Self-portrait. d, 120c, Sunflowers, detail, diff. e, 150c, Vase with Fourteen Sunflowers. f, 175c, Joseph Roulin.
500c, Sunflowers, detail, diff.

2005, June 16 ***Perf. 13x13½***
1067 A313 Block of 6, #a-f 10.00 10.00

Souvenir Sheet

1068 A313 500c multi 8.00 8.00

Otrobanda Section of Willemstad, 300th Anniv. (in 2007) — A314

No. 1069: a, 100c, Breedestraat. b, 150c, Wharf area. c, 285c, Rifwater. d, 500c, Brionplein bus stop.

2005, July 28 ***Perf. 13½x13***
1069 A314 Block of 4, #a-d 12.00 12.00

See Nos. 1108-1111, 1157-1160.

Fruit — A315

2005, Aug. 31
1070 Block of 10 15.00 15.00
a. A315 25c Papaya .50 .50
b. A315 45c Pomegranates .65 .65
c. A315 70c Mango .80 .80
d. A315 75c Bananas .90 .90
e. A315 85c Cashews 1.00 1.00
f. A315 97c Soursops 1.05 1.05
g. A315 145c Tamarinds 1.60 1.60
h. A315 193c Watermelons 2.00 2.00
i. A315 270c Gennips 3.00 3.00
j. A315 300c Sea grapes 3.25 3.25

See Nos. 1247-1256.

Worldwide Fund for Nature (WWF) — A316

No. 1071: a, 51c, Blushing star coral. b, 148c, Rose coral. c, 270c, Smooth flower coral. d, 750c, Symmetrical brain coral.

2005, Sept. 29
1071 A316 Block of 4, #a-d 14.00 14.00

Musical Instruments A317

Designs: 55c, Bandoneon. 97c, Bagpipe, vert. 145c, Vina. 195c, Samisen, vert. 240c, Shofar. 285c, Kaha di òrgel, vert.

2005, Nov. 8 ***Perf. 13½x13, 13x13½***
1072-1077 A317 Set of 6 13.00 13.00

A318

Santa Claus and: 10c, Children's hands. 97c, Children, horiz. 148c, Ornament, horiz. 580c, Chair.

Perf. 13x13½, 13½x13
2005, Nov. 17
1078-1081 A318 Set of 4 9.50 9.50

Christmas.

A319

Designs: 97c, Aerial view of St. Elizabeth Hospital, Willemstad. 145c, Stained glass window in hospital chapel. 300c, Entrance to first community hospital.

2005, Dec. 2 ***Perf. 13x13½***
1082-1084 A319 Set of 3 6.25 6.25

St. Elizabeth Hospital, 150th anniv.

New Year 2006 (Year of the Dog) — A320

Chinese character and: 100c, Porcelain dogs. 149c, Various dog breeds.
500c, Dog and zodiac animals.

2006, Jan. 30 ***Perf. 13½x13***
1085-1086 A320 Set of 2 3.25 3.25

Souvenir Sheet

1087 A320 500c multi 5.75 5.75

Equines — A321

No. 1088: a, Turkmenian Kulan. b, Rhineland heavy draft horse. c, Donkey. d, Mule. e, Hanoverian and Arabian horses.

Perf. 13¼x12¾
2006, Feb. 24 Litho.
1088 Horiz. strip of 5 14.00 14.00
a. A321 50c multi .65 .65
b. A321 100c multi 1.05 1.05
c. A321 149c multi 1.60 1.60
d. A321 285c multi 3.00 3.00
e. A321 550c multi 6.00 6.00

Frogs — A322

Designs: 55c, Hyla cinerea. 100c, Dendrobates tinctorius. 149c, Dendrobates azureus. 405c, Epipedobates tricolor.

2006, Mar. 10 ***Perf. 13¼x12¾***
1089-1092 A322 Set of 4 9.50 9.50

Butterflies — A323

Designs: 24c, Danaus chrysippus. 53c, Prepona praeneste. 100c, Caligo uranus. 149c, Ituna lamirus. 285c, Euphaedra gausape. 335c, Morpho hecuba.

2006, Apr. 7
1093-1098 A323 Set of 6 11.50 11.50

Orchids — A324

No. 1099: a, Brassolaeliocattleya Susan Harry M. G. R. b, Miltoniopsis Jean Sabourin. c, Promenaea xanthina Sylvan Sprite. d, Paphiopedilum Streathamense Wedgewood, vert. e, Cattleya chocoensis Linden, vert. f, Disa kewensis Rita Helen, vert.

Perf. 13¼x12¾, 12¾x13¼ (vert. stamps)
2006, Apr. 26
1099 Block of 6 22.50 22.50
a. A324 153c multi 1.90 1.90
b. A324 240c multi 2.60 2.60
c. A324 285c multi 3.25 3.25
d. A324 295c multi 3.25 3.25
e. A324 380c multi 4.00 4.00
f. A324 500c multi 5.25 5.25

Automobiles A325

Designs: 51c, 1976 MGB. 100c, 1963 Studebaker Avanti. 149c, 1953 Pegaso Cabriolet. 153c, 1939 Delage Aerosport. 195c, 1924 Hispano-Suiza Boulogne. 750c, 1903 Pierce Arrow Motorette.

2006, May 10 ***Perf. 13¼x12¾***
1100-1105 A325 Set of 6 16.00 16.00

Washington 2006 World Philatelic Exhibition — A326

No. 1106: a, 100c, Mailboxes of United States and Netherlands Antilles. b, 100c, Queen Emma Bridge, Curaçao, George Washington Bridge, New York and New Jersey. c, 149c, UPU emblem. d, 149c, Fokker F18-Snip, Fokker F4 airplanes.

405c, U.S. Capitol, Palace of the Governor of the Netherlands Antilles.

2006, May 26
1106 A326 Block of 4, #a-d 5.75 5.75

Souvenir Sheet

1107 A326 405c multi 4.75 4.75

Otrobanda Type of 2005

Designs: 100c, Hoogstraat. 149c, Emmabrug. 335c, Pasa Kontrami. 500c, Seaman's Home.

2006, June 16
1108-1111 A314 Set of 4 11.50 11.50

Greetings — A327

Designs: 52c, Bless you. 55c, Love. 77c, All the best. 95c, Regards. 1.00g, Go for it. 1.49g, Tolerance. 1.53g, Positivism. 2.85g, Keep on going. 3.35g, Success. 4.05g, Be good.

2006, July 31
1112-1121 A327 Set of 10 18.50 18.50

See No. 1239-1245.

Birds — A328

No. 1122: a, Taeniopygia guttata. b, Parus caeruleus, vert. c, Pitta genus. d, Pyrrhula pyrrhula, vert. e, Calospiza fastuosa. f, Cosmopsarus regius, vert. g, Coracias caudatus, vert. h, Merops apiaster, vert. i, Icterus nigrogularis. j, Dendrocopus major, vert. k, Amazona barbadensis. l, Alcedo atthis, vert.

Perf. 13¼x12¾, 12¾x13¼ (vert. stamps)

2006, Aug. 18

1122	Block of 12	9.50	9.50
a.-b.	A328 5c Either single	.60	.60
c.-d.	A328 35c Either single	.60	.60
e.-f.	A328 60c Either single	.60	.60
g.-h.	A328 75c Either single	.65	.65
i.-j.	A328 85c Either single	.75	.75
k.-l.	A328 100c Either single	.90	.90

Miniature Sheets

Personalized Stamps — A329

Nos. 1123 and 1124: a, Dog, "Thank you." b, Flower, "Missing you." c, Hearts, "Love you." d, Cat, "Hello." e, Teddy bear, "Hugs & kisses." f, Dolphin, "Wish you were here."

Perf. 13¼x13¾

2006, Aug. 26 **Litho.**

Stamps Inscribed "Local Mail"

1123 A329 (1g) Sheet of 6, #a-f, + 6 labels 11.50 11.50

Stamps Inscribed "International Mail"

1124 A329 (1.49g) Sheet of 6, #a-f, + 6 labels 17.00 17.00

On day of issue, No. 1123 sold for 10g, and No. 1124 sold for 15g. Labels could be personalized. Labels shown are generic.

Rembrandt (1606-69), Painter A330

No. 1125: a, 70c, The Nightwatch (detail of girl). b, 100c, De Staalmeesters. c, 153c, The Jewish Bride (detail). d, 285c, Self-portrait.
550c, The Nightwatch (detail of men).

Perf. 12¾x13¼

2006, Sept. 28 **Litho.**
1125 A330 Block of 4, #a-d 7.50 7.50

Souvenir Sheet

1126 A330 550c multi 7.00 7.00

Souvenir Sheet

Royal Visit of Queen Beatrix A331

No. 1127 — Various photos of Queen Beatrix with background colors of: a, 149c, Red. b, 285c, Blue. c, 335c, Yellow. d, 750c, Orange.

2006, Nov. 13 ***Perf. 13¼x12¾***
1127 A331 Sheet of 4, #a-d 17.00 17.00

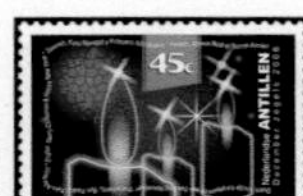

Christmas — A332

Designs: 45c, Candles. 100c, Bells. 149c, Candles. 215c, Bells. 285c, Steeple. 380c, Flower.

2006, Nov. 15
1128-1133 A332 Set of 6 13.00 13.00

Fauna — A333

No. 1134: a, Cacatua leadbeateri leadbeateri. b, Aptenocytes patagonica. c, Pan troglodytes. d, Stenella longirostris. e, Anolis lineatus and Cordia sebestina, horiz. f, Passerina ciris. g, Dryas lulia. h, Bombay cat. i, Epinephelus guttatus, horiz. j, Panthera leo, horiz. k, Pomeranian dog. l, Hawksbill turtle, horiz.

Perf. 12¾x13¼, 13¼x12¾

2007, Jan. 26 **Litho.**

1134	Block of 12	15.50	15.50
a.	A333 3c multi	.40	.40
b.	A333 25c multi	.45	.45
c.	A333 53c multi	.65	.65
d.	A333 60c multi	.75	.75
e.	A333 80c multi	.90	.90
f.	A333 81c multi	.90	.90
g.	A333 95c multi	1.10	1.10
h.	A333 106c multi	1.20	1.20
i.	A333 145c multi	1.60	1.60
j.	A333 157c multi	1.60	1.60
k.	A333 161c multi	1.60	1.60
l.	A333 240c multi	2.50	2.50

New Year 2007 (Year of the Pig) — A334

Designs: 104c, Berkshire pig. 155c, Wart hog.
500c, Pig, vert.

2007, Feb. 20 ***Perf. 13¼x12¾***
1135-1136 A334 Set of 2 3.00 3.00

Souvenir Sheet

Perf. 12¾x13¼

1137 A334 500c multi 5.75 5.75

Islands — A335

Designs: 1c, Flag of Bonaire, divers and marine life. 2c, Flag of Curaçao, royal poinciana flowers. 3c, Flag of Saba, The Bottom. 4c, Flag of Statia (St. Eustatius), cannons at Fort Orange. 5c, Flag of St. Maarten, cruise ship and pier. 104c, Map of Bonaire, flamingos, horiz. 285c, Map of Curaçao, Chobolobo Landhouse, laraha tree, horiz. 335c, Map of Saba, houses, horiz. 405c, Map of Statia, oil storage tanks, horiz. 500c, Map of St. Maarten, Guavaberry Emporium, horiz.

Perf. 12¾x13¼, 13¼x12¾

2007, Mar. 1

1138	A335	1c multi	.25	.25
1139	A335	2c multi	.25	.25
1140	A335	3c multi	.25	.25
1141	A335	4c multi	.25	.25
1142	A335	5c multi	.25	.25
1143	A335	104c multi	1.25	1.25
1144	A335	285c multi	3.50	3.50
1145	A335	335c multi	4.00	4.00
1146	A335	405c multi	4.75	4.75
1147	A335	500c multi	6.00	6.00
	Nos. 1138-1147 (10)		20.75	20.75

See Nos. 1221-1226.

Ananzi the Spider — A336

No. 1148 — Ananzi with: a, Turtle. b, Shark. c, Parrot. d, Cow. e, Dog. f, Goat. g, Chicken. h, Donkey.

2007, Mar. 21 ***Perf. 13¼x12¾***
1148 Block of 8 10.00 10.00
a.-h. A336 104c Any single 1.25 1.25

Saba Lace Designs — A337

Various lace designs with background colors of: 59c, Red. 80c, Green. 95c, Blue. 104c, Red. 155c, Green. 159c, Blue.

2007, Apr. 20 ***Perf. 12¾x13¼***
1149-1154 A337 Set of 6 7.50 7.50

Marine Life — A338

No. 1155: a, School of fish and sea floor. b, Portuguese man-of-war. c, Coral reef. d, Sea turtle. e, Sea anemones. f, Fish.

2007, May 22

1155	Block of 6	18.00	18.00
a.	A338 104c multi	1.00	1.00
b.	A338 155c multi	1.45	1.45
c.	A338 195c multi	1.75	1.75
d.	A338 335c multi	3.25	3.25
e.	A338 405c multi	3.75	3.75
f.	A338 525c multi	4.75	4.75

Fruits and Vegetables — A339

No. 1156: a, Grapes, Brussels sprouts, tomatoes, peppers and bananas. b, Pumpkins. c, Cucumber, tomatoes, corn, leeks. d, Strawberries, orange, peaches, pineapple. e, Avocados, horiz. f, Lemons, horiz. g, Peppers, corn, potato, mushrooms, horiz. h, Mangos, horiz.

Perf. 12¾x13¼, 13¼x12¾

2007, June 19

1156	Block of 8	11.50	11.50
a.	A339 10c multi	.30	.30
b.	A339 25c multi	.30	.30
c.	A339 35c multi	.40	.40
d.	A339 65c multi	.70	.70
e.	A339 95c multi	1.00	1.00
f.	A339 145c multi	1.60	1.60
g.	A339 275c multi	2.75	2.75
h.	A339 350c multi	3.50	3.50

Otrabanda Type of 2005

Designs: 104c, Brionplein Square. 155c, Jopi Building and Hotel Otrabanda. 285c, Kura Hulanda. 380c, Luna Blou.

2007, July 26 ***Perf. 13¼x12¾***
1157-1160 A314 Set of 4 9.50 9.50

Nature A340

No. 1161: a, 30c, Nautilus shell. b, 65c, Turtles on beach. c, 70c, Grasshopper. d, 75c, Cactus. e, 85c, Swamp. f, 95c, Bird on cactus. g, 104c, Surf spray at rocks. h, 145c, Plants near water. i, 250c, Rainbow in rainforest. j, 285c, Sun on horizon.

Perf. 12¾x 13¼

2007, Aug. 22 **Litho.**
1161 A340 Block of 10, #a-j 13.00 13.00

Paintings by Dutch Artists A341

No. 1162: a, 104c, Portrait of a Man (probably Nicolaes Hasselaer), by Frans Hals. b, 104c, Wedding of Isaak Abrahamsz Massa and Beatrix van der Lean, by Hals. c, 155c, The Merry Drinker, by Hals. d, 155c, Serenade, by Judith Leyster.
550c, The Meagre Company, by Hals, horiz.

2007, Sept. 20 ***Perf. 12¾x13¼***
1162 A341 Block of 4, #a-d 7.00 7.00

Souvenir Sheet
Perf. 13¼x12¾

1163 A341 550c multi 6.25 6.25

Dutch Royalty A342

No. 1164: a, 50c, Queen Emma (1858-1934). b, 104c, Queen Wilhelmina (1880-1962). c, 155c, Queen Juliana (1909-2004). d, 285c, Queen Beatrix. e, 380c, Princess Máxima. f, 550c, Princess Catharina-Amalia.

2007, Oct. 10 ***Perf. 12¾x13¼***
1164 A342 Block of 6, #a-f 15.50 15.50

Christmas and New Year — A343

Designs: 48c, Candle. 104c, Gifts under Christmas tree. 155c, Musical notes and song lyrics, horiz. 215c, "2008" above "2007," horiz.

Perf. 12¾x13¼, 13¼x12¾
2007, Nov. 15 **Litho.**
1165-1168 A343 Set of 4 5.25 5.25

Mailboxes A344

No. 1169 — Various mailboxes with panel color of: a, 20c, Yellow. b, 104c, Green. c, 240c, Light blue. d, 285c, Lilac. e, 380c, Orange. f, 500c, Brown.

2007, Dec. 3 ***Perf. 12¾x13¼***
1169 A344 Block of 6, #a-f 15.50 15.50

Lighthouses A345

No. 1170: a, Fort Oranje, Bonaire. b, Malmok, Bonaire. c, Noordpunt, Curaçao. d, Klein Curaçao. e, Willemstoren, Bonaire. f, Bullenbaai, Curaçao.

2008, Jan. 21
1170 A345 158c Block of 6, #a-f 12.00 12.00

New Year 2008 (Year of the Rat) — A346

Designs: 106c, Stylized rat. 158c, Rat. 500c, Rat on branch, horiz.

2008, Feb. 7 ***Perf. 12¾x13¼***
1171-1172 A346 Set of 2 3.00 3.00

Souvenir Sheet
Perf. 13¼x12¾

1173 A346 500c multi 5.50 5.50

Dutch Royalty A347

No. 1174: a, 75c, Princess Catharina-Amalia. b, 100c, Princess, diff. c, 125c, Crown Prince Willem-Alexander. d, 250c, Crown Prince, diff. e, 375c, Queen Beatrix. f, 500c, Queen, diff.

2008, Feb. 28 ***Perf. 12¾x13¼***
1174 A347 Block of 6, #a-f 15.50 15.50

Global Warming A348

No. 1175: a, 50c, Smokestacks. b, 75c, Polar bear. c, 125c, Windmills. d, 250c, Beach and lighthouse.

2008, Mar. 20 ***Perf. 13¼x12¾***
1175 A348 Block of 4, #a-d 6.25 6.25

2008 Summer Olympics, Beijing A349

No. 1176: a, 25c, Runner. b, 35c, Gymnast on rings. c, 75c, Swimmer. d, 215c, Cyclist.

2008, Apr. 1 ***Perf. 12¾x13¼***
1176 A349 Block of 4, #a-d 4.00 4.00

Stamp Passion Philatelic Exhibition, the Netherlands A350

No. 1177: a, 75c, Netherlands Antilles #C14. b, 100c, Netherlands Antilles #29. c, 125c, Netherlands Antilles #CB19. d, 250c, Netherlands #O32. e, 375c, Netherlands #134. f, 500c, Netherlands Antilles #187.

2008, Apr. 11
1177 A350 Block of 6, #a-f 14.00 14.00

Images of stamps shown on Nos. 1177a, 1177c and 1177e are distorted.

Catholic Diocese of Netherlands Antilles and Aruba, 50th Anniv. — A351

Designs: 59c, Chapel of Alto Vista, Aruba. 106c, Cross at Seru Largu, Bonaire. 158c, St. Ann Church, Curaçao. 240c, Sacred Heart Church, Saba. 285c, Roman Catholic Church of Oranjestad, St. Eustatius. 335c, Mary Star of the Sea Church, St. Maarten.

2008, Apr. 28
1178-1183 A351 Set of 6 11.50 11.50

Dolls Depicting Women Doing Work A352

No. 1184: a, 145c, Pounding corn (Batidó di maíshi den pilon). b, 145c, Selling fish (Bendedó di piská). c, 145c, Baking fish (Hasadó di masbangu riba bleki). d, 145c, Roasting coffee beans (Totadó di kòfi). e, 155c, Scrubbing clothes on scrub board (Labadera). f, 155c, Carrying basket of clothes (Labadó di paña na laman). g, 155c, Grinding corn on coral (Muladó di maíshi chikí riba pieda). h, 155c, Weaving hat (Trahadó di sombré).

2008, May 15
1184 A352 Block of 8, #a-h 11.50 11.50

Paintings by Johannes Vermeer (1632-75) — A353

No. 1185: a, 145c, Little Street. b, 145c, Girl with Pearl Earring. c, 155c, Woman in Blue Reading Letter. d, 155c, The Love Letter. 500c, The Milkmaid.

2008, June 23
1185 A353 Sheet of 4, #a-d, + 2 labels 7.50 7.50

Souvenir Sheet

1186 A353 500c multi 5.75 5.75

Windows — A354

Various windows.

2008, July 8 ***Perf. 13¾***

1187 A354 5c multi .50 .50
1188 A354 106c multi, vert. 1.60 1.60
1189 A354 285c multi, vert., diff. 3.25 3.25
a. Souvenir sheet of 5, # 1187-1189, Aruba #330, Netherlands #1311, + etiquette 15.00 15.00

Nos. 1188-1189 were only available in No. 1189a. No. 1187 also was available in Aruba No. 332a and in Netherlands Nos. 1313a and 1313b.

Shells — A355

No Country Name — A355a

Designs: 20c, Cypraea zebra. 40c, Charonia variegata. 65c, Calliostoma armillata. 106c, Strombus gigas. 158c, Pina carnea. 285c, Olivia sayana. 335c, Natica canrena. 405c, Voluta musica.

Perf. 13¼x12¾

2008, Sept. 19 **Litho.**

1190 A355 20c multi 1.00 1.00
1191 A355 40c multi 1.00 1.00
1192 A355 65c multi 1.00 1.00
1193 A355a 106c multi, without country name 1.10 1.10
a. With country name 3.00 3.00
1194 A355 158c multi 1.60 1.60
1195 A355 285c multi 3.00 3.00
1196 A355 335c multi 3.25 3.25
1197 A355 405c multi 4.00 4.00
Nos. 1190-1197 (8) 15.95 15.95

African Animals A356

No. 1198: a, 75c, Giraffes, vert. b, 150c, Elephants. c, 175c, Cheetahs. d, 250c, Zebras.
No. 1199, Impalas, vert.

Perf. 13¼x12¾, 12¾x13¼ (vert. stamps)

2008, Oct. 2

1198 A356 Block of 4, #a-d 7.50 7.50

Souvenir Sheet

1199 A356 250c multi 3.00 3.00

Christmas and New Year's Day — A357

Designs: 50c, Plate of basil. 106c, Flowers. 158c, Fishermen in boat. 215c, Dock.

Perf. 13¼x12¾

2008, Nov. 14 **Litho.**

1200-1203 A357 Set of 4 5.50 5.50

Traditional Costumes — A358

No. 1204: a, 100c, Antillean girl. b, 104c, Dutch boy. c, 155c, Japanese girl.

2008, Nov. 27 ***Perf. 12¾x13¼***

1204 A358 Horiz. strip of 3, #a-c 4.00 4.00

Birds — A359

No. 1205: a, Kasuaris (cassowary). b, Struisvogel (ostrich). c, Pinguin (penguin). d, Kalkoen (wild turkey). e, Aalscholver (cormorant), horiz. f, Mandarijneend (Mandarin duck), horiz. g, Putter-distelvink (goldfinch), horiz. h, Groene reiger (green heron), horiz.

Perf. 12¾x13¼, 13¼x12¾ (horiz. stamps)

2008, Dec. 12

1205 A359 158c Block of 8, #a-h 14.00 14.00

Flowers — A360

No. 1206: a, Nelumbo nucifera. b, Chrysanthemum leucanthemum. c, Hepatica nobilis. d, Cistus incanus. e, Alamanda. f, Wise portia.

2009, Jan. 26 **Litho.** ***Perf. 13¼x12¾***

1206 Block of 6 16.00 16.00
a. A360 75c multi .70 .70
b. A360 150c multi 1.10 1.10
c. A360 200c multi 1.60 1.60
d. A360 225c multi 2.10 2.10
e. A360 350c multi 3.50 3.50
f. A360 500c multi 5.00 5.00

New Year 2009 (Year of the Ox) — A361

Chinese character and: 110c, Outline of ox. 168c, Ox, horiz.

Perf. 12¾x13¼, 13¼x12¾

2009, Feb. 19

1207-1208 A361 Set of 2 3.00 3.00

Butterflies — A362

No. 1209: a, 25c, Lycaena phlaeas. b, 35c, danaus plexippus. c, 50c, Nymphalis antiopa. d, 105c, Carterocephalus palaemon. e, 115c, Inachis io. f, 155c, Phyciodes tharos. g, 185c, Papilio glaucus. h, 240c, Dryas iulia. i, 315c, Libytheana carinenta. j, 375c, Melanis pixe. k, 400c, Asterocampa celtis. l, 1000c, Historis acheronta.

2009, Mar. 2 ***Perf. 13¼x12¾***

1209 A362 Block of 12, #a-l 32.00 32.00

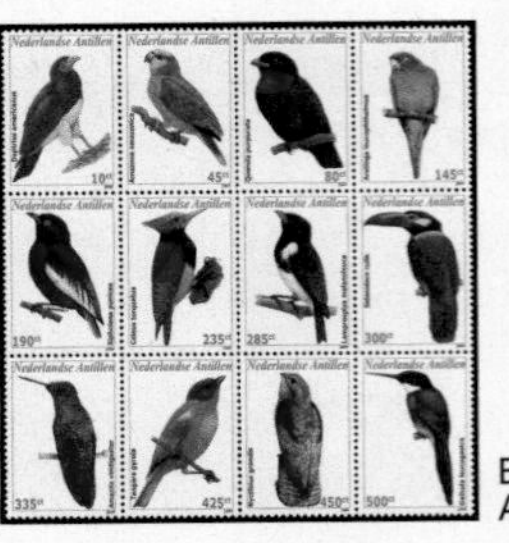

Birds A363

No. 1210: a, 10c, Daptrius americanus. b, 45c, Amazona amazonica. c, 80c, Querula purpurata. d, 145c, Aratinga leucophthalmus. e, 190c, Xipholena punicea. f, 235c, Celeus torquatus. g, 285c, Lamprospiza melanoleuca. h, 300c, Selenidera culik. i, 335c, Amazila viridigaster. j, 425c, Tangara gyrola. k, 450c, Nyctibius grandis. l, 500c, Galbula leucogastra.

2009, Apr. 20 ***Perf. 12¾x13¼***

1210 A363 Block of 12, #a-l 32.00 32.00

Telecommunications and Posts Department, Cent. — A364

Designs: 59c, Ship, telegraph operator. 110c, Person on telephone, room with radio and television. 164c, Person at computer, satellite dish, street scene.

2009, May 18 ***Perf. 13¼x12¾***

1211-1213 A364 Set of 3 3.50 3.50

Pianos — A365

Pianos manufactured by: 175c, J. B. & Sons, 1796. 225c, J. Schantz, 1818, vert. 250c, Steinway-Welt, 1927, vert. 350c, Yamaha, 2007.

Perf. 13¼x12¾, 12¾x13¼

2009, June 1

1214-1217 A365 Set of 4 11.50 11.50

Nos. 1214-1217 were printed in a sheet of 8 containing two of each stamp, with a central label.

Miniature Sheets

A366

A367

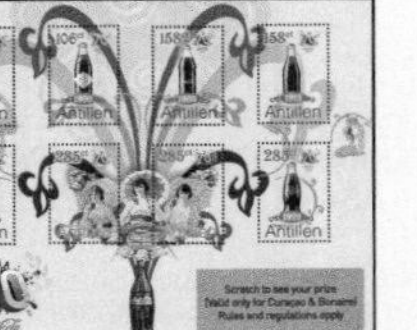

Coca-Cola Bottling on Curaçao, 70th Anniv. — A368

No. 1218 — Fria soft drinks: a, No bottle shown. b, Bottle with pink drink, parts of blue balls at UL and bottom. c, Bottle with purple drink, parts of red ball at UL and purple ball at right. d, Bottle with yellow drink, parts of green ball at UL and purple ball at LR. e, Bottle with orange drink, parts of purple ball at UL and red ball at LL. f, Bottle with red drink, parts of purple ball at UL, blue ball at LR. g, Bottle with pale pink drink, part of red ball at LR. h, Bottle with yellow-green drink, part of orange ball at LR.

No. 1219: a, Coca-Cola advertisement showing couple on beach and bottle. b, Women around counter with two Coca-Cola advertisements. c, Coca-Cola building with awning at left. d, Man at vending machine. e, Man and automobile in front of building with Coca-Cola advertisement, vert. f, Two men holding bottles of Coca-Cola. g, Men and women around a counter. h, Delivery truck.

No. 1220: a, 106c, 1899 Coca-Cola bottle. b, 106c, 1900 Coca-Cola bottle. c, 158c, 1905 Coca-Cola bottle. d, 158c, 1913 Coca-Cola bottle. e, 158c, 1915 Coca-Cola bottle. f, 285c, Woman holding glass of Coca-Cola and blue-striped umbrella. g, 285c, Woman holding glass of Coca-Cola and yellow umbrella. h, 285c, 1923 Coca-Cola bottle.

Perf. 12¾x13¼, 13¼x12¾

2008, Dec. 23 **Litho.**

1218 A366 106c Sheet of 8, #a-h 8.50 8.50
1219 A367 158c Sheet of 8, #a-h 13.00 13.00
1220 A368 Sheet of 8, #a-h 15.00 15.00
Nos. 1218-1220 (3) 36.50 36.50

Islands Type of 2007

Designs: 30c, Flag of Bonaire, divers and marine life. 59c, Map of Statia, oil storage tanks, horiz. 110c, Flag of Curaçao, royal poinciana flowers. 164c, Flag of St. Maarten, cruise ship and pier. 168c, Map of bonaire, flamingos, horiz. 285c, Map of Saba, houses, horiz.

Perf. 12¾x13¼, 13¼x12¾

2009, Jan.

1221 A335 30c multi 1.00 1.00
1222 A335 59c multi 1.00 1.00
1223 A335 110c multi 1.40 1.40
1224 A335 164c multi 1.60 1.60
1225 A335 168c multi 1.75 1.75
1226 A335 285c multi 3.00 3.00
Nos. 1221-1226 (6) 9.75 9.75

Souvenir Sheet

Birds A369

No. 1227: a, 5g, Celeus undatus. b, 10g, Todopleura fusca.

2009, July 20 ***Perf. 13¼x12¾***

1227 A369 Sheet of 2, #a-b 15.00 15.00

Sailing Ships A370

No. 1228: a, 1c, Merchantman, 200. b, 2c, Caravel, 1490. c, 3c, Naos, 1492. d, 4c, Constant, 1605. e, 5c, Merchant ship, 1620. f, 80c, Vasa, 1628. g, 220c, Hoys, 1730. h, 275c, Bark, 1750. i, 385c, Schooner, 1838. j, 475c, Sailing rig, 1884. k, 500c, Fifie, 1903. l, 750c, Junk, 1938.

2009, Aug. 31

1228 A370 Block of 12, #a-l 28.00 28.00

Snakes A371

No. 1229: a, 275c, Bothriopsis bilineata. b, 325c, Bothriechis schlegelii. c, 340c, Agkistrodon piscivorous. d, 390c, Erythrolamprus aesculapii. e, 420c, Atropoides mexicanus. f, 450c, Bothriechis nigroviridis.

2009, Oct. 5
1229 A371 Block of 6, #a-f 26.00 26.00

Aviation Pioneers — A372

Designs: 59c, Freddy Johnson (1932-2001). 110c, Norman Chester Wathey (1925-2001). 164c, José Dormoy (1925-2007).

Perf. 13¼x12¾
2009, Nov. 10 Litho.
1230-1232 A372 Set of 3 3.50 3.50

Airplanes — A373

No. 1233: a, Wright Flyer, 1903. b, DST Skysleeper, 1935. c, Cessna 170, 1948. d, Lockheed Constellation, 1943. e, De Havilland Comet, 1949. f, BAC Super VC10, 1962.

2009, Nov. 16

1233	Block of 6	21.00	21.00
a.	A373 55c multi	1.00	1.00
b.	A373 100c multi	1.20	1.20
c.	A373 205c multi	2.00	2.00
d.	A373 395c multi	4.00	4.00
e.	A373 645c multi	6.00	6.00
f.	A373 800c multi	7.00	7.00

Hanukkah A374

Christmas A375

Kwanzaa A376

New Year's Day A377

2009, Nov. 30 ***Perf. 12¾x13¼***

1234	A374 50c multi	.50	.50
1235	A375 110c multi	1.10	1.10
1236	A376 168c multi	1.75	1.75
1237	A377 215c multi	2.25	2.25
	Nos. 1234-1237 (4)	5.60	5.60

Fruit — A378

2009, Dec. 28 Litho.

1238	Block of 8 + label	20.00	20.00
a.	A378 20c Sapodilla	1.00	1.00
b.	A378 45c Pineapple	1.00	1.00
c.	A378 125c Mamey sapote	1.30	1.30
d.	A378 145c Avocado	1.60	1.60
e.	A378 160c Mangosteen	1.60	1.60
f.	A378 210c Rambutan	2.00	2.00
g.	A378 295c Pomelo	3.00	3.00
h.	A378 1000c Watermelon	9.00	9.00

Greetings Type of 2006

Designs: 32c, Bless you. 60c, Love. 81c, All the best. 87c, Regards. 1.06g, Go for it. 1.57g, Tolerance. 1.61g, Positivism.

2009 ***Perf. 13¼x12¾***
1239-1245 A327 Set of 7 10.00 10.00

Flowers A379

No. 1246: a, 50c, Opuntia basilaris. b, 75c, Aristolochiaceae. c, 125c, Protea cynaroides. d, 175c, Louisiana iris. e, 200c, Spontaneous frangipani. f, 250c, Red azaleas. g, 300c, English Heritage rose. h, 350c, Aquilegia. i, 475c, Octavia Hill rose. j, 500c, Tea rose.

2010, Jan. 25 Litho. ***Perf. 13¼x12¾***
1246 A379 Block of 10, #a-j 26.00 26.00

Fruit Type of 2005

2010, Feb. 1 Litho. ***Perf. 13¼x12¾***

1247	A315	1c Papaya	.30	.30
1248	A315	5c Pomegranates	.30	.30
1249	A315	30c Mangos	.30	.30
1250	A315	59c Bananas	.60	.60
1251	A315	79c Cashews	.80	.80
1252	A315	111c Soursops	1.10	1.10
1253	A315	164c Tamarinds	1.75	1.75
1254	A315	170c Watermelons	1.75	1.75
1255	A315	199c Gennips	2.00	2.00
1256	A315	285c Sea grapes	3.00	3.00
		Nos. 1247-1256 (10)	11.90	11.90

New Year 2010 (Year of the Tiger) — A380

Designs: 111c, Tiger cub. 164c, Tiger and cub. 170c, White tiger.

2010, Feb. 1 ***Perf. 12¾x13¼***
1257-1259 A380 Set of 3 5.00 5.00

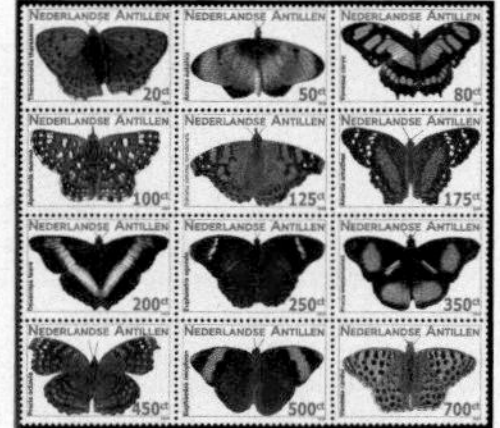
Butterflies — A381

No. 1260: a, 20c, Thersamonia thersamon. b, 50c, Acraea natalica. c, 80c, Vanessa carye. d, 100c, Apodemia mormo. e, 125c, Siproeta stelenes meridionalis. f, 175c, Anartia amathea. g, 200c, Doxocopa laure. h, 250c, Euphaedra uganda. i, 350c, Precis westermannii. j, 450c, Precis octavia. k, 500c, Euphaedra neophron. l, 700c, Vanessa cardui.

2010, Mar. 1 ***Perf. 13¼x12¾***
1260 A381 Block of 12, #a-l 34.00 34.00

Paintings by Vincent Van Gogh — A382

Designs: 200c, Self-portrait, 1888. 400c, Agostina Segatori, 1887. 500c, Arlesian Woman, 1888. 700c, Emperor Moth, 1889.

2010, Apr. 7 ***Perf. 12¾x13¼***

1261	A382	200c multi	4.00	4.00
1262	A382	400c multi	4.50	4.50
1263	A382	500c multi	5.50	5.50
1264	A382	700c multi	6.75	6.75
		Nos. 1261-1264 (4)	20.75	20.75

Nos. 1261-1264 were printed in sheets of 8 containing two of each stamp with a central label.

Birds A383

No. 1265: a, 75c, Pipra aureola. b, 150c, Neopelma chrysocephalum. c, 200c, Oxyruncus cristatus. d, 225c, Automolus rufipileatus. e, 350c, Empidonomus varius. f, 500c, Veniliornis sanguineus.

2010, May 10
1265 A383 Block of 6, #a-f 18.50 18.50

Ships A384

No. 1266 — Inscriptions: a, 100c, Osberg, 800. b, 125c, Dromon, 910. c, 175c, Cocca, 1500. d, 200c, Mary, 1661. e, 250c, Houtport, 1700. f, 300c, Santissima Trinidad, 1769. g, 350c, Vrachtschip, 1800. h, 400c, Amistad, 1839. i, 450c, Oorlogsschip, 1840. j, 650c, Nederlands schip, 1850.

Perf. 13¼x12¾
2010, June 14 Litho.
1266 A384 Block of 10, #a-j 33.00 33.00

Netherlands Antilles Stamps — A385

No. 1267: a, 25c, #109. b, 50c, #140. c, 100c, #77. d, 250c, #144. e, 275c, #290. f, 300c, #75. g, 400c, #C34. h, 600c, #200.

No. 1268: a, 700c, #204. b, 800c, #141.

2010, July 19 ***Perf. 12¾x13¼***
1267 A385 Block of 8, #a-h 22.50 22.50

Souvenir Sheet

1268 A385 Sheet of 2, #a-b 17.00 17.00

Image of stamp on No. 1267d is distorted.

TeleCuraçao, 50th Anniv. — A386

Television showing: 59c, Cameraman. 111c, Transmission tower. 164c, 50th anniversary emblem.

2010, Aug. 2 Litho. ***Perf. 13¼x12¾***
1269-1271 A386 Set of 3 3.75 3.75

Pocket Watches — A387

No. 1272 — Watches made by: a, Ulysse, 1890. b, Hampden, 1910. c, Elgin, 1924. d, Illinois, 1928. e, Vacheron, 1955.

2010, Sept. 6 ***Perf. 12¾x13¼***

1272	Horiz. strip of 5	14.00	14.00
a.	A387 125c multi	2.00	2.00
b.	A387 175c multi	2.00	2.00
c.	A387 250c multi	2.50	2.50
d.	A387 300c multi	3.00	3.00
e.	A387 350c multi	3.00	3.00

On Oct. 10, 2010, the Netherlands Antilles was dissolved, being replaced by three entities: Caribbean Netherlands, Curaçao and St. Martin.

SEMI-POSTAL STAMPS

Catalogue values for unused stamps in this section are for Never Hinged items.

Nos. 132, 133 and 135 Surcharged in Black

1947, Dec. 1 Unwmk. ***Perf. 12½***

B1	A26	1½c + 2½c on 6c	1.05	1.00
B2	A26	2½c + 5c on 10c	1.05	1.00
B3	A26	5c + 7½c on 15c	1.05	1.00
		Nos. B1-B3 (3)	3.15	3.00

The surtax was for the National Inspanning Welzijnszorg in Nederlandsch Indie, relief organization for Netherlands Indies.

Curaçao Children
SP1 SP2

Design: Nos. B6, B9, Girl.

1948, Nov. 3 Photo. ***Perf. 12½x12***

B4	SP1	6c + 10c ol brn	2.50	1.60
B5	SP2	10c + 15c brt red	2.50	1.60
B6	SP2	12½c + 20c Prus grn	2.50	1.75
B7	SP1	15c + 25c brt bl	2.50	1.75
B8	SP2	20c + 30c red brn	2.50	1.90
B9	SP2	25c + 35c purple	2.50	1.90
		Nos. B4-B9 (6)	15.00	10.50

The surtax was for child welfare and the White/Yellow Cross Foundation.

Leapfrog — SP4

Designs: 5c+2½c, Flying kite. 6c+2½c, Girls swinging. 12½c+5c, "London Bridge." 25c+10c, Rolling hoops.

Perf. 14½x13½

1951, Aug. 16 **Unwmk.**

No.	Type	Description	Unused	Used
B10	SP4	1½c + 1c pur	11.50	4.25
B11	SP4	5c + 2½c brn	11.50	4.25
B12	SP4	6c + 2½c blue	11.50	4.25
B13	SP4	12½c + 5c red	11.50	4.25
B14	SP4	25c + 10c dl grn	11.50	4.25
		Nos. B10-B14 (5)	57.50	21.25

The surtax was for child welfare.

Ship and Gull — SP5

Designs: 6c+4c, Sailor and lighthouse. 12½c+7c, Prow of sailboat. 15c+10c, Ships. 25c+15c, Ship, compass and anchor.

1952, July 16 ***Perf. 13x14***

No.	Type	Description	Unused	Used
B15	SP5	1½c + 1c dk grn	9.50	1.90
B16	SP5	6c + 4c choc	16.50	4.25
B17	SP5	12½c + 7c red vio	12.00	4.25
B18	SP5	15c + 10c dp bl	14.00	5.00
B19	SP5	25c + 15c red	13.00	3.75
		Nos. B15-B19 (5)	65.00	19.15

The surtax was for the seamen's welfare fund.

No. 226 Surcharged in Black

1953, Feb. 21

No.	Type	Description	Unused	Used
B20	A45	22½c + 7½c on 1½g	2.40	1.25

The surtax was for flood relief in the Netherlands.

Tribulus Cistoides — SP6

Flowers: 7½c+5c, Yellow hibiscus. 15c+5c, Oleander. 22½c+7½c, Cactus. 25c+10c, Red hibiscus.

1955, May 17 Photo. ***Perf. 14x13***

Flowers in Natural Colors

No.	Type	Description	Unused	Used
B21	SP6	1½c + 1c bl grn & dk bl	3.00	.95
B22	SP6	7½c + 5c dp ultra	4.00	1.90
B23	SP6	15c + 5c ol grn	4.00	2.25
B24	SP6	22½c + 7½c dk bl	4.00	1.90
B25	SP6	25c + 10c ind & gray	4.00	1.90
		Nos. B21-B25 (5)	19.00	8.90

The surtax was for child welfare.

Prince Bernhard and Queen Juliana — SP7

1955, Oct. 19 ***Perf. 11x12***

No.	Type	Description	Unused	Used
B26	SP7	7½c + 2½c rose brn	.40	.30
B27	SP7	22½c + 7½c dp bl	1.20	.95

Royal visit to the Netherlands Antilles, Oct. 1955.
Surtax paid for a gift.

Lord Baden-Powell SP8

1957, Feb. 22 ***Perf. 14x13½***

No.	Type	Description	Unused	Used
B28	SP8	6c + 1½c org yel	.95	.45
B29	SP8	7½c + 2½c dp grn	.95	.45
B30	SP8	15c + 5c red	.95	.45
		Nos. B28-B30 (3)	2.85	1.35

50th anniv. of the Boy Scout movement.

Soccer Player — SP9

Map of Central America and the Caribbean — SP10

Designs: 15c+5c, Goalkeeper catching ball. 22½c+7½c, Men playing soccer.

1957, Aug. 6 ***Perf. 12x11, 11x12***

No.	Type	Description	Unused	Used
B31	SP9	6c + 2½c org	1.90	.70
B32	SP10	7½c + 5c dk red	1.90	1.00
B33	SP9	15c + 5c brt bl grn	1.90	1.00
B34	SP9	22½c + 7½c brt bl	1.90	1.00
		Nos. B31-B34 (4)	7.60	3.70

8th Central American and Caribbean Soccer Championships, Aug. 11-25.
Surtax was for organizing costs.

American Kestrel — SP11

Birds: 7½+1½c, Yellow oriole. 15+2½c, Common ground doves. 22½+2½c, Brown-throated parakeet.

1958, Apr. 15 Photo. ***Perf. 13½x14***

No.	Type	Description	Unused	Used
B35	SP11	2½c + 1c multi	1.75	.95
B36	SP11	7½c + 1½c multi	1.75	.95
B37	SP11	15c + 2½c multi	1.75	.95
B38	SP11	22½c + 2½c multi	1.75	.95
		Nos. B35-B38 (4)	7.00	3.80

The surtax was for child welfare.

Flag and Map — SP12

1958, Dec. 1 Litho. ***Perf. 13½***

Cross in Red

No.	Type	Description	Unused	Used
B39	SP12	6c + 2c red brn	.95	.45
B40	SP12	7½c + 2½c bl grn	.95	.45
B41	SP12	15c + 5c org yel	.95	.45
B42	SP12	22½c + 7½c blue	.95	.45
		Nos. B39-B42 (4)	3.80	1.80

The surtax was for the Red Cross.

Community House, Zeeland — SP13

Historic buildings: 7½c+2½c, Molenplein. 15c+5c, Saba, vert. 22½c+7½c, Scharlooburg. 25c+7½c, Community House, Brievengat.

Perf. 14x13½, 13½x14

1959, Sept. 16 **Litho.**

No.	Type	Description	Unused	Used
B43	SP13	6c + 1½c multi	1.40	.90
B44	SP13	7½c + 2½c multi	1.40	.90
B45	SP13	15c + 5c multi	1.40	.90
B46	SP13	22½c + 7½c multi	1.40	.90
B47	SP13	25c + 7½c multi	1.40	.90
		Nos. B43-B47 (5)	7.00	4.50

The surtax went to the Foundation for the Preservation of Historical Monuments.

Fish — SP14

Designs. 10c+2c, SCUBA diver with spear gun, vert. 25c+5c, Two fish.

1960, Aug. 24 Photo. ***Perf. 13½***

No.	Type	Description	Unused	Used
B48	SP14	10c + 2c sapphire	1.50	.85
B49	SP14	20c + 3c multi	1.75	1.15
B50	SP14	25c + 5c blk, brt pink & dk bl	1.75	1.15
		Nos. B48-B50 (3)	5.00	3.15

The surtax was for the fight against cancer.

Infant — SP15

Designs: 10c+3c, Girl and doll. 20c+6c, Boy on beach. 25c+8c, Children in school.

1961, July 24 Litho. ***Perf. 13½x14***

Designs in Black

No.	Type	Description	Unused	Used
B51	SP15	6c + 2c lt yel grn	.55	.30
B52	SP15	10c + 3c rose red	.55	.30
B53	SP15	20c + 6c yellow	.55	.30
B54	SP15	25c + 8c orange	.55	.30
		Nos. B51-B54 (4)	2.20	1.20

The surtax was for child welfare.

Globe and Knight — SP16

1962, May 2 ***Perf. 13½x14½***

No.	Type	Description	Unused	Used
B55	SP16	10c + 5c green	1.10	.65
B56	SP16	20c + 10c carmine	1.10	.65
B57	SP16	25c + 10c dk bl	1.10	.65
		Nos. B55-B57 (3)	3.30	1.95

Intl. Candidates Chess Tournament, Willemstad, May-June.

No. 248 Surcharged

1963, Mar. 21

No.	Type	Description	Unused	Used
B58	A56	20c + 10c crimson & gray	.50	.50

FAO "Freedom from Hunger" campaign.

Child and Flowers — SP17

Designs: 6c+3c, Three girls and flowers, horiz. 10c+5c, Girl with ball and trees, horiz. 20c+10c, Three boys with flags, horiz. 25c+12c, Singing boy.

Perf. 14½x13½, 13½x14½

1963, Oct. 23 Photo. **Unwmk.**

No.	Type	Description	Unused	Used
B59	SP17	5c + 2c multi	.40	.25
B60	SP17	6c + 3c multi	.40	.25
B61	SP17	10c + 5c multi	.40	.25
B62	SP17	20c + 10c multi	.40	.25
B63	SP17	25c + 12c multi	.40	.25
		Nos. B59-B63 (5)	2.00	1.25

Surtax for child welfare.

Bougainvillea SP18

Designs: 10c+5c, Wild rose. 20c+10c, Chalice flower. 25c+11c, Bellisima.

1964, Oct. 21 ***Perf. 14x13***

Flowers in Natural Colors

No.	Type	Description	Unused	Used
B64	SP18	6c + 3c bl vio & blk	.40	.25
B65	SP18	10c + 5c yel brn, yel & blk	.40	.25
B66	SP18	20c + 10c dull red & blk	.40	.25
B67	SP18	25c + 11c citron & brn	.40	.25
		Nos. B64-B67 (4)	1.60	1.00

The surtax was for child welfare.

Sea Anemones and Star Coral — SP19

Corals: 6c+3c, Blue cup sponges. 10c+5c, Green cup sponges. 25c+11c, Basket sponge, knobbed brain coral and reef fish.

1965, Nov. 10 Photo. ***Perf. 14x13½***

No.	Type	Description	Unused	Used
B68	SP19	6c + 3c multi	.25	.25
B69	SP19	10c + 5c multi	.25	.25
B70	SP19	20c + 10c multi	.35	.25
B71	SP19	25c + 11c multi	.35	.25
		Nos. B68-B71 (4)	1.20	1.00

The surtax was for child welfare.

ICEM Type of Netherlands

1966, Jan. 31 Photo. ***Perf. 14x13***

No.	Type	Description	Unused	Used
B72	SP181	35c + 15c brn & dl yel	.25	.25

The surtax was for the Intergovernmental Committee for European Migration (ICEM). The message on the stamps was given and signed by Queen Juliana.

Girl Cooking — SP20

Youth at Work: 10c+5c, Nurse's aide with infant. 20c+10c, Young metalworker. 25c+11c, Girl ironing.

1966, Nov. 15 ***Perf. 13½***

No.	Type	Description	Unused	Used
B73	SP20	6c + 3c multi	.25	.25
B74	SP20	10c + 5c multi	.25	.25
B75	SP20	20c + 10c multi	.25	.25
B76	SP20	25c + 11c multi	.25	.25
		Nos. B73-B76 (4)	1.00	1.00

The surtax was for child welfare.

Helping Hands Supporting Women — SP21

1967, July 4 Litho. ***Perf. 13x14***

No.	Type	Description	Unused	Used
B77	SP21	6c + 3c bl & blk	.25	.25
B78	SP21	10c + 5c brt pink & blk	.25	.25
B79	SP21	20c + 10c lilac	.25	.25
B80	SP21	25c + 11c dk bl	.25	.25
		Nos. B77-B80 (4)	1.00	1.00

The surtax was for various social and cultural institutions.

Nanzi the Spider and the Tiger — SP22

Nanzi Stories (Folklore): 6c+3c, Princess Longnose, vert. 10c+5c, The Turtle and the Monkey. 25c+11c, Adventure of Shon Arey, vert.

Perf. 14x13, 13x14

1967, Nov. 15 **Photo.**

No.	Type	Description	Unused	Used
B81	SP22	6c + 3c dk red, pink & org	.25	.25
B82	SP22	10c + 5c vio bl & org	.25	.25
B83	SP22	20c + 10c grn & org	.25	.25
B84	SP22	25c + 11c brt bl & org	.25	.25
		Nos. B81-B84 (4)	1.00	1.00

The surtax was for child welfare.

Lintendans (Dance) and Koeoekoe House — SP23

1968, May 29 Litho. *Perf. 14x13*

B85	SP23	10c + 5c multi	.25	.25
B86	SP23	15c + 5c multi	.25	.25
B87	SP23	20c + 10c multi	.25	.25
B88	SP23	25c + 10c multi	.25	.25
		Nos. B85-B88 (4)	1.00	1.00

The surtax was for various social and cultural institutions.

Boy and Pet Cat — SP24

Designs: 6c+3c, Boy and goat. 10c+5c, Girl and poodle. 25c+11c, Girl and duckling.

1968, Nov. 13 Photo. *Perf. 13½*

B89	SP24	6c + 3c multi	.40	.25
B90	SP24	10c + 5c multi	.40	.25
B91	SP24	20c + 10c multi	.40	.25
B92	SP24	25c + 11c multi	.40	.25
		Nos. B89-B92 (4)	1.60	1.00

The surtax was for child welfare.

Carnival Headpiece — SP25

Folklore: 15c+5c, Harvest-home festival. 20c+10c, Feast of St. John (dancers & cock). 25c+10c, "Dande" New Year's celebration.

1969, July 23 Litho. *Perf. 13½*

B93	SP25	10c + 5c multi	.30	.25
B94	SP25	15c + 5c multi	.30	.25
B95	SP25	20c + 10c multi	.35	.30
B96	SP25	25c + 10c multi	.35	.30
		Nos. B93-B96 (4)	1.30	1.10

The surtax was for various social and cultural institutions.

Boy Playing Guitar — SP26

Designs: 10c+5c, Girl with English flute. 20c+10c, Boy playing the marimula. 25c+11c, Girl playing the piano.

1969, Nov. 3 Litho. *Perf. 14x13*

B97	SP26	6c + 3c org & vio	.40	.30
B98	SP26	10c + 5c yel & brt grn	.40	.35
B99	SP26	20c + 10c bl & car	.40	.35
B100	SP26	25c + 11c pink & brn	.40	.35
		Nos. B97-B100 (4)	1.60	1.35

The surtax was for child welfare.

Printing Press and Quill — SP27

Mass Media: 15c+5c, Filmstrip and reels. 20c+10c, Horn and radio mast. 25c+10c, Television antenna and eye focused on globe.

1970, July 14 Litho. *Perf. 13½*

B101	SP27	10c + 5c multi	.40	.35
B102	SP27	15c + 5c multi	.40	.35
B103	SP27	20c + 10c multi	.40	.35
B104	SP27	25c + 10c multi	.40	.35
		Nos. B101-B104 (4)	1.60	1.40

The surtax was for various social and cultural institutions.

Mother and Child — SP28

Designs: 10c+5c, Girl holding piggy bank. 20c+10c, Boys wrestling (Judokas). 25c+11c, Youth carrying small boy on his shoulders.

1970, Nov. 16 *Perf. 13½x14*

B105	SP28	6c + 3c multi	.40	.30
B106	SP28	10c + 5c multi	.40	.30
B107	SP28	20c + 10c multi	.40	.30
B108	SP28	25c + 11c multi	.40	.30
		Nos. B105-B108 (4)	1.60	1.20

The surtax was for child welfare.

Charcoal Burner — SP29

Kitchen Utensils: 15c+5c, Earthenware vessel for water. 20c+10c, Baking oven. 25c+10c, Soup plate, stirrer and kneading stick.

1971, May 12 *Perf. 14x13½*

B109	SP29	10c + 5c multi	.50	.40
B110	SP29	15c + 5c multi	.50	.40
B111	SP29	20c + 10c multi	.50	.40
B112	SP29	25c + 10c multi	.50	.40
		Nos. B109-B112 (4)	2.00	1.60

Surtax was for various social and cultural institutions.

Homemade Dolls and Comb — SP30

Homemade Toys: 20c+10c, Carts. 30c+15c, Musical top made from calabash.

1971, Nov. 16 *Perf. 13½x14*

B113	SP30	15c + 5c multi	.55	.50
B114	SP30	20c + 10c multi	.55	.50
B115	SP30	30c + 15c multi	.55	.50
		Nos. B113-B115 (3)	1.65	1.50

Surtax was for child welfare.

Steel Band — SP31

Designs: 20c+10c, Harvest festival (Seu). 30c+15c, Tambu dancers.

1972, May 16

B116	SP31	15c + 5c multi	.80	.65
B117	SP31	20c + 10c multi	.80	.65
B118	SP31	30c + 15c multi	.80	.65
		Nos. B116-B118 (3)	2.40	1.95

Surtax was for various social and cultural institutions.

Child at Play on Ground — SP32

Designs: 20c+10c, Child playing in water. 30c+15c, Child throwing ball into air.

1972, Nov. 14 Litho. *Perf. 14x13*

B119	SP32	15c + 5c multi	.65	.65
B120	SP32	20c + 10c multi	.65	.65
B121	SP32	30c + 15c multi	.65	.65
		Nos. B119-B121 (3)	1.95	1.95

Surtax was for child welfare.

Pedestrian Crossing, Traffic Sign — SP33

Designs: 15c+7c, School crossing. 40c+20c, Traffic light, road and car.

1973, Apr. 9 Litho. *Perf. 13x14*

B122	SP33	12c + 6c multi	.80	.65
B123	SP33	15c + 7c multi	.80	.65
B124	SP33	40c + 20c multi	.80	.65
		Nos. B122-B124 (3)	2.40	1.95

Surtax was for various social and cultural institutions.

"1948-73" — SP34

20c+10c, Children. 30c+15c, Mother & child.

1973, Nov. 19 Litho. *Perf. 14x13*

B125	SP34	15c + 5c multi	.60	.60
B126	SP34	20c + 10c multi	.60	.60
a.		Min. sheet, 2 ea #B125-B126	3.25	3.00
B127	SP34	30c + 15c multi	.70	.70
		Nos. B125-B127 (3)	1.90	1.90

Child Welfare semi-postal stamps, 25th anniv.

Girl Combing her Hair — SP35

15c+7c, Young people listening to rock music. 40c+20c, Drummer, symbolizing rock music.

1974, Apr. 9 Litho. *Perf. 14x13*

B128	SP35	12c + 6c multi	.90	.70
B129	SP35	15c + 7c multi	.90	.70
B130	SP35	40c + 20c multi	.90	.70
		Nos. B128-B130 (3)	2.70	2.10

Surtax was for various social and cultural institutions.

Child, Saw and Score — SP36

Designs: 20c+10c, Footprints in circle. 30c+15c, Moon and sun. Each design includes score of a children's song.

1974, Nov. 12 Litho. *Perf. 13x14*

B131	SP36	15c + 5c multi	.90	.60
B132	SP36	20c + 10c multi	.90	.60
B133	SP36	30c + 15c multi	.90	.60
		Nos. B131-B133 (3)	2.70	1.80

Surtax was for child welfare.

Carved Stone Grid, Flower Pot SP37

Jewish Tombstone, Mordecai's Procession SP38

Design: 40c+20c, Ornamental stone from facade of Jewish House, 1728.

1975, Mar. 21 Litho. *Perf. 13x14*

B134	SP37	12c + 6c multi	.60	.60
B135	SP38	15c + 7c multi	.60	.60
B136	SP37	40c + 20c multi	.60	.60
		Nos. B134-B136 (3)	1.80	1.80

Surtax was for various social and cultural institutions.

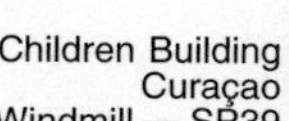

Children Building Curaçao Windmill — SP39

Designs: 20c+10c, Girl molding clay animal. 30c+15c, Children drawing picture.

1975, Nov. 12 Litho. *Perf. 14x13*

B137	SP39	15c + 5c multi	.60	.60
B138	SP39	20c + 10c multi	.60	.60
B139	SP39	30c + 15c multi	.60	.60
		Nos. B137-B139 (3)	1.80	1.80

Surtax was for child welfare.

Carrying a Child — SP40

Designs: Different ways of carrying a child. 40c+18c is vertical.

Perf. 14x13, 13x14

1976, Oct. 4 Litho.

B140	SP40	20c + 10c multi	.60	.60
B141	SP40	25c + 12c multi	.60	.60
B142	SP40	40c + 18c multi	.60	.60
		Nos. B140-B142 (3)	1.80	1.80

Surtax was for child welfare.

Composite: Aces of Hearts, Clubs, Diamonds and Spades — SP41

Designs: 25c+12c, "King" and inscription. 40c+18c, Hand holding cards; map of Aruba as ace of hearts, horiz.

Perf. 13x14, 14x13

1977, May 6 Litho.

B143	SP41	20c + 10c red & blk	.50	.35
B144	SP41	25c + 12c multi	.50	.35
a.		Min. sheet, 2 ea #B143-B144	1.40	1.10
B145	SP41	40c + 18c multi	.65	.45
		Nos. B143-B145 (3)	1.65	1.15

Central American and Caribbean Bridge Championships, Aruba.

Souvenir Sheet

1977, May 26 *Perf. 13½x14*

B146	SP41	Sheet of 3	3.50	2.50

Amphilex 77 International Philatelic Exhibition, Amsterdam, May 26-June 5. No. B146 contains 3 stamps similar to Nos. B143-B145 with bright green background.

Children and Toys — SP42

Children playing with fantasy animals.

1977, Oct. 25 Litho. *Perf. 14x13*

B147	SP42	15c + 5c multi	.35	.25
B148	SP42	20c + 10c multi	.45	.35
B149	SP42	25c + 12c multi	.55	.45
B150	SP42	40c + 18c multi	.65	.45
a.		Min. sheet, 2 ea #B148, B150	2.40	1.60
		Nos. B147-B150 (4)	2.00	1.50

Surtax was for child welfare.

Water Skiing — SP43

Designs: 20c+10c, Sailing. 25c+12c, Soccer. 40c+18c, Baseball.

1978, Mar. 31 Litho. *Perf. 13x14*

B151 SP43 15c + 5c multi .25 .25
B152 SP43 20c + 10c multi .25 .25
B153 SP43 25c + 12c multi .25 .25
B154 SP43 40c + 18c multi .25 .25
Nos. B151-B154 (4) 1.00 1.00

Surtax was for sports. Tete-beche gutter pairs exist.

Red Cross — SP44

1978, Sept. 19 Litho. *Perf. 14x13*

B155 SP44 55c + 25c red & blk .40 .40
a. Souv. sheet of 3, perf. 13½x13 2.00 1.60

Henri Dunant (1828-1910), founder of Red Cross. Surtax for the Red Cross.
Tete-beche gutter pairs exist.

Roller Skating — SP45

Children's Activities: 20c+10c, Kite flying. 25c+12c, Playing marbles. 40c+ 18c, Bicycling.

1978, Nov. 7 Litho. *Perf. 13x14*

B156 SP45 15c + 5c multi .45 .35
B157 SP45 20c + 10c multi .50 .40
a. Min. sheet, 2 ea #B156-B157 1.75 1.50
B158 SP45 25c + 12c multi .55 .45
B159 SP45 40c + 18c multi .60 .50
Nos. B156-B159 (4) 2.10 1.70

Surtax was for child welfare.

Carnival King — SP46

25th Aruba Carnival: 75c+20c, Carnival Queen and coat of arms.

1979, Feb. 20 Litho. *Perf. 13x14*

B160 SP46 40c + 10c multi .50 .45
B161 SP46 75c + 20c multi .75 .70

Regatta Emblem — SP47

Designs: 35c+10c, Race. 40c+15c, Globe and yacht, horiz. 55c+25c, Yacht, birds and sun.

Perf. 13x14, 14x13

1979, May 16 Litho.

B162 SP47 15c + 5c multi .25 .25
B163 SP47 35c + 10c multi .35 .30
B164 SP47 40c + 15c multi .45 .35
B165 SP47 55c + 25c multi .55 .40
a. Souv. sheet of 4, #B162-B165 1.75 1.50
Nos. B162-B165 (4) 1.60 1.30

12th International Sailing Regatta, Bonaire. #B164 in souvenir sheet is perf 13x14.

Volunteer Corps Type, 1979

15c+10c, Soldiers, 1929 and 1979. 40c+20c, Soldier guarding oil refinery, Guard emblem.

1979, July 4 Litho. *Perf. 13x14*

B166 A124 15c + 10c multi .35 .30
B167 A124 40c + 20c multi .45 .40

Girls Reading Book, IYC Emblem — SP48

IYC Emblem and Children's Drawings: 25c+12c, Infant and cat. 35c+15c, Girls walking under palm trees. 50c+20c, Children wearing adult clothing.

1979, Oct. 24 Litho. *Perf. 13x14*

B168 SP48 20c + 10c multi .35 .35
B169 SP48 25c + 12c multi .40 .35
B170 SP48 35c + 15c multi .45 .40
a. Souv. sheet, 2 ea #B168, B170 1.50 1.60
B171 SP48 50c + 20c multi .55 .50
Nos. B168-B171 (4) 1.75 1.60

International Year of the Child. Surtax for child welfare.

Fort Church Type of 1980

Designs: 20c+10c, Brass chandelier, 1909, horiz. 50c+25c, Pipe organ.

Perf. 14x13, 13x14

1980, Jan. 9 Litho.

B172 A128 20c + 10c multi .35 .35
B173 A128 50c + 25c multi .45 .45

Volleyball, Olympic Rings — SP49

Designs: 25c+10c, Woman gymnast. 30c+15c, Male gymnast. 60c+25c, Basketball.

1980, June 25 Litho. *Perf. 13x14*

B174 SP49 25c + 10c multi .35 .30
B175 SP49 30c + 15c multi .40 .35
B176 SP49 45c + 20c multi .55 .50
B177 SP49 60c + 25c multi .65 .55
a. Souvenir sheet of 6, 3 each #B174, B177, perf. 14x13½ 2.25 1.90
Nos. B174-B177 (4) 1.95 1.70

22nd Summer Olympic Games, Moscow, July 19-Aug. 3.

St. Maarten Landscape — SP50

Children's Drawings: 30c+15c, House in Bonaire. 40c+20c, Child at blackboard. 60c+25c, Dancers, vert.

Perf. 14x13, 13x14

1980, Oct. 22 Litho.

B178 SP50 25c + 10c multi .40 .25
B179 SP50 30c + 15c multi .50 .40
B180 SP50 40c + 20c multi .55 .45
B181 SP50 60c + 25c multi .65 .45
a. Souvenir sheet of 6+ 4 labels, 3 each #B178, B181 3.00 2.25
Nos. B178-B181 (4) 2.10 1.55

Surtax was for child welfare. #B178 in souvenir sheet is perf 13x14.

Girl Using Sign Language — SP51

Designs: 25c+10c, Blind woman. 30c+15c, Man in wheelchair. 45c+20c, Infant in walker.

1981, Apr. 7 Litho. *Perf. 13x14*

B182 SP51 25c + 10c multi .45 .40
B183 SP51 30c + 15c multi .50 .50
B184 SP51 45c + 20c multi .65 .65
B185 SP51 60c + 25c multi .75 .70
Nos. B182-B185 (4) 2.35 2.25

International Year of the Disabled. Surtax was for handicapped children.

Tennis Player — SP52

1981, May 27 Litho. *Perf. 13x14*

B186 SP52 30c + 15c shown .60 .50
B187 SP52 50c + 20c Diving .80 .60
B188 SP52 70c + 25c Boxing 1.00 .80
a. Min. sheet of 3, #B186-B188 2.50 2.50
Nos. B186-B188 (3) 2.40 1.90

Surtax was for sporting events.

Den Mother and Cub Scout — SP53

Scouting in Netherlands Antilles, 50th Anniv.: 70c+25c, van der Maarel, national founder. 1g+50c, Ronde Klip (headquarters).

1981, Sept. 16 Litho. *Perf. 14x13*

B189 SP53 45c + 20c multi .95 .75
B190 SP53 70c + 25c multi 1.20 .95
B191 SP53 1g + 50c multi 1.60 1.35
a. Min. sheet of 3, #B189-B191, perf. 13½x13 4.00 3.25
Nos. B189-B191 (3) 3.75 3.05

Surtax was for various social and cultural institutions.

Girl and Teddy Bear — SP54

Designs: 35c+15c, Mother and child. 45c+20c, Two children. 55c+25c, Boy and cat.

1981, Oct. 21 Litho. *Perf. 13x14*

B192 SP54 35c + 15c multi .50 .45
B193 SP54 45c + 20c multi .60 .50
B194 SP54 55c + 25c multi .75 .65
a. Min. sheet, 2 ea #B192, B194 2.50 2.00
B195 SP54 85c + 40c multi 1.10 .95
Nos. B192-B195 (4) 2.95 2.55

Surtax for child welfare.

Fencing — SP55

1982, Feb. 17 Litho. *Perf. 14x13*

B196 SP55 35c + 15c shown .75 .50
B197 SP55 45c + 20c Judo 1.00 .60
B198 SP55 70c + 35c Soccer 1.25 .95
a. Miniature sheet of 2 + label 3.50 2.00
B199 SP55 85c + 40c Bicycling 1.50 1.10
Nos. B196-B199 (4) 4.50 3.15

Surtax was for sporting events.

Girl Playing Accordion — SP56

1982, Oct. 20 Litho.

B200 SP56 35c + 15c shown .85 .50
B201 SP56 75c + 35c Guitar 1.40 1.00
B202 SP56 85c + 40c Violin 1.60 1.10
a. Min. sheet of 3, #B200-B202 4.00 3.25
Nos. B200-B202 (3) 3.85 2.60

Surtax for child welfare.

Traditional House, Saba — SP57

1982, Nov. 17 Litho.

B203 SP57 35c + 15c shown .95 .65
B204 SP57 75c + 35c Aruba 1.40 .95
B205 SP57 85c + 40c Curaçao 1.40 .95
a. Souv. sheet of 3, #B203-B205 4.00 3.25
Nos. B203-B205 (3) 3.75 2.55

Surtax was for various social and cultural institutions.

High Jump — SP58

No. B207, Weight lifting. No. B208, Wind surfing.

1983, Feb. 22 Litho.

B206 SP58 35c + 15c shown .75 .60
B207 SP58 45c + 20c multi 1.10 .75
B208 SP58 85c + 40c multi 1.75 1.20
Nos. B206-B208 (3) 3.60 2.55

Surtax was for sporting events.

Child with Lizard — SP59

No. B210, Child with insects. No. B211, Child with animal.

1983, Oct. 18 Litho. *Perf. 13x14*

B209 SP59 45c + 20c shown 1.00 .75
B210 SP59 55c + 25c multi 1.25 .90
B211 SP59 100c + 50c multi 2.00 1.50
a. Souv. sheet of 3, #B209-B211 4.50 3.25
Nos. B209-B211 (3) 4.25 3.15

Surtax was for Childrens' Charity.

Pre-Columbian Artifacts — SP60

1983, Nov. 22 Litho. *Perf. 13x14*

B212 SP60 45c + 20c multi 1.00 .85
B213 SP60 55c + 25c multi 1.25 1.00
B214 SP60 85c + 40c multi 1.50 1.10
B215 SP60 100c + 50c multi 1.90 1.50
Nos. B212-B215 (4) 5.65 4.45

Curaçao Baseball Federation, 50th Anniv. — SP61

1984, Mar. 27 Litho. *Perf. 14x13*

B216 SP61 25c + 10c Catching 1.20 .50
B217 SP61 45c + 20c Batting 1.70 .85
B218 SP61 55c + 25c Pitching 2.10 1.05
B219 SP61 85c + 40c Running 2.40 1.30
a. Min. sheet of 3, #B217-B219 6.00 3.75
Nos. B216-B219 (4) 7.40 3.70

Surtax was for baseball fed., 1984 Olympics.

Microphones, Radio — SP62

Designs: 55c+25c, Radio, record player. 100c+50c, Record players.

1984, Apr. 24 Litho. *Perf. 14x13*

B220 SP62 45c + 20c multi 1.45 .90
B221 SP62 55c + 25c multi 1.75 1.15
B222 SP62 100c + 50c multi 2.10 1.60
Nos. B220-B222 (3) 5.30 3.65

Surtax was for social and cultural institutions.

Boy Reading — SP63

Designs: 55c+25c, Parents reading to children. 100c+50c, Family worship.

1984, Nov. 7 Litho. *Perf. 13x14*

B223 SP63 45c + 20c multi 1.05 .90
B224 SP63 55c + 25c multi 1.35 1.15
B225 SP63 100c + 50c multi 1.75 1.45
a. Souv. sheet of 3, #B223-B225 4.50 3.75
Nos. B223-B225 (3) 4.15 3.50

Surtax was for children's charity.

Soccer Players — SP64

1985, Mar. 27 Litho. *Perf. 14x13*

B226 SP64 10c + 5c multi .60 .35
B227 SP64 15c + 5c multi .65 .40
B228 SP64 45c + 20c multi 1.15 .85
B229 SP64 55c + 25c multi 1.40 1.05
B230 SP64 85c + 40c multi 1.90 1.45
Nos. B226-B230 (5) 5.70 4.10

The surtax was for sporting events.

Intl. Youth Year — SP65

No. B231, Youth, computer keyboard. No. B232, Girl listening to music. No. B233, Youth breakdancing.

1985, Apr. 29 Litho.

B231 SP65 45c + 20c multi 1.20 .90
B232 SP65 55c + 25c multi 1.60 1.15
B233 SP65 100c + 50c multi 2.25 1.60
Nos. B231-B233 (3) 5.05 3.65

Surtax for youth, social and cultural organizations.

Children — SP66

No. B234, Eskimo. No. B235, African. No. B236, Asian. No. B237, Dutch. No. B238, American Indian.

1985, Oct. 16 Litho. *Perf. 13x14*

B234 SP66 5c + 5c multi .45 .25
B235 SP66 10c + 5c multi .55 .30
B236 SP66 25c + 10c multi .80 .45
B237 SP66 45c + 20c multi 1.40 .80
B238 SP66 55c + 25c multi 1.40 .95
a. Souv. sheet of 3, #B236-B238 4.00 2.25
Nos. B234-B238 (5) 4.60 2.75

Surtax for child welfare.

Sports — SP67

No. B239, Running. No. B240, Horse racing. No. B241, Car racing. No. B242, Soccer.

1986, Feb. 19 Litho. *Perf. 13x14*

B239 SP67 15c + 5c multi 1.05 .45
B240 SP67 25c + 10c multi 1.25 .65
B241 SP67 45c + 20c multi 1.60 .85
B242 SP67 55c + 25c multi 1.75 1.05
Nos. B239-B242 (4) 5.65 3.00

Surtax for the natl. Sports Federation.

Handicrafts — SP68

1986, Apr. 29

B243 SP68 30c + 15c Painting 1.05 .60
B244 SP68 45c + 20c Sculpting 1.25 .65
B245 SP68 55c + 25c Ceramics 1.50 .90
Nos. B243-B245 (3) 3.80 2.15

Surtax for Curaçao Social & Cultural Care.

Sports — SP69

1986, Oct. 15 Litho. *Perf. 13x14*

B246 SP69 20c + 10c Soccer .70 .40
B247 SP69 25c + 15c Tennis .90 .45
B248 SP69 45c + 20c Judo 1.05 .65
B249 SP69 55c + 25c Baseball 1.25 .85
a. Min. sheet of 2, #B248-B249 2.60 1.60
Nos. B246-B249 (4) 3.90 2.35

Surtax for the natl. Sports Foundation.

Social and Cultural Programs — SP70

No. B250, Musicians. No. B251, Handicapped. No. B252, Pavilion.

1987, Mar. 11 Litho.

B250 SP70 35c + 15c multi .80 .55
B251 SP70 45c + 25c multi 1.25 .65
B252 SP70 85c + 40c multi 1.60 1.05
Nos. B250-B252 (3) 3.65 2.25

Surtax for the Jong Wacht (Youth Guard) and the natl. Red Cross.

Boy in Various Stages of Growth — SP71

1987, Oct. 21 Litho. *Perf. 14x13*

B253 SP71 40c +15c Infant 1.00 .65
B254 SP71 55c +25c Toddler 1.25 .85
B255 SP71 115c +50c Boy 1.60 1.15
a. Souv. sheet of 3, #B253-B255 4.25 2.75
Nos. B253-B255 (3) 3.85 2.65

Surtax benefited Child Care programs.

Queen Emma Bridge, Cent. — SP72

55c+25c, Bridge, vert. 115c+55c, View of Willemstad Harbor and quay. 190c+60c, Flags of the Netherlands, Antilles and US, Leonard B. Smith, engineer.

1988, May 9 *Perf. 13x14, 14x13*

B256 SP72 55c +25c multi 1.15 .60
B257 SP72 115c +55c multi 1.75 1.10
B258 SP72 190c +60c multi 3.00 2.00
Nos. B256-B258 (3) 5.90 3.70

Surtax for social and cultural purposes.

Youth Care Campaign — SP73

No. B259, Girl, television. No. B260, Boy, portable stereo. No. B261, Girl, computer.

1988, Oct. 26 Litho. *Perf. 14x13*

B259 SP73 55c +25c multi 1.05 .65
B260 SP73 65c +30c multi 1.15 .80
B261 SP73 115c +55c multi 1.60 1.15
a. Souv. sheet of 3, #B259-B261 5.25 2.75
Nos. B259-B261 (3) 3.80 2.60

Surtax for child welfare.

Curaçao Stamp Assoc., 50th Anniv. SP75

Designs: 30c+10c, Type A25 and No. 461 under magnifying glass. 55c+20c, Simulated stamp (learning to use tongs). 80c+30c, Barn owl, album, magnifying glass, tongs.

1989, Jan. 18 Litho. *Perf. 13x14*

B264 30c +10c multi 1.25 .55
B265 55c +20c multi 1.25 .85
B266 80c +30c multi 1.25 .95
a. SP75 Strip of 3, #B264-B266 3.75 3.00

No. B266a has a continuous design. Surtaxed for welfare organizations.

Child and Nature — SP76

No. B267, Girl, boy, tree. No. B268, Playing on beach. No. B269, Father and child.
No. B270, At the beach, diff.

1989, Oct. 25 Litho. *Perf. 14x13*

B267 SP76 40c +15c multi 1.00 .60
B268 SP76 65c +30c multi 1.15 .80
B269 SP76 115c +55c multi 1.75 1.30
Nos. B267-B269 (3) 3.90 2.70

Souvenir Sheet

B270 SP76 155c +75c multi 3.75 2.10

Surtax for child welfare.

Natl. Girl Scout Movement, 60th Anniv. SP77

Totolika, 60th Anniv. SP78

Natl. Boy Scout Movement, 60th Anniv. — SP79

1990, Mar. 7 Litho. *Perf. 13x14*

B271 SP77 30c +10c multi .80 .55
B272 SP78 40c +15c multi 1.05 .75
B273 SP79 155c +65c multi 3.00 2.50
Nos. B271-B273 (3) 4.85 3.80

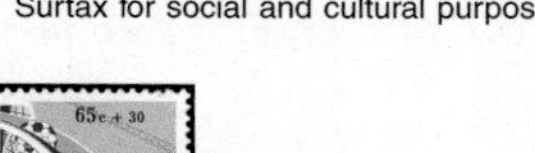

Parents' and Friends Association of Persons with a Mental Handicap (Totolika).
Surtax for social and cultural purposes.

SP80

1990, June 13 Litho. *Perf. 13x14*

B274 SP80 65c +30c multi 1.15 .75

Sport Unie Brion Trappers Soccer Club. Exists in tete-beche gutter pairs.

Anti-drug Campaign — SP81

1990, June 13

B275 SP81 115c +55c multi 1.75 1.35

Exists in tete-beche gutter pairs.

Youth Care Campaign — SP82

No. B276, Bees, flowers. No. B277, Dolphins. No. B278, Donkey, bicycle. No. B279, Goat, house. No. B280, Rabbit. No. B281, Lizard, moon.

1990, Oct. 31 Litho. *Perf. 14x13*

B276 SP82 30c +5c multi .70 .40
B277 SP82 55c +10c multi 1.05 .60
B278 SP82 65c +15c multi 1.15 .80
B279 SP82 100c +20c multi 1.75 1.20
B280 SP82 115c +25c multi 1.90 1.30
B281 SP82 155c +55c multi 3.25 2.10
Nos. B276-B281 (6) 9.80 6.40

Surtax for child welfare.
See Nos. B285-B288.

Social and Cultural Care — SP83

Designs: 30c+10c, Youth philately. 65c+25c, St. Vincentius Brass Band, 50th anniv. 155c+55c, Curaçao Community Center Federation.

1991, Apr. 3 Litho. *Perf. 14x13*

B282 SP83 30c +10c multi .85 .60
B283 SP83 65c +25c multi 1.35 1.00
B284 SP83 155c +55c multi 3.00 2.25
Nos. B282-B284 (3) 5.20 3.85

Youth Care Campaign Type of 1990

Fight illiteracy: 40c+15c, Octopus holding numbers and letters. 65c+30c, Birds, blackboard. 155c+65c, Turtle telling time. No. B288a, Owl, flag. b, Books, bookworms. c, Seahorse.

1991, Oct. 31 Litho. *Perf. 14x13*

B285 SP82 40c +15c multi 1.15 .80
B286 SP82 65c +30c multi 1.45 1.35
B287 SP82 155c +65c multi 3.00 3.00
Nos. B285-B287 (3) 5.60 5.15

Souvenir Sheet

Imperf

B288 Sheet of 3 6.25 5.00
a. SP82 55c +25c multi 2.00 1.60
b. SP82 100c +35c multi 2.00 1.60
c. SP82 115c +50c multi 2.00 1.60

Surtax for child welfare.

SP84

1992 Summer Olympics, Barcelona: a, 30c + 10c, Triangle and oval. b, 55c + 25c, Globe showing location of Netherland Antilles, flag. c, 115c + 55c, Emblem of Netherlands Antilles Olympic Committee.

1992, Mar. 4 Litho. *Perf. 13x14*

B289 SP84 Strip of 3, #a.-c. 4.50 3.75

Netherlands Antilles Olympic Committee, 60th Anniv.

SP85

No. B290, Spaceship. No. B291, Robot. No. B292, Extraterrestrial.
No. B293, Extraterrestrial, diff.

1992, Oct. 28 Litho. *Perf. 13x14*

B290	SP85	30c +10c multi	.65	.50
B291	SP85	70c +30c multi	1.15	1.15
B292	SP85	100c +40c multi	1.75	1.60
		Nos. B290-B292 (3)	3.55	3.25

Souvenir Sheet

B293	SP85	155c +70c multi	3.50	3.25

Surtax for child welfare.

SP86

Designs: 65c+25c, Fire safety, child playing with blocks. 90c+35c, Child fastening auto safety belt, vert. 175c+75c, Child wearing flotation equipment while swimming. 35c+15c, Alert child studying.

Perf. 14x13, 13x14

1993, Oct. 27 Litho.

B294	SP86	65c +25c multi	1.25	1.05
B295	SP86	90c +35c multi	1.50	1.35
B296	SP86	175c +75c multi	3.00	2.75
		Nos. B294-B296 (3)	5.75	5.15

Souvenir Sheet

Perf. 13½x13

B297	SP86	35c +15c Sheet of 5 + label	5.00	5.00

Surtax for child welfare.

Intl. Year of the Family — SP87

No. B298, Woman, baby. No. B299, Daughter, father. No. B300, Grandparents.
No. B301, Intl. emblem.

1994, Oct. 26 Litho. *Perf. 13x14*

B298	SP87	35c +15c multi	.60	.55
B299	SP87	65c +25c multi	1.10	1.05
B300	SP87	90c +35c multi	2.00	1.75
		Nos. B298-B300 (3)	3.70	3.35

Souvenir Sheet

B301	SP87	175c +75c multi	3.75	3.75

Surtax for the benefit of the Antillean Youth Care Federation.

Slave Rebellion in Curaçao, Bicent. — SP88

Designs: 30c+10c, Monument, bird with outstretched wings. 45c+15c, Bird, bell tower.

1995, Aug. 17 Litho. *Perf. 14x13*

B302	SP88	30c +10c multi	.75	.65
B303	SP88	45c +15c multi	1.15	1.00

Youth Philately — SP89

Stamp drawings by children from: 65c+25c, Curaçao, Bonaire. 75c+35c, St. Maarten, St. Eustatius, Saba.

1995, Aug. 17

B304	SP89	65c +25c multi	1.40	1.05
B305	SP89	75c +35c multi	1.50	1.20

Nos. 516-517, 544 Surcharged in Red Brown

1995, Sept. 22 Litho. *Perf. 14x13*

B306	A148	65c +65c on #516	1.75	1.60
B307	A148	75c +75c on #517	2.00	1.75
B308	A148	1g +1g on #544	2.40	2.25
		Nos. B306-B308 (3)	6.15	5.60

Surcharge for hurricane relief.

Child Welfare Stamps — SP91

Promotion of Children's Good Deeds: 35c+15c, Helping elderly across street. 65c+25c, Reading newspaper to blind person. 90c+35c, Caring for younger sibling. 175c+75c, Giving flowers to sick person.

1995, Oct. 25 Litho. *Perf. 14x13*

B309	SP91	35c +15c multi	.65	.60
B310	SP91	65c +25c multi	1.15	1.05
B311	SP91	90c +35c multi	1.45	1.35
B312	SP91	175c +75c multi	3.00	2.75
		Nos. B309-B312 (4)	6.25	5.75

Surtax for various youth organizations.

Child Welfare Stamps — SP92

UNICEF, 50th anniv.: 40c+15c, Child wandering streets. 75c+25c, Child labor in Asia. 110c+45c, Child in wartime (former Yugoslavia), vert. 225c+100c, Caribbean poverty, vert.

Perf. 14x13, 13x14

1996, Oct. 23 Litho.

B313	SP92	40c +15c multi	.75	.65
B314	SP92	75c +25c multi	1.30	1.20
B315	SP92	110c +45c multi	1.90	1.75
B316	SP92	225c +100c multi	4.00	3.75
		Nos. B313-B316 (4)	7.95	7.35

Social and Cultural Care Stamps — SP93

Designs: 40c+15c, Curaçao Foundation for the cure and resettlement of ex-prisoners, 50th anniv. 75c+30c, ABVO (General Union of Public Servants), 60th anniv. 85+40c, 110c+50c, Red Cross Corps section, Curaçao, 65th anniv.

1997, Jan. 16 Litho. *Perf. 13x14*

B317	SP93	40c +15c multi	.90	.65
B318	SP93	75c +30c multi	1.30	1.20
B319	SP93	85c +40c multi	1.60	1.60
B320	SP93	110 +50c multi	1.90	1.75
		Nos. B317-B320 (4)	5.70	5.20

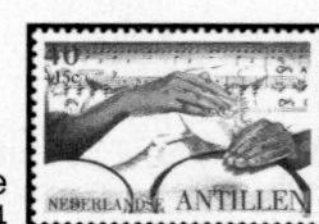

Child Welfare Stamps — SP94

Musical notes, musical instruments: 40c+15c, Drums. 75c+25c, Piano. 110c+45c, Flute. 225c+100c, Guitar.

1997, Oct. 22 Litho. *Perf. 14x13*

B321	SP94	40c +15c multi	.80	.65
B322	SP94	75c +25c multi	1.20	1.15
B323	SP94	110c +45c multi	2.00	1.75
B324	SP94	225c +100c multi	3.00	2.50
		Nos. B321-B324 (4)	7.00	6.05

Social and Cultural Care — SP95

No. B325, Curacao Museum, 50th anniv. No. B326, Seawater Desalination, 70th anniv. 75c+25c, Water area, Lac Cai Bonaire, vert. 85c+40c, Water area, Klein-Bonaire, vert.

Perf. 14x13, 13x14

1998, Mar. 9 Litho.

B325	SP95	40c +15c multi	.85	.70
B326	SP95	40c +15c multi	.85	.70
B327	SP95	75c +25c multi	1.45	1.30
B328	SP95	85c +40c multi	1.90	1.75
		Nos. B325-B328 (4)	5.05	4.45

Child Welfare Stamps — SP96

Universal Rights of the Child: 40c+15c, Child holding cutouts representing family. 75c+25c, Children eating watermelon. 110c+45c, Handicapped children drawing pictures. 225c+100c, Children holding cans with string to play telephone.

1998, Oct. 28 Litho. *Perf. 13x14*

B329	SP96	40c +15c multi	.85	.70
B330	SP96	75c +25c multi	1.30	1.20
B331	SP96	110c +45c multi	2.00	1.90
B332	SP96	225c +100c multi	4.25	4.00
		Nos. B329-B332 (4)	8.40	7.80

Buildings — SP97

Willemstad buildings on World Heritage List: 40c+15c, Houses, Ijzerstraat neighborhood, horiz. 75c+30c, Postal Museum. 110c+50c, "Bridal Cake" building, Scharloo area, horiz.

Perf. 14x13, 13x14

1999, Sept. 28 Litho.

B333	SP97	40c +15c multi	.80	.70
B334	SP97	75c +30c multi	1.45	1.30
B335	SP97	110c +50c multi	2.10	1.90
		Nos. B333-B335 (3)	4.35	3.90

Sports — SP98

1999, Oct. 27 *Perf. 13x14*

B336	SP98	40c +15c Basketball	1.30	.80
B337	SP98	75c +25c Golf	1.75	1.30
B338	SP98	110c +45c Fencing	2.60	1.90
B339	SP98	225c +100c Tennis	4.75	4.00
		Nos. B336-B339 (4)	10.40	8.00

Social and Cultural Care — SP99

Designs: 75c+30c, Children playing. 110c+50c, Chemistry lesson. 225c+100c, Arithmetic lesson, vert.

Perf. 14x13, 13x14

2000, Apr. 28 Litho.

B340-B342	SP99	Set of 3	8.25	7.00

Youth Care — SP100

Designs: 40c+15c, Child reaching up, vert. 75c+25c, Children learning with computers. 110c+45c, Children playing with toy boat. 225c+100c, Children and map, vert.

Perf. 13x14, 14x13

2000, Oct. 25 Litho.

B343-B346	SP100	Set of 4	9.50	8.75

Caribbean Postal Union, 5th Anniv. — SP101

Designs: 75c+25c, Pen, emblem. 110c+45c, Emblem. 225c+100c, Globe, emblem.

2001, May 21 Litho. *Perf. 13¼x13¾*

B347-B349	SP101	Set of 3	10.00	8.25

Youth Care — SP102

Designs: 40c+15c, Boy feeding baby. 75c+25c, Girls dancing, vert. 110c+45c, Boy pushing woman in wheelchair, vert.

Perf. 13½x12¾, 12¾x13½

2001, Oct. 24 Litho.

B350-B352	SP102	Set of 3	6.25	5.75

2002 World Cup Soccer Championships, Japan and Korea — SP103

Soccer player with: 95c+35c, Ball of flags. 145c+55c, Ball with map. 240c+110c, Ball.

2002, June 25 Litho. *Perf. 12¾x14*

B353-B355	SP103	Set of 3	11.00	10.00

Youth Care — SP104

"Dialogue among civilizations:" 50c+15c, Lion and fish. 95c+35c, Kangaroo and iguana. 145c+55c, Goat and penguin. 240c+110c, Lizard and toucan.

2002, Oct. 24 *Perf. 14x12¾*

B356-B359	SP104	Set of 4	11.25	11.25

Miniature Sheet

Maps of the Netherlands Antilles — SP105

No. B360: a, 25c+10c, Portion of 1688 map by Hendrick Doncker showing Curaçao and Bonaire. b, 30c+15c, Portion of Doncker map showing St. Maarten, Saba and St. Eustatius, vert. c, 55c+25c, Modern map of Curaçao and Bonaire. d, 85c+35c, Modern map of St. Maarten, Saba and St. Eustatius, vert. e, 95c+40c, Modern map of Caribbean Islands.

Perf. 14x12¾, 12¾x14 (vert. stamps)
2003, Mar. 19 Litho.
B360 SP105 Sheet of 5, #a-e 7.50 7.00

Miniature Sheet

Youth Care SP106

No. B361: a, 50c+15c, Boy taking shower. b, 95c+35c, Girl with umbrella. c, 145c+55c, Boy with watering can. d, 240c+110c, Hands in water from open faucet.

2003, Oct. 22 Litho. *Perf. 13x14*
B361 SP106 Sheet of 4, #a-d 9.50 8.50

Intl. Year of Fresh Water.

Youth Care — SP107

No. B362: a, Boy, girl, slave huts. b, Girl, Autonomy Monument. c, Boy, girl, broken stone walls built by slaves. d, Boy, girl, wall of plantation house. e, Boy, preamble of Netherlands Constitution.

2004, Oct. 20 *Perf. 13½x13*

B362		Horiz. strip of 5	8.25	8.25
a.	SP107	50c +15c multi	.75	.75
b.-c.	SP107	95c +35c either single	1.50	1.50
d.-e.	SP107	145c +55c either single	2.25	2.25

Autonomy of the Netherlands Antilles, 50th anniv. (Nos. B362b, B362e), Intl. Year Commemorating the Struggle Against Slavery and its Abolition (Nos. B362a, B362c, B362d).

Intl. Year of Sports and Physical Education — SP108

Designs: 55c+20c, Soccer. 97c+36c, Table tennis. 148c+56c, Tennis. 240c+110c, Baseball.

2005, Dec. 24 Litho. *Perf. 13x13½*
B363-B366 SP108 Set of 4 9.50 9.50

Youth Care — SP109

Hatted globes showing: 55c+20c, North and South America. 100c+45c, Africa. 149c+61c, Europe, Africa and Asia. 285c+125c, Africa and Asia.

2006, Oct. 23 Litho. *Perf. 12¾x13¼*
B367-B370 SP109 Set of 4 8.25 8.25

Youth Care — SP110

Family: 59c+26c, Praying at dinner table. 104c+46c, Respecting flag. 155c+65c, As baseball team. 285c+125c, Studying together.

2007, Oct. 24 Litho. *Perf. 13¼x12¾*
B371-B374 SP110 Set of 4 8.25 8.25

Youth Care — SP111

Potato: 59c+26c, As potato farmer. 1.06g+46c, Peeling potatoes. 1.58g+65c, Eating French fries. 2.85g+1.25g, Family.

2008, Oct. 23 Litho. *Perf. 12¾x13¼*
B375-B378 SP111 Set of 4 9.00 9.00

Intl. Year of the Potato.

Youth Care — SP112

Designs: 59c+26c, Galileo Galilei and silhouette of boy. 110c+45c, Silhouettes of stargazers and telescope. 168c+75c, Silhouettes of children watching space shuttle. 285c+125c, Men walking on Moon.

2009, Oct. 26 Litho. *Perf. 12¾x13¼*
B379-B382 SP112 Set of 4 8.50 8.50

Intl. Year of Astronomy.

AIR POST STAMPS

Regular Issues of 1915-22 Surcharged in Black

Perf. 12½
1929, July 6 Typo. Unwmk.

C1	A13	50c on 12½c red	18.00	21.00
C2	A13	1g on 20c blue	18.00	21.00
C3	A13	2g on 15c ol grn	45.00	52.50
		Nos. C1-C3 (3)	81.00	94.50

Excellent forgeries exist.

Allegory, "Flight" — AP1

1931-39 Engr.

C4	AP1	10c Prus grn ('34)	.25	.25
C5	AP1	15c dull blue ('38)	.40	.25
C6	AP1	20c red	1.00	.25
C7	AP1	25c gray ('38)	.80	.90
C8	AP1	30c yellow ('39)	.40	.40
C9	AP1	35c dull blue	1.20	1.15
C10	AP1	40c green	.80	.55
C11	AP1	45c orange	2.00	2.00
C12	AP1	50c lake ('38)	1.20	.60
C13	AP1	60c brown vio	.80	.40
C14	AP1	70c black	6.50	2.00
C15	AP1	1.40g brown	4.00	5.00
C16	AP1	2.80g bister	5.00	5.25
		Nos. C4-C16 (13)	24.35	19.00

No. C6 Surcharged in Black

1934, Aug. 25
C17 AP1 10c on 20c red 20.00 15.00

Catalogue values for unused stamps in this section, from this point to the end of the section, are for Never Hinged items.

Map of the Atlantic — AP2

Plane over Islands — AP3

Map of Curaçao, Aruba and Bonaire — AP4

Planes — AP5

Plane — AP6

1942, Oct. 20 *Perf. 13x13½*

C18	AP2	10c grn & bl	.80	.25
C19	AP3	15c rose car & yel grn	.80	.25
C20	AP4	20c red brn & grn	.80	.25
C21	AP5	25c dp ultra & org brn	.80	.25
C22	AP6	30c red & lt vio	.80	.75
C23	AP2	35c dk vio & ol grn	1.20	.55
C24	AP3	40c gray ol & chnt	1.60	.55
C25	AP4	45c dk red & blk	.80	.25
C26	AP5	50c vio & blk	2.00	.25
C27	AP6	60c lt yel brn & dl bl	3.25	1.15
C28	AP2	70c red brn & Prus bl	3.25	1.15
C29	AP3	1.40g bl vio & sl grn	20.00	2.10
C30	AP4	2.80g int bl & lt bl	28.00	5.75
C31	AP5	5g rose lake & sl grn	45.00	19.00
C32	AP6	10g grn & red brn	52.50	28.00
		Nos. C18-C32 (15)	161.60	60.50

For surcharges see Nos. CB9-CB12.

Plane and Post Horn AP7

DC-4 above Waves AP8

1947 Photo. *Perf. 12½x12*

C32A	AP7	6c gray blk	.65	.25
C33	AP7	10c deep red	.65	.25
C33A	AP7	12½c plum	.90	.25
C34	AP7	15c deep blue	.90	.30
C35	AP7	20c dl yel grn	1.10	.35
C36	AP7	25c org yel	1.10	.25
C37	AP7	30c lilac gray	1.35	.55
C38	AP7	35c org red	1.35	.70
C39	AP7	40c blue grn	1.35	.70
C40	AP7	45c brt violet	1.60	1.05
C41	AP7	50c carmine	1.60	.25
C42	AP7	60c brt blue	2.10	.65
C43	AP7	70c brown	3.75	1.50

Engr.
Perf. 12x12½

C44	AP8	1.50g black	2.75	.90
C45	AP8	2.50g dk car	15.50	4.00
C46	AP8	5g green	32.00	8.25
C47	AP8	7.50g dk blue	130.00	95.00
C48	AP8	10g dk red vio	82.50	34.00
C49	AP8	15g red org	110.00	95.00
C50	AP8	25g chocolate	110.00	95.00
		Nos. C32A-C50 (20)	501.15	339.20

AIR POST SEMI-POSTAL STAMPS

Flags of the Netherlands and the House of Orange with Inscription "Netherlands Shall Rise Again" — SPAP1

Engr. & Photo.
1941, Dec. 11 Unwmk. *Perf. 12*

CB1	SPAP1	10c + 10c multi	32.00	26.00
CB2	SPAP1	15c + 25c multi	32.00	26.00
CB3	SPAP1	20c + 25c multi	32.00	26.00
CB4	SPAP1	25c + 25c multi	32.00	26.00
CB5	SPAP1	30c + 50c multi	32.00	26.00
CB6	SPAP1	35c + 50c multi	32.00	26.00
CB7	SPAP1	40c + 50c multi	32.00	26.00
CB8	SPAP1	50c +100c multi	32.00	26.00
		Nos. CB1-CB8 (8)	256.00	208.00

The surtax was used by the Prince Bernhard Committee to purchase war material for the Netherlands' fighting forces in Great Britain.

Catalogue values for unused stamps in this section, from this point to the end of the section, are for Never Hinged items.

Nos. C29-C32 Surcharged in Black

1943, Dec. 1 *Perf. 13x13½*

CB9	AP3	40c + 50c on 1.40g	9.00	8.25
CB10	AP4	45c + 50c on 2.80g	9.00	8.25
CB11	AP5	50c + 75c on 5g	9.00	8.25
CB12	AP6	60c + 100c on 10g	9.00	8.25
		Nos. CB9-CB12 (4)	36.00	33.00

The surtax was for the benefit of prisoners of war. These stamps were not sold to the public in the normal manner. All were sold in sets by advance subscription, the majority to philatelic speculators.

On No. CB9 overprint reads: "Voor / Krijgsgevangenen."

Princess Juliana — SPAP2

Engr. & Photo.
1944, Aug. 16 *Perf. 12*
Frame in carmine & deep blue, cross in carmine

CB13	SPAP2	10c + 10c lt brn	2.75	2.50
CB14	SPAP2	15c + 25c turq grn	2.75	2.50
CB15	SPAP2	20c + 25c dk ol gray	2.75	2.50
CB16	SPAP2	25c + 25c slate	2.75	2.50
CB17	SPAP2	30c + 50c sepia	2.75	2.50
CB18	SPAP2	35c + 50c chnt	2.75	2.50
CB19	SPAP2	40c + 50c grn	2.75	2.50
CB20	SPAP2	50c + 100c dk vio	2.75	2.50
		Nos. CB13-CB20 (8)	22.00	20.00

The surtax was for the Red Cross.

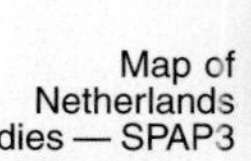

Map of Netherlands Indies — SPAP3

Map of Netherlands SPAP4

Photo. & Typo.
1946, July 1 *Perf. 11x11½*

CB21	SPAP3	10c + 10c	1.75	1.60
CB22	SPAP3	15c + 25c	1.75	1.60
CB23	SPAP3	20c + 25c	1.75	1.60
CB24	SPAP3	25c + 25c	1.75	1.60
CB25	SPAP3	30c + 50c	1.75	1.60
a.		Double impression of denomination	400.00	475.00
CB26	SPAP3	35c + 50c	1.75	1.60
CB27	SPAP3	40c + 75c	1.75	1.60
CB28	SPAP3	50c + 100c	1.75	1.60
CB29	SPAP4	10c + 10c	1.75	1.60
CB30	SPAP4	15c + 25c	1.75	1.60
CB31	SPAP4	20c + 25c	1.75	1.60
CB32	SPAP4	25c + 25c	1.75	1.60
CB33	SPAP4	30c + 50c	1.75	1.60
CB34	SPAP4	35c + 50c	1.75	1.60
CB35	SPAP4	40c + 75c	1.75	1.60
CB36	SPAP4	50c + 100c	1.75	1.60
		Nos. CB21-CB36 (16)	28.00	25.60

The surtax on Nos. CB21 to CB36 was for the National Relief Fund.

POSTAGE DUE STAMPS

D1

Type I — 34 loops. "T" of *"BETALEN"* over center of loop, top branch of "E" of *"TE"* shorter than lower branch.

Type II — 33 loops. "T" of *"BETALEN"* over center of two loops.

Type III — 32 loops. "T" of *"BETALEN"* slightly to the left of loop, top of first "E" of *"BETALEN"* shorter than lower branch.

Value in Black

1889 Unwmk. Typo. ***Perf. 12½***

Type III

No.	Type	Description	Unused	Used
J1	D1	2½c green	3.00	4.50
J2	D1	5c green	3.00	2.60
J3	D1	10c green	35.00	34.00
J4	D1	12½c green	400.00	210.00
J5	D1	15c green	28.00	22.50
J6	D1	20c green	16.00	11.50
J7	D1	25c green	200.00	150.00
J8	D1	30c green	14.00	11.50
J9	D1	40c green	18.00	11.50
J10	D1	50c green	40.00	30.00

Nos. J1-J10 were issued without gum.

Type I

No.	Type	Description	Unused	Used
J1a	D1	2½c	5.00	4.50
J2a	D1	5c	40.00	30.00
J3a	D1	10c	45.00	35.00
J4a	D1	12½c	450.00	225.00
J5a	D1	15c	32.00	22.50
J6a	D1	20c	80.00	57.50
J7a	D1	25c	600.00	350.00
J8a	D1	30c	80.00	67.50
J9a	D1	40c	80.00	67.50
J10a	D1	50c	50.00	37.50

Type II

No.	Type	Description	Unused	Used
J1b	D1	2½c	8.00	5.75
J2b	D1	5c	200.00	170.00
J3b	D1	10c	45.00	42.50
J4b	D1	12½c	475.00	260.00
J5b	D1	15c	32.00	26.00
J6b	D1	20c	450.00	425.00
J7b	D1	25c	*1,600.*	*1,600.*
J8b	D1	30c	450.00	375.00
J9b	D1	40c	450.00	375.00
10b	D1	50c	60.00	75.00

D2

1892-98 Value in Black ***Perf. 12½***

No.	Type	Description	Unused	Used
J11	D2	2½c green (III)	.80	1.15
J12	D2	5c green (III)	1.20	1.60
J13	D2	10c green (III)	2.00	1.90
J14	D2	12½c green (III)	2.00	1.90
J15	D2	15c green (III) ('95)	3.00	1.90
J17	D2	25c green (III)	12.00	1.15
		Nos. J11-J17 (6)	21.00	9.60

Type I

No.	Type	Description	Unused	Used
J11a	D2	2½c	.80	1.15
J12a	D2	5c	3.00	2.60
J13a	D2	10c	3.00	2.25
J14a	D2	12½c	2.40	1.90
J16	D2	20c green ('95)	4.00	1.90
J17a	D2	25c	12.00	1.90
J18	D2	30c green ('95)	40.00	34.00
J19	D2	40c green ('95)	50.00	34.00
J20	D2	50c green ('95)	50.00	34.00

Type II

No.	Type	Description	Unused	Used
J11b	D2	2½c	20.00	20.00
J12b	D2	5c	1.20	1.60
J13b	D2	10c	2.00	1.90
J14b	D2	12½c	8.00	7.50
J17b	D2	25c	*10.00*	*9.50*
		Nos. J11b-J17b (5)	41.20	40.50

The editors would like to see documented evidence of existence the following: 15c type I; 15c, 20c, 30c, 40c, 50c type II; 20c type III.

Nos. J18-J20 are printed on porous paper.

Type I

On Yellowish or White Paper

Value in Color of Stamp

1915 ***Perf. 12½, 13½x12½***

No.	Type	Description	Unused	Used
J21	D2	2½c green	.65	.75
J22	D2	5c green	.65	.75
J23	D2	10c green	.65	.75
J24	D2	12½c green	.80	1.15
J25	D2	15c green	1.45	1.60
J26	D2	20c green	.80	1.60
J27	D2	25c green	.25	.40
J28	D2	30c green	3.00	3.75
J29	D2	40c green	3.00	3.75
J30	D2	50c green	2.00	3.00
		Nos. J21-J30 (10)	13.25	17.50

1944 ***Perf. 11½***

No.	Type	Description	Unused	Used
J23a	D2	10c yellow green	40.00	37.50
J24a	D2	12½c yellow green	40.00	30.00
J27a	D2	25c yellow green	100.00	3.75
		Nos. J23a-J27a (3)	180.00	71.25

Nos. J23a-J27a designs are 18x22½mm; Nos. J21-J30 designs are 18x21½mm.

Type of 1915

Type I

Value in Color of Stamp

Perf. 13½x13

1948-49 Unwmk. Photo.

No.	Type	Description	Unused	Used
J31	D2	2½c bl grn ('48)	2.40	3.00
J32	D2	5c bl grn ('48)	2.40	3.00
J33	D2	10c blue green	10.00	10.50
J34	D2	12½c blue green	10.00	5.25
J35	D2	15c blue green	17.00	34.00
J36	D2	20c blue green	17.00	34.00
J37	D2	25c blue green	2.60	.75
J38	D2	30c blue green	17.00	34.00
J39	D2	40c blue green	17.00	34.00
J40	D2	50c blue green	17.00	34.00
		Nos. J31-J40 (10)	112.40	192.50

Catalogue values for unused stamps in this section, from this point to the end of the section, are for Never Hinged items.

D3

1953-59 Photo.

No.	Type	Description	Unused	Used
J41	D3	1c dk blue grn ('59)	.25	.40
J42	D3	2½c dk blue grn	.60	.75
J43	D3	5c dk blue grn	.25	.40
J44	D3	6c dk blue grn ('59)	.75	.90
J45	D3	7c dk blue grn ('59)	.75	.90
J46	D3	8c dk blue grn ('59)	.75	.90
J47	D3	9c dk blue grn ('59)	.75	.90
J48	D3	10c dk blue grn	.30	.40
J49	D3	12½c dk blue grn	.30	.40
J50	D3	15c dk blue grn	.75	.90
J51	D3	20c dk blue grn	.75	.90
J52	D3	25c dk blue grn	.60	.25
J53	D3	30c dk blue grn	1.60	1.90
J54	D3	35c dk blue grn ('59)	1.60	1.90
J55	D3	40c dk blue grn	1.60	1.90
J56	D3	45c dk blue grn ('59)	1.60	1.90
J57	D3	50c dk blue grn	1.60	1.90
		Nos. J41-J57 (17)	14.80	17.50

NETHERLANDS INDIES

'ne-thər-lən͵dz 'in-dēs

(Dutch Indies, Indonesia)

LOCATION — East Indies
GOVT. — Dutch colony
AREA — 735,268 sq. mi.
POP. — 76,000,000 (estimated 1949)
CAPITAL — Jakarta (formerly Batavia)

Netherlands Indies consisted of the islands of Sumatra, Java, the Lesser Sundas, Madura, two thirds of Borneo, Celebes, the Moluccas, western New Guinea and many small islands.

Netherlands Indies changed its name to Indonesia in 1948. The Netherlands transferred sovereignty on Dec. 28, 1949, to the Republic of the United States of Indonesia (see "Indonesia"), except for the western part of New Guinea (see "Netherlands New Guinea"). The Republic of Indonesia was proclaimed Aug. 15, 1950.

100 Cents = 1 Gulden
100 Sen = 1 Rupiah (1949)

Catalogue values for unused stamps in this country are for Never Hinged items, beginning with Scott 250 in the regular postage section, Scott B57 in the semi-postal section, and Scott J43 in the postage due section.

Values for unused stamps are for examples with original gum as defined in the catalogue introduction. Very fine examples of No. 2 will have perforations touching the frameline on one or more sides due to the narrow spacing of the stamps on the plates. Stamps with perfs clear of the framelines on all four sides are scarce and will command higher prices.

Watermarks

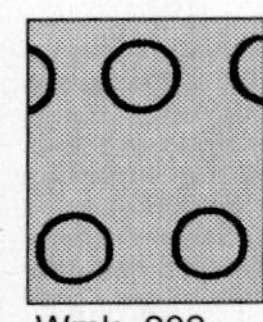

Wmk. 202 — Circles

Wmk. 228 — Small Crown and C of A Multiple

King William III — A1

Unwmk.

1864, Apr. 1 Engr. ***Imperf.***

No.	Type	Description	Unused	Used
1	A1	10c lake	325.00	100.00

1868 ***Perf. 12½x12***

No.	Type	Description	Unused	Used
2	A1	10c lake	1,250.	180.00

Privately perforated examples of No. 1 sometimes are mistaken for No. 2.

King William III — A2

ONE CENT:
Type I — "CENT" 6mm long.
Type II — "CENT" 7½mm long.

Perf. 11½x12, 12½, 12½x12, 13x14, 13½, 14, 13½x14

1870-88 Typo.

No.	Type	Description	Unused	Used
3	A2	1c sl grn, type I	20.00	8.00
a.		Perf. 13x14, small holes	16.00	6.50
4	A2	1c sl grn, type II	9.75	2.40
5	A2	2c red brown	13.00	5.00
a.		2c fawn	13.00	5.00
6	A2	2c violet brn	100.00	120.00
7	A2	2½c orange	65.00	30.00
8	A2	5c pale green	97.50	6.50
a.		Perf. 14, small holes	90.00	11.00
b.		Perf. 13x14, small holes	115.00	8.00
9	A2	10c orange brn	40.00	.40
a.		Perf. 14, small holes	35.00	.80
b.		Perf. 13x14, small holes	57.50	3.25
10	A2	12½c gray	9.75	3.25
a.		Perf. 12½x12		1,900.
11	A2	15c bister	40.00	3.00
a.		Perf. 13x14, small holes	57.50	4.00
12	A2	20c ultra	145.00	3.75
a.		Perf. 14, small holes	120.00	4.50
b.		Perf. 13x14, small holes	160.00	5.75
13	A2	25c dk violet	50.00	1.60
b.		Perf. 13x14, small holes	57.50	4.75
c.		Perf. 14, large holes	800.00	220.00
14	A2	30c green	65.00	5.00
15	A2	50c carmine	40.00	1.50
a.		Perf. 14, small holes	34.00	4.00
b.		Perf. 13x14, small holes	50.00	3.25
c.		Perf. 14, large holes	42.50	4.00
16	A2	2.50g green & vio	110.00	26.00
b.		Perf. 14, small holes	100.00	28.00
c.		Perf. 14, large holes	100.00	28.00
		Nos. 3-16 (14)	805.00	216.40

Imperforate examples of Nos. 3-16 are proofs. The 1c red brown and 2c yellow are believed to be bogus.

"Small hole" varieties have the spaces between the holes wider than the diameter of the holes.

Numeral of Value — A3

1883-90 ***Perf. 12½ Large Holes***

No.	Type	Description	Unused	Used
17	A3	1c slate grn ('88)	1.20	.25
a.		Perf. 12½x12	3.00	1.60
18	A3	2c brown ('84)	1.20	.25
a.		Perf. 12½x12	3.00	.80
b.		Perf. 11½x12	80.00	50.00
19	A3	2½c yellow	1.20	.80
a.		Perf. 12½x12	3.00	1.60
b.		Perf. 11½x12	24.00	24.00
20	A3	3c lilac ('90)	2.00	.25
21	A3	5c green ('87)	14.50	.40
a.		Perf. 12½, small holes	60.00	26.00
22	A3	5c ultra ('90)	14.50	.25
		Nos. 17-22 (6)	34.60	2.20

For surcharges and overprint see Nos. 46-47, O4.

Queen Wilhelmina — A4

1892-97 ***Perf. 12½***

No.	Type	Description	Unused	Used
23	A4	10c orange brn ('95)	8.00	.40
24	A4	12½c gray ('97)	12.00	*32.50*
25	A4	15c bister ('95)	20.00	2.40
26	A4	20c ultra ('93)	60.00	1.60
27	A4	25c violet	35.00	2.00
28	A4	30c green ('94)	50.00	3.75
29	A4	50c carmine ('93)	40.00	2.00
30	A4	2.50g org brn & ultra	140.00	45.00
		Nos. 23-30 (8)	365.00	89.65

For overprints see Nos. O21-O27.

Netherlands Nos. 67-69, 74, 77, 80 Surcharged in Black

1900, July 1

No.	Type	Description	Unused	Used
31	A11	10c on 10c gray lil	5.00	.25
32	A11	12½c on 12½c blue	5.00	.60
33	A11	15c on 15c yel brn	5.00	.60
34	A11	20c on 20c yel grn	22.00	.60
35	A11	25c on 25c car & bl	16.00	.60
36	A11	50c on 50c brnz grn & red brn	35.00	1.20

Netherlands No. 84 Surcharged in Black

1902 ***Perf. 11½x11***

No.	Type	Description	Unused	Used
37	A12	2.50g on 2½g brn lil	70.00	20.00
a.		Perf. 11	72.50	24.00
		Nos. 31-37 (7)	158.00	23.85

A6

1902-09 ***Perf. 12½***

No.	Type	Description	Unused	Used
38	A6	½c violet	.80	.25
39	A6	1c olive grn	.80	.25
a.		Booklet pane of 6		
b.		Complete booklet, 4 #39a	*24.00*	
40	A6	2c yellow brn	4.00	.25
41	A6	2½c green	2.40	.25
a.		Booklet pane of 6		
42	A6	3c orange	4.00	1.20
43	A6	4c ultra ('09)	14.00	8.50
44	A6	5c rose red	6.00	.25
a.		Booklet pane of 6		
45	A6	7½c gray ('08)	4.00	.40
		Nos. 38-45 (8)	36.00	11.35

For overprints see Nos. 63-69, 81-87, O1-O9.

Nos. 18, 20 Surcharged

1902

No.	Type	Description	Unused	Used
46	A3	½c on 2c yel brn	.25	.25
a.		Double surcharge	160.00	160.00
47	A3	2½c on 3c violet	.25	.25
a.		Double surcharge	*1,800.*	

Queen Wilhelmina — A9

1903-08

48 A9 10c slate 5.00 .25
a. Booklet pane of 6
b. Complete booklet, 4 #48a *2,000.*
49 A9 12½c deep blue ('06) 2.40 .25
a. Booklet pane of 6
b. Complete booklet, #39a, #41a, #44a, #49a; 2 #48a *2,000.*
50 A9 15c chocolate ('06) 10.00 2.00
a. Ovptd. with 2 horiz. bars 2.00 .80
51 A9 17½c bister ('08) 4.00 .25
52 A9 20c grnsh slate 2.40 1.60
53 A9 20c olive grn ('05) 32.00 .80
54 A9 22½c brn & ol grn ('08) 4.00 .30
55 A9 25c violet ('04) 16.00 .30
56 A9 30c orange brn 34.00 .40
57 A9 50c red brown ('04) 32.00 .40
Nos. 48-57 (10) 141.80 6.55

For overprints and surcharges see Nos. 58, 70-78, 88-96, 139, O10-O18.

No. 52 Surcharged in Black

Type I

Type II

Two Types of "10":
Type I — Skinny 1 with almost straight flag.
Type II — Fat 1 with rising flag.

1905, July 6

58 A9 10c on 20c grnsh slate 3.00 1.20
a. Type II 4.75 4.75

Queen Wilhelmina — A10

1905-12 Engr. *Perf. 11x11½*

59 A10 1g dp claret ('06) 65.00 .40
a. Perf. 11½x11 65.00 .75
b. Perf. 11 80.00 6.00
60 A10 1g dl lil, *bl* ('12) 60.00 8.00
a. Perf. 11 72.50 *57.50*
61 A10 2½g slate bl ('05) 77.50 2.00
a. Perf. 11½ 77.50 2.00
b. Perf. 11½x11 80.00 2.00
c. Perf. 11 900.00
62 A10 2½g sl bl, *bl* ('12) 120.00 40.00
a. Perf. 11 130.00 92.50
Nos. 59-62 (4) 322.50 50.40

Sheets of Nos. 60 & 62 were soaked in an indigo solution.

For overprints and surcharge see Nos. 79-80, 97-98, 140, O19-O20.

Overprint Reading Up

Previous Issues Overprinted

1908, July 1

63 A6 ½c violet .60 .30
64 A6 1c olive grn .60 .30
65 A6 2c yellow brn 2.00 3.00
66 A6 2½c green 1.20 .30
67 A6 3c orange 1.20 1.20
68 A6 5c rose red 3.25 .40
69 A6 7½c gray 3.00 3.00
70 A9 10c slate 1.20 .25
71 A9 12½c dp blue 10.00 2.40
72 A9 15c choc (#50a) 5.00 4.00
73 A9 17½c bister 2.25 2.00
74 A9 20c olive grn 10.00 2.40
75 A9 22½c brn & ol grn 8.00 7.00
76 A9 25c violet 8.00 .40
77 A9 30c orange brn 16.00 2.25
78 A9 50c red brown 8.00 .80
79 A10 1g dull lilac (#59) 60.00 6.00
b. Perf. 11½x11 60.00 6.00
c. Perf. 11 80.00 8.00
80 A10 2½g slate blue (#61b) 100.00 65.00
Nos. 63-80 (18) 240.30 101.00

The above stamps were overprinted for use in the territory outside of Java and Madura, stamps overprinted "Java" being used in these latter places.

The 15c is overprinted, in addition, with two horizontal lines, 2½mm apart.

Overprint Reading Down

63a A6 ½c .80 *6.00*
64a A6 1c .80 *4.00*
65a A6 2c 4.00 *8.00*
66a A6 2½c 1.60 *4.00*
67a A6 3c 35.00 *90.00*
68a A6 5c 4.00 *3.25*
70a A9 10c 1.20 *4.00*
71a A9 12½c 6.00 *12.00*
72a A9 15c 32.50 *75.00*
74a A9 20c 12.00 20.00
75a A9 22½c *2,200.* *2,800.*
76a A9 25c 8.00 12.00
77a A9 30c 14.00 32.50
78a A9 50c 10.00 24.00
79a A10 1g 200.00 240.00
d. Double overprint 180.00 200.00
80a A10 2½g *2,800.* *4,000.*

Overprinted

1908, July 1

81 A6 ½c violet .25 .25
b. Double overprint 600.00
82 A6 1c olive grn .60 .40
83 A6 2c yellow brn 2.40 2.60
84 A6 2½c green 1.60 .25
85 A6 3c orange 1.20 1.00
86 A6 5c rose red 2.40 .25
87 A6 7½c gray 2.00 1.75
88 A9 10c slate 1.40 .25
89 A9 12½c deep blue 2.00 .80
b. Dbl. ovpt., one inverted 150.00 150.00
90 A9 15c choc (on No. 50a) 3.75 3.75
91 A9 17½c bister 2.00 .80
92 A9 20c olive grn 10.00 .80
93 A9 22½c brn & ol grn 5.25 3.00
94 A9 25c violet 5.25 .40
95 A9 30c orange brn 28.00 3.00
96 A9 50c red brown 20.00 .80
97 A10 1g dull lilac (#59a) 50.00 3.25
b. Perf. 11 52.50 4.00
98 A10 2½g slate blue (#61b) 72.50 60.00
Nos. 81-98 (18) 210.60 83.35

Inverted Overprint

81a A6 ½c 1.25 *4.00*
82a A6 1c .75 *4.00*
83a A6 2c 3.00 *12.00*
84a A6 2½c 3.25 *8.00*
85a A6 3c 28.00 40.00
86a A6 5c 3.00 6.00
88a A9 10c 1.60 *4.00*
89a A9 12½c 4.00 8.00
90a A9 15c 4.00 *16.00*
92a A9 20c 16.00 16.00
94a A9 25c 6.00 *16.00*
95a A9 30c 28.00 40.00
96a A9 50c 20.00 28.00
97a A10 1g Perf. 11 160.00 220.00
98a A10 2½g *2,800.* *4,000.*

A11

Queen Wilhelmina
A12 A13

Typo., Litho. (#114A)

1912-40 *Perf. 12½*

101 A11 ½c lt vio .25 .25
102 A11 1c olive grn .25 .25
103 A11 2c yellow brn .60 .25
104 A11 2c gray blk ('30) .60 .25
105 A11 2½c green 1.40 .25
106 A11 2½c lt red ('22) .80 .25
107 A11 3c yellow .60 .25
108 A11 3c green ('29) 1.20 .25
109 A11 4c gray blue 1.20 .25
110 A11 4c dp grn ('28) 1.20 .25
111 A11 4c yellow ('30) 8.00 5.00
112 A11 5c rose 1.25 .25
113 A11 5c green ('22) 1.20 .25
114 A11 5c chlky bl ('28) .80 .25
114A A11 5c ultra ('40) .80 .30
115 A11 7½c bister .80 .25
116 A11 10c lilac ('22) 2.00 .25
117 A12 10c car rose ('14) 1.20 .25
118 A12 12½c dull bl ('14) 1.10 .25
119 A12 12½c red ('22) 1.10 .30
120 A12 15c blue ('29) 8.00 .25
121 A12 17½c red brn ('15) 1.10 .25
122 A12 20c green ('15) 2.00 .25
123 A12 20c blue ('22) 2.00 .25
124 A12 20c orange ('32) 14.00 .30
125 A12 22½c orange ('15) 2.00 .25
126 A12 25c red vio ('15) 2.00 .80
127 A12 30c slate ('15) 2.00 .25
128 A12 32½c vio & red ('22) 2.00 .25
129 A12 35c org brn ('29) 7.25 .60
130 A12 40c green ('22) 4.00 .25

Perf. 11½

Engr.

131 A13 50c green ('13) 6.00 .25
a. Perf. 11x11½ 6.00 .25
b. Perf. 12½ 6.00 .40
c. Vert. pair, imperf. betwn. *1,600.*
132 A13 60c dp blue ('22) 6.00 .25
133 A13 80c orange ('22) 6.00 .30
134 A13 1g brown ('13) 6.00 .25
a. Perf. 11x11½ 6.00 .30
135 A13 1.75g dk vio, perf, 12½ ('31) 20.00 2.00
136 A13 2½g car ('13) 16.00 .50
a. Perf. 11x11½ 16.00 4.00
b. Perf. 12½ 16.00 .70
Nos. 101-136 (37) 132.70 17.10

For surcharges and overprints see Nos. 137-138, 144-150, 102a-123a, 158, 194-195, B1-B3, C1-C5.

Water Soluble Ink

Some values of types A11 and A12 and late printings of types A6 and A9 are in soluble ink. The design disappears when immersed in water.

Nos. 105, 109, 54, 59 Surcharged

No. 137

No. 138

No. 139

No. 140

1917-18 Typo. *Perf. 12½*

137 A11 ½c on 2½c .30 .30
138 A11 1c on 4c ('18) .55 .55
139 A9 17½c on 22½c ('18) 2.00 .75
a. Inverted surcharge 350.00 725.00

Perf. 11x11½

140 A10 30c on 1g ('18) 6.50 1.75
a. Perf. 11½x11 130.00 120.00
Nos. 137-140 (4) 9.35 3.35

Nos. 121, 125, 131, 134 Surcharged in Red or Blue

On A12

On A13

Two types of 32½c on 50c:
I — Surcharge bars spaced as in illustration.
II — Bars more closely spaced.

1922, Jan. *Perf. 12½*

144 A12 12½c on 17½c (R) .75 .25
145 A12 12½c on 22½c (R) .75 .25
146 A12 20c on 22½c (Bl) .75 .25
a. Double overprint *1,800.*

Perf. 11½, 11x11½

147 A13 32½c on 50c (Bl) (I, perf. 11½) 1.50 .25
a. Type II, perf. 11½ 10.00 .25
b. Type I, perf. 11x11½ 1,000. 6.00
c. Type II, perf. 11x11½ 20.00 1.60
148 A13 40c on 50c (R) 4.00 .45
149 A13 60c on 1g (Bl) 6.50 .40
150 A13 80c on 1g (R) 8.00 1.20
Nos. 144-150 (7) 22.25 3.05

Stamps of 1912-22 Overprinted in Red, Blue, Green or Black

a

b

No. 145a

1922, Sept. 18 Typo. *Perf. 12½*

102a A11(a) 1c ol grn (R) 8.00 8.00
103a A11(a) 2c yel brn (Bl) 8.00 8.00
106a A11(a) 2½c lt red (G) 57.50 *65.00*
107a A11(a) 3c yellow (R) 8.00 8.00
109a A11(a) 4c ultra (R) 32.50 40.00
113a A11(a) 5c green (R) 12.00 8.00
115a A11(a) 7½c drab (Bl) 8.00 8.00
116a A11(a) 10c lilac (Bk) 65.00 92.50
145a A12(b) 12½c on 22½c org (Bl) 8.00 8.00
121a A12(b) 17½c red brn (Bk) 8.00 8.00
123a A12(b) 20c blue (Bk) 8.00 8.00
Nos. 102a-123a (11) 223.00 261.50

Issued to publicize the 3rd Netherlands Indies Industrial Fair at Bandoeng, Java.

Nos. 102a-123a were sold at a premium for 3, 4, 5, 6, 8, 9, 10, 12½, 15, 20 and 22½ cents respectively.

Queen Wilhelmina — A15

1923, Aug. 31 Engr. *Perf. 11½*

151 A15 5c myrtle green .25 .25
a. Perf. 11½x11 *1,000.* 125.00
b. Perf. 11x11½ 4.00 .75
152 A15 12½c rose .25 .25
a. Perf. 11x11½ 1.25 .25
b. Perf. 11½x11 1.75 .75
c. Vert. pair, imperf. btwn. *1,000.*
153 A15 20c dark blue .75 .25
a. Perf. 11½x11 4.00 .75
154 A15 50c red orange 2.00 .75
a. Perf. 11x11½ 6.00 1.25
b. Perf. 11½x11 3.00 .90
c. Perf. 11 6.00 1.25
155 A15 1g brown vio 4.50 .75
a. Perf. 11½x11 8.00 .80

156	A15	2½g gray black	40.00	40.00
157	A15	5g orange brown	125.00	140.00
		Nos. 151-157 (7)	172.75	182.25

25th anniversary of the assumption of the government of the Netherlands by Queen Wilhelmina, at the age of 18.

No. 123 Surcharged

1930, Dec. 13 Typo. *Perf. 12½*

158	A12	12½c on 20c bl (R)	.80	.25
a.		Inverted surcharge	375.00	725.00

Prince William I, Portrait by Van Key — A16

1933, Apr. 18 Photo.

163	A16	12½c deep orange	1.60	.40

400th anniv. of the birth of Prince William I, Count of Nassau and Prince of Orange, frequently referred to as William the Silent.

Rice Field Scene A17

Queen Wilhelmina A18

Queen Wilhelmina — A19

1933-37 Unwmk. *Perf. 11½x12½*

164	A17	1c lilac gray ('34)	.25	.25
165	A17	2c plum ('34)	.25	.25
166	A17	2½c bister ('34)	.25	.25
167	A17	3c yellow grn ('34)	.25	.25
168	A17	3½c dark gray ('37)	.25	.25
169	A17	4c dk olive ('34)	1.00	.25
170	A17	5c ultra ('34)	.25	.25
171	A17	7½c violet ('34)	1.00	.25
172	A17	10c ver ('34)	1.90	.25
173	A18	10c ver ('37)	.60	.25
174	A18	12½c dp org ('34)	.60	.25
a.		12½c light orange, perf. 12½ ('33)	8.00	.40
175	A18	15c ultra ('34)	.60	.25
176	A18	20c plum ('34)	.80	.25
177	A18	25c blue grn ('34)	2.25	.25
178	A18	30c lilac gray ('34)	3.75	.25
179	A18	32½c bister ('34)	8.00	8.00
180	A18	35c violet ('34)	6.00	2.10
181	A18	40c yel grn ('34)	3.00	.25
182	A18	42½c yellow ('34)	3.00	1.25

1934, Jan 16 *Perf. 12½*

183	A19	50c lilac gray	6.00	.25
184	A19	60c ultra	6.00	.80
185	A19	80c vermilion	8.00	1.20
186	A19	1g violet	8.00	.40
187	A19	1.75g yellow grn	20.00	13.50
188	A19	2.50g plum	20.00	2.00
		Nos. 164-188 (25)	102.00	33.50

See Nos. 200-225. For overprints and surcharges see Nos. 271-275, B48, B57.

Water Soluble Ink

Nos. 164-188 and the first printing of No. 163 have soluble ink and the design disappears when immersed in water.

Nos. C6-C7, C14, C9-C10 Surcharged in Black

a

b

1934 Typo. *Perf. 12½x11½, 12½*

189	AP1(a)	2c on 10c	.75	.45
190	AP1(a)	2c on 20c	.75	.25
191	AP3(b)	2c on 30c	.75	1.20
192	AP1(a)	42½c on 75c	7.00	.25
193	AP1(a)	42½c on 1.50g	7.00	.40
		Nos. 189-193 (5)	16.25	2.55

Nos. 127-128 Surcharged with New Value in Red or Black

1937, Sept. *Perf. 12½*

194	A12	10c on 30c (R)	3.00	.25
a.		Double surcharge	675.00	2,400.
195	A12	10c on 32½c (Bk)	3.00	.35

Wilhelmina — A20

Perf. 12½x12

1938, Aug. 30 Photo. Wmk. 202

196	A20	2c dull purple	.25	.25
197	A20	10c car lake	.25	.25
198	A20	15c royal blue	1.25	1.25
199	A20	20c red orange	.75	.40
		Nos. 196-199 (4)	2.50	2.15

40th anniv. of the reign of Queen Wilhelmina.

Types of 1933-37

1938-40 Photo. *Perf. 12½x12*

200	A17	1c lilac gray ('39)	.40	*.80*
201	A17	2c plum ('39)	.25	.25
202	A17	2½c bister ('39)	.75	.75
203	A17	3c yellow grn ('39)	1.50	1.50
205	A17	4c gray ol ('39)	1.50	1.50
206	A17	5c ultra ('39)	.25	.25
a.		Perf. 12x12½	1.50	.75
207	A17	7½c violet ('39)	3.00	1.50
208	A18	10c ver ('39)	.25	.25
210	A18	15c ultra ('39)	.25	.25
211	A18	20c plum ('39)	.25	.25
a.		Perf. 12x12½	1.50	.75
212	A18	25c blue grn ('39)	24.00	24.00
213	A18	30c lilac gray ('39)	10.00	5.00
215	A18	35c violet ('39)	5.75	1.60
216	A18	40c dp yel grn ('40)	5.75	.25

Perf. 12½

218	A19	50c lilac gray ('40)	275.00	
219	A19	60c ultra ('39)	14.00	8.00
220	A19	80c ver ('39)	75.00	65.00
221	A19	1g violet ('39)	30.00	4.00
223	A19	2g Prus green	26.00	14.00
225	A19	5g yellow brn	24.00	14.00
		Nos. 200-216,219-225 (19)	222.90	143.15

The note following No. 188 applies also to this issue.

The 50c was sold only at the philatelic window in Amsterdam.

War Dance of Nias Island A23

Legong Dancer of Bali A24

Wayang Wong Dancer of Java A25

Padjogé Dancer, Southern Celebes A26

Dyak Dancer of Borneo — A27

1941 Unwmk. *Perf. 12½*

228	A23	2½c rose violet	.60	.80
229	A24	3c green	.60	.80
230	A25	4c olive green	.50	.80
231	A26	5c blue	.25	.25
232	A27	7½c dark violet	.60	.35
		Nos. 228-232 (5)	2.55	3.00

See Nos. 279-280, 293, N38.

Imperfs. are printers waste.

A28

Queen Wilhelmina A28a

1941 *Perf. 12½*

Size: 18x22¾mm

234	A28	10c red orange	.80	.40
a.		Perf. 13½	.40	.40
235	A28	15c ultra	4.00	4.00
236	A28	17½c orange	2.00	2.00
237	A28	20c plum	40.00	120.00
238	A28	25c Prus green	50.00	1.75
239	A28	30c olive bis	7.00	3.25
240	A28	35c purple	160.00	*400.00*
241	A28	40c yellow grn	18.50	8.00

Perf. 13½

Size: 20½x26mm

242	A28	50c car lake	7.25	1.60
243	A28	60c ultra	6.50	1.60
244	A28	80c red orange	6.50	1.60
245	A28	1g purple	6.50	.80
246	A28	2g Prus green	20.00	2.40
247	A28	5g bis, perf. 12½	350.00	*3,000.*
248	A28	10g green	42.50	24.00

Size: 26x32mm

249	A28a	25g orange	260.00	160.00
		Nos. 234-249 (16)	981.55	*3,731.*

Nos. 242-246 come with pin-perf 13½.

Small hole, large hole, comb and line perforation varieties exist.

Nos. 242-246 exist on thick paper in darker colors. These are proofs.

The 10c comes in two types: 1¼mm between "10" and "CENT," and 1¾mm.

For overprints and surcharge see Nos. 276-278, J43-J46.

Catalogue values for unused stamps in this section, from this point to the end of the section, are for Never Hinged items.

Rice Fields — A29

Barge on Java Lake — A30

University of Medicine, Batavia — A31

Palms on Shore — A32

Plane over Bromo Volcano — A33

Queen Wilhelmina A34 A35

1945-46, Oct. 1 Engr. *Perf. 12*

250	A29	1c green	.60	.25
251	A30	2c rose lilac	.60	.35
252	A31	2½c dull lilac	.60	.25
253	A32	5c blue	.40	.25
254	A33	7½c olive gray	.80	.25
255	A34	10c red brown	.40	.25
256	A34	15c dark blue	.40	.25
257	A34	17½c rose lake	.40	.25
258	A34	20c sepia	.40	.25
259	A34	30c slate gray	.40	.25
260	A35	60c gray black	.80	.25
261	A35	1g blue green	1.20	.25
262	A35	2½g red orange	3.75	.75
		Nos. 250-262 (13)	10.75	3.85

For surcharge see No. 304.

Issued: 15c, 1946, others 10/1/45.

Railway Viaduct Near Soekaboemi A36

Dam and Power Station A37

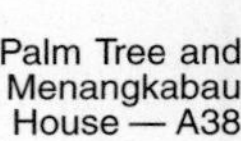

Palm Tree and Menangkabau House — A38

Huts on Piles A39

Buddhist Stupas A40

Perf. 14½x14

1946 Typo. Wmk. 228

263	A36	1c dark green	.35	.25
264	A37	2c black brown	.35	.25
265	A38	2½c scarlet	.35	.25
266	A39	5c indigo	.35	.25
267	A40	7½c ultra	.35	.25
		Nos. 263-267 (5)	1.75	1.25

Nos. 265, 267, 263 Surcharged

1947, Sept. 25

268	A38	3c on 2½c scar	.35	.25
269	A40	3c on 7½c ultra	.35	.25
a.		Double surcharge	200.00	200.00
270	A36	4c on 1c dk green	.35	.25
		Nos. 268-270 (3)	1.05	.75

No. 219 Surcharged with New Value and Bars in Red

1947, Sept. 25 Wmk. 202 *Perf. 12½*

271	A19	45c on 60c ultra	1.45	1.00

Nos. 212, 218 and 220 Overprinted "1947" in Red or Black

1947, Sept. 25 *Perf. 12½x12, 12½*

272 A18 25c blue green (R) .40 .25
a. Unwmkd. 260.00
273 A19 50c lilac gray (R) .80 .35
274 A19 80c vermilion 1.20 1.20
a. Unwmkd. 500.00 240.00
Nos. 272-274 (3) 2.40 1.80

Bar above "1947" on No. 274.

Nos. 174, 241, 246 and Type of 1941 Overprinted "1947" in Black

Perf. 12½, 12½x12 (2g)

1947, Sept. 25 **Unwmk.**

275 A18 12½c deep orange .40 .25
276 A28 40c yellow green .80 .25
277 A28 2g Prus green 4.00 1.40
278 A28 5g bister 11.00 9.75
Nos. 275-278 (4) 16.20 11.65

The overprint is vertical on Nos. 276-278.

Dancer Types of 1941, 1945

1948, May 13 **Litho.** *Perf. 12½*

279 OS21 3c rose red .25 .25
280 A24 4c dull olive grn .25 .25

Queen Wilhelmina — A41

1948 **Photo.** *Perf. 12½*

Size: 18x22mm

281 A41 15c red orange .80 2.00
282 A41 20c brt blue .30 .30
283 A41 25c dk green .30 .30
284 A41 40c dp yellow grn .30 .30
285 A41 45c plum .60 .80
286 A41 50c red brown .50 .30
287 A41 80c brt red .60 .60

Perf. 13

Size: 20½x26mm

288 A41 1g deep violet .30 .30
a. Perf. 12½ x 12 1.20 .60
289 A41 10g green 32.50 15.00
290 A41 25g orange 60.00 60.00
Nos. 281-290 (10) 96.20 79.90

See Nos. 291-292. For overprints see Nos. 294-303.

Wilhelmina Type of 1948 Inscribed "1898-1948"

1948, Aug. 31 *Perf. 12½x12*

Size: 21x26½mm

291 A41 15c orange .40 .40
292 A41 20c ultra .40 .30

Reign of Queen Wilhelmina, 50th anniv.

Dancer Type of 1941

1948, Sept. **Photo.** *Perf. 12½*

293 A27 7½c olive bister .80 .75

Juliana Type of Netherlands 1948

Perf. 14½x13½

1948, Sept. 25 **Wmk. 202**

293A A75 15c red orange .50 .35
293B A75 20c deep ultra .50 .35

Investiture of Queen Juliana, Sept. 6, 1948.

Indonesia

Nos. 281 to 287 Overprinted in Black

Two types of overprint:
I — Shiny ink, bar 1.8mm wide. By G. C. T. van Dorp & Co.
II — Dull ink, bar 2.2mm. By G. Kolff & Co.

1948 *Perf. 12½*

294 A41 15c red orange (I) 1.75 .25
a. Type II .95 .25
295 A41 20c bright blue (I) .25 .25
a. Type II .50 .25
296 A41 25c dark green (I) .25 .25
a. Type II .25 .25
297 A41 40c dp yel grn (I) .25 .25
298 A41 45c plum ('49) (II) 1.10 .90
299 A41 50c red brn ('49) (II) .25 .25
300 A41 80c bright red (I) 1.00 .25
a. Type II 1.10 .25

Nos. 288-290 Overprinted in Black

Two Bars

Perf. 12½x12

301 A41 1g deep violet 1.25 .25
a. As #301, with three bars 8.00 .35
b. Perf. 13 2.75 .30

Perf. 13

302 A41 10g green 92.50 30.00
303 A41 25g orange 125.00 57.50
Nos. 294-303 (10) 223.60 90.15

Same Overprint in Black on No. 262

1949 **Engr.** *Perf. 12*

Bars 28½mm long

304 A35 2½g red orange 52.50 9.75

A42

Tjandi Puntadewa Temple Entrance, East Java A43

Detail, Temple of the Dead, Bedjuning, Bali A44

Menangkabau House, Sumatra A45

Toradja House, Celebes A46

Designs: 5r, 10r, 25r, Temple entrance.

Perf. 12½, 11½

1949 **Unwmk.** **Photo.**

307 A42 1s gray .30 .25
a. Perf. 11½ .60 .80
308 A42 2s claret .60 .25
a. Perf. 11½ 30.00 *30.00*
309 A42 2½s olive brown .30 .25
a. Perf. 11½ .30 .25
310 A42 3s rose pink .60 .25
a. Perf. 11½ 1.50 1.40
311 A42 4s green .60 .60
312 A42 5s blue .30 .25
a. Perf. 11½ 1.10 .25
313 A42 7½s dark green .60 .25
a. Perf. 11½ 1.10 .60
314 A42 10s violet .30 .25
a. Perf. 11½ *475.00*
315 A42 12½s brt red 1.90 .25
a. Perf. 11½ 2.25 1.75
316 A43 15s rose red .30 .25
a. Perf. 12½ 1.75 .60
317 A43 20s gray black .30 .25
a. Perf. 12½ .95 .25
318 A43 25s ultra .30 .25
a. Perf. 12½ .95 .25
319 A44 30s brt red 1.10 .25
a. Perf. 12½ 1.10 .25
320 A44 40s gray green .60 .25
a. Perf. 12½ .30 .25
321 A44 45s claret .60 3.75
a. Perf. 12½ 2.75 .50
322 A45 50s orange brn .60 .25
a. Perf. 12½ 1.50 .25
323 A45 60s brown .80 1.90
a. Perf. 12½ 1.50 .25
324 A45 80s scarlet 1.15 .25
a. Perf. 12½ 4.00 .25

The 4s is perf. 12½. The 25s, 30s, 40s, 50s, 60s come both 12½ and 11½, same values.

Perf. 12½, 12¼

325 A46 1r purple .80 .25
a. Perf. 12¼ .80 .25
326 A46 2r gray green 4.75 .25
a. Perf. 12¼ 4.75 .25
327 A46 3r red violet 95.00 .25
328 A46 5r dk brown 67.50 .40
329 A46 10r gray 82.50 1.90
330 A46 25r orange brn .80 1.90
Nos. 307-330 (24) 262.60 14.95

Nos. 307-330 remained on sale in Indonesia Republic post offices until May 23, 1958, and were valid for postage until June 30, 1958.
For surcharge, see Indonesia Nos. 335-358.
Nos. 325-330 exist with both large and small holes.

Globe and Arms of Bern — A48

1949, Oct. 1 *Perf. 12½*

331 A48 15s bright red 1.15 .40
332 A48 25s ultra 1.15 .40

Nos. 307-330 remained on sale in Indonesia Republic post offices until May 23, 1958, and were valid for postage until June 30, 1958. 75th anniv. of UPU.
See Indonesia (republic) for subsequent listings.

SEMI-POSTAL STAMPS

Regular Issue of 1912-14 Surcharged in Carmine

1915, June 10 **Unwmk.** *Perf. 12½*

B1 A11 1c + 5c ol grn 4.50 4.50
B2 A11 5c + 5c rose 4.50 4.50
B3 A12 10c + 5c rose 7.25 7.25
Nos. B1-B3 (3) 16.25 16.25

Surtax for the Red Cross.

Bali Temple SP1

Watchtower SP2

Menangkabau Compound — SP3

Borobudur Temple, Java — SP4

Perf. 11½x11, 11x11½

1930, Dec. 1 **Photo.**

B4 SP1 2c (+ 1c) vio & brn 1.00 .80
B5 SP2 5c (+ 2½c) dk grn & brn 4.75 2.50
B6 SP3 12½c (+ 2½c) dp red & brn 3.25 .50
B7 SP4 15c (+ 5c) ultra & brn 5.75 5.75
Nos. B4-B7 (4) 14.75 9.55

Surtax for youth care.

Farmer and Carabao — SP5

5c, Fishermen. 12½c, Dancers. 15c, Musicians.

1931, Dec. 1 **Engr.** *Perf. 12½*

B8 SP5 2c (+ 1c) olive bis 3.00 2.00
B9 SP5 5c (+ 2½c) bl grn 4.25 3.75
B10 SP5 12½c (+ 2½c) dp red 3.25 .55
B11 SP5 15c (+ 5c) dl bl 8.25 7.00
Nos. B8-B11 (4) 18.75 13.30

The surtax was for the aid of the Leper Colony at Salatiga.

Weaving — SP9

5c, Plaiting rattan. 12½c, Woman batik dyer. 15c, Coppersmith.

1932, Dec. 1 **Photo.** *Perf. 12½*

B12 SP9 2c (+ 1c) dp vio & bis .40 .40
B13 SP9 5c (+ 2½c) dp grn & bis 2.50 2.00
B14 SP9 12½c (+ 2½c) brt rose & bis .85 .30
B15 SP9 15c (+ 5c) bl & bis 3.25 3.00
Nos. B12-B15 (4) 7.00 5.70

The surtax was donated to the Salvation Army.

Woman and Lotus — SP13

Designs: 5c, "The Light that Shows the Way." 12½c, YMCA emblem. 15c, Jobless man.

1933, Dec. 1 *Perf. 12½*

B16 SP13 2c (+ 1c) red vio & ol bis .65 .30
B17 SP13 5c (+ 2½c) grn & ol bis 2.25 1.90
B18 SP13 12½c (+ 2½c) ver & ol bis 2.50 .30
B19 SP13 15c (+ 5c) bl & ol bis 2.75 2.00
Nos. B16-B19 (4) 8.15 4.50

The surtax was for the Amsterdam Young Men's Society for Relief of the Poor in Netherlands Indies.

Dowager Queen Emma — SP17

1934, Sept. 15 *Perf. 13x14*

B20 SP17 12½c (+ 2½c) blk brn 1.25 .45

Issued in memory of the late Dowager Queen Emma of Netherlands. The surtax was for the Anti-Tuberculosis Society.

A Pioneer at Work — SP18

Designs: 5c, Cavalryman rescuing wounded native. 12½c, Artilleryman under fire. 15c, Bugler.

1935 *Perf. 12½*

B21 SP18 2c (+ 1c) dp mag & bis 1.25 1.00
B22 SP18 5c (+ 2½c) grn & bis 3.25 2.25
B23 SP18 12½c (+ 2½c) red org & bis 3.25 .25
B24 SP18 15c (+ 5c) brt bl & bis 4.50 4.50
Nos. B21-B24 (4) 12.25 8.00

The surtax was for the Indies Committee of the Christian Military Association for the East and West Indies.

Child Welfare Work — SP22

1936, Dec. 1 **Size: 23x20mm**

B25 SP22 2c (+ 1c) plum 1.00 .60

Size: 30x26½mm

B26 SP22 5c (+ 2½c) gray vio 1.25 1.10
B27 SP22 7½c (+ 2½c) dk vio 1.25 1.25
B28 SP22 12½c (+ 2½c) red org 1.25 .30
B29 SP22 15c (+5c) brt bl 2.00 1.75
Nos. B25-B29 (5) 6.75 5.00

Surtax for Salvation Army.

Boy Scouts — SP23

1937, May 1

B30 SP23 7½c + 2½c dk ol brn 1.25 1.00
B31 SP23 12½c + 2½c rose car 1.25 .50

Fifth Boy Scout World Jamboree, Vogelenzang, Netherlands, July 31-Aug. 13, 1937. Surtax for Netherlands Indies Scout Association.

Sifting Rice — SP24

Designs: 3½c, Mother and children. 7½c, Plowing with carabao team. 10c, Carabao team and cart. 20c, Native couple.

1937, Dec. 1

B32 SP24 2c (+ 1c) dk brn & org 1.10 .80
B33 SP24 3½c (+ 1½c) gray 1.10 .80
B34 SP24 7½c (+ 2½c) Prus grn & org 1.25 .95
B35 SP24 10c (+ 2½c) car & org 1.25 .25
B36 SP24 20c (+ 5c) brt bl 1.25 1.10
Nos. B32-B36 (5) 5.95 3.90

Surtax for the Public Relief Fund for indigenous poor.

Modern Plane — SP28

Design: 20c, Plane nose facing left.

Wmk. 202

1938, Oct. 15 **Photo.** *Perf. 12½*

B36A SP28 17½c (+5c) olive brn .85 .85
B36B SP28 20c (+5c) slate .85 .55

10th anniversary of the Dutch East Indies Royal Air Lines (K. N. I. L. M.).
Surtax for the Aviation Fund in the Netherlands Indies.

Nun and Child
SP29 SP30

Designs: 7½c, Nurse examining child's arm. 10c, Nurse bathing baby. 20c, Nun bandaging child's head.

1938, Dec. 1 **Wmk. 202** *Perf. 12½*

B37 SP29 2c (+ 1c) vio .60 .45

Perf. 11½x12

B38 SP30 3½c (+ 1½c) brt grn 1.00 .90

Perf. 12x11½

B39 SP30 7½c (+ 2½c) cop red .80 .85
B40 SP30 10c (+ 2½c) ver .90 .25
B41 SP30 20c (+ 5c) brt ultra 1.00 .95
Nos. B37-B41 (5) 4.30 3.40

The surtax was for the Central Mission Bureau in Batavia.

Social Workers SP34

Indonesian Nurse Tending Patient SP35

European Nurse Tending Patient — SP36

Perf. 13x11½, 11½x13

1939, Dec. 1 **Photo.**

B42 SP34 2c (+ 1c) purple .25 .25
B43 SP35 3½c (+ 1½c) bl grn & pale bl grn .30 .25
B44 SP34 7½c (+ 2½c) cop brn .25 .25
B45 SP35 10c (+ 2½c) scar & pink 1.40 .80
B46 SP36 10c (+ 2½c) scar 1.40 .80
B47 SP36 20c (+ 5c) dk bl .40 .35
Nos. B42-B47 (6) 4.00 2.70

No. B44 shows native social workers.
Nos. B45 and B46 were issued se-tenant vertically and horizontally. The surtax was used for the Bureau of Social Service.

No. 174 Surcharged in Brown

1940, Dec. 2 **Unwmk.** *Perf. 12x12½*

B48 A18 10c + 5c on 12½c dp org 1.10 .40

SP37

Netherlands coat of arms and inscription "Netherlands Shall Rise Again"

1941, May 10 **Litho.** *Perf. 12½*

B49 SP37 5c + 5c multi .25 .25
B50 SP37 10c + 10c multi .25 .25
B51 SP37 1g + 1g multi 9.00 6.75
Nos. B49-B51 (3) 9.50 7.25

The surtax was used to purchase fighter planes for Dutch pilots fighting with the Royal Air Force in Great Britain.

SP38

Designs: 2c, Doctor and child, 3½c, Rice eater. 7½c, Nurse and patient. 10c, Nurse and children. 15c, Basket weaver.

1941, Sept. 22 **Photo.**

B52 SP38 2c (+ 1c) yel grn .60 .55
B53 SP38 3½c (+ 1½c) vio brn 4.00 3.50
B54 SP38 7½c (+ 2½c) vio 3.25 2.75
B55 SP38 10c (+ 2½c) dk red .90 .25
B56 SP38 15c (+ 5c) saph 9.50 6.00
Nos. B52-B56 (5) 18.25 13.05

The surtax was used for various charities.

Catalogue values for unused stamps in this section, from this point to the end of the section, are for Never Hinged items.

Indonesia

No. 208 Surcharged in Black

Perf. 12½x12

1948, Feb. 2 **Wmk. 202**

B57 A18 15c + 10c on 10c .25 .25
a. Inverted surcharge 210.00 210.00

The surtax was for war victims and other charitable purposes.

AIR POST STAMPS

Regular Issues of 1913-1923 Surcharged in Black or Blue

Nos. 119 & 126 Surcharged

No. 133 Surcharged

No. 134 Surcharged

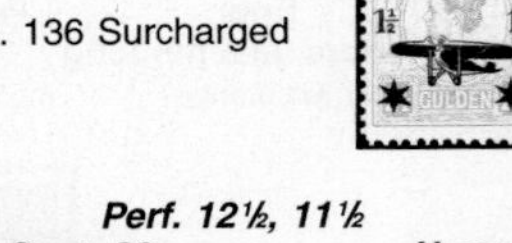

No. 136 Surcharged

Perf. 12½, 11½

1928, Sept. 20 **Unwmk.**

C1 A12 10c on 12½c red 1.25 1.25
C2 A12 20c on 25c red vio 3.00 3.00
C3 A13 40c on 80c org 3.00 3.00
C4 A13 75c on 1g brn (Bl) 1.25 1.25
C5 A13 1½g on 2½g car 8.00 8.00
Nos. C1-C5 (5) 16.50 16.50

On Nos. C4 and C5 there are stars over the original values and the airplane is of different shape. On No. C3 there are no bars under "OST."

Planes over Temple — AP1

1928, Dec. 1 **Litho.** *Perf. 12½x11½*

C6 AP1 10c red violet .40 .25
C7 AP1 20c brown 1.00 .75
C8 AP1 40c rose 1.20 .75
C9 AP1 75c green 3.25 .25
C10 AP1 1.50g orange 6.25 .75
Nos. C6-C10 (5) 12.10 2.75

For surcharges see Nos. 189-190, 192-193, C11-C12, C17.

No. C8 Surcharged in Black or Green

1930-32

C11 AP1 30c on 40c rose 2.00 .25
C12 AP1 30c on 40c rose (G) ('32) 2.40 .25

Pilot at Controls of Plane — AP2

1931, Apr. 1 **Photo.** *Perf. 12½*

C13 AP2 1g blue & brown 16.00 *18.00*

Issued for the first air mail flight from Java to Australia.

Landscape and Garudas — AP3

1931, May

C14 AP3 30c red violet 3.25 .25
C15 AP3 4½g bright blue 9.00 3.25
C16 AP3 7½g yellow green 12.00 4.50
Nos. C14-C16 (3) 24.25 8.00

For surcharge see No. 191.

No. C10 Surcharged in Blue

1932, July 21 *Perf. 12½x11½*

C17 AP1 50c on 1.50g org 3.25 .60
a. Inverted surcharge *2,200.* *2,800.*

Airplane — AP4

1933, Oct. 18 **Photo.** *Perf. 12½*

C18 AP4 30c deep blue 1.50 1.50

MARINE INSURANCE STAMPS

Floating Safe Attracting Gulls MI1

Floating Safe with Night Flare MI2

Artistic Fantasy of Floating Safe — MI3

Perf. 11½

1921, Nov. 1 **Unwmk.** **Engr.**

GY1 MI1 15c slate green 12.50 *60.00*
GY2 MI1 60c rose 12.50 *90.00*
GY3 MI1 75c gray brn 12.50 *120.00*
GY4 MI2 1.50g dark blue 37.50 *325.00*
GY5 MI2 2.25g org brn 45.00 *475.00*
GY6 MI3 4½g black 80.00 *800.00*
GY7 MI3 7½g red 100.00 *925.00*
Nos. GY1-GY7 (7) 300.00 *2,795.*

POSTAGE DUE STAMPS

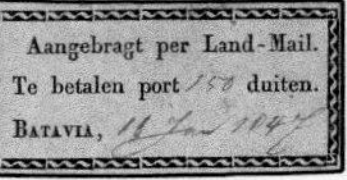

Aangebragt per Land-Mail.
Te betalen port 150 duiten.
Batavia, 17 Jan 1847

D1

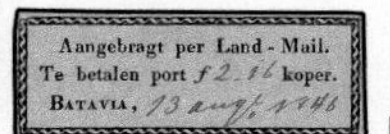

D2

1845-46 Unwmk. Typeset *Imperf.*
Bluish Paper

J1	D1	black ('46)	*1,650.*	
J2	D2	black	*2,000.*	
a.		"Maill" instead of "Mail"	*3,200.*	

D3

1874 Typo. *Perf. 12½x12, 13x14*

J3	D3	5c ocher	300.00	275.00
J4	D3	10c green, *yel*	240.00	155.00
J5	D3	15c ocher, *org*	40.00	24.00
a.		Perf. 11½x12	65.00	65.00
J6	D3	20c green, *blue*	60.00	24.00
a.		Perf. 11½x12	110.00	45.00
		Nos. J3-J6 (4)	640.00	478.00

D4

Type I — 34 loops. "T" of "Betalen" over center of loop, top branch of "E" of "Te" shorter than lower branch.

Type II — 33 loops. "T" of "Betalen" over center of two loops.

Type III — 32 loops. "T" of "Betalen" slightly to the left of loop, top branch of first "E" of "Betalen" shorter than lower branch.

Type IV — 37 loops and letters of "PORT" larger than in the other three types.

Value in Black

Perf. 11½x12, 12½, 12½x12, 13½

1882-88 Type III

J7	D4	2½c carmine	.75	1.25
J8	D4	5c carmine	.75	.75
J9	D4	10c carmine	4.00	4.00
J10	D4	15c carmine	4.00	3.25
J11	D4	20c carmine	100.00	.75
J12	D4	30c carmine	3.75	4.50
J13	D4	40c carmine	2.40	3.25
J14	D4	50c deep salmon	1.25	1.60
J15	D4	75c carmine	1.25	1.60
		Nos. J7-J15 (9)	118.15	20.95

Type I

J7a	D4	2½c carmine	.75	1.60
J8a	D4	5c carmine	.75	1.25
J9a	D4	10c carmine	5.00	6.00
J10a	D4	15c carmine	5.00	5.75
J11a	D4	20c carmine	120.00	1.25
J12a	D4	30c carmine	6.00	8.00
J13a	D4	40c carmine	2.40	3.25
J14a	D4	50c deep salmon	2.00	2.40
J15a	D4	75c carmine	1.25	2.00
		Nos. J7a-J15a (9)	143.15	31.50

Type II

J7b	D4	2½c carmine	.75	2.00
J8b	D4	5c carmine	.75	1.25
J9b	D4	10c carmine	6.00	6.00
J10b	D4	15c carmine	6.00	6.00
J11b	D4	20c carmine	120.00	3.25
J12b	D4	30c carmine	10.00	10.00
J13b	D4	40c carmine	3.25	4.00
J14b	D4	50c deep salmon	2.00	2.50
J15b	D4	75c carmine	1.60	2.50
		Nos. J7b-J15b (9)	150.35	37.50

Type IV

J7c	D4	2½c carmine	4.00	6.00
J8c	D4	5c carmine	2.00	6.00
J9c	D4	10c carmine	27.50	40.00
J10c	D4	15c carmine	24.00	27.50
J11c	D4	20c carmine	250.00	12.50
J13c	D4	40c carmine	4.00	6.00
J14c	D4	50c deep salmon	16.00	*24.00*
J15c	D4	75c carmine	2.50	6.00
		Nos. J7c-J15c (8)	330.00	128.00

D5

1892-95 Type I *Perf. 12½*

J16	D5	10c carmine	2.50	.40
J17	D5	15c carmine ('95)	22.00	3.00
J18	D5	20c carmine	5.50	.25
		Nos. J16-J18 (3)	30.00	3.65

Type III

J16a	D5	10c dull red	5.00	3.00
J18a	D5	20c dull red	6.00	2.00

Type II

J16b	D5	10c dull red	16.00	16.00
J18b	D5	20c dull red	10.00	10.00

1906-09 Type I

J19	D5	2½c carmine ('08)	1.60	.30
J20	D5	5c carmine ('09)	5.00	.25
J21	D5	30c carmine	30.00	10.00
J22	D5	40c carmine ('09)	26.00	3.25
J23	D5	50c carmine ('09)	18.00	1.60
J24	D5	75c carmine ('09)	34.00	5.25
		Nos. J19-J24 (6)	114.60	20.65

Value in Color of Stamp

1913-39 *Perf. 12½*

J25	D5	1c salmon ('39)	.25	*25.00*
J26	D5	2½c salmon	.25	.25
J27	D5	3½c salmon ('39)	.25	*25.00*
J28	D5	5c salmon	.25	.25
J29	D5	7½c salmon ('22)	.25	.25
J30	D5	10c salmon	.25	.25
J31	D5	12½c salmon ('22)	3.25	.40
J32	D5	15c salmon	3.25	.40
J33	D5	20c salmon	.25	.25
J34	D5	25c salmon ('22)	.25	.25
J35	D5	30c salmon	.25	.25
J36	D5	37½c salmon ('30)	18.00	20.00
J37	D5	40c salmon	.25	.25
J38	D5	50c salmon	2.40	.25
J39	D5	75c salmon	3.25	2.40
		Nos. J25-J39 (15)	32.65	75.45

Thick White Paper
Invisible Gum
Numerals Slightly Larger

1941 Litho. *Perf. 12½*

J25a	D5	1c light red	.75	*12.00*
J28a	D5	5c light red	.75	12.00
J30a	D5	10c light red	8.00	24.00
J32a	D5	15c light red	1.00	12.00
J33a	D5	20c light red	.80	12.00
J35a	D5	30c light red	1.25	12.00
J37a	D5	40c light red	1.00	12.00
		Nos. J25a-J37a (7)	13.55	96.00

No. J36 Surcharged with New Value

1937, Oct. 1 Unwmk. *Perf. 12½*

J40	D5	20c on 37½c salmon	.80	.40

D6

1939-40

J41	D6	1g salmon	6.00	8.00
J42	D6	1g blue ('40)	.40	*4.00*
a.		1g lt bl, thick paper, invisible gum	.80	*12.00*

Catalogue values for unused stamps in this section, from this point to the end of the section, are for Never Hinged items.

Nos. 234, 237 and 241 Surcharged or Overprinted in Black

1946, Mar. 11 Photo.

J43	A28	2½c on 10c red org	1.25	1.25
J44	A28	10c red orange	2.00	2.00
J45	A28	20c plum	6.00	6.00
J46	A28	40c yellow green	45.00	45.00
		Nos. J43-J46 (4)	54.25	54.25

D7

Perf. 14½x14

1946, Aug. 14 Wmk. 228 Typo.

J47	D7	1c purple	.75	1.25
J48	D7	2½c brn org	2.00	2.00
J49	D7	3½c ultra	.75	1.25
J50	D7	5c red orange	.75	1.25
J51	D7	7½c Prus green	.75	1.25
J52	D7	10c deep magenta	.75	1.25
J53	D7	20c light ultra	.75	1.25
J54	D7	25c olive	.75	1.25
J55	D7	30c red brown	1.25	1.50
J56	D7	40c yellow grn	1.25	1.50
J57	D7	50c yellow	1.60	1.50
J58	D7	75c aqua	1.60	1.50
J59	D7	100c apple green	1.60	1.50
		Nos. J47-J59 (13)	14.55	18.25

1948 Litho. Unwmk. *Perf. 12½*

J59A	D7	2½c brown orange	1.25	*2.00*

OFFICIAL STAMPS

Regular Issues of 1883-1909 Overprinted

Perf. 12½

1911, Oct. 1 Typo. Unwmk.

O1	A6	½c violet	1.00	8.00
O2	A6	1c olive grn	.25	.80
O3	A6	2c yellow brn	.25	.25
O4	A6	2½c yellow	.75	.75
O5	A6	2½c blue grn	2.00	2.00
O6	A6	3c orange	.65	.65
O7	A6	4c ultra	.25	.25
O8	A6	5c rose red	1.20	1.00
b.		Double overprint	*1,600.*	*400.00*
O9	A6	7½c gray	3.00	3.00
O10	A9	10c slate	.25	.25
O11	A9	12½c deep blue	3.00	3.00
O12	A9	15c chocolate	1.00	1.00
a.		Overprinted with two bars	40.00	*120.00*
b.		As "a," "Dienst" inverted	50.00	
O13	A9	17½c bister	4.00	3.00
O14	A9	20c olive grn	1.00	.65
O15	A9	22½c brn & ol grn	4.00	4.00
O16	A9	25c violet	2.40	2.00
O17	A9	30c orange brn	1.25	.75
O18	A9	50c red brown	16.00	10.00
O19	A10	1g dull lilac	4.00	2.00
O20	A10	2½g slate blue	34.00	35.00
		Nos. O1-O20 (20)	80.25	78.35

The overprint reads diagonally downward on Nos. O1-O3 and O5-O9.

Overprint Inverted

O1a	A6	½c	60.00	*120.00*
O2a	A6	1c	4.00	*20.00*
O3a	A6	2c	4.00	*20.00*
O5a	A6	2½c	12.00	*28.00*
O6a	A6	3c	120.00	*40.00*
O8a	A6	5c	4.00	*20.00*
O10a	A9	10c	4.00	*8.00*
O11a	A9	12½c	40.00	*60.00*
O14a	A9	20c	200.00	60.00
O16a	A9	25c	*1,400.*	*1,400.*
O17a	A9	30c	200.00	120.00
O18a	A9	50c	40.00	32.50
O19a	A10	1g	*575.00*	*1,000.*
O20a	A10	2½g	240.00	*650.00*

Regular Issue of 1892-1894 Overprinted

1911, Oct. 1

O21	A4	10c orange brn	2.40	1.60
O22	A4	12½c gray	4.00	*12.00*
O23	A4	15c bister	4.00	4.00
O24	A4	20c blue	4.00	2.40
O25	A4	25c lilac	16.00	10.00
O26	A4	50c carmine	4.00	2.00
O27	A4	2.50g org brn & bl	67.50	65.00
		Nos. O21-O27 (7)	101.90	97.00

Inverted Overprints

O21a	A4	10c	*15.00*	*50.00*
O22a	A4	12½c	*425.00*	*400.00*
O23a	A4	15c	*425.00*	*325.00*
O24a	A4	20c	*165.00*	*175.00*
O25a	A4	25c	*800.00*	*900.00*
O26a	A4	50c	*15.00*	*75.00*
O27a	A4	2.50g	*1,150.*	*1,450.*

Handstamped overprints exist on Nos. O21, O26, O27. Handstamps differ from machine overprints in that the ink is flatter, the quality is poorer, and the "D" is usually slightly angled. The machined printed overprints are always parallel.

A handstamped "D" exists on regular-issue No. 28; however, this was created in limited quantities and was never issued. Value, $2,200.

OCCUPATION STAMPS

Issued under Japanese Occupation

During the Japanese occupation of the Netherlands Indies, 1942-45, the occupation forces applied a great variety of overprints to supplies of Netherlands Indies stamps of 1933-42. A few typical examples are shown above.

Most of these overprinted stamps were for use in limited areas, such as Java, Sumatra, Bangka and Billiton, etc. The anchor overprints were applied by the Japanese naval authorities for areas under their control.

For a time, stamps of Straits Settlements and some of the Malayan states, with Japanese overprints, were used in Sumatra and the Riouw archipelago. Stamps of Japan without overprint were also used in the Netherlands Indies during the occupation.

For Use in Java and Sumatra

100 Sen (Cents) = 1 Rupee (Gulden)

Globe Showing Japanese Empire — OS1

Farmer Plowing Rice Field — OS2

Mt. Semeru, Java's Highest Active Volcano — OS3

Bantam Bay, Northwest Java — OS4

Values in Sen

Perf. 12½

1943, Mar. 9 Unwmk. Litho.

N1	OS1	2s red brown	2.50	4.25
N2	OS2	3½s carmine	1.75	1.25
N3	OS3	5s green	5.00	1.25
N4	OS4	10s light blue	15.00	2.50
		Nos. N1-N4 (4)	24.25	9.25

Issued to mark the anniversary of Japan's "Victory" in Java.

For Use in Java (also Sumatra, Borneo and Malaya)

Javanese Dancer OS5

Javanese Puppet OS6

Buddha Statue, Borobudur OS7

Map of Java OS8

Sacred Dancer of Djokja Palace, and Borobudur OS9

Bird of Vishnu, Map of Java and Mt. Semeru OS10

Plowing with Carabao OS11

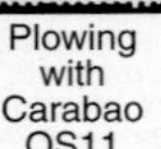

Terraced Rice Fields OS12

Values in Cents, Sen or Rupees

1943-44 Unwmk. *Perf. 12½*

N5 OS5 3½c rose red 2.00 1.00
N6 OS6 5s yellow grn 3.50 .80
N7 OS7 10c dk blue 4.00 .60
N8 OS8 20c olive brn 1.40 .80
N9 OS9 40c rose lilac 3.50 1.20
N10 OS10 60c red orange 2.50 1.20
N11 OS11 80s fawn ('44) 4.50 3.75
N12 OS12 1r violet ('44) 22.50 3.00
Nos. N5-N12 (8) 43.90 12.35

Indies Soldier — OS13

1943, Apr.

N13 OS13 3½c rose 11.00 10.00
N14 OS13 10c blue 35.00 4.25

Issued to commemorate reaching the postal savings goal of 5,000,000 gulden.

For Use in Sumatra

Batak Tribal House OS14

Menangkabau House OS15

Plowing with Carabao OS16

Nias Island Scene OS17

Carabao Canyon — OS18

1943 Unwmk. *Perf. 12½*

N15 OS14 1c olive green .55 1.00
N16 OS14 2c brt yel grn .55 1.00
N17 OS14 3c bluish green .55 1.00
N18 OS15 3½c rose red 2.10 1.00
N19 OS15 4c ultra 1.25 1.00
N20 OS15 5c red orange 1.50 1.00
N21 OS16 10c blue gray 4.75 .50
N22 OS16 20c orange brn 1.00 .50
N23 OS17 30c red violet 2.25 1.00
N24 OS17 40c dull brown 2.50 1.00
N25 OS18 50c bister brn 2.50 2.50
N26 OS18 1r lt blue vio 35.00 5.00
Nos. N15-N26 (12) 54.50 16.50

For Use in the Lesser Sunda Islands, Molucca Archipelago and Districts of Celebes and South Borneo Controlled by the Japanese Navy

Japanese Flag, Island Scene OS19

Mt. Fuji, Kite, Flag, Map of East Indies OS20

Values in Cents and Gulden

1943 Wmk. 257 Typo. *Perf. 13*

N27 OS19 2c brown 1.25 *11.50*
N28 OS19 3c yellow grn 1.25 *10.50*
N29 OS19 3½c brown org 4.00 *10.50*
N30 OS19 5c blue .80 *3.75*
N31 OS19 10c carmine 1.00 *3.75*
N32 OS19 15c ultra 1.20 *10.00*
N33 OS19 20c dull violet 1.75 *3.75*

Engr.

N34 OS20 25c orange 6.00 *11.50*
N35 OS20 30c blue 6.00 *6.25*
N36 OS20 50c slate green 8.50 *9.00*
N37 OS20 1g brown lilac 37.50 *20.00*
Nos. N27-N37 (11) 69.25 *100.50*

Issued under Nationalist Occupation

Menari Dancer of Amboina — OS21

Perf. 12½

1945, Aug. Photo. Unwmk.

N38 OS21 2c carmine .25 .35

This stamp was prepared in 1941 or 1942 by Netherlands Indies authorities as an addition to the 1941 "dancers" set, but was issued in 1945 by the Nationalists (Indonesian Republic). It was not recognized by the Dutch. Exists imperforate.

NETHERLANDS NEW GUINEA

'ne-t̲h̲ər-lənˌdˌz 'nü 'gi-nē

(Dutch New Guinea)

LOCATION — Western half of New Guinea, southwest Pacific Ocean
GOVT. — Former Overseas Territory of the Netherlands
AREA — 151,789 sq. mi.
POP. — 730,000 (est. 1958)
CAPITAL — Hollandia

Netherlands New Guinea came under temporary United Nations administration Oct. 1, 1962, when stamps of this territory overprinted "UNTEA" were introduced to replace issues of Netherlands New Guinea. See West New Guinea (West Irian) in Vol. 6.

100 Cents = 1 Gulden

Catalogue values for all unused stamps in this country are for Never Hinged items.

A1

A2

Queen Juliana — A3

Perf. 12½x13½

1950-52 Unwmk. Photo.

1 A1 1c slate blue .35 .25
2 A1 2c deep org .35 .25
3 A1 2½c olive brn .50 .25
4 A1 3c deep plum 1.75 1.60
5 A1 4c blue grn 1.75 1.25
6 A1 5c ultra 3.50 .25
7 A1 7½c org brown .55 .25
8 A1 10c purple 1.75 .25
9 A1 12½c crimson 1.75 1.60

Perf. 13½x12½

10 A2 15c brown org 2.50 .75
11 A2 20c blue 1.15 .25
12 A2 25c orange red 1.15 .25
13 A2 30c dp blue ('52) 10.00 .40
14 A2 40c blue grn 1.75 .25
15 A2 45c brown ('52) 5.50 .80
16 A2 50c deep orange 1.50 .25
17 A2 55c brown blk ('52) 10.00 .60
18 A2 80c purple 12.00 3.00

Engr. *Perf. 12½x12*

19 A3 1g red 15.00 .40
20 A3 2g yellow brn ('52) 12.00 1.40
21 A3 5g dk olive grn 17.50 1.40
Nos. 1-21 (21) 102.30 15.70

For surcharges see Nos. B1-B3.

Bird of Paradise A4

Queen Victoria Crowned Pigeon A5

Queen Juliana — A6

10c, 15c, 20c, Bird of Paradise with raised wings.

Photo.; Litho. (Nos. 24, 26, 28)

1954-60 *Perf. 12½x12*

22 A4 1c ver & yel ('58) .40 .25
23 A4 5c choc & yel .40 .25
24 A5 7c org red, bl & brn vio ('59) .55 .35
25 A4 10c aqua & red brn .40 .25
26 A5 12c grn, bl & brn vio ('59) .55 .35
27 A4 15c dp yel & red brn .40 .25
28 A5 17c brn vio & bl ('59) .55 .25
29 A4 20c lt bl grn & red brn ('56) 1.20 .60
30 A6 25c red .40 .25
31 A6 30c deep blue .55 .25
32 A6 40c dp orange ('60) 2.50 2.00
33 A6 45c dk olive ('58) 1.20 1.25
34 A6 55c dk blue grn .75 .25
35 A6 80c dl gray vio 1.60 .40
36 A6 85c dk vio brn ('56) 2.00 .55
37 A6 1g plum ('59) 5.25 2.25
Nos. 22-37 (16) 18.70 9.75

Stamps overprinted "UNTEA" are listed under West Irian in Vol. 6.
For surcharges see Nos. B4-B6.

Papuan Watching Helicopter — A7

1959, Apr. 10 Photo. *Perf. 11½x11*

38 A7 55c red brown & blue 1.75 1.00

1959 expedition to the Star Mountains of New Guinea.

Mourning Woman — A8

1960, Apr. 7 Unwmk. *Perf. 13x14*

39 A8 25c blue .75 .60
40 A8 30c yellow bister .75 .60

World Refugee Year, 7/1/59-6/30/60.

Council Building — A9

1961, Apr. 5 Litho. *Perf. 11x11½*

41 A9 25c bluish green .30 *.40*
42 A9 30c rose .30 *.40*

Inauguration of the New Council.

School Children Crossing Street — A10

Design: 30c, Men looking at traffic sign.

1962, Mar. 16 Photo. *Perf. 14x13*

43 A10 25c dp blue & red .40 .40
44 A10 30c brt green & red .40 .40

Need for road safety.

Queen Juliana and Prince Bernhard — A11

1962, Apr. 28 Unwmk. *Perf. 14x13*

45 A11 55c olive brown .40 *.50*

Silver wedding anniv.

Tropical Beach — A12

Design: 30c, Palm trees on beach.

1962, July 18 *Perf. 14x13*

46 A12 25c multicolored .30 *.40*
47 A12 30c multicolored .30 *.40*

5th So. Pacific Conf., Pago Pago, July 1962.

SEMI-POSTAL STAMPS

Regular Issue of 1950-52 Surcharged in Black

Perf. 12½x13½

1953, Feb. 9 Unwmk. Photo.

B1 A1 5c + 5c ultra 12.00 9.50

Perf. 13½x12½

B2 A2 15c + 10c brn org 12.00 9.50
B3 A2 25c + 10c org red 12.00 9.50
Nos. B1-B3 (3) 36.00 28.50

The tax was for flood relief work in the Netherlands.

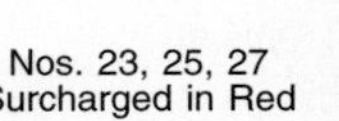

Nos. 23, 25, 27 Surcharged in Red

1955, Nov. 1 ***Perf. 12½x12***

B4 A4 5c + 5c 1.75 1.50
B5 A4 10c + 10c 1.75 1.50
B6 A4 15c + 10c 1.75 1.50
Nos. B4-B6 (3) 5.25 4.50

The surtax was for the Red Cross.

Leprosarium — SP1

10c+5c, 30c+10c, Young Papuan and huts.

Perf. 12x12½

1956, Dec. 15 Unwmk. Photo.

B7 SP1 5c + 5c dk slate grn 1.25 .95
B8 SP1 10c + 5c brn violet 1.25 .95
B9 SP1 25c + 10c brt blue 1.25 .95
B10 SP1 30c + 10c ocher 1.25 .95
Nos. B7-B10 (4) 5.00 3.80

The surtax was for the fight against leprosy.

Papuan Girl and Beach Scene — SP2

10c+5c, 30c+10c, Papuan boy and pile dwelling.

1957, Oct. 1 ***Perf. 12½x12***

B11 SP2 5c + 5c maroon 1.25 .95
B12 SP2 10c + 5c slate grn 1.25 .95
B13 SP2 25c + 10c brown 1.25 .95
B14 SP2 30c + 10c dark blue 1.25 .95
Nos. B11-B14 (4) 5.00 3.80

The surtax was to fight infant mortality.

Ancestral Image, North Coast New Guinea — SP3

Design: 10c+5c, 30c+10c, Bowl in form of human figure, Asmat-Papua.

1958, Oct. 1 Litho. ***Perf. 12½x12***

B15 SP3 5c + 5c bl, blk & red 1.25 .95
B16 SP3 10c + 5c rose lake, blk, red & yel 1.25 .95
B17 SP3 25c + 10c bl grn, blk & red 1.25 .95
B18 SP3 30c + 10c ol gray, blk, red & yel 1.25 .95
Nos. B15-B18 (4) 5.00 3.80

The surtax was for the Red Cross.

Bignonia — SP4

Flowers: 10c+5c, Orchid. 25c+10c, Rhododendron. 30c+10c, Gesneriacea.

1959, Nov. 16 Photo. ***Perf. 12½x13***

B19 SP4 5c + 5c car rose & grn .80 .70
B20 SP4 10c + 5c ol, yel & lil .80 .70
B21 SP4 25c + 10c red, org & grn .80 .70
B22 SP4 30c + 10c vio & grn .80 .70
Nos. B19-B22 (4) 3.20 2.80

Birdwing — SP5

Various Butterflies.

Perf. 13x12½

1960, Sept. 1 Unwmk. Litho.

B23 SP5 5c + 5c lt bl, blk, emer & yel 1.40 1.25
B24 SP5 10c + 5c sal, blk & bl 1.40 1.25
B25 SP5 25c + 10c yel, blk & org red 1.40 1.25
B26 SP5 30c + 10c lt grn, brn & yel 1.40 1.25
Nos. B23-B26 (4) 5.60 5.00

Surtax for social care.

Rhinoceros Beetle and Coconut Palm Leaf — SP6

Beetles & leaves of host plants: 10c+5c, Ectocemus 10-maculatus Montri, a primitive weevil. 25c+10c, Stag beetle. 30c+10c, Tortoise beetle.

1961, Sept. 15 ***Perf. 13x12½***

Beetles in Natural Colors

B27 SP6 5c + 5c deep org .70 .50
B28 SP6 10c + 5c lt ultra .70 .50
B29 SP6 25c + 10c citron .70 .50
B30 SP6 30c + 10c green .70 .50
Nos. B27-B30 (4) 2.80 2.00

Surtax for social care.

Crab — SP7

Designs: 10c+5c, Lobster, vert. 25c+10c, Spiny lobster, vert. 30c+10c, Shrimp.

Perf. 14x13, 13x14

1962, Sept. 17 Unwmk.

B31 SP7 5c + 5c red, grn, brn & yel .30 .25
B32 SP7 10c + 5c Prus bl & yel .30 .25
B33 SP7 25c + 10c multicolored .30 .25
B34 SP7 30c + 10c bl, org red & yel .35 .30
Nos. B31-B34 (4) 1.25 1.05

The surtax on Nos. B19-B34 went to various social works organizations.

POSTAGE DUE STAMPS

D1

Perf. 13½x12½

1957 Photo. Unwmk.

J1 D1 1c vermilion .50 .45
J2 D1 5c vermilion 1.25 *1.10*
J3 D1 10c vermilion 2.75 *2.50*
J4 D1 25c vermilion 3.25 2.90
J5 D1 40c vermilion 3.25 2.90
J6 D1 1g blue 5.25 *5.25*
Nos. J1-J6 (6) 16.25 15.10

NEVIS

'nē-vəs

LOCATION — West Indies, southeast of Puerto Rico

GOVT. — A former presidency of the Leeward Islands Colony (British)

AREA — 36 sq. mi.

POP. — 8,794 (1991)

Nevis stamps were discontinued in 1890 and replaced by those of the Leeward Islands. From 1903 to 1956 stamps of St. Kitts-Nevis and Leeward Islands were used concurrently. From 1956 to 1980 stamps of St. Kitts-Nevis were used. While still a part of St. Kitts-Nevis, Nevis started issuing stamps in 1980.

See Leeward Islands and St. Kitts-Nevis.

12 Pence = 1 Shilling
100 Cents = 1 Dollar

Catalogue values for unused stamps in this country are for Never Hinged items, beginning with Scott 100 in the regular postage section and Scott O1 in the officials section.

Unused examples of Nos. 1-8 almost always have no original gum, and they are valued without gum. These stamps with original gum are worth more. Other issues are valued with original gum as defined in the catalogue introduction. Very fine examples of Nos. 1-8, will have perforations touching the design on at least one side due to the narrow spacing of the stamps on the plates. Stamps with perfs clear of the design on all four sides are scarce and will command higher prices.

Medicinal Spring
A1 A2

A3

A4

1861 Unwmk. Engr. ***Perf. 13***

Bluish Wove Paper

1 A1 1p lake rose 325.00 140.00
2 A2 4p dull rose 950.00 200.00
3 A3 6p gray 775.00 260.00
4 A4 1sh green 1,100. 250.00

Grayish Wove Paper

5 A1 1p lake rose 115.00 60.00
6 A2 4p dull rose 170.00 80.00
7 A3 6p lilac gray 175.00 65.00
8 A4 1sh green 400.00 95.00

1867 White Wove Paper ***Perf. 15***

9 A1 1p red 67.50 55.00
10 A2 4p orange 155.00 25.00
11 A4 1sh yellow green 925.00 125.00
12 A4 1sh blue green 325.00 45.00

Laid Paper

13 A4 1sh yel green *25,000.* 6,750.
Manuscript cancel 3,000.

No. 13 values are for stamps with design cut into on one or two sides.

1876 Wove Paper Litho.

14 A1 1p rose 35.00 25.00
14A A1 1p red 45.00 30.00
b. 1p vermilion 45.00 45.00
c. Imperf., pair *1,900.*
d. Half used as ½p on cover *4,500.*
15 A2 4p orange 190.00 45.00
a. Imperf.
b. Vert. pair, imperf. between *12,750.*
16 A3 6p olive gray 250.00 250.00
17 A4 1sh gray green 100.00 *125.00*
a. 1sh dark green 135.00 *175.00*
b. Horiz. strip of 3, perf. all around & imperf. btwn. *20,000.*

Perf. 11½

18 A1 1p vermilion 65.00 60.00
a. Horiz. pair, imperf. btwn.
b. Half used as ½p on cover *4,500.*
c. Imperf., pair 1,200.
Nos. 14-18 (6) 685.00 535.00

Queen Victoria — A5

1879-80 Typo. Wmk. 1 ***Perf. 14***

19 A5 1p violet ('80) 90.00 55.00
a. Diagonal half used as ½p on cover *1,500.*
20 A5 2½p red brown 175.00 100.00

1882-90 Wmk. Crown and CA (2)

21 A5 ½p green ('83) 14.00 *27.50*
22 A5 1p violet 125.00 50.00
a. Half used as ½p on cover 900.00
23a A5 1p carmine ('84) 20.00 20.00
24 A5 2½p red brown 140.00 55.00
25 A5 2½p ultra ('84) 24.00 27.50
26 A5 4p blue 400.00 55.00
27 A5 4p gray ('84) 25.00 10.00
28 A5 6p green ('83) 500.00 400.00
29 A5 6p brown org ('86) 27.50 *77.50*
30 A5 1sh violet ('90) 125.00 *225.00*
Nos. 21-30 (10) 1,401. *947.50*

Half of No. 22 Surcharged in Black or Violet

1883

31 A5 ½p on half of 1p 1,100. 60.00
a. Double surcharge 450.00
b. Unsevered pair *7,500.*
c. Surcharged on half of 1p revenue stamp 600.00
32 A5 ½p on half of 1p (V) 1,250. 55.00
a. Double surcharge 450.00
b. Unsevered pair *7,500.* 850.00
c. Surcharged on half of 1p revenue stamp 600.00

Surcharge reads up or down.

Catalogue values for unused stamps in this section, from this point to the end of the section, are for Never Hinged items.

St. Kitts-Nevis Nos. 357-369 Ovptd.

Perf. 14½x14

1980, June 23 Litho. Wmk. 373

100 A61 5c multicolored .25 .25
101 A61 10c multicolored .25 .25
102 A61 12c multicolored .25 .30
103 A61 15c multicolored .25 .25
104 A61 25c multicolored .25 .25
a. Unwatermarked 1.00 *1.75*
105 A61 30c multicolored .25 .25
106 A61 40c multicolored .30 .30
107 A61 45c multicolored .65 .50
108 A61 50c multicolored .30 .30
109 A61 55c multicolored .40 .25
110 A61 $1 multicolored .30 .30
a. Unwatermarked 2.50 *5.00*
111 A61 $5 multicolored 1.00 1.00
112 A61 $10 multicolored 2.00 1.50
Nos. 100-112 (13) 6.45 5.70

The bars cover "St. Christopher" and "Anguilla."

80th Birthday of Queen Mother Elizabeth — A6

1980, Sept. 4 ***Perf. 14***

113 A6 $2 multicolored .40 .50

Ships and Boats — A6a

5c, Nevis lighter. 30c, Local fishing boat. 55c, *Caona.* $3, Windjammer's S.V. *Polynesia.*

1980, Oct. 8

114 A6a 5c multicolored .25 .25
115 A6a 30c multicolored .25 .25
116 A6a 55c multicolored .25 .25

Size: 38x52mm

No.	Type	Value	Description	Unused	Used
117	A6a	$3	multicolored	.55	.55
a.			Perf. 12½x12	.55	.55
b.			Booklet pane of 3 #117a	1.75	1.75
			Nos. 114-117 (4)	1.30	1.30

No. 117b separated into three parts by roulettes running vert. through the margin surrounding the stamps. For overprint see No. 538.

Christmas — A7

1980, Nov. 20 ***Perf. 14***

No.	Type	Value	Description	Unused	Used
118	A7	5c	Mother and child	.30	.30
119	A7	30c	Heralding angel	.30	.30
120	A7	$2.50	Three kings	.60	.60
			Nos. 118-120 (3)	1.20	1.20

A8

Landmarks — A9

5c, Charlestown Pier. 10c, Court House & Library. 15c, New River Mill. 20c, Nelson Museum. 25c, St. James' Parish Church. 30c, Nevis Lane. 40c, Zetland Plantation. 45c, Nisbet Plantation. 50c, Pinney's Beach. 55c, Eva Wilkin's Studio. $1, Nevis at dawn. $2.50, Ft. Charles ruins. $5, Old Bath House. $10, Nisbet's Beach.

1981, Feb. 5

No Date Imprint Below Design

No.	Type	Value	Description	Unused	Used
121	A8	5c	multicolored	.25	.25
122	A8	10c	multicolored	.25	.25
123	A9	15c	multicolored	.25	.25
124	A9	20c	multicolored	.25	.25
125	A9	25c	multicolored	.25	.25
126	A9	30c	multicolored	.25	.25
127	A9	40c	multicolored	.25	.25
128	A9	45c	multicolored	.25	.25
129	A9	50c	multicolored	.25	.25
130	A9	55c	multicolored	.30	.30
131	A9	$1	multicolored	.55	.55
132	A9	$2.50	multicolored	.75	.75
133	A9	$5	multicolored	1.25	1.25
134	A9	$10	multicolored	2.50	2.50
			Nos. 121-134 (14)	7.60	7.60

For surcharges see Nos. 169-181.

1982, June 9

Inscribed "1982" Below Design

No.	Type	Value	Description	Unused	Used
121a	A8	5c	multicolored	.30	.30
122a	A8	10c	multicolored	.30	.30
123a	A9	15c	multicolored	.25	.25
124a	A9	20c	multicolored	.25	.25
125a	A9	25c	multicolored	.25	.25
126a	A9	30c	multicolored	.25	.25
127a	A9	40c	multicolored	.25	.25
128a	A9	45c	multicolored	.25	.25
129a	A9	50c	multicolored	.25	.25
130a	A9	55c	multicolored	.30	.30
131a	A9	$1	multicolored	.55	.55
132a	A9	$2.50	multicolored	.75	.75
133a	A9	$5	multicolored	1.25	1.25
134a	A9	$10	multicolored	2.50	2.50
			Nos. 121a-134a (14)	7.70	7.70

1983

Inscribed "1983" Below Design

No.	Type	Value	Description	Unused	Used
124b	A9	20c	multicolored	.50	.25
125b	A9	25c	multicolored	.50	.25
126b	A9	30c	multicolored	.50	.25
127b	A9	40c	multicolored	.50	.25
128b	A9	45c	multicolored	.50	.25
129b	A9	50c	multicolored	.50	.25
130b	A9	55c	multicolored	.50	.25
132b	A9	$2.50	multicolored	1.25	1.00
			Nos. 124b-132b (8)	4.75	2.75

Prince Charles, Lady Diana, Royal Yacht Charlotte — A9a

Prince Charles and Lady Diana A9b

No. 135, Couple, *Royal Caroline*. No. 136, Couple. No. 137, Couple, *Royal Sovereign*. No. 139, Couple, HMY *Britannia*.

1981, June 23 Wmk. 373 ***Perf. 14***

No.	Type	Value	Description	Unused	Used
135	A9a	55c	multicolored	.25	.25
a.			Bklt. pane of 4, perf. 12, unwmkd.	.90	.90
136	A9b	55c	multicolored	.25	.25
137	A9a	$2	multicolored	.50	.50
138	A9b	$2	like No. 136	.50	.50
a.			Bklt. pane of 2, perf. 12, unwmkd.	1.40	1.40
139	A9a	$5	multicolored	1.10	1.10
140	A9b	$5	like No. 136	1.10	1.10
			Nos. 135-140 (6)	3.70	3.70

Souvenir Sheet

1981, Dec. 14 ***Perf. 12***

No.	Type	Value	Description	Unused	Used
141	A9b	$4.50	like No. 136	1.75	1.75

Stamps of the same denomination issued in sheets of 7 (6 type A9a and 1 type A9b).

For surcharges see Nos. 453-454.

Butterflies — A10

5c, Zebra. 30c, Malachite. 55c, Southern dagger tail. $2, Large orange sulphur.

1982, Feb. 16 ***Perf. 14***

No.	Type	Value	Description	Unused	Used
142	A10	5c	multicolored	.30	.30
143	A10	30c	multicolored	.30	.30
144	A10	55c	multicolored	.30	.30
145	A10	$2	multicolored	1.40	1.40
			Nos. 142-145 (4)	2.30	2.30

For overprint see No. 452.

1983, June 8

30c, Tropical chequered skipper. 55c, Caribbean buckeye, vert. $1.10, Common long-tailed skipper, vert. $2, Mimic.

No.	Type	Value	Description	Unused	Used
146	A10	30c	multicolored	.50	.50
147	A10	55c	multicolored	.50	.50
148	A10	$1.10	multicolored	.75	.75
149	A10	$2	multicolored	1.00	1.00
			Nos. 146-149 (4)	2.75	2.75

21st Birthday of Princess Diana, July 1 — A11

30c, Caroline of Brunswick. 55c, Brunswick arms. $5, Diana.

1982, June 22 ***Perf. 13½x14***

No.	Type	Value	Description	Unused	Used
150	A11	30c	multi	.25	.25
151	A11	55c	multi	.30	.30
152	A11	$5	multi	1.20	1.20
			Nos. 150-152 (3)	1.75	1.75

For surcharge see No. 449.

Nos. 150-152 Overprinted "ROYAL BABY"

1982, July 12

No.	Type	Value	Description	Unused	Used
153	A11	30c	multicolored	.25	.25
154	A11	55c	multicolored	.35	.35
155	A11	$5	multicolored	1.25	1.25
			Nos. 153-155 (3)	1.85	1.85

Birth of Prince William of Wales, June 21.

Scouting, 75th Anniv. — A12

1982, Aug. 18

No.	Type	Value	Description	Unused	Used
156	A12	5c	Cycling	.35	.35
157	A12	30c	Running	.45	.45
158	A12	$2.50	Building campfire	.90	.90
			Nos. 156-158 (3)	1.70	1.70

For overprints see Nos. 447, 455.

Christmas A13

Illustrations by youths — 15c, Eugene Seabrookes. 30c, Kharenzabeth Glasgow. $1.50, David Grant. $2.50, Leonard Huggins. Nos. 159-160 vert.

1982, Oct. 20 ***Perf. 13½x14, 14x13½***

No.	Type	Value	Description	Unused	Used
159	A13	15c	multicolored	.35	.35
160	A13	30c	multicolored	.35	.35
161	A13	$1.50	multicolored	.45	.45
162	A13	$2.50	multicolored	.85	.85
			Nos. 159-162 (4)	2.00	2.00

Coral — A14

15c, Tube sponge. 30c, Stinging coral. 55c, Flower coral. $3, Sea rod, red fire sponge.

1983, Jan. 12 ***Perf. 14***

No.	Type	Value	Description	Unused	Used
163	A14	15c	multicolored	.25	.25
164	A14	30c	multicolored	.40	.40
165	A14	55c	multicolored	.40	.40
166	A14	$3	multicolored	1.20	1.20
a.			Souvenir sheet of 4, #163-166	2.50	2.50
			Nos. 163-166 (4)	2.25	2.25

For overprints see Nos. 446, 448.

Commonwealth Day — A15

55c, HMS *Boreas* off Nevis. $2, Lord Nelson, *Boreas*.

1983, Mar. 14

No.	Type	Value	Description	Unused	Used
167	A15	55c	multicolored	.40	.40
168	A15	$2	multicolored	1.00	1.00

Nos. 121a and 123a-134a Ovptd.

No. 169

No. 170-181

1983, Sept. 19

No.	Type	Value	Description	Unused	Used
169	A8	5c	multicolored	.25	.25
c.			Overprint larger with serifed letters	1.25	*2.25*
170	A9	15c	multicolored	.25	.25
171	A9	20c	multicolored	.25	.25
172	A9	25c	multicolored	.25	.25
173	A9	30c	multicolored	.25	.25
174	A9	40c	multicolored	.25	.30
175	A9	45c	multicolored	.30	.40
176	A9	50c	multicolored	.30	.40
177	A9	55c	multicolored	.35	.45
178	A9	$1	multicolored	.45	.45
179	A9	$2.50	multicolored	.45	.70
180	A9	$5	multicolored	.55	.85
181	A9	$10	multicolored	.75	1.10
			Nos. 169-181 (13)	4.65	5.90

The overprints on Nos. 169a and 169c were applied locally.

Nos. 121, 123-127, 130-134 Ovptd.

1983

No.	Type	Value	Description	Unused	Used
169a	A8	5c	multicolored, larger ovpt.	15.00	12.00
170a	A9	15c	multicolored	42.50	42.50
171a	A9	20c	multicolored	6.00	6.00
172a	A9	25c	multicolored	6.00	6.00
173a	A9	30c	multicolored	1.10	1.10
174a	A9	40c	multicolored	1.00	1.00
177a	A9	55c	multicolored	1.00	1.00
178a	A9	$1	multicolored	1.00	1.00
179a	A9	$2.50	multicolored	1.40	1.40
180a	A9	$5	multicolored	2.50	2.50
181a	A9	$10	multicolored	4.50	4.50
			Nos. 169a-181a (11)	82.00	79.00

Nos. 124b-132b and Additional values inscribed "1983" Ovptd.

1983

No.	Type	Value	Description	Unused	Used
170b	A9	15c	multicolored	1.75	1.00
171b	A9	20c	multicolored	1.75	1.00
172b	A9	25c	multicolored	1.75	1.00
173b	A9	30c	multicolored	1.75	1.00
174b	A9	40c	multicolored	1.75	1.00
175b	A9	45c	multicolored	1.75	1.00
176b	A9	50c	multicolored	1.75	1.00
177b	A9	55c	multicolored	1.75	1.00
178b	A9	$1	multicolored	2.25	1.25
179b	A9	$2.50	multicolored	1.75	1.00
180b	A9	$5	multicolored	3.00	3.00
181b	A9	$10	multicolored	6.00	6.00
			Nos. 170b-181b (12)	27.00	19.25

1st Manned Flight, Bicent. — A16

10c, Montgolfier Balloon, 1783, vert. 45c, Lindbergh's Sikorsky S-38 carrying mail, 1929. 50c, Beechcraft Twin Bonanza. $2.50, Sea Harrier, 1st operational V/STOL fighter.

1983, Sept. 28 Wmk. 380

No.	Type	Value	Description	Unused	Used
182	A16	10c	multicolored	.25	.25
183	A16	45c	multicolored	.25	.25
184	A16	50c	multicolored	.25	.25
185	A16	$2.50	multicolored	.75	.75
a.			Souvenir sheet of 4, #182-185	1.75	1.75
			Nos. 182-185 (4)	1.50	1.50

Christmas A17

1983, Nov. 7

No.	Type	Value	Description	Unused	Used
186	A17	5c	Nativity	.25	.25
187	A17	30c	Shepherds, flock	.25	.25
188	A17	55c	Angels	.25	.25
189	A17	$3	Youths	.90	.90
a.			Souvenir sheet of 4, #186-189	1.60	1.60
			Nos. 186-189 (4)	1.65	1.65

Leaders of the World

Large quantities of some Leaders of the World issues were sold at a fraction of face value when the printer was liquidated.

A18

Leaders of the World: Locomotives — No. 190, 1882 Class Wee Bogie, UK. No. 191, 1968 JNR Class EF81, Japan. No. 192, 1878 Snowdon Ranger, UK. No. 193, 1927 P.O. Class 5500, France. No. 194, 1859 Connor Single Class. No. 195, 1904 Large Belpaire Passenger, UK. No. 196, 1829 Stourbridge Lion, US. No. 197, 1934 Cock O' The North. No. 198, 1945 County of Oxford, GB. No. 199, 1940 SNCF Class 240P, France. No. 200, 1851 Comet, UK. No. 201, 1904 County Class, UK. No. 202, 1926 JNR Class 7000, Japan. No. 203, 1877 Nord L'Outrance, France. No. 204, 1919 CM St.P&P Bipolar, US. No. 205, 1897 Palatinate Railway Class P3, Germany. No. 206, 1908 Class 8H, UK. No. 207, 1927 King George V. No. 208, 1951 Britannia. No. 209, 1924 Pendennis Castle. No. 210, 1960 Evening Star. No. 211, 1934 Stanier Class 5, GB. No. 212, 1946 Winston Churchill Battle of Britain. No. 213, 1935 Mallard A4. No. 214, 1899 Q.R. Class PB-15, Australia. No. 215, 1836 C&St.L Dorchester, Canada. No. 216, 1953 U.P. Gas Turbine, US. No. 217, 1969 U.P. Centennial Class, US. No. 218, 1866 No. 23 Class A, UK. No. 219, 1955 NY, NH & HR FL9, US. No. 220, 1837 B&O Lafayette, US. No. 221, 1964 JNR Shin-Kansen, Japan. No. 222, 1928 DRG Class 64, Germany. No. 223, 1882 D&RGR Class C-16, US.

1983-86 Litho. Unwmk. *Perf. 12½*
Se-tenant Pairs, #a.-b.
a. — Side and front views.
b. — Action scene.

190 A18 1c multicolored .25 .25
191 A18 5c multicolored .25 .25
192 A18 5c multicolored .25 .25
193 A18 10c multicolored .25 .25
194 A18 15c multicolored .25 .25
195 A18 30c multicolored .25 .25
196 A18 30c multicolored .25 .25
197 A18 45c multicolored .25 .25
198 A18 55c multicolored .25 .25
199 A18 60c multicolored .25 .25
200 A18 60c multicolored .25 .25
201 A18 60c multicolored .25 .25
202 A18 60c multicolored .25 .25
203 A18 75c multicolored .25 .25
204 A18 75c multicolored .25 .25
205 A18 75c multicolored .25 .25
206 A18 90c multicolored .25 .25
207 A18 $1 multicolored .30 .30
208 A18 $1 multicolored .30 .30
209 A18 $1 multicolored .30 .30
210 A18 $1 multicolored .30 .30
211 A18 $1 multicolored .30 .30
212 A18 $1 multicolored .30 .30
213 A18 $1 multicolored .30 .30
214 A18 $1 multicolored .30 .30
215 A18 $1 multicolored .30 .30
216 A18 $1.50 multicolored .45 .45
217 A18 $1.50 multicolored .45 .45
218 A18 $2 multicolored .60 .60
219 A18 $2 multicolored .60 .60
220 A18 $2 multicolored .60 .60
221 A18 $2.50 multicolored .85 .85
222 A18 $2.50 multicolored .85 .85
223 A18 $3 multicolored .85 .85
Nos. 190-223 (34) 12.20 12.20

Issued: #190, 200, 218, 4/26/85; #191, 193, 199, 221, 10/29/84; #192, 195, 201, 203, 214, 222, 7/26/85; #194, 197, 202, 204, 215, 217, 220, 223, 10/1/86; #196, 205, 216, 219, 1/30/86; #198, 206-213, 11/10/83.

British Monarchs, Scenes from History — A20

#258a, Boer War. #258b, Queen Victoria. #259a, Signing of the Magna Carta. #259b, King John. #260a, Victoria, diff. #260b, Osborne House. #261a, John, diff. #261b, Newark Castle, Nottinghamshire. #262a, Battle of Dettingen. #262b, King George II. #263a, George II, diff. #263b, Bank of England, 1732. #264a, George II's coat of arms. #264b, George II, diff. #265a, John's coat of arms. #265b, John, diff. #266a, Victoria's coat of arms. #266b, Victoria, diff.

1984

258 A20 5c Pair, #a.-b. .25 .25
259 A20 5c Pair, #a.-b. .25 .25
260 A20 50c Pair, #a.-b. .25 .25
261 A20 55c Pair, #a.-b. .25 .25
262 A20 60c Pair, #a.-b. .25 .25
263 A20 75c Pair, #a.-b. .25 .25
264 A20 $1 Pair, #a.-b. .25 .25
265 A20 $2 Pair, #a.-b. .60 .60
266 A20 $3 Pair, #a.-b. .50 .50
Nos. 258-266 (9) 2.85 2.85

Issued: #258, 260, 262-264, 266, 4/11; others, 11/20.

Tourism — A22

No. 276, Golden Rock Inn. No. 277, Rest Haven Inn. No. 278, Cliffdwellers Hotel. No. 279, Pinney's Beach Hotel.

1984, May 16 Wmk. 380 *Perf. 14*

276 A22 55c multicolored .40 .40
277 A22 55c multicolored .40 .40
278 A22 55c multicolored .40 .40
279 A22 55c multicolored .40 .40
Nos. 276-279 (4) 1.60 1.60

Seal of the Colony — A22a

1984, June 8 Wmk. 380 *Perf. 14*

279A A22a $15 dull red 2.00 *5.25*

Tourism Type of 1984

No. 280, Croney's Old Manor Hotel. No. 281, Montpelier Plantation Inn. No. 282, Nisbet's Plantation Inn. No. 283, Zetland Plantation Inn.

1985, Feb. 12

280 A22 $1.20 multicolored .65 .65
281 A22 $1.20 multicolored .65 .65
282 A22 $1.20 multicolored .65 .65
283 A22 $1.20 multicolored .65 .65
Nos. 280-283 (4) 2.60 2.60

A23

Leaders of the World: Classic cars — No. 285, 1932 Cadillac V16 Fleetwood Convertible, US. No. 286, 1935 Delahaye Type 35 Cabriolet, France. No. 287, 1916 Packard Twin Six Touring Car, US. No. 288, 1929 Lagonda Speed Model Touring Car, GB. No. 289, 1958 Ferrari Testarossa, Italy. No. 290, 1934 Voisin Aerodyne, France. No. 291, 1912 Sunbeam Coupe De L'Auto, GB. No. 292, 1936 Adler Trumpf, Germany. No. 293, 1886 Daimler 2-Cylinder, Germany. No. 294, 1930 Riley Brooklands Nine, UK. No. 295, 1967 Jaguar E-Type 4.2 Liter, GB. No. 296, 1970 Porsche 911 S Targa, Germany. No. 297, 1948 Cisitalia Pinnifarina Coupe, Italy. No. 298, 1885 Benz Three-wheeler, Germany. No. 299, 1966 Alfa Romeo GTA, Italy. No. 300, 1947 Volkswagen Beetle, Germany. No. 301, 1963 Buick Riviera. No. 302, 1947 MG TC, GB. No. 303, 1960 Cooper Climax, UK. No. 304, 1957 Maserati Tipo 250F, Italy. No. 305, 1913 Pierce Arrow Type 66, US. No. 306, 1904 Ford 999, US. No. 307, 1980 Porsche 928S, Germany. No. 308, 1910 Oldsmobile Limited, US. No. 309, 1951 Jaguar C-Type, UK. No. 310, 1928 Willys-Knight 66A, US. No. 311, 1933 MG K3 Magnette, GB. No. 312, 1937 Lincoln Zephyr, US. No. 313, 1937 ERA 1.5 l B Type, UK. No. 314, 1953 Studebaker Starliner, US. No. 315, 1926 Pontiac 2-door, US. No. 316, 1966 Cobra Roadster 289, US. No. 317, 1930 MG M-Type Midget, UK. No. 318, 1966 Aston Martin DB6 Hardtop, GB. No. 319, 1932 Pierce Arrow V12, US. No. 320, 1971 Rolls Royce Corniche, UK. No. 321, 1953 Chevrolet Corvette, US. No. 322, 1919 Cunningham V-8, US.

1984-86 Unwmk. *Perf. 12½*
Se-tenant Pairs, #a.-b.
a. — Side and front views.
b. — Action scene.

285 A23 1c multicolored .25 .25
286 A23 1c multicolored .25 .25
287 A23 5c multicolored .25 .25
288 A23 5c multicolored .25 .25
289 A23 5c multicolored .25 .25
290 A23 10c multicolored .25 .25
291 A23 10c multicolored .25 .25
292 A23 10c multicolored .25 .25
293 A23 15c multicolored .25 .25
294 A23 15c multicolored .25 .25
295 A23 30c multicolored .25 .25
296 A23 35c multicolored .25 .25
297 A23 35c multicolored .25 .25
298 A23 45c multicolored .25 .25
299 A23 45c multicolored .25 .25
300 A23 50c multicolored .25 .25
301 A23 50c multicolored .25 .25
302 A23 55c multicolored .25 .25
303 A23 60c multicolored .25 .25
304 A23 60c multicolored .25 .25
305 A23 60c multicolored .25 .25
306 A23 75c multicolored .25 .25
307 A23 75c multicolored .25 .25
308 A23 75c multicolored .25 .25
309 A23 $1 multicolored .30 .30
310 A23 $1 multicolored .30 .30
311 A23 $1.15 multicolored .35 .35
312 A23 $1.50 multicolored .40 .40
313 A23 $1.50 multicolored .40 .40
314 A23 $1.75 multicolored .45 .45
315 A23 $2 multicolored .55 .55
316 A23 $2.50 multicolored .70 .70
317 A23 $2.50 multicolored .70 .70
318 A23 $3 multicolored .75 .75
319 A23 $3 multicolored .75 .75
320 A23 $3 multicolored .75 .75
321 A23 $3 multicolored .75 .75
322 A23 $3 multicolored .75 .75
Nos. 285-322 (38) 13.90 13.90

Issued: #285, 287, 293, 296, 298, 302, 316, 318, 7/25/84; #286, 289-290, 301, 303, 306, 317, 320, 2/20/85; #288, 295, 300, 319, 10/23/84; #291, 297, 307, 311-312, 315, 10/4/85; #292, 303, 308-309, 313, 321, 1/30/86; #294, 299, 305, 310, 314, 322, 8/15/86.

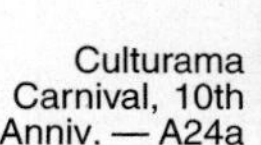

Culturama Carnival, 10th Anniv. — A24a

30c, Carpentry. 55c, Weaving mats and baskets. $1, Ceramics. $3, Carnival queen, folk dancers.

Wmk. 380
1984, Aug. 1 Litho. *Perf. 14*

361 A24a 30c multicolored .25 .25
362 A24a 55c multicolored .25 .25
363 A24a $1 multicolored .25 .25
364 A24a $3 multicolored .65 .65
Nos. 361-364 (4) 1.40 1.40

Flowers — A24b

5c, Yellow bell. 10c, Plumbago. 15c, Flamboyant. 20c, Eyelash orchid. 30c, Bougainvillea. 40c, Hibiscus. 50c, Night-blooming cereus. 55c, Yellow mahoe. 60c, Spider lily. 75c, Scarlet cordia. $1, Shell ginger. $3, Blue petrea. $5, Coral hibiscus. $10, Passion flower.

1984, Aug. 8
No Date Imprint Below Design

365 A24b 5c multi .25 .25
366 A24b 10c multi .25 .25
367 A24b 15c multi .25 .25
368 A24b 20c multi .25 .25
a. Inscribed "1986" .80 .35
369 A24b 30c multi .25 .25
370 A24b 40c multi .25 .25
a. Inscribed "1986" .50 .35
371 A24b 50c multi .25 .25
372 A24b 55c multi .25 .25
373 A24b 60c multi .30 .30
374 A24b 75c multi .35 .35
375 A24b $1 multi .30 .40
376 A24b $3 multi .60 1.10
377 A24b $5 multi 1.10 2.00
378 A24b $10 multi 2.25 3.50
Nos. 365-378 (14) 6.90 9.65

Nos. 368a and 370a issued 7/23/86.

Independence of St. Kitts and Nevis, 1st Anniv. — A26

15c, Picking cotton. 55c, Hamilton House. $1.10, Self-sufficiency in food production. $3, Pinney's Beach.

1984, Sept. 18

379 A26 15c multi .25 .25
380 A26 55c multi .25 .25
381 A26 $1.10 multi .40 .40
382 A26 $3 multi .70 1.00
Nos. 379-382 (4) 1.60 1.90

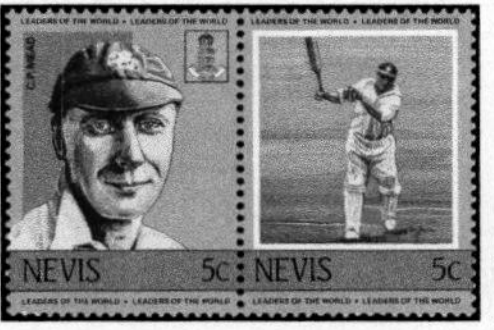

Leaders of the World A27

Cricket players and team emblems and match scenes: No. 383, C.P. Mead, England. No. 384, J.D. Love, Yorkshire. No. 385, S.J. Dennis, Yorkshire. No. 386, J.B. Statham, England. No. 387, Sir Learie Constantine, West Indies. No. 388, B.W. Luckhurst, Kent. No. 389, Sir Leonard Hutton, England. No. 390, B.L. D'Oliveira, England.

Pairs, #a.-b.

1984 Unwmk. *Perf. 12½*

383 A27 5c multicolored .25 .25
384 A27 5c multicolored .25 .25
385 A27 15c multicolored .25 .25
386 A27 25c multicolored .25 .25
387 A27 55c multicolored .25 .25
388 A27 55c multicolored .25 .25
389 A27 $2.50 multicolored .50 1.25
390 A27 $2.50 multicolored .50 1.25
Nos. 383-390 (8) 2.50 4.00

Issued: #383, 386, 389, 10/23; others, 11/20.

Christmas A29

Musicians from local bands: 15c, Flutist and drummer of the Honeybees Band. 40c, Guitar and barhow players of the Canary Birds Band. 60c, Shell All Stars steel band. $3, Choir, organist, St. John's Church, Fig Tree.

1984, Nov. 2 Wmk. 380 *Perf. 14*

399-402 A29 Set of 4 2.25 2.25

Birds — A30

1985, Mar. 19

403 A30 20c Broad-winged hawk 1.10 .25
404 A30 40c Red-tailed hawk 1.25 .35
405 A30 60c Little blue heron 1.25 .45
406 A30 $3 Great white heron 2.75 2.25
Nos. 403-406 (4) 6.35 3.30

Leaders of the World A31

Birds: #407a, Painted bunting. #407b, Golden-crowned kinglet. #408a, Eastern bluebird. #408b, Northern cardinal. #409a, Common flicker. #409b, Western tanager. #410a, Belted kingfisher. #410b, Mangrove cuckoo. #411a, Yellow warbler. #411b, Cerulean warbler. #412a, Sage thrasher. #412b, Evening grosbeak. #413a, Burrowing owl. #413b, Long-eared owl. #414a, Blackburnian warbler. #414b, Northern oriole.

1985 Unwmk. *Perf. 12½*

407 A31 1c Pair, #a.-b. .25 .25
408 A31 5c Pair, #a.-b. .25 .25
409 A31 40c Pair, #a.-b. .40 .40
410 A31 55c Pair, #a.-b. .45 .45
411 A31 60c Pair, #a.-b. .50 .50
412 A31 60c Pair, #a.-b. .50 .50
413 A31 $2 Pair, #a.-b. 1.50 1.50
414 A31 $2.50 Pair, #a.-b. 1.75 1.75
Nos. 407-414 (8) 5.60 5.60

John J. Audubon, ornithologist, birth bicent.
Issued: 1c, 40c, #412, $2.50, 6/3; others, 3/25.

Girl Guides, 75th Anniv. — A32

15c, Troop, horiz. 60c, Uniforms, 1910, 1985. $1, Lord and Lady Baden-Powell. $3, Princess Margaret.

1985, June 17 Wmk. 380 *Perf. 14*

423 A32 15c multicolored .25 .25
424 A32 60c multicolored .25 .25
425 A32 $1 multicolored .35 .35
426 A32 $3 multicolored .90 1.25
Nos. 423-426 (4) 1.75 2.10

Queen Mother Elizabeth A33

#427a, 432a, Black hat, white plume. #427b, 432b, Blue hat, pink feathers. #428a, Blue hat. #428b, Tiara. #429a, Violet & blue hat. #429b, Blue hat. #430a, 433a, Light blue hat. #430b, 433b, Black hat. #431a, As a child, c. 1910. #431b, Queen consort, c. 1945.

1985, July 31 Unwmk. *Perf. 12½*

427 A33 45c Pair, #a.-b. .25 .25
428 A33 75c Pair, #a.-b. .30 .30
429 A33 $1.20 Pair, #a.-b. .55 .55
430 A33 $1.50 Pair, #a.-b. .70 .70
Nos. 427-430 (4) 1.80 1.80

Souvenir Sheets

431 A33 $2 Sheet of 2, #a.-b. 2.00 2.00
432 A33 $3.50 Sheet of 2, #a.-b. 2.00 2.00
433 A33 $6 Sheet of 2, #a.-b. 4.00 4.00

Issued: #432-433, 12/27; others, 7/31.
For overprints see No. 450.

Great Western Railway, 150th Anniv. A34

Railway engineers and their achievements: #438a, Isambard Brunel. #438b, Royal Albert Bridge, 1859. #439a, William Dean. #439b, *Lord of the Isles,* 1895. #440a, *Lode Star,* 1907. #440b, G.J. Churchward. #441a, Pendennis Castle Class, 1924. #441b, C.B. Collett.

1985, Aug. 31

438 A34 25c Pair, #a.-b. .25 .25
439 A34 50c Pair, #a.-b. .30 .30
440 A34 $1 Pair, #a.-b. .50 .50
441 A34 $2.50 Pair, #a.-b. 1.30 1.30
Nos. 438-441 (4) 2.35 2.35

Nos. 163, 157, 164, 151, 427, 144, 139-140 and 158 Ovptd. or Srchd. "CARIBBEAN ROYAL VISIT 1985" in 2 or 3 Lines

Perf. 14, 12½ (45c)

1985, Oct. 23 Wmk. as Before

446 A14 15c No. 163 1.00 1.00
447 A12 30c No. 157 2.00 2.00
448 A14 30c No. 164 1.00 1.00
449 A11 40c on 55c No. 151 2.25 2.25
450 A33 45c Pair, #a.-b. 3.00 3.00
452 A10 55c No. 144 2.25 2.25
453 A9a $1.50 on $5 No. 139 3.75 3.75
454 A9b $1.50 on $5 No. 140 13.00 *16.00*
455 A12 $2.50 No. 158 4.00 4.00
Nos. 446-455 (9) 32.25 35.25

Christmas — A36

Anglican, Roman Catholic and Methodist churches — 10c, St. Paul's, Charlestown. 40c, St. Theresa, Charlestown. 60c, Methodist Church, Gingerland. $3, St. Thomas, Lowland.

1985, Nov. 5 Wmk. 380 *Perf. 15*

456 A36 10c multicolored .25 .25
457 A36 40c multicolored .30 .30
458 A36 60c multicolored .40 .40
459 A36 $3 multicolored 1.25 1.25
Nos. 456-459 (4) 2.20 2.20

Spitfire Fighter Plane, 50th Anniv. A37

$1, Prototype K.5054, 1936. $2.50, Mk.1A, 1940. $3, Mk.XII, 1944. $4, Mk.XXIV, 1948. $6, Seafire Mk.III.

1986, Mar. 24 Unwmk. *Perf. 12½*

460 A37 $1 multi .30 .30
461 A37 $2.50 multi .70 .70
462 A37 $3 multi .80 .80
463 A37 $4 multi 1.20 1.20
Nos. 460-463 (4) 3.00 3.00

Souvenir Sheet

464 A37 $6 multi 3.00 3.00

No. 464 exists imperf. Value, $12.50 unused.

Discovery of America, 500th Anniv. (in 1992) — A38

#465a, American Indian. #465b, Columbus trading with Indians. #466a, Columbus's coat of arms. #466b, Breadfruit. #467a, Galleons. #467b, Columbus.

1986, Apr. 11

465 A38 75c Pair, #a.-b. .90 .90
466 A38 $1.75 Pair, #a.-b. 2.25 2.25
467 A38 $2.50 Pair, #a.-b. 3.25 3.25
Nos. 465-467 (3) 6.40 6.40

Souvenir Sheet

468 A38 $6 Columbus, diff. 6.50 6.50

Printed in continuous designs picturing various maps of Columbus's voyages.

Queen Elizabeth II, 60th Birthday A39

Various portraits.

1986, Apr. 21

472 A39 5c multicolored .25 .25
473 A39 75c multicolored .25 .25
474 A39 $2 multicolored .50 .50
475 A39 $8 multi, vert. 2.00 2.00
Nos. 472-475 (4) 3.00 3.00

Souvenir Sheet

476 A39 $10 multicolored 6.00 6.00

1986 World Cup Soccer Championships, Mexico — A40

1c, Character trademark. 2c, Brazilian player. 5c, Danish player. 10c, Brazilian, diff. 20c, Denmark vs. Spain. 30c, Paraguay vs. Chile. 60c, Italy vs. W. Germany. 75c, Danish team. $1, Paraguayan team. $1.75, Brazilian team. $3, Italy vs. England. $6, Italian team.

Size of 75c, $1, $1.75, $6: 56x35½mm

Perf. 15, 12½ (75c, $1, $1.75, $6)

1986, May 16

477 A40 1c multicolored .25 .25
478 A40 2c multicolored .25 .25
479 A40 5c multicolored .25 .25
480 A40 10c multicolored .25 .25
481 A40 20c multicolored .25 .25
482 A40 30c multicolored .25 .25
483 A40 60c multicolored .35 .35
484 A40 75c multicolored .50 .50
485 A40 $1 multicolored .70 .70
486 A40 $1.75 multicolored .80 .80
487 A40 $3 multicolored 1.30 1.30
488 A40 $6 multicolored 2.50 2.50
Nos. 477-488 (12) 7.65 7.65

Souvenir Sheets

Perf. 12½

489 A40 $1.50 like $1.75 1.90 1.90
490 A40 $2 like $6 2.10 2.10

Perf. 15

491 A40 $2 like 20c 2.10 2.10
492 A40 $2.50 like 60c 2.50 2.50
493 A40 $4 like 30c 3.50 3.50

Nos. 478-483 and 487 vert.

Local Industry — A41

1986, July 18 Wmk. 380 *Perf. 14*

494 A41 15c Textile .35 .35
495 A41 40c Carpentry .50 .50
496 A41 $1.20 Agriculture 1.40 1.40
497 A41 $3 Fishing 3.25 3.25
Nos. 494-497 (4) 5.50 5.50

A42

Wedding of Prince Andrew and Sarah Ferguson A43

#498a, Andrew. #498b, Sarah. #499a, Andrew at the races, horiz. #499b, Andrew in Africa, horiz.

1986, July 23 Unwmk. *Perf. 12½*

498 A42 60c Pair, #a.-b. .40 .40
499 A42 $2 Pair, #a.-b. 1.25 1.25

Souvenir Sheet

500 A43 $10 Couple on Balcony 4.00 4.00

Printed in vert. and horiz. pairs.
For overprints see Nos. 521-522.

Coral — A44

1986, Sept. 8 Wmk. 380 *Perf. 15*

503 A44 15c Gorgonia .25 .25
504 A44 60c Fire coral .30 .30
505 A44 $2 Elkhorn coral .90 .90
506 A44 $3 Feather star 1.20 1.20
Nos. 503-506 (4) 2.65 2.65

A45

Statue of Liberty, Cent. A46

15c, Statue, World Trade Center. 25c, Statue, tall ship. 40c, Under renovation (front). 60c, Renovation (side). 75c, Statue, Operation Sail. $1, Tall ship. $1.50, Renovation (arm, head). $2, Ship flying Liberty flag. $2.50, Statue, Manhattan. $3, Workers on scaffold.

$3.50, Statue at dusk. $4, Head. $4.50, Torch struck by lightning. $5, Torch, blazing sun.

All stamps are vertical except the $1 & $2.

1986, Oct. 28 Unwmk. *Perf. 14*

507 A45 15c multicolored .25 .25
508 A45 25c multicolored .25 .25
509 A45 40c multicolored .25 .25
510 A45 60c multicolored .40 .40
511 A45 75c multicolored .50 .50
512 A45 $1 multicolored .65 .65
513 A45 $1.50 multicolored .85 .85
514 A45 $2 multicolored 1.10 1.10
515 A45 $2.50 multicolored 1.25 1.25
516 A45 $3 multicolored 1.60 1.60
Nos. 507-516 (10) 7.10 7.10

Souvenir Sheets

517 A46 $3.50 multicolored 2.10 2.10
518 A46 $4 multicolored 2.25 2.25
519 A46 $4.50 multicolored 2.50 2.50
520 A46 $5 multicolored 2.75 2.75

Nos. 498-499 Ovptd. "Congratulations to T.R.H. The Duke & Duchess of York"

1986, Nov. 17 *Perf. 12½*

521 A42 60c Pair, #a.-b. .45 .45
522 A42 $2 Pair, #a.-b. 1.50 1.50

Sports — A47

1986, Nov. 21 *Perf. 14*

525 A47 10c Sailing .30 .30
526 A47 25c Netball .30 .30
527 A47 $2 Cricket 2.00 2.00
528 A47 $3 Basketball 3.00 3.00
Nos. 525-528 (4) 5.60 5.60

Christmas A48

Churches: 10c, St. George's Anglican Church, Gingerland. 40c, Methodist Church, Fountain. $1, Charlestown Methodist Church. $5, Wesleyan Holiness Church, Brown Hill.

1986, Dec. 8

529 A48 10c multicolored .25 .25
530 A48 40c multicolored .30 .30
531 A48 $1 multicolored .75 .75
532 A48 $5 multicolored 2.75 2.75
Nos. 529-532 (4) 4.05 4.05

US Constitution — A49

Christening of the Hamilton, 1788 — A50

US Constitution, bicent. and 230th anniv. of the birth of Alexander Hamilton: 40c, Alexander Hamilton, Hamilton House. 60c, Hamilton. $2, George Washington and members of the 1st presidential cabinet.

1987, Jan. 11

533 A49 15c shown .25 .25
534 A49 40c multicolored .30 .30
535 A49 60c multicolored .45 .45
536 A49 $2 multicolored 1.10 1.10
Nos. 533-536 (4) 2.10 2.10

Souvenir Sheet

537 A50 $5 shown 7.50 7.50

No. 117 Overprinted

1987, Feb. 20 **Wmk. 373**
538 A6a $3 multicolored 1.50 1.50

A51

1987, Mar. 11 **Wmk. 380**
539 A51 15c Fig Tree Church .35 .35
540 A51 60c Frances Nisbet .75 .75
541 A51 $1 HMS *Boreas* 1.25 1.25
542 A51 $3 Capt. Nelson 3.00 3.00
Nos. 539-542 (4) 5.35 5.35

Souvenir Sheet

543 Sheet of 2, #542, 543a 5.25 5.25
a. A51 $3 like No. 540 3.50 3.50

Wedding of Capt. Horatio Nelson and Frances Nisbet, Bicent.

A52

#544a, Queen angelfish. #544b, Blue angelfish. #545a, Blue thum. #545b, Red thum. #546a, Red hind. #546b, Rock hind. #547a, Coney Butterfish. #547b, Coney butterfish, diff.

1987, July 22 **Unwmk.** ***Perf. 15***
544 A52 60c Pair, #a.-b. .70 .70
545 A52 $1 Pair, #a.-b. 1.25 1.25
546 A52 $1.50 Pair, #a.-b. 1.75 1.75
547 A52 $2.50 Pair, #a.-b. 3.00 3.00
Nos. 544-547 (4) 6.70 6.70

Mushrooms — A53

15c, Panaeolus antillarum. 50c, Pycnoporus sanguineus. $2, Gymnopilus chrysopellus. $3, Cantharellus cinnabarinus.

1987, Oct. 16 **Wmk. 384** ***Perf. 14***
552 A53 15c multicolored .40 .40
553 A53 50c multicolored 1.00 1.00
554 A53 $2 multicolored 2.50 2.50
555 A53 $3 multicolored 3.00 3.00
Nos. 552-555 (4) 6.90 6.90

Christmas A54

1987, Dec. 4 ***Perf. 14½***
556 A54 10c Rag doll .25 .25
557 A54 40c Coconut boat .25 .25
558 A54 $1.20 Sandbox cart .50 .50
559 A54 $5 Two-wheeled cart 2.00 2.00
Nos. 556-559 (4) 3.00 3.00

Sea Shells — A55

1988, Feb. 15 ***Perf. 14x14½***
560 A55 15c Hawk-wing conch .30 .30
561 A55 40c Roostertail conch .40 .40
562 A55 60c Emperor helmet .50 .50
563 A55 $2 Queen conch 1.30 1.30
564 A55 $3 King helmet 1.75 1.75
Nos. 560-564 (5) 4.25 4.25

Intl. Red Cross and Red Crescent Organizations, 125th Annivs. — A56

Activities: 15c, Visiting the sick and the elderly. 40c, First aid training. 60c, Wheelchairs for the disabled. $5, Disaster relief.

1988, June 20 ***Perf. 14½x14***
565 A56 15c multicolored .25 .25
566 A56 40c multicolored .25 .25
567 A56 60c multicolored .35 .35
568 A56 $5 multicolored 2.50 2.50
Nos. 565-568 (4) 3.35 3.35

1988 Summer Olympics, Seoul — A57

1988, Aug. 26 ***Perf. 14***
569 Strip of 4 3.00 3.00
a. A57 10c Runner at starting block .25 .25
b. A57 $1.20 Leaving block .55 .55
c. A57 $2 Full stride .95 .95
d. A57 $3 Crossing finish line 1.40 1.40
e. Souvenir sheet of 4, #569a-569d 3.00 3.00

Printed se-tenant in a continuous design. Stamps in No. 569e are 23½x36½.

Independence, 5th Anniv. — A58

1988, Sept. 19 **Wmk. 373** ***Perf. 14½***
570 A58 $5 multicolored 2.50 2.50

Common Design Types pictured following the introduction.

Lloyds of London
Common Design Type

Designs: 15c, Act of Parliament incorporating Lloyds, 1871. 60c, *Cunard Countess* in Nevis Harbor, horiz. $2.50, Space shuttle, deployment of satellite in space, horiz. $3, *Viking Princess* on fire in the Caribbean, 1966.

1988, Oct. 31 **Wmk. 384** ***Perf. 14***
571 CD341 15c multicolored .45 .45
572 CD341 60c multicolored .90 .90
573 CD341 $2.50 multicolored 2.50 2.50
574 CD341 $3 multicolored 4.50 4.50
Nos. 571-574 (4) 8.35 8.35

Christmas Flowers — A59

1988, Nov. 7 ***Perf. 14½***
575 A59 15c Poinsettia .25 .25
576 A59 40c Tiger claws .25 .25
577 A59 60c Sorrel flower .35 .35
578 A59 $1 Christmas candle .60 .60
579 A59 $5 Snow bush 2.40 2.40
Nos. 575-579 (5) 3.85 3.85

Battle of Frigate Bay, 1782 — A60

Exhibition emblem & maps. #580a-580c in a continuous design.

1989, Apr. 17 ***Perf. 14***
580 A60 Strip of 3 3.75 3.75
a. 50c multicolored .30 .30
b. $1.20 multicolored .80 .80
c. $2 multicolored 1.40 1.40

Size: 34x47mm
Perf. 14x13½

581 A60 $3 Map of Nevis, 1764 3.00 3.00

French revolution bicent., PHILEXFRANCE '89.

Nocturnal Insects and Frogs — A61

1989, May 15
582 A61 10c Cicada .30 .30
583 A61 40c Grasshopper .50 .50
584 A61 60c Cricket .85 .85
585 A61 $5 Tree frog 4.50 4.50
a. Souvenir sheet of 4, #582-585 7.00 7.00
Nos. 582-585 (4) 6.15 6.15

Moon Landing, 20th Anniv.
Common Design Type

Apollo 12: 15c, Vehicle Assembly Building, Kennedy Space Center. 40c, Crew members Charles Conrad Jr., Richard Gordon and Alan Bean. $2, Mission emblem. $3, Moon operation in the Sun's glare. $6, Buzz Aldrin deploying passive seismic experiment package on the lunar surface, Apollo 11 mission.

1989, July 20 ***Perf. 14x13½***
Size of Nos. 587-588: 29x29mm
586 CD342 15c multicolored .25 .25
587 CD342 40c multicolored .25 .25
588 CD342 $2 multicolored 1.25 1.25
589 CD342 $3 multicolored 1.75 1.75
Nos. 586-589 (4) 3.50 3.50

Souvenir Sheet

590 CD342 $6 multicolored 4.00 4.00

Queen Conchs *(Strombus gigas)* — A62

1990, Jan. 31
591 A62 10c shown .35 .35
592 A62 40c Conch, diff .65 .65
593 A62 60c Conch, diff 1.50 1.50
594 A62 $1 Conch, diff 2.25 2.25
Nos. 591-594 (4) 4.75 4.75

Souvenir Sheet

595 A62 $5 Fish and coral 5.75 5.75

World Wildlife Fund.

Wyon Portrait of Victoria — A63

40c, Engine-turned background. 60c, Heath's engraving. $4, Inscriptions added. $5, Completed design.

Perf. 14x15
1990, May 3 **Litho.** **Unwmk.**
596 A63 15c brn, blk, tan .25 .25
597 A63 40c grn, blk, lt grn .30 .30
598 A63 60c blk, gray .50 .50
599 A63 $4 blue, blk, lt blue 2.75 2.75
Nos. 596-599 (4) 3.80 3.80

Souvenir Sheet

600 A63 $5 multicolored 4.50 4.50

Penny Black, 150th anniv. No. 600 for Stamp World London '90.

A64

1990, May 3 ***Perf. 13½***
601 A64 15c brown .25 .25
602 A64 40c deep green .30 .30
603 A64 60c violet .50 .50
604 A64 $4 bright ultra 3.25 3.25
Nos. 601-604 (4) 4.30 4.30

Souvenir Sheet

605 A64 $5 gray, lake & buff 5.50 5.50

Penny Black 150th anniversary and commemoration of the Thurn & Taxis postal service.

Crabs — A65

Designs include UPAE and discovery of America anniversary emblems.

1990, June 25 **Litho.** ***Perf. 14***
606 A65 5c Sand fiddler .25 .25
607 A65 15c Great land crab .25 .25
608 A65 20c Blue crab .30 .30
609 A65 40c Stone crab .40 .40
610 A65 60c Mountain crab .60 .60
611 A65 $2 Sargassum crab 1.40 1.40
612 A65 $3 Yellow box crab 2.00 2.00
613 A65 $4 Spiny spider crab 2.75 2.75
Nos. 606-613 (8) 7.95 7.95

Souvenir Sheets

614 A65 $5 Wharf crab 4.00 4.00
615 A65 $5 Sally lightfoot 4.00 4.00

Queen Mother 90th Birthday
A66 A67

1990, July 5
616 A66 $2 shown 1.25 1.25
617 A67 $2 shown 1.25 1.25
618 A66 $2 Queen Consort, diff. 1.25 1.25
a. Strip of 3, #616-618 3.75 3.75

Souvenir Sheet

619 A67 $6 Coronation Portrait, diff. 4.00 4.00

Nos. 616-618 printed in sheet of 9.

A68

Players from participating countries.

1990, Oct. 1 **Litho.** ***Perf. 14***
620 A68 10c Cameroun .25 .25
621 A68 25c Czechoslovakia .25 .25
622 A68 $2.50 England 2.00 2.00
623 A68 $5 West Germany 4.00 4.00
Nos. 620-623 (4) 6.50 6.50

Souvenir Sheets

624	A68	$5 Spain	3.50	3.50
625	A68	$5 Argentina	3.50	3.50

World Cup Soccer Championships, Italy.

A69

Christmas (Orchids): 10c, Cattleya deckeri. 15c, Epidendrum ciliare. 20c, Epidendrum fragrans. 40c, Epidendrum ibaguense. 60c, Epidendrum latifolium. $1.20, Maxillaria conferta. $2, Epidendrum strobiliferum. $3, Brassavola cucullata. $5, Rodriguezia lanceolata.

Unwmk.

1990, Nov. 19 Litho. *Perf. 14*

626	A69	10c multicolored	.30	.30
627	A69	15c multicolored	.30	.30
628	A69	20c multicolored	.30	.30
629	A69	40c multicolored	.45	.45
630	A69	60c multicolored	.70	.70
631	A69	$1.20 multicolored	1.30	1.30
632	A69	$2 multicolored	2.25	2.25
633	A69	$3 multicolored	3.00	3.00
		Nos. 626-633 (8)	8.60	8.60

Souvenir Sheet

634	A69	$5 multicolored	7.00	7.00

Peter Paul Rubens (1577-1640), Painter — A70

Details from The Feast of Achelous: 10c, Pitchers. 40c, Woman at table. 60c, Two women. $4, Achelous feasting. $5, Complete painting, horiz.

1991, Jan. 14 Litho. *Perf. 13½*

635	A70	10c multicolored	.30	.30
636	A70	40c multicolored	.50	.50
637	A70	60c multicolored	.80	.80
638	A70	$4 multicolored	3.75	3.75
		Nos. 635-638 (4)	5.35	5.35

Souvenir Sheet

639	A70	$5 multicolored	5.25	5.25

Butterflies A71

5c, Gulf fritillary. 10c, Orion. 15c, Dagger wing. 20c, Red anartia. 25c, Caribbean buckeye. 40c, Zebra. 50c, Southern dagger tail. 60c, Silver spot. 75c, Doris. $1, Mimic. $3, Monarch. $5, Small blue grecian. $10, Tiger. $20, Flambeau.

1991, Mar. *Perf. 14*

No Date Imprint Below Design

640	A71	5c multicolored	.25	.25
641	A71	10c multicolored	.25	.25
642	A71	15c multicolored	.25	.25
643	A71	20c multicolored	.25	.25
644	A71	25c multicolored	.25	.25
645	A71	40c multicolored	.35	.35
646	A71	50c multicolored	.50	.50
647	A71	60c multicolored	.55	.55
648	A71	75c multicolored	.65	.65
649	A71	$1 multicolored	.90	.90
650	A71	$3 multicolored	2.75	2.75
651	A71	$5 multicolored	4.50	4.50
652	A71	$10 multicolored	9.00	9.00
653	A71	$20 multicolored	18.00	18.00
		Nos. 640-653 (14)	38.45	38.45

For overprints see Nos. O41-O54.

1992, Mar. 1 "1992" Below Design

640a	A71	5c multicolored	.25	.25
641a	A71	10c multicolored	.25	.25
642a	A71	15c multicolored	.25	.25
643a	A71	20c multicolored	.25	.25
644a	A71	25c multicolored	.30	.25
645a	A71	40c multicolored	.40	.25
646a	A71	50c multicolored	.50	.50
648b	A71	75c multicolored	.65	.65
648A	A71	80c multicolored	1.50	1.50
649a	A71	$1 multicolored	.90	.90
650a	A71	$3 multicolored	2.75	2.75
651a	A71	$5 multicolored	4.50	4.50
652a	A71	$10 multicolored	9.00	9.00
653a	A71	$20 multicolored	18.00	18.00
		Nos. 640a-653a (14)	39.50	39.30

1994 "1994" Below Design

640b	A71	5c multicolored	.40	.40
641b	A71	10c multicolored	.40	.40
644b	A71	25c multicolored	.40	.40
646b	A71	50c multicolored	.40	.40
648Ab	A71	80c multicolored	1.75	1.75
		Nos. 640b-648Ab (5)	3.35	3.35

Space Exploration-Discovery Voyages — A72

15c, Viking Mars lander. 40c, Apollo 11 liftoff. 60c, Skylab. 75c, Salyut 6. $1, Voyager 1. $2, Venera 7. $4, Gemini 4. $5, Luna 3.

No. 662, Sailing ship, vert. No. 663, Columbus' landfall.

1991, Apr. 22 Litho. *Perf. 14*

654	A72	15c multi	.25	.25
655	A72	40c multi	.30	.30
656	A72	60c multi	.45	.45
657	A72	75c multi	.55	.55
658	A72	$1 multi	.75	.75
659	A72	$2 multi	1.25	1.25
660	A72	$4 multi	2.50	2.50
661	A72	$5 multi	3.25	3.25
		Nos. 654-661 (8)	9.30	9.30

Souvenir Sheet

662	A72	$6 multi	5.00	5.00
663	A72	$6 multi	5.00	5.00

Discovery of America, 500th anniv. (in 1992) (No. 663).

Miniature Sheet

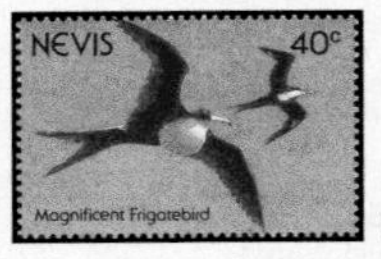

Birds — A73

Designs: a, Magnificent frigatebird. b, Roseate tern. c, Red-tailed hawk. d, Zenaida dove. e, Bananaquit. f, American kestrel. g, Grey kingbird. h, Prothonotary warbler. i, Blue-hooded euphonia. j, Antillean crested hummingbird. k, White-tailed tropicbird. l, Yellow-bellied sapsucker. m, Green-throated carib. n, Purple-throated carib. o, Black-bellied tree duck. p, Ringed kingfisher. q, Burrowing owl. r, Ruddy turnstone. s, Great white heron. t, Yellow-crowned night heron.

1991, May 28

664	A73	40c Sheet of 20, #a.-t.	16.00	16.00

Souvenir Sheet

665	A73	$6 Great egret	11.00	11.00

Royal Family Birthday, Anniversary

Common Design Type

No. 674, Elizabeth, Philip. No. 675, Charles, Diana & family.

1991, July 5 Litho. *Perf. 14*

666	CD347	10c multicolored	.30	.30
667	CD347	15c multicolored	.30	.30
668	CD347	40c multicolored	.45	.45
669	CD347	50c multicolored	.60	.60
670	CD347	$1 multicolored	1.00	1.00
671	CD347	$2 multicolored	1.75	1.75
672	CD347	$4 multicolored	3.75	3.75
673	CD347	$5 multicolored	4.50	4.50
		Nos. 666-673 (8)	12.65	12.65

Souvenir Sheets

674	CD347	$5 multicolored	5.50	5.50
675	CD347	$5 multicolored	5.50	5.50

10c, 50c, $1, Nos. 673, 675, Charles and Diana, 10th Wedding Anniv. Others, Queen Elizabeth II 65th birthday.

Japanese Trains — A74

Locomotives: 10c, C62 Steam, vert. 15c, C56 Steam. 40c, Streamlined C55, steam. 60c, Class 1400 Steam. $1, Class 485 bonnet type rail diesel car, vert. $2, C61 Steam, vert. $3, Class 485 express train. $4, Class 7000 electric train. No. 684, D51 Steam. No. 685, Hikari bullet train.

1991, Aug. 12

676-683	A74	Set of 8	13.50	13.50

Souvenir Sheets

684-685	A74	$5 Set of 2	11.00	11.00

Phila Nippon '91.

Christmas — A75

Paintings by Albrecht Durer: 10c, Mary Being Crowned by an Angel. 40c, Mary with the Pear. 60c, Mary in a Halo. $3, Mary with the Crown of Stars and Scepter. No. 690, The Holy Family. No. 691, Mary at the Yard Gate.

1991, Dec. 20 Litho. *Perf. 13½*

686	A75	10c yel green & blk	.25	.25
687	A75	40c org brown & blk	.30	.30
688	A75	60c blue & black	.45	.45
689	A75	$3 brt magenta & blk	1.90	1.90
		Nos. 686-689 (4)	2.90	2.90

Souvenir Sheets

690	A75	$6 black	5.00	5.00
691	A75	$6 black	5.00	5.00

A76

Mushrooms: 15c, Marasmius haematocephalus. 40c, Psilocybe cubensis. 60c, Hygrocybe acutoconica. 75c, Hygrocybe occidentalis. $1, Boletellus cubensis. $2, Gymnopilus chrysopellus. $4, Cantharellus cinnabarinus. $5, Chlorophyllum molybdites. No. 700, Our Lady of the Snows (8 mushrooms). No. 701, Our Lady of the Snows (4 mushrooms), diff.

1991, Dec. 20 Litho. *Perf. 14*

692-699	A76	Set of 8	10.00	10.00

Souvenir Sheet

700-701	A76	$6 Set of 2	10.00	10.00

Queen Elizabeth II's Accession to the Throne, 40th Anniv.

Common Design Type

1992, Feb. 26 Litho. *Perf. 14*

702	CD348	10c multicolored	.25	.25
703	CD348	40c multicolored	.30	.30
704	CD348	$1 multicolored	.75	.75
705	CD348	$5 multicolored	3.25	3.25
		Nos. 702-705 (4)	4.55	4.55

Souvenir Sheets

706	CD348	$6 Queen, people on beach	4.50	4.50
707	CD348	$6 Queen, seashell	4.50	4.50

A77

Gold medalists: 20c, Monique Knol, France, cycling. 25c, Roger Kingdom, US, 110-meter hurdles. 50c, Yugoslavia, water polo. 80c, Anja Fichtel, West Germany, foil. $1, Said Aouita, Morocco, 5000-meters. $1.50, Yuri Sedykh, USSR, hammer throw. $3, Yelena Shushunova, USSR, gymnastics. $5, Vladimir Artemov, USSR, gymnastics. No. 716, Florence Griffith-Joyner, US, 100-meter dash. No. 717, Naim Suleymanoglu, Turkey, weight lifting.

1992, May 7 Litho. *Perf. 14*

708-715	A77	Set of 8	10.50	10.50

Souvenir Sheets

716-717	A77	$6 Set of 2	7.25	7.25

1992 Summer Olympics, Barcelona. All athletes except those on $1 and $1.50 won gold medals in 1988. No. 715 incorrectly spelled "Valimir."

Spanish Art — A78

Designs: 20c, Landscape, by Mariano Fortuny, vert. 25c, Dona Juana la Loca, by Francisco Pradilla Ortiz. 50c, Idyll, by Fortuny, vert. 80c, Old Man in the Sun, by Fortuny, vert. $1, $2, The Painter's Children in the Japanese Salon (different details), vert., by Fortuny. $3, Still Life (Sea Bream and Oranges), by Luis Eugenio Melendez. $5, Still Life (Box of Sweets, Pastry, and Other Objects), by Melendez, vert. No. 726, Moroccans by Fortuny. No. 727, Bullfight, by Fortuny.

Perf. 13x13½, 13½x13

1992, June 1 Litho.

718-725	A78	Set of 8	10.00	10.00

Size: 120x95mm

Imperf

726-727	A78	$6 Set of 2	6.50	6.50

Granada '92.

A79

1992, July 6 *Perf. 14*

728	A79	20c Early compass	.50	.50
729	A79	50c Manatee	.50	.50
730	A79	80c Green turtle	.80	.80
731	A79	$1.50 Santa Maria	1.40	1.40
732	A79	$3 Queen Isabella	2.75	2.75
733	A79	$5 Pineapple	4.75	4.75
		Nos. 728-733 (6)	10.70	10.70

Souvenir Sheets

734	A79	$6 Storm petrel, horiz.	5.50	5.50
735	A79	$6 Pepper, horiz.	5.50	5.50

Discovery of America, 500th anniv. World Columbian Stamp Expo '92, Chicago.

A80

1992, Aug. 24 *Perf. 14½*

736	A80	$1 Coming ashore	.80	.80
737	A80	$2 Natives, ships	1.50	1.50

Discovery of America, 500th anniv. Organization of East Caribbean States.

Wolfgang Amadeus Mozart, Bicent. of Death (in 1991) — A81

1992, Oct. Litho. *Perf. 14*

738	A81	$3 multicolored	3.00	3.00

Souvenir Sheet

739	A81	$6 Don Giovanni	5.25	5.25

Mickey's Portrait Gallery — A82

10c, Minnie Mouse, 1930. 15c, Mickey Mouse. 40c, Donald Duck. 80c, Mickey Mouse, 1930. $1, Daisy Duck. $2, Pluto. $4, Goofy. $5, Goofy, 1932.

No. 748, Plane Crazy. No. 749, Mickey, Home Sweet Home, horiz.

1992, Nov. 9 Litho. *Perf. 13½x14*

No.	Type	Description	Unused	Used
740	A82	10c multicolored	.25	.25
741	A82	15c multicolored	.35	.35
742	A82	40c multicolored	.45	.45
743	A82	80c multicolored	.75	.75
744	A82	$1 multicolored	1.00	1.00
745	A82	$2 multicolored	1.75	1.75
746	A82	$4 multicolored	3.50	3.50
747	A82	$5 multicolored	4.00	4.00
		Nos. 740-747 (8)	12.05	12.05

Souvenir Sheet

Perf. 14x13½

No.	Type	Description	Unused	Used
748	A82	$6 multicolored	6.00	6.00
749	A82	$6 multicolored	6.00	6.00

Christmas — A83

Details or entire paintings: 20c, The Virgin and Child Between Two Saints, by Giovanni Bellini. 40c, The Virgin and Child Surrounded by Four Angels, by Master of the Castello Nativity. 50c, Virgin and Child Surrounded by Angels with St. Frediano and St. Augustine, by Fra Filippo Lippi. 80c, The Virgin and Child Between St. Peter and St. Sebastian, by Giovanni Bellini. $1, The Virgin and Child with St. Julian and St. Nicholas of Myra, by Lorenzo Di Credi. $2, Saint Bernardino and a Female Saint Presenting a Donor to Virgin and Child, by Francesco Bissolo. $4, Madonna and Child with Four Cherubs, Ascribed to Barthel Bruyn. $5, The Virgin and Child, by Quentin Metsys.

No. 758, The Virgin and Child Surrounded by Two Angels, by Perugino. No. 759, Madonna and Child with the Infant St. John and Archangel Gabriel, by Sandro Botticelli.

1992, Nov. 16 Litho. *Perf. 13½x14*

No.	Type	Description	Unused	Used
750-757	A83	Set of 8	10.00	10.00

Souvenir Sheet

No.	Type	Description	Unused	Used
758-759	A83	$6 Set of 2	9.50	9.50

Empire State Building, New York City — A84

1992, Oct. 28 Litho. *Perf. 14*

No.	Type	Description	Unused	Used
760	A84	$6 multicolored	5.00	5.00

Postage Stamp Mega Event '92, New York City.

A85

A89

A86

A87

A88

A90

A92

A91

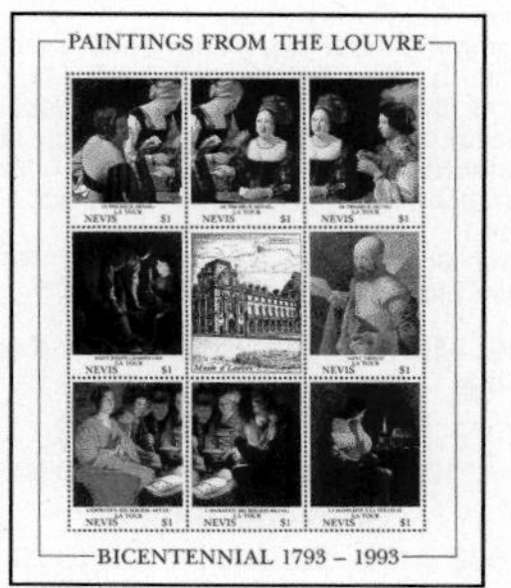

Anniversaries and Events — A93

Designs: 15c, Japanese launch vehicle H-2. 50c, Hindenburg on fire, 1937. 75c, Charles de Gaulle, Konrad Adenauer. No. 764, Horatio Nelson Museum, Nevis. No. 765, Red Cross emblem, Nevis. No. 766, America's Cup yacht *Resolute*, 1920, vert. No. 767, St. Thomas Anglican Church. No. 768, Care Bear, butterfly and flower. No. 770, Blue whale. No. 771, WHO, ICN, FAO emblems, graph showing population growth. vert. No. 772, Lion, Lion's Intl. emblem. No. 773, John F. Kennedy, Adenauer. No. 774, Lebaudy, first flying machine with mechanical engine. No. 775, Soviet Energia launch vehicle SL-17.

Elvis Presley: No. 776a, Portrait. b, With guitar. c, With microphone.

Details or entire paintings, by Georges de La Tour: No. 777a, The Cheater (left). b, The Cheater (center). c, The Cheater (right). d, St. Joseph, the Carpenter. e, Saint Thomas. f, Adoration of the Shepherds (left). g, Adoration of the Shepherds (right). h, La Madeleine a La Veilleuse.

No. 778, Care Bear, palm tree, vert. No. 779, Manned maneuvering unit in space. No. 780, Count Zeppelin taking off from Goppingen for Friedrichshafen. No. 781, Adenauer. No. 782, America's Cup yacht. No. 783, The Angel Departing from the Family of Tobias, by Rembrandt.

1993 Litho. *Perf. 14*

No.	Type	Description	Unused	Used
761	A85	15c multicolored	.25	.25
762	A86	50c multicolored	.40	.40
763	A87	75c multicolored	.80	.80
764	A88	80c multicolored	.90	.90
765	A88	80c multicolored	.90	.90
766	A89	80c multicolored	.60	.60
767	A88	80c multicolored	.60	.60
768	A90	80c multicolored	.60	.60
770	A88	$1 multicolored	.75	.75
771	A91	$3 multicolored	3.50	3.50
772	A85	$3 multicolored	3.00	3.00
773	A87	$5 multicolored	3.00	3.00
774	A86	$5 multicolored	3.50	3.50
775	A85	$5 multicolored	3.50	3.50

Perf. 14

No.	Type	Description	Unused	Used
776	A92	$1 Strip of 3, #a.-c.	2.25	2.25
		Nos. 761-776 (15)	24.55	24.55

Miniature Sheet

Perf. 12

No.	Type	Description	Unused	Used
777	A93	$1 Sheet of 8, #a.-h. + label	8.50	8.50

Souvenir Sheets

Perf. 14

No.	Type	Description	Unused	Used
778	A90	$2 multicolored	2.00	2.00
779	A85	$6 multicolored	5.25	5.25
780	A86	$6 multicolored	5.25	5.25
781	A87	$6 multicolored	5.50	5.50
782	A89	$6 multicolored	4.00	4.00

Perf. 14½

No.	Type	Description	Unused	Used
783	A92	$6 multicolored	6.00	6.00

Intl. Space Year (#761, 775, 779). Count Zeppelin, 75th anniv. of death (#762, 774, 780). Konrad Adenauer, 25th anniv. of death (#763, 773, 781). Anglican Church in Nevis, 150th anniv. Opening of Horatio Nelson Museum (#764). Nevis and St. Kitts Red Cross, 50th anniv. (#765). America's Cup yacht race (#766, 782). (#767). Lions Intl., 75th anniv. (#772). Earth Summit, Rio de Janeiro (#768, 770, 778). Intl. Conference on Nutrition, Rome (#771). Elvis Presley, 15th death anniv. (in 1992) (#776). Louvre Art Museum, bicent. (#777, 783).

Nos. 779-781 have continuous designs.

No. 783 contains one 55x89mm stamp.

Issued: No. 767, Mar.; others, Jan. 14.

Tropical Flowers — A94

1993, Mar. 26 Litho. *Perf. 14*

No.	Type	Description	Unused	Used
784	A94	10c Frangipani	.25	.25
785	A94	25c Bougainvillea	.25	.25
786	A94	50c Allamanda	.50	.50
787	A94	80c Anthurium	.80	.80
788	A94	$1 Ixora	1.00	1.00
789	A94	$2 Hibiscus	2.00	2.00
790	A94	$4 Shrimp plant	4.00	4.00
791	A94	$5 Coral vine	5.00	5.00
		Nos. 784-791 (8)	13.80	13.80

Souvenir Sheets

No.	Type	Description	Unused	Used
792	A94	$6 Lantana	4.50	4.50
793	A94	$6 Petrea	4.50	4.50

Butterflies — A95

10c, Antillean blue. 25c, Cuban crescent-spot. 50c, Ruddy daggerwing. 80c, Little yellow. $1, Atala. $1.50, Orange-barred giant sulphur. $4, Tropic queen. $5, Malachite.

No. 802, Polydamas swallowtail. No. 803, West Indian Buckeye.

1993, May 17 Litho. *Perf. 14*

No.	Type	Description	Unused	Used
794	A95	10c multicolored	.30	.30
795	A95	25c multicolored	.30	.30
796	A95	50c multicolored	.60	.60
797	A95	80c multicolored	.90	.90
798	A95	$1 multicolored	1.00	1.00
799	A95	$1.50 multicolored	1.40	1.40
800	A95	$4 multicolored	4.00	4.00
801	A95	$5 multicolored	5.00	5.00
		Nos. 794-801 (8)	13.50	13.50

Souvenir Sheets

No.	Type	Description	Unused	Used
802	A95	$6 multicolored	5.75	5.75
a.		Ovptd. in sheet margin	5.00	5.00
803	A95	$6 multicolored	5.75	5.75
a.		Ovptd. in sheet margin	5.00	5.00

Location of Hong Kong '94 emblem on Nos. 802a-803a varies.

Nos. 802a, 803a issued Feb. 18, 1994.

Miniature Sheet

Coronation of Queen Elizabeth II, 40th Anniv. — A96

Designs: a, 10c, Official coronation photograph. b, 80c, Queen, wearing Imperial Crown of State. c, $2, Queen, sitting on throne during ceremony. d, $4, Prince Charles kissing mother's hand.

$6, Portrait, "Riding on Worcran in the Great Park at Windsor," by Susan Crawford, 1977.

1993, June 2 Litho. *Perf. 13½x14*

No.	Type	Description	Unused	Used
804	A96	Sheet, 2 ea #a.-d.	10.00	10.00

Souvenir Sheet

Perf. 14

No.	Type	Description	Unused	Used
805	A96	$6 multicolored	4.00	4.00

No. 805 contains one 28x42mm stamp.

Independence of St. Kitts and Nevis, 10th Anniv. — A97

Designs: 25c, Natl. flag, anthem. 80c, Brown pelican, map of St. Kitts and Nevis.

1993, Sept. 19 Litho. *Perf. 13½*

No.	Type	Description	Unused	Used
807	A97	25c multicolored	.50	.50
808	A97	80c multicolored	1.50	1.50

1994 World Cup Soccer Championships, US — A98

Soccer players: 10c, Garaba, Hungary; Platini, France. 25c, Maradona, Argentina; Bergomi, Italy. 50c, Fernandez, France; Rats, Russia. 80c, Munoz, Spain. $1, Elkjaer, Denmark; Goicoechea, Spain. $2, Coelho, Brazil; Tigana, France. $3, Troglio, Argentina; Alejnikov, Russia. No. 816, $5, Karas, Poland; Costa, Brazil.

Each $5: No. 817, Belloumi, Algeria. No. 818, Steven, England, vert.

1993, Nov. 9 Litho. *Perf. 14*

No.	Type	Description	Unused	Used
809-816	A98	Set of 8	10.00	10.00

Souvenir Sheets

No.	Type	Description	Unused	Used
817-818	A98	Set of 2	16.00	16.00

Christmas — A99

Works by Albrecht Durer: 20c, Annunciation of Mary. 40c, The Nativity. 50c, Holy Family on a Grassy Bank. 80c, The Presentation of Christ in the Temple. $1, Virgin in Glory on the Crescent. $1.60, The Nativity, diff. $3, Madonna and Child. $5, The Presentation of Christ in the Temple (detail).

Each $6: No. 827, Mary with Child and the Long-Tailed Monkey, by Durer. No. 828, The Rest on the Flight into Egypt, by Fragonard, horiz.

1993, Nov. 30 *Perf. 13*

No.	Type	Description	Unused	Used
819-826	A99	Set of 8	10.00	10.00

Souvenir Sheets

No.	Type	Description	Unused	Used
827-828	A99	Set of 2	16.00	16.00

Tuff Mickey A100

Disney's Mickey Mouse playing: 10c, Basketball. 50c, Volleyball. $1, Soccer. $5, Boxing.

No. 837, $6, Tug-of-war. No. 838, Ringing carnival bell with hammer, vert.

Disney's Minnie Mouse: 25c, Welcome to my island, vert. 80c, Sunny and snappy, vert. $1.50, Happy hoopin', vert. $4, Jumping for joy, vert.

Perf. 14x13½, 13½x14

1994, Mar. 15 **Litho.**

829 A100 10c multicolored .25 .25
830 A100 25c multicolored .25 .25
831 A100 50c multicolored .55 .55
832 A100 80c multicolored .80 .80
833 A100 $1 multicolored .90 .90
834 A100 $1.50 multicolored 1.10 1.00
835 A100 $4 multicolored 3.00 3.00
836 A100 $5 multicolored 3.75 3.75
Nos. 829-836 (8) 10.60 10.50

Souvenir Sheets

837 A100 $6 multicolored 6.00 6.00
838 A100 $6 multicolored 6.00 6.00

Hummel Figurines — A101

Designs: 5c, Umbrella Girl. 25c, For Father. 50c, Apple Tree Girl. 80c, March Winds. $1, Have the Sun in Your Heart. $1.60, Blue Belle. $2, Winter Fun. $5, Apple Tree Boy.

1994, Apr. 6 **Litho.** ***Perf. 14***

839-846 A101 Set of 8 10.00 10.00
845a Souv. sheet, #839, 843-845 3.50 3.50
846a Souv. sheet, #840-842, 846 5.75 5.75

Beekeeping A102

Designs: 50c, Beekeeper cutting wild nest of bees. 80c, Group of beekeepers, 1987. $1.60, Decapping frames of honey. $3, Queen bee rearing.
$6, Queen bee, worker bees, woman extracting honey.

1994, June 13 **Litho.** ***Perf. 14***

847-850 A102 Set of 4 7.75 7.75

Souvenir Sheet

851 A102 $6 multicolored 8.00 8.00
a. Ovptd. in sheet margin 5.75 5.75

No. 851a Overprinted "2nd Caribbean Beekeeping Congress / August 14-18, 2000" in sheet margin. Issued 8/14/00.
Issued: No. 851a, 8/17/00.

Miniature Sheet

Cats A103

Designs: a, Blue point Himalayan. b, Black & white Persian. c, Cream Persian. d, Red Persian. e, Persian. f, Persian black smoke. g, Chocolate smoke Persian. h, Black Persian.
Each $6: No. 853, Brown tabby Persian. No. 854, Silver tabby Persian.

1994, July 20

852 A103 80c Sheet of 8, #a.-h. 8.25 8.25

Souvenir Sheets

853-854 A103 Set of 2 19.00 19.00

A104

Marine Life — A104a

Designs: 10c, Striped burrfish. 25c, Black coral, white & yellow, vert. 40c, Black coral, white & red, vert. 50c, Black coral, yellow & green, vert. 80c, Black coral, spiral-shaped, vert. $1, Blue-striped grunt. $1.60, Blue angelfish. $3, Cocoa damselfish.
No. 864a, Flameback angelfish. b, Reef bass. c, Honey gregory. d, Saddle squirrelfish. e, Cobalt chromis. f, Cleaner goby. g, Slendertail cardinalfish. h, Royal gramma.
Each $6: No. 865, Sailfish, vert. No. 866, Blue marlin.

1994, July 25 **Litho.** ***Perf. 14***

856-863 A104 Set of 8 7.25 7.25
860a Strip of 4, #857-860 3.75 3.75
860b Min. sheet, 3 each #857-860 11.50 11.50

Miniature Sheet of 8

864 A104a 50c #a.-h. 8.50 8.50
i. Ovptd. in sheet margin 3.75 3.75

Souvenir Sheets

865-866 A104a Set of 2 19.00 19.00

Nos. 857-860, World Wildlife Fund. No. 864i overprinted in sheet margin with PHILAKOREA '94 emblem.
Issued: #864i, 8/16; #860b, 7/25.

Local Architecture A105

Designs: 25c, Residence, Barnes Ghaut Village. 50c, House above grocery store, Newcastle. $1, Treasury Building, Charlestown. $5, House above supermarket, Charlestown. $6, Apartment houses.

1994, Aug. 22

867-870 A105 Set of 4 7.25 7.25

Souvenir Sheet

871 A105 $6 multicolored 4.75 4.75

Order of the Caribbean Community A106

First award recipients: 25c, William Demas, economist, Trinidad and Tobago. 50c, Sir Shridath Ramphal, statesman, Guyana. $1, Derek Walcott, writer, Nobel Laureate, St. Lucia.

1994, Sept. 1

872-874 A106 Set of 3 3.00 3.00

Miniature Sheet of 8

PHILAKOREA '94 — A107

Folding screen, longevity symbols embroidered on silk, Late Choson Dynasty: a, #1. b, #2. c, #3. d, #4. e, #5. f, #6. g, #7. h, #8.

1994 **Litho.** ***Perf. 14***

875 A107 50c #a.-h. 6.00 6.00

Christmas — A108

Different details from paintings: 20c, 40c, 50c, $5, The Virgin Mary as Queen of Heaven, by Jan Provost. 80c, $1, $1.60, $3, Adoration of the Magi, by Workshop of Hugo van der Goes.
No. 884, The Virgin Mary as Queen of Heaven (complete). $6, Adoration of the Magi (complete).

1994, Dec. 1 **Litho.** ***Perf. 14***

876-883 A108 Set of 8 8.00 8.00

Souvenir Sheets

884 A108 $5 multicolored 4.25 4.25
885 A108 $6 multicolored 5.00 5.00

Disney Valentines A109

Designs: 10c, Mickey, Minnie. 25c, Donald, Daisy. 50c, Pluto, Fifi. 80c, Clarabelle, Horace Horsecollar. $1, Pluto, Figaro. $1.50, Polly, Peter Penguin. $4, Prunella Pullet, Hick Rooster. $5, Jenny Wren, Cock Robin.
Each $6: No. 894, Minnie, vert. No. 895, Daisy, vert.

1995, Feb. 14 **Litho.** ***Perf. 14x13½***

886-893 A109 Set of 8 10.00 10.00

Souvenir Sheets

Perf. 13½x14

894-895 A109 Set of 2 10.00 10.00

Birds — A110

Designs: 50c, Hooded merganser. 80c, Green-backed heron. $2, Double crested cormorant. $3, Ruddy duck.
Hummingbirds: No. 900a, Rufous-breasted hermit. b, Purple-throated carib. c, Green mango. d, Bahama woodstar. e, Hispaniolan emerald. f, Antillean crested. g, Green-throated carib. h, Antillean mango. i, Vervian. j, Jamaican mango. k, Cuban emerald. l, Blue-headed.
Each $6: No. 901, Black skimmer. No. 902, Snowy plover.

1995, Mar. 30 **Litho.** ***Perf. 14***

896-899 A110 Set of 4 3.75 3.75

Miniature Sheet of 12

900 A110 50c #a.-l. 10.50 10.50

Souvenir Sheets

901-902 A110 Set of 2 10.00 10.00

Dogs — A111

Designs: 25c, Pointer. 50c, Old Danish pointer. $1, German short-haired pointer. $2, English setter.
No. 907a, Irish setter. b, Weimaraner. c, Gordon setter. d, Britanny spaniel. e, American cocker spaniel. f, English cocker spaniel. g, Labrador retriever. h, Golden retriever. i, Flat-coated retriever.
Each $6: #908, Bloodhound. #909, German shepherd.

1995, May 23 **Litho.** ***Perf. 14***

903-906 A111 Set of 4 3.75 3.75

Miniature Sheet of 9

907 A111 80c #a.-i. 11.00 11.00

Souvenir Sheets

908-909 A111 Set of 2 11.00 11.00

Cacti — A112

Designs: 40c, Schulumbergera truncata. 50c, Echinocereus pectinatus. 80c, Mammillaria zelmanniana alba. $1.60, Lobivia hertriehiana. $2, Hamatocatcus setispinus. $3, Astrophytum myriostigma.
Each $6: No. 916, Opuntia robusta. No. 917, Rhipsalidopsis gaertneri.

1995, June 20 **Litho.** ***Perf. 14***

910-915 A112 Set of 6 6.50 6.50

Souvenir Sheets

916-917 A112 Set of 2 10.00 10.00

Miniature Sheets of 6 or 8

End of World War II, 50th Anniv. A113

Famous World War II Personalities: No. 918: a, Clark Gable. b, Audie Murphy. c, Glenn Miller. d, Joe Louis. e, Jimmy Doolittle. f, John Hersey. g, John F. Kennedy. h, Jimmy Stewart.
Planes: No. 919: a, F4F Wildcat. b, F4U-1A Corsair. c, Vought SB2U Vindicator. d, F6-F Hellcat. e, SDB Dauntless. f, TBF-1 Avenger.
Each $6: No. 920, Jimmy Doolittle, vert. No. 921, Fighter plane landing on aircraft carrier.

1995, July 20

918 A113 $1.25 #a.-h. + label 10.00 10.00
919 A113 $2 #a.-f. + label 11.00 11.00

Souvenir Sheets

920-921 A113 Set of 2 15.00 15.00

UN, 50th Anniv. A114

People of various races: No. 922a, $1.25, Two men, child. b, $1.60, Man wearing turban, man with beard, woman. c, $3, Two men in business suits, woman.
$6, Nelson Mandela.

1995, July 20 **Litho.** ***Perf. 14***

922 A114 Strip of 3, #a.-c. 4.00 4.00

Souvenir Sheet

923 A114 $6 multicolored 4.25 4.25

No. 922 is a continuous design.

1995 Boy Scout Jamboree, Holland — A115

Scouts in various activities: No. 924a, $1, Two wearing backpacks. b, $2, One holding rope, one wearing backpack. c, $4, One crossing rope bridge, one looking at map, natl. flag.
$6, Scout in kayak.

1995, July 20

924 A115 Strip of 3, #a.-c. 5.00 5.00

Souvenir Sheet

925 A115 $6 multicolored 5.50 5.50

No. 924 is a continuous design.

Rotary Intl., 90th Anniv. — A116

Designs: $5, Rotary emblem, natl. flag.
$6, Rotary emblem, beach.

1995, July 20

926 A116 $5 multicolored 3.75 3.75

Souvenir Sheet

927 A116 $6 multicolored 4.50 4.50

Queen Mother, 95th Birthday A117

No. 928: a, Drawing. b, Pink hat. c, Formal portrait. d, Green blue hat.
$6, Wearing crown jewels.

1995, July 20 ***Perf. 13½x14***
928 A117 $1.50 Block or strip of 4, #a.-d. 4.50 4.50

Souvenir Sheet

928E A117 $6 multicolored 4.75 4.75

No. 928 was issued in sheets of 2.
Sheets of Nos. 928 and 928E exist with margins overprinted with black border and text "In Memoriam 1900-2002."

FAO, 50th anniv. A118

No. 929a, 40c, Woman with tan sari over head. b, $2, FAO emblem, two infants. c, $3, Woman with blue sari over head.
$6, Man with hands around hoe handle.

1995, July 20 ***Perf. 14***
929 A118 Strip of 3, #a.-c. 4.25 4.25

Souvenir Sheet

930 A118 $6 multicolored 4.75 4.75

No. 929 is a continuous design.

Miniature Sheet of 9

Nobel Prize Recipients — A119

No. 931: a, Emil A. von Behring, medicine, 1901. b, Wilhelm Roentgen, physics, 1901. c, Paul J.L. Heyse, literature, 1910. d, Le Duc Tho, peace, 1973. e, Yasunari Kawabata, 1968. f, Tsung-Dao Lee, physics, 1957. g, Werner Heisenberg, physics, 1932. h, Johannes Stark, physics, 1919. i, Wilhelm Wien, physics, 1911.
$6, Kenzaburo Oe, literature, 1994.

1995, July 20
931 A119 $1.25 #a.-i. 9.50 9.50

Souvenir Sheet

932 A119 $6 multicolored 4.75 4.75

Souvenir Sheet

American Eagle Service, 10th Anniv. — A120

a, 80c, President's Club Emblem. b, $3, Airplane over beach.

1995, Aug. 28 **Litho.** ***Perf. 14***
933 A120 Sheet of 2, #a.-b. 3.50 3.50

Miniature Sheet of 16

Marine Life A121

No. 934: a, Great egrets. b, 17th cent. ship. c, Marlin. d, Herring gulls. e, Nassau groupers. f, Manta ray. g, Leopard shark, hammerhead shark. h, Hourglass dolphins. i, Spanish hogfish. j, Jellyfish, sea horses. k, Angel fish. l, Hawsbill turtle. m, Octopus vulgaris (i, j, m). n, Moray eel (o). o, Queen angelfish, butterflyfish. p, Ghost crab, sea star.
Each $6: No. 935, Nassau grouper. No. 936, Queen angelfish, vert.

1995, Sept. 1
934 A121 50c #a.-p. 9.00 9.00

Souvenir Sheets

935-936 A121 Set of 2 11.00 11.00

Singapore '95 (#935-936).

Natl. Telephone Co., SKANTEL Ltd., 10th Anniv. — A122

Designs: $1, Repairman working on telephone. $1.50, Company sign on building.
$5, Front of SKANTEL's Nevis office, horiz.

1995, Oct. 23 **Litho.** ***Perf. 14***
937 A122 $1 multicolored .90 .90
938 A122 $1.50 multicolored 1.25 1.25

Souvenir Sheet

939 A122 $5 multicolored 4.25 4.25

Christmas Paintings, by Duccio di Buoninsegna (1250-1318) A123

Details or entire paintings: 20c, Rucellai Madonna and Child. 50c, Border angel from Rucellai Madonna facing left. 80c, Madonna and Child. $1, The Annuniciation. $1.60, Madonna and Child. $3, Border angel from Rucellai Madonna facing right.
No. 946, Nativity with Prophets Isiah and Ezekiel. No. 947, Crevole Madonna.

1995, Dec. 1 **Litho.** ***Perf. 13½x14***
940-945 A123 Set of 6 7.00 7.00

Souvenir Sheets

946 A123 $5 multicolored 4.50 4.50
947 A123 $6 multicolored 5.25 5.25

Four Seasons Resort, 5th Anniv. — A124

Designs: 25c, Beach, resort buildings. 50c, Sailboats on beach. 80c, Golf course. $2, Premier Simeon Daniel laying cornerstone.
$6, Lounge chair on beach, sunset.

1996, Feb. 14 **Litho.** ***Perf. 14***
948-951 A124 Set of 4 2.50 2.50

Souvenir Sheet

952 A124 $6 multicolored 4.25 4.25

New Year 1996 (Year of the Rat) — A125

Rat, various plant life, with olive margin: Nos. 953: a, Looking up at butterfly. b, Crawling left. c, Looking up at horsefly. d, Looking up at dragonfly.
Nos. 954a-954d: like Nos. 953a-953d, with yellow brown margin.
$3, Berries above rat.

1996, Feb, 28
953 A125 $1 Block of 4, #a.-d. 3.00 3.00

Miniature Sheet

954 A125 $1 Sheet of 4, #a.-d. 3.00 3.00

Souvenir Sheet

955 A125 $3 multicolored 3.00 3.00

No. 953 was issued in sheets of 16 stamps.

Pagodas of China — A126

#956: a, Qian Qing Gong, 1420, Beijing. b, Qi Nian Dian, Temple of Heaven, Beijing. c, Zhongnanhai, Beijing. d, Da Zing Hall, Shenyang Palace. e, Temple of the Sleeping Buddha, Beijing. f, Huang Qiong Yu, Alter of Heaven, Beijing. g, Grand Bell Temple, Beijing. h, Imperial Palace, Beijing. i, Pu Tuo Temple.
$6, Summer Palace of emperor Wan Yanliang, 1153, Beijing, vert.

1996, May 15 **Litho.** ***Perf. 14***
956 A126 $1 Sheet of 9, #a.-i. 6.25 6.25

Souvenir Sheet

957 A126 $6 multicolored 4.00 4.00

CHINA '96, 9th Asian Intl. Philatelic Exhibition (#956).

Queen Elizabeth II, 70th Birthday — A127

Queen wearing: a, Blue dress, pearls. b, Formal white dress. c, Purple dress, hat.
$6, In uniform at trooping of the color.

1996, May 15 **Litho.** ***Perf. 13½x14***
958 A127 $2 Strip of 3, #a.-c. 3.75 3.75

Souvenir Sheet

959 A127 $6 multicolored 3.75 3.75

No. 958 was issued in sheets of 9 stamps with each strip in a different order.

1996 Summer Olympic Games, Atlanta — A128

Designs: 25c, Ancient Greek athletes boxing. 50c, Mark Spitz, gold medalist, swimming, 1972. 80c, Siegbert Horn, kayak singles gold medalist, 1972. $3, Siegestor Triumphal Arch, Munich, vert.
Pictures inside gold medals: No. 964, vert.: a, Jim Thorpe. b, Glenn Morris. c, Bob Mathias. d, Rafer Johnson. e, Bill Toomey. f, Nikolay Avilov. g, Bruce Jenner. h, Daley Thompson. i, Christian Schenk.
Each $5: No. 965, Willi Holdorf, vert. No. 966, Hans-Joachim Walde, silver medal, vert.

1996, May 28 ***Perf. 14***
960-963 A128 Set of 4 3.50 3.50
964 A128 $1 Sheet of 9, #a.-i. 6.75 6.75

Souvenir Sheets

965-966 A128 Set of 2 12.00 12.00

Olymphilex '96 (#965).

UNESCO, 50th Anniv. A129

25c, Cave paintings, Tassili N'Ajjer, Algeria. $2, Tikal Natl. Park, Guatemala, vert. $3, Temple of Hera at Samos, Greece.
$6, Pueblo, Taos, US.

1996, July 1 **Litho.** ***Perf. 14***
967-969 A129 Set of 3 4.50 4.50

Souvenir Sheet

970 A129 $6 multicolored 4.25 4.25

UNICEF, 50th Anniv. — A130

25c, Children reading book. 50c, Girl receiving innoculation. $4, Faces of young people.
$6, Girl, vert.

1996, July 1
971-973 A130 Set of 3 4.25 4.25

Souvenir Sheet

974 A130 $6 multicolored 4.25 4.25

Disney's Sweethearts A131

Designs: a, Pocahontas, John Smith, Flit. b, Mowgli, The Girl, Kaa. c, Belle, Beast, Mrs. Potts, Chip. d, Cinderella, Prince Charming, Jaq. e, Pinocchio, Dutch Girl Marionette, Jiminy Cricket. f, Grace Martin, Henry Coy. g, Snow White, Prince. h, Aladdin, Jasmine, Abu. i, Pecos Bill, Slue Foot Sue.
Each $6: No. 977, Sleeping Beauty, Prince Phillip, vert. No. 978, Ariel, Eric.

Perf. 14x13½, 13½x14

1996, June 17 **Litho.**
975 A131 $2 Sheet of 9, #a.-i. 17.50 17.50

Souvenir Sheets

977-978 A131 Set of 2 11.00 11.00

A number has been reserved for an additional sheet with this set.

American Academy of Ophthalmology, Cent. — A132

1996, July 1 **Litho.** ***Perf. 14***
979 A132 $5 multicolored 4.00 4.00

Flowers — A133

Designs: 25c, Rothmannia longiflora. 50c, Gloriosa simplex. $2, Catharanthus roseus. $3, Plumbago auriculata.
No. 984: a, Monodora myristica. b, Giraffa camelopardalis. c, Adansonia digitata. d, Ansellia gigantea. e, Geissorhiza rochensis. f, Arctotis venusta. g, Gladiohis cardinalis. h, Eucomis bicolor. i, Protea obtusifolia.
$5, Stelitzia reginae.

1996, Sept. 24 Litho. *Perf. 14*
980-983 A133 Set of 4 4.25 4.25
984 A133 $1 Sheet of 9, #a.-i. 6.75 6.75

Souvenir Sheet

985 A133 $5 multicolored 3.75 3.75

Christmas A134

Designs: 25c, Western meadowlark, vert. 50c, American goldfinch. 80c, Santa in sleigh, reindeer. $1, Western meadowlark, diff., vert. $1.60, Mockingbird, vert. $5, Yellow-rumped caleque.
Each $6: No. 992, Macaw. No. 993, Vermilion flycatcher.

1996, Dec. 2 Litho. *Perf. 14*
986-991 A134 Set of 6 6.75 6.75

Souvenir Sheets

992-993 A134 Set of 2 8.50 8.50

New Year 1997 (Year of the Ox) A135

Painting, "Five Oxen," by Han Huang: a, 50c. b, 80c. c, $1.60. d, $2.

1997, Jan. 16 Litho. *Perf. 14x15*
994 A135 Sheet of 4, #a.-d. + label 4.00 4.00

A136

Pandas: a, Eating leaves on branch. b, Face, eating. c, Paws holding object. d, Hanging upside down. e, Lying between tree branch. f, Climbing tree.
$5, Mother, cub.

1997, Feb. 12 Litho. *Perf. 14*
995 A136 $1.60 Sheet of 6, #a.-f. 9.50 9.50

Souvenir Sheet

996 A136 $5 multicolored 3.75 3.75
Hong Kong '97.

A137

Cricket Players: 25c, Elquemedo Willet. 80c, Stuart Williams. $2, Keith Arthurton.
Each $5: No. 1000, Willet, Arthurton, Williams, 1990 Nevis team. No. 1001, Williams, Arthurton, 1994 West Indies team, vert.

1997, May 1 Litho. *Perf. 14*
997-999 A137 Set of 3 2.25 2.25

Souvenir Sheets

1000-1001 A137 Set of 2 7.00 7.00

Queen Elizabeth II, Prince Philip, 50th Wedding Anniv. — A138

No. 1002: a, Queen Elizabeth II. b, Royal arms. c, Prince, Queen in red hat. d, Queen in blue coat, Prince. e, Caernarfon Castle. f, Prince Philip.
$5, Queen wearing crown.

1997, May 29 Litho. *Perf. 14*
1002 A138 $1 Sheet of 6, #a.-f. 5.00 5.00

Souvenir Sheet

1003 A138 $5 multicolored 3.75 3.75

Paintings by Hiroshige (1797-1858) A139

No. 1004: a, Scattered Pines, Tone River. b, Nakagawa River Mouth. c, Niijuku Ferry. d, Horie and Nekozane. e, View of Konodai and the Tone River. f, Maple Trees at Mama, Tekona Shrine & Bridge.
Each $6: No. 1005, Mitsumata Wakarenofuchi. No. 1006, Moto-Hachinan Shrine, Sunamura.

1997, May 29 *Perf. 13½x14*
1004 A139 $1.60 Sheet of 6, #a.-f. 7.00 7.00

Souvenir Sheets

1005-1006 A139 Set of 2 8.00 8.00

Paul Harris (1868-1947), Founder of Rotary Intl. — A140

$2, Literacy promotion, portrait of Harris.
$5, Rotary Village Corps coaching soccer for youths in Chile.

1997, May 29 *Perf. 14*
1007 A140 $2 multicolored 1.75 1.75

Souvenir Sheet

1008 A140 $5 multicolored 3.75 3.75

Heinrich von Stephan (1831-97) A141

No. 1009: a, Russian Reindeer Post, 1859. b, Von Stephan, UPU emblem. c, Steamboat, City of Cairo, 1800's.
$5, Portrait of Von Stephan, Bavarian postal messenger, 1640.

1997, May 29
1009 A141 $1.60 Sheet of 3, #a.-c. 3.25 3.25

Souvenir Sheet

1010 A141 $5 multicolored 3.50 3.50
PACIFIC 97.

Butterflies and Moths — A142

10c, Crimson speckled. 25c, Purple emperor. 50c, Regent skipper. 80c, Provence burnet moth. $1, Common wall butterfly. $4, Cruiser butterfly.
No. 1017: a, Red-lined geometrid. b, Boisduval's autumnal moth. c, Blue pansy. d, Common clubtail. e, Tufted jungle queen. f, Lesser marbled fritillary. g, Peacock royal. h, Emperor gum moth. i, Orange swallow-tailed moth.
Each $5: No. 1018, Jersey tiger. No. 1019, Japanese emperor.

1997, May 12 Litho. *Perf. 14*
1011-1016 A142 Set of 6 5.50 5.50
1017 A142 $1 Sheet of 9, #a.-i. 7.25 7.25

Souvenir Sheets

1018-1019 A142 Set of 2 7.50 7.50

Souvenir Sheet

Mother Goose A143

1997, May 29
1020 A143 $5 Boy, two pigeons 3.75 3.75

Golf Courses of the World — A144

Designs: a, Augusta National, U.S. b, Cabo Del Sol, Mexico. c, Cypress Point, U.S. d, Lost City, South Africa. e, Moscow Country Club, Russia. f, New South Wales, Australia. g, Royal Montreal, Canada. h, St. Andrews, Scotland. i, Four Seasons Resort, Nevis.

1997, July 15
1021 A144 $1 Sheet of 9, #a.-i. 7.25 7.25

Mushrooms — A145

Designs: 25c, Cantharellus cibarius. 50c, Stropharia aeruginosa. $3, Lactarius turpis. $4, Entoloma Jypeatum.
No. 1026: a, Suillus luteus. b, Amanita musearia. c, Lactarius rufus. d, Amanita rubescens. e, Armillaria mellea. f, Russula sardonia.
No. 1027: a, Boletus edulis. b, Pholiota lenta. c, Cortinarius bolaris. d, Coprinus picaceus. e, Amanita phalloides. f, Cystolepiota aspera.
Each $5: No. 1028, Gymnopilus junonius. No. 1029, Galerina mutabilis, philiota auriuella.

1997, Aug. 12 Litho. *Perf. 13*
1022-1025 A145 Set of 4 6.00 6.00

Sheets of 6

1026 A145 80c #a.-f. 3.75 3.75
1027 A145 $1 #a.-f. 4.50 4.50

Souvenir Sheets

1028-1029 A145 Set of 2 8.00 8.00

Diana, Princess of Wales (1961-97) — A146

Various portraits.

1997, Sept. 19 Litho. *Perf. 14*
1030 A146 $1 Sheet of 9, #a.-i. 7.00 7.00

Trains — A147

Designs: 10c, New Pacific type, Victorian Government Railways, Australia. 50c, Express locomotive, Imperial Government Railways, Japan. 80c, Turbine driven locomotive, London, Midland & Scottish Railway. $1, Electric passenger & freight locomotive, Swiss Federal Railways. $2, 3 cylinder compound express locomotive, London, Midland, Scottish Railway. $3, Express locomotive Kestrel, Great Northern Railway, Ireland.
No. 1037: a, 2-8-2 Mikado, Sudan Government Railways. b, Mohammed Ali El Kebir locomotive, Egyptian State Railways. c, "Schools" class locomotive, Southern Railway. d, Drum Battery Train, Great Southern Railways, Ireland. e, "Pacific" express locomotive, German State Railways. f, Mixed traffic locomotive, Canton-Hankow Railway, China.
Each $5: No. 1038, "King" class express, Great Western Railway. No. 1039, High pressure locomotive, London, Midland and Scottish Railway.

1997, Sept. 29 Litho. *Perf. 14*
1031-1036 A147 Set of 6 6.00 6.00
1037 A147 $1.50 Sheet of 6, #a.-f. 7.00 7.00

Souvenir Sheets

1038-1039 A147 Set of 2 7.75 7.75

Christmas — A148

Entire paintings or details: 20c, 25c, Diff. details from Selection of Angels, by Durer. 50c, Andromeda and Perseus, by Rubens. 80c, $1.60, Diff. details from Astronomy, by Raphael. $5, Holy Trinity, by Raphael.
Each $5: No. 1046, Ezekiel's Vision, by Raphael, horiz. No. 1047, Justice, by Rapahel, horiz.

1997, Nov. 26 Litho. *Perf. 14*
1040-1045 A148 Set of 6 6.50 6.50

Souvenir Sheets

1046-1047 A148 Set of 2 7.00 7.00

New Year 1998 (Year of the Tiger) A149

Tigers: No. 1048: a, Jumping right. b, Looking back over shoulder. c, Jumping left. d, Looking forward.
No. 1049, Tiger, vert.

1998, Jan. 19 Litho. *Perf. 14*
1048 A149 80c Sheet of 4, #a.-d. 4.00 4.00

Souvenir Sheet

1049 A149 $2 multicolored 2.25 2.25

Social Security of St. Kitts and Nevis, 20th Anniv. — A150

Designs: 30c, Logo, vert. $1.20, Front of Social Security building.
$6, Social Security staff, Charlestown, Nevis.

1998, Feb. 2 Litho. *Perf. 13*
1050 A150 30c multicolored .30 .30
1051 A150 $1.20 multicolored .90 .90

Souvenir Sheet

Perf. 13½x13

1052 A150 $6 multicolored 4.50 4.50

No. 1052 contains one 56x36mm stamp.

Fruit — A151

1998, Mar. 9 *Perf. 14*

No Year Imprint Below Design

1053 A151	5c	Soursop	.25	.25
1054 A151	10c	Carambola	.25	.25
1055 A151	25c	Guava	.25	.25
1056 A151	30c	Papaya	.25	.25
1057 A151	50c	Mango	.40	.40
1058 A151	60c	Golden apple	.45	.45
1059 A151	80c	Pineapple	.60	.60
1060 A151	90c	Watermelon	.70	.70
1061 A151	$1	Bananas	.75	.75
1062 A151	$1.80	Orange	1.40	1.40
1063 A151	$3	Honeydew	2.25	2.25
1064 A151	$5	Cantaloupe	3.75	3.75
1065 A151	$10	Pomegranate	7.50	7.50
1066 A151	$20	Cashew	15.00	15.00
Nos. 1053-1066 (14)			33.80	33.80

For overprints see #O55-O66.

2000, Mar. 22

Inscribed "2000" Below Design

1054a A151	10c	multicolored	.25	.25
1056a A151	30c	multicolored	.40	.25
1059a A151	80c	multicolored	.90	.60
1062a A151	$1.80	multicolored	1.75	1.40
1064a A151	$5	multicolored	4.00	4.00
1065a A151	$10	multicolored	7.50	7.50
Nos. 1054a-1065a (6)			14.80	14.00

Endangered Species — A152

Designs: 30c, Fish eagle. 80c, Summer tangers. 90c, Orangutan. $1.20, Tiger. $2, Cape pangolin. $3, Moatzin.

No. 1073: a, Chimpanzee. b, Keel-billed toucan. c, Chaco peccary. d, Spadefoot toad. e, Howler monkey. f, Alaskan brown bear. g, Koala. h, Brown pelican. i, Iguana.

Each $5: No. 1074, Mandrill. No. 1075, Polar bear.

1998, Mar. 31 **Litho.** *Perf. 14*

1067-1072 A152 Set of 6 6.50 6.50
1073 A152 $1 Sheet of 9, #a.-i. 7.00 7.00

Souvenir Sheets

1074-1075 A152 Set of 2 8.50 8.50

Aircraft — A153

Designs: 10c, Boeing 747 200B. 90c, Cessna 185 Skywagon. $1.80, McDonnell Douglas DC-9 SO. $5, Airbus A300 B4.

No. 1080: a, Northrop B-2A. b, Lockheed SR-71A. c, Beechcraft T-44A. d, Sukhoi Su-27UB. e, Hawker Siddeley (BAe) Harrier GR.MK1. f, Boeing E-3A Sentry. g, Convair B-36H. h, IAI Kfir C2.

Each $5: No. 1081, Lockheed F-117A. No. 1082, Concorde G-BOAA.

1998, May 19 **Litho.** *Perf. 14*

1076-1079 A153 Set of 4 5.75 5.75
1080 A153 $1 Sheet of 8, #a.-h. 6.00 6.00

Souvenir Sheets

1081-1082 A153 Set of 2 7.75 7.75

Nos. 1081-1082 each contain 1 57x42mm stamp.

Chaim Topol Portraying Tevye from "Fiddler on the Roof" — A154

1998, May 17 **Litho.** *Perf. 13½*

1083 A154 $1.60 multicolored 1.75 1.75

Israel '98. Issued in sheets of 6.

A155

A155a

Voice of Nevis (VON) Radio, 10th Anniv. — A155b

20c, Logo of Nevis Broadcasting Co., vert. 30c, Evered "Webbo" Herbert, station manager at controls. $1.20, Exterior of offices and studios.

$5, Merritt Herbert, managing director, opening ceremony, 1988.

1998, June 18 *Perf. 14*

1084 A155 20c blk & vio .25 .25
1085 A155a 30c multicolored .50 .50
1086 A155a $1.20 multicolored .85 .85

Souvenir Sheet

1087 A155b $5 multicolored 3.50 3.50

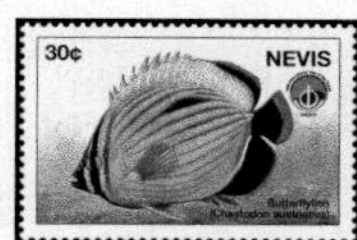

Intl. Year of the Ocean — A156

30c, Butterflyfish. 80c, Bicolor cherub. $1.20, Silver badgerfish. $2, Asfur angelfish.

No. 1092, vert: a, Copperbanded butterflyfish. b, Forcepsfish. c, Double-saddled butterflyfish. d, Blue surgeonfish. e, Orbiculate batfish. f, Undulated triggerfish. g, Rock beauty. h, Flamefish. i, Queen angelfish.

No. 1093: a, Pygama cardinal fish. b, Wimplefish. c, Long-nosed filefish. d, Oriental sweetlips. e, Blue spotted boxfish. f, Blue stripe angelfish. g, Goldrim tang. h, Royal gramma. i, Common clownfish.

Each $5: No. 1094, Longhorned cowfish, vert. No. 1095, Red-faced batfish, vert.

1998, Aug. 18 **Litho.** *Perf. 14*

1088-1091 A156 Set of 4 5.75 5.75
1092 A156 90c Sheet of 9, #a.-i. 6.25 6.25
1093 A156 $1 Sheet of 9, #a.-i. 7.00 7.00

Souvenir Sheets

1094-1095 A156 Set of 2 8.75 8.75

Princess Diana (1961-97) — A157

1998, Oct. 15 **Litho.** *Perf. 14*

1096 A157 $1 multicolored .75 .75

No. 1096 was issued in sheets of 6.

Mahatma Gandhi (1869-1948) — A158

Portraits: No. 1097, In South Africa, 1914. No. 1098, At Downing Street, London.

1998, Oct. 15

1097 A158 $1 multicolored 1.00 1.00
1098 A158 $1 multicolored 1.00 1.00

Nos. 1097-1098 were each issued in sheets of 6.

Royal Air Force, 80th Anniv. — A159

Aircraft — #1100: a, Panavia Tornado F3 ADV. b, Panavia Tornado F3 IDV. c, Tristar K Mk1 Tanker refueling Panavia Tornado. d, Panavia Tornado GRI.

Each $5: No. 1101, Wessex helicopter, fighter plane. No. 1102, Early aircraft, birds.

1998, Oct. 15 **Litho.** *Perf. 14*

1100 A159 $2 Sheet of 4, #a.-d. 7.00 7.00

Souvenir Sheets

1101-1102 A159 Set of 2 9.25 9.25

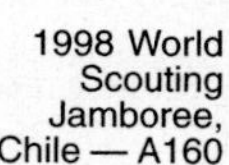

1998 World Scouting Jamboree, Chile — A160

Designs: a, Four Boy Scouts from around the world. b, Boy Scout accompanying Gettysburg veterans, 1913. c, First black troop, Virginia, 1928.

1998, Oct. 15

1103 A160 $3 Sheet of 3, #a.-c. 7.00 7.00

Independence, 15th Anniv. — A161

Design: Prime Minister Kennedy Simmonds receiving constitutional instruments from Princess Margaret, Countess of Snowden.

1998, Oct. 15 **Litho.** *Perf. 14*

1104 A161 $1 multicolored 1.10 1.10

Organization of American States, 50th Anniv. — A162

1998, Oct. 15 *Perf. 14*

1105 A162 $1 multicolored .90 .90

Enzo Ferrari (1898-1988), Automobile Manufacturer — A163

No. 1106: a, 365 California. b, Pininfarina's P6. c, 250 LM.

$5, 212 Export Spyder.

1998, Oct. 15

1106 A163 $2 Sheet of 3, #a.-c. 5.50 5.50

Souvenir Sheet

1107 A163 $5 multicolored 4.75 4.75

No. 1107 contains one 91x35mm stamp.

Christmas A164

Designs: 25c, Kitten, Santa. 60c, Kitten, ornament. 80c, Kitten in sock, vert. 90c, Puppy, presents. $1, Cherub sleeping, birds. $3, Child making snowball, vert.

Each $5: No. 1114, Family, vert. No. 1115, Two dogs.

1998, Nov. 24 **Litho.** *Perf. 14*

1108-1113 A164 Set of 6 5.25 5.25

Souvenir Sheets

1114-1115 A164 Set of 2 7.75 7.75

New Year 1999 (Year of the Rabbit) A165

Color of pairs of rabbits — #1116: a, brown & gray. b, brown & white. c, brown. d, white & black spotted.

$5, Adult white rabbit, 3 bunnies.

1999, Jan. 4 **Litho.** *Perf. 14*

1116 A165 $1.60 Sheet of 4, #a.-d. 5.25 5.25

Souvenir Sheet

1117 A165 $5 multicolored 4.50 4.50

No. 1117 contains one 58x47mm stamp.

Disney Characters Playing Basketball — A166

Basketball in background — #1118, each $1: a, Mickey in green. b, Donald. c, Minnie. d, Goofy. e, One of Donald's nephews. f, Goofy, Mickey. g, Mickey in purple. h, Huey, Dewey, Louie.

Green & white background — #1119, each $1: a, Mickey in purple. b, Goofy. c, Minnie in puple. d, Mickey in yellow & gray. e, Minnie in yellow. f, Donald. g, Donald & Mickey. h, One of Donald's nephews.

No. 1120, $5, Minnie, green bow, horiz. No. 1121, $5, Minnie, purple bow, horiz. No. 1122, $6, Mickey in purple, horiz. No. 1123, $6, Mickey in yellow, horiz.

Perf. 13½x14, 14x13½

1998, Dec. 24 **Litho.**

Sheets of 8, #a-h

1118-1119 A166 Set of 2 15.00 15.00

Souvenir Sheets

1120-1121 A166 Set of 2 8.00 8.00
1122-1123 A166 Set of 2 10.00 10.00

Mickey Mouse, 70th anniv.

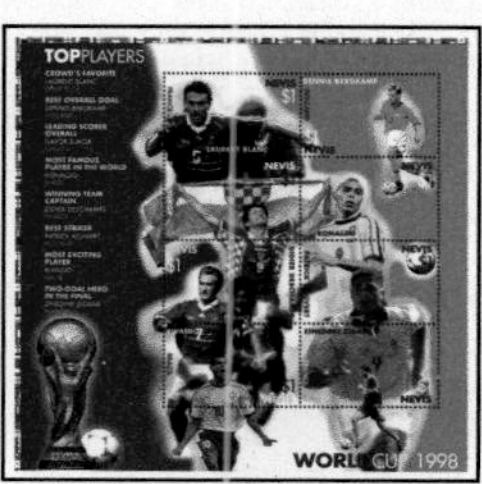

1998 World Cup Soccer Players — A167

No. 1124: a, Laurent Blanc, France. b, Dennis Bergkamp, Holland. c, David Sukor, Croatia. d, Ronaldo, Brazil. e, Didier Deschamps, France. f, Patrick Kluivert, Holland. g, Rivaldo, Brazil. h, Zinedine Zidane, France.

$5, Zinedine Zidane, close-up.

1999, Jan. 18 *Perf. 13½*

1124 A167 $1 Sheet of 8, #a.-h. 5.50 5.50

Souvenir Sheet

1125 A167 $5 multicolored 4.00 4.00

Australia '99, World Stamp Expo — A168

Dinosaurs: 30c, Kritosaurus. 60c, Oviraptor. 80c, Eustreptospondylus. $1.20, Tenontosaurus. $2, Ouranosaurus. $3, Muttaburrasaurus.

No. 1132, $1.20: a, Edmontosaurus. b, Avimimus. c, Minmi. d, Segnosaurus. e, Kentrosaurus. f, Deinonychus.

No. 1133, #1.20: a, Saltasaurus. b, Compsoganthus c, Hadrosaurus. d, Tuojiangosaurus. e, Euoplocephalus. f, Anchisaurus.

Each $5: #1134, Triceratops. #1135, Stegosaurus.

1999, Feb. 22 Litho. *Perf. 14*

1126-1131 A168 Set of 6 6.00 6.00

Sheets of 6, #a-f

1132-1133 A168 Set of 2 11.00 11.00

Souvenir Sheets

1134-1135 A168 Set of 2 7.50 7.50

World Leaders of the 20th Century — A169

No. 1136: a, Emperor Haile Selassie (1892-1975), Ethiopia. b, Selassie, Ethiopian warriors, flag. c, David Ben-Gurion (1886-1973), Prime Minister of Israel. d, Ben-Gurion, Israeli flag. e, Pres. Franklin Roosevelt (1882-1945), Eleanor Roosevelt (1884-1962), UN emblem. f, Roosevelts campaigning, US GI in combat. g, Mao Tse-tung (1893-1976), Chinese leader, 1934 Long March. h, Poster of Mao, soldier.

Each $5: No. 1137, Gandhi. No. 1138, Nelson Mandela.

1999, Mar. 8

1136 A169 90c Sheet of 8, #a.-h. 6.75 6.75

Souvenir Sheets

1137-1138 A169 Set of 2 8.00 8.00

Nos. 1136b-1136c, 1136f-1136g are each 53x38mm.

Birds — A170

No. 1139, each $1.60: a, Yellow warbler. b, Common yellowthroat. c, Painted bunting. d, Belted kingfisher. e, American kestrel. f, Northern oriole.

No. 1140, each $1.60: a, Malachite kingfisher. b, Lilac-breasted roller. c, Swallow-tailed bee-eater. d, Eurasian jay. e, Black-collared apalis. f, Gray-backed camaroptera.

Each $5: No. 1141, Banaquit. No. 1142, Ground scraper thrush, vert.

1999, May 10 Litho. *Perf. 14*

Sheets of 6, #a-f

1139-1140 A170 Set of 2 15.00 15.00

Souvenir Sheets

1141-1142 A170 Set of 2 8.00 8.00

Orchids — A171

Designs: 20c, Phaius hybrid, vert. 25c, Cuitlauzina pendula, vert. 50c, Bletilla striata, vert. 80c, Cymbidium "Showgirl," vert. $1.60, Zygopetalum crinitium. $3, Dendrobium nobile.

No. 1149, vert, each $1: a, Cattleya pumpernickel. b, Odontocidium Arthur Elle. c, Neostylis Lou Sneary. d, Phalaenopsis Aprodite. e, Arkundina graminieolia. f, Cymbidium Hunter's Point. g, Rynchoatylis coelestis. h, Cymbidium Elf's castle.

No. 1150, vert, each $1: a, Cattleya intermedia. b, Cattleya Sophia Martin. c, Phalaenopsis Little Hal. d, Laeliocattleya alisal "Rodeo." e, Laelia lucasiana fournieri. f, Cymbidium Red beauty. g, Sobralia sp. h, Promenaea xanthina.

Each $5: No. 1151, Philippine wind orchid. No. 1152, Dragon's mouth.

1999, June 15 Litho. *Perf. 14*

1143-1148 A171 Set of 6 5.50 5.50

Sheets of 8, #a-h

1149-1150 A171 14.50 14.50

Souvenir Sheets

1151-1152 A171 Set of 2 8.00 8.00

Wedding of Prince Edward and Sophie Rhys-Jones — A172

No. 1153, each $2: a, Sophie in checked suit. b, Couple walking across grass. c, Sophie in black hat, suit, d, Prince Edward in white shirt.

No. 1154, each $2: a, Couple standing in front of building. b, Sophie wearing large hat. c, Sophie in black dress. d, Edward in striped shirt.

Each $5: No. 1155, Couple posing for engagement photo, horiz. No. 1156, Edward kissing Sophie, horiz.

1999, June 19 Litho. *Perf. 14¼*

Sheets of 4, #a-d

1153-1154 A172 Set of 2 11.00 11.00

Souvenir Sheets

1155-1156 A172 Set of 2 7.00 7.00

IBRA '99, World Stamp Exhibition, Nuremberg — A173

Beuth 2-2-2 locomotive and: 30c, Baden #1. 80c, Brunswick #1.

Sailing ship Kruzenshstern and: 90c, Bergedorf #2 & #1a. $1, Bremen #1.

$5, Regensburg air post label on cover.

1999, July 1 *Perf. 14x14½*

1157-1160 A173 Set of 4 2.50 2.50

Souvenir Sheet

1161 A173 $5 multicolored 3.50 3.50

Souvenir Sheets

PhilexFrance '99, World Philatelic Exhibition — A174

Trains: No. 1162, $5: First Class Carriage, 1837. No. 1163, $5: 141.R Mixed Traffic 2-8-2, 1949.

1999, July 1 *Perf. 14x13½*

1162-1163 A174 Set of 2 8.25 8.25

Paintings by Hokusai (1760-1849) A175

Details or entire paintings — #1164: a, (Five) Women Returning Home at Sunset. b, The Blind. c, (Four) Women Returning Home at Sunset. d, A Young Man on a White Horse. e, The Blind (man with beard). f, A Peasant Crossing a Bridge.

No. 1165: a, Poppies (one in bloom). b, The Blind (man with goatee). c, Poppies. d, Abe No Nakamaro Gazing at the Moon from a Terrace. e, The Blind. f, Cranes on a Snowy Pine.

Each $5: No. 1166, Carp in a Waterfall. No. 1167, A Rider in the Snow.

1999, July 1 *Perf. 13½x14*

Sheets of 6

1164 A175 $1 #a.-f. 4.25 4.25

1165 A175 $1.60 #a.-f. 6.75 6.75

Souvenir Sheets

1166-1167 A175 Set of 2 7.75 7.75

Culturama Festival, 25th Anniv. — A176

Designs: 30c, Steel drummers. 80c, Clowns. $1.80, Masqueraders with "Big Drum." No. 1171, $5, String band.

No. 1172, Masquerade dancers.

1999, July 1 Litho. *Perf. 14*

1168-1171 A176 Set of 4 5.50 5.50

Souvenir Sheet

1172 A176 $5 multicolored 3.75 3.75

No. 1172 contains one 51x38mm stamp.

Queen Mother — A177

Queen Mother (b. 1900): No. 1173: a, In bridal gown, 1923. b, With Princess Elizabeth, 1926. c, With King George VI in World War II. d, Wearing hat, 1983.

$6, Wearing tiara, 1957.

Gold Frames

1999, Aug. 4 Sheet of 4 *Perf. 14*

1173 A177 $2 #a.-d., + label 5.50 5.50

Souvenir Sheet

Perf. 13¾

1174 A177 $6 multicolored 4.25 4.25

No. 1174 contains one 38x51mm stamp.

See Nos. 1287-1288.

Christmas — A178

30c, Adoration of the Magi, by Albrecht Durer. 90c, Canigiani Holy Family, by Raphael. $1.20, The Nativity, by Durer. $1.80, Madonna Surrounded by Angels, by Peter Paul Rubens. $3, Madonna Surrounded by Saints, by Rubens.

$5, Madonna and Child by a Window, by Durer, horiz.

1999, Nov. 12 Litho. *Perf. 14*

1175-1179 A178 Set of 5 5.50 5.50

Souvenir Sheet

1180 A178 $5 multicolored 3.75 3.75

Millennium — A179

Scenes of Four Seasons Resort: a, Aerial view. b, Palm tree, beach. c, Golf course. d, Couple on beach.

1999 Litho. *Perf. 14¼x13¾*

1181 A179 30c Sheet of 4, #a.-d. .90 .90

Flowers — A180

Various flowers making up a photomosaic of Princess Diana.

1999, Dec. 31 Litho. *Perf. 13¾*

1182 A180 $1 Sheet of 8, #a.-h. 6.00 6.00

New Year 2000 (Year of the Dragon) A181

No. 1183: a, Dragon showing 9 claws. b, Dragon showing 10 claws. c, Dragon showing 5 claws. d, Dragon showing 8 claws.

$5, Dragon, vert.

2000, Feb. 5 *Perf. 14*

1183 A181 $1.60 Sheet of 4, #a.-d. 4.25 4.25

Souvenir Sheet

Perf. 13¾

1184 A181 $5 multi 4.00 4.00

No. 1184 contains one 38x50mm stamp.

Millennium — A182

No. 1185 — Highlights of 1700-1750: a, Jonathan Swift writes "Gulliver's Travels." b, Manchu Dynasty flourishes in China. c, Bartolomeo Cristofori invents piano. d, Capt. William Kidd hanged for piracy. e, Astronomer William Herschel born. f, George I succeeds Queen Anne as British ruler. g, Russian treaty with China. h, Bubonic plague hits Austria and Germany. i, Kaigetsudo paints "Standing Woman." j, Queen Anne ascends to English throne. k, Anders Celsius invents centigrade scale for thermometer. l, Vitus Bering discovers Alaska and Aleutian Islands. m, Edmond Halley predicts return of comet. n, John and Charles Wesley found Methodism movement. o, Isaac Newton publishes "Opticks." p, England and Scotland form Great Britain (60x40mm). q, Johann Sebastian Bach composes "The Well-Tempered Clavier."

No. 1186 — Highlights of the 1990s: a, Boris Yeltsin becomes prime minister of Russian Federation. b, Gulf War begins. c, Civil War in Bosnia. d, Signing of the Oslo Accords. e, John Major, Albert Reynolds search for peace in Northern Ireland. f, F.W. De Klerk, Nelson Mandela end apartheid in South Africa. g, Cal Ripken, Jr. breaks record for most consecutive baseball games played. h, Kobe, Japan earthquake. i, Inca girl, believed to be 500 years old, found in ice. j, Sojourner beams back images from Mars. k, Dr. Ian Wilmot clones sheep "Dolly." l, Princess Diana dies in car crash. m, Hong Kong returned to China. n, Septuplets born and survive. o, Guggenheim Museum in Bilbao, Spain completed. p, Countdown to year 2000 (60x40mm). q, Pres. William J. Clinton impeached.

2000, Jan. 4 Litho. *Perf. 12¾x12½*

Sheets of 17

1185 A182 30c #a.-q., + label 6.75 6.75

1186 A182 50c #a.-q., + label 10.00 10.00

Misspellings and historical inaccuracies abound on Nos. 1185-1186.

Tropical Fish — A183

Designs: 30c, Spotted scat. 80c, Platy variatus. 90c, Emerald betta. $4, Cowfish.

No. 1191, each $1: a, Oriental sweetlips. b, Royal gramma. c, Threadfin butterflyfish. d, Yellow tang. e, Bicolor angelfish. f, Catalina goby. g, False cleanerfish. h, Powder blue surgeon.

No. 1192, each $1: a, Sailfin tang. b, Black-capped gramma. c, Majestic snapper. d, Purple firefish. e, Clown trigger. f, Yellow longnose. g, Clown wrasse. h, Yellow-headed jawfish.

Each $5: No. 1193, Clown coris. No. 1194, Clown killifish.

2000, Mar. 27 ***Perf. 14***

1187-1190 A183 Set of 4 5.50 5.50

Sheets of 8, #a.-h.

1191-1192 A183 Set of 2 13.50 13.50

Souvenir Sheets

1193-1194 A183 Set of 2 8.50 8.50

Dogs — A184

Designs: 10c, Miniature pinscher. 20c, Pyrenean mountain dog. 30c, Welsh Springer spaniel. 80c, Alaskan malamute. $2, Bearded collie. $3, Amercian cocker spaniel.

No. 1201, horiz.: a, Beagle. b, Basset hound. c, St. Bernard. d, Rough collie. e, Shih tzu. f, American bulldog.

No. 1202, horiz.: a, Irish red and white setter. b, Dalmatian. c, Pomeranian. d, Chihuahua. e, English sheepdog. f, Samoyed.

Each $5: No. 1203, Leonberger. No. 1204, Longhaired miniature dachshund, horiz.

2000, May 1 **Litho.** ***Perf. 14***

1195-1200 A184 Set of 6 5.25 5.25
1201 A184 90c Sheet of 6, #a-f 4.50 4.50
1202 A184 $1 Sheet of 6, #a-f 5.00 5.00

Souvenir Sheets

1203-1204 A184 Set of 2 8.50 8.50

100th Test Match at Lord's Ground — A185

Designs: $2, Elquemede Willett. $3, Keith Arthurton.

$5, Lord's Ground, horiz.

2000, June 10

1205-1206 A185 Set of 2 4.00 4.00

Souvenir Sheet

1207 A185 $5 multi 4.00 4.00

First Zeppelin Flight, Cent. A186

No. 1208: a, LZ-129. b, LZ-1. c, LZ-11.

$5, LZ-127.

2000, June 10 ***Perf. 14***

1208 A186 $3 Sheet of 3, #a-c 7.00 7.00

Souvenir Sheet

Perf. 14¼

1209 A186 $5 multi 4.25 4.25

No. 1208 contains three 38x25mm stamps.

Berlin Film Festival, 50th Anniv. A187

No. 1210: a, Rani Radovi. b, Salvatore Giuliano. c, Schoenzeit für Füchse. d, Shirley MacLaine. e, Simone Signoret. f, Sohrab Shahid Saless.

$5, Komissar.

2000, June 10 ***Perf. 14***

1210 A187 $1.60 Sheet of 6, #a-f 7.00 7.00

Souvenir Sheet

1211 A187 $5 multi 4.00 4.00

Spacecraft — A188

No. 1212, each $1.60: a, Mars IV probe. b, Mars Water. c, Mars 1. d, Viking. e, Mariner 7. f, Mars Surveyor.

No. 1213, each $1.60: a, Mariner 9. b, Mars 3. c, Mariner 4. d, Planet B. e, Mars Express Lander. f, Mars Express.

Each $5: No. 1214, Mars Observer. No. 1215, Mars Climate Observer, vert.

2000, June 10 **Sheets of 6, #a-f**

1212-1213 A188 Set of 2 15.00 15.00

Souvenir Sheets

1214-1215 A188 Set of 2 8.00 8.00

Souvenir Sheets

2000 Summer Olympics, Sydney — A189

No. 1216: a, Gisela Mauermeyer. b, Uneven bars. c, Wembley Stadium, London, and British flag. d, Ancient Greek horse racing.

2000, June 10

1216 A189 $2 Sheet of 4, #a-d 5.00 5.00

Albert Einstein (1879-1955) — A190

No. 1217: a, Sticking out tongue. b, Riding bicycle. c, Wearing hat.

2000, June 10

1217 A190 $2 Sheet of 3, #a-c 5.50 5.00

Public Railways, 175th Anniv. — A191

No. 1218: a, Locomotion No. 1, George Stephenson. b, Trevithick's 1804 drawing of locomotive.

2000, June 10

1218 A191 $3 Sheet of 2, #a-b 4.75 4.75

Johann Sebastian Bach (1685-1750) — A192

2000, June 10

1219 A192 $5 multi 4.25 4.25

Prince William, 18th Birthday A193

No. 1220: a, Reaching to shake hand. b, In ski gear. c, With jacket open. d, In sweater.

$5, In suit and tie.

2000, June 21 ***Perf. 14***

1220 A193 $1.60 Sheet of 4, #a-d 4.25 4.25

Souvenir Sheet

Perf. 13¾

1221 A193 $5 multi 4.00 4.00

No. 1220 contains four 28x42mm stamps.

Souvenir Sheets

Bob Hope, Entertainer — A194

No. 1222: a, Wearing Air Force Ranger uniform. b, With Sammy Davis, Jr. c, With wife, Dolores. d, On golf course. e, In suit behind microphone. f, Walking.

2000, July 10 ***Perf. 14***

1222 A194 $1 Sheet of 6, #a-f 5.75 5.75

Mike Wallace, Broadcast Journalist — A195

2000, July 10 ***Perf. 13¾***

1223 A195 $5 multi 4.00 4.00

Carifesta VII — A196

Designs: 30c, Emblem. 90c, Festival participants. $1.20, Dancer.

2000, Aug. 17 ***Perf. 14***

1224-1226 A196 Set of 3 2.25 2.25

Monarchs — A197

No. 1227: a, King Edward III of England, 1327-77. b, Holy Roman Emperor Charles V (Charles I of Spain), 1520-56. c, Holy Roman Emperor Joseph II of Austria-Hungary, 1780-90. d, King Henry II of Germany, 1002-24. e, King Louis IV of France, 936-54. f, King Louis II of Bavaria, 1864-86.

$5, King Louis IX of France, 1226-70.

2000, Aug. 1 **Litho.** ***Perf. 13¾***

1227 A197 $1.60 Sheet of 6, #a-f 8.00 8.00

Souvenir Sheet

1228 A197 $5 multi 4.25 4.25

David Copperfield, Magician — A198

2000, Aug. 10 ***Perf. 14***

1229 A198 $1.60 multi 2.00 2.00

Printed in sheets of 4.

Female Singing Groups A199

Singers from the Angels (a-c, blue background), Dixie Cups (d-f, yellow background) and Martha Reeves and the Vandellas (g-i, pink background): a, Record half. b, Woman with long hair. c, Woman with hand on chin. d, Record half. e, Woman with mole on cheek. f, Woman, no mole. g, Record half. h, Woman, not showing teeth. i, Woman showing teeth.

2000, Aug. 10

1230 A199 90c Sheet of 9, #a-i 6.25 6.25

Butterflies A200

Designs: 30c, Zebra. 80c, Julia. $1.60, Small flambeau. $5, Purple mort bleu.

No. 1235, $1: a, Ruddy dagger. b, Common morpho. c, Banded king shoemaker. d, Figure of eight. e, Grecian shoemaker. f, Mosaic.

No. 1236, $1: a, White peacock. b, Hewitson's blue hairstreak. c, Tiger pierid. d, Gold drop helicopsis. e, Cramer's mesene. f, Red-banded pereute.

No. 1237, $5, Common mechanitis. No. 1238, $5, Hewitson's pierella.

2001, Mar. 22

1231-1234 A200 Set of 4 6.00 6.00

Sheets of 6, #a-f

1235-1236 A200 Set of 2 9.50 9.50

Souvenir Sheets

1237-1238 A200 Set of 2 7.75 7.75

Flowers — A201

Designs: 30c, Golden elegance oriental lily. 80c, Frangipani. $1.60, Garden zinnia. $5, Rose elegance lily.

No. 1243, 90c: a, Star of the march. b, Tiger lily. c, Mont Blanc lily. d, Torch ginger. e, Cattleya orchid. f, Saint John's wort.

No. 1244, $1: a, Culebra. b, Rubellum lily. c, Silver elegance oriental lily. d, Chinese hibiscus. e, Tiger lily. f, Royal poinciana.

No. 1245, $1.60: a, Epiphyte. b, Enchantment lily. c, Glory lily. d, Purple granadilla. e, Jacaranda. f, Shrimp plant.

No. 1246, $5, Dahlia. No. 1247, $5, Bird of Paradise.

2000, Oct. 30

1239-1242 A201 Set of 4 6.00 6.00

Sheets of 6, #a-f

1243-1245 A201 Set of 3 17.00 17.00

Souvenir Sheets

1246-1247 A201 Set of 2 7.75 7.75

The Stamp Show 2000, London (Nos. 1243-1247).

Christmas — A203

Designs: 30c, The Coronation of the Virgin, by Diego Velazquez, vert. 80c, The Immaculate Conception, by Velazquez, vert. 90c, Madonna and Child, by Titian. $1.20, Madonna and Child With St. John the Baptist and St. Catherine, by Titian.

$6, Madonna and Child With St. Catherine, by Titian.

2000, Dec. 4 Litho. *Perf. 13½*

1249-1252 A203 Set of 4 2.40 2.40

Souvenir Sheet

1253 A203 $6 multi 4.50 4.50

New Year 2001 (Year of the Snake) A204

No. 1254: a, Snake coiled on branch, facing right. b, Snake coiled on branch, facing left. c, Snake on ground, facing right. d, Snake on ground, facing left.

$5, Snake raising head.

2001, Jan. 4 *Perf. 14*

1254 A204 $1.60 Sheet of 4, #a-d 5.00 5.00

Souvenir Sheet

1255 A204 $5 multi 4.00 4.00

195th Annual Leeward Islands Methodist Church District Conference — A205

Churches: a, Charlestown. b, Jessups. c, Clifton. d, Trinity. e, Combermere. f, Gingerland. g, New River.

2001, Jan. 23

1256 A205 50c Sheet of 7, #a-g 2.50 2.50

Garden of Eden A206

No. 1257, $1.60: a, Red-crested woodpecker, unicorn. b, African elephant. c, Siberian tiger. d, Greater flamingo, Adam and Eve. e, Hippopotamus. f, Harlequin frog.

No. 1258, $1.60: a, Giraffe. b, Rainbow boa constrictor. c, Mountain cottontail rabbit. d, Bluebuck antelope. e, Red fox. f, Box turtle.

No. 1259, $5, Bald eagle. No. 1260, $5, Blue and gold macaw, vert. No. 1261, $5, Toucan, vert. No. 1262, $5, Koala, vert.

2001, Jan. 31 *Perf. 14*

Sheets of 6, #a-f

1257-1258 A206 Set of 2 14.50 14.50

Souvenir Sheets

1259-1262 A206 Set of 4 15.00 15.00

Mushrooms — A207

Designs: 20c, Clavulinopsis corniculata. 25c, Cantharellus cibarius. 50c, Chlorociboria aeruginascens. 80c, Auricularia auricula judae. $2, Peziza vesiculosa. $3, Mycena acicula.

No. 1269, $1: a, Entoloma incanum. b, Entoloma nitidum. c, Stropharia cyanea. d, Otidea onotica. e, Aleuria aurantia. f, Mitrula paludosa. g, Gyromitra esculenta. h, Helvella crispa. i, Morchella semilibera.

No. 1270, $5, Omphalotus olearius. No. 1271, $5, Russula sardonia.

2001, May 15 Litho. *Perf. 14*

1263-1268 A207 Set of 6 5.50 5.50

1269 A207 $1 Sheet of 9, #a-i 7.50 7.50

Souvenir Sheets

1270-1271 A207 Set of 2 8.25 8.25

Tale of Prince Shotoku A208

No. 1272, $2: a, Conception of Prince Shotoku. b, At six. c, At ten. d, At eleven.

No. 1273, $2: a, At sixteen (soldiers at gate). b, At sixteen (soldiers on horseback). c, At thirty-seven. d, At forty-four.

2001, May 31 *Perf. 13¾*

Sheets of 4, #a-d

1272-1273 A208 Set of 2 12.00 12.00

Phila Nippon '01, Japan.

Queen Victoria (1819-1901) — A209

No. 1274: a, Prince Albert. b, Queen Victoria (flower in hair). c, Alexandrina Victoria. d, Duchess of Kent. e, Queen Victoria (as old woman). f, Prince of Wales.

$5, Queen Victoria (with tiara).

2001, July 9 Litho. *Perf. 14*

1274 A209 $1.20 Sheet of 6, #a-f 5.50 5.50

Souvenir Sheet

1275 A209 $5 multi 3.75 3.75

Queen Elizabeth II, 75th Birthday A210

No. 1276: a, Blue hat. b, Tiara. c, Yellow hat. d, Tan hat. e, Red hat. f, No hat.

$5, Blue hat, diff.

2001, July 9

1276 A210 90c Sheet of 6, #a-f 4.00 4.00

Souvenir Sheet

1277 A210 $5 multi 3.75 3.75

Flags of the Caribbean Community — A211

No. 1278: a, Antigua & Barbuda. b, Bahamas. c, Barbados. d, Belize. e, Dominica. f, Grenada. g, Guyana. h, Jamaica. i, Montserrat. j, St. Kitts & Nevis. k, St. Lucia. l, Surinam. m, St. Vincent & the Grenadines. n, Trinidad & Tobago.

2001, Dec. 3 Litho. *Perf. 14*

1278 A211 90c Sheet of 14, #a-n 11.00 11.00

Christmas A212

Flowers: 30c, Christmas candle, vert. 90c, Poinsettia. $1.20, Snowbush. $3, Tiger claw, vert.

2001, Dec. 3

1279-1282 A212 Set of 4 4.25 4.25

2002 World Cup Soccer Championships, Japan and Korea — A213

No. 1283, $1.60: a, Moracana Stadium, Brazil, 1950. b, Ferenc Puskas, 1954. c, Luis Bellini, 1958. d, Mauro, 1962. e, Cap, 1966. f, Banner, 1970.

No. 1284, $1.60: a, Passarella, 1978. b, Dino Zoff, 1982. c, Azteca Stadium, Mexico, 1986. d, San Siro Stadium, Italy, 1990. e, Dennis Bergkamp, Netherlands, 1994. f, Stade de France, 1998.

No. 1285, $5, Head from Jules Rimet Cup, 1930. No. 1286, $5, Head and globe from World Cup trophy, 2002.

2001, Dec. 10 *Perf. 13¾x14¼*

Sheets of 6, #a-f

1283-1284 A213 Set of 2 13.00 13.00

Souvenir Sheets

Perf. 14½x14¼

1285-1286 A213 Set of 2 7.25 7.25

Queen Mother Type of 1999 Redrawn

No. 1287: a, In bridal gown, 1923. b, With Princess Elizabeth, 1926. c, With King George VI in World War II. d, Wearing hat, 1983.

$6, Wearing tiara, 1957.

2001, Dec. 13 *Perf. 14*

Yellow Orange Frames

1287 A177 $2 Sheet of 4, #a-d, + label 6.00 6.00

Souvenir Sheet

Perf. 13¾

1288 A177 $6 multi 4.50 4.50

Queen Mother's 101st birthday. No. 1288 contains one 38x51mm stamp with a bluer background than that found on No. 1174. Sheet margins of Nos. 1287-1288 lack embossing and gold arms and frames found on Nos. 1173-1174.

Reign of Queen Elizabeth II, 50th Anniv. A214

No. 1289: a, Queen with Prince Philip. b, Prince Philip. c, Queen with yellow dress. d, Queen touching horse.
$5, Queen with Prince Philip, diff.

2002, Feb. 6 ***Perf. 14¼***
1289 A214 $2 Sheet of 4, #a-d 5.75 5.75

Souvenir Sheet

1290 A214 $5 multi 3.75 3.75

New Year 2002 (Year of the Horse) A215

Horse paintings by Ren Renfa: a, Brown and white horse. b, Horse with ribs showing. c, Horse with tassel under neck. d, Gray horse.

2002, Mar. 4 ***Perf. 13¼***
1291 A215 $1.60 Sheet of 4, #a-d 4.50 4.50

Insects, Birds and Whales A216

No. 1292, $1.20: a, Beechey's bee. b, Banded king shoemaker butterfly. c, Streaked sphinx caterpillar. d, Hercules beetle. e, South American palm beetle. f, Giant katydid.
No. 1293, $1.60: a, Roseate spoonbill. b, White-tailed tropicbird. c, Ruby-throated tropicbird. d, Black skimmer. e, Black-necked stilt. f, Mourning dove.
No. 1294, $1.60: a, Sperm whale. b, Sperm and killer whales. c, Minke whales. d, Fin whale. e, Blainville's beaked whale. f, Pygmy sperm whale.
No. 1295, $5, Click beetle. No. 1296, $5, Royal tern. No. 1297, $5, Humpback whale, vert.

2002, Aug. 15 **Litho.** ***Perf. 14***

Sheets of 6, #a-f

1292-1294 A216 Set of 3 21.00 21.00

Souvenir Sheets

1295-1297 A216 Set of 3 12.00 12.00

APS Stampshow (#1293).

United We Stand — A217

2002, Aug. 26
1298 A217 $2 multi 1.50 1.50

Printed in sheets of 4.

2002 Winter Olympics, Salt Lake City — A218

Designs: No. 1299, $2, Figure skating. No. 1300, $2, Freestyle skiing.

2002, Aug. 26
1299-1300 A218 Set of 2 3.00 3.00
a. Souvenir sheet, #1299-1300 3.25 3.25

Intl. Year of Mountains — A219

No. 1301: a, Mt. Assiniboine, Canada. b, Mt. Atitlán, Guatemala. c, Mt. Adams, US. d, Matterhorn, Switzerland and Italy. e, Mt. Dhaulagiri, Nepal. f, Mt. Chamlang, Nepal.
$5, Mt. Kvaenangen, Norway.

2002, Aug. 26
1301 A219 $2 Sheet of 6, #a-f 8.50 8.50

Souvenir Sheet

1302 A219 $5 multi 3.50 3.50

Ecotourism — A220

No. 1303: a, Horseback riding on beach. b, Windsurfing. c, Pinney's Beach. d, Cross-country hike. e, Robert T. Jones Golf Course. f, Scuba safaris.
$5, Coral reef snorkeling.

2002, Aug. 26
1303 A220 $1.60 Sheet of 6, #a-f 8.00 8.00

Souvenir Sheet

1304 A220 $5 multi 3.75 3.75

20th World Scout Jamboree, Thailand — A221

No. 1305: a, Scouts in two canoes. b, Scouts in one canoe. c, Scout on rope bridge. d, Scouts in inflatable rafts.
$5, Scout working on leatherwork project.

2002, Aug. 26
1305 A221 $2 Sheet of 4, #a-d 6.00 6.00

Souvenir Sheet

1306 A221 $5 multi 3.75 3.75

Souvenir Sheet

Artwork of Eva Wilkin (1898-1989) — A222

No. 1307: a, Unnamed painting of windmill. b, Nevis Peak (sepia toned). c, Fig Tree Church. d, Nevis Peak (full color).

2002, Sept. 23
1307 A222 $1.20 Sheet of 4, #a-d 3.75 3.75

Japanese Art — A223

No. 1308: a, Golden Pheasants and Loquat, by Shoei Kano. b, Flowers and Birds of the Four Seasons (snow-covered branches), by Koson Ikeda. c, Pheasants and Azaleas, by Kano. d, Flowers and Birds of the Four Seasons (tree and hill), by Ikeda.
No. 1309, $3: a, Flying bird from Birds and Flowers of Summer and Autumn, by Terutada Shikibu. b, Red flower, from Birds and Flowers of Summer and Autumn, by Shikibu
No. 1310, $3: a, White flower from Birds and Flowers of Summer and Autumn, by Shikibu. b, Perched bird from Birds and Flowers of Summer and Autumn, by Shikibu.
No. 1311, $3, horiz.: a, Bird facing right, from Two Birds on Willow and Peach Trees, by Buson Yosa. b, Bird facing left, from Two Birds on Willow and Peach Trees, by Yosa.
No. 1312, $5, Golden Pheasants Among Rhododendrons, by Baiitsu Yamamoto. No. 1313, $5, Muskrat and Camellias, by Neko Jako, horiz.

2002 ***Perf. 14x14¾***
1308 A223 $2 Sheet of 4, #a-d 6.00 6.00

Sheets of 2, #a-b

Perf. 13¾

1309-1311 A223 Set of 3 13.50 13.50

Souvenir Sheets

1312-1313 A223 Set of 2 7.50 7.50

No. 1308 contains four 29x80mm stamps.

2002 World Cup Soccer Championship Quarterfinal Matches — A224

No. 1314, $1.20: a, Claudio Reyna and Torsten Frings. b, Michael Ballack and Eddie Pope. c, Sebastian Kehl and Brian McBride. d, Puyol and Eul Yong Lee. e, Jin Cheul Choi and Gaizka Mendieta. f, Juan Valeron and Jin Cheul Choi.
No. 1315, $1.60: a, Emile Heskey and Edmilson. b, Rivaldo and Sol Campbell. c, Ronaldinho and Nicky Butt. d, Ilhan Mansiz and Omar Daf. e, Hasan Sas and Papa Bouba Diop. f, Lamine Diatta and Hakan Sukur.
No. 1316, $3: a, Sebastian Kehl. b, Frankie Hejduk.
No. 1317, $3: a, Hong Myung Bo. b, Gaizka Mendieta.
No. 1318, $3: a, David Beckham and Roque Junior. b, Paul Scholes and Rivaldo.
No. 1319, $3: a, Alpay Ozalan. b, Khalilou Fadiga.

2002, Nov. 4 **Litho.** ***Perf. 13¼***

Sheets of 6, #a-f

1314-1315 A224 Set of 2 12.50 12.50

Souvenir Sheets of 2, #a-b

1316-1319 A224 Set of 4 18.00 18.00

Christmas — A225

Religious art: 30c, Madonna and Child Enthroned with Saints, by Perugino. 80c, Adoration of the Magi, by Domenico Ghirlandaio. 90c, San Zaccaria Altarpiece, by Giovanni Bellini. $1.20, Presentation at the Temple, by Bellini. $5, Madonna and Child, by Simone Martini.
$6, Maestà, by Martini.

2002, Nov. 4 ***Perf. 14¼***
1320-1324 A225 Set of 5 6.25 6.25

Souvenir Sheet

Perf. 14x14¼

1325 A225 $6 multi 4.50 4.50

New Year 2003 (Year of the Ram) — A226

2003, Feb. 10 ***Perf. 14x13¾***
1326 A226 $2 multi 2.50 2.50

Printed in sheets of 4.

Pres. John F. Kennedy (1917-63) — A227

No. 1327, $2: a, Robert and Edward Kennedy. b, John F. Kennedy. c, Joseph P., Jr., and John F. Kennedy as children. d, Robert and John F. Kennedy.
No. 1328, $2: a, Taking oath of office, 1961. b, At cabinet oath ceremony, 1961. c, With Russian foreign minister Andrei Gromyko, 1963. d, Cuban Missile Crisis, 1962.

2003, Mar. 10 **Litho.** ***Perf. 14***

Sheets of 4, #a-d

1327-1328 A227 Set of 2 12.00 12.00

Elvis Presley (1935-77) — A228

2003, Mar. 10 **Litho.** ***Perf. 14***
1329 A228 $1.60 multi 1.60 1.60

Printed in sheets of 6.

First Non-Stop Solo Transatlantic Flight, 75th Anniv. — A229

No. 1330, $2: a, Ryan Airlines crew attaches wing to fuselage of the Spirit of St. Louis. b, Charles Lindbergh, Donald Hall and President of Ryan Flying Co. c, Lindbergh planning flight. d, Hall designing Spirit of St. Louis.

No. 1331, $2: a, Hall. b, Lindbergh. c, Automobile towing Spirit of St. Louis from Ryan factory. d, Spirit of St. Louis being towed at Curtiss Field.

2003, Mar. 10 **Sheets of 4, #a-d**
1330-1331 A229 Set of 2 12.00 12.00

Princess Diana (1961-97) — A230

No. 1332: a, Wearing light blue and white dress. b, Wearing light green dress, pearl necklace. c, Wearing black gown. d, Wearing black and white hat and pearls.
$5, Wearing black dress and necklace.

2003, Mar. 10 ***Perf. 12¼***
1332 A230 $2 Sheet of 4, #a-d 6.00 6.00

Souvenir Sheet

1333 A230 $5 multi 3.75 3.75

Marlene Dietrich (1901-92) — A231

No. 1334: a, With cigarette, country name at right. b, With cigarette, country name at left. c, Close-up. d, Wearing hat and white jacket.
$5, Wearing dress.

2003, Mar. 10 ***Perf. 14***
1334 A231 $1.60 Sheet, #a-b, 2 each #c-d 6.75 6.75

Souvenir Sheet

1335 A231 $5 multi 3.75 3.75

Coronation of Queen Elizabeth II, 50th Anniv. — A232

No. 1336: a, Queen as young woman. b, Queen as older woman. c, Queen wearing glasses.
$5, Queen wearing tiara.

2003, May 13
1336 A232 $3 Sheet of 3, #a-c 7.00 7.00

Souvenir Sheet

1337 A232 $5 multi 4.25 4.25

Prince William, 21st Birthday A233

No. 1338: a, Wearing suit, showing teeth. b, Wearing suit. c, Wearing sweater.
$5, Wearing suit, diff.

2003, May 13
1338 A233 $3 Sheet of 3, #a-c 7.00 7.00

Souvenir Sheet

1339 A233 $5 multi 4.00 4.00

Powered Flight, Cent. A234

No. 1340: a, A. V. Roe triplane. b, A. V. Roe Type D biplane. c, Avro Type F. d, Avro 504.
$5, Avro 561.

2003, May 13
1340 A234 $1.80 Sheet of 4, #a-d 5.75 5.75

Souvenir Sheet

1341 A234 $5 multi 4.00 4.00

Teddy Bears, Cent. (in 2002) A235

No. 1342: a, Abraham Lincoln bear. b, Napoleon bear. c, King Henry VIII bear. d, Charlie Chaplin bear.
$5, Baseball bear.

2003, May 13 ***Perf. 13¼***
1342 A235 $2 Sheet of 4, #a-d 5.50 5.50

Souvenir Sheet

1343 A235 $5 multi 3.75 3.75

Tour de France Bicycle Race, Cent. A236

No. 1344: a, Gustave Garrigou, 1911. b, Odile Defraye, 1912. c, Philippe Thys, 1913. d, Thys, 1914.
$5, François Faber.

2003, May 13
1344 A236 $2 Sheet of 4, #a-d 7.00 7.00

Souvenir Sheet

1345 A236 $5 multi 5.50 5.50

General Motors Automobiles — A237

No. 1346, $2 — Cadillacs: a, 1933 355-C V8 sedan. b, 1953 Eldorado. c, 1977 Coupe de Ville. d, 1980 Seville Elegante.

No. 1347, $2 — Corvettes: a, 1970. b, 1974. c, 1971. d, 1973.

No. 1348, $5, 1954 Cadillac. No. 1349, $5, 1997 C5 Corvette.

2003, May 13
Sheets of 4, #a-d
1346-1347 A237 Set of 2 12.00 12.00

Souvenir Sheets

1348-1349 A237 Set of 2 7.50 7.50

Orchids — A238

Designs: 20c, Phalaenopsis joline, vert. $1.20, Vanda thonglor, vert. No. 1352, $2, Potinara. $3, Lycaste aquila.

No. 1354, $2: a, Brassolaelia cattleya. b, Cymbidium claricon. c, Calanthe vestita. d, Odontoglossum crispum.
$5, Odontioda brocade.

2003, Oct. 24 ***Perf. 14***
1350-1353 A238 Set of 4 5.00 5.00
1354 A238 $2 Sheet of 4, #a-d 6.25 6.25

Souvenir Sheet

1355 A238 $5 multi 4.00 4.00

Butterflies A239

Designs: 30c, Perisama bonplandii. 90c, Danaus formosa. $1, Amauris vashti. $3, Lycorea ceres.

No. 1360: a, Kallima rumia. b, Nessaea ancaeus. c, Callicore cajetani. d, Hamadryas guatemalena.
$5, Euphaedra medon.

2003, Oct. 24
1356-1359 A239 Set of 4 4.25 4.25
1360 A239 $2 Sheet of 4, #a-d 6.25 6.25

Souvenir Sheet

1361 A239 $5 multi 4.00 4.00

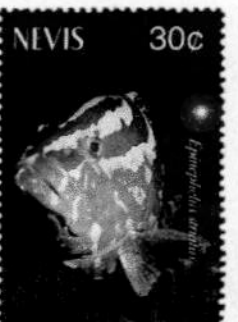

Marine Life — A240

Designs: 30c, Epinephelus striatus, vert. 80c, Acropora, vert. 90c, Myripristis hexagona. No. 1365, $5, Trichechus manatus.

No. 1366: a, Lioices latus. b, Chelmon rostratus. c, Epinephelus merra. d, Acanthurus coeruleus.

No. 1367, $5, Haemulon sciurus.

2003, Oct. 24
1362-1365 A240 Set of 4 5.50 5.50
1366 A240 $2 Sheet of 4, #a-d 6.25 6.25

Souvenir Sheet

1367 A240 $5 multi 4.00 4.00

A241

Christmas — A241a

Designs: 30c, Madonna of the Magnificat, by Botticelli. 90c, Madonna with the Long Neck, by Il Parmigianino. $1.20, Virgin and Child With St. Anne, by Leonardo da Vinci. $5, Madonna and Child and Scenes from the Life of St. Anne, by Filippo Lippi.
$6, Conestabile Madonna, by Raphael.

2003, Nov. 5 ***Perf. 14¼***
1368-1371 A241 Set of 4 5.00 5.00

Souvenir Sheet

1372 A241a $6 multi 4.25 4.25

World AIDS Day — A242

National flag, AIDS ribbon and: 90c, Stylized men. $1.20, Map.

2003, Dec. 1 ***Perf. 14***
1373-1374 A242 Set of 2 1.75 1.75

New Year 2004 (Year of the Monkey) — A243

Designs: $1.60, Monkey King and Chinese text. $3, Monkey King.

2004, Feb. 16 **Litho.** ***Perf. 13¼***
1375 A243 $1.60 red & black 1.25 1.25

Souvenir Sheet
Perf. 13¼x13

1376 A243 $3 multi 2.75 2.75

No. 1375 printed in sheets of 4. No. 1376 contains one 30x40mm stamp.

Girl Guides in Nevis, 50th Anniv. — A244

Designs: 30c, Badges. 90c, Guide and guide leader, horiz. $1.20, Lady Olave Baden-Powell. $5, Guides wearing t-shirts.

2004, Feb. 22 ***Perf. 14***
1377-1380 A244 Set of 4 5.50 5.50

Paintings in the Hermitage, St. Petersburg, Russia A245

Designs: 30c, Still Life with a Drapery, by Paul Cézanne. 90c, The Smoker, by Cézanne, vert. $2, Girl with a Fan, by Pierre Auguste Renoir, vert. No. 1384, $5, Grove, by André Derain, vert.

No. 1385, Lady in the Garden (Sainte Adresse), by Claude Monet.

2004, Mar. 4 ***Perf. 13¼***
1381-1384 A245 Set of 4 6.25 6.25

Imperf
Size: 94x74mm

1385 A245 $5 multi 3.75 3.75

Paintings by Norman Rockwell (1894-1978) — A246

No. 1386, vert.: a, The Morning After. b, Solitaire. c, Easter Morning. d, Walking to Church.
$5, The Graduate.

2004, Mar. 4 ***Perf. 13¼***
1386 A246 $2 Sheet of 4, #a-d 6.00 6.00

Souvenir Sheet

1387 A246 $5 multi 4.00 4.00

Paintings by Pablo Picasso (1881-1973) — A247

No. 1388, $2: a, Woman with a Hat. b, Seated Woman. c, Portrait of Nusch Eluard. d, Woman in a Straw Hat.
No. 1389, $2: a, L'Arlésienne. b, The Mirror. c, Repose. d, Portrait of Paul Eluard.
No. 1390, Portrait of Nusch Eluard, diff. No. 1391, Reclining Woman with a Book, horiz.

2004, Mar. 4 ***Perf. 13¼***

Sheets of 4, #a-d

1388-1389 A247 Set of 2 12.00 12.00

Imperf

1390 A247 $5 shown 4.00 4.00

Size: 100x75mm

1391 A247 $5 multi 4.00 4.00

ASDA Mega-Event, New York (#1389).

A248

Marilyn Monroe A249

No. 1393 — Placement of stamp on sheet: a, UL. b, UR. c, LL. d, LR.

2004, June 17 ***Perf. 13½x13¼***
1392 A248 60c multi .70 .70

Perf. 13¼

1393 A249 $2 Sheet of 4, #a-d 6.00 6.00

John Denver (1943-97), Musician — A250

Placement of stamp on sheet: a, Top left. b, Top right. c, Bottom left. d, Bottom right.

2004, June 17 ***Perf. 13¾x13½***
1394 A250 $1.20 Sheet of 4, #a-d 3.75 3.75

2004 Summer Olympics, Athens — A251

Designs: 30c, Commemorative medal, 1968 Mexico City Olympics. 90c, Pentathlon. $1.80, Avery Brundage, Intl. Olympic Committee President. $3, Women's tennis, 1920 Antwerp Olympics, horiz.

2004, Sept. 7 **Litho.** ***Perf. 14¼***
1395-1398 A251 Set of 4 4.50 4.50

Intl. Year of Peace A252

No. 1399: a, Country name at right, dove's feet not visible. b, Country name at left. c, Country name at right, dove's feet visible.

2004, Sept. 7
1399 A252 $3 Sheet of 3, #a-c 7.00 7.00

Souvenir Sheet

Deng Xiaoping (1904-97), Chinese Leader — A253

2004, Sept. 7 ***Perf. 14***
1400 A253 $5 multi 4.00 4.00

D-Day, 60th Anniv. A254

No. 1401: a, HMCS Penetang. b, Landing Craft Infantry (Large). c, LCT (6). d, Landing Craft Tank (Rocket). e, Landing Barge Kitchen. f, Battleship Texas.
$6, HMS Scorpion.

2004, Sept. 7
1401 A254 $1.20 Sheet of 6, #a-f 5.50 5.50

Souvenir Sheet

1402 A254 $6 multi 4.50 4.50

Arthur and Friends A255

No. 1403 — Characters reading: a, Brain. b, Sue Ellen. c, Buster. d, Francine. e, Muffy. f, Binky.
No. 1404, $2 — Characters, with purple background: a, Arthur. b, D. W. c, Francine, looking right. d, Buster, diff.
No. 1405, $2 — Characters, with lilac background: a, Binky, diff. b, Sue Ellen, diff. c, Brain, diff. d, Francine, looking left.

2004, June 17 **Litho.** ***Perf. 14¼***
1403 A255 $1 Sheet of 6, #a-f 4.50 4.50

Sheets of 4, #a-d

1404-1405 A255 Set of 2 12.00 12.00

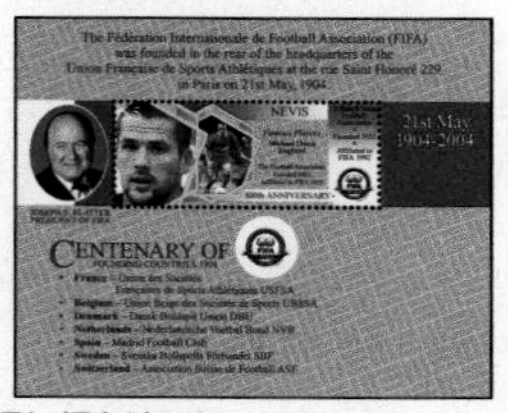

FIFA (Fédération Internationale de Football Association), Cent. — A256

Jason Berkley Joseph, Soccer Player A257

No. 1406: a, Nery Pumpido. b, Gary Lineker. c, Thomas Hassler. d, Sol Campbell.
No. 1407, Michael Owen.

2004, Nov. 29 ***Perf. 12¾x12½***
1406 A256 $2 Sheet of 4, #a-d 6.00 6.00

Souvenir Sheets

1407 A256 $5 multi 4.00 4.00
1408 A257 $5 multi 4.00 4.00

Marginal inscription on No. 1408, "100th Anniversary World Cup Soccer" is incorrect as the first World Cup was held in 1930.

Elvis Presley (1935-77) — A258

No. 1409 — Wearing checked shirt: a, Blue background. b, Bright red violet background.
No. 1410 — Color of sweater: a, Red. b, Orange yellow. c, Blue. d, Blue green. e, Red violet. f, Bright green.

2004, Nov. 29 ***Perf. 13½x13¼***
1409 A258 $1.20 Pair, #a-b 3.50 3.50
1410 A258 $1.20 Sheet of 6, #a-f 5.50 5.50

No. 1409 printed in sheets of 3 pairs.

Christmas — A259

Paintings by Norman Rockwell: 25c, Santa's Good Boys. 30c, Ride 'em Cowboy. 90c, Christmas Sing Merrilie. No. 1414, $5, The Christmas Newsstand.
No. 1415, $5, Is He Coming.

2004, Dec. 1 ***Perf. 12***
1411-1414 A259 Set of 4 5.00 5.00

Imperf

Size: 63x73mm

1415 A259 $5 multi 3.75 3.75

Locomotives, 200th Anniv. — A260

No. 1416: a, Steam Idyll, Indonesia. b, 2-8-2, Syria. c, Narrow gauge Mallet 0-4-4-0T, Portugal. d, Western Pacific Bo-Bo Road Switcher, US.
$5, LMS 5305, Great Britain.

2004, Dec. 13 ***Perf. 13¼x13½***
1416 A260 $3 Sheet of 4, #a-d 9.00 9.00

Souvenir Sheet

1417 A260 $5 multi 4.50 4.50

Reptiles and Amphibians — A261

No. 1418: a, Gekko gecko. b, Eyelash viper. c, Green iguana. d, Whistling frog.
$5, Hawksbill turtle.

2005, Jan. 10 ***Perf. 14***
1418 A261 $1.20 Sheet of 4, #a-d 4.50 4.50

Souvenir Sheet

1419 A261 $5 multi 4.50 4.50

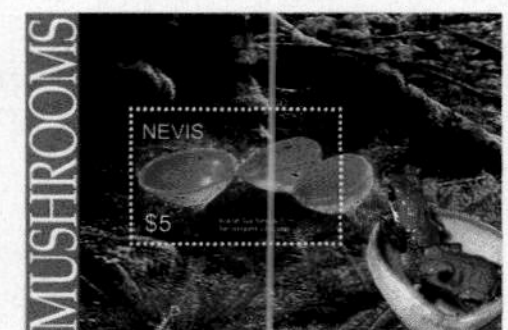

Mushrooms — A262

No. 1420: a, Xeromphalina campanella. b, Calvatia sculpta. c, Mitrula elegans. d, Aleuria aurantia.
$5, Scarlet cup.

2005, Jan. 10
1420 A262 $2 Sheet of 4, #a-d 7.00 7.00

Souvenir Sheet

1421 A262 $5 multi 4.50 4.50

Hummingbirds — A263

No. 1422: a, Rufous hummingbird. b, Green-crowned brilliant. c, Ruby-throated hummingbird. d, Purple-throated Carib.
$5, Magnificent hummingbird.

2005, Jan. 10 **Litho.** ***Perf. 14***
1422 A263 $2 Sheet of 4, #a-d 7.00 7.00

Souvenir Sheet

1423 A263 $5 multi 4.50 4.50

Sharks A264

No. 1424: a, Zebra shark. b, Caribbean reef shark. c, Blue shark. d, Bronze whaler.
$5, Blacktip reef shark.

2005, Jan. 10

1424	A264	$2 Sheet of 4, #a-d	7.00	7.00

Souvenir Sheet

1425	A264	$5 multi	4.50	4.50

Artist's Depictions of Hawksbill Turtles — A265

Artist: 30c, Leon Silcott. 90c, Kris Liburd. $1.20, Alice Webber. $5, Jeuaunito Huggins.

2005, Jan. 10

1426-1429	A265	Set of 4	6.00	6.00

Souvenir Sheet

New Year 2005 (Year of the Rooster) A266

No. 1430: a, Rooster, blue green background. b, Rooster silhouette, light green background. c, Rooster silhouette, blue background. d, Rooster, red violet background.

2005, Jan. 17 ***Perf. 12***

1430	A266	75c Sheet of 4, #a-d	2.50	2.50

Friedrich von Schiller (1759-1805), Writer — A267

No. 1431: a, Schiller, country name in pink. b, Schiller, country name in blue. c, Schiller's birthplace, Marbach, Germany.
$5, Statue of Schiller, Chicago.

2005, May 16 ***Perf. 12¾***

1431	A267	$3 Sheet of 3, #a-c	6.00	6.00

Souvenir Sheet

1432	A267	$5 multi	3.50	3.50

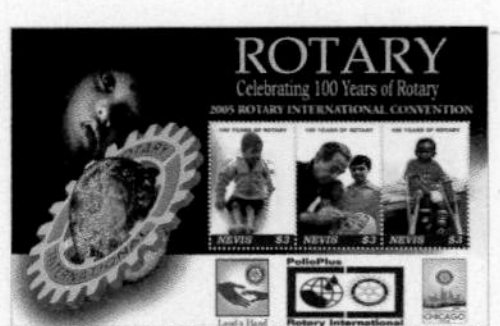

Rotary International, Cent. — A268

No. 1433, vert.: a, Barefoot child. b, Vaccination of child. c, Child with crutches and braces.
$5, Woman and children.

2005, May 16

1433	A268	$3 Sheet of 3, #a-c	6.00	6.00

Souvenir Sheet

1434	A268	$5 multi	3.50	3.50

Hans Christian Andersen (1805-75), Author — A269

No. 1435: a, The Little Mermaid. b, Thumbelina. c, The Snow Queen. d, The Emperor's New Clothes.
$6, Andersen.

2005, May 16

1435	A269	$2 Sheet of 4, #a-d	6.00	6.00

Souvenir Sheet

1436	A269	$6 multi	4.50	4.50

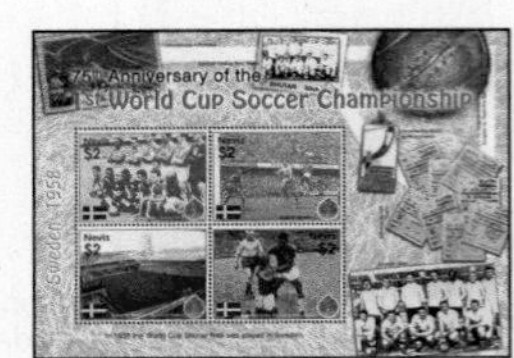
World Cup Soccer Championships, 75th Anniv. — A270

No. 1437: a, Brazil, 1958 champions. b, Scene from 1958 Brazil-Sweden final. c, Rasunda Stadium, Stockholm. d, Pele.
$5, 1958 Brazil team celebrating victory.

2005, May 16 **Litho.**

1437	A270	$2 Sheet of 4, #a-d	6.00	6.00

Souvenir Sheet

1438	A270	$5 multi	3.75	3.75

End of World War II, 60th Anniv. A271

No. 1439, $2: a, Gen. Charles de Gaulle. b, Gen. George S. Patton. c, Field Marshal Bernard Montgomery. d, Liberation of concentration camps. e, Political cartoon about end of war.

No. 1440, $2, horiz. — VJ Day: a, Flight crew of the Enola Gay. b, Atomic bomb mushroom cloud. c, Souvenir of Japanese surrender ceremony. d, Japanese delegation on USS Missouri. e, Gen. Douglas MacArthur speaking at surrender ceremony.

2005, May 16 ***Perf. 12¾***

Sheets of 5, #a-e

1439-1440	A271	Set of 2	16.50	16.50

Battle of Trafalgar, Bicent. — A272

Various ships and: 30c, Admiral William Cornwallis. 90c, Capt. Maurice Suckling. $1.20, Fleet Admiral Earl Howe. $3, Sir John Jervis.
$5, Earl Howe on the quarterdeck of the Queen Charlotte.

2005, May 16 ***Perf. 12¾***

1441-1444	A272	Set of 4	5.00	5.00

Souvenir Sheet

Perf. 12

1445	A272	$5 multi	4.25	4.25

A273

Prehistoric Animals — A274

Designs: 30c, Tyrannosaurus rex. No. 1447, $5, Hadrosaur.

No. 1448, $1.20: a, Apatosaurus. b, Camarasaurus. c, Iguanodon. d, Edmontosaurus. e, Centrosaurus. f, Euoplocephalus.

No. 1449, $1.20: a, Ouranosaurus. b, Parasaurolophus. c, Psittacosaurus. d, Stegosaurus. e, Scelidosaurus. f, Hypsilophodon.

No. 1450, $1.20, vert.: a, Deinotherium. b, Platybelodon. c, Palaeoloxodon. d, Arsinotherium. e, Procoptodon. f, Macrauchenia.

No. 1451, $5, Brontotherium. No. 1452, $5, Daspletosaurus. No. 1453, $5, Pliosaur.

2005, June 7 ***Perf. 12¾***

1446-1447	A273	Set of 2	4.25	4.25

Sheets of 6, #a-f

1448-1450	A274	Set of 3	16.50	16.50

Souvenir Sheets

1451-1453	A274	Set of 3	11.50	11.50

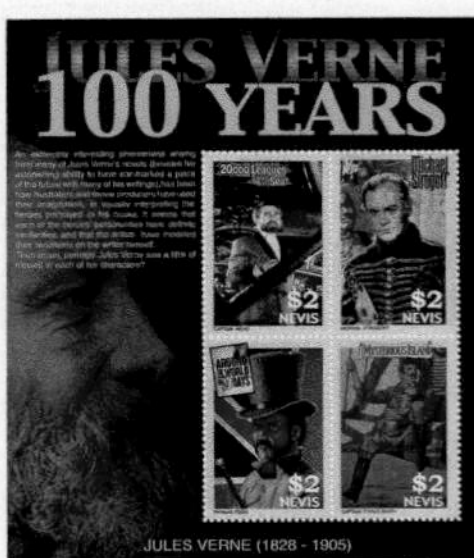

Jules Verne (1828-1905), Writer — A275

No. 1454 — Story characters: a, Captain Nemo, *20,000 Leagues Under the Sea*. b, Michael Strogoff, *Michael Strogoff*. c, Phileas Fogg, *Around the World in 80 Days*. d, Captain Cyrus Smith, *Mysterious Island*.
$5, Pat Boone, actor in movie, *Journey to the Center of the Earth*.

2005, June 17

1454	A275	$2 Sheet of 4, #a-d	6.50	6.50

Souvenir Sheet

1455	A275	$5 multi	4.25	4.25

2005 National Topical Stamp Show, Milwaukee (#1455).

Vatican City No. 66 A276

Pope John Paul II (1920-2005) A277

2005, July 12 ***Perf. 13x13¼***

1456	A276	90c multi	1.00	1.00

Perf. 13½x13¼

1457	A277	$4 multi	4.50	4.50

National Basketball Association Players — A278

Designs: No. 1458, $1, Shareef-Abdur Rahim (shown), Portland Trail Blazers. No. 1459, $1, Shaun Livingston, Los Angeles Clippers. No. 1460, $1, Vince Carter, New Jersey Nets. No. 1461, $1, Rasheed Wallace, Detroit Pistons.

No. 1462: a, Theo Ratliff, Portland Trail Blazers. b, Portland Trail Blazers emblem.

2005, July 26 ***Perf. 14***

1458-1461	A278	Set of 4	3.00	3.00
1462	A278	$1 Sheet, 10 #1462a, 2 #1462b	9.00	9.00

Souvenir Sheet

Sun Yat-sen (1866-1925), Chinese Leader — A279

No. 1463: a, Wearing blue suit, harbor in background. b, Wearing suit and tie. c, Wearing blue suit, statue in background. d, Wearing brown red suit.

2005, Aug. 19 **Litho.** ***Perf. 14***

1463	A279	$2 Sheet of 4, #a-d	5.00	5.00

Taipei 2005 Intl. Stamp Exhibition.

Christmas — A280

Designs: 25c, Madonna and the Angels, by Fra Angelico. 30c, Madonna and the Child, by Fra Filippo Lippi. 90c, Madonna and Child, by Giotto. $4, Madonna of the Chair, by Raphael.
$5, Adoration of the Magi, by Giovanni Batista Tiepolo, horiz.

2005, Dec. 1 ***Perf. 13½***

1464-1467	A280	Set of 4	4.75	4.75

Souvenir Sheet

1468	A280	$5 multi	4.25	4.25

U.S. Forest Service, Cent. (in 2005) — A281

No. 1469, vert.: a, Eldorado National Forest, California. b, Pisgah National Forest, North Carolina. c, Chattahoochee-Oconee National Forests, Georgia. d, Nantahala National Forest, North Carolina. e, Bridger-Teton National Forest, Wyoming. f, Mount Hood National Forest, Oregon.

No. 1470, $6, Klamath National Forest, California. No. 1471, $6, The Source Rain Forest Walk, Nevis, vert.

2006, Jan. 3
1469 A281 $1.60 Sheet of 6, #a-f 7.25 7.25

Souvenir Sheets

1470-1471 A281 Set of 2 9.00 9.00

A Dog, by Ren Xun — A282

2006, Jan. 3
1472 A282 75c multi .80 .80

New Year 2006 (Year of the Dog). Printed in sheets of 4.

Queen Elizabeth II, 80th Anniv. A283

No. 1473 — Queen wearing: a, Black hat with feather. b, No hat. c, Tiara. d, White hat. $5, As young woman.

2006, Mar. 20 Litho. *Perf. 13¼*
1473 A283 $2 Sheet of 4, #a-d 6.50 6.50

Souvenir Sheet

1474 A283 $5 multi 4.00 4.00

2006 Winter Olympics, Turin A284

Designs: 25c, U.S. #1796. 30c, Italy #705. 90c, Italy #707. $1.20, Emblem of 1980 Lake Placid Winter Olympics, vert. $4, Italy #708. $5, Emblem of 1956 Cortina d'Ampezzo Winter Olympics.

Perf. 14¼ (25c, $1.20), 13¼
2006, Apr. 24
1475-1480 A284 Set of 6 8.75 8.75

Mohandas K. Gandhi (1869-1948), Humanitarian A285

2006, May 27 *Perf. 12x11½*
1481 A285 $3 multi 3.00 3.00

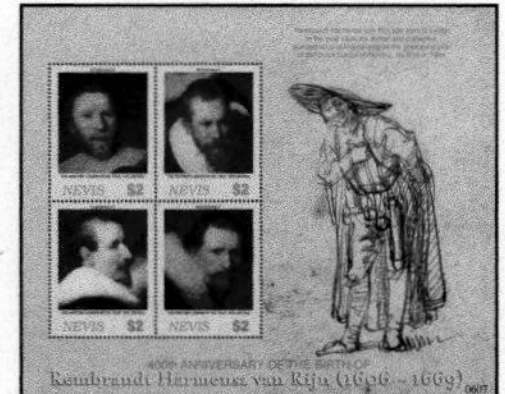

Rembrandt (1606-69), Painter — A286

No. 1482 — Various men from The Anatomy Lesson of Dr. Tulp.
$6, Bald-headed Old Man.

2006, June 23 *Perf. 13¼*
1482 A286 $2 Sheet of 4, a-d 6.00 6.00

Imperf
Size: 70x100mm

1483 A286 $6 multi 4.50 4.50

Miniature Sheets

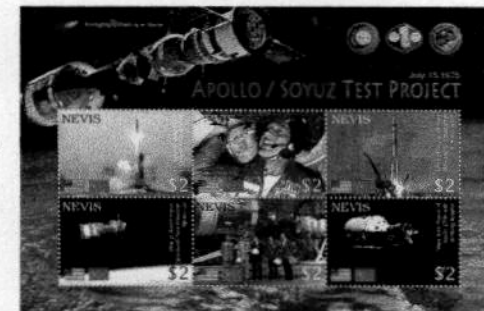

Space Achievements — A287

No. 1484 — Apollo-Soyuz: a, Liftoff of Saturn IB rocket . b, Astronaut Donald K. Slayton, Cosmonaut Aleksei A. Leonov. c, Liftoff of Soyuz 19. d, Soyuz in space. e, American and Soviet crews, model of docked spacecraft. f, Apollo in space.
No. 1485 — Viking I: a, Liftoff of Titan Centaur rocket. b, Viking I in flight. c, Model of Viking I on Mars. d, Mars.

2006, Sept. 11 *Perf. 13¼*
1484 A287 $2 Sheet of 6, #a-f 9.50 9.50
1485 A287 $3 Sheet of 4, #a-d 9.50 9.50

Christmas A288

Designs: 25c, Charlestown Christmas tree. 30c, Snowman decoration. 90c, Reindeer decorations. $4, Christmas tree and gifts, vert.
$6, Santa Claus and children.

2006, Dec. 8
1486-1489 A288 Set of 4 4.25 4.25

Souvenir Sheet

1490 A288 $6 multi 4.50 4.50

Scouting, Cent. — A289

Designs: $3, Flags, Map of Great Britain and Ireland. $5, Flags, bird, map, horiz.

2007, Jan. 29 Litho. *Perf. 13¼*
1491 A289 $3 multi 2.25 2.25

Souvenir Sheet

1492 A289 $5 multi 3.75 3.75

No. 1491 printed in sheets of 4.

Miniature Sheet

Marilyn Monroe (1926-62), Actress — A290

No. 1493 — Monroe: a, With head tilted. b, Wearing necklace. c, With lips closed. d, Wearing sash.

2007, Jan. 29
1493 A290 $2 Sheet of 4, #a-d 6.50 6.50

Cricket World Cup — A291

Designs: 90c, Cricket World Cup emblem, flag of St. Kitts and Nevis, map of Nevis. $2, Emblem and Runako Morton.
$6, Emblem.

2007, May 1 *Perf. 14*
1494-1495 A291 Set of 2 2.25 2.25

Souvenir Sheet

1496 A291 $6 multi 4.50 4.50

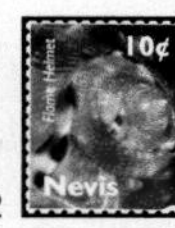

Shells — A292

Designs: 10c, Flame helmet. 25c, Rooster tail conch. 30c, Beaded periwinkle. 60c, Emperor helmet. 80c, Scotch bonnet. 90c Milk conch. $1, Beaded periwinkle, diff. $1.20, Alphabet cone. $1.80, Measled cowrie. $3, King helmet. $5, Atlantic hairy triton. $10, White-lined mitre. $20, Reticulated cowrie.

2007, July 5 *Perf. 12½x13¼*
1497 A292 10c multi .25 .25
1498 A292 25c multi .25 .25
1499 A292 30c multi .30 .30
1500 A292 60c multi .50 .50
1501 A292 80c multi .65 .65
1502 A292 90c multi .75 .75
1503 A292 $1 multi .80 .80
1504 A292 $1.20 multi 1.00 1.00
1505 A292 $1.80 multi 1.50 1.50
1506 A292 $3 multi 2.40 2.40
1507 A292 $5 multi 4.00 4.00
1508 A292 $10 multi 7.25 7.25
1509 A292 $20 multi 14.50 14.50
Nos. 1497-1509 (13) 34.15 34.15

Worldwide Fund for Nature (WWF) — A293

No. 1510 — Rainbow parrotfish: a, Facing left, white coral above fish. b, Two parrotfish. c, Facing left, ocean floor below fish. d, Facing right.

2007, July 23 *Perf. 13½*
1510 Strip of 4 4.00 4.00
a.-d. A293 $1.20 Any single .95 .95
e. Miniature sheet, 2 each #1510a-1510d 7.75 7.75

Flowers A294

No. 1511: a, Wild cilliment. b, Jumbie beads. c, Wild sage. d, Blood flower.
$6, Pink trumpet.

2007, July 23 *Perf. 13¼*
1511 A294 $2 Sheet of 4, #a-d 6.00 6.00

Souvenir Sheet

1512 A294 $6 multi 4.25 4.25

Butterflies — A295

No. 1513: a, Zetides swallowtail. b, Hahnel's Amazon swallowtail. c, Haitian mimic. d, Marbled white.
$6, Three-tailed tiger swallowtail.

2007, July 23
1513 A295 $2 Sheet of 4, #a-d 6.25 6.25

Souvenir Sheet

1514 A295 $6 multi 4.75 4.75

Miniature Sheet

Elvis Presley (1935-77) — A296

No. 1515 — Various photographs of Presley with: a, Denomination in white, country name in violet, laces showing on shirt. b, Denomination in blue. c, Denomination in bister. d, Denomination and country name in pink. e, Denomination in white, country name in pink. f, Denomination in white, country name in violet, laces not showing on shirt.

2007, Aug. 13
1515 A296 $1.20 Sheet of 6, #a-f 5.00 5.00

Princess Diana (1961-97) — A297

No. 1516: a, With head on hands. b, Wearing black dress. c, Wearing pink jacket. d, Wearing white dress.
$6, Wearing hat.

2007, Aug. 13
1516 A297 $2 Sheet of 4, #a-d 5.50 5.50

Souvenir Sheet

1517 A297 $6 multi 4.25 4.25

Miniature Sheets

Concorde — A298

No. 1518, $1.20 — Concorde with portions of globe in background: a, Western United States. b, Central United States. c, Atlantic Ocean and Eastern Canada. d, Central Pacific Ocean. e, Central America. f, Northeastern South America.
No. 1519, $1.20 — Concorde with: a, Green frame, white denomination. b, Red frame, blue denomination. c, Green frame, yellow denomination. d, Red frame, yellow denomination. e, Green frame, blue denomination. f, Red frame, white denomination.

2007, Aug. 13 Litho. *Perf. 13¼*
Sheets of 6, #a-f

1518-1519 A298 Set of 2 11.00 11.00

Pope Benedict XVI — A299

2007, Oct. 24

1520 A299 $1 multi .90 .90

Printed in sheets of 8.

Miniature Sheet

Wedding of Queen Elizabeth II and Prince Philip, 60th Anniv. A300

No. 1521 — Couple: a, Queen wearing tiara. b, Waving. c, Wearing feathered hats. d, In gilded coach, Queen in blue, waving. e, In coach, Queen with red hat, waving. f, On balcony, Queen waving.

2007, Oct. 24

1521 A300 $1.20 Sheet of 6, #a-f 6.00 6.00

Miniature Sheet

Inauguration of Pres. John F. Kennedy, 46th Anniv. — A301

No. 1522: a, Jacqueline Kennedy. b, John F. Kennedy, hands at side. c, John F. Kennedy, clapping. d, Vice president Lyndon B. Johnson.

2007, Nov. 28

1522 A301 $3 Sheet of 4, #a-d 8.00 8.00

First Helicopter Flight, Cent. — A302

No. 1523, horiz.: a, Westland Sea King. b, Schweizer N330TT. c, Sikorsky R-4/R-5. d, PZL Swidnik.
$6, MIL V-12.

2007, Nov. 28

1523 A302 $3 Sheet of 4, #a-d 9.00 9.00

Souvenir Sheet

1524 A302 $6 multi 4.50 4.50

Paintings by Qi Baishi (1864-1957) — A303

No. 1525: a, Begonias and Rock. b, Mother and Child. c, Fish and Bait. d, Solitary Hero.
$6, Chrysanthemums and Insects.

2007, Nov. 28 ***Perf. 12½***

1525 A303 $3 Sheet of 4, #a-d 8.00 8.00

Souvenir Sheet

Perf. 13¼

1526 A303 $6 multi 4.00 4.00

No. 1525 contains four 32x80mm stamps.

Christmas — A304

Paintings: 25c, The Rest on the Flight Into Egypt, by Federico Barocci. 30c, The Annunciation, by Barocci. 90c, The Annunciation, by Cavalier d'Arpino. $4, The Rest on the Flight Into Egypt, by Francesco Mancini.
$5, The Virgin and Child Between Saints Peter and Paul and the Twelve Magistrates of the Rota, by Antoniazzo Romano.

2007, Dec. 3 ***Perf. 11¼x11½***

1527-1530 A304 Set of 4 4.25 4.25

Souvenir Sheet

Perf. 13½

1531 A304 $5 multi 3.75 3.75

Miniature Sheet

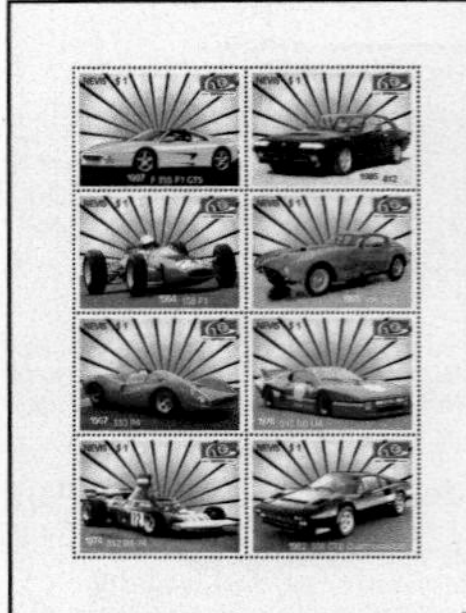

Ferrari Automobiles, 60th Anniv. — A305

No. 1532: a, 1997 F 355 F1 GTS. b, 1985 412. c, 1964 158 F1. d, 1953 375 MM. e, 1967 330 P4. f, 1978 512 BB LM. g, 1974 312 B3-74. h, 1982 308 GTB Quattrovalvole.

2007, Dec. 10 ***Perf. 13¼***

1532 A305 $1 Sheet of 8, #a-h 6.00 6.00

Miniature Sheet

2008 Summer Olympics, Beijing — A306

No. 1533: a, Cycling. b, Kayaking. c, Sailing. d, Equestrian.

2008, Mar. 8 **Litho.** ***Perf. 12¾***

1533 A306 $2 Sheet of 4, #a-d 6.00 6.00

Israel 2008 Intl. Philatelic Exhibition — A307

No. 1534 — Sites in Israel: a, Mt. Masada. b, Red Sea and mountains. c, Dead Sea. d, Sea of Galilee.
$5, Mt. Hermon.

2008, May 21 **Litho.** ***Perf. 11½x11¼***

1534 A307 $1.50 Sheet of 4, #a-d 4.50 4.50

Souvenir Sheet

1535 A307 $5 multi 3.75 3.75

32nd America's Cup Yacht Races A308

No. 1536 — Various yachts: a, $1.20. b, $1.80. c, $3. d, $5.

2007, Dec. 31 **Litho.** ***Perf. 13½***

1536 A308 Block of 4, #a-d 8.25 8.25

No. 1536 was not made available until late 2008.

Miniature Sheets

A309

Muhammad Ali, Boxer — A310

No. 1537 — Ali: a, In ring with fists at side. b, In ring, opponent at right. c, In ring, opponent punching. d, With arm on ropes. e, With arms raised. f, Receiving trophy.
No. 1538 — Ali: a, Facing left, face in background. b, With microphones, at bottom. c, Facing left, with microphone at left. d, With large microphone at LL.

2008, Sept. 3 **Litho.** ***Perf. 11½x12***

1537 A309 $1.80 Sheet of 6, #a-f 7.75 7.75

Perf. 13¼

1538 A310 $2 Sheet of 4, #a-d 6.00 6.00

Miniature Sheet

Elvis Presley (1935-77) — A311

No. 1539 — Presley with guitar: a, Microphone at right, both hands on guitar. b, Microphone at left, hand on neck of guitar. c, With audience at LL. d, Microphone at left, no hands shown. e, Wearing blue shirt. f, Microphone at right, with hands off guitar.

2008, Sept. 3 ***Perf. 13¼***

1539 A311 $1.80 Sheet of 6, #a-f 8.00 8.00

Miniature Sheet

Visit to New York of Pope Benedict XVI A312

No. 1540 — Pope Benedict XVI and background with: a, Gray spot to left of "N" in "Nevis." b, Left half of United Nations emblem. c, Right half of United Nations Emblem. d, Gray spot between "E" and "V" in "Nevis."

2008, Sept. 17

1540 A312 $2 Sheet of 4, #a-d 6.25 6.25

Geothermal Well — A313

2008, Sept. 19 ***Perf. 11½***

1541 A313 $5 multi 4.50 4.50

Independence, 25th anniv.

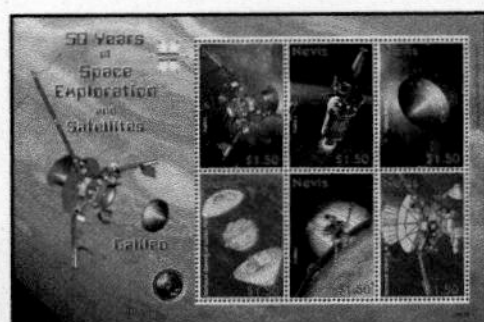

A314

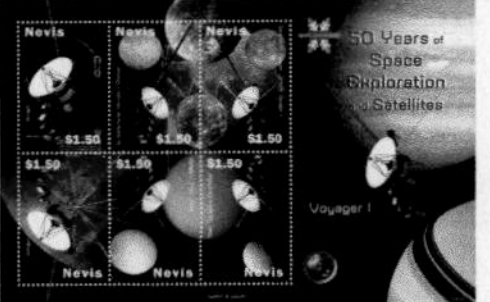

Space Exploration, 50th Anniv. — A315

No. 1542: a, Galileo spacecraft with arms extended, stars in background. b, Galileo on booster rocket. c, Galileo probe. d, Technical drawing of Galileo probe. e, Galileo, planet and moon. f, Technical drawing of Galileo.
No. 1543: a, Voyager 1 and ring diagram. b, Io, Ganymede, Voyager 1 and Callisto. c, Ganymede, Europa, Callisto and Voyager 1. d, Voyager 1 and radiating line diagram. e, Voyager 1, Titan and Dione. f, Titan, Voyager 1 and Enceladus.
No. 1544: a, Technical drawing of Apollo 11 command module. b, Saturn V rocket on launch pad. c, Edwin E. Aldrin on Moon. d, Technical drawing of Apollo 11 lunar module.
No. 1545: a, Van Allen radiation belt. b, Technical drawing of Explorer 1. c, James Van Allen. d, Explorer 1 above Earth.

2008, Dec. 3 ***Perf. 13¼***

1542 A314 $1.50 Sheet of 6, #a-f 7.00 7.00
1543 A315 $1.50 Sheet of 6, #a-f 7.00 7.00
1544 A314 $2 Sheet of 4, #a-d 6.25 6.25
1545 A315 $2 Sheet of 4, #a-d 6.25 6.25

Christmas A316

Traditional holiday foods: 25c, Roast pig. 30c, Fruit cake. 80c, Pumpkin pie. 90c, Sorrel drink. $2, Fruit cake, diff.
$6, Baked ham and turkey, vert.

2008, Dec. 5 ***Perf. 11½***

1546-1550 A316 Set of 5 3.25 3.25

Souvenir Sheet

1551 A316 $6 multi 4.75 4.75

Miniature Sheet

Inauguration of U.S. President Barack Obama — A317

No. 1552 — Pres. Obama and, in background: a, Window. b, Flag and chair. c, White House and flowers. d, Chair.

2009, Jan. 20 **Litho.** ***Perf. 11½x12***

1552 A317 $3 Sheet of 4, #a-d 8.25 8.25

Agricultural Open Day, 15th Anniv. — A318

Designs: 25c, Fruits and packaged foods. 30c, Fruits. 90c, Goats. $5, Workers propagating plants.
$6, Entertainment at fair.

2009, Mar. 26 *Perf. 11½*

1553-1556 A318 Set of 4 5.00 5.00

Souvenir Sheet

Perf. 13½

1557 A318 $6 multi 4.75 4.75

No. 1557 contains one 51x37mm stamp.

Miniature Sheets

A319

China 2009 World Stamp Exhibition, Luoyang — A320

No. 1558 — Olympic Sports: a, Shooting. b, Field hockey. c, Taekwondo. d, Softball.
No. 1559 — Emperor Hsuan-yeh (Kangxi) (1654-1722): a, Wearing blue robe. b, Wearing Robe with blue sleeves. c, Wearing robe with yellow sleeves. d, At desk.

2009, Apr. 10 *Perf. 14x14¾*

1558 A319 $1.40 Sheet of 4, #a-d 4.25 4.25

Perf. 12¾x12½

1559 A320 $1.40 Sheet of 4, #a-d 4.25 4.25

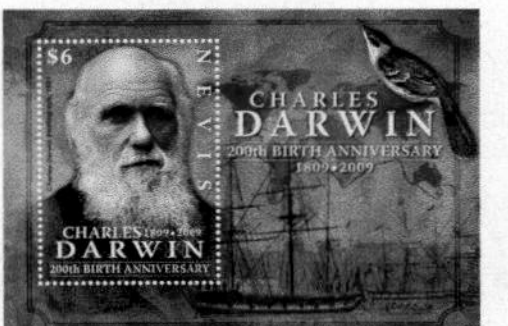

Charles Darwin (1809-82), Naturalist — A321

No. 1560, horiz.: a, Marine iguana. b, Statue of Darwin, Shrewsbury, England. c, Platypus. d, Vampire bat. e, Painting of Darwin by George Richmond. f, Large ground finch.
$6, 1881 colorized photograph of Darwin

2009, June 15 *Perf. 11½*

1560 A321 $2 Sheet of 6, #a-f 9.00 9.00

Souvenir Sheet

Perf. 13¼

1561 A321 $6 multi 4.50 4.50

No. 1560 contains six 40x30mm stamps.

Dolphins and Whales A322

No. 1562: a, Amazon River dolphin. b, Indus river dolphin. c, Atlantic white-sided dolphin. d, La Plata dolphin. e, Peale's dolphin. f, White-beaked dolphin.
No. 1563: a, Long-finned pilot whale. b, Short-finned pilot whale.
No. 1564: a, Killer whale. b, Pygmy killer whale.

2009, June 15 *Perf. 13¼*

1562 A322 $2 Sheet of 6, #a-f 9.00 9.00

Souvenir Sheets

1563 A322 $3 Sheet of 2, #a-b 4.75 4.75
1564 A322 $3 Sheet of 2, #a-b 4.75 4.75

Souvenir Sheets

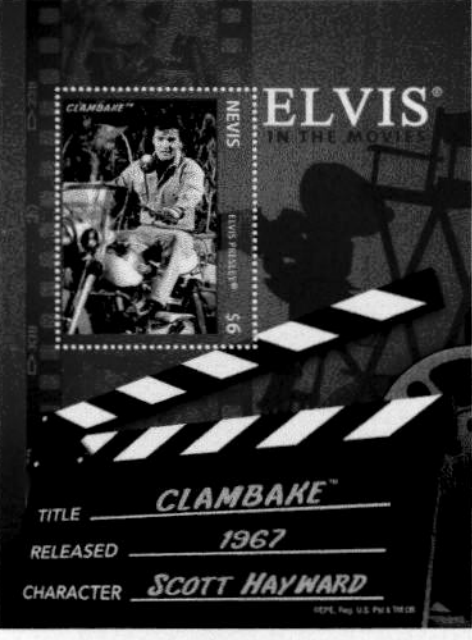

A323

A324

A325

Elvis Presley (1935-77) — A326

2009, June 15 *Perf. 13¼*

1565 A323 $6 multi 4.50 4.50
1566 A324 $6 multi 4.50 4.50
1567 A325 $6 multi 4.50 4.50
1568 A326 $6 multi 4.50 4.50
Nos. 1565-1568 (4) 18.00 18.00

Miniature Sheet

The Three Stooges A328

No. 1570: a, Moe Howard, Curly Howard and Larry Fine. b, Curly Howard. c, Moe Howard. d, Larry Fine.

2009, Aug. 20 *Perf. 11½*

1570 A328 $2.50 Sheet of 4, #a-d 7.25 7.25

Miniature Sheet

Pope Benedict XVI A329

No. 1571 — Pope Benedict XVI: a, Wearing miter, brown frame. b, Wearing miter, bister frame. c, Wearing zucchetto and eyeglasses, brown frame. d, Wearing zucchetto and eyeglasses, bister frame.

2009, Aug. 20

1571 A329 $3 Sheet of 4, #a-d 9.00 9.00

Miniature Sheets

A330

Michael Jackson (1958-2009) — A331

No. 1572 — Jackson with country name in: a, Blue. b, Yellow. c, Lilac. d, Red.
No. 1573 — Jackson: a, With microphone near mouth, hands raised. b, With arms extended to side. c, Holding microphone. d, With people in background.

Perf. 11¼x11½

2009, Sept. 25 **Litho.**

1572 A330 $2 Sheet of 4, #a-d 6.00 6.00

Perf. 11½x12

1573 A331 $3 Sheet of 4, #a-d 8.50 8.50

Worldwide Fund for Nature (WWF) — A332

No. 1574 — Caribbean reef squid with denomination in: a, Pink and blue. b, Pink. c, Orange and red. d, Green and blue.

2009, Dec. 1 *Perf. 13¼*

1574 Strip or block of 4 6.25 6.25
a.-d. A332 $2 Any single 1.50 1.50
e. Sheet of 8, 2 each #1574a-1574d 12.00 12.00

Flowers — A333

Designs: 25c, Genipa americana. 50c, Clusia rosea. 80c, Browallia americana. 90c, Bidens alba. $1, Begonia odorata. $5, Jatropha gossypiifolia.
No. 1581: a, Crantzia cristata. b, Selaginella flabellata. c, Hibiscus tiliaceus. d, Heliconia psittacorum.

2009, Dec. 1 **Litho.** *Perf. 13x13¼*

1575-1580 A333 Set of 6 6.75 6.75
1581 A333 $2.50 Sheet of 4, #a-d 8.00 8.00

Christmas A334

Designs: 25c, Magi on camels. 30c, Holy Family. 90c, Magus and camel in stars. $5, Holy Family and angels.

2009, Dec. 7 **Litho.** *Perf. 14¾x14¼*

1582-1585 A334 Set of 4 5.00 5.00

First Man on the Moon, 40th Anniv. A335

No. 1586: a, Astronaut Neil Armstrong, Saturn V rocket. b, Astronauts Edwin "Buzz" Aldrin and Michael Collins. c, Apollo 11 command module, Moon. d, Apollo 11 lunar module leaving Moon.
$6, Armstrong and lunar module.

2009, Dec. 30 **Litho.** *Perf. 11½x12*

1586 A335 $2.50 Sheet of 4, #a-d 8.00 8.00

Souvenir Sheet

Perf. 11½x11¼

1587 A335 $6 multi 5.00 5.00

Intl. Year of Astronomy.

Miniature Sheet

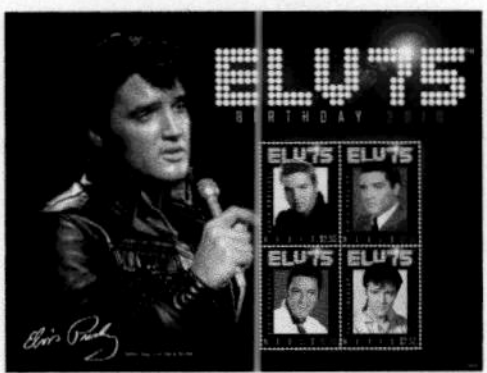

Elvis Presley (1935-77) — A336

No. 1588 — Presley wearing: a, Black jacket. b, Brown suit and blue shirt. c, White shirt with red neckerchief. d, Blue shirt.

2010, Mar. 2 **Litho.** *Perf. 12x11½*

1588 A336 $2.50 Sheet of 4, #a-d 7.25 7.25

Ferrari Race Cars and Parts — A337

No. 1589, $1.25: a, Engine diagram of 1947 125 S. b, 1947 125 S.
No. 1590, $1.25: a, Engine of 1951 500 F2. b, 1951 500 F2.
No. 1591, $1.25: a, Exhaust pipe of 1953 553 F2. b, 1953 553 F2.
No. 1592, $1.25: a, Engine of 1957 Dino 156 F2. b, 1957 Dino 156 F2.

2010, Mar. 2 ***Perf. 12***
Vert. Pairs, #a-b
1589-1592 A337 Set of 4 8.00 8.00

Mushrooms — A338

Designs: 25c, Psilocybe guilartensis. 80c, Alboleptonia flavifolia. $1, Agaricus sp. $5, Psilocybe caerulescens.
No. 1597: a, Psilocybe portoricensis. b, Boletus ruborculus. c, Psilocybe plutonia (one). d, Alboleptonia largentii. e, Psilocybe plutonia (three). f, Collybia aurea.

2010, Mar. 24 **Litho.** ***Perf. 11½***
1593-1596 A338 Set of 4 5.25 5.25
1597 A338 $1.50 Sheet of 6, #a-f 6.75 6.75

A339

A340

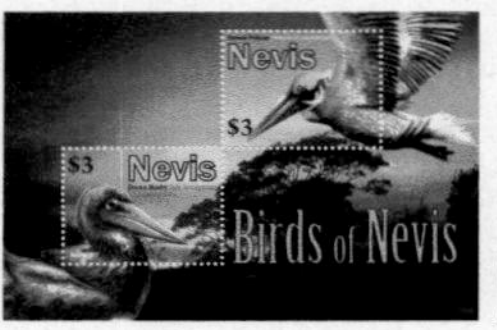
Birds A341

Designs: 30c, Great blue heron. 90c, Magnificent frigatebird. $1, Masked booby. $5, Great egret.
No. 1602: a, White-tailed tropicbird. b, Audubon's shearwater. c, Red-billed tropicbird. d, Leach's storm petrel.
No. 1603: a, Brown pelican. b, Brown booby.

2010, May 21 ***Perf. 11½***
1598-1601 A339 Set of 4 6.00 6.00
1602 A340 $2 Sheet of 4, #a-d 6.50 6.50

Souvenir Sheet
Perf. 11½x12
1603 A341 $3 Sheet of 2, #a-b 5.00 5.00

Miniature Sheets

A342

Election of Pres. John F. Kennedy, 50th Anniv. A343

No. 1604 — Denomination in red: a, Kennedy. b, USSR Premier Nikita Khrushchev. c, Khrushchev on sofa. d, Kennedy on sofa.
No. 1605 — Denomination in white: a, Pres. Richard M. Nixon, color photograph. b, Kennedy, color photograph. c, Kennedy, black-and-white photograph. d, Nixon, black-and-white photograph.

2010, May 21 **Litho.** ***Perf. 13¼***
1604 A342 $3 Sheet of 4, #a-d 8.50 8.50
1605 A343 $3 Sheet of 4, #a-d 8.50 8.50

Girl Guides, Cent. A344

No. 1606: a, Four Girl Guides and adult leader. b, Four Girl Guides. c, Girl Guide climbing rock. d, Three Girl Guides.
$6, Four Girl Guides, vert.

2010, May 21 ***Perf. 11½x12***
1606 A344 $3 Sheet of 4, #a-d 9.00 9.00

Souvenir Sheet
Perf. 11¼x11½
1607 A344 $6 multi 4.50 4.50

A345

Whales A346

Designs: $1.20, Minke whale. $1.80, Northern right whale. $3, Fin whale. $5, Sei whale. $6, Blue whale.

2010, July 14 ***Perf. 13x13¼***
1608-1611 A345 Set of 4 9.00 9.00

Souvenir Sheet
1612 A346 $6 multi 5.00 5.00

Souvenir Sheet

Sea Mammals — A347

No. 1613: a, Caribbean monk seal. b, West Indian manatee.

2010, July 14
1613 A347 $3 Sheet of 2, #a-b 5.00 5.00

Miniature Sheet

John F. Kennedy's 1960 US Presidential Campaign Buttons — A348

No. 1614: a, "Vote Kennedy for President." b, "For President John F. Kennedy." c, "Kennedy Johnson." d, "America Needs Kennedy Johnson."

2010, Sept. 8 ***Perf.***
1614 A348 $2 Sheet of 4, #a-d 6.50 6.50

Orchids A349

No. 1615, horiz.: a, Heart-lipped brassavola. b, Waunakee Sunset. c, Moss-loving cranichis. d, Longclaw orchid. e, Golden yellow cattleya. f, Fat Cat.
$6, Von Martin's brassavola.

2010, Sept. 8 ***Perf. 11½x12***
1615 A349 $2 Sheet of 6, #a-f 9.50 9.50

Souvenir Sheet
Perf. 11½
1616 A349 $6 multi 5.00 5.00

Henri Dunant (1828-1910), Founder of Red Cross — A350

No. 1617 — Dunant and: a, Bertha von Suttner. b, Victor Hugo. c, Charles Dickens. d, Harriet Beecher Stowe.
$6, Dunant and scene of abolition of slavery in Washington, DC.

2010, Sept. 8 ***Perf. 13x13¼***
1617 A350 $2.50 Sheet of 4, #a-d 7.50 7.50

Souvenir Sheet
1618 A350 $6 multi 4.50 4.50

A351

Princess Diana (1961-97) — A352

No. 1619 — Princess Diana wearing: a, Black hat, black jacket. b, Black and white hat, white dress. c, Tiara.
$3, White dress, no hat.

2010, Dec. 6 ***Perf. 12***
1619 A351 $2 Vert. strip of 3, #a-c 4.50 4.50
1620 A352 $3 multi 2.25 2.25

No. 1619 was printed in sheets containing 2 of each stamp. No. 1620 was printed in sheets of 4.

Christmas — A353

Paintings: 30c, Annunciation, by Paolo Uccello. 90c, The Altarpiece of the Rose Garlands, by Albrecht Dürer. $1.80, Like 30c. $2, Sistine Madonna, by Raphael. $2.30, Like $2. $3, The Adoration of the Magi, by Giotto di Bondone.

2010, Dec. 6 ***Perf. 12***
1621-1626 A353 Set of 6 8.00 8.00

A354

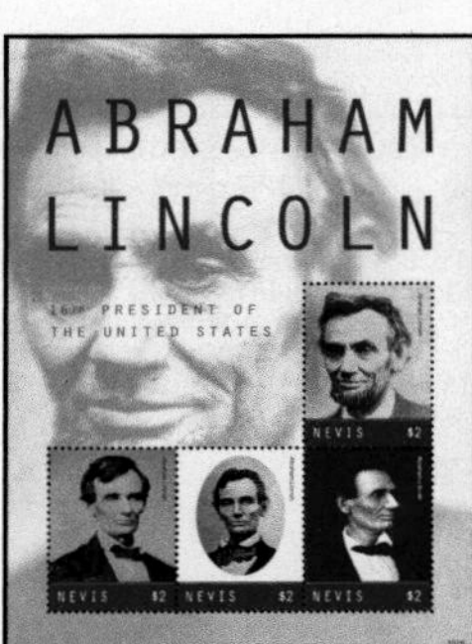
Pres. Abraham Lincoln (1809-65) — A355

No. 1628 — Lincoln: a, With buff background. b, With gray background. c, Oval photograph. d, With black background.

2010, Dec. 10 ***Perf. 11½***
1627 A354 $2 black 1.50 1.50
1628 A355 $2 Sheet of 4, #a-d 6.00 6.00

Bank of Nevis — A356

Designs: 30c, Old building. $5, New building.

2010, Dec. 9 **Litho.** ***Perf. 11¼x11½***
1629-1630 A356 Set of 2 4.00 4.00

Pope John Paul II (1920-2005) — A357

Pope John Paul II wearing: $3, Miter. $4, Red hat.

2010, Dec. 10 ***Perf. 14x14¾***
1631-1632 A357 Set of 2 5.00 5.00

No. 1631 was printed in sheets of 4; No. 1632, in sheets of 3.

Elvis Presley (1935-77) — A358

Presley wearing: No. 1633, $3, Black jacket, white shirt. No. 1634, $3, Red shirt.

2010, Dec. 10

1633-1634	A358	Set of 2	4.00	4.00

Nos. 1633-1634 each were printed in sheets of 4.

2010 World Cup Soccer Championships, South Africa — A359

No. 1635, $1.50: a, Marek Hamsik. b, Giovanni Van Bronckhorst. c, Robert Vittek. d, Eljero Elia. e, Miroslav Stoch. f, Dirk Kuyt.

No. 1636, $1.50: a, Lucio. b, Alexis Sanchez. c, Dani Alves. d, Arturo Vidal. e, Gilberto Silva. f, Rodrigo Tello.

No. 1637, $1.50: a, Liedson. b, Xavi Hernandez. c, Simao. d, Jasper Juinen. e, Cristiano Ronaldo. f, David Villa.

No. 1638, $1.50: a, Paulo Da Silva. b, Yoshito Okubo. c, Edgar Barreto. d, Yuichi Komano. e, Cristian Riveros. f, Yasuhito Endo.

No. 1639, $1.50: a, Netherlands coach Bert van Marwijk. b, Joris Mathijsen.

No. 1640, $1.50: a, Brazil coach Dunga. b, Kaka.

No. 1641, $1.50: a, Spain coach Vicente del Bosque. b, Sergio Ramos.

No. 1642, $1.50: a, Paraguay coach Gerardo Martino. b, Roque Santa Cruz.

2010, Dec. 10 ***Perf. 12***

Sheets of 6, #a-f

1635-1638	A359	Set of 4	27.00	27.00

Souvenir Sheets of 2, #a-b

1639-1642	A359	Set of 4	10.00	10.00

Trip to India of U.S. President Barack Obama — A360

No. 1643: a, Barack and Michelle Obama leaving Air Force One. b, Pres. Obama addressing Indian students in Mumbai. c, Pres. Obama signing Mumbai terrorist attacks condolence book. d, Pres. Obama and Indian Prime Minister Manmohan Singh. $6, Pres. Obama addressing Indian students in Mumbai, horiz.

2010, Dec. 10 ***Perf. 14¼x14¾***

1643	A360	$3 Sheet of 4, #a-d	9.00	9.00

Souvenir Sheet

Perf. 14¾x14¼

1644	A360	$6 multi	4.50	4.50

Indipex 2011, New Delhi.

Engagement of Prince William and Catherine Middleton — A361

No. 1645: a, Arms of Prince William (38mm diameter). b, Buckingham Palace (86x40mm arc-shaped). c, Catherine Middleton, black-and-white photo (86x40mm arc-shaped). d, Prince William, black-and-white photo (86x40mm arc-shaped).

No. 1646: a, Couple (86x40mm arc-shaped). b, Catherine Middleton, color photo (86x40mm arc-shaped). c, Prince William, color photo (86x40mm arc-shaped). $6, Couple, diff.

2010, Dec. 30 ***Perf. 13***

1645	A361	$3 Sheet of 4, #a-d	9.00	9.00
1646	A361	$3 Sheet of 4, #1645a, 1646a-1646c	9.00	9.00

Souvenir Sheet

Perf. 11½x11¼

1647	A361	$6 multi	4.50	4.50

No. 1647 contains one 40x30mm stamp.

Miniature Sheets

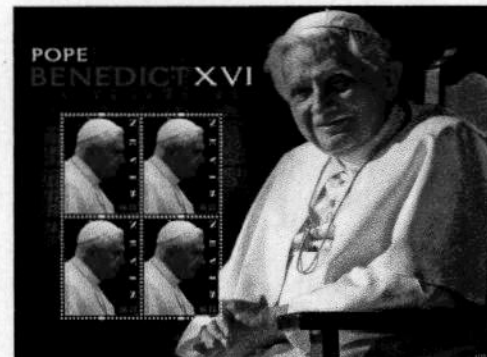

A362

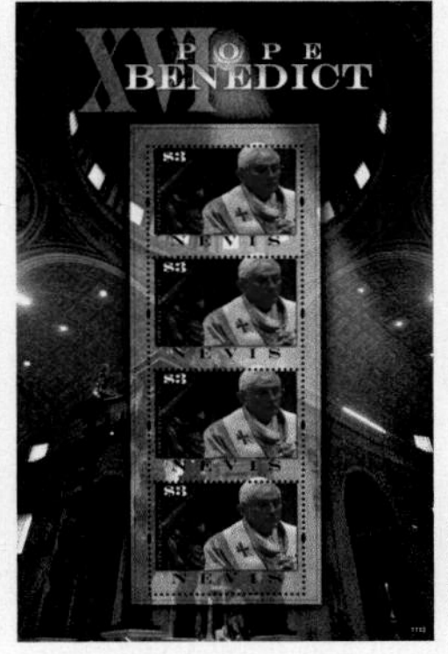

Pope Benedict XVI A363

No. 1648 — Pope Benedict XVI with: a, Part of white stole outside frame line at LR. b, Black areas outside of frame line.

No. 1649 — Pope Benedict with: a, Windows under "N," "V" and "S" in country name. b, Protruding corner of ceiling to left of "N" in country name. c, White area under "N" in country name. d, Cross and head of statue under "V" of country name.

2011, Mar. 30 ***Perf. 13 Syncopated***

1648	A362	$3 Sheet of 4, #1648a, 3 #1648b	9.00	9.00
1649	A363	$3 Sheet of 4, #a-d	9.00	9.00

Mohandas K. Gandhi (1869-1948), Indian Nationalist — A364

Gandhi and: No. 1650, $3, Orange panel at bottom. No. 1651, $3, Red brown panel at left.

2011, Mar. 30 ***Perf. 12***

1650-1651	A364	Set of 2	5.00	5.00

Nos. 1650-1651 each were printed in sheets of 4.

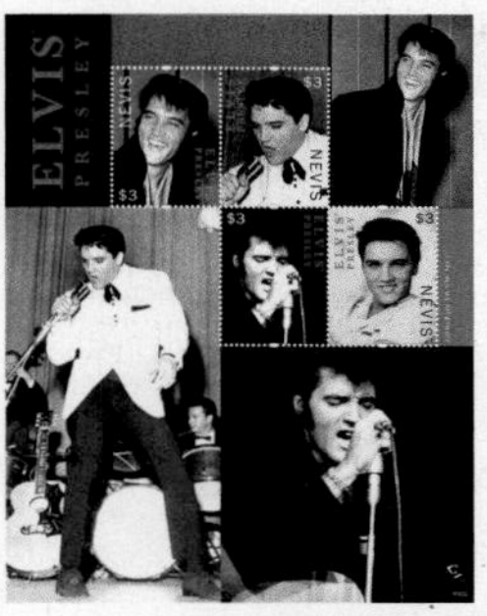

A365

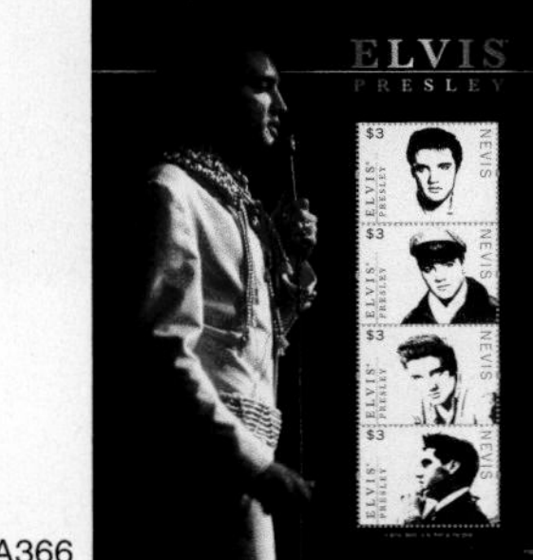

A366

A367

A368

A369

Elvis Presley (1935-77) — A370

No. 1652 — Presley and: a, Country name in white at UL. b, Country name in black at LR, Presley holding microphone. c, No country name. d, Country name in black at LL, no microphone shown.

No. 1653 — Presley: a, Head and neck only. b, Wearing hat. c, Wearing jacket. d, Touching his chin.

2011, Mar. 30 ***Perf. 13 Syncopated***

1652	A365	$3 Sheet of 4, #a-d	9.00	9.00
1653	A366	$3 Sheet of 4, #a-d	9.00	9.00

Souvenir Sheets

Perf. 12½

1654	A367	$6 multi	4.50	4.50
1655	A368	$6 multi	4.50	4.50
1656	A369	$6 multi	4.50	4.50
1657	A370	$6 multi	4.50	4.50
		Nos. 1654-1657 (4)	18.00	18.00

Miniature Sheets

Cats A371

No. 1658, $2.50: a, Maine Coon cat. b, Norwegian Forest cat. c, Ragdoll cat. d, Turkish Angora cat.

No. 1659: $2.50: a, Russian Blue cat. b, Siamese cat. c, Abyssinan cat. d, Bombay cat.

2011, Apr. 4 ***Perf. 12***

Sheets of 4, #a-d

1658-1659	A371	Set of 2	15.00	15.00

Butterflies — A372

No. 1660: a, Meadow argus. b, Gulf fritillary. c, Eastern tiger swallowtail. d, Gabb's checkerspot. e, Indian leafwing. f, Blue diadem.

$6, Monarch butterfly.

2011, Apr. 4 ***Perf. 13 Syncopated***

1660	A372	$2 Sheet of 6, #a-f	10.00	10.00

Souvenir Sheet

Perf. 12

1661	A372	$6 multi	5.00	5.00

British Royalty — A373

Designs: No. 1662, Prince Philip.

No. 1663 — Queen Elizabeth II wearing: a, White dress. b, Lilac dress.

No. 1664, King George V. No. 1665, King George VI.

2011, Apr. 4 ***Perf. 13 Syncopated***

1662	A373	$2 multi	1.50	1.50
1663	A373	$2 Pair, #a-b	3.00	3.00
1664	A373	$3 multi	2.25	2.25
1665	A373	$3 multi	2.25	2.25
		Nos. 1662-1665 (4)	9.00	9.00

Nos. 1662, 1664-1665 each were printed in sheets of 4. No. 1663 was printed in sheet containing two pairs.

Miniature Sheets

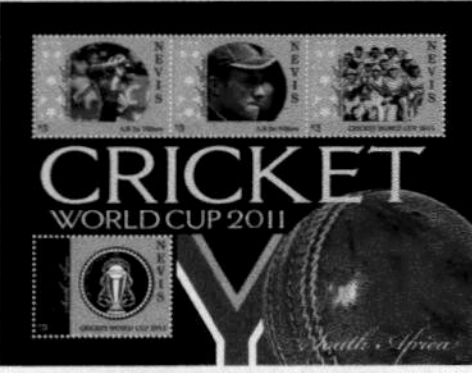

2011 Cricket World Cup, India, Bangladesh and Sri Lanka — A374

No. 1666 — Inscribed "South Africa," with dull orange background: a, A. B. De Villiers batting. b, Close-up of De Villiers. c, Posed photograph of South Africa team. d, Cricket World Cup.

No. 1667 — Inscribed "South Africa," with orange background: a, Like #1666a. b, Like #1666b. c, South Africa team celebrating. d, Like #1666d.

No. 1668 — Inscribed "Pakistan," with olive green background: a, Shoaib Akhtar running. b, Close-up of Akhtar. c, Pakistan team. d Like #1666d.

No. 1669 — Inscribed "Sri Lanka," with red brown background: a, Kumar Sangakkara on cricket pitch. b, Close-up of Sangakkara. c, Sri Lanka team. d, Like #1666d.

No. 1670 — Inscribed "West Indies," with dark red background: a, Chris Gayle holding on cricket bat. b, Close-up of Gayle. c, West Indies team. d, Like #1666d.

2011, Apr. 4 ***Perf. 12***

1666 A374 $3 Sheet of 4, #a-d 9.00 9.00
1667 A374 $3 Sheet of 4, #a-d 9.00 9.00
1668 A374 $3 Sheet of 4, #a-d 9.00 9.00
1669 A374 $3 Sheet of 4, #a-d 9.00 9.00
1670 A374 $3 Sheet of 4, #a-d 9.00 9.00
Nos. 1666-1670 (5) 45.00 45.00

Wedding of Prince William and Catherine Middleton — A375

No. 1671: a, Groom facing right. b, Bride waving.

No. 1672: a, Bride. b, Groom facing forward. c, Couple in coach, facing left, groom waving.

No. 1673: a, Couple standing. b, Couple in coach, facing right, groom waving.

2011, Apr. 29 **Litho.** ***Perf. 12***

1671 A375 $3 Pair, #a-b 4.50 4.50
1672 A375 $3 Sheet of 4, #1672a-1672b, 2 #1672c 9.00 9.00

Souvenir Sheet

1673 A375 $6 Sheet of 2, #a-b 9.00 9.00

No. 1671 was printed in sheets containing two pairs.

Miniature Sheets

Pres. Abraham Lincoln (1809-65) — A376

No. 1674, $2: a, Union soldier. b, Civil War era illustration with shield, books, wounded snake. c, Union soldiers in trenches. d, Lincoln.

No. 1675, $2 — Lincoln and quotes: a, "Government of the people, by the people, for the people shall not perish from the Earth." b, "The best way to destroy an enemy is to make him a friend." c, "A house divided against itself cannot stand." d, "Avoid popularity if you would have peace."

2011, June 20 ***Perf. 13 Syncopated***

Sheets of 4, #a-d

1674-1675 A376 Set of 2 12.00 12.00

U.S. Civil War, 150th anniv.

Miniature Sheets

Princess Diana (1961-97) — A377

No. 1676, $2 — Red panel, Princess Diana: a, Facing forward, wearing dress with dark collar. b, Wearing sailor's cap. c, Facing left, wearing striped blouse. d, Wearing maroon hat.

No. 1677, $2 — Yellow panel, Princess Diana wearing: a, Purple jacket. b, Black and white hat. c, Black jacket. d, Red dress.

2011, June 20 ***Perf. 12***

Sheets of 4, #a-d

1676-1677 A377 Set of 2 12.00 12.00

A378

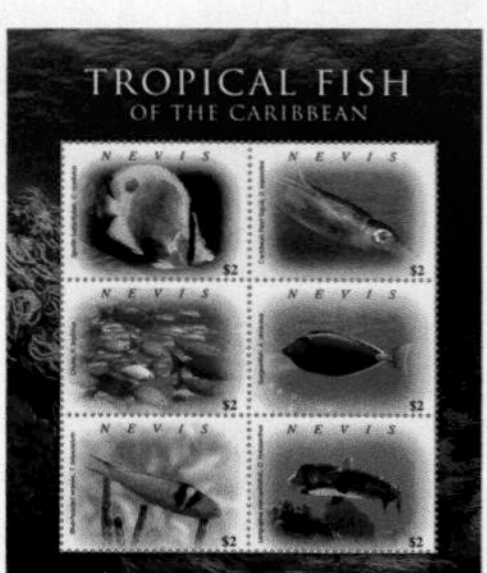

A379

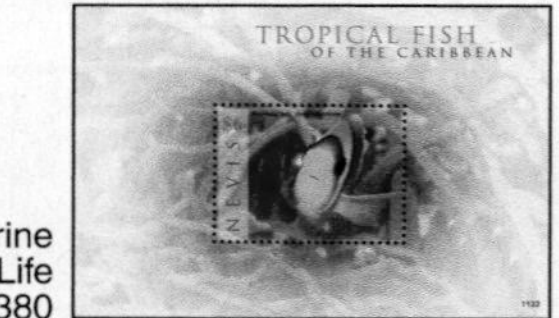

Marine Life A380

Designs: 10c, Blue stripe grunt. 30c, Red hind. 40c, Red snapper. $5, Old wife.

No. 1682: a, Spotfin butterflyfish. b, Caribbean reef squid. c, Chubs. d, Surgeonfish. e, Blue-headed wrasse. f, Long-spine porcupinefish.

$6, Anemonefish.

2011, July 6 ***Perf. 12***

1678-1681 A378 Set of 4 4.50 4.50
1682 A379 $2 Sheet of 6, #a-f 9.00 9.00

Souvenir Sheet

1683 A380 $6 multi 4.50 4.50

Shells — A381

Designs: 20c, Scaphella junonia. 30c, Strombus gigas. $1.80, Busycon contrarium. $5, Arca zebra.

No. 1688: a, Charonia variegata. b, Cypraea aurantium. c, Cyphoma gibbosa. d, Chicoreus articulatus.

No. 1689, $6, Thais deltoidea. No. 1690, $6, Cittarium pica.

2011, July 25 ***Perf. 12***

1684-1687 A381 Set of 4 6.00 6.00

Perf. 13 Syncopated

1688 A381 $2.50 Sheet of 4, #a-d 8.00 8.00

Souvenir Sheets

1689-1690 A381 Set of 2 10.00 10.00

Pres. John F. Kennedy (1917-63) — A382

No. 1691 — Kennedy: a, In front of window next to other man. b, With lectern visible. c, With other man in front of microphones. d, Greeting youths.

$6, Kennedy on path shoveled in snow.

2011, Aug. 29 ***Perf. 12***

1691 A382 $3 Sheet of 4, #a-d 9.00 9.00

Souvenir Sheet

1692 A382 $6 multi 4.75 4.75

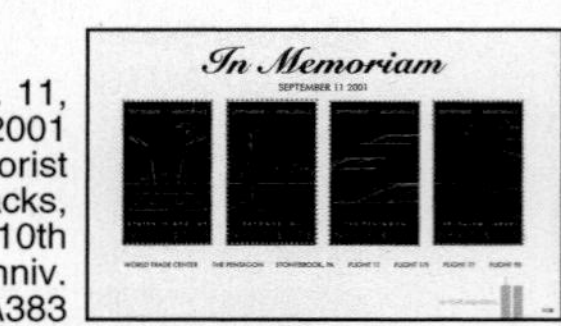

Sept. 11, 2001 Terrorist Attacks, 10th Anniv. A383

No. 1693 — Memorials at: a, Staten Island, New York. b, Bayonne, New Jersey. c, Pentagon. d, Jerusalem, Israel.

$6, Ground Zero Reflecting Pools.

2011, Sept. 9 **Litho.**

1693 A383 $2.75 Sheet of 4, #a-d 8.25 8.25

Souvenir Sheet

1694 A383 $2.75 multi 4.75 4.75

Miniature Sheet

Inter Milan Soccer Team A384

No. 1695: a, Team photo, 1910. b, Giorgio Muggiani, team founder. c, Angelo Moratti, past president of team. d, Heleno Herrera, coach. e, Team celebrating 2011 TIM Cup championship. f, Giacinto Facchetti, player and team president. g, Sandro Mazzola, player. h, Mario Corso, player. i, Luis Suarez, player.

2011, Sept. 13 ***Perf. 12¾***

1695 A384 $1.50 Sheet of 9, #a-i 10.00 10.00

A385

Dogs A386

No. 1696: a, Alaskan malamute. b, Yorkshire terrier. c, Black Labrador retriever. d, Dachshund.

$6, Beagle.

2011, Oct. 14 ***Perf. 13 Syncopated***

1696 A385 $2.75 Sheet of 4, #a-d 8.50 8.50

Souvenir Sheet

1697 A386 $6 multi 4.75 4.75

Christmas — A387

Paintings by Melchior Broederlam: 25c, Annunciation. 30c, Visitation. 90c, Presentation in the Temple. $5, Flight into Egypt.

2011, Nov. 7 ***Perf. 12***

1698-1701 A387 Set of 4 4.75 4.75

Reptiles A388

No. 1702: a, Anegada ground iguana. b, Antilles racer. c, Brown anole. d, Lesser Antillean iguana.

$6, Anegada ground iguana, horiz.

2011, Nov. 14 **Litho.** ***Perf. 12***

1702 A388 $3 Sheet of 4, #a-d 9.00 9.00

Souvenir Sheet

Perf. 12½

1703 A388 $6 multi 4.75 4.75

No. 1703 contains one 51x38mm stamp.

Miniature Sheets

First Man in Space, 50th Anniv. A389

No. 1704 — Planets: a, Neptune. b, Uranus. c, Earth and Mars. d, Venus and Mercury. e, Jupiter. f, Saturn.

No. 1705 — Phases of the Moon: a, Full (country name in black). b, Waxing gibbous ("N" of country name in white). c, First quarter ("NE" and part of "V" of country name in white). d, Waxing crescent (country name in white).

2011, Dec. 16 ***Perf. 12½x12***

1704 A389 $2 Sheet of 6, #a-f 9.50 9.50

Perf. 13

1705 A389 $3 Sheet of 4, #a-d 9.50 9.50

No. 1705 contains four 35mm diameter stamps.

Sinking of the Titanic, Cent. A390

No. 1706: a, Stowaway on rope. b, Grand Staircase of the Olympic. c, Titanic at Southampton dock. d, Reading and writing room.

$6, Titanic sinking.

2012, Feb. 8 ***Perf. 13 Syncopated***

1706 A390 $3 Sheet of 4, #a-d 9.00 9.00

Souvenir Sheet

Perf. 12

1707 A390 $6 multi 4.50 4.50

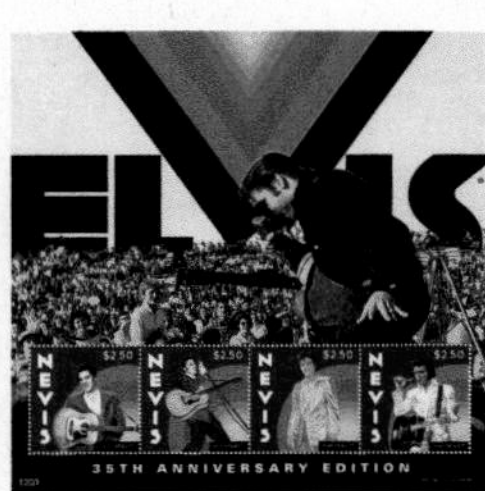

Elvis Presley (1935-77) — A391

No. 1708 — Presley: a, With guitar and gray suit, no microphone. b, With guitar, gray suit, microphone on stand. c, With beige suit. d, With guitar, white suit, holding microphone.
$9, Presley in gray suit playing guitar.

2012, Mar. 26 ***Perf. 12***
1708 A391 $2.50 Sheet of 4, #a-d 7.50 7.50

Souvenir Sheet

Perf. 13¼

1709 A391 $9 multi 6.75 6.75

Medicinal Spring A392

Nevis Coat of Arms A393

2012, June 14 ***Perf. 11¼***
1710 A392 $100 multi 75.00 75.00
1711 A393 $150 multi 110.00 110.00

Reign of Queen Elizabeth II, 60th Anniv. A394

No. 1712 — Various photographs of Queen Elizabeth II with denomination at: a, LR. b, LL. c, UR. d, UL.
$10, Queen Elizabeth II wearing tiara.

2012, July 25 ***Perf. 13¾***
1712 A394 $3 Sheet of 4, #a-d 9.50 9.50

Souvenir Sheet

1713 A394 $10 multi 8.00 8.00

Charles Dickens (1812-70), Writer — A395

Designs: $3.50, Dickens.
No. 1715: a, Books by Dickens. b, Dickens, diff.

2012, Aug. 7 **Litho.**
1714 A395 $3.50 multi 2.60 2.60

Souvenir Sheet

1715 A395 $4.50 Sheet of 2, #a-b 6.75 6.75

No. 1714 was printed in sheets of 4.

Miniature Sheet

Stingrays A396

No. 1716: a, Caribbean whiptail. b, Lesser electric ray. c, Giant manta ray. d, Southern stingray. e, Spotted eagle ray.

2012, Aug. 7 ***Perf. 12***
1716 A396 $3 Sheet of 5, #a-e 12.00 12.00

Illustrations From *Peter Pan,* by James M. Barrie (1860-1937) — A397

No. 1717 — Various illustrations with upper panel in: a, Green. b, Yellow green. c, Dull brown. d, Blue.
$6, Yellow green panel at right.

2012, Aug. 9 ***Perf. 13 Syncopated***
1717 A397 $3 Sheet of 4, #a-d 9.00 9.00

Souvenir Sheet

1718 A397 $6 multi 4.50 4.50

Miniature Sheet

Butterflies — A398

No. 1719: a, Hamadryas amphinome. b, Lycorea halia atergatis. c, Marpesia eleuchea bahamensis. d, Pyrisitia proterpia, with antennae. e, Pyrisitia proterpia, without antennae. f, Pyrrhocalles antiqua.

2012, Nov. 28 ***Perf. 12***
1719 A398 $2.50 Sheet of 6, #a-f 12.00 12.00

Beetles A399

No. 1720: a, Lema biornata. b, Lema splendida. c, Lema minuta. d, Lema dorsalis.
No. 1721: a, Stilodes heydeni. b, Stilodes leoparda.

2012, Nov. 28 ***Perf. 13¾***
1720 A399 $2.50 Sheet of 4, #a-d 7.50 7.50

Souvenir Sheet

1721 A399 $4 Sheet of 2, #a-b 6.00 6.00

Painting of the Sistine Chapel Ceiling by Michelangelo, 500th Anniv. — A400

No. 1722 — Details from Ancestors of Christ: a, Man with hand at face. b, Woman, man and infant. c, Woman kissing child. d, Woman and naked child at right.
$9, The Creation of Adam, horiz.

2012, Nov. 28 ***Perf. 13¾***
1722 A400 $3.50 Sheet of 4, #a-d 10.50 10.50

Souvenir Sheet

Perf. 12

1723 A400 $9 multi 6.75 6.75

No. 1723 contains one 80x30mm stamp.

Souvenir Sheets

Elvis Presley (1935-77) — A401

Presley: No. 1724, $9, Playing guitar, purple frame, country name in red. No. 1725, $9, With two women, black frame and country name. No. 1726, $9, With band, playing guitar, red frame and country name. No. 1727, $9, Holding microphone, red frame and country name. No. 1728, $9, Holding microphone, gray frame and country name.

2012, Nov. 28 ***Perf. 12¾***
1724-1728 A401 Set of 5 34.00 34.00

Christmas — A402

Paintings by Caravaggio: 25c, Adoration of the Shepherds. 30c, Annunciation. 90c, Holy Family with St. John the Baptist. $1, Nativity with St. Francis and St. Lawrence. $3, Rest on the Flight into Egypt. $5, Madonna of the Rosary.

2012, Nov. 28 **Litho.**
1729-1734 A402 Set of 6 7.75 7.75

Coronation of Queen Elizabeth II, 60th Anniv. — A403

No. 1735 — Queen Elizabeth II: a, Holding orb. b, Wearing blue hat. c, Wearing pink hat. d, Wearing sash.
$9, Queen Elizabeth II wearing crown, waving.

2013, Apr. 13 ***Perf. 13 Syncopated***
1735 A403 $3.25 Sheet of 4, #a-d 9.75 9.75

Souvenir Sheet

1736 A403 $9 multi 6.75 6,75

Miniature Sheets

Crossword Puzzles, Cent. — A404

No. 1737, $2 — Stamps with green panels and numbered squares: a, 1-5, 14, 17, 20, 23-25. b, 6-9, 15, 18, 21, 26-27. c, 10-13, 16, 19, 22. d, 28-29, 32-33, 37, 42, 45-48. e, 30, 34-36, 38, 43, 49-50. f, 31, 39-41, 44, 51. g, 52, 57, 60, 66, 69. h, 53-54, 58, 61-63, 67, 70. i, 55-56, 59, 64-65, 68, 71.
No. 1738, $2 — Stamps with red panels and numbered squares: a, 1-5, 14, 17, 20, 22, 23. b, 6-9, 15, 18, 21, 24. c, 10-13, 16, 19. d, 25, 29, 32-33, 37, 40-43. e, 26-27, 30, 34, 44. f, 28, 31, 35-36, 38-39, 45. g, 46-47, 49, 52, 56, 59. h, 48, 50-51, 53, 57, 60. i, 54-55, 58, 61.

2013, Apr. 3 ***Perf. 13¾***

Sheets of 9, #a-i

1737-1738 A404 Set of 2 25.00 25.00

On Nos. 1737-1738, crossword puzzle clues are in sheet margins and puzzle answers are printed on the backs of the stamps.

Personalizable Stamp — A405

2013, Apr. 22 ***Perf. 14x14¾***
1739 A405 $3 multi 2.25 2.25

No. 1739 was printed in sheets of 9 and presumably could be personalized for an extra fee.

World Radio Day A406

No. 1740 — Radio antennae and concentric circles with United Nations emblem at: a, UL. b, UR. c, LL. d, LR.
$8, Radio antenna, concentric circles, United Nations emblem at LL.

2013, Apr. 25 ***Perf. 12***
1740 A406 $3 Sheet of 4, #a-d 9.00 9.00

Souvenir Sheet

1741 A406 $8 multi 6.00 6.00

Hummingbirds — A407

No. 1742: a, Antillean mango. b, Ruby-throated hummingbird. c, Purple-throated carib. d, Long-billed starthroat.
No. 1743: a, Green-throated carib. b, Tufted coquette.

2013, Apr. 25 ***Perf. 13¾***
1742 A407 $3.25 Sheet of 4, #a-d 10.50 10.50

Souvenir Sheet

1743 A407 $4.50 Sheet of 2, #a-b 7.50 7.50

Nos. 1742 and 1743 exist imperf. Value, set $25.

Bees A408

No. 1744: a, Bicyrtes quadrifasciatus. b, Bembix americana. c, Ammophila apicalis. d, Ectemnius continuus.
$8, Bicyrtes quadrifasciatus, diff.

2013, Apr. 25 ***Perf. 12***
1744 A408 $4 Sheet of 4, #a-d 12.00 12.00

Souvenir Sheet

1745 A408 $8 multi 6.00 6.00

Fruit A409

No. 1746: a, Lemon. b, Persimmons. c, Yellow plum. d, Oranges.
$9, Peach, vert.

2013, June 3 ***Perf. 13¾***
1746 A409 $3.25 Sheet of 4, #a-d 9.75 9.75

Souvenir Sheet
Perf. 12½

1747 A409 $9 multi 6.75 6.75

No. 1747 contains one 38x51mm stamp.

Turtles A410

No. 1748: a, Desert tortoise. b, African helmeted turtle. c, Redbelly turtle. d, Red-eared slider.
$9, Gulf Coast box turtle.

2013, June 3 ***Perf. 13 Syncopated***
1748 A410 $3.25 Sheet of 4, #a-d 9.75 9.75

Souvenir Sheet

1749 A410 $9 multi 6.75 6.75

Parrots A411

No. 1750: a, Imperial amazon. b, Cuban amazon. c, Hispanolian parrot. d, St. Vincent amazon.
$9, St. Lucia amazon, vert.

2013, June 3 ***Perf. 13¾***
1750 A411 $3.25 Sheet of 4, #a-d 9.75 9.75

Souvenir Sheet
Perf. 12½

1751 A411 $9 multi 6.75 6.75

No. 1751 contains one 38x51mm stamp.

Election of Pope Francis A412

No. 1752 — Pope Francis: a, Waving, orange background. b, Waving, black background. c, Facing right. d, On balcony with assistant.
$9, Pope Francis, assistant with microphone.

2013, June 3 ***Perf. 14***
1752 A412 $3.25 Sheet of 4, #a-d 9.75 9.75

Souvenir Sheet
Perf. 12½

1753 A412 $9 multi 6.75 6.75

No. 1753 contains one 38x51mm stamp.

Souvenir Sheet

Elvis Presley (1935-77) — A413

Litho., Margin Embossed
2013, July 8 ***Imperf.***
Without Gum

1754 A413 $20 black 16.00 16.00

Birth of Prince George of Cambridge — A414

No. 1755: a, Duke and Duchess of Cambridge, Prince George. b, Prince George. c, Duchess of Cambridge, Prince George. d, Duke of Cambridge, Prince George.
No. 1756: a, Duke and Duchess of Cambridge, Prince George, diff. b, Prince George, diff.

2013, Sept. 10 Litho. ***Perf. 12x12½***
1755 A414 $3.25 Sheet of 4, #a-d 9.75 9.75

Souvenir Sheet

1756 A414 $4.75 Sheet of 2, #a-b 7.00 7.00

Flora of Thailand A415

No. 1757: a, Pineapple. b, Papayas. c, Red pineapple. d, Plumeria. e, Magnolia. f, Camellia.
$9, Bromeliad, vert.

2013, Aug. 26 Litho. ***Perf. 13¾***
1757 A415 $2.50 Sheet of 6, #a-f 10.50 10.50

Souvenir Sheet
Perf. 12½

1758 A415 $9 multi 6.25 6.25

Thailand 2013 World Stamp Exhibition, Bangkok. No. 1758 contains one 38x51mm stamp.

Insects A416

No. 1759: a, Citrus root weevil. b, West Indian firetail. c, Catarina. d, Field cricket.
$9, Biting black fly.

2013, Sept. 17 Litho. ***Perf. 12½***
1759 A416 $3.50 Sheet of 4, #a-d 10.50 10.50

Souvenir Sheet

1760 A416 $9 multi 6.25 6.25

Independence, 30th Anniv. — A417

Designs: 30c, Soldiers handling flag. $5, National anthem, vert. (30x50mm). $10, Soldiers on parade.
$9, Map of St. Kitts and Nevis, vert.

Perf. 12½x13¼, 12 ($5)
2013, Sept. 19 **Litho.**
1761-1763 A417 Set of 3 10.50 10.50

Souvenir Sheet
Perf. 13¼x12½

1764 A417 $9 multi 6.25 6.25

Christmas — A418

Paintings by Carlo Crivelli: 30c, Adoration of the Shepherds. 90c, Christ Blessing. $2, Immaculate Conception. $5, Madonna d'Ancona.

2013, Dec. 2 **Litho.** ***Perf. 12½***
1765-1768 A418 Set of 4 6.25 6.25

Fish — A419

Designs: 10c, Barred hogfish. 15c, Bluefaced angelfish (Pomacanthus xanthometopon). 20c, Comb grouper. 30c, Spotfin hogfish. 90c, Yellow jack. $1, Broadbarred firefish. $1.20, Queen angelfish. $2, Stoplight parrotfish. $3, Tiger grouper. $5, Titan triggerfish. $10, Blue-striped grunt. $20, Flameback angelfish.

2013, Dec. 4 **Litho.** ***Perf. 13¾***

1769	A419	10c	multi	.25	.25
1770	A419	15c	multi	.25	.25
1771	A419	20c	multi	.25	.25
1772	A419	30c	multi	.25	.25
1773	A419	90c	multi	.65	.65
1774	A419	$1	multi	.75	.75
1775	A419	$1.20	multi	.90	.90
1776	A419	$2	multi	1.50	1.50
1777	A419	$3	multi	2.25	2.25
1778	A419	$5	multi	3.75	3.75
1779	A419	$10	multi	7.50	7.50
1780	A419	$20	multi	15.00	15.00
	Nos. 1769-1780 (12)			33.30	33.30

A420

A421

A422

Nelson Mandela (1918-2013), President of South Africa — A423

No. 1782 — Mandela: a, Wearing blue and white shirt with AIDS ribbon below top button. b, Wearing black and white shirt, person in background. c, Waving. d, Wearing black and white shirt.

2013, Dec. 15 Litho. *Perf. 13¾*

1781 A420 $4 multi 3.00 3.00
1782 A421 $4 Sheet of 4, #a-d 11.50 11.50

Souvenir Sheets

1783 A422 $14 multi 10.00 10.00
1784 A423 $14 multi 10.00 10.00

No. 1781 was printed in sheets of 4.

Coffee A424

No. 1785: a, Cup of coffee. b, Leaves and roasted beans. c, Coffee berries.
$9, Roasted bean.

2013, Nov. 18 Litho. *Perf. 12½*

1785 A424 $3.75 Sheet of 3, #a-c 8.25 8.25

Souvenir Sheet

1786 A424 $9 multi 6.50 6.50

2013 Brasiliana Intl. Philatelic Exhibition, Rio de Janeiro.

Modern Art A425

No. 1787, $3.50: a, Charles au Jersey Rayé, by Henri Evenepoel. b, Harlequin with Guitar, by Juan Gris. c, Katedrala, by Frantisek Kupka.
No. 1788, $3.50: a, Madras Rouge, by Henri Matisse. b, Nude with a Parrot, by George Bellows. c, The Old Guitarist, by Pablo Picasso.
No. 1789, $9, Senecio, by Paul Klee. No. 1790, $9, Udnie, by Francis Picabia.

2014, Jan. 3 Litho. *Perf. 12¾*

Sheets of 3, #a-c

1787-1788 A425 Set of 2 15.50 15.50

Souvenir Sheets

1789-1790 A425 Set of 2 13.50 13.50

Alexander Hamilton (1755-1804), First U.S. Treasury Secretary — A426

Designs: 30c, Portrait of Hamilton. 90c, Statue of Hamilton, U.S. Treasury Building. $10, Parchment scrolls.
$9, Nevis Heritage Center, horiz.

2014, Jan. 11 Litho. *Perf. 14*

1791-1793 A426 Set of 3 8.25 8.25

Souvenir Sheet

Perf. 12

1794 A426 $9 multi 6.50 6.50

No. 1794 contains one 50x30mm stamp.

Miniature Sheets

2014 Winter Olympics, Sochi, Russia — A427

No. 1795: a, Ice hockey stick and puck. b, Luge. c, Snowboard. d, Biathlon skis and rifle. e, Bobsled. f, Curling stone.
No. 1796, vert.: a, Ski jumping. b, Speed skating. c, Alpine skiing. d, Figure skating.

2014, Mar. 5 Litho. *Perf. 12*

1795 A427 $3.15 Sheet of 6, #a-f 14.00 14.00
1796 A427 $4.75 Sheet of 4, #a-d 14.00 14.00

No. 1796 contains four 30x50mm stamps.

World War I, Cent. A428

No. 1797, $3.15: a, Recruitment station, Trafalgar Square, London, 1914. b, Man wearing body armor, 1915. c, French machine gunners take position, 1917. d, Fort Brady, 1915. e, World War I photographer, 1917. f, Medical officer in a gas mask, 1915.
No. 1798, $3.15 — War posters from: a, France, 1915. b, Great Britain, 1914. c, United States, 1914. d, Germany, 1914. e, Australia, 1914. f, Italy, 1914.
No. 1799, $5: a, French soldiers in a trench at Berry-au-Bac, 1914. b, French soldier standing in the entrance to a trench, 1914.
No. 1800, $5 — War recruitment posters from: a, Great Britain, 1914. b, United States, 1917.

2014, Mar. 5 Litho. *Perf. 12¾*

Sheets of 6, #a-f

1797-1798 A428 Set of 2 27.00 27.00

Souvenir Sheets of 2, #a-b

1799-1800 A428 Set of 2 14.00 14.00

Characters from *Downton Abbey* Television Series — A429

No. 1801: a, Anna. b, Ivy. c, Daisy. d, Alfred Nugent.
$9, Tom Branson and Lady Sybil Crawley, horiz.

2014, Mar. 5 Litho. *Perf. 14*

1801 A429 $3.25 Sheet of 4, #a-d 9.75 9.75

Souvenir Sheet

1802 A429 $9 multi 6.75 6.75

Worldwide Fund for Nature (WWF) — A430

Nos. 1803 and 1804 — Caribbean reef shark: a, One shark, nose pointing to UR. b, Two sharks and fish. c, One shark with nose pointing to UL and fish. d, One shark with nose pointing left and fish.

2014, Apr. 2 Litho. *Perf. 14*

1803 A430 $2.50 Block or vert. strip of 4, #a-d 7.50 7.50
1804 A430 $2.75 Block or vert. strip of 4, #a-d 8.25 8.25

Berlin Wall Graffiti Art A431

No. 1805: a, Dove, ball and chain. b, Pink stylized face. c, Reproduction of inner left cover of Pink Floyd's *The Wall* album (Marching hammers and broken wall). d, Soldier and barbed wire. e, Hand with upraised, chained thumb. f, Hands at prison window, chain.
No. 1806: a, Two stylized heads. b, Reproduction of inner right cover of Pink Floyd's *The Wall* album (mother, teacher and creature).

2014, June 23 Litho. *Perf. 12¾*

1805 A431 $3 Sheet of 6, #a-f 13.50 13.50

Souvenir Sheet

1806 A431 $5 Sheet of 2, #a-b 7.50 7.50

Fall of Berlin Wall, 25th anniv.

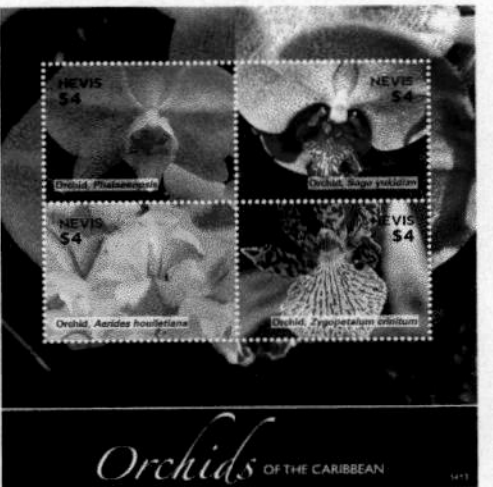

Orchids A432

No. 1807: a, Phalaenopsis. b, Phalaenopsis Sogo Yukidian. c, Aerides houlettiana. d, Zygopetalum crinitum.
No. 1808: a, Laelia gouldiana. b, Miltonia regnellii. c, Epidendrum fulgens. d, Cattleya alaorii.
No. 1809, vert.: a, Pink phalaenopsis, diff. b, Miltonia. No. 1810, vert.: a, Yellow phalaenopsis. b, Miltoniopsis.

2014, July 7 Litho. *Perf. 14*

1807 A432 $4 Sheet of 4, #a-d 12.00 12.00
1808 A432 $4 Sheet of 4, #a-d 12.00 12.00

Souvenir Sheet

1809 A432 $9 Sheet of 2, #a-b 13.50 13.50
1810 A432 $9 Sheet of 2, #a-b 13.50 13.50

Nevis Financial Services Department, 30th Anniv. — A433

Background color: 30c, Purple. $2, Greenish blue. $5, Blue.

2014, June 20 Litho. *Perf. 13¼*

1811-1813 A433 Set of 3 5.50 5.50

Dogs A434

No. 1814, $3.25: a, Great Dane. b, Komondor. c, Kuvasz. d, St. Bernard.
No. 1815, $3.25: a, Italian greyhound. b, Pomeranian. c, Chihuahua. d, Japanese chin.
No. 1816, $5: a, Newfoundland. b, Alaskan malamute.
No. 1817, $5: a, Mini pinshcer. b, Chinese crested.

2014, Aug. 14 Litho. *Perf. 14*

Sheets of 4, #a-d

1814-1815 A434 Set of 2 19.50 19.50

Souvenir Sheets of 2, #a-b

1816-1817 A434 Set of 2 15.00 15.00

A435

Prince George of Cambridge — A436

No. 1818 — Prince George wearing: a, Blue and white striped shirt. b, White shirt.
No. 1819, $9.50, Prince George (shown). No. 1820, $9.50, Prince George (close-up).

2014, Aug. 14 Litho. *Perf. 14*

1818 A435 $3.25 Vert. pair, #a-b 5.00 5.00

Souvenir Sheets

Perf. 12

1819-1820 A436 Set of 2 14.00 14.00

No. 1818 was printed in sheets containing three pairs. One example of No. 1818b has a different background, showing the shirt and tie of Prince William.

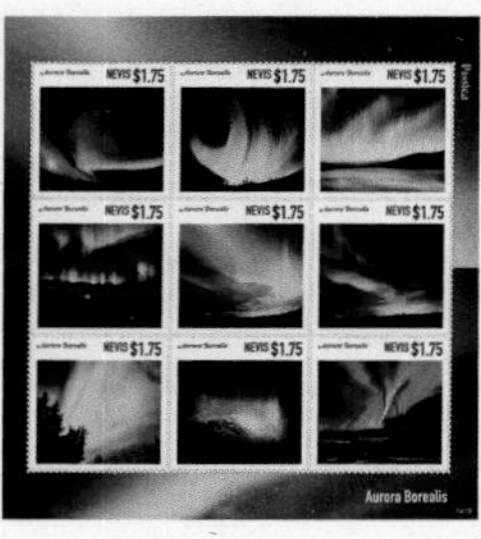
Aurora Borealis A437

No. 1821, Various depictions of the Aurora Borealis, as shown.
$10, Aurora Borealis, diff.

2014, Sept. 3 Litho. *Perf. 13¾*

1821 A437 $1.75 Sheet of 9, #a-i 12.00 12.00

Souvenir Sheet

1822 A437 $10 multi 7.50 7.50

Macaws A438

No. 1823, $3.25: a, Blue and yellow macaw. b, Red-shouldered macaw. c, Red-fronted macaw. d, Green-winged macaw.
No. 1824, $3.25: a, Indigo macaw. b, Hyacinth macaw. c, Blue-headed macaw. d, Great green macaw.
No. 1825, $5: a, Scarlet macaaw. b, Golden-collared macaw.
No. 1826, $5: a, Blue and yellow macaw, diff. b, Blue-throated macaw.

2014, Sept. 3 Litho. *Perf. 14*

Sheets of 4, #a-d

1823-1824 A438 Set of 2 19.50 19.50

Souvenir Sheets of 2, #a-b

1825-1826 A438 Set of 2 15.00 15.00

Ducks — A439

No. 1827, $3.25: a, Marbled duck. b, Tufted duck. c, Barrow's goldeneye. d, King eider.
No. 1828, $3.25: a, Wood duck. b, Rosy-billed pochard. c, Puna teal. d, Maned duck.
No. 1829, $10, Indian whistling ducks, vert. No. 1830, $10, Yellow-billed ducks, vert.

2014, Sept. 4 Litho. *Perf. 13¾*

Sheets of 4, #a-d

1827-1828 A439 Set of 2 19.50 19.50

Souvenir Sheets

Perf. 12

1829-1830 A439 Set of 2 15.00 15.00

Nos. 1829-1830 each contain one 30x40mm stamp.

A440

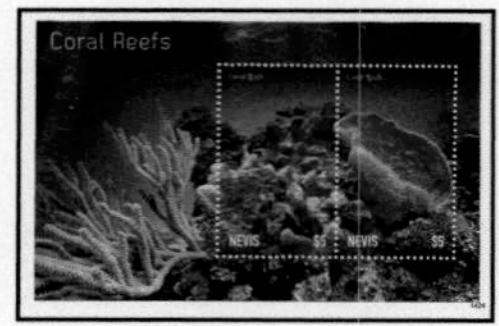
Coral Reefs A441

Various corals and fish, as shown.

2014, Sept. 4 Litho. *Perf. 12*

1831 A440 $3.25 Sheet of 8. #a-h 19.50 19.50

Souvenir Sheet

1832 A441 $5 Sheet of 2, #a-b 7.50 7.50

Visit of Pope Francis to Israel — A442

Designs: $1.25, Pope Francis seated with Israeli President Shimon Peres.
No. 1834 — Pope Francis: a, Standing at Church of the Holy Sepulchre. b, Kneeling at Church of the Holy Sepulchre. c, At Yad Vashem Holocaust Museum. d, At Dome of the Rock.
No. 1835, $9.50, Pope Francis facing left. and praying at Yad Vashem Holocaust Museum. No. 1836, $9.50, Pope Francis facing right and praying at the Wailing Wall.

2014, Oct. 14 Litho. *Perf. 14*

1833 A442 $1.25 multi .95 .95

Perf. 12

1834 A442 $3.25 Sheet of 4, #a-d 9.75 9.75

Souvenir Sheets

1835-1836 A442 Set of 2 14.00 14.00

Cicely Tyson, Actress — A443

2014, Jan. 1 Litho. *Perf. 14*

1837 A443 $3.25 multi 2.40 2.40

No. 1837 was printed in sheets of 4.

40th Culturama Festival — A444

Designs: $5, Crowd watching perfomers. No. 1839, $10, Dancers and crowd.
No. 1840, $10, King Meeko and King Dis and Dat, musicians.

2014, Aug. 1 Litho. *Perf. 13¼x12½*

1838-1839 A444 Set of 2 11.00 11.00

Souvenir Sheet

Perf. 12x12½

1840 A444 $10 multi 7.50 7.50

Paintings A445

No. 1841, $3.50: a, The Artist's Daughter, by Camille Pissarro. b, Yellow Roses in a Vase, by Gustave Caillebotte. c, Kitten, by Franz Marc.
No. 1842, $3.50: a, Clump of Chrysanthemums, by Caillebotte. b, Woman Combing Her Hair, by Edgar Degas. c, Still Life with a Curtain, by Paul Gauguin.
No. 1843, $10, Road in Maine, by Edward Hopper. No. 1844, $10, Baby Reaching for an Apple, by Mary Cassatt.

2014, Oct. 14 Litho. *Perf. 12¾x12½*

Sheets of 3, #a-c

1841-1842 A445 Set of 2 15.50 15.50

Size:100x100mm

Imperf

1843-1844 A445 Set of 2 15.00 15.00

Christmas — A446

Paintings by Raphael: 30c, Madonna of Foligno. 90c, The Transfiguration. $2, Madonna of Loreto. $5, Madonna del Baldacchino.

2014, Oct. 24 Litho. *Perf. 12½*

1845-1848 A446 Set of 4 6.00 6.00

Steam Locomotives of 1857 — A447

No. 1849, $3.25: a, Queen Class of Engines. b, Fourth and Fifth Lots Coupled. c, Eight Feet Passenger Engine. d, Third Lot Coupled.
No. 1850, $3.25: a, Five Feet Tank Engine. b, Sixth and Seventh Lots Coupled. c, Bogie Engine. d, Six Feet Tank Engine.
No. 1851, $10, Seven Feet Coupled Engine. No. 1852, $10, 6 Feet 6 Inches Coupled.

2014, Nov. 3 Litho. *Perf. 12*

Sheets of 4, #a-d

1849-1850 A447 Set of 2 19.50 19.50

Souvenir Sheets

1851-1852 A447 Set of 2 15.00 15.00

A448

Whales and Dolphins A449

No. 1853, Various photographs of killer whale, as shown.
No. 1854, Various photographs of humpback whale, as shown.
No. 1855, $10, Pygmy killer whale. No. 1856, $10, Sperm whale.

Perf. 13 Syncopated

2014, Dec. 16 Litho.

1853 A448 $3.15 Sheet of 6, #a-f 14.00 14.00

1854 A449 $3.25 Sheet of 4, #a-d 9.75 9.75

Souvenir Sheets

1855-1856 A449 Set of 2 15.00 15.00

Rosetta Mission A450

No. 1857: a, Philae landing on Comet 67P. b, Philae passing Earth. c, Philae passing Mars. d, Philae break away.
$10, Philae's descent to Comet 67P.

2015, Jan. 1 Litho. *Perf. 13¾*

1857 A450 $3.25 Sheet of 4, #a-d 9.75 9.75

Souvenir Sheet

1858 A450 $10 multi 7.50 7.50

Prehistoric Mammals — A451

No. 1859, $3.25: a, Daeodon. b, Pseudaelurus. c, Stenomylus. d, Amebelodon.
No. 1860, $3.25: a, Megacerops. b, Synthetoceras. c, Merychyrus. d, Prosthennops.
No. 1861, $10, Saber-toothed cat. No. 1862, $10, Woolly mammoth.

2015, Jan. 21 Litho. *Perf. 14*

Sheets of 4, #a-d

1859-1860 A451 Set of 2 19.50 19.50

Souvenir Sheets

Perf. 12

1861-1862 A451 Set of 2 15.00 15.00

Volcanoes — A452

No. 1863: a, Klyuchevskoy Volcano, Russia (80x30mm). b, Popocatépetl Volcano, Mexico (40x30mm). c, Kamchatka Volcano, Russia (40x60mm). d, Kilauea Volcano, U.S. (40x30mm). e, Nevis Peak, Nevis (40x30mm). f, Yasur Volcano, Vanuatu (40x30mm).
$10, Mt. Fuji, Japan.

2015, Mar. 2 Litho. *Perf. 14*

1863 A452 $3.15 Sheet of 6, #a-f 14.00 14.00

Souvenir Sheet

Perf. 12

1864 A452 $10 multi 7.50 7.50

No. 1864 contains one 65x32mm triangular stamp.

Birds A453

No. 1865: a, Scarlet ibis on tree branch. b, Greater flamingo. c, Scarlet ibis on rock with wings extended. d, Roseate spoonbill. e, Scarlet ibis on rock looking left. f, Caribbean flamingo.
$10, Caribbean flamingo, diff.

2015, Mar. 2 Litho. *Perf. 14*

1865 A453 $4 Sheet of 6, #a-f 18.00 18.00

Souvenir Sheet

1866 A453 $10 multi 7.50 7.50

No. 1866 contains one 30x80mm stamp.

Loggerhead Sea Turtles — A454

No. 1867, Various photographs.
$10, Loggerhead sea turtle, diff.

2015, Mar. 24 Litho. *Perf. 14*

1867 A454 $3.15 Sheet of 6, #a-f 14.00 14.00

Souvenir Sheet

Perf. 12

1868 A454 $10 multi 7.50 7.50

Pope Benedict XVI A455

No. 1869: a, Pope Benedict XVI on balcony with arms extended. b, Pope Benedict XVI wearing red zucchetto. c, Smoke announcing election of Pope Benedict XVI. d, Crowd at inauguration of Pope Benedict XVI. e, Pope Benedict XVI wearing miter. f, Pope Benedict XVI wearing white zucchetto.
$10, Pope Benedict XVI seated.

2015, Mar. 24 Litho. *Perf. 14*

1869 A455 $3.15 Sheet of 6, #a-f 14.00 14.00

Souvenir Sheet

Perf. 12

1870 A455 $10 multi 7.50 7.50

Hubble Space Telescope, 25th Anniv. — A456

No. 1871: a, Hubble Space Telescope above Earth. b, Crab Nebula. c, Rings of Saturn. d, Orion Nebula. e, Comet. f, Astronaut repairing telescope. g, Mars. h, Hubble Space Telescope, Earth at LL corner. i, NGC 3603. j, NGC 6543. k, Neptune. l, A moon in front of Jupiter.
$10, Hubble Space Telescope, diff.

2015, Mar. 24 Litho. *Perf. 14*

1871 A456 $1.60 Sheet of 12, #a-l 14.50 14.50

Souvenir Sheet

Perf. 12½

1872 A456 $10 multi 7.50 7.50

No. 1872 contains one 51x38mm stamp.

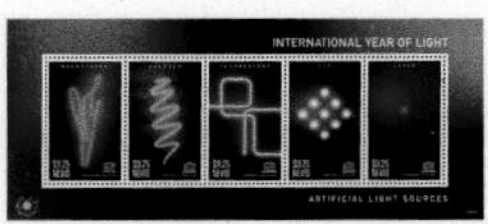

International Year of Light — A457

No. 1873 — UNESCO emblem, light and inscription: a, Incandescent. b, Halogen. c, Fluorescent. d, LED. e, Laser.
$10, UNESCO emblem and "2015 / International / Year of / Light."

2015, Apr. 15 Litho. *Perf. 12*

1873 A457 $3.25 Sheet of 5, #a-e 12.00 12.00

Souvenir Sheet

Perf. 12¾

1874 A457 $10 multi 7.50 7.50

No. 1874 contains one 38x51mm stamp.

English Lighthouses — A458

No. 1875: a, Roker Pier Lighthouse. b, Beachy Head Lighthouse. c, New Lighthouse at Dungeness. d, Smeaton's Tower. e, St. Catherine's Lighthouse. f, Flamborough Head Lighthouse.
$10, Needles Lighthouse.

2015, Apr. 15 Litho. *Perf. 14*

1875 A458 $3.15 Sheet of 6, #a-f 14.00 14.00

Souvenir Sheet

1876 A458 $10 multi 7.50 7.50

Europhilex Stamp Exhibition, London.

2015 Cricket World Cup, Australia and New Zealand — A459

Designs: $4, Hagley Oval, Christchurch, New Zealand.
$10, Cricket World Cup, vert.

2015, May 4 Litho. *Perf. 14*

1877 A459 $4 multi 3.00 3.00

Souvenir Sheet

Perf. 12

1878 A459 $10 multi 7.50 7.50

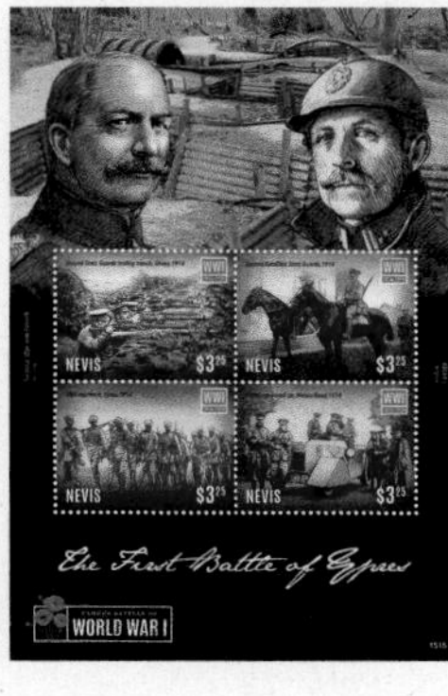

First Battle of Ypres, Cent. (in 2014) A460

No. 1879: a, Second Scots Guards testing trench, Ghent. b, Second Battalion Scots Guards. c, Sikh Regiment, Ypres. d, Naval armored car, Menin Road.
$10, British medics aid wounded comrade.

2015, Nov. 1 Litho. *Perf. 12*

1879 A460 $3.25 Sheet of 4, #a-d 9.75 9.75

Souvenir Sheet

Perf. 12½

1880 A460 $10 multi 7.50 7.50

No. 1880 contains one 51x38mm stamp.

Christmas — A461

Paintings by Bartolomé Esteban Murillo: 30c, The Annunciation. 90c, Nativity. $2, Madonna and Child. $5, Adoration of the Shepherds.

2015, Nov. 2 Litho. *Perf. 14*

1881-1884 A461 Set of 4 6.00 6.00

Queen Elizabeth II, Longest-Reigning British Monarch — A462

No. 1885 — Various photographs of Queen Elizabeth II with denomination in: a, Magenta. b, Turquoise green. c, Violet gray. d, Ochre, e, Black. f, Gray.
$10, Queen Elizabeth II wearing pink and white dress.

2015, Nov. 25 Litho. *Perf. 14*

1885 A462 $3.15 Sheet of 6, #a-f 14.00 14.00

Souvenir Sheet

Perf. 12¾

1886 A462 $10 multi 7.50 7.50

No. 1886 contains one 38x51mm stamp.

Flowers A463

No. 1887: a, Royal poinciana. b, Hibiscus. c, Bromeliad. d, Paper flower. e, Moth orchid. f, Flamingo flower.
$10, Red palulu, vert.

2015, Dec. 7 Litho. *Perf. 14*

1887 A463 $3.15 Sheet of 6, #a-f 14.00 14.00

Souvenir Sheet

Perf. 12

1888 A463 $10 multi 7.50 7.50

No. 1888 contains one 30x50mm stamp.

Bank of Nevis Limited, 30th Anniv. — A464

Designs: 30c, Bank building. 90c, Bank building, diff. $5, Sir Simeon Daniel (1934-2012), premier of Nevis, bank founder, vert.

2015, Dec. 9 Litho. *Perf. 14*

1889-1891 A464 Set of 3 4.75 4.75

Kingfishers — A465

No. 1892: a, Belted kingfisher. b, Ringed kingfisher. c, Green and rufous kingfisher. d, Green kingfisher, showing breast. e, Amazon kingfisher. f, Green kingfisher, showing back.
$10, Belted kingfisher in flight.

2015, Dec. 17 Litho. *Perf. 13¾*

1892 A465 $3.15 Sheet of 6, #a-f 14.00 14.00

Souvenir Sheet

1893 A465 $10 multi 7.50 7.50

Visit of Pope Francis to New York City A466

No. 1894, Various photographs of Pope Francis, as shown.
$10, Pope Francis looking forward with left arm raised.

2015, Dec. 17 Litho. *Perf. 14*

1894 A466 $3.15 Sheet of 6, #a-f 14.00 14.00

Souvenir Sheet

Perf. 12

1895 A466 $10 multi 7.50 7.50

1896 Olympic Champions — A467

No. 1896: a, Herman Weingärtner, horizontal bar. b, Carl Schuhmann, horse vault. c, Thomas Burke, 100-meter and 400-meter race. d, Thomas Curtis, 100-meter hurdles.
$10, Alfred Flatow, parallel bars.

2015, Dec. 21 Litho. *Perf. 14*

1896 A467 $3.25 Sheet of 4, #a-d 9.75 9.75

Souvenir Sheet

Perf. 12½

1897 A467 $10 multi 7.50 7.50

No. 1897 contains one 38x51mm stamp.

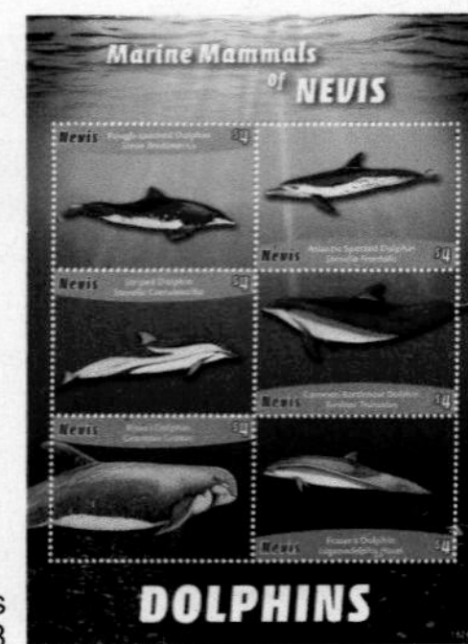

Dolphins A468

No. 1898: a, Rough-toothed dolphin. b, Atlantic spotted dolphin. c, Striped dolphin. d, Common bottlenose dolphin. e, Risso's dolphin. f, Fraser's dolphin.
$10, Short-beaked common dolphin.

2016, Jan. 28 Litho. *Perf. 14*

1898 A468 $4 Sheet of 6, #a-f 18.00 18.00

Souvenir Sheet

Perf. 12

1899 A468 $10 multi 7.50 7.50

No. 1899 contains one 80x30mm stamp.

Shells A469

No. 1900: a, King venus. b, Channeled duck clam. c, Sunrise tellin. d, Calico clam.
$10, Royal comb venus, horiz.

2016, Jan. 28 Litho. *Perf. 13¾*

1900 A469 $4 Sheet of 4, #a-d 12.00 12.00

Souvenir Sheet

Perf. 12½

1901 A469 $10 multi 7.50 7.50

No. 1901 contains one 51x38mm stamp.

Queen Elizabeth II, 90th Birthday A470

No. 1902: a, Queen Elizabeth II wearing pearl necklace (30x40mm). b, Queen Elizabeth II wearing long earring, looking left (30x40mm). c, Queen Elizabeth II wearing teardrop earrings (30x40mm). d, Queen Elizabeth II and Prince Philip (30x40mm). e, Queen Elizabeth II in 1970 (30x80mm).
$13, Queen Elizabeth II in 1987.

2016, Apr. 1 Litho. *Perf. 14*

1902 A470 $3.25 Sheet of 5, #a-e 12.00 12.00

Souvenir Sheet

Perf. 12

1903 A470 $13 multi 9.75 9.75

No. 1903 contains one 30x50mm stamp.

2016 World Stamp Show, New York A471

No. 1904 — New York City landmarks: a, Central Park. b, Statue of Liberty. c, Grand Central Terminal. d, Brooklyn Bridge.
$8, New York skyline.

2016, Apr. 29 Litho. *Perf. 12*

1904 A471 $4 Sheet of 4, #a-d 12.00 12.00

Souvenir Sheet

Perf. 14

1905 A471 $8 multi 6.00 6.00

No. 1905 contains one 60x80mm stamp.

September 11, 2001 Terrorist Attacks, 15th Anniv. — A472

No. 1906: a, Flag on World Trade Center rubble. b, World Trade Center. c, New York firefighters at World Trade Center. d, Pentagon 9/11 Memorial. e, Flight 93 National Memorial. f, 9/11 Memorial, Staten Island, New York.
No. 1907: a, Flag hanging from Pentagon. b, Pentagon. c, World Trade Center, diff. d, Tribute in Light.
$14, Tribute in Light, diff.

2016, May 26 Litho. *Perf. 13¾*

1906 A472 $3.25 Sheet of 6, #a-f 14.50 14.50

1907 A472 $3.50 Sheet of 4, #a-d 10.50 10.50

Souvenir Sheet

1908 A472 $14 multi 10.50 10.50

William Shakespeare (1564-1616), Writer — A473

No. 1909: a, Shakespeare's birthplace, Stratford-on-Avon, England. b, Shakespeare. c, Oberon, Titania and Puck with Fairies Dancing, painting by Henry Fuseli. d, Pity, painting by William Blake. e, Hamlet and His Father's Ghost, painting by Blake. f, Macbeth Consulting the Vision of the Armed Head, painting by Fuseli.
$12, Shakespeare, diff.

2016, June 1 Litho. *Perf. 12½*

1909 A473 $3.15 Sheet of 6, #a-f 14.00 14.00

Souvenir Sheet

Perf.

1910 A473 $12 multi 9.00 9.00

No. 1910 contains one 33x43mm oval stamp.

Pres. Barack Obama's Visit to Saudi Arabia A474

No. 1911: a, Pres. Obama, U.S. flag (40x60mm). b, Pres. Obama behind microphone (80x30mm). c, King Salman of Saudi Arabia (40x60mm). d, Pres. Obama and King Salman standing in front of emblem (40x30mm). e, Pres. Obama and King Salman walking (40x30mm).
No. 1912: a, Pres. Obama, U.S. flag. b, King Salman, Saudi Arabia flag.

2016, Oct. 18 Litho. *Perf. 14*

1911 A474 $4 Sheet of 5, #a-e 15.00 15.00

Souvenir Sheet

Perf. 12½

1912 A474 $7 Sheet of 2, #a-b 10.50 10.50

No. 1912 contains two 38x51mm stamps.

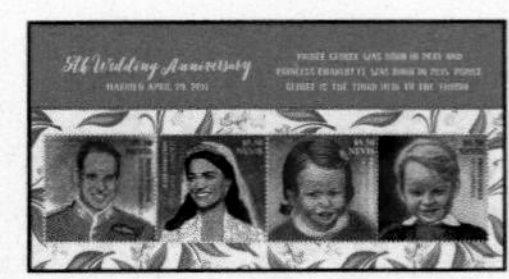

Duke and Duchess of Cambridge, 5th Wedding Anniversary — A475

No. 1913: a, Duke of Cambridge. b, Duchess of Cambridge. c, Princess Charlotte. d, Prince George.
$10, Duke and Duchess of Cambridge kissing at wedding, vert.

2017, Mar. 14 Litho. *Perf. 13¾*

1913 A475 $5.50 Sheet of 4, #a-d 16.50 16.50

Souvenir Sheet

Perf. 12½

1914 A475 $10 multi 7.50 7.50

No. 1914 contains one 38x51mm stamp.

Princess Diana (1961-97) — A476

No. 1915 — Princess Diana: a, With Princes William and Harry, horse. b, Carrying Prince Harry. c, With Princes William and Harry on fence. d, Leaning over Prince William's shoulder. e, With Princes William and Harry, wearing suits. f, With hands together talking to Prince William.
No. 1916 — Princess Diana, Princes Charles, William and Harry with: a, Building in background. b, Trees in background.

2017, Apr. 14 Litho. *Perf. 14*

1915 A476 $3.50 Sheet of 6, #a-f 15.50 15.50

Souvenir Sheet

1916 A476 $7.50 Sheet of 2, #a-b 11.00 11.00

Star Trek Television Shows, 50th Anniv. (in 2016) — A477

No. 1917 — Scenes from *Star Trek: The Next Generation* episodes: a, The Pegasus. b, Unification II. c, Q Who. d, Deja Q. e, Rascals. f, All Good Things. . .
$12, Scene from Darmok episode.

2017, Apr. 24 Litho. *Perf. 12*

1917 A477 $4 Sheet of 6, #a-f 18.00 18.00

Souvenir Sheet

Perf. 12½

1918 A477 $12 multi 9.00 9.00

No. 1918 contains one 51x38mm stamp.

Ancient Ruins A478

No. 1919: a, Stonehenge, England. b, Amphitheater of El Djem, Tunisia. c, Bagan, Burma. d, Petra, Jordan. e, Ellora Caves, India. f, Moai, Easter Island, Chile.
$10, Machu Picchu, Peru.

2017, June 7 Litho. *Perf. 12*

1919 A478 $3.50 Sheet of 6, #a-f 15.50 15.50

Souvenir Sheet

1920 A478 $10 multi 7.50 7.50

A479

A480

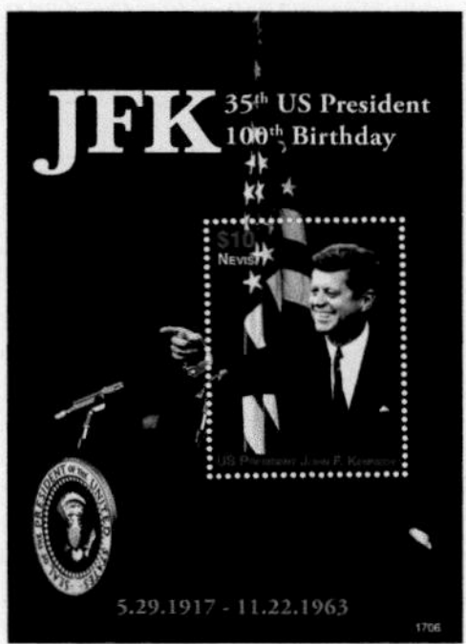

Pres. John F. Kennedy (1917-63) — A481

No. 1921: a, $5, Pres. Kennedy facing forward. b, $6, Pres. Kennedy facing right. c, $8, Pres. Kennedy facing left. d, $10, Pres. Kennedy and wife, Jacqueline.
No. 1922, vert. — Pres. Kennedy: a, Seated at desk. b, Pointing. c, Wearing Navy cap. d, Facing left.
No. 1923, Pres. Kennedy and U.S. flag, vert.

2017, June 7 Litho. *Perf. 13¾*
1921 A479 Sheet of 4, #a-d 21.50 21.50

Perf. 14

1922 A480 $5.50 Sheet of 4, #a-d 16.50 16.50

Souvenir Sheet

1923 A481 $10 multi 7.50 7.50

Piping Plovers A482

No. 1924: a, Chick (entire bird). b, Adult (head).
$10, Two birds, vert.

2017, June 22 Litho. *Perf.*
1924 A482 $7.50 Sheet of 2, #a-b 11.00 11.00

Souvenir Sheet

Perf. 12½

1925 A482 $10 multi 7.50 7.50

No. 1925 contains one 38x51mm stamp.

Animals A483

No. 1926: a, Naked mole rat. b, Cydno longwing butterfly. c, Saint Croix sheep. d, Asian garden dormouse.
$15, Cave cricket, vert.

2017, Apr. 14 Litho. *Perf. 12¾*
1926 A483 $4 Sheet of 4, #a-d 12.00 12.00

Souvenir Sheet

1927 A483 $15 multi 11.00 11.00

Miniature Sheets

Tree Flowers A484

No. 1928, $5.50: a, Tulip tree. b, Royal poinciana. c, Shaving brush tree. d, Geiger tree.
No. 1929, $5.50: a, Golden shower tree. b, Jacaranda. c, Japanese cherry. d, Southern magnolia.

2017, June 22 Litho. *Perf. 14*

Sheets of 4, #a-d

1928-1929 A484 Set of 2 32.50 32.50

Miniature Sheet

Brown Pelicans A485

No. 1930: a, One pelican in flight. b, Two pelicans in flight. c, Pelican on rock, denomination in black. d, Pelican, denomination in yellow. e, Juvenile pelican facing left. f, Pelican hatchling and egg.

2017, Sept. 28 Litho. *Perf. 13¾*
1930 A485 $4 Sheet of 6, #a-f 18.00 18.00

70th Wedding Anniversary of Queen Elizabeth II and Prince Philip — A486

No. 1931: a, Couple, bride waving. b, Couple with attendants. c, Couple passing line of people. d, Formal photograph of couple.
$12, Couple with family and attendants.

2017, Sept. 28 Litho. *Perf. 14*
1931 A486 $6 Sheet of 4, #a-d 18.00 18.00

Souvenir Sheet

1932 A486 $12 multi 9.00 9.00

No. 1932 contains one 80x30mm stamp.

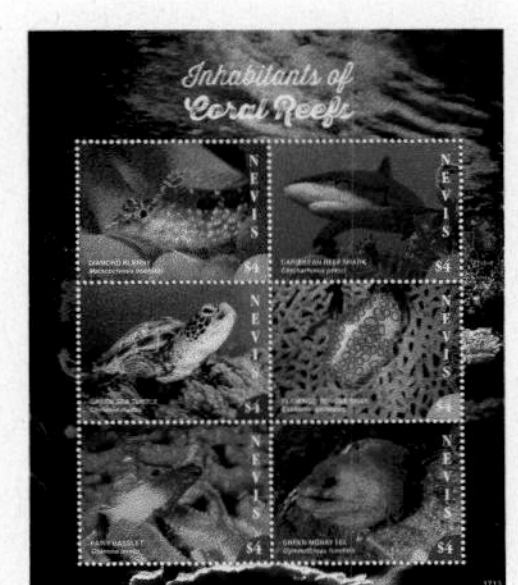

Inhabitants of Coral Reefs — A487

No. 1933: a, Diamond blenny. b, Caribbean reef shark. c, Green sea turtle. d, Flamingo tongue snail. e, Fairy basslet. f, Green moray eel.
No. 1934, $12, Longsnout seahorse, vert.
No. 1935, $12, Green sea turtle, vert.

2017, Dec. 4 Litho. *Perf. 14*
1933 A487 $4 Sheet of 6, #a-f 18.00 18.00

Souvenir Sheets

1934-1935 A487 Set of 2 18.00 18.00

Nevis Beaches A488

No. 1936: a, $2, Long Haul Beach. b, $4, Pinney's Beach. c, $6, Nisbet Beach. d, $8, Newcastle Beach.
No. 1937: a, $7, Pinney's Beach, diff. b, $8, Oualie Beach.

2017, Dec. 22 Litho. *Perf. 13¼*
1936 A488 Sheet of 4, #a-d 15.00 15.00

Souvenir Sheet

Perf. 12½x13¼

1937 A488 Sheet of 2, #a-b 11.00 11.00

No. 1937 contains two 40x30mm stamps.

Miniature Sheet

British Royalty A489

No. 1938: a, Queen Elizabeth II. b, Duke and Duchess of Cambridge. c, Prince George and Princess Charlotte of Cambridge. d, Prince Harry and fiancée Meghan Markle.

2018, Jan. 24 Litho. *Perf. 12½x13¼*
1938 A489 $7 Sheet of 4, #a-d 21.00 21.00

Swans A490

No. 1939: a, $4, Black-necked swan. b, $5.50, Trumpeter swan. c, $6, Mute swan. d, $6.50, Black swan.
No. 1940, vert.: a, $7, Tundra swan. b, $9, Coscoroba swan.

2018, Apr. 23 Litho. *Perf. 14*
1939 A490 Sheet of 4, #a-d 16.50 16.50

Souvenir Sheet

Perf. 12½

1940 A490 Sheet of 2, #a-b 12.00 12.00

No. 1940 contains two 38x51mm stamps.

Geckos A491

No. 1941: a, $4, Crested gecko. b, $5.50, Madagascar day gecko. c, $6, Tokay gecko. d, $6.50, Kuhl's flying gecko.
No. 1942: a, $7, William's dwarf gecko. b, $9, Leopard gecko.

2018, Apr. 23 Litho. *Perf. 14*
1941 A491 Sheet of 4, #a-d 16.50 16.50

Souvenir Sheet

Perf. 12½

1942 A491 Sheet of 2, #a-b 12.00 12.00

No. 1942 contains two 51x38mm stamps.

Souvenir Sheet

Red Squirrel A492

No. 1943 — Various photographs of red squirrel: a, $4. b, $5. c, $6.

2018, May 4 Litho. *Perf.*
1943 A492 Sheet of 3, #a-c 11.00 11.00

Coronation of Queen Elizabeth II, 65th Anniv. — A493

No. 1944 — Various photographs of Queen Elizabeth II wearing crown, as shown.
No. 1945 — Queen Elizabeth II: a, Sitting in coach. b, Waving.

2018, May 4 Litho. *Perf. 12*
1944 A493 $5 Sheet of 3, #a-c 11.00 11.00

Souvenir Sheet

Perf. 12½

1945 A493 $7.50 Sheet of 2, #a-b 11.00 11.00

No. 1945 contains two 38x51mm stamps.

Planets and Moons A494

No. 1946, $5.50: a, Phobos. b, Mars. c, Deimos.
No. 1947: a, $5, Mercury, Venus, Earth. b, $6, Mars, Jupiter. c, $7, Saturn, Uranus, Neptune.
No. 1948: a, $8, Moon. b, $9, Earth.

2018, May 4 Litho. *Perf. 12½*

Sheets of 3, #a-c

1946-1947 A494 Set of 2 25.50 25.50

Souvenir Sheet

1948 A494 Sheet of 2, #a-b 12.50 12.50

Miniature Sheet

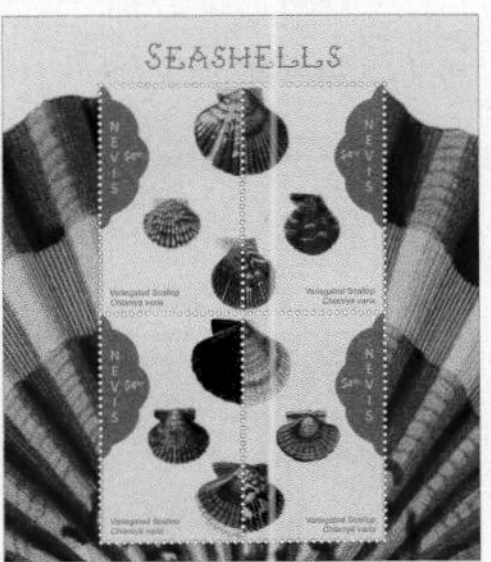

Variegated Scallops — A495

Various shells, as shown.

2018, May 24 Litho. *Perf. 12*
1949 A495 $4.50 Sheet of 4, #a-d 13.50 13.50

Miniature Sheet

Elvis Presley (1935-77) — A496

No. 1950 — Various photographs of Presley: a, Playing guitar, both hands visible, black background. b, Playing guitar, red background. c, Singing without guitar. d, Playing guitar, one arm visible, black background.

2018, May 24 Litho. *Perf. 14*
1950 A496 $6.80 Sheet of 4, #a-d 20.00 20.00

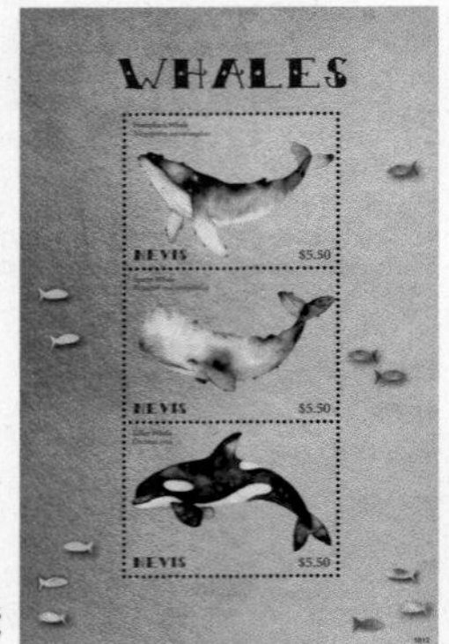

Whales A497

No. 1951: a, Humpback whale. b, Sperm whale. c, Killer whale.
$10, Blue whale, vert.

2018, May 24 Litho. *Perf. 12½*
1951 A497 $5.50 Sheet of 3, #a-c 12.50 12.50

Souvenir Sheet

1952 A497 $10 multi 7.50 7.50

Souvenir Sheet

Pres. Donald Trump at G7 Meeting, Rome A498

No. 1953: a, Leaders of G7 nations standing in front of flags. b, Pres. Trump and Italian Pres. Sergio Mattarella. c, Leaders seated at table.

2018, June 5 Litho. *Perf. 14*
1953 A498 $5.50 Sheet of 3, #a-c 12.50 12.50

Miniature Sheet

Fish A499

No. 1954: a, Moorish idol. b, Black tang. c, Flame angelfish. d, Northern red snapper. e, Pelagic porcupine fish. f, Yellow longnose butterflyfish.

2018, June 5 Litho. *Perf. 12*
1954 A499 $4 Sheet of 6, #a-f 18.00 18.00

Hummingbirds — A500

No. 1955: a, Antillean crested hummingbird. b, Green-throated carib. c, Blue-headed hummingbird. d, Purple-throated carib.
$10, White-bellied emerald hummingbird.

2018, June 5 Litho. *Perf. 12*
1955 A500 $4 Sheet of 4, #a-d 12.00 12.00

Souvenir Sheet
Perf. 12½

1956 A500 $10 multi 7.50 7.50

No. 1956 contains one 38x51mm stamp.

Miniature Sheet

Moths A501

No. 1957: a, $3, Pease blossom moth. b, $3.50, Orange moth. c, $4, Peppered moth. d, $4.50, Large emerald moth. e, $5, Brimstone moth. f, $5.50, Treble-bar moth.

2018, June 27 Litho. *Perf. 13¾*
1957 A501 Sheet of 6, #a-f 19.00 19.00

Sharks A502

No. 1958: a, $5.50, Shortfin mako shark. b, $6, Tiger shark. c, $6.50, Great white shark. d, $7, Bull shark.
$10, Smooth hammerhead shark.

2018, June 29 Litho. *Perf. 12½x12*
1958 A502 Sheet of 4, #a-d 18.50 18.50

Souvenir Sheet
Perf. 12½x13¼

1959 A502 $10 multi 7.50 7.50

No. 1959 contains one 80x30mm stamp.

Barbara Bush (1925-2018), U.S. First Lady — A503

No. 1960 — Mrs. Bush and: a, $5, Her husband, Pres. George H. W. Bush. b, $5, First Lady Hillary Clinton. c, $6, First Ladies Rosalynn Carter, Betty Ford, Nancy Reagan and Hillary Clinton. d, $6, Pres. Barack Obama and his wife, Michelle.
$10, Mrs. Bush, vert.

2018, June 29 Litho. *Perf. 13½*
1960 A503 Sheet of 4, #a-d 16.50 16.50

Souvenir Sheet
Perf. 13½x12½

1961 A503 $10 multi 7.50 7.50

No. 1961 contains one 30x40mm stamp.

British Royalty and Their Newborn Children A504

No. 1962: a, Duke and Duchess of Cambridge with Prince Louis. b, Prince Charles and Princess Diana with Prince William. c, Queen Elizabeth II with Prince Charles. d, King George V and Queen Mother with Princess Elizabeth.

2018, June 29 Litho. *Perf. 12½*
1962 A504 $5.50 Sheet of 4, #a-d 16.50 16.50

Souvenir Sheet

Wedding of Prince Harry and Meghan Markle A505

No. 1963 — Couple with: a, $5, Steps in background (40x30mm). b, $5, Black background (40x30mm). c, $6, Steps in background (40x60mm).

2018, June 29 Litho. *Perf. 12½x12*
1963 A505 Sheet of 3, #a-c 12.00 12.00

Concorde — A506

No. 1964: a, Air France Concorde, 1973. b, Two-person camera crew watching Air France Concorde take off, 1976. c, Five people watching Air France Concorde taking off, 1976. d, Air France Concorde, 2003.
$10, Queen Elizabeth II and Prince Philip on Concorde stairway, 1977.

2018, July 1 Litho. *Perf. 12½x12*
1964 A506 $5 Sheet of 4, #a-d 15.00 15.00

Souvenir Sheet
Perf. 12½x13¼

1965 A506 $10 multi 7.50 7.50

No. 1965 contains one 80x30mm stamp.

Prince George of Cambridge, 5th Birthday — A507

No. 1966: a, $4, Prince George as infant, with parents, Duke and Duchess of Cambridge. b, $5, Prince George. c, $6, Prince George in arms of his father.
No. 1967, horiz.: a, Prince George as infant, with parents and dog. b, Prince George with dog.

2018, July 1 Litho. *Perf. 13¼x12½*
1966 A507 Sheet of 3, #a-c 11.00 11.00

Souvenir Sheet
Perf. 12½x13¼

1967 A507 $8 Sheet of 2, #a-b 12.00 12.00

A508

Wedding of Prince Harry and Meghan Markle A509

No. 1968: a, Couple in coach, waving. b, Couple kissing. c, Couple holding hands on steps. d, Couple with people in background.
No. 1969: a, Couple kissing. b, Couple waving.

2018, July 17 Litho. *Perf. 12*
1968 A508 $5 Sheet of 4, #a-d 15.00 15.00

Souvenir Sheet

1969 A509 $8 Sheet of 2, #a-b 12.00 12.00

Miniature Sheet

Donkeys A510

No. 1970 — Various photographs: a, $1. b, $1.50. c, $2. d, $2.50. e, $3.

2018, Oct. 22 Litho. *Perf. 12*
1970 A510 Sheet of 5, #a-e 7.50 7.50

Miniature Sheet

Visit of Pres. Donald Trump to Windsor Castle
A511

No. 1971: a, $4, Pres. Trump and Queen Elizabeth II inspecting troops. b, $5, Pres. Trump, his wife, Melania, and Queen Elizabeth II. c, $6, Pres. Trump, his wife, and Queen Elizabeth II, diff. d, $7, Pres. Trump, his wife, Queen Elizabeth II and Sir Andrew Ford.

2018, Oct. 22 Litho. *Perf. 12*
1971 A511 Sheet of 4, #a-d 16.50 16.50

Christmas — A512

Words from Christmas music: 30c, Deck The Halls With Boughs Of Holly. 90c, Sweet Chiming Christmas Bells. $2, Beautiful Star Of Bethlehem. $5, Oh Christmas Tree, Oh Christmas Tree, How Lovely Are Thy Branches.
$10, Ho, Ho, Ho, How Will Santa Get Here.

2018, Dec. 5 Litho. *Perf. 12½*
1972-1975 A512 Set of 4 6.25 6.25

Souvenir Sheet

1976 A512 $10 multi 7.50 7.50

Souvenir Sheets

Butterflies — A513

No. 1977: a, $4, Jamaican ringlet butterfly (35x35mm). b, $5, Red-splashed sulphur butterfly (35x35mm). c, $6, Poey's black swallowtail butterflies (70x35mm).
No. 1978: a, $7, Cuban mimic butterfly (70x35mm). b, $8, Gundlach's swallowtail butterflies (70x35mm).

2018, Dec. 5 Litho. *Perf. 13¾*
1977 A513 Sheet of 3, #a-c 11.00 11.00
1978 A513 Sheet of 2, #a-b 11.00 11.00

Miniature Sheet

Mohandas K. Gandhi (1869-1948), Indian Nationalist Leader — A514

No. 1979 — Various photographs of Gandhi: a, $4. b, $5. c, $6. d, $7.

2018, Dec. 20 Litho. *Perf. 14*
1979 A514 Sheet of 4, #a-d 16.50 16.50

Red-Footed Tortoise — A515

No. 1980 — Various photographs of Red-footed tortoises: a, $4. b, $5. c, $6. d, $7.
$10, Tortoise, diff.

2018, Dec. 20 Litho. *Perf. 14*
1980 A515 Sheet of 4, #a-d 16.50 16.50

Souvenir Sheet

Perf. 12½

1981 A515 $10 multi 7.50 7.50

No. 1981 contains one 51x38mm stamp.

Paintings by Leonardo da Vinci (1452-1519) — A516

No. 1982: a, $4, Ginevra de'Benci. b, $5, Lady with an Ermine. c, $6, La Belle Ferronnière.
$10, Mona Lisa.

2019, Feb. 11 Litho. *Perf. 12*
1982 A516 Sheet of 3, #a-c 11.00 11.00

Size: 80x130mm

Imperf

1983 A516 $10 multi 7.50 7.50

Miniature Sheet

Pigeons and Doves
A517

No. 1984: a, $4, White-tipped dove. b, $5, Ruddy ground dove. c, $6, Pale-vented pigeon. d, $7, Rock pigeon.

2019, Mar. 16 Litho. *Perf. 12½*
1984 A517 Sheet of 4, #a-d 16.50 16.50

Royal Poinciana Flowers — A518

No. 1985: a, $4, Tree. b, $5, Blossom. c, $6, Cluster of flowers. d, $7, Cluster of flowers, diff.
$14, Tree, diff.

2019, Mar. 16 Litho. *Perf. 14*
1985 A518 Sheet of 4, #a-d 16.50 16.50

Souvenir Sheet

Perf. 12½

1986 A518 $14 multi 10.50 10.50

No. 1986 contains one 51x38mm stamp.

First Man on the Moon, 50th Anniv.
A519

No. 1987: a, $4, Apollo 11 mission patch and itinerary. b, $5, Astronaut Edwin "Buzz" Aldrin on Moon. c, $6, Astronaut Neil Armstrong. d, $7, Apollo 11 astronauts in space suits.
$11, Sketches of heads of Apollo 11 astronauts.

2019, May 25 Litho. *Perf. 14*
1987 A519 Sheet of 4, #a-d 16.50 16.50

Souvenir Sheet

Perf. 12

1988 A519 $11 multi 8.25 8.25

No. 1988 contains one 50x30mm stamp.

Red Lionfish
A520

No. 1989 — Red lionfish facing: a, $5, Right. b, $5, Left. c, $6, Left, black background. d, $6, Left, blue background.
$14, Red lionfish, diff.

2019, July 1 Litho. *Perf. 12*
1989 A520 Sheet of 4, #a-d 16.50 16.50

Souvenir Sheet

Perf. 12¾

1990 A520 $14 multi 10.50 10.50

No. 1990 contains one 51x38mm stamp.

Details of London's Victoria Monument, by Thomas Brock — A521

No. 1991: a, $3, Justice. b, $4, Truth. c, $5, Motherhood. d, $6, Queen Victoria Enthroned.
No. 1992: a, $3, Progress. b, $4, Agriculture. c, $5, Peace. d, $6, Manufacture.
$14, Winged Victory.

2019, July 1 Litho. *Perf. 14*
1991 A521 Sheet of 4, #a-d 13.50 13.50
1992 A521 Sheet of 4, #a-d 13.50 13.50

Souvenir Sheet

Perf. 12

1993 A521 $14 multi 10.50 10.50

Miniature Sheet

Leonard Bernstein (1918-90), Conductor — A522

No. 1994 — Bernstein: a, Conducting orchestra. b, Wearing shirt with open collar. c, Writing. d, Wearing turtle-neck sweater.

2019, July 7 Litho. *Perf. 14*
1994 A522 $6 Sheet of 4, #a-d 18.00 18.00

Atlantic Spotted Dolphins
A523

No. 1995: a, Two dolphins facing right. b, Head of dolphin facing left. c, One dolphin facing right. d, Two dolphins facing left.
$14, Head of dolphin facing right.

2019, July 7 Litho. *Perf. 14*
1995 A523 $4 Sheet of 4, #a-d 12.00 12.00

Souvenir Sheet

Perf. 12½

1996 A523 $14 multi 10.50 10.50

No. 1996 contains one 51x38mm stamp.

Miniature Sheet

Birth of Archie Mountbatten-Windsor — A524

No. 1997: a, $4, Duke and Duchess of Sussex with infant. b, $5, Duke of Sussex. c, $6, Duke and Duchess of Sussex. d, $7, Duke and Duchess of Sussex with infant, diff.

2019, July 10 Litho. *Perf. 12*
1997 A524 Sheet of 4, #a-d 16.50 16.50

Orchids
A525

No. 1998: a, $4, Guarianthe skinneri. b, $5, Papilionanthe Miss Joaquim. c, $6, Prosthechea cochleata. d, $7, Cattleya labiata.
$14, Unnamed orchids.

2019, July 31 Litho. *Perf. 14*
1998 A525 Sheet of 4, #a-d 16.50 16.50

Souvenir Sheet

Perf. 12½

1999 A525 $14 multi 10.50 10.50

Singpex 2019 International Stamp Exhibition, Singapore. No. 1999 contains one 51x38mm stamp.

Angelfish A526

No. 2000: a, $1, Gray angelfish. b, $2, Royal angelfish. c, $3, French angelfish. d, $4, Juvenile French angelfish. e, $5, Queen angelfish. f, $7, Queen angelfish, diff.
$14, Emperor angelfish, vert.

2020, Jan. 6 Litho. *Perf. 12½*
2000 A526 Sheet of 6, #a-f 16.50 16.50

Souvenir Sheet
Perf. 12

2001 A526 $14 multi 10.50 10.50

No. 2001 contains one 30x40mm stamp.

Marine Life A527

No. 2002: a, $2, Wolffish. b, $3, Equal sea star. c, $4, Purple sea urchin. d, $5, Mountain crab.
$14, Ornate butterflyfish, vert.

2020, Jan. 6 Litho. *Perf. 14*
2002 A527 Sheet of 4, #a-d 10.50 10.50

Souvenir Sheet
Perf. 12

2003 A527 $14 multi 10.50 10.50

Rabbits A528

No. 2004: a, Pygmy rabbit facing right. b, Angora rabbit. c, Holland lop rabbit. d, Pygmy rabbit facing left.
$14, Angora rabbit, diff., vert.

2020, Jan. 6 Litho. *Perf. 13¾*
2004 A528 $5 Sheet of 4, #a-d 15.00 15.00

Souvenir Sheet
Perf. 12½

2005 A528 $14 multi 10.50 10.50

No. 2005 contains one 38x51mm stamp.

Arrival in Massachusetts of the Pilgrims, 400th Anniv. — A529

No. 2006: a, Myles Standish (c. 1584-1656), military adviser to Plymouth Colony. b, Pilgrim settlers. c, William Bradford (1590-1657), governor of Plymouth Colony. d, Landing of the Pilgrims. e, Embarkation of the Pilgrims. f, The Mayflower Compact.
$14, Mayflower in Plymouth Harbor, by William Halsall (1841-1919), vert.

2020, May 20 Litho. *Perf. 14*
2006 A529 $4 Sheet of 6, #a-f 18.00 18.00

Souvenir Sheet
Perf. 12

2007 A529 $14 multi 10.50 10.50

A530

Starfish A531

No. 2008: a, Crown of thorns starfish. b, Granulated sea star. c, Ocher sea star. d, Giant spined star. e, Egyptian sea star.
$14, Blue starfish.

2020, Nov. 2 Litho. *Perf. 14*
2008 A530 $4.50 Sheet of 5, #a-e 17.00 17.00

Souvenir Sheet
Perf. 13¾

2009 A531 $14 multi 10.50 10.50

A532

Tree Frogs A533

No. 2010: a, Squirrel tree frog. b, Cuban tree frog. c, Gray tree frog. d, Red-eyed tree frog.
$14, Two tree frogs.

2020, Nov. 2 Litho. *Perf. 13¾*
2010 A532 $5.50 Sheet of 4, #a-d 16.50 16.50

Souvenir Sheet
Perf. 14

2011 A533 $14 multi 10.50 10.50

Dorje Chang Buddha III, Religious Leader — A534

2020, Dec. 28 Litho. *Perf. 13¼*
2012 A534 $5 multi 3.75 3.75

Miniature Sheet

Tribute to Workers During the COVID-19 Pandemic — A535

No. 2013: a, Doctor holding globe. b, World map on computer, gloved hand. c, Hospital gurneys. d, Health care worker, hands holding vials of blood.

2020, Dec. 28 Litho. *Perf. 14*
2013 A535 $5 Sheet of 4, #a-d 15.00 15.00

Miniature Sheet

Victory in Europe in World War II (V-E Day), 75th Anniv. A536

No. 2014: a, Alfred Jodl (1890-1946), chief of German Armed Forces High Command. b, Harry S. Truman (1884-1972), U.S. President. c, Soldiers at Arc de Triomphe, Paris. d, Franklin D. Roosevelt (1882-1945), U.S. President. e, Winston Churchill (1874-1965), British Prime Minister.

2020, Dec. 28 Litho. *Perf. 12*
2014 A536 $4.50 Sheet of 5, #a-e 17.00 17.00

Paintings by Raphael (1483-1520) — A537

No. 2015: a, Portrait of Elisabetta Gonzaga, c. 1504. b, Portrait of Pope Julius II, c. 1512. c, Portrait of Bindo Altoviti, c. 1514. d, Portrait of Baldassaare Castiglione, c. 1515.
$5, Self-portrait, c. 1504-06.

2020, Dec. 28 Litho. *Perf. 14*
2015 A537 $5.50 Sheet of 4, #a-d 16.50 16.50

Souvenir Sheet
Perf. 12½

2016 A537 $5 multi 3.75 3.75

No. 2016 contains one 38x51mm stamp that has the incorrect inscription of "Sistine Madonna, 1512."

Miniature Sheet

New Year 2021 (Year of the Ox) A538

No. 2017: a, Red ox with raised leg facing right. b, Head of red ox. c, Red ox with raised leg facing left. d, White ox with raised leg facing right. e, Head of white ox. f, White ox with raised leg facing left.

2020, Dec. 28 Litho. *Perf. 14*
2017 A538 $3 Sheet of 6, #a-f 13.50 13.50

A539

Anas Carolensis — A540

No. 2018 — Photograph of green-winged teal by: a, Unattributed photographer. b, Outriggr. c, Rudolphous. d, Trachemys.
$14, Three ducks.

2021, Jan. 20 Litho. *Perf. 14*
2018 A539 $5.50 Sheet of 4, #a-d 16.50 16.50

Souvenir Sheet
Perf. 12½

2019 A540 $14 multi 10.50 10.50

A541

Phoenicopterus Roseus — A542

No. 2020 — Photograph of greater flamingo: a, Facing right, black background. b, Facing right, in water. c, Facing left. d, Facing left, photograph by Max Benningfield.
$14, Two greater flamingos with heads in water.

2021, Jan. 20 Litho. *Perf. 14*
2020 A541 $5.50 Sheet of 4, #a-d 16.50 16.50

Souvenir Sheet

2021 A542 $14 multi 10.50 10.50

A543

Sea Turtles A544

No. 2022 — Drawings of sea turtles with: a, Head at right, denomination at LR. b, Denomination at UL. c, Denomination at LL. d, Head at center, denomination at LR.
No. 2023 — Drawings of sea turtles with head at: a, Right. b, Left.

2021, Jan. 20 Litho. *Perf. 14*
2022 A543 $5.50 Sheet of 4, #a-d 16.50 16.50

Souvenir Sheet

2023 A544 $8 Sheet of 2, #a-b 12.00 12.00

A545

95th Birthday of Queen Elizabeth II
A546

No. 2024 — Image of Queen Elizabeth II from: a, 2007 (30x40mm). b, 2006 (30x40mm). c, 1962 (30x80mm). d, 2012, wearing light blue jacket and hat (30x40mm). e, 2012, wearing tiara and ceremonial robe (30x40mm).
$14, Queen Elizabeth II wearing protective face mask.

2021, Mar. 14 Litho. *Perf. 14*
2024 A545 $4.95 Sheet of 5, #a-e 18.50 18.50

Souvenir Sheet
Perf. 12½

2025 A546 $14 multi 10.50 10.50

Joseph R. Biden, Jr., 46th President of the United States — A547

No. 2026 — Pres. Biden: a, Behind lectern with Presidential seal. b, With white background. c, With blue background. d, Holding mug. e, With wife, Jill and grandchildren Robert and Natalie. f, Behind microphones at the Pentagon.
$14.60, Pres. Biden behind microphones, vert.

2021 Litho. *Perf. 14*
2026 A547 $4.60 Sheet of 6, #a-f 20.50 20.50

Souvenir Sheet
Perf. 12½

2027 A547 $14.60 multi 11.00 11.00

Issued: No. 2026, 3/15; No. 2027, 3/14. No. 2027 contains one 38x51mm stamp.

Prince Philip (1921-2021) — A548

No. 2028: a, Prince Philip and Princess Elizabeth on wedding day. b, Prince Philip and Queen Elizabeth II. c, Prince Philip wearing hat. d, Prince Philip without hat.
$14, Pallbearers at coffin of Prince Philip.

2021 Litho. *Perf. 14*
2028 A548 $5.50 Sheet of 4, #a-d 16.50 16.50

Souvenir Sheet
Perf. 12

2029 A548 $14 multi 10.50 10.50

The date of issue reported for Nos. 2028-2029 is April. 9, 2021, the date of Prince Philip's death. No. 2029 contains one 50x30mm stamp.

Miniature Sheet

Elvis Presley (1935-77) — A549

No. 2030 — Presley: a, Wearing blue and gray shirt. b, Looking left, one eye visible. c, Wearing white jacket. d, Singing. e, Looking left, both eyes visible.

2021, July 5 Litho. *Perf. 14*
2030 A549 $4.50 Sheet of 5, #a-e 17.00 17.00

10th Wedding Anniversary of the Duke and Duchess of Cambridge — A550

No. 2031: a, Duke and Duchess of Cambridge, Duke with legs crossed. b, Duke and Duchess, Duchess wearing hat. c, Duke and Duchess, Duke holding umbrella. d, Queen Elizabeth II and Duchess of Cambridge.
$14, Duke and Duchess on wedding day.

2021, July 5 Litho. *Perf. 14*
2031 A550 $5.50 Sheet of 4, #a-d 16.50 16.50

Souvenir Sheet
Perf. 12½

2032 A550 $14 multi 10.50 10.50

No. 2032 contains one 51x38mm stamp.

3rd Wedding Anniversary of the Duke and Duchess of Sussex — A551

No. 2031: a, $5, Duke and Duchess of Sussex, Duchess wearing striped dress. b, $5, Duke and Duchess, Duchess wearing hat. c, $6, Duke and Duchess, Duchess waving. d, $6, Queen Elizabeth II and Duchess of Sussex.
$14, Duke and Duchess looking skyward at Royal Air Force ceremony.

2021, July 5 Litho. *Perf. 14*
2033 A551 Sheet of 4, #a-d 16.50 16.50

Souvenir Sheet

2034 A551 $14 multi 10.50 10.50

Miniature Sheet

Centenarians — A552

No. 2035: a, Nathan Sutton. b, Mary Browne. c, Eliza Liburd Jeffers. d, Gwendolyn Clarke.

2021, Nov. 5 Litho. *Perf. 13¼x13½*
2035 A552 30c Sheet of 4, #a-d .90 .90

Edible Mushrooms — A553

No. 2036: a, Shiitake mushrooms. b, Black truffles. c, Enoki mushrooms. d, Chanterelle mushrooms. e, Oyster mushrooms. f, Saffron milk cap.
$14, Caesar's mushrooms, vert.

2021, Nov. 8 Litho. *Perf. 14*
2036 A553 $4 Sheet of 6, #a-f 18.00 18.00

Souvenir Sheet
Perf. 12½

2037 A553 $14 multi 10.50 10.50

No. 2037 contains one 38x51mm stamp.

Macaws
A554

No. 2038: a, Glaucous macaw. b, Blue and yellow macaw. c, Green-winged macaw. d, Red-shouldered macaw. e, Great green macaw. f, Lear's macaw.
No. 2039: a, Cuban macaw. b, Red-fronted macaw.

2021, Nov. 8 Litho. *Perf. 14*
2038 A554 $3.50 Sheet of 6, #a-f 15.50 15.50

Souvenir Sheet

2039 A554 $8 Sheet of 2, #a-b 12.00 12.00

Butterflyfish — A555

No. 2040: a, Foureye butterflyfish. b, Pacific double-saddle butterflyfish. c, Threadfin butterflyfish. d, Lined butterflyfish. e, Bluecheek butterflyfish. f, Atoll butterflyfish. g, Eritrean butterflyfish. h, Longnose butterflyfish.
No. 2041: a, Millet butterflyfish. b, Fourspot butterflyfish.

2021, Nov. 8 Litho. *Perf. 14*
2040 A555 $3.50 Sheet of 8, #a-h 21.00 21.00

Souvenir Sheet

2041 A555 $8 Sheet of 2, #a-b 12.00 15.50

Sharks
A556

No. 2042: a, Caribbean reef shark. b, Bull shark. c, Blacktip reef shark. d, Silky shark. e, Pelagic thresher shark. f, Galapagos shark. g, Caribbean sharpnose shark. h, Night shark.
No. 2043: a, Australian sharpnose shark. b, Crocodile shark.

2021, Nov. 8 Litho. *Perf. 14*
2042 A556 $3.50 Sheet of 8, #a-h 21.00 21.00

Souvenir Sheet

2043 A556 $8 Sheet of 2, #a-b 12.00 15.50

Flight of Apollo 15, 50th Anniv.
A557

No. 2044: a, U.S. Navy divers leaving helicopter to secure Apollo 15 capsule in Pacific Ocean. b, Apollo 15 crew members James B. Irwin, Alfred M. Worden and David R. Scott. c, Apollo 15 on launch pad. d, Picture of Moon taken from Apollo 15. e, Drawing of deployment of Particles and Fields Subsatellite. f, Model of Apollo 15 Lunar Module on Moon.
$14, Scott's spacesuit on display at the Smithsonian Institution, vert.

2021, Dec. 1 Litho. *Perf. 14*
2044 A557 $4 Sheet of 6, #a-f 18.00 18.00

Souvenir Sheet
Perf. 12½

2045 A557 $14 multi 10.50 10.50

No. 2045 contains one 38x51mm stamp.

Reign of Queen Elizabeth II (1926-2022), 70th Anniv. — A558

No. 2046 — Photograph of Queen Elizabeth II: a, Wearing tiara and sash. b, Wearing pink jacket and hat. c, Wearing light blue jacket and hat. d, Holding infant. e, Wearing white jacket and hat.
$12.70, Queen Elizabeth II wearing gown and tiara.

2022, Feb. 6 Litho. *Perf. 14*
2046 A558 $3.70 Sheet of 5, #a-e 14.00 14.00

Souvenir Sheet
Perf. 12½

2047 A558 $12.70 multi 9.50 9.50

No. 2047 contains one 38x51mm stamp.

Skyscrapers — A559

No. 2048: a, Burj Khalifa, Dubai, United Arab Emirates. b, Taipei 101, Taipei, Republic of China. c, One World Trade Center, New York City. d, Lakhta Center, St. Petersburg, Russia. e, Q1 Tower, Gold Coast, Australia. f, Gran Torre Santiago, Santiago, Chile.
$14, Willis Tower, Chicago, Illinois.

2022, Mar. 7 Litho. *Perf. 14*
2048 A559 $4 Sheet of 6, #a-f 18.00 18.00

Souvenir Sheet
Perf. 12
2049 A559 $14 multi 10.50 10.50

No. 2049 contains one 30x60mm stamp.

Chlorocebus Pygerythrus — A560

No. 2050 — Various depictions of Vervet monkeys, as shown.
$14, Two Vervet monkeys, horiz.

2022, July 6 Litho. *Perf. 14*
2050 A560 $4 Sheet of 6, #a-f 18.00 18.00

Souvenir Sheet
Perf. 12½
2051 A560 $14 multi 10.50 10.50

No. 2051 contains one 51x38mm stamp.

Delonix Regia A561

No. 2052 — Various depictions of Poinicana flowers, as shown.
$14, Poinciana flowers, horiz.

2022, July 6 Litho. *Perf. 13¾*
2052 A561 $3 Sheet of 6, #a-f 13.50 13.50

Souvenir Sheet
Perf. 12½
2053 A561 $14 multi 10.50 10.50

No. 2053 contains one 51x38mm stamp.

40th Birthday of Prince William A562

No. 2054 — Photograph of: a, Prince William, 2011. b, Prince William and Queen Elizabeth II, 2017. c, Prince William and his wife, Catherine, 2016. d, Prince William and his mother, Princess Diana, 1986. e, Prince William, 2016.
$14, Prince William, Princess Diana and Queen Elizabeth II, 1989, horiz.

2022, July 11 Litho. *Perf. 13¾*
2054 A562 $4.50 Sheet of 5, #a-e 17.00 17.00

Souvenir Sheet
Perf. 12½
2055 A562 $14 multi 10.50 10.50

No. 2055 contains one 51x38mm stamp.

Fruits A565

No. 2059: a, Mango. b, Papaya. c, Tamarind. d, Strawberry. e, Black zapote. f, Pomegranate.
$14, Red Delicious apple.

2022, Oct. 10 Litho. *Perf. 14*
2059 A565 $3 Sheet of 6, #a-f 13.50 13.50

Souvenir Sheet
2060 A565 $14 multi 10.50 10.50

King Charles III A566

No. 2061 — King Charles III: a, With his son, Prince William. b, Alone, without hat. c, Alone, with hat. d, With his mother, Queen Elizabeth II.
$14, King Charles III as younger man wearing bow tie, horiz.

2022, Oct. 17 Litho. *Perf. 13¾*
2061 A566 $5.50 Sheet of 4, #a-d 16.50 16.50

Souvenir Sheet
Perf. 14
2062 A566 $14 multi 10.50 10.50

No. 2062 contains one 40x30mm stamp.

Miniature Sheet

Centenarians — A567

No. 2063: a, Bertram Roach, badge not visible. b, Roach wearing badge. c, Clarence Hendrickson, without hat. d, Hendrickson, wearing hat.

Perf. 13¼x12½
2022, Nov. 28 Litho.
2063 A567 30c Sheet of 4, #a-d .90 .90

Clownfish — A568

No. 2064: a, Saddleback clownfish. b, Maroon clownfish. c, Clark's clownfish. d, Cinnamon clownfish. e, Tomato clownfish. f, Pink skunk clownfish.
$14, True percula clownfish.

2022, Dec. 1 Litho. *Perf. 14*
2064 A568 $3.50 Sheet of 6, #a-f 15.50 15.50

Souvenir Sheet
Perf. 12
2065 A568 $14 multi 10.50 10.50

Visit of Pres. Joseph R. Biden, Jr. to Poland A569

No. 2066 — Pres. Biden: a, At lectern. b, With Polish Pres. Andrzej Duda, photographer in background. c, Departing Air Force One. d, With Pres. Duda, painting in background.
$14, Presidents Biden and Duda inspecting troops, horiz.

2022, Dec. 5 Litho. *Perf. 14*
2066 A569 $5 Sheet of 4, #a-d 15.00 15.00

Souvenir Sheet
Perf. 12½
2067 A569 $14 multi 10.50 10.50

No. 2067 contains one 51x38mm stamp.

OFFICIAL STAMPS

Catalogue values for unused stamps in this section are for Never Hinged items.

Nos. 103-112 Ovptd. "OFFICIAL"

Perf. 14½x14
1980, July 30 Litho. Wmk. 373

O1	A61	15c multicolored	.25	.25
O2	A61	25c multicolored	.25	.25
O3	A61	30c multicolored	.25	.25
O4	A61	40c multicolored	.25	.25
O5	A61	45c multicolored	.25	.25
O6	A61	50c multicolored	.25	.25
O7	A61	55c multicolored	.25	.25
O8	A61	$1 multicolored	.30	.30
O9	A61	$5 multicolored	1.50	1.50
O10	A61	$10 multicolored	2.50	2.50
		Nos. O1-O10 (10)	6.05	6.05

Inverted or double overprints exist on some denominations.

Nos. 123-134 Ovptd. "OFFICIAL"

1981, Mar. *Perf. 14*

O11	A9	15c multicolored	.25	.25
O12	A9	20c multicolored	.25	.25
O13	A9	25c multicolored	.25	.25
O14	A9	30c multicolored	.25	.25
O15	A9	40c multicolored	.25	.25
O16	A9	45c multicolored	.25	.25
O17	A9	50c multicolored	.25	.25
O18	A9	55c multicolored	.25	.25
O19	A9	$1 multicolored	.35	.35
O20	A9	$2.50 multicolored	.80	.80
O21	A9	$5 multicolored	1.50	1.50
O22	A9	$10 multicolored	2.50	2.50
		Nos. O11-O22 (12)	7.15	7.15

Nos. 135-140 Ovptd. or Surcharged "OFFICIAL" in Blue or Black

1983, Feb. 2

O23	A9a	45c on $2 #137	.30	.30
O24	A9b	45c on $2 #138	.30	.30
O25	A9a	55c #135	.40	.40
O26	A9b	55c #136	.40	.40
O27	A9a	$1.10 on $5 #139 (Bk)	.80	.80
O28	A9b	$1.10 on $5 #140 (Bk)	.80	.80
		Nos. O23-O28 (6)	3.00	3.00

Inverted or double overprints exist on some denominations.

Nos. 367-378 Ovptd. "OFFICIAL"

1985, Jan. 2 Wmk. 380

O29	A24b	15c multicolored	.30	.30
O30	A24b	20c multicolored	.30	.30
O31	A24b	30c multicolored	.30	.30
O32	A24b	40c multicolored	.30	.30
O33	A24b	50c multicolored	.35	.35
O34	A24b	55c multicolored	.35	.35
O35	A24b	60c multicolored	.35	.35
O36	A24b	75c multicolored	.45	.45
O37	A24b	$1 multicolored	.65	.65
O38	A24b	$3 multicolored	1.90	1.90
O39	A24b	$5 multicolored	3.25	3.25
O40	A24b	$10 multicolored	6.50	6.50
		Nos. O29-O40 (12)	15.00	15.00

Nos. 640-646, 648-653 Ovptd. "OFFICIAL"

1993 Litho. *Perf. 14*

O41	A71	5c multicolored	.30	.30
O42	A71	10c multicolored	.30	.30
O43	A71	15c multicolored	.30	.30
O44	A71	20c multicolored	.30	.30
O45	A71	25c multicolored	.30	.30
O46	A71	40c multicolored	.35	.35
O47	A71	50c multicolored	.50	.50
O48	A71	75c multicolored	.70	.70
O49	A71	80c multicolored	.75	.75
O50	A71	$1 multicolored	.95	.95
O51	A71	$3 multicolored	2.75	2.75
O52	A71	$5 multicolored	4.75	4.75
O53	A71	$10 multicolored	9.25	9.25
O54	A71	$20 multicolored	18.00	18.00
		Nos. O41-O54 (14)	39.50	39.50

Dated "1992."

Nos. 1055-1066 Ovptd. "OFFICIAL"

1999, Mar. 22 Litho. *Perf. 14*

O55	A151	25c multicolored	.25	.25
O56	A151	30c multicolored	.25	.25
O57	A151	50c multicolored	.40	.40

O58 A151 60c multicolored .45 .45
O59 A151 80c multicolored .60 .60
O60 A151 90c multicolored .70 .70
O61 A151 $1 multicolored .75 .75
O62 A151 $1.80 multicolored 1.40 1.40
O63 A151 $3 multicolored 2.25 2.25
O64 A151 $5 multicolored 3.75 3.75
O65 A151 $10 multicolored 7.50 7.50
O66 A151 $20 multicolored 15.00 15.00
Nos. O55-O66 (12) 33.30 33.30

NEW BRITAIN

'nü 'bri-tən

LOCATION — South Pacific Ocean, northeast of New Guinea
GOVT. — Australian military government
AREA — 13,000 sq. mi. (approx.)
POP. — 50,600 (est.)
CAPITAL — Rabaul

The island Neu-Pommern, a part of former German New Guinea, was captured during World War I by Australian troops and named New Britain. Following the war it was mandated to Australia and designated a part of the Mandated Territory of New Guinea. See German New Guinea, North West Pacific Islands and New Guinea.

12 Pence = 1 Shilling

Stamps of German New Guinea, 1900, Surcharged

Kaiser's Yacht "The Hohenzollern"
A3 A4

First Setting

Surcharge lines spaced 6mm on 1p-8p, 4mm on 1sh-5sh

Unwmk.

Perf. 14, 14½

1 A3 1p on 3pf brown 750.00 *875.00*
2 A3 1p on 5pf green 95.00 *200.00*
3 A3 2p on 10pf car 100.00 *260.00*
4 A3 2p on 20pf ultra 100.00 *200.00*
a. "2d." dbl., "G.R.I." omitted 6,000.
b. Inverted surcharge 16,500.
5 A3 2½p on 10pf car 105.00 *220.00*
6 A3 2½p on 20pf ultra 120.00 *250.00*
a. Inverted surcharge
7 A3 3p on 25pf org & blk, *yel* 375.00 *475.00*
8 A3 3p on 30pf org & blk, *sal* 475.00 *525.00*
a. Double surcharge *15,000.* *15,000.*
b. Triple surcharge
9 A3 4p on 40pf lake & black 475.00 *625.00*
a. Double surcharge 4,100. *5,000.*
b. Inverted surcharge *16,250.*
c. "4d." omitted
10 A3 5p on 50pf pur & blk, *sal* 850.00 *1,100.*
a. Double surcharge *16,250.*
11 A3 8p on 80pf lake & blk, *rose* 1,050. *1,650.*
a. No period after "8d" *4,600.*
b. Surcharged "G.R.I. 4d" (error) *15,250.*
12 A4 1sh on 1m car 5,500. *4,750.*
13 A4 2sh on 2m blue 3,750. *4,500.*
a. Surcharged "G.R.I. 5s" (error) *45,000.*
b. Surcharged "G.R.I. 2d" corrected by handstamped "s" *55,000.*
14 A4 3sh on 3m blk vio 6,000. *7,750.*
a. No period after "I" 14,000. *14,000.*
15 A4 5sh on 5m slate & car 14,000. *16,500.*
a. No period after "I" 18,500. 23,000.
b. Surcharged "G.R.I. 1s" (error) *87,500.*

"G.R.I." stands for Georgius Rex Imperator.

Second Setting

Surcharge lines spaced 5mm on 1p-8p, 5½mm on 1sh-5sh

1914, Dec. 16

16 A3 1p on 3pf brown 110.00 *120.00*
a. Double surcharge 1,500. *1,850.*
b. "I" for "1" 825.00
c. "1" with straight top serif 160.00 190.00
d. Inverted surcharge 6,000. —
e. "4" for "1" *17,500.*
f. Small "1" 350.00
g. Double surcharge, one inverted *8,000.*
17 A3 1p on 5pf green 37.50 *55.00*
a. Double surcharge 5,250.
b. "G. I. R." *13,000.* *14,000.*
c. "d" inverted 3,750.
d. No periods after "G R I" *11,000.*
e. Small "1" 140.00 210.00
f. "1d" double —
g. No period after "1d"
h. Triple surcharge
18 A3 2p on 10pf car 50.00 *65.00*
a. Double surcharge *16,250.* *16,250.*
b. Dbl. surch., one inverted *13,000.*
c. Surcharged "G. I. R., 3d" (error) *13,000.*
d. Surcharged "1d" (error) *12,500.* *12,500.*
e. Period before "G" *11,000.*
f. No period after "2d" 200.00 *275.00*
g. Inverted surcharge
h. "2d" double, one inverted
j. Pair, #18, 20 *30,000.*
19 A3 2p on 20pf ultra 50.00 *75.00*
a. Double surcharge 3,500. *5,250.*
b. Double surch., one inverted 5,000. *6,500.*
c. "R" inverted *9,250.*
d. Surcharged "1d" (error) *13,000.* *14,000.*
f. Inverted surcharge 11,500. *13,500.*
h. Pair, one without surcharge 25,000.
i. Vertical pair, #19, 21 20,000. 23,000.
20 A3 2½p on 10pf car 250.00 375.00
21 A3 2½p on 20pf ultra 2,100. *2,500.*
a. Double surcharge, one invtd.
b. "2½" triple
c. Surcharged "3d" in pair with normal *42,500.*
22 A3 3p on 25pf org & blk, *yel* 190.00 *275.00*
a. Double surcharge *11,000.* *13,000.*
b. Inverted surcharge *11,000.* *13,000.*
c. "G. R. I." only
d. "G. I. R."
e. Pair, one without surcharge *15,000.*
f. Surcharged "G. I. R., 5d" (error)
g. Surcharged "1d" (error) *22,000.*
23 A3 3p on 30pf org & blk, *sal* 175.00 *240.00*
a. Double surcharge 4,000. *4,600.*
b. Double surcharge, one invtd. 4,500. *5,500.*
c. "d" inverted
d. Surcharged "1d" (error) *12,000.* *16,000.*
e. Triple surcharge
g. Double inverted surcharge *13,000.* *14,000.*
h. Pair, one without surcharge *14,000.*
24 A3 4p on 40pf lake & blk 185.00 *300.00*
a. Double surcharge 3,500. —
b. Double surcharge, both invtd. *13,000.*
c. Double surcharge, one invtd. 5,250.
d. Inverted surcharge 9,250.
e. Surcharged "1d" (error) 9,000.
f. "1" on "4"
g. As "e," inverted *20,000.*
h. Surcharge "G.R.I. 3d," double (error) *27,500.*
i. No period after "I" 3,500.
25 A3 5p on 50pf pur & blk, *sal* 350.00 *400.00*
a. Double surcharge 4,500. *5,500.*
b. Double surcharge, one invtd. *10,500.* *10,500.*
c. "5" omitted
d. Inverted surcharge 10,000. *10,000.*
e. Double inverted surcharge 13,000. *14,000.*
f. "G. I. R."
g. Surcharge "G.R.I. 3d" (error) *23,000.*
26 A3 8p on 80pf lake & blk, *rose* 475.00 *650.00*
a. Double surcharge 7,000. *8,250.*
b. Double surcharge, one invtd. 7,000. *8,250.*
c. Triple surcharge 9,500. *10,000.*
d. No period after "8d"
e. Inverted surcharge *14,000.* 14,000.
f. Surcharged "3d" (error) *18,500.* *18,500.*
27 A4 1sh on 1m car 5,250. *8,250.*
a. No period after "I" *12,000.*
28 A4 2sh on 2m bl 5,500. *8,750.*
a. Surcharged "5s" (error)
b. Double surcharge
c. No period after "I" *13,000.*
29 A4 3sh on 3m blk vio 10,000. *16,250.*
a. No periods after "R I"
b. "G.R.I." double *45,000.*
29C A4 5sh on 5m sl & car *42,500.* *45,000.*
d. No periods after "R I"
e. Surcharged "1s"

Nos. 18-19 Surcharged with Large "1"

1915, Jan.

29F A3 1(p) on 2p on 10pf carmine *32,500.* *30,000.*
29G A3 1(p) on 2p on 20pf ultramarine *30,000.* *17,500.*

Same Surcharge on Stamps of Marshall Islands

1914

30 A3 1p on 3pf brn 110.00 *170.00*
a. Inverted surcharge 9,250.
31 A3 1p on 5pf green 90.00 *130.00*
a. Double surcharge 3,800. *5,000.*
b. No period after "d"
c. Inverted surcharge 5,250.
32 A3 2p on 10pf car 27.50 *50.00*
a. Double surcharge 3,800.
b. Double surcharge, one invtd. 5,500.
c. Surcharge sideways 10,500.
d. No period after "2d"
e. No period after "G" 875.00
f. Inverted surcharge 7,000.
33 A3 2p on 20 pf ultra 30.00 *50.00*
a. No period after "d" 80.00 *150.00*
b. Double surcharge 4,000. 5,250.
c. Double surcharge, one invtd. *9,750.* *10,500.*
d. Inverted surcharge *11,000.* *11,000.*
e. "I" omitted
34 A3 3p on 25pf org & blk, *yel* 475.00 *600.00*
a. Double surcharge 4,250. *5,000.*
b. Double surcharge, one invtd. 4,700.
c. No period after "d" 925.00 1,250.
d. Inverted surcharge 13,000.
35 A3 3p on 30pf org & blk, *sal* 475.00 *600.00*
a. No period after "d" 925.00 1,200.
b. Inverted surcharge 9,000. 9,500.
c. Double surcharge 7,000.
d. Double surcharge, one invtd.
36 A3 4p on 40pf lake & blk 175.00 *250.00*
a. No period after "d" 475.00 *700.00*
b. Double surcharge 7,000. *8,000.*
c. "4d" omitted
d. "1d" on "4d"
e. No period after "R"
f. Inverted surcharge 11,000.
g. Surcharged "1d" (error) *17,500.*
h. Surcharged "G.R.I. 3d" (error)
37 A3 5p on 50pf pur & blk, *sal* 300.00 *375.00*
a. "d" omitted 2,250.
b. Double surcharge *10,500.*
c. "5d" double
d. Inverted surcharge *16,500.*
38 A3 8p on 80pf lake & blk, *rose* 525.00 775.00
a. Inverted surcharge *11,500.*
b. Double surcharge *10,000.*
c. Double surcharge, one invtd.
d. Triple surcharge *16,500.*
e. Double surcharge, both inverted *13,250.* *14,000.*
39 A4 1sh on 1m car 4,100. *5,500.*
a. Double surcharge *45,000.*
b. Dbl. surch., one with "s1" for "1s"
c. No period after "I" 6,500. 9,250.
d. Additional surcharge "1d" *50,000.*
40 A4 2sh on 2m blue 2,000. 4,500.
a. Double surcharge, one invtd. *45,000.* *45,000.*
b. Double surcharge *45,000.*
c. Large "S"
d. No period after "I" 3,750. *6,500.*
41 A4 3sh on 3m blk vio 6,500. *9,750.*
a. Double surcharge *42,500.* *45,000.*
b. No period after "I" 8,750.
c. No period after "R I"
d. Inverted surcharge
42 A4 5sh on 5m sl & car *14,000.* *15,000.*
a. Double surcharge, one invtd. *75,000.*

See Nos. 44-45.

A5

Surcharged in Black on Registration Label

Town Name in Sans-Serif Letters

1914 ***Perf. 12***

43 A5 3p black & red (Rabaul) 300.00 *350.00*
a. Double surcharge (Rabaul) 5,500. *7,000.*
44 A5 3p black & red (Friedrich Wilhelmshaven) 275.00 *875.00*
45 A5 3p black & red (Herbertshohe) 325.00 *875.00*
46 A5 3p black & red (Kawieng) 350.00 *700.00*
a. Double surcharge
47 A5 3p black & red (Kieta) 500.00 *875.00*
a. Pair, one without surcharge *16,500.*
48 A5 3p black & red (Manus) 325.00 *925.00*
a. Double surcharge *9,250.*
49 A5 3p black & red (Deulon) 27,500. *30,000.*
50 A5 3p black & red (Stephansort) *4,500.*

Nos. 44, 46 and 48 exist with town name in letters with serifs. The varieties Deutsch-Neuguinea, Deutsch Neu-Guinea, etc., are known. For detailed listings see the *Scott Classic Specialized Catalogue of Stamps and Covers.*

Nos. 32-33 Surcharged with Large "1"

1915

51 A3 1p on 2p on 10pf 275. 300.
a. "1" double *16,500.*
b. "1" inverted *20,000.* *20,000.*
52 A3 1p on 2p on 20pf 4,000. 2,750.
a. "1" inverted *20,000.* *20,000.*

The stamps of Marshall Islands surcharged "G. R. I." and new values in British currency were all used in New Britain and are therefore listed here.

Stamps of Marshall Islands Surcharged

Surcharge lines spaced 6mm apart

53 A3 1p on 3pf brown *3,750.*
a. Inverted surcharge *16,000.*
54 A3 1p on 5pf green *3,750.*
a. Inverted surcharge *16,500.*
55 A3 2p on 10pf car *4,750.*
56 A3 2p on 20pf ultra *4,250.*
a. Inverted surcharge *17,000.*
57 A3 2½p on 10pf car *30,000.*
58 A3 2½p on 20pf ultra *45,000.*
59 A3 3p on 25pf org & blk, *yel* *7,000.*
60 A3 3p on 30pf org & blk, *sal* *7,000.*
61 A3 4p on 40pf lake & blk *7,000.*
a. Inverted surcharge *18,000.*
62 A3 5p on 50pf pur & blk, *sal* *6,500.*
63 A3 8p on 80pf lake & blk, *rose* *7,500.*
a. Inverted surcharge *20,000.*

Surcharge lines spaced 5½mm apart

64 A4 1sh on 1m car *17,500.*
a. Large "S" *22,500.*
65 A4 2sh on 2m bl *14,500.*
a. Large "S" *20,000.*
66 A4 3sh on 3m blk vi-ol *30,000.*
a. Large "S" *40,000.*
67 A4 5sh on 5m sl & car *45,000.*
a. Large "S" *52,500.*

OFFICIAL STAMPS

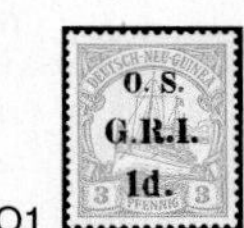

O1

German New Guinea Nos. 7-8 Surcharged

1915 **Unwmk.** ***Perf. 14***

O1 O1 1p on 3pf brown 36.00 *80.00*
a. Double surcharge 5,500.
O2 O1 1p on 5pf green 110.00 *150.00*

NEW CALEDONIA

'nü ˌka-lə-'dō-nyə

LOCATION — Island in the South Pacific Ocean, east of Queensland, Australia
GOVT. — French Overseas Territory
AREA — 7,172 sq. mi.
POP. — 197,361 (1999 est.)
CAPITAL — Noumea

Dependencies of New Caledonia are the Loyalty Islands, Isle of Pines, Huon Islands and Chesterfield Islands.

100 Centimes = 1 Franc

Catalogue values for unused stamps in this country are for Never Hinged items, beginning with Scott 252 in the regular postage section, Scott B10 in the semi-postal section, Scott C14 in the airpost section, Scott J32 in the postage due section, and Scott O1 in the official section.

Watermark

Wmk. 385

Napoleon III — A1

1859 Unwmk. Litho. *Imperf.*
Without Gum

1 A1 10c black 250.00 250.00

Fifty varieties. Counterfeits abound. See No. 315.

Type of French Colonies, 1877 Surcharged in Black

Nos. 2-5 Nos. 6-7

1881-83

2 A8 5c on 40c red, *straw* ('82) 425.00 425.00
a. Inverted surcharge 1,600. 1,600.
b. Double surcharge 1,350.
c. Double surcharge, both inverted 1,900. 1,900.
3 A8 05c on 40c red, *straw* ('83) 40.00 40.00
4 A8 25c on 35c dp vio, *yel* 300.00 300.00
a. Inverted surcharge 950.00 950.00
5 A8 25c on 75c rose car, *rose* ('82) 400.00 400.00
a. Inverted surcharge 1,250. 1,250.

1883-84

6 A8 5c on 40c red, *straw* ('84) 26.50 26.50
a. Inverted surcharge 26.50 26.50
7 A8 5c on 75c rose car, *rose* ('83) 52.50 52.50
a. Inverted surcharge 75.00 75.00

In type "a" surcharge, the narrower-spaced letters measure 14½mm, and an early printing of No. 4 measures 13½mm. Type "b" letters measure 18mm.

French Colonies No. 59 Surcharged in Black

No. 8

Nos. 9-10

1886 *Perf. 14x13½*

8 A9 5c on 1fr 32.50 26.50
a. Inverted surcharge 45.00 45.00
b. Double surcharge 200.00 200.00
c. Double surcharge, one inverted 225.00 225.00
9 A9 5c on 1fr 32.50 30.00
a. Inverted surcharge 60.00 60.00
b. Double surcharge 200.00 200.00
c. Double surcharge, one inverted 225.00 225.00

French Colonies No. 29 Surcharged

Imperf

10 A8 5c on 1fr 10,000. 11,500.

Types of French Colonies, 1877-86, Surcharged in Black

Nos. 11, 13

No. 12

1891-92 *Imperf.*

11 A8 10c on 40c red, *straw* ('92) 45.00 40.00
a. Inverted surcharge 42.50 37.50
b. Double surcharge 100.00 100.00
c. Double surcharge, one inverted 190.00 190.00
d. No period after "10c" 125.00 125.00

Perf. 14x13½

12 A9 10c on 30c brn, *bis* 25.00 22.50
a. Inverted surcharge 25.00 22.50
b. Double surcharge 67.50 67.50
c. Double surcharge, inverted 60.00 60.00
d. Double surcharge, one inverted 100.00 100.00
13 A9 10c on 40c red, *straw* ('92) 26.00 26.00
a. Inverted surcharge 26.00 26.00
b. No period after "10c" 60.00 60.00
c. Double surcharge 67.50 67.50
d. Double surcharge, one inverted 110.00 100.00
Nos. 11-13 (3) 96.00 88.50

Variety "double surcharge, one inverted" exists on Nos. 11-13. Value slightly higher than for "double surcharge."

Types of French Colonies, 1877-86, Handstamped in Black — g

1892 *Imperf.*

16 A8 20c red, *grn* 350.00 *400.00*
a. Inverted surcharge 850.00 900.00
17 A8 35c violet, *org* 75.00 75.00
a. Pair, one stamp without surcharge 950.00
18 A8 40c red, *straw* *1,500.*
19 A8 1fr bronz grn, *straw* 300.00 300.00

The 1c, 2c, 4c and 75c of type A8 are believed not to have been officially made or actually used.

1892 *Perf. 14x13½*

23 A9 5c green, *grnsh* 19.00 15.00
a. Pair, one stamp without overprint 600.00
24 A9 10c blk, *lavender* 140.00 82.50
25 A9 15c blue 110.00 60.00
a. Pair, one stamp without overprint 825.00
26 A9 20c red, *grn* 110.00 60.00
27 A9 25c yellow, *straw* 30.00 22.50
28 A9 25c black, *rose* 110.00 37.50
29 A9 30c brown, *bis* 90.00 75.00
30 A9 35c violet, *org* 240.00 190.00
a. Inverted overprint 650.00
b. Pair, one stamp without overprint 1,350.
32 A9 75c carmine, *rose* 225.00 190.00
a. Pair, one stamp without overprint 1,350.
33 A9 1fr bronz grn, *straw* 190.00 175.00
Nos. 23-33 (10) 1,264. 907.50

The note following No. 19 also applies to the 1c, 2c, 4c and 40c of type A9.

Surcharged in Blue or Black — h

1892-93 *Imperf.*

34 A8 10c on 1fr brnz grn, *straw* (Bl) *5,250. 4,500.*

Perf. 14x13½

35 A9 5c on 20c red, *grn* (Bk) 27.50 22.50
a. Inverted surcharge 125.00 125.00
b. Double surcharge 82.50 100.00
36 A9 5c on 75c car, *rose* (Bk) 22.50 16.50
a. Inverted surcharge 125.00 125.00
b. Double surcharge 82.50 82.50
37 A9 5c on 75c car, *rose* (Bl) 18.50 15.00
a. Inverted surcharge 125.00 125.00
b. Double surcharge 82.50 82.50
38 A9 10c on 1fr brnz grn, *straw* (Bk) 21.00 15.00
a. Inverted surcharge 600.00 600.00
39 A9 10c on 1fr brnz grn, *straw* (Bl) 22.50 21.00
a. Inverted surcharge 125.00 125.00
b. Double surcharge 85.00 85.00
Nos. 35-39 (5) 112.00 90.00

Navigation and Commerce — A12

1892-1904 Typo. *Perf. 14x13½*
Name of Colony in Blue or Carmine

40 A12 1c black, *blue* 1.10 1.10
41 A12 2c brown, *buff* 1.90 1.90
42 A12 4c claret, *lav* 2.50 2.25
43 A12 5c green, *grnsh* 4.00 1.90
44 A12 5c yellow green ('00) 2.25 1.50
45 A12 10c blk, *lavender* 9.00 5.25
46 A12 10c rose red ('00) 11.00 1.50
47 A12 15c bl, quadrille paper 30.00 3.50
48 A12 15c gray ('00) 20.00 1.50
49 A12 20c red, *grn* 20.00 10.50
50 A12 25c black, *rose* 25.00 6.75
51 A12 25c blue ('00) 22.00 10.50
52 A12 30c brown, *bis* 25.00 13.50
53 A12 40c red, *straw* 26.00 13.50
54 A12 50c carmine, *rose* 67.50 37.50
55 A12 50c brn, *az* (name in car) ('00) 125.00 85.00
56 A12 50c brn, *az* (name in bl) ('04) 65.00 42.50
57 A12 75c violet, *org* 37.50 26.50
58 A12 1fr bronz grn, *straw* 45.00 26.50
Nos. 40-58 (19) 539.75 293.15

Perf. 13½x14 stamps are counterfeits.
For overprints and surcharges see Nos. 59-87, 117-121.

Nos. 41-42, 52, 57-58 Surcharged in Black

j

1900-01

59 A12 (h) 5c on 2c ('01) 22.50 19.00
a. Double surcharge 140.00 140.00
b. Inverted surcharge 125.00 125.00
Never hinged 210.00
60 A12 (h) 5c on 4c 4.50 4.50
a. Inverted surcharge 82.50 82.50
b. Double surcharge 87.50 87.50
61 A12 (j) 15c on 30c 5.25 4.50
a. Inverted surcharge 75.00 75.00
b. Double surcharge 67.50 67.50
62 A12 (j) 15c on 75c ('01) 20.00 17.50
a. Pair, one without surcharge —
b. Inverted surcharge 130.00 130.00
c. Double surcharge 140.00 140.00
63 A12 (j) 15c on 1fr ('01) 26.50 26.50
a. Double surcharge 175.00 175.00
b. Inverted surcharge 175.00 175.00
Nos. 59-63 (5) 78.75 72.00

Nos. 52-53 Surcharged in Black

k

1902

64 A12 (k) 5c on 30c 10.50 9.00
a. Inverted surcharge 52.50 52.50
65 A12 (k) 15c on 40c 10.50 8.25
a. Inverted surcharge 52.50 52.50

Jubilee Issue

Stamps of 1892-1900 Overprinted in Blue, Red, Black or Gold

1903

66 A12 1c blk, *lil bl* (Bl) 3.00 3.00
a. Inverted overprint *290.00 290.00*
67 A12 2c brown, *buff* (Bl) 5.25 4.50
68 A12 4c claret, *lav* (Bl) 7.50 6.00
a. Double overprint *375.00 375.00*
69 A12 5c dk grn, *grnsh* (R) 7.50 4.50
70 A12 5c yellow green (R) 10.00 9.00
71 A12 10c blk, *lav* (R) 19.00 16.00
72 A12 10c blk, *lav* (double G & Bk) 11.50 9.00
73 A12 15c gray (R) 15.00 11.50
74 A12 20c red, *grn* (Bl) 22.00 19.00
75 A12 25c blk, *rose* (Bl) 19.50 19.00
a. Double overprint 325.00
76 A12 30c brown, *bis* (R) 26.50 22.50
77 A12 40c red, *straw* (Bl) 34.00 30.00
78 A12 50c car, *rose* (Bl) 60.00 52.50
a. Pair, one without overprint *300.00*
79 A12 75c vio, *org* (Bk) 77.50 72.50
a. Dbl. ovpt. in blk and red *500.00*
80 A12 1fr brnz grn, *straw* (Bl) 120.00 115.00
a. Dbl. ovpt., one in red *525.00 525.00*
Nos. 66-80 (15) 438.25 394.00

With Additional Surcharge of New Value in Blue

(a) (b)

(c)

81 A12 (a) 1c on 2c #67 1.90 1.90
a. Numeral double *115.00 115.00*
b. Numeral only 400.00
82 A12 (b) 2c on 4c #68 3.50 3.50
83 A12 (a) 4c on 5c #69 2.25 2.25
a. Small "4" *650.00 650.00*
84 A12 (c) 4c on 5c #70 3.00 3.00
a. Pair, one without numeral
85 A12 (b) 10c on 15c #73 3.00 3.00
86 A12 (b) 15c on 20c #74 3.75 3.75
87 A12 (b) 20c on 25c #75 9.00 9.00
Nos. 81-87 (7) 26.40 26.40

50 years of French occupation.
Surcharge on Nos. 81-83, 85-86 is horizontal, reading down.
There are three types of numeral on No. 83. The numeral on No. 84 is identical with that of No. 83a except that its position is upright.
Nos. 66-87 are known with "I" of "TENAIRE" missing.

Kagu A16

Landscape A17

Ship — A18

1905-28 Typo. *Perf. 14x13½*

88 A16 1c blk, *green* .30 .30
89 A16 2c red brown .30 .30
90 A16 4c bl, *yel* .45 .45
91 A16 5c pale green .55 .55
92 A16 5c dl bl ('21) .40 .40
93 A16 10c carmine 1.90 1.25
94 A16 10c green ('21) .75 .75
95 A16 10c red, *pink* ('25) .85 .85
96 A16 15c violet .90 .85
97 A17 20c brown .55 .55
98 A17 25c blue, *grn* 1.05 .60
99 A17 25c red, *yel* ('21) .75 .75
100 A17 30c brn, *org* 1.40 .85
101 A17 30c dp rose ('21) 2.50 2.50
102 A17 30c org ('25) .60 .60
103 A17 35c blk, *yellow* .75 .75
104 A17 40c car, *grn* 1.25 1.05
105 A17 45c vio brn, *lav* .75 .75
106 A17 50c red, *org* 3.25 3.00
107 A17 50c dk bl ('21) 1.75 1.75
108 A17 50c gray ('25) 1.05 1.05
109 A17 65c dp bl ('28) .90 .90

110 A17 75c ol grn, *straw* .85 .70
111 A17 75c bl, *bluish* ('25) .90 .90
112 A17 75c violet ('27) 1.15 1.15
113 A18 1fr bl, *yel grn* 1.30 1.05
114 A18 1fr dp bl ('25) 1.90 1.90
115 A18 2fr car, *bl* 3.50 2.25
116 A18 5fr blk, *straw* 6.75 6.75
Nos. 88-116 (29) 39.30 35.50

See Nos. 311, 317a. For surcharges see Nos. 122-135, B1-B3, Q1-Q3.

Nos. 96, 98, 103, 106, 113 and 115, pasted on cardboard and handstamped "TRESORIER PAYEUR DE LA NOUVELLE CALEDONIE" were used as emergency currency in 1914.

Stamps of 1892-1904 Surcharged in Carmine or Black

1912
117 A12 5c on 15c gray (C) 1.50 *1.90*
a. Inverted surcharge 210.00 210.00
118 A12 5c on 20c red, *grn* 1.50 *1.90*
119 A12 5c on 30c brn, *bis* (C) 2.25 *3.00*
120 A12 10c on 40c red, *straw* 3.25 *3.25*
121 A12 10c on 50c brn, *az* (C) 3.25 *4.25*
Nos. 117-121 (5) 11.75 14.30

Two spacings between the surcharged numerals are found on Nos. 117 to 121. For detailed listings, see the *Scott Classic Specialized Catalogue of Stamps and Covers.*

No. 96 Surcharged in Brown

1918
122 A16 5c on 15c violet 1.90 1.90
a. Double surcharge 75.00 75.00
b. Inverted surcharge 45.00 45.00

The color of the surcharge on No. 122 varies from red to dark brown.

No. 96 Surcharged

1922
123 A16 5c on 15c vio (R) .60 .60
a. Double surcharge 75.00 75.00

Stamps and Types of 1905-28 Surcharged in Red or Black

No. 124

No. 127

1924-27
124 A16 25c on 15c vio .75 .75
a. Double surcharge 75.00
b. Double surcharge, one inverted 110.00
125 A18 25c on 2fr car, *bl* .85 .85
126 A18 25c on 5fr blk, *straw* .90 .90
a. Double surcharge 125.00 125.00
b. Triple surcharge 225.00 210.00
127 A17 60c on 75c grn (R) .75 .75
128 A17 65c on 45c red brn 2.00 2.00
129 A17 85c on 45c red brn 2.00 2.00
130 A17 90c on 75c dp rose 1.05 1.05
131 A18 1.25fr on 1fr dp bl (R) .90 .90
132 A18 1.50fr on 1fr dp bl, *bl* 1.60 1.60
133 A18 3fr on 5fr red vio 2.10 2.10
134 A18 10fr on 5fr ol, *lav* (R) 7.50 7.50
135 A18 20fr on 5fr vio rose, *org* 14.50 14.50
Nos. 124-135 (12) 34.90 34.90

Issue years: Nos. 125-127, 1924. Nos. 124, 128-129, 1925. Nos. 131, 134, 1926. Nos. 130, 132-133, 135, 1927.

Bay of Palétuviers Point — A19

Landscape with Chief's House — A20

Admiral de Bougainville and Count de La Pérouse — A21

1928-40 **Typo.**
136 A19 1c brn vio & ind .30 .25
137 A19 2c dk brn & yel grn .30 .25
137B A19 3c brn vio & ind .30 .30
138 A19 4c org & Prus grn .30 .25
139 A19 5c Prus bl & dp ol .45 .45
140 A19 10c gray lil & dk brn .30 .30
141 A19 15c yel brn & dp bl .55 .55
142 A19 20c brn red & dk brn .55 .55
143 A19 25c dk grn & dk brn .70 .55
144 A20 30c ol grn & grn .60 .60
145 A20 35c blk & brt vio .90 .90
146 A20 40c brt red & olvn .55 .55
147 A20 45c dp bl & red org 1.60 1.30
147A A20 45c bl grn & dl grn 1.05 1.05
148 A20 50c vio & brn .85 .85
149 A20 55c vio bl & car 3.50 2.25
150 A20 60c vio bl & car .75 .75
151 A20 65c org brn & bl 1.30 1.15
152 A20 70c dp rose & brn .60 .60
153 A20 75c Prus bl & ol gray 1.40 1.15
154 A20 80c red brn & grn 1.15 1.00
155 A20 85c grn & brn 2.00 1.30
156 A20 90c dp red & brt red 1.30 .90
157 A20 90c ol grn & rose red 1.05 1.05
158 A21 1fr dp ol & sal red 7.25 4.25
159 A21 1fr rose red & dk car 2.25 1.75
160 A21 1fr brn red & grn 1.05 1.05
161 A21 1.10fr grn & brn 12.00 12.00
162 A21 1.25fr brn red & grn 1.20 1.20
163 A21 1.25fr rose red & dk car 1.15 1.15
164 A21 1.40fr dk bl & red org 1.20 1.20
165 A21 1.50fr dp bl & bl .90 .90
166 A21 1.60fr dp grn & brn 1.35 1.35
167 A21 1.75fr dk bl & red org 1.05 1.05
168 A21 1.75fr violet bl 1.50 1.05
169 A21 2fr red org & brn .90 .75
170 A21 2.25fr vio bl 1.20 1.20
171 A21 2.50fr brn & lt brn 1.75 1.75
172 A21 3fr mag & brn .75 .75
173 A21 5fr dk bl & brn 1.15 1.15
174 A21 10fr vio & brn, *pnksh* 1.30 1.30
175 A21 20fr red & brn, *yel* 2.75 2.75
Nos. 136-175 (42) 63.05 55.45

The 35c in Prussian green and dark green without overprint is listed as Wallis and Futuna No. 53a.

Issue years: 35c, 70c, 85c, #162, 167, 1933; 55c, 80c, #159, 168, 1938; #157, 163, 2.25fr, 1939; 3c, 60c, 1.40fr, 1.60fr, 2.50fr, 147A, 160, 1940; others, 1928.

For overprints see #180-207, 217-251, Q4-Q6.

Common Design Types pictured following the introduction.

Colonial Exposition Issue
Common Design Types

1931 **Engr.** ***Perf. 12½***
Country Name Typo. in Black
176 CD70 40c dp green 6.00 6.00
177 CD71 50c violet 6.00 6.00
178 CD72 90c red orange 6.00 6.00
179 CD73 1.50fr dull blue 6.00 6.00
Nos. 176-179 (4) 24.00 24.00

Paris-Nouméa Flight Issue
Regular Issue of 1928 Overprinted

1932 ***Perf. 14x13½***
180 A20 40c brt red & ol 475.00 *500.00*
181 A20 50c vio & brn 475.00 *500.00*

Arrival on Apr. 5, 1932 at Nouméa, of the French aviators, Verneilh, Dévé and Munch.

Excellent forgeries exist of #180-181.

Types of 1928-33 Overprinted in Black or Red

1933
182 A19 1c red vio & dl bl 6.50 *7.00*
183 A19 2c dk brn & yel grn 6.50 *7.00*
184 A19 4c dl org & Prus bl 6.50 *7.00*
185 A19 5c Prus grn & ol (R) 6.50 *7.00*
186 A19 10c gray lil & dk brn (R) 6.50 *7.00*
187 A19 15c yel brn & dp bl (R) 6.50 *7.00*
188 A19 20c brn red & dk brn 6.50 *7.00*
189 A19 25c dk grn & dk brn (R) 6.50 *7.00*
190 A20 30c gray grn & bl grn (R) 6.75 *7.50*
191 A20 35c blk & lt vio 6.75 *7.50*
192 A20 40c brt red & olvn 6.75 *7.00*
193 A20 45c dp bl & red org 6.75 *7.50*
194 A20 50c vio & brn 6.75 *7.00*
195 A20 70c dp rose & brn 7.50 *8.00*
196 A20 75c Prus bl & ol gray (R) 7.50 *8.00*
197 A20 85c grn & brn 7.50 *8.00*
198 A20 90c dp red & brt red 9.50 *10.00*
199 A21 1fr dp ol & sal red 9.50 *10.00*
200 A21 1.25fr brn red & grn 9.50 *10.00*
201 A21 1.50fr dp bl & bl (R) 9.50 *10.00*
202 A21 1.75fr dk bl & red org 9.50 *10.00*
203 A21 2fr red org & brn 9.50 *10.00*
204 A21 3fr mag & brn 9.50 *10.00*
205 A21 5fr dk bl & brn (R) 9.50 *10.00*
206 A21 10fr vio & brn, *pnksh* 10.00 *11.00*
207 A21 20fr red & brn, *yel* 10.00 *11.00*
Nos. 182-207 (26) 204.25 218.50

1st anniv., Paris-Noumea flight. Plane centered on Nos. 190-207.

Paris International Exposition Issue
Common Design Types

1937 **Engr.** ***Perf. 13***
208 CD74 20c dp vio 2.75 2.75
209 CD75 30c dk grn 2.75 2.75
210 CD76 40c car rose 2.75 2.75
211 CD77 50c dk brn & bl 2.75 2.75
212 CD78 90c red 2.75 2.75
213 CD79 1.50fr ultra 2.75 2.75
Nos. 208-213 (6) 16.50 16.50

Colonial Arts Exhibition Issue
Souvenir Sheet
Common Design Type

1937 ***Imperf.***
214 CD78 3fr sepia 22.50 *34.00*

New York World's Fair Issue
Common Design Type

1939 ***Perf. 12½x12***
215 CD82 1.25fr car lake 1.60 1.60
216 CD82 2.25fr ultra 1.75 1.75

Nouméa Roadstead and Marshal Pétain

1941 **Engr.** ***Perf. 12½x12***
216A A21a 1fr bluish green .75
216B A21a 2.50fr dark blue .75

Nos. 216A-216B were issued by the Vichy government in France, but were not placed on sale in the colony.

For surcharges, see Nos. B12A-B12B.

Types of 1928-40 Overprinted in Black

1941 ***Perf. 14x13½***
217 A19 1c red vio & dl bl 13.50 13.50
218 A19 2c dk brn & yel grn 13.50 13.50
219 A19 3c brn vio & ind 13.50 13.50
220 A19 4c dl org & Prus bl 13.50 13.50
221 A19 5c Prus bl & dp ol 13.50 13.50
222 A19 10c gray lil & dk brn 13.50 13.50
223 A19 15c yel brn & dp bl 18.00 18.00
224 A19 20c brn red & dk brn 18.00 18.00
225 A19 25c dk grn & dk brn 18.00 18.00
226 A20 30c gray grn & bl grn 18.00 18.00
227 A20 35c blk & brt vio 18.00 18.00
228 A20 40c brt red & olvn 18.00 18.00
229 A20 45c bl grn & dl grn 18.00 18.00
230 A20 50c vio & brn 18.00 18.00
231 A20 55c vio bl & car 18.00 18.00
232 A20 60c vio bl & car 18.00 18.00
233 A20 65c org brn & bl 18.00 18.00
234 A20 70c dp rose & brn 18.00 18.00
235 A20 75c Prus bl & ol gray 18.00 18.00
236 A20 80c red brn & grn 18.00 18.00
237 A20 85c grn & brn 18.00 18.00
238 A20 90c dp red & brt red 18.00 18.00
239 A21 1fr rose red & dk car 18.00 18.00
240 A21 1.25fr brn red & grn 18.00 18.00
241 A21 1.40fr dk bl & red org 18.00 18.00
242 A21 1.50fr dp bl & bl 18.00 18.00
243 A21 1.60fr dp grn & brn 18.00 18.00
244 A21 1.75fr dk bl & red org 18.00 18.00
245 A21 2fr red org & brn 18.00 18.00
246 A21 2.25fr vio bl 18.00 18.00
247 A21 2.50fr brn & lt brn 22.00 19.50
248 A21 3fr mag & brn 22.00 19.50
249 A21 5fr dk bl & brn 22.00 19.50
250 A21 10fr vio & brn, *pnksh* 22.00 22.00
251 A21 20fr red & brn, *yel* 23.50 23.50
Nos. 217-251 (35) 624.50 617.00
Set, never hinged 875.00

Issued to note this colony's affiliation with the "Free France" movement.

Catalogue values for unused stamps in this section, from this point to the end of the section, are for Never Hinged items.

Kagu — A22

1942 **Photo.** ***Perf. 14½x14***
252 A22 5c brown .40 .25
253 A22 10c dk gray bl .45 .30
254 A22 25c emerald .70 .30
255 A22 30c red org .70 .45
256 A22 40c dk slate grn .70 .45
257 A22 80c dl red brn .70 .45
258 A22 1fr rose vio .90 .70
259 A22 1.50fr red .90 .70
260 A22 2fr gray blk 1.30 1.10
261 A22 2.50fr brt ultra 1.30 1.10
262 A22 4fr dl vio 1.30 1.10
263 A22 5fr bister 1.30 1.10

264 A22 10fr dp brn 1.60 1.50
265 A22 20fr dp grn 2.50 2.25
Nos. 252-265 (14) 14.75 11.75

Types of 1928 Without "RF"

1944 Typo. *Perf. 14x13½*
265A A19 10c gray lil & dk brn .75
265B A20 60c vio bl & car 1.50

Nos. 265A-265B were issued by the Vichy government in France, but were not placed on sale in the colony.

Stamps of 1942 Surcharged in Carmine or Black

1945-46 Unwmk. *Perf. 14½x14*
266 A22 50c on 5c (C) ('46) 1.60 1.50
267 A22 60c on 5c (C) 1.60 1.50
268 A22 70c on 5c (C) 1.60 1.50
269 A22 1.20fr on 5c (C) .85 .75
270 A22 2.40fr on 25c .85 .75
271 A22 3fr on 25c ('46) 1.00 .75
272 A22 4.50fr on 25c 1.90 1.10
273 A22 15fr on 2.50fr (C) 2.60 2.00
Nos. 266-273 (8) 12.00 9.85

Eboue Issue
Common Design Type

1945 Engr. *Perf. 13*
274 CD91 2fr black .90 .90
275 CD91 25fr Prus grn 2.50 2.10

Kagus — A23

Ducos Sanatorium A24

Porcupine Isle — A25

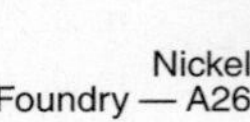
Nickel Foundry — A26

"Towers of Notre Dame" A27

Chieftain's House A28

1948 Unwmk. Photo. *Perf. 13½x13*
276 A23 10c yel & gray brn .30 .30
277 A23 30c bl grn & gray brn .30 .30
278 A23 40c org & gray brn .30 .30
279 A24 50c pink & gray blk .60 .45
280 A24 60c yel & brn .60 .60
281 A24 80c pale bl grn & bl grn .60 .60
282 A25 1fr brn, vio & org .75 .60
283 A25 1.20fr brn & bl .75 .60
284 A25 1.50fr dk bl & yel .90 .70
285 A26 2fr turq grn & brnsh blk .75 .60
286 A26 2.40fr car & peach 1.20 .85
287 A26 3fr pale org & vio 7.50 2.00
288 A26 4fr lt bl & dk bl 2.10 1.00
289 A27 5fr sal & dk vio 2.75 1.10
290 A27 6fr yel & brn 2.75 1.60
291 A27 10fr pale org & dk bl 2.75 1.60
292 A28 15fr red brn & bl gray 3.50 1.75
293 A28 20fr vio & yel 3.50 2.25
294 A28 25fr dk bl & pale org 4.50 3.50
Nos. 276-294 (19) 36.40 20.70

Military Medal Issue
Common Design Type

1952 Engr. & Typo. *Perf. 13*
295 CD101 2fr multi 6.50 6.00

Admiral Bruni d'Entrecasteaux and his Two Frigates — A29

Designs: 2fr, Msgr. Douarre and Cathedral of Nouméa. 6fr, Admiral Dumont d'Urville and map. 13fr, Admiral Auguste Febvrier-Despointes and Nouméa roadstead.

1953, Sept. 24 Engr.
296 A29 1.50fr org brn & dp claret 7.25 5.50
297 A29 2fr ind & aqua 6.00 3.50
298 A29 6fr dk brn, bl & car 11.00 6.00
299 A29 13fr bl grn & dk grnsh bl 12.50 7.00
Nos. 296-299 (4) 36.75 22.00

Centenary of the presence of the French in New Caledonia.

"Towers of Notre Dame" A30

Coffee A31

1955, Nov. 21 Unwmk. *Perf. 13*
300 A30 2.50fr dk brn, ultra & grn 1.90 1.05
301 A30 3fr grn, ultra & red brn 8.25 4.00
302 A31 9fr vio bl & indigo 3.00 1.05
Nos. 300-302 (3) 13.15 6.10

FIDES Issue
Common Design Type

Design: Dumbea Dam.

1956, Oct. 22 Engr. *Perf. 13x12½*
303 CD103 3fr grn & bl 1.90 1.10

Flower Issue
Common Design Type

Designs: 4fr, Xanthostemon. 15fr, Hibiscus.

1958, July 7 Photo. *Perf. 12x12½*
304 CD104 4fr multi 2.75 1.25
305 CD104 15fr grn, red & yel 5.25 1.75

Imperforates

Most stamps of New Caledonia from 1958 onward exist imperforate, in trial colors, or in small presentation sheets in which the stamps are printed in changed colors.

Human Rights Issue
Common Design Type

1958, Dec. 10 Engr. *Perf. 13*
306 CD105 7fr car & dk bl 2.00 1.50

Brachyrus Zebra A32

Lienardella Fasciata A33

Designs: 10fr, Glaucus and Spirographe. 26fr, Fluorescent corals.

1959, Mar. 21 Engr. *Perf. 13*
307 A32 1fr lil gray & red brn .75 .55
308 A33 3fr bl, grn & red 1.75 .60
309 A32 10fr dk brn, Prus bl & org brn 2.50 1.00
310 A33 26fr multi 4.50 4.50
Nos. 307-310 (4) 9.50 6.65

Types of 1859, 1905 and

Girl Operating Check Writer — A34

Telephone Receiver and Exchange — A35

Port-de-France (Nouméa) in 1859 — A36

Designs: 9fr, Wayside mailbox and mail bus, vert. 33fr, like 19fr without stamps.

Perf. 13½x13, 13

1960, May 20 Unwmk.
311 A16 4fr red 1.00 .55
312 A34 5fr claret & org brn 1.20 .75
313 A36 9fr dk grn & brn 1.20 .75
314 A35 12fr bl & blk 1.50 .90
315 A1 13fr slate blue 3.75 2.00
316 A36 19fr bl grn, dl grn & red 3.75 1.25
317 A36 33fr Prus bl & dl red 4.00 2.75
a. Souv. sheet of 3, #315, 311, 317 + label 12.50 12.50
Nos. 311-317 (7) 16.40 8.95

Cent. of postal service and stamps in New Caledonia.

No. 317a has label between 4fr and 33fr stamps.

Melanesian Sailing Canoes — A37

Designs: 4fr, Spear fisherman, vert. 5fr, Sail Rock and sailboats, Noumea.

1962, July 2 Engr. *Perf. 13*
318 A37 2fr slate grn, ultra & brn 1.10 .55
319 A37 4fr brn, car & grn 1.40 .55
320 A37 5fr sepia, grn & bl 1.75 .75
Nos. 318-320 (3) 4.25 1.85

See Nos. C29-C32.

Map of Australia and South Pacific A37a

1962, July 18 Photo. *Perf. 13x12*
321 A37a 15fr multi 3.00 1.90

Fifth South Pacific Conf., Pago Pago, 1962.

Air Currents over Map of New Caledonia and South Pacific, Barograph and Compass Rose — A38

1962, Nov. 5 *Perf. 12x12½*
322 A38 50fr multi 7.50 6.00

3rd regional assembly of the World Meteorological Association, Noumea, November 1962.

Wheat Emblem and Globe — A38a

1963, Mar. 21 Engr. *Perf. 13*
323 A38a 17fr choc & dk bl 3.50 1.75

FAO "Freedom from Hunger" campaign.

Relay Race — A39

Perf. 12½

1963, Aug. 29 Unwmk. Photo.
324 A39 1fr shown 1.20 .60
325 A39 7fr Tennis 1.75 .90
326 A39 10fr Soccer 2.40 1.50
327 A39 27fr Javelin 4.25 2.75
Nos. 324-327 (4) 9.60 5.75

South Pacific Games, Suva, Aug. 29-Sept. 7.

Red Cross Centenary Issue
Common Design Type

1963 Sept. 2 Engr. *Perf. 13*
328 CD113 37fr bl, gray & car 8.00 6.75

Human Rights Issue
Common Design Type

1963, Dec. 10 Unwmk. *Perf. 13*
329 CD117 50fr sl grn & dp claret 7.00 6.00

Bikkia Fritillarioides — A40

Flowers: 1fr, Freycinettia Sp. 3fr, Xanthostemon Francii. 4fr, Psidiomyrtus locellatus. 5fr, Callistemon suberosum. 7fr, Montrouziera sphaeroidea, horiz. 10fr, Ixora collina, horiz. 17fr, Deplanchea speciosa.

Photogravure; Lithographed (2fr, 3fr)

1964-65 *Perf. 13x12½*
330 A40 1fr multi 1.00 .55
331 A40 2fr multi 1.00 .60
332 A40 3fr multi 1.60 .75
333 A40 4fr multi ('65) 3.00 .90
334 A40 5fr multi ('65) 3.75 1.25
335 A40 7fr multi 4.75 1.60
336 A40 10fr multi 5.50 1.75
337 A40 17fr multi 8.50 4.25
Nos. 330-337 (8) 29.10 11.65

Sea Squirts — A41

Design: 10fr, Alcyonium catalai. 17fr, Shrimp (hymenocera elegans).

1964-65 Engr. *Perf. 13*
338 A41 7fr dk bl, red org & brn 1.75 1.00
339 A41 10fr dk red & dk vio bl ('65) 2.75 1.10
340 A41 17fr dk bl, red brn & grn 4.75 2.50
Nos. 338-340 (3) 9.25 4.60

Nouméa Aquarium. See Nos. C41-C43.

Philatec Issue
Common Design Type

1964, Apr. 9 Unwmk. *Perf. 13*
341 CD118 40fr dk vio, grn & choc 6.50 6.50

De Gaulle's 1940 Poster "A Tous les Francais" — A42

1965, Sept. 20 Engr. *Perf. 13*
342 A42 20fr red, bl & blk 12.50 8.25

25th anniv. of the rallying of the Free French.

Amedee Lighthouse — A43

1965, Nov. 25
343 A43 8fr dk vio bl, bis & grn 2.60 1.00

Centenary of the Amedee lighthouse.

Games' Emblem — A44

1966, Mar. 1 Engr. *Perf. 13*
344 A44 8fr dk red, brt bl & blk 1.50 .90

2nd So. Pacific Games, Nouméa, Dec. 1966.

Red-throated Parrot Finch — A45

Design: 3fr, Giant imperial pigeon.

1966, Oct. 10 Litho. *Perf. 13x12½*
Size: 22x37mm
345 A45 1fr green & multi 3.00 1.50
346 A45 3fr citron & multi 5.00 1.90

See #361-366, 380-381, C48-C49A, C70-C71.

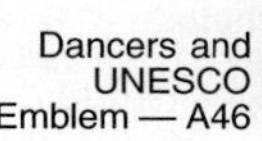

Dancers and UNESCO Emblem — A46

1966, Nov. 4 Engr. *Perf. 13*
347 A46 16fr pur, ocher & grn 2.40 1.40

20th anniv. of UNESCO.

High Jump and Games' Emblem — A47

1966, Dec. 8 Engr. *Perf. 13*
348 A47 17fr shown 3.00 1.25
349 A47 20fr Hurdling 4.25 2.10
350 A47 40fr Running 5.50 2.40
351 A47 100fr Swimming 9.50 6.25
a. Souv. sheet of 4, #348-351 + label 35.00 35.00
Nos. 348-351 (4) 22.25 12.00

2nd So. Pacific Games, Nouméa, Dec. 8-18.

Lekine Cliffs — A48

1967, Jan. 14 Engr. *Perf. 13*
352 A48 17fr brt grn, ultra & sl grn 2.40 2.00

Magenta Stadium, Nouméa — A49

Design: 20fr, Ouen Toro Municipal Swimming Pool, Nouméa.

1967, June 5 Photo. *Perf. 12x13*
353 A49 10fr multi 1.50 .85
354 A49 20fr multi 3.50 1.60

ITY Emblem, Beach at Nouméa — A50

1967, June 19 Engr. *Perf. 13*
355 A50 30fr multi 4.75 2.60

Issued for International Tourist Year, 1967.

19th Century Mailman — A51

1967, July 12
356 A51 7fr dk car, bl grn & brn 3.00 1.40

Issued for Stamp Day.

Papilio Montrouzieri A52

Butterflies: 9fr, Polyura clitarchus. 13fr, 15fr, Hypolimnas bolina, male and female respectively.

1967-68 Engr. *Perf. 13*
Size: 36x22mm
357 A52 7fr lt grn, blk & ultra 4.75 1.25
358 A52 9fr brn, lil & ind ('68) 5.75 1.50
359 A52 13fr vio bl, brn org & dk brn 7.00 2.50
360 A52 15fr dk brn, bl & yel 10.00 4.50
Nos. 357-360,C51-C53 (7) 58.50 24.25

Issued: 9fr, 3/26/68; others, 8/10/67.

Bird Type of 1966

Birds: 1fr, New Caledonian grass warbler. 2fr, New Caledonia whistler. 3fr, New Caledonia white-throated pigeon. 4fr, Kagus. 5fr, Crested parakeet. 10fr, Crow honey-eater.

1967-68 Photo. *Perf. 13x12½*
Size: 22x37mm
361 A45 1fr multi 1.50 1.00
362 A45 2fr multi 2.00 1.25
363 A45 3fr multi 2.50 1.40
364 A45 4fr grn & multi 4.00 2.50
365 A45 5fr lt yel & multi 7.00 3.25
366 A45 10fr pink & multi 12.00 4.25
Nos. 361-366 (6) 29.00 13.65

Issued: #364-366, 12/16/67; others 5/14/68.

WHO Anniversary Issue
Common Design Type

1968, May 4 Engr. *Perf. 13*
367 CD126 20fr mar, vio & dk bl grn 4.00 2.25

Ferrying Mail Truck Across Tontouta River, 1900 — A53

1968, Sept. 2 Engr. *Perf. 13*
368 A53 9fr dk red brn, grn & ultra 3.75 1.60

Issued for Stamp Day, 1968.

Human Rights Year Issue
Common Design Type

1968, Aug. 10 Engr. *Perf. 13*
369 CD127 12fr sl grn, dp car & org yel 2.75 1.50

Conus Geographus A54

1968, Nov. 9 Engr. *Perf. 13*
Size: 36x22mm
370 A54 10fr dk brn, brt bl & gray 4.25 2.25
Nos. 370,C58-C60 (4) 37.75 13.50

Car on Road — A55

1968, Dec. 26 Engr. *Perf. 13*
371 A55 25fr dp bl, sl grn & hn brn 7.50 3.75

2nd Automobile Safari of New Caledonia.

Cattle Dip — A56

1969, May 10 Engr. *Perf. 13*
Size: 36x22mm
372 A56 9fr shown 2.50 1.00
373 A56 25fr Cattle branding 3.50 1.75
Nos. 372-373,C64 (3) 13.00 6.00

Cattle breeding in New Caledonia.

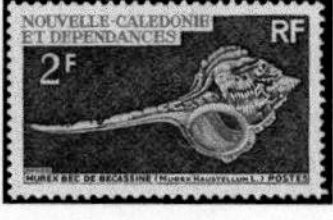
Murex Haustellum A57

Sea Shells: 5fr, Venus comb. 15fr, Murex ramosus.

1969, June 21 Engr. *Perf. 13*
Size: 35½x22mm
374 A57 2fr ver, bl & brn 1.75 .90
375 A57 5fr dl red, pur & beige 3.75 1.20
376 A57 15fr ver, dl grn & gray 6.00 2.40
Nos. 374-376,C65 (4) 35.50 16.00

Judo — A58

1969, Aug. 7 Engr. *Perf. 13*
Size: 36x22mm
377 A58 19fr shown 3.75 1.90
378 A58 20fr Boxers 3.75 1.90
Nos. 377-378,C66-C67 (4) 19.50 8.80

3rd South Pacific Games. Port Moresby, Papua and New Guinea, Aug. 13-23.

ILO Issue
Common Design Type

1969, Nov. 24 Engr. *Perf. 13*
379 CD131 12fr org, brn vio & brn 2.25 1.10

Bird Type of 1966

15fr, Friarbird. 30fr, Sacred kingfisher.

1970, Feb. 19 Photo. *Perf. 13*
Size: 22x37mm
380 A45 15fr yel grn & multi 8.25 3.25
381 A45 30fr pale salmon & multi 12.00 5.50
Nos. 380-381,C70-C71 (4) 59.75 22.75

UPU Headquarters Issue
Common Design Type

1970, May 20 Engr. *Perf. 13*
382 CD133 12fr brn, gray & dk car 3.00 1.50

Porcelain Sieve Shell — A59

Designs: 1fr, Strombus epidromis linne, vert. No. 385, Strombus variabilis swainson, vert. 21fr, Mole porcelain shell.

1970 Size: 22x36mm, 36x22mm
383 A59 1fr bl grn & multi 2.25 .75
384 A59 10fr car & multi 5.25 1.50
385 A59 10fr blk & multi 6.75 2.40
386 A59 21fr bl grn, red brn & dk brn 10.00 4.00
Nos. 383-386,C73-C76 (8) 64.50 25.65

See Nos. 395-396, C89-C90.

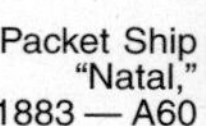

Packet Ship "Natal," 1883 — A60

1970, July 23 Engr. *Perf. 13*
387 A60 9fr Prus bl, blk & brt grn 4.00 1.40

Issued for Stamp Day.

Dumbea Railroad Post Office — A61

1971, Mar. 13 Engr. *Perf. 13*
388 A61 10fr red, slate grn & blk 5.00 2.00

Stamp Day, 1971.

Racing Yachts A62

1971, Apr. 17 Engr. *Perf. 13*
389 A62 16fr bl, Prus bl & sl grn *5.00* 3.00

Third sailing cruise from Whangarei, New Zealand, to Nouméa.

Morse Recorder, Communications Satellite — A63

1971, May 17 Engr. *Perf. 13*
390 A63 19fr red, lake & org 4.00 1.25

3rd World Telecommunications Day.

Weight Lifting — A64

1971, June 24 Engr. *Perf. 13*
391 A64 11fr shown 2.50 1.00
392 A64 23fr Basketball 3.75 1.50
Nos. 391-392,C82-C83 (4) 18.00 8.75

4th South Pacific Games, Papeete, French Polynesia, Sept. 8-19.

De Gaulle Issue
Common Design Type

Designs: 34fr, Pres. de Gaulle, 1970. 100fr, Gen. de Gaulle, 1940.

1971, Nov. 9
393 CD134 34fr dk pur & blk 8.00 3.75
394 CD134 100fr dk pur & blk 15.00 8.00

Sea Shell Type of 1970

Designs: 1fr, Scorpion conch, vert. 3fr, Common spider conch., vert.

1972, Mar. 4 Engr. *Perf. 13*
Size: 22x36mm
395 A59 1fr vio & dk brn 2.00 .70
396 A59 3fr grn & ocher 3.00 .80
Nos. 395-396,C89-C90 (4) 19.50 8.50

Carved Wooden Pillow — A66

1fr, Doorpost, Goa. 5fr, Monstrance. 12fr, Tchamba mask.

1972-73 Photo. *Perf. 12½x13*

397 A66 1fr multi ('73) 1.75 .40
398 A66 2fr shown 1.75 .65
399 A66 5fr multi 2.00 .80
400 A66 12fr multi 5.00 1.25
Nos. 397-400,C102-C103 (6) 18.00 6.10

Objects from Nouméa Museum.
Issued: 2fr-15fr, 8/5.

Chamber of Commerce Emblem — A67

1972, Dec. 16

401 A67 12fr blk, yel & brt bl 1.75 .90

Junior Chamber of Commerce, 10th anniv.

Tchamba Mask — A68

1973, Mar. 15 Engr. *Perf. 13*

402 A68 12fr lilac 8.25 2.00
a. Booklet pane of 5 200.00

No. 402 issued in booklets only.
See No. C99.

Black-back Butterflyfish (Day) — A69

1973, June 23 Photo. *Perf. 13x12½*

403 A69 8fr shown 2.50 1.00
404 A69 14fr same fish (night) 3.75 1.50
Nos. 403-404,C105 (3) 11.25 4.50

Nouméa Aquarium.

Emblem — A70

1973, July 21 *Perf. 13*

405 A70 20fr grn, yel & vio bl 2.25 .80

School Coordinating Office, 10th anniv.

"Nature Protection" A72

1974, June 22 Photo. *Perf. 13x12½*

406 A72 7fr multi 1.50 .55

Scorched Landscape — A73

1975, Feb. 7 Photo. *Perf. 13*

407 A73 20fr multi 2.25 1.10

"Prevent brush fires."

Calanthe Veratrifolia — A74

Design: 11fr, Liperanthus gigas.

1975, May 30 Photo. *Perf. 13*

408 A74 8fr pur & multi 3.00 1.00
409 A74 11fr dk bl & multi 3.50 1.00
Nos. 408-409,C125 (3) 12.50 4.25

Orchids. See Nos. 425-426.

Festival Emblem — A75

1975, Sept. 6 Photo. *Perf. 12½x13*

410 A75 12fr ultra, org & yel 2.00 .70

Melanesia 2000 Festival.

Birds in Flight — A76

1975, Oct. 18 Photo. *Perf. 13½x13*

411 A76 5fr ocher, yel & blk 1.75 .55

Nouméa Ornithological Society, 10th anniversary.

Georges Pompidou — A77

1975, Dec. 6 Engr. *Perf. 13*

412 A77 26fr dk grn, blk & sl 3.25 1.25

Pompidou (1911-74), president of France.

Sea Birds — A78

Perf. 13x12½, 12½x13

1976, Feb. 26 Photo.

413 A78 1fr Brown booby 1.25 .45
414 A78 2fr Blue-faced booby 1.75 .70
415 A78 8fr Red-footed booby, vert. 3.00 1.10
Nos. 413-415 (3) 6.00 2.25

Festival Emblem — A79

1976, Mar. 13 Litho. *Perf. 12½*

416 A79 27fr bl, org & blk 2.50 .90

Rotorua 1976, South Pacific Arts Festival, New Zealand.

Lion and Lions Emblem — A80

1976, Mar. 13 Photo. *Perf. 12½x13*

417 A80 49fr multi 5.00 2.00

Lions Club of Nouméa, 15th anniversary.

Music Pavilion A81

Design: 30fr, Fountain, vert.

1976, July 3 Litho. *Perf. 12½*

418 A81 25fr multi 1.75 .70
419 A81 30fr blue & multi 2.25 1.00

Old Nouméa.

Polluted Shore A82

1976, Aug. 21 Photo. *Perf. 13*

420 A82 20fr dp bl & multi 2.50 .90

Nature protection.

South Pacific People — A83

1976, Oct. 23 Photo. *Perf. 13*

421 A83 20fr bl & multi 2.25 .90

16th South Pacific Commission Conference, Nouméa, Oct. 1976.

Giant Grasshopper A84

1977, Feb. 21 Engr. *Perf. 13*

422 A84 26fr shown 2.00 1.25
423 A84 31fr Beetle and larvae 3.00 1.40

Ground Satellite Station, Nouméa A85

1977, Apr. 16 Litho. *Perf. 13*

424 A85 29fr multi 2.75 1.10

Orchid Type of 1975

Designs: 22fr, Phajus daenikeri. 44fr, Dendrobium finetianum.

1977, May 23 Photo. *Perf. 13*

425 A74 22fr brn & multi 3.75 1.25
426 A74 44fr bl & multi 4.25 1.90

Mask, Palms, "Stamps" A86

1977, June 25 Photo. *Perf. 13*

427 A86 35fr multi 2.00 1.00

Philately in school, Philatelic Exhibition, La Perouse Lyceum, Nouméa.

Trees — A87

1977, July 23 Photo. *Perf. 13*

428 A87 20fr multi 1.50 .75

Nature protection.

Congress Emblem A88

1977, Aug. 6 Photo. *Perf. 13*

429 A88 200fr multi 9.25 5.50

French Junior Economic Chambers Congress, Nouméa.

Young Frigate Bird — A89

Black-naped Tern — A89a

Sooty Terns — A89b

1977-78 Photo. *Perf. 13*

430 A89 16fr multi 5.75 1.00
431 A89a 22fr multi 2.25 1.10
432 A89b 40fr multi 3.75 1.50
Nos. 430-432,C138 (4) 17.75 5.20

Issued: 16fr, 9/17/77; 22fr, 40fr, 2/11/78.

Mare and Foal — A90

1977, Nov. 19 Engr. ***Perf. 13***
433 A90 5fr multi 2.00 .55

10th anniversary of the Society for Promotion of Caledonian Horses.

Araucaria Montana — A91

1978, Mar. 17 Photo. ***Perf. 12½x13***
434 A91 16fr multi 1.25 .55

See No. C149.

Halityle Regularis — A92

1978, May 20 Photo. ***Perf. 13***
436 A92 10fr vio bl & multi 1.60 .45

Nouméa Aquarium.

Stylized Turtle and Globe — A93

1978, May 20
437 A93 30fr multi 3.00 1.10

Protection of the turtle.

Flying Fox — A94

1978, June 10
438 A94 20fr multi 4.50 1.50

Nature protection.

Maurice Leenhardt — A95

1978, Aug. 12 Engr. ***Perf. 13***
439 A95 37fr multi 2.00 1.25

Pastor Maurice Leenhardt (1878-1954).

Soccer Player, League Emblem — A96

1978, Nov. 4 Photo. ***Perf. 13***
440 A96 26fr multi 4.50 2.50

New Caledonia Soccer League, 50th anniversary.

Lifu Island — A97

1978, Dec. 9 Litho. ***Perf. 13***
441 A97 33fr multi 2.25 1.75

Petroglyph, Mère — A98

1979, Jan. 27 Engr. ***Perf. 13***
442 A98 10fr brick red 1.40 .55

Map of Ouvea — A99

Design: 31fr, Map of Mare Island, horiz.

Perf. 12½x13, 13x12½

1979, Feb. 17 Photo.
443 A99 11fr multi 1.25 .55
444 A99 31fr multi 1.75 .75

House at Artillery Point A100

1979, Apr. 28 Photo. ***Perf. 13***
445 A100 20fr multi 2.00 1.50

Auguste Escoffier — A101

1979, July 21 Engr. ***Perf. 12½x13***
446 A101 24fr multi 1.50 1.50

Auguste Escoffier Hotel School.

Regatta and Games Emblem — A102

1979, Aug. 11 Photo. ***Perf. 13***
447 A102 16fr multi 2.00 .70

6th South Pacific Games, Suva, Fiji, Aug. 27-Sept. 8.

Agathis Ovata — A103

Design: 34fr, Cyathea intermedia.

1979, Oct. 20 Photo. ***Perf. 13x12½***
448 A103 5fr shown 1.50 .35
449 A103 34fr multicolored 2.00 .75

Pouembout Rodeo — A104

1979, Oct. 27 Engr. ***Perf. 13x12½***
450 A104 12fr multi 1.75 .55

Bantamia Merleti — A105

1979, Dec. 1 Photo. ***Perf. 13x11½***
451 A105 23fr multi 1.75 .70

Fluorescent corals from Nouméa Aquarium.

Map of Pine Tree Island, Fishermen with Nets — A106

1980, Jan. 12 Photo. ***Perf. 13x12½***
452 A106 23fr multi 1.60 .45

Hibbertia Virotii — A107

Design: 12fr, Grevillea meisneri.

1980, Apr. 19 Photo. ***Perf. 13x12½***
453 A107 11fr multicolored 1.40 .65
454 A107 12fr multicolored 1.40 .65

Philately at School — A108

1980, May 10 Litho. ***Perf. 12½***
455 A108 30fr multi 1.75 .55

Prevention of Traffic Accidents — A109

1980, July 5 Photo. ***Perf. 13x12½***
456 A109 15fr multi 1.20 .35

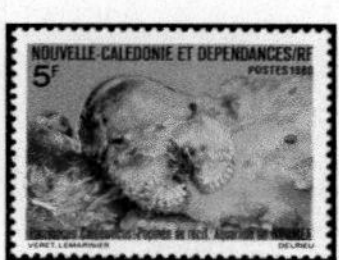

Parribacus Caledonicus A110

Noumea Aquarium Crustacea: 8fr, Panulirus versicolor.

1980, Aug. 23 Litho. ***Perf. 13x13½***
457 A110 5fr multi .75 .35
458 A110 8fr multi 1.00 .55

Solar Energy — A111

1980, Oct. 11 Photo. ***Perf. 13x12½***
459 A111 23fr multi 1.50 .70

Manta Birostris — A112

25fr, Carcharhinus amblyrhnchos.

1981, Feb. 18 Photo. ***Perf. 13x12½***
460 A112 23fr shown 2.50 .90
461 A112 25fr multicolored 2.50 .90

Belep Islands — A113

1981, Mar. 4
462 A113 26fr multi 1.25 .55

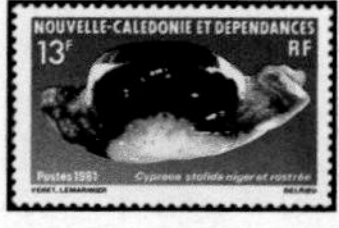

Cypraea Stolida — A114

1fr, Cymbiola rossiniana, vert. 2fr, Connus floccatus, vert.

1981, June 17 Photo. ***Perf. 13***
463 A114 1fr multicolored .95 .50
464 A114 2fr multicolored 1.00 .65
465 A114 13fr shown 1.90 .75
Nos. 463-465 (3) 3.85 1.90

See Nos. 470-471.

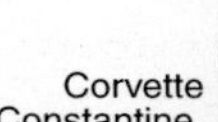

Corvette Constantine, 1854 — A115

25fr, Aviso le Phoque, 1853.

1981, July 22 Engr. ***Perf. 13***
466 A115 10fr shown 1.40 .55
467 A115 25fr multicolored 2.10 1.10

See Nos. 476-477.

Intl. Year of the Disabled — A116

1981, Sept. 2 Litho. ***Perf. 12½***
468 A116 45fr multicolored 1.90 .85

Nature Preservation — A117

1981, Nov. 7 Photo. ***Perf. 13***
469 A117 28fr multicolored 2.25 .90

Marine Life Type of 1981

1982, Jan. 20 Photo. ***Perf. 13x13½***
470 A114 13fr Calappa calappa 1.50 .80
471 A114 25fr Etisus splendidus 2.25 1.10

Chalcantite A118

1982, Mar. 17 Photo. ***Perf. 13x13½***
472 A118 15fr shown 2.25 1.10
473 A118 30fr Anorthosite 3.00 1.10

Melaleuca Quinquenervia
A119

20fr, Savannah trees, vert.

1982, June 23 Photo. *Perf. 13*
474 A119 20fr multicolored 1.25 .70
475 A119 29fr shown 1.50 .70

Ship Type of 1981

44fr, Barque Le Cher. 59fr, Naval dispatch vessel Kersaint.

1982, July 7 Engr.
476 A115 44fr multicolored 2.10 1.00
477 A115 59fr multicolored 2.75 1.00

Ateou Tribe Traditional House — A120

1982, Oct. 13 Photo. *Perf. 13½x13*
478 A120 52fr multicolored 1.75 .90

Grey's Ptilope — A121

Design: 35fr, Caledonian loriquet.

1982, Nov. 6
479 A121 32fr shown 1.75 .70
480 A121 35fr multicolored 2.00 .90

Central Education Coordination Office — A122

1982, Nov. 27 Litho. *Perf. 13½x13*
481 A122 48fr Boat 1.75 .75

Bernheim Library, Noumea
A123

1982, Dec. 15 Engr. *Perf. 13*
482 A123 36fr multicolored 1.10 .55

Caledonian Orchids — A123a

10fr, Dendrobium oppositifolium. 15fr, Dendrobium munificum. 29fr, Dendrobium fractiflexum.

1983, Feb. 16 Photo. *Perf. 13x13½*
482A A123a 10fr multicolored .75 .35
482B A123a 15fr multicolored 1.10 .45
482C A123a 29fr multicolored 1.75 .90
Nos. 482A-482C (3) 3.60 1.70

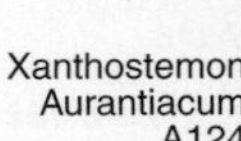

Xanthostemon Aurantiacum
A124

1fr, Crinum asiaticum. 2fr, Xanthostemon aurantiacum. 4fr, Metrosideros demonstrans, vert.

1983, Mar. 23 Litho. *Perf. 13*
483 A124 1fr multicolored .45 .35
484 A124 2fr multicolored .45 .65
485 A124 4fr multicolored .45 .35
Nos. 483-485 (3) 1.35 1.35

25th Anniv. of Posts and Telecommunications Dept. — A125

Telephones and post offices.

1983, Apr. 30 Litho. *Perf. 13*
486 A125 30fr multicolored 1.10 .45
487 A125 40fr multicolored 1.20 .75
488 A125 50fr multicolored 1.75 .80
a. Souvenir sheet of 3 11.00 10.00
b. Strip of 3, #486-488 5.50 5.50

No. 488a contains Nos. 486-488 with changed background colors.

Local Snakes — A126

Designs: 31fr, Laticauda laticauda. 33fr, Laticauda colubrina.

1983, June 22 Photo. *Perf. 13*
489 A126 31fr multicolored 1.75 .75
490 A126 33fr multicolored 2.00 .85

A127

1983, Aug. 10 Engr.
491 A127 16fr Volleyball 1.25 .65

7th South Pacific Games, Sept.

Nature Protection — A128

1983, Oct. 12 Photo. *Perf. 12½*
492 A128 56fr multi 2.00 1.00

Birds of Prey — A129

34fr, Tyto Alba Lifuensis, vert. 37fr, Pandion Haliaetus.

1983, Nov. 16 Litho. *Perf. 13*
493 A129 34fr multicolored 2.00 .95
494 A129 37fr multicolored 2.50 1.25

Local Shells — A130

5fr, Conus chenui. 15fr, Conus moluccensis. 20fr, Conus optimus.

1984, Jan. 11 Litho. & Engr.
495 A130 5fr multicolored 1.00 .60
496 A130 15fr multicolored 1.10 .60
497 A130 20fr multicolored 1.40 .80
Nos. 495-497 (3) 3.50 2.00

See Nos. 521-522.

Steamers — A131

1984, Feb. 8 Engr.
498 A131 18fr St. Joseph 1.00 .65
499 A131 31fr St. Antoine 1.50 .85

Arms of Noumea — A132

1984, Apr. 11 Litho. *Perf. 12½x13*
500 A132 35fr multi 1.25 .65

See No. 546, 607, C214.

Environmental Preservation — A133

1984, May 23 *Perf. 13*
501 A133 65fr Island scene 2.25 .90

Orchids
A134

16fr, Diplocaulobium ou-hinnae. 38fr, Acianthus atepalus.

1984, July 18 Litho. *Perf. 12*
502 A134 16fr multicolored 1.50 .75
503 A134 38fr multicolored 2.00 1.10

Cent. of Public Schooling
A135

1984, Oct. 11 Litho. *Perf. 13½x13*
504 A135 59fr Schoolhouse 2.00 .90

Kagu — A137

1985-86 Engr. *Perf. 13*
511 A137 1fr brt bl .60 .60
512 A137 2fr green .60 .60
513 A137 3fr brt org .60 .60
514 A137 4fr brt grn .60 .60
515 A137 5fr dp rose lil .60 .60
516 A137 35fr crimson 1.25 .90
517 A137 38fr vermilion 1.25 1.00
518 A137 40fr brt rose ('86) 1.40 .70
Nos. 511-518 (8) 6.90 5.60

Issued: 1, 2, 5, 38fr, 5/22; 3, 4, 35fr, 2/13; 40fr, 7/30.

See types A179, A179a. For redrawn stamp of type A137, see No. 1296a.

Sea Shell Type of 1984
Lithographed and Engraved

1985, Feb. 27 *Perf. 13*
521 A130 55fr Conus bullatus 1.50 .90
522 A130 72fr Conus lamberti 2.00 1.40

25th World Meteorological Day — A138

17fr, Radio communication, storm.

1985, Mar. 20 Litho.
523 A138 17fr multicolored .85 .85

Red Cross, Medicine Without Frontiers
A139

1985, Apr. 10 *Perf. 12½*
524 A139 41fr multicolored 1.50 .80

Telephone Switching Center Inauguration
A140

1985, Apr. 24
525 A140 70fr E 10 B installation 1.75 1.00

Marguerite La Foa Suspension Bridge — A141

1985, May 10 Engr. *Perf. 13*
526 A141 44fr brt bl & red brn 1.75 .90

Historical Preservation Association.

Le Cagou Philatelic Society
A142

1985, June 15 Litho.
527 A142 220fr multicolored 5.75 4.00
a. Souvenir sheet, perf. 12½ 8.50 8.50

No. 527a sold for 230fr.

4th Pacific Arts Festival — A143

1985, July 3 *Perf. 13½*
Black Overprint
528 A143 55fr multicolored 1.50 1.00
529 A143 75fr multicolored 2.25 1.40

Not issued without overprint. Festival was transferred to French Polynesia.

Intl. Youth Year
A144

1985, July 24 Litho. *Perf. 13*
530 A144 59fr multicolored 2.00 .80

Amedee Lighthouse Electrification A145

1985, Aug. 13
531 A145 89fr multicolored 2.25 1.10

Environmental Conservation — A146

1985, Sept. 18
532 A146 100fr Planting trees 2.50 1.10

Birds — A147

1985, Dec. 18 ***Perf. 12½***
533 A147 50fr Poule sultane 1.75 1.00
534 A147 60fr Merle caledonien 2.75 1.10

Noumea Aquarium — A148

10fr, Pomacanthus imperator. 17fr, Rhinopias aphanes.

1986, Feb. 19 Litho. ***Perf. 12½x13***
535 A148 10fr multicolored .55 .35
536 A148 17fr multicolored .75 .60

Kanumera Bay, Isle of Pines A149

1986, Mar. 26 Litho. ***Perf. 12½***
537 A149 50fr shown 1.25 .70
538 A149 55fr Inland village 1.40 .80

See Nos. 547-548, 617-618.

Geckos — A150

20fr, Bavayia sauvagii. 45fr, Rhacodactylus leachianus.

1986, Apr. 16 ***Perf. 12½x13***
539 A150 20fr multicolored 1.10 .75
540 A150 45fr multicolored 1.50 .85

1986 World Cup Soccer Championships, Mexico — A151

1986, May 28 ***Perf. 13***
541 A151 60fr multicolored 1.50 1.00

1st Pharmacy in New Caledonia, 120th Anniv. A152

1986, June 25 Litho. ***Perf. 13***
542 A152 80fr multicolored 2.25 1.25

Orchids — A153

44fr, Coelogynae licastioides. 58fr, Calanthe langei.

1986, July 16 ***Perf. 12½x13***
543 A153 44fr multicolored 1.50 .80
544 A153 58fr multicolored 1.75 .90

STAMPEX '86, Adelaide A154

1986, Aug. 4 ***Perf. 12½***
545 A154 110fr Bird 3.00 1.40

Arms Type of 1984

1986, Oct. 11 Litho. ***Perf. 13½***
546 A132 94fr Mont Dore 3.00 1.10

Landscape Type of 1986

40fr, West landscape, vert. 76fr, South Landscape.

1986, Oct. 29 Litho. ***Perf. 12½***
547 A149 40fr multicolored 1.10 .70
548 A149 76fr multicolored 1.75 .80

Flowers — A156

Niponthes vieillardi, Syzygium ngayense, Archidendropsis Paivana, Scavola balansae.

1986, Nov. 12 ***Perf. 12½***
549 A156 73fr multicolored 1.90 .90

Nature Protection Assoc.

A157

1986, Nov. 26 ***Perf. 13x12½***
550 A157 350fr Emblem 8.00 4.25

Noumea Lions Club, 25th anniv.

A158

Paintings: 74fr, Moret Point, by A. Sisley. 140fr, Butterfly Chase, by B. Morisot.

1986, Dec. 23 Litho. ***Perf. 13***
551 A158 74fr multicolored 2.25 1.40
552 A158 140fr multicolored 4.00 1.60

America's Cup — A159

1987, Jan. 28 ***Perf. 13½***
553 A159 30fr Challenge France 1.50 .90
554 A159 70fr French Kiss 1.90 1.10

Plants, Butterflies A160

46fr, Anona squamosa, Graphium gelon. 54fr, Albizzia granulosa, Polyura gamma.

1987, Feb. 25 Litho. ***Perf. 13x12½***
555 A160 46fr multicolored 2.50 .90
556 A160 54fr multicolored 3.00 1.50

Pirogues — A161

1987, May 13 Engr. ***Perf. 13x12½***
557 A161 72fr from Isle of Pines 1.75 1.00
558 A161 90fr from Ouvea 2.25 1.25

New Town Hall, Mont Dore — A162

1987, May 23 Litho. ***Perf. 12½x13***
559 A162 92fr multicolored 2.10 1.00

Seashells — A163

1987, June 24 ***Perf. 13***
560 A163 28fr Cypraea moneta 1.00 .65
561 A163 36fr Cypraea martini 1.50 .70

8th South Pacific Games — A164

1987, July 8 ***Perf. 12½x13***
562 A164 40fr multicolored 1.25 .55

A165

1987, July 22 ***Perf. 13½***
563 A165 270fr multicolored 5.75 2.75

Soroptimist Int'l. 13th Convention, Melbourne, July 26-31.

Birds — A166

18fr, Zosterops xanthochroa. 21fr, Falco peregrinus nesiotes, vert.

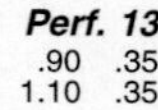

1987, Aug. 26 ***Perf. 13***
564 A166 18fr multicolored .90 .35
565 A166 21fr multicolored 1.10 .35

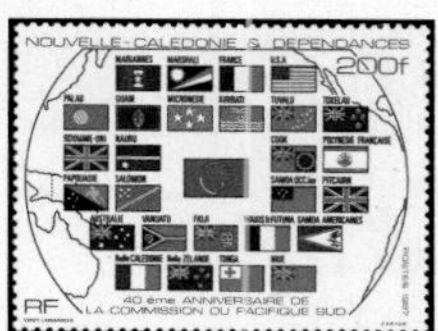

South Pacific Commission, 40th Anniv. — A167

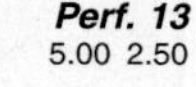

1987, Oct. 14 Litho. ***Perf. 13***
566 A167 200fr multicolored 5.00 2.50

Philately at School — A168

1987, Oct. 21 ***Perf. 12½***
567 A168 15fr multicolored .90 .50

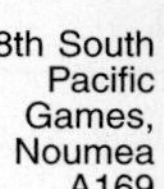

8th South Pacific Games, Noumea A169

1987, Dec. 8 Litho. ***Perf. 12½***
568 A169 20fr Golf 1.25 .50
569 A169 30fr Rugby 1.75 1.20
570 A169 100fr Long jump 3.00 1.25
Nos. 568-570 (3) 6.00 2.95

Map, Ships, La Perouse A170

1988, Feb. 10 Engr. ***Perf. 13***
571 A170 36fr dark rose lil 1.50 .70

Disappearance of La Perouse expedition, 200th anniv., and Jean-Francois de Galaup (1741-1788), Comte de La Perouse.

A171

Design: French University of the South Pacific at Noumea and Papeete.

1988, Feb. 24 Litho. ***Perf. 13x12½***
572 A171 400fr multicolored 9.25 4.25

Tropical Fish — A172

30fr, Pomacanthus semicirculatus. 46fr, Glyphidodontops cyaneus.

1988, Mar. 23 Litho. ***Perf. 13***
573 A172 30fr multicolored 1.10 .55
574 A172 46fr multicolored 1.50 .80

Intl. Red Cross and Red Crescent Organizations, 125th Annivs. — A173

1988, Apr. 27
575 A173 300fr multicolored 7.50 3.75

Regional Housing — A174

Designs: 19fr, Mwaringou, Canala Region, vert. 21fr, Nathalo, Lifou.

1988, Apr. 13 Engr. *Perf. 13*
576 A174 19fr emer grn, brt blue & red brn .85 .50
577 A174 21fr brt blue, emer grn & red brn .85 .50

Medicinal Plants — A175

1988, May 18 Litho. *Perf. 13x12½*
578 A175 28fr Ochrosia elliptica 1.10 .55
579 A175 64fr Rauvolfia levenetii 2.10 1.10

No. 579 is airmail.

Living Fossils A176

51fr, Gymnocrinus richeri.

1988, June 11 *Perf. 13*
580 A176 51fr multicolored 2.25 .90

Bourail Museum and Historical Soc. A177

1988, June 25 Litho. *Perf. 13*
581 A177 120fr multi 3.00 1.60

SYDPEX '88 — A178

Designs: No. 582, La Perouse aboard *La Boussole,* gazing through spyglass at the First Fleet in Botany Bay, Jan. 24, 1788. No. 583, Capt. Phillip and crew ashore on Botany Bay watching the approach of La Perouse's ships *La Boussole* and *L'Astrolabe.*

1988, July 30 Litho. *Perf. 13x12½*
582 A178 42fr multi 1.50 .90
583 A178 42fr multi 1.50 .90
a. Souvenir sheet of 2, #582-583, perf. 13x13½ 4.75 4.25
b. Strip of 2, #582-583 + label 3.50 3.00

No. 583a sold for 120fr.

Kagu — A179

1988-90 Engr. *Perf. 13*
584 A179 1fr bright blue .50 .25
585 A179 2fr green .50 .25
586 A179 3fr bright orange .75 .25
587 A179 4fr bright green .75 .25
588 A179 5fr deep rose lilac 1.00 .25
589 A179 28fr orange 1.00 .25
590 A179 40fr bright rose 1.10 .25
Nos. 584-590 (7) 5.60 1.75

Issued: 40fr, 8/10/88; 1fr, 4fr, 1/25/89; 2fr, 3fr, 5fr, 4/19/89; 28fr, 1/15/90.

See Type A137. For redrawn stamp of type A179, see No. 1296b.

Kagu — A179a

1990-93 Engr. *Perf. 13*
591 A179a 1fr dark blue .25 .25
592 A179a 2fr bright green .25 .25
593 A179a 3fr brt yel org .30 .25
594 A179a 4fr dark green .30 .25
595 A179a 5fr bright violet .30 .25
596 A179a 9fr blue black .35 .25
597 A179a 12fr orange .40 .25
598 A179a 40fr lilac rose 1.00 .25
599 A179a 50fr red 1.40 .30
Nos. 591-599 (9) 4.55 2.30

Issued: 50fr, 9/5/90; 1fr-5fr, 1/9/91; 40fr, 1/15/92; 9fr, 12fr, 1/25/93.

See Type A137 and Nos. 675, 683. For surcharge see No. 685. For redrawn stamp of type A179a, see No. 1296c.

1988 Summer Olympics, Seoul A180

1988, Sept. 14 *Perf. 12½x12*
600 A180 150fr multi 4.00 2.00

Pasteur Institute, Noumea, Cent. — A181

1988, Sept. 28 Engr. *Perf. 13*
601 A181 100fr blk, brt ultra & dark red 2.50 1.25

Writers A182

72fr, Georges Baudoux (1870-1949). 73fr, Jean Mariotti (1901-1975).

1988, Oct. 15 Engr. *Perf. 13*
602 A182 72fr multicolored 2.00 1.00
603 A182 73fr multicolored 2.00 1.00

No. 603 is airmail.

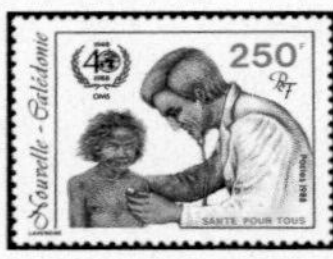

WHO, 40th Anniv. — A183

1988, Nov. 16 Litho. *Perf. 13x12½*
604 A183 250fr multi 6.00 2.75

Art Type of 1984 Without "ET DEPENDANCES"

Paintings by artists of the Pacific: 54fr, *Land of Men,* by L. Bunckley. 92fr, *The Latin Quarter,* by Marik.

1988, Dec. 7
605 AP113 54fr multi 2.25 1.00
606 AP113 92fr multi 3.00 1.40

Arms Type of 1984 Without "ET DEPENDANCES"

1989, Feb. 22 Litho. *Perf. 13½*
607 A132 200fr Koumac 4.50 2.00

Indigenous Flora — A184

80fr, Parasitaxus ustus, vert. 90fr, Tristaniopsis guillainii.

1989, Mar. 22 Litho. *Perf. 13½*
608 A184 80fr multicolored 2.00 1.10
609 A184 90fr multicolored 2.50 1.40

Marine Life — A185

1989, May 17 Litho. *Perf. 12½x13*
610 A185 18fr Plesionika 1.10 .60
611 A185 66fr Ocosia apia 1.90 1.00
612 A185 110fr Latiaxis 2.75 1.60
Nos. 610-612 (3) 5.75 3.20

See Nos. 652-653.

French Revolution, Bicent. — A186

40fr, Liberty. 58fr, Equality. 76fr, Fraternity. 180fr, Liberty, Equality, Fraternity.

1989, July 7 Litho. *Perf. 13½*
613 A186 40fr multi 1.75 .60
614 A186 58fr multi 1.75 .75
615 A186 76fr multi 1.75 1.00
Nos. 613-615 (3) 5.25 2.35

Souvenir Sheet

616 A186 180fr multi 5.50 5.50

Nos. 614-616 are airmail.

Landscape Type of 1986 Without "ET DEPENDANCES"

64fr, La Poule rookery, Hienghene. 180fr, Ouaieme ferry.

1989, Aug. 23 Litho. *Perf. 13*
617 A149 64fr multicolored 1.50 .75
618 A149 180fr multicolored 4.00 1.60

No. 617 is airmail.

Carved Bamboo — A187

Litho. & Engr.

1989, Sept. 27 *Perf. 12½x13*
619 A187 70fr multicolored 1.75 .70

See No. C216.

A188

1989, Oct. 25 Litho. *Perf. 13*
620 A188 350fr multicolored 8.50 3.50

Hobie-Cat 14 10th World Championships, Nov. 3, Noumea.

Natl. Historical Soc., 20th Anniv. A189

Cover of *Moeurs: Superstitions of New Caledonians,* cover of book on Melanesian oral literature and historians G. Pisier, R.P. Neyret and A. Surleau.

1989, Nov. 3 Engr.
621 A189 74fr brown & black 2.00 .80

Ft. Teremba A190

1989, Nov. 18 Engr.
622 A190 100fr bl grn & dk org 2.50 1.40

Marguerite Historical Preservation Soc.

Impressionist Paintings — A191

Designs: 130fr, The Escape of Rochefort, by Manet. 270fr, Self-portrait, by Courbet.

1989, Dec. 6 Litho. *Perf. 13½*
623 A191 130fr multicolored 3.25 1.90
624 A191 270fr multicolored 7.50 4.00

Fr. Patrick O'Reilly (1900-1988), Writer — A192

1990, Jan. 24 Engr. *Perf. 13x13½*
625 A192 170fr blk & plum 4.25 1.90

Grasses and Butterflies A193

Various Cyperacea costularia and Paratisiphone lyrnessa: 18fr, Female. 50fr, Female, diff. 94fr, Male.

1990, Feb. 21 Litho. *Perf. 13½*
626 A193 18fr shown 1.90 .60
627 A193 50fr multicolored .90 .50
628 A193 94fr multicolored 3.25 1.25
Nos. 626-628 (3) 6.05 2.35

Nos. 626 and 628 are airmail.

A194

1990, Mar. 16 Engr. *Perf. 12½x13*
629 A194 85fr Kanakan money 1.90 .80
630 A194 140fr money, diff. 3.50 1.40

A195

1990, Mar. 16 Litho. *Perf. 13x13½*
631 A195 230fr multicolored 5.25 2.50

Jade and mother of pearl exhibition, New Caledonian Museum.

Noumea Aquarium — A196

10fr, Phyllidia ocellata. 42fr, Chromodoris kuniei, vert.

1990, Apr. 25 *Perf. 13x12½, 12½x13*
632 A196 10fr multicolored .45 .45
633 A196 42fr multicolored 1.50 .70

Petroglyphs — A197

1990, July 11 Engr. *Perf. 13*
634 A197 40fr Neounda 1.25 .55
635 A197 58fr Kassducou 1.75 .90

No. 635 is airmail.

Meeting Center of the Pacific A198

1990, July 25 Litho. *Perf. 13*
636 A198 320fr multicolored 7.00 3.00

World Cup Soccer Championships, Italy — A199

1990, May 30 Litho. *Perf. 13*
637 A199 240fr multicolored 6.00 3.00

Flowers — A200

105fr, Gardenia aubryi. 130fr, Hibbertia baudouinii.

1990, Nov. 7 *Perf. 13x12½*
638 A200 105fr multicolored 2.50 1.25
639 A200 130fr multicolored 3.00 2.00

La Maison Celieres by M. Petron — A201

365fr, Le Mont-Dore de Jade by C. Degroiselle.

1990, Dec. 5 *Perf. 12½*
640 A201 110fr multicolored 2.50 1.25
641 A201 365fr multicolored 9.00 2.75

No. 640 is airmail.

Writers — A202

Designs: #642, Louise Michel (1830-1905). #643, Charles B. Nething (1867-1947).

1991, Mar. 20 Engr. *Perf. 13*
642 125fr rose lil & bl 3.00 1.50
643 125fr brn & bl 3.00 1.50
a. A202 Pair, #642-643 + label 6.50 6.00

Native Huts — A203

1991, May 15 Litho. *Perf. 12*
644 A203 12fr Houailou .75 .40
645 A203 35fr Hienghene 1.00 .60

Maps of the Provinces — A204

1991, June 17 Litho. *Perf. 13½*
646 A204 45fr Northern 1.00 .45
647 A204 45fr Island 1.00 .45
648 A204 45fr Southern 1.00 .45
a. Strip of 3, #646-648 3.50 3.25

Orchids A205

55fr, Dendrobium biflorum. 70fr, Dendrobium closterium.

1991, July 24 Litho. *Perf. 13*
649 A205 55fr multicolored 1.60 .80
650 A205 70fr multicolored 2.25 1.00

French Institute of Scientific Research A206

1991, Aug. 26
651 A206 170fr multicolored 3.75 1.75

Marine Life Type of 1989

60fr, Monocentris japonicus. 100fr, Tristigenys niphonia.

1991, Aug. 26 Litho. *Perf. 12*
652 A185 60fr multicolored 1.50 .80
653 A185 100fr multicolored 2.50 1.10

9th South Pacific Games, Papua New Guinea — A207

1991, Sept. 6 *Perf. 12½*
654 A207 170fr multicolored 3.50 1.50

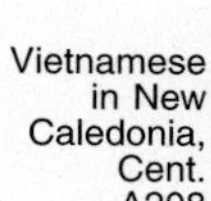

Vietnamese in New Caledonia, Cent. A208

1991, Sept. 8 Engr. *Perf. 13x12½*
655 A208 300fr multicolored 6.50 2.50

Lions Club of New Caledonia, 30th Anniv. — A209

1991, Oct. 5 Litho. *Perf. 12½*
656 A209 192fr multicolored 5.50 2.75

First Commercial Harvesting of Sandalwood, 150th Anniv. A210

1991, Oct. 23 Engr. *Perf. 13*
657 A210 200fr multicolored 5.25 2.75

Phila Nippon '91 — A211

Plants and butterflies: 8fr, Phillantus, Eurema hecabe. 15fr, Pipturus incanus, Hypolimnas octocula. 20fr, Stachytarpheta urticaefolia, Precis villida. 26fr, Malaisia scandens, Cyrestis telamon.

Butterflies: No. 662a, Cyrestis telamon, vert. b, Hypolimnas octocula, vert. c, Eurema hecabe, vert. d, Precis villida, vert.

1991, Nov. 16 Litho. *Perf. 12½*
658 A211 8fr multicolored .30 .25
659 A211 15fr multicolored .35 .35
660 A211 20fr multicolored .45 .35
661 A211 26fr multicolored .70 .45
a. Strip of 4, #658-661 + label 2.75 2.50

Souvenir Sheet

662 A211 75fr Sheet of 4, #a.-d. 12.00 12.00

Central Bank for Economic Cooperation, 50th Anniv. — A212

Designs: No. 663, Nickel processing plant, dam. No. 664, Private home, tourist hotels.

1991, Dec. 2 Litho. *Perf. 13*
663 76fr multicolored 1.90 1.00
664 76fr multicolored 1.90 1.00
a. A212 Pair, #663-664 + label 4.00 4.00

Preservation of Nature A213

15fr, Madeleine waterfalls.

1992, Mar. 25 Litho. *Perf. 13*
665 A213 15fr multicolored .60 .45
a. Souv. sheet, perf. 12½ 4.00 4.00

No. 665a sold for 150fr.

Immigration of First Japanese to New Caledonia, Cent. — A214

1992, June 11 Litho. *Perf. 13x12½*
666 95fr yellow & multi 2.25 1.25
667 95fr gray & multi 2.25 1.25
a. A214 Pair, #666-667 + label 4.50 4.50

Arrival of American Armed Forces, 50th Anniv. A215

1992, Aug. 13
668 A215 50fr multicolored 1.50 .60

Lagoon Protection A216

1993, Feb. 23 Litho. *Perf. 13*
669 A216 120fr multicolored 2.75 1.25

Kagu Type of 1990

1993-94 Engr. *Perf. 13*
675 A179a 55fr red 2.00 1.25
676 A179a (60fr) claret 1.50 .60

Self-Adhesive
Litho.
Die Cut Perf. 10

681 A179a 5fr bright lilac 1.40 1.40
a. Bklt. pane, 8+8, gutter btwn. 22.50
683 A179a 55fr red 3.50 3.50
a. Bklt. pane, 8+8, gutter btwn. 57.50

Issued: Nos. 675, 683, 4/7/93; No. 676, 1/27/94; No. 681, 2/94.

No. 676 sold for 60fr on day of issue.

By their nature, Nos. 681a, 683a are complete booklets. The peelable paper backing serves as a booklet cover.

No. 599 Surcharged

1993 Engr. *Perf. 13*
685 A179a 55fr on 50fr red 1.40 .70

Philately in School — A217

1993, Apr. 7 Litho. *Perf. 13½*
686 A217 25fr multicolored .60 .30

For overprint see No. 690.

Miniature Sheet of 13

Town Coats of Arms — A218

Designs: a, Bourail. b, Noumea. c, Canala. d, Kone. e, Paita. f, Dumbea. g, Koumac. h, Ponerhouen. i, Kaamoo Hyehen. j, Mont Dore. k, Thio. l, Kaala-Gomen. m, Touho.

1993, Dec. 10 Litho. *Perf. 13½*
687 A218 70fr #a.-m., + 2 labels 40.00 40.00

Souvenir Sheet

Hong Kong '94 — A219

Wildlife: a, Panda. b, Kagu.

1994, Feb. 18 Litho. *Perf. 13*
688 A219 105fr Sheet of 2, #a.-b. 8.25 8.25

First Postal Delivery Route, 50th Anniv. A220

1994, Apr. 28 Engr. *Perf. 13*
689 A220 15fr multicolored .50 .25

No. 686 Ovptd. in Blue

1994, Apr. 22 Litho. *Perf. 13½*
690 A217 25fr multicolored .70 .35

Headquarters of New Caledonian Post Office — A222

1994, June 25 Litho. *Perf. 13½x13*
691 Strip of 4, #a.-d. 8.00 8.00
a. A222 30fr 1859 .75 .45
b. A222 60fr 1936 1.50 .80
c. A222 90fr 1967 2.10 1.40
d. A222 120fr 1993 3.00 1.75

Pacific Sculpture — A223

1994, June 25 Litho. *Perf. 13x13½*
693 A223 60fr multicolored 1.50 .70

Chambeyronia Macrocarpa — A224

1994, July 7 Litho. *Perf. 13x13½*
694 A224 90fr multicolored 2.25 1.10

No. J46 Overprinted With Bar Over "Timbre Taxe"

1994, Aug. 8 Litho. *Perf. 13*
696 D5 5fr multicolored 17.50 —

Stag — A227

1994, Aug. 14 Litho. *Perf. 13½*
697 A227 150fr multicolored 3.50 1.60

Jacques Nervat, Writer — A228

1994, Sept. 15 *Perf. 13x13½*
698 A228 175fr multicolored 4.00 1.90

Frigate Nivose — A229

No. 699, 30fr, Ship at sea. No. 700, 30fr, Ship along shore. No. 701, 30fr, Ship docked. No. 702, 60fr, Painting of frigate, map of island, ship's crest. No. 703, 60fr, Ship's bell. No. 704, 60fr, Sailor looking at ship.

1994, Oct. 7 Litho. *Perf. 13½*
Booklet Stamps

699 A229 30fr multicolored 1.10 .45
700 A229 30fr multicolored 1.10 .45
701 A229 30fr multicolored 1.10 .35
702 A229 60fr multicolored 1.75 .80
703 A229 60fr multicolored 1.75 .80
704 A229 60fr multicolored 1.75 .80
a. Booklet pane, #699-704 9.00
Booklet, 4 #704a 40.00

Philately at School — A230

1994, Nov. 4 Litho. *Perf. 13½*
705 A230 30fr multicolored .90 .35

For overprint see No. 749

Christmas — A231

Top of bell starts below: a, Second "o." b, Third "e." c, "a." d, "C." e, Second "e."

1994, Dec. 17
706 Strip of 5 4.75 4.25
a.-e. A231 30fr Any single .85 .55

Nos. 706a-706e differ in location of the red ball, yellow bell and statue. No.706 is designed for stereoscopic viewing.

Le Monde Newspaper, 50th Anniv. — A232

1994, Dec. 17
707 A232 90fr multicolored 2.75 1.60

Louis Pasteur (1822-95) A233

1995, Feb. 13 Litho. *Perf. 13*
708 A233 120fr No. 601 2.75 1.40

Charles de Gaulle (1890-1970) A234

Litho. & Embossed

1995, Mar. 28 *Perf. 13*
709 A234 1000fr blue & gold 18.00 15.00

Teacher's Training College for the French Territories in the Pacific — A235

1995, Apr. 24 Litho. *Perf. 13*
710 A235 100fr multicolored 2.25 1.25

See French Polynesia No. 656 and Wallis & Futuna No. C182.

Sylviornis Neo-Caledonia, Fossil Bird — A236

1995, May 16 Litho. *Perf. 13x13½*
711 A236 60fr multicolored 1.75 .70

10th Sunshine Triathlon A237

1995, May 26 Engr. *Perf. 13x12½*
712 A237 60fr multicolored 1.50 .90

Creation of the CFP Franc, 1945 — A238

Top of tree at left points to: a, Second "e." b, Second "l." c, First "l." d, First "e."

1995, June 8 Litho. *Perf. 13x13½*
713 A238 10fr Strip of 4, #a.-d. 1.50 1.50

Nos. 713a-713d show coin rotating clockwise with trees, hut at different locations. No. 713 is designed for stereoscopic viewing.

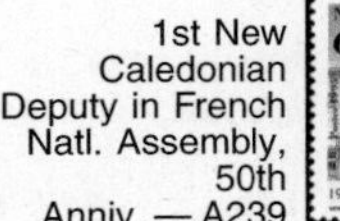
1st New Caledonian Deputy in French Natl. Assembly, 50th Anniv. — A239

1995, June 8 *Perf. 13½*
714 A239 60fr multicolored 1.50 .70

End of World War II, 50th Anniv. — A240

1995, June 8 *Perf. 13x13½*
715 A240 90fr multicolored 1.50 .60

UN, 50th Anniv. — A241

1995, June 8
716 A241 90fr multicolored 2.25 .90

Sebertia Acuminata A242

1995, July 28 Litho. *Perf. 13x13½*
717 A242 60fr multicolored 1.50 .60

Singapore '95 — A243

Sea birds: 5fr, Anous stolidus. 10fr, Larus novaehollandiae. 20fr, Sterna dougallii. 35fr, Pandion haliaetus. 65fr, Sula sula. 125fr, Fregata minor.

1995, Aug. 24 Litho. *Perf. 13x13½*
718 A243 5fr multicolored .30 .25
719 A243 10fr multicolored .35 .25
720 A243 20fr multicolored .40 .25
721 A243 35fr multicolored .80 .55
722 A243 65fr multicolored 1.40 1.10
723 A243 125fr multicolored 3.00 1.60
a. Souvenir sheet, #718-723 + label 7.50 7.50
Nos. 718-723 (6) 6.25 4.00

10th South Pacific Games — A244

1995, Aug. 24
724 A244 90fr multicolored 2.10 1.10

Sculpture, The Lizard Man, by Dick Bone — A248

1995, Oct. 25 Litho. *Perf. 13*
730 A248 65fr multicolored 1.25 .75

Gargariscus Prionocephalus A249

1995, Dec. 15 Litho. *Perf. 13*
731 A249 100fr multicolored 2.25 1.00

Francis Carco (1886-1958), Poet & Novelist — A250

1995, Nov. 15 Litho. *Perf. 13x13½*
732 A250 95fr multicolored 2.25 1.25

Ancient Pottery — A251

1996, Apr. 12 Litho. *Perf. 13*
733 A251 65fr multicolored 1.60 .90

Endemic Rubiaceous Plants — A252

Designs: 65fr, Captaincookia margaretae. 95fr, Ixora cauliflora.

1996, Apr. 17
734 A252 65fr multicolored 1.50 .60
735 A252 95fr multicolored 2.10 .90

7th Va'a (Outrigger Canoe) World Championship, Noumea, New Caledonia
A253

Designs: a, 30fr, Islander standing on shore with early version of canoe. b, 65fr, Early single-hull canoe with islanders. c, 95fr, Early catamaran, people rowing. d, 125fr, Modern racing canoe.

1996, May 10 Litho. *Perf. 13*
736 A253 Strip of 4, #a.-d. 6.50 6.50

No. 736 is a continuous design.

CHINA '96 — A254

Marine life: 25fr, Halieutaea stellata. 40fr, Perotrochus deforgesi. 65fr, Mursia musorstomia. 125fr, Metacrinus levii.

1996, May 18
737 A254 25fr multicolored .55 .35
738 A254 40fr multicolored .85 .65
739 A254 65fr multicolored 1.50 .90
740 A254 125fr multicolored 2.75 1.60
Nos. 737-740 (4) 5.65 3.50

Nos. 737-740 were each issued in sheets of 10 + 5 labels.

On Nos. 737-740 portions of the design were applied by a thermographic process producing a shiny, raised effect.

737a Booklet pane of 6 5.00
738a Booklet pane of 6 6.50
739a Booklet pane of 6 12.50
740a Booklet pane of 6 25.00
Complete booklet, #737a-740a 49.00

CAPEX '96 — A255

Orchids: 5fr, Sarcochilus koghiensis. 10fr, Phaius robertsii. 25fr, Megastylis montana. 65fr, Dendrobium macrophyllum. 95fr, Dendrobium virotii. 125fr, Ephemerantha comata.

1996, June 25 Litho. *Perf. 13*
741 A255 5fr multicolored .30 .25
742 A255 10fr multicolored .40 .25
743 A255 25fr multicolored .65 .35
744 A255 65fr multicolored 1.40 .65
745 A255 95fr multicolored 2.25 1.00
746 A255 125fr multicolored 2.50 1.25
a. Booklet pane of 6, #741-746 7.75
Souvenir booklet, 4 #746a 38.00
Nos. 741-746 (6) 7.50 3.75

Nos. 741-746 were each issued in sheets of 10 + 5 labels.

No. 705 Ovptd. with UNICEF Emblem in Blue

1996, Sept. 12 Litho. *Perf. 13½*
749 A230 30fr multicolored .75 .45

UNICEF, 50th anniv.

Ordination of the First Melanesian Priests — A258

1996, Oct. 9 Litho. *Perf. 13*
750 A258 160fr multicolored 3.50 1.90

Portions of the design on No. 750 were applied by a thermographic process producing a shiny, raised effect.

7th Festival of South Pacific Arts — A259

Designs: 100fr, Dancer, face carving. 105fr, Wood carvings of women. 200fr, Painting by Paula Boi. 500fr, Gaica Dance, Lifou.

1996, Oct. 9
751 A259 100fr multicolored 2.25 1.25
752 A259 105fr multicolored 2.25 1.25
753 A259 200fr multicolored 4.00 2.25
754 A259 500fr multicolored 9.00 5.75
Nos. 751-754 (4) 17.50 10.50

No. 751 is airmail.

French Pres. Francois Mitterrand (1916-96)
A260

1997, Mar. 14 Litho. *Perf. 13*
755 A260 1000fr multicolored 18.00 11.00

Alphonse Daudet (1840-97), Writer — A261

Designs: No. 756, "Letters from a Windmill." No. 757, "Le Petit Chose." No. 758, "Tartarin of Tarascon." No. 759, Daudet writing.

1997, May 14 *Perf. 13*
756 A261 65fr multicolored 1.50 1.50
757 A261 65fr multicolored 1.50 1.50
758 A261 65fr multicolored 1.50 1.50
759 A261 65fr multicolored 1.50 1.50
a. Souvenir sheet, #756-759 6.50 6.50

Henri La Fleur, First Senator of New Caledonia
A262

1997, June 12 Litho. *Perf. 13*
760 A262 105fr multicolored 2.40 1.25

Insects — A263

Designs: a, Tectocoris diophthalmus. b, Kanakia gigas. c, Aenetus cohici.

1997, June 25 Litho. *Perf. 13x12½*
761 A263 65fr Strip of 3, #a.-c. 4.50 4.00

Jacques Iekawe (1946-92), First Melanesian Prefect
A264

1997, July 23 Litho. *Perf. 13*
762 A264 250fr multicolored 5.00 2.50

Kagu — A265

1997, Aug. 13 Engr. *Perf. 13*
763 A265 95fr blue 2.10 1.25

See Nos. 772-773C, 878-879, 897. For redrawn stamp of type A265, see No. 1296d.

Horse Racing — A266

No. 764, Harness racing. No. 765, Thoroughbred racing.

1997, Sept. 20 Litho. *Perf. 13*
764 A266 65fr multicolored 1.75 .80
765 A266 65fr multicolored 1.75 .80

Early Engraving of "View of Port de France" (Noumea)
A267

Photo. & Engr.
1997, Sept. 22 *Perf. 13x12½*
766 A267 95fr multicolored 2.00 1.25

See No. 802.

A268

1997, Sept. 22 Litho. *Perf. 13*
767 A268 150fr multicolored 3.00 1.75

First Melanesian election, 50th anniv.

Hippocampus Bargibanti — A269

1997, Nov. 3 Litho. *Perf. 13½x13*
768 A269 100fr multicolored 2.25 1.50

5th World Conf. on Fish of the Indo-Pacific. Issued in sheets of 10+5 labels.

South Pacific Arts — A270

Designs: a, Doka wood carvings. b, Beizam dance mask. c, Abstract painting of primative life by Yvette Bouquet.

1997, Nov. 3 *Perf. 13*
769 A270 100fr Strip of 3, #a.-c. 6.00 6.00

Christmas
A271

Designs: 95fr, Santa on surfboard pulled by dolphins. 100fr, Dolphin with banner in mouth.

1997, Nov. 17
770 A271 95fr multicolored 2.00 1.00
771 A271 100fr multicolored 2.00 1.00

Nos. 770-771 issued in sheets of 10+5 labels.

Kagu Type of 1997

1997-98 Engr. *Perf. 13*
772 A265 30fr orange 1.00 .35
773 A265 (70fr) red 1.60 .75

Booklet Stamps
Self-Adhesive
Litho.
Serpentine Die Cut 11

773A A265 (70fr) red 2.00 .45
b. Booklet pane of 10 22.50

Engr.
Serpentine Die Cut 6¾ Vert.

773C A265 (70fr) red — —
d. Booklet pane of 10 —

The peelable paper backing of No. 773A serves as a booklet cover.

Issued: 30fr, 1997; No. 773A, 1/2/98; No. 773C, 2004.

A272

Mushrooms: #774, Lentinus tuber-regium. #775, Volvaria bombycina. #776, Morchella anteridiformis.

1998, Jan. 22 Litho. *Perf. 13*
774 A272 70fr multicolored 1.40 .80
775 A272 70fr multicolored 1.40 .80
776 A272 70fr multicolored 1.40 .80
Nos. 774-776 (3) 4.20 2.40

A273

Artifacts from Territorial Museum: 105fr, Mask, Northern Region. 110fr, "Dulon" door frame pillar, Central Region.

1998, Mar. 17 Litho. *Perf. 13*
777 A273 105fr multicolored 2.00 1.10
778 A273 110fr multicolored 2.10 1.10

Paul Gauguin (1848-1903) A274

1998, May 15 Litho. *Perf. 13*
779 A274 405fr multicolored 8.00 5.00

1998 World Cup Soccer Championships, France — A280

1998, June 5 Photo. *Perf. 12½*
787 A280 100fr multicolored 2.00 1.25

A281

Jean-Marie Tjibaou Cultural Center — A282

Designs: 30fr, "Mitimitia," artwork by Fatu Feu'u. No. 789, Jean-Marie Tjibaou (1936-89), Melanesian political leader. No. 790, Exterior view of building, vert. 105fr, "Man Bird," painting by Mathias Kauage.

1998, June 21 Litho. *Perf. 13x13½*
788 A281 30fr multicolored .75 .35
a. Booklet pane of 6 4.50
789 A281 70fr multicolored 1.50 .85
a. Booklet pane of 6 9.00
790 A281 70fr multicolored 1.50 .85
a. Booklet pane of 6 9.00
791 A282 105fr multicolored 2.25 1.25
a. Booklet pane of 6 15.00
Complete booklet, #788a, 789a, 790a, 791a 40.00
Nos. 788-791 (4) 6.00 3.30

Abolition of Slavery, 150th Anniv. A283

1998, July 21 Engr. *Perf. 13*
792 A283 130fr multicolored 2.50 1.50

Postman, Dogs — A284

1998, Aug. 20 Litho. *Perf. 13*
793 A284 70fr multicolored 1.75 .85

Arab Presence in New Caledonia, Cent. — A285

1998, Sept. 4
794 A285 80fr multicolored 1.75 1.00

A286

Vasco da Gama's Voyage to India, 500th Anniv. — A287

No. 795: a, Port in India. b, Da Gama at Cape of Good Hope, ships at sea. c, Da Gama meeting with Indians. d, Da Gama's picture in crest.

No. 796: a, Map of route. b, Vasco da Gama. c, Ship at anchor.

1998, Sept. 4
795 A286 100fr Strip of 4, #a.-d. 8.00 8.00

Souvenir Sheet

796 A287 70fr Sheet of 3, #a.-c. 5.00 5.00

Portugal '98 Intl. Philatelic Exhibition.

A288

Litho. & Engr.

1998, Sept. 25 *Perf. 12½x13*
797 A288 110fr multicolored 2.25 2.25

Vincent Bouquet (1893-1971), High Chief.

A289

World Wildlife Fund — Kagu: 5fr, Male. 10fr, Female. 15fr, Two in grass. 70fr, Two in dirt, one ruffling feathers.

1998, Oct. 20 Litho. *Perf. 13*
798 A289 5fr multicolored .30 .25
799 A289 10fr multicolored .40 .25
800 A289 15fr multicolored .60 .25
801 A289 70fr multicolored 1.75 1.25
Nos. 798-801 (4) 3.05 2.00

Early Engraving Type of 1997

1998, Nov. 4 Engr. *Perf. 13x12½*
802 A267 155fr Nou Island 3.00 2.00

Universal Declaration of Human Rights, 50th Anniv. — A290

1998, Nov. 4 Engr. *Perf. 13*
803 A290 70fr blk, bl & bl grn 1.75 1.40

Columnar Pine — A291

1998, Nov. 5 Litho. *Perf. 13x13½*
804 A291 100fr shown 2.25 2.00
805 A291 100fr Coast, forest 2.25 2.00

A292

Post and Telecommunications, 40th Anniv.: #806, Switchboard, bicycle, early post office. #807, Cell phone, microwave relay, motorcycle.

1998, Nov. 27 Litho. *Perf. 13½x13*
806 A292 70fr multicolored 1.60 1.60
807 A292 70fr multicolored 1.60 1.60
a. Pair, #806-807 + label 3.50 3.50

A293

Underwater scenes (Greetings Stamps): No. 808, Fish, coral forming flower, Happy Anniversary. No. 809, Fish up close, Happy New Year. No. 810, Open treasure chest, Best Wishes. No. 811, Fish, starfish forming Christmas tree, Merry Christmas.

1998, Dec. 1
808 A293 100fr multicolored 2.00 1.50
809 A293 100fr multicolored 2.00 1.50
810 A293 100fr multicolored 2.00 1.50
811 A293 100fr multicolored 2.00 1.50
Nos. 808-811 (4) 8.00 6.00

Monument to the Disappearance of the Ship Monique, 20th Anniv. — A294

1998, Dec. 1 *Perf. 13*
812 A294 130fr multicolored 2.75 2.00

Arachnids A295

Designs: No. 813, Argiope aetherea. No. 814, Barycheloides alluvviophilus. No. 815, Latrodectus hasselti. No. 816, Crytophora moluccensis.

1999, Mar. 19 Litho. *Perf. 13x13½*
813 A295 70fr multicolored 1.60 1.40
814 A295 70fr multicolored 1.60 1.40
815 A295 70fr multicolored 1.60 1.40
816 A295 70fr multicolored 1.60 1.40
Nos. 813-816 (4) 6.40 5.60

Carcharodon Megalodon — A296

Designs: 100fr, Fossil tooth of megalodon. No. 818: a, Shark swimming with mouth open, vert. b, Comparison of shark to man and carcharodon carcharias. c, Fossil tooth on bottom of ocean.

1999, Mar. 19 *Perf. 12½*
817 A296 100fr multicolored 2.25 1.50

Souvenir Sheet

Perf. 13

818 A296 70fr Sheet of 3, #a.-c. 4.50 4.50

Nos. 818a is 30x40mm and 818b is 40x30mm.

Australia '99, World Stamp Expo (#818).

Paul Bloc (1883-1970), Writer — A297

1999, Apr. 23 Engr. *Perf. 13x12½*
819 A297 105fr grn, bl grn & brn 2.25 1.50

Traditional Musical Instruments — A298

1999, May 20 Litho. *Perf. 13½x13*
820 A298 30fr Bwanjep .75 .60
821 A298 70fr Sonnailles 1.50 1.40
822 A298 100fr Flutes 2.25 2.00
Nos. 820-822 (3) 4.50 4.00

11th South Pacific Games, Guam — A299

1999, May 20 *Perf. 13x13¼*
823 A299 5fr Track & field .30 .25
824 A299 10fr Tennis .30 .25
825 A299 30fr Karate .75 .60
826 A299 70fr Baseball 1.50 1.40
Nos. 823-826 (4) 2.85 2.50

Overseas Transport Squadron 52, Humanitarian Missions — A300

1999, June 18 *Perf. 13*
827 A300 135fr multicolored 2.75 1.75

Escoffier Hotel Catering and Business School, Noumea, 20th Anniv. — A301

Designs: No. 828, Building, computer. No. 829, Building, chef's hat.

1999, June 17 Litho. *Perf. 13*
828 A301 70fr multicolored 1.40 1.00
a. Pair + central label 3.00 2.50
829 A301 70fr multicolored 1.40 1.00
a. Pair + central label 3.00 2.50

New Caledonia's First Postage Stamp, 140th Anniv. — A302

Designs: No. 830, #1.
No. 831: a, Two #1. b, #1, diff. c, #1 up close. d, like #830. e, Design A265, image of Napolean III from #1, "1999."

1999, July 2 Photo. *Perf. 13¼*
830 A302 70fr multicolored 1.75 1.40

Souvenir Sheet
Perf. 12

831	Sheet of 5	27.50	27.50
a.	A302 100fr Engraved	2.50	2.50
b.	A302 100fr Litho., thermograph	2.50	2.50
c.	A302 100fr Litho.	2.50	2.50
d.	A302 100fr Litho. & embossed	2.50	2.50
e.	A302 700fr Litho., hologram	15.00	15.00

Nos. 831a-831d are each 36x28mm. No. 831e is 44x35mm. Portions of the design on No. 831b were applied by a thermographic process producing a shiny, raised effect. No. 831e contains a holographic image. Soaking in water may affect the hologram.
PhilexFrance '99 (#831).

Tourism — A303

1999, Sept. 28 Litho. *Perf. 13¼*

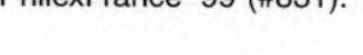

832	A303	5fr Fish, vegetables	.30	.25
833	A303	30fr Lobster dish	.75	.55
834	A303	70fr Tourist huts	1.50	1.25
835	A303	100fr Hotel pool	2.25	1.90
		Nos. 832-835 (4)	4.80	3.95

Ratification of Noumea Accord, 1998 — A304

1999, Nov. 10 Litho. *Perf. 13x13½*
836 A304 70fr multi 1.75 1.25

Aji Aboro Dance — A305

1999, Nov. 10
837 A305 70fr multi 1.50 1.25

Château Hagen A306

1999, Nov. 18 *Perf. 13*
838 A306 155fr multi 3.50 2.75

Nature Protection A307

1999, Dec. 7
839 A307 30fr multi .75 .50

Greetings A308

Designs: No. 840, "Joyeux Noel." No. 841, "Félicitations." No. 842, "Bon Anniversaire." No. 843, "Meilleurs Voeux 2000."

1999, Dec. 20

840	A308	100fr multi	2.00	1.50
841	A308	100fr multi	2.00	1.50
842	A308	100fr multi	2.00	1.50
843	A308	100fr multi	2.00	1.50
		Nos. 840-843 (4)	8.00	6.00

Amédée Lighthouse — A309

2000, Mar. 7 Litho. *Perf. 13½x12*
844 A309 100fr multi 2.25 1.60

Ship Emile Renouf A310

2000, Apr. 19 Engr. *Perf. 13x13¼*
845 A310 135fr multi 3.50 2.25

Painting by Giles Subileau A311

2000, June 15 Litho. *Perf. 13*
846 A311 155fr multi 3.00 2.25

Souvenir Sheet

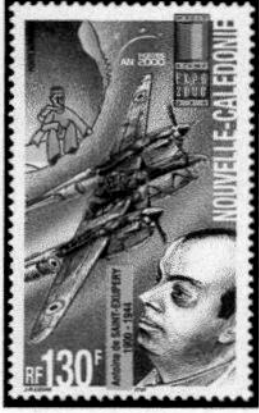

New Year 2000 (Year of the Dragon) A312

Denomination: a, at R. b, at L.

2000, June 15
847 A312 105fr Sheet of 2, #a-b 5.00 4.50

Antoine de Saint-Exupéry (1900-44), Aviator, Writer — A313

2000, July 7
848 A313 130fr multi 3.00 2.75

World Stamp Expo 2000, Anaheim.

Noumea Aquarium — A314

Designs: No. 849, Hymenocera elegans. No. 850, Fluorescent corals. No. 851, Chelinus undulatus.

2000, July 7 *Perf. 13x13¼*
849-851 A314 70fr Set of 3 5.50 3.50

Mangrove Heart — A315

2000, Aug. 10 Photo. *Perf. 13*
852 A315 100fr multi 2.50 1.40

Value is for copy with surrounding selvage.

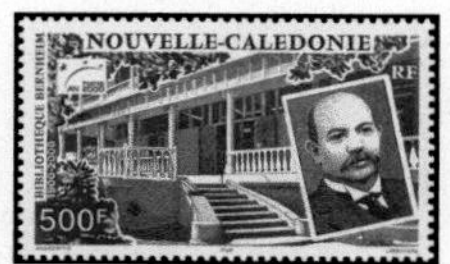

2000 Summer Olympics, Sydney — A316

Designs: 10fr, Archery. 30fr, Boxing. 80fr, Cycling. 100fr, Fencing.

2000, Sept. 15 Litho. *Perf. 13x13¼*
853-856 A316 Set of 4 4.50 4.50

Lucien Bernheim (1856-1917), Library Founder, and Bernheim Library, Cent. — A317

2000, Oct. 24 Engr. *Perf. 13*
857 A317 500fr multi 11.00 7.25

A318

8th Pacific Arts Festival A319

Kanak money and background colors of: 90fr, Orange. 105fr, Dark blue.
Festival emblem and works of art — No. 860: a, White denomination at UL, "RF" at UR. b, White denomination and "RF" at UL. c, Yellow denomination. d, White denomination at UR.

2000, Oct. 24 *Perf. 13x13¼*
858-859 A318 Set of 2 4.50 3.00

Souvenir Sheet

860 A319 70fr Sheet of 4, #a-d 6.25 6.25

Red Cross — A320

2000, Nov. 9 Litho. *Perf. 13¼x13*
861 A320 100fr multi 2.25 2.00

Queen Hortense (1848-1900) — A321

2000, Nov. 9 Engr. *Perf. 12½x13*
862 A321 110fr multi 2.50 2.25

Northern Province Landscapes — A322

a, Fisherman in canoe. b, Motorboat near beach and cliffs. c, Fisherman on raft.

2000, Nov. 9 Litho. *Perf. 13x13¼*
863 A322 Horiz. strip of 3 6.50 6.50
a.-c. 100fr Any single 2.00 1.50

Philately in School — A323

Children's art by: a, Kévyn Pamoiloun. b, Lise-Marie Samanich. c, Alexandre Mandin.

2000, Nov. 14 *Perf. 13¼x13*
864 A323 Horiz. strip of 3 4.50 3.50
a.-c. 70fr Any single 1.40 1.10

Christmas, Holy Year 2000 — A324

2000, Dec. 19 *Perf. 13*
865 A324 100fr multi 2.00 1.60

Portions of the design were applied by a thermographic process producing a shiny, raised effect.

Greetings — A325

Kagu and: No. 866, "Meilleurs voeux de bonheur." No. 867, "Vive les vacances." No. 868, Félicitations.

2000, Dec. 19 *Perf. 13¼x13*
866-868 A325 100fr Set of 3 6.75 6.00

No. 868 printed se-tenant with two labels.

New Year 2001 (Year of the Snake) — A326

Designs: 100fr, Snake on beach, snake wearing robe.
No. 870: a, Snake in flowers. b, Snake in city.

2001, Feb. 15 Litho. *Perf. 13*
869 A326 100fr multi 2.50 2.00

Souvenir Sheet
Perf. 13½x13

870 A326 70fr Sheet of 2, #a-b 4.25 4.25

Size of Nos. 870a-870b: 30x40mm.

Sailing Ship France II — A327

2001, Apr. 18 Engr. *Perf. 13x13¼*
871 A327 110fr multi 2.50 2.25

Noumea Aquarium — A328

Nautilus macromphalus: a, Conjoined pair. b, Anatomical cross-section. c, Pair separated.

2001, May 22 Litho.
872 A328 Horiz. strip of 3 7.00 7.00
a.-c. 100fr Any single 2.25 1.50

Corvus Moneduliodes and Tools — A329

2001, June 14 *Perf. 13*
873 A329 70fr multi 1.60 1.50

Operation Cetacean — A330

No. 874: a, Pair of Megaptera novaeangliae underwater. b, Whales breaching surface.

2001, July 18 *Perf. 13x13¼*
874 A330 Horiz. pair with central label 5.00 5.00
a.-b. 100fr Any single 2.25 1.50

See Vanuatu Nos. 785-787.

The Keeper of Gaia, the Eden, by Ito Waia — A331

Vision From Oceania, by Jipé Le-Bars A332

2001, Aug. 22 *Perf. 13*
875 A331 70fr multi 1.60 1.25
876 A332 110fr multi 2.25 2.00

Year of Dialogue Among Civilizations A333

2001, Sept. 19 Litho. *Perf. 13x13¼*
877 A333 265fr multi 6.50 5.50

Kagu Type of 1997

2001 Engr. *Perf. 13*
878 A265 100fr bright blue 2.50 2.50

Self-Adhesive
Litho.
Serpentine Die Cut 11

879 A265 100fr bright blue 2.75 2.50
a. Booklet pane of 10 32.50

Issued: No. 878, 9/23; No. 879, 9/20.

For surcharge see No. 972.

The Lonely Boatman, by Marik A334

2001, Oct. 11 Litho. *Perf. 13*
880 A334 110fr multi 2.25 2.25

Underwater Observatory A335

2001, Oct. 11
881 A335 135fr multi 2.75 1.25

Qanono Church, Lifou A336

2001, Oct. 11
882 A336 500fr multi 10.00 8.00

Fernande Le Riche (1884-1967), Novelist — A337

2001, Nov. 8
883 A337 155fr brown & blue 3.00 3.00

First Olympic Gold Medal Won by a New Caledonian A338

2001, Nov. 8 *Perf. 13x13¼*
884 A338 265fr multi 5.50 5.00

Kitesurfing — A339

2001, Nov. 16 *Perf. 13*
885 A339 100fr multi 2.50 2.00

"The Book, My Friend" Literacy Campaign — A340

2001, Nov. 27 *Perf. 13x13¼*
886 A340 70fr multi 1.75 1.40

Lifou Scenes — A341

No. 887: a, Easo. b, Jokin.

2001, Nov. 27 *Perf. 13¼x13*
887 A341 100fr Vert. pair, #a-b 4.75 4.50

Greetings — A342

Flying fox and: No. 888, 100fr, Joyeux Noel (Merry Christmas). No. 889, 100fr, Meilleurs voeux (Best wishes). No. 890, 100fr, Vive la fete (Long live the holiday).

2001, Dec. 7 *Perf. 13x13¼*
888-890 A342 Set of 3 6.50 6.00

New Year 2002 (Year of the Horse) A343

Designs: 100fr, Horse, other zodiac animals.

No. 892, vert.: a, Horse. b, Seahorse.

2002, Feb. 7 *Perf. 13*
891 A343 100fr multi 2.50 2.25

Souvenir Sheet

892 A343 70fr Sheet of 2, #a-b 3.50 3.25

Love — A344

2002, Feb. 13
893 A344 100fr multi 2.50 2.00

Value is for stamp with surrounding selvage.

Cricket A345

2002, Mar. 20 Litho. *Perf. 13*
894 A345 100fr multi 2.50 2.00

Ancient Hatchet — A346

2002, Mar. 20 Litho.
895 A346 505fr multi 11.00 10.00

Portions of the design were applied by a thermographic process producing a shiny, raised effect.

Hobie Cat 16 World Championships — A347

2002, Apr. 1 Litho. *Perf. 13*
896 A347 70fr multi 1.75 1.40

Kagu Type of 1997

2002, Apr. 15 Engr. *Perf. 13*
897 A265 5fr purple .30 .25

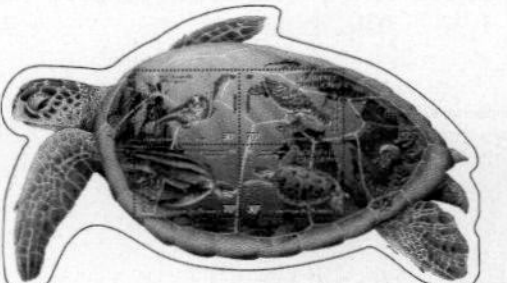

2002 World Cup Soccer Championships, Japan and Korea — A348

2002, May 15 Photo.
898 A348 100fr multi 2.75 2.00

Values are for stamp with surrounding selvage.

Souvenir Sheet

Turtles at Noumea Aquarium — A349

No. 899: a, 30fr, Caretta caretta. b, 70fr, Eretmochelys imbricat. c, 70fr, Dermochelys coriacea. d, 30fr, Chelonia mydas.

2002, May 15 Litho. *Perf. 13x13¼*
899 A349 Sheet of 4, #a-d 4.75 4.75
e. As #899, with inscription added in margin 4.75 4.75

Issued: No. 899e, 10/24/03. Inscription in margin of No. 899e reads "Coupe du monde 2003 / Champion du monde."

Corvette Alcmene and Map — A350

2002, June 13 Engr. *Perf. 13x13¼*
900 A350 210fr multi 4.75 4.00

Coffee — A351

No. 901: a, Coffee plant and beans. b, Bean roasters. c, Coffee makers, woman, cup of coffee.

2002, June 13 Litho.
901 A351 Horiz. strip of 3 5.00 5.00
a.-c. 70fr Any single 1.50 1.40

No. 901 was impregnated with coffee scent.

Edmond Caillard (1912-91), Astronomer A352

2002, June 26 **Engr.**
902 A352 70fr multi 1.75 1.50

Statue of Emma Piffault (1861-77), by Michel Rocton — A353

2002, July 17 **Litho.** ***Perf. 13¼x13***
903 A353 10fr multi .40 .25

Noumea Circus School — A354

2002, Aug. 30 ***Perf. 13***
904 A354 70fr multi 1.75 1.40

Illustrations From Books by Jean Mariotti A355

2002, Sept. 18
905 A355 70fr multi 1.60 1.40

Operation Cetacean — A356

No. 906: a, Adult and young of Physeter macrocephalus. b, Physeter macrocephalus and squid.

2002, Sept. 18 ***Perf. 13x13¼***
906 A356 Horiz. pair with central label 4.75 4.75
a.-b. 100fr Either single 2.25 2.00

See Norfolk Island No. 783.

Intl. Year of Mountains A357

2002, Nov. 7 **Litho.** ***Perf. 13***
907 A357 100fr multi 2.50 2.00

Christmas and New Year's Day — A358

2002, Nov. 7
908 A358 100fr multi 2.25 2.00

Bourail Fort Powder Magazine — A359

2002, Nov. 7 **Engr.** ***Perf. 13x12½***
909 A359 1000fr multi 20.00 18.00

Mel Me Mec, by Adrien Trohmae A360

2002, Nov. 28 **Litho.** ***Perf. 13***
910 A360 100fr multi 2.50 2.00

New Year 2003 (Year of the Ram) — A361

2003, Jan. 29
911 A361 100fr multi 2.50 2.00

Printed in sheets of 10 + 2 labels. See No. 1251h.

Valentine's Day — A362

2003, Jan. 29 **Photo.** ***Perf. 13***
912 A362 100fr multi 2.50 2.00

Values are for stamps with surrounding selvage.

Jubilee Issue, Cent. — A363

2003 **Litho.** ***Perf. 13¼x13***
913 A363 70fr No. 77 1.75 1.40

Booklet Stamp

Size: 19x25mm

913A A363 70fr No. 77 1.75 1.40
b. Booklet pane of 10 17.50 —

Issued: No. 913, 2/7. No. 913A, 8/20.

Kagu — A364

2003 **Engr.** ***Perf. 13***
914 A364 10fr green .30 .25
915 A364 15fr brown .35 .25
916 A364 30fr orange .80 .60
917 A364 (70fr) red 1.50 1.40
Nos. 914-917 (4) 2.95 2.50

Booklet Stamps

Litho. & Embossed

Perf. 13¼x13¾

918 A364 70fr gray & silver 1.75 1.40
a. Booklet pane of 10 17.50 —
Complete booklet, #913Ab, 918a 35.00

Engr.

Serpentine Die Cut 6¾ Vert.

Self-Adhesive

919 A364 (70fr) red 1.90 1.40
a. Booklet pane of 10 20.00

Issued: Nos. 914-917, 2/7; No. 918, 8/20; No. 919, 5/15.

See Nos. 938, 965-966, 985-986, 1007, 1070. For redrawn stamp of type A364, see No. 1296e.

Fish at Nouméa Aquarium — A365

No. 920: a, Epinephelus maculatus. b, Plectropomus leopardus. c, Cromileptes altivelis.

2003, Apr. 9 **Photo.** ***Perf. 12¾***
920 A365 70fr Horiz. strip of 3, #a-c 5.00 4.00

Greater Nouméa High School A366

2003, May 14 **Litho.** ***Perf. 13***
921 A366 70fr multi 1.50 1.40

Operation Cetacean — A367

No. 922: a, Dugong swimming (79x29mm). b, Dugong feeding (40x29mm).

2003, June 11 ***Perf. 13x13¼***
922 A367 100fr Horiz. pair, #a-b 5.00 4.00

12th South Pacific Games, Suva, Fiji — A368

Designs: 5fr, Trapshooting. 30fr, Rugby. 70fr, Squash.

2003, June 11
923-925 A368 Set of 3 2.50 2.10

Man Picking Fruit From a Tree, by Paul Gauguin (1848-1903) A369

2003, June 25 **Photo.** ***Perf. 13***
926 A369 100fr multi 2.50 1.90

Aircalin, 20th Anniv. A370

2003, July 9 **Litho.**
927 A370 100fr multi 2.50 1.90

Governor Paul Feillet (1857-1903) — A371

2003, July 9 **Engr.** ***Perf. 12½x13***
928 A371 100fr dk blue & ol grn 2.00 1.50

Souvenir Sheet

Paintings by Paul Gauguin A372

No. 929: a, Study of Heads of Tahitian Women. b, Still Life with Maori Statuette.

2003, Aug. 20 **Litho.** ***Perf. 13***
929 A372 100fr Sheet of 2, #a-b 5.00 4.50

German Shepherd A373

2003, Oct. 8
930 A373 105fr multi 2.50 2.10

Le Phoque, Le Prony and Le Catinat in Balade Roadstead, 1853 A374

2003, Oct. 8 **Engr.** ***Perf. 13x12½***
931 A374 110fr multi 2.75 2.10

Robert Tatin d'Avesnières (1925-82), Painter A375

2003, Oct. 8 **Litho.** ***Perf. 13***
932 A375 135fr multi 3.25 2.60

Souvenir Sheet

Geckos A376

No. 933: a, 30fr, Bavayia cyclura. b, 30fr, Rhacodactylus chahoua. c, 70fr, Rhacodactylus ciliatus. d, 70fr, Eurydactylodes vieillardi.

2003, Oct. 8 ***Perf. 13x13¼***
933 A376 Sheet of 4, #a-d 5.50 5.50

Ouen Island A377

2003, Nov. 6 ***Perf. 13***
934 A377 100fr multi 2.50 1.90

Merry Christmas and Happy New Year — A378

2003, Nov. 6
935 A378 100fr multi 2.50 1.90

New Year 2004 (Year of the Monkey) A379

Designs: 70fr, Monkeys, Hong Kong skyline. No. 937: a, Tiger and woman. b, Monkey on horse.

2004, Jan. 30 **Litho.** ***Perf. 13***
936 A379 70fr multi 1.75 1.50

Souvenir Sheet
Perf. 13¼x13
Litho. With Foil Application

937 A379 100fr Sheet of 2, #a-b 5.00 5.00

2004 Hong Kong Stamp Expo. No. 937 contains two 30x40mm stamps.

Kagu Type of 2003

2004, Feb. 11 Engr. *Perf. 13*
938 A364 100fr blue 2.50 2.10

For surcharge see No. 973.

Love — A380

2004, Feb. 11 Photo.
939 A380 100fr multi 2.50 2.10

Values are for stamps with surrounding selvage.

Stamp Day A381

2004, May 15 Litho.
940 A381 105fr multi 2.50 2.10

Railroads in New Caledonia A382

2004, May 15 Engr. *Perf. 13x12½*
941 A382 155fr multi 3.50 3.00

Rays — A383

No. 942: a, Dasyatis kuhlii. b, Aetobatus narinari. c, Taeniura meyeni.

2004, May 15 Litho. *Perf. 13x13¼*
942 A383 Horiz. strip of 3 7.25 7.25
a.-c. 100fr Any single 2.25 2.00

Souvenir Sheet

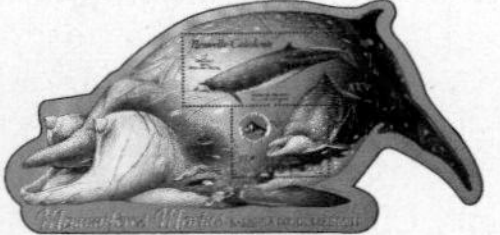

Mesoplodon Densirostris — A384

No. 943: a, Male (79x29mm). b, Female (40x29mm).

2004, May 15
943 A384 100fr Sheet of 2, #a-b 5.00 5.00

Operation Cetacean.

Flowers — A385

No. 944: a, Oxera sulfurea. b, Turbina inopinata. c, Gardenia urvillei.

2004, June 26
944 A385 Horiz. strip of 3 7.25 7.25
a.-c. 100fr Any single 2.25 2.00

Sandalwood A386

Designs: 200fr, Sandalwood sculpture, house.
No. 946: a, Fruit and flowers. b, Sandalwood oil extraction machinery. c, Flowerpot.

2004, June 26 *Perf. 13*
945 A386 200fr multi 4.75 4.25

Souvenir Sheet
Perf. 13x13¼

946 A386 100fr Sheet of 3, #a-c 7.25 7.25

No. 946 contains three 40x29mm stamps.

Noumea, 150th Anniv. A387

2004, July 8 Litho. *Perf. 13*
947 A387 70fr multi 1.60 1.50

Miniature Sheet

Cats A388

No. 948: a, Mixed breed. b, Oriental. c, Persian. d, Birman. e, European. f, Abyssinian.

2004, July 25
948 A388 100fr Sheet of 6, #a-f 14.50 12.50

2004 Summer Olympics, Athens — A389

Designs: No. 949, 70fr, Women's rhythmic gymnastics. No. 950, 70fr, Women's 4x400m relay. No. 951, 70fr, Beach volleyball.

2004, Aug. 5 *Perf. 13x13¼*
949-951 A389 Set of 3 5.00 4.50

Symposium on French Research in the Pacific — A390

No. 952: a, Butterfly, hut. b, Dolphin, woman.

2004, Aug. 10 *Perf. 13*
952 A390 Pair 4.75 4.75
a.-b. 100fr Either single 2.25 2.00

Belep Island and Walla Bay A391

2004, Nov. 10
953 A391 100fr multi 2.50 2.25

Tradimodernition, by Nathalie Deschamps — A392

2004, Nov. 10
954 A392 505fr multi 12.00 11.00

Christmas A393

2004, Dec. 8
955 A393 100fr multi 2.50 2.25

A394

New Year 2005 (Year of the Rooster) A395

No. 957: a, Rooster. b, Monkey.

2005, Feb. 9 Litho. *Perf. 13*
956 A394 100fr multi 2.50 2.25

Souvenir Sheet
Perf. 13¼x13

957 A395 100fr Sheet of 2, #a-b 4.75 4.50

Rotary International, Cent. — A396

2005, Feb. 23 Photo. *Perf. 12½*
958 A396 110fr multi 2.75 2.50

Values are for stamps with surrounding selvage.

Francophone Week — A397

2005, Mar. 17 Litho. *Perf. 13x13¼*
959 A397 135fr multi 3.25 3.00

Printed in sheets of 10 + 5 labels. See Wallis & Futuna Islands No. 600.

20th International Triathlon, Noumea A398

2005, Apr. 22 Litho. *Perf. 13*
960 A398 80fr multi 2.00 1.75

Coastal Tour Ship A399

2005, May 21
961 A399 75fr multi 1.90 1.60

New Caledonian Railways A400

2005, May 21
962 A400 745fr multi 18.00 15.00

Dolphins A401

No. 963: a, Stenella attenuata. b, Turciop truncatus. c, Stenella longirostris.

2005, May 21 *Perf. 13x13¼*
963 A401 Horiz. strip of 3 7.75 7.75
a.-c. 100fr Any single 2.25 2.00

For surcharge, see No. 971.

Souvenir Sheet

Sharks A402

No. 964: a, Carcharinus melanopterus. b, Nebrius ferrugineus.

2005, July 20 *Perf. 13*
964 A402 110fr Sheet of 2, #a-b 5.25 4.50

Kagu Type of 2003

2005, Aug. 10 Engr. *Perf. 13*
965 A364 1fr sky blue .25 .25
966 A364 3fr brt yel green .60 .25

Luengoni Beach, Lifou A403

2005, Aug. 24 Litho.
967 A403 85fr multi 2.00 1.75

Parakeets A404

Designs: No. 968, 75fr, Eunymphicus uvaeensis. No. 969, 75fr, Eunymphicus cornutus. No. 970, 75fr, Cyanoramphus saisseti.

2005, Aug. 24 *Perf. 13x13¼*
968-970 A404 Set of 3 5.50 4.75

No. 963 Surcharged in Silver

and Nos. 878 and 938 Surcharged

Methods and Perfs as Before

2005

971 Horiz. strip of 3 (#963) 7.00 7.00
a.-c. A401 100fr +10fr Any single 2.25 2.25
972 A265 100fr +10fr bright blue (#878) 2.25 2.25
973 A364 100fr +10fr blue (#938) 2.25 2.25
Nos. 971-973 (3) 11.50 11.50

Issued: No. 971, July. Nos. 972-973, Oct.

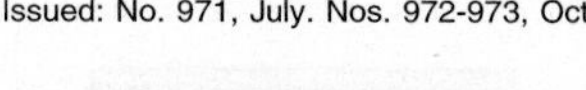

World Health Organization West Pacific Region Conference, Noumea — A405

2005, Sept. 14 Litho. *Perf. 13x13¼*
974 A405 150fr multi 3.75 3.00

World Peace Day — A406

2005, Sept. 21 *Perf. 13¼x13*
975 A406 85fr multi 2.00 1.75

Governor Eugène du Bouzet (1805-67) — A407

2005, Nov. 10 Engr.
976 A407 500fr multi 12.50 10.00

Petroglyphs A408

Designs: No. 977, 120fr, Enclosed crosses. No. 978, 120fr, Petroglyph, Balade. No. 979, 120fr, Ouaré Petroglyph, Hienghène.

2005, Nov. 10 *Perf. 13x12¾*
977-979 A408 Set of 3 8.75 7.25

Common Destiny, Artwork by Ito Waia and Adjé — A409

2005, Dec. 7 Litho. *Perf. 13*
980 A409 190fr multi 4.75 4.00

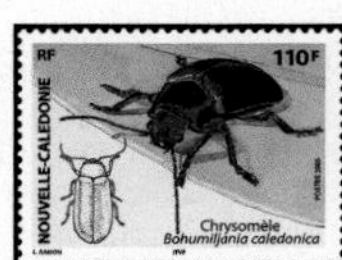

Insects — A410

Designs: No. 981, 110fr, Bohumiljania caledonica. No. 982, 110fr, Bohumiljania humboldti. No. 983, 110fr, Cazeresia montana.

2005, Dec. 7 *Perf. 13x13¼*
981-983 A410 Set of 3 8.00 6.75

Christmas — A411

2005, Dec. 8 *Perf. 13¼x13*
984 A411 110fr multi 2.75 2.25

Kagu Type of 2003

2006 Engr. *Perf. 13*
985 A364 110fr dk blue gray 2.75 2.25

Booklet Stamp
Self-Adhesive
Serpentine Die Cut 6¾ Vert.

986 A364 110fr dk blue gray 2.75 2.25
a. Booklet pane of 10 30.00

Issued: No. 985, 1/18. No. 986, June.

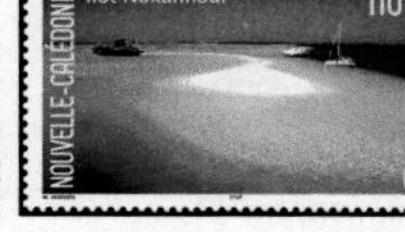

Nokanhoui Islet A412

2006, Mar. 9 Litho. *Perf. 13*
987 A412 110fr multi 2.75 2.25

Automobiles — A413

No. 988: a, 1903 Georges Richard. b, 1925 Renault NN. c, 1925 Citroen Tréfle.

2006, Mar. 23 *Perf. 13x13¼*
988 A413 Horiz. strip of 3 8.00 8.00
a.-c. 110fr Any single 2.50 2.25

New Caledonian Red Cross, 60th Anniv. — A414

2006, Apr. 12 Litho. *Perf. 13¼x13*
989 A414 75fr red & black 1.90 1.60

Conus Geographus — A415

2006, Apr. 12 Litho. *Perf. 13*
990 A415 150fr multi 3.75 3.25

11th World Congress on Pain, New Caledonia, 2005. Portions of the design were applied by a thermographic process producing a shiny, raised effect.

Arrival of French Colonists, 80th Anniv. A416

2006, May 23 Engr. *Perf. 13x12¾*
991 A416 180fr multi 4.50 3.75

2006 World Cup Soccer Championships, Germany — A417

2006, June 8 Litho. *Perf. 13*
992 A417 110fr multi 2.75 2.25

BirdLife International — A418

Designs: No. 993, 75fr, Charmosyna diadema. No. 994, 75fr, Aegotheles savesi. No. 995, 75fr, Gallirallus lafresnayanis.

2006, June 17 *Perf. 13¼x13*
993-995 A418 Set of 3 5.50 4.75

Souvenir Sheet

Endangered Birds — A419

No. 996: a, Charmosyna diadema. b, Aegotheles savesi, vert. c, Gallirallus lafresnayanis.

2006, June 17
996 A419 110fr Sheet of 3, #a-c 8.00 7.00

Creeper Flowers — A420

No. 997: a, Artia balansae. b, Oxera brevicalyx. c, Canavalia favieri.

2006, June 17 *Perf. 13x13¼*
997 A420 Horiz. strip of 3 8.00 8.00
a.-c. 110fr Any single 2.50 2.25

Mobile Post Office A421

2006, Aug. 5 Engr. *Perf. 13x12¾*
998 A421 75fr multi 1.75 1.60

Stamp Day.

New Caledonian Evacuee Voluntary Aid Association, 25th Anniv. — A422

2006, Aug. 5 Litho. *Perf. 13¼x13*
999 A422 85fr multi 2.00 1.90

17th South Pacific Regional Environment Program Conference, Noumea — A423

2006, Sept. 11 Litho. *Perf. 13*
1000 A423 190fr multi 4.00 4.00

Nakale 7547 Locomotive of New Caledonia Railroad A424

2006, Sept. 19 Engr. *Perf. 13x13¼*
1001 A424 320fr multi 6.75 6.75

Kaneka Music, 20th Anniv. — A425

2006, Nov. 8 Litho. *Perf. 13x13½*
1002 A425 75fr multi 1.90 1.75

Mobilis Mobile Phone Service, 10th Anniv. A426

2006, Nov. 8 *Perf. 13*
1003 A426 75fr multi 1.90 1.75

Wooden Players Puppet Theater, 30th Anniv. A427

2006, Nov. 8
1004 A427 280fr multi 7.00 6.25

Christmas A428

Litho. & Engr.

2006, Nov. 9 *Perf. 13*
1005 A428 110fr multi 2.75 2.50

Lizard Man, Sculpture by Joseph Poukiou — A429

2006, Dec. 13 Litho.
1006 A429 110fr multi 2.75 2.40

Kagu Type of 2003

2007, Jan. 25 Engr. *Perf. 13*
1007 A364 5fr purple .35 .25

New Year 2007 (Year of the Pig) — A430

2007, Feb. 6 Litho. *Perf. 13*
1008 A430 110fr multi 2.50 2.50

Printed in sheets of 10 + central label. See No. 1251j.

General Secretariat of the South Pacific Community, 60th Anniv. — A431

2007, Feb. 6
1009 A431 120fr multi 2.75 2.75

Audit Office, Bicent. — A432

2007, Mar. 17 Engr. *Perf. 13¼*
1010 A432 110fr multi 2.50 2.50

Treaty of Rome, 50th Anniv. — A433

2007, May 10 Litho. *Perf. 13x13¼*
1011 A433 110fr multi 2.50 2.50

13th South Pacific Games, Samoa A434

2007, June 13 Litho. *Perf. 13*
1012 A434 75fr multi 1.75 1.75

Submarine Cable Between Noumea and Sydney A435

2007, June 13 Litho. & Engr.
1013 A435 280fr multi 6.50 6.50

Fish — A436

Designs: 35fr, Siganus lineatus. 75fr, Lutianus adetii. 110fr, Naso unicornis.

2007, June 13 Litho. *Perf. 13x13½*
1014-1016 A436 Set of 3 5.00 5.00

Natl. Sea Rescue Society, 40th Anniv. A437

2007, Aug. 3 *Perf. 13*
1017 A437 75fr multi 1.75 1.75

BirdLife International A438

Endangered birds: 35fr, Gymnomyza aubryana. 75fr, Coracina analis. 110fr, Rhynochetos jubatus.

2007, Aug. 3 *Perf. 13x13¼*
1018-1020 A438 Set of 3 5.00 5.00

A439

A440

A441

A442

A443

A444

A445

A446

A447

Mailboxes A448

2007, Aug. 3 *Perf. 13¼x13, 13x13¼*

1021	Booklet pane of 10	17.50	17.50
a.	A439 75fr multi	1.75	1.75
b.	A440 75fr multi	1.75	1.75
c.	A441 75fr multi	1.75	1.75
d.	A442 75fr multi	1.75	1.75
e.	A443 75fr multi	1.75	1.75
f.	A444 75fr multi	1.75	1.75
g.	A445 75fr multi	1.75	1.75
h.	A446 75fr multi	1.75	1.75
i.	A447 75fr multi	1.75	1.75
j.	A448 75fr multi	1.75	1.75
	Complete booklet, #1021	17.50	

Stamp Day.

Souvenir Sheet

Kagu Philatelic Club, 60th Anniv. A449

No. 1022: a, Magnifying glass over New Caledonia #262 on cover. b, Kagu.

Litho. & Silk Screened

2007, Aug. 3 *Perf. 13x13¼*
1022 A449 110fr Sheet of 2, #a-b 5.00 5.00

Season of New Hebrides Culture in New Zealand A450

2007, Aug. 16 Litho. *Perf. 13*
1023 A450 190fr multi 4.50 4.50

New Aquarium of New Caledonia — A451

No. 1024 — Entrance of new aquarium and: a, Gymnothorax polyranodon (40x30mm). b, Entrance of old aquarium. (80x30mm). c, Monodactylus argenteus (40x30mm). d, Negaprion brevirostris (40x30mm). e, Pseudanthias bicolor (40x30mm).

2007, Aug. 31 *Perf. 13x13¼*
1024 A451 110fr Booklet pane of 5, #a-e 13.00 13.00
Complete booklet, 2 #1024 26.00

2007 Rugby World Cup, France — A452

2007, Sept. 5 Photo. *Perf.*
1025 A452 110fr multi 2.60 2.60

Jules Repiquet (1874-1960), Governor of New Caledonia, 1914-23 — A453

2007, Oct. 10 Engr. *Perf. 13x13¼*
1026 A453 320fr multi 7.75 7.75

Tropical Fruits — A454

Designs: 35fr, Bananas and passion fruits. 75fr, Vanilla beans, vert. 110fr, Pineapples and lychees.

Perf. 13x13¼, 13¼x13

2007, Nov. 8 Litho.
1027-1029 A454 Set of 3 5.50 5.50

The banana, vanilla bean and pineapple portions of these stamps are covered with scratch-and-sniff coatings having those fragrances.

La Montagnarde Locomotive, New Caledonian Railways — A455

2007, Nov. 8 Engr. *Perf. 13x13¼*
1030 A455 400fr multi 10.00 10.00

Tao Waterfall — A456

2007, Nov. 8 Litho. *Perf. 13*
1031 A456 110fr multi 2.75 2.75

The Damned, Performance by Najib Guerfi Dance Company — A457

2007, Nov. 8
1032 A457 110fr multi 2.75 2.75

Birth Announcement A458

2007, Nov. 8 *Perf. 13x13¼*
1033 A458 110fr multi 2.75 2.75

New Year's Greetings A459

2007, Nov. 8
1034 A459 110fr multi 2.75 2.75

Rooftop Totem — A460

2007, Dec. 5 Litho. *Perf. 13*
1035 A460 110fr multi 2.75 2.75

New Year 2008 (Year of the Rat) — A461

2008, Feb. 6 Litho. *Perf. 13*
1036 A461 110fr multi 3.00 3.00

See No. 1251a.

Academic Palms, Bicent. A462

Litho. & Embossed

2008, Mar. 17 *Perf. 13x13¼*
1037 A462 110fr multi 3.00 3.00

Tjibaou Cultural Center, 10th Anniv. — A463

2008, June 14 Litho. *Perf. 13*
1038 A463 120fr multi 3.25 3.25

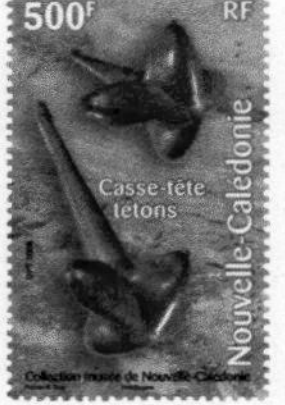

Matignon Accords, 20th Anniv. A464

2008, June 14
1039 A464 430fr multi 11.50 11.50

Kanak Ax — A465

2008, June 14
1040 A465 500fr multi 13.50 13.50

BirdLife International A466

Endangered birds: No. 1041, 110fr, Pterodroma leucoptera. No. 1042, 110fr, Pseudobulweria rostrata. No. 1043, 110fr, Nesofregatta fuliginosa.

2008, June 14 *Perf. 13x13¼*
1041-1043 A466 Set of 3 8.75 8.75

Fruit — A467

Designs: No. 1044, 110fr, Citrus nobilis. No. 1045, 110fr, Mangifera indica. No. 1046, 110fr, Carica papaya.

2008, June 14
1044-1046 A467 Set of 3 8.75 8.75

2008 Summer Olympics, Beijing — A468

Designs: No. 1047, 75fr, Weight lifting. No. 1048, 75fr, Table tennis. No. 1049, 75fr, Taekwondo.

2008, July 31
1047-1049 A468 Set of 3 5.75 5.75

Office of Posts and Telecommunications, 50th Anniv. — A469

Designs: No. 1050, 75fr, New Caledonia #314, dish antennas, cable, map of South Pacific. No. 1051, 75fr, New Caledonia #311, savings card, person at computer. No. 1052, 75fr, New Caledonia #C106, mailbox, mail sorter.

2008, July 31
1050-1052 A469 Set of 3 5.75 5.75

Miniature Sheet

Telecommunications History — A470

No. 1053: a, Telegraph. b, Radio telephone. c, Satellite and antenna. d, Fiber-optic cables and flowers.

2008, July 31 *Perf. 13¼x13*
1053 A470 75fr Sheet of 4, #a-d 7.50 7.50

Kagu A471

Serpentine Die Cut 6¾x7¾

2008 Self-Adhesive Litho.
1054 A471 (75fr) red & multi 4.50 4.50
1055 A471 110fr blue & multi 5.25 5.25

Nos. 1054 and 1055 each were issued in sheets of 20 and 25. Sheets of 20 of each stamp sold for 3800fr and 4500fr, respectively, and sheets of 25 sold for 4125fr and 5000fr, respectively. The left part of the stamp, which cannot be separated from the stamp, could be personalized if desired. The left part of the stamp shown has a generic image that was utilized if a customer did not provide an image for personalization.

Koné Fort A472

2008, Oct. 3 Engr. *Perf. 13x12¾*
1056 A472 220fr multi 5.00 5.00

Fifth French Republic, 50th Anniv. A473

2008, Oct. 14 *Perf. 13x13¼*
1057 A473 290fr blue & red 6.25 6.25

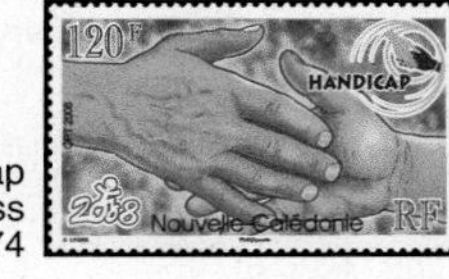

Handicap Awareness A474

2008, Nov. 6 Litho. *Perf. 13*
1058 A474 120fr multi 2.60 2.60

Diahot River — A475

No. 1059 — View of river with denomination color of: a, Green. b, Blue violet.

2008, Nov. 6
1059 A475 Horiz. pair + central label 5.00 5.00
a.-b. 110fr Either single 2.50 2.50

Christmas — A476

2008, Nov. 6 *Perf. 13¼x13*
1060 A476 110fr multi 2.50 2.50

14th Pacific Games, New Caledonia — A477

2008, Dec. 12 *Perf. 13*
1061 A477 110fr multi 2.50 2.50

Miniature Sheet

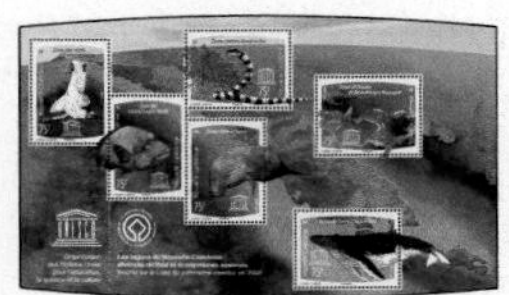

New Caledonia Lagoons UNESCO World Heritage Site — A478

No. 1062: a, Birds from Entrecasteaux Reefs Zone. b, Snake from Northeastern Coastal Zone, horiz. c, Sea turtles from Beautemps-Beaupré Zone, horiz. d, Fish from Great Northern Lagoon Zone. e, Dugong from Western Coastal Zone. f, Whale from Great Southern Lagoon Zone, horiz.

Perf. 13¼x13, 13x13¼ (horiz. stamps)

2008, Dec. 12
1062 A478 75fr Sheet of 6, #a-f 10.50 10.50

Fish — A479

No. 1063 — Fish sold at local fish markets: a, Lethrinus atkinsoni. b, Chlorurus microrhinos. c Lethrinus nebulosus.

2009, Mar. 25 Litho. *Perf. 13x13¼*
1063 A479 Horiz. strip of 3 5.00 5.00
a.-c. 75fr Any single 1.60 1.60

New Year 2009 (Year of the Ox) — A480

2009, Apr. 8 *Perf. 13*
1064 A480 75fr multi 1.75 1.75

See No. 1251b for stamp dated "2019."

Souvenir Sheet

New Year 2009 (Year of the Ox) A481

No. 1065 — Ox: a, Standing. b, Charging.

2009, Apr. 8 Litho. *Perf. 13*
1065 A481 110fr Sheet of 2, #a-b 5.00 5.00

The Turtle Bearer, Sculpture by Tein Thavouvace A482

2009, May 14 Litho. *Perf. 13*
1066 A482 180fr multi 4.25 4.25

BirdLife International — A483

No. 1067 — Terns: a, Sterna nereis. b, Sterna sumatrana. c, Sterna dougalli.

2009, June 10 *Perf. 13x13¼*
1067 A483 Horiz. strip of 3 5.25 5.25
a.-c. 75fr Any single 1.75 1.75

Jean-Pierre Jeunet Cinema, La Foa, 10th Anniv. — A484

2009, June 26 *Perf. 13*
1068 A484 75fr multi 1.75 1.75

Third France-Oceania Summit, Noumea — A485

No. 1069 — Earth in: a, Hands. b, Flower.

2009, July 16
1069 A485 110fr Pair, #a-b 5.25 5.25

Kagu Type of 2003
Serpentine Die Cut 7½ Vert.

2009, July **Litho.**

Booklet Stamp
Self-Adhesive

1070 A364 (75fr) red 1.75 1.75
a. Booklet pane of 10 17.50

A486

Kagu — A487

2009, Aug. 6 **Engr.** ***Perf. 13***
1071 A486 5fr purple .30 .25
1072 A486 10fr green .30 .25
a. Dated "2014" .30 .25
1073 A486 (75fr) red 1.75 1.75
1074 A486 110fr dark blue 2.60 2.60

Litho. With Three-Dimensional Plastic Affixed
Perf. 16
Self-Adhesive

1075 A487 500fr multi 12.00 12.00

Litho.
Serpentine Die Cut 7½ Vert.
Booklet Stamp

1076 A486 (75fr) red 1.75 1.75
a. Booklet pane of 10 17.50
b. As #1076, serpentine die cut 6¾ vert., with "Phil@poste" printer's inscription at bottom 1.60 1.60
c. Booklet pane of 10 #1076b 16.00
d. As "b," dated "2014" 1.75 1.75
e. Booklet pane of 10 #1076d 17.50
f. As "b," dated "2016" 1.40 1.40
g. Booklet pane of 10 #1076f 14.00
Nos. 1071-1076 (6) 18.70 18.60

No. 1075 printed in sheets of 4.
Issued: Nos. 1076b, 1076c, June 2010; Nos. 1076d, 1076e, July 2014.
See No. 1131. For redrawn stamp of type A486, see No. 1296f.

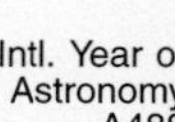

Intl. Year of Astronomy A488

2009, Aug. 6 **Litho.** ***Perf. 13***
1077 A488 110fr multi 2.60 2.60

Miniature Sheet

New Caledonia Postal Service, 150th Anniv. — A489

No. 1078 — Modes of mail delivery: a, Coach. b, Horse, vert. c, Automobile. d, Mail deliverer on foot, vert.

2009, Aug. 6 ***Perf. 13¼***
1078 A489 110fr Sheet of 4, #a-d 10.50 10.50

Society for Historical Research, 40th Anniv. A490

2009, Aug. 6 **Engr.** ***Perf. 13x13¼***
1079 A490 75fr multi 1.75 1.75

Personalized Stamps — A490a

Serpentine Die Cut 6¾x8

2009, Sept. **Litho.**

Self-Adhesive

1079A A490a (75fr) red & multi — —
1079B A490a 110fr blue & multi — —

Nos. 1079A and 1079B were issued in sheets of 20 and 25. The personalized part of the stamp is at left. The illustration is that of a generic image used for both No. 1079A and 1079B. Sheets with other personalized images sold for more than the face value.

14th Pacific Games, New Caledonia — A491

2009, Nov. 5 **Litho.** ***Perf. 13***
1080 A491 75fr multi 1.90 1.90

Western Coastal Zone of Lagoons of New Caledonia UNESCO World Heritage Site — A492

2009, Nov. 5
1081 A492 75fr multi 1.90 1.90

Christmas A493

2009, Nov. 5 ***Perf. 13x13¼***
1082 A493 110fr multi 2.75 2.75

Canala Barracks A494

2009, Nov. 5 **Engr.**
1083 A494 120fr multi 3.00 3.00

Maritime History Museum, Noumea, 10th Anniv. A495

No. 1084: a, Ships and museum. b, Ship and map.

2009, Nov. 5 **Litho.**
1084 A495 75fr Horiz. pair, #a-b 3.75 3.75

A496

Tontouta River A497

2009, Nov. 5 ***Perf. 13***
1085 Horiz. pair + central label 5.50 5.50
a. A496 110fr multi 2.75 2.75
b. A497 110fr multi 2.75 2.75

Women and Children, by Micheline Néporon — A498

2010, Mar. 8 **Litho.** ***Perf. 13***
1086 A498 110fr multi 2.50 2.50

Intl. Women's Day.

Champlain Alliance, 25th Anniv. — A499

2010, Mar. 18 ***Perf. 13x13¼***
1087 A499 110fr multi 2.50 2.50

Fish — A500

No. 1089 — Fish sold at local fish markets: a, Acanthocybium solandri. b, Thunnus albacares. c, Coryphaena hippurus.

2010, Mar. 18
1088 A500 Horiz. strip of 3 5.25 5.25
a.-c. 75fr multi 1.75 1.75

New Year 2010 (Year of the Tiger) — A501

2010, Mar. 18 ***Perf. 13***
1089 A501 110fr multi 2.50 2.50

See No. 1251c.

Dumbea River — A502

No. 1090: a, River bends. b, Canoers on river, bridge.

2010, Mar. 18
1090 A502 Horiz. pair + central label 5.00 5.00
a.-b. 110fr Either single 2.50 2.50

14th Va'a (Outrigger Canoe) World Championships, Anse Vata Bay — A503

2010, May 3 **Litho.** ***Perf. 13x13¼***
1091 A503 75fr multi 1.75 1.75

French Pavilion, Expo 2010, Shanghai A504

2010, June 14 ***Perf. 13***
1092 A504 110fr multi 2.40 2.40

Mueo Fort A505

2010, Aug. 5 **Engr.** ***Perf. 13x13¼***
1093 A505 75fr multi 1.75 1.75

2010 Youth Olympics, Singapore A506

2010, Aug. 5 **Litho.** ***Perf. 13***
1094 A506 75fr multi 1.75 1.75

St. Joseph's Cathedral, Noumea — A507

2010, Aug. 5 **Litho. & Engr.**
1095 A507 1000fr multi 22.50 22.50

Nickel Mining A508

No. 1096: a, Open-pit mine. b, Smelter. c, Ship transport.

Litho. With Foil Application

2010, Aug. 5 ***Perf. 13x12¾***
1096 A508 75fr Horiz. strip of 3, #a-c 5.00 5.00

Miniature Sheet

Flora and Fauna of Grandes Fougères Park A509

No. 1097: a, Pteropus ornatus. b, Ducula goliath. c, Cyathea sp. d, Calanthe langel.

2010, Aug. 5 Litho. *Perf. 13¼x13*
1097 A509 110fr Sheet of 4, #a-d 9.75 9.75

14th Pacific Games, New Caledonia A510

2010, Aug. 27 *Perf. 13*
1098 A510 75fr multi 1.60 1.60

Fourth Melanesian Arts Festival A511

2010, Sept. 8
1099 A511 180fr multi 4.00 4.00

Governor Henri Sautot (1885-1963) A512

2010, Sept. 16 Engr. *Perf. 13x13¼*
1100 A512 250fr multi 6.00 6.00

New Caledonia's alliance with Free France, 70th anniv.

Road Safety — A513

Designs: No. 1101, 75fr, Car with drunk driver. No. 1102, 75fr, Woman with baby stroller in crosswalk escaping speeding motorcyclist.

2010, Oct. 13 Litho. *Perf. 13x13¼*
1101-1102 A513 Set of 2 3.50 3.50

Great Northern Lagoon UNESCO World Heritage Site A514

2010, Nov. 3 *Perf. 13*
1103 A514 75fr multi 1.75 1.75

New Caledonia House, Paris A515

2010, Nov. 3
1104 A515 110fr multi 2.50 2.50

Intl. Year of Biodiversity — A516

2010, Nov. 3 *Perf. 13¼*
1105 A516 110fr multi 2.50 2.50

Christmas A517

2010, Nov. 3 *Perf. 13x13¼*
1106 A517 110fr multi 2.50 2.50

New Year 2011 (Year of the Rabbit) — A518

2011, Feb. 2 *Perf. 13*
1107 A518 110fr multi 2.50 2.50

Printed in sheets of 10 + central label. See No. 1251f.

Inauguration of Digital High Definition Television Transmission A519

2011, Feb. 2 *Perf. 13x13¼*
1108 A519 75fr multi 1.75 1.75

14th Pacific Games, New Caledonia — A520

2011, Mar. 17 *Perf. 13*
1109 A520 110fr multi 2.75 2.75

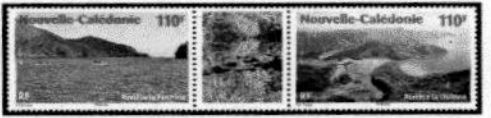
Rivers — A521

No. 1110: a, Pourina River. b, Ouinné River.

2011, Mar. 17 Litho.
1110 A521 Horiz. pair + central label 5.50 5.50
a.-b. 110fr Either single 2.75 2.75

Transcaledonian Adventure Race, 20th Anniv. — A522

2011, June 23 *Perf. 13x13¼*
1111 A522 75fr multi 1.75 1.75

Podoserpula Miranda — A523

2011, June 23 *Perf. 13¼x13*
1112 A523 110fr multi 2.60 2.60

Ouégoa Fort A524

2011, Aug. 5 Engr. *Perf. 13x13¼*
1113 A524 75fr multi 1.90 1.90

Ouvea and Beautemps-Beaupré Lagoon Area UNESCO World Heritage Site — A525

2011, Aug. 5 Litho. *Perf. 13*
1114 A525 75fr multi 1.90 1.90

Intl. Year of Forests A526

2011, Aug. 5
1115 A526 120fr multi 3.00 3.00

Miniature Sheet

Rivière Bleue Provincial Park — A527

No. 1116: a, Syzygium acre. b, Montrouziera gabriellae. c, Waterfall. d, Rhynochetos jubatus.

2011, Aug. 5 Photo. *Perf. 13¼x13*
1116 A527 110fr Sheet of 4, #a-d 11.00 11.00

Kanak Traditional Games — A528

2011, Aug. 27 Litho. *Perf. 13x13¼*
1117 A528 75fr multi 1.75 1.75

Souvenir Sheet

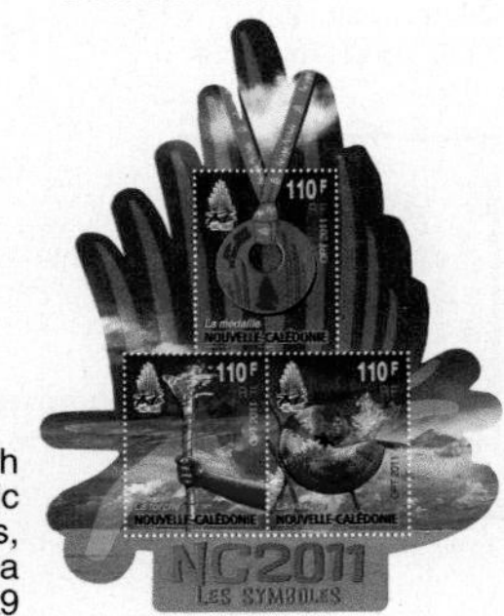
14th Pacific Games, Noumea A529

No. 1118 — Emblem and: a, Medal. b, Torch. c, Flame basin.

Photo. Photo & Embossed (#1118a)
2011, Aug. 27 *Perf. 13¼x13*
1118 A529 110fr Sheet of 3, #a-c 7.75 7.75

Ruins and Chimney of Nimba Sugar Factory, Dumbea A530

2011, Nov. 3 Engr. *Perf. 13x13¼*
1119 A530 450fr multi 10.50 10.50

Animals and Scenery — A531

Designs: No. 1120, 110fr, Cerf rusa (rusa deer). No. 1121, 110fr, Tricot rayé (striped jersey snake). No. 1122, 110fr, Lindéralique Cliffs. No. 1123, 110fr, Ilôt Canard, vert.

Perf. 13x13¼, 13¼x13
2011, Nov. 3 Litho.
1120-1123 A531 Set of 4 10.50 10.50

Christmas — A532

2011, Nov. 3 *Perf. 13¼x13*
1124 A532 110fr multi 2.60 2.60

Jacques Lafleur (1932-2010), Politician — A533

2011, Dec. 1 Engr. *Perf. 12¼x13*
1125 A533 1000fr multi 22.50 22.50

New Year 2012 (Year of the Dragon) — A534

2012, Jan. 23 Litho. *Perf. 13*
1126 A534 75fr multi 1.75 1.75

Printed in sheets of 10 + central label. See No. 1251e for stamp dated "2019."

St. Valentine's Day — A535

2012, Jan. 23
1127 A535 110fr multi 2.50 2.50

Values are for stamps with surrounding selvage.

Voh, 120th Anniv. A536

No. 1128: a, Coffee plantation. b, Mine.

2012, Jan. 23 *Perf. 13x13¼*
1128 A536 110fr Horiz. pair, #a-b 5.00 5.00

Southern Backpacking Trail — A537

2012, Mar. 5 *Perf. 13¼x13*
1129 A537 110fr multi 2.50 2.50

Ouaménie Sugar Works Chimney — A538

2012, May 4 Engr. *Perf. 12¼x13*
1130 A538 750fr multi 16.00 16.00

Kagu Type of 2009

2012, June 5 Engr. *Perf. 13*
1131 A486 30fr orange .65 .65
a. Dated "2014" .60 .60

Nudibranchs A539

Designs: 75fr, Glossodoris cruenta. 85fr, Halgerda sp., vert. 120fr, Noumea catalai.

Perf. 13x13¼, 13¼x13

2012, July 6 Litho.
1132-1134 A539 Set of 3 5.75 5.75

Souvenir Sheet

Japanese Presence on New Caledonia, 120th Anniv. — A540

No. 1135: a, Memorial. b, Nickel miner with pick, horiz. c, Mine worker with ore cart, horiz.

Perf. 13¼x13, 13x13¼

2012, July 6 Photo.
1135 A540 110fr Sheet of 3, #a-c 6.75 6.75

Amborella Trichopoda — A541

2012, Aug. 6 Litho. *Perf. 13¼x13*
1136 A541 180fr multi 4.00 4.00

2012 Paralympics, London — A542

Designs: No. 1137, 75fr, Wheelchair race. No. 1138, 75fr, Shot put.

2012, Aug. 6 *Perf. 13x13¼*
1137-1138 A542 Set of 2 3.25 3.25

Local Scenes A543

Designs: No. 1139, 110fr, Bonhomme de Bourail rock formation. No. 1140, 110fr, Hut made of coconut palm fronds, Maré. No. 1141, 110fr, Mouth of Koumac River. No. 1142, 110fr, Cowboys and cattle.

2012, Aug. 6 *Perf. 13*
1139-1142 A543 Set of 4 9.50 9.50

Souvenir Sheet

Michel Corbasson Zoo and Forest, Noumea, 50th Anniv. — A544

No. 1143: a, Rhacodactylus leachianus. b, Corvus moneduloides. c, Pittosporum tanianum.

2012, Sept. 25 *Perf. 13¼x13*
1143 A544 110fr Sheet of 3, #a-c 7.25 7.25

National Tree Planting Campaign A545

2012, Sept. 26 *Perf. 13*
1144 A545 75fr multi 1.60 1.60

3G Technology A546

2012, Sept. 26 *Perf. 13x13¼*
1145 A546 280fr multi 6.00 6.00

Whales in Great Southern Lagoon Zone A547

2012, Nov. 9 *Perf. 13*
1146 A547 75fr multi 1.60 1.60

Mangrove Forest — A548

2012, Nov. 9 Litho.
1147 A548 75fr multi 1.60 1.60

Christmas A549

2012, Nov. 9 *Perf. 13x13¼*
1148 A549 110fr multi 2.40 2.40

New Year 2013 (Year of the Snake) — A550

2013, Feb. 7 Litho. *Perf. 13*
1149 A550 110fr multi 2.40 2.40

See No. 1251d.

Encastreaux Reefs Area A551

2013, Mar. 7
1150 A551 110fr multi 2.40 2.40

Opening of La Tontouta Intl. Airport, Noumea A552

2013, Mar. 19
1151 A552 110fr multi 2.40 2.40

Bacouya Sugar Factory Chimney A553

2013, May 13 Engr. *Perf. 13x12¼*
1152 A553 120fr multi 2.75 2.75

Red Cross South Pacific Regional Intervention Platform — A554

2013, June 7 Litho. *Perf. 13*
1153 A554 75fr multi 1.75 1.75

Opening of Calédoscope, New Philatelic Office — A555

2013, June 7 Litho. *Perf. 14½*
1154 A555 75fr multi 1.75 1.75

Naso Unicornis — A556

2013, June 7 Engr. *Perf. 13*
1155 A556 110fr blue 2.50 2.50

Marine Life in Lagoons — A557

No. 1156: a, Plectorpomus leopardus, Epinephelus polyphekadion. b, Carcharhinus amblyrhynchos. c, Scomberomorus commerson. d, Chelonia mydas. e, Caranx melampygus. f, Tridacna maxima, Forcipiger flavissimus. g, Chromis viridis. h, Panulirus penicillatus. i, Myripristis berndti. j, Lutjanus kasmira.

Serpentine Die Cut 11

2013, June 8 Litho.

Self-Adhesive

1156 Booklet pane of 10 25.00
a.-j. A557 110fr Any single 2.50 2.50

Re-opening of Maritime History Museum A558

2013, June 28 Litho. *Perf. 13*
1157 A558 110fr multi 2.40 2.40

Opening of Nouville Penitentiary Museum A559

2013, Aug. 7 Litho. *Perf. 13*
1158 A559 280fr multi 6.25 6.25

Birth of a Girl — A560

Birth of a Boy — A561

2013, Aug. 8 Litho. *Perf. 13¼x13*
1159 A560 110fr multi 2.50 2.50
1160 A561 110fr multi 2.50 2.50

World Swimming Championships for the Intellectually Disabled, Dumbea — A562

2013, Aug. 19 Litho. *Perf. 13*
1161 A562 120fr multi 2.75 2.75

Captaincookia Tree — A563

2013, Sept. 9 Litho. *Perf. 13¼x13*
1162 A563 85fr multi 1.90 1.90

Pouembout Dovecote — A564

2013, Sept. 9 Litho. *Perf. 13¼x13*
1163 A564 180fr multi 4.00 4.00

Wildlife and Landscapes A565

Designs: 85fr, Fruit bat and bougainvillea flowers. 110fr, 500-Franc Note Beach, Hienghène. 190fr, Warrior's Leap, Maré Island, vert. 250fr, Thio and Bota Méré, vert.

Perf. 13x13¼, 13¼x13

2013, Nov. 6 Litho.
1164-1167 A565 Set of 4 14.50 14.50

Beekeeping — A566

No. 1168: a, Jars of honey, honeydipper, flower, beekeeper checking hives. b, Bees and hives.

2013, Nov. 6 Litho. *Perf. 13*
1168 A566 110fr Horiz. pair, #a-b 5.00 5.00

Miniature Sheet

Orchids A567

No. 1169: a, Eria karicouyensis. b, Earina deplanchei, vert. c, Eriaxis rigida, vert. d, Dendrobium poissonianum.

Perf. 13x13¼, 13¼x13
2013, Sept. 10 Litho.
1169 A567 110fr Sheet of 4, #a-d 10.00 10.00

Christmas A568

2013, Nov. 6 Litho. *Perf. 13x13¼*
1170 A568 110fr multi 2.50 2.50

Miniature Sheet

New Banknotes — A569

No. 1171: a, 75fr, 500-franc banknote. b, 75fr, 1000-franc banknote. c, 110fr, 5000-franc banknote. d, 110fr, 10,000-franc banknote.

Litho. & Silk-screened
2014, Jan. 20 *Perf. 13x12¾*
1171 A569 Sheet of 4, #a-d 8.50 8.50

New Year 2014 (Year of the Horse) — A570

2014, Feb. 3 Litho. *Perf. 13*
1172 A570 110fr multi 2.50 2.50

No. 1172 was printed in sheets of 10 + central label. See No. 1251g.

Exhibition at Tjibaou Cultural Center of Kanak Art — A571

2014, Mar. 15 Litho. *Perf. 12¾x13*
1173 A571 110fr multi 2.60 2.60

North and East Coastal Zone UNESCO World Heritage Site — A572

2014, Apr. 22 Litho. *Perf. 13¼x13*
1174 A572 110fr multi 2.60 2.60

Veteran's Center, Noumea, 50th Anniv. — A573

2014, May 16 Litho. *Perf. 13x13¼*
1175 A573 150fr multi 3.50 3.50

Cajoulle House, Koné A574

2014, May 16 Engr. *Perf. 13x13¼*
1176 A574 750fr multi 17.00 17.00

World Blood Donor Day — A575

2014, June 6 Litho. *Perf. 13*
1177 A575 110fr multi 2.50 2.50

Landscapes and Wildlife — A576

Designs: 75fr, Koné Coral Reef. 110fr, Golden damselfish (poisson-demoiselle), horiz. 120fr, Horned parakeet (perruche), horiz. 190fr, Drowned Forest (La Fôret Noyée).

Perf. 13¼x13, 13x13¼
2014, June 6 Litho.
1178-1181 A576 Set of 4 11.50 11.50

Marine Rescue Service, 10th Anniv. A577

Litho. & Engr.
2014, Sept. 8 *Perf. 13*
1182 A577 110fr multi 2.40 2.40

Souvenir Sheet

Flora and Fauna of the Mining Scrubland — A578

No. 1183: a, Red-throated parrotfinch (Diamant psittaculaire). b, Grevillea gillivrayi, vert. c, Deplanchea sessilifolia.

Perf. 13x13¼, 13¼x13
2014, Sept. 8 Photo.
1183 A578 110fr Sheet of 3, #a-c 7.00 7.00

Murraya Paniculata Bonsai, by Jean-Jacques Mahuteau — A579

2014, Oct. 6 Litho. *Perf. 13¼x13*
1184 A579 150fr multi 3.25 3.25

Isle of Pines Penitentiary A580

2014, Oct. 6 Engr. *Perf. 13x12½*
1185 A580 280fr multi 6.00 6.00

Papilio Montrouzieri A581

Litho. & Embossed With Foil Application
2014, Nov. 6 *Perf. 13½*
1186 A581 180fr multi 3.75 3.75

Niaouli Flowers and Oil Distillation A582

2014, Nov. 6 Litho. *Perf. 13*
1187 A582 190fr multi 4.00 4.00

No. 1187 is impregnated with a niaouli scent.

Kanak Weaving — A583

Litho. & Embossed
2014, Nov. 6 *Perf. 13*
1188 A583 250fr multi 5.25 5.25

Christmas A584

2014, Nov. 6 Litho. *Perf. 13x13¼*
1189 A584 110fr multi 2.40 2.40

New Year 2015 (Year of the Goat) — A585

2015, Feb. 19 Litho. *Perf. 13*
1190 A585 110fr multi 2.10 2.10

No. 1190 was printed in sheets of 10 + central label.

Dick Ukeiwe (1928-2013), Senator — A586

2015, Feb. 19 Engr. *Perf. 13¼*
1191 A586 500fr dark blue & brown 9.25 9.25

Pittosporum Tanianum — A587

2015, Mar. 19 Litho. *Perf. 13x13¼*
1192 A587 120fr multi 2.25 2.25

Kô Salt Marshes, Poingam A588

2015, Apr. 22 Litho. *Perf. 13*
1193 A588 450fr multi 8.50 8.50

Children's Art — A589

Designs: No. 1194, Wildlife, by Eliot-Louis Hatterer.

No. 1195, horiz.: a, Building, tree and Sun, by Emmanuelle Hnawang. b, Flower and snake, by Thomas Bodeouarou.

2015, June 5 Litho. *Perf. 13¼x13*
1194 A589 75fr multi 1.40 1.40

Perf. 13x13¼
1195 Horiz. pair + central label 2.80 2.80
a.-b. A589 75fr Either single 1.40 1.40

World War I, Cent. — A590

No. 1196 — Military medals and: a, Soldiers boarding the Sontay. b, Battle of the Serre. c, Soldiers returning home on the El Kantara.

2015, June 5 Litho. *Perf. 13x13¼*
1196 Horiz. strip of 3 2.00 2.00
a.-c. A590 35fr Any single .65 .65

Souvenir Sheet

Birds A591

No. 1197: a, Nycticorax caledonicus. b, Egretta sacra albolineata, horiz. c, Egretta novaehollandiae nana.

Perf. 13¼x13, 13x13¼
2015, June 5 Litho.
1197 A591 110fr Sheet of 3, #a-c 6.25 6.25

Maxat, First Yam Farming Cycle A592

2015, July 20 Litho. *Perf. 13*
1198 A592 110fr multi 2.10 2.10

New Caledonia Ornithological Society, 50th Anniv. — A593

2015, Aug. 5 Litho. *Perf. 13*
1199 A593 180fr multi 3.50 3.50

Château Escande, Poya A594

2015, Sept. 15 Engr. *Perf. 13x12½*
1200 A594 750fr multi 14.00 14.00

First Lighting of Amédée Lighthouse, 150th Anniv. — A595

2015, Nov. 5 Litho. *Perf. 13*
1201 A595 110fr multi 2.00 2.00

Flowers — A596

No. 1202: a, Arthroclianthus deplanchei. b, Thiollierea campanulata. c, Xanthostemon aurantiacus. d, Deplanchea speciosa. e, Xanthostemon sulfureus. f, Deplanchea sessifolia. g, Boronella pancheri. h, Artia balansae. i, Virotia angustifolia. j, Arthroclianthus microbotrys.

Serpentine Die Cut 11
2015, Nov. 5 Litho.
Self-Adhesive
1202 Booklet pane of 10 20.00
a.-j. A596 110fr Any single 2.00 2.00

Miniature Sheet

Turtles A597

No. 1203 — Inscriptions: a, Tortue bonne écaille. b, Tortue grosse tête. c, Tortue verte, horiz. d, Tortue luth, horiz.

2015, Nov. 5 Photo. *Perf. 13½x13*
1203 A597 110fr Sheet of 4, #a-d 8.00 8.00

Christmas — A598

Litho. & Thermographed
2015, Nov. 5 *Perf. 13 on 3 Sides*
1204 A598 110fr multi 2.00 2.00

New Year 2016 (Year of the Monkey) — A599

2016, Feb. 8 Litho. *Perf. 13*
1205 A599 110fr multi 2.00 2.00

No. 1205 was printed in sheets of 10 + central label. See No. 1251i.

Conifers and Palm Trees A600

2016, Mar. 14 Litho. *Perf. 13*
1206 A600 120fr multi 2.40 2.40

Tiga Island A601

2016, Apr. 14 Litho. *Perf. 13*
1207 A601 110fr multi 2.10 2.10

Marriage — A602

2016, May 12 Litho. *Perf. 13x13¼*
1208 A602 75fr multi 1.40 1.40

Statue of Kanak Soldier of World War I — A603

2016, June 3 Litho. *Perf. 13*
1209 A603 110fr multi 2.10 2.10

Shell Engraved by Convict — A604

Litho. & Silk-Screened
2016, June 10 *Perf. 13x13¼*
1210 A604 75fr multi 1.40 1.40

Fiber Optic Communications A605

2016, June 10 Litho. *Perf. 13x13¼*
1211 A605 75fr multi 1.40 1.40

Natural Park of the Coral Sea — A606

2016, June 10 Litho. *Perf. 13*
1212 A606 110fr multi 2.10 2.10

Astronomy in New Caledonia A607

2016, Aug. 5 Litho. *Perf. 14¼x14*
1213 A607 450fr multi 8.50 8.50

Janisel House, Pouébo — A608

2016, Sept. 12 Litho. *Perf. 13x13¼*
1214 A608 110fr multi 2.10 2.10

Dr. René Catala (1901-88), Biologist — A609

2016, Sept. 12 Litho. *Perf. 13*
1215 A609 120fr multi + label 2.25 2.25

Horat, Second Yam Farming Cycle A610

2016, Oct. 10 Litho. *Perf. 13*
1216 A610 120fr multi 2.25 2.25

Ocean Liner Le Calédonien A611

2016, Nov. 3 Litho. *Perf. 13*
1217 A611 110fr multi 2.00 2.00

Miniature Sheet

Items With Spirals A612

No. 1218: a, Hippocampus kuda (seahorse). b, Spirobranchus giganteus (Christmas tree worms), horiz. c, Cyathea intermedia (tree fern). d, Nautilus macromphalus (nautilus), horiz.

2016, Nov. 3 Litho. *Perf. 13¼*
1218 A612 110fr Sheet of 4, #a-d 8.00 8.00

Kagu — A613

2016, Nov. 3 Litho. *Perf. 13*
Background Color
1219 A613 5fr red lilac .30 .25
a. Dated "2018" .30 .25
b. Dated "2019" .30 .25
1220 A613 10fr light green .30 .25
a. Dated "2018" .30 .25
b. Dated "2019" .30 .25
1221 A613 30fr cerise .55 .55
a. Dated "2018" .60 .60
b. Dated "2019" .55 .55
Nos. 1219-1221 (3) 1.15 1.05

Booklet Stamps
Self-Adhesive
Serpentine Die Cut 6¾ Vert.
1222 A613 (75fr) dark red 1.40 1.40
a. Booklet pane of 10 14.00
b. As No. 1222, dated "2018" 1.50 1.50
c. Booklet pane of 10 #1222b 15.00
d. As #1222, dated "2019" 1.40 1.40
e. Booklet pane of 10 #1222d 14.00
1223 A613 (120fr) yel orange 2.25 2.25
a. Booklet pane of 10 22.50

Issued: No. 1219a, 4/5/18; Nos. 1220a, 1221a, 4/10/18; Nos. 1219b, 1220b, 1221b, 8/9/19; Nos. 1222b, 1222c, 4/18/18; Nos. 1222d, 1222e, 9/15/19.

For redrawn stamp of type A613, see No. 1296g.

Christmas and New Year's Day — A614

2016, Nov. 3 Litho. *Perf. 13x13¼*
1224 A614 110fr multi 2.00 2.00

New Year 2017 (Year of the Rooster) — A615

2017, Feb. 1 Litho. *Perf. 13¼*
1225 A615 75fr multi 1.40 1.40

No. 1225 was printed in sheets of 10 + central label. See No. 1251l for stamp dated "2019."

Roger Gervolino (1909-91), Politician A616

2017, Mar. 14 Engr. *Perf. 13*
1226 A616 1000fr dk blue & dk brn 18.00 18.00

Stork Delivering Baby, Star at Upper Left — A617

Stork Delivering Baby, Heart at Upper Left — A618

2017, May 4 Litho. *Perf. 13x13¼*
1227 A617 110fr multi, unscratched panel 2.10 2.10
Scratched panel 1.75
1228 A618 110fr multi, unscratched panel 2.10 2.10
Scratched panel 1.75

Gold scratch-off panels hide inscriptions "un garçon" (a boy) on No. 1227, and "une fille" (a girl) on No. 1228.

Mixed Battalion of the Pacific, Cent. — A619

2017, May 15 Litho. *Perf. 13*
1229 A619 120fr multi 2.25 2.25

Lions Clubs International, Cent. — A620

2017, July 6 Litho. *Perf. 13¼x13*
1230 A620 75fr multi 1.50 1.50

Steamer Natal — A621

2017, July 7 Litho. *Perf. 13*
1231 A621 110fr multi 2.25 2.25

Buildings A622

No. 1232: a, Beaumont House, Moindou. b, Round houses, Isle of Pines.

2017, July 7 Litho. *Perf. 13x13¼*
1232 A622 75fr Horiz. pair, #a-b, + central label 3.00 3.00

Noumea Carnival — A623

2017, Sept. 15 Litho. *Perf. 13x13¼*
1233 A623 75fr multi 1.50 1.50

Miniature Sheet

Birds of Prey A624

No. 1234: a, Pandion cristatus. b, Circus approximans. c, Accipiter haplochrous. d, Haliastur sphenurus.

2017, Oct. 17 Photo. *Perf. 13¼x13*
1234 A624 110fr Sheet of 4, #a-d 8.75 8.75

Kagu Philatelic Club, 70th Anniv. — A625

2017, Nov. 8 Litho. *Perf. 13x13¼*
1235 A625 75fr multi 1.50 1.50

Wênit, Third Yam Farming Cycle — A626

2017, Nov. 9 Litho. *Perf. 13*
1236 A626 75fr multi 1.50 1.50

Caves and Water Holes — A627

No. 1237 — Inscriptions: a, Grotte de Koumac. b, Pléiades du Nord. c, Trou Feuillet. d, Trou bleu. e, Trou d'eau à la Rivière Bleue. f, Trou d'eau d'Anawa. g, Grotte de la Reine Hortense. h, Aquarium naturel. i, Trou de Bone. j, Grotte du Diable.

Serpentine Die Cut 11
2017, Nov. 9 Litho.
Self-Adhesive

1237 Booklet pane of 10 22.50
a.-j. A627 110fr Any single 2.25 2.25

Christmas — A628

2017, Nov. 9 Litho. *Perf. 13¼x13*
1238 A628 110fr multi 2.25 2.25

New Year 2018 (Year of the Dog) — A629

2018, Feb. 16 Litho. *Perf. 13*
1239 A629 75fr multi 1.60 1.60

No. 1239 was printed in sheets of 10 + central label. See No. 1251k for stamp dated "2019."

New Caledonian Battalion's Capture of Vesles-et-Caumont, France, Cent. — A630

2018, Apr. 10 Litho. *Perf. 13*
1240 A630 75fr multi 1.50 1.50

Tjibaou Cultural Center, 20th Anniv. A631

2018, May 7 Litho. *Perf. 13*
1241 A631 110fr multi 2.25 2.25

Kuyiuk Huuda, Fourth Yam Farming Cycle — A632

2018, June 8 Litho. *Perf. 13*
1242 A632 110fr multi 2.25 2.25

Steamship Dupleix 1 — A633

2018, June 8 Litho. *Perf. 13*
1243 A633 110fr multi 2.25 2.25

Buildings A634

No. 1244: a, Great Chief's hut, Poindimié. b, Albaret House, Canala.

2018, June 8 Litho. *Perf. 13x13¼*
1244 A634 110fr Horiz. pair, #a-b, + central label 4.25 4.25

Bancoule Worm Eating Festival, Farino — A635

2018, Sept. 7 Litho. *Perf. 13x13¼*
1245 A635 75fr multi 1.50 1.50

Horse Breeder's Promotion Unit (UPRA), 20th Anniv. — A636

2018, Sept. 13 Litho. *Perf. 13x13¼*
1246 A636 75fr multi 1.50 1.50

Fauna — A637

No. 1247: a, Triops intermedius. b, Callismilax bouabouiensis. c, Tuba valkyrie.

2018, Nov. 7 Litho. *Perf. 13x13¼*
1247 Horiz. strip of 3 4.50 4.50
a.-c. A637 75fr Any single 1.50 1.50

Women's Handball Players A638

2018, Nov. 8 Litho. *Perf. 13*
1248 A638 110fr multi 2.10 2.10

Miniature Sheet

Pollinators — A639

No. 1249: a, Gymnomyza aubryana. b, Pteropus ornatus, horiz. c, Apis mellifera mellifera, horiz. d, Eurema hecabe novaecalidoniae.

Perf. 13¼x13, 13x13¼ (horiz. stamps)
2018, Nov. 8 Photo.
1249 A639 110fr Sheet of 4, #a-d 8.50 8.50

Michel Rocard (1930-2016), Politician — A640

2018, Nov. 8 Engr. *Perf. 13*
1250 A640 1000fr multi 19.00 19.00

Matignon-Oudinot Accords, 30th anniv.

New Year Types of 2003-17
Miniature Sheet
2019, Feb. 5 Litho. *Perf. 13*
Dated "2019"

1251	Sheet of 12	18.00	18.00
a.	A461 75fr Rat	1.50	1.50
b.	A480 75fr Ox	1.50	1.50
c.	A501 75fr Tiger	1.50	1.50
d.	A550 75fr Snake	1.50	1.50
e.	A534 75fr Dragon	1.50	1.50
f.	A518 75fr Rabbit	1.50	1.50
g.	A570 75fr Horse	1.50	1.50
h.	A361 75fr Goat	1.50	1.50
i.	A599 75fr Monkey	1.50	1.50
j.	A430 75fr Pig	1.50	1.50
k.	A629 75fr Dog	1.50	1.50
l.	A615 75fr Rooster	1.50	1.50

Turtle in Lagoon — A641

2019, Mar. 14 Litho. *Perf. 13¼x13*
1252 A641 110fr multi 2.10 2.10

Lagoons of New Caledonia as UNESCO World Heritage Site, 10th anniv.

Disabled Athletes A642

2019, June 7 Litho. *Perf. 13*
1253 A642 120fr multi 2.40 2.40

Packet Boat Le Polynésie A643

2019, June 7 Litho. *Perf. 13*
1254 A643 110fr multi 2.10 2.10

South Pacific Community Headquarters, Noumea — A644

2019, Aug. 9 Litho. *Perf. 13*
1255 A644 75fr multi 1.40 1.40

South Pacific Community headquarters in Noumea, 70th anniv.

Return of New Caledonian World War I Soldiers, Cent. — A645

2019, Sept. 13 Litho. *Perf. 13*
1256 A645 75fr multi 1.40 1.40

Avocado Festival, Maré — A646

2019, Oct. 10 Litho. *Perf. 13¼x13*
1257 A646 110fr multi 2.10 2.10

Buildings A647

No. 1258: a, Roh hut, Maré. b, House of Samuel MacFarlane, Lifou.

2019, Oct. 10 Litho. *Perf. 13x13¼*
1258 A647 110fr Horiz. pair, #a-b, + central label 4.25 4.25

Hand on Braille Book, Emma Meyer (1910-87), Founder of Valentin Haüy Association in New Caledonia A648

Litho. & Embossed

2019, Nov. 6 *Perf. 13*
1259 A648 75fr multi 1.40 1.40

Valentin Haüy Association in New Caledonia, 40th anniv.

Fort Constantine, Colonial Hospital, Gaston Bourret Hospital and Bourret (1875-1917), Microbiologist — A649

2019, Nov. 6 Litho. *Perf. 13x13¼*
1260 A649 120fr multi 2.25 2.25

Pilou Mine Chimney — A650

2019, Nov. 6 Engr. *Perf. 13*
1261 A650 1000fr multi 18.50 18.50

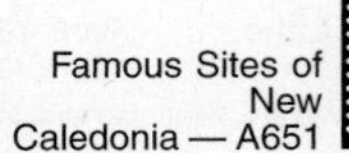

Famous Sites of New Caledonia — A651

No. 1262: a, University of New Caledonia. b, Church, Vao. c, Kanak hut. d, Chicken of Hienghène rock formation. e, Place Feillet Bandstand. f, Tjibaou Cultural Center.

Serpentine Die Cut 11

2020, Jan. 13 Litho.

Self-Adhesive

1262 Booklet pane of 6 12.00
a.-f. A651 110fr Any single 2.00 2.00

10th Pacific Island Biodiversity Conservation Conference, Noumea — A652

2020, July 1 Litho. *Perf. 13¼x13*
1263 A652 (210fr) multi 4.00 4.00

Love — A653

Design: Sea Fans Resembling People Kissing.

2020, July 1 Litho. *Perf. 13x13¼*
1264 A653 (210fr) multi 4.00 4.00

Ship and Bernard Brou (1922-2009), Historian — A654

2020, July 17 Litho. *Perf. 13*
1265 A654 140fr multi 2.75 2.75

New Caledonia Society for Historic Studies, 50th anniv.

Pôle Espoir Judo League — A655

2020, July 17 Litho. *Perf. 13¼x13*
1266 A655 140fr multi 2.75 2.75

Aircalin Airbus A330neo — A656

2020, July 17 Litho. *Perf. 13x13¼*
1267 A656 (140fr) multi 2.75 2.75

Mushrooms A657

No. 1268: a, Panus lecomtei. b, Ryvardenia campyla.

2020, Sept. 7 Litho. *Perf. 13x13¼*
1268 Horiz. pair + central label 5.50 5.50
a.-b. A657 140fr Either single 2.75 2.75

International Organization of La Francophonie, 50th Anniv. — A658

2020, Sept. 16 Litho. *Perf. 13x13¼*
1269 A658 210fr multi 4.25 4.25

Pouembout Solar Farm A659

2020, Oct. 20 Litho. *Perf. 13*
1270 A659 (210fr) multi 4.25 4.25

Jacques Chirac (1932-2019), President and Prime Minister of France — A660

2020, Nov. 4 Litho. *Perf. 13*
1271 A660 840fr multi 17.00 17.00

Christmas A661

2020, Nov. 4 Litho. *Perf. 13x13¼*
1272 A661 (210fr) multi 4.25 4.25

Kagu
A662 A663

2021, Mar. 22 Litho. *Perf. 13*
1273 A662 (180fr) red & black 3.75 3.75
1274 A663 (260fr) violet & black 5.25 5.25

Mushrooms A664

No. 1275: a, Aseroe arachnoidea. b, Ophiocordyceps sp.

2021, May 3 Litho. *Perf. 13x13¼*
1275 Horiz. pair + central label 7.50 7.50
a.-b. A664 (180fr) Either single 3.75 3.75

New Caledonian Society for the Safeguarding of Nature, 50th Anniv. — A665

2021, May 6 Litho. *Perf. 13*
1276 A665 260fr multi + label 5.50 5.50

Tabou Lighthouse — A666

2021, Aug. 17 Litho. *Perf. 13¼x13*
1277 A666 (260fr) multi 5.25 5.25

New Pacific Franc Coins A667

Litho. & Embossed

2021, Sept. 1 *Perf. 13*
1278 A667 (180fr) multi 3.75 3.75

Mandarin Oranges — A668

2021, Sept. 14 Litho. *Perf. 13x13¼*
1279 A668 (180fr) multi 3.50 3.50

Mandarin Orange Fair, Canala, 25th anniv. No. 1279 is impregnated with a mandarin orange scent.

Environmental Protection A669

No. 1280: a, Hands and kauri tree. b, Hands, ship, sea cucumbers.

2021, Oct. 15 Litho. *Perf. 13*
1280 A669 (260fr) Vert. pair, #a-b 10.00 10.00

Pan American Airways Boeing B-314 Clippers — A670

2021, Nov. 15 Litho. *Perf. 13x13¼*
1281 A670 260fr multi 5.00 5.00

Mamie Fogliani (1939-2020), Restauranteur and Market Owner — A671

2021, Dec. 17 Litho. *Perf. 13*
1282 A671 (180fr) multi 3.50 3.50

New Caledonia Youth Rugby Hope Academy A672

2022, Jan. 25 Litho. *Perf. 13*
1283 A672 260fr multi 5.00 5.00

Mushrooms A673

No. 1284: a, Ileodictyon sp. b, Anthracophyllum archeri.

2022, Apr. 11 Litho. *Perf. 13x13¼*
1284 Horiz. pair + central label 6.50 6.50
a.-b. A673 (180fr) Either single 3.25 3.25

Earth Day — A674

2022, Apr. 22 Litho. *Perf. 13¼x13*
1285 A674 (180fr) multi 3.25 3.25

Cap N'Dua Lighthouse — A675

2022, July 22 Litho. *Perf. 13¼x13*
1286 A675 (310fr) multi 5.50 5.50

UTA Boeing 747-400 "Big Boss" — A676

2022, July 22 Litho. *Perf. 13x13¼*
1287 A676 310fr multi 5.50 5.50

Peace Statue, Place de la Paix, Nouméa — A677

2022, Sept. 20 Litho. *Perf. 13¼x13*
1288 A677 210fr multi 3.50 3.50

Miniature Sheet

Old Automobiles — A678

No. 1289: a, Willys Jeep. b, Cadillac Eldorado. c, Peugeot 504. d, Volkswagen Beetle Cabriolet.

2022, Sept. 20 Litho. *Perf. 13x13¼*
1289 A678 (310fr) Sheet of 4, #a-d 20.00 20.00

Christmas — A679

2022, Nov. 15 Litho. *Perf. 13¼x13*
1290 A679 (310fr) multi 5.50 5.50

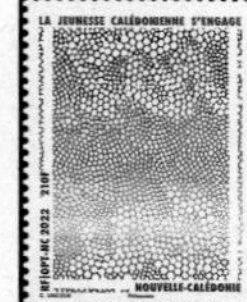
Art by Camille Lincoln — A680

2022, Nov. 15 Litho. *Perf. 13¼x13*
1291 A680 210fr multi 3.75 3.75

Kagu — A681

2022, Nov. 15 Litho. *Perf. 13*
1292 A681 (210fr) red 3.75 3.75

Booklet Stamp
Self-Adhesive
Serpentine Die Cut 6¾ Vert.

1293 A681 (210fr) red 3.75 3.75
a. Booklet pane of 10 37.50

See No. 1297. For stamp of type A681 with denomination, see No. 1296h.

Environmental Protection — A682

No. 1294: a, Giant crested gecko. b, Coral reef fauna.

2022, Dec. 6 Litho. *Perf. 13¼x13*
1294 A682 (310fr) Pair, #a-b 11.00 11.00

Agroforestry on Maré Island — A683

2023, May 30 Litho. *Perf. 13x13¼*
1295 A683 (230fr) multi 4.25 4.25

Kagu Types of 1985-2022 Redrawn

2023, May 30 Litho. *Perf. 13*
1296 Booklet pane of 8 3.75 —
a. A137 20fr yellow orange .35 .35
b. A179 20fr yellow orange .35 .35
c. A179a 20fr yellow orange .35 .35
d. A265 20fr yellow orange .35 .35
e. A364 30fr brt lilac rose .55 .55
f. A486 30fr brt lilac rose .55 .55
g. A613 30fr brt lilac rose .55 .55
h. A681 30fr brt lilac rose .55 .55

Nos. 1296a-1296h have inscriptions added to the designs that give the year and designer of the original issue of that stamp type, with some stamps having other inscriptions moved or added.

Kagu Type of 2022 Inscribed "International"

2023, July 21 Litho. *Perf. 13*
1297 A681 (340fr) dark blue 6.50 6.50

UTA Caravelle — A684

2023, July 21 Litho. *Perf. 13x13¼*
1298 A684 340fr multi 6.50 6.50

Amédée Lighthouse A685

2023, July 21 Litho. *Perf. 13x13¼*
1299 A685 (340fr) multi 6.50 6.50

Jean Lèques (1931-2022), First President of New Caledonia A686

2023, Sept. 15 Engr. *Perf. 13x13¼*
1300 A686 460fr multi 8.25 8.25

West Coast of New Caledonia — A687

2023, Oct. 10 Litho. *Perf. 13¼x13*
1301 A687 (230fr) multi 4.25 4.25

Nickel Industry Environmental Protection — A688

2023, Nov. 8 Litho. *Perf. 13*
1302 A688 230fr multi 4.25 4.25

Door Light A689

Kanak Money A690

Tobacco Pot and Lid — A691

2023, Nov. 8 Litho. *Perf. 13¼x13*
1303 Horiz. strip of 3 19.00 19.00
a. A689 340fr multi 6.25 6.25
b. A690 340fr multi 6.25 6.25
c. A691 340fr multi 6.25 6.25

Exhibit of Kanak art and artifacts at Quai Branly Museum, Paris, 10th anniv.

A692

A693

Selection of Lagoons of New Caledonia as UNESCO World Heritage Site, 15th Anniv. — A694

2023, Nov. 8 Litho. *Perf. 13x13¼*
1304 Vert. strip of 3 19.00 19.00
a. A692 (340fr) multi 6.25 6.25
b. A693 (340fr) multi 6.25 6.25
c. A694 (340fr) multi 6.25 6.25

SEMI-POSTAL STAMPS

No. 93 Surcharged

1915 Unwmk. *Perf. 14x13½*
B1 A16 10c + 5c carmine 1.50 1.50
a. Inverted surcharge 75.00 75.00
b. Cross omitted 100.00 —
c. Double surcharge 160.00 160.00

Regular Issue of 1905 Surcharged

1917
B2 A16 10c + 5c rose 1.50 1.30
a. Double surcharge 130.00 —
B3 A16 15c + 5c violet 1.50 1.40

Curie Issue
Common Design Type

1938, Oct. 24 *Perf. 13*
B4 CD80 1.75fr + 50c brt ultra 16.50 17.50

French Revolution Issue
Common Design Type

1939, July 5 Photo.
Name and Value Typo. in Black
B5 CD83 45c + 25c green 13.50 13.50
B6 CD83 70c + 30c brown 13.50 13.50
B7 CD83 90c + 35c red org 13.50 13.50
B8 CD83 1.25fr + 1fr rose pink 13.50 13.50
B9 CD83 2.25fr + 2fr blue 13.50 13.50
Nos. B5-B9 (5) 67.50 67.50

Catalogue values for unused stamps in this section, from this point to the end of the section, are for Never Hinged items.

Common Design Type and

Dumont d'Urville's ship, "Zélée" SP2

New Caledonian Militiaman SP3

1941 Photo. *Perf. 13½*
B10 SP2 1fr + 1fr red 2.25
B11 CD86 1.50fr + 3fr maroon 2.25
B12 SP3 2.50fr + 1fr dk blue 2.25
Nos. B10-B12 (3) 6.75

Nos. B10-B12 were issued by the Vichy government in France, but were not placed on sale in New Caledonia.

Nos. 216A-216B Srchd. in Black or Red

1944 Engr. *Perf. 12½x12*
B12A 50c + 1.50fr on 2.50fr deep blue (R) 1.00
B12B + 2.50fr on 1fr green 1.25

Colonial Development Fund.

Nos. B12A-B12B were issued by the Vichy government in France, but were not placed on sale in New Caledonia.

Red Cross Issue
Common Design Type

1944 *Perf. 14½x14*
B13 CD90 5fr + 20fr brt scar 1.50 1.50

The surtax was for the French Red Cross and national relief.

Tropical Medicine Issue
Common Design Type

1950, May 15 Engr. *Perf. 13*

B14 CD100 10fr + 2fr red brn & sepia 6.75 5.25

The surtax was for charitable work.

AIR POST STAMPS

Seaplane Over Pacific Ocean — AP1

1938-40 Unwmk. Engr. *Perf. 13*

C1 AP1 65c deep violet 1.00 1.00
a. "65c" omitted 225.00
C2 AP1 4.50fr red 1.60 1.60
C3 AP1 7fr dk bl grn ('40) 1.15 .85
C4 AP1 9fr ultra 3.00 2.60
C5 AP1 20fr dk org ('40) 2.25 2.25
C6 AP1 50fr black ('40) 3.75 3.25
Nos. C1-C6 (6) 12.75 11.55

Type of 1938-40 Without "RF"

1942-43

C6A AP1 65c deep violet .30
C6B AP1 4.50fr red .30
C6C AP1 5fr yellow brown .55
C6D AP1 9fr ultramarine .45
C6E AP1 10fr brown lilac 1.00
C6F AP1 20fr dark orange 1.60
C6G AP1 50fr black 1.75
Nos. C6A-C6G (7) 5.95

Nos. C6A-C6G were issued by the Vichy government in France, but were not placed on sale in New Caledonia.

Common Design Type

1942 Unwmk. *Perf. 14½x14*

C7 CD87 1fr dk orange .70 .70
C8 CD87 1.50fr brt red .70 .70
C9 CD87 5fr brown red .70 .70
C10 CD87 10fr black 1.10 .70
C11 CD87 25fr ultra 1.40 1.25
C12 CD87 50fr dk green 2.00 1.25
C13 CD87 100fr plum 2.25 2.00
Nos. C7-C13 (7) 8.85 7.30

Eagle — AP1a

1944 *Perf. 13*

C13A AP1a 100fr blue grn 1.50

No. C13A was issued by the Vichy government in France, but was not placed on sale in New Caledonia.

Catalogue values for unused stamps in this section, from this point to the end of the section, are for Never Hinged items.

Victory Issue
Common Design Type

1946, May 8 Engr. *Perf. 12½*

C14 CD92 8fr brt ultra 1.50 1.25

Chad to Rhine Issue
Common Design Types

1946, June 6

C15 CD93 5fr black 1.75 1.60
C16 CD94 10fr carmine 1.75 1.60
C17 CD95 15fr dk blue 1.75 1.60
C18 CD96 20fr orange brn 1.75 1.60
C19 CD97 25fr olive grn 2.40 2.00
C20 CD98 50fr dk rose vio 4.00 3.50
Nos. C15-C20 (6) 13.40 11.90

St. Vincent Bay — AP2

Planes over Islands — AP3

View of Nouméa AP4

Perf. 13x12½, 12½x13

1948, Mar. 1 Photo. Unwmk.

C21 AP2 50fr org & rose vio 6.00 4.00
C22 AP3 100fr bl grn & sl bl 10.50 4.50
C23 AP4 200fr brown & yel 16.50 8.50
Nos. C21-C23 (3) 33.00 17.00

UPU Issue
Common Design Type

1949, Nov. 21 Engr. *Perf. 13*

C24 CD99 10fr multicolored 7.50 5.00

Liberation Issue
Common Design Type

1954, June 6

C25 CD102 3fr indigo & ultra 7.50 5.00

Conveyor for Nickel Ore — AP5

1955, Nov. 21 Unwmk. *Perf. 13*

C26 AP5 14fr indigo & sepia 4.00 1.50

Rock Formations, Bourail AP6

1959, Mar. 21

C27 AP6 200fr lt bl, brn & grn 34.00 15.00

Yaté Dam — AP7

1959, Sept. 21 Engr.

C28 AP7 50fr grn, brt bl & sepia 7.50 4.50

Dedication of Yaté Dam.

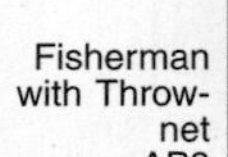

Fisherman with Throw-net AP8

Skin Diver Shooting Bumphead Surgeonfish AP9

20fr, Nautilus shell. 100fr, Yaté rock.

1962 Unwmk. *Perf. 13*

C29 AP8 15fr red, Prus grn & sep 4.75 2.25
C30 AP9 20fr dk sl grn & org ver 9.50 3.75
C31 AP9 25fr red brn, gray & bl 9.50 4.50
C32 AP9 100fr dk brn, dk bl & sl grn 16.00 11.50
Nos. C29-C32 (4) 39.75 22.00

Telstar Issue
Common Design Type

1962, Dec. 4 Unwmk. *Perf. 13*

C33 CD111 200fr dk bl, choc & grnsh bl 25.00 18.50

Nickel Mining, Houailou AP10

1964, May 14 Photo.

C34 AP10 30fr multi 4.00 2.50

Isle of Pines AP11

1964, Dec. 7 Engr. *Perf. 13*

C35 AP11 50fr dk bl, sl grn & choc 5.75 2.60

Marine Life — AP12

Designs: 27fr, Paracanthurus teuthis (fish). 37fr, Phyllobranchus.

1964, Dec. 21 Photo.

C36 AP12 27fr multicolored 7.50 3.50
C37 AP12 37fr multicolored 9.00 5.00

Issued to publicize the Nouméa Aquarium.

Greco-Roman Wrestling — AP13

1964, Dec. 28 Engr.

C38 AP13 10fr brt grn, pink & blk 18.00 15.00

18th Olympic Games, Tokyo, Oct. 10-25.

Nimbus Weather Satellite over New Caledonia — AP14

1965, Mar. 23 Photo. *Perf. 13x12½*

C39 AP14 9fr multi 3.75 3.00

Fifth World Meteorological Day.

ITU Issue
Common Design Type

1965, May 17 Engr. *Perf. 13*

C40 CD120 40fr lt bl, lil rose & red brn 10.00 8.00

Coris Angulata (Young Fish) AP15

15fr, Adolescent fish. 25fr, Adult fish.

1965, Dec. 6 Engr. *Perf. 13*

C41 AP15 13fr red org, ol bis & blk 4.00 1.50
C42 AP15 15fr ind, sl grn & bis 6.00 2.00
C43 AP15 25fr ind & yel grn 8.00 4.00
Nos. C41-C43 (3) 18.00 7.50

Issued to publicize the Nouméa Aquarium.

French Satellite A-1 Issue
Common Design Type

Designs: 8fr, Diamant rocket and launching installations. 12fr, A-1 satellite.

1966, Jan. 10 Engr. *Perf. 13*

C44 CD121 8fr rose brn, ultra & Prus bl 2.00 1.60
C45 CD121 12fr ultra, Prus bl & rose brn 3.00 3.00
a. Strip of 2, #C44-C45 + label 7.00 7.00

French Satellite D-1 Issue
Common Design Type

1966, May 16 Engr. *Perf. 13*

C46 CD122 10fr dl bl, ocher & sep 2.25 2.00

Port-de-France, 1866 — AP16

1966, June 2

C47 AP16 30fr dk red, bl & ind 4.25 3.00

Port-de-France changing name to Nouméa, cent.

Bird Type of Regular Issue

Designs: 27fr, Uvea crested parakeet. 37fr, Scarlet honey eater. 50fr, Two cloven-feathered doves.

1966-68 Photo. *Perf. 13*

Size: 26x46mm

C48 A45 27fr pink & multi 7.50 4.00
C49 A45 37fr grn & multi 10.00 5.00

Size: 27x48mm

C49A A45 50fr multi ('68) 13.00 7.50
Nos. C48-C49A (3) 30.50 16.50

Issued: 27fr, 37fr, Oct. 10; 50fr, May 14.

Sailboats and Map of New Caledonia-New Zealand Route — AP17

1967, Apr. 15 Engr. *Perf. 13*

C50 AP17 25fr brt grn, dp ultra & red 6.75 3.75

2nd sailboat race from Whangarei, New Zealand, to Nouméa, New Caledonia.

Butterfly Type of Regular Issue

Butterflies: 19fr, Danaus plexippus. 29fr, Hippotion celerio. 85fr, Delias elipsis.

1967-68 Engr. *Perf. 13*

Size: 48x27mm

C51 A52 19fr multi ('68) 6.50 3.00
C52 A52 29fr multi ('68) 9.50 4.00
C53 A52 85fr red, dk brn & yel 15.00 7.50
Nos. C51-C53 (3) 31.00 14.50

Issued: 85fr, Aug. 10; others, Mar. 26.

Jules Garnier, Garnierite and Mine AP18

1967, Oct. 9 Engr. *Perf. 13*
C54 AP18 70fr bl gray, brn & yel grn 9.00 5.25

Discovery of garnierite (nickel ore), cent.

Lifu Island AP19

1967, Oct. 28 Photo. *Perf. 13*
C55 AP19 200fr multi 14.00 7.50

Skier, Snowflake and Olympic Emblem AP20

1967, Nov. 16 Engr. *Perf. 13*
C56 AP20 100fr brn red, sl grn & brt bl 14.00 7.50

10th Winter Olympic Games, Grenoble, France, Feb. 6-18, 1968.

Sea Shell Type of Regular Issue

Designs: 39fr, Conus lienardi. 40fr, Conus cabriti. 70fr, Conus coccineus.

1968, Nov. 9 Engr. *Perf. 13*
C58 A54 39fr bl grn, brn & gray 8.25 2.75
C59 A54 40fr blk, brn red & ol 8.25 3.00
C60 A54 70fr brn, pur & gray 17.00 5.50
Nos. C58-C60 (3) 33.50 11.25

Maré Dancers — AP21

1968, Nov. 30 Engr. *Perf. 13*
C61 AP21 60fr grn, ultra & hn brn 7.50 5.00

World Map and Caudron C 600 "Aiglon" AP22

1969, Mar. 24 Engr. *Perf. 13*
C62 AP22 29fr lil, dk bl & dk car 5.00 2.25

Stamp Day and honoring the 1st flight from Nouméa to Paris of Henri Martinet & Paul Klein, Mar. 24, 1939.

Concorde Issue
Common Design Type

1969, Apr. 17 Engr. *Perf. 13*
C63 CD129 100fr sl grn & brt grn 27.50 20.00

Cattle Type of Regular Issue

Design: 50fr, Cowboy and herd.

1969, May 10 Engr. *Perf. 13*
Size: 48x27mm
C64 A56 50fr sl grn, dk brn & red brn 7.00 3.25

Sea Shell Type of Regular Issue, 1969

Design: 100fr, Black murex.

1969, June 21 Engr. *Perf. 13*
Size: 48x27mm
C65 A57 100fr lake, bl & blk 24.00 11.50

Sports Type of 1969

30fr, Woman diver. 39fr, Shot put, vert.

1969, Aug. 7 Engr. *Perf. 13*
Size: 48x27mm, 27x48mm
C66 A58 30fr dk brn, bl & blk 5.25 2.00
C67 A58 39fr dk ol, brt grn & ol 6.75 3.00

Napoleon in Coronation Robes, by François P. Gerard — AP23

1969, Oct. 2 Photo. *Perf. 12½x12*
C68 AP23 40fr lil & multi 14.00 10.00

200th birth anniv. of Napoleon Bonaparte (1769-1821).

Air France Plane over Outrigger Canoe AP24

1969, Oct. 2 Engr. *Perf. 13*
C69 AP24 50fr slate grn, sky bl & choc 5.50 3.25

20th anniversary of the inauguration of the Nouméa to Paris airline.

Bird Type of Regular Issue

39fr, Emerald doves. 100fr, Whistling kite.

1970, Feb. 19 Photo. *Perf. 13*
Size: 27x48mm
C70 A45 39fr multi 13.50 4.00
C71 A45 100fr multi 26.00 10.00

Planes Circling Globe and Paris-Nouméa Route — AP25

1970, May 6 Engr. *Perf. 13*
C72 AP25 200fr vio, org brn & grnsh bl 17.50 9.75

10th anniversary of the Paris to Nouméa flight: "French Wings Around the World."

Shell Type of Regular Issue, 1970

22fr, Strombus sinautus humphrey, vert. 33fr, Argus porcelain shell. 34fr, Strombus vomer, vert. 60fr, Card porcelain shell.

1970 Engr. *Perf. 13*
Size: 27x48mm, 48x27mm
C73 A59 22fr lt bl & multi 7.25 3.00
C74 A59 33fr red brn & grnsh bl 9.00 4.50
C75 A59 34fr vio & multi 9.00 3.50
C76 A59 60fr emer & red brn 15.00 6.00
Nos. C73-C76 (4) 40.25 17.00

See Nos. C89-C90.

Bicyclists on Map of New Caledonia AP26

1970, Aug. 20 Engr. *Perf. 13*
C77 AP26 40fr bl, ultra & choc 6.75 3.25

The 4th Bicycling Race of New Caledonia.

Mt. Fuji and Monorail Train AP27

45fr, Map of Japan and Buddha statue.

1970, Sept. 3 Photo. *Perf. 13x12½*
C78 AP27 20fr blk, bl & yel grn 4.50 1.90
C79 AP27 45fr mar, lt bl & ol 6.00 3.25

EXPO '70 International Exposition, Osaka, Japan, Mar. 15-Sept. 13.

Racing Yachts — AP28

1971, Feb. 23 Engr. *Perf. 13*
C80 AP28 20fr grn, blk & ver 3.75 1.25

First challenge in New Zealand waters for the One Ton Cup ocean race.

Lt. Col. Broche and Map of Mediterranean — AP29

1971, May 5 Photo. *Perf. 12½*
C81 AP29 60fr multi 7.50 4.00

30th anniversary of Battalion of the Pacific.

Pole Vault AP30

1971, June 24 Engr. *Perf. 13*
C82 AP30 25fr shown 3.75 2.00
C83 AP30 100fr Archery 8.00 4.25

4th South Pacific Games, Papeete, French Polynesia, Sept. 8-19.

Port de Plaisance, Nouméa AP31

1971, Sept. 27 Photo. *Perf. 13*
C84 AP31 200fr multi 16.00 7.00

Golden Eagle and Pilot's Leaflet — AP32

1971, Nov. 20 Engr. *Perf. 13*
C85 AP32 90fr dk brn, org & indigo 8.25 3.75

1st flight New Caledonia — Australia with Victor Roffey piloting the Golden Eagle, 40th anniv.

Skiing and Sapporo '72 Emblem AP33

1972, Jan. 22 Engr. *Perf. 13*
C86 AP33 50fr brt bl, car & sl grn 6.00 2.75

11th Winter Olympic Games, Sapporo, Japan, Feb. 3-13.

South Pacific Commission Headquarters, Nouméa — AP34

1972, Feb. 5 Photo.
C87 AP34 18fr bl & multi 2.25 .85

South Pacific Commission, 25th anniv.

St. Mark's Basilica, Venice AP35

1972, Feb. 5 Engr.
C88 AP35 20fr lt grn, bl & grn 4.25 1.25

UNESCO campaign to save Venice.

Shell Type of Regular Issue, 1970

Designs: 25fr, Orange spider conch, vert. 50fr, Chiragra spider conch, vert.

1972, Mar. 4 Engr. *Perf. 13*
Size: 27x48mm
C89 A59 25fr dp car & dk brn 6.50 3.00
C90 A59 50fr grn, brn & rose car 8.00 4.00

Breguet F-ALMV and Globe AP36

1972, Apr. 5 Engr. *Perf. 13*
C91 AP36 110fr brt rose lil, bl & grn 8.00 6.00

40th anniversary of the first Paris-Nouméa flight, Mar. 9-Apr. 5, 1932.

Round House and Festival Emblem — AP37

1972, May 13
C92 AP37 24fr org, bl & brn 3.00 1.50

So. Pacific Festival of Arts, Fiji, May 6-20.

Hurdles and Olympic Rings AP38

1972, Sept. 2 Engr. *Perf. 13*
C93 AP38 72fr vio, bl & red lil 7.50 3.75

20th Olympic Games, Munich, Aug. 26-Sept. 11.

New Post Office, Noumea AP39

1972, Nov. 25 Engr. *Perf. 13*
C94 AP39 23fr brn, brt bl & grn 2.25 1.00

Molière and Scenes from Plays AP40

1973, Feb. 24 Engr. *Perf. 13*
C95 AP40 50fr multi 7.50 2.75

300th anniversary of the death of Molière (Jean Baptiste Poquelin, 1622-1673), French actor and playwright.

Woodlands AP41

Designs: 18fr, Palm trees on coast, vert. 21fr, Waterfall, vert.

1973, Feb. 24 Photo.
C96 AP41 11fr gold & multi 2.00 1.00
C97 AP41 18fr gold & multi 3.00 1.50
C98 AP41 21fr gold & multi 4.00 1.50
Nos. C96-C98 (3) 9.00 4.00

Concorde — AP42

1973, Mar. 15 Engr. *Perf. 13*
C99 AP42 23fr blue 12.50 5.00
a. Booklet pane of 5 250.00

No. C99 issued in booklets only.

El Kantara in Panama Canal AP43

1973, Mar. 24 Engr. *Perf. 13*
C100 AP43 60fr brn, yel grn & blk 7.50 3.25

50th anniversary of steamship connection Marseilles to Nouméa through Panama Canal.

Sun, Earth, Wind God and Satellite AP44

1973, Mar. 24
C101 AP44 80fr multi 7.00 2.75

Centenary of intl. meteorological cooperation and 13th World Meteorological Day.

Museum Type of Regular Issue

Designs: 16fr, Carved arrows and arrowhead. 40fr, Carved entrance to chief's house.

1973, Apr. 30 Photo. *Perf. 12½x13*
C102 A66 16fr multi 3.00 1.00
C103 A66 40fr multi 4.50 2.00

DC-10 over Map of Route Paris to Nouméa AP45

1973, May 26 Engr. *Perf. 13*
C104 AP45 100fr brn, ultra & sl grn 7.50 3.50

First direct flight by DC-10, Nouméa to Paris.

Fish Type of Regular Issue

32fr, Old and young olive surgeonfish.

1973, June 23 Photo. *Perf. 13x12½*
C105 A69 32fr multi 5.00 2.00

Coach, 1880 — AP46

1973, Sept. 22 Engr. *Perf. 13*
C106 AP46 15fr choc, bl & sl grn 2.50 1.25

Stamp Day 1973.

Landscape AP47

West Coast Landscapes: 8fr, Rocky path, vert. 26fr, Trees on shore.

1974, Feb. 23 Photo. *Perf. 13*
C107 AP47 8fr gold & multi 1.60 .90
C108 AP47 22fr gold & multi 2.25 1.40
C109 AP47 26fr gold & multi 3.75 1.50
Nos. C107-C109 (3) 7.60 3.80

Anse-Vata, Scientific Center, Nouméa AP48

1974, Mar. 23 Photo. *Perf. 13x12½*
C110 AP48 50fr multi 3.25 2.00

Ovula Ovum — AP49

1974, Mar. 23
C111 AP49 3fr shown 1.50 .55
C112 AP49 32fr Hydatina 4.00 1.10
C113 AP49 37fr Dolium perdix 4.50 2.10
Nos. C111-C113 (3) 10.00 3.75

Nouméa Aquarium.

Capt. Cook, Map of Grande Terre and "Endeavour" AP50

Designs: 25fr, Jean F. de la Perouse, his ship and map of Grande Terre. 28fr, French sailor, 18th century, on board ship, vert. 30fr, Antoine R. J. d'Entrecasteaux, ship and map. 36fr, Dumont d'Urville, ship and map of Loyalty Islands.

1974, Sept. 4 Engr. *Perf. 13*
C114 AP50 20fr multi 2.00 1.00
C115 AP50 25fr multi 3.00 1.60
C116 AP50 28fr multi 4.00 1.60
C117 AP50 30fr multi 5.00 2.00
C118 AP50 36fr multi 9.00 2.50
Nos. C114-C118 (5) 23.00 8.70

Discovery and exploration of New Caledonia and Loyalty Islands.

UPU Emblem and Symbolic Design AP51

1974, Oct. 9 Engr. *Perf. 13*
C119 AP51 95fr multi 6.00 2.75

Centenary of Universal Postal Union.

Abstract Design AP52

1974, Oct. 26 Photo. *Perf. 13*
C120 AP52 80fr bl, blk & org 5.00 2.00

ARPHILA 75, Philatelic Exhibition, Paris, June 6-16, 1975.

Hôtel Chateau-Royal, Nouméa — AP53

1975, Jan. 20 Photo. *Perf. 13*
C121 AP53 22fr multi 2.25 1.25

Cricket AP54

Designs: 25fr, Bougna ceremony (food offering). 31fr, Pilou dance.

1975, Apr. 5 Photo. *Perf. 13*
C122 AP54 3fr bl & multi 1.25 .45
C123 AP54 25fr olive grn & multi 2.50 .70
C124 AP54 31fr yel grn & multi 3.00 1.10
Nos. C122-C124 (3) 6.75 2.25

Tourist publicity.

Orchid Type of 1975

Design: 42fr, Eriaxis rigida.

1975, May 30
C125 A74 42fr grn & multi 6.00 2.25

Globe as "Flower" with "Stamps" and leaves — AP55

1975, June 7 Engr. *Perf. 13*
C126 AP55 105fr multi 7.00 2.75

ARPHILA 75 International Philatelic Exhibition, Paris, June 6-16.

Discus and Games' Emblem AP56

50fr, Volleyball and Games' emblem.

1975, Aug. 23 Photo. *Perf. 13x12½*
C127 AP56 24fr emer, pur & dk bl 2.00 1.00
C128 AP56 50fr multi 3.50 2.00

5th South Pacific Games, Guam, Aug. 1-10.

Concorde AP57

1976, Jan. 21 Engr. *Perf. 13*
C129 AP57 147fr car & ultra 12.00 7.00

First commercial flight of supersonic jet Concorde, Paris-Rio de Janeiro, Jan. 21.
For surcharge see No. C141.

Telephones 1876 and 1976, Satellite — AP58

1976, Apr. 12 Photo. *Perf. 13*
C130 AP58 36fr multi 3.50 1.25

Centenary of first telephone call by Alexander Graham Bell, Mar. 10, 1876.

Battle Scene AP59

1976, June 14 Engr. *Perf. 13*
C131 AP59 24fr red brn & ver 2.75 1.25

American Bicentennial.

Runners and Maple Leaf — AP60

1976, July 24 Engr. *Perf. 13*
C132 AP60 33fr car, vio & brn 2.25 1.25

21st Olympic Games, Montreal, Canada, July 17-Aug. 1.

Whimsical Bird as Student and Collector — AP61

1976, Aug. 21 Photo.
C133 AP61 42fr multi 3.50 1.50

Philately in School, Philatelic Exhibition in La Perouse Lyceum, Nouméa.

Old City Hall, Nouméa AP62

Design: 125fr, New City Hall, Nouméa.

1976, Oct. 22 Photo. *Perf. 13*
C134 AP62 75fr multi 5.00 2.75
C135 AP62 125fr multi 7.25 3.25

Lagoon, Women and Festival Symbols — AP63

1977, Jan. 15 Photo. *Perf. 13x12½*
C136 AP63 11fr multi 2.00 1.00

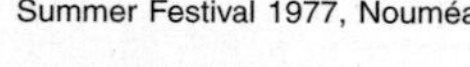

Summer Festival 1977, Nouméa.

Training Children in Toy Cars AP64

1977, Mar. 12 Litho. *Perf. 13*
C137 AP64 50fr multi 3.00 1.60

Road safety training.

Bird Type of 1977

Design: 42fr, Male frigate bird, horiz.

1977, Sept. 17 Photo. *Perf. 13*
C138 A89 42fr multi 6.00 1.60

Magenta Airport and Routes AP65

Design: 57fr, La Tontouta airport.

1977, Oct. 22 Litho. *Perf. 13*
C139 AP65 24fr multi 1.75 1.00
C140 AP65 57fr multi 3.50 2.00

No. C129 Surcharged in Violet Blue

1977, Nov. 22 Engr. *Perf. 13*
C141 AP57 147fr car & ultra 14.00 9.00

Concorde, 1st commercial flight Paris-NY.

Old Nouméa, by H. Didonna AP66

Valley of the Settlers, by Jean Kreber AP67

1977, Nov. 26 Photo. *Perf. 13*
C142 AP66 41fr gold & multi 3.00 1.50

Engr.

C143 AP67 42fr red brn & dk brn 3.00 1.50

"Underwater Carnival," Aubusson Tapestry AP68

1978, June 17 Photo. *Perf. 13*
C144 AP68 105fr multi 5.50 2.25

"The Hare and the Tortoise" AP69

1978, Aug. 19 Photo. *Perf. 13x13½*
C145 AP69 35fr multi 4.50 1.50

School philately.

Bourail School Children, Map and Conus Shell AP70

1978, Sept. 30 Engr. *Perf. 13*
C146 AP70 41fr multi 3.00 1.25

Promotion of topical philately in Bourail public schools.

Old and New Candles — AP71

1978, Oct. 28 Photo. *Perf. 13*
C147 AP71 36fr multi 2.00 .75

Third Caledonian Senior Citizens' Day.

Faubourg Blanchot, by Lacouture AP72

1978, Nov. 25 Photo. *Perf. 13*
C148 AP72 24fr multi 1.75 1.00

Type of 1978

Design: 42fr, Amyema scandens, horiz.

1978, Mar. 17 *Perf. 13x12½*
C149 A91 42fr multi 3.50 1.60

Orbiting Weather Satellites, WMO Emblem — AP73

1979, Mar. 24 Photo. *Perf. 13*
C150 AP73 53fr multi 2.50 1.25

First world-wide satellite system in the atmosphere.

Ships and Emblem — AP74

1979, Mar. 31 Engr.
C151 AP74 49fr multi 2.10 1.10

Chamber of Commerce and Industry, centenary.

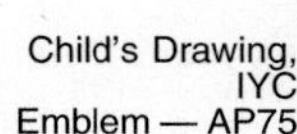

Child's Drawing, IYC Emblem — AP75

1979, Apr. 21 Photo. *Perf. 13*
C152 AP75 35fr multi 2.10 1.10

International Year of the Child.

Surf Casting — AP76

Design: 30fr, Swordfish fishing.

1979, May 26 Litho. *Perf. 12½*
C153 AP76 29fr multi 2.00 1.00
C154 AP76 30fr multi 2.00 1.00

Port-de-France, 1854, and de Montravel — AP77

1979, June 16 Engr. *Perf. 13*
C155 AP77 75fr multi 4.25 2.25

125th anniversary of Noumea, formerly Port-de-France, founded by L. Tardy de Montravel.

The Eel Queen, Kanaka Legend — AP78

1979, July 7 Photo. *Perf. 13*
C156 AP78 42fr multi 3.00 1.75

Nature protection.

Map of New Caledonia, Postmark, Five Races AP79

1979, Aug. 18 Photo. *Perf. 13*
C157 AP79 27fr multi 1.75 .90

New Caledonian youth and philately.

Orstom Center, Noumea, Orstom Emblem AP80

1979, Sept. 17 Photo. *Perf. 13*
C158 AP80 25fr multi 1.75 1.00

Old Post Office, Noumea, New Caledonia No. 1, Hill — AP81

1979, Nov. 17 Engr.
C159 AP81 150fr multi 5.25 2.00

Sir Rowland Hill (1795-1879), originator of penny postage.

Pirogue — AP82

1980, Jan. 26 Engr. *Perf. 13*
C160 AP82 45fr multi 1.75 .90

Rotary Intl., 75th Anniv. AP83

1980, Feb. 23 Photo. *Perf. 13*
C161 AP83 100fr multi 4.50 1.60

Man Holding Dolphinfish AP84

39fr, Fishermen, sail fish, vert.

1980, Mar. 29 Photo. *Perf. 13x12½*
C162 AP84 34fr shown 1.75 1.00
C163 AP84 39fr multicolored 2.50 1.25

Coral Seas Air Rally AP85

1980, June 7 Engr. *Perf. 13*
C164 AP85 31fr multi 1.75 .90

Carved Alligator, Boat AP86

1980, June 21 Photo.
C165 AP86 27fr multi 1.50 .55

South Pacific Arts Festival, Port Moresby, Papua New Guinea.

New Caledonian Kiwanis, 10th Anniversary AP87

1980, Sept. 10 Photo. *Perf. 13*
C166 AP87 50fr multi 1.90 .90

View of Old Noumea AP88

1980, Oct. 25 Photo. *Perf. 13½*
C167 AP88 33fr multi 1.60 .90

Charles de Gaulle, 10th Anniversary of Death — AP89

1980, Nov. 15 Engr. *Perf. 13*
C168 AP89 120fr multi 6.00 3.50

Fluorescent Coral, Noumea Aquarium AP90

1980, Dec. 13 Photo. *Perf. 13x13½*
C169 AP90 60fr multi 3.00 1.10

Xeronema Moorei — AP91

51fr, Geissois pruinosa.

1981, Mar. 18 Photo. *Perf. 13x12½*
C170 AP91 38fr shown 1.50 1.25
C171 AP91 51fr multicolored 2.00 1.40

Yuri Gagarin and Vostok I — AP92

20th Anniversary of First Space Flights: 155fr, Alan B. Shepard, Freedom 7.

1981, Apr. 8 Engr. *Perf. 13*
C172 AP92 64fr multi 2.75 1.10
C173 AP92 155fr multi 4.50 2.10
a. Souv. sheet of 2, #C172-C173 15.00 15.00

No. C173a sold for 225fr.

40th Anniv. of Departure of Pacific Batallion AP93

1981, May 5 Photo. *Perf. 13*
C174 AP93 29fr multi 3.00 1.10

Ecinometra Mathaei — AP94

51fr, Prionocidaris verticillata.

1981, Aug. 5 Photo. *Perf. 13x13½*
C175 AP94 38fr shown 1.50 .80
C176 AP94 51fr multicolored 2.25 .95

No. 4, Post Office Building — AP95

1981, Sept. 16 Photo. *Perf. 13x13½*
C177 AP95 41fr multi 1.75 .90

Stamp Day.

Old Noumea Latin Quarter — AP96

1981, Oct. 14 Photo. *Perf. 13½*
C178 AP96 43fr multi 1.75 .75

New Caledonia to Australia Airmail Flight by Victor Roffey, 50th Anniv. — AP97

1981, Nov. 21 Engr. *Perf. 13*
C179 AP97 37fr multi 1.50 .75

Rousette — AP98

1982, Feb. 24 Engr. *Perf. 13*
C180 AP98 38fr shown 1.50 .75
C181 AP98 51fr Kagu 2.00 .85

See Nos. C188B-C188C.

50th Anniv. of Paris-Noumea Flight — AP99

250fr, Pilots, map, plane.

1982, Apr. 5 Engr. *Perf. 13*
C182 AP99 250fr multi 7.00 3.50

Scouting Year — AP100

1982, Apr. 21 Photo. *Perf. 13½x13*
C183 AP100 40fr multi 1.50 .80

PHILEXFRANCE '82 Intl. Stamp Show, Paris, June 11-21 — AP101

1982, May 12 Engr. *Perf. 13*
C184 AP101 150fr multi 3.25 2.00

1982 World Cup — AP102

1982, June 9 Photo. *Perf. 13x13½*
C185 AP102 74fr multi 2.10 1.00

French Overseas Possessions Week, Sept. 18-25 — AP103

100fr, Map, kagu, citizens.

1982, Sept. 17 *Perf. 13x12½*
C186 AP103 100fr multicolored 2.75 1.00

Gypsum, Poya Mines — AP104

59fr, Silica gel, Kone mine.

1983, Jan. 15 Photo. *Perf. 13x13½*
C187 AP104 44fr shown 2.50 1.10
C188 AP104 59fr multicolored 3.50 1.40

World Communications Year — AP104a

Design: WCY emblem, map, globe.

1983, Mar. 9 Litho. *Perf. 13*
C188A AP104a 170fr multi 4.00 1.50

Aircraft Type of 1982

46fr, Pou-du-Ciel. 61fr, L'Aiglon Caudron.

1983, July 6 Engr. *Perf. 13*
C188B AP98 46fr multi 1.50 .75
C188C AP98 61fr multi 2.50 1.25

Temple and Dancers AP105

1983, July 20 Litho. *Perf. 12½x12*
C189 AP105 47fr multi 1.50 .80

BANGKOK '83 Intl. Stamp Show, Aug. 4-13.

Ouehoulle Tribe, Straw Hut — AP106

1983, Sept. 7 Litho. *Perf. 13*
C190 AP106 76fr multi 2.25 1.10

Loyalty Islander by the Shore, by R. Mascart — AP107

Paintings: 350fr, The Guitarist from Mare Island, by P. Neilly.

1983, Dec. 7 Photo. *Perf. 13*
C191 AP107 100fr multi 3.75 1.75
C192 AP107 350fr multi 9.00 5.25

Noumea Aquarium Fish — AP108

46fr, Amphiprion clarkii. 61fr, Centropyge bicolor.

1984, Mar. 7 Photo. *Perf. 13*
C193 AP108 46fr multi 2.25 .90
C194 AP108 61fr multi 2.75 1.25

Local Plants — AP109

51fr, Araucaria columnaris. 67fr, Pritchardiopsis jeanneneyi.

1984, Apr. 25 Litho. *Perf. 12½x13*
C195 AP109 51fr multi 2.00 .90
C196 AP109 67fr multi 2.75 1.25

1984 Summer Olympics AP110

1984, June 20 Photo. *Perf. 13½x13*
C197 AP110 50fr Swimming 1.75 1.10
C198 AP110 83fr Wind surfing 3.50 1.60
C199 AP110 200fr Running 6.00 2.75
Nos. C197-C199 (3) 11.25 5.45

Ausipex '84 — AP111

1984, Sept. 21 Engr. *Perf. 13*
C200 AP111 150fr Exhibition Hall 4.50 2.25
a. Souvenir sheet 6.00 6.00

Se-tenant with label showing exhibition emblem. No. C200a contains No. C200 in changed colors.

Army Day — AP112

1984, Oct. 27 Litho. *Perf. 13½x13*
C201 AP112 51fr multi 1.60 1.00

Woman Fishing for Crabs, by Mme. Bonnet de Larbogne AP113

Painting: 300fr, Cook Discovering New Caledonia, by Pilioko.

1984, Nov. 8 Litho. *Perf. 13x12½*
C202 AP113 120fr multi 3.50 1.75
C203 AP113 300fr multi 8.00 4.50

See Nos. 605-606.

Transpac Dragon Rapide, Map — AP114

1985, Oct. 2 Litho. *Perf. 13½*
C204 AP114 80fr multi 2.50 1.25

Internal air services, 30th anniv.

UN, 40th Anniv. — AP115

Perf. 12½x13
1985, Oct. 25 Wmk. 385
C205 AP115 250fr multi 5.50 2.00

Jules Garnier High School — AP116

1985, Nov. 13 Unwmk. *Perf. 13*
C206 AP116 400fr multi 10.00 4.25

Paris-Noumea Scheduled Flights, 30th Anniv. — AP117

1986, Jan. 6

C207 AP117 72fr multi 2.25 1.25

Nou Island Livestock Warehouse AP118

1986, June 14 Engr. *Perf. 13*

C208 AP118 230fr Prus bl, sep & brn 5.25 2.75

ATR-42 Inaugural Service — AP119

1986, Aug. 13 Litho. *Perf. 12½x13*

C209 AP119 18fr multi .90 .75

STOCKHOLMIA '86 — AP120

1986, Aug. 29 Engr. *Perf. 13*

C210 AP120 108fr No. 1 3.00 1.50

Natl. Assoc. of Amateur Radio Operators, 25th Anniv. — AP121

1987, Jan. 7 Litho. *Perf. 12½*

C211 AP121 64fr multi 1.75 .85

Nature Conservation, Fight Noise Pollution AP122

1987, Mar. 25 Litho. *Perf. 13x12½*

C212 AP122 150fr multi 4.00 1.75

French Cricket Federation AP123

1987, Nov. 25 Litho. *Perf. 12½*

C213 AP123 94fr multi 2.50 1.75

Arms Type of 1984

1988, Jan. 13 *Perf. 12½x13*

C214 A132 76fr Dumbea 2.50 1.00

Rotary Intl. Anti-Polio Campaign AP124

1988, Oct. 26 Litho. *Perf. 13½*

C215 AP124 220fr multi 5.25 2.75

Bamboo Type of 1989

Litho. & Engr.

1989, Sept. 27 *Perf. 12½x13*

C216 A187 44fr multi 1.25 .65

De Gaulle's Call For French Resistance, 50th Anniv. — AP125

1990, June 20 Litho. *Perf. 12½*

C217 AP125 160fr multicolored 4.00 1.75

Military Cemetery, New Zealand — AP126

Auckland 1990: #C219, Brigadier William Walter Dove.

1990, Aug. 24 *Perf. 13*

C218 AP126 80fr multi 2.00 1.00

C219 AP126 80fr multi 2.00 1.00

a. Pair, #C218-C219 + label 4.50 4.50

Souvenir Sheet

New Zealand 1990 AP126a

1990, Aug. 25 Litho. *Perf. 13x12½*

C219B AP126a 150fr multi 6.00 5.00

Crustaceans — AP127

30fr, Munidopsis sp. Orstom. 60fr, Lyreidius tridentatus.

1990, Oct. 17 Litho. *Perf. 12½x13*

C220 AP127 30fr multi 1.00 .55

C221 AP127 60fr multi 2.00 1.10

30th South Pacific Conference AP128

1990, Oct. 29 Litho. *Perf. 13*

C222 AP128 85fr multicolored 2.10 1.10

Gen. Charles de Gaulle (1890-1970) — AP129

1990, Nov. 21 Engr. *Perf. 13*

C223 AP129 410fr dk blue 9.00 3.50

Scenic Views AP130

1991, Feb. 13 Litho. *Perf. 13*

C224 AP130 36fr Fayawa-Ouvea Bay .90 .50

C225 AP130 90fr shown 2.40 1.25

See No. C246.

New Caledonian Cricket Players by Marcel Moutouh AP131

Design: 435fr, Saint Louis by Janine Goetz.

1991, Dec. 18 *Perf. 13x12½*

C226 AP131 130fr multicolored 3.00 2.00

C227 AP131 435fr multicolored 10.00 5.00

See Nos. C236, C242, C260.

Blue River Nature Park AP132

1992, Feb. 6 Litho. *Perf. 12½*

C228 AP132 400fr multicolored 9.25 4.75

a. Souvenir sheet of 1 10.50 10.50

No. C228a sold for 450fr and was issued 2/5/92.

Native Pottery — AP133

Photo. & Engr.

1992, Apr. 9 *Perf. 12½x13*

C229 AP133 25fr black & orange .75 .30

Expo '92, Seville — AP134

1992, Apr. 25 Litho. *Perf. 13*

C230 AP134 10fr multicolored .35 .25

Discovery of America, 500th Anniv. — AP135

#C234: a, Erik the Red, Viking longship. b, Columbus, coat of arms. c, Amerigo Vespucci.

1992, May 22 Litho. *Perf. 13½*

C231 AP135 80fr Pinta 2.00 1.00

C232 AP135 80fr Santa Maria 2.00 1.00

C233 AP135 80fr Nina 2.00 1.00

a. Strip of 3, #C231-C233 6.00 6.00

b. Bklt. pane of 3, #C231-C233 10.00 10.00

Souvenir Sheet

Perf. 12½

C234 AP135 110fr Sheet of 3, #a.-c. 10.00 10.00

World Columbian Stamp Expo '92, Chicago. No. C234 sold for 360fr.

1992 Summer Olympics, Barcelona AP136

260fr, Synchronized swimming.

1992, July 25 *Perf. 13*

C235 AP136 260fr multi 6.75 3.25

Painters of the Pacific Type of 1991

Design: 205fr, Wahpa, by Paul Mascart

1992, Sept. 28 Litho. *Perf. 12½x13*

C236 AP131 205fr multicolored 5.00 2.50

Australian Bouvier — AP138

1992, Oct. 4 *Perf. 12*

C237 AP138 175fr multicolored 5.25 2.40

Exploration of New Caledonian Coast by Chevalier d'Entrecasteaux, Bicent. — AP139

1992, Nov. 18 Engr. *Perf. 13*

C238 AP139 110fr bl grn, ocher & olive grn 3.00 1.25

Shells — AP140

30fr, Amalda fuscolingua. 50fr, Cassis abbotti.

1992, Nov. 26 Litho. *Perf. 13½x13*

C239 AP140 30fr multi 1.00 .35

C240 AP140 50fr multi 1.50 .75

The vignettes on Nos. C239-C240 were applied by a thermographic process, producing a shiny, raised effect.

AP141

Comic Strip Characters from "La Brousse en Folie," by Bernard Berger: a, Dede. b. Torton Marcel in Mimine II. c, Tathan. d, Joinville.

1992, Dec. 9 Litho. *Perf. 13½*

C241 AP141 80fr Strip of 4, #a.-d. 8.50 8.50

Painters of the Pacific Type of 1991

Design: 150fr, Noumea, 1890, by Gaston Roullet (1847-1925).

1993, Mar. 25 Litho. *Perf. 13x12½*
C242 AP131 150fr multicolored 3.50 1.75

Extraction of Attar from Niaouli Flowers (Melaleuca Quinquenervia), Cent. — AP142

1993, Apr. 28 *Perf. 13*
C243 AP142 85fr multicolored 2.00 1.00

Nicolaus Copernicus (1473-1543) AP143

1993, May 5 Engr. *Perf. 13*
C244 AP143 110fr multicolored 3.00 1.25

Polska '93.

Noumea Temple, Cent. — AP144

1993, June 16 Litho. *Perf. 12½x13*
C245 AP144 400fr multicolored 8.00 4.50

Scenic Views Type of 1991

1993, July 8 Litho. *Perf. 13*
C246 AP130 85fr Malabou 2.00 1.00

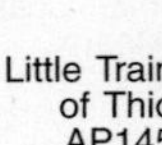

Little Train of Thio AP145

1993, July 24 Engr. *Perf. 13*
C247 AP145 115fr multicolored 3.00 1.40

AP146

1993, Aug. 18 Litho.
C248 AP146 100fr multicolored 2.50 1.10

Henri Rochefort (1831-1913), writer.

Bangkok '93 — AP147

No. C249, Vanda coerulea. No. C250, Megastylis paradoxa. 140fr, Royal Palace, Bangkok, horiz.

1993, Oct. 1 *Perf. 13½*
C249 AP147 30fr multicolored 1.00 .35
C250 AP147 30fr multicolored 1.00 .35

Souvenir Sheet

Perf. 13

C251 AP147 140fr multicolored 3.50 3.50

No. C251 contains one 52x40mm stamp.

Air Caledonia, 10th Anniv. AP148

1993, Oct. 9 *Perf. 13*
C252 AP148 85fr multicolored 2.25 1.10

New Caledonia-Australia Telephone Cable, Cent. — AP149

1993, Oct. 15 Engr. *Perf. 13x12½*
C253 AP149 200fr blue & black 4.75 2.25

Oxpleurodon Orbiculatus AP150

1993, Oct. 15 Litho. *Perf. 13½*
C254 AP150 250fr multicolored 6.00 2.75

Portions of the design on No. C254 were applied by a thermographic process producing a shiny, raised effect.

Tontouta Airport, Noumea, 25th Anniv. AP151

1993, Nov. 29 Litho. *Perf. 13*
C255 AP151 90fr multicolored 2.25 1.00

Christmas AP152

1993, Dec. 9 Litho.
C256 AP152 120fr multicolored 3.00 1.25

Portions of the design on No. C256 were applied by a thermographic process producing a shiny, raised effect.

New Year 1994 (Year of the Dog) — AP153

1994, Feb. 18 Litho. *Perf. 13*
C257 AP153 60fr multicolored 1.75 .85

Hong Kong '94.

First Airbus A340 Flight, Paris-Noumea — AP154

1994, Mar. 31 Litho. *Die Cut 8*
Self-Adhesive
C258 AP154 90fr multicolored 2.75 1.25

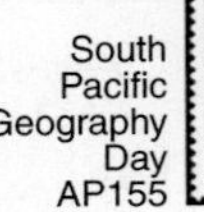
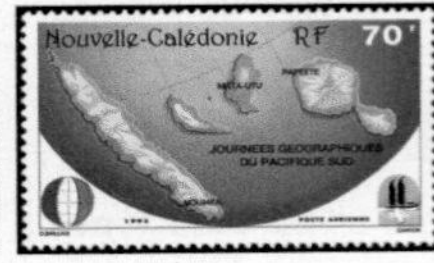

South Pacific Geography Day AP155

1994, May 10 Litho. *Perf. 13*
C259 AP155 70fr multicolored 1.75 .85

See Wallis and Futuna No. C177.

Painters of the Pacific Type of 1991

Design: 120fr, Legende du Poulpe, by Micheline Neporon.

1994, June 24 Litho. *Perf. 13*
C260 AP131 120fr multicolored 2.75 1.40

Pottery, Museum of Noumea — AP156

1994, July 6 Litho. *Perf. 12½x13*
C261 AP156 95fr multicolored 2.25 1.10

1994 World Cup Soccer Championships, U.S. — AP156a

1994, July 12 Litho. *Perf. 13*
C261A AP156a 105fr multicolored 2.50 1.50

Intl. Year of the Family — AP157

PHILAKOREA '94 — AP158

Korean cuisine: No. C263a, Rice, celery, carrots, peppers. b, Lettuce, cabbage, garlic. c, Onions. d, Shrimp, oysters.

1994, Aug. 17 *Perf. 13½x13*
C262 AP157 60fr multicolored 2.25 1.00

Souvenir Sheet

Perf. 12½

C263 Sheet of 4 4.75 4.75
a.-d. AP158 35fr any single 1.10 1.00

Research Ship Atalante AP159

1994, Aug. 26 *Perf. 13*
C264 AP159 120fr multicolored 2.75 1.50

Masons in New Caledonia, 125th Anniv. AP160

1994, Sept. 16 *Perf. 13*
C265 AP160 350fr multicolored 8.00 3.75

Participation in First European Stamp Show AP161

1994, Oct. 15 Litho. *Perf. 13*
C266 AP161 90fr Island 2.00 1.00
C267 AP161 90fr Herding cattle 2.00 1.00
a. Pair, #C266-C267 + label 4.50 4.50

ORSTOM, 50th Anniv. AP162

1994, Nov. 14 Photo. *Perf. 13*
C268 AP162 95fr multicolored 2.50 1.25

Tiebaghi Mine AP163

1994, Nov. 24 Litho.
C269 AP163 90fr multicolored 2.75 1.00

South Pacific Tourism Year — AP164

1995, Mar. 15 Litho. *Perf. 13½*
C270 AP164 90fr multicolored 3.00 1.00

35th South Pacific Conference, Noumea AP165

1995, Oct. 25 Litho. *Perf. 13*
C271 AP165 500fr multicolored 9.00 5.00

Kanak Dances — AP166

1995, Dec. 8 Litho. *Perf. 13x13½*
C272 AP166 95fr Ouaré 2.25 1.00
C273 AP166 100fr Pothé 2.50 1.00

Mekosuchus Inexpactatus AP167

1996, Feb. 23 Litho. *Perf. 13x13½*
C274 AP167 125fr multicolored 2.75 1.50

Indonesian Centenary — AP168

1996, July 20
C275 AP168 130fr multicolored 3.00 3.00

Louis Brauquier (1900-76), Writer — AP169

1996, Aug. 7 Litho. *Perf. 12½*
C276 AP169 95fr multicolored 2.25 1.10

Ile Nou Ground Station, 20th Anniv. — AP170

125fr, Guglielmo Marconi, telegraph wires.

1996, Sept. 26 Litho. *Perf. 13*
C277 AP170 95f multicolored 2.25 1.10
C278 AP170 125fr multicolored 2.75 1.50
a. Pair, #C277-C278 + label 5.00 5.00

Radio, cent. (#C278).

Regional Views AP171

1996, Nov. 7 Litho. *Perf. 13*
C279 AP171 95fr Great reef 2.25 1.10
C280 AP171 95fr Mount Koghi 2.25 1.10
a. Pair, #C279-C280 + label 4.75 4.75

50th Autumn Philatelic Salon.

Christmas — AP172

1996, Nov. 25 *Perf. 13½x13*
C281 AP172 95fr multicolored 2.25 1.10

Horned Turtle Meiolania AP173

1997, Jan. 8 Litho. *Perf. 13*
C282 AP173 95fr multicolored 2.25 1.25

Portions of the design were applied by a thermographic process producing a shiny, raised effect.

South Pacific Commission, 50th Anniv. — AP174

1997, Feb. 7 Litho. *Perf. 13X13½*
C283 AP174 100fr multicolored 2.25 1.10

Hong Kong '97 — AP175

New Year 1997 (Year of the Ox) — #C285: a, Water buffalo pulling plow. b, Cattle in pasture.

1997, Feb. 12 *Perf. 13*
C284 AP175 95fr multicolored 2.50 1.10

Sheet of 2
Perf. 13x13½
C285 AP175 75fr #a.-b. 3.50 3.25

No. C285 contains two 40x30mm stamps.

Melanesian Pottery — AP176

Lapita pottery c. 1200-1000 B.C.: No. C286, With stylized faces. No. C287, With labyrinth pattern.

1997, May 14 Litho. *Perf. 13*
C286 AP176 95fr multicolored 2.25 2.25
C287 AP176 95fr multicolored 2.25 2.25

TRAPAS, French Airlines in the South Pacific, 1947-50 AP177

Airplane, emblem, map showing: No. C288, Australia, New Herbrides, Suva, Tahiti, New Zealand. No. C289, Koumac, Poindimie, Noumea, Isle of Pines.

Photo. & Engr.
1997, Aug. 12 *Perf. 13*
C288 AP177 95fr multicolored 2.10 2.10
C289 AP177 95fr multicolored 2.10 2.10
a. Pair, #C288-C289 4.25 4.25

Regular Paris-Noumea Air Service, 50th Anniv. — AP178

1999, Sept. 29 Photo. *Perf. 13x12½*
C290 AP178 100fr multicolored 2.50 2.00

Inauguration of Noumea-Osaka Air Service — AP179

2001, Oct. 11 Litho. *Perf. 13*
C291 AP179 110fr multi 2.25 2.25

AIR POST SEMI-POSTAL STAMPS

French Revolution Issue
Common Design Type
Unwmk.
1939, July 5 Photo. *Perf. 13*
Name and Value Typo. in Orange
CB1 CD83 4.50fr + 4fr brn blk 34.00 34.00

Father & Child — SPAP1

1942, June 22 Engr. *Perf. 13*
CB2 SPAP1 1.50fr + 3.50fr green 2.25
CB3 SPAP1 2fr + 6fr yel brn 2.25

Native children's welfare fund.
Nos. CB2-CB3 were issued by the Vichy government in France, but were not placed on sale in New Caledonia.

Colonial Education Fund
Common Design Type
1942, June 22
CB4 CD86a 1.20fr + 1.80fr blue & red 2.25

No. CB4 was issued by the Vichy government in France, but was not placed on sale in New Caledonia.

POSTAGE DUE STAMPS

For a short time in 1894, 5, 10, 15, 20, 25 and 30c postage stamps (Nos. 43, 45, 47, 49, 50 and 52) were overprinted with a "T" in an inverted triangle and used as Postage Due stamps.

French Colonies Postage Due Stamps Overprinted in Carmine, Blue or Silver

1903 Unwmk. *Imperf.*
J1 D1 5c blue (C) 3.75 3.75
J2 D1 10c brown (C) 11.50 11.50
J3 D1 15c yel grn (C) 22.50 11.50
J4 D1 30c carmine (Bl) 19.00 15.00
J5 D1 50c violet (Bl) 65.00 22.50
J6 D1 60c brn, *buff* (Bl) 260.00 95.00
J7 D1 1fr rose, *buff* (S) 42.50 26.00
b. Double overprint 225.00 225.00
J8 D1 2fr red brn (Bl) 1,300. 1,300.
Nos. J1-J8 (8) 1,724. 1,485.

Nos. J1 to J8 are known with the "I" in "TENAIRE" missing.
Fifty years of French occupation.

Men Poling Boat — D2

1906 Typo. *Perf. 13½x14*
J9 D2 5c ultra .70 *.75*
J10 D2 10c vio brn, *buff* .70 *.75*
J11 D2 15c greenish blue 1.00 *1.10*
J12 D2 20c blk, *yellow* 1.00 *1.10*
J13 D2 30c carmine 1.35 *1.50*
J14 D2 50c ultra, *cream* 2.25 2.25
J15 D2 60c olive brn, *azure* 1.50 *1.90*
J16 D2 1fr blue green 2.25 *2.75*
Nos. J9-J16 (8) 10.75 *12.10*

Type of 1906 Issue Surcharged

1926-27
J17 D2 2fr on 1fr vio 5.75 *6.25*
J18 D2 3fr on 1fr org brn 5.75 *6.25*

Malayan Sambar — D3

1928 Typo.
J19 D3 2c sl bl & dp brn .30 *.40*
J20 D3 4c brn red & bl grn .45 *.60*
J21 D3 5c red org & bl blk .60 *.75*
J22 D3 10c brt rose & Prus bl .60 *.75*
J23 D3 15c dp gray grn & scar .60 *.75*
J24 D3 20c mar & ol grn 1.05 *1.10*
J25 D3 25c bis brn & sl bl .75 *.90*
J26 D3 30c bl grn & ol grn 1.05 *1.10*
J27 D3 50c lt brn & dk red 1.35 *1.50*
J28 D3 60c mag & brt rose 1.35 *1.50*
J29 D3 1fr dl bl & Prus grn 1.75 *1.90*
J30 D3 2fr dk red & ol grn 1.90 *2.25*
J31 D3 3fr violet & brn 2.75 *3.00*
Nos. J19-J31 (13) 14.50 *16.50*

Catalogue values for unused stamps in this section, from this point to the end of the section, are for Never Hinged items.

D4

1948 Unwmk. Photo. *Perf. 13*
J32 D4 10c violet .30 .30
J33 D4 30c brown .40 .40
J34 D4 50c blue green .60 .60
J35 D4 1fr orange .60 .60
J36 D4 2fr red violet .75 .75
J37 D4 3fr red brown .75 .75
J38 D4 4fr dull blue 1.10 1.10
J39 D4 5fr henna brown 1.10 1.10
J40 D4 10fr slate green 1.75 1.75
J41 D4 20fr violet blue 2.40 2.40
Nos. J32-J41 (10) 9.75 9.75

Bat — D5

1983 Litho. *Perf. 13*
J42 D5 1fr multi .30 .25
J43 D5 2fr multi .30 .30
J44 D5 3fr multi .30 .30
J45 D5 4fr multi .45 .45
J46 D5 5fr multi .55 .55
J47 D5 10fr multi .75 .75
J48 D5 20fr multi .90 .90
J49 D5 40fr multi 1.40 1.40
J50 D5 50fr multi 1.75 1.75
Nos. J42-J50 (9) 6.70 6.65

For overprint see No. 696.

MILITARY STAMPS

Stamps of the above types, although issued by officials, were unauthorized and practically a private speculation.

OFFICIAL STAMPS

Catalogue values for unused stamps in this section are for Never Hinged items.

Ancestor Pole — O1

Various carved ancestor poles.

1959 Unwmk. Typo. *Perf. 14x13*
O1 O1 1fr org yel .45 .45
O2 O1 3fr lt bl grn .45 .45
O3 O1 4fr purple .60 .60
O4 O1 5fr ultra .75 .75
O5 O1 9fr black 1.00 1.00
O6 O1 10fr brt vio 1.40 1.40
O7 O1 13fr yel grn 1.50 1.50
O8 O1 15fr lt bl 2.00 2.00
O9 O1 24fr red lilac 2.40 2.40
O10 O1 26fr deep org 2.75 2.75
O11 O1 50fr green 5.75 5.75

O12	O1	100fr chocolate	11.00	11.00
O13	O1	200fr red	20.00	20.00
		Nos. O1-O13 (13)	50.05	50.05

Carved Wooden Pillow — O2

Vignette: Green, Red Brown (2, 29, 31, 35, 38, 65, 76fr), Brown (40fr), Blue (58fr)

1973-87 Photo. *Perf. 13*

O14	O2	1fr yellow	.30	.30
O14A	O2	2fr green ('87)	.30	.25
O15	O2	3fr tan	.45	.45
O16	O2	4fr pale violet	.60	.60
O17	O2	5fr lilac rose	.60	.60
O18	O2	9fr light blue	1.00	1.00
O19	O2	10fr orange	1.10	1.10
O20	O2	11fr bright lilac ('76)	.60	.60
O21	O2	12fr bl grn ('73)	1.25	1.25
O22	O2	15fr green ('76)	.70	.70
O23	O2	20fr rose ('76)	.75	.75
O24	O2	23fr red ('80)	1.00	1.00
O25	O2	24fr Prus bl ('76)	1.00	1.00
O25A	O2	25fr gray ('81)	1.30	1.30
O26	O2	26fr yellow ('76)	1.05	1.05
O26A	O2	29fr dl grn ('83)	1.30	1.30
O26B	O2	31fr yellow ('82)	1.40	1.40
O26C	O2	35fr yellow ('84)	1.50	1.50
O27	O2	36fr dp lil rose ('76)	1.30	1.30
O27A	O2	38fr tan	1.50	1.50
O27B	O2	40fr blue ('87)	1.30	1.30
O28	O2	42fr bister ('76)	1.50	1.50
O29	O2	50fr blue ('76)	1.50	1.50
O29A	O2	58fr blue grn ('87)	1.75	1.75
O29B	O2	65fr lilac ('84)	1.90	1.90
O29C	O2	76fr brt yel ('87)	2.25	2.25
O30	O2	100fr red ('76)	2.75	2.75
O31	O2	200fr orange ('76)	5.00	5.00
		Nos. O14-O31 (28)	36.95	36.90

PARCEL POST STAMPS

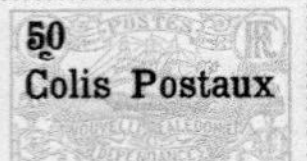

Type of Regular Issue of 1905-28 Srchd. or Ovptd.

1926 Unwmk. *Perf. 14x13½*

Q1	A18	50c on 5fr olive, *lav*	1.30	1.90
Q2	A18	1fr deep blue	1.75	2.75
Q3	A18	2fr car, *bluish*	2.10	3.00
		Nos. Q1-Q3 (3)	5.15	7.65

Regular Issue of 1928 Overprinted

1930

Q4	A20	50c violet & brown	1.30	1.90
Q5	A21	1fr dp ol & sal red	1.75	2.75
Q6	A21	2fr red org & brn	2.10	3.00
		Nos. Q4-Q6 (3)	5.15	7.65

NEW GUINEA

'nü 'gi-nē

LOCATION — On an island of the same name in the South Pacific Ocean, north of Australia.
GOVT. — Mandate administered by Australia
AREA — 93,000 sq. mi.
POP. — 675,369 (1940)
CAPITAL — Rabaul

The territory occupies the northeastern part of the island and includes New Britain and other nearby islands. It was formerly a German possession and should not be confused with British New Guinea (Papua) which is in the southeastern part of the same island, nor Netherlands New Guinea. For previous issues see German New Guinea, New Britain, North West Pacific Islands. Issues for 1952 and later are listed under Papua.

12 Pence = 1 Shilling
20 Shillings = 1 Pound

Native Huts — A1

1925-28 Engr. Unwmk. *Perf. 11*

1	A1	½p orange	2.75	8.00
2	A1	1p yellow green	2.75	6.25
3	A1	1½p vermilion ('26)	3.75	3.00
4	A1	2p claret	7.25	5.00
5	A1	3p deep blue	8.00	4.50
6	A1	4p olive green	15.00	26.00
7	A1	6p yel bister ('28)	6.50	55.00
a.		6p light brown	22.50	55.00
b.		6p olive bister ('27)	15.00	52.50
8	A1	9p deep violet	15.00	50.00
9	A1	1sh gray green	17.50	30.00
10	A1	2sh red brown	35.00	55.00
11	A1	5sh olive bister	55.00	75.00
12	A1	10sh dull rose	120.00	200.00
13	A1	£1 grnsh gray	210.00	325.00
		Nos. 1-13 (13)	498.50	842.75

For overprints see Nos. C1-C13, O1-O9.

Bird of Paradise — A2

1931, Aug. 2

18	A2	1p light green	4.50	7.50
19	A2	1½p red	5.75	11.50
20	A2	2p violet brown	5.75	2.50
21	A2	3p deep blue	5.75	5.50
22	A2	4p olive green	7.50	32.50
23	A2	5p slate green	9.00	24.00
24	A2	6p bister	8.00	25.00
25	A2	9p dull violet	9.50	21.00
26	A2	1sh bluish gray	7.00	17.00
27	A2	2sh red brown	11.50	50.00
28	A2	5sh olive brown	47.50	62.50
29	A2	10sh rose red	120.00	150.00
30	A2	£1 gray	250.00	300.00
		Nos. 18-30 (13)	491.75	709.00

10th anniversary of Australian Mandate.
For overprints see #C14-C27, O12-O22.

Type of 1931 without date scrolls

A2a

1932-34 *Perf. 11*

31	A2a	1p light green	8.00	.25
32	A2a	1½p violet brown	8.00	20.00
33	A2a	2p red	5.50	.25
34	A2a	2½p dp grn ('34)	7.50	27.50
35	A2a	3p gray blue	8.00	1.25
36	A2a	3½p magenta ('34)	15.00	22.50
37	A2a	4p olive green	7.00	7.00
38	A2a	5p slate green	7.25	.80
39	A2a	6p bister	7.50	5.50
40	A2a	9p dull violet	11.00	27.50
41	A2a	1sh bluish gray	7.00	11.50
42	A2a	2sh brown lake	5.00	19.00
43	A2a	5sh olive brown	32.50	50.00
44	A2a	10sh rose red	60.00	80.00
45	A2a	£1 gray	120.00	110.00
		Nos. 31-45 (15)	309.25	383.05

For overprints see #46-47, C28-C43, O23-O35. See footnote following C43.

Silver Jubilee Issue

Stamps of 1932-34 Overprinted

1935, June 27 Glazed Paper

46	A2	1p green	1.10	.85
47	A2	2p red	3.25	.85
		Set, never hinged	6.50	

King George VI — A3

1937, May 18 Engr.

48	A3	2p salmon rose	.30	1.60
49	A3	3p blue	.30	1.90
50	A3	5p green	.35	1.90
51	A3	1sh brown violet	.45	2.50
		Nos. 48-51 (4)	1.40	7.90
		Set, never hinged	2.50	

Coronation of George VI and Queen Elizabeth.

AIR POST STAMPS

Regular Issues of 1925-28 Overprinted

1931, June *Perf. 11*

C1	A1	½p orange	1.75	9.50
C2	A1	1p yellow green	1.75	5.75
C3	A1	1½p vermilion	1.40	8.50
C4	A1	2p claret	1.40	8.00
C5	A1	3p deep blue	2.00	15.00
C6	A1	4p olive green	1.40	10.00
C7	A1	6p light brown	2.00	16.00
C8	A1	9p deep violet	3.50	19.00
C9	A1	1sh gray green	3.50	19.00
C10	A1	2sh red brown	8.00	50.00
C11	A1	5sh ol bister	22.50	75.00
C12	A1	10sh light red	92.50	120.00
C13	A1	£1 grnsh gray	170.00	290.00
		Nos. C1-C13 (13)	311.70	645.75

Type of Regular Issue of 1931 (Nos. 18-30) Overprinted

1931, Aug.

C14	A2	½p orange	3.75	3.75
C15	A2	1p light green	4.50	7.50
C16	A2	1½p red	4.25	11.50
C17	A2	2p violet brown	4.25	3.50
C18	A2	3p deep blue	7.00	7.00
C19	A2	4p olive green	7.00	7.00
C20	A2	5p slate green	7.00	12.50
C21	A2	6p bister	8.00	30.00
C22	A2	9p dull violet	9.00	17.00
C23	A2	1sh bluish gray	8.50	17.00
C24	A2	2sh red brown	18.00	55.00
C25	A2	5sh olive brown	47.50	80.00
C26	A2	10sh rose red	87.50	140.00
C27	A2	£1 gray	150.00	290.00
		Nos. C14-C27 (14)	366.25	681.75

10th anniversary of Australian Mandate.

Same Overprint on Type of Regular Issue of 1932-34 (Nos. 31-45)

1932-34 *Perf. 11*

C28	A2	½p orange	.65	1.75
C29	A2	1p light green	1.40	2.50
C30	A2	1½p violet brown	2.00	11.50
C31	A2	2p red	2.00	.35
C32	A2	2½p dp grn ('34)	8.75	2.75
C33	A2	3p gray blue	3.75	3.50
C34	A2	3½p mag ('34)	5.25	3.75
C35	A2	4p olive green	5.00	11.50
C36	A2	5p slate green	8.00	8.50
C37	A2	6p bister	5.00	17.00
C38	A2	9p dull violet	7.00	10.00
C39	A2	1sh bluish gray	7.00	12.50
C40	A2	2sh red brown	14.00	55.00
C41	A2	5sh olive brown	55.00	65.00
C42	A2	10sh rose red	100.00	92.50
C43	A2	£1 gray	87.50	62.50
		Nos. C28-C43 (16)	312.30	360.60

No. C28 exists without overprint, but is believed not to have been issued in this condition. Value $200.

Plane over Bulolo Goldfield — AP1

1935, May 1 Engr. Unwmk.

C44	AP1	£2 violet	350.00	160.00
C45	AP1	£5 green	750.00	550.00

AP2

1939, Mar. 1

C46	AP2	½p orange	2.50	9.25
C47	AP2	1p green	2.00	5.00
C48	AP2	1½p vio brown	2.50	19.00
C49	AP2	2p red orange	5.00	4.00
C50	AP2	3p dark blue	11.00	21.00
C51	AP2	4p ol bister	9.00	9.75
C52	AP2	5p slate grn	8.50	4.50
C53	AP2	6p bister brn	25.00	30.00
C54	AP2	9p dl violet	27.50	45.00
C55	AP2	1sh sage grn	27.50	32.50
C56	AP2	2sh car lake	50.00	75.00
C57	AP2	5sh ol brown	110.00	160.00
C58	AP2	10sh rose red	350.00	425.00
C59	AP2	£1 grnsh gray	90.00	150.00
		Nos. C46-C59 (14)	720.50	990.00
		Set, never hinged	1,200.	

OFFICIAL STAMPS

Regular Issue of 1925 Overprinted

1925-29 Unwmk. *Perf. 11*

O1	A1	1p yellow green	5.00	5.00
O2	A1	1½p vermilion ('29)	6.25	19.00
O3	A1	2p claret	3.25	4.25
O4	A1	3p deep blue	6.00	10.00
O5	A1	4p olive green	5.00	9.75
O6	A1	6p yel bister ('29)	8.00	40.00
a.		6p olive bister	29.00	40.00
O7	A1	9p deep violet	4.50	40.00
O8	A1	1sh gray green	6.25	40.00
O9	A1	2sh red brown	42.50	70.00
		Nos. O1-O9 (9)	86.75	238.00

Nos. 18-28 Overprinted

1931, Aug. 2

O12	A2	1p light green	12.00	14.00
O13	A2	1½p red	12.00	13.50
O14	A2	2p violet brown	12.00	8.00
O15	A2	3p deep blue	7.50	7.00
O16	A2	4p olive green	7.00	9.75
O17	A2	5p slate green	11.50	13.50
O18	A2	6p bister	16.00	19.00
O19	A2	9p dull violet	18.00	32.50
O20	A2	1sh bluish gray	18.00	32.50
O21	A2	2sh red brown	45.00	80.00
O22	A2	5sh olive brown	110.00	200.00
		Nos. O12-O22 (11)	269.00	429.75

10th anniversary of Australian Mandate.

Same Overprint on Nos. 31-43

1932-34

O23	A2	1p light green	19.00	20.00
O24	A2	1½p violet brown	19.00	20.00
O25	A2	2p red	19.50	3.75
O26	A2	2½p dp green ('34)	10.00	12.50
O27	A2	3p gray blue	11.50	42.50
O28	A2	3½p magenta ('34)	8.00	10.00
O29	A2	4p olive green	21.00	32.50
O30	A2	5p slate green	10.00	30.00
O31	A2	6p bister	25.00	55.00
O32	A2	9p dull violet	16.00	50.00
O33	A2	1sh bluish gray	17.50	32.50
O34	A2	2sh red brown	40.00	85.00
O35	A2	5sh olive brown	140.00	190.00
		Nos. O23-O35 (13)	356.50	583.75

NEW HEBRIDES, BRITISH

'nü 'he-brə-ˌdēz

LOCATION — A group of islands in the South Pacific Ocean northeast of New Caledonia
GOVT. — Condominium under the joint administration of Great Britain and France
AREA — 5,790 sq. mi.
POP. — 100,000 (est. 1976)
CAPITAL — Vila (Port-Vila)

Stamps were issued by both Great Britain and France. In 1911 a joint issue bore the coats of arms of both countries. The British stamps bore the arms of Great Britain and the value in British currency on the right and the French arms and value at the left. On the French stamps the positions were reversed. After World War II when the franc dropped in value, both series were sold for their value in francs.

New Hebrides became the independent state of Vanuatu in 1980.

12 Pence = 1 Shilling
100 Centimes = 1 Franc
100 Centimes = 1 Hebrides Franc (FNH) (1977)

French issues (inscribed "Nouvelles Hebrides") follow after No. J20.

Catalogue values for unused stamps in this country are for Never Hinged items, beginning with Scott 62 in the regular postage section, Scott J11 in the postage due section.

British Issues

Stamps of Fiji, 1903- 06, Overprinted

1908-09 Wmk. 2 *Perf. 14*
Colored Bar Covers "FIJI" on #2-6, 9

1 A22 ½p grn & pale grn ('09) 60.00 *87.50*
2 A22 2p vio & orange 1.50 *1.75*
3 A22 2½p vio & ultra, *bl* 1.50 *1.75*
4 A22 5p vio & green 1.60 *3.25*
5 A22 6p vio & car rose 3.75 *3.50*
6 A22 1sh grn & car rose 145.00 *300.00*
Nos. 1-6 (6) 213.35 *397.75*

Wmk. Multiple Crown and CA (3)

7 A22 ½p gray green 1.00 *5.00*
8 A22 1p carmine .80 *1.00*
a. Pair, one without overprint *10,000.*
9 A22 1sh grn & car rose ('09) 25.00 *4.25*
Nos. 7-9 (3) 26.80 *10.25*

Nos. 2-6, 9 are on chalk-surfaced paper.

Stamps of Fiji, 1904- 11, Overprinted in Black or Red

1910, Dec. 15

10 A22 ½p green 3.50 *25.00*
11 A22 1p carmine 11.00 *8.50*
12 A22 2p gray 1.00 *3.00*
13 A22 2½p ultra 1.10 *6.00*
14 A22 5p violet & ol grn 2.25 *5.50*
15 A22 6p violet 2.50 *7.50*
16 A22 1sh black, *grn* (R) 3.00 *7.50*
Nos. 10-16 (7) 24.35 *63.00*

Nos. 14-16 are on chalk-surfaced paper.

Native Idols — A1

1911, July 25 Engr. Wmk. 3

17 A1 ½p pale green 1.00 *1.75*
18 A1 1p red 4.00 2.00
19 A1 2p gray 7.00 3.00
20 A1 2½p ultramarine 4.75 *5.75*
21 A1 5p olive green 4.50 *6.00*
22 A1 6p claret 3.00 *5.00*
23 A1 1sh black, *green* 2.75 *12.00*
24 A1 2sh violet, *blue* 22.50 *20.00*
25 A1 5sh green, *yel* 32.50 *50.00*
Nos. 17-25 (9) 82.00 *105.50*

See Nos. 33-37. For surcharges see Nos. 26-29, 38-39, French Issues No. 36.

Surcharged

1920-21

26 A1 1p on 5p ol grn ('21) 10.00 *60.00*
a. Inverted surcharge 4,500.
27 A1 1p on 1sh blk, *grn* 4.00 *13.00*
28 A1 1p on 2sh vio, *blue* 1.50 *10.00*
29 A1 1p on 5sh grn, *yel* 1.25 *10.00*

On French Issue No. 16

30 A2 2p on 40c red, *yel* ('21) 2.00 *22.00*
Nos. 26-30 (5) 18.75 *115.00*

French Issue No. 27

Wmk. R F in Sheet

31 A2 2p on 40c red, *yel* ('21) 125.00 *700.00*

The letters "R.F." are the initials of "Republique Francaise." They are large double-lined Roman capitals, about 120mm high. About one-fourth of the stamps in each sheet show portions of the watermark, the other stamps are without watermark.

No. 26a is considered by some to be printers' waste.

Type of 1911 Issue

1921, Oct. Wmk. 4

33 A1 1p rose red 2.50 *14.50*
34 A1 2p gray 4.00 *45.00*
37 A1 6p claret 14.00 *80.00*
Nos. 33-37 (3) 20.50 *139.50*

For surcharge see No. 40.

Stamps of 1911-21 Surcharged with New Values as in 1920-21

1924, May 1 Wmk. 3

38 A1 1p on ½p pale green 4.00 *22.50*
39 A1 5p on 2½p ultra 7.50 *27.50*
a. Inverted surcharge 3,500.

Wmk. 4

40 A1 3p on 1p rose red 4.50 *10.00*
Nos. 38-40 (3) 16.00 *60.00*

No. 39a is considered by some to be printers' waste.

A3

The values at the lower right denote the currency and amount for which the stamps were to be sold. The English stamps could be bought at the French post office in French money.

1925 Engr.

41 A3 ½p (5c) black 1.25 *20.00*
42 A3 1p (10c) green 1.00 *17.50*
43 A3 2p (20c) grnsh gray 1.75 *2.75*
44 A3 2½p (25c) brown 1.00 *14.00*
45 A3 5p (50c) ultra 3.25 *2.75*
46 A3 6p (60c) claret 4.00 *15.00*
47 A3 1sh (1.25fr) blk, *grn* 3.50 *18.00*
48 A3 2sh (2.50fr) vio, *bl* 6.25 *20.00*
49 A3 5sh (6.25fr) grn, *yel* 6.25 *27.50*
Nos. 41-49 (9) 28.25 *137.50*

Beach Scene — A5

1938, June 1 Wmk. 4 *Perf. 12*

50 A5 5c green 1.75 *4.00*
51 A5 10c dark orange 2.00 *2.00*
52 A5 15c violet 2.50 *3.00*
53 A5 20c rose red 2.75 *3.25*
54 A5 25c brown 1.50 *2.75*
55 A5 30c dark blue 3.00 2.50
56 A5 40c olive green 3.25 *5.50*
57 A5 50c brown vio 1.25 *1.50*
58 A5 1fr car, *emerald* 6.50 *9.00*
59 A5 2fr dk blue, *emer* 22.50 22.50
60 A5 5fr red, *yellow* 40.00 50.00
61 A5 10fr violet, *blue* 125.00 80.00
Nos. 50-61 (12) 212.00 186.00
Set, never hinged 300.00

Catalogue values for unused stamps in this section, from this point to the end of the section, are for Never Hinged items.

Common Design Types pictured following the introduction.

UPU Issue

Common Design Type

1949, Oct. 10 Engr. *Perf. 13½*

62 CD309 10c red orange .35 *.90*
63 CD309 15c violet .35 *1.00*
64 CD309 30c violet blue .40 *1.10*
65 CD309 50c brown violet .50 *1.25*
Nos. 62-65 (4) 1.60 *4.25*

Outrigger Canoes with Sails — A6

Designs: 25c, 30c, 40c and 50c, Native Carving. 1fr, 2fr and 5fr, Island couple.

1953, Apr. 30 *Perf. 12½*

66 A6 5c green 1.00 *1.25*
67 A6 10c red 1.10 .35
68 A6 15c yellow 1.10 .25
69 A6 20c ultramarine 1.10 .25
70 A6 25c olive .90 .25
71 A6 30c light brown .90 .25
72 A6 40c black brown 1.10 .40
73 A6 50c violet 1.40 .50
74 A6 1fr deep orange 5.75 1.75
75 A6 2fr red violet 6.00 *9.00*
76 A6 5fr scarlet 9.00 *22.50*
Nos. 66-76 (11) 29.35 *36.75*

Coronation Issue

Common Design Type

1953, June 2 *Perf. 13½x13*

77 CD312 10c car & black .75 .60

Discovery of New Hebrides, 1606 — A7

20c, 50c, Britannia, Marianne, Flags & Mask.

Perf. 14½x14

1956, Oct. 20 Photo. Wmk. 4

78 A7 5c emerald .25 .25
79 A7 10c scarlet .25 .25
80 A7 20c dp ultra .25 .25
81 A7 50c redsh pur .25 .25
Nos. 78-81 (4) 1.00 1.00

50th anniv. of the establishment of the Anglo-French Condominium.

Port Vila and Iririki Islet — A8

Designs: 25c, 30c, 40c, 50c, Tropical river and spear fisherman. 1fr, 2fr, 5fr, Woman drinking from coconut (inscribed: "Franco-British Alliance 4th March 1947").

1957, Sept. 3 Engr. *Perf. 13½x13*

82 A8 5c green .45 *1.00*
83 A8 10c red .40 .25
84 A8 15c orange yellow .55 *1.00*
85 A8 20c ultramarine .45 .25
86 A8 25c olive .50 .25
87 A8 30c light brown .50 .25
88 A8 40c sepia .50 .25
89 A8 50c violet .75 .25
90 A8 1fr orange 1.10 1.10
91 A8 2fr rose lilac 4.50 2.75
92 A8 5fr black 10.00 5.50
Nos. 82-92 (11) 19.70 12.85

Freedom from Hunger Issue

Common Design Type

Perf. 14x14½

1963, Sept. 2 Photo. Wmk. 314

93 CD314 60c green .60 .25

Red Cross Centenary Issue

Common Design Type with Royal Cipher and "RF" Replacing Queen's Portrait

1963, Sept. 2 Litho. *Perf. 13*

94 CD315 15c black & red .40 .25
95 CD315 45c ultra & red .60 .25

Copra Industry — A9

Designs: 5c, Manganese loading, Forari Wharf. 10c, Cacao. 20c, Map of New Hebrides, tuna, marlin, ships. 25c, Striped triggerfish. 30c, Pearly nautilus (mollusk). 40c, 60c, Turkeyfish. 50c, Lined tang (fish). 1fr, Cardinal honey-eater and hibiscus. 2fr, Buff-bellied flycatcher. 3fr, Thicket warbler. 5fr, White-collared kingfisher.

Wmk. 314 (10c, 20c, 40c, 60c, 3fr); Unwmkd. (others)
Perf. 12½ (10c, 20c, 40c, 60c); 14 (3fr); 13 (others)
Photo. (10c, 20c, 40c, 60c, 3fr); Engraved (others)

1963-67

96 A9 5c Prus bl, pur brn & cl ('66) 1.75 .50
a. 5c prus blue & claret ('72) 45.00 37.50
97 A9 10c brt grn, org brn & dk brn ('65) .25 .25
98 A9 15c dk pur, yel & brn .25 .25
99 A9 20c brt blue, gray & cit ('65) .55 .25
100 A9 25c vio, rose lil & org brn ('66) .75 .50
101 A9 30c lilac, brn & cit 1.00 .75
102 A9 40c dk bl & ver ('65) 1.25 1.50
103 A9 50c Prus bl, yel & green 1.10 .80
103A A9 60c dk bl & ver ('67) 1.00 .50
104 A9 1fr blue grn, blk & red ('66) 3.00 3.50
105 A9 2fr ol, blk & brn 4.00 2.00
106 A9 3fr org grn, brt grn & blk ('65) 10.00 7.00
107 A9 5fr indigo, dp bl & gray ('67) 15.00 *20.00*
Nos. 96-107 (13) 39.90 37.80

For surcharge see No. 141.

ITU Emblem CD317

Perf. 11x11½

1965, May 17 Litho. Wmk. 314

108 CD317 15c ver & ol bister .25 .25
109 CD317 60c ultra & ver .40 .25

Intl. Cooperation Year Issue

Common Design Type with Royal Cipher and "RF" Replacing Queen's Portrait

1965, Sept. 24 *Perf. 14½*

110 CD318 5c blue grn & claret .25 .25
111 CD318 55c lt violet & green .25 .25

Churchill Memorial Issue

Common Design Type with Royal Cipher and "RF" Replacing Queen's Portrait

1966, Jan. 24 Photo. *Perf. 14*

112 CD319 5c multicolored .30 .25
113 CD319 15c multicolored .50 .25
114 CD319 25c multicolored .75 .25
115 CD319 30c multicolored .75 .25
Nos. 112-115 (4) 2.30 1.00

World Cup Soccer Issue

Common Design Type with Royal Cipher and "RF" Replacing Queen's Portrait

1966, July 1 Litho. *Perf. 14*

116 CD321 20c multicolored .30 .30
117 CD321 40c multicolored .70 .70

WHO Headquarters Issue

Common Design Type with Royal Cipher and "RF" Replacing Queen's Portrait

1966, Sept. 20 Litho. *Perf. 14*

118 CD322 25c multicolored .25 .25
119 CD322 60c multicolored .50 .25

UNESCO Anniversary Issue

Common Design Type with Royal Cipher and "RF" Replacing Queen's Portrait

1966, Dec. 1 Litho. *Perf. 14*

120 CD323 15c "Education" .35 .35
121 CD323 30c "Science" .60 .60
122 CD323 45c "Culture" .95 .95
Nos. 120-122 (3) 1.90 1.90

Coast Watchers A11

25c, Map of South Pacific war zone, US Marine and Australian soldier. 60c, Australian cruiser Canberra. 1fr, Flying fortress taking off from Bauer Field, & view of Vila.

Perf. 14x13

1967, Sept. 26 Photo. Wmk. 314

123 A11 15c lt blue & multi .25 .25
124 A11 25c yellow & multi .30 .30
125 A11 60c multicolored .75 .75
126 A11 1fr pale salmon & multi 1.00 1.00
Nos. 123-126 (4) 2.30 2.30

25th anniv. of the Allied Forces' campaign in the South Pacific War Zone.

Globe and World Map — A12

Designs: 25c, Ships La Boudeuse and L'Etoile and map of Bougainville Strait. 60c, Louis Antoine de Bougainville, ship's figurehead and bougainvillaea.

1968, May 23 Engr. *Perf. 13*

127 A12 15c ver, emer & dull vio .25 .25
128 A12 25c ultra, olive & brn .25 .25
129 A12 60c magenta, grn & brn .30 .25
Nos. 127-129 (3) .80 .75

200th anniv. of Louis Antoine de Bougainville's (1729-1811) voyage around the world.

Concorde Airliner — A13

Design: 60c, Concorde, sideview.

1968, Oct. 9 Litho. *Perf. 14x13½*

130 A13 25c vio bl, red & lt bl .30 .25
131 A13 60c red, ultra & black .60 .50

Development of the Concorde supersonic airliner, a joint Anglo-French project to produce a high speed plane.

Kauri Pine — A14

Perf. 14x14½

1969, June 30 Wmk. 314

132 A14 20c brown & multi .30 .30

New Hebrides timber industry. Issued in sheets of 9 (3x3) on simulated wood grain background.

Relay Race, French and British Flags — A15

Design: 1fr, Runner at right.

Perf. 12½x13

1969, Aug. 13 Photo. Unwmk.

133 A15 25c ultra, car, brn & gold .25 .25
134 A15 1fr brn, car, ultra & gold .25 .25

3rd South Pacific Games, Port Moresby, Papua and New Guinea, Aug. 13-23.

Land Diver, Pentecost Island — A16

Designs: 15c, Diver in starting position on tower. 1fr, Diver nearing ground.

Wmk. 314

1969, Oct. 15 Litho. *Perf. 12½*

135 A16 15c yellow & multi .25 .25
136 A16 25c pink & multi .25 .25
137 A16 1fr gray & multi .25 .25
Nos. 135-137 (3) .75 .75

UPU Headquarters and Monument, Bern — A17

Unwmk.

1970, May 20 Engr. *Perf. 13*

138 A17 1.05fr org, lilac & slate .30 .30

Opening of the new UPU Headquarters, Bern.

Charles de Gaulle — A18

1970, July 20 Photo. *Perf. 13*

139 A18 65c brown & multi .25 .25
140 A18 1.10fr dp blue & multi .75 .75

30th anniv. of the rallying to the Free French.
For overprints see Nos. 144-145.

No. 99 Surcharged

1970, Oct. 15 Wmk. 314 *Perf. 12½*

141 A9 35c on 20c multi .30 .30

Virgin and Child, by Giovanni Bellini — A19

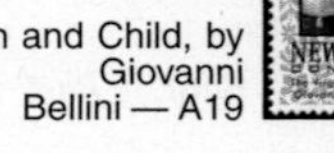

Christmas: 50c, Virgin and Child, by Giovanni Cima.

Perf. 14½x14

1970, Nov. 30 Litho. Wmk. 314

142 A19 15c tan & multi .25 .25
143 A19 50c lt green & multi .25 .25

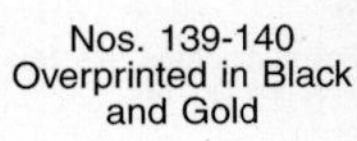

Nos. 139-140 Overprinted in Black and Gold

Unwmk.

1971, Jan. 19 Photo. *Perf. 13*

144 A18 65c brown & multi .25 .25
145 A18 1.10fr dp blue & multi .35 .35

In memory of Gen. Charles de Gaulle (1890-1970), President of France.

Soccer A20

Design: 65c, Basketball, vert.

1971, July 13 Photo. *Perf. 12½*

146 A20 20c multicolored .25 .25
147 A20 65c multicolored .25 .25

4th South Pacific Games, Papeete, French Polynesia, Sept. 8-19.

Kauri Pine, Cone and Arms of Royal Society — A21

Perf. 14½x14

1971, Sept. 7 Litho. Wmk. 314

148 A21 65c multicolored .30 .30

Royal Society of London for the Advancement of Science expedition to study vegetation and fauna, July 1-October.

Adoration of the Shepherds, by Louis Le Nain — A22

Design: 50c, Adoration of the Shepherds, by Jacopo Tintoretto.

1971, Nov. 23 *Perf. 14x13½*

149 A22 25c lt green & multi .25 .25
150 A22 50c lt blue & multi .25 .25

Christmas. See Nos. 167-168.

Drover Mk III — A23

Airplanes: 25c, Sandringham seaplane. 30c, Dragon Rapide. 65c, Caravelle.

Perf. 13½x13

1972, Feb. 29 Photo. Unwmk.

151 A23 20c lt green & multi .25 .25
152 A23 25c ultra & multi .25 .25
153 A23 30c orange & multi .45 .45
154 A23 65c dk blue & multi .90 .90
Nos. 151-154 (4) 1.85 1.85

Headdress, South Malekula A24

Baker's Pigeon A25

Artifacts: 15c, Slit gong and carved figure, North Ambrym. 1fr, Carved figures, North Ambrym. 3fr, Ceremonial headdress, South Malekula.

Birds: 20c, Red-headed parrot-finch. 35c, Chestnut-bellied kingfisher. 2fr, Green palm lorikeet.

Sea shells: 25c, Cribraria fischeri. 30c, Oliva rubrolabiata. 65c, Strombus plicatus. 5fr, Turbo marmoratus.

1972, July 24 Photo. *Perf. 12½x13*

155 A24 5c plum & multi .25 .25
156 A25 10c blue & multi .25 .25
157 A24 15c red & multi .30 .40
158 A25 20c org brown & multi .35 .50
159 A24 25c dp blue & multi .50 .80
160 A24 30c dk green & multi .65 .85
161 A25 35c gray bl & multi .70 1.10
162 A24 65c dk green & multi 1.25 3.75
163 A24 1fr orange & multi 2.00 3.00
164 A25 2fr multicolored 4.50 4.50
165 A24 3fr yellow & multi 5.75 6.75
166 A24 5fr pink & multi 9.00 13.50
Nos. 155-166 (12) 25.50 35.65

For overprints and surcharges see #181-182, 217-228.

Christmas Type of 1971

Designs: 25c, Adoration of the Magi (detail), by Bartholomaeus Spranger. 70c, Virgin and Child, by Jan Provoost.

Perf. 14x13½

1972, Sept. 25 Litho. Wmk. 314

167 A22 25c lt green & multi .25 .25
168 A22 70c lt blue & multi .25 .25

Silver Wedding Issue, 1972

Common Design Type

Design: Elizabeth II and Prince Philip.

1972, Nov. 20 Photo. *Perf. 14x14½*

169 CD324 35c vio black & multi .25 .25
170 CD324 65c olive & multi .25 .25

Dendrobium Teretifolium — A26

Orchids: 30c, Ephemerantha comata. 35c, Spathoglottis petri. 65c, Dendrobium mohlianum.

1973, Feb. 26 Litho. *Perf. 14*

171 A26 25c blue vio & multi .40 .25
172 A26 30c multicolored .60 .35
173 A26 35c violet & multi .75 .45
174 A26 65c dk green & multi 1.25 .60
Nos. 171-174 (4) 3.00 1.65

New Wharf, Vila — A27

Design: 70c, New wharf, horiz.

1973, May 14 Wmk. 314

175 A27 25c multicolored .25 .25
176 A27 70c multicolored .30 .30

New wharf at Vila, finished Nov. 1972.

Wild Horses, Tanna Island — A28

70c, Yasur Volcano, Tanna.

Perf. 13x12½

1973, Aug. 13 Photo. Unwmk.

177	A28	35c shown	.45	.45
178	A28	70c multicolored	1.25	.90

Mother and Child, by Marcel Moutouh — A29

Christmas: 70c, Star over Lagoon, by Tatin d'Avesnieres.

Perf. 14x13½

1973, Nov. 19 Litho. Wmk. 314

179	A29	35c tan & multi	.25	.25
180	A29	70c lilac rose & multi	.25	.25

Nos. 161 and 164 Overprinted in Red or Black

Perf. 12½x13

1974, Feb. 11 Photo. Unwmk.

181	A25	35c multicolored (R)	.35	.25
182	A25	2fr multicolored (B)	.75	.60

Visit of British Royal Family, Feb. 11-12.

Pacific Dove — A30

Designs: 35c, Night swallowtail. 70c, Green sea turtle. 1.15fr, Flying fox.

1974, Feb. 11 *Perf. 13x12½*

183	A30	25c gray & multi	.75	.25
184	A30	35c gray & multi	1.10	.30
185	A30	70c gray & multi	1.90	1.00
186	A30	1.15fr gray & multi	3.25	1.75
		Nos. 183-186 (4)	7.00	3.30

Nature conservation.

Old Post Office, Vila — A31

Design: 70c, New Post Office.

1974, May 6 Unwmk. *Perf. 12*

187	A31	35c blue & multi	.25	.25
188	A31	70c red & multi	.25	.25
a.		Pair, #187-188	.50	.50

Opening of New Post Office, May, 1974.

Capt. Cook and Tanna Island — A32

#190, William Wales, & boat landing on island. #191, William Hodges painting islanders & landscape. 1.15fr, Capt. Cook, "Resolution" & map of New Hebrides.

Wmk. 314

1974, Aug. 1 Litho. *Perf. 13*

Size: 40x25mm

189	A32	35c multicolored	1.50	1.00
190	A32	35c multicolored	1.50	1.00
191	A32	35c multicolored	1.50	1.00
a.		Strip of 3, #189-191	4.75	*5.50*

Perf. 11

Size: 58x34mm

192	A32	1.15fr lilac & multi	3.00	3.00
		Nos. 189-192 (4)	7.50	6.00

Bicentenary of the discovery of the New Hebrides by Capt. Cook. No. 191a has continuous design.

Exchange of Letters, UPU Emblem — A33

Perf. 13x12½

1974, Oct. 9 Photo. Unwmk.

193	A33	70c multicolored	.30	.30

Centenary of Universal Postal Union.

Nativity, by Gerard van Honthorst A34

Christmas: 35c, Adoration of the Kings, by Velazquez, vert.

Wmk. 314

1974, Nov. 14 Litho. *Perf. 13½*

194	A34	35c multicolored	.25	.25
195	A34	70c multicolored	.25	.25

Charolais Bull — A35

1975, Apr. 29 Engr. *Perf. 13*

196	A35	10fr multicolored	10.00	*20.00*

For surcharge see No. 229.

A36

1975, Aug. 5 Litho. *Perf. 14x13½*

197	A36	25c Kayak race	.25	.25
198	A36	35c Camp cooks	.25	.25
199	A36	1fr Map makers	.65	.65
200	A36	5fr Fishermen	4.50	4.50
		Nos. 197-200 (4)	5.65	5.65

Nordjamb 75, 14th Boy Scout Jamboree, Lillehammer, Norway, July 29-Aug. 7.

A37

Christmas (After Michelangelo): 35c, Pitti Madonna. 70c, Bruges Madonna. 2.50fr, Taddei Madonna.

Perf. 14½x14

1975, Nov. 11 Litho. Wmk. 373

201	A37	35c ol green & multi	.25	.25
202	A37	70c brown & multi	.45	.45
203	A37	2.50fr blue & multi	1.40	1.40
		Nos. 201-203 (3)	2.10	2.10

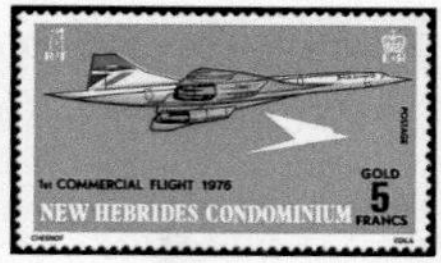

Concorde, British Airways Colors and Emblem A38

Unwmk.

1976, Jan. 30 Typo. *Perf. 13*

204	A38	5fr blue & multi	7.50	7.50

First commercial flight of supersonic jet Concorde from London to Bahrain, Jan. 21.

Telephones, 1876 and 1976 — A39

Designs: 70c, Alexander Graham Bell. 1.15fr, Nouméa earth station and satellite.

1976, Mar. 31 Photo. *Perf. 13*

205	A39	25c black, car & blue	.30	.30
206	A39	70c black & multi	.40	.40
207	A39	1.15fr black, org & vio bl	1.00	1.00
		Nos. 205-207 (3)	1.70	1.70

Centenary of first telephone call by Alexander Graham Bell, Mar. 10, 1876.

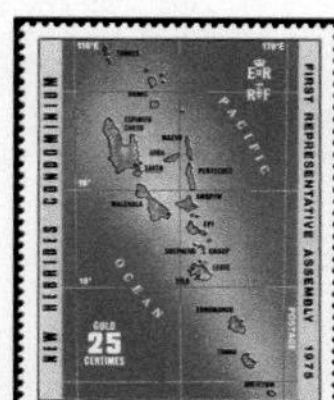

Map of New Hebrides — A40

View of Santo — A41

Design: 2fr, View of Vila.

1976, June 29 Photo. *Perf. 13*

208	A40	25c blue & multi	.30	.30
209	A41	1fr multicolored	.70	.70
210	A41	2fr multicolored	1.50	1.50
		Nos. 208-210 (3)	2.50	2.50

Opening of First Representative Assembly, June 29 (25c); first Santo Municipal Council (1fr); first Vila Municipal Council (2fr).

See Nos. 263-264 for types of design A40 surcharged.

Flight into Egypt, by Francisco Vieira Lusitano — A42

Christmas (Portuguese 16th Cent. Paintings): 70c, Adoration of the Shepherds. 2.50fr, Adoration of the Kings.

Wmk. 373

1976, Nov. 8 Litho. *Perf. 14*

211	A42	35c purple & multi	.25	.25
212	A42	70c blue & multi	.25	.25
213	A42	2.50fr lt green & multi	.60	.60
		Nos. 211-213 (3)	1.10	1.10

Queen's Visit, 1974 — A43

70c, Imperial state crown. 2fr, The blessing.

1977, Feb. 7 *Perf. 14x13½*

214	A43	35c lt green & multi	.25	.25
215	A43	70c blue & multi	.25	.25
216	A43	2fr pink & multi	.25	.25
		Nos. 214-216 (3)	.75	.75

25th anniv. of the reign of Elizabeth II.

Nos. 155-166, 196 Surcharged

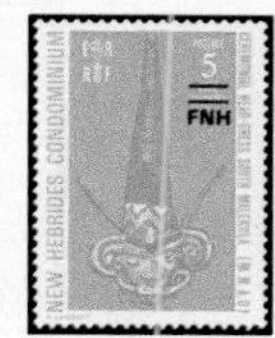

Paris Overprints

Perf. 12½x13

1977, July 1 Photo. Unwmk.

217	A24	5fr on 5c multi	.50	*.60*
218	A25	10fr on 10c multi	.80	.40
219	A24	15fr on 15c multi	.65	*1.75*
220	A25	20fr on 20c multi	1.30	.60
221	A24	25fr on 25c multi	1.75	2.00
222	A24	30fr on 30c multi	1.75	1.25
223	A25	35fr on 35c multi	1.75	1.50
224	A24	40fr on 65c multi	1.50	1.50
225	A24	50fr on 1fr multi	1.10	2.00
226	A25	70fr on 2fr multi	6.75	1.00
227	A24	100fr on 3fr multi	1.20	*4.00*
228	A24	200fr on 5fr multi	5.50	*14.00*

Wmk. 314

Engr. *Perf. 13*

229	A35	500fr on 10fr multi	15.00	17.50
		Nos. 217-229 (13)	39.55	48.10

Nos. 155//166, 196 Surcharged with New Value, "FNH" and Bars

FNH a — FNH b — FNH c — 25 FNH d

Port Vila Overprints

Two settings of 35fr and 200fr surcharges: type 1, 1.4mm between new value and "FNH"; type 2, 2.1mm between value and "FNH."

Perf. 12½x13

1977-78 Photo. Unwmk.

217a A24 5fr on 5c (a) .60 .25
218a A25 10fr on 10c (b) .85 .25
219a A24 15fr on 15c (c) 2.00 1.00
221a A24 25fr on 25c (d) 60.00 24.00
222a A24 30fr on 30c (d) 275.00 75.00
223a A25 35fr on 35c (d), type 1 3.50 .90
b. Type 2 6.00 1.20
224a A24 40fr on 65c (d) 1.75 .65
225a A24 50fr on 1fr (d) 50.00 30.00
227a A24 100fr on (d) 50.00 *30.00*
228a A24 200fr on 5fr (d), type 1 20.00 15.00
b. Type 2 — —
229a A35 500fr on 10fr (d) 22.50 16.00
Nos. 217a-229a (11) 486.20 193.05

The 50fr and 100fr values were sold only through the philatelic bureau.

Issued: 10fr, 7/10; 15fr, 7/18; 5fr, 8/10; #228a, 8/22; 25fr, 30fr, #223a, 9/10; 40fr, 9/12; 500fr, 9/14; #223b, 1/6/78; #228b, 1/13/78.

Erromango and Kaori Tree — A44

Designs: 10fr, Archipelago and man making copra. 15fr, Espiritu Santo Island and cattle. 20fr, Efate Island and Post Office, Vila. 25fr, Malakula Island and headdresses. 30fr, Aoba and Maewo Islands and pig tusks. 35fr, Pentecost Island and land diving. 40fr, Tanna Island and Prophet John Frum's Red Cross. 50fr, Shepherd Island and canoe with sail. 70fr, Banks Island and dancers. 100fr, Ambrym Island and carvings. 200fr, Aneityum Island and decorated baskets. 500fr, Torres Islands and fishing with bow and arrow.

1977-78 Wmk. 373 Litho. *Perf. 14*

238 A44 5fr multicolored .25 .25
239 A44 10fr multicolored .25 .25
240 A44 15fr multicolored .25 .25
241 A44 20fr multicolored .30 .30
242 A44 25fr multicolored .40 .40
243 A44 30fr multicolored .50 .50
244 A44 35fr multicolored .55 .55
245 A44 40fr multicolored .60 .60
246 A44 50fr multicolored 1.25 .75
247 A44 70fr multicolored 1.50 *2.00*
248 A44 100fr multicolored 1.75 1.25
249 A44 200fr multicolored 2.50 2.50
250 A44 500fr multicolored 5.50 7.50
Nos. 238-250 (13) 15.60 17.10

Issue dates: 5fr, 20fr, 50fr, 100fr, 200fr, Sept. 7; 15fr, 25fr, 30fr, 40fr, Nov. 23, 1977; 10fr, 35fr, 70fr, 500fr, May 9, 1978.

Tempi Madonna, by Raphael — A45

Christmas: 15fr, Virgin and Child, by Gerard David. 30fr, Virgin and Child, by Pompeo Batoni.

1977, Dec. 8 Litho. *Perf. 12*

251 A45 10fr multicolored .25 .25
252 A45 15fr multicolored .25 .25
253 A45 30fr multicolored .30 .30
Nos. 251-253 (3) .80 .80

British Airways Concorde over New York City — A46

20fr, British Airways Concorde over London. 30fr, Air France Concorde over Washington. 40fr, Air France Concorde over Paris.

1978, May 9 Wmk. 373 *Perf. 14*

254 A46 10fr multicolored .85 .50
255 A46 20fr multicolored 1.10 1.10
256 A46 30fr multicolored 1.50 1.50
257 A46 40fr multicolored 1.75 1.75
Nos. 254-257 (4) 5.20 4.85

Concorde, 1st commercial flight, Paris to NYC.

Elizabeth II Coronation Anniversary Issue

Common Design Types
Souvenir Sheet

1978, June 2 Unwmk. *Perf. 15*

258 Sheet of 6 1.75 1.75
a. CD326 40fr White horse of Hanover .25 .25
b. CD327 40fr Elizabeth II .25 .25
c. CD328 40fr Gallic cock .25 .25

No. 258 contains 2 se-tenant strips of Nos. 258a-258c, separated by horizontal gutter with commemorative and descriptive inscriptions and showing central part of coronation procession with coach.

Virgin and Child, by Dürer — A47

Dürer Paintings: 15fr, Virgin and Child with St. Anne. 30fr, Virgin and Child with Goldfinch. 40fr, Virgin and Child with Pear.

Perf. 14x13½

1978, Dec. 1 Litho. Wmk. 373

259 A47 10fr multicolored .25 .25
260 A47 15fr multicolored .25 .25
261 A47 30fr multicolored .25 .25
262 A47 40fr multicolored .25 .25
Nos. 259-262 (4) 1.00 1.00

Christmas and 450th death anniv. of Albrecht Dürer (1471-1528), German painter.

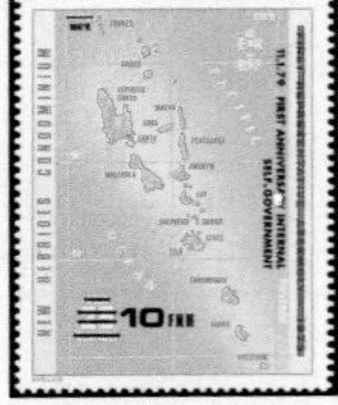

No. 208 and Type of 1976 Surcharged

Longitude changed to "166E."

1979, Jan. 11 Photo. *Perf. 13*

263 A40 10fr on 25c bl & multi .25 .25
264 A40 40fr on 25c lt grn & multi .25 .25

1st anniv. of Internal Self-Government.

New Hebrides No. 50 — A48

Rowland Hill and New Hebrides Stamps: 20fr, No. 136. 40fr, No. 43.

1979, Sept. 10 Litho. *Perf. 14*

265 A48 10fr multicolored .25 .25
266 A48 20fr multicolored .25 .25
a. Souvenir sheet of 2 .90 .90
267 A48 40fr multicolored .40 .40
Nos. 265-267 (3) .90 .90

Sir Rowland Hill (1795-1879), originator of penny postage. No. 266a contains New Hebrides, British, No. 266, and French, No. 286; margin shows Mulready envelope.

Arts Festival — A49

Designs: 10fr, Clubs and spears. 20fr, Ritual puppet. 40fr, Headdress.

1979, Nov. 16 Wmk. 373 *Perf. 14*

268 A49 5fr multicolored .25 .25
269 A49 10fr multicolored .25 .25
270 A49 20fr multicolored .25 .25
271 A49 40fr multicolored .40 .40
Nos. 268-271 (4) 1.15 1.15

Church, IYC Emblem — A50

IYC Emblem, Children's Drawings: 10fr, Father Christmas. 20fr, Cross and Bible, vert. 40fr, Stars, candle and Santa Claus, vert.

1979, Dec. 4 *Perf. 13x13½*

272 A50 5fr multicolored .25 .25
273 A50 10fr multicolored .25 .25
274 A50 20fr multicolored .25 .25
275 A50 40fr multicolored .35 .35
Nos. 272-275 (4) 1.10 1.10

Christmas; Intl. Year of the Child.

White-bellied Honeyeater A51

1980, Feb. 27 Litho. *Perf. 14*

276 A51 10fr shown .85 .25
277 A51 20fr Scarlet robins 1.10 .45
278 A51 30fr Yellow white-eyes 1.50 .65
279 A51 40fr Fan-tailed brush cuckoo 1.75 .85
Nos. 276-279 (4) 5.20 2.20

New Hebrides stamps were replaced in 1980 by those of Vanuatu.

POSTAGE DUE STAMPS

British Issues

Type of 1925 Overprinted

1925, June Engr. Wmk. 4 *Perf. 14*

J1 A3 1p (10c) green 37.50 1.25
J2 A3 2p (20c) gray 40.00 1.25
J3 A3 3p (30c) carmine 40.00 3.25
J4 A3 5p (50c) ultra 45.00 5.50
J5 A3 10p (1fr) car, *blue* 52.50 6.50
Nos. J1-J5 (5) 215.00 17.75

Values for Nos. J1-J5 are for toned stamps.

Regular Stamps of 1938 Overprinted in Black

1938, June 1 *Perf. 12*

J6 A5 5c green 20.00 *32.50*
J7 A5 10c dark orange 20.00 *32.50*
J8 A5 20c rose red 22.50 *50.00*
J9 A5 40c olive green 27.50 *57.50*
J10 A5 1fr car, *emerald* 35.00 *67.50*
Nos. J6-J10 (5) 125.00 *240.00*

Catalogue values for unused stamps in this section, from this point to the end of the section, are for Never Hinged items.

Regular Stamps of 1953 Overprinted in Black

1953, Apr. 30 *Perf. 12½*

J11 A6 5c green 4.75 *13.50*
J12 A6 10c red 2.25 *11.00*
J13 A6 20c ultramarine 6.00 *20.00*
J14 A6 40c black brown 8.50 *37.50*
J15 A6 1fr deep orange 5.50 *45.00*
Nos. J11-J15 (5) 27.00 *127.00*

Same on Nos. 82-83, 85, 88 and 90

1957, Sept. 3 *Perf. 13½x13*

J16 A8 5c green .25 *1.00*
J17 A8 10c red .35 *1.25*
J18 A8 20c ultramarine .75 *1.50*
J19 A8 40c sepia 1.00 *2.50*
J20 A8 1fr orange 2.00 *3.50*
Nos. J16-J20 (5) 4.35 *9.75*

NEW HEBRIDES, FRENCH

'nü 'he-brə-ˌdēz

LOCATION — A group of islands in the South Pacific Ocean lying north of New Caledonia

GOVT. — Condominium under the joint administration of Great Britain and France

AREA — 5,790 sq. mi.

POP. — 100,000 (est. 1976)

CAPITAL — Port-Vila (Vila)

Postage stamps are issued by both Great Britain and France. In 1911 a joint issue was made bearing the coats of arms of both countries. The British stamps bore the coat of arms of Great Britain and the value in British currency on the right and the French coat of arms and values at the left. On the French stamps the positions were reversed. This resulted in some confusion when the value of the French franc decreased following World War I but the situation was corrected by arranging that both series of stamps be sold for their value as expressed in French currency.

12 Pence = 1 Shilling
100 Centimes = 1 Franc
New Hebrides Franc (FNH) — 1977

Catalogue values for unused stamps in this country are for Never Hinged items, beginning with Scott 79 in the regular postage section, Scott J16 in the postage due section.

French Issues

Stamps of New Caledonia, 1905, Overprinted in Black or Red

Nos. 1-4

No. 5

1908 Unwmk. *Perf. 14x13½*

1 A16 5c green 13.50 *5.00*
2 A16 10c rose 13.50 *4.75*
3 A17 25c blue, *grnsh* (R) 9.50 *4.00*
4 A17 50c carmine, *org* 8.50 *6.50*
5 A18 1fr bl, *yel grn* (R) 29.00 *22.50*
Nos. 1-5 (5) 74.00 *42.75*

For overprints and surcharges see #6-10, 33-35.

Stamps of 1908 with Additional Overprint

1910

6 A16 5c green 8.00 *3.00*
7 A16 10c rose 8.00 *1.75*
8 A17 25c blue, *grnsh* (R) 3.50 *4.50*
9 A17 50c red, *org* 12.00 *27.50*
10 A18 1fr bl, *yel grn* (R) 30.00 *22.50*
Nos. 6-10 (5) 61.50 *59.25*

A2

Perf. 14

1911, July 12 Engr. Wmk. 3

11 A2 5c pale green 1.00 *3.00*
12 A2 10c red .55 *1.10*
13 A2 20c gray 2.00 *3.00*

14 A2 25c ultramarine 2.75 *7.00*
15 A2 30c vio, *yellow* 6.50 *6.50*
16 A2 40c red, *yellow* 4.00 *7.50*
17 A2 50c olive green 4.00 *7.50*
18 A2 75c brn orange 7.00 *30.00*
19 A2 1fr brn red, *bl* 6.00 *7.00*
20 A2 2fr violet 12.00 *22.50*
21 A2 5fr brn red, *grn* 14.00 *47.50*
Nos. 11-21 (11) 59.80 *142.60*

For surcharges see Nos. 36-37, 43 and British issue No. 30.

1912 Wmk. R F in Sheet

22 A2 5c pale green 1.75 *5.50*
23 A2 10c red 1.75 *6.00*
24 A2 20c gray 2.10 *2.40*
25 A2 25c ultramarine 2.50 *5.00*
26 A2 30c vio, *yellow* 2.50 *17.00*
27 A2 40c red, *yellow* 24.00 *80.00*
28 A2 50c olive green 18.00 *35.00*
29 A2 75c brn orange 9.00 *42.50*
30 A2 1fr brn red, *bl* 9.00 *10.00*
31 A2 2fr violet 9.25 *50.00*
32 A2 5fr brn red, *grn* 32.50 *57.50*
Nos. 22-32 (11) 112.35 310.90

In the watermark, "R F" (République Française initials) are large double-lined Roman capitals, about 120mm high. About one-fourth of the stamps in each sheet show parts of the watermark. The other stamps are without watermark.

For surcharges see Nos. 38-42 and British issue No. 31.

No. 9 Surcharged

No. 8 Surcharged

1920 Unwmk. *Perf. 14x13½*

33 A17 5c on 50c red, *org* 2.50 *22.00*
34 A17 10c on 25c bl, *grnsh* .75 *1.50*

Same Surcharge on No. 4

35 A17 5c on 50c car, *org* 800.00 *1,000.*

British Issue No. 21 and French Issue No. 15 Surcharged

1921 Wmk. 3 *Perf. 14*

36 A1 10c on 5p ol grn 16.00 *50.00*
37 A2 20c on 30c vio, *yel* 15.00 *65.00*

Nos. 27 and 26 Surcharged

1921 Wmk. R F in Sheet

38 A2 5c on 40c red, *yel* 27.50 *100.00*
39 A2 20c on 30c vio, *yel* 11.50 *80.00*

Stamps of 1910-12 Surcharged with New Values as in 1920-21

1924

40 A2 10c on 5c pale grn 2.75 11.00
41 A2 30c on 10c red 2.75 3.00
42 A2 50c on 25c ultra 4.50 20.00

Wmk. 3

43 A2 50c on 25c ultra 45.00 *110.00*
Nos. 40-43 (4) 55.00 144.00

A4

The values at the lower right denote the currency and amount for which the stamps were to be sold. The stamps could be purchased at the French post office and used to pay postage at the English rates.

1925 Engr. Wmk. R F in Sheet

44 A4 5c (½p) black .90 *13.00*
45 A4 10c (1p) green 1.00 *9.00*
46 A4 20c (2p) grnsh gray 4.25 *3.75*
47 A4 25c (2½p) brown 1.50 *9.00*
48 A4 30c (3p) carmine 1.75 *18.00*
49 A4 40c (4p) car, *org* 3.25 *16.00*
50 A4 50c (5p) ultra 2.00 *11.00*
51 A4 75c (7½p) bis brn 1.75 *22.00*
52 A4 1fr (10p) car, *blue* 3.00 *14.50*
53 A4 2fr (1sh 8p) gray vio 2.75 37.50
54 A4 5fr (4sh) car, *grnsh* 5.00 *37.50*
Nos. 44-54 (11) 27.15 *191.25*

For overprints see Nos. J1-J5.

Beach Scene — A6

1938 *Perf. 12*

55 A6 5c green 3.00 *9.75*
56 A6 10c dark orange 3.25 *3.25*
57 A6 15c violet 3.25 *8.00*
58 A6 20c rose red 3.25 *5.50*
59 A6 25c brown 6.50 *7.75*
60 A6 30c dark blue 6.50 *8.00*
61 A6 40c olive grn 3.50 *14.50*
62 A6 50c brown violet 3.50 *5.50*
63 A6 1fr dk car, *grn* 4.00 *8.50*
64 A6 2fr blue, *grn* 27.50 *42.50*
65 A6 5fr red, *yellow* 40.00 *67.50*
66 A6 10fr vio, *blue* 87.50 *145.00*
Nos. 55-66 (12) 191.75 *325.75*
Set, never hinged 375.00

For overprints see Nos. 67-78, J6-J15.

Stamps of 1938 Ovptd. in Black

1941

67 A6 5c green 1.25 *25.00*
68 A6 10c dark orange 3.50 *24.00*
69 A6 15c violet 5.50 *40.00*
70 A6 20c rose red 15.50 *30.00*
71 A6 25c brown 16.50 *40.00*
72 A6 30c dark blue 17.00 *35.00*
73 A6 40c olive green 17.00 *40.00*
74 A6 50c brn violet 14.50 *35.00*
75 A6 1fr dk car, *grn* 14.50 *37.50*
76 A6 2fr blue, *grn* 13.50 *37.50*
77 A6 5fr red, *yellow* 11.00 *37.50*
78 A6 10fr vio, *blue* 10.00 *40.00*
Nos. 67-78 (12) 139.75 421.50
Set, never hinged 245.00

Catalogue values for unused stamps in this section, from this point to the end of the section, are for Never Hinged items.

UPU Issue

Common Design Type

Wmk. RF in Sheet

1949 Engr. *Perf. 13½x14*

79 CD309 10c red orange 1.90 *2.75*
80 CD309 15c violet 3.25 *4.50*
81 CD309 30c violet blue 3.50 *5.00*
82 CD309 50c brown violet 6.75 *9.75*
Nos. 79-82 (4) 15.40 *22.00*

Some stamps in each sheet show part of the watermark; others show none.

Common Design Types pictured following the introduction.

A8

5c, 10c, 15c, 20c, Canoes with sails. 25c, 30c, 40c, 50c, Native carving. 1fr, 2fr, 5fr, Natives.

1953 *Perf. 12½*

83 A8 5c green .60 *.75*
84 A8 10c red .60 *.75*
85 A8 15c yellow .60 *.75*
86 A8 20c ultramarine 1.15 *1.90*
87 A8 25c olive .80 *1.25*
88 A8 30c light brown 1.75 *2.75*
89 A8 40c black brown 2.00 *3.25*
90 A8 50c violet 2.25 *3.75*
91 A8 1fr deep orange 8.00 *12.50*
92 A8 2fr red violet 21.00 *35.00*
93 A8 5fr scarlet 37.50 *60.00*
Nos. 83-93 (11) 76.25 *122.65*

For overprints see Nos. J16-J20.

Discovery of New Hebrides, 1606 — A9

20c, 50c, Britannia, Marianne, Flags and Mask.

Perf. 14½x14

1956, Oct. 20 Unwmk. Photo.

94 A9 5c emerald 1.10 1.10
95 A9 10c crimson 1.25 1.25
96 A9 20c ultramarine 1.25 1.25
97 A9 50c purple 2.00 2.00
Nos. 94-97 (4) 5.60 5.60

50th anniv. of the establishment of the Anglo-French Condominium.

Port Vila and Iririki Islet — A10

Designs: 25c, 30c, 40c, 50c, Tropical river and spear fisherman. 1fr, 2fr, 5fr, Woman drinking from coconut (inscribed: "Alliance Franco-Britannique 4 Mars 1947").

Wmk. RF in Sheet

1957 Engr. *Perf. 13½x13*

98 A10 5c green .60 *1.25*
99 A10 10c red .90 *.85*
100 A10 15c orange yel 1.00 *1.50*
101 A10 20c ultramarine 1.25 *1.50*
102 A10 25c olive 1.25 *1.25*
103 A10 30c light brown 1.60 *1.75*
104 A10 40c sepia 1.90 *2.25*
105 A10 50c violet 2.40 *3.25*
106 A10 1fr orange 6.50 *9.00*
107 A10 2fr rose lilac 14.00 *20.00*
108 A10 5fr black 27.00 *39.00*
Nos. 98-108 (11) 58.40 *81.60*

For overprints see Nos. J21-J25.

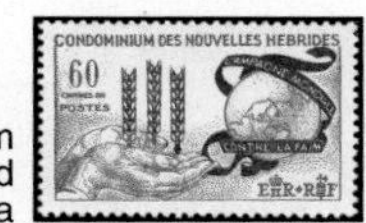
Wheat Emblem and Globe — A10a

1963, Sept. 2 Unwmk. *Perf. 13*

109 A10a 60c org brn & slate grn 16.00 16.00

FAO "Freedom from Hunger" campaign.

Centenary Emblem — A11

1963, Sept. 2 Unwmk.

110 A11 15c org, gray & car 11.00 11.00
111 A11 45c bis, gray & car 16.50 16.50

Centenary of International Red Cross.

Copra Industry — A12

Designs: 5c, Manganese loading, Forari Wharf. 10c, Cacao. 20c, Map of New Hebrides, tuna, marlin and ships. 25c, Striped triggerfish. 30c, Nautilus. 40c, 60c, Turkeyfish (pterois volitans). 50c, Lined tang (fish). 1fr, Cardinal honeyeater and hibiscus. 2fr, Buff-bellied flycatcher. 3fr, Thicket warbler. 5fr, White-collared kingfisher.

Perf. 12½ (10c, 20c, 40c, 60c); 14 (3fr); 13 (others)

Photo. (10c, 20c, 40c, 60c, 3fr); Engr. (others)

1963-67 Unwmk.

112 A12 5c Prus bl, pur brn & cl ('66) .60 .60
a. 5c prus blue & claret ('72) 57.50 *60.00*
113 A12 10c brt grn, org brn & dk brn ("RF" at left) ('65) 1.75 1.75
114 A12 15c dk pur, yel & brn .70 .70
115 A12 20c brt bl, gray & cit ("RF" at left) ('65) 2.60 2.60
116 A12 25c vio, rose lil & org brn ('66) .70 .70
117 A12 30c lil, brn & citron 5.25 5.25
118 A12 40c dk bl & ver ('65) 4.75 4.75
119 A12 50c Prus bl, yel & grn 4.25 4.25
119A A12 60c dk bl & ver ('67) 1.60 1.60
120 A12 1fr bl grn, blk & red ('66) 3.25 3.25
121 A12 2fr ol, blk & brn 15.00 15.00
122 A12 3fr org brn, brt grn & blk ("RF" at left) ('65) 14.00 14.00
123 A12 5fr ind, dp bl & gray ('67) 25.00 25.00
Nos. 112-123 (13) 79.45 79.45

See #146-148. For surcharge see #160.

Telegraph, Syncom Satellite and ITU Emblem — A13

1965, May 17 Unwmk. *Perf. 13*

124 A13 15c red brn, lt bl & bl grn 9.25 7.25
125 A13 60c dp bl grn, red & indigo 23.00 20.00

ITU, centenary.

Intl. Cooperation Year Issue

Common Design Type with Royal Cipher and "RF" Replacing Queen's Portrait

1965, Oct. 24 Litho. *Perf. 14½*

126 CD318 5c blue grn & claret 4.00 4.00
127 CD318 55c lt violet & grn 8.00 8.00

International Cooperation Year.

Churchill Memorial Issue

Common Design Type with Royal Cipher and "RF" Replacing Queen's Portrait

1966, Jan. 24 Photo. *Perf. 14*

Design in Black, Gold and Carmine Rose

128 CD319 5c brt blue .80 .80
129 CD319 15c green 1.20 1.20
130 CD319 25c brown 2.60 2.60
131 CD319 30c violet 3.75 3.75
Nos. 128-131 (4) 8.35 8.35

World Cup Soccer Issue

Common Design Type with Royal Cipher and "RF" Replacing Queen's Portrait

1966, July 1 Litho. *Perf. 14*

132 CD321 20c multicolored 2.75 2.75
133 CD321 40c multicolored 4.25 4.25

WHO Headquarters Issue

Common Design Type with Royal Cipher and "RF" Replacing Queen's Portrait

1966, Sept. 20 Litho. *Perf. 14*

134 CD322 25c multicolored 3.75 3.75
135 CD322 60c multicolored 4.75 4.75

UNESCO Anniversary Issue

Common Design Type with Royal Cipher and "RF" Replacing Queen's Portrait

1966, Dec. 1 Litho. *Perf. 14*

136 CD323 15c "Education" 1.50 1.50
137 CD323 30c "Science" 3.00 3.00
138 CD323 45c "Culture" 3.25 3.25
Nos. 136-138 (3) 7.75 7.75

US Marine, Australian Soldier and Map of South Pacific War Zone A19

Designs: 15c, The coast watchers. 60c, Australian cruiser Canberra. 1fr, Flying fortress taking off from Bauer Field, and view of Vila.

Perf. 14x13

1967, Sept. 26 Photo. Unwmk.

139 A19 15c lt blue & multi 1.00 1.00
140 A19 25c yellow & multi 1.25 1.25
141 A19 60c multicolored 2.00 2.00
142 A19 1fr pale salmon & multi 2.50 2.50
Nos. 139-142 (4) 6.75 6.75

25th anniv. of the Allied Forces' campaign in the South Pacific War Zone.

L. A. de Bougainville, Ship's Figurehead and Bougainvillea A20

15c, Globe & world map. 25c, Ships La Boudeuse & L'Etoile & map of Bougainville Strait.

1968, May 23 Engr. *Perf. 13*

143 A20 15c ver, emer & dl vio .45 .45
144 A20 25c ultra, ol & brn .65 .65
145 A20 60c mag, grn & brn 1.15 1.15
Nos. 143-145 (3) 2.25 2.25

200th anniv. of Louis Antoine de Bougainville's (1729-1811) voyage around the world.

Type of 1963-67 Redrawn, "E II R" at left, "RF" at Right

Designs as before.

1968, Aug. 5 Photo. *Perf. 12½*

146 A12 10c brt grn, org brn & dk brn 1.00 1.00
147 A12 20c brt bl, gray & citron 1.40 1.40

Perf. 14

148 A12 3fr org brn, brt grn & blk 9.50 9.50
Nos. 146-148 (3) 11.90 11.90

On Nos. 113, 115 and 122 "RF" is at left and "E II R" is at right.

For surcharge see No. 160.

Concorde Supersonic Airliner — A21

Design: 25c, Concorde seen from above.

1968, Oct. 9 Litho. *Perf. 14x13½*

149 A21 25c vio bl, red & lt bl 2.40 2.00
150 A21 60c red, ultra & blk 5.25 4.00

Development of the Concorde supersonic airliner, a joint Anglo-French project.

Kauri Pine — A22

1969, June 30 *Perf. 14½x14*

151 A22 20c brown & multi .55 .55

New Hebrides timber industry. Issued in sheets of 9 (3x3) on simulated wood grain background.

Relay Race, British and French Flags — A23

1969, Aug. 13 Photo. *Perf. 12½x13*

152 A23 25c shown .75 .75
153 A23 1fr Runner at right 1.50 1.50

3rd South Pacific Games, Port Moresby, Papua and New Guinea, Aug. 13-23.

Land Diver at Start, Pentecost Island — A24

1969, Oct. 15 Litho. *Perf. 12½*

154 A24 15c shown .50 .50
155 A24 25c Diver in mid-air .60 .60
156 A24 1fr Diver near ground 2.00 2.00
Nos. 154-156 (3) 3.10 3.10

Land divers of Pentecost Island.

UPU Headquarters and Monument, Bern — A25

1970, May 20 Engr. *Perf. 13*

157 A25 1.05fr org, lilac & slate 1.00 1.00

New UPU Headquarters, Bern.

Charles de Gaulle — A26

1970, July 20 Photo. *Perf. 13*

158 A26 65c brown & multi 1.60 1.60
159 A26 1.10fr dp blue & multi 2.25 2.25

Rallying of the Free French, 30th anniv.

For overprints see Nos. 163-164.

No. 147 Surcharged

1970, Oct. 15 Photo. *Perf. 12½*

160 A12 35c on 20c multi .50 *.60*

Virgin and Child, by Giovanni Bellini — A27

50c, Virgin and Child, by Giovanni Cima.

1970, Nov. 30 Litho. *Perf. 14½x14*

161 A27 15c tan & multi .30 .25
162 A27 50c lt grn & multi .65 .40

Christmas. See Nos. 186-187.

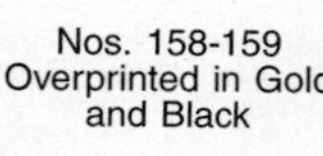

Nos. 158-159 Overprinted in Gold and Black

1971, Jan. 19 Photo. *Perf. 13*

163 A26 65c brown & multi .85 .85
164 A26 1.10fr dp blue & multi 1.90 1.90

In memory of Gen. Charles de Gaulle (1890-1970), President of France.

Soccer A28

Design: 65c, Basketball, vert.

1971, July 13 Photo. *Perf. 12½*

165 A28 20c multicolored .75 .75
166 A28 65c multicolored 1.25 1.25

4th South Pacific Games, Papeete, French Polynesia, Sept. 8-19.

Breadfruit Tree and Fruit, Society Arms — A29

Perf. 14½x14

1971, Sept. 7 Litho. Unwmk.

167 A29 65c multicolored 1.75 1.75

Expedition of the Royal Society of London for the Advancement of Science to study vegetation and fauna, July 1-October.

Adoration of the Shepherds, by Louis Le Nain — A30

Christmas: 50c, Adoration of the Shepherds, by Jacopo Tintoretto.

1971, Nov. 23 *Perf. 14x13½*

168 A30 25c lt green & multi .60 .60
169 A30 50c lt blue & multi .90 .90

Drover Mk III — A31

Airplanes: 25c, Sandringham seaplane. 30c, Dragon Rapide. 65c, Caravelle.

1972, Feb. 29 Photo. *Perf. 13½x13*

170 A31 20c lt green & multi .90 .90
171 A31 25c ultra & multi 1.00 1.00
172 A31 30c orange & multi 1.10 1.10
173 A31 65c dk blue & multi 3.25 3.25
Nos. 170-173 (4) 6.25 6.25

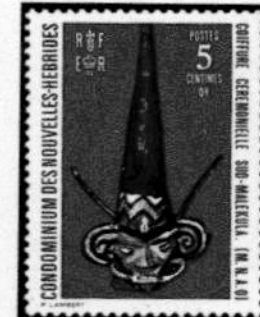

Headdress, South Malekula A32

Baker's Pigeon A33

Artifacts: 15c, Slit gong and carved figure, North Ambrym. 1fr, Carved figures, North Ambrym. 3fr, Ceremonial headdress, South Malekula.

Birds: 20c, Red-headed parrot-finch. 35c, Chestnut-bellied kingfisher. 2fr, Green palm lorikeet.

Sea Shells: 25c, Cribraria fischeri. 30c, Oliva rubrolabiata. 65c, Strombus plicatus. 5fr, Turbo marmoratus.

1972, July 24 Photo. *Perf. 12½x13*

174 A32 5c plum & multi .30 *.80*
175 A33 10c blue & multi 1.75 *1.40*
176 A32 15c red & multi .30 .80
177 A33 20c org brn & multi 2.00 1.20
178 A32 25c dp blue & multi 1.40 1.30
179 A32 30c dk green & multi 1.40 *1.40*
180 A33 35c gray bl & multi 2.40 2.00
181 A32 65c dk green & multi 3.00 2.40
182 A32 1fr orange & multi 2.25 *3.50*
183 A33 2fr multicolored 19.00 12.00
184 A32 3fr yellow & multi 8.00 *14.00*
185 A32 5fr pink & multi 20.00 *24.00*
Nos. 174-185 (12) 61.80 *64.80*

For overprints see Nos. 200-201. For surcharges see Nos. 236-247.

Christmas Type of 1970

Christmas: 25c, Adoration of the Magi (detail), by Bartholomaeus Spranger. 70c, Virgin and Child, by Jan Provoost.

1972, Sept. 25 Litho. *Perf. 14x13½*

186 A27 25c lt green & multi .60 .60
187 A27 70c lt blue & multi .90 .90

Silver Wedding Issue

Common Design Type With Royal Cipher and "RF" (at Right)

Design: Elizabeth II and Prince Philip.

Perf. 14x14½

1972, Nov. 20 Photo. Wmk. 314

188 CD324 35c violet blk & multi .50 .50
189 CD324 65c olive & multi .75 .75

Dendrobium Teretifolium — A35

Orchids: 30c, Ephemerantha comata. 35c, Spathoglottis petri. 65c, Dendrobium mohlianum.

Unwmk.

1973, Feb. 26 Litho. *Perf. 14*

190 A35 25c blue vio & multi 1.75 1.75
191 A35 30c multicolored 1.75 1.75
192 A35 35c violet & multi 2.50 2.50
193 A35 65c dk green & multi 5.00 5.00
Nos. 190-193 (4) 11.00 11.00

New Wharf, Vila — A36

1973, May 14 Litho. *Perf. 14*

194 A36 25c shown .90 .90
195 A36 70c New Wharf, horiz. 1.60 1.60

New wharf at Vila, completed Nov. 1972.

Wild Horses, Tanna — A37

Design: 70c, Yasur Volcano, Tanna.

1973, Aug. 13 Photo. *Perf. 13x13½*

196 A37 35c multicolored 2.75 2.75
197 A37 70c multicolored 3.50 3.50

Christmas — A38

35c, Mother and Child, by Marcel Moutouh. 70c, Star over Lagoon, by Tatin D'Avesnieres.

1973, Nov. 19 Litho. *Perf. 14x13½*

198	A38	35c tan & multi	.60	.60
199	A38	70c lil rose & multi	.90	.90

Nos. 180, 183 Overprinted in Red or Black

1974, Feb. 11 Photo. *Perf. 12½x13*

200	A33	35c multi (R)	2.40	.90
201	A33	2fr multi (B)	7.00	6.00

Visit of British Royal Family, Feb. 15-16.

Pacific Dove — A39

Designs: 35c, Night swallowtail. 70c, Green sea turtle. 1.15fr, Flying fox.

1974, Feb. 11 *Perf. 13x12½*

202	A39	25c gray & multi	3.75	2.40
203	A39	35c gray & multi	4.50	2.00
204	A39	70c gray & multi	5.50	4.00
205	A39	1.15fr gray & multi	6.25	7.75
		Nos. 202-205 (4)	20.00	16.15

Nature conservation.

Old Post Office, Vila A40

Design: 70c, New Post Office.

Unwmk.

1974, May 6 Photo. *Perf. 12*

206	A40	35c blue & multi	.60	.50
207	A40	70c red & multi	1.10	.90
a.		Pair, #206-207	2.25	2.25

Opening of New Post Office, May, 1974.

Capt. Cook and Tanna Island — A41

Designs: No. 209, William Wales and boat landing on island. No. 210, William Hodges painting islanders and landscape. 1.15fr, Capt. Cook, "Resolution" and map of New Hebrides.

1974, Aug. 1 Litho. *Perf. 13*

Size: 40x25mm

208	A41	35c multicolored	3.75	2.25
209	A41	35c multicolored	3.75	2.25
210	A41	35c multicolored	3.75	2.25
a.		Strip of 3, #208-210	14.50	14.50

Size: 58x34mm

Perf. 11

211	A41	1.15fr lilac & multi	6.00	6.00

Bicentenary of the discovery of the New Hebrides by Capt. James Cook.

No. 210a has a continuous design.

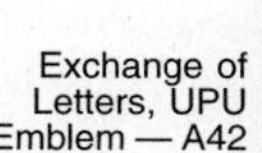

Exchange of Letters, UPU Emblem — A42

1974, Oct. 9 Photo. *Perf. 13x12½*

212	A42	70c multicolored	1.50	1.50

Centenary of Universal Postal Union.

Nativity, by Gerard Van Honthorst A43

Christmas: 35c, Adoration of the Kings, by Velazquez, vert.

1974, Nov. 14 Litho. *Perf. 13½*

213	A43	35c multicolored	.50	.50
214	A43	70c multicolored	1.00	1.00

Charolais Bull — A44

1975, Apr. 29 Engr. *Perf. 13*

215	A44	10fr multicolored	22.00	*24.00*

For surcharge see No. 248.

Nordjamb Emblem, Kayaks — A45

1975, Aug. 5 Litho. *Perf. 14x13½*

216	A45	25c shown	.60	.50
217	A45	35c Camp cooks	.80	.70
218	A45	1fr Map makers	1.60	1.60
219	A45	5fr Fishermen	8.00	8.00
		Nos. 216-219 (4)	11.00	10.80

Nordjamb 75, 14th Boy Scout Jamboree, Lillehammer, Norway, July 29-Aug. 7.

Pitti Madonna, by Michelangelo — A46

Christmas (After Michelangelo): 70c, Bruges Madonna. 2.50fr, Taddei Madonna.

1975, Nov. 11 Litho. *Perf. 14½x14*

220	A46	35c multicolored	.50	.50
221	A46	70c brown & multi	.75	.75
222	A46	2.50fr blue & multi	3.25	3.25
		Nos. 220-222 (3)	4.50	4.50

Concorde, Air France Colors and Emblem A47

1976, Jan. 30 Typo. *Perf. 13*

223	A47	5fr blue & multi	15.00	15.00

1st commercial flight of supersonic jet Concorde from Paris to Rio, Jan. 21.

Telephones, 1876 and 1976 — A48

Designs: 70c, Alexander Graham Bell. 1.15fr, Nouméa Earth Station and satellite.

1976, Mar. 31 Photo. *Perf. 13*

224	A48	25c black, car & bl	.45	.45
225	A48	70c black & multi	1.40	1.40
226	A48	1.15fr blk, org & vio bl	1.90	1.90
		Nos. 224-226 (3)	3.75	3.75

Centenary of first telephone call by Alexander Graham Bell, Mar. 10, 1876.

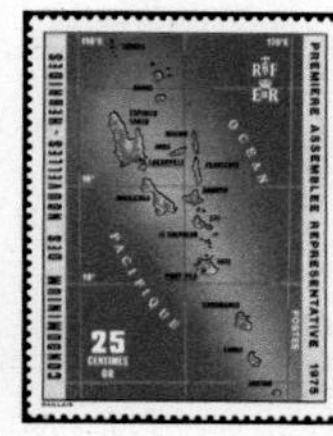

Map of New Hebrides — A49

View of Luganville (Santo) — A50

Design: 2fr, View of Vila.

1976, June 29 Unwmk. *Perf. 13*

227	A49	25c blue & multi	.55	.45
228	A50	1fr multicolored	1.25	1.00
229	A50	2fr multicolored	3.00	3.00
		Nos. 227-229 (3)	4.80	4.45

Opening of first Representative Assembly, June 29, 1976 (25c); first Luganville (Santo) Municipal Council (1fr); first Vila Municipal Council (2fr).

Nos. 228-229 exist with lower inscription reading "Premiere Assemblée Representative 1975" instead of "Premiere Municipalite de Luganville" on 1fr and "Premiere Municipalite de Port-Vila" on 2fr.

For surcharges, see No. 283-284.

Flight into Egypt, by Francisco Vieira Lusitano — A51

Portuguese 16th Cent. Paintings: 70c, Adoration of the Shepherds. 2.50fr, Adoration of the Kings.

1976, Nov. 8 Litho. *Perf. 14*

230	A51	35c purple & multi	.60	.50
231	A51	70c blue & multi	.85	.75
232	A51	2.50fr multicolored	2.60	2.60
		Nos. 230-232 (3)	4.05	3.85

Christmas 1976.

Queen's Visit, 1974 — A52

70c, Imperial State crown. 2fr, The blessing.

1977, Feb. 7 Litho. *Perf. 14x13½*

233	A52	35c lt green & multi	.45	.30
234	A52	70c blue & multi	.70	.65
235	A52	2fr pink & multi	1.35	1.35
		Nos. 233-235 (3)	2.50	2.30

Reign of Queen Elizabeth II, 25th anniv.

Nos. 174-185, 215 Surcharged

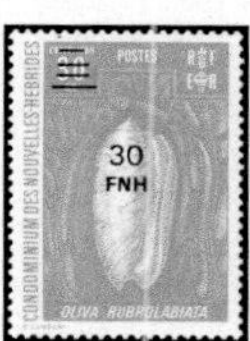

Paris Overprints

1977, July 1 Photo. *Perf. 12½x13*

236	A32	5fr on 5c multi	2.10	1.75
237	A33	10fr on 10c multi	3.50	1.50
238	A32	15fr on 15c multi	1.75	1.50
239	A33	20fr on 20c multi	3.75	1.75
240	A32	25fr on 25c multi	3.50	2.00
241	A32	30fr on 30c multi	3.50	2.50
242	A33	35fr on 35c multi	5.50	4.00
243	A32	40fr on 65c multi	4.25	3.00
244	A32	50fr on 1fr multi	2.75	*3.00*
245	A33	70fr on 2fr multi	9.00	4.00
246	A32	100fr on 3fr multi	3.75	*6.00*
247	A32	200fr on 5fr multi	12.00	*20.00*

Engr.

Perf. 13

248	A44	500fr on 10fr multi	24.00	*42.50*
		Nos. 236-248 (13)	79.35	*93.50*

Nos. 174/185, 215 Surcharged with New Value, "FNH" and Bars

FNH FNH FNH 25 FNH

a b c d

Port Vila Overprints

Two settings of 35fr and 200fr surcharges: type 1, 1.4mm between new value and "FNH"; type 2, 2.1mm between value and "FNH."

Perf. 12½x13

1977-78 Photo. Unwmk.

236a	A32	5fr on 5c (a)	*1.00*	*1.00*
237a	A33	10fr on 10c (b)	*1.25*	*1.25*
238a	A32	15fr on 15c (c)	*2.50*	*2.50*
240a	A32	25fr on 25c (d)	*190.00*	*190.00*
241a	A32	30fr on 30c (d)	*210.00*	*210.00*
242a	A33	35fr on 35c (d), type 1	*5.50*	*5.50*
b.		Type 2	*37.50*	*22.50*
243a	A32	40fr on 65c (d)	*7.00*	*7.00*
244a	A32	50fr on 1fr multi	*16.00*	*16.00*
245a	A33	70fr on 2fr multi	*26.00*	*26.00*
246a	A32	100fr on 3fr multi	*32.50*	*32.50*
247a	A32	200fr on 5fr (d), type 1	*65.00*	*65.00*
b.		Type 2	*75.00*	*75.00*
248a	A44	500fr on 10fr (d)	*100.00*	*100.00*
		Nos. 236a-248a (12)	656.75	656.75

The 50fr, 70fr and 100fr values were sold only through the philatelic bureau.

Issued: 15fr, 7/18; 10fr, 7/20; 5fr, 8/10#247a, 8/22; 25fr, 30fr, #242a, 9/10; 40fr, 9/12; 500fr, 9/14; #242b, 1/6/78; #247b, 1/13/78.

Espiritu Santo and Cattle — A53

Designs: 5fr, Erromango Island and Kaori tree. 10fr, Archipelago and man making copra. 20fr, Efate Island and Post Office, Vila. 25fr, Malakula Island and headdresses. 30fr, Aoba and Maewo Islands and pig tusks. 35fr, Pentecost Island and land diving. 40fr, Tanna Island and Prophet John Frum's Red Cross. 50fr, Shepherd Island and canoe with sail. 70fr, Banks Island and dancers. 100fr, Ambrym Island and carvings. 200fr, Aneityum Island and decorated baskets. 500fr, Torres Islands and fishing with bow and arrow.

1977-78 Litho. *Perf. 14*

258 A53 5fr multicolored .30 .25
259 A53 10fr multicolored .40 .40
260 A53 15fr multicolored .50 .50
261 A53 20fr multicolored .60 .60
262 A53 25fr multicolored .75 .75
263 A53 30fr multicolored 1.00 1.00
264 A53 35fr multicolored 1.10 1.10
265 A53 40fr multicolored 1.25 1.25
266 A53 50fr multicolored 1.50 1.50
267 A53 70fr multicolored 2.40 3.25
268 A53 100fr multicolored 3.50 3.50
269 A53 200fr multicolored 6.75 6.75
270 A53 500fr multicolored 14.00 14.00
Nos. 258-270 (13) 34.05 34.85

Issued: 5fr, 20fr, 50fr, 100fr, 200fr, 9/7/77; 15fr, 25fr, 30fr, 40fr, 11/23/77; 10fr, 35fr, 70fr, 500fr, 5/9/78.

Tempi Madonna, by Raphael — A54

Christmas: 15fr, Virgin and Child, by Gerard David. 30fr, Virgin and Child, by Pompeo Batoni.

1977, Dec. 8 Litho. *Perf. 12*

271 A54 10fr multicolored .35 .35
272 A54 15fr multicolored .50 .35
273 A54 30fr multicolored .90 .90
Nos. 271-273 (3) 1.75 1.60

British Airways Concorde over New York — A55

Designs: 20fr, British Airways Concorde over London. 30fr, Air France Concorde over Washington. 40fr, Air France Concorde over Paris.

1978, May 9 Litho. *Perf. 14*

274 A55 10fr multicolored 2.60 2.60
275 A55 20fr multicolored 2.60 2.60
276 A55 30fr multicolored 2.60 2.60
277 A55 40fr multicolored 2.60 2.60
Nos. 274-277 (4) 10.40 10.40

Elizabeth II Coronation Anniversary Issue

Common Design Types

Souvenir Sheet

1978, June 2 Litho. *Perf. 15*

278 Sheet of 6 3.50 3.50
a. CD326 40fr White Horse of Hanover .25 .25
b. CD327 40fr Elizabeth II .25 .25
c. CD328 40fr Gallic cock .25 .25

No. 278 contains 2 se-tenant strips of Nos. 278a-278c, separated by horizontal gutter with commemorative and descriptive inscriptions and showing central part of coronation procession with coach.

Virgin and Child, by Dürer — A58

Christmas, Paintings by Albrecht Durer (1471-1528): 15fr, Virgin and Child with St. Anne. 30fr, Virgin and Child with Goldfinch. 40fr, Virgin and Child with Pear.

1978, Dec. 1 Litho. *Perf. 14x13½*

279 A58 10fr multicolored .30 .25
280 A58 15fr multicolored .50 .50
281 A58 30fr multicolored .85 .85
282 A58 40fr multicolored 1.90 1.40
Nos. 279-282 (4) 3.55 3.00

No. 227 and Type of 1976 Surcharged

1979, Jan. 11 Photo. *Perf. 13*

283 A49 10fr on 25c bl & multi 1.00 1.00
284 A49 40fr on 25c lt grn & multi 1.90 1.90

First anniv. of Internal Self-Government.

New Hebrides No. 155 and Hill Statue — A59

Rowland Hill and New Hebrides Stamps: 10fr, No. 55. 40fr, No. 46.

1979, Sept. 10 Litho. *Perf. 14*

285 A59 10fr multicolored .30 .25
286 A59 20fr multicolored .35 .25
287 A59 40fr multicolored .75 .60
Nos. 285-287 (3) 1.40 1.10

Sir Rowland Hill (1795-1879), originator of penny postage. A souvenir sheet containing No. 286 and British issue No. 266 is listed as No. 266a under New Hebrides, British issues.

Arts Festival — A60

Designs: 10fr, Clubs and spears. 20fr, Ritual puppet. 40fr, Headdress.

1979, Nov. 16 Litho. *Perf. 14*

288 A60 5fr multicolored .55 .55
289 A60 10fr multicolored .55 .55
290 A60 20fr multicolored .55 .55
291 A60 40fr multicolored .55 .55
Nos. 288-291 (4) 2.20 2.20

Church, IYC Emblem — A61

IYC Emblem, Children's Drawings: 10fr, Father Christmas. 20fr, Cross and Bible, vert. 40fr, Stars, candle and Santa Claus, vert.

1979, Dec. 4 *Perf. 13x13½*

292 A61 5fr multicolored .30 .30
293 A61 10fr multicolored .50 .50
294 A61 20fr multicolored 1.00 1.00
295 A61 40fr multicolored 1.75 1.75
Nos. 292-295 (4) 3.55 3.55

Christmas; Intl. Year of the Child.

White-bellied Honeyeater A62

20fr, Scarlet robins. 30fr, Yellow white-eyes. 40fr, Fan-tailed brush cuckoo.

1980, Feb. 27 Litho. *Perf. 14*

296 A62 10fr shown .85 .85
297 A62 20fr multi 1.40 1.60
298 A62 30fr multi 2.60 2.60
299 A62 40fr multi 3.25 3.25
Nos. 296-299 (4) 8.10 8.30

Stamps of Vanuatu replaced those of New Hebrides in 1980.

POSTAGE DUE STAMPS

French Issues

Nos. 45-46, 48, 50, 52 Overprinted

1925 Wmk. R F in Sheet *Perf. 14*

J1 A4 10c green 50.00 4.75
J2 A4 20c greenish gray 50.00 4.75
J3 A4 30c carmine 50.00 4.75
J4 A4 50c ultramarine 50.00 4.75
J5 A4 1fr carmine, *blue* 50.00 4.75
Nos. J1-J5 (5) 250.00 23.75

Nos. 55-56, 58, 61, 63 Overprinted

1938 *Perf. 12*

J6 A6 5c green 11.00 *65.00*
J7 A6 10c dark orange 12.50 *65.00*
J8 A6 20c rose red 14.50 *70.00*
J9 A6 40c olive green 30.00 *140.00*
J10 A6 1fr dark car, *green* 35.00 *160.00*
Nos. J6-J10 (5) 103.00 *500.00*

Nos. J6-J10 Overprinted like Nos. 67-78

1941

J11 A6 5c green 11.00 *42.50*
J12 A6 10c dark orange 11.00 *42.50*
J13 A6 20c rose red 11.00 *42.50*
J14 A6 40c olive green 13.00 *42.50*
J15 A6 1fr dk car, *green* 12.00 *42.50*
Nos. J11-J15 (5) 58.00 *212.50*

Catalogue values for unused stamps in this section, from this point to the end of the section, are for Never Hinged items.

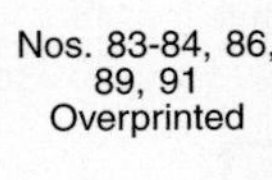

Nos. 83-84, 86, 89, 91 Overprinted

1953 Unwmk. *Perf. 12½*

J16 A8 5c green 4.75 *10.00*
J17 A8 10c red 6.25 *14.00*
J18 A8 20c ultramarine 11.00 *24.00*
J19 A8 40c black brown 15.00 *44.00*
J20 A8 1fr deep orange 22.00 *48.00*
Nos. J16-J20 (5) 59.00 *140.00*

Nos. 98-99, 101, 104, 106 Overprinted "TIMBRE-TAXE"

Wmk. R F in Sheet

1957 Engr. *Perf. 13½x13*

J21 A10 5c green 1.10 *2.75*
J22 A10 10c red 1.40 *3.50*
J23 A10 20c ultramarine 1.60 *4.25*
J24 A10 40c sepia 6.25 *15.00*
J25 A10 1fr orange 15.00 *35.00*
Nos. J21-J25 (5) 25.35 *60.50*

NEW REPUBLIC

'nü ri-'pə-blik

LOCATION — In South Africa, located in the northern part of the present province of Natal
GOVT. — A former Republic
CAPITAL — Vryheid

New Republic was created in 1884 by Boer adventurers from Transvaal who proclaimed Dinizulu king of Zululand and claimed as their reward a large tract of country as their own, which they called New Republic. This area was excepted when Great Britain annexed Zululand in 1887, but New Republic became a part of Transvaal in 1888 and was included in the Union of South Africa.

12 Pence = 1 Shilling
20 Shillings = 1 Pound

New Republic stamps were individually handstamped on gummed and perforated sheets of paper. Naturally many of the impressions are misaligned and touch or intersect the perforations. Values are for stamps with good color and, for Nos. 37-64, sharp embossing. The alignment does not materially alter the value of the stamp.

A1

Handstamped

1886-87 Unwmk. *Perf. 11½*

1 A1 1p violet, *yel* 20.00 22.50
a. "d" omitted, in pair with normal 2,750.
1A A1 1p black, *yel* *3,250.*
2 A1 2p violet, *yel* 22.50 *27.50*
a. "d" omitterd 4,750.
b. Without date *42.50* 50.00
c. Tête-bêche pair —
3 A1 3p violet, *yel* 50.00 *60.00*
a. Double impression
b. "d" omitted (Oct. 13 '86) *4,750.*
c. Tete-beche pair —
4 A1 4p violet, *yel* 85.00
a. Without date
b. "4d" omitted, in pair with normal *3,000.*
5 A1 6p violet, *yel* 65.00 *70.00*
a. Double impression
b. "6d" omitted in pair with normal —
6 A1 9p violet, *yel* 125.00
7 A1 1sh violet, *yel* 125.00
a. "1/S" 800.00
b. "1s" omitted in pair with normal —
8 A1 1/6 violet, *yel* 120.00
a. Without date
b. "1s6d" 600.00
c. as "b", tete-beche pair —
d. as "b", "d" omitted 150.00
9 A1 2sh violet, *yel* 75.00
a. tete-beche pair 875.00
10 A1 2sh6p violet, *yel* 190.00
a. Without date
b. "2/6" 190.00
11 A1 4sh violet, *yel*
a. "4/s" 825.00
12 A1 5sh violet, *yel* 55.00 *65.00*
a. Without date —
b. "s" omitted, in pair with normal 3,500.
13 A1 5/6 violet, *yel* 300.00
a. "5s6d" 550.00
14 A1 7sh6p violet, *yel* 175.00
a. "7/6" 250.00
15 A1 10sh violet, *yel* 225.00 *275.00*
a. Tete-beche pair —
16 A1 10sh6p violet, *yel* 250.00
b. "d" omitted 225.00
16A A1 13sh violet, *yel* 600.00
17 A1 £1 violet, *yel* 150.00
a. Tete-beche pair 650.00
18 A1 30sh violet, *yel* 150.00
a. tete-beche pair 750.00

Granite Paper

19 A1 1p violet, *gray* 30.00 *35.00*
a. "d" omitted 750.00
b. "1" omitted in pair with normal —
20 A1 2p violet, *gray* 22.50 *25.00*
a. "ZUID AFRIKA" omitted
b. "d" omitted *1,350.*
c. "2d." omitted in pair with normal —
21 A1 3p violet, *gray* 40.00 37.50
a. tete-beche pair 375.00
22 A1 4p violet, *gray* 55.00 *60.00*
23 A1 6p violet, *gray* 95.00 *95.00*
a. "6" omitted in pair with normal *2,750.*
24 A1 9p violet, *gray* 150.00
25 A1 1sh violet, *gray* 45.00 50.00
a. tete-beche pair 425.00
b. "1s." omitted in pair with normal 2,750.
26 A1 1sh6p violet, *gray* 125.00
a. tete-beche pair 750.00
b. "1/6" 190.00
c. "d" omitted —
27 A1 2sh violet, *gray* 150.00
a. "2s." omitted in pair with normal *3,250.*

No.	Type	Description	Unused	Used
28	A1	2sh6p violet, *gray*	3,500.	
a.		"2/6"	250.00	
29	A1	4sh violet, *gray*	525.00	
30	A1	5sh6p violet, *gray*	425.00	
a.		"5/6"	325.00	
b.		As "a," "/" omitted	—	
c.		As "a," "6" omitted	4,500.	
31	A1	7/6 violet, *gray*	325.00	
a.		7s. 6d violet gray	450.00	
32	A1	10sh violet, *gray*	225.00	225.00
a.		tete-beche pair	525.00	
f.		"s" omitted	—	
32B	A1	10sh 6p vio, *gray*	275.00	
c.		Without date	—	
d.		tete-beche pair	—	
e.		"d" omitted	600.00	
33	A1	12sh violet, *gray*	450.00	
34	A1	13sh violet, *gray*	550.00	
35	A1	£1 violet, *gray*	375.00	
36	A1	30sh violet, *gray*	325.00	

Same with Embossed Arms

No.	Type	Description	Unused	Used
37	A1	1p violet, *yel*	22.50	25.00
a.		Arms inverted	30.00	35.00
b.		Arms tete-beche, pair	125.00	135.00
c.		tete-beche pair	950.00	
38	A1	2p violet, *yel*	27.50	30.00
a.		Arms inverted	30.00	35.00
39	A1	4p violet, *yel*	80.00	85.00
a.		Arms inverted	125.00	87.50
b.		Arms tete-beche, pair	350.00	
40	A1	6p violet, *yel*	375.00	

Granite Paper

No.	Type	Description	Unused	Used
41	A1	1p violet, *gray*	30.00	30.00
a.		Imperf. vert., pair		
b.		Arms inverted	40.00	45.00
c.		Arms tete-beche, pair	550.00	
42	A1	2p violet, *gray*	30.00	30.00
a.		Imperf. horiz., pair		
b.		Arms inverted	55.00	65.00
c.		Arms tete-beche, pair	550.00	

There were several printings of the above stamps and the date upon them varies from "JAN 86" and "7 JAN 86" to "20 JAN 87."

Nos. 7, 8, 10, 13, 14, 26, 28 and 30 have the denomination expressed in two ways. Example: "1s 6d" or "1/6."

A2

1887 — Arms Embossed

No.	Type	Description	Unused	Used
43	A2	3p violet, *yel*	27.50	27.50
a.		Arms inverted	30.00	32.50
b.		tete-beche pair	375.00	450.00
c.		Imperf. vert., pair		
d.		Arms omitted		
e.		Arms tete-beche, pair	225.00	
f.		Arms sideways	375.00	
44	A2	4p violet, *yel*	20.00	20.00
a.		Arms inverted	25.00	25.00
45	A2	6p violet, *yel*	17.50	17.50
a.		Arms inverted	50.00	50.00
b.		Arms omitted	95.00	
c.		Arms tete-beche, pair	375.00	
46	A2	9p violet, *yel*	17.50	20.00
a.		Arms inverted	250.00	
b.		Arms tete-beche, pair	425.00	
47	A2	1sh violet, *yel*	20.00	20.00
a.		Arms inverted	75.00	
b.		Arms omitted		
48	A2	1sh6p violet, *yel*	55.00	45.00
49	A2	2sh violet, *yel*	42.50	45.00
a.		Arms inverted	65.00	60.00
b.		Arms omitted	150.00	
50	A2	2sh6p violet, *yel*	40.00	40.00
a.		Arms inverted	45.00	45.00
50B	A2	3sh violet, *yel*	65.00	65.00
c.		Arms inverted	80.00	80.00
d.		Arms tete-beche, pair	600.00	
51	A2	4sh violet, *yel*	650.00	
a.		Arms omitted	—	
b.		"4/s"	65.00	65.00
c.		As "b," arms omitted	275.00	
51D	A2	4/s violet, *yel*		
a.		Arms omitted		
52	A2	5sh violet, *yel*	60.00	60.00
a.		Imperf. vert., pair		
b.		Arms inverted	—	175.00
53	A2	5sh6p violet, *yel*	30.00	35.00
54	A2	7sh6p violet, *yel*	35.00	37.50
a.		Arms inverted	125.00	
b.		Arms tete-beche, pair	—	
55	A2	10sh violet, *yel*	32.50	35.00
a.		Arms inverted	40.00	
b.		Arms omitted	135.00	90.00
c.		Imperf. vert., pair		
d.		Arms tete-beche, pair	150.00	
56	A2	10sh6p violet, *yel*	30.00	32.50
a.		Imperf. vert., pair		
b.		Arms inverted	55.00	
c.		Arms omitted		
57	A2	£1 violet, *yel*	75.00	85.00
a.		Arms inverted	80.00	
b.		tete-beche pair	650.00	750.00
57C	A2	£15 violet, *yel*		50,000.
58	A2	30sh violet, *yel*	225.00	

Granite Paper

No.	Type	Description	Unused	Used
59	A2	1p violet, *gray*	32.50	20.00
a.		Arms omitted	150.00	150.00
b.		Arms inverted	30.00	30.00
c.		Imperf. vert., pair		
d.		tete-beche pair	650.00	
e.		Arms tete-beche, pair	—	
f.		Arms sideways	—	
60	A2	2p violet, *gray*	20.00	20.00
a.		Arms omitted	135.00	125.00
b.		Arms inverted	55.00	55.00
c.		tete-beche pair	425.00	
d.		Arms tete-beche, pair	—	
61	A2	3p violet, *gray*	35.00	35.00
a.		Arms inverted	65.00	65.00
b.		tete-beche pair	450.00	
c.		Arms tete-beche, pair	—	
62	A2	4p violet, *gray*	30.00	27.50
a.		Arms inverted	110.00	
b.		Tete-beche, pair	375.00	
c.		Arms tete-beche, pair	300.00	
63	A2	6p violet, *gray*	35.00	35.00
a.		Arms inverted	110.00	
64	A2	1sh6p violet, *gray*	50.00	42.50
a.		Arms inverted	175.00	
b.		Arms tete-beche, pair	475.00	
65	A2	2/6 violet, *gray*	—	1,150.
		Nos. 59-64 (6)	202.50	180.00

These stamps were valid only in New Republic.

All these stamps may have been valid for postage but bona-fide canceled examples of any but the 1p and 2p stamps are quite rare.

A £15 violet stamp on yellow paper exists with what is believed to be a fiscal cancel. Value, $50,000.

NEW ZEALAND

'nü 'zē-lənd

LOCATION — Group of islands in the south Pacific Ocean, southeast of Australia
GOVT. — Self-governing dominion of the British Commonwealth
AREA — 107,241 sq. mi.
POP. — 4,820,000 (2020 est.)
CAPITAL — Wellington

12 Pence = 1 Shilling
20 Shillings = 1 Pound
100 Cents = 1 Dollar (1967)

Catalogue values for unused stamps in this country are for Never Hinged items, beginning with Scott 246 in the regular postage section, Scott AR99 in the postal-fiscal section, Scott B9 in the semi-postal section, Scott J21 in the postage due section, Scott O92 in the officials section, Scott OY29 in the Life Insurance Department section, and Scott L1 in Ross Dependency.

Watermarks

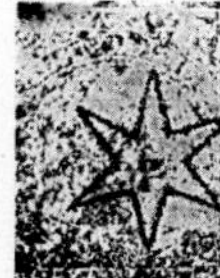
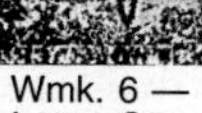
Wmk. 6 — Large Star

Wmk. 59 — N Z

Wmk. 60 — Lozenges

This watermark includes the vertical word "INVICTA" once in each quarter of the sheet.

Wmk. 61 — N Z and Star Close Together

Wmk. 62 — N Z and Star Wide Apart

On watermark 61 the margins of the sheets are watermarked "NEW ZEALAND POSTAGE" and parts of the double-lined letters of these words are frequently found on the stamps. It occasionally happens that a stamp shows no watermark whatever.

Wmk. 63 — Double-lined N Z and Star

Wmk. 64 — Small Star Only

Wmk. 253 — Multiple N Z and Star

Wmk. 387

Values for unused stamps are for examples with original gum as defined in the catalogue introduction.

Very fine examples of the perforated issues between Nos. 7a-69, AR1-AR30, J1-J11, OY1-OY9 and P1-P4 will have perforations touching the framelines or design on one or more sides due to the narrow spacing of the stamps on the plates and imperfect perforating methods.

The rouletted and serrate rouletted stamps of the same period rarely have complete roulettes and are valued as sound and showing partial roulettes. Stamps with complete roulettes range from very scarce to very rare, are seldom traded, and command great premiums.

Victoria — A1

London Print
Wmk. 6

1855, July 20 — Engr. — *Imperf.*

White Paper

No.	Type	Description	Unused	Used
1	A1	1p dull carmine	85,000.	20,000.
2	A1	2p deep blue	40,000.	775.
3	A1	1sh yellow green	55,000.	6,000.
a.		Half used as 6p on cover		42,500.

The blueing of Nos. 2 and 3 was caused by chemical action in the printing process.

Auckland Print

1855-58 — Blue Paper — Unwmk.

No.	Type	Description	Unused	Used
4	A1	1p orange red	14,000.	2,200.
5	AI	2p blue ('56)	4,000.	325.
6	AI	1sh green ('58)	50,000.	4,250.
a.		Half used as 6p on cover		27,500.

Nos. 4-6 may be found with parts of the papermaker's name in double-lined letters.

1857-61 — Unwmk.

Thin Hard or Thick Soft White Paper

No.	Type	Description	Unused	Used
7	A1	1p orange ('58)	4,000.	825.
e.		1p org vermilion, Wmk. 6 ('56)		36,000.
8	A1	2p blue ('58)	1,450.	200.
9	A1	6p brown ('59)	3,000.	325.
e.		6p bister brown ('59)	4,250.	600.
f.		6p chestnut ('59)	5,000.	650.
h.		6p pale brown	2,850.	350.
10	A1	1sh blue grn ('61)	18,500.	2,250.
e.		1sh emerald ('58)	22,000.	1,850.

No. 7e is identical to a shade of No. 7. The only currently known example is a pair on a cover front. To qualify as No. 7e, a stamp must be on piece or on cover with a cancellation dated prior to 1862.

1859 — *Pin Rouletted 9-10*

No.	Type	Description	Unused	Used
7a	A1	1p dull orange		6,000.
8a	A1	2p blue		3,800.
9a	A1	6p brown		4,600.
10a	A1	1sh greenish blue		8,250.

1859 — *Serrate Rouletted 16, 18*

No.	Type	Description	Unused	Used
7b	A1	1p dull orange		5,500.
8b	A1	2p blue		4,100.
9b	A1	6p brown		3,800.
g.		6p chestnut		7,750.
10b	A1	1sh greenish blue		7,000.

Value for No. 10b is for a damaged stamp.

1859 — *Rouletted 7*

No.	Type	Description	Unused	Used
7c	A1	1p dull orange	9,750.	5,500.
f.		Pair, imperf between		—
8c	A1	2p blue	8,250.	3,500.
9c	A1	6p brown	7,750.	4,750.
l.		Pair, imperf. between	27,500.	13,000.
10c	A1	1sh greenish blue	—	5,750.
10d	A1	1sh emerald green	—	5,250.

Roulettes are seldom complete or intact. Values for Nos. 7c to 10d are for stamps with partial roulettes.

1862 — *Perf. 13*

No.	Type	Description	Unused	Used
7d	A1	1p orange vermilion		8,000.
8d	A1	2p blue	8,250.	3,800.
9d	A1	6p brown		7,000.

See No. 26.

1862-63 — Wmk. 6 — *Imperf.*

No.	Type	Description	Unused	Used
11	A1	1p orange ver	1,050.	275.00
d.		1p carmine vermilion ('63)	475.00	300.00
e.		1p vermilion	800.00	275.00
12	A1	2p deep blue	950.00	100.00
d.		2p slate blue	2,000.	200.00
e.		Double impression		4,250.
g.		2p blue, worn plate	950.00	95.00
13	A1	3p brn lil ('63)	750.00	95.00
14	A1	6p red brn ('63)	1,700.	115.00
d.		6p black brown	2,000.	130.00
e.		6p brown ('63)	2,100.	125.00
15	A1	1sh yellow green	2,500.	375.00
d.		1sh deep green	2,750.	650.00

See No. 7e.

1862 — *Pin Rouletted 9-10*

No.	Type	Description	Unused	Used
12a	A1	2p deep blue	—	3,100.
14a	A1	6p black brown	—	4,250.

1862		Serrate Rouletted 16, 18		
11b	A1	1p orange vermilion	11,500.	2,400.
12b	A1	2p blue	—	1,500.
13b	A1	3p brown lilac	6,000.	1,850.
14b	A1	6p black brown	—	2,250.
15b	A1	1sh yellow green		4,500.

1862		Rouletted 7		
11c	A1	1p vermilion	4,750.	850.
12c	A1	2p blue	3,750.	500.
13c	A1	3p brown lilac	3,800.	900.
14c	A1	6p red brown	3,500.	525.
15c	A1	1sh green	4,500.	950.

The 1p, 2p, 6p and 1sh come in two or more shades.

1863		Perf. 13		
16	A1	1p carmine ver	2,500.	425.00
17	A1	2p blue, no plate wear	2,500.	450.00
18	A1	3p brown lilac	3,250.	525.00
19	A1	6p red brown	1,500.	120.00
c.		As "b," horiz. pair, imperf. btwn.		—
20	A1	1sh green	2,850.	375.00

The 1p, 2p, 6p and 1sh come in two or more shades. See the *Scott Classic Specialized Catalogue*.

1862	Unwmk. Pelure Paper	Imperf.		
21	A1	1p vermilion	15,000.	2,750.
b.		Rouletted 7		6,500.
c.		Serrate perf.13		11,000.
22	A1	2p pale dull ultra	5,250.	1,000.
c.		2p gray blue	7,000.	1,000.
23	A1	3p brown lilac	*50,000.*	
24	A1	6p black brown	3,300.	400.
b.		Rouletted 7	4,250.	*525.*
c.		Serrate rouletted 15	—	*6,000.*
d.		Serrate rouletted 13		*6,250.*
25	A1	1sh dp yel grn	14,500.	1,100.
b.		1sh deep green	14,500.	*1,250.*
c.		Rouletted 7	15,000.	*2,500.*
d.		Serrate rouletted 15		*5,000.*
e.		"Y" rouletted 18		*5,000.*

No. 23 was never placed in use.

1863		Perf. 13		
21a	A1	1p vermilion	15,000.	3,500.
22a	A1	2p gray blue	9,000.	1,100.
b.		2p pale dull ultramarine	8,000.	1,100.
24a	A1	6p black brown	8,000.	400.
25a	A1	1sh deep green	14,000.	2,100.

1863	Unwmk. Thick White Paper	Perf. 13		
26	A1	2p dull dark blue	3,750.	900.
a.		Imperf.	2,000.	1,150.
b.		Pin Roulette 9-10		*2,500.*

Nos. 26 and 26a differ from 8 and 8d by a white patch of wear at right of head.

1864	Wmk. 59	Imperf.		
27	A1	1p carmine ver	950.	325.
28	A1	2p blue	1,750.	275.
29	A1	6p red brown	5,250.	750.
30	A1	1sh green	3,250.	350.

1864		Rouletted 7		
27a	A1	1p carmine vermilion	6,250.	4,000.
28a	A1	2p blue	2,500.	775.
29a	A1	6p deep red brown	7,250.	3,100.
30a	A1	1sh green	4,250.	1,150.

1864		Perf. 12½		
27B	A1	1p carmine ver	12,000.	5,000.
28B	A1	2p blue	450.	80.
29B	A1	6p red brown	625.	70.
30B	A1	1sh dp yel green	7,750.	3,100.

1864		Perf. 13		
27C	A1	1p carmine ver	11,500.	5,250.
d.		"Y" roulette 18		*7,000.*
28C	A1	2p blue	1,250.	210.
30C	A1	1sh yellow green	2,600.	800.
d.		Horiz. pair, imperf. btwn.		*45,000.*
e.		Perf. 6½x13		4,750.

1864-71	Wmk. 6	Perf. 12½		
31	A1	1p vermilion	225.00	42.50
a.		1p orange ('71)	600.00	95.00
b.		1p pale org & ver	275.00	42.50
c.		1p Imperf. pair	4,500.	2,750.
d.		1p Vert. pair, imperf. btwn.		
32	A1	2p blue	225.00	22.00
a.		2p blue, worn plate	325.00	30.00
b.		Horiz. pair, imperf. btwn. (#32)		*5,250.*
c.		Perf. 10x12½		19,000.
d.		Imperf., pair (#32)	*3,250.*	*2,250.*
e.		indigo ('65), plate II	325.00	*75.00*
f.		As "e", horiz. pair, imperf. btwn.		
33	A1	3p lilac	165.00	35.00
a.		3p mauve	850.00	90.00
b.		Imperf. pair (#33)	*4,500.*	*2,000.*
c.		As "a", imperf. pair	*5,000.*	*2,000.*
d.		3p brown lilac	2,600.	800.00
34	A1	4p deep rose ('65)	3,250.	275.00
35	A1	4p yellow ('65)	250.00	130.00
a.		4p orange yellow	*2,350.*	1,000.
36	A1	6p red brown	325.00	27.50
a.		6p brown	375.00	42.50
b.		Horiz. pair, imperf. btwn.	3,000.	3,000.
c.		Imperf. pair	2,250.	3,250.
37	A1	1sh yellow green	325.00	125.00
c.		Imperf., pair	5,500.	4,250.

The 1p, 2p and 6p come in two or more shades.

Imperforate examples of the 1p pale orange, worn plate; 2p dull blue and 6p dull chocolate brown are official reprints. Value, each $100.

1871	Wmk. 6	Perf. 10		
38	A1	1p deep brown	950.00	130.00

1871		Perf. 12½		
39	A1	1p brown	250.00	55.00
a.		Imperf., pair	3,500.	2,250.
b.		Vert. pair, imperf. horiz.	3,500.	5,750.
40	A1	2p orange	190.00	31.00
a.		2p vermilion	225.00	35.00
b.		Imperf., pair	3,000.	*4,750.*
41	A1	6p blue	500.00	75.00
		Nos. 39-41 (3)	940.00	161.00

1871		Perf. 10x12½		
42	A1	1p brown	425.00	55.00
43	A1	2p orange	300.00	42.50
44	A1	6p blue	2,400.	575.00
c.		Vert. pair, imperf. btwn.	*6,000.*	—
d.		Horiz. pair, imperf. vert.		—
		Nos. 42-44 (3)	3,125.	672.50

1873	Wmk. 59	Perf. 12½		
45	A1	1p brown		11,000.
46	A1	2p vermilion	1,600.	400.00
a.		Imperf., pair	*4,750.*	

1873	Unwmk.	Perf. 12½		
47	A1	1p brown	1,150.	260.00
48	A1	2p vermilion	160.00	60.00
49	A1	4p yellow orange	225.00	*2,100.*

The watermark "T.H. SAUNDERS" in double-line capitals falls on 32 of the 240 stamps in a sheet. The 1p and 2p also are known with script "WT & CO" watermark.

1873		Wmk. 60		
50	A1	2p vermilion	*3,500.*	925.

A2

A3

A4

A5

A6

A7

1874	Typo. Wmk. 62	Perf. 12½		
51	A2	1p violet	120.00	15.50
a.		Bluish paper	240.00	45.00
b.		Imperf. pair		1,750.
c.		Perf. 12x12½	1,650.	400.00
52	A3	2p rose	120.00	9.00
a.		Bluish paper	240.00	42.50
b.		Perf. 12	1,300.	210.00
c.		Perf. 12x12½	1,300.	350.00
53	A4	3p brown	210.00	85.00
a.		Bluish paper	400.00	110.00
54	A5	4p claret	315.00	75.00
a.		Bluish paper	625.00	125.00
55	A6	6p blue	275.00	13.50
a.		Bluish paper	475.00	60.00
56	A7	1sh green	625.00	40.00
a.		Bluish paper	1,150.	200.00
		Nos. 51-56 (6)	1,665.	238.00

1874		Perf. 12½, 10		
51f	A2	1p violet	175.00	45.00
g.		Bluish paper	275.00	65.00
52f	A3	2p rose	250.00	95.00
g.		Bluish paper	600.00	110.00
53f	A4	3p brown	225.00	90.00
g.		Bluish paper	425.00	125.00
54f	A5	4p claret	850.00	165.00
g.		Bluish paper	425.00	125.00
55f	A6	6p blue	325.00	55.00
g.		Bluish paper	475.00	110.00
56f	A7	1sh green	700.00	150.00
g.		Bluish paper	1,200.	275.00
h.		Vert. pair, imperf. between		*6,750.*

1878		Perf. 12x11½		
51i	A2	1p violet	65.00	9.00
52i	A3	2p rose	70.00	8.00
54i	A5	4p claret	210.00	60.00
55i	A6	6p blue	140.00	12.50
56i	A7	1sh green	225.00	50.00

1875	Wmk. 6	Perf. 12½		
57	A2	1p violet	2,000.	310.00
58	A3	2p rose	775.00	45.00

A8

1878	Wmk. 62	Perf. 12x11½		
59	A8	2sh deep rose	750.00	450.00
60	A8	5sh gray	800.00	500.00

No. 60 has numeral "5" in each of the four spandrels.

Beware of cleaned fiscally used examples of Nos. 59-60.

A9

A10

A11

A12

A13

A14

A15

Perf. 10, 11, 11½, 12, 12½ and Compound

1882-98				
61	A9	1p rose	9.00	.25
a.		Vert. pair, imperf. horiz.	*1,100.*	
b.		Perf. 12x11½	55.00	7.50
c.		Perf. 12½	500.00	305.00
d.		Imperf., pair	*1,100.*	
62	A10	2p violet	16.00	1.00
a.		Vert. pair, imperf. btwn.	*950.00*	
b.		Perf. 12½	500.00	500.00
c.		Imperf., pair	*1,000.*	
63	A11	3p orange	60.00	9.50
a.		3p yellow ('99)	62.50	15.00
64	A12	4p blue grn ('97)	62.50	5.00
a.		Perf. 10x11 ('96)	110.00	13.50
65	A13	6p brown	82.50	8.50
b.		6p brown, thin coarse paper ('98)	140.00	14.50
66	A14	8p blue ("98)	85.00	65.00
67	A15	1sh red brown ('97)	120.00	14.00
d.		Vert. pair, imperf. btwn.	*1,800.*	
		Nos. 61-67 (7)	435.00	103.25

See #87. For overprints see #O1-O2, O5, O7-O8.

A15a

A16

A17

1891-95				
67A	A15a	½p black ('95)	9.00	.25
b.		Perf. 12x11½	45.00	*90.00*
68	A16	2½p ultramarine	57.50	4.25
a.		Perf. 12½	550.00	550.00
69	A17	5p olive gray ('99)	75.00	40.00
		Nos. 67A-69 (3)	141.50	44.50

In 1893 advertisements were printed on the backs of Nos. 61-67, 68-69.

See #86C. For overprints see #O3-O4, O9.

Mt. Cook
A18

Lake Taupo
A19

Pembroke Peak
A20

Mt. Earnslaw, Lake Wakatipu (Incorrect Spelling on Stamp)
A21

Mt. Earnslaw, Lake Wakatipu (Correct Spelling on Stamp)
A22

Huia, Sacred Birds
A23

White Terrace, Rotomahana
A24

Otira Gorge and Mt. Ruapehu
A25

Kiwi
A26

Maori Canoe
A27

Pink Terrace, Rotomahana
A28

Kea & Kaka (Hawk-billed Parrots)
A29

Milford Sound
A30

Mt. Cook
A31

Perf. 12 to 16

1898, Apr. 5	Engr.	Unwmk.		
70	A18	½p lilac gray	9.00	1.65
a.		Horiz. or vert. pair, imperf. btwn.	1,750.	1,450.
71	A19	1p yel brn & bl	6.00	.75
a.		Horiz. or vert. pair, imperf. btwn.	1,350.	1,350.
b.		Imperf. pair	950.00	850.00
72	A20	2p rose brown	57.50	.30
a.		Horiz. pair, imperf. vert.	650.00	
b.		Vert. pair, imperf. btwn.	1,300.	
73	A21	2½p bl *(Wakitipu)*	16.00	*47.50*
74	A22	2½p bl *(Wakatipu)*	50.00	9.00
75	A23	3p orange brn	35.00	9.00
76	A24	4p rose	17.00	*21.00*
77	A25	5p red brown	95.00	200.00
a.		5p violet brown	65.00	*25.00*
78	A26	6p green	85.00	50.00
79	A27	8p dull blue	75.00	50.00
80	A28	9p lilac	70.00	42.50
81	A29	1sh dull red	100.00	30.00
a.		Pair, imperf. between	5,250.	

82 A30 2sh blue green 275.00 160.00
a. Vert. pair, imperf. btwn. 5,500. 5,250.
83 A31 5sh vermilion 375.00 *525.00*
Nos. 70-83 (14) 1,266. *1,147.*

The 5sh stamps are often found with revenue cancellations that are embossed or show a crown on the top of a circle. These are worth much less.

See Nos. 84, 88-89, 91-98, 99B, 102, 104, 106-107, 111-112, 114-121, 126-128, 1508-1521. For overprint see No. O10.

A32 A33

1900 Wmk. 63 *Perf. 11*

Thick Soft Wove Paper

84 A18 ½p green 9.00 2.00
85 A32 1p carmine rose 14.00 .25
a. 1p lake 50.00 6.50
b. 1p crimson 14.00 .25
c. As "b," pair, imperf. btwn. 1,650. 1,750.
d. As "c," horiz. pair, imperf. vert. 650.00
86 A33 2p red violet 15.00 .75
a. Pair, imperf. btwn. 1,450.
Nos. 84-86 (3) 38.00 3.00

Nos. 84 and 86 are re-engravings of Nos. 70 and 72 and are slightly smaller.

See No. 110. For Handstamp see No. O18.

A34

1899-1900 Wmk. 63

86C A15a ½p black ('00) 9.00 *18.00*
87 A10 2p violet ('00) 30.00 20.00

Unwmk.

88 A22 2½p blue 21.00 4.00
a. Horiz. pair, imperf. vert. 1,500.
b. Vert. pair, imperf. btwn. 650.00 —
89 A23 3p org brown 27.50 2.50
a. Horiz. pair, imperf. vert. 700.00
b. Horiz. pair, imperf. btwn. 1,525.
90 A34 4p yel brn & bl ('00) 6.50 4.00
91 A25 5p red brown 50.00 9.00
a. 5p violet brown 60.00 9.00
b. Pair, imperf. between *3,250.*
92 A26 6p green 70.00 *75.00*
93 A26 6p rose ('00) 50.00 8.50
a. 6p carmine 50.00 8.00
d. As #93, horiz. pair, imperf. vert. 600.00
g. As #93, horiz. pair, imperf. btwn. 1,400.
94 A27 8p dark blue 50.00 20.00
95 A28 9p red lilac 60.00 37.50
96 A29 1sh red 70.00 11.00
97 A30 2sh blue green 215.00 60.00
98 A31 5sh vermilion 300.00 400.00
Revenue cancel 27.50
Nos. 86C-98 (13) 959.00 669.50

See #113. For overprints see #O11-O15.

The 5sh stamps are often found with revenue cancellations that are embossed or show a crown on the top of a circle. These are worth much less.

"Commerce" — A35

1901, Jan. 1 Unwmk. *Perf. 12 to 16*

99 A35 1p carmine 7.00 4.50

Universal Penny Postage.

See Nos. 100, 103, 105, 108, 129. For overprint see Nos. 121a, O16, O18, O24, O32, and Aitutaki No. 2. Compare design A35 with A42.

Boer War Contingent — A36

1901 Wmk. 63 *Perf. 11*

Thick Soft Paper

99B A18 ½p green 14.00 7.50
c. Pair, imperf. btwn. 650.00
100 A35 1p carmine 10.00 .40
a. Horiz. pair, imperf. vert. 425.00 350.00
101 A36 1½p brown org 10.00 4.00
a. Vert. pair, imperf. horiz. 1,200.
b. As "d," imperf. pair 1,250.
c. Horiz. pair, imperf. vert. 1,300.
Nos. 99B-101 (3) 34.00 11.90

Perf. 14

99Bd A18 ½p green 24.00 7.00
100c A35 1p carmine 70.00 23.00
d. Horiz. pair, imperf. vert. 350.00

Perf. 14x11

99Be A18 ½p green 12.00 16.50
100e A35 1p carmine 300.00 125.00

Perf. 11x14

99Bf A18 ½p green 14.00 27.50
100f A35 1p carmine 2,400. 925.00

Perf. 11, 14 mixed

99Bg A18 ½p green 60.00 90.00
100g A35 1p carmine 300.00 125.00

No. 101 was issued to honor the New Zealand forces in the South African War.

See No. 109.

Thin Hard Paper

Perf. 14

102 A18 ½p green 42.50 42.50
a. Horiz. pair, imperf. vert. 400.00
103 A35 1p carmine 18.00 8.00
a. Horiz. pair, imperf. vert. 300.00
b. Vert. pair, imperf. horiz. 300.00

Perf. 11

102c A18 ½p green 95.00 125.00
103c A35 1p carmine 165.00 145.00

Perf. 14x11

102d A18 ½p green 50.00 70.00
103d A35 1p carmine 35.00 20.00

Perf. 11x14

102e A18 ½p green 26.00 55.00
103e A35 1p carmine 10.00 4.00

Perf. 11, 14 mixed

102f A18 ½p green 70.00 105.00
103f A35 1p carmine 82.50 87.50

1902 Unwmk. *Perf. 14*

104 A18 ½p green 35.00 8.50
105 A35 1p carmine 12.50 4.25

Perf. 11

104a A18 ½p green 200.00 210.00

Perf. 14x11

104b A18 ½p green 145.00 210.00
105b A35 1p carmine 125.00 145.00

Perf. 11x14

104c A18 ½p green 200.00 350.00
105c A35 1p carmine 145.00 200.00

Perf. 11, 14 mixed

104d A18 ½p green 175.00 250.00
105d A35 1p carmine 130.00 175.00

1902 *Perf. 11*

Thin White Wove Paper

106 A26 6p rose red 65.00 80.00
a. Watermarked letters 120.00 130.00

The sheets of No. 106 are watermarked with the words "LISBON SUPERFINE" in two lines, covering 10 stamps. Value, block of 10 *$4,000.*

1902-07 Wmk. 61 *Perf. 14*

107 A18 ½p green 9.00 2.75
a. Horiz. pair, imperf. vert. 300.00
108 A35 1p carmine 4.25 .25
d. Horiz. pair, imperf. vert. 200.00
e. Vert. pair, imperf. horiz. 200.00
f. Booklet pane of 6 275.00
109 A36 1½p brn org ('07) 25.00 *55.00*
110 A33 2p dull vio ('03) 12.00 2.75
111 A22 2½p blue 30.00 5.00
112 A23 3p org brown 32.50 8.00
a. Horiz. pair, imperf. vert. 1,000.
113 A34 4p yel brn & bl 10.00 4.50
a. Horiz. pair, imperf. vert. 650.00
b. Vert. pair, imperf. horiz. 650.00
114 A25 5p red brown 40.00 16.00
115 A26 6p rose red 60.00 9.00
116 A27 8p steel blue 45.00 11.50
117 A28 9p red violet 45.00 8.00
118 A29 1sh pale red 175.00 60.00
119 A30 2sh green 150.00 32.50
120 A31 5sh deep red 240.00 *300.00*
Nos. 107-120 (14) 877.75 515.25

The unique example of No. 113 with inverted center is used and is in the New Zealand National Philatelic Collection.

1902-03 *Perf. 11*

107e A18 ½p green 70.00 *120.00*
108k A35 1p carmine *800.00 800.00*
111e A22 2½p blue 35.00 11.00
112e A23 3p yellow brown 37.50 3.50
113e A34 4p yel brn & bl 6.00 *75.00*
f. Horiz. pair, imperf. vert. *650.00*
114e A25 5p deep brown 55.00 7.50
115e A26 6p rose 40.00 8.00
h Horiz. pair, imperf. vert. 850.00
116e A27 8p deep blue 55.00 11.50
g. Horiz. pair, imperf. vert. 2,000.
h. Vert. pair, imperf. horiz. 2,000.
117e A28 9p red violet 70.00 11.00
118e A29 1sh orange red 75.00 7.50
119e A30 2sh blue green 190.00 42.50
120e A31 5sh vermilion 275.00 *375.00*
Nos. (12) 1,709. 1,473.

1902-07 *Perf. compound 11 and 14*

107i A18 ½p green, perf. 14x11 ('02) 30.00 *125.00*
j. Perf 11x14 30.00 *90.00*
108l A35 1p carmine, perf 14x11 ('02) 100.00 *125.00*
m. Perf. 11x14 150.00 *150.00*
109i A36 1½p chestnut ('07) *1,600.*
110i A33 2p dull violet ('03) *500.00 400.00*
112i A23 3p orange brown *1,000. 750.00*
113i A34 4p yel brn & blue ('03) *450.00 450.00*
114i A25 5p red brown ('06) *1,800. 1,500.*
115i A26 6p rose carmine ('07) *450.00 450.00*
116i A27 8p steel blue ('07) *1,500. 1,500.*
117i A28 9p red violet ('06) *1,750. 1,600.*
120i A31 5sh deep red ('06) *3,500. 3,250.*

1903-07 *Perf. mixed 11 and 14*

107k A18 ½p green 40.00 *77.50*
108o A35 1p carmine 35.00 *55.00*
109k A36 1½p chestnut ('07) *1,600.*
110k A33 2p dull violet ('03) *450.00* 325.00
112k A23 3p orange brown ('06) *1,000. 750.00*
113k A34 4p yel brn & blue ('03) *425.00 450.00*
114k A25 5p red brown ('06) *1,400. 200.00*
115k A26 6p rose carmine ('07) *450.00 450.00*
116k A27 8p steel blue ('07) *1,500. 1,500.*
117k A28 9p red violet ('06) *1,650. 1,600.*
119k A30 2sh blue green ('06) *1,750. 1,800.*
120k A31 5sh deep red ('06) *3,500. 3,250.*

Wmk. 61 is normally sideways on 3p, 5p, 6p, 8p and 1sh. The 6p exists with wmk. upright. The 1sh exists with wmk. upright and inverted.

See No. 129. For overprints see Nos. O17-O22.

The 5sh stamps are often found with revenue cancellations that are embossed or show a crown on the top of a circle. These are worth much less.

1903 Unwmk. *Perf. 11*

Laid Paper

121 A30 2sh blue green 225.00 *250.00*

No. 108a Overprinted in Green: "King Edward VII Land" in Two Lines Reading Up

1908, Jan. 15 Wmk. 61 *Perf. 14*

121A A35 1p rose carmine 600.00 67.50
b. Double overprint *1,600.*

In 1908 a quantity of the 1p carmine (A35) was overprinted "King Edward VII Land" and taken on a Shackleton expedition to the Antarctic. Because of the weather Shackleton landed at Victoria Land instead. The stamp was never sold to the public at face value.

Similar conditions prevailed for the 1909-12 ½p green and 1p carmine overprinted "VICTORIA LAND." See Nos. 130D, 131D.

Christchurch Exhibition Issue

Arrival of the Maoris — A37

Maori Art — A38

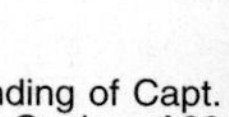

Landing of Capt. Cook — A39

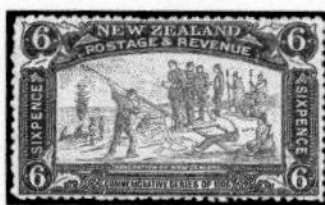

Annexation of New Zealand — A40

Wmk. 61

1906, Nov. Typo. *Perf. 14*

122 A37 ½p emerald 33.50 *37.50*
123 A38 1p vermilion 27.50 27.50
124 A39 3p blue & brown 100.00 *120.00*
125 A40 6p gray grn & rose 300.00 *400.00*
Nos. 122-125 (4) 461.00 *585.00*

Designs of 1902-07 Issue, but smaller

1907-08 Engr. *Perf. 14x15*

126 A23 3p orange brown 60.00 17.00
127 A26 6p carmine rose 70.00 15.00
128 A29 1sh orange red 250.00 35.00
Nos. 126-128 (3) 380.00 67.00

Perf. 14x13, 13½ Compound

126a A23 3p orange brown 72.50 47.50
127a A26 6p carmine red 425.00 190.00
128a A29 1sh orange red 190.00 85.00

Perf. 14

126b A23 3p orange brown 120.00 40.00
127b A26 6p carmine red 67.50 15.00

The small stamps are about 21mm high, those of 1898-1902 about 23mm.

Type of 1902 Redrawn

1908 Typo. *Perf. 14x14½*

129 A35 1p carmine 40.00 1.00

REDRAWN, 1p: The lines of shading in the globe are diagonal and the other lines of the design are generally thicker than on No. 108.

Edward VII A41

"Commerce" A42

1909-16 *Perf. 14x14½*

130 A41 ½p yellow green 7.50 .50
a. Booklet pane of 6 *250.00*
b. Booklet pane 5 + label *900.00*
c. Imperf., pair 300.00
131 A42 1p carmine 2.25 .25
a. Imperf., pair 375.00
b. Booklet pane of 6 225.00

Perf. 14x14½

Engr.

Various Frames

132 A41 2p mauve 25.00 6.75
133 A41 3p orange brown 25.00 1.40
134 A41 4p red orange 30.00 26.00
135 A41 4p yellow ('12) 25.00 15.00
136 A41 5p red brown 22.00 3.75
137 A41 6p carmine rose ('10) 47.50 1.75
138 A41 8p deep blue 21.00 2.90
139 A41 1sh vermilion ('10) 85.00 9.50
Nos. 130-139 (10) 290.25 67.80

Perf. 14

133a A41 3p orange brown ('10) 65.00 25.00
134a A41 4p red orange ('10) 27.50 18.00
136a A41 5p red brown 32.50 5.00
137a A41 6p carmine rose 55.00 12.00
138a A41 8p deep blue ('16) 70.00 *120.00*
d. No wmk. 150.00 *240.00*
139a A41 1sh vermilion 85.00 17.50

Perf. 14x13½

133b A41 3p orange brown 95.00 *160.00*
c. Vert. pair, perf. 14x13½ and 14x14½ 310.00 *600.00*
136b A41 5p red brown 24.00 3.75
c. Vert. pair, perf. 14x13½ and 14x14½ 200.00 *210.00*
137b A41 6p carmine rose 95.00 *160.00*
c. Vert. pair, perf. 14x13½ and 14x14½ 310.00 *750.00*
138b A41 8p deep blue 62.50 4.00
c. Vert. pair, perf. 14x13½ and 14x14½ *200.00* 200.00

See No. 177. For overprints see Nos. 130d-131d, 130e-137e, O33-O37, O49, O54; Cook Islands No. 49.

Nos. 130-131 Overprinted in Black in Two Lines

1911-13

130D A41 ½p yellow green ('13) *1,100.* *1,100.*
131D A42 1p carmine 75.00 *150.00*

See note after No. 121A.
Issue dates: 1p, Feb. 9; ½p, Jan. 18, 1913.

Stamps of 1909 Overprinted in Black

1913

130E A41 ½p yellow green 30.00 *40.00*
131E A42 1p carmine 35.00 *45.00*
133E A41 3p orange brown 250.00 *400.00*
137E A41 6p carmine rose 300.00 *500.00*
Nos. 130E-137E (4) 615.00 985.00

This issue was valid only within New Zealand and to Australia from Dec. 1, 1913, to Feb. 28, 1914. The Auckland Stamp Collectors Club inspired this issue.

King George V — A43

1915, July 30 Typo. Perf. 14x15

144 A43 ½p yellow green 1.60 .25
a. Perf. 14 ('27) 3.25 .40
b. Booklet pane of 6 *160.00*

See Nos. 163-164, 176, 178. For overprints see Nos. O41, O45-O46, MR1; Cook Islands No. 48.

A44

A45

1915-22 Engr. Perf. 14x13½

145 A44 1½p gray 4.25 2.00
a. Perf. 14x14½ 5.50 2.00
b. Vert. pair, both perfs 39.00 *110.00*
146 A45 2p purple 14.00 *37.50*
a. Perf. 14x14½ 7.75 *55.00*
b. Vert. pair, both perfs 30.00 *175.00*
147 A45 2p org yel ('16) 8.75 *30.00*
a. Perf. 14x14½ 8.75 *30.00*
b. Vert. pair, both perfs 23.00 *275.00*
148 A44 2½p dull blue 9.00 7.50
a. Perf. 14x14½ 10.00 *35.00*
b. Vert. pair, both perfs 45.00 *200.00*
149 A45 3p violet brown 12.50 2.25
a. Vert. pair, both perfs 55.00 *150.00*
b. Perf. 14x14½ 13.00 2.25
150 A45 4p org yel 7.00 *47.50*
a. Vert. pair, both perfs 30.00 *275.00*
b. Perf. 14x14½ 7.00 *47.50*
151 A45 4p purple ('16) 17.50 .65
a. Perf. 14x14½ 9.25 .65
b. Vert. pair, both perfs 65.00 *165.00*
c. 4p blackish violet ('26) 55.00 15.00
d. Vert. pair, top stamp imperf, bottom stamp perf 3 sides *1,500.*
e. As "c," perf. 14x14½ 10.00 .55
f. As "c," vert. pair, both perfs *10.00* .55
152 A44 4½p dark green 25.00 *26.00*
a. Perf. 14x14½ 15.00 *60.00*
b. Vert. pair, both perfs 2,500. *190.00*

153 A45 5p lt blue ('22) 19.00 2.25
a. Imperf., pair 200.00 200.00
b. Perf. 14x14½ 13.00 *17.50*
c. Vert. pair, both perfs 90.00 *275.00*
154 A45 6p carmine rose 12.00 .55
a. Horiz. pair, imperf. vert. *1,500.*
b. Perf. 14x14½ 12.00 .65
c. Vert. pair, both perfs 70.00 *155.00*
155 A44 7½p red brown 22.50 *26.00*
a. Perf. 14x14½ ('20) 12.00 *90.00*
b. Vert. pair, both perfs 55.00 *250.00*
156 A45 8p blue ('21) 21.50 *45.00*
a. Perf. 14x14½ 9.50 *60.00*
b. Vert. pair, both perfs 42.50 *200.00*
157 A45 8p red brn ('22) 35.00 4.00
158 A45 9p olive green 30.00 5.00
a. Imperf., pair *1,500.*
b. Perf. 14x14½ 16.50 *32.50*
c. Vert. pair, both perfs 82.50 *250.00*
159 A45 1sh vermilion 30.00 2.25
a. Imperf., pair *2,250.*
b. Perf. 14x14½ 15.00 .55
c. Vert. pair, both perfs 82.50 *300.00*
Nos. 145-159 (15) 268.00 238.45

Nos. 151c and 153 exist with the perf varieties reversed. These are rare. No. 157 only comes perf. 14x13½.

For overprints see Nos. O47-O48, O50-O53; Cook Islands Nos. 53-60.

A46

A47

No. 160 No. 161

The engr. stamps have a background of geometric lathe-work; the typo. stamps have a background of crossed dotted lines.

Type A43 has three diamonds at each side of the crown, type A46 has two, and type A47 has one.

1916-19 Typo. Perf. 14x15

160 A46 1½p gray black 15.00 1.00
161 A47 1½p gray black 9.00 .60
162 A47 1½p brown org ('18) 4.00 .75
a. Perf. 14 ('29) 10.00 *45.00*
163 A43 2p yellow 3.00 .25
a. Perf. 14 ('29) 3.50 .25
164 A43 3p chocolate ('19) 12.00 1.60
a. Perf. 14 ('29) 9.50 4.00
Nos. 160-164 (5) 43.00 4.20

In 1916 the 1½, 2, 3 and 6p of the 1915-16 issue and the 8p of the 1909 issue were printed on paper intended for the long rectangular stamps of the 1902-07 issue. In this paper the watermarks are set wide apart, so that the smaller stamps often show only a small part of the watermark or miss it altogether.

For overprints see Nos. O42-O44; Cook Islands Nos. 50-52.

Victory Issue

"Peace" and British Lion — A48

Peace and Lion — A49

Maori Chief — A50

British Lion — A51

"Victory" A52

King George V, Lion and Maori Fern at Sides A53

1920, Jan. 27 Perf. 14

165 A48 ½p yellow green 5.00 3.00
166 A49 1p carmine 3.50 .65
167 A50 1½p brown orange 5.00 .55
168 A51 3p black brown 17.00 17.00
169 A52 6p purple 25.00 25.00
170 A53 1sh vermilion 35.00 *55.00*
Nos. 165-170 (6) 90.50 101.20

No. 165 Surcharged in Red

1922, Mar.

174 A48 2p on ½p yellow green 6.00 1.75

Map of New Zealand — A54

1923 Typo. Perf. 14x15

175 A54 1p carmine rose 3.00 .70

Restoration of Penny Postage. The paper varies from thin to thick.

Types of 1909-15
N Z and Star "watermark" printed on back, usually in blue

1925 Unwmk. Perf. 14x14½

176 A43 ½p yellow green 3.50 *3.50*
177 A42 1p carmine 3.50 .90
178 A43 2p yellow 20.00 *62.50*
Nos. 176-178 (3) 27.00 *66.90*

Exhibition Buildings — A55

1925, Nov. 17 Wmk. 61

Surface Tinted Paper

179 A55 ½p yel green, *grnsh* 4.50 *7.50*
180 A55 1p car rose, *pink* 4.75 *6.75*
181 A55 4p red violet, *lilac* 45.00 *92.50*
Nos. 179-181 (3) 54.25 *106.75*

Dunedin Exhibition.

George V in Admiral's Uniform A56

In Field Marshal's Uniform A57

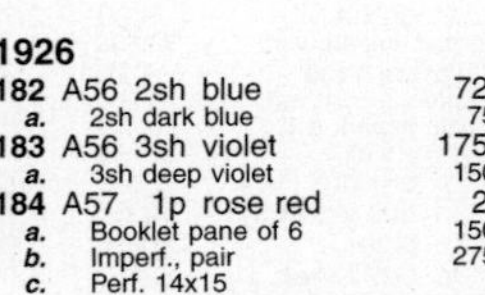

1926 Perf. 14

182 A56 2sh blue 72.50 35.00
a. 2sh dark blue 75.00 75.00
183 A56 3sh violet 175.00 170.00
a. 3sh deep violet 150.00 *200.00*
184 A57 1p rose red 2.40 .25
a. Booklet pane of 6 150.00
b. Imperf., pair 275.00
c. Perf. 14x15 .85 .55
Nos. 182-184 (3) 249.90 205.25

For overprints see Nos. O55-O56 and Cook Islands Nos. 74-75.

Pied Fantail and Clematis A58

Kiwi and Cabbage Palm A59

Maori Woman Cooking in Boiling Spring A60

Maori Council House (Whare) A61

Mt. Cook and Mountain Lilies A62

Maori Girl Wearing Tiki A63

Mitre Peak A64

Striped Marlin A65

Harvesting A66

Tuatara A67

Maori Panel from Door A68

Tui or Parson Bird A69

Capt. Cook Landing at Poverty Bay — A70

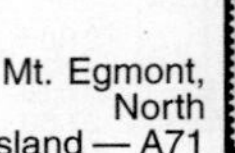

Mt. Egmont, North Island — A71

Perf. 13½-14x13½, 13-14x13½ (189, 192, 197, 198), 13½x14 (193), 14x14½ (195), 14 (191)

1935, May 1 Engr. Wmk. 61

185 A58 ½p bright green .80 .60
186 A59 1p copper red 1.00 .90
c. Perf. 13½x14 85.00 55.00
186A A59 1p copper red, re-engraved 9.00 3.25
b. Booklet pane of 6 + ad labels 90.00
187 A60 1½p red brown 8.25 *13.00*
a. Perf. 13½x14 5.50 9.75
188 A61 2p red orange 2.50 1.40
189 A62 2½p dull blue & dk brown 10.00 *21.50*
a. Perf. 13½x14 6.50 15.50
190 A63 3p chocolate 25.00 2.50
191 A64 4p blk brn & blk 7.50 2.50
192 A65 5p violet blue 31.00 25.00
a. Perf. 13½x14 55.00 31.00
193 A66 6p red 17.00 7.50
194 A67 8p dark brown 10.00 *13.00*

Litho.

Size: 18x21½mm

195 A68 9p blk & scar 27.50 5.25

Engr.

196 A69 1sh dk sl green 23.00 13.00
197 A70 2sh olive green 50.00 31.00
a. Perf. 13½x14 62.50 35.00
198 A71 3sh yel brn & brn black 42.50 42.50
a. Perf. 13½x14 42.50 42.50
Nos. 185-198 (15) 265.05 182.90
Set, never hinged 575.00

On No. 186A, the horizontal lines in the sky are much darker.

The 2½p, 5p, 2sh and 3sh are perf. 13½ vertically; perf. 13-14 horizontally on each stamp.

See Nos. 203-216, 244-245. For overprints see Nos. O58-O71, O90.

Silver Jubilee Issue

Queen Mary and King George V — A72

1935, May 7 *Perf. 11x11½*

199 A72 ½p dp blue grn .50 .50
200 A72 1p dark car rose .50 .50
201 A72 6p scarlet 22.00 *27.50*
Nos. 199-201 (3) 23.00 *28.50*
Set, never hinged 35.00

25th anniv. of the reign of King George V.

Types of 1935

Perf. 13½-14x13½

1936-42 **Wmk. 253**

203 A58 ½p bright green .80 .25
204 A59 1p copper red 1.00 .25
205 A60 1½p red brown 4.00 3.00
206 A61 2p red orange .25 .25
a. Perf. 14 13.00 13.00
b. Perf. 14x14½-15 18.00 18.00
c. Perf. 12½ 2.00 .25
207 A62 2½p dull blue & dk brn 1.50 *6.00*
a. Perf. 14 2.50 3.25
b. Perf. 13-14x13½ 5.25 *13.00*
208 A63 3p chocolate 23.50 1.50
209 A64 4p blk brn & blk 3.25 .65
a. Perf. 12½ 17.50 13.00
b. Perf. 14 70.00 145.00
c. Perf. 14x14¼ 2.00 .35
210 A65 5p violet blue 3.25 .80
a. Perf. 12½ 22.00 5.25
b. Perf. 13-14x13½ 13.00 2.00
211 A66 6p red, perf. 13½x14 10.00 .80
a. Perf. 12½ 2.50 3.25
b. Perf. 14½x14 2.00 .25
212 A67 8p dark brown 2.50 *3.25*
a. Perf. 12½ 2.50 1.50
b. Perf. 14x14½ 2.00 .80

Litho.

Size: 18x21½mm

213 A68 9p gray & scar, perf.14x15 4.00 4.00
a. 9p black & scarlet, perf. 14x14½ 32.50 4.25

Engr.

214 A69 1sh dk sl grn 3.50 .25
a. Perf. 12½ 35.00 20.50
215 A70 2sh olive green 6.50 1.50
a. Perf. 13½x14 225.00 4.00
b. Perf. 12½ 20.00 3.25
c. Perf. 13-14x13½ 42.50 5.25
216 A71 3sh yel brn & blk brn 7.25 4.00
a. Perf. 12½ ('41) 45.00 50.00
b. Perf. 13-14x13½ 27.50 10.00
Nos. 203-216 (14) 71.30 26.50
Set, never hinged 135.00

Perf. 13-14x13½ is perforated 13 on half of each horizontal side and 14 on the other half.

Wool Industry — A73

Butter Industry — A74

Sheep Farming — A75

Apple Industry — A76

Shipping — A77

1936, Oct. 1 **Wmk. 61** *Perf. 11*

218 A73 ½p emerald .25 .30
a. Perf. 12½ .25 .30
219 A74 1p red .25 .30
220 A75 2½p deep blue 2.50 *3.25*
221 A76 4p dark purple 2.50 *3.25*
222 A77 6p red brown 2.75 *3.25*
Nos. 218-222 (5) 8.25 *10.35*
Set, never hinged 13.25

Congress of the Chambers of Commerce of the British Empire held in New Zealand.

Queen Elizabeth and King George VI — A78

Perf. 13½x13

1937, May 13 **Wmk. 253**

223 A78 1p rose carmine .25 .25
224 A78 2½p dark blue .50 *.65*
225 A78 6p vermilion 1.00 *1.35*
Nos. 223-225 (3) 1.75 *2.25*
Set, never hinged 3.00

Coronation of George VI and Elizabeth.

A79

A80

1938-44 **Engr.** *Perf. 13½*

226 A79 ½p emerald 3.25 .25
226B A79 ½p brown org ('41) .25 .25
227 A79 1p rose red 2.75 .25
227A A79 1p lt blue grn ('41) .25 .25
228 A80 1½p red brown 13.50 2.40
228B A80 1½p red ('44) .25 .25
228C A80 3p blue ('41) .25 .25
Nos. 226-228C (7) 20.50 3.90
Set, never hinged 39.00

See Nos. 258-264. For surcharges and overprints see Nos. 242-243, 279, 285, O72-O74, O88-O89, O92-O97.

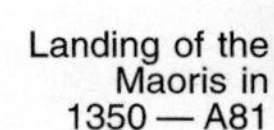

Landing of the Maoris in 1350 — A81

Captain Cook, His Map of New Zealand, 1769, H.M.S. Endeavour — A82

Victoria, Edward VII, George V, Edward VIII and George VI — A83

Abel Tasman, Ship, and Chart of West Coast of New Zealand A84

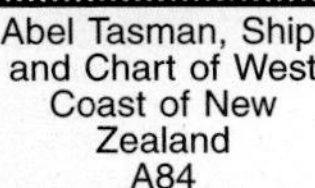

Treaty of Waitangi, 1840 A85

Pioneer Settlers Landing on Petone Beach, 1840 — A86

The Progress of Transport A87

H.M.S. "Britomart" at Akaroa A88

Route of Ship Carrying First Shipment of Frozen Mutton to England — A89

Maori Council — A90

Gold Mining in 1861 and Modern Gold Dredge A91

Giant Kauri A92

Perf. 13½x14 (236), 13x13½, 14x13½ (233)

1940, Jan. 2 **Engr.** **Wmk. 253**

229 A81 ½p dk blue green .30 .25
230 A82 1p scarlet & sepia .65 .25
231 A83 1½p brt vio & ultra .40 .25
232 A84 2p blk brn & Prus grn 1.10 .25
233 A85 2½p dk bl & myr grn 1.10 .70
234 A86 3p dp plum & dk vio 3.25 .40
235 A87 4p dk red vio & vio brn 3.75 1.35
236 A88 5p brown & lt bl 3.25 2.40
237 A89 6p vio & brt grn 5.75 .70
238 A90 7p org red & black 3.75 *6.50*
239 A90 8p org red & black 6.25 2.75
240 A91 9p dp org & olive 6.50 6.75
241 A92 1sh dk sl grn & ol 22.00 4.00
Nos. 229-241 (13) 58.05 26.55
Set, never hinged 110.00

Centenary of British sovereignty established by the treaty of Waitangi.

Imperfs of #229-241 exist. These probably are plate proofs.

For surcharge and overprints see Nos. 246, O76-O86.

Nos. 226 and 228 Surcharged in Black

1941 **Wmk. 253** *Perf. 13½*

242 A79 1p on ½p emerald .60 .25
243 A80 2p on 1½p red brn .60 .25
Set, never hinged 2.25

Type of 1935 Redrawn

1941 **Typo.** **Wmk. 61** *Perf. 14x15*

Size: 17½x20½mm

244 A68 9p int black & scarlet 75.00 35.00

Wmk. 253

245 A68 9p int black & scarlet 3.00 3.00
Set, never hinged 156.00

Catalogue values for unused stamps in this section, from this point to the end of the section, are for Never Hinged items.

No 231 Srchd. in Black

1944 *Perf. 13½x13*

246 A83 10p on 1½p brt vio & ultra .45 1.00

Peace Issue

Lake Matheson A93

Parliament House, Wellington A94

St. Paul's Cathedral, London A95

The Royal Family A96

Badge of Royal New Zealand Air Force — A97

New Zealand Army Overseas Badge — A98

Badge of Royal Navy — A99

New Zealand Coat of Arms A100

Knight, Window of Wellington Boys' College A101

Natl. Memorial Campanile, Wellington A103

Southern Alps and Chapel Altar A102

Engr.; Photo. (1½p, 1sh)

Perf. 13x13½, 13½x13

1946, Apr. 1 **Wmk. 253**

247 A93 ½p choc & grn .25 *.60*
248 A94 1p emerald .25 .25
249 A95 1½p scarlet .25 .25
250 A96 2p rose violet .25 .25
251 A97 3p dk grn & ultra .25 .25
252 A98 4p brn org & ol grn .30 .25
253 A99 5p ultra & grn .25 .25
254 A100 6p org red & red brn .35 .25
255 A101 8p brown lake & blk .35 .25
256 A102 9p black & brt bl .35 .60
257 A103 1sh gray black .50 .45
Nos. 247-257 (11) 3.35 3.65

Return to peace at the close of WWII. Imperfs exist from the printer's archives.

George VI Type of 1938 and

King George VI — A104

1947 **Engr.** *Perf. 13½*

258 A80 2p red org .30 .25
260 A80 4p rose lilac .65 .25
261 A80 5p gray 1.00 .25
262 A80 6p rose red 1.00 .25
263 A80 8p deep violet 1.30 .25
264 A80 9p sepia 1.90 .25

Perf. 14

265 A104 1sh rose car & chnt 1.90 .25
266 A104 1sh3p ultra & chnt 3.25 .40
267 A104 2sh gray grn & org brn 6.50 .60
268 A104 3sh gray blk & chnt 13.50 2.50
Nos. 258-268 (10) 31.30 5.25

Nos. 265-267 have watermark either upright or sideways. On No. 268 watermark is always sideways.
For overprints see Nos. O98-O99.

"John Wickliffe" and "Philip Laing" — A105

Cromwell, Otago A106

First Church, Dunedin A107

University of Otago — A108

1948, Feb. 23 ***Perf. 13½***

269 A105 1p green & blue .25 .25
270 A106 2p brown & green .25 .25
271 A107 3p violet .25 .25
272 A108 6p brt rose & gray blk .35 .35
Nos. 269-272 (4) 1.10 1.10

Otago Province settlement, cent.

A Royal Visit set of four was prepared but not issued. Examples of the 3p have appeared in the stamp market.

A109

Black Surcharge

Wmk. 253

1950, July 28 Typo. ***Perf. 14***

273 A109 1½p rose red .40 .40

No. 273 was not issued without surcharge. See Nos. 367, 404A-404D, AR46-69.

Cathedral at Christchurch A110

"They Passed this Way" A111

3p, John Robert Godley. 6p, Canterbury University College. 1sh, View of Timaru.

1950, Nov. 20 Engr. ***Perf. 13x13½***

274 A110 1p dl gray grn & blue .35 .35
275 A111 2p car & red org .35 .35
276 A110 3p indigo & blue .35 .35
277 A111 6p brown & blue .50 .50
278 A111 1sh claret & blue .70 .70
Nos. 274-278 (5) 2.25 2.25

Centenary of the founding of Canterbury Provincial District.
Imperfs of #274-278 exist.

No. 227A Surcharged in Black

1952, Dec. ***Perf. 13½***

279 A79 3p on 1p lt blue green .30 .25

Coronation Issue

Buckingham Palace and Elizabeth II A112

Queen Elizabeth II A113

Westminster Abbey — A114

Crown and royal scepter — A114a

Designs: 4p, Queen Elizabeth and state coach.

Perf. 13x12½, 14x14½ (3p, 8p)
Engr., Photo. (3p, 8p)

1953, May 25

280 A112 2p ultramarine .30 .25
281 A113 3p brown .30 .25
282 A112 4p carmine .50 *.70*
283 A114 8p slate black .85 *1.35*
284 A114a 1sh6p vio blue & pur 1.35 *2.00*
Nos. 280-284 (5) 3.30 *4.55*

See Nos. 1869-1873.

No. 226B Surcharged in Black

1953, Sept. ***Perf. 13½***

285 A79 1p on ½p brown orange .40 .25

Queen Elizabeth II A115

Queen Elizabeth II and Duke of Edinburgh A116

Perf. 12½x13½, 13½x13

1953, Dec. 9 **Engr.**

286 A115 3p lilac .25 .25
287 A116 4p deep blue .25 .25

Visit of Queen Elizabeth II and the Duke of Edinburgh.

A117

A118

A119

1953-57 ***Perf. 13½***

288 A117 ½p gray .25 *.30*
289 A117 1p orange .25 .25
290 A117 1½p rose brown .25 .25
291 A117 2p blue green .25 .25
292 A117 3p red .25 .25
293 A117 4p blue .35 .30
294 A117 6p rose violet 1.10 .75
295 A117 8p rose car .80 .60
296 A118 9p emer & org brn 1.20 .30
297 A118 1sh car & blk 1.25 .25
298 A118 1sh6p blue & blk 2.40 .30
298A A118 1sh9p org & blk 5.00 1.25
298B A119 2sh6p redsh brn 37.50 5.25
299 A119 3sh blue green 16.00 .65
300 A119 5sh rose car 37.50 4.75
301 A119 10sh vio blue 75.00 25.00
Nos. 288-301 (16) 179.35 40.70

The 1½p was issued in 1953; 1sh9p and 2sh6p in 1957; all others in 1954.

No. 298A exists on both ordinary and chalky paper.
Two dies of the 1sh differ in shading on the sleeve.
Imperfs of Nos. 298B-301 and tete-beche pairs of Nos. 301 and 312 exist from the printer's archives.
See Nos. 306-312. For surcharge see No. 320.

Maori Mailman A120

Queen Elizabeth II A121

Douglas DC-3 — A122

Perf. 13½ (2p), 14 (3p), 13 (4p)

1955, July 18 **Wmk. 253**

302 A120 2p deep grn & brn .25 .25
303 A121 3p claret .25 .25
304 A122 4p ultra & black .30 *.40*
Nos. 302-304 (3) .80 .90

Cent. of New Zealand's 1st postage stamps.

Type of 1953-54 Redrawn

1955-59 Wmk. 253 ***Perf. 13½***

306 A117 1p orange ('56) .50 .25
307 A117 1½p rose brown 1.25 .45
308 A117 2p bl grn ('56) .50 .25
309 A117 3p vermilion ('56) .50 .25
310 A117 4p blue ('58) 3.00 .70
311 A117 6p purple 4.25 .25
312 A117 8p brown red ('59) 5.00 5.00
Nos. 306-312 (7) 15.00 7.15

The numeral has been enlarged and the ornament in the lower right corner omitted.
Nos. 306, 308-310 exist on both ordinary and chalky paper.
Imperfs exist.
For surcharges see Nos. 319, 354.

Whalers of Foveaux Strait — A123

"Agriculture" with Cow and Sheep A124

Notornis (Takahe) A125

1956, Jan. ***Perf. 13x12½, 13 (8p)***

313 A123 2p deep green .30 .25
314 A124 3p sepia .25 .25
315 A125 8p car & blue vio 1.20 1.20
Nos. 313-315 (3) 1.75 1.70

Southland centennial.

Lamb and Map of New Zealand A126

Lamb, S. S. "Dunedin" and Refrigeration Ship A127

Perf. 14x14½, 14½x14

1957, Feb. 15 **Photo.**

316 A126 4p bright blue .80 *.85*
317 A127 8p vermilion 1.50 *1.75*

New Zealand Meat Export Trade, 75th anniv.

Sir Truby King — A128

1957, May 14 Engr. ***Perf. 13***

318 A128 3p rose red .25 .25

Plunket Society, 50th anniversary.
Imperfs exist. These probably are plate proofs.

Nos. 307, 290 Surcharged

1958, Jan. 15 ***Perf. 13½***

319 A117 2p on 1½p (#307) .35 .25
a. Small surcharge .25 .25
320 A117 2p on 1½p (#290) 170.00 *200.00*
a. Small surcharge —

Surcharge measures 9½mm vert. on Nos. 319-320; 9mm on No. 319a-320a. Diameter of dot 4½mm on Nos. 319-320; 3¾mm on No. 319a-320a.
Counterfeits exist.

Sir Charles Kingsford-Smith and "Southern Cross" — A129

Perf. 14x14½

1958, Aug. 27 Engr. Wmk. 253

321 A129 6p brt violet blue .45 *.60*

1st air crossing of the Tasman Sea, 30th anniv. See footnote under No. 2322.
See Australia No. 310.

Nelson Diocese Seal — A129a

1958, Sept. 29 ***Perf. 13***

322 A129a 3p carmine rose .25 .25

Centenary of Nelson City.
Imperfs exist. These probably are plate proofs.

Statue of "Pania," Napier A130

Gannet Sanctuary, Cape Kidnappers A131

Design: 8p, Maori shearing sheep.

Perf. 13½x14½, 14½x14

1958, Nov. 3 Photo. Wmk. 253

323 A130 2p yellow green .25 .25
324 A131 3p ultramarine .25 .25
325 A130 8p red brown 1.40 *1.60*
Nos. 323-325 (3) 1.90 2.10

Centenary of Hawkes Bay province.

Jamboree Kiwi Badge — A132

1959, Jan. 5 Engr. ***Perf. 13***

326 A132 3p car rose & brown .25 .25

Pan-Pacific Scout Jamboree, Auckland, Jan. 3-10.

"Endeavour" at Ship Cove — A133

Designs: 3p, Shipping wool at Wairau bar, 1857. 8p, Salt Industry, Grassmere.

1959, Mar. 2 Photo. *Perf. 14½x14*

327 A133 2p green .25 .25
328 A133 3p dark blue .25 .25
329 A133 8p brown 1.40 *1.60*
Nos. 327-329 (3) 1.90 2.10

Centenary of Marlborough Province.

The Explorer — A134

Westland Centennial: 3p, The Gold Digger. 8p, The Pioneer Woman.

1960, May 16 *Perf. 14x14½*

330 A134 2p green .25 .25
331 A134 3p orange .30 .25
332 A134 8p gray 2.00 *2.75*
Nos. 330-332 (3) 2.55 3.25

Manuka Flower A135

Timber Industry A136

Tiki A137

Maori Rock Drawing A138

Butter Making — A139

Designs: 1p, Karaka flower. 2p, Kaka Beak Flower. 2½p, Titoki flower. 3p, Kowhai flower. 4p, Hibiscus. 5p, Mountain daisy. 6p, Clematis. 7p, Koromiko flower. 8p, Rata flower. 9p, Flag. 1sh3p, Rainbow trout. 1sh9p, Plane spraying farmland. 3sh, Ngauruhoe Volcano, Tongariro National Park. 5sh, Sutherland Falls. 10sh, Tasman Glacier, Mount Cook. £1, Pohutu Geyser.

Perf. 14½x14, 14x14½

1960-66 Photo. Wmk. 253

333 A135 ½p dp car, grn & pale bl .25 .25
b. Green omitted 475.00
c. Pale blue omitted 350.00 275.00
334 A135 1p brn, org & grn .25 .25
b. Orange omitted 675.00 400.00
c. Perf. 14½x13, wmkd. sideways 1.50 *2.75*
335 A135 2p grn, rose car, blk & yel .25 .25
b. Black omitted 550.00
c. Yellow omitted 600.00
336 A135 2½p blk, grn, red & brn .25 .25
a. Brown omitted 300.00
b. Green & red omitted 950.00
c. Green omitted 400.00
d. Red omitted 850.00 850.00
337 A135 3p Prus bl, yel, brn & grn .25 .25
b. Yellow omitted 200.00
c. Brown omitted 250.00
d. Green omitted 350.00
e. Perf. 14½x13, wmkd. sideways 1.50 *2.75*
338 A135 4p bl, grn, yel & lil .25 .25
a. Yellow omitted 900.00
b. Lilac omitted 650.00 500.00
339 A135 5p pur, blk, yel & grn .25 .25
a. Yellow omitted 425.00 350.00

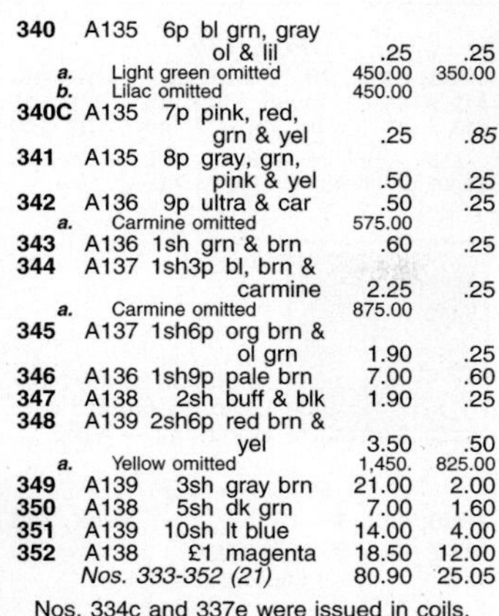

340 A135 6p bl grn, gray ol & lil .25 .25
a. Light green omitted 450.00 350.00
b. Lilac omitted 450.00
340C A135 7p pink, red, grn & yel .25 *.85*
341 A135 8p gray, grn, pink & yel .50 .25
342 A136 9p ultra & car .50 .25
a. Carmine omitted 575.00
343 A136 1sh grn & brn .60 .25
344 A137 1sh3p bl, brn & carmine 2.25 .25
a. Carmine omitted 875.00
345 A137 1sh6p org brn & ol grn 1.90 .25
346 A136 1sh9p pale brn 7.00 .60
347 A138 2sh buff & blk 1.90 .25
348 A139 2sh6p red brn & yel 3.50 .50
a. Yellow omitted 1,450. 825.00
349 A139 3sh gray brn 21.00 2.00
350 A138 5sh dk grn 7.00 1.60
351 A139 10sh lt blue 14.00 4.00
352 A138 £1 magenta 18.50 12.00
Nos. 333-352 (21) 80.90 25.05

Nos. 334c and 337e were issued in coils.

Only on chalky paper: 2½p, 5p, 7p. On ordinary and chalky paper: 1p, 3p, 4p, 6p, 1sh9p, 2sh, 3sh, 5sh, 10sh. Others on ordinary paper only.

Issued: 2p, 4p, 1sh, 1sh3p, 1sh6p, 1sh9p, 2sh, 2sh6p, 3sh, 5sh, 10sh, £1, 7/11/60; ½p, 1p, 3p, 6p, 8p, 9p, 9/1/60; 2½p, 11/1/61; 5p, 5/14/62; 7p, 3/16/66; #334c, 11/63; #337e, 10/3/63.

See Nos. 360-361, 382-404.

Adoration of the Shepherds, by Rembrandt — A140

Perf. 11½x12

1960, Nov. 1 Wmk. 253

353 A140 2p dp brn & red, *cream* .30 .25
a. Red omitted *450.00 450.00*

Christmas. See No. 355.

No. 309 Surcharged with New Value and Bars

Two types of surcharge:
Type I — "2½d" is 5½mm wide.
Type II — "2½d" is 5mm wide.

1961, Sept. 1 Engr. *Perf. 13½*

354 A117 2½p on 3p vermilion, I .40 .25
a. Type II .40 .25

Christmas Type of 1960

2½p, Adoration of the Magi, by Dürer.

1961, Oct. 16 Photo. *Perf. 14½x14*
Size: 30x34mm

355 A140 2½p multicolored .25 .25

Morse Key and Port Hills, Lyttelton, 1862 — A141

Design: 8p, Teleprinter and tape, 1962.

1962, June 1 Wmk. 253

356 A141 3p dk brn & grn .25 .25
a. Green omitted 3,000.
357 A141 8p dk red & gray 1.10 1.40
a. Imperf., pair 2,600.
b. Gray omitted 2,300.

Centenary of the New Zealand telegraph.

Madonna in Prayer by Sassoferrato — A142

1962, Oct. 15 *Perf. 14½x14*

358 A142 2½p multicolored .25 .25

Christmas.

Holy Family by Titian — A143

1963, Oct. 14 Photo. *Perf. 12½*

359 A143 2½p multicolored .25 .25
a. Imperf., pair *300.00*
b. Yellow omitted *500.00*

Christmas.

Types of 1960-62

1sh9p, Plane spraying farmland. 3sh, Ngauruhoe volcano, Tongariro National Park.

1963-64 *Perf. 14½x14*

360 A136 1sh9p brt blue, grn & yel 2.75 .50
361 A139 3sh bl, grn & bis 4.50 1.50

Issued: 1sh9p, 11/4/63; 3sh, 4/1/64.

Old and New Engines — A144

1sh9p, Express train and Mt. Ruapehu.

1963, Nov. 25 *Perf. 14*

362 A144 3p multicolored .30 .25
a. Blue (sky) omitted *550.00*
363 A144 1sh9p bl, blk, yel & carmine 2.60 3.00
a. Carmine (value) omitted *2,500.*

Centenary of New Zealand Railways.

Cable Around World and Under Sea — A144a

1963, Dec. 3 Unwmk. *Perf. 13½*

364 A144a 8p yel, car, blk & bl 1.90 *2.75*

Opening of the Commonwealth Pacific (telephone) cable service (COMPAC).

See Australia No. 381.

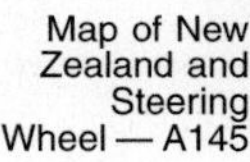

Map of New Zealand and Steering Wheel — A145

Perf. 14½x14

1964, May 1 Wmk. 253

365 A145 3p multicolored .25 .25

National Road Safety Campaign.

Rev. Samuel Marsden Conducting First Christian Service, Rangihoua Bay, Christmas 1814 — A146

1964, Oct. 12 *Perf. 14x13½*

366 A146 2½p multicolored .25 .25

Christmas.

Postal-Fiscal Type of 1950

1964, Dec. 14 Typo. *Perf. 14*
Black Surcharge

367 A109 7p rose red .40 *.70*

ANZAC Issue

Anzac Cove, Gallipoli — A147

Design: 5p, Anzac Cove and poppy.

Perf. 12½

1965, Apr. 14 Unwmk. Photo.

368 A147 4p light brown .25 .25
369 A147 5p green & red .25 *.40*

50th anniv. of the landing of the Australian and New Zealand Army Corps, ANZAC, at Gallipoli, Turkey, Apr. 25, 1915.

ITU Emblem, Old and New Communication Equipment A148

Perf. 14½x14

1965, May 17 Photo. Wmk. 253

370 A148 9p lt brown & dk blue .40 *.90*

Centenary of the ITU.

Sir Winston Spencer Churchill (1874-1965) — A148a

1965, May 24 Unwmk. *Perf. 13½*

371 A148a 7p lt blue, gray & blk .25 *.50*

See Australia No. 389.

Provincial Council Building, Wellington A149

Perf. 14½x14

1965, July 26 Photo. Wmk. 253

372 A149 4p multicolored .25 .25

Centenary of the establishment of Wellington as seat of government. The design is from a water color by L. B. Temple, 1867.

ICY Emblem — A150

1965, Sept. 28 Litho. *Perf. 14*

373 A150 4p ol bister & dk red .25 .25

International Cooperation Year.

"The Two Trinities" by Murillo — A151

1965, Oct. 11 Photo. *Perf. 13½x14*

374 A151 3p multicolored .25 .25
a. Gold omitted 1,500.

Christmas.

Parliament House, Wellington and Commonwealth Parliamentary Association Emblem — A152

Designs: 4p, Arms of New Zealand and Queen Elizabeth II. 2sh, Wellington from Mt. Victoria.

1965, Nov. 30 Unwmk. *Perf. 14*

375 A152 4p multicolored .25 .25
a. Blue omitted *1,000.*
376 A152 9p multicolored 1.20 1.20
377 A152 2sh multicolored 5.75 5.75
a. Red omitted *950.00*
Nos. 375-377 (3) 7.20 7.20

11th Commonwealth Parliamentary Assoc. Conf.

Scout Emblem, Maori Pattern — A153

Perf. 14x14½

1966, Jan. 5 Photo. Wmk. 253

378 A153 4p green & gold .25 .25
a. Gold omitted *1,100.*

4th National Scout Jamboree, Trentham.

Virgin with Child, by Carlo Maratta — A154

1966, Oct. 3 Wmk. 253 *Perf. 14*

379 A154 3p multicolored .25 .25
a. Red omitted *350.00*

Christmas.

Queens Victoria and Elizabeth II — A155

New Zealand PO Savings Bank cent.: 9p, Reverse of half sovereign, 1867, and 1967 dollar.

Perf. 14x14½

1967, Feb. 3 Photo. Wmk. 253

380 A155 4p plum, gold & black .25 .25
381 A155 9p dk grn, bl, blk, sil & gold .25 *.35*

Decimal Currency

Types of 1960-62

Designs: ½c, Manuka flower. 1c, Karaka flower. 2c, Kaka beak flower. 2½c, Kowhai flower. 3c, Hibiscus. 4c, Mountain daisy. 5c, Clematis. 6c, Koromiko flower. 7c, Rata flower. 7½c, Brown trout. 8c, Flag. 10c, Timber industry. 15c, Tiki. 20c, Maori rock drawing. 25c, Butter making. 28c, Fox Glacier, Westland National Park. 30c, Ngauruhoe Volcano, Tongarino National Park. 50c, Sutherland Falls. $1, Tasman Glacier, Mount Cook. $2, Pohutu Geyser.

Wmk. 253, Unwmkd. (#400)

1967-70 Photo. *Various Perfs.*

382 A135 ½c multicolored .25 .25
a. Pale blue omitted *325.00*
383 A135 1c multicolored .25 .25
a. Booklet pane of 5 + label 2.25
384 A135 2c multicolored .25 .25
385 A135 2½c multicolored .25 .25
a. Dark blue omitted *3,750.*
386 A135 3c multicolored .25 .25
387 A135 4c multicolored .25 .25
388 A135 5c multicolored .25 .25
389 A135 6c multicolored .25 *.25*
390 A135 7c multicolored .30 *.25*
391 A137 7½c multicolored .25 .25
392 A136 8c ultra & car .30 .25
a. Red omitted *1,200.*
393 A136 10c grn & brn .40 .25
394 A137 15c org brn & slate grn .50 .40
395 A137 15c grn, sl grn & red ('68) .75 .25
396 A138 20c buff & black 1.25 .25
397 A139 25c brown & yel 1.25 *1.25*
398 A138 28c multi ('68) .90 .30
399 A139 30c multicolored 2.90 .75
400 A139 30c multi ('70) 9.00 3.00
401 A138 50c dark green 2.90 .75
402 A139 $1 blue 12.00 4.25
403 A138 $2 magenta 12.00 12.00
404 A138 $2 multi ('68) 30.00 19.00
Nos. 382-404 (23) 76.70 45.20

Perf. 13½x14: ½c to 3c, 5c, 7c. Perf. 14½x14: 4c, 6c, 8c, 10c, 25c, 30c, $1.

Perf. 13½: 7½c. Perf. 14x14½: 15c, 20c, 28c, 50c, $2.

Issued: 7½c, 8/29/67; No. 395, 3/19/68; 28c, 7/30/68; No. 404, 12/10/68; No. 400, 1970; others, 7/10/67.

The 7½c was issued to commemorate the centenary of the brown trout's introduction to New Zealand, and retained as part of the regular series.

No. 395 has been redrawn. The "c" on No. 395 lacks serif; No. 394 has serif.

No. 391 exists with watermarks either sideways or upright.

Coat of Arms — A155a

Decimal Currency

1967, July 10 Wmk. 253 *Perf. 14*

404A A155a $4 purple 6.00 2.00
404B A155a $6 green 6.00 4.00
a. Unwmk. ('87) 9.00 4.50
404C A155a $8 light blue 8.00 4.75
a. Unwmk. ('87) 9.50 *12.00*
404D A155a $10 dark blue 10.00 *4.00*
a. Unwmk. ('87) 11.00 9.00
Nos. 404A-404D (4) 30.00 14.75

See Nos. AR46-AR69.

Adoration of the Shepherds, by Poussin — A156

Perf. 13½x14

1967, Oct. 3 Photo. Wmk. 253

405 A156 2½c multicolored .25 .25

Christmas.

Sir James Hector — A157

Design: 4c, Mt. Aspiring, aurora australis and Southern Cross.

1967, Oct. 10 Litho. *Perf. 14*

406 A157 4c multicolored .25 .25
407 A157 8c multicolored .40 *.55*

Centenary of the Royal Society of New Zealand to Promote Science.

Maori Bible — A158

1968, Apr. 23 Litho. *Perf. 13½*

408 A158 3c multicolored .25 .25
a. Gold omitted *160.00*

Publication of the Bible in Maori, cent.

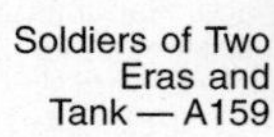

Soldiers of Two Eras and Tank — A159

10c, Airmen of two eras, insigne & plane. 28c, Sailors of two eras, insigne & battleships.

1968, May 7 *Perf. 14x13½*

409 A159 4c multicolored .25 .25
410 A159 10c multicolored .50 .50
411 A159 28c multicolored 1.50 1.50
Nos. 409-411 (3) 2.25 2.25

Issued to honor the Armed Services.

"Universal Suffrage" A160

Human Rights Flame A161

Perf. 13½

1968, Sept. 19 Photo. Unwmk.

412 A160 3c ol grn, lt bl & grn .25 .25
413 A161 10c dp grn, yel & red .30 .30

75th anniv. of universal suffrage in New Zealand; Intl. Human Rights Year.

Adoration of the Holy Child, by Gerard van Honthorst — A162

Perf. 14x14½

1968, Oct. 1 Wmk. 253

414 A162 2½c multicolored .25 .25

Christmas.

Romney Marsh Sheep and Woolmark on Carpet — A163

Designs: 7c, Trawler and catch. 8c, Apples and orchard. 10c, Radiata pines and stacked lumber. 20c, Cargo hoist and grazing cattle. 25c, Dairy farm in Taranaki, Mt. Egmont and crated dairy products.

Wmk. 253 (10c, 18c, 25c); others Unwmkd.

Perf. 13½; 14½x14 (10c, 25c)

1968-69 Litho.; Photo. (10c, 25c)

415 A163 7c multi ('69) .50 .50
416 A163 8c multi ('69) .80 .80
417 A163 10c multi .50 .25
a. Green omitted *950.00*
418 A163 18c multi ('69) 1.40 .25
419 A163 20c multi ('69) 1.25 .25
420 A163 25c multi 3.50 .60
Nos. 415-420 (6) 7.95 2.65

ILO Emblem — A164

Perf. 14½x14

1969, Feb. 11 Photo. Wmk. 253

421 A164 7c scarlet & black .50 .50

50th anniv. of the ILO.

Supreme Court Building, Auckland — A165

Designs: 10c, Law Society Coat of Arms. 18c, "Justice" from memorial window of the University of Canterbury Hall, Christchurch.

1969, Apr. 8 Litho. *Perf. 13½*

422 A165 3c multicolored .25 .25
423 A165 10c multicolored .40 .40
424 A165 18c multicolored .70 .70
Nos. 422-424 (3) 1.35 1.35

Centenary of New Zealand Law Society.

Otago University — A166

Design: 10c, Conferring degree and arms of the University, horiz.

1969, June 3

425 A166 3c multicolored .25 .25
426 A166 10c multicolored .50 .50

Centenary of the University of Otago.

Oldest House in New Zealand, Kerikeri — A167

Design: 6c, Bay of Islands.

1969, Aug. 18 Litho. Wmk. 253

427 A167 4c multicolored .30 .30
428 A167 6c multicolored .75 .75

Early European settlements in New Zealand on the 150th anniv. of the founding of Kerikeri, the oldest existing European settlement.

Nativity, by Federico Fiori — A168

Perf. 13½x14

1969, Oct. 1 Photo. Wmk. 253

429 A168 2½c multicolored .25 .25

Unwmk.

430 A168 2½c multicolored .25 .25

Christmas.

Capt. Cook, Transit of Venus and Octant — A169

Designs: 6c, Joseph Banks and bark Endeavour. 18c, Dr. Daniel Solander and matata branch (rhabdothamnus solandri). 28c, Queen Elizabeth II and map showing Cook's chart of 1769.

1969, Oct. 9 *Perf. 14½x14*

431 A169 4c dk bl, blk & brt rose .25 .25
a. Imperf., pair 425.00
432 A169 6c sl grn & choc 1.40 *1.40*
433 A169 18c choc, sl grn & black 2.00 2.00
434 A169 28c dk ultra, blk & brt rose 3.75 *3.75*
a. Souv. sheet of 4, #431-434 18.50 18.50
Nos. 431-434 (4) 7.40 7.40

Cook's landing in New Zealand, bicent.

Child Drinking Milk, and Cattle — A170

7c, Wheat and child with empty bowl, vert.

1969, Nov. 18 Photo. *Perf. 13*

435 A170 7c multicolored 1.25 1.25
436 A170 8c multicolored 1.25 1.25

25th anniv. of CORSO (Council of Organizations for Relief Services Overseas).

Cardigan Bay — A171

1970, Jan. 28 Unwmk. *Perf. 11½*

Granite Paper

437 A171 10c multicolored .40 .40

Return to New Zealand from the US of Cardigan Bay, 1st standard bred light-harness race horse to win a million dollars in stake money.

Glade Copper Butterfly A172

Scarlet Parrotfish A173

New Zealand Coat of Arms and Queen Elizabeth II — A174

Maori Fishhook — A175

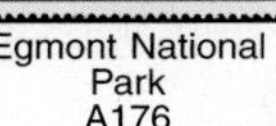

Egmont National Park A176

Hauraki Gulf Maritime Park A177

Designs: 1c, Red admiral butterfly. 2c, Tussock butterfly. 2½c, Magpie moth. 3c, Lichen moth. 4c, Puriri moth. 6c, Sea horses. 7c, Leatherjackets (fish). 7½c, Garfish. 8c, John dory (fish). 18c, Maori club. 20c, Maori tattoo pattern. 30c, Mt. Cook National Park (chamois). 50c, Abel Tasman National Park. $1, Geothermal power plant. $2, Helicopter over field, molecule (agricultural technology).

1970-71 Wmk. 253 *Perf. 13½x13*

438	A172	½c ultra & multi	.25	.25
439	A172	1c dp bis & multi	.25	.25
a.		Bklt. pane of 3 + 3 labels ('71)	2.50	
b.		Red omitted	275.00	
440	A172	2c ol grn & multi	.25	.25
a.		Black omitted	400.00	
441	A172	2½c yel & multi	.25	.25
442	A172	3c brown & multi	.25	.25
443	A172	4c dk brown & multi	.25	.25
a.		Bright green omitted	250.00	110.00
444	A173	5c dk green & multi	.35	.25
445	A173	6c dp car & multi	.45	.25
446	A173	7c brn red & multi	.50	.25
447	A173	7½c dk vio & multi	.70	.50
448	A173	8c blue grn & multi	.50	.25

Perf. 14½x14

449	A174	10c dk bl, sil, red & ultra	.45	.25

Perf. 14x13, 13x14

450	A175	15c brick red, sal & blk	.45	.25
a.		Brick red omitted	700.00	
451	A177	18c yel grn, blk & red brn	.55	.25
452	A175	20c yel brn & blk	.60	.25

Nos. 439, 442 and 443 exist with watermark either sideways or upright.

Perf. 13½x12½
Unwmk.

453	A176	23c bl, grn & blk	.60	.25

Litho.
Perf. 13½

454	A177	25c gray & multi	.70	.25
a.		Perf. 14 ('76)	.60	.25
455	A177	30c tan & multi	.70	.25
a.		Perf. 14 ('76)	2.75	2.00

Photo.
Perf. 13½x12½

456	A176	50c sl grn & multi	.80	.25
a.		Apple grn omitted	27.50	
b.		Buff omitted	55.00	
c.		Slate grn omitted	350.00	

Perf. 11½
Granite Paper

457	A175	$1 lt ultra & multi	1.90	.40
458	A175	$2 ol & multi	3.75	1.60
		Nos. 438-458 (21)	14.50	7.00

The 10c for the visit of Queen Elizabeth II, Prince Philip and Princess Anne.

Issued: 10c, 3/12/70; ½c-4c, 9/2/70; 5c-8c, 11/4/70; 15c-20c, 1/20/71; 25c-50c, 9/1/71; $1-$2, 4/14/71; 23c, 12/1/71.

See Nos. 533-546. For surcharge see No. 480.

EXPO '70 Emblem, Geyser Restaurant A178

Designs: 8c, EXPO '70 emblem and New Zealand Pavilion. 18c, EXPO '70 emblem and bush walk (part of N.Z. exhibit).

Perf. 13x13½
1970, Apr. 8 Photo. Unwmk.

459	A178	7c multicolored	.75	.75
460	A178	8c multicolored	.75	.75
461	A178	18c multicolored	1.50	1.50
		Nos. 459-461 (3)	3.00	3.00

EXPO '70 Intl. Expo., Osaka, Japan.

UN Headquarters, New York — A179

UN, 25th anniv.: 10c, Plowing toward the sun and "25" with laurel.

1970, June 24 Litho. *Perf. 13½*

462	A179	3c multicolored	.25	.25
463	A179	10c yellow & red	.50	.50

Adoration, by Correggio A180

Tower, Catholic Church, Sockburn A181

Christmas: 3c, Holy Family, stained glass window, First Presbyterian Church, Invercargill.

1970, Oct. 1 Unwmk. *Perf. 12½*

464	A180	2½c multicolored	.25	.25
465	A180	3c multicolored	.25	.25
a.		Green omitted	275.00	
466	A181	10c silver, org & blk	.45	.45
		Nos. 464-466 (3)	.95	.95

Chatham Islands Mollymawk A182

1970, Dec. 2 Photo. *Perf. 13x13½*

467	A182	1c Chatham Islands lily	.25	.25
468	A182	2c shown	.25	.25

G Clef, Emblem and Spinning Wheel — A183

Rotary Emblem and Map of New Zealand — A184

1971, Feb. 10 Photo. *Perf. 13x13½*

469	A183	4c multicolored	.25	.25
470	A184	10c lemon, dk blue & gold	.50	.50

50th anniv. of Country Women's Inst. (4c) and Rotary Intl. in New Zealand (10c).

Ocean Racer — A185

8c, One Ton Cup and blueprint of racing yacht.

1971, Mar. 3 Litho. *Perf. 13½x13*

471	A185	5c blue, blk & red	.25	.25
472	A185	8c ultra & black	.70	.70

First challenge in New Zealand waters for the One Ton Cup ocean race.

Coats of Arms — A186

1971, May 12 Photo. *Perf. 13x13½*

473	A186	3c Palmerston North	.25	.25
474	A186	4c Auckland	.25	.25
475	A186	5c Invercargill	.40	.40
		Nos. 473-475 (3)	.90	.90

Centenary of New Zealand cities.

Map of Antarctica A187

1971, June 9 Photo. *Perf. 13x13½*

476	A187	6c dk blue, pur & grn	1.05	.70

10th anniv. of the Antarctic Treaty pledging peaceful uses of and scientific cooperation in Antarctica.

Child on Swing — A188

1971, June 9 *Perf. 13½x13*

477	A188	7c yellow & multi	.75	.75

25th anniv. of UNICEF.

A189

1971, July 14 *Perf. 11½*

478	A189	8c Radar Station	.70	.70
479	A189	10c Satellite	.70	.70

Opening of New Zealand's 1st satellite Earth station near Warkworth.

No. 441 Surcharged

1971 Wmk. 253 *Perf. 13½x13*

480	A172	4c on 2½c multi	.40	.25
a.		Narrow bars	.25	.25

Surcharge typographed on No. 480, photogravure or typographed on No. 480a.

Holy Night, by Carlo Maratta A190

The Three Kings A191

Christmas: 4c, Annunciation, stained glass window, St. Luke's Anglican Church, Havelock North.

Perf. 13x13½
1971, Oct. 6 Photo. Unwmk.

481	A190	3c orange & multi	.25	.25
482	A191	4c multicolored	.25	.25
483	A191	10c dk blue & multi	.50	.50
		Nos. 481-483 (3)	1.00	1.00

World Rose Convention — A192

1971, Nov. 3 *Perf. 11½*

484	A192	2c Tiffany rose	.25	.25
485	A192	5c Peace rose	.35	.35
486	A192	8c Chrysler Imperial rose	.75	.75
		Nos. 484-486 (3)	1.35	1.35

Rutherford and Alpha Particles Passing Atomic Nucleus — A193

7c, Lord Rutherford, by Sir Oswald Birley, and formula of disintegration of nitrogen atom.

1971, Dec. 1 Litho. *Perf. 13½x13*

487	A193	1c gray & multi	.25	.25
488	A193	7c bister & multi	.75	.75

Centenary of the birth of Ernest Lord Rutherford (1871-1937), physicist.

Benz, 1895 — A194

Vintage Cars: 4c, Oldsmobile, 1904. 5c, Model T Ford, 1914. 6c, Cadillac service car, 1915. 8c, Chrysler, 1924. 10c, Austin 7, 1923.

1972, Feb. 2 *Perf. 14x14½*

489	A194	3c car rose & multi	.25	.25
490	A194	4c brt lilac & multi	.25	.25
491	A194	5c brt pur & multi	.25	.25
492	A194	6c dl bl grn & multi	.40	.40
493	A194	8c vio blue & multi	.60	.60
494	A194	10c sepia & multi	.70	.70
		Nos. 489-494 (6)	2.45	2.45

13th International Vintage Car Rally, New Zealand, Feb. 1972.

Asian-Oceanic Postal Union — A195

Designs: 3c, Wanganui City arms and Drurie Hill tower, vert. 5c, De Havilland DH89 and Boeing 737 planes, vert. 8c, French frigate and Maori palisade at Moturoa, vert. 10c, Stone cairn at Kaeo (site of first Methodist mission).

1972, Apr. 5 *Perf. 13x14, 14x13*

495	A195	3c gray & multi	.30	.30
496	A195	4c red org & multi	.30	.30
497	A195	5c dp turq bl & multi	.45	.45
498	A195	8c dp olive & multi	1.20	1.20
499	A195	10c bister & multi	1.40	1.40
		Nos. 495-499 (5)	3.65	3.65

Cent. of Council government at Wanganui (3c); 10th anniv. of Asian-Oceanic Postal Union (4c); 25th anniv. of Nat. Airways Corp. (5c); bicent. of the landing by Marion du Fresne at the Bay of Islands (8c); 150th anniv. of the Methodist Church in New Zealand (10c).

Black Scree Cotula — A196

Alpine Plants: 6c, North Is. edelweiss. 8c, Haast's buttercup. 10c, Brown mountain daisy.

1972, June 7 Litho. *Perf. 13x14*

500 A196 4c orange & multi .40 .40
501 A196 6c dp blue & multi .70 .70
502 A196 8c rose lilac & multi 1.10 1.10
503 A196 10c brt yel grn & multi 1.60 1.60
Nos. 500-503 (4) 3.80 3.80

Madonna and Child, by Murillo — A197

Christmas: 5c, Resurrection, stained-glass window, St. John's Methodist Church, Levin. 10c, Pohutukawa (New Zealand's Christmas flower).

1972, Oct. 4 Photo. *Perf. 11½*

504 A197 3c gray & multi .25 .25
505 A197 5c gray & multi .25 .25
506 A197 10c gray & multi .65 .65
Nos. 504-506 (3) 1.15 1.15

New Zealand Lakes — A198

1972, Dec. 6 Photo. Unwmk.

507 A198 6c Waikaremoana 1.00 1.00
508 A198 8c Hayes 1.25 1.25
509 A198 18c Wakatipu 2.10 *2.10*
510 A198 23c Rotomahana 3.00 *3.00*
Nos. 507-510 (4) 7.35 7.35

Old Pollen Street — A199

Coal Mining and Landscape A200

Cloister, University of Canterbury A201

Forest, Birds and Lake — A202

Rowing and Olympic Emblems — A203

Progress Chart — A204

1973, Feb. 7 Litho. *Perf. 13½x13*

511 A199 3c ocher & multi .25 .25
512 A200 4c blue & multi .25 .25
513 A201 5c multicolored .25 .25
514 A202 6c blue & multi .50 .50
515 A203 8c multicolored .60 .60
516 A204 10c blue & multi .60 .60
Nos. 511-516 (6) 2.45 2.45

Centenaries of Thames and Westport Boroughs (3c, 4c); centenary of the Univ. of Canterbury, Christchurch (5c); 50th anniv. of Royal Forest and Bird Protection Soc. (6c); success of New Zealand rowing team at 20th Olympic Games (8c); 25th anniv. of the Economic Commission for Asia and the Far East (ECAFE, 10c).

Class W Locomotive, 1889 — A205

New Zealand Steam Locomotives: 4c, Class X, 1908. 5c, "Passchendaele" Ab Class. 10c, Ja Class, last steam locomotive.

1973, Apr. 4 Litho. *Perf. 14½*

517 A205 3c lt green & multi .25 .25
518 A205 4c lil rose & multi .25 .25
519 A205 5c lt blue & multi .50 .50
520 A205 10c cream & multi 2.10 2.00
Nos. 517-520 (4) 3.10 3.00

Maori Woman and Child, by Hodgkins — A206

Paintings by Frances Hodgkins: 8c, The Hill Top. 10c, Barn in Picardy. 18c, Self-portrait, Still Life.

1973, June 6 Photo. *Perf. 12x11½*

521 A206 5c multicolored .25 .25
522 A206 8c multicolored .75 .75
523 A206 10c multicolored .75 .75
524 A206 18c multicolored 1.25 1.25
Nos. 521-524 (4) 3.00 3.00

Christmas in New Zealand — A207

Christmas: 3c, Tempi Madonna, by Raphael. 5c, Three Kings, stained-glass window, St. Theresa's R.C. Church, Auckland.

1973, Oct. 3 Photo. *Perf. 12½x13½*

525 A207 3c gold & multi .25 .25
526 A207 5c gold & multi .25 .25
527 A207 10c gold & multi .50 .50
Nos. 525-527 (3) 1.00 1.00

Mt. Ngauruhoe — A208

6c, Mitre Peak. 18c, Mt. Sefton, horiz. 23c, Burnett Range, horiz.

Perf. 13x13½, 13½x13

1973, Dec. 5 Photo.

528 A208 6c multi .60 .60
529 A208 8c shown .90 .90
530 A208 18c multi 1.60 1.60
531 A208 23c multi 1.90 1.90
Nos. 528-531 (4) 5.00 5.00

Types of 1970-71

Designs as before.

Perf. 13½x13

1973-76 Photo. Unwmk.

533 A172 1c multicolored .60 *1.00*
a. Bklt. pane of 3 + 3 labels ('74) 2.50
534 A172 2c multicolored .30 .25
536 A172 3c multicolored .50 .50
537 A172 4c multicolored .45 .25
538 A173 5c multicolored .60 .60
539 A173 6c multicolored 1.50 1.50
540 A173 7c multicolored 4.00 2.75
542 A173 8c multicolored 4.75 3.50

Perf. 14x13½

543 A174 10c multicolored 1.25 .25

Perf. 13x14, 14x13

544 A175 15c multicolored .50 .50
545 A177 18c multicolored 2.00 .60
546 A175 20c yel brn & blk .80 .80
Nos. 533-546 (12) 17.25 12.50

Issued: 2c, 10c, 6/73; 1c, 4c, 6c, 9/7/73; 5c, 1973; 3c, 7c, 8c, 18c, 20c, 1974; 15c, 8/2/76.
For surcharges see Nos. 630-631.

Hurdles and Games' Emblem — A209

Designs: 5c, Paraplegic ballplayer. 10c, Bicycling. 18c, Rifle shooting. 23c, Lawn bowling. 4c, 10c, 18c and 23c stamps also show Commonwealth Games' emblem.

1974, Jan. 9 Litho. *Perf. 13x13½*

547 A209 4c yellow & multi .25 .25
548 A209 5c violet & black .25 .25
549 A209 10c brt red & multi .40 .40
550 A209 18c brown & multi .60 .60
551 A209 23c yel green & multi .80 .80
Nos. 547-551 (5) 2.30 2.30

10th British Commonwealth Games, Christchurch, 1/24-2/2. #548 for the 4th Paraplegic Games, Dunedin, 1/10-20.

Souvenir Sheet

New Zealand Day A210

1974, Feb. 6 Litho. *Perf. 13*

552 A210 Sheet of 5 1.60 1.60
a. 4c Treaty House, Waitangi .25 .25
b. 4c Parliament extension buildings .25 .25
c. 4c Signing Treaty of Waitangi .25 .25
d. 4c Queen Elizabeth II .25 .25
e. 4c Integrated school .25 .25

New Zealand Day (Waitangi Day). No. 552 has marginal inscription and imprint.

"Spirit of Napier" Fountain A211

Clock Tower, Bern A212

Design: 8c, UPU emblem.

1974, Apr. 3 Photo. *Perf. 11½*

553 A211 4c blue green & multi .25 .25
554 A212 5c brown & multi .25 .25
555 A212 8c lemon & multi .60 .60
Nos. 553-555 (3) 1.10 1.10

Centenaries of Napier (4c); UPU (5c, 8c).

Boeing Seaplane, 1919 — A213

Designs: 4c, Lockheed Electra, 1937. 5c, Bristol freighter, 1958. 23c, Empire S30 flying boat, 1940.

1974, June 5 Litho. *Perf. 14x13*

556 A213 3c multicolored .25 .25
557 A213 4c multicolored .30 .30
558 A213 5c multicolored .30 .30
559 A213 23c multicolored 1.90 1.90
Nos. 556-559 (4) 2.75 2.75

Development of New Zealand's air transport.

Adoration of the Kings, by Conrad Witz — A214

Christmas: 5c, Angels, stained glass window, St. Paul's Church, Wellington. 10c, Christmas lily (lilium candidum).

1974, Oct. 2 Photo. *Perf. 11½*
Granite Paper

560 A214 3c olive & multi .25 .25
561 A214 5c lilac & multi .25 .25
562 A214 10c orange & multi .50 .50
Nos. 560-562 (3) 1.00 1.00

Offshore Islands — A215

1974, Dec. 4 Photo. *Perf. 13½x13*

563 A215 6c Great Barrier .40 .40
564 A215 8c Stewart .60 .60
565 A215 18c White .85 .85
566 A215 23c The Brothers 1.00 1.00
Nos. 563-566 (4) 2.85 2.85

Child Using Walker — A216

Farm Woman and Children — A217

IWY Symbol — A218

Otago Medical School — A219

1975, Feb. 5 Litho. *Perf. 13½x13*

567 A216 3c orange & multi .25 .25
568 A217 5c green & multi .25 .25
569 A218 10c blue & multi .30 *.30*
570 A219 18c multicolored .50 *.50*
Nos. 567-570 (4) 1.30 1.30

New Zealand Crippled Children's Soc., 40th anniv. (3c); Women's Division Federated Farmers of N. Z., 50th anniv. (5c); IWY (10c); Otago Medical School cent. (18c).

Scow "Lake Erie," 1873 — A220

Historic Sailing Ships: 5c, Schooner "Herald," 1826. 8c, Brigantine "New Zealander," 1828. 10c, Topsail schooner "Jessie Kelly," 1866. 18c, Barque "Tory," 1834. 23c, Clipper "Rangitiki," 1863.

1975, Apr. 2 Litho. *Perf. 13½x13*

571 A220 4c vermilion & blk .25 .25
572 A220 5c grnsh blue & blk .25 .25
573 A220 8c yellow & black .40 .40
574 A220 10c yellow grn & blk .50 .50
575 A220 18c brown & black .65 .65
576 A220 23c dull lilac & blk .85 .85
Nos. 571-576 (6) 2.90 2.90

State Forest Parks — A221

1975, June 4 Photo. *Perf. 13½x13*

577 A221 6c Lake Sumner .50 .50
578 A221 8c North West Nelson .75 .75
579 A221 18c Kaweka .90 .90
580 A221 23c Coromandel 1.40 1.40
Nos. 577-580 (4) 3.55 3.55

Virgin and Child, by Zanobi Machiavelli (1418-1479) — A222

Stained Glass Window, Greendale Methodist/Presbyterian Church — A223

Christmas: 10c, Medieval ships and doves.

Perf. 13½x14, 14x13½

1975, Oct. 1 Photo.

581 A222 3c multicolored .25 .25
582 A223 5c multicolored .25 .25
583 A223 10c multicolored .45 .45
Nos. 581-583 (3) .95 .95

Sterling Silver — A224

Roses: 2c, Lilli Marlene. 3c, Queen Elizabeth. 4c, Super star. 5c, Diamond jubilee. 6c, Cresset. 7c, Michele Meilland. 8c, Josephine Bruce. 9c, Iceberg.

1975, Nov. 26 Photo. *Perf. 14½x14*

584 A224 1c multicolored .25 .25
585 A224 2c orange & multi .25 .25
586 A224 3c ultra & multi .25 .25
a. Perf. 14½ ('79) .25 .25
587 A224 4c purple & multi .25 .25
588 A224 5c brown & multi .25 .25
589 A224 6c multicolored ('76) .25 .25
a. Perf. 14½ .50 .50
590 A224 7c multicolored ('76) .25 .25
a. Perf. 14½ .80 .50
591 A224 8c yellow & multi ('76) .25 .25
a. Perf. 14½ .80 .50
592 A224 9c blue & multi .25 .25
Nos. 584-592 (9) 2.25 2.25

For surcharges see Nos. 693, 695, 718.

Family and Mothers' League Emblem — A225

Designs: 7c, "Weight, measure, temperature and capacity." 8c, 1st emigrant ship "William Bryan" and Mt. Egmont. 10c, Maori and Caucasian women and YWCA emblem. 25c, Telecommunications network on Goode's equal area projection.

1976, Feb. 4 Litho. *Perf. 14*

593 A225 6c yel olive & multi .25 .25
594 A225 7c reddsh pur & multi .25 .25
595 A225 8c red & multi .25 .25
596 A225 10c yellow & multi .25 .25
597 A225 25c tan & multi .50 .50
Nos. 593-597 (5) 1.50 1.50

League of Mothers of New Zealand, 50th anniv. (6c); Metric conversion, 1976 (7c); cent. of New Plymouth (8c); YWCA in New Zealand, 50th anniv. (10c); cent. of link into intl. telecommunications network (25c).

Gig — A226

Farm Vehicles: 7c, Thornycroft truck. 8c, Scandi wagon. 9c, Traction engine. 10c, Wool wagon. 25c, One-horse cart.

1976, Apr. 7 Litho. *Perf. 14x13½*

598 A226 6c dk olive & multi .25 .25
599 A226 7c gray & multi .25 .25
600 A226 8c dk blue & multi .50 .25
601 A226 9c maroon & multi .40 .30
602 A226 10c brown & multi .40 .30
603 A226 25c multicolored .60 .60
Nos. 598-603 (6) 2.40 1.95

Purakaunui Falls — A227

Waterfalls: 14c, Marakopa Falls. 15c, Bridal Veil Falls. 16c, Papakorito Falls.

1976, June 2 Photo. *Perf. 11½*

604 A227 10c blue & multi .25 .25
605 A227 14c lilac & multi .60 .60
606 A227 15c ocher & multi .50 .50
607 A227 16c multicolored .75 .75
Nos. 604-607 (4) 2.10 2.10

Nativity, Carved Ivory, Spain, 16th Century — A228

Christmas: 11c, Risen Christ, St. Joseph's Church, Grey Lynn, Auckland, horiz. 18c, "Hark the Herald Angels Sing," horiz.

Perf. 14x14½, 14½x14

1976, Oct. 6 Photo.

608 A228 7c ocher & multi .25 .25
609 A228 11c ocher & multi .35 .35
610 A228 18c ocher & multi .45 .45
Nos. 608-610 (3) 1.05 1.05

Maripi (Carved Wooden Knife) — A229

Maori Artifacts: 12c, Putorino, carved flute. 13c, Wahaika, hardwood club. 14c, Kotiate, violin-shaped weapon.

1976, Nov. 24 Photo. *Perf. 11½*

Granite Paper

611 A229 11c multicolored .25 .25
612 A229 12c multicolored .25 .25
613 A229 13c multicolored .25 .25
614 A229 14c multicolored .25 .25
Nos. 611-614 (4) 1.00 1.00

Arms of Hamilton A230

Automobile Assoc. Emblem A231

Designs: No. 616, Arms of Gisborne. No. 617, Arms of Masterton. No. 619, Emblem of Royal Australasian College of Surgeons.

1977, Jan. 19 Litho. *Perf. 13x13½*

615 A230 8c multicolored .25 .25
616 A230 8c multicolored .25 .25
617 A230 8c multicolored .25 .25
a. Strip of 3, #615-617 .75 *.75*
618 A231 10c multicolored .25 *.35*
619 A230 10c multicolored .25 *.35*
a. Pair, #618-619 .50 *.70*
Nos. 615-619 (5) 1.25 *1.45*

Centenaries of Hamilton, Gisborne and Masterton (cities); 75th anniv. of the New Zealand Automobile Assoc. and 50th anniv. of the Royal Australasian College of Surgeons.

Souvenir Sheet

Queen Elizabeth II, 1976 — A232

Designs: Various portraits.

1977, Feb. Photo. *Perf. 14x14½*

620 A232 Sheet of 5 1.25 *1.40*
a.-e. 8c single stamp .25 .25
f. Sheet imperf. *1,350.*

25th anniv. of the reign of Elizabeth II.

Physical Education, Maori Culture A233

Education Dept., Geography, Science A234

#623, Special school for the deaf; kindergarten. #624, Language class. #625, Home economics, correspondence school, teacher training.

1977, Apr. 6 Litho. *Perf. 13x13½*

621 A233 8c shown .40 .40
622 A234 8c shown .40 .40
623 A233 8c multicolored .40 .40
624 A234 8c multicolored .40 .40
625 A233 8c multicolored .40 .40
a. Strip of 5, #621-625 2.50 *2.60*
Nos. 621-625 (5) 2.00 2.00

Cent. of Education Act, establishing Dept. of Education.

Karitane Beach — A235

Seascapes and beach scenes: 16c, Ocean Beach, Mount Maunganui. 18c, Piha Beach. 30c, Kaikoura Coast.

1977, June 1 Photo. *Perf. 14½*

626 A235 10c multicolored .25 .25
627 A235 16c multicolored .30 .30
628 A235 18c multicolored .30 .30
629 A235 30c multicolored .40 .35
Nos. 626-629 (4) 1.25 1.20

Nos. 536-537 Surcharged with New Value and Heavy Bar

1977 Unwmk. *Perf. 13½x13*

630 A172 7c on 3c multicolored .35 .35
631 A172 8c on 4c multicolored .35 .35

Holy Family, by Correggio A236

Window, St. Michael's and All Angels Church A237

Partridge in a Pear Tree — A238

1977, Oct. 5 Photo. *Perf. 11½*

632 A236 7c multicolored .25 .25
633 A237 16c multicolored .30 .30
634 A238 23c multicolored .50 .50
Nos. 632-634 (3) 1.05 1.05

Christmas.

Merryweather Manual Pump, 1860 — A239

Fire Fighting Equipment: 11c, 2-wheel hose reel and ladder, 1880. 12c, Shand Mason Steam Fire Engine, 1873. 23c, Chemical fire engine, 1888.

1977, Dec. 7 Litho. *Perf. 14x13½*

635 A239 10c multicolored .25 .25
636 A239 11c multicolored .25 .25
637 A239 12c multicolored .25 .25
638 A239 23c multicolored .30 .30
Nos. 635-638 (4) 1.05 1.05

A240

A240a

Parliament Building, Wellington — A241

1977-82 Photo. *Perf. 14½*

648 A240 10c ultra & multi .25 .25
a. Perf. 14½x14 .75 .50

Perf. 14½x14

649 A240a 24c blue & lt green .30 .25
a. Perf. 13x12½ .45 .25

Perf. 13

650 A241 $5 multicolored 4.75 3.50
Nos. 648-650 (3) 5.30 4.00

Issued: No. 648, 2/79; No. 648a, 12/7/77; $5, 12/2/81; No. 649, 4/1/82; No. 649a, 12/13/82.

For surcharge see No. 694.

A242

Coil Stamps

1978 Photo. *Perf. 13½x13*

651 A242 1c red lilac .25 .25
652 A242 2c orange .25 .25
653 A242 5c brown .25 .25

Perf. 14½x14

654 A242 10c ultramarine .25 .25
Nos. 651-654 (4) 1.00 1.00

Issue dates: 10c, May 3; others, June 9.

Ashburton A244

Stratford A245

Old Telephone A246

Bay of Islands A247

1978, Feb. 1 Litho. *Perf. 14*

656 A244 10c multicolored .25 .25
657 A245 10c multicolored .25 .25
a. Pair, #656-657 .50 .50
658 A246 12c multicolored .25 .25
659 A247 20c multicolored .30 .30
Nos. 656-659 (4) 1.05 1.05

Cent. of the cities of Ashburton, Stratford, the NZ Telephone Co. and Bay of Islands County.

Lincoln Univ. College of Agriculture, Cent. — A248

Designs: 10c, Students and Ivey Hall. 12c, Grazing sheep. 15c, Mechanical fertilization. 16c, Furrow, plow and tractor. 20c, Combine harvester. 30c, Grazing cattle.

1978, Apr. 26 *Perf. 14½*

660 A248 10c multicolored .25 .25
661 A248 12c multicolored .25 .25
662 A248 15c multicolored .25 .25
663 A248 16c multicolored .25 .25
664 A248 20c multicolored .25 .25
665 A248 30c multicolored .30 .30
Nos. 660-665 (6) 1.55 1.55

Maui Gas Drilling Platform — A249

The sea and its resources: 15c, Fishing boat. 20c, Map of New Zealand and 200-mile limit. 23c, Whale and bottle-nosed dolphins. 35c, Kingfish, snapper, grouper and squid.

1978, June 7 Litho. *Perf. 13½x14*

666 A249 12c multicolored .25 .25
667 A249 15c multicolored .25 .25
668 A249 20c multicolored .25 .25
669 A249 23c multicolored .30 .30
670 A249 35c multicolored .45 .45
Nos. 666-670 (5) 1.50 1.50

Christmas — A250

Designs: 7c, Holy Family, by El Greco, vert. 16c, All Saints Church, Howick. 23c, Beach scene.

1978, Oct. 4 Photo. *Perf. 11½*

671 A250 7c gold & multi .25 .25
672 A250 16c gold & multi .30 .30
673 A250 23c gold & multi .35 .35
Nos. 671-673 (3) .90 .90

Sea Shells — A251

20c, Paua (Haliotis Iris). 30c, Toheroa (paphies ventricosa). 40c, Coarse dosinia (dosinia anus). 50c, Spiny murex (poirieria zelandica).

1978, Nov. 29 Photo. *Perf. 13x12½*

674 A251 20c multicolored .25 .25
675 A251 30c multicolored .30 .25
676 A251 40c multicolored .45 .30
677 A251 50c multicolored .55 .40
Nos. 674-677 (4) 1.55 1.20

See Nos. 696-697.

Julius Vogel — A252

19th cent. NZ statesmen: No. 679, George Grey. No. 680, Richard John Seddon.

1979, Feb. 7 Litho. *Perf. 13x13½*

678 A252 10c light & dark brown .25 .25
679 A252 10c light & dark brown .25 .25
680 A252 10c light & dark brown .25 .25
a. Strip of 3, #678-680 1.10 1.10

Riverlands Cottage, Blenheim A253

Early NZ Architecture: 12c, Mission House, Waimate North, 1831-32. 15c, The Elms, Anglican Church Mission, Tauranga, 1847. 20c, Provincial Council Buildings, Christchurch, 1859.

1979, Apr. 4 *Perf. 13½x13*

681 A253 10c multicolored .25 .25
682 A253 12c multicolored .25 .25
683 A253 15c black & gray .25 .25
684 A253 20c multicolored .25 .25
Nos. 681-684 (4) 1.00 1.00

Whangaroa Harbor — A254

Small Harbors: 20c, Kawau Island. 23c, Akaroa Harbor, vert. 35c, Picton Harbor, vert.

Perf. 13x13½, 13½x13

1979, June 6 **Photo.**

685 A254 15c multicolored .25 .25
686 A254 20c multicolored .25 .25
687 A254 23c multicolored .25 .25
688 A254 35c multicolored .40 .40
Nos. 685-688 (4) 1.15 1.15

IYC — A255

1979, June 6 Litho. *Perf. 14*

689 A255 10c Children playing .25 .25

Virgin and Child, by Lorenzo Ghiberti — A256

Christmas: 25c, Christ Church, Russell, 1835. 35c, Pohutukawa ("Christmas") tree.

1979, Oct. 3 Photo. *Perf. 11½*

690 A256 10c multicolored .25 .25
691 A256 25c multicolored .35 .35
692 A256 35c multicolored .45 .45
Nos. 690-692 (3) 1.05 1.05

Nos. 591a, 648 and 589a Surcharged

1979, Sept. *Perf. 14½, 14½x14 (14c)*

693 A224 4c on 8c multi .25 .25
694 A240 14c on 10c multi .25 .25
695 A224 17c on 6c multi .25 .25
Nos. 693-695 (3) .75 .75

Shell Type of 1978

$1, Scallop (pecten novaezelandiae). $2, Circular saw (astraea heliotropium).

1979, Nov. 26 Photo. *Perf. 13x12½*

696 A251 $1 multicolored 1.25 .25
697 A251 $2 multicolored 2.40 .75

Debating Chamber, House of Parliament — A257

1979, Nov. 26 Litho. *Perf. 14x13½*

698 A257 14c shown .25 .25
699 A257 20c Mace, black rod .25 .25
700 A257 30c Wall hanging .40 .40
Nos. 698-700 (3) .90 .90

25th Commonwealth Parliamentary Conference, Wellington, Nov. 26-Dec. 2.

NZ No. 1 — A258

1980, Feb. 7 Litho. *Perf. 14x13½*

701 A258 14c shown .25 .25
702 A258 14c No. 2 .25 .25
703 A258 14c No. 3 .25 .25
a. Souvenir sheet of 3, #701-703 2.00 2.00
b. Strip of 3, #701-703 .75 .75

NZ postage stamps, 125th anniv. No. 703a publicizes Zeapex '80 Intl. Stamp Exhib., Auckland, Aug. 23-31; it sold for 52c, of which 10c went to exhib. fund.

Maori Wood Carving, Tudor Towers — A259

Earina Autumnalis and Thelymitra Venosa — A260

Tractor Plowing, Golden Plow Trophy — A261

1980, Feb. 7 *Perf. 14½*

704 A259 17c multicolored .25 .25
705 A260 25c multicolored .30 .30
706 A261 30c multicolored .30 .30
Nos. 704-706 (3) .85 .85

Rotorua cent.; Intl. Orchid Conf., Auckland, Oct.; World Plowing Championship, Christchurch, May.

Ewelme Cottage, Parnell, 1864 — A262

Early NZ Architecture: 17c, Broadgreen, Nelson, 1855. 25c, Courthouse, Oamaru, 1822, 30c, Government Buildings, Wellington, 1877.

1980, Apr. 2 Litho. *Perf. 13½x13*

707 A262 14c multicolored .25 .25
708 A262 17c multicolored .25 .25
709 A262 25c multicolored .30 .30
710 A262 30c multicolored .30 .30
Nos. 707-710 (4) 1.10 1.10

Harbors — A263

1980, June 4 Photo. *Perf. 13x13½*

711 A263 25c Auckland .30 .20
712 A263 30c Wellington .35 .35
713 A263 35c Lyttelton .40 .40
714 A263 50c Port Chalmers .65 .65
Nos. 711-714 (4) 1.70 1.60

Madonna and Child with Cherubim, by Andrea della Robbia — A264

25c, St. Mary's Church, New Plymouth. 35c, Picnic.

1980, Oct. 1 Photo. *Perf. 12*

715 A264 10c shown .25 .25
716 A264 25c multi .30 .30
717 A264 35c multi .40 .40
Nos. 715-717 (3) .95 .95

Christmas.

No. 590 Surcharged

1980, Sept. 29 Photo. *Perf. 14½x14*

718 A224 20c on 7c multicolored .25 .25

Te Heu Heu Tukino IV, Ngati Tuwharetoa Tribal Chief — A265

Maori Leaders: 25c, Te Hau-Takiri Wharepapa. 35c, Princess Te Puea Herangi. 45, Apirana Ngata. 60c, Hakopa Te Ata-o-tu.

1980, Nov. 26 *Perf. 13*

719 A265 15c multicolored .25 .25
720 A265 25c multicolored .25 .25
721 A265 35c multicolored .35 .35
722 A265 45c multicolored .55 .55
723 A265 60c multicolored .60 .60
Nos. 719-723 (5) 2.00 2.00

Henry A. Feilding, Borough Emblem — A266

1981, Feb. 4 Litho. *Perf. 14½*

724 A266 20c multicolored .30 .25

Borough of Feilding centenary.

IYD — A267

1981, Feb. 4

725 A267 25c orange & black .35 .35

Family and Dog — A268

25c, Grandparents. 30c, Parents reading to children. 35c, Family outing.

1981, Apr. 1 Litho. *Perf. 13*

726 A268 20c shown .25 .25
727 A268 25c multi .30 .30
728 A268 30c multi .35 .35
729 A268 35c multi .40 .40
Nos. 726-729 (4) 1.30 1.30

Shotover River — A269

30c, Kaiauai River, vert. 35c, Mangahao River, vert. 60c, Cleddau River.

1981, June 3 Photo. *Perf. 13½*

730 A269 30c multi .35 .35
731 A269 35c multi .40 .40
732 A269 40c shown .50 .50
733 A269 60c multi .65 .65
Nos. 730-733 (4) 1.90 1.90

Prince Charles and Lady Diana — A270

No. 735, St. Paul's Cathedral.

1981, July 29 Litho. *Perf. 14½*
734 A270 20c shown .30 .25
735 A270 20c multi .30 .25
a. Pair, #734-735 .60 .60

Royal Wedding.

Golden Tainui — A271

Christmas: 14c, Madonna and Child, by Marco d'Oggiono, 15th cent. 30c, St. John's Church, Wakefield.

1981, Oct. Photo. *Perf. 11½*
Granite Paper
736 A271 14c multicolored .25 .25
737 A271 30c multicolored .30 .30
738 A271 40c multicolored .45 .45
Nos. 736-738 (3) 1.00 1.00

SPCA Centenary A272

Intl. Science Year A273

Centenaries: No. 739, Tauranga. No. 740, Hawera. 30c, Frozen meat exports.

1982, Feb. 3 Litho. *Perf. 14½*
739 A272 20c multicolored .25 .25
740 A272 20c multicolored .25 .25
a. Pair, #739-740 .60 .60
741 A272 25c multicolored .30 .30
742 A273 30c multicolored .40 .40
743 A273 35c multicolored .45 .45
Nos. 739-743 (5) 1.65 1.65

Alberton Farmhouse, Auckland, 1867 — A274

25c, Caccia Birch, Palmerston North, 1893. 30c, Dunedin Railway Station, 1904. 35c, PO, Ophir, 1886.

1982, Apr. 7 Litho.
744 A274 20c shown .25 .25
745 A274 25c multicolored .30 .30
746 A274 30c multicolored .45 .45
747 A274 35c multicolored .45 .45
Nos. 744-747 (4) 1.45 1.45

Summer, Kaiteriteri — A275

40c, Autumn, Queenstown. 45c, Winter, Mt. Ngauruhoe. 70c, Spring, Wairarapa.

1982, June 2 Photo. *Perf. 13½*
748 A275 35c shown .40 .40
749 A275 40c multicolored .45 .45
750 A275 45c multicolored .50 .50
751 A275 70c multicolored .85 .85
Nos. 748-751 (4) 2.20 2.20

Madonna with Child and Two Angels, by Piero di Cosimo — A276

Christmas: 35c, Rangiatea Maori Church, Otaki. 45c, Surf life-saving patrol.

1982, Oct. 6 Photo. *Perf. 14*
752 A276 18c multicolored .25 .25
753 A276 35c multicolored .35 .35
754 A276 45c multicolored .60 .60
Nos. 752-754 (3) 1.20 1.20

Nephrite A277

Fruit Export A278

1982-83 Litho.
755 A277 1c shown .25 .25
a. Perf 13x12½ .40 .40
756 A277 2c Agate .25 .25
a. Perf 13x12½ 1.25 1.25
757 A277 3c Iron pyrites .25 .25
758 A277 4c Amethyst .25 .25
759 A277 5c Carnelian .25 .25
760 A277 9c Native sulphur .25 .25
761 A278 10c Grapes .25 .25
762 A278 20c Citrus fruit .30 .25
763 A278 30c Nectarines .40 .25
764 A278 40c Apples .60 .25
765 A278 50c Kiwifruit .70 .25
Nos. 755-765 (11) 3.75 2.75

Issued: A277, Dec. 1; A278, Dec. 7, 1983.

Native Birds — A279

1985-89 *Perf. 14½*
766 A279 30c Kakapo .50 .25
767 A279 45c Falcon 1.00 .50
768 A279 $1 Kokako 1.00 .45
769 A279 $2 Black Robin 2.50 .70
a. Souvenir sheet of one 11.00 11.00
770 A279 $3 Stitchbird 4.00 2.75
770A A279 $4 Saddleback 4.75 3.25
Nos. 766-770A (6) 13.75 7.90

No. 769a for PHILEXFRANCE '89 and has margin picturing progressive proofs of No. 769. No. 769a sold for $3.50.

Issued: $1, $2, 4/24; $3, $4, 4/23/86; 30c, 45c, 5/1/86; No. 769a, 7/7/89.

See Nos. 830-835, 919-933.

Salvation Army in NZ Cent. A280

Univ. of Auckland Cent. A281

NZ-Australia Closer Economic Relationship Agreement — A282

Introduction of Rainbow Trout Cent. A283

WCY A284

Perf. 14, 14x13½ (35c)
1983, Feb. 2 Litho.
771 A280 24c multicolored .30 .30
772 A281 30c multicolored .40 .40
773 A282 35c multicolored .50 .50
774 A283 40c multicolored .60 .60
775 A284 45c multicolored .60 .60
Nos. 771-775 (5) 2.40 2.40

A285

24c, Queen Elizabeth II. 35c, Maori rock painting. 40c, Wool industry logos. 45c, Arms.

1983, Mar. 14 Litho. *Perf. 14*
776 A285 24c multicolored .40 .40
777 A285 35c multicolored .45 .45
778 A285 40c multicolored .55 .55
779 A285 45c multicolored .60 .60
Nos. 776-779 (4) 2.00 2.00

Commonwealth Day.

Island Bay, by Rita Angus (1908-1970) — A286

Landscapes.

1983, Apr. 6 Litho. *Perf. 14½*
780 A286 24c shown .40 .40
781 A286 30c Central Otago .40 .40
782 A286 35c Wanaka .50 .50
783 A286 45c Tree, Greymouth .60 .60
Nos. 780-783 (4) 1.90 1.90

Lake Matheson — A287

Perf. 13½x13, 13x13½
1983, June 1 Photo.
784 A287 35c Mt. Egmont, vert. .40 .40
785 A287 40c Cooks Bay, vert. .50 .50
786 A287 45c shown .60 .60
787 A287 70c Lake Alexandrina .95 .95
Nos. 784-787 (4) 2.45 2.45

Christmas 1983 — A288

18c, Holy Family of the Oak Tree, by Raphael. 35c, St. Patrick's Church, Greymouth. 45c, Star, poinsettias.

1983, Oct. 5 Photo. *Perf. 12*
788 A288 18c multicolored .25 .25
789 A288 35c multicolored .45 .45
790 A288 45c multicolored .70 .70
Nos. 788-790 (3) 1.40 1.40

Antarctic Research A289

1984, Feb. 1 Litho. *Perf. 13½x13*
791 A289 24c Geology .35 .35
792 A289 40c Biology .55 .55
793 A289 58c Glaciology .90 .90
794 A289 70c Meteorology 1.00 1.00
a. Souvenir sheet of 4, #791-794 3.00 3.00
Nos. 791-794 (4) 2.80 2.80

Ferry Mountaineer, Lake Wakatipu, 1879 — A290

40c, Waikana, Otago Harbor, 1909. 58c, Britannia, Waitemata Harbor, 1885. 70c, Wakatere, Firth of Thames, 1896.

1984, Apr. 4 Litho. *Perf. 13½*
795 A290 24c shown .40 .40
796 A290 40c multicolored .60 .60
797 A290 58c multicolored .80 .80
798 A290 70c multicolored 1.00 1.00
Nos. 795-798 (4) 2.80 2.80

Skier, Mount Hutt — A291

1984, June 6 Litho. *Perf. 13½x13*
799 A291 35c shown .50 .50
800 A291 40c Coronet Peak .60 .60
801 A291 45c Turoa .60 .60
802 A291 70c Whakapapa 1.00 1.00
Nos. 799-802 (4) 2.70 2.70

Hamilton's Frog — A292

1984, July 11 *Perf. 13½*
803 A292 24c shown .35 .25
804 A292 24c Great barrier skink .35 .25
a. Pair, #803-804 .80 .80
805 A292 30c Harlequin gecko .40 .40
806 A292 58c Otago skink .90 .90
807 A292 70c Gold-striped gecko 1.00 1.00
Nos. 803-807 (5) 3.00 2.80

No. 804a has continuous design.

Christmas A293

Designs: 18c, Adoration of the Shepherds, by Lorenzo Di Credi. 35c, Old St. Paul's Church, Wellington, vert. 45c, Bell, vert.

Perf. 13½x14, 14x13½
1984, Sept. 26 Photo.
808 A293 18c multicolored .25 .25
809 A293 35c multicolored .35 .35
810 A293 45c multicolored .50 .50
Nos. 808-810 (3) 1.10 1.10

Military History — A294

24c, South Africa, 1901. 40c, France, 1917. 58c, North Africa, 1942. 70c, Korea & South-east Asia, 1950-72.

1984, Nov. 7 Litho. *Perf. 15x14*
811 A294 24c multi .40 .40
812 A294 40c multi .60 .60
813 A294 58c multi .80 .80
814 A294 70c multi 1.00 1.00
a. Souvenir sheet of 4, #811-814 3.00 3.00
Nos. 811-814 (4) 2.80 2.80

St. John Ambulance Assoc. Cent. in NZ — A295

1985, Jan. 16 Litho. *Perf. 14*
815 A295 24c multicolored .40 .40
816 A295 30c multicolored .40 .40
817 A295 40c multicolored .60 .60
Nos. 815-817 (3) 1.40 1.40

Early Transportation A296

24c, Nelson Horse Tram, 1862. 30c, Graham's Town-Steam, 1871. 35c, Dunedin Cable Car, 1881. 40c, Auckland Electric, 1902. 45c, Wellington Electric, 1904. 58c, Christchurch Electric, 1905.

1985, Mar. 6 Litho. *Perf. 13½*
818 A296 24c multicolored .40 .25
819 A296 30c multicolored .40 .40
820 A296 35c multicolored .50 .50
821 A296 40c multicolored .60 .60
822 A296 45c multicolored .60 .60
823 A296 58c multicolored .80 .80
Nos. 818-823 (6) 3.30 3.15

Bridges — A297

35c, Shotover. 40c, Alexandra. 45c, South Rangitikei, vert. 70c, Twin Bridges, vert.

1985, June 12 Photo. *Perf. 11½*
824 A297 35c multicolored .45 .45
825 A297 40c multicolored .50 .50
826 A297 45c multicolored .65 .65
827 A297 70c multicolored .90 .90
Nos. 824-827 (4) 2.50 2.50

Bird Type of 1985 and

Elizabeth II — A298

1985-89 Litho. *Perf. 14½x14*
828 A298 25c multicolored .50 .40
829 A298 35c multicolored .70 .60

Perf. 14½
830 A279 40c Blue duck .65 .25
Complete booklet, 10 #830 6.50
831 A279 60c Brown teal 1.00 .65
832 A279 70c Paradise shelduck 1.05 .75
a. Souvenir sheet of 1 *10.00 10.00*
835 A279 $5 Takahe 7.00 6.00
Nos. 828-835 (6) 10.90 8.65

Size of 70c, 22x27mm.
No. 832a for World Stamp Expo '89. Sold for $1.50.
Issued: 25c, 35c, 7/1/85; 40c, 60c, 2/2/87; 70c, 6/7/88; $5, 4/20/88; #832a, 11/17/89.

Christmas — A301

Carol "Silent Night, Holy Night," by Joseph Mohr (1792-1848), Austrian clergyman.

Perf. 13½x12½
1985, Sept. 18 Litho.
836 A301 18c Stable .25 .25
837 A301 40c Shepherds .55 .55
838 A301 50c Angels .60 .60
Nos. 836-838 (3) 1.40 1.40

Navy Ships — A302

25c, Philomel, 1914-1947. 45c, Achilles, 1936-1946. 60c, Rotoiti, 1949-1965. 75c, Canterbury, 1971-.

1985, Nov. 6 Litho. *Perf. 13½*
839 A302 25c multicolored .40 .25
840 A302 45c multicolored .75 .75
841 A302 60c multicolored 1.00 1.00
842 A302 75c multicolored 1.25 1.25
a. Souvenir sheet of 4, #839-842 4.00 *4.00*
Nos. 839-842 (4) 3.40 3.25

Police Force Act, Cent. — A303

Designs: a, Radio operators, 1940-1985. b, Mounted policeman, 1890, forensic specialist in mobile lab, 1985. c, Police station, 1895, policewoman and badge, 1985. d, 1920 motorcycle, 1940s car, modern patrol cars and graphologist. e, Original Mt. Cook Training Center and modern Police College, Poriria.

1986, Jan. 15 *Perf. 14½x14*
843 Strip of 5 2.40 1.90
a.-e. A303 25c any single .40 .25

Intl. Peace Year — A304

1986, Mar. 5 *Perf. 13½x13*
844 25c Tree .35 .25
845 25c Dove .35 .25
a. A304 Pair, #844-845 .80 .70

Motorcycles A305

35c, 1920 Indian Power Plus. 45c, 1927 Norton CS1. 60c, 1930 BSA Sloper. 75c, 1915 Triumph Model H.

1986, Mar. 5
846 A305 35c multicolored .50 .50
847 A305 45c multicolored .60 .60
848 A305 60c multicolored .80 .80
849 A305 75c multicolored 1.00 1.00
Nos. 846-849 (4) 2.90 2.90

Knight's Point — A306

1986, June 11 Litho. *Perf. 14*
850 A306 55c shown .65 .65
851 A306 60c Beck's Bay .70 .70
852 A306 65c Doubtless Bay .75 .75
853 A306 80c Wainui Bay .80 .80
a. Miniature sheet of one 1.90 1.90
Nos. 850-853 (4) 2.90 2.90

No. 853a sold for $1.20. Surtax benefited the "NZ 1990" executive committee.
No. 853a exists with Stockholmia '86 emblem. This sheet was sold only at the exhibition.

The Twelve Days of Christmas — A307

1986, Sept. 17 Photo. *Perf. 14½*
854 A307 25c First day .35 .25
855 A307 55c Second .55 .55
856 A307 65c Third .90 .90
Nos. 854-856 (3) 1.80 1.70

Music — A308

1986, Nov. 5 Litho. *Perf. 14½x14*
857 A308 30c Conductor .45 .30
858 A308 60c Brass band .70 .70
859 A308 80c Highland pipe band .95 .95
860 A308 $1 Country music 1.20 1.20
Nos. 857-860 (4) 3.30 3.15

Tourism — A309

60c, Boating. 70c, Aviation. 80c, Camping. 85c, Windsurfing. $1.05, Mountain climbing. $1.30, White water rafting.

1987, Jan. 14 *Perf. 14½x14*
861 A309 60c multi .75 .75
862 A309 70c multi .90 .90
863 A309 80c multi 1.00 1.00
864 A309 85c multi 1.10 1.10
865 A309 $1.05 multi 1.25 1.25
866 A309 $1.30 multi 1.50 1.50
Nos. 861-866 (6) 6.50 6.50

Blue Water Classics — A310

40c, Southern Cross Cup. 80c, Admiral's Cup. $1.05, Kenwood Cup. $1.30, America's Cup.

1987, Feb. 2 *Perf. 14x14½*
867 A310 40c multi .60 .35
868 A310 80c multi 1.00 1.00
869 A310 $1.05 multi 1.25 1.25
870 A310 $1.30 multi 1.50 1.50
Nos. 867-870 (4) 4.35 4.10

Vesting Day — A311

a, Motor vehicles, plane. b, Train, bicycle.

1987, Apr. 1 Litho. *Perf. 13½*
871 A311 Pair 1.35 1.35
a.-b. 40c any single .50 .40

Establishment of NZ Post Ltd., Apr. 1, replacing the NZ PO.

Royal NZ Air Force, 50th Anniv. — A312

Designs: 40c, Avro 626, Wigram Airfield, c. 1937. 70c, P-40 Kittyhawks. 80c, Sunderland seaplane. 85c, A4 Skyhawks.

1987, Apr. 15 *Perf. 14x14½*
872 A312 40c multicolored .60 .60
873 A312 70c multicolored 1.00 1.00
874 A312 80c multicolored 1.10 1.10
875 A312 85c multicolored 1.25 1.25
a. Souvenir sheet of 4, #872-875 4.75 4.75
b. As "a," ovptd. with CAPEX '87 emblem in margin 13.00 *15.00*
Nos. 872-875 (4) 3.95 3.95

Natl. Parks System, Cent. — A313

1987, June 17 Litho. *Perf. 14½*
876 A313 70c Urewera .85 .85
877 A313 80c Mt. Cook .90 .90
878 A313 85c Fiordland 1.00 1.00
879 A313 $1.30 Tongariro 1.75 1.75
a. Souvenir sheet of one 3.75 3.75
b. As "a," ovptd. with CAPEX '87 emblem in margin 13.00 *15.00*
Nos. 876-879 (4) 4.50 4.50

No. 879a sold for $1.70 to benefit the NZ 1990 World Phil. Exhib., Auckland.

Christmas Carols — A314

35c, Hark! The Herald Angels Sing. 70c, Away in a Manger. 85c, We Three Kings of Orient Are.

1987, Sept. 16 Litho. *Perf. 14x14½*
880 A314 35c multi .50 .40
881 A314 70c multi .90 .90
882 A314 85c multi 1.25 1.25
Nos. 880-882 (3) 2.65 2.55

Maori Fiber Art — A315

1987, Nov. 4 Litho. *Perf. 12*
883 A315 40c Knot .55 .45
884 A315 60c Binding .75 .75
885 A315 80c Plait .95 .95
886 A315 85c Flax fiber 1.00 1.00
Nos. 883-886 (4) 3.25 3.15

Royal Phil. Soc. of NZ, Cent. A316

Portrait of Queen Victoria by Chalon A317

Queen Elizabeth II and: No. 887, No. 61 (blue background). No. 888, No. 62 (red background).

1988, Jan. 13 *Perf. 14x14½*
887 A316 40c multicolored .55 .55
888 A316 40c multicolored .55 .55
a. Pair, #887-888 1.25 1.25

Souvenir Sheet
889 A317 $1 multicolored 2.75 2.75
a. Overprinted with SYDPEX '88 emblem in margin 30.00 30.00

NZ Electrification, Cent. — A318

1988, Jan. 13 *Perf. 14x14½*
890 A318 40c Geothermal .45 .45
891 A318 60c Thermal .60 .60
892 A318 70c Gas .75 .75
893 A318 80c Hydroelectric 1.00 1.00
Nos. 890-893 (4) 2.80 2.80

Maori Rafter Paintings — A319

1988, Mar. 2 Litho. *Perf. 14½*
894 A319 40c Mangopare .65 .65
895 A319 40c Koru .65 .65
896 A319 40c Raupunga .65 .65
897 A319 60c Koiri .95 .95
Nos. 894-897 (4) 2.90 2.90

Greetings Messages — A320

1988, May 18 Litho. *Perf. 13½x13*
Booklet Stamps
898 A320 40c Good luck .75 .75
899 A320 40c Keeping in touch .75 .75
900 A320 40c Happy birthday .75 .75

Size: 41x27mm
901 A320 40c Congratulations .75 .75
902 A320 40c Get well soon .75 .75
a. Bklt. pane of 5, #898-902 4.25

Landscapes — A321

1988, June 8 *Perf. 14½*

903	A321 70c Milford Track	.80	.80
904	A321 80c Heaphy Track	.85	.85
905	A321 85c Copland Track	.95	.95
906	A321 $1.30 Routeburn Track	1.50	1.50
a.	Miniature sheet of one	3.00	3.00
	Nos. 903-906 (4)	4.10	4.10

No. 906a sold for $1.70 to benefit the exhibition.

NEW ZEALAND 1990
Souvenir Sheets

Four souvenir sheets were sold by the New Zealand post to benefit NEW ZEALAND 1990 World Stamp Exhibition. They each contain three $1 and one $2 "stamps" picturing antarctic scenes. They are not valid for postage.

Australia Bicentennial A322

Caricature: Kiwi and koala around campfire.

1988, June 21

907	A322 40c multicolored	.55	.55

See Australia No. 1086.

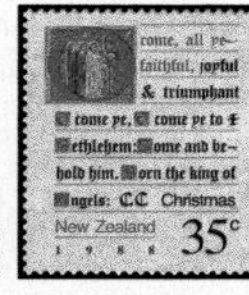

Christmas Carols — A323

Illuminated manuscripts: 35c, O, Come All Ye Faithful, by John Francis Wade, 1742. 70c, Hark! the Herald Angels Sing. 80c, Ding Dong! Merrily on High. 85c, The First Noel, first published in Davies & Gilbert's Some Ancient Christmas Carols, 1832.

1988, Sept. 14 **Litho.** *Perf. 14½*

908	A323 35c multicolored	.55	.40
909	A323 70c multicolored	.95	.95
910	A323 80c multicolored	1.00	1.00
911	A323 85c multicolored	1.10	1.10
	Nos. 908-911 (4)	3.60	3.45

New Zealand Heritage — A324

The Land. Paintings by 19th cent. artists: 40c, Lake Pukaki, 1862, by John Gully. 60c, On the Grass Plain Below Lake Arthur, 1846, by William Fox. 70c, View of Auckland, 1873, by John Hoyte. 80c, Mt. Egmont from the Southward, 1840, by Charles Heaphy. $1.05, Anakiwa, Queen Charlotte Sound, 1871, by John Kinder. $1.30, White Terraces, Lake Rotomahana, 1880, by Charles Barraud.

1988, Oct. 5 **Litho.** *Perf. 14x14½*

912	A324 40c multicolored	.50	.25
913	A324 60c multicolored	.70	.70
914	A324 70c multicolored	.90	.90
915	A324 80c multicolored	1.00	1.00
916	A324 $1.05 multicolored	1.20	1.20
917	A324 $1.30 multicolored	1.40	1.40
	Nos. 912-917 (6)	5.70	5.45

Kiwi — A325

1988, Oct. 19 **Engr.** *Perf. 14½*

918	A325 $1 green	2.50	2.50
a.	Booklet pane of 6	15.00	
b.	Litho.	2.50	2.50

Value is for stamp with surrounding selvage. No. 918 issued in booklets only.

No. 918b is from No. 1161a.

See Nos. 1027, 1161, 1445, 1635, 1787, 2368-2370.

Bird Type of 1985

5c, Spotless crake. 10c, Banded dotterel. 20c, Yellowhead. 30c, Silvereye. 40c, Brown kiwi. 45c, Rock wren. 50c, Kingfisher. 60c, Spotted shag. No. 927, Fiordland crested penguin. No. 928, New Zealand falcon. 90c, South Island robin. $10, Little spotted kiwi.

1988-95 **Litho.** *Perf. 14½x14*
Sizes: $10, 26x31½mm, Others, 22x27mm

919	A279 5c multi	.25	.25
920	A279 10c multi	.25	.25
921	A279 20c multi	.30	.25
a.	Perf. 13½	.75	.75
922	A279 30c multi	.45	.25
923	A279 40c multi	.60	.25
	Complete booklet, 10 #923	6.50	
c.	Perf. 13½x13	2.50	2.50
924	A279 45c multi	.70	.25
b.	Booklet pane of 10	7.00	
925	A279 50c multi	.70	.35
926	A279 60c multi	.85	.60
a.	Sheet of 8, #919-926	5.00	5.00
b.	Perf. 13½	7.00	7.00
927	A279 80c multi	1.10	.70
	Complete booklet, 10 #927 + 10 etiquettes	11.00	
928	A279 80c multi	1.10	.70
	Complete booklet, 10 #928	11.00	
c.	Perf. 12 on 3 sides	4.00	4.00
d.	As "c," booklet pane of 10	45.00	
	Complete booklet, #928d	47.50	
929	A279 90c multi	1.40	1.25
930	A279 $10 multi	9.50	6.75
d.	Souv. sheet of 1	20.00	20.00

Self-Adhesive
Die Cut Perf 11½

931	A279 40c like #923	.80	.50
932	A279 45c like #924	.70	.55

Die Cut Perf 10½x11

933	A279 45c like #924	.70	.55
	Nos. 919-933 (15)	19.40	13.45

No. 933 has a darker blue background than No. 932 and has perf "teeth" at the corners while No. 932 does not. Perf "teeth" on the top and left side are staggered to line up with perf "holes" on the bottom and right on No. 933. "Teeth" line up with "teeth" on No. 932.

PHILAKOREA '94 (#926a). POST'X '95 Postal Exhibition (#930d).

Issued: $10, 4/19/89; #931, 4/17/91; 5c, #924, 932, 7/1/91; #933, 1991; #928, 3/31/93; #926a, 8/16/94; #930d, 2/3/95; #921a, 926b, 9/22/95; #923c, 11/8/89; others, 11/2/88.

Whales of the Southern Oceans — A326

60c, Humpback. 70c, Killer. 80c, Southern right. 85c, Blue. $1.05, Southern bottlenose. $1.30, Sperm.

1988, Nov. 2 **Litho.** *Perf. 13½*

936	A326 60c multi	.95	.95
937	A326 70c multi	1.00	1.00
938	A326 80c multi	1.10	1.10
939	A326 85c multi	1.25	1.25
940	A326 $1.05 multi	1.50	1.50
941	A326 $1.30 multi	1.90	1.90
	Nos. 936-941 (6)	7.70	7.70

Wildflowers — A327

1989, Jan. 18 **Litho.** *Perf. 14½*

942	A327 40c Clover	.55	.55
943	A327 60c Lotus	.80	.80
944	A327 70c Montbretia	1.00	1.00
945	A327 80c Wild ginger	1.20	1.20
	Nos. 942-945 (4)	3.55	3.55

Authors — A328

Portraits: 40c, Katherine Mansfield (1888-1923). 60c, James K. Baxter (1926-1972). 70c, Bruce Mason (1921-1982). 80c, Ngaio Marsh (1899-1982).

1989, Mar. 1 **Litho.** *Perf. 12½*

946	A328 40c multicolored	.45	.45
947	A328 60c multicolored	.65	.65
948	A328 70c multicolored	.70	.70
949	A328 80c multicolored	.80	.80
	Nos. 946-949 (4)	2.60	2.60

New Zealand Heritage — A329

The people.

1989, May 17 *Perf. 14x14½*

950	A329 40c Moriori	.60	.35
951	A329 60c Prospectors	.85	.85
952	A329 70c Land settlers	.70	.70
953	A329 80c Whalers	.85	.85
954	A329 $1.05 Missionaries	.95	.95
955	A329 $1.30 Maori	1.25	1.25
	Nos. 950-955 (6)	5.20	4.95

Trees — A330

1989, June 7

956	A330 80c Kahikatea	.90	.90
957	A330 85c Rimu	1.00	1.00
958	A330 $1.05 Totara	1.25	1.25
959	A330 $1.30 Kauri	1.50	1.50
a.	Miniature sheet of one	3.50	3.50
	Nos. 956-959 (4)	4.65	4.65

No. 959a sold for $1.80. Surtax benefited the "NZ 1990" executive committee.

Christmas — A331

Star of Bethlehem illuminating settings: 35c, View of One Tree Hill from a bedroom window. 65c, A shepherd overlooking snow-capped mountains. 80c, Boats in harbor. $1, Earth.

1989, Sept. 13 **Litho.** *Perf. 14½*

960	A331 35c multicolored	.40	.25
a.	Booklet pane of 10	5.50	
961	A331 65c multicolored	.75	.75
962	A331 80c multicolored	.95	.95
963	A331 $1 multicolored	1.10	1.10
	Nos. 960-963 (4)	3.20	3.05

New Zealand Heritage — A332

The sea.

1989, Oct. 11 **Litho.** *Perf. 14x14½*

964	A332 40c Windsurfing	.50	.25
965	A332 60c Fishing	.70	.70
966	A332 65c Swordfish	.90	.90
967	A332 80c Harbor	1.00	1.00
968	A332 $1 Gulls over coast	1.25	1.25
969	A332 $1.50 Container ship	1.90	1.90
	Nos. 964-969 (6)	6.25	6.00

14th Commonwealth Games, Auckland, Jan. 24-Feb. 3, 1990 — A333

No. 970, Emblem. No. 971, Goldie character trademark. No. 972, Gymnastics. No. 973, Weight lifting. No. 974, Swimming. No. 975, Cycling. No. 976, Lawn bowling. No. 977, Hurdles.

1989, Nov. 8 *Perf. 14½*

970	A333 40c multi	.50	.50
971	A333 40c multi	.50	.50
a.	Souvenir sheet of 2, #970-971, sailboats ('90)	2.75	2.75
b.	As "a," stadium ('90)	2.75	2.75
972	A333 40c multi	.50	.50
973	A333 50c multi	.60	.60
974	A333 65c multi	.75	.75
975	A333 80c multi	.95	.95
976	A333 $1 multi	1.10	1.10
977	A333 $1.80 multi	1.90	1.90
	Nos. 970-977 (8)	6.80	6.80

Air New Zealand, 50th Anniv. — A334

1990, Jan. 17 *Perf. 13½x14½*

978	A334 80c multicolored	1.00	.80

Souvenir Sheet

Treaty of Waitangi, 150th Anniv. A335

Painting by Leonard Mitchell: a, Maori chief signing the treaty. b, Chief Hone Heke shaking hand of Lt.-Gov. William Hobson.

1990, Jan. 17 *Perf. 13½*

979	A335 Sheet of 2	3.00	3.00
a.-b.	40c any single	1.10	1.10

New Zealand Heritage — A336

The Ships: No. 980, Polynesian double-hulled canoe, c. 1000. No. 981, Endeavour. No. 982, Tory. No. 983, Crusader. No. 984, Edwin Fox. No. 985, Arawa.

1990, Mar. 7 **Litho.** *Perf. 14x14½*

980	A336 40c multi	.60	.25
981	A336 50c multi	.75	.75
a.	Souvenir sheet of 1	*20.00*	*20.00*
982	A336 60c multi	.90	.90
983	A336 80c multi	1.40	1.40
984	A336 $1 multi	1.50	1.50
985	A336 $1.50 multi	2.00	2.00
	Nos. 980-985 (6)	7.15	6.80

No. 981a for Stamp World London '90. Sold for $1.30. Issued May 3.

Miniature Sheet

Orchids — A337

Designs: a, Sun. b, Spider. c, Winika. d, Greenhood. e, Odd-leaved orchid.

1990, Apr. 18 Litho. *Perf. 14½*

986 Sheet of 5 7.50 7.50
a.-d. A337 40c any single 1.00 1.00
e. A337 80c multicolored 2.00 2.00

No. 986 sold for $4.90. Surcharge for the intl. stamp exhibition, Auckland, Aug. 24-Sept 2. Imperf. sheets were available only in season tickets which were sold for $25. Value, $42.50.

New Zealand Heritage — A338

The Achievers: 40c, Grace Neill (1846-1926), nurse, journalist. 50c, Jean Batten (1909-1982), aviator. 60c, Katherine Sheppard (1848-1934), social worker. 80c, Richard Pearse (1877-1953), inventor. $1, Gov.-Gen. Bernard Freyberg (1889-1963). $1.50, Peter Buck (1877-1951), cabinet minister.

1990, May 16 Litho. *Perf. 14x14½*

987 A338 40c multicolored .65 .30
988 A338 50c multicolored .80 .80
989 A338 60c multicolored .95 .95
990 A338 80c multicolored 1.25 1.25
991 A338 $1 multicolored 1.50 1.50
992 A338 $1.50 multicolored 1.75 1.75
Nos. 987-992 (6) 6.90 6.55

Akaroa Harbor — A339

Early Settlements: $1, Durie Hill, Wanganui River. $1.50, Mt. Victoria, Wellington. $1.80, Rangitoto Island, Takapuna Beach, Auckland.

1990, June 13 Litho. *Perf. 14½*

993 A339 80c multicolored 1.00 1.00
994 A339 $1 multicolored 1.40 1.40
995 A339 $1.50 multicolored 2.25 2.25
996 A339 $1.80 multicolored 2.50 2.50
a. Souvenir sheet of 1 4.25 4.25
Nos. 993-996 (4) 7.15 7.15

No. 996a sold for $2.30. Surtax for world philatelic expo, New Zealand '90.

New Zealand Heritage — A340

The Maori: 40c, Legend of Rangi and Papa. 50c, Maori feather cloak. 60c, Song. 80c, Maori tattoo. $1, War canoe prow. $1.50, Maori war dance.

1990, Aug. 24 Litho. *Perf. 14*

997 A340 40c multicolored .55 .30
998 A340 50c multicolored .65 .65
999 A340 60c multicolored .75 .75
1000 A340 80c multicolored .85 .85
1001 A340 $1 multicolored 1.25 1.25
1002 A340 $1.50 multicolored 1.75 1.75
Nos. 997-1002 (6) 5.80 5.55

Souvenir Sheet

First Postage Stamps, 150th Anniv. A341

Designs: a, Victoria. b, Edward VII. c, George V. d, Edward VIII. e, George VI. f, Elizabeth II.

1990, Aug. 29 Engr. *Perf. 14½x14*

1003 A341 40c Sheet of 6 5.25 5.25
a.-f. any single .75 .75

Christmas — A342

Various angels.

1990, Sept. 12 Litho. *Perf. 14*

1004 A342 40c multicolored .55 .40
1005 A342 $1 multicolored 1.25 .25
1006 A342 $1.50 multicolored 2.00 1.25
1007 A342 $1.80 multicolored 2.25 2.00
Nos. 1004-1007 (4) 6.05 3.90

Antarctic Petrel — A343

50c, Wilson's storm petrel. 60c, Snow petrel. 80c, Antarctic fulmar. $1, Chinstrap penguin. $1.50, Emperor penguin.

1990, Nov. 7 *Perf. 13½x13*

1008 A343 40c shown .65 .35
1009 A343 50c multicolored .80 .70
1010 A343 60c multicolored .95 .85
1011 A343 80c multicolored 1.25 1.10
1012 A343 $1 multicolored 1.60 1.60
1013 A343 $1.50 multicolored 2.40 2.25
Nos. 1008-1013 (6) 7.65 6.85

Sheep — A344

1991, Jan. 23 Litho. *Perf. 14½*

1014 A344 40c Coopworth .55 .25
1015 A344 60c Perendale .80 .80
1016 A344 80c Corriedale 1.00 1.00
1017 A344 $1 Drysdale 1.25 1.25
1018 A344 $1.50 South Suffolk 1.75 1.75
1019 A344 $1.80 Romney 2.00 2.00
Nos. 1014-1019 (6) 7.35 7.05

Map, Royal Albatross, Designs from Moriori House, Moriori Man, Nikau Palm, Tree Carving — A345

Design: 80c, Map, sailing ship, carving, petroglyph, Moriori house, Tommy Solomon, last full-blooded Moriori.

1991, Mar. 6 Litho. *Perf. 13½*

1020 A345 40c shown .65 .55
1021 A345 80c multicolored 1.25 1.10

Discovery of the Chatham Islands, Bicent.

New Zealand Football (Soccer) Assoc., Cent. — A346

Designs: a, Goal. b, 5 players, referee.

1991, Mar. 6

1022 Pair 2.50 2.50
a.-b. A346 80c any single 1.25 1.25

Tuatara — A347

Designs: No. 1023, Juvenile. No. 1024, In burrow. No. 1025, Female. No. 1026, Male.

1991, Apr. 17 Litho. *Perf. 14½*
Denomination Color

1023 A347 40c gray blue .80 .80
1024 A347 40c dark brown .80 .80
1025 A347 40c olive green .80 .80
1026 A347 40c orange brown .80 .80
Nos. 1023-1026 (4) 3.20 3.20

Kiwi Type of 1988

1991, Apr. 17 Engr. *Perf. 14½*

1027 A325 $1 red 1.60 1.25
a. Litho. 1.75 1.50

Value is for stamp with surrounding selvage. No. 1027a is from Nos.1161a, 1635a.

Happy Birthday A348

Thinking of You A349

No. 1028, Clown face. No. 1029, Balloons. No. 1030, Birthday hat. No. 1031, Present. No. 1032, Cake & candles. No. 1033 Cat, front paws on window sill. No. 1034, Cat, slippers. No. 1035, Cat, alarm clock. No. 1036, Cat sitting on window sill. No. 1037, Cat walking by door.

1991, May 15 Litho. *Perf. 14x13½*
Size of Nos. 1031-1032, 1036-1037: 41x27mm

1028 A348 40c multi .90 .90
1029 A348 40c multi .90 .90
1030 A348 40c multi .90 .90
1031 A348 40c multi .90 .90
1032 A348 40c multi .90 .90
a. Bklt. pane of 5, #1028-1032 6.00
1033 A349 40c shown .90 .90
1034 A349 40c multi .90 .90
1035 A349 40c multi .90 .90
1036 A349 40c multi .90 .90
1037 A349 40c multi .90 .90
a. Bklt. pane of 5, #1033-1037 6.00
Nos. 1028-1037 (10) 9.00 9.00

See Nos. 1044-1053.

Rock Formations — A350

40c, Punakaiki Rocks. 50c, Moeraki Boulders. 80c, Organ Pipes. $1, Castle Hill. $1.50, Te Kaukau Point. $1.80, Ahuriri River Clay Cliffs.

1991, June 12 Litho. *Perf. 14½*

1038 A350 40c multicolored .60 .35
1039 A350 50c multicolored .75 .75
1040 A350 80c multicolored 1.10 1.10
1041 A350 $1 multicolored 1.25 1.25
1042 A350 $1.50 multicolored 2.00 2.00
1043 A350 $1.80 multicolored 2.25 2.25
Nos. 1038-1043 (6) 7.95 7.70

Greetings Types

1991, July 1 Litho. *Perf. 14x13½*
Size of Nos. 1047-1048, 1052-1053: 41x27mm

1044 A348 45c like #1028 .80 .80
1045 A348 45c like #1029 .80 .80
1046 A348 45c like #1030 .80 .80
1047 A348 45c like #1031 .80 .80
1048 A348 45c like #1032 .80 .80
a. Bklt. pane of 5, #1044-1048 5.00
1049 A349 45c like #1033 .80 .80
1050 A349 45c like #1034 .80 .80
1051 A349 45c like #1035 .80 .80
1052 A349 45c like #1036 .80 .80
1053 A349 45c like #1037 .80 .80
a. Bklt. pane of 5, #1049-1053 5.00
Nos. 1044-1053 (10) 8.00 8.00

1991 Rugby World Cup — A351

1991, Aug. 21 Litho. *Perf. 14½x14*

1054 A351 80c Children's 1.00 1.00
1055 A351 $1 Women's 1.25 1.25
1056 A351 $1.50 Senior 2.00 2.00
1057 A351 $1.80 All Blacks 2.25 2.25
a. Souvenir sheet of 1 4.00 4.00
b. As "a," with Phila Nippon '91 emblem in margin 15.00 15.00
Nos. 1054-1057 (4) 6.50 6.50

No. 1057a sold for $2.40 to benefit philatelic trust for hobby support.

Christmas — A352

No. 1058, Shepherds. No. 1059, Wise men, camels. No. 1060, Mary, Baby Jesus. No. 1061, Wise man, gift. No. 1062, Star. No. 1063, Crown. No. 1064, Angel.

1991, Sept. 18 Litho. *Perf. 13½x14*

1058 A352 45c multi .55 .55
1059 A352 45c multi .55 .55
1060 A352 45c multi .55 .55
1061 A352 45c multi .55 .55
a. Block of 4, #1058-1061 3.00 3.00
1062 A352 65c multi .90 .90
1063 A352 $1 multi 1.50 1.50
1064 A352 $1.50 multi 2.00 2.00
Nos. 1058-1064 (7) 6.60 6.60

Butterflies — A354

$1, Forest ringlet. $2, Southern blue. $3, Yellow admiral. $4, Common copper. $5, Red admiral.

1991-2008 Litho. *Perf. 14¼*

1075 A354 $1 multi 1.40 1.10
a. Perf. 14x14½ on 3 sides 5.00 5.00
b. Booklet pane of 5 + 5 labels Perf. 14x14½ on 3 sides 25.00
Complete booklet, #1075b 25.00
c. Perf. 13¾x14¼ 2.00 2.00
1076 A354 $2 multi 3.00 2.25
a. Perf. 13¾x14¼ 12.00 12.00
1077 A354 $3 multi 4.00 3.50
a. Souvenir sheet of 1 10.00 10.00
b. Perf. 13¾x14¼ 12.00 12.00
1078 A354 $4 multi 5.00 3.00
a. Perf. 13¾x14¼ 7.00 5.25
b. Perf. 14 ('08) 6.25 4.50
1079 A354 $5 multi 6.50 5.00
a. Perf. 13¾x14¼ 8.50 6.00
Nos. 1075-1079 (5) 19.90 14.85

No. 1077a issued later for Phila Nippon '91.
Issued: #1075, 1075a, 1076, 1077, 11/6/91; $4-$5, 1/25/95; #1075b, 9/1/95; #1078a, 10/97; #1079a, 10/9/96; #1075c, 1076a, 11/6/96; #1077b, Aug. 1996.

Mount Cook A356

Engraved with Foil Application
Perf. 14½x15

1994, Feb. 18 Wmk. 387

1084 A356 $20 gold & blue 22.50 15.00

1992 America's Cup Competition A357

45c, KZ7 Kiwi Magic, 1987. 80c, KZ1 New Zealand, 1988. $1, America, 1851. $1.50, New Zealand, 1992.

Perf. 14x14½
1992, Jan. 22 Litho. Unwmk.

1085 A357 45c multicolored .60 .25
1086 A357 80c multicolored .95 .95
1087 A357 $1 multicolored 1.25 1.25
1088 A357 $1.50 multicolored 1.90 1.90
Nos. 1085-1088 (4) 4.70 4.35

Sighting of New Zealand by Abel Tasman, 350th Anniv. — A358

1992, Mar. 12 ***Perf. 13½x14½***

No.	Type	Description	Unused	Used
1089	A358	45c Heemskerck	.60	.30
1090	A358	80c Zeehaen	1.00	1.00
1091	A358	$1 Santa Maria	1.40	1.40
1092	A358	$1.50 Pinta and Nina	1.90	1.90
a.		Souvenir sheet of 2, #1091-1092, Perf. 14x14½	8.00	8.00
		Nos. 1089-1092 (4)	4.90	4.60

Discovery of America, 500th anniv. (#1091-1092).

Issue date: No. 1092a, May 22. World Columbian Stamp Expo (#1092a).

1992 Summer Olympics, Barcelona A359

1992, Apr. 3 **Litho.** ***Perf. 13½***

No.	Type	Description	Unused	Used
1093	A359	45c Runners	.70	.60

Antarctic Seals — A360

45c, Weddell seal. 50c, Crabeater seal. 65c, Leopard seal. 80c, Ross seal. $1, Southern elephant seal. $1.80, Hooker's sea lion.

1992, Apr. 8 ***Perf. 14x13½***

No.	Type	Description	Unused	Used
1094	A360	45c multi	.70	.60
1095	A360	50c multi	.80	.70
1096	A360	65c multi	1.00	.85
1097	A360	80c multi	1.25	1.00
1098	A360	$1 multi	1.60	1.40
1099	A360	$1.80 multi	2.75	2.50
		Nos. 1094-1099 (6)	8.10	7.05

1992 Summer Olympics, Barcelona A361

1992, May 13 **Litho.** ***Perf. 13½***

No.	Type	Description	Unused	Used
1100	A361	45c Cycling	.65	.40
1101	A361	80c Archery	1.00	1.00
1102	A361	$1 Equestrian	1.25	1.25
1103	A361	$1.50 Board sailing	1.90	1.90
a.		Souvenir sheet of 4, #1100-1103, perf 14x14½	5.75	5.75
b.		No. 1103a overprinted	11.50	11.50
		Nos. 1100-1103 (4)	4.80	4.55

No. 1103b overprint consists of World Columbian Stamp Expo emblem in sheet margin. Issue date: No. 1103b, May 22.

Glaciers — A362

45c, Glacier ice. 50c, Tasman glacier. 80c, Snowball glacier. $1, Brewster glacier. $1.50, Fox glacier. $1.80, Franz Josef glacier.

1992, June 12

No.	Type	Description	Unused	Used
1104	A362	45c multicolored	.60	.30
1105	A362	50c multicolored	.70	.70
1106	A362	80c multicolored	.85	.85
1107	A362	$1 multicolored	1.25	1.25
1108	A362	$1.50 multicolored	1.90	1.90
1109	A362	$1.80 multicolored	2.10	2.10
		Nos. 1104-1109 (6)	7.40	7.10

Camellias — A363

45c, Grand finale. 50c, Showa-no-sakae. 80c, Sugar dream. $1, Night rider. $1.50, E.G. Waterhouse. $1.80, Dr. Clifford Parks.

1992, July 8 ***Perf. 14½***

No.	Type	Description	Unused	Used
1110	A363	45c multicolored	.60	.30
1111	A363	50c multicolored	.70	.70
1112	A363	80c multicolored	.90	.90
1113	A363	$1 multicolored	1.25	1.25
1114	A363	$1.50 multicolored	1.90	1.90
1115	A363	$1.80 multicolored	2.10	2.10
		Nos. 1110-1115 (6)	7.45	7.15

Scenic Views of New Zealand — A364

No. 1116, Tree, hills. No. 1117, Hills, stream. No. 1118, Hills, mountain tops. No. 1119, Glacier. No. 1120, Trees, green hills. No. 1121, Tree branch, rapids. No. 1122, Rocky shoreline. No. 1123, Fjord. No. 1124, Glacial runoff. No. 1125, Vegetation, stream.

1992, Sept. 1 **Litho.** ***Perf. 14x14½***

Booklet Stamps

No.	Type	Description	Unused	Used
1116	A364	45c multicolored	.65	.65
1117	A364	45c multicolored	.65	.65
1118	A364	45c multicolored	.65	.65
1119	A364	45c multicolored	.65	.65
1120	A364	45c multicolored	.65	.65
1121	A364	45c multicolored	.65	.65
1122	A364	45c multicolored	.65	.65
1123	A364	45c multicolored	.65	.65
1124	A364	45c multicolored	.65	.65
1125	A364	45c multicolored	.65	.65
a.		Bklt. pane of 10, #1116-1125	8.75	
		Nos. 1116-1125 (10)	6.50	6.50

No. 1125a has continous design.

Christmas — A365

No. 1126, Two reindeer over village. No. 1127, Two reindeer pulling Santa's sleigh. No. 1128, Christmas tree in window. No. 1129, Two children looking out window. 65c, Fireplace, stockings. $1, Church. $1.50, People beneath pohutukawa tree at beach.

1992, Sept. 16 ***Perf. 14½***

No.	Type	Description	Unused	Used
1126	A365	45c multicolored	.50	.50
1127	A365	45c multicolored	.50	.50
1128	A365	45c multicolored	.50	.50
1129	A365	45c multicolored	.50	.50
a.		Block of 4, #1126-1129	2.50	2.50
1130	A365	65c multicolored	.75	.75
1131	A365	$1 multicolored	1.00	1.00
1132	A365	$1.50 multicolored	1.75	1.75
		Nos. 1126-1132 (7)	5.50	5.50

No. 1129a has continous design.

A366

The Emerging Years: The 1920s: 45c, Flaming youth. 50c, Birth of broadcasting. 80c, All Blacks rugby player. $1, The swaggie. $1.50, Motorcar brings freedom. $1.80, Arrival of the air age.

1992, Nov. 4 **Litho.** ***Perf. 13½***

No.	Type	Description	Unused	Used
1133	A366	45c multicolored	.50	.25
1134	A366	50c multicolored	.55	.35
1135	A366	80c multicolored	.85	.85
1136	A366	$1 multicolored	1.10	1.10
1137	A366	$1.50 multicolored	1.75	1.75
1138	A366	$1.80 multicolored	2.00	2.00
		Nos. 1133-1138 (6)	6.75	6.30

Royal Doulton Ceramics — A367

45c, Character jug, "Old Charley." 50c, Plate from "Bunnykins" series. 80c, Maori art tea ware. $1, Hand painted "Ophelia" plate. $1.50, Burslem figurine of St. George. $1.80, Salt glazed vase.

1993, Jan. 20 **Litho.** ***Perf. 13***

No.	Type	Description	Unused	Used
1139	A367	45c multicolored	.50	.25
1140	A367	50c multicolored	.55	.55
1141	A367	80c multicolored	.85	.85
1142	A367	$1 multicolored	1.10	1.10
1143	A367	$1.50 multicolored	1.60	1.60
1144	A367	$1.80 multicolored	1.90	1.90
a.		Souvenir sheet of 1	2.50	2.50
		Nos. 1139-1144 (6)	6.50	6.25

A368

The Emerging Years: The 1930's: 45c, Buttons and bows, the new femininity. 50c, The Great Depression. 80c, Race horse, Phar Lap. $1, State housing. $1.50, Free milk for schools. $1.80, The talkies.

1993, Feb. 17 **Litho.** ***Perf. 14½x14***

No.	Type	Description	Unused	Used
1145	A368	45c multicolored	.55	.25
1146	A368	50c multicolored	.60	.60
1147	A368	80c multicolored	.95	.95
1148	A368	$1 multicolored	1.10	1.10
1149	A368	$1.50 multicolored	1.60	1.60
1150	A368	$1.80 multicolored	1.90	1.90
		Nos. 1145-1150 (6)	6.70	6.40

Woman Suffrage, Cent. — A369

45c, First vote. 80c, War work. $1, Child care. $1.50, Contemporary women.

1993, Mar. 31 **Litho.** ***Perf. 13½***

No.	Type	Description	Unused	Used
1151	A369	45c multicolored	.55	.25
1152	A369	80c multicolored	.85	.85
1153	A369	$1 multicolored	1.10	1.10
1154	A369	$1.50 multicolored	2.25	2.25
		Nos. 1151-1154 (4)	4.75	4.45

Thermal Wonders — A370

45c, Champagne Pool. 50c, Boiling mud, Rotorua. 80c, Emerald Pool. $1, Hakereteke Falls. $1.50, Warbrick Terrace. $1.80, Pohutu Geyser.

1993, May 5 **Litho.** ***Perf. 12***

No.	Type	Description	Unused	Used
1155	A370	45c multicolored	.55	.25
1156	A370	50c multicolored	.65	.65
1157	A370	80c multicolored	1.00	1.00
1158	A370	$1 multicolored	1.10	1.10
1159	A370	$1.50 multicolored	1.50	1.50
1160	A370	$1.80 multicolored	2.00	2.00
a.		Souvenir sheet of 1	3.50	3.50
		Nos. 1155-1160 (6)	6.80	6.50

No. 1160a inscribed with Bangkok '93 emblem in sheet margin. Issue date: No. 1160a, Oct. 1.

Kiwi Type of 1988

1993, June 9 **Engr.** ***Perf. 14½***

No.	Type	Description	Unused	Used
1161	A325	$1 blue	1.40	1.40
a.		Souv. sheet of 3, #918b, 1027a, 1161	8.50	8.50
b.		Litho.	2.25	1.75
c.		Souv. sheet of 3, #918b, 1027a, 1161b	6.00	6.00

Taipei '93, Asian Intl. Stamp Exhibition (#1161a), Hong Kong '94 (#1161c).

Value is for stamp with surrounding selvage.

Issued: #1161a, 8/14/93; #1161c, 2/18/94.

See No. 1635a.

Species Unique to New Zealand — A371

Designs: No. 1162, Yellow-eyed penguin, Hector's dolphin, New Zealand fur seal. 1162A, Taiko, Mt. Cook lily, blue duck. 1162B, Giant snail, rock wren, Hamilton's frog. 1162C, Kaka, Chatham Island pigeon, giant weta.

No. 1163, Tusked weta.

1993, June 9 **Litho.** ***Perf. 14x14½***

No.	Type	Description	Unused	Used
1162	A371	45c multicolored	.80	.80
1162A	A371	45c multicolored	.80	.80
1162B	A371	45c multicolored	.80	.80
1162C	A371	45c multicolored	.80	.80
d.		As #1162-1162C, block of 4	4.00	4.00
1163	A371	45c multicolored	.80	.80
a.		Booklet pane of 10	8.00	—
		Complete booklet	8.50	
		Nos. 1162-1163 (5)	4.00	4.00

World Wildlife Fund.

Nos. 1162-1162C were issued both in sheets containing individual designs and in sheets containing the four values setenant (#1162d).

Christmas — A372

Christmas designs: No. 1164, Flowers from pohutukawa tree, denomination at UL. No. 1165, Like #1164, denomination at UR. No. 1166, Present with yellow ribbon, denomination at LL. No. 1167, Present with red ribbon, denomination at LR. $1.00, Ornaments, cracker, sailboats. $1.50, Wreath, sailboats, present.

1993, Sept. 1 **Litho.** ***Perf. 14½x14***

No.	Type	Description	Unused	Used
1164	A372	45c multicolored	.60	.60
1165	A372	45c multicolored	.60	.60
1166	A372	45c multicolored	.60	.60
1167	A372	45c multicolored	.60	.60
a.		Block of 4, #1164-1167	2.50	2.50
1168	A372	$1 multicolored	1.25	1.10
1169	A372	$1.50 multicolored	2.00	1.75
		Nos. 1164-1169 (6)	5.65	5.25

Booklet Stamps

Perf. 12

No.	Type	Description	Unused	Used
1164a	A372	45c multicolored	1.00	1.00
1165a	A372	45c multicolored	1.00	1.00
1166a	A372	45c multicolored	1.00	1.00
1167b	A372	45c multicolored	1.00	1.00
c.		Bklt. pane, 2 ea #1166a, 1167b, 3 ea #1164a-1165a	17.00	

At least one edge of No. 1167c is guillotined.

Fish — A373

Designs: No. 1170, Paua (#1175). No. 1171, Greenshell mussels. No. 1172, Terakihi (#1171). No. 1173, Salmon (#1172). No. 1174, Southern bluefin tuna, albacore tuna, kahawai (#1173). No. 1175, Rock lobster (#1171). No. 1176, Snapper (#1177). No. 1177, Grouper ("Groper," #1178). No. 1178, Orange roughy (#1179). No. 1179, Squid, hoki, oreo dory (#1173, #1174, #1178).

1993, Sept. 1 ***Perf. 13½***

Booklet Stamps

No.	Type	Description	Unused	Used
1170	A373	45c multicolored	.90	.90
1171	A373	45c multicolored	.90	.90
1172	A373	45c multicolored	.90	.90
1173	A373	45c multicolored	.90	.90
1174	A373	45c multicolored	.90	.90
1175	A373	45c multicolored	.90	.90
1176	A373	45c multicolored	.90	.90
1177	A373	45c multicolored	.90	.90
1178	A373	45c multicolored	.90	.90
1179	A373	45c multicolored	.90	.90
a.		Booklet pane of 10, #1170-1179 + 2 labels	11.00	
		Nos. 1170-1179 (10)	9.00	9.00

Nos. 1179a has continuous design.

Dinosaurs — A374

1993, Oct. 1

No.	Type	Description	Unused	Used
1180	A374	45c Sauropod	.60	.50
1181	A374	80c Pterosaur	1.10	1.10
1182	A374	$1 Ankylosaur	1.25	1.25
1183	A374	$1.20 Mauisaurus	1.50	1.50
1184	A374	$1.50 Carnosaur	1.60	1.60
a.		Souvenir sheet of 1, perf. 14½x14	2.00	2.00
b.		As "a," inscribed with Bangkok '93 emblem	3.00	2.75
		Nos. 1180-1184 (5)	6.05	5.95

Booklet Stamp

Size: 25½x23½mm

Perf. 12

No.	Type	Description	Unused	Used
1185	A374	45c Carnosaur, sauropod	.70	.55
a.		Booklet pane of 10 + 2 labels	7.00	7.00

The 1940s — A375

Designs: 45c, New Zealand at war. 50c, Crop dusting. 80c, State produces hydroelectricity. $1, New Zealand Marching Assoc. $1.50, The American invasion. $1.80, Victory.

1993, Nov. 3 Litho. *Perf. 14*

1186 A375 45c multicolored .65 .30
1187 A375 50c multicolored .75 .75
1188 A375 80c multicolored 1.10 1.10
1189 A375 $1 multicolored 1.40 1.40
1190 A375 $1.50 multicolored 2.00 2.00
1191 A375 $1.80 multicolored 2.25 2.25
Nos. 1186-1191 (6) 8.15 7.80

Outdoor Adventure Sports — A376

45c, Bungy jumping. 80c, Trout fishing. $1, Jet boating, horiz. $1.50, Tramping. $1.80, Heli-skiing.

1994, Jan. 19 Litho. *Perf. 12*

1192 A376 45c multicolored .60 .30
1193 A376 80c multicolored .95 .95
1194 A376 $1 multicolored 1.25 1.25
1195 A376 $1.50 multicolored 1.75 1.75
1196 A376 $1.80 multicolored 2.00 2.00
a. Souvenir sheet of 1 3.75 3.75
Nos. 1192-1196 (5) 6.55 6.25

No. 1196a inscribed in sheet margin with Hong Kong '94 emblem and text in English and Chinese. Issue date: No. 1196a, Feb. 18.

White Water Rafting — A377

1994, Jan. 19 Litho. *Perf. 12*

Booklet Stamp

1197 A377 45c multicolored .55 .55
a. Booklet pane of 10 + 4 labels 6.00

Whitbread Trans-Global Yacht Race — A378

1994, Jan. 19 *Perf. 15*

1198 A378 $1 Endeavour 1.40 1.40

Used value is for stamp with complete selvage.

The 1950's — A379

Designs: 45c, Rock and roll. 80c, Conquest of Mt. Everest. $1, Aunt Daisy, "Good Morning Everybody." $1.20, Royal visit, 1953. $1.50, Opo, the Friendly Dolphin. $1.80, The Coat Hanger (Auckland Harbor Bridge.)

1994, Mar. 24 Litho. *Perf. 14*

1199 A379 45c multicolored .60 .30
1200 A379 80c multicolored .95 .95
1201 A379 $1 multicolored 1.25 1.25
1202 A379 $1.20 multicolored 1.50 1.50
1203 A379 $1.50 multicolored 1.75 1.75
1204 A379 $1.80 multicolored 2.25 2.25
Nos. 1199-1204 (6) 8.30 8.00

Scenic Views of the Four Seasons A380

Designs: 45c, Winter, Mt. Cook, Mt. Cook lily. 70c, Spring, Lake Hawea, kowhai flower. $1.50, Summer, Opononi, pohutukawa flower. $1.80, Autumn, Mt. Cook, Lake Pukaki, puriri flower.

1994, Apr. 27 *Perf. 12*

1205 A380 45c multicolored .50 .30
1206 A380 70c multicolored .85 .85
1207 A380 $1.50 multicolored 1.25 1.25
1208 A380 $1.80 multicolored 1.75 1.75
a. Strip of 4, #1205-1208 5.00 5.00
Nos. 1205-1208 (4) 4.35 4.15

Paua Shell A381

Pavlova Dessert A382

Jandals A383

Bush Shirt A384

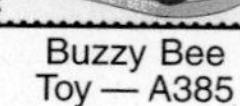

Buzzy Bee Toy — A385

Kiwi Fruit — A386

Kiwiana: #1211, Hokey pokey ice cream. #1212, Fish and chips. #1216, Black singlet, gumboots. #1217, Rugby shoes, ball.

1994, Apr. 27 Litho. *Perf. 12*

Booklet Stamps

1209 A381 45c shown .80 .80
1210 A382 45c shown .80 .80
1211 A381 45c multicolored .80 .80
1212 A382 45c multicolored .80 .80
1213 A383 45c shown .80 .80
1214 A384 45c shown .80 .80
1215 A385 45c shown .80 .80
1216 A384 45c multicolored .80 .80
1217 A385 45c multicolored .80 .80
1218 A386 45c shown .80 .80
a. Booklet pane of 10, #1209-1218 10.00
Nos. 1209-1218 (10) 8.00 8.00

Maori Myths — A387

Designs: 45c, Maui pulls up Te Ika (the fish). 80c, Rona is snatched up by Marama (moon). $1, Maui attacks Tuna (eel). $1.20, Tane separates Rangi (sky) and Papa (earth). $1.50, Matakauri slays Giant of Wakatipu. $1.80, Panenehu shows Koura (crayfish) to Tangaroa.

1994, June 8 *Perf. 13*

1219 A387 45c multicolored .65 .35
1220 A387 80c multicolored .95 .95
1221 A387 $1 multicolored 1.25 1.25
1222 A387 $1.20 multicolored 1.50 1.50
1223 A387 $1.50 multicolored 1.90 1.90
1224 A387 $1.80 multicolored 2.25 2.25
Nos. 1219-1224 (6) 8.50 8.20

First Manned Moon Landing, 25th Anniv. — A388

1994, July 20 Litho. *Perf. 12*

1225 A388 $1.50 multicolored 2.25 2.25

No. 1225 has a holographic image. Soaking in water may affect the hologram.

People Reaching People — A389

Serpentine Die Cut 11

1994, July 20 Photo.

Self-Adhesive

1226 A389 45c multicolored .60 .50
a. Arrow partially covering hole in "B," serpentine die cut 11¼ *2.00* .75

No. 1226a issued Aug. 1995.

See No. 1311.

Wild Animals — A390

No. 1227, Hippopotamus. No. 1228, Spider monkey. No. 1229, Giant panda. No. 1230, Polar bear. No. 1231, African elephant. No. 1232, White rhinoceros. No. 1233, African lion. No. 1234, Plains zebra. No. 1235, Giraffe. No. 1236, Siberian tiger.

1994, Aug. 16 Litho. *Perf. 14*

1227 A390 45c multicolored .80 .80
1228 A390 45c multicolored .80 .80
1229 A390 45c multicolored .80 .80
1230 A390 45c multicolored .80 .80
1231 A390 45c multicolored .80 .80
1232 A390 45c multicolored .80 .80
1233 A390 45c multicolored .80 .80
1234 A390 45c multicolored .80 .80
1235 A390 45c multicolored .80 .80
1236 A390 45c multicolored .80 .80
a. Block of 10, #1227-1236 10.00 10.00
b. Souvenir sheet of 6, #1229-1231, 1233, 1235-1236 4.50 4.50
Nos. 1227-1236 (10) 8.00 8.00

PHILAKOREA '94 (#1236b). Nos. 1227-1236 printed in sheets of 100. Because of the design of these sheets, blocks or strips of Nos. 1227-1236 exist in 10 different arrangements. Value assigned to No. 1236a applies to all arrangements.

Christmas — A391

Designs: No. 1237, Children, Nativity scene. 70c, Magi, father, child. 80c, Carolers, stained glass window. $1, Carolers, Christmas tree. $1.50, Children, candles. $1.80, Father, mother, infant.

No. 1243, Children, Christmas tree, Santa.

1994, Sept. 21 Litho. *Perf. 14*

1237 A391 45c multicolored .60 .50
1238 A391 70c multicolored .90 .90
1239 A391 80c multicolored 1.10 1.10
1240 A391 $1 multicolored 1.25 1.25
a. Souv. sheet, 1 ea #1237-1240 4.00 4.00
1241 A391 $1.50 multicolored 1.50 1.50
1242 A391 $1.80 multicolored 1.75 1.75
Nos. 1237-1242 (6) 7.10 7.00

Booklet Stamp

Size: 30x25mm

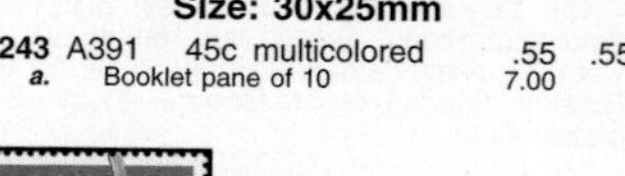

1243 A391 45c multicolored .55 .55
a. Booklet pane of 10 7.00

Cricket in New Zealand, Cent. A392

Beach Cricket A393

No. 1248: a, Woman with striped bathing suit in ocean. b, Person on bodyboard in ocean. c, Child holding float toy at water's edge. d, Boy with beach ball. e, Man holding ice cream cone. f, Beach umbrella at LL. g, Man in blue and red shorts holding cricket bat. h, Woman with cap holding cricket bat. i, Child with pail and shovel. j, Sunbather reading newspaper.

1994, Nov. 2 *Perf. 13½*

1244 A392 45c Batting .60 .40
1245 A392 80c Bowling 1.10 .80
1246 A392 $1 Wicketkeeping 1.25 1.25
1247 A392 $1.80 Fielding 2.00 2.00
Nos. 1244-1247 (4) 4.95 4.45

Perf. 12

1248 45c Bklt. pane of 10 8.00 8.00
a.-j. A393 Any single .70 .55

New Zealand at Night — A394

1995, Feb. 22 Litho. *Perf. 12*

1249 A394 45c Auckland .65 .30
1250 A394 80c Wellington 1.00 .60
1251 A394 $1 Christchurch 1.40 1.00
1252 A394 $1.20 Dunedin 1.60 1.60
1253 A394 $1.50 Rotorua 1.75 1.75
1254 A394 $1.80 Queenstown 2.00 2.00
a. Souv. sheet of 6, #1249-1254 25.00 25.00
Nos. 1249-1254 (6) 8.40 7.25

Singapore '95, Jakarta '95 (#1254a). Issued: No. 1254a, 9/1/95.

Golf Courses — A395

1995, Mar. 22 Litho. *Perf. 14*

1255 A395 45c Waitangi .65 .35
1256 A395 80c New Plymouth 1.00 1.00
1257 A395 $1.20 Rotorua 1.50 1.50
1258 A395 $1.80 Queenstown 2.50 2.50
Nos. 1255-1258 (4) 5.65 5.35

Environmental Protection — A396

No. 1259, Native fauna, flora. No. 1260, Plant native trees, shrubs. No. 1261, Protect marine mammals. No. 1262, Conserve power, water. No. 1263, Enjoy natural environment. No. 1264, Control animal pests. No. 1265, Eliminate noxious plants. No. 1266, Return undersized catches. No. 1267, Control air, water quality. No. 1268, Dispose of trash properly.

1995, Mar. 22

1259 A396 45c multicolored .65 .65
1260 A396 45c multicolored .65 .65
1261 A396 45c multicolored .65 .65
1262 A396 45c multicolored .65 .65
1263 A396 45c multicolored .65 .65
1264 A396 45c multicolored .65 .65
1265 A396 45c multicolored .65 .65
1266 A396 45c multicolored .65 .65
1267 A396 45c multicolored .65 .65
1268 A396 45c multicolored .65 .65
a. Booklet pane, #1259-1268 7.50
Complete booklet, #1268a 8.00
Nos. 1259-1268 (10) 6.50 6.50

Maori Language — A397

Designs: 45c, Treasured Language Nest. 70c, Sing to awaken the spirit. 80c, Acquire knowledge through stories. $1, The welcoming call. $1.50, Recite the genealogies that link people. $1.80, Tell the lore of the people.

1995, May 3 Litho. *Perf. 13½*
1269 A397 45c multicolored .60 .25
1270 A397 70c multicolored .90 .90
1271 A397 80c multicolored 1.10 1.10
1272 A397 $1 multicolored 1.25 1.25
1273 A397 $1.50 multicolored 2.00 2.00
1274 A397 $1.80 multicolored 2.25 2.25
Nos. 1269-1274 (6) 8.10 7.75

Asian Development Bank, 28th Meeting of the Board of Governors, Auckland — A398

Design: $1.50, Pacific Basin Economic Council, 28th Intl. Meeting, Auckland.

1995, May 3
1275 A398 $1 Map shown 1.25 1.25
1276 A398 $1.50 Map of Pacific 2.00 2.00

Team New Zealand, 1995 America's Cup Winner — A399

1995, May 16 *Perf. 12*
1277 A399 45c Black Magic yacht .70 .60

Rugby League, Cent. — A400

Designs: No. 1278, Club Rugby League, Lion Red Cup. No. 1282, Trans Tasman. $1, Mini League. $1.50, George Smith, Albert Baskerville, Early Rugby League. $1.80, Intl. Rugby League, Courtney Intl. Goodwill Trophy.

1995, July 26 Litho. *Perf. 14*
1278 A400 45c multicolored .65 .25
1279 A400 $1 multicolored 1.40 1.40
1280 A400 $1.50 multicolored 2.10 2.10
1281 A400 $1.80 multicolored 2.50 2.50
a. Souvenir sheet of 1 3.00 3.00
Nos. 1278-1281 (4) 6.65 6.25

Booklet Stamp
Perf. 12 on 3 Sides
1282 A400 45c multicolored .60 .60
a. Booklet pane of 10 7.00
Complete booklet, #1282a 7.00

#1281a exists imperf from a "Limited Edition" album.

From 1995 onward, New Zealand Post has released a series of "Limited Edition" albums in editions of 2,000. Some contain souvenir sheets unique to these albums.

Farm Animals — A401

1995 Litho. *Perf. 14x14½*
Booklet Stamps
1283 A401 40c Sheep .50 .50
1284 A401 40c Deer .50 .50
1285 A401 40c Horses .50 .50
1286 A401 40c Cattle .50 .50
1287 A401 40c Goats .50 .50
1288 A401 40c Turkey .50 .50
1289 A401 40c Ducks .50 .50
1290 A401 40c Chickens .50 .50
1291 A401 40c Pigs .50 .50
1292 A401 40c Border collie .50 .50
a. Bklt. pane of 10, #1283-1292 6.25
Complete booklet 6.75
1293 A401 45c Sheep .75 .75
1294 A401 45c Deer .75 .75
1295 A401 45c Horses .75 .75
1296 A401 45c Cattle .75 .75
1297 A401 45c Goats .75 .75
1298 A401 45c Turkey .75 .75
1299 A401 45c Ducks .75 .75
1300 A401 45c Chickens .75 .75
1301 A401 45c Pigs .75 .75
1302 A401 45c Border collie .75 .75
a. Bklt. pane of 10, #1293-1302 8.25
Complete booklet, #1302a 8.75
b. Souvenir sheet of 5, #1298-1302, perf. 12 4.25 4.25
Nos. 1283-1302 (20) 12.50 12.50

Singapore '95 (#1302b).
#1302b exists imperf.
Issued: #1302a, 9/1/95; #1292a, 10/2/95.

Christmas — A402

Stained glass windows: 40c, 45c, Archangel Gabriel. No. 1309A, Angel with trumpet. 70c, Mary. 80c, Shepherds. $1, Madonna and Child. $1.50, Two wise men. $1.80, One wise man.

1995 *Perf. 12*
1303 A402 40c multi .60 .25
1304 A402 45c multi .65 .35
1305 A402 70c multi .95 .95
1306 A402 80c multi 1.00 1.00
1307 A402 $1 multi 1.25 1.25
1308 A402 $1.50 multi 2.25 2.25
1309 A402 $1.80 multi 2.50 2.50
Nos. 1303-1309 (7) 9.20 8.55

Booklet Stamp
Size: 25x30mm
Perf. 14½x14
1309A A402 40c multi .55 .55
b. Booklet pane of 10 6.50
Complete booklet, #1309b 6.50

Issued: 45c-$1.80, 9/1; #1303, 10/2; #1309A, 11/9.
Nos. 1303-1309 exist in a souvenir sheet from a "Limited Edition" pack.

Nuclear Disarmament — A403

1995, Sept. 1 Litho. *Perf. 13½*
1310 A403 $1 multicolored 1.40 1.40

People Reaching People Type of 1994
Serpentine Die Cut 11
1995, Oct. 2 Photo.
Self-Adhesive
1311 A389 40c multicolored 2.00 1.00
a. Arrow partially covering hole in "B," serpentine die cut 11¼ 1.00 1.00

No. 1311a, Nov. 1995.

Scenic Views

Mitre Peak — A404

1995, Oct. 2 Litho. *Perf. 13½*
1312 A404 40c multicolored .65 .55
a. Perf 12 1.25 .90
b. As "a," miniature sheet of 10 12.50

Southpex '96 Stamp Show (No. 1312a).
See Nos. 1345-1360, 1405, 1412, 1636-1640, 1679-1680, 1909, 1929.

UN, 50th Anniv. — A405

1995, Oct. 4 *Perf. 14½*
1313 A405 $1.80 multicolored 2.50 2.50

Famous Living New Zealanders A406

Person, career field: 40c, Dame Kiri Te Kanawa, performing arts. 80c, Charles Upham, service, business, development. $1, Barry Crump, fine arts, literature. $1.20, Sir Brian Barratt-Boyes, science, medicine, education. $1.50, Dame Whina Cooper, community leader, social campaigner. $1.80, Sir Richard Hadlee, sports.

1995, Oct. 4 *Perf. 12*
1314 A406 40c multicolored .90 .45
1315 A406 80c multicolored 1.10 .85
1316 A406 $1 multicolored 1.25 1.25
1317 A406 $1.20 multicolored 1.50 1.50
1318 A406 $1.50 multicolored 2.00 2.00
1319 A406 $1.80 multicolored 2.50 2.50
Nos. 1314-1319 (6) 9.25 8.55

Nos. 1314-1319 issued with se-tenant tab inscribed "STAMP / MONTH / OCTOBER / 1995."

Commonwealth Heads of Government Meeting, Auckland — A407

Designs: 40c, Fern, sky, globe, $1.80, Fern, sea, national flag.

1995, Nov. 9 Litho. *Perf. 14*
1320 A407 40c multicolored .65 .50
1321 A407 $1.80 multicolored 2.75 2.50

Racehorses A408

40c, Kiwi. 80c, Rough Habit. $1, Blossom Lady. $1.20, Il Vicolo. $1.50, Horlicks. $1.80, Bonecrusher.

1996, Jan. 24 Litho. *Perf. 13½x14*
1322 A408 40c multi .75 .25
1323 A408 80c multi 1.00 1.00
1324 A408 $1 multi 1.25 1.25
1325 A408 $1.20 multi 1.75 1.75
1326 A408 $1.50 multi 2.00 2.00
1327 A408 $1.80 multi 2.50 2.50
Nos. 1322-1327 (6) 9.25 8.75

Souvenir Booklet
1328 A408 multicolored *19.00*

No. 1328 contains one booklet pane of Nos. 1322-1327, perf. 14, and individual panes of 1 each Nos. 1322-1327.

Maori Crafts — A409

1996, Feb. 21 Litho. *Perf. 14x13½*
1329 A409 40c Basket .45 .25
1330 A409 80c Weapon .85 .85
1331 A409 $1 Embroidery 1.10 1.10
1332 A409 $1.20 Greenstone 1.50 1.50
1333 A409 $1.50 Gourd 1.75 1.75
a. Souvenir sheet of 3, #1329, 1330, 1333, perf. 13 5.50 5.50
1334 A409 $1.80 Cloak 2.00 2.00
Nos. 1329-1334 (6) 7.65 7.45

No. 1333a for Hong Kong '97. Issued 2/12/97.

Seashore — A410

Designs: No. 1335, Black-backed gull. No. 1336, Sea cucumber, spiny starfish. No. 1337, Common shrimp. No. 1338, Gaudy nudibranch. No. 1339, Large rock crab, clingfish. No. 1340, Snake skin chiton, red rock crab. No. 1341, Estuarine triplefin, cat's eye shell. No. 1342, Cushion star, sea horse. No. 1343, Blue-eyed triplefin, yaldwyn's triplefin. No. 1344, Common octopus.

1996, Feb. 21 *Perf. 14x14½*
Booklet Stamps
1335 A410 40c multicolored .55 .55
1336 A410 40c multicolored .55 .55
1337 A410 40c multicolored .55 .55
1338 A410 40c multicolored .55 .55
1339 A410 40c multicolored .55 .55
1340 A410 40c multicolored .55 .55
1341 A410 40c multicolored .55 .55
1342 A410 40c multicolored .55 .55
1343 A410 40c multicolored .55 .55
1344 A410 40c multicolored .55 .55
a. Booklet pane, Nos. 1335-1344 6.50
Complete booklet, No. 1344a 6.75
Nos. 1335-1344 (10) 5.50 5.50

No. 1344a has a continuous design.

Serpentine Die Cut 11½
1996, Aug. 7 Litho.
Booklet Stamps
Self-Adhesive
1344B A410 40c like #1335 2.10 2.10
1344C A410 40c like #1336 2.10 2.10
1344D A410 40c like #1337 2.10 2.10
1344E A410 40c like #1338 2.10 2.10
1344F A410 40c like #1339 2.10 2.10
1344G A410 40c like #1340 2.10 2.10
1344H A410 40c like #1341 2.10 2.10
1344I A410 40c like #1342 2.10 2.10
1344J A410 40c like #1343 2.10 2.10
1344K A410 40c like #1344 2.10 2.10
l. Bklt pane, #1344B-1344K 24.00
Nos. 1344B-1344K (10) 21.00 21.00

No. 1344Kl is a complete booklet. The peelable paper backing serves as a booklet cover.

Scenic Views Type of 1995

5c, Mt. Cook, horiz. 10c, Champagne Pool, horiz. 20c, Cape Reinga, horiz. 30c, Mackenzie Country, horiz. 50c, Mt. Ngauruhoe, horiz. 60c, Lake Wanaka. 70c, Giant Kauri-Tane Mahuta. 80c, Doubtful Sound. 90c, Waitomo Limestone Cave.
No. 1354, Tory Channel, Marlborough Sounds. No. 1355, Lake Wakatipu. No. 1356, Lake Matheson. No. 1357, Fox Glacier. No. 1358, Mt. Egmont, Taranaki. No. 1359, Piercy Island, Bay of Islands. No. 1354-1359 horiz.

1996, Mar. 27 Litho. *Perf. 13½*
1345 A404 5c multicolored .25 .25
1346 A404 10c multicolored .25 .25
1347 A404 20c multicolored .25 .25
1348 A404 30c multicolored .35 .35
1349 A404 50c multicolored .50 .50
a. Souv. sheet of 4, #1346-1349 3.00 3.00
1350 A404 60c multicolored .70 .70
1351 A404 70c multicolored .80 .80
1352 A404 80c multicolored 1.00 1.00
1353 A404 90c multicolored 1.25 1.25
a. Souv. sheet of 4, #1350-1353 6.50 6.50
Nos. 1345-1353 (9) 5.35 5.35

CHINA '96 (#1349a). CAPEX '96 (#1353a.)
See No. 1405.

Serpentine Die Cut 11¼
1996, May 1 Photo.
Size: 26x21mm
Self-Adhesive
1354 A404 40c multicolored .55 .55
1355 A404 40c multicolored .55 .55
1356 A404 40c multicolored .55 .55
1357 A404 40c multicolored .55 .55
1358 A404 40c multicolored .55 .55
1359 A404 40c multicolored .55 .55
a. Strip of 6, Nos. 1354-1359 3.50 3.50
k. Sheet of 10, #1356, 1359, 2 each #1354-1355, 1357-1358 *27.50*
l. Sheet of 10, #1355, 1358, 2 each #1354, 1356-1357, 1359 *27.50*

m. Sheet of 10, #1354, 1357, 2 each #1355-1356, 1358-1359 — 27.50
Nos. 1354-1359 (6) — 3.30 3.30

Serpentine Die Cut 10x9¾

1998, Jan. 14 **Litho.**

Booklet Stamps

Size: 26x21mm

Self-Adhesive

1359B A404 40c like #1358 .55 .55
1359C A404 40c like #1357 .55 .55
1359D A404 40c like #1359 .55 .55
1359E A404 40c like #1356 .55 .55
1359F A404 40c like #1354 .55 .55
h. "Marlborough Sounds" omitted 17.50
1359G A404 40c like #1355 .55 .55
i. Booklet pane, #1359D, 1359F, 1359Fh, 1359G, 2 #1359B-1359C, 1359E 19.00
j. Booklet pane #1359D, 1359G, 2 each #1359B, 1359C, 1359E, 1359F 5.50
n. Coil strip of 6, #1359B-1359G 3.60
Nos. 1359B-1359G (6) 3.30 3.30

No. 1359Gi is a complete booklet.

Serpentine Die Cut 11½

1996, Aug. 7 **Litho.**

Size: 33x22mm

Self-Adhesive

Design: $1, Pohutukawa tree, horiz.

1360 A404 $1 multicolored 1.40 1.40
a. Booklet pane of 5 7.00

By its nature No. 1360a is a complete booklet. The peelable paper backing serves as a booklet cover. The outside of the cover contains 5 peelable international airpost labels.

Rescue Services — A411

40c, Fire service, ambulance. 80c, Civil defense. $1, Air sea rescue. $1.50, Air ambulance, rescue helicopter. $1.80, Mountain rescue, Red Cross.

1996, Mar. 27 ***Perf. 14½x15***

1361 A411 40c multicolored .60 .45
1362 A411 80c multicolored 1.00 1.00
1363 A411 $1 multicolored 1.25 1.25
1364 A411 $1.50 multicolored 2.00 2.00
1365 A411 $1.80 multicolored 2.50 2.50
Nos. 1361-1365 (5) 7.35 7.20

Wildlife — A412

Designs: 40c, Yellow-eyed penguin, vert. 80c, Royal albatross. $1, White heron. $1.20, Sperm whale. $1.50, Fur seal, vert. $1.80, Bottlenose dolphin, vert.

1996, May 1 **Litho.** ***Perf. 14***

1366 A412 40c multicolored .70 .50
1367 A412 80c multicolored 1.25 .90
1368 A412 $1 multicolored 1.40 1.40
1369 A412 $1.20 multicolored 1.50 1.50
1370 A412 $1.50 multicolored 1.75 1.75
a. Sheet of 2, #1368, 1370 6.50 6.50
1371 A412 $1.80 multicolored 2.00 2.00
a. Sheet of 2, #1367, 1371 5.00 5.00
b. Block, #1366-1371, + 2 labels 9.50 9.50
Nos. 1366-1371 (6) 8.60 8.05

No. 1370a for CHINA '96. Issued May 18. No. 1371a for Taipei '96. Issued Oct. 2.

New Zealand Symphony Orchestra, 50th Anniv. A413

1996, July 10 **Litho.** ***Perf. 15x14½***

1372 A413 40c Violin .60 .50
1373 A413 80c French horn 1.10 1.10

1996 Summer Olympics, Atlanta — A414

1996, July 10 ***Perf. 14½***

1374 A414 40c Swimming .75 .30
1375 A414 80c Cycling 1.40 1.40
1376 A414 $1 Athletics 1.50 1.50
1377 A414 $1.50 Rowing 1.75 1.75
1378 A414 $1.80 Yachting 2.00 2.00
a. Sheet of 5, #1374-1378 8.00 8.00
Nos. 1374-1378 (5) 7.40 6.95

Used value is for stamp with complete selvage.

A miniature sheet containing #1374-1378, both perf and imperf within the sheet, exists. This comes from a "Limited Edition" collectors' pack.

See No. 1383.

A415

Motion pictures, cent.: 40c, Hinemoa. 80c, Broken Barrier. $1.50, Goodbye Pork Pie. $1.80, Once Were Warriors.

1996, Aug. 7 **Litho.** ***Perf. 14½x15***

1379 A415 40c multicolored .60 .35
1380 A415 80c multicolored 1.10 1.10
1381 A415 $1.50 multicolored 1.75 1.75
1382 A415 $1.80 multicolored 2.00 2.00
Nos. 1379-1382 (4) 5.45 5.20

Nos. 1379-1382 are printed se-tenant with scratch and win labels for a contest available to New Zealand residents. Values 25% more with unscratched labels attached.

1996 Summer Olympics Type

Design: Danyon Loader, swimmer, Blyth Tait, horseman, 1996 gold medalists from New Zealand.

1996, Aug. 28 **Litho.** ***Perf. 14½***

1383 A414 40c multicolored .65 .65

Used value is for stamp with complete selvage.

Leaves in selvage printed in six different patterns.

Beehive Ballot Box — A416

1996, Sept. 4 ***Perf. 12***

1384 A416 40c multicolored .65 .50

Mixed member proportional election, 1966. No. 1384 was issued in sheets of 10.

Christmas — A417

Scenes from the Christmas story: No. 1385, Following the star. 70c, Shepherd finding baby in manger. 80c, Angel's announcement to shepherd. $1, The Nativity. $1.50, Journey to Bethlehem. $1.80, The annunciation.

No. 1391, Adoration of the Magi. No. 1392, Heavenly host praising God.

1996, Sept. 4 ***Perf. 14***

1385 A417 40c multicolored .60 .30
1386 A417 70c multicolored 1.00 1.00
1387 A417 80c multicolored 1.10 1.10
1388 A417 $1 multicolored 1.25 1.25
1389 A417 $1.50 multicolored 1.75 1.75
1390 A417 $1.80 multicolored 2.00 2.00
Nos. 1385-1390 (6) 7.70 7.40

Size: 29x24mm

Self-Adhesive

Serpentine Die Cut 11½

1391 A417 40c multicolored .65 .55
a. Booklet pane 10 6.50
1392 A417 40c multicolored .65 .55

By its nature No. 1391a is a complete booklet. The peelable paper backing serves as a booklet cover.

Extinct Birds — A418

No. 1393, 40c, Adzebill. 80c, Laughing owl. $1, Piopio. $1.20, Huia. $1.50, Giant eagle. $1.80, Giant moa. No. 1399, 40c, Stout-legged wren.

1996, Oct. 2 **Litho.** ***Perf. 13½***

1393 A418 40c multi .60 .45
1394 A418 80c multi 1.10 1.10
1395 A418 $1 multi 1.50 1.50
1396 A418 $1.20 multi 1.60 1.60
1397 A418 $1.50 multi 2.00 2.00
1398 A418 $1.80 multi 2.25 2.25
a. Souvenir sheet 3.00 3.00
b. As "a," with added inscription 4.50 4.50
Nos. 1393-1398 (6) 9.05 8.90

Size: 29x24mm

Self-Adhesive

Serpentine Die Cut 11½

1399 A418 40c multi .65 .55
a. Booklet pane of 10 6.50

Inscriptions on backs of Nos. 1393-1398 describe each species. By its nature No. 1399a is a complete booklet. The peelable backing serves as a booklet cover.

No. 1398b contains Taipei '96 exhibition emblem in sheet margin.

Scenic Gardens — A419

Designs: 40c, Seymour Square Gardens, Blenheim. 80c, Pukekura Park Gardens, New Plymouth. $1, Wintergarden, Auckland. $1.50, Botanic Gardens, Christchurch. $1.80, Marine Parade Gardens, Napier.

1996, Nov. 13 **Litho.** ***Perf. 13½***

1400 A419 40c multicolored .55 .45
1401 A419 80c multicolored 1.00 1.00
1402 A419 $1 multicolored 1.25 1.25
1403 A419 $1.50 multicolored 1.75 1.75
1404 A419 $1.80 multicolored 2.25 2.25
Nos. 1400-1404 (5) 6.80 6.70

New Zealand Post produced and distributed three souvenir sheets as rewards for purchases made from the post office during 1996. The sheets were not available through normal philatelic channels. The sheets are inscribed "NEW ZEALAND POST / Best of 1996" and the Stamp Points emblem. Each sheet contains 3 stamps; #1327, 1365, 1334; #1378, 1382, 1371; #1390, 1404, 1398.

Scenic Views Type of 1995

Serpentine Die Cut 11½

1996, Nov. 1 **Litho.**

Size: 21x26mm

Self-Adhesive

1405 A404 80c like No. 1352 1.10 1.10
a. Booklet pane of 10 12.50

By its nature No. 1405a is a complete booklet. The peelable paper backing serves as a booklet cover. The outside of the cover contains 10 peelable international airpost labels.

Cattle — A420

40c, Holstein-Friesian. 80c, Jersey. $1, Simmental. $1.20, Ayrshire. $1.50, Angus. $1.80, Hereford.

1997, Jan. 15 ***Perf. 14x14½***

1406 A420 40c multi .65 .30
1407 A420 80c multi 1.10 1.10
1408 A420 $1 multi 1.50 1.40
1409 A420 $1.20 multi 1.60 1.60
1410 A420 $1.50 multi 1.90 1.90
a. Souvenir sheet of 3, #1407, 1408, 1410 8.50 8.50
1411 A420 $1.80 multi 2.10 2.10
Nos. 1406-1411 (6) 8.85 8.40

No. 1410a for Hong Kong '97. Issued 2/12/97.

Souvenir Sheets

The 1997 sheets contain: Nos. 1411, 1418, 1434; Nos. 1440, 1444, 1451; Nos. 1445, 1457, 1475.

See note following No. 1404.

Scenic Views Type of 1995

1997, Feb. 12 **Litho.** ***Perf. 13½***

Size: 37x32mm

1412 A404 $10 Mt. Ruapehu 10.00 8.00

Discoverers A421

40c, James Cook. 80c, Kupe. $1, Maui, vert. $1.20, Jean de Surville, vert. $1.50, Dumont d'Urville. $1.80, Abel Tasman.

1997, Feb. 12 ***Perf. 14***

1413 A421 40c multicolored .75 .50
1414 A421 80c multicolored 1.10 1.10
1415 A421 $1 multicolored 1.40 1.40
1416 A421 $1.20 multicolored 1.75 1.75
1417 A421 $1.50 multicolored 2.25 2.25
1418 A421 $1.80 multicolored 2.50 2.50
Nos. 1413-1418 (6) 9.75 9.50

#1413-1418 exist in sheet of 6 created for a hard-bound millennium book that sold for $129.

"Wackiest Letterboxes" — A422

Serpentine Die Cut 11¼

1997, Mar. 19 **Litho.**

Self-Adhesive

Booklet Stamps

1419 A422 40c Log house .55 .55
1420 A422 40c Owl .55 .55
1421 A422 40c Whale .55 .55
1422 A422 40c "Kilroy is Back" .55 .55
1423 A422 40c House of twigs .55 .55
1424 A422 40c Scottish piper .55 .55
1425 A422 40c Diving helmet .55 .55
1426 A422 40c Airplane .55 .55
1427 A422 40c Water faucet .55 .55
1428 A422 40c Painted buildings .55 .55
a. Bklt. pane of 10, #1419-1428 7.00
b. Sheet of 10, #1419-1428 17.00
Nos. 1419-1428 (10) 5.50 5.50

By its nature No. 1428a is a complete booklet. The peelable paper backing serves as a booklet cover.

Vineyards A423

40c, Central Otago. 80c, Hawke's Bay. $1, Marlborough. $1.20, Canterbury, Waipara. $1.50, Gisborne. $1.80, Auckland, Waiheke.

1997, Mar. 19 *Perf. 14*

1429 A423 40c multicolored .50 .30
 a. Booklet pane of 1 .65
1430 A423 80c multicolored 1.10 1.10
 a. Booklet pane of 1 1.10
1431 A423 $1 multicolored 1.40 1.40
 a. Booklet pane of 1 1.40
1432 A423 $1.20 multicolored 1.60 1.60
 a. Booklet pane of 1 1.60
1433 A423 $1.50 multicolored 2.00 2.00
 a. Booklet pane of 1 2.00
 b. Souvenir sheet of 3, #1429, 1431, 1433 9.25 9.25
1434 A423 $1.80 multicolored 2.40 2.40
 a. Booklet pane of 1 2.40
 b. Bklt. pane of 6, #1429-1434 9.25
 Complete booklet, #1429a, 1430a, 1431a, 1432a, 1433a, 1434a, 1434b 19.00
 Nos. 1429-1434 (6) 9.00 8.80

No. 1433b for PACIFIC 97. Issued: 5/29.

Pigeon Mail Service, Cent. — A424

Design: 1899 local stamp.

1997, May 7 **Litho.** *Perf. 14*

1435 A424 40c red .65 .65
1436 A424 80c blue 1.25 1.25
 a. Souv. sheet, 2 ea #1435-1436 10.50 10.50
 b. As "a," diff. inscription 6.00 6.00

No. 1436a for PACIFIC 97. Issued: 5/29.
No. 1436b was inscribed in sheet margin for AUPEX '97 National Stamp Exhibition, Auckland. Issued 11/13.

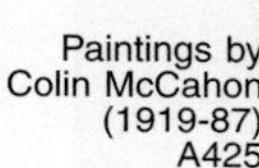

Paintings by Colin McCahon (1919-87) A425

Designs: 40c, The Promised Land, 1948. $1, Six Days in Nelson and Canterbury, 1950. $1.50, Northland Panels, 1958. $1.80, Moby Dick is sighted off Muriwai Beach, 1972.

1997, May 7

1437 A425 40c multicolored .65 .30
1438 A425 $1 multicolored 1.25 1.25
1439 A425 $1.50 multicolored 2.00 2.00
1440 A425 $1.80 multicolored 2.25 2.25
 Nos. 1437-1440 (4) 6.15 5.80

See Nos. 1597-1600.

Fly Fishing — A426

Designs: 40c, Red setter fly, rainbow trout. $1, Grey ghost fly, sea-run brown trout. $1.50, Twilight beauty fly, brook trout. $1.80, Hare & copper fly, brown trout.

1997, June 18 **Litho.** *Perf. 13*

1441 A426 40c multicolored .60 .40
1442 A426 $1 multicolored 1.50 1.50
1443 A426 $1.50 multicolored 2.00 2.00
1444 A426 $1.80 multicolored 2.25 2.25
 a. Souv. sheet of 2, #1441, 1444 6.00 6.00
 Nos. 1441-1444 (4) 6.35 6.15

No.1444a issued 5/13/98 for Israel '98 World Stamp Exhibition, Tel Aviv.

Kiwi Type of 1988

1997, Aug. 6 **Litho.** *Perf. 14½*

1445 A325 $1 violet 1.25 1.25

Value is for stamp with surrounding selvage. Selvage comes with and without gold sunbursts.
See No. 1635a.

Scenic Trains — A426a

Name of train, area scene, map of train route: 40c, Overlander, Paremata, Wellington, Wellington-Auckland. 80c, Trans-Alpine, Southern Alps, Christchurch-Greymouth. $1, Southerner, Canterbury, Invercargill-Christchurch. $1.20, Coastal Pacific, Kaikoura Coast, Christchurch-Picton. $1.50, Bay Express, Central Hawke's Bay, Wellington-Napier. $1.80, Kaimai Express, Tauranga Harbor, Tauranga-Auckland.

1997, Aug. 6 *Perf. 14x14½*

1446 A426a 40c multicolored .60 .40
1447 A426a 80c multicolored 1.10 1.00
1448 A426a $1 multicolored 1.25 1.25
1449 A426a $1.20 multicolored 1.50 1.50
1450 A426a $1.50 multicolored 2.00 2.00
 a. Sheet of 3, #1447-1448, 1450 7.50 7.50
1451 A426a $1.80 multicolored 2.25 2.25
 Nos. 1446-1451 (6) 8.70 8.40

No. 1450a issued 5/13/98 for Israel '98 World Stamp Exhibition, Tel Aviv.
Nos. 1446-1451 exist in a sheet of 6 from a "Limited Edition" album.

Christmas — A427

Scenes from first Christian service, Rangihoua Bay, and words from Christmas carol, "Te Harinui:" No. 1452, Samuel Marsden's ship, Active. 70c, Marsden preaching from pulpit. 80c, Marsden extending hand to local chiefs. $1, Mother, children from Rangihoua. $1.50, Maori and Pakeha hands, Marsden's memorial cross. $1.80, Pohutukawa flowers, Rangihoua Bay. No. 1458, Cross marking spot of service, flowers, bay.

1997, Sept. 3 **Litho.** *Perf. 14*

1452 A427 40c multicolored .60 .25
1453 A427 70c multicolored .90 .90
1454 A427 80c multicolored 1.00 1.00
1455 A427 $1 multicolored 1.25 1.25
1456 A427 $1.50 multicolored 1.75 1.75
1457 A427 $1.80 multicolored 2.00 2.00
 a. Block of 6, #1452-1457 10.00 10.00
 Nos. 1452-1457 (6) 7.50 7.15

Self-Adhesive

Size: 30x24mm

Serpentine Die Cut 10

1458 A427 40c multicolored .50 .50
 a. Booklet pane of 10 6.50

By its nature No. 1458a is a complete booklet. The peelable paper backing serves as a booklet cover.

"Creepy Crawlies" — A428

Serpentine Die Cut 11¼

1997, Oct. 1 **Litho.**

Booklet Stamps

1459 A428 40c Huhu beetle .55 .55
1460 A428 40c Giant land snail .55 .55
1461 A428 40c Giant weta .55 .55
1462 A428 40c Giant dragonfly .55 .55
1463 A428 40c Peripatus .55 .55
1464 A428 40c Cicada .55 .55
1465 A428 40c Puriri moth .55 .55
1466 A428 40c Veined slug .55 .55
1467 A428 40c Katipo .55 .55
1468 A428 40c Flaxweevil .55 .55
 a. Booklet pane, #1459-1468 6.25
 b. Sheet of 10, #1459-1468 10.00
 Nos. 1459-1468 (10) 5.50 5.50

By its nature No. 1468a is a complete booklet. The peelable paper backing serves as a booklet cover.

China-New Zealand Stamp Expo — A429

1997, Oct. 9 *Perf. 14*

1469 40c Rosa rugosa .65 .50
1470 40c Aotearoa-New Zealand .65 .50
 a. A429 Pair, #1469-1470 1.40 1.10
 b. Souvenir sheet, #1470a 2.00 2.00
 c. As "b," diff. inscription 2.00 2.00

No. 1470c inscribed in gold and black in sheet margin for Shanghai 1997 Intl. Stamp & Coin Expo. Issued: 11/19/97.
See People's Republic of China Nos. 2797-2798.

Queen Elizabeth II and Prince Philip, 50th Wedding Anniv. — A430

1997, Nov. 12 **Litho.** *Perf. 12*

1471 A430 40c multicolored .65 .45

Issued in sheets of 10.

Cartoonists A431

"Kiwis Taking on the World:" 40c, Kiwi flying on bee, by Garrick Tremain. $1, Kiwi using world as egg and having it for breakfast, by Jim Hubbard. $1.50, Kiwi in yacht race against the world, by Eric Heath. $1.80, Man with chain saw, trees on mountainside cut as peace symbol, by Burton Silver.

1997, Nov. 12 *Perf. 14*

1472 A431 40c multicolored .65 .30
1473 A431 $1 multicolored 1.25 1.25
1474 A431 $1.50 multicolored 1.75 1.75
1475 A431 $1.80 multicolored 2.50 2.50
 Nos. 1472-1475 (4) 6.15 5.80

Performing Arts — A432

1998, Jan. 14 **Litho.** *Perf. 13½*

1476 A432 40c Modern dance .60 .35
 a. Booklet pane of 1 .60
1477 A432 80c Music 1.00 .95
 a. Booklet pane of 1 1.00
 b. Perf 14 2.50 2.50
1478 A432 $1 Opera 1.25 1.25
 a. Booklet pane of 1 1.25
1479 A432 $1.20 Theater 1.50 1.50
 a. Booklet pane of 1 1.50
1480 A432 $1.50 Song 2.00 2.00
 a. Booklet pane of 1 2.00
1481 A432 $1.80 Ballet 2.25 2.25
 a. Booklet pane of 1 2.25
 b. Bklt. pane of 6, #1476-1481 11.00
 Complete booklet, 1 each #1476a-1481a, 1481b 22.50
 c. Perf 14 5.50 5.50
 Nos. 1476-1481 (6) 8.60 8.30

Museum of New Zealand Te Papa Tongarewa A433

40c, People at entrance. $1.80, Waterfront location.

1998, Feb. 11 **Litho.** *Perf. 14*

1482 A433 40c multicolored .50 .45
1483 A433 $1.80 multicolored 2.00 2.00

Souvenir Sheets

The 1998 sheets contain: Nos. 1489, 1483, 1481; Nos. 1491, 1521, 1525; Nos. 1531, 1537, 1562.
See note following No. 1404.

Domestic Cat — A434

1998, Feb. 11 *Perf. 13½*

1484 A434 40c Moggy .55 .30
1485 A434 80c Burmese 1.00 1.00
1486 A434 $1 Birman 1.10 1.10
1487 A434 $1.20 British blue 1.25 1.25
1488 A434 $1.50 Persian 1.75 1.75
1489 A434 $1.80 Siamese 2.25 2.25
 a. Souvenir sheet of 3, #1484, #1486, #1489 6.00 6.00
 Nos. 1484-1489 (6) 7.90 7.65

Memorial Statues — A435

40c, "With Great Respect to the Mehmetcik, Gallipoli" (Turkish soldier carrying wounded ANZAC). $1.80, "Mother with Children," Natl. War Memorial, Wellington.

1998, Mar. 18 **Litho.** *Perf. 13½*

1490 A435 40c multicolored .50 .40
1491 A435 $1.80 multicolored 2.00 2.00

See Turkey Nos. 2695-2696.

New Zealand's Multi-cultural Society — A436

Designs: 40c, The Maori. 80c, British/European settlers, 1840-1914. $1, Fortune seekers, 1800-1920. $1.20, Post-war British/European migrants, 1945-70. $1.50, Pacific Islanders, from 1960. $1.80, Asian arrivals, 1980s-90s.

1998, Mar. 18 *Perf. 14*

1492 A436 40c multicolored .55 .25
1493 A436 80c multicolored 1.10 .90
1494 A436 $1 multicolored 1.40 1.10
1495 A436 $1.20 multicolored 1.50 1.50
1496 A436 $1.50 multicolored 1.75 1.75
1497 A436 $1.80 multicolored 2.00 2.00
 Nos. 1492-1497 (6) 8.30 7.50

Nos. 1492-1497 exist in sheet of 6 created for a hard-bound millennium book that sold for $129.

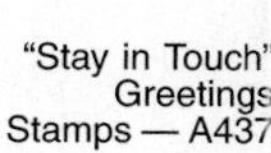

"Stay in Touch" Greetings Stamps — A437

Designs: No. 1498, Young and older person hugging, vert. No. 1499, Middle-aged couple wading in water at beach, vert. No. 1500, Characters giving "high five," vert. No. 1501, Stylized boy pointing way to old woman, vert. No. 1502, Cartoon of woman with tears embracing man. No. 1503, Couple kissing. No. 1504, Older couple with faces together. No. 1505, Two boys arm in arm in swimming pool. No. 1506, Stylized couple, clouds. No. 1507, Stylized couple seated on sofa.

Die Cut Perf. 10x10¼, 10¼x10

1998, Apr. 15 **Litho.**

Booklet Stamps

Self-Adhesive

1498 A437 40c multicolored .80 .80
1499 A437 40c multicolored .80 .80
1500 A437 40c multicolored .80 .80
1501 A437 40c multicolored .80 .80
 a. Sheet of 4, #1498-1501 5.00
1502 A437 40c multicolored .80 .80
1503 A437 40c multicolored .80 .80
1504 A437 40c multicolored .80 .80
1505 A437 40c multicolored .80 .80
1506 A437 40c multicolored .80 .80

1507 A437 40c multicolored .80 .80
a. Booklet pane, #1498-1507 10.00
b. Sheet of 6, #1502-1507 8.00
Nos. 1498-1507 (10) 8.00 8.00

The peelable paper backing of No. 1507a serves as a booklet cover.

Types of 1898

1998, May 20 Litho. *Perf. 14x14½*
1508 A18 40c Mt. Cook .55 .55
1509 A19 40c Lake Taupo .55 .55
1510 A20 40c Pembroke Peak .55 .55
1511 A23 40c Huia .55 .55
1512 A24 40c White Terrace .55 .55
1513 A26 40c Kiwi .55 .55
1514 A27 40c Maori canoe .55 .55
1515 A29 40c Hawk-billed parrots .55 .55

Perf. 14½
1516 A21 80c Wakatipu 1.00 1.00
1517 A22 80c Wakatipu 1.00 1.00
a. Souvenir sheet of 2, 1516-1517 4.75 4.75
1518 A25 $1 Otira Gorge 1.25 1.25
1519 A28 $1.20 Pink Terrace 1.50 1.50
1520 A30 $1.50 Milford Sound 1.75 1.75
a. Sheet of 2, #1517, 1520 4.00 4.00
1521 A31 $1.80 Mt. Cook 2.00 2.00
Nos. 1508-1521 (14) 12.90 12.90

No. 1517a issued 8/7/98 for Tarapex '98, Natl. Stamp Exhibition.
No. 1520a issued 10/23/98 for Italia '98.

Paintings by Peter McIntyre A438

Designs: 40c, Wounded at Cassino, 1944. $1, The Cliffs of Rangitikei, c. 1958. $1.50, Maori Children, King Country, 1963. $1.80, The Anglican Church, Kakahi, 1972.

1998, June 24 Litho. *Perf. 13½*
1522 A438 40c multicolored .45 .30
1523 A438 $1 multicolored 1.10 1.10
1524 A438 $1.50 multicolored 1.60 1.60
1525 A438 $1.80 multicolored 1.90 1.90
a. Souvenir sheet, #1524-1525, perf 14 6.00 6.00
Nos. 1522-1525 (4) 5.05 4.90

No. 1525a issued 10/23/98 for Italia '98.
Nos. 1524-1525 exist in an imperf souvenir sheet from a "Limited Edition" album.

Scenic Skies A439

40c, Cambridge. 80c, Lake Wanaka. $1, Mt. Maunganui. $1.20, Kaikoura. $1.50, Whakatane. $1.80, Lindis Pass.

1998, July 29 Litho. *Perf. 14½*
1526 A439 40c multi .60 .25
1527 A439 80c multi 1.10 .90
1528 A439 $1 multi 1.25 1.10
1529 A439 $1.20 multi 1.40 1.40
1530 A439 $1.50 multi 2.00 2.00
1531 A439 $1.80 multi 2.25 2.25
a. Souv. sheet of 2, #1526, 1531 3.75 3.75
Nos. 1526-1531 (6) 8.60 7.90

No. 1531a issued 3/19/99 for Australia '99 World Stamp Expo.

Christmas — A440

Designs: 40c, Madonna and Child. 70c, Shepherds approaching nativity scene. 80c, Joseph, Mary, Christ Child. $1, Magus. $1.50, Magi with gifts. $1.80, Angel telling shepherds about Messiah.

1998, Sept. 2 Litho. *Perf. 13x14*
1532 A440 40c multicolored .55 .25
1533 A440 70c multicolored .90 .80
1534 A440 80c multicolored 1.10 .90
1535 A440 $1 multicolored 1.25 1.25
1536 A440 $1.50 multicolored 1.75 1.75
1537 A440 $1.80 multicolored 2.00 2.00
Nos. 1532-1537 (6) 7.55 6.95

Self-adhesive
Size: 24x30mm
Serpentine Die Cut 11½
1538 A440 40c multicolored .50 .40
a. Booklet pane of 10 6.50

No. 1538a is a complete booklet. The peelable paper backing serves as a booklet cover.

Marine Life — A441

1998, Oct. 7 Litho. *Perf. 14*
1539 A441 40c Moonfish .45 .45
1540 A441 40c Mako shark .45 .45
1541 A441 40c Yellowfin tuna .45 .45
1542 A441 40c Giant squid .45 .45
a. Block of 4, #1539-1542 2.50 2.50
1543 A441 80c Striped marlin .90 .90
1544 A441 80c Porcupine fish .90 .90
a. Souvenir sheet of 4, #1539-1540, #1543-1544 5.25 5.25
1545 A441 80c Eagle ray .90 .90
1546 A441 80c Sandager's wrasse .90 .90
a. Block of 4, #1543-1546 4.75 4.75
b. Souvenir sheet of 4, #1541-1542, 1545-1546 8.00 8.00
Nos. 1539-1546 (8) 5.40 5.40

No. 1544a issued 3/19/99 for Australia '99, World Stamp Expo. No. 1546b was issued 7/2/99 for PhilexFrance '99, World Philatelic Exhibition.
#1539-1546 exist in sheets of 8 from a "Limited Edition" album.

Famous Town Icons
A442 A443

Designs: No. 1547, L&P bottle, Paeroa. No. 1548, Carrot, Ohakune. No. 1549, Brown trout, Gore. No. 1550, Crayfish, Kaikoura. No. 1551, Sheep shearer, Te Kuiti. No. 1552, Pania of the Reef, Napier. No. 1553, Paua shell, Riverton. No. 1554, Kiwifruit, Te Puke. No. 1555, Border collie, Tekapo. No. 1556, Cow, Hawera.

Serpentine Die Cut 11½
1998, Oct. 7 Litho.
Self-Adhesive
1547 A442 40c multicolored .50 .25
1548 A442 40c multicolored .50 .25
1549 A443 40c multicolored .50 .25
1550 A443 40c multicolored .50 .25
1551 A443 40c multicolored .50 .25
1552 A443 40c multicolored .50 .25

Size: 25x30mm
1553 A443 40c multicolored .50 .25
1554 A443 40c multicolored .50 .25
1555 A443 40c multicolored .50 .25
1556 A443 40c multicolored .50 .25
a. Sheet of 10, #1547-1556 11.50
b. Booklet pane, #1547-1556 6.00
Nos. 1547-1556 (10) 5.00 2.50

No. 1556b is a complete booklet. The peelable paper backing serves as a booklet cover.

Urban Transformation A444

1998, Nov. 11 Litho. *Perf. 14x14½*
1557 A444 40c Wellington .60 .35
1558 A444 80c Auckland 1.00 .65
1559 A444 $1 Christchurch 1.10 1.10
1560 A444 $1.20 Westport 1.40 1.40
1561 A444 $1.50 Tauranga 1.75 1.75
1562 A444 $1.80 Dunedin 2.25 2.25
Nos. 1557-1562 (6) 8.10 7.50

#1557-1562 exist in sheet of 6 created for a hard-bound Millennium book that sold for $129.

Native Tree Flowers — A445

40c, Kotukutuku. 80c, Poroporo. $1, Kowhai. $1.20, Weeping broom. $1.50, Teteaweka. $1.80, Southern rata.

1999, Jan. 13 Litho. *Perf. 14½x14*
1563 A445 40c multi .50 .25
1564 A445 80c multi .85 .85
a. Souv. sheet of 2, #1563-1564 3.75 3.75
1565 A445 $1 multi 1.10 1.10
1566 A445 $1.20 multi 1.30 1.30
1567 A445 $1.50 multi 1.60 1.60
1568 A445 $1.80 multi 2.00 2.00
Nos. 1563-1568 (6) 7.35 7.10

No. 1564a was issued 8/21/99 for China 1999 World Philatelic Exhibition.
Nos. 1567-1568 exist in a souvenir sheet from a "Limited Edition" album.

Souvenir Sheets
The 1999 sheets contain: Nos. 1568, 1572, 1578; Nos. 1584, 1600, 1607; Nos. 1613, 1620, 1627.
See note following No. 1404.

Art Deco Buildings — A446

40c, Civic Theatre, Auckland. $1, Masonic Hotel, Napier. $1.50, Medical and Dental Offices, Hastings. $1.80, Buller County Offices, Westport.

1999, Feb. 10 Litho. *Perf. 14*
1569 A446 40c multicolored .70 .25
1570 A446 $1 multicolored 1.75 1.00
1571 A446 $1.50 multicolored 1.75 1.75
1572 A446 $1.80 multicolored 2.00 2.00
Nos. 1569-1572 (4) 6.20 5.00

Popular Pets — A447

Designs: 40c, Labrador puppy. 80c, Netherland dwarf rabbit. $1, Rabbit, tabby kitten. $1.20, Lamb. $1.50, Welsh pony. $1.80, Budgies.

1999, Feb. 10
1573 A447 40c multicolored .50 .35
1574 A447 80c multicolored 1.00 .60
1575 A447 $1 multicolored 1.25 1.25
a. Souvenir sheet, #1573-1575 4.25 4.25
b. Souvenir sheet, #1573, 1575 5.50 5.50
1576 A447 $1.20 multicolored 1.50 1.50
1577 A447 $1.50 multicolored 1.75 1.75
1578 A447 $1.80 multicolored 2.25 2.25
Nos. 1573-1578 (6) 8.25 7.70

New Year 1999, Year of the Rabbit (#1575a).
No. 1575b was issued 8/21/99 for China 1999 World Philatelic Exhibition.

Nostalgia A448

1999, Mar. 10 Litho. *Perf. 14*
1579 A448 40c Toys .70 .25
1580 A448 80c Food 1.00 1.00
1581 A448 $1 Transport 1.25 1.25
1582 A448 $1.20 Household 1.50 1.50
1583 A448 $1.50 Collectibles 1.75 1.75
1584 A448 $1.80 Garden 2.00 2.00
Nos. 1579-1584 (6) 8.20 7.75

#1579-1584 exist in sheet of 6 created for a hard-bound Millennium book that sold for $129.

Victoria University of Wellington, Cent. — A449

1999, Apr. 7 Litho. *Perf. 14*
1585 A449 40c multicolored .55 .45

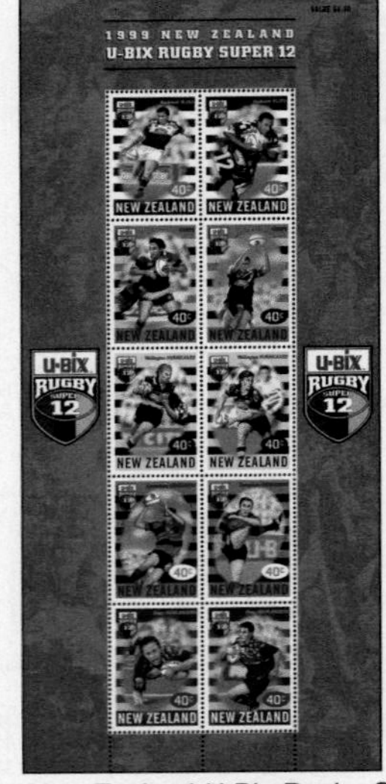

1999 New Zealand U-Bix Rugby Super 12 — A450

Auckland Blues: a, Kicking ball. b, Running with ball.
Chiefs: c, Being tackled. d, Catching ball.
Wellington Hurricanes: e, Being tackled. f, Passing.
Canterbury Crusaders: g, Catching ball. h, Kicking ball.
Otago Highlanders: i, Falling down with ball. j, Running with ball.

1999, Apr. 7 *Perf. 14½*
1586 A450 40c Sheet of 10, #a.-j. 13.50 13.50

Booklet Stamps
Self-Adhesive
Die Cut Perf. 12
1587 A450 40c like #1586a .60 .45
1588 A450 40c like #1586b .60 .45
a. Bklt. pane, 5 ea #1587-1588 6.50
1589 A450 40c like #1586c .60 .45
1590 A450 40c like #1586d .60 .45
a. Bklt. pane, 5 ea #1589-1590 6.50
1591 A450 40c like #1586e .60 .45
1592 A450 40c like #1586f .60 .45
a. Bklt. pane, 5 ea #1591-1592 6.50
1593 A450 40c like #1586g .60 .45
1594 A450 40c like #1586h .60 .45
a. Bklt. pane, 5 ea #1593-1594 6.50
1595 A450 40c like #1586i .60 .45
1596 A450 40c like #1586j .60 .45
a. Bklt. pane, 5 ea #1595-1596 6.50

Nos. 1587-1588, 1589-1590, 1591-1592, 1593-1594, 1595-1596 were also issued as pairs without surrounding selvage.
Nos. 1588a, 1590a, 1592a, 1594a and 1596a are all complete booklets.

Paintings Type of 1997

Paintings by Doris Lusk: 40c, The Lake, Tuai, 1948. $1, The Pumping Station, 1958. $1.50, Arcade Awning, St. Mark's Square, Venice (2), 1976. $1.80, Tuan St. II, 1982.

1999, June 16 Litho. *Perf. 14*
1597 A425 40c multicolored .60 .25
1598 A425 $1 multicolored 1.25 1.25
1599 A425 $1.50 multicolored 1.60 1.60
1600 A425 $1.80 multicolored 2.25 2.25
a. Souv. sheet of 2, #1597, 1600 5.00 5.00
Nos. 1597-1600 (4) 5.70 5.35

No. 1600a was issued 7/2/99 for PhilexFrance '99, World Philatelic Exhibition.

Asia-Pacific Economic Cooperation (APEC) — A451

1999, July 21 Litho. *Perf. 14*

1601 A451 40c multicolored .50 .45

Scenic Walks — A452

Designs: 40c, West Ruggedy Beach, Stewart Island. 80c, Ice Lake, Butler Valley, Westland. $1, Tonga Bay, Abel Tasman Natl. Park. $1.20, East Matakitaki Valley, Nelson Lakes Natl. Park. $1.50, Great Barrier Island. $1.80, Mt. Taranaki/Egmont.

1999, July 28

1602	A452	40c multicolored	.50	.25
a.		Booklet pane of 1	.55	
1603	A452	80c multicolored	.85	.85
a.		Booklet pane of 1	.95	
1604	A452	$1 multicolored	1.10	1.10
a.		Booklet pane of 1	1.20	
1605	A452	$1.20 multicolored	1.40	1.40
a.		Booklet pane of 1	1.50	
1606	A452	$1.50 multicolored	2.00	2.00
a.		Booklet pane of 1	2.25	
1607	A452	$1.80 multicolored	2.25	2.25
a.		Booklet pane of 1	2.50	
b.		Bklt. pane of 6, #1602-1607	11.00	
		Complete booklet, 1 each #1602a-1607a, 1607b	22.50	
c.		Souvenir sheet of 1	3.50	3.50
		Nos. 1602-1607 (6)	8.10	7.85

Issued: No. 1607c, 10/1.

Christmas — A453

40c, Baby in manger. 80c, Virgin Mary. $1.10, Joseph and Mary. $1.20, Angel with harp. $1.50, Shepherds. $1.80, Three Magi. No. 1614, Baby in manger.

1999, Sept. 8 Litho. *Perf. 13*

1608	A453	40c multicolored	.50	.25
1609	A453	80c multicolored	1.00	1.00
1610	A453	$1.10 multicolored	1.40	1.40
1611	A453	$1.20 multicolored	1.50	1.50
1612	A453	$1.50 multicolored	1.75	1.75
1613	A453	$1.80 multicolored	2.00	2.00
		Nos. 1608-1613 (6)	8.15	7.90

Self-Adhesive

Size: 23x27mm

Die Cut Perf. 9½x10

1614	A453	40c multicolored	.50	.25
a.		Booklet pane of 10	6.00	

No. 1614a is a complete booklet.

Yachting — A454

1999, Oct. 20 Litho. *Perf. 14*

1615	A454	40c P Class	.60	.25
1616	A454	80c Laser	1.00	.85
1617	A454	$1.10 18-foot skiff	1.25	1.25
1618	A454	$1.20 Hobie Cat	1.40	1.40
1619	A454	$1.50 Racing yacht	1.60	1.60
1620	A454	$1.80 Cruising yacht	1.90	1.90
a.		Souvenir sheet of 6, #1615-1620	8.50	8.50
		Nos. 1615-1620 (6)	7.75	7.25

Nos. 1615-1620 exist in an imperf souvenir sheet from a "Limited Edition" album.

Self-Adhesive

Size: 25x30mm

Die Cut Perf. 9½x10

1621	A454	40c Optimist	.45	.40
a.		Booklet pane of 10	6.00	

No. 1621a is a complete booklet.

Millennium A455

New Zealanders Leading the Way: 40c, Women, ballot box. 80c, Airplane of Richard Pearse, pioneer aviator. $1.10, Lord Ernest Rutherford, physicist. $1.20, Jet boat. $1.50, Sir Edmund Hillary, Mt. Everest. $1.80, Anti-nuclear protesters.

1999, Nov. 17 Litho. *Perf. 14x14¼*

1622	A455	40c multicolored	.60	.25
1623	A455	80c multicolored	1.10	.60
1624	A455	$1.10 multicolored	1.50	1.50
1625	A455	$1.20 multicolored	1.60	1.60
1626	A455	$1.50 multicolored	1.75	1.75
1627	A455	$1.80 multicolored	2.00	2.00
		Nos. 1622-1627 (6)	8.55	7.70

Nos. 1622-1627 exist in sheet of 6 created for a hard-bound millennium book that sold for $129.

Year 2000 — A456

2000, Jan. 1 Litho. *Perf. 14¼*

1628	A456	40c multi	.65	.45
a.		Miniature sheet of 10	6.50	4.50

No. 1628 exists in a sheet of 6 created for a hard-bound Millennium book that sold for $129.

The third stamp in the left column on No. 1628a is missing the map and sun emblem between the time and country name.

New Year 2000 (Year of the Dragon) — A457

Spirits and guardians: 40c, Araiteuru. 80c, Kurangaituku. $1.10, Te Hoata and Te Pupu. $1.20, Patupaiarehe. $1.50, Te Ngararahuarau. $1.80, Tuhirangi.

2000, Feb. 9 Litho. *Perf. 14*

1629	A457	40c multi	.60	.25
1630	A457	80c multi	.90	.45
1631	A457	$1.10 multi	1.25	1.25
1632	A457	$1.20 multi	1.50	1.50
1633	A457	$1.50 multi	1.75	1.75
1634	A457	$1.80 multi	2.25	2.25
a.		Souv. sheet of 2, #1633-1634	5.25	5.25
		Nos. 1629-1634 (6)	8.25	7.45

Nos. 1631-1632 exist in a souvenir sheet from a "Limited Edition" album.

Kiwi Type of 1988

2000, Mar. 6 Litho. *Perf. 14½*

1635	A325	$1.10 gold	1.50	1.50
a.		Souv. sheet, #918b, 1027a, 1161b, 1445, 1635	8.25	8.25

Used value is for stamp with complete selvage.

#1635a issued 7/7 for World Stamp Expo 2000, Anaheim.

The 2000 sheets contain: #1694, 1635, 1671; #1662, 1634, 1638; #1677, 1665, 1656. See note following #1404.

Scenic Views Type of 1995

$1, Taiaroa Head. $1.10, Kaikoura Coast. $2, Great Barrier Is. $3, Cape Kidnappers.

2000 Litho. *Perf. 13¼x13½*

Size: 27x22mm

1636	A404	$1 multi	1.50	1.00
1637	A404	$1.10 multi	1.60	1.10
1638	A404	$2 multi	2.25	1.75
1639	A404	$3 multi	2.75	2.50
a.		Souv. sheet, #1636, 1638-1639	9.00	9.00
		Nos. 1636-1639 (4)	8.10	6.35

Self-Adhesive

Booklet Stamp

Die Cut Perf 10x9¾

1640	A404	$1.10 Like #1637	1.50	1.10
a.		Booklet, 5 #1640 + 5 etiquettes	8.75	

The Stamp Show 2000, London (No. 1639a).

Issued: #1639a, 5/22; #1640, 4/3; others, 3/6.

New Zealand Popular Culture — A458

Kiwi with: #1641, Insulated cooler. #1642, Pipis. #1643, Inflatable beach cushion. #1644, Chocolate fish. #1645, Beach house and surf board. #1646, Barbecue. #1647, Ug boots. #1648, Anzac biscuit. #1649, Hot dog. #1650, Meat pie.

Die Cut Perf. 9¾x10

2000, Apr. 3 Litho.

Booklet Stamps

Self-Adhesive

1641	A458	40c multi	.50	.25
1642	A458	40c multi	.50	.25
1643	A458	40c multi	.50	.25
1644	A458	40c multi	.50	.25
1645	A458	40c multi	.50	.25
1646	A458	40c multi	.50	.25
1647	A458	40c multi	.50	.25
1648	A458	40c multi	.50	.25
1649	A458	40c multi	.50	.25
1650	A458	40c multi	.50	.25
a.		Booklet, #1641-1650	5.75	
b.		Sheet, #1641-1650	5.75	
		Nos. 1641-1650 (10)	5.00	2.50

No. 1650b has plain backing paper.

Automobiles — A459

40c, Volkswagen Beetle. 80c, Ford Zephyr MK I. $1.10, Morris Mini MK II. $1.20, Holden HQ Kingswood. $1.50, Honda Civic EB2. $1.80, Toyota Corolla.

2000, June 1 *Perf. 14*

1651	A459	40c claret	.55	.35
a.		Booklet pane of 1	.55	
1652	A459	80c blue	.90	.65
a.		Booklet pane of 1	.90	
1653	A459	$1.10 brown	1.25	1.25
a.		Booklet pane of 1	1.25	
1654	A459	$1.20 green	1.50	1.50
a.		Booklet pane of 1	1.50	
1655	A459	$1.50 olive grn	2.00	2.00
a.		Booklet pane of 1	2.00	
1656	A459	$1.80 violet	2.25	2.25
a.		Booklet pane of 1	2.25	
b.		Booklet pane, #1651-1656	9.00	
		Booklet, #1651a-1656a, 1656b	18.00	
		Nos. 1651-1656 (6)	8.45	8.00

A miniature sheet containing #1651-1656, both perf and imperf within the sheet, exists. This comes from a "Limited Edition" album.

Scenic Reflections A460

Designs: 40c, Lake Lyndon. 80c, Lake Wakatipu. $1.10, Mt. Ruapehu. $1.20, Rainbow Mountain Scenic Reserve. $1.50, Tairua Harbor. $1.80, Lake Alexandrina.

2000, July 7 Litho. *Perf. 14*

1657	A460	40c multi	.60	.35
1658	A460	80c multi	1.10	.55
1659	A460	$1.10 multi	1.25	1.00
1660	A460	$1.20 multi	1.50	1.50
1661	A460	$1.50 multi	1.75	1.75
1662	A460	$1.80 multi	2.00	2.00
a.		Souvenir Sheet, #1657, 1662	4.00	4.00
		Nos. 1657-1662 (6)	8.20	7.15

No. 1662a issued 10/5/00 for Canpex 2000 Stamp Exhibition, Christchurch.

Queen Mother's 100th Birthday — A461

Queen Mother in: 40c, 1907. $1.10, 1966. $1.80, 1997.

2000, Aug. 4

1663	A461	40c multi	.60	.35
1664	A461	$1.10 multi	1.25	1.00
1665	A461	$1.80 multi	2.50	2.00
a.		Souvenir sheet, #1663-1665	4.25	4.25
		Nos. 1663-1665 (3)	4.35	3.35

Sports — A462

2000, Aug. 4 *Perf. 14x14¼*

1666	A462	40c Rowing	.60	.35
1667	A462	80c Equestrian	1.00	.55
1668	A462	$1.10 Cycling	1.50	1.00
1669	A462	$1.20 Triathlon	1.50	1.50
1670	A462	$1.50 Lawn bowling	1.75	1.75
1671	A462	$1.80 Netball	2.00	2.25
		Nos. 1666-1671 (6)	8.35	7.40

2000 Summer Olympics, Sydney (Nos. 1666-1669).

Christmas A463

Designs: 40c, Madonna and child. 80c, Mary, Joseph and donkey. $1.10, Baby Jesus, cow, lamb. $1.20, Archangel. $1.50, Shepherd and lamb. $1.80, Magi.

2000, Sept. 6 *Perf. 14*

1672	A463	40c multi	.60	.25
1673	A463	80c multi	1.00	.60
1674	A463	$1.10 multi	1.40	1.40
1675	A463	$1.20 multi	1.60	1.60
1676	A463	$1.50 multi	1.75	1.75
1677	A463	$1.80 multi	2.00	2.00
		Nos. 1672-1677 (6)	8.35	7.60

Self-Adhesive

Size: 30x25mm

Serpentine Die Cut 11¼x11

1678	A463	40c multi	.60	.25
a.		Booklet of 10	6.50	

Issued: No. 1678a, 11/1/00.

Scenic Views Type of 1995

Designs: 90c, Rangitoto Island. $1.30, Lake Camp, South Canterbury.

2000 Litho. *Perf. 13¼x13½*

Size: 27x22mm

1679	A404	90c multi	1.25	.75
1680	A404	$1.30 multi	1.75	1.10
a.		Souvenir sheet, #1636-1637, 1679-1680	6.00	6.00

Issued: Nos. 1679-1680, 10/2/00; No. 1680a, 3/16/01. 2001: A Stamp Odyssey Philatelic Exhibition, Invercargill (#1680a).

Teddy Bears and Dolls — A464

Designs: 40c+5c, Teddy bear "Geronimo," by Rose Hill. 80c+5c, Antique French and wooden Schoenhut dolls. $1.10, Chad Valley bear. $1.20, Doll "Poppy," by Debbie Pointon. $1.50, Teddy bears "Swanni," by Robin Rive, and "Dear John," by Rose Hill. $1.80, Doll "Lia," by Gloria Young, and teddy bear.

2000, Oct. 5 *Perf. 14½x14¾*

1681	A464	40c +5c multi	.65	.40
1682	A464	80c +5c multi	1.25	.70
a.		Souvenir sheet, #1681-1682	2.75	2.75
1683	A464	$1.10 multi	1.40	1.40
1684	A464	$1.20 multi	1.60	1.60
1685	A464	$1.50 multi	1.75	1.75
1686	A464	$1.80 multi	2.00	2.00
a.		Block of 6, #1681-1686	9.50	9.50

Coil Stamp
Size: 30x25mm
Self-Adhesive
Serpentine Die Cut 11¼

1687	A464	40c +5c multi	.55	.40

Endangered Birds — A465

Designs: No. 1688, Lesser kestrel. No. 1689, Orange fronted parakeet. 80c, Black stilt. $1.10, Stewart Island fernbird. $1.20, Kakapo. $1.50, North Island weka. $1.80, Okarito brown kiwi.

2000, Nov. 4 ***Perf. 14***

1688	A465	40c multi	.60	.35
1689	A465	40c multi	.60	.35
a.		Pair, #1688-1689	1.75	1.75
1690	A465	80c multi	1.25	.90
1691	A465	$1.10 multi	1.40	1.40
1692	A465	$1.20 multi	1.50	1.50
1693	A465	$1.50 multi	1.75	1.75
1694	A465	$1.80 multi	2.00	2.00
a.		Souvenir sheet, #1693-1694	5.75	5.75
		Nos. 1688-1694 (7)	9.10	8.25

Nos. 1689-1690 exist in a souvenir sheet from a "Limited Edition" album.

Issued: No. 1694a, 2/1/01. Hong Kong 2001 Stamp Exhibition (#1694a). See France Nos. 2790-2791.

Penny Universal Postage, Cent. — A466

Methods of mail delivery: a, Steamship. b, Horse-drawn coach. c, Early mail truck. d, Paddle steamer. e, Railway traveling post office. f, Airplane with front cargo hatch. g, Bicycle. h, Tractor trailer. i, Airplane with side cargo hatch. j, Computer mouse.

2001, Jan. 1

1695		Sheet of 10	7.00	7.00
a.-j.		A466 40c Any single	.60	.60
k.		As No. 1695, with Belgica 2001 sheet margin	7.00	7.00

No. 1695k has no perforations running through sheet margin.

Marine Reptiles — A467

Designs: 40c, Green turtle. 80c, Leathery turtle. 90c, Loggerhead turtle. $1.30, Hawksbill turtle. $1.50, Banded sea snake. $2, Yellow-bellied sea snake.

2001, Feb. 1

1696	A467	40c multi	.75	.25
1697	A467	80c multi	1.10	.65
1698	A467	90c multi	1.25	1.25
1699	A467	$1.30 multi	1.75	1.75
1700	A467	$1.50 multi	2.00	2.00
1701	A467	$2 multi	2.25	2.25
a.		Souvenir sheet, #1700-1701	5.00	5.00
		Nos. 1696-1701 (6)	9.10	8.15

New Year 2001 (Year of the snake) (#1701a).

Flowers — A468

2001, Mar. 7

1702	A468	40c Camellia	.55	.35
1703	A468	80c Siberian iris	.90	.55
1704	A468	90c Daffodil	1.10	1.10
1705	A468	$1.30 Chrysanthemum	1.50	1.50
1706	A468	$1.50 Sweet pea	1.75	1.75
1707	A468	$2 Petunia	2.50	2.50
a.		Souvenir sheet, #1702-1707	8.25	8.25
		Nos. 1702-1707 (6)	8.30	7.75

No. 1707a exists imperf from a "Limited Edition" album.

Art From Nature — A469

2001, Apr. 4 **Litho.** ***Perf. 14¼***

1708	A469	40c Greenstone	.55	.35
1709	A469	80c Oamaru stone	.90	.55
1710	A469	90c Paua	1.10	1.10
1711	A469	$1.30 Kauri gum	1.50	1.50
1712	A469	$1.50 Flax	1.75	1.75
1713	A469	$2 Fern	2.50	2.50
		Nos. 1708-1713 (6)	8.30	7.75

Within sheets of 25 printed for each stamp are four blocks of four showing a circular design, made by rotating each stamp design 90 degrees.

Aircraft — A470

Designs: 40c, Douglas DC-3. 80c, Fletcher FU24 Topdresser. 90c, De Havilland DH82A Tiger Moth. $1.30, Fokker FVIIb/3m. $1.50, De Havilland DH100 Vampire. $2, Boeing & Westervelt Seaplane.

2001, May 2 ***Perf. 14x14¼***

1714	A470	40c multi	.60	.35
a.		Booklet pane of 1	.60	
1715	A470	80c multi	.90	.65
a.		Booklet pane of 1	.90	
1716	A470	90c multi	1.25	1.25
a.		Booklet pane of 1	1.25	
1717	A470	$1.30 multi	1.50	1.50
a.		Booklet pane of 1	1.50	
1718	A470	$1.50 multi	1.75	1.75
a.		Booklet pane of 1	1.75	
1719	A470	$2 multi	2.50	2.50
a.		Booklet pane of 1	2.50	
b.		Booklet pane, #1714-1719	10.00	
		Booklet, #1714a-1719a, 1719b	20.00	
		Nos. 1714-1719 (6)	8.50	8.00

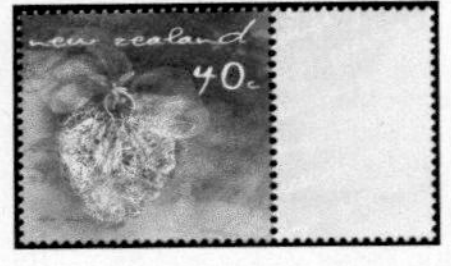

Greetings A471

No. 1720: a, Heart. b, Balloons. c, Flower. d, Gift. e, Trumpet.

No. 1721: a, Candles. b, Stars. c, Roses and candle. d, Picture frame. e, Letter and fountain pen.

2001, June 6 ***Perf. 14½x14***

1720		Vert. strip of 5 + 5 labels	2.75	2.75
a.-e.		A471 40c Any single + label	.50	.50
1721		Vert. strip of 5 + 5 labels	5.75	5.75
a.-e.		A471 90c Any single + label	.90	.90

Labels could be personalized on sheets that sold for $15.95 and $27.95 respectively.

Government Tourist Office, Cent. — A472

Designs: 40c, Bungee jumper, Queenstown. 80c, Canoeing on Lake Rotoiti. 90c, Sightseers on Mt. Alfred. $1.30, Fishing in Glenorchy River. $1.50, Kayakers in Abel Tasman Natl. Park. $2, Hiker in Fiordland Natl. Park.

2001 **Litho.** ***Perf. 14¼***

1722	A472	40c multi	.50	.25
1723	A472	80c multi	.90	.90
1724	A472	90c multi	1.10	1.10
1725	A472	$1.30 multi	1.50	1.50
1726	A472	$1.50 multi	1.75	1.75
1727	A472	$2 multi	2.25	2.25
a.		Souvenir sheet, #1726-1727	6.00	6.00

Size: 26x21mm
Serpentine Die Cut 11¼x11
Self-Adhesive

1728	A472	40c multi	.60	.50
a.		Booklet of 10 + 10 etiquettes	6.50	
1729	A472	90c multi	1.25	1.25
a.		Booklet of 10 + 10 etiquettes	14.00	
1730	A472	$1.50 multi	2.25	2.25
a.		Horiz. strip, #1728-1730	4.50	
b.		Booklet of 5 + 5 etiquettes	12.00	

Coil Stamp
Size: 26x21mm
Self-Adhesive
Serpentine Die Cut 10x9¾

1730C	A472	40c Like #1722	.55	.35
		Nos. 1722-1730C (10)	12.65	12.10

Phila Nippon '01, Japan (No. 1727a). Issued: No. 1727a, 8/1; others, 7/4.

A sheet containing 3 each of Nos. 1722-1727 was included in a book that sold for $69.95.

Christmas — A473

Designs: 40c, In Excelsis Gloria. 80c, Away in the Manger. 90c, Joy to the World. $1.30, Angels We Have Heard on High. $1.50, O Holy Night. $2, While Shepherds Watched Their Flocks.

2001, Sept. 5 ***Perf. 13¼x13¾***

1731	A473	40c multi	.60	.25
1732	A473	80c multi	1.10	.50
1733	A473	90c multi	1.25	1.25
1734	A473	$1.30 multi	1.50	1.50
1735	A473	$1.50 multi	1.75	1.75
1736	A473	$2 multi	2.00	2.00

Size: 21x26mm
Serpentine Die Cut 9¾x10
Self-Adhesive

1737	A473	40c multi	.65	.25
a.		Booklet of 10	6.50	
		Nos. 1731-1737 (7)	8.85	7.50

Issued: No. 1737a, 11/7/01.

Visit of Queen Elizabeth II, Oct. 2001 — A474

Queen in past visits: 40c, Arriving for opening of Parliament, 1953. 80c, With crowd, 1970. 90c, With crowd, 1977. $1.30, With crowd, 1986. $1.50, At Commonwealth Games, 1990. $2, 2001 portrait.

2001, Oct. 3 **Litho.** ***Perf. 14***

1738	A474	40c multi	.65	.35
1739	A474	80c multi	1.10	.60
1740	A474	90c multi	1.25	1.25
1741	A474	$1.30 multi	1.50	1.50
1742	A474	$1.50 multi	1.75	1.75
1743	A474	$2 multi	2.25	2.25
a.		Horiz. strip, #1738-1743	8.50	8.50
		Nos. 1738-1743 (6)	8.50	7.70

Nos. 1738-1743 exist in a souvenir sheet from a "Limited Edition" album. Nos. 1738-1743 also exist imperf.

Penguins — A475

Designs: 40c, Rockhopper. 80c, Little blue. 90c, Snares crested. $1.30, Erect-crested. $1.50, Fiordland crested. $2, Yellow-eyed.

2001, Nov. 7 ***Perf. 14¼***

1744	A475	40c multi	.75	.40
1745	A475	80c multi	1.10	.60
1746	A475	90c multi	1.25	1.25
1747	A475	$1.30 multi	1.75	1.75
1748	A475	$1.50 multi	2.00	2.00
1749	A475	$2 multi	2.25	2.25
		Nos. 1744-1749 (6)	9.10	8.25

Filming in New Zealand of The Lord of the Rings Trilogy A476

Scenes from "The Lord of the Rings: The Fellowship of the Ring:" 40c, Gandalf the Gray and Saruman the White, vert. 80c, Lady Galadriel, vert. 90c, Sam Gamgee and Frodo Baggins. $1.30, Guardian of Rivendell, vert. $1.50, Strider, vert. $2, Boromir, son of Denethor.

Perf. 14½x14, 14x14½

2001, Dec. 4 **Litho.**

1750	A476	40c multi	.75	.50
a.		Souvenir sheet of 1	2.25	1.75
b.		Sheet of 10 #1750	7.50	—
1751	A476	80c multi	1.75	1.75
a.		Souvenir sheet of 1	4.00	3.50
1752	A476	90c multi	2.00	2.00
a.		Souvenir sheet of 1	4.75	4.00
1753	A476	$1.30 multi	2.75	2.75
a.		Souvenir sheet of 1	6.50	5.75
1754	A476	$1.50 multi	3.00	3.00
a.		Souvenir sheet of 1	7.50	6.50
1755	A476	$2 multi	4.00	4.00
a.		Souvenir sheet of 1	11.00	8.75
b.		Souvenir sheet, #1754-1755	8.00	8.00
c.		Souvenir sheet, #1750, 1753, 1755	9.50	9.50

Self-Adhesive
Serpentine Die Cut 10x10¼, 10¼x10
Size: 22x33mm, 33x22mm

1756	A476	40c multi	.85	.85
1757	A476	80c multi	2.00	2.00
1758	A476	90c multi	2.25	2.25
1759	A476	$1.30 multi	3.00	3.00
1760	A476	$1.50 multi	3.25	3.25
1761	A476	$2 multi	4.25	4.25
a.		Pane, #1756-1761	*16.00*	
b.		Booklet pane, #1757, 1759-1761, 4 #1756, 2 #1758	*35.00*	
		Nos. 1750-1761 (12)	29.85	29.60

Issued: No. 1755b, 8/30/02; No. 1755c, 4/5/02. Other values, 12/4/01.

No. 1755b issued for Amphilex 2002 World Stamp Exhibition, Amsterdam; No. 1755c issued for Northpex 2002.

See Nos. 1835-1846, 1897-1908.

New Year 2002 (Year of the Horse) — A477

Champion race horses: 40c, Christian Cullen. 80c, Lyell Creek. 90c, Yulestar. $1.30, Sunline. $1.50, Ethereal. $2, Zabeel.

2002, Feb. 7 ***Perf. 14***

1762	A477	40c multi	.55	.35
1763	A477	80c multi	.90	.90
1764	A477	90c multi	1.10	1.10
1765	A477	$1.30 multi	1.50	1.50
1766	A477	$1.50 multi	1.75	1.75
a.		Souvenir sheet, #1765-1766	4.50	4.50
1767	A477	$2 multi	2.50	2.50
		Nos. 1762-1767 (6)	8.30	8.10

Fungi — A478

Designs: 40c, Hygrocybe rubrocarnosa. 80c, Entoloma hochstetteri. 90c, Aseroe rubra. $1.30, Hericium coralloides. $1.50, Thaxterogaster porphyreus. $2, Ramaria aureorhiza.

2002, Mar. 6 **Litho.** ***Perf. 14***

1768	A478	40c multi	.60	.40
1769	A478	80c multi	1.10	.60
1770	A478	90c multi	1.25	1.25
1771	A478	$1.30 multi	1.75	1.75
1772	A478	$1.50 multi	2.00	2.00
1773	A478	$2 multi	2.25	2.25
a.		Souvenir sheet, #1768-1773	9.00	9.00
		Nos. 1768-1773 (6)	8.95	8.25

No. 1773a exists as an imperforate souvenir sheet from a "Limited Edition" album.

A479

A480

Architectural Heritage A481

Designs: 40c, War Memorial Museum, Auckland. 80c, Stone Store, Kerikeri. 90c, Arts Center, Christchurch. $1.30, Government buildings, Wellington. $1.50, Railway Station, Dunedin. $2, Sky Tower, Auckland.

2002, Apr. 3 Litho. *Perf. 14½x14*

1774 A479 40c multi .65 .30
a. Booklet pane of 1 .65 —
1775 A480 80c multi 1.10 .75
a. Booklet pane of 1 1.10 —
1776 A481 90c multi 1.25 1.00
a. Booklet pane of 1 1.25 —
1777 A481 $1.30 multi 1.50 1.50
a. Booklet pane of 1 1.50 —
1778 A480 $1.50 multi 1.75 1.75
a. Booklet pane of 1 1.75 —
1779 A479 $2 multi 2.00 2.00
a. Booklet pane of 1 2.00 —
b. Block of 6, #1774-1779 10.00 10.00
c. Booklet pane, #1779b 11.00 —
Booklet, #1774a-1779a, 1779c 20.00
Nos. 1774-1779 (6) 8.25 7.30

Booklet containing Nos. 1774a-1779a, 1779c sold for $16.95.

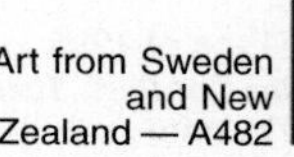

Art from Sweden and New Zealand — A482

Designs: No. 1780, Maori basket, by Willa Rogers, New Zealand. No. 1781, Starfish Vessel, by Graeme Priddle, New Zealand. 80c, Catch II, by Raewyn Atkinson, New Zealand. 90c, Silver brooch, by Gavin Hithings, New Zealand. $1.30, Glass towers, by Emma Camden, New Zealand. $1.50, Pacific Rim, by Merilyn Wiseman. $2, Rain Forest, glass vase by Ola Höglund, Sweden.

Litho. & Engr. (#1780, 1786), Litho.
Perf. 12½x12¾ (#1780, 1786), 14

2002, May 2

1780 A482 40c multi .60 .35
1781 A482 40c multi .60 .35
1782 A482 80c multi 1.10 .65
1783 A482 90c multi 1.25 1.25
1784 A482 $1.30 multi 1.50 1.50
1785 A482 $1.50 multi 1.75 1.75
1786 A482 $2 multi 2.00 2.00
Nos. 1780-1786 (7) 8.80 7.85

See Sweden No. 2440.

Nos. 1780-1786 exist in a souvenir sheet from a "Limited Edition" album.

Kiwi Type of 1988

2002, June 5 Litho. *Perf. 14½*

1787 A325 $1.50 brown 2.00 1.50
a. Souvenir sheet of 3 7.00 7.00

Used value is for stamp with complete selvage.

Issued: No. 1787a, 11/12/10. Palmpex 2010 Stamp Show, Palmerston North (No. 1787a).

Queen Mother Elizabeth (1900-2002) — A483

2002, June 5 *Perf. 14¼*

1788 A483 $2 multi 2.25 2.00

Children's Book Festival Stamp Design Contest Winners — A484

Art by: No. 1789, Anna Poland, Cardinal McKeefry School, Wellington. No. 1790, Hee Su Kim, Glendowie Primary School, Auckland. No. 1791, Jayne Bruce, Rangiora Borough School, Rangiora. No. 1792, Teigan Stafford-Bush (bird), Ararimu School, Auckland. No. 1793, Hazel Gilbert, Gonville School, Wanganui. No. 1794, Gerard Mackle, Temuka High School, Temuka. No. 1795, Maria Rodgers, Salford School, Invercargill. No. 1796, Paul Read (hand and ball), Ararimu School, Auckland. No. 1797, Four students, Glendene Primary School, Auckland. No. 1798, Olivia Duncan, Takapuna Normal Intermediate School, Auckland.

2002, June 5 *Perf. 14*

1789 A484 40c multi .80 .80
1790 A484 40c multi .80 .80
1791 A484 40c multi .80 .80
1792 A484 40c multi .80 .80
1793 A484 40c multi .80 .80
1794 A484 40c multi .80 .80
1795 A484 40c multi .80 .80
1796 A484 40c multi .80 .80
1797 A484 40c multi .80 .80
1798 A484 40c multi .80 .80
a. Block of 10, #1789-1798 10.00 10.00
b. Sheet of 10, #1789-1798 11.00 11.00
Nos. 1789-1798 (10) 8.00 8.00

Scenic Coastlines — A485

Designs: 40c, Tongaporutu Cliffs, Taranaki. 80c, Lottin Point, East Cape. 90c, Curio Bay, Catlins. $1.30, Kaikoura Coast. $1.50, Meybille Bay, West Coast. $2, Papanui Point, Raglan.

2002, July 3 *Perf. 14*

1799 A485 40c multi .50 .30
1800 A485 80c multi 1.00 .60
1801 A485 90c multi 1.25 1.25
1802 A485 $1.30 multi 1.50 1.50
1803 A485 $1.50 multi 1.75 1.75
1804 A485 $2 multi 2.10 2.10

Size: 28x22mm
Self-Adhesive
Serpentine Die Cut 10x9¾

1805 A485 40c multi .55 .55
a. Booklet pane of 10 6.50
b. Serpentine die cut 11 .70 .70
c. Booklet pane of 10 #1805b 7.50
1806 A485 90c multi 1.25 1.25
a. Booklet pane of 10 14.00
1807 A485 $1.50 multi 2.40 1.50
a. Booklet pane of 5 12.00
b. Coil strip of 3, #1805-1807 4.50

Coil Stamp
Size: 28x22mm
Self-Adhesive
Die Cut Perf. 12¾

1808 A485 40c multi .55 .40
Nos. 1799-1808 (10) 12.85 11.20

Christmas — A487

Church interiors: 40c, Saint Werenfried Catholic Church, Waihi Village, Tokaannu. 80c, St. David's Anglican Church, Christchurch. 90c, Orthodox Church of the Transfiguration of Our Lord, Masterton. $1.30, Cathedral of the Holy Spirit, Palmerston North. $1.50, Cathedral of St. Paul, Wellington. $2, Cathedral of the Blessed Sacrament, Christchurch.

2002, Sept. 4 *Perf. 14¼*

1812 A487 40c multi .50 .25
1813 A487 80c multi 1.00 .45
1814 A487 90c multi 1.25 1.00
1815 A487 $1.30 multi 1.75 1.75
1816 A487 $1.50 multi 2.00 2.00
1817 A487 $2 multi 2.25 2.25

Coil Stamp
Size: 21x26mm
Self-Adhesive
Die Cut Perf. 13x12¾

1818 A487 40c multi .55 .25

Booklet Stamp
Size: 21x26mm
Self-Adhesive
Die Cut Perf 9¾x10

1818A A487 40c Like No. 1818 .55 .25
b. Booklet pane of 10 6.50
Nos. 1812-1818A (8) 9.85 8.20

Issued: No. 1818A, 11/6/02.

Boats — A488

Designs: 40c, KZ1. 80c, High 5. 90c, Gentle Spirit. $1.30, NorthStar. $1.50, OceanRunner. $2, Salperton.

2002, Oct. 2 Litho. *Perf. 14*

1819 A488 40c multi .60 .35
1820 A488 80c multi 1.00 .65
1821 A488 90c multi 1.10 1.10
1822 A488 $1.30 multi 1.50 1.50
1823 A488 $1.50 multi 2.00 2.00
1824 A488 $2 multi 2.25 2.25
a. Souvenir sheet, #1819-1824 9.00 9.00
Nos. 1819-1824 (6) 8.45 7.85

No. 1824a exists an an imperforate souvenir sheet from a "Limited Edition" album.

2003 America's Cup Yacht Races — A489

Scenes from 2000 America's Cup finals: $1.30, Black Magic next to Luna Rossa. $1.50, Aerial view. $2, Black Magic passing Luna Rossa.

2002

1825 A489 $1.30 multi 1.75 1.50
1826 A489 $1.50 multi 2.00 2.00
1827 A489 $2 multi 2.25 2.25
a. Souvenir sheet, #1825-1827 7.50 7.50
b. As "a," with Stampshow Melbourne 02 ovpt. in margin 7.00 7.00
Nos. 1825-1827 (3) 6.00 5.75

Issued: No. 1827b, 10/4; others 10/2.

Vacation Homes — A490

Various vacation homes with denominations over: No. 1828, Paua shell. No. 1829, Sunflower. No. 1830, Life preserver. No. 1831, Fish hook. No. 1832, Fish. No. 1833, Flower bouquet.

2002, Nov. 6 Litho. *Perf. 14*

1828 A490 40c multi .70 .55
1829 A490 40c multi .70 .55
1830 A490 40c multi .70 .55
1831 A490 40c multi .70 .55
1832 A490 40c multi .70 .55
1833 A490 40c multi .70 .55
Nos. 1828-1833 (6) 4.20 3.30

Nativity, by Pseudo Ambrogio di Baldese A491

2002, Nov. 21 *Perf. 14¼x14*

1834 A491 $1.50 multi 2.10 1.75

See Vatican City No. 1232.

The Lord of the Rings Type of 2001

Scenes from *The Lord of the Rings: The Two Towers:* 40c, Aragorn and Eowyn. 80c, Orc raider. 90c, Gandalf the White, vert. $1.30, The Easterlings. $1.50, Frodo captured, vert. $2, Shield Maiden of Rohan.

2002, Dec. 4 *Perf. 14x14½, 14½x14*

1835 A476 40c multi .65 .40
a. Souvenir sheet of 1 1.00 .65
1836 A476 80c multi 1.40 1.40
a. Souvenir sheet of 1 2.00 2.00
1837 A476 90c multi 1.50 1.50
a. Souvenir sheet of 1 2.25 2.25
1838 A476 $1.30 multi 2.25 2.25
a. Souvenir sheet of 1 3.25 3.25
1839 A476 $1.50 multi 2.50 2.50
a. Souvenir sheet of 1 3.75 3.75
1840 A476 $2 multi 3.25 3.25
a. Souvenir sheet of 1 4.25 4.25
Set of 6 souvenir sheets of 1 each, #1835a//1840a 16.50

Self-Adhesive
Size: 34x23mm, 23x34mm
Serpentine Die Cut 10¼x10, 10x10¼

1841 A476 40c multi .65 .40
1842 A476 80c multi 1.25 1.25
1843 A476 90c multi 1.40 1.40
1844 A476 $1.30 multi 2.10 2.10
1845 A476 $1.50 multi 2.40 2.40
1846 A476 $2 multi 3.25 3.25
a. Pane, #1841-1846 11.00
b. Booklet pane, #1842, 1844-1846, 2 #1843, 4 #1841 14.50
Nos. 1835-1846 (12) 22.60 22.10

The 2002 sheets contain: #1767, 1773, 1779, 1785, 1787, 1804, 1817, 1830, B170. See note following #1404.

2003 America's Cup Yacht Races — A492

Designs: 40c, Yacht and sail with sponsor's advertisements. 80c, Yachts circling. 90c, Yachts racing.

2003, Jan. 8 Litho. *Perf. 14*

1847 A492 40c multi .50 .35
1848 A492 80c multi 1.10 1.10
1849 A492 90c multi 1.25 1.25
a. Souvenir sheet of 3, #1847-1849 3.25 3.25
Nos. 1847-1849 (3) 2.85 2.70

New Year 2003 (Year of the Ram) — A493

Designs: 40c, Sheep in high country. 90c, Sheep leaving pen. $1.30, Sheepdog and sheep. $1.50, Shearer. $2, Shearing gang.

2003, Feb. 5 Litho. *Perf. 14*

1850 A493 40c multi .55 .35
1851 A493 90c multi 1.00 .65
1852 A493 $1.30 multi 1.50 1.50
1853 A493 $1.50 multi 2.00 2.00
1854 A493 $2 multi 2.50 2.50
a. Souvenir sheet of 2, #1852, 1854 4.00 4.00
Nos. 1850-1854 (5) 7.55 7.00

Royal New Zealand Ballet, 50th Anniv. — A494

Scenes from productions of: 40c, Carmina Burana, 1971, vert. 90c, Papillon, 1989. $1.30, Cinderella, 2000, vert. $1.50, FrENZy, 2001, vert. $2, Swan lake, 2002.

2003, Mar. 5 Litho. *Perf. 14*

1855 A494 40c multi .55 .40
1856 A494 90c multi 1.10 .75
1857 A494 $1.30 multi 1.50 1.50
1858 A494 $1.50 multi 2.00 2.00
1859 A494 $2 multi 2.50 2.50
a. Souvenir sheet, #1855, 1856, 1859 6.50 6.50
Nos. 1855-1859 (5) 7.65 7.15

No. 1859a issued for Bangkok 2003 World Philatelic Exhibition.

Nos. 1855-1859 exist in a souvenir sheet from a "Limited Edition" album.

Military Uniforms, Medals and Insignia — A495

No. 1860: a, Forest ranger, 1860s. b, Napier naval artillery volunteer officer, 1890s. c, Amuri mounted rifles officer, 1900-10. d, Mounted Rifles, South Africa, 1898-1902. e, Staff officer, France, 1918. f, Petty officer, 1914-18. g, Infantry, France, 1916-18. h, Engineer, 1939-45. i, Matron, RNZN Hospital, 1940s. j, WAAC, Egypt, 1942. k, Bomber pilot, Europe, 1943. l, Fighter pilot, Pacific, 1943. m, WAAF driver, 1943. n, Gunner, Korea, 1950-53. o, Petty officer, 1950s. p, SAS, Malaya, 1955-57. q, Canberra Pilot, 1960. r, Infantry, Viet Nam, 1960s. s, UN Peacekeeper, East Timor, 2000. t, Peace Monitor, Bougainville, 2001.

2003, Apr. 2 Litho. *Perf. 14*

1860 Sheet of 20 20.00 20.00
a.-t. A495 40c Any single .65 .45
u. Booklet pane, 2 each #a-d 6.00 —
v. Booklet pane, 2 each #e-h 6.00 —
w. Booklet pane, 2 each #i-l 6.00 —
x. Booklet pane, 2 each #m-p 6.00 —
y. Booklet pane, 2 each #q-t 6.00 —
Complete booklet, #u-y 30.00

Tourist Attractions — A496

Designs: 50c, Ailsa Mountains. $1, Coromandel Peninsula. $1.50, Arrowtown. $2, Tongariro National Park. $5, Castlepoint.

2003, May 7 Litho. *Perf. 13¼x13½*

1861 A496 50c multi .65 .40
1862 A496 $1 multi 1.30 .90
1863 A496 $1.50 multi 1.75 1.40
1863A A496 $1.50 multi 1.75 1.40
1864 A496 $2 multi 2.75 2.00
1865 A496 $5 multi 5.75 4.75

Self-Adhesive

Serpentine Die Cut 10x9½

1866 A496 $1.50 multi 2.00 1.50
a. Booklet pane of 5 11.00
1866B A496 $1.50 As #1866, vignette 26mm wide 2.10 2.00
c. Booklet pane of 5 #1866b + 10 etiquettes 12.00
Nos. 1861-1866 (7) 15.95 12.35

Nos. 1861-1865 exist with silver fern leaf overprints from a limited printing.

Nos. 1866b, 1866c issued 3/27/07. Vignette of No. 1866 is 27mm wide. No. 1863A issued 2007.

Nos. 1863A and 1866B show a person on the sidewalk in front of the door of the house in the foreground (above the zero in the denomination). The person is not found on Nos. 1863 and 1866.

See Nos. 1926-1928B, 1972-1977, 2062-2067, 2129-2137, 2222, 2238, 2257-2263, 2316-2322, 2392, 2405-2409.

Ascent of Mt. Everest, 50th Anniv. — A497

Designs: No. 1867, Sir Edmund Hillary, Mt. Everest. No. 1868, Tenzing Norgay, climbers on mountain.

2003, May 29 *Perf. 14*

1867 A497 40c multi .95 .95
1868 A497 40c multi .95 .95
a. Pair, #1867-1868 2.00 2.00

Nos. 1867-1868 exist in a miniature sheet of 10. Value, $15.

Coronation Type of 1953

Perf. 14x14½, 14½x14

2003, June 4 Litho.

1869 A112 40c Like #280 .60 .30
1870 A113 90c Like #281 1.10 .75
1871 A112 $1.30 Like #282 1.75 1.75
1872 A114 $1.50 Like #283 2.00 2.00
1873 A112 $2 Like #284 2.25 2.25
Nos. 1869-1873 (5) 7.70 7.05

Nos. 1869-1873 exist in a souvenir sheet from a "Limited Edition" album.

Test Rugby, Cent. — A498

Designs: 40c, New Zealand vs. South Africa, 1937. 90c, New Zealand vs. Wales, 1963. $1.30, New Zealand vs. Australia, 1985. No.1877, New Zealand vs. France, 1986. No. 1878, All Blacks jersey. $2, New Zealand vs. England, 1997.

2003, July 2 *Perf. 14*

1874 A498 40c multi .65 .35
1875 A498 90c multi 1.25 .80
1876 A498 $1.30 multi 1.75 1.75
1877 A498 $1.50 multi 2.00 2.00
1878 A498 $1.50 multi 2.00 2.00
1879 A498 $2 multi 2.25 2.25
a. Souvenir sheet, #1874-1879 10.00 10.00
b. Sheet, #1877-1879 7.00 7.00
c. Souvenir sheet, #1878-1879 6.00 6.00
Nos. 1874-1879 (6) 9.90 9.15

No. 1879b issued 11/7 for Welpex 2003 Stampshow, Wellington. No. 1879b sold for $6.

No. 1879c issued 1/30/04 for 2004 Hong Kong Stamp Expo (#1879c).

Waterways A499

Designs: 40c, Papaaroha, Coromandel Peninsula. 90c, Waimahana Creek, Chatham Islands. $1.30, Blue Lake, Central Otago. $1.50, Waikato River, Waikato. $2, Hooker River, Canterbury.

2003, Aug. 6 Litho. *Perf. 14¼*

1880 A499 40c multi .55 .35
1881 A499 90c multi 1.00 .90
1882 A499 $1.30 multi 1.75 1.75
1883 A499 $1.50 multi 2.00 2.00
1884 A499 $2 multi 2.25 2.25
Nos. 1880-1884 (5) 7.55 7.25

Antique Automobiles A500

Designs: 40c, 1895 Benz Velo. 90c, 1903 Oldsmobile. $1.30, 1911 Wolseley. $1.50, 1915 Talbot. $2, 1915 Ford Model T.

2003, Sept. 3 Litho. *Perf. 13x13¼*

1885 A500 40c multi .60 .40
1886 A500 90c multi 1.10 .95
1887 A500 $1.30 multi 1.75 1.75
1888 A500 $1.50 multi 2.00 2.00
1889 A500 $2 multi 2.25 2.25
Nos. 1885-1889 (5) 7.70 7.35

Christmas — A501

Tree decorations: 40c, Christ child. 90c, Dove. $1.30, Geometric (candles). $1.50, Bells. $2, Angel.

$1, Geometric (fleur-de-lis).

2003, Oct. 1 *Perf. 13½*

1890 A501 40c multi .60 .25
1891 A501 90c multi 1.10 .75
1892 A501 $1.30 multi 1.75 1.75
1893 A501 $1.50 multi 2.00 2.00
1894 A501 $2 multi 2.25 2.25

Self-Adhesive

Serpentine Die Cut 9½x10

Size: 21x26mm

1895 A501 40c multi .60 .40
a. Booklet pane of 10 6.50
1896 A501 $1 multi 1.25 1.25
a. Booklet pane of 8 + 8 etiquettes 13.00
Nos. 1890-1896 (7) 9.55 8.65

The Lord of the Rings Type of 2001

Scenes from *The Lord of the Rings: The Return of the King:* 40c, Legolas, vert. 80c, Frodo, vert. 90c, Merry and Pippin. $1.30, Aragorn, vert. $1.50, Gandalf the White, vert. $2, Gollum.

2003, Nov. 5 *Perf. 14½x14, 14x14½*

1897 A476 40c multi .65 .40
a. Souvenir sheet of 1 .90 .90
1898 A476 80c multi 1.10 1.10
a. Souvenir sheet of 1 1.50 1.50
1899 A476 90c multi 1.25 1.25
a. Souvenir sheet of 1 2.00 2.00
1900 A476 $1.30 multi 2.00 2.00
a. Souvenir sheet of 1 2.25 2.25
1901 A476 $1.50 multi 2.25 2.25
a. Souvenir sheet of 1 2.75 2.75
1902 A476 $2 multi 2.50 2.50
a. Souvenir sheet of 1 3.75 3.75
Set of 6 souvenir sheets of 1 each, #1897a-1902a 13.25

Self-Adhesive

Size: 23x34mm, 34x23mm

Serpentine Die Cut 10x10¼, 10¼x10

1903 A476 40c multi .65 .45
1904 A476 80c multi 1.10 1.00
1905 A476 90c multi 1.40 1.10
1906 A476 $1.30 multi 2.00 2.00
1907 A476 $1.50 multi 2.25 2.25
1908 A476 $2 multi 2.50 2.50
a. Pane, #1903-1908 10.00
b. Booklet pane, #1904, 1906-1908, 2 #1905, 4 #1903 14.00
Nos. 1897-1908 (12) 19.65 18.80

The 2003 sheets contain: #1854, 1859, 1864, 1873, 1879, 1884, 1889, 1894, 1902. See note following #1404.

Scenic Views Type of 1995

Serpentine Die Cut 10x9¾

2004, Jan. 28 Litho.

Booklet Stamp

Size: 26x21mm

Self-Adhesive

1909 A404 10c Like #1346 .40 .40
a. Booklet pane, 10 #1359F, 4 #1909 8.00

Zoo Animals — A502

Designs: 40c, Hamadryas baboon. 90c, Malayan sun bear. $1.30, Red panda. $1.50, Ring-tailed lemur. $2, Spider monkey.

2004, Jan. 28 Litho. *Perf. 13¼x13*

1910 A502 40c multi .60 .50
1911 A502 90c multi 1.25 1.25
1912 A502 $1.30 multi 2.00 2.00
1913 A502 $1.50 multi 2.25 2.25
1914 A502 $2 multi 2.50 2.50
a. Souvenir sheet, #1913-1914 5.00 5.00

Nos. 1910-1914 exist in a souvenir sheet from a "Limited Edition" album.

Self-Adhesive

Size: 21x26mm

Coil Stamp

Die Cut Perf. 12¾x12½

1915 A502 40c multi .60 .55

Booklet Stamp

Serpentine Die Cut 11¼

1916 A502 40c multi .60 .55
a. Booklet pane of 10 6.50
Nos. 1910-1916 (7) 9.80 9.60

New Year 2004 (Year of the Monkey) (#1914a).

Rugby Sevens — A503

Designs: 40c, New Zealand Sevens. 90c, Hong Kong Sevens. $1.50, Hong Kong Stadium. $2, Westpac Stadium, Wellington.

2004, Feb. 25 Litho. *Perf. 14x14¼*

1917 A503 40c multi .60 .45
1918 A503 90c multi 1.25 1.25
1919 A503 $1.50 multi 1.75 1.75
1920 A503 $2 multi 2.75 2.75
a. Souvenir sheet, #1917-1920 7.00 7.00
b. Souvenir sheet, #1877, 1878, 1920 7.00 7.00
Nos. 1917-1920 (4) 6.35 6.20

No. 1920b issued 6/26 for Le Salon du Timbre 2004, Paris.

See Hong Kong Nos. 1084-1087.

Parliament, 150th Anniv. — A504

Designs: 40c, Parliament Building, Auckland, 1854. 90c, Parliament Buildings, Wellington (Provincial Chambers), 1865. $1.30, Parliament Buildings, Wellington, 1899. $1.50, Parliament House, Wellington, 1918. $2, Beehive, Wellington, 1977.

2004, Mar. 3 *Perf. 14½x14¼*

1921 A504 40c blk & purple .60 .45
1922 A504 90c blk & violet 1.25 1.10
1923 A504 $1.30 blk & gray 1.75 1.75
1924 A504 $1.50 blk & blue 2.00 2.00
1925 A504 $2 blk & green 2.50 2.50
a. Souvenir sheet, #1921-1925 9.75 9.75
Nos. 1921-1925 (5) 8.10 7.80

See No. 1935.

Tourist Attractions Type of 2003

Designs: 45c, Kaikoura. $1.35, Church of the Good Shepherd, Lake Tekapo.

Perf. 13¼x13½

2004, Mar. 22 Litho.

1926 A496 45c multi .60 .60

Perf. 14x14½

1927 A496 $1.35 multi 2.00 2.00
a. Perf. 13½ ('06) 2.10 2.10

Self-Adhesive

Serpentine Die Cut 11¼x11

1928 A496 45c multi .70 .70
a. Booklet pane of 10 7.00

Coil Stamp

1928B A496 45c multi .70 .70
Nos. 1926-1928B (4) 4.00 4.00

Country name on No. 1928B has an unserifed font, with horizontal bars in "e," and a symmetrical "w."

No. 1927a issued 8/2006.

Scenic Views Type of 1995

2004, Apr. 5 *Die Cut Perf. 10x9½*

Size: 27x22mm

Self-Adhesive

1929 A404 90c Like #1679 1.10 1.10
a. Booklet pane of 10 11.00

Historic Farm Equipment A505

Designs: 45c, Kinnard Haines tractor. 90c, Fordson F tractor with plow. $1.35, Burrell traction engine. $1.50, Threshing mill. $2, Duncan's seed drill.

2004, Apr. 5 *Perf. 14*

1930 A505 45c multi .65 .40
a. Booklet pane of 1, perf. 14x13¼ .90 —
1931 A505 90c multi 1.25 .75
a. Booklet pane of 1, perf. 14x13¼ 1.75 —
1932 A505 $1.35 multi 2.00 2.00
a. Booklet pane of 1, perf. 14x13¼ 2.75 —
1933 A505 $1.50 multi 2.25 2.25
a. Booklet pane of 1, perf. 14x13¼ 3.00 —
1934 A505 $2 multi 2.50 2.50
a. Booklet pane of 1, perf. 14x13¼ 4.00 —
b. Booklet pane of 5, #1930-1934, perf. 14x13¼ 10.00 —
Complete booklet, #1930a, 1931a, 1932a, 1933a, 1934a, 1934b 25.00
Nos. 1930-1934 (5) 8.65 7.90

The complete booklet sold for $19.95.

Parliament Type of 2004

2004, May 5 *Perf. 14½x14¼*

1935 A504 45c Like #1921 .65 .65

World of Wearable Art Awards Show — A506

Designs: 45c, Dragon Fish. 90c, Persephone's Descent. $1.35, Meridian. $1.50, Taunga Ika. $2, Cailleach Na Mara (Sea Witch).

2004, May 5 ***Perf. 14***

1936	A506	45c multi	.65	.35
1937	A506	90c multi	1.10	.85
1938	A506	$1.35 multi	1.75	1.75
1939	A506	$1.50 multi	2.00	2.00
1940	A506	$2 multi	2.50	2.50
		Nos. 1936-1940 (5)	8.00	7.45

Strips of 5 exist from a special sheet.. Exists imperf. Value, strip with tabs, $32.50

New Zealanders A507

Designs: No. 1941, Man outside of Pungarehu Post Office. No. 1942, Children on horse. No. 1943, Elderly man and woman in front of house.

2004, Feb. Litho. ***Die Cut Perf. 13½***

Booklet Stamps

Self-Adhesive

1941	A507	$1.50 multi	5.00	5.00
1942	A507	$1.50 multi	5.00	5.00
1943	A507	$1.50 multi	5.00	5.00
a.		Booklet pane, 2 each #1941-1943, 6 etiquettes and 10 stickers	30.00	
		Complete booklet, #1943a	30.00	
		Nos. 1941-1943 (3)	15.00	15.00

Wild Food A508

Designs: No. 1944, Mountain oysters. No. 1945, Huhu grubs. No. 1946, Possum paté.

2004, Feb. **Booklet Stamps**

Self-Adhesive

1944	A508	$1.50 multi	5.00	5.00
1945	A508	$1.50 multi	5.00	5.00
1946	A508	$1.50 multi	5.00	5.00
a.		Booklet pane, 2 each #1944-1946, 6 etiquettes and 6 stickers	30.00	
		Complete booklet, #1946a	30.00	
		Nos. 1944-1946 (3)	15.00	15.00

New Zealand Post Emblem A509

2004, Feb. **Booklet Stamps**

Self-Adhesive

1947	A509	$1.50 blue & red	*6.00*	*6.00*
1948	A509	$1.50 red	*6.00*	*6.00*
1949	A509	$1.50 green & red	*6.00*	*6.00*
a.		Booklet pane, 2 each #1947-1949, 6 etiquettes	*35.00*	
		Complete booklet, #1949a	*35.00*	
		Nos. 1947-1949 (3)	*18.00*	*18.00*

Country name is at bottom on No. 1948. A pane of eight stamps containing two each of Nos. 1947-1949 and two $1.50 purple and red stamps similar to No. 1948 came unattached in a folder together with a set of four markers, a sheet of decorative magnets and two sheets of self-adhesive plastic stickers. The pane of eight was not available without purchasing the other non-stamp items, which sold as a package for $19.95.

Flowers — A510

Designs: 45c, Magnolia "Vulcan." 90c, Helleborus "Unnamed Hybrid." $1.35, Nerine "Anzac." $1.50, Rhododendron "Charisma." $2, Delphinium "Sarita."

2004, June 2 ***Perf. 13¼x13¾***

1950	A510	45c multi	.65	.35
1951	A510	90c multi	1.25	.75
1952	A510	$1.35 multi	1.75	1.75
1953	A510	$1.50 multi	2.00	2.00
1954	A510	$2 multi	2.25	2.25
a.		Souvenir sheet, #1950-1954	8.75	8.75
		Nos. 1950-1954 (5)	7.90	7.10

The 45c stamp in the souvenir sheet was impregnated with a floral scent.

Numeral — A511

Serpentine Die Cut 5¾

2004, June 28 **Litho.**

Booklet Stamp

Self-Adhesive

1955	A511	5c multi	1.40	1.40
a.		Booklet pane of 10	14.00	

Postage Advertising Labels

In 2004, New Zealand Post began issuing "Postage Advertising Labels," which have the New Zealand Post emblem and curved side panel found on type A511. These stamps have various vignettes and denominations and were designed in conjunction with various private parties who contracted for and purchased the entire print run of these stamps. Though valid for domestic postage only as most of these stamps lack a country name, none of these stamps were made available to the general public by New Zealand Post.

In 2006, a limited number of Postal Advertising Labels began to be sold at face value by New Zealand Post when new contracts with the private parties were written. These agreements allowed New Zealand Post to print more items than the private party desired and to sell the overage to collectors.

Scene Locations from *The Lord of the Rings* Movie Trilogy — A512

Designs: Nos. 1956, 1965, Skippers Canyon. Nos. 1957, 1964, Skippers Canyon (Ford of Bruinden) with actors. Nos. 1958, 1967, Mount Olympus. No. 1959, 1966, Mount Olympus (South of Rivendell) with actors. No. 1960, Erewhon. No. 1961, Erewhon (Edoras) with actors. No. 1962, Tongariro National Park. No. 1963, Tongariro National Park (Emyn Muil) with actors.

2004, July 7 ***Perf. 14***

1956	A512	45c multi	.65	.65
1957	A512	45c multi	.65	.65
a.		Vert. pair, #1956-1957	1.40	1.40
1958	A512	90c multi	1.25	1.25
1959	A512	90c multi	1.25	1.25
a.		Vert. pair, #1958-1959	2.75	2.75
1960	A512	$1.50 multi	2.25	2.25
1961	A512	$1.50 multi	2.25	2.25
a.		Vert. pair, #1960-1961	4.75	4.75
b.		Souvenir sheet, #1958-1961	7.25	7.25
1962	A512	$2 multi	3.00	3.00
1963	A512	$2 multi	3.00	3.00
a.		Vert. pair, #1962-1963	6.50	6.50
b.		Horiz. block of 8, #1956-1963	15.50	15.50
c.		Souvenir sheet, #1956-1963	15.50	15.50

No. 1963c exists imperf from a "Limited Edition" album.

Self-Adhesive

Serpentine Die Cut 11¼

Size: 30x25mm

1964	A512	45c multi	.60	.60
1965	A512	45c multi	.60	.60
1966	A512	90c multi	1.25	1.25
1967	A512	90c multi	1.25	1.25
a.		Block of 4, #1964-1967	4.00	
b.		Booklet pane, 3 each #1964-1965, 2 each #1966-1967	9.25	
		Nos. 1956-1967 (12)	18.00	18.00

No. 1961b issued 8/28. World Stamp Championship (No. 1961b).

2004 Summer Olympics, Athens — A513

Gold medalists: 45c, John Walker, 1500 meters, Montreal, 1976. 90c, Yvette Williams, long jump, Helsinki, 1952. $1.50, Ian Ferguson and Paul MacDonald, 500 meters kayak doubles, Seoul, 1988. $2, Peter Snell, 800 meters, Rome, 1960.

Litho. with 3-Dimensional Plastic Affixed

Serpentine Die Cut 10¾

2004, Aug. 2 **Self-Adhesive**

1968	A513	45c multi	.65	.50
1969	A513	90c multi	1.00	.80
1970	A513	$1.50 multi	1.75	1.75
1971	A513	$2 multi	2.25	2.25
a.		Horiz. strip of 4, #1968-1971	7.00	
		Nos. 1968-1971 (4)	5.65	5.30

Tourist Attractions Type of 2003

Designs: No. 1972, Lake Wakatipu, Queenstown. No. 1973, Kaikoura. No. 1974, Bath House, Rotorua. No. 1975, Pohutu Geyser, Rotorua. No. 1976, Mitre Peak, Milford Sound. No. 1977, Hawke's Bay.

2004-05 Litho. ***Perf. 13¼x13½***

1972	A496	$1.50 multi	1.90	1.90
a.		Perf. 14x14¼	1.90	1.90
1973	A496	$1.50 multi	1.90	1.90
1974	A496	$1.50 multi	1.90	1.90
1975	A496	$1.50 multi	1.90	1.90
a.		Souvenir sheet, #1973, 1975	5.00	5.00
1976	A496	$1.50 multi	1.90	1.90
a.		Perf. 14x14¼	1.90	1.90
b.		Souvenir sheet, #1972a, 1976a	4.50	4.50
1977	A496	$1.50 multi	1.90	1.90
a.		Souvenir sheet, #1639, 1977	7.25	7.25
		Nos. 1972-1977 (6)	11.40	11.40

Issued: Nos. 1972-1977, 8/28; No. 1977a, 10/29 for Baypex 2004; No. 1975a, 8/18/05 for Taipei 2005 Stamp Exhibition; Nos. 1972a, 1976a, 1976b, 8/3/07. Bangkok 2007 Asian International Stamp Exhibition (#1976b).

A514

Christmas — A515

Designs: 45c, Candle, wine bottle, turkey, ham. 90c, Hangi. $1, Christmas cards, fruit cake. $1.35, Barbecued shrimp. $1.50, Wine bottle, pie and salad. $2, Candelabra, pavlova and plum pudding.

2004, Oct. 4 ***Perf. 14¼***

1978	A514	45c multi	.60	.25
1979	A514	90c multi	1.25	.50
1980	A514	$1.35 multi	1.50	1.50
1981	A514	$1.50 multi	1.75	1.75
1982	A514	$2 multi	2.50	2.50
		Nos. 1978-1982 (5)	7.60	6.50

Self-Adhesive

Serpentine Die Cut 9½x10

1983	A515	45c multi	.60	.40
a.		Booklet pane of 10	7.00	
1984	A515	90c multi	1.10	1.00
1985	A515	$1 multi	1.40	1.40
a.		Booklet pane of 8 + 8 etiquettes	13.00	
b.		Horiz. strip, #1983-1985	3.75	3.75
		Nos. 1983-1985 (3)	3.10	2.80

Extreme Sports — A516

Designs: 45c, Whitewater rafting. 90c, Snow sports. $1.35, Skydiving. $1.50, Jet boating. $2, Bungy jumping.

2004, Dec. 1 ***Perf. 14***

1986	A516	45c multi	.55	.25
a.		Booklet pane of 1	.75	—
1987	A516	90c multi	1.00	.65
a.		Booklet pane of 1	1.50	—
1988	A516	$1.35 multi	1.50	1.50
a.		Booklet pane of 1	2.00	—
1989	A516	$1.50 multi	1.75	1.75
a.		Booklet pane of 1	2.50	—
1990	A516	$2 multi	2.75	2.75
a.		Booklet pane of 1	3.25	—
b.		Booklet pane, #1986-1990	12.00	—
		Complete booklet, #1986a, 1987a, 1988a, 1989a, 1990a, 1990b	24.00	
		Nos. 1986-1990 (5)	7.55	6.90

Complete booklet sold for $14.95.

The 2004 sheets contain: #1914, 1920, 1925, 1934, 1940, 1954, 1962, 1982, 1990. See note following #1404.

Farm Animals — A517

Designs: 45c, Ewe (with horns) and lambs. 90c, Scottish border collies. $1.35, Pigs. $1.50, Rooster and chicken. $2, Rooster and chicken, diff.

2005, Jan. 12 ***Perf. 14***

1991	A517	45c multi	.60	.45
1992	A517	90c multi	1.25	.75
1993	A517	$1.35 multi	1.50	1.50
1994	A517	$1.50 multi	1.75	1.75
1995	A517	$2 multi	2.75	2.75
a.		Horiz. strip, #1991-1995	10.00	10.00
b.		Souvenir sheet, #1994-1995	5.25	5.25
		Nos. 1991-1995 (5)	7.85	7.20

Nos. 1991-1995 exist in a souvenir sheet from a "Limited Edition" album.

Self-Adhesive

Size: 22x27mm

Serpentine Die Cut 11x11¼

1996	A517	45c multi	.50	.60
a.		Booklet pane of 10	6.50	

New Year 2005 (Year of the Cock) (No. 1995b).

Community Groups — A518

Designs: No. 1997, Canoeists, YMCA emblem. No. 1998, Three people holding cement, Rotary International emblem. No. 1999, People building track bed, Lions International emblem. No. 2000, Four people jumping, YMCA emblem. No. 2001, People building wall, Rotary International emblem. No. 2002, Miniature train, Lions International emblem.

2005, Feb. 2 **Litho.** ***Perf. 14***

1997	A518	45c multi	.50	.40
1998	A518	45c multi	.50	.40
1999	A518	45c multi	.50	.40
2000	A518	$1.50 multi	2.00	2.00
a.		Horiz. pair, #1997, 2000, + central label	3.00	3.00
b.		Miniature sheet, 3 #2000a	8.00	8.00
2001	A518	$1.50 multi	2.00	2.00
a.		Horiz. pair, #1998, 2001, + central label	3.00	3.00
b.		Miniature sheet, 3 #2001a	8.00	8.00
2002	A518	$1.50 multi	2.00	2.00
a.		Horiz. pair, #1999, 2002, + central label	3.00	3.00

b.	Miniature sheet, #2000a, 2001a, 2002a	8.00	8.00
c.	Miniature sheet, 3 #2002a	8.25	8.25
	Nos. 1997-2002 (6)	7.50	7.20

New Zealand Postage Stamps, 150th Anniv. — A519

2005, Mar. 2 Litho. *Perf. 14*

2003	A519	45c No. 1	.60	.35
2004	A519	90c No. P1	1.10	.75
2005	A519	$1.35 No. OY5	1.50	1.50
2006	A519	$1.50 No. 83	1.75	1.75
2007	A519	$2 No. 99	2.75	2.75
a.		Souvenir sheet, #2003-2007	8.75	8.75
		Nos. 2003-2007 (5)	7.70	7.10

2005, Apr. 6 Litho. *Perf. 14*

2008	A519	45c No. 123a	.60	.60
2009	A519	90c No. B3	1.10	.75
2010	A519	$1.35 No. C7	1.50	1.50
2011	A519	$1.50 No. 256	1.75	1.75
2012	A519	$2 No. 301	2.75	2.75
a.		Souvenir sheet, #2008-2012	8.75	8.75
b.		Souvenir sheet, #2007, 2012	6.50	6.50
		Nos. 2008-2012 (5)	7.70	7.35

No. 2012b issued 4/21 for Pacific Explorer 2005 World Stamp Expo, Sydney.

Size: 25x30mm

Self-Adhesive

Coil Stamps

Serpentine Die Cut 12¾

2013	A519	45c No. 123a	.55	.55
2014	A519	90c No. B3	1.00	1.00
a.		Horiz. pair, #2013-2014	2.25	

Booklet Stamps

Serpentine Die Cut 11x11¼

2015	A519	45c No. 123a	.60	.50
a.		Booklet pane of 10	7.00	
2016	A519	90c No. B3	1.10	1.10
a.		Booklet pane of 10	12.00	
		Nos. 2013-2016 (4)	3.25	3.15

2005, June 1 Litho. *Perf. 14*

2017	A519	45c No. 369	.60	.25
2018	A519	90c No. 918	1.10	.75
2019	A519	$1.35 No. 989	1.50	1.50
2020	A519	$1.50 No. 1219	1.75	1.75
a.		Souvenir sheet, #2006, 2011, 2020	7.25	7.25
2021	A519	$2 No. 1878	2.75	2.75
a.		Souvenir sheet, #2017-2021	10.00	10.00
		Nos. 2017-2021 (5)	7.70	7.00

No. 2020a issued 11/17 for New Zealand 2005 National Stamp Show, Auckland.

A miniature sheet containing Nos. 2003-2012 and 2017-2021 was sold only with a commemorative book.

Cafés — A520

2005, May 4 Litho. *Die Cut*

Self-Adhesive

2022	A520	45c 1910s	.60	.35
2023	A520	90c 1940s	1.25	.75
2024	A520	$1.35 1970s	1.50	1.50
2025	A520	$1.50 1990s	2.00	2.00
2026	A520	$2 2005	2.75	2.75
a.		Horiz. strip, #2022-2026	10.00	
		Nos. 2022-2026 (5)	8.10	7.35

Rugby Team Shirts — A521

Shirts of: Nos. 2027, 2029, All Blacks. Nos. 2028, 2030, British & Irish Lions.

2005, June 1 *Die Cut*

Self-Adhesive

2027	A521	45c multi	.55	.55
2028	A521	45c multi	.55	.55
a.		Horiz. pair, #2027-2028	1.30	
2029	A521	$1.50 multi	2.00	2.00
2030	A521	$1.50 multi	2.00	2.00
a.		Horiz. pair, #2029-2030	4.50	
		Nos. 2027-2030 (4)	5.10	5.10

Miniature Sheet

Greetings Stamps — A522

No. 2031: a, Kiwi. b, Pohutukawa flower. c, Champagne flutes. d, Balloons. e, Wedding rings. f, Gift. g, Baby's hand. h, New Zealand on globe. i, Kiwi. j, Fern.

2005, July 6 *Perf. 14*

2031	A522	Sheet of 10	12.50	12.50
a.-g.		45c Any single	.60	.50
h.		$1.50 multi	2.10	1.75
i.-j.		$2 Either single	3.00	3.00
k.		Sheet of 20 #2031a + 20 labels	25.00	—
l.		Sheet of 20 #2031b + 20 labels	25.00	—
m.		Sheet of 20 #2031c + 20 labels	25.00	—
n.		Sheet of 20 #2031d + 20 labels	25.00	—
o.		Sheet of 20 #2031e + 20 labels	25.00	—
p.		Sheet of 20 #2031f + 20 labels	25.00	—
q.		Sheet of 20 #2031g + 20 labels	25.00	—
r.		Sheet of 20 #2031h + 20 labels	50.00	—
s.		Sheet of 20 #2031i + 20 labels	70.00	—
t.		Sheet of 20 #2031j + 20 labels	70.00	—

Nos. 2031k-2031q each sold for $19.95; No. 2031r sold for $44.95; Nos. 2031s-2031t each sold for $54.95.

Examples of Nos. 2031a and 2031h without the "2005" year date were produced in sheets of 20 stamps + 20 labels for the Washington 2006 World Philatelic Exhibition and sold only at that show.

See Nos. 2070, 2120.

Worldwide Fund for Nature (WWF) — A523

Kakapo and text: No. 2032, "Nocturnal bird living on the forest floor." No. 2033, "Endangered — only 86 known surviving." No. 2034, "Relies heavily on camouflage for defence." No. 2035, "Night Parrot unique to New Zealand."

2005, Aug. 3

2032	A523	45c multi	.70	.70
2033	A523	45c multi	.70	.70
2034	A523	45c multi	.70	.70
2035	A523	45c multi	.70	.70
a.		Strip of 4, #2032-2035	2.75	2.75
		Nos. 2032-2035 (4)	2.80	2.80

A524

Christmas — A525

Designs: 45c, Baby Jesus. 90c, Mary and Joseph. $1.35, Shepherd and sheep. $1.50, Magi. $2, Star of Bethlehem.

2005 Litho. *Perf. 14¼*

2036	A524	45c multi	.60	.30
2037	A524	90c multi	1.10	.70
2038	A524	$1.35 multi	1.50	1.50
2039	A524	$1.50 multi	1.75	1.75
2040	A524	$2 multi	2.75	2.75
a.		Horiz. strip, #2036-2040	9.50	9.50
		Nos. 2036-2040 (5)	7.70	7.00

Booklet Stamps

Size: 22x27mm

Self-Adhesive

Serpentine Die Cut 11x11¼

2041	A524	45c multi	.65	.55
a.		Booklet pane of 10	7.00	
2042	A525	$1 multi	1.40	1.40
a.		Booklet pane of 10	14.00	

Issued: $1, 10/5; Nos. 2036-2041, 11/2.

Premiere of Movie, *King Kong* — A526

Characters: 45c, King Kong. 90c, Carl Denham. $1.35, Ann Darrow. $1.50, Jack Driscoll. $2, Darrow and Driscoll.

2005, Oct. 19 *Perf. 14¾*

2043	A526	45c multi	.70	.70
2044	A526	90c multi	1.40	1.40
2045	A526	$1.35 multi	2.10	2.10
2046	A526	$1.50 multi	2.40	2.40
2047	A526	$2 multi	3.25	3.25
a.		Horiz. strip, #2043-2047	10.00	10.00
b.		Souvenir sheet, #2047a	10.00	10.00
		Nos. 2043-2047 (5)	9.85	9.85

Premiere of Film *Narnia: The Lion, The Witch and the Wardrobe* — A527

Designs: 45c, Lucy and the Wardrobe. 90c, Lucy, Edmund, Peter and Susan, horiz. $1.35, White Witch and Edmund, horiz. $1.50, Frozen Army. $2, Aslan and Lucy, horiz.

Perf. 14x14¼, 14¼x14

2005, Dec. 1 Litho.

2048	A527	45c multi	.70	.70
a.		Souvenir sheet of 1	1.00	1.00
2049	A527	90c multi	1.40	1.40
a.		Souvenir sheet of 1	1.90	1.90
2050	A527	$1.35 multi	2.10	2.10
a.		Souvenir sheet of 1	3.00	3.00
2051	A527	$1.50 multi	2.40	2.40
a.		Souvenir sheet of 1	3.25	3.25
2052	A527	$2 multi	3.25	3.25
a.		Souvenir sheet of 1	4.25	4.25
		Nos. 2048-2052 (5)	9.85	9.85
		Set of 5 souvenir sheets of 1 each, #2048a//2052a	13.40	13.40

Self-Adhesive

Serpentine Die Cut 12½x12, 12x12½

2053	Sheet of 5	10.00	
a.	A527 45c multi, 26x37mm	.70	.70
b.	A527 90c multi, 37x26mm	1.40	1.40
c.	A527 $1.35 multi, 37x26mm	2.10	2.10
d.	A527 $1.50 multi, 26x37mm	2.40	2.40
e.	A527 $2 multi, 37x26mm	3.25	3.25

Nos. 2048a-2052a sold as a set for $8.70.

The 2005 sheets contain: #2003, 2006, 2007, 2008, 2011, 2012, 2017, 2020, 2021. See note following #1404.

New Year 2006 (Year of the Dog) — A528

Designs: 45c, Labrador retriever. 90c, German shepherd. $1.35, Jack Russell terrier. $1.50, Golden retriever. $2, Huntaway.

Litho. & Embossed

2006, Jan. 4 *Perf. 14*

2054	A528	45c multi	.60	.30

Litho.

2055	A528	90c multi	1.10	1.10
2056	A528	$1.35 multi	1.50	1.50
2057	A528	$1.50 multi	2.00	2.00
2058	A528	$2 multi	2.75	2.75
a.		Souvenir sheet, #2057-2058	5.75	5.75
		Nos. 2054-2058 (5)	7.95	7.65

No. 2058a exists imperf in a limited edition album.

Self-Adhesive

Size: 25x30mm Coil Stamp

Coil Stamp

Die Cut Perf. 12¾

2059	A528	45c multi	.65	.55

Booklet Stamp

Serpentine Die Cut 11x11¼

2060	A528	45c multi	.65	.55
a.		Booklet pane of 10	7.00	

Hawke's Bay Earthquake, 75th Anniv. — A529

No. 2061: a, Napier before the earthquake. b, Aerial view of the devastation (denomination at left). c, Aerial view of the devastation (denomination at right). d, Fire service. e, HMS Veronica. f, HMS Veronica sailors. g, Red Cross. h, Rescue services. i, Devastation. j, Medical services. k, Emergency mail flights. l, Refugees. m, Emergency accommodation. n, Makeshift cooking facilities. o, Community spirit. p, Refugees evacuated by train. q, Building industry. r, A new Art Deco city. s, Celebrations. t, Hawke's Bay region today.

2006, Feb. 3 Litho. *Perf. 14*

2061	A529	Sheet of 20	14.00	14.00
a.-t.		45c Any single	.70	.70
u.		Booklet pane, 2 each #2061a-2061c	4.75	—
v.		Booklet pane, 2 each #2061r-2061t	4.75	—
w.		Booklet pane, 2 each #2061d-2061f	4.75	—
x.		Booklet pane, 2 each #2061g-2061h + 2 labels	3.25	—
y.		Booklet pane, 2 each #2061i, 2061k, 2061p	4.75	—
z.		Booklet pane, 2 each #2061j, 2061l, 2061m	4.75	—
aa.		Booklet pane, 2 each #2061n, 2061o, 2061q	4.75	—
		Complete booklet, #2061u-2061aa	32.50	

Complete booklet sold for $19.95.

Tourist Attractions Type of 2003

Designs: No. 2062, Franz Josef Glacier, West Coast. No. 2063, Halfmoon Bay, Stewart Island. No. 2064, Cathedral Cove, Coromandel. No. 2065, Mount Taranaki. No. 2066, Huka Falls, Taupo. No. 2067, Lake Wanaka.

2006, Mar. 1 *Perf. 13¼x13½*

2062	A496	$1.50 multi	2.00	2.00
2063	A496	$1.50 multi	2.00	2.00
2064	A496	$1.50 multi	2.00	2.00
2065	A496	$1.50 multi	2.00	2.00
2066	A496	$1.50 multi	2.00	2.00
2067	A496	$1.50 multi	2.00	2.00
		Nos. 2062-2067 (6)	12.00	12.00

Queen Elizabeth II, 80th Birthday — A530

Litho. & Embossed with Foil Application

2006, Apr. 21 *Perf. 13½*

2068	A530	$5 dk bl & multi	8.00	8.00
a.		$5 Prussian blue & multi	8.00	8.00
b.		Souvenir sheet, #2068a, Jersey #1215a	27.50	27.50

Printed in sheets of 4.

No. 2068b sold for $17.50. See Jersey No. 1215.

Miniature Sheet

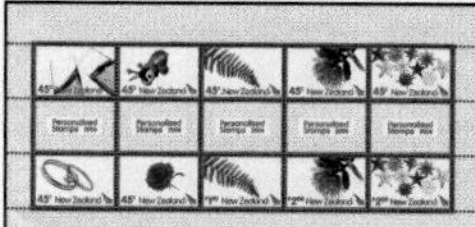

Greetings Stamps — A531

No. 2069: a, Champagne flutes. b, Child's toy. c, Fern. d, Pohutukawa flower. e, Stars. f, Wedding and engagement rings. g, Rose. h, Fern. i, Pohutukawa flower. j, Stars.

2006, May 3 Litho. *Perf. 14*

2069 A531 Sheet of 10 + 5 labels 14.00 14.00
- *a.-g.* 45c Any single .70 .70
- *h.* $1.50 multi 2.40 2.40
- *i.-j.* $2 Either single 3.25 3.25
- *k.* Souvenir sheet, #2069i, 2 #2069h 8.00 8.00
- *l.* Sheet of 20 #2069h + 20 labels 67.50 —
- *m.* Sheet of 20 #2069i + 20 labels 82.50 —
- *n.* Sheet of 20 #2069j + 20 labels 82.50 —

No. 2069k issued 11/16. Belgica'06 World Philatelic Exhibition, Brussels (#2069k).

Nos. 2069l-2069n issued 2007. No. 2069l sold for $44.90; Nos. 2069m and 2069n, each sold for $54.90. Labels could be personalized

A sheet of 20 #2069c + 20 labels depicting New Zealand's America's Cup Emirates Team yacht sold for $19.90. Labels on this sheet could not be personalized.

See Nos. 2138, 2292, 2326-2327, 2412.

Greetings Type of 2005 Redrawn

Souvenir Sheet

No. 2070: a, Like #2031i, without "2005" year date. b, Like #2031j, without "2005" year date.

2006, May 27 Litho. *Perf. 14*

2070 Sheet of 2 + central label 6.50 6.50
- *a.-b.* A522 $2 Either single 3.25 3.25
- *c.* Souvenir sheet, #2070a-2070b 6.75 6.75

Washington 2006 World Philatelic Exhibition.

No. 2070c issued 11/2. Kiwipex 2006 National Stamp Exhibition, Christchurch (#2070c). No. 2070c lacks label, and sold for $5, with the extra $1 going to the NZ Philatelic Foundation.

A set of five gummed stamps, a self-adhesive coil stamp and a self-adhesive booklet stamp depicting Traditional Maori Performing Arts was prepared for release on June 7, 2006 but was withdrawn on June 2. Some mail orders for these stamps were fulfilled and shipped out inadvertantly prior to the June 7 issue date, but apparently no examples were sold over post office counters. Used examples are also known, but there is no evidence of sale of any of these stamps over post office counters.

Renewable Energy — A532

Designs: 45c, Wind farm, Tararua. 90c, Roxburgh Hydroelectric Dam. $1.35, Biogas facility, Waikato. $1.50, Geothermal Power Station, Wairakei. $2, Solar panels on Cape Reinga Lighthouse, vert.

2006, July 5

2071	A532	45c multi	.70	.70
2072	A532	90c multi	1.40	1.40
2073	A532	$1.35 multi	2.10	2.10
2074	A532	$1.50 multi	2.40	2.40
2075	A532	$2 multi	3.25	3.25
		Nos. 2071-2075 (5)	9.85	9.85

Fruits and Vegetables — A533

Slogan "5 + a day," and: 45c+5c, Tomatoes and "5." 90c+10c, Oranges and "+." $1.35, Onions and "a" (30x30mm). $1.50, Kiwi fruit and "Day," horiz. $2, Radicchio and hand.

2006, Aug. 2 Litho. *Perf. 14*

2076	A533	45c +5c multi	.70	.70
2077	A533	90c +10c multi	1.40	1.40
2078	A533	$1.35 multi	2.10	2.10
2079	A533	$1.50 multi	2.40	2.40
2080	A533	$2 multi	3.25	3.25
a.		Souvenir sheet, #2076-2080	10.00	10.00
		Nos. 2076-2080 (5)	9.85	9.85

Self-Adhesive

Size: 24x29mm

Serpentine Die Cut 9¾x10

2081 A533 45c +5c multi .70 .70

New Zealand Gold Rush — A534

Designs: 45c, Gold panner, c. 1880. 90c, Miners, Kuranui Creek, c. 1868, horiz. $1.35, Chinese miners, Tuapeka, c. 1900, horiz. $1.50, Gold escort coach, Roxburgh, 1901, horiz. $2, Dunedin harbor, c. 1900, horiz.

2006, Sept. 9 *Perf. 14*

2082	A534	45c multi	.70	.70
2083	A534	90c multi	1.40	1.40
2084	A534	$1.35 multi	2.10	2.10
2085	A534	$1.50 multi	2.40	2.40
2086	A534	$2 multi	3.25	3.25
		Nos. 2082-2086 (5)	9.85	9.85

Souvenir Sheet

Litho. With Foil Application

2087 Sheet of 5 10.00 10.00
- *a.* A534 45c gold & multi .70 .70
- *b.* A534 90c gold & multi 1.40 1.40
- *c.* A534 $1.35 gold & multi 2.10 2.10
- *d.* A534 $1.50 gold & multi 2.40 2.40
- *e.* A534 $2 gold & multi 3.25 3.25

Portions of the design of Nos. 2082 and 2087a are printed with a thermochromic ink that changes color when warmed that is applied by a thermographic process producing a shiny, raised effect.

No. 2087 exists imperf in a limited edition album.

Christmas — A535

Children's art by: Nos. 2088, 2098, Hanna McLachlan. No. 2089, Isla Hewitt. No. 2090, Caitlin Davidson. No. 2091, Maria Petersen. No. 2092, Deborah Yoon. No. 2093, Hannah Webster. 90c, Pierce Higginson. $1.35, Rosa Tucker. $1.50, Sylvie Webby. $2, Gemma Baldock.

2006, Oct. 4 Litho. *Perf. 14¼*

2088	A535	45c multi	.70	.70
2089	A535	45c multi	.70	.70
2090	A535	45c multi	.70	.70
2091	A535	45c multi	.70	.70
2092	A535	45c multi	.70	.70
2093	A535	45c multi	.70	.70
a.		Miniature sheet, #2088-2093	4.25	4.25
b.		Horiz. strip of 5, #2089-2093	3.50	3.50
2094	A535	90c multi	1.40	1.40
2095	A535	$1.35 multi	2.10	2.10
2096	A535	$1.50 multi	2.40	2.40
2097	A535	$2 multi	3.25	3.25
		Nos. 2088-2097 (10)	13.35	13.35

Self-Adhesive

Size: 21x26mm

Serpentine Die Cut 9¾x10

2098	A535	45c multi	.70	.70
a.		Booklet pane of 10	7.00	
2099	A535	$1.50 multi	2.40	2.40
a.		Horiz. pair, #2098-2099	3.00	
b.		Booklet pane of 10	24.00	

No. 2099b sold for $13.50.

Summer Festivals — A536

Designs: 45c, Dragon boat racing. 90c, Race day. $1.35, Teddy Bears' Picnic. $1.50, Outdoor concerts. $2, Jazz festivals.

2006, Nov. 1 *Perf. 14¼*

2100	A536	45c multi	.70	.70
2101	A536	90c multi	1.40	1.40
2102	A536	$1.35 multi	2.10	2.10
2103	A536	$1.50 multi	2.40	2.40
2104	A536	$2 multi	3.25	3.25
a.		Horiz. strip of 5, #2100-2104	10.00	10.00
b.		Miniature sheet, #2104a	10.00	10.00
		Nos. 2100-2104 (5)	9.85	9.85

The 2006 sheets contain: #2058, 2061e, 2066, 2069i, 2075, 2080, 2086, 2097, 2104. See note following #1404.

Scott Base, Antarctica, 50th Anniv. — A537

Designs: 45c, Opening ceremony, 1957. 90c, Scott Base, 1990. $1.35, Aerial view, 2000. $1.50, Sign, 2003-04. $2, Aerial view, 2005.

2007, Jan. 20 *Perf. 14¼x14*

2105	A537	45c multi	.70	.70
a.		Souvenir sheet of 1	1.00	1.00
2106	A537	90c multi	1.40	1.40
a.		Souvenir sheet of 1	1.90	1.90
2107	A537	$1.35 multi	2.10	2.10
a.		Souvenir sheet of 1	2.75	2.75
2108	A537	$1.50 multi	2.40	2.40
a.		Souvenir sheet of 1	3.50	3.50
2109	A537	$2 multi	3.25	3.25
a.		Souvenir sheet of 1	4.50	4.50
		Nos. 2105-2109 (5)	9.85	9.85

Nos. 2105a-2109a sold as a set for $8.70. The souvenir sheets exist overprinted in a limited edition album.

New Year 2007 (Year of the Pig) — A538

Pig breeds: 45c, Kunekune. 90c, Kunekune, diff. $1.35, Arapawa. $1.50, Auckland Island. $2, Kunekune, diff.

2007, Feb. 7 *Perf. 14½x14*

2110	A538	45c multi	.70	.70
2111	A538	90c multi	1.40	1.40
2112	A538	$1.35 multi	2.10	2.10
2113	A538	$1.50 multi	2.40	2.40
2114	A538	$2 multi	3.25	3.25
a.		Souvenir sheet, #2113-2114	5.75	5.75

Nos. 2111-2112 exist in a souvenir sheet in a limited edition album.

Indigenous Animals — A539

Designs: 45c, Tuatara. 90c, Kiwi. $1.35, Hamilton's frog. $1.50, Yellow-eyed penguin. $2, Hector's dolphin.

Serpentine Die Cut

2007, Mar. 7 Litho.

Self-Adhesive

2115	A539	45c multi	.65	.65
2116	A539	90c multi	1.25	1.25
2117	A539	$1.35 multi	1.90	1.90
2118	A539	$1.50 multi	2.10	2.10
2119	A539	$2 multi	2.75	2.75
a.		Horiz. strip of 5, #2115-2119	8.65	

Greetings Type of 2005 Redrawn

Souvenir Sheet

2007, Mar. 30 Litho. *Perf. 14*

2120 Sheet , #2075, 2120a 6.00 6.00
- *a.* A531 $2 Like #2069i, without "2006" year date 3.00 3.00

Northland 2007 National Stamp Exhibition, Whangarei.

Centenaries A540

Designs: No. 2121, Scouts and Lieutenant Colonel David Cossgrove, founder of scouting movement in New Zealand. No. 2122, Infant, nurse, Dr. Frederic Truby King, founder of Plunket Society. No. 2123, Rugby players, Hercules "Bumper" Wright, first team captain. No. 2124, Sister of Compassion teaching children, Suzanne Aubert, founder of Sisters of Compassion. $1, Plunket Society emblem, family. $1.50, Sisters of Compassion emblem, women reading book. No. 2127, New Zealand Rugby League emblem, rugby players. No. 2128, Scouting emblem, scouts.

2007, Apr. 24 *Perf. 14*

2121	A540	50c multi	.75	.75
2122	A540	50c multi	.75	.75
2123	A540	50c multi	.75	.75
2124	A540	50c multi	.75	.75
a.		Horiz. strip of 4, #2121-2124	4.00	4.00
2125	A540	$1 multi	1.50	1.50
2126	A540	$1.50 multi	2.25	2.25
2127	A540	$2 multi	3.00	3.00
2128	A540	$2 multi	3.00	3.00
a.		Block of 8, #2121-2128	12.75	12.75
b.		Horiz. pair, #2127-2128	9.00	9.00

Tourist Attractions Type of 2003

Designs: 5c, Whakarewarewa geothermal area. 10c, Central Otago. 20c, Rainbow Falls, Northland. 50c, Lake Coleridge. $1, Rangitoto Island. $2.50, Abel Tasman National Park. $3, Tongaporutu, Taranaki.

2007, May 9 *Perf. 13¼x13½*

2129	A496	5c multi	.25	.25
2130	A496	10c multi	.25	.25
2131	A496	20c multi	.30	.30
2132	A496	50c multi	.75	.75
2133	A496	$1 multi	1.50	1.50
2134	A496	$2.50 multi	3.75	3.75
2135	A496	$3 multi	4.50	4.50
		Nos. 2129-2135 (7)	11.30	11.30

Self-Adhesive

Serpentine Die Cut 10x9½

2136	A496	50c multi	.75	.75
a.		Booklet pane of 10	7.50	
2137	A496	$1 multi	1.50	1.50
a.		Horiz. pair, #2136-2137	2.25	2.25
b.		Booklet pane of 10	15.00	

Greetings Type of 2006 Redrawn

No. 2138: a, Child's toy. b, Pohutukawa flower. c, Wedding and engagement rings. d, Fern. e, Champagne flutes. f, Rose. g, Stars.

2007, May 9 *Perf. 14*

2138 A531 Sheet of 7 + 8 labels 5.25 5.25
- *a.-g.* 50c Any single .75 .75
- *h.* Sheet of 20 #2138a + 20 labels 32.50 —
- *i.* Sheet of 20 #2138b + 20 labels 32.50 —
- *j.* Sheet of 20 #2138c + 20 labels 32.50 —
- *k.* Sheet of 20 #2138d + 20 labels 32.50 —
- *l.* Sheet of 20 #2138e + 20 labels 32.50 —
- *m.* Sheet of 20 #2138f + 20 labels 32.50 —
- *n.* Sheet of 20 #2138g + 20 labels 32.50 —

Nos. 2138h-2138n each sold for $20.90.

Southern Skies and Observatories A541

Designs: 50c, Southern Cross, Stardome Observatory. $1, Pleiades, McLellan Mt. John Observatory. $1.50, Trifid Nebula, Ward Observatory. $2, Southern Pinwheel, MOA telescope, Mt. John Observatory. $2.50, Large Magellanic Cloud, Southern African Large Telescope.

2007, June 6 *Perf. 13x13¼*

2139	A541	50c multi	.80	.80
a.		Perf. 14	1.00	1.00
b.		Booklet pane of 1 #2139a	1.00	—
2140	A541	$1 multi	1.60	1.60
a.		Perf. 14	2.00	2.00
b.		Booklet pane of 1 #2140a	2.00	—
2141	A541	$1.50 multi	2.40	2.40
a.		Perf. 14	3.00	3.00
b.		Booklet pane of 1 #2141a	3.00	—
2142	A541	$2 multi	3.00	3.00
a.		Perf. 14	4.25	4.25
b.		Booklet pane of 1 #2142a	4.25	—
2143	A541	$2.50 multi	3.75	3.75
a.		Perf. 14	5.25	5.25
b.		Booklet pane of 1 #2143a	5.25	—

c. Booklet pane of 5, #2139a-2143a 15.50 —
Complete booklet, #2139b, 2140b, 2141b, 2142b, 2143b, 2143c 31.00
d. Souvenir sheet, #2142a, 2143a 6.75 6.75
Nos. 2139-2143 (5) 11.55 11.55

No. 2143d issued 8/31. Huttpex 2007 Stampshow (#2143d).

Miniature Sheet

New Zealand Slang A542

No. 2144 — Designs: a, "Good as gold," gold nugget. b, "Sweet as," kiwi fruit. c, "She'll be right," hand with thumb up. d, "Hissy fit," insect. e, "Sparrow fart," sun in sky. f, "Cuz," kiwi bird. g, "Away laughing," sandals. h, "Tiki tour," road sign. i, "Away with the fairies," cookies. j, "Wop-wops," house. k, "Hard yakka," shirt. l, "Cods wollop," fish. m, "Boots and all," rugby ball and athletic shoes. n, "Shark and taties," fish and chips. o, "Knackered," boots. p, "Laughing gear," mug. q, "Everyman and his dog," dog. r, "Bit of a dag," sheep. s, "Dreaded lurgy," box of tissues. t, "Rark up," hand pointing.

2007, July 4 ***Perf. 14***
2144 A542 Sheet of 20 16.00 16.00
a.-t. 50c Any single .80 .80

Portions of the design were covered with a thermographic ink that allowed printing below (definitinons of the slang phrases) to appear when the ink was warmed.

Technical Innovations by New Zealanders A543

Designs: 50c, Gallagher electric fence. $1, Spreadable butter. $1.50, Mountain buggy. $2, Hamilton jet boat. $2.50, Tranquilizer gun.

2007, Aug. 1
2145 A543 50c multi .75 .75
2146 A543 $1 multi 1.50 1.50
2147 A543 $1.50 multi 2.25 2.25
2148 A543 $2 multi 3.00 3.00
2149 A543 $2.50 multi 3.75 3.75
Nos. 2145-2149 (5) 11.25 11.25

Nos. 2145-2149 exist in a souvenir sheet in a limited edition album.

Wedding of Queen Elizabeth II and Prince Philip, 60th Anniv. — A544

Queen and Prince: 50c, In 2007. $2, On wedding day, 1947.

2007, Sept. 5 **Litho.** ***Perf. 14***
2150 A544 50c multi .70 .70
2151 A544 $2 multi 2.75 2.75
a. Souvenir sheet, #2150-2151 3.50 3.50

Christmas — A545

Children's art by: 50c, Sione Vao. $1, Reece Cateley. $1.50, Emily Wang. $2, Alexandra Eathorne. $2.50, Jake Hooper.

2007, Oct. 3 ***Perf. 14¼***
2152 A545 50c multi .80 .80
2153 A545 $1 multi 1.50 1.50
2154 A545 $1.50 multi 2.40 2.40
2155 A545 $2 multi 3.00 3.00
2156 A545 $2.50 multi 4.00 4.00
Nos. 2152-2156 (5) 11.70 11.70

Size: 25x30mm

Self-Adhesive

Coil Stamps

Die Cut Perf. 13x12¾

2157 A545 50c multi .80 .80
2158 A545 $1.50 multi 2.40 2.40
a. Horiz. pair, #2157-2158 3.25

Booklet Stamps

Serpentine Die Cut 11x11¼

2159 A545 50c multi .80 .80
a. Booklet pane of 10 8.00
2160 A545 $1.50 multi 2.10 2.10
a. Booklet pane of 10 21.00

No. 2160a sold for $13.50.

Miniature Sheet

Greetings Stamps — A546

No. 2161: a, "Go You Good Thing." b, "Look Who It Is." c, "Love Always." d, "Thanks a Million." e, "We've Got News." f, "Wish You Were Here." g, "Time to Celebrate." h, "Kia Ora." i, "You Gotta Love Christmas." j, Chinese characters.

2007, Nov. 7 ***Perf. 14***
2161 A546 Sheet of 10 + 5 labels 13.00 13.00
a.-f. 50c Any single .75 .75
g.-h. $1 Either single 1.50 1.50
i. $1.50 multi 2.40 2.40
j. $2 multi 3.00 3.00
k. Sheet of 20 #2161c + 20 labels 32.50 —
l. Sheet of 20 #2161d + 20 labels 32.50 —
m. Sheet of 20 #2161e + 20 labels 32.50 —
n. Sheet of 20 #2161f + 20 labels 32.50 —
o. Sheet of 20 #2161g + 20 labels 47.50 —
p. Sheet of 20 #2161h + 20 labels 47.50 —
q. Sheet of 20 #2161i + 20 labels 70.00 —
r. Sheet of 20 #2161j + 20 labels 85.00 —
s. As #2161h, perf 13¼x13½ (2224b) 1.25 1.25
t. As #2161j, perf 13¼x13½ (2224b) 2.40 2.40

Nos. 2161k-2161n each sold for $20.90; Nos. 2161o-2161p, for $30.90; No. 2161q, for $44.90; No. 2161r, for $54.90. Labels were personalizable on Nos. 2161k-2161r. Issued: Nos. 2161s, 2161t, 4/1/09.

The 2007 sheets contain: #2114, 2109, 2142; #2127, 2128, 2148; #2155, 2151, 2161j. See note following #1404.

Reefs — A547

Marine life from: 50c, Dusky Sound, Fiordland. $1, Mayor Island, Bay of Plenty. $1.50, Fiordland. $2, Volkner Rocks, White Island, Bay of Plenty.

2008, Jan. 9 **Litho.** ***Perf. 13x13¼***
2162 A547 50c multi .80 .80
2163 A547 $1 multi 1.60 1.60
2164 A547 $1.50 multi 2.40 2.40
2165 A547 $2 multi 3.25 3.25
a. Souvenir sheet, #2162-2165 8.25 8.25
Nos. 2162-2165 (4) 8.05 8.05

Self-Adhesive

Size: 26x21mm

Serpentine Die Cut 11¼

2166 A547 50c multi .80 .80
a. Booklet pane of 10 8.00
2167 A547 $1 multi 1.60 1.60
a. Horiz. pair, #2166-2167 2.40
b. Booklet pane of 10 #2167 16.00

Pocket Pets — A548

2008, Feb. 7 ***Perf. 14***
2168 A548 50c Rabbits .80 .80
2169 A548 $1 Guinea pigs 1.60 1.60
2170 A548 $1.50 Rats 2.40 2.40
2171 A548 $2 Mice 3.25 3.25
a. Souvenir sheet, #2170-2171 5.75 5.75
b. As #2171, perf. 13½x13¼ 3.25 3.25
c. Souvenir sheet, #2161j, 2171b 6.50 6.50

New Year 2008 (Year of the Rat), No. 2171a.
Nos. 2171b, 2171c issued 3/7. Taipei 2008 International Stamp Exhibition (#2171c).

Weather Extremes — A549

Designs: No. 2172, Drought, Gisborne, 1998. No. 2173, Wind, Auckland, 2007. $1, Storm, Wellington, 2001. $1.50, Flooding, Hikurangi, 2007. $2, Snow storm, Southland, 2001. $2.50, Heat, Matarangi, 2005.

2008, Mar. 5 **Litho.** ***Perf. 14***
2172 A549 50c multi .80 .80
2173 A549 50c multi .80 .80
2174 A549 $1 multi 1.60 1.60
2175 A549 $1.50 multi 2.40 2.40
2176 A549 $2 multi 3.25 3.25
2177 A549 $2.50 multi 4.00 4.00
Nos. 2172-2177 (6) 12.85 12.85

Nos. 2172-2177 exist in a souvenir sheet in a limited edition album.

Australian and New Zealand Army Corps (ANZAC) — A550

Designs: No. 2178, Dawn Parade. No. 2179, Soldiers at Gallipoli, 1915. $1, Soldiers at Western Front, 1916-18. $1.50, Chalk kiwi made by soldiers, England, 1919. $2, Soldier's Haka dance, Egypt, 1941. $2.50, Soldiers in Viet Nam, 1965-71.

2008, Apr. 2
2178 A550 50c multi .80 .80
a. Booklet pane of 1 1.00 —
2179 A550 50c multi .80 .80
a. Booklet pane of 1 1.00 —
2180 A550 $1 multi 1.60 1.60
a. Booklet pane of 1 2.00 —
2181 A550 $1.50 multi 2.40 2.40
a. Booklet pane of 1 3.00 —
b. Souvenir sheet, #2179-2181 3.50 3.50
2182 A550 $2 multi 3.25 3.25
a. Booklet pane of 1 4.00 —
2183 A550 $2.50 multi 4.00 4.00
a. Booklet pane of 1 5.00 —
b. Booklet pane of 6, #2178-2183 16.00 —
Complete booklet, #2178a, 2179a, 2180a, 2181a, 2182a, 2183a, 2183b 32.00
Nos. 2178-2183 (6) 12.85 12.85

No. 2181b issued 10/20. End of World War I, 90th anniv. (#2181b).

Maori King Movement, 150th Anniv. — A551

Various unnamed artworks by Fred Graham and English text: 50c, "There is but one eye of the needle. . ." $1.50, "Taupiri is the mountain. . ." $2.50, "After I am gone. . .," horiz.

2008, May 2 **Litho.** ***Perf. 14***
2184 A551 50c multi .80 .80
2185 A551 $1.50 multi 2.40 2.40
2186 A551 $2.50 multi 4.00 4.00
Nos. 2184-2186 (3) 7.20 7.20

Premiere of Film, *The Chronicles of Narnia: Prince Caspian* A552

Designs: 50c, The Pevensie children. $1, Queen Susan. $1.50, High King Peter. $2, Prince Caspian.

2008, May 7 ***Perf. 14½x14***
2187 A552 50c multi .80 .80
a. Souvenir sheet of 1 1.10 1.10
2188 A552 $1 multi 1.60 1.60
a. Souvenir sheet of 1 2.25 2.25
2189 A552 $1.50 multi 2.40 2.40
a. Souvenir sheet of 1 3.25 3.25
2190 A552 $2 multi 3.25 3.25
a. Souvenir sheet of 1 4.50 4.50
Nos. 2187-2190 (4) 8.05 8.05

Nos. 2187a-2190a were sold as a set for $7.

Matariki (Maori New Year) — A553

Inscriptions: No. 2191, Ranginui. No. 2192, Te Moana nui a Kiwa. $1, Papatuanuku. $1.50, Whakapapa. $2, Takoha. $2.50, Te Tau Hou.

2008, June 5 **Litho.** ***Perf. 14***
2191 A553 50c multi .80 .80
2192 A553 50c multi .80 .80
2193 A553 $1 multi 1.60 1.60
2194 A553 $1.50 multi 2.40 2.40
2195 A553 $2 multi 3.25 3.25
a. Souvenir sheet, #2192, 2194, 2195 6.50 6.50
2196 A553 $2.50 multi 4.00 4.00
a. Miniature sheet, #2191-2196, perf. 13½x13¼ 13.00 13.00
Nos. 2191-2196 (6) 12.85 12.85

No. 2195a issued 9/18. Vienna Intl. Postage Stamp Exhibition (#2195a).
No. 2196a exists as an imperf miniature sheet from a limited edition album.

2008 Summer Olympics, Beijing A554

2008, July 2 ***Perf. 14¼***
2197 A554 50c Rowing .80 .80
2198 A554 50c Cycling .80 .80
2199 A554 $1 Kayaking 1.60 1.60
2200 A554 $2 Running 3.00 3.00
Nos. 2197-2200 (4) 6.20 6.20

Compare with Type SP82.

Miniature Sheet

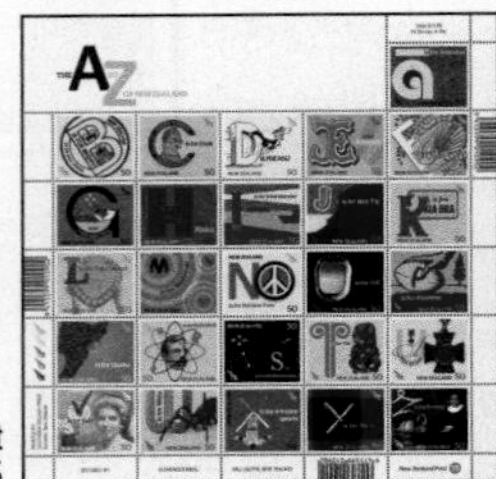

Alphabet A555

No. 2201 — Inscriptions: a, A is for Aotearoa (Maori name for New Zealand). b, B is for Beehive (Parliament Building). c, C is for Cook (Capt. James Cook). d, D is for Dog (comic strip character). e, E is for Edmonds (Thomas J. Edmonds, cookbook producer). f, F is for Fantail (bird). g, G is for Goodnight Kiwi (cartoon). h, H is for Haka (Maori dance). i, I is for Interislander (ferry). j, J is for Jelly tip (ice cream bar). k, K is for Kia ora. l, L is for Log O'Wood (rugby trophy). m, M is for Mudpools. n, N is for Nuclear free. o, O is for O.E. (overseas experience). p, P is for Pinetree (Colin "Pinetree" Meads, rugby player). q, Q is for Quake. r, R is for Rutherford (Sir Ernest Rutherford, chemist and physicist). s, S is for Southern Cross (constellation). t, T is for Tiki (rock carving). u, U is for Upham (Capt. Charles Upham, war hero). v, V is for Vote. w,

W is for Weta (insect). x, X is for X-treme sports. y, Y is for Yarn. z, Z is for Zeeland (Dutch province for which New Zealand was named).

2008, Aug. 6 ***Perf. 14¼***
2201 A555 Sheet of 26 18.50 18.50
a.-z. 50c Any single .70 .70

North Island Main Trunk Line, Cent. — A556

Designs: 50c, Last spike ceremony, Manganui-o-te-Ao, 1908. $1, Locomotive at Taumarunui Station, 1958. $1.50, Train on Makatote Viaduct, 1963. $2, Train on Raurimi Spiral, 1964. $2.50, Train on Hapuawhenua Viaduct, 2003.

2008, Sept. 3 **Litho.** ***Perf. 14***
2202 A556 50c multi .70 .70
2203 A556 $1 multi 1.40 1.40
2204 A556 $1.50 multi 2.00 2.00
2205 A556 $2 multi 2.75 2.75
2206 A556 $2.50 multi 3.50 3.50
Nos. 2202-2206 (5) 10.35 10.35

Christmas — A557

Winning art in children's stamp design competition: 50c, Sheep With Stocking Cap, by Kirsten Fisher-Marsters. $2, Pohutukawa and Koru, by Tamara Jenkin. $2.50, Kiwi and Pohutukawa, by Molly Bruhns.

2008, Oct. 1 ***Perf. 14¼***
2207 A557 50c multi .70 .70
2208 A557 $2 multi 2.75 2.75
2209 A557 $2.50 multi 3.25 3.25
Nos. 2207-2209 (3) 6.70 6.70

Christmas — A558

Designs: 50c, Nativity. $1, Holy Family. $1.50, Madonna and Child.

2008, Oct. 1 ***Perf. 14¼***
2210 A558 50c multi .70 .70
2211 A558 $1 multi 1.40 1.40
2212 A558 $1.50 multi 2.00 2.00
Nos. 2210-2212 (3) 4.10 4.10

Size: 21x26mm
Self-Adhesive
Coil Stamps
Die Cut Perf. 12¾

2213 A558 50c multi .70 .70
2214 A558 $1.50 multi 2.00 2.00
a. Horiz. pair, #2213-2214 2.75

Booklet Stamps
Serpentine Die Cut 11¼

2215 A558 50c multi .70 .70
a. Booklet pane of 10 7.00
2216 A558 $1.50 multi 2.00 2.00
a. Booklet pane of 10 20.00
Nos. 2213-2216 (4) 5.40 5.40

Sir Edmund Hillary (1919-2008), Mountaineer — A559

New Zealand flag and: 50c, Hillary. $1, Hillary and Tenzing Norgay on Mt. Everest, 1953. $1.50, Hillary on Trans-Antarctic Expedition, 1958. $2, Hillary with Nepalese people, 1964. $2.50, Hillary at Order of the Garter ceremony, 1995.

2008, Nov. 5 **Litho.** ***Perf. 14¾***
2217 A559 50c multi .60 .60
a. Perf. 14 .75 .75
2218 A559 $1 multi 1.25 1.25
a. Perf. 14 1.50 1.50
2219 A559 $1.50 multi 1.75 1.75
2220 A559 $2 multi 2.40 2.40
2221 A559 $2.50 multi 3.00 3.00
a. Perf. 14 3.75 3.75
b. Souvenir sheet, #2217a, 2218a, 2221a, + specimen of #1084 6.00 6.00
Nos. 2217-2221 (5) 9.00 9.00

Timpex 2009 National Stamp Exhibition, Timaru (Nos. 2217a, 2218a, 2221a-b); Issued 10/16/09.

Tourist Attractions Type of 2003
Souvenir Sheet

No. 2222: a, Like #2065, without year date. b, Like #2135, without year date.

2008, Nov. 7 ***Perf. 13¼x13½***
2222 Sheet of 2 5.50 5.50
a. A496 $1.50 multi 1.75 1.75
b. A496 $3 multi 3.75 3.75

Tarapex 2008 Philatelic Exhibition, New Plymouth.

The 2008 sheets contain: #2165, 2171, 2177; #2183, 2186, 2196; #2206, 2212, 2221. See note following #1404.

New Year 2009 (Year of the Ox) — A560

Designs: 50c, Chinese character for "ox." $1, Ox. $2, Chinese lanterns and Auckland Harbor Bridge.

2009, Jan. 7 ***Perf. 13¼x13***
2223 A560 50c multi .60 .60
2224 A560 $1 multi 1.25 1.25
a. Perf. 13¼x13½ 1.25 1.25
b. Souvenir sheet, #2161s, 2161t, 2224a 5.00 5.00
2225 A560 $2 multi 2.40 2.40
a. Souvenir sheet, #2223-2225 4.25 4.25
Nos. 2223-2225 (3) 4.25 4.25

China 2009 World Stamp Exhibition, Luoyand (#2224b). Issued: Nos. 2224a, 2224b, 4/1.

Lighthouses A561

Designs: 50c, Pencarrow Lighthouse. $1, Dog Island Lighthouse. $1.50, Cape Brett Lighthouse. $2, Cape Egmont Lighthouse. $2.50, Cape Reinga Lighthouse.

2009, Jan. 7 ***Perf. 13x13¼***
2226 A561 50c multi .60 .60
2227 A561 $1 multi 1.25 1.25
2228 A561 $1.50 multi 1.75 1.75
2229 A561 $2 multi 2.40 2.40
2230 A561 $2.50 multi 3.00 3.00
Nos. 2226-2230 (5) 9.00 9.00

Motor Sports Champions A562

Designs: 50c, Scott Dixon. $1, Bruce McLaren. $1.50, Ivan Mauger. $2, Denny Hulme. $2.50, Hugh Anderson.

2009, Feb. 4 **Litho.** ***Perf. 14***
2231 A562 50c multi .50 .50
2232 A562 $1 multi 1.00 1.00
2233 A562 $1.50 multi 1.50 1.50
2234 A562 $2 multi 2.10 2.10
2235 A562 $2.50 multi 2.60 2.60
a. Sheet, #2231-2235 7.75 7.75
Nos. 2231-2235 (5) 7.70 7.70

Self-Adhesive
Size: 26x21mm
Serpentine Die Cut 10x9¾

2236 A562 50c multi .50 .50
a. Booklet pane of 10 5.00
2237 A562 $1 multi 1.00 1.00
a. Booklet pane of 10 10.00
b. Horiz. pair, #2236-2237 1.50

Tourist Attractions Type of 2003

2009, Mar. 4 **Litho.** ***Perf. 13¼x13½***
2238 Sheet of 2 #2238a 3.00 3.00
a. A496 $1.50 Like #2062, without year date 1.50 1.50

Intl. Polar Year.

Giants of New Zealand A563

Designs: 50c, Giant moa. $1, Colossal squid. $1.50 Southern right whale. $2, Giant eagle. $2.50, Giant weta.

2009, Mar. 4 ***Perf. 14½***
2239 A563 50c multi .75 .75
2240 A563 $1 multi 1.50 1.50
2241 A563 $1.50 multi 2.00 2.00
2242 A563 $2 multi 2.50 2.50
2243 A563 $2.50 multi 3.00 3.00
a. Miniature sheet, #2239-2243 8.00 8.00
Nos. 2239-2243 (5) 9.75 9.75

Australian and New Zealand Army Corps (ANZAC) — A564

Poppy and: No. 2244, Funeral procession of the Unknown Warrior. No. 2245, New Zealand Maori Pioneer Battalion, World War I. $1, New Zealand No. 75 Squadron of the Royal Air Force, World War II. $1.50, HMS Achilles, World War II. $2, Kayforce soldiers, Korean War. $2.50, ANZAC Battalion, Vietnam War.

2009, Apr. 1 **Litho.** ***Perf. 13½x13¼***
2244 A564 50c multi .60 .60
a. Perf. 14 .70 .70
b. Booklet pane of 1 #2244a .70 —
2245 A564 50c multi .60 .60
a. Perf. 14 .70 .70
b. Booklet pane of 1 #2245a .70 —
2246 A564 $1 multi 1.25 1.25
a. Perf. 14 1.50 1.50
b. Booklet pane of 1 #2246a 1.50 —
2247 A564 $1.50 multi 1.75 1.75
a. Perf. 14 2.25 2.25
b. Booklet pane of 1 #2247a 2.25 —
2248 A564 $2 multi 2.40 2.40
a. Perf. 14 3.00 3.00
b. Booklet pane of 1 #2248a 3.00 —
2249 A564 $2.50 multi 3.00 3.00
a. Perf. 14 3.75 3.75
b. Booklet pane of 1 #2249a 3.75 —
c. Booklet pane of 6, #2244a, 2245a, 2246a, 2247a, 2248a, 2249a 12.00 —
Complete booklet, #2244b, 2245b, 2246b, 2247b, 2248b, 2249b, 2249c 24.00
Nos. 2244-2249 (6) 9.60 9.60

Complete booklet sold for $19.90.

Auckland Harbour Bridge, 50th Anniv. — A565

Various views of bridge with inscription: 50c, Opening Day 1959. $1, Our Bridge 2009. $1.50, Our Icon 1961. $2, Our Link 2009.

2009, May 1 ***Perf. 13½x13¼***
2250 A565 50c multi .60 .60
2251 A565 $1 multi 1.25 1.25
2252 A565 $1.50 multi 1.75 1.75
2253 A565 $2 multi 2.25 2.25
Nos. 2250-2253 (4) 5.85 5.85

Self-Adhesive
Serpentine Die Cut 9½x10

2254 A565 50c multi .60 .60

Miniature Sheets

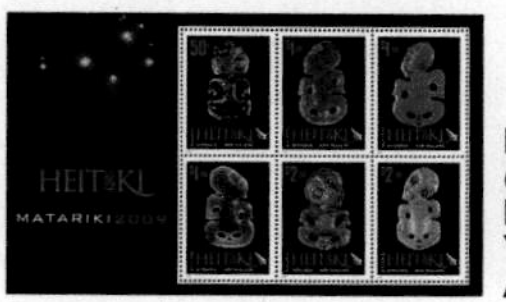

Matariki (Maori New Year) A566

Nos. 2255 and 2256 — Various heitikis: a, Heitiki in Te Maori Exhibition. b, Heitiki carved by Raponi. c, Corian heitiki carved by Rangi Kipa. d, Female greenstone heitiki. e, Heitiki in Museum of New Zealand. f, Whalebone heitiki carved by Rangi Hetet.

Perf. 13¼x13½

2009, June 24 **Litho.**
2255 A566 Sheet of 6 11.50 11.50
a. 50c multi .60 .60
b. $1 multi 1.25 1.25
c. $1.50 multi 1.90 1.90
d. $1.80 multi 2.25 2.25
e. $2 multi 2.50 2.50
f. $2.30 multi 3.00 3.00

Self-Adhesive
Serpentine Die Cut 10x9½

2256 A566 Sheet of 6 11.50 11.50
a. 50c multi .60 .60
b. $1 multi 1.25 1.25
c. $1.50 multi 1.90 1.90
d. $1.80 multi 2.25 2.25
e. $2 multi 2.50 2.50
f. $2.30 multi 3.00 3.00

Tourist Attractions Type of 2003

Designs: 30c, Tolaga Bay. $1.80, Russell. $2.30, Lake Wanaka. $2.80, Auckland. $3.30, Rakaia River. $4, Wellington.

2009, July 1 ***Perf. 13¼x13½***
2257 A496 30c multi .40 .40
2258 A496 $1.80 multi 2.25 2.25
2259 A496 $2.30 multi 3.00 3.00
2260 A496 $2.80 multi 3.50 3.50
2261 A496 $3.30 multi 4.25 4.25
2262 A496 $4 multi 5.00 5.00
Nos. 2257-2262 (6) 18.40 18.40

Self-Adhesive
Serpentine Die Cut 10x9½

2263 A496 $1.80 multi 2.25 2.25
a. Booklet pane of 5 11.50

Miniature Sheet

Tiki Tour of New Zealand A567

No. 2264 — Parts of map of New Zealand and: a, Signpost and lighthouse, Cape Reinga, fisherman and red snapper, Tane Mahuta, quill pen, Stone Store, Kerikeri. b, Bird, boat on Hole in the Rock tour, dolphin. c, White heron, Maori snaring the Sun. d, Bird, airplane, yachts. e, Rangitoto Island volcano, Sky tower, Auckland, L&P Bottle, Paeroa, bird, surf boat, hibiscus, car and trailer. f, Fishing boat and marlin. g, Balloons, Maori canoe, bull playing rugby. h, Balloon, rower, statue of sheep shearer, Te Kuiti, trout, kiwifruit, Maori carving, Rotorua Mud Pools. i, Pohutukawa tree blossom, meeting house, surfer, horse and rider. j, Maui gas rig, Mt. Taranaki, hang glider, Wind Wand sculpture. k, Rubber boot, apple, pear, windmills, Waimarie River cruise boat, highway sign, Viking helmet, giant kiwi. l, Tractor and wagon, gannet, Pania of the Reef, Napier. m, Westport Municipal Building, statue, Greymouth, Pancake Rocks, Punakaiki. n, Mussel, fisherman, grapes, glass blowers and bottle. o, Birds, statue of Richard Seddon, daffodil, windsurfer, Cook Strait ferry, Golden Shears, Masterton, Westpac Stadium, Wellington. p, Mount Cook lily, bulldozer lifting coal, statue of Mackenzie sheep dog, Lake Tekapo. q, Red deer, punt on Avon River, trailer for selling crayfish, French flags, Chalice, sculpture by Neil Dawson, Christchurch. r, Birds, boat, whale, fish. s, Crayfish, black robin, fishing boat. t, Kayakers, skier, mountains, jetboat on Shotover River. u, Kea, biplane, clams, Museum, Oamaru, clock, Alexandra. v, Kakapo, Museum, Invercargill, Burt Munro motorcycle, musician at Country and Western Festival, Gore. w, Moeraki Boulders, Larnach Castle, Dunedin, curler, seal. x, Stewart Island shag, blue cod, Chain sculpture, Oban.

2009, Aug. 5 ***Perf. 14¼***
2264 A567 Sheet of 24 + label 16.00 16.00
a.-x. 50c Any single .65 .65

Kiwistamps — A568

Designs: No. 2265, Cricket ball, bails and wickets. No. 2266, Kiwi fruit. No. 2267, Highway route sign. No. 2268, Wind turbine and man with broken umbrella. No. 2269, Rotary lawn mower. No. 2270, Trailer. No. 2271, Wall decorations (three birds). No. 2272, Fish and chips. No. 2273, Jacket on barbed-wire fence. No. 2274, Hot dog and barbecue.

Serpentine Die Cut 9¾x10

2009, Sept. 7 Litho.

Self-Adhesive

2265 A568 (50c) multi .75 .75
a. Serpentine die cut 11x11¼ .75 .75
b. As "a," with silver text .75 .75
c. Serpentine die cut 10x9¾ .75 .75
d. As "c," with silver text .75 .75
2266 A568 (50c) multi .75 .75
a. Serpentine die cut 11x11¼ .75 .75
b. As "a," with silver text .75 .75
c. Serpentine die cut 10x9¾ .75 .75
d. As "c," with silver text .75 .75
2267 A568 (50c) multi .75 .75
a. Serpentine die cut 11x11¼ .75 .75
b. As "a," with silver text .75 .75
c. Serpentine die cut 10x9¾ .75 .75
d. As "c," with silver text .75 .75
2268 A568 (50c) multi .75 .75
a. Serpentine die cut 11x11¼ .75 .75
b. As "a," with silver text .75 .75
c. Serpentine die cut 10x9¾ .75 .75
d. As "c," with silver text .75 .75
2269 A568 (50c) multi .75 .75
a. Serpentine die cut 11x11¼ .75 .75
b. As "a," with silver text .75 .75
c. Serpentine die cut 10x9¾ .75 .75
d. As "c," with silver text .75 .75
2270 A568 (50c) multi .75 .75
a. Serpentine die cut 11x11¼ .75 .75
b. As "a," with silver text .75 .75
c. Serpentine die cut 10x9¾ .75 .75
d. As "c," with silver text .75 .75
2271 A568 (50c) multi .75 .75
a. Serpentine die cut 11x11¼ .75 .75
b. As "a," with silver text .75 .75
c. Serpentine die cut 10x9¾ .75 .75
d. As "c," with silver text .75 .75
2272 A568 (50c) multi .75 .75
a. Serpentine die cut 11x11¼ .75 .75
b. As "a," with silver text .75 .75
c. Serpentine die cut 10x9¾ .75 .75
d. As "c," with silver text .75 .75
2273 A568 (50c) multi .75 .75
a. Serpentine die cut 11x11¼ .75 .75
b. As "a," with silver text .75 .75
c. Serpentine die cut 10x9¾ .75 .75
d. As "c," with silver text .75 .75
2274 A568 (50c) multi .75 .75
a. Serpentine die cut 11x11¼ .75 .75
b. As "a," with silver text .75 .75
c. Serpentine die cut 10x9¾ .75 .75
d. As "c," with silver text .75 .75
e. Block of 10, #2265-2274 7.50
f. Booklet pane of 10, #2265a-2274a 7.50
g. Booklet pane of 10, #2265b-2274b 7.50
h. Vert. coil strip of 10, #2265-2274 7.50
Nos. 2265-2274 (10) 7.50 7.50

A569

A570

Christmas — A571

Designs: Nos. 2275, 2281, Adoration of the Shepherds. No. 2276, Chair and Pohutukawa Tree, by Felix Wang. $1, Holy Family. $1.80, Adoration of the Magi. $2.30, New Zealand Pigeon, by Dannielle Aldworth. $2.80, Child, Gifts and Christmas Tree, by Apurv Bakshi.

2009, Oct. 7 Litho. *Perf. 14¼*

2275 A569 50c multi .75 .75
2276 A570 50c multi .75 .75
2277 A569 $1 multi 1.50 1.50
2278 A569 $1.80 multi 2.60 2.60
2279 A570 $2.30 multi 3.50 3.50
2280 A570 $2.80 multi 4.00 4.00
Nos. 2275-2280 (6) 13.10 13.10

Self-Adhesive

Serpentine Die Cut 10x9½

2281 A571 50c multi .75 .75
a. Booklet pane of 10 7.50
2282 A571 $1.80 multi 2.60 2.60
a. Booklet pane of 10 26.00
b. Horiz. pair, #2281-2282 3.50

No. 2282a sold for $15.

Sir Peter Blake (1948-2001), Yachtsman — A572

Photograph of Blake and New Zealand flag with inscription at lower right: 50c, Inspirational leader. $1, Yachtsman. $1.80, Record breaker. $2.30, Passionate Kiwi. $2.80, Environmentalist.

2009, Nov. 25 *Perf. 13¼x13½*

2283 A572 50c multi .75 .75
2284 A572 $1 multi 1.50 1.50
2285 A572 $1.80 multi 2.60 2.60
2286 A572 $2.30 multi 3.25 3.25
2287 A572 $2.80 multi 4.00 4.00
a. Souvenir sheet, #2283-2287 12.50 12.50
Nos. 2283-2287 (5) 12.10 12.10

The 2009 sheets contain: #2230, 2225, 2235; #2249, 2243, 2253; #2256f, 2278, 2287. See note following #1404.

New Year 2010 (Year of the Tiger) — A573

Designs: 50c, Chinese character for "tiger." $1, Tiger. $1.80 Tiger's head. $2.30, Bird and Wellington Beehive.

2010, Jan. 6 *Perf. 14*

2288 A573 50c multi .70 .70
a. Perf. 13½ .70 .70
2289 A573 $1 multi 1.40 1.40
a. Perf. 13½ 1.40 1.40
2290 A573 $1.80 multi 2.60 2.60
a. Perf. 13½ 2.60 2.60
2291 A573 $2.30 multi 3.25 3.25
a. Perf. 13½ 3.25 3.25
b. Souvenir sheet, #2288a-2291a 8.00 8.00
Nos. 2288-2291 (4) 7.95 7.95

Greetings Type of 2006 Redrawn Without Silver Frames

No. 2292: a, Heitiki. b, Champagne flutes. c, Wedding and engagement rings. d, Pohutukawa flower.

2010, Feb. 10 Litho. *Perf. 15x14½*

2292 Sheet of 4 + 2 labels 12.50 12.50
a. A531 $1.80 multi 2.60 2.60
b.-d. A531 $2.30 Any single 3.25 3.25
e. Sheet of 20 #2292a + 20 labels 72.50 72.50
f. Sheet of 20 #2292b + 20 labels 85.00 85.00
g. Sheet of 20 #2292c + 20 labels 85.00 85.00
h. Sheet of 20 #2292d + 20 labels 85.00 85.00

Labels are not personalizable on No. 2292.

No. 2292e sold for $50.90. Nos. 2292f-2292h each sold for $60.90. Labels could be personalized on Nos. 2292e-2292h.

Prehistoric Animals A574

Designs: 50c, Allosaurus. $1, Anhanguera. $1.80, Titanosaurus. $2.30, Moanasaurus. $2.80, Mauisaurus.

2010, Mar. 3 Litho. *Perf. 14¾*

2293 A574 50c multi .70 .70
2294 A574 $1 multi 1.40 1.40
2295 A574 $1.80 multi 2.50 2.50
2296 A574 $2.30 multi 3.25 3.25
2297 A574 $2.80 multi 4.00 4.00
Nos. 2293-2297 (5) 11.85 11.85

Self-Adhesive

Serpentine Die Cut 10x9¾

2298 Sheet of 5 12.00
a. A574 50c multi .70 .70
b. A574 $1 multi 1.40 1.40
c. A574 $1.80 multi 2.50 2.50
d. A574 $2.30 multi 3.25 3.25
e. A574 $2.80 multi 4.00 4.00

ANZAC Remembrance A575

Designs: No. 2299, Silhouette of soldier. No. 2300, Gallipoli veterans marching on ANZAC Day, 1958. $1, Posthumous Victoria Cross ceremony for Te Moana-nui-a-Kiwa, 1943. $1.80, Nurses placing wreath in Cairo cemetery on ANZAC Day, 1940. $2.30, Unveiling of ANZAC War Memorial, Port Said, Egypt, 1932. $2.80, Veteran visiting Sangro War Cemetery, Italy, 2004.

2010, Apr. 7 Litho. *Perf. 13½x13¼*

2299 A575 50c multi .75 .75
a. Perf. 14 .80 .80
b. Booklet pane of 1, perf. 14 .80 —
2300 A575 50c multi .75 .75
a. Perf. 14 .80 .80
b. Booklet pane of 1, perf. 14 .80 —
2301 A575 $1 multi 1.50 1.50
a. Perf. 14 1.60 1.60
b. Booklet pane of 1, perf. 14 1.60 —
2302 A575 $1.80 multi 2.60 2.60
a. Perf. 14 3.00 3.00
b. Booklet pane of 1, perf. 14 3.00 —
2303 A575 $2.30 multi 3.25 3.25
a. Perf. 14 3.75 3.75
b. Booklet pane of 1, perf. 14 3.75 —
2304 A575 $2.80 multi 4.00 4.00
a. Perf. 14 4.50 4.50
b. Booklet pane of 1, perf. 14 4.50 —
c. Booklet pane of 6, #2299a-2304a 14.50 —
Complete booklet, #2299b-2304b, 2304c 29.00
d. Souvenir sheet of 3, #2299a, 2303a, 2304a 9.25 9.25
Nos. 2299-2304 (6) 12.85 12.85

Complete booklet sold for $19.90.

Issued: No. 2304d, 4/30. London 2010 Festival of Stamps (No. 2304d).

Expo 2010, Shanghai — A576

Designs: 50c, Pohutukawas and peonies. $1, Kaitiaki and Fu Dog. $1.80, Tane and Pan Gu. $2.30, Auckland and Shanghai. $2.80, Heitiki and Cong.

2010, Apr. 30 Litho. *Perf. 14*

2305 A576 50c multi .75 .75
2306 A576 $1 multi 1.50 1.50
2307 A576 $1.80 multi 2.60 2.60
2308 A576 $2.30 multi 3.50 3.50
2309 A576 $2.80 multi 4.25 4.25
a. Horiz. strip of 5, #2305-2309 13.00 13.00
b. Sheet of 5, #2305-2309, without back printing 13.00 13.00
Nos. 2305-2309 (5) 12.60 12.60

Maori Rugby, Cent. — A577

Designs: 50c, Centenary jersey. $1.80, Centenary emblem.

2010, June 9

2310 A577 50c multi .70 .70
2311 A577 $1.80 multi 2.50 2.50
a. Souvenir sheet of 2, #2310-2311 3.25 3.25

Traditional Maori Kites — A578

Designs: 50c, Manu Aute. $1, Manu Patiki, vert. $1.80, Manu Taratahi, vert. $2.30, Upoko Tangata.

2010, June 9

2312 A578 50c multi .70 .70
2313 A578 $1 multi 1.40 1.40
2314 A578 $1.80 multi 2.50 2.50
2315 A578 $2.30 multi 3.25 3.25
a. Souvenir sheet of 4, #2312-2315 8.00 8.00
Nos. 2312-2315 (4) 7.85 7.85

Tourist Attractions Type of 2003

Designs: $1.20, Mitre Peak, Milford Sound. $1.90, Queenstown. $2.40, Lake Rotorua. $2.90, Kaikoura. $3.40, Christchurch.

2010, Aug. 4 *Perf. 13¼x13½*

2316 A496 $1.20 multi 1.75 1.75
2317 A496 $1.90 multi 2.75 2.75
2318 A496 $2.40 multi 3.50 3.50
a. Souvenir sheet of 3, #2316-2318 8.50 8.50
2319 A496 $2.90 multi 4.25 4.25
2320 A496 $3.40 multi 5.00 5.00
a. Souvenir sheet of 2, #2319-2320, #321 9.00 9.00
Nos. 2316-2320 (5) 17.25 17.25

Self-Adhesive

Serpentine Die Cut 10x9½

2321 A496 $1.20 multi 1.75 1.75
a. Booklet pane of 10 17.50
2322 A496 $1.90 multi 2.75 2.75
a. Booklet pane of 5 14.00

Issued: No. 2318a, 2/12/11. Indipex 2011 (#2318a). Christchurch 2016 Stamp & Postcard Exhibition (No. 2320a). Issued: No. 2320a, 11/18/16. No. 2320a contains a lithographed perf. 14½ reproduction of No. 321 that is not valid for postage.

Emblem of All Blacks Rugby Team — A579

2010, Aug. 4 *Perf. 13½x13¼*

2323 A579 60c black .90 .90
2324 A579 $1.90 black 2.75 2.75
a. Miniature sheet of 6 60.00 60.00

Souvenir Sheet

2325 Sheet of 4, #2323, 2324, 2325a, 2325b 7.50 7.50
a. A579 60c black, 32x17mm, perf. 15x14½ .90 .90
b. A579 $1.90 black, 32x17mm, perf. 15x14½ .90 .90
c. Sheet of 20 #2325a + 20 labels 34.00 34.00
d. Sheet of 20 #2325b + 20 labels 77.50 77.50

2011 Rugby World Cup victory of New Zealand rugby team (No. 2324a). Issued: No. 2324a, 10/28/11. No. 2324a sold for $19.90.

No. 2325c sold for $22.90. No. 2325d sold for $52.90. Labels could be personalized on Nos. 2325c-2325d. In 2011, No. 2325c was made available for the same price with labels that could not be personalized.

See Nos. 2410-2411, 2519-2521.

Greetings Stamps Type of 2006 Without Silver Frames

No. 2326: a, Champagne flutes. b, Child's toy. c, Fern. d, Pohutukawa flower. e, Wedding and engagement rings. f, Rose. g, Heitiki. h, Teddy bear.

No. 2327: a, Heitiki. b, Champagne flutes. c, Wedding and engagement rings. d, Pohutukawa flower.

2010, Sept. 9 *Perf. 15x14½*

2326 A531 Sheet of 8 + 4 labels 7.25 7.25
a.-h. 60c Any single .90 .90
i. Sheet of 20 #2326a + 20 labels 34.00 34.00
j. Sheet of 20 #2326b + 20 labels 34.00 34.00
k. Sheet of 20 #2326c + 20 labels 34.00 34.00
l. Sheet of 20 #2326d + 20 labels 34.00 34.00
m. Sheet of 20 #2326e + 20 labels 34.00 34.00
n. Sheet of 20 #2326f + 20 labels 34.00 34.00
o. Sheet of 20 #2326g + 20 labels 34.00 34.00
p. Sheet of 20 #2326h + 20 labels 34.00 34.00
2327 A531 Sheet of 4 + 2 labels 13.50 13.50
a. $1.90 multi 2.75 2.75
b.-d. $2.40 Any single 3.50 3.50
e. Sheet of 20 #2327a + 20 labels 77.50 77.50
f. Sheet of 20 #2327b + 20 labels 92.50 92.50

g. Sheet of 20 #2327c + 20 labels 92.50 92.50
h. Sheet of 20 #2327d + 20 labels 92.50 92.50

Nos. 2326i-2326p each sold for $22.90. No. 2327e sold for $52.90. Nos. 2327f-2327h each sold for $62.90. Labels could be personalized on Nos. 2326i-2326p, 2327e-2327h.

Emblem of 2011 Rugby World Cup — A580

2010, Sept. 9 ***Perf. 13½x13¼***

2328 A580 60c multi .90 .90
2329 A580 $1.90 multi 2.75 2.75

Souvenir Sheet

2330 Sheet of 4, #2328, 2329, 2330a, 2330b 7.50 7.50
a. A580 60c multi, 32x17mm, perf. 15x14½ .90 .90
b. A580 $1.90 multi, 32x17mm, perf. 15x14½ .90 .90
c. Sheet of 20 #2330a + 20 labels 34.00 34.00
d. Sheet of 20 #2330b + 20 labels 77.50 77.50

No. 2330c sold for $22.90. No. 2330d sold for $52.90. Labels could be personalized on Nos. 2330c-2330d. In 2011, No. 2330c was made available for the same price with labels that could not be personalized.

Miniature Sheet

"A Slice of Heaven" A581

No. 2331: a, Tane Mahuta kauri tree, Stone Store, Kerikeri, Waitangi Treaty Grounds, boat at dock. b, Carter Fountain, Oriental Bay, buildings. c, The Octagon, St. Paul's Cathedral, Dunedin. d, Cruise ship, Princes Wharf, Auckland. e, The Beehive, Wellington. f, Sky Tower, Auckland Ferry Terminal. g, Obelisk on grave of Sir John Logan Campbell on One Tree Hill, cable car, buildings. h, Mount Ruapehu (volcano), punts on Avon River, Christchurch. i, Fairfield Bridge, hot-air balloons over Basin Reserve Cricket Grounds, Wellington. j, Christchurch Cathedral, Bridge of Remembrance. k, Horse racing track. l, Road, small town, war memorial, sheep in field. m, Mountain climbers with flag on Mt. Cook, ski plane, helicopter. n, Farm house, storage shed, plowed field, cows in pasture, shore of Lake Taupo. o, Lake Taupo, Huka Falls. p, Champagne Pool, geyser, mud pool. q, Rugby field. r, TSS Earnslaw on Lake Wakatipu, parasailers, Queenstown. s, Biplane and glider over ski and golf resort. t, Suspension bridge over river, river mouth. u, Trailer park near beach, Moeraki Boulders. v, Line of boatsheds, Tihati Bay. w, Farmhouse, barn, tractor, silos. x, House, sheep pens, truck. y, Nugget Point Lighthouse, whale.

2010, Oct. 6 ***Perf. 14¼***

2331 A581 Sheet of 25 22.50 22.50
a.-y. 60c Any single .90 .90

Christmas — A582

New Zealand Christmas stamps of the past: 60c, #353. $1.20, #465. $1.90, #692. $2.40, #790. $2.90, #1672.

2010, Oct. 20 ***Perf. 13¼x13½***

Stamps Without White Frames

2332 A582 60c multi .95 .95
2333 A582 $1.20 multi 1.90 1.90
2334 A582 $1.90 multi 3.00 3.00
2335 A582 $2.40 multi 4.00 4.00
2336 A582 $2.90 multi 4.75 4.75
Nos. 2332-2336 (5) 14.60 14.60

Stamps With White Frames

Coil Stamps

Self-Adhesive

Size: 21x26mm

Die Cut Perf. 12¾

2337 A582 60c multi .95 .95
2338 A582 $1.90 multi 3.00 3.00
a. Horiz. pair, #2337-2338 4.00

Booklet Stamps

Serpentine Die Cut 11¼

2339 A582 60c multi .95 .95
a. Booklet pane of 10 9.50
2340 A582 $1.90 multi 3.00 3.00
a. Booklet pane of 10 30.00
Nos. 2337-2340 (4) 7.90 7.90

New Zealand Christmas stamps, 50th anniv. No. 2339a sold for $5.40 and No. 2340a sold for $16.

Volunteer Lifeguard Clubs, Cent. — A583

Designs: 60c, Surf lifeguard and beach flag. $1.20, Lifeguards on inflatable rescue boat. $1.90, Lifeguards on ski paddlers. $2.40, Lifeguards on surf boat. $2.90, Lifeguards marching on beach.

2010, Nov. 3 ***Perf. 13x13¼***

2341 A583 60c multi .95 .95
2342 A583 $1.20 multi 1.90 1.90
2343 A583 $1.90 multi 3.00 3.00
2344 A583 $2.40 multi 4.00 4.00
2345 A583 $2.90 multi 4.75 4.75
Nos. 2341-2345 (5) 14.60 14.60

The 2010 sheets contain: #2291, 2297, 2304; #2309, 2315, B198; #2319, 2336, 2345. See note following #1404.

New Year 2011 (Year of the Rabbit) — A584

Designs: 60c, Chinese character for "rabbit." $1.20, Paper-cut rabbit. $1.90, Rabbit. $2.40, Kite, Christchurch Cathedral.

2011, Jan. 12 **Litho.** ***Perf. 13½x13***

2346 A584 60c multi .95 .95
2347 A584 $1.20 multi 1.90 1.90
2348 A584 $1.90 multi 3.00 3.00
2349 A584 $2.40 multi 3.75 3.75
a. Souvenir sheet, #2346-2349 9.75 9.75
Nos. 2346-2349 (4) 9.60 9.60

Miniature Sheets

Kapa Haka A585

Nos. 2350 and 2351: a, Whakaeke. b, Poi. c, Waiata-a-ringa. d, Haka. e, Whakawatea. f, Moteatea.

2011, Feb. 17 ***Perf. 13¼x13½***

2350 A585 Sheet of 6 15.00 15.00
a.-b. 60c Either single .90 .90
c. $1.20 multi 1.90 1.90
d. $1.90 multi 3.00 3.00
e. $2.40 multi 3.75 3.75
f. $2.90 multi 4.50 4.50

Self-Adhesive

Serpentine Die Cut 10x9½

2351 A585 Sheet of 6 15.00 15.00
a.-b. 60c Either single .90 .90
c. $1.20 multi 1.90 1.90
d. $1.90 multi 3.00 3.00
e. $2.40 multi 3.75 3.75
f. $2.90 multi 4.50 4.50

Kiwistamps — A586

Designs: Nos. 2352, 2357, Hokey pokey ice cream cone. Nos. 2353, 2358, Kiwi crossing road sign. Nos. 2354, 2359, People on beach. Nos. 2355, 2360, Trout fisherman. Nos. 2356, 2361, Mountain biking.

Serpentine Die Cut 10x9¾

2011, Mar. 23 **Litho.**

Self-Adhesive

Coil Stamps

2352 A586 (60c) multi .95 .95
2353 A586 (60c) multi .95 .95
2354 A586 (60c) multi .95 .95
2355 A586 (60c) multi .95 .95
2356 A586 (60c) multi .95 .95
a. Horiz. strip of 5, #2352-2356 4.75
Nos. 2352-2356 (5) 4.75 4.75

Booklet Stamps

Serpentine Die Cut 11

2357 A586 (60c) multi .95 .95
2358 A586 (60c) multi .95 .95
2359 A586 (60c) multi .95 .95
2360 A586 (60c) multi .95 .95
2361 A586 (60c) multi .95 .95
a. Booklet pane of 10, 2 each #2357-2361 9.50
Nos. 2357-2361 (5) 4.75 4.75

Wedding of Prince William and Catherine Middleton — A587

Prince William and Catherine Middleton with Prince William wearing: No. 2362, Suit and tie. No. 2363, Sweater.

2011, Mar. 23 ***Perf. 14½x14¾***

2362 A587 $2.40 multi 3.75 3.75
2363 A587 $2.40 multi 3.75 3.75
a. Horiz. pair, #2362-2363 7.50 7.50
b. Souvenir sheet of 2, #2362-2363 7.50 7.50

New Zealand's Victoria Cross Recipients — A588

No. 2364: a, Charles Heaphy. b, William James Hardham. c, Cyril Royston Guyton Bassett. d, Donald Forrester Brown. e, Samuel Frickleton. f, Leslie Wilton Andrew. g, Henry James Nicholas. h, Richard Charles Travis. i, Samuel Forsyth. j, Reginald Stanley Judson. k, Harry John Laurent. l, James Crichton. m, John Gildroy Grant. n, James Edward Allen Ward. o, Charles Hazlitt Upham. p, Alfred Clive Hulme. q, John Daniel Hinton. r, Keith Elliott.s, Moana-nui-a-Kiwa Ngarimu. t, Lloyd Allen Trigg. u, Leonard Henry Trent. v, Bill Henry Apiata (medal only).

2011, Apr. 14 ***Perf. 13¼x13½***

2364 Miniature sheet of 22 22.00 22.00
a.-v. A588 60c Any single 1.00 1.00

Miniature Sheet

Life Beyond the Coast A589

No. 2365: a, Humpback whale. b, White-faced storm petrel, horiz. c, John Dory, horiz. d, Yellowfin tuna, horiz. e, Kingfish, horiz. f, Hammerhead shark, horiz. g, Snapper, horiz. h, Arrow squid, horiz. i, Lord Howe coralfish. j, Orange roughy, horiz. k, Yellow moray eel, horiz. l, King crab.

Serpentine Die Cut 10x9½, 9½x10

2011, May 4 **Self-Adhesive**

2365 A589 Sheet of 12 15.50
a.-j. 60c Any single .95 .95
k.-l. $1.90 Either single 3.00 3.00

Miniature Sheet

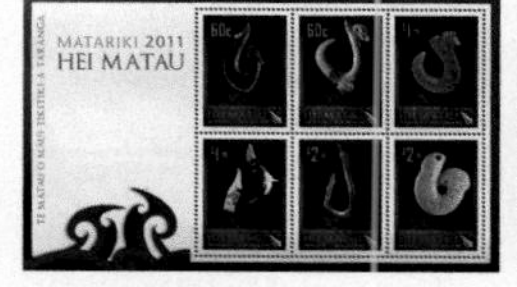

Matariki (Maori New Year) A590

Nos. 2366 and 2367 -- Various hei mataus (decorative fish hooks): a, Green pounamu fish hook by Lewis Gardiner. b, White whalebone fish hook, c. 1500-1800, in Museum of New Zealand. c, Inanga fish hook, c. 1800, in Museum of New Zealand. d, Pounamu, whalebone, feathers and flax fiber fish hook by Gardiner. e, Wooden fish hook, c. 1800, in Auckland War Memorial Museum. f, Whalebone fish hook, c. 1750-1850, in Museum of New Zealand.

2011, June 1 **Litho.** ***Perf. 13¼x13½***

2366 A590 Sheet of 6 16.00 16.00
a.-b. 60c Either single 1.00 1.00
c. $1.20 multi 2.00 2.00
d. $1.90 multi 3.25 3.25
e. $2.40 multi 4.00 4.00
f. $2.90 multi 4.75 4.75

Self-Adhesive

Serpentine Die Cut 10x9½

2367 A590 Sheet of 6 16.00 16.00
a.-b. 60c Either single 1.00 1.00
c. $1.20 multi 2.00 2.00
d. $1.90 multi 3.25 3.25
e. $2.40 multi 4.00 4.00
f. $2.90 multi 4.75 4.75

Kiwi Type of 1988

2011 **Litho.** ***Perf. 14½***

2368 A325 $1.20 black 2.00 2.00
2369 A325 $1.90 silver 3.25 3.25
a. Souvenir sheet, #2369, 2 #2324 9.75 9.75
2370 A325 $2.40 blue 4.00 4.00
a. Horiz. strip of 3, #2368-2370 9.25 9.25
b. Souvenir sheet of 3, #2368-2370 8.75 8.75
Nos. 2368-2370 (3) 9.25 9.25

Issued: Nos. 2368-2370, 7/6; No. 2369a, 7/28. No. 2370b, 11/11. Philanippon 2011 World Stamp Exhibition, Yokohama (#2369a). China 2011 Intl. Stamp Exhibition, Wuxi, China (#2370b).

Values for Nos. 2368-2370 are for stamps with surrounding selvage.

Miniature Sheet

Numbers A591

No. 2371 — Maori words for numbers and stylized numbers: a, 1 (State Highway 1 sign). b, 2 (2 beach sandals). c, 3 (sea gull, Cook Strait ferry). d, 4 (stars in Southern Cross, sailboat) e, 5 (child with backpack). f, 6 (hand, cricket umpire). g, 7 (netball goal and players). h, 8 (barbed wire, tractor). i, 9 (woman in fancy clothes, race horse). j, 10 (guitar). k, 11 (legs of soccer player). l, 12 (oyster shell, tongue, plate of oysters). m, 13 (Lamington cakes). n, 14 (dolphins, outrigger canoes in national parks). o, 15 (hand on rugby ball). p, 16 (dice hanging from rear-view mirror). q, 17 (Capt. James Cook and year of his arrival in New Zealand). r, 18 (bird on statue, ballot circles, Parliament building). s, 19 (surf board and wave). t, 20 (parrot with crown). u, 21 (key and streamers).

2011, Aug. 10 ***Perf. 14***

2371 A591 Sheet of 21 21.00 21.00
a.-u. 60c Any single 1.00 1.00

Webb Ellis Cup, Trophy of Rugby World Cup — A592

Litho. With 3-Dimensional Plastic Affixed

Serpentine Die Cut 10¼

2011, Sept. 7 **Self-Adhesive**

2372 A592 $15 multi 25.00 25.00

The New Zealand Experience — A593

Designs: No. 2373, Backpacker, paraglider, camp, hikers, mountains. No. 2374, Sailboaters, motor boat, sailboarder. $1.20, Fisherman and fish. $1.90, Maoris. $2.40, Skier, helicopter. $2.90, Bungee jumper, whitewater raft, hot air balloon.

2011, Sept. 7 **Litho.** ***Perf. 14***

2373 A593 60c multi .95 .95
2374 A593 60c multi .95 .95
2375 A593 $1.20 multi 1.90 1.90
2376 A593 $1.90 multi 3.00 3.00
2377 A593 $2.40 multi 3.75 3.75
2378 A593 $2.90 multi 4.50 4.50
a. Souvenir sheet of 6, #2373-2378 15.50 15.50
Nos. 2373-2378 (6) 15.05 15.05

A594

Christmas — A595

Star of Bethlehem and: 60c, Baby Jesus and livestock. $1.20, Angel appearing to shepherds. $1.90, Holy Family. $2.40, Adoration of the Shepherds. $2.90, Adoration of the Magi.

2011, Nov. 2 **Litho.** ***Perf. 14¼***

2379 A594 60c multi .95 .95
2380 A594 $1.20 multi 1.90 1.90
2381 A594 $1.90 multi 3.00 3.00
2382 A594 $2.40 multi 4.00 4.00
2383 A594 $2.90 multi 4.75 4.75
Nos. 2379-2383 (5) 14.60 14.60

Self-Adhesive

Serpentine Die Cut 9¾x10

2384 A595 60c multi .95 .95
2385 A595 $1.90 multi 3.00 3.00
a. Booklet pane of 10 30.00
2386 A595 $2.40 multi 4.00 4.00
a. Horiz. sheet of 3, #2384-2386 8.00
b. Booklet pane of 10 40.00

Booklet Stamp

Serpentine Die Cut 11¼

2387 A595 60c multi .95 .95
a. Booklet pane of 10 9.50
Nos. 2384-2387 (4) 8.90 8.90

Nos. 2385a and 2386b sold for $17.10 and $21.60, respectively. A se-tenant strip of Nos. 2379-2383 was not put on sale but was a reward for standing order customers.

The 2011 sheets contain: #2349, 2362, 2350f; #2364v, B202, 2366f; #2378, 2370, 2383. See note following #1404.

New Year 2012 (Year of the Dragon) — A596

Designs: 60c, Chinese character for "dragon." $1.20, Dragon. $1.90, Dragon lantern. $2.40, Dunedin Railroad Station, swallows.

2012, Jan. 5 **Litho.** ***Perf. 13¼x13½***

2388 A596 60c multi 1.00 1.00
2389 A596 $1.20 multi 2.00 2.00
2390 A596 $1.90 multi 3.25 3.25
2391 A596 $2.40 multi 4.00 4.00
a. Souvenir sheet of 4, #2388-2391 10.50 10.50
b. Souvenir sheet of 3, #2388, 2390, 2391 8.25 8.25
Nos. 2388-2391 (4) 10.25 10.25

Issued: No. 2391b, 11/2. 2012 Beijing Intl. Stamp and Coin Expo (#2391b).

Tourist Attractions Type of 2003

Serpentine Die Cut 10x9½

2012, Feb. 1 **Litho.**

Self-Adhesive

2392 A496 $2.40 Lake Rotorua 4.00 4.00
a. Booklet pane of 5 + 2 etiquettes 20.00
b. Dated "2010" 3.25 3.25
c. Booklet pane of 5 #2392b + 2 etiquettes 16.50

Issued: Nos. 2392b, 2392c, 2015.

Native Trees — A597

Designs: 60c, Pohutukawa. $1.20, Cabbage tree. $1.90, Kowhai. $2.40, Nikau. $2.90, Manuka.

2012, Feb. 1 ***Perf. 13¼x13½***

2393 A597 60c multi 1.00 1.00
2394 A597 $1.20 multi 2.00 2.00
2395 A597 $1.90 multi 3.25 3.25
2396 A597 $2.40 multi 4.00 4.00
a. Souvenir sheet of 3, #2393, 2395, 2396 8.25 8.25
2397 A597 $2.90 multi 5.00 5.00
a. Souvenir sheet of 5, #2393-2397 15.50 15.50
Nos. 2393-2397 (5) 15.25 15.25

Issued: No. 2396a, 6/18. Indonesia 2012 World Stamp Championship and Exhibition, Jakarta (#2396a).

Miniature Sheet

Royal New Zealand Air Force, 75th Anniv. A598

No. 2398 — Inscriptions: a, The Beginning. b, Air Training corps. c, WWII Europe. d, Women's Auxiliary Air Force. e, WWII Pacific. f, Aerial Topdressing. g, Territorial Air Force. h, Sout East Asia. i, ANZAC. j, Naval Support. k, Transport. l, Peacekeeping. m, Search and Rescue. n, Remembrance. o, The Future.

2012, Mar. 15 ***Perf. 14½***

2398 A598 Sheet of 15 15.00 15.00
a.-o. 60c Any single 1.00 1.00
p. Booklet pane of 4, 2 each #2398a-2398b 4.50 —
q. Booklet pane of 4, 2 each #2398c-2398d 4.50 —
r. Booklet pane of 4, 2 each #2398e-2398f 4.50 —
s. Booklet pane of 4, 2 each #2398g-2398h 4.50 —
t. Booklet pane of 4, 2 each #2398i-2398j 4.50 —
u. Booklet pane of 4, 2 each #2398k-2398l 4.50 —
v. Booklet pane of 4, 2 each #2398m, 2398o 4.50 —
w. Booklet pane of 2 #2398n 2.25 —
Complete booklet, #2398p-2398w 34.00

Complete booklet sold for $19.90.

Reign of Queen Elizabeth II, 60th Anniv. — A599

Photographs of: No. 2399, Queen, 2012. No. 2400, Queen and Prince Philip, 2012. $1.40, Queen and Prince Philip, 1986. $1.90, Queen and Prince Philip, 1981. $2.40, Queen and Prince Philip, 1977. $2.90, Queen, 1953.

Litho. With Foil Application

2012, May 9 ***Perf. 13¼x13½***

2399 A599 70c multi 1.10 1.10
2400 A599 70c multi 1.10 1.10
2401 A599 $1.40 multi 2.25 2.25
2402 A599 $1.90 multi 3.00 3.00
2403 A599 $2.40 multi 3.75 3.75
2404 A599 $2.90 multi 4.50 4.50
a. Souvenir sheet of 6, #2399-2404 16.00 16.00
b. Souvenir sheet of 3, #2399, 2402, 2404 9.25 9.25
Nos. 2399-2404 (6) 15.70 15.70

Issued: No. 2404b, 10/12. 2012 New Zealand National Stamp Exhibition, Blenheim (#2404b).

Tourist Attractions Type of 2003

Designs: $1.40, Cape Reinga Lighthouse. $2.10, Stewart Island. $3.50, Lake Matheson.

2012, May 23 **Litho.** ***Perf. 13¼x13½***

2405 A496 $1.40 multi 2.25 2.25
2406 A496 $2.10 multi 3.25 3.25
2407 A496 $3.50 multi 5.50 5.50
Nos. 2405-2407 (3) 11.00 11.00

Self-Adhesive

Serpentine Die Cut 10x9½

2408 A496 $1.40 multi 2.25 2.25
a. Booklet pane of 10 22.50
2409 A496 $2.10 multi 3.25 3.25
a. Booklet pane of 5 16.50
b. Horiz. pair, #2408-2409 5.50

All Blacks Type of 2010

2012, May 23 ***Perf. 13½x13¼***

2410 A579 70c black 1.10 1.10

Souvenir Sheet

2411 Sheet of 2, #2410, 2411a 2.25 2.25
a. A579 70c black, 32x17mm, perf. 15x14½ 1.10 1.10

Greetings Stamps Type of 2006 Without Silver Frames

No. 2412: a, Champagne flutes. b, Child's toy. c, Fern. d, Pohutukawa flower. e, Wedding and engagement rings. f, Rose. g, Heitiki. h, Tedddy bear.

2012, June 6 ***Perf. 15x14½***

2412 A531 Sheet of 8 + 4 labels 9.00 9.00
a.-h. 70c Any single 1.10 1.10

Miniature Sheets

Maori Rock Art A600

Nos. 2413 and 2414: a, Pouakai, Pareora. b, Tiki, Maerewhenua. c, Mohiki, Opihi. d, Te Puawaitanga, Waitaki. e, Tiki, Te Ana a Wai. f, Taniwha, Opihi.

2012, June 6 ***Perf. 13½x13¼***

2413 A600 Sheet of 6 16.00 16.00
a.-b. 70c Either single 1.10 1.10
c. $1.40 multi 2.25 2.25
d. $1.90 multi 3.00 3.00
e. $2.40 multi 3.75 3.75
f. $2.90 multi 4.50 4.50

Self-Adhesive

Serpentine Die Cut 9½x10

2414 A600 Sheet of 6 16.00 16.00
a.-b. 70c Either single 1.10 1.10
c. $1.40 multi 2.25 2.25
d. $1.90 multi 3.00 3.00
e. $2.40 multi 3.75 3.75
f. $2.90 multi 4.50 4.50

Miniature Sheet

Tiki Tour of New Zealand A601

No. 2415 — Places named on map of New Zealand: a, Cape Reinga, Ninety Mile Beach, Kaitaia. b, Whangarei, Bay of Islands. c, Cape Brett. d, Lion Rock. e, Auckland, Hamilton, Tauranga. f, White Island, East Cape. g, Mt. Taranaki, New Plymouth, Hawera. h, Rotorua, Taupo, Palmerston North. i, Gisborne, Napier. j, No place names (fish, boat, waves). k, Westport, Greymouth. l, Golden Bay, Nelson, Cook Strait, Kaikoura. m, Wellington, Castlepoint. n, Chatham Islands. o, Mitre Peak, Milford Sound. p, Queenstown, Aoraki (Mount Cook), Timaru. q, Christchurch, Ashburton. r, Gore, Invercargill, Foveaux Strait, Stewart Island. s, Dunedin. t, Taiaroa Head.

2012, July 4 ***Perf. 14¼***

2415 A601 Sheet of 20 22.00 22.00
a.-t. 70c Any single 1.10 1.10

Samoan Head Combs — A602

Designs: 70c, Fu'a. $1.40, Niu. $1.90, Maota. $2.40, Tatau. $2.90, Malumalu.

2012, Aug. 1 ***Perf. 14***

2416 A602 70c multi 1.25 1.25
2417 A602 $1.40 multi 2.40 2.40
2418 A602 $1.90 multi 3.25 3.25
2419 A602 $2.40 multi 4.00 4.00
2420 A602 $2.90 multi 4.75 4.75
a. Souvenir sheet of 5, #2416-2420 16.00 16.00
Nos. 2416-2420 (5) 15.65 15.65

Ships — A603

Designs: 70c, Aramoana. $1.40, Waka. $1.90, Earnslaw. $2.40, Dunedin. $2.90, Rotomahana.

2012, Sept. 5

2421 A603 70c multi 1.25 1.25
2422 A603 $1.40 multi 2.25 2.25
2423 A603 $1.90 multi 3.25 3.25
2424 A603 $2.40 multi 4.00 4.00
2425 A603 $2.90 multi 4.75 4.75
a. Souvenir sheet of 5, #2421-2425 15.50 15.50
Nos. 2421-2425 (5) 15.50 15.50

A604

Christmas — A605

Designs: 70c, Holy Family. $1.40, Adoration of the Shepherds. $1.90, Angel. $2.40 Adoration of the Magi. $2.90, Magi and camels.

2012, Oct. 3 ***Perf. 14***

2426	A604 70c multi		1.25	1.25
2427	A604 $1.40 multi		2.25	2.25
2428	A604 $1.90 multi		3.25	3.25
2429	A604 $2.40 multi		4.00	4.00
2430	A604 $2.90 multi		4.75	4.75
	Nos. 2426-2430 (5)		15.50	15.50

Self-Adhesive

Serpentine Die Cut 11x11¼

2431	A605 70c multi	1.25	1.25
a.	Booklet pane of 10	12.50	
2432	A605 $1.90 multi	3.25	3.25
a.	Booklet pane of 10 + 10 etiquettes	32.50	
2433	A605 $2.40 multi	4.00	4.00
a.	Booklet pane of 10 + 10 etiquettes	40.00	
b.	Horiz. sheet of 3, #2431-2433	8.50	
	Nos. 2431-2433 (3)	8.50	8.50

Nos. 2432 and 2433 are air mail. No. 2432a sold for $17.10. No. 2433a sold for $21.60.

Premiere of Movie *The Hobbit: An Unexpected Journey*

A606 A607

Characters: 70c, Bilbo Baggins. $1.40, Gollum. $1.90, Gandalf, horiz. $2.10, Thorin Oakenshield, horiz. $2.40, Radagast. $2.90, Elrond.

2012, Nov. 1 ***Perf. 14½x14, 14x14½***

2434	A606 70c multi	1.25	1.25
a.	Souvenir sheet of 1	1.50	1.50
2435	A606 $1.40 multi	2.40	2.40
a.	Souvenir sheet of 1	3.00	3.00
2436	A606 $1.90 multi	3.25	3.25
a.	Souvenir sheet of 1	4.00	4.00
2437	A606 $2.10 multi	3.50	3.50
a.	Souvenir sheet of 1	4.50	4.50
2438	A606 $2.40 multi	4.00	4.00
a.	Souvenir sheet of 1	5.00	5.00
2439	A606 $2.90 multi	4.75	4.75
a.	Souvenir sheet of 1	6.25	6.25
	Nos. 2434-2439 (6)	19.15	19.15

Self-Adhesive

Serpentine Die Cut 11¼

2440	Sheet of 6	19.50	
a.	A607 70c multi	1.25	1.25
b.	A607 $1.40 multi	2.40	2.40
c.	A607 $1.90 multi	3.25	3.25
d.	A607 $2.10 multi	3.50	3.50
e.	A607 $2.40 multi	4.00	4.00
f.	A607 $2.90 multi	4.75	4.75
g.	Booklet pane of 10, #2440c-2440f, 4 #2440a, 2 #2440b	25.50	

Nos. 2434a-2439a sold as a set of 6 sheets for $14.40.

New Year 2013 (Year of the Snake) — A608

Designs: 70c, Chinese character for "snake." $1.40, Snake. $1.90, Snake on lantern. $2.40, Lanterns and Skyline Gondola, Queenstown.

2013, Jan. 9 ***Perf. 13¼x13***

2441	A608 70c multi	1.25	1.25
2442	A608 $1.40 multi	2.40	2.40
2443	A608 $1.90 multi	3.25	3.25
2444	A608 $2.40 multi	4.00	4.00
a.	Souvenir sheet of 4, #2441-2444	11.00	11.00
	Nos. 2441-2444 (4)	10.90	10.90

Ferns — A609

Designs: 70c, Hen and chickens fern. $1.40, Kidney fern. $1.90, Colenso's hard fern. $2.40, Umbrella fern. $2.90, Silver fern.

2013, Feb. 7 ***Perf. 13x13¼***

2445	A609 70c multi	1.25	1.25
2446	A609 $1.40 multi	2.40	2.40
2447	A609 $1.90 multi	3.25	3.25
2448	A609 $2.40 multi	4.00	4.00
2449	A609 $2.90 multi	5.00	5.00
a.	Souvenir sheet of 5, #2445-2449	16.00	16.00
b.	Souvenir sheet of 2, #2448-2449, perf. 13½	13.00	13.00
	Nos. 2445-2449 (5)	15.90	15.90

Issued: No. 2449b, 9/13. Upper Hutt 2013 National Stamp Show (#2449b). No. 2449b sold for $7.80, with $2.50 of that amount going to the Philatelic Trust.

Children's Books by Margaret Mahy (1936-2012) A610

Designs: 70c, A Lion in the Meadow. $1.40, A Summery Saturday Morning. $1.90, The Word Witch. $2.40, The Great White Man-Eating Shark. $2.90, The Changeover.

2013, Mar. 13 ***Perf. 14***

2450	A610 70c multi	1.25	1.25
2451	A610 $1.40 multi	2.40	2.40
2452	A610 $1.90 multi	3.25	3.25
2453	A610 $2.40 multi	4.00	4.00
2454	A610 $2.90 multi	4.75	4.75
a.	Souvenir sheet of 5, #2450-2454	16.00	16.00
	Nos. 2450-2454 (5)	15.65	15.65

New Zealand Defense Force Missions Abroad — A611

Mission in: No. 2455, Afghanistan. No. 2456, Timor. 140c, Solomon Islands. 190c, Bosnia and Herzegovina. 240c, Antarctica. 290c, Korea.

2013, Apr. 10

2455	A611 70c multi	1.25	1.25
a.	Booklet pane of 1	1.25	1.25
2456	A611 70c multi	1.25	1.25
a.	Booklet pane of 1	1.25	1.25
2457	A611 140c multi	2.40	2.40
a.	Booklet pane of 1	2.40	2.40
2458	A611 190c multi	3.25	3.25
a.	Booklet pane of 1	3.25	3.25
2459	A611 240c multi	4.00	4.00
a.	Booklet pane of 1	4.00	4.00
2460	A611 290c multi	5.00	5.00
a.	Booklet pane of 1	5.00	5.00
b.	Booklet pane of 6, #2455-2460	17.50	—
	Complete booklet, #2455a, 2456a, 2457a, 2458a, 2459a, 2460a, 2460b	35.00	
	Nos. 2455-2460 (6)	17.15	17.15

Complete booklet sold for $19.90.

Coronation of Queen Elizabeth II, 60th Anniv. — A612

Depictions of Queen Elizabeth II used on New Zealand currency by: No. 2461, Mary Gillick, 1953. No. 2462, Gillick, re-engraved in 1956. $1.40, Arnold Machin, 1967. $1.90, James Berry, 1979. $2.40, Raphael Maklouf, 1986. $2.90, Ian Rank-Broadley, 1999.

Litho. & Embossed With Foil Application

2013

2461	A612 70c multi	1.25	1.25
2462	A612 70c multi	1.25	1.25
2463	A612 $1.40 multi	2.25	2.25
2464	A612 $1.90 multi	3.00	3.00
2465	A612 $2.40 multi	4.00	4.00
2466	A612 $2.90 multi	4.75	4.75
a.	Souvenir sheet of 6, #2461-2466	16.50	16.50
b.	Souvenir sheet of 3, #2461, 2463, 2466	8.25	8.25
	Nos. 2461-2466 (6)	16.50	16.50

Australia 2013 World Stamp Exhibition, Melbourne (#2466b). Issued: Nos. 2461-2466, 2466a, 5/8; No. 2466b, 5/10.

Miniature Sheets

Matariki (Maori New Year) A613

Nos. 2467 and 2468 — Koru patterns: a, Piko. b, Manu Tukutuku. c, Nguru. d, Pataka. e, Kotiate. f, Patiki.

2013, June 5 Litho. ***Perf. 13¾x13½***

2467	A613 Sheet of 6	16.50	16.50
a.-b.	70c Either single	1.25	1.25
c.	$1.40 multi	2.25	2.25
d.	$1.90 multi	3.00	3.00
e.	$2.40 multi	4.00	4.00
f.	$2.90 multi	4.75	4.75

Self-Adhesive

Serpentine Die Cut 9½x10

2468	A613 Sheet of 6	16.50	16.50
a.-b.	70c Either single	1.25	1.25
c.	$1.40 multi	2.25	2.25
d.	$1.90 multi	3.00	3.00
e.	$2.40 multi	4.00	4.00
f.	$2.90 multi	4.75	4.75

Honey Bees — A614

Designs: 70c, Bee collecting nectar. 140c, Bees at hive entrance. 190c, Bees on honeycomb. 240c, Apiarist collecting honey. 290c, Harvested honeycomb.

2013, July 3 ***Perf. 14***

2469	A614 70c multi	1.25	1.25
2470	A614 140c multi	2.25	2.25
2471	A614 190c multi	3.00	3.00
2472	A614 240c multi	4.00	4.00
2473	A614 290c multi	4.75	4.75
a.	Souvenir sheet of 5, #2469-2473	15.50	15.50
	Nos. 2469-2473 (5)	15.25	15.25

Classic Travel Posters — A615

No. 2474 — Travel poster depicting: a, Woman in bathing suit, Napier Carnival. b, Fishing boat and fish. c, Tree fern. d, Rata blossom, Franz Josef Glacier. e, Fisherman in river. f, Wellington. g, Contrail of TEAL Airlines emblem going through mouth of Maori carving, mountains. h, Queenstown. i, Timaru by the Sea. j, Lake and mountains. k, Man reaching for hand, Tauranga. l, Kea. m, Bus touring the Southern Alps. n, Marlborough Sounds. o, Sheep drover on horse, sheep herd, dog. p, Basket weaver. q, Skier at Mt. Cook. r, Mt. Egmont. s, Maori statues, mountains, geyser. t, Swimmers at Blue Baths, Rotorua.

2013, Aug. 7 ***Perf. 14x14½***

2474	A615 Sheet of 20	22.00	22.00
a.-t.	70c Any single	1.10	1.10

Coastlines and Lighthouses — A616

Designs: 70c, Castlepoint. $1.40, Nugget Point. $1.90, East Cape. $2.40, Pencarrow Head. $2.90, Cape Campbell.

2013, Sept. 4 ***Perf. 13¼x13½***

2475	A616 70c multi	1.10	1.10
2476	A616 $1.40 multi	2.25	2.25
2477	A616 $1.90 multi	3.00	3.00
2478	A616 $2.40 multi	4.00	4.00
2479	A616 $2.90 multi	4.75	4.75
a.	Souvenir sheet of 5, #2475-2479	15.50	15.50
	Nos. 2475-2479 (5)	15.10	15.10

Birth of Prince George of Cambridge — A617

Designs: 70c, Duke, Duchess of Cambridge, Prince George. $1.90, Duke of Cambridge holding Prince George. $2.40, Duke, Duchess of Cambridge, Prince George, diff. $2.90, Duchess of Cambridge holding Prince George.

2013, Sept. 11 ***Perf. 14¾***

2480	A617 70c multi	1.25	1.25
2481	A617 $1.90 multi	3.25	3.25
2482	A617 $2.40 multi	4.00	4.00
2483	A617 $2.90 multi	4.75	4.75
a.	Horiz. strip of 4, #2480-2483	13.50	13.50
	Nos. 2480-2483 (4)	13.25	13.25

A618

Christmas — A619

Designs: 70c, Child receiving gift. $1.40, Christmas lunch. $1.90, Children decorating Christmas tree. $2.40, Children playing cricket on beach. $2.90, People singing Christmas carols.

2013, Oct. 2 ***Perf. 14¼***

2484	A618 70c multi	1.25	1.25
2485	A618 $1.40 multi	2.40	2.40
2486	A618 $1.90 multi	3.25	3.25
2487	A618 $2.40 multi	4.00	4.00
2488	A618 $2.90 multi	5.00	5.00
	Nos. 2484-2488 (5)	15.90	15.90

Self-Adhesive

Serpentine Die Cut 9½x10¼

2489	Sheet of 3	8.50	
a.	A619 70c multi	1.25	1.25
b.	A619 $1.90 multi	3.25	3.25
c.	A619 $2.40 multi	4.00	4.00
d.	Booklet pane of 10 #2489a	12.50	
e.	Booklet pane of 10 #2489b	32.50	
f.	Booklet pane of 10 #2489c	40.00	

No. 2489a doesn not have a blue airmail panel at the bottom of the stamp. No. 2489e sold for $17.10. No. 2489f sold for $21.60.

Premiere of Movie *The Hobbit: The Desolation of Smaug*

A620 A621

Designs: 70c, Thorin Oakenshield. $1.40, Gandalf. $1.90, Tauriel, horiz. $2.10, Bilbo Baggins, horiz. $2.40, Legolas Greenleaf. $2.90, Bard the Bowman.

2013, Nov. 1 ***Perf. 14½x14, 14x14½***

2490	A620 70c multi	1.25	1.25
a.	Souvenir sheet of 1	1.50	1.50
2491	A620 $1.40 multi	2.40	2.40
a.	Souvenir sheet of 1	3.00	3.00
2492	A620 $1.90 multi	3.25	3.25
a.	Souvenir sheet of 1	4.00	4.00
2493	A620 $2.10 multi	3.50	3.50
a.	Souvenir sheet of 1	4.50	4.50
2494	A620 $2.40 multi	4.00	4.00
a.	Souvenir sheet of 1	5.00	5.00

2495 A620 $2.90 multi 5.00 5.00
a. Souvenir sheet of 1 6.25 6.25
Nos. 2490-2495 (6) 19.40 19.40

Self-Adhesive

Serpentine Die Cut 10¼x10, 10x10¼

2496 Sheet of 6 19.50
a. A621 70c multi 1.25 1.25
b. A621 $1.40 multi 2.40 2.40
c. A621 $1.90 multi 3.25 3.25
d. A621 $2.10 multi 3.50 3.50
e. A621 $2.40 multi 4.00 4.00
f. A621 $2.90 multi 5.00 5.00
g. Booklet pane of 10, #2496c-2496f, 4 #2496a, 2 #2496b 26.00

Nos. 2490a-2495a were sold as a set for $14.40.

New Year 2014 (Year of the Horse) — A622

Designs: 70c, Chinese character for "horse." $1.40, Horse. $1.90, Horse jumping over hurdle. $2.40, Rotorua Museum, Chinese lantern.

2014, Jan. 8 Litho. *Perf. 13½x13*

2497 A622 70c multi 1.25 1.25
2498 A622 $1.40 multi 2.40 2.40
2499 A622 $1.90 multi 3.25 3.25
2500 A000 $2.40 multi 4.00 4.00
a. Souvenir sheet of 4, #2497-2500 11.00 11.00
Nos. 2497-2500 (4) 10.90 10.90

Seaweeds — A623

Map of New Zealand and: 70c, Hormosira banksii. $1.40, Landsburgia quercifolia. $1.90, Caulerpa brownii. $2.40, Marginariella boryana. $2.90, Pterocladia lucida.

2014, Feb. 5 Litho. *Perf. 14*

2501 A623 70c multi 1.25 1.25
a. Perf. 13¼x13½ 1.25 1.25
2502 A623 $1.40 multi 2.40 2.40
a. Perf. 13¼x13½ 2.40 2.40
2503 A623 $1.90 multi 3.25 3.25
a. Perf. 13¼x13½ 3.25 3.25
2504 A623 $2.40 multi 4.00 4.00
a. Perf. 13¼x13½ 4.00 4.00
2505 A623 $2.90 multi 5.00 5.00
a. Perf. 13¼x13½ 5.00 5.00
b. Souvenir sheet of 5, #2501a-2505a 16.00 16.00
Nos. 2501-2505 (5) 15.90 15.90

Houses — A624

Designs: 70c, Colonial cottage. $1.40, Villa. $1.90, Californian bungalow. $2.40, Art Deco. $2.90, State house.

2014, Mar. 5 Litho. *Perf. 14*

2506 A624 70c multi 1.25 1.25
2507 A624 $1.40 multi 2.40 2.40
2508 A624 $1.90 multi 3.25 3.25
2509 A624 $2.40 multi 4.00 4.00
2510 A624 $2.90 multi 5.00 5.00
a. Souvenir sheet of 5, #2506-2510 15.90 5.00
Nos. 2506-2510 (5) 15.90 15.90

World War II Poster Art — A625

Posters inscribed: No. 2511, Duty Calls the Youth of New Zealand. No. 2512, Help Farm for Victory. $1.40, The Air Force Needs Men! $1.90, Navy Week. $2.40, Army Week. $2.90, Taringa Whakarongo!

2014, Apr. 2 Litho. *Perf. 14¾*

2511 A625 70c multi 1.25 1.25
a. Perf. 13 1.25 1.25
b. Booklet pane of 1, #2511a 1.25 —
2512 A625 70c multi 1.25 1.25
a. Perf. 13 1.25 1.25
b. Booklet pane of 1, #2512a 1.25 —
2513 A625 $1.40 multi 2.40 2.40
a. Perf. 13 2.40 2.40
b. Booklet pane of 1, #2513a 2.40 —
2514 A625 $1.90 multi 3.25 3.25
a. Perf. 13 3.25 3.25
b. Booklet pane of 1, #2514a 3.25 —
2515 A625 $2.40 multi 4.00 4.00
a. Perf. 13 4.00 4.00
b. Booklet pane of 1, #2515a 4.00 —
2516 A625 $2.90 multi 5.00 5.00
a. Perf. 13 5.00 5.00
b. Booklet pane of 1, #2516a 5.00 —
c. Booklet pane of 6, #2511a-2516a 17.50 —
Complete booklet, #2511b, 2512b, 2513b, 2514b, 2515b, 2516b, 2516c 35.00
Nos. 2511-2516 (6) 17.15 17.15

Complete booklet sold for $19.90.

Visit to New Zealand of Duke and Duchess of Cambridge and Prince George — A626

Various photos of Duke, Duchess and Prince.

2014, Apr. 7 Litho. *Perf. 14½*

2517 A626 70c multi 1.25 1.25
2518 A626 $2.40 multi 4.25 4.25

All Blacks Type of 2010

2014, May 7 Litho. *Perf. 13½x13¼*

2519 A579 80c black 1.40 1.40
2520 A579 $2.50 black 4.25 4.25

Souvenir Sheet

2521 Sheet of 4, #2519, 2520, 2521a, 2521b 11.50 11.50
a. A579 80c black, 32x17mm, perf. 15x14½ 1.40 1.40
b. A579 $2.50 black, 32x17mm, perf. 15x14½ 4.25 4.25

Tourist Attractions — A627

Designs: 60c, Franz Josef Glacier. $1.60, Moeraki Boulders. $2, Mount Taranaki. $2.50, Pancake Rocks. $3.60, Waikato River.

2014, May 7 Litho. *Perf. 13¼*

2522 A627 60c multi 1.00 1.00
2523 A627 $1.60 multi 2.75 2.75
2524 A627 $2.50 multi 4.25 4.25
2525 A627 $3.60 multi 6.25 6.25
Nos. 2522-2525 (4) 14.25 14.25

Self-Adhesive

Serpentine Die Cut 10x9½

2526 A627 $2 multi 3.50 3.50
a. Booklet pane of 5 17.50
2527 A627 $2.50 multi 4.25 4.25
a. Pair, #2526-2527 7.75
b. Booklet pane of 5 21.50

See Nos. 2644-2651, 2729-2730, 2800-2803, 2863-2867, 3026. Compare types A627 and A738.

Miniature Sheets

Personalized Stamps — A628

No. 2528: a, Wedding rings. b, Fern fiddlehead. c, "Love." d, Champagne flutes. e, Teddy bear. f, Pohutukawa flowers. g, Cupcake with birthday candles. h, Bunch of balloons.

No. 2529: a, Wedding rings. b, Fern fiddlehead. c, Champagne flutes. d, Pohutukawa flowers.

2014, May 7 Litho. *Perf. 15x14½*

2528 A628 Sheet of 8 + 4 labels 11.50 11.50
a.-h. 80c Any single 1.40 1.40
2529 A628 Sheet of 4 + 2 labels 15.50 15.50
a.-b. $2 Either single 3.50 3.50
c.-d. $2.50 Either single 4.25 4.25

Miniature Sheets

Matariki A629

Nos. 2530 and 2531 — Maori art depicting the story of Papatuanuku and Ranginui: a, Te Wehenga o Rangi Raua ko Papa, by Cliff Whiting, b, Rangi and Papa, by Phil Mokaraka Berry. c, Te Whakamamae o te Wehenga, by Kura Te Waru Rewiri. d, The Separtation of Rangi and Papa, by Fred Graham, horiz. e, The Children of Rangi and Papa, by Pauline Kahurangi Yearbury, horiz. f, The Ranginui Doorway, by Robert Jahnke, horiz.

2014, June 4 Litho. *Perf. 13½*

2530 A629 Sheet of 6 18.50 18.50
a.-b. 80c Either single 1.40 1.40
c. $1.40 multi 2.40 2.40
d. $2 multi 3.50 3.50
e. $2.50 multi 4.25 4.25
f. $3 multi 5.25 5.25

Self-Adhesive

Serpentine Die Cut 10x9½ (vert. stamps), 9½x10 (horiz. stamps)

2531 A629 Sheet of 6 18.50
a.-b. 80c Either single 1.40 1.40
c. $1.40 multi 2.40 2.40
d. $2 multi 3.50 3.50
e. $2.50 multi 4.25 4.25
f. $3 multi 5.25 5.25

Miniature Sheet

Landmarks — A630

No. 2532: a, Sculptures of peaches, Cromwell. b, Kiwi statue, Otorohanga. c, Kiwi fruit slice statue, Te Puke. d, Lemon and Paeroa bottle statue, Paeroa. e, Deer statue, Mossburn. f, Surfer statue, Colac Bay. g, Carrot statue, Ohakune. h, Fish statue, Rakaia. i, Sheep building, Tirau. j, Gumboot sculpture, Taihape. k, Chain sculpture, Raikura. l, Statue of boy and bottlenose dolphin, Opononi. m, Dog statue, Hunterville. n, Bicycle sculpture, Taupo. o, Sandfly sculpture, Pukekura. p, Sculpture of man and dog, Feilding. q, Clydesdale horses sculptures, Clinton. r, Sculpture of bread loaves, Manaia.

2014, July 2 Litho. *Perf. 14½*

2532 A630 Sheet of 18 + label 25.50 25.50
a.-r. 80c Any single 1.40 1.40

World War I, Cent. — A631

Designs: No. 2533, Lord Kitchener. No. 2534, Poster for military training. No. 2535, Announcement of war. No. 2536, Melville Mirfin in military uniform. No. 2537, Photograph of Mirfin family. No. 2538, Departure of troop ships. No. 2539, Training camp. No. 2540, Street scene, Karaka Bay. No. 2541, Letter from Mirfin from Samoa. No. 2542, New Zealand soldiers in Egypt.

2014, July 29 Litho. *Perf. 14½*

2533 A631 80c multi 1.40 1.40
a. Booklet pane of 1 2.00 —
2534 A631 80c multi 1.40 1.40
a. Booklet pane of 1 2.00 —
2535 A631 80c multi 1.40 1.40
a. Booklet pane of 1 2.00 —
2536 A631 80c multi 1.40 1.40
a. Booklet pane of 1 2.00 —
2537 A631 80c multi 1.40 1.40
a. Booklet pane of 1 2.00 —
2538 A631 80c multi 1.40 1.40
a. Booklet pane of 1 2.00 —
b. Booklet pane of 6, #2533-2538 12.00 —
c. Block of 6, #2533-2538 8.50 8.50
d. Souvenir sheet, #2533-2538 8.50 8.50
2539 A631 $2 multi 3.50 3.50
a. Booklet pane of 1 5.00 —
2540 A631 $2 multi 3.50 3.50
a. Booklet pane of 1 5.00 —
b. Horiz. pair, #2539-2540 7.00 7.00
2541 A631 $2.50 multi 4.25 4.25
a. Booklet pane of 1 6.25 —
2542 A631 $2.50 multi 4.25 4.25
a. Booklet pane of 1 6.25 —
b. Booklet pane of 4, #2539-2542 22.50 —
Complete booklet, #2533a, 2534a, 2535a, 2536a, 2537a. 2538a, 2538b, 2539a, 2540a, 2541a, 2542a, 2542b 69.00
c. Horiz. pair, #2541-2542 8.50 8.50
d. Souvenir sheet of 4, #2539-2542 15.50 15.50
e. Souvenir sheet of 10, #2533-2542 24.00 24.00
f. Souvenir sheet of 3, #2538, 2539, 2542 12.50 12.50
Nos. 2533-2542 (10) 23.90 23.90

Issued: No. 2542f, 11/14. Baypex 2014 National Stamp Exhibition, Hawke's Bay (No. 2542f). No. 2542f sold for $7.80 with surtax going to the Philatelic Trust. Complete booklet sold for $39.90. See Nos. 2574-2683, 2633-2642, 2715-2724, 2782-2791.

Endangered Seabirds — A632

Designs: 80c, Antipodean albatross. $1.40, New Zealand fairy tern. $2, Chatham Island shag. $2.50, Black-billed gull. $3, Chatham Island taiko.

2014, Sept. 3 Litho. *Perf. 14*

2543 A632 80c multi 1.25 1.25
a. Perf. 13½x13¼ 1.25 1.25
2544 A632 $1.40 multi 2.25 2.25
a. Perf. 13½x13¼ 2.25 2.25
2545 A632 $2 multi 3.25 3.25
a. Perf. 13½x13¼ 3.25 3.25
2546 A632 $2.50 multi 4.00 4.00
a. Perf. 13½x13¼ 4.00 4.00
2547 A632 $3 multi 4.75 4.75
a. Perf. 13½x13¼ 4.75 4.75
b. Souvenir sheet of 5, #2543a, 2544a, 2545a, 2546a, 2547a 15.50 15.50
Nos. 2543-2547 (5) 15.50 15.50

The silhouettes of birds were printed with thermochromic ink, which disappeared when warmed.

A633

Christmas — A634

Children in Nativity play depicting: 80c, Mary and Jesus. $1.40, Joseph. $2, Wise Man. $2.50, Angel. $3, Shepherd.

2014, Oct. 1 Litho. *Perf. 14*

2548 A633 80c multi 1.25 1.25
2549 A633 $1.40 multi 2.25 2.25
2550 A633 $2 multi 3.25 3.25
2551 A633 $2.50 multi 4.00 4.00
2552 A633 $3 multi 4.75 4.75
Nos. 2548-2552 (5) 15.50 15.50

Self-Adhesive

Serpentine Die Cut 10x9½

2553 Sheet of 3 8.50
a. A634 80c multi 1.25 1.25
b. A634 $2 multi 3.25 3.25
c. A634 $2.50 multi 4.00 4.00
d. Booklet pane of 10 #2553a 12.50
e. Booklet pane of 10 #2553b 32.50
f. Booklet pane of 10 #2553c 40.00

Nos. 2553b and 2553c are airmail. No. 2553e sold for $18. No. 2553f sold for $22.50.

Souvenir Sheet

Premiere of Movie *The Hobbit: The Battle of the Five Armies*
A635

Design: Characters from movie in costume.

2014, Oct. 15 Litho. *Perf. 14¾x14½*

2554	A635 Sheet of 2		5.25	5.25
a.	80c multi		1.25	1.25
b.	$2.50 multi		4.00	4.00

Nos. 2554a and 2554b were each available in sheets of 20 + 20 personalizable labels.

Premiere of Movie *The Hobbit: The Battle of the Five Armies*
A636 A637

Designs: 80c, Smaug. $1.40, Bilbo Baggins. $2, Gandalf, horiz. $2.10, Thranduil, horiz. Nos. 2559, 2562e, Bard the Bowman. $3, Tauriel. No. 2561, Door to Bag End.

Perf. 14½x14, 14x14½

2014, Nov. 12 Litho.

2555	A636 80c multi	1.25	1.25
a.	Souvenir sheet of 1	1.60	1.60
2556	A636 $1.40 multi	2.25	2.25
a.	Souvenir sheet of 1	2.75	2.75
2557	A636 $2 multi	3.00	3.00
a.	Souvenir sheet of 1	4.00	4.00
2558	A636 $2.10 multi	3.25	3.25
a.	Souvenir sheet of 1	4.25	4.25
2559	A636 $2.50 multi	4.00	4.00
a.	Souvenir sheet of 1	5.00	5.00
2560	A636 $3 multi	4.75	4.75
a.	Souvenir sheet of 1	5.75	5.75

Litho. & Thermography

2561	A636 $2.50 multi	4.00	4.00
a.	Souvenir sheet of 1	5.00	5.00
	Nos. 2555-2561 (7)	22.50	22.50

Self-Adhesive

Litho.

Serpentine Die Cut 10¼x10, 10x10¼

2562	Sheet of 6	18.50	
a.	A637 80c multi	1.25	1.25
b.	A637 $1.40 multi	2.25	2.25
c.	A637 $2 multi	3.00	3.00
d.	A637 $2.10 multi	3.25	3.25
e.	A637 $2.50 multi	4.00	4.00
f.	A637 $3 multi	4.75	4.75
g.	Booklet pane of 10, #2562c-2562f, 4 #2562a, 2 #2562b	24.50	

Particles of wood from the movie set are embedded in the thermographic ink on No. 2561. Nos. 2555a-2561a sold as a set for $17.80.

New Year 2015 (Year of the Sheep) — A638

Designs: 80c, Chinese character for "sheep." $1.40, Sheep in paper-cut design. $2, Sheep and fence, New Zealand. $2.50, Church of the Good Shepherd, Tekapo, and Chinese kite.

2015, Jan. 14 Litho. *Perf. 14*

2563	A638 80c multi	1.25	1.25
a.	Perf. 13¼x13½	1.25	1.25
2564	A638 $1.40 multi	2.10	2.10
a.	Perf. 13¼x13½	2.10	2.10
2565	A638 $2 multi	3.00	3.00
a.	Perf. 13¼x13½	3.00	3.00
2566	A638 $2.50 multi	3.75	3.75
a.	Perf. 13¼x13½	3.75	3.75
b.	Souvenir sheet of 4, #2563a-2566a	10.50	10.50
	Nos. 2563-2566 (4)	10.10	10.10

Air New Zealand, 75th Anniv.
A639

Designs: 80c, Short S-30 Flying Boat on first Auckland-Sydney flight, 1940. $1.40, Airplanes, Stewardess Margaret Gould, child, pilot, 1948. $2, Tasman Empire Airways Ltd. 1951-60 Coral Route baggage label. $2.50, Children and flight attendant, 1977. $3, Air New Zealand Boeing 787-9 taking off.

2015, Jan. 14 Litho. *Perf. 14¾*

2567	A639 80c multi	1.25	1.25
2568	A639 $1.40 multi	2.10	2.10
2569	A639 $2 multi	3.00	3.00
2570	A639 $2.50 multi	3.75	3.75
2571	A639 $3 multi	4.50	4.50
a.	Souvenir sheet of 5, #2567-2571	15.00	15.00
	Nos. 2567-2571 (5)	14.60	14.60

Souvenir Sheet

Treaty of Waitangi, 175th Anniv. — A640

Perf. 14x14½

2015, Feb. 4 Litho. Wmk. 387

2572	A640 $2.50 multi	3.75	3.75

Miniature Sheet

2015 ICC Cricket World Cup Tournament, Australia and New Zealand — A641

No. 2573 — Tournament emblem on cricket ball with flag of competing team: a, India (dark blue ball, red stitching). b, England (white ball, red stitching). c, South Africa (green ball, orange stitching). d, Pakistan (yellow green ball, yellow stitching). e, United Arab Emirates (gray ball, red stitching). f, Sri Lanka (dark blue ball, yellow stitching). g, West Indies (red violet ball, orange stitching). h, Afghanistan (blue ball, red stitching). i, Ireland (green ball, blue stitching). j, Bangladesh (red ball, green stitching). k, Australia (yellow ball, black stitching). l, New Zealand (gray ball, black stitching). m, Zimbabwe (red ball, white stitching). n, Scotland (deep blue ball, blue stitching).

Unwmk.

2015, Feb. 4 Litho. *Die Cut*

Self-Adhesive

2573	A641 Sheet of 14	17.50	
a.-n.	80c Any single	1.25	1.25

World War I, Cent. Type of 2014

Designs: No. 2574, Evelyn Brooke, nurse. No. 2575, Postcard from Egypt. No. 2576, Landing at Anzac Cove. No. 2577, Chunuk Bair. No. 2578, Casualties return. No. 2579, Marquette Memorial. No. 2580, The Sapper and His Donkey, painting by Horace Moore-Jones. No. 2581, War census poster. No. 2582, Hospital ship Maheno. No. 2583, An Enduting Bond, poster by Otho Hewett.

2015, Mar. 23 Litho. *Perf. 14½*

2574	A631 80c multi	1.25	1.25
a.	Booklet pane of 1	1.75	—
2575	A631 80c multi	1.25	1.25
a.	Booklet pane of 1	1.75	—
2576	A631 80c multi	1.25	1.25
a.	Booklet pane of 1	1.75	—
2577	A631 80c multi	1.25	1.25
a.	Booklet pane of 1	1.75	—
2578	A631 80c multi	1.25	1.25
a.	Booklet pane of 1	1.75	—
2579	A631 80c multi	1.25	1.25
a.	Booklet pane of 1	1.75	—
b.	Booklet pane of 6, #2574-2579	10.50	—
c.	Block of 6, #2574-2579	7.50	7.50
d.	Souvenir sheet of 6, #2574-2579	7.50	7.50
2580	A631 $2 multi	3.00	3.00
a.	Booklet pane of 1	4.50	—
2581	A631 $2 multi	3.00	3.00
a.	Booklet pane of 1	4.50	—
b.	Horiz. pair, #2580-2581	6.00	6.00
2582	A631 $2.50 multi	3.75	3.75
a.	Booklet pane of 1	5.50	—
b.	Souvenir sheet of 3, #2576, 2580, 2582	7.25	7.25
2583	A631 $2.50 multi	3.75	3.75
a.	Booklet pane of 1	5.50	—
b.	Booklet pane of 4, #2580-2583	20.00	—
	Complete booklet, #2574a, 2575a, 2576a, 2577a, 2578a, 2579a, 2579b, 2580a, 2581a, 2582a, 2583a, 2583b	61.00	
c.	Horiz. pair, #2582-2583	7.50	7.50
d.	Souvenir sheet of 4, #2580-2583	13.50	13.50
e.	Souvenir sheet of 10, #2574-2583	21.00	21.00
	Nos. 2574-2583 (10)	21.00	21.00

Complete booklet sold for $39.90.
Issued: No. 2582b, 10/23/15. 2015, Capital Stamp Show, Wellington, (No. 2582b).

Australian and New Zealand Army Corps, Cent. — A642

Soldier and bugler with bugler facing: 80c, Right. $2, Left.

2015, Apr. 7 Litho. *Perf. 14½x14*

2584	A642 80c multi	1.25	1.25
2585	A642 $2 multi	3.00	3.00
a.	Souvenir sheet of 2, #2584-2585	4.25	4.25

See Australia Nos. 4271-4274.

Shells — A643

Designs: 80c, Silver paua. $1.40, Scott's murex. $2, Golden volute. $2.50, Fan shell. $3, Opal top shell.

2015, May 6 Litho. *Perf. 14*

2586	A643 80c multi	1.25	1.25
a.	Perf. 13¼x13½	1.25	1.25
2587	A643 $1.40 multi	2.10	2.10
a.	Perf. 13¼x13½	2.10	2.10
2588	A643 $2 multi	3.00	3.00
a.	Perf. 13¼x13½	3.00	3.00
2589	A643 $2.50 multi	3.75	3.75
a.	Perf. 13¼x13½	3.75	3.75
2590	A643 $3 multi	4.50	4.50
a.	Perf. 13¼x13½	4.50	4.50
b.	Souvenir sheet of 5, #2586a-2590a	15.00	15.00
	Nos. 2586-2590 (5)	14.60	14.60

Miniature Sheets

Matariki (Maori New Year) A644

Nos. 2591 and 2592 — Kowhaiwhai: a, Digiwhaiwhai, by Johnson Witehira. b, Tenei Au Tenei Au, by Kura Te Waru Rewiri. c, Haki, by Kylie Tiuka. d, Banner Moon, by Buck Nin, horiz. e, Part of Te Hatete o Te Reo Series, by Ngatai Taepa, horiz. f, Taona Marama, by Sandy Adsett, horiz.

2015, June 3 Litho. *Perf. 14*

2591	A644 Sheet of 6	14.50	14.50
a.-b.	80c Either single	1.10	1.10
c.	$1.40 multi	1.90	1.90
d.	$2 multi	2.75	2.75
e.	$2.50 multi	3.50	3.50
f.	$3 multi	4.00	4.00

Self-Adhesive

Serpentine Die Cut 10x9½ (vert. stamps), 9½x10 (horiz. stamps)

2592	A644 Sheet of 6	14.50	14.50
a.-b.	80c Either single	1.10	1.10
c.	$1.40 multi	1.90	1.90
d.	$2 multi	2.75	2.75
e.	$2.50 multi	3.50	3.50
f.	$3 multi	4.00	4.00

Miniature Sheet

Popular New Zealand Foods A645

No. 2593: a, Aspargaus rolls. b, Kiwi onion dip. c, Puha and pork. d, Bluff oyster. e, Meat loaf. f, Hokey pokey ice cream. g, Shrimp cocktail. h, Cheese rolls. i, Pikelets. j, Lamington cake. k, Mince on toast. l, Whitebait fritters. m, Curried egg. n, Saveloy sausage and sauce. o, Bacon and egg pie. p, Pavlova. q, Fairy bread. r, Mouse trap.

2015, July 1 Litho. *Perf. 14¼x14¾*

2593	A645 Sheet of 18	20.00	20.00
a.-r.	80c Any single	1.10	1.10

UNESCO World Heritage Sites — A646

Designs: 80c, Emerald Lakes, Tongariro National Park. $1.40, Franz Josef Glacier, Te Wahipounamu-South West New Zealand. $2, Enderby Island, New Zealand Sub-Antarctic Islands. $2.20, Mount Ngauruhoe, Tongariro National Park. $2.50, Lake Mackenzie, Te Wahipounamu-South West New Zealand. $3, Campbell Island, New Zealand Sub-Antarctic Islands.

2015, Aug. 5 Litho. *Perf. 14*

2594	A646 80c multi	1.00	1.00
2595	A646 $1.40 multi	1.75	1.75
2596	A646 $2 multi	2.50	2.50
2597	A646 $2.20 multi	2.75	2.75
2598	A646 $2.50 multi	3.25	3.25
2599	A646 $3 multi	3.75	3.75
a.	Souvenir sheet of 6, #2594-2599	15.00	15.00
	Nos. 2594-2599 (6)	15.00	15.00

Parliament House, Wellington — A647

2015, Aug. 14 Litho. *Perf. 14¼*

2600	A647 $2.50 multi	3.25	3.25
a.	Souvenir sheet of 3, #2600, Australia #4331, Singapore #1743	5.75	5.75

See Australia Nos. 4331-4333, Singapore Nos. 1743-1745.
No. 2600a sold for $4.50 and was released for Singapore 2015 International Stamp Exhibition.

All Blacks Rugby Team Uniform Shirt A648

Litho. With Fabric Affixed

2015, Sept. 2 *Perf. 13¼x13½*

2601	A648 $15 multi	19.00	19.00

No. 2601 was sold individually in a folder.

Queen Elizabeth II, Longest-Reigning British Monarch — A649

Photograph of Queen Elizabeth II from: No. 2602, 1950s. No. 2603, 1960s. $1.40, 1970s. $2, 1980s. $2.20, 1990s. $2.50, 2000s. $3, 2010s.

2015, Oct. 7 Litho. *Perf. 14¾x14¼*

No.	Description	Unused	Used
2602	A649 80c multi	1.10	1.10
2603	A649 80c multi	1.10	1.10
2604	A649 $1.40 multi	1.90	1.90
2605	A649 $2 multi	2.75	2.75
2606	A649 $2.20 multi	3.00	3.00
2607	A649 $2.50 multi	3.50	3.50
2608	A649 $3 multi	4.00	4.00
a.	Souvenir sheet of 7, #2602-2608	17.50	17.50
	Nos. 2602-2608 (7)	17.35	17.35

A650

Christmas — A651

Stained-glass windows: 80c, Angel, St. Mark's Church, Carterton. $1.40, Dove, St. Aidan's Anglican Church, Remuera. $2, Madonna and Child, St. Mary's-in-Holy Trinity Cathedral, Parnell. $2.50, Pohutukawa flower, Christchurch Hospital Nurses Memorial Chapel. $3, Wise Men, St. Benedict's Church, Auckland.

2015, Nov. 4 Litho. *Perf. 14*

No.	Description	Unused	Used
2609	A650 80c multi	1.10	1.10
2610	A650 $1.40 multi	1.90	1.90
2611	A650 $2 multi	2.75	2.75
2612	A650 $2.50 multi	3.50	3.50
2613	A650 $3 multi	4.00	4.00
	Nos. 2609-2613 (5)	13.25	13.25

Miniature Sheet
Translucent Paper

No.	Description	Unused	Used
2614	Sheet of 5	13.50	13.50
a.	A650 80c multi	1.10	1.10
b.	A650 $1.40 multi	1.90	1.90
c.	A650 $2 multi	2.75	2.75
d.	A650 $2.50 multi	3.50	3.50
e.	A650 $3 multi	4.00	4.00

Self-Adhesive
Serpentine Die Cut 9½x10

No.	Description	Unused	Used
2615	A651 80c multi	1.10	1.10
a.	Booklet pane of 10	9.00	
2616	A651 $2 multi	2.75	2.75
a.	Booklet pane of 10 + 10 etiquettes	27.50	
2617	A651 $2.50 multi	3.50	3.50
a.	Booklet pane of 10 + 10 etiquettes	35.00	
b.	Horiz. strip of 3, #2615-2617	7.50	
	Nos. 2615-2617 (3)	7.35	7.35

No. 2616a sold for $18. No. 2617a sold for $22.50.

New Year 2016 (Year of the Monkey) — A652

Designs: 80c, Chinese character for "monkey." $1.40, Monkey in paper-cut design. $2, Monkey hanging from branch. $2.50, Bar-tailed godwit and Monkey Island.

2016, Jan. 13 Litho. *Perf. 14*

No.	Description	Unused	Used
2618	A652 80c multi	1.10	1.10
a.	Perf. 13¼x13½	1.10	1.10
2619	A652 $1.40 multi	1.90	1.90
a.	Perf. 13¼x13½	1.90	1.90
2620	A652 $2 multi	2.60	2.60
a.	Perf. 13¼x13½	2.60	2.60
2621	A652 $2.50 multi	3.25	3.25
a.	Perf. 13¼x13½	3.25	3.25
b.	Souvenir sheet of 4, #2618a-2621a	9.00	9.00
	Nos. 2618-2621 (4)	8.85	8.85

Returned and Services' Association, Cent. — A653

Inscription: 80c, The returned. $1.40, The poppy. $2, Supporting those who served. $2.20, At the RSA. $2.50, The badge. $3, We will remember them.

2016, Feb. 3 Litho. *Perf. 14¼x14¾*

No.	Description	Unused	Used
2622	A653 80c multi	1.10	1.10
2623	A653 $1.40 multi	1.90	1.90
2624	A653 $2 multi	2.75	2.75
2625	A653 $2.20 multi	3.00	3.00
2626	A653 $2.50 multi	3.50	3.50
2627	A653 $3 multi	4.00	4.00
a.	Souvenir sheet of 6, #2622-2627	16.50	16.50
	Nos. 2622-2627 (6)	16.25	16.25

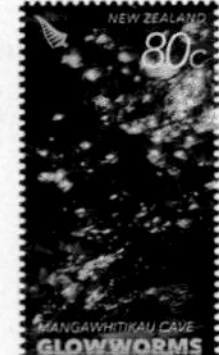

A654

Glowworms — A655

Glowworms from: 80c, Mangawhitikau Cave. $1.40, Nikau Cave. $2, Ruakuri Cave. $2.50, Waipu Cave.

2016, Mar. 2 Litho. *Perf. 14½x14*

No.	Description	Unused	Used
2628	A654 80c multi	1.10	1.10
2629	A654 $1.40 multi	1.90	1.90
2630	A654 $2 multi	2.75	2.75
2631	A654 $2.50 multi	3.50	3.50
a.	Souvenir sheet of 4, #2628-2631	9.25	9.25
	Nos. 2628-2631 (4)	9.25	9.25

Self-Adhesive
Serpentine Die Cut 10x9½

No.	Description	Unused	Used
2632	A655 $2 multi	2.75	2.75
a.	Booklet pane of 10	27.50	

No. 2632 was issued with backing paper with and without printing on the reverse.

World War I, Cent. Type of 2014

Designs: No. 2633, Solomon Isaacs, member of New Zealand Expeditionary Force. No. 2634, Pioneer Battalion. No. 2635, Inscriptions in Arras Tunnels. No. 2636, Newspaper story announcing introduction of conscription. No. 2637, New Zealand troops in the Middle East. No. 2638, Troops in trenches during the Somme Offensive. No. 2639, First ANZAC Day. No. 2640, Soldiers away from the front at Bloomsbury Square headquarters of New Zealand Expeditionary Force. No. 2641, Battle of Jutland. No. 2642, The home front (Kaikoura, New Zealand Post Office).

2016, Apr. 6 Litho. *Perf. 14½*

No.	Description	Unused	Used
2633	A631 80c multi	1.10	1.10
a.	Booklet pane of 1	1.60	—
2634	A631 80c multi	1.10	1.10
a.	Booklet pane of 1	1.60	—
2635	A631 80c multi	1.10	1.10
a.	Booklet pane of 1	1.60	—
2636	A631 80c multi	1.10	1.10
a.	Booklet pane of 1	1.60	—
2637	A631 80c multi	1.10	1.10
a.	Booklet pane of 1	1.60	—
2638	A631 80c multi	1.10	1.10
a.	Booklet pane of 1	1.60	—
b.	Booklet pane of 6, #2633-2638	9.50	—
c.	Block of 6, #2633-2638	6.60	6.60
d.	Souvenir sheet, #2633-2638	6.60	6.60
2639	A631 $2 multi	2.75	2.75
a.	Booklet pane of 1	4.00	—
2640	A631 $2 multi	2.75	2.75
a.	Booklet pane of 1	4.00	—
b.	Horiz. pair, #2639-2640	5.50	5.50
2641	A631 $2.50 multi	3.50	3.50
a.	Booklet pane of 1	5.00	—
2642	A631 $2.50 multi	3.50	3.50
a.	Booklet pane of 1	5.00	—
b.	Booklet pane of 4, #2639-2642	17.50	—
	Complete booklet, #2633a, 2634a, 2635a, 2636a, 2637a, 2638a, 2638b, 2639a, 2640a, 2641a, 2642a, 2642b	55.00	
c.	Horiz. pair, #2641-2642	7.00	7.00
d.	Souvenir sheet of 4, #2639-2642	12.50	12.50
e.	Souvenir sheet of 10, #2633-2642	19.50	19.50
	Nos. 2633-2642 (10)	19.10	19.10

Complete booklet sold for $39.90.

Souvenir Sheet

Queen Elizabeth II, 90th Birthday A656

No. 2643: a, Infant Princess Elizabeth with King George VI and Queen Mother Elizabeth, 1926, Princess Elizabeth with infant Prince Charles, 1949, Queen Elizabeth II on visit to New Zealand, 1995. b, Princess Elizabeth as young girl, 1936, Queen Elizabeth II opening New Zealand's Parliament, 1963, Queen Elizabeth II on visit to New Zealand, 2002. d, Princess Elizabeth in wedding dress, 1947, Queen Elizabeth II on visit to New Zealand, 1977, Queen Elizabeth II attending ANZAC centenary commemorations, 2015.

Litho. With 3-Dimensional Plastic Affixed

2016, May 4 *Die Cut*

Self-Adhesive

No.	Description	Unused	Used
2643	A656 Sheet of 3	21.00	21.00
a.-c.	$5 Any single	7.00	7.00

Tourist Attractions Type of 2014

Designs: 40c, Church of the Good Shepherd, Lake Tekapo. 80c, Chatham Islands. $2.20, Awaroa Bay, Abel Tasman Scenic Reserve. $2.70, Vineyard, Marlborough. $3.30, Dunedin Railway Station. $3.80, Te Mata Peak, Hawke's Bay.

2016, May 18 Litho. *Perf. 13¼x13½*

No.	Description	Unused	Used
2644	A627 40c multi	.55	.55
2645	A627 80c multi	1.10	1.10
2646	A627 $2.20 multi	3.00	3.00
2647	A627 $2.70 multi	3.75	3.75
2648	A627 $3.30 multi	4.50	4.50
2649	A627 $3.80 multi	5.25	5.25
	Nos. 2644-2649 (6)	18.15	18.15

Self-Adhesive
Serpentine Die Cut 10x9½

No.	Description	Unused	Used
2650	A627 $2.20 multi	3.00	3.00
a.	Booklet pane of 5	15.00	
2651	A627 $2.70 multi	3.75	3.75
a.	Horiz. pair, #2650-2651	6.75	
b.	Booklet pane of 5	19.00	

For self-adhesive version of $3.80 stamp, see No. 3026.

Miniature Sheets

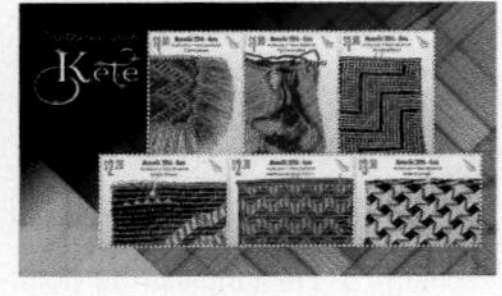

Matariki (Maori New Year) A657

Nos. 2652 and 2653 — Kete woven by: a, Cori Marsters. b, Pip Devonshire. c, Te Atiwei Ririnui. d, Audra Potaka, horiz. e, Matthew McIntyre Wilson, horiz. f, Sonia Snowden, horiz.

2016, June 1 Litho. *Perf. 13½*

No.	Description	Unused	Used
2652	A657 Sheet of 6	17.00	17.00
a.-b.	$1 Either single	1.40	1.40
c.	$1.80 multi	2.50	2.50
d.	$2.20 multi	3.00	3.00
e.	$2.70 multi	3.75	3.75
f.	$3.30 multi	4.50	4.50

Self-Adhesive
Serpentine Die Cut 10x9½ (vert. stamps), 9½x10 (horiz. stamps)

No.	Description	Unused	Used
2653	A657 Sheet of 6	17.00	17.00
a.-b.	$1 Either single	1.40	1.40
c.	$1.80 multi	2.50	2.50
d.	$2.20 multi	3.00	3.00
e.	$2.70 multi	3.75	3.75
f.	$3.30 multi	4.50	4.50

Miniature Sheet

Personalized Stamps — A658

No. 2654: a and i, Wedding rings. b and h, Fern fiddlehead. c, "Love." d, Champagne flutes. e, Teddy bear. f and j, Pohutukawa flowers. g, Bunch of balloons.

2016, June 22 Litho. *Perf. 15x14½*

No.	Description	Unused	Used
2654	A658 Sheet of 10 + 5 labels	21.00	21.00
a.-g.	$1 Any single	1.50	1.50
h.-i.	$2.20 Either single	3.25	3.25
j.	$2.70 multi	4.00	4.00

See No. 2799.

Track — A659

Boxing A660

Canoeing A661

Swimming A662

Equestrian A663

Field Hockey A664

Triathlon A665

Cycling A666

Rowing A667

Sailing A668

2016, July 6 Litho. *Perf. 14¼*

No.	Description	Unused	Used
2655	A659 $1 multi	1.50	1.50
2656	A660 $1 multi	1.50	1.50
2657	A661 $1 multi	1.50	1.50
2658	A662 $1 multi	1.50	1.50
2659	A663 $1 multi	1.50	1.50
2660	A664 $1 multi	1.50	1.50
2661	A665 $1 multi	1.50	1.50
2662	A666 $1 multi	1.50	1.50
2663	A667 $1 multi	1.50	1.50
2664	A668 $1 multi	1.50	1.50
a.	Block of 10, #2655-2664	15.00	15.00
b.	Souvenir sheet of 10, #2655-2664	15.00	15.00

A669

Designs: No. 2665, Natalie Rooney, women's trap shooting silver medalist. No. 2666, Women's rugby sevens team, silver medalist. No. 2667, Eric Murray and Hamish Bond, men's rowing pair gold medalists. No. 2668, Luuka Jones, women's kayaking single slalom silver medalist. No. 2669, Ethan Mitchell, Sam Webster and Eddie Dawkins, men's team sprint track cycling silver medalists. No. 2670, Genevieve Behrent and Rebecca Scown, women's rowing pair silver medalists. No. 2671, Valerie Adams, women's shot put silver medalist. No. 2672, Mahe Drysdale, men's single scull rowing gold medalist. No. 2673, Lisa Carrington, women's 200-meter single kayaking sprint gold medalist. No. 2674, Sam Meech, men's Laser class sailing bronze medalist. No. 2675, Lisa Carrington, women's 500-meter single kayaking sprint bronze medalist. No. 2676, Jo Aleh and Polly Powrie, women's 470 class sailing silver medalists. No. 2677, Peter Burling and Blair Tuke, men's 49er class sailing gold medalists. No. 2678, Molly Meech and Alex Maloney, women's 49erFX class sailing silver medalists. No. 2679, Tomas Walsh, men's shot put bronze medalist. No. 2680, Eliza McCartney, women's pole vault bronze medalist. No. 2681, Lydia Ko, women's golf silver medalist. No. 2682, Nick Willis, men's 1500-meter race bronze medalist.

2016 Litho. *Perf. 14¼*

2665 A669 $1 multi 1.50 1.50
2666 A669 $1 multi 1.50 1.50
2667 A669 $1 multi 1.50 1.50
2668 A669 $1 multi 1.50 1.50
2669 A669 $1 multi 1.50 1.50
2670 A669 $1 multi 1.50 1.50
2671 A669 $1 multi 1.50 1.50
2672 A669 $1 multi 1.50 1.50
2673 A669 $1 multi 1.50 1.50
2674 A669 $1 multi 1.50 1.50
2675 A669 $1 multi 1.50 1.50
2676 A669 $1 multi 1.50 1.50
2677 A669 $1 multi 1.50 1.50
2678 A669 $1 multi 1.50 1.50
2679 A669 $1 multi 1.50 1.50
2680 A669 $1 multi 1.50 1.50
2681 A669 $1 multi 1.50 1.50
2682 A669 $1 multi 1.50 1.50
a. Souvenir sheet of 18, #2665-2682 27.00 27.00
Nos. 2665-2682 (18) 27.00 27.00

New Zealand medalists at the 2016 Summer Olympics, Rio de Janeiro.

Issued: No. 2665, 8/8; Nos. 2666-2669, 8/12; Nos. 2670-2672, 8/15; Nos. 2673-2674, 8/18; Nos. 2675-2679, 8/19; Nos. 2680-2682, 2682a, 8/22.

Miniature Sheet

"It's a Kiwi Thing" A670

No. 2683 — Inscriptions: a, At that moment Trev had a bit of an idea. b, I'll have a trim decaf latte with a twist and a . . . c, Breaking the tackle in the big game. d, The traditional Kiwi sand-wich. e, Gone but not forgotten 2011-2014. f, A kea ate my car. g, Catching a glimpse of our national bird. h, A cool splash followed by a hot dash. i, Water skiing on Lake Taupo. j, Another smooth landing in the capital. k, At this time of year we'd be lucky to see a whale . . . l, Another successful day's whitebaiting. m, Just a friendly game of beach cricket. n, Always blow on the pie.

2016, Sept. 7 Litho. *Perf. 14¼x14½*

2683 A670 Sheet of 14 21.00 21.00
a.-n. $1 Any single 1.50 1.50

Royal New Zealand Navy, 75th Anniv. A671

Designs: No. 2684, Sailors from HMS Neptune. No. 2685, Ship in Korean conflict. $1.80, Woman sailor using sextant. $2.20, Ship and helicopter supporting United Nations peacekeepers. $2.70, Sailor in Christchurch disaster relief efforts. $3.30, Sailor with his children.

2016, Oct. 5 Litho. *Perf. 14½x14¼*

2684 A671 $1 multi 1.50 1.50
2685 A671 $1 multi 1.50 1.50
2686 A671 $1.80 multi 2.75 2.75
2687 A671 $2.20 multi 3.25 3.25
2688 A671 $2.70 multi 4.00 4.00
2689 A671 $3.30 multi 5.00 5.00
a. Souvenir sheet of 6, #2684-2689 18.00 18.00
Nos. 2684-2689 (6) 18.00 18.00

Souvenir Sheet

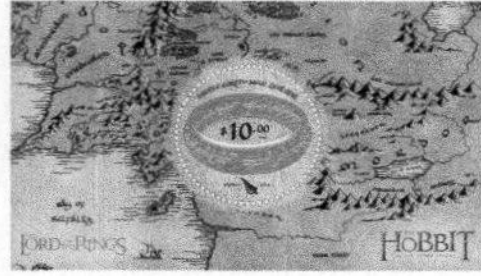

The One Ring From *The Lord of the Rings* A672

Litho. & Embossed With Foil Application

2016, Oct. 19 *Perf.*

2690 A672 $10 multi 15.50 15.50

No. 2690 sold for $10.50.

A673

Christmas — A674

Designs: $1, Infant Jesus. $1.80, Joseph. $2.20, Shepherd. $2.70, Virgin Mary. $3.30, Magus.

2016, Nov. 2 Litho. *Perf. 14x14¼*

2691 A673 $1 multi 1.50 1.50
2692 A673 $1.80 multi 2.75 2.75
2693 A673 $2.20 multi 3.25 3.25
2694 A673 $2.70 multi 4.00 4.00
2695 A673 $3.30 multi 5.00 5.00
a. Souvenir sheet of 5, #2691-2695 16.50 16.50
Nos. 2691-2695 (5) 16.50 16.50

Self-Adhesive

Serpentine Die Cut 9½x10

2696 A674 $1 multi 1.50 1.50
a. Booklet pane of 10 15.00
2697 A674 $2.20 multi 3.25 3.25
a. Booklet pane of 10 + 10 labels 32.50
2698 A674 $2.70 multi 4.00 4.00
a. Booklet pane of 10 + 10 labels 40.00
b. Horiz. strip of 3, #2696-2698 11.50
Nos. 2696-2698 (3) 8.75 8.75

No. 2697a sold for $19.80, No. 2698a, for $24.30.

New Year 2017 (Year of the Rooster) — A675

Designs: $1, Chinese character for "rooster." $1.80, Paper-cut rooster. $2.20, Rooster. $2.70, Auckland War Memorial Museum, Chinese lantern.

2017, Jan. 11 Litho. *Perf. 13¼x13*

2699 A675 $1 multi 1.50 1.50
2700 A675 $1.80 multi 2.60 2.60
2701 A675 $2.20 multi 3.25 3.25
2702 A675 $2.70 multi 4.00 4.00
a. Souvenir sheet of 4, #2699-2702 11.50 11.50
Nos. 2699-2702 (4) 11.35 11.35

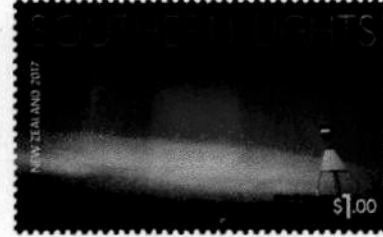

Southern Lights — A676

Various depictions of Southern Lights (Aurora Australis) from Mackenzie Basin.

2017, Feb. 8 Litho. *Perf. 14½x14*

2703 A676 $1 multi 1.40 1.40
2704 A676 $1.80 multi 2.60 2.60
2705 A676 $2 multi 3.00 3.00
2706 A676 $2.20 multi 3.25 3.25
2707 A676 $2.70 multi 4.00 4.00
2708 A676 $3.30 multi 4.75 4.75
Nos. 2703-2708 (6) 19.00 19.00

Miniature Sheet

Litho. With Foil Application

2709 Sheet of 6 19.00 19.00
a. A676 $1 Like #2703 1.40 1.40
b. A676 $1.80 Like #2704 2.60 2.60
c. A676 $2 Like #2705 3.00 3.00
d. A676 $2.20 Like #2706 3.25 3.25
e. A676 $2.70 Like #2707 4.00 4.00
f. A676 $3.30 Like #2708 4.75 4.75

Freshwater Fish — A677

Designs: $1, Lowland longjaw galaxias. $1.80, Redfin bully. $2.20, Longfin eel. $2.70, Lamprey. $3.30, Torrentfish.

2017, Mar. 1 Litho. *Perf. 14x14½*

2710 A677 $1 multi 1.40 1.40
2711 A677 $1.80 multi 2.60 2.60
2712 A677 $2.20 multi 3.25 3.25
2713 A677 $2.70 multi 4.00 4.00
2714 A677 $3.30 multi 4.75 4.75
a. Souvenir sheet of 5, #2710-2714 16.00 16.00
Nos. 2710-2714 (5) 16.00 16.00

World War I, Cent. Type of 2014

Designs: No. 2715, Ellen Knight, mother who lost three sons in World War I. No. 2716, New Zealand officers near Beersheba mosque. No. 2717, Postmarks of Sling Camp, England. No. 2718, Tank at Battle of Messines. No. 2719, Hospital staffers in plastic surgery operating room. No. 2720, People looking at graves at Passchendaele battlefield. No. 2721, Soldiers marching at Battle of Messines. No. 2722, Notice of closing of New Zealand bars at 6 o'clock. No. 2723, SS Port Kembla, sunk off New Zealand coast. No. 2724, Women working at Census and Statistics Office Military Service Section.

2017, Apr. 5 Litho. *Perf. 14½*

2715 A631 $1 multi 1.40 1.40
a. Booklet pane of 1 1.75 —
2716 A631 $1 multi 1.40 1.40
a. Booklet pane of 1 1.75 —
2717 A631 $1 multi 1.40 1.40
a. Booklet pane of 1 1.75 —
2718 A631 $1 multi 1.40 1.40
a. Booklet pane of 1 1.75 —
2719 A631 $1 multi 1.40 1.40
a. Booklet pane of 1 1.75 —
2720 A631 $1 multi 1.40 1.40
a. Booklet pane of 1 1.75 —
b. Booklet pane of 6, #2715-2720 11.00 —
c. Block of 6, #2715-2720 8.50 8.50
d. Souvenir sheet, #2715-2720 8.50 8.50
2721 A631 $2.20 multi 3.25 3.25
a. Booklet pane of 1 4.00 —
2722 A631 $2.20 multi 3.25 3.25
a. Booklet pane of 1 4.00 —
b. Vert. pair, #2721-2722 6.50 6.50
2723 A631 $2.70 multi 3.75 3.75
a. Booklet pane of 1 4.75 —
2724 A631 $2.70 multi 3.75 3.75
a. Booklet pane of 1 4.75 —
b. Booklet pane of 4, #2721-2724 17.50 —
Complete booklet, #2715a, 2716a, 2717a, 2718a, 2719a, 2720a, 2720b, 2721a, 2722a, 2723a, 2724a, 2724b 57.00
c. Vert. pair, #2723-2724 7.50 7.50
d. Souvenir sheet of 4, #2721-2724 14.00 14.00
e. Souvenir sheet of 10, #2715-2724 22.50 22.50
Nos. 2715-2724 (10) 22.40 22.40

Complete booklet sold for $39.90.

Miniature Sheet

British and Irish Lions Rugby Team's 2017 Tour of New Zealand A678

No. 2725 — Lion from team emblem and parts of map of New Zealand showing: a, Whangarei area. b, Auckland area. c, Hamilton area. d, Rotorua area. e, Wellington area. f, Christchurch area. g, Dunedin area.

2017, May 3 Litho. *Perf. 14x14¼*

2725 A678 Sheet of 7 28.00 28.00
a.-g. $2.70 Any single 4.00 4.00

Opening of He Tohu Exhibition at National Library, Wellington A679

Historic and modern people and text: $1, Declaration of Independence of the United Tribes of New Zealand, 1835. $2, Treaty of Waitangi, 1840. $2.20, Women's Suffrage Petition, 1893.

2017, May 17 Litho. *Perf. 14x14¼*

2726 A679 $1 multi 1.40 1.40
2727 A679 $2 multi 3.00 3.00
2728 A679 $2.20 multi 3.25 3.25
Nos. 2726-2728 (3) 7.65 7.65

Tourist Attractions Type of 2014

Designs: $2.30, Mangamaunu, Kaikoura. $4.30, Manu Bay, Raglan.

2017, June 7 Litho. *Perf. 13¼x13½*

2729 A627 $2.30 multi 3.50 3.50
2730 A627 $4.30 multi 6.25 6.25

Surfing Areas A681

Designs: $1, Piha Bar, Piha. $2.20, Manu Bay, Raglan. $2.30, Surf Highway 45, Taranaki. $2.70, Mangamaunu, Kaikoura. $3.30, Aramoana Spit, Dunedin.

2017, June 7 Litho. *Perf. 14x14½*

2731 A681 $1 multi 1.50 1.50
2732 A681 $2.20 multi 3.25 3.25
2733 A681 $2.30 multi 3.50 3.50
2734 A681 $2.70 multi 4.00 4.00
2735 A681 $3.30 multi 5.00 5.00
a. Souvenir sheet of 5, #2731-2735 17.50 17.50
Nos. 2731-2735 (5) 17.25 17.25

A682

A683

A684

A685

A686

Victory of Emirates Team New Zealand in 2017 America's Cup Yacht Race — A687

2017, July 3 Litho. *Perf. 13½x13¼*

2736 Sheet of 6	29.00	29.00
a. A682 $2.70 multi	4.75	4.75
b. A683 $2.70 multi	4.75	4.75
c. A684 $2.70 multi	4.75	4.75
d. A685 $2.70 multi	4.75	4.75
e. A686 $2.70 multi	4.75	4.75
f. A687 $2.70 multi	4.75	4.75

No. 2736 sold for $19.90.

Miniature Sheet

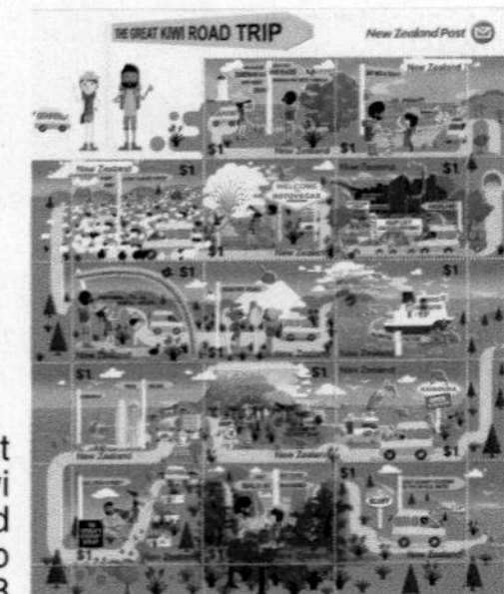

Great Kiwi Road Trip A688

No. 2737 — Tourists and: a, Lighthouse and seven directional signs. b, Directional sign for 90 Mile Beach. c, Three directional signs for Sheep. d, "Welcome to Rotovegas" sign. e, Directional sign for Auckland. f, Directional sign for Taumatawhakatangihangakoauauotamateaturipukakapikimaungahoronukupokaiwhenuakitanatahu. g, Directional sign for Dessert Road. h, Directional signs for Wellington and Picton. i, Three directional signs for Sumner Beach, Togs and Undies. j, "Welcome to the West Coast" sign. k, Kaikoura sign. l, Directional sign for Baldwin Street. m, Waterfalls and four directional signs. n, Directional sign for best oysters.

2017, July 12 Litho. *Perf. 14½x14*

2737 A688 Sheet of 14	21.00	21.00
a.-n. $1 Any single	1.50	1.50

Native Birds — A689

Designs: $1, Campbell Island teal. $2.20, Black stilt. $2.30, North Island kaka. $2.70, South Island saddleback. $3.30, Northern New Zealand dotterel.

2017, Aug. 2 Litho. *Perf. 14½x14*

2738 A689 $1 multi	1.50	1.50
a. Perf. 14¼x14	1.50	1.50
2739 A689 $2.20 multi	3.25	3.25
a. Perf. 14¼x14	3.25	3.25
2740 A689 $2.30 multi	3.50	3.50
a. Perf. 14¼x14	3.50	3.50
b. Souvenir sheet of 3, #2738-2740	7.75	7.75
2741 A689 $2.70 multi	4.00	4.00
a. Perf. 14¼x14	4.00	4.00
2742 A689 $3.30 multi	4.75	4.75
a. Perf. 14¼x14	4.75	4.75
b. Souvenir sheet of 5, #2738a-2742a	17.00	17.00
Nos. 2738-2742 (5)	17.00	17.00

Royalpex 2017 National Stamp Exhibition, Hamilton (No. 2740b). Issued: No. 2740b, 11/24.

Miniature Sheet

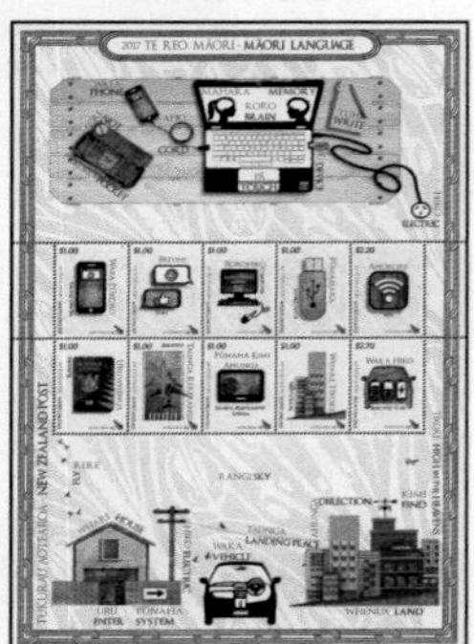

Maori Language — A690

No. 2743 — English and Maori words for modern objects: a, Mobile phone. b, Text. c, Computer. d, Flash drive. e, Passport. f, Airport. g, Global positioning system. h, Skyscraper. i, Wifi. j, Electric car.

2017, Sept. 6 Litho. *Perf. 13¼*

2743 A690 Sheet of 10	18.50	18.50
a.-h. $1 Any single	1.40	1.40
i. $2.20 multi	3.25	3.25
j. $2.70 multi	4.00	4.00

Herbs and Vegetables — A691

Designs: Nos. 2744, 2750a, Basil. Nos. 2745, 2750b, Carrots. $2.20, Parsley. $2.30, Chives. $2.70, Broccoli. $3.30, Lettuce.

Perf. 14x14¼ on 3 sides, Rouletted 9½ on diagonal sides

2017, Oct. 4 Litho.

2744 A691 $1 multi	1.40	1.40
2745 A691 $1 multi	1.40	1.40
2746 A691 $2.20 multi	3.25	3.25
2747 A691 $2.30 multi	3.50	3.50
2748 A691 $2.70 multi	4.00	4.00
2749 A691 $3.30 multi	4.75	4.75
Nos. 2744-2749 (6)	18.30	18.30

Miniature Sheet
Stamps With Circle and "Plant Me" at Bottom

2750 Sheet of 6	18.50	18.50
a.-b. A691 $1 Either single	1.40	1.40
c. A691 $2.20 multi	3.25	3.25
d. A691 $2.30 multi	3.50	3.50
e. A691 $2.70 multi	4.00	4.00
f. A691 $3.30 multi	4.75	4.75

Examples of No. 2750 sold in New Zealand had seeds affixed to the bottom of each stamp. The stamps could be planted so the seeds could sprout. International purchasers of No. 2750 were only sent examples without seeds affixed.

70th Wedding Anniversary of Queen Elizabeth II and Prince Philip — A692

Designs: $1, Engagement photograph. $2, Wedding photograph. $2.20, Queen Elizabeth II, Prince Philip and their children. $2.30, Queen Elizabeth II and Prince Philip. $2.70, Queen Elizabeth II, Princes, Philip, Charles, William, Harry, Duchess of Cambridge and Princess Charlotte. $3.30, Queen Elizabeth II and Prince Philip, diff.

Litho. With Foil Application

2017, Nov. 20 *Perf. 14¼*

2751 A692 $1 sil & multi	1.40	1.40
2752 A692 $2 sil & multi	2.75	2.75
2753 A692 $2.20 sil & multi	3.00	3.00
2754 A692 $2.30 sil & multi	3.25	3.25
2755 A692 $2.70 sil & multi	3.75	3.75
2756 A692 $3.30 sil & multi	4.50	4.50
a. Souvenir sheet of 6, #2751-2756	19.00	19.00
Nos. 2751-2756 (6)	18.65	18.65

A693

Christmas — A694

Quilled: $1, Angel. $2.20, Christmas ornament. $2.30, Star. $2.70, Bell. $3.30, Wreath.

2017, Dec. 6 Litho. *Perf. 14¼*

2757 A693 $1 multi	1.50	1.50
2758 A693 $2.20 multi	3.25	3.25
2759 A693 $2.30 multi	3.25	3.25
2760 A693 $2.70 multi	4.00	4.00
2761 A693 $3.30 multi	4.75	4.75
a. Souvenir sheet of 5, #2757-2761	17.00	17.00
Nos. 2757-2761 (5)	16.75	16.75

Self-Adhesive

Serpentine Die Cut 9½x10

2762 A694 $1 multi	1.50	1.50
a. Booklet pane of 10	15.00	
2763 A694 $2.20 multi	3.25	3.25
a. Booklet pane of 10	32.50	
2764 A694 $2.70 multi	4.00	4.00
a. Booklet pane of 10	40.00	
b. Horiz. strip of 3, #2762-2764	8.75	
Nos. 2762-2764 (3)	8.75	8.75

Nos. 2763 and 2764 are airmail. No. 2763a sold for $19.80. No. 2764a sold for $24.30.

New Year 2018 (Year of the Dog) — A695

Designs: $1, Chinese character for "dog." $2.20, Paper-cut dog. $2.70, Dog and sheep. $3.30, Sheepdog Memorial, Lake Tekapo and birds.

2018, Jan. 10 Litho. *Perf. 13¼x13*

2765 A695 $1 multi	1.50	1.50
2766 A695 $2.20 multi	3.25	3.25
2767 A695 $2.70 multi	4.00	4.00
2768 A695 $3.30 multi	5.00	5.00
a. Souvenir sheet of 4, #2765-2768	14.00	14.00
Nos. 2765-2768 (4)	13.75	13.75

New Zealand in Space — A696

No. 2769: a, Electron rocket being delivered to launch pad. b, Rocket on launch pad. c, Humanity Star satellite. d, Aerial view of launch facility. e, Rocket launch. f, Satellite in space.

2018, Jan. 25 Litho. *Perf. 13½x13¼*

2769 Sheet of 6	29.50	29.50
a. A696 $1 multi	2.00	2.00
b. A696 $2 multi	4.25	4.25
c. A696 $2.20 multi	4.50	4.50
d. A696 $2.70 multi	5.75	5.75
e. A696 $3 multi	6.25	6.25
f. A696 $3.30 multi	6.75	6.75

No. 2769 sold for $19.90.

Bicycle Trails — A697

Designs: No. 2770, $1, Alps 2 Ocean Trail. No. 2771, $1, Mountains to Sea Trail. $2, Otago Central Rail Trail. $2.20, Old Ghost Road. $2.70, Queen Charlotte Track. $3.30, Timber Trail.

2018, Feb. 7 Litho. *Perf. 14x14½*

2770 A697 $1 multi	1.50	1.50
2771 A697 $1 multi	1.50	1.50
2772 A697 $2 multi	3.00	3.00
2773 A697 $2.20 multi	3.25	3.25
2774 A697 $2.70 multi	4.00	4.00
2775 A697 $3.30 multi	4.75	4.75
a. Souvenir sheet of 6, #2770-2775	18.00	18.00
Nos. 2770-2775 (6)	18.00	18.00

Wahine Ferry Disaster, 50th Anniv. — A698

Inscription: No. 2776, $1, World's Finest Drive-on Vessel. No. 2777, $1, Wahine in Trouble. $2, Waiting to Abandon Ship. $2.20, Lifeboats Make Land. $2.70, Hundreds Rescued From Wellington Harbor. $3.30, Aranui Passes Wahine Wreck.

2018, Mar. 7 Litho. *Perf. 14½x14*

2776 A698 $1 multi	1.50	1.50
2777 A698 $1 multi	1.50	1.50
2778 A698 $2 multi	3.00	3.00
2779 A698 $2.20 multi	3.25	3.25
2780 A698 $2.70 multi	4.00	4.00
2781 A698 $3.30 multi	4.75	4.75
a. Souvenir sheet of 6, #2776-2781	18.00	18.00
Nos. 2776-2781 (6)	18.00	18.00

World War I, Cent. Type of 2014

Designs: No. 2782, Private Arthur Gordon (1895-1978), advocate for disabled veterans. No. 2783, Hundred Days Offensive. No. 2784, Medicine Depot for treating victims of influenza pandemic. No. 2785, Demobilized soldier in New Zealand with family. No. 2786, Resettlement of veterans. No. 2787, Sopwith Camel biplane in air battle. No. 2788, Auckland Town Hall with lights celebrating armistice. No. 2789, Return of Maori Battalion. No. 2790, New Zealand soldiersat Le Quesnoy on stained-glass window of St. Andrew's Anglican Church, Cambridge, England. No. 2791, Emblem of War Amputees' Association.

2018, Apr. 4 Litho. *Perf. 14½*

2782 A631 $1 multi	1.50	1.50
a. Booklet pane of 1	1.90	—
2783 A631 $1 multi	1.50	1.50
a. Booklet pane of 1	1.90	—
2784 A631 $1 multi	1.50	1.50
a. Booklet pane of 1	1.90	—
2785 A631 $1 multi	1.50	1.50
a. Booklet pane of 1	1.90	—
2786 A631 $1 multi	1.50	1.50
a. Booklet pane of 1	1.90	—
2787 A631 $1 multi	1.50	1.50
a. Booklet pane of 1	1.90	—
b. Block of 6, #2782-2787	9.00	9.00
c. Souvenir sheet of 6, #2782-2787	9.00	9.00
2788 A631 $2.20 multi	3.25	3.25
a. Booklet pane of 1	4.00	—
b. Booklet pane of 6, #2782-2786, 2788	13.00	—
2789 A631 $2.20 multi	3.25	3.25
a. Booklet pane of 1	4.00	—
b. Horiz. pair, #2788-2789	6.50	6.50
2790 A631 $2.70 multi	4.00	4.00
a. Booklet pane of 1	5.00	—
2791 A631 $2.70 multi	4.00	4.00
a. Booklet pane of 1	5.00	—
b. Booklet pane of 4, #2787, 2789-2791	16.00	—
Complete booklet, #2782a, 2783a, 2784a, 2785a, 2786a. 2787a, 2788a, 2788b, 2789a, 2790a, 2791a, 2791b	58.50	
c. Horiz. pair, #2790-2791	8.00	8.00
d. Souvenir sheet of 4, #2788-2791	14.50	14.50
e. Souvenir sheet of 10, #2782-2791	23.50	23.50
Nos. 2782-2791 (10)	23.50	23.50

Complete booklet sold for $39.90.

Earthquake Reconstruction — A699

Designs: No. 2792, Construction on a seaside road. No. 2793, Helicopter above worker on hillside. $2, Dumptruck and excavator at construction site. $2.20, Construction of wall. $2.70, Finished rail bridge. $3.30, Freight train.

2018, May 2 Litho. *Perf. 14½x14*

2792 A699 $1 multi	1.40	1.40
2793 A699 $1 multi	1.40	1.40
2794 A699 $2 multi	2.75	2.75
2795 A699 $2.20 multi	3.25	3.25
2796 A699 $2.70 multi	3.75	3.75
2797 A699 $3.30 multi	4.75	4.75
a. Souvenir sheet of 6, #2792-2797	17.50	17.50
Nos. 2792-2797 (6)	17.30	17.30

Miniature Sheet

Wedding of Prince Harry and Meghan Markle A700

No. 2798: a, Color engagement photograph. b, Couple in wedding attire holding hands. c, Black-and-white engagement photograph. d, Couple kissing. e, Couple at wedding ceremony with Archbishop of Canterbury. f, Couple waving.

2018, May 21 Litho. *Perf. 14¼*

2798 A700 Sheet of 6	28.00	28.00
a.-f. $2.70 Any single	4.50	4.50

No. 2798 sold for $19.90.

Personalized Stamps Type of 2016
Miniature Sheet

No. 2799: a and i, Wedding rings. b and h, Fern fiddlehead. c, "Love." d, Champagne flutes. e, Teddy bear. f and j, Pohutukawa flowers. g, Bunch of balloons.

2018, June 6 Litho. *Perf. 15x14½*

2799 A658 Sheet of 10 + 5 labels 21.00 21.00
a.-g. $1.20 Any single 1.60 1.60
h.-i. $2.40 Either single 3.25 3.25
j. $3 multi 4.00 4.00

Tourist Attractions Type of 2014

Designs: $2.40, Mount Maunganui, Tauranga. $3, Tongaporutu, Taranaki. $4.40, Lake Te Anau, Fiordland.

2018, June 6 Litho. *Perf. 13¼x13½*

2800 A627 $2.40 multi 3.25 3.25
2801 A627 $4.40 multi 6.00 6.00

Self-Adhesive
Serpentine Die Cut 10x9½

2802 A627 $2.40 multi 3.25 3.25
a. Booklet pane of 5 16.50
2803 A627 $3 multi 4.00 4.00
a. Booklet pane of 5 + 2 etiquettes 20.00
b. Horiz. pair, #2802-2803 7.25
c. Dated "2022" 4.00 4.00
d. Booklet pane of 5 #2803c + 2 etiquettes 20.00

Issued: No. 2803c, 6/1/22.

Miniature Sheets

Legend of Maui and the Fish A702

Nos. 2804 and 2805: a, Eyes. b, Prow of waka. c, Hand holding jawbone. d, Fish. e, Curved triangles over land. f, Map of New Zealand.

2018, June 6 Litho. *Perf. 13¼x13½*

2804 A702 Sheet of 6 17.00 17.00
a.-c. $1.20 Any single 1.60 1.60
d. $2.40 multi 3.25 3.25
e. $3 multi 4.00 4.00
f. $3.60 multi 4.75 4.75

Self-Adhesive
Serpentine Die Cut 10x9½

2805 A702 Sheet of 6 17.00 17.00
a.-c. $1.20 Any single 1.60 1.60
d. $2.40 multi 3.25 3.25
e. $3 multi 4.00 4.00
f. $3.60 multi 4.75 4.75

Kiwis — A703

Designs: No. 2806, Brown kiwi. No. 2807, Great spotted kiwi. $2.40, Little spotted kiwi. $3, Tokoeka. $3.60, Rowi.

2018, July 4 Litho. *Perf. 14¾*

2806 A703 $1.20 multi 1.75 1.75
a. Booklet pane of 6 10.50 —
Complete booklet, #2806a 10.50
2807 A703 $1.20 multi 1.75 1.75
2808 A703 $2.40 multi 3.25 3.25
a. Souvenir sheet of 3, #2806-2808, with Asian International Stamp Exhibition emblem in sheet margin 7.75 7.75
b. As "a," with Thailand 2018 World Stamp Expo emblem in sheet margin 8.00 8.00
2809 A703 $3 multi 4.25 4.25
2810 A703 $3.60 multi 5.00 5.00
a. Souvenir sheet of 5, #2806-2810 16.00 16.00
Nos. 2806-2810 (5) 16.00 16.00

Values are for stamps with surrounding selvage.

Issued: No. 2808a, 9/21; No. 2808b, 12/3. 2018 Asian International Stamp Exhibition, Macao (#2808a); Thailand 2018 World Stamp Expo (#2808b). Nos. 2808a, 2808b each sold for $5.80.

Animals Native to New Zealand Threatened by Predators A704

Designs: No. 2811, Tui, stitchbird, saddleback, building, car, couple in beach chairs. No. 2812, White herons, blue ducks, kingfisher, Hochstetter's frog, couple on bicycles. $2.40, Tuatara, jewelled gecko, red admiral butterfly, weka, family on picnic. $3, Whitehead, tomtit, North Island robin, Forbes' parakeet, people at outdoor tables. $3.60, Owl, giant snail, kiwi, giant weta, people in house.

2018, Aug. 1 Litho. *Perf. 14½x14*

2811 A704 $1.20 multi 1.75 1.75
a. Perf. 14 2.00 2.00
2812 A704 $1.20 multi 1.75 1.75
a. Perf. 14 2.00 2.00
2813 A704 $2.40 multi 3.25 3.25
a. Perf. 14 3.75 3.75
b. Souvenir sheet of 3, #2811a, 2812a, 2813a 7.75 7.75
2814 A704 $3 multi 4.25 4.25
a. Souvenir sheet of 3, #2811, 2812, 2814 9.00 9.00
2815 A704 $3.60 multi 5.00 5.00
a. Souvenir sheet of 5, #2811-2815 16.00 16.00
Nos. 2811-2815 (5) 16.00 16.00

Issued: No. 2813b, 9/21; No. 2814a, 12/3. 2018 Asian International Stamp Exhibition, Macao (#2813b); Thailand 2018 World Stamp Expo (#2814a). No. 2813b sold for $5.80; No. 2814a sold for $6.40.

Woman Suffrage, 125th Anniv. A705

Designs: No. 2816, Kate Sheppard (1848-1934), suffragette. No. 2817, Camellia.

2018, Sept. 5 Litho. *Perf. 14¼x14*

2816 $3 multi 4.00 4.00
2817 $3 multi 4.00 4.00
a. A705 Horiz. pair, #2816-2817 8.00 8.00
b. Souvenir sheet of 2, #2816-2817 8.00 8.00

Miniature Sheet

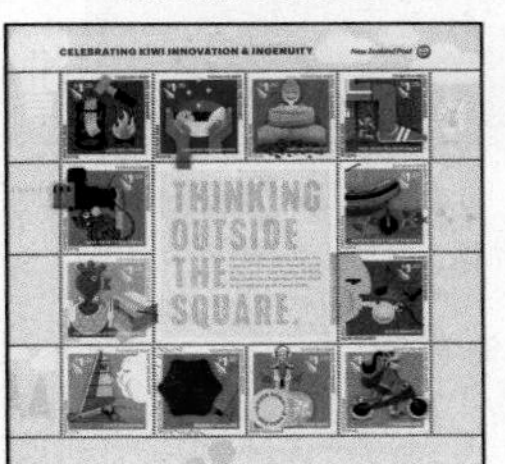

Innovations by New Zealanders — A706

No. 2818: a, Log splitter, invented by Ayla Hutchinson. b, Lifepod incubator, invented by Sir Ray Avery. c, Instant coffee, invented by David Strang. d, Jogging movement, popularized by Arthur Lydard. e, Self-resetting traps, invented by Stu Barr, Robbie van Dam and Craig Bond. f, Retractable boat wheels, invented by Maurice Bryham. g, Automatic chicken feeder, invented by Bill Kirkham. h, Referee's whistle, invented by William Harrington Atack. i, Land yacht, invented by Paul Beckett. j, Wind-resistant umbrella, invented by Greig Brebner. k, Child-proof medicine bottle caps, invented by Claudio Petronelli. l, 3-stage bike, invented by Rich Latham.

2018, Sept. 5 Litho. *Perf. 14½*

2818 A706 Sheet of 12 + central label 19.50 19.50
a.-l. $1.20 Any single 1.60 1.60

End of World War I, Cent. — A707

Designs: No. 2819, Old and modern Air Force aviators. No. 2820, Medical Corps nurse from World War I and modern doctor. $2.40, Old and modern Army soldiers. $3, Old and modern Navy sailors. $3.60, Poppy.

2018, Oct. 1 Litho. *Perf. 14¼*

2819 A707 $1.20 multi 1.60 1.60
2820 A707 $1.20 multi 1.60 1.60
2821 A707 $2.40 multi 3.25 3.25
2822 A707 $3 multi 4.00 4.00
a. Souvenir sheet of 3, #2819, 2821, 2822 13.00 13.00
2823 A707 $3.60 multi 4.75 4.75
a. Souvenir sheet of 5, #2819-2823 15.50 15.50
Nos. 2819-2823 (5) 15.20 15.20

Issued: No. 2822a, 11/9. Armistice Stamp Show, Dunedin (No. 2822a). No. 2822a sold for $9.10 with $2.50 going to the Philatelic Trust.

Miniature Sheet

Royal Visit of the Duke and Duchess of Sussex A708

No. 2824: a, Duchess of Sussex touching heads with New Zealand man at welcoming ceremony. b, Black-and-white photograph of Duke and Duchess of Sussex. c, Duke of Sussex holding child's toy. d, Duke of Sussex reviewing troops. e, Duke and Duchess of Sussex with crowd in background. f, Duke and Duchess of Sussex with building pillar in background.

2018, Oct. 30 Litho. *Perf. 14¼x14½*

2824 A708 Sheet of 6 27.00 27.00
a.-f. $3 Any single 4.50 4.50

No. 2824 sold for $19.90.

Christmas — A709

Designs: Nos. 2825, 2830a, 2831, Virgin Mary. Nos. 2826, 2830b, 2832, Holy Family. $2.40, Christmas angel. $3, Magi with infant Jesus. $3.60, Shepherd.

2018, Nov. 7 Litho. *Perf. 14*

2825 A709 $1.20 multi 1.75 1.75
2826 A709 $1.20 multi 1.75 1.75
a. Horiz. pair, #2825-2826 3.50 3.50
2827 A709 $2.40 multi 3.50 3.50
2828 A709 $3 multi 4.25 4.25
2829 A709 $3.60 multi 5.00 5.00
Nos. 2825-2829 (5) 16.25 16.25

Miniature Sheet
Litho. With Foil Application

2830 Sheet of 5 16.50 16.50
a.-b. A709 $1.75 Either single 1.75 1.75
c. A709 $2.40 gold & multi 3.50 3.50
d. A709 $3 gold & multi 4.25 4.25
e. A709 $3.60 gold & multi 5.00 5.00

Self-Adhesive
Size: 25x30mm
Litho.
Serpentine Die Cut 9¾x10¼

2831 A709 $1.20 multi 1.75 1.75
2832 A709 $1.20 multi 1.75 1.75
a. Booklet pane of 10, 5 each #2831-2832 17.50

With Added Blue International Air Inscription

2833 A709 $2.40 multi 3.50 3.50
a. Booklet pane of 10 + 10 stickers 35.00
2834 A709 $3 multi 4.25 4.25
a. Booklet pane of 10 + 10 stickers 42.50
b. Horiz. strip of 4, #2831-2834 11.50
Nos. 2831-2834 (4) 11.25 11.25

No. 2833a sold for $21.60. No. 2834a sold for $27.

New Year 2019 (Year of the Pig) — A710

Designs: $1.20, Chinese character for "pig." $2.40, Paper-cut pig. $3, Arapawa pig. $3.60, State Highway 85, the "Pig Route".

2019, Jan. 16 Litho. *Perf. 13¼x13*

2835 A710 $1.20 multi 1.75 1.75
2836 A710 $2.40 multi 3.50 3.50
2837 A710 $3 multi 4.25 4.25
2838 A710 $3.60 multi 5.00 5.00
a. Souvenir sheet of 4, #2835-2838 14.50 14.50
Nos. 2835-2838 (4) 14.50 14.50

Native Alpine Flowers — A711

Designs: No. 2839, Mountain buttercups. No. 2840, Penwiper plant. No. 2841, Black scree button daisies. $2.40, Woollyheads. $3, Mount Cook lilies. $3.60, Moss-dwelling forget-me-nots.

2019, Feb. 13 Litho. *Perf. 14*

2839 A711 $1.20 multi 1.75 1.75
a. Perf. 13½ 2.25 2.25
2840 A711 $1.20 multi 1.75 1.75
2841 A711 $1.20 multi 1.75 1.75
a. Perf. 13½ 2.25 2.25
2842 A711 $2.40 multi 3.25 3.25
a. Perf. 13½ 4.50 4.50
b. Souvenir sheet of 3, #2839a, 2841a, 2842a 9.00 9.00
2843 A711 $3 multi 4.25 4.25
2844 A711 $3.60 multi 5.00 5.00
a. Souvenir sheet of 6, #2839-2844 18.00 18.00
Nos. 2839-2844 (6) 17.75 17.75

China 2019 World Stamp Exhibition, Wuhan (No. 2842b). Issued; No. 2842b, 6/11. No. 2842b sold for $6.80. On each of the seven days of the China 2019 World Stamp Exhibition, 300 examples were offered for sale of No. 2842b with an overprint added in the the sheet margin at lower right noting the day of the show on which it was sold and a serial number.

Views From Lighthouses A712

Drawing of and view from: No. 2845, Pouto Lighthouse. No. 2846, Manukau Heads Lighthouse. No. 2847, Baring Head Lighthouse. $2.40, French Pass Lighthouse. $3, Nugget Point Lighthouse. $3.60, Puysegur Point Lighthouse.

2019, Mar. 6 Litho. *Perf. 14¼x14*

2845 A712 $1.20 multi 1.75 1.75
2846 A712 $1.20 multi 1.75 1.75
2847 A712 $1.20 multi 1.75 1.75
a. Souvenir sheet of 3, #2845-2847 4.25 4.25
2848 A712 $2.40 multi 3.25 3.25
2849 A712 $3 multi 4.25 4.25
2850 A712 $3.60 multi 5.00 5.00
a. Souvenir sheet of 6, #2845-2850 18.00 18.00
Nos. 2845-2850 (6) 17.75 17.75

Issued: No. 2847a, 3/19/20. New Zealand 2020 International Stamp Exhibition, Auckland (No. 2847a).

ANZAC Day Dawn Service A713

Dawn service at: No. 2851, Auckland. No. 2852, Kaikoura. No. 2853, Stewart Island. $2.40, Scott Base, Antarctica. $3, Whangarei. $3.60, Dannevirke.

2019, Apr. 3 Litho. *Perf. 14x14½*

2851 A713 $1.20 multi 1.75 1.75
2852 A713 $1.20 multi 1.75 1.75
2853 A713 $1.20 multi 1.75 1.75
2854 A713 $2.40 multi 3.25 3.25
2855 A713 $3 multi 4.25 4.25
2856 A713 $3.60 multi 5.00 5.00
a. Souvenir sheet of 6, #2851-2856 18.00 18.00
Nos. 2851-2856 (6) 17.75 17.75

Space Pioneers — A714

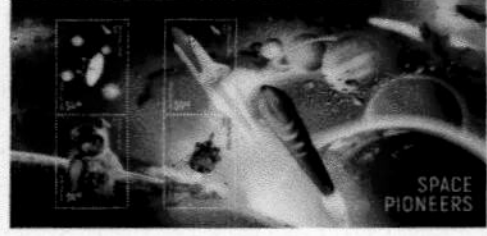

Space Missions A715

Designs: No. 2857, Beatrice Hill Tinsley (1941-81), cosmologist. No. 2858, Alan Gilmore and Pamela Kilmartin, astronomers. $2.40, Charles Gifford (1861-1948), astronomer. $3, Albert Jones (1920-2013), visual astronomer. $3.60, Sir William Pickering (1910-2004), rocket scientist.

No. 2862: a, Space probe and stars. b, Space Shuttle. c, Astronaut on Moon. d, Lunar Module lifting off from Moon.

2019, May 1 Litho. *Perf. 14½*

2857 A714 $1.20 multi 1.60 1.60
2858 A714 $1.20 multi 1.60 1.60
2859 A714 $2.40 multi 3.25 3.25
2860 A714 $3 multi 4.00 4.00
2861 A714 $3.60 multi 4.75 4.75
a. Vert. strip of 5, #2857-2861 15.50 15.50
Nos. 2857-2861 (5) 15.20 15.20

Miniature Sheet

Litho. With Lenticular Lens Affixed

Perf. 14x14¼

2862 A715 Sheet of 4 21.00 21.00
a.-d. $4 Any single 5.25 5.25

Crushed meteorites were added to the ink used to print the circle around the portraits on Nos. 2857-2861.

Tourist Attractions Type of 2014

Designs: $2.60, Escarpment Walkway, Paekakariki. $3.30, Dunedin Railway Station. $3.90, Banks Peninsula, Canterbury. $4.50, Shotover River Valley, Otago.

2019, June 5 Litho. *Perf. 13¼x13½*

2863 A627 $2.60 multi 3.50 3.50
2864 A627 $3.90 multi 5.25 5.25
2865 A627 $4.50 multi 6.00 6.00
Nos. 2863-2865 (3) 14.75 14.75

Self-Adhesive

Serpentine Die Cut 10x9¾

2866 A627 $2.60 multi 3.50 3.50
a. Booklet pane of 5 + 2 etiquettes 17.50
2867 A627 $3.30 multi 4.50 4.50
a. Booklet pane of 5 + 2 etiquettes 22.50
b. Horiz. pair, #2866-2867 on paper without back printing 8.00

A716

A717

A718

A719

A720

A721

A722

Legend of Kupe, the Great Navigator A723

2019, June 5 Litho. *Perf. 14¼*

2868 Block of 8 14.00 14.00
a. A716 $1.30 multi 1.75 1.75
b. A717 $1.30 multi 1.75 1.75
c. A718 $1.30 multi 1.75 1.75
d. A719 $1.30 multi 1.75 1.75
e. A720 $1.30 multi 1.75 1.75
f. A721 $1.30 multi 1.75 1.75
g. A722 $1.30 multi 1.75 1.75
h. A723 $1.30 multi 1.75 1.75
i. Sheet of 8, #2868a-2868h 14.00 14.00
j. Souvenir sheet of 4, #2868a, 2868b, 2868c, 2868e 6.25 6.25

Issued: No. 2868j, 3/19/20. New Zealand 2020 International Stamp Exhibition, Auckland (No. 2868j).

Paintings by Colin McCahon (1919-87) A724

Paintings: No. 2869, I Am, 1954. No. 2870, Titirangi Landscape, 1954. $2.60, The Angel of the Annunciation, 1947, vert. $3.30, Red and Black Landscape, 1959, vert. $4, The First Waterfall, 1964, vert.

2019, July 3 Litho. *Perf. 14¼*

2869 A724 $1.30 multi 1.75 1.75
2870 A724 $1.30 multi 1.75 1.75
2871 A724 $2.60 multi 3.50 3.50
2872 A724 $3.30 multi 4.50 4.50
2873 A724 $4 multi 5.25 5.25
a. Souvenir sheet of 5, #2869-2873 17.00 17.00
Nos. 2869-2873 (5) 16.75 16.75

Sir Edmund Hillary (1919-2008), Mountaineer A725

No. 2874 — Various images of Hillary and inscription: a. Hillary Ridge, Aoraki/Mount Cook. b, Mount Everest. c, South Pole Expedition. d, Himalayan Trust. e, Ocean to Sky, India.

2019, July 23 Litho. *Perf. 14¼*

2874 Horiz. strip of 5 8.75 8.75
a.-e. A725 $1.30 Any single 1.75 1.75

Miniature Sheet

Rock Formations — A726

No. 2875: a, Kaiaraara. b, Lion Rock. c, Elephant Rock. d, Te Hoho Rock. e, Castlepoint Reef. f, Motukiekie. g, Tunnel Beach. h, Punakaiki. i, Anapai Bay.

2019, Aug. 7 Litho. *Perf. 14¼*

2875 A726 Sheet of 9 15.00 15.00
a.-i. $1.30 Any single 1.60 1.60

Te Araroa Trail — A727

Designs: No. 2876, Ninety Mile Beach, Northland. No. 2877, Karamu Walkway, Waikato. No. 2878, Tongariro Alpine Crossing. $2.60, Nelson Lakes, Tasman. $3.30, Stag Saddle, Canterbury. $4, Lake Hawea, Otago.

2019, Sept. 4 Litho. *Perf. 14¼*

2876 A727 $1.30 multi 1.60 1.60
2877 A727 $1.30 multi 1.60 1.60
2878 A727 $1.30 multi 1.60 1.60
2879 A727 $2.60 multi 3.25 3.25
2880 A727 $3.30 multi 4.25 4.25
2881 A727 $4 multi 5.00 5.00
a. Souvenir sheet of 6, #2876-2881 17.50 17.50
Nos. 2876-2881 (6) 17.30 17.30

Emblems of All Blacks Rugby Team A728

No. 2882 — Emblem from: a, 1905. b, 1921. c, 1924. d, 1967. e, 1986. f, 2003.

Perf. 13¾x13¼

2019, Sept. 20 Litho.

2882 A728 Sheet of 6 19.50 19.50
a.-f. $2.60 Any single 3.25 3.25

Paintings by Michel Tuffery on 250th Anniv. of Encounter of the Maori and British Explorers — A729

Designs: No. 2883, Birds and Maori boats. No. 2884, British sailor on ship and Maori on shore. $2.60, Daniel Solander (1733-82), naturalist, and Te Maro. $3.30, Maori and British ship in harbor. $4, Captain James Cook (1728-79).

2019, Oct. 2 Litho. *Perf. 14*

2883 A729 $1.30 multi 1.75 1.75
2884 A729 $1.30 multi 1.75 1.75
2885 A729 $2.60 multi 3.50 3.50
2886 A729 $3.30 multi 4.25 4.25
2887 A729 $4 multi 5.25 5.25
a. Souvenir sheet of 5, #2883-2887 16.50 16.50
Nos. 2883-2887 (5) 16.50 16.50

A730

Christmas — A731

Designs: Nos. 2888, 2893, Madonna and Child. Nos. 2889, 2894, St. Joseph. Nos. 2890, 2895, Shepherd playing flute. Nos. 2891, 2896, Magi. No. 2892, $4, Angel.

2019, Nov. 6 Litho. *Perf. 14¼x14*

2888 A730 $1.30 multi 1.75 1.75
2889 A730 $1.30 multi 1.75 1.75
a. Horiz. pair, #2888-2889 3.50 3.50
2890 A730 $2.60 multi 3.50 3.50
2891 A730 $3.30 multi 4.25 4.25
2892 A730 $4 multi 5.25 5.25
a. Souvenir sheet of 5, #2888-2892 16.50 16.50

Self-Adhesive

Serpentine Die Cut 9½x10

2893 A731 $1.30 multi 1.75 1.75
2894 A731 $1.30 multi 1.75 1.75
a. Booklet pane of 10, 5 each #2893-2894 17.50
2895 A731 $2.60 multi 3.50 3.50
a. Booklet pane of 10 + 10 etiquettes 35.00
2896 A731 $3.30 multi 4.25 4.25
a. Booklet pane of 10 + 10 etiquettes 42.50
b. Horiz. strip of 4, #2893-2896 11.50
Nos. 2893-2896 (4) 11.25 11.25

Nos. 2895-2896 are airmail. No. 2895a sold for $23.40 and No. 2896a sold for $29.70.

Miniature Sheet

Visit to New Zealand of Prince Charles and Duchess of Cornwall A732

No. 2897: a, Prince Charles. b, Prince Charles reviewing troops. c, Prince Charles and Duchess of Cornwall at wreath-laying ceremony. d, Duchess of Cornwall and Prince Charles. e, Prince Charles and Duchess of Cornwall wearing ceremonial robes. f, Duchess of Cornwall.

2019, Nov. 22 Litho. *Perf. 14½x15*

2897 A732 Sheet of 6 26.50 26.50
a.-b. $1.30 Either single 2.40 2.40
c.-d. $2.60 Either single 4.75 4.75
e.-f. $3.30 Either single 6.00 6.00

No. 2897 sold for $19.90.

New Year 2020 (Year of the Rat) — A733

Designs: $1.30, Chinese character for "rat." $2.60, Paper-cut rat. $3.30, Rat and ship. $4, Sky Tower, Auckland.

2019-20 Litho. *Perf. 13¼x13*

2898 A733 $1.30 multi 1.75 1.75
a. Perf. 13¼x13½ 1.50 1.50
2899 A733 $2.60 multi 3.50 3.50
a. Perf. 13¼x13½ 3.00 3.00
2900 A733 $3.30 multi 4.50 4.50
a. Perf. 13¼x13½ 4.00 4.00
b. Souvenir sheet of 3, #2898a, 2899a, 2900a 8.50 8.50
2901 A733 $4 multi 5.50 5.50
a. Souvenir sheet of 4, #2898-2901 15.50 15.50
Nos. 2898-2901 (4) 15.25 15.25

Issued: Nos. 2898-2901, 2901a, 12/4; Nos. 2898a, 2899a, 2900a, 2900b, 3/19/20. New Zealand 2020 International Stamp Exhibition, Auckland (No. 2900b).

Moths — A734

Designs: No. 2902, Notoreas blax. No. 2903, Notoreas casanova. No. 2904, Notoreas edwardsi. $2.60, Notoreas mechanitis. $3.30, Notoreas "Wellington Coast." $4, Notoreas "Kaitorete Spit."

2020, Feb. 5 Litho. *Perf. 14*

Background Color

2902 A734 $1.30 bright blue 1.60 1.60
2903 A734 $1.30 bright green 1.60 1.60
2904 A734 $1.30 bright yellow 1.60 1.60
2905 A734 $2.60 bright orange 3.25 3.25
2906 A734 $3.30 bright pink 4.25 4.25
2907 A734 $4 bright lilac 5.00 5.00
a. Souvenir sheet of 6, #2902-2907 17.50 17.50
Nos. 2902-2907 (6) 17.30 17.30

Parakeets — A735

Designs: No. 2908, Yellow-crowned parakeet. No. 2909, Orange-fronted parakeet. $2.60, Red-crowned parakeet. $3.30, Forbes' parakeet. $4, Antipodes Island parakeet.

2020, Mar. 4 Litho. *Perf. 14½x14*

2908 A735 $1.30 multi 1.50 1.50
2909 A735 $1.30 multi 1.50 1.50
2910 A735 $2.60 multi 3.00 3.00
2911 A735 $3.30 multi 4.00 4.00
2912 A735 $4 multi 4.75 4.75
a. Souvenir sheet of 5, #2908-2912 15.00 15.00
Nos. 2908-2912 (5) 14.75 14.75

Souvenir Sheet

New Zealand 2020 International Stamp Exhibition, Auckland — A736

No. 2913 — Exhibition emblem, lifebuoy, and: a, Auckland Harbour Bridge, sailboats in distance. b, Auckland Harbour Bridge, sailboats in foreground. c, Auckland skyline.

2020, Mar. 19 Litho. *Perf. 14*

2913 A736 Sheet of 3 6.00 6.00
a.-b. $1.30 Either single 1.50 1.50
c. $2.60 multi 3.00 3.00

End of World War II, 75th Anniv. A737

No. 2914 — Inscriptions: a, Mobilizing the nation. b, HMS Achilles. c, Fighter pilots. d, Retreat from Crete. e, 28th (Maori) Battalion. f, Women's War Service Auxiliary. g, Railway construction in Africa. h, At rest in the Pacific. i, American servicemen in Wellington. j, Merchant Marine. k, Bomber Command. l, Air raid drill in Auckland. m, Home Guard. n, Monte Cassino. o, Peace celebration in Wellington.

2020, May 18 Litho. *Perf. 14¼x14*

2914 Miniature sheet of 15 24.00 24.00
a.-o. A737 $1.30 Any single 1.60 1.60
p. Booklet pane of 2 #2914a 3.25 —
q. Booklet pane of 2 #2914b 3.25 —
r. Booklet pane of 2 #2914c 3.25 —
s. Booklet pane of 2 #2914d 3.25 —
t. Booklet pane of 2 #2914e 3.25 —
u. Booklet pane of 2 #2914f 3.25 —
v. Booklet pane of 2 #2914g 3.25 —
w. Booklet pane of 2 #2914h 3.25 —
x. Booklet pane of 2 #2914i 3.25 —
y. Booklet pane of 2 #2914j 3.25 —
z. Booklet pane of 2 #2914k 3.25 —
aa. Booklet pane of 2 #2914l 3.25 —
ab. Booklet pane of 2 #2914m 3.25 —
ac. Booklet pane of 2 #2914n 3.25 —
ad. Booklet pane of 2 #2914o 3.25 —
Complete bookleet, #2914p-2914ad 49.00

Complete booklet sold for $39.90.

Scenery — A738

Designs: $4, Island Bay, Wellington. $10, Aoraki Mount Cook.

2020, June 3 Litho. *Perf. 13¼x13½*

2915 A738 $4 multi 5.25 5.25
2916 A738 $10 multi 13.00 13.00

Compare types A627 and A738. See Nos. 2922-2925, 2966, 2968-2969, 3024-3025, 3084-3089.

For self-adhesive stamp like No. 2916, see No. 3089.

The Four Winds — A739

Various designs.

2020, June 3 Litho. *Perf. 14¼x14*

2917 A739 $1.40 multi 1.90 1.90
2918 A739 $2.70 multi 3.50 3.50
2919 A739 $3.30 multi 4.25 4.25
2920 A739 $4 multi 5.25 5.25
a. Souvenir sheet of 4, #2917-2920 15.00 15.00
Nos. 2917-2920 (4) 14.90 14.90

Baked Goods — A740

No. 2921: a, Anzac biscuits. b, Pavlova. c, Churchill slices. d, Cheese rolls. e, Lolly cakes. f, Neenish tarts, g, Lamingtons. h, Cheese scones. i, Custard squares. j, Chocolate crackles. k, Ginger biscuits. l, Melting moments. m, Louise cakes, n, Afghans. o, Banana cake.

2020, July 1 Litho. *Perf. 13¾x14¼*

2921 Miniature sheet of 15 28.50 28.50
a.-o. A740 $1.40 Any single 1.90 1.90

Scenery Type of 2020

Designs: $3.50, Fitzroy Bay, Marlborough Sounds. $4.20, Waterfall on Whanganui River. $4.70, Mount Ngauruhoe.

2020, Aug. 5 Litho. *Perf. 13¼x13½*

2922 A738 $3.50 multi 4.75 4.75
2923 A738 $4.20 multi 5.75 5.75
2924 A738 $4.70 multi 6.50 6.50
Nos. 2922-2924 (3) 17.00 17.00

Booklet Stamp
Self-Adhesive

Serpentine Die Cut 10x9¾

2925 A738 $3.50 multi 4.75 4.75
a. Booklet pane of 5 + 2 etiquettes 24.00
b. Single stamp on backing paper without back printing 4.75

Paintings of New Zealand Armed Forces in World War II by Peter McIntyre (1910-95) — A741

Artwork: $1.40, General Hospital, Crete, 1941. $2.70, Building the Railway to Tobruk, 1941. $3.50, The Grant Tanks Go Into Action, El Alamein, 1942. $4, Medical Officer Attending Wounded Germans After Final Surrender in Tunisia, 1943.

2020, Aug. 5 Litho. *Perf. 14½*

2926 A741 $1.40 multi 1.90 1.90
2927 A741 $2.70 multi 3.75 3.75
2928 A741 $3.50 multi 4.75 4.75
2929 A741 $4 multi 5.50 5.50
a. Souvenir sheet of 4, #2926-2929 16.00 16.00
Nos. 2926-2929 (4) 15.90 15.90

Maori Language Week — A742

Maori words: $1.40, Aroha (love). $2.70, Whanau (family). $3.50, Tane (man). $4, Wahine (woman).

2020, Sept. 2 Litho. *Perf. 14x14¼*

2930 A742 $1.40 multi 1.90 1.90
2931 A742 $2.70 multi 3.50 3.50
2932 A742 $3.50 multi 4.75 4.75
2933 A742 $4 multi 5.25 5.25
a. Souvenir sheet of 4, #2930-2933 15.50 15.50
Nos. 2930-2933 (4) 15.40 15.40

2020 Summer Olympics, Tokyo — A743

Designs: No. 2934, Track. No. 2935, Surfing. No. 2936, Pole vault, horiz. $2.70, Field hockey, horiz. $3.50, Rugby sevens. $4, Shot put.

Perf. 14½x14, 14x14½

2020, Oct. 7 Litho.

2934 A743 $1.40 multi 1.90 1.90
2935 A743 $1.40 multi 1.90 1.90
2936 A743 $1.40 multi 1.90 1.90
2937 A743 $2.70 multi 3.75 3.75
2938 A743 $3.50 multi 4.75 4.75
2939 A743 $4 multi 5.25 5.25
a. Souvenir sheet of 6, #2934-2939 19.50 19.50
Nos. 2934-2939 (6) 19.45 19.45

First appearance of a New Zealand team at Summer Olympics, cent. The 2020 Summer Olympics was postponed to 2021 because of the coronavirus pandemic.

A744

Christmas — A745

Stained-glass windows depicting: $1.40, Angel. $2.70, Madonna and Child. $3.50, Star. $4, Magus.

2020, Nov. 4 Litho. *Perf. 14¼x14*

2940 A744 $1.40 multi 2.00 2.00
2941 A744 $2.70 multi 3.75 3.75
2942 A744 $3.50 multi 5.00 5.00
2943 A744 $4 multi 5.75 5.75
a. Souvenir sheet of 4, #2940-2943 16.50 16.50
Nos. 2940-2943 (4) 16.50 16.50

Self-Adhesive

Serpentine Die Cut 9¾x10

2944 A745 $1.40 multi 2.00 2.00
a. Booklet pane of 10 20.00
2945 A745 $2.70 multi 3.75 3.75
a. Booklet pane of 10 + 10 etiquettes 37.50
2946 A745 $3.50 multi 5.00 5.00
a. Booklet pane of 10 + 10 etiquettes 50.00
b. Horiz. strip of 3, #2944-2946 11.00
Nos. 2944-2946 (3) 10.75 10.75

New Year 2020 (Year of the Ox) — A746

Designs: $1.40, Faces of child and ox. $2.70, Ox and two children. $3.50, Child with toy ox. $4, Ox, child and apples.

2020, Dec. 2 Litho. *Perf. 13¼x13½*

2947 A746 $1.40 dp ultra & pink 2.00 2.00
2948 A746 $2.70 red & pink 4.00 4.00
2949 A746 $3.50 dp ultra & pink 5.00 5.00
2950 A746 $4 red & pink 5.75 5.75
a. Souvenir sheet of 4, #2947-2950 17.00 17.00
Nos. 2947-2950 (4) 16.75 16.75

Passage of Homosexual Law Reform Bill, 35th Anniv. — A747

2021, Feb. 3 Litho. *Perf. 14*

2951 A747 $1.40 multi 2.10 2.10

Miniature Sheet

Holiday at Home A748

No. 2952: a, Surfer and Mount Taranaki. b, Hiker and kiwis, Stewart Island. c, Telescope and Church of the Good Shepherd, Tekapo. d, Dolphins and building, Akaroa. e, Snorkelers and Treaty House, Treaty Grounds, Waitangi. f, Castlepoint Lighthouse, Wairarapa. g, Automobile, woman at Hamilton Gardens, Hamilton. h, Canoers and Bridge to Nowhere, Whanganui. i, Boats, fisherman on pier, Marlborough Sounds.

2021, Feb. 3 Litho. *Perf. 14¼x14*

2952 A748 Sheet of 9 19.00 19.00
a.-i. $1.40 Any single 2.10 2.10

Royal New Zealand Yacht Squadron, 150th Anniv. — A749

New Zealand yachts victorious in international competitions: $1.40, Te Rehutai, 2020. $2.70, Steinlager II, 1989. $3.50, Rainbow II, 1969. $4, Rainbow I, 1898.

2021, Mar. 3 Litho. *Perf. 14x14½*

2953 A749 $1.40 multi 2.10 2.10
2954 A749 $2.70 multi 4.00 4.00
2955 A749 $3.50 multi 5.25 5.25
2956 A749 $4 multi 6.00 6.00
a. Souvenir sheet of 4, #2953-2956 17.50 17.50
Nos. 2953-2956 (4) 17.35 17.35

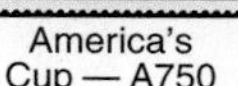

America's Cup — A750

Aerial View of Te Rehutai — A751

Te Rehutai — A752

Top of Te Rehutai Sails — A753

Te Rehutai and Auckland Skyline — A754

Te Rehutai — A755

Perf. 14¼x14¾

2021, Mar. 17 **Litho.**

2957 Sheet of 6 29.00 29.00
a. A750 $2.70 multi 4.75 4.75
b. A751 $2.70 multi 4.75 4.75
c. A752 $2.70 multi 4.75 4.75
d. A753 $2.70 multi 4.75 4.75
e. A754 $2.70 multi 4.75 4.75
f. A755 $2.70 multi 4.75 4.75

Victory of Te Rehutai in 2021 America's Cup Yacht Race. No. 2957 sold for $19.90.

Queen Elizabeth II, 95th Birthday — A756

Designs: Manuka flower and various photographs of Queen Elizabeth II.

2021, Apr. 7 **Litho.** ***Perf. 14***

2958 A756 $1.40 multi 2.00 2.00
2959 A756 $2.70 multi 3.75 3.75
2960 A756 $3.50 multi 5.00 5.00
2961 A756 $4 multi 5.75 5.75
a. Souvenir sheet of 4, #2958-2961 16.50 16.50
Nos. 2958-2961 (4) 16.50 16.50

Botanical Art by Sarah Featon (1848-1927) — A757

Designs: $1.40, Clematis paniculata. $2.70, Corynocarpus laevigatus. $3.50, Clianthus puniceus. $4, Pleurophyllum speciosum.

2021, May 5 **Litho.** ***Perf. 13¼x13½***

2962 A757 $1.40 multi 2.00 2.00
2963 A757 $2.70 multi 4.00 4.00
2964 A757 $3.50 multi 5.25 5.25
2965 A757 $4 multi 5.75 5.75
a. Souvenir sheet of 4, #2962-2965 17.00 17.00
Nos. 2962-2965 (4) 17.00 17.00

Scenery Type of 2020

Designs: $2.80, Auckland. $3.60, Bridge over Waikato River. $4.10, Castle Hill, Canterbury.

2021, June 2 **Litho.** ***Perf. 13¼x13½***

2966 A738 $4.10 multi 5.75 5.75

Self-Adhesive

Serpentine Die Cut 10x9¾

2968 A738 $2.80 multi 4.00 4.00
a. Booklet pane of 5 + 2 etiquettes 20.00
2969 A738 $3.60 multi 5.00 5.00
a. Booklet pane of 5 + 2 etiquettes 25.00
b. Horiz. pair, #2968-2969 on backing paper without back printing 9.00

Kayaking A758

Cycling A759

Skiing A760

Hiking A761

Camping with Recreational Vehicle — A762

Serpentine Die Cut 10x9¾

2021, June 2 **Litho.**

Self-Adhesive

2970 A758 ($1.50) multi 2.10 2.10
2971 A759 ($1.50) multi 2.10 2.10
2972 A760 ($1.50) multi 2.10 2.10
2973 A761 ($1.50) multi 2.10 2.10
2974 A762 ($1.50) multi 2.10 2.10
a. Horiz. coil strip of 5, #2970-2974 10.50
b. Booklet pane of 10, 2 each #2970-2974 21.00
Nos. 2970-2974 (5) 10.50 10.50

Family of Light — A763

Various designs.

2021, June 2 **Litho.** ***Perf. 14x14¼***

2975 A763 $1.50 multi 2.10 2.10
2976 A763 $2.80 multi 4.00 4.00
2977 A763 $3.60 multi 5.00 5.00
2978 A763 $4.10 multi 5.75 5.75
a. Souvenir sheet of 4, #2975-2978 17.00 17.00
Nos. 2975-2978 (4) 16.85 16.85

Matariki (Maori New Year).

A764

A765

A766

A767

A768

Curved Lines — A769

2021, July 2 **Litho.** ***Perf. 14¼***

2979 Sheet of 6 21.50 21.50
a. A764 $1.50 multi 2.10 2.10
b. A765 $1.50 multi 2.10 2.10
c. A766 $1.50 multi 2.10 2.10
d. A767 $2.80 multi 4.00 4.00
e. A768 $3.60 multi 5.00 5.00
f. A769 $4.10 multi 5.75 5.75

Rebranding and new emblem of NZPost.

Souvenir Sheet

Prince Philip (1921-2021) — A770

2021, Aug. 4 **Litho.** ***Perf. 14x14¼***

2980 A770 $3.60 multi 5.25 5.25

2020 Paralympics, Tokyo — A771

Designs: $1.50, Sophie Pascoe. $2.80, Cameron Leslie. $3.60, Emma Foy and Hannah Van Kampen. $4.10, "Spirit of Gold."

2021, Aug. 4 **Litho.** ***Perf. 14***

2981 A771 $1.50 black & gold 2.10 2.10
2982 A771 $2.80 black & gold 4.00 4.00
2983 A771 $3.60 black & gold 5.25 5.25
2984 A771 $4.10 black & gold 5.75 5.75
a. Souvenir sheet of 4, #2981-2984 17.50 17.50
Nos. 2981-2984 (4) 17.10 17.10

The 2020 Paralympics were postponed until 2021 because of the COVID-19 pandemic.

Home of Bilbo and Frodo Baggins — A772

Frodo and Samwise Gamgee Hiding From Black Rider — A773

Frodo, Samwise and Aragorn Elessar II at the Prancing Pony A774

Arwen Undómiel A775

Balrog — A776

The Fellowship at the Gates of Argonath — A777

2021 **Litho.** ***Perf. 14x14½***

2985 A772 $1.50 multi 2.10 2.10
a. Souvenir sheet of 1 2.10 2.10
2986 A773 $1.50 multi 2.10 2.10
a. Souvenir sheet of 1 2.10 2.10
2987 A774 $1.50 multi 2.10 2.10
a. Souvenir sheet of 1 2.10 2.10
2988 A775 $2.80 multi 4.00 4.00
a. Souvenir sheet of 1 4.00 4.00
2989 A776 $3.60 multi 5.25 5.25
a. Souvenir sheet of 1 5.25 5.25
2990 A777 $4.10 multi 5.75 5.75
a. Souvenir sheet of 1 5.75 5.75
b. Souvenir sheet of 2, #2989-2990 11.00 11.00
Nos. 2985-2990 (6) 21.30 21.30

Movie *The Lord of the Rings: The Fellowship of the Ring*, 20th anniv.; Royalpex 2021, (No. 2990b). Issued: Nos. 2985-2990, 2985a-2990a, 9/1. No. 2990b, 9/10.

Diwali A778

Designs: $1.50, Oil lamp. $2.80, Sparkler. $3.60, Woman's hands holding plate of laddus. $4.10, Lotus flower.

2021, Oct. 7 **Litho.** ***Perf. 14x14¼***

2991 A778 $1.50 multi 2.25 2.25
2992 A778 $2.80 multi 4.00 4.00
2993 A778 $3.60 multi 5.25 5.25
2994 A778 $4.10 multi 6.00 6.00
a. Souvenir sheet of 4, #2991-2994 17.50 17.50
Nos. 2991-2994 (4) 17.50 17.50

The New Zealand Post Philatelic Bureau sent out se-tenant blocks of 4 of Nos. 2991-2994 that were removed from a rejected printing of No. 2994a rather than sending out singles from sheets of 25 of each stamp.

A779

Christmas — A780

Designs: $1.50, Angel. $2.80, Baby Jesus. $3.60, Shepherd. $4.10, Magus.

2021, Nov. 3 **Litho.** ***Perf. 14¼x14***

2995 A779 $1.50 multi 2.10 2.10
2996 A779 $2.80 multi 4.00 4.00
2997 A779 $3.60 multi 5.00 5.00
2998 A779 $4.10 multi 5.75 5.75
a. Souvenir sheet of 4, #2995-2998 17.00 17.00
Nos. 2995-2998 (4) 16.85 16.85

Self-Adhesive

Serpentine Die Cut 9¾x10

2999 A780 $1.50 multi 2.10 2.10
a. Booklet pane of 10 21.00
3000 A780 $2.80 multi 4.00 4.00
a. Booklet pane of 10 + 10 etiquettes 40.00
3001 A780 $3.60 multi 5.00 5.00
a. Booklet pane of 10 + 10 etiquettes 50.00
b. Strip of 3, #2999-3001 11.50
Nos. 2999-3001 (3) 11.10 11.10

New Year 2022 (Year of the Tiger) — A781

Chinese child with: $1.50, Tiger, coins, bowls. $2.80, Tiger, Chinese lanterns. $3.60, Tiger, bowls, bamboo. $4.10, Tiger mask, firecrackers.

2021, Dec. 1 **Litho.** ***Perf. 14x14¼***

3002 A781 $1.50 green & pink 2.10 2.10
3003 A781 $2.80 red & pink 4.00 4.00
3004 A781 $3.60 green & pink 5.00 5.00
3005 A781 $4.10 red & pink 5.75 5.75
a. Souvenir sheet of 4, #3002-3005 17.00 17.00
Nos. 3002-3005 (4) 16.85 16.85

19th Century Ships — A782

Designs: $1.50, European ships trading with Maori and Pakeha at Tata Beach, 1843. $2.80, Whalers from the Charles W. Morgan whaling in Cloudy Bay, 1852. $3.60, The Mataura sailing from England to New Zealand, 1879. $4.10, The Felicity and the Blind Bay hookers, at Nelson, 1889.

2022, Feb. 2 **Litho.** ***Perf. 14¼x14***

3006 A782 $1.50 multi 2.10 2.10
3007 A782 $2.80 multi 3.75 3.75
3008 A782 $3.60 multi 5.00 5.00
3009 A782 $4.10 multi 5.50 5.50
a. Souvenir sheet of 4, #3006-3009 16.50 16.50
Nos. 3006-3009 (4) 16.35 16.35

Armistice Day Poppy Appeal, Cent. — A783

Armistice Day poppies to support veterans from: $1.50, 1922. $2.80, 1960s or 1970s. $3.60, 1978. $4.10, 2015. $4.90, 2020.

2022, Mar. 2 Litho. *Perf. 13¼x13½*

3010 A783 $1.50 multi 2.10 2.10
3011 A783 $2.80 multi 4.00 4.00
3012 A783 $3.60 multi 5.00 5.00
3013 A783 $4.10 multi 5.75 5.75
3014 A783 $4.90 multi 6.75 6.75
a. Souvenir sheet of 5, #3010-3014 24.00 24.00
Nos. 3010-3014 (5) 23.60 23.60

Souvenir Sheet

New Zealand Symphony Orchestra, 75th Anniv. — A784

2022, Mar. 2 Litho. *Perf. 13¼x13½*

3015 A784 Sheet of 2 8.00 8.00
a. $1.50 Harp 2.10 2.10
b. $4.10 French horn 5.75 5.75

Eid — A785

Various Arabic inscriptions.

2022, Apr. 6 Litho. *Perf. 14¼x14*

3016 A785 $1.50 gold & green 2.00 2.00
3017 A785 $2.80 gold & blue 4.00 4.00
3018 A785 $3.60 gold & purple 5.00 5.00
3019 A785 $6.50 gold & green 9.00 9.00
a. Souvenir sheet of 4, #3016-3019 20.00 20.00
Nos. 3016-3019 (4) 20.00 20.00

Matariki (Maori New Year) — A786

Designs: $1.50, Tawhirimatea throwing his eyes into the sky. $2.80, Head of Tawhirimatea. $3.60, Stars of the Pleiades in sky, horiz. $4.10, Tawhirimatea in sky with stars, horiz.

2022, May 4 Litho. *Perf. 14*

3020 A786 $1.50 multi 2.00 2.00
3021 A786 $2.80 multi 3.75 3.75
3022 A786 $3.60 multi 4.75 4.75
3023 A786 $4.10 multi 5.50 5.50
a. Souvenir sheet of 4, #3020-3023 16.00 16.00
Nos. 3020-3023 (4) 16.00 16.00

Tourist Attractions and Scenery Types of 2014-20

Designs: $3.80, Te Mata Peak, Hawke's Bay. $5.10, Sarjeant Gallery, Whanganui. $6.70, Whanganui.

2022, June 1 Litho. *Perf. 13¼x13½*

3024 A738 $5.10 multi 6.75 6.75
3025 A738 $6.70 multi 8.75 8.75

Self-Adhesive

Serpentine Die Cut 10x9½

3026 A627 $3.80 multi 5.00 5.00
a. Booklet pane of 5 + 2 etiquettes on backing paper with back printing 25.00

No. 3026 was printed in the booklet pane and also was made available on a translucent backing paper without back printing.

Te Aho o Te Kura Pounamu (The Correspondence School), Wellington, Cent. — A787

Designs: $1.70, Early students, Wairarapa, 1930s. $3, Rider on horse collecting mail bag, Aoraki Mt. Cook, 1950s. $3.80, Boy receiving schoolwork, Arapito, 1960s. $6.70, Lighthouse lessons, Tiritiri Matangi, 1970s.

2022, June 1 Litho. *Perf. 14¼x14*

3027 A787 $1.70 multi 2.25 2.25
3028 A787 $3 multi 4.00 4.00
3029 A787 $3.80 multi 5.00 5.00
3030 A787 $6.70 multi 8.75 8.75
a. Souvenir sheet of 4, #3027-3030 20.00 20.00
Nos. 3027-3030 (4) 20.00 20.00

Tiaki Care for New Zealand Promise — A788

No. 3031 — Inscription at lower right: a, Protect nature. b, Keep NZ clean. c, Drive carefully. d, Be prepared. e, Show respect. f, Tiaki care for New Zealand.

2022, June 1 Litho. *Perf. 13½x13¼*

3031 Sheet of 6 25.00 25.00
a.-b. A788 $1.70 Either single 2.25 2.25
c. A788 $3 black 4.00 4.00
d. A788 $3.80 black 5.00 5.00
e. A788 $4.30 black 5.50 5.50
f. A788 $4.50 black 6.00 6.00

IHC Art Award-Winning Works by New Zealanders with Intellectual Disabilities — A789

Designs: $1.70, Aeroplane, by 2021 winner, Matthew Tonkin. $3, Colorful Unicorn, by 2020 winner, Katie McMillan. $3.80, My Nani as a Maori Girl, by 2019 winner, Malachi Oldridge. $5.10, Looking Out from the Inside, by 2018 winner, Charlize Wilson.

2022, July 6 Litho. *Perf. 14*

3032 A789 $1.70 multi 2.25 2.25
3033 A789 $3 multi 3.75 3.75
3034 A789 $3.90 multi 5.00 5.00
3035 A789 $5.10 multi 6.50 6.50
a. Souvenir sheet of 4, #3032-3035 17.50 17.50
Nos. 3032-3035 (4) 17.50 17.50

Gandalf, the White Wizard — A790

Attack of the Warg Riders — A791

Gollum at the Forbidden Pool — A792

Battle of Helm's Deep — A793

Last March of the Ents — A794

The Tales That Really Mattered — A795

2022 Litho. *Perf. 14x14½*

3036 A790 $1.70 multi 2.00 2.00
a. Souvenir sheet of 1 2.00 2.00
3037 A791 $1.70 multi 2.00 2.00
a. Souvenir sheet of 1 2.00 2.00
3038 A792 $3 multi 3.50 3.50
a. Souvenir sheet of 1 3.50 3.50
3039 A793 $3.80 multi 4.50 4.50
a. Souvenir sheet of 1 4.50 4.50
b. Souvenir sheet of 2, #3038-3039 9.50 9.50
3040 A794 $4.30 multi 5.00 5.00
a. Souvenir sheet of 1 5.00 5.00
3041 A795 $4.50 multi 5.25 5.25
a. Souvenir sheet of 1 5.25 5.25
b. Souvenir sheet of 2, #3040-3041 10.50 10.50
Nos. 3036-3041 (6) 22.25 22.25

Movie *The Lord of the Rings: The Two Towers,* 20th anniv., Wellington Philatelic Society 100 Stamp Show (No. 3041b). New Zealand 2023 Intl. Stamp Exhibition, Auckland (No. 3039b). No. 3039b sold for $7.80, with $1 of that going to the Philatelic Trust.

Issued: Nos. 3036-3041, 3036a-3041a, 9/7; No. 3041b, 11/11; No. 3039b, 5/4/23.

Emblem of the Black Ferns, New Zealand's National Women's Rugby Team — A796

2022, Oct. 5 Litho. *Perf. 14¼x14½*

3042 Sheet of 6, #3042b-3042e, 2 #3042a 22.50 22.50
a. A796 $1.70 multi 2.00 2.00
b. A796 $3 multi 3.50 3.50
c. A796 $3.80 multi 4.50 4.50
d. A796 $4.30 multi 5.00 5.00
e. A796 $4.50 multi 5.25 5.25

Christmas

A797 A798

Designs: $1.70, Christmas star and kakabeak flowers. $3, Christmas candle, toetoe and raupo. $3.80, New Zealand fantail, poroporo flowers and berries. $4.30, Christmas bell and manuka flowers. $4.50, New Zealand pigeon, kowhai flowers.

2022, Oct. 5 Litho. *Perf. 14*

3043 A797 $1.70 sil & multi 2.00 2.00
3044 A797 $3 sil & multi 3.50 3.50
3045 A797 $3.80 sil & multi 4.50 4.50
3046 A797 $4.30 sil & multi 5.00 5.00
3047 A797 $4.50 sil & multi 5.25 5.25
a. Souvenir sheet of 5, #3043-3047 20.50 20.50
Nos. 3043-3047 (5) 20.25 20.25

Self-Adhesive

Serpentine Die Cut 9¾x10

3048 A798 $1.70 sil & multi 2.00 2.00
a. Booklet pane of 10 20.00
3049 A798 $3 sil & multi 3.50 3.50
a. Booklet pane of 10 + 10 etiquettes 35.00
3050 A798 $3.80 sil & multi 4.50 4.50
a. Booklet pane of 10 + 10 etiquettes 45.00
b. Strip of 3, #3048-3050 10.00
Nos. 3048-3050 (3) 10.00 10.00

Women in Science — A799

Designs: $1.70, Lucy Moore (1906-87), botanist. $3, Joan Wiffen (1922-2009), paleontologist. $3.80, Beatrice Hill Tinsley (1941-81), astronomer and cosmologist. $4.30, Makereti Papakura (1873-1930), ethnographer.

2022, Nov. 2 Litho. *Perf. 13½x13¾*

3051 A799 $1.70 multi 2.10 2.10
3052 A799 $3 multi 3.75 3.75
3053 A799 $3.80 multi 4.75 4.75
3054 A799 $4.30 multi 5.50 5.50
a. Souvenir sheet of 4, #3051-3054 16.50 16.50
Nos. 3051-3054 (4) 16.10 16.10

New Year 2023 (Year of the Rabbit) — A800

Chinese child with: $1.70, Head of rabbit, cherries. $3, Another child, rabbit and ball. $3.80, Platter, peaches, rabbit and incense sticks. $6.70, Another child, rabbit, tree in pot.

2022, Dec. 7 Litho. *Perf. 13¼x13½*

3055 A800 $1.70 multi 2.25 2.25
3056 A800 $3 multi 3.75 3.75
3057 A800 $3.80 multi 4.75 4.75
3058 A800 $6.70 multi 8.50 8.50
a. Souvenir sheet of 4, #3055-3058 19.50 19.50
Nos. 3055-3058 (4) 19.25 19.25

Katherine Mansfield (1888-1923), Writer — A801

Mansfield and: $1.70, Typewriter, and "I'm a writer first and a woman after." $3, Fan, and "I want to be all that I am capable of becoming." $3.80, Plant, and "To be alive and . . . a writer is enough." $4.30, House, and "Risk! Risk anything! Care no more for the opinions of others."

2023, Feb. 1 Litho. *Perf. 14¼*

3059 A801 $1.70 multi 2.25 2.25
3060 A801 $3 multi 4.00 4.00
3061 A801 $3.80 multi 5.00 5.00
3062 A801 $4.30 multi 5.50 5.50
a. Souvenir sheet of 4, #3059-3062 17.00 17.00
Nos. 3059-3062 (4) 16.75 16.75

Premiere of Movie *Avatar: The Way of Water* A802

Designs: No. 3063, Tulkun breaching surface of water. No. 3064, Rider on skimwing. $3, Woodsprite and riders on mountain banshees. $3.80, Ilus. $4.30, Neytiri. $4.50, Rider on mountain banshee.

2023, Mar. 1 Litho. *Perf. 14¼x14*

3063 A802 $1.70 multi 2.25 2.25
a. Souvenir sheet of 1 2.25 2.25
3064 A802 $1.70 multi 2.25 2.25
a. Souvenir sheet of 1 2.25 2.25
3065 A802 $3 multi 3.75 3.75
a. Souvenir sheet of 1 3.75 3.75
3066 A802 $3.80 multi 4.75 4.75
a. Souvenir sheet of 1 4.75 4.75
3067 A802 $4.30 multi 5.50 5.50
a. Souvenir sheet of 1 5.50 5.50
3068 A802 $4.50 multi 5.75 5.75
a. Souvenir sheet of 1 5.75 5.75
b. Souvenir sheet of 2, #3064, 3068 8.75 8.75
Nos. 3063-3068 (6) 24.25 24.25

New Zealand 2023 Intl. Stamp Exhibition, Auckland (No. 3068b). No. 3068b, issued on 5/4/23, sold for $7.20, with $1 of that going to the Philatelic Trust.

Characters From Children's Book, *Hairy Maclary From Donaldson's Dairy,* by Lynley Dodd — A803

Designs: No. 3069, Hairy Maclary. No. 3070, Hercules Morse. $3, Bottomley Potts. $3.80, Muffin McLay. $4.30, Bitzer Maloney. 4.50, Schnitzel von Krumm.

2023, Mar. 1 Litho. *Perf. 14¼x14*

3069	A803 $1.70 multi	2.25	2.25
3070	A803 $1.70 multi	2.25	2.25
3071	A803 $3 multi	3.75	3.75
a.	Souvenir sheet of 3, #3069-3071	9.00	9.00
3072	A803 $3.80 multi	4.75	4.75
3073	A803 $4.30 multi	5.50	5.50
3074	A803 $4.50 multi	5.75	5.75
a.	Souvenir sheet of 6, #3069-3074	24.50	24.50
	Nos. 3069-3074 (6)	24.25	24.25

New Zealand 2023 Intl. Stamp Exhibition, Auckland (No. 3071a). No. 3071a, issued on 5/4/23, sold for $7.40, with $1 of that going to the Philatelic Trust.

Royal Forest and Bird Protection Society of New Zealand, Cent. — A804

Designs: $1.70, Birds. $3, Lizard, bat and flowers. $3.80, Bird, whale, tree and mushrooms. $4.30, Butterflies, snail and flowers.

2023, Apr. 5 Litho. *Perf. 13¼x13½*

3075	A804 $1.70 multi	2.10	2.10
3076	A804 $3 multi	3.75	3.75
3077	A804 $3.80 multi	4.75	4.75
3078	A804 $4.30 multi	5.25	5.25
a.	Souvenir sheet of 4, #3075-3078	16.00	16.00
	Nos. 3075-3078 (4)	15.85	15.85

King Charles III — A805

King Charles III: $1.70, Wearing Maori kiwi feather cloak on visit to New Zealand, 2015. $3, With Queen Consort Camilla. $3.80, Wearing blue suit. $4.30, Wearing pinstripe suit.

2023 Litho. *Perf. 14¼*

3079	A805 $1.70 pur & multi	2.10	2.10
3080	A805 $3 gray & multi	3.75	3.75
3081	A805 $3.80 brn & multi	4.75	4.75
3082	A805 $4.30 red & multi	5.25	5.25
a.	Souvenir sheet of 4, #3079-3082	16.00	16.00
b.	Souvenir sheet of 2, #3080, 3082	10.00	10.00
	Nos. 3079-3082 (4)	15.85	15.85

Issued: Nos. 3079-3082, 3082a, 5/3; No. 3082b, 5/4. New Zealand 2023 Intl. Stamp Exhibition, Auckland (No. 3082b). No. 3082b sold for $8.30, with $1 of that going to the Philatelic Trust.

Coronation of King Charles III — A806

No. 3083 — King Charles III: a, Praying. b, Holding Sword of State. c, Seated, holding scepters. d, Standing, holding orb and scepter. e, Waving. f, With Queen Consort Camilla, waving.

2023, May 8 Litho. *Perf. 14¼x14½*

3083	Miniature sheet of 6	22.50	22.50
a.-b.	A806 $1.70 Either single	2.10	2.10
c.-d.	A806 $3 Either single	3.75	3.75
e.-f.	A806 $4.30 Either single	5.25	5.25

Scenery Type of 2020

Designs: $3.30, Emerald Lakes, Tongariro Crossing. $4, Island Bay, Wellington. $4.60, Routeburn Track. $5.30, Te Urewera. $6.90, Abel Tasman National Park.

2023, June 7 Litho. *Perf. 13¼x13½*

3084	A738 $3.30 multi	4.25	4.25
3085	A738 $4.60 multi	5.75	5.75
3086	A738 $5.30 multi	6.50	6.50
3087	A738 $6.90 multi	8.50	8.50
	Nos. 3084-3087 (4)	25.00	25.00

Self-Adhesive

Serpentine Die Cut 10x9¾

3088	A738 $3.30 multi	4.25	4.25
a.	Booklet pane of 5 + 2 etiquettes	21.50	
3089	A738 $4 multi	5.00	5.00
a.	Booklet pane of 5 + 2 etiquettes	25.00	
b.	Horiz. pair, #3088-3089	9.25	

For $4 stamp with water-activated gum, see No. 2916.

New Zealand Post Tractor Trailer — A807

New Zealand Post Van — A808

New Zealand Post Van — A809

New Zealand Post Van — A810

Aerial View of New Zealand Post Tractor Trailer — A811

Serpentine Die Cut 10x9¾

2023, July 1 Litho.

Coil Stamps Self-Adhesive

3090	A807 ($2) multi	2.50	2.50
3091	A808 ($2) multi	2.50	2.50
3092	A809 ($2) multi	2.50	2.50
3093	A810 ($2) multi	2.50	2.50
3094	A811 ($2) multi	2.50	2.50
a.	Horiz. coil strip of 5, #3090-3094	12.50	
	Nos. 3090-3094 (5)	12.50	12.50

Souvenir Sheet

2023 Women's World Cup Soccer Championships, Australia and New Zealand — A812

No. 3095: a, Women soccer players. b, Women's World Cup, vert.

2023, July 5 Litho. *Perf. 14¼*

3095	A812 Sheet of 2	9.00	9.00
a.	$3.30 multi	4.00	4.00
b.	$4 multi	5.00	5.00

Miniature Sheet

Toys From the Middle of the 20th Century A813

No. 3096: a, World War II hospital ship. b, Hercules tractor. c, Fun Ho! racing car. d, Lines Bros. dump truck. e, Luvme teddy bear. f, Wooden train. g, Paper doll. h, H. E. Ramsey Mary Lou doll. i, Pedigree Maori doll.

2023, July 5 Litho. *Perf. 14¼x14*

3096	A813 Sheet of 9	22.50	22.50
a.-i.	$2 Any single	2.50	2.50

Pets — A814

Designs: $2, Dog named Spencer. $3.30, Cat named Zita. $4, Parrot named Kea. $5.30, Sheep named Oh-Good.

2023, Aug. 2 Litho. *Perf. 14x14¼*

3097	A814 $2 multi	2.40	2.40
3098	A814 $3.30 multi	4.00	4.00
3099	A814 $4 multi	4.75	4.75
3100	A814 $5.30 multi	6.25	6.25
a.	Souvenir sheet of 4, #3097-3100	17.50	17.50
	Nos. 3097-3100 (4)	17.40	17.40

Souvenir Sheet

Issuance of No. P1, 150th Anniv. A815

2023, Aug. 2 Litho. *Perf. 14¼x14*

3101	A815 $6.90 multi	8.25	8.25

Queen Elizabeth II (1926-2022) — A816

Photographs of Queen Elizabeth taken on visits to New Zealand in: No. 3102, 1953-54. No. 3103, 1977. No. 3104, 1974. No. 3105, 2002. No. 3106, 2002. $4.60, 2006.

2023, Sept. 6 Litho. *Perf. 14¼x14*

Denomination Color

3102	A816 $2 light green	2.40	2.40
3103	A816 $2 orange brown	2.40	2.40
3104	A816 $2 pink	2.40	2.40
3105	A816 $3.30 blue	4.00	4.00
3106	A816 $3.30 yellow	4.00	4.00
3107	A816 $4.60 blue green	5.50	5.50
a.	Souvenir sheet of 6, #3102-3107	21.00	21.00
	Nos. 3102-3107 (6)	20.70	20.70

Christmas — A817

Gift with ribbon and: $2, Clematis flowers, Star of Bethlehem. $3.30, Pohutukawa flowers, Christmas tree. $4, Silver fern, dove. $4.60, Hebe flowers, angel.

2023, Oct. 4 Litho. *Perf. 13¾x13¼*

3108	A817 $2 multi	2.40	2.40
3109	A817 $3.30 multi	4.00	4.00
3110	A817 $4 multi	4.75	4.75
3111	A817 $4.60 multi	5.50	5.50
a.	Souvenir sheet of 4, #3108-3111	17.00	17.00
	Nos. 3108-3111 (4)	16.65	16.65

Self-Adhesive

Serpentine Die Cut 9¾x10

3112	A817 $2 multi	2.40	2.40
a.	Booklet pane of 10	24.00	
3113	A817 $3.30 multi	4.00	4.00
a.	Booklet pane of 10	40.00	
3114	A817 $4 multi	4.75	4.75
a.	Booklet pane of 10	47.50	
b.	Strip of 3, #3112-3114	11.50	
	Nos. 3112-3114 (3)	11.15	11.15

Lair of Shelob A818

Arwen A819

Shieldmaiden of Rohan — A820

Army of the Dead A821

Gandalf and the Moth A822

"The Ring is Mine" A823

2023, Nov. 1 Litho. *Perf. 14¼x14*

3115	A818 $2 multi	2.40	2.40
a.	Souvenir sheet of 1	2.40	2.40
3116	A819 $2 multi	2.40	2.40
a.	Souvenir sheet of 1	2.40	2.40
3117	A820 $3.30 multi	4.00	4.00
a.	Souvenir sheet of 1	4.00	4.00
3118	A821 $3.30 multi	4.00	4.00
a.	Souvenir sheet of 1	4.00	4.00
3119	A822 $4 multi	4.75	4.75
a.	Souvenir sheet of 1	4.75	4.75
3120	A823 $4.60 multi	5.50	5.50
a.	Souvenir sheet of 1	5.50	5.50
	Nos. 3115-3120 (6)	23.05	23.05

Movie *The Lord of the Rings: The Return of the King,* 20th anniv.

New Year 2024 (Year of the Dragon) — A824

Various children and dragons.

2023, Dec. 6 Litho. *Perf. 13¼x13¾*

Background Color

3121	A824 $2 pink	2.60	2.60
3122	A824 $3.30 green	4.25	4.25
3123	A824 $4 yellow	5.25	5.25
3124	A824 $6.90 light blue	8.75	8.75
a.	Souvenir sheet of 4, #3121-3124	21.00	21.00
	Nos. 3121-3124 (4)	20.85	20.85

Marine Life of New Zealand Marine Reserves — A825

Designs: $2, Clown nudibranch, Taputeranga Marine Reserve. $3.30, Red coral, Te Awaaatu Channel Marine Reserve. $4, Sea sponge, Cape Rodney-Okakari Poing Marine Reserve. $4.60, Biscuit star, Ulva Island-Te Wharawhara Marine Reserve.

2024, Feb. 7 Litho. *Perf. 14¼x14*

3125	A825 $2 multi		2.50	2.50
3126	A825 $3.30 multi		4.00	4.00
3127	A825 $4 multi		5.00	5.00
3128	A825 $4.60 multi		5.75	5.75
a.	Souvenir sheet of 4, #3125-3128		17.50	17.50
	Nos. 3125-3128 (4)		17.25	17.25

Games Developed in New Zealand A826

Designs: No. 3129, Bloons TD 6. No. 3130, Depth. $3.30, Dredge. $4.60, Mini Metro. $5.30, Into the Dead.

2024, Mar. 6 Litho. *Perf. 14x14¼*

3129	A826 $2 multi	2.40	2.40
3130	A826 $2 multi	2.40	2.40
3131	A826 $3.30 multi	4.00	4.00
3132	A826 $4.60 multi	5.50	5.50
3133	A826 $5.30 multi	6.50	6.50
a.	Souvenir sheet of 5, #3129-3133	21.00	21.00
	Nos. 3129-3133 (5)	20.80	20.80

POSTAL-FISCAL STAMPS

In 1881 fiscal stamps of New Zealand of denominations over one shilling were made acceptable for postal duty. Values for canceled stamps are for postal cancellations. Denominations above £5 appear to have been used primarily for fiscal purposes.

Queen Victoria
PF1 PF2

Perf. 11, 12, 12½

1882 Typo. Wmk. 62

AR1	PF1	2sh blue	125.00	20.00
AR2	PF1	2sh6p dk brown	125.00	20.00
AR3	PF1	3sh violet	225.00	25.00
AR4	PF1	4sh brown vio	325.00	40.00
AR5	PF1	4sh red brn	275.00	40.00
AR6	PF1	5sh green	325.00	40.00
AR7	PF1	6sh rose	500.00	65.00
AR8	PF1	7sh ultra	550.00	150.00
AR9	PF1	7sh6p ol gray	1,500.	500.00
AR10	PF1	8sh dull blue	525.00	125.00
AR11	PF1	9sh org red	900.00	300.00
AR12	PF1	10sh red brn	350.00	75.00

1882-90

AR13	PF2	15sh dk grn	1,500.	400.00
AR15	PF2	£1 rose	700.00	150.00
AR16	PF2	25sh blue		—
AR17	PF2	30sh brown		—
AR18	PF2	£1 15sh yellow		—
AR19	PF2	£2 purple		—

PF3

PF4

AR20	PF3	£2 10sh red brn		—
AR21	PF3	£3 yel green		—
AR22	PF3	£3 10sh rose		—
AR23	PF3	£4 ultra		—
AR24	PF3	£4 10sh ol brn		—
AR25	PF3	£5 dark blue		—
AR26	PF4	£6 org red		—
AR27	PF4	£7 brn red		—
AR28	PF4	£8 green		—
AR29	PF4	£9 rose		—
AR30	PF4	£10 blue		—
AR30A	PF4	£20 yellow	—	—

No. AR31

With "COUNTERPART" at Bottom

1901

AR31	PF1	2sh6p brown	300.00	*400.00*

Perf. 11, 14, 14½x14

1903-15 Wmk. 61

AR32	PF1	2sh blue ('07)	80.00	12.00
AR33	PF1	2sh6p brown	80.00	12.00
AR34	PF1	3sh violet	175.00	14.00
AR35	PF1	4sh brn red	200.00	30.00
AR36	PF1	5sh grn ('06)	225.00	30.00
AR37	PF1	6sh rose	375.00	50.00
AR38	PF1	7sh dull blue	400.00	80.00
AR39	PF1	7sh6p ol gray ('06)	1,500.	400.00
AR40	PF1	8sh dk blue	450.00	75.00
AR41	PF1	9sh dl org ('06)	600.00	200.00
AR42	PF1	10sh dp clar	250.00	50.00
AR43	PF2	15sh blue grn	1,350.	350.00
AR44	PF2	£1 rose	500.00	150.00

Perf. 14½

AR45	PF2	£2 dp vio ('25)	600.00	150.00
a.		Perf. 14	700.00	150.00
		Nos. AR32-AR45 (14)	6,785.	1,603.

For overprints see Cook Islands Nos. 67-71.

Coat of Arms — PF5

1931-39 Wmk. 61 *Perf. 14*

Type PF5 (Various Frames)

AR46	1sh3p lemon	30.00	40.00
AR47	1sh3p org ('32)	8.00	9.00
AR48	2sh6p brown	16.00	5.25
AR49	4sh dull red ('32)	17.00	7.50
AR50	5sh green	21.00	12.50
AR51	6sh brt rose ('32)	37.50	15.00
AR52	7sh gray blue	32.50	25.00
AR53	7sh6p olive gray ('32)	75.00	92.50
AR54	8sh dark blue	50.00	37.50
AR55	9sh dull ver	52.50	32.50
AR56	10sh dark car	27.50	10.50
AR57	12sh6p brn vio ('35)	250.00	250.00
AR58	15sh ol grn ('32)	70.00	42.50
AR59	£1 pink ('32)	75.00	22.50
AR60	25sh turq bl ('38)	550.00	600.00
AR61	30sh dk brn ('36)	300.00	200.00
AR62	35sh yel ('37)	6,000.	*7,500.*
AR63	£2 vio ('33)	400.00	70.00
AR64	£2 10sh dk red ('36)	400.00	*550.00*
AR65	£3 lt grn ('32)	400.00	210.00
AR66	£3 10sh rose ('39)	2,250.	2,250.
AR67	£4 light blue	400.00	175.00
AR68	£4 10sh dk ol gray ('39)	2,500.	2,500.
AR69	£5 dk blue ('32)	400.00	100.00

For overprints see Cook Islands Nos. 80-83.

No. AR62 Surcharged in Black

35/-

1939 *Perf. 14*

AR70	PF5 35sh on 35sh yel	500.00	350.00

Type PF5 Surcharged in Black

1940

AR71	3sh6p on 3sh6p dl green	28.50	21.00
AR72	5sh6p on 5sh6p rose lilac	60.00	57.50
AR73	11sh on 11sh pale yellow	125.00	150.00
AR74	22sh on 22sh scar	275.00	350.00
	Nos. AR71-AR74 (4)	488.50	578.50

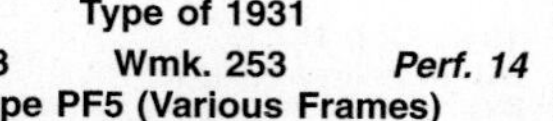

Type of 1931

1940-58 Wmk. 253 *Perf. 14*

Type PF5 (Various Frames)

AR75	1sh3p orange	5.75	.60
AR76	2sh6p brown	5.75	.60
AR77	4sh dull red	6.75	.60
AR78	5sh green	11.50	.90
AR79	6sh brt rose	20.00	4.00
AR80	7sh gray bl	20.00	6.75
AR81	7sh6p ol gray ('50)	70.00	*70.00*
AR82	8sh dk blue	45.00	25.00
AR83	9sh orange ('46)	50.00	30.00
AR84	10sh dk carmine	25.00	3.25
AR85	15sh olive ('45)	55.00	20.00
AR86	£1 pink('45)	29.00	8.50
a.	Perf. 14x13½ ('58)	32.50	15.00
AR87	25sh blue ('46)	500.00	*550.00*
AR88	30sh choc ('46)	250.00	200.00
AR89	£2 violet ('46)	100.00	60.00
AR90	£2 10sh dk red ('51)	400.00	*525.00*
AR91	£3 lt grn ('46)	150.00	125.00
AR92	£3 10sh rose ('48)	2,300.	*2,500.*
AR93	£4 lt blue ('52)	150.00	160.00
AR94	£5 dk blue ('40)	175.00	150.00

Type PF5 Surcharged in Black

1942-45 Wmk. 253

AR95	3sh6p on 3sh6p grn	12.50	8.00
AR96	5sh6p on 5sh6p rose lil ('44)	26.00	8.50
AR97	11sh on 11sh yel	67.50	52.50
AR98	22sh on 22sh car ('45)	325.00	*275.00*
	Nos. AR95-AR98 (4)	431.00	344.00

Catalogue values for unused stamps in this section, from this point to the end of the section, are for Never Hinged items.

Type of 1931 Redrawn Surcharged in Black

1953 Typo.

AR99	PF5 3sh6p on 3sh6p green	32.50	35.00

Denomination of basic stamp is in small, sans-serif capitals without period after "sixpence."

Type of 1931

1955 Wmk. 253 *Perf. 14*

Denomination in Black

AR100	PF5 1sh3p orange	2.75	.90

1956 Denomination in Blue

AR101	PF5 1sh3p orange yel	17.50	14.50

For decimal-currency postage stamps of design No. PF5, see Nos. 404A-404D, 404Ba, 404Ca, 404Da.

1967, July 10 *Perf. 14*

AR102	PF5 $4 purple	10.00	2.50
AR103	PF5 $6 green	9.00	4.00
AR104	PF5 $8 light blue	12.00	5.50
AR105	PF5 $10 dark blue	17.00	6.50
	Nos. AR102-AR105 (4)	48.00	18.50

1987 Unwmk.

AR103a	PF5 $6 green	9.00	9.00
AR104a	PF5 $8 light blue	12.00	12.00
AR105a	PF5 $10 dark blue	15.00	15.00
	Nos. AR103a-AR105a (3)	36.00	36.00

SEMI-POSTAL STAMPS

Nurse — SP1

Inscribed: "Help Stamp out Tuberculosis, 1929"

Wmk. 61

1929, Dec. 11 Typo. *Perf. 14*

B1	SP1 1p + 1p scarlet	12.50	*20.00*

Nurse — SP2

Inscribed: "Help Promote Health, 1930"

1930, Oct. 29

B2	SP2 1p + 1p scarlet	30.00	*45.00*

Boy — SP3

1931, Oct. 31 *Perf. 14½x14*

B3	SP3 1p + 1p scarlet	100.00	90.00
B4	SP3 2p + 1p dark blue	100.00	75.00

Hygeia, Goddess of Health — SP4

1932, Nov. 18 Engr. *Perf. 14*

B5	SP4 1p + 1p carmine	22.50	*30.00*
	Never hinged	55.00	

Road to Health — SP5

1933, Nov. 8

B6	SP5 1p + 1p carmine	15.00	*20.00*
	Never hinged	35.00	

Crusader — SP6

1934, Oct. 25 *Perf. 14x13½*

B7	SP6 1p + 1p dark carmine	12.50	*20.00*
	Never hinged	25.00	

Child at Bathing Beach — SP7

1935, Sept. 30 *Perf. 11*

B8	SP7 1p + 1p scarlet	3.00	3.25
	Never hinged	5.00	

Catalogue values for unused stamps in this section, from this point to the end of the section, are for Never Hinged items.

Anzac — SP8

1936, Apr. 27

B9	SP8 ½p + ½p green	.70	*2.00*
B10	SP8 1p + 1p red	.70	*1.60*

21st anniv. of Anzac landing at Gallipoli.

"Health" — SP9

1936, Nov. 2
B11 SP9 1p + 1p red 2.00 *4.25*

Boy Hiker — SP10

1937, Oct. 1
B12 SP10 1p + 1p red 3.00 *4.00*

Children at Play — SP11

Perf. 14x13½

1938, Oct. 1 **Wmk. 253**
B13 SP11 1p + 1p red 6.25 3.25

Children at Play — SP12

Black Surcharge

1939, Oct. 16 **Wmk. 61** ***Perf. 11½***
B14 SP12 1p on ½p + ½p grn 5.00 5.00
B15 SP12 2p on 1p + 1p scar 5.00 5.00

Children at Play — SP12a

1940, Oct. 1
B16 SP12a 1p + ½p green 16.00 17.50
B17 SP12a 2p + 1p org brown 16.00 17.50

The surtax was used to help maintain children's health camps.

Nos. B16-B17 Overprinted in Black

1941, Oct. 4 ***Perf. 11½***
B18 SP12a 1p + ½p green 3.00 *3.50*
B19 SP12a 2p + 1p org brown 3.00 *3.50*

Children in Swing — SP13

1942, Oct. 1 **Engr.**
B20 SP13 1p + ½p green .35 *1.10*
B21 SP13 2p + 1p dp org brown .35 *1.10*

Imperf plate proofs on card exist for #B22-B27, B32-B33, B38-B39, B46-B48, B59-B60. Imperfs exist for B44-B45, B49-B51. These are from the printer's archives.

Princess Elizabeth SP14

Design: 1p+1/2p, Princess Margaret Rose.

1943, Oct. 1 **Wmk. 253** ***Perf. 12***
B22 SP14 1p + ½p dark green .25 .40
a. Vert. pair, imperf. between 12,500.
B23 SP14 2p + 1p red brown .25 .40
a. Vert. pair, imperf. between 12,500.

Princesses Margaret Rose and Elizabeth — SP16

1944, Oct. 9 ***Perf. 13½***
B24 SP16 1p + ½p dp bl grn .35 .45
B25 SP16 2p + 1p chalky blue .35 .35

Peter Pan Statue, London — SP17

1945, Oct. 1
B26 SP17 1p + ½p gray grn & bis brn .25 .35
B27 SP17 2p + 1p car & ol bis .25 .35

Soldier Helping Child over Stile — SP18

1946, Oct. 24 ***Perf. 13½x13***
B28 SP18 1p + ½p dk grn & org brn .25 .35
B29 SP18 2p + 1p dk brn & org brn .25 .35

Statue of Eros, London — SP19

1947, Oct. 1 **Engr.** ***Perf. 13x13½***
B30 SP19 1p + ½p deep green .25 .35
B31 SP19 2p + 1p scarlet .25 .35

Children's Health Camp — SP20

1948, Oct. 1 ***Perf. 13½x13***
B32 SP20 1p + ½p blue grn & ultra .25 .35
B33 SP20 2p + 1p red & dk brn .25 .35

Nurse and Child — SP21

1949, Oct. 3 **Photo.** ***Perf. 14x14½***
B34 SP21 1p + ½p deep green .30 .35
B35 SP21 2p + 1p ultramarine .30 .35

Princess Elizabeth and Prince Charles — SP22

1950, Oct. 2
B36 SP22 1p + ½p green .25 .35
B37 SP22 2p + 1p violet brown .25 .35

Racing Yachts — SP23

Perf. 13½x13

1951, Nov. 1 **Engr.** **Wmk. 253**
B38 SP23 1½p + ½p red & yel .25 *.35*
B39 SP23 2p + 1p dp grn & yel .25 .35

Princess Anne SP24

Prince Charles SP25

Perf. 14x14½

1952, Oct. 1 **Wmk. 253** **Photo.**
B40 SP24 1½p + ½p crimson .25 .35
B41 SP25 2p + 1p brown .25 .35

Girl Guides Marching SP26

Boy Scouts at Camp SP27

1953, Oct. 7
B42 SP26 1½p + ½p bright blue .25 .35
B43 SP27 2p + 1p deep green .25 .35

The border of No. B43 consists of Morse code reading "Health" at top and bottom and "New Zealand" on each side. On No. B42 the top border line is replaced by "Health" in Morse code.

Young Mountain Climber Studying Map — SP28

1954, Oct. 4 **Engr.** ***Perf. 13½***
B44 SP28 1½p + ½p pur & brn .25 *.35*
B45 SP28 2p + 1p vio gray & brn .25 *.35*

Child's Head — SP29

1955, Oct. 3 **Wmk. 253** ***Perf. 13***
B46 SP29 1½p + ½p brn org & sep .25 *.35*
B47 SP29 2p + 1p grn & org brn .25 *.35*
B48 SP29 3p + 1p car & sepia .25 .35
Nos. B46-B48 (3) .75 1.05

Children Picking Apples — SP30

1956, Sept. 24
B49 SP30 1½p + ½p chocolate .25 *.35*
B50 SP30 2p + 1p blue green .25 *.35*
B51 SP30 3p + 1p dk car .25 .35
Nos. B49-B51 (3) .75 1.05

Life-Saving Team — SP31

3p+1p, Children playing and boy in canoe.

1957, Sept. 25 ***Perf. 13½***
B52 SP31 2p + 1p emer & blk .25 .35
a. Miniature sheet of 6 7.25 *25.00*
B53 SP31 3p + 1p car & ultra .25 .35
a. Miniature sheet of 6 7.25 *25.00*

The watermark is sideways on Nos. B52a and B53a. In a second printing, the watermark is upright; values double.

Girls' Life Brigade Cadet — SP32

Design: 3p+1p, Bugler, Boys' Brigade.

1958, Aug. 20 **Photo.** ***Perf. 14x14½***
B54 SP32 2p + 1p green .25 .45
a. Miniature sheet of 6 5.00 *25.00*
B55 SP32 3p + 1p dl ultra .25 .45
a. Miniature sheet of 6 5.00 *25.00*

75th anniv. of the founding of the Boys' Brigade.

The surtax on this and other preceding semi-postals was for the maintenance of children's health camps.

Globes and Red Cross Flag — SP33

1959, June 3 ***Perf. 14½x14***
B56 SP33 3p + 1p ultra & car .25 .25
a. Red Cross omitted *2,000.*

The surtax was for the Red Cross.

Gray Teal (Tete) — SP34

Design: 3p+1p, Pied stilt (Poaka).

1959, Sept. 16 ***Perf. 14x14½***
B57 SP34 2p + 1p pink, blk, yel & gray .60 .75
a. Miniature sheet of 6 6.00 *20.00*
B58 SP34 3p + 1p blue, black & pink .60 .75
a. Miniature sheet of 6 6.00 *20.00*
b. Pink omitted *160.00*

Sacred Kingfisher (Kotare) — SP35

Design: 3p+1p, NZ pigeon (Kereru).

1960, Aug. 10 **Engr.** ***Perf. 13x13½***
B59 SP35 2p + 1p grnsh blue & sepia .60 .85
a. Min. sheet of 6, perf. 11½x11 13.00 *22.50*
B60 SP35 3p + 1p org & sepia .60 .85
a. Min. sheet of 6, perf. 11½x11 13.00 *22.50*

Type of 1959

Birds: 2p+1p, Great white egret (Kotuku). 3p+1p, New Zealand falcon (Karearea).

1961, Aug. 2 **Wmk. 253**

B61 SP34 2p + 1p pale lil & blk .60 .80
  a. Miniature sheet of 6 13.00 *22.50*
B62 SP34 3p + 1p yel grn & blk brn .60 .80
  a. Miniature sheet of 6 13.00 *22.50*

Type of 1959

Birds: 2½p+1p, Red-fronted parakeet (Kakariki). 3p+1p, Saddleback (Tieke).

1962, Oct. 3 **Photo.** ***Perf. 15x14***

B63 SP34 2½p + 1p lt bl, blk, grn & org .60 .80
  a. Miniature sheet of 6 20.00 *27.50*
B64 SP34 3p + 1p salmon, blk, grn & org .60 .80
  a. Miniature sheet of 6 20.00 *27.50*
  b. Orange omitted *2,750.*

Prince Andrew — SP36

Design: 3p+1p, Prince without book.

1963, Aug. 7 **Engr.** ***Perf. 14***

B65 SP36 2½p + 1p ultra .35 .80
  a. Miniature sheet of 6 13.00 *22.50*
B66 SP36 3p + 1p rose car .35 .25
  a. Miniature sheet of 6 13.00 *22.50*

Red-billed Gull (Tarapunga) SP37

Design: 3p+1p, Blue penguin (Korora).

1964, Aug. 5 **Photo.** ***Perf. 14***

B67 SP37 2½p + 1p lt bl, pale yel, red & blk .45 .75
  a. Miniature sheet of 8 22.50 *35.00*
  b. Red omitted 325.00 225.00
  c. Yellow omitted
B68 SP37 3p + 1p blue, yel & blk .45 .75
  a. Miniature sheet of 8 22.50 *35.00*

Kaka — SP38

Design: 4p+1p, Fantail (Piwakawaka).

1965, Aug. 4 ***Perf. 14x14½***

B69 SP38 3p + 1p gray, red, brn & yellow .60 .85
  a. Miniature sheet of 6 11.00 *27.50*
B70 SP38 4p + 1p yel, blk, emer & brn .60 .85
  a. Miniature sheet of 6 11.00 *27.50*
  b. As No. B70, green omitted *2,000.* *2,000.*

Bellbird & Bough of Kowhai Tree — SP39

4p+1p, Flightless rail (Weka) and fern.

1966, Aug. 3 **Photo.** **Wmk. 253**

B71 SP39 3p + 1p lt bl & multi .60 .85
  a. Miniature sheet of 6 9.00 *25.00*
B72 SP39 4p + 1p lt grn & multi .60 .85
  a. Miniature sheet of 6 9.00 *25.00*
  b. Brown omitted *2,250.*

National Team Rugby Player and Boy — SP40

Design: 3c+1c, Man and boy placing ball for place kick, horiz.

1967, Aug. 2 ***Perf. 14½x14, 14x14½***

B73 SP40 2½c + 1c multi .25 .25
  a. Miniature sheet of 6 10.00 *20.00*
B74 SP40 3c + 1c multi .25 .25
  a. Miniature sheet of 6 10.00 *20.00*

Boy Running and Olympic Rings — SP41

3c+1c, Girl swimming and Olympic rings.

1968, Aug. 7 ***Perf. 14½x14***

B75 SP41 2½c + 1c multi .25 .25
  a. Miniature sheet of 6 9.50 *22.50*
  b. As No. B75, blue omitted *400.00*
B76 SP41 3c + 1c multi .25 .25
  a. Miniature sheet of 6 9.50 *22.50*
  b. Red omitted, from No. B76a *3,350.* *2,000.*
  c. Dark blue omitted, from No. B76a *2,250.*

Boys Playing Cricket SP42

Dr. Elizabeth Gunn SP43

Design: 3c+1c, playing cricket.

Perf. 13½x13, 13x13½

1969, Aug. 6 **Litho.** **Unwmk.**

B77 SP42 2½c + 1c multi .45 .75
  a. Miniature sheet of 6 10.00 *25.00*
B78 SP42 3c + 1c multi .45 .75
  a. Miniature sheet of 6 10.00 *25.00*
B79 SP43 4c + 1c multi .45 *2.50*
  Nos. B77-B79 (3) 1.35 4.00

50th anniv. of Children's Health Camps, founded by Dr. Elizabeth Gunn.

Boys Playing Soccer — SP44

2½c+1c, Girls playing basketball, vert.

1970, Aug. 5 **Unwmk.** ***Perf. 13½***

B80 SP44 2½c + 1c multi .30 .80
  a. Miniature sheet of 6 10.00 *26.00*
B81 SP44 3c + 1c multi .30 .80
  a. Miniature sheet of 6 10.00 *26.00*

Hygienist and Child — SP45

Designs: 3c+1c, Girls playing hockey. 4c+1c, Boys playing hockey.

1971, Aug. 4 **Litho.** ***Perf. 13½***

B82 SP45 3c + 1c multicolored .50 .75
  a. Miniature sheet of 6 10.00 *22.50*
B83 SP45 4c + 1c multicolored .50 .75
  a. Miniature sheet of 6 10.00 *22.50*
B84 SP45 5c + 1c multicolored 1.00 *2.25*
  Nos. B82-B84 (3) 2.00 3.75

50th anniv. of School Dental Service (No. B84).

Boy Playing Tennis — SP46

Design: 4c+1c, Girl playing tennis.

1972, Aug. 2 **Litho.** ***Perf. 13x13½***

B85 SP46 3c + 1c gray & lt brn .35 .60
  a. Miniature sheet of 6 9.50 *20.00*
B86 SP46 4c + 1c red brn, yel & gray .35 .60
  a. Miniature sheet of 6 9.50 *20.00*

Prince Edward — SP47

1973, Aug. 1 **Photo.**

B87 SP47 3c + 1c grn & brn .35 .60
  a. Miniature sheet of 6 9.00 *20.00*
B88 SP47 4c + 1c dk red & blk .35 .60
  a. Miniature sheet of 6 9.00 *20.00*

Children with Cat and Dog — SP48

Designs: 4c+1c, Girl with dogs and cat. 5c+1c, Children and dogs.

1974, Aug. 7 **Litho.** ***Perf. 13½x14***

B89 SP48 3c + 1c multicolored .25 .60
B90 SP48 4c + 1c multicolored .30 .60
  a. Miniature sheet of 10 20.00 *40.00*
B91 SP48 5c + 1c multicolored 1.10 1.75
  Nos. B89-B91 (3) 1.65 2.95

Girl Feeding Lamb — SP49

Designs: 4c+1c, Boy with hen and chicks. 5c+1c, Boy with duck and duckling.

1975, Aug. 6 **Litho.** ***Perf. 14x13½***

B92 SP49 3c + 1c multicolored .25 .35
B93 SP49 4c + 1c multicolored .25 .35
  a. Miniature sheet of 10 15.00 *40.00*
B94 SP49 5c + 1c multicolored .75 *1.75*
  Nos. B92-B94 (3) 1.25 2.45

Boy and Piebald Pony — SP50

Designs: 8c+1c, Farm girl and calf. 10c+1c, 2 girls watching nest-bound thrush.

1976, Aug. 4 **Litho.** ***Perf. 13½x14***

B95 SP50 7c + 1c multicolored .25 .35
B96 SP50 8c + 1c multicolored .25 .35
B97 SP50 10c + 1c multicolored .45 *.90*
  a. Min. sheet, 2 each #B95-B97 4.25 *6.00*
  Nos. B95-B97 (3) .95 1.60

Girl and Bluebird — SP51

8c+2c, Boy & frog. 10c+2c, Girl & butterfly.

1977, Aug. 3 **Litho.** ***Perf. 13½x14***

B98 SP51 7c + 2c multi .25 .60
B99 SP51 8c + 2c multi .25 .65
B100 SP51 10c + 2c multi .50 *1.10*
  a. Miniature sheet of 6 2.50 *6.50*
  Nos. B98-B100 (3) 1.00 2.35

No. B100a contains 2 each of Nos. B98-B100 in 2 strips of continuous design.

NZ No. B1 SP52

Heart Surgery SP53

1978, Aug. 2 **Litho.** ***Perf. 13½x14***

B101 SP52 10c + 2c multi .35 .40
B102 SP53 12c + 2c multi .35 .45
  a. Min. sheet, 3 ea #B101-B102 1.40 *4.00*

50th Health Stamp issue (No. B101) and National Heart Foundation (No. B102).

No. B102a exists in two printings: with "HARRISON & SONS LTD., LONDON" imprint at bottom left margin (valued) and with imprint more centered across three bottom stamps (apparently very scarce). Both varieties are known on first day covers.

Demoiselle Fish — SP54

Designs: No. B104, Sea urchin. 12c+2c, Underwater photographer and red mullet, vert.

1979, July 25 ***Perf. 13½x13, 13x13½***

B103 SP54 10c + 2c multi .35 .70
B104 SP54 10c + 2c multi .35 .70
  a. Pair, #B103-B104 .70 1.25
B105 SP54 12c + 2c multi .35 .70
  a. Min. sheet, 2 ea #B103-B105 1.50 *2.75*
  Nos. B103-B105 (3) 1.05 2.10

Children Surf Casting — SP55

No. B107, Wharf Fishing. B108, Underwater fishing.

1980, Aug. 6 **Litho.** ***Perf. 13½x13***

B106 SP55 14c + 2c shown .35 .95
B107 SP55 14c + 2c multi .35 .95
  a. Pair, #B106-B107 .70 1.75
B108 SP55 17c + 2c multi .35 .65
  a. Min. sheet, 2 ea #B106-B108 1.90 *3.25*
  Nos. B106-B108 (3) 1.05 2.55

Boy and Girl at Rock Pool — SP56

1981, Aug. 5 **Litho.** ***Perf. 14½***

B109 SP56 20c + 2c Girl, starfish .30 .75
B110 SP56 20c + 2c Boy fishing .30 .75
  a. Pair, #B109-B110 .60 1.50
B111 SP56 25c + 2c shown .30 .40
  a. Min. sheet, 2 ea #B109-B111 1.50 3.50
  Nos. B109-B111 (3) .90 1.90

Cocker Spaniel — SP57

1982, Aug. 4 **Litho.** ***Perf. 13x13½***

B112 SP57 24c + 2c Labrador .90 1.10
B113 SP57 24c + 2c Border collie .90 1.10
  a. Pair, #B112-B113 1.90 2.25

B114 SP57 30c + 2c shown .90 1.10
a. Min. sheet, 2 each #B112-B114, perf. 14x13½ 5.00 7.50
Nos. B112-B114 (3) 2.70 3.30

Persian Cat — SP58

1983, Aug. 3 Litho. *Perf. 14½*
B115 SP58 24 + 2c Tabby .70 .85
B116 SP58 24 + 2c Siamese .70 .85
a. Pair, #B115-B116 1.40 1.75
B117 SP58 30 + 2c shown .95 1.10
a. Min. sheet, 2 ea #B115-B117 3.00 3.50
Nos. B115-B117 (3) 2.35 2.80

Thoroughbreds SP59

1984, Aug. 1 Litho. *Perf. 13½x13*
B118 SP59 24c + 2c Clydesdales .60 .85
B119 SP59 24c + 2c Shetlands .60 .85
a. Pair, #B118-B119 1.25 1.75
B120 SP59 30c + 2c shown .60 .85
a. Min. sheet, 2 ea #B118-B120 2.50 3.75
Nos. B118-B120 (3) 1.80 2.55

Health — SP60

Princess Diana and: No. B121, Prince William. No. B122, Prince Henry. No. B123, Princes Charles, William and Henry.

1985, July 31 Litho. *Perf. 13½*
B121 SP60 25c + 2c multi 1.00 1.50
B122 SP60 25c + 2c multi 1.00 1.50
a. Pair, #B121-B122 2.10 3.00
B123 SP60 35c + 2c multi 1.00 1.50
a. Min. sheet, 2 ea #B121-B123 4.75 7.00
Nos. B121-B123 (3) 3.00 4.50

Surtax for children's health camps.

Children's Drawings — SP61

No. B125, Children playing. No. B126, Skipping rope, horiz.

1986, July 30 Litho. *Perf. 14½x14*
B124 SP61 30c + 3c shown .50 .75
B125 SP61 30c + 3c multi .50 .75
a. Pair, #B124-B125 1.00 1.50
B126 SP61 45c + 3c multi .75 .90
a. Min. sheet, 2 ea #B124-B126 3.50 4.00
Nos. B124-B126 (3) 1.75 2.40

Surtax for children's health camps.
No. B126a exists with Stockholmia '86 emblem. This sheet was sold only at the exhibition.

Children's Drawings — SP62

1987, July 29 Litho. *Perf. 14½*
B127 SP62 40c + 3c shown .90 1.75
B128 SP62 40c + 3c Swimming .90 1.75
a. Pair, #B127-B128 1.90 3.50
B129 SP62 60c + 3c Riding horse, vert. 1.50 7.75
a. Min. sheet, 2 ea #B127-B129 6.50 11.00
Nos. B127-B129 (3) 3.30 11.25

Surtax benefited children's health camps.

1988 Summer Olympics, Seoul — SP63

1988, July 27 Litho. *Perf. 14½*
B130 SP63 40c + 3c Swimming .70 .80
B131 SP63 60c + 3c Running .95 1.25
B132 SP63 70c + 3c Rowing 1.10 1.25
B133 SP63 80c + 3c Equestrian 1.25 1.60
a. Souv. sheet of 4, #B130-B133 4.00 5.00
Nos. B130-B133 (4) 4.00 4.90

Children's Health — SP64

Designs: No. B134, Duke and Duchess of York, Princess Beatrice. No. B135, Duchess, princess. No. B136, Princess.

1989, July 23
B134 SP64 40c + 3c multi .90 1.75
B135 SP64 40c + 3c multi .90 1.75
a. Pair, #B134-B135 1.90 3.50
B136 SP64 80c + 3c multi 1.60 2.00
a. Min. sheet, 2 ea #B134-B136 6.75 8.75
b. As "a," overprinted with World Stamp Expo '89 emblem in margin 17.50 17.50
Nos. B134-B136 (3) 3.40 5.50

Athletes — SP65

40c+5c, Jack Lovelock (1910-1949), runner. 80c+5c, George Nepia (1905-1986), rugby player.

1990, July 25 Litho. *Perf. 14½x14*
B137 SP65 40c +5c multi .60 .95
B138 SP65 80c +5c multi 1.25 1.60
a. Min. sheet, 2 ea #B137-B138 3.75 4.25

Hector's Dolphin — SP66

1991, July 24 Litho. *Perf. 14½*
B139 SP66 45c +5c 3 Swimming 1.00 1.40
B140 SP66 80c +5c 2 Jumping 1.40 2.25
a. Souv. sheet, 2 ea #B139-B140 5.75 7.50

Surtax benefited children's health camps.

Anthony F. Wilding (1883-1915), Tennis Player — SP67

Design: No. B142, C.S. "Stewie" Dempster (1903-1974), cricket player.

1992, Aug. 12 Litho. *Perf. 14x13½*
B141 SP67 45c +5c multi 1.10 1.40
B142 SP67 80c +5c multi 1.40 1.75
a. Souv. sheet, 2 each #B141-B142, perf. 14½ 4.50 6.25

Surtax for children's health camps.

SP68

1993, July 21 Litho. *Perf. 13½x14*
B143 SP68 45c +5c Boy, puppy .80 1.00
B144 SP68 80c +5c Girl, kitten 1.40 1.75
a. Souvenir sheet, 2 each #B143-B144, perf. 14½ 4.50 5.00
b. As "a," inscribed in sheet margin 7.00 7.00

Surtax for children's health camps.

No. B144b inscribed with "TAIPEI '93" emblem.
Issue date: No. B144b, Aug. 14.

SP69

Children's Health Camps, 75th Anniv.: No. B145, #B15, Children playing with ball. No. B146, #B34, Nurse holding child. No. B147, #B79, Children reading. 80c+5c, #B4, Boy.

1994, July 20 Litho. *Perf. 14*
B145 SP69 45c +5c multi .80 .90
B146 SP69 45c +5c multi .80 .90
B147 SP69 45c +5c multi .80 .90
B148 SP69 80c +5c multi 1.40 1.40
a. Souv. sheet of 4, #B145-B148 4.50 5.00
Nos. B145-B148 (4) 3.80 4.10

Surtax for children's health camps.

Children's Health Camps — SP70

Designs: 45c+5c, Boy on skateboard. 80c+5c, Child on bicycle.

1995, June 21 Litho. *Perf. 14½*
B149 SP70 45c +5c multi .85 1.25
B150 SP70 80c +5c multi 2.10 2.10
a. Souv. sheet, 2 ea #B149-B150 4.75 5.75
b. As "a," with added inscription 8.00 8.00

No. B150b inscribed with Stampex '95 emblem in sheet margin.
Surtax for children's health camps.

SP71

Children's Health: Nos. B151, B153, Infant buckled into child safety seat. 80c, Child holding adult's hand on pedestrian crossing.

1996, June 5 Litho. *Perf. 14x13½*
B151 SP71 40c +5c multi .80 .95
B152 SP71 80c +5c multi 1.40 1.50
a. Souvenir sheet, 2 each Nos. B151-B152, perf. 14x14½ 4.00 4.00
b. As "a" with added inscription 5.50 5.50

Self-Adhesive
Serpentine Die Cut 11½
B153 SP71 40c +5c multi .60 .85

No. B152b inscribed with CAPEX '96 emblem in sheet margin.

SP72

Original Design
1996, June 5 Litho. *Perf. 14x13½*
B154 SP72 40c +5c multi *1,000.* 1,200.

Self-Adhesive
Serpentine Die Cut 11½
B155 SP72 40c +5c multi 1,750. 1,750.

Nos. B154 and B155 were withdrawn before issue by New Zealand Post. Slightly over 1,000 examples of No. B154 and 500 examples of No. B155 were sold in error by two post offices within three days of June 5. A total of 402 examples of the souvenir sheet containing No. B154 were made available by the printer, but none were sold at post offices.
The stamps were withdrawn because the inclusion of the stuffed animal indicated that the infant was improperly belted into the vehicle.

Children's Health — SP73

Children's designs of "Healthy Living:" No. B156, Child on beach. 80c+5c, Child riding horse on waterfront. No. B158, Mosaic of person collecting fruit from tree, vert.

1997, June 18 Litho. *Perf. 14*
B156 SP73 40c +5c multi .80 .85
B157 SP73 80c +5c multi 1.40 1.40

Souvenir Sheet
B157A Sheet of 3, #B156-B157, B157Ab 3.50 3.50
b. SP73 40c +5c like #B158 2.00 2.00

Size: 25x36mm
Self-Adhesive
Serpentine Die Cut 10½
B158 SP73 40c +5c multi .75 .70

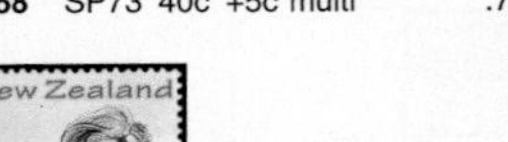

Children's Water Safety — SP74

Designs: 40c+5c, Child in life jacket. 80c+5c Child learning to swim.

1998, June 24 Litho. *Perf. 13½*
B159 SP74 40c +5c multicolored .75 .60
B160 SP74 80c +5c multicolored 1.40 1.40
a. Sheet, 2 each #B159-B160 4.25 4.25

Size: 25x38mm
Self-Adhesive
Serpentine Die Cut 11½
B161 SP74 40c +5c multicolored .75 .45

Children's Health — SP75

Scenes from children's books: #B162, Hairy Maclary's Bone, by Lynley Dodd. #B163, Lion in the Meadow, by Margaret Mahy. 80c+5c, Greedy Cat, by Joy Cowley.

Serpentine Die Cut 10¼
1999, June 16 Litho.
Self-Adhesive (#B162)
B162 SP75 40c +5c multi .75 .60

Perf. 14¼
B163 SP75 40c +5c multi .75 .60
B164 SP75 80c +5c multi 1.40 1.40

Souvenir Sheet
B165 Sheet of 3, #B163-B164, B165a 3.50 3.50
a. SP75 40c +5c like #B162 2.00 2.00

Nos. B162, B165a are 37x26mm.

For 2000 semi-postals, see Nos. 1681, 1682, 1682a and 1687.

Children's Health — SP76

Designs: No. B166, Four cyclists. 90c+5c, Cyclist in air. No. B168, Cyclist riding through puddle.

2001, Aug. 1 Litho. *Perf. 14*
B166 SP76 40c +5c multi .75 .60
a. Sheet of 10 7.50 7.50
B167 SP76 90c +5c multi 1.50 1.40
a. Souvenir sheet, #B166-B167 2.10 2.10

Size: 30x25mm
Serpentine Die Cut 10x9¾
Self-Adhesive
B168 SP76 40c +5c multi .60 .60
Nos. B166-B168 (3) 2.85 2.60

Healthy Living — SP77

Designs: B169, 40c+5c, Fruits. 90c+5c, Vegetables.
No. B171a, Fruits, diff. B172, Fruits diff. (like B171a).

2002, Aug. 7 ***Perf. 14¼x14***

B169 SP77 40c +5c multi .75 .60
B170 SP77 90c +5c multi 1.50 1.50

Souvenir Sheet

B171 Sheet, #B169-B170, B171a 3.50 3.50
a. SP77 40c +5c multi (21x26mm) 2.00 2.00

Coil Stamp
Size: 21x26mm
Self-Adhesive
Serpentine Die Cut 9¾x10

B172 SP77 40c +5c multi .75 .50

Children's Health — SP78

Designs: No. B173, 40c+5c, Children on swings. 90c+5c, Child with ball, girl playing hopscotch.
Nos. B175a, B176, 40c+ 5c, Girl on monkey bars.

2003, Aug. 6 **Litho.** ***Perf. 14***

B173 SP78 40c +5c multi .75 .55
B174 SP78 90c +5c multi 1.50 1.50

Souvenir Sheet

B175 Sheet, #B173-B174, B175a 3.50 3.50
a. SP78 40c +5c multi (21x26mm), perf. 14½x14 2.00 2.00

Coil Stamp
Size: 21x26mm
Self-Adhesive
Serpentine Die Cut 9¾x10

B176 SP78 40c +5c multi .75 .55

Children's Health — SP79

Designs: No. B177, Children playing with beach ball in water. No. B178, People in boat. Nos. B179a, B180, People fishing.

2004, Sept. 1 **Litho.** ***Perf. 14***

B177 SP79 45c +5c multi .75 .65
B178 SP79 90c +5c multi 1.50 1.50

Souvenir Sheet

B179 Sheet, #B177-B178, B179a 3.50 3.50
a. SP79 45c +5c multi (22x27mm), perf. 14¼x14 2.00 2.00

Self-Adhesive
Size: 22x27mm
Serpentine Die Cut 9½x10

B180 SP79 45c +5c multi .75 .65

Children's Health — SP80

Designs: No. B181, Girl and horse. 90c+5c, Boy and rabbit. Nos. B183a, B184, Children and dog.

2005, Aug. 3 **Litho.** ***Perf. 14***

B181 SP80 45c +5c multi .75 .65
B182 SP80 90c +5c multi 1.50 1.50
B183 Souvenir sheet, #B181-B182, B183a 3.50 3.50
a. SP80 45c +5c multi, 20x25mm, perf. 14½x14 2.00 2.00

Self-Adhesive
Size: 20x25mm
Serpentine Die Cut 9½x10

B184 SP80 45c +5c multi .75 .65

Children's Health — SP81

Designs: No. B185, Girl releasing dove. $1+10c, Boy with origami bird. Nos. B187a, B188, Two children, peace lily (25x30mm).

2007, Sept. 5 **Litho.** ***Perf. 14***

B185 SP81 50c +10c multi .85 .85
a. Perf. 13½ .85 .85
B186 SP81 $1 +10c multi 1.50 1.50
a. Perf. 13½ 1.50 1.50

Souvenir Sheet

B187 Sheet, #B185-B186, B187a 3.75 3.75
a. SP81 50c +10c multi, perf. 14½x14 2.50 2.50
b. As "a," perf. 14½x13½x14½x14 2.00 2.00
c. Souvenir sheet, #B185a, B186a, B187b 3.25 3.25

Self-Adhesive
Serpentine Die Cut 9½x10

B188 SP81 50c +10c multi .85 .85

Surtax for Children's Health Camps.

Children's Health SP82

Child: No. B189, Cycling. $1+10c, Kayaking. Nos. B191a, B192, Running.

2008, July 2 **Litho.** ***Perf. 14¼***

B189 SP82 50c +10c multi .75 .75
B190 SP82 $1 +10c multi 1.50 1.50

Souvenir Sheet

B191 Sheet, #B189-B190, B191a 4.00 4.00
a. SP82 50c +10c multi (36x36mm), perf. 14x14½ 1.75 1.75

Self-Adhesive
Serpentine Die Cut 9¾
Size: 34x34mm

B192 SP82 50c +10c multi .95 .95

Surtax for Children's Health Camps.

Children's Health Stamps, 80th Anniv. — SP83

Stamps in color: No. B193, #B151. $1+10c, #B5. Nos. B195a, B196, #B23.

2009, Sept. 7 **Litho.** ***Perf. 13¼x13½***

B193 SP83 50c +10c multi .90 .90
a. Perf. 14 1.00 1.00
B194 SP83 $1 +10c multi 1.60 1.60
a. Perf. 14 1.75 1.75

Souvenir Sheet

B195 Sheet, #B193a, B194a, B195a 3.75 3.50
a. SP83 50c+10c multi, perf. 14½x14, 22x27mm 2.00 2.00

Self-Adhesive
Serpentine Die Cut 9½x10
Size: 21x26mm

B196 SP83 50c +10c multi .90 .90

Surtax for Children's Health Camps.

Butterflies SP84

Designs: No. B197, Monarch butterfly. $1+10c, Tussock butterfly. Nos. B199a, B200, Boulder copper butterfly, vert. (25x30mm).

2010, July 7 **Litho.** ***Perf. 14***

B197 SP84 50c + 10c multi .75 .75
B198 SP84 $1 +10c multi 1.50 1.50

Souvenir Sheet

B199 Sheet of 3, #B197-B198, B199a 3.75 3.75
a. SP84 50c +10c multi 1.50 1.50

Self-Adhesive
Serpentine Die Cut 9½x10

B200 SP84 50c +10c multi 1.00 1.00

Surtax for Children's Health Camps.

Flightless Birds — SP85

Designs: No. B201, Kiwi. $1.20+10c, Kakapo. Nos. B203a, B204, Takahe, vert. (25x30mm).

2011, July 6 **Litho.** ***Perf. 14***

B201 SP85 60c + 10c multi 1.10 1.10
B202 SP85 $1.20 +10c multi 2.25 2.25

Souvenir Sheet

B203 Sheet of 3, #B201-B202, B203a 5.00 5.00
a. SP85 60c +10c multi 1.60 1.60

Self-Adhesive
Serpentine Die Cut 9½x10

B204 SP85 60c +10c multi 1.25 1.25

Surtax for Children's Health Camps.

New Zealand Sea Lions — SP86

Designs: No. B205, Sea lion pup. $1.40+10c, Adolescent male sea lion. Nos. B207a, B208, Head of sea lion pup, vert. (23x27mm).

2012, Aug. 1 ***Perf. 14***

B205 SP86 70c + 10c multi 1.25 1.25
B206 SP86 $1.40 +10c multi 2.50 2.50

Souvenir Sheet

B207 Sheet of 3, #B205-B206, B207a 5.75 5.75
a. SP86 70c +10c multi 2.00 2.00

Self-Adhesive
Serpentine Die Cut 9½x10

B208 SP86 70c +10c multi 1.40 1.40

Surtax for New Zealand Foundation for Child and Family Health and Development.

Children and Farm Pets — SP87

Designs: No. B209, Boy and lamb. $1.40 + 10c, Girl and piglets. Nos. B211a, B212, Boy and goat (22x27mm).

2013, Sept. 4 ***Perf. 14***

B209 SP87 70c +10c multi 1.25 1.25
a. Perf. 13½ 1.25 1.25
B210 SP87 $1.40 +10c multi 2.40 2.40
a. Perf. 13½ 2.40 2.40

Souvenir Sheet
Perf. 13½

B211 Sheet of 3, #B209a, B210a, B211a 5.00 5.00
a. SP87 70c +10c multi 1.25 1.25

Self-Adhesive
Serpentine Die Cut 9½x10

B212 SP87 70c +10c multi 1.25 1.25

Surtax for Stand Children's Services.

Children and Vegetables — SP88

Designs: No. B213, Girl and carrots. $1.40 + 10c, Boy and apples. Nos. B215a, B216, Boy and pumpkin.

2014, Sept. 3 **Litho.** ***Perf. 14***

B213 SP88 80c +10c multi 1.40 1.40
a. Perf. 13½ 1.40 1.40
B214 SP88 $1.40 +10c multi 2.40 2.40
a. Perf. 13½ 2.40 2.40

Souvenir Sheet

B215 Sheet of 3, #B213a, B214a, B215a 5.25 5.25
a. SP88 80c +10c multi (22x27mm) 1.40 1.40

Self-Adhesive
Size: 21x26mm

B216 SP88 80c +10c multi 1.40 1.40

Surtax for Stand Children's Services Tu Maia Whanau.

Children and Sun Protection — SP89

Designs: No. B217, Girl under beach umbrella. $1.40+10c, Girl wearing hat with ear flaps putting sun screen on hands. $2+10c, Girl with large hat over head. Nos. B220a, B221, Boy, large pair of sunglasses.

2015, Sept. 2 **Litho.** ***Perf. 14***

B217 SP89 80c +10c multi 1.25 1.25
a. Perf. 13¼x13½ 1.25 1.25
B218 SP89 $1.40 +10c multi 1.90 1.90
a. Perf. 13¼x13½ 1.90 1.90
B219 SP89 $2 +10c multi 2.75 2.75
a. Perf. 13¼x13½ 2.75 2.75
Nos. B217-B219 (3) 5.90 5.90

Miniature Sheet

B220 Sheet of 4, #B217a, B218a, B219a, B220a 7.25 7.25
a. SP89 80c+10c multi, perf. 13¾x13½, 25x30mm 1.25 1.25

Self-Adhesive
Size: 25x30mm
Serpentine Die Cut 9½x10

B221 SP89 80c +10c multi 1.25 1.25

Surtax for Stand Children's Services Tu Maia Whanau.

Children's Health — SP90

Designs: $1+10c, Child with rugby ball, child holding end of rope. $1.80+10c, Children playing tug-of-war. $2.20+10c, Child holding end of rope, children stretching.

2016, Sept. 7 **Litho.** ***Perf. 14¼***

B222 SP90 $1 +10c multi 1.60 1.60
B223 SP90 $1.80 +10c multi 2.75 2.75
B224 SP90 $2.20 +10c multi 3.50 3.50
a. Horiz. strip of 3, #B222-B224 8.00 8.00
b. Souvenir sheet of 3, #B222-B224 8.00 8.00
Nos. B222-B224 (3) 7.85 7.85

Surtax for Stand Children's Services Tu Maia Whanau.

Theodore Bear on Ladder — SP91

Hay Hay Teddy Bear — SP92

Lubert Bear Wearing Sweater — SP93

Teddy Bear in Mailbox — SP94

Little Ted Bear Wearing Poppy — SP95

Frontliner Bear With Face Mask — SP96

2020, May 20 Litho. ***Perf. 14¼x14½***

B225	Miniature sheet of 6	19.00	19.00
a.	SP91 $1.30 multi	2.00	2.00
b.	SP92 $1.30 multi	2.00	2.00
c.	SP93 $1.30 multi	2.00	2.00
d.	SP94 $2.60 multi	4.25	4.25
e.	SP95 $2.60 multi	4.25	4.25
f.	SP96 $2.60 multi	4.25	4.25

No. B225 sold for $14.70, with $3 going to the Red Cross.

AIR POST STAMPS

Plane over Lake Manapouri — AP1

Perf. 14x14½
1931, Nov. 10 Typo. Wmk. 61

C1	AP1 3p chocolate	27.50	22.50
a.	Perf. 14x15	150.00	*500.00*
C2	AP1 4p dark violet	27.50	27.50
C3	AP1 7p orange	30.00	27.50
	Nos. C1-C3 (3)	85.00	77.50

Most examples of No. C1a are poorly centered.

Type of 1931 Surcharged in Red

1931, Dec. 18 ***Perf. 14x14½***

C4	AP1 5p on 3p yel green	20.00	25.00

Type of 1931 Overprinted in Dark Blue

1934, Jan. 17

C5	AP1 7p bright blue	50.00	55.00

1st official air mail flight between NZ and Australia.

Airplane over Landing Field — AP2

1935, May 4 Engr. ***Perf. 14***

C6	AP2 1p rose carmine	1.10	.80
C7	AP2 3p dark violet	5.75	3.75
C8	AP2 6p gray blue	11.50	5.75
	Nos. C6-C8 (3)	18.35	10.30
	Set, never hinged	40.00	

SPECIAL DELIVERY STAMPS

SD1

Perf. 14x14½,14x15
1903-26 Typo. Wmk. 61

E1	SD1 6p purple & red ('26)	60.00	40.00
a.	6p violet & red, perf. 11	70.00	50.00

Mail Car — SD2

1939, Aug. 16 Engr. ***Perf. 14***

E2	SD2 6p violet gray	1.75	6.00

POSTAGE DUE STAMPS

D1

Wmk. 62
1899, Dec. 1 Typo. ***Perf. 11***

J1	D1 ½p green & red	8.00	*19.00*
a.	No period after "D"	75.00	60.00
J2	D1 1p green & red	12.50	2.10
J3	D1 2p green & red	40.00	6.25
J4	D1 3p green & red	20.00	6.00
J5	D1 4p green & red	42.50	25.00
J6	D1 5p green & red	45.00	*60.00*
J7	D1 6p green & red	45.00	*60.00*
J8	D1 8p green & red	110.00	*150.00*
J9	D1 10p green & red	175.00	*225.00*
J10	D1 1sh green & red	140.00	100.00
J11	D1 2sh green & red	225.00	*300.00*
	Nos. J1-J11 (11)	863.00	953.35
	Set, never hinged	1,650.	

Nos. J1-J11 may be found with N. Z. and D. varying in size.

D2

1902, Feb. 28 Unwmk.

J12	D2 ½p gray grn & red	3.00	7.50

Wmk. 61

J13	D2 ½p gray grn & red	3.00	2.10
J14	D2 1p gray grn & red	12.00	4.00
J15	D2 2p gray grn & red	150.00	150.00

1904-28 ***Perf. 14, 14x14½***

J16	D2 ½p green & car	3.75	4.25
J17	D2 1p green & car	7.00	1.00
J18	D2 2p green & car	9.00	3.50
J19	D2 3p grn & rose ('28)	50.00	25.00
	Nos. J16-J19 (4)	69.75	33.75

N Z and Star printed on the back in Blue

1925 Unwmk. ***Perf. 14x14½, 14x15***

J20	D2 ½p green & rose	4.00	*26.00*
J21	D2 2p green & rose	9.00	*35.00*

Catalogue values for unused stamps in this section, from this point to the end of the section, are for Never Hinged items.

D3

1939 Wmk. 61 Typo. ***Perf. 15x14***

J22	D3 ½p turquoise green	13.00	*9.00*
J23	D3 1p rose pink	5.00	.60
J24	D3 2p ultramarine	9.00	1.75
J25	D3 3p brown orange	26.00	29.00
	Nos. J22-J25 (4)	53.00	40.35

1945-49 Wmk. 253

J27	D3 1p rose pink ('49)	5.00	25.00
J28	D3 2p ultramarine ('47)	7.00	9.00
J29	D3 3p brown orange	15.00	5.75
	Nos. J27-J29 (3)	27.00	39.75

The use of postage due stamps was discontinued in Sept., 1951.

WAR TAX STAMP

No. 144 Overprinted in Black

Perf. 14x14½
1915, Sept. 24 Wmk. 61

MR1	A43 ½p green	2.10	.60

OFFICIAL STAMPS

Regular Issues of 1882-92 Overprinted & Handstamped

1892 Wmk. 62 ***Perf as Before***
Rose or Magenta Handstamp

O1	A9 1p rose	*600.*	
O2	A10 2p violet	*800.*	
O3	A16 2½p ultramarine	*700.*	
O4	A17 5p olive gray	*1,000.*	
O5	A13 6p brown	*1,200.*	

Violet Handstamp

O6	N1 ½p rose	*1,000.*	
O7	A9 1p rose	*600.*	
O8	A10 2p violet		

Handstamped on No. 67A in Rose
1899 ***Perf. 10, 10x11***

O9	A15a ½p black	*600.*	

Handstamped on No. 79 in Violet
Unwmk. ***Perf. 14, 15***

O10	A27 8p dull blue	*1,200.*	

Hstmpd. on Stamps of 1899-1900 in Violet

1902 ***Perf. 11***

O11	A22 2½p blue	*650.*	
O12	A23 3p org brown	*1,000.*	
O13	A25 5p red brown	*900.*	
O14	A27 8p dark blue	*1,000.*	

Green Handstamp

O15	A25 5p red brown	*900.*	

Handstamped on Stamp of 1901 in Violet
Wmk. 63 ***Perf. 11***

O16	A35 1p carmine	*600.*	

Handstamped on Stamps of 1902-07 in Violet or Magenta
1905-07 Wmk. 61 ***Perf. 11, 14***

O17	A18 ½p green	*600.*	
O18	A35 1p carmine	*600.*	
O19	A22 2½p blue	*700.*	
O20	A25 5p red brown		
O21	A27 8p deep blue		
O22	A30 2sh blue green	*5,000.*	

The "O. P. S. O." handstamp is usually struck diagonally, reading up, but on No. O19 it also occurs horizontally. The letters stand for "On Public Service Only."

Overprinted in Black

On Stamps of 1902-07
1907 ***Perf. 14, 14x13, 14x14½***

O23	A18 ½p green	12.00	2.00
O24	A35 1p carmine	12.00	1.00
a.	Booklet pane of 6	110.00	
O25	A33 2p violet	20.00	2.00
O26	A23 3p orange brn	60.00	6.00
O27	A26 6p carmine rose	250.00	40.00
a.	Horiz. pair, imperf. vert.	*925.00*	
O28	A29 1sh brown red	125.00	25.00
O29	A30 2sh blue green	175.00	150.00
a.	Horiz. pair, imperf. vert.	*1,400.*	
O30	A31 5sh vermilion	350.00	350.00
	Nos. O23-O30 (8)	1,004.	576.00

On No. 127
Perf. 14x13, 14x14½

O31	A26 6p carmine rose	325.00	65.00

On No. 129
1909 ***Perf. 14x14½***

O32	A35 1p car (redrawn)	90.00	3.00

On Nos. 130-131, 133, 137, 139
1910 ***Perf. 14, 14x13½, 14x14½***

O33	A41 ½p yel grn	10.00	1.00
a.	Inverted overprint		1,600.
O34	A42 1p carmine	3.75	.25
O35	A41 3p org brn	20.00	2.00
O36	A41 6p car rose	30.00	10.00
O37	A41 1sh vermilion	70.00	40.00
	Nos. O33-O37 (5)	133.75	53.25

For 3p see note on perf varieties following No. 139.

On Postal-Fiscal Stamps Nos. AR32, AR36, AR44

1911-14

O38	PF1 2sh blue ('14)	75.00	52.50
O39	PF1 5sh green ('13)	125.00	*200.00*
O40	PF2 £1 rose	1,000.	625.00
	Nos. O38-O40 (3)	1,200.	877.50

On Stamps of 1909-19
Perf. 14x13½, 14x14½, 14x15]
1915-19 Typo.

O41	A43 ½p green	1.60	.25
O42	A46 1½p gray black ('16)	8.00	3.00
O43	A47 1½p gray black ('16)	5.75	1.00
O44	A47 1½p brown org ('19)	5.75	.60
O45	A43 2p yellow ('17)	5.75	.50
O46	A43 3p chocolate ('19)	16.00	1.50

Engr.

O47	A45 3p vio brn ('16)	8.00	1.50
O48	A45 6p car rose ('16)	12.00	1.00
O49	A41 8p dp bl (R) ('16)	20.00	*30.00*
O50	A45 1sh vermilion ('16)	7.50	2.25
a.	1sh orange	15.00	*20.00*
	Nos. O41-O50 (10)	90.35	*41.60*

For 8p see note on perf varieties following No. 139.

1922 On No. 157

O51	A45 8p red brown	125.00	*200.00*

1925 On Nos. 151, 158

O52	A45 4p purple	20.00	4.25
O53	A45 9p olive green	45.00	42.50

On No. 177
1925 ***Perf. 14x14½***

O54	A42 1p carmine	5.00	5.00

On Nos. 184, 182
1927-28 Wmk. 61 ***Perf. 14, 14½x14***

O55	A57 1p rose red	2.50	.25
O56	A56 2sh blue	125.00	140.00

On No. AR50
1933 ***Perf. 14***

O57	PF5 5sh green	450.00	450.00

Nos. 186, 187, 196 Overprinted in Black

1936 *Perf. 14x13½, 13½x14, 14*

O58 A59 1p copper red 2.00 1.40
O59 A60 1½p red brown 14.00 *30.00*
O60 A69 1sh dark slate grn 30.00 *52.50*
Nos. O58-O60 (3) 46.00 83.90
Set, never hinged 120.00

Same Overprint Horizontally in Black or Green on Stamps of 1936

Perf. 12½, 13½, 13x13½, 14x13½, 13½x14, 14

1936-42 **Wmk. 253**

O61 A58 ½p brt grn ('37) 1.50 5.25
O62 A59 1p copper red 3.00 .60
O63 A60 1½p red brown 4.00 5.25
O64 A61 2p red org ('38) 1.00 .25
Never hinged 250.00
O65 A62 2½p dk gray & dk brown 8.00 24.00
O66 A63 3p choc ('38) 27.50 4.00
O67 A64 4p blk brn & blk 5.00 1.10
O68 A66 6p red ('37) 5.75 .35
O68B A67 8p dp brn ('42) 8.50 20.00
O69 A68 9p blk & scar (G) ('38) 80.00 45.00
O70 A69 1sh dk slate grn 14.00 1.60
a. Perf. 12½ ('42) 27.50 1.75

Overprint Vertical

O71 A70 2sh ol grn ('37) 24.00 8.50
a. Perf. 12½ ('42) 90.00 25.00
Nos. O61-O71 (12) 182.25 115.90
Set, never hinged 550.00

Same Overprint Horizontally in Black on Nos. 226, 227, 228

1938

O72 A79 ½p emerald 5.75 1.75
O73 A79 1p rose red 7.25 .30
O74 A80 1½p red brn 37.50 10.50
Nos. O72-O74 (3) 50.50 12.55
Set, never hinged 95.00

Same Overprint on No. AR50

1938 **Wmk. 61** *Perf. 14*

O75 PF5 5sh green 75.00 47.50

Nos. 229-235, 237, 239-241 Overprinted in Red or Black

Perf. 13½x13, 13x13½, 14x13½

1940 **Wmk. 253**

O76 A81 ½p dk bl grn (R) .60 .75
a. "ff" joined 29.00 70.00
O77 A82 1p scar & sepia 2.25 .30
a. "ff" joined 29.00 70.00
O78 A83 1½p brt vio & ultra 1.10 *4.25*
O79 A84 2p blk brn & Prus grn 2.25 .30
a. "ff" joined 35.00 70.00
O80 A85 2½p dk bl & myr grn 1.40 4.50
a. "ff" joined 29.00 77.50
O81 A86 3p dp plum & dk vio (R) 5.75 .95
a. "ff" joined 24.00 55.00
O82 A87 4p dk red vio & vio brn 14.50 1.60
a. "ff" joined 70.00 92.50
O83 A89 6p vio & brt grn 14.50 1.60
a. "ff" joined 40.00 80.00
O84 A90 8p org red & blk 14.50 13.00
a. "ff" joined 40.00 110.00
O85 A91 9p dp org & olive 5.75 5.75
O86 A92 1sh dk sl grn & ol 35.00 5.25
Nos. O76-O86 (11) 97.60 38.25
Set, never hinged 190.00

Nos. 227A, 228C Overprinted in Black

1941 **Wmk. 253** *Perf. 13½*

O88 A79 1p light blue green .30 .30
O89 A80 3p blue .75 .30
Set, never hinged 2.25

Same Overprint on No. 245

1944 *Perf. 14x15*

Size: 17¼x20¼mm

O90 A68 9p int black & scar 20.00 17.00
Never hinged 60.00

Same Overprint on No. AR78

Perf. 14

O91 PF5 5sh green 12.00 7.00
Never hinged 20.00

Catalogue values for unused stamps in this section, from this point to the end of the section, are for Never Hinged items.

Same Ovpt. on Stamps of 1941-47

1946-51 *Perf. 13½, 14*

O92 A79 ½p brn org ('46) 1.75 1.25
O92B A80 1½p red 5.75 1.25
O93 A80 2p orange .90 .30
O94 A80 4p rose lilac 4.00 1.25
O95 A80 6p rose carmine 5.75 1.25
O96 A80 8p deep violet 10.00 4.50
O97 A80 9p chocolate 11.50 5.75
O98 A104 1sh dk car rose & chestnut 11.50 1.75
O99 A104 2sh dk grn & brn org 26.00 8.50
Nos. O92-O99 (9) 77.15 25.80

Queen Elizabeth II — O1

Perf. 13½x13

1954, Mar. 1 **Engr.** **Wmk. 253**

O100 O1 1p orange 1.10 .50
O101 O1 1½p rose brown 4.25 5.75
O102 O1 2p green .45 .25
O103 O1 3p red .45 .25
O104 O1 4p blue 1.10 .60
O105 O1 9p rose carmine 10.50 2.50
O106 O1 1sh rose violet 1.10 .25
Nos. O100-O106 (7) 18.95 10.10

Exist imperf.

Nos. O102, O101 Surcharged

1959-61

O107 O1 2½p on 2p green ('61) 1.10 1.75
O108 O1 6p on 1½p rose brn .60 1.25

Exist imperf.

1963, Mar. 1

O109 O1 2½p dark olive 4.00 1.75
O111 O1 3sh slate 47.50 57.50

Exist imperf.

LIFE INSURANCE

Lighthouses — LI1

Perf. 10, 11, 10x11, 12x11½

1891, Jan. 2 **Typo.** **Wmk. 62**

OY1 LI1 ½p purple 110.00 7.00
OY2 LI1 1p blue 80.00 2.00
OY3 LI1 2p red brown 150.00 4.25
OY4 LI1 3p chocolate 425.00 22.50
OY5 LI1 6p green 550.00 70.00
OY6 LI1 1sh rose pink 800.00 140.00
Nos. OY1-OY6 (6) 2,115. 245.75

Stamps from outside rows of the sheets sometimes lack watermark.

1903-04 **Wmk. 61** *Perf. 11, 14x11*

OY7 LI1 ½p purple 120.00 7.00
OY8 LI1 1p blue 75.00 1.10
OY9 LI1 2p red brown 200.00 10.00
Nos. OY7-OY9 (3) 395.00 18.10

Lighthouses — LI2

1905-32 *Perf. 11, 14, 14x14½*

OY10 LI2 ½p yel grn ('13) 1.40 .90
OY11 LI2 ½p green ('32) 5.75 2.75
OY12 LI2 1p blue ('06) 375.00 29.00
OY13 LI2 1p dp rose ('13) 9.75 1.10
OY14 LI2 1p scarlet ('31) 4.25 2.00
OY15 LI2 1½p gray ('17) 14.00 4.25
OY16 LI2 1½p brn org ('19) 1.75 1.40
OY17 LI2 2p red brown 2,750. 200.00
OY18 LI2 2p violet ('13) 20.00 17.00
OY19 LI2 2p yellow ('21) 6.00 6.00
OY20 LI2 3p ocher ('13) 29.00 20.00
OY21 LI2 3p choc ('31) 11.00 26.00
OY22 LI2 6p car rose ('13) 20.00 26.00
OY23 LI2 6p pink ('31) 20.00 45.00
Nos. OY10-OY23 (14) 3,268. 381.40

#OY15, OY16 have "POSTAGE" at each side.

Stamps from outside rows of the sheets sometimes lack watermark.

1946-47 **Wmk. 253** *Perf. 14x15*

OY24 LI2 ½p yel grn ('47) 1.90 1.90
OY25 LI2 1p scarlet 1.40 1.25
OY26 LI2 2p yellow 2.25 *15.00*
OY27 LI2 3p chocolate 10.50 *30.00*
OY28 LI2 6p pink ('47) 8.50 *25.00*
Nos. OY24-OY28 (5) 24.55 73.15
Set, never hinged 42.50

Catalogue values for unused stamps in this section, from this point to the end of the section, are for Never Hinged items.

New Zealand Lighthouses

Castlepoint — LI3

Taiaroa — LI4

Cape Palliser LI5

Cape Campbell LI6

Eddystone (England) LI7

Stephens Island LI8

The Brothers LI9

Cape Brett LI10

Perf. 13½x13, 13x13½

1947-65 **Engr.** **Wmk. 253**

OY29 LI3 ½p dk grn & red orange 1.75 1.70
OY30 LI4 1p ol brn & blue 1.75 1.10
OY31 LI5 2p int bl & gray .90 .90
OY32 LI6 2½p ultra & blk ('63) 11.00 15.00
OY33 LI7 3p red vio & bl 3.50 .75
OY34 LI8 4p dk brn & org 4.50 1.75
a. Wmkd. sideways ('65) 4.50 16.00
OY35 LI9 6p dk brn & bl 4.25 2.50
OY36 LI10 1sh red brn & bl 4.25 3.50
Nos. OY29-OY36 (8) 31.90 27.20

Set first issued Aug. 1, 1947.

Exist imperf.

Nos. OY30, OY32-OY33, OY34a, OY35-OY36 and Types Surcharged

No. OY37

No. OY38

Perf. 13½x13, 13x13½

1967-68 **Engr.** **Wmk. 253**

OY37 LI4 1c on 1p 2.50 4.75
a. Wmkd. upright ('68) 1.10 4.75
OY38 LI6 2c on 2½p 11.00 16.00
OY39 LI7 2½c on 3p, wmkd. upright 1.75 5.50
a. Watermarked sideways ('68) 2.75 5.50
OY40 LI8 3c on 4p 5.25 6.25
OY41 LI9 5c on 6p .85 7.00
OY42 LI10 10c on 1sh, wmkd. sideways .85 4.75
a. Watermarked upright 2.40 11.50
Nos. OY37-OY42 (6) 22.20 44.25

The surcharge is different on each stamp and is adjusted to obliterate old denomination. One dot only on 2½c.

Set first issued July 10, 1967.

Moeraki Point Lighthouse — LI11

Lighthouses: 2½c, Puysegur Point, horiz. 3c, Baring Head. 4c, Cape Egmont, horiz. 8c, East Cape. 10c, Farewell Spit. 15c, Dog Island.

Perf. 13x13½, 13½x13, 14 (8c, 10c)

1969-76 **Litho.** **Unwmk.**

OY43 LI11 ½c pur, bl & yel .75 2.00
OY44 LI11 2½c yel, ultra & grn .60 1.40
OY45 LI11 3c org brn & brn .60 .85
OY46 LI11 4c lt ultra, org & ol brn .60 1.10
OY47 LI11 8c multicolored .60 3.25
OY48 LI11 10c multicolored .40 3.25
OY49 LI11 15c multicolored .40 2.40
a. Perf. 14 ('78) 1.00 2.50
Nos. OY43-OY49 (7) 3.95 14.25

Cent. of Government Life Insurance Office.

Issued: #OY47-OY48, 11/17/76; others 3/27/69.

No. OY44 Srchd.

Perf. 13½x13

1978, Mar. 8 **Litho.** **Wmk. 253**

OY50 LI11 25c on 2½c multi .85 2.00

Lighthouse LI12

1981, June 3 **Litho.** *Perf. 14½*

OY51 LI12 5c multicolored .25 .25
OY52 LI12 10c multicolored .25 .25
OY53 LI12 20c multicolored .25 .25
OY54 LI12 30c multicolored .30 .30
OY55 LI12 40c multicolored .35 .35
OY56 LI12 50c multicolored .35 .50
Nos. OY51-OY56 (6) 1.75 1.90

Government Life Insurance Stamps have been discontinued.

NEWSPAPER STAMPS

Queen Victoria — N1

Wmk. 59

1873, Jan. 1 Typo. *Perf. 10*

P1 N1 ½p rose 140.00 47.50
a. Perf. 12½x10 160.00 75.00
b. Perf. 12½ 210.00 75.00

The "N Z" watermark is widely spaced and intended for larger stamps. About a third of the stamps in each sheet are unwatermarked. They are worth a slight premium.

For overprint, see No. O6.

1875, Jan. Wmk. 64 *Perf. 12½*

P3 N1 ½p rose 25.00 5.00
a. Pair, imperf. between 800.00 500.00
b. Perf. 12 70.00 12.50

1892 Wmk. 62 *Perf. 12½*

P4 N1 ½p bright rose 11.00 1.50
a. Unwatermarked 20.00 10.00

ROSS DEPENDENCY

Catalogue values for unused stamps in this section are for Never Hinged items.

H.M.S. Erebus and Mount Erebus — A1

Ernest H. Shackleton and Robert F. Scott A2

Map Showing Location of Ross Dependency A3

Queen Elizabeth II — A4

Perf. 14, 13 (A4)

1957, Jan. 11 Engr. Wmk. 253

L1 A1 3p dark blue 3.00 1.25
L2 A2 4p dark carmine 3.00 1.25
L3 A3 8p ultra & car rose 3.00 1.25
L4 A4 1sh6p dull violet 3.00 1.25
Nos. L1-L4 (4) 12.00 5.00

1967, July 10

L5 A1 2c dark blue 21.00 15.00
L6 A2 3c dark carmine 12.00 10.00
L7 A3 7c ultra & car rose 12.00 10.00
L8 A4 15c dull violet 12.00 10.00
Nos. L5-L8 (4) 57.00 45.00

Skua — A5

Scott Base — A6

Designs: 4c, Hercules plane unloading at Williams Field. 5c, Shackleton's hut, Cape Royds. 8c, Naval supply ship Endeavour unloading. 18c, Tabular ice floe.

Perf. 13x13½

1972, Jan. 18 Litho. Unwmk.

L9 A5 3c lt bl, blk & gray 1.00 1.75
L10 A5 4c black & violet .25 1.75
L11 A5 5c rose lil, blk & gray .25 1.75
L12 A5 8c blk, dk gray & brn .25 1.75

Perf. 14½x14

L13 A6 10c slate grn, brt grn & blk .25 1.90
a. Perf. 14½x13½ ('79) .70 1.75
L14 A6 18c pur & black .25 1.90
a. Perf. 14½x13½ ('79) 1.60 3.00
Nos. L9-L14 (6) 2.25 10.80

25th Anniv. of Scott Base — A7

5c, Adelie penguins. 10c, Tracked vehicles. 30c, Field party, Upper Taylor Valley. 40c, Vanda Station. 50c, Scott's hut, Cape Evans, 1911.

1982, Jan. 20 Litho. *Perf. 15½*

L15 A7 5c multicolored 1.40 1.60
L16 A7 10c multicolored .25 .75
L17 A7 20c shown .25 .75
L18 A7 30c multicolored .25 .45
L19 A7 40c multicolored .25 .45
L20 A7 50c multicolored .25 .45
Nos. L15-L20 (6) 2.65 4.45

Wildlife — A8

5c, South polar skua. 10c, Snow petrel chick. 20c, Black-browed albatross. 45c, Emperor penguins. 50c, Chinstrap penguins. 70c, Adelie penguins. 80c, Elephant seals. $1, Leopard seal. $2, Weddell seal. $3, Crabeater seal pup.

1994-95 Litho. *Perf. 13½*

L21 A8 5c multicolored .25 .25
L22 A8 10c multicolored .25 .25
L23 A8 20c multicolored .30 .30
L23A A8 40c like No. 24 .65 .65
L24 A8 45c multicolored .70 .70
L25 A8 50c multicolored .80 .80
L26 A8 70c multicolored 1.10 1.10
L27 A8 80c multicolored 1.25 1.25
L28 A8 $1 multicolored 1.60 1.60
L29 A8 $2 multicolored 3.25 3.25
L30 A8 $3 multicolored 4.75 4.75
Nos. L21-L30 (11) 14.90 14.90

Issued: 40c, 10/2/95; others, 11/2/94.

Antarctic Explorers — A9

Explorer, ships: 40c, James Cook, Resolution & Adventure. 80c, James Clark Ross, Erebus & Terror. $1, Roald Amundsen, Fram. $1.20, Robert Falcon Scott, Terra Nova. $1.50, Ernest Henry Shackleton, Endurance. $1.80, Richard Evelyn Byrd, Floyd Bennett (airplane).

1995, Nov. 9 Litho. *Perf. 14½*

L31 A9 40c multicolored .65 .65
L32 A9 80c multicolored 1.25 1.25
L33 A9 $1 multicolored 1.60 1.60
L34 A9 $1.20 multicolored 1.90 1.90
L35 A9 $1.50 multicolored 2.40 2.40
L36 A9 $1.80 multicolored 2.75 2.75
Nos. L31-L36 (6) 10.55 10.55

Antarctic Landscapes — A10

Designs: 40c, Inside ice cave, vert. 80c, Base of glacier, vert. $1, Glacier ice fall, vert. $1.20, Climbers on crater rim. $1.50, Pressure ridges. $1.80, Fumarole ice tower.

1996, Nov. 13 Litho. *Perf. 14*

L37 A10 40c multicolored .65 .65
L38 A10 80c multicolored 1.25 1.25
L39 A10 $1 multicolored 1.60 1.60
L40 A10 $1.20 multicolored 1.90 1.90
L41 A10 $1.50 multicolored 2.40 2.40
L42 A10 $1.80 multicolored 2.75 2.75
Nos. L37-L42 (6) 10.55 10.55

Antarctic Sea Birds — A11

40c, Snow petrel. 80c, Cape petrel. $1, Antarctic prion. $1.20, Antarctic fulmar. $1.50, Antarctic petrel. $1.80, Antarctic tern.

1997, Nov. 12 Litho. *Perf. 14*

L43 A11 40c multi .65 .65
L44 A11 80c multi 1.25 1.25
L45 A11 $1 multi 1.75 1.50
L46 A11 $1.20 multi 2.25 2.00
L47 A11 $1.50 multi 2.50 2.25
L48 A11 $1.80 multi 3.00 15.00
Nos. L43-L48 (6) 11.40 22.65
L48A Block of 6, #L45, L48, L48b-L48e 20.00 20.00
b. A11 40c As #L43, without WWF emblem .90 .90
c. A11 80c As #L44, without WWF emblem 1.75 1.75
d. A11 $1.20 As #L46, without WWF emblem 2.75 2.75
e. A11 $1.50 As #L47, without WWF emblem 3.50 3.50

World Wildlife Fund. Nos. L43-L44, L46-L47 have WWF emblem. Nos. L45 and L48 do not have emblem.

Ice Formations — A12

Designs: 40c, Sculptured sea ice. 80c, Glacial tongue. $1, Stranded tabular iceberg. $1.20, Autumn at Cape Evans. $1.50, Sea ice in summer thaw. $1.80, Sunset on tabular icebergs.

1998, Nov. 11 Litho. *Perf. 14*

L49 A12 40c multicolored .65 .65
L50 A12 80c multicolored 1.25 1.25
L51 A12 $1 multicolored 1.60 1.60
L52 A12 $1.20 multicolored 1.90 1.90
L53 A12 $1.50 multicolored 2.40 2.40
L54 A12 $1.80 multicolored 2.75 2.75
a. Block of 6, #L49-L54 15.00 15.00
Nos. L49-L54 (6) 10.55 10.55

Night Skies — A13

Designs: 40c, Sea smoke, McMurdo Sound. 80c, Alpenglow, Mt. Erebus. $1.10, Sunset, Black Island. $1.20, Pressure ridges, Ross Sea. $1.50, Evening light, Ross Island. $1.80, Mother of pearl clouds, Ross Island.

1999, Nov. 17 Litho. *Perf. 14*

L55 A13 40c multicolored .65 .65
L56 A13 80c multicolored 1.25 1.25
L57 A13 $1.10 multicolored 1.75 1.75
L58 A13 $1.20 multicolored 1.90 1.90
L59 A13 $1.50 multicolored 2.40 2.40
L60 A13 $1.80 multicolored 2.75 2.75
Nos. L55-L60 (6) 10.70 10.70

Antarctic Transportation A14

Designs: 40c, RNZAF C130 Hercules. 80c, Hagglunds BV206 All-terrain carrier. $1.10, Tracked 4x4 motorbike. $1.20, ASV Track truck. $1.50, Squirrel helicopter. $1.80, Elan Skidoo.

2000, Nov. 4 Litho. *Perf. 14*

L61 A14 40c multi .65 .65
L62 A14 80c multi 1.25 1.25
L63 A14 $1.10 multi 1.75 1.75
L64 A14 $1.20 multi 1.90 1.90
L65 A14 $1.50 multi 2.40 2.40
L66 A14 $1.80 multi 2.75 2.75
Nos. L61-L66 (6) 10.70 10.70

Penguins Type of 2001 of New Zealand

Designs: 40c, Emperor. 80c, Adelie. 90c, Emperor, diff. $1.30, Adelie, diff. $1.50, Emperor, diff. $2, Adelie, diff.

2001, Nov. 7 *Perf. 14¼*

L67 A475 40c multi .65 .65
L68 A475 80c multi 1.25 1.25
L69 A475 90c multi 1.40 1.40
L70 A475 $1.30 multi 2.10 2.10
L71 A475 $1.50 multi 2.40 2.40
L72 A475 $2 multi 3.25 3.25
Nos. L67-L72 (6) 11.05 11.05

Discovery Expedition of Capt. Robert Falcon Scott, 1901-04 — A15

Designs: 40c, Three men with sleds. 80c, HMS Discovery. 90c, HMS Discovery trapped in ice. $1.30, Edward Wilson, Ernest Shackleton and sleds. $1.50, Explorers with flags and dog. $2, Base hut.

2002, Nov. 6 Litho. *Perf. 14*

L73 A15 40c multi .65 .65
L74 A15 80c multi 1.25 1.25
L75 A15 90c multi 1.40 1.40
L76 A15 $1.30 multi 2.10 2.10
L77 A15 $1.50 multi 2.40 2.40
L78 A15 $2 multi 3.25 3.25
Nos. L73-L78 (6) 11.05 11.05

Marine Life — A16

Designs: 40c, Odontaster validus. 90c, Beroe cucumis. $1.30, Macroptychaster accrescens. $1.50, Sterechinus neumayeri. $2, Perkinsiana littoralis.

2003, Oct. 1 Litho. *Perf. 13x13¼*

L79 A16 40c multi .65 .65
L80 A16 90c multi 1.40 1.40
L81 A16 $1.30 multi 2.10 2.10
L82 A16 $1.50 multi 2.40 2.40
L83 A16 $2 multi 3.25 3.25
Nos. L79-L83 (5) 9.80 9.80

Emperor Penguins and Map of Antarctica — A17

Various pictures of penguins.

2004, Nov. 3 Litho. *Perf. 13¼x14*

Color of Denomination

L84 A17 45c yellow orange .70 .70
L85 A17 90c dark brown 1.40 1.40
L86 A17 $1.35 lilac 2.10 2.10
L87 A17 $1.50 red brown 2.40 2.40
L88 A17 $2 gray blue 3.25 3.25
Nos. L84-L88 (5) 9.85 9.85

Photographs A18

Designs: 45c, Dry Valleys, by Craig Potton. 90c, Emperor Penguins, by Andris Apse. $1.35, Fur Seal, by Mark Mitchell. $1.50, Captain Scott's Hut, by Colin Monteath. $2. Minke Whale, by Kim Westerskov.

2005, Nov. 2 Litho. *Perf. 13¼*

L89 A18 45c multi .70 .70
L90 A18 90c multi 1.40 1.40
L91 A18 $1.35 multi 2.10 2.10
L92 A18 $1.50 multi 2.40 2.40
L93 A18 $2 multi 3.25 3.25
Nos. L89-L93 (5) 9.85 9.85

A sheet containing Nos. L89-L93 was in a limited edition album.

New Zealand Antarctic Program, 50th Anniv. — A19

Designs: 45c, Biologist. 90c, Hydrologist. $1.35, Geologist. $1.50, Meteorologist. $2, Marine biologist.

2006, Nov. 1 Litho. *Perf. 14*

L94	A19	45c multi	.70	.70
L95	A19	90c multi	1.40	1.40
L96	A19	$1.35 multi	2.10	2.10
L97	A19	$1.50 multi	2.40	2.40
L98	A19	$2 multi	3.25	3.25
		Nos. L94-L98 (5)	9.85	9.85

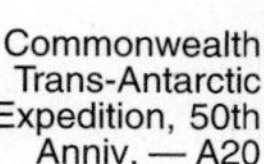

Commonwealth Trans-Antarctic Expedition, 50th Anniv. — A20

Designs: 50c, Man and Beaver airplane. $1, Man and sled. $1.50, Sled dogs. $2, TE20 Ferguson tractor. $2.50, HMNZS Endeavour.

2007, Nov. 7 Litho. *Perf. 14*

L99	A20	50c multi	.80	.80
L100	A20	$1 multi	1.50	1.50
L101	A20	$1.50 multi	2.40	2.40
L102	A20	$2 multi	3.25	3.25
L103	A20	$2.50 multi	4.00	4.00
a.		Souvenir sheet, #L102-L103	7.25	7.25
		Nos. L99-L103 (5)	11.95	11.95

1907-09 British Antarctic Expedition — A21

Designs: 50c, Departure of Nimrod from Lyttleton. $1, Expedition Hut, Cape Royds. $1.50, First vehicle on Antarctica. $2, First men to reach South Magnetic Pole. $2.50, First ascent of Mt. Erebus.

2008, Nov. 5 Litho. *Perf. 13½x13¼*

L104	A21	50c multi	.80	.80
L105	A21	$1 multi	1.50	1.50
L106	A21	$1.50 multi	2.40	2.40
L107	A21	$2 multi	3.25	3.25
L108	A21	$2.50 multi	4.00	4.00
		Nos. L104-L108 (5)	11.95	11.95

Signing of Antarctic Treaty, 50th Anniv. — A22

Mountains and: 50c, Map of Antarctica. $1, Penguins. $1.80, Scientist and equipment. $2.30, Flags. $2.80, Seal.

Perf. 13¼x13½

2009, Nov. 25 Litho.

L109	A22	50c multi	.75	.75
L110	A22	$1 multi	1.50	1.50
L111	A22	$1.80 multi	2.60	2.60
L112	A22	$2.30 multi	3.25	3.25
L113	A22	$2.80 multi	4.00	4.00
		Nos. L109-L113 (5)	12.10	12.10

Whales A23

Designs: 60c, Sperm whale. $1.20, Minke whale. $1.90, Sei whale. $2.40, Killer whale. $2.90, Humpback whale.

2010, Nov. 17 Litho. *Perf. 15x14¾*

L114	A23	60c multi	.95	.95
L115	A23	$1.20 multi	1.90	1.90
L116	A23	$1.90 multi	3.00	3.00
L117	A23	$2.40 multi	3.75	3.75
L118	A23	$2.90 multi	4.50	4.50
a.		Souvenir sheet of 5, #L114-L118	14.50	14.50
		Nos. L114-L118 (5)	14.10	14.10

Race to the South Pole — A24

Map of Antarctica and: 60c, Roald Amundsen and ship, Fram. $1.20, Men of Amundsen's expedition. $1.90, Robert Falcon Scott and ship Terra Nova. $2.40, Men of Scott expedition, cross on cairn. $2.90, Flags of United Kingdom and Norway.

2011, Nov. 2 *Perf. 13½x13¼*

L119	A24	60c multi	.95	.95
L120	A24	$1.20 multi	1.90	1.90
L121	A24	$1.90 multi	3.00	3.00
L122	A24	$2.40 multi	4.00	4.00
a.		Souvenir sheet of 2, #L121-L122	10.00	10.00
L123	A24	$2.90 multi	4.75	4.75
a.		Souvenir sheet of 5, #L119-L123	15.00	15.00
		Nos. L119-L123 (5)	14.60	14.60

Issued: No. L122a, 1/14/12. Christchurch Philatelic Society Centennial Stamp and Postcard Exhibition (#L122a).

Antarctic Landscapes A25

Designs: 70c, Mount Erebus. $1.40, Beardmore Glacier. $1.90, Lake Vanda. $2.40, Cape Adare. $2.90, Ross Ice Shelf.

2012, Nov. 21

L124	A25	70c multi	1.25	1.25
L125	A25	$1.40 multi	2.40	2.40
L126	A25	$1.90 multi	3.25	3.25
L127	A25	$2.40 multi	4.00	4.00
L128	A25	$2.90 multi	4.75	4.75
a.		Souvenir sheet of 5, #L124-L128	16.00	16.00
		Nos. L124-L128 (5)	15.65	15.65

Antarctic Food Web — A26

Designs: 70c, Antarctic krill. $1.40, Lesser snow petrel. $1.90, Adélie penguin. $2.40, Crabeater seal. $2.90, Blue whale.

2013, Nov. 20 Litho. *Perf. 14*

L129	A26	70c multi	1.25	1.25
L130	A26	$1.40 multi	2.40	2.40
L131	A26	$1.90 multi	3.25	3.25
L132	A26	$2.40 multi	4.00	4.00
L133	A26	$2.90 multi	4.75	4.75
a.		Souvenir sheet of 5, #L129-L133	16.00	16.00
		Nos. L129-L133 (5)	15.65	15.65

Penguins — A27

Designs: 80c, Emperor penguins. $1.40, Adélie penguin. $2, Macaroni penguins. $2.50, Gentoo penguin and eggs. $3, Chinstrap penguin.

2014, Nov. 19 Litho. *Perf. 14½*

L134	A27	80c multi	1.25	1.25
L135	A27	$1.40 multi	2.25	2.25
L136	A27	$2 multi	3.25	3.25
L137	A27	$2.50 multi	4.00	4.00
L138	A27	$3 multi	4.75	4.75
a.		Souvenir sheet of 1 + label	4.75	4.75
b.		Souvenir sheet of 5, #L134-L138	15.50	15.50
		Nos. L134-L138 (5)	15.50	15.50

Values for Nos. L134-L138 are for stamps with surrounding selvage. See Greenland No. 679a.

Imperial Trans-Antarctic Expedition, Cent. — A28

Designs: No. L139, S.Y. Endurance. No. L140, Ocean Camp. $1.40, Expedition members in boat going from Elephant Island to South Georgia. $2, S.Y. Aurora. $2.50, Expedition members laying depots. $3, Rescue of the Ross Sea Party.

2015, Nov. 4 Litho. *Perf. 14x14½*

L139	A28	80c multi	1.10	1.10
L140	A28	80c multi	1.10	1.10
L141	A28	$1.40 multi	1.90	1.90
a.		Souvenir sheet of 3, #L139-L141	4.25	4.25
L142	A28	$2 multi	2.75	2.75
L143	A28	$2.50 multi	3.50	3.50
L144	A28	$3 multi	4.00	4.00
a.		Souvenir sheet of 3, #L142-L144	10.50	10.50
		Nos. L139-L144 (6)	14.35	14.35

Creatures of the Antarctic Sea Floor — A29

Designs: $1, Stalked crinoid. $1.80, Sea star. $2.20, Sponge. $2.70, Hydroid. $3.30, Sea spider.

2016, Nov. 16 Litho. *Perf. 14½x14*

L145	A29	$1 multi	1.40	1.40
L146	A29	$1.80 multi	2.60	2.60
L147	A29	$2.20 multi	3.25	3.25
L148	A29	$2.70 multi	4.00	4.00
L149	A29	$3.30 multi	4.75	4.75
a.		Souvenir sheet of 5, #L145-L149	16.00	16.00
		Nos. L145-L149 (5)	16.00	16.00

Historic Huts and Items Found In Them — A30

Designs: $1, Captain Robert Falcon Scott's Discovery Hut. $2, Box, bottle, kettle and crate in Discovery Hut. $2.20, Sir Ernest Shackleton's Nimrod Hut. $2.30, Stove, kettles and canister in Nimrod Hut. $2.70, Scott's Terra Nova Hut. $3.30, Letter, bottles and pencils in Terra Nova Hut.

2017, Sept. 20 Litho. *Perf. 14½*

L150	A30	$1 multi	1.40	1.40
L151	A30	$2 multi	3.00	3.00
L152	A30	$2.20 multi	3.25	3.25
L153	A30	$2.30 multi	3.50	3.50
L154	A30	$2.70 multi	4.00	4.00
L155	A30	$3.30 multi	4.75	4.75
a.		Souvenir sheet of 6, #L150-L155	20.00	20.00
		Nos. L150-L155 (6)	19.90	19.90

Aircraft A31

Designs: No. L156, Royal New Zealand Air Force Auster T7C. No. L157, Royal New Zealand Air Force DHC-2 Beaver. No. L158, Royal New Zealand Air Force C130 Hercules. $2.40, Royal New Zealand Air Force Boeing 757. $3, Southern Lakes Helicopters AS350 B3 Squirrel. $3.60, Kenn Borek Air DHC6 Twin Otter.

2018, Nov. 7 Litho. *Perf. 14¼x14*

L156	A31	$1.20 multi	1.75	1.75
L157	A31	$1.20 multi	1.75	1.75
L158	A31	$1.20 multi	1.75	1.75
L159	A31	$2.40 multi	3.50	3.50
L160	A31	$3 multi	4.25	4.25
L161	A31	$3.60 multi	5.00	5.00
a.		Souvenir sheet of 6, #L156-L161	18.00	18.00
		Nos. L156-L161 (6)	18.00	18.00

Ship and Carsten Borchgrevink (1864-1934), Explorer A32

Fruitcake and Cape Adare Cabin — A33

Toothbrush and Men in Cape Adare Cabin — A34

Primus Stove and Penguins Near Cape Adare Cabin — A35

Artist and Watercolor of Dead Bird — A36

2019, Sept. 18 Litho. *Perf. 14½x14*

L162	A32	$1.30 multi	1.60	1.60
L163	A33	$1.30 multi	1.60	1.60
L164	A34	$2.60 multi	3.25	3.25
L165	A35	$3.30 multi	4.25	4.25
L166	A36	$4 multi	5.00	5.00
a.		Souvenir sheet of 5, #L162-L166	16.00	16.00
		Nos. L162-L166 (5)	15.70	15.70

The fern emblem and "Ross Dependency" inscription on Nos, L162-L166 and L166a were printed in a clear ink that is difficult to see.

Seasonal Views of Scott Base — A37

Designs: $1.40, Aurora Australis over Scott Base in winter. $2.70, Sunrise at Scott Base in spring. $3.50, Sunset at Scott Base in summer. $4, Twilight at Scott Base in autumn.

2020, Oct. 7 Litho. *Perf. 13½x13¼*

L167	A37	$1.40 multi	1.90	1.90
L168	A37	$2.70 multi	3.75	3.75
L169	A37	$3.50 multi	4.75	4.75
L170	A37	$4 multi	5.25	5.25
a.		Souvenir sheet of 4, #L167-L170	16.00	16.00
		Nos. L167-L170 (4)	15.65	15.65

Portions of the designs of Nos. L167-L170 and L170a were covered with thermochromic ink, which changes color when warmed.

Megafauna — A38

Designs: $1.50, Weddell seal. $2.80, Minke whale. $3.60, Skua. $4.10, Emperor penguins.

2021, Sept. 1 Litho. *Perf. 13¼x13½*

L171	A38	$1.50 multi	2.10	2.10
L172	A38	$2.80 multi	4.00	4.00
L173	A38	$3.60 multi	5.25	5.25
L174	A38	$4.10 multi	5.75	5.75
a.		Souvenir sheet of 4, #L171-L174	17.50	17.50
		Nos. L171-L174 (4)	17.10	17.10

Ice Science — A39

Designs: $1.70, Scientist studying microbial communities in sea ice. $3, Chart of supercool measurements. $3.80, Helicopter with ice and snow thickness measuring device. $4.30, Platelet ice research.

2022, Nov. 2 Litho. *Perf. 14*

L175	A39	$1.70	multi	2.10	2.10
L176	A39	$3	multi	3.75	3.75
L177	A39	$3.80	multi	4.75	4.75
L178	A39	$4.30	multi	5.50	5.50
a.	Souvenir sheet of 4, #L175-L178			16.50	16.50
	Nos. L175-L178 (4)			16.10	16.10

Scott Base — A40

Various photographs of Scott Base.

2023, Sept. 6 Litho. *Perf. 14½x14*

L179	A40	$2	multi	2.40	2.40
L180	A40	$3.30	multi	4.00	4.00
L181	A40	$4	multi	4.75	4.75
L182	A40	$4.60	multi	5.50	5.50
a.	Souvenir sheet of 4, #L179-L182			17.00	17.00
	Nos. L179-L182 (4)			16.65	16.65

NICARAGUA

ˌni-kə-ˈrä-gwə

LOCATION — Central America, between Honduras and Costa Rica
GOVT. — Republic
AREA — 50,439 sq. mi.
POP. — 6,630,000 (2020 est.)
CAPITAL — Managua

100 Centavos = 1 Peso
100 Centavos = 1 Córdoba (1913)

Catalogue values for unused stamps in this country are for Never Hinged items, beginning with Scott 689 in the regular postage section, Scott C261 in the airpost section, Scott CO37 in the airpost official section, and Scott RA60 in the postal tax section.

ISSUES OF THE REPUBLIC

Watermarks

Wmk. 117 — Liberty Cap

Wmk. 209 — Multiple Ovals

Liberty Cap on Mountain Peak; From Seal of Country — A1

Unwmk.

1862, Dec. 2 Engr. *Perf. 12*

Yellowish Paper

1	A1	2c	dark blue	75.00	20.00
2	A1	5c	black	150.00	60.00

Designs of Nos. 1-2 measure 22½x18½mm. Perforations are invariably rough.

Values are for stamps without gum. Examples with gum sell for more. Nos. 1-2 were canceled only by pen.

There is one reported cover of No. 1, two of No. 2.

See No. C509.

A2

A3

1869-71 White Paper

3	A1	1c	bister ('71)	3.00	1.25
4	A1	2c	blue	3.00	1.25
5	A1	5c	black	100.00	1.00
6	A2	10c	vermilion	4.00	1.75
7	A3	25c	green	7.50	4.00
	Nos. 3-7 (5)			117.50	9.25

Designs of Nos. 3-7 measure 22½x19mm. Perforations are clean cut.

There are two reported covers of No. 5, five of No. 7.

1878-80 *Rouletted 8½*

8	A1	1c	brown	2.00	1.25
9	A1	2c	blue	2.00	1.25
10	A1	5c	black	50.00	1.00
11	A2	10c	ver ('80)	2.50	1.50
12	A3	25c	green ('79)	2.50	4.00
	Nos. 8-12 (5)			59.00	9.00

Most values exist on thicker soft paper.

Stamps with letter/numeral cancellations other than "3 G," "6 M," "9 C" sell for more.

Nos. 3-12 were reprinted in 1892. The corresponding values of the two series are printed in the same shades which is not usually true of the originals. They are, however, similar to some of the original shades and the only certain test is comparison. Originals have thin white gum; reprints have rather thick yellowish gum. Value 50c each. Unused examples of Nos. 3-12 without gum should be presumed to be reprints. Nos. 5 and 10 unused are extremely scarce and should be purchased with original gum and should be expertized.

Seal of Nicaragua — A4

1882, Aug.-1888 Engr. *Perf. 12*

13	A4	1c	green	.25	.25
14	A4	2c	carmine	.25	.25
15	A4	5c	blue	.30	.25
16	A4	10c	dull violet	.40	*.75*
17	A4	15c	yellow	.80	*25.00*
18	A4	20c	slate gray	1.60	*5.00*
19	A4	50c	dull violet ('88)	2.25	*25.00*
	Nos. 13-19 (7)			5.85	*56.50*

Used Values

of Nos. 13-120 are for stamps with genuine cancellations applied while the stamps were valid. Various counterfeit cancellations exist.

Locomotive and Telegraph Key — A5

1890 Engr.

20	A5	1c	yellow brown	.40	—
21	A5	2c	vermilion	.40	—
22	A5	5c	deep blue	.40	—
23	A5	10c	lilac gray	.40	—
24	A5	20c	red	.40	—
25	A5	50c	purple	.40	—
26	A5	1p	brown	.40	—
27	A5	2p	dark green	.40	—
28	A5	5p	lake	.40	—
29	A5	10p	orange	.40	—
	Nos. 20-29 (10)			4.00	

The issues of 1890-1899 were printed by the Hamilton Bank Note Co., New York, to the order of N. F. Seebeck who held a contract for stamps with the government of Nicaragua. Reprints were made, for sale to collectors, of the 1896, 1897 and 1898, postage, postage due and official stamps. See notes following those issues.

For overprints see Nos. O1-O10.

Perforation Varieties

Imperfs and part perfs of all the Seebeck issues, Nos. 20-120, exist for all except originals of the 1898 issue, Nos. 99-109M.

Goddess of Plenty — A6

1891 Engr.

30	A6	1c	yellow brn	.40	—
31	A6	2c	red	.40	—
32	A6	5c	dk blue	.40	—
33	A6	10c	slate	.40	—
34	A6	20c	plum	.40	—
35	A6	50c	purple	.40	—
36	A6	1p	black brn	.40	—
37	A6	2p	green	.40	—
38	A6	5p	brown red	.40	—
39	A6	10p	orange	.40	—
	Nos. 30-39 (10)			4.00	

For overprints see Nos. O11-O20.

Columbus Sighting Land — A7

1892 Engr.

40	A7	1c	yellow brn	.40	—
41	A7	2c	vermilion	.40	—
42	A7	5c	dk blue	.40	—
43	A7	10c	slate	.40	—
44	A7	20c	plum	.40	—
45	A7	50c	purple	.40	—
46	A7	1p	brown	.40	—
47	A7	2p	blue grn	.40	—
48	A7	5p	rose lake	.40	—
49	A7	10p	orange	.40	—
	Nos. 40-49 (10)			4.00	

Commemorative of the 400th anniversary of the discovery of America by Columbus.

Stamps of the 1892 design were printed in other colors than those listed and overprinted "Telegrafos". The 1c blue, 10c orange, 20c slate, 50c plum and 2p vermilion are telegraph stamps which did not receive the overprint.

For overprints see Nos. O21-O30.

Arms — A8

1893 Engr.

51	A8	1c	yellow brn	.40	—
52	A8	2c	vermilion	.40	—
53	A8	5c	dk blue	.40	—
54	A8	10c	slate	.40	—
55	A8	20c	dull red	.40	—
56	A8	50c	violet	.40	—
57	A8	1p	dk brown	.40	—
58	A8	2p	blue green	.40	—
59	A8	5p	rose lake	.40	—
60	A8	10p	orange	.40	—
	Nos. 51-60 (10)			4.00	

The 1c blue and 2c dark brown are telegraph stamps which did not receive the "Telegrafos" overprint.

For overprints see Nos. O31-O41.

"Victory" — A9

1894 Engr.

61	A9	1c	yellow brn	.40	*.30*
62	A9	2c	vermilion	.40	*.30*
63	A9	5c	dp blue	.40	*.30*
64	A9	10c	slate	.40	*.30*
65	A9	20c	lake	.40	*2.00*
66	A9	50c	purple	.40	*5.00*
67	A9	1p	brown	.40	*9.50*
68	A9	2p	green	.40	*17.50*
69	A9	5p	brown red	.40	*45.00*
70	A9	10p	orange	.40	*45.00*
	Nos. 61-70 (10)			4.00	125.20

There were three printings of this issue. Only the first is known postally used. Unused values are for the third printing.

Used values are for stamps with "DIRECCION" cancels in black that were removed from post office new year cards.

Specialists believe the 25c yellow green, type A9, is a telegraph denomination never issued for postal purposes. Stamps in other colors are telegraph stamps without the usual "Telegrafos" overprint.

For overprints see Nos. O42-O51.

Coat of Arms — A10

1895 Engr.

71	A10	1c	yellow brn	.40	.30
72	A10	2c	vermilion	.40	.30
73	A10	5c	deep blue	.40	.25
74	A10	10c	slate	.40	.25
75	A10	20c	claret	.40	*.75*
76	A10	50c	light violet	50.00	*5.00*
77	A10	1p	dark brown	.40	*5.00*
78	A10	2p	deep green	.40	*8.00*
79	A10	5p	brown red	.40	*11.00*
80	A10	10p	orange	.40	
	Nos. 71-80 (10)			53.60	

Frames of Nos. 71-80 differ for each denomination.

A 50c violet blue exists. Its status is questioned. Value 40c.

There was little proper use of No. 80. Canceled examples are almost always c-t-o or have faked cancels.

For overprints see Nos. O52-O71.

Map of Nicaragua — A11

1896 Engr.

81	A11	1c	violet	.30	*1.00*
82	A11	2c	blue grn	.30	*.50*
83	A11	5c	brt rose	.30	*.30*
84	A11	10c	blue	.50	*.50*
85	A11	20c	bister brn	3.00	*4.00*
86	A11	50c	blue gray	.60	*8.00*
87	A11	1p	black	.75	*11.00*
88	A11	2p	claret	.75	*15.00*
89	A11	5p	deep blue	.75	*15.00*
	Nos. 81-89 (9)			7.25	*55.30*

There were two printings of this issue. Only the first is known postally used. Unused values are for the second printing.

See italic note after No. 109M.

For overprints see Nos. O82-O117.

Wmk. 117

89A	A11	1c	violet	3.75	.90
89B	A11	2c	bl grn	3.75	1.25
89C	A11	5c	brt rose	15.00	.40
89D	A11	10c	blue	25.00	.90
89E	A11	20c	bis brn	22.50	4.25
89F	A11	50c	bl gray	42.50	*9.00*
89G	A11	1p	black	37.50	*12.50*
89H	A11	2p	claret	50.00	*18.00*
89I	A11	5p	dp bl	100.00	*40.00*

Same, dated 1897

1897 Engr. Unwmk.

90	A11	1c	violet	.50	.50
91	A11	2c	bl grn	.50	.60
92	A11	5c	brt rose	.50	.30
93	A11	10c	blue	6.25	.75
94	A11	20c	bis brn	2.50	*3.75*
95	A11	50c	bl gray	9.00	*9.50*
96	A11	1p	black	9.00	*15.00*
97	A11	2p	claret	20.00	*19.00*
98	A11	5p	dp bl	20.00	*42.50*
	Nos. 90-98 (9)			68.25	*91.90*

See italic note after No. 109M.

Wmk. 117

98A	A11	1c	violet	14.00	.50
98B	A11	2c	bl grn	14.00	.50
98C	A11	5c	brt rose	20.00	.40
98D	A11	10c	blue	22.50	.90
98E	A11	20c	bis brn	22.50	4.25
98F	A11	50c	bl gray	22.50	*8.00*
98G	A11	1p	black	25.00	*16.00*
98H	A11	2p	claret	25.00	*25.00*
98I	A11	5p	dp bl	125.00	*50.00*
	Nos. 98A-98I (9)			290.50	*105.55*

Coat of Arms of "Republic of Central America" — A12

1898 Engr. Wmk. 117

99	A12	1c	brown	.40	.40
100	A12	2c	slate	.40	.40
101	A12	4c	red brown	.40	.50
102	A12	5c	olive green	40.00	22.50
103	A12	10c	violet	15.00	.60
104	A12	15c	ultra	.40	1.50
105	A12	20c	blue	10.00	2.00
106	A12	50c	yellow	10.00	*9.50*
107	A12	1p	violet blue	.40	*16.00*

108	A12	2p brown	19.00	*22.50*
109	A12	5p orange	25.00	*32.50*
		Nos. 99-109 (11)	121.00	*108.40*

Unwmk.

109A	A12	1c brown	1.25	.30
109B	A12	2c slate	1.25	
109D	A12	4c red brown	2.25	.60
109E	A12	5c olive green	25.00	.25
109G	A12	10c violet	25.00	.60
109H	A12	15c ultra	25.00	
109I	A12	20c blue	25.00	
109J	A12	50c yellow	25.00	
109K	A12	1p deep ultra	25.00	
109L	A12	2p olive brown	25.00	
109M	A12	5p orange	25.00	
		Nos. 109A-109M (11)	204.75	

The paper of Nos. 109A to 109M is slightly thicker and more opaque than that of Nos. 81 to 89 and 90 to 98. The 5c and 10c also exist on very thin, semi-transparent paper.

Many reprints of Nos. 81-98, 98F-98H, 99-109M are on thick, porous paper, with and without watermark. The watermark is sideways. Paper of the originals is thinner for Nos. 81-109 but thicker for Nos. 109A-109M. Value 40c each.

In addition, reprints of Nos. 81-89 and 90-98 exist on thin paper, but with shades differing slightly from those of originals.

For overprints see Nos. O118-O128.

"Justice" — A13

1899 **Litho.**

110	A13	1c gray grn	.40	*.35*
111	A13	2c brown	.40	*.25*
112	A13	4c dp rose	.40	*.40*
113	A13	5c dp bl	.40	*.25*
114	A13	10c buff	.40	*.30*
115	A13	15c chocolate	.40	*.65*
116	A13	20c dk grn	.40	*.75*
117	A13	50c brt rose	.40	*3.00*
118	A13	1p red	.40	*8.50*
119	A13	2p violet	.40	*20.00*
120	A13	5p lt bl	.40	*25.00*
		Nos. 110-120 (11)	4.40	*59.45*

Nos. 110-120 exist imperf. and in horizontal pairs imperf. between.

Nos. 110-111, 113 exist perf 6x12 due to defective perforating equipment.

For overprints see Nos. O129-O139.

Mt. Momotombo — A14

Imprint: "American Bank Note Co. NY"

1900, Jan. 1 **Engr.**

121	A14	1c plum	.65	.25
122	A14	2c vermilion	.65	.25
123	A14	3c green	.90	.25
124	A14	4c ol grn	1.25	.25
125	A14	5c dk bl	4.00	.25
126	A14	6c car rose	14.00	5.00
127	A14	10c violet	7.00	.25
128	A14	15c ultra	8.00	.65
129	A14	20c brown	8.00	.65
130	A14	50c lake	7.00	1.10
131	A14	1p yellow	12.00	4.00
132	A14	2p salmon	10.00	2.25
133	A14	5p black	10.00	3.00
		Nos. 121-133 (13)	83.45	18.15

Used values for #123, 126, 130-133 are for canceled to order examples.

See Nos. 159-161. For overprints and surcharges see Nos. 134-136, 144-151, 162-163, 175-178, O150-O154, 1L1-1L13, 1L16-1L19, 1L20, 2L1-2L10, 2L16-2L24, 2L36-2L39.

Mt. Momotombo — A14a

1902 **White Wove Paper** ***Imperf.***

Size: 55x52mm

133A	A14a	5c blue
133B	A14a	10c red violet
133C	A14a	20c brown
133D	A14a	30c black green
133E	A14a	50c red

51x51mm

133F	A14a	2c dk red, *buff*
133G	A14a	4c red brown, *buff*

Nos. 133A-133G are documented on covers postmarked from 1902-04. Specimen pairs and blocks are from sheets of 35 (Nos. 133A-133E) or 28 (Nos. 133F-133G) sold in the 1990 American Bank Note Company archives sale. Nos. 133A-133G are not cutouts from similar postal envelopes issued in 1900. They can be distinguished from postal stationery cutouts by their size, and unlike postal staationery cutouts, the stamps are square in which the image is centered. The mesh is perpendicular with the sides.

Nos. 131-133 Surcharged in Black or Red

1901, Mar. 5

134	A14	2c on 1p yel org	5.00	4.50
	a.	Bar below date	16.00	*9.00*
	b.	Inverted surcharge		*35.00*
	c.	Double surcharge		*50.00*
135	A14	10c on 5p blk (R)	12.00	4.50
	a.	Bar below date	17.50	8.00
136	A14	20c on 2p salmon	7.50	7.50
	a.	Bar below date	14.00	10.00
		Nos. 134-136 (3)	24.50	16.50

A 2c surcharge on No. 121, the 1c plum, was not put on sale, though some are known used from a few sheets distributed by the post office to "government friends." Value, *$250.*

The 2c on 1p yellow without ornaments is a reprint.

Postage Due Stamps of 1900 Overprinted in Black or Gold

1901, Mar.

137	D3	1c plum	4.50	3.50
138	D3	2c vermilion	4.50	3.50
139	D3	5c dk bl	6.00	3.50
140	D3	10c pur (G)	8.50	8.50
	a.	Double overprint	14.00	14.00
141	D3	20c org brn	10.00	10.00
142	D3	30c dk grn	10.00	6.50
143	D3	50c lake	8.50	4.00
	a.	"1091" for "1901"	35.00	35.00
	b.	"Correo"	37.50	
		Nos. 137-143 (7)	52.00	39.50

In 1904 an imitation of this overprint was made to fill a dealer's order. The date is at top and "Correos" at bottom. The overprint is printed in black, sideways on the 1c and 2c and upright on the 5c and 10c. Some examples of the 2c were further surcharged "1 Centavo." None of these stamps was ever regularly used.

Nos. 126, 131-133 Surcharged

1901, Oct. 20 **Black Surcharge**

144	A14	3c on 6c rose	12.00	5.00
	a.	Bar below value	13.00	5.50
	b.	Inverted surcharge	14.00	8.00
	c.	Double surcharge	14.00	8.00
	d.	Double surch., one inverted	25.00	25.00
145	A14	4c on 6c rose	8.00	6.00
	a.	Bar below value	9.00	6.50
	b.	"1 cent" instead of "4 cent"	11.00	8.00
	c.	Double surcharge	20.00	20.00
146	A14	5c on 1p yellow	6.00	4.00
	a.	Three bars below value	7.00	5.00
	b.	Ornaments at each side of "1901"	30.00	4.50
	c.	Double surcharge, one in red	17.50	15.00
147	A14	10c on 2p salmon	6.50	4.00
	a.	Inverted surcharge	30.00	27.50
	b.	Double surcharge		

Blue Surcharge

148	A14	3c on 6c rose	9.00	4.50
	a.	Bar below value	10.00	5.50
	b.	Double surcharge	11.00	8.00
149	A14	4c on 6c rose	12.00	5.00
	a.	Bar below value	13.00	7.50
	b.	"1 cent" instead of "4 cent"	20.00	10.00
	c.	Inverted surcharge	25.00	20.00

Red Surcharge

150	A14	5c on 1p yel org	8.00	6.50
	a.	Three bars below value	10.00	7.00
	b.	Ornaments at each side of "1901"	10.00	7.00
	c.	Inverted surcharge	20.00	12.00
	d.	Double surcharge, inverted	22.50	17.50
151	A14	20c on 5p black	5.50	3.50
	a.	Inverted surcharge	20.00	16.00
	b.	Double surcharge	22.50	22.50
	c.	Triple surcharge		
		Nos. 144-151 (8)	67.00	38.50

In 1904 a series was surcharged as above, but with "Centavos" spelled out. About the same time No. 122 was surcharged "1 cent." and "1901," "1902" or "1904." All of these surcharges were made to fill a dealer's order and none of the stamps was regularly issued or used.

Postage Due Stamps of 1900 Overprinted in Black

1901, Oct.

152	D3	1c red violet	1.00	.40
	a.	Ornaments at each side of the stamp	10.00	.65
	b.	Ornaments at each side of "1901"	1.10	.65
	c.	"Correos" in italics	1.50	1.50
	d.	Double overprint	14.00	14.00
153	D3	2c vermilion	.75	.40
	a.	Double overprint	8.50	5.50
154	D3	5c dark blue	1.00	.60
	a.	Double overprint, one inverted		
	b.	Double overprint	7.00	7.00
155	D3	10c purple	1.00	.60
	b.	Double overprint	10.00	10.00
	c.	Double overprint, one inverted	12.00	12.00
156	D3	20c org brn	1.50	1.25
	b.	Double overprint	7.00	7.00
157	D3	30c dk grn	1.00	1.10
	a.	Double overprint	9.00	9.00
	b.	Inverted overprint	19.00	19.00
158	D3	50c lake	1.00	1.10
	a.	Triple overprint	25.00	25.00
	b.	Double overprint	16.00	16.00
		Nos. 152-158 (7)	7.25	5.45

One stamp in each group of 25 has the 2nd "o" of "Correos" italic. Value twice normal.

Momotombo Type of 1900

Without Imprint

1902 **Litho.** ***Perf. 14***

159	A14	5c blue	.50	.40
	a.	Imperf., pair	3.75	
160	A14	5c carmine	.50	.40
	a.	Imperf., pair	3.75	
161	A14	10c violet	1.50	.40
	a.	Imperf., pair	3.75	
		Nos. 159-161 (3)	2.50	1.20

No. 161 was privately surcharged 6c, 1p and 5p in black in 1903. Not fully authorized but known postally used. Value of c-t-o peso denominations, $5 each.

Nos. 121 and 122 Surcharged in Black

1902, Oct. ***Perf. 12***

162	A14	15c on 2c ver	4.00	.75
	a.	Double surcharge	32.50	
	b.	Blue surcharge	90.00	
163	A14	30c on 1c plum	3.00	2.25
	a.	Double surcharge	12.00	
	b.	Inverted surcharge	27.50	

Counterfeits of No. 163 exist in slightly smaller type.

President José Santos Zelaya — A15

1903, Jan. **Engr.**

167	A15	1c emer & blk	.45	.50
168	A15	2c rose & blk	1.00	.50
169	A15	5c ultra & blk	.50	.50
170	A15	10c yel & blk	.50	*.85*
171	A15	15c lake & blk	1.75	*2.00*
172	A15	20c vio & blk	1.75	*2.00*
173	A15	50c ol & blk	1.75	*5.00*
174	A15	1p red brn & blk	2.00	*6.00*
		Nos. 167-174 (8)	9.70	*17.35*

10th anniv. of 1st election of Pres. Zelaya.

The so-called color errors-1c orange yellow and black, 2c ultramarine and black, 5c lake and black and 10c emerald and black-were also delivered to postal authorities. They were intended for official use though not issued as such. Value, $4 each.

No. 161 Surcharged in Blue

Nos. 175-176

No. 177

1904-05

175	A14	5c on 10c vio ('05)	1.75	.40
	a.	Inverted surcharge	5.50	3.00
	b.	Without ornaments	2.00	.70
	c.	Character for "cents" inverted	1.75	.40
	d.	As "b," inverted		
	e.	As "c," inverted	2.75	2.75
	f.	Double surcharge	25.00	8.00
	g.	"5" omitted	2.75	2.75
176	A14	15c on 10c vio ('05)	.90	.40
	a.	Inverted surcharge	4.00	1.40
	b.	Without ornaments	2.00	1.40
	c.	Character for "cents" inverted	2.50	1.10
	d.	As "b," inverted		
	e.	As "c," inverted	5.00	1.75
	f.	Imperf.	7.00	
	h.	As "a," imperf.	10.00	9.00
	i.	Double surcharge	16.00	14.00
177	A14	15c on 10c vio	4.50	2.75
	a.	Inverted surcharge	7.00	6.00
	b.	"Centcvos"	7.00	4.50
	c.	"5" of "15" omitted	12.50	
	d.	As "b," inverted	8.50	8.50
	e.	Double surcharge	11.00	11.00
	f.	Double surcharge, inverted	13.00	13.00
	g.	Imperf., pair	9.00	9.00
		Nos. 175-177 (3)	7.15	3.55

There are two settings of the surcharge on No. 175. In the 1st the character for "cents" and the figure "5" are 2mm apart and in the 2nd 4mm.

The 2c vermilion, No. 122, with surcharge "1 cent. / 1904" was not issued.

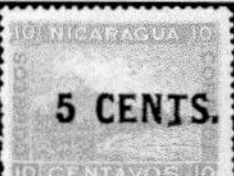

No. 161 Surcharged in Black

1905, June

178	A14	5c on 10c violet	.60	.40
	a.	Inverted surcharge	13.50	10.00
	b.	Double surcharge	4.50	4.50
	c.	Surcharge in blue	*75.00*	

Coat of Arms — A18

Imprint: "American Bank Note Co. NY"

1905, July 25 **Engr.** ***Perf. 12***

179	A18	1c green	.40	.40
180	A18	2c car rose	.40	.40
181	A18	3c violet	.60	.60
182	A18	4c org red	.60	.60
183	A18	5c blue	.60	.60
184	A18	6c slate	.80	.80
185	A18	10c yel brn	1.10	1.10
186	A18	15c brn olive	1.00	1.00
187	A18	20c lake	.80	.80
188	A18	50c orange	4.00	4.00
189	A18	1p black	2.00	2.00
190	A18	2p dk grn	2.00	2.00
191	A18	5p violet	2.50	2.50
		Nos. 179-191 (13)	16.80	16.80

See Nos. 202-208, 237-248. For overprints and surcharges see Nos. 193-201, 212-216, 235-236, 249-265, O187-O198, O210-O222, 1L21-1L62, 1L73-1L95, 1LO1-1LO3, 2L26-2L35, 2L42-2L46, 2L48-2L72, 2LO1-2LO4.

Nos. 179-184 and 191 Surcharged in Black or Red Reading Up or Down

1906-08

193 A18 10c on 2c car rose (up) 7.00 4.50
a. Surcharge reading down 13.00 13.00
194 A18 10c on 3c vio (up) .80 .40
a. "¢" normal 2.75 1.35
b. Double surcharge 4.50 4.50
c. Double surch., up and down 7.00 5.00
d. Pair, one without surcharge 9.50
e. Surcharge reading down .40 .40
195 A18 10c on 4c org red (up) ('08) *35.00 20.00*
a. Surcharge reading down *32.50 26.00*
196 A18 15c on 1c grn (up) .60 .40
a. Double surcharge 7.50 7.50
b. Dbl. surch., one reading down 11.00 11.00
c. Surcharge reading down .70 .40
197 A18 20c on 2c car rose (down) ('07) .50 .40
a. Double surcharge 13.00 13.00
b. Surcharge reading up 37.50 32.50
c. "V" omitted 10.00 10.00
198 A18 20c on 5c bl (down) .90 .50
a. Surcharge reading up 35.00
199 A18 50c on 6c sl (R) (down) .80 .50
a. Double surcharge
b. Surcharge reading up 30.00 30.00
c. Yellow brown surcharge .80 .40
200 A18 1p on 5p vio (down) ('07) 42.50 25.00
Nos. 193-200 (8) *88.10 51.70*

There are several settings of these surcharges and many varieties in the shapes of the figures, the spacing, etc.

Surcharged in Red Vertically Reading Up

1908, May

201 A18 35c on 6c slate 3.50 2.25
a. Double surcharge (R) 25.00
b. Double surcharge (R + Bk) 65.00
c. Carmine surcharge 3.50 2.25

Arms Type of 1905

Imprint: "Waterlow & Sons, Ltd."

1907, Feb. ***Perf. 14 to 15***

202 A18 1c green .70 .40
203 A18 2c rose .80 .25
204 A18 4c brn org 2.00 .30
205 A18 10c yel brn 3.00 .25
206 A18 15c brn olive 4.50 .90
207 A18 20c lake 8.00 1.25
208 A18 50c orange 20.00 4.25
Nos. 202-208 (7) 39.00 7.60

Nos. 202-204, 207-208 Surcharged in Black or Blue (Bl) Reading Down

1907-08

212 A18 10c on 2c rose 1.50 .50
a. Double surcharge 10.00
b. "Vale" only 22.50
c. Surcharge reading up 14.00 6.50
213 A18 10c on 4c brn org (up) ('08) 2.25 .85
a. Double surcharge 10.00
b. Surcharge reading down 10.00
214 A18 10c on 20c lake ('08) 3.25 1.40
b. Surcharge reading up 80.00
215 A18 10c on 50c org (Bl) ('08) 2.00 .60
216 A18 15c on 1c grn ('08) 32.50 4.00
Nos. 212-216 (5) 41.50 7.35

Several settings of this surcharge provide varieties of numeral font, spacing, etc.

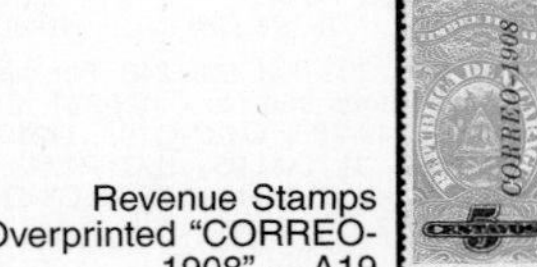

Revenue Stamps Overprinted "CORREO-1908" — A19

1908, June

217 A19 5c yel & blk .75 .40
a. "CORROE" 2.75 2.75
b. Overprint reading down 7.00
c. Double overprint 13.00
218 A19 10c lt bl & blk .75 .25
a. Double overprint 4.50 4.50
b. Overprint reading down .50 .40
c. Double overprint, up and down 13.00 13.00
219 A19 1p yel brn & blk .75 *2.00*
a. "CORROE" 10.00 *12.00*
220 A19 2p pearl gray & blk .75 *2.50*
a. "CORROE" 10.00 10.00
Nos. 217-220 (4) 3.00 *5.15*

The overprint exists on a 5p in green (value $200) and on a 50p in black (value $300).

Revenue Stamps Surcharged Vertically Reading Up in Red (1c, 15c), Blue (2c), Green (4c, 5c) or Orange (35c)

221 A19 1c on 5c yel & blk .40 .25
a. "1008" 2.00 *3.00*
b. "8908" 2.00 *3.00*
c. Surcharge reading down 4.00 4.00
d. Double surcharge 4.00 4.00
222 A19 2c on 5c yel & blk .50 .30
b. "ORRE0" 1.75 1.75
c. "1008" 1.75 1.75
d. "8908" 2.50 *5.50*
f. Double surcharge 7.00 7.00
g. Double surcharge, one inverted 7.00 7.00
h. Surcharge reading down 9.00 9.00
223 A19 4c on 5c yel & blk .65 .35
a. "ORRE0" 3.50 *7.50*
b. "1008" 2.00 2.00
c. "8908" 2.00 2.00
224 A19 15c on 50c ol & blk .60 .40
a. "1008" 4.00 *11.50*
b. "8908" 4.00 4.00
c. Surcharge reading down 10.00 10.00
225 A19 35c on 50c ol & blk 4.00 1.00
a. Double surcharge, one inverted 12.00 12.00
b. Surcharge reading down 12.00 12.00
c. Double surcharge, one in black
Nos. 221-225 (5) 6.15 2.30

For surcharges and overprints see Nos. 225D-225H, 230-234, 266-278, 1L63-1L72A, 1L96-1L106, 2L47.

Revenue Stamps Surcharged Vertically Reading Up in Blue, Black or Orange

1908, Nov.

225D A19 2c on 5c yel org & blk (Bl) 20.00 15.00
e. "9c" instead of "2c" 75.00 75.00
225F A19 10c on 50c ol & blk (Bk) *850.00 325.00*
g. Double surcharge *425.00*
225H A19 35c on 50c ol & blk (O) 17.50 10.00

In this setting there are three types of the character for "cents."

Revenue Stamps Overprinted or Surcharged in Various Colors

No. 226

No. 227

1908, Dec.

226 2c org (Bk) 3.50 2.00
a. Double overprint 6.00 6.00
b. Overprint reading up 5.00 5.00
227 4c on 2c org (Bk) 1.75 .90
a. Surcharge reading up 5.00 5.00
b. Blue surcharge 80.00 80.00
228 5c on 2c org (Bl) 1.50 .60
a. Surcharge reading up 6.00 6.00
229 10c on 2c org (G) 1.50 .30
a. "1988" for "1908" 4.00 3.00
b. Surcharge reading up 5.00 5.00
c. "¢" inverted 4.00 4.00
d. Double surcharge 7.50
Nos. 226-229 (4) 8.25 3.80

Two printings of No. 229 exist. In the first, the initial of "VALE" is a small capital, and in the second a large capital.

The overprint "Correos-1908." 35mm long, handstamped on 1c blue revenue stamp of type A20, is private and fraudulent.

Revenue Stamps Surcharged in Various Colors

1909, Feb. **Color: Olive & Black**

230 A19 1c on 50c (V) 4.00 1.90
231 A19 2c on 50c (Br) 7.00 2.40
232 A19 4c on 50c (G) 7.00 3.50
233 A19 5c on 50c (C) 4.00 2.10
a. Double surcharge 12.50 12.50
234 A19 10c on 50c (Bk) 1.10 .90
Nos. 230-234 (5) 23.10 10.80

Nos. 230 to 234 are found with three types of the character for "cents."

Nos. 190 and 191 Surcharged in Black

1909, Mar. ***Perf. 12***

235 A18 10c on 2p dk grn 20.00 12.00
236 A18 10c on 5p vio *100.00 70.00*

There are three types of the character for "cents."

Arms Type of 1905

Imprint: "American Bank Note Co. NY"

1909, Mar.

237 A18 1c yel grn .50 .30
238 A18 2c vermilion .50 .30
239 A18 3c red org .50 .30
240 A18 4c violet .50 .30
241 A18 5c dp bl .50 .30
242 A18 6c gray brn 4.50 1.50
243 A18 10c lake 1.25 .30
244 A18 15c black 1.25 .30
245 A18 20c brn olive 1.25 .30
246 A18 50c dp grn 1.90 .40
247 A18 1p yellow 1.90 .40
248 A18 2p car rose 1.50 .40
Nos. 237-248 (12) 16.05 5.10

Nos. 239 and 244, Surcharged in Black or Red

1910, July

249 A18 2c on 3c red org 2.75 1.10
250 A18 10c on 15c blk (R) 1.25 .30
a. "VLEA" 3.50 2.00
b. Double surcharge 17.50 17.50

There are two types of the character for "cents."

Nos. 239, 244, 245 Surcharged in Black or Red

1910

252 A18 2c on 3c (Bk) 1.50 1.25
a. Double surcharge 6.00 6.00
b. Pair, one without surcharge
c. "Vale" omitted 10.00 10.00
254 A18 5c on 20c (R) .50 .30
a. Double surcharge (R) 6.00 5.00
b. Inverted surcharge (R) 10.00 *32.50*
c. Black surcharge 100.00
d. Double surcharge (Bk) 140.00
e. Inverted surcharge (Bk) 110.00
255 A18 10c on 15c (Bk) 1.10 .30
a. "c" omitted 2.00 1.10
b. "10c" omitted 2.50 1.50
c. Inverted surcharge 4.00 4.00
d. Double surcharge 6.00 6.00
e. Double surch., one inverted 14.00 *18.50*
Nos. 252-255 (3) 3.10 1.85

There are several minor varieties in this setting, such as italic "L" and "E" and fancy "V" in "VALE," small italic "C," and italic "I" for "1" in "10."

Nos. 239, 244, 246 and 247, Surcharged in Black

1910, Dec. 10

256 A18 2c on 3c red org .85 .45
a. Without period 1.00 .75
b. Inverted surcharge 6.00 6.00
c. Double surcharge 6.00 6.00
257 A18 10c on 15c blk 2.00 .75
a. Without period 3.50 1.25
b. Double surcharge 6.00 3.00
c. Inverted surcharge 10.00 *18.00*
258 A18 10c on 50c dp grn 1.25 .40
a. Without period 1.50 .75
b. Double surcharge 10.00 *26.00*
c. Inverted surcharge 3.00 3.00
259 A18 10c on 1p yel .90 .40
a. Without period 1.25 .75
b. Double surcharge 3.00 3.00
Nos. 256-259 (4) 5.00 2.00

The 15c on 50c deep green is a telegraph stamp from which the "Telegrafos" overprint was omitted. It appears to have been pressed into postal service, as all examples are used with postal cancels. Value $450.

Nos. 240, 244-248 Surcharged in Black

Surcharge as on Nos. 256-259 but lines wider apart.

1911, Mar.

260 A18 2c on 4c vio .30 .25
a. Without period .35 .30
b. Double surcharge 3.50 3.00
c. Double surcharge, inverted 4.00 4.00
d. Double surcharge, one invtd. 9.00 *17.50*
e. Inverted surcharge 10.00 *18.50*
261 A18 5c on 20c brn ol .30 .25
a. Without period .60 .50
b. Double surcharge 2.50 2.50
c. Inverted surcharge 2.50 2.00
d. Double surcharge, one invtd. 6.00 6.00
262 A18 10c on 15c blk .40 .25
a. Without period 1.00 .50
b. "Yale" 12.00 12.00
c. Double surcharge 3.00 3.00
d. Inverted surcharge 3.00 3.00
e. Double surch., one inverted 5.00 4.00
f. Double surch., both inverted 12.00 12.00
263 A18 10c on 50c dp grn .25 .25
a. Without period 1.00 .50
b. Double surcharge 3.00 2.50
c. Double surcharge, one invtd. 5.00 4.00
d. Inverted surcharge 5.00 5.00
264 A18 10c on 1p yel 1.50 .40
a. Without period 2.00 1.50
b. Double surcharge 4.00 4.00
c. Double surcharge, one invtd. 7.50
265 A18 10c on 2p car rose .60 .50
a. Without period 2.00 1.50
b. Double surcharge 2.50 2.50
c. Double surcharge, one invtd. 6.00 6.00
d. Inverted surcharge 6.00 6.00
Nos. 260-265 (6) 3.35 1.90

Revenue Stamps Surcharged in Black

1911, Apr. 10 ***Perf. 14 to 15***

266 A19 2c on 5p dl bl 1.30 *1.25*
a. Without period 1.25 *1.50*
b. Double surcharge 2.50 2.00
267 A19 2c on 5p ultra .40 *.40*
a. Without period .75 *1.25*
b. Double surcharge *3.50*
268 A19 5c on 10p pink .75 .40
a. Without period 1.50 1.00
b. "cte" for "cts" 1.50 1.00
c. Double surcharge 4.00 4.00
d. Inverted surcharge 2.50 2.50
269 A19 10c on 25c lilac .75 .40
a. Without period 1.00 .75
b. "cte" for "cts" 2.00 2.00
c. Inverted surcharge 4.00 4.00
d. Double surcharge 2.50 2.50
e. Double surcharge, one inverted 4.00 4.00
270 A19 10c on 2p gray .40 .40
a. Without period 1.00 .75
b. "cte" for "cts" 1.60 1.00
c. Double surcharge 5.00 5.00
d. Double surcharge, one inverted 4.00 3.00
271 A19 35c on 1p brown .40 .40
a. Without period 1.00 .75
b. "cte" for "cts" 2.00 2.00
c. "Corre" 5.00 5.00
d. Double surcharge 2.50 2.50
e. Double surcharge, one inverted 2.50 2.50
f. Double surcharge inverted 3.00 3.00
g. Inverted surcharge *5.00*
Nos. 266-271 (6) 4.00 3.25

These surcharges are in settings of twenty-five. One stamp in each setting has a large square period after "cts" and two have no period. One of the 2c has no space between "02" and "cts" and one 5c has a small thin "s" in "Correos."

Surcharged in Black

1911, June

272 A19 5c on 2p gray 1.50 1.00
a. Inverted surcharge 6.00 5.00

In this setting one stamp has a large square period and another has a thick up-right "c" in "cts."

Surcharged in Black

1911, June 12

273 A19 5c on 25c lilac 1.50 1.25
274 A19 5c on 50c ol grn 5.00 5.00
275 A19 5c on 5p blue 7.00 7.00
276 A19 5c on 5p ultra 7.50 6.00
a. Inverted surcharge 45.00
277 A19 5c on 50p ver 6.25 5.00
278 A19 10c on 50c ol grn 1.50 .50
Nos. 273-278 (6) 28.75 24.75

This setting has the large square period and the thick "c" in "cts." Many of the stamps have no period after "cts." Owing to broken type and defective impressions letters sometimes appear to be omitted.

A21

Revenue Stamps Surcharged on the Back in Black

a

b

Railroad coupon tax stamps (1st class red and 2nd class blue) are the basic stamps of Nos. 279-294. They were first surcharged for revenue use in 1903 in two types: I — "Timbre Fiscal" and "ctvs." II — "TIMBRE FISCAL" and "cents" (originally intended for use in Bluefields).

1911, July

279 A21 (a) 2c on 5c on 2c bl .40 .40
a. New value in yellow on face 6.00 6.00
b. New value in black on face 10.00 5.00
c. New value in red on face *100.00*
d. Inverted surcharge .75
e. Double surch., one inverted 7.50 7.50
f. "TIMBRE FISCAL" in black .75 .75
280 A21 (b) 2c on 5c on 2c bl .40 .40
a. New value in yellow on face 3.00 3.00
b. New value in black on face 9.00 4.00
c. New value in red on face *100.00*
d. Inverted surcharge .90 1.00
e. Double surch., one inverted 7.50 7.50
f. "TIMBRE FISCAL" in black 1.00 1.00
281 A21 (a) 5c on 5c on 2c bl .40 .40
a. Inverted surcharge 2.00 2.00
b. "TIMBRE FISCAL" in black 1.00 1.00
c. New value in yellow on face
282 A21 (b) 5c on 5c on 2c bl .40 .40
a. Inverted surcharge 2.00 2.00
b. "TIMBRE FISCAL" in black 1.00 1.00
c. New value in yellow on face
283 A21 (a) 10c on 5c on 2c bl .40 .40
a. Inverted surcharge 2.00 2.00
b. "TIMBRE FISCAL" in black 1.00 1.00
c. New value in yellow on face *100.00*
d. Double surcharge 6.00 6.00
284 A21 (b) 10c on 5c on 2c bl .40 .40
a. Inverted surcharge 2.00 2.00
b. "TIMBRE FISCAL" in black 1.00 1.00
c. Double surcharge 6.00 6.00
d. New value in yellow on face *110.00*

285 A21 (a) 15c on 10c on 1c red .40 .40
a. Inverted surcharge 1.00 1.25
b. "Timbre Fiscal" double 5.00
286 A21 (b) 15c on 10c on 1c red .40 .40
a. Inverted surcharge 1.00 1.00
b. "Timbre Fiscal" double 5.00
Nos. 279-286 (8) 3.20 3.20

These surcharges are in settings of 20. For listing, they are separated into small and large figures, but there are many other varieties due to type and arrangement.

The colored surcharges on the face of the stamps were trial printings. These were then surcharged in black on the reverse. The olive yellow surcharge on the face of the 2c was later applied to prevent use as a 5c revenue stamps. Other colors known on the face are orange and green. Forgeries exist.

For overprints and surcharges see Nos. 287-294, O223-O244, 1L107-1L108.

Surcharged on the Face in Black

1911, Oct.

287 A21 2c on 10c on 1c red 6.50 6.50
a. Inverted surcharge 1.40 1.40
b. Double surcharge 10.00 10.00
288 A21 20c on 10c on 1c red 4.50 4.50
a. Inverted surcharge 5.25 5.00
289 A21 50c on 10c on 1c red 5.25 4.50
a. Inverted surcharge 10.00 10.00
Nos. 287-289 (3) 16.25 15.50

There are two varieties of the figures "2" and "5" in this setting.

Surcharged on the Back in Black

1911, Nov.

289B A21 5c on 10c on 1c red 37.50
c. Inverted surcharge 20.00
289D A21 10c on 10c on 1c red 12.50
e. Inverted surcharge 24.00

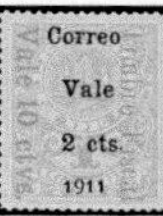

Surcharged on the Face

1911, Dec.

Dark Blue Postal Surcharge

290 A21 2c on 10c on 1c red .40 .40
a. Inverted surcharge 2.50 2.50
b. Double surcharge 5.00 5.00
291 A21 5c on 10c on 1c red .40 .40
a. Double surcharge 2.50 2.50
b. Inverted surcharge 2.50 2.50
292 A21 10c on 10c on 1c red .40 .40
a. Inverted surcharge 2.50 2.50
b. Double surcharge 2.50 2.50
c. "TIMBRE FISCAL" on back 3.50 3.50

Black Postal Surcharge

293 A21 10c on 10c on 1c red 1.50 1.00
a. Inverted surcharge 7.00 7.00
b. New value surch. on back 12.00 12.00

Red Postal Surcharge

293C A21 5c on 5c on 2c blue 1.40 1.25
d. "TIMBRE FISCAL" in black 2.50 1.75
e. "5" omitted 3.75 3.75
f. Inverted surcharge 4.75 4.75
Nos. 290-293C (5) 4.10 3.45

Bar Overprinted on No. O234 in Dark Blue

294 A21 10c on 10c on 1c red 1.25 1.00
a. Inverted surcharge 2.50 2.50
b. Bar at foot of stamp 5.00 5.00

Nos. 290-294 each have three varieties of the numerals in the surcharge.

"Liberty" — A22

Coat of Arms — A23

1912, Jan. Engr. *Perf. 14, 15*

295 A22 1c yel grn .30 .25
296 A22 2c carmine .40 .25
297 A22 3c yel brn .30 .25
298 A22 4c brn vio .30 .25
299 A22 5c blue & blk .25 .25
300 A22 6c olive bister .30 .80
301 A22 10c red brn .25 .25
302 A22 15c vio .25 .25
303 A22 20c red .25 .25
304 A22 25c blue grn & blk .30 .25
305 A23 35c grn & chnt 2.00 1.50
306 A22 50c lt blue 1.00 .40
307 A22 1p org 1.40 2.00
308 A22 2p dark blue grn 1.50 2.25
309 A22 5p blk 3.50 3.50
Nos. 295-309 (15) 12.30 12.70

For overprints and surcharges see Nos. 310-324, 337A-348, 395-396, O245-O259.

No. 305 Surcharged in Violet

1913, Mar.

310 A23 15c on 35c .40 .40
a. "ats" for "cts" 7.50 6.00

Stamps of 1912 Surcharged in Red or Black

1913-14

311 A22 ½c on 3c yel brn (R) .40 .35
a. "Corooba" 2.50 2.50
b. "do" for "de" 2.50 2.50
c. Inverted surcharge 22.50
312 A22 ½c on 15c vio (R) .25 .25
a. "Corooba" 1.00 1.00
b. "do" for "de" 1.25 1.25
313 A22 ½c on 1p org .75 .25
a. "VALB" 3.00 *5.00*
b. "ALE" 4.00 3.50
c. "LE" 6.00 5.00
d. "VALE" omitted 3.50 3.50
314 A22 1c on 3c yel brn .95 .60
315 A22 1c on 4c brn vio .75 .25
316 A22 1c on 50c lt blue .25 .25
317 A22 1c on 5p blk .25 .25
318 A22 2c on 4c brn vio .35 .25
a. "do" for "de" 3.00 *12.00*
319 A22 2c on 20c red 3.50 *4.50*
a. "do" for "de" 17.50 12.50
320 A22 2c on 25c blue grn & blk .35 .25
a. "do" for "de" 3.50 2.50
321 A23 2c on 35c grn & chnt .25 .40
a. "9131" 4.00 *7.50*
b. "do" for "de" 2.50 2.00
322 A22 2c on 50c lt blue .25 .25
a. "do" for "de" 2.00 *4.00*
323 A22 2c on 2p dark blue grn .25 .25
a. "VALB" 1.25 .75
b. "ALE" 2.50 1.25
c. "VALE" omitted 6.00
d. "VALE" and "dos" omitted 6.00
324 A22 3c on 6c olive bis .25 .25
a. "VALB" *35.00*
Nos. 311-324 (14) 8.80 8.35

Nos. 311, 312 surcharged in black were not regularly issued.

Surcharged on Zelaya Issue of 1912

325 Z2 ½c on 2c ver 1.00 *1.25*
a. "Corooba" 2.00 1.25
b. "do" for "de" 1.25 1.25
326 Z2 1c on 3c org brn .80 .25
327 Z2 1c on 4c car .80 .25
328 Z2 1c on 6c red brn .65 .25
329 Z2 1c on 20c dark vio .80 .25
330 Z2 1c on 25c grn & blk .80 .25
331 Z2 2c on 1c yel grn ('14) 11.00 1.25
a. "Centavos" 7.50 1.50
332 Z2 2c on 25c grn & blk 3.75 *3.00*
333 Z2 5c on 35c brn & blk .65 .25
334 Z2 5c on 50c ol grn .65 .25
a. Double surcharge 22.50

335 Z2 6c on 1p org .80 .25
336 Z2 10c on 2p org brn 1.50 .25
337 Z2 1p on 5p dk bl grn 1.00 .40
Nos. 325-337 (13) 24.20 8.15

On No. 331 the surcharge has a space of 2½mm between "Vale" and "dos."

Space between "Vale" and "dos" 2½mm instead of 1mm, "de Cordoba" in different type.

1914, Feb.

337A A22 2c on 4c brn vio 27.50 4.00
b. "Ccntavos" 12.00
337C A22 2c on 20c red 13.00 1.25
d. "Ccntavos" 4.00
337E A22 2c on 25c bl grn & blk 6.00
f. "Ccntavos" 12.00
337G A23 2c on 35c grn & chnt 8.50
h. "Ccntavos" 15.00
337I A22 2c on 50c lt bl 22.50 4.00
j. "Ccntavos" 10.00

No. 310 with Additional Surcharge

1913, Dec.

337K A23 ½c on 15c on 35c *300.00*

The word "Medio" is usually in heavy-faced, shaded letters. It is also in thinner, unshaded letters and in letters from both fonts mixed.

No. 310 Surcharged in Black and Violet

338 A23 ½c on 15c on 35c .40 .40
a. Double surcharge 3.50
b. Inverted surcharge 3.50
c. Surcharged on No. 305 12.00
339 A23 1c on 15c on 35c .40 .40
a. Double surcharge 4.00

Official Stamps of 1912 Surcharged

1914, Feb.

340 A22 1c on 25c lt bl .40 .40
a. Double surcharge 9.00
341 A23 1c on 35c lt bl .40 .40
a. "0.10" for "0.01" 10.00 10.00
341B A22 1c on 50c lt bl *200.00*
342 A22 1c on 1p lt bl .40 .40
342A A22 2c on 20c lt bl *200.00 150.00*
b. "0.12" for "0.02"
343 A22 2c on 50c lt bl .40 .40
a. "0.12" for "0.02" 150.00
344 A22 2c on 2p lt bl .40 .40
345 A22 2c on 5p lt bl *250.00*
346 A22 5c on 5p lt bl .40 .40

Red Surcharge

347 A22 5c on 1p lt bl *140.00*
348 A22 5c on 5p lt bl *500.00*

National Palace, Managua A24

León Cathedral A25

Various Frames

1914, May 13 Engr. *Perf. 12*

349 A24 ½c lt blue .85 .35
350 A24 1c dk green .85 .35
351 A25 2c red orange .85 .35
352 A24 3c red brown 1.25 .40
353 A25 4c scarlet 1.25 .55
354 A24 5c gray black .45 .35
355 A25 6c black brn 9.00 7.50
356 A25 10c orange yel .85 .35
357 A24 15c dp violet 5.75 2.75
358 A25 20c slate 11.00 7.50
359 A24 25c orange 1.50 .60
360 A25 50c pale blue 1.40 .55
Nos. 349-360 (12) 35.00 21.60

In 1924 the 5c, 10c, 25c, 50c were issued in slightly larger size, 27x22¾mm. The original set was 26x22½mm.

No. 356 with overprint "Union Panamericana 1890-1940" in green is of private origin.

See Nos. 408-415, 483-495, 513-523, 652-664. For overprints and surcharges see Nos. 361-394, 397-400, 416-419, 427-479, 500,

540-548, 580-586, 600-648, 671-673, 684-685, C1-C3, C9-C13, C49-C66, C92-C105, C121-C134, C147-C149, C155-C163, C174-C185, CO1-CO24, O260-O294, O296-O319, O332-O376, RA1-RA5, RA10-RA11, RA26-RA35, RA39-RA40, RA44, RA47, RA52.

No. 355 Surcharged in Black

1915, Sept.

361 A25 5c on 6c blk brn 1.50 .40
a. Double surcharge 7.00 7.00

Stamps of 1914 Surcharged in Black or Red

1918-19 **New Value in Figures**

362 A24 1c on 3c red brn 6.50 2.25
a. Double surch., one invtd. 12.50
363 A25 2c on 4c scarlet 32.50 22.50
364 A24 5c on 15c dp vio (R) 7.50 1.50
a. Double surcharge 12.00
364C A24 5c on 15c dp vio 350.00

Surcharged in Black

365 A25 2c on 20c slate 110.00 60.00
a. "ppr" for "por" *500.00* *300.00*
b. Double surcharge *300.00*
c. "Cordobo" *500.00* *300.00*
365D A25 5c on 20c slate — *200.00*
e. Double surcharge (Bk + R) *300.00*
f. "Cordobo" *300.00*

The surcharge on No. 365 is in blue black, and that on No. 365D usually has an admixture of red.

Used only at Bluefields and Rama.

Surcharged in Black, Red or Violet

New Value in Words

366 A25 ½c on 6c blk brn 4.00 1.50
a. "Meio" 15.00
b. Double surcharge 12.00
367 A25 ½c on 10c yellow 2.50 .40
a. "Val" for "Vale" 3.00
b. "Codoba" 3.00
c. Inverted surcharge 5.00
d. Double surch., one inverted 10.00
368 A24 ½c on 15c dp vio 2.50 .60
a. Double surcharge 7.50
b. "Codoba" 4.00
c. "Meio" 6.00
369 A24 ½c on 25c orange 5.00 2.00
a. Double surcharge 8.00
e. Double surch., one inverted 6.00
370 A25 ½c on 50c pale bl 2.50 .40
a. "Meio" 6.00
b. Double surcharge 5.00
c. Double surch., one inverted 7.00
371 A25 ½c on 50c pale bl (R) 4.50 1.50
a. Double surcharge 10.00
372 A24 1c on 3c red brn 3.00 .40
a. Double surcharge 3.50
373 A25 1c on 6c blk brn 12.50 3.50
a. Double surcharge 9.00
374 A25 1c on 10c yellow 24.00 8.00
a. "nu" for "un" 22.50
375 A24 1c on 15c dp vio 4.50 .75
a. Double surcharge 10.00
b. "Codoba" 6.00
376 A25 1c on 20c slate *200.00* *100.00*
a. Black surch. normal and red surch. invtd. *150.00*
b. Double surch., red & black *150.00*
c. Blue surcharge *200.00*
377 A25 1c on 20c sl (V) 110.00 70.00
a. Double surcharge (V + Bk) *150.00*
378 A25 1c on 20c sl (R) 2.50 .40
a. Double surch., one inverted
b. "Val" for "Vale" 3.50 3.00
379 A24 1c on 25c orange 4.50 1.00
a. Double surcharge 11.00
380 A25 1c on 50c pale bl 14.00 4.50
a. Double surcharge 17.50
381 A25 2c on 4c scarlet 3.50 .40
a. Double surcharge 10.00
b. "centavo" 5.00
c. "Val" for "Vale"
382 A25 2c on 6c blk brn 24.00 8.00
a. "Centavoss"
b. "Cordobas"
383 A25 2c on 10c yellow 24.00 4.50
a. "centavo"
384 A25 2c on 20c sl (R) 13.00 3.25
a. "pe" for "de" 15.00
b. Double surch., red & blk 27.50
c. "centavo" 12.00
d. Double surcharge (R) 17.50
385 A24 2c on 25c orange 5.50 .40
a. "Vle" for "Vale" 7.50
b. "Codoba" 7.50
c. Inverted surcharge 10.00
386 A25 5c on 6c blk brn 10.00 4.25
a. Double surcharge 13.50
387 A24 5c on 15c dp vio 3.50 .60
a. "cincoun" for "cinco" 15.00
b. "Vle" for "Vale" 12.50
c. "Codoba" 12.50
Nos. 366-387 (22) 479.50 216.35

No. 378 is surcharged in light red and brown red: the latter color is frequently offered as the violet surcharge (No. 377).

Official Stamps of 1915 Surcharged in Black or Blue

1919-21

388 A24 1c on 25c lt blue 1.50 .40
a. Double surcharge 10.00
b. Inverted surcharge 12.00
389 A25 2c on 50c lt blue 1.50 .40
a. "centavo" 4.00 4.00
b. Double surcharge 12.00
390 A25 10c on 20c lt blue 1.40 .40
a. "centavos" 5.00 5.00
b. Double surcharge 8.00
390F A25 10c on 20c lt bl (Bl) 65.00 65.00
Nos. 388-390 (3) 4.40 1.20

There are numerous varieties of omitted, inverted and italic letters in the foregoing surcharges.

No. 358 Surcharged in Black

Types of the numerals

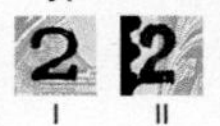

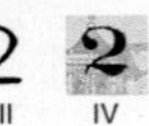

I II III IV

V VI VII VIII

I II III IV

V VI VII VIII

1919, May

391 A25 2c on 20c (I) *200.00* *150.00*
a. Type II 195.00
b. Type III
c. Type IV
d. Type VI
e. Type VIII
392 A25 5c on 20c (I) 110.00 50.00
a. Type II 110.00 45.00
b. Type III 125.00 55.00
c. Type IV 125.00 50.00
d. Type V 140.00 60.00
e. Type VI 140.00 60.00
f. Type VII 400.00 250.00
h. Double surch., one inverted

No. 358 Surcharged in Black

393 A25 2 Cents on 20c (I) *200.00* *150.00*
a. Type II
b. Type III
c. Type IV
d. Type V
e. Type VI
f. Type VII
393G A25 5 Cents on 20c sl, (VIII) 140.00 55.00

Nos. 391-393G used only at Bluefields and Rama.

No. 351 Surcharged in Black

1920, Jan.

394 A25 1c on 2c red org 1.50 .40
a. Inverted surcharge 10.00
b. Double surcharge

No. 394 stamps with uppercase "VALE" in surcharge are believed to be unauthorized surcharges.

Official Stamps of 1912 Overprinted in Carmine

1921, Mar.

395 A22 1c lt blue 1.50 .60
a. "Parricular" 5.00 5.00
b. Inverted overprint 10.00
396 A22 5c lt blue 1.50 .40
a. "Parricular" 5.00 5.00

Official Stamps of 1915 Surcharged in Carmine

1921, May

397 A25 ½c on 2c light blue .50 .40
a. "Mddio" 2.50 2.50
398 A25 ½c on 4c light blue 1.25 .40
a. "Mddio" 2.50 2.50
399 A24 1c on 3c light blue 1.25 .40
Nos. 397-399 (3) 3.00 1.20

No. 354 Surcharged in Red

1921, Aug.

400 A24 ½c on 5c gray blk .75 .75

Trial printings of this stamp were surcharged in yellow, black and red, and yellow and red. Some of these were used for postage.

Gen. Manuel José Arce — A26

José Cecilio del Valle — A27

Miguel Larreinaga A28

Gen. Fernando Chamorro A29

Gen. Máximo Jérez A30

Gen. Pedro Joaquín Chamorro A31

Rubén Darío — A32

1921, Sept. **Engr.**

401 A26 ½c lt bl & blk 1.60 1.60
402 A27 1c grn & blk 1.60 1.60
403 A28 2c rose red & blk 1.60 1.60
404 A29 5c ultra & blk 1.60 1.60
405 A30 10c org & blk 1.60 1.60
406 A31 25c yel & blk 1.60 1.60
407 A32 50c vio & blk 1.60 1.60
Nos. 401-407 (7) 11.20 11.20

Centenary of independence.

For overprints and surcharges see Nos. 420-421, RA12-RA16, RA19-RA23.

Types of 1914 Issue

1922 **Various Frames**

408 A24 ½c green .40 .40
409 A24 1c violet .40 .40
410 A25 2c car rose .40 .40
411 A24 3c ol gray .45 .40
411A A25 4c vermilion .50 .40
412 A25 6c red brn .40 .40
413 A24 15c brown .50 .40
414 A25 20c bis brn .90 .40
415 A25 1cor blk brn 1.40 2.00
Nos. 408-415 (9) 5.35 5.20

In 1924 Nos. 408-415 were issued in slightly larger size, 27x22¾mm. The original set was 26x22½mm.

Nos. 408, 410 exist with signature controls. See note before No. 600. Same values.

No. 356 Surcharged in Black

1922, Nov.

416 A25 1c on 10c org yel 1.00 .40
417 A25 2c on 10c org yel 1.00 .40

Nos. 354 and 356 Surcharged in Red

1923, Jan.

418 A24 1c on 5c gray blk 1.25 .40
419 A25 2c on 10c org yel 1.25 .40
a. Inverted surcharge

Nos. 401 and 402 Overprinted in Red

1923

420 A26 ½c lt blue & blk 7.50 7.50
421 A27 1c green & blk 2.50 .85
a. Double overprint 7.50

Francisco Hernández de Córdoba — A33

1924 **Engr.**

422 A33 1c deep green 2.50 .30
423 A33 2c carmine rose 2.50 .30
424 A33 5c deep blue 2.00 .30
425 A33 10c bister brn 2.00 .60
Nos. 422-425 (4) 9.00 1.50

Founding of León & Granada, 400th anniv.

For overprint & surcharges see #499, 536, O295.

Stamps of 1914-22 Overprinted

Black, Red or Blue Overprint

1927, May 3

427 A24 ½c green (Bk) .40 .40
428 A24 1c violet (R) .40 .40
a. Double overprint 3.00 3.00
428B A24 1c violet (Bk) 85.00 55.00
429 A25 2c car rose (Bk) .40 .40
a. Inverted overprint 5.00
b. Double overprint 5.00
430 A24 3c ol gray (Bk) 1.25 1.25
a. Inverted overprint 5.00
b. Double overprint 6.00

c. Double ovpt., one inverted 10.00 10.00
430D A24 3c ol gray (Bl) 8.00 3.25
431 A25 4c ver (Bk) 16.00 13.00
a. Inverted overprint 30.00
432 A24 5c gray blk (R) 1.25 .40
a. Inverted overprint 7.50
432B A24 5c gray blk (Bk) .75 .40
c. Double ovpt., one inverted 8.00
d. Double overprint 8.00
433 A25 6c red brn (Bk) 13.00 11.00
a. Inverted overprint 17.50
b. Double overprint 27.50
c. "1297" for "1927" *250.00*
434 A25 10c yellow (Bl) .65 .40
a. Double overprint 12.50
b. Double ovpt., one inverted 10.00
435 A24 15c brown (Bk) 6.00 2.50
436 A25 20c bis brn (Bk) 6.00 2.50
a. Double overprint 17.50
437 A24 25c orange (Bk) 27.50 5.00
438 A25 50c pale bl (Bk) 7.50 3.00
439 A25 1cor blk brn (Bk) 15.00 9.00
Nos. 427-439 (16) 189.10 107.90

Most stamps of this group exist with tall "1" in "1927." Counterfeits exist of normal stamps and errors of Nos. 427-478.

1927, May 19 Violet Overprint

440 A24 ½c green .40 .40
a. Inverted overprint 2.00 2.00
b. Double overprint 2.00 2.00
441 A24 1c violet .40 .40
a. Double overprint 2.00 2.00
442 A25 2c car rose .40 .40
a. Double overprint 2.00 2.00
b. "1927" double 5.00
d. Double ovpt., one inverted 2.00 2.00
443 A24 3c ol gray .40 .40
a. Inverted overprint 6.00
b. Overprinted "1927" only 12.00
c. Double ovpt., one inverted 9.00
444 A25 4c vermilion 37.50 27.50
a. Inverted overprint 75.00
445 A24 5c gray blk 1.00 .40
a. Double overprint, one inverted 6.00
446 A25 6c red brn 37.50 27.50
a. Inverted overprint 75.00
447 A25 10c yellow .40 .40
a. Double overprint 2.00 2.00
448 A24 15c brown .75 .40
a. Double overprint 5.00
b. Double overprint, one inverted 8.00
449 A25 20c bis brn .40 .40
a. Double overprint
450 A24 25c orange .40 .40
451 A25 50c pale bl .40 .40
a. Double ovpt., one inverted 4.00 4.00
452 A25 1cor blk brn .75 .40
a. Double overprint 3.00
b. "1927" double 5.00
c. Double ovpt., one inverted 6.00
Nos. 440-452 (13) 80.70 59.40

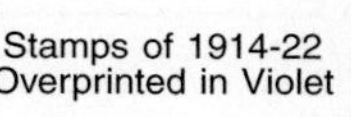

Stamps of 1914-22 Overprinted in Violet

1928, Jan. 3

453 A24 ½c green .40 .40
a. Double overprint 3.00
b. Double overprint, one inverted 4.00
454 A24 1c violet .40 .40
a. Inverted overprint 2.00
b. Double overprint 2.00
c. Double overprint, one inverted 2.00
d. "928" for "1928" 2.50 2.50
455 A25 2c car rose .40 .40
a. Inverted overprint 2.00
b. Double overprint 2.00
c. "1928" omitted 5.00
d. "928" for "1928" 2.50
e. As "d," inverted
f. "19" for "1928"
456 A24 3c ol gray .40 .40
457 A25 4c vermilion .40 .40
458 A24 5c gray blk .40 .40
a. Double overprint 5.00
b. Double overprint, one inverted 5.00
459 A25 6c red brn .40 .40
460 A25 10c yellow .40 .40
a. Double overprint 2.50
c. Inverted overprint
461 A24 15c brown .40 .40
462 A25 20c bis brn .50 .40
a. Double overprint
463 A24 25c orange .75 .40
a. Double overprint, one inverted 4.00
464 A25 50c pale bl 1.25 .40
465 A25 1cor blk brn 1.25 .40
Nos. 453-465 (13) 7.35 5.20

Stamps of 1914-22 Overprinted in Violet

1928, June 11

466 A24 ½c green .40 .40
467 A24 1c violet .40 .40
a. "928" omitted
469 A24 3c ol gray .75 .40
a. Double overprint 6.00

470 A25 4c vermilion .40 .40
471 A24 5c gray blk .40 .40
a. Double overprint 4.00
472 A25 6c red brn .40 .40
a. Double overprint 5.00
473 A25 10c yellow .50 .40
474 A24 15c brown 1.75 .40
a. Double overprint
475 A25 20c bis brn 2.00 .40
476 A24 25c orange 2.00 .40
a. Double overprint, one inverted 6.00
477 A25 50c pale bl 2.00 .40
478 A25 1cor blk brn 5.00 2.50
a. Double overprint 10.00
Nos. 466-478 (12) 16.00 6.90

No. 410 with above overprint in black was not regularly issued.

No. 470 with Additional Surcharge in Violet

1928

479 A25 2c on 4c ver 1.25 .40
a. Double surcharge 9.00

A34

Inscribed: "Timbre Telegrafico"

1928 Red Surcharge

480 A34 1c on 5c bl & blk .40 .40
a. Double surcharge 5.00
b. Double surcharge, one inverted
481 A34 2c on 5c bl & blk .40 .40
a. Double surcharge 5.00
482 A34 3c on 5c bl & blk .40 .40
Nos. 480-482 (3) 1.20 1.20

Stamps similar to Nos. 481-482, but with surcharge in black and with basic stamp inscribed "Timbre Fiscal," are of private origin.

See designs A36, A37, A44, PT1, PT4, PT6, PT7.

Types of 1914 Issue

1928 Various Frames

483 A24 ½c org red .40 .25
484 A24 1c orange .40 .25
485 A25 2c green .40 .25
486 A24 3c dp vio .40 .25
487 A25 4c brown .40 .25
488 A24 5c yellow .40 .25
489 A25 6c lt bl .40 .25
490 A25 10c dk bl .90 .25
491 A24 15c car rose 1.40 .50
492 A25 20c dk grn 1.40 .50
493 A24 25c blk brn 27.50 6.00
494 A25 50c bis brn 3.25 1.00
495 A25 1cor dl vio 6.25 3.00
Nos. 483-495 (13) 43.50 13.00

No. 425 Overprinted in Violet

1929

499 A33 10c bis brn .75 .60

No. 408 Overprinted in Red

1929

500 A24 ½c green (R) .40 .40
a. Inverted overprint 5.50
b. Double overprint 5.00
c. Double overprint, one inverted 5.00

A36

Telegraph Tax Stamp Surcharged Vertically in Red

1929

504 A36 1c on 5c bl & blk (R) .40 .40
a. Inverted surcharge 3.00
b. Surcharged "0.10" for "0.01" 3.00
c. "0.0" instead of "0.01" 5.00
509 A36 2c on 5c bl & blk (R) .40 .40
a. Double surcharge 2.50
b. Double surcharge, one inverted 3.50
c. Inverted surcharge 5.00

Telegraph Tax Stamp Surcharged Vertically in Red

510 A36 2c on 5c bl & blk (R) 22.50 1.25
a. Dbl. surcharge, one inverted 25.00

A37

Surcharged in Red

511 A37 1c on 10c dk grn & blk (R) .40 .40
a. Double surcharge
512 A37 2c on 5c bl & blk (R) .40 .40
Nos. 504-512 (5) 24.10 2.85

The varieties tall "1" in "0.01" and "O$" for "C$" are found in this surcharge.

Nos. 500, 504, 509-512 and RA38 were surcharged in red and sold in large quantities to the public. Surcharges in various other colors were distributed only to a favored few and not regularly sold at the post offices.

Types of 1914 Issue

1929-31 Various Frames

513 A24 1c ol grn .40 .40
514 A24 3c lt bl .40 .40
515 A25 4c dk bl ('31) .40 .40
516 A24 5c ol brn .40 .40
517 A25 6c bis brn ('31) .50 .40
518 A25 10c lt brn ('31) .60 .40
519 A24 15c org red ('31) .90 .40
520 A25 20c org ('31) 1.25 .40
521 A24 25c dk vio .25 .40
522 A25 50c grn ('31) .50 .40
523 A25 1cor yel ('31) 4.50 1.25
Nos. 513-523 (11) 10.10 5.25

Nos. 513-523 exist with signature controls. See note before No. 600. Same values.

New Post Office at Managua — A38

1930, Sept. 15 Engr.

525 A38 ½c olive gray 1.25 1.25
526 A38 1c carmine 1.25 1.25
527 A38 2c red org .90 .90
528 A38 3c orange 1.75 1.75
529 A38 4c yellow 1.75 1.75
530 A38 5c ol grn 2.25 2.25
531 A38 6c bl grn 2.25 2.25
532 A38 10c black 2.75 2.75
533 A38 25c dp bl 5.50 5.50
534 A38 50c ultra 9.00 9.00
535 A38 1cor dp vio 25.00 25.00
Nos. 525-535 (11) 53.65 53.65

Opening of the new general post office at Managua. The stamps were on sale on day of issuance and for an emergency in April, 1931.

No. 499 Surcharged in Black and Red

1931, May 29

536 A33 2c on 10c bis brn .50 1.60
a. Red surcharge omitted 2.50
b. Red surcharge double 5.00
c. Red surcharge inverted 6.00
d. Red surcharge double, one invtd.

Surcharge exists in brown.

Types of 1914-31 Issue Overprinted

1931, June 11

540 A24 ½c green .40 .40
a. Double overprint 2.00
b. Double ovpt., one inverted 1.40
c. Inverted overprint .80

541 A24 1c ol grn .40 .40
a. Double overprint 2.00
b. Double ovpt., one inverted 1.40
c. Inverted overprint
542 A25 2c car rose .40 .40
a. Double overprint 2.00
b. Double ovpt., both inverted 2.50
c. Inverted overprint 1.40
543 A24 3c lt bl .40 .40
a. Double overprint .80
b. Double ovpt., one inverted 1.40
c. Inverted overprint 1.40
544 A24 5c yellow 4.00 2.25
545 A24 5c ol brn 1.25 .25
a. Double overprint 4.50
b. Inverted overprint 4.50
546 A24 15c org red 1.50 .40
a. Double overprint 3.50
547 A24 25c blk brn 12.00 6.50
a. Double overprint 13.00 7.00
b. Inverted overprint 13.00 7.00
548 A24 25c dk vio 4.50 2.50
a. Double overprint 10.00
Nos. 540-548 (9) 24.85 13.50

Counterfeits exist of the scarcer values. The 4c brown and 6c light blue with this overprint are bogus.

Managua P.O. Before and After Earthquake — A40

1932, Jan. 1 Litho. *Perf. 11½*

Soft porous paper, Without gum

556 A40 ½c emerald 1.50
557 A40 1c yel brn 1.90
558 A40 2c dp car 1.50
559 A40 3c ultra 1.50
560 A40 4c dp ultra 1.50
561 A40 5c yel brn 1.60
562 A40 6c gray brn 1.60
563 A40 10c yel brn 2.50
564 A40 15c dl rose 3.75
565 A40 20c orange 3.50
566 A40 25c dk vio 2.50
567 A40 50c emerald 2.50
568 A40 1cor yellow 6.25
Nos. 556-568 (13) 32.10

Issued in commemoration of the earthquake at Managua, Mar. 31, 1931. The stamps were on sale on Jan. 1, 1932, only. The money received from this sale was for the reconstruction of the Post Office building and for the improvement of the postal service. Many shades exist.

Sheets of 10.

Reprints are on thin hard paper and do not have the faint horiz. ribbing that is on the front or back of the originals. Fake cancels abound. Value 75 cents each.

See Nos. C20-C24. For overprints and surcharges see Nos. C32-C43, C47-C48.

Rivas Railroad Issue

"Fill" at El Nacascolo — A41

1c, Wharf at San Jorge. 5c, Rivas Station. 10c, San Juan del Sur. 15c, Train at Rivas Station.

1932, Dec. 17 Litho. *Perf. 12*

Soft porous paper

570 A41 1c yellow 16.00
a. 1c ocher 18.00
571 A41 2c carmine 16.00
572 A41 5c blk brn 16.00
573 A41 10c olive brown 16.00
574 A41 15c yellow 16.00
a. 15c deep orange 18.00
Nos. 570-574 (5) 80.00

Inauguration of the railroad from San Jorge to San Juan del Sur. On sale only on Dec. 17, 1932.

Sheets of 4, without gum. See #C67-C71.

Reprints exist on five different papers ranging from thick soft light cream to thin very hard paper and do not have the faint horiz. ribbing that is normally on the front or back of the originals. Originals are on very white paper. Value of reprints, $5 each.

Leon-Sauce Railroad Issue

Bridge No. 2 at Santa Lucia — A42

Designs: 1c, Environs of El Sauce. 5c, Santa Lucia. 10c, Works at Km. 64. 15c, Rock cut at Santa Lucia.

1932, Dec. 30 *Perf. 12*

Soft porous paper

575 A42 1c orange 16.00
576 A42 2c carmine 16.00
577 A42 5c blk brn 16.00
578 A42 10c olive brown 16.00
579 A42 15c orange 16.00
Nos. 575-579 (5) 80.00

Inauguration of the railroad from Leon to El Sauce. On sale only on Dec. 30, 1932.

Sheets of 4, without gum. See #C72-C76.

Reprints exist on thin hard paper and do not have the faint horiz. ribbing that is on the front or back of the originals. Value $5 each.

Nos. 514-515, 543 Surcharged in Red

1932, Dec. 10
580 A24 1c on 3c lt bl (514) .40 .40
a. Double surcharge 3.50
581 A24 1c on 3c lt bl (543) 4.00 3.50
582 A25 2c on 4c dk bl (515) .40 .40
a. Double surcharge 2.50
Nos. 580-582 (3) 4.80 4.30

Nos. 514, 516, 545 and 518 Surcharged in Black or Red

1933
583 A24 1c on 3c lt bl (Bk) (514) .40 .40
a. "Censavo" 4.00 2.25
b. Double surcharge, one inverted 4.00
584 A24 1c on 5c ol brn (R) (516) .40 .40
a. Inverted surcharge 25.00
b. Double surcharge
585 A24 1c on 5c ol brn (R) (545) 6.50 5.00
a. Red surcharge double 12.00
586 A25 2c on 10c lt brn (Bk) (518) .40 .40
a. Double surcharge 7.00 2.50
b. Inverted surcharge 5.00 3.50
c. Double surcharge, one inverted 5.00 2.50
Nos. 583-586 (4) 7.70 6.20

On No. 586 "Vale Dos" measures 13mm and 14mm.

No. 583 with green surcharge and No. 586 with red surcharge are bogus.

Flag of the Race Issue

Flag with Three Crosses for Three Ships of Columbus — A43

1933, Aug. 3 **Litho.** ***Rouletted 9***

Without gum

587 A43 ½c emerald 2.25 2.25
588 A43 1c green 1.90 1.90
589 A43 2c red 1.90 1.90
590 A43 3c dp rose 1.90 1.90
591 A43 4c orange 1.90 1.90
592 A43 5c yellow 2.25 2.25
593 A43 10c dp brn 2.25 2.25
594 A43 15c dk brn 2.25 2.25
595 A43 20c vio bl 2.25 2.25
596 A43 25c dl bl 2.25 2.25
597 A43 30c violet 5.50 5.50
598 A43 50c red vio 5.50 5.50
599 A43 1cor ol brn 5.50 5.50
Nos. 587-599 (13) 37.60 37.60

Commemorating the raising of the symbolical "Flag of the Race"; also the 441st anniversary of the sailing of Columbus for the New World, Aug. 3, 1492. Printed in sheets of 10.

See Nos. C77-C87, O320-O331.

In October, 1933, various postage, airmail and official stamps of current issues were overprinted with facsimile signatures of the Minister of Public Works and the Postmaster-General. These overprints are control marks.

Nos. 410 and 513 Overprinted in Black

1935 *Perf. 12*
600 A24 1c ol grn .40 .40
a. Inverted overprint 1.40 1.60
b. Double overprint 1.40 1.60
c. Double overprint, one inverted 1.60 1.60
601 A25 2c car rose .40 .40
a. Inverted overprint 1.60
b. Double overprint 1.60
c. Double overprint, one inverted 4.50
d. Double overprint, both inverted 2.50 2.25

No. 517 Surcharged in Red as in 1932

1936, June
602 A25 ½c on 6c bis brn .40 .40
a. "Ccentavo" .80 .80
b. Double surcharge 3.50 3.50

Regular Issues of 1929-35 Overprinted in Blue

1935, Dec.
603 A25 ½c on 6c bis brn .65 .40
604 A24 1c ol grn (#600) .80 .40
605 A25 2c car rose (#601) .80 .40
a. Black overprint inverted 6.00
606 A24 3c lt bl .80 .40
607 A24 5c ol brn 1.00 .40
608 A25 10c lt brn 1.60 .80
Nos. 603-608 (6) 5.65 2.80

Nos. 606-608 have signature control overprint. See note before No. 600.

Same Overprint in Red

1936, Jan.
609 A24 ½c dk grn .50 .40
610 A25 ½c on 6c bis brn (602) .50 .40
a. Double surch., one inverted 6.00 6.00
611 A24 1c ol grn (513) .50 .40
612 A24 1c ol grn (600) .50 .40
613 A25 2c car rose (410) 1.00 .40
614 A25 2c car rose (601) .50 .40
a. Black overprint inverted 12.00 2.50
b. Black ovpt. double, one invtd. 12.00 3.50
615 A24 3c lt bl .50 .40
616 A25 4c dk bl .50 .40
617 A24 5c ol brn .50 .40
618 A25 6c bis brn .50 .40
619 A25 10c lt brn 1.00 .40
620 A24 15c org red .50 .40
621 A25 20c orange 1.60 .40
622 A24 25c dk vio .50 .40
623 A25 50c green .70 .40
624 A25 1cor yellow .80 .40
Nos. 609-624 (16) 10.60 6.40

Red or blue "Resello 1935" overprint may be found inverted or double. Red and blue overprints on same stamp are bogus.

Nos. 615-624 have signature control overprint. See note before No. 600.

Regular Issues of 1922-29 Overprinted in Carmine

1936, May
625 A24 ½c green .40 .40
626 A24 1c olive green .40 .40
627 A25 2c carmine rose .50 .40
628 A24 3c light blue .40 .40
Nos. 625-628 (4) 1.70 1.60

No. 628 has signature control overprint. See note before No. 600.

Nos. 514, 516 Surcharged in Black

1936, June
629 A24 1c on 3c lt bl .40 .40
a. "1396" for "1936" 1.00 1.00
b. "Un" omitted 4.50 1.40
c. Inverted surcharge 1.60 1.20
d. Double surcharge 1.60 1.60
630 A24 2c on 5c ol brn .40 .40
a. "1396" for "1936" 1.40 1.40
b. Double surcharge 3.50 3.50

Regular Issues of 1929-31 Surcharged in Black or Red

1936
631 A24 ½c on 15c org red (R) .35 .35
a. Double surcharge 4.00
632 A25 1c on 4c dk bl (Bk) .35 .35
633 A24 1c on 5c ol brn (Bk) .35 .35
634 A25 1c on 6c bis brn (Bk) .40 .35
a. "1939" instead of "1936" 2.50 1.60
635 A24 1c on 15c org red (Bk) .35 .35
a. "1939" instead of "1936" 2.50 1.60
636 A25 1c on 20c org (Bk) .35 .35
a. "1939" intead of "1936" 2.50 1.60
b. Double surcharge 4.00
637 A25 1c on 20c org (R) .35 .35
638 A25 2c on 10c lt brn (Bk) .35 .35
639 A24 2c on 15c org red (Bk) 1.00 .80
640 A25 2c on 20c org (Bk) .50 .35
641 A24 2c on 25c dk vio (R) .35 .35
642 A24 2c on 25c dk vio (Bk) .35 .35
a. "1939" instead of "1936" 2.50 1.60
643 A25 2c on 50c grn (Bk) .35 .35
a. "1939" instead of "1936" 2.50 1.60
644 A25 2c on 1 cor yel (Bk) .35 .35
a. "1939" instead of "1936" 2.50 1.60
645 A25 3c on 4c dk bl (R) .65 .50
a. "1939" instead of "1936" 2.50 1.60
b. "s" of "Centavos" omitted and "r" of "Tres" inverted 2.50
Nos. 631-645 (15) 6.40 5.85

Nos. 634, 639, 643-644 exist with and without signature controls. Same values, except for No. 639, which is rare without the signature control. Nos. 635-636, 642, 645 do not have signature controls. Others have signature controls only. See note before No. 600.

Regular Issues of 1929-31 Overprinted in Black

No. 646

No. 648, Script Control Mark

1936, Aug.
646 A24 3c lt bl .65 .40
647 A24 5c ol brn .45 .40
648 A25 10c lt brn 1.00 4.00
Nos. 646-648 (3) 2.10 4.80

A44

1936, Oct. 19 **Red Surcharge**
649 A44 1c on 5c grn & blk .40 .40
650 A44 2c on 5c grn & blk .40 .40

Types of 1914

1937, Jan. 1 **Engr.**
652 A24 ½c black .75 .40
653 A24 1c car rose .75 .40
654 A25 2c dp bl .75 .40
655 A24 3c chocolate .75 .40
656 A25 4c yellow .75 .40
657 A24 5c org red .75 .40
658 A25 6c dl vio .75 .40
659 A25 10c ol grn .75 .40
660 A24 15c green .75 .40
661 A25 20c red brn .75 .40
663 A25 50c brown .75 .40
664 A25 1cor ultra 1.50 .40
Nos. 652-664 (12) 9.75 4.80

See note after No. 360.

Mail Carrier — A45

Designs: 1c, Mule carrying mail. 2c, Mail coach. 3c, Sailboat. 5c, Steamship. 7½c, Train.

1937, Dec. **Litho.** ***Perf. 11***
665 A45 ½c green .35 .35
666 A45 1c magenta .35 .35
667 A45 2c brown .35 .35
668 A45 3c purple .35 .35
669 A45 5c blue .35 .35
670 A45 7½c red org .65 .65
Nos. 665-670 (6) 2.40 2.40

75th anniv. of the postal service in Nicaragua.

Nos. 665-670 exists printed on several different kinds of paper: medium thick porous white paper, a thinner whitish toned paper, and a thin hard brownish tone paper.

Nos. 665-670 were also issued in sheets of 4. Value, set of sheets $25.

The miniature sheets are ungummed, and also exist imperf. and part-perf.

Nos. 359, 663 and 664 Surcharged in Red

1938 *Perf. 12*
671 A24 3c on 25c org .40 .40
672 A25 5c on 50c brn .40 .40
a. "e" of "Vale" omitted 1.60 1.00
673 A25 6c on 1cor ultra .40 .40
Nos. 671-673 (3) 1.20 1.20

No. 672 has a script signature control and the surcharge is in three lines.

Dario Park — A46

1939, Jan. **Engr.** ***Perf. 12½***
674 A46 1½c yel grn .90 .50
675 A46 2c dp rose .90 .50
676 A46 3c brt bl .90 .50
677 A46 6c brn org .90 .50
678 A46 7½c dp grn .90 .50
679 A46 10c blk brn .90 .50
680 A46 15c orange .90 .50
681 A46 25c lt vio .90 .50
682 A46 50c brt yel grn .90 .50
683 A46 1cor yellow 1.90 .50
Nos. 674-683 (10) 10.00 5.00

Nos. 660 and 661 Surcharged in Red

1939 *Perf. 12*
684 A24 1c on 15c grn .40 .40
a. Inverted surcharge 2.00 2.00
685 A25 1c on 20c red brn .40 .40

No. C236 Surcharged in Carmine

1941 **Unwmk.** ***Perf. 12***
686 AP14 10c on 1c brt grn .65 .40
a. Double surcharge 10.00 2.50
b. Inverted surcharge 10.00 2.50

Rubén Darío — A47

1941, Dec. Engr. *Perf. 12½*

687 A47 10c red .80 .40
Nos. 687,C257-C260 (5) 4.00 2.00

25th anniversary of the death of Rubén Darío, poet and writer.

No. C236 Surcharged in Carmine

1943 *Perf. 12*

688 AP14 10c on 1c brt grn 4.00 .40
a. Inverted surcharge 10.00
b. Double surcharge 10.00

Catalogue values for unused stamps in this section, from this point to the end of the section, are for Never Hinged items.

"Victory" — A48

1943, Dec. 8 Engr.

689 A48 10c vio & cerise .40 .40
690 A48 30c org brn & cerise .50 .40

2nd anniv. of Nicaragua's declaration of war against the Axis. See Nos. C261-C262.

Columbus and Lighthouse — A49

1945, Sept. 1 Unwmk. *Perf. 12½*

691 A49 4c dk grn & blk .40 .30
692 A49 6c org & blk .40 .30
693 A49 8c dp rose & blk .50 .35
694 A49 10c bl & blk .55 .40
Nos. 691-694,C266-C271 (10) 8.00 5.70

Issued in honor of the discovery of America by Columbus and the Columbus Lighthouse near Ciudad Trujillo, Dominican Republic.

Franklin D. Roosevelt, Philatelist A50

Roosevelt Signing Declaration of War Against Japan A51

8c, F. D. Roosevelt, Winston Churchill. 16c, Gen. Henri Giraud, Roosevelt, de Gaulle & Churchill. 32c, Stalin, Roosevelt, Churchill. 50c, Sculptured head of Roosevelt.

Engraved, Center Photogravure

1946, June 15 Unwmk. *Perf. 12½*

Frame in Black

695 A50 4c sl grn .40 .30
696 A50 8c violet .40 .30
697 A51 10c ultra .40 .30
698 A50 16c rose red .55 .30
699 A50 32c org brn .40 .30
700 A51 50c gray .40 .30
Nos. 695-700,C272-C276 (11) 15.30 11.55

Issued to honor US Pres. Franklin D. Roosevelt (1882-1945). See Nos. C272-C276.

Buildings A56

Designs: 4c, Metropolitan Cathedral, Managua. 5c, Sanitation Building. 6c, Municipal Building.10c, Projected Provincial Seminary. 75c, Communications Building.

1947, Jan. 10 Frame in Black

701 A56 4c carmine .45 .30
702 A56 5c blue .45 .30
703 A56 6c green .45 .30
704 A56 10c olive .45 .30
705 A56 75c golden brn .55 .30
Nos. 701-705,C277-C282 (11) 8.40 4.65

Centenary of the founding of the city of Managua. See Nos. C277-C282.

San Cristóbal Volcano — A61

Designs: 3c, Tomb of Rubén Dario. 4c, Grandstand. 5c, Soldiers' monument. 6c, Sugar cane. 8c, Tropical fruit. 10c, Cotton industry. 20c, Horse race. 30c, Nicaraguan coffee. 50c, Steer. 1cor, Agriculture.

Engraved, Center Photogravure

1947, Aug. 29 Frame in Black

706 A61 2c orange .35 .30
707 A61 3c violet .35 .30
708 A61 4c gray .35 .30
709 A61 5c rose car .75 .30
710 A61 6c green .40 .30
711 A61 8c org brn .55 .30
712 A61 10c red .75 .30
713 A61 20c brt ultra 2.60 .50
714 A61 30c rose lilac 2.00 .50
715 A61 50c dp claret 4.25 .95
716 A61 1cor brn org 1.50 .50
Nos. 706-716,C283-C295 (24) 43.45 29.55

The frames differ for each denomination.
For surcharge see No. 769.

Softball — A62

Boy Scout, Badge and Flag — A63

Designs: 3c, Pole vault. 4c, Diving. 5c, Bicycling. 10c, Proposed stadium. 15c, Baseball. 25c, Boxing. 35c, Basketball. 40c, Regatta. 60c, Table tennis. 1 cor, Soccer. 2 cor, Tennis.

1949, July 15 Photo. *Perf. 12*

717 A62 1c henna brn .50 .25
718 A63 2c ultra .90 .25
719 A63 3c bl grn .50 .25
720 A62 4c dp claret .35 .25
721 A63 5c orange .70 .25
722 A62 10c emerald .70 .25
723 A62 15c cerise 1.00 .25
724 A63 25c brt bl 1.00 .25
725 A63 35c olive grn 1.90 .25
726 A62 40c violet 2.75 .30
727 A62 60c olive gray 3.25 .40
728 A62 1cor scarlet 4.50 1.25
729 A62 2cor red vio 7.25 2.50
Nos. 717-729 (13) 25.30 6.70
Nos. 717-729,C296-C308 (26) 62.75 17.25

10th World Series of Amateur Baseball, 1948.

Each denomination was also issued in a souvenir sheet containing four stamps and marginal inscriptions. Value, set of 13 sheets, $395.

Rowland Hill — A64

Designs: 25c, Heinrich von Stephan. 75c, UPU Monument. 80c, Congress medal, obverse. 4cor, as 80c, reverse.

1950, Nov. 23 Engr. *Perf. 13*

Frame in Black

730 A64 20c car lake .35 .25
731 A64 25c yel grn .35 .25
732 A64 75c ultra .70 .25
733 A64 80c green .35 .25
734 A64 4cor blue 1.40 .80
Nos. 730-734 (5) 3.15 1.80
Nos. 730-734,C309-C315,CO45-CO50 (18) 17.30 9.45

75th anniv. (in 1949) of the UPU.
Each denomination was also issued in a souvenir sheet containing 4 stamps. Size: 115x123mm. Value, set of 5 sheets, $30.
For surcharge see #771.

Queen Isabella I A65

Ships of Columbus A66

Designs: 98c, Santa Maria. 1.20cor, Map. 1.76cor, Portrait facing left.

1952, June 25 *Perf. 11½*

735 A65 10c lilac rose .30 .25
736 A66 96c deep ultra .90 .75
737 A65 98c carmine .95 .75
738 A65 1.20cor brown 1.10 .90
739 A65 1.76cor red violet 1.50 1.25
a. Souvenir sheet of 5, #735-739 12.00 8.00
Nos. 735-739 (5) 4.75 3.90
Nos. 735-739,C316-C320 (10) 19.75 13.90

Queen Isabella I of Spain, 500th birth anniv.

ODECA Flag — A67

Designs: 5c, Map of Central America. 6c, Arms of ODECA. 15c, Presidents of Five Central American Republics. 50c, ODECA Charter and Flags.

1953, Apr. 15 *Perf. 13½x14*

740 A67 4c dk bl .40 .40
741 A67 5c emerald .40 .40
742 A67 6c lt brn .40 .40
743 A67 15c lt ol grn .40 .40
744 A67 50c blk brn .40 .40
Nos. 740-744,C321-C325 (10) 7.85 5.85

Founding of the Organization of the Central American States (ODECA).
For surcharge see #767.

Pres. Carlos Solorzano — A68

Presidents: 6c, Diego Manuel Chamorro. 8c, Adolfo Diaz. 15c, Gen. Anastasio Somoza. 50c, Gen. Emiliano Chamorro.

Heads in Gray Black

Engr. (frames); Photo. (heads)

1953, June 25 *Perf. 12½*

745 A68 4c dk car rose .40 .40
746 A68 6c dp ultra .40 .40
747 A68 8c brown .40 .40
748 A68 15c car rose .40 .40
749 A68 50c bl grn .40 .40
Nos. 745-749,C326-C338 (18) 13.80 7.30

For surcharges see Nos. 768, 853.

Sculptor and UN Emblem — A69

4c, Arms of Nicaragua. 5c, Globe. 15c, Candle & Charter. 1cor, Flags of Nicaragua & UN.

Perf. 13½

1954, Apr. 30 Engr. Unwmk.

750 A69 3c olive .30 .25
751 A69 4c olive green .30 .25
752 A69 5c emerald .30 .25
753 A69 15c deep green 1.20 .25
754 A69 1cor blue green 1.40 .30
Nos. 750-754,C339-C345 (12) 17.40 7.30

UN Organization.

Capt. Dean L. Ray, USAF — A70

Designs: 2c, Sabre jet plane. 3c, Plane, type A-20. 4c, B-24 bomber. 5c, Plane, type AT-6. 15c, Gen. Anastasio Somoza. 1cor, Air Force emblem.

Frame in Black

Engraved; Center Photogravure

1954, Nov. 5 *Perf. 13*

755 A70 1c gray .45 .25
756 A70 2c gray .45 .25
757 A70 3c dk gray grn .45 .25
758 A70 4c orange .45 .25
759 A70 5c emerald .45 .25
760 A70 15c aqua .45 .25
761 A70 1cor purple .45 .25
Nos. 755-761,C346-C352 (14) 11.10 4.10

National Air Force.

Rotary Slogans and Wreath A71

Map of the World and Rotary Emblem A72

20c, Handclasp, Rotary emblem & globe. 35c, Flags of Nicaragua & Rotary. 90c, Paul P. Harris.

1955, Aug. 30 Photo. *Perf. 11½*

Granite Paper.

762 A71 15c dp orange .60 .35
763 A71 20c dk olive grn .60 .35
764 A71 35c red violet .60 .35
765 A72 40c carmine .60 .35
766 A71 90c black & gray 1.10 .35
a. Souvenir sheet of 5, #762-766 6.50 4.25
Nos. 762-766,C353-C362 (15) 8.90 5.25

50th anniversary of Rotary International.
For surcharges see Nos. 770, 772, 876.

Issues of 1947-55 Surcharged in Various Colors

Perf. 13½x14, 12½, 11½, 13

Engraved, Photogravure

1956, Feb. 4 Unwmk.

767 A67 5c on 6c lt brn .40 .35
768 A68 5c on 6c ultra & gray blk (Ult) .40 .35
769 A61 5c on 8c blk & org brn .40 .35
770 A71 15c on 35c red vio (G) .40 .35
771 A64 15c on 80c blk & grn .40 .35
772 A71 15c on 90c blk & gray (Bl) .40 .35
Nos. 767-772,C363-C366 (10) 9.15 4.65

Spacing of surcharge varies to fit shape of stamps.
National Exhibition, Feb. 4-16, 1956.

Gen. Máximo Jerez — A73

Battle of San Jacinto — A74

10c, Gen. Fernando Chamorro. 25c, Burning of Granada. 50c, Gen. José Dolores Estrada.

Perf. 12½x12, 12, 12½

1956, Sept. 14 **Engr.**

773 A73 5c brown .40 .35
774 A73 10c dk car rose .40 .35
775 A74 15c blue gray .40 .35
776 A74 25c brt red .40 .35
777 A73 50c brt red vio .80 .35
Nos. 773-777,C367-C371 (10) 9.45 5.20

National War, cent.

Boy Scout — A75

Designs: 15c, Cub Scout. 20c, Boy Scout. 25c, Lord Baden-Powell. 50c, Joseph A. Harrison.

Perf. 13½x14

1957, Apr. 9 **Photo.** **Unwmk.**

778 A75 10c violet & ol .50 .35
779 A75 15c dp plum & gray blk .50 .35
780 A75 20c ultra & brn .50 .35
781 A75 25c dl red brn & dp bluish grn .50 .35
782 A75 50c red & olive .50 .35
a. Souvenir sheet of 5, #778-782, imperf. 7.00 4.00
Nos. 778-782,C377-C386 (15) 11.15 5.50

Centenary of the birth of Lord Baden-Powell, founder of the Boy Scouts.
For surcharge see #C754.

Pres. Luis A. Somoza — A76

Portrait in Dark Brown

1957, July 2 ***Perf. 14x13½***

783 A76 10c brt red .35 .25
784 A76 15c deep blue .35 .25
785 A76 35c rose violet .35 .25
786 A76 50c brown .40 .25
787 A76 75c gray green .90 .55
Nos. 783-787,C387-C391 (10) 8.40 5.55

President Luis A. Somoza.

Leon Cathedral A77

Bishop Pereira y Castellon A78

Designs: 5c, Managua Cathedral. 15c, Archbishop Lezcano y Ortega. 50c, De la Merced Church, Granada. 1cor, Father Mariano Dubon.

Centers in Olive Gray

1957, July 12 ***Perf. 13½x14, 14x13½***

788 A77 5c dull green .35 .25
789 A78 10c dk purple .35 .25
790 A78 15c dk blue .40 .25
791 A77 20c dk brown .50 .25
792 A77 50c dk slate grn .55 .25
793 A78 1cor dk violet 1.40 .30
Nos. 788-793,C392-C397 (12) 10.20 3.60

Honoring the Catholic Church in Nicaragua.

M. S. Honduras — A79

5c, Gen. Anastasio Somoza & freighter. 6c, M. S. Guatemala. 10c, M. S. Salvador. 15c, Ship between globes. 50c, Globes & ship.

1957, Oct. 15 **Litho.** ***Perf. 14***

794 A79 4c green, bl & blk .65 .25
795 A79 5c multi .65 .25
796 A79 6c red, bl & blk .65 .25
797 A79 10c brn, bl grn & blk .65 .25
798 A79 15c dk car, ultra & ol brn .65 .25
799 A79 50c violet, bl & mar 1.90 .75
Nos. 794-799,C398-C403 (12) 14.15 6.10

Issued to honor Nicaragua's Merchant Marine. For surcharge see No. C691.

Melvin Jones and Lions Emblem — A80

Designs: 5c, Arms of Central American Republics. 20c, Dr. Teodoro A. Arias. 50c, Edward G. Barry. 75c, Motto and emblem. 1.50 cor, Map of Central America.

Emblem in Yellow, Red and Blue

1958, May 8 **Unwmk.** ***Perf. 14***

800 A80 5c blue & multi .40 .25
801 A80 10c blue & org .40 .25
802 A80 20c blue & olive .40 .25
803 A80 50c blue & lilac .40 .25
804 A80 75c blue & pink .55 .25
805 A80 1.50cor blue, gray ol & sal .90 .45
a. Souvenir sheet of 6, #800-805 4.50 2.50
Nos. 800-805,C410-C415 (12) 9.90 4.70

17th convention of Lions Intl. of Central America, May, 1958.
For overprnts and surchargse see Nos. 1104H, C686.

St. Jean Baptiste De La Salle — A81

Christian Brothers: 5c, Arms of La Salle. 10c, School, Managua, horiz. 20c, Bro. Carlos. 50c, Bro. Antonio. 75c, Bro. Julio. 1cor, Bro. Argeo.

1958, July 13 **Photo.** ***Perf. 14***

806 A81 5c car, bl & yel .35 .25
807 A81 10c emer, blk & ultra .35 .25
808 A81 15c red brn, bis & blk .35 .25
809 A81 20c car, bis & blk .35 .25
810 A81 50c org, bis & brn blk .35 .25
811 A81 75c bl, lt grn & dk brn .35 .25
812 A81 1cor vio, bis & grnsh blk .55 .30
Nos. 806-812,C416-C423 (15) 13.55 5.65

For surcharges see Nos. C539A, C755-C756.

UN Emblem and Globe — A82

15c, UNESCO building. 25c, 45c, "UNESCO." 40c, UNESCO building and Eiffel tower.

1958, Dec. 15 **Litho.** ***Perf. 11½***

813 A82 10c brt pink & bl .40 .25
814 A82 15c blue & brt pink .40 .25
815 A82 25c green & brn .40 .25
816 A82 40c red org & blk .40 .25
817 A82 45c dk bl & rose lil .40 .25
818 A82 50c brown & grn .40 .25
a. Miniature sheet of 6, #813-818 2.00 .75
Nos. 813-818,C424-C429 (12) 11.35 5.00

UNESCO Headquarters in Paris opening, Nov. 3.

Pope John XXIII and Cardinal Spellman — A83

Designs: 10c, Spellman coat of arms. 15c, Cardinal Spellman. 20c, Human rosary and Cardinal, horiz. 25c, Cardinal with Ruben Dario order.

1959, Nov. 26 **Unwmk.** ***Perf. 12½***

819 A83 5c grnsh bl & brn .40 .25
820 A83 10c yel, bl & car .40 .25
821 A83 15c dk grn, blk & dk car .40 .25
822 A83 20c yel, dk bl & grn .40 .25
823 A83 25c ultra, vio & mag .40 .25
a. Min. sheet of 5, #819-823, perf. or imperf. 4.00 2.00
Nos. 819-823,C430-C436 (12) 8.95 4.65

Cardinal Spellman's visit to Managua, Feb. 1958.
For surcharges see #C638, C747, C752.

Abraham Lincoln — A84

Center in Black

1960, Jan. **Engr.** ***Perf. 13x13½***

824 A84 5c car ver .45 .30
825 A84 10c green .45 .30
826 A84 15c dp orange .45 .30
827 A84 1cor plum .45 .30
828 A84 2cor ultra .45 .30
a. Souv. sheet of 5, #824-828, imperf. 1.50 1.00
Nos. 824-828,C437-C442 (11) 8.65 4.60

150th anniv. of the birth of Abraham Lincoln.
For surcharges see Nos. C500, C539, C637, C680, C753.

Nos. 824-828 Overprinted in Red

1960, Sept. 19 **Center in Black**

829 A84 5c deep carmine .40 .30
830 A84 10c green .40 .30
831 A84 15c deep orange .40 .30
832 A84 1cor plum .40 .30
833 A84 2cor ultra .65 .40
Nos. 829-833,C446-C451 (11) 12.80 6.10

Issued for the Red Cross to aid earthquake victims in Chile.

Gen. Tomas Martinez and Pres. Luis A. Somoza — A85

5c, Official decrees. 10c, Two envelopes.

Perf. 13½

1961, Aug. 29 **Unwmk.** **Litho.**

834 A85 5c grnsh bl & lt brn .80 .40
835 A85 10c green & lt brn .80 .40
836 A85 15c pink & brn .80 .40
Nos. 834-836 (3) 2.40 1.20

Cent. (in 1960) of the postal rates regulation.

Arms of Nueva Segovia — A86

Coats of Arms: 3c, León. 4c, Managua. 5c, Granada. 6c, Rivas.

Arms in Original Colors; Black Inscriptions

1962, Nov. 22 ***Perf. 12½x13***

837 A86 2c pink .45 .40
838 A86 3c lt blue .45 .40
839 A86 4c pale lilac .45 .40
840 A86 5c yellow .45 .40
841 A86 6c buff .45 .40
Nos. 837-841,C510-C514 (10) 7.20 4.60

For surcharge see #854.

No. RA73 Overprinted in Red: "CORREOS"

1964 **Photo.** ***Perf. 11½***

842 PT13 5c gray, red & org .75 .40
a. Inverted overprint

Nos. RA66-RA75 Overprinted

1965 **Photo.** ***Perf. 11½***

Orchids in Natural Colors

843 PT13 5c pale lilac & grn 1.10 .45
844 PT13 5c yellow & grn 1.10 .45
845 PT13 5c pink & grn 1.10 .45
846 PT13 5c pale vio & grn 1.10 .45
847 PT13 5c lt grnsh bl & red 1.10 .45
848 PT13 5c buff & lil 1.10 .45
849 PT13 5c yel grn & brn 1.10 .45
850 PT13 5c gray & red 1.10 .45
851 PT13 5c lt blue & dk bl 1.10 .45
852 PT13 5c lt green & brn 1.10 .45
Nos. 843-852 (10) 11.00 4.50

Seventh Central American Scout Camporee at El Coyotete. This overprint was also applied to each stamp on souvenir sheet No. C386a. Value, $15.
Use of Nos. 843-852 for postage was authorized by official decree.

Nos. 746 and 841 Surcharged with New Value and "RESELLO"

1968, May **Engr.** ***Perf. 12½***

853 A68 5c on 6c dp ultra & gray blk 1.00 1.00

Litho. ***Perf. 12½x13***

854 A86 5c on 6c multi 1.00 1.00

Nos. RA66-RA67, RA69 and RA71 Overprinted

1969 **Photo.** ***Perf. 11½***

Orchids in Natural Colors

855 PT13 5c pale lil & grn 1.25 .75
856 PT13 5c yellow & grn 1.25 .75
857 PT13 5c pale vio & grn 1.25 .75
858 PT13 5c buff & lilac 1.25 .75
Nos. 855-858 (4) 5.00 3.00

Nos. RA66-RA75 Overprinted

1969 **Photo.** ***Perf. 11½***

Orchids in Natural Colors

859 PT13 5c pale lil & grn 1.00 .45
860 PT13 5c yellow & grn 1.00 .45
861 PT13 5c pink & grn 1.00 .45
862 PT13 5c pale vio & grn 1.00 .45
863 PT13 5c lt grnsh bl & red 1.00 .45
864 PT13 5c buff & lil 1.00 .45
865 PT13 5c yel grn & brn 1.00 .45
866 PT13 5c gray & red 1.00 .45
867 PT13 5c lt & dk blue 1.00 .45
868 PT13 5c lt grn & brn 1.00 .45
Nos. 859-868 (10) 10.00 4.50

International Labor Organization, 50th anniv.

Pelé, Brazil — A87

Soccer Players: 10c, Ferenc Puskás, Hungary. 15c, Sir Stanley Matthews, England. 40c, Alfredo di Stefano, Argentina. 2cor, Giacinto Facchetti, Italy. 3cor, Lev Yashin, USSR. 5cor, Franz Beckenbauer, West Germany.

1970, May 11 Litho. *Perf. 13½*

869 A87	5c multicolored	.40	.40
870 A87	10c multicolored	.40	.40
871 A87	15c multicolored	.40	.40
872 A87	40c multicolored	.40	.40
873 A87	2cor multicolored	1.25	.75
874 A87	3cor multicolored	1.60	.90
875 A87	5cor multicolored	2.40	1.25
	Nos. 869-875,C712-C716 (12)	15.55	10.15

Issued to honor the winners of the 1970 poll for the International Soccer Hall of Fame. Names of players and their achievements printed in black on back of stamps.

For surcharges and overprint see Nos. 899-900, C786-C788.

No. 766 Surcharged & Overprinted in Black

1971, Mar. Photo. *Perf. 11*

876 A71 30c on 90c blk & gray *210.00 100.00*

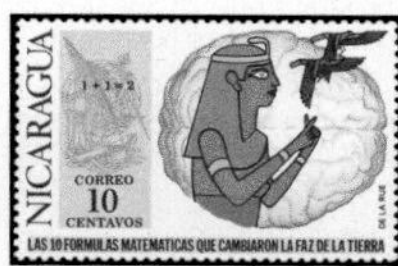
Egyptian Using Fingers to Count — A88

Symbolic Designs of Scientific Formulas: 15c, Newton's law (gravity). 20c, Einstein's theory (relativity). 1cor, Tsiolkovski's law (speed of rockets). 2cor, Maxwell's law (electromagnetism).

1971, May 15 Litho. *Perf. 13½*

877 A88	10c lt bl & multi	.95	.40
878 A88	15c lt bl & multi	.95	.40
879 A88	20c lt bl & multi	1.10	.50
880 A88	1cor lt bl & multi	3.50	1.10
881 A88	2cor lt bl & multi	7.75	2.25
	Nos. 877-881,C761-C765 (10)	26.50	9.75

Mathematical equations which changed the world. On the back of each stamp is a descriptive paragraph.

See Nos. C761-C765.

Symbols of Civilization, Peace Emblem with Globe — A89

1971, Sept. 6 Litho. *Perf. 14*

882 A89	10c blk & bl	.45	.40
883 A89	15c vio bl, bl & blk	.45	.40
884 A89	20c brn bl & blk	.45	.40
885 A89	40c emer, bl & blk	.55	.40
886 A89	50c mag, bl & blk	.80	.45
887 A89	80c org, bl & blk	1.10	.60
888 A89	1cor ol, bl & blk	1.40	.75
889 A89	2cor vio, bl & blk	3.00	1.75
	Nos. 882-889 (8)	8.20	5.15

"Is there a formula for peace?" issue.

Moses with Tablets of the Law, by Rembrandt — A90

The Ten Commandments (Paintings): 15c, Moses and the Burning Bush, by Botticelli (I). 20c, Jephthah's Daughter, by Degas, (II), horiz. 30c, St. Vincent Ferrer Preaching in Verona, by Domenico Morone (III). 35c, The Nakedness of Noah, by Michelangelo (IV), horiz. 40c, Cain and Abel, by Francesco Trevisani (V), horiz. 50c, Potiphar's wife, by Rembrandt (VI). 60c, Isaac Blessing Jacob, by Gerbrand van den Eeckhout (VII), horiz. 75c, Susanna and the Elders, by Rubens (VIII), horiz.

1971, Nov. 1 *Perf. 11*

890 A90	10c yel brn & multi	.35	.35
891 A90	15c yel brn & multi	.35	.35
892 A90	20c yel brn & multi	.35	.35
893 A90	30c yel brn & multi	.35	.35
894 A90	35c yel brn & multi	.35	.35
895 A90	40c yel brn & multi	.35	.35
896 A90	50c yel brn & multi	.45	.45
897 A90	60c yel brn & multi	.85	.65
898 A90	75c yel brn & multi	1.80	1.00
	Nos. 890-898,C776-C777 (11)	10.45	5.80

Descriptive inscriptions printed in gray on back of stamps.

Nos. 873-874 Surcharged

1972, Mar. 20 Litho. *Perf. 13½*

899 A87	40c on 2cor multi	.40	.25
900 A87	50c on 3cor multi	.45	.25
	Nos. 899-900,C786-C788 (5)	4.40	2.70

20th Olympic Games, Munich, 8/26-9/10.

Nos. RA66-RA69, RA71-RA74 Overprinted in Blue

1972, July 29 Photo. *Perf. 11½*

Granite Paper

901 PT13	5c (#RA66)	1.10	.40
902 PT13	5c (#RA67)	1.10	.40
903 PT13	5c (#RA68)	1.10	.40
904 PT13	5c (#RA69)	1.10	.40
905 PT13	5c (#RA71)	1.10	.40
906 PT13	5c (#RA72)	1.10	.40
907 PT13	5c (#RA73)	1.10	.40
908 PT13	5c (#RA74)	1.10	.40
	Nos. 901-908 (8)	8.80	3.20

Gown by Givenchy, Paris — A91

1973, July 26 Litho. *Perf. 13½*

909 A91	1cor shown	.50	.25
910 A91	2cor Hartnell, London	.80	.50
911 A91	5cor Balmain, Paris	2.00	1.20
	Nos. 909-911,C839-C844 (9)	8.10	3.45

Gowns by famous designers, modeled by Nicaraguan women. Inscriptions on back printed on top of gum give description of gown in Spanish and English.

Nos. 909-911 in perf. 11, see No. C844a.

Christmas — A92

2c, 5c, Virginia O'Hanlon writing letter, father. 3c, 15c, letter. 4c, 20c, Virginia, father reading letter.

1973, Nov. 15 Litho. *Perf. 15*

912 A92	2c multicolored	.40	.25
913 A92	3c multicolored	.40	.25
914 A92	4c multicolored	.40	.25
915 A92	5c multicolored	.40	.25
916 A92	15c multicolored	.40	.25
917 A92	20c multicolored	.40	.25
	Nos. 912-917,C846-C848 (9)	7.95	4.35

Sir Winston Churchill (1874-1965) — A93

Designs: 2c, Churchill speaking. 3c, Military planning. 4c, Cigar, lamp. 5c, Churchill with Roosevert and Stalin. 10c, Churchill walking ashore from landing craft.

1974, Apr. 30 *Perf. 14½*

918 A93	2c multicolored	.40	.25
919 A93	3c multicolored	.40	.25
920 A93	4c multicolored	.40	.25
921 A93	5c multicolored	.40	.25
922 A93	10c multicolored	.40	.25
	Nos. 918-922,C849-C850 (7)	7.85	4.40

World Cup Soccer Championships, Munich — A94

Scenes from previous World Cup Championships with flags and scores of finalists.

1974, May 8 *Perf. 14½*

923 A94	1c 1930	.40	.25
924 A94	2c 1934	.40	.25
925 A94	3c 1938	.40	.25
926 A94	4c 1950	.40	.25
927 A94	5c 1954	.40	.25
928 A94	10c 1958	.40	.25
929 A94	15c 1962	.40	.25
930 A94	20c 1966	.40	.25
931 A94	25c 1970	.40	.25
	Nos. 923-931,C853 (10)	9.85	8.50

For overprint see No. C856.

A95

Wild Flowers and Cacti: 2c, Hollyhocks. 3c, Paguira insignis. 4c, Morning glory. 5c, Pereschia autumnalis. 10c, Cultivated morning glory. 15c, Hibiscus. 20c, Pagoda tree blossoms.

1974, June 11 Litho. *Perf. 14*

932 A95	2c grn & multi	.40	.25
933 A95	3c grn & multi	.40	.25
934 A95	4c grn & multi	.40	.25
935 A95	5c grn & multi	.40	.25
936 A95	10c grn & multi	.40	.25
937 A95	15c grn & multi	.40	.25
938 A95	20c grn & multi	.40	.25
	Nos. 932-938,C854-C855 (9)	9.30	5.25

Nicaraguan Stamps — A96

1974, July 10 *Perf. 14½*

939 A96	2c No. 670	.35	.25
940 A96	3c No. 669	.35	.25
941 A96	4c No. C110, horiz.	.35	.25
942 A96	5c No. 667	.35	.25
943 A96	10c No. 666	.35	.25
944 A96	20c No. 665	.35	.25
	Nos. 939-944,C855A-C855C (9)	8.90	5.40

UPU, Cent.

Four-toed Anteater — A97

Designs: 2c, Puma. 3c, Raccoon. 4c, Ocelot. 5c, Kinkajou. 10c, Coypu. 15c, Peccary. 20c, Tapir.

1974, Sept. 10 Litho. *Perf. 14½*

946 A97	1c multi	.35	.25
947 A97	2c multi	.35	.25
948 A97	3c multi	.35	.25
949 A97	4c multi	.35	.25
950 A97	5c multi	.35	.25
951 A97	10c multi	.35	.25
952 A97	15c multi	.35	.25
953 A97	20c multi	.35	.25
	Nos. 946-953,C857-C858 (10)	8.55	5.50

Wild animals from San Diego and London Zoos.

Prophet Zacharias, by Michelangelo — A98

Works of Michelangelo: 2c, The Last Judgment. 3c, The Creation of Adam, horiz. 4c, Sistine Chapel. 5c, Moses. 10c, Mouscron Madonna. 15c, David. 20c, Doni Madonna.

1974, Dec. 15

954 A98	1c dp rose & multi	.60	.30
955 A98	2c yellow & multi	.60	.30
956 A98	3c sal & multi	.60	.30
957 A98	4c blue & multi	.60	.30
958 A98	5c tan & multi	.60	.30
959 A98	10c multicolored	.60	.30
960 A98	15c multicolored	.60	.30
961 A98	20c blue & multi	.60	.30
	Nos. 954-961,C859-C862 (12)	16.50	7.65

Christmas 1974 and 500th birth anniversary of Michelangelo Buonarroti (1475-1564), Italian painter, sculptor and architect.

Giovanni Martinelli, Othello — A99

Opera Singers and Scores: 2c, Tito Gobbi, Simone Boccanegra. 3c, Lotte Lehmann, Der Rosenkavalier. 4c, Lauritz Melchior, Parsifal. 5c, Nellie Melba, La Traviata. 15c, Jussi Bjoerling, La Bohème. 20c, Birgit Nilsson, Turandot.

1975, Jan. 22 *Perf. 14x13½*

962 A99	1c rose lil & multi	.45	.25
963 A99	2c brt bl & multi	.45	.25
964 A99	3c yel & multi	.45	.25
965 A99	4c dl bl & multi	.45	.25
966 A99	5c org & multi	.45	.25
967 A99	15c lake & multi	.45	.25
968 A99	20c gray & multi	.45	.25
	Nos. 962-968,C863-C870 (15)	13.85	5.20

Famous opera singers.

Jesus Condemned — A100

Stations of the Cross: 2c, Jesus Carries the Cross. 3c, Jesus falls the first time. 4c, Jesus meets his mother. 5c, Simon of Cyrene carries the Cross. 15c, St. Veronica wipes Jesus' face. 20c, Jesus falls the second time. 25c,

Jesus meets the women of Jerusalem. 35c, Jesus falls the third time. Designs from Leon Cathedral.

1975, Mar. 20 *Perf. 14½*

969 A100 1c ultra & multi .50 .25
970 A100 2c ultra & multi .50 .25
971 A100 3c ultra & multi .50 .25
972 A100 4c ultra & multi .50 .25
973 A100 5c ultra & multi .50 .25
974 A100 15c ultra & multi .50 .25
975 A100 20c ultra & multi .50 .25
976 A100 25c ultra & multi .50 .25
977 A100 35c ultra & multi .50 .25
Nos. 969-977,C871-C875 (14) 11.20 4.65

Easter 1975.

The Spirit of 76, by Archibald M. Willard — A101

Designs: 2c, Pitt Addressing Parliament, by K. A. Hickel. 3c, The Midnight Ride of Paul Revere, horiz. 4c, Statue of George III Demolished, by W. Walcutt, horiz. 5c, Boston Massacre. 10c, Colonial coin and seal, horiz. 15c, Boston Tea Party, horiz. 20c, Thomas Jefferson, by Rembrandt Peale. 25c, Benjamin Franklin, by Charles Willson Peale. 30c, Signing Declaration of Independence, by John Trumbull, horiz. 35c, Surrender of Cornwallis, by Trumbull, horiz.

1975, Apr. 16 *Perf. 14*

978 A101 1c buff & multi .40 .25
979 A101 2c buff & multi .30 .25
980 A101 3c buff & multi .40 .25
981 A101 4c buff & multi .40 .25
982 A101 5c buff & multi .40 .25
983 A101 10c buff & multi .40 .25
984 A101 15c buff & multi .40 .25
985 A101 20c buff & multi .40 .25
986 A101 25c buff & multi .40 .25
987 A101 30c buff & multi .40 .25
988 A101 35c buff & multi .40 .25
Nos. 978-988,C876-C879 (15) 13.40 7.15

American Bicentennial. See Nos. C876-C879.

Scouts Saluting Flag, Scout Emblems A102

2c, Two-men canoe. 3c, Scouts of various races shaking hands. 4c, Scout cooking. 5c, Entrance to Camp Nicaragua. 20c, Group discussion.

1975, Aug. 15 *Perf. 14½*

989 A102 1c multi .40 .25
990 A102 2c multi .40 .25
991 A102 3c multi .40 .25
992 A102 4c multi .40 .25
993 A102 5c multi .40 .25
994 A102 20c multi .40 .25
Nos. 989-994,C880-C883 (10) 8.45 4.30

Nordjamb 75, 14th World Boy Scout Jamboree, Lillehammer, Norway, July 29-Aug. 7.

Pres. Somoza, Map and Arms of Nicaragua — A103

1975, Sept. 10 *Perf. 14*

995 A103 20c multi .55 .30
996 A103 40c org & multi .55 .30
Nos. 995-996,C884-C886 (5) 13.70 6.10

Reelection of Pres. Anastasio Somoza D.

King's College Choir, Cambridge A104

Famous Choirs: 2c, Einsiedeln Abbey. 3c, Regensburg. 4c, Vienna Choir Boys. 5c, Sistine Chapel. 15c, Westminster Cathedral. 20c, Mormon Tabernacle.

1975, Nov. 15 *Perf. 14½*

997 A104 1c silver & multi .45 .25
998 A104 2c silver & multi .45 .25
999 A104 3c silver & multi .45 .25
1000 A104 4c silver & multi .45 .25
1001 A104 5c silver & multi .45 .25
1002 A104 15c silver & multi .45 .25
1003 A104 20c silver & multi .45 .25
Nos. 997-1003,C887-C890 (11) 8.75 3.90

Christmas 1975.

The Chess Players, by Ludovico Carracci — A105

History of Chess: 2c, Arabs Playing Chess, by Delacroix. 3c, Cardinals Playing Chess, by Victor Marais-Milton. 4c, Albrecht V of Bavaria and Anne of Austria Playing Chess, by Hans Muelich, vert. 5c, Chess Players, Persian manuscript, 14th century. 10c, Origin of Chess, Indian miniature, 17th century. 15c, Napoleon Playing Chess at Schönbrunn, by Antoni Uniechowski, vert. 20c, The Chess Game, by J. E. Hummel.

1976, Jan. 8 *Perf. 14½*

1004 A105 1c brn & multi .40 .25
1005 A105 2c lt vio & multi .40 .25
1006 A105 3c ocher & multi .40 .25
1007 A105 4c multi .40 .25
1008 A105 5c multi .40 .25
1009 A105 10c multi .40 .25
1010 A105 15c blue & multi .40 .25
1011 A105 20c ocher & multi .40 .25
Nos. 1004-1011,C891-C893 (11) 9.70 5.00

Olympic Rings, Danish Crew A107

Winners, Rowing and Sculling Events: 2c, East Germany, 1972. 3c, Italy, 1968. 4c, Great Britain, 1936. 5c, France, 1952. 35c, US, 1920, vert.

1976, Sept. 7 **Litho.** *Perf. 14*

1022 A107 1c blue & multi .30 .25
1023 A107 2c blue & multi .30 .25
1024 A107 3c blue & multi .30 .25
1025 A107 4c blue & multi .30 .25
1026 A107 5c blue & multi .30 .25
1027 A107 35c blue & multi .30 .25
Nos. 1022-1027,C902-C905 (10) 13.85 8.25

Candlelight A108

#1028, The Smoke Signal, by Frederic Remington. #1029, Space Signal Monitoring Center. #1031, Edison's laboratory & light bulb. #1032, Agriculture, 1776. #1033, Agriculture, 1976. #1034, Harvard College, 1726. #1035, Harvard University, 1976. #1036, Horse-drawn carriage. #1037, Boeing 747.

1976, May 25 **Litho.** *Perf. 13½*

1028 A108 1c gray & multi .25 .25
1029 A108 1c gray & multi .25 .25
a. Pair, #1028-1029 .60 .45
1030 A108 2c gray & multi .25 .25
1031 A108 2c gray & multi .25 .25
a. Pair, #1030-1031 .60 .45
1032 A108 3c gray & multi .25 .25
1033 A108 3c gray & multi .25 .25
a. Pair, #1032-1033 .60 .45
1034 A108 4c gray & multi .25 .25
1035 A108 4c gray & multi .25 .25
a. Pair, #1034-1035 .60 .45
1036 A108 5c gray & multi .25 .25
1037 A108 5c gray & multi .25 .25
a. Pair, #1036-1037 .60 .45
Nos. 1028-1037,C907-C912 (16) 5.60 4.80

American Bicentennial, 200 years of progress.

Mauritius No. 2 — A109

Rare Stamps: 2c, Western Australia #3a. 3c, Mauritius #1. 4c, Jamaica #83a. 5c, US #C3a. 10c, Basel #3L1. 25c, Canada #387a.

1976, Dec. *Perf. 14*

1038 A109 1c multi .40 .25
1039 A109 2c multi .40 .25
1040 A109 3c multi .40 .25
1041 A109 4c multi .40 .25
1042 A109 5c multi .40 .25
1043 A109 10c multi .40 .25
1044 A109 25c multi .40 .25
Nos. 1038-1044,C913-C917 (12) 10.30 4.40

Back inscriptions printed on top of gum describe illustrated stamp.

Zeppelin in Flight — A110

1c, Zeppelin in hangar. 3c, Giffard's dirigible airship, 1852. 4c, Zeppelin on raising stilts coming out of hangar. 5c, Zeppelin ready for take-off.

1977, Oct. 31 **Litho.** *Perf. 14½*

1045 A110 1c multi .40 .25
1046 A110 2c multi .40 .25
1047 A110 3c multi .40 .25
1048 A110 4c multi .40 .25
1049 A110 5c multi .40 .25
Nos. 1045-1049,C921-C924 (9) 10.95 6.00

75th anniversary of Zeppelin.

Lindbergh, Map of Nicaragua A111

2c, Spirit of St. Louis, map of Nicaragua. 3c, Lindbergh, vert. 4c, Spirit of St. Louis & NYC-Paris route. 5c, Lindbergh & Spirit of St. Louis. 20c, Lindbergh, NYC-Paris route & plane.

1977, Nov. 30

1050 A111 1c multi .40 .25
1051 A111 2c multi .40 .25
1052 A111 3c multi .40 .25
1053 A111 4c multi .40 .25
1054 A111 5c multi .40 .25
1055 A111 20c multi .40 .25
Nos. 1050-1055,C926-C929 (10) 11.00 4.95

Charles A. Lindbergh's solo transatlantic flight from NYC to Paris, 50th anniv.

Nutcracker Suite — A112

1c, Christmas party. 2c, Dancing dolls. 3c, Clara and Snowflakes. 4c, Snowflake and prince. 5c, Snowflake dance. 15c, Sugarplum fairy and prince. 40c, Waltz of the flowers. 90c, Chinese tea dance. 1cor, Bonbonnière. 10cor, Arabian coffee dance.

1977, Dec. 12

1056 A112 1c multi .40 .25
1057 A112 2c multi .40 .25
1058 A112 3c multi .40 .25
1059 A112 4c multi .40 .25
1060 A112 5c multi .40 .25
1061 A112 15c multi .40 .25
1062 A112 40c multi .40 .25
1063 A112 90c multi .40 .25
1064 A112 1cor multi .60 .30
1065 A112 10cor multi 6.00 3.00
Nos. 1056-1065 (10) 9.80 5.30

Christmas 1977. See No. C931.

Mr. and Mrs. Andrews, by Gainsborough A113

Paintings: 2c, Giovanna Bacelli, by Gainsborough. 3c, Blue Boy by Gainsborough. 4c, Francis I, by Titian. 5c, Charles V in Battle of Muhlberg, by Titian. 25c, Sacred Love, by Titian.

1978, Jan. 11 **Litho.** *Perf. 14½*

1066 A113 1c multi .35 .25
1067 A113 2c multi .35 .25
1068 A113 3c multi .35 .25
1069 A113 4c multi .35 .25
1070 A113 5c multi .35 .25
1071 A113 25c multi .35 .25
Nos. 1066-1071,C932-C933 (8) 10.10 5.75

Thomas Gainsborough (1727-1788), 250th birth anniv.; Titian (1477-1576), 500th birth anniv.

Gothic Portal, Lower Church, Assisi — A114

Designs: 2c, St. Francis preaching to the birds. 3c, St. Francis, painting. 4c, St. Francis and Franciscan saints, 15th century tapestry. 5c, Portiuncola, cell of St. Francis, now in church of St. Mary of the Angels, Assisi. 15c, Blessing of St. Francis for Brother Leo (parchment). 25c, Stained-glass window, Upper Church of St. Francis, Assisi.

1978, Feb. 23 **Litho.** *Perf. 14½*

1072 A114 1c red & multi .40 .25
1073 A114 2c brt grn & multi .40 .25
1074 A114 3c bl grn & multi .40 .25
1075 A114 4c ultra & multi .40 .25
1076 A114 5c rose & multi .40 .25
1077 A114 15c yel & multi .40 .25
1078 A114 25c ocher & multi .40 .25
Nos. 1072-1078,C935-C936 (9) 8.15 3.75

St. Francis of Assisi (1182-1266), 750th anniversary of his canonization, and in honor of Our Lady of the Immaculate Conception, patron saint of Nicaragua.

Passenger and Freight Locomotives A115

Locomotives: 2c, Lightweight freight. 3c, American. 4c, Heavy freight Baldwin. 5c, Light freight and passenger Baldwin. 15c, Presidential coach.

1978, Apr. 7 **Litho.** *Perf. 14½*

1079 A115 1c lil & multi .30 .25
1080 A115 2c rose lil & multi .30 .25
1081 A115 3c lt bl & multi .30 .25
1082 A115 4c ol & multi .45 .25
1083 A115 5c yel & multi .45 .25
1084 A115 15c dp org & multi .60 .25
Nos. 1079-1084,C938-C940 (9) 11.25 5.90

Centenary of Nicaraguan railroads.

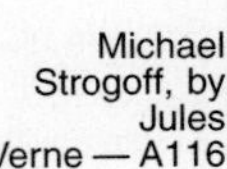

Michael Strogoff, by Jules Verne — A116

Jules Verne Books: 2c, The Mysterious Island. 3c, Journey to the Center of the Earth (battle of the sea monsters). 4c, Five Weeks in a Balloon.

1978, Aug. **Litho.** *Perf. 14½*

1085 A116 1c multi .35 .25
1086 A116 2c multi .35 .25
1087 A116 3c multi .35 .25
1088 A116 4c multi .35 .25
Nos. 1085-1088,C942-C943 (6) 7.30 4.35

Jules Verne (1828-1905), science fiction writer.

Montgolfier Balloon — A117

1c, Icarus. 3c, Wright Brothers' Flyer A. 4c, Orville Wright at control of Flyer, 1908.

Perf. 14½, horiz.

1978, Sept. 29 **Litho.**

1089 A117 1c multi, horiz. .40 .25
1090 A117 2c multi .40 .25
1091 A117 3c multi, horiz. .40 .25
1092 A117 4c multi .40 .25
Nos. 1089-1092,C945-C946 (6) 6.00 3.30

History of aviation & 75th anniv. of 1st powered flight.

Ernst Ocwirk and Alfredo Di Stefano — A118

Soccer Players: 25c, Ralf Edstroem and Oswaldo Piazza.

1978, Oct. 25 **Litho.** ***Perf. 13½x14***

1093 A118 20c multicolored .40 .25
1094 A118 25c multicolored .40 .25
Nos. 1093-1094,C948-C949 (4) 4.20 2.50

11th World Soccer Cup Championship, Argentina, June 1-25. See No. C950.

St. Peter, by Goya — A119

Paintings: 15c, St. Gregory, by Goya.

1978, Dec. 12 **Litho.** ***Perf. 13½x14***

1095 A119 10c multi .35 .25
1096 A119 15c multi .35 .25
Nos. 1095-1096,C951-C952 (4) 5.35 2.95

Christmas 1978. See No. C953.

San Cristobal Volcano and Map — A120

Designs: No. 1098, Lake Cosiguina. No. 1099, Telica Volcano. No. 1100, Lake Jiloa.

1978, Dec. 29 ***Perf. 14x13½***

1097 A120 5c multi .40 .25
1098 A120 5c multi .40 .25
a. Pair, #1097-1098 .95 .50
1099 A120 20c multi .40 .25
1100 A120 20c multi .40 .25
a. Pair, #1099-1100 .95 .50
Nos. 1097-1100,C954-C961 (12) 7.80 5.30

Volcanos, lakes and their locations.

Overprinted in Silver or Red — A120a

Overprint reads: 1979 / ANO DE LA LIBERACION / OLYMPIC RINGS / PARTICIPACION NICARAGUA / OLIMPIADAS 1980 / Litografia Nacional, Portugal symbol

International Year of the Child: 20c, Carousel. 90c, Playing soccer. 2cor, Collecting stamps. 2.20cor, Playing with model train, plane. 10cor, Playing baseball.

1980, Apr. 7 **Litho.** ***Perf. 13¾x14¼***

Overprinted in Silver

1101 A120a 20c multi *10.00 10.00*
e. Red ovpt. *10.00 10.00*
1101A A120a 90c multi *10.00 10.00*
f. Red ovpt. *10.00 10.00*
1101B A120a 2cor multi *10.00 10.00*
g. Red ovpt. *10.00 10.00*
1101C A120a 2.20cor multi *10.00 10.00*
h. Red ovpt. *10.00 10.00*
1101D A120a 10cor multi *10.00 10.00*
i. Red ovpt. *10.00 10.00*
Nos. 1101-1101D (5) *50.00 50.00*

Overprinted for Year of Liberation and 1980 Olympic Games.

Nos. 1101-1101D, 1101e-1101i were not issued without overprint.

Nos. 1101A-1101D are airmail.

Overprinted in Red or Silver — A120b

Overprint reads like Nos. 1101-1101D

Designs: 20c, North American Indian messenger. 35c, Post rider on horse. 1cor, Prestamp cover to London, horiz. 1.80cor, Sir Rowland Hill (1795-1897), postal reformer. 2.20cor, Block of six of Great Britain #1, horiz. 5cor, Nicaragua Zeppelin cover to Germany, horiz.

1980, Apr. 7 **Litho.** ***Perf. 14½***

Overprinted in Red

1102 A120b 20c multi *11.00 11.00*
f. Silver overprint *11.00 11.00*
1102A A120b 35c multi *11.00 11.00*
g. Silver overprint *11.00 11.00*
1102B A120b 1cor multi *11.00 11.00*
h. Silver overprint *11.00 11.00*
1102C A120b 1.80cor multi *11.00 11.00*
i. Silver overprint *11.00 11.00*
1102D A120b 2.20cor multi *11.00 11.00*
j. Silver overprint *11.00 11.00*
1102E A120b 5cor multi *11.00 11.00*
k. Silver overprint *11.00 11.00*
Nos. 1102-1102E (6) *66.00 66.00*

Overprinted for Year of Liberation and 1980 Olympic Games. Nos. 1102-1102E, 1102f-1102k were not issued without overprint. Nos. 1102C-1102E are airmail.

Stamps of Type A120b With Different Overprints

Overprinted in Red — A120c

Overprinted in Silver — A120d

Designs of unoverprinted stamps as Nos. 1102-1102E.

1980 **Litho.** ***Perf. 14½***

Overprinted in Red

1102L A120c 20c multi — —
1102M A120c 35c multi — —
1102N A120c 1cor multi — —

Overprinted in Silver

1102O A120d 1.80cor multi — —
1102P A120d 2.20cor multi — —
1102Q A120d 5cor multi — —

Issued: Nos. 1102L-1102Q, 9/30/80. Nos. 1102L-1102Q were not issued without overprint. Nos. 1102O-1102Q are airmail.

Overprinted in Silver or Red — A120c

Overprint reads: 1979 / ANO DE LA LIBERACION / OLYMPIC RINGS / PARTICIPACION NICARAGUA / OLIMPIADAS 1980 / Litografia Nacional, Portugal symbol

Albert Einstein and: 5c, Albert Schweitzer. 10c, Theory of Relativity; 15c, Trylon & Perisphere, NY World's Fair, 1939. 20c, J. Robert Oppenheimer. 25c, Wailing Wall, Jerusalem. 1cor, Nobel Prize Medal. 2.75cor, Spaceship, radio telescope antenna. 10cor, Mohandas K. Gandhi and Taj Mahal.

1980, Apr. 7 **Litho.** ***Perf. 14¾***

Overprinted in Silver

1103 A120c 5c multi
h. Red ovpt. *5.75 5.75*
1103A A120c 10c multi — —
i. Red ovpt. *5.75 5.75*
1103B A120c 15c multi
j. Red ovpt. *5.75 5.75*
1103C A120c 20c multi
k. Red ovpt. *5.75 5.75*
1103D A120c 25c multi
l. Red ovpt. *5.75 5.75*
1103E A120c 1cor multi
m. Red ovpt. *5.75 5.75*
1103F A120c 2.75cor multi
n. Red ovpt. *5.75 5.75*
Nos. 1103-1103F (7) *5.50 5.50*

Overprinted in Red

1103G A120c 10cor multi — —

Overprinted for Intl. Year of the Child, Year of Liberation and 1980 Olympic Games.

Nos. 1103-1103F were not issued without overprint. Nos. 1103E-1103G are airmail. No. 1103G was only issued with red overprint.

1st Anniv. of the Revolution — A120d

Sandino portrait and: 40c, Rigoberto Lopez Perez. 75c, Street fighters. 1cor, Literacy Logo, Intl. Solidarity with Nicaragua, vert. 1.25cor, German Pomares Ordonez, jungle fighters. 1.85cor, Crowd celebrating, vert. 2.50cor, Carlos Fonseca, campfire, FSLN. 5cor, Map of Central America, Flag of Nicarauga, vert. 10cor, Literacy statement, rural scene.

1980, July 19 **Litho.** ***Perf. 14***

1104 A120d 40c multi *1.20 1.20*
1104A A120d 75c multi *1.20 1.20*
1104B A120d 1cor multi *1.20 1.20*
1104C A120d 1.25cor multi *1.20 1.20*
1104D A120d 1.85cor multi *1.20 1.20*
1104E A120d 2.50cor multi *1.20 1.20*
1104F A120d 5cor multi *1.20 1.20*
Nos. 1104-1104F (7) *8.40 8.40*

Souvenir Sheet

Perf. 14½x14¼

1104G A120d 10cor multi *8.50 8.50*

No. 805a Overprinted in Black and Silver

A120e

Methods and Perfs. As Before

1980, Sept. 30

1104H A120e Sheet of 6 105.00 —
i. 5c multi — —
j. 10c multi — —
k. 20c multi — —
l. 50c multi — —
m. 75c multi — —
n. 1.50cor multi — —

Intl. Year of the Child Type of 1980 Overprinted in Black — A120f

Overprint reads: 1980 ANO DE LA ALFABETIZACION and Litografia Nacional, Portugal symbol

Perf. 13¾x14¼

1980, Dec. 20 **Litho.**

1106 A120f 20c like #1101 *7.50 7.50*
1106A A120f 90c like #1101A *7.50 7.50*
1106B A120f 2cor like #1101B *7.50 7.50*
1106C A120f 2.20cor like #1101C *7.50 7.50*
1106D A120f 10cor like #1101D *7.50 7.50*
Nos. 1106-1106D (5) 37.50 37.50

Souvenir Sheet

1106E A120f 10cor on 15cor, like #C970b *7.25 7.25*

Nos. 1106-1106D were not issued without overprint. Nos. 1106A-1106D are airmail.

No. 1106E was not issued without the surcharge, however it does not have an overprint.

Einstein Type of 1980

Overprinted in Gold and Black: 1980 ANO DE LA ALFABETIZACION, Litografia Nacional, Portugal symbol and

A120g

Additional overprints read: No. 1107, YURI GAGARIN / 12/IV/1961 / LER HOMBRE EN EL ESPACIO. No. 1107A, Space Shuttle and LUNABA 1981. No. 1107B, Space Shuttle. Nos. 1107C, 1107E, 1107F, 1980 ANO DE LA ALFABETIZACION and Litografia Nacional, Portugal symbol. No. 1107D, Apollo XI / 16/VII/1969 / LER HONBRE A LA LUNA. No. 1107G, Einstin and Gandhi, with LUNOJOD 1 Overprint. No. 1107H, Einstin holding clipboard, with Space Shuttle, LUNABA 1981, PLANETA SATURNO 1980 and VOYAGER overprints.

1981, May 15 **Litho.** ***Perf. 14½***

1107 A120g 5c like #1103 — —
1107A A120g 10c like #1103A — —
1107B A120g 15c like #1103B — —
1107C A120g 20c like #1103C — —
1107D A120g 25c like #1103D — —
1107E A120g 1cor like #1103E — —
1107F A120g 2.75cor like #1103F — —
1107G A120g 10cor multi — —
Nos. 1107-1107G (10) 100.00 —

Souvenir Sheet

Perf. 14¾

1107H A120g 10cor on 20cor multi 100.00 —

Nos. 1107-1107H were not issued without overprint. Nos. 1107E-1107H are airmail.

Souvenir Sheet

Quetzal A121

1981, May 18 **Litho.** ***Perf. 13***

1108 A121 10cor multi 2.50 1.25

WIPA 1981 Phil. Exhib., Vienna, May 22-31.

1982 World Cup — A122

Various soccer players and stadiums.

1981, June 25 ***Perf. 12x12½***

1109	A122	5c multi	.45	.25
1109A	A122	20c multi	.45	.25
1109B	A122	25c multi	.45	.25
1109C	A122	30c multi	.45	.25
1109D	A122	50c multi	.45	.25
1109E	A122	4cor multi	.95	.25
1109F	A122	5cor multi	1.20	.30
1109G	A122	10cor multi	2.25	.80
		Nos. 1109-1109G (8)	6.65	2.60

Souvenir Sheet

Perf. 13

1109H	A122	10cor multi	3.50	1.50

2nd Anniv. of Revolution A123

1981, July 19 ***Perf. 12½x12***

1110	A123	50c Adult education	.55	.25
		Nos. 1110,C975E-C975G (4)	10.55	1.20

20th Anniv. of the FSLN — A124

1981, July 23

1111	A124	50c Armed citizen	.60	.40

See No. C976.

Postal Union of Spain and the Americas, 12th Congress, Managua A125

1981, Aug. 10

1112	A125	50c Mailman	.60	.40
		Nos. 1112,C977-C979 (4)	3.00	1.70

Natl. Literacy Campaign, 1st Anniv. — A125a

Designs: 5c, "S"ahino, man counting on fingers. 20c, "A"rmadillo, children marching. 30c, "N"utria, teacher with 2 women. 40c, "D"anto, teacher with 5 people.60c, "I"guana, teacher with 3 adults, hut. 6cor, "N"icaragua, map of Nicaragua with graph. 9cor, "O"so hormiguera, UNESCO Krupskaya medal.

1981, August **Litho.** ***Perf. 14***

1113	A125a	5c multi		
1113A	A125a	10c multi		
1113B	A125a	30c multi		
1113C	A125a	40c multi		
1113D	A125a	60c multi		
1113E	A125a	6cor multi		
1113F	A125a	9cor multi		
		Nos. 1113-1113F (7)	29.00	5.00

Aquatic Flowers (Nymphaea...) A126

1981, Sept. 15 ***Perf. 12½***

1114	A126	50c Capensis	.35	.25
1115	A126	1cor Daubenyana	.35	.25
1116	A126	1.20cor Marliacea	.35	.25
1117	A126	1.80cor GT Moore	.50	.25
1118	A126	2cor Lotus	.55	.25
1119	A126	2.50cor BG Berry	.75	.30
		Nos. 1114-1119,C981 (7)	9.35	2.45

Tropical Fish — A127

50c, Cheirodon axelrodi. 1cor, Poecilia reticulata. 1.85cor, Anostomus anostomus. 2.10cor, Corydoras arcuatus. 2.50cor, Cynolebias nigripinnis.

1981, Oct. 19

1120	A127	50c multicolored	.35	.25
1121	A127	1cor multicolored	.35	.25
1122	A127	1.85cor multicolored	.70	.25
1123	A127	2.10cor multicolored	.95	.25
1124	A127	2.50cor multicolored	1.20	.30
		Nos. 1120-1124,C983-C984 (7)	9.30	1.90

Dryocopus Lineatus — A128

1.20cor, Ramphastos sulfuratus, horiz. 1.80cor, Aratinga finschi, horiz. 2cor, Ara macao.

1981, Nov. 30 ***Perf. 12½***

1125	A128	50c multi	.50	.25
1126	A128	1.20cor multi	.70	.25
1127	A128	1.80cor multi	.90	.25
1128	A128	2cor multi	1.10	.25
		Nos. 1125-1128,C986-C988 (7)	8.20	2.45

Space Communications A129

Various communications satellites.

1981, Dec. 15 ***Perf. 13x12½***

1129	A129	50c multi	.40	.25
1130	A129	1cor multi	.40	.25
1131	A129	1.50cor multi	.40	.25
1132	A129	2cor multi	.75	.25
		Nos. 1129-1132,C989-C991 (7)	8.55	1.90

Vaporcito 93 — A130

1cor, Vulcan Iron Works, 1946. 1.20cor, 1911. 1.80cor, Hoist & Derrick, 1909. 2cor, U-10B, 1956. 2.50cor, Ferrobus, 1945.

1981, Dec. 30 ***Perf. 12½***

1133	A130	50c multi	.30	.25
1134	A130	1cor multi	.35	.25
1135	A130	1.20cor multi	.40	.25
1136	A130	1.80cor multi	.65	.25
1137	A130	2cor multi	.75	.25
1138	A130	2.50cor multi	1.00	.30
		Nos. 1133-1138,C992 (7)	9.70	2.30

No. 1136 is inscribed "Hoist & Derriel."

1982 World Cup — A131

Designs: Various soccer players. 3.50cor horiz.

1982, Jan. 25

1139	A131	5c multi	.35	.25
1140	A131	20c multi	.35	.25
1141	A131	25c multi	.35	.25
1142	A131	2.50cor multi	.55	.35
1143	A131	3.50cor multi	.75	.35
		Nos. 1139-1143,C993-C994 (7)	9.45	2.55

Cocker Spaniels A132

20c, German shepherds. 25c, English setters. 2.50cor, Brittany spaniels.

1982, Feb. 18

1144	A132	5c multi	.40	.25
1145	A132	20c multi	.40	.25
1146	A132	25c multi	.40	.25
1147	A132	2.50cor multi	1.25	.40
		Nos. 1144-1147,C996-C998 (7)	8.60	2.25

Dynamine Myrrhina — A133

1.20cor, Eunica alcmena. 1.50cor, Callizona acesta. 2cor, Adelpha leuceria.

1982, Mar. 26

1148	A133	50c multi	.40	.25
1149	A133	1.20cor multi	.50	.25
1150	A133	1.50cor multi	.65	.25
1151	A133	2cor multi	.70	.25
		Nos. 1148-1151,C1000-C1002 (7)	8.50	2.00

Satellite — A134

Designs: Various satellites. 5c, 50c, 1.50cor, 2.50cor horiz.

1982, Apr. 12

1152	A134	5c multi	.40	.25
1153	A134	15c multi	.40	.25
1154	A134	50c multi	.40	.25
1155	A134	1.50cor multi	.40	.25
1156	A134	2.50cor multi	.60	.25
		Nos. 1152-1156,C1003-C1004 (7)	6.60	2.15

UPU Membership Centenary A135

1982, May 1 **Litho.** ***Perf. 13***

1157	A135	50c Mail coach	.65	.25
1158	A135	1.20cor Ship	.65	.25
		Nos. 1157-1158,C1005-C1006 (4)	4.40	1.45

14th Central American and Caribbean Games (Cuba '82) — A136

1982, May 13

1159	A136	10c Bicycling	.45	.25
1160	A136	15c Swimming, horiz.	.45	.25
1161	A136	25c Basketball	.45	.25
1162	A136	50c Weight lifting	.45	.25
		Nos. 1159-1162,C1007-C1009 (7)	7.30	2.35

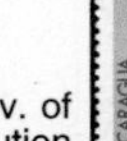

3rd Anniv. of Revolution A137

1982, July 19

1163	A137	50c multi	.60	.25
		Nos. 1163,C1012-C1014 (4)	6.05	1.55

George Washington (1732-1799) — A138

19th Century Paintings. 50c, Mount Vernon. 1cor, Signing the Constitution, horiz. 2cor, Riding through Trenton.

Size of 50c: 45x35mm.

Perf. 13x12½, 12½x13

1982, June 20 **Litho.**

1164	A138	50c multicolored	.40	.25
1165	A138	1cor multicolored	.40	.25
1166	A138	2cor multicolored	.85	.25
		Nos. 1164-1166,C1015-C1018 (7)	8.35	2.40

Flower Arrangement, by R. Penalba — A139

Paintings: 50c, Masked Dancers, by M. Garcia, horiz. 1cor, The Couple, by R. Perez. 1.20cor, Canales Valley, by A. Mejias, horiz. 1.85cor, Portrait of Mrs. Castellon, by T. Jerez. 2cor, Street Vendors, by L. Cerrato. 10cor, Cock Fight, by Gallos P. Ortiz.

1982, Aug. 17 ***Perf. 13***

1167	A139	25c multi	.40	.25
1168	A139	50c multi	.40	.25
1169	A139	1cor multi	.40	.25
1170	A139	1.20cor multi	.40	.25
1171	A139	1.85cor multi	.45	.25
1172	A139	2cor multi	.45	.25
		Nos. 1167-1172,C1019 (7)	8.50	2.30

Souvenir Sheet

1173	A139	10cor multi	2.25	1.00

No. 1173 contains one 36x28mm stamp.

George Dimitrov, First Pres. of Bulgaria A140

50c, Lenin, Dimitrov, 1921.

1982, Sept. 9

1174	A140	50c multicolored	.70	.25
		Nos. 1174,C1020-C1021 (3)	2.70	.95

26th Anniv. of End of Dictatorship A141

50c, Ausberto Narvaez. 2.50cor, Cornelio Silva.

1982, Sept. 21 ***Perf. 13x12½***

1175	A141	50c multi	.40	.25
1176	A141	2.50cor multi	.90	.30
		Nos. 1175-1176,C1022-C1023 (4)	4.45	1.55

Ruins, Leon Viejo — A142

1cor, Ruben Dario Theater and Park. 1.20cor, Independence Plaza, Granada. 1.80cor, Corn Island. 2cor, Santiago Volcano crater, Masaya.

1982, Sept. 25 ***Perf. 13***

1177 A142 50c multi .40 .25
1178 A142 1cor multi .40 .25
1179 A142 1.20cor multi .40 .25
1180 A142 1.80cor multi .45 .25
1181 A142 2cor multi .45 .25
Nos. 1177-1181,C1024-C1025 (7) 7.35 1.85

Karl Marx (1818-1883) — A143

1982, Oct. 4 ***Perf. 12½***

1182 A143 1cor Marx, birthplace .35 .25

Se-tenant with label showing Communist Manifesto titlepage. See No. C1026.

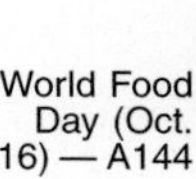

World Food Day (Oct. 16) — A144

50c, Picking fruit. 1cor, Farm workers, vert. 2cor, Cutting sugar cane. 10cor, Emblems.

1982, Oct. 10 ***Perf. 13***

1183 A144 50c multicolored .35 .25
1184 A144 1cor multicolored .35 .25
1185 A144 2cor multicolored .80 .25
1186 A144 10cor multicolored 4.25 1.25
Nos. 1183-1186 (4) 5.75 2.00

Discovery of America, 490th Anniv. — A145

50c, Santa Maria. 1cor, Nina. 1.50cor, Pinta. 2cor, Columbus, fleet.

1982, Oct. 12 ***Perf. 12½x13***

1187 A145 50c multi .40 .25
1188 A145 1cor multi .40 .25
1189 A145 1.50cor multi .75 .25
1190 A145 2cor multi 1.00 .30
Nos. 1187-1190,C1027-C1029 (7) 8.70 2.40

A146

50c, Lobelia laxiflora. 1.20cor, Bombacopsis quinata. 1.80cor, Mimosa albida. 2cor, Epidendrum alatum.

1982, Nov. 13 ***Perf. 12½***

1191 A146 50c multi .40 .25
1192 A146 1.20cor multi .40 .25
1193 A146 1.80cor multi .50 .25
1194 A146 2cor multi .50 .25
Nos. 1191-1194,C1031-C1033 (7) 8.10 2.00

A147

10c, Coral snake. 50c, Iguana, horiz. 2cor, Lachesis muta, horiz.

1982, Dec. 10 ***Perf. 13***

1195 A147 10c multi .35 .25
1196 A147 50c multi .35 .25
1197 A147 2cor multi 1.10 .25
Nos. 1195-1197,C1034-C1037 (7) 10.60 2.05

Telecommunications Day — A148

50c, Radio transmission station. 1cor, Telcor building, Managua.

1982, Dec. 12 **Litho.** ***Perf. 12½***

1198 A148 50c multicolored .75 .25
1199 A148 1cor multicolored .75 .25

50c airmail.

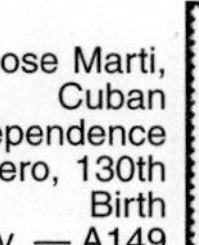

Jose Marti, Cuban Independence Hero, 130th Birth Anniv. — A149

1983, Jan. 28 ***Perf. 13***

1200 A149 1cor multi .90 .25

Boxing — A150

1cor, Gymnast. 1.50cor, Running. 2cor, Weightlifting. 4cor, Women's discus. 5cor, Basketball. 6cor, Bicycling.
15cor, Sailing.

1983, Jan. 31 ***Perf. 12½***

1201 A150 50c shown .40 .25
1202 A150 1cor multi .40 .25
1203 A150 1.50cor multi .40 .25
1204 A150 2cor multi .90 .25
1205 A150 4cor multi 1.75 .30
1206 A150 5cor multi 2.40 .40
1207 A150 6cor multi 2.75 .50
Nos. 1201-1207 (7) 9.00 2.20

Souvenir Sheet

Perf. 13

1208 A150 15cor multi 4.25 2.00

23rd Olympic Games, Los Angeles, July 28-Aug. 12, 1984. Nos. 1205-1208 airmail. No. 1208 contains one 31x39mm stamp.

Local Flowers — A151

No. 1209, Bixa orellana. No. 1210, Brassavola nodosa. No. 1211, Cattleya lueddemanniana. No. 1212, Cochlospermum spec. No. 1213, Hibiscus rosa-sinensis. No. 1214, Laella spec. No. 1215, Malvaviscus arboreus. No. 1216, Neomarica coerulea. No. 1217, Plumeria rubra. No. 1218, Senecio spec. No. 1219, Sobralla macrantha. No. 1220, Stachytarpheta indica. No. 1221, Tabebula ochraceae. No. 1222, Tagetes erecta. No. 1223, Tecoma stans. No. 1224, Thumbergia alata.

1983, Feb. 5 ***Perf. 12½***

1209 A151 1cor black .75 .25
1210 A151 1cor olive green .75 .25
1211 A151 1cor olive grey .75 .25
1212 A151 1cor apple green .75 .25
1213 A151 1cor brown rose .75 .25
1214 A151 1cor deep magenta .75 .25
1215 A151 1cor blue green .75 .25
1216 A151 1cor ultramarine .75 .25
1217 A151 1cor dull vermilion .75 .25
1218 A151 1cor brown ochre .75 .25
1219 A151 1cor deep purple .75 .25
1220 A151 1cor light blue .75 .25
1221 A151 1cor bluish violet .75 .25
1222 A151 1cor orange yellow .75 .25
1223 A151 1cor bright magenta .75 .25
1224 A151 1cor dp turq grn .75 .25
Nos. 1209-1224 (16) 12.00 4.00

See #1515-1530, 1592-1607, 1828-1843.

Visit of Pope John Paul II — A152

50c, Peace banner. 1cor, Map, girl picking coffee beans. 4cor, Pres. Rafael Rivas, Pope. 7cor, Pope, Managua Cathedral.
15cor, Pope, vert.

1983, Mar. 4 ***Perf. 13***

1225 A152 50c multicolored .35 .25
1226 A152 1cor multicolored .35 .25
1227 A152 4cor multicolored 2.00 .60
1228 A152 7cor multicolored 3.75 1.00
Nos. 1225-1228 (4) 6.45 2.10

Souvenir Sheet

1229 A152 15cor multicolored 6.75 2.50

Nos. 1227-1229 airmail. No. 1229 contains one 31x39mm stamp.

Nocturnal Moths — A153

15c, Xilophanes chiron. 50c, Protoparce ochus. 65c, Pholus lasbruscae. 1cor, Amphypterus gannascus. 1.50cor, Pholus licaon. 2cor, Agrius cingulata. 10cor, Rothschildia jurulla, vert.

1983, Mar. 10

1230 A153 15c multi .35 .25
1231 A153 50c multi .35 .25
1232 A153 65c multi .70 .25
1233 A153 1cor multi .80 .25
1234 A153 1.50cor multi .95 .25
1235 A153 2cor multi 1.00 .25
1236 A153 10cor multi 4.25 .80
Nos. 1230-1236 (7) 8.40 2.30

No. 1236 airmail.

26th Anniv. of the Anti-Somoza Movement A154

Various monuments and churches — 50c, Church of Subtiava, Leon. 1cor, La Immaculata Castle, Rio San Juan. 2cor, La Recoleccion Church, Leon, vert. 4cor, Ruben Dario monument, Managua, vert.

1983, Mar. 25 ***Perf. 12½***

1237 A154 50c multi .40 .25
1238 A154 1cor multi .40 .25
1239 A154 2cor multi 1.10 .25
1240 A154 4cor multi 2.10 .40
Nos. 1237-1240 (4) 4.00 1.15

Nos. 1237-1239 has "correos" above date. No. 1240 has "aereo" above date.

Railroad Cars — A155

15c, Passenger. 65c, Freight. 1cor, Tank. 1.50cor, Ore. 4cor, Rail bus. 5cor, Dump truck. 7cor, Rail bus, diff.

1983, Apr. 15

1241 A155 15c multi .40 .25
1242 A155 65c multi .40 .25
1243 A155 1cor multi .40 .25
1244 A155 1.50cor multi .40 .25
1245 A155 4cor multi 1.30 .30
1246 A155 5cor multi 1.60 .40
1247 A155 7cor multi 2.25 .50
Nos. 1241-1247 (7) 6.75 2.20

Nos. 1245-1247 airmail.

Red Cross Flood Rescue A156

1cor, Putting patient in ambulance. 4cor, 1972 earthquake & fire rescue. 5cor, Nurse examining soldier, 1979 Liberation War.

1983, May 8 ***Perf. 13***

1248 A156 50c multi .40 .25
1249 A156 1cor multi .40 .25
1250 A156 4cor multi 2.00 .40
1251 A156 5cor multi 2.25 .40
Nos. 1248-1251 (4) 5.05 1.30

4cor, 5cor airmail. 4cor vert.

World Communications Year — A157

1983, May 17

1252 A157 1cor multi .90 .40

9th Pan-American Games, Aug. — A158

15c, Baseball. 50c, Water polo. 65c, Running. 1cor, Women's basketball, vert. 2cor, Weightlifting, vert. 7cor, Fencing. 8cor, Gymnastics.
15cor, Boxing.

1983, May 30 **Litho.** ***Perf. 13***

1253 A158 15c multi .35 .25
1254 A158 50c multi .35 .25
1255 A158 65c multi .35 .25
1256 A158 1cor multi .35 .25
1257 A158 2cor multi 1.00 .25
1258 A158 7cor multi 3.25 .55
1259 A158 8cor multi 3.75 .65
Nos. 1253-1259 (7) 9.40 2.45

Souvenir Sheet

1260 A158 15cor multi 3.50 1.50

Nos. 1258-1260 airmail. No. 1260 contains one 39x31mm stamp.

4th Anniv. of Revolution A159

1cor, Port of Corinto. 2cor, Telecommunications Bldg., Leon.

1983, July 19 **Litho.** ***Perf. 12½***

1261 A159 1cor multicolored .55 .25
1262 A159 2cor multicolored 1.10 .25

Founders of FSLN (Sandinista Party) — A160

1983, July 23 **Litho.** ***Perf. 13***

1263 A160 50c multi .40 .25
1264 A160 1cor multi .45 .25
1265 A160 4cor multi, vert. 2.00 .35
Nos. 1263-1265 (3) 2.85 .85

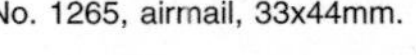

No. 1265, airmail, 33x44mm.

Simon Bolivar, 200th Birth Anniv. — A161

50c, Bolivar and Sandino. 1cor, Bolivar on horseback, vert.

1983, July 24 Litho. *Perf. 12½*
1266 A161 50c multicolored .40 .25
1267 A161 1cor multicolored 1.40 .25

14th Winter Olympic Games, Sarajevo, Yugoslavia, Feb. 8-19, 1984 — A162

50c, Speed skating. 1cor, Slalom. 1.50cor, Luge. 2cor, Ski jumping. 4cor, Ice dancing. 5cor, Skiing. 6cor, Biathlon.

1983, Aug. 5 Litho. *Perf. 13*
1268 A162 50c multi .40 .40
1269 A162 1cor multi .40 .40
1270 A162 1.50cor multi .40 .40
1271 A162 2cor multi 1.10 .40
1272 A162 4cor multi 1.30 .40
1273 A162 5cor multi 1.60 .40
1274 A162 6cor multi 2.10 .50
Nos. 1268-1274 (7) 7.30 2.90

Souvenir Sheet

1983, Aug. 25 Litho. *Perf. 13*
1275 A162 15cor Hockey 5.25 2.50

No. 1275 contains one 39x32mm stamp. Nos. 1272-1275 airmail.

Chess Moves — A163

1983, Aug. 20 Litho. *Perf. 13*
1276 A163 15c Pawn .40 .40
1277 A163 65c Knight .40 .40
1278 A163 1cor Bishop .40 .40
1279 A163 2cor Castle 1.20 .40
1280 A163 4cor Queen 2.00 .40
1281 A163 5cor King 2.40 .40
1282 A163 7cor Player 2.75 .55
Nos. 1276-1282 (7) 9.55 2.95

Nos. 1280-1282 airmail.

Archaeological Finds — A164

1983, Aug. 20 *Perf. 13x12½*
1283 A164 50c Stone figurine .40 .40
1284 A164 1cor Covered dish .40 .40
1285 A164 2cor Vase 1.20 .40
1286 A164 4cor Platter 2.00 .40
Nos. 1283-1286 (4) 4.00 1.60

No. 1286 airmail.

Madonna of the Chair, by Raphael (1483-1517) — A165

Paintings: 1cor, The Eszterhazy Madonna. 1.50cor, Sistine Madonna. 2cor, Madonna of the Linnet. 4cor, Madonna of the Meadow. 5cor, La Belle Jardiniere. 6cor, Adoration of the Kings. 15cor, Madonna de Foligno. 4, 5, 6, 15cor airmail.

1983, Sept. 15
1287 A165 50c multi .40 .25
1288 A165 1cor multi .40 .25
1289 A165 1.50cor multi .40 .25
1290 A165 2cor multi 1.00 .25
1291 A165 4cor multi 1.75 .35
1292 A165 5cor multi 2.00 .40
1293 A165 6cor multi 2.50 .45
Nos. 1287-1293 (7) 8.45 2.20

Souvenir Sheet

1984, Sept. 15 Litho. *Perf. 13*
1293A A165 15cor multi 5.00 2.25

Mining Industry Nationalization A166

1cor, Pouring molten metal. 4cor, Mine headstock, workers.

1983, Oct. 2 *Perf. 13*
1294 A166 1cor multicolored .40 .25
1295 A166 4cor multicolored 1.10 .40

4cor airmail.

Ship-to-Shore Communications — A167

1983, Oct. 7 *Perf. 12½*
1296 A167 1cor shown .40 .25
1297 A167 4cor Radio tower, view 3.00 .40

FRACAP '83, Federation of Central American and Panamanian Radio Amateurs Cong., Oct. 7-9.

Agrarian Reform — A168

1983, Oct. 16
1298 A168 1cor Tobacco .40 .25
1299 A168 2cor Cotton .90 .25
1300 A168 4cor Corn 1.60 .25
1301 A168 5cor Sugar cane 1.80 .35
1302 A168 6cor Cattle 2.50 .40
1303 A168 7cor Rice paddy 2.75 .45
1304 A168 8cor Coffee beans 3.00 .55
1305 A168 10cor Bananas 3.75 .65
Nos. 1298-1305 (8) 16.70 3.15

See Nos. 1531-1538, 1608-1615.

Fire Engine — A169

Various Fire Engines.

1983, Oct. 17 *Perf. 13*
1306 A169 50c multi .35 .25
1307 A169 1cor multi .35 .25
1308 A169 1.50cor multi .35 .25
1309 A169 2cor multi 1.20 .25
1310 A169 4cor multi 2.00 .35
1311 A169 5cor multi 2.40 .40
1312 A169 6cor multi 2.75 .45
Nos. 1306-1312 (7) 9.40 2.20

Nos. 1308-1311 airmail.

Nicaraguan-Cuban Solidarity — A170

1cor, José Marti, Gen. Sandino. 4cor, Education, health, industry.

1983, Oct. 24
1313 A170 1cor multicolored .45 .25
1314 A170 4cor multicolored 1.40 .40

4cor airmail.

A171

Christmas (Adoration of the Kings Paintings by): 50c, Hugo van der Goes. 1 cor, Ghirlandaio. 2cor, El Greco. 7cor, Konrad von Soest. 7cor airmail.

1983, Dec. 1
1315 A171 50c multi .40 .25
1316 A171 1cor multi .40 .25
1317 A171 2cor multi .65 .25
1318 A171 7cor multi 2.60 .40
Nos. 1315-1318 (4) 4.05 1.15

A172

1984, Jan. 10
1319 A172 50c Biathlon .40 .25
1320 A172 50c Bobsledding .40 .25
1321 A172 1cor Speed skating .40 .25
1322 A172 1cor Slalom .40 .25
1323 A172 4cor Downhill skiing 1.90 .35
1324 A172 5cor Ice dancing 2.10 .40
1325 A172 10cor Ski jumping 3.75 .75
Nos. 1319-1325 (7) 9.35 2.50

Souvenir Sheet

1326 A172 15cor Hockey 4.00 1.75

1984 Winter Olympics. No. 1326 contains one 31x39mm stamp. Nos. 1323-1326 airmail.

Domestic Cats — A173

No. 1327, Chinchilla. No. 1328, Long-haired Angel. No. 1329, Red tabby. No. 1330, Tortoiseshell. No. 1331, Siamese. No. 1332, Blue Burmese. No. 1333, Silver long-haired.

1984, Feb. 15 *Perf. 12½*
1327 A173 50c multicolored .35 .25
1328 A173 50c multicolored .35 .25
1329 A173 1cor multicolored .90 .25
1330 A173 2cor multicolored 1.50 .25
1331 A173 3cor multicolored 1.30 .30
1332 A173 4cor multicolored 2.10 .40
1333 A173 7cor multicolored 4.25 .60
Nos. 1327-1333 (7) 10.75 2.30

Nos. 1331, 1333 airmail.

Augusto Cesar Sandino (d. 1934) — A174

1984, Feb. 21
1334 A174 1cor Arms .40 .25
1335 A174 4cor Portrait 2.00 .40

4cor airmail.

Intl. Women's Day — A175

1984, Mar. 8
1336 A175 1cor Blanca Arauz .90 .25

Bee-pollinated Flowers — A176

No. 1337, Poinsettia. No. 1338, Sunflower. No. 1339, Antigonan leptopus. No. 1340, Cassia alata. No. 1341, Bidens pilosa. No. 1342, Althea rosea. No. 1343, Rivea corymbosa.

1984, Mar. 20
1337 A176 50c multicolored .40 .25
1338 A176 50c multicolored .40 .25
1339 A176 1cor multicolored .40 .25
1340 A176 1cor multicolored .40 .25
1341 A176 3cor multicolored 1.60 .25
1342 A176 4cor multicolored 2.40 .35
1343 A176 5cor multicolored 2.75 .40
Nos. 1337-1343 (7) 8.35 2.00

Nos. 1341-1343 airmail.

Space Annivs. — A177

No. 1344, Soyuz 6,7,8, 1969. No. 1345, Soyuz 6,7,8, diff. No. 1346, Apollo 11, 1969. No. 1347, Luna 1, 1959. No. 1348, Luna 2, 1959. No. 1349, Luna 3, 1959. No. 1350, Painting by Koroliov, 1934.

1984, Apr. 20
1344 A177 50c multicolored .40 .25
1345 A177 50c multicolored .40 .25
1346 A177 1cor multicolored .40 .25
1347 A177 2cor multicolored 1.00 .25
1348 A177 3cor multicolored 1.40 .25
1349 A177 4cor multicolored 1.75 .35
1350 A177 9cor multicolored 3.75 .50
Nos. 1344-1350 (7) 9.10 2.10

Nos. 1348-1350 airmail.

Noli Me Tangere, by Correggio — A178

No. 1352, Madonna of San Girolamo. No. 1353, Allegory of the Virtues. No. 1354, Allegory of Placer. No. 1355, Ganimedes. No. 1356, Danae. No. 1357, Leda.
No. 1358, St. John the Evangelist.

1984, May 17 Litho. *Perf. 12½*
1351 A178 50c shown .40 .25
1352 A178 50c multicolored .40 .25
1353 A178 1cor multicolored .40 .25
1354 A178 2cor multicolored .70 .25
1355 A178 3cor multicolored 1.00 .25
1356 A178 5cor multicolored 1.60 .40
1357 A178 8cor multicolored 2.60 .65
Nos. 1351-1357 (7) 7.10 2.30

Souvenir Sheet

1358 A178 15cor multicolored 4.50 1.75

No. 1358 contains one 31x39mm stamp. Nos. 1355-1358 airmail.

Vintage Cars — A179

No. 1359, Abadal, 1914. No. 1360, Daimler, 1886, vert. No. 1361, Ford, 1903, vert. No. 1362, Renault, 1899, vert. No. 1363, Rolls Royce, 1910. No. 1364, Metallurgique, 1907. No. 1365, Bugatti Mode 40.

1984, May 18
1359 A179 1cor multicolored .35 .25
1360 A179 1cor multicolored .35 .25
1361 A179 2cor multicolored 1.10 .25
1362 A179 2cor multicolored 1.10 .25

1363 A179 3cor multicolored 1.50 .25
1364 A179 4cor multicolored 1.80 .35
1365 A179 7cor multicolored 3.00 .60
Nos. 1359-1365 (7) 9.20 2.20

Birth sesquicentennial of Gottlieb Daimler. Nos. 1363-1365 airmail.

1984 Summer Olympics — A180

1984, July 6
1366 A180 50c Volleyball .35 .25
1367 A180 50c Basketball .35 .25
1368 A180 1cor Field hockey .35 .25
1369 A180 2cor Tennis 1.00 .25
1370 A180 3cor Soccer 1.50 .25
1371 A180 4cor Water polo 1.90 .35
1372 A180 9cor Net ball 4.25 .70
Nos. 1366-1372 (7) 9.70 2.30

Souvenir Sheet
Perf. 13

1373 A180 15cor Baseball 5.50 2.00

No. 1373 contains one 40x31mm stamp. Nos. 1370-1373 airmail and horiz.

5th Anniv. of Revolution A181

1984, July 19
1374 A181 50c Construction .40 .25
1375 A181 1cor Transportation .40 .25
1376 A181 4cor Agriculture 1.25 .35
1377 A181 7cor Govt. building 2.45 .55
Nos. 1374-1377 (4) 4.50 1.40

Nos. 1376-1377 airmail.

UNESCO Nature Conservation Campaign A182

50c, Children dependent on nature. 1cor, Forest. 2cor, River. 10cor, Seedlings, field, vert.

1984, Aug. 3 ***Perf. 12½x13, 13x12½***
1378 A182 50c multicolored .40 .25
1379 A182 1cor multicolored .40 .25
1380 A182 2cor multicolored .65 .25
1381 A182 10cor multicolored 2.75 .80
Nos. 1378-1381 (4) 4.20 1.55

No. 1381 airmail.

Nicaraguan Red Cross, 50th Anniv. A183

1984, Sept. 16 ***Perf. 12½x12***
1382 A183 1cor Air ambulance .40 .25
1383 A183 7cor Battle field 3.60 .55

No. 1383 airmail.

History of Baseball A184

Portraits and national colors: #1384, Ventura Escalante, Dominican Republic. #1385, Daniel Herrera, Mexico. #1386, Adalberto Herrera, Venezuela. #1387, Roberto Clemente, Puerto Rico. #1388, Carlos Colas, Cuba. #1389, Stanley Cayasso, Nicaragua. #1390, Babe Ruth, US.

1984, Oct. 25 **Litho.** ***Perf. 12½***
1384 A184 50c multi .40 .25
1385 A184 50c multi .40 .25
1386 A184 1cor multi .60 .25
1387 A184 1cor multi .60 .25
1388 A184 3cor multi 1.50 .25
1389 A184 4cor multi 2.25 .25
1390 A184 5cor multi 2.75 .35
Nos. 1384-1390 (7) 8.50 1.85

Nos. 1388-1390 are airmail.

Tapirus Bairdii — A185

1984, Dec. 28 ***Perf. 13***
1391 A185 25c In water .65 .25
1392 A185 25c In field .65 .25
1393 A185 3cor Baring teeth 1.40 .25
1394 A185 4cor Female and young 1.90 .25
Nos. 1391-1394 (4) 4.60 1.00

Wildlife conservation. Nos. 1393-1394 are airmail. Compare with type A202.

1986 World Cup Soccer Championships, Mexico — A186

Evolution of soccer.

1985, Jan. 20
1395 A186 50c 1314 .40 .25
1396 A186 50c 1500 .40 .25
1397 A186 1cor 1846 .40 .25
1398 A186 1cor 1872 .40 .25
1399 A186 2cor 1883 .40 .25
1400 A186 4cor 1890 1.75 .25
1401 A186 6cor 1953 2.60 .30
Nos. 1395-1401 (7) 6.35 1.80

Souvenir Sheet
Perf. 12½

1402 A186 10cor 1985 5.00 2.25

Nos. 1399-1402 are airmail. No. 1402 contains one 40x32mm stamp.

Mushrooms — A187

No. 1403, Boletus calopus. No. 1404, Strobilomyces retisporus. No. 1405, Boletus luridus. No. 1406, Xerocomus illudens. No. 1407, Gyrodon merulioides. No. 1408, Tylopilus plumbeoviolaceus. No. 1409, Gyroporus castaneus.

1985, Feb. 20
1403 A187 50c multicolored .40 .25
1404 A187 50c multicolored .40 .25
1405 A187 1cor multicolored .40 .25
1406 A187 1cor multicolored .40 .25
1407 A187 4cor multicolored 1.90 .25
1408 A187 5cor multicolored 2.10 .25
1409 A187 8cor multicolored 3.75 .40
Nos. 1403-1409 (7) 9.35 1.90

Nos. 1406-1409 are airmail.

Postal Union of the Americas and Spain, 13th Congress — A188

UPAE emblem and: 1cor, Chasqui, mail runner and map of Realejo-Nicaragua route. 7cor, Monoplane and Nicaraguan air network.

1985, Mar. 11 ***Perf. 12½x13***
1410 A188 1cor multi 1.00 .25
1411 A188 7cor multi 3.50 .40

No. 1411 is airmail.

Locomotives A189

1985, Apr. 5 ***Perf. 12½***
1412 A189 1cor Electric .35 .25
1413 A189 1cor Steam .35 .25
1414 A189 9cor Steam, diff. 1.60 .25
1415 A189 9cor Tram 1.60 .25
1416 A189 15cor Steam, diff. 2.75 .40
1417 A189 21cor Steam, diff. 4.00 .35
Nos. 1412-1417 (6) 10.65 1.75

Souvenir Sheet
Perf. 13

1418 A189 42cor Steam, diff. 8.00 5.75

German Railroads, 150th Anniv. #1418 also for 100th anniv. of Nicaraguan railroads. #1418 contains one 40x32mm stamp. #1414-1418 are airmail.

Motorcycle Cent. — A190

1985, Apr. 30 **Litho.** ***Perf. 12½***
1419 A190 50c F.N., 1928 .35 .35
1420 A190 50c Douglas, 1928 .35 .35
1421 A190 1cor Puch, 1938 .75 .40
1422 A190 2cor Wanderer, 1939 1.00 .40
1423 A190 4cor Honda, 1949 2.10 .40
1424 A190 5cor BMW, 1984 2.90 .40
1425 A190 7cor Honda, 1984 3.50 .40
Nos. 1419-1425 (7) 10.95 2.70

Nos. 1419-1425 se-tenant with labels picturing manufacturers' trademarks. Nos. 1422-1425 are airmail.

Flowers — A194

No. 1454, Metelea quirosii. No. 1455, Ipomea nil. No. 1456, Lysichitum americanum. No. 1457, Clusia sp. No. 1458, Vanilla planifolia. No. 1459, Stemmadenia obovata.

1985, May 20 **Litho.** ***Perf. 13***
1454 A194 50c multicolored .35 .25
1455 A194 50c multicolored .35 .25
1456 A194 1cor multicolored .75 .25
1457 A194 2cor multicolored 1.40 .25
1458 A194 4cor multicolored 2.75 .35
1459 A194 7cor multicolored 5.00 .60
a. Miniature sheet of 6, #1454-1459 10.50
Nos. 1454-1459 (6) 10.60 1.95

Nos. 1457-1459 are airmail.
Stamps in No. 1459a do not have white border.

End of World War II, 40th Anniv. — A195

9.50cor, German army surrenders. 28cor, Nuremberg trials, horiz.

1985, May ***Perf. 12x12½, 12½x12***
1460 A195 9.50cor multi 1.25 .35
1461 A195 28cor multi 2.75 1.00

No. 1461 is airmail.

Lenin, 115th Birth Anniv. — A196

Design: 21cor, Lenin speaking to workers.

1985, June **Litho.** ***Perf. 12x12½***
1462 A196 4cor multicolored .75 .25
1463 A196 21cor multicolored 3.75 1.10

Souvenir Sheet

Argentina '85 — A197

1985, June 5 **Litho.** ***Perf. 13***
1464 A197 75cor multicolored 15.00 5.00

World Stamp Exposition.

Birds — A198

No. 1465, Ring-neck pheasant. No. 1466, Chicken. No. 1467, Guinea hen. No. 1468, Goose. No. 1469, Turkey. No. 1470, Duck.

1985, Aug. 25
1465 A198 50c multi .35 .25
1466 A198 50c multi .35 .25
1467 A198 1cor multi .60 .25
1468 A198 2cor multi 1.10 .25
1469 A198 6cor multi 3.50 .60
1470 A198 8cor multi 4.25 .80
Nos. 1465-1470 (6) 10.15 2.40

Intl. Music Year — A199

No. 1471, Luis A. Delgadillo, vert. No. 1473, Parade. No. 1474, Managua Cathedral. No. 1475, Masked dancer. No. 1476, Parade, diff.

1985, Sept. 1
1471 A199 1cor multicolored .35 .25
1472 A199 1cor shown .35 .25
1473 A199 9cor multicolored 1.75 .35
1474 A199 9cor multicolored 1.75 .35
1475 A199 15cor multicolored 2.60 .55
1476 A199 21cor multicolored 3.50 .75
Nos. 1471-1476 (6) 10.30 2.50

Nos. 1473-1476 are airmail.

Natl. Fire Brigade, 6th Anniv. — A200

No. 1477, Fire station. No. 1478, Fire truck. No. 1480, Ambulance. No. 1481, Airport fire truck. No. 1482, Waterfront fire. No. 1483, Hose team, fire.

1985, Oct. 18

1477	A200	1cor multi	.35	.30
1478	A200	1cor multi	.35	.30
1479	A200	1cor shown	.35	.30
1480	A200	3cor multi	.35	.30
1481	A200	9cor multi	1.90	.35
1482	A200	15cor multi	3.00	.50
1483	A200	21cor multi	4.50	.75
a.		Min. sheet of 7, #1474-1483 + 2 labels	12.00	
		Nos. 1477-1483 (7)	10.80	2.80

Stamps from No. 1483a have orange borders. Nos. 1480-1483 are airmail. Nos. 1477-1483 exist imperf, Value, $140.

Halley's Comet — A201

No. 1484, Edmond Halley. No. 1485, Map of comet's track, 1910. No. 1486, Tycho Brahe's observatory. No. 1487, Astrolabe, map. No. 1488, Telescopes. No. 1489, Telescope designs.

1985, Nov. 26

1484	A201	1cor multicolored	.35	.25
1485	A201	3cor multicolored	.70	.25
1486	A201	3cor multicolored	.70	.25
1487	A201	9cor multicolored	1.75	.25
1488	A201	15cor multicolored	2.90	.40
1489	A201	21cor multicolored	4.00	.60
		Nos. 1484-1489 (6)	10.40	2.00

Nos. 1487-1489 are airmail.

Tapirus Bairdii — A202

1985, Dec. 30

1490	A202	1cor Eating	.65	.40
1491	A202	3cor Drinking	1.00	.40
1492	A202	5cor Grazing in field	1.60	.40
1493	A202	9cor With young	3.25	.40
		Nos. 1490-1493 (4)	6.50	1.60

Nos. 1491-1493 are airmail.

Roses A203

1986, Jan. 15 ***Perf. 12½***

1494	A203	1cor Spinosissima	.35	.25
1495	A203	1cor Canina	.35	.25
1496	A203	3cor Eglanteria	.75	.25
1497	A203	5cor Rubrifolia	.75	.25
1498	A203	9cor Foetida	.75	.25
1499	A203	100cor Rugosa	7.50	1.10
		Nos. 1494-1499 (6)	10.45	2.35

Nos. 1497-1499 are airmail.

Birds — A204

No. 1500, Colibri topacio. No. 1501, Paraulata picodorado. No. 1502, Troupial. No. 1503, Vereron pintado. No. 1504, Tordo ruisenor. No. 1505, Buho real. No. 1506, Gran kiskadee.

1986, Feb. 10 ***Perf. 13x12½***

1500	A204	1cor multi	.35	.25
1501	A204	3cor multi	.60	.25
1502	A204	3cor multi	.60	.25
1503	A204	5cor multi	.60	.25
1504	A204	10cor multi	.90	.25
1505	A204	21cor multi	1.75	.25
1506	A204	75cor multi	6.00	1.10
		Nos. 1500-1506 (7)	10.80	2.60

Nos. 1504-1506 are airmail.

A205

World Cup Soccer Championships, Mexico: Soccer players and pre-Columbian artifacts. No. 1514, Player's foot, ball.

1986, Mar. 20 ***Perf. 12½***

Shirt Colors

1507	A205	1cor blue & yel	.35	.25
1508	A205	1cor yel & green	.35	.25
1509	A205	3cor blue & white	.35	.25
1510	A205	3cor red & white	.35	.25
1511	A205	5cor red	.35	.25
1512	A205	9cor blk & yel	.35	.25
1513	A205	100cor red & grn	5.50	1.10
		Nos. 1507-1513 (7)	7.60	2.60

Souvenir Sheet

Perf. 13

1514	A205	100cor multicolored	4.25	1.25

Nos. 1509-1514 are airmail.

Flower Type of 1983

1986, Mar. **Litho.** ***Perf. 12½***

1515	A151	5cor like #1209	.90	.40
1516	A151	5cor like #1210	.90	.40
1517	A151	5cor like #1211	.90	.40
1518	A151	5cor like #1212	.90	.40
1519	A151	5cor like #1213	.90	.40
1520	A151	5cor like #1214	.90	.40
1521	A151	5cor like #1215	.90	.40
1522	A151	5cor like #1216	.90	.40
1523	A151	5cor like #1217	.90	.40
1524	A151	5cor like #1218	.90	.40
1525	A151	5cor like #1219	.90	.40
1526	A151	5cor like #1220	.90	.40
1527	A151	5cor like #1221	.90	.40
1528	A151	5cor like #1222	.90	.40
1529	A151	5cor like #1223	.90	.40
1530	A151	5cor like #1224	.90	.40
		Nos. 1515-1530 (16)	14.40	6.40

Agrarian Reform Type of 1983

1986, Apr. 15 ***Perf. 12½***

1531	A168	1cor dk brown	.35	.25
1532	A168	9cor purple	.35	.25
1533	A168	15cor rose violet	.65	.25
1534	A168	21cor dk car rose	1.00	.25
1535	A168	33cor orange	1.60	.35
1536	A168	42cor green	2.00	.45
1537	A168	50cor brown	2.50	.55
1538	A168	100cor blue	5.00	1.10
		Nos. 1531-1538 (8)	13.45	3.45

Writers — A207

No. 1539, Alfonso Cortes. No. 1540, Salomon de la Selva. No. 1541, Azarias H. Pallais. No. 1542, Ruben Dario. No. 1543, Pablo Neruda. No. 1544, Alfonso Reyes. No. 1545, Pedro Henriquez Urena.

1986, Apr. 23 ***Perf. 12½x13***

1539	A207	1cor multicolored	.35	.25
1540	A207	3cor multicolored	.35	.25
1541	A207	3cor multicolored	.35	.25
1542	A207	5cor multicolored	.35	.25
1543	A207	9cor multicolored	.55	.25
1544	A207	15cor multicolored	.75	.25
1545	A207	100cor multicolored	6.00	1.10
		Nos. 1539-1545 (7)	8.70	2.60

Nos. 1544-1545 are airmail.

Nuts & Fruits — A208

No. 1546, Maranon (cashew). No. 1547, Zapote. No. 1548, Pitahaya. No. 1549, Granadilla. No. 1550, Anona. No. 1551, Melocoton (starfruit). No. 1552, Mamey.

1986, June 20 ***Perf. 12x12½***

1546	A208	1cor multicolored	.35	.25
1547	A208	1cor multicolored	.35	.25
1548	A208	3cor multicolored	.60	.25
1549	A208	3cor multicolored	.60	.25
1550	A208	5cor multicolored	.60	.25
1551	A208	21cor multicolored	1.50	.25
1552	A208	100cor multicolored	6.75	1.10
		Nos. 1546-1552 (7)	10.75	2.60

FAO, 40th Anniv. Nos. 1550-1552 are airmail.

Lockheed L-1011 Tristar — A209

Airplanes: No. 1554, YAK 40. No. 1555, BAC 1-11. No. 1556, Boeing 747. 9cor, A-300. 15cor, TU-154. No. 1559, Concorde, vert. No. 1560, Fairchild 340.

1986, Aug. 22 ***Perf. 12½***

1553	A209	1cor multicolored	.35	.25
1554	A209	1cor multicolored	.35	.25
1555	A209	3cor multicolored	.35	.25
1556	A209	3cor multicolored	.65	.25
1557	A209	9cor multicolored	.80	.25
1558	A209	15cor multicolored	1.00	.25
1559	A209	100cor multicolored	7.50	1.10
		Nos. 1553-1559 (7)	11.00	2.60

Souvenir Sheet

Perf. 13

1560	A209	100cor multicolored	5.50	3.75

Stockholmia '86. No. 1560 contains one 40x32mm stamp.

Nos. 1557-1560 airmail.

A210

A210a

Discovery of America, 500th Anniv. (in 1992) — A210b

No. 1561, 1 of Columbus' ships. No. 1562, 2 of Columbus' ships. No. 1563, Juan de la Cosa. No. 1564, Columbus. No. 1565, Ferdinand, Isabella. No. 1566, Columbus before throne.

1986, Oct. 12 ***Perf. 12½x12***

1561	A210	1cor multi	.30	.25
1562	A210	1cor multi	.30	.25
a.		Pair, #1561-1562	.80	.60
b.		Souv. sheet of 2, #1561-1562	1.25	.50

Perf. 12x12½

1563	A210a	9cor multi	.45	.25
1564	A210a	9cor multi	.45	.25
a.		Pair, #1563-1564	1.10	.75
1565	A210b	21cor multi	1.20	.25
1566	A210b	100cor multi	5.00	1.10
a.		Pair, #1565-1566	8.00	4.00
b.		Souv. sheet of 4, #1563-1566	14.00	7.00
		Nos. 1561-1566 (6)	7.70	2.35

Nos. 1563-1566 are airmail. Nos. 1564a, 1566a have continuous design.

Butterflies — A211

No. 1567, Theritas coronata. No. 1568, Charayes nitebis. No. 1569, Salamis cacta. No. 1570, Papilio maacki. No. 1571, Euphaedro cyparissa. No. 1572, Palaeochrysophonus hippothoe. No. 1573, Ritra aurea.

1986, Dec. 12 ***Perf. 12½***

1567	A211	10cor multi	.75	.25
1568	A211	15cor multi	1.20	.25
1569	A211	15cor multi	1.20	.25
1570	A211	15cor multi	1.20	.25
1571	A211	25cor multi	1.90	.30
1572	A211	25cor multi	1.90	.30
1573	A211	30cor multi	2.60	.35
		Nos. 1567-1573 (7)	10.75	1.95

Nos. 1568-1573 are airmail.

Ruben Dario Order of Cultural Independence A212

Dario Order Winning Writers: No. 1574, Ernesto Mejia Sanchez. No. 1575, Fernando Gordillo C. No. 1576, Francisco Perez Estrada. 30cor, Julio Cortazar. 60cor, Enrique Fernandez Morales.

1987, Jan. 18 **Litho.** ***Perf. 13***

1574	A212	10cor multicolored	.30	.25
1575	A212	10cor multicolored	.30	.25
1576	A212	10cor multicolored	.30	.25
1577	A212	15cor multicolored	.40	.25
1578	A212	30cor multicolored	.80	.30
1579	A212	60cor multicolored	1.75	.65
a.		Strip of 6, #1574-1579	5.25	2.50
b.		Min. sheet of 6, #1574-1579	6.25	3.50

1988 Winter Olympics, Calgary — A213

#1580, Speed skating. #1581, Ice hockey. #1582, Women's figure skating. #1583, Ski jumping. 20cor, Biathalon. 30cor, Slalom skiing. 40cor, Downhill skiing. 110cor, Ice hockey, diff., horiz.

1987, Feb. 3 ***Perf. 13***

1580	A213	10cor multi	.90	.25
1581	A213	10cor multi	.90	.25
1582	A213	15cor multi	1.20	.25
1583	A213	15cor multi	1.20	.25
1584	A213	20cor multi	1.50	.25
1585	A213	30cor multi	2.10	.30
1586	A213	40cor multi	3.25	.40
		Nos. 1580-1586 (7)	11.05	1.95

Souvenir Sheet

Perf. 12½

1587	A213	110cor multi	5.50	3.75

Nos. 1582-1587 are airmail. No. 1587 contains one 40x32mm stamp.

Children's Welfare Campaign — A214

No. 1588, Growth & development. No. 1589, Vaccination. No. 1590, Rehydration. No. 1591, Breastfeeding.

1987, Mar. 18 *Perf. 13*

1588 A214 10cor multi .35 .25
1589 A214 25cor multi .65 .30
1590 A214 30cor multi 1.90 .35
1591 A214 50cor multi 6.50 .60
Nos. 1588-1591 (4) 9.40 1.50

Nos. 1589-1591 are airmail. For surcharges, see Nos. 1674A-1674D.

Flower Type of 1983

No. 1592, Bixa orellana. No. 1593, Brassavola nodosa. No. 1594, Cattleya luedemanniana. No. 1595, Cochlospermum spec. No. 1596, Hibiscus rosa-sinensis. No. 1597, Laelia spec. No. 1598, Malvaviscus arboreus. No. 1599, Neomarica coerulea. No. 1600, Plumeria rubra. No. 1601, Senecio spec. No. 1602, Sobralla macrantha. No. 1603, Stachytarpheta indica. No. 1604, Tabebula ochraceae. No. 1605, Tagetes erecta. No. 1606, Tecoma stans. No. 1607, Thumbergia alata.

1987, Mar. 25 *Perf. 12½*

1592 A151 10cor black .70 .30
1593 A151 10cor olive green .70 .30
1594 A151 10cor olive grey .70 .30
1595 A151 10cor apple green .70 .30
1596 A151 10cor brown rose .70 .30
1597 A151 10cor deep magenta .70 .30
1598 A151 10cor blue green .70 .30
1599 A151 10cor ultramarine .70 .30
1600 A151 10cor dull vermilion .70 .30
1601 A151 10cor brown ochre .70 .30
1602 A151 10cor deep purple .70 .30
1603 A151 10cor light blue .70 .30
1604 A151 10cor bluish violet .70 .30
1605 A151 10cor orange yellow .70 .30
1606 A151 10cor bright magenta .70 .30
1607 A151 10cor dp turq grn .70 .30
Nos. 1592-1607 (16) 11.20 4.80

Agrarian Reform Type of 1983 Inscribed "1987"

Designs: No. 1608, Tobacco. No. 1609, Cotton. 15cor, Corn. 25cor, Sugar. 30cor, Cattle. 50cor, Coffee Beans. 60cor, Rice. 100cor, Bananas.

1987, Mar. 25 *Perf. 12½*

1608 A168 10cor dk brown .60 .30
1609 A168 10cor purple .60 .30
1610 A168 15cor rose violet .90 .30
1611 A168 25cor dk car rose 1.40 .35
1612 A168 30cor orange 1.75 .45
1613 A168 50cor brown 2.75 .65
1614 A168 60cor green 3.50 .90
1615 A168 100cor blue 5.50 1.40
Nos. 1608-1615 (8) 17.00 4.65

77th Interparliamentary Conf., Managua — A215

1987, Apr. 27

1616 A215 10cor multicolored .80 .30

Prehistoric Creatures A216

1987, May 25 *Perf. 13*

1617 A216 10cor Mammoth .65 .30
1618 A216 10cor Dimetrodon .65 .30
1619 A216 10cor Triceratops .65 .30
1620 A216 15cor Dinichthys 1.00 .30
1621 A216 15cor Uintaterium 1.00 .30
1622 A216 30cor Pteranodon 2.25 .30
1623 A216 40cor Tilosaurus 3.00 .30
Nos. 1617-1623 (7) 9.20 2.10

Nos. 1620-1623 are airmail.

CAPEX '87 — A217

Various tennis players in action: No. 1624, Male player. No. 1625, Female player serving. No. 1626, Male player at net. No. 1627, Female player at line, racquet at left side. No. 1628, Female player, racquet behind her ready to hit ball. No. 1629, Female player, both hands on racquet above head. No. 1630, Male player, one hand hold racquet above head.
No. 1631, Doubles partners, vert.

1987, June 2 *Perf. 13*

1624 A217 10cor multi .55 .30
1625 A217 10cor multi .55 .30
1626 A217 15cor multi 1.00 .30
1627 A217 15cor multi 1.00 .30
1628 A217 20cor multi 1.10 .30
1629 A217 30cor multi 2.00 .30
1630 A217 40cor multi 3.00 .40
Nos. 1624-1630 (7) 9.20 2.20

Souvenir Sheet

Perf. 12½

1631 A217 110cor multi 5.50 3.75

Nos. 1626-1631 are airmail. No. 1631 contains one 32x40mm stamp.

Dogs — A218

No. 1632, Doberman pinscher. No. 1633, Bull Mastiff. No. 1634, Japanese Spaniel. No. 1635, Keeshond. No. 1636, Chihuahua. No. 1637, St. Bernard. No. 1638, West Gotha spitz.

1987, June 25 *Perf. 13*

1632 A218 10cor multicolored .50 .30
1633 A218 10cor multicolored .50 .30
1634 A218 15cor multicolored 1.00 .30
1635 A218 15cor multicolored 1.00 .30
1636 A218 20cor multicolored 1.40 .30
1637 A218 30cor multicolored 2.00 .30
1638 A218 40cor multicolored 3.00 .40
Nos. 1632-1638 (7) 9.40 2.20

Nos. 1634-1638 are airmail.

Cacti — A219

No. 1639, Lophocereus schottii. No. 1640, Opuntia acanthocarpa. No. 1641, Echinocereus engelmanii. No. 1642, Lemaireocereus thurberi. No. 1643, Saguaros. No. 1644, Opuntia fulgida. No. 1645, Opuntia ficus.

1987, July 25 *Perf. 12½*

1639 A219 10cor multicolored .70 .30
1640 A219 10cor multicolored .70 .30
1641 A219 10cor multicolored .70 .30
1642 A219 20cor multicolored 1.50 .30
1643 A219 20cor multicolored 1.50 .30
1644 A219 30cor multicolored 2.40 .30
1645 A219 50cor multicolored 3.75 .50
Nos. 1639-1645 (7) 11.25 2.30

Nos. 1642-1645 are airmail.

10th Pan American Games, Indianapolis A220

No. 1646, High jump. No. 1647, Volleyball. No. 1648, Sprinter. No. 1649, Gymnastics. No. 1650, Baseball. No. 1651, Synchronized swimming. No. 1652, Weightlifting.
110cor, Rhythmic gymnastics.

1987, Aug. 7 *Perf. 13*

1646 A220 10cor multi .65 .30
1647 A220 10cor multi .65 .30
1648 A220 15cor multi 1.20 .30
1649 A220 15cor multi 1.20 .30
1650 A220 20cor multi 1.50 .30
1651 A220 30cor multi 2.40 .45
1652 A220 40cor multi 3.25 .60
Nos. 1646-1652 (7) 10.85 2.55

Souvenir Sheet

1653 A220 110cor multi 5.25 3.50

Nos. 1648-1653 are airmail. No. 1653 contains one 32x40mm stamp. Nos. 1651-1653 are vert.

Satellites A221

1987, Oct. 4

1654 A221 10cor Sputnik .70 .35
1655 A221 10cor Cosmos .70 .35
1656 A221 15cor Proton 1.00 .35
1657 A221 25cor Meteor 1.75 .35
1658 A221 25cor Luna 1.75 .35
1659 A221 30cor Electron 1.90 .35
1660 A221 50cor Mars 1 3.25 .60
Nos. 1654-1660 (7) 11.05 2.70

Cosmonauts' Day. Nos. 1656-1660 are airmail.

Fish — A222

Designs: No. 1661, Tarpon atlanticus. No. 1662, Cichlasoma managuense. No. 1663, Atractoteus tropicus. No. 1664, Astyana fasciatus. No. 1665, Cichlasoma citrimellum. 20cor, Cichlosoma dowi. 50cor, Caracharhinus nicaraguensis.

1987, Oct. 18 *Perf. 12½*

1661 A222 10cor multicolored .70 .40
1662 A222 10cor multicolored .70 .40
1663 A222 10cor multicolored .70 .40
1664 A222 15cor multicolored 1.20 .40
1665 A222 15cor multicolored 1.20 .40
1666 A222 20cor multicolored 1.60 .40
1667 A222 50cor multicolored 4.25 .40
Nos. 1661-1667 (7) 10.35 2.80

Nos. 1663-1667 are airmail.

October Revolution, 70th Anniv. — A223

Designs: 30cor, Cruiser Aurora, horiz. 50cor, USSR natl. arms.

1987, Nov. 7 *Perf. 13*

1668 A223 10cor multicolored .60 .40
1669 A223 30cor multicolored 1.40 .40
1670 A223 50cor multicolored 2.40 .60
Nos. 1668-1670 (3) 4.40 1.40

Nos. 1669-1670 are airmail.

Christmas Paintings by L. Saenz — A224

10cor, Nativity. 20cor, Adoration of the Magi. 25cor, Adoration of the Magi, diff. 50cor, Nativity, diff.

1987, Nov. 15 *Perf. 13*

1671 A224 10cor multicolored 1.00 .40
1672 A224 20cor multicolored 1.40 .40
1673 A224 25cor multicolored 1.60 .40
1674 A224 50cor multicolored 3.25 .40
Nos. 1671-1674 (4) 7.25 1.60

Nos. 1588-1591 Surcharged

Methods and Perfs As Before

1987, Dec. 26

1674A A214 400cor on 10cor #1588 — 5.00
1674B A214 600cor on 50cor #1591 — —
1674C A214 1000cor on 25cor #1589 — —
1674D A214 5000cor on 30cor #1590 — —
Nos. 1674A-1674D (4) *80.00 80.00*

1988 Winter Olymmpics, Calgary — A225

No. 1675, Biathlon. No. 1676, Cross-country skiing, vert. No. 1677, Hockey, vert. No. 1678, Women's figure skating, vert. No. 1679, Slalom skiing, vert. No. 1680, Ski jumping. No. 1681, Men's downhill skiing, vert.
No. 1682, Pairs figure skating.

1988, Jan. 30 **Litho.** *Perf. 12½*

1675 A225 10cor multicolored .45 .30
1676 A225 10cor multicolored .45 .30
1677 A225 15cor multicolored 1.00 .30
1678 A225 20cor multicolored 1.50 .30
1679 A225 25cor multicolored 2.00 .30
1680 A225 30cor multicolored 2.25 .40
1681 A225 40cor multicolored 3.00 .50
Nos. 1675-1681 (7) 10.65 2.40

Souvenir Sheet

Perf. 13

1682 A225 100cor multicolored 5.50 3.75

Nos. 1675-1681 printed with se-tenant label showing Canadian flag and wildlife.
No. 1682 contains one 40x32mm stamp.

Nicaraguan Journalists Assoc., 10th Anniv. — A226

Design: 5cor, Churches of St. Francis Xavier and Fatima, and speaker addressing journalists, horiz.

1988, Feb. 10

1683 A226 1cor shown 1.25 .25
1684 A226 5cor multicolored 3.75 .40

No. 1684 is airmail.

1988 Summer Olympics, Seoul — A227

1988, Feb. 28

1685 A227 10cor Gymnastics .50 .30
1686 A227 10cor Basketball .50 .30
1687 A227 15cor Volleyball .95 .30
1688 A227 20cor Long jump 1.50 .30
1689 A227 25cor Soccer 1.90 .30
1690 A227 30cor Water polo 2.00 .40
1691 A227 40cor Boxing 3.50 .55
Nos. 1685-1691 (7) 10.85 2.45

Souvenir Sheet

1692 A227 100cor Baseball 5.50 3.75

No. 1692 contains one 40x32mm stamp.

European Soccer Championships, Essen — A228

Designs: Various soccer players in action.

1988, Apr. 14 ***Perf. 13x12½, 12½x13***

1693	A228	50c multicolored	.70	.25
1694	A228	1cor multicolored	.70	.25
1695	A228	2cor multi, vert.	.80	.25
1696	A228	3cor multi, vert.	1.40	.25
1697	A228	4cor multi, vert.	1.90	.25
1698	A228	5cor multi, vert.	2.50	.35
1699	A228	6cor multicolored	3.00	.40
		Nos. 1693-1699 (7)	11.00	2.00

Souvenir Sheet

Perf. 13

1700	A228	15cor multi, vert.	5.50	3.75

Nos. 1695-1700 are airmail. No. 1700 contains one 32x40mm stamp.

Sandinista Revolution, 9th Anniv. — A229

1988, July 19 ***Perf. 13***

1701	A229	1cor shown	.60	.25
1702	A229	5cor Volcanoes, dove	2.40	.30

No. 1702 is airmail.

Animals A230

10c, Bear, cub. 15c, Lion, cubs. 25c, Spaniel, pups. 50c, Wild boars. 4cor, Cheetah, cubs. 7cor, Hyenas. 8cor, Fox, kit.
15cor, House cat, kittens, vert.

1988, Mar. 3 ***Perf. 13x12½***

1703	A230	10c multi	.40	.25
1704	A230	15c multi	.40	.25
1705	A230	25c multi	.40	.25
1706	A230	50c multi	.40	.25
1707	A230	4cor multi	1.90	.35
1708	A230	7cor multi	2.75	.70
1709	A230	8cor multi	3.50	.80
		Nos. 1703-1709 (7)	9.75	2.85

Souvenir Sheet

Perf. 12½

1710	A230	15cor multi	5.50	3.75

Nos. 1707-1710 are airmail. No. 1710 contains one 32x40mm stamp.

Helicopters — A231

1988, June 1 ***Perf. 12½x12***

1711	A231	4cor B-206B-JRIII	.50	.25
1712	A231	12cor BK-117A-3	.50	.25
1713	A231	16cor B-360	1.10	.25
1714	A231	20cor 109-MRII	1.25	.25
1715	A231	24cor S-61	1.75	.25
1716	A231	28cor SA-365N-D2	2.00	.25
1717	A231	56cor S-76	2.60	.50
		Nos. 1711-1717 (7)	9.70	2.00

Souvenir Sheet

Perf. 13

1718	A231	120cor NH-90	5.50	3.75

Nos. 1712-1718 are airmail. No. 1718 contains one 40x32mm stamp.

Shells — A232

4cor, Strombus pugilis. 12cor, Polymita picta. 16cor, Architectonica maximum. 20cor, Pectens laqueatus. 24cor, Guildfordia triumphans. 28cor, Ranella pustulosa. 50cor, Trochus maculatus.

1988, Sept. 20 ***Perf. 13***

1719	A232	4cor multicolored	.50	.40
1720	A232	12cor multicolored	.60	.40
1721	A232	16cor multicolored	1.00	.40
1722	A232	20cor multicolored	1.40	.40
1723	A232	24cor multicolored	1.75	.40
1724	A232	28cor multicolored	1.90	.40
1725	A232	50cor multicolored	3.50	.40
		Nos. 1719-1725 (7)	10.65	2.80

Nos. 1720-1725 are airmail.

Insects — A233

4cor, Chrysina macropus. 12cor, Plusiotis victoriana. 16cor, Ceratotrupes bolivari. 20cor, Gymnetosoma stellata. 24cor, Euphoria lineoligera. 28cor, Euphoria candezei. 50cor, Sulcophanaeus chryseicollis.

1988, Nov. 10

1726	A233	4cor multicolored	.50	.40
1727	A233	12cor multicolored	.75	.40
1728	A233	16cor multicolored	1.00	.40
1729	A233	20cor multicolored	1.50	.40
1730	A233	24cor multicolored	1.75	.40
1731	A233	28cor multicolored	2.00	.40
1732	A233	50cor multicolored	3.25	.40
		Nos. 1726-1732 (7)	10.75	2.80

Nos. 1727-1732 are airmail.

Heroes of the Revolution — A234

Designs: 4cor, Casimiro Sotelo Montenegro. 12cor, Ricardo Morales Aviles. 16cor, Silvio Mayorga Delgado. 20cor, Pedro Arauz Palacios. 24cor, Oscar A. Turcios Chavarrias. 28cor, Julio C. Buitrago Urroz. 50cor, Jose B. Escobar Perez. 100cor, Eduardo E. Contreras Escobar.

1988, Aug. 27 ***Perf. 12½x12***

1733	A234	4cor sky blue	.60	.40
1734	A234	12cor red lilac	.60	.40
1735	A234	16cor yel grn	.70	.40
1736	A234	20cor org brown	1.00	.40
1737	A234	24cor brown	1.10	.40
1738	A234	28cor purple	1.30	.40
1739	A234	50cor henna brn	2.40	.50
1740	A234	100cor plum	4.75	.95
		Nos. 1733-1740 (8)	12.45	3.85

Nos. 1734-1740 are airmail.

Flowers — A235

Designs: 4cor, Acacia baileyana. 12cor, Anigozanthos manglesii. 16cor, Telopia speciosissima. 20cor, Eucalyptus ficifolia. 24cor, Boronia heterophylla. 28cor, Callistemon speciosus. 30cor, Nymphaea caerulea, horiz. 50cor, Clianthus formosus.

1988, Aug. 30 ***Perf. 13***

1741	A235	4cor multicolored	.60	.40
1742	A235	12cor multicolored	.85	.40
1743	A235	16cor multicolored	1.10	.40
1744	A235	20cor multicolored	1.40	.40
1745	A235	24cor multicolored	1.75	.40
1746	A235	28cor multicolored	1.90	.40
1747	A235	30cor multicolored	2.10	.40
1748	A235	50cor multicolored	1.80	.40
		Nos. 1741-1748 (8)	11.50	3.20

Nos. 1742-1748 are airmail.

Pre-Columbian Art — A236

Designs: 4cor, Zapotec funeral urn. 12cor, Mochica ceramic kneeling man. 16cor, Mochica ceramic head. 20cor, Taina ceramic vase. 28cor, Nazca cup, horiz. 100cor, Inca pipe, horiz.
120cor, Aztec ceramic vessel, horiz.

1988, Oct. 12 ***Perf. 12x12½, 12½x12***

1749	A236	4cor multi + label	.55	.35
1750	A236	12cor multi + label	.75	.35
1751	A236	16cor multi + label	1.00	.35
1752	A236	20cor multi + label	1.25	.35
1753	A236	28cor multi + label	1.75	.35
1754	A236	100cor multi + label	6.00	1.00
		Nos. 1749-1754 (6)	11.30	2.75

Souvenir Sheet

Perf. 13x13½

1755	A236	120cor multicolored	5.50	3.75

Discovery of America, 500th anniv. (in 1992). Nos. 1750-1755 are airmail. No. 1755 contains one 40x32mm stamp.

Publication of Blue, by Ruben Dario, Cent. — A237

1988, Oct. 12 ***Perf. 12x12½***

1756	A237	25cor multi + label	3.00	.40

No. 1756 is airmail.

Tourism A238

4cor, Pochomil. 12cor, Granada. 20cor, Olof Palme Convention Center. 24cor, Masaya Volcano Natl. Park. 28cor, La Boquita. 30cor, Xiloa. 50cor, Hotels of Managua.
160cor, Montelimar.

1989, Feb. 5 ***Perf. 12½x12***

1757	A238	4cor multicolored	.50	.40
1758	A238	12cor multicolored	.70	.40
1759	A238	20cor multicolored	1.30	.40
1760	A238	24cor multicolored	1.30	.40
1761	A238	28cor multicolored	1.80	.40
1762	A238	30cor multicolored	1.90	.40
1763	A238	50cor multicolored	3.50	.40
		Nos. 1757-1763 (7)	11.00	2.80

Souvenir Sheet

Perf. 13

1764	A238	160cor multicolored	6.50	3.75

Nos. 1758-1764 are airmail. No. 1764 contains one 40x32mm stamp.

French Revolution, Bicentennial A240

Designs: 50cor, Procession of the Estates General, Versailles. 300cor, Oath of the Tennis Court. 600cor, 14th of July, vert. 1000cor, Dancing Around the Liberty Tree. 2000cor, Liberty Guiding the People, vert. 3000cor, Storming the Bastille. 5000cor, Lafayette Swearing Allegiance to the Constitution, vert. 9000cor, La Marsiellaise, vert.

Perf. 12½x13 (50cor), 13x12½ (600, 2000cor), 12½

1989, July 14

Sizes: 50cor, 40x25mm

600cor, 2000cor, 33x44mm

1773	A240	50cor multicolored	.45	.30
1774	A240	300cor shown	.45	.30
1775	A240	600cor multicolored	.60	.30
1776	A240	1000cor multicolored	.90	.30
1777	A240	2000cor multicolored	1.60	.30
1778	A240	3000cor multicolored	2.60	.40
1779	A240	5000cor multicolored	4.00	.65
		Nos. 1773-1779 (7)	10.60	2.55

Souvenir Sheet

Perf. 12½

1780	A240	9000cor multicolored	6.25	4.50

Philexfrance '89. #1774-1780 are airmail. #1780 contains one 32x40mm stamp.

Currency Reform

Currency reform took place Mar. 4, 1990. Until stamps in the new currency were issued, mail was to be handstamped "Franqueo Pagado," (Postage Paid). Stamps were not used again until Apr. 25, 1991. Nos. 1781-1812 were prepared but not issued prior to the currency reform and were sold by the post office without postal validity. Used values are for CTO stamps.

Ships — A241

Stamp World London '90: 500cor, Director. 1000cor, Independence. 3000cor, Orizaba. 5000cor, SS Lewis. 10,000cor, Golden Rule. 30,000cor, Santiago de Cuba. 100,000cor, North Star.
75,000cor, Bahia de Corinto.

1990, Apr. 3 ***Perf. 12½x12***

1781	A241	500cor shown	.40	.30
1782	A241	1000cor multi	.40	.30
1783	A241	3000cor multi	.50	.30
1784	A241	5000cor multi	.75	.30
1785	A241	10,000cor multi	1.25	.40
1786	A241	30,000cor multi	2.40	.50
1787	A241	100,000cor multi	3.50	.65
		Nos. 1781-1787 (7)	9.20	2.75

Souvenir Sheet

Perf. 12½

1788		75,000cor multi	6.00	4.00

World Cup Soccer Championships, Italy — A242

Designs: Various soccer players in action.

1990, Apr. 30 ***Perf. 13***

1789	A242	500cor shown	.35	.25
1790	A242	1000cor multi	.35	.25
1791	A242	3000cor multi	.50	.30
1792	A242	5000cor multi	.85	.35
1793	A242	10,000cor multi	1.40	.50
1794	A242	30,000cor multi	2.40	.60
1795	A242	100,000cor multi	3.50	.75
		Nos. 1789-1795 (7)	9.35	3.00

Souvenir Sheet

Perf. 12½

1796	A242	75,000cor multi	5.00	2.50

1992 Winter Olympics, Albertville A243

Designs: 500cor, Ski jumping. 1000cor, Downhill skiing. 3000cor, Figure skating, vert. 5000cor, Speed skating, vert. 10,000cor, Biathlon, vert. 30,000cor, Cross country skiing, vert. 100,000cor, Ice hockey, vert.
75,000cor, Two-man bobsled, vert.

1990, July 25 ***Perf. 13***

1797	A243	500cor shown	.70	.55
1798	A243	1000cor multi	.70	.55
1799	A243	3000cor multi	.90	.75
1800	A243	5000cor multi	1.90	.85
1801	A243	10,000cor multi	2.50	1.30
1802	A243	30,000cor multi	4.50	1.65
1803	A243	100,000cor multi	7.00	1.85
		Nos. 1797-1803 (7)	18.20	7.50

Souvenir Sheet

Perf. 12½

1804	A243	75,000cor multi	5.50	2.50

1992 Summer Olympics, Barcelona — A244

Designs: 500cor, Javelin. 1000cor, Steeplechase. 3000cor, Handball. 5000cor, Basketball. 10,000cor, Gymnastics. 30,000cor, Cycling. 100,000cor, Boxing, horiz.
75,000cor, Soccer.

1990, Aug. 10 ***Perf. 13***

1805	A244	500cor shown	.70	.55
1806	A244	1000cor multi	.70	.55
1807	A244	3000cor multi	.90	.75
1808	A244	5000cor multi	1.90	.85
1809	A244	10,000cor multi	2.50	1.30
1810	A244	30,000cor multi	4.50	1.65
1811	A244	100,000cor multi	7.00	1.85
		Nos. 1805-1811 (7)	18.20	7.50

Souvenir Sheet

1812	75,000cor multi	5.50	2.50

Birds — A245

Designs: No. 1813, Apteryx owenii. No. 1814, Notornis mantelli. 10c, Cyanoramphus novaezelandiae. 20c, Gallirallus australis. 30c, Rhynochetos jubatus, vert. 60c, Nestor notabilis. 70c, Strigops habroptilus.
1.50cor, Cygnus atratus.

1990, Aug. 14 **Litho.** ***Perf. 12½***

1813	A245	5c multicolored	.40	.25
1814	A245	5c multicolored	.40	.25
1815	A245	10c multicolored	.40	.25
1816	A245	20c multicolored	1.00	.25
1817	A245	30c multicolored	1.50	.30
1818	A245	60c multicolored	3.00	.65
1819	A245	70c multicolored	3.50	.75
		Nos. 1813-1819 (7)	10.20	2.70

Souvenir Sheet

1820	A245	1.50cor multicolored	5.25	3.75

New Zealand '90, Intl. Philatelic Exhibition.

Fauna A246

No. 1821, Panthera onca. No. 1822, Felis pardalis, vert. No. 1823, Atelles geoffrogi, vert. No. 1824, Tapirus bairdi. No. 1825, Dasypus novencintus. No. 1826, Canis latrans. No. 1827, Choloepus hoffmanni.

1990, Oct. 10

1821	A246	5c multicolored	.45	.25
1822	A246	5c multicolored	.45	.25
1823	A246	10c multicolored	.45	.25
1824	A246	20c multicolored	.95	.25
1825	A246	30c multicolored	1.60	.30
1826	A246	60c multicolored	3.00	.65
1827	A246	70c multicolored	3.75	.75
		Nos. 1821-1827 (7)	10.65	2.70

FAO, 45th anniv.

Flower Type of 1983 Redrawn Without Date

1991, Apr. 24 **Litho.** ***Perf. 14x13½***

Size: 19x22mm

1828	A151	1cor like #1220	.65	.25
1829	A151	2cor like #1212	1.25	.25
1830	A151	3cor like #1218	1.60	.25
1831	A151	4cor like #1219	2.50	.25
1832	A151	5cor like #1217	3.10	.25
1833	A151	6cor like #1210	3.60	.25
1834	A151	7cor like #1216	4.25	.25
1835	A151	8cor like #1215	5.00	.25
1836	A151	9cor like #1211	5.50	.25
1837	A151	10cor like #1221	8.25	.25
1838	A151	11cor like #1214	7.00	.25
1839	A151	12cor like #1222	7.25	.25
1840	A151	13cor like #1213	8.00	.25
1841	A151	14cor like #1224	8.50	.25
1842	A151	15cor like #1223	9.50	.25
1843	A151	16cor like #1209	10.25	.25
		Nos. 1828-1843 (16)	86.20	4.00

Dr. Pedro Joaquin Chamorro — A247

1991, Apr. 25 ***Perf. 14½x14***

1844	A247	2.25cor multicolored	1.90	.45

1990 World Cup Soccer Championships, Italy — A248

Designs: No. 1845, Two players. No. 1846, Four players, vert. 50c, Two players, referee. 1cor, Germany, five players, vert. 1.50cor, One player, vert. 3cor, Argentina, five players, vert. 3.50cor, Italian players.
7.50cor, German team with trophy.

1991, July 16 ***Perf. 14x14½, 14½x14***

1845	A248	25c multicolored	.60	.25
1846	A248	25c multicolored	.60	.25
1847	A248	50c multicolored	.60	.25
1848	A248	1cor multicolored	.95	.25
1849	A248	1.50cor multicolored	1.30	.30
1850	A248	3cor multicolored	3.00	.60
1851	A248	3.50cor multicolored	3.25	.70
		Nos. 1845-1851 (7)	10.30	2.60

Souvenir Sheet

1852	A248	7.50cor multicolored	5.00	1.50
a.		Overprinted in sheet margin ('93)	5.00	1.60

No. 1852a overprint reads "COPA DE FOOTBALL / U.S.A. '94."

Butterflies — A249

Designs: No. 1853, Prepona praeneste. No. 1854, Anartia fatima. 50c, Eryphanis aesacus. 1cor, Heliconius melpomene. 1.50cor, Chlosyne janais. 3cor, Marpesia iole. 3.50cor, Metamorpha epaphus.
7.50cor, Morpho peleides.

1991, July 16 ***Perf. 14½x14***

1853	A249	25c multicolored	.35	.25
1854	A249	25c multicolored	.35	.25
1855	A249	50c multicolored	.60	.25
1856	A249	1cor multicolored	.90	.30
1857	A249	1.50cor multicolored	1.30	.45
1858	A249	3cor multicolored	2.90	.95
1859	A249	3.50cor multicolored	3.00	1.05
		Nos. 1853-1859 (7)	9.40	3.50

Souvenir Sheet

1860	A249	7.50cor multicolored	5.00	2.10

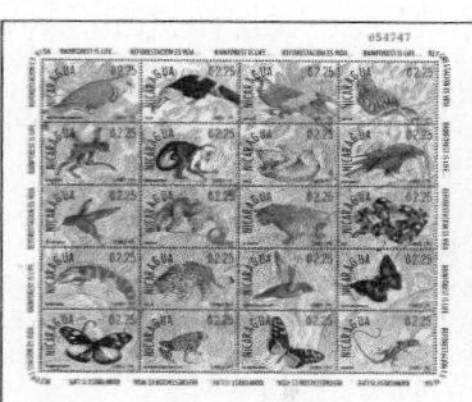

Fauna of Rainforest — A250

No. 1861 a, Yellow-headed amazon. b, Toucan. c, Scarlet macaw (lapa roja). d, Quetzal. e, Spider monkey (mono arana). f, Capuchin monkey. g, Sloth (cucala). h, Oropendola. i, Violet sabrewing (colibri violeta). j, Tamandua. k, Jaguarundi. l, Boa constrictor. m, Iguana. n, Jaguar. o, White-necked jacobin. p, Doxocopa clothilda. q, Dismorphia deione. r, Golden arrow-poison frog (rana venenosa). s, Calithomia hezia. t, Chameleon.

1991, Aug. 7 **Litho.** ***Perf. 14x14½***

1861	A250	2.25cor Sheet of 20, #a.-t.	35.00	15.00

America Issue — A251

2.25cor, Concepcion volcano.

1990, Oct. 12 ***Perf. 14½x14***

1862	A251	2.25cor multi	2.00	.55

Orchids — A252

Designs: No. 1863, Isochilus major. No. 1864, Cycnoches ventricosum. 50c, Vanilla odorata. 1cor, Helleriella nicaraguensis. 1.50cor, Barkeria spectabilis. 3cor, Maxillaria hedwigae. 3.50cor, Cattleya aurantiaca.
7.50cor, Psygmorchis pusilla, vert.

1991 **Litho.** ***Perf. 14x14½***

1863	A252	25c multicolored	.55	.25
1864	A252	25c multicolored	.55	.25
1865	A252	50c multicolored	.55	.25
1866	A252	1cor multicolored	.80	.25
1867	A252	1.50cor multicolored	1.30	.25
1868	A252	3cor multicolored	2.40	.50
1869	A252	3.50cor multicolored	3.00	.55
		Nos. 1863-1869 (7)	9.15	2.30

Souvenir Sheet

Perf. 14½x14

1870	A252	7.50cor multicolored	4.75	1.50

Locomotives of South America — A253

Various steam locomotives.

1991, Apr. 21 ***Perf. 14½x14***

1871	A253	25c	Bolivia	.55	.25
1872	A253	25c	Peru	.55	.25
1873	A253	50c	Argentina	.55	.25
1874	A253	1.50cor	Chile	1.30	.25
1875	A253	2cor	Colombia	1.75	.30
1876	A253	3cor	Brazil	2.40	.50
1877	A253	3.50cor	Paraguay	2.90	.55
			Nos. 1871-1877 (7)	10.00	2.35

Souvenir Sheets

1878	A253	7.50cor	Nicaragua	5.00	3.00
1879	A253	7.50cor	Guatemala	5.00	3.00

Birds — A254

Designs: 50c, Eumomota supercilliosa. 75c, Trogon collaris. 1cor, Electron platyrhynchum. 1.50cor, Teleonema filicauda. 1.75cor, Tangara chilensis, horiz. No. 1885, Pharomachrus mocino. No. 1886, Phlegopsis nigromaculata. No. 1887, Hylophylax naevioides, horiz. No. 1888, Aulacorhynchus haematopygius, horiz.

1991 ***Perf. 14½x14, 14x14½***

1880	A254	50c multicolored	.55	.25
1881	A254	75c multicolored	.65	.25
1882	A254	1cor multicolored	.80	.25
1883	A254	1.50cor multicolored	1.40	.25
1884	A254	1.75cor multicolored	1.50	.30
1885	A254	2.25cor multicolored	2.00	.35
1886	A254	2.25cor multicolored	2.00	.35
		Nos. 1880-1886 (7)	8.90	2.00

Souvenir Sheets

1887	A254	7.50cor multicolored	4.50	3.00
1888	A254	7.50cor multicolored	4.50	3.00

Paintings by Vincent Van Gogh — A255

Designs: No. 1889, Head of a Peasant Woman Wearing a Bonnet. No. 1890, One-Eyed Man. 50c, Self-Portrait. 1cor, Vase with Carnations and Other Flowers. 1.50cor, Vase with Zinnias and Geraniums. 3cor, Portrait of Pere Tanguy. 3.50cor, Portrait of a Man, horiz.
7.50cor, Path Lined with Poplars, horiz.

1991 ***Perf. 14x13½, 13½x14***

1889	A255	25c multicolored	.50	.25
1890	A255	25c multicolored	.50	.25
1891	A255	50c multicolored	.60	.25
1892	A255	1cor multicolored	.80	.25
1893	A255	1.50cor multicolored	1.25	.25
1894	A255	3cor multicolored	2.50	.50
1895	A255	3.50cor multicolored	2.60	.55
		Nos. 1889-1895 (7)	8.75	2.30

Size: 128x102mm

Imperf

1896	A255	7.50cor multicolored	4.75	1.25

Phila Nippon '91 — A256

Designs: 25c, Golden Hall. 50c, Phoenix Hall. 1cor, Bunraku puppet head. 1.50cor, Japanese cranes. 2.50cor, Himeji Castle. 3cor, Statue of the Guardian. 3.50cor, Kabuki warrior. 7.50cor, Vase.

1991 ***Perf. 14x14½***

1897	A256	25c multicolored	.50	.25
1898	A256	50c multicolored	.50	.25
1899	A256	1cor multicolored	.90	.25
1900	A256	1.50cor multicolored	1.30	.25
1901	A256	2.50cor multicolored	1.90	.40
1902	A256	3cor multicolored	2.40	.50
1903	A256	3.50cor multicolored	2.75	.55
		Nos. 1897-1903 (7)	10.25	2.45

Souvenir Sheet

1904	A256	7.50cor multicolored	5.00	3.00

Inscriptions are switched on 50c and 2.50cor.

Child's Drawing — A257

1991

1905	A257	2.25cor multicolored	1.75	.45

Central American Bank of Economic Integration, 30th Anniv. — A258

1991, Aug. 1 Litho. *Perf. 14*

1906 A258 1.50cor multicolored 1.50 .50

No. 1906 printed with se-tenant label.

Discovery of America, 500th Anniv. (in 1992) — A259

1991, Oct. 12 *Perf. 14½x14*

1907 A259 2.25cor Columbus' fleet 2.00 .75

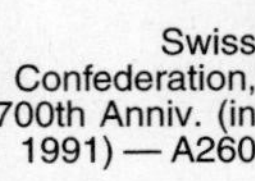

Swiss Confederation, 700th Anniv. (in 1991) — A260

1992, Aug. 1 Litho. *Perf. 14x14½*

1908 A260 2.25cor black & red 2.00 .75

Contemporary Art — A261

Designs: No. 1909, Pitcher, by Jose Ortiz. No. 1910, Black jar, by Lorenza Pineda Cooperative, vert. 50c, Vase, by Elio Gutierrez, vert. 1cor, Christ on Cross, by Jose de Los Santos, vert. 1.50cor, Sculpture of family, by Erasmo Moya, vert. 3cor, Bird and fish, by Silvio Chavarria Cooperative. 3.50cor, Filigree jar, by Maria de Los Angeles Bermudez, vert. 7.50cor, Masks by Jose Flores.

Perf. 14x14½, 14½x14

1992, Sept. 17 Litho.

1909 A261 25c multicolored .50 .25
1910 A261 25c multicolored .50 .25
1911 A261 50c multicolored .50 .25
1912 A261 1cor multicolored .85 .25
1913 A261 1.50cor multicolored 1.25 .30
1914 A261 3cor multicolored 2.50 .65
1915 A261 3.50cor multicolored 3.00 .75
Nos. 1909-1915 (7) 9.10 2.70

Imperf

Size: 100x70mm

1916 A261 7.50cor multicolored 5.00 1.60

Miniature Sheet

Fauna and Flora of Rainforest — A262

No. 1917: a, Colibri magnifico (b). b, Aguila arpia (f). c, Orchids. d, Toucan, Mariposa morpho. e, Quetzal (i). f, Guardabarranco (g, k). g, Mono aullador (howler monkey). h, Perezoso (sloth). i, Mono ardilla (squirrel monkey). j, Guacamaya (macaw) (n). k, Boa esmeralda, Tanagra escarlata (emerald boa, scarlet tanager). l, Rana flecha venenosa (arrow frog). m, Jaguar. n, Oso hormiguero (anteater) (o). o, Ocelot. p, Coati.

1992, Nov. 12 *Perf. 14½x14*

1917 A262 1.50cor Sheet of 16, #a.-p. 21.50 6.00

1992 Winter Olympics, Albertville A263

No. 1918, Ice hockey. No. 1919, 4-man bobsled. No. 1920, Combined slalom, vert. No. 1921, Speed skating. No. 1922, Cross-country skiing. No. 1923, Double luge. No. 1924, Ski jumping, vert. No. 1925, Slalom.

Perf. 14x14½, 14½x14

1992, Sept. 17

1918 A263 25c multi .55 .25
1919 A263 25c multi .55 .25
1920 A263 50c multi .55 .25
1921 A263 1cor multi .60 .25
1922 A263 1.50cor multi 1.30 .30
1923 A263 3cor multi 3.00 .65
1924 A263 3.50cor multi 3.10 .75
Nos. 1918-1924 (7) 9.65 2.70

Imperf

Size: 100x70mm

1925 A263 7.50cor multi 4.75 1.60
a. Overprinted ('93) 4.75 1.60

No. 1925a overprint reads "JUEGOS PRE OLIMPICOS DE INVIERNO / LILLEHAMMER, NORUEGA."

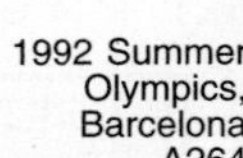

1992 Summer Olympics, Barcelona A264

No. 1926, Javelin. No. 1927, Fencing. No. 1928, Basketball. No. 1929, 1500-meter race. No. 1930, Long jump. No. 1931, Women's 10,000-meter race. No. 1932, Equestrian. No. 1933, Canoeing

Perf. 14x14½, 14½x14

1992, Sept. 17 Litho.

1926 A264 25c multi .50 .25
1927 A264 25c multi .50 .25
1928 A264 50c multi .50 .25
1929 A264 1.50cor multi 1.30 .30
1930 A264 2cor multi 1.75 .40
1931 A264 3cor multi 2.50 .65
1932 A264 3.50cor multi 3.00 .75
Nos. 1926-1932 (7) 10.05 2.85

Imperf

Size: 96x68mm

1933 A264 7.50cor multi 5.00 1.60
a. Overprinted ('93) 4.75 1.60

Nos. 1927-1932 are vert. Dated 1991.

No. 1933a overprint reads "JUEGOS PRE OLIMPICOS DE VERANO / ATLANTA, GA. / ESTADOS UNIDOS DE AMERICA."

Father R. M. Fabretto and Children — A265

1992, Nov. 12 Litho. *Perf. 14x14½*

1934 A265 2.25cor multicolored 1.75 .50

Nicaraguan Natives, by Claudia Gordillo — A266

1992, Nov. 12

1935 A266 2.25cor black & brn 1.75 .50

Nicaraguan Caciques, by Milton Jose Cruz — A267

1992, Nov. 12

1936 A267 2.25cor multicolored 1.60 .50

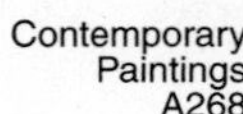

Contemporary Paintings A268

Paintings by: No. 1937, Alberto Ycaza, vert. No. 1938, Alejandro Arostegui, vert. 50c, Bernard Dreyfus. 1.50cor, Orlando Sobalvarro. 2cor, Hugo Palma. 3cor, Omar D'Leon. 3.50cor, Carlos Montenegro, vert. 7.50cor, Federico Nordalm.

Perf. 14½x14, 14x14½

1992, Nov. 12

1937 A268 25c multicolored .50 .25
1938 A268 25c multicolored .50 .25
1939 A268 50c multicolored .50 .25
1940 A268 1.50cor multicolored 1.20 .30
1941 A268 2cor multicolored 1.75 .40
1942 A268 3cor multicolored 2.40 .65
1943 A268 3.50cor multicolored 2.90 .75
Nos. 1937-1943 (7) 9.75 2.85

Imperf

Size: 100x70mm

1944 A268 7.50cor multicolored 4.75 1.60

Monument to Columbus, Rivas — A269

1993, Mar. 22 *Perf. 14½x14*

1945 A269 2.25cor multicolored 1.75 .50

UPAEP issue. Dated 1992.

Catholic Religion in Nicaragua, 460th Anniv. — A270

Designs: 25c, Eucharistic gonfalon. 50c, Statue of Virgin Mary. 1cor, Document, 1792-93. 1.50cor, Baptismal font. 2cor, Statue of Madonna and Child. 2.25cor, Monsignor Diego Alvarez Osario. 3cor, Christ on cross.

1993, Mar. 22

1946 A270 25c multicolored .50 .25
1947 A270 50c multicolored .50 .25
1948 A270 1cor multicolored .80 .25
1949 A270 1.50cor multicolored 1.30 .30
1950 A270 2cor multicolored 1.75 .40
1951 A270 2.25cor multicolored 1.95 .50
1952 A270 3cor multicolored 2.60 .65
Nos. 1946-1952 (7) 9.40 2.60

Dated 1992.

A271

Archdiocese of Managua: a, 3cor, Cathedral of the Immaculate Conception. b, 4cor, Cross, map.

1993, Apr. 30

1953 A271 Pair, #a.-b. 5.00 1.75

Dated 1992.

A272

Player, country: 50c, Brolin, Sweden. No. 1955, Karas, Poland; Costa, Brazil. No. 1956, Bossis, Platini, France. 1.50cor, Schumacher, Germany. 2cor, Zubizarreta, Spain. 2.50cor, Matthaeus, Germany; Maradona, Argentina. 3.50cor, Robson, England; Santos, Portugal. 10cor, Biyik, Cameroun; Valderrama, Colombia.

1994, Jan. 28 Litho. *Perf. 14*

1954 A272 50c multicolored .50 .25
1955 A272 1cor multicolored .75 .25
1956 A272 1cor multicolored .75 .25
1957 A272 1.50cor multicolored 1.30 .30
1958 A272 2cor multicolored 1.60 .40
1959 A272 2.50cor multicolored 2.10 .55
1960 A272 3.50cor multicolored 3.00 .75
Nos. 1954-1960 (7) 10.00 2.75

Souvenir Sheet

1961 A272 10cor multicolored 6.25 2.00

1994 World Cup Soccer Championships, US.

Sonatina, by Alma Iris Prez A272a

1993, Oct. 29 Litho. *Perf. 13½x14*

1961A A272a 3cor multicolored 1.90 1.00

Butterflyfish — A273

No. 1962: a, Chaetodon lunula. b, Chaetodon rainfordi. c, Chaetodon reticulatus. d, Chaetodon auriga. e, Heniochus acuminatus. f, Coradion fulvocinctus. g, Chaetodon speculum. h, Chaetodon lineolatus. i, Chaetodon bennetti. j, Chaetodon melanotus. k, Chaetodon aureus. l. Chaetodon ephippium. m, Hemitaurichthys polylepis. n, Chaetodon semeion. o, Chaetodon kleinii. p, Chelmon rostratus.

1993, Nov. 18 Litho. *Perf. 14*

1962 Sheet of 16 21.50 7.50
a.-p. A273 1.50cor Any single .75 .30
q. Inscribed with Bangkok '93 emblem in sheet margin 19.50 7.50
r. Inscribed with Indopex '93 emblem in sheet margin 19.50 7.50
s. Inscribed with Taipei '93 emblem in sheet margin 19.50 7.50

Issue date: No. 1962, Nov. 1, 1993.

No. 1962 is without any show emblem in sheet margin.

1994 Winter Olympics, Lillehammer, 1996 Summer Olympics, Atlanta — A274

No. 1963, Downhill skiing. No. 1964, Four-man bobsled. No. 1965, Swimming. No. 1966, Diving. No. 1967, Speed skating. No. 1968, Race walking. No. 1969, Hurdles. No. 1970, Ski jumping. No. 1971, Women's gymnastics. No. 1972, Women's figure skating. No. 1973, Pairs figure skating. No. 1974, Javelin. No. 1975, Biathlon. No. 1976, Running.

No. 1977, Torch, hands. No. 1978, Flags.

1993, Nov. 18

1963 A274 25c multicolored .45 .25
1964 A274 25c multicolored .45 .25
1965 A274 25c multicolored .45 .25
1966 A274 25c multicolored .45 .25
1967 A274 50c multicolored .45 .25
1968 A274 50c multicolored .45 .25
1969 A274 1cor multicolored .75 .25
1970 A274 1.50cor multicolored 1.25 .30
1971 A274 1.50cor multicolored 1.25 .30
1972 A274 2cor multicolored 1.50 .40
1973 A274 3cor multicolored 2.40 .65
1974 A274 3cor multicolored 2.40 .65
1975 A274 3.50cor multicolored 2.75 .75
1976 A274 3.50cor multicolored 2.75 .75
Nos. 1963-1976 (14) 17.75 5.55

Souvenir Sheets

1977 A274 7.50cor multicolored 4.75 1.50
1978 A274 7.50cor multicolored 4.75 1.50

1994 Winter Olympics (#1963-1964, 1967, 1970, 1972-1973, 1975, 1978). Others, 1996 Summer Olympics.

Pan-American Health Organization, 90th Anniv. — A275

1993, June 16 ***Perf. 14½***
1979 A275 3cor multicolored 2.25 .65

Organization of American States, 23rd General Assembly A276

1993, June 7 ***Perf. 13½x14***
1980 A276 3cor multicolored 2.25 .65

Christmas A276a

Paintings: 1cor, Holy Family, by unknown painter. 4cor, Birth of Christ, by Lezamon.

1994, Feb. 23 Litho. ***Perf. 13½x14***
1980A A276a 1cor multicolored .70 .25
1980B A276a 4cor multicolored 2.60 .70

Fauna and Flora of Rainforest — A277

No. 1981: a, Bromeliacae. b, Tilmatura dupontii. c, Anolis biporcatus (b). d, Fulgara laternaria. e, Bradypus. f, Spizaetus ornatus. g, Cotinga amabilis. h, Bothrops schlegelii. i, Odontoglossum. j, Agalychnis callidryas. k, Heliconius spaho. l, Passiflora vitifolia.
No. 1982, Dasyprocta punctata. No. 1983, Melinaea lilis.

1994, Jan. 20 ***Perf. 14***
1981 A277 2cor Sheet of 12, #a.-l. 20.00 7.50

Souvenir Sheets

1982 A277 10cor multicolored 5.25 1.75
1983 A277 10cor multicolored 5.25 1.75

Hong Kong '94 — A278

No. 1984 — Butterflies: a, Callicore patelina. b, Chlosyne narva. c, Anteos maerula. d, Marpesia petreus. e, Pierella helvetia. f, Eurytides epidaus. g, Heliconius doris. h, Smyrna blomfildia. i, Eueides lybia. j, Adelpha heraclea. k, Heliconius hecale. l, Parides montezuma. m, Morpho polyphemus. n, Eresia alsina. o, Prepona omphale. p, Morpho granadensis.

1994, Feb. 18 Litho. ***Perf. 14***
1984 A278 1.50cor Sheet of 16, #a.-p. 20.00 6.00

Astronomers A279

No. 1985 — Copernicus and: a, Satellite. b, Tycho Brahe (1546-1601), making observations. c, Galileo probe, Galileo. d, Isaac Newton, Newton telescope. e, Giotto probe to Halley's comet, Edmund Halley. f, James Bradley (1693-1762), Grenwich Observatory. g, 1793 telescope, William Herschel (1738-1822). h, John Goodricke (1764-86), stellar eclipse. i, Gottingen observatory, Karl Fredrich Gauss (1777-1855). j, Friedrich Bessell (1784-1846), astronomical instrument. k, Harvard College Observatory, William Granch (1783-1859). l, George B. Airy (1801-92), stellar disc. m, Lowell Observatory, Flagstaff, Arizona, Percival Lowell (1855-1916). n, George A. Halle (1868-1938), solar spectrograph. o, Space telescope, Edwin Hubble (1889-1953). p, Gerard Kuiper (1905-73), Uranus' moon Miranda.
10cor, Nicolas Copernicus, interstellar probe.

1994, Apr. 4
1985 A279 1.50cor Sheet of 16, #a.-p. 19.00 4.50

Souvenir Sheet

1986 A279 10cor multicolored 5.50 2.00

Automotive Anniversaries — A280

No. 1987: a, 1886 Benz three-wheel car. b, 1909 Benz Blitzen. c, 1923 Mercedes Benz 24/100/140. d, 1928 Mercedes Benz SSK. e, 1934 Mercedes Benz Cabriolet 500k. f, 1949 Mercedes Benz 170S. g, 1954 Mercedes Benz W196. h, 1954 Mercedes Benz 300SL. i, 1896 Ford four-wheel car. j, 1920 Ford taxi. k, 1928 Ford Roadster. l, 1932 Ford V-8. m, 1937 Ford 78 (V-8). n, 1939 Ford 91 Deluxe Tudor Sedan. o, 1946 Ford V-8 Sedan Coupe. p, 1958 Ford Custom 300.
10cor, Henry Ford (1863-1947), 1903 Ford Model A; Karl Benz (1844-1929), 1897 Benz 5CH.

1994, Apr. 5
1987 A280 1.50cor Sheet of 16, #a.-p. 19.00 4.50

Souvenir Sheet

1988 A280 10cor multicolored 5.25 2.00

First Benz four-wheeled vehicle, cent. (Nos. 1987a-1987h). First Ford gasoline engine, cent. (Nos. 1987i-1987p).

Graf Zeppelin — A281

No. 1989 — Graf Zeppelin and: a, Dr. Hugo Eckener, Count Zeppelin (inside cabin). b, New York City, 1928. c, Tokyo, 1929. d, San Simeon, California, 1929. e, Col. Charles Lindbergh, Dr. Hugo Eckener, 1929. f, Moscow, 1930. g, Paris, 1930. h, Cairo, 1931. i, Arctic waters. j, Rio de Janeiro, 1932. k, London, 1935. l, St. Peter's Basilica, Vatican City. m, Swiss Alps. n, Brandenburg Gate. o, Eckener in control room. p, Ernest A. Lehman, DO-X.
No. 1990, Graf Zeppelin, Count Zeppelin. No. 1991, Zeppelin, Eckener.

1994, Apr. 6
1989 A281 1.50cor Sheet of 16. #a.-p. 19.00 4.50

Souvenir Sheets

1990 A281 10cor multicolored 5.25 1.75
1991 A281 10cor multicolored 5.25 1.75

Dr. Hugo Eckener (1868-1954) (#1991).

Contemporary Crafts — A282

Designs: No. 1992, 50c, Basket weaving, by Rosalia Sevilla, horiz. No. 1993, 50c, Wood carving, by Julio Lopez. No. 1994, 1cor, Woman carrying sack, by Indiana Robleto. No. 1995, 1cor, Church, by Auxiliadora Bush. 2.50cor, Carving, by Jose de Los Santos. 3cor, Costumed doll with horse's head, by Ines Gutierrez de Chong. 4cor, Ceramic container, by Elio Gutierrez.
10cor, Metate, by Saul Carballo.

Perf. 13½x14, 14x13½

1994, Feb. 15 Litho.
1992-1998 A282 Set of 7 9.25 2.00

Imperf

Size: 96x66mm

1999 A282 10cor multicolored 5.25 1.60

Dated 1993.

Stone Carvings, Chontal Culture — A283

Color of inscription tablet: No. 2000, 50c, Yellow. No. 2001, 50c, Yellow brown. No. 2002, 1cor, Green. No. 2003, 1cor, Yellow green. 2.50cor, Greenish blue. 3cor, Blue. 4cor, Grey green.
10cor, Two stone totems seen against landscape painting.

1994, Feb. 23 ***Perf. 14***
2000-2006 A283 Set of 7 9.25 2.00

Imperf

Size: 96x66mm

2007 A283 10cor multicolored 5.25 1.60

Dated 1993.

Contemporary Art — A284

Designs: No. 2008, 50c, Lady Embroidering, by Guillermo Rivas Navas. No. 2009, 50c, Virgin of Nicaragua, by Cella Lacayo. No. 2010, 1cor, The Dance, by June Beer. No. 2011, 1cor, Song of Peace, by Alejandro Canales. 2.50cor, Fruits, by Genaro Lugo, horiz. 3cor, Figures and Fragments, by Leonel Vanegas. 4cor, Eruption of Volcano of Water, by Asilia Guillen, horiz.
10cor, Still life, by Alejandro Alonso Rochi.

1994, Mar. 15 ***Perf. 14x13½, 13½x14***
2008-2014 A284 Set of 7 9.25 2.00

Imperf

Size: 96x66mm

2015 A284 10cor multicolored 5.25 1.60

Dated 1993.

Prominent Nicaraguan Philatelists — A285

Designs: 1cor, Gabriel Horvilleur (1907-91). 3cor, Jose S. Cuadra A. (1932-92). 4cor, Alfredo Pertz (1864-1948).

1994, Apr. 18 Litho. ***Perf. 14***
2016-2018 A285 Set of 3 5.25 1.40

Dated 1993.

First Tree Conference of Nicaragua A286

1994, June 5 ***Perf. 14x13½***
2019 A286 4cor multicolored 2.40 .70

Souvenir Sheets

Reported Alien Sightings A287

Date and location of sighting: No. 2020, 60cor, July 21, 1991, Missouri. No. 2021, 60cor, July 28, 1965, Argentina. No. 2022, 60cor, Aug. 21, 1955, Kentucky. No. 2023, 60cor, Oct. 25, 1973, Pennsylvania. No. 2024, 60cor, Sept. 19, 1961, New Hampshire. No. 2025, 60cor, Nov. 7, 1989, Kansas. No. 2026, 60cor, Sept. 26, 1976, Grand Canary Island. No. 2027, 60cor, May 8, 1973, Texas.

1994, May 25 Litho. ***Perf. 14***
2020-2027 A287 Set of 8 *225.00 75.00*

Sheet margins of Nos. 2020-2027 have inscriptions in English, but also exist with inscriptions in Spanish.

Sacred Art — A288

Designs: No. 2028, 50c, Pulpit, Cathedral of Leon. No. 2029, 50c, Statue of Saint Ann, Chinandega Parish. No. 2030, 1cor, Statue of St. Joseph, San Pedro Parish, Rivas. No. 2031, 1cor, Statue of St. James, Jinotepe Parish. 2.50cor, Chalice, Subtiava Temple, Leon. 3cor, Processional cross, Nequinohoma Parish, Masaya. 4cor, Crucifix, Temple of Miracles, Managua.
10cor, Silver frontal, San Pedro Parish, Rivas.

1994, July 11 Litho. ***Perf. 14***
2028-2034 A288 Set of 7 9.25 2.25

Size: 96x66mm

Imperf

2036 A288 10cor multicolored 5.00 1.75

No. 2035 is unassigned.

A289

1994, July 4 Litho. ***Perf. 14***
2037 A289 3cor multicolored 1.90 1.00

Intl. Conference of New or Restored Democracies.

A290

1994, Aug. 2

2038 A290 4cor multicolored 2.40 1.50

32nd World Amateur Baseball Championships.

PHILAKOREA '94 — A291

No. 2039: a, Soraksan. b, Statue of Kim Yu-Shin. c, Solitary Rock. d, Waterfall, Hallasan Valley. e, Mirukpong and Pisondae. f, Chonbuldong Valley. g, Bridge of the Seven Nymphs. h, Piryong Falls.

No. 2040, Boy on first birthday, gifts of fruit.

1994, Aug. 16

2039 A291 1.50cor Sheet of 8, #a.-h. 9.50 4.00

Souvenir Sheet

2040 A291 10cor multicolored 4.75 3.00

Dinosaurs A292

No. 2041: a, Tyrannosaurus rex. b, Plateosaurus (f-g). c, Pteranodon (b). d, Camarasaurus (c). e, Euplocephalus. f, Sacuanjoche. g, Deinonychus (h). h, Chasmosaurus (d). i, Dimorphodon. j, Ametriorhynchids (i). k, Ichthyosaurus (j). l, Pterapsis, Compsognathus. m, Cephalopod. n, Archelon (o). o, Griphognatus, Gyroptychius. p, Plesiosaur (o), Navtiloid.

1994, Sept. 1

2041 A292 1.50cor Sheet of 16, #a.-p. 20.00 8.50

1994 World Cup Soccer Championships, US — A293

Players: a, Rai. b, Freddy Rincon. c, Luis Garcia. d, Thomas Dooley. e, Franco Baresi. f, Tony Meola. g, Enzo Francescoli. h, Roy Wegerle.

No. 2043, 10cor, Faustino Asprilla. No. 2044, 10cor, Adolfo Valencia, horiz.

1994, Sept. 19

2042 A293 3cor Sheet of 8, #a.-h. 14.00 7.50

Souvenir Sheets

2043-2044 A293 Set of 2 10.50 6.00

D-Day, 50th Anniv. — A294

No. 2045: a, British fighter plane. b, C-47 transports dropping paratroopers. c, HMS Mauritius bombards Houlgate. d, Mulberry artificial harbor. e, Churchill tank. f, Landing craft approaching beach.

1994, Sept. 26

2045 A294 3cor Sheet of 6, #a.-f. 10.00 6.00

Ruben Dario National Theater, 25th Anniv. — A295

1994, Sept. 30

2046 A295 3cor multicolored 1.60 1.00

A296

Intl. Olympic Committee, Cent. — A297

Gold Medalists: No. 2047, Cassius Clay (Muhammad Ali), boxing, 1960. No. 2048, Renate Stecher, track, 1972, 1976. 10cor, Claudia Pechstein, speed skating, 1994.

1994, Oct. 3

2047 A296 3.50cor multicolored 2.25 1.25

2048 A296 3.50cor multicolored 2.25 1.25

Souvenir Sheet

2049 A297 10cor multicolored 5.25 3.25

La Carreta Nagua, by Erick Joanello Montoya — A298

1994, Oct. 19

2050 A298 4cor multicolored 2.40 1.25

Motion Pictures, Cent. — A299

No. 2051 — Film and director: a, The Kid, Charlie Chaplin. b, Citizen Kane, Orson Welles. c, Lawrence of Arabia, David Lean. d, Ivan the Terrible, Sergei Eisenstein. e, Metropolis, Fritz Lang. f, The Ten Commandments, Cecil B. DeMille. g, Gandhi, Richard Attenborough. h, Casablanca, Michael Curtis. i, Platoon, Oliver Stone. j, The Godfather, Francis Ford Coppola. k, 2001: A Space Odyssey, Stanley Kubrick. l, The Ocean Depths, Jean Renoir.

No. 2052, Gone With the Wind, Victor Fleming.

1994, Nov. 14

2051 A299 2cor Sheet of 12, #a.-l. 17.00 8.00

Souvenir Sheet

2052 A299 15cor multicolored 8.00 5.00

Wildlife — A300

No. 2053: a, Nyticorax nyticorax. b, Ara macao. c, Bulbulcus ibis. d, Coragyps atratus. e, Epicrates cenchria. f, Cyanerpes cyaneus. g, Ortalis vetula. h, Bradypus griseus. i, Felis onca. j, Anhinga anhinga. k, Tapirus bairdi. l, Myrmecophaga jubata. m, Iguana iguana. n, Chelydra serpentina. o, Dendrocygna autumnalis. p, Felis paradalis.

1994, Oct. 31

2053 A300 2cor Sheet of 16, #a.-p. 23.00 10.00

First Manned Moon Landing, 25th Anniv. A301

No. 2054: a, Docking command, lunar modules. b, Lift-off. c, Entering lunar orbit. d, Footprint on moon. e, Separation of first stage. f, Trans-lunar insertion. g, Lander descending toward moon. h, Astronaut on moon.

No. 2055, 10cor, Astronaut saluting, flag. No. 2056, 10cor, Astronauts in quarantine, horiz.

1994, Oct. 17

2054 A301 3cor Sheet of 8, #a.-h. 14.00 8.00

Souvenir Sheets

2055-2056 A301 Set of 2 9.50 6.50

Nos. 2055-2056 each contain one 29x47mm stamp.

Contemporary Paintings by Rodrigo Penalba — A302

Designs: 50c, Discovery of America. 1cor, Portrait of Maurice. 1.50cor, Portrait of Franco. 2cor, Portrait of Mimi Hammer. 2.50cor, Seated Woman. 3cor, Still Life, horiz. 4cor, Portrait of Maria Augusta. 15cor, Entrance to Anticoli.

1994, Nov. 15

2057-2063 A302 Set of 7 9.75 4.75

Size: 66x96mm

Imperf

2064 A302 15cor multicolored 6.75 4.75

Domestic Cats — A303

No. 2065: a, Chocolate point Himalayan. b, Red Somalian. c, American long hair. d, Russian blue. e, Scottish folded ear. f, Persian chinchilla. g, Egyptian mau. h, Manx blue cream. i, Burmese blue Malaysian. j, Balinesian seal point. k, Oriental long-haired blue. l, Persian chinchilla cameo. m, Angora. n, Siamese. o, Burmese seal point. p, Mixed red.

15cor, Golden shoulder Persian.

1994, Dec. 20 Litho. *Perf. 14*

2065 A303 1.50cor Sheet of 16, #a.-p. 18.00 8.00

Souvenir Sheet

2066 A303 15cor multicolored 6.75 5.00

No. 2066 contains one 38x51mm stamp.

Wild Fowl — A304

No. 2067 — Penelopina nigra: a, 50c, Male, female on tree branch. b, 1cor, Head of male, male on tree branch. c, 2.50cor, Head of female, female on tree branch. d, 3cor, Male spreading wings, female.

No. 2068, Heads of male and female Penelopina nigra. No. 2069, Anhinga anhinga.

1994, Dec. 20 Litho. *Perf. 14*

2067 A304 Vert. strip of 4, #a.-d. 13.00 2.25

Souvenir Sheets

2068 A304 15cor multi 6.75 7.00

2069 A304 15cor multi 6.75 5.50

World Wildlife Fund (#2067).

No. 2067 was issued in minature sheets of 3 strips.

Sculpture — A305

Designs: 50c, Truth, by Aparicio Arthola. 1cor, Owl, by Orlando Sobalvarro. 1.50cor, Small Music Player, by Noel Flores Castro. 2cor, Exodus II, by Miguel Angel Abarca. 2.50cor, Raza, by Fernando Saravia. 3cor, Dolor Incognito, by Edith Gron. 4cor, Heron, by Ernesto Cardenal.

No. 2077, 15cor, Atlante, by Jorge Navas Cordonero. No. 2078, 15cor, Motherhood, by Rodrigo Penalba.

1995, Feb. 23 Litho. *Perf. 14½*

2070-2076 A305 Set of 7 9.75 4.50

Size: 66x96mm

Imperf

2077-2078 A305 Set of 2 13.50 9.00

Historic Landmarks A306

Designs: 50c, Animas Chapel, Granada, vert. 1cor, San Francisco Convent, Granada. 1.50cor, Santiago Tower, Leon, vert. 2cor, Santa Ana Church, Nindiri. 2.50cor, Santa Ana Church, Nandaime, vert. 3cor, Lion Gate, Granada. 4cor, Castle of the Immaculate Conception, Rio San Juan.

15cor, Hacienda San Jacinto, Managua.

1995 Litho. *Perf. 14*

2079-2085 A306 Set of 7 9.75 4.50

Size: 96x66mm

2086 A306 15cor multicolored 6.75 4.50

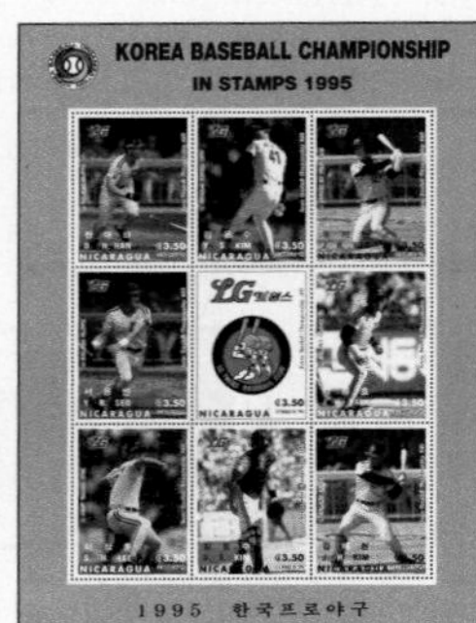

Korean Baseball Championships — A307

No. 2087, 3.50cor — LG Twins: No. 2087a, D.H. Han. b, Y.S. Kim. c, J.H. Yoo. d, Y.B. Seo. e, Team logo. f, J.H. Park. g, S.H. Lee. h, D.S. Kim. i, J.H. Kim.

No. 2088, 3.50cor — Samsung Lions: a, J.L. Ryu. b, S.Y. Kim. c, S.R. Kim. d, B.C. Dong. e, Team logo. f, K.W. Kang. g, C.S. Park. h, J.H. Yang. i, T.H. Kim.

No. 2089, 3.50cor — SBW Raiders: a, H.J. Park. b, K.J. Cho. c, K.T. Kim. d, W.H. Kim. e, Team logo. f, I.H. Baik. g, S.K. Park. h, K.L. Kim. i, J.S. Park.

No. 2090, 3.50cor — Doosan OB Bears: a, M.S. Lee. b, C.S. Park. c, H.S. Lim. d, K.W. Kim. e, Team logo. f, J.S. Kim. g, T.H. Kim. h, H.S. Kim. i, S.J. Kim.

No. 2091, 3.50cor — Pacific Dolphins: a, M.W. Jung. b, K.K. Kim. c, H.J. Kim. d, M.T. Chung. e, Team logo. f, B.W. An. g, D.G. Yoon. h, S.D. Choi. i, D.K. Kim.

No. 2092, 3.50cor — Hanwha Eagles: a, J.H. Jang. b, Y.D. Han. c, K.D. Lee. d, J.S. Park. e, Team logo. f, M.C. Jeong. g, J.W. Song. h, J.G. Kang. i, D.S. Koo.

No. 2093, 3.50cor — Lotte Giants: a, H.K. Yoon. b, D.H. Park. c, H.K. Joo. d, E.G. Kim. e,

Team logo. f, J.T. Park. g, P.S. Kong. h, J.S. Yeom. i, M.H. Kim.

No. 2094, 3.50cor — Haitai Tigers: a, D.Y. Sun. b, J.B. Lee. c, J.S. Kim. d, S.H. Kim. e, Team logo. f, G.C. Lee. g, G.H. Cho. h, S.H. Kim. i, S.C. Lee.

1995, Mar. 25 Litho. *Perf. 14*

Sheets of 9, #a-i

2087-2094 A307 Set of 8 140.00 77.50

Nature Paintings — A308

Designs: 1cor, Advancing Forward, by Maria Jose Zamora. 2cor, Natural Death, by Rafael Castellon. 4cor, Captives of Water, by Alvaro Gutierrez.

1995, Apr. 4 Litho. *Perf. 14*

2095-2097 A308 Set of 3 4.50 2.25

British-Nicaragua Expedition, San Juan River — A309

1995, May 5

2098 A309 4cor multicolored 2.25 1.25

Boaco Festival A310

1995, May 10

2099 A310 4cor multicolored 2.25 1.25

Printed with se-tenant label.

Contemporary Paintings, by Armando Morales — A311

Designs: 50c, Ferry Boat. 1cor, Oliverio Castañeda, vert. 1.50cor, Sitting Nude, vert. 2cor, Señoritas at the Port of Cabeza. 2.50cor, The Automobile and Company, vert. 3cor, Bullfight, vert. 4cor, Still life.

15cor, Woman Sleeping.

1995, Oct. 31 Litho. *Perf. 14*

2100-2106 A311 Set of 7 10.00 4.50

Size: 96x66mm

2107 A311 15cor multicolored 7.25 4.50

Louis Pasteur (1822-95) — A312

1995, Sept. 28 Litho. *Perf. 14*

2108 A312 4cor multicolored 2.25 1.25

First Place in Childrens' Painting Contest — A313

Nature scene, by Brenda Jarquin Gutierrez.

1995, Oct. 9

2109 A313 3cor multicolored 1.90 .90

Animals — A314

No. 2110: a, Crocodile. b, Opossum. c, Zahina. d, Guardatinale. e, Frog. f, Iguana. g, Macaw. h, Capybara. i, Vampire bat.

No. 2111, 15cor, Jaguar, vert. No. 2112, 15cor, Eagle, vert.

1995, Oct. 9

2110 A314 2.50cor Sheet of 9, #a.-i. 15.00 6.75

Souvenir Sheets

2111-2112 A314 Set of 2 14.50 9.00

Issued: #2112, 4/15; #2110-2111, 10/9.

FAO, 50th Anniv. — A315

1995, Oct. 16

2113 A315 4cor multicolored 2.25 1.25

UN, 50th Anniv. — A316

No. 2114: a, 3cor, UN flag, doves, rainbow. b, 4cor, Rainbow, lion, lamb. c, 5cor, Rainbow, dove on soldier's helmet.

No. 2115, Children holding hands under sun, dove.

1995, Oct. 31

2114 A316 Strip of 3, #a.-c. 7.00 3.75

Souvenir Sheet

2115 A316 10cor multicolored 5.00 3.00

No. 2114 is a continuous design.

Rotary Intl., 90th Anniv. — A317

1995, Nov. 17

2116 A317 15cor Paul Harris, logo 7.25 4.50

Souvenir Sheet

2117 A317 25cor Old, new logos 11.50 7.50

Butterflies, Moths — A318

No. 2118: a, Cyrestis camillus. b, Salamis cacta. c, Charaxes castor. d, Danaus formosa. e, Graphium ridleyanus. f, Hewitsonia boisduvali. g, Charaxes zoolina. h, Kallima cymodoce i, Precis westermanni. j, Papilo antimachus. k, Cymothoe sangaris. l, Papillo zalmoxis.

No. 2119, Danaus formosa, vert.

1995, Nov. 17

2118 A318 2.50cor Sheet of 12, #a.-l. 19.00 9.00

Souvenir Sheet

2119 A318 15cor multicolored 7.25 4.50

1996 Summer Olympics, Atlanta — A319

No. 2120: a, Michael Jordan. b, Heike Henkel. c, Linford Christie. d, Vitaly Chtcherbo. e, Heike Drechsler. f, Mark Tewksbury.

Pierre de Coubertin and: No. 2121, 20cor, Javelin thrower, horiz. No. 2122, 20cor, Runner.

1995, Dec. 1 Litho. *Perf. 14*

2120 A319 5cor Sheet of 6, #a.-f. 16.00 9.00

Souvenir Sheets

2121-2122 A319 Set of 2 19.00 12.00

John Lennon (1940-80) — A320

1995, Dec. 8

2123 A320 2cor multicolored 1.75 .60

Issued in sheets of 16.

Trains — A321

Designs: No. 2124, 2cor, Mombasa mail train, Uganda. No. 2125, 2cor, Steam locomotive, East Africa. No. 2126, 2cor, Electric locomotive, South Africa. No. 2127, 2cor, Beyer-Garrat steam locomotive, South Africa. No. 2128, 2cor, Beyer-Garrat steam locomotive, Rhodesia. No. 2129, 2cor, Class 30 steam locomotive, East Africa.

No. 2130: a, New York Central & Hudson River RR 4-4-0, #999, US. b, Australian Class 638, 4-6-2, Pacific. c, Baldwin 2-10-2, Bolivia. d, Vulcan 4-8-4, China. e, Paris-Orleans 4-6-2 Pacific, France. f, Class 062, 4-6-4, Japan.

No. 2131, 15cor, Siberian cargo train. No. 2132, 15cor, Midland 4-4-0 train, Great Britain. No. 2133, 15cor, Soviet steam locomotive.

1995, Dec. 11

2124-2129 A321 Set of 6 8.50 3.75

Miniature Sheet

2130 A321 4cor Sheet of 6, #a.-f. 14.00 7.25

Souvenir Sheets

2131-2133 A321 Set of 3 21.00 13.50

#2131-2133 each contain one 85x28mm stamp.

Establishment of Nobel Prize Fund, Cent. — A322

No. 2134: a, Otto Meyerhof, medicine, 1922. b, Léon Bourgeois, peace, 1920. c, James Franck, physics, 1925. d, Leo Esaki, physics, 1973. e, Miguel Angel Asturias, literature, 1967. f, Henri Bergson, literature, 1927. g, Friedrich Bergius, chemistry, 1931. h, Klaus von Klitzing, physics, 1985. i, Eisaku Sato, Japan, peace, 1974.

No. 2135: a, Wilhelm C. Roentgen, physics, 1901. b, Theodor Mommsen, literature, 1902. c, Philipp E.A. von Lenard, physics, 1905. d, Walther H. Nernst, chemistry, 1920. e, Hans Spemann, medicine, 1935. f, Jean Paul Sartre, literature, 1964. g, T.S. Eliot, literature, 1948. h, Albert Camus, literature, 1957. i, Ludwig Quidde, peace, 1927. j, Werner Heisenberg, physics, 1932. k, Joseph Brodsky, literature, 1987. l, Carl von Ossietzky, peace, 1935.

No. 2136, 15cor, Sin-itiro Tomonaga, physics, 1965. No. 2137, 15cor, Johannes Stark, physics, 1919. No. 2138, 15cor, Oscar Arias Sánchez, peace, 1987.

1995, Dec. 11

2134 A322 2.50cor Sheet of 9, #a.-i. 14.50 6.75

2135 A322 2.50cor Sheet of 12, #a.-l. 1.90 9.00

Souvenir Sheets

2136-2138 A322 Set of 3 21.00 13.50

Orchids — A323

No. 2139: a, Cattleya dowinana. b, Odontoglossum maculatum. c, Barkeria lindleyana. d, Rossioglossum grnde. e, Brassavpia digbyana. f, Miltonia schroederiana. g, Ondidium ornithorhynchum. h, Odontoglossum cervantesii. i, Chysis tricostata.

No. 2140: a, Lycaste auburn. b, Lemboglossum cordatum. c, Cyrtochilum macranthum. d, Miltassia Aztec "Nalo." e, Masdevaltia ignea. f, Oncidium sniffen "Jennifer Dauro." g, Brassolaeliocattleya Alma Kee. h, Ascocenda blue boy. i, Phalaenopsis.

15cor, Odontogiossum uro-skinneri.

1995, Dec. 15

2139 A323 2.50cor Sheet of 9, #a.-i. 15.00 6.75

2140 A323 3cor Sheet of 9, #a.-i. 16.00 8.25

Souvenir Sheet

2141 A323 15cor multicolored 7.25 4.50

World War II, 50th Anniv. — A324

No. 2142: a, Patton's troops crossing the Rhine. b, Churchill, Roosevelt, and Stalin at Yalta. c, US flag being raised at Iwo Jima. d, Marine infantry taking possession of Okinawa. e, US troops greeting Russian troops at Torgau. f, Liberation of concentration camps. g, Signing UN Charter, June 1945. h, Ships arriving at Tokyo after war's end.

10cor, German Bf-109 fighter plane.

1996, Jan. 24 Litho. *Perf. 14*

2142 A324 3cor Sheet of 8, #a.-h. + label 15.00 7.25

Souvenir Sheet

2143 A324 10cor multicolored 5.00 3.00

Miniature Sheet

Exotic Birds — A325

No. 2144: a, Paradisiaea apoda. b, Dryocopus galeatus. c, Psarisomus dalhousiae (g). d, Psarocolius montezuma. e, Halcyon pileata. f, Calocitta formosa. g, Ara chloroptera. h, Platycercus eximius. i, Polyplectron emphanum. j, Cariama cristata. k, Opisthocomus hoatzin. l, Coracias cyanogaster.

10cor, Dryocopus galeatus.

1996, Feb. 1

2144 A325 2cor Sheet of 12, #a.-l. 17.00 7.25

Souvenir Sheet

2145 A325 10cor multicolored 5.00 3.00

Town of Rivas, 275th Anniv. A326

1995, Sept. 23 Litho. *Perf. 14*

2146 A326 3cor multi +label 1.80 .90

Christmas A327

1995, Dec. 8

2147 A327 4cor multicolored 2.25 1.25

20th Century Writers — A328

No. 2148 — Writer, country flag: a, C. Drummond de Andrade (1902-87), Brazil. b, Cesar Vallejo (1892-1938), Peru. c, J. Luis Borges (1899-1986), Argentina. d, James Joyce (1882-1941), Italy. e, Marcel Proust (1871-1922), France. f, William Faulkner (1897-1962), US. g, Vladmir Maiakovski (1893-1930), Russia. h, Ezra Pound (1885-1972), US. i, Franz Kafka (1883-1924), Czechoslovakia. j, T.S. Eliot (188-1965), United Kingdom. k, Rainer Rilke (1875-1926), Austria. l, Federico G. Lorca (1898-1936), Spain.

1995, Oct. 15 ***Perf. 14½x14***

2148 A328 3cor Sheet of 12, #a.-l. 22.00 12.50

Classic Sailing Ships — A329

No. 2149, 2.50cor: a, Mayflower, England. b, Young America, US. c, Preussen, Germany. d, Lateen-rigged pirate ship, Caribbean Sea. e, Cutty Sark, England. f, Square-rigged pirate ship, Caribbean Sea. g, Galeón, Spain. h, The Sun King, France. i, Santa Maria, Spain.

No. 2150, 2.50cor: a, HMS Bounty, England. b, The President, US. c, Prince William, Holland. d, Flying Cloud, US. e, Markab, Nile River, Egypt. f, Europa, Holland. g, Vasa, Sweden. h, Foochow junk, China. i, San Gabriel, Portugal.

No. 2151, 15cor, Passat, Germany. No. 2152, 15cor, Japanese junk, vert.

1996, Jan. 10 **Litho.** ***Perf. 14***

Sheets of 9, #a-i

2149-2150 A329 Set of 2 29.00 13.50

Souvenir Sheets

2151-2152 A329 Set of 2 14.50 9.00

Visit of Pope John Paul II — A330

1996, Feb. 7

2153 A330 5cor multicolored 2.75 1.50

Puppies — A331

Various breeds: No. 2154, 1cor, Holding red leash in mouth. No. 2155, 1cor, With red bandanna around neck. No. 2156, 2cor, Spaniel playing with ball. No. 2157, 2cor, With dog biscuit in mouth. No. 2158, 3cor, Akita. No. 2159, 3cor, Bull dog. No. 2160, 4cor, With newspaper in mouth. No. 2161, 4cor, Dalmatian with cat.

No. 2162, 16cor, Bending down on front paws. No. 2163, 16cor, Poodle.

1996, Mar. 6

2154-2161 A331 Set of 8 13.00 7.25

Souvenir Sheets

2162-2163 A331 Set of 2 15.00 9.50

Famous Women A332

No. 2164: a, Indira Gandhi. b, Mme. Chiang Kai-shek. c, Mother Teresa. d, Marie Curie. e, Margaret Thatcher. f, Eleanor Roosevelt. g, Eva Perón. h, Golda Meir. i, Violeta Barrios de Chamorro.

No. 2165, 15cor, Jacqueline Kennedy Onassis, vert. No. 2166, 15cor, Aung San Suu Kyi, vert. No. 2167, 15cor, Valentina Tereshkova, vert.

1996, Mar. 8 ***Perf. 14x13½***

2164 A332 2.50cor Sheet of 9, #a.-i. 14.50 7.25

Souvenir Sheets

Perf. 13½x14

2165-2167 A332 Set of 3 22.00 13.50

Members of Baseball's Hall of Fame — A333

No. 2168 — Player, year inducted: a, Lou Gehrig, 1944. b, Rogers Hornsby, 1946. c, Mike Schmidt, 1995. d, Honus Wagner, 1936. e, Ty Cobb, 1936. f, Roberto Clemente, 1973. g, Babe Ruth, 1936. h, Johnny Bench, 1987. i, Tom Seaver, 1993.

10cor, Reggie Jackson, 1993.

1996, Mar. 15 **Litho.** ***Perf. 13½x14***

2168 A333 4cor Sheet of 9, #a.-i. 21.00 14.00

Souvenir Sheet

2169 A333 10cor multicolored 9.75 9.25

1996 Summer Olympics, Atlanta — A334

Designs: 1cor, Takehide Nakatani, Japan. 2cor, Olympic Stadium, Tokyo, 1964. 3cor, Al Oerter, US, vert. 10cor, Discus thrower from ancient games.

No. 2174, 2.50cor, vert. — Gold medal winners in boxing: a, Andrew Maynard, U.S. b, Rudi Fink, Germany. c, Peter Lessov, Bulgaria. d, Angel Herrera, Cuba. e, Patrizio Oliva, Italy. f, Armando Martinez, Cuba. g, Slobodan Kacar, Yugoslavia. h, Teofilo Stevenson, Cuba. i, George Foreman, U.S.

No. 2175, 2.50cor — Events: a, Basketball. b, Baseball. c, Boxing. d, Long jump. e, Judo. f, Team handball. g, Volleyball. h, Water polo. i, Tennis.

25cor, Cassius Clay (Muhammad Ali), US.

1996, Mar. 28 ***Perf. 14***

2170-2173 A334 Set of 4 9.25 7.25

Sheets of 9, #a-i

2174-2175 A334 Set of 2 29.00 20.00

Souvenir Sheet

2176 A334 25cor multicolored 12.00 11.00

Race Horses — A335

Carousel Horses A336

Race horses: 1cor, "Wave." 2cor, "Charming Traveler." 2.50cor, "Noble Vagabond." No. 2180, 3cor, "Golden Dancer," vert. No. 2181, 3cor, "Wave Runner." No. 2182, 4cor, "Ebony Champion." No. 2183, 4cor, "Wave Tamer."

Antique carousel horses: No. 2184a, Persian light infantry horse, 18th cent. b, Italian parade horse, 15th cent. c, German armored horse, 15th cent. d, Turkish light infantry horse, 17th cent.

16cor, "Proud Heart." 25cor, German armored horse, 16th cent.

1996, Apr. 15

2177-2183 A335 Set of 7 12.00 6.00

2184 A336 2cor Sheet of 4, #a.-d. 6.75 2.50

Souvenir Sheets

2185 A335 16cor multi 7.75 6.50

2186 A336 25cor multi 10.75 7.50

Marine Life — A337

No. 2187, 2.50cor: a, Butterflyfish (d). b, Barracuda (a). c, Manatee. d, Jellyfish. e, Octopus (b, d, f, g, h). f, Small yellow-striped fish. g, Lemon shark. h, Striped fish. i, Red fish.

No. 2188, 2.50cor: a, Reef shark. b, Diver, hammerhead shark (c, e). c, Moray eel (f). d, Macrela ojos de caballo (a, b, e). e, Hammerhead shark. f, Butterflyfish. g, Mediterranean grouper. h, Octopus, diff. i, Manta ray.

No. 2189, 20cor, Angelfish. No. 2190, 20cor, Saddleback butterflyfish.

1996, Apr. 29 **Litho.** ***Perf. 14***

Sheets of 9, #a-i

2187-2188 A337 Set of 2 29.00 14.50

Souvenir Sheets

2189-2190 A337 Set of 2 19.00 13.00

Chinese Lunar Calendar A338

Year signs: a, Rat. b, Ox. c, Tiger. d, Hare. e, Dragon. f, Snake. g, Horse. h, Sheep. i, Monkey. j, Rooster. k, Dog. l, Boar.

1996, May 6

2191 A338 2cor Sheet of 12, #a.-l. 15.00 6.50

China'96.

Central American Integration System (SICA) — A339

1996, May 8 ***Perf. 14½***

2192 A339 5cor multicolored 2.75 1.60

20th Century Events — A340

No. 2193: a, Russian revolution, 1917. b, Chinese revolution, 1945. c, Creation of the UN, 1945. d, Tearing down the Berlin Wall, 1989. e, World War I, vert. f, Creation of the State of Israel, 1948, vert. g, World War II, vert. h, 2nd Vatican Council, 1962-65, vert. i, Atom bombing of Hiroshima, 1945. j, Viet Nam War, 1962-73. k, Persian Gulf War, 1991. l, End of Apartheid, 1991.

1996 ***Perf. 14***

2193 A340 3cor Sheet of 12, #a.-l. + label 22.00 11.50

Souvenir Sheet

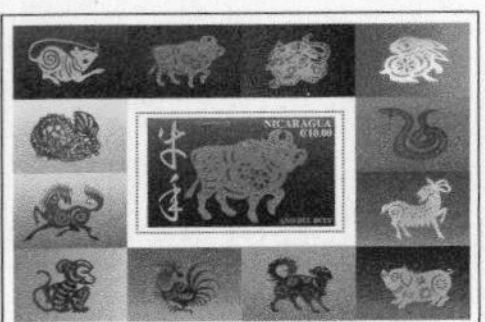

New Year 1997 (Year of the Ox) A341

1996 **Litho.** ***Perf. 15x14***

2194 A341 10cor multicolored 5.00 3.00

Wuhan Huanghelou A342

1996, May 20 **Litho.** ***Perf. 14***

2195 A342 4cor multicolored 2.25 1.50

China '96. No. 2195 was not available until March 1997. No. 2195 comes in a souvenir sheet of 1.

Red Parrot, by Ernesto Cardenal — A343

1996, June 5 **Litho.** ***Perf. 14½x14***

2196 A343 4cor multicolored 1.75 1.25

Friendship Between Nicaragua and Republic of China — A344

Designs: 10cor, Painting, "Landscape with Bags," by Fredrico Nordalm, vert. 20cor, Dr. Lee Teng-Hui, Pres. of Republic of China and Violeta Barrios de Chamorro, President of Nicaragua.

Perf. 14½x14, 14x14½

1996, June 26 **Litho.**

2197 A344 10cor multicolored 3.25 1.75

2198 A344 20cor multicolored 5.75 3.50

Violeta Barrios de Chamorro, President, 1990-96 — A345

Serpentine Die Cut

1997, Jan. 27 **Litho.**

Self-Adhesive

2199 A345 3cor multicolored 1.25 .90

a. Booklet pane of 9 + 2 labels 11.50

The peelable paper backing serves as a booklet cover.

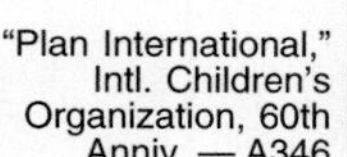

"Plan International," Intl. Children's Organization, 60th Anniv. — A346

1997, Feb. 24 *Serpentine Die Cut*

Self-Adhesive

2200 A346 7.50cor multicolored 2.50 2.25
a. Booklet pane of 12 31.00

The peelable paper backing serves as a booklet cover.

"Iberoamerica," Spanish-America Art Exhibition — A347

Painting, "Night with Two Figures," by Alejandro Aróstegui.

1998, May 8 *Perf. 13½*

2201 A347 7.50cor multicolored 2.60 2.00

Butterflies A348

No. 2202: a, Metamorpha stelenes. b, Erateina staudingeri. c, Premolis semirufa. d, Heliconius eisini. e, Phoebis phlea. f, Dione juno. g, Helicopis cupido. h, Catonephele numili. i, Anteos clorinde.

No. 2203, 25cor, Thecla coronata. No. 2204, 25cor, Ufefheisa bela.

1999, Mar. 15 **Litho.** *Perf. 14*

2202 A348 2.50cor Sheet of 9, #a.-i. 10.75 5.00

Souvenir Sheets

2203-2204 A348 Set of 2 17.00 15.50

Dated 1996.

Fauna of Central America — A349

No. 2205, 2cor: a, Red banded parrot. b, Sloth. c, Porcupine. d, Toucan. e, Howler monkey. f, Anteater. g, Kinkajou. h, Owl monkey. i, Red-footed land turtle. j, Red deer. k, Armadillo. l, Paca.

No. 2206, 2cor: a, Vulture. b, Tarantula. c, Palm viper. d, Ocelot. e, Fighting spider. f, Large fruit bat. g, Jaguar. h, Venomous tree frog. i, Viper. j, Grison. k, Rattlesnake. l, Puma.

No. 2207, 25cor, Tapir. No. 2208, 25cor, Caiman.

1999, Mar. 15 **Sheets of 12, #a-l**

2205-2206 A349 Set of 2 20.00 9.00

Souvenir Sheets

2207-2208 A349 Set of 2 14.50 9.00

Dated 1996.

Endangered Species — A350

No. 2209, 2.50cor: a, Owls, gorilla. b, Cheetahs. c, Giraffes. d, Gazelle, elephants. e, Elephants. f, Lion, okapi. g, Rhinoceros. h, Hippopotamus. i, Lion.

No. 2210, 2.50cor, vert: a, Lemurs. b, Blue gliding parrot. c, Toucan. d, Boa. e, Jaguar. f, Margay. g, Loris. h, White egret. i, Armadillo.

No. 2211, 2.50cor, vert: a, Prezwalski horse. b, Red deer. c, Zebra. d, Golden lion monkey. e, African elephant. f, Black bear. g, Tiger. h, Orangutan. i, Snow leopard.

25cor, Chimpanzee. 25.50cor, Panda, vert.

1999, Mar. 15 **Sheets of 9, #a-i**

2209-2211 A350 Set of 3 26.00 14.00

Souvenir Sheets

2212 A350 25cor multi 6.75 4.50
2213 A350 25.50cor multi 7.75 4.75

Dated 1996.

India's Independence, 50th Anniv. — A351

1998, Aug. 13 **Litho.** *Perf. 14½*

2214 A351 3cor blue & multi 1.00 .50
2215 A351 9cor brn yel & multi 2.00 1.50

Dated 1997.

Nature Reserves and Natl. Parks — A352

Designs: 1.50cor, Mombacho Volcano Nature Reserve. 2.50cor, La Flor Wildlife Refuge. 3cor, Zapatera Archipelago Natl. Park. 3.50cor, Miraflor Nature Reserve. 5cor, Cosigüina Volcano Natl. Park. 6.50cor, Masaya Volcano Natl. Park. 7.50cor, Juan Venado Island Nature Reserve. 8cor, Escalante Chacocente River Wildlife Refuge. 10cor, Protected Areas, Natl. Park System.

12cor, Trees, first Biosphere Reserve.

1998, Aug. 20 *Perf. 10½*

2216 A352 1.50cor multicolored .50 .25
2217 A352 2.50cor multicolored .10 .45
2218 A352 3cor multicolored 1.00 .50
2219 A352 3.50cor multicolored 1.25 .60
2220 A352 5cor multicolored 1.75 .85
2221 A352 6.50cor multicolored 2.25 1.10
2222 A352 7.50cor multicolored 2.60 1.25
2223 A352 8cor multicolored 2.90 1.40
2224 A352 10cor multicolored 3.75 1.75
Nos. 2216-2224 (9) 16.10 8.15

Size: 65x95mm

Imperf

2225 A352 12cor multicolored 3.75 2.00

National Museum, Cent — A353

1998, Aug. 25

2226 A353 3.50cor Footprints 1.50 .60

Paintings by Rodrigo Peñalba (1908-1979) — A354

Designs: 2.50cor, "Descendimiento." 3.50cor, "Victoria y Piere With Child." 5cor, "Motherhood."

10cor, "El Güegüense."

1998, Aug. 26 *Perf. 10½*

2227 A354 2.50cor multicolored 1.10 .45
2228 A354 3.50cor multicolored 1.40 .60
2229 A354 5cor multicolored 2.10 .85
Nos. 2227-2229 (3) 4.60 1.90

Size: 95x65mm

Imperf

2230 A354 10cor multicolored 3.25 1.75

Child's Painting, "Children Love Peace" — A355

1998, Aug. 28 *Perf. 14½*

2231 A355 50c multicolored 1.50 .25

Dated 1997.

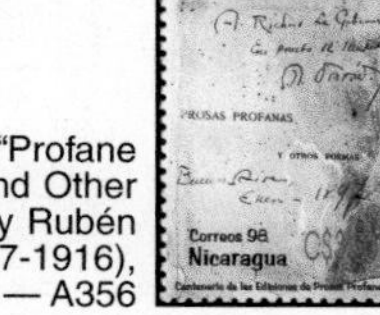

Publishing of "Profane Prose and Other Poems," by Rubén Darío (1867-1916), Cent. — A356

1998, Sept. 11 *Perf. 10½*

2232 A356 3.50cor shown 1.40 .60
2233 A356 5cor Portrait 1.95 .85

Naturaleza '98 — A357

Painting by Bayron Gómez Chavarría.

1998, Sept. 25

2234 A357 3.50cor multicolored 1.50 .60

World Stamp Day — A358

1998, Oct. 9

2235 A358 6.50cor multicolored 2.25 1.10

Dialogue of Nicaragua — A359

1998, Oct. 12

2236 A359 5cor multicolored 1.80 .85

Famous Nicaraguan Women — A360

America issue: 3.50cor, Lolita Soriano de Guerrero (b. 1922), writer. 7.50cor, Violeta Barrios de Chamorro (b. 1929), former president.

1998, Oct. 16

2237 A360 3.50cor multicolored 1.25 .60
2238 A360 7.50cor multicolored 2.75 1.25

Universal Declaration of Human Rights, 50th Anniv. — A361

1998, Dec. 10 *Perf. 13½*

2239 A361 12cor multicolored 3.75 2.10

Christmas A362

Nativity scenes: 50c, Molded miniature, vert. 1cor, Drawing on pottery, vert. 2cor, Adoration of the Magi. 3cor, Painting.

7.50cor, Painting of angel over modern village.

1998, Dec. 14 *Perf. 14*

2240 A362 50c multicolored .70 .25
2241 A362 1cor multicolored .70 .25
2242 A362 2cor multicolored .95 .35
2243 A362 3cor multicolored 1.40 .50
Nos. 2240-2243 (4) 3.75 1.35

Size: 95x64mm

Imperf

2244 A362 7.50cor multicolored 2.60 1.25

Dated 1997.

Managua Earthquake, 25th Anniv. (in 1997) — A363

Designs: 3cor, Managua in 1997, vert. 7.50cor, Devastation after earthquake in 1972.

10.50cor, Buildings toppling, clock, vert.

1998, Dec. 23

2245 A363 3cor multicolored 1.25 .50
2246 A363 7.50cor multicolored 2.75 1.25

Souvenir Sheet

2247 A363 10.50cor multicolored 3.75 1.75

Dated 1997.

Diana, Princess of Wales (1961-97) — A364

Designs: 5cor, Wearing hat. 7.50cor, Wearing tiara. 10cor, Wearing white dress.

1999, Apr. 29 **Litho.** *Perf. 13½*

2248-2250 A364 Set of 3 7.25 3.75

Nos. 2248-2250 were each issued in sheets of 6.

Butterflies A365

Designs: 3.50cor, Papilionidae ornithoptera. 8cor, Nymphalidae cepheuptychia. 12.50cor, Pieridae phoebis.

No. 2254: a, Nymphalidae eryphanis. b, Nymphalidae callicore. c, Nymphalidae hypolimmas. d, Nymphalidae precis. e, Papilionidae troides. f, Nymphalidae cithaerias. g, Papilionidae parides. h, Nymphalidae heliconius. i, Nymphalidae morpho.

15cor, Papilionidae papilio.

1999, Apr. 30 *Perf. 14*

2251-2253 A365 Set of 3 8.00 4.25
2254 A365 9cor Sheet of 9, #a.-i. 26.00 14.00

Souvenir Sheet

2255 A365 15cor multicolored 4.50 3.25

Sailing Ships A366

Paintings: 2cor, Eagle, 1851, US. 4cor, Contest, 1800, US. 5cor, Architect, 1847, US. 10cor, Edward O'Brien, 1863, UK.

No. 2260, vert: a, HMS Rodney, 1830, UK. b, Boyne, 1700's, Great Britain. c, Castor, 1800's, UK. d, Mutin, 1800's, UK. e, Britainnia, 1820, UK. f, Gouden Leeuw, 1600, Holland. g, Hercules, 1600, Holland. h, Resolution, 1667, Great Britain. i, Royal George, 1756, Great Britain. j, Vanguard, 1700's, Great Britain. k, Prince Royal, 1600, Great Britain. l, Zeven Provincien, 1600, Holland.

No. 2261, 15cor, Pamir, 1905, US. No. 2262, 15cor, Great Expedition, 1700's, Great Britain.

1999, May 31 Litho. *Perf. 14x13½*

2256-2259 A366 Set of 4 7.75 3.75

Perf. 14½x14¼

2260 A366 3cor Sheet of 12, #a.-l. 15.00 6.50

Souvenir Sheets

Perf. 13½x14

2261-2262 A366 Set of 2 9.25 5.50

No. 2260 contains twelve 28x36mm stamps.

Flora and Fauna — A367

Designs: 5cor, Anteos clorinde. 6cor, Coereba flaveola. No. 2265, 7.50cor, Rynchops niger. No. 2266, 7.50cor, Chaetodon striatus.

No. 2267, vert: a, Palm tree. b, Phaethon lepturus. c, Cinclocerthia ruficauda. d, Myadestes genibarbis. e, Rosa sinesis. f, Cyanophala bicolor. g, Delphinus delphis. h, Anolis carolinensis (l). i, Dynastes tityus. j, Heliconia psittacorum. k, Iguana iguana (j). l, Propona meander.

No. 2268, 10cor, Ceryle torquata, vert. No. 2269, 10cor, Anisotremus virginicus.

1999, June 14 *Perf. 14x14¼*

2263-2266 A367 Set of 4 10.00 4.75

Perf. 14¼x14

2267 A367 5cor Sheet of 12, #a.-l. 22.00 11.00

Souvenir Sheet

2268-2269 A367 Set of 2 6.50 4.50

No. 2267 l is inscribed 3cor, but the editors believe the sheet was sold as sheet of 5cor stamps.

Birds — A368

Designs: 5cor, Eudyptes chrysocome. 5.50cor, Spheniscus magellanious. 6cor, Pygoscelis antarctica. 7.50cor, Magadyptes antipodes.

No. 2274, horiz.: a, Phalacrocorax punctatus featherstoni. b, Phalacrocorax bougainvillii. c, Anhinga anhinga. d, Phalacrocorax punctatus punctatus. e, Phalacrocorax sulcirostris. f, Pelecanus occidentalis.

No. 2275, 12cor, Aptenodytes forsteri, horiz. No. 2276, 12cor, Pygoscelis papua.

1999, May 25 Litho. *Perf. 14*

2270-2273 A368 Set of 4 6.00 4.00

2274 A368 6cor Sheet of 6, #a.-f. 13.00 6.00

Souvenir Sheets

2275-2276 A368 Set of 2 12.00 4.00

Dated 1998.

Dinosaurs A369

No. 2277: a, Sordes. b, Dimorphodon. c, Anurognathus. d, Rhamphorhynchus. e, Pterodaustro. f, Pteranodon.

No. 2278: a, Macroplata. b, Coelurus. c, "Stegosaurus." d, "Corythosaurus." e, Thadeosaurus. f, "Brachisaurus."

No. 2279, 12cor, Platecarpus. No. 2280, 12cor, Pterodactylus.

1999, June 1 Litho. *Perf. 14*

2277 A369 5cor Sheet of 6, #a.-f. 11.50 5.00

2278 A369 6cor Sheet of 6, #a.-f. 12.50 6.00

Souvenir Sheets

2279-2280 A369 Set of 2 7.50 5.25

Dated 1998. Stamp inscriptions on Nos. 2278c, 2278d and 2278f, and perhaps others, are incorrect or misspelled.

Trains — A370

Designs: 1cor, U25B, Rock Island Line. 5cor, C-630 Santa Fe Railroad. 6.50cor, Class D. D. 40 AX, Union Pacific Railroad. 7.50cor, F Series B. B. EMD, Maryland Department of Transportation.

No. 2285: a, CR Alco RS11. b, Metra EMD F40. c, British Columbia Railways GF6C. d, Amtrak AEM7. e, C-40-9, Norfolk Southern. f, C-630, Reading Railroad.

No. 2286: a, British Columbia Railways GF6C, diff. b, Indian Railways WDM C-C. c, Class 421, Australia. d, Class M821, Australia. e, LRC B.B., Via Canada. f, GM Class X, Victorian Railways, Australia.

No. 2287, 15cor, Queen Victoria. No. 2288, 15cor, Donald Smith driving last spike of Trans-Canada Railway, vert.

1999, June 28 Litho. *Perf. 14*

2281-2284 A370 Set of 4 7.50 3.25

2285 A370 5cor Sheet of 6, #a.-f. 11.50 5.00

2286 A370 6cor Sheet of 6, #a.-f. 12.50 6.00

Souvenir Sheets

2287-2288 A370 Set of 2 9.25 5.00

Dated 1998. Stamp inscription on No. 2284, and perhaps others, is misspelled.

Mushrooms and Insects — A371

No. 2289: a, Tricholoma ustaloides, leaf beetle. b, Tricholoma pardinum, grasshopper. c, Amanita echinocephala, crickets. d, Tricholoma saponaceum, red-tipped clearwing moth. e, Amanita inaurata, hanging scorpionfly. f, Amanita rubescens, assassin bug.

No. 2290: a, Amanita citrina, banded agrion. b, Cryoptotrama asprata, clouded yellow butterfly. c, Amanita gemmata, mayfly. d, Catathelasma imperiale, variable reed beetle. e, Collybia fusipes, black swallowtail caterpillar. f, Collybia butyracea, South African savannah grasshopper.

No. 2291, 12.50cor, Tricholomopsis rutilans, lesser cloverleaf weevil. No. 2292, 12.50cor, Tricholoma virgatum, rose weevil.

1999, Oct. 27 Litho. *Perf. 13¼x13½*

2289 A371 5.50cor Sheet of 6, #a.-f. 11.00 9.00

2290 A371 7.50cor Sheet of 6, #a.-f. 16.00 12.50

Souvenir Sheets

2291-2292 A371 Set of 2 8.00 7.50

Dated 1998.

Ballooning — A372

No. 2293, 12cor: a, Solo Spirit 3. b, Emblem of Breitling Orbiter 3, first balloon to make non-stop circumnavigation, 1999. c, ICO Global.

No. 2294, 12cor: a, Breitling Orbiter 3 over mountains. b, Leonardo da Vinci. c, Brian Jones and Bertrand Piccard, pilots of Breitling Orbiter 3.

No. 2295, 12cor: a, Tiberius Cavallo. b, Breitling Orbiter 3 on ground. c, Piccard and Jones, diff.

No. 2296, 12cor: a, Jones. b, Breitling Orbiter 3 in flight. c, Piccard.

No. 2297, 25cor, Jean-Francois Pilatre de Rozier. No. 2298, 25cor, Jean-Pierre Blanchard. No. 2299, 25cor, Madame Thible. No. 2300, 25cor, J. A. C. Charles.

1999, Nov. 12 *Perf. 13½x13¼*

Sheets of 3, #a-c

2293-2296 A372 Set of 4 42.50 24.00

Souvenir Sheets

2297-2300 A372 Set of 4 37.50 16.00

Dated 1998.

Orchids — A373

Designs: 2cor, Cattleya, skinneri. 4cor, Lycaste aromatica. 5cor, Odontoglossum cervantesii. 10cor, Brassia verrucosa.

No. 2305, 3cor: a, Odontoglossum rossii. b, Cattleya aurantiaca. c, Encyclia cordigera. d, Phragmipedium bessae. e, Brassavola nodosa. f, Cattleya forbesii.

No. 2306, 3cor: a, Barkeria spectabilis. b, Dracula erythrochaete. c, Cochleanthes discolor. d, Encyclia cochleata. e, Lycaste aromatica. f, Brassia maculata.

No. 2307, 25cor, Odontoglossum rossii, diff. No. 2308, 25cor, Phragmipedium longifolium.

1999, Nov. 10

2301-2304 A373 Set of 4 7.75 4.25

Sheets of 6, #a.-f.

2305-2306 A373 Set of 2 16.00 7.25

Souvenir Sheets

2307-2308 A373 Set of 2 14.50 8.00

Rubén Darío Natl. Theater, 30th Anniv. — A374

1999, Dec. 6 *Perf. 13¼x13½*

2309 A374 7.50cor multi 2.60 1.50

Inter-American Development Bank, 40th Anniv. — A375

1999, Nov. 18 *Perf. 13¼*

2310 A375 7.50cor multi 2.60 1.50

America Issue, A New Millennium Without Arms — A376

1999, Nov. 25 *Perf. 13½*

2311 A376 7.50cor multi 2.60 1.50

Japanese-Nicaraguan Friendship — A377

Designs: a, 3.50cor, Fishing boats, Puertos Cabezas. b, 9cor, Hospital. c, 5cor, Combine in field. d, 6cor, Japanese school. e, 7.50cor, Bridge on Pan-American Highway. f, 8cor, Aqueduct.

1999, Nov. 12 *Perf. 13x13¼*

2312 A377 Sheet of 6, #a.-f. 12.50 10.00

UPU, 125th Anniv. — A378

1999, Dec. 20 Litho. *Perf. 13½*

2313 A378 7.50cor multi 2.50 1.40

Cities of Granada and León, 475th Anniv. — A379

No. 2314 — Granada: a, City Hall. b, Guadalupe Church. c, Buildings on central square. d, Houses with porches. e, House of the Leones. f, El Consulado Street.

No. 2315 — León: a, Cathedral. b, Municipal theater. c, La Recolección Church. d, Rubén Dario Museum. e, Post and Telegraph office. f, Cural de Subtiava house.

1999, Dec. 13 *Perf. 13x13½*

2314 A379 3.50cor Sheet of 6, #a.-f. 8.00 6.00

2315 A379 7.50cor Sheet of 6, #a.-f. 16.00 12.00

Dogs and Cats — A380

Designs: 1cor, Azawakh. 2cor, Chihuahua. 2.50cor, Chocolate colorpoint Birman, horiz. 3cor, Norwegian Forest cat, horiz.

No. 2320: a, Clumber spaniel. b, Australian shepherd. c, German wire-haired pointer. d, Unnnamed. e, Ibizan hound. f, Norwegian elkhound.

No. 2321, horiz.: a, Blue European Shorthair. b, Turkish Angora. c, Red Tiffany. d, Persian. e, Calico Shorthair. f, Russian Blue.

No. 2322, 12cor, Braque du Bourbonnais. No. 2323, 12cor, Burmese, horiz.

Perf. 13¾x13½, 13½x13¾

2000, July 20 Litho.

2316-2319 A380 Set of 4 4.25 2.40

2320 A380 6cor Sheet of 6, #a-f 8.50 6.25

2321 A380 6.50cor Sheet of 6, #a-f 10.50 6.75

Souvenir Sheets

2322-2323 A380 Set of 2 7.50 6.50

No. 2322 contains one 42x56mm stamp; No. 2323 contains one 56x42mm stamp.

Trains — A381

Designs: 3cor, Class 470 APT-P, Great Britain. 4cor, X-2000, Sweden. 5cor, XPT, Australia. 10cor, High speed train, Great Britain.

No. 2328: a, Metro North B-25-7. b, Long Island Railroad EMD DE30. c, EMD F40 PHM-2C. d, Pennsylvania Railroad GG1. e, New Jersey Transit MK GP40 FH-2. f, Amtrak EMD F59 PHI.

No. 2329: a, DM-3, Sweden. b, EW 165, New Zealand. c, Class 87, Great Britain. d, Class 40, Great Britain. e, GE 6/6, Switzerland. f, Class 277, Spain.

No. 2330, Metra EMD P69PN-AC. No. 2331, Class 44, Great Britain.

2000, Aug. 21 Litho. *Perf. 14*

2324-2327 A381 Set of 4 8.00 6.00

Sheets of 6, #a-f

2328-2329 A381 3cor Set of 2 16.00 10.00

Souvenir Sheets

2330-2331 A381 25cor Set of 2 14.50 14.00

Marine Life — A382

Designs: 3.50cor, Great white shark. 5cor, Humpback whale. 6cor, Sea turtle. 9cor, Sperm whale.

No. 2336, 7.50cor: a, Puffer fish. b, Manta ray. c, Black grouper. d, Tiger grouper. e, Golden-tailed eel. f, Atlantic squid.

No. 2337, 7.50cor: a, Hawksbill turtle. b, Moon jellyfish. c, Caribbean reef shark. d, Turtle. e, Spotted dolphin. f, Southern sting ray.

No. 2338, Tiger shark. No. 2339, Spotted dolphins.

2000, Aug. 22 ***Perf. 14***

2332-2335 A382 Set of 4 8.25 6.25

Sheets of 6, #a-f

2336-2337 A382 Set of 2 23.00 17.50

Souvenir Sheets

2338-2339 A382 25cor Set of 2 14.50 14.00

Queen Mother, 100th Birthday A383

No. 2340: a, As young woman. b, In 1970. c, With King George VI. d, As old woman.

Litho. (Margin Embossed)

2000, July 25 ***Perf. 14***

2340 A383 10cor Sheet of 4, #a-d + label 12.00 11.00

Souvenir Sheet

Perf. 13¾

2341 A383 25cor In 1948 7.50 7.50

No. 2341 contains one 38x51mm stamp.

History of Aviation A384

No. 2342, 7.50cor: a, Montgolfier balloon (blue background), vert. b, Hawker Hart. c, Lysander. d, Bleriot and Fox Moth, vert. e, Harrier. f, VC10.

No. 2343, 7.50cor: a, Montgolfier balloon (tan background), vert. b, Bristol F2B. c, Jet Provost. d, Avro 504K and Redwing II trainer, vert. e, Hunter. f, Wessex.

No. 2344, 25cor, Spartan Arrow (top) and Tiger Moth. No. 2345, 25cor, Tiger Moth (top) and Spartan Arrow.

2000, July 27 Litho. ***Perf. 14½x14***

Sheets of 6, #a-d

2342-2343 A384 Set of 2 30.00 25.00

Souvenir Sheets

2344-2345 A384 Set of 2 14.50 14.00

Size of Nos. 2342a, 2342d, 2343a, 2343d: 41x60mm.

Birds — A385

Designs: 5cor, Cotinga amabilis. 7.50cor, Galbula ruficauda. 10cor, Guiraca caerulea. 12.50cor, Momotus momota.

No. 2350: a, Ara macao. b, Amazona ochrocephala. c, Chloroceryle americana. d, Archilocus colubris. e, Pharamachrus mocinno. f, Ramphastos sulfuratus. g, Coereba flaveola. h, Piculus rubiginosus. i, Passerina ciris. j, Busarellus nigricollis.

No. 2351, 25cor, Aulacorhynchus prasinus. No. 2352, 25cor, Ceryle alcyon.

2000, Aug. 23 ***Perf. 14***

2346-2349 A385 Set of 4 10.25 8.25

2350 A385 3cor Sheet of 10, #a-j 13.00 8.25

Souvenir Sheets

2351-2352 A385 Set of 2 14.50 14.00

Space Exploration — A386

No. 2353, 5cor: a, Donald K. Slayton. b, M. Scott Carpenter. c, Walter M. Schirra. d, John H. Glenn, Jr. e, L. Gordon Cooper. f, Virgil I. Grissom. g, Mercury Redsone 3 rocket. h, Alan B. Shepard.

No. 2354, 5cor, horiz.: a, Recovery of Mercury 8. b, View of Earth from space. c, Carpenter in life raft. d, Shepard in water. e, USS Intrepid. f, Friendship 7. g, Mercury 9 splashdown. h, Recovery of Mercury 6.

No. 2355, 25cor, Glenn, diff. No. 2356, 25cor, Shepard, horiz.

2000, Aug. 25 **Litho.**

Sheets of 8, #a-h

2353-2354 A386 Set of 2 29.00 20.00

Souvenir Sheets

2355-2356 A386 Set of 2 14.50 13.50

Millennium — A387

No. 2357: a, Pope Leo XIII. b, Rerum Novarum. c, Pope Pius X. d, Revision of ecclesiatic music. e, Pope Benedict XV. f, Canonization of Joan of Arc. g, Pope Pius XI. h, Establishment of Radio Vatican. i, Pope John XXIII. j, Peace symbol. k, Pope Paul VI. l, Arms of Paul VI. m, Pope John Paul I. n, Lamb and cross. o, Pope John Paul II. p, Globe, hands holding dove.

No. 2358, 25cor, John XXIII. No. 2359, 25cor, John Paul II.

2000, Sept. 7 ***Perf. 13¼***

2357 A387 3cor Sheet of 16, #a-p + label 21.00 16.00

Souvenir Sheets

2358-2359 A387 Set of 2 14.50 14.00

No. 2357 contains sixteen 30x40mm stamps.

Butterflies — A388

No. 2360, 8cor: a, Catonephele numilla esite. b, Marpesia marcella. c, Heliconius hecalesia. d, Actinote thalia anteas. e, Doxocopa larentia cherubina. f, Napeogenes tolosa mombachoensis.

No. 2361, 9cor: a, Heliconius cydno galanthus. b, Nessaea agiaura. c, Godyris zavaleta sosunga. d, Caligo atreus dionysos. e, Morpho amatonte. f, Eryphanis polyxena lycomedon.

No. 2362, 25cor, Papilio garamas. No. 2363, 25cor, Cithaerias menander.

2000, Sept. 27 ***Perf. 14***

Sheets of 6, #a-f

2360-2361 A388 Set of 2 33.00 27.50

Souvenir Sheets

2362-2363 A388 Set of 2 14.50 14.00

20th Century National Leaders A389

No. 2364, 5cor: a, Kemal Ataturk, dam. b, Ataturk, Turkish flag, horiz. c, John F. Kennedy, wife Jacqueline, Soviet missiles, horiz. d, John F. Kennedy, rocket. e, Winston Churchill, bomb explosion. f, Churchill, airplane, horiz. g, Jomo Kenyatta, tribesman, animals, horiz. h, Kenyatta, Mt. Kenya.

No. 2365, 5cor: a, Indira Gandhi. b, Indira Gandhi, soldier, elephant, horiz. c, Ronald Reagan, airplanes, horiz. d, Reagan, American flags. e, Lenin. f, Lenin, hammer and sickle, horiz. g, Charles de Gaulle, Eiffel Tower, horiz. h, De Gaulle, monument.

No. 2366, 25cor, Chiang Kai-shek. No. 2367, 25cor, Theodore Roosevelt.

2000, Oct. 5 ***Perf. 14***

Sheets of 8, #a-h

2364-2365 A389 Set of 2 29.00 21.00

Souvenir Sheets

2366-2367 A389 Set of 2 14.50 13.50

Horizontal stamps are 56x42mm.

Lions Intl. A390

No. 2368, horiz.: a, Melvin Jones and other founding members, Chicago, 1917. b, Old headquarters building, Chicago. c, Helen Keller and dog. d, UN Secretary General Kofi Annan greeting Lions Intl. Pres. Kajit Hadananda. e, Jones and globe. f, André de Villiers, winner of 1998-99 Peace Poster contest.

2000, Oct. 26 **Litho.**

2368 A390 5cor Sheet of 6, #a-f 14.50 11.50

Souvenir Sheet

2369 A390 25cor Melvin Jones 7.25 6.75

Rotary Intl. A391

No. 2370: a, Clowns and child in Great Britain. b, Polio vaccination in Egypt. c, Burkina Faso natives at well. d, School for girls in Nepal. e, Assisting the disabled in Australia. f, Discussing problem of urban violence.

2000, Oct. 26 ***Perf. 14***

2370 A391 7cor Sheet of 6, #a-f 11.00 8.25

Souvenir Sheet

2371 A391 25cor Rotary emblem 7.25 7.00

Campaign Against AIDS — A392

2000, Dec. 1 **Litho.** ***Perf. 13¼***

2372 A392 7.50cor multi 2.10 1.60

Third Conference of States Signing Ottawa Convention A393

Designs: 7.50cor, People, world map. 10cor, People opposing land mines on globe.

2001, Sept. 18 ***Perf. 13x13½***

2373-2374 A393 Set of 2 4.25 3.25

Miniature Sheet

Bridges Built With Japanese Assistance — A394

No. 2375: a, 6.50cor, Tamarindo Bridge. b, 7.50cor, Ochomogo Bridge. c, 9cor, Gil González Bridge. d, 10cor, Las Lajas Bridge. e, 12cor, Río Negro Bridge.

2001, Oct. 23 ***Perf. 13x13¼***

2375 A394 Sheet of 5, #a-e, + label 9.50 8.25

World Post Day — A395

2001, Nov. 21 ***Perf. 13½***

2376 A395 6.50cor multi 1.80 1.40

Dated 2000.

America Issue — Old Léon Ruins, UNESCO World Heritage Site — A396

2001, Nov. 23 ***Perf. 13½***

2377 A396 10cor multi 2.40 2.00

Order of Piarists in Nicaragua, 50th Anniv. — A397

Perf. 13¼x13½

2001, Nov. 27 **Litho.**

2378 A397 7cor multi 1.75 1.40

Dated 2000.

Miniature Sheet

Endangered Wildlife — A398

No. 2379: a, 5cor, Rhamphastos swaisonii. b, 6.50cor, Amazona auropalliata. c, 8cor, Buteo magnirostris. d, 9cor, Atteles geoffroyi. 10cor, Leopardus wiedii. 12cor, Puma concolor.

2001, Nov. 27 ***Perf. 13¼x13***
2379 A398 Sheet of 6, #a-f 9.75 7.50

Dated 2000.

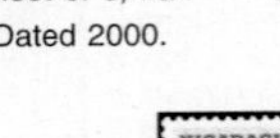

SOS Children's Villages, 50th Anniv. — A399

2001, Dec. 6 ***Perf. 13¼x13½***
2380 A399 5.50cor multi 1.50 1.00

Dated 2000.

Miguel Cardinal Obando Bravo — A400

2002, Jan. 3 Litho. ***Perf. 13½***
2381 A400 6.50cor multi 1.75 1.25

Souvenir Sheet

Friendship Between Nicaragua and People's Republic of China — A401

No. 2382: a, 3cor, President's House, Managua. b, 7.50cor, Ministry of Foreign Affairs Building, Managua.

2002, Jan. 4 Litho. ***Perf. 13x13¼***
2382 A401 Sheet of 2, #a-b 2.50 2.00

Visit of UN Secretary General Kofi Annan to Nicaragua — A402

2002, Mar. 15 Litho. ***Perf. 13¼***
2383 A402 14cor multi 2.75 2.50

Sister Maria Romero — A403

2002, Apr. 9 ***Perf. 13x13¼***
2384 A403 7.50cor multi 2.00 1.50

Discovery of Nicaragua, 500th Anniv. — A404

Design: 12cor, Natives watching ships on horizon, vert.

2002, Sept. 12 Litho. ***Perf. 13x13¼***
2385 A404 7.50cor shown 2.00 1.50

Souvenir Sheet

Perf. 13¼x13
2386 A404 12cor multi 3.25 2.00

America Issue - Youth, Education and Literacy — A405

2002, Nov. 29 Litho. ***Perf. 13¼x13***
2387 A405 7.50cor multi 2.00 1.75

Canonization of St. Josemaría Escrivá de Balaguer — A406

2002, Nov. 28 ***Perf. 13x13¼***
2388 A406 2.50cor multi 1.00 .50

Port of Corinto — A407

2002, Dec. 10
2389 A407 5cor multi 1.50 1.00

Managua Earthquake, 30th Anniv. — A408

Pictures of earthquake damage: 3.50cor, Avenida del Mercado Central. 7.50cor, Managua Cathedral, vert.

Perf. 13¼x13½, 13½x13¼
2002, Dec. 13
2390-2391 A408 Set of 2 3.25 2.50

Visit of Grand Duke Henri and Princess Maria Teresa of Luxembourg — A409

2003, Feb. 5 ***Perf. 13¼x13***
2392 A409 12cor multi 3.00 2.50

Paintings — A410

Designs: 3cor, En Diriamba de Nicaragua, Capturaronme Amigo, by Roger Pérez de la Rocha. 5cor, San Gabriel Arcangel, by Orlando Sobalvarro. 6.50cor, Ava Fénix, by Alejandro Aróstegui. 7.50cor, Abstracción de Frutas, by Leonel Vanegas. 8cor, Suite en Turquesa y Azules, by Bernard Dreyfus, horiz. 9cor, Ana III, by Armando Morales, horiz. 10cor, Coloso IV, by Arnoldo Guillén, horiz.

Perf. 14x13½, 13½x14
2003, Oct. 23 Litho.
2393-2399 A410 Set of 7 11.50 10.00

Souvenir Sheet

Pontificate of Pope John Paul II, 25th Anniv. — A411

No. 2400: a, 3cor, Pope wearing zucchetto. b, 10cor, Pope wearing miter.

2003, Oct. 28 Litho. ***Perf. 13¼x13***
2400 A411 Sheet of 2, #a-b 3.25 2.50

Christian Brothers (La Salle Order) in Nicaragua, Cent. — A412

Designs: 3cor, San Juan de Dios Hospice, horiz. 5cor, Brother Octavio de Jesús. 6.50cor, Brother Bodrán Marie. 7.50cor, Brother Agustin Hervé. 9cor, Brother Vauthier de Jesús. 10cor, Father Mariano Dubón.
12cor, St. Jean-Baptiste de la Salle.

Perf. 13½x14, 14x13½
2003, Nov. 14 Litho.
2401-2406 A412 Set of 6 9.50 7.00

Souvenir Sheet

2407 A412 12cor multi 2.75 2.50

Insects A413

No. 2408, 6.50cor: a, Fulgora laternaria. b, Acraephia perspicillata. c, Copidocephala guttata. d, Pterodictya reticularis. e, Phrictus quinquepartitus. f, Odontoptera carrenoi.
No. 2409, 8cor: a, Golofa pizarro. b, Phaneus pyrois. c, Plusiotis aurigans. d, Polyphylla concurrens. e, Dynastes hercules septentrionalis. f, Phaneus demon excelsus.

2003, Nov. 19 ***Perf. 13x13½***
Sheets of 6, #a-f
2408-2409 A413 Set of 2 20.00 16.00

Contemporary Crafts — A414

Designs: 3cor, Marble sculpture, vert. 5cor, Dolls. 6.50cor, Balsa wood fish and birds. 7.50cor, Cord and jipijapa hats. 8cor, Ceramics. 9cor, Saddle. 10cor, Clay rendition of Léon Cathedral.

Perf. 14x13½, 13½x14
2003, Nov. 20
2410-2416 A414 Set of 7 11.50 8.50

Lake and River Mail Steamships A415

Designs: 3cor, Victoria. 5cor, Irma. 6.50cor, Hollenbeck. 7.50cor, Managua.

2003, Nov. 28 ***Perf. 13½x14***
2417-2420 A415 Set of 4 5.50 4.00

America Issue - Flora and Fauna — A416

Designs: 10cor, Corytophanes cristatus. 12.50cor, Guaiacum sanctum.

2003, Dec. 4 ***Perf. 13x13¼***
2421-2422 A416 Set of 2 4.75 4.00

San Juan del Sur, 150th Anniv. — A417

2003, Dec. 9 Litho.
2423 A417 10cor multi 2.25 1.75

Miniature Sheet

Toyota Motor Vehicles A418

No. 2424: a, 1936 Model AA. b, 1936 Model AB Phaeton. c, 1947 Model SA. d, 1951 Model BJ. e, 1955 Model Crown RSD. f, 1958 Model FJ28VA.

2003, Dec. 11
2424 A418 7.50cor Sheet of 6, #a-f 9.00 6.75

Publication of Tierras Solares, by Rubén Darío, Cent. — A419

2004, June 22 ***Perf. 13x13¼***
2425 A419 10cor multi 2.25 1.75

Flora — A420

Designs: 3cor, Tabebuia rosea. 5cor, Cassia fistula. 6.50cor, Delonix regia.

2004, June 24
2426-2428 A420 Set of 3 4.00 3.25

America Issue - Environmental Protection A421

Designs: No. 2429, 7.50cor, Bosawas Río Bocay Biosphere Reserve. No. 2430, 7.50cor, Cerro Kilambé Nature Reserve.

2004, June 30
2429-2430 A421 Set of 2 3.75 3.25

2004 Summer Olympics, Athens — A422

Designs: 7.50cor, Track athletes. 10cor, Swimmers. 12cor, Rifleman.

2004, Aug. 13 ***Perf. 13¼x13***
2431-2433 A422 Set of 3 6.25 5.00

Central American Student's Games, Managua — A423

Designs: 3cor, Judo. 5cor, Soccer, baseball. 6.50cor, High jump, swimming.

2004, Sept. 17
2434-2436 A423 Set of 3 4.25 3.00

Birds — A424

Designs: 5cor, Selenidera spectabilis. 6.50cor, Nycticorax nycticorax. 7.50cor, Caracara plancus. 10cor, Myiozetetes similis.

2004, Sept. 28 **Litho.**
2437-2440 A424 Set of 4 7.00 5.00

Granada Railroad Station — A425

2004, Oct. 8 ***Perf. 13x13¼***
2441 A425 3cor multi 1.00 .50

Tourist Attractions A426

Designs: No. 2442, 7.50cor, Río Tapou, Río San Juan Forest Refuge. No. 2443, 7.50cor, Mombacho Volcano Natural Reserve.

2004, Oct. 12
2442-2443 A426 Set of 2 3.50 2.50

Contemporary Paintings — A427

Designs: 3cor, Frutas Ocultas, by Federico Nordalm. 7.50cor, Nicaraguapa, by Efrén Medina, vert. 10cor, Bambues, by Genaro Lugo.

2004, Nov. 4 ***Perf. 13x13¼, 13¼x13***
2444-2446 A427 Set of 3 5.00 3.75

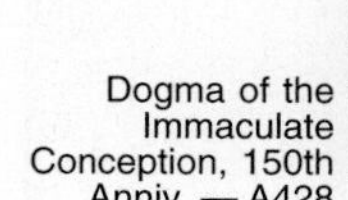

Dogma of the Immaculate Conception, 150th Anniv. — A428

2004, Dec. 6 ***Perf. 13¼x13***
2447 A428 3cor multi 1.30 1.00

Pablo Neruda (1904-73), Poet — A429

2004, Dec. 16
2448 A429 7.50cor multi 1.75 1.25

Publication of *Songs of Life and Hope,* by Rubén Darío, Cent. — A430

2005, Feb. 7 **Litho.** ***Perf. 13¼x13½***
2449 A430 7.50col multi + label 1.80 1.40

Souvenir Sheet

Nicaragua — Japan Diplomatic Relations, 70th Anniv. — A431

No. 2450: a, 3col, Adult volunteer teaching student. b, 7.50col, Momotombo Volcano. c, 10col, Vado Bridge, Bocana de Paiwas. d, 12col, Flowers.

2005, Feb. 21 ***Perf. 13x13¼***
2450 A431 Sheet of 4, #a-d 7.00 5.50

Orchids — A432

Designs: 3.50cor, Eleanthus hymeniformis. 5cor, Laelia superbens. 6.50cor, Cattleya aurentiaca. 7.50cor, Bletia roezlii. 10cor, Dimerandra emarginata. 12cor, Epidendrum wercklei.
25cor, Cyhysis tricostata.

2005 **Litho.** ***Perf. 13¼x13***
2451-2456 A432 Set of 6 9.25 6.75

Souvenir Sheet

2457 A432 25cor multi 4.25 3.75

Endangered Reptiles and Amphibians A433

Designs: 3cor, Dendrobates pumilio. 6.50cor, Drymodius melanotropis. 7.50cor, Cochranella granulosa. 10cor, Bolitoglossa mombachoensis. 12cor, Caiman crocodilus. 15cor, Polychrus gutturosus.
25cor, Lepidochelys olivacea.

2005 **Litho.** ***Perf. 13x13¼***
2458-2463 A433 Set of 6 10.50 8.50

Souvenir Sheet

2464 A433 25cor multi 4.25 3.75

Intl. Year of Microcredit — A434

2005 **Litho.** ***Perf. 13¼x13***
2465 A434 3.50cor multi 1.10 .45

Europa Stamps, 50th Anniv. — A435

Designs: Nos. 2466, 2470a, 14cor, Morpho peleides. Nos. 2467, 2470b, 14cor, Amazona autumnalis. Nos. 2468, 2470c, 15cor, Rubén Dario Monument. Nos. 2469, 2470d, 25cor, Antigua Cathedral, Managua.

2005, Dec. 12 ***Perf. 13¾x13½***
2466-2469 A435 Set of 4 12.00 10.00

Souvenir Sheet

Imperf

2470 A435 Sheet of 4, #a-d 14.50 13.50

No. 2470 contains four 40x30mm stamps.

Souvenir Sheet

Second Intl. Poetry Festival, Granada A436

No. 2471: a, 4.50cor, Jose Coronel Urtecho (1906-94), poet. b, 7cor, Guadalupe Church, 1856. c, 10cor, Church of St. Francis. d, 12cor, Joaquin Pasos (1914-47), poet.

2006 **Litho.** ***Perf. 14***
2471 A436 Sheet of 4, #a-d 6.75 5.25

Environmental Protection A437

Designs: 4.50cor, Casmerodius albus. 11.50cor, Amazilia tzacatl. 13.50cor, Jacana spinosa. 14.50cor, Mico River.

2007 **Litho.** ***Perf. 13x13¼***
2472-2475 A437 Set of 4 8.50 7.00

Gen. Augusto C. Sandino (1893-1934) — A438

Various photographs of Sandino: 8.50cor, 10.50cor, 12.50cor.

2007 ***Perf. 13¼x13***
2476-2478 A438 Set of 3 6.50 5.25

Land Mine Clearance Program, 15th Anniv. — A439

2007 **Litho.** ***Perf. 13x13¼***
2479 A439 19cor multi 3.75 3.25

Literacy Campaign, 27th Anniv. — A440

Various literacy campaign workers and students: 1cor, 2cor, 2.50cor, 4.50cor.

2007 ***Perf. 13¼x13***
2480-2483 A440 Set of 4 3.75 2.10

Second Edition of "Cantos de Vida y Esperanza," by Rubén Darío — A441

Designs: 4cor, Baptismal font, León Cathedral. 10cor, Photograph of Darío at age 5. 13.50cor, Birthplace of Darío, monument. 16cor, Portrait of Darío as diplomat in Spain.

2007, May 4 **Litho.** ***Perf. 13¼x13***
2484-2487 A441 Set of 4 8.50 7.00

Port Facilities — A442

Designs: 1cor, Port of Corinto. 2cor, Port of Rama. 5cor, Port of Granada. 10cor, Port of San Juan del Sur. 15cor, Port of Sandino. 25cor, Salvador Allende Port.

2009, Apr. 28 **Litho.** ***Perf. 10½***
2488-2493 A442 Set of 6 10.50 8.25

Gen. Augusto C. Sandino (1895-1934) — A443

Designs: No. 2494, 10cor, Sandino and wife, Blanca Aráuz. No. 2495, 10cor, Statue of Sandino.

2009, May 18 **Litho.** ***Perf. 10½***
2494-2495 A443 Set of 2 4.25 3.50

Víctor Raúl Haya de la Torre (1895-1979), President of Peruvian Constitutional Assembly — A444

2009, May 27 **Litho.** ***Perf. 10½***
2496 A444 12cor multi 2.40 1.90

Nicaraguan Social Security Institute, 50th Anniv. — A445

50th anniversary emblem and: 4cor, Nurse examining child. 14cor, Hands, map of Nicaragua. 16cor, Elderly women. 25cor, Workman wearing air filter.

2009, July 30 **Litho.** ***Perf. 10½***
2497-2500 A445 Set of 4 11.50 9.00

A446

Sandinista Revolution, 30th Anniv. — A447

Designs: 4cor, General Augusto C. Sandino. 5cor, Victory celebration, July 19, 1979. 60cor, Soldier.

2009, July 30

2501	A446	4cor multi	.75	.75
2502	A446	5cor multi	1.50	1.00
2503	A447	60cor multi	10.50	9.75
		Nos. 2501-2503 (3)	12.75	11.50

Caribbean Coast Autonomy Law, 22nd Anniv. — A448

Designs: 6.50cor, Creole children. 10cor, Map and Mayagna people. 14cor, Garifuna people, vert. 60cor, Dancers wrapping ribbons around pole.

2009, Oct. 9 **Litho.** ***Perf. 10½***
2504-2507 A448 Set of 4 16.00 14.00

Central American Court of Justice, 17th Anniv. — A449

2009
2508 A449 25cor multi 3.25 2.75

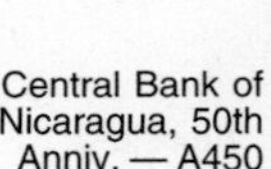

Central Bank of Nicaragua, 50th Anniv. — A450

Designs: No. 2509, 15cor, 50th anniversary emblem. No. 2510, 15cor, Nicaraguan banknotes.

2010, Jan. 6
2509-2510 A450 Set of 2 4.25 3.25

National Assembly, 25th Anniv. — A451

2010, Jan. 9
2511 A451 60cor multi 9.75 9.25

Venezuelan Independence, Bicent. — A452

2010
2512 A452 60cor multi 4.25 4.00

Mexican Revolution, Cent. — A453

Mexican Independence, Bicent. — A454

2010 ***Imperf.***

2513	A453	10cor multi	2.00	1.75
2514	A454	13.50cor multi	3.00	2.60

Miniature Sheet

Ecuadoran Independence, Bicent. — A455

No. 2515: a, 50c, Manuel Rodríguez de Quiroga. b, 4cor, Eugenio de Santa Cruz y Espejo. c, 5cor, Juan Salinas. d, 6.50cor, José Joaquín Olmedo. e, 10cor, Juan Pio Montufar.

2010 ***Perf. 10½***
2515 A455 Sheet of 5, #a-e, + label 5.25 3.00

Postal Union of the Americas, Spain and Portugal (UPAEP), Cent. — A456

2011, Sept. 1
2516 A456 12cor multi 2.50 1.90

Bernardo O'Higgins (1778-1842), Chilean General — A457

2011
2517 A457 15cor multi 2.10 1.75

José de San Martín (1778-1850), Argentine General — A458

2011
2518 A458 25cor multi 3.25 2.75

Argentine independence, bicent.

Souvenir Sheet

Preservation of Polar Regions and Glaciers — A459

2011 **Litho.**
2519 A459 50.50cor multi 8.75 8.00

Miniature Sheet

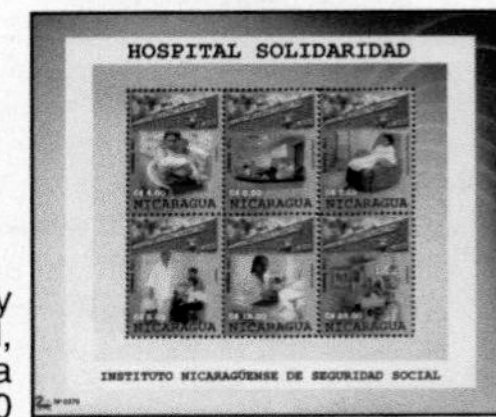

Solidarity Hospital, Managua A460

No. 2520: a, 4cor, Woman in chair holding infant in neo-natal unit. b, 6.50cor, Nurse's station. c, 7.50cor, Woman in chair receiving chemotherapy. d, 8cor, Pediatrician, mother and child. e, 12cor, Woman sitting on hospital bed holding infant. f, 25cor, Pediatrics unit equipment.

2011 ***Perf. 10½***
2520 A460 Sheet of 6, #a-f 13.50 10.50

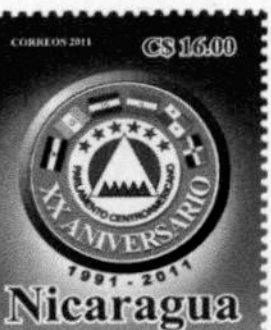

Central American Parliament, 20th Anniv. — A461

2011, Aug. 9 **Litho.** ***Perf. 10½***
2521 A461 16cor multi 3.00 3.00

Colombian Independence, Bicent. (in 2010) — A462

2012, Feb. 29 **Litho.** ***Perf. 10½***
2522 A462 50.50cor multi 5.50 5.25

Dated 2011.

Paintings — A463

Designs: No. 2523, 50c, La Embarcacíon, by Leonel Vanegas. No. 2524, 50c, La Princesa Está Triste, by Vanegas. No. 2525, 1cor, La Montaña Mágica, by Leoncio Sáenz. No. 2426, 1cor, La Gigantona I, by Sáenz. No. 2527, 2cor, No Olvides Monimbó, by Roger Pérez de la Rocha. No. 2528, 2cor, Campesinas, by Pérez de la Rocha. 10cor, Amanecer, by Arnoldo Guillén. 13.50cor, Esta Tierra ni se Vende, ni se Rinde, Guillén. 15cor, Metamorfosis de las Mujeres del Cua, by Orlando Sobalvarro. 16cor, Verano, by Sobalvarro.

2012, Sept. 6
2523-2532 A463 Set of 10 10.75 7.25

Miniature Sheet

San Juan River A464

No. 2533: a, 1cor, El Castillo. b, 4cor, River and its shores. c, 5cor, Crocodylus acutus. d, 10cor, Ctenosaura similis. e, 14cor, Mellisuga helenae. f, 50cor, Egretta alba.

2012, Sept. 6
2533 A464 Sheet of 6, #a-f 12.50 10.00

Miniature Sheet

Diplomatic Relations Between Nicaragua and South Korea, 50th Anniv. — A465

No. 2534: a, 4cor, Solar panels. b, 5cor, Water pump, Juigalpa. c, 13.50cor, Machinery in factory. d, 25cor, Building in free trade zone.

2012, Sept. 30
2534 A465 Sheet of 4, #a-d 6.50 5.50

Souvenir Sheet

Cádiz Constitution (First Spanish Constitution), Bicent. — A466

2012, Oct. 16
2535 A466 100cor multi 12.50 12.00

Souvenir Sheet

Spanish Agency for Intl. Development Cooperation, 25th Anniv. — A467

2013, Nov. 21 **Litho.** ***Perf. 10½***
2536 A467 25cor multi 3.25 2.75

America Issue — A468

Flags and Hugo Chávez (1954-2013), President of Venezuela: 5cor, Waving. 10cor, Holding map of South America.

2014, Mar. 5 **Litho.** ***Perf. 10½***
2537-2538 A468 Set of 2 3.50 2.25

Miniature Sheet

International Day of Older Persons — A469

No. 2539: a, 50c, Man using computer. b, 1cor, Man and woman with guitars. c, 4cor, Teacher and students in classroom. d, 7cor, Dancers. e, 13.50cor, Women holding greeting cards. f, 20cor, People exercising.

2015, Oct. 1 **Litho.** ***Perf. 10½***
2539 A469 Sheet of 6, #a-f 7.00 3.50

Rubén Darío (1867-1916), Poet — A470

2015, Oct. 15 **Litho.** ***Perf. 13½***
2540 A470 60cor multi 5.75 4.50

Tourism — A471

Designs: 50c, Icon of St. Dominic de Guzmán (1170-1221), patron saint of Managua. 1cor, Icon of St. Geronimo, patron saint of Masaya. 2cor, Nacatamal. 3cor, Baho. 4cor, Black ceramics of Jinotega. 5cor, Carved balsa wood birds. 6.50cor, Palo de Mayo dancers. 13.50cor, El Güegüense street theater performance.

2017, Oct. 1 **Litho.** ***Perf. 11¾***
2541-2548 A471 Set of 8 *18.00 16.00*

Miniature Sheet

Managua, 200th Anniv. — A472

No. 2549: a, 1cor, Nicaraguan Institute of Social Security Building, 2019. b, 1.50cor, Nicaraguan Institute of Social Security Building, 1956. c, 3cor, National Stadium, 2017. d, 5cor, National Stadium, 1948. e, 6cor, Rubén Darío National Theater, 2019. f, 10cor, Rubén Darío National Theater, 1969. g, 20cor, Communications Building, 2019. h, 30cor, Communications Building, 1931.

2019, May 21 **Litho.** ***Perf. 13½x13***
2549 A472 Sheet of 8, #a-h *14.00 8.25*

Central Bank of Nicaragua, 60th Anniv. — A473

Denominations: 5cor, 10cor, 20cor, 60cor.

2020, Feb. 29 **Litho.** ***Perf. 13x13¼***
2550-2553 A473 Set of 4 *5.75 5.75*

Miniature Sheet

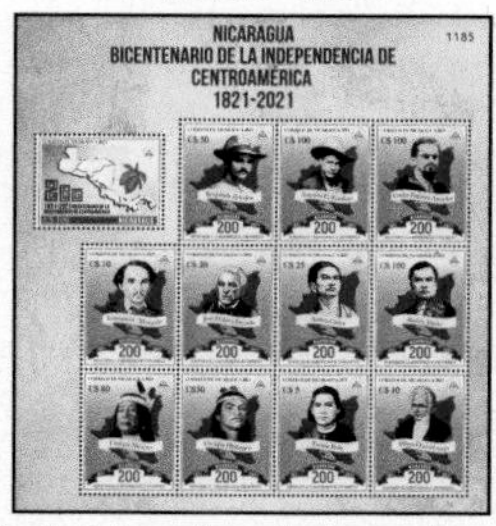

Central American Independence, 200th Anniv. — A474

No. 2554 — Nicaraguan coat of arms and: a, 5cor, Tomás Ruiz (1777-1819), priest and lawyer. b, 10cor, Enmanuel Mongalo (1834-72), teacher and military hero. c, 10cor, Miguel Larreynaga (1772-1847), judge and minister of finance. d, 20cor, José Dolores Estrada (1792-1869), military hero. e, 25cor, Andrés Castro (1831-82), military hero. f, 50cor, Benjamín Zeladón (1879-1912), general and President of Nicaragua. g, 50cor, Cacique Diriangén (c. 1497-c. 1524), leader of rebellions against Spanish colonizers. h, 80cor, Cacique Nicarao (fl. 16th century), chief of the Niquiranos. i, 100cor, Augusto C. Sandino (1895-1934), leader of rebellion against United States occupation of Nicaragua. j, 100cor, Carlos Fonseca Amador (1936-76), founder of Sandinista National Liberation Front. k, 100cor, Rubén Darío (1867-1916), poet. l, 100cor, Map of Central America, cacao pod, horiz.

Perf. 13¼x13, 13x13¼ (#2554l)
2021, Sept. 30 **Litho.**
2554 A474 Sheet of 12, #a-l *37.00 37.00*

AIR POST STAMPS

Counterfeits exist of almost all scarce surcharges among Nos. C1-C66.

Regular Issues of 1914-28 Overprinted in Red

1929 **Unwmk.** ***Perf. 12***
C1 A24 25c orange 1.75 1.75
a. Double overprint, one inverted 50.00
b. Inverted overprint 50.00
c. Double overprint 50.00
C2 A24 25c blk brn 2.25 2.25
a. Double overprint, one inverted 50.00
b. Double overprint 50.00
c. Inverted overprint 30.00

Issued: No. C1, July 17; No. C2, May 12 (used on May 15 first-flight covers).

There are numerous varieties in the setting of the overprint. The most important are: Large "1" in "1929" and large "A" in "Aereo" and "P. A. A."

Similar Overprint on Regular Issue of 1929 in Red

1929, Sept. 1
C3 A24 25c dk vio 1.25 .75
a. Double overprint 50.00
b. Inverted overprint 50.00
c. Double overprint, one inverted 50.00
Nos. C1-C3 (3) 5.25 4.75

The stamps in the bottom row of the sheet have the letters "P. A. A." larger than usual.

Similar overprints, some including an airplane, have been applied to postage issues of 1914-20, officials of 1926 and Nos. 401-407. These are, at best, essays.

Airplanes over Mt. Momotombo AP1

1929, Dec. 15 **Engr.**
C4 AP1 25c olive blk 1.25 1.25
C5 AP1 50c blk brn 1.50 1.50
C6 AP1 1cor org red 2.25 2.25
Nos. C4-C6 (3) 5.00 5.00

See Nos. C18-C19, C164-C168. For surcharges and overprints see Nos. C7-C8, C14-C17, C25-C31, C106-C120, C135-C146, C150-C154, C169-C173, CO25-CO29.

No. C4 Surcharged in Red or Black

1930, May 15
C7 AP1 15c on 25c ol blk (R) 1.00 .40
a. "$" inverted 3.50
b. Double surcharge (R + Bk) 7.00
c. As "b," red normal, blk invtd. 7.00
d. Double red surch., one inverted 7.00
C8 AP1 20c on 25c ol blk (Bk) 1.25 .60
a. "$" inverted 7.00
b. Inverted surcharge 15.00

Nos. C1, C2 and C3 Surcharged in Green

1931, June 7
C9 A24 15c on 25c org 70.00 50.00
C10 A24 15c on 25c blk brn 120.00 100.00
C11 A24 15c on 25c dk vio 15.00 15.00
c. Inverted surcharge 47.50
C12 A24 20c on 25c dk vio 10.00 10.00
c. Inverted surcharge 100.00
d. Double surcharge 100.00
C13 A24 20c on 25c blk brn *375.00*

No. C13 was not regularly issued.

"1391"

C9a A24 15c on 25c
C10a A24 15c on 25c
C11a A24 15c on 25c 60.00
d. As "a," inverted 400.00
C12a A24 20c on 25c *75.00*
e. As "a," inverted 400.00
g. As "a," double 400.00
C13a A24 20c on 25c

"1921"

C9b A24 15c on 25c
C10b A24 15c on 25c 400.00
C11b A24 15c on 25c 60.00
e. As "b," inverted 400.00
C12b A24 20c on 25c *100.00*
f. As "b," inverted 400.00
h. As "b," double 400.00
C13b A24 20c on 25c

Nos. C8, C4-C6 Surcharged in Blue

1931, June
C14 AP1 15c on 20c on 25c 26.00 9.00
b. Blue surcharge inverted 37.50
c. "$" in blk, surch. invtd. 50.00
d. Blue surch. dbl., one invtd. 30.00
C15 AP1 15c on 25c 5.50 5.50
b. Blue surcharge inverted 100.00
c. Double surch., one invtd. 25.00
C16 AP1 15c on 50c 40.00 40.00
C17 AP1 15c on 1cor 100.00 100.00
Nos. C14-C17 (4) 171.50 154.50

"1391"

C14a AP1 15c on 20c on 25c 50.00
C15a AP1 15c on 25c 30.00
C16a AP1 15c on 50c 80.00
C17a AP1 15c on 1cor 225.00
Nos. C14a-C17a (4) 385.00

Momotombo Type of 1929

1931, July 8
C18 AP1 15c deep violet .40 .40
C19 AP1 20c deep green .40 .40

Managua Post Office Before and After Earthquake — AP2

Without gum, Soft porous paper

1932, Jan. 1 **Litho.** ***Perf. 11***
C20 AP2 15c lilac 1.50 *1.25*
a. 15c violet 22.50
b. Vert. pair, imperf. btwn. 35.00
C21 AP2 20c emerald 2.00 2.00
b. Horizontal pair, imperf. between 35.00
C22 AP2 25c yel brn 6.50 6.50
b. Vertical pair, imperf. between 60.00
C23 AP2 50c yel brn 8.00 8.00
C24 AP2 1cor dp car 12.00 12.00
a. Vert. or horiz. pair, imperf. btwn. 80.00
Nos. C20-C24 (5) 30.00

Sheets of 10. See note after No. 568.

For overprint and surcharges see #C44-C46.

Reprints: see note following No. 568. Value $1 each.

Nos. C5 and C6 Surcharged in Red or Black

1932, July 12 ***Perf. 12***
C25 AP1 30c on 50c (Bk) 1.50 1.50
a. "Valc" 25.00
b. Double surcharge 15.00
c. Double surch., one inverted 15.00
d. Period omitted after "O" 25.00
e. As "a," double 300.00
C26 AP1 35c on 50c (R) 1.50 1.50
a. "Valc" 30.00
b. Double surcharge 12.00
c. Double surch., one inverted 12.00
d. As "a," double 300.00
C27 AP1 35c on 50c (Bk) 35.00 35.00
a. "Valc" 250.00
C28 AP1 40c on 1cor (Bk) 1.75 1.75
a. "Valc" 25.00
b. Double surcharge 15.00
c. Double surch., one inverted 15.00
d. Inverted surcharge 15.00
e. As "a," inverted 300.00
f. As "a," double 300.00
C29 AP1 55c on 1cor (R) 1.75 1.75
a. "Valc" 25.00
b. Double surcharge 12.00
c. Double surch., one inverted 12.00
d. Inverted surcharge 12.00
e. As "a," inverted 300.00
f. As "a," double 300.00
Nos. C25-C29 (5) 41.50 41.50

No. C18 Overprinted in Red

1932, Sept. 11
C30 AP1 15c dp vio 70.00 70.00
a. "Aereo" 150.00 150.00
b. Invtd. "m" in "Septiembre" 150.00

International Air Mail Week.

No. C6 Surcharged

1932, Oct. 12
C31 AP1 8c on 1 cor org red 20.00 20.00
a. "1232" 30.00 30.00
b. 2nd "u" of "Inauguracion" is an "n" 30.00 30.00

Inauguration of airmail service to the interior.

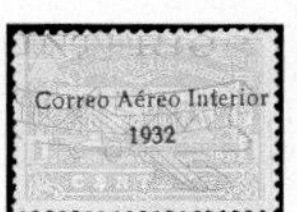

Regular Issue of 1932 Overprinted in Red

1932, Oct. 24 ***Perf. 11½***

Without Gum

C32 A40 1c yel brn 20.00 20.00
a. Inverted overprint 125.00 125.00
C33 A40 2c carmine 20.00 20.00
a. Inverted overprint 125.00 125.00
b. Double overprint 100.00 100.00
C34 A40 3c ultra 9.50 9.50
a. Inverted overprint 150.00 150.00
b. As "a," vert. pair, imperf. btwn. 500.00
C35 A40 4c dp ultra 9.50 9.50
a. Inverted overprint 125.00 125.00
b. Double overprint 100.00 100.00
c. Vert. or horiz. pair, imperf. btwn. 300.00
C36 A40 5c yel brn 9.50 9.50
a. Inverted overprint 125.00 125.00
b. Vert. pair, imperf. btwn. 75.00
C37 A40 6c gray brn 9.50 9.50
a. Inverted overprint 100.00 100.00
C38 A40 50c green 9.00 9.00
a. Inverted overprint 125.00 125.00

C39 A40 1cor yellow 9.50 9.50
a. Inverted overprint 125.00 125.00
b. Horiz. pair, imperf. btwn. 200.00
Nos. C32-C39 (8) 96.50 96.50

Nos. 564, C20-C21 exist overprinted as C32-C39. The editors believe they were not regularly issued.

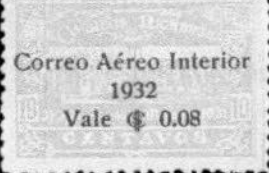

Surcharged in Red

1932, Oct. 24

C40 A40 8c on 10c yel brn 9.00 9.00
a. Inverted surcharge 125.00 125.00
C41 A40 16c on 20c org 9.00 9.00
a. Inverted surcharge 125.00 125.00
C42 A40 24c on 25c dp vio 9.00 9.00
a. Inverted surcharge 125.00 125.00
b. Horiz. pair, imperf. vert. 300.00

Surcharged in Red as No. C40 but without the word "Vale"

C43 A40 8c on 10c yel brn 45.00 45.00
a. Inverted surcharge 125.00 125.00
b. Horiz. pair, imperf. vert. 300.00

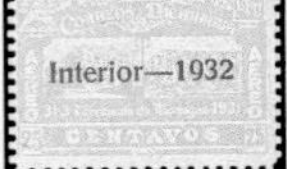

No. C22 Overprinted in Red

1932, Oct. 24

C44 AP2 25c yel brn 8.00 8.00
a. Inverted overprint 125.00 125.00

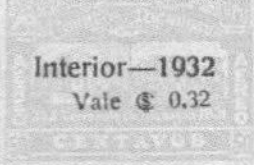

Nos. C23 and C24 Surcharged in Red

1932, Oct. 24

C45 AP2 32c on 50c yel brn 9.50 9.50
a. Inverted surcharge 125.00 125.00
b. "Interior-1932" inverted 150.00 150.00
c. "Vale $0.32" inverted 150.00 150.00
d. Horiz. pair, imperf. btwn. 200.00
C46 AP2 40c on 1cor car 7.00 7.00
a. Inverted surcharge 125.00 125.00
b. "Vale $0.40" inverted 200.00 200.00

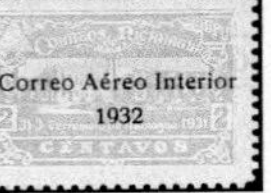

Nos. 557-558 Overprinted in Black

1932, Nov. 16

C47 A40 1c yel brn 25.00 22.50
a. "1232" 45.00 45.00
b. Inverted overprint 125.00 125.00
c. Double ovpt., one invtd. 125.00 125.00
d. As "a," inverted 500.00
C48 A40 2c dp car 20.00 17.50
a. "1232" 45.00 45.00
b. Inverted overprint 125.00 125.00
c. As "a," inverted 500.00

Excellent counterfeits exist of Nos. C27, C30-C48. Forged overprints and surcharges as on Nos. C32-C48 exist on reprints of Nos. C20-C24.

Regular Issue of 1914-32 Surcharged in Black

1932 *Perf. 12*

C49 A25 1c on 2c brt rose .70 .30
C50 A24 2c on 3c lt bl .70 .30
C51 A25 3c on 4c dk bl .70 .30
C52 A24 4c on 5c gray brn .70 .30
C53 A25 5c on 6c ol brn .70 .30
C54 A25 6c on 10c lt brn .70 .30
a. Double surcharge 25.00
C55 A24 8c on 15c org red .70 .30
C56 A25 16c on 20c org .70 .35
C57 A24 24c on 25c dk vio 2.75 1.00
C58 A24 25c on 25c dk vio 2.75 1.00
a. Double surcharge 25.00
C59 A25 32c on 50c grn 2.75 1.25
C60 A25 40c on 50c grn 3.25 1.40
C61 A25 50c on 1cor yel 4.75 2.25
C62 A25 1cor on 1cor yel 7.25 3.00
Nos. C49-C62 (14) 29.10 12.35

Nos. C49-C62 exist with inverted surcharge.

In addition to C49 to C62, four other stamps, Type A25, exist with this surcharge:
40c on 50c bister brown, black surcharge.
1cor on 2c bright rose, black surcharge.
1cor on 1cor yellow, red surcharge.
1cor on 1cor dull violet, black surcharge.
The editors believe they were not regularly issued.

Surcharged on Nos. 548, 547

1932

C65 A24 24c on 25c dk vio 45.00 45.00
C66 A24 25c on 25c blk brn 50.00 50.00

Counterfeits of Nos. C65 and C66 are plentiful.

Rivas Railroad Issue

La Chocolata Cut — AP3

El Nacascola — AP4

Designs: 25c, Cuesta cut. 50c, Mole of San Juan del Sur. 1cor, View of El Estero.

1932, Dec. **Litho.**

Soft porous paper

C67 AP3 15c dk vio 20.00 20.00
C68 AP4 20c grn 20.00 20.00
C69 AP4 25c dk brn 20.00 20.00
C70 AP4 50c blk brn 20.00 20.00
C71 AP4 1cor rose red 20.00 20.00
Nos. C67-C71 (5) 100.00

Inauguration of the railroad from San Jorge to San Juan del Sur, Dec. 18, 1932. Printed in sheets of 4, without gum.

Reprints: see note following No. 574. Value, $6 each.

Leon-Sauce Railroad Issue

"Fill" at Santa Lucia River AP5

Designs: 15c, Bridge at Santa Lucia. 25c, Malpaicillo Station. 50c, Panoramic view. 1cor, San Andres.

1932, Dec. 30 **Soft porous paper**

C72 AP5 15c purple 20.00
C73 AP5 20c bl grn 20.00
C74 AP5 25c lt brn 20.00
C75 AP5 50c dk brn 20.00
C76 AP5 1cor ver 20.00
Nos. C72-C76 (5) 100.00

Inauguration of the railroad from Leon to El Sauce, 12/30/32. Sheets of 4, without gum.

Reprints: see note following No. 579. Value, $6 each.

Flag of the Race Issue

1933, Aug. 3 **Litho.** ***Rouletted 9***

Without gum

C77 A43 1c dk brn 1.50 1.50
C78 A43 2c red vio 1.50 1.50
C79 A43 4c violet 2.50 2.25
C80 A43 5c dl bl 2.25 2.25
C81 A43 6c vio bl 2.25 2.25
C82 A43 8c dp brn .70 .70
C83 A43 15c ol brn .70 .70
C84 A43 20c yellow 2.25 2.25
a. Horiz. pair, imperf. btwn. 15.00
b. Horiz. pair, imperf. vert. 15.00
C85 A43 25c orange 2.25 2.25
C86 A43 50c rose 2.25 2.25
C87 A43 1cor green 11.00 11.00
Nos. C77-C87 (11) 29.15 28.90

See note after No. 599. Printed in sheets of 10.

Reprints exist, shades differ from postage and official stamps.

Imperf., Pairs

C78a A43 2c 14.00
C79a A43 4c 10.00
C81a A43 6c 10.00
C82a A43 8c 10.00
C83a A43 15c 10.00
C87a A43 1cor 30.00

AP7

1933, Nov. ***Perf. 12***

C88 AP7 10c bis brn 1.60 1.60
a. Vert. pair, imperf. between 35.00
C89 AP7 15c violet 1.25 1.25
a. Vert. pair, imperf. between 37.50
C90 AP7 25c red 1.50 1.50
a. Horiz. pair, imperf. between 22.50
C91 AP7 50c dp bl 1.60 1.60
Nos. C88-C91 (4) 5.95 5.95

Intl. Air Post Week, Nov. 6-11, 1933. Printed in sheets of 4. Counterfeits exist.

Stamps and Types of 1928-31 Surcharged in Black

1933, Nov. 3

C92 A25 1c on 2c grn .35 .35
C93 A24 2c on 3c ol gray .35 .35
C94 A25 3c on 4c car rose .35 .35
C95 A24 4c on 5c lt bl .35 .35
C96 A25 5c on 6c dk bl .35 .35
C97 A25 6c on 10c ol brn .35 .35
C98 A24 8c on 15c bis brn .35 .35
C99 A25 16c on 20c brn .35 .35
C100 A24 24c on 25c ver .35 .35
C101 A24 25c on 25c org .35 .35
C102 A25 32c on 50c vio .35 .35
C103 A25 40c on 50c grn .35 .35
C104 A25 50c on 1cor yel .50 .20
C105 A25 1cor on 1cor org red 1.00 *1.00*
Nos. C92-C105 (14) 5.70 5.40

Nos. C100, C102-C105 exist without script control overprint. Value, each $1.50.

Type of Air Post Stamps of 1929 Surcharged in Black

1933, Oct. 28

C106 AP1 30c on 50c org red *2.00* .40
C107 AP1 35c on 50c lt bl *2.00* .40
C108 AP1 40c on 1cor yel *5.00* .40
C109 AP1 55c on 1cor grn *4.00* .40
Nos. C106-C109 (4) *13.00* 1.60

No. C19 Surcharged in Red

1934, Mar. 31

C110 AP1 10c on 20c grn .40 .40
a. Inverted surcharge 15.00
b. Double surcharge, one inverted 15.00
c. "Ceutroamericano" 10.00

No. C110 with black surcharge is believed to be of private origin.

No. C4 Surcharged in Red

1935, Aug.

C111 AP1 10c on 25c ol blk .40 .40
a. Small "v" in "vale" (R) 5.00
b. "centrvos" (R) 5.00
c. Double surcharge (R) 25.00
d. Inverted surcharge (R) 25.00
g. As "a," inverted 400.00
h. As "a," double 400.00

No. C111 with blue surcharge is believed to be private origin.

The editors do not recognize the Nicaraguan air post stamps overprinted in red "VALIDO 1935" in two lines and with or without script control marks as having been issued primarily for postal purposes.

Nos C4-C6, C18-C19 Overprinted Vertically in Blue, Reading Up:

1935-36

C112 AP1 15c dp vio 1.00 1.00
C113 AP1 20c dp grn 1.75 1.75
C114 AP1 25c ol blk 2.25 2.25
C115 AP1 50c blk brn 5.00 5.00
C116 AP1 1cor org red 40.00 40.00
Nos. C112-C116 (5) 50.00 50.00

Same Overprint on Nos. C106-C109 Reading Up or Down

C117 AP1 30c on 50c org red 1.50 1.40
C118 AP1 35c on 50c lt bl 6.50 6.50
C119 AP1 40c on 1cor yel 6.50 6.50
C120 AP1 55c on 1cor grn 6.50 6.50
Nos. C117-C120 (4) 21.00 20.90
Nos. C112-C120 (9) 71.00 70.90

Same Overprint in Red on Nos. C92-C105

1936

C121 A25 1c on 2c grn .40 .40
C122 A24 2c on 3c ol gray .40 .40
C123 A25 3c on 4c car rose .40 .40
C124 A24 4c on 5c lt bl .40 .40
C125 A25 5c on 6c dk bl .40 .40
C126 A25 6c on 10c ol brn .40 .40
C127 A24 8c on 15c bis brn .40 .40
C128 A25 16c on 20c brn .40 .40
C129 A24 24c on 25c ver .50 .40
C130 A24 25c on 25c org .40 .40
C131 A25 32c on 50c vio .40 .40
C132 A25 40c on 50c grn 1.00 1.00
C133 A25 50c on 1cor yel .85 .40
C134 A25 1cor on 1cor org red 3.50 3.50
Nos. C121-C134 (14) 9.85 9.30

Nos. C121 to C134 are handstamped with script control mark.

Overprint Reading Down on No. C110

C135 AP1 10c on 20c grn *350.00*

This stamp has been extensively counterfeited.

Overprinted in Red on Nos. C4 to C6, C18 and C19

C136 AP1 15c dp vio .55 .40
C137 AP1 20c dp grn 1.25 .60
C138 AP1 25c ol blk 1.25 .55
C139 AP1 50c blk brn 1.00 .55
C140 AP1 1cor org red 3.25 .55

On Nos. C106 to C109

C141 AP1 30c on 50c org red 2.25 .60
C142 AP1 35c on 50c lt bl 2.25 .40
C143 AP1 40c on 1cor yel 2.25 .55
C144 AP1 55c on 1cor grn 2.25 .50

Same Overprint in Red or Blue on No. C111 Reading Up or Down

C145 AP1 10c on 25c, down 3.00 .45
a. "Centrvos" 25.00
C146 AP1 10c on 25c (Bl), up 6.00 1.00
a. "Centrvos" 25.00
Nos. C136-C146 (11) 25.30 6.15

Overprint on No. C145 is at right, on No. C146 in center.

Nos. C92, C93 and C98 Overprinted in Black

1936

C147 A25 1c on 2c grn 2.00 .40
C148 A24 2c on 3c ol gray 2.00 .40
a. "Resello 1936" dbl., one invtd. 7.50
C149 A24 8c on 15c bis brn 2.00 .40
Nos. C147-C149 (3) 6.00 1.20

With script control handstamp.

Nos. C5 and C6 Surcharged in Red

1936, Nov. 26

C150 AP1 15c on 50c blk brn .40 .40
C151 AP1 15c on 1cor org red .40 .40

Nos. C18 and C19 Overprinted in Carmine

1936, July 2

C152 AP1 15c dp vio .60 .40
C153 AP1 20c dp grn .60 .40

Overprint reading up or down.

No. C4 Surcharged and Overprinted in Red

C154 AP1 10c on 25c olive blk .50 .40
a. Surch. and ovpt. inverted 3.50

Same Overprint in Carmine on Nos. C92 to C99

C155 A25 1c on 2c green .75 .40
C156 A24 2c on 3c olive gray 4.00 2.00
C157 A25 3c on 4c car rose .75 .40
C158 A24 4c on 5c light blue .75 .40
C159 A25 5c on 6c dark blue .75 .40
C160 A25 6c on 10c olive brn .75 .40
C161 A24 8c on 15c bister brn .75 .40
C162 A25 16c on 20c brown .75 .40
Nos. C154-C162 (9) 9.75 5.20

No. 518 Overprinted in Black

C163 A25 10c lt brn .75 .40
a. Overprint inverted 3.50
b. Double overprint 3.50

Two fonts are found in the sheet of #C163.

Momotombo Type of 1929

1937

C164 AP1 15c yel org 1.00 .40
C165 AP1 20c org red 1.00 .40
C166 AP1 25c black 1.00 .40
C167 AP1 50c violet 1.00 .40
C168 AP1 1cor orange 4.50 .40
Nos. C164-C168 (5) 8.50 2.00

Surcharged in Black

1937

C169 AP1 30c on 50c car rose 3.75 .40
C170 AP1 35c on 50c olive grn 3.75 .40
C171 AP1 40c on 1cor green 3.75 .40
C172 AP1 55c on 1cor blue 3.75 .40
Nos. C169-C172 (4) 15.00 1.60

No. C168 Surcharged in Violet

1937 Unwmk. *Perf. 12*

C173 AP1 10c on 1cor org .45 .40
a. "Centauos" 10.00

No. C98 with Additional Overprint "1937"

C174 A24 8c on 15c bis brn .65 .40
a. "1937" double 6.50

Nos. C92-C102 with Additional Overprint in Blue reading "HABILITADO 1937"

C175 A25 1c on 2c grn .90 .40
a. Blue overprint double 3.50
C176 A24 2c on 3c ol gray .90 .40
a. Double surch., one inverted 3.50
C177 A25 3c on 4c car rose .90 .40
C178 A24 4c on 5c lt bl .90 .40
C179 A25 5c on 6c dk bl .90 .40
C180 A25 6c on 10c ol brn .90 .40
C181 A24 8c on 15c bis brn .90 .40
a. "Habilitado 1937" double 4.50
C182 A25 16c on 20c brn .90 .40
a. Double surcharge 3.50
C183 A24 24c on 25c ver .90 .40
C184 A24 25c on 25c org .90 .40
C185 A25 32c on 50c vio .90 .40
Nos. C175-C185 (11) 9.90 4.40

Map of Nicaragua AP8

For Foreign Postage

1937, July 30 Engr.

C186 AP8 10c green .40 .40
C187 AP8 15c dp bl .40 .40
C188 AP8 20c yellow .40 .40
C189 AP8 25c bl vio .40 .40
C190 AP8 30c rose car .40 .40
C191 AP8 50c org yel .50 .40
C192 AP8 1cor ol grn 1.00 .40
Nos. C186-C192 (7) 3.50 2.80

Presidential Palace — AP9

For Domestic Postage

C193 AP9 1c rose car .40 .40
C194 AP9 2c dp bl .40 .40
C195 AP9 3c ol grn .40 .40
C196 AP9 4c black .40 .40
C197 AP9 5c dk vio .40 .40
C198 AP9 6c chocolate .40 .40
C199 AP9 8c bl vio .40 .40
C200 AP9 16c org yel .40 .40
C201 AP9 24c yellow .40 .40
C202 AP9 25c yel grn .40 .40
Nos. C193-C202 (10) 4.00 4.00

No. C201 with green overprint "Union Panamericana 1890-1940" is of private origin.

Managua — AP10

Designs: 15c, Presidential Palace. 20c, Map of South America. 25c, Map of Central America. 30c, Map of North America. 35c, Lagoon of Tiscapa, Managua. 40c, Road Scene. 45c, Park. 50c, Another park. 55c, Scene in San Juan del Sur. 75c, Tipitapa River. 1cor, Landscape.

Wmk. 209

1937, Sept. 17 Typo. *Perf. 11*

Center in Dark Blue

C203 AP10 10c yel grn 2.25 1.20
C204 AP10 15c orange 2.25 1.40
C205 AP10 20c red 1.75 1.00
C206 AP10 25c vio brn 1.75 1.00
a. Center, double impression —
C207 AP10 30c bl grn 1.75 1.00
a. Great Lakes omitted 40.00 40.00
C208 AP10 35c lemon .75 .45
C209 AP10 40c green .75 .40
C210 AP10 45c brt vio .75 .35
C211 AP10 50c rose lil .75 .35
a. Vert. pair, imperf. btwn. 140.00
C212 AP10 55c lt bl .75 .35
C213 AP10 75c gray grn .75 .35

Center in Brown Red

C214 AP10 1cor dk bl 1.75 .50
Nos. C203-C214 (12) 16.00 8.35

150th anniv. of the Constitution of the US.

Diriangen AP11

Designs: 4c, 10c, Nicarao. 5c, 15c, Bartolomé de Las Casas. 8c, 20c, Columbus.

For Domestic Postage
Without gum

1937, Oct. 12 Unwmk. *Perf. 11*

C215 AP11 1c green .50 .50
C216 AP11 4c brn car .50 .50
C217 AP11 5c dk vio .50 .50
a. Without imprint .40
C218 AP11 8c dp bl .50 .50
a. Without imprint .50

For Foreign Postage
Wmk. 209
With Gum

C219 AP11 10c lt brn .50 .50
C220 AP11 15c pale bl .50 .50
a. Without imprint 1.00
C221 AP11 20c pale rose .50 .50
Nos. C215-C221 (7) 3.50 3.50

Nos. C215-C221 printed in sheets of 4.

Imperf., Pairs

C215a AP11 1c .50 .50
C216a AP11 4c .50 .50
C217b AP11 5c .50 .50
C217c AP11 5c Without imprint
C218b AP11 8c .50 .50
C218c AP11 8c Without imprint
C219a AP11 10c .50 .50
C220b AP11 15c .50 .50
C220c AP11 15c Without imprint
C221a AP11 20c .50 .50

Gen. Tomas Martinez AP11a

Design: 10c-50c, Gen. Anastasio Somoza.

For Domestic Postage
Without Gum

Perf. 11½, Imperf.

1938, Jan. 18 Typo. Unwmk.

Center in Black

C221B AP11a 1c orange *.50 .50*
C221C AP11a 5c red vio *.50 .50*
C221D AP11a 8c dk bl *.50 .50*
C221E AP11a 16c brown *.50 .50*
f. Sheet of 4, 1c, 5c, 8c, 16c *3.50 3.50*

For Foreign Postage

C221G AP11a 10c green *.50 .50*
C221H AP11a 15c dk bl *.50 .50*
C221J AP11a 25c violet *.50 .50*
C221K AP11a 50c carmine *.50 .50*
m. Sheet of 4, 10c, 15c, 25c, 50c *3.50 3.50*
Nos. C221B-C221K (8) *4.00 4.00*

75th anniv. of postal service in Nicaragua. Printed in sheets of four.

Stamps of type AP11a exist in changed colors and with inverted centers, double centers and frames printed on the back. These varieties were private fabrications.

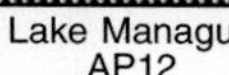
Lake Managua AP12

President Anastasio Somoza AP13

For Domestic Postage

1939 Unwmk. Engr. *Perf. 12½*

C222 AP12 2c dp bl .40 .40
C223 AP12 3c green .40 .40
C224 AP12 8c pale lil .40 .40
C225 AP12 16c orange .40 .40
C226 AP12 24c yellow .40 .40
C227 AP12 32c dk grn .40 .40
C228 AP12 50c dp rose .40 .40

For Foreign Postage

C229 AP13 10c brown .40 .40
C230 AP13 15c dk bl .40 .40
C231 AP13 20c org yel .40 .40
C232 AP13 25c dk pur .40 .40
C233 AP13 30c lake .40 .40
C234 AP13 50c dp org .40 .40
C235 AP13 1cor dk ol grn .40 .40
Nos. C222-C235 (14) 5.60 5.60

For Domestic Postage

Will Rogers and View of Managua AP14

Designs: 2c, Rogers standing beside plane. 3c, Leaving airport office. 4c, Rogers and US Marines. 5c, Managua after earthquake.

1939, Mar. 31 Engr. *Perf. 12*

C236 AP14 1c brt grn .40 .40
C237 AP14 2c org red .40 .40
C238 AP14 3c lt ultra .40 .40
C239 AP14 4c dk bl .40 .40
C240 AP14 5c rose car .40 .40
Nos. C236-C240 (5) 2.00 2.00

Will Rogers' flight to Managua after the earthquake, Mar. 31, 1931.

For surcharges see Nos. 686, 688.

Pres. Anastasio Somoza in US House of Representatives AP19

President Somoza and US Capitol AP20

President Somoza, Tower of the Sun and Trylon and Perisphere AP21

For Domestic Postage

1940, Feb. 1

C241 AP19 4c red brn .40 .40
C242 AP20 8c blk brn .40 .40
C243 AP19 16c grnsh bl .40 .40
C244 AP20 20c brt plum .40 .40
C245 AP21 32c scarlet .40 .40

For Foreign Postage

C246 AP19 25c dp bl .40 .40
C247 AP19 30c black .40 .40
C248 AP20 50c rose pink .45 .40
C249 AP21 60c green .50 .40
C250 AP19 65c dk vio brn .50 .40
C251 AP19 90c ol grn .65 .40
C252 AP21 1cor violet 1.00 .40
Nos. C241-C252 (12) 5.90 4.80

Visit of Pres. Somoza to US in 1939.

For surcharge see No. C636.

L. S. Rowe, Statue of Liberty, Nicaraguan Coastline, Flags of 21 American Republics, US Shield and Arms of Nicaragua — AP22

1940, Aug. 2 Engr. *Perf. 12½*

C253 AP22 1.25cor multi 2.00 1.00

50th anniversary of Pan American Union.

For overprint see No. C493.

First Nicaraguan Postage Stamp and Sir Rowland Hill — AP23

1941, Apr. 4

C254 AP23 2cor brown 2.50 .80
C255 AP23 3cor dk bl 8.25 1.40
C256 AP23 5cor carmine 22.50 3.50
Nos. C254-C256 (3) 33.25 5.70

Centenary of the first postage stamp.
Nos. C254-C256 imperf. are proofs.

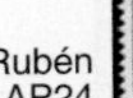

Rubén Darío — AP24

1941, Dec. 23

C257	AP24	20c pale lil	.50	.40
C258	AP24	35c yel grn	.60	.40
C259	AP24	40c org yel	.80	.40
C260	AP24	60c lt bl	1.30	.40
		Nos. C257-C260 (4)	3.20	1.60

25th anniversary of the death of Rubén Dario, poet and writer.

Catalogue values for unused stamps in this section, from this point to the end of the section, are for Never Hinged items.

Victory Type

1943, Dec. 8 ***Perf. 12***

C261	A48	40c dk bl grn & cer	.75	.40
C262	A48	60c lt bl & cer	.95	.40

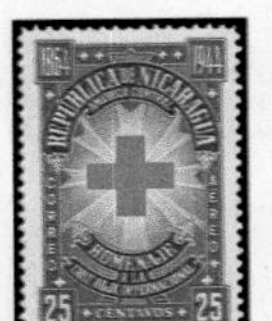

Red Cross AP26

Cross and Globes AP27

Red Cross Workers — AP28

1944, Oct. 12 ***Engr.***

C263	AP26	25c red lil & car	.80	.30
C264	AP27	50c ol brn & car	1.20	.55
C265	AP28	1cor dk bl grn & car	2.40	2.00
		Nos. C263-C265 (3)	4.40	2.85

International Red Cross Society, 80th anniv.

Caravels of Columbus and Columbus Lighthouse AP29

Landing of Columbus AP30

1945, Sept. 1 ***Perf. 12½***

C266	AP29	20c dp grn & gray	.35	.35
C267	AP29	35c dk car & blk	.50	.30
C268	AP29	75c ol grn & rose pink	.70	.40
C269	AP29	90c brick red & aqua	1.10	.75
C270	AP29	1cor blk & pale bl	1.25	.30
C271	AP30	2.50cor dk bl & car rose	2.25	2.25
		Nos. C266-C271 (6)	6.15	4.35

Issued in honor of the discovery of America by Columbus and the Columbus Lighthouse near Ciudad Trujillo, Dominican Republic.

Roosevelt Types

Designs: 25c, Franklin D. Roosevelt and Winston Churchill. 75c, Roosevelt signing declaration of war against Japan. 1cor, Gen. Henri Giraud, Roosevelt, Gen. Charles de Gaulle and Churchill. 3cor, Stalin, Roosevelt and Churchill. 5cor, Sculptured head of Roosevelt.

Engraved, Center Photogravure

1946, June 15 ***Perf. 12½***

Frame in Black

C272	A50	25c orange	.35	.30
a.		Horiz. pair, imperf. btwn.	225.00	
b.		Imperf., pair	175.00	
C273	A51	75c carmine	.35	.30
a.		Imperf., pair	175.00	
C274	A50	1cor dark green	.55	.40
C275	A50	3cor violet	5.00	3.75
C276	A51	5cor greenish blue	6.50	5.00
		Nos. C272-C276 (5)	12.75	9.75

Issued to honor Franklin D. Roosevelt.

Projected Provincial Seminary — AP36

Designs: 20c, Communications Building. 35c, Sanitation Building. 90c, National Bank. 1cor, Municipal Building. 2.50cor, National Palace.

1947, Jan. 10 ***Frame in Black***

C277	AP36	5c violet	.45	.30
a.		Imperf., pair	125.00	
C278	AP36	20c gray grn	.45	.30
C279	AP36	35c orange	.45	.30
C280	AP36	90c red lil	.70	.30
C281	AP36	1cor brown	1.00	.45
C282	AP36	2.50cor rose lil	3.00	1.50
		Nos. C277-C282 (6)	6.05	3.15

City of Managua centenary.

Rubén Darío Monument AP42

Designs: 6c, Tapir. 8c, Stone Highway. 10c, Genizaro Dam. 20c, Detail of Dario Monument. 25c, Sulphurous Lake of Nejapa. 35c, Mercedes Airport. 50c, Prinzapolka River delta. 1cor, Tipitapa Spa. 1.50cor, Tipitapa River. 5cor, United States Embassy. 10cor, Indian fruit vendor. 25cor, Franklin D. Roosevelt Monument.

Engraved, Center Photogravure

1947, Aug. 29 **Unwmk.** ***Perf. 12½***

C283	AP42	5c dk bl grn & rose car	.30	.25
C284	AP42	6c blk & yel	.30	.25
C285	AP42	8c car & ol	.30	.25
C286	AP42	10c brn & bl	.30	.25
C287	AP42	20c bl vio & org	.35	.30
C288	AP42	25c brn red & emer	.40	.35
C289	AP42	35c gray & bis	.35	.30
C290	AP42	50c pur & sep	.30	.25
C291	AP42	1cor blk & lil rose	.90	.75
C292	AP42	1.50cor red brn & aqua	.60	.80
C293	AP42	5cor choc & car rose	7.50	6.25
C294	AP42	10cor vio & dk brn	6.00	5.00
C295	AP42	25cor dk bl grn & yel	12.00	10.00
		Nos. C283-C295 (13)	29.60	25.00

The frames differ for each denomination. For surcharge see No. C750.

Tennis — AP43

Designs: 2c, Soccer. 3c, Table tennis. 4c, Proposed stadium. 5c, Regatta. 15c, Basketball. 25c, Boxing. 30c, Baseball. 40c, Bicycling. 75c, Diving. 1cor, Pole vault. 2cor, Boy Scouts. 5cor, Softball.

1949, July **Photo.** ***Perf. 12***

C296	AP43	1c cerise	.40	.25
C297	AP43	2c ol gray	.40	.25
C298	AP43	3c scarlet	.40	.25
C299	AP43	4c dk bl gray	.40	.25
C300	AP43	5c aqua	.40	.25
C301	AP43	15c bl grn	.40	.25
C302	AP43	25c red vio	3.25	.30
C303	AP43	30c red brn	3.00	.30
C304	AP43	40c violet	.80	.30
C305	AP43	75c magenta	8.25	2.75
C306	AP43	1cor lt bl	10.00	1.40
C307	AP43	2cor brn ol	4.25	1.75
C308	AP43	5cor lt grn	5.50	2.25
a.		Set of 13 souv. sheets of 4	*475.00*	*450.00*
		Nos. C296-C308 (13)	37.45	10.55

10th World Series of Amateur Baseball, 1948.

Rowland Hill — AP44

Designs: 20c, Heinrich von Stephan. 25c, First UPU Bldg. 30c, UPU Bldg., Bern. 85c, UPU Monument. 1.10cor, Congress medal, obverse. 2.14cor, as 1.10cor, reverse.

1950, Nov. 23 **Engr.** ***Perf. 13***

Frames in Black

C309	AP44	16c cerise	.35	.25
C310	AP44	20c orange	.35	.25
C311	AP44	25c gray	.35	.25
C312	AP44	30c cerise	.55	.25
C313	AP44	85c dk bl grn	1.00	.65
C314	AP44	1.10cor chnt brn	2.00	.45
C315	AP44	2.14cor ol grn	3.00	2.25
		Nos. C309-C315 (7)	7.60	4.35

75th anniv. (in 1949) of the UPU.

Each denomination was also issued in a souvenir sheet containing four stamps and marginal inscriptions. Size: 126x114mm. Value, set of 7 sheets, $35.

For surcharges see Nos. C501, C758.

Queen Isabela I Type

Designs: 2.30cor, Portrait facing left. 2.80cor, Map. 3cor, Santa Maria. 3.30cor, Columbus' ships. 3.60cor, Portrait facing right.

1952, June 25 **Unwmk.** ***Perf. 11½***

C316	A65	2.30cor rose car	3.00	2.00
C317	A65	2.80cor red org	2.75	1.75
C318	A65	3cor green	3.00	2.00
C319	A66	3.30cor lt bl	3.00	2.00
C320	A65	3.60cor yel grn	3.25	2.25
a.		Souv. sheet of 5, #C316-C320	14.00	14.00
		Nos. C316-C320 (5)	15.00	10.00

For overprint see No. C445.

Arms of ODECA — AP47

Designs: 25c, ODECA Flag. 30c, Presidents of five Central American countries. 60c, ODECA Charter and Flags. 1cor, Map of Central America.

1953, Apr. 15 ***Perf. 13½x14***

C321	AP47	20c red lil	.90	.40
C322	AP47	25c lt bl	.90	.40
C323	AP47	30c sepia	.90	.40
C324	AP47	60c dk bl grn	.90	.40
C325	AP47	1cor dk vio	2.25	2.25
		Nos. C321-C325 (5)	5.85	3.85

Founding of the Organization of Central American States (ODECA).

Leonardo Arguello — AP48

Presidents: 5c, Gen. Jose Maria Moncada. 20c, Juan Bautista Sacasa. 25c, Gen. Jose Santos Zelaya. 30c, Gen. Anastasio Somoza. 35c, Gen. Tomas Martinez. 40c, Fernando Guzman. 45c, Vicente Cuadra. 50c, Pedro Joaquin Chamorro. 60c, Gen. Joaquin Zavala. 85c, Adan Cardenas. 1.10cor, Evaristo Carazo. 1.20cor, Roberto Sacasa.

Engraved (frames); Photogravure (heads)

1953, June 25 ***Perf. 12½***

Heads in Gray Black

C326	AP48	4c dp car	.75	.40
C327	AP48	5c dp org	.75	.40
C328	AP48	20c dk Prus bl	.75	.40
C329	AP48	25c blue	.75	.40
C330	AP48	30c red brn	.75	.40
C331	AP48	35c dp grn	.75	.40
C332	AP48	40c dk vio brn	.75	.40
C333	AP48	45c olive	.75	.40
C334	AP48	50c carmine	.90	.40
C335	AP48	60c ultra	.90	.40
C336	AP48	85c brown	1.20	.40
C337	AP48	1.10cor purple	1.40	.45
C338	AP48	1.20cor ol bis	1.40	.45
		Nos. C326-C338 (13)	11.80	5.30

For surcharges see Nos. C363-C364, C757.

Torch and UN Emblem — AP49

Designs: 4c, Raised hands. 5c, Candle and charter. 30c, Flags of Nicaragua and UN. 2cor, Globe. 3cor, Arms of Nicaragua. 5cor, Type A69 inscribed "Aereo."

1954, Apr. 30 **Engr.** ***Perf. 13½***

C339	AP49	3c rose pink	.30	.25
C340	AP49	4c dp org	.30	.25
C341	AP49	5c red	.30	.25
C342	AP49	30c cerise	1.60	.25
C343	AP49	2cor magenta	2.40	1.00
C344	AP49	3cor org brn	4.25	1.75
C345	AP49	5cor brn vio	4.75	2.25
		Nos. C339-C345 (7)	13.90	6.00

Honoring the United Nations.

For overprint & surcharge see #C366, C443.

Capt. Dean L. Ray, USAF — AP50

Designs: 15c, Sabre jet plane. 20c, Air Force emblem. 25c, National Air Force hangars. 30c, Gen. A. Somoza. 50c, AT-6's in formation. 1cor, Plane, type P-38.

Frame in Black

Engraved; Center Photogravure

1954, Nov. 5 ***Perf. 13***

C346	AP50	10c gray	.95	.25
C347	AP50	15c gray	.95	.25
C348	AP50	20c claret	.95	.25
C349	AP50	25c red	.95	.25
C350	AP50	30c ultra	.95	.25
C351	AP50	50c blue	1.80	.60
C352	AP50	1cor green	1.40	.50
		Nos. C346-C352 (7)	7.95	2.35

Issued to honor the National Air Force.

Rotary Intl. Type

Designs: 1c, 1cor, Paul P. Harris. 2c, 50c, Handclasp, Rotary emblem and globe. 3c, 45c, Map of world and Rotary emblem. 4c, 30c, Rotary slogans and wreath. 5c, 25c, Flags of Nicaragua and Rotary.

Perf. 11½

1955, Aug. 30 **Unwmk.** **Photo.**

Granite Paper

C353	A71	1c vermilion	.50	.35
C354	A71	2c ultra	.50	.35
C355	A72	3c pck grn	.50	.35
C356	A71	4c violet	.50	.35
C357	A71	5c org brn	.50	.35
C358	A71	25c brt grnsh bl	.50	.35
C359	A71	30c dl pur	.50	.35
C360	A72	45c lil rose	.70	.35
C361	A71	50c lt bl grn	.50	.35
C362	A71	1cor ultra	.70	.35
a.		Souv. sheet of 5, #C358-C362	11.00	11.00
		Nos. C353-C362 (10)	5.40	3.50

For surcharge see No. C365.

Nos. C331, C333, C360, C345 Surcharged in Green or Black

Engraved, Photogravure

1956, Feb. 4 ***Perf. 13½x13, 11½***

C363	AP48	30c on 35c (G)	1.00	.35
C364	AP48	30c on 45c (G)	1.00	.35
C365	A72	30c on 45c	1.00	.35
C366	AP49	2cor on 5cor	3.75	1.50
		Nos. C363-C366 (4)	6.75	2.55

National Exhibition, Feb. 4-16, 1956.

See note after No. 772.

Gen. Jose D. Estrada AP53

The Stoning of Andres Castro AP54

1.50 cor, Emanuel Mongalo. 2.50 cor, Battle of Rivas. 10 cor, Com. Hiram Paulding.

1956, Sept. 14 Engr. *Perf. 12½*

C367 AP53 30c dk car rose .40 .35
C368 AP54 60c chocolate .40 .35
C369 AP53 1.50cor green .40 .35
C370 AP54 2.50cor dk ultra .85 .40
C371 AP53 10cor red org 5.00 2.00
Nos. C367-C371 (5) 7.05 3.45

Centenary of the National War.

For overprint and surcharge see #C444, C751.

President Somoza — AP55

1957, Feb. 1 Photo. *Perf. 14x13½*
Various Frames: Centers in Black

C372 AP55 15c gray blk .35 .25
C373 AP55 30c indigo .35 .25
C374 AP55 2cor purple 1.40 1.00
C375 AP55 3cor dk grn 2.75 2.00
C376 AP55 5cor dk brn 4.25 3.25
Nos. C372-C376 (5) 9.10 6.75

President Anastasio Somoza, 1896-1956.

Type of Regular Issue and

Handshake and Globe — AP56

Designs: 4c, Scout emblem, globe and Lord Baden-Powell. 5c, Cub Scout. 6c, Crossed flags and Scout emblem. 8c, Scout symbols. 30c, Joseph A. Harrison. 40c, Pres. Somoza receiving decoration at first Central American Camporee. 75c, Explorer Scout. 85c, Boy Scout. 1cor, Lord Baden-Powell.

1957, Apr. 9 Unwmk. *Perf. 13½x14*

C377 AP56 3c red org & ol .85 .35
C378 A75 4c dk brn & dk Prus grn .85 .35
C379 A75 5c grn & brn .85 .35
C380 A75 6c pur & ol .85 .35
C381 A75 8c grnsh blk & red .85 .35
C382 A75 30c Prus grn & gray .85 .35
C383 AP56 40c dk bl & grysh blk .85 .35
C384 A75 75c mar & brn .85 .35
C385 A75 85c red & gray .85 .35
C386 A75 1cor dl red brn & sl grn 1.00 .60
a. Souv. sheet of 5, #C382-C386, imperf. 4.00 4.00
Nos. C377-C386 (10) 8.65 3.75

Centenary of the birth of Lord Baden-Powell, founder of the Boy Scouts.

No. C386a with each stamp overprinted "CAMPOREE SCOUT 1965" was issued in 1965 along with Nos. 843-852. Value, sheet $10.

For surcharge see No. C754.

Pres. Luis A. Somoza — AP57

1957, July 2 *Perf. 14x13½*
Portrait in Dark Brown

C387 AP57 20c dp bl .45 .25
C388 AP57 25c lil rose .45 .25
C389 AP57 30c blk brn .45 .25
C390 AP57 40c grnsh bl .45 .25
C391 AP57 2cor brt vio 4.25 3.00
Nos. C387-C391 (5) 6.05 4.00

Issued to honor President Luis A. Somoza.

Church Types of Regular Issue

Designs: 30c, Archbishop Lezcano y Ortega. 60c, Managua Cathedral. 75c, Bishop Pereira y Castellon. 90c, Leon Cathedral. 1.50cor, De la Merced Church, Granada. 2cor, Father Mariano Dubon.

1957, July 16 Unwmk.
Centers in Olive Gray

C392 A78 30c dk grn .55 .25
C393 A77 60c chocolate .55 .25
C394 A78 75c dk bl .55 .25
C395 A77 90c brt red .85 .30
C396 A77 1.50cor Prus grn 1.75 .40
C397 A78 2cor brt pur 2.40 .60
Nos. C392-C397 (6) 6.65 2.05

Merchant Marine Type of 1957

Designs: 25c, M. S. Managua. 30c, Ship's wheel and map. 50c, Pennants. 60c, M. S. Costa Rica. 1 cor, M. S. Nicarao. 2.50 cor, Flag, globe & ship.

1957, Oct. 24 Litho. *Perf. 14*

C398 A79 25c ultra grysh bl & gray .65 .25
C399 A79 30c red brn, gray & yel .65 .25
C400 A79 50c vio, ol gray & bl .75 .30
C401 A79 60c lake, grnsh bl & blk .95 .35
C402 A79 1cor crim, brt bl & blk 1.25 .45
C403 A79 2.50cor blk, bl & red brn 4.75 2.50
Nos. C398-C403 (6) 9.00 4.10

For surcharge see No. C691.

Fair Emblem — AP58

Designs: 30c, 2cor, Arms of Nicaragua. 45c, 10cor, Pavilion of Nicaragua, Brussels.

1958, Apr. 17 Unwmk. *Perf. 14*

C404 AP58 25c bluish grn, blk & yel .40 .25
C405 AP58 30c multi .40 .25
C406 AP58 45c bis, bl & blk .40 .25
C407 AP58 1cor pale brn, lt bl & blk .40 .25
C408 AP58 2cor multi .75 .30
C409 AP58 10cor pale bl, lil & brn 2.60 1.60
a. Souv. sheet of 6, #C404-C409 13.50 12.00
Nos. C404-C409 (6) 4.95 2.90

World's Fair, Brussels, Apr. 17-Oct. 19.

Lions Type of Regular Issue

Designs: 30c, Dr. Teodoro A. Arias. 60c, Arms of Central American Republics. 90c, Edward G. Barry. 1.25cor, Melvin Jones. 2cor, Motto and emblem. 3cor, Map of Central America.

1958, May 8 Litho.
Emblem in Yellow, Red and Blue

C410 A80 30c bl & org .40 .25
C411 A80 60c multi .40 .25
C412 A80 90c blue .70 .30
C413 A80 1.25cor bl & ol 1.00 .40
C414 A80 2cor bl & grn 1.75 .70
C415 A80 3cor bl, lil & pink 2.60 1.10
a. Souv. sheet of 6, #C410-C415 6.50 4.25
Nos. C410-C415 (6) 6.85 3.00

For overprints and surcharges see Nos. C686, C971P.

Christian Brothers Type of 1958

Designs: 30c, Arms of La Salle. 60c, School, Managua, horiz 85c, St. Jean Baptiste De La Salle. 90c, Bro. Carlos. 1.25cor, Bro. Julio. 1.50cor, Bro. Antonio. 1.75cor, Bro. Argeo. 2cor, Bro. Eugenio.

1958, July 13 Photo. *Perf. 14*

C416 A81 30c bl, car & yel .40 .25
C417 A81 60c gray, brn & lil .75 .25
C418 A81 85c red, bl & grnsh blk .75 .30
C419 A81 90c ol grn, ocher & blk 1.10 .35
C420 A81 1.25cor car, ocher & blk 1.50 .50
C421 A81 1.50cor lt grn, gray & vio blk 1.75 .55
C422 A81 1.75cor brn, bl & grnsh blk 1.90 .65
C423 A81 2cor ol grn, gray & vio blk 2.75 1.00
Nos. C416-C423 (8) 10.90 3.85

For surcharges see Nos. C539A, C755-C756.

UNESCO Building, Paris — AP59

75c, 5cor, "UNESCO." 90c, 3cor, UNESCO building, Eiffel tower. 1cor, Emblem, globe.

Perf. 11½
1958, Dec. 15 Unwmk. Litho.

C424 AP59 60c magenta & bl .70 .25
C425 AP59 75c bl grn & org brn .70 .25
C426 AP59 90c lt brn & blue grn .70 .25
C427 AP59 1cor ultra & magenta .70 .25
C428 AP59 3cor blk & org 2.40 1.00
C429 AP59 5cor rose lil & dk bl 3.75 1.50
a. Min. sheet of 6, #C424-C429 7.00 4.50
Nos. C424-C429 (6) 8.95 3.50

UNESCO Headquarters Opening in Paris, Nov. 3.

For overprints see Nos. C494-C499.

Type of Regular Issue, 1959 and

Nicaraguan, Papal and US Flags — AP60

Designs: 35c, Pope John XXIII and Cardinal Spellman. 1cor, Spellman coat of arms. 1.05cor, Cardinal Spellman. 1.50cor, Human rosary and Cardinal, horiz. 2cor, Cardinal with Ruben Dario order.

1959, Nov. 26 *Perf. 12½*

C430 AP60 30c vio bl, yel & red .40 .25
C431 A83 35c dp org & grnsh blk .40 .25
C432 A83 1cor yel, bl & car .40 .25
C433 A83 1.05cor red, blk & dk car 1.00 .40
C434 A83 1.50cor dk bl & yel 1.00 .40
C435 A83 2cor multi 1.25 .60
C436 AP60 5cor multi 2.50 1.25
a. Min. sheet of 7, #C430-C436, perf. or imperf. 8.00 5.00
Nos. C430-C436 (7) 6.95 3.40

Visit of Cardinal Spellman to Managua, Feb. 1958.

For overprints and surcharges see #C538, C638, C747, C752, C971.

Type of Lincoln Regular Issue and

AP61

Perf. 13x13½, 13½x13
1960, Jan. 21 Engr. Unwmk.
Portrait in Black

C437 A84 30c indigo .45 .30
C438 A84 35c brt car .45 .30
C439 A84 70c plum .45 .30
C440 A84 1.05cor emerald .45 .30
C441 A84 1.50cor violet 1.10 .40
C442 AP61 5cor int blk & bis 3.50 1.50
a. Souv. sheet of 6, #C437-C442, imperf. 6.50 4.50
Nos. C437-C442 (6) 6.40 3.10

150th anniv. of the birth of Abraham Lincoln.

For overprints and surcharges see Nos. C446-C451, C500, C539, C637, C680, C753, C971W.

Nos. C343, C370 and C318 Overprinted

1960, July 4 Engr.

C443 AP49 2cor magenta 1.30 .70
C444 AP54 2.50cor dk ultra 1.30 .75
C445 A65 3cor green 1.90 1.10
Nos. C443-C445 (3) 4.50 2.55

10th anniversary of the Philatelic Club of San Jose, Costa Rica.

Nos. C437-C442 Overprinted in Red

Perf. 13x13½, 13½x13
1960, Sept. 19 Unwmk.
Center in Black

C446 A84 30c indigo .65 .30
C447 A84 35c brt car .65 .30
C448 A84 70c purple .65 .30
C449 A84 1.05cor emerald .95 .30
C450 A84 1.50cor violet 1.90 .80
C451 AP61 5cor int blk & bis 5.75 2.50
Nos. C446-C451 (6) 10.55 4.50

Issued for the Red Cross to aid earthquake victims in Chile. The overprint on No. C451 is horizontal and always inverted.

People and World Refugee Year Emblem — AP62

5cor, Crosses, globe and WRY emblem.

1961, Dec. 30 Litho. *Perf. 11x11½*

C452 AP62 2cor multi .75 .30
C453 AP62 5cor multi 1.25 .65
a. Souv. sheet of 2, #C452-C453 3.00 2.50

World Refugee Year, July 1, 1959-June 30, 1960.

Consular Service Stamps Surcharged in Red, Black or Blue — AP63

Unwmk.
1961, Feb. 21 Engr. *Perf. 12*
Red Marginal Number

C454 AP63 20c on 50c dp bl (R) .80 .40
C455 AP63 20c on 1cor grnsh blk (R) .80 .40
C456 AP63 20c on 2cor grn (R) .80 .40
C457 AP63 20c on 3cor dk car .80 .40
C458 AP63 20c on 5cor org (Bl) .80 .40
C459 AP63 20c on 10cor vio (R) .80 .40
C460 AP63 20c on 20cor red brn (R) .80 .40
C461 AP63 20c on 50cor brn (R) .80 .40
C462 AP63 20c on 100cor mag .80 .40
Nos. C454-C462 (9) 7.20 3.60

See Nos. CO51-CO59, RA63-RA64.

Charles L. Mullins, Anastasio Somoza and Franklin D. Roosevelt AP64

Standard Bearers with Flags of Nicaragua and Academy AP65

Designs: 25c, 70c, Flags of Nicaragua and Academy. 30c, 1.05cor, Directors of Academy: Fred T. Cruse, LeRoy Bartlett, Jr., John F. Greco, Anastasio Somoza Debayle, Francisco Boza, Elias Monge. 40c, 2cor, Academy Emblem. 45c, 5cor, Anastasio Somoza Debayle and Luis Somoza Debayle.

Perf. 11x11½, 11½x11
1961, Feb. 24 Litho. Unwmk.

C463 AP64 20c rose, gray & buff .60 .40
C464 AP65 25c bl, red & blk .60 .40
C465 AP64 30c bl, gray & yel .60 .40
C466 AP65 35c multi .60 .40
C467 AP65 40c multi .60 .40
C468 AP64 45c pink, gray & buff .60 .40
a. Min. sheet of 6, #C463-C468, imperf. 1.50 1.00
C469 AP64 60c brn, gray & buff .60 .40
C470 AP65 70c multi .60 .40
C471 AP64 1.05cor clar, gray & yel .60 .40
C472 AP65 1.50cor multi .60 .40
C473 AP65 2cor multi .75 .40

C474 AP64 5cor gray & buff 1.75 .40
a. Min. sheet of 6, #C469-C474, imperf. 6.50 4.00
Nos. C463-C474 (12) 8.50 4.80

20th anniversary (in 1959) of the founding of the Military Academy of Nicaragua.

In 1977, Nos. C468a and C474a were overprinted in black: "1927-1977 50 ANIVERSARIO / Guardia Nacional de Nicaragua." Value, $7.50 for both.

For surcharges see Nos. C692, C748, C759.

Emblem of Junior Chamber of Commerce — AP66

Designs: 2c, 15c, Globe showing map of Americas, horiz. 4c, 35c, Globe and initials, horiz. 5c, 70c, Chamber credo. 6c, 1.05cor, Handclasp. 10c, 5cor, Regional map.

Perf. 11x11½, 11½x11

1961, May 16 **Unwmk.**

C475 AP66 2c multi .65 .40
C476 AP66 3c yel & blk .65 .40
C477 AP66 4c multi .65 .40
C478 AP66 5c crim & blk .65 .40
C479 AP66 6c brn, yel & blk .65 .40
C480 AP66 10c org, blk & lt bl .65 .40
C481 AP66 15c bl, blk & grn .65 .40
C482 AP66 30c bl & blk .65 .40
C483 AP66 35c multi .65 .40
C484 AP66 70c yel, blk & crim .65 .40
C485 AP66 1.05cor multi .65 .40
C486 AP66 5cor multi 1.50 .40
Nos. C475-C486 (12) 8.65 4.80

13th Regional Congress of the Junior Chamber of Commerce of Nicaragua and the Intl. Junior Chamber of Commerce.

The imperforates of Nos. C475-C486 were not authorized.

For overprints and surcharges see Nos. C504-C508, C537, C634, C687, C749.

Rigoberto Cabezas AP67

Map of Costa Rica and View of Cartago AP68

Designs: 45c, Newspaper. 70c, Building. 2cor, Cabezas quotation. 10cor, Map of lower Nicaragua with Masaya area.

1961, Aug. 29 **Litho.** ***Perf. 13½***

C487 AP67 20c org & dk bl .60 .40
C488 AP68 40c lt bl & claret .60 .40
C489 AP68 45c citron & brn .60 .40
C490 AP68 70c beige & grn .60 .40
C491 AP68 2cor pink & dk bl 1.80 .40
C492 AP68 10cor grnsh bl & cl 3.50 1.10
Nos. C487-C492 (6) 7.70 3.10

Centenary of the birth of Rigoberto Cabezas, who acquired the Mosquito Territory (Atlantic Littoral) for Nicaragua.

No. C253 Overprinted in Red: "Convención Filatélica-Centro-América-Panama-San Salvador-27 Julio 1961"

1961, Aug. 23 **Engr.** ***Perf. 12½***

C493 AP22 1.25cor multi .90 .65
a. Inverted overprint 75.00

Central American Philatelic Convention, San Salvador, July 27.

Nos. C424-C429 Overprinted in Red

1961 **Litho.** ***Perf. 11½***

C494 AP59 60c magenta & bl .40 .40
C495 AP59 75c bl grn & org brn .50 .40
C496 AP59 90c lt brn & blue grn .50 .40
C497 AP59 1cor ultra & magenta .50 .40
C498 AP59 3cor blk & org 1.10 .65
C499 AP59 5cor rose lil & dk bl 4.50 1.75
Nos. C494-C499 (6) 7.50 4.00

Issued in memory of Dag Hammarskjold, Secretary General of the United Nations, 1953-61.

Nos. C314 and C440 Surcharged in Red

Perf. 13x13½, 13

1962, Jan. 20 **Engr.**

C500 A84 1cor on 1.05cor .80 .40
C501 AP44 1cor on 1.10cor .80 .40

UNESCO Emblem and Crowd — AP69

Design: 5cor, UNESCO and UN Emblems.

Unwmk.

1962, Feb. 26 **Photo.** ***Perf. 12***

C502 AP69 2cor multi .75 .25
C503 AP69 5cor multi 1.50 .70
a. Souv. sheet of 2, #C502-C503, imperf. 2.00 1.50

15th anniv. (in 1961) of UNESCO. For overprint, see No. C971H, C971K.

Nos. C480 and C483-C486 Overprinted

Perf. 11x11½, 11½x11

1962, July **Litho.**

C504 AP66 10c multi .50 .25
C505 AP66 35c multi .70 .25
C506 AP66 70c multi .90 .30
C507 AP66 1.05cor multi 1.20 .45
C508 AP66 5cor multi 1.90 1.40
Nos. C504-C508 (5) 5.20 2.65

WHO drive to eradicate malaria.

Souvenir Sheet

Stamps and Postmarks of 1862 — AP69a

1962, Sept. 9 **Litho.** ***Imperf.***

C509 AP69a 7cor multi 3.25 2.75

Cent. of Nicaraguan postage stamps. For overprint, see Nos. C971Y-C971Z.

Arms Type of Regular Issue, 1962

30c, Nueva Segovia. 50c, León. 1cor, Managua. 2cor, Granada. 5cor, Rivas.

1962, Nov. 22 ***Perf. 12½x13***

Arms in Original Colors; Black Inscriptions

C510 A86 30c rose .75 .40
C511 A86 50c salmon .75 .40
C512 A86 1cor lt grn .75 .40
C513 A86 2cor gray .90 .40
C514 A86 5cor lt bl 1.80 1.00
Nos. C510-C514 (5) 4.95 2.60

Liberty Bell — AP70

1963, May 15 **Litho.** ***Perf. 13x12***

C515 AP70 30c lt bl, blk & ol bis .80 .40

Sesquicentennial of the 1st Nicaraguan declaration of Independence (in 1961).

Paulist Brother Comforting Boy — AP71

60c, Nun comforting girl. 2cor, St. Vincent de Paul and St. Louisa de Marillac, horiz.

1963, May 15 **Photo.** ***Perf. 13½***

C516 AP71 60c gray & ocher .55 .40
C517 AP71 1cor salmon & blk .70 .40
C518 AP71 2cor crimson & blk 1.20 .40
Nos. C516-C518 (3) 2.45 1.20

300th anniv. of the deaths of St. Vincent de Paul and St. Louisa de Marillac (in 1960).

Map of Central America — AP72

Lithographed and Engraved

1963, Aug. 2 **Unwmk.** ***Perf. 12***

C519 AP72 1cor bl & yel .80 .40

Issued to honor the Federation of Central American Philatelic Societies.

Cross over World — AP73

1963, Aug. 6

C520 AP73 20c yel & red .80 .40

Vatican II, the 21st Ecumenical Council of the Roman Catholic Church.

Wheat and Map of Nicaragua — AP74

Design: 25c, Dead tree on parched earth.

1963, Aug. 6

C521 AP74 10c lt grn & grn .80 .40
C522 AP74 25c yel & dk brn .80 .40

FAO "Freedom from Hunger" campaign.

Boxing — AP75

Lithographed and Engraved

1963, Dec. 12 **Unwmk.** ***Perf. 12***

C523 AP75 2c shown .65 .25
C524 AP75 3c Running .65 .25
C525 AP75 4c Underwater .65 .25
C526 AP75 5c Soccer .65 .25
C527 AP75 6c Baseball .65 .25
C528 AP75 10c Tennis .65 .25
C529 AP75 15c Bicycling .65 .25
C530 AP75 20c Motorcycling .65 .25
C531 AP75 35c Chess .65 .25
C532 AP75 60c Deep-sea fishing .75 .30
C533 AP75 1cor Table tennis 1.00 .40
C534 AP75 2cor Basketball 2.00 .80
C535 AP75 5cor Golf 5.00 2.00
Nos. C523-C535 (13) 14.60 5.75

Publicizing the 1964 Olympic Games.

For overprints and surcharge see Nos. C553-C558, C635.

Central American Independence Issue

Flags of Central American States — AP75a

1964, Sept. 15 **Litho.** ***Perf. 13x13½***

Size: 27x43mm

C536 AP75a 40c multi .80 .40

Nos. C479, C430, C437 and C416 Surcharged in Black or Red

a

b

1964 **Litho.** ***Perf. 11½x11***

C537 AP66 (a) 5c on 6c .90 .40

Perf. 12½

C538 AP60 (a) 10c on 30c 1.80 .40

Engr.

Perf. 13x13½

C539 A84 (a) 15c on 30c (R) 2.25 .40

Photo.

Perf. 14

C539A A81 (b) 20c on 30c .90 .40
Nos. C537-C539A (4) 5.85 1.60

Floating Red Cross Station — AP76

Designs: 5c, Alliance for Progress emblem, vert. 15c, Highway. 20c, Plowing with tractors, and sun. 25c, Housing development. 30c, Presidents Somoza and Kennedy and World Bank Chairman Eugene Black. 35c, Adult education. 40c, Smokestacks.

1964, Oct. 15 **Litho.** ***Perf. 12***

C540 AP76 5c yel, brt bl, grn & gray .40 .40
C541 AP76 10c multi .40 .40
C542 AP76 15c multi .40 .40
C543 AP76 20c org brn, yel & blk .40 .40
C544 AP76 25c multi .40 .40
C545 AP76 30c dk bl, blk & brn .40 .40
C546 AP76 35c lil rose, dk red & blk .40 .40
C547 AP76 40c dp car, blk & yel 4.00 .40
Nos. C540-C547 (8) 6.80 3.20

Alliance for Progress.

For surcharges see Nos. C677, C693.

Map of Central America and Central American States — AP77

Designs (Map of Central America and): 25c, Grain. 40c, Cogwheels. 50c, Heads of cattle.

1964, Nov. 30 Litho. *Perf. 12*

C548 AP77 15c ultra & multi .80 .40
C549 AP77 25c multi .80 .40
C550 AP77 40c multi .80 .40
C551 AP77 50c multi .80 .40
Nos. C548-C551 (4) 3.20 1.60

Central American Common Market.
For surcharge see No. C678.

Nos. C523-C525, C527 and C533-C534 Overprinted: "OLIMPIADAS / TOKYO-1964"

Lithographed and Engraved

1964, Dec. 19 Unwmk. *Perf. 12*

C553 AP75 2c multi .40 .25
C554 AP75 3c multi .40 .25
C555 AP75 4c multi .40 .25
C556 AP75 6c multi .40 .25
C557 AP75 1cor multi 3.75 2.00
C558 AP75 2cor multi 5.00 2.50
Nos. C553-C558 (6) 10.35 5.50

18th Olympic Games, Tokyo, Oct. 10-25.

Blood Transfusion — AP78

Designs: 20c, Volunteers and priest rescuing wounded man. 40c, Landscape during storm. 10cor, Red Cross over map of Nicaragua.

1965, Jan. 28 Litho. *Perf. 12*

C559 AP78 20c yel, blk & red .50 .40
C560 AP78 25c red, blk & ol bis .50 .40
C561 AP78 40c grn, blk & red .50 .40
C562 AP78 10cor multi 3.50 1.10
Nos. C559-C562 (4) 5.00 2.30

Centenary (in 1963) of the Intl. Red Cross.

Stele — AP79

Antique Indian artifacts: 5c, Three jadeite statuettes, horiz. 15c, Dog, horiz. 20c, Talamanca pendant. 25c, Decorated pottery bowl and vase, horiz. 30c, Stone pestle and mortar on animal base. 35c, Three statuettes, horiz. 40c, Idol on animal pedestal. 50c, Decorated pottery bowl and vase. 60c, Vase and metate (tripod bowl), horiz. 1cor, Metate.

Perf. 13½x13, 13x13½

1965, Mar. 24 Litho. Unwmk.

Black Margin and Inscription

C563 AP79 5c yel & multi .75 .40
C564 AP79 10c multi .75 .40
C565 AP79 15c multi .75 .40
C566 AP79 20c sal & dk brn .75 .40
C567 AP79 25c lil & multi .75 .40
C568 AP79 30c lt grn & multi .75 .40
C569 AP79 35c multi .75 .40
C570 AP79 40c cit & multi .75 .40
C571 AP79 50c ocher & multi .75 .40
C572 AP79 60c multi .75 .40
C573 AP79 1cor car & multi 1.00 .40
Nos. C563-C573 (11) 8.50 4.40

For surcharges see Nos. C596-597, C679, C688-C690.

Pres. John F. Kennedy (1917-63) — AP80

Photogravure & Lithographed

1965, Apr. 28 *Perf. 12½x13½*

C574 AP80 35c blk & brt grn .45 .25
C575 AP80 75c blk & brt pink .65 .25
C576 AP80 1.10cor blk & dk bl .90 .40
C577 AP80 2cor blk & yel brn 2.25 1.00
Nos. C574-C577 (4) 4.25 1.90
Set of 4 souvenir sheets 17.00 12.00

Nos. C574-C577 each exist in souvenir sheets containing one imperf. block of 4.
For surcharge see No. C760.

Andrés Bello — AP81

1965, Oct. 15 Litho. *Perf. 14*

C578 AP81 10c dk brn & red brn .75 .25
C579 AP81 15c ind & lt bl .75 .25
C580 AP81 45c blk & dl lil .75 .25
C581 AP81 80c blk & yel grn .75 .25
C582 AP81 1cor dk brn & yel .75 .25
C583 AP81 2cor blk & gray .85 .30
Nos. C578-C583 (6) 4.60 1.55

Centenary of the death of Andrés Bello (1780?-1864), Venezuelan writer and educator.

Winston Churchill — AP82

Winston Churchill: 35c, 1cor, Broadcasting, horiz. 60c, 3cor, On military inspection. 75c, As young officer.

1966, Feb. 7 Unwmk. *Perf. 14*

C584 AP82 20c cer & blk .40 .40
C585 AP82 35c dk ol grn & blk .40 .40
C586 AP82 60c brn & blk .40 .40
C587 AP82 75c rose red .50 .40
C588 AP82 1cor vio blk .75 .40
C589 AP82 2cor lil & blk 1.40 .40
a. Souv. sheet of 4 2.75 1.40
C590 AP82 3cor ind & blk 2.10 .40
Nos. C584-C590 (7) 5.95 2.80

Sir Winston Spencer Churchill (1874-1965), statesman and World War II leader.

No. C589a contains four imperf. stamps similar to Nos. C586-C589 with simulated perforations.

Pope John XXIII — AP83

35c, Pope Paul VI. 1cor, Archbishop Gonzalez y Robleto. 2cor, St. Peter's, Rome. 3cor, Arms of Pope John XXIII & St. Peter's.

1966, Dec. 15 Litho. *Perf. 13*

C591 AP83 20c multi .65 .40
C592 AP83 35c multi .65 .40
C593 AP83 1cor multi .65 .40
C594 AP83 2cor multi 1.10 .40
C595 AP83 3cor multi 1.60 .50
Nos. C591-C595 (5) 4.65 2.10

Closing of the Ecumenical Council, Vatican II.

Nos. C571-C572 Surcharged in Red

1967 *Perf. 13x13½, 13½x13*

C596 AP79 10c on 50c multi .80 .40
C597 AP79 15c on 60c multi .80 .40

Rubén Dario and Birthplace AP84

Portrait and: 10c, Monument, Managua. 20c, Leon Cathedral, site of Dario's tomb. 40c, Centaurs. 75c, Swans. 1cor, Roman triumphal march. 2cor, St. Francis and the Wolf. 5cor, "Faith" defeating "Death."

1967, Jan. 18 Litho. *Perf. 13*

C598 AP84 5c lt brn, tan & blk .65 .40
C599 AP84 10c org, pale org & blk .65 .40
C600 AP84 20c vio, lt bl & blk .65 .40
C601 AP84 40c grn, dk grn & blk .65 .40
a. Souv. sheet of 4, #C598-C601 1.75 1.75
C602 AP84 75c ultra, pale bl & blk .65 .40
C603 AP84 1cor red, pale red & blk .65 .40
C604 AP84 2cor rose pink, car & blk .80 .40
C605 AP84 5cor dp ultra, vio bl, & blk 1.80 .40
a. Souv. sheet of 4, #C602-C605 6.75 6.75
Nos. C598-C605 (8) 6.50 3.20

Rubén Dario (pen name of Felix Rubén Garcia Sarmiento, 1867-1916), poet, newspaper correspondent and diplomat.
Sheets were issued perf. and imperf.

Megalura Peleus — AP85

Designs: Various butterflies. 5c, 10c, 30c, 35c, 50c and 1cor are vertical.

1967, Apr. 20 Litho. *Perf. 14*

C606 AP85 5c multi .40 .40
C607 AP85 10c multi .40 .40
C608 AP85 15c multi .45 .40
C609 AP85 20c multi .80 .40
C610 AP85 25c multi 1.00 .40
C611 AP85 30c multi 1.20 .40
C612 AP85 35c multi 1.25 .40
C613 AP85 40c multi 1.50 .40
C614 AP85 50c multi 1.60 .40
C615 AP85 60c multi 2.00 .80
C616 AP85 1cor multi 3.25 .80
C617 AP85 2cor multi 7.00 4.00
Nos. C606-C617 (12) 20.85 9.20

Com. James McDivitt and Maj. Edward H. White — AP86

Gemini 4 Space Flight: 10c, 40c, Rocket launching and astronauts. 15c, 75c, Edward H. White walking in space. 20c, 1cor, Recovery of capsule.

1967, Sept. 20 Litho. *Perf. 13*

C618 AP86 5c red & multi .80 .40
C619 AP86 10c org & multi .80 .40
C620 AP86 15c multi .80 .40
C621 AP86 20c multi .80 .40
C622 AP86 35c ol & multi .80 .40
C623 AP86 40c ultra & multi .80 .40
C624 AP86 75c brn & multi .80 .40
C625 AP86 1cor multi .80 .40
Nos. C618-C625 (8) 6.40 3.20

Saquanjoche, National Flower of Nicaragua — AP87

National Flowers: No. C626, White nun orchid, Guatemala. No. C627, Rose, Honduras. No. C629, Maquilishuat, Salvador. No. C630, Purple guaria orchid, Costa Rica.

1967, Nov. 22 Litho. *Perf. 13½*

C626 AP87 40c multi 1.25 .40
C627 AP87 40c multi 1.25 .40
C628 AP87 40c multi 1.25 .40
C629 AP87 40c multi 1.25 .40
C630 AP87 40c multi 1.25 .40
a. Strip of 5, #C626-C630 6.75 2.00

5th anniversary of the General Treaty for Central American Economic Integration.

Presidents of Nicaragua and Mexico — AP88

Designs: 40c Pres. Gustavo Diáz Ordaz of Mexico and Pres. René Schick of Nicaragua signing statement, horiz. 1cor, President Diáz.

1968, Feb. 28 Litho. *Perf. 12½*

C631 AP88 20c black .80 .40
C632 AP88 40c slate grn .80 .40
C633 AP88 1cor dp brn .80 .40
Nos. C631-C633 (3) 2.40 1.20

Issued to commemorate the visit of the President of Mexico, Gustavo Diáz Ordaz.

Nos. C479, C527, C242, C440 and C434 Surcharged in Black, Red (#C637) or Yellow (#C638)

1968, May Litho.; Engr.

C634 AP66 5c on 6c multi .80 .40
C635 AP75 5c on 6c multi .80 .40
C636 AP20 5c on 8c blk brn .80 .40
C637 A84 1cor on 1.05cor emer & blk .80 .40
C638 A83 1cor on 1.50cor dk bl & yel .80 .40
Nos. C634-C638 (5) 4.00 2.00

Mangos — AP89

1968, May 15 Litho. *Perf. 14*

C639 AP89 5c shown .45 .40
C640 AP89 10c Pineapples .45 .40
C641 AP89 15c Orange .45 .40
C642 AP89 20c Papaya .50 .40
C643 AP89 30c Bananas .50 .40
C644 AP89 35c Avocado .95 .40
C645 AP89 50c Watermelon .95 .40
C646 AP89 75c Cashews .95 .40
C647 AP89 1cor Sapodilla .95 .40
C648 AP89 2cor Cacao 1.80 .40
Nos. C639-C648 (10) 7.95 4.00

The Last Judgment, by Michelangelo AP90

Paintings: 10c, The Crucifixion, by Fra Angelo, horiz. 35c, Madonna with Child and St. John, by Raphael. 2cor, The Disrobing of Christ, by El Greco. 3cor, The Immaculate Conception, by Murillo. 5cor, Christ of St. John of the Cross, by Salvador Dali.

1968, July 22 Litho. *Perf. 12½*

C649 AP90 10c gold & multi .55 .40
C650 AP90 15c gold & multi .55 .40
C651 AP90 35c gold & multi .55 .40
C652 AP90 2cor gold & multi 1.00 .40
C653 AP90 3cor gold & multi 1.50 .55
Nos. C649-C653 (5) 4.15 2.15

Miniature Sheet

C654 AP90 5cor gold & multi 3.25 2.75

Nos. C649-C652 Overprinted: "Visita de S.S. Paulo VI C.E. de Bogota 1968"

1968, Oct. 25 Litho. *Perf. 12½*

C655 AP90 10c gold & multi .60 .40
C656 AP90 15c gold & multi .60 .40
C657 AP90 35c gold & multi .60 .40
C658 AP90 2cor gold & multi 1.20 .40
Nos. C655-C658 (4) 3.00 1.60

Visit of Pope Paul VI to Bogota, Colombia, Aug. 22-24. The overprint has 3 lines on the 10c stamp and 5 lines on others.

Basketball — AP91

Sports: 15c, Fencing, horiz. 20c, Diving. 35c, Running. 50c, Hurdling, horiz. 75c, Weight lifting. 1cor, Boxing, horiz. 2cor, Soccer.

1968, Nov. 28 Litho. *Perf. 14*

C659 AP91 10c multi .65 .40
C660 AP91 15c org red, blk & gray .65 .40
C661 AP91 20c multi .65 .40
C662 AP91 35c multi .65 .40
C663 AP91 50c multi .65 .40
C664 AP91 75c multi .65 .40
C665 AP91 1cor yel & multi .75 .40
C666 AP91 2cor gray & multi 2.10 .80
a. Souv. sheet of 4, #C663-C666 3.75 2.50
Nos. C659-C666 (8) 6.75 3.60

19th Olympic Games, Mexico City, 10/12-27.

Cichlasoma Citrinellum AP92

Fish: 15c, Cichlasoma nicaraguensis. 20c, Carp. 30c, Gar (lepisosteus tropicus). 35c, Swordfish. 50c, Phylipnus dormitor, vert. 75c, Tarpon atlanticus, vert. 1cor, Eulamia nicaraguensis, vert. 2cor, Sailfish, vert. 3cor, Sawfish, vert.

Perf. 13½x13, 13x13½

1969, Mar. 12 Litho.

C667 AP92 10c vio bl & multi 1.00 .40
C668 AP92 15c org & multi 1.00 .40
C669 AP92 20c grn & multi 1.00 .40
C670 AP92 30c pur & multi 1.00 .40
C671 AP92 35c yel & multi 1.00 .40
C672 AP92 50c brn & multi 1.00 .40
C673 AP92 75c ultra & multi 1.00 .40
C674 AP92 1cor org & multi 1.00 .40
C675 AP92 2cor dk bl & multi 1.75 .40
C676 AP92 3cor multi 2.60 .40
a. Min. sheet of 4, #C673-C676 6.25 5.00
Nos. C667-C676 (10) 12.35 4.00

Nos. C544, C549, C567 and C439 Srchd. in Black or Red

No. C678

No. C680

1969, Mar. Litho. *Perf. 12, 13½x13*

C677 AP76 10c on 25c multi .80 .40
C678 AP77 10c on 25c multi .80 .40
C679 AP79 15c on 25c multi .80 .40

Engr.

C680 A84 50c on 70c (R) .80 .40
Nos. C677-C680 (4) 3.20 1.60

Size of 50c surcharge: 11½x9mm.

View, Exhibition Tower and Emblem — AP93

1969, May 30 Litho. *Perf. 13½x13*

C681 AP93 30c dk vio bl & red .60 .40
C682 AP93 35c blk & red .60 .40
C683 AP93 75c car rose & vio bl .60 .40
C684 AP93 1cor dp plum & blk .60 .40
C685 AP93 2cor dk brn & blk 1.50 .40
a. Souv. sheet of 4, #C681-C682, C684-C685 4.00 2.50
Nos. C681-C685 (5) 3.90 2.00

HEMISFAIR 1968 Exhibition.

Nos. C410, C482, C567-C569, C399, C465, C546 Srchd. in Black or Red

1969 Litho. *Perfs. as before*

C686 A80 10c on 30c multi 1.00 .40
C687 AP66 10c on 30c bl & blk (R) 1.00 .40
C688 AP79 10c on 25c multi 1.00 .40
C689 AP79 10c on 30c multi 1.00 .40
C690 AP79 15c on 35c multi (R) 1.00 .40
C691 A79 20c on 30c multi 1.00 .40
C692 AP64 20c on 30c multi 1.00 .40
C693 AP76 20c on 35c multi 1.00 .40
Nos. C686-C693 (8) 8.00 3.20

Products of Nicaragua AP94

5c, Minerals (miner). 10c, Fishing. 15c, Bananas. 20c, Timber (truck). 35c, Coffee. 40c, Sugar cane. 60c, Cotton. 75c, Rice and corn. 1cor, Tobacco. 2cor, Meat.

1969, Sept. 22 Litho. *Perf. 13x13½*

C694 AP94 5c gold & multi .80 .40
C695 AP94 10c gold & multi .80 .40
C696 AP94 15c gold & multi .80 .40
C697 AP94 20c gold & multi .80 .40
C698 AP94 35c gold & multi .80 .40
C699 AP94 40c gold & multi .80 .40
C700 AP94 60c gold & multi .80 .40
C701 AP94 75c gold & multi .80 .40
C702 AP94 1cor gold & multi .80 .40
C703 AP94 2cor gold & multi 1.00 .40
Nos. C694-C703 (10) 8.20 4.00

Woman Carrying Jar, Conference Emblem — AP95

1970, Feb. 26 Litho. *Perf. 13½x14*

C704 AP95 10c multi .65 .40
C705 AP95 15c grn & multi .65 .40
C706 AP95 20c ultra & multi .65 .40
C707 AP95 35c multi .65 .40
C708 AP95 50c multi .65 .40
C709 AP95 75c multi .65 .40
C710 AP95 1cor lil & multi 1.10 .40
C711 AP95 2cor multi 2.00 .50
Nos. C704-C711 (8) 7.00 3.30

8th Inter-American Conf. on Savings & Loans.

Soccer Type of Regular Issue and

Flags of Participating Nations, World Cup, 1970 — AP96

Soccer Players: 20c, Djalma Santos, Brazil. 80c, Billy Wright, England. 4cor, Jozef Bozsik, Hungary. 5cor, Bobby Charlton, England.

1970, May 11 Litho. *Perf. 13½*

C712 A87 20c multi .55 .40
C713 A87 80c multi .70 .40
C714 AP96 1cor multi .95 .60
C715 A87 4cor multi 3.00 2.00
C716 A87 5cor multi 3.50 2.25
Nos. C712-C716 (5) 8.70 5.65

Issued to honor the winners of the 1970 poll for the International Soccer Hall of Fame. No. C714 also publicizes the 9th World Soccer Championships for the Jules Rimet Cup, Mexico City, May 30-June 21, 1970.

Names of players and their achievements printed in black on back of stamps.

For overprint and surcharges see Nos. C786-788.

EXPO Emblem, Mt. Fuji and Torii — AP97

1970, July 5 Litho. *Perf. 13½x14*

C717 AP97 25c multi .45 .40
C718 AP97 30c multi .45 .40
C719 AP97 35c multi .45 .40
C720 AP97 75c multi .70 .45
C721 AP97 1.50cor multi 1.00 .65
C722 AP97 3cor multi 2.10 1.25
a. Souv. sheet of 3, #C720-C722, imperf. 2.00 1.25
Nos. C717-C722 (6) 5.15 3.55

EXPO '70 International Exhibition, Osaka, Japan, Mar. 15-Sept. 13, 1970. For overprint, see No. C972.

Moon Landing, Apollo 11 Emblem and Nicaragua Flag — AP98

Apollo 11 Emblem, Nicaragua Flag and: 40c, 75c, Moon surface and landing capsule. 60c, 1cor, Astronaut planting US flag.

1970, Aug. 12 Litho. *Perf. 14*

C723 AP98 35c multi .65 .40
C724 AP98 40c multi .65 .40
C725 AP98 60c pink & multi .65 .40
C726 AP98 75c yel & multi .65 .40
C727 AP98 1cor vio & multi 1.00 .40
C728 AP98 2cor org & multi 1.50 .40
Nos. C723-C728 (6) 5.10 2.40

Man's 1st landing on the moon, July 20, 1969. See note after US No. C76.

Franklin D. Roosevelt — AP99

Roosevelt Portraits: 15c, 1cor, as stamp collector. 20c, 50c, 2cor, Full face.

1970, Oct. 12

C729 AP99 10c blk & bluish blk .75 .40
C730 AP99 15c blk & brn vio .75 .40
C731 AP99 20c blk & ol grn .75 .40
C732 AP99 35c blk & brn vio .75 .40
C733 AP99 50c brown .75 .40
C734 AP99 75c blue .75 .40
C735 AP99 1cor rose red .75 .40
C736 AP99 2cor black .75 .40
Nos. C729-C736 (8) 6.00 3.20

Franklin Delano Roosevelt (1882-1945).

Christmas 1970 — AP100

Paintings: Nos. C737, C742, Annunciation, by Matthias Grunewald. Nos. C738, C743, Nativity, by El Greco. Nos. C739, C744, Adoration of the Magi, by Albrecht Dürer. Nos. C740, C745, Virgin and Child, by J. van Hemessen. Nos. C741, C746, Holy Shepherd, Portuguese School, 16th century.

1970, Dec. 1 Litho. *Perf. 14*

C737 AP100 10c multi .80 .40
C738 AP100 10c multi .80 .40
C739 AP100 10c multi .80 .40
C740 AP100 10c multi .80 .40
C741 AP100 10c multi .80 .40
C742 AP100 15c multi .80 .40
C743 AP100 20c multi .80 .40
C744 AP100 35c multi .80 .40
C745 AP100 75c multi .80 .40
C746 AP100 1cor multi .80 .40
Nos. C737-C746 (10) 8.00 4.00

Nos. C737-C741 printed se-tenant.

Issues of 1947-67 Surcharged

1971, Mar.

C747 A83 25c on 1.05cor, #C433 .55 .40
C748 AP64 10c on 1.05cor, #C471 .55 .40
C749 AP66 10c on 1.05cor, #C485 .55 .40
C750 AP42 15c on 1.50cor, #C292 .80 .40
C751 AP53 15c on 1.50cor, #C369 .80 .40
C752 A83 15c on 1.50cor, #C434 .80 .40
C753 A84 15c on 1.50cor, #C441 .80 .40
C754 A75 20c on 85c, #C385 1.00 .50
C755 A81 20c on 85c, #C418 1.00 .50
C756 A81 25c on 90c, #C419 1.40 .70
C757 AP48 30c on 1.10cor, #C337 1.50 .85
C758 AP44 40c on 1.10cor, #C314 2.25 1.10
C759 AP65 40c on 1.50cor, #C472 2.25 1.10
C760 AP80 1cor on 1.10cor, #C576 5.50 2.75
Nos. C747-C760 (14) 19.75 10.30

The arrangement of the surcharge differs on each stamp.

Mathematics Type of Regular Issue

Symbolic Designs of Scientific Formulae: 25c, Napier's law (logarithms). 30c, Pythagorean theorem (length of sides of right-angled triangle). 40c, Boltzman's equation (movement of gases). 1cor, Broglie's law (motion of particles of matter). 2cor, Archimedes' principle (displacement of mass).

1971, May 15 Litho. *Perf. 13½*

C761 A88 25c lt bl & multi .95 .40
C762 A88 30c lt bl & multi 1.10 .50
C763 A88 40c lt bl & multi 1.60 .55
C764 A88 1cor lt bl & multi 1.60 1.40
C765 A88 2cor lt bl & multi 7.00 2.25
Nos. C761-C765 (5) 12.25 5.10

On the back of each stamp is a descriptive paragraph.

Montezuma Oropendola — AP101

Birds: 15c, Turquoise-browed motmot. 20c, Magpie-jay. 25c, Scissor-tailed flycatchers. 30c, Spot-breasted oriole, horiz. 35c, Rufous-naped wren. 40c, Great kiskadee. 75c, Red-legged honeycreeper, horiz. 1cor, Great-tailed grackle, horiz. 2cor, Belted kingfisher.

1971, Oct. 15 Litho. *Perf. 14*

C766 AP101 10c multi 1.25 .40
C767 AP101 15c multi 1.25 .40
C768 AP101 20c gray & multi 1.25 .40
C769 AP101 25c multi 1.25 .40
C770 AP101 30c multi 1.25 .40
C771 AP101 35c multi 1.50 .40
C772 AP101 40c multi 1.50 .40
C773 AP101 75c yel & multi 1.75 .40
C774 AP101 1cor org & multi 2.25 .40
C775 AP101 2cor org & multi 3.75 .40
Nos. C766-C775 (10) 17.00 4.00

Ten Commandments Type of Regular Issue

Designs: 1cor, Bathsheba at her Bath, by Rembrandt (IX). 2cor, Naboth's Vineyard, by James Smetham (X).

1971, Nov. 1 *Perf. 11*

C776 A90 1cor yel brn & multi 2.00 .60
C777 A90 2cor yel brn & multi 3.25 1.00

Descriptive inscriptions printed in gray on back of stamps.

U Thant, Anastasio Somoza, UN Emblem — AP102

1972, Feb. 15 *Perf. 14x13½*

C778 AP102 10c pink & mar .70 .40
C779 AP102 15c green .70 .40
C780 AP102 20c blue .70 .40
C781 AP102 25c rose claret .70 .40
C782 AP102 30c org & brn .70 .40
C783 AP102 40c gray & sl grn .70 .40
C784 AP102 1cor ol grn .70 .40
C785 AP102 2cor brown 1.40 .40
Nos. C778-C785 (8) 6.30 3.20

25th anniv. of the United Nations (in 1970).

Nos. C713, C715, C716 Surcharged or Overprinted Like Nos. 899-900

1972, Mar. 20 **Litho.** *Perf. 13½*

C786 A87 20c on 80c multi .65 .35
C787 A87 60c on 4cor multi .65 .35
C788 A87 5cor multi 2.25 1.50
Nos. C786-C788 (3) 3.55 2.20

20th Olympic Games, Munich, 8/26-9/11.

Ceramic Figure, Map of Nicaragua AP103

Pre-Columbian ceramics (700-1200 A.D.) found at sites indicated on map of Nicaragua.

1972, Sept. 16 **Litho.** *Perf. 14x13½*

C789 AP103 10c blue & multi .75 .40
C790 AP103 15c blue & multi .75 .40
C791 AP103 20c blue & multi .75 .40
C792 AP103 25c blue & multi .75 .40
C793 AP103 30c blue & multi .75 .40
C794 AP103 35c blue & multi .75 .40
C795 AP103 40c blue & multi .75 .40
C796 AP103 50c blue & multi .75 .40
C797 AP103 60c blue & multi .75 .40
C798 AP103 80c blue & multi .75 .40
C799 AP103 1cor blue & multi .75 .40
C800 AP103 2cor blue & multi 1.10 .40
Nos. C789-C800 (12) 9.35 4.80

Lord Peter Wimsey, by Dorothy L. Sayers — AP104

Designs (Book and): 10c, Philip Marlowe, by Raymond Chandler. 15c, Sam Spade, by Dashiell Hammett. 20c, Perry Mason, by Erle S. Gardner. 25c, Nero Wolfe, by Rex Stout. 35c, Auguste Dupin, by Edgar Allan Poe. 40c, Ellery Queen, by Frederick Dannay and Manfred B. Lee. 50c, Father Brown, by G. K. Chesterton. 60c, Charlie Chan, by Earl Derr Biggers. 80c, Inspector Maigret, by Georges Simenon. 1cor, Hercule Poirot, by Agatha Christie. 2cor, Sherlock Holmes, by A. Conan Doyle.

1972, Nov. 13 **Litho.** *Perf. 14x13½*

C801 AP104 5c blue & multi .70 .25
C802 AP104 10c blue & multi .70 .25
C803 AP104 15c blue & multi .70 .25
C804 AP104 20c blue & multi .70 .25
C805 AP104 25c blue & multi .70 .25
C806 AP104 35c blue & multi 1.00 .25
C807 AP104 40c blue & multi 1.00 .25
C808 AP104 50c blue & multi 1.20 .30
C809 AP104 60c blue & multi 1.60 .40
C810 AP104 80c blue & multi 2.10 .50
C811 AP104 1cor blue & multi 2.75 .65
C812 AP104 2cor blue & multi 5.50 1.25
Nos. C801-C812 (12) 18.65 4.85

50th anniv. of INTERPOL, intl. police organization. Designs show famous fictional detectives. Inscriptions on back, printed on top of gum, give thumbnail sketch of character and author.

Shepherds Following Star — AP105

Legend of the Christmas Rose: 15c, Adoration of the kings and shepherds. 20c, Shepherd girl alone crying. 35c, Angel appears to girl. 40c, Christmas rose (Helleborus niger). 60c, Girl thanks angel. 80c, Girl and Holy Family. 1cor, Girl presents rose to Christ Child. 2cor, Adoration.

1972, Dec. 20

C813 AP105 10c multi .70 .25
C814 AP105 15c multi .70 .25
C815 AP105 20c multi .70 .25
C816 AP105 35c multi .70 .25
C817 AP105 40c multi .70 .25
C818 AP105 60c multi .70 .25
C819 AP105 80c multi .70 .25
C820 AP105 1cor multi .70 .25
C821 AP105 2cor multi 1.40 .30
a. Souv. sheet of 9, #C813-C821 7.00 1.75
Nos. C813-C821 (9) 7.00 2.30

Christmas 1972.

No. C821a exists with red marginal overprint, "TERREMOTO DESASTRE," for the Managua earthquake of Dec. 22-23, 1972. It was sold abroad, starting in Jan. 1973. Value, $7.

Sir Walter Raleigh, Patent to Settle New World AP106

Events and Quotations from Contemporary Illustrations: 15c, Mayflower Compact, 1620. 20c, Acquittal of Peter Zenger, 1735, vert. 25c, William Pitt, 1766, vert. 30c, British revenue stamp for use in America No. RM31, vert. 35c, "Join or Die" serpent, 1768. 40c, Boston Massacre and State House, 1770, vert. 50c, Boston Tea Party and 3p coin, 1774. 60c, Patrick Henry, 1775, vert. 75c, Battle scene ("Our cause is just, our union is perfect," 1775). 80c, Declaration of Independence, 1776. 1cor, Liberty Bell, Philadelphia. 2cor, Seal of US, 1782, vert.

1973, Feb. 22 **Photo.** *Perf. 13½*

C822 AP106 10c olive & multi .65 .25
C823 AP106 15c olive & multi .65 .25
C824 AP106 20c olive & multi .65 .25
C825 AP106 25c olive & multi .65 .25
C826 AP106 30c olive & multi .65 .25
C827 AP106 35c ol, gold & blk .85 .25
C828 AP106 40c olive & multi .85 .25
C829 AP106 50c olive & multi .85 .35
C830 AP106 60c olive & multi .95 .35
C831 AP106 75c olive & multi 1.20 .40
C832 AP106 80c olive & multi 1.20 .40
C833 AP106 1cor olive & multi 1.90 .50
C834 AP106 2cor olive & multi 3.50 1.00
Nos. C822-C834 (13) 14.55 4.75

Inscriptions on back, printed on top of gum, give brief description of subject and event.

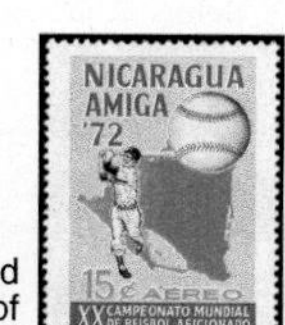

Baseball, Player and Map of Nicaragua — AP107

1973, May 25 **Litho.** *Perf. 13½x14*

C835 AP107 15c multi .70 .25
C836 AP107 20c multi .70 .25
C837 AP107 40c multi .70 .25
C838 AP107 10cor multi 5.00 1.50
a. Souvenir sheet of 4 16.50 15.00
Nos. C835-C838 (4) 7.10 2.25

20th International Baseball Championships, Managua, Nov. 15-Dec. 5, 1972. No. C838a contains 4 stamps similar to Nos. C835-C838 with changed background colors (15c, olive; 20c, gray; 40c, lt. green; 10cor, lilac), and 5 labels.

Fashion Type of 1973

10c, Lourdes Nicaragua. 15c, Halston, New York. 20c, Pino Lancetti, Rome. 35c, Madame Ges, Paris. 40c, Irene Galitzine, Rome. 80c, Pedro Rodriguez, Barcelona.

1973, July 26 **Litho.** *Perf. 13½*

C839 A91 10c multicolored .80 .25
C840 A91 15c multicolored .80 .25
C841 A91 20c multicolored .80 .25
C842 A91 35c multicolored .80 .25
C843 A91 40c multicolored .80 .25
C844 A91 80c multicolored .80 .25
a. Souv. sheet of 9, #909-911, C839-C844, perf. 11 + 3 labels 2.40 5.50
Nos. C839-C844 (6) 4.80 1.50

Inscriptions on back printed on top of gum give description of gown in Spanish and English.

Type of Air Post Semi-Postal Issue

Design: 2cor, Pediatric surgery.

1973, Sept. 25

C845 SPAP1 2cor multi 2.75 .40
Nos. C845,CB1-CB11 (12) 7.80 3.60

Planned Children's Hospital. Inscription on back, printed on top of gum gives brief description of subject shown.

See Nos. CB1-CB11.

Christmas Type

1cor, Virginia O'Hanlon writing letter, father. 2cor, Letter. 4cor, Virginia, father reading letter.

1973, Nov. 15 **Litho.** *Perf. 15*

C846 A92 1cor multicolored .80 .45
C847 A92 2cor multicolored 1.75 .90
C848 A92 4cor multicolored 3.00 1.50
a. Souvenir sheet of 3, #C846-C848, perf. 14½ 3.50 4.00
Nos. C846-C848 (3) 5.55 2.85

Churchill Type

No. C851, Silhouette, Parliament. No. C852, Silhouette, #10 Downing St. 5cor, Showing "V" sign. 6cor, "Bulldog" Churchill protecting England.

1974, Apr. 30 *Perf. 14½*

C849 A93 5cor multicolored 2.60 1.40
C850 A93 6cor multicolored 3.25 1.75

Souvenir Sheets

Perf. 15

C851 A93 4cor blk, org & bl 2.90 1.40
C852 A93 4cor blk, org, & grn 2.90 1.40

Nos. C851-C852 contain one 28x42mm stamp.

World Cup Type

Scenes from previous World Cup Championships with flags and scores of finalists.

1974, May 8 *Perf. 14½*

C853 A94 10cor Flags of participants 6.25 6.25

Souvenir Sheets

C853A A94 4cor like No. 928 4.00 1.10
C853B A94 5cor like No. 930 5.00 1.40

For overprint see No. C856.

Flower Type of 1974

Wild Flowers and Cacti: 1 cor, Centrosema. 3 cor, Night-blooming cereus.

1974, June 11 **Litho.** *Perf. 14*

C854 A95 1cor green & multi 2.00 1.00
C855 A95 3cor green & multi 4.50 2.50

Nicaraguan Stamps Type

1974, July 10 *Perf. 14½*

C855A A96 40c #835 .65 .40
C855B A96 3cor #C313, horiz. 2.40 1.25
C855C A96 5cor #734 3.75 2.25
Nos. C855A-C855C (3) 6.80 3.90

Souvenir Sheet

Imperf

C855D Sheet of 3 15.00
e. A96 1cor #665 1.50
f. A96 2cor #C110, horiz. 2.75
g. A96 4cor Globe, stars 7.00

UPU, Cent.

No. C853 Ovptd.

1974, July 12

C856 A94 10cor Flags 3.25 2.25

Animal Type of 1974

3cor, Colorado deer. 5cor, Jaguar.

1974, Sept. 10 **Litho.** *Perf. 14½*

C857 A97 3cor multi 1.75 1.00
C858 A97 5cor multi 4.00 2.50

Christmas Type of 1974

Works of Michelangelo: 40c, Madonna of the Stairs. 80c, Pitti Madonna. 2cor, Pietà. 5cor, Self-portrait.

1974, Dec. 15

C859 A98 40c multi 1.90 .50
C860 A98 80c multi 1.90 .50
C861 A98 2cor multi 2.40 1.25
C862 A98 5cor multi 5.50 3.00
Nos. C859-C862 (4) 11.70 5.25

An imperf. souvenir sheet with simulated perfs exists containing 2cor and 5cor stamps. Value, $4. This imperforate sheet was overprinted with Literacy Year and 1980 Summer Olympic inscriptions and illustrations on 9/26/80.

Opera Type of 1975

Opera Singers and Scores: 25c, Rosa Ponselle, Norma. 35c, Giuseppe de Luca, Rigoletto. 40c, Joan Sutherland, La Figlia del Reggimento. 50c, Ezio Pinza, Don Giovanni. 60c, Kirsten Flagstad, Tristan and Isolde. 80c, Maria Callas, Tosca. 2cor, Fyodor Chaliapin, Boris Godunov. 5cor, Enrico Caruso, La Juive.

1975, Jan. 22 *Perf. 14x13½*

C863 A99 25c grn & multi .65 .35
C864 A99 35c multi .65 .35
C865 A99 40c multi .65 .35
C866 A99 50c org & multi .65 .35
C867 A99 60c rose & multi .65 .35
C868 A99 80c lake & multi .80 .35
C869 A99 2cor sep & multi 1.90 .35
C870 A99 5cor multi 4.75 1.00
a. Souvenir sheet of 3 13.50 10.00
Nos. C863-C870 (8) 10.70 3.45

No. C870a contains one each of Nos. C869-C870 and a 1cor with design and colors of No. C868. Exists imperf.

Easter Type of 1975

Stations of the Cross: 40c, Jesus stripped of his clothes. 50c, Jesus nailed to the Cross. 80c, Jesus dies on the Cross. 1cor, Descent from the Cross. 5cor, Jesus laid in the tomb.

1975, Mar. 20 *Perf. 14½*

C871 A100 40c ultra & multi .50 .25
C872 A100 50c ultra & multi .50 .25
C873 A100 80c ultra & multi .70 .25
C874 A100 1cor ultra & multi 1.00 .25
C875 A100 5cor ultra & multi 4.00 1.40
Nos. C871-C875 (5) 6.70 2.40

American Bicentennial Type of 1975

Designs: 40c, Washington's Farewell, 1783. 50c, Washington Addressing Continental Congress by J. B. Stearns. 2cor, Washington Arriving for Inauguration. 5cor, Statue of Liberty and flags of 1776 and 1976. 40c, 50c, 2cor, horiz.

1975, Apr. 16 *Perf. 14*

C876 A101 40c tan & multi .65 .25
C877 A101 50c tan & multi .80 .30
C878 A101 2cor tan & multi 2.40 .85
C879 A101 5cor tan & multi 5.25 3.00
Nos. C876-C879 (4) 9.10 4.40

Perf. and imperf. 7cor souvenir sheets exist. Value, $8. These sheets were overprinted with Literacy Year and 1980 Winter Olympic inscriptions and illustrations on 9/26/80.

See Nos. 978-988.

Nordjamb 75 Type of 1975

Designs (Scout and Nordjamb Emblems and): 35c, Camp. 40c, Scout musicians. 1cor, Campfire. 10cor, Lord Baden-Powell.

1975, Aug. 15 *Perf. 14½*

C880 A102 35c multi .55 .25
C881 A102 40c multi .55 .25
C882 A102 1cor multi .70 .30
C883 A102 10cor multi 4.25 2.00
Nos. C880-C883 (4) 6.05 2.80

Two airmail souvenir sheets of 2 exist. One, perf., contains 2cor and 3cor with designs of Nos. 992 and 990. The other, imperf., contains 2cor and 3cor with designs of Nos. 993 and C882. Size: 125x101mm. Value, pair $19. These sheets were overprinted with Literacy Year and International Year of the Child inscriptions and illustrations on 9/26/80.

Pres. Somoza Type of 1975

1975, Sept. 10 *Perf. 14*

C884 A103 1cor vio & multi .35 .25
C885 A103 10cor bl & multi 4.00 1.75
C886 A103 20cor multi 8.25 3.50
Nos. C884-C886 (3) 12.60 5.50

Choir Type of 1975

Famous Choirs: 50c, Montserrat Abbey. 1cor, St. Florian Choir Boys. 2cor, Choir Boys of the Wooden Cross, vert. 5cor, Boys and

Pope Paul VI (Pueri Cantores International Federation).

1975, Nov. 15 *Perf. 14½*
C887 A104 50c sil & multi .45 .25
C888 A104 1cor sil & multi .45 .25
C889 A104 2cor sil & multi .95 .40
C890 A104 5cor sil & multi 3.75 1.25
Nos. C887-C890 (4) 5.60 2.15

A 10cor imperf. souvenir sheet exists (Oberndorf Memorial Chapel Choir and score of "Holy Night-Silent Night"). Value, $12.50.

Chess Type of 1976

Designs: 40c, The Chess Players, by Thomas Eakins. 2cor, Bobby Fischer and Boris Spasski in Reykjavik, 1972. 5cor, Shakespeare and Ben Johnson Playing Chess, by Karel van Mander.

1976, Jan. 8 *Perf. 14½*
C891 A105 40c multi .40 .25
C892 A105 2cor vio & multi 2.10 .75
C893 A105 5cor multi 4.00 2.00
Nos. C891-C893 (3) 6.50 3.00

A souvenir sheet contains one each of Nos. C892-C893, perf. and imperf. Size: 143x67mm. Value, pair $11.

Olympic Winner Type 1976

Winners, Rowing and Sculling Events: 55c, USSR, 1956, 1960, 1964, vert. 70c, New Zealand, 1972, vert. 90c, New Zealand, 1968. 10cor, Women's rowing crew, US, 1976, vert. 20cor, US, 1956.

1976, Sept. 7 Litho. *Perf. 14*
C902 A107 55c bl & multi .35 .25
C903 A107 70c bl & multi .35 .25
C904 A107 90c bl & multi .35 .25
C905 A107 20cor bl & multi 11.00 6.00
Nos. C902-C905 (4) 12.05 6.75

Souvenir Sheet

C906 A107 10cor multi 8.50 5.00

No. C906 for the 1st participation of women in Olympic rowing events, size of stamp: 37x50mm.

The overprint "Republica Democratica Alemana Vencedor en 1976" was applied in 1976 to No. C905 in black in 3 lines and to the margin of No. C906 in gold in 2 lines.

Bicentennial Type of 1976

American Bicentennial Emblem and: #C907, Philadelphia, 1776. #C908, Washington, 1976. #C909, John Paul Jones' ships. #C910, Atomic submarine. #C911, Wagon train. #C912, Diesel train.

1976, May 25 Litho. *Perf. 13½*
C907 A108 80c multi .25 .25
C908 A108 80c multi .25 .25
a. Pair, #C907-C908 .75 .60
C909 A108 2.75cor multi .50 .40
C910 A108 2.75cor multi .50 .40
a. Pair, #C909-C910 2.25 1.75
C911 A108 4cor multi .80 .50
C912 A108 4cor multi .80 .50
a. Pair, #C911-C912 4.00 3.00
Nos. C907-C912 (6) 3.10 2.30

A souvenir sheet contains two 10cor stamps showing George Washington and Gerald R. Ford with their families. Size: 140x111mm. Value, $9.50.

Rare Stamps Type of 1976

Rare Stamps: 40c, Hawaii #1. 1cor, Great Britain #1. 2cor, British Guiana #13. 5cor, Honduras #C12. 10cor, Newfoundland #C1.

1976, Dec. *Perf. 14*
C913 A109 40c multi .40 .25
C914 A109 1cor multi .55 .25
C915 A109 2cor multi .80 .25
C916 A109 5cor multi 2.25 .65
C917 A109 10cor multi 3.50 1.25
Nos. C913-C917 (5) 7.50 2.65

Inscriptions on back printed on top of gum give description of illustrated stamp.

A 4cor imperf. souvenir sheet shows 1881 Great Britain-Nicaragua combination cover. Size: 140x101mm. Value, $2.50. This sheet was overprinted with Literacy Year and International Year of the Child inscriptions and illustrations on 9/26/80.

Olga Nuñez de Saballos AP108

Designs: 1cor, Josefa Toledo de Aguerri. 10cor, Hope Portocarrero de Somoza.

1977, Feb. Litho. *Perf. 13½*
C918 AP108 35c multi .35 .25
C919 AP108 1cor red & multi .35 .25
C920 AP108 10cor multi 3.25 1.75
Nos. C918-C920 (3) 3.95 2.25

Famous Nicaraguan women and for International Women's Year (in 1975).

Zeppelin Type of 1977

Designs: 35c, Ville de Paris airship. 70c, Zeppelin "Schwaben." 3cor, Zeppelin in flight. 10cor, Vickers "Mayfly" before take-off. 20cor, Zeppelin with leadlines extended.

1977, Oct. 31 Litho. *Perf. 14½*
C921 A110 35c multi .40 .25
C922 A110 70c multi .40 .25
C923 A110 3cor multi 1.90 .75
C924 A110 10cor multi 6.25 3.50
Nos. C921-C924 (4) 8.95 4.75

Souvenir Sheet

C925 A110 20cor multi 15.00 7.50

No. C925 exists imperf.
For overprints, see Nos. C974-C974A,

Lindbergh Type of 1977

Designs: 55c, Lindbergh's plane approaching Nicaraguan airfield, 1928. 80c, Spirit of St. Louis and map of New York-Paris route. 2cor, Plane flying off Nicaragua's Pacific Coast. 10cor, Lindbergh flying past Momotombo Volcano on way to Managua. 20cor, Spirit of St. Louis.

1977, Nov. 30
C926 A111 55c multi .40 .25
C927 A111 80c multi .40 .25
C928 A111 2cor multi 1.30 .45
C929 A111 10cor multi 6.50 2.50
Nos. C926-C929 (4) 8.60 3.45

Souvenir Sheet

C930 A111 20cor multi 15.00 7.50

For overprint, see Nos. C973-C973A.

Christmas Type of 1977
Souvenir Sheet

Design: 20cor, Finale of Nutcracker Suite.

1977, Dec. 12
C931 A112 20cor multi 9.00 4.50

Painting Type of 1978

Rubens Paintings: 5cor, Hippopotamus and Crocodile Hunt. 10cor, Duke de Lerma on Horseback. 20cor, Self-portrait.

1978, Jan. 11 Litho. *Perf. 14½*
C932 A113 5cor multi 2.75 1.25
C933 A113 10cor multi 5.25 3.00

Souvenir Sheet

C934 A113 20cor multi 10.00 5.00

Peter Paul Rubens (1577-1640), 400th birth anniversary.

St. Francis Type of 1978

Designs: 80c, St. Francis and the wolf. 10cor, St. Francis, painting. 20cor, Our Lady of Conception, statue in Church of El Viejo.

1978, Feb. 23 Litho. *Perf. 14½*
C935 A114 80c lt brn & multi .60 .25
C936 A114 10cor bl & multi 4.75 1.75

Souvenir Sheet

C937 A114 20cor multi 10.00 5.00

For overprint, see No, C971N-C971O.

Railroad Type of 1978

Locomotives: 35c, Light-weight American. 4cor, Heavy Baldwin. 10cor, Juniata, 13-ton. 20cor, Map of route system.

1978, Apr. 7 Litho. *Perf. 14½*
C938 A115 35c lt grn & multi .95 .40
C939 A115 4cor dp org & multi 2.90 1.50
C940 A115 10cor cit & multi 5.00 2.50
Nos. C938-C940 (3) 8.85 4.40

Souvenir Sheet

C941 A115 20cor multi 16.00 8.00

Jules Verne Type of 1978

Designs: 90c, 20,000 Leagues under the Sea. 10cor, Around the World in 80 Days. 20cor, From the Earth to the Moon.

1978, Aug. Litho. *Perf. 14½*
C942 A116 90c multi .65 .35
C943 A116 10cor multi 5.25 3.00

Souvenir Sheet

C944 A116 20cor multi 9.75 5.00

Aviation History Type of 1978

Designs: 55c, Igor Sikorsky in his helicopter, 1913, horiz. 10cor, Space shuttle, horiz. 20cor, Flyer III, horiz.

1978, Sept. 29 Litho. *Perf. 14½*
C945 A117 55c multi .65 .30
C946 A117 10cor multi 3.75 2.00

Souvenir Sheet

C947 A117 20cor multi 40.00 20.00

Soccer Type of 1978

Soccer Players: 50c, Denis Law and Franz Beckenbauer. 5cor, Dino Zoff and Pelé. 20cor, Dominique Rocheteau and Johan Neeskens.

1978, Oct. 25 Litho. *Perf. 13½x14*
C948 A118 50c multi .40 .25
C949 A118 5cor multi 3.00 1.75

Souvenir Sheet

C950 A118 20cor multi 10.00 5.00

Christmas Type of 1978

Paintings: 3cor, Apostles John and Peter, by Dürer. 10cor, Apostles Paul and Mark, by Dürer. 20cor, Virgin and Child with Garlands, by Dürer.

1978, Dec. 12 Litho. *Perf. 13½x14*
C951 A119 3cor multi .90 .45
C952 A119 10cor multi 3.75 2.00

Souvenir Sheet

C953 A119 20cor multi 8.00 4.00

Volcano Type of 1978

Designs: No. C954, Cerro Negro Volcano. No. C955, Lake Masaya. No. C956, Momotombo Volcano. No. C957, Lake Asososca. No. C958, Mombacho Volcano. No. C959, Lake Apoyo. No. C960, Concepcion Volcano. No. C961, Lake Tiscapa.

1978, Dec. 29 *Perf. 14x13½*
C954 A120 35c multi .40 .25
C955 A120 35c multi .40 .25
a. Pair, #C549-C955 .80 .40
C956 A120 90c multi .40 .25
C957 A120 90c multi .40 .25
a. Pair, #C956-C957 .90 .45
C958 A120 1cor multi .40 .25
C959 A120 1cor multi .40 .25
a. Pair, #C958-C959 1.00 .50
C960 A120 10cor multi 1.90 1.40
C961 A120 10cor multi 1.90 1.40
a. Pair, #C960-C961 6.50 5.00
Nos. C954-C961 (8) 6.20 4.30

Bernardo O'Higgins — AP109

1979, Mar. 7 Litho. *Perf. 14*
C962 AP109 20cor multi 4.75 3.25

Bernardo O'Higgins (1778-1842), Chilean soldier and statesman.

Red Ginger and Rubythroated Hummingbird AP110

Designs: 55c, Orchid. 70c, Poinsettia. 80c, Flower and bees. 2cor, Lignum vitae and blue morpho butterfly. 4cor, Cattleya.

1979, Apr. 6 Litho. *Perf. 14x13½*
C963 AP110 50c multi .65 .25
C964 AP110 55c multi .65 .25
C965 AP110 70c multi .65 .25
C966 AP110 80c multi .65 .25
C967 AP110 2cor multi 1.75 .30
C968 AP110 4cor multi 6.50 .50
Nos. C963-C968 (6) 10.85 1.80

Endangered Turtles Overprinted in Red — AP110a

Overprint reads: 1979 / ANO DE LA LIBERACION / OLYMPIC RINGS / PARTICIPACION NICARAGUA / OLIMPIADAS 1980 / Litografia Nacional, Portugal symbol

Turtles: 90c, Loggerhead. 2cor, Correoso. 2.20cor, Ridley. 10cor, Pico Halcón.

1980, Apr. 7 Litho. *Perf. 14¼x13¾*
C969 AP110a 90c multi *19.00 19.00*
C969A AP110a 2cor multi *19.00 19.00*
C969B AP110a 2.20cor multi *19.00 19.00*
C969C AP110a 10cor multi *19.00 19.00*
Nos. C969-C969C (4) *76.00 76.00*

Overprinted for Year of Liberation and 1980 Olympic Games.

Nos. C969-C969C were not issued without overprints.

Souvenir Sheet

Intl. Year of the Child — AP110b

Designs: a, 5cor, like #1101C. b, 15cor, Dr. Hermann Gmeiner.

1980, May 3 Litho. *Perf. 14½*
C970 AP110b Sheet of 2, #a-b. *85.00* —

No. C970 exists imperf.

Souvenir Sheet

Endangered Turtles Overprinted in Red and Blue — AP110c

No. C970C: d, 5cor, Correoso turtle. e, 15cor, Green (verde) turtle.

1980, May 3 Litho. *Perf. 13¼x13*
C970C AP110c Sheet of 2, #d-e — —

Overprinted for Year of Liberation and 1980 Olympic Games. No. C970C was not issued without overprints.

Souvenir Sheet

AP110d

No. C970F: g, 6cor, Albert Einstein (1879-1955), physicist. h, 15cor, Einstein and Mohandas K, Gandhi (1869-1948), Indian nationalist leader.

1980, May 3 Litho. *Perf. 13½*
C970F AP110d Sheet of 2, #g-h — —

Souvenir Sheet

Sir Rowland Hill and Nicaragua No. 1 — AP110e

1980, May 3 Litho. *Imperf.*
C970I AP110e 20cor multi — —

Souvenir Sheet

Sir Rowland Hill and Indigenous Messenger — AP110f

1980, May 3 Litho. *Perf. 14½*
C970J AP110f 20cor multi — —

No. C436a Overprinted in Black and Silver

AP110g

Methods and Perfs. As Before
1980, Sept. 26
C971 AP110g Sheet of 7 — —
a. 30c multi — —
b. 35c multi — —
c. 1cor multi — —
d. 1.05cor multi — —
e. 1.50cor multi — —
f. 2cor multi — —
g. 5cor multi — —

No. C503a Overprinted

AP110h

Methods and Perfs. As Before
1980, Sept. 26
Black and Silver Overprint in Sheet Margin
C971H AP110h Sheet of 2 — —
i. 2col multi — —
j. 5col multi — —

Dark Blue and Gold Overprint in Sheet Margin
C971K AP110h Sheet of 2 — —
l. 2col multi — —
m. 5col multi — —

No. C937 Overprinted
Souvenir Sheet

AP110i

1980, Sept. 26 Litho. *Perf. 14½*
Overprnted in Black and Silver
C971N AP110i 20cor multi — —

Overprnted in Black, Gold and Silver
C971O AP110i 20cor multi — —

No. C415a Overprinted in Blue and Silver

AP110j

Methods and Perfs. As Before
1980, Sept. 30
C971P AP110j Sheet of 6 — —
q. 30c multi — —
r. 60c multi — —
s. 90c multi — —
t. 1.25cor multi — —
u. 2cor multi — —
v. 3cor multi — —

No. C442a Overprinted in Black and Red

AP110k

Methods and Perfs. As Before
1980, Sept. 30
C971W AP110k Sheet of 6, #C437-C441, C971Lm — —
x. 5cor multi with overprint — —

No. C509 Overprinted in Red, Black and Silver

AP110l

Methods and Perfs. As Before
1980, Sept. 30
Overprinted in Red, Black and Silver, With Vostok 1 at Left
C971Y AP110l 7cor multi — —

Overprinted in Red, Black and Silver, With Apollo 11 at Left
C971Z AP110l 7cor multi — —

No. C722a Overprinted in Black, Red and Silver

AP110m

Methods and Perfs. As Before
1980, Sept. 30
C972 AP110m Sheet of 3 — —
a. 75c multi — —
b. 1.50cor multi — —
c. 3cor multi — —

No. C930 Overprinted in Gold, Purple and Green, Blue & Orange Brown

A111

1980, Sept. 30 *Perf. 14½*
C973 A111 20cor multi 44.00 —

No. C930 Overprinted in Silver, Black and Green, Blue & Orange Brown
C973A A111 20cor multi — —

No. C925 Overprinted

AP111a

Methods and Perfs. As Before
1980, Sept. 30
Overprinted in Dark Blue and Silver
C974 AP111a 20cor multi — —

Overprinted in Dark Blue and Gold
C974A AP111a 20cor multi — —

Nos. C974 and C974A exist imperforate.

Souvenir Sheet

AP111d

Overprint reads: 1980 ANO DE LA ALFABETIZACION / 1980 MOSCU and Litografia Nacional, Portugal symbol

1980, Dec. 20 Litho. *Perf. 14½*
Overprinted & Surcharged in Black & Silver
C974F AP111d 10cor on 20cor multi 22.00 —

Overprinted & surcharged for Literacy Year.

No. 974F was not issued without surcharge.

Numbers have been reserved for 6 additional stamps in this set. The editors would like to examine these stamps.

Endangered Turtles Type of 1980 Overprinted in Red — AP111e

Overprint reads: 1980 ANO DE LA ALFABETIZACION and Litografia Nacional, Portugal symbol

No. C975D, Green (Verde) turtle.

1981, May 15 Litho. *Perf. 14¼x13¾*
C975 AP111e 90c like #C969 8.00 —
C975A AP111e 2cor like #C969A 8.00 —
C975B AP111e 2.20cor like #C969B 8.00 —
C975C AP111e 10cor like #C969C 8.00 —
Nos. C975-C975C (4) 32.00

Souvenir Sheet
C975D AP111e 5cor on 20cor multi 100.00 —

Overprinted for Literacy Year.

Nos. C975-C975D were not issued without overprints and surcharge.

Revolution Type of 1981

1981, July 19 Litho. *Perf. 12½x12*
C975E A123 2.10cor March 1.50 .25
C975F A123 3cor Construction 2.50 .25
C975G A123 6cor Health programs 6.00 .45
Nos. C975E-C975G (3) 10.00 .95

FSLN Type of 1981

1981, July 23
C976 A124 4cor Founder 2.40 .40

Postal Union Type of 1981

1981, Aug. 10
C977 A125 2.10cor Pony express .60 .40
C978 A125 3cor Headquarters .70 .40
C979 A125 6cor Members' flags 1.10 .50
Nos. C977-C979 (3) 2.40 1.30

1300th Anniv. of Bulgaria AP112

1981, Sept. 2 *Imperf.*
C980 AP112 10cor multi 3.00 1.00

Size: 96x70mm.

Aquatic Flower Type of 1981

10cor, Nymphaea gladstoniana.

1981, Sept. 15 *Perf. 12½*
C981 A126 10cor multi 6.50 .90

Souvenir Sheet

Panda Bear AP113

1981, Oct. 9 *Perf. 13*
C982 AP113 10cor multi 5.50 2.00

Philatokyo Stamp Exhibition, Tokyo.

Tropical Fish Type of 1981

3.50cor, Pterolebias longipinnis. 4cor, Xiphophorus helleri.

1981, Oct. 19 *Perf. 12½*
C983 A127 3.50cor multi 2.50 .30
C984 A127 4cor multi 3.25 .30

Souvenir Sheet

Frigate AP114

1981, Nov. 2 *Perf. 13*
C985 AP114 10cor multi 3.50 1.00

Espamer '81 Stamp Exhibition, Buenos Aires, Nov. 13-22.

Bird Type of 1981

3cor, Trogon massena. 4cor, Campylopterus hemileucurus, horiz. 6cor, Momotus momota.

1981, Nov. 30 *Perf. 12½*
C986 A128 3cor multicolored 1.00 .30
C987 A128 4cor multicolored 1.25 .40
C988 A128 6cor multicolored 2.75 .75
Nos. C986-C988 (3) 5.00 1.45

Satellite Type of 1981

1981, Dec. 15 *Perf. 13x12½*
C989 A129 3cor multi 1.60 .25
C990 A129 4cor multi 2.25 .30
C991 A129 5cor multi 2.75 .35
Nos. C989-C991 (3) 6.60 .90

Railroad Type of 1981

1981, Dec. 30 *Perf. 12½*
C992 A130 6cor Ferrobus, 1967 6.25 .75

World Cup Type of 1982

1982, Jan. 25
C993 A131 4cor multi 2.10 .30
C994 A131 10cor multi, horiz. 5.00 .80

Souvenir Sheet

Perf. 13

C995 A131 10cor multi 4.00 1.60

No. C995 contains one 39x31mm stamp.

Dog Type of 1982

1982, Feb. 18
C996 A132 3cor Boxers 1.50 .30
C997 A132 3.50cor Pointers 1.90 .30
C998 A132 6cor Collies 2.75 .50
Nos. C996-C998 (3) 6.15 1.10

Intl. ITU Congress AP115

1982, Mar. 12
C999 AP115 25cor multi 4.00 2.25

Butterfly Type of 1982

3cor, Parides iphidamas. 3.50cor, Consul hippona. 4cor, Morpho peleides.

1982, Mar. 26
C1000 A133 3cor multi 1.75 .30
C1001 A133 3.50cor multi 2.00 .30
C1002 A133 4cor multi 2.50 .40
Nos. C1000-C1002 (3) 6.25 1.00

Satellite Type of 1982

1982, Apr. 12
C1003 A134 5cor multi, horiz. 2.00 .40
C1004 A134 6cor multi 2.40 .50

UPU Type of 1982

1982, May 1 Litho. *Perf. 13*
C1005 A135 3.50cor Train .85 .25
C1006 A135 10cor Jet 2.25 .70

Sports Type of 1982

2.50cor, Women's volleyball, vert. 3cor, Boxing. 9cor, Soccer. 10cor, Baseball, vert.

1982, May 13
C1007 A136 2.50cor multi .90 .25
C1008 A136 3cor multi 1.10 .30
C1009 A136 9cor multi 3.50 .80
Nos. C1007-C1009 (3) 5.50 1.35

Souvenir Sheet

C1010 A136 10cor multi 5.50 2.50

No. C1010 contains one 29x36mm stamp.

Souvenir Sheet

PHILEXFRANCE '82 Intl. Stamp Exhibition, Paris, June 11-21 — AP116

1982, June 9 *Perf. 13x12½*
C1011 AP116 15cor multi 5.50 1.25

Revolution Type of 1982

Symbolic doves. 2.50cor, 4cor vert.

1982, July 19 *Perf. 13*
C1012 A137 2.50cor multi 1.10 .30
C1013 A137 4cor multi 1.75 .40
C1014 A137 6cor multi 2.60 .60
Nos. C1012-C1014 (3) 5.45 1.30

Washington Type of 1982

2.50cor, Crossing the Delaware. 3.50cor, At Valley Forge. 4cor, Battle of Trenton. 6cor, Washington in Princeton.

Perf. 12½x13, 13x12½

1982, June 20 Litho.
C1015 A138 2.50cor multi, horiz. 1.10 .30
C1016 A138 3.50cor multi, horiz. 1.40 .35
C1017 A138 4cor multi 1.60 .40
C1018 A138 6cor multi 2.60 .60
Nos. C1015-C1018 (4) 6.70 1.65

Painting Type of 1982

9cor, Seated Woman, by A. Morales.

1982, Aug. 17 *Perf. 13*
C1019 A139 9cor multi 6.00 .80

Dimitrov Type of 1982

2.50cor, Dimitrov, Yikov, Sofia, 1946. 4cor, Portrait, flag.

1982, Sept. 9
C1020 A140 2.50cor multi .90 .30
C1021 A140 4cor multi 1.10 .40

Dictatorship Type of 1982

4cor, Rigoberto Lopez Perez. 6cor, Edwin Castro.

1982, Sept. 21 *Perf. 13x12½*
C1022 A141 4cor multi 1.25 .40
C1023 A141 6cor multi 1.90 .60

Tourism Type of 1982

2.50cor, Coyotepe Fortress, Masaya. 3.50cor, Velazquez Park, Managua.

1982, Sept. 25 *Perf. 13*
C1024 A142 2.50cor multi 2.25 .30
C1025 A142 3.50cor multi 3.00 .30

Marx Type of 1982

4cor, Marx, Highgate Monument.

1982, Oct. 4 *Perf. 12½*
C1026 A143 4cor multi 1.75 .35

Discovery of America Type of 1982

2.50cor, Trans-atlantic voyage. 4cor, Landing of Columbus. 7cor, Death of Columbus. 10cor, Columbus' fleet.

1982, Oct. 12 *Perf. 12½x13*
C1027 A145 2.50cor multi 1.25 .25
C1028 A145 4cor multi 1.90 .40
C1029 A145 7cor multi 3.00 .70
a. Sheet, 2 each #1187-1190, C1027-C1029, + 2 labels 16.00 —
Nos. C1027-C1029 (3) 6.15 1.35

Souvenir Sheet

Perf. 13

C1030 A145 10cor multi 5.50 1.10

No. C1030 contains one 31x39mm stamp.

Flower Type of 1982

2.50cor, Pasiflora foetida. 3.50cor, Clitoria sp. 5cor, Russelia sarmentosa.

1982, Nov. 13 *Perf. 12½*
C1031 A146 2.50cor multi 1.80 .25
C1032 A146 3.50cor multi 2.00 .30
C1033 A146 5cor multi 2.50 .45
Nos. C1031-C1033 (3) 6.30 1.00

Reptile Type of 1982

2.50cor, Turtle, horiz. 3cor, Boa constrictor. 3.50cor, Crocodile, horiz. 5cor, Sistrurus catenatus, horiz.

1982, Dec. 10 *Perf. 13*
C1034 A147 2.50cor multi 1.80 .25
C1035 A147 3cor multi 1.90 .30
C1036 A147 3.50cor multi 2.10 .30
C1037 A147 5cor multi 3.00 .45
Nos. C1034-C1037 (4) 8.80 1.30

Non-aligned States Conference, Jan. 12-14 — AP117

1983, Jan. 10 Litho. *Perf. 12½x13*
C1038 AP117 4cor multi 1.40 .40

Geothermal Electricity Generating Plant, Momotombo Volcano AP118

1983, Feb. 25 *Perf. 13*
C1039 AP118 2.50cor multi .90 .40

Souvenir Sheet

TEMBAL '83 Philatelic Exhibition, Basel, Switzerland — AP119

1983, May 21 Litho. *Perf. 13*
C1040 AP119 15cor Chamoix 3.50 1.40

Souvenir Sheet

1st Nicaraguan Philatelic Exhibition — AP120

10cor, Nicaragua Airlines jet.

1983, July 17 Litho. *Perf. 13*
C1041 AP120 10cor multi 3.00 1.40

Armed Forces — AP121

4cor, Frontier guards, watch dog.

1983, Sept. 2 Litho. *Perf. 13*
C1042 AP121 4cor multi 1.10 .40

Souvenir Sheet

BRASILIANA '83 Intl. Stamp Show, Rio de Janeiro, July 29-Aug. 7 — AP122

1983
C1043 AP122 15cor Jaguar 5.50 1.75

Cuban Revolution, 25th Anniv. — AP122a

6cor, Castro, Guevara, flag.

1984, Jan. 1 Litho. *Perf. 13*
C1043A AP122a 4cor shown 1.25 .40
C1043B AP122a 6cor multi 1.75 .60

Souvenir Sheet

Cardinal Infante Don Fernando, by Diego Velazquez — AP123

1984, May 2 Litho. *Perf. 13*
C1044 AP123 15cor multi 4.25 1.25

ESPANA '84.

Souvenir Sheet

Hamburg '84 AP124

1984, June 19 Litho. *Perf. 13*
C1045 AP124 15cor Dirigible 4.25 1.25

1984 UPU Congress AP125

15cor, Mail transport.

1984, June 24 *Perf. 12½*
C1046 AP125 15cor multi 6.25 1.00

Souvenir Sheet

Expofilnic '84 (2nd Natl. Stamp Exhibition) — AP126

15cor, Communications Museum.

1984, July 15
C1047 AP126 15cor multi 3.00 1.00

Souvenir Sheet

Ausipex '84 AP127

1984, Sept. 21
C1048 AP127 15cor Explorer ship 3.00 1.00

Souvenir Sheet

OLYMPHILEX '85 — AP128

1985, Mar. 18 Litho. *Perf. 12½*
C1049 AP128 15cor Bicycle race 2.50 .75

Souvenir Sheet

ESPAMER '85, Havana, Mar. 19-24 — AP129

10cor, Crocodylus rhombifer.

1985, Mar. 19
C1050 AP129 10cor multi 5.50 .75

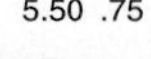

Victory of Sandanista Revolution, 6th Anniv. — AP134

1985, July 19 Litho. *Perf. 12½*
C1125 AP134 9cor Soldier, flag 1.40 .60
C1126 AP134 9cor Sugar mill 1.40 .60

Benjamin Zeledon, Birth Cent. — AP135

1985, Oct. 4 Litho. *Perf. 12½*
C1127 AP135 15cor multicolored 3.00 .40

Henri Dunant (1828-1910), Founder of Red Cross AP136

15cor, Dunant, air ambulance.

1985, Oct. 10 *Perf. 12½x12*
C1128 AP136 3cor shown .40 .25
C1129 AP136 15cor multi 1.40 .45
a. Pair, #C1128-C1129 + label 3.10 1.50

Nicaraguan Stamps, 125th Anniv. — AP137

1986, May 22 *Perf. 12½x13*
C1130 AP137 30cor No. C1 1.25 .30
C1131 AP137 40cor No. 174 1.60 .40
C1132 AP137 50cor No. 48 2.00 .50
C1133 AP137 100cor No. 1 3.50 1.10
Nos. C1130-C1133 (4) 8.35 2.30

Intl. Peace Year — AP138

1986, July 19 *Perf. 12½*
C1134 AP138 5cor shown .85 .25
C1135 AP138 10cor Globe, dove .85 .25

Carlos Fonseca, 10th Death Anniv. AP139

1986, Aug. 11 Litho. *Perf. 12½*
C1136 AP139 15cor multicolored .95 .40

Formation of the Sandinista Front, 25th anniv.

AP140

1986, Nov. 20 *Perf. 13*
C1137 AP140 15cor Rhinoceros 1.00 .35
C1138 AP140 15cor Zebra 1.00 .35
C1139 AP140 25cor Elephant 1.40 .50
C1140 AP140 25cor Giraffe 1.40 .50
C1141 AP140 50cor Mandrill 2.90 1.00
C1142 AP140 50cor Tiger 2.90 1.00
Nos. C1137-C1142 (6) 10.60 3.70

AP141

World Cup Soccer Championships, Mexico: Various soccer players and natl. flags.

1986, Dec. 20 *Perf. 13*

Shirt Colors

C1143 AP141 10cor blue .85 .25
C1144 AP141 10cor blk & white .85 .25
C1145 AP141 10cor blue & white .85 .25
C1146 AP141 15cor pink & white 1.20 .25
C1147 AP141 15cor grn & blk 1.20 .25
C1148 AP141 25cor blk & white, red 1.90 .30
C1149 AP141 50cor grn & yel, red, horiz. 2.10 .55
Nos. C1143-C1149 (7) 8.95 2.10

Souvenir Sheet

Perf. 12½

C1150 AP141 100cor blk & white, bl & white 5.50 1.10

Vassil Levski, 150th Birth Anniv. — AP142

1987, Apr. 18 *Perf. 13*
C1151 AP142 30cor multicolored 1.50 .40

Intl. Year of Shelter for the Homeless AP143

Design: 30cor, Housing, diff.

1987, Aug. 2
C1152 AP143 20cor multicolored 1.00 .25
C1153 AP143 30cor multicolored 1.80 .35

For surcharges, see Nos. C1160B-C1160C.

Souvenir Sheet

Berlin, 750th Anniv. AP144

1987, Sept. 25 Litho. *Perf. 13*
C1154 AP144 130cor multi 4.50 1.00

Discovery of America, 500th Anniv. (in 1992) — AP145

No. C1155, Indian village. No. C1156, Sailing ships. No. C1157, Battle in village. No. C1158, Battle, prisoners. No. C1159, Spanish town. No. C1160, Cathedral.

1987, Oct. 12 *Perf. 13*
C1155 AP145 15cor multicolored 1.10 .25
C1156 AP145 15cor multicolored 1.10 .25
C1157 AP145 20cor multicolored 1.40 .25
C1158 AP145 30cor multicolored 2.10 .30
C1159 AP145 40cor multicolored 3.00 .40
C1160 AP145 50cor multicolored 3.50 .50
a. Min. sheet of 6, #C1155-C1160 12.50 7.00
Nos. C1155-C1160 (6) 12.20 1.95

Nos. C1152-C1153 Surcharged

Methods and Perfs As Before

1987, Dec. 26
C1160B AP143 200cor on 20cor 250.00 250.00
C1160C AP143 3000cor on 30cor 250.00 250.00
Nos. C1160B-C1160C (2) 500.00

Cuban Revolution, 30th Anniv. — AP146

1989, Jan. 1 *Perf. 13*
C1161 AP146 20cor multicolored 1.75 .40

AP147

Designs: Various soccer players in action.

1989, Feb. 20 *Perf. 13x12½*
C1162 AP147 100cor multi .55 .25
C1163 AP147 200cor multi .55 .25
C1164 AP147 600cor multi .55 .25
C1165 AP147 1000cor multi .90 .25
C1166 AP147 2000cor multi 1.60 .45
C1167 AP147 3000cor multi 2.75 .40
C1168 AP147 5000cor multi 4.00 .65
Nos. C1162-C1168 (7) 10.90 2.50

Souvenir Sheet

Perf. 13

C1169 AP147 9000cor multi 5.50 2.25

World Cup Soccer Championships, Italy. No. C1169 contains one 32x40mm stamp.

AP148

Design: 9000cor, Concepcion Volcano.

1989, July 19 *Perf. 13*
C1170 AP148 300cor multi .80 .40

Souvenir Sheet

C1171 AP148 9000cor multi 7.75 2.25

Sandinista Revolution, 10th Anniv. No. C1171 contains one 40x32mm stamp.

AP149

Birds: 100cor, Anhinga anhinga. 200cor, Elanoides forficatus. 600cor, Eumomota superciliosa. 1000cor, Setophaga picta. 2000cor, Taraba major, horiz. 3000cor, Onychorhynchus mexicanus. 5000cor, Myrmotherula axillaris, horiz. 9000cor, Amazona ochrocephala.

1989, July 18 *Perf. 13x12½, 12½x13*
C1172 AP149 100cor multi .45 .25
C1173 AP149 200cor multi .45 .25
C1174 AP149 600cor multi .45 .25
C1175 AP149 1000cor multi .75 .25
C1176 AP149 2000cor multi 1.60 .30
C1177 AP149 3000cor multi 2.60 .45
C1178 AP149 5000cor multi 4.50 .75
Nos. C1172-C1178 (7) 10.80 2.50

Souvenir Sheet

Perf. 13

C1179 AP149 9000cor multi 5.50 2.00

Brasiliana '89. No. C1179 contains one 32x40mm stamp.

AP150

Designs: 50cor, Downhill skiing. 300cor, Ice hockey. 600cor, Ski jumping. 1000cor, Pairs figure skating. 2000cor, Biathalon. 3000cor, Slalom skiing. 5000cor, Cross country skiing. 9000cor, Two-man luge.

1989, Mar. 25 *Perf. 13*
C1180 AP150 50cor multi 1.10 .25
C1181 AP150 300cor multi 1.10 .25
C1182 AP150 600cor multi 1.10 .25

C1183 AP150 1000cor multi 1.10 .25
C1184 AP150 2000cor multi 1.90 .25
C1185 AP150 3000cor multi 2.10 .25
C1186 AP150 5000cor multi 2.40 .25
Nos. C1180-C1186 (7) 10.80 1.75

Souvenir Sheet

C1187 AP150 9000cor multi 5.50 2.00

1992 Winter Olympics, Albertville. No. C1187 contains one 32x40mm stamp.

AP151

Designs: 100cor, Water polo. 200cor, Running. 600cor, Diving. 1000cor, Gymnastics. 2000cor, Weight lifting. 3000cor, Volleyball. 5000cor, Wrestling. 9000cor, Field hockey.

1989, Apr. 23

C1188 AP151 100cor multi 1.10 .25
C1189 AP151 200cor multi 1.10 .25
C1190 AP151 600cor multi 1.10 .25
C1191 AP151 1000cor multi 1.10 .25
C1192 AP151 2000cor multi 1.90 .25
C1193 AP151 3000cor multi 2.10 .25
C1194 AP151 5000cor multi 2.40 .25
Nos. C1188-C1194 (7) 10.80 1.75

Souvenir Sheet

C1195 AP151 9000cor multi 5.50 .45

1992 Summer Olympics, Barcelona. No. C1195 contains one 32x40mm stamp.

AP152

1989, Oct. 12

C1196 AP152 2000cor Vase 1.50 .30

Discovery of America, 500th Anniv. (in 1992).

Currency Reform

Currency reform took place Mar. 4, 1990. Until stamps in the new currency were issued, mail was to be handstamped "Franqueo Pagado," (Postage Paid). Stamps were not used again until Apr. 25, 1991. Nos. C1197-C1203 were prepared but not issued prior to the currency reform and were sold by the post office without postal validity. Used values are for CTO stamps.

Mushrooms — AP153

Designs: 500cor, Morchella esculenta. 1000cor, Boletus edulis. 5000cor, Lactarius deliciosus. 10,000cor, Panellus stipticus. 20,000cor, Craterellus cornucopioides. 40,000cor, Cantharellus cibarius. 50,000cor, Armillariella mellea.

1990, July 15 ***Perf. 13***

C1197 AP153 500cor multi .45 .25
C1198 AP153 1000cor multi .65 .25
C1199 AP153 5000cor multi 1.00 .25
C1200 AP153 10,000cor multi 1.60 .25
C1201 AP153 20,000cor multi 1.90 .40
C1202 AP153 40,000cor multi 2.40 .50
C1203 AP153 50,000cor multi 2.90 .60
Nos. C1197-C1203 (7) 10.90 2.50

AIR POST SEMI-POSTAL STAMPS

Children and weight chart SPAP1

Designs: 10c+5c, Mrs. Somoza and Children's Hospital. 15c+5c, Incubator and Da Vinci's "Child in Womb." 20c+5c, Smallpox vaccination. 30c+5c, Water purification. 35c+5c, 1cor+50c, like 10c+5c. 50c+10c, Antibiotics. 60c+15c, Malaria control. 70c+10c, Laboratory. 80c+20c, Gastroenteritis (sick and well babies).

1973, Sept. 25 Litho. ***Perf. 13½x14***

CB1 SPAP1 5c + 5c multi .25 .25
CB2 SPAP1 10c + 5c multi .25 .25
CB3 SPAP1 15c + 5c multi .30 .25
CB4 SPAP1 20c + 5c multi .30 .25
CB5 SPAP1 30c + 5c multi .30 .25
CB6 SPAP1 35c + 5c multi .30 .25
CB7 SPAP1 50c + 10c multi .30 .25
CB8 SPAP1 60c + 15c multi .50 .30
CB9 SPAP1 70c + 10c multi .75 .30
CB10 SPAP1 80c + 20c multi .85 .40
CB11 SPAP1 1cor + 50c multi .95 .45
Nos. CB1-CB11 (11) 5.05 3.20

The surtax was for hospital building fund.

See No. C845. Inscriptions on back, printed on top of gum give brief description of subjects shown.

AIR POST OFFICIAL STAMPS

OA1

"Typewritten" Overprint on #O293

1929, Aug. Unwmk. ***Perf. 12***

CO1 OA1 25c orange 50.00 45.00

Excellent counterfeits of No. CO1 are plentiful.

Official Stamps of 1926 Ovptd. in Dark Blue

1929, Sept. 15

CO2 A24 25c orange .50 .50
a. Inverted overprint 25.00 25.00
b. Double overprint 25.00 25.00
CO3 A25 50c pale blue .75 .75
a. Inverted overprint 25.00 25.00
b. Double overprint 25.00 25.00
c. Double overprint, one inverted 25.00

Nos. 519-523 Overprinted in Black

1932, Feb.

CO4 A24 15c org red .40 .40
a. Inverted overprint 25.00
b. Double overprint 25.00 25.00
c. Double overprint, one invtd. 25.00 25.00
CO5 A25 20c orange .45 .45
a. Double overprint 25.00
CO6 A24 25c dk vio .45 .45
CO7 A25 50c green .55 .55
CO8 A25 1cor yellow 1.00 1.00
Nos. CO4-CO8 (5) 2.85 2.85

Nos. CO4-CO5, CO7-CO8 exist with signature control overprint. Value, each, $2.50.

No. 547 Overprinted

CO9 A24 25c blk brn 75.00 75.00

The varieties "OFICAL", "OFIAIAL" and "CORROE" occur in the setting and are found on each stamp of the series.

Counterfeits of No. CO9 are plentiful.

Stamp No. CO4 with overprint "1931" in addition is believed to be of private origin.

Type of Regular Issue of 1914 Overprinted

1933

CO10 A24 25c olive .40 .40
CO11 A25 50c ol grn .40 .40
CO12 A25 1cor org red .40 .40

On Stamps of 1914-28

CO13 A24 15c dp vio .40 .40
CO14 A25 20c dp grn .40 .40
Nos. CO10-CO14 (5) 2.00 2.00

Nos. CO10-CO14 exist without signature control mark. Value, each $2.50.

Air Post Official Stamps of 1932-33 Ovptd. in Blue

1935

CO15 A24 15c dp vio 1.00 .80
CO16 A25 20c dp grn 2.00 1.60
CO17 A24 25c olive 3.00 2.50
CO18 A25 50c ol grn 35.00 30.00
CO19 A25 1cor org red 40.00 37.50
Nos. CO15-CO19 (5) 81.00 72.40

Overprinted in Red

CO20 A24 15c dp vio .50 .40
CO21 A25 20c dp grn .50 .40
CO22 A24 25c olive .50 .40
CO23 A25 50c ol grn 1.75 .80
CO24 A25 1cor org red 1.75 .80
Nos. CO20-CO24 (5) 5.00 2.80

Nos. CO15 to CO24 are handstamped with script control mark. Counterfeits of blue overprint are plentiful.

The editors do not recognize the Nicaraguan air post Official stamps overprinted in red "VALIDO 1935" in two lines and with or without script control marks as having been issued primarily for postal purposes.

Nos. C164-C168 Overprinted in Black

1937

CO25 AP1 15c yel org 1.00 .55
CO26 AP1 20c org red 1.00 .60
CO27 AP1 25c black 1.00 .70
CO28 AP1 50c violet 1.00 .70
CO29 AP1 1cor orange 1.00 .70
Nos. CO25-CO29 (5) 5.00 3.25

Pres. Anastasio Somoza — OA2

1939, Feb. 7 Engr. ***Perf. 12½***

CO30 OA2 10c brown .40 .40
CO31 OA2 15c dk bl .40 .40
CO32 OA2 20c yellow .40 .40
CO33 OA2 25c dk pur .40 .40
CO34 OA2 30c lake .40 .40
CO35 OA2 50c dp org 1.00 .65
CO36 OA2 1cor dk ol grn 2.00 1.25
Nos. CO30-CO36 (7) 5.00 3.90

Catalogue values for unused stamps in this section, from this point to the end of the section, are for Never Hinged items.

Mercedes Airport OA3

Designs: 10c, Sulphurous Lake of Nejapa. 15c, Ruben Dario Monument. 20c, Tapir. 25c, Genizaro Dam. 50c, Tipitapa Spa. 1cor, Stone Highway. 2.50cor, Franklin D. Roosevelt Monument.

Engraved, Center Photogravure
1947, Aug. 29
Various Frames in Black

CO37 OA3 5c org brn .80 .25
CO38 OA3 10c blue .80 .25
CO39 OA3 15c violet .80 .25
CO40 OA3 20c red org .80 .25
CO41 OA3 25c blue .80 .25
CO42 OA3 50c car rose .80 .25
CO43 OA3 1cor slate 1.20 .45
CO44 OA3 2.50cor red brn 3.50 1.25
Nos. CO37-CO44 (8) 9.50 3.20

Rowland Hill — OA4

Designs: 10c, Heinrich von Stephan. 25c, 1st UPU Bldg. 50c, UPU Bldg., Bern. 1cor, UPU Monument. 2.60cor, Congress medal, reverse.

1950, Nov. 23 Engr. ***Perf. 13***

Frames in Black

CO45 OA4 5c rose vio .50 .25
CO46 OA4 10c dp grn .50 .25
CO47 OA4 25c rose vio .50 .25
CO48 OA4 50c dp org .50 .25
CO49 OA4 1cor ultra .55 .30
CO50 OA4 2.60cor gray blk 4.00 2.00
Nos. CO45-CO50 (6) 6.55 3.30

75th anniv. (in 1949) of the UPU.

Each denomination was also issued in a souvenir sheet containing four stamps and marginal inscriptions. Size: 121x96mm. Value, set of 6 sheets, $35.

Consular Service Stamps Surcharged "Oficial Aéreo" and New Denomination in Red, Black or Blue

1961, Nov. Unwmk. Engr. ***Perf. 12***

Red Marginal Number

CO51 AP63 10c on 1cor grnsh blk (R) .60 .25
CO52 AP63 15c on 20cor red brn (R) .60 .25
CO53 AP63 20c on 100cor mag .60 .25
CO54 AP63 25c on 50c dp bl (R) .60 .25
CO55 AP63 35c on 50cor brn (R) .60 .25
CO56 AP63 50c on 3cor dk car .60 .25
CO57 AP63 1cor on 2cor grn (R) .60 .25
CO58 AP63 2cor on 5cor org (Bl) 1.00 .40
CO59 AP63 5cor on 10cor vio (R) 2.75 1.00
Nos. CO51-CO59 (9) 7.95 3.15

POSTAGE DUE STAMPS

D1

1896 Unwmk. Engr. ***Perf. 12***

J1 D1 1c orange .50 *1.25*
J2 D1 2c orange .50 *1.25*
J3 D1 5c orange .50 *1.25*
J4 D1 10c orange .50 *1.25*
J5 D1 20c orange .50 *1.25*
J6 D1 30c orange .50 *1.25*
J7 D1 50c orange .50 *1.50*
Nos. J1-J7 (7) 3.50 *9.00*

Wmk. 117

J8 D1 1c orange 1.00 *1.50*
J9 D1 2c orange 1.00 *1.50*
J10 D1 5c orange 1.00 *1.50*
J11 D1 10c orange 1.00 *1.50*
J12 D1 20c orange 1.25 *1.50*
J13 D1 30c orange 1.00 *1.50*
J14 D1 50c orange 1.00 *1.50*
Nos. J8-J14 (7) 7.25 *10.50*

1897 Unwmk.

J15 D1 1c violet .50 *1.50*
J16 D1 2c violet .50 *1.50*
J17 D1 5c violet .50 *1.50*
J18 D1 10c violet .50 *1.50*
J19 D1 20c violet 1.25 *2.00*
J20 D1 30c violet .50 *1.50*
J21 D1 50c violet .50 *1.50*
Nos. J15-J21 (7) 4.25 *11.00*

Wmk. 117

J22 D1 1c violet .50 *1.50*
J23 D1 2c violet .50 *1.50*
J24 D1 5c violet .50 *1.50*
J25 D1 10c violet .50 *1.50*
J26 D1 20c violet 1.00 *2.00*
J27 D1 30c violet .50 *1.50*
J28 D1 50c violet .50 *1.50*
Nos. J22-J28 (7) 4.00 *11.00*

Reprints of Nos. J8-J28 are on thick, porous paper. Color of 1896 reprints, reddish orange; or 1897 reprints, reddish violet. On watermarked reprints, liberty cap is sideways. Value 40c each.

D2

1898 Litho. Unwmk.

J29 D2 1c blue green .40 *2.00*
J30 D2 2c blue green .40 *2.00*
J31 D2 5c blue green .40 *2.00*
J32 D2 10c blue green .40 *2.00*
J33 D2 20c blue green .40 *2.00*
J34 D2 30c blue green .40 *2.00*
J35 D2 50c blue green .40 *2.00*
Nos. J29-J35 (7) 2.80 *14.00*

1899

J36 D2 1c carmine .40 *2.00*
J37 D2 2c carmine .40 *2.00*
J38 D2 5c carmine .40 *2.00*
J39 D2 10c carmine .40 *2.00*
J40 D2 20c carmine .40 *2.00*
J41 D2 50c carmine .40 *2.00*
Nos. J36-J41 (6) 2.40 *12.00*

Some denominations are found in se-tenant pairs.

Various counterfeit cancellations exist on #J1-J41.

D3

1900 Engr.

J42 D3 1c plum .75
J43 D3 2c vermilion .75
J44 D3 5c dk bl .75
J45 D3 10c purple .75
J46 D3 20c org brn .75
J47 D3 30c dk grn 1.50
J48 D3 50c lake 1.50
Nos. J42-J48 (7) 6.75

Nos. J42-J48 were not placed in use as postage due stamps. They were only issued with "Postage" overprints. See Nos. 137-143, 152-158, O72-O81, 2L11-2L15, 2L25, 2L40-2L41.

OFFICIAL STAMPS

Types of Postage Stamps Overprinted in Red Diagonally Reading up

1890 Unwmk. Engr. *Perf. 12*

O1 A5 1c ultra .40 .40
O2 A5 2c ultra .40 .40
O3 A5 5c ultra .40 .40
O4 A5 10c ultra .40 .40
O5 A5 20c ultra .40 .45
O6 A5 50c ultra .40 .75
O7 A5 1p ultra .40 *1.25*
O8 A5 2p ultra .40 *1.60*
O9 A5 5p ultra .40 *2.40*
O10 A5 10p ultra .40 *4.00*
Nos. O1-O10 (10) 4.00 *12.05*

All values of the 1890 issue are known without overprint and most of them with inverted or double overprint, or without overprint and imperforate. There is no evidence that they were issued in these forms.

Official stamps of 1890-1899 are scarce with genuine cancellations. Forged cancellations are plentiful.

Overprinted Vertically Reading Up

1891 Litho.

O11 A6 1c green .40 .40
O12 A6 2c green .40 .40
O13 A6 5c green .40 .40
O14 A6 10c green .40 .40
O15 A6 20c green .40 .50
O16 A6 50c green .40 *1.10*
O17 A6 1p green .40 *1.25*
O18 A6 2p green .40 *1.30*
O19 A6 5p green .40 *2.40*
O20 A6 10p green .60 *4.00*
Nos. O11-O20 (10) 4.20 *12.15*

All values of this issue except the 2c and 5p exist without overprint and several with double overprint. They are not known to have been issued in this form.

Many of the denominations may be found in se-tenant pairs.

Overprinted in Dark Blue

1892 Engr.

O21 A7 1c yellow brown .40 .40
O22 A7 2c yellow brown .40 .40
O23 A7 5c yellow brown .40 .40
O24 A7 10c yellow brown .40 .40
O25 A7 20c yellow brown .40 .50
O26 A7 50c yellow brown .40 *1.00*
O27 A7 1p yellow brown .40 *1.25*
O28 A7 2p yellow brown .40 *1.60*
O29 A7 5p yellow brown .40 *2.40*
O30 A7 10p yellow brown .40 *4.00*
Nos. O21-O30 (10) 4.00 *12.35*

The 2c and 1p are known without overprint and several values exist with double or inverted overprint. These probably were not regularly issued.

Commemorative of the 400th anniversary of the discovery of America by Christopher Columbus.

Overprinted in Red

1893 Engr.

O31 A8 1c slate .40 .40
O32 A8 2c slate .40 .40
O33 A8 5c slate .40 .40
O34 A8 10c slate .40 .40
O35 A8 20c slate .40 .50
O36 A8 25c slate .40 .75
O37 A8 50c slate .40 .85
O38 A8 1p slate .40 *1.00*
O39 A8 2p slate .40 *2.00*
O40 A8 5p slate .40 *2.50*
O41 A8 10p slate .40 *5.50*
Nos. O31-O41 (11) 4.40 *14.70*

The 2, 5, 10, 20, 25, 50c and 5p are known without overprint but probably were not regularly issued. Some values exist with double or inverted overprints.

Overprinted in Black

1894

O42 A9 1c orange .40 .40
O43 A9 2c orange .40 .40
O44 A9 5c orange .40 .40
O45 A9 10c orange .40 .40
O46 A9 20c orange .40 .50
O47 A9 50c orange .40 .75
O48 A9 1p orange .40 *1.50*
O49 A9 2p orange .40 *2.00*
O50 A9 5p orange 2.00 *3.00*
O51 A9 10p orange 2.00 *4.00*
Nos. O42-O51 (10) 7.20 *13.35*

Reprints are yellow.

Overprinted in Dark Blue

1895

O52 A10 1c green .40 .40
O53 A10 2c green .40 .40
O54 A10 5c green .40 .40
O55 A10 10c green .40 .40
O56 A10 20c green .40 .50
O57 A10 50c green .40 *1.00*
O58 A10 1p green .40 *1.50*
O59 A10 2p green .40 *2.00*
O60 A10 5p green .40 *3.00*
O61 A10 10p green .40 *4.00*
Nos. O52-O61 (10) 4.00 *13.60*

Wmk. 117

O62 A10 1c green .40
O63 A10 2c green .40
O64 A10 5c green .40
O65 A10 10c green .40
O66 A10 20c green .40
O67 A10 50c green .40
O68 A10 1p green .40
O69 A10 2p green .40
O70 A10 5p green .40
O71 A10 10p green .40

Nos. O62-O71 probably exist only as reprints. Value, each 30¢.

Postage Due Stamps of Same Date Handstamped in Violet

1896 Unwmk.

O72 D1 1c orange 7.00
O73 D1 2c orange 7.00
O74 D1 5c orange 5.00
O75 D1 10c orange 5.00
O76 D1 20c orange 10.00
Nos. O72-O76 (5) 34.00

Wmk. 117

O77 D1 1c orange 7.00
O78 D1 2c orange 7.00
O79 D1 5c orange 4.00
O80 D1 10c orange 4.00
O81 D1 20c orange 4.00
Nos. O77-O81 (5) 26.00

Nos. O72-O81 were handstamped in rows of five. Several handstamps were used, one of which had the variety "Oftcial." Most varieties are known inverted and double.

Forgeries exist.

Types of Postage Stamps Overprinted in Red

1896 Unwmk.

O82 A11 1c red 2.50 3.00
O83 A11 2c red 2.50 3.00
O84 A11 5c red 2.50 3.00
O85 A11 10c red 2.50 3.00
O86 A11 20c red 3.00 3.00
O87 A11 50c red 5.00 *5.00*
O88 A11 1p red 12.00 *12.00*
O89 A11 2p red 12.00 *12.00*
O90 A11 5p red 16.00 *16.00*
Nos. O82-O90 (9) 58.00 *60.00*

Wmk. 117

O91 A11 1c red 3.00 3.50
O92 A11 2c red 3.00 3.50
O93 A11 5c red 3.00 3.50
O94 A11 10c red 3.00 3.50
O95 A11 20c red 5.00 5.00
O96 A11 50c red 3.00 *5.00*
O97 A11 1p red 14.00 *14.00*
O98 A11 2p red 16.00 *16.00*
O99 A11 5p red 25.00 *25.00*
Nos. O91-O99 (9) 75.00 *79.00*

Used values for Nos. O88-O90, O97-O99 are for CTO examples. Postally used examples are not known.

Same, Dated 1897

1897 Unwmk.

O100 A11 1c red 3.00 3.00
O101 A11 2c red 3.00 3.00
O102 A11 5c red 3.00 2.50
O103 A11 10c red 3.00 3.00
O104 A11 20c red 3.00 4.00
O105 A11 50c red 5.00 *5.00*
O106 A11 1p red 12.00 *12.00*
O107 A11 2p red 12.00 *12.00*
O108 A11 5p red 16.00 *16.00*
Nos. O100-O108 (9) 60.00 *60.50*

Wmk. 117

O109 A11 1c red 5.00 5.00
O110 A11 2c red 5.00 5.00
O111 A11 5c red 5.00 5.00
O112 A11 10c red 10.00 10.00
O113 A11 20c red 10.00 10.00
O114 A11 50c red 12.00 *12.00*
O115 A11 1p red 20.00 *20.00*
O116 A11 2p red 20.00 *20.00*
O117 A11 5p red 20.00 *20.00*
Nos. O109-O117 (9) 107.00 *107.00*

Reprints of Nos. O82-O117 are described in notes after No. 109M. Value 30¢ each.

Used values for Nos. O106-O108, O115-O117 are for CTO examples. Postally used examples are not known.

Overprinted in Blue

1898 Unwmk.

O118 A12 1c carmine 3.25 3.25
O119 A12 2c carmine 3.25 3.25
O120 A12 4c carmine 3.25 3.25
O121 A12 5c carmine 2.50 2.50
O122 A12 10c carmine 4.00 4.00
O123 A12 15c carmine 6.00 6.00
O124 A12 20c carmine 6.00 6.00
O125 A12 50c carmine 8.50 *8.50*
O126 A12 1p carmine 11.00 *11.00*
O127 A12 2p carmine 11.00 *11.00*
O128 A12 5p carmine 11.00 *11.00*
Nos. O118-O128 (11) 69.75 *69.75*

Stamps of this set with sideways watermark 117 or with black overprint are reprints. Value 30¢ each.

Used values for Nos. O126-O128 are for CTO examples. Postally used examples are not known.

Overprinted in Dark Blue

1899

O129 A13 1c gray grn .40 *1.00*
O130 A13 2c bis brn .40 *1.00*
O131 A13 4c lake .40 *1.00*
O132 A13 5c dk bl .40 .50
O133 A13 10c buff .40 *1.00*
O134 A13 15c chocolate .40 *2.00*
O135 A13 20c dk grn .40 *3.00*
O136 A13 50c car rose .40 *3.00*
O137 A13 1p red .40 *10.00*
O138 A13 2p violet .40 *10.00*
O139 A13 5p lt bl .40 *15.00*
Nos. O129-O139 (11) 4.40 *47.50*

Counterfeit cancellations on Nos. O129-O139 are plentiful.

"Justice" -- O5

1900 Engr.

O140 O5 1c plum .60 .60
O141 O5 2c vermilion .50 .50
O142 O5 4c ol grn .60 .60
O143 O5 5c dk bl 1.25 .45
O144 O5 10c purple 1.25 .35
O145 O5 20c brown .90 .35
O146 O5 50c lake 1.25 .50
O147 O5 1p ultra 3.50 2.50
O148 O5 2p red org 4.00 4.00
O149 O5 5p grnsh blk 5.00 5.00
Nos. O140-O149 (10) 18.85 14.85

For surcharges see Nos. O155-O157.

Nos. 123, 161 Surcharged in Black

1903 *Perf. 12, 14*

O150 A14 1c on 10c violet .40 .40
a. "Centovo" 1.00
b. "Contavo" 1.00
c. With ornaments .40 .40
d. Inverted surcharge 1.00
e. "1" omitted at upper left 2.00
O151 A14 2c on 3c green .40 .40
a. "Centovos" 1.00
b. "Contavos" 1.00
c. With ornaments .35
d. Inverted surcharge 1.00

O152 A14 4c on 3c green 1.25 1.25
a. "Centovos" 2.50
b. "Contavos" 2.50
c. With ornaments 2.50
d. Inverted surcharge
O153 A14 4c on 10c violet 1.25 1.25
a. "Centovos" 2.50
b. "Contavos" 2.50
c. With ornaments 2.00
d. Inverted surcharge
O154 A14 5c on 3c green .40 .40
a. "Centovos" 1.00
b. "Contavos" 1.00
c. With ornaments .40 .40
d. Double surcharge 2.00
e. Inverted surcharge
Nos. O150-O154 (5) 3.70 3.70

These surcharges are set up to cover 25 stamps. Some of the settings have bars or pieces of fancy border type below "OFICIAL." There are 5 varieties on #O150, 3 on #O151, 1 each on #O152, O153, O154.

In 1904 #O151 was reprinted to fill a dealer's order. This printing lacks the small figure at the upper right. It includes the variety "OFICILA." At the same time the same setting was printed in carmine on official stamps of 1900, 1c on 10c violet and 2c on 1p ultramarine. Also the 1, 2 and 5p official stamps of 1900 were surcharged with new values and the dates 1901 or 1902 in various colors, inverted, etc. It is doubtful if any of these varieties were ever in Nicaragua and certain that none of them ever did legitimate postal duty.

No. O145 Surcharged in Black

1904 *Perf. 12*
O155 O5 10c on 20c brn .40 .40
a. No period after "Ctvs" 1.00 .75
O156 O5 30c on 20c brn .40 .40
O157 O5 50c on 20c brn .50 .35
a. Lower "50" omitted 2.50 2.50
b. Upper figures omitted 2.50 2.50
c. Top left and lower figures omitted 3.50 3.50
Nos. O155-O157 (3) 1.30 1.15

Coat of Arms — O6

1905, July 25 **Engr.**
O158 O6 1c green .40 .40
O159 O6 2c rose .40 .40
O160 O6 5c blue .40 .40
O161 O6 10c yel brn .40 .40
O162 O6 20c orange .40 .40
O163 O6 50c brn ol .40 .40
O164 O6 1p lake .40 .40
O165 O6 2p violet .40 .40
O166 O6 5p gray blk .40 .40
Nos. O158-O166 (9) 3.60 3.60

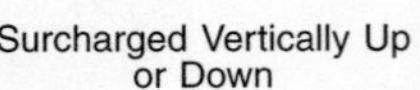
Surcharged Vertically Up or Down

1907
O167 O6 10c on 1c grn .75 .75
O168 O6 10c on 2c rose 25.00 22.50
O169 O6 20c on 2c rose 22.50 *26.00*
O170 O6 50c on 1c grn 1.50 1.50
O171 O6 50c on 2c rose 22.50 *23.00*

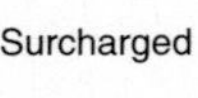
Surcharged

O172 O6 1p on 2c rose 1.50 1.50
O173 O6 2p on 2c rose 1.50 1.50
O174 O6 3p on 2c rose 1.50 1.50
O175 O6 4p on 2c rose
O176 O6 4p on 5c blue 2.25 2.25

The setting for this surcharge includes various letters from wrong fonts, the figure "1" for "I" in "Vale" and an "I" for "1" in "$1.00."

Surcharged

O177 O6 20c on 1c green 1.00 1.00
a. Double surcharge 5.00 5.00
Nos. O167-O174,O176-O177 (10) 80.00 81.50

The preceding surcharges are vertical, reading both up and down.

Revenue Stamps Surcharged

O7

1907 *Perf. 14 to 15*
O178 O7 10c on 2c org (Bk) .40 .40
O179 O7 35c on 1c bl (R) .40 .40
a. Inverted surcharge 3.00 3.00
O180 O7 70c on 1c bl (V) .40 .40
a. Inverted surcharge 3.00 3.00
O181 O7 70c on 1c bl (O) .40 .40
a. Inverted surcharge 3.00 3.00
O182 O7 1p on 2c org (G) .40 .40
a. Inverted surcharge 14.00 14.00
O183 O7 2p on 2c org (Br) .40 .40
O184 O7 3p on 5c brn (Bl) .40 .40
O185 O7 4p on 5c brn (G) .40 .40
a. Double surcharge 3.00 3.00
O186 O7 5p on 5c brn (G) .40 .40
a. Inverted surcharge 3.50 3.50
Nos. O178-O186 (9) 3.60 3.60

Letters and figures from several fonts were mixed in these surcharges.
See Nos. O199-O209.

No. 202 Surcharged

1907, Nov.
Black or Blue Black Surcharge
O187 A18 10c on 1c grn 15.00 15.00
O188 A18 15c on 1c grn 15.00 20.00
O189 A18 20c on 1c grn 15.00 15.00
O190 A18 50c on 1c grn 15.00 20.00

Red Surcharge
O191 A18 1(un)p on 1c grn 14.00 15.00
O192 A18 2(dos)p on 1c grn 14.00 15.00
Nos. O187-O192 (6) 88.00 100.00

No. 181 Surcharged

1908 **Yellow Surcharge** *Perf. 12*
O193 A18 10c on 3c vio 15.00 15.00
O194 A18 15c on 3c vio 15.00 15.00
O195 A18 20c on 3c vio 15.00 15.00
O196 A18 35c on 3c vio 15.00 15.00
O197 A18 50c on 3c vio 15.00 15.00
Nos. O193-O197 (5) 75.00 75.00

Black Surcharge
O198 A18 35c on 3c vio 210.00 *210.00*

Revenue Stamps Surcharged like 1907 Issue Dated "1908"

1908 *Perf. 14 to 15*
O199 O7 10c on 1c bl (V) .75 .50
a. Inverted surcharge 3.50 3.50
O200 O7 35c on 1c bl (Bk) .75 .50
a. Inverted surcharge 3.50 3.50
b. Double surcharge 4.00 4.00
O201 O7 50c on 1c bl (R) .75 .50
O202 O7 1p on 1c bl (Br) 40.00 40.00
a. Inverted surcharge 65.00 65.00
O203 O7 2p on 1c bl (G) .90 .75
O204 O7 10c on 2c org (Bk) 1.10 .65
O205 O7 35c on 2c org (R) 1.10 .65
a. Double surcharge 3.50
O206 O7 50c on 2c org (Bk) 1.10 .65
O207 O7 70c on 2c org (Bl) 1.10 .65
O208 O7 1p on 2c org (G) 1.10 .65
O209 O7 2p on 2c org (Br) 1.10 .65
Nos. O199-O209 (11) 49.75 46.15

There are several minor varieties in the figures, etc., in these surcharges.

Nos. 243-248 Overprinted in Black

1909 *Perf. 12*
O210 A18 10c lake .40 .40
a. Double overprint 2.50 2.50
O211 A18 15c black .60 .50
O212 A18 20c brn ol 1.00 .75
O213 A18 50c dp grn 1.50 1.00
O214 A18 1p yellow 1.75 1.25
O215 A18 2p car rose 6.50 2.00
Nos. O210-O215 (6) 11.75 5.90

Overprinted in Black

1910
O216 A18 15c black 1.50 1.25
a. Double overprint 4.00 4.00
O217 A18 20c brn ol 2.50 2.00
O218 A18 50c dp grn 2.50 2.00
O219 A18 1p yellow 2.75 2.50
a. Inverted overprint 16.00 7.50
O220 A18 2p car rose 4.00 3.00
Nos. O216-O220 (5) 13.25 10.75

Nos. 239-240 Surcharged in Black

No. O221

No. O222

1911
O221 A18 5c on 3c red org 10.00 6.00
O222 A18 10c on 4c vio 12.00 5.00
a. Double surcharge 24.00 24.00
b. Pair, one without new value 35.00

Revenue Stamps Surcharged in Black

1911, Nov. *Perf. 14 to 15*
O223 A21 10c on 10c on 1 red org 3.00 3.00
a. Inverted surcharge 4.50
b. Double surcharge 4.50
O224 A21 15c on 10c on 1 red org 3.00 3.00
a. Inverted surcharge 5.00
b. Double surcharge 4.50
O225 A21 20c on 10c on 1 red org 3.00 3.00
a. Inverted surcharge 5.00
O226 A21 50c on 10c on 1 red org 3.75 3.75
a. Inverted surcharge 4.50
O227 A21 1p on 10c on 1 red org 5.00 *7.00*
a. Inverted surcharge 6.00
O228 A21 2p on 10c on 1 red org 5.50 *10.00*
a. Inverted surcharge 7.50
b. Double surcharge 7.50
Nos. O223-O228 (6) 23.25 29.75

Surcharged in Black

1911, Nov.
O229 A21 10c on 10c on 1 red org 22.50
O230 A21 15c on 10c on 1 red org 22.50
O231 A21 20c on 10c on 1 red org 22.50
O232 A21 50c on 10c on 1 red org 16.00
Nos. O229-O232 (4) 83.50

Surcharged in Black

1911, Dec.
O233 A21 5c on 10c on 1 red org 4.50 *6.00*
a. Double surcharge 7.50
b. Inverted surcharge 7.50
c. "5" omitted 6.00
O234 A21 10c on 10c on 1 red org 5.50 *7.00*
O235 A21 15c on 10c on 1 red org 6.00 *7.50*
O236 A21 20c on 10c on 1 red org 6.50 *8.50*
O237 A21 50c on 10c on 1 red org 7.50 *10.00*
Nos. O233-O237 (5) 30.00 39.00

Nos. O233 to O237 have a surcharge on the back like Nos. 285 and 286 with "15 cts" obliterated by a heavy horizontal bar.

Surcharged Vertically in Black

1912
O238 A21 5c on 10c on 1 red org 10.00 10.00
O239 A21 10c on 10c on 1 red org 10.00 10.00
O240 A21 15c on 10c on 1 red org 10.00 10.00
O241 A21 20c on 10c on 1 red org 10.00 10.00
O242 A21 35c on 10c on 1 red org 10.00 10.00
O243 A21 50c on 10c on 1 red org 10.00 10.00
O244 A21 1p on 10c on 1 red org 10.00 10.00
Nos. O238-O244 (7) 70.00 70.00

Nos. O238 to O244 are printed on Nos. 285 and 286 but the surcharge on the back is obliterated by a vertical bar.

Types of Regular Issue of 1912 Overprinted in Black

1912 *Perf. 12*
O245 A22 1c light blue .40 .40
O246 A22 2c light blue .40 .40
O247 A22 3c light blue .40 .40
O248 A22 4c light blue .40 .40
O249 A22 5c light blue .40 .40
O250 A22 6c light blue .40 .40
O251 A22 10c light blue .40 .40
O252 A22 15c light blue .40 .40
O253 A22 20c light blue .40 .40
O254 A22 25c light blue .40 .40
O255 A23 35c light blue .40 .40
O256 A22 50c light blue 3.75 2.00
O257 A22 1p light blue .65 .45
O258 A22 2p light blue .75 .55
O259 A22 5p light blue 1.00 .75
Nos. O245-O259 (15) 10.55 8.15

On the 35c the overprint is 15½mm wide, on the other values it is 13mm.

Types of Regular Issue of 1914 Overprinted in Black

1915, May
O260 A24 1c light blue .40 .40
O261 A25 2c light blue .40 .40
O262 A24 3c light blue .40 .40
O263 A25 4c light blue .40 .40
O264 A24 5c light blue .40 .40
O265 A25 6c light blue .40 .40
O266 A25 10c light blue .40 .40
O267 A24 15c light blue .40 .40
O268 A25 20c light blue .40 .40
O269 A24 25c light blue .40 .40
O270 A25 50c light blue .60 .60
Nos. O260-O270 (11) 4.60 4.60

Regular Issues of 1914-22 Overprinted in Red

1925
O271 A24 ½c dp grn .40 .40
a. Double overprint 2.50 2.50
O272 A24 1c violet .40 .40
O273 A25 2c car rose .40 .40
O274 A24 3c ol grn .40 .40
O275 A25 4c vermilion .40 .40
a. Double overprint 4.00 4.00
O276 A24 5c black .40 .40
a. Double overprint 4.00 4.00
O277 A25 6c red brn .40 .40
O278 A25 10c yellow .40 .40
a. Double overprint 4.25 4.25
O279 A24 15c red brn .40 .40
O280 A25 20c bis brn .50 .50
O281 A24 25c orange .60 .60
a. Inverted overprint 60.00 40.00
O282 A25 50c pale bl .75 .75
a. Double overprint 20.00 20.00
Nos. O271-O282 (12) 5.45 5.45

Type II overprint has "f" and "i" separated. Comes on Nos. O272-O274 and O276.

Regular Issues of 1914-22 Overprinted in Black

1926
O283 A24 ½c dk grn .40 .40
O284 A24 1c dp vio .40 .40
O285 A25 2c car rose .40 .40
O286 A24 3c ol gray .40 .40
O287 A25 4c vermilion .40 .40
O288 A24 5c gray blk .40 .40
O289 A25 6c red brn .40 .40
O290 A25 10c yellow .40 .40
O291 A24 15c dp brn .40 .40
O292 A25 20c bis brn .40 .40
O293 A24 25c orange .40 .40
O294 A25 50c pale bl .40 .40
Nos. O283-O294 (12) 4.80 4.80

No. 499 Surcharged in Red & Black

1931
O295 A33 5c on 10c bis brn .50 .40

Nos. 517-518 Overprinted in Red

1931
O296 A25 6c bis brn .50 .40
O297 A25 10c lt brn .50 .40

Nos. 541, 543, 545 With Additional Overprint in Red

O298 A24 1c ol grn .50 .50
O299 A24 3c lt bl .50 .50
a. "OFICIAL" inverted .80 .80
O300 A24 5c gray brn .50 .50
a. "1931" double .80 .80
Nos. O298-O300 (3) 1.50 1.50

Regular Issues of 1914-31 Overprinted in Black

1932, Feb. 6
O301 A24 1c ol grn .25 .25
a. Double overprint 1.40 1.40
O302 A25 2c brt rose .25 .25
a. Double overprint 1.40 1.40
O303 A24 3c lt bl .25 .25
a. Double overprint .50 .50
O304 A25 4c dk bl .25 .25
O305 A24 5c ol brn .25 .25
O306 A25 6c bis brn .25 .25
a. Double overprint 2.00 2.00
O307 A25 10c lt brn .30 .25
O308 A24 15c org red .40 .25
a. Double overprint 2.25 2.25
O309 A25 20c orange .70 .35
O310 A24 25c dk vio 2.00 .50
O311 A25 50c green .25 .25
O312 A25 1cor yellow .25 .25
Nos. O301-O312 (12) 5.40 3.35

With Additional Overprint in Black

1932, Feb. 6
O313 A24 1c ol grn 5.50 5.50
O314 A25 2c brt rose 6.50 6.50
a. Double overprint 8.25 8.25
O315 A24 3c lt bl 5.00 5.00
O316 A24 5c ol brn 5.00 5.00
O317 A24 15c org red .75 .75
O318 A24 25c blk brn .75 .75
O319 A24 25c dk vio 1.50 1.50
Nos. O313-O319 (7) 25.00 25.00

The variety "OFIAIAL" occurs once in each sheet of Nos. O301 to O319 inclusive.

Despite the 1932 release date, the "1931" overprint on Nos. O313-O319 is correct.

Flag of the Race Issue

1933, Aug. 9 Litho. *Rouletted 9*
Without gum
O320 A43 1c orange 1.25 1.25
O321 A43 2c yellow 1.25 1.25
O322 A43 3c dk brn 1.25 1.25
O323 A43 4c dp brn 1.25 1.25
O324 A43 5c gray brn 1.25 1.25
O325 A43 6c dp ultra 1.50 1.50
O326 A43 10c dp vio 1.50 1.50
O327 A43 15c red vio 1.50 1.50
O328 A43 20c dp grn 1.50 1.50
O329 A43 25c green 2.50 2.50
O330 A43 50c carmine 3.00 3.00
O331 A43 1cor red 5.00 5.00
Nos. O320-O331 (12) 22.75 22.75

See note after No. 599.
Reprints of Nos. O320-O331 exist.
A 25c dull blue exists. Its status is questioned.

Regular Issue of 1914-31 Overprinted in Red

1933, Nov. *Perf. 12*
O332 A24 1c ol grn .40 .40
O333 A25 2c brt rose .40 .40
O334 A24 3c lt bl .40 .40
O335 A25 4c dk bl .40 .40
O336 A24 5c ol brn .40 .40
O337 A25 6c bis brn .40 .40
O338 A25 10c lt brn .40 .40
O339 A24 15c red org .40 .40
O340 A25 20c orange .40 .40
O341 A24 25c dk vio .40 .40
O342 A25 50c green .40 .40
O343 A25 1cor yellow .40 .40
Nos. O332-O343 (12) 4.80 4.80

Nos. O332-O343 exist with or without signature control overprint. Values are the same.

Nos. O332-O343 Overprinted in Blue

1935, Dec.
O344 A24 1c ol grn .65 .40
O345 A25 2c brt rose .65 .50
O346 A24 3c lt bl 1.60 .50
O347 A25 4c dk bl 1.60 1.60
O348 A24 5c ol brn 1.60 1.60
O349 A25 6c bis brn 2.00 2.00
O350 A25 10c lt brn 2.00 2.00
O351 A24 15c org red 27.50 27.50
O352 A25 20c orange 27.50 27.50
O353 A24 25c dk vio 27.50 27.50
O354 A25 50c green 27.50 27.50
O355 A25 1cor yellow 27.50 27.50
Nos. O344-O355 (12) 147.60 146.10

Nos. O344-O355 have signature control overprints. Counterfeits of overprint abound.

Nos. O332-O343 Overprinted in Red

1936, Jan.
O356 A24 1c ol grn .40 .40
O357 A25 2c brt rose .40 .40
O358 A24 3c lt bl .40 .40
a. Double overprint
O359 A25 4c dk bl .40 .40
O360 A24 5c ol brn .40 .40
O361 A25 6c bis brn .40 .40
O362 A25 10c lt brn .40 .40
O363 A24 15c org red .40 .40
O364 A25 20c orange .40 .40
O365 A24 25c dk vio .40 .40
O366 A25 50c green .40 .40
O367 A25 1cor yellow .55 .55
Nos. O356-O367 (12) 4.95 4.95

Nos. O356-O367 have signature control overprints.

Nos. 653 to 655, 657, 659 660, 662 to 664 Overprinted in Black

1937
O368 A24 1c car rose .65 .55
O369 A25 2c dp bl .65 .55
O370 A24 3c chocolate .65 .55
O371 A24 5c org red .95 .55
O372 A25 10c ol grn 1.75 .90
O373 A24 15c green 2.10 1.10
O374 A24 25c orange 2.60 1.40
O375 A25 50c brown 3.75 1.75
O376 A25 1cor ultra 7.00 2.75
Nos. O368-O376 (9) 20.10 10.10

Islands of the Great Lake — O9

1939, Jan. Engr. *Perf. 12½*
O377 O9 2c rose red .65 .25
O378 O9 3c lt bl .65 .25
O379 O9 6c brn org .65 .25
O380 O9 7½c dp grn .65 .25
O381 O9 10c blk brn .65 .25
O382 O9 15c orange .65 .25
O383 O9 25c dk vio 1.00 .25
O384 O9 50c brt yel grn 2.60 .75
Nos. O377-O384 (8) 7.50 2.50

POSTAL TAX STAMPS

Official Stamps of 1915 Surcharged in Black

1921, July Unwmk. *Perf. 12*
RA1 A24 1c on 5c lt bl 1.50 .60
RA2 A25 1c on 6c lt bl .65 .40
a. Double surcharge, one inverted
RA3 A25 1c on 10c lt bl 1.00 .40
a. Double surcharge 3.50 3.50
RA4 A24 1c on 15c lt bl 1.50 .40
a. Double surcharge, one inverted 5.00 5.00
Nos. RA1-RA4 (4) 4.65 1.80

"R de C" signifies "Reconstruccion de Comunicaciones." The stamps were intended to provide a fund for rebuilding the General Post Office which was burned in April, 1921. One stamp was required on each letter or parcel, in addition to the regular postage. In the setting of one hundred there are five stamps with antique "C" and twenty-one with "R" and "C" smaller than in the illustration. One or more stamps in the setting have a dotted bar, as illustrated over No. 388, instead of the double bar.

The use of the "R de C" stamps for the payment of regular postage was not permitted.

Official Stamp of 1915 Overprinted in Black

1921, July
RA5 A24 1c light blue 6.00 1.75

This stamp is known with the dotted bar as illustrated over No. 388, instead of the double bar.

Coat of Arms — PT1

1921, Sept. Red Surcharge
RA6 PT1 1c on 1c ver & blk .40 .40
RA7 PT1 1c on 2c grn & blk .40 .40
a. Double surcharge 3.00 3.00
b. Double surcharge, one inverted 4.00 4.00
RA8 PT1 1c on 4c org & blk .40 .40
a. Double surcharge 4.00 4.00
RA9 PT1 1c on 15c dk bl & blk .40 .40
a. Double surcharge 3.00 3.00
Nos. RA6-RA9 (4) 1.60 1.60

PT2

1922, Feb. Black Surcharge
RA10 PT2 1c on 10c yellow .40 .40
a. Period after "de" .50 .40
b. Double surcharge 2.00 2.00
c. Double inverted surcharge 3.75 3.75
d. Inverted surcharge 3.00 3.00
e. Without period after "C" 1.00 1.00

No. 409 Overprinted in Black

1922
RA11 A24 1c violet .40 .40
a. Double overprint 2.00 2.00

This stamp with the overprint in red is a trial printing.

Nos. 402, 404-407 Surcharged in Black

1922, June
RA12 A27 1c on 1c grn & blk .75 .75
RA13 A29 1c on 5c ultra & blk .75 .75
RA14 A30 1c on 10c org & blk .75 .40
RA15 A31 1c on 25c yel & blk .75 .30
a. Inverted surcharge 5.00 5.00
RA16 A32 1c on 50c vio & blk .30 .25
a. Double surcharge 4.00 4.00
Nos. RA12-RA16 (5) 3.30 2.45

PT3

Surcharge in Red or Dark Blue

1922, Oct. *Perf. 11½*
RA17 PT3 1c yellow (R) .40 .40
a. No period after "C" 1.00 1.00
RA18 PT3 1c violet (DBl) .40 .40
a. No period after "C" 1.00 1.00

Surcharge is inverted on 22 out of 50 of No. RA17, 23 out of 50 of No. RA18.

See No. RA24.

Nos. 403-407 Surcharged in Black

1923 *Perf. 12*
RA19 A28 1c on 2c rose red & black .50 .45
RA20 A29 1c on 5c ultra & blk .55 .40
RA21 A30 1c on 10c org & blk .40 .40
RA22 A31 1c on 25c yel & blk .40 .40
RA23 A32 1c on 50c vio & blk .40 .40
Nos. RA19-RA23 (5) 2.25 2.05

The variety no period after "R" occurs twice on each sheet.

Red Surcharge
Wmk. Coat of Arms in Sheet
Perf. 11½
RA24 PT3 1c pale blue .40 .40

Type of 1921 Issue

Without Surcharge of New Value

Unwmk.

RA25 PT1 1c ver & blk .40 .40
a. Double overprint, one inverted 3.00 3.00

No. 409 Overprinted in Blue

1924

RA26 A24 1c violet .40 .40
a. Double overprint 8.00 8.00

There are two settings of the overprint on No. RA26, with "1924" 5½mm or 6½mm wide.

No. 409 Overprinted in Blue

1925

RA27 A24 1c violet .40 .40

No. 409 Overprinted in Blue

1926

RA28 A24 1c violet .40 .40

No. RA28 Overprinted in Various Colors

1927

RA29 A24 1c vio (R) .40 .40
a. Double overprint (R) 2.50 2.50
b. Inverted overprint (R) 3.00 3.00
RA30 A24 1c vio (V) .40 .40
a. Double overprint 2.50 2.50
b. Inverted overprint 2.50 2.50
RA31 A24 1c vio (Bl) .40 .40
a. Double overprint 5.00 5.00
RA32 A24 1c vio (Bk) .40 .40
a. Double ovpt., one invtd. 4.25 4.25
b. Double overprint 4.25 4.25

Same Overprint on No. RA27

RA33 A24 1c vio (Bk) 25.00 25.00
Nos. RA29-RA33 (5) 26.60 26.60

No. RA28 Overprinted in Violet

1928

RA34 A24 1c violet .40 .40
a. Double overprint 2.00 2.00
b. "928" 1.00 1.00

Similar to No. RA34 but 8mm space between "Resello" and "1928"

Black Overprint

RA35 A24 1c violet .40 .40
a. "1828" 2.00 2.00

PT4

Inscribed "Timbre Telegrafico"

Horiz. Srch. in Black,
Vert. Srch. in Red

RA36 PT4 1c on 5c bl & blk .60 .40
a. Comma after "R" 1.25 1.25
b. No period after "R" 1.25 1.25
c. No periods after "R" and "C" 1.25 1.25

("CORREOS" at right) — PT5

1928 Engr. *Perf. 12*

RA37 PT5 1c plum .40 .40

See Nos. RA41-RA43. For overprints see Nos. RA45-RA46, RA48-RA51.

PT6

1929 Red Surcharge

RA38 PT6 1c on 5c bl & blk .40 .40
a. Inverted surcharge 3.00 3.00
b. Double surcharge 2.00 2.00
c. Double surcharge, one inverted 2.00 2.00
d. Period after "de" 1.25 1.25
e. Comma after "R" 1.25 1.25

See note after No. 512.

Regular Issue of 1928 Overprinted in Blue

RA39 A24 1c red orange .40 .40

No. RA39 exists both with and without signature control overprint.

An additional overprint, "1929" in black or blue on No. RA39, is fraudulent.

No. 513 Overprinted in Red

1929

RA40 A24 1c ol grn .40 .40
a. Double overprint .75 .75

No. RA40 is known with overprint in black, and with overprint inverted. These varieties were not regularly issued, but copies have been canceled by favor.

Type of 1928 Issue Inscribed at right "COMUNICACIONES"

1930-37

RA41 PT5 1c carmine .40 .40
RA42 PT5 1c orange ('33) .40 .40
RA43 PT5 1c green ('37) .40 .40
Nos. RA41-RA43 (3) 1.20 1.20

No. RA42 has signature control. See note before No. 600.

No. RA39 Overprinted in Black

1931

RA44 A24 1c red orange .40 .40
a. "1931" double overprint .40 .40
b. "1931" double ovpt., one invtd. .40 .40

No. RA44 exists with signature control overprint. See note before No. 600. Value is the same.

No. RA42 Overprinted Vertically, up or down, in Black

1935

RA45 PT5 1c orange .40 .40
a. Double overprint 1.00 1.00
b. Double ovpt., one inverted

No. RA45 and RA45a Overprinted Vertically, Reading Down, in Blue

RA46 PT5 1c orange .50 .40
a. Black overprint double 2.00 2.00

Same Overprint in Red on Nos. RA39, RA42 and RA45

RA47 A24 1c red org (#RA39) *50.00 50.00*
RA48 PT5 1c org (#RA42) .40 .40
RA49 PT5 1c org (#RA45) .40 .40
a. Black overprint double .80 .80

Overprint is horizontal on No. RA47 and vertical, reading down, on Nos. RA48-RA49.

No. RA48 exists with signature control overprint. See note before No. 600. Same values.

No. RA42 Overprinted Vertically, Reading Down, in Carmine

1935 Unwmk. *Perf. 12*

RA50 PT5 1c orange .40 .40

No. RA45 with Additional Overprint "1936", Vertically, Reading Down, in Red

1936

RA51 PT5 1c orange .50 .40

No. RA39 with Additional Overprint "1936" in Red

RA52 A24 1c red orange 1.00 .40

No. RA52 exists only with script control mark.

PT7

1936 Vertical Surcharge in Red

RA53 PT7 1c on 5c grn & blk .40 .40
a. "Cenavo" 1.40 1.40
b. "Centavos" 1.40 1.40

Horizontal Surcharge in Red

RA54 PT7 1c on 5c grn & blk .40 .40
a. Double surcharge 1.40 1.40

Baseball Player — PT8

1937 Typo. *Perf. 11*

RA55 PT8 1c carmine .60 .40
RA56 PT8 1c yellow .60 .40
RA57 PT8 1c blue .60 .40
RA58 PT8 1c green .60 .40
b. Sheet of 4, #RA55-RA58 8.00 3.00
Nos. RA55-RA58 (4) 2.40 1.60

Issued for the benefit of the Central American Caribbean Games of February 1938 in Panama City, Panama.

Control mark in red is variously placed. See dark oval below "OLIMPICO" in illustration.

Tête bêche Pairs

RA55a PT8 1c 1.25 1.25
RA56a PT8 1c 1.25 1.25
RA57a PT8 1c 1.25 1.25
RA58a PT8 1c 1.25 1.25
Nos. RA55a-RA58a (4) 5.00 5.00

Catalogue values for unused stamps in this section, from this point to the end of the section, are for Never Hinged items.

Proposed Natl. Stadium, Managua — PT9

1949 Photo. *Perf. 12*

RA60 PT9 5c greenish blue .80 .40
a. Souvenir sheet of 4 5.00 5.00

10th World Series of Amateur Baseball, 1948. The tax was used toward the erection of a national stadium at Managua.

Type Similar to 1949, with "Correos" omitted

1952

RA61 PT9 5c magenta .80 .40

The tax was used toward the erection of a national stadium at Managua.

PT10

1956 Engr. *Perf. 12½x12*

RA62 PT10 5c deep ultra .80 .40

The tax was used for social welfare.

PT11

PT11a

Surcharged in Red or Black

1959 Unwmk. *Perf. 12*

Red Marginal Number

RA63 PT11 5c on 50c vio bl (R) .80 .40
RA64 PT11a 5c on 50c vio bl (B) .80 .40

Nos. RA63-RA64 are surcharged on consular revenue stamps. Surcharge reads "Sobre Tasa Postal CO.O5." Vertical surcharge on No. RA63, horizontal on No. RA64.

Jesus and Children — PT12

1959 Photo. *Perf. 16*

RA65 PT12 5c ultra .80 .40

Hexisia Bidentata — PT13

Orchids: No. RA67, Schomburgkia tibicinus. No. RA68, Stanhopea ecornuta. No. RA69, Lycaste macrophylla. No. RA70, Maxillaria tenuifolia. No. RA71, Cattleya skinneri. No. RA72, Cycnoches egertonianum. No. RA73, Bletia roezlii. No. RA74, Sobralia pleiantha. No. RA75, Oncidium cebolleta and ascendens.

1962, Feb. Photo. *Perf. 11½*

Granite Paper

Orchids in Natural Colors

RA66 PT13 5c rose lil & grn .65 .40
RA67 PT13 5c yel & gray bl .65 .40
RA68 PT13 5c pink & bl grn .65 .40
RA69 PT13 5c lil & brn ol .65 .40
RA70 PT13 5c turq bl & red .65 .40
RA71 PT13 5c pale sal & vio .65 .40
RA72 PT13 5c yel grn & dk brn .65 .40
RA73 PT13 5c gray & red .65 .40
RA74 PT13 5c lt bl & indigo .65 .40
RA75 PT13 5c turq grn & red brn .65 .40
Nos. RA66-RA75 (10) 6.50 4.00

For overprints see #842-852, 855-868, 901-908.

Exist imperf. Value, each pair $100.

PROVINCE OF ZELAYA

(Bluefields)

A province of Nicaragua lying along the eastern coast. Special postage stamps for this section were made necessary because for a period two currencies, which differed materially in value, were in use in Nicaragua. Silver money was used in Zelaya and Cabo Gracias a Dios while the rest of Nicaragua used paper money. Later the money of the entire country was placed on a gold basis.

Dangerous counterfeits exist of most of the Bluefields overprints.

Regular Issues of 1900-05 Handstamped in Black (4 or more types)

1904-05 **Unwmk.** ***Perf. 12, 14***

On Engraved Stamps of 1900

1L1 A14 1c plum 1.50 .75
1L2 A14 2c vermilion 1.50 .75
1L3 A14 3c green 2.00 1.50
1L4 A14 4c ol grn 11.00 9.00
1L5 A14 15c ultra 3.00 2.00
1L6 A14 20c brown 3.00 2.00
1L7 A14 50c lake 10.50 9.00
1L8 A14 1p yellow 21.00
1L9 A14 2p salmon 30.00 30.00
1L10 A14 5p black 37.50 40.00
Nos. 1L1-1L10 (10) 121.00
Nos. 1L1-1L7 (7) 25.00

On Lithographed Stamps of 1902

1L11 A14 5c blue 3.00 .75
1L12 A14 5c carmine 1.90 .90
1L13 A14 10c violet 1.50 .75
Nos. 1L11-1L13 (3) 6.40 2.40

On Postage Due Stamps Overprinted "1901 Correos"

1L14 D3 20c brn (No. 156) 4.50 1.90
1L15 D3 50c lake (No. 158) — —

On Surcharged Stamps of 1904-05

1L16 A14 5c on 10c (#175) 1.50 1.10
1L17 A14 5c on 10c (#178) 6.00 6.50
1L18 A14 15c on 10c vio (#176) 1.50 1.50
1L19 A14 15c on 10c vio (#177) 14.00 4.50
Nos. 1L16-1L19 (4) 23.00 13.60

On Surcharged Stamp of 1901

1L20 A14 20c on 5p blk 18.00 3.00

On Regular Issue of 1905

1906-07 ***Perf. 12***

1L21 A18 1c green .40 .40
1L22 A18 2c car rose .40 .40
1L23 A18 3c violet .40 .40
1L24 A18 4c org red .45 .45
1L25 A18 5c blue .40 .40
1L26 A18 10c yel brn 3.00 1.50
1L27 A18 15c brn ol 4.50 1.75
1L28 A18 20c lake 9.00 7.50
1L29 A18 50c orange 35.00 30.00
1L30 A18 1p black 30.00 27.50
1L31 A18 2p dk grn 37.50
1L32 A18 5p violet 45.00
Nos. 1L21-1L32 (12) 166.05
Nos. 1L21-1L30 (10) 70.30

On Surcharged Stamps of 1906-08

1L33 A18 10c on 3c vio .40 .40
1L34 A18 15c on 1c grn .50 .50
1L35 A18 20c on 2c rose 3.50 3.50
1L36 A18 20c on 5c bl 1.50 1.50
1L37 A18 50c on 6c sl (R) 3.00 3.00
Nos. 1L33-1L37 (5) 8.90 8.90

Handstamped

Stamps with the above overprints were made to fill dealers' orders but were never regularly issued or used. Stamps with similar overprints handstamped are bogus.

Surcharged Stamps of 1906 Overprinted in Red, Black or Blue

1L38 A18 15c on 1c grn (R) 2.75 2.75
a. Red overprint inverted
1L39 A18 20c on 2c rose (Bk) 1.90 1.90
1L40 A18 20c on 5c bl (R) 3.00 3.00
1L41 A18 50c on 6c sl (Bl) 14.00 14.00
Nos. 1L38-1L41 (4) 21.65 21.65

Stamps of the 1905 issue overprinted as above No. 1L38 or similarly overprinted but with only 2¼mm space between "B" and "Dpto. Zelaya" were made to fill dealers' orders but not placed in use.

No. 205 Handstamped in Black

Perf. 14 to 15

1L42 A18 10c yel brn 24.00 24.00

Stamps of 1907 Overprinted in Red or Black

1L43 A18 15c brn ol (R) 3.00 3.00
1L44 A18 20c lake .90 .90
a. Inverted overprint 11.00 11.00

With Additional Surcharge

1L45 A18 5c brn org .50 .45
a. Inverted surcharge 7.50 7.50

With Additional Surcharge

1L46 A18 5c on 4c brn org 12.00 12.00

On Provisional Postage Stamps of 1907-08 in Black or Blue

1L47 A18 10c on 2c rose (Bl) 4.50 4.50
1L48 A18 10c on 2c rose *300.00*
1L48A A18 10c on 4c brn org *300.00*
1L49 A18 10c on 20c lake 3.00 3.00
1L50 A18 10c on 50c org (Bl) 3.00 2.25

Arms Type of 1907 Overprinted in Black or Violet

1907

1L51 A18 1c green .40 .40
1L52 A18 2c rose .40 .40
1L53 A18 3c violet .40 .40
1L54 A18 4c brn org .45 .45
1L55 A18 5c blue 4.50 2.25
1L56 A18 10c yel brn .40 .40
1L57 A18 15c brn ol .75 .40
1L58 A18 20c lake .75 .45
1L59 A18 50c orange 2.25 1.50
1L60 A18 1p blk (V) 2.25 1.50
1L61 A18 2p dk grn 2.25 1.90
1L62 A18 5p violet 3.75 2.25
Nos. 1L51-1L62 (12) 18.55 12.30

Nos. 217-225 Overprinted in Green

1908

1L63 A19 1c on 5c yel & blk (R) .45 .40
1L64 A19 2c on 5c yel & blk (Bl) .45 .40
1L65 A19 4c on 5c yel & blk (G) .45 .40
a. Overprint reading down 11.00 11.00
b. Double overprint, reading up and down 18.00 18.00
1L66 A19 5c yel & blk .45 .45
a. "CORROE" 4.50
b. Double overprint 11.00 11.00
c. Double overprint, reading up and down 19.00 19.00
d. "CORREO 1908" double 15.00 15.00
1L67 A19 10c lt bl & blk .50 .50
a. Ovpt. reading down .50 .50
b. "CORREO 1908" triple 37.50
1L68 A19 15c on 50c ol & blk (R) .90 .90
a. "1008" 4.50
b. "8908" 4.50
1L69 A19 35c on 50c ol & blk 1.40 1.40
1L70 A19 1p yel brn & blk 1.90 1.90
a. "CORROE" 12.00 12.00
1L71 A19 2p pearl gray & blk 2.25 2.25
a. "CORROE" 15.00 15.00
Nos. 1L63-1L71 (9) 8.75 8.60

Overprinted Horizontally in Black or Green

1L72 A19 5c yel & blk 9.00 7.50
1L72A A19 2p pearl gray & blk (G) *300.00*

On Nos. 1L72-1L72A, space between "B" and "Dpto. Zelaya" is 13mm.

Nos. 237-248 Overprinted in Black

Imprint: "American Bank Note Co. NY"

1909 ***Perf. 12***

1L73 A18 1c yel grn .25 .25
1L74 A18 2c vermilion .25 .25
a. Inverted overprint
1L75 A18 3c red org .25 .25
1L76 A18 4c violet .25 .25
1L77 A18 5c dp bl .30 .25
a. Inverted overprint 9.00 9.00
b. "B" inverted 7.50 7.50
c. Double overprint 12.00 12.00
1L78 A18 6c gray brn 4.50 3.00
1L79 A18 10c lake .30 .30
a. "B" inverted 9.00 9.00
1L80 A18 15c black .45 .40
a. "B" inverted 11.00 11.00
b. Inverted overprint 12.00 12.00
c. Double overprint 14.00 14.00
1L81 A18 20c brn ol .50 .50
a. "B" inverted 19.00 19.00
1L82 A18 50c dp grn 1.50 1.50
1L83 A18 1p yellow 5.00 2.25
1L84 A18 2p car rose 6.00 3.00
a. Double overprint 27.50 27.50
Nos. 1L73-1L84 (12) 19.55 12.20

One stamp in each sheet has the "o" of "Dpto." sideways.

Overprinted in Black

1910

1L85 A18 3c red org .40 .40
1L86 A18 4c violet .40 .40
a. Inverted overprint 14.00 14.00
1L87 A18 15c black 4.50 2.25
1L88 A18 20c brn ol .25 .30
1L89 A18 50c dp grn .30 .40
1L90 A18 1p yellow .30 .45
a. Inverted overprint 7.50
1L91 A18 2p car rose .40 .75
Nos. 1L85-1L91 (7) 6.55 4.95

No. 243 Overprinted and Surcharged in Black, Green & Carmine

1910

1L92 A18 5c on 10c lake 3.75 3.00

There are three types of the letter "B." It is stated that this stamp was used exclusively for postal purposes and not for telegrams.

No. 247 Surcharged in Black

1911

1L93 A18 5c on 1p yellow .75 .75
a. Double surcharge 14.00
1L94 A18 10c on 1p yellow 1.50 1.50
1L95 A18 15c on 1p yellow .75 .75
a. Inverted surcharge 9.00
b. Double surcharge 9.00
c. Double surcharge, one invtd. 9.00
Nos. 1L93-1L95 (3) 3.00 3.00

Revenue Stamps Surcharged in Black

Perf. 14 to 15

1L96 A19 5c on 25c lilac .75 1.10
a. Without period 1.50 1.50
b. Inverted surcharge 9.00 9.00
1L97 A19 10c on 1p yel brn 1.10 .75
a. Without period 2.00 2.00
b. "01" for "10" 9.00 7.50
c. Inverted surcharge 13.00 13.00

Surcharged in Black

1L98 A19 5c on 1p yel brn 1.50 1.50
a. Without period 3.75
b. "50" for "05" 14.00 14.00
c. Inverted surcharge 15.00 15.00
1L99 A19 5c on 10p pink 1.50 1.50
a. Without period 2.25 2.25
b. "50" for "05" 11.00 11.00
1L100 A19 10c on 1p yel brn 82.50 82.50
a. Without period 95.00 95.00
1L101 A19 10c on 25p grn .75 .75
a. Without period 2.25 2.25
b. "1" for "10" 7.50
1L102 A19 10c on 50p ver 11.00 11.00
a. Without period 16.00 16.00
b. "1" for "10" 22.50
Nos. 1L98-1L102 (5) 97.25 97.25

With Additional Overprint "1904"

1L103 A19 5c on 10p pink 14.00 14.00
a. Without period 24.00 24.00
b. "50" for "05" 110.00 110.00
1L104 A19 10c on 2p gray .75 .75
a. Without period 1.90
b. "1" for "10" 7.50
1L105 A19 10c on 25p grn 92.50
a. Without period 100.00
1L106 A19 10c on 50p ver 7.50 7.50
a. Without period 14.00
b. "1" for "10" 18.00
c. Inverted surcharge

The surcharges on Nos. 1L96 to 1L106 are in settings of twenty-five. One stamp in each setting has a large square period after "cts" and another has a thick upright "c" in that word. There are two types of "1904".

No. 293C Overprinted

1911

1L107 A21 5c on 5c on 2 bl (R) 32.50
a. "5" omitted 37.50
b. Red overprint inverted 40.00
c. As "a" and "b" 47.50

Same Overprint On Nos. 290, 291, 292 and 289D with Lines of Surcharge spaced 2½mm apart Reading Down

No.	Type	Description	Unused	Used
1L107D	A21	2c on 10c on 1 red	*250.00*	
e.		Overprint reading up	*250.00*	
1L107F	A21	5c on 10c on 1 red	*150.00*	
1L107G	A21	10c on 10c on 1 red (#292)	*200.00*	
1L108	A21	10c on 10c on 1 red (#289D)	*200.00*	

Locomotive — Z2

1912 Engr. *Perf. 14*

No.	Type	Description	Unused	Used
1L109	Z2	1c yel grn	1.50	.50
1L110	Z2	2c vermilion	1.25	.25
1L111	Z2	3c org brn	1.50	.45
1L112	Z2	4c carmine	1.50	.30
1L113	Z2	5c dp bl	1.50	.45
1L114	Z2	6c red brn	9.00	3.50
1L115	Z2	10c slate	1.50	.30
1L116	Z2	15c dl lil	1.50	.60
1L117	Z2	20c bl vio	1.50	.60
1L118	Z2	25c grn & blk	2.25	.80
1L119	Z2	35c brn & blk	3.00	1.25
1L120	Z2	50c ol grn	3.00	1.25
1L121	Z2	1p orange	4.00	1.75
1L122	Z2	2p org brn	7.50	3.25
1L123	Z2	5p dk bl grn	18.00	7.50
		Nos. 1L109-1L123 (15)	58.50	22.75

The stamps of this issue were for use in all places on the Atlantic Coast of Nicaragua where the currency was on a silver basis.

For surcharges see Nos. 325-337.

OFFICIAL STAMPS

Regular Issue of 1909 Overprinted in Black

1909 Unwmk. *Perf. 12*

No.	Type	Description	Unused	Used
1LO1	A18	20c brn ol	15.00	12.00
a.		Double overprint	30.00	

No. O216 Overprinted in Black

No.	Type	Description	Unused	Used
1LO2	A18	15c black	15.00	10.00

Same Overprint on Official Stamp of 1911

1911

No.	Type	Description	Unused	Used
1LO3	A18	5c on 3c red org	22.50	17.50

CABO GRACIAS A DIOS

A cape and seaport town in the extreme northeast of Nicaragua. The name was coined by Spanish explorers who had great difficulty finding a landing place along the Nicaraguan coast and when eventually locating this harbor expressed their relief by designating the point "Cape Thanks to God." Special postage stamps came into use for the same reasons as the Zelaya issues. See Zelaya.

Dangerous counterfeits exist of most of the Cabo Gracias a Dios overprints. Special caution should be taken with double and inverted handstamps of Nos. 2L1-2L25, as most are counterfeits. Expert opinion is required.

Regular Issues of 1900-04 Handstamped in Violet

On Engraved Stamps of 1900

1904-05 Unwmk. *Perf. 12, 14*

No.	Type	Description	Unused	Used
2L1	A14	1c plum	2.25	1.10
2L2	A14	2c vermilion	4.50	1.25
2L3	A14	3c green	10.00	4.50
2L4	A14	4c ol grn	9.75	9.75
2L5	A14	15c ultra	35.00	22.50
2L6	A14	20c brown	3.00	2.25
		Nos. 2L1-2L6 (6)	64.50	41.35

On Lithographed Stamps of 1902

No.	Type	Description	Unused	Used
2L7	A14	5c blue	24.00	24.00
2L8	A14	10c violet	24.00	24.00

On Surcharged Stamps of 1904

No.	Type	Description	Unused	Used
2L9	A14	5c on 10c vio	22.50	22.50
2L10	A14	15c on 10c vio		

On Postage Due Stamps

Violet Handstamp

No.	Type	Description	Unused	Used
2L11	D3	20c org brn (#141)	5.00	1.25
2L12	D3	20c org brn (#156)	3.50	1.25
2L13	D3	30c dk grn (#157)	14.00	14.00
2L14	D3	50c lake (#158)	3.75	.75
		Nos. 2L11-2L14 (4)	26.25	17.25

Black Handstamp

No.	Type	Description	Unused	Used
2L15	D3	30c dk grn (#157)	25.00	25.00

Stamps of 1900-05 Handstamped in Violet

On Engraved Stamps of 1900

No.	Type	Description	Unused	Used
2L16	A14	1c plum	2.75	2.25
2L17	A14	2c vermilion	27.50	25.00
2L18	A14	3c green	37.50	30.00
2L19	A14	4c ol grn	40.00	37.50
2L20	A14	15c ultra	45.00	45.00
		Nos. 2L16-2L20 (5)	152.75	139.75

On Lithographed Stamps of 1902

No.	Type	Description	Unused	Used
2L22	A14	5c dk bl	95.00	50.00
2L23	A14	10c violet	27.50	24.00

On Surcharged Stamp of 1904

No.	Type	Description	Unused	Used
2L24	A14	5c on 10c vio		

On Postage Due Stamp

No.	Type	Description	Unused	Used
2L25	D3	20c org brn (#141)		

The editors have no evidence that stamps with this handstamp were issued. Examples were sent to the UPU and covers are known.

Stamps of 1900-08 Handstamped in Violet

1905 On Stamps of 1905

No.	Type	Description	Unused	Used
2L26	A18	1c green	1.10	1.10
2L27	A18	2c car rose	1.50	1.50
2L28	A18	3c violet	1.50	1.50
2L29	A18	4c org red	3.75	3.75
2L30	A18	5c blue	1.50	1.10
2L31	A18	6c slate	3.75	3.75
2L32	A18	10c yel brn	3.00	1.90
2L33	A18	15c brn ol	4.50	4.50
2L34	A18	1p black	20.00	20.00
2L35	A18	2p dk grn	35.00	35.00
		Nos. 2L26-2L35 (10)	75.60	74.10

Magenta Handstamp

No.	Type	Description	Unused	Used
2L26a	A18	1c	3.75	3.00
2L27a	A18	2c	3.00	2.75
2L28a	A18	3c	3.75	3.00
2L30a	A18	5c	7.50	6.00
2L33a	A18	15c	13.50	11.00
		Nos. 2L26a-2L33a (5)	31.50	25.75

On Stamps of 1900-04

No.	Type	Description	Unused	Used
2L36	A14	5c on 10c vio	14.00	14.00
2L37	A14	10c violet	125.00	
2L38	A14	20c brown	12.00	12.00
2L39	A14	20c on 5p blk	95.00	95.00

On Postage Due Stamps Overprinted "Correos"

No.	Type	Description	Unused	Used
2L40	D3	20c org brn (#141)	9.00	9.00
2L41	D3	20c org brn (#156)	5.00	4.50

On Surcharged Stamps of 1906-08

No.	Type	Description	Unused	Used
2L42	A18	10c on 3c vio	*250.00*	
2L43	A18	20c on 5c blue	10.00	10.00
2L44	A18	50c on 6c slate	24.00	24.00

On Stamps of 1907

Perf. 14 to 15

No.	Type	Description	Unused	Used
2L44A	A18	2c rose	*250.00*	
2L45	A18	10c yel brn	*100.00*	*75.00*
2L46	A18	15c brn ol	*90.00*	*75.00*

On Provisional Stamp of 1908 in Magenta

No.	Type	Description	Unused	Used
2L47	A19	5c yel & blk	7.50	7.50

Stamps with the above large handstamp in black instead of violet, are bogus. There are also excellent counterfeits in violet.

The foregoing overprints being handstamped are found in various positions, especially the last type.

Stamps of 1907 Type A18, Overprinted in Black or Violet

1907

No.	Type	Description	Unused	Used
2L48	A18	1c green	.50	.30
a.		Vert. pair, imperf. btwn.	—	
2L49	A18	2c rose	.50	.30
2L50	A18	3c violet	.50	.30
a.		Vert. pair, imperf. btwn.	*350.00*	
2L51	A18	4c brn org	.75	.40
2L52	A18	5c blue	.90	.50
2L53	A18	10c yel brn	.75	.40
2L54	A18	15c brn ol	1.25	.75
2L55	A18	20c lake	1.25	.75
2L56	A18	50c orange	3.50	1.50
2L57	A18	1p blk (V)	3.75	1.90
2L58	A18	2p dk grn	5.25	2.25
2L59	A18	5p violet	7.50	3.75
		Nos. 2L48-2L59 (12)	26.40	13.10

Nos. 237-248 Overprinted in Black

Imprint: American Bank Note Co.

1909 *Perf. 12*

No.	Type	Description	Unused	Used
2L60	A18	1c yel grn	.40	.40
2L61	A18	2c vermilion	.40	.40
2L62	A18	3c red org	.40	.40
2L63	A18	4c violet	.40	.40
2L64	A18	5c dp bl	.40	.60
2L65	A18	6c gray brn	8.00	8.00
2L66	A18	10c lake	.80	.75
2L67	A18	15c black	1.20	.90
2L68	A18	20c brn ol	1.50	*4.00*
2L69	A18	50c dp grn	3.75	2.50
2L70	A18	1p yellow	4.25	4.00
2L71	A18	2p car rose	7.50	5.75
		Nos. 2L60-2L71 (12)	29.00	28.10

No. 199 Overprinted Vertically

No.	Type	Description	Unused	Used
2L72	A18	50c on 6c slate (R)	15.00	15.00

CABO GRACIAS A DIOS OFFICIAL STAMPS

Official Stamps of 1907 Overprinted in Red or Violet

1907

No.	Type	Description	Unused	Used
2LO1	A18	10c on 1c green	*60.00*	
2LO2	A18	15c on 1c green	*75.00*	
2LO3	A18	20c on 1c green	*100.00*	
2LO4	A18	50c on 1c green	*125.00*	

NIGER

'nī-jər

LOCATION — Northern Africa, directly north of Nigeria
GOVT. — Republic
AREA — 458,075 sq. mi.
POP. — 24,210,000 (2020 est.)
CAPITAL — Niamey

The colony, formed in 1922, was originally a military territory. The Republic of the Niger was proclaimed December 18, 1958. In the period between issues of the colony and the republic, stamps of French West Africa were used. Full independence from France was proclaimed August 3, 1960.

100 Centimes = 1 Franc

Catalogue values for unused stamps in this country are for Never Hinged items, beginning with Scott 91 in the regular postage section, Scott B14 in the semi-postal section, Scott C14 in the airpost section, Scott J22 in the postage due section, and Scott O1 in the official section.

Watermark

Wmk. 385

Stamps of Upper Senegal and Niger Type of 1914, Overprinted

In the overprint, normal spacing between the words "DU" and "NIGER" is 2½mm. In one position (72) of all sheets in the first printing, the space between the two words is 3mm.

1921-26 Unwmk. Perf. 13½x14

No.	Type	Description	Unused	Used
1	A4	1c brn vio & vio	.25	*.40*
2	A4	2c dk gray & dl vio	.25	*.40*
3	A4	4c black & blue	.35	*.50*
4	A4	5c ol brn & dk brn	.30	*.50*
5	A4	10c yel grn & bl grn	1.60	*2.00*
6	A4	10c mag, *bluish* ('26)	.95	*1.20*
7	A4	15c red brn & org	.40	*.55*
8	A4	20c brn vio & blk	.35	*.50*
9	A4	25c blk & bl grn	.80	*.80*
10	A4	30c red org & rose	2.75	*3.50*
11	A4	30c bl grn & red org ('26)	.80	*.80*
12	A4	35c rose & violet	.95	*1.20*
13	A4	40c gray & rose	.95	*1.20*
14	A4	45c blue & ol brn	1.40	*1.40*
15	A4	50c ultra & bl	.80	*1.20*
16	A4	50c dk gray & bl vio ('25)	1.60	*1.60*
17	A4	60c org red ('26)	1.40	*2.00*
18	A4	75c yel & ol brn	1.40	*1.60*
19	A4	1fr dk brn & dl vio	1.60	*2.00*
20	A4	2fr green & blue	1.60	*2.00*
21	A4	5fr violet & blk	2.75	*4.00*
		Nos. 1-21 (21)	23.25	*29.35*

Types of 1921 Surcharged in Black or Red

1922-26

No.	Type	Description	Unused	Used
22	A4	25c on 15c red brn & org ('25)	.95	.80
a.		Multiple surcharge	260.00	
b.		"25c" inverted	140.00	
23	A4	25c on 2fr grn & bl (R) ('24)	.90	.80
24	A4	25c on 5fr vio & blk (R) ('24)	.95	.80
a.		Double surcharge	225.00	
25	A4	60c on 75c vio,*pnksh*	.90	*1.20*
26	A4	65c on 45c bl & ol brn ('25)	2.75	*3.50*
27	A4	85c on 75c yel & ol brn ('25)	2.75	*3.50*
28	A4	1.25fr on 1fr dp bl & lt bl (R) ('26)	1.10	*1.20*
a.		Surcharge omitted	260.00	
b.		As "a," in pair with unsurcharged stamp	1,700.	
		Nos. 22-28 (7)	10.30	11.80

Nos. 22-24 are surcharged "25c," No. 28, "1f25." Nos. 25-27 are surcharged like illustration.

Drawing Water from Well
A2

Zinder Fortress
A4

Boat on Niger River — A3

Perf. 13x14, 13½x14, 14x13, 14x13½

1926-40 Typo.

No.	Type	Description	Unused	Used
29	A2	1c lil rose & ol	.25	*.40*
30	A2	2c dk gray & dl red	.25	*.40*
31	A2	3c red vio & ol gray ('40)	.25	*.40*
32	A2	4c amber & gray	.25	*.40*
33	A2	5c ver & yel grn	.25	*.40*
34	A2	10c dp bl & Prus bl	.25	*.40*
35	A2	15c gray grn & yel grn	.55	*.80*
36	A2	15c gray lil & lt red ('28)	.40	.40
37	A3	20c Prus grn & ol brn	.40	*.55*
38	A3	25c black & dl red	.40	.50
39	A3	30c bl grn & yel grn	.80	*1.20*
40	A3	30c yel & red vio ('40)	.30	*.50*
41	A3	35c brn org & turq bl, *bluish*	.80	*1.20*
42	A3	35c bl grn & dl grn ('38)	1.20	*1.60*
43	A3	40c red brn & slate	.40	*.50*
44	A3	45c yel & red vio	1.60	*1.90*
45	A3	45c bl grn & dl grn ('40)	.30	*.50*
46	A3	50c scar & grn, *grnsh*	.40	.40
47	A3	55c dk car & brn ('38)	2.00	2.00
48	A3	60c dk car & brn ('40)	.55	*.70*
49	A3	65c ol grn & rose	.40	*.55*
50	A3	70c ol grn & rose ('40)	2.00	*2.50*
51	A3	75c grn & vio, *pink*	2.00	*2.25*
a.		Center and value double	225.00	
52	A3	80c cl & ol grn ('38)	1.60	*2.00*
53	A3	90c brn red & ver	1.60	*1.90*
54	A3	90c brt rose & yel grn ('39)	2.00	*2.40*
55	A4	1fr rose & yel grn	8.00	8.75
56	A4	1fr dk red & red org ('38)	2.00	*2.40*
57	A4	1fr grn & red ('40)	.80	.80
58	A4	1.10fr ol brn & grn	4.00	*6.50*
59	A4	1.25fr grn & red ('33)	2.40	2.40
60	A4	1.25fr dk red & red org ('39)	.80	*1.20*
61	A4	1.40fr red vio & dk brn ('40)	.80	*1.50*
62	A4	1.50fr dp bl & pale bl	.55	*.70*
63	A4	1.60fr ol brn & grn ('40)	1.75	*2.00*
64	A4	1.75fr red vio & dk brn ('33)	1.60	2.40
65	A4	1.75fr dk bl & vio bl ('38)	1.25	*1.60*
66	A4	2fr red org & ol brn	.30	*.50*
67	A4	2.25fr dk bl & vio bl ('39)	1.20	*1.60*
68	A4	2.50fr blk brn ('40)	1.20	*1.60*
69	A4	3fr dl vio & blk ('27)	.55	*.80*
70	A4	5fr vio brn & blk, *pink*	.80	*1.20*
71	A4	10fr chlky bl & mag	1.60	*2.00*
72	A4	20fr yel grn & red org	1.60	*2.00*
		Nos. 29-72 (44)	52.40	*66.70*

For surcharges see Nos. B7-B10.

Common Design Types pictured following the introduction.

Colonial Exposition Issue

Common Design Types

1931 Typo. Perf. 12½

Name of Country in Black

No.	Type	Description	Unused	Used
73	CD70	40c deep green	4.75	4.75
74	CD71	50c violet	4.75	4.75
75	CD72	90c red orange	5.50	5.50
76	CD73	1.50fr dull blue	5.50	5.50
		Nos. 73-76 (4)	20.50	20.50

Paris International Exposition Issue

Common Design Types

1937 Perf. 13

No.	Type	Description	Unused	Used
77	CD74	20c deep violet	1.90	1.90
78	CD75	30c dark green	1.90	1.90
79	CD76	40c car rose	1.90	1.90
80	CD77	50c dark brown	1.50	1.50
81	CD78	90c red	1.50	1.50
82	CD79	1.50fr ultra	1.90	1.90
		Nos. 77-82 (6)	10.60	10.60

Colonial Arts Exhibition Issue

Souvenir Sheet

Common Design Type

1937 Imperf.

No.	Type	Description	Unused	Used
83	CD74	3fr magenta	9.50	*14.00*

Caillie Issue

Common Design Type

1939 Perf. 12½x12

No.	Type	Description	Unused	Used
84	CD81	90c org brn & org	.35	.35
85	CD81	2fr brt violet	1.00	1.00
86	CD81	2.25fr ultra & dk bl	1.00	1.00
		Nos. 84-86 (3)	2.35	2.35

New York World's Fair Issue

Common Design Type

1939, May 10

No.	Type	Description	Unused	Used
87	CD82	1.25fr car lake	.80	1.40
88	CD82	2.25fr ultra	.80	1.40

Zinder Fortress and Marshal Pétain — A5

1941 Unwmk. Engr. Perf. 12x12½

No.	Type	Description	Unused	Used
89	A5	1fr green	.35	
90	A5	2.50fr dark blue	.35	
		Set, never hinged	1.75	

Nos. 89-90 were issued by the Vichy government in France, but were not placed on sale in Niger.

For surcharges, see Nos. B13A-B13B.

See French West Africa No. 68 for additional stamp inscribed "Niger" and "Afrique Occidentale Francaise."

Catalogue values for unused stamps in this section, from this point to the end of the section, are for Never Hinged items.

Republic of the Niger

Giraffes — A6

1fr, 2fr, Crested cranes. 5fr, 7fr, Saddle-billed storks. 15fr, 20fr, Barbary sheep. 25fr, 30fr, Giraffes. 50fr, 60fr, Ostriches. 85fr, 100fr, Lion.

1959-60 Unwmk. Engr. Perf. 13

No.	Type	Description	Unused	Used
91	A6	1fr multi	.35	.25
92	A6	2fr multi	.35	.25
93	A6	5fr blk, car & ol	.55	.25
94	A6	7fr grn, blk & red	.65	.25
95	A6	15fr grnsh bl & dk brn	.25	.25
96	A6	20fr vio, blk & ind	.25	.25
97	A6	25fr multi	.35	.25
98	A6	30fr multi	.45	.30
99	A6	50fr ind & org brn	5.00	.65
100	A6	60fr dk brn & emer	7.00	.90
101	A6	85fr org brn & bis	2.50	.80
102	A6	100fr bis & yel grn	3.25	1.10
		Nos. 91-102 (12)	20.95	5.50

Issue years: #97, 1959; others, 1960.
For surcharge see No. 103.

Imperforates

Most stamps of the republic exist imperforate in issued and trial colors, and also in small presentation sheets in issued color.

No. 102 Surcharged

1960

No.	Type	Description	Unused	Used
103	A6	200fr on 100fr	15.00	15.00

Niger's independence.

C.C.T.A. Issue

Common Design Type

1960 Engr. Perf. 13

No.	Type	Description	Unused	Used
104	CD106	25fr buff & red brn	.85	.45

Emblem of the Entente — A6a

1960, May 29 Photo. Perf. 13x13½

No.	Type	Description	Unused	Used
105	A6a	25fr multi	.85	.55

1st anniversary of the Entente (Dahomey, Ivory Coast, Niger and Upper Volta).

Pres. Diori Hamani — A7

1960, Dec. 18 Engr. Perf. 13

No.	Type	Description	Unused	Used
106	A7	25fr ol bis & blk	.60	.35

2nd anniversary of the proclamation of the Republic of the Niger.

Manatee — A8

1962, Jan. 29 Unwmk. Perf. 13

No.	Type	Description	Unused	Used
107	A8	50c grn & dk sl grn	.40	.25
108	A8	10fr red brn & dk grn	.65	.25

Abidjan Games Issue

Common Design Type

25fr, Basketball & Soccer. 85fr, Track, horiz.

1962, May 26 Photo. Perf. 12x12½

No.	Type	Description	Unused	Used
109	CD109	15fr multi	.40	.25
110	CD109	25fr multi	.60	.30
111	CD109	85fr multi	1.60	.70
		Nos. 109-111 (3)	2.60	1.25

African-Malgache Union Issue

Common Design Type

1962, Sept. 8 Perf. 12½x12

No.	Type	Description	Unused	Used
112	CD110	30fr multi	.80	.50

Pres. Diori Hamani and Map of Niger in Africa — A10

1962, Dec. 18 Photo. ***Perf. 12½x12***
113 A10 25fr multi .60 .30

Woman Runner — A11

15fr, Swimming, horiz. 45fr, Volleyball.

Unwmk.

1963, Apr. 11 Engr. ***Perf. 13***
114 A11 15fr brt bl & dk brn .40 .25
115 A11 25fr dk brn & red .60 .30
116 A11 45fr grn & blk 1.10 .50
Nos. 114-116 (3) 2.10 1.05

Friendship Games, Dakar, Apr. 11-21.

Woodworker — A12

10fr, Tanners, horiz. 25fr, Goldsmith. 30fr, Mat makers, horiz. 85fr, Decoy maker.

Perf. 12x12½, 12½x12

1963, Aug. 30 Photo.
117 A12 5fr brn & multi .25 .25
118 A12 10fr dk grn & multi .35 .25
119 A12 25fr blk & multi .60 .30
120 A12 30fr vio & multi .90 .35
121 A12 85fr dk bl & multi 2.00 .90
Nos. 117-121,C26 (6) 7.10 3.65

Berberi (Nuba) Woman's Costume — A13

Costume Museum, Niamey A14

Costumes: 20fr, Hausa woman. 25fr, Tuareg woman. 30fr, Tuareg man. 60fr, Djerma woman.

Perf. 12x12½, 12½x12

1963, Oct. 15 Photo.
122 A13 15fr multi .35 .25
123 A13 20fr blk & bl .50 .25
124 A13 25fr multi .70 .30
125 A13 30fr multi .75 .30
126 A13 60fr multi 1.75 .70
127 A14 85fr multi 2.00 .80
Nos. 122-127 (6) 6.05 2.60

Man, Globe and Scales — A15

Unwmk.

1963, Dec. 10 Engr. ***Perf. 13***
128 A15 25fr lt ol grn, ultra & brn org .80 .30

15th anniversary of the Universal Declaration of Human Rights.

Parkinsonia Aculeata — A16

Plumeria Rubra — A16a

Flowers: 10fr, Russelia equisetiformis. 15fr, Red sage (lantana). 20fr, Argyreia nervosa. 25fr, Luffa cylindrica. 30fr, Hibiscus rosa sinensis. 50fr, Catharanthus roseus. 60fr, Caesalpinia pulcherrima.

1964-65 Photo. ***Perf. 13½x13***
129 A16 5fr dk red, grn & yel .75 .35
130 A16 10fr multi .60 .35
131 A16 15fr multi 1.00 .50
132 A16 20fr multi 1.00 .50
133 A16 25fr multi 1.00 .50
134 A16 30fr multi 1.25 .55
135 A16a 45fr multi ('65) 2.25 .95
136 A16a 50fr dk red, brt pink & grn ('65) 2.25 .95
137 A16a 60fr multi ('65) 4.00 1.25
Nos. 129-137 (9) 14.10 5.90

On No. 135 "PLUMERIA" is spelled incorrectly.

Solar Flares and IQSY Emblem — A17

1964, May 12 Engr. ***Perf. 13***
138 A17 30fr dp org, vio & blk .70 .45

International Quiet Sun Year, 1964-65.

Mobile Medical Unit — A18

30fr, Mobile children's clinic. 50fr, Mobile women's clinic. 60fr, Outdoor medical laboratory.

1964, May 26
139 A18 25fr bl, org & ol .45 .25
140 A18 30fr multi .55 .25
141 A18 50fr vio, org & bl .85 .30
142 A18 60fr grnsh bl, org & dk brn .95 .40
Nos. 139-142 (4) 2.80 1.20

Nigerian mobile health education organization, OMNES (Organisation Médicale Mobile Nigérienne d'Education Sanitaire).

Cooperation Issue
Common Design Type

1964, Nov. 7 Unwmk. ***Perf. 13***
143 CD119 50fr vio, dk brn & org .80 .40

Tuareg Tent of Azawak — A19

Designs: 20fr, Songhai house. 25fr, Wogo and Kourtey tents. 30fr, Djerma house. 60fr, Huts of Sorkawa fishermen. 85fr, Hausa town house.

1964-65 Engr.
144 A19 15fr ultra, dl grn & red brn .25 .25
145 A19 20fr multi .30 .25
146 A19 25fr Prus bl, dk brn & org brn .40 .25
147 A19 30fr multi ('65) .50 .30
148 A19 60fr red, grn & bis ('65) 1.10 .30
149 A19 85fr multi ('65) 1.60 .50
Nos. 144-149 (6) 4.15 1.85

Leprosy Examination — A20

1964, Dec. 15 Photo. ***Perf. 13x12½***
150 A20 50fr multi .80 .50

Issued to publicize the fight against leprosy.

Abraham Lincoln — A21

1965, Apr. 3 ***Perf. 13x12½***
151 A21 50fr vio bl, blk, & ocher .80 .50

Centenary of death of Abraham Lincoln.

Teaching with Radio and Pictures A22

Designs: 25fr, Woman studying arithmetic: "A better life through knowledge." 30fr, Adult education class. 50fr, Map of Niger and 5 tribesmen, "Literacy for adults."

1965, Apr. 16 Engr. ***Perf. 13***
152 A22 20fr dk bl, dk brn & ocher .40 .25
153 A22 25fr sl grn, brn & ol brn .50 .25
154 A22 30fr red, sl grn & vio brn .60 .30
155 A22 50fr dp bl, brn & vio brn .85 .40
Nos. 152-155 (4) 2.35 1.20

Issued to promote adult education and "a better life through knowledge."

Ader Portable Telephone — A23

Designs: 30fr, Wheatstone telegraph interrupter. 50fr, Early telewriter.

1965, May 17 Unwmk. ***Perf. 13***
156 A23 25fr red brn, dk grn & ind .60 .30
157 A23 30fr lil, slate grn & red .70 .30
158 A23 50fr red, slate grn & pur 1.00 .50
Nos. 156-158 (3) 2.30 1.10

International Telecommunication Union, cent.

Runner — A24

Designs: 10fr, Hurdler, horiz. 20fr, Pole vaulter, horiz. 30fr, Long jumper.

1965, July 1 Engr. ***Perf. 13***
159 A24 10fr brn, ocher & blk .25 .25
160 A24 15fr gray, brn & red .45 .25
161 A24 20fr dk grn, brn & vio bl .60 .25
162 A24 30fr maroon, brn & grn .70 .30
Nos. 159-162 (4) 2.00 1.05

African Games, Brazzaville, July 18-25.

Radio Interview and Club Emblem — A25

45fr, Recording folk music, vert. 50fr, Group listening to broadcast, vert. 60fr, Public debate.

1965, Oct. 1 Engr. ***Perf. 13***
163 A25 30fr brt vio, emer & red brn .40 .25
164 A25 45fr blk, car & buff .55 .25
165 A25 50fr dk car, bl & lt brn .70 .30
166 A25 60fr bis, ultra & brn .80 .35
Nos. 163-166 (4) 2.45 1.15

Issued to promote radio clubs.

Water Cycle — A26

1966, Feb. 28 Engr. ***Perf. 13***
167 A26 50fr vio, ocher & bl .90 .40

Hydrological Decade, 1965-74.

Carvings, Mask and Headdresses A27

50fr, Carvings and wall decorations. 60fr, Carvings and arch. 100fr, Architecture and handicraft.

1966, Apr. 12
168 A27 30fr red brn, blk & brt grn .55 .40
169 A27 50fr brt bl, ocher & pur .80 .40
170 A27 60fr car lake, dl pur & yel brn .90 .55
171 A27 100fr brt red, bl & blk 1.75 .95
Nos. 168-171 (4) 4.00 2.30

Intl. Negro Arts Festival, Dakar, Senegal, Apr. 1-24.

Soccer Player — A28

50fr, Goalkeeper, horiz. 60fr, Player kicking ball.

1966, June 17 Engr. ***Perf. 13***
172 A28 30fr dk brn, brt bl & rose red .65 .30
173 A28 50fr bl, choc & emer .80 .40
174 A28 60fr bl, lil & brn .95 .50
Nos. 172-174 (3) 2.40 1.20

8th World Soccer Cup Championship, Wembley, England, July 11-30.

Color Guard — A29

20fr, Parachutist, horiz. 45fr, Tanks, horiz.

Perf. 12½x13, 13x12½

1966, Aug. 23 Photo.
175 A29 20fr multi .40 .25
176 A29 30fr multi .50 .25
177 A29 45fr multi .70 .35
Nos. 175-177 (3) 1.60 .85

5th anniv. of the National Armed Forces.

Cow Receiving Injection — A30

1966, Sept. 26 Litho. ***Perf. 12½x13***
178 A30 45fr org brn, bl & blk 1.25 .60

Campaign against cattle plague.

UNESCO Emblem — A31

1966, Nov. 4 Litho. *Perf. 13x12½*
179 A31 50fr multi .70 .40

20th anniversary of UNESCO.

Cement Works Malbaza — A32

Designs: 10fr, Furnace, vert. 20fr, Electric center. 50fr, Handling of raw material.

1966, Dec. 17 Engr. *Perf. 13*
180 A32 10fr ind, brn & org .30 .25
181 A32 20fr dk ol grn & dl bl .50 .25
182 A32 30fr bl, gray & red brn .50 .25
183 A32 50fr ind, bl & brn .70 .35
Nos. 180-183 (4) 2.00 1.10

Redbilled Hornbill — A33

Birds: 2fr, Pied kingfisher. 30fr, Barbary shrike. 45fr, 65fr, Little weaver and nest. 70fr, Chestnut-bellied sand grouse.

1967-81 Engr. *Perf. 13*
184 A33 1fr red, sl grn & dk brn .70 .35
185 A33 2fr brn, brt grn & blk .70 .35
186 A33 30fr multi 4.00 .70
187 A33 45fr multi 1.90 .40
188 A33 65fr multi ('81) 3.25 .85
189 A33 70fr multi 3.25 .70
Nos. 184-189 (6) 13.80 3.35

Issued: 1fr, 2fr, 30fr, 2/8; 45fr, 70fr, 11/18; 65fr, 9/81. See #237.

Villard-de-Lans and Olympic Emblem — A34

Olympic Emblem and Mountains: 45fr, Autrans and ski jump. 60fr, Saint Nizier du Moucherotte and ski jump. 90fr, Chamrousse and course for downhill and slalom races.

1967, Feb. 24
190 A34 30fr grn, ultra & brn .50 .25
191 A34 45fr grn, ultra & brn .70 .40
192 A34 60fr grn, ultra & brn .95 .50
193 A34 90fr grn, ultra & brn 1.40 .75
Nos. 190-193 (4) 3.55 1.90

10th Winter Olympic Games, Grenoble, 1968.

Lions Emblem and Family — A35

1967, Mar. 4
194 A35 50fr dk grn, brn red & ultra 1.00 .40

Lions International, 50th anniversary.

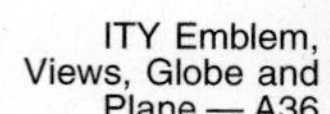

ITY Emblem, Views, Globe and Plane — A36

1967, Apr. 28 Engr. *Perf. 13*
195 A36 45fr vio, brt grn & red lil .70 .35

International Tourist Year, 1967.

1967 Jamboree Emblem and Scouts — A37

Designs (Jamboree Emblem and): 45fr, Scouts gathering from all directions, horiz. 80fr, Campfire.

1967, May 25 Engr. *Perf. 13*
196 A37 30fr mar, Prus bl & ol .55 .25
197 A37 45fr org, vio bl & brn ol .75 .30
198 A37 80fr multi 1.50 .75
Nos. 196-198 (3) 2.80 1.30

12th Boy Scout World Jamboree, Farragut State Park, Idaho, Aug. 1-9.

Red Cross Aides Carrying Sick Man — A38

Designs: 50fr, Nurse, mother and infant. 60fr, Physician examining woman.

1967, July 13 Engr. *Perf. 13*
199 A38 45fr blk, grn & car .65 .30
200 A38 50fr grn, blk & car .90 .50
201 A38 60fr blk, grn & car 1.25 .55
Nos. 199-201 (3) 2.80 1.35

Issued for the Red Cross.

Europafrica Issue

Map of Europe and Africa — A39

1967, July 20 Photo. *Perf. 12½x12*
202 A39 50fr multi .80 .35

Women and UN Emblem — A40

1967, Oct. 21 Engr. *Perf. 13*
203 A40 50fr brn, brt bl & yel .80 .40

UN Commission on Status of Women.

Monetary Union Issue
Common Design Type

1967, Nov. 4 Engr. *Perf. 13*
204 CD125 30fr grn & dk gray .55 .25

A41

Design: Human Rights Flame, Globe, People and Statue of Liberty.

1968, Feb. 19 Engr. *Perf. 13*
205 A41 50fr brn, indigo & brt bl .80 .40

International Human Rights Year.

Woman Dancing and WHO Emblem — A42

1968, Apr. 8 Engr. *Perf. 13*
206 A42 50fr brt bl, blk & red brn 1.00 .40

20th anniv. of WHO.

Gray Hornbill — A43

Birds: 10fr, Woodland kingfisher. 15fr, Senegalese coucal. 20fr, Rose-ringed parakeets. 25fr, Abyssinian roller. 50fr, Cattle egret.

Dated "1968"

1968, Nov. 15 Photo. *Perf. 12½x13*
207 A43 5fr dk grn & multi .60 .40
208 A43 10fr grn & multi .70 .40
209 A43 15fr bl vio & multi 1.25 .40
210 A43 20fr pink & multi 1.25 .50
211 A43 25fr ol & multi 2.00 .60
212 A43 50fr pur & multi 2.75 1.50
Nos. 207-212 (6) 8.55 3.80

See Nos. 233-236, 316.

ILO Emblem and "Labor Supporting the World" — A44

1969, Apr. 22 Engr. *Perf. 13*
213 A44 30fr yel grn & dk car .50 .25
214 A44 50fr dk car & yel grn .65 .40

50th anniv. of the World Labor Organization.

Red Crosses, Mother and Child — A45

Designs: 50fr, People, globe, red crosses, horiz. 70fr, Man with gift parcel and red crosses.

1969, May 5 Engr. *Perf. 13*
215 A45 45fr bl, red & brn ol .80 .25
216 A45 50fr dk grn, red & gray .80 .40
217 A45 70fr ocher, red & dk brn 1.25 .60
Nos. 215-217 (3) 2.85 1.25

50th anniv. of the League of Red Cross Societies.

Mouth and Ear — A46

1969, May 20 Photo. *Perf. 12½x12*
218 A46 100fr multi 1.25 .60

First (cultural) Conference of French-speaking Community at Niamey.

National Administration College — A47

1969, July 8 Photo. *Perf. 12½x12*
219 A47 30fr emer & dp org .70 .30

Development Bank Issue
Common Design Type

1969, Sept. 10 Engr. *Perf. 13*
220 CD130 30fr pur, grn & ocher .70 .30

ASECNA Issue
Common Design Type

1969, Dec. 12 Engr. *Perf. 12*
221 CD132 100fr car rose 1.40 .70

Classical Pavilion, National Museum — A48

Pavilions, National Museum: 45fr, Temporary exhibitions. 50fr, Audio-visual. 70fr, Nigerian musical instruments. 100fr, Craftsmanship.

1970, Feb. 23 Engr. *Perf. 13*
222 A48 30fr brt bl, sl grn & brn .40 .25
223 A48 45fr emer, Prus bl & brn .60 .25
224 A48 50fr sl grn, vio bl & brn .65 .25
225 A48 70fr brn, sl grn & lt bl .95 .45
226 A48 100fr sl grn, vio bl & brn 1.40 .60
Nos. 222-226 (5) 4.00 1.80

Map of Africa and Vaccination Gun — A49

1970, Mar. 31 Engr. *Perf. 13*
227 A49 50fr ultra, dp yel grn & mag .80 .40

Issued to commemorate the 100 millionth smallpox vaccination in West Africa.

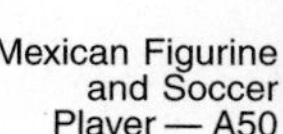

Mexican Figurine and Soccer Player — A50

Designs: 70fr, Figurine, globe and soccer ball. 90fr, Figurine and 2 soccer players.

1970, Apr. 25
228 A50 40fr dk brn, red lil & emer .75 .35
229 A50 70fr red brn, bl & plum 1.05 .50
230 A50 90fr blk & red 1.40 .70
Nos. 228-230 (3) 3.20 1.55

9th World Soccer Championship for the Jules Rimet Cup, Mexico City, 5/29-6/21.

UPU Headquarters Issue
Common Design Type

1970, May 20 Engr. *Perf. 13*
231 CD133 30fr brn, dk gray & dk red .50 .25
232 CD133 60fr vio bl, dk car & vio 1.00 .35

Bird Types of 1967-68

Birds: 5fr, Gray hornbill. 10fr, Woodland kingfisher. 15fr, Senegalese coucal. 20fr, Rose-ringed parakeets. 40fr, Red bishop.

Dated "1970"

1970-71 Photo. *Perf. 13*
233 A43 5fr multi ('71) .45 .25
234 A43 10fr multi ('71) .45 .25
235 A43 15fr multi ('71) .75 .25
236 A43 20fr multi ('71) 1.00 .30

Engr.

237 A33 40fr multi 3.25 1.00
Nos. 233-237 (5) 5.90 2.05

Issue dates: 40fr, Dec. 9; others Jan. 4.

World Map with Niamey in Center — A51

1971, Mar. 3 Photo. *Perf. 12½x12*
238 A51 40fr brn & multi .90 .40

First anniversary of founding of the cooperative agency of French-speaking countries.

For overprint see No. 289.

Scout Emblem, Merit Badges, Mt. Fuji, Japanese Flag — A52

Designs: 40fr, Boy Scouts and flags, vert. 45fr, Map of Japan, Boy Scouts and compass rose, vert. 50fr, Tent and "Jamboree."

1971, July 5 Engr. *Perf. 13*

239 A52 35fr rose lil, dp car & org .55 .25
240 A52 40fr dk pur, grn & mar .60 .25
241 A52 45fr ultra, cop red & grn .80 .30
242 A52 50fr multi .90 .35
Nos. 239-242 (4) 2.85 1.15

13th Boy Scout World Jamboree, Asagiri Plain, Japan, Aug. 2-10.

Maps of Europe and Africa — A53

1971, July 29 Photo. *Perf. 13x12*

243 A53 50fr lt bl & multi .90 .40

Renewal of the agreement on economic association between Europe and Africa, 2nd anniv.

Broad-tailed Whydah — A54

1971, Aug. 17 *Perf. 12½x12*

244 A54 35fr yel grn & multi 4.00 1.25

See No. 443.

Garaya, Haoussa — A55

Stringed Instruments of Niger: 25fr, Gouroumi, Haoussa. 30fr, Molo, Djerma. 40fr, Godjie, Djerma-Sonrai. 45fr, Inzad, Tuareg. 50fr, Kountigui, Sonrai.

1971-72 Engr. *Perf. 13*

245 A55 25fr red, emer & brn .50 .25
246 A55 30fr emer, pur & brn .55 .25
247 A55 35fr brn red, emer & ind .60 .40
248 A55 40fr emer, org & dk brn .70 .45
249 A55 45fr Prus bl, grn & bis .95 .50
250 A55 50fr blk, red & brn 1.25 .60
Nos. 245-250 (6) 4.55 2.45

Issued: 35, 40, 45fr, 10/13/71; others, 6/16/72.

UNICEF Emblem, Children of 4 Races — A56

1971, Dec. 11 Photo. *Perf. 11*

251 A56 50fr multi .80 .50

25th anniversary of UNICEF.

Star with Globe, Book, UNESCO Emblem — A57

Design: 40fr, Boy reading, UNESCO emblem, sailing ship, plane, mosque.

1972, Mar. 27 Engr. *Perf. 13*

252 A57 35fr mag & emer .25 .25
253 A57 40fr dk car & Prus bl .75 .30

International Book Year 1972.

Cattle Egret — A58

1972, July 31 Photo. *Perf. 12½x12*

254 A58 50fr tan & multi 5.25 2.75

See No. 425.

Cattle at Salt Pond of In-Gall — A59

40fr, Cattle wading in pond.

1972, Aug. 25 *Perf. 13*

255 A59 35fr shown .85 .40
256 A59 40fr multicolored 1.25 .45

Salt cure for cattle.
For surcharge see No. 282.

Lottery Drum — A60

1972, Sept. 18

257 A60 35fr multi .80 .40

6th anniversary of the national lottery.

West African Monetary Union Issue
Common Design Type

Design: 40fr, African couple, city, village and commemorative coin.

1972, Nov. 2 Engr. *Perf. 13*

258 CD136 40fr brn, lil & gray .65 .30

Dromedary Race — A61

Design: 40fr, Horse race.

1972, Dec. 15 Engr. *Perf. 13*

259 A61 35fr brt bl, dk red & brn .90 .50
260 A61 40fr sl grn, mar & brn 1.25 .70

Pole Vault, Map of Africa — A62

Map of Africa and: 40fr, Basketball. 45fr, Boxing. 75fr, Soccer.

1973, Jan. 15 Engr. *Perf. 13*

261 A62 35fr claret & multi .40 .25
262 A62 40fr grn & multi .45 .25
263 A62 45fr red & multi .55 .30
264 A62 75fr dk bl & multi .90 .40
Nos. 261-264 (4) 2.30 1.20

2nd African Games, Lagos, Nigeria, 1/7-18.

Knight, Pawn, Chessboard — A63

1973, Feb. 16 Engr. *Perf. 13*

265 A63 100fr dl red, sl grn & bl 4.00 1.25

World Chess Championship, Reykjavik, Iceland, July-Sept. 1972.

Abutilon Pannosum — A64

Rare African Flowers: 45fr, Crotalaria barkae. 60fr, Dichrostachys cinerea. 80fr, Caralluma decaisneana.

1973, Feb. 26 Photo. *Perf. 12x12½*

266 A64 30fr dk vio & multi .75 .40
267 A64 45fr red & multi .90 .40
268 A64 60fr ultra & multi 1.25 .50
269 A64 80fr ocher & multi 1.75 .65
Nos. 266-269 (4) 4.65 1.95

Interpol Emblem — A65

1973, Mar. 13 Typo. *Perf. 13x12½*

270 A65 50fr brt grn & multi .90 .40

50th anniversary of International Criminal Police Organization (INTERPOL).

Dr. Hansen, Microscope and Petri Dish — A66

1973, Mar. 29 Engr. *Perf. 13*

271 A66 50fr vio bl, sl grn & dk brn 1.25 .50

Centenary of the discovery by Dr. Armauer G. Hansen of the Hansen bacillus, the cause of leprosy.

Nurse Treating Infant, UN and Red Cross Emblems — A67

1973, Apr. 3 Engr. *Perf. 13*

272 A67 50fr red, bl & brn .80 .30

25th anniversary of WHO.

Crocodile — A68

Animals from W National Park: 35fr, Elephant. 40fr, Hippopotamus. 80fr, Wart hog.

1973, June 5 Typo. *Perf. 12½x13*

273 A68 25fr gray & blk .90 .25
274 A68 35fr blk, gold & gray 1.25 .30
275 A68 40fr red, lt bl & blk 1.25 .35
276 A68 80fr multi 2.50 .50
Nos. 273-276 (4) 5.90 1.40

Eclipse over Mountains — A69

1973, June 21 Engr. *Perf. 13*

277 A69 40fr dk vio bl .75 .40

Solar eclipse, June 30, 1973.

Palominos A70

Horses: 75fr, French trotters. 80fr, English thoroughbreds. 100fr, Arabian thoroughbreds.

1973, Aug. 1 Photo. *Perf. 13x12½*

278 A70 50fr ultra & multi 1.00 .45
279 A70 75fr gray & multi 1.40 .55
280 A70 80fr emer & multi 1.75 .70
281 A70 100fr ocher & multi 2.25 .90
Nos. 278-281 (4) 6.40 2.60

No. 255 Srchd. and Ovptd. in Ultramarine

1973, Aug. 16 *Perf. 13*

282 A59 100fr on 35fr multi 1.75 1.10

African solidarity in drought emergency.

Diesel Engine and Rudolf Diesel — A71

Designs: Various Diesel locomotives.

1973, Sept. 7 *Perf. 13x12½*

283 A71 25fr gray, choc & Prus bl .75 .25
284 A71 50fr sl bl, gray & dk grn 1.40 .45
285 A71 75fr red lil, sl bl & gray 1.75 .65
286 A71 125fr brt grn, vio bl & car 3.00 1.20
Nos. 283-286 (4) 6.90 2.55

Rudolf Diesel (1858-1913), inventor of an internal combustion engine, later called Diesel engine.

African Postal Union Issue
Common Design Type

1973, Sept. 12 Engr. *Perf. 13*

287 CD137 100fr ol, dk car & sl grn .90 .60

TV Set, Map of Niger, Children — A72

1973, Oct. 1 Engr. *Perf. 13*

288 A72 50fr car, ultra & brn .90 .40

Educational television.

Type of 1971 Overprinted

1973, Oct. 12 Photo. *Perf. 13*

289 A51 40fr red & multi .90 .30

3rd Conference of French-speaking countries, Liège, Sept. 15-Oct. 14.

Apollo of Belvedère — A73

Classic Sculpture: No. 291, Venus of Milo. No. 292, Hercules. No. 293, Atlas.

1973, Oct. 15 **Engr.**

290 A73 50fr brn & sl grn 1.25 .50
291 A73 50fr rose car & pur 1.25 .50
292 A73 50fr red brn & dk brn 1.25 .50
293 A73 50fr red brn & blk 1.25 .50
Nos. 290-293 (4) 5.00 2.00

Beehive, Bees and Globes — A74

1973, Oct. 31 **Engr.** ***Perf. 13***

294 A74 40fr dl red, ocher & dl bl .75 .30

World Savings Day.

Tcherka Songhai Blanket A75

Design: 35fr, Kounta Songhai blanket, vert.

Perf. 12½x13, 13x12½

1973, Dec. 17 **Photo.**

295 A75 35fr brn & multi .80 .40
296 A75 40fr brn & multi .80 .45

Textiles of Niger.

WPY Emblem, Infant and Globe — A76

1974, Mar. 4 **Engr.** ***Perf. 13***

297 A76 50fr multi .70 .35

World Population Year 1974.

Locomotives, 1938 and 1948 — A77

75fr, Locomotive, 1893. 100fr, Locomotives, 1866 and 1939. 150fr, Locomotives, 1829.

1974, May 24 **Engr.** ***Perf. 13***

298 A77 50fr shown .95 .40
299 A77 75fr multicolored 1.50 .55
300 A77 100fr multicolored 2.10 .85
301 A77 150fr multicolored 3.25 1.40
Nos. 298-301 (4) 7.80 3.20

Map and Flags of Members — A78

1974, May 29 **Photo.** ***Perf. 13x12½***

302 A78 40fr bl & multi .80 .40

15th anniversary of the Council of Accord.

Marconi Sending Radio Signals to Australia A79

1974, July 1 **Engr.** ***Perf. 13***

303 A79 50fr pur, bl & dk brn .80 .40

Centenary of the birth of Guglielmo Marconi (1874-1937), Italian inventor and physicist.

Hand Holding Sapling — A80

1974, Aug. 2 **Engr.** ***Perf. 13***

304 A80 35fr multi .75 .40

National Tree Week.

Camel Saddle — A81

Design: 50fr, 3 sculptured horses, horiz.

1974, Aug. 20 **Engr.** ***Perf. 13***

305 A81 40fr ol brn, bl & red .65 .30
306 A81 50fr ol brn, bl & red .80 .40

Chopin and Polish Eagle — A82

Design: No. 308, Ludwig van Beethoven and allegory of Ninth Symphony.

1974

307 A82 100fr multi 2.10 .80
308 A82 100fr multi 2.10 .80

125th anniversary of the death of Frederic Chopin (1810-1849), composer and 150th anniversary of Beethoven's Ninth Symphony, composed 1823.

Issue dates: #307, Sept. 4; #308, Sept. 19.

Don-Don Drum — A83

1974, Nov. 12 **Engr.** ***Perf. 13***

309 A83 60fr multi 1.25 .55

Tenere Tree, Compass Rose and Caravan A84

1974, Nov. 24 **Engr.** ***Perf. 13***

310 A84 50fr multi 2.50 1.25

Tenere tree, a landmark in Sahara Desert, first death anniversary.

Satellite over World Weather Map — A85

1975, Mar. 23 **Litho.** ***Perf. 13***

311 A85 40fr bl, blk & red .65 .30

World Meteorological Day, Mar. 23, 1975.

"City of Truro," English, 1903 — A86

Locomotives and Flags: 75fr, "5.003," Germany, 1937. 100fr, "The General," United States, 1863. 125fr, "Electric BB 15.000," France, 1971.

1975, Apr. 24 **Typo.** ***Perf. 13***

312 A86 50fr org & multi 1.40 .35
313 A86 75fr yel grn & multi 1.75 .50
314 A86 100fr lt bl & multi 2.40 .80
315 A86 125fr multi 3.00 1.00
Nos. 312-315 (4) 8.55 2.65

Bird Type of 1968 Dated "1975"

1975, Apr. **Photo.** ***Perf. 13***

316 A43 25fr ol & multi 2.00 .65

Zabira Leather Bag — A87

Handicrafts: 40fr, Damier tapestry. 45fr, Vase. 60fr, Gourd flask.

1975, May 28 **Litho.** ***Perf. 12½***

317 A87 35fr dp bl & multi .35 .25
318 A87 40fr dp grn & multi .50 .30
319 A87 45fr brn & multi .70 .40
320 A87 60fr dp org & multi 1.00 .45
Nos. 317-320 (4) 2.55 1.40

Mother and Child, IWY Emblem — A88

1975, June 9 **Engr.** ***Perf. 13***

321 A88 50fr claret, brn & bl .80 .40

International Women's Year 1975.

Dr. Schweitzer and Lambarene Hospital A89

1975, June 23 **Engr.** ***Perf. 13***

322 A89 100fr brn, grn & blk 1.75 .80

Dr. Albert Schweitzer (1875-1965), medical missionary.

Peugeot, 1892 — A90

Early Autos: 75fr, Daimler, 1895. 100fr, Fiat, 1899. 125fr, Cadillac, 1903.

1975, July 16 **Engr.** ***Perf. 13***

323 A90 50fr rose & vio bl 1.05 .40
324 A90 75fr bl & vio brn 1.60 .50
325 A90 100fr brt grn & mag 2.25 .80
326 A90 125fr brick red & brt grn 2.75 .90
Nos. 323-326 (4) 7.65 2.60

Sun, Tree and Earth — A91

1975, Aug. 2 **Engr.** ***Perf. 13***

327 A91 40fr multi .80 .40

National Tree Week.

Boxing — A92

Designs: 35fr, Boxing, horiz. 45fr, Wrestling, horiz. 50fr, Wrestling.

1975, Aug. 25 **Engr.** ***Perf. 13***

328 A92 35fr blk, org & brn .45 .25
329 A92 40fr bl grn, brn & blk .50 .30
330 A92 45fr blk, brt bl & brn .75 .40
331 A92 50fr red, brn & blk .80 .45
Nos. 328-331 (4) 2.50 1.40

Lion's Head Tetradrachm, Leontini, 460 B.C. — A93

Greek Coins: 75fr, Owl tetradrachm, Athens, 500 B.C. 100fr, Crab didrachm, Himera, 480 B.C. 125fr, Minotaur tetradrachm, Gela, 460 B.C.

1975, Sept. 12 **Engr.** ***Perf. 13***

332 A93 50fr red, dl bl & blk 1.00 .30
333 A93 75fr lil, brt bl & blk 1.40 .40
334 A93 100fr bl, org & blk 1.75 .60
335 A93 125fr grn, pur & blk 2.50 .80
Nos. 332-335 (4) 6.65 2.10

Starving Family — A94

45fr, Animal skeletons. 60fr, Truck bringing food.

1975, Oct. 21 **Engr.** ***Perf. 13x12½***

336 A94 40fr multi .80 .35
337 A94 45fr ultra & brn .80 .35
338 A94 60fr grn, org & dk bl .85 .45
Nos. 336-338 (3) 2.45 1.15

Fight against drought.

Niger River Crossing A95

Designs: 45fr, Entrance to Boubon camp. 50fr, Camp building.

1975, Nov. 10 **Litho.** ***Perf. 12½***

339 A95 40fr multi .70 .30
340 A95 45fr multi .75 .30
341 A95 50fr multi .80 .40
Nos. 339-341 (3) 2.25 1.00

Tourist publicity.

Teacher and Pupils — A96

Each stamp has different inscription in center.

1976, Jan. 12 Photo. *Perf. 13*

342 A96 25fr ol & multi .25 .25
343 A96 30fr vio bl & multi .25 .25
344 A96 40fr multi .25 .25
345 A96 50fr multi .40 .25
346 A96 60fr multi .50 .25
Nos. 342-346 (5) 1.65 1.25

Literacy campaign 1976.
For overprints see Nos. 371-375.

12th Winter Olympic Games, Innsbruck A97

1976, Feb. 20 Litho. *Perf. 14x13½*

347 A97 40fr Ice hockey .40 .25
348 A97 50fr Luge .55 .30
349 A97 150fr Ski jump 1.35 .65
Nos. 347-349,C266-C267 (5) 6.30 3.20

Satellite, Telephone, ITU Emblem — A98

1976, Mar. 10 Litho. *Perf. 13*

350 A98 100fr org, bl & vio bl 1.25 .65

Centenary of first telephone call by Alexander Graham Bell, Mar. 10, 1876.

WHO Emblem, Red Cross Truck, Infant — A99

1976, Apr. 7 Engr. *Perf. 13*

351 A99 50fr multi .75 .30

World Health Day 1976.

Statue of Liberty and Washington Crossing the Delaware A100

50fr, Statue of Liberty and call to arms.

1976, Apr. 8 Litho. *Perf. 14x13½*

352 A100 40fr multi .30 .25
353 A100 50fr multi .40 .25
Nos. 352-353,C269-C271 (5) 6.05 2.45

American Bicentennial.

The Army Helping in Development — A101

Design: 50fr, Food distribution, vert.

Perf. 12½x13, 13x12½

1976, Apr. 15 Litho.

354 A101 50fr multi .45 .25
355 A101 100fr multi .90 .45

National Armed Forces, 2nd anniv. of take-over.

Europafrica Issue

Maps, Concorde, Ship and Grain — A102

1976, June 9 Litho. *Perf. 13*

356 A102 100fr multi 1.25 .55

Road Building — A103

Design: 30fr, Rice cultivation.

1976, June 26 *Perf. 12½*

357 A103 25fr multi .25 .25
358 A103 30fr multi .40 .25

Community labor.

Motobecane 125, France A104

Motorcycles: 75fr, Norton Challenge, England. 100fr, BMW 90 S, Germany. 125fr, Kawasaki 1000, Japan.

1976, July 16 Engr. *Perf. 13*

359 A104 50fr vio bl & multi .70 .30
360 A104 75fr dp grn & multi 1.00 .40
361 A104 100fr dk brn & multi 1.50 .70
362 A104 125fr slate & multi 1.75 .90
Nos. 359-362 (4) 4.95 2.30

Boxing — A105

Designs: 50fr, Basketball. 60fr, Soccer. 80fr, Cycling, horiz. 100fr, Judo, horiz.

1976, July 17 Litho. *Perf. 14*

363 A105 40fr multi .50 .30
364 A105 50fr multi .60 .30
365 A105 60fr multi .70 .30
366 A105 80fr multi .80 .30
367 A105 100fr multi 1.10 .35
Nos. 363-367 (5) 3.70 1.55

21st Summer Olympic games, Montreal. See No. C279.

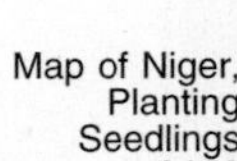

Map of Niger, Planting Seedlings A106

Designs: 50fr, Woman watering seedling, vert. 60fr, Women planting seedlings, vert.

1976, Aug. 1 Litho. *Perf. 12½x13*

368 A106 40fr org & multi .45 .25
369 A106 50fr yel & multi .55 .30
370 A106 60fr grn & multi .70 .40
Nos. 368-370 (3) 1.70 .95

Reclamation of Sahel Region.

Nos. 342-346 Overprinted: "JOURNEE / INTERNATIONALE / DE L'ALPHABETISATION"

1976, Sept. 8 Photo. *Perf. 13*

371 A96 25fr ol & multi .25 .25
372 A96 30fr vio bl & multi .25 .25
373 A96 40fr multi .35 .25
374 A96 50fr multi .45 .25
375 A96 60fr multi .45 .30
Nos. 371-375 (5) 1.75 1.30

Literacy campaign.

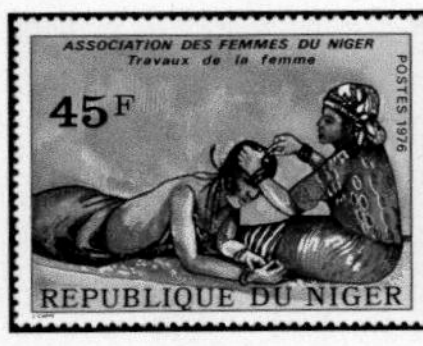
Hairdresser A107

Designs: 40fr, Woman weaving straw, vert. 50fr, Women potters, vert.

1976, Oct. 6 *Perf. 13*

376 A107 40fr buff & multi .45 .25
377 A107 45fr bl & multi .50 .25
378 A107 50fr red & multi .70 .30
Nos. 376-378 (3) 1.65 .80

Niger Women's Association.

Rock Carvings — A108

Archaeology: 50fr, Neolithic sculptures. 60fr, Dinosaur skeleton.

1976, Nov. 15 Photo. *Perf. 13x12½*

379 A108 40fr blk, sl & yel 2.50 .55
380 A108 50fr blk, red & bis 2.75 .55
381 A108 60fr buff, blk & org brn 5.50 .80
Nos. 379-381 (3) 10.75 1.90

Benin Head — A109

Weaver, Dancers and Musicians A110

1977, Jan. 15 Engr. *Perf. 13*

382 A109 40fr dk brn .45 .25
383 A110 50fr gray bl 1.00 .40

2nd World Black and African Festival, Lagos, Nigeria, Jan. 15-Feb. 12.

First Aid, Student, Blackboard and Plow — A111

Designs: Inscriptions on blackboard differ on each denomination.

1977, Jan. 23 Photo. *Perf. 12½x13*

384 A111 40fr multi .40 .25
385 A111 50fr multi .50 .30
386 A111 60fr multi .70 .40
Nos. 384-386 (3) 1.60 .95

Literacy campaign.

Midwife — A112

Design: 50fr, Midwife examining newborn.

1977, Feb. 23 Litho. *Perf. 13*

387 A112 40fr multi .45 .25
388 A112 50fr multi .75 .35

Village health service.

Titan Rocket Launch — A113

80fr, Viking orbiter near Mars, horiz.

1977, Mar. 15 Litho. *Perf. 14*

389 A113 50fr multi .45 .25
390 A113 80fr multi .75 .30
Nos. 389-390,C283-C285 (5) 4.70 1.85

Viking Mars project.
For overprints see #497-498, C295-C297.

Marabous A114

Design: 90fr, Harnessed antelopes.

1977, Mar. 18 Engr. *Perf. 13*

391 A114 80fr multi 2.00 1.00
392 A114 90fr multi 2.25 1.00

Nature protection.

Weather Map, Satellite, WMO Emblem — A115

1977, Mar. 23

393 A115 100fr multi 1.25 .65

World Meteorological Day.

Group Gymnastics A116

50fr, High jump. 80fr, Folk singers.

1977, Apr. 7 Litho. *Perf. 13x12½*

394 A116 40fr dl yel & multi .45 .25
395 A116 50fr bl & multi .60 .30
396 A116 80fr org & multi .75 .35
Nos. 394-396 (3) 1.80 .90

2nd Tahoua Youth Festival, Apr. 7-14.

Red Cross, WHO Emblems and Children A117

1977, Apr. 25 Engr. ***Perf. 13***
397 A117 80fr lil, org & red .85 .40

World Health Day: "Immunization means protection of your children."

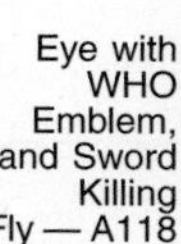

Eye with WHO Emblem, and Sword Killing Fly — A118

1977, May 7
398 A118 100fr ver, lt bl & bluish blk 1.25 .65

Fight against onchocerciasis, a roundworm infection, transmitted by flies, causing blindness.

Guirka Tahoua Dance — A119

50fr, Mailfilafili Gaya. 80fr, Naguihinayan Loga.

1977, June 7 Photo. ***Perf. 13x12½***
399 A119 40fr multi .55 .30
400 A119 50fr multi .75 .40
401 A119 80fr multi 1.10 .55
Nos. 399-401 (3) 2.40 1.25

Popular arts and traditions.

Cavalry A120

Traditional chief's cavalry, different groups.

1977, July 7 Litho. ***Perf. 13x12½***
402 A120 40fr multi .70 .40
403 A120 50fr multi .80 .45
404 A120 60fr multi 1.20 .60
Nos. 402-404 (3) 2.70 1.45

Planting and Cultivating A121

1977, Aug. 10
405 A121 40fr multi .65 .30

Reclamation of Sahel Region.

Albert John Luthuli Peace A122

Designs: 80fr, Maurice Maeterlinck, literature. 100fr, Allan L. Hodgkin, medicine. 150fr, Albert Camus, literature. 200fr, Paul Ehrlich, medicine.

1977, Aug. 20 Litho. ***Perf. 14***
406 A122 50fr multi .40 .25
407 A122 80fr multi .50 .25
408 A122 100fr multi .75 .25
409 A122 150fr multi 1.25 .40
410 A122 200fr multi 1.60 .55
Nos. 406-410 (5) 4.50 1.70

Nobel prize winners. See No. C287.

Mao Tse-tung — A123

1977, Sept. 9 Engr. ***Perf. 13***
411 A123 100fr blk & red 3.75 1.75

Argentina '78 Emblem, Soccer Players and Coach, Vittorio Pozzo, Italy — A124

Designs (Argentina '78 emblem, soccer players and coach): 50fr, Vincente Feola, Spain. 80fr, Aymore Moreira, Portugal. 100fr, Sir Alf Ramsey, England. 200fr, Helmut Schoen, Germany. 500fr, Sepp Herberger, Germany.

1977, Oct. 12 Litho. ***Perf. 13½***
412 A124 40fr multi .40 .25
413 A124 50fr multi .50 .25
414 A124 80fr multi .65 .25
415 A124 100fr multi 1.10 .35
416 A124 200fr multi 1.75 .65
Nos. 412-416 (5) 4.40 1.75

Souvenir Sheet

417 A124 500fr multi 4.25 1.75

World Cup Soccer championship, Argentina '78.
For overprints see Nos. 453-458.

Horse's Head, Parthenon and UNESCO Emblem A125

1977, Nov. 12 Engr. ***Perf. 13***
418 A125 100fr multi 1.75 .80

Woman Carrying Water Pots — A126

Design: 50fr, Women pounding corn.

1977, Nov. 23 Photo. ***Perf. 12½x13***
419 A126 40fr multi .50 .25
420 A126 50fr red & multi .65 .30

Niger Women's Association.

Crocodile's Skull, 100 Million Years Old — A127

Design: 80fr, Neolithic flint tools.

1977, Dec. 14 ***Perf. 13***
421 A127 50fr multi 1.50 .65
422 A127 80fr multi 2.00 .90

Raoul Follereau and Lepers — A128

40fr, Raoul Follereau and woman leper, vert.

1978, Jan. 28 Engr. ***Perf. 13***
423 A128 40fr multi .45 .25
424 A128 50fr multi .65 .40

25th anniversary of Leprosy Day. Follereau (1903-1977) was "Apostle to the Lepers" and educator of the blind.

Bird Type of 1972 Redrawn

1978, Feb. Photo. ***Perf. 13***
425 A58 50fr tan & multi 2.50 1.00

No. 425 is dated "1978" and has only designer's name in imprint. No. 254 has printer's name also.

Assumption, by Rubens — A129

Rubens Paintings: 70fr, Rubens and Friends, horiz. 100fr, History of Marie de Medici. 150fr, Alathea Talbot and Family. 200fr, Marquise de Spinola. 500fr, Virgin and St. Ildefonso.

1978, Feb. 25 Litho. ***Perf. 14***
426 A129 50fr multi .40 .25
427 A129 70fr multi .45 .25
428 A129 100fr multi .85 .30
429 A129 150fr multi 1.25 .40
430 A129 200fr multi 1.80 .50
Nos. 426-430 (5) 4.75 1.70

Souvenir Sheet
Perf. 13½

431 A129 500fr gold & multi 5.00 1.60

Peter Paul Rubens (1577-1640), 400th birth anniversary.

Shot Put — A130

1978, Mar. 22 Photo. ***Perf. 13***
432 A130 40fr shown .30 .25
433 A130 50fr Volleyball .40 .25
434 A130 60fr Long jump .45 .30
435 A130 100fr Javelin .80 .40
Nos. 432-435 (4) 1.95 1.20

Natl. University Games' Championships.

First Aid and Red Crosses — A131

1978, May 13 **Litho.**
436 A131 40fr red & multi .40 .25

Niger Red Cross.

Goudel Earth Station — A132

1978, May 23
437 A132 100fr multi .85 .40

Soccer Ball, Flags of Participants A133

Argentina '78 Emblem and: 50fr, Ball in net. 100fr, Globe with South America, Soccer field. 200fr, Two players, horiz. 300fr, Player and globe.

1978, June 18 Litho. ***Perf. 13½***
438 A133 40fr multi .30 .25
439 A133 50fr multi .50 .25
440 A133 100fr multi .75 .35
441 A133 200fr multi 1.50 .70
Nos. 438-441 (4) 3.05 1.55

Souvenir Sheet

442 A133 300fr multi 2.50 1.25

11th World Cup Soccer Championship, Argentina, June 1-25.

Bird Type of 1971 Redrawn

1978, June Photo. ***Perf. 13***
443 A54 35fr bl & multi 3.25 .90

No. 443 has no year date, nor Delrieu imprint.

Post Office, Niamey A134

Design: 60fr, Post Office, different view.

1978, Aug. 12 **Litho.**
444 A134 40fr multi .40 .25
445 A134 60fr multi .60 .30

Goudel Water Works — A135

1978, Sept. 25 Photo. ***Perf. 13***
446 A135 100fr multi 1.00 .55

Giraffe — A136

Animals and Wildlife Fund Emblem: 50fr, Ostrich. 70fr, Cheetah. 150fr, Oryx, horiz. 200fr, Addax, horiz. 300fr, Hartebeest, horiz.

1978, Nov. 20 Litho. ***Perf. 15***
447 A136 40fr multi *1.10* .50
448 A136 50fr multi *2.00* .60
449 A136 70fr multi *2.75* .80
450 A136 150fr multi *5.75* 1.40
451 A136 200fr multi *9.00* 2.00
452 A136 300fr multi *12.00* 2.75
Nos. 447-452 (6) *32.60* 8.05

Endangered species.

Nos. 412-417 Overprinted in Silver

a

b

c

d

e

1978, Dec. 1 *Perf. 13½*

453	A124(a)	40fr multi	.40	.25
454	A124(b)	50fr multi	.55	.25
455	A124(c)	80fr multi	.85	.30
456	A124(d)	100fr multi	1.00	.40
457	A124(e)	200fr multi	2.10	1.00
		Nos. 453-457 (5)	4.90	2.20

Souvenir Sheet

458	A124(e)	500fr multi	4.50	1.75

Winners, World Soccer Cup Championship, Argentina, June 1-25.

Tinguizi — A137

Musicians: No. 460, Dan Gourmou. No. 461, Chetima Ganga, horiz.

1978, Dec. 11 **Litho.** *Perf. 13*

459	A137	100fr multi	1.10	.55
460	A137	100fr multi	1.10	.55
461	A137	100fr multi	1.10	.55
		Nos. 459-461 (3)	3.30	1.65

Virgin Mary, by Dürer — A138

50fr, The Homecoming, by Honoré Daumier (1808-79). 150fr, 200fr, 500fr, Virgin and Child, by Albrecht Dürer (1471-1528), diff.

1979, Jan. 31 **Litho.** *Perf. 13½*

462	A138	50fr multi	.70	.25
463	A138	100fr multi	.75	.30
464	A138	150fr multi	1.25	.40
465	A138	200fr multi	1.75	.60
		Nos. 462-465 (4)	4.45	1.55

Souvenir Sheet

466	A138	500fr multi	4.75	1.60

Solar Panels and Tank A139

Design: 40fr, Tank and panels on roof, vert.

1979, Feb. 28 *Perf. 12½x12, 12x12½*

467	A139	40fr multi	.45	.25
468	A139	50fr multi	.55	.30

Hot water from solar heat.

Children with Building Blocks A140

Children and IYC Emblem: 100fr, Reading books. 150fr, With model plane.

1979, Apr. 10 **Litho.** *Perf. 13½*

469	A140	40fr multi	.40	.25
470	A140	100fr multi	.80	.30
471	A140	150fr multi	1.60	.50
		Nos. 469-471 (3)	2.80	1.05

International Year of the Child.

The Langa, Traditional Sport — A141

Design: 50fr, The langa, diff.

1979, Apr. 10 **Litho.** *Perf. 12½x12*

472	A141	40fr multi	.45	.25
473	A141	50fr multi	.55	.30

Rowland Hill, Mail Truck and France No. 8 — A142

Designs (Hill and): 100fr, Canoes and Austria #P4. 150fr, Air Niger plane and US #122. 200fr, Streamlined mail train and Canada type A6. 400fr, Electric train and Niger #51.

1979, June 6 **Litho.** *Perf. 14*

474	A142	40fr multi	.50	.25
475	A142	100fr multi	1.00	.30
476	A142	150fr multi	1.50	.40
477	A142	200fr multi	1.80	.55
		Nos. 474-477 (4)	4.80	1.50

Souvenir Sheet

478	A142	400fr multi	4.00	1.50

Sir Rowland Hill (1795-1879), originator of penny postage.

Zabira Handbag and Niger No. 135 — A143

Design: 150fr, Heads with communications waves, world map, UPU emblem and satellite.

1979, June 8 **Litho.** *Perf. 12x12½*

479	A143	50fr multi	1.25	.60

Engr. *Perf. 13*

480	A143	150fr brt red & ultra	3.25	1.60

Philexafrique II, Libreville, Gabon, June 8-17. Nos. 479, 480 each printed in sheets of 10 and 5 labels showing exhibition emblem.

Djermakoye Palace A144

1979, Sept. 26 **Litho.** *Perf. 13x12½*

481	A144	100fr multi	.90	.50

Bororo Festive Headdress A145

60fr, Bororo women's traditional costumes.

Perf. 13x12½, 12½x13

1979, Sept. 26

482	A145	45fr multi	.45	.30
483	A145	60fr multi, vert.	.55	.35

Annual Bororo Festival.

Olympic Emblem, Flame and Boxers A146

Designs: 100fr, 150fr, 250fr, 500fr, Olympic emblem, flame and boxers, diff.

1979, Oct. 6 *Perf. 13½*

484	A146	45fr multi	.40	.25
485	A146	100fr multi	.85	.30
486	A146	150fr multi	1.30	.40
487	A146	250fr multi	2.25	.65
		Nos. 484-487 (4)	4.80	1.60

Souvenir Sheet

488	A146	500fr multi	4.00	1.75

Pre-Olympic Year.

John Alcock, Arthur Whitten Brown, Vickers-Vimy Biplane A147

1979, Sept. 3 *Perf. 13½*

489	A147	100fr multi	1.25	.50

First Transatlantic flight, 60th anniversary.

Road and Traffic Safety A148

1979, Nov. 20 **Litho.** *Perf. 12½*

490	A148	45fr multi	.45	.30

Four-Man Bobsledding, Lake Placid '80 Emblem A149

Lake Placid '80 Emblem and: 60fr, Downhill skiing. 100fr, Speed skating. 150fr, Two-man bobsledding. 200fr, Figure skating. 300fr, Cross-country skiing.

1979, Dec. 10 *Perf. 14½*

491	A149	40fr multi	.30	.25
492	A149	60fr multi	.45	.25
493	A149	100fr multi	.80	.30
494	A149	150fr multi	1.25	.45
495	A149	200fr multi	1.75	.75
		Nos. 491-495 (5)	4.55	2.00

Souvenir Sheet

496	A149	300fr multi	2.75	1.10

13th Winter Olympic Games, Lake Placid, NY, Feb. 12-24, 1980.

For overprints see Nos. 501-506.

Nos. 389, 390 Overprinted in Silver or Black

1979, Dec. 20 **Litho.** *Perf. 14*

497	A113	50fr multi (S)	.40	.25
498	A113	80fr multi	.70	.30
		Nos. 497-498,C295-C296 (4)	3.95	2.10

Apollo 11 moon landing, 10th anniv. See #C297.

Court of Sultan of Zinder A150

1980, Mar. 25 **Litho.** *Perf. 13x12½*

499	A150	45fr shown	.40	.25
500	A150	60fr Sultan's court, diff.	.50	.25

Nos. 491-496 Overprinted

(a)

(b)

(c)

(d)

(e)

(f)

1980, Mar. 31 Litho. *Perf. 14½*

501 A149 (a) 40fr multi .30 .25
502 A149 (b) 60fr multi .45 .25
503 A149 (c) 100fr multi .85 .40
504 A149 (d) 150fr multi 1.25 .50
505 A149 (e) 200fr multi 1.75 .70
Nos. 501-505 (5) 4.60 2.10

Souvenir Sheet

506 A149 (f) 300fr multi 2.50 1.50

Javelin, Olympic Rings — A151

90fr, Walking. 100fr, High jump, horiz. 300fr, Marathon runners, horiz.
500fr, High jump, horiz.

1980, Apr. 17

507 A151 60fr shown .55 .25
508 A151 90fr multi .85 .25
509 A151 100fr multi .95 .30
510 A151 300fr multi 2.50 .80
Nos. 507-510 (4) 4.85 1.60

Souvenir Sheet

511 A151 500fr multi 4.00 1.50

22nd Summer Olympic Games, Moscow, July 19-Aug. 3.
For overprints see Nos. 527-531.

Man Smoking Cigarette, Runner — A152

1980, Apr. 7 *Perf. 13*

512 A152 100fr multi 1.00 .50

World Health Day; fight against cigarette smoking.

Health Year — A153

1980, May 15 Photo. *Perf. 13x12½*

513 A153 150fr multi 1.25 .65

Shimbashi-Yokohama Locomotive — A154

60fr, American type. 90fr, German Reichsbahn series 61. 100fr, Prussian Staatsbahn P2. 130fr, L'Aigle.
425fr, Stephenson's Rocket.

1980, June Litho. *Perf. 12½*

514 A154 45fr shown .55 .30
515 A154 60fr multicolored .80 .35
516 A154 90fr multicolored 1.05 .50
517 A154 100fr multicolored 1.40 .65
518 A154 130fr multicolored 1.75 .85
Nos. 514-518 (5) 5.55 2.65

Souvenir Sheet

519 A154 425fr multicolored 7.50 2.25

For overprint see No. 674.

Steve Biko, 4th Anniversary of Death — A155

1980, Sept. 12 Litho. *Perf. 13*

520 A155 150fr org & blk 1.40 .70

Soccer Players A156

Designs: Various soccer scenes.

1980, Oct. 15 *Perf. 12½*

521 A156 45fr multi .30 .25
522 A156 60fr multi .40 .25
523 A156 90fr multi .70 .25
524 A156 100fr multi .80 .30
525 A156 130fr multi .90 .35
Nos. 521-525 (5) 3.10 1.40

Souvenir Sheet

526 A156 425fr multi 4.00 1.25

World Soccer Cup 1982.

Nos. 507-511 Overprinted in Gold with Winner's Name and Country

1980, Sept. 27 Litho. *Perf. 14½*

527 A151 60fr multi .45 .25
528 A151 90fr multi .70 .30
529 A151 100fr multi .80 .35
530 A151 300fr multi 2.40 1.10
Nos. 527-530 (4) 4.35 2.00

Souvenir Sheet

531 A151 500fr multi, horiz. 4.00 2.50

African Postal Union, 5th Anniversary — A157

1980, Dec. 24 Photo. *Perf. 13½*

532 A157 100fr multi .90 .50

Terra Cotta Kareygorou Head — A158

Designs: Terra Cotta Kareygorou Statues, 5th-12th cent. 45fr, 150fr, horiz.

1981, Jan. 23 Litho. *Perf. 13*

533 A158 45fr multi .35 .25
534 A158 60fr multi .55 .25
535 A158 90fr multi .70 .35
536 A158 150fr multi 1.30 .60
Nos. 533-536 (4) 2.90 1.45

Ostrich — A159

1981, Mar. 17 Litho. *Perf. 12½*

537 A159 10fr shown 1.20 .30
538 A159 20fr Oryx .45 .30
539 A159 25fr Gazelle .45 .30
540 A159 30fr Great bustard 2.00 .60
541 A159 60fr Giraffe .85 .40
542 A159 150fr Addax 2.00 .80
Nos. 537-542 (6) 6.95 2.70

7th Anniv. of the F.A.N. — A160

1981, Apr. 14 Litho. *Perf. 13*

543 A160 100fr multi .90 .45

One-armed Archer — A161

1981, Apr. 24 Engr.

544 A161 50fr shown .70 .30
545 A161 100fr Draftsman 1.25 .60

Intl. Year of the Disabled.

Scene from Mahalba Ballet, 1980 Youth Festival, Dosso — A162

1981, May 17 Litho.

546 A162 100fr shown .80 .40
547 A162 100fr Ballet, diff. .80 .40

Prince Charles and Lady Diana, Coach — A163

Designs: Couple and coaches.

1981, July 15 Litho. *Perf. 14½*

548 A163 150fr multi 1.10 .45
549 A163 200fr multi 1.40 .65
550 A163 300fr multi 2.00 .80
Nos. 548-550 (3) 4.50 1.90

Souvenir Sheet

551 A163 400fr multi 3.25 1.50

Royal wedding.
For overprints see Nos. 595-598.

Hegira 1500th Anniv. — A164

1981, July 15 *Perf. 13½x13*

552 A164 100fr multi .90 .45

Alexander Fleming (1881-1955) — A165

1981, Aug. 6 Engr. *Perf. 13*

553 A165 150fr multi 2.10 .95

25th Intl. Letter Writing Week, Oct. 6-12 A167

1981, Oct. 9 Surcharged in Black

554 A167 65fr on 40fr multi .55 .30
555 A167 85fr on 60fr multi .75 .50

Nos. 554-555 not issued without surcharge.

World Food Day — A168

1981, Oct. 16 Litho.

556 A168 100fr multi .90 .45

Espana '82 World Cup Soccer A169

Designs: Various soccer players.

1981, Nov. 18 Litho. *Perf. 14x13½*

557 A169 40fr multi .30 .25
558 A169 65fr multi .50 .25
559 A169 85fr multi .60 .25
560 A169 150fr multi 1.10 .45
561 A169 300fr multi 2.00 .90
Nos. 557-561 (5) 4.50 2.10

Souvenir Sheet

562 A169 500fr multi 4.00 1.75

For overprints see Nos. 603-608.

75th Anniv. of Grand Prix — A170

Designs: Winners and their cars — 20fr, Peugeot, 1912. 40fr, Bugatti, 1924. 65fr, Lotus-Climax, 1962. 85fr, Georges Boillot, 1912. 150fr, Phil Hill, 1960.
450fr, Race.

1981, Nov. 30 *Perf. 14*

563 A170 20fr multicolored .40 .25
564 A170 40fr multicolored .55 .25
565 A170 65fr multicolored .80 .25
566 A170 85fr multicolored 1.00 .50
567 A170 150fr multicolored 1.60 .80
Nos. 563-567 (5) 4.35 2.05

Souvenir Sheet

568 A170 450fr multicolored 5.25 1.75

For overprint see No. 675.

Christmas 1981 — A171

Designs: Virgin and Child paintings.

1981, Dec. 24

569 A171 100fr Botticelli .80 .35
570 A171 200fr Botticini 1.40 .75
571 A171 300fr Botticelli, diff. 2.40 1.00
Nos. 569-571 (3) 4.60 2.10

School Gardens — A172

1982, Feb. 19 Litho. *Perf. 13x13½*

572 A172 65fr shown .55 .30
573 A172 85fr Garden, diff. .70 .45

L'Estaque, by Georges Braque (1882-1963) A173

Anniversaries: 120fr, Arturo Toscanini (1867-1957), vert. 140fr, Fruit on a Table, by Edouard Manet (1832-1883). 300fr, George Washington (1732-99), vert. 400fr, Goethe (1749-1832), vert. Nos. 579-580, 21st birthday of Diana, Princess of Wales (portraits), vert.

1982, Mar. 8 Litho. ***Perf. 13***

574 A173 120fr multi 1.15 .45
575 A173 140fr multi 1.60 .50
576 A173 200fr multi 2.75 .75
577 A173 300fr multi 3.25 1.15
578 A173 400fr multi 4.00 1.50
579 A173 500fr multi 5.00 2.00
Nos. 574-579 (6) 17.75 6.35

Souvenir Sheet

580 A173 500fr multi 4.00 1.75

Palace of Congress A174

1982, Mar. 17

581 A174 150fr multi 1.25 .70

7th Youth Festival, Agadez — A175

65fr, Martial arts, horiz. 100fr, Wrestling.

1982, Apr. 7 ***Perf. 12½***

582 A175 65fr multicolored .50 .30
583 A175 100fr multicolored .90 .50

Reafforestation Campaign — A176

1982, Apr. 16 ***Perf. 13***

584 A176 150fr Tree planting 1.20 .50
585 A176 200fr Trees, Desert 1.60 .80

For overprints see Nos. 668-669.

Scouting Year — A177

65fr, Canoeing, two boys sitting. 85fr, Scouts in rubber boat. 130fr, Canoeing, two boys standing. 200fr, Rafting.
400fr, Beach scene.

1982, May 13

586 A177 65fr multi .60 .25
587 A177 85fr multi .85 .30
588 A177 130fr multi 1.25 .45
589 A177 200fr multi 1.75 .75
Nos. 586-589 (4) 4.45 1.75

Souvenir Sheet

590 A177 400fr multi 3.25 1.75

For overprint see No. 673.

A178

1982, June 6

591 A178 100fr multi .90 .45

13th Meeting of Islamic Countries Foreign Affairs Ministers, Niamey, Aug. 20-27.

West African Economic Community — A179

1982, June 28

592 A179 200fr Map 1.40 .85

Fishermen in Canoe — A180

1982, July 18 ***Perf. 13x12½***

593 A180 65fr shown .60 .35
594 A180 85fr Bringing in nets .80 .40

Nos. 548-551 Overprinted in Blue: "NAISSANCE ROYALE 1982"

1982, Aug. 4 ***Perf. 14½***

595 A163 150fr multi .95 .50
596 A163 200fr multi 1.20 .70
597 A163 300fr multi 2.10 1.00
Nos. 595-597 (3) 4.25 2.20

Souvenir Sheet

598 A163 400fr multi 2.75 1.50

Flautist, by Norman Rockwell — A181

85fr, Clerk. 110fr, Teacher and Pupil. 150fr, Girl Shopper.

1982, Sept. 10 Litho. ***Perf. 14***

599 A181 65fr shown .50 .30
600 A181 85fr multi .70 .30
601 A181 110fr multi .90 .40
602 A181 150fr multi 1.25 .55
Nos. 599-602 (4) 3.35 1.55

Nos. 557-562 Overprinted with Past and Present Winners in Black on Silver

1982, Sept. 28 ***Perf. 14x13½***

603 A169 40fr multi .30 .25
604 A169 65fr multi .45 .25
605 A169 85fr multi .55 .30
606 A169 150fr multi 1.20 .45
607 A169 300fr multi 2.25 1.10
Nos. 603-607 (5) 4.75 2.35

Souvenir Sheet

608 A169 500fr multi 4.00 2.75

Italy's victory in 1982 World Cup.

ITU Plenipotentiaries Conference, Nairobi, Sept. — A182

1982, Sept. 28 ***Perf. 13***

609 A182 130fr black & blue 1.00 .50

Laboratory Workers — A183

Various laboratory workers.

1982, Nov. 9 Litho. ***Perf. 13***

610 A183 65fr multi .65 .35
611 A183 115fr multi .90 .55

Self-sufficiency in Food Production — A184

1983, Feb. 16 Litho. ***Perf. 13½x13***

612 A184 65fr Rice harvest .70 .35
613 A184 85fr Planting rice, vert. .95 .45

Grand Ducal Madonna, by Raphael — A185

Raphael Paintings: 65fr, Miraculous Catch of Fishes. 100fr, Deliverance of St. Peter. 150fr, Sistine Madonna. 200fr, Christ on the Way to Calvary. 300fr, Deposition. 400fr, Transfiguration. 500fr, St. Michael Slaying the Dragon.

1983, Mar. 30 Litho. ***Perf. 14***

614 A185 65fr multi, vert. .50 .25
615 A185 85fr multi .60 .25
616 A185 100fr multi, vert. .80 .25
617 A185 150fr multi 1.10 .40
618 A185 200fr multi 1.40 .55
619 A185 300fr multi, vert. 2.00 .80
620 A185 400fr multi 3.00 1.10
621 A185 500fr multi 4.00 1.25
Nos. 614-621 (8) 13.40 4.85

African Economic Commission, 25th Anniv. — A186

1983, Mar. 18 ***Perf. 12½x13***

622 A186 120fr multi .95 .45
623 A186 200fr multi 1.50 .85

Army Surveyors — A187

1983, Apr. 14 ***Perf. 13x12½***

624 A187 85fr shown .35 .40
625 A187 150fr Road building .65 .75

Agadez Court — A188

1983, Apr. 26 Litho. ***Perf. 13x12½***

626 A188 65fr multi .45 .25

Mail Van — A189

1983, June 25 **Litho.**

627 A189 65fr Van .45 .40
628 A189 100fr Van, map .80 .45

Palestine Solidarity — A190

1983, Aug. 21 Litho. ***Perf. 12½***

629 A190 65fr multi .65 .30

Intl. Literacy Year — A191

Various adult education classes. 65fr, 150fr vert.

Perf. 13½x14½, 14½x13½

1983, Sept. 8 **Litho.**

630 A191 40fr multi .35 .25
631 A191 65fr multi .45 .25
632 A191 85fr multi .60 .30
633 A191 100fr multi .75 .40
634 A191 150fr multi 1.25 .80
Nos. 630-634 (5) 3.40 2.00

7th Ballet Festival of Dosso Dept. — A192

Various dancers.

1983, Oct. 7 ***Perf. 14½x13½***

635 A192 65fr multi .50 .35
636 A192 85fr multi .70 .45
637 A192 120fr multi 1.10 .60
Nos. 635-637 (3) 2.30 1.40

World Communications Year — A193

80fr, Post Office, mail van. 120fr, Sorting mail. 150fr, Emblem, vert.

1983, Oct. 18 ***Perf. 13x12½, 12½x13***

638 A193 80fr multi .60 .45
639 A193 120fr multi .85 .50
640 A193 150fr multi 1.25 .60
Nos. 638-640 (3) 2.70 1.55

Solar Energy For Television — A194

1983, Nov. 26 ***Perf. 13***

641 A194 85fr Antenna .60 .40
642 A194 130fr Car 1.00 .45

Local Butterflies A195

75fr, Hypolimnas misippus. 120fr, Papilio demodocus. 250fr, Vanessa antiopa. 350fr, Charesex jasius. 500fr, Danaus chrisippus.

1983, Dec. 9 *Perf. 12½*

643	A195	75fr multicolored	.90	.40
644	A195	120fr multicolored	1.25	.50
645	A195	250fr multicolored	2.25	.90
646	A195	350fr multicolored	3.00	1.25
647	A195	500fr multicolored	4.75	1.60
		Nos. 643-647 (5)	12.15	4.65

SAMARIYA Natl. Development Movement — A196

1984, Jan. 18 **Litho.** *Perf. 13x13½*

648 A196 80fr multi .60 .40

Alestes Bouboni — A197

1984, Mar. 28 **Litho.** *Perf. 13*

649 A197 120fr multi 3.25 .80

Military Pentathlon — A198

1984, Apr. 10

650	A198	120fr Hurdles	.85	.45
651	A198	140fr Shooting	1.00	.65

Radio Broadcasting Building Opening — A199

1984, May 14 **Litho.** *Perf. 13*

652 A199 120fr multi .90 .45

25th Anniv. of Council of Unity — A200

1984, May 29 *Perf. 12½*

653	A200	65fr multi	.55	.35
654	A200	85fr multi	.75	.45

Renault, 1902 — A201

80fr, Paris. 100fr, Gottlieb Daimler. 120fr, Three-master Jacques Coeur. 150fr, Barque Bosphorus. 250fr, Delage D8. 300fr, Three-master Comet. 400fr, Maybach Zeppelin.

Vintage cars (#656, 658, 660, 662) & ships.

1984, June 12 *Perf. 12½*

655	A201	80fr multicolored	.60	.30
656	A201	100fr multicolored	.75	.40
657	A201	120fr multicolored	.75	.40
658	A201	140fr shown	1.00	.50
659	A201	150fr multicolored	1.10	.60
660	A201	250fr multicolored	1.90	.75
661	A201	300fr multicolored	2.00	.75
662	A201	400fr multicolored	3.00	1.00
		Nos. 655-662 (8)	11.10	4.70

1984 UPU Congress — A202

1984, June 20 **Engr.** *Perf. 13x12½*

663 A202 300fr Ship, emblems 3.00 1.75

Ayerou Market Place — A203

1984, July 18 **Litho.** *Perf. 12½*

664	A203	80fr shown	.80	.55
665	A203	120fr River scene	1.25	.70

Vipere Echis Leucogaster A204

1984, Aug. 16 *Perf. 13x12½*

666 A204 80fr multi 1.05 .55

West African Union, CEAO, 10th Anniv. — A205

1984, Oct. 26 **Litho.** *Perf. 13½*

667 A205 80fr multi .65 .40

UN Disarmament Campaign, 20th Anniv. — A205a

1984, Oct. 31 *Perf. 13*

667A	A205a	400fr brt grn & blk	2.75	1.50
667B	A205a	500fr brt bl & blk	3.25	2.00

Nos. 584-585 Overprinted "Aide au Sahel 84"

1984 **Litho.** *Perf. 13*

668	A176	150fr multi	1.40	.75
669	A176	200fr multi	1.60	1.10

World Tourism Organization, 10th Anniv. — A206

1985, Jan. 2 **Litho.** *Perf. 12½*

670 A206 110fr WTO emblem .90 .45

Infant Survival Campaign — A207

85fr, Breastfeeding. 110fr, Weighing child, giving liquids.

1985, Jan. 28 **Litho.** *Perf. 12½*

671	A207	85fr multi	.70	.35
672	A207	110fr multi	.90	.50

Nos. 590, 519 and 568 Overprinted with Exhibitions in Red

Souvenir Sheets

Perf. 13, 12½, 14

1985, Mar. 11 **Litho.**

673	A177	400fr MOPHILA '85 / HAMBOURG	4.50	4.50
674	A154	425fr TSUKUBA EXPO '85	4.50	4.50
675	A170	450fr ROME, ITALIA '85 emblem	4.50	4.50

See Nos. C356-C357.

Technical & Cultural Cooperation Agency, 15th Anniv. — A208

1985, Mar. 20 *Perf. 13*

676 A208 110fr vio, brn & car rose .80 .45

8th Niamey Festival — A209

Gaya Ballet Troupe. No. 678 vert.

1985, Apr. 8 *Perf. 12½x13, 13x12½*

677	A209	85fr multi	.60	.40
678	A209	110fr multi	.75	.55
679	A209	150fr multi	1.10	.70
		Nos. 677-679 (3)	2.45	1.65

Intl. Youth Year A210

Authors and scenes from novels: 85fr, Jack London (1876-1916). 105fr, Joseph Kessel (1898-1979). 250fr, Herman Melville. 450fr, Rudyard Kipling.

1985, Apr. 29 *Perf. 13*

680	A210	85fr multi	.75	.35
681	A210	105fr multi	.80	.40
682	A210	250fr multi	2.00	1.00
683	A210	450fr multi	3.50	1.75
		Nos. 680-683 (4)	7.05	3.50

PHILEXAFRICA '85, Lome, Togo — A211

1985, May 6 *Perf. 13x12½*

684	A211	200fr Tree planting	1.50	1.10
685	A211	200fr Industry	1.50	1.10
a.		Pair, Nos. 684-685 + label	4.25	4.25

Victor Hugo and His Son Francois, by A. de Chatillon — A212

1985, May 22 *Perf. 12½*

686 A212 500fr multi 4.00 2.00

Europafrica A213

1985, June 3 *Perf. 13*

687 A213 110fr multi 1.00 .50

World Wildlife Fund A214

50fr, 60fr, Addax. 85fr, 110fr, Oryx.

1985, June 15

688	A214	50fr Head, vert.	*3.25*	*.65*
689	A214	60fr Grazing	*4.25*	*.85*
690	A214	85fr Two adults	*5.00*	*1.05*
691	A214	110fr Head, vert.	*6.50*	*1.25*
		Nos. 688-691 (4)	*19.00*	*3.80*

Environ-destroying Species — A215

85fr, Oedaleus sp. 110fr, Dysdercus volkeri. 150fr, Tolyposporium ehrenbergii, Sclerospora graminicola, horiz. 210fr, Passer luteus. 390fr, Quelea quelea.

1985, July 1 *Perf. 13x12½, 12½x13*

692	A215	85fr multi	1.00	.40
693	A215	110fr multi	1.10	.45
694	A215	150fr multi	1.75	.65
695	A215	210fr multi	2.50	1.00
696	A215	390fr multi	4.75	1.90
		Nos. 692-696 (5)	11.10	4.40

Official Type of 1988 and

Cross of Agadez — A216

1985-94 **Engr.** *Perf. 13*

697	A216	85fr green	.75	.40
698	O2	110fr brown	1.00	.50
699	A216	125fr blue green	—	
700	A216	175fr emerald	—	
701	A216	210fr orange	—	—

Issued: 85fr, 110fr, 7/85; 125fr, 175fr, 210fr, 5/15/94.

Natl. Independence, 25th Anniv. — A217

1985, Aug. 3 **Litho.** *Perf. 13x12½*

707 A217 110fr multi 1.00 .50

Protected Trees — A218

Designs: 30fr, No. 711, Adansonia digitata and pod, vert. 85fr, 210fr, Acacia albida. No. 710, 390fr, Adansonia digitata, diff. Nos. 708-710 inscribed "DES ARBRES POUR LE NIGER."

1985 *Perf. 13x12½, 12½x13*

708	A218	30fr grn & multi	.55	.40
709	A218	85fr brn & multi	.85	.50
710	A218	110fr mag & multi	1.20	.60
711	A218	110fr blk & multi	1.05	.55
712	A218	210fr blk & multi	1.75	1.10
713	A218	390fr blk & multi	3.75	1.75
		Nos. 708-713 (6)	9.15	4.90

Issued: #708-710, 10/1; #711-713, 8/19.

Niamey-Bamako Motorboat Race — A219

110fr, Boats on Niger River. 150fr, Helicopter, competitor. 250fr, Motorboat, map.

1985, Sept. 16 *Perf. 13½*

714 A219 110fr multicolored .80 .40
715 A219 150fr multicolored 1.10 .60
716 A219 250fr multicolored 2.00 1.00
Nos. 714-716 (3) 3.90 2.00

Mushrooms A220

85fr, Boletus. 110fr, Hypholoma fasciculare. 200fr, Coprinus comatus. 300fr, Agaricus arvensis. 400fr, Geastrum fimbriatum.

1985, Oct. 3

717 A220 85fr multicolored .80 .35
718 A220 110fr multicolored 1.10 .40
719 A220 200fr multicolored 1.90 .75
720 A220 300fr multicolored 3.25 1.25
721 A220 400fr multicolored 4.25 1.75
Nos. 717-721 (5) 11.30 4.50

Nos. 717-719 vert.

PHILEXAFRICA '85, Lome, Togo — A221

No. 722, Village water pump. No. 723, Children playing dili.

1985, Oct. 21 *Perf. 13x12½*

722 A221 250fr multicolored 2.00 1.25
723 A221 250fr multicolored 2.00 1.25
a. Pair, Nos. 722-723 4.50 4.50

61st World Savings Day — A222

1985, Oct. 31 *Perf. 12½x13*

724 A222 210fr multi 1.50 .90

European Music Year — A223

Traditional instruments.

1985, Nov. 4 *Perf. 13½*

725 A223 150fr Gouroumi, vert. 1.25 .80
726 A223 210fr Gassou 1.75 1.25
727 A223 390fr Algaita, vert. 3.00 1.75
Nos. 725-727 (3) 6.00 3.80

Souvenir Sheet

Perf. 12½

728 A223 500fr Biti 4.00 4.00

Civil Statutes Reform — A224

1986, Jan. 2 Litho. *Perf. 13x12½*

729 A224 85fr Natl. identity card .65 .40
730 A224 110fr Family services .85 .50

Traffic Safety — A225

1986, Mar. 26 Litho. *Perf. 12½x13*

731 A225 85fr Obey signs .65 .40
732 A225 110fr Speed restriction .85 .50

Artists — A226

60fr, Oumarou Ganda, filmmaker. 85fr, Ida Na Dadaou, entertainer. 100fr, Dan Gourmou, entertainer. 130fr, Koungoui, comedian.

1986, Apr. 11 *Perf. 12½*

733 A226 60fr multi .45 .30
734 A226 85fr multi .60 .40
735 A226 100fr multi .75 .50
736 A226 130fr multi 1.00 .55
Nos. 733-736 (4) 2.80 1.75

Hunger Relief Campaign, Trucks of Hope A227

85fr, Relief supply truck. 110fr, Mother, child, vert.

1986, Aug. 27 Litho. *Perf. 12½*

737 A227 85fr multicolored .75 .40
738 A227 110fr multicolored 1.00 .50

Intl. Solidarity Day — A228

200fr, Nelson Mandela and Walter Sisulu, Robben Island prison camp. 300fr, Mandela.

1986, Oct. 8 *Perf. 13½*

739 A228 200fr multi 1.80 .90
740 A228 300fr multi 2.75 1.40

FAO, 40th Anniv. — A229

50fr, Cooperative peanut farm. 60fr, Fight desert encroachment. 85fr, Irrigation management. 100fr, Breeding livestock. 110fr, Afforestation.

1986, Oct. 16 *Perf. 13*

741 A229 50fr multicolored .40 .30
742 A229 60fr multicolored .45 .30
743 A229 85fr multicolored .60 .40
744 A229 100fr multicolored .75 .40
745 A229 110fr multicolored 1.00 .40
Nos. 741-745 (5) 3.20 1.80

Improved Housing for a Healthier Niger — A230

1987, Feb. 26 Litho. *Perf. 13½*

746 A230 85fr Albarka .75 .30
747 A230 110fr Mai Sauki .95 .50

Insects Protecting Growing Crops — A231

1987, Mar. 26 *Perf. 13x12½*

748 A231 85fr Sphodromantis 1.00 .50
749 A231 110fr Delta 1.50 .60
750 A231 120fr Cicindela 1.75 .85
Nos. 748-750 (3) 4.25 1.95

Liptako-Gourma Telecommunications Link Inauguration — A232

1987, Apr. 10 *Perf. 13½*

751 A232 110fr multi .85 .55

Samuel Morse — A233

120fr, Telegraph key, operator, horiz. 350fr, Receiver, horiz.

1987, May 21 Litho. *Perf. 12x12½*

752 A233 120fr multicolored .75 .40
753 A233 200fr shown 1.50 .75
754 A233 350fr multicolored 3.00 1.50
Nos. 752-754 (3) 5.25 2.65

Invention of the telegraph, 150th anniv.

1988 Seoul Summer Olympics — A234

1987, July 15

755 A234 85fr Tennis .55 .40
756 A234 110fr Pole vault .85 .40
757 A234 250fr Soccer 2.00 .85
Nos. 755-757 (3) 3.40 1.65

Souvenir Sheet

758 A234 500fr Running 4.00 2.75

1988 Winter Olympics, Calgary A235

85fr, Ice hockey. 110fr, Speed skating. 250fr, Pairs figure skating. 500fr, Downhill skiing.

1987, July 28 Litho. *Perf. 12½*

759 A235 85fr multi .60 .35
760 A235 110fr multi .85 .40
761 A235 250fr multi 2.00 .85
Nos. 759-761 (3) 3.45 1.60

Souvenir Sheet

762 A235 500fr multi 4.00 2.75

For overprints see Nos. 783-785.

African Games, Nairobi A236

1987, Aug. 5 *Perf. 13*

763 A236 85fr Runners .60 .35
764 A236 110fr High jump .75 .40
765 A236 200fr Hurdles 1.50 .75
766 A236 400fr Javelin 3.00 1.50
Nos. 763-766 (4) 5.85 3.00

Natl. Tourism Office, 10th Anniv. — A237

85fr, Chief's stool, scepter, vert. 110fr, Nomad, caravan, scepter. 120fr, Moslem village. 200fr, Bridge over Niger River.

1987, Sept. 10 *Perf. 13½*

767 A237 85fr multicolored .50 .40
768 A237 110fr multicolored 1.00 .45
769 A237 120fr multicolored 1.00 .45
770 A237 200fr multicolored 1.75 .85
Nos. 767-770 (4) 4.25 2.15

Aga Khan Architecture Prize, 1986 A238

85fr, Yaama Mosque, dawn. 110fr, At night. 250fr, In daylight.

1987, Oct. 7 *Perf. 13*

771 A238 85fr multi .60 .30
772 A238 110fr multi .80 .40
773 A238 250fr multi 2.00 1.00
Nos. 771-773 (3) 3.40 1.70

Niamey Court of Appeal — A239

1987, Nov. 17 *Perf. 13x12½*

774 A239 85fr multi .60 .30
775 A239 110fr multi .80 .40
776 A239 140fr multi 1.10 .55
Nos. 774-776 (3) 2.50 1.25

Christmas 1987 — A240

Paintings: 110fr, The Holy Family with Lamb, by Raphael. 500fr, The Adoration of the Magi, by Hans Memling (c. 1430-1494).

Wmk. 385

1987, Dec. 24 Litho. *Perf. 12½*

777 A240 110fr multi 1.00 .50

Souvenir Sheet

778 A240 500fr multi 4.00 2.50

No. 778 is airmail.

Modern Services for a Healthy Community A241

1988, Jan. 21 *Perf. 13*

779 A241 85fr Water drainage .95 .55
780 A241 110fr Sewage 1.10 .70
781 A241 165fr Garbage removal 1.90 .95
Nos. 779-781 (3) 3.95 2.20

Dan-Gourmou Prize — A242

1988, Feb. 16 Litho. *Perf. 13½*

782 A242 85fr multi 1.25 .70

Natl. modern music competition.

Nos. 759-761 Ovptd. "Medaille d'or" and Name of Winner in Gold

1988, Mar. 29 *Perf. 12½*

783 A235 85fr USSR .60 .40
784 A235 110fr Gusafson, Sweden .80 .50
785 A235 250fr Gordeeva and Grinkov, USSR 2.00 1.20
Nos. 783-785 (3) 3.40 2.10

New Market Building, Niamey — A243

1988, Apr. 9 Litho. *Perf. 13x12½*

786 A243 85fr multi .80 .40

WHO 40th Anniv., Universal Immunization Campaign A244

1988, May 26 Litho. *Perf. 12½x13*

787 A244 85fr Mother and child .65 .40
788 A244 110fr Visiting doctor .90 .45

Organization for African Unity (OAU), 25th Anniv. — A245

1988, June 28 *Perf. 12½*

789 A245 85fr multi .70 .35

Construction of a Sand Break to Arrest Desert Encroachment A246

1988, Sept. 27 Litho. *Perf. 12½x13*

790 A246 85fr multi 1.10 .55

Intl. Red Cross and Red Crescent Organizations, 125th Annivs. — A247

1988, Oct. 26 *Perf. 13x12½*

791 A247 85fr multi .65 .35
792 A247 110fr multi .85 .45

Niger Press Agency — A248

1989, Jan. 31 Litho. *Perf. 12½*

793 A248 85fr blk, org & grn .70 .35

Fight Against AIDS — A249

1989, Feb. 28 *Perf. 13½*

794 A249 85fr multi .70 .40
795 A249 110fr multi .90 .50

Intl. Maritime Organization, 30th Anniv. — A250

1989, Mar. 29 Litho. *Perf. 12½x13*

796 A250 100fr multi .90 .45
797 A250 120fr multi 1.20 .55

FAN Seizure of Government, 15th Anniv. — A251

85fr, Gen. Ali Saibou. 110fr, Raising of the flag.

1989, Apr. 14

798 A251 85fr multi .60 .30
799 A251 110fr multi .80 .40

PHILEXFRANCE '89 — A252

100fr, Eiffel Tower. 200fr, Simulated stamps.

1989, July 1 Litho. *Perf. 13*

800 A252 100fr multi .80 .45
801 A252 200fr multi 1.60 .80

French Revolution, Bicent. A253

250fr, Planting a tree for liberty.

1989, July 1

802 A253 250fr multicolored 2.25 1.10

Zinder Regional Museum — A253a

Perf. 14¾x14¼

1989, Aug. 23 Litho.

802A A253a 85fr multicolored *20.00 20.00*

African Development Bank, 25th Anniv. — A254

1989, Aug. 30 Litho. *Perf. 13½*

803 A254 100fr multicolored .80 .40

Communication and Postal Organization of West Africa (CAPTEAO), 30th Anniv. — A255

1989, July 3 Litho. *Perf. 13½*

804 A255 85fr multicolored .70 .35

Verdant Field, Field After Locust Plague A256

1989, Oct. 1 Litho. *Perf. 13*

805 A256 85fr multicolored 1.25 .60

Lumiere Brothers, Film Pioneers A256a

Designs: 150fr, Auguste Lumiere (1862-1954). 250fr, Louis Lumiere (1864-1948).

1989, Nov. 21 Litho. *Perf. 13½*

805A A256a 150fr multicolored 1.50 .75
805B A256a 250fr multicolored 2.25 1.00
805C A256a 400fr multicolored 3.75 1.75
Nos. 805A-805C (3) 7.50 3.50

Rural Development Council, 30th Anniv. — A256b

1989 Litho. *Perf. 15x14*

805D A256b 75fr multicolored *20.00*

Flora — A257

10fr, Russelia equisetiformis. 20fr, Argyreia nervosa. 30fr, Hibiscus rosa-sinensis. 50fr, Catharanthus roseus. 100fr, Cymothoe sangaris, horiz.

1989, Dec. 12 Litho. *Perf. 13*

806 A257 10fr multicolored .25 .25
807 A257 20fr multicolored .25 .25
808 A257 30fr multicolored .25 .25
809 A257 50fr multicolored .45 .25
810 A257 100fr multicolored 1.00 .40
Nos. 806-810 (5) 2.20 1.40

Dunes of Temet — A257a

1989 Litho. *Perf. 15x14*

810A A257a 145fr Caravan *55.00 45.00*
810B A257a 165fr shown *55.00 45.00*

Pan-African Postal Union, 10th Anniv. — A258

1990, Jan. 18 *Perf. 12½*

811 A258 120fr multicolored 1.00 .50

Intl. Literacy Year — A259

1990, Feb. 27 *Perf. 13½x13*

812 A259 85fr shown .65 .35
813 A259 110fr Class, diff. .95 .45

Islamic Conference Organization, 20th anniv. — A260

1990, Mar. 15 *Perf. 13x12½*

814 A260 85fr OCI emblem .70 .35

U.S. Congressman Mickey Leland — A261

1990, Mar. 29 Litho. *Perf. 13½*

815 A261 300fr multicolored 2.40 1.25
816 A261 500fr multicolored 4.00 2.00

Leland died Aug. 7, 1989 in a plane crash on a humanitarian mission.

Natl. Development Society, 1st Anniv. — A262

1990, May 15 Litho. *Perf. 13½*

817 A262 85fr multicolored .70 .35

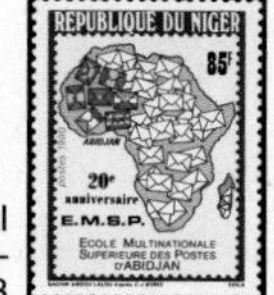

Multinational Postal School, 20th Anniv. — A263

1990, May 31 *Perf. 13x12½*

818 A263 85fr multicolored .80 .40

1992 Summer Olympics, Barcelona A263a

1990, June 4 Litho. *Perf. 13½*

818A A263a 85fr Gymnastics .65 .30
818B A263a 110fr Hurdles .85 .40
818C A263a 250fr Running 2.00 1.00
818D A263a 400fr Equestrian 3.00 1.50
818E A263a 500fr Long jump 4.00 2.00
Nos. 818A-818E (5) 10.50 5.20

Souvenir Sheet

818F A263a 600fr Cycling 4.75 2.75

Nos. 818D-818F are airmail.

Independence, 30th Anniv. — A264

1990, Aug. 3 *Perf. 12½*
819 A264 85fr gray grn & multi .65 .35
820 A264 110fr buff & multi .95 .50

UN Development Program, 40th Anniv. — A265

1990, Oct. 24 **Litho.** *Perf. 13½*
821 A265 100fr multicolored .80 .40

A266

Butterflies and Mushrooms — A266a

Designs: 85fr, Amanita rubescens. 110fr, Graphum pylades. 200fr, Pseudacraea hostilia. 250fr, Russula virescens. 400fr, Boletus impolitus. 500fr, Precis octavia. 600fr, Cantharellus cibarius & pseudacraea boisduvali.

1991, Jan. 15 **Litho.** *Perf. 13½*
822 A266 85fr multicolored .65 .30
823 A266 110fr multicolored .75 .40
824 A266 200fr multicolored 1.20 .80
825 A266 250fr multicolored 2.25 1.00
826 A266 400fr multicolored 3.25 1.50
827 A266 500fr multicolored 3.50 1.60
Nos. 822-827 (6) 11.60 5.60

Souvenir Sheet

828 A266a 600fr multicolored 5.00 5.00

Nos. 826-828 are airmail. No. 828 contains one 30x38mm stamp.

Palestinian Uprising — A267

1991, Mar. 30 **Litho.** *Perf. 12½*
829 A267 110fr multicolored 1.00 .45

Christopher Columbus (1451-1506) — A268

Hypothetical portraits and: 85fr, Santa Maria. 110fr, Frigata, Portuguese caravel, 15th cent. 200fr, Four-masted caravel, 16th cent. 250fr, Estremadura, Spanish caravel, 1511. 400fr, Vija, Portuguese caravel, 1600. 500fr, Pinta. 600fr, Nina.

1991, Mar. 19 **Litho.** *Perf. 13½*
830 A268 85fr multicolored .75 .35
831 A268 110fr multicolored .90 .40
832 A268 200fr multicolored 1.60 .70
833 A268 250fr multicolored 2.00 .90
834 A268 400fr multicolored 3.25 1.25
835 A268 500fr multicolored 3.75 1.60
Nos. 830-835 (6) 12.25 5.20

Souvenir Sheet

835A A268 600fr multicolored 5.00 5.00

Nos. 834-835A are airmail.

Timia Falls — A269

African Tourism Year — A270

Designs: 85fr, Boubon Market, horiz. 130fr, Ruins of Assode, horiz.

1991, July 10
836 A269 85fr multicolored .70 .30
837 A269 110fr multicolored .95 .45
838 A269 130fr multicolored 1.10 .50
839 A270 200fr multicolored 1.75 .85
Nos. 836-839 (4) 4.50 2.10

Anniversaries and Events — A270a

85fr, Chess players Anatoly Karpov and Garry Kasparov. 110fr, Race car drivers Ayrton Senna and Alain Prost. 200fr, An official swears allegiance to the constitution, Honoré-Gabriel Riqueti (Comte de Mirabeau). 250fr, Gen. Dwight D. Eisenhower, Winston Churchill, Field Marshal Bernard Montgomery and Republic P-4D Thunderbolt. 400fr, Charles de Gaulle and Konrad Adenauer. 500fr, German Chancellor Helmut Kohl, Brandenburg Gate. 600fr, Pope John Paul II's visit to Africa.

1991, July 15 **Litho.** *Perf. 13½*
839A A270a 85fr multicolored .45 .25
839B A270a 110fr multicolored .60 .25
839C A270a 200fr multicolored 1.10 .35
839D A270a 250fr multicolored 6.00 1.25
839E A270a 400fr multicolored 2.25 .80
839F A270a 500fr multicolored 2.75 .90
839G A270a 600fr multicolored 5.00 5.00
Nos. 839A-839G (7) 18.15 8.80

French Revolution, bicent. (#839C). Franco-German Cooperation Agreement, 28th anniv. (#839E). #839E is airmail & exists in a souvenir sheet of 1. German reunification (#839F). Nos. 839F and 839G are airmail and exist in souvenir sheets of 1.

For surcharge see No. 865.

Women's Hairstyles — A271

1991
840 A271 85fr multicolored .95 .35
841 A271 110fr multicolored 1.25 .45
842 A271 165fr multicolored 1.90 .70
843 A271 200fr multicolored 2.10 .85
Nos. 840-843 (4) 6.20 2.35

Transportation — A271a

Design: 85fr, Earth Resources Satellite, ERS-1, Japan; 110fr, EXOS-D satellite for observation of the Aurora Borealis, Japan; 200fr, Louis Favre (1826-1879), Congo-Ocean locomotive BB 415; 250fr, Congo-Ocean locomotive BB.BB.301; 400fr, Locomotive BB 302; 500fr, Anglo-French Concorde, F117 stealth fighter, US. 600fr, George Nagelmacker (1845-1905), Orient Express.

1991, Oct. 15 **Litho.** *Perf. 13½x13¼*
843A A271a 85fr multi .45 .25
843B A271a 110fr multi .60 .25
843C A271a 200fr multi 2.25 .35
843D A271a 250fr multi 2.75 .40
843E A271a 400fr multi 4.00 .55
843F A271a 500fr multi 2.75 .50
Nos. 843A-843F (6) 12.80 2.30

Souvenir Sheet

843G A271a 600fr multi 4.75 4.75

Nos. 843E-843G are airmail. Nos. 843A-843F exist in souvenir sheets of one. A souvenir sheet of 3 containing Nos. 843A-843B, 843F exists.

Natl. Conference of Niger — A272

1991, Dec. 17 **Litho.** *Perf. 12½*
844 A272 85fr multicolored .70 .35

House Built Without Wood — A273

1992, May 25 **Litho.** *Perf. 12½*
845 A273 85fr multicolored .75 .40

World Population Day — A274

Designs: 85fr, Assembling world puzzle. 110fr, Globe on a kite string.

1992, July 11 **Litho.** *Perf. 12½*
846 A274 85fr multicolored .70 .40
847 A274 110fr multicolored .90 .50

Discovery of America, 500th Anniv. A275

1992, Sept. 16 *Perf. 13*
848 A275 250fr multicolored 2.25 1.10

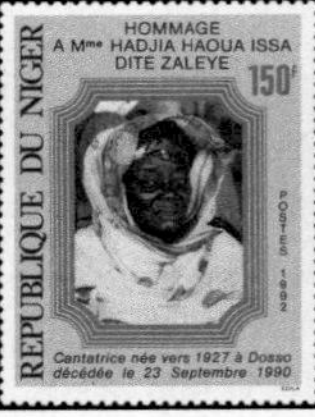

Hadjia Haoua Issa (1927-1990), Singer — A276

1992, Sept. 23 *Perf. 12½x13*
849 A276 150fr multicolored 1.25 .65

Intl. Conference on Nutrition, Rome — A277

1992 **Litho.** *Perf. 12½*
850 A277 145fr tan & multi 1.40 .60
851 A277 350fr blue & multi 3.00 1.50

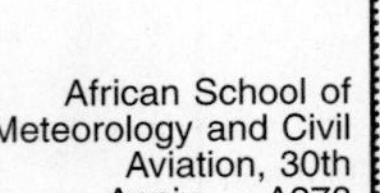

African School of Meteorology and Civil Aviation, 30th Anniv. — A278

1993, Feb. 7 *Perf. 13½*
852 A278 110fr bl, grn & blk .90 .45

Environmental Protection — A279

1993, June 26 **Litho.** *Perf. 12½*
853 A279 85fr salmon & multi .75 .40
854 A279 165fr green & multi 1.50 .75

World Population Day — A280

110fr, Buildings, person with globe as head, tree.

1993, July 11 **Litho.** *Perf. 13½*
855 A280 85fr multicolored .70 .35
856 A280 110fr multicolored .90 .45

Holy City of Jerusalem A281

1993, Nov. 8 **Litho.** *Perf. 13x12½*
857 A281 110fr multicolored 1.00 .45

Artisans at Work — A282b

1994 **Litho.** *Perf. 13x13¼*
857D A282b 125fr Tailor 20.00 —
857E A282b 175fr Weaver, vert. 20.00 —

Nelson Mandela, F.W. De Klerk, Winners of 1993 Nobel Peace Prize — A282

1994, Feb. 11 **Litho.** *Perf. 13*
858 A282 270fr multicolored 1.10 .55

A282a

A282b

Landscapes — A282c

1994 **Litho.** ***Perf. 12½***

858A	A282a	85fr multi	—	
858B	A282b	110fr multi	—	
858C	A282c	165fr multi	—	

Cultural Cooperation & Technique Agency, 25th Anniv. — A283

1995 **Litho.** ***Perf. 13½x13***

859	A283	100fr multicolored	.50	.25

Animals Used for Transportation A284

500fr, Donkey cart. 1000fr, Man, saddled horse.

1995 ***Perf. 13x13½***

860	A284	500fr multi	1.60	.95
861	A284	1000fr multi	4.00	2.25

Economic Community of West African States (ECOWAS), 20th Anniv. — A285

1995 **Litho.** ***Perf. 13½***

862	A285	125fr multicolored	.70	.35

Cattle Ranching — A286

Design: 300fr, Irrigating fields.

1995 ***Perf. 13½x13***

863	A286	125fr shown	.60	.35
864	A286	300fr multicolored	1.20	.65

Souvenir Sheet of No. 839E Ovptd.

1995, Nov. 8 **Litho.** ***Perf. 13½***

865	A270a	400fr multicolored	*6.75*	*5.00*

African Development Bank, 30th Anniv. — A287

1995 **Litho.** ***Perf. 14***

866	A287	300fr green & red	1.25	.70

Boy Scouts — A288

350fr, Robert Baden-Powell. 500fr, Scout saluting.

1996 ***Perf. 13½***

867	A288	350fr multicolored	1.25	.75
868	A288	500fr multicolored	1.75	1.20

Nos. 867-868 exist imperf. and in souvenir sheets of 1 both perf. and imperf.

UN, UNICEF, 50th Anniv. — A289

Designs: 150fr, Child with head bandaged, UNICEF emblem. 225fr, Boy carrying bowl of food on head, dove, globes. 475fr, Woman, boy playing on artillery piece, space station Mir. 550fr, Boy, race car driver Michael Schumacher, UNICEF emblem.

1996

869	A289	150fr multicolored	.70	.35
870	A289	225fr multicolored	1.00	.50
871	A289	475fr multicolored	2.25	1.10
a.		Sheet of 2, #870-871 + label	*11.00*	*5.50*
872	A289	550fr multicolored	2.50	1.25
a.		Sheet of 2, #869, 872 + label	*11.00*	*5.50*
		Nos. 869-872 (4)	6.45	3.20

Entertainers A290

No. 873, Bob Marley. No. 874, Janis Joplin. No. 874A, Madonna. No. 875, Jerry Garcia. No. 876, Elvis Presley. No. 877, Marilyn Monroe. No. 878, John Lennon. No. 879, Monroe, diff. No. 880, Presley, diff.

No. 881, Presley, diff. No. 882, Monroe, diff.

1996

873	A290	175fr multicolored	.65	.45
874	A290	300fr multicolored	1.00	.90
874A	A290	400fr multicolored	1.40	1.20
875	A290	600fr multicolored	2.25	1.75
876	A290	700fr multicolored	2.50	2.10
877	A290	700fr multicolored	2.50	2.10
878	A290	750fr multicolored	3.00	2.25
879	A290	800fr multicolored	3.00	2.40
880	A290	800fr multicolored	3.00	2.40
		Nos. 873-880 (9)	19.30	15.55

Souvenir Sheets

881	A290	2000fr multicolored	6.75	6.00
882	A290	2000fr multicolored	6.75	6.00

Nos. 873-882 exist imperf. and in souvenir sheets of 1 both perf. and imperf.

No. 874A exists in a souvenir sheet of 1.

Butterflies — A291

Boy Scout Jamboree emblem and: 150fr, Chrysiridia riphearia. 200fr, Palla ussheri. 750fr, Mylothris chloris. 800fr, Papilo dardanus.

1996 **Litho.** ***Perf. 13½***

883	A291	150fr multicolored	.60	.35
884	A291	200fr multicolored	.80	.50
885	A291	750fr multicolored	2.60	2.25
886	A291	800fr multicolored	2.75	2.40
		Nos. 883-886 (4)	6.75	5.50

Nos. 883-886 exist imperf. and in souvenir sheets of 1 both perf. and imperf.

Wild Animals — A292

Boy Scout Jamboree emblem, Rotary emblem and: 150fr, Erythrocebus patas. 200fr, Panthera pardus. 900fr, Balearica regulorum. 1000fr, Alcelaphus buselaphus.
2000fr, Panthera leo.

1996

887	A292	150fr multicolored	.55	.35
888	A292	200fr multicolored	.70	.55
889	A292	900fr multicolored	2.75	2.50
890	A292	1000fr multicolored	3.25	2.75
		Nos. 887-890 (4)	7.25	6.15

Souvenir Sheet

891	A292	2000fr multicolored	6.75	5.75

Nos. 887-890 exist in souvenir sheets of 1.

Rotary International A292a

Designs: 200fr, Boy holding fruits and vegetables. 700fr, Girl holding sheaves of grain.

1996 **Litho.** ***Perf. 13½***

891A	A292a	200fr multicolored	.70	.55
891B	A292a	700fr multicolored	2.75	1.90

Intl. Red Cross and Lions Intl. — A293

Designs: 250fr, Jean-Henri Dunant as young man. 300fr, Lions Intl. emblems, boy with books. 400fr, Dunant as old man. 600fr, Older boy carrying younger boy, Lions Intl. emblems.

1996 **Litho.** ***Perf. 13½***

892	A293	250fr multicolored	.90	.60
893	A293	300fr multicolored	1.05	.55
894	A293	400fr multicolored	1.50	1.25
895	A293	600fr multicolored	2.25	1.75
		Nos. 892-895 (4)	5.70	4.15

Traditional Musical Instruments — A294

1996 **Litho.** ***Perf. 13½***

896	A294	125fr violet & multi	.50	.30
897	A294	175fr pink & multi	.70	.45

Sports — A295

1996

898	A295	300fr Golf	1.05	.70
899	A295	500fr Tennis	1.75	1.40
900	A295	700fr Table tennis	2.60	1.80
		Nos. 898-900 (3)	5.40	3.90

Nos. 898-900 exist in souvenir sheets of one.

1996 Summer Olympic Games, Atlanta — A296

Designs: 250fr, Track & field. 350fr, Women's gymnastics, table tennis. 400fr, Tennis, swimming. 600fr, Hurdles, pole vault.
1500fr, Men's track and field.

1996 **Litho.** ***Perf. 13½***

901	A296	250fr multicolored	.90	.60
902	A296	350fr multicolored	1.25	1.05
903	A296	400fr multicolored	1.50	1.25
904	A296	600fr multicolored	2.10	1.80
		Nos. 901-904 (4)	5.75	4.70

Souvenir Sheet

904A	A296	1500fr multicolored	5.75	5.75

Souvenir Sheet

CHINA '96 A297

Statues from Yunguang Grottoes, Datong, China: a, Head of Buddha. b, Side view.

1996

905	A297	140fr Sheet of 2, #a.-b.	1.75	1.75

1998 Winter Olympic Games, Nagano — A298

1996

906	A298	85fr Hockey	.40	.30
907	A298	200fr Downhill skiing	.90	.50
908	A298	400fr Slalom skiing	1.75	1.00
909	A298	500fr Pairs figure skating	2.25	1.25
		Nos. 906-909 (4)	5.30	3.05

Nos. 906-909 were not issued without metallic blue overprint on stamps dated 1991. Nos. 908-909 are airmail.

Nos. 906-909 exist with red metallic overprint. A 600fr souvenir sheet with red metallic overprint exists in limited quantities.

Formula I Race Car Drivers — A299

Designs: 450fr, Jacques Villeneuve. 2000fr, Ayrton Senna (1960-94).

1996

910	A299	450fr multicolored	1.60	1.00

Souvenir Sheet

911	A299	2000fr multicolored	6.75	6.00

No. 910 exists in souvenir sheet of 1. No. 911 contains one 39x57mm stamp.

Tockus Nasutus — A300

Coracias Abyssinica A301

Designs: 15fr, Psittacula krameri. 25fr, Coracias abyssinica. 35fr, Bulbucus ibis.

1996 Litho. *Perf. 13½x13*

912	A300	5fr multi	6.75	2.50
912A	A300	15fr multi	6.75	2.50
912B	A300	25fr multi	10.00	5.00
912C	A300	35fr multi	6.75	2.50

Perf. 13

913	A301	25fr multi		
914	A301	35fr multi		

Compare type A300 to types A301 and A309.

1998 Winter Olympic Games, Nagano, Japan — A302

1996 Litho. *Perf. 13x13½*

915	A302	125fr Ice hockey	.90	.30
916	A302	175fr Slalom skiing	.65	.35
917	A302	700fr Pairs figure skating	2.75	1.50
918	A302	800fr Speed skating	3.00	1.75
		Nos. 915-918 (4)	7.30	3.90

Souvenir Sheet

919	A302	1500fr Downhill skiing	6.00	6.00

No. 919 contains one 57x51mm stamp.
Nos. 915-918 exist in souvenir sheets of 1.

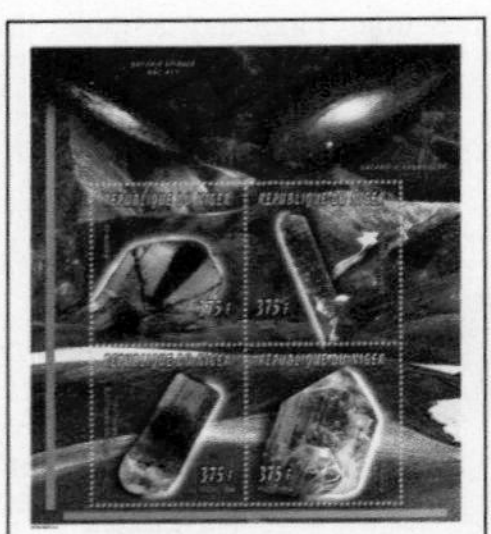

Minerals — A303

No. 920: a, Brookite. b, Elbaite indicolite. c. Elbaite rubellite verdelite. d, Olivine.

No. 921: a, Topaz. b, Autunite. c, Leucite. d, Struvite.

1996 Litho. *Perf. 13½*

920	A303	375fr Sheet of 4, #a.-d.	5.25	5.25
921	A303	500fr Sheet of 4, #a.-d.	6.50	6.50

Souvenir Sheet

922	A303	2000fr Pyrargyrite	6.50	6.50

No. 922 contains one 42x39mm stamp.

World Driving Champion Michael Schumacher — A304

Schumacher: a, Grand Prix of Spain. b, In race car in pit. c, Ahead of another car. d, Behind another car.

1996 Litho. *Perf. 13½*

923	A304	375fr Sheet of 4, #a.-d.	5.50	5.50

German Soccer Team, Euro '96 Champions — A305

No. 924: a, Oliver Bierhoff, player jumping up. b, Bierhoff, player holding up arms. c, ChancellorHelmut Kohl, Queen Elizabeth II, Klinsmann. d, Stadium, Mathias Sammer. logos.

1996 Litho. *Perf. 13½*

924	A305	400fr Sheet of 4, #a.-d.	5.75	5.75

Dinosaurs — A306

No. 925: a, Ouranosaurus. b, Spinosaurus. c, Polacanthus. d, Deinonychus.

No. 926: a, Camptosaurus. b, Allosaurus. c, Nodosaurus. d, Kritosaurus.

2000fr, Protoceratops, oviraptor, horiz.

1996

925	A306	300fr Sheet of 4, #a.-d.	7.00	7.00
926	A306	450fr Sheet of 4, #a.-d.	11.00	11.00

Souvenir Sheet

927	A306	2000fr multicolored	7.00	7.00

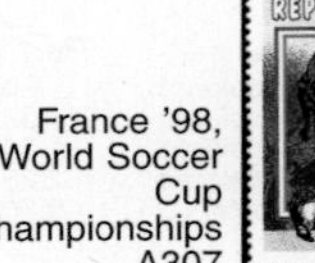

France '98, World Soccer Cup Championships A307

World Cup Trophy and: 125fr, American player. 175fr, Brazilian player. 750fr, Italian player. 1000fr, German player.

1500fr, Player in action scene.

1996

928	A307	125fr multicolored	.45	.35
929	A307	175fr multicolored	.60	.50
930	A307	750fr multicolored	2.60	2.10
931	A307	1000fr multicolored	3.50	2.75
		Nos. 928-931 (4)	7.15	5.70

Souvenir Sheet

932	A307	1500fr multicolored	5.75	5.75

No. 932 contains one 57x51mm stamp.

New Year 1997 (Year of the Ox) A308

1997 Litho. *Perf. 13½*

933	A308	500fr shown	2.00	1.00
934	A308	500fr Riding three oxen	2.00	1.00

Nos. 933-934 exist in souvenir sheets of 1, design extending to perfs on No. 933.

Birds — A309

5fr, Tockus nasutus. 15fr, Psittacula kramer. 25fr, Coracias abyssinica. 35fr, Bulbucus ibis.

1997 Litho. *Perf. 13½*

935	A309	5fr multicolored	.30	.25
936	A309	15fr multicolored	.30	.25
937	A309	25fr multicolored	.30	.25
938	A309	35fr multicolored	.30	.25
		Nos. 935-938 (4)	1.20	1.00

See No. 1050.

19th Dakar-Agades-Dakar Rally — A310

Designs: 125fr, Truck, child in traditional dress. 175fr, Ostrich, three-wheel vehicle. 300fr, Camel, heavy-duty support truck. 500fr, Motorcycles.

1997

939	A310	125fr multicolored	.55	.30
940	A310	175fr multicolored	.80	.40
941	A310	300fr multicolored	1.20	.75
942	A310	500fr multicolored	1.90	1.25
a.		Souvenir sheet, #939-942	4.50	4.50
b.		Strip of 4, #939-942	4.50	4.50

Deng Xiaoping (1904-97), Chinese Leader — A311

Designs: a, Deng, flag, eating at table, Deng as young man. b, Farming with oxen, Deng holding girl, flag. c, Flag, Deng with soldiers, camp. d, Deng bathing, ships in port, combining grain, launching space vehicle. e, Huts, heavy equipment vehicle, men working. f, Airplane, man holding up flask, operating room, Deng.

1997

943	A311	150fr Sheet of 6, #a.-f.	3.25	3.25

Diana, Princess of Wales (1961-97) — A312

No. 944: Various portraits performing humanitarin deeds, on world tours, with various figures.

No. 945: Various portraits in designer dresses.

No. 946: With Mother Teresa (in margin).

1997, Sept. 30 Litho. *Perf. 13½*

944	A312	180fr Sheet of 9, #a.-i.	6.50	4.00
945	A312	180fr Sheet of 9, #a.-i.	6.50	4.00

Souvenir Sheets

946	A312	2000fr multicolored	7.25	5.00
947	A312	4000fr multicolored	14.00	14.00

No. 947 contains one 40x46mm stamp depicting Princess Diana in red coat, holding bouquet.

A number of other stamps and souvenir sheets having similar type fonts depicting Princess Diana exist. These were declared to be not authorized by Niger postal authorites.

Famous Americans — A313

No. 948 — Various portraits: a-b, John F. Kennedy. c-d, Pres. Bill Clinton.

No. 949 — Various pprtraits: a, Kennedy. b, Dr. Martin Luther King (1929-68). c-d, Clinton.

2000fr, John F. Kennedy.

1997 Litho. *Perf. 13½*

948	A313	350fr Sheet of 4, #a.-d.	4.75	3.00
949	A313	400fr Sheet of 4, #a.-d.	5.75	5.75

Souvenir Sheet

950	A313	2000fr multicolored	6.75	6.75

No. 950 contains one 42x60mm stamp.

Stars of American Cinema — A314

No. 951: a, Eddie Murphy. b, Elizabeth Taylor. c, Bruce Willis. d, James Dean. e, Clint Eastwood. f, Elvis Presley. g, Michelle Pfeiffer. h, Marilyn Monroe. i, Robert Redford.

1997 Litho. *Perf. 13½*

951	A314	300fr Sheet of 9, #a.-i.	9.50	9.50

Communications — A315

No. 952: a, 80fr, Satellite transmission, radios. b, 100fr, Computers. c, 60fr, Cellular phone transmission around world. d, 120fr, Hand holding car phone. e, 180fr, Satellite, earth. f, 50fr, Transmission tower, cellular phone.

1997

952	A315	Sheet of 6, #a.-f.	2.25	2.25

Prof. Abdou Moumouni Dioffo — A316

1997 Litho. *Perf. 13½x13*

953 A316 125fr multicolored — —

Methods of Transportation — A317

Bicycles, motorcycles: No. 954: a, Jan Ullrich, 1997 Tour de France winner, Eiffel Tower. b, Diana 250, Harley Davidson. c, MK VIII motorcycle, bicycles of 1819, 1875. d, Brands Match Motorcycle Race, Great Britain.

Modern locomotives, country flags: No. 955: a, Pendolino ETR 470, Italy. b, Rame TGV 112, France. c, Eurostar, France, Belgium, UK. d, Intercity Express ICE train, Germany.

Early locomotives, country flags: No. 956: a, Trevithick, UK. b, Pacific North Chapelon, France. c, Buddicom, UK, France. d, PLM "C", France.

Trains of Switzerland: No. 957: a, Crocodile, St. Gothard. b, RE 460. c, Red Streak, RAE 2/4 1001. d, Limmat.

Classic cars, modern sports cars: No. 958: a, Mercedes 300 SL Gullwing, Mercedes E320 Cabriolet. b, Aston Martin V8, Aston Martin DBR2. c. Ferrari F50, Ferrari 250 GT Berlinette. d, Ford Thunderbird, Ford GT40.

Air flight: No. 959: a, Clement Ader's Avion 111, dirigible R101. b, Concorde jet, X36 NASA/MCDD prototype. c, Aile volante FW900, Airbus A340. d, Gaudron GIII, Montgolfier's balloon.

Space travel: No. 960: a, HII rocket, Japan, Copernicus. b, Galileo, Ariane rocket. c, Space shuttle, Neil Armstrong. d, Yuri Gagarin, orbital space station, Soyuz.

1500fr, Swiss train, RE 4/4 II 11349, vert. No. 962, Hubble Space Telescope, Concorde jet. No. 963, TGV mail train, 1958 Chevrolet Corvette.

1997 Litho. *Perf. 13½*

954 A317 300fr Sheet of 4, #a.-d. 4.00 4.00
955 A317 350fr Sheet of 4, #a.-d. 4.75 4.75
956 A317 375fr Sheet of 4, #a.-d. 4.75 4.75
957 A317 400fr Sheet of 4, #a.-d. 5.75 5.75
958 A317 450fr Sheet of 4, #a.-d. 5.75 5.75
959 A317 500fr Sheet of 4, #a.-d. 6.50 6.50
960 A317 600fr Sheet of 4, #a.-d. 7.25 7.25

Souvenir Sheets

961 A317 1500fr multicolored 5.75 5.75
962 A317 2000fr multicolored 6.75 6.75
963 A317 2000fr multicolored 6.75 6.75

Swiss Railroad, 150th anniv. (#957, #961). Nos. 961-963 each contain one 50x60mm stamp.

Diana, Princess of Wales (1961-97) — A318

Various portraits.

1500fr, Wearing red dress. No. 966, Wearing blue dress.

1997 Litho. *Perf. 13½*

964 A318 250fr Sheet of 9, #a.-i. 8.00 8.00
964J A318 300fr Sheet of 9, #k.-s. 9.50 9.50

Souvenir Sheets

965 A318 1500fr multicolored 5.25 5.25
966 A318 2000fr multicolored 7.00 7.00

Nos. 965-966 contain one 42x60mm stamp.

Man in Space A319

No. 967: a, John Glenn, Mercury capsule. b, Cassini/Huygens satellite. c, Laika, first dog in space, Sputnik 2. d, Valentina Tereshkova, first woman in space, Vostok 6. e. Edward White, first American to walk in space, Gemini 4. f, Alexi Leonov, first Soviet to walk in space. g, Luna 9. h, Gemini capsule docked to Agena.

No. 968: a, Skylab space station. b, Pioneer 13, Venus 2. c, Giotto probe, Halley's Comet. d, Apollo-Soyuz mission. e, Mariner 10. f, Viking 1. g, Venera 11. h, Surveyor 1.

No. 969, 2000fr, Yuri Gagarin, first man in space, Sergei Korolev, RD107 rocket. No. 970, 2000fr, John F. Kennedy, Apollo 11, Neil Armstrong, first man to set foot on the moon.

1997 Litho. *Perf. 13½*

967 A319 375fr Sheet of 8 + label 8.00 8.00
968 A319 450fr Sheet of 8 + label 9.00 9.00

Souvenir Sheets

969-970 A319 Set of 2 12.00 12.00

Nos. 969-970 each contain one 42x60mm stamp.

Pres. Ibrahim Mainassara-Bare A320

1997 Litho. & Embossed *Perf. 13½*

971 A320 500fr gold & multi 1.75 1.75

Scouting, Intl., 90th Anniv. (in 1997) — A321

No. 972 — Scout and: a, Lion. b, Rhinoceros. c, Giraffe. d, Elephant.

No. 972E — Girl Scout: f, Building bird house. g, Examining flower with magnifying glass. h, Identifying flower from book. i, Playing with bird.

No. 973: a, Butterfly. b, Bird with berries in mouth. c, Bird. d, Brown & white butterfly.

No. 974: a, Holding up rock to light. b, Using magnifying glass. c, Looking at rock. d, On hands and knees.

No. 975 — Scout, mushroom, with background color of: a, Yellow. b, White. c, Pink. d, Green.

2000fr, Robert Baden-Powell, Scouts chasing butterflies, mushroom.

1998 Litho.

972 A321 350fr Sheet of 4, #a.-d. 4.75 4.75
972E A321 400fr Sheet of 4, #f.-i. 5.50 5.50
973 A321 450fr Sheet of 4, #a.-d. 6.50 6.50
974 A321 500fr Sheet of 4, #a.-d. 7.00 7.00
975 A321 600fr Sheet of 4, #a.-d. 8.00 8.00

Souvenir Sheet

975E A321 2000fr multicolored 7.00 7.00

Greenpeace A322

No. 976 — Turtles: a, Being caught in net. b, One swimming right. c, Mating. d, One swimming left.

1998

976 A322 400fr Block of 4, #a-d 8.00 8.00
e. Souvenir sheet, #976 16.00 16.00

Sheets overprinted "CHINA 99 World Philatelic Exhibition" are not authorized.

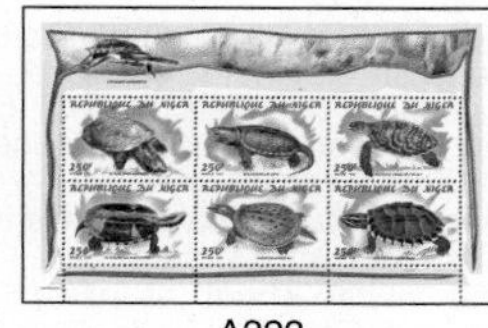

A323

No. 977 — Turtles: a, Pelomedusa subruta. b, Megacephalum shiui. c, Eretmochelus imbricata. d, Platycephala platycephala. e, Spinifera spinifera. f, Malayemys subtrijuga.

No. 978 — Raptors: a, Aquila uerreauxii. b, Asia otus. c, Bubo bubo. d, Surnia ulula. e, Asio flammeus. f, Falco biarnicus.

No. 979 — Orchids: a, Oeceoclades saundersiana. b, Paphiopedilum venustum. c, Maxillaria picta. d, Masdevallia triangularis. e, Zugopetalum. f, Encyllia nemoralis.

No. 980 — Butterflies: a, Danaus plexippus. b, Leto venus. c, Callioratis millari. d, Hippotion celerio. e, Euchloron megaera. f, Teracotona euprepia.

No. 981 — Mushrooms: a, Phaeolepotia aurea. b, Disciotis venosa. c, Gomphidius glutinosus. d, Amanita vaginata. e, Tremellodon gelatinosum. f, Voluariella voluacea.

1998, Sept. 29 Litho. *Perf. 13½*

977 A323 250fr Sheet of 6, #a.-f. 5.50 5.50
978 A323 300fr Sheet of 6, #a.-f. 6.50 6.50
979 A323 350fr Sheet of 6, #a.-f. 7.25 7.25
980 A323 400fr Sheet of 6, #a.-f. 8.00 8.00
981 A323 450fr Sheet of 6, #a.-f. 9.75 8.75

Marine Life A324

No. 982: a, Tursiops truncatus. b, Phocoenoides dalli. c, Sousa teuszii. d, Stegostoma fasciatum. e, Delphinus delphis, balaenoptera musculus. f, Carcharodon carcharias. g, Argonauta argo, heterodontus portusjacksoni. h, Mitsukurina owstoni. i, Sphyrna mokarran. j, Homarus gammarus, prostheceraeus vittatus. k, Glossodoris valenciennesi, cephalopodes decapodes. l, Nemertien anople, elysia viridis.

1998, Sept. 29 Litho. *Perf. 13½*

982 A324 175fr Sheet of 12, #a-l 8.00 8.00

World Wildlife Fund — A325

Gazella dorcas: No. 983, Doe, fawn. No. 984, Adult lying down. No. 985, Two adults standing still. No. 986 Adult walking.

1998

983 A325 250fr multicolored 1.40 .85
984 A325 250fr multicolored 1.40 .85
985 A325 250fr multicolored 1.40 .85
986 A325 250fr multicolored 1.40 .85
a. Se-tenant block of 4 8.00 8.00
b. Souvenir sheet, #983-986 40.00 40.00
Nos. 983-986 (4) 5.60 3.40

Similar items without WWF emblem are not authorized.

Pope John Paul II — A326

Various portraits of pontiff thoughout his life.

1998, Sept. 29 Litho. *Perf. 13½*

987 A326 250fr Sheet of 9, #a.-i. 8.00 8.00

Souvenir Sheet

988 A326 2000fr multicolored 7.25 7.25

No. 988 contains one 57x51mm stamp.

Frank Sinatra (1915-98) — A327

Various portraits.

1998

989 A327 300fr Sheet of 9, #a.-i. 9.75 9.75

Explorers — A328

No. 990: a, Juan Sebastian del Cano (1476-1526), commander of vessel that completed circumnavigation of globe. b, Globe, sailing ships. c, Ferdinand Magellan (1480-1521).

No. 991 — Vasco da Gama (1469-1524): a. Portrait. b, Angels, explorers, soldiers, flag. c, Sailing ship, da Gama's tomb, Lisbon.

No. 992 — Aviator Roland Garros (1888-1918): a, Arriving at Utrecht. b, Flying across Mediterranean, 1913. c, Portrait.

1998, Sept. 29

990 A328 350fr Sheet of 3, #a.-c. 3.75 3.75
991 A328 400fr Sheet of 3, #a.-c. 4.50 4.50
992 A328 450fr Sheet of 3, #a.-c. 4.75 4.75

Nos. 990b, 991b, 992b are 60x51mm.

Jacques-Yves Cousteau (1910-97), Environmentalist — A329

No. 993: a, Whales. b, Fish, diver, whales, sled dog team. c, Portrait of Cousteau surrounded by ship, explorers in polar region, whale, fish.

No. 994: a, Cousteau, children, bird. b, Ship, marine life. c, Cousteau in diving gear, fish.

1998, Sept. 29

993 A329 500fr Sheet of 3, #a.-c. 5.75 5.75
994 A329 600fr Sheet of 3, #a.-c. 6.50 6.50

Nos. 993b and 994b are 60x51mm.

1998 World Cup Soccer Championships, France — A330

No. 995: a, Emmanuel Petit. b, Zinedine Zidane. c, Fabien Barthez. d, Lilian Thuram. e, Didier Deschamps. f, Youri Djorkaeff. g, Marcel Desailly, Christian Karembeu. h, Bixente Lizarazu. i, Frank Leboeuf, Stephane Guivarc'h.

1998

995 A330 250fr Sheet of 9, #a.-i. 8.50 8.50

A331

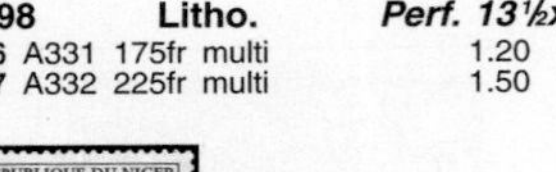

FIMA Niger '98 African Fashion Festival — A332

1998 **Litho.** *Perf. 13½x13*

996 A331 175fr multi 1.20 .75
997 A332 225fr multi 1.50 .75

Flowers — A333

Designs: 10fr, Roses and anemone. 20fr, Asystasia vogeliana, horiz. 30fr, Agrumes, horiz. 40fr, Angraecum sesquipedale. 45fr, Dissotis rotundifolia. 50fr, Hibiscus rosa-sinensis. 100fr, Datura.

1998 **Litho.** *Perf. 13¼x13½*

997A	A333	10fr multi	—	—
997B	A333	20fr multi	—	8.00
997C	A333	30fr multi	—	8.00
997D	A333	40fr multi	—	—
997E	A333	45fr multi	—	8.00
998	A333	50fr multi	—	—
999	A333	100fr multi	24.00	8.00

A number of items inscribed "Republique du Niger" were not authorized by Niger postal authorities. These include:

Dated 1996: Overprinted 500fr souvenir sheet for 20th anniv. first commercial flight of the Concorde.

Dated 1998: Martin Luther King, Jr., 2000fr souvenir sheet;

Ferrari automobile, 2000fr stamp and souvenir sheet;

Trains, 650fr sheet of 4, 2500fr souvenir sheet, two 3000fr souvenir sheets;

Titanic, 650fr sheet of 4, four 650fr souvenir sheets, 2500fr souvenir sheet;

Paintings by Toulouse-Lautrec, Gauguin, Renoir, Matisse, Delacroix, Van Gogh, sheets of nine 250fr, 300fr, 375fr 400fr, 425fr, 500fr stamps, sheet of three 725fr Matisse stamps, 200fr, Delacroix souvenir sheet;

French and Italian performers, sheet of nine 675fr stamps;

Sailing vessels, sheets of four 525fr, 875fr stamps;

Events of the 20th Century, 3 sheets of nine 225fr stamps, 2 sheets of nine 375fr stamps, 3 sheets of nine 500fr stamps, fourteen 225fr souvenir sheets, three 2000fr souvenir sheets;

Space events of the 20th Century, two 2000fr souvenir sheets;

Papal visits, sheet of nine 500fr stamps, sheet of two 1500fr stamps;

Cats, sheetlet of 5 stamps, various denominations, 500fr souvenir sheet;

African Music, sheet of nine 225fr stamps;

Pinocchio, sheet of nine 200fr stamps;

Dated 1999: History of the Cinema (Marilyn Monroe), sheet of nine 275fr stamps, 2000fr souvenir sheet;

History of American Cinema (various actors), sheet of nine 400fr stamps;

John F. Kennedy, Jr., sheet of nine 500fr stamps;

Sheets of nine stamps of various denominations depicting Cats, Panda, Dinosaurs, Kennedy Space Center, Mushrooms, Butterflies, Eagles, Tiger Woods, Chess Pieces (2 different sheets);

Sheets of six stamps of various denominations depicting Butterflies, Cartoon Network Cartoon Characters.

Additional issues may be added to this list.

Wildlife — A334

Designs: No. 1000, 180fr, Tiger, Rotary emblem, vert. No. 1001, 250fr, Tigers, Lions emblem. No. 1002, 375fr, Tiger, Scouting, scouting jamboree emblems. 500fr, Owl, vert.

No. 1003, vert. — Rotary emblem and: a, Lions. b, Leopard. c, Red-headed cranes. d, Owl. e, Buzzards. f, Gazelles (long horns). g, Elands (twisted horns). h, Antelope (short horns).

No. 1004 — Lions emblem and: a, Lion, looking left. b, Lion, lioness. c, Lion reclining. d, Leopards. e, Leopard on rock. f, Lion, looking right. g, Lion in grass. h, Lion cub.

No. 1005 — Scouting and scouting jamboree emblems and: a, Leopard, mouth open. b, Leopard overlooking plains. c, Leopard looking right. d, Cat. e, Pair of leopards. f, Leopard and trees. g, Leopard reclining. h, Leopard standing on rock.

1000fr, Tiger in water, horiz. 2500fr, Leopards.

1998 **Litho.** *Perf. 13½*

1000-1002 A334 Set of 3
1003 A334 180fr Sheet of 9, #a-h, 1000
1004 A334 250fr Sheet of 9, #a-h, 1001
1005 A334 375fr Sheet of 9, #a-h, 1002

Souvenir Sheets

1005I A334 500fr multi — —
1006 A334 1000fr multi
1007 A334 2500fr multi

New Year 1998, Year of the Tiger, Nos. 1000-1002, 1006. Nos. 1006-1007 each contain one 46x40mm stamp.

No. 1005I contains one 40x46mm stamp. Italia '98 Intl. Philatelic Exhibition (No. 1005I).

Jerry Garcia A335

No. 1008: a, In brown shirt. b, In blue shirt, with flower. c, In yellow shirt. d, in green shirt. e, With fists clenched. f, In blue shirt. g, In black jacket. h, Holding glasses. i, In black shirt, with black guitar strap.

1998

1008 A335 350fr Sheet of 9, #a-i 10.00 10.00

Dogs and Birds A336

No. 1009, 100fr — Scouting emblem and: a, Beagle, butterfly. b, Airedale terrier, Italia 98 emblem. c, Doberman pinscher, butterfly. d, Small white dog, Italia emblem. e, Husky pup, Concorde. f, White Eskimo dog, Italia emblem. g, Dalmatian, butterfly. h, Retriever, butterfly. i, Pit bull, butterfly.

No. 1010, 300fr — a-i, Scouting jamboree emblem and various penguins.

No. 1011, 500fr — a-i, Various parrots.

1999 **Sheets of 9, #a-i**

1009-1011 A336 Set of 3 *15.00 15.00*

Intl. Year of the Ocean (No. 1010). Dated 1998.

Sailing A337

No. 1012: a, Sailboat, lighthouse. b, Man, woman in sailboat. c, Sailor, large waves. d, Yachts racing.

1999

1012 A337 750fr Sheet of 4, #a-d

Dated 1998. Sheets of four 525fr and 875fr stamps were not authorized by Niger Post.

Trains A338

Various trains. Sheets of 4, each stamp denominated: 225fr, 325fr, 375fr, 500fr.

1999 **Sheets of 4, #a-d**

1013-1017 A338 Set of 5

Dated 1998. PhilexFrance 99 (#1017). A sheet of four similar stamps with 650fr denominations, 750fr souvenir sheet, 2500fr souvenir sheet, and two 3000fr souvenir sheets were not authorized by Niger Post.

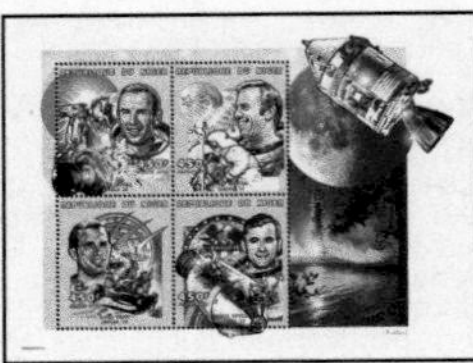

Astronauts — A339

No. 1018, 450fr: a, James Lovell. b, Alan Shepard. c, David Scott. d, John Young.

No. 1019, 500fr: a, Neil Armstrong. b, Michael Collins. c, Edwin Aldrin. d, Alan Bean.

No. 1020, 600fr: a, Walter Schirra. b, Robert Crippen. c, Thomas Stafford. d, Owen Garriott.

No. 1021, 750fr: a, John Glenn. b, Gordon Cooper. c, Scott Carpenter. d, Virgil Grissom.

2000fr, Collins, Armstrong and Aldrin.

1999 **Sheets of 4, #a-d**

1018-1021 A339 Set of 4 *35.00 35.00*

Souvenir Sheet

1022 A339 2000fr multi *8.00 8.00*

No. 1022 contains one 56x51mm stamp.

Chess A340

No. 1023, 350fr: a, Tigran Petrosian. b, Robert Fischer. c, Boris Spassky. d, Viktor Korchnoi. e, Garry Kasparov. f, Anatoly Karpov.

No. 1024, 400fr: a, Richard Reti. b, Alexander Alekhine. c, Max Euwe. d, Paul Keres. e, Mikhail Botvinnik. f, Mikhail Tal.

No. 1025, 500fr: a, Philidor. b, Adolf Anderssen. c, Joseph Henry Blackburne. d, Emanuel Lasker. e, Frank Marshall. f, José Raul Capablanca.

2000fr, head of Kasparov, Leo Tolstoy playing chess.

1999 **Sheets of 6, #a-f**

1023-1025 A340 Set of 3 *30.00 30.00*

Souvenir Sheet

1026 A340 2000fr multi *9.00 9.00*

Nos. 1023-1025 each contain six 51x36mm stamps. Dated 1998.

Baseball Players A341

No. 1027, 200fr, Various views of Lou Gehrig.

No. 1028, 250fr, Various views of Ty Cobb.

Nos. 1029, 1031, Gehrig, diff. Nos. 1030, 1032, Cobb, diff.

1999 Sheets of 9, #a-i
1027-1028 A341 Set of 2 *19.00 19.00*

Souvenir Sheets

1029-1030 A341 1500fr Set of 2 *15.00 15.00*
1031-1032 A341 2000fr Set of 2 *15.00 15.00*

Animals and Mushrooms — A342

No. 1033, 300fr: a, Snake. b, Tortoise. c, Scorpion. d, Lizard.
No. 1034, 400fr: a, Vulture. b, Gray cuckoo. c, Jackdaw. d, Turtle dove.
No. 1035, 600fr: a, Ham the chimpanzee. b, Laika the dog. c, Cat. d, Spider.
No. 1036, 750fr: a, Nymphalidae palla. b, Nymphalidae perle. c, Nymphalidae diademebleu. d, Nymphalidae pirate.
No. 1037, 1000fr: a, Cliotcybe rouge brique. b, Lactaire a odeur de camphre. c, Strophaire vert-de-gris. d, Lepiote a ecailles aigues.
Illustration reduced.

1999, Nov. 23 Sheets of 4, #a-d
1033-1037 A342 Set of 5 *50.00 50.00*

Council of the Entente, 40th Anniv. — A343

1999, May 29 Litho. *Perf. 13x13¼*
1039 A343 175fr multi 1.75 1.75

An additional stamp was issued in this set. The editors would like to examine any examples.

First French Stamps, 150th Anniv. — A344

Litho. With Hologram Applied

1999, Oct. 7 *Perf. 13*
1040 A344 200fr France Type A1 1.50 1.50

Fire Fighting Equipment — A345

No. 1041 — Automobiles: a, Bugatti Type 37. b, Chevrolet Corvette. c, Lotus Elise. d, Ferrari 550 Maranello.
No. 1042: a, Canadair airplane. b, Hook and ladder truck. c, Water pumper of middle ages. d, 1914 pumper.
No. 1043 — Trains: a, Union Pacific, 1869. b, Prussian State Railway P8, 1905. c, Pennsylvania Railroad T1, 1942. d, German Railways Series 015, 1962.
No. 1044 — Airplanes: a, De Havilland Comet. b, Airbus A340. c, Boeing 747. d, Concorde.
No. 1045 — Trains: a, Diesel-electric locomotive. b, Bullet train, Japan. c, Thalys. d, X2000, China.
No. 1046 — Spacecraft: a, Atlas rocket, Mercury capsule. b, RD-107 Soyuz. c, Saturn V rocket, Apollo capsule. d, Space shuttle.

1999, Nov. 23 Litho. *Perf. 13½*
1041 A345 450fr Sheet of 4, #a-d *10.00 10.00*
1042 A345 500fr Sheet of 4, #a-d *11.50 11.50*
1043 A345 600fr Sheet of 4, #a-d *13.00 13.00*
1044 A345 650fr Sheet of 4, #a-d *14.50 14.50*
1045 A345 750fr Sheet of 4, #a-d *16.00 16.00*
1046 A345 800fr Sheet of 4, #a-d *12.50 12.50*

Intl. Anti-Desertification Day — A346

Designs: 150fr, Trenches. 200fr, Men in field. 225fr, Trees in desert.

2000, June 17 Litho. *Perf. 13½*
1047-1049 A346 Set of 3 — —

Bird Type of 1997

2000, June 20 *Perf. 13¼*
1050 A309 150fr Psittacula krameri 1.25 1.25

2000 Summer Olympics, Sydney — A347

No. 1051: a, 50fr, Men's singles, badminton. b, 50fr, Men's doubles, badminton. c, 50fr, Softball. d, 50fr, Men's floor exercises. e, 50fr, Women's singles, badminton. f, 50fr, Women's doubles, badminton. g, 50fr, Baseball. h, 50fr, Men's long horse vault. i, 50fr, Women's cycling. j, 50fr, Women's pursuit cycling. k, 50fr, Women's road race cycling. l, 50fr, Women's shot put. m, 900fr, Men's singles, table tennis. n, 900fr, Men's doubles, table tennis. o, 900fr, Women's singles, table tennis. p, 900fr, Women's doubles, table tennis.
No. 1052: a, 100fr, Women's freestyle swimming. b, 100fr, Women's butterfly. c, 100fr, Men's prone rifle. d, 100fr, Women's sport pistol. e, 100fr, Women's 3-meter diving. f, 100fr, Women's 10-meter diving. g, 100fr, Women's three-position rifle. h, 100fr, Women's double trap. i, 100fr, Women's beach volleyball. j, 100fr, Women's volleyball. k, 100fr, Women's handball. l, 100fr, Men's sailboarding. m, 700fr, Women's kayak singles. n, 700fr, Women's kayak pairs. o, 700fr, Women's kayak fours. p, 700fr, Women's eight-oared shell with coxswain.

2000, July 27 Litho.

Sheets of 16, #a-p

1051-1052 A347 Set of 2 *70.00 70.00*

Modern and Prehistoric Fauna — A348

No. 1053, 200fr — Butterflies: a, Epiphora bauhiniae. b, Cymothoe sangaris. c, Cyrestris camillus. d, Precis clelia. e, Precis octavia amestris. f, Nudaurelia zambesina.
No. 1054, 200fr — Insects: a, Stenocara eburnea. b, Chalcocoris anchorago. c, Scarabaeus aeratus. d, Pseudocreobotra wahlbergi. e, Schistocera gregaria. f, Anopheles gambiae.
No. 1055, 225fr — Prehistoric winged animals: a, Sordes pilosus. b, Quetzalcoatlus. c, Dimorphodon. d, Podopteryx. e, Archaeopteryx. f, Pteranodon.
No. 1056, 225fr — Birds: a, Bec-en-sabot. b, Euplecte ingnicolore. c, Spreo royal. d, Calao trompette. e, Pseudocanari parasite. f, Gonolek rouge et noir.
No. 1057, 400fr — Cats: a, Egyptian mau. b, Domestic. c, African wildcat. d, Chat dore. e, Chat a pieds noirs. f, Chat des sables.
No. 1058, 400fr — Dogs: a, Chien du pharaon. b, Saluki. c, Rhodesian ridgeback. d, Beagle. e, Spitz. f, Basenji.
No. 1059, 450fr — Modern and prehistoric African animals: a, Proconsul africanus. b, Chimpanzee. c, Metamynodon planifrons. d, Black rhinoceros. e, Hyrachius eximus. f, White rhinoceros.
No. 1060, 450fr — Modern and prehistoric African animals: a, Canis familiaris. b, Black and white basenji. c, Hipparion mediterraneum. d, Burchell zebra. e, Moeritherium. f, African elephant.
No. 1061, 475fr — Modern and prehistoric reptiles: a, Palaeobatrachus. b, African frog. c, Metoposaurus. d, Salamander. e, Tylosaurus. f, Varan du Nil.
No. 1062, 475fr — Modern and prehistoric African animals: a, Basilosaurus. b, Solalie du Cameroun. c, Mesosaurus. d, Cordylus giganteus. e, Sarcosuchus. f, Nile crocodile

2000, Oct. 27 *Perf. 13¼*

Sheets of 6, #a-f

1053-1062 A348 Set of 10 *120.00 120.00*

2002 World Cup Soccer Championships, Japan and Korea — A349

No. 1063, 400fr: a, Castro. b, Orsi. c, Piola. d, Ghiggia.
No. 1064, 400fr: a, Morlock. b, Pele. c, Amarildo. d, Hurst.
No. 1065, 400fr: a, Jairzinho. b, Müller. c, Kempes. d, Rossi.
No. 1066, 400fr: a, Burruchaga. b, Brehme. c, Dunga. d, Petit.

2001, Jan. 16 Sheets of 4, #a-d
1063-1066 A349 Set of 4 24.00 24.00

Dated 2000.

Universal Postal Union, 125th Anniv. (in 1999) A350

No. 1067, 150fr — Ships: a, Transat, Citta di Catania. b, Great Eastern, Julius Caesar. c, Caledonia, Mercury. d, Braganza, Westland.
No. 1068, 225fr — Vehicles: a, Horse-drawn omnibus, postal bus. b, 1899 automobile, rural omnibus. c, 1904 van, postal automobile and bicycle. d, 1906 automobile, Swiss postal bus.
No. 1069, 450fr — Trains: a, 25NC Modder Kimberley locomotive, CDJR diesel. b, Pacific Karoo, Budd diesel. c, 141 Maghreb locomotive, EAR Diesel-electric locomotive. d, 230 Series 6 C.G.A., Postal TGV train.
No. 1070, 500fr — Airplanes: a, Late-28, Super Constellation. b, Douglas DC-4, Nord Atlas. c, Boeing 707, Concorde. d, Boeing 747, Airbus A3XX.
No. 1071, 550fr — Spacecraft: a, 1934 postal rocket, Asian telecommunications satellite. b, Space capsules. c, Apollo 15, Astra 1 H telecommunications satellite. d, Voyager, Space Station and shuttle.
No. 1072, 700fr — Trains: a, 230 locomotive, Senegal, 141 locomotive, Tanganyika. b, 141 locomotive, Niger. 242 locomotive, South Africa. c, 130+031 locomotive, Ivory Coast, Garrat 242+242. d, 040 locomotive, Cameroun, 14R locomotive.

2001, Jan. 16 *Perf. 13¼*

Sheets of 4, #a-d

1067-1072 A350 Set of 6 47.50 47.50

Dated 2000.

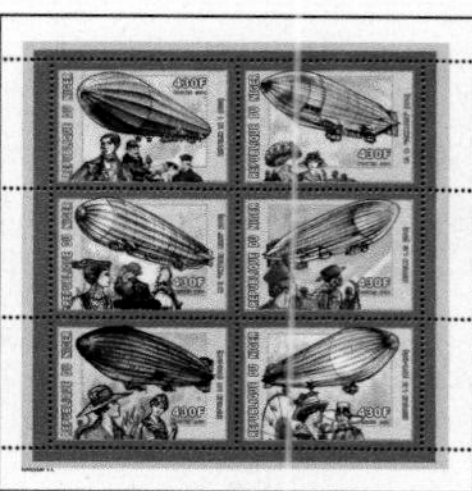

Zeppelins and Satellites — A351

No. 1073, 430fr — Zeppelins: a, LZ-1. b, LZ-10 Schwaben. c, LZ II Viktoria Luise. d, L-30. e, L-11. f, L-59.
No. 1074, 460fr — Zeppelins: a, LZ-120 Bodensee. b, L-72 Dixmude. c, LZ-127 Graf Zeppelin. d, LZ-129 Hindenburg. e, LZ-130. f, D-LZFN.
No. 1075, 750fr, vert. — Satellites: a, Meteosat. b, GOMS. c, GMS. d, Insat 1A. e, GOES. f, FY-2.

2001, June 20 Litho.

Sheets of 6, #a-f

1073-1075 A351 Set of 3 40.00 40.00

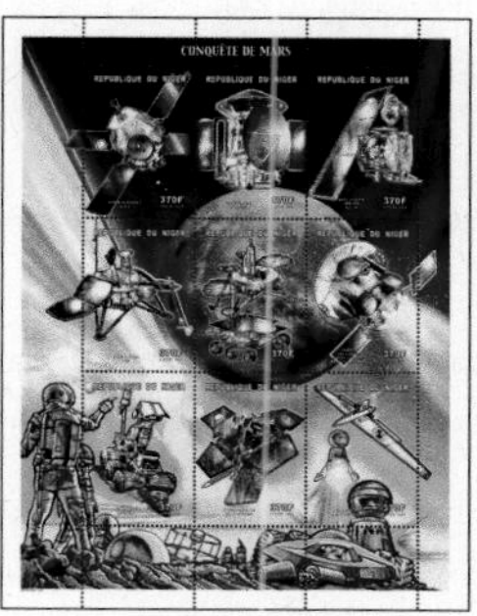

Space Exploration — A352

No. 1076, 370fr — Conquest of Mars: a, Mariner 9. b, Mars 3. c, Mars Climate Orbiter. d, Mars Lander. e, Mars Rover. f, Netlander. g, Robot on Mars. h, Beagle 2. i, Ames Research plane for Mars.
No. 1077, 390fr — Orbital and Lunar Exploration: a, Yuri Gagarin, Vostok capsule. b, John Glenn, Mercury capsule. c, Space shuttle. d, Alan Shepard, Apollo 14. e, Neil Armstrong, Apollo 11. f, Charles Conrad, Apollo 12. g, Edward White, Gemini 4. h, James Irwin, Apollo 15. i, Lunar base and shuttle.
No. 1078, 490fr — Planetary and Interstellar Exploration: a, Pioneer 10. b, Mariner 10. c, Venera 13. d, Pioneer 13, Venus 2. e, Probe for detecting "Big Bang." f, Interstellar spacecraft. g, Inhabited space station. h, Giotto probe, Astronaut on comet. i, Galileo probe.

2001, June 20 Litho.

Sheets of 9, #a-i

1076-1078 A352 Set of 3 45.00 45.00

African History A353

No. 1079, 390fr: a, Gahna Empire, 10th cent. b, Kankou Moussa, Emperor of Mali, 1324. c, Sankore, University of Tombouctou, 15th cent. d, Sonni Ali Ber, Songhai Emperor. e, Bantu migrations, 15th and 16th cents. f, Slave trade, 1513.
No. 1080, 490fr: a, Ramses II, 1301-1235 B.C., Battle of Qadesh. b, Mummification. c, Religion. d, Instruction. e, Justice. f, Artisans.
No. 1081, 530fr: a, Djoser, Third Dynasty, 2650 B.C. b, Rahotep and wife, Fourth Dynasty, 2570 B.C. c, Cheops and Pyramid, Fourth Dynasty, 2600 B.C. d, Chephren, Fourth Dynasty, 2500 B.C. e, Akhenaton and Nefertiti, 18th Dynasty, 1372-1354 B.C. f, Tutankhamen, 18th Dynasty, 1354-1346 B.C.

2001, July 24 Litho.

Sheets of 6, #a-f

1079-1081 A353 Set of 3 35.00 35.00

Air Chiriet A354

2001 *Perf. 13x13¼*
1082 A354 150fr multi 1.00 1.00

Intl. Volunteers Year — A355

2001
1083 A355 150fr multi 1.00 1.00

Birds, Butterflies, Meteorites, and Mushrooms — A356

No. 1084, 530fr — Birds: a, Falco peregrinus. b, Falco biarmicus. c, Vultur gryphus.
No. 1085, 575fr — Butterflies: a, Junonia orithya. b, Salamis parhassus. c, Amauris echeria.
No. 1086, 750fr — Meteorites: a, P. Pallas, 1772. b, Iron meteorite. c, Bouvante rock.
No. 1087, 825fr — Mushrooms: a, Otidea onotica. b, Lentinus sajor-caju. c, Pleurotus luteoalbus.

2002, Apr. 24 *Perf. 13¼*
Sheets of 3, #a-c
1084-1087 A356 Set of 4 26.00 26.00

Souvenir sheets of 1 of each of the individual stamps exist.

Cow's Head — A357

2002, Sept. 17 Litho. *Perf. 13¼*
1088 A357 50fr multi .50 .50

Toubou Spears — A358

2002, Sept. 17 Litho. *Perf. 13x12½*
1089 A358 100fr multi *7.50 7.50*

Birds A359

2002, Sept. 17 Litho. *Perf. 13*
1090 A359 225fr multi 1.10 1.10

Hippopotamus in Captivity — A360

Boudouma Cow — A361 Boudouma Calf — A362

2003, Dec. 3 Litho. *Perf. 13x13¼*
1091 A360 100fr multi *.60 .60*
Perf. 13
1092 A361 150fr multi *.80 .80*
Perf. 13¼
1093 A362 225fr multi *1.10 1.10*
Nos. 1091-1093 (3) *2.50 2.50*

Values for No. 1092 are for stamps with surrounding selvage.

Pottery A363

Camel and Rider — A364

2004 *Perf. 13x13¼*
1094 A363 150fr multi *10.00 10.00*
Perf. 13
1095 A364 1000fr multi *5.00 5.00*

Values for No. 1095 are for stamps with surrounding selvage.

In Universal Postal Union Circular 388, issued Nov. 28, 2005, Niger postal officials declared illegal additional items bearing the inscription "Republique du Niger." As this circular contains a somewhat unintelligible list of items which lacks specifics as to denominations found on the illegal items or the sizes of sheets, some of the items may be duplicative of items mentioned in the note on illegal stamps following No. 999. Also, because of the lack of clarity of the list, some catalogued items may now be items cited as "illegal" in Circular 388. The text of this circular can be seen on the UPU's WNS website.

Emblem of 2005 Francophone Games — A365

2005, May 12 Litho. *Perf. 13x13¼*
1096 A365 150fr multi *4.00 4.00*

World Summit on the Information Society, Tunis — A366

2005, May 26 *Perf. 13¼*
1097 A366 225fr multi *7.50 7.50*

Mascot of 2005 Francophone Games A367

2005, Aug. 22 *Perf. 13*
1098 A367 225fr multi *4.00 4.00*

Léopold Sédar Senghor (1906-2001), First President of Senegal — A368

2006, Apr. 6 Litho. *Perf. 12¾*
1099 A368 175fr multi *2.50 2.50*

Pres. Tandja Mamadou — A369

2006, July 14
1100 A369 750fr multi 3.50 3.50

Boubou Hama (1906-82), Writer — A370

Background colors: 150fr, Green. 175fr, Orange brown. 325fr, Light blue.

2006, Sept. 23 Litho. *Perf. 13x12¾*
1101-1103 A370 Set of 3 *10.00 10.00*

Messenger From Madaoua — A371

2006, Nov. 6 Litho. *Perf. 13x12¾*
1104 A371 25fr multi —

Dated 2004.

24th UPU Congress, Geneva, Switzerland A373

2007, Nov. 9 Litho. *Perf. 13*
1106 A373 500fr multi 3.50 3.50

Values are for stamps with surrounding selvage. UPU Congress was moved to Geneva after political violence in Nairobi, Kenya.

Wildlife — A374

Designs: 200fr, Giraffes. 400fr, Addax. 600fr, Ostriches.

2007, Nov. 9 *Perf. 12¾*
1107-1109 A374 Set of 3 5.50 5.50

Grain Grinding — A375

Bororo Dance — A376

Chief's Guard — A377

2008, Aug. 8 *Perf. 12¾*
1110 A375 100fr multi .45 .45
1111 A376 350fr multi 1.60 1.60
1112 A377 1000fr multi 4.75 4.75
Nos. 1110-1112 (3) 6.80 6.80

Women At Well — A378

Hunters A379

2009, Nov. 20 *Perf. 13*
1113 A378 300fr multi 1.40 1.40
1114 A379 450fr multi 2.10 2.10

Baobab Tree — A380

Téra-téra Blanket — A381

Women's Hairstyles — A382

2010, June 4 *Perf. 12¾*
1115 A380 500fr multi 1.90 1.90
Perf. 13
1116 A381 700fr multi 2.60 2.60
Perf. 13¼
1117 A382 1500fr multi 5.50 5.50
Nos. 1115-1117 (3) 10.00 10.00

Values for No. 1116 are for stamps with surrounding selvage.

Independence, 50th Anniv. — A383

2010, June 30 ***Perf. 13***

1118 A383 1000fr multi 4.00 4.00

Hut of Sultan Usman Dan Fodio (1754-1817) A384

Lété Island — A385

2011, May 30 ***Perf. 12¾***

1119 A384 175fr multi .80 .80
1120 A385 320fr multi 1.40 1.40

Violet de Galmi Onions — A386

Djado Ruins — A387

Gen. Salou Djibo, Head of State of Niger — A388

2011, Oct. 19

1121 A386 500fr multi 2.10 2.10
1122 A387 735fr multi 3.25 3.25
1123 A388 1000fr multi 4.25 4.25
Nos. 1121-1123 (3) 9.60 9.60

Worldwide Fund for Nature (WWF) — A389

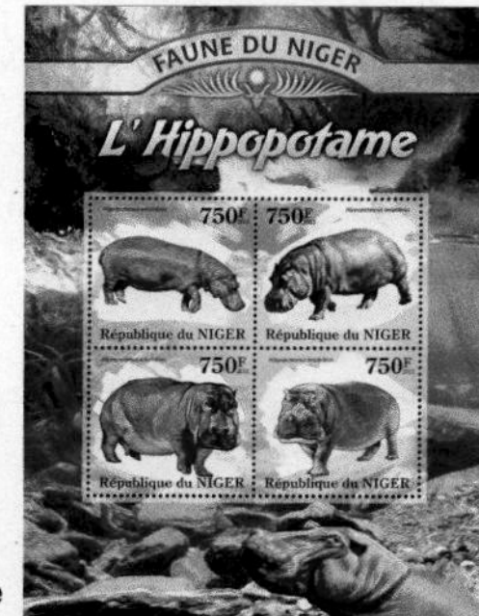
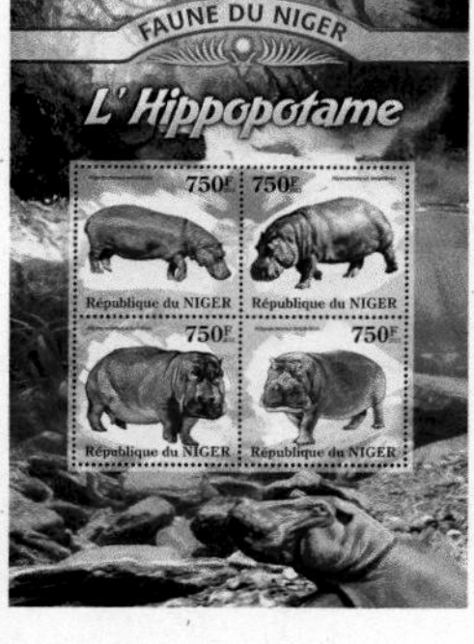

Wildlife A390

No. 1124 — Giraffa camelopardalis peralta with: a, WWF emblem at LR, animal name at UR. b, WWF emblem at UL, animal name at bottom. c, WWF emblem at LR, animal name at UL. d, WWF emblem at UR, animal name at bottom.

No. 1125, 750fr — Hippopotamus amphibius: a, Denomination at UR, head down, facing right. b, Denomination at UL. c, Denomination at UR, head up at right. d, Denomination at UR, head up at left.

No. 1126, 750fr — Syncerus caffer: a, Denomination at UR, animal name at UL. b, Denomination at UL, animal name at top, animal facing right. c, Denomination at UL, animal name at top, animal facing left. d, Denomination at UR, animal name at LL.

No. 1127, 750fr — Foxes: a, Vulpes rueppellii, animal name at UL. b, Vulpes zerda, animal name at UL, end of name even with top of denomination. c, Vulpes zerda, animal name at left, end of name lower than denomination. d, Vulpes rueppellii, animal name at LR.

No. 1128, 750fr — Hyenas: a, Crocuta crocuta, animal name at LL. b, Hyaena hyaena, animal name at UR. c, Hyaena hyaena, animal name at UL. d, Crocuta crocuta, animal name at top.

No. 1129, 750fr — Antelopes: a, Oryx dammah. b, Ammotragus lervia. c, Nanger dama. d, Tragelaphus eurycerus.

No. 1130, 750fr — Primates: a, Galago senegalensis. b, Chlorocebus tantalus. c, Erythrocebus patas. d, Papio anubis.

No. 1131, 750fr — Bats: a, Eidolon helvum. b, Micropteropus pusillus. c, Lavia frons. d, Nycteris thebaica.

No. 1132, 750fr — Lions and leopards: a, Male Panthera leo. b, One Panthera pardus. c, Two Panthera pardus. d, Two female Panthera leo.

No. 1133, 750fr — Wildcats: a, Felis silvestris lybica. b, Felis margarita. c, Leptailurus serval. d, Felis margarita airensis.

No. 1134, 750fr — Lycaon pictus: a, Denomination at UR, animal name at UL. b, Denomination at UL, animal name at UR. c, Denomination at UL, animal name at top center. d, Denomination at UR, animal name at top center.

No. 1135, 750fr — Loxodonta africana: a, Denomination at right center, animal name at UL. b, Denomination at UR, animal name at UL. c, Denomination at UL, animal name at left. d, Denomination at UR, animal name at right center.

No. 1136, 750fr — Trichechus senegalensis: a, Animal name at UL, left flipper above "b" in "République." b, Animal name at UL, right flipper above "d" in "du." c, Animal name at UL, right fin above space between "République" and "du." d, Animal name at LL.

No. 1137, 750fr — Owls: a, Scotopelia peli. b, Glaucidium perlatum. c, Otus senegalensis. d, Ptilopsis leucotis.

No. 1138, 750fr — Doves: a, Colombar waalia. b, Oena capensis. c, Columba guinea. d, Columba arquatrix.

No. 1139, 750fr — Parrots: a, Poicephalus robustus. b, Psittacula krameri, animal name below denomination. c, Psittacula krameri, animal name to left of denomination. d, Psittacus erithacus, Psittacula krameri.

No. 1140, 750fr — Birds: a, Chalcomitra senegalensis. b, Hedydipna platurus. c, Cinnyris pulchella. d, Cinnyris cupreus.

No. 1141, 750fr — Water birds: a, Ardea cinerea in flight. b, Ardeola rufiventris. c, Ardea cinerea with fish. d, Ardea goliath.

No. 1142, 750fr — Birds of prey: a, Circaetus cinereus. b, Hieraaetus pennatus. c, Aquila rapax. d, Aquila pomarina.

No. 1143, 750fr — Butterflies: a, Pinacopteryx eriphia. b, Colotis antevippe with orange wing tips. c, Colotis antevippe with yellow and black coloratiion. d, Zizeeria knysna.

No. 1144, 750fr — Butterflies: a, Catopsilia florella. b, Coeliades forestan. c, Acraea neobule. d, Hypolimnas misippus.

No. 1145, 750fr — Fish: a, Hemichromis fasciatus. b, Fundulosoma thierryi. c, Aphyosemion bitaeniatum. d, Arnoldichthys spilopterus.

No. 1146, 750fr — Turtles: a, Psammobates geometricus. b, Pelomedusa subrufa. c, Pelusios niger. d, Astrochelys yniphora.

No. 1147, 750fr — Crocodiles: a, Crocodylus niloticus, animal name at UL. b, Crocodylus cataphractus, denomination at UL. c, Crocodylus cataphractus, denomination at UR. d, Crocodylus niloticus, animal name at LL.

No. 1148, 750fr — Snakes: a, Dasypeltis sahelensis. b, Dromophis praeornatus. c, Dromophis lineatus. d, Dasypeltis gansi.

No. 1149, 2500fr, Giraffa camelopardalis peralta, diff. No. 1150, 2500fr, Hippopotamus amphibius, diff. No. 1151, 2500fr, Syncerus caffer, diff. No. 1152, 2500fr, Vulpes rueppellii, diff. No. 1153, 2500fr, Crocuta crocuta, diff. No. 1154, 2500fr, Ammotragus lervia, diff. No. 1155, 2500fr, Papio anubis, diff. No. 1156, 2500fr, Micropteropus pusillus, diff. No. 1157, 2500fr, Panthera pardus, diff. No. 1158, 2500fr, Caracal caracal. No. 1159, 2500fr, Lycaon pictus, diff. No. 1160, 2500fr, Loxodonta africana, diff. No. 1161, 2500fr, Trichechus senegalensis, diff. No. 1162, 2500fr, Bubo ascalaphus. No. 1163, 2500fr, Colombar waalia, diff. No. 1164, 2500fr, Psittacus erithacus, diff. No. 1165, 2500fr, Cinnyris coccinigastrus. No. 1166, 2500fr, Ardea cinerea, diff. No. 1167, 2500fr, Falco naumanii. No. 1168, 2500fr, Spialia spio. No. 1169, 2500fr, Danaus chysippus. No. 1170, 2500fr, Oreochromis aureus. No. 1171, 2500fr, Pelusios sinuatus. No. 1172, 2500fr, Crocodylus niloticus, diff. No. 1173, 2500fr, Atracaspis microlepidota.

2013, Mar. 1 ***Perf. 13¼x13***

1124 Strip of 4 12.00 12.00
a.-d. A389 750fr Any single 3.00 3.00
e. Souvenir sheet of 8, 2 each #1124a-1124d, + 2 labels 24.00 24.00

Sheets of 4, #a-d

Perf. 13¼

1125-1148 A390 Set of 24 285.00 285.00

Souvenir Sheets

1149-1173 A390 Set of 25 250.00 250.00

Pres. Issoufou Mahamadou A391

2013, Mar. 8 ***Perf. 13¼x13***

1174 A391 500fr multi 2.00 2.00

A392

No. 1175, 500fr — Mahatma Gandhi (1869-1948), Indian independence leader: a, On Russia #3639, denomination at LR. b, On cover of *Time* magazine, denomination at LL. c, Denomination at UR. d, With hands together, denomination at UL.

No. 1176, 500fr — Yang Liwei, Chinese astronaut, and Shenzhou 5 with: a, Denomination at LR. b, Denomination at LL. c, Denomination at UR. d, Denomination at UL.

No. 1177, 675fr — Pope Benedict XVI with: a, Denomination at LR. b, Denomination at LL. c, Denomination at UR. d, Denomination at UL.

No. 1178, 675fr — Garry Kasparov, chess champion, and chess pieces with: a, Denomination at LR. b, Denomination at LL. c, Denomination at UR. d, Denomination at UL.

No. 1179, 675fr — Cat breeds: a, Cymric. b, Maine coon cat. c, Persian. d, Oriental.

No. 1180, 675fr — Small dog breeds: a, Chihuahua. b, Spitz. c, Russian toy terrier. d, Yorkshire terrier.

No. 1181, 750fr — Paintings by Albrecht Dürer (1471-1528): a, Portrait of Barbara Dürer, denomination at LR. b, Nativity, denomination at LL. c, Young Hare, denomination at UR. d, Feast of the Rosary, denomination at UL.

No. 1182, 750fr — Paintings by Paul Signac (1863-1935): a, Calvados, denomination at LR. b, Road to Gennevilliers, denomination at LL. c, The Gas Tanks at Clichy, denomination at UR. d, The Railroad at Bois Colombes, denomination at UL.

No. 1183, 750fr — Paintings by Joan Miró (1893-1983): a, Carneval d'Arlequin, denomination at LR. b, Catalan Landscape (The Hunter), denomination at LL. c, Circus, denomination at UR. d, The Poetess, denomination at UL.

No. 1184, 750fr — Bobby Fischer (1943-2008), chess champion: a, On Iceland #1203, denomination at LR. b, On cover of *Life* magazine, denomination at LL. c, With chess pieces, denomination at UR. d, With chess pieces, denomination at UL.

No. 1185, 750fr — Audrey Hepburn (1929-93), actress: a, Wearing red dress. b, With Peter O'Toole. c, With Cary Grant. d, With Gregory Peck.

No. 1186, 750fr — Ancient Egyptian monuments: a, Sculpted head of Amenhotep III. Temple of Horus. b, Bust of Nefertiti. c, Sphinx and Pyramids. d, Pyramids.

No. 1187, 750fr — Lighthouses: a, Biloxi Lighthouse, U.S. b, Rotesand Lighthouse, Germany. c, Execution Rocks Lighthouse, U.S. d, Coney Island Lighthouse, U.S.

No. 1188, 750fr — Cessation of Concorde flights, 10th anniv.: a, Concorde, Buckingham Palace, Queen Elizabeth II, Prince Philip. b, Concorde, Heathrow Airport, Brian Trubshaw, pilot. c, Concorde, Tower Bridge, British flag. d, Concorde, Arc de Triomphe, French flag.

No. 1189, 750fr — Space Shuttle Columbia disaster, 10th anniv.: a, Explosion. b, Columbia, map of U.S.. c, Memorial to Columbia astronauts. d, Columbia on launch pad.

No. 1190, 750fr — Tour de France bicycle race, cent.: a, Lucien Petit-Breton. b, Philippe Thys. c, Greg LeMond. d, Cadel Evans.

No. 1191, 750fr — 2013 African Cup of Nations soccer tournament: a, Two players, denomination at LR. b, One player, denomination at LL. c, One player, denomination at UR. d, Two players, denomination at UL.

No. 1192, 750fr — 2014 Winter Olympics, Sochi: a, Luge. b, Figure skating. c, Ice hockey. d, Speed skating.

No. 1193, 750fr — Dinosaurs: a, Jobaria tiguidensis. b, Afrovenator abakensis. c, Spinophorosaurus nigerensis. d, Suchomimus tenerensis.

No. 1194, 825fr — Paintings by Vincent van Gogh (1853-90): a, Portrait of Postman Joseph Roulin, denomination at LR. b, Self-portrait, Agostina Segatori Sitting in the Cafe du Tambourin, denomination at LL. c, Self-portrait, Olive Trees, denomination at UR. d, The Drinkers, denomination at UL.

No. 1195, 825fr — Hamadou Djibo Issaka, Nigerien rower at 2012 Summer Olympics: a, Denomination at LR. b, Denomination at LL. c, Denomination at UR. d, Denomination at UL.

No. 1196, 825fr — Scouting: a, Scouts building bridge, denomination at LR. b, Scout at campfire, denomination at LL. c, Map, Scout with pocket watch. d, Scouts erecting tents, denomination at UL.

No. 1197, 825fr — Rotary International Flood Aid to Niger: a, Denomination at LR. b, Denomination at LL. c, Denomination at UR. d, Denomination at UL.

No. 1198, 825fr — Scenes from the Djado Plateau: a, Denomination at LR. b, Denomination at LL. c, Denomination at UR. d, Denomination at UL.

No. 1199, 825fr — Minerals of Niger: a, Diamond, denomination at LR. b, Gold, denomination at LL. c, Tin, denomination at UR. d, Silver, denomination at UL.

No. 1200, 2000fr, Gandhi, diff. No. 1201, 2000fr, Yang Liwei and Shenzhou 5, diff. No. 1202, 2000fr, Pope Benedict XVI, diff. No. 1203, 2000fr, Kasparov, diff. No. 1204, 2000fr, Cymric cat, diff. No. 1205, 2000fr, Papillon. No. 1206, 2500fr, Adoration of the Magi, by Dürer. No. 1207, 2500fr, Evening Calm, Concarneau, by Signac. No. 1208, 2500fr, Women and Birds at Sunrise, by Miró. No. 1209, 2500fr, Fischer, diff. No. 1210, 2500fr, Hepburn and husband, Mel Ferrer. No. 1211, 2500fr, Bust of Nefertiti, diff. No. 1212, 2500fr, Mohegan Lighthouse, U.S. No. 1213, 2500fr, Concorde and London. No. 1214, 2500fr, Crew of Space Shuttle Columbia flight STS-107. No. 1215, 2500fr, Bradley Wiggins, cyclist. No. 1216, 2500fr, Two soccer players, diff. No. 1217, 2500fr, Freestyle skiing. No. 1218, 2500fr, Kryptops palaios. No. 1219, 3000fr, Pietà, by van Gogh. No. 1220, 3000fr, Issaka, diff. No. 1221, 3000fr, Scouts and tent. No. 1222, 3000fr, Map of Niger, Rotary International emblem, child and Gaston Kaba, Niamey Rotary president. No. 1223, 3000fr, Djado Plateau rock painting. No. 1224, 3000fr, Salt, map of Niger.

2013, Apr. 15 ***Perf. 13¼***

Sheets of 4, #a-d

1175-1199 A392 Set of 25 290.00 290.00

Souvenir Sheets

1200-1224 A392 Set of 25 250.00 250.00

A393

No. 1225, 750fr — Yuri Gagarin (1934-68), first man in space: a, Blue panel, Gagarin without cap at left. b, Red panel, Gagarin wearing space helmet at left. c, Red panel, Gagarin wearing military cap at left. d, Blue panel, Gagarin wearing military cap.

No. 1226, 750fr — Space tourism: a, International Space Station, XCOR Lynx Mark II. b, WhiteKnightTwo, SpaceShipOne. c, SpaceShipTwo. d, International Space Station, Astrium Suborbital Space Plane.

No. 1227, 750fr — Steam trains: a, South African Class 26. b, LNER Peppercorn Class A1 60163 Tornado. c, LB&SCR Class B4. d, Reading Blue Mountain & Northern Railway 425.

No. 1228, 750fr — High-speed trains: a, Acela Express, New York City skyline. b, Chinese CRH380A UEM, Yongdinghe Bridge, Beijing. c, Maglev train, Shanghai. d, Alfa train, Lisbon, Portugal skyline.

No. 1229, 750fr — Ships and lighthouses: a, Barque Europa, 2007. b, Mahatao Lighthouse, Philippines. c, Amerigo Vespucci, 1976. d, Isle of May Lighthouse, Scotland.

No. 1230, 750fr — French airplanes: a, Concorde. b, Dassault Rafale. c, Breguet 14. d, Dassault Mirage F1.

No. 1231, 750fr — Fire trucks: a, SACFS Isuzu 800. b, Atego Mercedes-Benz LF 10/6 Ziegler. c, Valdosta, Georgia Airport E-7 fire truck. d, Kronenburg MAC 11.

No. 1232, 750fr — Motorcycles and actors: a, 1953 Triumph Thunderbird, Marlon Brando. b, 1955 Triumph TR5, James Dean, Marilyn Monroe. c, 1934 Harley-Davidson RL, Clark Gable. d, 1940 Indian Four Cylinder, Steve McQueen.

No. 1233, 750fr — Elvis Presley (1935-77), with panel color of: a, Blue. b, Purple. c, Olive green. d, Red.

No. 1234, 750fr — Marilyn Monroe (1926-62), with panel color of: a, Prussian blue. b, Red. c, Violet. d, Brown orange.

No. 1235, 750fr — 60th anniv. of coronation of Queen Elizabeth II, with panel color of: a, Blue. b, Red. c, Green. d, Brown orange.

No. 1236, 750fr — Pope Francis, with panel color of: a, Blue. b, Brown orange. c, Green. d, Red.

No. 1237, 750fr — Dr. Albert Schweitzer (1875-1965), 1952 Nobel Peace laureate, with panel color of: a, Dark brown. b, Prussian blue. c, Dark blue. d, Brown orange.

No. 1238, 750fr — Louis Pasteur (1822-95), microbiologist, with panel colors of: a, Brown. b, Prussian blue. c, Dark blue. d, Brown orange.

No. 1239, 750fr — Mao Zedong (1893-1976), Chinese Communist leader: a, Holding book at right, gray panel. b, Clapping at right, brown orange panel. c, Holding book at right, brown orange panel. d, With raised arm at right, gray panel.

No. 1240, 750fr — Table tennis players: a, Zhang Jike. b, Ding Ning. c, Ma Long. d, Xu Xin.

No. 1241, 750fr — Paul Cézanne (1839-1906), painter, and: a, Compotier, Pitcher and Fruit, 1894. b, Mont Saint-Victoire and Chateau Noir, 1904-06. c, Lac d'Annecy, 1896. d, Apples and Oranges, 1899.

No. 1242, 750fr — Pierre-Auguste Renoir (1841-1919), painter, and: a, Luncheon of the Boating Party, 1881. b, La Grenouillère, 1869. c, Chestnut Tree in Bloom, 1881. d, Madame Georges Charpentier and Her Children, 1878.

No. 1243, 750fr — Volcanoes and minerals: a, Chaíten Volcano, Chile, Vanadinite. b, Popocatépetl, Mexico, Calcite. c, Tungurahua, Ecuador, Hemimorphite. d, Redoubt Volcano, Alaska, Calcite and hematite.

No. 1244, 750fr — Dolphins and shells: a, Lagenorhynchus obscurus. b, Turbinella pyrum. c, Cymbiola vespertilio. d, Tursiops truncatus.

No. 1245, 750fr — Owls and mushrooms: a, Tyto alba, unnamed mushrooms. b, Gomphidus glutinosus, unnamed owl. c, Bubo virginianus, unnamed mushrooms. d, Sarcodon imbricatus, unnamed owl.

No. 1246, 750fr — Orchids and butterflies: a, Encyclia vitellina, unnamed butterflies. b, Papilio maackii, unnamed orchid. c, Vanda sanderiana, unnamed butterflies. d, Bhutanitis lidderdalii, unnamed orchid.

No. 1247, 750fr — Year of the Horse: a, Horse, brown orange panel. b, Two horses, blue panel. c, Two horses, purple panel. d, Horse, black panel.

No. 1248, 2500fr, Gagarin, diff. No. 1249, 2500fr, Richard Branson, SpaceShip Two. No. 1250, 2500fr, Southern Railway Class Ps-4. No. 1251, 2500fr, Shinkansen Series 800, Japan. No. 1252, 2500fr, Fastnet Lighthouse, Ireland, and ship. No. 1253, 2500fr, Blériot XI. No. 1254, 2500fr, Oshkosh Striker T-3000. No. 1255, 2500fr, 1964 Triumph Tiger 100, Bob Dylan. No. 1256, 2500fr, Presley, diff. No. 1257, 2500fr, Monroe, diff. No. 1258, 2500fr, Queen Elizabeth II, diff. No. 1259, 2500fr, Pope Francis, diff. No. 1260, 2500fr, Schweitzer, diff. No. 1261, 2500fr, Pasteur, diff. No. 1262, 2500fr, Mao Zedong, diff. No. 1263, 2500fr, Timo Boll, table tennis player. No. 1264, 2500fr, Cézanne, Mont Sainte-Victoire, 1885-87. No. 1265, 2500fr, Renoir, Ball at the Moulin de la Galette, 1876. No. 1266, 2500fr, Mount Etna, Italy, Pyrite. No. 1267, 2500fr, Stenella coeruleoalba. No. 1268, 2500fr, Strix aluco, unnamed mushrooms. No. 1269, 2500fr, Atrophaneura hector, unnamed orchid. No. 1270, 2500fr, Horse, diff.

2013, July 1 Litho. *Perf. 13¼*

Sheets of 4, #a-d

1225-1247 A393 Set of 23 275.00 275.00

Souvenir Sheets

1248-1270 A393 Set of 23 230.00 230.00

2013 China International Collection Expo (Nos. 1239, 1262).

Photography by Sergey Tkachenko and Russian Philatelic Items — A394

No. 1271 — Photograph and: a, Post card depicting Graf Zeppelin. b, Russia #C24. c, Russia #C21. d, Russia #C20.

2500fr, Photograph and Russia #6016.

2013, July 1 Litho. *Perf. 12¾x13¼*

1271 A394 750fr Sheet of 4, #a-d 12.00 12.00

Souvenir Sheet

1272 A394 2500fr multi 10.00 10.00

Souvenir Sheet

Mao Zedong (1893-1976), Chinese Communist Leader — A395

2013, July 1 Litho. *Perf. 12¾x13¼*

On Wood Veneer

Self-Adhesive

1273 A395 6500fr multi 26.00 26.00

Souvenir Sheet

Peng Liyuan, Singer and Wife of Xi Jinping, President of People's Republic of China — A396

2013, July 1 Litho. *Perf. 12¾x13¼*

On Wood Veneer

Self-Adhesive

1274 A396 6500fr multi 26.00 26.00

Cooperation Between Niger and Algeria A397

Perf. 12¾x13¼

2013, Sept. 10 Litho.

1275 A397 1060fr multi 4.50 4.50

A398

No. 1276, 500fr — Chinese high-speed trains: a, Maglev. b, CRH5. c, Bombardier. d, CRH6A.

No. 1277, 500fr — Shenzhou 10: a, Astronaut Wang Yaping, Shenzhou 10. b, Astronaut Nie Haisheng, Shenzhou 10. c, Astronaut Zhang Xiaoguang, rocket on launch pad. d, Shenzhou 10 and emblem.

No. 1278, 675fr — Nanger Dama: a, Head of gazelle facing left, gazelle in background. b, Gazelle leaping. c, Gazelle resting. d, Adult and juvenile gazelles.

No. 1279, 675fr — African mammals: a, Equus burchelli. b, Phacochoerus africanus. c, Hippopotamus amphibius. d, Alcelaphus buselaphus caama.

No. 1280, 675fr — Wildcats: a, Caracal caracal. b, Leptailurus serval. c, Acinonyx jubatus. d, Panthera pardus.

No. 1281, 750fr — Whales: a, Megaptera novaeangliae. b, Balaenoptera borealis. c, Balaenoptera musculus. d, Eschrichtius robustus.

No. 1282, 750fr — Apis mellifera and flowers: a, Chaenomeles japonica. b, Tanacetum parthenium. c, Paeonia cambessedesii. d, Odontoglossum rossii.

No. 1283, 750fr — Birds: a, Halcyon malimbica. b, Caprimulgus eximius. c, Scopus umbretta. d, Musophaga violacea.

No. 1284, 750fr — Reptiles: a, Python regius. b, Crocodylus niloticus. c, Varanus griseus. d, Trionyx triunguis.

No. 1285, 750fr — Campaign against malaria: a, Red Cross worker feeling head of sick child. b, Children under mosquito netting, mosquito at right. c, Children under mosquito netting, mosquito at left. d, Red Cross worker wearing gloves treating sick child.

No. 1286, 750fr — Prehistoric man: a, Homo georgicus. b, Homo neanderthalensis. c, Homo tyrolensis. d, Homo erectus.

No. 1287, 750fr — Military aircraft: a, Argentine Air Force Douglas A-4 Skyhawk. b, Iranian Air Force F14 Tomcat. c, U.S. Air Force Northrop Grumman RQ-4 Global Hawk. d, U.S. Air Force Lockheed Martin F35B Stealth fighter.

No. 1288, 750fr — Special transportation: a, BMW R1200RT police motorcycle. b, Agusta A-109 K2 helicopter ambulance. c, Pierce Arrow 105-foot X-ladder fire truck. d, Chevrolet C4500 ambulance.

No. 1289, 750fr — Famous cricket players: a, Inzamam-ul-Haq. b, Malcolm Marshall. c, Sanath Jayasuriya. d, Sachin Tendulkar.

No. 1290, 750fr — Pierre de Coubertin (1863-1937), founder of International Olympic Committee, and: a, Runner. b, High jumper. c, Wrestlers. d, Gymnast.

No. 1291, 750fr — Giuseppe Verdi (1813-1901), composer, and performers from opera: a, Rigoletto. b, Hermani. c, Macbeth. d, La Pucelle d'Orléans (Giovanna d'Arco).

No. 1292, 750fr — Richard Wagner (1813-83), composer, and performers from opera: a, Lohengrin. b, Tristan and Isolde. c, The Mastersingers of Nuremberg (Les Maîtres Chanteurs de Nuremberg). d, The Flying Dutchman (Le Vaisseau Fantôme).

No. 1293, 750fr — Nelson Mandela (1918-2013), President of South Africa, and: a, Princess Diana. b, Dove. c, Michael Jackson. d, Bill Gates.

No. 1294, 750fr — Pope John Paul II (1920-2005): a, Waving. b, Seated. c, Seated holding crucifix. d, Standing and praying.

No. 1295, 750fr — Grace Kelly (1929-82), actress and Princess of Monaco: a, Wearing red dress in background. b, In scene from *To Catch a Thief,* 1955. c, In scene from *Dial M for Murder,* 1954. d, Wearing blue dress in background.

No. 1296, 750fr — Paintings by Francisco Goya (1746-1828): a, Witches' Sabbath, 1798. b, The Grape Harvest, 1787. c, The Parasol, 1777. d, Gaspar Melchor de Jovellanos, 1798.

No. 1297, 750fr — Paintings by American Impressionists: a, The Hammock, by Joseph DeCamp. b, Five O'Clock, by Guy Rose. c, Madonna of the Apples, by Joseph Kleitsch. d, Marjorie and Little Edmund, by Edmund C. Tarbell.

No. 1298, 750fr — Paintings by Pablo Picasso (1881-1973): a, Woman at Fountain, 1901. b, Still Life with a Bull's Skull, 1939. c, Science and Charity, 1897. d, The Red Armchair, 1931 (incorrect inscription).

No. 1299, 750fr — Birth of Prince George of Cambridge: a, Prince Charles, Princess Diana and Prince William. b, Duke and Duchess of Cambridge with Prince George outside hospital. c, Duke and Duchess of Cambridge with Prince George in nursery. d, Princess Diana, Princes William and Harry.

No. 1300, 875fr — Rotary International emblem and: a, Paul P. Harris (1868-1947), founder of Rotary International, Acraea neobule. b, Polio virus. c, Rotarians giving baby polio vaccine, Hypolimnas misippus. d, Hands touching, Colotis danae.

No. 1301, 2000fr, CRH3 train. No. 1302, 2000fr, Nanger dama, diff. No. 1303, 2000fr, Ceratotherium simum. No. 1304, 2000fr, Panthera leo. No. 1305, 2500fr, Wang Yaping, Shenzhou 10, diff. No. 1306, 2500fr, Orcinus orca. No. 1307, 2500fr, Apis mellifera, Raphanus sativus. No. 1308, 2500fr, Halcyon chelicuti. No. 1309, 2500fr, Geochelone sulcata. No. 1310, 2500fr, Red Cross emblem, medical worker giving child an injection. No. 1311, 2500fr, Homo neanderthalensis, cave drawing. No. 1312, 2500fr, Russian Air Force Sukhoi PAK FA. No. 1313, 2500fr, Ford F150 fire truck. No. 1314, 2500fr, Cricket player Andrew Flintoff. No. 1315, 2500fr, Coubertin, meeting of International Olympic Committee. No. 1316, 2500fr, Verdi. No. 1317, 2500fr, Wagner. No. 1318, 2500fr, Mandela and Queen Elizabeth II. No. 1319, 2500fr, Popes John Paul II and Benedict XVI. No. 1320, 2500fr, Kelly. No. 1321, 2500fr, Two Boys with a Giant Mastiff, by Goya. No. 1322, 2500fr, Spring on the Riviera, by Rose. No. 1323, 2500fr, Bullfight, by Picasso. No. 1324, 2500fr, Duke and Duchess of Cambridge, Prince George, vert. No. 1325, 3000fr, Harris, Rotary International emblem, Charaxes jasius.

2013, Sept. 30 Litho. *Perf. 13¼*

Sheets of 4, #a-d

1276-1300 A398 Set of 25 300.00 300.00

Souvenir Sheets

1301-1325 A398 Set of 25 255.00 255.00

A399

A400

A401

Chinese Chang'e 3 Mission to the Moon A402

Perf. 12¾x13¼

2013, Dec. 20 Litho.

1326 Horiz. strip of 4 13.00 13.00
- *a.* A399 750fr multi 3.25 3.25
- *b.* A400 750fr multi 3.25 3.25
- *c.* A401 750fr multi 3.25 3.25
- *d.* A402 750fr multi 3.25 3.25

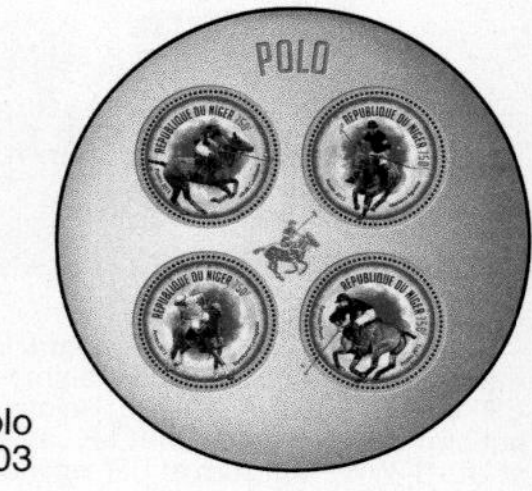

Polo A403

No. 1327 — Polo players on horses: a, Adolfo Cambiaso. b, Mariano Aguerre. c, Bartolomé Castagnola. d, Facundo Pieres.

2500fr, Polo player on horse.

2013, Dec. 20 Litho. *Perf.*

1327 A403 750fr Sheet of 4, #a-d 13.00 13.00

Souvenir Sheet

1328 A403 2500fr multi 10.50 10.50

A404

No. 1329, 750fr — Pan troglodytes: a, Sitting on rock. b, Sitting next to tree, looking forward. c, Adult and juvenile. d, Sitting on branch looking left.

No. 1330, 750fr — Dugong dugon with Latin name: a, At LL, animal facing left. b, At UR, animal facing forward. c, At UR, with animal's head touching sea floor. d, At LL, with animal looking forward.

No. 1331, 750fr — Dolphins: a, Tursiops truncatus, Latin name at LR. b, Two Tursiops truncatus, Latin name at LL. c, Two Tursiops truncatus, Latin name at UR. d, Two Delphinus delphi.

No. 1332, 750fr — Tropical fish: a, Chelmon rostratus. b, Pygoplites diacanthus. c, Chaetodon auriga. d, Amphiprion ocellaris.

No. 1333, 750fr — Turtles: a, Geochelone sulcata. b, Chelonoidis denticulata. c, Geochelone nigra. d, Trachemys scripta elegans.

No. 1334, 750fr — Dinosaurs: a, Diceratops. b, Dicraeosaurus. c, Diplodocus. d, Tyrannosaurus.

No. 1335, 750fr — Endangered animals: a, Eretmochelys imbricata. b, Ailuropoda melanoleuca. c, Loxodonta cyclotis. d, Panthera pardus orientalis.

No. 1336, 750fr — Climate change: a, Arctocephalus gazella on shore. b, Ursus maritimus in water. c, Giraffa camelopardalis in water. d, Odobenus rosmarus on ice.

No. 1337, 750fr — Orchids: a, Paphiopedilum callosum. b, Cattleya auera. c, Cattleya labiata. d, Miltonia spectabilis.

No. 1338, 750fr — Mushrooms: a, Macrolepiota procera. b, Sarcodon imbricatus. c, Cantharellus cibarius. d, Leccinum aurantiacum.

No. 1339, 750fr — Minerals: a, Jasper. b, Amethyst. c, Malachite. d, Smoky quartz.

No. 1340, 750fr — Lighthouses: a, Rubjerg Knude Lighthouse, Denmark. b, Green Cape Lighthouse, Australia (incorrect inscription on stamp). c, Fingal Head Lighthouse, Australia (incorrect inscription on stamp). d, Hov Fyr Lighthouse, Denmark.

No. 1341, 750fr — Windmills in: a, Campo de Criptana, Spain. b, Kuzelov, Czech Republic. c, Kinderdijk, Netherlands. d, Volendam, Netherlands.

No. 1342, 750fr — Japanese high-speed trains: a, E3 Series Shinkansen. b, 700 Series Shinkansen. c, E2 Series Shinkansen. d, E3 R1 Akita Shinkansen.

No. 1343, 750fr — Fire trucks: a, Ural. b, 1938 Quad. c, Magirus-Deutz LF 16-TS. d, Steam-driven wagon.

No. 1344, 750fr — Ferrari automobiles: a, F40. b, 458. c, FF. d, "Enzo Ferrari".

No. 1345, 750fr — Chess: a, White piece tilting wooden king on white square. b, White and black queens. c, Timer. d, Player holding white piece tilting wooden king on black square.

No. 1346, 750fr — Campaign against AIDS: a, Women wearing head covering, child. b, Mother and infant meeting with doctor. c, Woman. d, Doctor examining infant held in woman's arms.

No. 1347, 750fr — Niger culture: a, Aerial view of desert village. b, Buildings in Agadez. c, Mural. d, Mountains in desert.

No. 1348, 750fr — Composers: a, Joseph Haydn (1732-1809). b, Johann Sebastian Bach (1685-1750). c, Robert Schumann (1810-56). d, Wolfgang Amadeus Mozart (1756-91).

No. 1349, 750fr — Paintings by Eugène Delacroix (1798-1863): a, Combat of Horsemen in the Countryside, 1824. b, The Dying Turk, 1825-30. c, Horse Frightened by a Storm, 1824. d, A Mortally Wounded Brigand Quenches His Thirst, 1825.

No. 1350, 750fr — Pope Benedix XVI with top inscription: a, In white on one line. b, In black on two lines. c, In white on two lines. d, In black on three lines.

No. 1351, 750fr — Nelson Mandela (1918-2013), President of South Africa: a, With hand clenched at LL. b, Waving. c, Saluting. d, With flag of South Africa.

No. 1352, 2500fr, Adult and juvenile Pan troglodytes, diff. No. 1353, 2500fr, Dugong dugon, diff. No. 1354, 2500fr, Tursiops truncatus, diff. No. 1355, 2500fr, Heniochus acuminatus. No. 1356, 2500fr, Chelonia mydas. No. 1357, 2500fr, Spinosaurus. No. 1358, 2500fr, Diceros bicornis. No. 1359, 2500fr, Pygoscelis papua. No. 1360, 2500fr, Oncidium altissimum. No. 1361, 2500fr, Boletus edulis. No. 1362, 2500fr, Chalcedony. No. 1363, 2500fr, Michigan City East Lighthouse, Michigan City, Indiana. No. 1364, 2500fr, Windmill at Lithuanian Ethnographic Museum. No. 1365, 2500fr, E3-2000 Series Shinkansen. No. 1366, 2500fr, Mercedes-Benz Zetros fire truck. No. 1367, 2500fr, Enzo Ferrari (1898-1988), automobile manufacturer. No. 1368, 2500fr, Chess board and timer. No. 1369, 2500fr, Two women, infant, red cross. No. 1370, 2500fr, Sahara Desert rock paintings. No. 1371, 2500fr, Ludwig van Beethoven (1770-1827), composer. No. 1372, 2500fr, The Combat of the Giaour and Hassan, by Delacroix. No. 1373, 2500fr, Pope Benedict XVI, diff. No. 1374, 2500fr, Mandela with fist raised. No. 1375, 2500fr, Mandela and flag of South Africa, diff.

2013, Dec. 20 Litho. *Perf. 13¼*

Sheets of 4, #a-d

1329-1351 A404 Set of 23 290.00 290.00

Souvenir Sheets

1352-1375 A404 Set of 24 250.00 250.00

Millet — A405

2014, Apr. 25 Litho. *Perf. 13¼x13*

1376 A405 35fr multi .25 .25

A406

No. 1377, 500fr — Jawaharlal Nehru (1889-1964), First Prime Minister of India, and: a, Panthera tigris tigris. b, Mahatma Gandhi (1869-1948), Indian nationalist leader (Nehru wearing hat). c, Pavo cristatus. d, Gandhi (Nehru without hat).

No. 1378, 500fr — Diplomatic relations between Niger and People's Republic of China, 40th anniv.: a, Flags of Niger and People's Republic of China, Great Wall of China, ruins of Djado, Niger. b, Flags, Niger Prime Minister Senyi Oumarou and Chinese President Hu Jintao shaking hands. c, Flags, Cheiffou Amadou and Wang Gang shaking hands. d, Flags, 2012 meeting of Presidents of Niger and People's Republic of China.

No. 1379, 675fr — Charles Lindbergh (1902-74), aviator, and airplane: a, Lindbergh wearing cap. b, Lindbergh wearing headgear and goggles, standing. c, Lindbergh without hat. d, Lindbergh wearing headgear and goggles, in cockpit.

No. 1380, 675fr — Louis Renault (1877-1944), automobile manufacturer: a, At right of car. b, Driving car. c, With head above car roof. d, At left of car.

No. 1381, 675fr — Giacomo Puccini (1858-1924), opera composer: a, Theater in background. b, Poster for *Tosca* in background. c, With Giuseppe Verdi (1813-1901). d, With character from *Turandot* in background.

No. 1382, 750fr — Jean-Philippe Rameau (1683-1764), composer, and: a, Cathedral of St. Benignus, Dijon, France. b, Dulcimer. c, Baroque lute. d, Harpsichord.

No. 1383, 750fr — Joséphine de Beauharnais (1763-1814), first wife of Napoleon Bonaparte: a, With head on chair, Napoleon standing. b, In her Malmaison bedroom. c, Standing, with Napoleon. d, Seated, her portrait in background.

No. 1384, 750fr — Charlie Chaplin (1889-1977), actor: a, Holding hat. b, With legs above head, holding cane. c, Reading. d, Touching bottom of shoe.

No. 1385, 750fr — Yuri Gagarin (1934-68), first man in space: a, Receiving flowers from girl. b, Wearing space helmet. c, Wearing military uniform, Vostok 1 in flight. d, Wearing space suit, no helmet.

No. 1386, 750fr — Pope Francis: a, Wearing miter, dove flying in background. b, With cardinals in background. c, Standing on platform, cardinals in background. d, Wearing zucchetto, dove flying in background.

No. 1387, 750fr — Joe DiMaggio (1914-99), baseball player, and his wife, Marilyn Monroe (1926-62), actress: a, DiMaggio wearing brown suit. b, DiMaggio wearing baseball uniform. c, Monroe alone. d, DiMaggio wearing green suit.

No. 1388, 750fr — Ayrton Senna (1960-94), race car driver: a, Driving blue race car. b, Holding trophy. c, Flag of Brazil in background. d, Driving yellow car.

No. 1389, 750fr — 2014 Winter Olympics, Sochi, Russia: a, Ski jumper. b, Figure skater. c, Ice hockey player. d, Snowboarder.

No. 1390, 750fr — 2014 World Cup Soccer Championships, Brazil: a, Player in blue shirt and player in green shirt. b, Player in yellow orange shirt. c, Player in light yellow shirt. d, Player in light blue shirt and player in light yellow shirt.

No. 1391, 750fr — Start of World War I, cent.: a, Carrier pigeon. b, Fokker Dr.I airplane of Manfred von Richtofen c, Renault Ft tank. d, German soldiers wearing gas masks.

No. 1392, 750fr — USS Nautilus, 60th anniv.: a, Entire ship at surface. b, Submarine submerging. c, Fore of submarine at surface. d, Submarine and wake.

No. 1393, 750fr — English Channel Tunnel, 20th anniv.: a, British Rail Class 92, flags of Great Britain and France. b, Eurotunnel Class 9, Eiffel Tower, flag of France. c, ICE3, Tower Bridge, flag of Great Britain. d, Eurostar Class 373, flags of Great Britain and France.

No. 1394, 750fr — Red List of Endangered Animals, 50th anniv.: a, Procolobus kirkii. b, Onychogalea fraenata. c, Gyps rueppellii. d, Balearica regulorum.

No. 1395, 2000fr, Nehru, Gandhi, flag of India. No. 1396, 2000fr, Prime Minister Oumarou shaking hands with Chinese Premier Wen Jiabao, flags of Niger and People's Republic of China. No. 1397, 2000fr, Lindbergh, map of transatlantic flight. No. 1398, 2000fr, Renault and tank. No. 1399, 2000fr, Puccini and poster for *La Bohàme.* No. 1400, 2500fr, Rameau and Baroque guitar. No. 1401, 2500fr, Napoleon Bonaparte and Josàphine de Beauharnais, diff. No. 1402, 2500fr, Chaplin in and out of stage makeup. No. 1403, 2500fr, Gagarin and Vostok 1, diff. No. 1404, 2500fr, Pope Francis and two cardinals. No. 1405, 2500fr, DiMaggio in baseball uniform. No. 1406, 2500fr, Senna and race car, diff. No. 1407, 2500fr, Biathlon. No. 1408, 2500fr, Two soccer players, diff. No. 1409, 2500fr, Assassination of Archduke Franz Ferdinand. No. 1410, 2500fr, Launch of USS Nautilus. No. 1411, 2500fr, Eurostar Class 320, map of English Channel Tunnel, flags of Great Britain and France. No. 1412, 2500fr, Panthera tigris sumatrae.

2014, Apr. 25 Litho. *Perf. 13¼*

Sheets of 4, #a-d

1377-1394 A406 Set of 18 215.00 215.00

Souvenir Sheets

1395-1412 A406 Set of 18 180.00 180.00

Works of Famous Artists A407

No. 1413, 750fr — Alphonse Mucha (1860-1939): a, Poster for F. Champenois, 1897. b, The Precious Stones Series, 1900. c, The Celebration of Svantovit on Rügen, 1912. d, Fate, 1920.

No. 1414, 750fr — Edvard Munch (1863-1944): a, Self-portrait with a Bottle of Wine, 1906. b, The Girls on the Bridge, 1901. c, Two Human Beings: The Lonely Ones, 1933-35. d, Separation, 1896.

No. 1415, 750fr — Frida Kahlo (1907-54): a, The Wounded Deer, 1946. b, Self-portrait Along the Border of Mexico and the United States, 1932. c, The Bride Frightened at Seeing Life Opened, 1944. d, The Two Fridas, 1939.

No. 1416, 750fr — Henri de Toulouse-Lautrec (1864-1901): a, Self-portrait in Front of a Mirror, 1883. b, Count Alphonse de Toulouse-Lautrec Driving a Four Horse Hitch, 1881. c, Portrait of Suzanne Valadon, 1888. d, In Bed, 1893.

No. 1417, 750fr — Salvador Dalí (1904-89): a, Apparition of a Face and Fruit Dish on a Beach, 1938. b, Atavism at Twilight, 1934. c, Metamorphosis of Narcissus, 1937. d, Paranoiac-Critical Solitude, 1935.

No. 1418, 750fr — Wassily Kandinsky (1866-1944): a, Autumn Landscape, 1911. b, Transverse Line, 1923. c, Green Emptyness, 1930. d, In Blue, 1925.

No. 1419, 750fr — William Hogarth (1697-1764): a, The Distrest Poet, 1729. b, The Life of a Libertine, 1732-35. c, The Graham Children, 1742. d, Marriage à la Mode: The Toilette, 1743-45.

No. 1420, 2500fr, Spring, by Mucha, 1896. No. 1421, 2500fr, Cendres, by Munch, 1924. No. 1422, 2500fr, Without Hope, by Kahlo, 1945. No. 1423, 2500fr, At the Moulin Rouge, by Toulouse-Lautrec, 1892-95. No. 1424, 2500fr, The Persistence of Memory, by Dalí, 1931. No. 1425, 2500fr, Murnau, A Village Street, by Kandinsky, 1908. No. 1426, 2500fr, Columbus Breaking the Egg, 1752.

2014, Apr. 25 Litho. *Perf. 13¼*

Sheets of 4, #a-d

1413-1419 A407 Set of 7 90.00 90.00

Souvenir Sheets

1420-1426 A407 Set of 7 75.00 75.00

A408

No. 1427, 750fr — St. John Paul II (1920-2005), and: a, St. Peter's Basilica, holding crucifix. b, Castel Sant'Angelo. c, St. Peter's Basilica, waving. d, Pope Francis.

No. 1428, 750fr — Deng Xiaoping (1904-97), paramount leader of People's Republic of China, and: a, Mao Zedong (1893-1976) and other Chinese leaders. b, City Skyline, flag of People's Republic of China. c, Chinese temple, flag of People's Republic of China. d, Mao Zedong.

No. 1429, 750fr — Postage stamps of various countries: a, Russia #6178, Tokelau #389. b, Australia #3563, Falkland Islands #1031. c, Australia #3562, Russia #7302. d, Australia #3561, Jamaica #1057.

No. 1430, 2500fr, St. John Paul II and his papal coat of arms. No. 1431, 2500fr, Deng Xiaoping, Mao Zedong, flowers, map of People's Republic of China. No. 1432, 2500fr, Australia #3564, Christmas Island #487a.

Litho. With Foil Application (#1427, 1430), Litho.

2014, June 25 *Perf. 13¼*

Sheets of 4, #a-d

1427-1429 A408 Set of 3 37.50 37.50

Souvenir Sheets

1430-1432 A408 Set of 3 32.00 32.00

Animals A409

No. 1433, 750fr — Ursus maritimus: a, Cub on adult polar bear. b, Adult polar bear on ice. c, Adult polar bear crossing gap in ice. d,Two polar bear cubs.

No. 1434, 750fr — Ailuropoda melanoleuca: a, Head and paws of giant panda. b, Giant panda sitting and eating. c, Giant panda reclining and eating. d, Giant panda climbing rock.

No. 1435, 750fr — Gorillas: a, Gorilla gorilla diehli. b, Gorilla gorilla gorilla. c, Gorilla beringei graueri. d, Gorilla gorilla.

No. 1436, 750fr — Rhinoceroses: a, Diceros bicornis. b, Rhinoceros unicornis. c, Dicerorhinus sumatrensis. d, Rhinoceros sondaicus.

No. 1437, 750fr — Bovids: a, Bubalus bubalis. b, Bos primigenius indicus. c, Ovis aries. d, Gazella dorcas.

No. 1438, 750fr — Sea lions: a, Otaria flavescens. b, Phocarctos hookeri. c, Adult and juvenile Zalophus californianus. d, One Zalophus californianus.

No. 1439, 750fr — Wild cats: a, Panthera leo. b, Panthera tigris tigris. c, Panthera onca. d, Acinonyx jubatus.

No. 1440, 750fr — Domesticated cats: a, Japanese bobtail. b, Himalayan. c, Munchkin. d, Singapura.

No. 1441, 750fr — Dogs: a, West Highland white terriers. b, Field spaniel. c, Parson Russell terriers. d, Basset hounds.

No. 1442, 750fr — Elephants: a, Three juvenile Loxodonta africana. b, Two adult Loxodonta africana. c, One Loxodonta africana. d, Elephas maximus.

No. 1443, 750fr — Horses: a, Bavarian Warmblood. b, East Bulgarian. c, Icelandic. d, Gypsy Cob.

No. 1444, 750fr — Dolphins: a, Delphinus delphis. b, Sotalia guianensis. c, Tursiops aduncus. d, Sousa chinensis.

No. 1445, 750fr — Orcinas orca: a, Dorsal fin at UR. b, Dorsal fin at UL. c, Backflipping. d, With open mouth.

No. 1446, 750fr — Fish: a, Parambassis ranga. b, Pterapogon kauderni. c, Centropyge loricula. d, Pterophyllum scalare.

No. 1447, 750fr — Owls: a, Megascops asio. b, Strix occidentalis. c, Bubo virginianus. d, Strix nebulosa.

No. 1448, 750fr — Birds of prey: a, Pithecophaga jefferyi. b, Accipiter soloensis. c, Elanus leucurus. d, Gypaetus barbatus.

No. 1449, 750fr — Water birds: a, Fratercula arctica. b, Ardea herodias. c, Aethia cristatella. d, Podiceps nigricollis nigricollis.

No. 1450, 750fr — Butterflies: a, Danaus plexippus. b, Siproeta epaphus. c, Talicada nyseus. d, Diaethria neglecta.

No. 1451, 750fr — Turtles: a, Chelydra serpentina. b, Terrapene carolina. c, Stigmochelys pardalis. d, Clemmys guttata.

No. 1452, 750fr — Varanus komodensis: a, Komodo dragon facing left. b, Komodo dragon, head and tail facing right, tongue extended. c, Komodo dragon, head facing right, tongue extended. d, Komodo dragon facing left, mouth open.

No. 1453, 750fr — Extinct animals: a, Megaladapis. b, Macrotis leucura. c, Pinguinus impennis. d, Diceros bicornis longipes.

No. 1454, 2500fr, Ursus maritimus, diff. No. 1455, 2500fr, Adult and juvenile Ailuropoda melanoleuca. No. 1456, 2500fr, Three Gorilla gorilla. No. 1457, 2500fr, Ceratotherium simum simum. No. 1458, 2500fr, Antilope cervicapra. No. 1459, 2500fr, Phocarctos hookeri and bird. No. 1460, 2500fr, Neofelis nebulosa. No. 1461, 2500fr, Abyssinian cat. No. 1462, 2500fr, Russian toy dogs. No. 1463, 2500fr, Loxodonta africana, diff. No. 1464, 2500fr, Marwari horse. No. 1465, 2500fr, Delphinus delphis, diff. No. 1466, 2500fr, Orcinus orca, diff. No. 1467, 2500fr, Pomacanthus annularis. No. 1468, 2500fr, Tyto alba. No. 1469, 2500fr, Harpia harpyja. No. 1470, 2500fr, Aix galericulata. No. 1471, 2500fr, Danaus plexippus, diff. No. 1472, 2500fr, Chelonia mydas. No. 1473, 2500fr, Varanus komodoensis, diff. No. 1474, 2500fr, Palaeopropithecus.

2014, June 25 Litho. *Perf. 13¼*

Sheets of 4, #a-d

1433-1453 A409 Set of 21 260.00 260.00

Souvenir Sheets

1454-1474 A409 Set of 21 220.00 220.00

Souvenir Sheet

Mei Lanfang (1894-1961), Chinese Opera Actor — A410

Perf. 12¾x13¼

2014, June 25 Litho.

Self-Adhesive On Silk

1475 A410 2500fr multi 10.50 10.50

2014 World Cup Soccer Championships, Brazil — A411

No. 1476: a, Emblem of 2014 World Cup, flag of Brazil with soccer ball in place of constellation in sky (150x80mm). b, World Cup (150x240mm). c, Flag of Brazil with soccer ball in place of constellation in sky, mascot of 2014 World Cup (150x80mm).

2014, June 25 Litho. *Perf. 13¼x13*

1476 Sheet of 3 + 40 labels 6.50 6.50
a.-c. A411 500fr Any single 2.10 2.10

SEMI-POSTAL STAMPS

Curie Issue

Common Design Type

1938 Unwmk. Engr. *Perf. 13*

B1 CD80 1.75fr + 50c brt ultra 16.50 16.50

French Revolution Issue

Common Design Type

1939 Photo. *Perf. 13*

Name and Value Typo. in Black

B2 CD83 45c + 25c grn 12.00 12.00
B3 CD83 70c + 30c brn 12.00 12.00
B4 CD83 90c + 35c red org 12.00 12.00
B5 CD83 1.25fr + 1fr rose pink 12.00 12.00
B6 CD83 2.25fr + 2fr blue 12.00 12.00
Nos. B2-B6 (5) 60.00 60.00

Stamps of 1926-38, Surcharged in Black

1941 *Perf. 14x13½, 13½x14*

B7 A3 50c + 1fr scar & grn, *grnsh* 3.25 3.25
B8 A3 80c + 2fr cl & ol grn 8.00 8.00
B9 A4 1.50fr + 2fr dp bl & pale bl 8.00 8.00
B10 A4 2fr + 3fr red org & ol brn 8.00 8.00
Nos. B7-B10 (4) 27.25 27.25

Common Design Type and

Colonial Cavalry SP1

Soldiers and Tank SP2

1941 Unwmk. Photo. *Perf. 13½*

B11 SP2 1fr + 1fr red 1.10
B12 CD86 1.50fr + 3fr claret 1.10
B13 SP1 2.50fr + 1fr blue 1.10
Nos. B11-B13 (3) 3.30
Set, never hinged 5.25

Nos. B11-B13 were issued by the Vichy government in France, but were not placed on sale in Niger.

Nos. 89-90 Surcharged in Black or Red

1944 Engr. *Perf. 12x12½*

B13A 50c + 1.50fr on 2.50fr deep blue (R) .45
B13B + 2.50fr on 1fr green .45
Set, never hinged 1.75

Colonial Development Fund.

Nos. B13A-B13B were issued by the Vichy government in France, but were not placed on sale in Niger.

Catalogue values for unused stamps in this section, from this point to the end of the section, are for Never Hinged items.

Republic of the Niger

Anti-Malaria Issue

Common Design Type

Perf. 12½x12

1962, Apr. 7 Engr. Unwmk.

B14 CD108 25fr + 5fr brn .75 .75

Freedom from Hunger Issue

Common Design Type

1963, Mar. 21 *Perf. 13*

B15 CD112 25fr + 5fr gray ol, red lil & brn .75 .75

Dome of the Rock — SP3

1978, Dec. 11 Litho. *Perf. 12½*

B16 SP3 40fr + 5fr multi .45 .30

Surtax was for Palestinian fighters and their families.

AIR POST STAMPS

Common Design Type

1940 Unwmk. Engr. *Perf. 12½x12*

C1 CD85 1.90fr ultra .35 .35
C2 CD85 2.90fr dk red .35 .35
C3 CD85 4.50fr dk gray grn .70 .70
C4 CD85 4.90fr yel bis .70 .70
C5 CD85 6.90fr dp org 1.40 1.40
Nos. C1-C5 (5) 3.50 3.50

Common Design Types

1942

C6 CD88 50c car & bl .30
C7 CD88 1fr brn & blk .35
C8 CD88 2fr multi .60
C9 CD88 3fr multi .60
C10 CD88 5fr vio & brn red .60

Frame Engraved, Center Typographed

C11 CD89 10fr multi .90
C12 CD89 20fr multi 1.25
C13 CD89 50fr multi 1.60
Nos. C6-C13 (8) 6.20
Set, never hinged 9.00

There is doubt whether Nos. C6-C13 were officially placed in use. They were issued by the Vichy government.

Catalogue values for unused stamps in this section, from this point to the end of the section, are for Never Hinged items.

Republic of the Niger

Wild Animals, W National Park — AP1

1960, Apr. 11 Engr. *Perf. 13*

C14 AP1 500fr multi 19.00 8.00

For overprint see No. C112.

Nubian Carmine Bee-eater AP2

1961, Dec. 18 Unwmk. *Perf. 13*

C15 AP2 200fr multi 8.50 3.25

UN Headquarters and Emblem, Niger Flag and Map — AP3

1961, Dec. 16

C20 AP3 25fr multi .60 .40
C21 AP3 100fr multi 2.00 1.35

Niger's admission to the United Nations.
For overprints see Nos. C28-C29.

Air Afrique Issue

Common Design Type

1962, Feb. 17 Unwmk. *Perf. 13*

C22 CD107 100fr multi 1.75 .90

Mosque at Agadez and UPU Emblem AP4

Designs: 85fr, Gaya Bridge. 100fr, Presidential Palace, Niamey.

1963, June 12 Photo. *Perf. 12½*

C23 AP4 50fr multi 1.00 .55
C24 AP4 85fr multi 1.75 .75
C25 AP4 100fr multi 1.75 .90
Nos. C23-C25 (3) 4.50 2.20

2nd anniv. of Niger's admission to the UPU.

Type of Regular Issue, 1963

Design: 100fr, Building boats (kadei), horiz.

1963, Aug. 30 *Perf. 12½x12*

Size: 47x27mm

C26 A12 100fr multi 3.00 1.60

African Postal Union Issue

Common Design Type

1963, Sept. 8 *Perf. 12½*

C27 CD114 85fr multi 1.25 .60

Nos. C20-C21 Overprinted in Red

1963, Sept. 30 Engr. *Perf. 13*

C28 AP3 25fr multi .80 .50
C29 AP3 100fr multi 1.90 .90

Centenary of International Red Cross.

White and Black before Rising Sun — AP5

1963, Oct. 25 Photo. *Perf. 12x13*

C30 AP5 50fr multi 3.50 2.50

See note after Mauritania No. C28.

Peanut Cultivation AP6

Designs: 45fr, Camels transporting peanuts to market. 85fr, Men closing bags. 100fr, Loading bags on truck.

1963, Nov. 5 **Engr.** ***Perf. 13***

C31 AP6 20fr grn, bl & red brn .60 .25
C32 AP6 45fr red brn, bl & grn 1.00 .40
C33 AP6 85fr multi 2.00 .70
C34 AP6 100fr red brn, ol bis & bl 2.25 1.00
a. Souv. sheet of 4, #C31-C34 6.00 6.00
Nos. C31-C34 (4) 5.85 2.35

To publicize Niger's peanut industry.

1963 Air Afrique Issue
Common Design Type

1963, Nov. 19 **Photo.** ***Perf. 13x12***

C35 CD115 50fr multi 1.00 .55

Telstar and Capricornus and Sagittarius Constellations — AP7

100fr, Relay satellite, Leo & Virgo constellations.

1964, Feb. 11 **Engr.** ***Perf. 13***

C36 AP7 25fr ol brn & bluish vio .50 .30
C37 AP7 100fr grn & dp claret 1.40 .85

Ramses II Holding Crook and Flail, Abu Simbel — AP8

1964, Mar. 9

C38 AP8 25fr bis brn & dl bl grn .80 .50
C39 AP8 30fr dk bl & org brn 1.25 .65
C40 AP8 50fr dp claret & dk bl 2.25 1.25
Nos. C38-C40 (3) 4.30 2.40

Issued to publicize the UNESCO world campaign to save historic monuments in Nubia.

Tiros I Weather Satellite over Globe and WMO Emblem AP9

1964, Mar. 23 **Unwmk.** ***Perf. 13***

C41 AP9 50fr emer, dk bl & choc 1.50 .75

4th World Meteorological Day, Mar. 23.

Rocket, Stars and "Stamp" AP10

1964, June 5 **Engr.**

C42 AP10 50fr dk bl & car red 1.25 .65

"PHILATEC," International Philatelic and Postal Techniques Exhibition, Paris, June 5-21, 1964.

Europafrica Issue, 1963
Common Design Type

50fr, European & African shaking hands, emblems of industry & agriculture.

1964, July 20 **Photo.** ***Perf. 12x13***

C43 CD116 50fr multi .85 .50

John F. Kennedy — AP11

Perf. 12½

1964, Sept. 25 **Unwmk.** **Photo.**

C44 AP11 100fr multi 1.90 1.25
a. Souvenir sheet of 4 8.50 8.50

President John F. Kennedy (1917-1963).

Discobolus and Discus Thrower — AP12

60fr, Water polo, horiz. 85fr, Relay race, horiz. 250fr, Torch bearer & Pierre de Coubertin.

1964, Oct. 10 **Engr.** ***Perf. 13***

C45 AP12 60fr red brn & sl grn 1.00 .50
C46 AP12 85fr ultra & red brn 1.50 .60
C47 AP12 100fr brt grn, dk red & sl 1.50 .70
C48 AP12 250fr yel brn, brt grn & sl 3.50 1.75
a. Min. sheet of 4, #C45-C48 10.50 10.50
Nos. C45-C48 (4) 7.50 3.55

18th Olympic Games, Tokyo, Oct. 10-25.

Pope John XXIII (1881-1963) AP13

1965, June 3 **Photo.** ***Perf. 12½x13***

C49 AP13 100fr multi 1.75 .80

Hand Crushing Crab — AP14

1965, July 15 **Engr.** ***Perf. 13***

C50 AP14 100fr yel grn, blk & brn 1.50 .85

Issued to publicize the fight against cancer.

Sir Winston Churchill — AP15

Perf. 12½x13

1965, Sept. 3 **Photo.** **Unwmk.**

C51 AP15 100fr multi 1.40 .85

Symbols of Agriculture, Industry, Education — AP16

1965, Oct. 24 **Engr.** ***Perf. 13***

C52 AP16 50fr henna brn, blk & ol .90 .50

International Cooperation Year, 1965.

Flags and Niamey Fair — AP17

1965, Dec. 10 **Photo.** ***Perf. 13x12½***

C53 AP17 100fr multi 1.40 .85

International Fair at Niamey.

Dr. Schweitzer, Crippled Hands and Symbols of Medicine, Religion and Music AP18

1966, Jan. 4 **Photo.** ***Perf. 12½x13***

C54 AP18 50fr multi 1.10 .55

Weather Survey Frigate and WMO Emblem AP19

1966, Mar. 23 **Engr.** ***Perf. 13***

C55 AP19 50fr brt rose lil, dl grn & dk vio bl 1.50 .60

6th World Meteorological Day, Mar. 23.

Edward H. White Floating in Space and Gemini IV — AP20

#C57, Alexei A. Leonov & Voskhod II.

1966, Mar. 30

C56 AP20 50fr dk red brn, blk & brt grn 1.00 .50
C57 AP20 50fr pur, slate & org 1.00 .50

Issued to honor astronauts Edward H. White and Alexei A. Leonov.

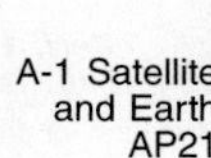

A-1 Satellite and Earth AP21

45fr, Diamant rocket and launching pad. 90fr, FR-1 satellite. 100fr, D-1 satellite.

1966, May 12 **Photo.** ***Perf. 13***

C58 AP21 45fr multi, vert. .75 .45
C59 AP21 60fr multi .90 .55
C60 AP21 90fr multi 1.10 .80
C61 AP21 100fr multi 1.75 1.00
Nos. C58-C61 (4) 4.50 2.80

French achievements in space.

Maps of Europe and Africa and Symbols of Industry — AP22

1966, July 20 **Photo.** ***Perf. 12x13***

C62 AP22 50fr multi .90 .45

Third anniversary of economic agreement between the European Economic Community and the African and Malgache Union.

Air Afrique Issue, 1966
Common Design Type

1966, Aug. 31 **Photo.** ***Perf. 13***

C63 CD123 30fr gray, yel grn & blk .70 .35

Voskhod 1 — AP23

Design: 100fr, Gemini 6 and 7.

1966, Oct. 14 **Engr.** ***Perf. 13***

C64 AP23 50fr multi .80 .45
C65 AP23 100fr multi 1.60 .80

Russian & American achievements in space.

Torii and Atom Destroying Crab — AP24

1966, Dec. 2 **Photo.** ***Perf. 13***

C66 AP24 100fr dp claret, brn, vio & bl grn 1.60 .80

9th Intl. Anticancer Cong., Tokyo, Oct. 23-29.

New Mosque, Niamey AP25

1967, Jan. 11 **Engr.** ***Perf. 13***

C67 AP25 100fr grn & brt bl 1.60 .80

Albrecht Dürer, Self-portrait AP26

Self-portraits: 100fr, Jacques Louis David. 250fr, Ferdinand Delacroix.

1967, Jan. 27 **Photo.** ***Perf. 12½***

C68 AP26 50fr multi 1.10 .70
C69 AP26 100fr multi 2.00 1.00
C70 AP26 250fr multi 4.50 2.25
Nos. C68-C70 (3) 7.60 3.95

See No. C98.

Maritime Weather Station — AP27

1967, Mar. 23 Engr. *Perf. 13*
C71 AP27 50fr brt bl, dk car rose & blk 1.50 .75

7th World Meteorological Day.

View of EXPO '67, Montreal AP28

1967, Apr. 28 Engr. *Perf. 13*
C72 AP28 100fr lil, brt bl & blk 1.25 .70

Issued for EXPO '67, International Exhibition, Montreal, Apr. 28-Oct. 27, 1967.

Audio-visual Center, Stylized Eye and People AP29

1967, June 22 Engr. *Perf. 13*
C73 AP29 100fr brt bl, pur & grn 1.25 .60

National Audio-Visual Center.

Konrad Adenauer (1876-1967), Chancellor of West Germany (1949-63) — AP30

1967, Aug. 11 Photo. *Perf. 12½*
C74 AP30 100fr dk bl, gray & sep 1.75 .70
a. Souv. sheet of 4 7.75 7.75

African Postal Union Issue, 1967
Common Design Type

1967, Sept. 9 Engr. *Perf. 13*
C75 CD124 100fr emer, red & brt lil 1.40 .60

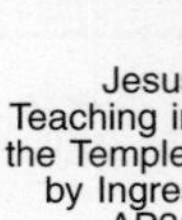

Jesus Teaching in the Temple, by Ingres AP31

Design: 150fr, Jesus Giving the Keys to St. Peter, by Ingres, vert.

1967, Oct. 2 Photo. *Perf. 12½*
C76 AP31 100fr multi 2.50 1.25
C77 AP31 150fr multi 3.50 1.75

Jean Dominique Ingres (1780-1867), French painter.

Children and UNICEF Emblem — AP32

1967, Dec. 11 Engr. *Perf. 13*
C78 AP32 100fr bl, brn & grn 1.50 1.00

21st anniv. of UNICEF.

O.C.A.M. Emblem AP33

1968, Jan. 12 Engr. *Perf. 13*
C79 AP33 100fr brt bl, grn & org 1.25 .55

Conf. of the Organization Communitée Afrique et Malgache (OCAM), Niamey, Jan. 1968.

Vincent van Gogh, Self-portrait AP34

Self-portraits: 50fr, Jean Baptiste Camille Corot. 150fr, Francisco de Goya.

1968, Jan. 29 Photo. *Perf. 12½*
C80 AP34 50fr multi 1.00 .45
C81 AP34 150fr multi 2.75 1.10
C82 AP34 200fr multi 4.50 1.75
Nos. C80-C82 (3) 8.25 3.30

See No. C98.

Breguet 27 — AP35

Planes: 80fr, Potez 25 on the ground. 100fr, Potez 25 in the air.

1968, Mar. 14 Engr. *Perf. 13*
C83 AP35 45fr ind, car & dk grn 1.00 .40
C84 AP35 80fr indigo, bl & brn 1.50 .75
C85 AP35 100fr sky bl, brn blk & dk grn 2.50 .90
Nos. C83-C85 (3) 5.00 2.05

25th anniversary of air mail service between France and Niger.

Splendid Glossy Starling AP36

Design: 100fr, Amethyst starling, vert.

1968-69 Photo. *Perf. 13*
C86 AP36 100fr gold & multi ('69) 5.50 1.10

Engr.
C87 AP36 250fr mag, sl grn & brt bl 3.25 1.40

See No. C255.

Dandy Horse, 1818, and Racer, 1968 AP37

1968, May 17 Engr. *Perf. 13*
C88 AP37 100fr bl grn & red 2.40 .80

150th anniversary of the invention of the bicycle.

Sheet Bend Knot AP37a

1968, July 20 Photo. *Perf. 13*
C89 AP37a 50fr gray, blk, red & grn .90 .45

Fifth anniversary of economic agreement between the European Economic Community and the African and Malgache Union.

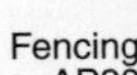

Fencing AP38

Designs: 100fr, Jackknife dive, vert. 150fr, Weight lifting, vert. 200fr, Equestrian.

1968, Sept. 10 Engr. *Perf. 13*
C90 AP38 50fr pur & blk .60 .40
C91 AP38 100fr choc, ultra & blk 1.10 .60
C92 AP38 150fr choc & org 1.60 .75
C93 AP38 200fr brn, emer & ind 2.25 1.50
a. Min. sheet of 4, #C90-C93 8.00 8.00
Nos. C90-C93 (4) 5.55 3.25

19th Olympic Games, Mexico City, 10/12-27.

No. C93a is folded down the vertical gutter separating Nos. C90-C91 se-tenant at left and Nos. C92-C93 se-tenant at right.

Robert F. Kennedy — AP39

#C95, John F. Kennedy. #C96, Rev. Dr. Martin Luther King, Jr. #C97, Mahatma Gandhi.

1968, Oct. 4 Photo. *Perf. 12½*
C94 AP39 100fr blk & pale org 1.25 .70
C95 AP39 100fr blk & aqua 1.40 .70
C96 AP39 100fr blk & bluish gray 1.25 .70
C97 AP39 100fr blk & yel 1.25 .70
a. Souv. sheet of 4, #C94-C97 6.75 6.75
Nos. C94-C97 (4) 5.15 2.80

Issued to honor proponents of non-violence.

PHILEXAFRIQUE Issue
Painting Type of 1968

Design: 100fr, Interior Minister Paré, by J. L. La Neuville (1748-1826).

1968, Oct. 25 Photo. *Perf. 12½*
C98 AP34 100fr multi 2.75 2.75

Issued to publicize PHILEXAFRIQUE, Philatelic Exhibition in Abidjan, Feb. 14-23, 1969. Printed with alternating light blue label.

Arms and Flags of Niger AP40

1968, Dec. 17 Litho. *Perf. 13*
C99 AP40 100fr multi 1.50 .70

10th anniv. of the proclamation of the Republic.

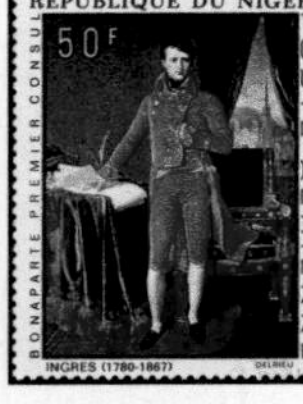

Bonaparte as First Consul, by Ingres — AP41

Paintings: 100fr, Napoleon Visiting the Plague House in Jaffa, by Antoine Jean Gros. 150fr, Napoleon on the Imperial Throne, by Jean Auguste Dominique Ingres. 200fr, Napoleon's March Through France, by Jean Louis Ernest Meissonier, horiz.

Perf. 12½x12, 12x12½
1969, Jan. 20 Photo.
C100 AP41 50fr multi 1.90 .95
C101 AP41 100fr grn & multi 3.00 1.50
C102 AP41 150fr pur & multi 4.00 1.75
C103 AP41 200fr brn & multi 6.00 3.00
Nos. C100-C103 (4) 14.90 7.20

Napoleon Bonaparte (1769-1821).

2nd PHILEXAFRIQUE Issue
Common Design Type

Designs: 50fr, Niger No. 41 and giraffes.

1969, Feb. 14 Engr. *Perf. 13*
C104 CD128 50fr slate, brn & org 3.00 1.90

Weather Observation Plane in Storm and Anemometer — AP42

1969, Mar. 23 Engr. *Perf. 13*
C105 AP42 50fr blk, brt bl & grn .90 .45

9th World Meteorological Day.

Panhard Levassor, 1900 AP43

Early Automobiles: 45fr, De Dion Bouton 8, 1904. 50fr, Opel, 1909. 70fr, Daimler, 1910. 100fr, Vermorel 12/16, 1912.

1969, Apr. 15 Engr. *Perf. 13*
C106 AP43 25fr gray, lt grn & bl grn .55 .30
C107 AP43 45fr gray, bl & vio .70 .30
C108 AP43 50fr gray, yel bis & brn 1.60 .40
C109 AP43 70fr gray, brt pink & brt lil 2.00 .65
C110 AP43 100fr gray, lem & sl grn 2.25 .90
Nos. C106-C110 (5) 7.10 2.55

Apollo 8 Trip around Moon — AP44

Embossed on Gold Foil
1969, Mar. 31 *Die-cut Perf. 10½*
C111 AP44 1000fr gold 18.50 18.50

US Apollo 8 mission, which put the 1st men into orbit around the moon, Dec. 21-27, 1968.

No. C14 Overprinted in Red

1969, July 25 Engr. *Perf. 13*
C112 AP1 500fr multi 7.50 7.50

See note after Mali No. C80.

Toys AP45

1969, Oct. 13 Engr. *Perf. 13*
C113 AP45 100fr bl, red brn & grn 1.40 .60

International Nuremberg Toy Fair.

Europafrica Issue

Links AP46

1969, Oct. 30 Photo.
C114 AP46 50fr vio, yel & blk .90 .50

Camels and Motor Caravan Crossing Desert AP47

100fr, Motor caravan crossing mountainous region. 150fr, Motor caravan in African village. 200fr, Map of Africa showing tour, Citroen B-2 tractor, African & European men shaking hands.

1969, Nov. 22 Engr. *Perf. 13*
C115 AP47 50fr lil, pink & brn .95 .40
C116 AP47 100fr dk car rose, lt bl & vio bl 2.00 .75
C117 AP47 150fr multi 2.50 1.25
C118 AP47 200fr sl grn, bl & blk 4.00 1.75
Nos. C115-C118 (4) 9.45 4.15

Black Tour across Africa from Colomb-Bechar, Algeria, to Mombassa, Dar es Salaam, Mozambique, Tananarive and the Cape of Good Hope.

EXPO '70 at Osaka — AP48

1970, Mar. 25 Photo. *Perf. 12½*
C119 AP48 100fr multi 1.50 .60

Issued to publicize EXPO '70 International Exhibition, Osaka, Japan, Mar. 15-Sept. 13.

Education Year Emblem and Education Symbols AP49

1970, Apr. 6 Engr. *Perf. 13*
C120 AP49 100fr plum, red & gray 1.25 .60

Issued for International Education Year.

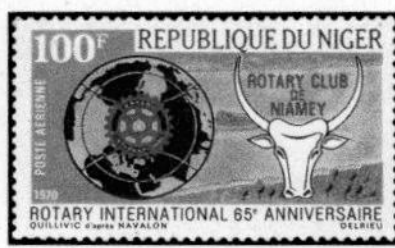

Rotary Emblem, Globe and Niamey Club Emblem AP50

1970, Apr. 30 Photo. *Perf. 12½*
C121 AP50 100fr gold & multi 1.60 .80

65th anniversary of Rotary International.

Modern Plane, Clement Ader and his Flying Machine AP51

Designs: 100fr, Joseph and Jacques Montgolfier, rocket and balloon. 150fr, Isaac Newton, planetary system and trajectories. 200fr, Galileo Galilei, spaceship and trajectories. 250fr, Leonardo da Vinci, his flying machine, and plane.

1970, May 11 Engr. *Perf. 13*
C122 AP51 50fr bl, cop red & sl 1.00 .40
C123 AP51 100fr cop red, bl & sl 1.75 .80
C124 AP51 150fr brn, grn & ocher 1.90 1.00
C125 AP51 200fr dk car rose, dp vio & bis 2.60 1.40
C126 AP51 250fr cop red, gray & pur 4.00 1.75
Nos. C122-C126 (5) 11.25 5.35

Pioneers of space research.
For overprints and surcharges see Nos. C129-C130, C141-C142.

Bay of Naples, Buildings, Mt. Vesuvius and Niger No. 97 — AP52

1970, May 5 Photo. *Perf. 12½*
C127 AP52 100fr multi 1.40 .60

Issued to publicize the 10th Europa Philatelic Exhibition, Naples, Italy, May 2-10.

TV Tube, Books, Microscope, Globe and ITU Emblem AP53

1970, May 16 Engr. *Perf. 13*
C128 AP53 100fr grn, brn & red 1.40 .70

Issued for World Telecommunications Day.

Nos. C123 and C125 Overprinted: "Solidarité Spatiale / Apollo XIII / 11-17 Avril 1970"

1970, June 6 Engr. *Perf. 13*
C129 AP51 100fr multi 1.25 .60
C130 AP51 200fr multi 2.25 .80

Abortive flight of Apollo 13, 4/11-17/70.

UN Emblem, Man, Woman and Doves AP54

1970, June 26 Photo. *Perf. 12½*
C131 AP54 100fr brt bl, dk bl & org 1.25 .60
C132 AP54 150fr multi 1.75 .90

25th anniversary of the United Nations.

European and African Men, Globe and Fleur-de-lis — AP55

Lithographed; Embossed on Gold Foil

1970, July 22 *Perf. 12½*
C133 AP55 250fr gold & ultra 4.00 4.00

French Language Cong., Niamey, Mar. 1970.

Europafrica Issue

European and African Women AP56

1970, July 29 Engr. *Perf. 13*
C134 AP56 50fr slate grn & dl red .85 .40

EXPO Emblem, Geisha and Torii — AP57

Design: 150fr, EXPO emblem, exhibition at night and character from Noh play.

1970, Sept. 16 Engr. *Perf. 13*
C135 AP57 100fr multi 1.10 .55
C136 AP57 150fr bl, dk brn & grn 1.60 .75

EXPO '70 International Exhibition, Osaka, Japan, Mar. 15-Sept. 13.

Gymnast on Parallel Bars — AP58

Sports: 100fr, Vaulting, horiz. 150fr, Flying jump, horiz. 200fr, Rings.

1970, Oct. 26 Engr. *Perf. 13*
C137 AP58 50fr brt bl .65 .40
C138 AP58 100fr brt grn 1.40 .70
C139 AP58 150fr brt rose lil 2.25 .95
C140 AP58 200fr red org 2.75 1.25
Nos. C137-C140 (4) 7.05 3.30

17th World Gymnastics Championships, Ljubljana, Oct. 22-27.

Nos. C124 and C126 Surcharged and Overprinted: "LUNA 16 - Sept. 1970 / PREMIERS PRELEVEMENTS / AUTOMATIQUES SUR LA LUNE"

1970, Nov. 5
C141 AP51 100fr on 150fr multi 1.50 .70
C142 AP51 200fr on 250fr multi 3.00 1.40

Unmanned moon probe of the Russian space ship Luna 16, Sept. 12-24.

Beethoven and Piano — AP59

Design: 150fr, Beethoven and dancers with dove, symbolic of Ode to Joy.

1970, Nov. 18 Photo. *Perf. 12½*
C143 AP59 100fr multi 1.60 .60
C144 AP59 150fr multi 2.40 .90

Ludwig van Beethoven (1770-1827), composer.

John F. Kennedy Bridge, Niamey AP60

1970, Dec. 18 Photo. *Perf. 12½*
C145 AP60 100fr multicolored 1.50 .65

Proclamation of the Republic, 12th anniv.

Gamal Abdel Nasser (1918-70), President of Egypt — AP61

Design: 200fr, Nasser with raised arm.

1971, Jan. 5 Photo. *Perf. 12½*
C146 AP61 100fr blk, org brn & grn 1.00 .50
C147 AP61 200fr grn, org & blk brn 1.75 .85

Charles de Gaulle — AP62

Embossed on Gold Foil

1971, Jan. 22 *Die-cut Perf. 10*
C148 AP62 1000fr gold *65.00 65.00*

In memory of Gen. Charles de Gaulle (1890-1970), President of France.

Olympic Rings and "Munich" AP63

1971, Jan. 29 Engr. *Perf. 13*
C149 AP63 150fr dk bl, rose lil & grn 1.90 .90

1972 Summer Olympic Games, Munich.

Landing Module over Moon — AP64

1971, Feb. 5 Engr. *Perf. 13*
C150 AP64 250fr ultra, sl grn & org 3.00 1.75

Apollo 14 mission, Jan. 31-Feb. 9.

Masks of Hate — AP65

200fr, People & 4-leaf clover (symbol of unity).

1971, Mar. 20 Engr. *Perf. 13*
C151 AP65 100fr red, sl & brt bl 1.10 .45
C152 AP65 200fr slate, red & grn 2.25 .85

Intl. Year against Racial Discrimination.

Map of Africa and Telecommunications System — AP66

1971, Apr. 6 Photo. *Perf. 12½*
C153 AP66 100fr grn & multi .90 .45

Pan-African telecommunications system.

African Mask and Japan No. 580 — AP67

Design: 100fr, Japanese actors, stamps of Niger, No. 95 on cover and No. 170.

1971, Apr. 23 Engr. *Perf. 13*
C154 AP67 50fr choc, brt grn & blk .90 .45
C155 AP67 100fr red brn & multi 1.50 .60

Philatokyo 71, Tokyo Philatelic Exposition, Apr. 19-29.

Longwood, St. Helena, by Carle Vernet AP68

Napoleon Bonaparte: 200fr, Napoleon's body on camp bed, by Marryat.

1971, May 5 Photo. *Perf. 13*
C156 AP68 150fr gold & multi 2.50 .75
C157 AP68 200fr gold & multi 3.50 1.25

Satellite, Waves and Earth — AP69

1971, May 17 Engr. *Perf. 13*
C158 AP69 100fr org, ultra & dk brn 1.50 .70

3rd World Telecommunications Day.

Olympic Rings, Athletes and Torch — AP70

Designs: 50fr, Pierre de Coubertin, discus throwers, horiz. 150fr, Runners, horiz.

1971, June 10
C159 AP70 50fr red & slate .80 .35
C160 AP70 100fr sl, brn & grn 1.25 .60
C161 AP70 150fr plum, bl & rose lil 2.10 1.10
Nos. C159-C161 (3) 4.15 2.05

75th anniv. of modern Olympic Games.

Astronauts and Landing Module on Moon — AP71

1971, July 26 Engr. *Perf. 13*
C162 AP71 150fr scar, pur & sl 1.90 1.00

US Apollo 15 moon mission, 7/26-8/7/71.

Charles de Gaulle — AP72

1971, Nov. 9 Photo. *Perf. 12½x12*
C163 AP72 250r multi 8.50 5.50

First anniversary of the death of Charles de Gaulle (1890-1970), president of France.

African Postal Union Issue, 1971
Common Design Type

Design: 100fr, Water carrier, cattle and UAMPT headquarters, Brazzaville, Congo.

1971, Nov. 13 Photo. *Perf. 13x13½*
C164 CD135 100fr blue & multi 1.25 .60

Al Hariri Holding Audience, Baghdad, 1237 AP73

Designs from Mohammedan Miniatures: 150fr, Archangel Israfil, late 14th century, vert. 200fr, Horsemen, 1210.

1971, Nov. 25 *Perf. 13*
C165 AP73 100fr multi 1.40 .60
C166 AP73 150fr multi 2.25 .95
C167 AP73 200fr multi 3.25 1.75
Nos. C165-C167 (3) 6.90 3.30

Louis Armstrong — AP74

Design: 150fr, Armstrong with trumpet.

1971, Dec. 6
C168 AP74 100fr multi 2.10 .75
C169 AP74 150fr multi 3.25 1.00

Armstrong (1900-71), American jazz musician.

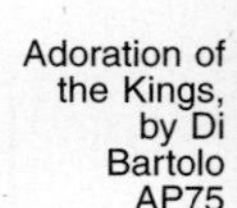

Adoration of the Kings, by Di Bartolo AP75

Christmas (Paintings): 150fr, Nativity, by Domenico Ghirlandaio, vert. 200fr, Adoration of the Shepherds, by Il Perugino.

1971, Dec. 24 Photo. *Perf. 13*
C170 AP75 100fr blk & multi 1.25 .55
C171 AP75 150fr blk & multi 2.00 .80
C172 AP75 200fr blk & multi 2.50 1.20
Nos. C170-C172 (3) 5.75 2.55

See Nos. C210-C212, C232-C234.

Presidents Pompidou and Diori Hamani, Flags of Niger and France AP76

1972, Jan. 22
C173 AP76 250fr multi 6.75 4.00

Visit of President Georges Pompidou of France, Jan. 1972.

Snowflakes, Olympic Torch and Emblem AP77

Design: 100fr, Torii made of ski poles and skis, and dwarf tree, vert.

1972, Jan. 27 Engr.
C174 AP77 100fr dk vio, grn & car 1.25 .55
C175 AP77 150fr dk vio, lil & red 1.90 .75
a. Souv. sheet of 2, #C174-C175 3.25 3.25

11th Winter Olympic Games, Sapporo, Japan, Feb. 3-13.

The Masked Ball, by Guardi AP78

50fr, 100fr, 150fr, Details from "The Masked Ball," by Francesco Guardi (1712-93); all vert.

1972, Feb. 7 Photo.
C176 AP78 50fr gold & multi 1.10 .50
C177 AP78 100fr gold & multi 1.75 .85
C178 AP78 150fr gold & multi 2.75 1.10
C179 AP78 200fr gold & multi 3.25 1.40
Nos. C176-C179 (4) 8.85 3.85

UNESCO campaign to save Venice. See Nos. C215-C216.

Johannes Brahms and "Lullaby" — AP79

1972, Mar. 17 Engr. *Perf. 13*
C180 AP79 100fr multicolored 2.10 .75

75th anniversary of death of Johannes Brahms (1833-1897), German composer.

Scout Sign and Tents — AP80

1972, Mar. 22
C181 AP80 150fr pur, org & slate bl 1.75 .75

World Boy Scout Seminar, Cotonou, Dahomey, March 1972.

Surgical Team, Heart-shaped Globe and Emblem — AP81

1972 Engr. *Perf. 13*
C182 AP81 100fr dp brn & car 1.40 .60

"Your heart is your health," World Health Day.

Famous Aircraft AP82

50fr, Bleriot XI Crossing English Channel. 75fr, Spirit of St. Louis crossing Atlantic. 100fr, 1st flight of Concorde supersonic jet.

1972, Apr. 24
C183 AP82 50fr shown 1.00 .40
C184 AP82 75fr multicolored 1.60 .55
C185 AP82 100fr multicolored 3.00 1.40
Nos. C183-C185 (3) 5.60 2.35

ITU Emblem, Satellite, Stars and Earth AP83

1972, May 17 Engr. *Perf. 13*
C186 AP83 100fr pur, car & blk 1.50 .60

4th World Telecommunications Day.

20th Olympic Games, Munich — AP84

50fr, Boxing and Opera House. 100fr, Broad jump & City Hall. 150fr, Soccer & Church of the Theatines, vert. 200fr, Running and Propylaeum.

1972, May 26
C187 AP84 50fr blue & grn .70 .30
C188 AP84 100fr yel grn & dk brn 1.00 .50
C189 AP84 150fr org red & dk brn 1.60 .70
C190 AP84 200fr violet & dk brn 2.10 .90
a. Min. sheet of 4, #C187-C190 5.75 5.75
Nos. C187-C190 (4) 5.40 2.40

For overprints see Nos. C196-C199.

"Alexander Graham Bell," Telephone AP85

1972, July 7
C191 AP85 100fr car, dk pur & slate 1.75 .60

Alexander Graham Bell (1847-1922), inventor of the telephone. Stamp pictures Samuel F. B. Morse.

Europafrica Issue

Stylized Maps of Africa and Europe — AP86

1972, July 29 **Engr.** ***Perf. 13***
C192 AP86 50fr red brn, bl & grn .60 .25

Mail Runner, UPU Emblem AP87

Designs: 100fr, Mail truck, UPU emblem. 150fr, Mail plane, UPU emblem.

1972, Oct. 9 **Engr.** ***Perf. 13***
C193 AP87 50fr multicolored .80 .40
C194 AP87 100fr multicolored 1.25 .65
C195 AP87 150fr multicolored 2.00 .95
Nos. C193-C195 (3) 4.05 2.00

Universal Postal Union Day.

Nos. C187-C190 Overprinted in Red or Violet Blue

(a)

(b)

(c)

(d)

1972, Nov. 10
C196 AP84(a) 50fr multi (R) .70 .40
C197 AP84(b) 100fr multi (R) 1.10 .55
C198 AP84(c) 150fr multi (VBl) 2.10 .90
C199 AP84(d) 200fr multi (R) 2.60 1.10
Nos. C196-C199 (4) 6.50 2.95

Gold medal winners in 20th Olympic Games: Emilio Correa, Cuba, welterweight boxing; Victor Saneev, USSR, triple jump; Poland, soccer; Frank Shorter, US, marathon.

Fables AP88

25fr, The Crow and The Fox. 50fr, The Lion and the Mouse. 75fr, The Monkey and the Leopard.

1972, Nov. 23
C200 AP88 25fr emer, blk & brn 1.25 .40
C201 AP88 50fr brt pink, bl grn & brn 1.75 .50
C202 AP88 75fr lt brn, grn & dk brn 2.75 .80
Nos. C200-C202 (3) 5.75 1.70

Jean de La Fontaine (1621-1695), French fabulist.

Astronauts on Moon AP89

1972, Dec. 12 **Photo.** ***Perf. 13***
C203 AP89 250fr multi 3.25 1.75

Apollo 17 US moon mission, Dec. 7-19.

Young Athlete — AP90

Design: 100fr, Head of Hermes.

1973, Feb. 7 **Engr.** ***Perf. 13***
C204 AP90 50fr dk car .60 .35
C205 AP90 100fr purple 1.25 .50

Treasures of antiquity.

Boy Scouts and Radio Transmission — AP91

Niger Boy Scouts: 50fr, Red Cross, first aid. 100fr, Scout and gazelle. 150fr, Scouts with gazelle and bird.

1973, Mar. 21 **Engr.** ***Perf. 13***
C206 AP91 25fr multicolored .40 .30
C207 AP91 50fr multicolored .75 .35
C208 AP91 100fr multicolored 1.25 .60
C209 AP91 150fr multicolored 1.60 .80
Nos. C206-C209 (4) 4.00 2.05

For overprints see Nos. C217-C218.

Christmas Type of 1971

Paintings: 50fr, Crucifixion, by Hugo van der Goes, vert. 100fr, Burial of Christ, by Cima da Conegliano. 150fr, Pietà, by Giovanni Bellini.

1973, Apr. 20 **Photo.** ***Perf. 13***
C210 AP75 50fr gold & multi .70 .30
C211 AP75 100fr gold & multi 1.40 .55
C212 AP75 150fr gold & multi 2.00 .80
Nos. C210-C212 (3) 4.10 1.65

Easter 1973.

Air Afrique Plane and Mail Truck AP92

1973, Apr. 30 **Engr.** ***Perf. 13***
C213 AP92 100fr brt grn, choc & car 1.60 .70

Stamp Day 1973.

WMO Emblem, Pyramids with Weather Symbols, Satellite — AP93

1973, May 7
C214 AP93 100fr multicolored 1.25 .55

Cent. of intl. meteorological cooperation.

Painting Type of 1972

Paintings by Delacroix: 150fr, Prowling lioness. 200fr, Tigress and cub.

1973, May 22 **Photo.** ***Perf. 13x12½***
C215 AP78 150fr blk & multi 2.75 1.40
C216 AP78 200fr blk & multi 4.50 2.25

175th anniversary of the birth of Ferdinand Delacroix (1798-1863), French painter.

Nos. C208-C209 Overprinted

1973, July 19 **Engr.** ***Perf. 13***
C217 AP91 100fr multi 1.25 .55
C218 AP91 150fr multi 1.75 .80

Boy Scout 24th World Jamboree, Nairobi, Kenya, July 16-21.

Head and City Hall, Brussels — AP93a

1973, Sept. 17 **Engr.** ***Perf. 13***
C219 AP93a 100fr multicolored 1.25 .80

Africa Weeks, Brussels, Sept. 15-30, 1973.

Men Emptying Cornucopia, FAO Emblem, People — AP94

1973, Nov. 2 **Engr.** ***Perf. 13***
C220 AP94 50fr ultra, pur & ver .90 .40

10th anniversary of the World Food Program.

AP95

Copernicus, Sputnik 1, Heliocentric System.

1973, Nov. 12
C221 AP95 150fr rose red, vio bl & brn 2.00 .90

AP96

1973, Nov. 22 **Photo.** ***Perf. 12½***
C222 AP96 100fr reddsh brn & multi 1.25 .60

Souvenir Sheet
Perf. 13

C223 AP96 200fr dp ultra & multi 2.40 2.40

10th anniv. of the death of Pres. John F. Kennedy.

Barge on Niger River AP97

Design: 75fr, Tug Baban Maza.

1974, Jan. 18 **Engr.** ***Perf. 13***
C224 AP97 50fr mar, vio bl & grn 1.00 .50
C225 AP97 75fr yel grn, bl & lil rose 1.40 .50

1st anniv. of the upstream voyage of the Flotilla of Hope.

Lenin — AP98

1974, Jan. 21
C226 AP98 50fr dk red brn 2.10 .60

Skiers — AP99

1974, Feb. 8 **Engr.** ***Perf. 11½x11***
C227 AP99 200fr bl, sepia & car 3.00 1.20

50th anniversary of the first Winter Olympic Games, Chamonix, France.

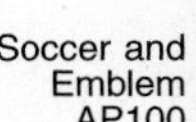

Soccer and Emblem AP100

Designs: Various views of soccer game.

1974, Apr. 8 **Engr.** ***Perf. 13***
C228 AP100 75fr vio & blk .85 .40
C229 AP100 150fr brn, lt & sl grn 1.75 .75
C230 AP100 200fr Prus bl, grn & brn 2.40 1.25
Nos. C228-C230 (3) 5.00 2.40

Souvenir Sheet

C231 AP100 250fr yel grn, brn & ol brn 3.25 3.25

World Soccer Championship, Munich, June 13-July 7.

For overprint see No. C239.

Christmas Type of 1971

Paintings: 50fr, Crucifixion, by Matthias Grunewald. 75fr, Avignon Pietà, attributed to Enguerrand Quarton. 125fr, Burial of Christ, by G. Isenmann.

1974, Apr. 12 **Litho.** ***Perf. 13x12½***
C232 AP75 50fr blk & multi .70 .35
C233 AP75 75fr blk & multi .95 .45
C234 AP75 125r blk & multi 1.60 .75
Nos. C232-C234 (3) 3.25 1.55

Easter 1974.

21st Chess Olympiad, Nice, June 6-30 — AP101

1974, June 3 **Engr.** ***Perf. 13***
C235 AP101 50fr Knights 2.10 .70
C236 AP101 75fr Kings 2.60 1.10

Astronaut and Apollo 11 Badge — AP102

1974, July 20 **Engr.** ***Perf. 13***
C237 AP102 150fr multi 1.60 .80

5th anniversary of the first manned moon landing.

Europafrica Issue

The Rhinoceros, by Pietro Longhi — AP103

1974, Aug. 10 **Photo.** ***Perf. 12½x13***
C238 AP103 250fr multi 7.25 4.00

No. C231 Overprinted in Red

Souvenir Sheet

1974, Sept. 27 **Engr.** ***Perf. 13***
C239 AP100 250fr multi 3.25 3.25

World Cup Soccer Championship, Munich, 1974, victory of German Federal Republic.

Caucasian Woman, Envelope, UPU Emblem and Jets — AP104

Designs (UPU emblem, Envelope and): 100fr, Oriental woman and trains. 150fr, Indian woman and ships. 200fr, Black woman and buses.

1974, Oct. 9 **Engr.** ***Perf. 13***
C240 AP104 50fr multi .75 .35
C241 AP104 100fr multi 1.40 .45
C242 AP104 150fr bl & multi 2.00 .75
C243 AP104 200fr multi 2.75 1.20
Nos. C240-C243 (4) 6.90 2.75

Centenary of Universal Postal Union.

Skylab over Africa — AP105

1974, Nov. 4 **Engr.** ***Perf. 13***
C244 AP105 100fr multi 1.25 .55

Virgin and Child, by Correggio AP106

150fr, Virgin and Child with St. Hilary, by Filippo Lippi. 200fr, Virgin and Child, by Murillo.

1974, Dec. 24 **Litho.** ***Perf. 12½x13***
C245 AP106 100fr multi 1.25 .45
C246 AP106 150fr multi 2.00 .70
C247 AP106 200fr multi 2.50 1.10
Nos. C245-C247 (3) 5.75 2.25

Christmas 1974. See Nos. C252-C254, C260-C262, C280-C282.

Apollo and Emblem — AP107

Designs (Emblem of Soyuz-Apollo Space Docking): 100fr, Docking in space over earth. 150fr, Soyuz in space.

1975, Jan. 31 **Engr.** ***Perf. 13***
C248 AP107 50fr bl & multi .55 .35
C249 AP107 100fr multi 1.10 .50
C250 AP107 150fr multi 1.90 .70
Nos. C248-C250 (3) 3.55 1.55

Russo-American space cooperation. For overprints see Nos. C263-C265.

Europafrica Issue

European and African Women, Globe — AP108

1975, Feb. 28 **Engr.** ***Perf. 13***
C251 AP108 250fr brn, lil & red 3.25 1.75

Painting Type of 1974

Easter: 75fr, Jesus in Garden of Olives, by Delacroix, horiz. 125fr, Crucifixion, by El Greco. 150fr, Resurrection, by Leonard Limosin.

Perf. 13x12½, 12½x13
1975, Mar. 27 **Litho.**
C252 AP106 75fr multi .85 .35
C253 AP106 125fr multi 1.60 .50
C254 AP106 150fr multi 2.00 .75
Nos. C252-C254 (3) 4.45 1.60

Bird Type of 1968-69 Dated "1975"

100fr, Cinnyricinclus leucogaster, vert.

1975, Apr. **Photo.** ***Perf. 13***
C255 AP36 100fr gold & multi 4.00 1.30

Lt. Col. Seyni Kountche AP109

1975, Apr. 15 **Litho.** ***Perf. 12½x13***
C256 AP109 100fr multi 1.40 .70

Military Government, first anniversary.

Shot Put, Maple Leaf, Montreal Olympic Emblem — AP110

Design: 200fr, Gymnast on rings, Canadian flag, Montreal Olympic emblem.

1975, Oct. 6 **Engr.** ***Perf. 13***
C257 AP110 150fr blk & red 1.40 .70
C258 AP110 200fr red & blk 2.00 1.00

Pre-Olympic Year 1975.

UN Emblem and Dove AP111

1975, Nov. 26 **Engr.** ***Perf. 13***
C259 AP111 100fr grn & bl 1.25 .50

United Nations, 30th anniversary.

Painting Type of 1974

50fr, Virgin of Seville, by Murillo. 75fr, Adoration of the Shepherds, by Tintoretto, horiz. 125fr, Virgin with Angels, Florentine, 15th cent.

1975, Dec. 24 **Litho.** ***Perf. 12½x13***
C260 AP106 50fr multi .65 .35
C261 AP106 75fr multi 1.00 .45
C262 AP106 125fr multi 1.60 .80
Nos. C260-C262 (3) 3.25 1.60

Christmas 1975.

Nos. C248-C250 Ovptd.

1975, Dec. 30 **Engr.** ***Perf. 13***
C263 AP107 50fr bl & multi .70 .25
C264 AP107 100fr multi .90 .55
C265 AP107 150fr multi 1.60 .90
Nos. C263-C265 (3) 3.20 1.70

Apollo-Soyuz link-up in space, July 17, 1975.

12th Winter Olympic Games Type, 1976

Designs: 200fr, Women's figure skating. 300fr, Biathlon. 500fr, Speed skating.

1976, Feb. 20 **Litho.** ***Perf. 14x13½***
C266 A97 200fr multi 1.60 .80
C267 A97 300fr multi 2.40 1.20

Souvenir Sheet

C268 A97 500fr multi 4.50 2.00

American Bicentennial Type, 1976

Design (Statue of Liberty and): 150fr, Joseph Warren, martyr at Bunker Hill. 200fr, John Paul Jones on the bridge of the "Bonhomme Richard." 300fr, Molly Pitcher, Monmouth battle heroine. 500fr, Start of the fighting.

1976, Apr. 8
C269 A100 150fr multi 1.20 .40
C270 A100 200fr multi 1.75 .70
C271 A100 300fr multi 2.40 .85
Nos. C269-C271 (3) 4.95 1.85

Souvenir Sheet

C272 A100 500fr multi 4.75 1.60

LZ-129 over Lake Constance — AP112

Designs: 50fr, LZ-3 over Würzburg. 150fr, LZ-9 over Friedrichshafen. 200fr, LZ-2 over Rothenburg, vert. 300fr, LZ-130 over Essen. 500fr, LZ-127 over the Swiss Alps.

1976, May 18 **Litho.** ***Perf. 11***
C273 AP112 40fr multi .50 .25
C274 AP112 50fr multi .60 .25
C275 AP112 150fr multi 1.75 .50
C276 AP112 200fr multi 2.00 .55
C277 AP112 300fr multi 3.00 .70
Nos. C273-C277 (5) 7.85 2.25

Souvenir Sheet

C278 AP112 500fr multi 5.00 2.00

75th anniversary of the Zeppelin.

Olympic Games Issue
Souvenir Sheet

1976, July 17 **Litho.** ***Perf. 14***
C279 A105 150fr Sprint 1.75 .80

Christmas Type of 1974

Paintings: 50fr, Nativity, by Rubens. 100fr, Virgin and Child, by Correggio. 150fr, Adoration of the Kings, by Gerard David, horiz.

1976, Dec. 24 **Litho.** ***Perf. 12½***
C280 AP106 50fr multi .60 .25
C281 AP106 100fr multi 1.25 .50
C282 AP106 150fr multi 2.00 .85
Nos. C280-C282 (3) 3.85 1.60

Christmas 1976.

Viking Mars Project Issue

100fr, Viking lander & nprobe, horiz. 150fr, Descent phases of Viking lander. 200fr, Titan rocket start for Mars. 400fr, Viking orbiter in flight.

1977, Mar. 15 **Litho.** ***Perf. 14***
C283 A113 100fr multi .80 .25
C284 A113 150fr multi 1.10 .45
C285 A113 200fr multi 1.60 .60
Nos. C283-C285 (3) 3.50 1.10

Souvenir Sheet

C286 A113 400fr multi 3.25 1.25

For overprints see Nos. C295-C297.

Nobel Prize Issue
Souvenir Sheet

Design: 500fr, Theodore Roosevelt, peace.

1977, Aug. 20 **Litho.** ***Perf. 14***
C287 A122 500fr multi 4.75 1.40

Games' Emblem, Wheels and Colors — AP113

150fr, Rings, colors and Games' emblem.

1978, July 13 **Litho.** ***Perf. 12½x13***
C288 AP113 40fr multi .40 .30
C289 AP113 150fr multi 1.40 .70

Third African Games, Algiers, July 13-28.

Emblem — AP114

1978, Oct. 6 **Litho.** ***Perf. 13***
C290 AP114 150fr multi 1.25 .70

Niger Broadcasting Company, 20th anniversary.

Philexafrique II — Essen Issue
Common Design Types

Designs: No. C291, Giraffes and Niger No. 92. No. C292, Eagle and Oldenburg No. 7.

1978, Nov. 1 **Litho.** ***Perf. 13x12½***
C291 CD138 100fr multi 2.25 1.40
C292 CD139 100fr multi 2.25 1.40
a. Pair, #C291-C292 + label 6.00 6.00

View of Campus and Laying Cornerstone AP115

1978, Dec. 11 **Litho.** ***Perf. 12½***
C293 AP115 100fr multi 2.00 .40

Islamic University of Niger.

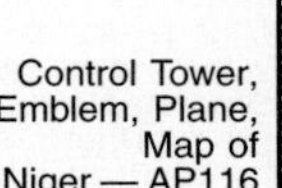

Control Tower, Emblem, Plane, Map of Niger — AP116

1979, Dec. 12 **Litho.** ***Perf. 12½***
C294 AP116 150fr multi 1.50 .80

ASECNA (Air Safety Board), 20th anniversary.

Nos. C284-C286 Overprinted in Silver or Black

1979, Dec. 20 **Litho.** ***Perf. 14***
C295 A113 150fr multi 1.25 .70
C296 A113 200fr multi (S) 1.60 .85

Souvenir Sheet

C297 A113 400fr multi 3.50 3.50

Apollo 11 moon landing, 10th anniversary.

Gaweye Hotel — AP117

1980, Jan. 10 **Litho.** ***Perf. 13***
C298 AP117 100fr multi .90 .45

Self-portrait, by Rembrandt AP118

Rembrandt Portraits: 90fr, Hendrickje at the Window. 100fr, Old Man. 130fr, Maria Trip. 200fr, Self-portrait, diff. 400fr, Saskia.

1981, Feb. 12 **Litho.** ***Perf. 12½***
C299 AP118 60fr multi .45 .25
C300 AP118 90fr multi .70 .25
C301 AP118 100fr multi .80 .30
C302 AP118 130fr multi 1.10 .40
C303 AP118 200fr multi 1.60 .40
C304 AP118 400fr multi 3.25 1.00
Nos. C299-C304 (6) 7.90 2.60

Apollo 11, 1969 AP119

Space Conquest: Views of Columbia space shuttle, 1981.

1981, Mar. 30 **Litho.** ***Perf. 12½***
C305 AP119 100fr multi .80 .30
C306 AP119 150fr multi 1.25 .35
C307 AP119 200fr multi 1.40 .45
C308 AP119 300fr multi 2.25 .75
Nos. C305-C308 (4) 5.70 1.85

Souvenir Sheet

C309 AP119 500fr multi 4.25 1.60

For overprint see No. C356.

Girl in a Room, by Picasso AP120

Picasso Birth Centenary: 60fr, Olga in an Armchair. 90fr, Family of Acrobats. 120fr, Three Musicians. 200fr, Paul on a Donkey. All vert.

1981, June 25 **Litho.** ***Perf. 12½***
C310 AP120 60fr multi .50 .25
C311 AP120 90fr multi .80 .30
C312 AP120 120fr multi 1.00 .40
C313 AP120 200fr multi 1.75 .60
C314 AP120 400fr multi 3.50 1.10
Nos. C310-C314 (5) 7.55 2.65

Christmas 1982 — AP121

Rubens Paintings — 200fr, Adoration of the Kings. 300fr, Mystical Marriage of St. Catherine. 400fr, Virgin and Child.

1982, Dec. 24 **Litho.** ***Perf. 14***
C315 AP121 200fr multi 1.50 .40
C316 AP121 300fr multi 2.25 .65
C317 AP121 400fr multi 3.00 .90
Nos. C315-C317 (3) 6.75 1.95

Manned Flight Bicentenary AP122

65fr, Montgolfiere balloon, 1783, vert. 85fr, Hydrogen balloon, 1783, vert. 200fr, Zeppelin. 250fr, Farman plane. 300fr, Concorde. 500fr, Apollo 11, vert.

1983, Jan. 24
C318 AP122 65fr multi .50 .25
C319 AP122 85fr multi .75 .25
C320 AP122 200fr multi 1.50 .40
C321 AP122 250fr multi 2.00 .60
C322 AP122 300fr multi 2.25 .70
C323 AP122 500fr multi 4.00 1.10
Nos. C318-C323 (6) 11.00 3.30

Pre-Olympic Year AP123

1983, May 25 **Litho.** ***Perf. 13***
C324 AP123 85fr Javelin .60 .25
C325 AP123 200fr Shot put 1.60 .55
C326 AP123 250fr Hammer, vert. 1.90 .70
C327 AP123 300fr Discus 2.40 .80
Nos. C324-C327 (4) 6.50 2.30

Souvenir Sheet

C328 AP123 500fr Shot put, diff. 4.00 1.50

For overprint see No. C357.

Christmas 1983 AP124

Botticelli Paintings — 120fr, Virgin and Child with Angels, vert. 350fr, Adoration of the Kings. 500fr, Virgin of the Pomegranate, vert.

Wmk. 385 Cartor

1983 **Litho.** ***Perf. 13***
C329 AP124 120fr multi .90 .35
C330 AP124 350fr multi 2.75 .75
C331 AP124 500fr multi 3.75 1.10
Nos. C329-C331 (3) 7.40 2.20

1984 Summer Olympics AP125

80fr, Sprint. 120fr, Pole vault. 140fr, High jump. 200fr, Triple jump, vert. 350fr, Long jump, vert.
500fr, 110-meter hurdles.

Unwmk.

1984, Feb. 22 **Litho.** ***Perf. 13***
C332 AP125 80fr multi .55 .25
C333 AP125 120fr multi .80 .25
C334 AP125 140fr multi 1.25 .40
C335 AP125 200fr multi 1.75 .40
C336 AP125 350fr multi 2.75 .90
Nos. C332-C336 (5) 7.10 2.20

Souvenir Sheet

C337 AP125 500fr multi 3.75 1.25

1984, Oct. 8 **Litho.**

Designs: Winners of various track events: 80fr, Carl Lewis, vert. 120fr, J. Cruz, vert. 140fr, A. Cova, vert. 300fr, Al Joyner, vert.
500fr, D. Mogenburg, high jump.

C338 AP125 80fr multi .55 .35
C339 AP125 120fr multi .90 .45
C340 AP125 140fr multi 1.00 .50
C341 AP125 300fr multi 2.10 1.10
Nos. C338-C341 (4) 4.55 2.40

Souvenir Sheet

C342 AP125 500fr multi 3.75 2.25

World Soccer Cup AP126

1984, Nov. 19 **Litho.** ***Perf. 13***
C345 AP126 150fr multi .90 .60
C346 AP126 250fr multi 1.60 1.05
C347 AP126 450fr multi 3.00 1.60
C348 AP126 500fr multi 3.25 1.90
Nos. C345-C348 (4) 8.75 5.15

Christmas 1984 — AP127

Paintings: 100fr, The Visitation, by Ghirlandajo. 200fr, Virgin and Child, by the Master of Santa Verdiana. 400fr, Virgin and Child, by J. Koning.

1984, Dec. 24 **Litho.** ***Perf. 13***
C349 AP127 100fr multi .80 .45
C350 AP127 200fr multi 1.60 .95
C351 AP127 400fr multi 3.25 1.40
Nos. C349-C351 (3) 5.65 2.80

Audubon Birth Bicentennial AP128

110fr, Himantopus mexicanus. 140fr, Phoenicopterus ruber, vert. 200fr, Fratercula arctica. 350fr, Sterna paradisaea, vert.

1985, Feb. 6 **Litho.** ***Perf. 13***
C352 AP128 110fr multi .90 .50
C353 AP128 140fr multi 1.40 .55
C354 AP128 200fr multi 1.75 .85
C355 AP128 350fr multi 3.25 1.40
Nos. C352-C355 (4) 7.30 3.30

Nos. C309, C328 Ovptd. in Silver with Exhibition Emblems

1985, Mar. 11 **Litho.** ***Perf. 12½, 13***
C356 AP119 500fr ARGENTINA '85 BUENOS AIRES 4.75 4.75
C357 AP123 500fr OLYMPHILEX '85 LAUSANNE 4.75 4.75

Religious Paintings by Bartolome Murillo (1617-1682) AP129

110fr, Virgin of the Rosary. 250fr, The Immaculate Conception. 390fr, Virgin of Seville.

1985, Dec. 19 **Litho.** ***Perf. 13***
C358 AP129 110fr multi .80 .45
C359 AP129 250fr multi 2.10 1.00
C360 AP129 390fr multi 3.50 1.60
Nos. C358-C360 (3) 6.40 3.05

Christmas 1985.

Halley's Comet AP130

110fr, Over Paris, 1910. 130fr, Over New York. 200fr, Giotto space probe. 300fr, Vega probe. 390fr, Planet A probe.

1985, Dec. 26
C361 AP130 110fr multi .80 .40
C362 AP130 130fr multi .90 .55
C363 AP130 200fr multi 1.60 .80
C364 AP130 300fr multi 2.25 1.20
C365 AP130 390fr multi 3.00 1.60
Nos. C361-C365 (5) 8.55 4.55

Martin Luther King, Jr. (1929-1968), Civil Rights Activist — AP131

1986, Apr. 28 **Litho.** *Perf. 13½*

C366 AP131 500fr multi 4.00 2.00

1986 World Cup Soccer Championships, Mexico — AP132

Various soccer plays, stamps and labels.

1986, May 21 *Perf. 13*
C367 AP132 130fr No. 228 .90 .40
C368 AP132 210fr No. 229 1.40 .70
C369 AP132 390fr No. 230 2.75 1.25
C370 AP132 400fr Aztec drawing 2.75 1.25
Nos. C367-C370 (4) 7.80 3.60

Souvenir Sheet

C371 AP132 500fr World Cup 3.75 2.25

Statue of Liberty, Cent. — AP133

300fr, Bartholdi, statue.

1986, June 19
C372 AP133 300fr multi 2.60 1.35

1988 Summer Olympics, Seoul — AP134

Olympic Rings, Pierre de Coubertin and: 85fr, One-man kayak, vert. 165fr, Crew racing. 200fr, Two-man kayak. 600fr, One-man kayak, diff., vert. 750fr, One-man kayak, diff., vert.

1988, June 22 **Litho.** *Perf. 13*
C373 AP134 85fr multi .60 .30
C374 AP134 165fr multi 1.15 .60
C375 AP134 200fr multi 1.50 .80
C376 AP134 600fr multi 4.25 2.25
Nos. C373-C376 (4) 7.50 3.95

Souvenir Sheet

C377 AP134 750fr multi 5.75 4.50

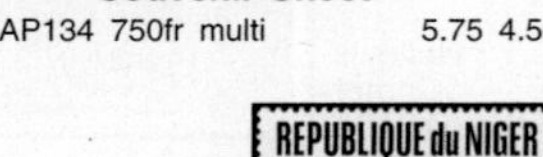

First Moon Landing, 20th Anniv. — AP135

200fr, Launch. 300fr, Crew. 350fr, Lunar experiments. 400fr, Raising flag.

1989, July 27 **Litho.** *Perf. 13*
C378 AP135 200fr multi 1.60 .75
C379 AP135 300fr multi 2.40 1.25
C380 AP135 350fr multi 2.75 1.40
C381 AP135 400fr multi 3.25 1.50
Nos. C378-C381 (4) 10.00 4.90

1990 World Cup Soccer Championships, Italy — AP136

Athletes & views or symbols of Italian cities.

1990, Mar. 6 **Litho.** *Perf. 13*
C382 AP136 130fr Florence .90 .45
C383 AP136 210fr Verona 1.50 .85
C384 AP136 500fr Bari 3.25 2.00
C385 AP136 600fr Rome 4.00 2.40
Nos. C382-C385 (4) 9.65 5.70

1992 Winter Olympics, Albertville AP138

110fr, Speed skating. 300fr, Ice hockey. 500fr, Downhill skiing. 600fr, Luge.

1991, Mar. 28 **Litho.** *Perf. 13*
C392 AP138 110fr multicolored .70 .35
C393 AP138 300fr multicolored 2.10 1.25
C394 AP138 500fr multicolored 3.50 2.00
C395 AP138 600fr multicolored 4.25 2.40
Nos. C392-C395 (4) 10.55 6.00

AIR POST SEMI-POSTAL STAMPS

Dahomey types SPAP1-SPAP3 inscribed Niger

Perf. 13½x12½, 13 (#CB3)

Photo, Engr. (#CB3)

1942, June 22
CB1 SPAP1 1.50fr + 3.50fr green .35 *5.00*
CB2 SPAP2 2fr + 6fr brown .35 *5.00*
CB3 SPAP3 3fr + 9fr car red .35 *5.00*
Nos. CB1-CB3 (3) 1.05 15.00
Set, never hinged 3.00

Native children's welfare fund.

Colonial Education Fund

Common Design Type

Perf. 12½x13½

1942, June 22 **Engr.**
CB4 CD86a 1.20fr + 1.80fr blue & red .35 *5.00*
Never hinged .90

POSTAGE DUE STAMPS

1914 Upper Senegal and Niger Postage Due Stamps Ovptd.

1921 **Unwmk.** *Perf. 14x13½*
J1 D1 5c green .75 *.95*
J2 D1 10c rose .75 *.95*
J3 D1 15c gray .75 *1.05*
J4 D1 20c brown .75 *1.05*
J5 D1 30c blue .75 *1.20*
J6 D1 50c black .75 *1.20*
J7 D1 60c orange 1.60 *2.00*
J8 D1 1fr violet 1.60 *2.00*
Nos. J1-J8 (8) 7.70 *10.40*

Caravansary Near Timbuktu — D2

1927 **Typo.**
J9 D2 2c dk bl & red .35 *.35*
J10 D2 4c ver & blk .35 *.35*
J11 D2 5c org & vio .35 *.35*
J12 D2 10c red brn & blk vio .35 *.35*
J13 D2 15c grn & org .35 .35
J14 D2 20c cer & ol brn .35 .70
J15 D2 25c blk & ol brn .35 *.70*
J16 D2 30c dl vio & blk 1.40 *1.40*
J17 D2 50c dp red, *grnsh* .70 *1.10*
J18 D2 60c gray vio & org, *bluish* .70 .70
J19 D2 1fr ind & ultra, *bluish* 1.00 *1.20*
J20 D2 2fr rose red & vio 1.10 *1.40*
J21 D2 3fr org brn & ultra 1.75 2.00
Nos. J9-J21 (13) 9.10 *10.95*

Catalogue values for unused stamps in this section, from this point to the end of the section, are for Never Hinged items.

Republic of the Niger

Cross of Agadez — D3

Native Metalcraft: 3fr, 5fr, 10fr, Cross of Iferouane. 15fr, 20fr, 50fr, Cross of Tahoua.

Perf. 12½

1962, July 1 **Unwmk.** **Photo.**
J22 D3 50c emerald .25 .25
J23 D3 1fr violet .25 .25
J24 D3 2fr slate green .25 .25
J25 D3 3fr lilac rose .25 .25
J26 D3 5fr green .25 .25
J27 D3 10fr orange .25 .25
J28 D3 15fr deep blue .25 .25
J29 D3 20fr carmine .25 .25
J30 D3 50fr chocolate .35 .35
Nos. J22-J30 (9) 2.35 2.35

1993 **Litho.** *Perf. 12½*

Designs as Before

Size: 50x50mm

J31 D3 5fr green .25 .25
J32 D3 10fr orange .25 .25
J33 D3 15fr blue .25 .25
J34 D3 20fr red .25 .25
J35 D3 50fr chocolate .40 .40
Nos. J31-J35 (5) 1.40 1.40

Imprint on Nos. J31-J35 is in black.

OFFICIAL STAMPS

Catalogue values for unused stamps in this section are for Never Hinged items.

Djerma Girl Carrying Jug — O1

Denomination in Black

Perf. 14x13½

1962-71 **Typo.** **Unwmk.**
O1 O1 1fr dark purple .25 .25
O2 O1 2fr yel grn .25 .25
O3 O1 5fr brt blue .25 .25
O4 O1 10fr deep red .25 .25
O5 O1 20fr vio blue .25 .25
O6 O1 25fr orange .25 .25
O7 O1 30fr light blue ('65) .30 .25
O8 O1 35fr pale grn ('71) .40 .30
O9 O1 40fr brown ('71) .40 .30
O10 O1 50fr black .40 .30
O11 O1 60fr rose red .60 .35
O12 O1 85fr blue green .90 .35
O13 O1 100fr red lilac .95 .35
O14 O1 200fr dark blue 2.00 .75
Nos. O1-O14 (14) 7.45 4.45

Djerma Girl Carrying Jug — O2

Denomination Same Color As Design

1988, Nov. **Photo. & Typo.** *Perf. 13*
O15 O2 5fr brt blue .25 .25
O16 O2 10fr henna brn .25 .25
O17 O2 20fr vio blue .25 .25
O18 O2 50fr greenish blk .55 .30

1989-96(?)
O19 O2 15fr bright yellow .25 .25
O20 O2 45fr orange .30 .25
O21 O2 85fr blue green — —
O22 O2 100fr red lilac — —

Issued: 15, 45fr, 3/89; 85, 100fr, 1996(?).
See No. 698.

Djerma Girl Carrying Jug Type of 1988

1995 ? **Litho.** *Perf. 13*

Denomination in Black

O24 O2 35fr dull green — —

Three additional stamps were issued in this set. The editors would like to examine any examples.

NIGER COAST PROTECTORATE

'nī-jər 'kōst prə-'tek-t̨ə-ˌrət

(Oil Rivers Protectorate)

LOCATION — West coast of Africa on Gulf of Guinea
GOVT. — British Protectorate

This territory was originally known as the Oil Rivers Protectorate, and its affairs were conducted by the British Royal Niger Company. The Company surrendered its charter to the Crown in 1899. In 1900 all of the territories formerly controlled by the Royal Niger Company were incorporated into the two protectorates of Northern and Southern Nigeria, the latter absorbing the area formerly known as Niger Coast Protectorate. In 1914 Northern and Southern Nigeria joined to form the Crown Colony of Nigeria. (See Nigeria, Northern Nigeria, Southern Nigeria and Lagos.)

12 Pence = 1 Shilling

Stamps of Great Britain, 1881-87, Overprinted in Black

1892 **Wmk. 30** *Perf. 14*
1 A54 ½p vermilion 22.50 13.00
2 A40 1p lilac 13.00 11.00
a. "OIL RIVERS" at top *10,000.*
b. Half used as ½p on cover *2,750.*
3 A56 2p green & car 40.00 9.50
a. Half used as 1p on cover *2,500.*
4 A57 2½p violet, *bl* 10.00 2.75
5 A61 5p lilac & blue 20.00 7.25
6 A65 1sh green 77.50 *100.00*
Nos. 1-6 (6) 183.00 143.50

For surcharges see Nos. 7-36, 50.

Dangerous forgeries exist of all surcharges.

No. 2 Surcharged in Red or Violet

1893
7 A40 ½p on half of 1p (R) 175. 160.
c. Unsevered pair 550. 500.
d. As "c," surcharge inverted and dividing line reversed *27,500.*
e. "½" omitted
f. Straight top to "1" in "½" 390. *400.*
g. Double surcharge in pair with normal *2,100.*
7A A40 ½p on half of 1p (V) *7,750.* *5,500.*
b. Surcharge double *27,500.*
c. Unsevered pair *20,000.* *17,500.*

Nos. 3-6 Handstamp Srchd. in Violet, Red, Carmine, Bluish Black, Deep Blue, Green or Black

1893 Wmk. 30 *Perf. 14*

8 A56 ½p on 2p (V) *525.* 325.
- *a.* Surcharge inverted *19,000.*
- *b.* Surcharge diagonal, inverted *18,500.*

9 A57 ½p on 2½p (V) 14,000.
10 A57 ½p on 2½p (R) 425. 275.
- *a.* Surcharge inverted *12,500.*
- *b.* Surcharge diagonal, inverted *14,500.*

11 A57 ½p on 2½p (C) *25,000. 24,500.*
12 A57 ½p on 2½p (B) *40,000.* —
13 A57 ½p on 2½p (G) 550.

14 A56 ½p on 2p (V) 500. 375.
15 A56 ½p on 2p (Bl) 2,200. 825.
16 A57 ½p on 2½p (V) *7,750.*
17 A57 ½p on 2½p (R) 650. *775.*
18 A57 ½p on 2½p (Bl) 475. 450.
19 A57 ½p on 2½p (G) 500. *550.*

20 A56 ½p on 2p (V) 550. 775.
- *a.* Surcharge inverted *17,500.*

21 A57 ½p on 2½p (R) 600. 475.
- *a.* Surcharge inverted *20,000.*
- *b.* Surcharge diagonal, inverted *8,250.*

22 A57 ½p on 2½p (C) 475. 500.
23 A57 ½p on 2½p (Bl Bk) *5,500.*
24 A57 ½p on 2½p (Bl) 475. *525.*
25 A57 ½p on 2½p (G) 325. 275.
- *a.* Surcharge diagonal, inverted

26 A57 ½p on 2½p (Bk) *4,750.*
- *a.* Surcharge inverted *15,500.*
- *b.* Surcharge diagonal, inverted *13,500.*

27 A57 ½p on 2½p (R) *10,000.*
28 A57 ½p on 2½p (G) 550. 500.

29 A56 1sh on 2p (V) 500. 425.
- *a.* Surcharge inverted *13,500.*
- *b.* Surcharge diagonal, inverted *12,500.*

30 A56 1sh on 2p (R) 825. *4,500.*
- *a.* Surcharge inverted *18,000.*

31 A56 1sh on 2p (Bk) *6,500.*
- *a.* Surcharge inverted *21,000.*

32 A56 5sh on 2d (V) *10,000. 11,500.*
- *a.* Surcharge inverted *55,000.*

33 A61 10sh on 5p (R) *7,250. 11,000.*
- *a.* Surcharge inverted *55,000.*

34 A65 20sh on 1sh (V) *165,000.*
- *a.* Surcharge inverted *190,000.*

35 A65 20sh on 1sh (R) *145,000.*
36 A65 20sh on 1sh (Bk) *145,000.*

The handstamped 1893 surcharges are known inverted, vertical, etc.

Queen Victoria
A8 A9

A10 A11

A12 A13

1893 Unwmk. *Perf. 12 to 15*

37 A8 ½p vermilion 9.00 *11.00*
38 A9 1p light blue 5.75 5.25
- *a.* Half used as ½p on cover 825.00

39 A10 2p green 22.00 20.00
- *a.* Half used as 1p on cover *1,000.*
- *b.* Horiz. pair, imperf. between *17,500.*

40 A11 2½p car lake 20.00 4.50
41 A12 5p gray lilac 24.00 15.00
- *a.* 5p lilac 16.50 24.00

42 A13 1sh black 15.50 16.00
Nos. 37-42 (6) 96.25 71.75

For surcharge see No. 49.

A15 A16

A17 A18

A19 A20

1894 Engr.

43 A15 ½p yel green 5.50 5.50
44 A16 1p vermilion 15.00 9.50
- *a.* 1p orange vermilion 25.00 17.50
- *b.* Diagonal half, used as ½p on cover 875.00

45 A17 2p car lake 35.00 7.25
- *a.* Half used as 1p on cover —

46 A18 2½p blue 10.00 4.50
47 A19 5p dp violet 14.00 6.00
48 A20 1sh black 70.00 8.50
Nos. 43-48 (6) 149.50 41.25

See #55-59, 61. For surcharges see #51-54.

Halves of Nos. 38, 3 & 44 Srchd. in Red, Blue, Violet or Black

No. 49

No. 50

Nos. 51-53

1894

49 A9 ½p on half of 1p (R) 1,300. 425.
- *a.* Inverted surcharge *15,500.*

Perf. 14
Wmk. 30

50 A56 1p on half of 2p (R) 1,950. 425.
- *a.* Double surcharge 7,250. 1,350.
- *b.* Inverted surcharge 2,250.

Perf. 12 to 15
Unwmk.

51 A16 ½p on half of 1p (Bl) 3,850. 550.
- *a.* Double surcharge

52 A16 ½p on half of 1p (V) 4,400. 775.
53 A16 ½p on half of 1p (Bk) *6,000. 1,100.*

This surcharge is found on both vertical and diagonal halves of the 1p.

No. 46 Surcharged in Black

1894

54 A18 ½p on 2½p blue 475. 275.
- *a.* Double surcharge 8,750. 2,500.

The surcharge is found in eight types. The "OIE" variety is broken type.

A27 A28

A29

1897-98 Wmk. 2

55 A15 ½p yel green 3.50 3.00
56 A16 1p vermilion 9.00 1.60
- *a.* 1p orange-vermilion 3.00 1.50

57 A17 2p car lake 4.75 2.50
58 A18 2½p blue 17.50 3.25
- *a.* 2½p slate blue 7.50 3.00

59 A19 5p dp violet 22.50 *90.00*
- *a.* 5p purple 13.00 *95.00*

60 A27 6p yel brn ('98) 8.00 *10.00*
61 A20 1sh black 17.50 *32.50*
62 A28 2sh6p olive bister 24.00 *90.00*
63 A29 10sh dp pur ('98) 140.00 *250.00*
- *a.* 10sh bright purple 135.00 *225.00*

Nos. 55-63 (9) 246.75 *482.85*

The stamps of Niger Coast Protectorate were superseded in Jan. 1900, by those of Northern and Southern Nigeria.

NIGERIA

nī-ˈjir-ē-ə

LOCATION — West coast of Africa, bordering on the Gulf of Guinea
GOVT. — Republic
AREA — 356,669 sq. mi.
POP. — 206,140,000 (2020 est.)
CAPITAL — Abuja

The colony and protectorate were formed in 1914 by the union of Northern and Southern Nigeria. The mandated territory of Cameroons (British) was also attached for administrative purposes. The Federation of Nigeria was formed in 1960. It became a republic in 1963. See Niger Coast Protectorate, Lagos, Northern Nigeria and Southern Nigeria.

12 Pence = 1 Shilling
20 Shillings = 1 Pound
100 Kobo = 1 Naira (1973)

Catalogue values for unused stamps in this country are for Never Hinged items, beginning with Scott 71 in the regular postage section, Scott B1 in the semi-postal section and Scott J1 in the postage due section.

Watermarks

Wmk. 335 — FN Multiple

Wmk. 379 — NIGERIA in Continuous Wavy Lines

King George V — A1

Numerals of 3p, 4p, 6p, 5sh and £1 of type A1 are in color on plain tablet.

Dies I and II are described at front of this volume.

Die I
Ordinary Paper
Wmk. Multiple Crown and CA (3)

1914-27 Typo. *Perf. 14*

1 A1 ½p green 5.50 .70
- *a.* Booklet pane of 6

2 A1 1p carmine 5.25 .25
- *a.* Booklet pane of 6
- *b.* 1p scarlet ('16) 16.00 .25

3 A1 2p gray 9.00 2.00
- *a.* 2p slate gray ('18) 10.00 .85

4 A1 2½p ultramarine 10.00 8.00
- *a.* 2½p dull blue ('15) 225.00

Chalky Paper

5 A1 3p violet, *yel* 1.60 3.00
6 A1 4p blk & red, *yel* 1.25 *6.00*
7 A1 6p dull vio & red vio 10.00 11.00
8 A1 1sh black, *green, white back* 2.25 *22.50*
- *a.* 1sh black, *yel grn* (white back) ('15) 1.40 *15.00*
- *b.* 1sh As "a," yellow green back ('15) 60.00 *60.00*
- *c.* As "a," blue green back ('15) 4.00 *9.50*
- *d.* As "c," ovpt. "SPECIMEN" 40.00
- *e.* 1sh black, "bl grn," pale olive back ('17) 42.50 *52.50*
- *f.* 1sh black, "emerald," pale olive back ('20) 8.00 *50.00*
- *g.* 1sh black, "emerald," emerald back ('20) 1.75 *15.00*

9 A1 2sh6p blk & red, *bl* 17.50 6.75
10 A1 5sh grn & red, *yel, white back* 25.00 *65.00*
11 A1 10sh grn & red, *bl grn, white back* 60.00 *175.00*
- *a.* 10sh bl grn & red, *bl grnr*, bl grn back ('15) 75.00 *100.00*
- *b.* As "a," ovpt. "SPECIMEN" 55.00
- *c.* 10sh grn & red, *blue grn*, pale olive back ('17) 11.00 *17.50*
- *d.* 10sh grn & red, *emerald*, pale olive back ('20) 160.00 *250.00*
- *e.* 10sh grn & red, *emerald*, emerald back ('20) 40.00 *120.00*

12 A1 £1 vio & blk, *red* 190.00 *260.00*
- *a.* Die II ('27) 275.00 *350.00*

Nos. 1-12 (12) 337.35 *560.20*

Surface-colored Paper

13 A1 3p violet, *yel* 3.50 *12.00*
14 A1 4p black & red, *yel* 1.60 *11.50*
15 A1 1sh black, *green* 1.60 *25.00*
- *a.* 1sh black, *emerald* *225.00*

16 A1 5sh grn & red, *yel* 21.00 *55.00*
17 A1 10sh grn & red, *grn* 50.00 *180.00*
Nos. 13-17 (5) 77.70 *283.50*

Die II

1921-33 Ordinary Paper Wmk. 4

18 A1 ½p green 6.50 .90
- *a.* Die I 1.25 .75

19 A1 1p carmine 1.75 .55
- *a.* Booklet pane of 6 27.50
- *b.* Die I 3.25 .35
- *c.* Booklet pane of 6, Die I 37.50

20 A1 1½p orange ('31) 9.25 .25
21 A1 2p gray 10.00 .40
- *a.* Die I 2.25 *8.00*
- *b.* Booklet pane of 6, Die I 55.00

22 A1 2p red brown ('27) 5.00 1.00
- *a.* Booklet pane of 6 60.00

23 A1 2p dk brown ('28) 5.50 .25
- *a.* Booklet pane of 6 50.00
- *b.* Die I ('32) 6.50 .75

24 A1 2½p ultra (die I) 1.50 *15.00*
25 A1 3p dp violet 11.00 1.10
- *a.* Die I ('24) 6.00 5.00

26 A1 3p ultra ('31) 12.00 1.25

Chalky Paper

27 A1 4p blk & red, *yel* 1.10 .60
a. Die I ('32) 4.00 5.00
28 A1 6p dull vio & red vio 8.00 *9.00*
a. Die I 14.00 *42.50*
29 A1 1sh black, *emerald* 8.00 2.25
30 A1 2sh6p blk & red, *bl* 10.00 *52.50*
a. Die I ('32) 50.00 *85.00*
31 A1 5sh green & red, *yel* ('26) 20.00 *80.00*
a. Die I ('32) 75.00 *250.00*
32 A1 10sh green & red, *emer* 75.00 *225.00*
a. Die I ('32) 140.00 *500.00*
Nos. 18-32 (15) 184.60 390.05

Silver Jubilee Issue
Common Design Type

1935, May 6 Engr. *Perf. 11x12*
34 CD301 1½p black & ultra 1.00 *1.50*
35 CD301 2p indigo & green 2.00 2.00
36 CD301 3p ultra & brown 3.50 *22.00*
37 CD301 1sh brown vio & ind 11.00 *47.50*
Nos. 34-37 (4) 17.50 *73.00*
Set, never hinged 24.00
Set, perf "SPECIMEN" 125.00

Wharf at Apapa — A2

Picking Cacao Pods — A3

Dredging for Tin A4

Timber A5

Fishing Village A6

Ginning Cotton A7

Minaret at Habe — A8

Fulani Cattle — A9

Victoria-Buea Road — A10

Oil Palms — A11

View of Niger at Jebba — A12

Nigerian Canoe — A13

1936, Feb. 1 *Perf. 11½x13*
38 A2 ½p green 1.50 1.40
39 A3 1p rose car .60 .40
40 A4 1½p brown 2.00 .40
a. Perf. 12½x13½ 85.00 5.00
41 A5 2p black .60 *.80*
42 A6 3p dark blue 2.00 1.50
a. Perf. 12½x13½ 150.00 27.50
43 A7 4p red brown 2.50 2.00
44 A8 6p dull violet .75 .75
45 A9 1sh olive green 1.75 *5.00*

Perf. 14
46 A10 2sh6p ultra & blk 10.00 *45.00*
47 A11 5sh ol grn & blk 25.00 *65.00*
48 A12 10sh slate & blk 90.00 *150.00*
49 A13 £1 orange & blk 150.00 *225.00*
Nos. 38-49 (12) 286.70 *497.25*
Set, never hinged 400.00
Set, perf "SPECIMEN" 300.00

Common Design Types pictured following the introduction.

Coronation Issue
Common Design Type

1937, May 12 *Perf. 11x11½*
50 CD302 1p dark carmine .50 *2.00*
51 CD302 1½p dark brown 1.25 *2.50*
52 CD302 3p deep ultra 1.50 *4.00*
Nos. 50-52 (3) 3.25 8.50
Set, never hinged 6.50

George VI — A14

Victoria-Buea Road — A15

Niger at Jebba — A16

1938-51 Wmk. 4 *Perf. 12*
53 A14 ½p deep green .25 .25
a. Perf. 11½ ('50) 1.40 *1.75*
54 A14 1p dk carmine .40 .30
55 A14 1½p red brown .25 .25
a. Perf. 11½ ('50) .25 .25
56 A14 2p black .25 *3.00*
57 A14 2½p orange ('41) .25 *3.00*
58 A14 3p deep blue .25 .25
59 A14 4p orange 32.50 4.00
60 A14 6p brown violet .30 .25
a. Perf. 11½ ('51) 1.40 .60
61 A14 1sh olive green .40 .25
a. Perf. 11½ ('50) .90 .25
62 A14 1sh3p turq blue ('40) .60 .70
a. Perf. 11½ ('50) 2.10 .70
63 A15 2sh6p ultra & blk ('51) 1.50 4.50
a. Perf. 13½ ('42) 2.25 *7.00*
b. Perf. 14 ('42) 2.00 *3.50*
c. Perf. 13x11½ 37.50 24.00
64 A16 5sh org & blk, perf. 13½ ('42) 4.50 *4.50*
a. Perf. 12 ('49) 5.50 4.00
b. Perf. 14 ('48) 6.75 3.00
c. Perf. 13x11½ 67.50 21.00

1944, Dec. 1 *Perf. 12*
65 A14 1p red violet .25 .30
a. Perf. 11½ ('50) .60 .60
66 A14 2p deep red .25 *3.00*
a. Perf. 11½ ('50) .35 *.70*
67 A14 3p black .25 *3.50*
68 A14 4p dark blue .25 *4.00*
Nos. 53-68 (16) 42.45 *32.05*
Set, never hinged 75.00

Issue date: Nos. 65a, 66a, Feb. 15.

Catalogue values for unused stamps in this section, from this point to the end of the section, are for Never Hinged items.

Peace Issue
Common Design Type

1946, Oct. 21 Engr. *Perf. 13½x14*
71 CD303 1½p brown .35 .25
72 CD303 4p deep blue .35 *2.50*

Silver Wedding Issue
Common Design Types

1948, Dec. 20 Photo. *Perf. 14x14½*
73 CD304 1p brt red violet .35 .30

Perf. 11½x11
Engraved; Name Typographed
74 CD305 5sh brown orange 17.50 *22.50*

UPU Issue
Common Design Types

Engr.; Name Typo. on 3p, 6p
Perf. 13½, 11x11½
1949, Oct. 10 Wmk. 4
75 CD306 1p red violet .25 .25
76 CD307 3p indigo .35 *3.50*
77 CD308 6p rose violet .80 *3.50*
78 CD309 1sh olive 1.40 *2.00*
Nos. 75-78 (4) 2.80 *9.25*

Coronation Issue
Common Design Type

1953, June 2 Engr. *Perf. 13½x13*
79 CD312 1½p brt grn & blk .40 .25

Manilla (Bracelet) Currency — A17

Olokun Head, Ife — A18

Designs: 1p, Bornu horsemen. 1½p, Peanuts, Kano City. 2p, Mining tin. 3p, Jebba Bridge over Niger River. 4p, Cocoa industry. 1sh, Logging. 2sh6p, Victoria harbor. 5sh, Loading palm oil. 10sh, Goats and Fulani cattle. £1, Lagos waterfront, 19th and 20th centuries.

1953, Sept. 1 *Perf. 14*
Size: 35½x22½mm
80 A17 ½p red org & blk .25 .25
81 A17 1p ol gray & blk .25 .25
82 A17 1½p blue green .50 .25
83 A17 2p bister & blk 4.00 .30
84 A17 3p purple & blk .50 .30
85 A17 4p ultra & black 2.50 .25
86 A18 6p blk & org brn .30 .25
87 A17 1sh brn vio & blk .50 .25
Size: 40½x24½mm
88 A17 2sh6p green & black 16.00 1.25
89 A17 5sh ver & black 5.50 1.40
90 A17 10sh red brn & blk 24.00 3.25
Size: 42x31½mm
91 A17 £1 violet & black 32.50 16.00
Nos. 80-91 (12) 86.80 24.00

Booklet panes of 4 of Nos. 80, 81, 84, 87 were issued in 1957. They are identical to margin blocks of 4 from sheets.

See No. 93.

No. 83 Overprinted in Black

1956, Jan. 28 Wmk. 4 *Perf. 13½*
92 A17 2p bister & black .40 .30

Visit of Queen Elizabeth II to Nigeria, Jan.-Feb., 1956.

Mining Tin Type of 1953

Two types:
I — Broken row of dots between "G" and miner's head.
II — Complete row of dots.

1956-57
93 A17 2p bluish gray (shades) (I) 3.25 2.00
b. 2p gray (shades) (II) 4.75 .40

Booklet pane of 4 of No. 93 was issued in 1957. See note after No. 91.

Ambas Bay, Victoria Harbor — A19

Wmk. 314
1958, Dec. 1 Engr. *Perf. 13½*
94 A19 3p purple & black .40 .30

Cent. of the founding of Victoria, Southern Cameroons.

1959, Mar. 14

3p, Lugard Hall, Kaduna. 1sh, Kano Mosque.

95 A19 3p purple & black .30 .25
96 A19 1sh green & black .75 .50

Attainment of self-government by the Northern Region, Mar. 15, 1959.

Federation of Nigeria

Federal Legislature — A20

3p, Man Paddling Canoe. 6p, Federal Supreme Court. 1sh3p, Map of Africa, dove and torch.

Wmk. 335
1960, Oct. 1 Photo. *Perf. 13½*
Size: 35x22mm
97 A20 1p carmine & black .25 .25
98 A20 3p blue & black .25 .25
99 A20 6p dk red brn & emer .25 .25
Size: 39½x23½mm
100 A20 1sh3p ultra & yellow .25 .25
Nos. 97-100 (4) 1.00 1.00

Nigeria's independence, Oct. 1, 1960.

Peanuts A21

Central Bank, Lagos A22

Designs: 1p, Coal miner. 1½p, Adult education. 2p, Potter. 3p, Oyo carver. 4p, Weaver. 6p, Benin mask. 1sh, Yellow-casqued hornbill. 1sh3p, Camel train and map. 5sh, Nigeria museum and sculpture. 10sh, Kano airport. £1, Lagos terminal.

Perf. 14½x14
1961, Jan. 1 Wmk. 335
101 A21 ½p emerald .30 *.60*
102 A21 1p purple .80 .30
a. Booklet pane of 6 5.00
103 A21 1½p rose red .80 *2.25*
104 A21 2p ultra .30 .30
105 A21 3p dk grn .40 .30
a. Booklet pane of 6 2.50
106 A21 4p blue .30 *2.00*
107 A21 6p blk & yel .80 .30
a. Booklet pane of 6 5.00
b. Yellow omitted 2,750. 1,300.
108 A21 1sh yel grn 4.00 .30
109 A21 1sh3p orange 1.50 .30
a. Booklet pane of 6 9.00
110 A22 2sh6p yellow & blk 2.75 .30
111 A22 5sh emer & blk 1.25 1.25
112 A22 10sh dp ultra & blk 3.75 3.75
113 A22 £1 dp car & blk 13.00 *14.00*
Nos. 101-113 (13) 29.95 25.95

For overprint see No. 198.

Globe and Train — A23

1961, July 25 Wmk. 335
114 A23 1p shown .25 .25
115 A23 3p Truck .25 .25
116 A23 1sh3p Plane .35 .35
117 A23 2sh6p Ship .80 .80
Nos. 114-117 (4) 1.65 1.65

Nigeria's admission to the UPU.

Coat of Arms — A24

Map and Natural Resources — A25

Designs: 6p, Eagle carrying banner. 1sh3p, Flying eagles forming flag. 2sh6p, Young couple looking at flag and government building.

Perf. 14½x14, 14x14½

1961, Oct. 1 Photo. Wmk. 335

118 A24 3p multicolored .25 .25
119 A25 4p org, yel grn & dk red .25 .25
120 A25 6p emerald .25 .25
121 A25 1sh3p ultra, emer & gray .25 .25
122 A25 2sh6p blue, emer & sep .50 .50
Nos. 118-122 (5) 1.50 1.50

First anniversary of independence.

Map of Africa and Staff of Aesculapius — A26

Map of Africa and: 3p, Lyre, book and scroll. 6p, Cogwheel. 1sh, Radio beacon. 1sh3p, Hands holding globe.

1962, Jan. 25 ***Perf. 14x14½***

123 A26 1p bister .25 .25
124 A26 3p deep magenta .25 .25
125 A26 6p blue green .25 .25
126 A26 1sh chestnut .25 .25
127 A26 1sh3p bright blue .25 .25
Nos. 123-127 (5) 1.25 1.25

Issued to honor the conference of heads of state of African and Malagasy Governments.

Malaria Eradication Emblem and Larvae — A27

Emblem and: 6p, Man with spray gun. 1sh3p, Plane spraying insecticide. 2sh6p, Microscope, retort and patient.

1962, Apr. 7 ***Perf. 14½***

128 A27 3p emer, brn & ver .25 .25
129 A27 6p lil rose & dk blue .25 .25
130 A27 1sh3p dk blue & lil rose .25 .25
131 A27 2sh6p yel brown & blue .30 .80
Nos. 128-131 (4) 1.05 1.55

WHO drive to eradicate malaria.

National Monument, Lagos — A28

Ife Bronze Head and Flag — A29

Perf. 14½x14, 14x14½

1962, Oct. 1 Wmk. 335 Photo.

132 A28 3p lt ultra & emer .25 .25
a. Emerald omitted 800.00 475.00
133 A29 5sh vio, emer & org red 1.25 1.25

Second anniversary of independence.

Fair Emblem — A30

Designs (horizontal): 6p, "Wheels of Industry." 1sh, Cornucopia, goods and trucks. 2sh6p, Oil derricks and tanker.

1962, Oct. 27 Wmk. 335

134 A30 1p brown olive & org .25 .25
135 A30 6p crimson & blk .25 .25
136 A30 1sh dp orange & blk .25 .25
137 A30 2sh6p dk ultra, yel & blk .30 .25
Nos. 134-137 (4) 1.05 1.00

Lagos Intl. Trade Fair, Oct. 27-Nov. 8.

Globe and Arrows — A31

4p, Natl. Hall & Commonwealth emblem, horiz. 1sh3p, Palm tree, emblem & doves.

1962, Nov. 5

138 A31 2½p sky blue .25 *1.00*
139 A31 4p dp rose & slate bl .25 .25
140 A31 1sh3p gray & yellow .25 .25
Nos. 138-140 (3) .75 1.50

8th Commonwealth Parliamentary Conf., Lagos.

Herdsman with Cattle — A32

Design: 6p, Tractor and corn, horiz.

1963, Mar. 21 Photo. ***Perf. 14½***

141 A32 3p olive green 1.10 .25
142 A32 6p brt lilac rose 1.40 .25

FAO "Freedom from Hunger" campaign.

US Mercury Capsule over Kano Tracking Station — A33

Design: 1sh3p, Syncom II satellite and US tracking ship "Kingsport," Lagos harbor.

1963, June 21 ***Perf. 14½***

143 A33 6p dk blue & yel grn .25 .25
144 A33 1sh3p black & dp green .30 .30

Peaceful uses of outer space.

Printed in sheets of 12 (4x3) with ornamental borders and inscriptions.

Nigerian and Greek Scouts Shaking Hands and Jamboree Emblem — A34

1sh, Scouts dancing around campfire.

1963, Aug. 1 Photo. ***Perf. 14***

145 A34 3p gray olive & red .30 .25
146 A34 1sh red & black .60 .60
a. Souvenir sheet of 2, #145-146 1.60 1.60

11th Boy Scout Jamboree, Marathon, Greece, Aug. 1963.

Republic

First Aid — A35

Designs: 6p, Blood donors and ambulances. 1sh3p, Helping the needy.

1963, Sept. 1 Wmk. 335 ***Perf. 14½***

147 A35 3p dk blue & red .35 .25
148 A35 6p dk green & red .55 .30
149 A35 1sh3p black & red 1.50 1.00
a. Souvenir sheet of 4, #149 12.00 12.00
Nos. 147-149 (3) 2.40 1.55

Cent. of the Intl. Red Cross.

Pres. Nnamdi Azikiwe and State House — A36

Designs: 1sh3p, President and Federal Supreme Court. 2sh6p, President and Parliament Building.

1963, Oct. 1 Unwmk. ***Perf. 14x13***

150 A36 3p dull grn & yel grn .25 .25
151 A36 1sh3p brown & bister .25 .25
a. Bister (head) omitted
152 A36 2sh6p vio bl & brt grnsh bl .25 .25
Nos. 150-152 (3) .75 .75

Independence Day, Oct. 1, 1963.

"Freedom of Worship" — A37

3p, Charter & broken whip, horiz. 1sh3p, "Freedom from Want." 2sh6p, "Freedom of Speech."

1963, Dec. 10 Wmk. 335 ***Perf. 13***

153 A37 3p vermilion .25 .25
154 A37 6p green .25 .25
155 A37 1sh3p deep ultra .25 .25
156 A37 2sh6p red lilac .30 .30
Nos. 153-156 (4) 1.05 1.05

15th anniv. of the Universal Declaration of Human Rights.

Queen Nefertari — A38

1964, Mar. 8 Photo. ***Perf. 14***

157 A38 6p shown .90 .35
158 A38 2sh6p Ramses II 1.75 2.25

UNESCO world campaign to save historic monuments in Nubia.

John F. Kennedy, US and Nigerian Flags — A39

1sh3p, Kennedy bust & laurel. 5sh, Kennedy coin (US), flags of US & Nigeria at half-mast.

1964, Aug. 20 Unwmk. ***Perf. 13x14***

159 A39 1sh3p black & lt vio .25 .25
160 A39 2sh6p multicolored .50 .50
161 A39 5sh multicolored .75 1.75
a. Souvenir sheet of 4 7.50 7.50
Nos. 159-161 (3) 1.50 2.50

Pres. John F. Kennedy (1917-63). No. 161a contains 4 imperf. stamps similar to No. 161 with simulated perforations.

Pres. Nnamdi Azikiwe A40

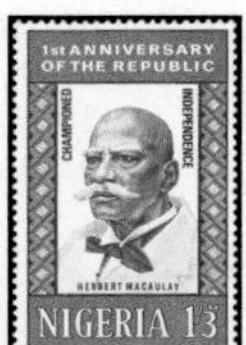

Herbert Macaulay A41

Design: 2sh6p, King Jaja of Opobo.

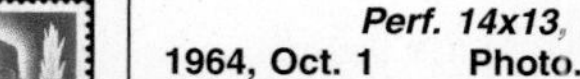

Perf. 14x13, 14

1964, Oct. 1 Photo. Unwmk.

162 A40 3p red brown .25 .25
163 A41 1sh3p green .25 .25
164 A41 2sh6p slate green .60 .60
Nos. 162-164 (3) 1.10 1.10

First anniversary of the Republic.

Boxing Gloves and Torch — A42

Hurdling A43

6p, High jump. 1sh3p, Woman runner, vert.

1964, Oct. ***Perf. 14½***

165 A42 3p olive grn & sepia .25 .25
166 A42 6p dk blue & emer .35 .35
167 A42 1sh3p olive & brown .55 .55

Perf. 14

168 A43 2sh6p orange red & brn 1.50 1.50
a. Souvenir sheet of 4 4.25 4.25
Nos. 165-168 (4) 2.65 2.65

18th Olympic Games, Tokyo, Oct. 10-25.

No. 168a contains 4 imperf. stamps similar to No. 168 with simulated perforations.

Mountain Climbing Scouts — A44

3p, Golden Jubilee emblem. 6p, Nigeria's Scout emblem & merit badges. 1sh3p, Lord Baden-Powell & Nigerian Boy Scout.

1965, Jan. Photo. ***Perf. 14½***

169 A44 1p brown .25 .25
170 A44 3p emer, blk & red .25 .25
171 A44 6p yel grn, red & blk .25 .25
172 A44 1sh3p sep, yel & dk grn .35 .75
a. Souvenir sheet of 4 6.50 6.50
Nos. 169-172 (4) 1.10 1.50

Founding of the Nigerian Boy Scouts, 50th anniv.

No. 172a contains four imperf. stamps similar to No. 172 with simulated perforation.

IQSY Emblem and Telstar, Map of Africa — A45

1sh3p, Explorer XII over map of Africa.

1965, Apr. 1 Unwmk. ***Perf. 14x13***

173 A45 6p grnsh bl & vio .25 .25
174 A45 1sh3p lilac & green .30 .30

Intl. Quiet Sun Year, 1964-65. Printed in sheets of 12 (4x3) with ornamental borders and inscriptions.

ITU Emblem, Drummer, Man at Desk and Telephone — A46

Cent. of the ITU: 1sh3p, ITU emblem and telecommunication tower, vert. 5sh, ITU emblem, Syncom satellite and map of Africa showing Nigeria.

Perf. 11x11½, 11½x11

1965, Aug. 2 Photo. Unwmk.

175 A46 3p ocher, red & blk .30 .25
176 A46 1sh3p ultra, grn & blk 1.50 1.50
177 A46 5sh multicolored 6.00 6.00
Nos. 175-177 (3) 7.80 7.75

ICY Emblem, Diesel Locomotive and Camel Caravan — A47

ICY Emblem and: 1sh, Students and hospital, Lagos. 2sh6p, Kainji Dam, Niger River.

Perf. 14x15

1965, Sept. 1 Wmk. 335

178	A47	3p orange, grn & car	3.50	.35
179	A47	1sh ultra, blk & yel	3.00	.50
180	A47	2sh6p ultra, yel & grn	10.00	7.50
		Nos. 178-180 (3)	16.50	8.35

Intl. Cooperation Year and 20th anniv. of the UN.

Stone Images, Ikom — A48

Designs: 3p, Carved frieze, horiz. 5sh, Seated man, Taba bronze.

Perf. 14x15, 15x14

1965, Oct. 1 Photo. Unwmk.

181	A48	3p ocher, blk & red	.25	.25
182	A48	1sh3p lt ultra, grn & red-dish brn	.25	.25
183	A48	5sh emer, dk brn & reddish brn	.50	1.25
		Nos. 181-183 (3)	1.00	1.75

Second anniversary of the Republic.

Elephants — A49

Designs: ½p, Lioness and cubs, vert. 1½p, Splendid sunbird. 2p, Weaverbirds. 3p, Cheetah. 4p, Leopard and cubs. 6p, Saddle-billed storks, vert. 9p, Gray parrots. 1sh, Kingfishers. 1sh3p, Crowned cranes. 2sh6p, Buffon's kobs (antelopes). 5sh, Giraffes. 10sh, Hippopotami, vert. £1, Buffalos.

"MAURICE FIEVET" below Design

Perf. 12x12½, 12½x12, 14x13½ (1p, 2p, 3p, 4p, 9p)

1965-66 Photo.

Size: 23x38mm, 38x23mm

184	A49	½p multicolored	1.00	*2.50*
185	A49	1p red & multi	.50	.25
186	A49	1½p lt blue & multi	8.00	*9.50*
187	A49	2p brt red & multi	3.75	.25
a.		White "2d" ('70)	4.50	2.50
188	A49	3p brt grn, yel & dl brn	1.25	.30
189	A49	4p lilac & multi	.30	.25
a.		Perf 12½x12	.60	*3.00*
b.		"4" 5mm wide ('71)	60.00	8.00
190	A49	6p violet & multi	2.10	.40
191	A49	9p blue & orange	3.00	.60

Perf. 12½

Size: 45x26mm, 26x45mm

192	A49	1sh gray & multi	5.00	.60
a.		Red omitted		
193	A49	1sh3p brt bl & multi	9.00	2.00
194	A49	2sh6p dk brn, yel & ocher	1.00	*2.00*
195	A49	5sh brn, yel & red brown	2.25	3.50
196	A49	10sh grnsh bl & multi	7.00	3.25
197	A49	£1 brt grn & multi	18.50	9.00
		Nos. 184-197 (14)	62.65	34.40

The designer's name, Maurice Fievet, appears at right or left, in small or large capitals. Nos. 187a and 189b have "MAURICE FIEVET" at right, 5mm wide. No. 187a has "2d" in white instead of yellow. No. 189b has "REPUBLIC" and "4d" larger, bolder.

Issued: ½p, 1p, 11/1/65; 2p, 4/1/66; 1½p, #189a, 6p, 1sh, 1sh3p, 2sh6p, 5sh, 10sh, 1£, 5/2/66; 3p, 9p, 10/17/66; 4p, 1966.

Nine values were overprinted "F. G. N./ F. G. N." (Federal Government of Nigeria) in 1968. They were not issued, but some were sold by accident in 1968. Later the Nigerian Philatelic Service sold examples, stating they were not postally valid. However, some were used by government agencies in 1969.

See Nos. 258-267.

No. 110 Overprinted in Red: "COMMONWEALTH / P.M. MEETING / 11. Jan. 1966"

Perf. 14½x14

1966, Jan. 11 Photo. Wmk. 335

198	A22	2sh6p yellow & black	.35	.35

Conf. of British Commonwealth Prime Ministers, Lagos.

YWCA Building, Lagos — A50

Unwmk.

1966, Sept. 1 Litho. *Perf. 14*

199	A50	4p yel, green & multi	.25	.25
200	A50	9p brt green & multi	.25	.50

60th anniv. of the Nigerian YWCA.

Lineman and Telephone — A51

Designs: 4p, Flag and letter carrying pigeon, vert. 2sh6p, Niger Bridge.

Perf. 14½x14, 14x14½

1966, Oct. 1 Photo. Wmk. 335

201	A51	4p green	.25	.25
202	A51	1sh6p lilac, blk & sep	.30	.50
203	A51	2sh6p multicolored	.70	1.75
		Nos. 201-203 (3)	1.25	2.50

Third anniversary of the Republic.

Book, Chemical Apparatus, Carved Head and UNESCO Emblem — A52

1966, Nov. 4 *Perf. 14½x14*

204	A52	4p dl org, mar & blk	.45	.25
205	A52	1sh6p bl grn, plum & blk	2.10	2.50
206	A52	2sh6p pink, plum & blk	2.90	6.00
		Nos. 204-206 (3)	5.45	8.75

20th anniv. of UNESCO.

Surveyors and Hydrological Decade Emblem — A53

Design: 2sh6p, Water depth gauge on dam and Hydrological Decade emblem, vert.

Perf. 14½x14, 14x14½

1967, Feb. 1 Photo. Wmk. 335

207	A53	4p multicolored	.25	.25
208	A53	2sh6p multicolored	.50	1.25

Hydrological Decade (UNESCO), 1965-74.

Weather Satellite Orbiting Earth — A54

1sh6p, Storm over land & sea & World Meteorological Organization emblem.

1967, Mar. 23 Photo. *Perf. 14½x14*

209	A54	4p dp ultra & brt rose	.25	.25
210	A54	1sh6p ultra & yellow	.65	.90

World Meteorological Day, March 23.

Eyo Masqueraders A55

1sh6p, Acrobat. 2sh6p, Stilt dancer, vert.

Perf. 11x11½, 11½x11

1967, Oct. 1 Photo. Unwmk.

211	A55	4p multicolored	.25	.25
212	A55	1sh6p turq bl & multi	.50	1.25
213	A55	2sh6p pale grn & multi	.75	2.50
		Nos. 211-213 (3)	1.50	4.00

4th anniversary of the Federal Republic.

Vaccination of Cattle — A56

1967, Dec. 1 *Perf. 14½x14*

214	A56	4p maroon & multi	.25	.25
215	A56	1sh6p ultra & multi	.70	*1.25*

Campaign to eradicate cattle plague.

Anopheles Mosquito and Sick Man — A57

20th anniv. of the WHO: 4p, WHO emblem and vaccination.

1968, Apr. 7 Litho. *Perf. 14*

216	A57	4p dp lil rose & blk	.25	.25
217	A57	1sh6p org yel & blk	.55	.80

Shackled Hands, Map of Nigeria and Human Rights Flame — A58

Design: 1sh6p, Flag of Nigeria and human rights flame, vert.

1968, July 1 Photo. *Perf. 14*

218	A58	4p dp blue, yel & blk	.25	.25
219	A58	1sh6p green, blk & red	.45	.80

International Human Rights Year.

Hand and Doves — A59

1968, Oct. 1 Unwmk. *Perf. 14*

220	A59	4p brt blue & multi	.25	.25
221	A59	1sh6p black & multi	.25	.25

5th anniversary of the Federal Republic.

Olympic Rings, Nigerian Flag and Athletes — A60

4p, Map of Nigeria and Olympic rings.

1968, Oct. 14 Photo. *Perf. 14*

222	A60	4p red, blk & emer	.25	.25
223	A60	1sh6p multicolored	.50	.35

19th Olympic Games, Mexico City, 10/12-27.

G.P.O., Lagos — A61

1969, Apr. 11 Unwmk. *Perf. 14*

224	A61	4p emerald & black	.25	.25
225	A61	1sh6p dk blue & black	.25	.40

Opening of the Nigerian Philatelic Service of the GPO, Lagos.

Gen. Yakubu Gowon and Victoria Zakari — A62

Perf. 13x13½

1969, Sept. 20 Litho. Unwmk.

226	A62	4p emerald & choc	.30	.25
227	A62	1sh6p emerald & black	.70	.45

Wedding of Yakubu Gowon, head of state of Nigeria, and Miss Victoria Zakari, Apr. 19, 1969.

Development Bank Emblem and "5" — A63

Design: 1sh6p, Emblem and rays.

1969, Oct. 18 Litho. *Perf. 14*

228	A63	4p dk bl, blk & org	.25	.25
229	A63	1sh6p dk pur, yel & blk	.35	*1.00*

African Development Bank, 5th anniv.

ILO Emblem — A64

50th anniv. of the ILO: 1sh6p, ILO emblem and world map.

1969, Nov. 15 Photo.

230	A64	4p purple & black	.25	.25
231	A64	1sh6p green & black	.65	*1.25*

Tourist Year Emblem and Musicians — A65

Designs: 4p, Olumo Rock and Tourist Year emblem, horiz. 1sh6p, Assob Falls.

1969, Dec. 30 Photo. *Perf. 14*

232	A65	4p blue & multi	.25	.25
233	A65	1sh emerald & black	.30	.30
234	A65	1sh6p multicolored	1.00	.85
		Nos. 232-234 (3)	1.55	1.40

International Year of African Tourism.

12-Spoke Wheel and Arms of Nigeria — A66

Designs: 4p, Map of Nigeria and tree with 12 fruits representing 12 tribes. 1sh6p, People bound by common destiny and map of Nigeria. 2sh, Torch with 12 flames and map of Africa, horiz.

Perf. 11½x11, 11x11½

1970, May 28 Photo. Unwmk.

235	A66	4p gold, blue & blk	.25	.25
236	A66	1sh gold & multi	.25	.25
237	A66	1sh6p green & black	.25	.25
238	A66	2sh bl, org, gold & black	.25	.25
		Nos. 235-238 (4)	1.00	1.00

Establishment of a 12-state administrative structure in Nigeria.

Opening of New UPU Headquarters, Bern — A67

1970, June 29 Unwmk. *Perf. 14*

239	A67	4p purple & yellow	.30	.25
240	A67	1sh6p blue & vio blue	.45	.35

UN Emblem and Charter — A68

25th anniv. of the UN: 1sh6p, UN emblem and headquarters, New York.

1970, Sept. 1 Photo. *Perf. 14*

241	A68	4p	brn org, buff & blk	.25	.25
242	A68	1sh6p	dk bl, gold & bis brn	.25	.25

Student — A69

Designs: 2p, Oil drilling platform. 6p, Durbar horsemen. 9p, Soldier and sailors raising flag. 1sh, Soccer player. 1sh6p, Parliament Building. 2sh, Kainji Dam. 2sh6p, Export products: Timber, rubber, peanuts, cocoa and palm produce.

1970, Sept. 30 Litho. *Perf. 14x13½*

243	A69	2p	blue & multi	.25	.25
244	A69	4p	blue & multi	.25	.25
245	A69	6p	blue & multi	.30	.25
246	A69	9p	blue & multi	.40	.25
247	A69	1sh	blue & multi	.40	.25
248	A69	1sh6p	blue & multi	.40	.40
249	A69	2sh	blue & multi	.50	.90
250	A69	2sh6p	blue & multi	.50	1.00
			Nos. 243-250 (8)	3.00	3.55

Ten years of independence.

Black and White Men Uprooting Racism — A70

Designs: 4p, Black and white school children and globe, horiz. 1sh6p, World map with black and white stripes. 2sh, Black and white men, shoulder to shoulder, horiz.

Perf. 13½x14, 14x13½

1971, Mar. 22 Photo. Unwmk.

251	A70	4p	multicolored	.25	.25
252	A70	1sh	yellow & multi	.25	.25
253	A70	1sh6p	blue, yel & blk	.25	.65
254	A70	2sh	multicolored	.25	1.25
			Nos. 251-254 (4)	1.00	2.40

Intl. year against racial discrimination.

Ibibio Mask, c. 1900 — A71

Nigerian Antiquities: 1sh3p, Bronze mask of a King of Benin, c. 1700. 1sh9p, Bronze figure of a King of Ife.

1971, Sept. 30 *Perf. 13½x14*

255	A71	4p	lt blue & black	.25	.25
256	A71	1sh3p	yellow bis & blk	.25	.35
257	A71	1sh9p	apple grn, dp grn & blk	.25	1.00
			Nos. 255-257 (3)	.75	1.60

Type of 1965-66 Redrawn

Imprint: "N.S.P. & M. Co. Ltd." Added to "MAURICE FIEVET"

Perf. 13x13½; 14x13½ (6p)

1969-72 Photo.

Size: 38x23mm

258	A49	1p	red & multi	3.00	2.25
259	A49	2p	brt red & multi	4.00	1.50
260	A49	3p	multi ('71)	.75	*2.00*
261	A49	4p	lilac & multi	8.50	.25
262	A49	6p	brt vio & multi ('71)	2.25	.25
263	A49	9p	dl bl & dp org ('70)	7.00	.50

Size: 45x26mm

264	A49	1sh	multi ('71)	3.00	.25
265	A49	1sh3p	multi ('71)	11.00	3.50
266	A49	2sh6p	multi ('72)	15.00	7.00
267	A49	5sh	multi ('72)	3.50	*17.50*
			Nos. 258-267 (10)	58.00	35.00

"Maurice Fievet" imprint on No. 259 exists in two lengths, 5mm and 5½mm.

"Maurice Fievet" imprint on No. 260 exists in two lengths, 5½mm and 8½mm.

UNICEF Emblem and Children — A72

UNICEF 25th anniv.: 1sh3p, Mother and child. 1sh9p, African mother carrying child on back.

1971, Dec. 11 *Perf. 14*

270	A72	4p	purple & yellow	.25	.25
271	A72	1sh3p	org, pur & plum	.25	*.45*
272	A72	1sh9p	blue & dk blue	.25	*.90*
			Nos. 270-272 (3)	.75	1.60

Satellite Earth Station — A73

Various views of satellite communications earth station, Lanlate, Nigeria. All horiz.

1971, Dec. 30 Photo. *Perf. 14*

273	A73	4p	multicolored	.25	.25
274	A73	1sh3p	blue, blk & grn	.25	.65
275	A73	1sh9p	orange & blk	.30	.95
276	A73	3sh	brt pink & blk	.55	1.75
			Nos. 273-276 (4)	1.35	3.60

Satellite communications earth station, Lanlate, Nigeria.

Fair Emblem — A74

Fair Emblem and: 1sh3p, Map of Africa, horiz. 1sh9p, Globe with map of Africa.

Perf. 13½x13, 13x13½

1972, Feb. 23 Litho.

277	A74	4p	multicolored	.25	.25
278	A74	1sh3p	dull pur, yel & gold	.25	*.40*
279	A74	1sh9p	orange, yel & blk	.25	*1.25*
			Nos. 277-279 (3)	.75	1.90

First All-Africa Trade Fair, Nairobi, Kenya, Feb. 23-Mar. 5.

Traffic — A75

Designs: 1sh3p, Traffic flow at circle. 1sh9p, Car and truck on road. 3sh, Intersection with lights and pedestrians.

1972, June 23 Photo. *Perf. 13x13½*

280	A75	4p	orange & blk	.45	.25
281	A75	1sh3p	lt blue & multi	1.40	.85
282	A75	1sh9p	emerald & multi	1.50	1.10
283	A75	3sh	yellow & multi	2.60	*3.00*
			Nos. 280-283 (4)	5.95	5.20

Introduction of right-hand driving in Nigeria, Apr. 2, 1972.

Nok Style Terra-cotta Head, Katsina Ala — A76

1sh3p, Roped bronze vessel, Igbo Ukwu. 1sh9p, Bone harpoon, Daima, horiz.

Perf. 13½x13, 13x13½

1972, Sept. 1 Litho.

284	A76	4p	dk blue & multi	.25	.25
285	A76	1sh3p	gold & multi	.40	*.50*
286	A76	1sh9p	dp blue & multi	.50	*1.50*
			Nos. 284-286 (3)	1.15	2.25

All-Nigeria Festival of the Arts, Kaduna, Dec. 9.

Games Emblem and Soccer — A77

Designs: 5k, Running. 18k, Table tennis. 25k, Stadium, vert.

1973, Jan. 8 Litho. *Perf. 13x13½*

287	A77	5k	lilac, blue & blk	.25	.25
288	A77	12k	multicolored	.35	.55
289	A77	18k	yellow & multi	.60	*1.10*
290	A77	25k	brown & multi	1.00	*1.50*
			Nos. 287-290 (4)	2.20	3.40

2nd All-Africa Games, Lagos, Jan. 7-18.

Hides and Skins — A78

Designs: 2k, Natural gas tanks. 3k, Cement works. 5k, Cattle ranching. 7k, Lumbermill. 8k, Oil refinery. 10k, Leopards, Yankari Game Reserve. 12k, New civic building. 15k, Sugar cane harvesting. 18k, Palm oil production, vert. 20k, Vaccine production. 25k, Modern docks. 30k, Argungu Fishing Festival, vert. 35k, Textile industry. 50k, Pottery, vert. 1n, Eko Bridge. 2n, Teaching Hospital, Lagos.

Imprint at left: "N S P & M Co Ltd"

6mm on Litho. Stamps, 5¼ mm on Photo. Stamps

Litho.; Photo. (50k)

1973-74 Unwmk. *Perf. 14*

291	A78	1k	multi, buff imprint	*.25*	*.25*
292	A78	2k	multi ('74)	*4.00*	*.90*
293	A78	3k	multi ('74)	*.25*	*.25*
294	A78	5k	grn & multi ('74)	*6.00*	*.90*
295	A78	7k	multicolored	*.35*	*1.25*
296	A78	8k	multicolored	*.40*	*.25*
297	A78	10k	multicolored	*6.00*	*.25*
298	A78	12k	multicolored	*.50*	*2.00*
299	A78	15k	multicolored	*.35*	*.60*
300	A78	18k	multicolored	*.55*	*.30*
301	A78	20k	multicolored	*.65*	*.30*
302	A78	25k	multicolored	*.85*	*.45*
303	A78	30k	multicolored	*.50*	*1.50*
304	A78	35k	multicolored	*6.00*	*4.00*
305	A78	50k	black background	*2.00*	*2.50*
306	A78	1n	multicolored	*1.00*	*.90*
307	A78	2n	multicolored	*1.00*	*2.25*
			Nos. 291-307 (17)	*30.65*	*18.85*

Imprint on 35k has periods.

Imprint at left: "N S P & M Co Ltd"

1973 Photo., Imprint 5¼mm

291a	A78	1k	multi, dk grn foliage	*1.00*	*.75*
291b	A78	1k	multi, brt grn foliage	*.25*	*.25*
292a	A78	2k	multicolored	*.35*	*.25*
294a	A78	5k	multi, emer fields	*.60*	*.75*
294b	A78	5k	multi, yel grn fields	*.50*	*.25*
297a	A78	10k	multicolored	*.75*	*.80*
298a	A78	12k	multicolored	*12.00*	*10.00*
300a	A78	18k	multicolored	*12.00*	*2.00*
301a	A78	20k	multicolored	*13.00*	*3.00*
303a	A78	30k	multicolored	*12.00*	*7.50*
305a	A78	50k	dk brn background	*.75*	*.90*
306a	A78	1n	multicolored	*2.00*	*4.00*
			Nos. 291a-306a (12)	*55.20*	*30.45*

Nos. 300a, 305a and 306a have periods in the imprint. The liquid in the flasks is gray on No. 301, black on No. 301a, and blue on No. 301b.

1975-80 Wmk. 379

291c	A78	1k	multi, dk grn foliage	*1.50*	*2.00*
292b	A78	2k	multi ('75)	*1.75*	*.25*
293a	A78	3k	multi ('75)	*.25*	*.25*
294c	A78	5k	emerald fields ('76)	*2.25*	*.25*
295a	A78	7k	multi ('80)	*3.50*	*3.50*
296a	A78	8k	multi ('76)	*1.75*	*2.00*

297b	A78	10k	multi ('76)	*2.00*	*.25*
299a	A78	15k	multicolored		*3.00*
300b	A78	18k	multi ('78)	*4.25*	*4.00*
301b	A78	20k	multi, pale pink table, door, windows ('79)	*3.25*	*3.50*
302a	A78	25k	multi, pur barges	*3.25*	*.25*
302b	A78	25k	multi, brn barges	*3.25*	*.25*
305b	A78	50k	dk brn background, grn imprint	*3.50*	*3.75*
307a	A78	2n	multicolored	*5.50*	*6.50*

OAU Headquarters A79

Designs: 18k, OAU flag, vert. 30k, Stairs leading to OAU emblem, vert.

1973, May 25 Litho. *Perf. 14*

308	A79	5k	blue & multi	.25	.25
309	A79	18k	olive grn & multi	.35	*.50*
310	A79	30k	lilac & multi	.55	*.80*
			Nos. 308-310 (3)	1.15	1.55

Org. for African Unity, 10th anniv.

WMO Emblem, Weather Vane — A80

1973, Sept. 4 Litho. *Perf. 13*

311	A80	5k	multicolored	.30	.25
312	A80	30k	multicolored	1.50	*2.25*

Cent. of intl. meteorological cooperation.

View of Ibadan University — A81

Designs: 12k, Campus, crest and graph showing growth, vert. 18k, Campus, students and crest. 30k, Teaching hospital.

1973, Nov. 17 *Perf. 14*

313	A81	5k	lt blue & multi	.25	.25
314	A81	12k	lilac & multi	.25	.30
315	A81	18k	orange & multi	.45	.40
316	A81	30k	blue, org & blk	.65	*.80*
			Nos. 313-316 (4)	1.60	1.75

University of Ibadan, 25th anniversary.

Growth of Mail, 1874-1974 — A82

12k, Nigerian Post emblem & Northern Nigeria #18A. 18k, Postal emblem & Lagos #1. 30k, Map of Nigeria &means of transportation.

1974, June 10 Litho. *Perf. 14*

317	A82	5k	green, black & org	.25	.25
318	A82	12k	green & multi	.55	.55
319	A82	18k	green, lilac & blk	.90	.90
320	A82	30k	black & multi	1.60	1.60
			Nos. 317-320 (4)	3.30	3.30

Centenary of first Nigerian postage stamps.

Globe and UPU Emblem — A83

UPU cent.: 18k, World map and means of transportation. 30k, Letters.

1974, Oct. 9

321	A83	5k	blue & multi	.25	.25
322	A83	18k	orange & multi	2.50	.60
323	A83	30k	brown & multi	2.00	1.75
			Nos. 321-323 (3)	4.75	2.60

Hungry and Well-fed Children — A84

Designs: 12k, Chicken farm, horiz. 30k, Irrigation project.

1974, Nov. 25 Litho. *Perf. 14*

324	A84	5k orange, blk & grn	.25	.25
325	A84	12k multicolored	.35	.50
326	A84	30k multicolored	.80	*1.50*
		Nos. 324-326 (3)	1.40	2.25

Freedom from Hunger.

A85

Map of Nigeria with Telex Network, Teleprinter — A86

1975, July 3 Litho. *Perf. 14*

327	A85	5k multicolored	.25	.25
328	A85	12k multicolored	.25	.25
329	A86	18k multicolored	.30	.30
330	A86	30k multicolored	.55	.55
		Nos. 327-330 (4)	1.35	1.35

Inauguration of Nigeria Telex Network.

Queen Amina of Zaria (1536-1566) — A87

1975, Aug. 18 Litho. *Perf. 14*

331	A87	5k multicolored	.25	.25
332	A87	18k multicolored	1.10	.90
333	A87	30k multicolored	1.40	*1.75*
		Nos. 331-333 (3)	2.75	2.90

International Women's Year.

Alexander Graham Bell — A88

Designs: 18k, Hands beating gong, modern telephone operator, horiz. 25k, Telephones, 1876, 1976.

1976, Mar. 10 Wmk. 379

334	A88	5k pink, black & ocher	.25	.25
335	A88	18k deep lilac & multi	.45	.55
336	A88	25k lt bl, vio bl & blk	.90	1.10
		Nos. 334-336 (3)	1.60	1.90

Centenary of first telephone call by Alexander Graham Bell, Mar. 10, 1876.

Children Going to School — A89

Designs: 5k, Child learning to write, horiz. 25k, Classroom.

1976, Sept. 20 Litho. *Perf. 14*

337	A89	5k multicolored	.25	.25
338	A89	18k multicolored	.55	.75
339	A89	25k multicolored	.70	1.00
		Nos. 337-339 (3)	1.50	2.00

Launching of universal primary education in 1976.

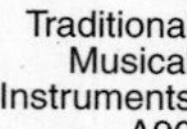

Traditional Musical Instruments A90

5k, Carved mask (festival emblem). 10k, Natl. Arts Theater, Lagos. 12k, Nigerian & African women's hair styles. 30k, Nigerian carvings.

1976-77 Wmk. 379

340	A90	5k black, gold & grn	.25	.25
341	A90	10k multicolored	.40	.40
342	A90	12k multicolored	.75	.75
343	A90	18k brown, ocher & blk	.90	.90
344	A90	30k multicolored	1.10	1.25
		Nos. 340-344 (5)	3.40	3.55

2nd World Black and African Festival of Arts and Culture, Lagos, Jan. 15-Feb. 12, 1977. Issued: 5k, 18k, 11/1; others 1/15/77.

Gen. Muhammed Broadcasting and Map of Nigeria — A91

Designs: 18k, Gen. Muhammed as Commander in Chief, vert. 30k, in battle dress, vert.

1977, Feb. 13 Litho. *Perf. 14*

345	A91	5k multicolored	.25	.25
346	A91	18k multicolored	.40	.40
347	A91	30k multicolored	.70	.70
		Nos. 345-347 (3)	1.35	1.35

Gen. Murtala Ramat Muhammed, Head of State and Commander in Chief, 1st death anniversary.

Scouts Clearing Street — A92

5k, Senior and Junior Boy Scouts saluting, vert. 25k, Scouts working on farm. 30k, African Scout Jamboree emblem, map of Africa.

1977, Apr. 1 Wmk. 379

348	A92	5k multicolored	.30	.30
349	A92	18k multicolored	.65	.65
350	A92	25k multicolored	.80	1.00
351	A92	30k multicolored	1.10	1.60
		Nos. 348-351 (4)	2.85	3.55

First All-Africa Boy Scout Jamboree, Sherehills, Jos, Nigeria, Apr. 2-8, 1977.

Trade Fair Emblem — A93

Emblem and: 5k, View of Fair grounds. 30k, Weaver and potter.

1977, Nov. 27 Litho. *Perf. 13*

352	A93	5k multicolored	.25	.25
353	A93	18k multicolored	.30	.30
354	A93	30k multicolored	.60	.60
		Nos. 352-354 (3)	1.15	1.15

1st Lagos Intl. Trade Fair, Nov. 27-Dec. 11.

Nigeria's 13 Universities A94

12k, Map of West African highways and telecommunications network. 18k, Training of technicians, and cogwheel. 30k, World map and map of Argentina with Buenos Aires.

1978, Apr. 28 Wmk. 379

355	A94	5k multicolored	.25	.25
356	A94	12k multicolored	.25	.25
357	A94	18k multicolored	.25	.25
358	A94	30k multicolored	.60	.60
		Nos. 355-358 (4)	1.35	1.35

Global Conf. on Technical Cooperation among Developing Countries, Buenos Aires.

Antenna and ITU Emblem — A95

1978, May 17 Litho. *Perf. 14*

359	A95	30k multicolored	.75	.75

10th World Telecommunications Day.

Students on Cassava Plantation — A96

"Operation Feed the Nation": 18k, Woman working in backyard vegetable garden. 30k, Plantain harvest, vert.

1978, July 7 Litho. *Perf. 14*

360	A96	5k multicolored	.25	.25
361	A96	18k multicolored	.30	.30
362	A96	30k multicolored	.50	.50
		Nos. 360-362 (3)	1.05	1.05

Mother Holding Sick Child — A97

Designs: 12k, Sick boy at health station. 18k, Vaccination of children. 30k, Syringe and WHO emblem, vert.

1978, Aug. 31 Wmk. 379

363	A97	5k multicolored	.25	.25
364	A97	12k multicolored	.30	.30
365	A97	18k multicolored	.45	.45
366	A97	30k multicolored	.75	.75
		Nos. 363-366 (4)	1.75	1.75

Global eradication of smallpox.

Bronze Horseman from Benin — A98

Nigerian antiquities: 5k, Nok terracotta figure from Bwari. 12k, Bronze snail and animal from Igbo-Ukwu. 18k, Bronze statue of a king of Ife.

1978, Oct. 27 Litho. *Perf. 14*

367	A98	5k multicolored	.25	.25
368	A98	12k multicolored, horiz.	.25	.25
369	A98	18k multicolored	.30	.30
370	A98	30k multicolored	.50	.50
		Nos. 367-370 (4)	1.30	1.30

Anti-Apartheid Emblem — A99

1978, Dec. 10 *Perf. 14*

371	A99	18k red, yellow & black	.35	.35

Anti-Apartheid Year.

Wright Brothers, Flyer A — A100

18k, Nigerian Air Force fighters in formation.

1978, Dec. 28

372	A100	5k multicolored	.30	.30
373	A100	18k multicolored	.60	.60

75th anniversary of powered flight.

Murtala Muhammed Airport — A101

1979, Mar. 15 Litho. *Perf. 14*

374	A101	5k bright blue & black	.50	.30

Inauguration of Murtala Muhammed Airport.

Young Stamp Collector — A102

1979, Apr. 11

375	A102	5k multicolored	.35	.25

Philatelic Week; Natl. Philatelic Service, 10th anniv.

Mother Nursing Child, IYC Emblem — A103

18k, Children at study. 25k, Children at play, vert.

1979, June 28 Wmk. 379 *Perf. 14*

376	A103	5k multicolored	.25	.25
377	A103	18k multicolored	.30	.30
378	A103	25k multicolored	.35	.35
		Nos. 376-378 (3)	.90	.90

International Year of the Child.

A104

Design: 10k, Preparation of audio-visual material. 30k, Adult education class.

1979, July 25 Photo. & Engr.

379	A104	10k multicolored	.25	.25
380	A104	30k multicolored	.40	.40

Intl. Bureau of Education, Geneva, 50th anniv.

Necom House, Lagos — A105

1979, Sept. 20 Litho. *Perf. 13½x14*

381	A105	10k multicolored	.30	.30

Intl. Radio Consultative Committee (CCIR) of the ITU, 50th anniv.

Trainees and Survey Equipment A106

1979, Dec. 12 Photo. *Perf. 14*

382	A106	10k multicolored	.30	.30

Economic Commission for Africa, 21st anniv.

Soccer Cup and Ball on Map of Nigeria — A107

1980, Mar. 8

383	A107	10k shown	.25	.25
384	A107	30k Player, vert.	.60	.60

12th African Cup of Nations Soccer Championship, Lagos and Ibadan, Mar.

Swimming, Moscow '80 Emblem — A108

10k, Wrestling, vert. 20k, Long jump, vert. 45k, Women's basketball, vert.

Litho. & Engr.

1980, July 19 *Perf. 14*

385 A108 10k multi .25 .25
386 A108 20k multi .25 .25
387 A108 30k shown .30 .30
388 A108 45k multi .35 .35
Nos. 385-388 (4) 1.15 1.15

22nd Summer Olympic Games, Moscow, July 19-Aug. 3.

Men Holding OPEC Emblem — A109

45k, Anniversary emblem, vert.

1980, Sept. 15 **Litho. & Engr.**

389 A109 10k shown .25 .25
390 A109 45k multi .75 .75

OPEC, 20th anniversary.

First Steam Locomotive in Nigeria — A110

20k, Unloading freight car. 30k, Freight train.

1980, Oct. 2 **Wmk. 379** *Perf. 14*

391 A110 10k shown .50 .50
392 A110 20k multi 1.40 1.40
393 A110 30k multi 2.10 2.10
Nos. 391-393 (3) 4.00 4.00

Nigerian Railway Corp., 75th anniv.

Technician Performing Quality Control Test — A111

1980, Oct. 14

394 A111 10k Scale, ruler, vert. .25 .25
395 A111 30k shown .45 .45

World Standards Day.

A112

Designs: 10k, Map of West Africa showing ECOWAS Members, Modes of Communication. 25k, Transportation. 30k, Map, cow, cocoa. 45k, Map, industrial symbols.

1980, Nov. 5 **Litho. & Engr.**

396 A112 10k multicolored .25 .25
396A A112 25k multicolored .30 .30
397 A112 30k multicolored .40 .40
398 A112 45k multicolored .55 .55
Nos. 396-398 (4) 1.50 1.50

Woman with Cane Sweeping — A113

30k, Amputee photographer.

Wmk. 379

1981, June 25 **Litho.** *Perf. 14*

399 A113 10k shown .25 .25
400 A113 30k multicolored .50 .50

Intl. Year of the Disabled.

World Food Day — A114

10k, Pres. Shenu Shagari. 25k, Produce, vert. 30k, Tomato crop, vert. 45k, Pig farm.

1981, Oct. 16 **Litho. & Engr.**

401 A114 10k multicolored .25 .25
402 A114 25k multicolored .30 .30
403 A114 30k multicolored .35 .35
404 A114 45k multicolored .50 .50
Nos. 401-404 (4) 1.40 1.40

Anti-apartheid Year — A115

30k, Soweto riot. 45k, Police hitting man, vert.

1981, Dec. 10 **Litho.**

405 A115 30k multicolored .40 .55
406 A115 45k multicolored .60 1.00

Scouting Year — A116

30k, Animal first aid. 45k, Baden-Powell, scouts.

1982, Feb. 22 **Litho.** *Perf. 14*

407 A116 30k multicolored .60 .65
408 A116 45k multicolored 1.10 1.25

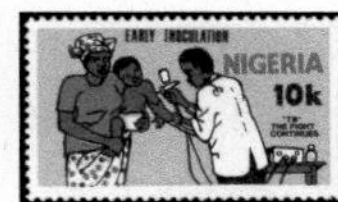

TB Bacillus Centenary A117

10k, Inoculation. 30k, Research. 45k, Patient being x-rayed, vert.

1982, Mar. 24 **Litho.** *Perf. 14*

409 A117 10k multicolored .30 .30
410 A117 30k multicolored .50 .60
411 A117 45k multicolored .80 1.40
Nos. 409-411 (3) 1.60 2.30

10th Anniv. of UN Conference on Human Environment A118

10k, Keep your environment clean. 20k, Check air pollution. 30k, Preserve natural environment. 45k, Reafforestation concerns all.

1982, June 10 **Litho.**

412 A118 10k multicolored .25 .25
413 A118 20k multicolored .25 .35
414 A118 30k multicolored .35 .50
415 A118 45k multicolored .60 .80
Nos. 412-415 (4) 1.45 1.90

Salamis Parnassus A119

20k, Papilio zalmoxis. 30k, Pachylophus beckeri. 45k, Papilio hesperus.

1982, Sept. 15 **Litho.**

416 A119 10k shown .35 .25
417 A119 20k multicolored .65 .55
418 A119 30k multicolored 1.00 1.00
419 A119 45k multicolored 1.50 1.40
Nos. 416-419 (4) 3.50 3.20

25th Anniv. of Natl. Museum — A120

10k, Statuettes, vert. 20k, Bronze leopard. 30k, Soapstone seated figure, vert. 45k, Wooden helmet mask.

1982, Nov. 18 **Wmk. 379**

420 A120 10k multicolored .25 .25
421 A120 20k multicolored .35 .35
422 A120 30k multicolored .40 .40
423 A120 45k multicolored .60 .60
Nos. 420-423 (4) 1.60 1.60

Family Day — A121

10k, Extended family, house, horiz. 30k, Family.

1983, Mar. 8 **Litho.** *Perf. 14*

424 A121 10k multicolored .25 .25
425 A121 30k multicolored .50 .50

Commonwealth Day — A122

10k, Satellite view, horiz. 25k, Natl. Assembly buildings, horiz. 30k, Oil exploration. 45k, Runners.

1983, Mar. 14

426 A122 10k multicolored .25 .25
427 A122 25k multicolored .35 .35
428 A122 30k multicolored .45 .45
429 A122 45k multicolored .55 .55
Nos. 426-429 (4) 1.60 1.60

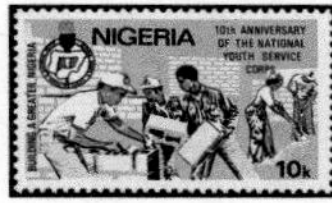

10th Anniv. of Natl. Youth Service Corps — A123

1983, May 25 **Litho.** *Perf. 14*

430 A123 10k Construction .25 .25
431 A123 25k Climbing wall, vert. .45 .45
432 A123 30k Marching, vert. .65 .65
Nos. 430-432 (3) 1.35 1.35

World Communications Year — A124

10k, Mailman, vert. 25k, Newspaper stand. 30k, Traditional horn messenger. 45k, TV news broadcast.

Wmk. 379

1983, July 22 **Litho.** *Perf. 14*

433 A124 10k multicolored .25 .25
434 A124 25k multicolored .35 .35
435 A124 30k multicolored .55 .55
436 A124 45k multicolored .45 .45
Nos. 433-436 (4) 1.60 1.60

World Fishery — A125

1983, Sept. 22 **Litho.** **Wmk. 379**

437 A125 10k Pink shrimp .30 .30
438 A125 25k Long neck croaker .40 .40
439 A125 30k Barracuda .50 .50
440 A125 45k Fishing technique .60 .60
Nos. 437-440 (4) 1.80 1.80

Boys' Brigade, 75th Anniv. — A126

10k, Boys, emblem, vert. 30k, Food production. 45k, Skill training.

1983, Oct. 14 *Perf. 14*

441 A126 10k multicolored .30 .30
442 A126 30k multicolored 1.50 1.50
443 A126 45k multicolored 2.25 2.25
Nos. 441-443 (3) 4.05 4.05

Fight Against Polio Campaign A127

1984, Feb. 29 **Litho.** *Perf. 14*

444 A127 10k Crippled boy, vert. .25 .25
445 A127 25k Vaccination .60 .60
446 A127 30k Healthy child, vert. .80 .80
Nos. 444-446 (3) 1.65 1.65

Hartebeests A128

10k, Waterbuck, vert. 30k, Buffalo. 45k, African golden monkey, vert.

1984, May 25 **Wmk. 379** *Perf. 14*

447 A128 10k multicolored .50 .30
448 A128 25k shown .45 .45
449 A128 30k multicolored .65 .65
450 A128 45k multicolored 1.00 1.00
Nos. 447-450 (4) 2.60 2.40

Central Bank of Nigeria, 25th Anniv. — A129

1984, July 2 **Wmk. 379**

451 A129 10k £1 note, 1968 .25 .25
452 A129 25k Bank .55 .55
453 A129 30k £5 note, 1959 .70 .70
Nos. 451-453 (3) 1.50 1.50

1984 Summer Olympics, Los Angeles — A130

Wmk. 379

1984, Aug. 9 **Litho.** *Perf. 14*

454 A130 10k Boxing .25 .25
455 A130 25k Discus .40 .40
456 A130 30k Weight lifting .50 .50
457 A130 45k Bicycling .75 .75
Nos. 454-457 (4) 1.90 1.90

African Development Bank, 20th Anniv. — A131

10k, Irrigation project, Lesotho. 25k, Bomi Hills roadway, Liberia. 30k, Education development, Seychelles. 45k, Coal mining & transportation, Niger. #459-461 horiz.

1984, Sept. 10

458 A131 10k multicolored .30 .30
459 A131 25k multicolored .55 .55
460 A131 30k multicolored .75 .75
461 A131 45k multicolored 1.20 1.20
Nos. 458-461 (4) 2.80 2.80

A132

A132a

A132b

A132c

Rare bird species: 10k, Pin-tailed whydah. 25k, Spur-winged plover. 30k, Red bishop. 45k, Francolin.

1984, Oct. 24

462	A132	10k multicolored	.75	.75
463	A132a	25k multicolored	1.25	1.25
464	A132b	30k multicolored	1.75	1.75
465	A132c	45k multicolored	2.75	2.75
		Nos. 462-465 (4)	6.50	6.50

Intl. Civil Aviation Organization, 40th Anniv. — A132d

45k, Jet circling Earth.

1984, Dec. 7 Litho. *Perf. 14*

465A	A132d	10k shown	.50	.50
465B	A132d	45k multicolored	2.00	2.00

Fight Against Indiscipline A133

20k, Encourage punctuality. 50k, Discourage bribery.

1985, Feb. 27

466	A133	20k multicolored	.30	.30
467	A133	50k multicolored	.90	.90

Intl. Youth Year — A134

20k, Sports, horiz. 50k, Nationalism. 55k, Service organizations.

1985, June 5

468	A134	20k multi	.25	.25
469	A134	50k multi	.60	.60
470	A134	55k multi	.70	.70
		Nos. 468-470 (3)	1.55	1.55

OPEC, 25th Anniv. — A135

1985, Sept. 15

471	A135	20k shown	.90	.90
472	A135	50k World map, horiz.	1.75	1.75

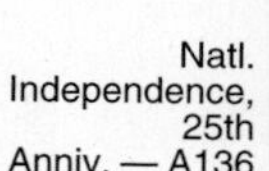

Natl. Independence, 25th Anniv. — A136

20k, Oil refinery. 50k, Map of states. 55k, Monument. 60k, Eleme Oil Refinery.

1985, Sept. 25

473	A136	20k multi	.25	.25
474	A136	50k multi	.60	.60
475	A136	55k multi	.65	.65
476	A136	60k multi	.75	.75
a.		Souvenir sheet of 4, #473-476	5.50	*5.50*
		Nos. 473-476 (4)	2.25	2.25

World Tourism Day — A137

20k, Waterfalls. 50k, Crafts, horiz. 55k, Carved calabashes, flag. 60k, Leather goods, rug.

1985, Sept. 27

477	A137	20k multi	.25	.25
478	A137	50k multi	.55	.55
479	A137	55k multi	.60	.60
480	A137	60k multi	.65	.65
		Nos. 477-480 (4)	2.05	2.05

UN, 40th Anniv. — A138

1985, Oct. 7

481	A138	20k Emblem, map, flag	.30	.30
482	A138	50k UN building, horiz.	.50	.50
483	A138	55k Emblem, horiz.	.80	.80
		Nos. 481-483 (3)	1.60	1.60

Admission of Nigeria to UN, 25th anniv.

African Reptiles — A139

1986, Apr. 15 Wmk. 379 *Perf. 14*

484	A139	10k Python	.30	.30
485	A139	20k Crocodile	.50	.50
486	A139	25k Gopher tortoise	.60	.60
487	A139	30k Chameleon	.70	.70
		Nos. 484-487 (4)	2.10	2.10

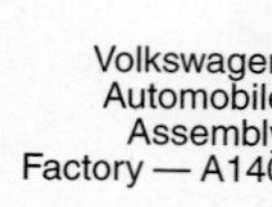

Volkswagen Automobile Assembly Factory — A140

Designs: 1k, Social worker with children, vert. 5k, Modern housing development. 10k, Modern method of harvesting coconuts, vert. 15k, Port activities. 20k, Tecoma stans, flower, vert. 25k, Medical care. 30k, Birom folk dancers. 35k, Telephone operators. 40k, Nkpokiti dancers, vert. 45k, Hibiscus. 50k, Modern p.o. 1n, Stone quarry. 2n, Technical education.

1986, June 16 Wmk. 379 *Perf. 14*

488	A140	1k multicolored	.45	.45
489	A140	2k multicolored	.45	.45
490	A140	5k multicolored	.30	.25
491	A140	10k multicolored	.30	.25
492	A140	15k multicolored	1.00	.25
493	A140	20k multicolored	.30	.25
494	A140	25k multicolored	.35	.45
494A	A140	30k multicolored	.55	.55
495	A140	35k multicolored	.35	.25
496	A140	40k multicolored	.35	.25
497	A140	45k multicolored	.35	.25
498	A140	50k multicolored	1.00	.60
499	A140	1n multicolored	.45	.40
500	A140	2n multicolored	.45	.45
		Nos. 488-500 (14)	6.65	5.10

Use of some denominations began as early as 1984. Date of issue of the 30k is not definite.

See Nos. 560A-560D, 615C.

Intl. Peace Year — A141

10k, Emblem. 20k, Hands touching globe.

1986, June 20 Litho. *Perf. 14*

501	A141	10k multi	.30	.30
502	A141	20k multi	.50	.50

Insects — A142

1986, July 14

503	A142	10k Goliath beetle	.35	.35
504	A142	20k Wasp	.80	.80
505	A142	25k Cricket	1.00	1.00
506	A142	30k Carpet beetle	1.25	1.25
a.		Souvenir sheet of 4, #503-506	5.75	5.75
		Nos. 503-506 (4)	3.40	3.40

Nos. 503-506 and 506a exist imperf. Values: 503-506, set $6; 506a, $12.

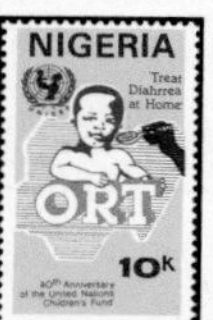

UNICEF, 40th Anniv. — A143

10k, Oral rehydration. 20k, Immunization. 25k, Breast-feeding. 30k, Mother playing with child.

1986, Nov. 11

507	A143	10k multicolored	.25	.25
508	A143	20k multicolored	.35	.35
509	A143	25k multicolored	.70	.70
510	A143	30k multicolored	.80	.80
		Nos. 507-510 (4)	2.10	2.10

UN Child Survival Campaign.

Institute of Intl. Affairs, 25th Anniv. — A144

20k, Intl. understanding, horiz.

1986, Dec. 13

511	A144	20k multi	.70	.70
512	A144	30k shown	.90	.90

Nos. 511-512 exist imperf. Value, set $2.50.

Seashells — A145

1987, Mar. 31

513	A145	10k Freshwater clam	1.25	1.25
514	A145	20k Periwinkle	1.50	1.50
515	A145	25k Bloddy cockle	1.75	1.75
516	A145	30k Mangrove oyster	2.00	2.00
		Nos. 513-516 (4)	6.50	6.50

A146

A147

10k, Blue pea but. 20k, Hibiscus. 25k, Acanthus montanus. 30k, Combretum racemosum.

1987, May 28

517	A146	10k multicolored	.25	.25
518	A146	20k multicolored	.25	.25
519	A147	25k multicolored	.25	.25
520	A147	30k multicolored	.25	.25
		Nos. 517-520 (4)	1.00	1.00

Hair Styles — A148

1987, Sept. 15 Wmk. 379 *Perf. 14*

521	A148	10k Doka	.30	.30
522	A148	20k Eting	.30	.30
523	A148	25k Agogo	.30	.30
524	A148	30k Goto	.30	.30
		Nos. 521-524 (4)	1.20	1.20

Intl. Year of Shelter for the Homeless — A149

20k, Homeless family. 30k, Moving to new home.

1987, Dec. 10 Litho.

525	A149	20k multicolored	.30	.25
526	A149	30k multicolored	.30	.25

A150

1988, Feb. 17 Litho. *Perf. 14*

527	A150	20k Help the Needy	.70	.50
528	A150	30k Care for the sick	1.10	.90

Intl. Red Cross and Red Crescent Organizations, 125th annivs.

A151

10k, Immunization. 20k, Map, globe, emblem. 30k, Mobile hospital.

1988, Apr. 7 Wmk. 379 *Perf. 14*

529	A151	10k multicolored	.30	.25
530	A151	20k multicolored	.60	.60
531	A151	30k multicolored	.70	.70
		Nos. 529-531 (3)	1.60	1.55

WHO, 40th anniv.

A152

20k, Emblem, map, 4 men.

1988, May 25

532	A152	10k shown	.30	.25
533	A152	20k multicolored	.30	.25

Organization of African Unity, 25th anniv.

Shrimp — A153

10k, Pink shrimp. 20k, Tiger shrimp. 25k, Deepwater roseshrimp. 30k, Estuarine prawn.

1988, June 2

534	A153	10k multicolored	.30	.30
535	A153	20k multicolored	.50	.50
536	A153	25k multicolored	.60	.60
537	A153	30k multicolored	.70	.70
a.		Miniature sheet of 4, #534-537	2.50	2.50
		Nos. 534-537 (4)	2.10	2.10

1988 Summer Olympics, Seoul — A154

1988, Sept. 6 Wmk. 379 *Perf. 14*

538	A154	10k Weight lifting	.30	.30
539	A154	20k Boxing	.30	.30
540	A154	30k Running, vert.	.30	.30
		Nos. 538-540 (3)	.90	.90

A155

A156

Nigerian Security Printing and Minting Co., Ltd., 25th Anniv. — A157

10k, Bank note production. 20k, Coin production. 25k, Products. 30k, Anniv. emblem.

1988, Oct. 28

541 A155 10k multicolored .35 .35
542 A155 20k multicolored .35 .35
543 A156 25k multicolored .35 .35
544 A157 30k multicolored .35 .35
Nos. 541-544 (4) 1.40 1.40

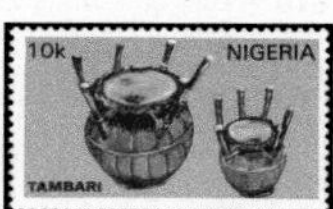

Traditional Musical Instruments A158

Wmk. 379

1989, June 29 Litho. *Perf. 14*

545 A158 10k Tambari .40 .40
546 A158 20k Kundung .40 .40
547 A158 25k Ibid .40 .40
548 A158 30k Dundun .40 .40
Nos. 545-548 (4) 1.60 1.60

African Development Bank, 25th Anniv. — A159

10k, Reservoir, Mali. 20k, Irrigation project, Gambia. 25k, Bank headquarters.

1989, Sept. 10

549 A159 10k multicolored .30 .25
550 A159 20k multicolored .30 .25
551 A159 25k multicolored .30 .25
552 A159 30k shown .30 .25
Nos. 549-552 (4) 1.20 1.00

Nos. 549-551 horiz.

Nigerian Girl Guides Assoc., 70th Anniv. — A160

1989, Sept. 16

553 A160 10k Campfire, horiz. .50 .50
554 A160 20k shown .50 .50

Traditional Costumes — A161

1989, Oct. 26

555 A161 10k Etubom .40 .40
556 A161 20k Fulfulde .40 .40
557 A161 25k Aso-ofi .40 .40
558 A161 30k Fuska Kura .40 .40
Nos. 555-558 (4) 1.60 1.60

Pan-African Postal Union, 10th Anniv. — A162

1990, Jan. 18

559 A162 10k shown .35 .35
560 A162 20k Map, delivery .40 .40

National Theater — A162a

20n, Ancient wall, Kano. 50n, Rock bridge. 100n, Ekpe masquerade, vert.

1990, May 23 Litho. *Perf. 14*

560A A162a 20n multicolored *13.00* 2.00
560B A162a 50n multicolored *9.00* 4.00
560C A162a 100n multicolored *7.00* 7.00
560D A162a 500n multicolored *37.50* 25.00
e. Perf. 13, unwatermarked (NSPMPLC inscription at LL) — —
Nos. 560A-560D (4) *66.50* 38.00

Postal counterfeits are known of No. 560B. Issued: No. 560De, 2010.

Pottery — A163

1990, May 24

561 A163 10k Oil lamp .25 .25
562 A163 20k Water pot .25 .25
563 A163 25k Musical pots .25 .25
564 A163 30k Water jug .25 .25
a. Sheet of 4, #561-564 with yellow frames, + 4 labels 1.75 1.75
Nos. 561-564 (4) 1.00 1.00

Inscriptions, including country name, denomination and descriptions vary widely in size and style.

Intl. Literacy Year — A164

1990, Aug. 8

565 A164 20k multicolored .30 .25
566 A164 30k multicolored .30 .25

A165 A166

1990, Sept. 14

567 A165 10k shown .25 .25
568 A166 20k Flags .25 .25
569 A165 25k Globe .25 .25
570 A166 30k shown .25 .25
Nos. 567-570 (4) 1.00 1.00

Organization of Petroleum Exporting Countries (OPEC), 30th anniv.

Wildlife — A167

20k, Grey parrot. 30k, Roan antelope. 1.50n, Grey-necked rock fowl. 2.50n, Mountain gorilla.

1990, Nov. 8

571 A167 20k multi .30 .30
572 A167 30k multi .40 .40
573 A167 1.50n multi 1.25 1.25
574 A167 2.50n multi 1.75 1.75
a. Souvenir sheet of 4, #571-574 4.25 4.25
Nos. 571-574 (4) 3.70 3.70

Inscriptions vary widely in size and style.

A168 A169

1991, Mar. 20

575 A168 10k Eradication .25 .25
576 A169 20k shown .25 .25
577 A168 30k Prevention .25 .25
Nos. 575-577 (3) .75 .75

Natl. Guineaworm Eradication Day.

A170

1991, May 26

578 A170 20k Progress .25 .25
579 A170 30k Unity .25 .25
580 A170 50k Freedom .25 .25
Nos. 578-580 (3) .75 .75

OAU Heads of State Meeting, Abiya.

ECOWAS Summit, Abuja — A171

1991, July 4

581 A171 20k Flags .45 .40
582 A171 50k Map of West Africa .45 .40

Economic Community of West African States.

Fish — A172

1991, July 10

583 A172 10k Electric catfish .30 .30
584 A172 20k Niger perch .45 .45
585 A172 30k Talapia .50 .50
586 A172 50k African catfish .60 .60
a. Souvenir sheet of 4, #583-586 2.75 2.75
Nos. 583-586 (4) 1.85 1.85

Telecom '91 — A173

1991, Oct. 7

587 A173 20k shown .25 .25
588 A173 50k multi, vert. .45 .45

Sixth World Forum and Exposition on Telecommunications, Geneva, Switzerland.

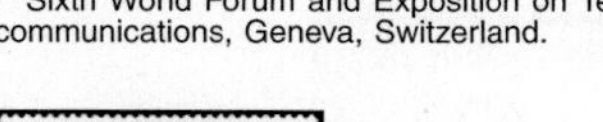

1992 Summer Olympics, Barcelona A174

1992, Jan. 24 Unwmk.

589 A174 50k Boxing .30 .30
590 A174 1n Running .30 .30
591 A174 1.50n Table tennis .40 .40
592 A174 2n Taekwondo .50 .50
a. Souvenir sheet of 4, #589-592, wmk. 379 3.50 3.50
Nos. 589-592 (4) 1.50 1.50

1992 Summer Olympics, Barcelona — A175

Wmk. 379

1992, Apr. 3 Litho. *Perf. 14*

593 A175 1.50n multicolored .55 .55

World Health Day — A176

Designs: 50k, Heart and blood pressure gauge. 1n, Globe and blood pressure guage. 1.50n, Heart in rib cage. 2n, Cross-section of heart.

1992, Apr. 7 Unwmk.

594 A176 50k multicolored .25 .25
595 A176 1n multicolored .25 .25
596 A176 1.50n multicolored .30 .30
597 A176 2n multicolored .40 .40
a. Souvenir sheet of 4, #594-597 1.50 1.50
Nos. 594-597 (4) 1.20 1.20

Intl. Institute of Tropical Agriculture, 25th Anniv. — A177

Designs: 50k, Plantain, vert. 1n, Food products. 1.50n, Harvesting cassava tubers, vert. 2n, Yam barn, vert.

1992, July 17

598 A177 50k multicolored .25 .25
599 A177 1n multicolored .25 .25
600 A177 1.50n grn, blk & brown .25 .25
601 A177 2n multicolored .30 .30
a. Souvenir sheet of 4, #598-601 2.40 2.40
Nos. 598-601 (4) 1.05 1.05

Olymphilex '92 — A178

1.50n, Stamp under magnifying glass.

Wmk. 379

1992, July 3 Litho. *Perf. 14*

602 A178 50k multicolored .25 .25
603 A178 1.50n multicolored .45 .45
a. Souvenir sheet of 2, #602-603 + 4 labels, unwmkd. 2.25 2.25

Maryam Babangida, Natl. Center for Women's Development
A179 A180

A180a

Designs: 50k, Emblem of Better Life Program. 1n, Women harvesting corn. 1.50n, Natl. Center, horiz. 2n, Woman using loom.

1992, Oct. 16

604 A179 50k multicolored .25 .25
605 A180 1n multicolored .25 .25
606 A180 1.50n multicolored .30 .30
607 A180a 2n multicolored .35 .35
Nos. 604-607 (4) 1.15 1.15

Traditional Dances — A181

Unwmk.

1992, Dec. 15 Litho. *Perf. 14*

608 A181 50k Sabada .25 .25
609 A181 1n Sato .25 .25
610 A181 1.50n Asian Ubo Ikpa .30 .30
611 A181 2n Dundun .35 .35
a. Souvenir sheet of 4, #608-611 2.25 2.25
Nos. 608-611 (4) 1.15 1.15

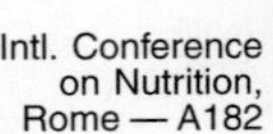

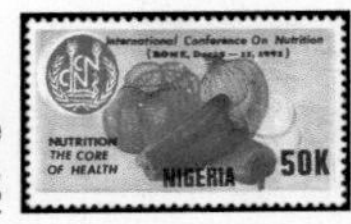

Intl. Conference on Nutrition, Rome — A182

1992, Dec. 1 Litho. *Perf. 14*

612 A182 50k Vegetables .25 .25
613 A182 1n Child eating .25 .25
614 A182 1.50n Fruits, vert. .30 .30
615 A182 2n Vegetables, diff. .35 .35
a. Souvenir sheet of 4, #611-615 2.75 2.75
Nos. 612-615 (4) 1.15 1.15

African Elephant — A182a

Stanley Crane — A182b

Lekki Beach — A182c

Roan Antelopes — A182d

Lion — A182e

1992-93 Litho. *Perf. 14*

615A A182a 1.50n multi 4.25 1.50
615B A182b 5n multi 5.00 1.00
615C A182c 10n multi 2.50 1.00
615D A182d 20n multi 9.00 4.00
615E A182e 30n multi 12.00 6.00
Nos. 615A-615E (5) 32.75 13.50

World Environment Day — A183

Designs: 1n, Clean environment ensures good health. 1.50n, Check water polution. 5n, Preserve your environment. 10n, Environment and nature.

1993, June 4 Litho. *Perf. 14*

616 A183 1n multicolored .25 .25
617 A183 1.50n multicolored .30 .30
618 A183 5n multicolored .80 .80
619 A183 10n multicolored 1.00 1.00
Nos. 616-619 (4) 2.35 2.35

Natl. Commission for Museums and Monuments, 50th Anniv. — A184

1n, Oni figure, vert. 1.50n, Queen Mother head, vert. 5n, Pendant. 10n, Nok head, vert.

1993, July 28 Litho. *Perf. 14*

620 A184 1n multi .25 .25
621 A184 1.50n multi .30 .30
622 A184 5n multi .45 .45
623 A184 10n multi .75 .75
Nos. 620-623 (4) 1.75 1.75

Orchids — A185

1n, Bulbophyllum distans. 1.50n, Eulophia cristata. 5n, Eulophia horsfalli. 10n, Eulophia quartiniana.

1993, Oct. 28 Litho. *Perf. 14*

624 A185 1n multicolored .30 .30
625 A185 1.50n multicolored .35 .35
626 A185 5n multicolored .60 .60
627 A185 10n multicolored 1.25 1.25
a. Souv. sheet of 4, #624-627 *3.50 3.50*
Nos. 624-627 (4) 2.50 2.50

No. 627a exists with perforations through either the bottom or top margins.

Intl. Year of the Family — A186

1.50n, Child abuse, classroom scene. 10n, Fending for the family, market scene.

1994, Mar. 30 Litho. *Perf. 14*

628 A186 1.50n multicolored .50 .50
629 A186 10n multicolored 1.10 1.10

Nigerian Philatelic Service, 25th Anniv. — A187

1n, #224. 1.50n, Bureau building. 5n, Map made of stamps. 10n, Counter staff, customers.

1994, Apr. 11

630 A187 1n multicolored .25 .25
631 A187 1.50n multicolored .30 .30
632 A187 5n multicolored .50 .50
633 A187 10n multicolored 1.20 1.20
Nos. 630-633 (4) 2.25 2.25

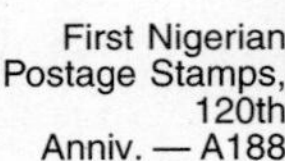

First Nigerian Postage Stamps, 120th Anniv. — A188

Designs: 1n, "I love stamps." 1.50n, "I collect stamps." 5n, Methods of transporting mail. 10n, Lagos type A1 on airmail envelope.

1994, June 10 Litho. *Perf. 14*

634 A188 1n multicolored .25 .25
635 A188 1.50n multicolored .30 .30
636 A188 5n multicolored .50 .50
637 A188 10n multicolored 1.20 1.20
Nos. 634-637 (4) 2.25 2.25

PHILAKOREA '94 — A189

1994, Aug. 16 Litho. *Perf. 14*

638 A189 30n multicolored 3.00 3.00
a. Souvenir sheet of 1, #638 5.50 5.50

Crabs — A190

1n, Geryon quinquedens. 1.50n, Spider crab. 5n, Red spider. 10n, Geryon maritae.

1994, Aug. 12 Litho. *Perf. 14*

639 A190 1n multi .25 .25
640 A190 1.50n multi .35 .35
641 A190 5n multi .75 .75
642 A190 10n multi 1.50 1.50
Nos. 639-642 (4) 2.85 2.85

African Development Bank, 30th Anniv. — A191

1.50n, Water treatment plant. 30n, Emblem, field.

1994, Sept. 16

643 A191 1.50n multi .25 .25
644 A191 30n multi 2.75 2.75

NIPOST/NITEL, 10th Anniv. — A192

Designs: 1n, Putting letter into mailbox, vert. 1.50n, Airmail letter. 5n, NIPOST, NITEL logos. 10n, Telephones, vert.

1995, Jan. 1 Litho. *Perf. 14*

645 A192 1n multicolored .25 .25
646 A192 1.50n multicolored .25 .25
647 A192 5n multicolored .40 .40
648 A192 10n multicolored .80 .80
Nos. 645-648 (4) 1.70 1.70

Family Support Program — A194

Designs: 1n, Feed the family. 1.50n, Monitoring child education. 5n, Caring for the family. 10n, Support agriculture.

1995, July 20 Litho. *Perf. 14*

653 A194 1n multicolored .25 .25
654 A194 1.50n multicolored .25 .25
655 A194 5n multicolored .40 .40
656 A194 10n multicolored .80 .80
Nos. 653-656 (4) 1.70 1.70

First Telephone in Nigeria, Cent. — A195

Designs: 1.50n, Dial telephone, c. 1919. 10n, Crank telephone, c. 1885.

1995, Oct. 9 Litho. *Perf. 14*

657 A195 1.50n multicolored .30 .30
658 A195 10n multicolored 1.10 1.10

FAO, 50th Anniv. — A196

1995, Oct. 16

659 A196 1.50n shown .25 .25
660 A196 30n Fishing boats 3.00 3.00

UN, 50th Anniv. — A197

Designs: 1n, Emblem of justice, vert. 1.50n, Against illegal dumping of toxic chemicals. 5n, Tourism. 10n, Peace-keeping soldiers.

1995, Oct. 24

661 A197 1n multicolored .25 .25
662 A197 1.50n multicolored .25 .25
663 A197 5n multicolored .40 .40
664 A197 10n multicolored .80 .80
Nos. 661-664 (4) 1.70 1.70

Niger Dock, 10th Anniv. — A198

5n, Overall view of dock. 10n, Boat being lifted. 20n, Boats in dock area. 30n, Boat on water.

1996, Apr. 29 Litho. *Perf. 14*

665 A198 5n multicolored .40 .40
666 A198 10n multicolored 1.00 1.00
667 A198 20n multicolored 1.75 1.75
668 A198 30n multicolored 2.50 2.50
Nos. 665-668 (4) 5.65 5.65

Economic Community of West African States (ECOWAS), 21st Anniv. — A199

5n, Developing agriculture and scientific research. 30n, Free movement of people.

1996, May 5 Litho. *Perf. 14*

669 A199 5n multicolored .50 .50
670 A199 30n multicolored 2.50 2.50

A200

1996, June 28

671 A200 5n Judo .40 .40
672 A200 10n Tennis 1.00 1.00
673 A200 20n Relay race 1.75 1.75
674 A200 30n Soccer 2.50 2.50
Nos. 671-674 (4) 5.65 5.65

1996 Summer Olympic Games, Atlanta.

Natl. Flag, Logo — A201

1996, Oct. 10 Litho. *Perf. 14*

675 A201 30n multicolored 3.00 3.00

Istanbul '96.

Mushrooms A202

Designs: 5n, Volvariella esculenta. 10n, Lentinus subnudus. 20n, Tricholoma lobayensis. 30n, Pleurotus tuber-regium.

1996, Nov. 19

676 A202 5n multicolored .50 .50
677 A202 10n multicolored .90 .90
678 A202 20n multicolored 2.10 2.10
679 A202 30n multicolored 3.00 3.00
Nos. 676-679 (4) 6.50 6.50

UNICEF, 50th Anniv. — A203

Designs: 5n, "Child's right to play," vert. 30n, "Educate the girl child."

1996, Dec. 10

680 A203 5n multicolored .50 .50
681 A203 30n multicolored 2.50 2.50

Mass Literacy Commission, 5th Anniv. — A204

Designs: 5n, "Teach one to teach one." 30n, "Education through co-operation."

1996, Dec. 30
682 A204 5n grn, blk & dk grn .45 .45
683 A204 30n grn, blk & dk grn 2.40 2.40

1998 World Cup Soccer Championships, France — A205

1998, June 10 Litho. *Perf. 13*
684 A205 5n shown .45 .45
685 A205 10n Player, vert. .90 .90
686 A205 20n Player, diff., vert. 1.60 1.60
687 A205 30n Two players 2.50 2.50
Nos. 684-687 (4) 5.45 5.45

ECOMOG (Military Co-operation Organization), 8th Anniv. — A206

Designs: 5n, Silhouette of ship. 30n, Flag colors of Gambia, Ghana, Guinea, Mali, Nigeria, Senegal, Sierra Leone. 50n, Flag colors of Gambia, Ghana, Nigeria, Guinea, Mali, Senegal, Sierra Leone, Niger, Ivory Coast, Benin, Burkina Faso.

1998, Nov. 30 Litho. *Perf. 14*
688 A206 5n multicolored .40 .40
689 A206 30n multicolored 2.40 2.40
690 A206 50n multicolored 4.00 4.00
Nos. 688-690 (3) 6.80 6.80

Nigerian Railroad, Cent. — A207

5n, Caged locomotive. 10n, Iddo Terminal. 20n, Locomotive. 30n, Passenger tram.

1999, Jan. 20 *Perf. 13*
691 A207 5n multicolored .40 .40
692 A207 10n multicolored .85 .85
693 A207 20n multicolored 1.75 1.75
694 A207 30n multicolored 2.50 2.50
Nos. 691-694 (4) 5.50 5.50

Rain Forest — A207a

1999, May 10 Litho. *Perf. 13*
694A A207a 10n multi — —

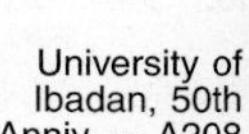

University of Ibadan, 50th Anniv. — A208

1998, Nov. 17 Litho. *Perf. 14*
695 A208 5n University building .50 .50
696 A208 30n "50," Crest 2.25 2.25

Federal Environmental Protection Agency, 10th Anniv. — A209

5n, Water resources. 10n, Natural resources. 20n, Endangered species. 30n, One earth, one family.

1999, June 8 Litho. *Perf. 13*
697 A209 5n multicolored .50 .50
698 A209 10n multicolored .75 .75
699 A209 20n multicolored 1.75 1.75
700 A209 30n multicolored 2.50 2.50
Nos. 697-700 (4) 5.50 5.50

NICON Insurance Corp., 30th Anniv. — A210

Emblem and: 5n, Airplane, ship, oil refinery, vert. 30n, Building.

Perf. 12¾x13, 13x12¾
1999, Aug. 31 Litho.
701 A210 5n multi .40 .40
702 A210 30n multi 2.00 2.00

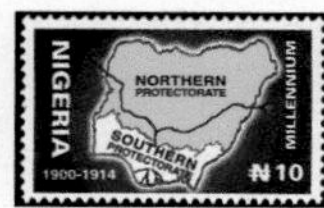

Millennium A211

Designs: 10n, Map of Northern and Southern Protectorates, 1900-14. 20n, Map of Nigeria, 1914. 30n, Coat of arms. 40n, Map of 36 states, 1996.

2000 Litho. *Perf. 13*
703-706 A211 Set of 4 2.10 2.10

World Meteorological Organization, 50th Anniv. — A212

Designs: 10n, Sunshine hour recorder, vert. 30n, Meteorological station.

2000 *Perf. 12¾x13, 13x12¾*
707-708 A212 Set of 2 1.00 1.00

Return to Democracy A213

Designs: 10n, Flag, "Freedom of the press," vert. 20n, Scales of justice. 30n, Legislative mace, vert. 40n, Pres. Olusegun Obasanjo, flag, vert.

2000 *Perf. 14¾*
709-712 A213 Set of 4 3.25 3.25
712a Souvenir sheet, #709-712 5.00 5.00

2000 Summer Olympics, Sydney — A214

Designs: 10n, Boxing. 20n, Weight lifting. 30n, Soccer. 40n, Soccer, diff.

2000, Sept. 7 Litho. *Perf. 13x12¾*
713-716 A214 Set of 4 3.25 3.25
716a Souvenir sheet, #713-716 + 4 labels 5.00 5.00

A215

Independence, 40th anniv.: 10n, Obafemi Awolowo (1909-87), promoter of federal constitution. 20n, Prime Minister Abubakar Tafawa Balewa (1912-66). 30n, Pres. Nnamdi Azikiwe (1904-96). 40n, Liquified gas refinery, horiz. 50n, Ship carrying exports, horiz.

Perf. 12¾x13, 13x12¾
2000, Sept. 27 Litho.
717-721 A215 Set of 5 3.75 3.75

A216

Fruit: 20n, Hug plum. 30n, White star apple. 40n, African breadfruit. 50n, Akee apple.

2001, Jan. 16 *Perf. 14*
722-725 A216 Set of 4 3.00 3.00

Nigeria Daily Times Newspaper, 75th Anniv. — A217

Designs: 20n, Corporate headquarters, Lagos. 30n, First issue. 40n, Daily Times complex, Lagos. 50n, Masthead.

2001, June 1 Litho. *Perf. 13x12¾*
726-729 A217 Set of 4 3.25 3.25

Fauna — A218

Designs: 10n, Broad-tailed paradise whydahs, vert. 15n, Fire-bellied woodpeckers, vert. 20n, Grant's zebras. 25n, Aardvark. 30n, Preuss's guenon, vert. 40n, Giant ground pangolin. 50n, Bonobo. 100n, Red-eared guenon, vert.

2001, June 15 *Perf. 14*
730 A218 10n multi .40 .25
731 A218 15n multi .50 .25
732 A218 20n multi .60 .35
a. Thinner inscriptions, perf. 13x13¼ ('05) .30 .30
733 A218 25n multi .70 .45
734 A218 30n multi .80 .60
735 A218 40n multi .90 .80
736 A218 50n multi 1.00 .90
a. Thinner inscriptions, perf. 13x13¼ ('05) .80 .80
737 A218 100n multi 2.50 2.00
a. Perf. 13¼x13 — —
Nos. 730-737 (8) 7.40 5.60

Inscriptions vary widely in size and style. Issued: Nos. 732a, 736a, 737a, 2005.

Year of Dialogue Among Civilizations — A219

2001, Oct. 9 Litho. *Perf. 13*
738 A219 20n multi .90 .90

New Millennium A220

Designs: 20n, Peace. 30n, Age of globalization. 40n, Reconciliation. 50n, Love.

2002, Feb. 13 Litho. *Perf. 13x12¾*
739-742 A220 Set of 4 3.00 3.00

Crops — A221

Designs: 20n, Kola nuts. 30n, Oil palm. 40n, Cassava. 50n, Corn, vert.

2002, May 10 *Perf. 13x12¾, 12¾x13*
743-746 A221 Set of 4 2.60 2.60

2002 World Cup Soccer Championships, Japan and Korea — A222

Emblem and: 20n, Nigerian player and opponent, vert. 30n, Globe and soccer balls, vert. 40n, Player's legs and ball. 50n, World Cup trophy, vert.

Perf. 12¾x13, 13x12¾
2002, June 14
747-750 A222 Set of 4 2.75 2.75

World AIDS Day — A223

Designs: 20n, Nurse, patient, flowers. 50n, AIDS counseling.

2003, May 3 Litho. *Perf. 13x12¾*
751-752 A223 Set of 2 1.70 1.70
752a Souvenir sheet, #751-752 3.50 3.50

A224

Universal basic education: 20n, Students. 50n, Student writing, horiz.

Perf. 12¾x13, 13x12¾
2003, Sept. 22 Litho.
753-754 A224 Set of 2 2.00 2.00

A225

Eighth All Africa Games: 20n, Runner. 30n, High jump, horiz. 40n, Taekwondo, horiz. 50n, Long jump

2003, Oct. 4
755-758 A225 Set of 4 2.50 2.50
758a Souvenir sheet, #755-758 + 4 labels 3.00 3.00

Worldwide Fund for Nature (WWF) — A226

Side-striped jackal: 20n, Adult and pups. 40n, Adult in grass. 80n, Two adults. 100n, Adult in grass, diff.

2003, Dec. 12 *Perf. 13x12¾*
759-762 A226 Set of 4 4.25 3.75
762a Block of 4, #759-762 4.75 4.75

Commonwealth Heads of Government Meeting, Abuja — A227

Emblem and: 20n, Map of Nigeria. 50n, Flag of Nigeria, vert.

Perf. 13x12¾, 12¾x13
2003, Dec. 7 Litho.
763-764 A227 Set of 2 2.00 2.00

2004 Summer Olympics, Athens — A228

Designs: 50n, Runners. 120n, Basketball.

2004, Aug. 18 Litho. *Perf. 12¾x13*
765-766 A228 Set of 2 3.00 3.00
766a Souvenir sheet of 2, #765-766, + 4 labels 25.00 25.00

No. 766a sold for 150n.

A229 A232

A230

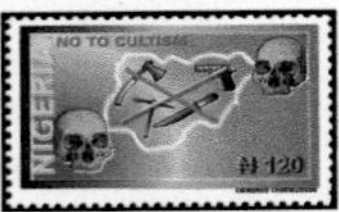
Winning Children's Stamp Art Contest Designs — A231

Perf. 12¾x13, 13x12¾

2004, Oct. 29 **Litho.**

767 A229 50n multi .75 .75
768 A230 90n multi 1.50 1.50
769 A231 120n multi 2.00 2.00
770 A232 150n multi 2.50 2.50
a. Souvenir sheet, #767-770, + 12 labels 7.00 7.00
Nos. 767-770 (4) 6.75 6.75

Rotary International, Cent. — A233

Designs: 50n, "100" with Rotary emblems for zeroes. 120n, Rotary emblem and world map.

2005, Aug. 9 **Litho.** ***Perf. 13x12¾***

771-772 Set of 2 3.50 3.50
772a A233 Horiz. pair, #771-772 3.50 3.50

Nigerian Postage Stamps, 131st Anniv. — A234

Designs: 50n, Text in simulated stamp. 90n, Map of Nigeria, simulated stamp. 120n, Map of Nigeria, years "1874" and "2005." 150n, Nigeria #118, 746, vert.

2005, Oct. 9 ***Perf. 13x12¾, 12¾x13***

773-776 A234 Set of 4 6.50 6.50

World Summit on the Information Society, Tunis — A235

Summit emblems, globe and: 20n, Nigeria Post emblem. 50n, Postman on motorcycle, vert. 120n, Like 20n.

Perf. 13x12¾, 12¾x13

2005, Nov. 4 **Litho.**

777-779 A235 Set of 3 3.50 3.50

Writers — A236

Designs: 20n, Prof. Chinua Achebe. 40n, Dr. Abubakar Imam (1911-81). 50n, Prof. Wole Soyinka.

2006, Jan. 18 ***Perf. 13x12¾***

780-782 A236 Set of 3 1.75 1.75

Scholars — A237

Designs: No. 783, 50n, No. 786, 100n, Prof. Ayodele Awojobi (1937-84), engineer. No. 784, 50n, No. 787, 120n, Prof. Gabriel Oyibo, mathematician. No. 785, 50n, No. 788, 150n, Philip Emeagwali, computer scientist.

2006, Jan. 18 ***Perf. 12¾x13***

783-788 A237 Set of 6 8.25 8.25

Dated 2005.

52nd Commonwealth Parliamentary Conference, Abuja — A238

Designs: No. 789, International Conference Center. No. 790, National Assembly Building.

No. 791: a, 20n, Like No. 789 with smaller-sized denomination in green and white. b, 50n, Like No. 790 with denomination in green.

2006, Sept. 4 **Litho.** ***Perf. 13x12¾***

789 A238 20n multi — —
790 A238 50n multi — —

Souvenir Sheet

Imperf

791 A238 Sheet of 2, #a-b — —

Queen Elizabeth II, 80th Birthday — A239

Designs: 20n, Queen at public ceremony, in pink hat. 50n, Queen in pink hat, vert.

2006, Oct. 9 **Litho.** ***Perf. 13***

792-793 A239 Set of 2 1.40 1.40

Agbani Darego, 2001 Miss World — A240

Darego and: 20n, Map of Nigeria. 50n, Map of world, horiz.

2006, Nov. 9

794-795 A240 Set of 2 1.10 1.10

Abuja, 30th Anniv. — A241

Designs: 20n, Gate, fireworks, palm trees, map of Nigeria. 50n, Emblem, hands beating drum, vert.

2006, Dec. 13

796-797 A241 Set of 2 1.10 1.10

143rd Extraordinary Conference of OPEC, Abuja — A242

2006, Dec. 14

798 A242 50n multi .80 .80

The editors have been shown numerous examples of this stamp on cover, but Nigerian postal authorities state that it was issued "strictly for the validation of documents, and not for postage," and that use of the stamp on mail was probably done out of ignorance.

Mungo Park (1771-1806), Explorer — A243

Park and: 20n, Monument. 50n, River, horiz.

2007, Mar. 29 **Litho.** ***Perf. 13***

799-800 A243 Set of 2 1.10 1.10

A244

2007, Mar. 29 **Litho.** ***Perf. 13***

801 A244 50n multi .80 .80
h. Sheet of 2 #801, imperf. — —

Second World Black and African festival of arts and culture, 30th Anniv.

24th UPU Congress — A244a

Ceremonial costumes: No. 801A, Fulani man. No. 801B, Igbo man and woman. No. 801C, South Zone man and woman. No. 801D, Tiv man and woman, horiz. No. 801E, 50n, Yoruba man and woman. No. 801F, North East Zone women.

Perf. 13x12¾, 12¾x13

2007, Oct. 9 **Litho.**

801A A244a 20n multi — —
801B A244a 20n multi — —
801C A244a 30n multi —
801D A244a 30n multi —
801E A244a 50n multi —
801F A244a 50n multi —
g. Souvenir sheet of 6, #801A-801F, imperf. — —

The 24th UPU Congress, scheduled to be held in Nairobi, was moved to Geneva, Switzerland, because of political unrest in Kenya.

A245

Cross river gorilla: 20n, Adult. 50n, Two adults, horiz. 100n, Adult and juvenile, horiz. 150n, Head.

2008, Mar. 26 **Litho.** ***Perf. 13***

802-805 A245 Set of 4 5.00 5.00

Worldwide Fund for Nature (WWF).

A246

Designs: 20n, Hands, money. 50n, Campaign to end violation of 419 law. 100n, Clasped hands.

2008, Apr. 10

806-808 A246 Set of 3 3.00 3.00
808a Souvenir sheet of 3, #806-808, imperf. — —

Economic & Financial Crimes Commission anti-corruption campaign.

Nos. 806-809 exist without printer's imprint. Their issue status is uncertain. Value, set $110.

2008 Summer Olympics, Beijing — A247

Designs: 20n, Runners at finish line. 50n, Soccer. 100n, Wrestling, vert.

2008, Aug. 8

809-811 A247 Set of 3 3.00 3.00

Federal Road Safety Commission, 20th Anniv. — A247a — 811A

2008, Nov. 13 **Litho.** ***Perf. 13***

811A A247a 50n multi 1.25 1.00

Nigerian Institute of Advanced Legal Studies — A248

2009, Sept. 4 **Litho.** ***Perf. 13***

812 A248 50n multi .65 .65

Pan-African Postal Union, 30th Anniv. — A248a

2010, Jan. 8 **Litho.** ***Perf. 13x12¾***

812A A248a 50n multi 1.00 1.00

Dated 2009.

Return to Democracy, 10th Anniv. — A249

Designs: No. 813, 50n, Nigerian flag, Pres. Umaru Musa Yar'Adua. No. 814, 50n, Mace, scales of justice, barrister's wig, vert.

Perf. 13x12¾, 12¾x13

2010, Apr. 6 **Litho.**

813-814 A249 Set of 2 1.75 1.75

Dated 2009.

GT Bank, 20th Anniv. — A250

Woman, globe, 20th anniversary emblem, bank emblem and background color of: 20n, Red. 50n, Gray. 100n, Pale yellow. 120n, Gray green.

2010, July 14 **Litho.** ***Perf. 13x12¾***

815-818 A250 Set of 4 5.50 5.50

Organization of Petroleum Exporting Countries, 50th Anniv. — A251

Designs: 50n, Oil droplet, 50th anniversary emblem. 120n, 50th anniversary emblem.

2010, Aug. 12 **Litho.** ***Perf. 12¾x13***

819-820 A251 Set of 2 3.00 3.00

A252

A252a

2010 World Cup Soccer Championships, South Africa — A252b

Design: 20n, Two soccer players and ball. 30n, Soccer ball, globe, World Cup, vert. 50n, Soccer players and stadium.

2010 ***Perf. 13x12¾, 12¾x13***

821	A252	20n	multi	.50	—
821A	A252a	30n	multi	1.00	—
821B	A252b	50n	multi	1.75	—

Terracotta Head — A253

Terracotta Head — A253a

Terracotta Head — A253b

Bronze Bowl — A254

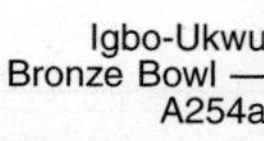

Igbo-Ukwu Bronze Bowl — A254a

Igbo-Ukwu Bronze Bowl — A254b

Slave Chain A255

Lander Brothers Anchorage A256

Lander Brothers Anchorage — A256a

Nok Terracotta Head A257

Monkey Colony, Lagwa-Mbaise A258

Lander Brothers Anchorage — A258a

Elephants, Yankari Game Reserve — A258b

Argungu Fishing Festival, Kebbi State A259

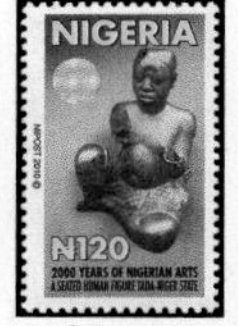
Seated Human Figurine A260

Lander Brothers Anchorage — A260a

Perf. 12¼x12½, 13 (Nos. 822A, 823A, 825A, 826, 827, 828), 12½x12¼ (Nos. 823B, 827A)

Litho. With Hologram Applied

2010-11

822	A253	20n	multi	.75	—
822A	A253a	20n	multi	—	—
822B	A253b	20n	multi	—	—
823	A254	30n	multi	—	—
823A	A254a	30n	multi	—	—
823B	A254b	30n	multi	—	—
824	A255	50n	multi	—	—
825	A256	50n	multi	—	—
825A	A256a	50n	multi	—	—
826	A257	50n	multi	—	—
827	A258	50n	multi	—	—
827A	A258a	50n	multi (round hologram)	—	—
827B	A258b	90n	multi	—	—
828	A259	100n	multi		4.00
829	A260	120n	multi	3.50	—

Litho.

Perf. 12¾x13

829A	A260a	50n	multi	20.00	20.00

Issued: No. 822A, 823A, 825A, 2011; No. 829A, 2010; others, 10/9/2010. No. 822A is dated 2010. No. 829A is dated 2009. Nos. 822B and 823B are dated 2010.

Independence, 50th Anniv. — A261

Nigerian arms and: 20n, Nigerian flag on pole, man holding pole with British flag, 50th anniv. emblem. 30n, Map and symbols of Nigeria. No. 832, 50n, Four men and Nigerian flag, 50th anniv. emblem, horiz. (77x22mm). No. 833, 50n, Photographs of Nigerian crops and industries, 50th anniv. emblem, horiz. (53x37mm).

Perf. 13, 13¼ (#832), 13¼x13 (#833)

2010 **Litho.**

830-833	A261	Set of 4	3.50	3.50

Federal Inland Revenue Service — A262

Emblem of Federal Inland Revenue Service and: 20n, Heart, map of Nigeria. 50n, Light bulb, water faucet. 100n, Taxcard.

2011 **Litho.** ***Perf. 13***

834	A262	20n	multi	.75	—
835	A262	50n	multi	1.25	—
836	A262	100n	multi	2.50	—

Dated 2009.

Benue State — A263

Map of Benue State and: 20n, Gugur Waterfall. 30n, Food basket. 50n, Senator Joseph Sawuan Tarka (1932-80). 100n, Benue Bridge.

2011 **Litho.** ***Perf. 13***

837-840	A263	Set of 4	4.50	4.50
840a		Souvenir sheet of 4, #837-840, imperf.	*14.00*	*14.00*

Nigerian Institute of Management, 50th Anniv. — A264

2011, Sept. 27

841	A264	50n	multi	1.00	1.00
a.		Souvenir sheet of 1, imperf.		—	—

Phila Africa 2012 Stamp Exhibition — A265

2012, Jan. 31

842	A265	50n	multi	1.00	1.00

An imperforate souvenir sheet of 1 sold for 400n.

Enugu, Cent. (in 2009) — A266

2012, Sept. 27 **Litho.** ***Perf. 12¾x13***

843	A266	50n	multi	—	—

Ahmadu Bello University, Zaria, 50th Anniv. — A267

50th Anniv. emblem and: Nos. 844, 848, Sir Ahmadu Bello (1910-66), Premier of Northern Nigeria. Nos. 845, 849, Ahmadu Bello University Senate Building, horiz. 90n, University crest. 120n, Shika brown chickens, horiz.

Litho. With Hologram Applied

2012, Nov. 24 ***Perf. 13***

844	A267	50n	multi	—	—
845	A267	50n	multi	—	—
846	A267	90n	multi	—	—
847	A267	120n	multi	—	—

Litho.

Perf. 13¼x14

Booklet Stamps

848	A267	50n	multi	—	—
849	A267	50n	multi	—	—
850	A267	90n	multi	—	—
851	A267	120n	multi	—	—
a.		Booklet pane of 4, #848-851		—	—
		Complete booklet, 3 #851a		—	

Diplomatic Relations Between Nigeria and Philippines, 50th Anniv. — A268

Flags of Philippines and Nigeria and: 50n, Coat of arms of Nigeria, daisy. 120n, Coat of arms of Philippines, sampaguita.

Litho. With Hologram Applied

2013, Dec. 24 ***Perf. 12¾x13¼***

853	A268	50n	multi	—	—
854	A268	120n	multi	—	—

See Philippines No. 3511.

Civilian Leaders of Nigerians A269

Designs: Nos. 855, 862a, 50n, Nnamdi Azikwe (1904-96), President and Governor-General. Nos. 856, 862b, 50n, Sir Abubakar Tafawa Balewa (1912-96), Prime Minister. Nos. 857, 862c, 50n, Alhajlaliyu Shehu Shagari, President. Nos. 858, 862d, 50n, Goodluck Ebele Jonathan, President. Nos. 859, 862e, 50n, Ernest Shonekan, President. Nos. 860, 862f, 50n, Olusegun Obasanjo, President. Nos. 861, 862g, 50n, Umaru Musa Yar'Adua (1951-2010), President.

Litho. With Hologram

2014, Nov. 27 ***Perf. 13½***

855-861	A269	Set of 7	—	—

Souvenir Sheet

Litho.

Imperf

862	A269	Sheet of 7, #a-g	—	—

Nigeria, Cent. — A270

Designs: Nos. 863, 867a, 50n, Fist, map of Nigeria. Nos. 864, 867b, 50n, People lifting map of Nigeria. Nos. 865, 867c, 100n, Chief Obafemi Awolowo (1909-87), Sir Ahmadu Bello (1910-66), Dr. Nnamdi Azikwe (1904-96). Nos, 866, 867d, 120n, Sir Frederick Lord Lugard (1858-1945), colonial administrator.

Litho. With Hologram

2014 ***Perf. 14***

863-866	A270	Set of 4	—	—

Souvenir Sheet

Litho.

Imperf

867	A270	Sheet of 4, #a-d	—	—

Famous Nigerian Buildings — A271

Designs: Nos. 868, 874a, 50n, Amalgamation House, Calabar. Nos. 869, 874b, 50n, Lord Lugard Court, Lokoja. Nos. 870, 874c, 50n, Seat of Administration of Lord Lugar (now Kogi State Government House), Lokoja. Nos. 871, 874d, 50n, National Assembly, Abuja, Nigeria #97. Nos. 872, 874e, 50n, Supreme Court, Abuja, Nigeria #98. Nos. 873, 874f, 50n, State House, Marina, Lagos, Presidential Villa, Abuja.

Litho. With Hologram

2014 ***Perf. 13½x13¾***

868-873 A271 Set of 6 — —

Souvenir Sheet

Litho.

Imperf

874 A271 Sheet of 6, #a-f — —

Nigeria, cent.

Economic Community of West African States (ECOWAS), 40th Anniv. — A272

2015, May 28 **Litho.** ***Perf. 13x13¼***

875 A272 50n multi — —

No. 875 comes in sheets of 25.

University of Nigeria, 55th Anniv. — A273

Designs: No. 876, 50n, University crest, emblem of West African University Games. No. 877, 50n, Prof. Benjamin C. Ozumba, University Vice-Chancellor, university crest and games emblem. 100n, Dr. George M. Johnson, first Vice-Chancellor, university crest and games emblem. 120n, Dr. Nnamdi Azikwe, founder, university crest and games emblem.

2015, Oct. 23 **Litho.** ***Perf. 14x13½***

876-879 A273 Set of 4 — —

879a Souvenir sheet of 4, #876-879, imperf. — —

University of Nigeria, host of 2015 West African University Games.

University of Nigeria Type of 2015

Designs: No. 879B, 50n, Like #876. No. 879C, 50n, Like #877. No. 879D, 100n, Like #878. No. 879E, 120n, Like #879.

Litho. With Hologram Affixed

2015, Oct. 23 ***Perf. 14x13½***

879B-879E A273 Set of 4 — —

Anti-Corruption Campaign A274

Inscriptions: No. 880, 50n, Say no to theft. No. 881, 50n, Say no to bunkering. No. 882, 50n, Say no to fraud. No. 883, 50n, Say no to bribery.

Litho. With Hologram

2016, Nov. 7 ***Perf. 12½x13¼***

880-883 A274 Set of 4 — —

883a Souvenir sheet of 4, #880-883 — —

Rivers State, 50th Anniv. — A275

Designs: Nos. 884, 888, 50n, Old Brick House, Port Harcourt. Nos. 885, 889, 50n, Aquatic resources of Rivers State. Nos. 886, 890, 50n, Point Block, Port Harcourt. Nos. 887, 891, 50n, Woman carrying basket on head, vert.

2018 **Litho.** ***Rouletted 6¾***

884-887 A275 Set of 4 — —

Perf. 13

888-891 A275 Set of 4 — —

Issued: Nos. 884-887, 5/29; No. 890, 12/6; Nos. 888-889, 891, 12/13.

African Drum Festival, Abeokuta — A276

Emblem and denomination in: 50n, Red (in LL). 100n, Green (in UR).

2019, Apr. 25 **Litho.** ***Perf. 13***

892-893 A276 Set of 2 — —

Mohandas K. Gandhi (1869-1948), Indian Nationalist Leader — A277

Litho. With Hologram Affixed

2019, Oct. 2 ***Perf. 13***

894 A277 100n multi — —

Litho.

Size: 45x33mm

Without Hologram

Perf. 10¾

895 A277 100n multi — —

Souvenir Sheet

Without Gum

896 A277 100n multi — —

a. Imperf. — —

No. 896 contains one 71x47mm stamp. No. 896a has simulated perforations. On Nos. 895 and 896, "N" in denomination lacks horizontal lines.

Sheikh Mujibur Rahman (1920-75), First President of Bangladesh A278

Litho. With Hologram Affixed

2020, Aug. 27 ***Perf. 13½x14***

897 A278 100n multi — —

Without Hologram

897A A278 100n multi — —

Souvenir Sheet

Without Gum

Litho.

Imperf

898 A278 100n multi — —

a. As #898, with windblown flags in sheet margin — —

b. As #898a, perf. 10½ — —

Nos. 898 and 898a contain one 65x47mm stamp with simulated perforations. Flags on sheet margin of No. 898 are not windblown.

Nigerian postal officials have declared as "illegal" items bearing the country name of Nigeria:

Sheets of five stamps depicting Mushrooms, Pope John Paul II.

Sheets of four stamps depicting the 500th anniversary of the Reformation.

30 sheets of four stamps, two stamps or one stamp with Space themes.

24 sheets of four stamps, two stamps or one stamp with Soccer and Olympic themes.

10 sheets of nine stamps depicting 2013 Formula 1 racing cars and drivers.

A279

Independence, 60th Anniv. — A280

2020, Dec. 30 **Litho.** ***Perf. 13***

899 A279 100n multi — —

900 A280 500n multi — —

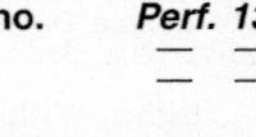

Law Making Abuja Capital of Nigeria, 45th Anniv. — A281

2021, Mar. 18 **Litho.** ***Perf. 13***

901 A281 100n multi — —

Special Agro-Industrial Processing Zones Program — A282

2022, Oct. 24 **Litho.** ***Perf. 13***

902 A282 250n multi — —

SEMI-POSTAL STAMPS

Catalogue values for unused stamps in this section are for Never Hinged items.

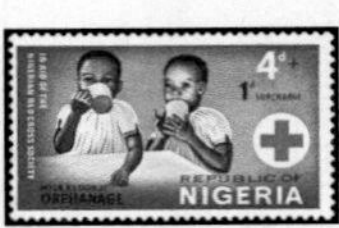

Children Drinking Milk at Orphanage SP1

Designs: 1sh6p+3p, Civilian first aid, vert. 2sh6p+3p, Military first aid.

1966, Dec. 1 **Photo.** ***Perf. 14½x14***

B1	SP1	4p + 1p pur, blk & red	.35	.35
B2	SP1	1sh6p + 3p multi	.80	.80
B3	SP1	2sh6p + 3p multi	1.25	1.25
		Nos. B1-B3 (3)	2.40	2.40

The surtax was for the Nigerian Red Cross.

Dr. Armauer G. Hansen — SP2

1973, July 30 **Litho.** ***Perf. 14***

B4 SP2 5k + 2k blk, brn & buff .50 *1.00*

Centenary of the discovery of the Hansen bacillus, the cause of leprosy. The surtax was for the Nigerian Anti-Leprosy Association.

Nigeria '99, FIFA World Youth Championships SP3

5n+5n, Soccer ball, FIFA emblem. 10n+5n, Throwing ball. 20n+5n, Kicking ball into goal. 30n+5n, Map of Nigeria. 40n+5n, FIFA emblem, eagle, soccer ball. 50n+5n, Tackling.

1999, Mar. 31 **Litho.** ***Perf. 13x14***

B5	SP3	5n +5n multi	.25	.25
B6	SP3	10n +5n multi	.30	.30
B7	SP3	20n +5n multi	.55	.55
B8	SP3	30n +5n multi	.65	.65
B9	SP3	40n +5n multi	.90	.90
B10	SP3	50n +5n multi	1.20	1.20
a.		Souvenir sheet of 6, #B5-B10	3.75	3.75
		Nos. B5-B10 (6)	3.85	3.85

Commissioning of Pan-African Postal Union Tower, Arusha, Tanzania — SP4

No. B12 — Design of No. B11 with red brown rectangular simulated perforations at: a, Bottom and right. b, Bottom and left. c, Top and right. d, Top and left.

2023, Sept. 2 **Litho.** ***Perf. 13***

Stamp With White Frame

B11 SP4 250n+5n multi — —

Stamps With Red Brown Rctangular Simulated Perforations

B12 Block of 4 + 16 surrounding labels — —

a.-d. SP4 250n+5n Any single — —

POSTAGE DUE STAMPS

Catalogue values for unused stamps in this section are for Never Hinged items.

D1

Perf. 14½x14

1959, Jan. 4 **Wmk. 4** **Litho.**

J1	D1	1p orange	.25	*1.00*
J2	D1	2p orange	.25	*1.25*
J3	D1	3p orange	.25	*1.75*
J4	D1	6p orange	.80	*6.25*
J5	D1	1sh black	1.25	*11.00*
		Nos. J1-J5 (5)	2.80	*21.25*

1961, Aug. 1 **Wmk. 335**

J6	D1	1p red	.25	*.40*
J7	D1	2p blue	.25	*.50*
J8	D1	3p emerald	.25	*.75*
J9	D1	6p yellow	.25	*2.00*
J10	D1	1sh dark blue	.40	*4.00*
		Nos. J6-J10 (5)	1.40	*7.65*

D2

Perf. 12½x13½

1973, May 3 **Litho.** **Unwmk.**

J11	D2	2k red	.25	.25
J12	D2	3k blue	.25	.25
J13	D2	5k orange	.25	.25
J14	D2	10k yellow green	.25	.25
		Nos. J11-J14 (4)	1.00	1.00

1987-94 ***Rouletted 9***

J15	D2	2k red	1.75	*2.50*
J16	D2	5k yellow	4.50	*5.00*
J17	D2	10k green	9.00	*10.00*
		Nos. J15-J17 (3)	15.25	*17.50*

D3

2004 **Litho.** ***Perf. 12¾***

J18	D3	20n yel green	*.75*	—
J19	D3	40n red	*.95*	—

NIUE

nē-ˈü-ˌā

LOCATION — Island in the south Pacific Ocean, northeast of New Zealand
GOVT. — Self-government, in free association with New Zealand
AREA — 100 sq. mi.
POP. — 1,708 (1997 est.)
CAPITAL — Alofi

Niue, also known as Savage Island, was annexed to New Zealand in 1901 with the Cook Islands. Niue achieved internal self-government in 1974.

12 Pence = 1 Shilling
20 Shillings = 1 Pound
100 Cents = 1 Dollar (1967)

Catalogue values for unused stamps in this country are for Never Hinged items, beginning with Scott 90 in the regular postage section, Scott B1 in the semi-postal section, Scott C1 in the air post section, and Scott O1 in the officials section.

Watermarks

Wmk. 61 — Single-lined NZ and Star Close Together

Wmk. 253 — NZ and Star

New Zealand No. 100 Handstamped in Green

1902 Wmk. 63 *Perf. 11*
Thick Soft Paper

No.	Type	Description	Unused	Used
1	A35	1p carmine	350.00	350.00

Stamps of New Zealand Surcharged in Carmine, Vermilion or Blue

1/2p

1p

2 1/2p

Perf. 14
Thin Hard Paper

No.	Type	Description	Unused	Used
3	A18	½p green (C)	8.50	*11.00*
a.		Inverted surcharge	375.00	*700.00*
b.		Double surcharge	1,400.	
4	A35	1p carmine (Bl), perf. 11x14	2.00	*5.00*
a.		No period after "PENI"	62.50	*80.00*
b.		Perf. 14	57.50	*62.50*
c.		As "a," perf. 14	600.00	700.00

Perf. 14
Wmk. 61

No.	Type	Description	Unused	Used
6	A18	½p green (V)	2.00	2.00
7	A35	1p carmine (Bl)	1.25	2.00
a.		No period after "PENI"	*10.00*	*21.00*
b.		Double surcharge	*2,000.*	*2,300.*

Perf. 11
Unwmk.

No.	Type	Description	Unused	Used
8	A22	2½p blue (C)	2.20	*7.00*
a.		No period after "PENI"	35.00	*75.00*
b.		Double surcharge	*2,000.*	*2,300.*

The surcharge on the ½ & 1p stamps is printed in blocks of 60. Two stamps in each block have a space between the "U" and "E" of "NIUE" and one of the 1p stamps has a broken "E" like an "F."

The 2½p blue stamp with surcharge in vermilion, formerly listed as No. 9, has been deleted, along with Nos. 9a and 9b. The editors are seeking evidence of its existence.

Blue Surcharge on Stamps of New Zealand, Types of 1898

e

f

g

h

1903 Wmk. 61 *Perf. 11*

No.	Type	Description	Unused	Used
10	A23(e)	3p yellow brown	11.00	5.50
11	A26(f)	6p rose	15.00	12.50
13	A29(g)	1sh brown red	40.00	*50.00*
a.		1sh scarlet	40.00	*50.00*
b.		1sh orange red	50.00	*52.50*
c.		As "b," surcharge "h" (error)	750.00	
		Nos. 10-13 (3)	66.00	*68.00*

Surcharged in Carmine or Blue on Stamps of New Zealand — j

1911-12 *Perf. 14, 14x14½*

No.	Type	Description	Unused	Used
14	A41(j)	½p yellow grn (C)	1.00	1.00
15	A41(f)	6p car rose (Bl)	2.50	*7.50*
16	A41(g)	1sh vermilion (Bl)	8.00	*55.00*
		Nos. 14-16 (3)	11.50	*63.50*

1915 *Perf. 14*

No.	Type	Description	Unused	Used
18	A22(d)	2½p dark blue (C)	26.00	*55.00*

Surcharged in Brown or Dark Blue on Stamps of New Zealand

1917 *Perf. 14x15*

No.	Type	Description	Unused	Used
19	A42	1p carmine (Br)	24.00	6.25
a.		No period after "PENI"	950.00	

Perf. 14x14½

No.	Type	Description	Unused	Used
20	A45(e)	3p violet brn (Bl)	55.00	125.00
a.		No period after "Pene"	950.00	
b.		Perf. 14x13½	75.00	150.00
c.		Vert. pair, #20 & 20b	225.00	

New Zealand Stamps of 1909-19 Overprinted in Dark Blue or Red — k

1917-20 Typo. *Perf. 14x15*

No.	Type	Description	Unused	Used
21	A43	½p yellow grn (R)	.80	*3.25*
22	A42	1p carmine (Bl)	11.00	*17.50*
23	A47	1½p gray black (R)	1.10	*3.25*
24	A47	1½p brown org (R)	1.00	*10.00*
25	A43	3p chocolate (Bl)	1.60	*40.00*

Engr.
Perf. 14x14½

No.	Type	Description	Unused	Used
26	A44	2½p dull blue (R)	1.50	*19.00*
a.		Perf. 14x13½	5.75	*22.50*
b.		Vert. pair, #26-26a	19.00	*72.50*
27	A45	3p violet brown (Bl)	1.75	*3.00*
a.		Perf. 14x13½	4.25	3.00
b.		Vert. pair, #27-27a	25.00	*50.00*
28	A45	6p car rose (Bl)	6.00	*26.00*
a.		Perf. 14x13½	12.50	*25.00*
b.		Vert. pair, #28-28a	32.50	*125.00*
29	A45	1sh vermilion (Bl)	6.00	*30.00*
a.		Perf. 14x13½	20.00	*42.50*
b.		Vert. pair, #29-29a	47.50	*135.00*
		Nos. 21-29 (9)	30.75	*152.00*

Same Overprint On Postal-Fiscal Stamps of New Zealand, 1906-15
Perf. 14, 14½ and Compound

1918-23

No.	Type	Description	Unused	Used
30	PF1	2sh blue (R)	18.00	*35.00*
31	PF1	2sh6p bn (Bl) ('23)	24.00	*55.00*
32	PF1	5sh green (R)	32.50	*67.50*
a.		Perf. 14	115.00	*125.00*
b.		Perf. 14½x14 ('29)	27.50	*60.00*
33	PF1	10sh red brn (Bl) ('23)	150.00	*185.00*
a.		Perf. 14½x14 ('27)	100.00	*165.00*
34	PF2	£1 rose (Bl) ('23)	185.00	*275.00*
a.		Perf. 14½x14 ('28)	165.00	*300.00*
		Nos. 30-34 (5)	409.50	*617.50*

Nos. 32b, 33a and 34a come on thick paper and in different color varieties.

Landing of Captain Cook A16

Avarua Waterfront A17

Capt. James Cook A18

Coconut Palm A19

Arorangi Village — A20

Avarua Harbor — A21

Unwmk.

1920, Aug. 23 Engr. *Perf. 14*

No.	Type	Description	Unused	Used
35	A16	½p yel grn & blk	4.25	*4.75*
36	A17	1p car & black	2.25	1.40
37	A18	1½p red & black	3.50	*18.00*
38	A19	3p pale blue & blk	2.50	*17.50*
39	A20	6p dp grn & red brn	6.25	*19.00*
a.		Center inverted	*1,000.*	
40	A21	1sh blk brn & blk	9.00	*19.00*
		Nos. 35-40 (6)	27.75	*79.65*

See Nos. 41-42. For surcharge see No. 48.

Types of 1920 Issue and

Rarotongan Chief (Te Po) — A22

Avarua Harbor — A23

1925-27 Wmk. 61

No.	Type	Description	Unused	Used
41	A16	½p yel grn & blk ('26)	4.00	*13.00*
42	A17	1p car & black	1.75	1.00
43	A22	2½p dk blue & blk ('27)	6.50	*16.00*
44	A23	4p dull vio & blk ('27)	12.50	*22.50*
		Nos. 41-44 (4)	24.75	*52.50*

New Zealand No. 182 Overprinted Type "k" in Red

1927

No.	Type	Description	Unused	Used
47	A56	2sh blue	18.00	*35.00*
a.		2sh dark blue	17.00	*50.00*

No. 37 Surcharged

1931 Unwmk. *Perf. 14*

No.	Type	Description	Unused	Used
48	A18	2p on 1½p red & blk	5.25	1.50

New Zealand Postal-Fiscal Stamps of 1931-32 Overprinted Type "k" in Blue or Red

1931, Nov. 12 Wmk. 61

No.	Type	Description	Unused	Used
49	PF5	2sh6p deep brown	4.50	*12.00*
50	PF5	5sh green (R)	40.00	*80.00*
51	PF5	10sh dark car	45.00	*130.00*
52	PF5	£1 pink ('32)	90.00	*180.00*
		Nos. 49-52 (4)	179.50	*402.00*

See Nos. 86-89D, 116-119.

Landing of Captain Cook A24

Capt. James Cook A25

Polynesian Migratory Canoe — A26

Islanders Unloading Ship — A27

View of Avarua Harbor A28

R.M.S. Monowai A29

King George V — A30

Perf. 13, 14 (4p, 1sh)

1932, Mar. 16 Engr. Unwmk.

No.	Type	Description	Unused	Used
53	A24	½p yel grn & blk	14.00	*25.00*
a.		Perf. 13x14x13x13	275.00	
54	A25	1p dp red & blk	1.10	1.25
55	A26	2p org brn & blk	8.50	*5.75*
a.		Perf. 14x13x13x13	150.00	*210.00*
56	A27	2½p indigo & blk	8.50	*80.00*
a.		Center inverted	325.00	
57	A28	4p Prus blue & blk	19.00	*70.00*
a.		Perf. 13	17.00	*72.50*
58	A29	6p dp org & blk	3.25	2.50
59	A30	1sh dull vio & blk	4.75	*7.25*
		Nos. 53-59 (7)	59.10	*191.75*

For types overprinted see Nos. 67-69.

1932-36 Wmk. 61 *Perf. 14*

No.	Type	Description	Unused	Used
60	A24	½p yel grn & blk	.50	*3.50*
61	A25	1p deep red & blk	.50	*2.25*
62	A26	2p brown & blk ('36)	.75	*1.75*
63	A27	2½p indigo & blk	.75	*4.50*
64	A28	4p Prus blue & blk	1.75	*4.50*
65	A29	6p org & blk ('36)	1.50	*.75*
66	A30	1sh dk vio & blk ('36)	12.50	*27.50*
		Nos. 60-66 (7)	18.25	*44.75*

See Nos. 77-82.

Silver Jubilee Issue

Types of 1932 Overprinted in Black or Red

1935, May 7 *Perf. 14*

No.	Type	Description	Unused	Used
67	A25	1p car & brown red	1.00	*3.50*
68	A27	2½p indigo & bl (R)	5.75	*15.00*
a.		Vert. pair, imperf. horiz.	200.00	
69	A29	6p dull org & dark grn	12.50	*12.50*
		Nos. 67-69 (3)	19.25	*31.00*
		Set, never hinged	22.50	

The vertical spacing of the overprint is wider on No. 69.

No. 68a is from proof sheets.

Coronation Issue

New Zealand Stamps of 1937 Overprinted in Black

Perf. 13½x13

1937, May 13 **Wmk. 253**

70 A78 1p rose carmine .30 .25
71 A78 2½p dark blue .30 *1.50*
72 A78 6p vermilion .30 .30
Nos. 70-72 (3) .90 *2.05*
Set, never hinged 1.00

George VI A31

Village Scene A32

Coastal Scene with Canoe — A33

1938, May 2 **Wmk. 61** ***Perf. 14***

73 A31 1sh dp violet & blk 6.00 *10.00*
74 A32 2sh dk red brown & blk 7.75 *22.50*
75 A33 3sh yel green & blue 22.50 *22.50*
Nos. 73-75 (3) 36.25 *55.00*
Set, never hinged 67.50

See Nos. 83-85.

Mt. Ikurangi behind Avarua — A34

Perf. 13½x14

1940, Sept. 2 **Engr.** **Wmk. 253**

76 A34 3p on 1½p rose vio & blk .45 .75
Never hinged .75

Examples without surcharge are from printer's archives. Value, $250 unused.

See Cook Islands No. 115.

Types of 1932-38

1944-46 **Wmk. 253** ***Perf. 14***

77 A24 ½p yel grn & blk .40 *6.50*
78 A25 1p dp red & blk ('45) .40 *4.75*
79 A26 2p org brn & blk ('46) 3.75 *15.00*
80 A27 2½p dk bl & blk ('45) .50 *3.75*
81 A28 4p Prus blue & blk 2.75 1.25
82 A29 6p dp orange & blk 1.40 1.75
83 A31 1sh dp vio & blk .85 2.00
84 A32 2sh brn car & blk ('45) 8.50 6.75
85 A33 3sh yel grn & bl ('45) 11.00 15.00
Nos. 77-85 (9) 29.55 56.75
Set, never hinged 45.00

New Zealand Postal-Fiscal Stamps Overprinted (narrow "E") in Blue or Red

1941-45 **Wmk. 61** ***Perf. 14***

86 PF5 2sh6p brown 65.00 *125.00*
87 PF5 5sh green (R) 140.00 *450.00*
88 PF5 10sh rose 85.00 *600.00*
89 PF5 £1 pink 125.00 *750.00*
Nos. 86-89 (4) 415.00 *1,925.*
Set, never hinged 850.00

Wmk. 253

89A PF5 2sh6p brown 2.75 *11.00*
89B PF5 5sh brt grn (R) 5.50 *19.00*
e. 5sh light yellow green, wmkd. sideways ('67) 10.00 *80.00*
89C PF5 10sh rose 37.50 *135.00*
89D PF5 £1 pink 40.00 *90.00*
Nos. 89A-89D (4) 85.75 *255.00*
Set, never hinged 150.00

No. 89Be exists in both line and comb perf.

Catalogue values for unused stamps in this section, from this point to the end of the section, are for Never Hinged items.

Peace Issue

New Zealand Nos. 248, 250, 254 and 255 Overprinted in Black or Blue

p

q

1946, June 4 ***Perf. 13x13½, 13½x13***

90 A94 (p) 1p emerald .40 .35
91 A96 (q) 2p rose violet (Bl) .40 .35
92 A100 (p) 6p org red & red brn .40 *.75*
93 A101 (p) 8p brn lake & blk (Bl) .50 *.75*
Nos. 90-93 (4) 1.70 *2.20*

Map of Niue A35

H.M.S. Resolution A36

Designs: 2p, Alofi landing. 3p, Thatched Dwelling. 4p, Arch at Hikutavake. 6p, Alofi bay. 9p, Fisherman. 1sh, Cave at Makefu. 2sh, Gathering bananas. 3sh, Matapa Chasm.

Perf. 14x13½, 13½x14

1950, July 3 **Engr.** **Wmk. 253**

94 A35 ½p red orange & bl .30 *2.25*
95 A36 1p green & brown 2.25 *3.25*
96 A36 2p red & blk 1.25 *3.25*
97 A36 3p blue vio & blue .30 .25
98 A36 4p brn vio & ol grn .30 .25
99 A36 6p brn org & bl grn 1.00 *1.25*
100 A35 9p dk brn & brn org .30 *1.40*
101 A36 1sh black & purple .30 .25
102 A35 2sh dp grn & brn org 7.50 *6.25*
103 A35 3sh black & dp blue 6.50 *7.50*
Nos. 94-103 (10) 20.00 *25.90*

For surcharges see Nos. 106-115.

Coronation Issue

Queen Elizabeth II — A36a

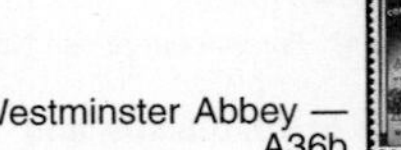

Westminster Abbey — A36b

1953, May 24 **Photo.** ***Perf. 14x14½***

104 A36a 3p brown 1.00 .75
105 A36b 6p slate black 1.25 .75

Nos. 94-103 Surcharged

Perf. 14x13½, 13½x14

1967, July 10 **Engr.** **Wmk. 253**

106 A35 ½c on ½p red org & blue .30 .25
107 A36 1c on 1p green & brn 1.00 .25
108 A36 2c on 2p rose car & blk .30 .25
109 A36 2½c on 3p bl vio & bl .30 .25
110 A36 3c on 4p brn vio & ol grn .30 .25
111 A36 5c on 6p brn org & grn .30 .25
112 A35 8c on 9p dk brn & brn org .30 .25
113 A36 10c on 1sh blk & pur .30 .25
114 A35 20c on 2sh dp grn & brn org .40 *1.25*
115 A35 30c on 3sh blk & dp bl .75 *1.25*
Nos. 106-115 (10) 4.25 4.50

The position of the numeral varies on each denomination. The surcharge on the ½c, 2½c, 8c, 10c and 20c contains one dot only.

New Zealand Arms — A37

Wmk. 253

1967, July 10 **Typo.** ***Perf. 14***

Black Surcharge

116 A37 25c yellow brown .30 .60
117 A37 50c green .75 .85
118 A37 $1 cerise .50 1.25
119 A37 $2 pale pink .50 2.00
Nos. 116-119 (4) 2.05 4.70

1967 ***Perf. 11***

116a A37 25c 6.50 18.50
117a A37 50c 6.50 19.50
118a A37 $1 8.00 13.50
119a A37 $2 9.00 14.50
Nos. 116a-119a (4) 30.00 66.00

The perf. 11 stamps were produced when a normal perforating machine broke down and 2,500 of each denomination were perforated on a treadle machine first used by the N.Z. Post Office in 1899.

Christmas Issues

Adoration of the Shepherds, by Poussin — A37a

Perf. 13½x14

1967, Oct. 3 **Photo.** **Wmk. 253**

120 A37a 2½c multicolored .30 .25

Nativity, by Federico Fiori — A37b

1969, Oct. 1 **Photo.** **Wmk. 253**

121 A37b 2½c multicolored .30 .25

Pua — A38

Flowers (except 20c): 1c, Golden shower. 2c, Flamboyant. 2½c, Frangipani. 3c, Niue crocus. 5c, Hibiscus. 8c, Passion fruit. 10c, Kamapui. 20c, Queen Elizabeth II. 30c, Tapeu orchid.

Perf. 12½x13

1969, Nov. 27 **Litho.** **Unwmk.**

122 A38 ½c green & multi .30 .25
123 A38 1c orange & multi .30 .25
124 A38 2c gray & multi .30 .25
125 A38 2½c bister & multi .30 .25
126 A38 3c blue & multi .30 .25
127 A38 5c ver & multi .30 .25
128 A38 8c violet & multi .30 .25
129 A38 10c yellow & multi .30 .25
130 A38 20c dk blue & multi 1.00 *1.75*
131 A38 30c olive grn & multi 2.00 *2.25*
Nos. 122-131 (10) 5.40 6.00

See Nos. 678.

Edible Crab — A39

Perf. 13½x12½

1969, Aug. 19 **Litho.**

132 A39 3c Kalahimu .30 .25
133 A39 5c Kalavi .30 .25
134 A39 30c Unga .40 .40
Nos. 132-134 (3) 1.00 .90

Christmas Issue

Adoration, by Correggio — A39a

1970, Oct. 1 **Litho.** ***Perf. 12½***

135 A39a 2½c multicolored .30 .25

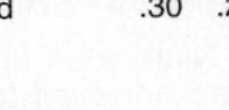

Plane over Outrigger Canoe — A40

Designs: 5c, Plane over ships in harbor. 8c, Civair plane over island.

1970, Dec. 9 **Litho.** ***Perf. 13½***

136 A40 3c multicolored .30 .25
137 A40 5c multicolored .30 .25
138 A40 8c multicolored .30 .30
Nos. 136-138 (3) .90 .80

Opening of Niue Airport.

Polynesian Triller (Heahea) — A41

Birds: 10c, Crimson-crowned fruit pigeon (kulukulu). 20c, Blue-crowned lory (henga).

1971, June 23 **Litho.** ***Perf. 13½x13***

139 A41 5c multicolored .30 .25
140 A41 10c multicolored .50 .25
141 A41 20c multicolored .85 .25
Nos. 139-141 (3) 1.65 .75

Christmas Issue

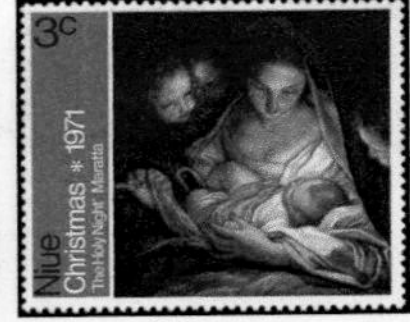

Holy Night, by Carlo Maratta A41a

1971, Oct. 6 **Photo.** ***Perf. 13x13½***

142 A41a 3c orange & multi .35 .25

People of Niue — A42

1971, Nov. 17

143 A42 4c Boy .30 .25
144 A42 6c Girl .30 .25
145 A42 9c Man .30 .35
146 A42 14c Woman .30 .70
Nos. 143-146 (4) 1.20 1.55

Octopus Lure and Octopus — A43

5c, Warrior and weapons. 10c, Sika (spear) throwing, horiz. 25c, Vivi dance, horiz.

1972, May 3 **Litho.** ***Perf. 13x13½***

147 A43 3c blue & multi .30 .25
148 A43 5c rose & multi .30 .25
149 A43 10c blue & multi .30 .25
150 A43 25c yellow & multi .30 .25
Nos. 147-150 (4) 1.20 1.00

So. Pacific Festival of Arts, Fiji, May 6-20.

Alofi Wharf — A44

South Pacific Commission Emblem and: 5c, Health service. 6c, School children. 18c, Cattle and dwarf palms.

1972, Sept. 6 Litho. *Perf. 13½x14*

151	A44	4c blue & multi	.30	.25
152	A44	5c blue & multi	.30	.25
153	A44	6c blue & multi	.30	.25
154	A44	18c blue & multi	.30	.25
		Nos. 151-154 (4)	1.20	1.00

So. Pacific Commission, 25th anniv.

Christmas Issue

Madonna and Child, by Murillo — A44a

1972, Oct. 4 Photo. *Perf. 11½*

155	A44a	3c gray & multi	.30	.25

Pempheris Oualensis — A45

Designs: Various fish.

Perf. 13½x13

1973, June 27 Litho. Unwmk.

156	A45	8c shown	.35	.35
157	A45	10c Cephalopholis	.35	.35
158	A45	15c Variola louti	.40	.40
159	A45	20c Etelis carbunculus	.45	.45
		Nos. 156-159 (4)	1.55	1.55

Flowers, by Jan Breughel — A46

Paintings of Flowers: 5c, by Hans Bollongier. 10c, by Rachel Ruysch.

1973, Nov. 21 Litho. *Perf. 13½x13*

160	A46	4c bister & multi	.30	.25
161	A46	5c orange brn & multi	.30	.25
162	A46	10c emerald & multi	.30	.25
		Nos. 160-162 (3)	.90	.75

Christmas.

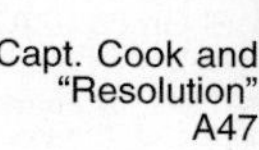

Capt. Cook and "Resolution" A47

Capt. Cook and: 3c, Cook's landing place and ship. 8c, Map of Niue. 20c, Administration Building and flag of 1774.

1974, June 20 Litho. *Perf. 13½x14*

163	A47	2c multicolored	.30	.25
164	A47	3c multicolored	.30	.25
165	A47	8c multicolored	.30	.30
166	A47	20c multicolored	.35	.55
		Nos. 163-166 (4)	1.25	1.35

Bicentenary of Cook's landing on Niue.

King Fataaiki A48

Annexation Day, Oct. 19, 1900 A49

Village Meeting — A50

Design: 10c, Legislative Assembly Building.

Perf. 14x13½, 13½x14

1974, Oct. 19 Litho.

167	A48	4c multicolored	.30	.25
168	A49	8c multicolored	.30	.25
169	A50	10c multicolored	.30	.25
170	A50	20c multicolored	.30	.25
		Nos. 167-170 (4)	1.20	1.00

Referendum for Self-government, 9/3/74.

Decorated Bicycle — A51

Christmas: 10c, Decorated motorcycle. 20c, Going to church by truck.

1974, Nov. 13 Litho. *Perf. 12½*

171	A51	3c green & multi	.30	.25
172	A51	10c dull blue & multi	.30	.25
173	A51	20c brown & multi	.30	.25
		Nos. 171-173 (3)	.90	.75

Children Going to Church — A52

Children's Drawings: 5c, Child on bicycle trailing balloons. 10c, Balloons and gifts hanging from tree.

1975, Oct. 29 Litho. *Perf. 14½*

174	A52	4c multicolored	.30	.25
175	A52	5c multicolored	.30	.25
176	A52	10c multicolored	.30	.25
		Nos. 174-176 (3)	.90	.75

Christmas.

Opening of Tourist Hotel — A53

Design: 20c, Hotel, building and floor plan.

1975, Nov. 19 Litho. *Perf. 14x13½*

177	A53	8c multicolored	.30	.25
178	A53	20c multicolored	.30	.25

Preparing Ground for Taro — A54

2c, Planting taro (root vegetable). 3c, Banana harvest. 4c, Bush plantation. 5c, Shellfish gathering. 10c, Reef fishing. 20c, Luku (fern) harvest. 50c, Canoe fishing. $1, Husking coconuts. $2, Hunting uga (land crab).

1976, Mar. 3 Litho. *Perf. 13½x14*

179	A54	1c multicolored	.30	.25
180	A54	2c multicolored	.30	.25
181	A54	3c multicolored	.30	.25
182	A54	4c multicolored	.30	.25
183	A54	5c multicolored	.30	.25
184	A54	10c multicolored	.30	.25
185	A54	20c multicolored	.30	.25
186	A54	50c multicolored	.30	.50
187	A54	$1 multicolored	.30	.75
188	A54	$2 multicolored	.75	1.00
		Nos. 179-188 (10)	3.45	4.00

See #222-231. For surcharges see #203-210.

Water Tower, Girl Drawing Water — A55

15c, Teleprinter & Niue radio station. 20c, Instrument panel, generator & power station.

1976, July 7 Litho. *Perf. 14x14½*

189	A55	10c multicolored	.30	.25
190	A55	15c multicolored	.30	.25
191	A55	20c multicolored	.30	.25
		Nos. 189-191 (3)	.90	.75

Technical achievements.

Christmas Tree (Flamboyant) and Administration Building — A56

Christmas: 15c, Avatele Church, interior.

1976, Sept. 15 Litho. *Perf. 14½*

192	A56	9c orange & multi	.30	.25
193	A56	15c orange & multi	.30	.25

Elizabeth II, Coronation Portrait, and Westminster Abbey A57

Design: $2, Coronation regalia.

1977, June 7 Photo. *Perf. 13½*

194	A57	$1 multicolored	.50	.50
195	A57	$2 multicolored	1.25	.75
a.		Souvenir sheet of 2, #194-195	2.00	2.00

25th anniv. of reign of Elizabeth II. Nos. 194-195 each printed in sheets of 5 stamps and label showing Niue flag and Union Jack.

For surcharge see No. 213.

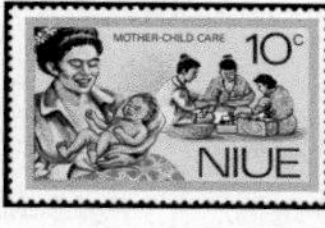

Mothers and Infants — A58

Designs: 15c, Mobile school dental clinic. 20c, Elderly couple and home.

1977, June 29 Litho. *Perf. 14½*

196	A58	10c multicolored	.30	.25
197	A58	15c multicolored	.30	.25
198	A58	20c multicolored	.30	.25
		Nos. 196-198 (3)	.90	.75

Personal (social) services.

For surcharges see Nos. 211-212.

Annunciation, by Rubens — A59

Rubens Paintings (details, Virgin and Child): 12c, Adoration of the Kings. 20c, Virgin with Garland. 35c, Holy Family.

1977, Nov. 15 Photo. *Perf. 13x13½*

199	A59	10c multicolored	.30	.25
200	A59	12c multicolored	.30	.25
201	A59	20c multicolored	.35	.50
202	A59	35c multicolored	.40	.80
a.		Souvenir sheet of 4, #199-202	1.75	1.75
		Nos. 199-202 (4)	1.35	1.80

Christmas and 400th birth anniversary of Peter Paul Rubens (1577-1640). Nos. 199-202 each printed in sheets of 6 stamps.

Stamps of 1976-77 Surcharged with New Value and 4 Bars in Black or Gold

Printing and Perforations as Before

1977, Nov. 15

203	A54	12c on 1c (#179)	.45	.25
204	A54	16c on 2c (#180)	.50	.30
205	A54	30c on 3c (#181)	.50	.40
206	A54	35c on 4c (#182)	.50	.45
207	A54	40c on 5c (#183)	.50	.50
208	A54	60c on 20c (#185)	.50	.50
209	A54	70c on $1 (#187)	.50	.50
210	A54	85c on $2 (#188)	.50	.60
211	A58	$1.10 on 10c (#196)	.50	.60
212	A58	$2.60 on 20c (#198)	.85	.65
213	A57	$3.20 on $2 (#195, G)	1.05	.75
		Nos. 203-213 (11)	6.35	5.50

"An Inland View in Atooi," by John Webber A60

Scenes in Hawaii, by John Webber: 16c, A View of Karakooa in Owyhee. 20c, An Offering Before Capt. Cook in the Sandwich Islands. 30c, Tereoboo, King of Owyhee, bringing presents (boats). 35c, Masked rowers in boat.

1978, Jan. 18 Photo. *Perf. 13½*

214	A60	12c gold & multi	.70	.35
215	A60	16c gold & multi	.75	.40
216	A60	20c gold & multi	.75	.50
217	A60	30c gold & multi	.85	.60
218	A60	35c gold & multi	.90	.65
a.		Souv. sheet, #214-218 + label	4.50	2.75
		Nos. 214-218 (5)	3.95	2.50

Bicentenary of Capt. Cook's arrival in Hawaii. Nos. 214-218 printed in sheets of 5 stamps and one label showing flags of Hawaii and Niue.

Descent from the Cross, by Caravaggio — A61

Easter: 20c, Burial of Christ, by Bellini.

1978, Mar. 15 Photo. *Perf. 13x13½*

219	A61	10c multicolored	.30	.25
220	A61	20c multicolored	.35	.25
a.		Souv. sheet, #219-220, perf. 13½	1.00	1.00

Nos. 219-220 issued in sheets of 8.

See Nos. B1-B2.

Souvenir Sheet

Elizabeth II — A62

1978, June 26 Photo. *Perf. 13*

221	A62	Sheet of 6	3.00	3.00
a.		$1.10 Niue and UK flags	.50	.75
b.		$1.10 shown	.50	.75
c.		$1.10 Queen's New Zealand flag	.50	.75
d.		Souvenir sheet of 3	2.25	2.25

25th anniv. of coronation of Elizabeth II. No. 221 contains 2 horizontal se-tenant strips of Nos. 221a-221c, separated by horizontal gutter showing coronation coach. No. 221d contains a vertical se-tenant strip of Nos. 221a-221c.

Type of 1977

12c, Preparing ground for taro. 16c, Planting taro. 30c, Banana harvest. 35c, Bush plantation. 40c, Shellfish gathering. 60c, Reef fishing. 75c, Luku (fern) harvest. $1.10, Canoe fishing. $3.20, Husking coconuts. $4.20, Hunting uga (land crab).

1978, Oct. 27 Litho. *Perf. 14*

222	A54	12c multicolored	.30	.25
223	A54	16c multicolored	.30	.25
224	A54	30c multicolored	.30	.25
225	A54	35c multicolored	.30	.25
226	A54	40c multicolored	.30	.25
227	A54	60c multicolored	.30	.35
228	A54	75c multicolored	.35	.40

229	A54	$1.10 multicolored	.45	.50
230	A54	$3.20 multicolored	1.25	1.50
231	A54	$4.20 multicolored	1.90	2.25
		Nos. 222-231 (10)	5.75	6.25

Celebration of the Rosary, by Dürer — A63

Designs: 30c, Nativity, by Dürer. 35c, Adoration of the Kings, by Dürer.

1978, Nov. 30 Photo. *Perf. 13*

232	A63	20c multicolored	.30	.30
233	A63	30c multicolored	.45	.45
234	A63	35c multicolored	.50	.50
a.		Souv. sheet, #232-234 + label	1.60	1.60
		Nos. 232-234 (3)	1.25	1.25

Christmas and 450th death anniversary of Albrecht Dürer (1471-1528). Nos. 232-234 each printed in sheets of 5 stamps and descriptive label.

See Nos. B3-B5.

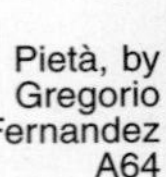

Pietà, by Gregorio Fernandez A64

Easter: 35c, Burial of Christ, by Pedro Roldan.

1979, Apr. 2

235	A64	30c multicolored	.35	.35
236	A64	35c multicolored	.40	.40
a.		Souvenir sheet of 2, #235-236	1.50	1.50

See Nos. B6-B7.

Child, by Franz Hals — A65

IYC (Emblem and Details from Paintings): 16c, Nurse and Child. 20c, Child of the Duke of Osuna, by Goya. 30c, Daughter of Robert Strozzi, by Titian. 35c, Children Eating Fruit, by Murillo.

1979, May 31 Photo. *Perf. 14*

237	A65	16c multicolored	*.30*	.25
238	A65	20c multicolored	.35	.35
239	A65	30c multicolored	.40	.40
240	A65	35c multicolored	.50	.50
a.		Souvenir sheet of 4, #237-240	2.10	2.10
		Nos. 237-240 (4)	1.55	1.50

See Nos. B8-B11.

Penny Black, Bath Mail Coach, Rowland Hill A66

30c, Basel #3L1 & Alpine village coach. 35c, US #1 & 1st US transatlantic mail ship. 50c, France #3 & French railroad mail car, 1849. 60c, Bavaria #1 & Bavarian mail coach.

1979, July 3 Photo. *Perf. 14*

241	A66	20c Pair, #a.-b.	.40	.40
242	A66	30c Pair, #a.-b.	.55	.55
243	A66	35c Pair, #a.-b.	.65	.65
244	A66	50c Pair, #a.-b.	1.00	1.00
245	A66	60c Pair, #a.-b.	1.10	1.10
c.		Souv. sheet of 10, #241-245 + 2 labels	4.25	4.25
		Nos. 241-245 (5)	3.70	3.70

Sir Rowland Hill (1795-1879), originator of penny postage.

For overprints and surcharges see Nos. 281-285, B16, B21, B26, B30, B33, B41.

Cook's Landing at Botany Bay — A68

18th Century Paintings: 30c, Cook's Men during a Landing on Erromanga. 35c, Resolution and Discovery in Queen Charlotte's Sound. 75c, Death of Capt. Cook on Hawaii, by Johann Zoffany.

1979, July 30 Photo. *Perf. 14*

251	A68	20c multicolored	.65	.30
252	A68	30c multicolored	.85	.40
253	A68	35c multicolored	1.10	.50
254	A68	75c multicolored	1.10	.90
a.		Souv. sheet, #251-254, perf. 13½	3.75	3.75
		Nos. 251-254 (4)	3.70	2.10

200th death anniv. of Capt. James Cook.

For surcharges see Nos. B18, B23, B28, B36.

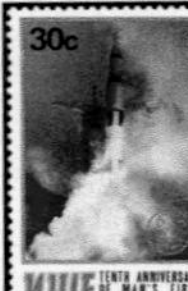

Apollo 11 Lift-off — A69

1979, Sept. 27 Photo. *Perf. 13½*

255	A69	30c shown	.35	.35
256	A69	35c Lunar module	.40	.40
257	A69	60c Splashdown	.70	.70
a.		Souvenir sheet of 3	1.90	1.90
		Nos. 255-257 (3)	1.45	1.45

Apollo 11 moon landing, 10th anniversary. No. 257a contains Nos. 255-257 in changed colors.

For surcharges see Nos. B24, B29, B35.

Virgin and Child, by P. Serra — A70

Virgin and Child by: 25c, R. di Mur. 30c, S. diG. Sasseta. 50c, J. Huguet.

1979, Nov. 29 Photo. *Perf. 13*

258	A70	20c multicolored	.30	.25
259	A70	25c multicolored	.30	.25
260	A70	30c multicolored	.30	.25
261	A70	50c multicolored	.30	.25
a.		Souvenir sheet of 4, #258-261	1.40	1.40
		Nos. 258-261 (4)	1.20	1.00

Christmas. See Nos. B12-B15. For surcharges see Nos. B19-B20, B25, B32.

Pietà, by Giovanni Bellini — A71

Easter (Pietà, Paintings by): 30c, Botticelli. 35c, Anthony Van Dyck.

1980, Apr. 2 Photo. *Perf. 13*

262	A71	25c multicolored	.30	.30
263	A71	30c multicolored	.35	.35
264	A71	35c multicolored	.40	.40
		Nos. 262-264 (3)	1.05	1.05

See Nos. B37-B40.

A72

#265a, Ceremonial Stool, New Guinea (shown). #265b, Ku-Tagwa plaque. #265c, Suspension hook. #265d, Ancestral board. #266a, Platform post. #266b, Canoe ornament. #266c, Carved figure. #266d, Woman and child. #267a, God A'a, statue. #267b, Tangaroa, statue. #267c, Ivory pendant. #267d, Tapa cloth. #268a, Maori feather box. #268b, Hei-tiki. #268c, House post. #268d, God Ku, feather image.

1980, July 30 Photo. *Perf. 13*

265	A72	20c Strip of 4, #a.-d.	.65	.65
266	A72	25c Strip of 4, #a.-d.	.80	.80
267	A72	30c Strip of 4, #a.-d.	.95	.95
268	A72	35c Strip of 4, #a.-d.	1.10	1.10

Souvenir Sheets of 4

e.	#265a, 266a, 267a, 268a	1.10	1.10
f.	#265b, 266b, 267b, 268b	1.10	1.10
g.	#265c, 266c, 267c, 268c	1.10	1.10
h.	#265d, 266d, 267d, 268d	1.10	1.10
	Nos. 265-268 (4)	3.50	3.50

3rd South Pacific Festival of Arts, Port Moresby, Papua New Guinea, June 30-July 12. Stamps in souvenir sheets have 2c surtax.

For surcharges see Nos. 626-629.

Nos. 241-250, Overprinted in Black on Silver

1980, Aug. 22 *Perf. 14*

281	A66	20c Pair, #a.-b.	.50	.50
282	A66	30c Pair, #a.-b.	.70	.70
283	A66	35c Pair, #a.-b.	.80	.80
284	A66	50c Pair, #a.-b.	1.10	1.10
285	A66	60c Pair, #a.-b.	1.40	1.40
		Nos. 281-285 (5)	4.50	4.50

ZEAPEX '80, New Zealand International Stamp Exhibition, Auckland, Aug. 23-31.

Queen Mother Elizabeth, 80th Birthday — A73

1980, Sept. 15 Photo. *Perf. 13x13½*

291	A73	$1.10 multicolored	.90	1.40

Souvenir Sheet

292	A73	$3 multicolored	2.00	2.00

No. 291 issued in sheets of 5 and label showing coad of arms.

A74

#293a, 100-meter dash. #293b, Allen Wells, England. #294a, 400-Meter freestyle. #294b, Ines Diers, DDR. #295a, Soling class yachting. #295b, Denmark. #296a, Soccer. #296b, Czechoslovakia.

1980, Oct. 30 Photo. *Perf. 14*

293	A74	20c Pair, #a.-b.	.45	.45
294	A74	25c Pair, #a.-b.	.50	.50
295	A74	30c Pair, #a.-b.	.60	.60
296	A74	35c Pair, #a.-b.	.70	.70
		Nos. 293-296 (4)	2.25	2.25

22nd Summer Olympic Games, Moscow, July 19-Aug. 3.

See No. B42.

Virgin and Child, by del Sarto — A76

Paintings of Virgin & Child, by Andrea del Sarto.

1980, Nov. 28 Photo. *Perf. 13x13½*

301	A76	20c multicolored	.25	.25
302	A76	25c multicolored	.25	.25
303	A76	30c multicolored	.25	.25
304	A76	35c multicolored	.25	.25
a.		Souvenir sheet of 4, #301-304	1.00	1.25
		Nos. 301-304 (4)	1.00	1.00

Christmas and 450th death anniversary of Andrea del Sarto.

See Nos. B43-B46.

A77

Golden Shower Tree — A77a

#317a, Phalaenopsis sp. #317b, Moth Orchid. #318a, Euphorbia pulcherrima. #318b, Poinsettia. #319a, Thunbergia alata. #319b, Black-eyed Susan. #320a, Cochlospermum hibiscoides. #320b, Buttercup tree. #321a, Begonia sp. #321b, Begonia. #322a, Plumeria sp. #322b, Frangipani. #323a, Sterlitzia reginae. #323b, Bird of paradise. #324a, Hibiscus syriacus. #324b, Rose of Sharon. #325a, Nymphaea sp. #325b, Water lily. #326a, Tibouchina sp. #326b, Princess flower. #327a, Nelumbo sp. #327b, Lotus. #328a, Hybrid hibiscus. #328b, Yellow hibiscus.

1981-82 Photo. *Perf. 13x13½*

317	A77	2c Pair, #a.-b.	.25	.25
318	A77	5c Pair, #a.-b.	.25	.25
319	A77	10c Pair, #a.-b.	.25	.25
320	A77	15c Pair, #a.-b.	.30	.30
321	A77	20c Pair, #a.-b.	.40	.40
322	A77	25c Pair, #a.-b.	.50	.50
323	A77	30c Pair, #a.-b.	.55	.55
324	A77	35c Pair, #a.-b.	.65	.65
325	A77	40c Pair, #a.-b.	.70	.70
326	A77	50c Pair, #a.-b.	1.00	1.00
327	A77	60c Pair, #a.-b.	1.10	1.10
328	A77	80c Pair, #a.-b.	1.60	1.60

Perf. 13½

329	A77a	$1 shown	1.00	1.00
330	A77a	$2 Orchid var.	2.00	2.00
331	A77a	$3 Orchid sp.	2.75	2.75
332	A77a	$4 Poinsettia	4.00	4.00
333	A77a	$6 Hybrid hibiscus	5.75	5.75
334	A77a	$10 Hibiscus rosa-sinensis	10.00	10.00
		Nos. 317-334 (18)	33.05	33.05

Issued: 2c, 5c, 10c, 15c, 20c, 25c, Apr. 2; 30c, 35c, 40c, 50c, 60c, 80c, May 26; $1, $2, $3, Dec. 9, 1981; $4, $6, $10, Jan. 15, 1982.

For surcharges and overprints see Nos. 406-409, 413E, 594-595, O14, O16, O19.

Jesus Defiled, by El Greco — A78

Easter (Paintings): 50c, Pieta, by Fernando Gallego. 60c, The Supper of Emaus, by Jacopo da Pontormo.

1981, Apr. 10 *Perf. 14*

337	A78	35c multicolored	.40	.40
338	A78	50c multicolored	.65	.65
339	A78	60c multicolored	.75	.75
		Nos. 337-339 (3)	1.80	1.80

See Nos. B47-B50.

Prince Charles and Lady Diana — A79

1981, June 26 Photo. *Perf. 14*

340	A79	75c Charles	.50	.50
341	A79	95c Lady Diana	.65	.65
342	A79	$1.20 shown	.90	.90
a.		Souvenir sheet of 3, #340-342	2.50	2.50
		Nos. 340-342 (3)	2.05	2.05

Royal Wedding. Nos. 340-342 each printed in sheets of 5 plus label showing St. Paul's Cathedral.

For overprints and surcharges see Nos. 357-359, 410, 412, 455, 596-598, B52-B55.

1982 World Cup Soccer — A80

No. 343: Players dribbling ball. No. 344, Players kicking ball (#a, b.), heading ball (#c.). No. 345, Players kicking ball (#a, b.), goalie (#c.)

1981, Oct. 16 Photo. *Perf. 13*

343	Strip of 3	.80	.80
a.-c.	A80 30c any single	.30	.25
344	Strip of 3	1.05	1.05
a.-c.	A80 35c any single	.35	.35
345	Strip of 3	1.20	1.20
a.-c.	A80 40c any single	.40	.40
	Nos. 343-345 (3)	3.05	3.05

See No. B51.

Christmas 1981 — A81

Rembrandt Paintings: 20c, Holy Family with Angels, 1645. 35c, Presentation in the Temple, 1631. 50c, Virgin and Child in Temple, 1629. 60c, Holy Family, 1640.

1981-82 Photo. *Perf. 14x13*

346	A81	20c multicolored	.35	.35
347	A81	35c multicolored	.80	.80
348	A81	50c multicolored	1.10	1.10
349	A81	60c multicolored	1.25	1.25
a.		Souvenir sheet of 4, #346-349	3.50	3.50
		Nos. 346-349 (4)	3.50	3.50

Souvenir Sheets

350	A81	80c + 5c like #346	.80	.80
351	A81	80c + 5c like #347	.80	.80
352	A81	80c + 5c like #348	.80	.80
353	A81	80c + 5c like #349	.80	.80

Surtax was for school children.
Issued: #346-349, 12/11; others, 1/22/82.

21st Birthday of Princess Diana — A82

1982, July 1 *Perf. 14*

354	A82	50c Charles	.50	.50
355	A82	$1.25 Wedding	1.25	1.25
356	A82	$2.50 Diana	2.25	2.25
a.		Souvenir sheet of 3, #354-356	6.00	6.00
		Nos. 354-356 (3)	4.00	4.00

Nos. 354-356 each printed in sheets of 5 plus label showing wedding day picture.
For overprints and surcharges see Nos. 359B-359D, 411, 413, 456.

Nos. 340-342a Overprinted

Type I Type II

Type III

1982, July 23 *Perf. 14*

357	A79	75c multi (I)	1.40	1.40
357A	A79	75c multi (II)	1.40	1.40
358	A79	95c multi (I)	1.75	1.75
358A	A79	95c multi (II)	1.75	1.75
359	A79	$1.20 multi (I)	2.25	2.25
359A	A79	$1.20 multi (II)	2.25	2.25
		Nos. 357-359A (6)	10.80	10.80

Souvenir Sheet

359B	A79	Sheet of 3, #a.-c.	7.50	7.50
a.		75c multi (III)	2.00	2.00
b.		95c multi (III)	2.00	2.00
c.		$1.20 multi (III)	2.00	2.00

Nos. 357/357A, 358/358A and 359/359A were printed in small sheets containing three stamps overprinted Type I, two overprinted type II and one label.

Birthday Type of 1982 Inscribed in Silver

1982 Photo. *Perf. 14*

359C	A82	50c like #354	.70	.70
359D	A82	$1.25 like #355	1.75	1.75
359E	A82	$2.50 like #356	3.25	3.25
a.		Souvenir sheet of 3	7.00	7.00
		Nos. 359C-359E (3)	5.70	5.70

Christmas A83

Princess Diana Holding Prince William and Paintings of Infants by: 40c, Bronzino (1502-1572). 52c, Murillo (1617-1682). 83c, Murillo, diff. $1.05, Boucher (1703-1770). Singles in No. 363a: 34x30mm, showing paintings only.

1982, Dec. 3 Photo. *Perf. 13½x14½*

360	A83	40c multicolored	1.20	1.20
361	A83	52c multicolored	1.40	1.40
362	A83	83c multicolored	2.40	2.40
363	A83	$1.05 multicolored	3.50	3.50
a.		Souvenir sheet of 4, #364-367	6.75	6.75
		Nos. 360-363 (4)	8.50	8.50

Souvenir Sheets

364	A83	80c + 5c like #360	2.40	2.40
365	A83	80c + 5c like #361	2.40	2.40
366	A83	80c + 5c like #362	2.40	2.40
367	A83	80c + 5c like #363	2.40	2.40

Nos. 364-367 each contain one 30x42mm stamp showing Royal family. Surtax was for children's funds.

Commonwealth Day — A84

No. 368, Flag, Premier Robert R. Rex. No. 369, Resolution, Adventurer. No. 370, Passion flower. No. 371, Lime branch.

1983, Mar. 14 Photo. *Perf. 13*

368	A84	70c multi	.75	.75
369	A84	70c multi	.75	.75
370	A84	70c multi	.75	.75
371	A84	70c multi	.75	.75
a.		Block of 4, #368-371	3.00	3.00

For overprints see Nos. 484-487.

Scouting Year — A85

1983, Apr. 28 Photo. *Perf. 13*

372	A85	40c Flag signals	.70	.70
373	A85	50c Tree planting	.80	.80
374	A85	83c Map reading	1.50	1.50
		Nos. 372-374 (3)	3.00	3.00

Souvenir Sheet

375		Sheet of 3	3.00	3.00
a.		A85 40c + 3c like 40c	.75	.75
b.		A85 50c + 3c like 50c	.80	.80
c.		A85 83c + 3c like 83c	1.30	1.30

Nos. 372-375 Overprinted in Black on Silver: "XV WORLD JAMBOREE CANADA"

1983, July 14 Photo.

376	A85	40c multicolored	.60	.60
377	A85	50c multicolored	.75	.75
378	A85	83c multicolored	1.15	1.15
		Nos. 376-378 (3)	2.50	2.50

Souvenir Sheet

379		Sheet of 3	2.75	2.75
a.		A85 40c + 3c multicolored	.60	.60
b.		A85 50c + 3c multicolored	.70	.70
c.		A85 83c + 3c multicolored	1.40	1.40

Save the Whales Campaign A86

1983, Aug. 15 *Perf. 13x14*

380	A86	12c Right whale	.90	.50
381	A86	25c Fin whale	1.30	.60
382	A86	35c Sei whale	1.75	.95
383	A86	40c Blue whale	2.00	1.10
384	A86	58c Bowhead whale	2.25	1.25
385	A86	70c Sperm whale	2.75	1.25
386	A86	83c Humpback whale	3.00	1.75
387	A86	$1.05 Lesser rorqual	3.75	1.90
388	A86	$2.50 Gray whale	5.00	3.25
		Nos. 380-388 (9)	22.70	12.55

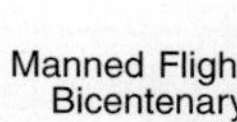

Manned Flight Bicentenary A87

25c, Montgolfier, 1783. 40c, Wright Bros. Flyer, 1903. 58c, Graf Zeppelin, 1928. 70c, Boeing 247, 1933. 83c, Apollo VIII, 1968. $1.05, Columbia space shuttle.

1983, Oct. 14 Photo. *Perf. 14*

389	A87	25c multicolored	.50	.50
390	A87	40c multicolored	.75	.75
391	A87	58c multicolored	1.25	1.25
392	A87	70c multicolored	1.75	1.75
393	A87	83c multicolored	2.10	2.10
394	A87	$1.05 multicolored	2.40	2.40
a.		Souvenir sheet of 6	5.50	5.50
		Nos. 389-394 (6)	8.75	8.75

No. 394a contains Nos. 389-394 inscribed "AIRMAIL."

Christmas — A87a

Paintings by Raphael (1483-1520): 30c, Garvagh Madonna, National Gallery, London. 40c, Granduca Madonna, Pitti Gallery, Florence. 58c, Goldfinch Madonna, Uffizi Gallery, Florence. 70c, Holy Family of Francis I, Louvre, Paris. 83c, Holy Family with Saints, Alte Pinakothek, Munich.

1983 Photo. *Perf. 14*

395	A87a	30c multicolored	.60	.60
396	A87a	40c multicolored	.80	.80
397	A87a	58c multicolored	1.20	1.20
398	A87a	70c multicolored	1.30	1.30
399	A87a	83c multicolored	1.60	1.60
		Nos. 395-399 (5)	5.50	5.50

Souvenir Sheets

Perf. 13½

400		Sheet of 5	4.00	4.00
a.		A87a 30c + 3c like #395	.40	.40
b.		A87a 40c + 3c like #396	.55	.55
c.		A87a 58c + 3c like #397	.80	.80
d.		A87a 70c + 3c like #398	.90	.90
e.		A87a 83c + 3c like #399	1.10	1.10
401	A87a	85c + 5c like #395	1.20	1.20
402	A87a	85c + 5c like #396	1.20	1.20
403	A87a	85c + 5c like #397	1.20	1.20
404	A87a	85c + 5c like #398	1.20	1.20
405	A87a	85c + 5c like #399	1.20	1.20

500th birth anniv. of Raphael.
Issued: #395-400, 11/25; #401-405, 12/29.

Nos. 323, 326-328, 341, 355, 342, 356 and 331 Surcharged in Black or Gold with One or Two Bars

1983, Nov. 30 Photo.

Pairs, #a.-b. (#406-409)

406	A77	52c on 30c	1.60	1.60
407	A77	58c on 50c	1.75	1.75
408	A77	70c on 60c	2.25	2.25
409	A77	83c on 80c	2.75	2.75
410	A79	$1.10 on 95c #341	1.60	1.60
411	A82	$1.10 on $1.25 #355 (G)	1.60	1.60
412	A79	$2.60 on $1.20 #342	4.00	4.00
413	A82	$2.60 on $2.50 #356 (G)	4.00	4.00
413A	A77a	$3.70 on $3 #331	5.50	5.50
		Nos. 406-413A (9)	25.05	25.05

World Communications Year — A88

1984, Jan. 23 Photo. *Perf. 13x13½*

414	A88	40c Telegraph sender	.45	.45
415	A88	52c Early telephone	.65	.65
416	A88	83c Satellite	1.10	1.10
a.		Souvenir sheet of 3, #414-416	2.00	2.00
		Nos. 414-416 (3)	2.20	2.20

Moth Orchid — A89

Golden Shower Tree — A90

25c, Poinsettia. 30c, Buttercup tree. 35c, Begonia. 40c, Frangipani. 52c, Bird of paradise. 58c, Rose of Sharon. 70c, Princess flower. 83c, Lotus. $1.05, Yellow hibiscus. $2.30, Orchid var. $3.90, Orchid sp. $5, Poinsettia, diff. $6.60, Hybrid hibiscus. $8.30, Hibiscus rosasinensis.

1984 *Perf. 13x13½*

417	A89	12c shown	.25	.25
418	A89	25c multicolored	.35	.35
419	A89	30c multicolored	.50	.50
420	A89	35c multicolored	.50	.50
421	A89	40c multicolored	.55	.55
422	A89	52c multicolored	.70	.70
423	A89	58c multicolored	.80	.80
424	A89	70c multicolored	1.00	1.00
425	A89	83c multicolored	1.10	1.10
426	A89	$1.05 multicolored	1.60	1.60
427	A90	$1.75 shown	1.60	1.60
428	A90	$2.30 multicolored	2.25	2.25
429	A90	$3.90 multicolored	3.50	3.50
430	A90	$5 multicolored	4.50	4.50
431	A90	$6.60 multicolored	6.00	6.00
431A	A90	$8.30 multicolored	8.00	8.00
		Nos. 417-431A (16)	33.20	33.20

Issued: #417-426, 2/20; #427-429, 5/10; others 6/18.
For overprints see #O1-O13, O15, O17-O18.

1984 Summer Olympics — A91

Designs: Greek pottery designs, 3rd cent. BC. 30c, 70c vert.

1984, Mar. 15 Photo. *Perf. 14*

432	A91	30c Discus	.45	.45
433	A91	35c Running	.50	.50
434	A91	40c Equestrian	.55	.55
435	A91	58c Boxing	.80	.80
436	A91	70c Javelin	.95	.95
		Nos. 432-436 (5)	3.25	3.25

For overprints and surcharges see #446-450, 480-483.

AUSIPEX '84, Australian Animals — A92

25c, Koala on gray branch. 35c, Koala sitting in curve of branch. 40c, Koala on green branch (yellow background). 58c, Koala on branch, arms stretched out in front. 70c, Koala on green branch (lt. blue green background). 83c, Kangaroo with joey, facing right. $1.05, Kangaroo with joey, facing left. $2.50, Kangaroo, tail in LR corner.

1984 Photo. *Perf. 14*

437 A92 25c gold & multi .30 .30
438 A92 35c gold & multi .40 .40
439 A92 40c gold & multi .65 .65
440 A92 58c gold & multi 1.00 1.00
441 A92 70c gold & multi 1.30 1.30
442 A92 83c gold & multi 1.50 1.50
443 A92 $1.05 gold & multi 1.75 1.75
444 A92 $2.50 gold & multi 4.00 4.00
Nos. 437-444 (8) 10.90 10.90

Souvenir Sheets

445 Sheet of 2 + label 5.00 5.00
a. A92 $1.75 Wallaby 2.50 2.50
b. A92 $1.75 Koala, diff. 2.50 2.50
c. Sheet, #437-441, 445b, perf 13½ 4.50 4.50
d. Sheet, #442-444, 445a, perf 13½ 6.50 6.50

Nos. 442-444 airmail.

Issued: #437-444, Aug. 24; $445, Sept. 20.

Nos. 432-436 Ovptd. with Event, Names of Gold Medalists, Country in Gold or Red

1984, Sept. 7 *Perf. 14*

446 A91 30c Danneberg .40 .40
447 A91 35c Coe (R) .50 .50
448 A91 40c Todd .55 .55
449 A91 58c Biggs .80 .80
450 A91 70c Haerkoenen 1.00 1.00
Nos. 446-450 (5) 3.25 3.25

10th Anniv. of Self Government A93

1984, Oct. 19 Photo. *Perf. 13*

451 A93 40c Niue flag .55 .55
452 A93 58c Niue map 1.00 1.00
453 A93 70c Ceremony 1.15 1.15
a. Souvenir sheet of 3, #451-453 2.50 2.50
Nos. 451-453 (3) 2.70 2.70

Souvenir Sheet

454 A93 $2.50 like 70c 2.50 2.50

For overprints and surcharges see Nos. 655-660.

Nos. 340, 354 Surcharged "Prince Henry / 15.9.84" and Bars and New Values in Red or Silver

1984, Oct. 22 Photo. *Perf. 14*

455 A79 $2 on 75c multi (R) 2.25 2.25
456 A82 $2 on 50c multi (S) 2.25 2.25

Nos. 455-456 issued in sheets of 5 + label.

Christmas — A94

Paintings: 40c, The Nativity, by A. Vaccaro. 58c, Virgin with Fly, anonymous. 70c, Adoration of the Shepherds, by B. Murillo. 83c, Flight into Egypt, by B. Murillo.

1984, Oct. 19 Photo. *Perf. 13x13½*

457 A94 40c multicolored .55 .55
458 A94 58c multicolored .80 .80
459 A94 70c multicolored 1.00 1.00
460 A94 83c multicolored 1.10 1.10
Nos. 457-460 (4) 3.45 3.45

Souvenir Sheets

461 Sheet of 4 3.25 3.25
a. A94 40c + 5c Like 40c .55 .55
b. A94 58c + 5c Like 58c .70 .70
c. A94 70c + 5c Like 70c .90 .90
d. A94 83c + 5c Like 83c 1.00 1.00

Perf. 13½

462 A94 95c + 10c Like 40c 1.25 1.25
463 A94 95c + 10c Like 58c 1.25 1.25
464 A94 95c + 10c Like 70c 1.25 1.25
465 A94 95c + 10c Like 83c 1.25 1.25

Audubon Birth Bicentenary — A95

Illustrations of North American bird species by artist/naturalist John J. Audubon: 40c, House wren. 70c, Veery. 83c, Grasshopper sparrow. $1.05, Henslow's sparrow. $2.50, Vesper sparrow.

1985, Apr. 15 Photo. *Perf. 14½*

466 A95 40c multicolored 1.50 1.50
467 A95 70c multicolored 2.00 2.00
468 A95 83c multicolored 2.75 2.75
469 A95 $1.05 multicolored 3.25 3.25
470 A95 $2.50 multicolored 7.50 7.50
Nos. 466-470 (5) 17.00 17.00

Souvenir Sheets

Perf. 14

471 A95 $1.75 like #466 2.50 2.50
472 A95 $1.75 like #467 2.50 2.50
473 A95 $1.75 like #468 2.50 2.50
474 A95 $1.75 like #469 2.50 2.50
475 A95 $1.75 like #470 2.50 2.50
Nos. 471-475 (5) 12.50 12.50

Queen Mother, 85th Birthday — A96

Designs: 70c, Wearing mantle of the Order of the Garter. $1.15, With Queen Elizabeth II. $1.50, With Prince Charles. $3, Writing letter.

1985, June 14 *Perf. 13½x13*

476 A96 70c multicolored 1.00 1.00
477 A96 $1.15 multicolored 1.25 1.25
478 A96 $1.50 multicolored 1.75 1.75
a. Souvenir sheet of 3 + label, #476-478 8.00 8.00
Nos. 476-478 (3) 4.00 4.00

Souvenir Sheet

Perf. 13½

479 A96 $3 multicolored 4.25 4.25

Nos. 476-478 issued in sheets of 5 plus label. No. 479 contains one 39x36mm stamp. No. 478a issued 8/4/86, for 86th birthday.

Nos. 432-433, 435-436 Overprinted "Mini South Pacific Games, Rarotonga" and Surcharged with Gold Bar and New Value in Black

1985, July 26 *Perf. 14*

480 A91 52c on 95c multi .55 .55
481 A91 83c on 58c multi 1.15 1.15
482 A91 95c on 35c multi 1.30 1.30
483 A91 $2 on 30c multi 2.50 2.50
Nos. 480-483 (4) 5.50 5.50

Nos. 368-371 Overprinted with Conference Emblem and: "Pacific Islands Conference, Rarotonga"

1985, July 26 *Perf. 13½x13*

484 A84 70c on #368 .75 .75
485 A84 70c on #369 .75 .75
486 A84 70c on #370 .75 .75
487 A84 70c on #371 .75 .75
a. Block of 4, #484-487 3.00 3.00

A97

Paintings of children: 58c, Portrait of R. Strozzi's Daughter, by Titian. 70c, The Fifer, by Manet. $1.15, Portrait of a Young Girl, by Renoir. $1.50, Portrait of M. Berard, by Renoir.

1985, Oct. 11 *Perf. 13*

488 A97 58c multicolored 1.75 1.75
489 A97 70c multicolored 2.00 2.00
490 A97 $1.15 multicolored 3.50 3.50
491 A97 $1.50 multicolored 4.50 4.50
Nos. 488-491 (4) 11.75 11.75

Souvenir Sheets

Perf. 13x13½

492 A97 $1.75 + 10c like #488 5.00 5.00
493 A97 $1.75 + 10c like #489 5.00 5.00
494 A97 $1.75 + 10c like #490 5.00 5.00
495 A97 $1.75 + 10c like #491 5.00 5.00

Intl. Youth Year.

A98

Christmas, Paintings (details) by Correggio: 58c, No. 500a, Virgin and Child. 85c, No. 500b, Adoration of the Magi. $1.05, No. 500c, Virgin and Child, diff. $1.45, No. 500d, Virgin and Child with St. Catherine.

1985, Nov. 29 Photo. *Perf. 13x13½*

496 A98 58c multicolored 1.25 1.25
497 A98 85c multicolored 2.25 2.25
498 A98 $1.05 multicolored 2.75 2.75
499 A98 $1.45 multicolored 3.75 3.75
Nos. 496-499 (4) 10.00 10.00

Souvenir Sheets

500 Sheet of 4 5.50 5.50
a.-d. A98 60c + 10c, any single 1.30 1.30

Imperf

501 A98 65c like #496 1.25 1.25
502 A98 95c like #497 1.75 1.75
503 A98 $1.20 like #498 2.50 2.50
504 A98 $1.75 like #499 3.50 3.50
Nos. 500-504 (5) 14.50 14.50

Nos. 501-504 each contain one 61x71mm stamp.

Halley's Comet A99

The Constellations, fresco by Giovanni De Vecchi, Farnesio Palace, Caprarola, Italy.

1986, Jan. 24 *Perf. 13½*

505 A99 60c multicolored .90 .90
506 A99 75c multicolored 1.10 1.00
507 A99 $1.10 multicolored 1.50 1.50
508 A99 $1.50 multicolored 2.40 2.40
Nos. 505-508 (4) 5.90 5.80

Souvenir Sheet

509 Sheet of 4 8.00 8.00
a. A99 95c like #505 2.00 2.00
b. A99 95c 95c like #506 2.00 2.00
c. A99 95c like #507 2.00 2.00
d. A99 95c like #508 2.00 2.00

A100

Elizabeth II, 60th Birthday: $1.10, No. 513a, Elizabeth and Prince Philip at Windsor Castle. $1.50, No. 513b, At Balmoral. $2, No. 513c, Elizabeth at Buckingham Palace. $3, Elizabeth seated and Prince Philip.

1986, Apr. 28 *Perf. 14½x13½*

510 A100 $1.10 multicolored 1.00 1.00
511 A100 $1.50 multicolored 1.50 1.50
512 A100 $2 multicolored 2.00 2.00
Nos. 510-512 (3) 4.50 4.50

Souvenir Sheets

513 Sheet of 3 2.75 2.75
a.-c. A100 75c any single .90 .90
514 A100 $3 multicolored 3.50 3.50

For surcharges see Nos. 546-547.

A101

AMERIPEX '86: #515a, Washington, US #1. #515b, Jefferson, Roosevelt, Lincoln.

1986, May 22 Photo. *Perf. 14*

515 A101 $1 Pair, #a.-b. 7.75 7.75

A102

Paintings: $1, Statue under construction, 1883, by Victor Dargaud. $2.50, Unveiling the Statue of Liberty, 1886, by Edmund Morand (1829-1901).

1986, July 4 *Perf. 13x13½*

517 A102 $1 multicolored 2.25 2.25
518 A102 $2.50 multicolored 5.50 5.50

Souvenir Sheet

519 Sheet of 2 4.00 4.00
a. A102 $1.25 like #517 2.00 2.00
b. A102 $1.25 like #518 2.00 2.00

Statue of Liberty, cent.

Wedding of Prince Andrew and Sarah Ferguson A103

Designs: $2.50, Portraits, Westminster Abbey. $5, Portraits.

1986, July 23 *Perf. 13½x13*

520 A103 $2.50 multicolored 4.00 4.00

Souvenir Sheet

521 A103 $5 Portraits 8.25 8.25

No. 520 printed in sheets of 4. No. 521 contains one 45x32mm stamp.

STAMPEX '86, Adelaide, Aug. 4-10 — A104

Birds — 40c, Egretta alba, vert. 60c, Emblema picta. 75c, Aprosmictus scapularis, vert. 80c, Malurus lamberti. $1, Falco peregrinus, vert. $1.65, Halcyon azurea. $2.20, Melopsittacus undulatus, vert. $4.25,

Perf. 13x13½, 13½x13

1986, Aug. 4 Photo.

522 A104 40c multi 1.10 1.10
523 A104 60c multi 1.60 1.60
524 A104 75c multi 2.25 2.25
525 A104 80c multi 2.50 2.50
526 A104 $1 multi 3.00 3.00
527 A104 $1.65 multi 4.75 4.75
528 A104 $2.20 multi 7.00 7.00
529 A104 $4.25 multi 13.00 13.00
Nos. 522-529 (8) 35.20 35.20

Christmas — A105

Paintings in the Vatican Museum: 80c, No. 534a, Virgin and Child, by Perugino (1446-1523). $1.15, No. 534b, Virgin of St. N. dei Frari, by Titian. $1.80, No. 534c, Virgin with Milk, by Lorenzo di Credi (1459-1537). $2.60,

$7.50, No. 534d, Foligno Madonna, by Raphael.

1986, Nov. 14 Litho. *Perf. 14*

530	A105	80c multi	1.60	1.60
531	A105	$1.15 multi	2.25	2.25
532	A105	$1.80 multi	4.00	4.00
533	A105	$2.60 multi	6.00	6.00
		Nos. 530-533 (4)	13.85	13.85

Souvenir Sheets

Perf. 13½

534	Sheet of 4	11.00	11.00
a.-d.	A105 $1.50 any single	2.75	2.75

Perf. 14½x13½

535	A105 $7.50 multi	12.00	12.00

For surcharges see Nos. B56-B61.

Souvenir Sheets

Statue of Liberty, Cent. — A106

Photographs: No. 536a, Tall ship, bridge. No. 536b, Workmen, flame from torch. No. 536c, Workman, flame, diff. No. 536d, Ships, New York City. No. 536e, Tall ship, sailboat, bridge. No. 537a, Statue, front. No. 537b, Statue, left side. No. 537c, Torch dismantled. No. 537d, Statue, right side. No. 537e, Welder.

1987, May 20

536	A106	Sheet of 5 + label	3.75	3.75
a.-e.		75c any single	.75	.75
537	A106	Sheet of 5 + label	3.75	3.75
a.-e.		75c any single, vert.	.75	.75

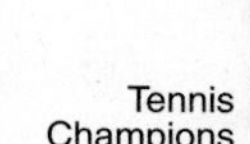

Tennis Champions A107

Olympic emblem, coin and: 80c, $1.15, $1.40, $1.80, Boris Becker. 85c, $1.05, $1.30, $1.75, Steffi Graf. Various action scenes.

1987

538	A107	80c multi	2.50	2.50
539	A107	85c multi	2.10	2.10
540	A107	$1.05 multi	2.50	2.50
541	A107	$1.15 multi	2.60	2.60
542	A107	$1.30 multi	2.50	2.50
543	A107	$1.40 multi	3.00	3.00
544	A107	$1.75 multi	3.00	3.00
545	A107	$1.80 multi	3.75	3.75
		Nos. 538-545 (8)	21.95	21.95

Issued: 80c, $1.15, $1.40, $1.80, 9/25; others, 10/20.

For overprints see Nos. 560-563.

Nos. 511-512 Surcharged "40th /WEDDING / ANNIV." with Denomination in Black on Gold

Perf. 14½x13½

1987, Nov. 20 Photo.

546	A100	$4.85 on $1.50 #511	6.00	6.00
547	A100	$4.85 on $2 #512	6.00	6.00

40th Wedding anniv. of Queen Elizabeth II and Prince Philip, Duke of Edinburgh.

Christmas A108

Paintings (details) by Albrecht Durer (Angel with Lute on 80c, $1.05, $2.80): 80c, No. 551a, The Nativity. $1.05, No. 551b, Adoration of the Magi. $2.80, No. 551c, $7.50, Celebration of the Rosary.

1987, Dec. 4 Photo. *Perf. 13½*

548	A108	80c multi	1.75	1.75
549	A108	$1.05 multi	2.25	2.25
550	A108	$2.80 multi	5.00	5.00
		Nos. 548-550 (3)	9.00	9.00

Souvenir Sheets

551	Sheet of 3	9.00	9.00
a.-c.	A108 $1.30 any single	3.00	3.00
552	A108 $7.50 multi	11.00	11.00

Size of Nos. 551a-551c: 49½x38½mm. No. 552 contains one 51x33mm stamp.

European Soccer Championships — A109

Highlights from Franz Beckenbauer's career: 20c, Match scene. 40c, German all-star team. 60c, Brussels, 1974. 80c, England, 1966. $1.05, Mexico, 1970. $1.30, Munich, 1974. $1.80, FC Bayern Munchen vs. Athletico Madrid.

1988, June 20 Litho. *Perf. 14*

553	A109	20c multi	.40	.40
554	A109	40c multi	.80	.80
555	A109	60c multi	1.25	1.25
556	A109	80c multi	1.60	1.60
557	A109	$1.05 multi	2.25	2.25
558	A109	$1.30 multi	3.00	3.00
559	A109	$1.80 multi	3.75	3.75
		Nos. 553-559 (7)	13.05	13.05

Nos. 539-540, 542 and 543 Ovptd.

a. "AUSTRALIA 24 JAN 88 / FRENCH OPEN 4 JUNE 88"

b. "WIMBLEDON 2 JULY 88 / U S OPEN 10 SEPT. 88"

c. "WOMEN'S TENNIS GRAND / SLAM: 10 SEPTEMBER 88"

d. "SEOUL OLYMPIC GAMES / GOLD MEDAL WINNER"

1988, Oct. 14 Litho. *Perf. 13½x14*

560	A107(a)	85c on No. 539	1.75	1.75
561	A107(b)	$1.05 on No. 540	2.25	2.25
562	A107(c)	$1.30 on No. 542	2.75	2.75
563	A107(d)	$1.75 on No. 543	3.75	3.75
		Nos. 560-563 (4)	10.50	10.50

Steffi Graf, 1988 Olympic gold medalist; opportunities for youth in sports.

Christmas — A110

Adoration of the Shepherds, by Rubens: 60c, Angels. 80c, Joseph and witness. $1.05, Madonna. $1.30, Christ child. $7.20, Entire painting.

1988, Oct. 28 Photo. *Perf. 13½*

564	A110	60c multi	1.40	1.40
565	A110	80c multi	2.40	2.40
566	A110	$1.05 multi	3.50	3.50
567	A110	$1.30 multi	4.00	4.00
		Nos. 564-567 (4)	11.30	11.30

Souvenir Sheet

568	A110	$7.20 multi	10.00	10.00

No. 568 contains one 40x50mm stamp.

First Moon Landing, 20th Anniv. — A111

Apollo 11: #a, Mission emblem and astronaut. #b, Earth, Moon and simplified flight plan. #c, Olive branch, Apollo 1 mission emblem and astronaut on Moon. Printed in continuous design.

1989, July 20 Photo. *Perf. 14*

571	A111	$1.50 Strip of 3, #a.-c.	14.50	14.50

Souvenir Sheet of 3

Perf. 13½x13

572	A111	$1.15 #a.-c.	8.00	8.00

Christmas A112

Details of Presentation in the Temple, 1631, by Rembrandt, Royal Cabinet of Paintings, The Hague: 70c, Priests. 80c, Madonna. $1.05, Joseph. $1.30, Christ child. $7.20, Entire painting.

1989, Nov. 22 Photo. *Perf. 13x13½*

573	A112	70c gold & multi	2.60	2.60
574	A112	80c gold & multi	2.75	2.75
575	A112	$1.05 gold & multi	3.50	3.50
576	A112	$1.30 gold & multi	4.50	4.50
		Nos. 573-576 (4)	13.35	13.35

Souvenir Sheet

Perf. 13½

577	A112	$7.20 gold & multi	13.50	13.50

No. 577 contains one 39x50mm stamp.

Emblem of the German Natl. Soccer Team and Signatures A113

Former team captains: 80c, Fritz Walter. $1.15, Franz Beckenbauer. $1.40, Uwe Seeler.

1990, Feb. 5 Photo. *Perf. 13½*

578	A113	80c multicolored	2.25	2.25
579	A113	$1.15 multicolored	2.60	2.60
580	A113	$1.40 multicolored	4.50	4.50
581	A113	$1.80 shown	5.25	5.25
		Nos. 578-581 (4)	14.60	14.60

1990 World Cup Soccer Championships, Italy.

First Postage Stamp, 150th Anniv. — A114

Paintings by Rembrandt showing letters: 80c, No. 586d, Merchant Maarten Looten (1632). $1.05, No. 586c, Rembrandt's son Titus holding pen (1655). $1.30, No. 586b, The Shipbuilder and his Wife (1633). $1.80, No. 586a, Bathsheba with King David's letter (1654).

1990, May 2 Photo. *Perf. 13½*

582	A114	80c multicolored	2.25	2.25
583	A114	$1.05 multicolored	3.00	3.00
584	A114	$1.30 multicolored	4.50	4.50
585	A114	$1.80 multicolored	6.00	6.00
		Nos. 582-585 (4)	15.75	15.75

Souvenir Sheet

586	Sheet of 4	11.00	11.00
a.-d.	A114 $1.50 any single	2.75	2.75

A115

1990, July 23 *Perf. 13x13½*

587	A115	$1.25 multicolored	5.00	5.00

Souvenir Sheet

588	A115	$7 multicolored	16.00	16.00

Queen Mother, 90th birthday.

A116

Christmas (Paintings): 70c, Adoration of the Magi by Bouts. 80c, Holy Family by Fra Bartolomeo. $1.05, The Nativity by Memling. $1.30, Adoration of the King by Pieter Bruegel, the Elder. $7.20, Virgin and Child Enthroned by Cosimo Tura.

1990, Nov. 27 Litho. *Perf. 14*

589	A116	70c multicolored	2.25	2.25
590	A116	80c multicolored	3.00	3.00
591	A116	$1.05 multicolored	3.50	3.50
592	A116	$1.30 multicolored	4.25	4.25
		Nos. 589-592 (4)	13.00	13.00

Souvenir Sheet

593	A116	$7.20 multicolored	13.00	13.00

No. 334 Overprinted in Silver

1990, Dec. 5 *Perf. 13x13½*

594	A77a	$10 multicolored	16.00	16.00

Birdpex '90, 20th Intl. Ornithological Congress, New Zealand.

No. 333 Overprinted "SIXTY FIFTH BIRTHDAY QUEEN ELIZABETH II"

1991, Apr. 22 Litho. *Perf. 13x13½*

595	A77a	$6 multicolored	8.00	8.00

Nos. 340-342 Overprinted in Black or Silver

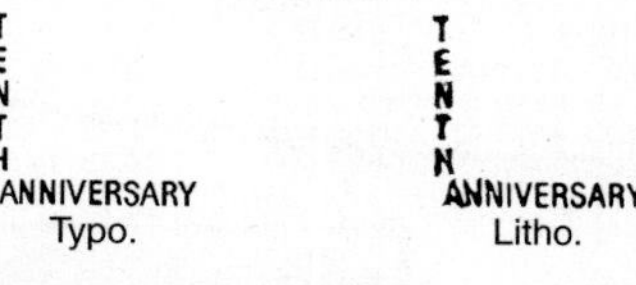

Typo. Litho.

1991, June 26 Photo. *Perf. 14*

596	A79	75c on #340 (S)	1.50	1.50
a.		Litho. overprint	1.50	1.50
597	A79	95c on #341	2.25	2.25
a.		Litho. overprint	2.25	2.25
598	A79	$1.20 on #342	3.25	3.25
a.		Litho. overprint	3.25	3.25
		Nos. 596-598 (3)	7.00	7.00
		Nos. 596a-598a (3)	7.00	7.00

Nos. 596-598 issued in miniature sheets of 5 with typo. overprint. Nos. 596a-598a issued in uncut panes of 4 miniature sheets of 5. Letters of typo. overprint are taller and thinner than litho. overprint.

Christmas — A117

Paintings: 20c, The Virgin and Child with Saints Jerome and Dominic, by Filippino Lippi. 50c, The Isenheim Altarpiece, The Virgin and Child, by Grunewald. $1, The Nativity, by Pittoni. $2, Adoration of the Kings, by Jan Brueghel, the Elder. $7, The Adoration of the Shepherds, by Reni.

1991, Nov. 11 Litho. *Perf. 14*

599	A117	20c multicolored	.50	.50
600	A117	50c multicolored	1.40	1.40
601	A117	$1 multicolored	3.00	3.00
602	A117	$2 multicolored	5.50	5.50
		Nos. 599-602 (4)	10.40	10.40

Souvenir Sheet

603	A117	$7 multicolored	11.00	11.00

Birds — A118

20c, Banded rail. 50c, Red-tailed tropicbird. 70c, Purple swamphen. $1, Pacific pigeon. $1.50, White-collared kingfisher. $2, Blue-crowned lory. $3, Crimson-crowned fruit dove. $5, Barn owl. $7, Longtailed cockoo. $10, Reef heron. $15, Polynesian triller.

1992-93 Litho. *Perf. 14x13½*

604 A118 20c multicolored .30 .30
605 A118 50c multicolored .70 .70
606 A118 70c multicolored 1.00 1.00
607 A118 $1 multicolored 1.50 1.50
608 A118 $1.50 multicolored 2.00 2.00
609 A118 $2 multicolored 2.75 2.75
610 A118 $3 multicolored 4.25 4.25
611 A118 $5 multicolored 6.50 6.50

Perf. 13

Size: 51x38mm

612 A118 $7 multicolored 8.50 8.50

Size: 49x35mm

613 A118 $10 multicolored 11.50 11.50
614 A118 $15 multicolored 18.00 18.00
Nos. 604-614 (11) 57.00 57.00

Issued $1.50, $2, 3/20; $3, 4/16; $5, 5/15; $7, 3/26/93; $10, 4/16/93; $15, 8/10/93; others, 2/92.

For overprints & surcharges see Nos. O20-O25, 676-677.

Discovery of America, 500th Anniv. A119

$2, Queen Isabella supports Columbus. $3, Columbus' fleet. $5, Columbus landing in America.

1992 Litho. *Perf. 13*

621 A119 $2 multicolored 2.55 2.55
622 A119 $3 multicolored 4.50 4.50
623 A119 $5 multicolored 7.50 7.50
Nos. 621-623 (3) 14.55 14.55

1992 Summer Olympics, Barcelona A120

No. 624: a, $10 coin, tennis player. b, Flags, torch. c, Gymnast, $10 coin. $5, Water polo player.

1992, July 22 Litho. *Perf. 13½x13*

624 A120 $2.50 Strip of 3, #a.-c. 17.00 17.00

Souvenir Sheet

625 A120 $5 multicolored 10.50 10.50

Nos. 265-268 Surcharged

1992, Sept. 30 Photo. *Perf. 13*

Strips of 4, #a.-d.

626 A72 $1 on 20c 4.75 4.75
627 A72 $1 on 25c 4.75 4.75
628 A72 $1 on 30c 4.75 4.75
629 A72 $1 on 35c 4.75 4.75
Nos. 626-629 (4) 19.00 19.00

6th South Pacific Festival of the Arts.

Christmas — A121

Design: Different details from St. Catherine's Mystic Marriage, by Hans Memling.

1992, Nov. 18 Litho. *Perf. 13½*

642 A121 20c multicolored .35 .35
643 A121 50c multicolored 1.00 1.00
644 A121 $1 multicolored 2.40 2.40
645 A121 $2 multicolored 4.00 4.00
Nos. 642-645 (4) 7.75 7.75

Souvenir Sheet

646 A121 $7 like #643 11.50 11.50

No. 646 contains one 39x48mm stamp.

Queen Elizabeth II's Accession to the Throne, 40th Anniv. — A122

Various portraits of Queen Elizabeth II.

1992, Dec. 7 *Perf. 14*

647 A122 70c multicolored .60 .60
648 A122 $1 multicolored 1.75 1.75
649 A122 $1.50 multicolored 3.50 3.50
650 A122 $2 multicolored 4.25 4.25
Nos. 647-650 (4) 10.10 10.10

Dolphins — A123

Designs: 20c, Rough-toothed dolphin. 50c, Fraser's dolphin. 75c, Pantropical spotted dolphin. $1, Risso's dolphin.

1993, Jan. 13 Litho. *Perf. 14*

651 A123 20c multicolored 1.25 .75
652 A123 50c multicolored 3.50 1.50
653 A123 75c multicolored 4.75 2.50
654 A123 $1 multicolored 6.00 4.50
Nos. 651-654 (4) 15.50 9.25

World Wildlife Fund.

Nos. 451-453 Ovptd.

1993, Mar. 15 Photo. *Perf. 13*

655 A93 40c on #451 multi .65 .65
656 A93 58c on #452 multi 1.25 1.25
657 A93 70c on #453 multi 1.75 1.75

Nos. 655-657 Surcharged

1993, Mar. 15

658 A93 $1 on 40c #655 3.25 3.25
659 A93 $1 on 58c #656 3.25 3.25
660 A93 $1 on 70c #657 3.25 3.25
Nos. 655-660 (6) 13.40 13.40

Queen Elizabeth II, 40th Anniv. of Coronation A124

1993, June 2 Litho. *Perf. 14*

661 A124 $5 multicolored 10.50 10.50

Christmas — A125

Details from Virgin of the Rosary, by Guido Reni: 20c, Infant Jesus. 70c, Cherubs. $1, Two men, one pointing upward. $1.50, Two men looking upward. $3, Madonna and child.

1993, Oct. 29 Litho. *Perf. 14*

662 A125 20c multicolored .30 .30
663 A125 70c multicolored 1.20 1.20
664 A125 $1 multicolored 1.75 1.75
665 A125 $1.50 multicolored 3.25 3.25

Size: 32x47mm

Perf. 13½

666 A125 $3 multicolored 6.00 6.00
Nos. 662-666 (5) 12.50 12.50

1994 World Cup Soccer Championships, U.S. — A126

1994, June 17 Litho. *Perf. 14*

667 A126 $4 multicolored 8.00 8.00

First Manned Moon Landing, 25th Anniv. A127

Designs: a, Flight to Moon, astronaut opening solar wind experiment lunar surface. b, Astronaut holding flag. c, Astronaut standing by lunar experiment package.

1994, July 20 Litho. *Perf. 14*

668 A127 $2.50 Tryptic, #a.-c. 20.00 20.00

Christmas A128

Entire paintings or details: No. 669a, The Adoration of the Kings, by Jan Gossaert. b, Madonna & Child with Saints John & Catherine, by Titian. c, The Holy Family and Shepherd, by Titian. d, Virgin & Child with Saints, by Gerard David.

No. 670: a-b, Adoration of the Shepherds, by N. Poussin. c, Madonna & Child with Saints Joseph & John, by Sebastiano. d, Adoration of the Kings, by Veronese.

1994, Nov. 28 Litho. *Perf. 14*

669 A128 70c Block of 4, #a.-d. 4.50 4.50
670 A128 $1 Block of 4, #a.-d. 7.00 7.00

Robert Louis Stevenson (1850-94), Writer — A129

a, Treasure Island. b, Dr. Jekyll and Mr. Hyde. c, Kidnapped. d, Stevenson, tomb, inscription.

1994, Dec. 14 *Perf. 15x14*

671 A129 $1.75 Block of 4, #a.-d. 15.00 15.00

Flowers — A130

1996, May 10 Litho. *Perf. 14½x14*

672 A130 70c Tapeu orchid .90 .90
673 A130 $1 Frangipani 1.40 1.40
674 A130 $1.20 Golden shower 1.60 1.60
675 A130 $1.50 Pua 2.10 2.10
Nos. 672-675 (4) 6.00 6.00

Nos. 606, 608 Surcharged

1996, Feb. 19 Litho. *Perf. 14x13½*

676 A118 50c on 70c #606 11.50 8.50
677 A118 $1 on $1.50 #608 13.50 10.50

Flower Type of 1969 Redrawn

Design: 20c, Hibiscus.

1996, Aug. 22 Litho. *Rouletted 7*

678 A38 20c red & green .45 .45

Yachting — A131

1996 Litho. *Perf. 14½*

679 A131 70c Jackfish 1.00 1.00
680 A131 $1 S/V Jennifer 1.40 1.40
681 A131 $1.20 Mikeva 2.00 2.00
682 A131 $2 Eye of the Wind 3.50 3.50
Nos. 679-682 (4) 7.90 7.90

Souvenir Sheet

Perf. 14

683 A131 $1.50 Desert Star 2.50 2.50

Issued: Nos. 679-682, 9/30/96. No. 683, 10/96 (Taipei '96). No. 683 contains one 30x30mm stamp.

Coral — A132

20c, Acropora gemmifera. 50c, Acropora nobilis. 70c, Goniopora lobata. $1, Stylaster. $1.20, Alveopora catalai. $1.50, Fungia scutaria. $2, Porites solida. $3, Millepora. $4, Pocillopora eydouxi. $5, Platygyra pini.

1996, Dec. 20 Litho. *Perf. 14*

684-693 A132 Set of 10 26.00 26.00

Souvenir Sheet

New Year 1997 (Year of the Ox) A133

1997, Feb. 10 Litho. *Perf. 13*

694 A133 $1.50 multicolored 2.50 2.50

Hong Kong '97.

Humpback Whale A134

20c, Whale in water. 50c, Killer whale. 70c, Minke whale. $1, Adult, young whale swimming upward. $1.20, Sperm whale. $1.50, Whale breaching.

1997 Litho. *Perf. 14*

695	A134	20c multi	.40	.40
696	A134	50c multi, vert.	1.05	1.05
697	A134	70c multi, vert.	1.40	1.40
698	A134	$1 multi, vert.	2.25	2.25
699	A134	$1.20 multi, vert.	2.60	2.60
700	A134	$1.50 multi, vert.	3.50	3.50
a.		Souvenir sheet, #695, 698, 700	4.25	4.25
		Nos. 695-700 (6)	11.20	11.20

Pacific '97 (#700a).
Issued: 20c, $1, $1.50, 5/29; others, 9/3.

Island Scenes — A135

Designs: a, Steps leading over island along inlet. b, Island, vegetagion, sky. c, Coral reef, undersea vegetation. d, Reef, vegetation, diff.

1997, Apr. 18 Litho. *Perf. 13½x14*

701 A135 $1 Block of 4, #a.-d. 5.50 5.50

Christmas — A136

Bouquets of various flowers.

1997, Nov. 26 Litho. *Perf. 14*

702	A136	20c deep plum & multi	.30	.30
703	A136	50c green & multi	.70	.70
704	A136	70c blue & multi	1.00	1.00
705	A136	$1 red & multi	1.50	1.50
		Nos. 702-705 (4)	3.50	3.50

Diana, Princess of Wales (1961-97)
Common Design Type

Various portraits: a, 20c. b, 50c. c, $1. d, $2.

1998, Apr. 29 Litho. *Perf. 14½x14*

706 CD355 Sheet of 4, #a.-d. 5.50 5.50

No. 706 sold for $3.70 + 50c, with surtax from international sales being donated to the Princess of Wales Memorial fund and surtax from national sales being donated to designated local charity.

Diving — A137

Designs: 20c, Two snorkeling beneath water's surface. 70c, One diver, coral. $1, Diving into underwater canyon, vert. $1.20, Two divers, coral. $1.50, Divers exploring underwater cavern.

Wmk. Triangles

1998, May 20 Litho. *Perf. 14½*

707	A137	20c multicolored	.40	.40
708	A137	70c multicolored	1.00	1.00
709	A137	$1 multicolored	1.40	1.40
710	A137	$1.20 multicolored	1.75	1.75
711	A137	$1.50 multicolored	2.40	2.40
		Nos. 707-711 (5)	6.95	6.95

Sea Birds — A138

Designs: 20c, Pacific black duck. 70c, Fairy tern. $1, Great frigatebird, vert. $1.20, Lesser golden plover. $2, Brown noddy.

Perf. 14½x14, 14x14½
Wmk. Triangles

1998, July 23 Litho.

712	A138	20c multicolored	.55	.55
713	A138	70c multicolored	1.20	1.20
714	A138	$1 multicolored	2.10	2.10
715	A138	$1.20 multicolored	2.40	2.40
716	A138	$2 multicolored	3.50	3.50
		Nos. 712-716 (5)	9.75	9.75

Shells — A139

Two views of various shells from the Pacific Ocean.

Perf. 14½

1998, Sept. 23 Litho. Unwmk.

717	A139	20c multicolored	.50	.50
718	A139	70c multicolored	1.15	1.15
719	A139	$1 multicolored	2.40	2.40
720	A139	$5 multicolored	7.50	7.50
		Nos. 717-720 (4)	11.55	11.55

Ancient Weapons A140

Perf. 14x14½

1998, Nov. 18 Litho. Unwmk.

721	A140	20c Clubs	.50	.50
722	A140	$1.20 Spears	1.50	1.50
723	A140	$1.50 Spears, diff.	1.90	1.90
724	A140	$2 Throwing stones	2.60	2.60
		Nos. 721-724 (4)	6.50	6.50

Nos. 722-723 are each 60x23mm.

Maritime Heritage A141

Designs: 70c, First migration of Niue Fekai. $1, Crew of Resolution discover Niue. $1.20, LMS John Williams. $1.50, Captain James Cook (1728-79).

1999, Feb. 24 Litho. *Perf. 14½x14*

725	A141	70c bright violet blue	.90	.90
726	A141	$1 bright violet blue	1.40	1.40
727	A141	$1.20 bright violet blue	1.75	1.75
728	A141	$1.50 bright violet blue	2.10	2.10
		Nos. 725-728 (4)	6.15	6.15

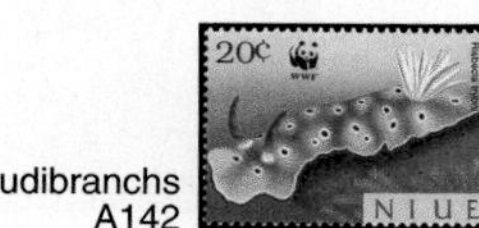

Nudibranchs A142

World Wide Fund for Nature: 20c, Risbecia tryoni. $1, Chromodoris lochi. $1.20, Chromodoris elizabethina. $1.50, Chromodoris bullocki.

1999, Mar. 17 Litho. *Perf. 14½*

729	A142	20c multicolored	.40	.40
730	A142	$1 multicolored	1.40	1.40
731	A142	$1.20 multicolored	1.50	1.50
732	A142	$1.50 multicolored	2.25	2.25
a.		Souv. sheet, 2 ea #729-732	11.50	11.50
		Nos. 729-732 (4)	5.55	5.55

Scenic Views — A143

$1, Togo Chasm, vert. $1.20, Matapa Chasm, vert. $1.50, Tufukia. $2, Talava Arches.

1999, June 16 Litho. *Perf. 14*

734	A143	$1 multicolored	1.40	1.40
735	A143	$1.20 multicolored	1.50	1.50
736	A143	$1.50 multicolored	1.90	1.90
737	A143	$2 multicolored	2.75	2.75
		Nos. 734-737 (4)	7.55	7.55

Woven Baskets — A144

Various styles and patterns: #738a, 20c. #738b, $1. #739a, 70c. #739b, $3.

1999, Sept. 18 Litho. *Perf. 12*

738	A144	Pair, a.-b.	2.00	2.00
739	A144	Pair, a.-b.	4.00	4.00

Nos. 738b, 739b are each 45x35mm.

Souvenir Sheet

Self-Government, 25th Anniv. — A145

Designs: a, 20c, Natives, boats. b, $5, Fish, tree, diver, child.

Litho. with Foil application

1999, Dec. 1 *Perf. 15x14¾*

740 A145 Sheet of 2, #a.-b 6.00 6.00

Millennium — A146

a, 20c, Man in outrigger canoe. b, 70c, Women pointing up. c, $4, Swimmers, bird, fish.

1999, Dec. 31 Litho. *Perf. 14¼x15*

741 A146 Strip of 3, #a.-c. 6.50 6.50

Birds and Flora — A147

20c, Purple-capped fruit dove, mamane. $1, Purple swamphen, fig. $1.20, Barn owl, koa. $2, Blue-crowned lory, ohia lehua.

2000, Apr. 5 Litho. *Perf. 13x13¼*

742-745 A147 Set of 4 6.50 6.50

Royal Birthdays — A148

Designs: $1.50, Queen Mother, 100th birthday, vert. $3, Prince William, 18th birthday, and Queen Mother.

2000, May 22 *Perf. 13¼x13, 13x13¼*

746-747 A148 Set of 2 4.50 4.50

2000 Summer Olympics, Sydney — A149

Designs: 50c, Pole vault. 70c, Diving. $1, Hurdles. $3, Gymnastics.

Perf. 13½x13¼

2000, Sept. 16 Litho.

748-751 A149 Set of 4 5.00 5.00

Dancers — A150

No. 752: a, Couple. b, Woman with red garments. c, Woman with white garments. d, Child with garments made of leaves.

2000, Nov. 22 Litho. *Perf. 13¼x13*

752		Horiz. strip of 4	5.00	5.00
a.	A150	20c multi	.30	.30
b.	A150	70c multi	.65	.65
c.	A150	$1.50 multi	1.30	1.30
d.	A150	$3 multi	2.75	2.75

Niue Postage Stamps, Cent. (in 2002) — A151

Designs: 70c, #1. $3, #34.

2001, Jan. 31

753-754 A151 Set of 2 3.25 3.25

Butterflies — A152

No. 755: a, Large green-banded blue. b, Leafwing. c, Cairns birdwing. d, Meadow argus.

2001, Mar. 22 *Perf. 13½x13¼*

755		Horiz. strip of 4	4.00	4.00
a.	A152	20c multi	.25	.25
b.	A152	70c multi	.60	.60
c.	A152	$1.50 multi	1.40	1.40
d.	A152	$2 multi	1.75	1.75

Turtles — A153

Designs: 50c, Green turtle hatching. $1, Hawksbill turtle. $3, Green turtle on beach.

2001, May 10

756-758 A153 Set of 3 4.00 4.00

Coconut Crabs — A154

Crab: 20c, In water. 70c, On beach. $1.50, Climbing tree. $3, With coconut.

2001, July 7 *Perf. 14*

759-762 A154 Set of 4 5.00 5.00

Annexation by New Zealand, Cent. — A155

Designs: $1.50, Building. $2, Man and woman.

2001, Oct. 19 Litho. *Perf. 13½x13¼*

763-764 A155 Set of 2 3.25 3.25

Christmas — A156

Designs: 20c, Magi. 70c, Dove. $1, Angel. $2, Star.

2001, Dec. 13 *Perf. 13x13¼*

765-768 A156 Set of 4 3.50 3.50
768a Horiz. strip, #765-768 3.50 3.50

No. 729 Surcharged

2002, July 7 **Litho.** *Perf. 14½*

769 A142 $10 on 20c multi *75.00 65.00*

Worldwide Fund for Nature (WWF) — A156a

Various depictions of small giant clam.

2002, Nov. 7 **Litho.** *Perf. 13¼x13*

769A Horiz. strip of 4 4.50 4.50
b. A156a 50c multi .60 .60
c. A156a 70c multi .75 .70
d. A156a $1 multi 1.10 1.10
e. A156a $1.50 multi 1.60 1.60
f. As #769Ab, without emblem — —
g. As #760Ac, without emblem — —
h. As #769Ad, without emblem — —
i. As #769Ae, without emblem — —
j. Souvenir sheet of 4, #769Ab-769Ae — —
k. Souvenir sheet of 4, #769Af-769Ai 10.00 —

A limited quantity of No. 769Ab received a $10 surcharge. Value, $145.

General Motors Automobiles — A157

No. 770, $1.50 — Cadillacs: a, 1953 Eldorado. b, 2002 Eldorado. c, 1967 Eldorado. d, 1961 Sedan de Ville.

No. 771, $1.50 — Corvettes: a, 1954 convertible. b, 1979. c, 1956 convertible. d, 1964 Stingray.

No. 772, $4, 1978 Cadillac Seville. No. 773, $4, 1979 Corvette.

2003 **Litho.** *Perf. 14*

Sheets of 4, #a-d

770-771 A157 Set of 2 24.00 24.00

Souvenir Sheets

772-773 A157 Set of 2 22.00 22.00

Issued: Nos. 770, 772, 8/25; Nos. 771, 773, 9/2.

Coronation of Queen Elizabeth II, 50th Anniv. — A158

No. 774: a, Wearing crown as younger woman. b, Wearing tiara. c, Wearing crown as older woman.

$4, Wearing hat.

2003, Sept. 2

774 A158 $1.50 Sheet of 3, #a-c 9.00 9.00

Souvenir Sheet

775 A158 $4 multi 9.00 9.00

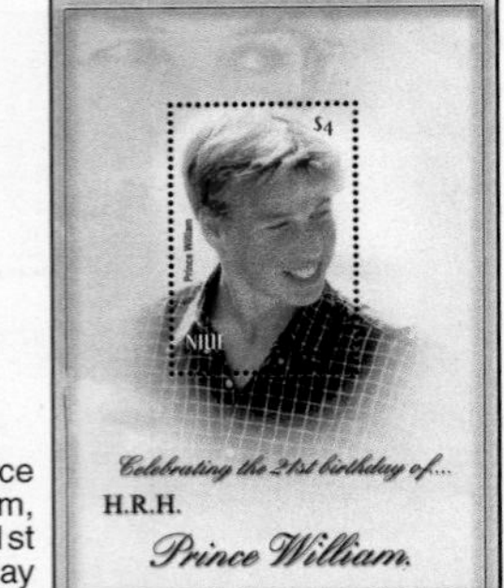

Prince William, 21st Birthday A159

No. 776: a, Wearing blue checked tie. b, Wearing shirt and jacket. c, Wearing striped shirt and tie.

$4, Wearing shirt.

2003, Sept. 2

776 A159 $1.50 Sheet of 3, #a-c 9.00 9.00

Souvenir Sheet

777 A159 $4 multi 8.50 8.50

Tour de France Bicycle Race, Cent. A160

No. 778: a, Nicholas Frantz, 1927. b, Frantz, 1928. c, Maurice de Waele, 1929. d, André Leducq, 1930.

$4, Leducq, 1930, diff.

2003, Sept. 2 *Perf. 13½x13¼*

778 A160 $1.50 Sheet of 4, #a-d 10.50 10.50

Souvenir Sheet

779 A160 $4 multi 8.75 8.75

Powered Flight, Cent. A161

No. 780: a, Boeing 737-200. b, Boeing Stratocruiser. c, Boeing Model SA-307B. d, Douglas DC-2. e, Wright Flyer I. f, De Havilland D.H.4A.

$4, Boeing 767.

2003, Sept. 2 *Perf. 14*

780 A161 80c Sheet of 6, #a-f 9.00 9.00

Souvenir Sheet

781 A161 $4 multi 9.00 9.00

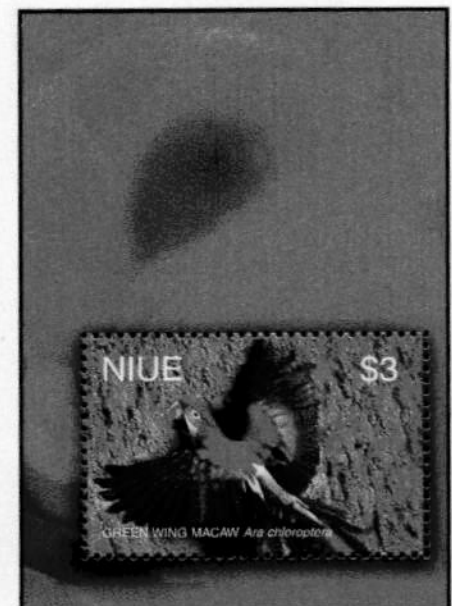

Birds, Butterflies and Fish A162

No. 782, $1.50, vert. — Birds: a, Wrinkled hornbill. b, Toco toucan. c, Roseate spoonbill. d, Blue and gold macaw.

No. 783, $1.50 — Butterflies: a, Agrias beata. b, Papilio blumei. c, Cethosia bibbis. d, Cressida cressida.

No. 784, $1.50 — Fish: a, Garibaldi fish. b, Golden damselfish. c, Squarespot anthias. d, Orange-fin anemonefish.

No. 785, $3, Green-wing macaw. No. 786, $3, Blue morpho butterfly. No. 787, $3, Maculosus angelfish.

Perf. 13½x13¼, 13¼x13½

2004, Aug. 16 **Litho.**

Sheets of 4, #a-d

782-784 A162 Set of 3 24.00 24.00

Souvenir Sheets

785-787 A162 Set of 3 12.00 12.00

Miniature Sheet

Intl. Year of Peace A163

No. 788: a, Lily. b, Thistle. c, Lily of the valley. d, Rose. e, Garland flower. f, Crocus. g, Lotus. h, Iris.

2004, Oct. 13 *Perf. 13½x13¼*

788 A163 75c Sheet of 8, #a-h 8.50 8.50

Miniature Sheet

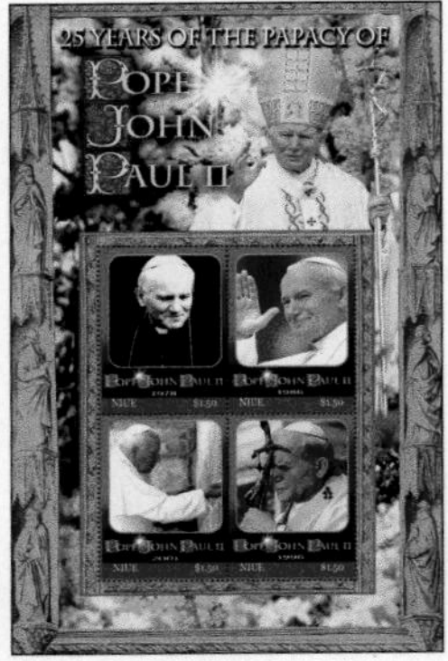

Election of Pope John Paul II, 25th Anniv. (in 2003) A164

No. 789 — Pope in: a, 1978. b, 1986. c, 2001. d, 1996.

2004, Oct. 13 *Perf. 13¼*

789 A164 $1.50 Sheet of 4, #a-d 8.50 8.50

D-Day, 60th Anniv. A165

No. 790: a, Allied Air Forces begin bombing German coastal batteries. b, Allied naval guns pound Atlantic Wall. c, Paratroopers drop over Normandy. d, Allies advance and the Germans begin to surrender.

$3, Assault troops disembark on the shores of Normandy.

2004, Oct. 13 *Perf. 13¼x13½*

790 A165 $1.50 Sheet of 4, #a-d 8.50 8.50

Souvenir Sheet

791 A165 $3 multi 4.50 4.50

Locomotives, 200th Anniv. — A166

No. 792: a, 520 Class 4-8-4, Australia. b, FEF-2 Class 4-8-4, US. c, Royal Scot Class 4-6-0, Great Britain. d, A4 Class 4-6-2, Great Britain.

$3, Class GS-4 4-8-4, US.

2004, Oct. 13

792 A166 $1.50 Sheet of 4, #a-d 8.50 8.50

Souvenir Sheet

793 A166 $3 multi 4.50 4.50

Pope John Paul II (1920-2005) A167

2005, Dec. 13 **Litho.** *Perf. 13¼*

794 A167 $2 multi 3.00 3.00

Printed in sheets of 4.

Rotary International, Cent. — A168

No. 795: a, Children. b, Paul P. Harris, Rotary founder. c, Carlo Ravizza, 1999-2000 Rotary International President.

$3, Dr. Jonas Salk, polio vaccine pioneer.

2005, Dec. 22

795 A168 $1.50 Sheet of 3, #a-c 6.50 6.50

Souvenir Sheet

796 A168 $3 multi 4.50 4.50

Pope Benedict XVI — A169

2005, Dec. 27

797 A169 $1.50 multi 2.25 2.25

Printed in sheets of 4.

Hans Christian Andersen (1805-75), Author — A170

No. 798 — Andersen and country name and denomination in: a, Lilac. b, Ocher. c, Red.

$3, Andersen facing left.

2005, Dec. 27

798 A170 $1.50 Sheet of 3, #a-c 6.50 6.50

Souvenir Sheet

799 A170 $3 multi 4.50 4.50

World Cup Soccer Championships, 75th Anniv. — A171

No. 800: a, Frank Bauman. b, Marcus Babbel. c, Dietmar Hamann.

$3, Christian Worns.

2005, Dec. 27

800 A171 $1.50 Sheet of 3, #a-c 6.50 6.50

Souvenir Sheet

801 A171 $3 multi 4.50 4.50

End of World War II, 60th Anniv. A172

No. 802, horiz.: a, Entertaining the troops in the Pacific. b, USS Argonaut sailors reading letters from home. c, Japan surrenders on USS Missouri. d, A toast to peace. e, Entertainment at sea. f, Welcoming peace.

No. 803: a, D-Day invasion, Normandy, France. b, Lt. Meyrick Clifton-James, double for Field Marshal Bernard Montgomery. c, RAF Hawker Typhoon over French coast. d, Allied war cemetery, St. Laurent-sur-Mer, France.

No. 804, $3, Sir Winston Churchill. No. 805, $3, Pres. Franklin D. Roosevelt.

2005, Dec. 27

802 A172 75c Sheet of 6, #a-f 6.75 6.75
803 A172 $1.25 Sheet of 4, #a-d 7.50 7.50

Souvenir Sheets

804-805 A172 Set of 2 9.00 9.00

Souvenir Sheets

National Basketball Association Players and Team Emblems — A173

No. 806, $4.50: a, LeBron James. b, Cleveland Cavaliers emblem.

No. 807, $4.50: a, Tim Duncan. b, San Antonio Spurs emblem.

No. 808, $4.50: a, Allen Iverson. b, Denver Nuggets emblem.

No. 809, $4.50: a, Kobe Bryant. b, Los Angeles Lakers emblem.

No. 810, $4.50: a, Tracy McGrady. b, Houston Rockets emblem.

No. 811, $4.50: a, Jermaine O'Neal. b, Indiana Pacers emblem.

Litho. & Embossed

2007, Feb. 4 ***Imperf.***

Without Gum

Sheets of 2, #a-b

806-811 A173 Set of 6 77.50 77.50

Miniature Sheet

Elvis Presley (1935-77) — A174

No. 812 — Presley: a, With hands resting on guitar. b, In green shirt, playing guitar. c, In brown red shirt, playing guitar. d, Holding guitar by neck.

2007, Feb. 15 Litho. ***Perf. 12¾***

812 A174 $1.50 Sheet of 4, #a-d 8.50 8.50

Miniature Sheets

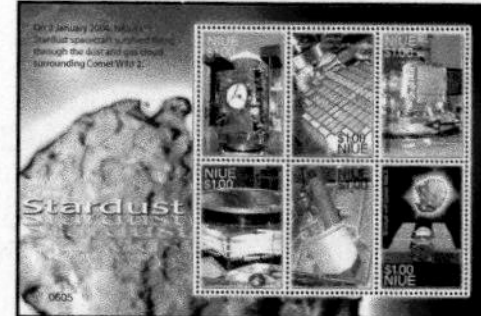

Space Achievements — A175

No. 813: a, Stardust probe at Kennedy Space Center. b, Stardust dust collector with aerogel. c, Stardust navigational camera. d, Stardust Whipple shield. e, Cometary and interstellar dust analyzer. f, Stardust and Comet Wild 2.

No. 814, horiz. — Artist's rendition of future projects: a, Astrobiology field laboratory. b, Deep-drill lander. c, Mars science laboratory. d, Phoenix lander.

2007, Feb. 15

813 A175 $1 Sheet of 6, #a-f 8.50 8.50
814 A175 $1.50 Sheet of 4, #a-d 8.50 8.50

Queen Elizabeth II, 80th Birthday (in 2006) A176

No. 815 — Dress color: a, Brown. b, Pink. c, Red. d, White.

$3, Purple.

2007, Feb. 15 ***Perf. 12¼x12***

815 A176 $1.50 Sheet of 4, #a-d 8.50 8.50

Souvenir Sheet

Perf. 13¼

816 A176 $3 multi 4.50 4.50

Rembrandt (1606-69), Painter — A177

Designs: 75c, Life Study of a Young Man Pulling a Rope. $1.25, Self-portrait. $1.50, Joseph Telling His Dreams. $2, The Blindness of Tobit.

$3, Christ in the Storm on the Lake of Galilee.

2007, Feb. 15 ***Perf. 12¼x12***

817-820 A177 Set of 4 8.25 8.25

Imperf

Size: 70x100mm

821 A177 $3 multi 4.75 4.75

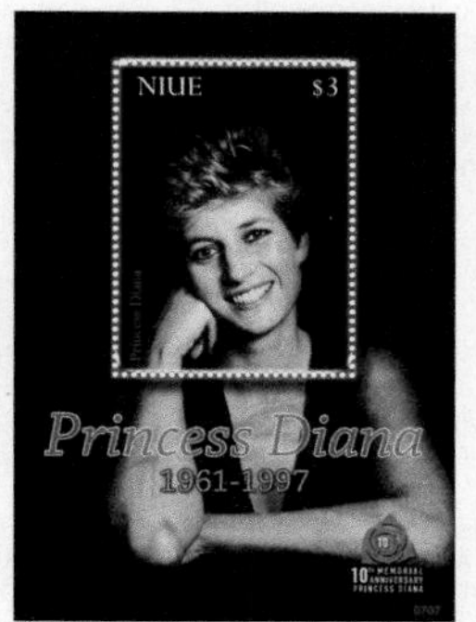

Princess Diana (1961-97) — A178

No. 822 — Diana wearing: a, Purple dress. b, Tiara and black dress. c, Green dress, close-up. d, Purple dress, close-up. e, Tiara, close-up. f, Green dress.

$3, Diana with head on hand.

2007, May 3 ***Perf. 13½x13¼***

822 A178 $1 Sheet of 6, #a-f 9.50 9.50

Souvenir Sheet

823 A178 $3 multi 4.75 4.75

Local Attractions, Flora and Fauna — A179

Designs: 20c, Palaha Cave. 70c, White pua flower. $1, Talava Natural Arch. $1.20, Avaiki Pool. $1.50, Coral rock spears. $2, Humpback whale. $3, Spinner dolphins.

2007, July 9 Litho. ***Perf. 14x14¾***

824 A179 20c multi .35 .35
825 A179 70c multi 1.20 1.20
826 A179 $1 multi 1.60 1.60
827 A179 $1.20 multi 2.00 2.00
828 A179 $1.50 multi 2.40 2.40
829 A179 $2 multi 3.25 3.25
830 A179 $3 multi 4.75 4.75
Nos. 824-830 (7) 15.55 15.55

Miniature Sheets

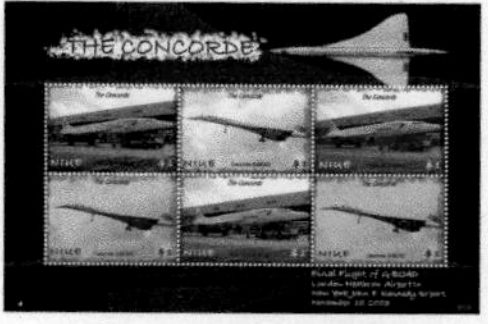

Concorde — A180

No. 831, $1: a, Concorde and hangar, blue tint. b, Concorde in air, normal tint. c, Concorde and hangar, red tint. d, Concorde in air, pink tint. e, Concorde and hangar, normal tint. f, Concorde in air, blue tint.

No. 832, $1: a, Concorde landing, yellow green frame. b, Concorde being towed, gray frame. c, Concorde landing, green gray frame. d, Concorde being towed, brown frame. e, Concorde landing, gray frame. f, Concorde being towed, blue frame.

2007, July 21 ***Perf. 13¼***

Sheets of 6, #a-f

831-832 A180 Set of 2 19.00 19.00

Wedding of Queen Elizabeth II and Prince Philip, 60th Anniv. A181

No. 833, vert.: a, Queen and Prince, "N" of "Niue" and denomination over white area, parts of flag in faded area between country name and denomination. b, Queen, "N" of "Niue" and denomination over white and blue areas. c, Queen, flower buds in faded area between country name and denomination. d, Queen and Prince, "N" of "Niue" and denomination over gray area, parts of flag in faded area between country name and denomination. e, Queen and Prince, country name and denomination over solid gray area. f, Queen, country name and denomination over solid gray area.

$3, Queen and Prince.

2007, July 21 ***Perf. 13¼***

833 A181 $1 Sheet of 6, #a-f 9.25 9.25

Souvenir Sheet

834 A181 $3 multi 4.25 4.25

Miniature Sheets

A182

Marilyn Monroe (1926-62), Actress — A183

Various portraits.

2007, Aug. 21

835 A182 $1.50 Sheet of 4, #a-d 8.50 8.50
836 A183 $1.50 Sheet of 4, #a-d 8.50 8.50

Jamestown, Virginia, 400th Anniv. — A184

No. 837: a, Marriage of John Rolfe to Pocahontas. b, First settlers reach Jamestown. c, Tobacco plant. d, Capt. John Smith. e, Jamestown Tercentenary Monument. f, Map of Jamestown.

$3, Queen Elizabeth II and Prince Philip at Jamestown.

2007, Aug. 21

837 A184 $1 Sheet of 6, #a-f 9.00 9.00

Souvenir Sheet

838 A184 $3 multi 4.50 4.50

Pope Benedict XVI — A185

2007, Dec. 3 Litho. ***Perf. 13¼***

839 A185 70c multi 1.25 1.25

Printed in sheets of 8.

Miniature Sheet

Ferrari Automobiles, 60th Anniv. — A186

No. 840: a, 1949 166 FL. b, 1991 512 TR. c, 2003 Challenge Stradale. d, 1988 F1 87/88C. e, 2007 F2007. f, Building with Ferrari sign.

2007, Dec. 10

840 A186 $1 Sheet of 6, #a-f 10.50 10.50

Tourism — A187

Designs: 10c, Coconut palm. 20c, Tropical sunset. 30c, Humpback whale. 50c, Rainbow over rainforest. $1, Hio Beach. $1.20, Talava Arches. $1.40, Limu Pools. $1.70, Limestone caves. $2, Snorkeling in Limu Pools. $3, Panoramic coastline. $5, Liku Caves.

Perf. 13½x13¼

2009, Sept. 14 **Litho.**

841 A187 10c multi .25 .25
842 A187 20c multi .30 .30
843 A187 30c multi .45 .45
844 A187 50c multi .75 .75
845 A187 $1 multi 1.50 1.50
846 A187 $1.20 multi 1.75 1.75
a. Miniature sheet of 6, #841-846, perf. 14 5.00 5.00
847 A187 $1.40 multi 2.00 2.00
848 A187 $1.70 multi 2.50 2.50
849 A187 $2 multi 3.00 3.00
850 A187 $3 multi 4.50 4.50

851 A187 $5 multi 7.25 7.25
a. Miniature sheet of 5, #847-851, perf. 14 19.50 19.50
Nos. 841-851 (11) 24.25 24.25

Christmas — A188

Stained-glass window depicting: 30c, Man facing right, Ekalesia Millennium Hall. 80c, Dove, Lakepa Ekalesia Church. $1.20, Chalice and bread, Lakepa Ekalesia Church. $1.40, Man facing left, Ekalesia Millennium Hall.

Perf. 13¼x13½

2009, Nov. 25 **Litho.**
852-855 A188 Set of 4 5.50 5.50
855a Souvenir sheet, #852-855 5.50 5.50

Butterflies A189

Designs: $1.40, Hypolimnas bolina. $1.70, Junonia villida, vert. (22x26mm). $2.40, Hypolimnas antilope.

2010, July 7 **Litho.** ***Perf. 14***
856-858 A189 Set of 3 8.00 8.00
858a Souvenir sheet of 3, #856-858 8.00 8.00

Christmas — A190

Designs: a, Annunciation. b, Journey to Bethlehem. c, Nativity. d, Adoration of the Shepherds.

2010, Oct. 20 ***Perf. 13¼x13½***
859 Horiz. strip of 4 12.00 12.00
a. A190 30c multicolored .45 .45
b. A190 $1.40 multicolored 2.10 2.10
c. A190 $2 multicolored 3.00 3.00
d. A190 $4 multicolored 6.00 6.00

Whales — A191

Designs: 80c, Whale's flukes. $1.20, Two whales raising heads out of water. $1.40, Calf breaching surface. $2, Mother and calf playing.

2010, Nov. 17 **Litho.** ***Perf. 14***
860-863 A191 Set of 4 8.50 8.50
863a Souvenir sheet, #860-863 8.50 8.50

Wedding of Prince William and Catherine Middleton — A192

No. 864: a, $2.40, Catherine Middleton. b, $3.40, Prince William.

2011, Mar. 23
864 A192 Horiz. pair, #a-b 9.25 9.25
c. Souvenir sheet, #864a-864b 9.25 9.25

Birds — A193

Designs: $1.70, Aplonis tabuensis. $2, Lalage maculosa, vert. (25x30mm). $2.40, Ptilinopus porphyraceus.

2011, July 6
865-867 A193 Set of 3 10.50 10.50
867a Souvenir sheet of 3, #865-867 10.50 10.50

Christmas — A194

Designs: 30c, Pacific sunset. $1.40, Matapa Chasm. $2, Coconut palms. $4, Centennial Church, Alofi.

2011, Nov. 16 ***Perf. 13¼x13½***
868-871 A194 Set of 4 12.00 12.00
871a Souvenir sheet of 4, #868-871 12.00 12.00

Shells — A195

Designs: $1.20, Map cowrie. $1.40, Geography cone. $1.70, Partridge tun. $2, Tiger cowrie.

2012, Apr. 11 ***Perf. 13½x13¼***
872-875 A195 Set of 4 10.50 10.50
875a Souvenir sheet of 4, #872-875 10.50 10.50

Reign of Queen Elizabeth II, 60th Anniv. — A196

Hibiscus flowers and photograph of Queen Elizabeth II from: $2.40, 1953. $3.40, 2012.

2012, May 23 ***Perf. 13¼x13½***
876-877 A196 Set of 2 9.00 9.00
877a Souvenir sheet of 2, #876-877 9.00 9.00
877b Horiz. pair, #876-877 9.00 9.00

Worldwide Fund For Nature (WWF) — A197

Various depictions of Giant sea fan: $1.20, $1.40, $1.70, $2.

2012, Sept. 5 ***Perf. 13½x13¼***
878-881 A197 Set of 4 10.50 10.50
881a Souvenir sheet of 4, #878-881 10.50 10.50

Christmas — A198

Designs: 30c, Angel and infant Jesus. $1.40, Holy Family. $2, Magi. $4, Shepherds.

2012, Nov. 21
882-885 A198 Set of 4 13.00 13.00

Niue Blue Butterfly — A199

Designs: $1.20, Male underside. $1.40, Male upperside. $1.70, Female underside. $2, Female upperside.

2013, Apr. 10 ***Perf. 13½***
886-889 A199 Set of 4 10.50 10.50
889a Souvenir sheet of 4, #886-889 10.50 10.50

Coronation of Queen Elizabeth II, 60th Anniv. — A200

Designs: $2.40, Queen Elizabeth II. $3.40, Queen Elizabeth II, Prince Philip, Princess Margaret, Queen Mother.

2013, May 8 ***Perf. 13¼x13½***
890-891 A200 Set of 2 9.25 9.25
891a Souvenir sheet of 2, #890-891 9.25 9.25

Christmas — A201

Designs: 30c, Dove. $1.40, Angel. $2, Star of Bethlehem. $4, Bells.

Perf. 13¼x13¾

2013, Nov. 20 **Litho.**
892-895 A201 Set of 4 13.00 13.00
895a Souvenir sheet of 4, #892-895 13.00 13.00

Traditional Dress — A202

Designs: 30c, Pulou (hat). $1.40, Pipi (belt). $2, Tiputa (poncho). $4, Patutiti (skirt).

2014, Apr. 23 **Litho.** ***Perf. 13½x13¼***
896-899 A202 Set of 4 13.50 13.50
899a Souvenir sheet of 4 #896-899 13.50 13.50

Fish — A203

Designs: 30c, Whitemouth moray. $1.40, Orangefin anemonefish. $2, Fire dartfish. $4, Longnose butterflyfish.

Perf. 13½x13¼

2014, June 18 **Litho.**
900-903 A203 Set of 4 13.50 13.50
903a Souvenir sheet of 4 #900-903 13.50 13.50

Island Views A204

Designs: 20c, Talava Arches. 30c, Mutalau. $1, Avaiki Caves. $1.20, Lakepa Village Church. $1.40, Golf course. $1.70, Huvalu Forest. $2, Tepa Point. $4, Togo Chasm.

2014, Oct. 18 **Litho.** ***Perf. 14x14¼***
904 A204 20c multi .35 .35
905 A204 30c multi .50 .50
906 A204 $1 multi 1.60 1.60
907 A204 $1.20 multi 1.90 1.90
908 A204 $1.40 multi 2.25 2.25
909 A204 $1.70 multi 2.75 2.75
910 A204 $2 multi 3.25 3.25
911 A204 $4 multi 6.25 6.25
Nos. 904-911 (8) 18.85 18.85

Christmas — A205

Various Christmas ornaments in: 30c Blue. $1.40, Red. $2, Green. $4, Purple.

Perf. 13¼x13½

2014, Dec. 10 **Litho.**
912-915 A205 Set of 4 12.00 12.00
915a Souvenir sheet of 4, #912-915 12.00 12.00

Haipo (Tapa Cloths) — A206

Various haipo designs: 30c, $1.40, $2, $4.

2015, Apr. 7 **Litho.** ***Perf. 13½***
916-919 A206 Set of 4 12.00 12.00
919a Souvenir sheet of 4, #916-919 12.00 12.00

Flora — A207

Designs: 30c, Hibiscus tiliaceus. $1.40, Fagraea Berteroana. $2, Alphitonia zizyphoides. $4, Cordyline fruticosa.

2015, June 3 **Litho.** ***Perf. 13½***
920-923 A207 Set of 4 10.50 10.50
923a Souvenir sheet of 4, #920-923 10.50 10.50

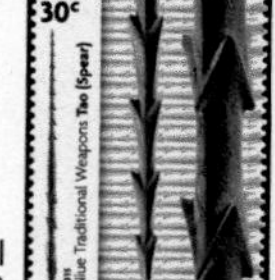

Traditional Weapons — A208

Designs: 30c, Spear. $1.40, Club. $3, Spear, diff. $4, Club, diff.

2015, Aug. 5 **Litho.** ***Perf. 13½***
924-927 A208 Set of 4 11.00 11.00
927a Souvenir sheet of 4, #924-927 11.00 11.00

Miniature Sheet

World War I, Cent. A209

No. 928: a, 20c, Life in Niue, pre-war. b, 30c, Soldiers at Narrow Neck Camp, Auckland. c, $1, Troops departing for war from Auckland. d, $1.20, Badge of New Zealand Pioneer Battalion, map of Egypt. e, $1.40, Trench in Armentières, France. f, $1.70, New Zealand Convalescent Hospital, Hornchurch, England. g, $2, Soldiers and nurses recovering in Auckland. h, $4, War Memorial, Niue.

2015, Oct. 13 **Litho.** ***Perf. 14x14½***
928 A209 Sheet of 8, #a-h 16.00 16.00

Christmas — A210

Carols: 30c, Silent Night. $1.40, Joy to the World. $2, Away in the Manger. $4, Deck the Halls.

2015, Nov. 25 Litho. *Perf. 14½*
929-932 A210 Set of 4 10.50 10.50
932a Souvenir sheet of 4, #929-932 10.50 10.50

Queen Elizabeth II, 90th Birthday — A211

Queen Elizabeth II: $2.40, As young child. $3.40, In 2016.

2016, May 4 Litho. *Perf. 13¼x13½*
933-934 A211 Set of 2 8.00 8.00
934a Souvenir sheet of 2, #933-934 8.00 8.00

Humpback Whale — A212

Designs: 30c, Whale with flukes above water. $1.40, Two whales exhaling. $2, Whale with head above water. $4, Whale breaching surface of water.

2016, Aug. 3 Litho. *Perf. 14x14¼*
935-938 A212 Set of 4 11.50 11.50
938a Souvenir sheet of 4, #935-938 11.50 11.50

Language Week — A213

Niuean phrases for: 30c, "Hello." $1.40, "How are you?" $2, "Nice to meet you." $4, "Goodbye."

2016, Oct. 5 Litho. *Perf. 13¼x13½*
939-942 A213 Set of 4 11.50 11.50
942a Souvenir sheet of 4, #939-942 11.50 11.50

Christmas — A214

Winning children's art in stamp design contest: 30c, Golden grouper, by Bailey Pasisi. $1.40, Family arriving for Christmas feast, by Bentley Poihenga. $2, Gift box, by Iva Tanevesi. $4, Family at Christmas, by Flornie R. Malinao.

2016, Dec. 7 Litho. *Perf. 14x14¼*
943-946 A214 Set of 4 11.00 11.00
946a Souvenir sheet of 4, #943-946 11.00 11.00

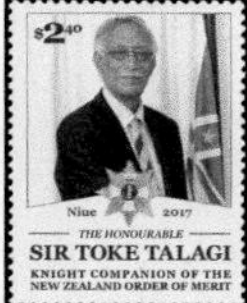

Awarding of Knight Companion of the New Zealand Order of Merit to Niue Premier Sir Toke Talagi — A215

Designs: $2.40, Talagi and Niue flag. $3.40, Talagi.

2017, Mar. 21 Litho. *Perf. 13½*
947-948 A215 Set of 2 8.25 8.25

Reptiles — A216

Designs: 30c, Mourning gecko. $1.40, Flat-tail sea snake. $2, Snake-eyed skink. $4, Pacific slender-toed gecko.

2017, Apr. 5 Litho. *Perf. 13½*
949-952 A216 Set of 4 11.00 11.00
952a Souvenir sheet of 4, #949-952 11.00 11.00

Walkways — A217

Designs: 30c, Matapa Chasm. $1.40, Avaiki Cave. $2, Anapala Chasm. $4, Talava Arches.

2017, July 12 Litho. *Perf. 13½*
953-956 A217 Set of 4 11.50 11.50
956a Souvenir sheet of 4, #953-956 11.50 11.50

Butterflyfish A218

Designs: 30c, Reticulate butterflyfish. $1.40, Bennett's butterflyfish. $2, Lined butterflyfish. $4, Acropora butterflyfish.

2017, Sept. 20 Litho. *Perf. 13½*
957-960 A218 Set of 4 11.00 11.00
960a Souvenir sheet of 4, #957-960 11.00 11.00

70th Wedding Anniversary of Queen Elizabeth II and Prince Philip — A219

Photographs of Queen Elizabeth II and Prince Philip: 30c, On wedding day, 1947. $1.40, With their children, 1960. $2, On vacation, 1972. $4, With family of Duke and Duchess of Cambridge at Trooping the Colors ceremony, 2017.

2017, Nov. 20 Litho. *Perf. 13¼*
961-964 A219 Set of 4 10.50 10.50
964a Souvenir sheet of 4, #961-964 10.50 10.50

Christmas — A220

Flowers: 30c, Frangipani. $1.40, Guava. $2, Hibiscus. $4, Papaya.

2017, Dec. 6 Litho. *Perf. 14x14¼*
965-968 A220 Set of 4 11.00 11.00
968a Souvenir sheet of 4, #965-968 11.00 11.00

Fruit Trees — A221

Designs: 30c, Lime. $1.40, Mango. $2, Avocado. $4, Coconut.

2018, Mar. 7 Litho. *Perf. 13¼x13½*
969-972 A221 Set of 4 11.50 11.50
972a Souvenir sheet of 4, #969-972 11.50 11.50

Wedding of Prince Harry and Meghan Markle — A222

Couple: 30c, Walking down steps. $1.40, Looking at each other. $2, Kissing on wedding day. $4, Holding hands on wedding day.

2018, May 21 Litho. *Perf. 13¼x13½*
973-976 A222 Set of 4 11.00 11.00
976a Souvenir sheet of 4, #973-976 11.00 11.00

Map of Niue A223

No. 977 — Map of Niue highlighting: a, 30c, Marine Reserve. b, $1.40, Coral reef. c, $2, International Airport. d, $4, Huvalu Conservation Area.

2018, Sept. 5 Litho. *Perf. 13¼x13½*
977 A223 Block of 4, #a-d 10.50 10.50
e. Souvenir sheet of 4, #977a-977d 10.50 10.50

Items From Taoga Niue Museum — A224

Designs: 30c, Woven tray. $1.40, Walking stick. $2, Close combat club. $4, Arrowroot grater.

2018, Oct. 19 Litho. *Perf. 13¼x13½*
978-981 A224 Set of 4 10.50 10.50
981a Souvenir sheet of 4, #978-981 10.50 10.50

Paintings by John Pule — A225

Paintings: 30c, Pia. $1.40, Hafata. $2, First Time Outside. $4, Kavaka.

2019, June 5 Litho. *Perf. 14x14¼*
982-985 A225 Set of 4 10.50 10.50
985a Souvenir sheet of 4, #982-985 10.50 10.50

First Man on the Moon, 50th Anniv. — A226

Designs: 30c, Apollo 11 on launchpad. $1.40, Launch of Apollo 11. $2, Astronaut on Moon. $4, Apollo 11 capsule in ocean.

2019, July 5 Litho. *Perf. 13¼x13½*
986-989 A226 Set of 4 10.00 10.00
989a Souvenir sheet of 4, #986-989 10.00 10.00

Queen Victoria (1819-1901) — A227

Roses and various depictions of Queen Victoria: 30c, $1.40, $2, $4.

2019, Oct. 16 Litho. *Perf. 14x14½*
990-993 A227 Set of 4 10.00 10.00
993a Souvenir sheet of 4, #990-993 10.00 10.00

Christmas — A228

Star of Bethlehem and: 30c, Angel, Mary and infant Jesus. $1.40, Magus. $2, Angel and shepherd. $4, Magus, shepherd, Mary and infant Jesus.

2019, Dec. 4 Litho. *Perf. 13¼x13½*
994-997 A228 Set of 4 10.50 10.50
997a Souvenir sheet of 4, #994-997 10.50 10.50

Woven Items — A229

Designs: 30c, Potu. $1.40, Kato with cover and straps. $2, Kato with strap. $4, Iliili.

2020, Apr. 16 Litho. *Perf. 13¼x13½*
998-1001 A229 Set of 4 9.50 9.50
1001a Souvenir sheet of 4, #998-1001 9.50 9.50

Boys' Brigade in Niue, 75th Anniv. — A230

Designs: 30c, Brigade emblem. $1.40, Emblem and 38 people. $2, Emblem and 13 people. $4, Emblem and 49 people.

2021, Apr. 7 Litho. *Perf. 13½*
1002-1005 A230 Set of 4 11.00 11.00
1005a Souvenir sheet of 4, #1002-1005 11.00 11.00

SEMI-POSTAL STAMPS

Catalogue values for unused stamps in this section are for Never Hinged items.

Easter Type of 1978
Souvenir Sheets

Designs: No. B1, Descent from the Cross, by Caravaggio. No. B2, Burial of Christ, by Bellini. Sheets show paintings from which stamp designs were taken.

1978, Mar. 15 Photo. *Perf. 13½*
B1 A61 70c + 5c multi 1.00 1.00
B2 A61 70c + 5c multi 1.00 1.00

Surtax was for school children in Niue.

Christmas Type of 1978
Souvenir Sheets

1978, Nov. 30 Photo. ***Perf. 13***

B3 A63 60c + 5c like #232 .90 .90
B4 A63 60c + 5c like #233 .90 .90
B5 A63 60c + 5c like #234 .90 .90
Nos. B3-B5 (3) 2.70 2.70

Surtax was for school children of Niue. The sheets show paintings from which designs of stamps were taken.

Easter Type of 1979
Souvenir Sheets

1979, Apr. 2

B6 A64 70c + 5c like #235 1.10 1.10
B7 A64 70c + 5c like #236 1.10 1.10

Surtax was for school children of Niue. The sheets show altarpiece from which designs of stamps were taken.

IYC Type of 1979
Souvenir Sheets

1979, May 31 Photo. ***Perf. 13***

B8 A65 70c + 5c like #237 .85 .85
B9 A65 70c + 5c like #238 .85 .85
B10 A65 70c + 5c like #239 .85 .85
B11 A65 70c + 5c like #240 .85 .85
Nos. B8-B11 (4) 3.40 3.40

Sheets show paintings from which designs of stamps were taken.

Christmas Type of 1979
Souvenir Sheets

1979, Nov. 29 Photo. ***Perf. 13***

B12 A70 85c + 5c like #258 .80 .80
B13 A70 85c + 5c like #259 .80 .80
B14 A70 85c + 5c like #260 .80 .80
B15 A70 85c + 5c like #261 .80 .80
Nos. B12-B15 (4) 3.20 3.20

Multicolored margins show entire paintings.

Nos. 241-245, 251-254, 255-257, 258-261 Srchd. in Black (2 lines) or Silver (3 lines)

1980, Jan. 25 Photo. ***Perf. 14, 13½***

B16 A66 20c + 2c Pair, #a-b .55 .55
B18 A68 20c + 2c multi (S) .30 .30
B19 A70 20c + 2c multi (S) .30 .30
B20 A70 25c + 2c multi (S) .40 .40
B21 A66 30c + 2c Pair, #a-b .80 .80
B23 A68 30c + 2c multi (S) .45 .45
B24 A69 30c + 2c multi (S) .45 .45
B25 A70 30c + 2c multi (S) .45 .45
B26 A66 35c + 2c Pair, #a-b 1.00 1.00
B28 A68 35c + 2c multi (S) .55 .55
B29 A69 35c + 2c multi (S) .55 .55
B30 A66 50c + 2c Pair, #a-b 1.20 1.20
B32 A70 50c + 2c multi (S) .65 .65
B33 A66 60c + 2c Pair, #a-b 1.40 1.40
B35 A69 60c + 2c multi (S) .80 .80
B36 A68 75c + 2c multi (S) 1.00 1.00
Nos. B16-B36 (16) 10.85 10.85

Easter Type of 1980
Souvenir Sheets

1980, Apr. 2 Photo. ***Perf. 13***

B37 Sheet of 3 1.05 1.05
a. A71 25c + 2c like #262 .30 .30
b. A71 30c + 2c like #263 .35 .35
c. A71 35c + 2c like #264 .40 .40

1980, Apr. 2

B38 A71 85c + 5c like #262 .75 .75
B39 A71 85c + 5c like #263 .75 .75
B40 A71 85c + 5c like #264 .75 .75
Nos. B38-B40 (3) 2.25 2.25

Surtax was for hurricane relief.

No. 245c Overprinted and Surcharged
Souvenir Sheet

1980, Aug. 22 Photo. ***Perf. 14***

B41 Sheet of 10 5.00 5.00
a. A66 20c + 2c pair .50 .50
b. A66 30c + 2c pair .65 .65
c. A66 35c + 2c pair .80 .80
d. A66 50c + 2c pair 1.25 1.25
e. A66 60c + 2c pair 1.60 1.60

ZEAPEX '80, New Zealand Intl. Stamp Exhib., Auckland, Aug. 23-31.

Nos. 293-296 Surcharged in Black
Souvenir Sheet

1980, Oct. 30 Photo. ***Perf. 14***

B42 Sheet of 8, #a.-h. 2.50 2.50

22nd Summer Olympic Games, Moscow, July 19-Aug. 3.

Christmas Type of 1980
Souvenir Sheets

1980, Nov. 28 Photo. ***Perf. 13½x13***

B43 A76 80c + 5c like #301 .75 .75
B44 A76 80c + 5c like #302 .75 .75
B45 A76 80c + 5c like #303 .75 .75
B46 A76 80c + 5c like #304 .75 .75
Nos. B43-B46 (4) 3.00 3.00

Nos. B43-B46 each contain one 31x39mm stamp.

Easter Type of 1981
Souvenir Sheets

1981, Apr. 10 Photo. ***Perf. 13½***

B47 Sheet of 3 1.75 1.75
a. A78 35c + 2c like #337 .40 .40
b. A78 50c + 2c like #338 .50 .50
c. A78 60c + 2c like #339 .60 .60
B48 A78 80c + 5c like #337 .75 .75
B49 A78 80c + 5c like #338 .75 .75
B50 A78 80c + 5c like #339 .75 .75
Nos. B47-B50 (4) 4.00 4.00

Soccer Type of 1981

1981, Oct. 16 Photo. ***Perf. 13***

B51 A80 Sheet of 9 3.25 3.25

#B51 contains #343-345 each with 3c surtax.

Nos. 340-342a Surcharged

1981, Nov. 3 Photo. ***Perf. 14***

B52 A79 75c + 5c like #340 1.00 1.00
B53 A79 95c + 5c like #341 1.25 1.25
B54 A79 $1.20 + 5c like #342 1.50 1.50
Nos. B52-B54 (3) 3.75 3.75

Souvenir Sheet

B55 Sheet of 3 4.50 4.50
a. A79 75c + 10c like #340 1.20 1.20
b. A79 95c + 10c like #341 1.40 1.40
c. A79 $1.20 + 10c like #342 1.75 1.75

Intl. Year of the Disabled. Surtax was for disabled.

Nos. 530-535 Surcharged in Black on Silver

1986, Nov. 21 Litho. ***Perf. 14***

B56 A105 80c + 10c multi 2.75 2.75
B57 A105 $1.15 + 10c multi 3.75 3.75
B58 A105 $1.80 + 10c multi 5.50 5.50
B59 A105 $2.60 + 10c multi 8.00 8.00
Nos. B56-B59 (4) 20.00 20.00

Souvenir Sheets

Perf. 13½

B60 Sheet of 4 18.00 18.00
a.-d. A105 $1.50 + 10c on #534a-534d 4.50 4.50

Perf. 14½x13½

B61 A105 $7.50 + 50c multi 18.00 18.00

No. B60 ovptd. "FIRST VISIT OF A POPE TO SOUTH PACIFIC" and "HIS HOLINESS POPE JOHN PAUL II" on margin. No. B61 ovptd. on margin only "Visit of Pope John Paul II, Nov 21-24 1986 / First Papal Visit to the South Pacific."

Souvenir Sheets

Aupex '97 Stamp Exhibition — SP1

1997, June 9 Litho. ***Perf. 14x15***

B62 SP1 $2 +20c like #1 3.75 3.75

Perf. 14½x15

B63 SP1 $2 +20c like #34 3.25 3.25

No. B63 contains one 31x60mm stamp.

AIR POST STAMPS

Catalogue values for unused stamps in this section are for Never Hinged items.

Type of 1977

Designs: 15c, Preparing ground for taro. 20c, Banana harvest. 23c, Bush plantation. 50c, Canoe fishing. 90c, Reef fishing. $1.35, Preparing ground for taro. $2.10, Shellfish gathering. $2.60, Luku harvest.

1979 Litho. ***Perf. 14***

C1 A54 15c gold & multi .30 .25
C2 A54 20c gold & multi .30 .25
C3 A54 23c gold & multi .30 .30
C4 A54 50c gold & multi .45 .45
C5 A54 90c gold & multi .70 .70
C6 A54 $1.35 gold & multi 1.10 1.10
C7 A54 $2.10 gold & multi 1.75 1.75
C8 A54 $2.60 gold & multi 2.25 2.25
C9 A54 $5.10 like #187 4.25 4.25
C10 A54 $6.35 like #188 5.50 5.50
Nos. C1-C10 (10) 16.90 16.80

Issue dates: Nos. C1-C5, Feb. 26. Nos. C6-C8, Mar. 30. C9-C10, May 28.

OFFICIAL STAMPS

Catalogue values for unused stamps in this section are for Never Hinged items.

Nos. 417-430, 332-334, 431-431A Ovptd. in Metallic Blue or Gold

Perf. 13½, 13½x13, 13x13½, 13

1985-87 Photo.

O1 A89 12c multi .30 .25
O2 A89 25c multi .30 .25
O3 A89 30c multi .30 .25
O4 A89 35c multi .30 .25
O5 A89 40c multi .30 .30
O6 A89 52c multi .40 .40
O7 A89 58c multi .50 .50
O8 A89 70c multi .55 .55
O9 A89 83c multi .65 .65
O10 A89 $1.05 multi .75 .75
O11 A90 $1.75 multi 1.50 1.50
O12 A90 $2.30 multi 2.50 2.50
O13 A90 $3.90 multi 4.75 4.75
O14 A77a $4 multi (G) 4.50 4.50
O15 A90 $5 multi 5.50 5.50
O16 A77a $6 multi ('87) (G) 10.00 10.00
O17 A90 $6.60 multi ('86) 7.00 7.00
O18 A90 $8.30 multi ('86) 9.00 9.00
O19 A77a $10 multi ('87) (G) 16.00 16.00
Nos. O1-O19 (19) 65.10 64.90

Nos. 604-613 Ovptd. in Gold

1993-94 Litho. ***Perf. 14x13½***

O20 A118 20c multicolored .30 .30
O21 A118 50c multicolored .55 .55
O22 A118 70c multicolored .80 .80
O23 A118 $1 multicolored 1.25 1.25
O24 A118 $1.50 multicolored 2.00 2.00
O25 A118 $2 multicolored 3.50 3.50
O26 A118 $3 multicolored 4.25 4.25
O27 A118 $5 multicolored 6.50 6.50
O28 A118 $7 multicolored 9.00 9.00
O29 A118 $10 multicolored 13.00 13.00
O30 A118 $15 multicolored 20.00 20.00
Nos. O20-O30 (11) 61.15 61.15

Nos. O20-O30 were not sold unused to local customers.

Issued: 20c-$2, 12/10/93; $3, $5, 4/27/94; $7, $10, 9/1/94; $15, 9/30/94.

NORFOLK ISLAND

'nor-fək 'ī-lənd

LOCATION — Island in the south Pacific Ocean, 900 miles east of Australia
GOVT. — Territory of Australia
AREA — 13½ sq. mi.
POP. — 1,905 (1999 est.)

12 Pence = 1 Shilling
100 Cents = 1 Dollar (1966)

Catalogue values for all unused stamps in this country are for Never Hinged items.

Watermark

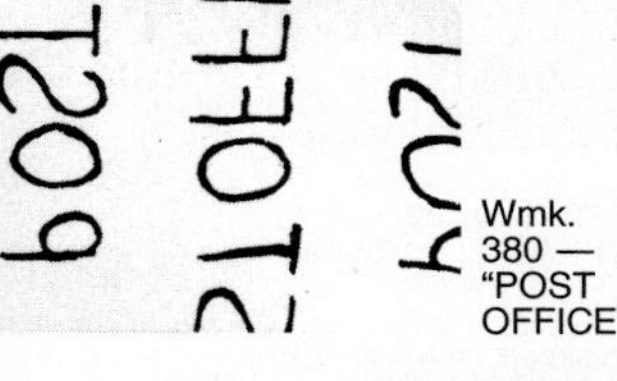

Wmk. 380 — "POST OFFICE"

View of Ball Bay — A1

Unwmk.

1947, June 10 Engr. *Perf. 14*

On Toned Paper

1 A1 ½p deep orange 1.35 .40
2 A1 1p violet .80 .40
3 A1 1½p bright green .80 .60
4 A1 2p red violet .90 .50
5 A1 2½p red 1.25 .50
6 A1 3p brown orange 1.10 .70
7 A1 4p rose lake 2.75 .70
8 A1 5½p slate 1.10 .70
9 A1 6p sepia 1.10 1.10
10 A1 9p lilac rose 2.00 1.25
11 A1 1sh gray green 1.10 1.10
12 A1 2sh olive bister 2.00 *2.75*
Nos. 1-12 (12) 16.25 10.70

Nos. 1-4 were reprinted in 1956-59 on white paper. Values, set: never hinged $125; used $200.

See Nos. 23-24.

The ½p, 1p, 1½p, 6p, and 1sh exist perf. 11 in different colors. These were not officially issued.

Warder's Tower A2

Airfield A3

Designs: 7½p, First Governor's Residence. 8½p, Barracks entrance. 10p, Salt House. 5sh, Bloody Bridge.

1953, June 10 *Perf. 14½*

13 A2 3½p rose brown 1.40 2.75
14 A3 6½p dark green 3.25 3.50
15 A3 7½p deep ultra 2.00 3.50
16 A2 8½p chocolate 2.40 4.75
17 A2 10p rose lilac 1.40 .75
18 A3 5sh dark brown 47.50 14.50
Nos. 13-18 (6) 57.95 29.75

See Nos. 35, 40. For surcharges see Nos. 21-22, 27. For types surcharged see Nos. 26, 28.

Original Norfolk Seal and First Settlers — A4

1956, June 8

19 A4 3p bluish green 2.00 1.40
20 A4 2sh violet 3.75 2.50

Cent. of the landing of the Pitcairn Islanders on Norfolk Island.

Two types of No. 20 exist on alternating stamps in each row: with and without a dot in the lower right corner.

Nos. 15 and 16 Surcharged with New Value and Bars

1958, July 1

21 A3 7p on 7½p dp ultra 1.75 *1.10*
22 A2 8p on 8½p choc 2.25 *1.40*

Ball Bay Type of 1947

1959, July 6 Engr. *Perf. 14*

23 A1 3p green 12.50 7.75
24 A1 2sh dark blue 13.00 8.25

A5

Australia #332 Surcharged in Red

1959, Dec. 7

25 A5 5p on 4p dk gray blue 1.75 1.25

No. 14 and Types of 1953 Surcharged with New Values and Bars

1960, Sept. 26 *Perf. 14½*

26 A2 1sh1p on 3½p dk bl 5.25 3.25
27 A3 2sh5p on 6½p dk grn 7.00 4.75
28 A3 2sh8p on 7½p dk brn 9.25 6.50
Nos. 26-28 (3) 21.50 14.50

Types of 1953 and

Island Hibiscus A6

Fairy Tern A7

Red-Tailed Tropic Bird — A8

Designs: 2p, Lagunaria patersonii (flowers). 5p, Lantana. 8p, Red hibiscus. 9p, Cereus and Queen Elizabeth II. 10p, Salt House. 1sh1p, Fringed hibiscus. 2sh, Providence petrel, vert. 2sh5p, Passion flower. 2sh8p, Rose apple. 5sh, Bloody Bridge.

1960-62 Unwmk. Engr. *Perf. 14½*

29 A6 1p blue green .25 .25
30 A6 2p gray grn & brt pink .30 .25
31 A7 3p brt green ('61) 1.00 .25
32 A6 5p lilac .85 .25
33 A6 8p vermilion 1.20 .40
34 A6 9p ultramarine 1.20 .40
35 A2 10p pale pur & brn ('61) 3.75 .80
36 A6 1sh1p dark red ('61) 1.20 .30
37 A6 2sh sepia ('61) 6.00 .80
38 A6 2sh5p dk purple ('62) 1.50 .35
39 A6 2sh8p green & sal ('62) 3.50 .45
40 A3 5sh green & gray ('61) 4.50 .60

Perf. 14½x14

41 A8 10sh green ('61) 40.00 30.00
Nos. 29-41 (13) 65.25 35.10

See #585-586. For surcharges see #71-82.

Map of Norfolk Island — A9

1960, Oct. 24 Engr. *Perf. 14*

42 A9 2sh8p rose violet 19.00 15.00

Introduction of local government for Norfolk Island.

Open Bible and Candle — A9a

1960, Nov. 21 *Perf. 14½*

43 A9a 5p bright lilac rose 4.00 4.00

Christmas.

Page from Book of Hours, 15th Century — A9b

1961, Nov. 20 *Perf. 14½x14*

44 A9b 5p slate blue 2.00 2.00

Nos. 43-44 were issued to mark the beginning and the end of the 350th anniversary year of the publication of the King James translation of the Bible.

Madonna and Child — A9c

1962, Nov. 19 *Perf. 14½*

45 A9c 5p blue 2.00 2.00

Christmas.

Overlooking Kingston A10

Dreamfish A11

Designs: 6p, Tweed trousers (fish). 8p, Kingston scene. 9p, "The Arches." 10p, Slaughter Bay. 11p, Trumpeter fish. 1sh, Po'ov (wrasse). 1sh6p, Queensland grouper. 2sh3p, Ophie (carangidae).

Perf. 14½x14

1962-64 Unwmk. Photo.

49 A10 5p multi ('64) .45 .35
50 A11 6p multi .60 .45
51 A10 8p multi ('64) .75 .50
52 A10 9p multi ('64) 1.00 .75
53 A10 10p multi ('64) 1.25 .95
54 A11 11p multi ('63) 1.75 .95
55 A11 1sh olive, bl & pink 2.00 1.30
57 A11 1sh3p bl, mar & grn ('63) 2.25 1.60
58 A11 1sh6p bl, brn & lil ('63) 2.50 2.00
60 A11 2sh3p dl bl, yel & red ('63) 3.00 2.25
Nos. 49-60 (10) 15.55 11.10

Star of Bethlehem — A11a

1963, Nov. 11 Engr. *Perf. 14½*

65 A11a 5p vermilion 1.50 1.25

Christmas.

Symbolic Pine Tree — A12

1964, July 1 Photo. *Perf. 13½x13*

66 A12 5p orange, blk & red 1.10 .85
67 A12 8p gray green, blk & red 1.40 1.15

50th anniv. of Norfolk Island as an Australian Territory.

Child Looking at Nativity Scene — A12a

1964, Nov. 9 *Perf. 13½*

68 A12a 5p multicolored 1.40 1.20

Christmas.

"Simpson and His Donkey" by Wallace Anderson — A12b

1965, Apr. 14 Photo. *Perf. 13½x13*

69 A12b 5p brt grn, sepia & blk .65 .55

ANZAC issue. See note after Australia No. 387.

Nativity — A12c

1965, Oct. 25 Unwmk. *Perf. 13½*

70 A12c 5p gold, blk, ultra & redsh brn .45 .45

Christmas. No. 70 is luminescent. See note after Australia No. 331.

Nos. 29-33 and 35-41 Surcharged in Black on Overprinted Metallic Rectangles

No. 74

Type IV

Two types of 1c on 1p:
I. Silver rectangle 4x5½mm.
II. Silver rectangle 5½x5¼mm.
Two types of $1 on 10sh:
III. Silver rectangle 7x6½mm.
IV. Silver rectangle 6x4mm.

Perf. 14½, 14½x14

1966, Feb. 14 Engr.

71 A6 1c on 1p bl grn (I) .25 .25
a. Type II .35 .25
72 A6 2c on 2p gray grn & brt pink .25 .25
73 A7 3c on 3p brt green .35 *.35*
74 A6 4c on 5p purple .25 .25
75 A6 5c on 8p vermilion .25 .25
76 A2 10c on 10p pale pur & brn .70 .70
77 A6 15c on 1sh1p dark red .30 .30
78 A6 20c on 2sh sepia 2.75 2.75
79 A6 25c on 2sh5p dk pur 1.10 1.10
80 A6 30c on 2sh8p grn & sal .75 .75
81 A3 50c on 5sh grn & gray 2.75 2.75
82 A8 $1 on 10sh green (III) 2.50 2.50
a. Type IV 5.25 2.50
Nos. 71-82 (12) 12.20 12.20

Headstone Bridge — A13

1966, June 27 Photo. *Perf. 14½*

88 A13 7c shown .25 .25
89 A13 9c Cemetery road .45 .40

St. Barnabas Chapel — A14

Design: 4c, Interior of St. Barnabas Chapel.

Perf. 14x14½

1966, Aug. 23 Photo. Unwmk.

97 A14 4c multicolored .25 .25
98 A14 25c multicolored .45 .30

Centenary of the Melanesian Mission.

Star over Philip Island — A15

1966, Oct. 24 Photo. *Perf. 14½*

99 A15 4c violet, grn, blue & sil .35 .25

Christmas.

H.M.S. Resolution, 1774 — A16

Ships: 2c, La Boussole and Astrolabe, 1788. 3c, Brig Supply, 1788. 4c, Sirius, 1790. 5c, The Norfolk, 1798. 7c, Survey cutter Mermaid, 1825. 9c, The Lady Franklin, 1853. 10c The Morayshire, 1856. 15c, Southern Cross, 1866. 20c, The Pitcairn, 1891. 25c, Norfolk Island whaleboat, 1895. 30c, Cable ship Iris, 1907. 50c, The Resolution, 1926. $1, S.S. Morinda, 1931.

1967-68 Photo. *Perf. 14x14½*

100 A16 1c multicolored .25 .25
101 A16 2c multicolored .25 .25
102 A16 3c multicolored .25 .25
103 A16 4c multicolored .40 .25
104 A16 5c multicolored .25 .25
105 A16 7c multicolored .25 .25
106 A16 9c multicolored .30 .25
107 A16 10c multicolored .40 .35
108 A16 15c multicolored .60 .55
109 A16 20c multicolored .90 .80
110 A16 25c multicolored 1.40 1.25
111 A16 30c multicolored 1.75 1.50
112 A16 50c multicolored 2.25 2.00
113 A16 $1 multicolored 3.50 3.25
Nos. 100-113 (14) 12.75 11.45

Issued: #100-103, 4/17; #104-107, 8/19; #108-110, 3/18/68; #111-113, 6/18/68.

Lions Intl., 50th Anniv. — A16a

1967, June 7 Photo. *Perf. 13½*

114 A16a 4c citron, blk & bl grn .30 .25

Printed on luminescent paper; see note after Australia No. 331.

John Adams' Prayer — A17

1967, Oct. 16 Photo. *Perf. 14x14½*

115 A17 5c brick red, blk & buff .40 .40

Christmas.

Queen Elizabeth II Type of Australia, 1966-67

Coil Stamps

Perf. 15 Horizontally

1968-71 Photo. Unwmk.

116 A157 3c brn org, blk & buff .25 .25
117 A157 4c blue grn, blk & buff .25 .25
118 A157 5c brt purple, blk & buff .25 .25
118A A157 6c dk red, brn, blk & buff .25 .25
Nos. 116-118A (4) 1.00 1.00

Issued: 6c, 8/2/71; others, 8/5/68.

DC-4 Skymaster and Lancastrian Plane — A18

1968, Sept. 25 *Perf. 14½x14*

119 A18 5c dk car, sky bl & ind .25 .25
120 A18 7c dk car, bl grn & sep .25 .25

21st anniv. of the Sydney to Norfolk Island air service by Qantas Airways.

Star and Hibiscus Wreath — A19

Photo.; Silver Impressed (Star)

1968, Oct. 24 *Perf. 14½x14*

121 A19 5c sky blue & multi .25 .25

Christmas.

Map of Pacific, Transit of Venus before Sun, Capt. Cook and Quadrant — A20

1969, June 3 Photo. *Perf. 14x14½*

122 A20 10c brn, ol, pale brn & yel .35 .25

Bicent. of the observation at Tahiti by Capt. James Cook of the transit of the planet Venus across the sun.

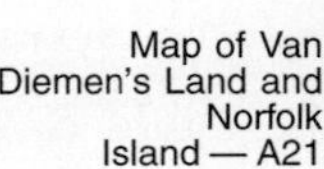

Map of Van Diemen's Land and Norfolk Island — A21

1969, Sept. 29 *Perf. 14x14½*

123 A21 5c multicolored .25 .25
124 A21 30c multicolored .45 .45

125th anniv. of the annexation of Norfolk Island by Van Diemen's Land (Tasmania).

Nativity (Mother-of-Pearl carving) — A22

1969, Oct. 27 Photo. *Perf. 14½x14*

125 A22 5c brown & multi .30 .25

Christmas.

Gerygone Modesta — A23

Birds of Norfolk Island from Book by Gregory Mathews: 1c, Petroica multicolor, vert. 2c, Pachycephala xanthoprocta, vert. 4c, Urodynamis taitensis. 5c, Cyanoramphus verticalis, vert. 7c, Diaphoropterus leucopygus, vert. 9c, Turdus poliocephalus. 10c, Ninox boobook royana, vert. 15c, Hemiphaga argetraea (extinct), vert. 20c, Zosterops albogularis. 25c, Nestor productus (extinct), vert. 30c, Rhipidura pelzelni. 45c, Aplonis fuscus. 50c, Platycercus elegans, vert. $1, Halcyon sanctus norfolkiensis.

Perf. 14x14½, 14½x14

1970-71 Photo. Unwmk.

126 A23 1c multicolored .25 .25
127 A23 2c multicolored .25 .30
128 A23 3c multicolored .25 .25
129 A23 4c multicolored .45 .30
130 A23 5c multicolored 1.15 .75
131 A23 7c multicolored .35 .25
132 A23 9c multicolored .50 .30
133 A23 10c multicolored 1.30 1.45
134 A23 15c multicolored 1.15 .70
135 A23 20c multicolored 5.25 3.25
136 A23 25c multicolored 1.75 1.15
137 A23 30c multicolored 5.25 2.60
138 A23 45c multicolored 2.25 1.25
139 A23 50c multicolored 2.75 2.00
140 A23 $1 multicolored 7.50 6.25
Nos. 126-140 (15) 30.40 21.05

Issued: 3c, 4c, 9c, 45c, 2/25; 1c, 7c, 10c, 25c, 7/22; 2c, 2c, 5c, 15c, 50c, 2/24/71; 20c, 30c, $1, 6/16/71.

Map of Australia, James Cook and Southern Cross — A24

Design: 10c, "Endeavour" entering Botany Bay, Apr. 29, 1770, and aborigine with spear. The 1776 portrait of James Cook on the 5c is by John Webber.

1970, Apr. 29 Photo. *Perf. 14x14½*

141 A24 5c multicolored .25 .25
142 A24 10c multicolored .25 .25

200th anniv. of Cook's discovery and exploration of the eastern coast of Australia.

First Christmas, Sydney Bay, 1788 — A25

1970, Oct. 15 Photo. *Perf. 14x14½*

143 A25 5c multicolored .25 .25

Christmas.

Bishop Patteson, Open Bible — A26

#145, Bible opened to Acts Chap. 7, martyrdom of St. Stephen, & knotted palm fronds. #146, Bishop Patteson, rose window of Melanesian Mission Chapel on Norfolk Island. #147, Cross erected at Nukapu where Patteson died & his arms.

1971, Sept. 20

144 A26 6c brown & multi .25 .25
145 A26 6c brown & multi .25 .25
a. Pair, #144-145 .55 .55
146 A26 10c purple & multi .25 .25
147 A26 10c purple & multi .25 .25
a. Pair, #146-147 .65 .65
Nos. 144-147 (4) 1.00 1.00

Centenary of the death of Bishop John Coleridge Patteson (1827-1871), head of the Melanesian mission.

Rose Window, St. Barnabas Chapel, Norfolk Island — A27

1971, Oct. 25 *Perf. 14x13½*

148 A27 6c dk vio blue & multi .25 .25

Christmas.

Map of South Pacific and Commission Flag — A28

1972, Feb. 7 *Perf. 14x14½*

149 A28 7c multicolored .30 .30

So. Pacific Commission, 25th anniv.

Stained-glass Window — A29

1972, Oct. 16 Photo. *Perf. 14x14½*

150 A29 7c dark olive & multi .25 .25

Christmas. The stained-glass window by Edward Coley Burne-Jones is in All Saints Church, Norfolk Island.

Cross, Church, Pines — A30

1972, Nov. 20

151 A30 12c multicolored .40 .40
a. Purple omitted *1,600.*

Centenary of All Saints Church, first built by Pitcairners on Norfolk Island.

"Resolution" in Antarctica A31

1973, Jan. 17 Photo. *Perf. 14½x14*

152 A31 35c multicolored 2.10 1.75

200th anniv. of the 1st crossing of the Antarctic Circle by Cook, Jan. 17, 1773.

Sleeping Child, and Christmas Tree — A32

Christmas: 35c, Star over lagoon.

1973, Oct. 22 Photo. *Perf. 14x14½*

153 A32 7c black & multi .30 .25
154 A32 12c black & multi .50 .30
155 A32 35c black & multi 1.60 1.10
Nos. 153-155 (3) 2.40 1.65

Protestant Clergyman's House — A33

Designs: 2c, Royal Engineer Office. 3c, Double quarters for free overseers. 4c, Guard House. 5c, Pentagonal Gaol entrance. 7c, Pentagonal Gaol, aerial view. 8c, Convict barracks. 10c, Officers' quarters, New Military Barracks. 12c, New Military Barracks. 14c, Beach stores. 15c, Magazine. 20c, Old Military Barracks, entrance. 25c, Old Military Barracks. 30c, Old stores, Crankmill. 50c, Commissariat stores. $1, Government House.

1973-75 Photo. *Perf. 14x14½*

156 A33 1c multicolored .25 .25
157 A33 2c multicolored .25 .25
158 A33 3c multicolored .30 *.30*
159 A33 4c multicolored .25 .25
160 A33 5c multicolored .25 .45
161 A33 7c multicolored .30 .30
162 A33 8c multicolored 1.20 1.20
163 A33 10c multicolored .45 .45
164 A33 12c multicolored .45 .45
165 A33 14c multicolored .45 *.45*
166 A33 15c multicolored 1.10 1.10
167 A33 20c multicolored .45 .45
168 A33 25c multicolored 1.10 1.10
169 A33 30c multicolored .45 .45

170 A33 50c multicolored .50 *.50*
171 A33 $1 multicolored .95 *.95*
Nos. 156-171 (16) 8.70 8.70

Issued: 1c, 5c, 10c, 50c, 11/19/73; 2c, 7c, 12c, 30c, 5/1/74; 4c, 14c, 20c, $1, 7/12/74; 3c, 8c, 15c, 25c, 2/19/75.

Map of Norfolk Island — A34

1974, Feb. 8 Photo. *Perf. 14x14½*
172 A34 7c red lilac & multi .50 .35
173 A34 25c dull blue & multi 1.10 1.00

Visit of Queen Elizabeth II and the Duke of Edinburgh, Feb. 11-12.

Gipsy Moth over Norfolk Island — A35

1974, Mar. 28 Litho. *Perf. 14x14½*
174 A35 14c multicolored 1.60 1.35

1st aircraft to visit Norfolk, Sir Francis Chichester's "Mme. Elijah," Mar. 28, 1931.

Capt. Cook — A36

Designs: 10c, "Resolution," by Henry Roberts. 14c, Norfolk Island pine, cone and seedling. 25c, Norfolk Island flax, by George Raper, 1790. Portrait of Cook on 7c by William Hodges, 1770.

1974, Oct. 8 Litho. *Perf. 14*
175 A36 7c multicolored .60 .60
176 A36 10c multicolored 1.50 1.50
177 A36 14c multicolored 1.25 1.25
178 A36 25c multicolored 1.25 1.25
Nos. 175-178 (4) 4.60 4.60

Bicentenary of the discovery of Norfolk Island by Capt. James Cook.

Nativity — A37

1974, Oct. 18 Photo. *Perf. 14*
179 A37 7c rose & multi .25 .25
180 A37 30c violet & multi 1.00 1.00

Christmas.

Norfolk Island Pine A38

15c, Off-shore islands. 35c, Crimson rosella and sacred kingfisher. 40c, Map showing Norfolk's location. Stamps in shape of Norfolk Island.

1974, Dec. 16 Litho. *Imperf.*
Self-adhesive
181 A38 10c brown & multi .35 .30
182 A38 15c dk blue & multi .50 .40
183 A38 35c dk purple & multi 1.25 1.05
184 A38 40c dk blue grn & multi 1.50 *2.10*
a. Souvenir sheet of 4 24.00 24.00
Nos. 181-184 (4) 3.60 3.85

Cent. of UPU. Stamps printed on peelable paper backing. No. 184a contains 4 imperf. stamps similar to Nos. 181-184 in reduced size on a background of map of Norfolk Island. Peelable paper backing shows beach scene on Norfolk Island.

Survey Cutter "Mermaid," 1825 — A39

Design: 35c, Kingston, 1835, after painting by Thomas Seller. Stamps outlined in shape of Norfolk Island map.

1975, Aug. 18 Litho. *Imperf.*
Self-adhesive
185 A39 10c multicolored .35 .30
186 A39 35c multicolored .70 .55

Sesquicentennial of 2nd settlement of Norfolk Island. Printed on peelable paper backing with green and black design and inscription.

Star over Norfolk Island Pine and Map — A40

1975, Oct. 6 Photo. *Perf. 14½x14*
187 A40 10c lt blue & multi .35 .30
188 A40 15c lt brown & multi .55 .45
189 A40 35c lilac & multi .75 .60
Nos. 187-189 (3) 1.65 1.35

Christmas.

Brass Memorial Cross — A41

Design: 60c, Laying foundation stone, 1875, and chapel, 1975, horiz.

Perf. 14½x14, 14x14½
1975, Nov. 24 Photo.
190 A41 30c multicolored .35 .35
191 A41 60c multicolored 1.00 .90

St. Barnabas Chapel, centenary.

Launching "Resolution" — A42

Design: 45c, "Resolution" under sail.

1975, Dec. 1 *Perf. 14x14½*
192 A42 25c multicolored .50 .45
193 A42 45c multicolored 1.25 .90

50th anniversary of launching of schooner "Resolution."

Bedford Flag, Charles W. Morgan Whaler — A43

Designs: 25c, Grand Union Flag, church interior. 40c, 15-stari flag, 1795, and plane over island, WWII. 45c, 13-star flag and California quail.

1976, July 5 Photo. *Perf. 14*
194 A43 18c multicolored .40 .35
195 A43 25c multicolored .40 .30
196 A43 40c multicolored .80 .75
197 A43 45c multicolored .90 .85
Nos. 194-197 (4) 2.50 2.25

American Bicentennial.

Bird in Flight, Brilliant Sun — A44

1976, Oct. 4 Photo. *Perf. 14*
198 A44 18c blue grn & multi .40 .30
199 A44 25c dp blue & multi .60 .50
200 A44 45c violet & multi 1.00 .80
Nos. 198-200 (3) 2.00 1.60

Christmas.

Bassaris Itea — A45

Butterflies and Moths: 2c, Utetheisa pulchelloides vaga. 3c, Agathia asterias jowettorum. 4c, Cynthia kershawi. 5c, Leucania loreyimima. 10c, Hypolimnas bolina nerina. 15c, Pyrrhorachis pyrrhogona. 16c, Austrocarea iocephala millsi. 17c, Pseudocoremia christiani. 18c, Cleora idiocrossa. 19c, Simplicia caeneusalis buffetti. 20c, Austrocidaria ralstonae. 30c, Hippotion scrofa. 40c, Papilio ilioneus. 50c, Tiracola plagiata. $1, Precis villida. $2, Cepora perimale.

1976-77 Photo. *Perf. 14*
201 A45 1c multicolored .25 .25
202 A45 2c multicolored .25 .25
203 A45 3c multicolored .25 .25
204 A45 4c multicolored .25 .25
205 A45 5c multicolored .25 .25
206 A45 10c multicolored .25 .25
207 A45 15c multicolored .25 .25
208 A45 16c multicolored .25 .25
209 A45 17c multicolored .30 .30
210 A45 18c multicolored .30 .30
211 A45 19c multicolored .30 .30
212 A45 20c multicolored .35 .35
213 A45 30c multicolored .45 .45
214 A45 40c multicolored .50 .50
215 A45 50c multicolored .65 .65
216 A45 $1 multicolored .70 .70
217 A45 $2 multicolored 1.10 1.10
Nos. 201-217 (17) 6.65 6.65

Issued: 1c, 5c, 10c, 16c, 18c, $1, 11/17; others, 1977.

View of Kingston — A46

1977, June 10
218 A46 25c multicolored .60 .50

25th anniv. of reign of Elizabeth II.

Hibiscus and 19th Century Whaler's Lamp — A47

1977, Oct. 4 Photo. *Perf. 14½*
219 A47 18c multicolored .25 .25
220 A47 25c multicolored .35 .25
221 A47 45c multicolored .65 .40
Nos. 219-221 (3) 1.25 .90

Christmas.

Capt. Cook, by Nathaniel Dance — A48

Designs: 25c, Discovery of Northern Hawaiian Islands (Cook aboard ship), horiz. 80c, British flag and Island, horiz.

1978, Jan. 18 Photo. *Perf. 14½*
222 A48 18c multicolored .35 .35
223 A48 25c multicolored .45 .35
224 A48 80c multicolored .85 .70
Nos. 222-224 (3) 1.65 1.40

Bicentenary of Capt. Cook's arrival in Hawaiian Islands.

World Guides Flag and Globe A49

Designs: 25c, Norfolk Guides' scarf badge and trefoil. 35c, Elizabeth II and trefoil. 45c, FAO Ceres medal with portrait of Lady Olive Baden-Powell, and trefoil. Stamps outlined in shape of Norfolk Island map.

1978, Feb. 22 Litho. *Imperf.*
Self-adhesive
225 A49 18c lt ultra & multi .35 .30
226 A49 25c yellow & multi .35 .30
227 A49 35c lt green & multi .45 .35
228 A49 45c yellow grn & multi .55 .45
Nos. 225-228 (4) 1.70 1.40

50th anniversary of Norfolk Island Girl Guides. Printed on peelable paper backing with green multiple pines and tourist publicity inscription.

St. Edward's Crown — A50

Design: 70c, Coronation regalia.

1978, June 29 Photo. *Perf. 14½*
229 A50 25c multicolored .45 .45
230 A50 70c multicolored .90 .90

25th anniv. of coronation of Elizabeth II.

Norfolk Island Boy Scouts, 50th Anniv. A51

Designs: 20c, Cliffs, Duncombe Bay, Scout Making Fire. 25c, Emily Bay, Philip and Nepean Islands from Kingston. 35c, Anson Bay, Cub and Boy Scouts. 45c, Sunset and Lord Baden-Powell. Stamps outlined in shape of Norfolk Island map.

1978, Aug. 22 Litho. *Imperf.*
Self-adhesive
231 A51 20c multicolored .40 .40
232 A51 25c multicolored .45 .45
233 A51 35c multicolored .65 .65
234 A51 45c multicolored .70 .70
Nos. 231-234 (4) 2.20 2.20

Printed on peelable paper backing with green multiple pines and tourist publicity inscription and picture.

Map of Bering Sea and Pacific Ocean, Routes of Discovery and Resolution A52

Design: 90c, Discovery and Resolution trapped in ice, by John Webber.

1978, Aug. 29 Photo. *Perf. 14½*
235 A52 25c multicolored .40 .40
236 A52 90c multicolored 1.00 1.00

Northernmost point of Cook's voyages.

Poinsettia and Bible — A53

Christmas: 30c, Native oak (flowers) and Bible. 55c, Hibiscus and Bible.

1978, Oct. 3 Photo. *Perf. 14½*
237 A53 20c multicolored .30 .30
238 A53 30c multicolored .40 .40
239 A53 55c multicolored .75 .75
Nos. 237-239 (3) 1.45 1.45

Capt. Cook, View of Staithes — A54

80c, Capt. Cook and view of Whitby harbor.

1978, Oct. 27
240 A54 20c multicolored .40 *.50*
241 A54 80c multicolored 1.10 *1.25*

Resolution, Map of Asia and Australia — A55

Designs: No. 243, Map of Hawaii and Americas, Cook's route and statue. No. 244, Capt. Cook's death. No. 245, Ships off Hawaii.

1979, Feb. 14 Photo. *Perf. 14½*
242 20c multicolored .25 .25
243 20c multicolored .25 .25
a. A55 Pair, #242-243 .60 .60
244 40c multicolored .60 .60
245 40c multicolored .60 .60
a. A55 Pair, #244-245 1.30 1.30
Nos. 242-245 (4) 1.70 1.70

Bicentenary of Capt. Cook's death.

Rowland Hill and Tasmania No. 1 — A56

Rowland Hill and: 30c, Great Britain No. 8. 55c, Norfolk Island No. 2.

1979, Aug. 27 *Perf. 14x14½*
246 A56 20c multicolored .30 .30
247 A56 30c multicolored .35 .35
248 A56 55c multicolored .45 .45
a. Souvenir sheet of 1 1.10 1.10
Nos. 246-248 (3) 1.10 1.10

Sir Rowland Hill (1795-1879), originator of penny postage.

Legislative Assembly — A57

1979, Aug. Photo. *Perf. 14½x14*
249 A57 $1 multicolored 1.10 1.10

First session of Legislative Assembly.

Map of Pacific Ocean, IYC Emblem — A58

1979, Sept. 25 Litho. *Perf. 15*
250 A58 80c multicolored .95 .95

International Year of the Child.

Emily Bay Beach A59

1979, Oct. 2 Photo. *Perf. 12½x13*
251 15c Beach .25 .25
252 20c Emily Bay .25 .25
253 30c Salt House .30 .30
a. Souv. sheet of 3, #251-253, perf. 14x14½ 1.50 *2.00*
b. A59 Strip of 3, #251-253 .80 .80

Christmas. #253b has continuous design.

Lions District Convention 1980 — A60

1980, Jan. 25 Litho. *Perf. 15*
254 A60 50c multicolored .70 .70

Rotary International, 75th Anniversary A61

1980, Feb. 21
255 A61 50c multicolored .60 .60
a. Black omitted *11,000.*

No. 255a is unique.

DH-60 "Gypsy Moth" — A62

1c, Hawker Siddeley HS-748. 3c, Curtiss P-40 Kittyhawk. 4c, Chance Vought Corsair. 5c, Grumman Avenger. 15c, Douglas Dauntless. 20c, Cessna 172. 25c, Lockheed Hudson. 30c, Lockheed PV-1 Ventura. 40c, Avro York. 50c, DC-3. 60c, Avro 691 Lancastrian. 80c, DC-4. $1, Beechcraft Super King Air. $2, Fokker Friendship. $5, Lockheed C-130 Hercules.

1980-81 Litho. *Perf. 14½*
256 A62 1c multicolored .25 .25
257 A62 2c multicolored .25 .25
258 A62 3c multicolored .25 .25
259 A62 4c multicolored .25 .25
260 A62 5c multicolored .25 .25
261 A62 15c multicolored .25 .25
262 A62 20c multicolored .30 .25
262A A62 25c multicolored .40 .35
263 A62 30c multicolored .50 .45
264 A62 40c multicolored .60 .50
265 A62 50c multicolored .75 .65
266 A62 60c multicolored .80 .70
267 A62 80c multicolored 1.25 1.10
268 A62 $1 multicolored 1.45 1.25
269 A62 $2 multicolored 1.75 1.60
270 A62 $5 multicolored 4.75 4.25
Nos. 256-270 (16) 14.05 12.60

Issued: 2, 3, 20c, $5, 3/25; 4, 5, 15c, $2, 8/19; 30, 50, 60, 80c, 1/13/81; 1, 25, 40c, $1, 3/3/81.

Queen Mother Elizabeth, 80th Birthday — A63

1980, Aug. 4 Litho. *Perf. 14½*
271 A63 22c multicolored .30 .30
272 A63 60c multicolored .70 .70

Red-tailed Tropic Birds — A64

22c, Adult and juvenile white terns. 35c, White-capped noddys. 60c, Two adult white terns.

1980, Oct. 28 Litho. *Perf. 14x14½*
273 A64 15c shown .25 .25
274 A64 22c multicolored .25 .25
275 A64 35c multicolored .40 .40
a. Strip of 3, #273-275 1.00 1.00
276 A64 60c multicolored .75 .75
Nos. 273-276 (4) 1.65 1.65

Christmas. No. 275a has continuous design.

Citizens Arriving at Norfolk Island — A65

1981, June 5 Litho. *Perf. 14½*
277 A65 5c Departure .25 .25
278 A65 35c shown .40 .40
279 A65 60c Settlement .70 .70
a. Souvenir sheet of 3, #277-279 1.50 1.50
Nos. 277-279 (3) 1.35 1.35

Pitcairn migration to Norfolk Island, 125th anniv.

Common Design Types pictured following the introduction.

Royal Wedding Issue
Common Design Type

1981, July 22 Litho. *Perf. 14*
280 CD331 35c Bouquet .40 .40
281 CD331 55c Charles .65 .65
282 CD331 60c Couple .70 .70
Nos. 280-282 (3) 1.75 1.75

Nos. 280-282 each se-tenant with decorative label.

Uniting Church of Australia — A66

24c, Seventh Day Adventist Church. 30c, Church of the Sacred Heart. $1, St. Barnabas Church.

1981, Sept. 15 Litho. *Perf. 14½*
283 A66 18c shown .25 .25
284 A66 24c multicolored .30 .30
285 A66 30c multicolored .35 .35
286 A66 $1 multicolored 1.10 1.10
Nos. 283-286 (4) 2.00 2.00

Christmas.

White-breasted Silvereye — A67

1981, Nov. 10 Litho. *Perf. 14½*
287 Strip of 5 2.75 2.75
a.-e. A67 35c any single .50 .50

Philip Island — A68

Views, Flora and Fauna: No. 288, Philip Isld. No. 289, Nepean Island.

1982, Jan. 12 Litho. *Perf. 14*
288 Strip of 5 1.50 1.50
a.-e. A68 24c any single .25 .25
289 Strip of 5 2.25 2.25
a.-e. A68 35c any single .40 .40

Sperm Whale — A69

55c, Southern right whale. 80c, Humpback whale.

1982, Feb. 23 Litho. *Perf. 14½*
290 A69 24c shown .50 .50
291 A69 55c multicolored 1.00 1.00
292 A69 80c multicolored 1.75 1.75
Nos. 290-292 (3) 3.25 3.25

Shipwrecks A70

1982 Litho. *Perf. 14½*
293 A70 24c Sirius, 1790 .40 .35
294 A70 27c Diocet, 1873 .40 .35
295 A70 35c Friendship, 1835 .65 .60
296 A70 40c Mary Hamilton, 1873 .70 .65
297 A70 55c Fairlie, 1840 .85 .75
298 A70 65c Warrigal, 1918 1.10 .95
Nos. 293-298 (6) 4.10 3.65

Christmas and 40th Anniv. of Aircraft Landing — A71

1982, Sept. 7 *Perf. 14*
299 A71 27c Supplies drop .35 .35
300 A71 40c Landing .60 .60
301 A71 75c Sharing supplies 1.15 1.15
Nos. 299-301 (3) 2.10 2.10

A72

British Army Uniforms, Second Settlement, 1839-1848: 27c, Battalion Company Officer, 50th Regiment, 1835-1842. 40c, Light Company Officer, 58th Reg., 1845. 55c, Private, 80th Bat., 1838. 65c, Bat. Company Officer, 11th Reg., 1847.

1982, Nov. 9 *Perf. 14½*
302 A72 27c multicolored .30 .30
303 A72 40c multicolored .55 .50
304 A72 55c multicolored .60 .55
305 A72 65c multicolored .80 .70
Nos. 302-305 (4) 2.25 2.05

Local Mushrooms — A73

Designs: 27c, Panaeolus papilonaceus. 40c, Coprinus domesticus. 55c, Marasmius niveus. 65c, Cymatoderma elegans.

1983, Mar. 29 Litho. *Perf. 14x13½*
306 A73 27c multicolored .40 .35
307 A73 40c multicolored .65 .55
308 A73 55c multicolored .80 .70
309 A73 65c multicolored 1.00 .90
Nos. 306-309 (4) 2.85 2.50

Manned Flight Bicentenary — A74

10c, Beech 18, aerial mapping. 27c, Fokker F-28. 45c, DC4. 75c, Sikorsky helicopter.

1983, July 12 Litho. *Perf. 14½x14*
310 A74 10c multicolored .25 .25
311 A74 27c multicolored .35 .30
312 A74 45c multicolored .75 .65
313 A74 75c multicolored 1.10 1.00
a. Souvenir sheet of 4, #310-313 2.75 2.50
Nos. 310-313 (4) 2.45 2.20

Christmas — A75

Stained-glass Windows by Edward Burne-Jones (1833-1898), St. Barnabas Chapel.

1983, Oct. 4 Litho. *Perf. 14*
314 A75 5c multicolored .25 .25
315 A75 24c multicolored .30 .30
316 A75 30c multicolored .35 .35
317 A75 45c multicolored .45 .45
318 A75 85c multicolored .90 .90
Nos. 314-318 (5) 2.25 2.25

World Communications Year — A76

ANZCAN Cable Station: 30c, Chantik, Cable laying Ship. 45c, Shore end. 75c, Cable Ship Mercury. 85c, Map of cable route.

1983, Nov. 15 Litho. *Perf. 14½x14*
319 A76 30c multicolored .30 .30
320 A76 45c multicolored .50 .50
321 A76 75c multicolored .90 .90
322 A76 85c multicolored 1.00 1.00
Nos. 319-322 (4) 2.70 2.70

Local Flowers — A77

1c, Myoporum obscurum. 2c, Ipomoea pes-caprae. 3c, Phreatia crassiuscula. 4c, Streblorrhiza speciosa. 5c, Rhopalostylis baueri. 10c, Alyxia gynopogon. 15c, Ungeria floribunda. 20c, Capparis nobilis. 25c, Lagunaria patersonia. 30c, Cordyline obtecta. 35c, Hibiscus insularis. 40c, Millettia australis. 50c, Jasminum volubile. $1, Passiflora aurantia. $3, Oberonia titania. $5, Araucaria heterophylla.

1984 Litho. *Perf. 14*
323 A77 1c multicolored .25 .25
324 A77 2c multicolored .25 .25
325 A77 3c multicolored .25 .25
326 A77 4c multicolored .25 .25
327 A77 5c multicolored .25 .25
328 A77 10c multicolored .25 .25
329 A77 15c multicolored .25 .25
330 A77 20c multicolored .30 .30
331 A77 25c multicolored .35 .35
332 A77 30c multicolored .45 .45
333 A77 35c multicolored .50 .50
334 A77 40c multicolored .55 .55
335 A77 50c multicolored .65 .65
336 A77 $1 multicolored 1.25 1.25
337 A77 $3 multicolored 4.00 4.00
338 A77 $5 multicolored 6.00 6.00
Nos. 323-338 (16) 15.80 15.80

Issued: 2-3, 10, 20-25, 40-50c, $5, 1/10; others 3/27.

Reef Fish — A78

30c, Painted morwong. 45c, Black-spot goatfish. 75c, Ring-tailed surgeon fish. 85c, Three-striped butterfly fish.

Perf. 13½x14
1984, Apr. 17 Litho. Wmk. 373
339 A78 30c multicolored .50 .50
340 A78 45c multicolored .65 .65
341 A78 75c multicolored 1.15 1.15
342 A78 85c multicolored 1.30 1.30
Nos. 339-342 (4) 3.60 3.60

Boobook Owl — A79

Designs: a, Laying eggs. b, Standing at treehole. c, Sitting on branch looking sideways. d, Looking head on. e, Flying.

Wmk. 373
1984, July 17 Litho. *Perf. 14*
343 Strip of 5 6.00 6.00
a.-e. A79 30c any single 1.20 1.20

AUSIPEX '84 A80

1984, Sept. 18 Litho. *Perf. 14½*
344 A80 30c Nos. 15 and 176 .40 .40
345 A80 45c First day cover .65 .65
346 A80 75c Presentation pack 1.25 1.25
a. Souvenir sheet of 3, #344-346 4.00 4.00
Nos. 344-346 (3) 2.30 2.30

Christmas — A81

5c, The Font. 24c, Church at Kingston, interior. 30c, Pastor and Mrs. Phelps. 45c, Phelps, Church of Chester. 85c, Phelps, Methodist Church, modern interior.

1984, Oct. 9 Litho. *Perf. 13½*
347 A81 5c multicolored .25 .25
348 A81 24c multicolored .40 .35
349 A81 30c multicolored .45 .40
350 A81 45c multicolored .70 .60
351 A81 85c multicolored 1.25 1.10
Nos. 347-351 (5) 3.05 2.70

Rev. George Hunn Nobbs, Death Cent. — A82

30c, As teacher. 45c, As minister. 75c, As chaplain. 85c, As community leader.

1984, Nov. 6 Litho. *Perf. 14x15*
352 A82 30c multicolored .40 .40
353 A82 45c multicolored .50 .50
354 A82 75c multicolored .90 .90
355 A82 85c multicolored 1.20 1.20
Nos. 352-355 (4) 3.00 3.00

Whaling Ships — A83

1985 Litho. *Perf. 13½x14*
356 A83 5c Fanny Fisher .25 .25
357 A83 15c Waterwitch .30 .30
358 A83 20c Canton .35 .35
359 A83 33c Costa Rica Packet .55 .55
360 A83 50c Splendid .80 .80
361 A83 60c Aladin 1.25 1.25
362 A83 80c California 1.50 1.50
363 A83 90c Onward 1.90 1.90
Nos. 356-363 (8) 6.90 6.90

Issued: 5c, 33c, 50c, 90c, 2/19; others 4/30.

Queen Mother 85th Birthday
Common Design Type

5c, Portrait, 1926. 33c, With Princess Anne. 50c, Photograph by N. Parkinson. 90c, Holding Prince Henry.
$1, With Princess Anne, Ascot Races.

Perf. 14½x14
1985, June 6 Litho. Wmk. 384
364 CD336 5c multicolored .25 .25
365 CD336 33c multicolored .45 .45
366 CD336 50c multicolored .65 .65
367 CD336 90c multicolored 1.40 1.40
Nos. 364-367 (4) 2.75 2.75

Souvenir Sheet
368 CD336 $1 multicolored 2.25 2.25

Intl. Youth Year — A84

Children's drawings.

1985, July 9 Litho. *Perf. 13½x14*
369 A84 33c Swimming .55 .50
370 A84 50c Nature walk .90 .85

Girl, Prize-winning Cow — A85

Designs: 90c, Embroidery, jam-making, baking, animal husbandry.

1985, Sept. 10 Litho. *Perf. 13½x14*
371 A85 80c multicolored 1.00 1.00
372 A85 90c multicolored 1.10 1.10
a. Souvenir sheet of 2, #371-372 3.00 3.00

Royal Norfolk Island Agricultural & Horticultural Show, 125th anniv.

Christmas — A86

27c, Three Shepherds. 33c, Journey to Bethlehem. 50c, Three Wise Men. 90c, Nativity.

1985, Oct. 3 *Perf. 13½*
373 A86 27c multicolored .35 .35
374 A86 33c multicolored .50 .50
375 A86 50c multicolored .65 .65
376 A86 90c multicolored 1.25 1.25
Nos. 373-376 (4) 2.75 2.75

Marine Life — A87

5c, Long-spined sea urchin. 33c, Blue starfish. 55c, Eagle ray. 75c, Moray eel.

1986, Jan. 14 *Perf. 13½x14*
377 A87 5c multicolored .25 .25
378 A87 33c multicolored .55 .55
379 A87 55c multicolored .95 .95
380 A87 75c multicolored 1.25 1.25
a. Souvenir sheet of 4, #377-380 4.00 4.00
Nos. 377-380 (4) 3.00 3.00

Halley's Comet A88

Designs: a, Giotto space probe. b, Comet.

1986, Mar. 11 *Perf. 15*
381 A88 Pair 3.25 3.25
a.-b. $1 any single 1.60 1.60

Se-tenant in continuous design.

AMERIPEX '86 A89

Designs: 33c, Isaac Robinson, US consul in Norfolk, 1887-1908, vert. 50c, Ford Model-T. 80c, Statue of Liberty.

1986, May 22 Litho. *Perf. 13½*
382 A89 33c multicolored .45 .45
383 A89 50c multicolored .70 .70
384 A89 80c multicolored 1.10 1.10
a. Souvenir sheet of #382-384 3.00 3.00
Nos. 382-384 (3) 2.25 2.25

Queen Elizabeth II, 60th Birthday — A90

Various portraits — 5c, As Princess. 33c, Contemporary photograph. 80c, Opening N.I. Golf Club. 90c, With Prince Philip.

1986, June 12
385 A90 5c multicolored .25 .25
386 A90 33c multicolored .60 .60
387 A90 80c multicolored 1.30 1.30
388 A90 90c multicolored 1.60 1.60
Nos. 385-388 (4) 3.75 3.75

Christmas — A91

1986, Sept. 23 Litho. *Perf. 13½x14*
389 A91 30c multicolored .50 .50
390 A91 40c multicolored .60 .60
391 A91 $1 multicolored 1.50 1.50
Nos. 389-391 (3) 2.60 2.60

Commission of Gov. Phillip, Bicent. — A92

36c, British prison, 1787. 55c, Transportation, Court of Assize. No. 394, Gov. meeting Home Society. No. 395, Gov. meeting Home Secretary. $1, Gov. Phillip, 1738-1814.

1986 Litho. *Perf. 14x13½*
392 A92 36c multicolored .80 .80
393 A92 55c multicolored 1.35 1.35
394 A92 90c multicolored 2.25 2.25
395 A92 90c multicolored 2.25 2.25
396 A92 $1 multicolored 3.25 3.25
Nos. 392-396 (5) 9.90 9.90

No. 395 was issued because No. 394 is incorrectly inscribed.
Issued: #395, Dec. 16; others, Oct. 14.
See #417-420, 426-436.

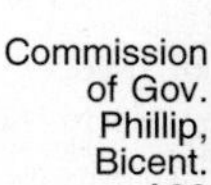

Commission of Gov. Phillip, Bicent. A93

1986, Dec. 16 *Perf. 13½*
397 A93 36c Maori chief .95 .95
398 A93 36c Bananas, taro .95 .95
399 A93 36c Stone tools .95 .95
400 A93 36c Polynesian outrigger .95 .95
Nos. 397-400 (4) 3.80 3.80

Pre-European occupation of the Island.

Island Scenery — A94

1c, Cockpit Creek Bridge. 2c, Cemetery Bay Beach. 3c, Guesthouse. 5c, Philip Island from Point Ross. 15c, Cattle grazing. 30c, Rock fishing. 37c, Old home. 40c, Shopping center. 50c, Emily Bay. 60c, Bloody Bridge. 80c, Pitcairner-style shop. 90c, Government House. $1, Melanesian Memorial Chapel. $2, Kingston convict settlement. $3, Ball Bay. $5, Northerly cliffs.

1987-88 Litho. *Perf. 13½*

401 A94 1c multicolored .25 .25
402 A94 2c multicolored .25 .25
403 A94 3c multicolored .25 .25
404 A94 5c multicolored .25 .25
405 A94 15c multicolored .25 .25
406 A94 30c multicolored .40 .40
407 A94 37c multicolored .50 .50
408 A94 40c multicolored .55 .55
409 A94 50c multicolored .65 .65
410 A94 60c multicolored .75 .75
411 A94 80c multicolored .95 .95
412 A94 90c multicolored 1.10 1.10
413 A94 $1 multicolored 1.25 1.25
414 A94 $2 multicolored 2.60 2.60
415 A94 $3 multicolored 4.00 4.00
416 A94 $5 multicolored 8.75 8.75
Nos. 401-416 (16) 22.75 22.75

Issued: 5c, 50c, 90c, $1, 2/17; 30c, 40c, 80c, $2, 4/17; 15c, 37c, 60c, $3, 7/27; 1c, 2c, 3c, $5, 5/17/88.

Bicentennial Type of 1986

Designs: 5c, Loading supplies at Deptford, England, 1787. No. 418, First Fleet sailing from Spithead (buoy in water). No. 419, Sailing from Spithead (ship flying British merchant flag). $1, Convicts below deck.

1987, May 13 Litho. *Perf. 14x13½*

417 A92 5c multicolored .45 .45
418 A92 55c multicolored 1.40 1.40
419 A92 55c multicolored 1.40 1.40
a. Pair, #418-419 3.00 3.00
420 A92 $1 multicolored 2.10 2.10
Nos. 417-420 (4) 5.35 5.35

No. 419a has a continuous design.

A96

World Wildlife Fund: Green parrot.

1987, Sept. 16 Unwmk.

421 Strip of 4 *14.00 14.00*
a. A96 5c Parrot facing right *2.25 2.25*
b. A96 15c Parrot, chick, egg *2.75 2.75*
c. A96 36c Parrots *3.75 3.75*
d. A96 55c Parrot facing left *5.00 5.00*

Christmas — A97

Children's party: 30c, Norfolk Island pine tree, restored convicts' settlement. 42c, Santa Claus, children opening packages. 58c, Santa, children, gifts in fire engine. 63c, Meal.

Perf. 13½x14

1987, Oct. 13 Litho. Wmk. 384

422 A97 30c multicolored .55 .55
423 A97 42c multicolored .80 .80
424 A97 58c multicolored 1.05 1.05
425 A97 63c multicolored 1.15 1.15
Nos. 422-425 (4) 3.55 3.55

Bicentennial Type of 1986

Designs: 5c, Lt. Philip Gidley King. No. 427, La Perouse and Louis XVI of France. No. 428, Gov. Phillip sailing in ship's cutter from Botany Bay to Port Jackson. No. 429, Flag raising on Norfolk Is. 55c, Lt. King and search party exploring the island. 70c, Landfall, Sydney Bay. No. 432, L'Astrolabe and La Boussole off coast of Norfolk. No. 433, HMS Supply. No. 434, Wrecking of L'Astrolabe off the Solomon Isls. No. 435, First Fleet landing at Sydney Cove. No. 436, First settlement, Sydney Bay, 1788.

1987-88 Litho. *Perf. 14x13½*

426 A92 5c multicolored .25 .25
427 A92 37c multicolored .80 .80
428 A92 37c multicolored .80 .80
429 A92 37c multicolored .80 .80
430 A92 55c multicolored 1.60 1.60
431 A92 70c multicolored 1.40 1.40
432 A92 90c multicolored 2.50 2.50
433 A92 90c multicolored 2.00 2.00
434 A92 $1 multicolored 2.50 2.50
435 A92 $1 multicolored 2.25 2.25
436 A92 $1 multicolored 2.25 2.25
Nos. 426-436 (11) 17.15 17.15

Visit of Jean La Perouse (1741-88), French navigator, to Norfolk Is. (Nos. 427, 432, 434); arrival of the First Fleet at Sydney Cove (Nos. 428, 435); founding of Norfolk Is. (Nos. 426, 429-431, 433, 436).

Issued: #427, 432, 434, Dec. 8, 1987; #428, 435, Jan. 25, 1988; others, Mar. 4, 1988.

SYDPEX '88, July 30-Aug. 7 — A98

Sydney-Norfolk transportation and communication links — No. 437, Air and sea transports, vert. No. 439, Telecommunications, vert.

Perf. 14x13½ 13½x14

1988, July 30 Litho.

437 A98 37c multicolored 1.15 1.15
438 A98 37c shown 1.15 1.15
439 A98 37c multicolored 1.15 1.15
a. Souvenir sheet of 3, #437-439 7.00 7.00
Nos. 437-439 (3) 3.45 3.45

No. 438 exists perf. 13½ within No. 439a.

Christmas — A99

1988, Sept. 27 Litho. *Perf. 14x13½*

440 A99 30c shown .60 .60
441 A99 42c Flowers, diff. .85 .85
442 A99 58c Trees, fish 1.20 1.20
443 A99 63c Trees, sailboats 1.20 1.20
Nos. 440-443 (4) 3.85 3.85

Convict Era Georgian Architecture, c. 1825-1850 — A100

Designs: 39c, Waterfront shop and boat shed. 55c, Royal Engineers' Building. 90c, Old military barracks. $1, Commissary and new barracks.

1988, Dec. 6 Litho. *Perf. 13½x14*

444 A100 39c multicolored .65 .65
445 A100 55c multicolored .95 .95
446 A100 90c multicolored 1.50 1.50
447 A100 $1 multicolored 1.75 1.75
Nos. 444-447 (4) 4.85 4.85

Indigenous Insects — A101

39c, Lamprima aenea. 55c, Insulascirtus nythos. 90c, Caedicia araucariae. $1, Thrincophora aridela.

Perf. 13½x14

1989, Feb. 14 Litho. Unwmk.

448 A101 39c multicolored .85 .85
449 A101 55c multicolored 1.15 1.15
450 A101 90c multicolored 1.75 1.75
451 A101 $1 multicolored 2.40 2.40
Nos. 448-451 (4) 6.15 6.15

Mutiny on the Bounty — A102

Designs: 5c, *Bounty's* landfall, Adventure Bay, Tasmania. 39c, Mutineers and Polynesian maidens, c. 1790. 55c, Cumbria, Christian's home county. $1.10, Capt. Bligh and crewmen cast adrift.

Perf. 13½

1989, Apr. 28 Litho. Unwmk.

452 A102 5c multicolored .60 .60
453 A102 39c multicolored 2.00 2.00
454 A102 55c multicolored 2.60 2.60
455 A102 $1.10 multicolored 4.00 4.00
Nos. 452-455 (4) 9.20 9.20

Souvenir Sheet

456 Sheet of 3 + label (#453, 456a-456b) 10.00 10.00
a. A102 90c Isle of Man No. 393 3.25 3.25
b. A102 $1 Pitcairn Isls. No. 321d 3.50 3.50

See Isle of Man Nos. 389-394 and Pitcairn Isls. Nos. 320-322.

Self-Government, 10th Anniv. — A103

41c, Flag. 55c, Ballot box. $1, Norfolk Is. Act of 1979. $1.10, Norfolk Island crest.

Perf. 14x13½

1989, Aug. 10 Litho. Unwmk.

457 A103 41c multicolored .80 .80
458 A103 55c multicolored .90 .90
459 A103 $1 multicolored 1.90 1.90
460 A103 $1.10 multicolored 2.00 2.00
Nos. 457-460 (4) 5.60 5.60

Natl. Red Cross, 75th Anniv. — A104

Perf. 13½x13

1989, Sept. 25 Litho. Unwmk.

461 A104 $1 dk ultra & dk red 3.50 3.50

Bounty Hymns — A105

Designs: 36c, "While nature was sinking in stillness to rest, The last beams of daylight show dim in the west." 60c, "There's a land that is fairer than day, And by faith we can see it afar." 75c, "Let the lower lights be burning, Send a gleam across the wave." 80c, "Oh, have you not heard of that beautiful stream That flows through our father's lands."

1989, Oct. 9 *Perf. 13½x14*

462 A105 36c multicolored .75 .75
463 A105 60c multicolored 1.50 1.50
464 A105 75c multicolored 2.10 2.10
465 A105 80c multicolored 2.10 2.10
Nos. 462-465 (4) 6.45 6.45

Radio Australia, 50th Anniv. — A106

41c, Announcer John Royle. 65c, Sound waves on map. $1.10, Jacko, the laughing kookaburra.

1989, Nov. 21 *Perf. 14x13½*

466 A106 41c multicolored 1.25 1.25
467 A106 65c multicolored 1.75 1.75
468 A106 $1.10 multicolored 2.60 2.60
Nos. 466-468 (3) 5.60 5.60

A107

Settlement of Pitcairn (The Norfolk Islanders): 70c, The *Bounty* on fire. $1.10, Armorial ensign of Norfolk.

Perf. 15x14½

1990, Jan. 23 Litho. Unwmk.

469 A107 70c multicolored 2.75 2.75
470 A107 $1.10 multicolored 3.00 3.00

Salvage Team at Work — A108

Designs: No. 471, HMS *Sirius* striking reef. No. 472, HMS *Supply* clearing reef. $1, Map of salvage sites, artifacts.

1990, Mar. 19 *Perf. 14x13½*

Size of Nos. 471-472: 40x27

471 A108 41c multicolored 1.60 1.60
472 A108 41c multicolored 1.60 1.60
a. Pair, #471-472 3.50 3.50
473 A108 65c shown 2.40 2.40
474 A108 $1 multicolored 2.60 2.60
Nos. 471-474 (4) 8.20 8.20

Wreck of HMS *Sirius*, 200th anniv. No. 472a has continuous design.

Lightering Cargo Ashore, Kingston A109

MV Ile de Lumiere A110

45c, La Dunkerquoise. 50c, Dmitri Mendeleev. 65c, Pacific Rover. 75c, Norfolk Trader. 80c, Roseville. 90c, Kalia. $1, HMS Bounty. $2, HMAS Success. $5, HMAS Whyalia.

1990-91 Litho. *Perf. 14x14½*

479 A109 5c shown .35 .35
480 A109 10c like #479 .35 .35

Perf. 14½

481 A110 45c multicolored .75 .75
482 A110 50c multicolored .85 .85
483 A110 65c multicolored 1.10 1.10
484 A110 70c shown 1.15 1.15
485 A110 75c multicolored 1.25 1.25
486 A110 80c multicolored 1.25 1.25
487 A110 90c multicolored 1.50 1.50
488 A110 $1 multicolored 1.60 1.60
489 A110 $2 multicolored 3.50 3.50
490 A110 $5 multicolored 8.75 8.75
Nos. 479-490 (12) 22.40 22.40

Issued: 5c, 10c, 70c, $2, 7/17/90; 45c, 50c, 65c, $5, 2/19/91; 75c, 80c, 90c, $1, 8/13/91.

Christmas — A111

38c, Island home. 43c, New post office. 65c, Sydney Bay, Kingston, horiz. 85c, Officers' Quarters, 1836, horiz.

1990, Sept. 25 Litho. *Perf. 14½*

491 A111 38c multicolored .70 .70
492 A111 43c multicolored .75 .75
493 A111 65c multicolored 1.75 1.75
494 A111 85c multicolored 1.90 1.90
Nos. 491-494 (4) 5.10 5.10

A112

Designs: 70c, William Charles Wentworth (1790-1872), Australian politician. $1.20, Thursday October Christian (1790-1831).

1990, Oct. 11 Litho. *Perf. 15x14½*
495 A112 70c brown 1.60 1.60
496 A112 $1.20 brown 2.50 2.50

Norfolk Island Robin
A113 A114

1990, Dec. 3 Litho. *Perf. 14½*
497 A113 65c multicolored 1.25 1.25
498 A113 $1 shown 2.00 2.00
499 A113 $1.20 multi, diff. 2.50 2.50
Nos. 497-499 (3) 5.75 5.75

Souvenir Sheet

500 Sheet of 2 6.50 6.50
a. A114 $1 shown 2.75 2.75
b. A114 $1 Two robins 2.75 2.75

Birdpex '90, 20th Intl. Ornithological Congress, New Zealand.

Ham Radio — A115

1991, Apr. 9 Litho. *Perf. 14½*
501 A115 43c Island map 1.25 1.25
502 A115 $1 World map 2.75 2.75
503 A115 $1.20 Regional location 2.75 2.75
Nos. 501-503 (3) 6.75 6.75

Museum Displays — A116

43c, Ship's bow, Sirius Museum, vert. 70c, House Museum. $1, Carronade, Sirius Museum. $1.20, Pottery, Archaeology Museum, vert.

1991, May 16 Litho. *Perf. 14½*
504 A116 43c multicolored 1.00 1.00
505 A116 70c multicolored 1.75 1.75
506 A116 $1 multicolored 1.90 1.90
507 A116 $1.20 multicolored 2.25 2.25
Nos. 504-507 (4) 6.90 6.90

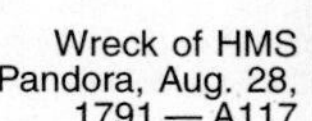

Wreck of HMS Pandora, Aug. 28, 1791 — A117

Design: $1.20, HMS Pandora searching for Bounty mutineers.

1991, July 2 Litho. *Perf. 13½x14*
508 A117 $1 shown 3.25 3.25
509 A117 $1.20 multicolored 3.75 3.75

Christmas — A118

1991, Sept. 23 Litho. *Perf. 14½*
510 A118 38c multicolored .65 .65
511 A118 43c multicolored .90 .90
512 A118 65c multicolored 1.40 1.40
513 A118 85c multicolored 1.75 1.75
Nos. 510-513 (4) 4.70 4.70

Start of World War II in the Pacific, 50th Anniv. — A119

1991, Dec. 9 Litho. *Perf. 14½*
514 A119 43c Tank and soldier 1.25 1.25
515 A119 70c B-17 2.25 2.25
516 A119 $1 War ships 3.00 3.00
Nos. 514-516 (3) 6.50 6.50

Discovery of America, 500th Anniv. — A120

45c, Columbus' Coat of Arms. $1.05, Santa Maria. $1.20, Columbus at globe.

1992, Feb. 11 Litho. *Perf. 14½*
517 A120 45c multicolored .85 .85
518 A120 $1.05 multicolored 2.00 2.00
519 A120 $1.20 multicolored 2.50 2.50
Nos. 517-519 (3) 5.35 5.35

A121

Designs: No. 520, Map of Coral Sea Battle area. No. 521, Battle area, Midway. No. 522, HMAS Australia. No. 523, Catalina PBY5. No. 524, USS Yorktown. No. 525, Dauntless dive bomber.

1992, May 4 Litho. *Perf. 14½*
520 A121 45c multicolored 1.00 1.00
521 A121 45c multicolored 1.00 1.00
522 A121 70c multicolored 1.75 1.75
523 A121 70c multicolored 1.75 1.75
524 A121 $1.05 multicolored 2.75 2.75
525 A121 $1.05 multicolored 2.75 2.75
Nos. 520-525 (6) 11.00 11.00

Battles of the Coral Sea and Midway, 50th anniv.

US Invasion of Guadalcanal, 50th Anniv. — A122

Designs: 45c, Troops landing on beach. 70c, Troops in battle. $1.05, Map, flags.

1992, Aug. 6 Litho. *Perf. 14½*
526 A122 45c multicolored 1.10 1.10
527 A122 70c multicolored 1.90 1.90
528 A122 $1.05 multicolored 3.25 3.25
Nos. 526-528 (3) 6.25 6.25

Christmas — A123

Scenes of Norfolk Island: 40c, Ball Bay, looking over Point Blackbourne. 45c, Headstone Creek. 75c, Ball Bay. $1.20, Rocky Point Reserve.

1992, Oct. 29 Litho. *Perf. 15x14½*
529 A123 40c multicolored .75 .75
530 A123 45c multicolored .85 .85
531 A123 75c multicolored 1.75 1.75
532 A123 $1.20 multicolored 2.50 2.50
Nos. 529-532 (4) 5.85 5.85

Tourism — A124

Tourist sites at Kingston: a, Boat shed, flaghouses. b, Old military barracks. c, All Saints Church. d, Officers quarters. e, Quality row.

1993, Feb. 23 Litho. *Perf. 14½*
533 A124 45c Strip of 5, #a.-e. 5.00 5.00

Emergency Services — A125

45c, Volunteer fire service. 70c, Rescue squad. 75c, St. John ambulance. $1.20, Police service.

1993, May 18 Litho. *Perf. 14½*
534 A125 45c multicolored 1.00 1.00
535 A125 70c multicolored 1.25 1.25
536 A125 75c multicolored 1.50 1.50
537 A125 $1.20 multicolored 2.75 2.75
Nos. 534-537 (4) 6.50 6.50

Nudibranchs A126

No. 538, Phyllidia ocellata. No. 539, Glaucus atlanticus. 75c, Bornella sp. 85c, Glossodoris rubroannolata. 95c, Halgerda willeyi. $1.05, Chromodoris amoena.

1993, July 7 Litho. *Perf. 14½*
538 A126 45c multicolored 1.00 1.00
539 A126 45c multicolored 1.25 1.25
540 A126 75c multicolored 1.40 1.40
541 A126 85c multicolored 1.60 1.60
542 A126 95c multicolored 1.75 1.75
543 A126 $1.05 multicolored 2.00 2.00
Nos. 538-543 (6) 9.00 9.00

No. 539 identified as "glauc."

A127

Designs: 70c, Maori patus. $1.20, First Maori map of New Zealand on paper, 1793.

1993, Oct. 28 Litho. *Perf. 14½*
544 A127 70c tan, buff & black 1.40 1.40
545 A127 $1.20 tan, buff & black 2.60 2.60

Cultural contact with New Zealand, bicent.

A128

1993, Oct. 28
546 A128 40c blue & multi .75 .75
547 A128 45c red & multi .85 .85
548 A128 75c green & multi 1.40 1.40
549 A128 $1.20 black & multi 2.25 2.25
Nos. 546-549 (4) 5.25 5.25

Early Pacific Explorers — A129

Explorer, ship: 5c, Vasco Nunez de Balboa, Barbara. 10c, Ferdinand Magellan, Victoria. 20c, Juan Sebastian de Elcano, Victoria. 50c, Alvaro de Saavedra, Florida. 70c, Ruy Lopez de Villalobos, San Juan. 75c, Miguel Lopez de Legaspi, San Lesmes. 80c, Sir Frances Drake, Golden Hinde. 85c, Alvaro de Mendana, Santiago. 90c, Pedro Fernandes de Quiros, San Pedro Paulo. $1, Luis Baez de Torres, San Perico. $2, Abel Tasman, Heemskerk. $5, William Dampier, Cygnet. No. 562, Golden Hinde (Francis Drake).

1994 Litho. *Perf. 14½*
550 A129 5c multicolored .30 .30
551 A129 10c multicolored .35 .35
552 A129 20c multicolored .60 .60
554 A129 50c multicolored .90 .90
556 A129 70c multicolored 1.10 1.10
557 A129 75c multicolored 1.25 1.25
558 A129 80c multicolored 1.25 1.25
559 A129 85c multicolored 1.40 1.40
560 A129 90c multicolored 1.60 1.60
560A A129 $1 multicolored 1.75 1.75
561 A129 $2 multicolored 3.50 3.50
561A A129 $5 multicolored 8.00 8.00
Nos. 550-561A (12) 22.00 22.00

Souvenir Sheet
Perf. 13

562 A129 $1.20 multicolored 3.75 3.75

No. 562 contains one 32x52mm stamp.

Issued: 50c, 70c, 75c, $2, No. 562, 2/8/94; 5c, 10c, 20c, $5, 5/3/94. 80c, 85c, 90c, $1, 7/26/94.

A130

Seabirds: a, Sooty tern. b, Red-tailed tropic bird. c, Australasian gannet. d, Wedge-tail shearwater. e, Masked booby.

1994, Aug. 17 Litho. *Perf. 14½x14*
565 A130 45c Strip of 5, #a.-e. 6.50 6.50
Booklet, 2 #565 14.00

A131

Christmas: 45c, Church, flowers, words from Pitcairn anthem. 75c, Stained glass windows, "To God be the glory." $1.20, Rainbow, ship, "Ship of Fame."

1994, Oct. 27 Litho. *Die Cut*
Self-Adhesive
566 A131 45c multicolored 1.20 1.20
567 A131 75c multicolored 1.40 1.40
568 A131 $1.20 multicolored 2.40 2.40
Nos. 566-568 (3) 5.00 5.00

Vintage Cars — A132

45c, 1926 Chevrolet. 75c, 1928 Model A Ford. $1.05, 1929 Model A A/C Ford truck. $1.20, 1930 Model A Ford.

1995, Feb. 7 Litho. *Perf. 14x14½*
569 A132 45c multicolored .65 .65
570 A132 75c multicolored 1.25 1.25
571 A132 $1.05 multicolored 1.75 1.75
572 A132 $1.20 multicolored 2.50 2.50
Nos. 569-572 (4) 6.15 6.15

Humpback Whales — A133

Perf. 14x14½, 14½x14
1995, May 9 Litho.
573 A133 45c Tail fluke 1.15 1.15
574 A133 75c Mother & calf 1.60 1.60
575 A133 $1.05 Breaching, vert. 2.25 2.25
Nos. 573-575 (3) 5.00 5.00

Souvenir Sheet
Perf. 14x14½

576 A133 $1.20 Bubble netting, vert. 4.00 4.00
a. Overprinted in gold & black 7.50 7.50

No. 576 contains one 30x50mm stamp and is a continuous design.

Overprint in margin of No. 576a has "Selamat Hari Merdeka" and JAKARTA '95 exhibition emblem.

Butterfly Fish — A134

Chaetodon: 5c, pelewensis. 45c, plebeius. $1.20, tricinctus. $1.50, auriga.

1995, June 15 Litho. *Perf. 14*

577 A134 5c multicolored .90 .90
578 A134 45c multicolored 1.40 1.40
579 A134 $1.20 multicolored 2.75 2.75
580 A134 $1.50 multicolored 3.25 3.25
Nos. 577-580 (4) 8.30 8.30

World War II Vehicles — A135

Designs: 5c, 1942 Intl. 4x4 refueler. 45c, 1942 Ford 5 passenger sedan. $1.20, 1942 Ford 3-ton tipper. $2, D8 Caterpillar with scraper.

1995, Aug. 8 Litho. *Perf. 14x15*
Black Vignettes

581 A135 5c brown & tan .50 .50
582 A135 45c blue & red lil 1.25 1.25
583 A135 $1.20 grn & org 2.60 2.60
584 A135 $2 red & gray 4.25 4.25
Nos. 581-584 (4) 8.60 8.60

Island Flower Type of 1960
1995, Sept. 1 Litho. *Rouletted 7*
Booklet Stamps

585 A6 5c like No. 30 .25 .25
a. Booklet pane of 18 + 3 labels 4.25
586 A6 5c like No. 33 .25 .25
a. Booklet pane of 18 + 3 labels 4.25
Complete booklet, 1 each #585a-586a 8.75

A136

Victory in the Pacific Day, 50th Anniv. A136a

Designs: 5c, Fighter plane en route. 45c, Sgt. T.C. Derrick, VC, vert. 75c, Gen. MacArthur, vert. $1.05, Girls at victory party.

1995, Sept. 1 Litho. *Perf. 12*

587 A136 5c multicolored .35 .35
588 A136 45c multicolored .80 .80
589 A136 75c multicolored 1.30 1.30
590 A136 $1.05 multicolored 2.00 2.00
Nos. 587-590 (4) 4.45 4.45

Litho. & Embossed

591 A136a $10 Medals 23.00 23.00

Singapore '95.

UN, 50th Anniv. — A137

45c, Dove. 75c, Christmas star. $1.05, Christmas candles. $1.20, Olive branch.

1995, Nov. 7 Litho. *Perf. 14½x14*

592 A137 45c multicolored .85 .85
593 A137 75c multicolored 1.20 1.20
594 A137 $1.05 multicolored 1.60 1.60
595 A137 $1.20 multicolored 2.10 2.10
Nos. 592-595 (4) 5.75 5.75

Christmas (#593-594).

Skinks and Geckos — A138

World Wildlife Fund: a, 5c, Skink crawling left. b, 45c, Skink crawling right. c, 5c, Gecko crawling right. d, 45c, Gecko crawling left, flower.

1996, Feb. 7 Litho. *Perf. 14½x15*

596 A138 Strip of 4, #a.-d. 3.00 3.00

No. 596 was issued in sheets of 4 strips with stamps in each strip in different order.

Royal Australian Air Force, 75th Anniv. — A139

1996, Apr. 22 Litho. *Perf. 14*

597 A139 45c Sopwith pup .85 .85
598 A139 45c Wirraway .85 .85
599 A139 75c F-111C 1.40 1.40
600 A139 85c F/A-18 Hornet 1.60 1.60
Nos. 597-600 (4) 4.70 4.70

Souvenir Sheet

New Year 1996 (Year of the Rat) A140

1996, May 17 Litho. *Perf. 12*

601 A140 $1 multicolored 2.60 2.60
a. With addl. inscription in sheet margin 5.00 5.00

No. 601a is inscribed in sheet margin with China '96 exhibition emblem.

Shells — A141

Designs: No. 602, Argonauta nodosa. No. 603, Janthina janthina. No. 604, Naticarius oncus. No. 605, Cypraea caputserpentis.

1996, July 2 Litho. *Perf. 14*

602 A141 45c multicolored .90 .90
603 A141 45c multicolored .90 .90
604 A141 45c multicolored .90 .90
605 A141 45c multicolored .90 .90
Nos. 602-605 (4) 3.60 3.60

Tourism — A142

1996, Sept. 17 Litho. *Perf. 13½x14*

606 A142 45c Shopping .70 .70
607 A142 75c Bounty day 1.10 1.10
608 A142 $2.50 Horse riding 3.50 3.50
609 A142 $3.70 Working the ship 5.25 5.25
Nos. 606-609 (4) 10.55 10.55

A143

Christmas: Cow, star, Bible verse, and: No. 610, Nativity scene. No. 611, Boats, boathouses. 75c, House, trees. 85c, Flowers, fruits.

1996, Nov. 5 Litho. *Perf. 15*

610 A143 45c multicolored .75 .75
611 A143 45c multicolored .75 .75
612 A143 75c multicolored 1.25 1.25
613 A143 85c multicolored 1.40 1.40
Nos. 610-613 (4) 4.15 4.15

A144

No. 614, Natl. Arms. No. 615, Natl. Seal.

1997, Jan. 22 Litho. *Roulette 7*

614 A144 5c yellow & green .35 .35
a. Booklet pane of 10 3.50
615 A144 5c tan & brown .35 .35
a. Booklet pane of 10 3.50
Complete booklet, 2 each #614a-615a 7.00

Souvenir Sheet

Beef Cattle A145

1997, Feb. 11 *Perf. 13½x13*

616 A145 $1.20 multicolored 2.75 2.75
a. Inscribed in sheet margin 30.00 25.00

No. 616a is inscribed with Hong Kong '97 exhibition emblem.

Butterflies — A146

Designs: 75c, Cepora perimale perimale. 90c, Danaus chrysippus petilia. $1, Danaus bamata bamata. $1.20, Danaus plexippus.

1997, Mar. 28 *Perf. 14½*

617 A146 75c multicolored 1.50 1.50
a. Black omitted, denomination and country name are missing 10,000.
618 A146 90c multicolored 1.75 1.75
619 A146 $1 multicolored 2.00 2.00
620 A146 $1.20 multicolored 2.50 2.50
Nos. 617-620 (4) 7.75 7.75

On No. 617a the denomination and country name are missing.

Dolphins A147

1997, May 29 Litho. *Perf. 14*

621 A147 45c Dusky dolphin 1.00 1.00
622 A147 75c Common dolphin 2.00 2.00

Souvenir Sheet

623 A147 $1.05 Dolphin, diff. 2.75 2.75
a. Inscribed in sheet margin 5.25 5.25

No. 623a is inscribed in sheet margin with PACIFIC 97 exhibition emblem.

First Norfolk Island Stamp, 50th Anniv. A148

Designs: $1, View of Ball Bay. $1.50, #4. $8, #12, view of Ball Bay.

1997, June 10 *Perf. 12*

624 $1.00 multicolored 1.25 1.25
625 $1.50 multicolored 2.00 2.00
a. A148 Pair, #624-625 3.50 3.50

Size: 90x45mm

626 A148 $8 multicolored 10.00 10.00

Queen Elizabeth II & Prince Philip, 50th Wedding Anniv. — A149

Designs: 20c, Queen. No. 628, Prince guiding 4-in-hand team. No. 629, Prince in formal suit, hat. 50c, Queen riding in royal coach. $1.50, Younger picture of Queen, Prince riding in carriage.

1997, Aug. 12 Litho. *Perf. 14½*

627 A149 20c multicolored .45 .45
628 A149 25c multicolored .50 .50
a. Pair, #627-628 1.00 1.00
629 A149 25c multicolored .50 .50
630 A149 50c multicolored 1.00 1.00
a. Pair, #629-630 1.60 1.60

Souvenir Sheet

631 A149 $1.50 multicolored 3.25 3.25

Souvenir Sheet

Return of Hong Kong to China A150

1997, Sept. 16 Litho. *Perf. 14*

632 A150 45c Royal Yacht Britannia 2.75 2.75

Greetings Stamps — A151

1997, Nov. 4 Litho. *Perf. 13x13½*

633 A151 45c Christmas .75 .75
634 A151 75c New Year's Eve 1.10 1.10
635 A151 $1.20 Valentine's Day 1.90 1.90
Nos. 633-635 (3) 3.75 3.75

Souvenir Sheet

Oriental Pearl TV Tower, Shanghai — A152

1997, Nov. 18 *Perf. 14½*

636 A152 45c multicolored 2.25 2.25

Shanghai '97, Intl. Stamp & Coin Expo.

Souvenir Sheet

New Year 1998 (Year of the Tiger) A153

1998, Feb. 12 Litho. *Perf. 12*

637 A153 45c multicolored 2.00 2.00

Paintings of Cats — A154

1998, Feb. 26 ***Perf. 14½***

638	A154	45c "Pepper"	.65	.65
639	A154	45c "Tabitha"	.65	.65
640	A154	75c "Midnight"	1.10	1.10
641	A154	$1.20 "Rainbow"	1.75	1.75
		Nos. 638-641 (4)	4.15	4.15

Island Scenes, by Brent Hilder — A155

Designs: No. 642, Penal Settlement, 1825-56. No. 643, First settlement, 1788-1814.

1998, Feb. 27 ***Rouletted 7***

642	A155	5c blue & black	.30	.30
a.		Booklet pane of 10	3.00	
643	A155	5c blue green & black	.30	.30
a.		Booklet pane of 10	3.00	
		Complete booklet, 2 each 1642a-1643a	12.00	

Diana, Princess of Wales (1961-97)

Common Design Type

#645: a, Wearing blue & white dress. b, Wearing pearl pendant earrings. c, In striped dress.

1998, Apr. 28 Litho. ***Perf. 14½x14***

644 CD355 45c multicolored 1.10 1.10

Sheet of 4

645 CD355 45c #a.-c., #644 4.50 4.50

No. 644 sold for $1.80 + 45c, with surtax from international sales being donated to the Princess Diana Memorial fund and surtax from national sales being dontated to designated local charity.

Reef Fish — A156

Designs: 10c, Tweed trousers. 20c, Conspicuous angelfish. 30c, Moon wrasse. 45c, Wide-stiped clownfish. 50c, Raccoon butterfly fish. 70c, Artooti. 75c, Splendid hawkfish. 85c, Scorpion fish. 90c, Orange fairy basslet. $1, Sweetlip. $3, Moorish idol. $4, Gold ribbon soapfish.

$1.20, Shark.

1998 Litho. ***Perf. 14½***

646	A156	10c multicolored	.25	.25
647	A156	20c multicolored	.30	.30
648	A156	30c multicolored	.45	.45
649	A156	45c multicolored	.60	.60
650	A156	50c multicolored	.70	.70
651	A156	70c multicolored	.95	.95
652	A156	75c multicolored	1.05	1.05
653	A156	85c multicolored	1.20	1.20
654	A156	90c multicolored	1.20	1.20
655	A156	$1 multicolored	1.40	1.40
656	A156	$3 multicolored	4.25	4.25
657	A156	$4 multicolored	5.75	5.75
		Nos. 646-657 (12)	18.10	18.10

Souvenir Sheet

Perf. 14x14½

658 A156 $1.20 multicolored 2.50 2.50

No. 658 contains 30x40mm stamp.

Issued: 10c, 30c, 50c, 75c, 90c, $1.20, $4, 5/5; others, 6/29.

16th Commonwealth Games, Kuala Lumpur — A157

Designs: 75c, Hammer throw, vert. 95c, Trap shooting. $1.05, Lawn bowling, vert.

85c, Flag bearer, vert.

1998, July 23 Litho. ***Perf. 14½***

659	A157	75c black & red	1.10	1.10
660	A157	95c black & violet blue	1.35	1.35
661	A157	$1.05 black & red lilac	1.40	1.40
		Nos. 659-661 (3)	3.85	3.85

Souvenir Sheet

662 A157 85c black & greenish blue 2.40 2.40

The Norfolk, Bicent. — A158

1998, Sept. 24 Litho. ***Perf. 13***

663 A158 45c multicolored 1.90 1.90

Souvenir Sheet

664 A158 $1.20 multicolored 3.00 3.00

Souvenir Sheet

Whales A159

1998, Oct. 23 Litho. ***Perf. 13½x14***

665 A159 $1.50 multicolored 4.25 4.25

See Namibia No. 919, South Africa No. 1095.

Christmas A160

Designs: 45c, "Peace on earth." 75c, "Joy to the World." $1.05, Doves, "A season of love." $1.20, Candle, "Light of the World."

1998, Nov. 10 ***Perf. 13x13½***

666	A160	45c multicolored	.65	.65
667	A160	75c multicolored	1.10	1.10
668	A160	$1.05 multicolored	1.50	1.50
669	A160	$1.20 multicolored	1.60	1.60
		Nos. 666-669 (4)	4.85	4.85

Airplanes — A161

No. 670, S23 Sandringham. No. 671, DC4 "Norfolk Trader."

1999, Jan. 28 Litho. ***Roulette 7***

Booklet Stamps

670	A161	5c dk grn & lake	.50	.50
a.		Booklet pane of 10	5.00	
671	A161	5c lake & dk grn	.50	.50
a.		Booklet pane of 10	5.00	
		Complete booklet, 2 ea #670a-671a	10.00	

Souvenir Sheet

New Year 1999 (Year of the Rabbit) A162

1999, Feb. 9 Litho. ***Perf. 14***

672	A162	95c multicolored	2.40	2.40
a.		With additional sheet margin inscription	4.00	4.00

No. 672a is inscribed in sheet margin with China '99 exhibition emblem. Issued: 8/23/99.

Trading Ship Resolution A163

Designs: No. 673, Under construction. No. 674, Launch day. No. 675, Emily Bay. No. 676, Cascade. No. 677, Docked at Auckland.

1999, Mar. 19 ***Perf. 13x13½***

Booklet Stamps

673	A163	45c multicolored	2.00	2.00
674	A163	45c multicolored	2.00	2.00
675	A163	45c multicolored	2.00	2.00
676	A163	45c multicolored	2.00	2.00
677	A163	45c multicolored	2.00	2.00
a.		Booklet pane, #673-677 + label	10.00	
		Complete booklet, #677a	10.00	

Australia '99, World Stamp Expo.

Souvenir Sheet

Pacific Black Duck A164

1999, Apr. 27 Litho. ***Perf. 14***

678 A164 $2.50 multicolored 4.75 4.75

IBRA '99, Intl. Philatelic Exhibition, Nuremberg, Germany.

Providence Petrel — A165

1999, May 27 Litho. ***Perf. 14½***

679	A165	75c In flight, vert.	1.90	1.90
680	A165	$1.05 Up close	2.75	2.75
681	A165	$1.20 Adult, young	3.00	3.00
		Nos. 679-681 (3)	7.65	7.65

Souvenir Sheet

Perf. 13

682 A165 $4.50 In flight 7.75 7.75

No. 682 contains one 35x51mm stamp.

See No. 710.

Roses — A166

1999, July 30 Litho. ***Perf. 14½x14***

683	A166	45c Cecile Brunner	.90	.90
684	A166	75c Green	1.25	1.25
685	A166	$1.05 David Buffett	2.00	2.00
		Nos. 683-685 (3)	4.15	4.15

Souvenir Sheet

686 A166 $1.20 A Country Woman 2.75 2.75

Handicrafts — A167

Designs: a, 45c, Pottery. b, 45c, Woodcarving. c, 75c, Quilting. d, $1.05, Weaving.

1999, Sept. 16 ***Perf. 14¼x14¾***

687 A167 Strip of 4, #a.-d. 4.25 4.25

Queen Mother's Century

Common Design Type

Queen Mother: No. 688, Inspecting bomb damage at Buckingham Palace, 1940. No. 689, With royal family at Abergeldy Castle, 1955. 75c, With Queen Elizabeth, Prince William, 94th birthday. $1.20, As colonel-in-chief of King's Regiment.

$3, With Amy Johnson, pilot of 1930 flight to Australia.

Wmk. 384

1999, Oct. 12 Litho. ***Perf. 13½***

688	CD358	45c multicolored	.70	.70
689	CD358	45c multicolored	.70	.70
690	CD358	75c multicolored	1.10	1.10
691	CD358	$1.20 multicolored	1.75	1.75
		Nos. 688-691 (4)	4.25	4.25

Souvenir Sheet

692 CD358 $3 multicolored 5.25 5.25

Melanesian Mission, 150th Anniv. — A168

Christmas: a, 45c, Bishop George Augustus Selwyndd. b, 45c, Bishop John Coleridge Patteson. c, 75c, Text. d, $1.05, Stained glass. e, $1.20, Southern Cross.

1999, Nov. 10 Litho. ***Perf. 14***

693 A168 Strip of 5, #a.-e. 7.50 7.50

See Solomon Islands No. 890.

Festivals — A169

No. 694, Thanksgiving. No. 695, Country music festival.

2000, Jan. 31 Litho. ***Roulette 5¾***

Booklet Stamps

694	A169	5c lav & blk	.25	.25
695	A169	5c blue & blk	.25	.25
a.		Booklet pane, 5 each #694-695	1.75	
		Complete booklet, 4 #695a	7.00	

Souvenir Sheet

New Year 2000 (Year of the Dragon) A170

2000, Feb. 7 Litho. ***Perf. 13¼***

696 A170 $2 multi 3.25 3.25

Fowl — A171

Designs: 45c, Domestic goose. 75c, Pacific black duck. $1.05, Mallard drake. $1.20, Aylesbury duck.

2000, Feb. 18 Litho. ***Perf. 14¼***

697	A171	45c multi	.85	.85
698	A171	75c multi	1.25	1.25
699	A171	$1.05 multi	1.75	1.75
700	A171	$1.20 multi	2.25	2.25
		Nos. 697-700 (4)	6.10	6.10

Anzac Day — A172

Monument and lists of war dead from: 45c, WWI. 75c, WWII and Korean War.

2000, Apr. 25 Litho. ***Perf. 14x14¾***

701-702 A172 Set of 2 2.40 2.40

Souvenir Sheets

Whaler Project A173

Designs: No. 703, shown. No. 704, As #703, with gold overprints for The Stamp Show 2000, London, and Crown Agents.

Perf. 14¼, Imperf. (#704)

2000, May 1

703-704 A173 $4 Set of 2 14.00 14.00

Bounty Day — A174

Designs: 45c, Capt. William Bligh. 75c, Fletcher Christian.

2000, June 8 ***Perf. 14¼***

705-706 A174 Set of 2 3.25 3.25

Eighth Festival of Pacific Arts, New Caledonia — A175

Designs: 45c, Pot and broom.

No. 708: a, 75c, Turtle and shells. $1.05, Paintings. $1.20, Spear, mask. $2, Decorated gourds.

2000, June 19 ***Die cut 9x9½***

Self-Adhesive

707 A175 45c multi 1.75 1.75

Souvenir Sheet

Perf. 13¾

Water-Activated Gum

708 A175 Sheet of 4, #a-d 9.00 9.00

No. 708 contains four 30x38mm stamps.

Souvenir Sheet

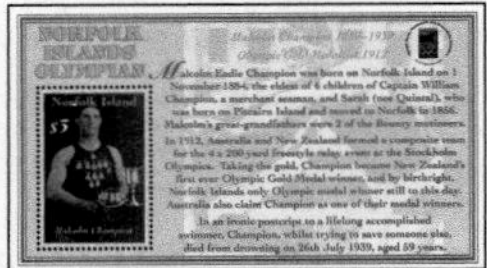

Malcolm Eadie Champion, 1912 Olympic Gold Medalist — A176

2000, Sept. 15 Litho. ***Perf. 14x14¼***

709 A176 $3 multi 5.75 5.75

Olymphilex 2000 Stamp Exhibition, Sydney.

Providence Petrel Type of 1999

Souvenir Sheet

2000, Oct. 5 ***Perf. 14½x14¾***

710 Sheet of 2 #710a 6.00 6.00
a. A165 $1.20 Like #681, 32x22mm, with white frame 3.75 3.75

Canpex 2000 Stamp Exhibition, Christchurch, New Zealand.

Christmas — A177

Words from "Silent Night" and: 45c, Sun. 75c, Candle. $1.05, Moon. $1.20, Stars.

2000, Oct. 20 ***Perf. 13¼x13***

711-714 A177 Set of 4 7.25 7.25

Millennium — A178

Children's art by: No. 715, 45c, Jessica Wong and Mardi Pye. No. 716, 45c, Roxanne Spreag. No. 717, 75c, Tara Grube. No. 718, 75c, Tom Greenwood.

2000, Nov. 26 ***Perf. 14¾x14½***

715-718 A178 Set of 4 7.50 7.50

Green Parrot — A179

2001, Jan. 26 ***Rouletted 5½***

Booklet Stamp

719 A179 5c green & red .25 .25
a. Booklet pane of 10 2.25
Booklet, 4 #719a 9.00

Tarler Bird — A180

Designs: $2.30, Norfolk island eel and tarler bird.

2001, Feb. 1 ***Perf. 13¼***

720 A180 45c multi 1.75 1.75

Imperf

Size: 110x70mm

721 A180 $2.30 multi 7.00 7.00

No. 720 issued in sheet of 5 + label. New Year 2001 (Year of the snake), Hong Kong 2001 Stamp Exhibition (#721).

Australian Federation, Cent. — A181

Pre-federation political cartoons from The Bulletin Magazine: No. 722, 45c, Promises, Promises! No. 723, 45c, The Gout of Federation. No. 724, 45c, The Political Garotters. No. 725, 45c, Tower of Babel. No. 726, 45c, Old Clothes. No. 727, 45c, The Federal Spirit. 75c, Australia Faces the Dawn. $1.05, The Federal Capital Question. $1.20, The Imperial Fowl Yard.

2001, Mar. 12 Litho. ***Perf. 14x14¾***

722-730 A181 Set of 9 8.50 8.50

Souvenir Sheet

2001 A Stamp Odyssey Stamp Show, Invercargill, New Zealand — A182

Blue portion of background at: a, Right. b, Left. c, Top.

2001, Mar. 16 ***Perf. 13***

731 A182 75c Sheet of 3, #a-c, + 3 labels 3.75 3.75

Bounty Day — A183

2001, June 8 ***Rouletted 6***

732 A183 5c green & black .25 .25
a. Booklet pane of 10 1.50
Booklet, 4 #732a 6.00

Tourism — A184

Perfume bottle and: 45c, Jasminium simplicifolium. 75c, Woman's face in perfume bottle. $1.05, Woman with roses. $1.20, Taylors Road. $1.50, Couple shopping for perfume.

$3, Woman and Norfolk pine trees.

2001, June 9 ***Perf. 13¼***

733 A184 45c multi 1.00 1.00
734 A184 75c multi 2.00 2.00
a. Booklet pane, #733-734 3.00 —
735 A184 $1.05 multi 2.00 2.00
736 A184 $1.20 multi 2.25 2.25
a. Booklet pane, #735-736 4.25 —
737 A184 $1.50 multi 3.25 2.75
a. Booklet pane of 1 3.25 —

Souvenir Sheet

738 A184 $3 multi 5.50 5.50

Booklet Stamp

Size: 154x97mm

Microrouletted at Left

739 A184 $3 Like #738 5.50 5.50
a. Booklet pane of 1 5.50 5.50
Booklet, #734a, 736a, 737a, 739a 16.00

Nos. 733-739 are impregnated with jasmine perfume. No. 738 contains one 60x72mm stamp.

No. 739 has perfume bottle at LR, country name moved on one line at UL, and is impregnated with jasmine perfume. No. 739a has binding stub at left. Booklet sold for $10 and includes postal card.

For overprint see No. 824.

Boats — A185

Designs: 45c, Whaler, vert. No. 741, $1, Rowers in boat. No. 742, $1, Motorboat, vert. $1.50, Men in cutter.

Perf. 14½x14¼, 14¼x14½

2001, Aug. 1 Litho.

740-743 A185 Set of 4 6.00 6.00

Coil Stamp

Self-Adhesive

Die Cut Perf. 14¼x14¾

744 A185 45c multi .90 .90

Peace Keepers in Japan — A186

No. 745: a, Australian soldiers playing cards. b, Soldiers with birthday cake.

No. 746: a, Soldiers on Christmas float. b, Soldiers controlling traffic.

2001, Sept. 9 ***Perf. 14½x14¾***

745 Pair with central label 3.00 3.00
a. A186 45c multi .90 .90
b. A186 $1 multi 2.10 2.10
746 Pair with central label 3.00 3.00
a. A186 45c multi .90 .90
b. A186 $1 multi 2.10 2.10

6th South Pacific Mini Games — A187

2001, Oct. 1 ***Rouletted 6***

747 A187 10c green & brown .30 .30
a. Booklet pane of 10 3.00 —
Booklet, 2 #747a 6.00

Two souvenir sheets publicizing the 6th South Pacific Mini-Games, featuring four 45c and four $1 values, respectively, were scheduled for release but were withdrawn from sale upon arrival in Norfolk, when serious design errors were discovered. A small quantity had previously been sold by Crown Agents. Value for pair of sheets, $150.

Christmas — A188

Christmas carols and flora: No. 748, 45c, Hark, the Herald Angels Sing, strawberry guava. No. 749, 45c, Deck the Halls, poinsettia. No., 750, $1, The First Noel, hibiscus. No. 751, $1, Joy to the World, Christmas croton. $1.50, We Wish You a Merry Christmas, Indian shot.

2001, Oct. 26 ***Perf. 12½***

748-752 A188 Set of 5 7.25 7.25

Sacred Kingfisher — A189

2002, Jan. 15 Litho. ***Rouletted 5¾***

Booklet Stamp

753 A189 10c aqua & dk bl .25 .25
a. Booklet pane of 10 2.50 —
Booklet, 2 #753a 5.00

Cliff Ecology — A190

Designs: 45c, Red-tailed tropicbird. No. 755, $1, White oak tree. No. 756, $1, White oak flower. $1.50, Eagle ray.

2002, Jan. 21 Unwmk. ***Perf. 13***

754-757 A190 Set of 4 7.25 7.25

Reign Of Queen Elizabeth II, 50th Anniv. Issue

Common Design Type

Designs: Nos. 758, 762a, 45c, Queen Mother with Princesses Elizabeth and Margaret, 1930. Nos. 759, 762b, 75c, Wearing scarf, 1977. Nos. 760, 762c, $1, Wearing crown, 1953. Nos. 761, 762d, $1.50, Wearing yellow hat, 2000. No. 762e, $3, 1955 portrait by Annigoni (38x50mm).

Perf. 14¼x14½, 13¾ (#762e)

2002, Feb. 6 Litho. Wmk. 373

With Gold Frames

758 CD360 45c multicolored .75 .75
759 CD360 75c multicolored 1.25 1.25
760 CD360 $1 multicolored 1.75 1.75
761 CD360 $1.50 multicolored 2.40 2.40
Nos. 758-761 (4) 6.15 6.15

Souvenir Sheet

Without Gold Frames

762 CD360 Sheet of 5, #a-e 9.75 9.75

The Age of Steam — A191

Perf. 14½x14¾

2002, Mar. 21 Litho. Unwmk.

763 A191 $4.50 multi 7.25 7.25

South Pacific Mini Games — A192

Designs: 50c, Track and field. $1.50, Tennis.

2002, Mar. 21 *Perf. 13¾x14¼*
764-765 A192 Set of 2 3.50 3.50

2002 Bounty Bowls Tournament — A193

2002, May 6 *Rouletted 6*

Booklet Stamp

766 A193 10c multi		.25	.25
a.	Booklet pane of 10	2.00	—
	Booklet, 2 #766a	4.00	

Phillip Island Flowers — A194

Designs: 10c, Streblorrhiza speciosa. 20c, Plumbago zeylanica. 30c, Canavalia rosea. 40c, Ipomoea pes-caprae. 45c, Hibiscus insularis. 50c, Solanum laciniatum. 95c, Phormium tenax. $1, Lobelia anceps. $1.50, Carpobrotus glaucescens. $2, Abutilon julianae. $3, Wollastonia biflora. $5, Oxalis corniculata.

2002 *Perf. 14½*

767	A194	10c multi	.25	.25
768	A194	20c multi	.30	.30
769	A194	30c multi	.45	.45
770	A194	40c multi	.55	.55
771	A194	45c multi	.60	.60
772	A194	50c multi	.70	.70
773	A194	95c multi	1.50	1.50
774	A194	$1 multi	1.60	1.60
775	A194	$1.50 multi	2.25	2.25
776	A194	$2 multi	3.25	3.25
777	A194	$3 multi	4.75	4.75
778	A194	$5 multi	7.50	7.50
		Nos. 767-778 (12)	23.70	23.70

Issued: 20c, 40c, 45c, 95c, $2, $5, 5/21; others 9/18.

2002 Commonwealth Games, Manchester, England — A195

Designs: 10c, Track and field, vert. 45c, Cycling. $1, Lawn bowling, vert. $1.50, Shooting.

2002, July 25
779-782 A195 Set of 4 6.00 6.00

Operation Cetacean — A196

No. 783: a, Sperm whale and calf. b, Sperm whale and squid.

2002, Sept. 18 *Perf. 14*

783	A196	Horiz. pair with central label	6.50	6.50
a.-b.		$1 Either single	3.25	3.25

See New Caledonia No. 906.

Christmas — A197

White tern: No. 784, 45c, Hatchling. No. 785, 45c, Bird on egg in nest. $1, Pair in flight. $1.50, One in flight.

2002, Nov. 12 **Litho.** *Perf. 14*
784-787 A197 Set of 4 6.50 6.50

Horses on Norfolk Island — A198

No. 788: a, Horses with riders near stable. b, Horses grazing. c, Show jumping. d, Horse racing. e, Horses pulling carriage.

2003, Jan. 14

788		Horiz. strip of 5	6.50	6.50
a.-c.	A198	45c Any single	.80	.80
d.-e.	A198	75c Either single	1.75	1.75

Year of the horse (in 2002).

Island Scenes A199

Photographs by Mary Butterfield: 50c, Buildings. 95c, Boat on beach. $1.10 Cattle grazing. $1.65 Tree near water.

2003, Mar. 18 *Perf. 14x14¼*
789-792 A199 Set of 4 7.50 7.50

See Nos. 805-808.

Day Lilies — A200

No. 793: a, Southern Prize. b, Becky Stone. c, Cameroons. d, Chinese Autumn. e, Scarlet Orbit. f, Ocean Rain. g, Gingerbread man. h, Pink Corduroy. i, Elizabeth Hinrichsen. j, Simply Pretty.

2003, June 10 **Litho.** *Perf. 14¼*

793		Block of 10	8.50	8.50
a.-j.	A200	50c Any single	.85	.85
		Complete booklet, #793	9.50	

Island Views A201

No. 794: a, Large trees at left, ocean. b, Beach. c, Rocks at shoreline. d, Cattle grazing.

2003, July 21 *Perf. 14*

794		Horiz. strip of 4 + 4 labels	6.25	6.25
a.-d.	A201	50c Any single + label	.95	.95

No. 794 was issued in sheets of five strips that had labels that could be personalized for an additional fee.

First Norfolk Island Writer's Festival — A202

No. 795: a, Maeve and Gil Hitch. b, Alice Buffett. c, Nan Smith. d, Archie Bigg. e, Colleen McCullough. f, Peter Clarke. g, Bob Tofts. h, Merval Hoare.

2003, July 21 *Perf. 14½*

795		Block of 8 + 2 labels	5.50	5.50
a.-d.	A202	10c Any single	.25	.25
e.-h.	A202	50c Any single	.75	.75

Souvenir Sheet

Coronation of Queen Elizabeth II, 50th Anniv. — A203

No. 796: a, 10c, Queen wearing crown. b, $3, Queen wearing hat.

2003, July 29 *Perf. 14½*
796 A203 Sheet of 2, #a-b 5.75 5.75

Christmas — A204

Designs: No. 797, 50c, Dove, rainbow, "Joy to the World." No. 798, 50c, Earth, "Peace on Earth." $1.10, Heart, "Give the gift of Love." $1.65, Candle, "Trust in Faith."

2003, Oct. 21 *Perf. 14¼x14*
797-800 A204 Set of 4 7.25 7.25

Powered Flight, Cent. — A205

Designs: 50c, Seaplane. $1.10, QANTAS airliner in flight. No. 803, $1.65, QANTAS airliner on ground.

No. 804, $1.65, Wright Flyer.

2003, Dec. 2 *Perf. 14x14¼*
801-803 A205 Set of 3 8.00 8.00

Souvenir Sheet

Perf. 14½x14

804 A205 $1.65 multi 8.25 8.25

No. 804 contains one 48x30mm stamp.

Limited quantities of No. 804 exist with an 85c surcharge and a 2004 Hong Kong Stamp Expo emblem in the margin. These were sold only at the exhibition. Value, mint never hinged or cto, $60.

Island Scenes Type of 2003

Designs: 50c, Houses, boat prow with foliage, vert. 95c, Waterfall, vert. $1.10, Cattle, vert. $1.65, Sea shore, vert.

2004, Feb. 10 **Litho.** *Perf. 14¼x14*
805-808 A199 Set of 4 8.00 8.00

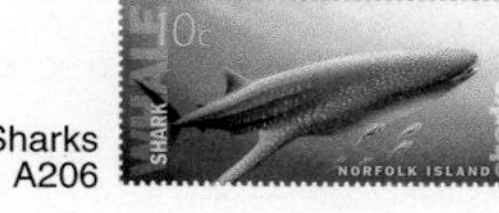

Sharks A206

Designs: 10c, Whale shark. 50c, Hammerhead shark. $1.10, Tiger shark. $1.65, Bronze whaler shark.

2004, Apr. 6 *Perf. 14¾*
809-812 A206 Set of 4 8.75 8.75

Spiders — A207

Designs: No. 813, 50c, Golden orb spider. No. 814, 50c, Community spider. $1, St. Andrew's cross spider. $1.65, Red-horned spider.

$1.50, Red-horned spider, diff.

2004, June 1 *Perf. 14½*
813-816 A207 Set of 4 6.75 6.75

Souvenir Sheet

Perf. 14½x14

817 A207 $1.50 multi 3.50 3.50

No. 817 contains one 47x40mm stamp.

Unloading of Ship Cargo A208

Designs: 50c, Men climbing on cargo nets. $1.10, Small boat with men and cargo. No. 820, $1.65, Two small boats.

No. 821, $1.65, Two small boats at dock.

2004, July 13 **Litho.** *Perf. 14¾*
818-820 A208 Set of 3 5.75 5.75

Souvenir Sheet

821 A208 $1.65 multi 3.50 3.50

Souvenir Sheet

Quota International, 25th Anniv. on Norfolk Island — A209

No. 822: a, 50c, Three children. b, $1.10, "We Care" on feet. c, $1.65, Child drawing "Quota" in sand.

2004, Aug. 16 *Perf. 14¼*
822 A209 Sheet of 3, #a-c 9.00 9.00

Day Lilies — A210

No. 823 — Hippeastrum varieties: a, Apple Blossom. b, Carnival. c, Cherry Blossom. d, Lilac Wonder. e, Millenium Star. f, Cocktail. g, Milady. h, Pacific Sunset. i, Geisha Girl. j, Lady Jane.

2004, Aug. 16 *Perf. 14½*

823		Block of 10	9.75	9.75
a.-j.	A210	50c Any single	.95	.95
		Complete booklet, #823	10.50	

No. 738 Overprinted in Silver

Souvenir Sheet

2004, Aug. **Litho.** *Perf. 13¼*
824 A184 $3 multi 12.00 12.00

No. 824 is impregnated with jasmine perfume.

Flora — A211

Designs: No. 825, Norfolk Island tree fern. No. 826, Norfolk Island palm.

2004, Sept. 28 *Rouletted 6*

Booklet Stamps

825 A211 10c bl grn & blk		.40	.30
a.	Booklet pane of 10	4.00	—
826 A211 10c yel & blk		.40	.25
a.	Booklet pane of 10	4.00	—
	Complete booklet, #825a, 826a	8.00	

Christmas — A212

Norfolk pine and words from: No. 827, 50c, Silent Night. No. 828, 50c, 'Twas the Night Before Christmas. $1.10, On the First Day of Christmas. $1.65, Oh, Holy Night.

2004, Oct. 26 *Perf. 14¼*
827-830 A212 Set of 4 6.25 6.25

Legislative Assembly, 25th Anniv. — A213

2004, Dec. 14 *Perf. 14*
831 A213 $5 multi 8.50 8.50

Worldwide Fund for Nature (WWF) — A214

Sacred kingfisher: No. 832, 50c, Two birds on tree branch. No. 833, 50c, Bird in flight with insect in beak. $1, Bird on branch. $2, Bird on branch, diff.

2004, Dec. 14

832-835	A214	Set of 4	7.25	7.25
835a	Miniature sheet, 2 each #832-835		14.00	14.00

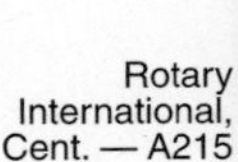

Rotary International, Cent. — A215

Emblem and: No. 836, 50c, Beach Carnival. No. 837, 50c, Tree planting, vert. $1.20, Paul Harris. $1.80, Rotary Youth Leadership Awards, vert.
$2, District 9910 ceremony.

2005, Feb. 23 Litho. *Perf. 14½*

836-839 A215 Set of 4 6.50 6.50

Souvenir Sheet

840 A215 $2 multi 4.00 4.00

No. 840 contains one 40x30mm stamp.

Items From Norfolk Island Museum — A216

Designs: No. 841, 50c, Teacup, 1856. No. 842, 50c, Salt cellar from HMAV Bounty, 1856. $1.10, Medicine cups, 1825-55. $1.65, Stoneware jar, 1825-55.

2005, Apr. 5

841-844 A216 Set of 4 7.25 7.25

Pacific Explorers — A217

Designs: 50c, Polynesian explorer, boat and fish. $1.20, Magellan's ship and bird. $1.80, Captain James Cook, ship and flower.
$2, Old map of world, horiz.

2005, Apr. 21 *Perf. 14*

845-847 A217 Set of 3 6.00 6.00

Souvenir Sheet

Perf. 14¾

848 A217 $2 multi 4.00 4.00

Pacific Explorer 2005 World Stamp Expo, Sydney. No. 848 contains one 46x32mm stamp.

Old Houses — A218

Designs: No. 849, 50c, Greenacres. No. 850, 50c, Branka House. $1.20, Ma Annas. $1.80, Naumai.

2005, June 16 Litho. *Perf. 14½*

849-852 A218 Set of 4 6.50 6.50

Sea Birds — A219

Designs: 10c, Red-tailed tropicbird. 50c, Australasian gannet. $1.50 Gray ternlet. $2, Masked booby. $5, White-necked petrel.
$4, Red-tailed tropicbird, horiz.

2005, Aug. 9

853-857 A219 Set of 5 17.00 17.00

Souvenir Sheet

858 A219 $4 multi 7.75 7.75

See Nos. 883-888. For surcharge, see No. 1044.

Hibiscus Varieties — A220

No. 859: a, Marjory Brown. b, Aloha. c, Pulau Tree. d, Ann Miller. e, Surfrider. f, Philip Island. g, Rose of Sharon. h, D. J. O'Brien. i, Elaine's Pride. j, Castle White. k, Skeleton Hibiscus. l, Pink Sunset.

2005, Aug. 30 *Perf. 14¼x14*

859	Block of 12	9.75	9.75
a.-l.	A220 50c Any single	.80	.80
	Complete booklet, #859	12.00	

Christmas A221

Designs: 50c, Anson Bay. $1.20, Cascade Bay. $1.80, Ball Bay.

2005, Oct. 25 Litho. *Perf. 14¼x14*

860-862 A221 Set of 3 5.75 5.75

Jazz Festival — A222

Designs: 50c, Drummer. $1.20, Saxophonist. $1.80, Guitarist.

2005, Dec. 6 *Perf. 14x14¼*

863-865 A222 Set of 3 5.75 5.75

Queen's Baton Relay for 2006 Commonwealth Games — A223

No. 866: a, 50c, Baton relay runner, boat's prow. b, $1.50, Baton.

2006, Jan. 16 Litho. *Perf. 14½x14¾*

866 A223 Horiz. pair, #a-b 3.50 3.50

2006 Commonwealth Games, Melbourne — A224

Norfolk Island flag and: 50c, Shooting. $1.50, Lawn bowling. $2, Squash.

2006, Mar. 14 Litho. *Perf. 14½*

867-869 A224 Set of 3 6.00 6.00

Pitcairn Migration, 150th Anniv. A225

Pitcairn Island history: No. 870, 50c, The Bounty at Portsmouth. No. 871, 50c, Collecting breadfruit at Tahiti. $1.20, The mutiny. $1.50, Burning of the Bounty at Pitcairn Island. $1.80, Pitcairners arrive at Norfolk Island, 1856.

2006, May 4 *Perf. 14x14½*

870-874 A225 Set of 5 8.75 8.75

Bounty Anniversary Day — A226

Designs: 10c, Re-enactment procession. 30c, Remembering old soldiers. No. 877, 50c, Honoring ancestors. No. 878, 50c, Community picnic. $4, Bounty Ball.

2006, June 7

875-879 A226 Set of 5 8.50 8.50

See Pitcairn Islands No. 643.

Traditional Hat Making A227

No. 880, 50c — Purple panel: a, Hat with flowers on brim. b, Hat with no flowers.
No. 881, 50c — Blue green panel: a, Hat with flowers on brim. b, Hat with feather at right.
No. 882, 50c — Green panel: a, Hat with flowers on brim. b, Hat with no flowers.

2006, June 7 *Perf. 15¼x14¾*

Horiz. Pairs, #a-b

880-882 A227 Set of 3 5.00 5.00

Sea Birds Type of 2005

Designs: 25c, White tern. 40c, Sooty tern. 70c, Black-winged petrel. $1, Black noddy. $3, Wedge-tailed shearwater.
$2.50, Sooty tern, diff.

2006, Aug. 9 *Perf. 14½*

883-887 A219 Set of 5 8.00 8.00

Souvenir Sheet

888 A219 $2.50 multi 5.50 5.50

Dogs — A228

Dogs named: 10c, Wal. 50c, Axel. $1, Wag. $2.65, Gemma.

2006, Sept. 12 *Perf. 14½*

889-892 A228 Set of 4 7.25 7.25

Norfolk Island Central School, Middlegate, Cent. A229

Designs: No. 893, $2, Sepia-toned photograph. No. 894, $2, Color photograph.

2006, Oct. 3

893-894 A229 Set of 2 7.00 7.00

Christmas A230

Ornaments showing: No. 895, 50c, Birds. No. 896, 50c, House. $1.20, Building. $1.80, Flower.

2006, Nov. 21 Litho.

Stamp + Label

895-898 A230 Set of 4 *11.00 11.00*

Weeds — A231

Designs: No. 899, 50c, Ageratina riparia. No. 900, 50c, Lantana camara. $1.20, Ipomoea cairica. $1.80, Solanum mauritianum.

2007, Feb. 6 *Perf. 14¼*

899-902 A231 Set of 4 6.00 6.00

Adventure Sports — A232

Designs: No. 903, 50c, Wind surfing. No. 904, 50c, Sea kayaking. $1.20, Mountain biking. $1.80, Surfing.

2007, Apr. 3 Litho. *Perf. 14½*

903-906 A232 Set of 4 6.50 6.50

Souvenir Sheet

Kentia Palm Seed Harvest A233

No. 907: a, Ladder and trees, vert. b, Dog and buckets of seeds. c, Man pouring seeds into box. d, Seeds on tree, vert.

Perf. 14 (14½ on Short Side Not Adjacent to Another Stamp)

2007, May 29

907 A233 50c Sheet of 4, #a-d, + central label 4.00 4.00

Ghosts — A234

Designs: 10c, Violinist, musical notes, building. 50c, Graveyard. $1, Female ghost on dock steps. $1.80, Ghosts on building steps.

2007, June 26 *Perf. 14½*

908-911 A234 Set of 4 6.00 6.00

Queen Victoria — A235

2007, July 31 *Die Cut*

Self-Adhesive

Booklet Stamp (10c)

912	A235 10c multi		.30	.30
a.	Booklet pane of 10		3.00	

Size: 21x28mm

913 A235 $5 multi 10.00 10.00

Queen Victoria Scholarship, 120th anniv.

13th South Pacific Games, Samoa — A236

Designs: 50c, Squash. $1, Golf. $1.20, Netball. $1.80, Running.
$2, Games emblem.

2007, Aug. 28 ***Perf. 14¼***
914-917 A236 Set of 4 7.50 7.50

Souvenir Sheet

918 A236 $2 multi 3.50 3.50

Closure of First Convict Settlement, Bicent. — A237

Designs: 10c, HMS Sirius and Supply off Kingston. 50c, Shipping signal, Kingston. $1.20, First settlement, Kingston. $1.80, Ship Lady Nelson leaving for Tasmania.

2007, Nov. 13
919-922 A237 Set of 4 6.25 6.25

Banyan Park Play Center — A238

Children and slogans: 50c, "Friendship." $1, "Community." $1.20, "Play, learn, grow together." $1.80, "Read books."

2007, Nov. 27 Litho. ***Perf. 14x14¼***
923-926 A238 Set of 4 7.00 7.00

Christmas A239

Items with Christmas lights: 50c, Christmas tree. $1.20, Building. $1.80, Rowboat.

2007, Nov. 27
927-929 A239 Set of 3 5.50 5.50

Automobiles A240

Designs: 50c, 1965 Ford Falcon XP. $1, 1952 Chevrolet Styleline. $1.20, 1953 Pontiac Silver Arrow. $1.80, 1971 Rolls Royce Silver Shadow.

2008, Feb. 5
930-933 A240 Set of 4 6.75 6.75

Norfolk Islanders With Pitcairn Islands Heritage — A241

Designs: 50c, Andre Nobbs. $1, Darlene Buffett. $1.20, Colin "Boonie" Lindsay Buffett. $1.80, Tania Grube.

2008, Apr. 4 Litho. ***Perf. 14½***
934-937 A241 Set of 4 6.75 6.75

Jewish Gravestones — A242

Gravestone of: 50c, Carl Hans Nathan Strauss. $1.20, Meta Kienhuize. $1.80, Johan Jacobus Kienhuize.
$2, Sally Kadesh.

2008, May 14 ***Perf. 14½***
938-940 A242 Set of 3 5.50 5.50

Souvenir Sheet

Perf. 13½

941 A242 $2 multi 3.50 3.50

2008 World Stamp Championship, Israel (#941). No. 941 contains one 30x40mm stamp.

Calves — A243

Designs: 50c, Limousin Cross. $1, Murray Grey. $1.20, Poll Hereford. $1.80, Brahman Cross.

2008, May 30 ***Perf. 14¼***
942-945 A243 Set of 4 7.00 7.00

St. John Ambulance, 25th Anniv. on Norfolk Island — A244

Designs: 30c, Past and present members. 40c, Re-enactment of treatment of accident victim at scene. 95c, Accident victim being placed in ambulance. $4, Accident victim entering hospital.

2008, June 27 ***Perf. 14½***
946-949 A244 Set of 4 8.75 8.75

Ferns A245

No. 950, 20c: a, Netted brakefern. b, Pteris zahlbrucknerianа.
No. 951, 50c: a, Robinsonia. b, Asplenium australasicum.
No. 952, 80c: a, Hanging fork fern. b, Tmesipteris norfolkensis.
No. 953, $2: a, King fern. b, Marattia salicina.

2008, Aug. 1 Litho. ***Perf. 14¼***

Horiz. Pairs, #a-b

950-953 A245 Set of 4 10.50 10.50

Ships Built On Norfolk Island — A246

Designs: 50c, Sloop Norfolk, 1798. $1.20, Schooner Resolution, 1925. $1.80, Schooner Endeavour, 1808.

2008, Sept. 2
954-956 A246 Set of 3 5.00 5.00

A247

Designs: 25c, Prison buildings. 55c, Gate and prison buildings. $1.75, Graveyard. $2.50, Building and walls.

2008, Oct. 27 Litho. ***Perf. 14½***
957-960 A247 Set of 4 7.00 7.00

Isles of Exile Conference, Norfolk Island.

A248

Christmas: 55c, Adoration of the Shepherds. $1.40, Madonna and Child. $2.05, Adoration of the Magi.

2008, Nov. 7 ***Perf. 14¼***
961-963 A248 Set of 3 5.50 5.50

Mosaics — A249

Designs: 5c, Fish. No. 965, 15c, Flower. 55c, Bird. $1.40, Tree.
No. 968, 15c, Turtle. No. 969, 15c, Starfish.

2009, Feb. 16 ***Perf. 14x14¼***
964-967 A249 Set of 4 3.00 3.00

Booklet Stamps

Self-Adhesive

Serpentine Die Cut 9½x10

968-969 A249 Set of 2 .75 .75
969a Booklet pane of 12, 6 each #968-969 4.25 4.25

Cattle Breeds — A250

Designs: 15c, Shorthorn. 55c, South Devon. $1.40, Norfolk Blue. $2.05, Lincoln Red. $5.00, Three calves.

2009, Apr. 24 Litho. ***Perf. 14x14¼***
970-973 A250 Set of 4 6.00 6.00

Souvenir Sheet

Perf. 14¼

974 A250 $5 multi 7.25 7.25

Mushrooms — A251

Designs: 15c, Gyrodon sp. 55c, Stereum ostrea. $1.40, Cymatoderma elegans. $2.05, Chlorophyllum molybdites.

2009, May 29 Litho. ***Perf. 14½x14***
975-978 A251 Set of 4 6.75 6.75
978a Souvenir sheet, #975-978 6.75 6.75
978b As "a," overprinted with Intl. Stamp & Coin Expo emblem and text in sheet margin in gold 8.25 8.25

Issued: No. 978b, 11/7/10.

Endangered Wildlife — A252

Designs: No. 979, Bridled nailtail wallaby. No. 980, Norfolk Island green parrot. No. 981, Subarctic fur seal. No. 982, Christmas Island blue-tailed skink. No. 983, Green turtle.

2009, Aug. 4 Litho. ***Perf. 14¾x14***

"Norfolk Island" Above Denomination

979 A252 55c multi .95 .95
980 A252 55c multi .95 .95
981 A252 55c multi .95 .95
982 A252 55c multi .95 .95
983 A252 55c multi .95 .95
a. Horiz. strip of 5, #979-983 4.75 4.75
Nos. 979-983 (5) 4.75 4.75

Miniature Sheet

984 A252 55c Sheet of 5, #980, Australia #3126, 3128-3130 5.00 5.00

See Australia Nos. 3126-3136. No. 984 is identical to Australia No. 3131. Australia No. 3127 is similar to No. 980, but has "Australia" above denomination.

Birds — A253

Designs: 15c, Gray fantail. 55c, Pacific robin, vert. $1.40, Golden whistler, vert. $2.05, Sacred kingfisher.

2009, Aug. 19 ***Perf. 14½***
985 A253 15c multi .25 .25
986 A253 55c multi .95 .95
Complete booklet, 10 #986 9.50
987 A253 $1.40 multi 2.40 2.40
988 A253 $2.05 multi 3.50 3.50
Nos. 985-988 (4) 7.10 7.10

Self-government, 30th Anniv. — A254

2009, Aug. 19 ***Perf. 14***
989 A254 $10 multi 15.00 15.00

Christmas — A255

Stained-glass windows depicting: 15c, St. Matthew. 50c, Roses. $1.45, Christ in Glory. $2.10, Saint with Chalice.

2009, Nov. 2 Litho. ***Perf. 14¼***
990-993 A255 Set of 4 7.75 7.75

Historical Artifacts — A256

Designs: 5c, China from second convict settlement, drawing of man and woman. 55c, Polynesian ivory fish hook, drawing of fishing boat. $1.10, Regimental badge, painting of soldiers. $1.45, Brass wall fitting from HMS Sirius shipwreck, drawing of shipwreck. $1.65, Bottles from convict settlement's Civil Hospital, drawing of treatment of an ill woman. $2.10, Bounty wedding ring, painting of the Bounty.

2010, Feb. 22 Litho. ***Perf. 14½***
994 A256 5c multi .25 .25
995 A256 55c multi 1.00 1.00
996 A256 $1.10 multi 1.10 1.10
997 A256 $1.45 multi 2.60 2.60
998 A256 $1.65 multi 3.00 3.00
999 A256 $2.10 multi 3.75 3.75
Nos. 994-999 (6) 11.70 11.70

See Nos. 1021-1026.

Cruise Ships — A257

Designs: 55c, Pacific Jewel. $1.45, Pacific Sun. $1.65, Pacific Pearl. $1.75, Pacific Dawn. $2.10, RMS Strathaird.

2010, Mar. 26 Litho. ***Perf. 14x14½***
1000-1004 A257 Set of 5 14.00 14.00

1856 Emigration of Pitcairn Islanders to Norfolk Island — A258

Ship Morayshire and: 55c, Pitcairn Island girls on Norfolk Island, 1857. $1.10, Passengers aboard ship, 1856. $1.45, Pitcairn Island men on Norfolk Island, 1861. $2.75, Naomi and Jane Nobbs.

2010, June 15 ***Perf. 13½x13¼***
1005-1008 A258 Set of 4 10.00 10.00

History of Whaling — A259

Designs: No. 1009, 60c, Blessing of the fleet. No. 1010, 60c, Launching of boats. $1.20, Cliff top navigational fires. $3, Products made from whales.

2010, Aug. 16 Litho. ***Perf. 14x14¼***
1009-1012 A259 Set of 4 10.00 10.00

Christmas — A260

Parrots and: 15c, Bells. 55c, Conifer sprig. 60c, Gift. $1.30, Christmas ornament.

2010, Oct. 18 Litho. ***Perf. 13¼x13½***
1013-1016 A260 Set of 4 5.25 5.25

2010 World Bowls Champion of Champions Lawn Bowling Tournament, Norfolk Island — A261

Designs: 60c, Woman holding trophy. $1.50, Man bowling. $2.20, Bowling balls.

2010, Nov. 23 Litho. ***Perf. 14***
1017-1019 A261 Set of 3 8.75 8.75

Souvenir Sheet

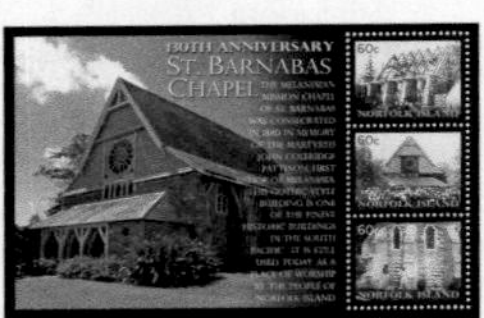

St. Barnabas Chapel, 130th Anniv. — A262

No. 1020: a, Chapel under construction. b, Congregation in front of chapel. c, Two men in front of chapel.

2010, Dec. 7 ***Perf. 14½x14***
1020 A262 60c Sheet of 3, #a-c 3.75 3.75

Historical Artifacts Type of 2010

Designs: 15c, Women, iron. 60c, Thursday October Christian and his mug. $1.20, Soldiers, bone dominoes. $1.50, Soldier in front of Civil Hospital, clay pipe and ceramic shards. $1.80, Woman and child, doll and doll's head. $3, People at Melanesian Mission, wooden and shell hair items.

2011, Feb. 22 ***Perf. 14½***
1021 A256 15c multi .30 .30
1022 A256 60c multi 1.25 1.25
1023 A256 $1.20 multi 2.50 2.50
1024 A256 $1.50 multi 3.00 3.00
1025 A256 $1.80 multi 3.75 3.75
1026 A256 $3 multi 6.25 6.25
Nos. 1021-1026 (6) 17.05 17.05

Shells — A263

Designs: 15c, Cirostrema zelebori, Canarium labiatum. 60c, Janthina janthina, Spirula spirula. $1.50, Conus capitaneus, Conus ebraeus. $1.80, Cypraea vitellus, Cypraea caputserpentis. $3, Nerita atramentosa, Neritina turrita.

2011, Apr. 21 Litho. ***Perf. 14½***
1027-1031 A263 Set of 5 15.00 15.00

Norfolk Island National Park, 25th Anniv. — A264

Park emblem and: 25c, Abutilon julianae. 60c, Hibiscus insularis. $1.55, Myoporum obscurum. $2.25, Meryta latifolia.

2011, June 24 ***Perf. 13½x13¼***
1032-1035 A264 Set of 4 10.00 10.00

Kingston and Arthur's Vale UNESCO World Heritage Site — A265

No. 1036: a, Guard House, 1796-1826. b, Graveyard, 1790s-1825. c, Government House, 1804-28. d, Pier Store, 1825. e, Crank Mill, 1827. f, Bloody Bridge, 1835. g, Commissariat Store, 1835. h, Kingston Pier, 1839. i, No. 9 Quality Row, 1839. j, Flaghouses, 1840s. k, New Jail, 1847. l, Royal Engineers Office, 1851.

2011, Aug. 1 ***Die Cut Perf. 9¾x10***
Self-Adhesive
1036 Booklet pane of 12 15.00
a.-l. A265 60c Any single 1.25 1.25

Norfolk Island Police Force, 80th Anniv. — A266

Designs: 60c, Mounted policeman on Bounty Day, c. 1933. $1.55, 1970s police car. $2.25, Policeman observing ship.

2011, Oct. 14 Litho. ***Perf. 13x13¼***
1037-1039 A266 Set of 3 9.25 9.25

Christmas — A267

Various flowers: 15c, 55c, 60c, $1.35.

2011, Oct. 14 ***Perf. 14½***
1040-1043 A267 Set of 4 5.50 5.50

No. 853 Surcharged in Brown and Black

Methods and Perfs As Before
2012, Feb. 13
1044 A219 $4 on 10c #853 8.75 8.75

Iconic Activities — A268

Designs: 60c, Collecting hi hi shells. 75c, Collecting whale bird eggs. $1.55, Fishing off the rocks. $2.75, Clifftop barbecue.

2012, Apr. 10 Litho. ***Die Cut***
Self-Adhesive
1045-1048 A268 Set of 4 11.50 11.50

Souvenir Sheet

Reign of Queen Elizabeth II, 60th Anniv. — A269

No. 1049: a, Commemorative plaque on Queen Elizabeth Avenue. b, Beacon at Queen Elizabeth Lookout. c, Decorated pine tree at Government House.

Litho. With Foil Application
2012, Aug. 20 ***Perf. 14½***
1049 A269 $1.60 Sheet of 3, #a-c 10.00 10.00

Sunshine Club, 51st Anniv. — A270

Designs: 60c, Baked goods. $1.60, Basket with bananas, flour and sugar. $1.65, Cook book and pie ingredients. $2.35, Hands.

2012, Oct. 19 Litho. ***Perf. 14***
1050-1053 A270 Set of 4 13.00 13.00

Christmas — A271

Various pearl inlays from pews in St. Barnabas Chapel and lyrics from Christmas carols: 15c, 55c, $1.55, $2.35.

2012, Nov. 1
1054-1057 A271 Set of 4 9.75 9.75

Airplanes Landing on Norfolk Island, 70th Anniv. — A272

No. 1058: a, Royal New Zealand Air Force Hudson Bomber. b, DC-3. c, Lancastrian. d, DC-4 Skymaster. e, Fokker F27 Friendship. f, Beechcraft Super King Air 200. g, Fokker F28 Fellowship. h, C-130 Hercules. i, BAe 146. j, Boeing 737-300. k, F/A-18 Hornet. l, Airbus A320.

Serpentine Die Cut 9¾x10
2012, Dec. 24
1058 Booklet pane of 12 15.00
a.-l. A272 60c Any single 1.25 1.25

Bell, All Saints Church, Kingston — A273

2013, Apr. 9 ***Perf. 14***
1059 A273 $5 multi 10.50 10.50

Norfolk Island Country Music Festival, 20th Anniv. — A274

Designs: 15c, Boots, Emily Bay Beach. 60c, Adam Harvey with guitar. $1.60, Guitar. $1.65, Dennis Marsh with guitar. $2.35, Street perfomer with guitar.

2013, May 20
1060-1064 A274 Set of 5 12.00 12.00

Shorelines A275

Designs: 15c, Ball Bay. 60c, Second Sands. 95c, Anson Bay. $1.20, Slaughter Bay. $1.70, Bumboras. $1.85, Emily Bay.

2013, Sept. 30 Litho. ***Perf. 13½***
1065 A275 15c multi .30 .30
1066 A275 60c multi 1.10 1.10
1067 A275 95c multi 1.90 1.90
1068 A275 $1.20 multi 2.25 2.25
1069 A275 $1.70 multi 3.25 3.25
1070 A275 $1.85 multi 3.50 3.50
Nos. 1065-1070 (6) 12.30 12.30

See Nos. 1079-1084.

Christmas — A276

Locally-made Christmas ornamentation: 15c, Wreath. 55c, Christmas tree made of driftwood. $1.10, Bird made of driftwood. $1.65, Three stars.

2013, Nov. 1 Litho. ***Perf. 14½***
1071-1074 A276 Set of 4 6.50 6.50

Trans-Tasman Freestyle Motocross Challenge A277

Flag of Norfolk Island and New Zealand motorcyclists performing stunts on motorcycle: 50c, Joe McNaughton. $1, McNaughton, diff. $1.50, McNaughton, diff. $1.60, Callum Shaw.

2013, Dec. 18 Litho. ***Perf. 13½***
1075-1078 A277 Set of 4 8.25 8.25

Shorelines Type of 2013

Designs: 5c, Cemetery Beach. 10c, Beefsteak. 25c, Crystal Pool. 70c, Cascade Bay. $1.75, Garnet Point. $2.60, Duncombe Bay.

2014, May 7 Litho. ***Perf. 13½***
1079 A275 5c multi .25 .25
1080 A275 10c multi .25 .25
1081 A275 25c multi .50 .50
1082 A275 70c multi 1.40 1.40
1083 A275 $1.75 multi 3.25 3.25
1084 A275 $2.60 multi 4.75 4.75
Nos. 1079-1084 (6) 10.40 10.40

Wearable Art — A278

Designs: 15c, Fishing for the Groom, by Wayne Boniface. 70c, Pasta Bella, by Boniface. $1.40, Flora Abunda Metallica, by Tony Gazzard., $1.50, Romeo and Julieta, by Julie Paris. $3.50, Bamboo Princess Warrior, by Robyn Butterfield.

2014, May 26 Litho. ***Perf. 14***
1085-1089 A278 Set of 5 13.50 13.50

Norfolk Island Pine — A279

Norfolk Island Pine and: 20c, Cottesloe Beach, Western Australia. 70c, Old Military Barracks, Kingston, Norfolk Island.

2014, July 22 Litho. *Perf. 14x14¾*
1090-1091 A279 Set of 2 1.75 1.75

See Australia Nos. 4145-4146.

Norfolk Island Quota International Club, 35th Anniv. — A280

Designs: 15c, Picnic table near Emily Bay. 70c, Telescope on Queen Elizabeth Lookout. $3.20, Family on bench overlooking ocean.

2014, Aug. 15 Litho. *Perf. 14*
1092-1094 A280 Set of 3 7.50 7.50

Souvenir Sheet

Red Cross on Norfolk Island, Cent. A281

2014, Sept. 29 Litho. *Perf. 14*
1095 A281 $3.50 multi 6.25 6.25

Tip of Norfolk Island Pine A282

Developing Norfolk Island Pine Cone A283

Norfolk Island Pine Seedling A284

Norfolk Island Pine Forest A285

Norfolk Island Pine Seeds A286

Norfolk Island Pine Branches A287

Shed Norfolk Island Pine Needles A288

Hollowed-out Norfolk Island Pine A289

Norfolk Island Pines A290

Norfolk Island Pine A291

Serpentine Die Cut 10¾x10
2014, Sept. 29 Litho.
Self-Adhesive

1096	Booklet pane of 10	12.50	
a.	A282 70c multi	1.25	1.25
b.	A283 70c multi	1.25	1.25
c.	A284 70c multi	1.25	1.25
d.	A285 70c multi	1.25	1.25
e.	A286 70c multi	1.25	1.25
f.	A287 70c multi	1.25	1.25
g.	A288 70c multi	1.25	1.25
h.	A289 70c multi	1.25	1.25
i.	A290 70c multi	1.25	1.25
j.	A291 70c multi	1.25	1.25

See No. 1109.

Quilts — A292

Designs: 15c, Memory Quilt, by Julie South. 70c, Sampler Quilt, by Kay Greenbury, Raewyn Maxwell, Rowena Massicks and Barbara Solomon. $1.40, Sunset at Puppy's Point, by Greenbury. $1.50, Southern Cross Shared, by Greenbury. $3.50, Storm at Sea, by Massicks.

2014, Oct. 17 Litho. *Perf. 14½*
1097-1101 A292 Set of 5 12.50 12.50

Christmas A293

Fabric designs by Sue Pearson depicting: 15c, Breadfruit leaves. 65c, Passion fruit flowers. $1.70, Turtles. $1.80, Taro leaves. $2.55, Hibiscus flowers.

2014, Nov. 3 Litho. *Perf. 14¼x14*
1102-1106 A293 Set of 5 12.00 12.00

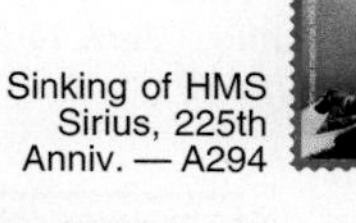

Sinking of HMS Sirius, 225th Anniv. — A294

No. 1107: a, Diver at underwater memorial. b, HMS Sirius, painting by John Allcott. c, The Melancholy Loss of HMS Sirius, painting by George Rapet. d, Cross belt plate from HMS Sirius. e, Capt. John Hunter of the HMS Sirius. f, Anchor of HMS Sirius. g, HMS Sirius, painting by Francis J. Bayldon. h, Carronades of HMS Sirius. i, Bronze shackle from HMS Sirius. j, Pantograph from HMS Sirius.

Serpentine Die Cut 10x10¾
2015, Mar. 19 Litho.
Self-Adhesive

1107	Booklet pane of 10	11.00	
a.-j.	A294 70c Any single	1.10	1.10

Souvenir Sheet

Battle of Gallipoli, Cent. A295

Litho. With Foil Application
2015, Apr. 24 *Perf. 13½*
1108 A295 $5 multi 8.00 8.00

Norfolk Island Pine Types of 2014

Designs as before.

Serpentine Die Cut 10¾x10
2015, June 1 Litho.
Self-Adhesive

1109	Booklet pane of 10	2.50	
a.	A282 15c multi	.25	.25
b.	A283 15c multi	.25	.25
c.	A284 15c multi	.25	.25
d.	A285 15c multi	.25	.25
e.	A286 15c multi	.25	.25
f.	A287 15c multi	.25	.25
g.	A288 15c multi	.25	.25
h.	A289 15c multi	.25	.25
i.	A290 15c multi	.25	.25
j.	A291 15c multi	.25	.25

Celebrities at Christmas in July Festival — A296

Designs: 25c, John Rowles, singer. 35c, Suzanne Prentice, singer. 45c, Normie Rowe, singer. $1.40, Glenn A. Baker, journalist and 2015 festival master of ceremonies. $1.95, Colleen McCullough (1937-2015), writer.

2015, July 13 Litho. *Perf. 14¼x14*
1110-1114 A296 Set of 5 6.50 6.50

Christmas — A297

Ornaments made from plant fibers: 15c, Bird. 65c, Star. $1.30, Fish. $1.70, Rings around glass balls, candle. $2.55, Netting around glass ball.

2015, Oct. 1 Litho. *Perf. 14½x14¾*
1115-1119 A297 Set of 5 9.00 9.00

Norfolk's Ocean Challenge Canoe Races A298

Various participants with panel color of: No. 1120, $1, Cerise. No. 1121, $1, Cobalt. $1.85, Green. $2.75, Gray blue.

2016, Jan. 14 Litho. *Perf. 14x14½*
1120-1123 A298 Set of 4 9.50 9.50

Phillip Island — A299

Designs: 15c, Building. 20c, Building, diff. No. 1126, $1, Building, diff. No. 1127, $1, Man, woman and building. $1.85, Building, diff. $2, Tree near cliff.

2016, Feb. 22 Litho. *Perf. 14½*
1124-1129 A299 Set of 6 9.00 9.00

Souvenir Sheet

Landing of Pitcairn Islanders on Norfolk Island, 160th Anniv. A300

2016, June 7 Litho. *Perf. 13½*
1130 A300 $5 multi 7.50 7.50

Sea Birds — A301

Designs: $1, Red-tailed tropicbird. $2, Masked booby.

2016, Sept. 20 Litho. *Perf. 14x14¾*
1131-1132 A301 Set of 2 4.75 4.75
1132a Souvenir sheet of 2, #1131-1132 4.75 4.75

Waterfalls — A302

Designs: $1, Cockpit Waterfall. $2, Cascade Creek Falls.

2017, Jan. 17 Litho. *Perf. 14¾x14*
1133-1134 A302 Set of 2 4.50 4.50
1134a Souvenir sheet of 2, #1133-1134 4.50 4.50

Flowers — A303

Designs: $1, Hibiscus insularis. $2, Lagunaria patersonia.

2017, July 18 Litho. *Perf. 14x14¾*
1135-1136 A303 Set of 2 5.00 5.00
1136a Souvenir sheet of 2, #1135-1136 5.00 5.00

UNESCO World Heritage Sites on Norfolk Island — A304

Designs: $1, New Jail. $2, Prisoners Barracks.

2017, Sept. 19 Litho. *Perf. 14¾x14*
1137-1138 A304 Set of 2 4.75 4.75
1138a Souvenir sheet of 2, #1137-1138 4.75 4.75

Norfolk Island Golf Club — A305

2018, Feb. 27 Litho. *Perf. 13¾x14*
1139 A305 $5 multi 7.75 7.75
a. Souvenir sheet of 1 7.75 7.75

Wrasses — A306

Designs: $1, Surge wrasse. $2, Luculent wrasse.

2018, Apr. 30 Litho. *Perf. 14x14¾*
1140-1141 A306 Set of 2 4.50 4.50
1141a Souvenir sheet of 2, #1140-1141 4.50 4.50

Crystal Pool — A307

Pool at: $1, High tide. $2, Low tide.

2018, July 17 Litho. *Perf. 14x14¾*
1142-1143 A307 Set of 2 4.50 4.50
1143a Souvenir sheet of 2, #1142-1143 4.50 4.50

Cruise Ships — A308

Designs: $1, Seven Seas Mariner. $2, Pacific Explorer.

2018, Sept. 18 Litho. ***Perf. 14x14¾***

1144-1145 A308 Set of 2 4.50 4.50
1145a Souvenir sheet of 2, #1144-1145 4.50 4.50

Pitcairn Settlement on Norfolk Island — A309

Pitcairn settlement on Norfolk Island and: $1, George Hunn Nobbs (1799-1884), missionary. $2, Queen Victoria (1819-1901).

2019, Jan. 22 Litho. ***Perf. 14x14¾***

1146-1147 A309 Set of 2 4.50 4.50
1147a Souvenir sheet of 2, #1146-1147 4.50 4.50

Cyathea Brownii — A310

Designs: $1, Curled frond tip. $2, Opened frond.

2019, Apr. 2 Litho. ***Perf. 14x14¾***

1148-1149 A310 Set of 2 4.25 4.25
1149a Souvenir sheet of 2, #1148-1149 4.25 4.25

Phillip Island Landscapes A311

Designs: $1, Boulders on hillside. $2, Forest.

2019, July 9 Litho. ***Perf. 14x14¾***

1150-1151 A311 Set of 2 4.25 4.25
1151a Souvenir sheet of 2, #1150-1151 4.25 4.25

Mutiny on the Bounty, 230th Anniv. — A312

Designs: $1, Captain William Bligh set adrift. $2, Mutineers (38x52mm).

2019, Sept. 24 Litho. ***Perf. 14x14¾***

1152-1153 A312 Set of 2 4.00 4.00
1153a Souvenir sheet of 2, #1152-1153 4.00 4.00

Botanical Art of the 1790s Attributed to John Doody — A313

Designs: $1.10, Lagunaria patersonia. $2.20, Ungeria floribunda.

2020, Jan. 14 Litho. ***Perf. 14¾x14***

1154-1155 A313 Set of 2 4.50 4.50
1155a Souvenir sheet of 2, #1154-1155 4.50 4.50

Norfolk Blue Cattle — A314

Designs: $1.10, Bull. $2.20, Cow and calf.

2020, June 2 Litho. ***Perf. 14¾x14***

1156-1157 A314 Set of 2 4.75 4.75
1157a Souvenir sheet of 2, #1156-1157 4.75 4.75

Fish — A315

Designs: $1.10, Bump-head sunfish. $2.20, Oarfish.

2020, July 14 Litho. ***Perf. 14¾x14***

1158-1159 A315 Set of 2 4.75 4.75
1159a Souvenir sheet of 2, #1158-1159 4.75 4.75

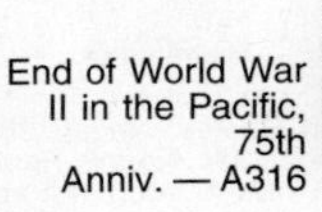

End of World War II in the Pacific, 75th Anniv. — A316

Designs: $1.10, Airplane. $2.20, Soldiers.

2020, Sept. 1 Litho. ***Perf. 14x14¾***

1160-1161 A316 Set of 2 5.00 5.00
1161a Souvenir sheet of 2, #1160-1161 5.00 5.00

Lizards — A317

Designs: $1.10, Lord Howe Island skink. $2.20, Lord Howe Island gecko.

2021, Feb. 9 Litho. ***Perf. 14x14¾***

1162-1163 A317 Set of 2 5.25 5.25
1163a Souvenir sheet of 2, #1162-1163 5.25 5.25

Land Snails — A318

Designs: $1.10, Greenwoodoconcha nux. $2.20, Duritropis albocarinata.

2021, June 22 Litho. ***Perf. 14x14¾***

1164-1165 A318 Set of 2 5.00 5.00
1165a Souvenir sheet of 2, #1164-1165 5.00 5.00

Model Ships Displayed at HMS Sirius Museum Site — A319

Model of: $1.10, HMS Sirius. $2.20, HMAT Supply.

2021, July 13 Litho. ***Perf. 14¾x14***

1166-1167 A319 Set of 2 5.00 5.00
1167a Souvenir sheet of 2, #1166-1167 5.00 5.00

Butterflies — A320

Designs: $1.10, Norfolk swallowtail butterfly. $2.20, Norfolk Island gull butterfly.

2021, Sept. 21 Litho. ***Perf. 14x14¾***

1168-1169 A320 Set of 2 5.00 5.00
1169a Souvenir sheet of 2, #1168-1169 5.00 5.00

Watercolors of Norfolk Island by John Eyre — A321

View of: $1.10, Sydney (now Kingston), c. 1805. $2.20, Queenborough, 1804.

2022, Jan. 19 Litho. ***Perf. 14x14¾***

1170-1171 A321 Set of 2 4.75 4.75
1171a Souvenir sheet of 2, #1170-1171 4.75 4.75

Norfolk Island Morepork — A322

Norfolk Island morepork: $1.10, On branch. $2.20, Head.

2022, June 21 Litho. ***Perf. 14¾x14***

1172-1173 A322 Set of 2 4.50 4.50
1173a Souvenir sheet of 2, #1172-1173 4.50 4.50

Art of George Raper (1769-96) — A323

Designs: $1.10, Map of south coast of Norfolk Island. $2.20, Snapper of Norfolk Island and map of Phillip Island.

2022, Sept. 13 Litho. ***Perf. 14x14¾***

1174-1175 A323 Set of 2 4.25 4.25
1175a Souvenir sheet of 2, #1174-1175 4.25 4.25

Extinct Birds — A324

Designs: $1.20, Norfolk Island pigeon. $2.40, Norfolk Island kaka.

2023, Jan. 31 Litho. ***Perf. 14x14¾***

1176-1177 A324 Set of 2 5.25 5.25
1177a Souvenir sheet of 2, #1176-1177 5.25 5.25

Norfolk Island Botanic Garden — A325

Designs: $1.20, Pepper tree and stairway. $2.40, Philip Island hibiscus and boardwalk.

2023, June 13 Litho. ***Perf. 14¾x14***

1178-1179 A325 Set of 2 5.00 5.00
1179a Souvenir sheet of 2, #1178-1179 5.00 5.00

Lookouts — A326

Designs: $1.20, Queen Elizabeth Lookout. $2.40, Captain Cook Lookout.

2023, July 25 Litho. ***Perf. 14x14¾***

1180-1181 A326 Set of 2 4.75 4.75
1181a Souvenir sheet of 2, #1180-1181 4.75 4.75

Humpback Whale — A327

Designs: $1.20, Whale reaching water. $2.40, Two whales underwater.

2024, Jan. 8 Litho. ***Perf. 14x14¾***

1182-1183 A327 Set of 2 4.75 4.75
1183a Souvenir sheet of 2, #1182-1183 4.75 4.75

NORTH BORNEO

'north 'bor-nē-,ō

LOCATION — Northeast part of island of Borneo, Malay archipelago
GOVT. — British colony
AREA — 29,388 sq. mi.
POP. — 470,000 (est. 1962)
CAPITAL — Jesselton

The British North Borneo Company administered North Borneo, under a royal charter granted in 1881, until 1946 when it became a British colony. Labuan (q.v.) became part of the new colony. As "Sabah," North Borneo joined with Singapore, Sarawak and Malaya to form the Federation of Malaysia on Sept. 16, 1963.

100 Cents = 1 Dollar

Quantities of most North Borneo stamps through 1912 have been canceled to order with an oval of bars. Values given for used stamps beginning with No. 6 are for those with this form of cancellation. Stamps from No. 6 through Nos. 159 and J31 that do not exist CTO have used values in italics. Stamps with dated town cancellations sell for much higher prices.

Catalogue values for unused stamps in this country are for Never Hinged items, beginning with Scott 238.

North Borneo

Coat of Arms — A1

1883-84 Unwmk. Litho. ***Perf. 12***

1 A1 2c brown 47.50 *75.00*
 a. Horiz. pair, imperf. btwn. 20,000.
2 A1 4c rose ('84) 65.00 *70.00*
3 A1 8c green ('84) 90.00 *60.00*
 Nos. 1-3 (3) 202.50 *205.00*

For surcharges see Nos. 4, 19-21.

No. 1 Surcharged in Black

4 A1 8c on 2c brown 500.00 *210.00*
 a. Double surcharge *6,000.*

Coat of Arms with Supporters
A4 A5

Perf. 14

6 A4 50c violet 225.00 40.00
7 A5 $1 red 185.00 19.00

1886 ***Perf. 14***

8 A1 ½c magenta 120.00 *200.00*
9 A1 1c orange *210.00 350.00*
 a. Imperf., pair 300.00
 b. Vert. pair, imperf horiz. 1,500.
10 A1 2c brown 47.50 42.50
 a. Horiz. pair, imperf. between 700.00
11 A1 4c rose 20.00 *55.00*
 a. Horiz. pair, imperf. between — 1,700.
12 A1 8c green 22.50 *50.00*
 a. Horiz. pair, imperf. between *900.00*
13 A1 10c blue 55.00 *65.00*
 a. Imperf., pair 375.00
 Nos. 8-13 (6) 475.00 *762.50*

Nos. 8, 11, 12 and 13 Surcharged or Overprinted in Black

b

c

d

1886
14 A1 (b) ½c magenta 225.00 *325.00*
15 A1 (c) 3c on 4c rose 130.00 *150.00*
16 A1 (d) 3c on 4c rose 1,800.
17 A1 (c) 5c on 8c green 140.00 *150.00*
a. Inverted surcharge 2,750.
18 A1 (b) 10c blue 300.00 *375.00*

On Nos. 2 and 3
Perf. 12
19 A1 (c) 3c on 4c rose 325.00 *375.00*
20 A1 (d) 3c on 4c rose — *16,000.*
a. Double surcharge, both types of "3" —
21 A1 (c) 5c on 8c green 325.00 *375.00*

British North Borneo

A9

1886 Unwmk. Litho. *Perf. 12*
22 A9 ½c lilac rose 400.00 *700.00*
23 A9 1c orange 250.00 *400.00*

Perf. 14
25 A9 ½c rose 4.75 *21.00*
a. ½c lilac rose *21.00* *50.00*
b. Imperf., pair 70.00
26 A9 1c orange 2.25 *16.00*
a. Imperf., pair 80.00
b. Vert. pair, imperf. btwn. 425.00
27 A9 2c brown 2.25 *16.00*
a. Imperf., pair 50.00
28 A9 4c rose 6.50 *19.00*
a. Cliché of 1c in plate of 4c 350.00 *1,300.*
b. Imperf., pair 65.00
c. As "a," imperf. in pair with #28 7,500.
d. Horiz. pair, imperf vert. 425.00
29 A9 8c green 30.00 *28.00*
a. Imperf., pair 55.00 *55.00*
30 A9 10c blue 15.00 *45.00*
a. Imperf., pair 55.00
b. Vert. pair, imperf btwn. 425.00
Nos. 25-30 (6) 60.75 *145.00*

For surcharges see Nos. 54-55.

A10

A11

A12

A13

31 A10 25c slate blue 475.00 25.00
a. Imperf., pair 475.00 50.00
32 A11 50c violet 475.00 25.00
a. Imperf., pair 550.00 50.00
33 A12 $1 red 400.00 24.00
a. Imperf., pair 600.00 50.00
34 A13 $2 sage green 700.00 30.00
a. Imperf., pair 600.00 55.00
Nos. 31-34 (4) 2,050. 104.00
Nos. 22-34 (12) 2,761. *1,349.*

See Nos. 44-47.

A14

1887-92 *Perf. 14*
35 A14 ½c rose 1.50 .60
a. ½c magenta 4.00 *3.00*
36 A14 1c orange 6.50 .50
37 A14 2c red brown 7.50 .50
b. As "a," horiz. pair imperf. between *425.00*
38 A14 3c violet 2.75 .50
39 A14 4c rose 14.50 .50
a. Horiz. pair, imperf. vert. *250.00*
40 A14 5c slate 3.00 .50
41 A14 6c lake ('92) 20.00 .50
42 A14 8c green 32.50 1.00
a. Horiz. pair, imperf. between
43 A14 10c blue 7.25 .50
Nos. 35-43 (9) 95.50 5.10

Exist imperf. Value $20 each, unused, $4.50 used. Forgeries exist, perf. 11½.

For surcharges see Nos. 52-53, 56-57.

Redrawn

25c. The letters of "BRITISH NORTH BORNEO" are 2mm high instead of 1½mm.

50c. The club of the native at left does not touch the frame. The 0's of "50" are flat at top and bottom instead of being oval.

$1.00. The spear of the native at right does not touch the frame. There are 14 pearls at each side of the frame instead of 13.

$2.00. "BRITISH" is 11mm long instead of 12mm. There are only six oars at the side of the dhow.

1888
44 A10 25c slate blue 115.00 .75
b. Horiz. pair, imperf. between *300.00*
c. Imperf., pair 500.00 22.50
45 A11 50c violet 135.00 .75
a. Imperf., pair 600.00 22.50
46 A12 $1 red 67.50 .75
a. Imperf., pair 450.00 22.50
47 A13 $2 sage green 250.00 1.50
a. Imperf., pair 750.00 25.00
Nos. 44-47 (4) 567.50 3.75

For surcharges see Nos. 50-51, 58.

A15

A16

1889
48 A15 $5 red violet 400.00 9.00
a. Imperf., pair 1,100. 80.00
49 A16 $10 brown 400.00 12.50
b. Imperf., pair 1,300. 90.00

No. 44 Surcharged in Red — e

1890
50 A10 2c on 25c slate blue 87.50 *100.00*
a. Inverted surcharge 450.00 *450.00*
b. With additional surcharge "2 cents" in black
51 A10 8c on 25c slate blue 135.00 *145.00*

Surcharged in Black On #42-43 — f

1891-92
52 A14 6c on 8c green 25.00 *11.00*
a. "c" of "cents" inverted 700.00 *750.00*
b. "cetns" 700.00 *750.00*
c. Inverted surcharge 500.00 *500.00*
53 A14 6c on 10c blue 210.00 *27.50*

On Nos. 29 and 30
54 A9 6c on 8c green 9,000. *4,750.*
55 A9 6c on 10c blue 67.50 *22.50*
a. Inverted surcharge 300.00 *300.00*
b. Double surcharge 1,500.
c. Triple surcharge 550.00

Nos. 39, 40 and 44 Surcharged in Red

1892
56 A14 1c on 4c rose 27.50 15.00
a. Double surcharge 1,650.
b. Surcharged on face & back *675.00*
57 A14 1c on 5c slate 8.00 6.50
58 A10 8c on 25c blue 185.00 *200.00*
Nos. 56-58 (3) 220.50 *221.50*

North Borneo

Dyak Chief — A21

Malayan Sambar
A22

Malay Dhow
A26

Sago Palm
A23

Saltwater Crocodile
A27

Argus Pheasant
A24

Mt. Kinabalu
A28

Coat of Arms
A25

Coat of Arms with Supporters
A29

A30

A31

A32

A33

A34

A35

Perf. 12 to 15 and Compound
1894 Engr. Unwmk.
59 A21 1c bis brn & blk 1.40 .50
a. Vert. pair, imperf. btwn. *950.00*
60 A22 2c rose & black 5.50 .75
a. Horiz. pair, imperf. btwn. *950.00* *950.00*
b. Vert. pair, imperf. btwn. *950.00* *950.00*
61 A23 3c vio & ol green 4.00 .55
a. Horiz. pair, imperf. btwn. — *850.00*
b. Vert. pair, imperf. btwn. 1,350.
62 A24 5c org red & blk 14.00 .75
a. Horiz. pair, imperf. btwn. 850.00
63 A25 6c brn ol & blk 4.50 .60
64 A26 8c lilac & black 6.50 .75
a. Vert. pair, imperf. btwn. 550.00 *350.00*
b. Horiz. pair, imperf. btwn. *750.00*
65 A27 12c ultra & black 47.50 3.00
a. 12c blue & black 30.00 2.75
66 A28 18c green & black 30.00 2.00
67 A29 24c claret & blue 25.00 2.00

Litho. *Perf. 14*
68 A30 25c slate blue 10.00 1.00
a. Imperf., pair 60.00 12.00
69 A31 50c violet 50.00 2.00
a. Imperf., pair 12.00
70 A32 $1 red 14.50 1.25
a. Perf. 14x11 300.00
b. Imperf., pair 47.50 12.00
71 A33 $2 gray green 27.50 2.75
a. Imperf., pair 18.00
72 A34 $5 red violet 275.00 17.50
a. Imperf., pair 925.00 65.00
73 A35 $10 brown 325.00 16.00
a. Imperf., pair 950.00 60.00
Nos. 59-73 (15) 840.40 51.40

For #68-70 in other colors see Labuan #63b-65b.

For surcharges & overprints see #74-78, 91-94, 97-102, 115-119, 130-135, 115-119, 150-151, 158-159, J1-J8. In other colors see Labuan #63-65, 93-95, 116-118, and 120.

No. 70 Surcharged in Black

1895, June
74 A32 4c on $1 red 7.00 1.25
a. Double surcharge 1,000.
75 A32 10c on $1 red 27.50 .60
76 A32 20c on $1 red 57.50 .60
77 A32 30c on $1 red 52.50 2.00
78 A32 40c on $1 red 65.00 2.00
Nos. 74-78 (5) 209.50 6.45

See No. 99.

A37

A38

A39

A40

A41

A42

A43

"Postal Revenue"
A44

No "Postal Revenue"
A45

Perf. 13 to 16 and Compound
1897-1900 Engr.
79 A37 1c bis brn & blk 12.00 .55
a. Horiz. pair, imperf. btwn. 600.00
80 A38 2c dp rose & blk 25.00 .55
81 A38 2c grn & blk ('00) 72.50 .60
82 A39 3c lilac & ol green 36.00 .55
83 A40 5c orange & black 125.00 .85
84 A41 6c ol brown & blk 57.50 .50
85 A42 8c brn lilac & blk 16.50 .75
86 A43 12c blue & black 160.00 1.50
87 A44 18c green & black 40.00 4.50
a. Vert. pair, imperf. btwn. *350.00*
b. Horiz. pair, imperf. vert. *95.00*
c. Imperf, pair *200.00*
88 A45 24c claret & blue 40.00 4.25
Nos. 79-88 (10) 584.50 14.60

For overprints and surcharges see Nos. 105-107, 109-112, 124-127, J9-J17, J20-J22, J24-J26, J28.

"Postage & Revenue"
A46 A47

1897

89 A46 18c green & black 135.00 1.75
90 A47 24c claret & blue 62.50 2.10

For surcharges & overprints see #95-96, 128-129, 113-114, J18-J19, J30-J31.

Stamps of 1894-97 Surcharged in Black

1899

91 A40 4c on 5c org & blk 40.00 *12.50*
92 A41 4c on 6c ol brn & blk 20.00 *25.00*
93 A42 4c on 8c brn lil & blk 16.00 *13.00*
94 A43 4c on 12c bl & blk 29.00 *15.00*
a. Horiz. pair, imperf. btwn. 850.00
b. Vert. pair, imperf. btwn. 950.00
95 A46 4c on 18c grn & blk 16.00 *18.00*
96 A47 4c on 24c cl & blue 25.00 *20.00*
a. Perf. 16 55.00 *55.00*
97 A30 4c on 25c sl blue 6.00 *10.00*
98 A31 4c on 50c violet 18.00 *18.00*
99 A32 4c on $1 red 6.25 *14.00*
100 A33 4c on $2 gray grn 6.25 *19.00*

"CENTS" 8½mm below "4"

101 A34 4c on $5 red vio 7.25 *18.00*
a. Normal spacing 170.00 *250.00*
102 A35 4c on $10 brown 7.25 *18.00*
a. Normal spacing 130.00 *250.00*
Nos. 91-102 (12) 197.00 *200.50*

No. 99 differs from No. 74 in the distance between "4" and "cents" which is 4¾mm on No. 99 and 3¾mm on No. 74.

Orangutan — A48

1899-1900 **Engr.**

103 A48 4c green & black 10.00 1.75
104 A48 4c dp rose & blk ('00) 40.00 .75

For overprints see Nos. 108, J13, J23.

Stamps of 1894-1900 Overprinted in Red, Black, Green or Blue — m

1901-05

105 A37 1c bis brn & blk (R) 4.00 .35
106 A38 2c grn & blk (R) 3.50 .35
107 A39 3c lil & ol grn (Bk) 2.00 .35
108 A48 4c dp rose & blk (G) 10.00 .35
109 A40 5c org & blk (G) 16.00 .35
110 A41 6c ol brn & blk (R) 4.50 .75
111 A42 8c brn & blk (Bl) 4.25 .55
a. Vert. pair, imperf. btwn. 425.00
112 A43 12c blue & blk (R) 60.00 1.50
113 A46 18c grn & blk (R) 15.00 1.40
114 A47 24c red & blue (Bk) 18.00 1.75
115 A30 25c slate blue (R) 3.00 .60
a. Inverted overprint 700.00
116 A31 50c violet (R) 3.00 .70
117 A32 $1 red (R) 20.00 3.75
118 A32 $1 red (Bk) 10.00 2.75
a. Double overprint 425.00
119 A33 $2 gray grn (R) 37.50 4.00
a. Double overprint 1,600.
Nos. 105-119 (15) 210.75 19.50

Nos. 110, 111 and 122 are known without period after "PROTECTORATE."
See Nos. 122-123, 150-151.

Bruang (Sun Bear) — A49

Railroad Train — A50

1902 **Engr.**

120 A49 10c slate & dk brn 130.00 3.25
a. Vertical pair, imperf. between 575.00
121 A50 16c yel brn & grn 150.00 3.75

Overprinted type "m" in Red or Black

122 A49 10c sl & dk brn (R) 75.00 1.10
a. Double overprint 900.00 350.00
123 A50 16c yel brn & grn (Bk) 150.00 2.50
Nos. 120-123 (4) 505.00 10.60

For overprints see Nos. J27, J29.

Stamps of 1894-97 Surcharged in Black

1904

124 A40 4c on 5c org & blk 50.00 14.00
125 A41 4c on 6c ol brn & blk 8.00 14.00
a. Inverted surcharge 350.00
126 A42 4c on 8c brn lil & blk 15.00 14.00
a. Inverted surcharge 350.00
127 A43 4c on 12c blue & blk 40.00 14.00
128 A46 4c on 18c grn & blk 16.00 14.00
129 A47 4c on 24c cl & bl 20.00 14.00
130 A30 4c on 25c sl blue 5.00 14.00
131 A31 4c on 50c violet 5.50 14.00
132 A32 4c on $1 red 7.00 14.00
133 A33 4c on $2 gray grn 10.50 14.00
134 A34 4c on $5 red vio 14.00 14.00
135 A35 4c on $10 brown 14.00 14.00
a. Inverted surcharge 2,750.
Nos. 124-135 (12) 205.00 168.00

Malayan Tapir A51

Traveler's Palm A52

Railroad Station A53

Meeting of the Assembly A54

Elephant and Mahout A55

Sumatran Rhinoceros A56

Natives Plowing — A57

Wild Boar — A58

Palm Cockatoo A59

Rhinoceros Hornbill A60

Banteng (Wild Ox)
A61 A62

Cassowary — A63

1909-22 **Unwmk.** **Engr.** ***Perf. 14***

Center in Black

136 A51 1c chocolate 7.00 .30
b. Perf. 13½ 47.50 .40
c. Perf. 15 47.50 .40
137 A52 2c green 1.00 .30
b. Perf. 15 3.25 .30
138 A53 3c deep rose 3.25 .30
b. Perf. 15 42.50 .55
139 A53 3c green ('22) 42.50 *.40*
140 A54 4c dull red 2.75 .30
b. Perf. 13½ *11.00* *10.50*
c. Perf. 15 21.00 .40
141 A55 5c yellow brn 16.00 .40
b. Perf. 15
142 A56 6c olive green 13.00 .30
b. Perf. 15 80.00 1.00
143 A57 8c rose 4.00 .60
b. Perf 15 *12.00*
144 A58 10c blue 45.00 2.00
b. Perf. 13½ —
c. Perf. 15 70.00 *6.50*
145 A59 12c deep blue 42.50 1.00
c. Perf. 15 *12.00*
146 A60 16c red brown 26.00 1.25
b. Perf. 13½ 30.00 6.50
147 A61 18c blue green 120.00 1.25
148 A62 20c on 18c bl grn (R) 7.00 .55
b. Perf. 15 250.00 *75.00*
149 A63 24c violet 28.00 1.75
Nos. 136-149 (14) 358.00 10.70

Issued: No. 139, 1922; others, July 1, 1909.
See No. 167-178.
For surcharges and overprints, see Nos. 160-162, 166, B1-B12, B14-B24, B31-B41, J32-J49. Nos. 136a-149a follow No. 162.

Nos. 72-73 Overprinted type "m" in Red

1910

150 A34 $5 red violet 325.00 9.00
151 A35 $10 brown 550.00 11.00
a. Double overprint
b. Inverted overprint 2,700. 450.00

A64

A65

1911 **Engr.** ***Perf. 14***

Center in Black

152 A64 25c yellow green 18.00 2.00
a. Perf. 15 19.00
b. Imperf., pair 55.00
153 A64 50c slate blue 18.00 2.25
a. Perf. 15 24.00 *22.50*
b. Imperf., pair 90.00
154 A64 $1 brown 18.00 4.00
a. Perf. 15 60.00 *8.00*
c. Imperf., pair 180.00
155 A64 $2 dk violet 75.00 5.00
156 A65 $5 claret 150.00 32.50
a. Perf. 13½ *150.00*
b. Imperf., pair 200.00
157 A65 $10 vermilion 500.00 90.00
a. Imperf., pair 475.00
Nos. 152-157 (6) 779.00 *135.75*

See #179-184. #152c-153c follow #162.
For overprint and surcharges see Nos. B13, B25-B30, B42-B47.

Nos. 72-73 Overprinted in Red

1912

158 A34 $5 red violet 1,500. 9.25
159 A35 $10 brown 1,800. 9.25

Nos. 158 and 159 were prepared for use but not regularly issued.

Nos. 138, 142 and 145 Surcharged in Black or Red

1916 **Center in Black** ***Perf. 14***

160 A53 2c on 3c dp rose 30.00 15.00
a. Inverted "S" 110.00 95.00
161 A56 4c on 6c ol grn (R) 30.00 20.00
a. Inverted "S" 110.00 100.00
162 A59 10c on 12c bl (R) 60.00 *70.00*
a. Inverted "S" 180.00 *190.00*
Nos. 160-162 (3) 120.00 105.00

Stamps and Types of 1909-11 Overprinted in Red or Blue

1922 **Center in Black**

136A A51 1c brown 20.00 *70.00*
137A A52 2c green 2.50 *25.00*
138A A53 3c deep rose (B) 16.00 *65.00*
140A A54 4c dull red (B) 3.75 *45.00*
141A A55 5c yel brown (B) 9.50 *65.00*
142A A56 6c olive green 9.50 *70.00*
143A A57 8c rose (B) 8.50 *42.50*
144A A58 10c gray blue 20.00 *65.00*
145A A59 12c deep blue 12.00 *45.00*
146A A60 16c red brown (B) 26.00 *75.00*
148A A62 20c on 18c bl grn 27.50 *90.00*
149A A63 24c violet 50.00 *75.00*
152C A64 25c yel green 12.00 *65.00*
153C A64 50c slate blue 17.50 *70.00*
Nos. 136A-153C (14) 234.75 *867.50*

Industrial fair, Singapore, 3/31-4/15/22.

No. 140 Surcharged in Black

1923

166 A54 3c on 4c dull red & blk 2.75 *6.00*
a. Double surcharge *1,300.*

Types of 1909-22 Issues

1926-28 **Engr.** ***Perf. 12½***

Center in Black

167 A51 1c chocolate 1.00 .70
168 A52 2c lake .85 .60
169 A53 3c green 3.00 .75
170 A54 4c dull red .50 .25
171 A55 5c yellow brown 6.00 3.50
172 A56 6c yellow green 10.00 .90
173 A57 8c rose 4.75 .50
174 A58 10c bright blue 4.25 .90
175 A59 12c deep blue 24.00 .80
176 A60 16c orange brn 37.50 *225.00*
177 A62 20c on 18c bl grn (R) 16.00 4.00
178 A63 24c dull violet 60.00 *170.00*
179 A64 25c yellow grn 16.00 5.50
180 A64 50c slate blue 25.00 *14.00*
181 A64 $1 brown 25.00 *500.00*
182 A64 $2 dark violet 85.00 *650.00*
183 A65 $5 deep rose 200.00 *1,300.*
184 A65 $10 dull vermilion 550.00 *1,500.*
Nos. 167-184 (18) 1,069. *4,377.*

Murut A66

Orangutan A67

Dyak — A68

Mt. Kinabalu — A69

Clouded Leopard — A70

Coat of Arms — A71

Arms with Supporters and Motto A72

Arms with Supporters A73

1931, Jan. 1 Engr. *Perf. 12½*

Center in Black

No.	Type	Description	Unused	Used
185	A66	3c blue green	1.50	*1.50*
186	A67	6c orange red	17.50	4.75
187	A68	10c carmine	4.50	*13.00*
188	A69	12c ultra	4.75	*8.00*
189	A70	25c deep violet	40.00	35.00
190	A71	$1 yellow green	27.50	*110.00*
191	A72	$2 red brown	47.50	*110.00*
192	A73	$5 red violet	160.00	*500.00*
		Nos. 185-192 (8)	303.25	*782.25*

50th anniv. of the North Borneo Co.

Buffalo Transport A74

Palm Cockatoo A75

Murut A76

Proboscis Monkey A77

Bajaus A78

Map of North Borneo and Surrounding Lands A79

Orangutan A80

Murut with Blowgun A81

Dyak — A82

River Scene — A83

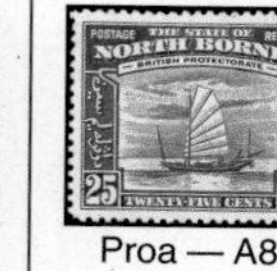
Proa — A84

Mt. Kinabalu — A85

Coat of Arms A86

Arms with Supporters A87

1939, Jan. 1 *Perf. 12½*

No.	Type	Description	Unused	Used
193	A74	1c red brn & dk grn	2.75	2.25
194	A75	2c Prus bl & red vio	3.25	2.25
195	A76	3c dk grn & sl blue	3.50	2.50
196	A77	4c rose vio & ol grn	8.50	.50
197	A78	6c dp cl & dk blue	7.75	14.00
198	A79	8c red	11.00	2.00
199	A80	10c olive grn & vio	26.00	7.00
200	A81	12c ultra & grn	27.50	8.00
201	A82	15c bis brn & brt bl grn	21.00	13.00
202	A83	20c ind & rose vio	14.50	7.00
203	A84	25c dk brn & bl grn	21.00	15.00
204	A85	50c purple & brn	22.50	14.00
205	A86	$1 car & brown	72.50	22.50
206	A86	$2 ol grn & pur	120.00	*150.00*
207	A87	$5 blue & indigo	350.00	*375.00*
		Nos. 193-207 (15)	711.75	635.00
		Set, never hinged	1,200.	

For overprints see #208-237, MR1-MR2, N1-N15, N16-N31.

Nos. 193 to 207 Overprinted in Black

1945, Dec. 17 Unwmk. *Perf. 12½*

No.	Type	Description	Unused	Used
208	A74	1c red brn & dk grn	9.50	2.25
209	A75	2c Prus bl & red vio	10.00	2.00
210	A76	3c dk grn & sl bl	.90	1.25
211	A77	4c rose vio & ol grn	12.00	*16.00*
212	A78	6c dp cl & dk bl	.90	1.25
213	A79	8c red	2.10	.75
214	A80	10c ol green & vio	2.10	.40
215	A81	12c ultra & green	4.25	3.50
216	A82	15c bis brn & brt bl grn	1.20	1.10
217	A83	20c ind & rose vio	4.25	2.50
218	A84	25c dk brn & bl grn	4.75	1.50
219	A85	50c purple & brn	3.00	2.50
220	A86	$1 carmine & brn	35.00	*40.00*
221	A86	$2 ol green & pur	35.00	*42.50*
a.		Double overprint	4,000.	
222	A87	$5 blue & indigo	18.00	18.00
		Nos. 208-222 (15)	142.95	135.50
		Set, never hinged	235.00	

"BMA" stands for British Military Administration.

Nos. 193 to 207 Ovptd. in Black or Carmine

1947

No.	Type	Description	Unused	Used
223	A74	1c red brn & dk grn	.25	1.00
224	A75	2c Prus bl & red vio	1.25	.80
225	A76	3c dk grn & sl bl (C)	.25	.80
226	A77	4c rose vio & ol grn	.50	.80
227	A78	6c dp cl & dk bl (C)	.25	.25
228	A79	8c red	.25	.25
229	A80	10c olive grn & vio	1.10	.35
230	A81	12c ultra & grn	2.40	2.75
231	A82	15c bis brn & brt bl grn	1.75	.30
232	A83	20c ind & rose vio	2.40	.85
233	A84	25c dk brn & bl grn	2.40	.50
234	A85	50c purple & brn	2.00	.85
235	A86	$1 carmine & brn	8.50	1.75
236	A86	$2 ol green & pur	11.50	*18.00*
237	A87	$5 blue & ind (C)	19.00	*25.00*
		Nos. 223-237 (15)	53.80	54.25
		Set, never hinged	80.00	

The bars obliterate "The State of" and "British Protectorate."

Catalogue values for unused stamps in this section, from this point to the end of the section, are for Never Hinged items.

Silver Wedding Issue

Common Design Types

Perf. 14x14½

1948, Nov. 1 Wmk. 4 Photo.

No.	Type	Description	Unused	Used
238	CD304	8c scarlet	.30	*.75*

Perf. 11½x11

Engraved; Name Typographed

No.	Type	Description	Unused	Used
239	CD305	$10 purple	35.00	*45.00*

Common Design Types pictured following the introduction.

UPU Issue

Common Design Types

Engr.; Name Typo. on 10c and 30c

1949, Oct. 10 *Perf. 13½, 11x11½*

No.	Type	Description	Unused	Used
240	CD306	8c rose carmine	.65	.25
241	CD307	10c chocolate	3.25	1.75
242	CD308	30c deep orange	1.50	1.75
243	CD309	55c blue	1.75	*2.75*
		Nos. 240-243 (4)	7.15	6.50

Mount Kinabalu — A88

Coconut Grove — A89

Designs: 2c, Musician. 4c, Hemp drying. 5c, Cattle at Kota Belud. 8c, Map. 10c, Logging. 15c, Proa at Sandakan. 20c, Bajau Chief. 30c, Suluk Craft. 50c, Clock tower. $1, Bajau horsemen. $2, Murut with blowgun. $5, Net fishing. $10, Arms.

Perf. 13½x14½, 14½x13½

1950, July 1 Photo.

No.	Type	Description	Unused	Used
244	A88	1c red brown	.25	*1.25*
245	A88	2c blue	.25	*.50*
246	A89	3c green	.25	.25
247	A89	4c red violet	.25	.25
248	A89	5c purple	.25	.25
249	A88	8c red	1.35	.85
250	A88	10c violet brn	1.90	.25
251	A88	15c brt ultra	2.10	.65
252	A88	20c dk brown	2.40	.25
253	A89	30c brown	6.00	.25
254	A89	50c cer *(Jessleton)*	1.90	4.75
255	A89	$1 red orange	6.50	1.75
256	A88	$2 dark green	16.00	*20.00*
257	A88	$5 emerald	26.00	*30.00*
258	A88	$10 gray blue	70.00	*90.00*
		Nos. 244-258 (15)	135.40	151.25

Redrawn

1952, May 1 *Perf. 14½x13½*

No.	Type	Description	Unused	Used
259	A89	50c cerise *(Jesselton)*	16.00	3.25

Coronation Issue

Common Design Type

1953, June 3 Engr. *Perf. 13½x13*

No.	Type	Description	Unused	Used
260	CD312	10c carmine & black	1.75	1.00

Types of 1950 with Portrait of Queen Elizabeth II

Perf. 13½x14½, 14½x13½

1954-57 Photo.

No.	Type	Description	Unused	Used
261	A88	1c red brown	.25	.30
262	A88	2c Prus blue ('56)	1.25	.25
263	A89	3c green ('57)	4.00	2.00
264	A89	4c magenta ('55)	1.75	.25
265	A89	5c purple	1.00	.25
266	A88	8c red	1.25	.30
267	A88	10c violet brown	.40	.25
268	A88	15c brt ultra ('55)	1.00	.25
269	A88	20c dk brown	.50	.25
270	A89	30c brown	3.25	.25
271	A89	50c cerise ('56)	6.25	.25
272	A89	$1 red orange ('55)	7.50	.25
273	A88	$2 dk green ('55)	15.00	1.25
274	A88	$5 emerald ('57)	12.50	*32.50*
275	A88	$10 gray blue ('57)	29.00	*35.00*
		Nos. 261-275 (15)	84.90	73.60

Issued: 10c, 3/1; 5c, 7/1; 20c, 30c, 8/3; 1c, 8c, 10/1; $1, 4/1/55; 4c, 15c, 5/16/55; $2, 10/1/55; 50c, 2/10/56; 2c, 6/1/56; 3c, $5, $10, 2/1/57.

In 1960, the 30c plate was remade, using a finer, smaller-dot (250) screen instead of the 200 screen. The background appears smoother. Value, $2.75 unused.

Borneo Railway, 1902 — A90

Comp. Arms — A91

15c, Proa (sailboat). 35c, Mount Kinabalu.

Perf. 13x13½, 13½x13

1956, Nov. 1 Engr. Wmk. 4

No.	Type	Description	Unused	Used
276	A90	10c rose car & blk	1.50	.40
277	A90	15c red brown & blk	.80	.30
278	A90	35c green & blk	.80	1.50
279	A91	$1 slate & blk	1.90	2.50
		Nos. 276-279 (4)	5.00	4.70

75th anniv. of the founding of the Chartered Company of North Borneo.

Malayan Sambar A92

Orangutan A93

Designs: 4c, Honey bear. 5c, Clouded leopard. 6c, Dusun woman with gong. 10c, Map of Borneo. 12c, Banteng (wild ox). 20c, Butterfly orchid. 25c, Rhinoceros. 30c, Murut with blowgun. 35c, Mount Kinabalu. 50c, Dusun with buffalo transport. 75c, Bajau horsemen. $2, Rhinoceros hornbill. $5, Crested wood partridge. $10, Coat of arms.

Perf. 13x12½, 12½x13

1961, Feb. 1 Wmk. 314 Engr.

No.	Type	Description	Unused	Used
280	A92	1c lt red brn & grn	.25	.25
281	A92	4c orange & olive	.90	.90
282	A92	5c violet & sepia	.30	.25
283	A92	6c bluish grn & sl	.75	.40
284	A92	10c rose red & lt grn	1.25	.25
285	A92	12c dull grn & brn	.50	.25
286	A92	20c ultra & bl grn	4.00	.25
287	A92	25c rose red & gray	1.25	*1.50*
288	A92	30c gray ol & sep	1.25	.25
289	A92	35c redsh brn & stl bl	2.50	2.25
290	A92	50c brn org & bl grn	2.25	.25
291	A92	75c red vio & sl bl	16.00	.90
292	A93	$1 yel grn & brn	14.00	.80
293	A93	$2 slate & brown	35.00	3.75
294	A93	$5 brn vio & grn	37.50	22.50
295	A93	$10 blue & car	50.00	50.00
		Nos. 280-295 (16)	167.70	84.75

For overprints, see Malaysia - Sabah Nos. 1-16.

Freedom from Hunger Issue

Common Design Type

1963, June 4 Photo. *Perf. 14x14½*

No.	Type	Description	Unused	Used
296	CD314	12c ultramarine	1.90	.75

SEMI-POSTAL STAMPS

Nos. 136-138, 140-146, 148-149, 152 Ovptd. in Carmine or Vermilion

1916 Unwmk. *Perf. 14*

Center in Black

No.	Type	Description	Unused	Used
B1	A51	1c chocolate	7.50	*35.00*
B2	A52	2c green	30.00	*80.00*
a.		Perf. 15	35.00	*80.00*
B3	A53	3c deep rose	27.50	*50.00*
B4	A54	4c dull red	7.25	*32.50*
a.		Perf. 15	275.00	*180.00*
B5	A55	5c yellow brown	50.00	*55.00*
B6	A56	6c olive green	70.00	*75.00*
a.		Perf. 15	225.00	225.00
B7	A57	8c rose	24.00	*60.00*
B8	A58	10c brt blue	55.00	*70.00*
B9	A59	12c deep blue	100.00	*100.00*
B10	A60	16c red brown	110.00	*110.00*
B11	A62	20c on 18c bl grn	55.00	*100.00*

B12 A63 24c violet 130.00 *130.00*

Perf. 15

B13 A64 25c yellow green 375.00 *425.00*
Nos. B1-B13 (13) 1,041. *1,323.*

All values exist with the vermilion overprint and all but the 4c with the carmine.

Of the total overprinting, a third was given to the National Philatelic War Fund Committee in London to be auctioned for the benefit of the wounded and veterans' survivors. The balance was lost en route from London to Sandakan when a submarine sank the ship. Very few were postally used.

Nos. 136-138, 140-146, 149, 152-157 Surcharged

1918 Center in Black *Perf. 14*

B14 A51 1c + 2c choc 3.50 *14.00*
B15 A52 2c + 2c green 1.00 *8.50*
B16 A53 3c + 2c dp rose 14.00 *19.00*
a. Perf. 15 30.00 *65.00*
B17 A54 4c + 2c dull red .70 *5.00*
a. Inverted surcharge 450.00
B18 A55 5c + 2c yel brn 8.00 *29.00*
B19 A56 6c + 2c olive grn 5.00 *29.00*
a. Perf. 15 225.00 *250.00*
B20 A57 8c + 2c rose 5.50 *11.00*
B21 A58 10c + 2c brt blue 8.00 *27.50*
B22 A59 12c + 2c deep bl 21.00 *55.00*
a. Inverted surcharge 700.00
B23 A60 16c + 2c red brn 22.50 *45.00*
B24 A63 24c + 2c violet 22.50 *45.00*
B25 A64 25c + 2c yel grn 12.00 *42.50*
B26 A64 50c + 2c sl blue 14.00 *42.50*
B27 A64 $1 + 2c brown 50.00 *55.00*
B28 A64 $2 + 2c dk vio 75.00 *95.00*
B29 A65 $5 + 2c claret 425.00 *650.00*
B30 A65 $10 + 2c ver 475.00 *700.00*
Nos. B14-B30 (17) 1,163. *1,873.*

On Nos. B14-B24 the surcharge is 15mm high, on Nos. B25-B30 it is 19mm high.

Nos. 136-138, 140-146, 149, 152-157 Surcharged in Red

1918 Center in Black

B31 A51 1c + 4c choc .60 *5.00*
B32 A52 2c + 4c green .65 *8.00*
B33 A53 3c + 4c dp rose 1.00 *3.75*
B34 A54 4c + 4c dull red .40 *4.75*
B35 A55 5c + 4c yel brn 2.00 *22.50*
B36 A56 6c + 4c olive grn 2.00 *12.00*
a. Vert. pair, imperf. btwn. 2,500.
B37 A57 8c + 4c rose 1.25 *9.50*
B38 A58 10c + 4c brt blue 3.75 *12.00*
B39 A59 12c + 4c dp blue 14.00 *14.00*
B40 A60 16c + 4c red brn 8.00 *16.00*
B41 A63 24c + 4c violet 11.00 *20.00*
B42 A64 25c + 4c yel grn 9.00 *50.00*
B43 A64 50c + 4c sl blue 15.00 *45.00*
a. Perf. 15 60.00
B44 A64 $1 + 4c brown 22.50 *60.00*
a. Perf. 15 *180.00*
B45 A64 $2 + 4c dk vio 55.00 *80.00*
B46 A65 $5 + 4c claret 300.00 *400.00*
B47 A65 $10 + 4c ver 375.00 *450.00*
Nos. B31-B47 (17) 821.15 *1,213.*

POSTAGE DUE STAMPS

Regular Issues Overprinted

On Nos. 60 to 67
Reading Up Vert. (V), or Horiz. (H)

1895, Aug. 1 Unwmk. *Perf. 14, 15*

J1 A22 2c rose & blk (V) 30.00 2.50
J2 A23 3c vio & ol grn (V) 6.00 1.25
J3 A24 5c org red & blk (V) 60.00 3.25
a. Period after "DUE" (V) 275.00
J4 A25 6c ol brn & blk (V) 20.00 2.75
J5 A26 8c lilac & blk (H) 50.00 3.00
a. Double ovpt. (H) *400.00*
J6 A27 12c blue & blk (H) 70.00 3.00
a. Double overprint (H) *325.00*
J7 A28 18c green & blk (V) 70.00 4.25
a. Ovpt. reading down 600.00 *350.00*
b. Overprinted horizontally 70.00 4.25
c. Same as "b" inverted 375.00 *400.00*
J8 A29 24c claret & bl (H) 40.00 4.00
Nos. J1-J8 (8) 346.00 24.00

1897 On Nos. 80 and 85

J9 A38 2c dp rose & blk (V) 8.50 1.50
a. Overprinted horizontally 23.00 *15.00*
J10 A42 8c brn lil & blk (H) 65.00 *80.00*
a. Period after "DUE" 30.00 *75.00*

On Nos. 81-88 and 104 Vertically reading up

1901

J11 A38 2c green & blk 75.00 .70
a. Overprinted horizontally 225.00
J12 A39 3c lilac & ol grn 32.00 .50
a. Period after "DUE" 70.00 *70.00*
J13 A48 4c dp rose & blk 70.00 .50
J14 A40 5c orange & blk 28.00 .90
a. Period after "DUE" 90.00
J15 A41 6c olive brn & blk 7.00 .50
J16 A42 8c brown & blk 9.00 .50
a. Overprinted horizontally 30.00
b. Period after "DUE" (H) 23.00 75.00
J17 A43 12c blue & blk 150.00 4.00
J18 A46 18c green & blk 80.00 4.00
J19 A47 24c red & blue 50.00 2.50
Nos. J11-J19 (9) 501.00 14.10

On Nos. 105-114, 122-123 Horizontally

1903-11 *Perf. 14*

J20 A37 1c bis brn & blk, period after "DUE" 4.50 55.00
a. Period omitted
J21 A38 2c green & blk 27.50 .30
a. Ovpt. vert., perf. 16 550.00 *275.00*
b. Perf 15 (ovpt. horiz.) 55.00 *55.00*
J22 A39 3c lilac & ol grn 7.00 .35
a. Ovpt. vert. 140.00 *140.00*
b. Perf. 15 (ovpt. horiz.) 50.00 *45.00*
J23 A48 4c dp rose & blk, perf. 15 11.00 2.00
a. "Postage Due" double 550.00 170.00
b. Perf. 14 21.00 1.00
J24 A40 5c orange & blk 45.00 .45
a. Ovpt. vert., perf. 15 250.00 *160.00*
b. Perf. 13½ (ovpt. horiz.)
c. Perf. 15 (ovpt. horiz.) 85.00 *35.00*
J25 A41 6c olive brn & blk 24.00 .40
a. "Postage Due" double *750.00*
b. "Postage Due" inverted 500.00 *125.00*
c. Perf. 16 90.00 *37.50*
J26 A42 8c brown & blk 27.50 .50
a. Overprint vertical 200.00 *125.00*
J27 A49 10c slate & brn 130.00 1.60
J28 A43 12c blue & blk 42.50 3.75
J29 A50 16c yel brn & grn 85.00 3.75
J30 A46 18c green & blk 17.50 1.50
a. "Postage Due" double *500.00* *100.00*
J31 A47 24c claret & blue 17.50 3.75
a. "Postage Due" double *350.00* *125.00*
b. Overprint vertical 325.00 *140.00*
Nos. J20-J31 (12) 439.00 73.35

On Nos. 137 and 139-146

1921-31 *Perf. 14, 15*

J32 A52 2c green & blk 27.50 *80.00*
a. Perf. 13½ 11.00 *75.00*
J33 A53 3c green & blk 5.25 *50.00*
J34 A54 4c dull red & blk 1.25 1.25
J35 A55 5c yel brn & blk 9.50 *30.00*
J36 A56 6c olive grn & blk 17.00 17.00
J37 A57 8c rose & blk 2.00 2.00
J38 A58 10c blue & blk 16.00 *19.00*
a. Perf. 15 120.00 *200.00*
J39 A59 12c dp vio & blk 70.00 55.00
J40 A60 16c red brn & blk 26.00 65.00
Nos. J32-J40 (9) 174.50 319.25

On Nos. 168 to 176

1926-28 *Perf. 12½*

J41 A52 2c lake & blk .75 *2.00*
J42 A53 3c green & blk 10.00 *32.50*
J43 A54 4c dull red & blk 3.25 *2.00*
J44 A55 5c yel brown & blk 8.50 *90.00*
J45 A56 6c yel green & blk 14.00 3.00
J46 A57 8c rose & black 11.00 *22.50*
J47 A58 10c brt blue & blk 12.00 *90.00*
J48 A59 12c dp blue & blk 32.50 *160.00*
J49 A60 16c org brn & blk 75.00 *225.00*
Nos. J41-J49 (9) 167.00 *627.00*

Crest of British North Borneo Company — D1

1939, Jan. 1 Engr. *Perf. 12½*

J50 D1 2c brown 4.25 *80.00*
J51 D1 4c carmine 4.75 *110.00*
J52 D1 6c dp rose violet 17.50 *150.00*
J53 D1 8c dk blue green 22.50 *300.00*
J54 D1 10c deep ultra 50.00 *450.00*
Nos. J50-J54 (5) 99.00 *1,090.*
Set, never hinged 160.00

WAR TAX STAMPS

Nos. 193-194 Overprinted

No. MR1

No. MR2

1941, Feb. 24 Unwmk. *Perf. 12½*

MR1 A74 1c red brn & dk grn 2.75 4.50
MR2 A75 2c Prus blue & red violet 11.00 4.75

For overprints see Nos. N15A-N15B.

OCCUPATION STAMPS

Issued under Japanese Occupation

Nos. 193-207 Handstamped in Violet or Black

On Nos. N1-N15B, the violet overprint is attributed to Jesselton, the black to Sandakan. Nos. N1-N15 are generally found with violet overprint, Nos. N15A-N15B with black.

1942 Unwmk. *Perf. 12½*

N1 A74 1c 200.00 *250.00*
N2 A75 2c 220.00 *300.00*
N3 A76 3c 175.00 *300.00*
N4 A77 4c 175.00 *300.00*
N5 A78 6c 200.00 *355.00*
N6 A79 8c 275.00 *210.00*
N7 A80 10c 250.00 *360.00*
N8 A81 12c 275.00 *525.00*
N9 A82 15c 220.00 *525.00*
N10 A83 20c 300.00 *650.00*
N11 A84 25c 300.00 *700.00*
N12 A85 50c 400.00 *775.00*
N13 A86 $1 440.00 *925.00*
N14 A86 $2 650.00 *1,250.*
N15 A87 $5 775.00 *1,350.*
Nos. N1-N15 (15) 4,855. *8,775.*

For overprints see Nos. N22a, N31a.

Same Overprint on Nos. MR1-MR2 in Black or Violet

1942

N15A A74 1c *750.00* *325.00*
N15B A75 2c *1,900.* *650.00*

Nos. 193 to 207 Overprinted in Black

1944, Sept. 30 Unwmk. *Perf. 12½*

N16 A74 1c 8.25 13.00
N17 A75 2c 8.25 10.00
a. On No. N2 300.00
N18 A76 3c 8.25 11.00
a. On. No. N3 400.00
N19 A77 4c 15.00 25.00
N20 A78 6c 12.00 7.00
N21 A79 8c 11.00 *18.50*
a. On No. N6 375.00
N22 A80 10c 9.25 *14.50*
a. On No. N7 425.00
N23 A81 12c 17.50 *14.50*
a. On No. N8 400.00
N24 A82 15c 17.50 *17.50*
a. On No. N9 450.00
N25 A83 20c 40.00 *60.00*
N26 A84 25c 40.00 *60.00*
N27 A85 50c 100.00 *130.00*
N28 A86 $1 150.00 *150.00*
Nos. N16-N28 (13) 437.00 *531.00*

Nos. N1 and 205 Surcharged in Black

No. N30

No. N31

1944, May

N30 A74 $2 on 1c *7,500.* *5,000.*
N31 A86 $5 on $1 7,000. 4,500.
a. On No. N13 10,000. 6,000.

Mt. Kinabalu OS1

Boat and Traveler's Palm OS2

1943, Apr. 29 Litho.

N32 OS1 4c dull rose red 30.00 60.00
N33 OS2 8c dark blue 25.00 55.00

Stamps of Japan, 1938-43, Overprinted in Black

1s, War factory girl. 2s, Gen. Maresuke Nogi. 3s, Power plant. 4s, Hyuga Monument and Mt. Fuji. 5s, Adm. Heihachiro Togo. 6s, Garambi Lighthouse, Formosa. 8s, Meiji Shrine, Tokyo. 10s, Palms and map of "Greater East Asia." 15s, Aviator saluting and Japanese flag. 20s, Mt. Fuji and cherry blossoms. 25s, Horyu Temple, Nara. 30s, Miyajima Torii, Itsukushima shrine. 50s, Golden Pavilion, Kyoto. 1y, Great Buddha, Kamakura. See Burma, Vol. 1, for illustrations of 2s, 3s, 5s, 8s, 20s and watermark. For others, see Japan.

Wmk. Curved Wavy Lines (257)

1944, Sept. 30 *Perf. 13*

N34 A144 1s orange brown 10.00 *35.00*
N35 A84 2s vermilion 9.00 *30.00*
N36 A85 3s green 10.00 *35.00*
N37 A146 4s emerald 17.00 *27.50*
N38 A86 5s brown lake 12.50 *30.00*
N39 A88 6s orange 15.00 *32.50*
N40 A90 8s dk purple & pale vio 11.00 *32.50*
N41 A148 10s crim & dull rose 15.00 *35.00*
N42 A150 15s dull blue 15.00 *32.50*
N43 A94 20s ultra 100.00 *125.00*
N44 A95 25s brown 80.00 *110.00*
N45 A96 30s peacock blue 200.00 *200.00*
N46 A97 50s olive 100.00 *100.00*
N47 A98 1y lt brown 100.00 *120.00*
Nos. N34-N47 (14) 694.50 *945.00*

The overprint translates "North Borneo."

OCCUPATION POSTAGE DUE STAMPS

Nos. J50-J51, J53 Handstamped in Black

1942, Sept. 30

NJ1 D1 2c brown 600. —
NJ2 D1 4c carmine 600. —
NJ3 D1 8c dk blue green 600. —

NORTHERN NIGERIA

ˈnor-t͟həˌrn nī-ˈjir-ē-ə

LOCATION — Western Africa
GOVT. — British Protectorate
AREA — 281,703 sq. mi.
POP. — 11,866,250
CAPITAL — Zungeru

In 1914 Northern Nigeria united with Southern Nigeria to form the Colony and Protectorate of Nigeria.

12 Pence = 1 Shilling
20 Shillings = 1 Pound

Victoria — A1

Numerals of 5p and 6p, types A1 and A2, are in color on plain tablet.

Wmk. Crown and C A (2)

1900, Mar. Typo. *Perf. 14*

No.	Type	Description	Unused	Used
1	A1	½p lilac & grn	8.75	*22.00*
2	A1	1p lilac & rose	5.75	5.50
3	A1	2p lilac & yel	16.00	*60.00*
4	A1	2½p lilac & blue	13.00	*45.00*
5	A1	5p lilac & brn	30.00	*70.00*
6	A1	6p lilac & vio	30.00	*50.00*
7	A1	1sh green & blk	32.50	*85.00*
8	A1	2sh6p green & blue	180.00	*550.00*
9	A1	10sh green & brn	325.00	*900.00*
		Nos. 1-9 (9)	641.00	*1,788.*

Edward VII — A2

1902, July 1

No.	Type	Description	Unused	Used
10	A2	½p violet & green	2.25	2.00
11	A2	1p vio & car rose	5.00	1.00
12	A2	2p violet & org	2.50	*3.00*
13	A2	2½p violet & ultra	2.00	*13.00*
14	A2	5p vio & org brn	7.00	*7.50*
15	A2	6p violet & pur	20.00	*8.00*
16	A2	1sh green & black	8.50	*8.50*
17	A2	2sh6p green & ultra	19.00	*75.00*
18	A2	10sh green & brown	55.00	*60.00*
		Nos. 10-18 (9)	121.25	*178.00*

1904, Apr. Wmk. 3

No.	Type	Description	Unused	Used
18A	A2	£25 green & car	*60,000.*	

No. 18A was available for postage but probably was used only for fiscal purposes.

1905

No.	Type	Description	Unused	Used
19a	A2	½p violet & grn	6.00	5.50
20a	A2	1p violet & car rose	6.00	1.25
21	A2	2p violet & org	19.00	*32.50*
22	A2	2½p violet & ultra	7.25	*10.00*
23	A2	5p violet & org brn	32.50	*85.00*
24	A2	6p violet & pur	29.00	*65.00*
25a	A2	1sh green & black	24.00	*55.00*
26a	A2	2sh6p green & ultra	45.00	*60.00*
		Nos. 19a-26a (8)	166.25	314.25

All values except the 2½p exist on ordinary and chalky papers. The less expensive values are given above. For detailed listings, see the *Scott Classic Specialized Catalogue of Stamps and Covers 1840-1940.*

1910-11 Ordinary Paper

No.	Type	Description	Unused	Used
28	A2	½p green	2.25	1.25
29	A2	1p carmine	5.75	1.25
30	A2	2p gray	9.50	*6.50*
31	A2	2½p ultra	4.25	*11.00*

Chalky Paper

No.	Type	Description	Unused	Used
32	A2	3p violet, *yel*	4.50	1.00
33	A2	5p vio & ol grn	6.00	*19.00*
34	A2	6p vio & red vio ('11)	6.00	*6.00*
a.		6p violet & deep violet	7.50	*28.00*
35	A2	1sh black, *green*	5.25	.75
36	A2	2sh6p blk & red, *bl*	19.00	*50.00*
37	A2	5sh grn & red, *yel*	29.00	*75.00*
38	A2	10sh grn & red, *grn*	55.00	*50.00*
		Nos. 28-38 (11)	146.50	221.75

George V — A3

For description of dies I and II, see A pages in front section of catalogue.

Die I

1912 Ordinary Paper

No.	Type	Description	Unused	Used
40	A3	½p green	4.50	1.00
41	A3	1p carmine	4.50	.60
42	A3	2p gray	6.75	*17.00*

Chalky Paper

No.	Type	Description	Unused	Used
43	A3	3p violet, *yel*	2.25	1.25
44	A3	4p blk & red, *yel*	1.25	*2.25*
45	A3	5p vio & ol grn	4.50	*20.00*
46	A3	6p vio & red vio	4.25	*4.50*
47	A3	9p violet & scar	2.25	*12.00*
48	A3	1sh blk, *green*	5.00	2.25
49	A3	2sh6p blk & red, *bl*	10.00	*55.00*
50	A3	5sh grn & red, *yel*	25.00	*90.00*
51	A3	10sh grn & red, *grn*	45.00	*50.00*
52	A3	£1 vio & blk, *red*	200.00	120.00
		Nos. 40-52 (13)	315.25	*375.85*

Numerals of 3p, 4p, 5p and 6p, type A3, are in color on plain tablet.

Stamps of Northern Nigeria were replaced in 1914 by those of Nigeria.

NORTHERN RHODESIA

ˈnor-t͟həˌrn rō-ˈdē-zhˌē-ˌə

LOCATION — In southern Africa, east of Angola and separated from Southern Rhodesia by the Zambezi River.
GOVT. — British Protectorate
AREA — 287,640 sq. mi.
POP. — 2,550,000 (est. 1962)
CAPITAL — Lusaka

Prior to April 1, 1924, Northern Rhodesia was administered by the British South Africa Company. It joined the Federation of Rhodesia and Nyasaland in 1953 and used its stamps in 1954-63. It resumed issuing its own stamps in December, 1963, after the Federation was dissolved. On Oct. 24, 1964, Northern Rhodesia became the independent republic of Zambia. See Rhodesia, Southern Rhodesia, Rhodesia and Nyasaland, Zambia.

12 Pence = 1 Shilling
20 Shillings = 1 Pound

Catalogue values for unused stamps in this country are for Never Hinged items, beginning with Scott 46 in the regular postage section and Scott J5 in the postage due section.

King George V
A1 A2

1925-29 Engr. Wmk. 4 *Perf. 12½*

No.	Type	Description	Unused	Used
1	A1	½p dk green	1.75	.80
2	A1	1p dk brown	1.75	.25
3	A1	1½p carmine	4.25	.30
4	A1	2p brown org	4.50	.25
5	A1	3p ultra	4.50	1.30
6	A1	4p dk violet	7.50	.50
7	A1	6p gray	9.00	.40
8	A1	8p rose lilac	9.00	*60.00*
9	A1	10p olive grn	9.00	*50.00*
10	A2	1sh black & org	4.75	2.25
11	A2	2sh ultra & brn	32.50	*50.00*
12	A2	2sh6p green & blk	26.00	*15.00*
13	A2	3sh indigo & vio	50.00	28.00
14	A2	5sh dk vio & gray	57.50	22.50
15	A2	7sh6p blk & lil rose	200.00	*325.00*
16	A2	10sh black & green	125.00	*100.00*
17	A2	20sh rose lil & red	375.00	*400.00*
		Nos. 1-17 (17)	922.00	*1,057.*

High values with revenue cancellations are inexpensive.

Issue dates: 3sh, 1929; others, Apr. 1.

Common Design Types pictured following the introduction.

Silver Jubilee Issue
Common Design Type

1935, May 6 *Perf. 13½x14*

No.	Type	Description	Unused	Used
18	CD301	1p olive grn & ultra	1.50	1.50
19	CD301	2p indigo & grn	2.75	2.00
20	CD301	3p blue & brown	4.25	*9.00*
21	CD301	6p brt vio & indigo	8.50	2.50
		Nos. 18-21 (4)	17.00	15.00
		Set, never hinged	26.00	

Coronation Issue
Common Design Type

1937, May 12 *Perf. 11x11½*

No.	Type	Description	Unused	Used
22	CD302	1½p dark carmine	.25	.25
23	CD302	2p yellow brown	.30	*.75*
24	CD302	3p deep ultra	.40	*1.25*
		Nos. 22-24 (3)	.95	2.25
		Set, never hinged	1.50	

King George VI — A3

1938-52 Wmk. 4 *Perf. 12½*

Size: 19x24mm

No.	Type	Description	Unused	Used
25	A3	½p green	.25	.25
26	A3	½p dk brn ('51)	1.40	*1.50*
a.		Perf. 12½x14	1.00	*6.00*
27	A3	1p dk brown	.25	.25
28	A3	1p green ('51)	.90	*2.25*
29	A3	1½p carmine	27.50	.75
a.		Horiz. pair, imperf. between	*30,000.*	
30	A3	1½p brn org ('41)	.30	.25
31	A3	2p brown org	27.50	1.75
32	A3	2p carmine ('41)	1.00	.50
33	A3	2p rose lilac ('51)	.40	*1.50*
34	A3	3p ultra	.45	.30
35	A3	3p red ('51)	.30	*3.00*
36	A3	4p dk violet	.30	.40
37	A3	4½p dp blue ('52)	1.75	*12.00*
38	A3	6p dark gray	.30	.25
39	A3	9p violet ('52)	1.75	*12.00*

Size: 21½x26¾mm

No.	Type	Description	Unused	Used
40	A3	1sh blk & brn org	2.50	.60
41	A3	2sh6p green & blk	8.00	7.00
42	A3	3sh ind & dk vio	14.00	*16.00*
43	A3	5sh violet & gray	14.50	*17.00*
44	A3	10sh black & green	16.00	*32.50*
45	A3	20sh rose lil & red	37.50	*75.00*
		Nos. 25-45 (21)	156.85	*185.05*
		Set, never hinged	275.00	

Catalogue values for unused stamps in this section, from this point to the end of the section, are for Never Hinged items.

Peace Issue
Common Design Type

1946, Nov. 26 Engr. *Perf. 13½x14*

No.	Type	Description	Unused	Used
46	CD303	1½p deep orange	1.00	*1.50*
a.		Perf. 13½	14.00	*13.00*
47	CD303	2p carmine	.25	*.50*

Silver Wedding Issue
Common Design Types

1948, Dec. 1 Photo. *Perf. 14x14½*

No.	Type	Description	Unused	Used
48	CD304	1½p orange	.30	.25

Perf. 11½x11

Engr.

No.	Type	Description	Unused	Used
49	CD305	20sh rose brown	100.00	90.00

UPU Issue
Common Design Types

Engr.; Name Typo. on 3p, 6p

Perf. 13½, 11x11½

1949, Oct. 10 Wmk. 4

No.	Type	Description	Unused	Used
50	CD306	2p rose carmine	.50	.50
51	CD307	3p indigo	2.00	*3.00*
52	CD308	6p gray	1.50	1.50
53	CD309	1sh red orange	1.00	*1.50*
		Nos. 50-53 (4)	5.00	*6.50*

A4

Designs: Victoria Falls and Railway Bridge, Cecil Rhodes and Elizabeth II.

1953, May 30 Engr. *Perf. 12x11*

No.	Type	Description	Unused	Used
54	A4	½p brown	.55	*1.25*
55	A4	1p green	.45	*1.25*
56	A4	2p deep claret	.80	.40
57	A4	4½p deep blue	.55	*4.00*
58	A4	1sh gray & orange	1.25	*4.25*
		Nos. 54-58 (5)	3.60	11.15

Cecil Rhodes (1853-1902).

Exhibition Seal — A5

1953, May 30 *Perf. 14x13½*

No.	Type	Description	Unused	Used
59	A5	6p purple	.70	*1.25*

Central African Rhodes Centenary Exhib.

Coronation Issue
Common Design Type

1953, June 2 *Perf. 13½x13*

No.	Type	Description	Unused	Used
60	CD312	1½p orange & black	.70	.25

Elizabeth II — A6

Perf. 12½x13½

1953, Sept. 15 Engr.

Size: 19x23mm

No.	Type	Description	Unused	Used
61	A6	½p dark brown	.65	.25
62	A6	1p green	.75	.25
63	A6	1½p brown orange	1.25	.25
64	A6	2p rose lilac	1.40	.25
65	A6	3p red	.80	.25
66	A6	4p dark violet	1.25	*2.00*
67	A6	4½p deep blue	1.50	*4.25*
68	A6	6p dark gray	1.25	.40
69	A6	9p violet	1.25	*4.25*

Size: 21x27mm

No.	Type	Description	Unused	Used
70	A6	1sh black & brn org	1.00	.25
71	A6	2sh6p green & blk	15.00	8.00
72	A6	5sh violet & gray	16.00	*15.00*
73	A6	10sh black & green	12.00	*32.50*
74	A6	20sh rose lilac & red	30.00	*37.50*
		Nos. 61-74 (14)	84.10	105.40

Coat of Arms — A7

Size: 23x19mm

Perf. 14½

1963, Dec. 1 Unwmk. Photo.

Arms in Black, Blue and Orange

No.	Type	Description	Unused	Used
75	A7	½p redsh lil & blk	.70	*1.00*
a.		Value omitted	1,100.	
b.		Orange (eagle) omitted	1,400.	
76	A7	1p turq bl & blk	1.50	.25
a.		Value omitted	12.50	
77	A7	2p red brn & blk	.70	.25
78	A7	3p orange & blk	.25	.25
a.		Bklt. pane of 4	1.00	
b.		Value omitted	120.00	
c.		Orange (eagle) omitted	*1,200.*	—
d.		Value and orange (eagle) omitted	325.00	
79	A7	4p green & blk	.70	.30
a.		Value omitted	130.00	
80	A7	6p ol grn & blk	1.00	.25
a.		Value omitted	800.00	
81	A7	9p dl org & blk	.70	*1.60*
a.		Value omitted	600.00	
b.		Value and orange (eagle) omitted	600.00	
82	A7	1sh dk gray & blk	.50	.25
83	A7	1sh3p mag & blk	2.25	.25

Perf. 13

Size: 27x23mm

No.	Type	Description	Unused	Used
84	A7	2sh ver & blk	2.50	*5.25*
85	A7	2sh6p claret & blk	2.50	2.25
86	A7	5sh dk car rose & blk	10.00	8.00
a.		Value omitted	*2,750.*	
87	A7	10sh brt pink & blk	17.00	*22.50*
88	A7	20sh Prus bl & blk	22.00	*40.00*
a.		Value omitted	1,100.	
		Nos. 75-88 (14)	62.30	*82.40*

Stamps of Northern Rhodesia were replaced by those of Zambia, starting Oct. 24, 1964.

POSTAGE DUE STAMPS

D1

1929 Typo. Wmk. 4 *Perf. 14*

J1 D1 1p black 3.00 *2.75*
a. Wmk. 4a (error) 7,000.
J2 D1 2p black 8.00 *3.50*
a. Bisected, used as 1d, on cover *850.00*
J3 D1 3p black 3.00 *27.50*
a. Crown in watermark missing 700.00
b. Wmk. 4a (error) 425.00
J4 D1 4p black 11.00 *42.50*
Nos. J1-J4 (4) 25.00 *76.25*

Catalogue values for unused stamps in this section, from this point to the end of the section, are for Never Hinged items.

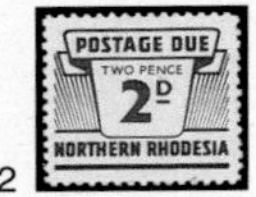

D2

1964 Unwmk. Litho. *Perf. 12½*

J5 D2 1p orange 3.00 *5.50*
J6 D2 2p dark blue 3.00 *4.50*
J7 D2 3p rose claret 3.00 *7.50*
J8 D2 4p violet blue 3.00 *13.00*
J9 D2 6p purple 9.50 *10.00*
J10 D2 1sh emerald 11.00 *30.00*
Nos. J5-J10 (6) 32.50 *70.50*

NORTH INGERMANLAND

'north 'iŋ-gər-mən-ˌland

LOCATION — In Northern Russia lying between the River Neva and Finland
CAPITAL — Kirjasalo

In 1920 the residents of this territory revolted from Russian rule and set up a provisional government. The new State existed only a short period as the revolution was quickly quelled by Soviet troops.

100 Pennia = 1 Markka

Arms — A1

Perf. 11½

1920, Mar. 21 Unwmk. Litho.

1 A1 5p green 2.75 *3.50*
2 A1 10p rose red 2.75 *3.50*
b. Horiz. pair, imperf. btwn. 50.00
3 A1 25p bister 2.75 *3.50*
b. Horiz. pair, imperf. btwn. 50.00
c. Vert. pair, imperf. btwn. 50.00
4 A1 50p dark blue 2.50 *3.50*
b. Horiz. pair, imperf. btwn. 75.00
5 A1 1m car & black 30.00 *42.50*
6 A1 5m lilac & black 175.00 160.00
7 A1 10m brown & blk 200.00 200.00
Nos. 1-7 (7) 415.75 *416.50*
Set, never hinged 1,100.

Well centered examples sell for twice the values shown.

Imperf., Pairs

1a A1 5p 45.00
2a A1 10p 100.00
3a A1 25p 50.00
4a A1 50p 50.00
5a A1 1m 65.00
6a A1 5m 200.00
7a A1 10m 350.00

Arms — A2

Peasant — A3

Plowing — A4

Milking — A5

Planting — A6

Ruins of Church — A7

Peasants Playing Zithers — A8

1920, Aug. 2

8 A2 10p gray grn & ultra 3.50 *7.00*
9 A3 30p buff & gray grn 3.50 *7.00*
a. Horiz. pair, imperf. btwn. 100.00
10 A4 50p ultra & red brn 3.50 *7.00*
11 A5 80p claret & slate 3.50 *7.00*
12 A6 1m red & slate 20.00 *45.00*
13 A7 5m dk vio & dl rose 8.25 *18.00*
14 A8 10m brn & violet 8.25 *18.00*
a. Center inverted 1,000.
Nos. 8-14 (7) 50.50 *109.00*
Set, never hinged 120.00

Counterfeits abound.

Nos. 8-14 exist imperf. Value for set in pairs, $200.

NORTH WEST PACIFIC ISLANDS

'north 'west pə-'si-fik 'ī-lənds

LOCATION — Group of islands in the West Pacific Ocean including a part of New Guinea and adjacent islands of the Bismarck Archipelago
GOVT. — Australian military government
AREA — 96,160 sq. mi.
POP. — 636,563

Stamps of Australia were overprinted for use in the former German possessions of Nauru and German New Guinea which Australian troops had captured. Following the League of Nations' decision which placed these territories under mandate to Australia, these provisional issues were discontinued. See German New Guinea, New Britain, Nauru and New Guinea.

12 Pence = 1 Shilling
20 Shillings = 1 Pound

Watermarks

Wmk. 8 — Wide Crown and Wide A

Wmk. 9 — Wide Crown and Narrow A

Wmk. 10 — Narrow Crown and Narrow A

Wmk. 11 — Multiple Crown and A

Stamps of Australia Overprinted — a

Type a: "P" of "PACIFIC" above "S" of "ISLANDS."

There are two varieties of the letter "S" in the Type "a" overprint. These occur in three combinations:1. both normal "S"; 2. 1st "S" with small head and long bottom stroke, 2nd "S" normal; 3.. both "S" with small head and long bottom stroke.

DESIGN A1
Die I — The inside frameline has a break at left, even with the top of the letters of the denomination.
Die II — The frameline does not show a break.
Die IV — As Die III, with a break in the top outside frameline above the "ST" of "AUSTRALIA." The upper right inside frameline has an incomplete corner.
Dies are only indicated when there are more than one for any denomination.

1915-16 Wmk. 8 *Perf. 12*

1 A1(a) 2p gray 25.00 *75.00*
2 A1(a) 2½p dark blue 5.00 *22.50*
3 A1(a) 3p ol bis, die I 25.00 *65.00*
a. Die II 385.00 *600.00*
b. Pair, #3, 3a 825.00 *1,200.*
c. Pair, die I and die II 2,500.
4 A1(a) 6p ultra 120.00 *130.00*
5 A1(a) 9p violet 60.00 *72.50*
6 A1(a) 1sh blue green 75.00 *77.50*
8 A1(a) 5sh yel & gray ('16) 2,750. *3,850.*
9 A1(a) 10sh pink & gray 170.00 *200.00*
Revenue cancel
10 A1(a) £1 ultra & brown *600.00* *775.00*
Nos. 1-6,8-10 (9) 3,830. *5,268.*

For surcharge see No. 27.

Wmk. Wide Crown and Narrow A (9)
Perf. 12, 14

ONE PENNY
Die I — Normal die, having outside the oval band with "AUSTRALIA" a white line and a heavy colored line.
Die Ia — As die I with a small white spur below the right serif at foot of the "1" in left tablet.
Dies are only indicated when there are more than one for any denomination.

11 A4(a) ½p emerald 3.25 *10.00*
a. Double overprint
12 A4(a) 1p car (Die I) 7.75 7.25
a. 1p carmine rose (Die I) 120.00 *150.00*
b. 1p carmine (Die Ia) 110.00 *145.00*
13 A1(a) 2p gray 20.00 *50.00*
14 A1(a) 2½p dk bl ('16) *30,000.* *30,000.*
16 A4(a) 4p orange 4.50 *17.50*
17 A4(a) 5p org brown 3.25 *19.00*
18 A1(a) 6p ultra 11.00 *13.00*
19 A1(a) 9p violet 17.50 *24.00*
20 A1(a) 1sh blue green 12.50 *27.50*
21 A1(a) 2sh brown 110.00 *130.00*
22 A1(a) 5sh yel & gray 82.50 *120.00*
Nos. 11-13,16-22 (10) 272.25 *418.25*

For surcharge see No. 28.

1915-16 Wmk. 10 *Perf. 12*

23 A1(a) 2p gray, die I 9.00 *32.50*
24 A1(a) 3p ol bis, die I 7.00 *15.00*
a. Die II 125.00 *190.00*
b. Pair, #24, 24a 350.00
25 A1(a) 2sh brown ('16) 45.00 *65.00*
26 A1(a) £1 ultra & brn ('16) 400.00 *525.00*
Nos. 23-26 (4) 461.00 *637.50*

Nos. 6 and 17 Surcharged

1918, May 23 Wmk. 8 *Perf. 12*

27 A1 1p on 1sh bl grn 125.00 100.00

Wmk. 9 *Perf. 14*

28 A4 1p on 5p org brn 110.00 100.00

Stamps of Australia Overprinted — b

Type "b": "P" of "PACIFIC" above space between "I" and "S" of "ISLANDS."

1918-23 Wmk. 10 *Perf. 12*

29 A1(b) 2p gray 8.50 *30.00*
a. Die II 13.50 *57.50*
30 A1(b) 2½p dk bl ('19) 6.50 *19.00*
a. "1" of fraction omitted *14,000.* *16,500.*
31 A1(b) 3p ol bis, die I 27.50 *30.00*
a. Die II 80.00 *100.00*
b. Pair, #31, 31a 500.00 *650.00*
32 A1(b) 6p ultra ('19) 7.50 *16.50*
a. 6p chalky blue 50.00 *75.00*
33 A1(b) 9p violet ('19) 11.50 *60.00*
34 A1(b) 1sh bl grn ('18) 16.50 *37.50*
a. 1sh emerald green 7.00 *32.50*
35 A1(b) 2sh brown 25.00 *42.50*
36 A1(b) 5sh yel & gray ('19) 75.00 *80.00*
37 A1(b) 10sh pink & gray ('19) 200.00 *275.00*
38 A1(b) £1 ultra & brn 4,500. *5,500.*
Nos. 29-37 (9) 378.00 *590.50*

1919 Wmk. 11 *Perf. 14*

39 A4(b) ½p emerald 5.00 *6.00*

1918-23 Wmk. 9

40 A4(b) ½p emerald 2.00 *4.00*
41 A4(b) 1p car red, die 1 4.25 1.75
a. 1p carmine red, die Ia 125.00 90.00
42 A4(b) 1p scar, die I, rough paper 1,000. 675.00
a. 1p rose red, die Ia, rough paper 1,000. 675.00
43 A4(b) 1p violet ('22) 2.75 *7.25*
44 A4(b) 2p orange 8.75 2.75
45 A4(b) 2p red ('22) 10.50 2.25
46 A4(b) 4p yel org 4.00 *17.50*
47 A4(b) 4p violet ('22) 22.50 *45.00*
a. "Four Penc" in thinner letters 900.00 *1,550.*
48 A4(b) 4p light ultra ('22) 12.50 *65.00*
a. "Four Penc" in thinner letters 1,000. *2,000.*
49 A4(b) 5p brown 4.25 *13.50*
Nos. 40-41,43-49 (9) 71.50 *159.00*

North West Pacific Islands stamps were largely used in New Britain. Some were used in Nauru. They were intended to serve the Bismarck Archipelago and other places.

NORWAY

'nor-ˌwā

LOCATION — Western half of the Scandinavian Peninsula in northern Europe
GOVT. — Kingdom
AREA — 125,051 sq. mi.
POP. — 5,420,000 (2020 est.)
CAPITAL — Oslo

120 Skilling = 1 Specie Daler
100 Ore = 1 Krone (1877)

Catalogue values for unused stamps in this country are for Never Hinged items, beginning with Scott 275 in the regular postage section, Scott B27 in the semi-postal section, and Scott O65 in the official section.

Watermarks

Wmk. 159 — Lion

Wmk. 160 — Post Horn

Coat of Arms — A1

Wmk. 159

1855, Jan. 1 Typo. *Imperf.*

1 A1 4s blue *4,250.* 165.
a. Double foot on right hind leg of lion 3,000.

Only a few genuine unused examples of No. 1 exist. Stamps often offered have had pen-markings removed. The unused catalogue value is for a stamp without gum. Stamps with original gum sell for much more.

No. 1 was reprinted in 1914 and 1924 unwatermarked. Lowest value reprint, $125.

ROULETTED REPRINTS

1963: No. 1, value $25; Nos. 2-5, 15, value each $15.
1966: Nos. 57, 70a, 100, 152, J1, O1. Value each $12.
1969: Nos. 69, 92, 107, 114, 128, J12. Value each $12.

King Oscar I — A2

1856-57 Unwmk. *Perf. 13*

2 A2 2s yellow ('57) 600.00 150.00
3 A2 3s lilac ('57) 250.00 50.00
4 A2 4s blue 240.00 13.00
a. Imperf. *7,500.*
b. Half used as 2s on cover —
5 A2 8s dull lake 1,450. 60.00

Nos. 2-5 were reprinted in 1914 and 1924, perf. 13½. Lowest valued reprint, $45 each.

Background of Crisscrossed Lines

A3

1863 Litho. *Perf. 14½x13½*

6 A3 2s yellow 750.00 250.00
7 A3 3s gray lilac 400.00 300.00
8 A3 4s blue 240.00 14.00
9 A3 8s rose 850.00 60.00
10 A3 24s brown 45.00 125.00
Nos. 6-10 (5) 2,285. 749.00

There are four types of the 2, 3, 8 and 24 skilling and eight types of the 4 skilling. See note on used value of No. 10 following No. 21.

No. 8 exists imperf. Value, unused $1,200.

Background of Vertical Lines

A4

1867-68 Typo.

11 A4 1s black, coarse impression ('68) 85.00 55.00
12 A4 2s orange 22.50 *55.00*
b. Vert. pair, imperf between —
13 A4 3s dl lil, coarse impression ('68) 450.00 160.00
14 A4 4s blue, thin paper 175.00 11.00
15 A4 8s car rose 600.00 55.00
a. 8s rose, clear impression 1,500. 425.00
Nos. 11-15 (5) 1,333. 336.00

See note on used value of #12 following #21.

For surcharges see Nos. 59-61, 149.

No. 15 was reprinted in 1914 and 1924, perf. 13½. Lowest valued reprint, $45.

Post Horn and Crown — A5

1872-75 Wmk. 160

16 A5 1s yel grn ('75) 12.00 *40.00*
a. 1s deep green ('73) 250.00 75.00
b. "E.EN" 25.00 *75.00*
d. Vert. pair, imperf between —
17 A5 2s ultra ('74) 14.00 *85.00*
a. 2s Prussian blue ('74) *15,000.* *4,750.*
b. 2s gray blue 11.00 *75.00*
18 A5 3s rose 60.00 12.00
a. 3s carmine 110.00 42.50
b. 3s carmine, *bluish* thin paper 240.00 30.00
19 A5 4s lilac, thin paper ('75) 15.00 *72.50*
a. 4s dark violet, *bluish*, thin paper 450.00 160.00
b. 4s brown violet, *bluish*, thin paper ('73) 500.00 190.00
c. 4s violet, *white*, thick paper ('73) 110.00 72.50
20 A5 6s org brn ('75) 500.00 72.50
21 A5 7s red brn ('73) 50.00 72.50
Nos. 16-21 (6) 651.00 354.50

In this issue there are 12 types each of Nos. 16, 17, 18 and 19; 12 types of No. 20 and 20 types of No. 21. The differences are in the words of value.

Nos. 10, 12, 16, 17, 19 and 21 were re-released in 1888 and used until March 31, 1908. Used values of these stamps are for examples canceled in this later period, usually with a two-ring cancellation. Examples bearing clear dated cancellations before 1888 are worth considerably more, as follows: No. 10 $300, No. 12 $140, No. 16 $125, No. 17 $175, No. 17b $350, No. 19 $300, No. 21 $140.

No. 21 exists imperf. Value, unused without gum $800.

No. 19 comes on thin and thick paper.

For surcharges see Nos. 62-63.

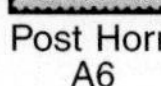

Post Horn A6

King Oscar II A7

"NORGE" in Sans-serif Capitals, Ring of Post Horn Shaded

1877-78

22 A6 1o drab 7.25 *8.00*
23 A6 3o orange 90.00 35.00
24 A6 5o ultra 30.00 12.00
a. 5o dull blue 500.00 125.00
b. 5o bright blue 300.00 60.00
c. No period after "Postfrim" 45.00 18.00
d. Retouched plate 150.00 25.00
e. As "c," retouched plate 225.00 27.50
25 A6 10o rose 120.00 3.50
b. Retouched plate 120.00 3.75
26 A6 12o lt green 120.00 24.00
27 A6 20o orange brn 350.00 12.00
28 A6 25o lilac 500.00 150.00
29 A6 35o bl grn ('78) 24.00 15.00
a. Retouched plate 250.00 110.00
30 A6 50o maroon 50.00 12.50
31 A6 60o dk bl ('78) 50.00 11.00
32 A7 1k gray grn & grn ('78) 30.00 12.50
33 A7 1.50k ultra & bl ('78) 60.00 50.00
34 A7 2k rose & mar ('78) 45.00 25.00
Nos. 22-34 (13) 1,476. 370.50

There are 6 types each of Nos. 22, 26 and 28 to 34; 12 types each of Nos. 23, 24, 25 and 27. The differences are in the numerals.

A 2nd plate of the 5o ultramarine has 100 types, the 10o, 200 types.

The retouch on 5o, 10o and 35o shows as a thin white line between crown and post horn.

Post Horn — A8

"NORGE" in Sans-serif Capitals, Ring of Horn Unshaded

1882-93 Wmk. 160 *Perf. 14½x13½*

35 A8 1o blk brn ('86) 17.50 *24.00*
a. No period after "Postfrim" 60.00 60.00
b. Small "N" in "NORGE" 60.00 60.00
36 A8 1o gray ('93) 15.00 30.00
37 A8 2o brown ('90) 4.50 *10.00*
38 A8 3o yellow ('89) 90.00 8.50
a. 3o orange ('83) 150.00 20.00
b. Perf. 13½x12½ ('93) 8,500. 2,500.
39 A8 5o bl grn ('89) 60.00 2.50
a. 5o gray green ('86) 85.00 5.00
b. 5o emerald ('88) 200.00 7.50
c. 5o yellow green ('91) 70.00 6.00
d. Perf. 13½x12½ ('93) *3,000.* *1,200.*
40 A8 10o rose 60.00 1.75
a. 10o rose red ('86) 60.00 1.75
b. 10o carmine ('91) 60.00 1.75
c. As "b," imperf. ('91) *3,000.* *2,750.*
41 A8 12o green ('84) 1,600. 400.00
42 A8 12o org brn ('84) 24.00 27.00
a. 12o bister brown ('83) 70.00 60.00
43 A8 20o brown 160.00 20.00
44 A8 20o blue ('86) 125.00 6.00
a. 20o ultramarine ('83) 600.00 30.00
b. No period after "Postfrim" ('85) 600.00 24.00
c. As "a," imperf. ('90) *2,500.* *3,000.*
d. 20o Prussian blue 225.00 21.00
45 A8 25o dull vio ('84) 15.00 16.00

Dies vary from 20 to 21mm high. Numerous types exist due to different production methods, including separate handmade dies for value figures. Many shades exist.

No. 42 and 42a Surcharged in Black

1888 *Perf. 14½x13½*

46 A8 2o on 12o org brn 3.00 *3.00*
a. 2o on 12o bister brown 3.00 3.00

Post Horn — A10

"NORGE" in Roman instead of Sans-serif capitals

Perf. 14½x13½

1893-1908 Wmk. 160

Size: 16x20mm

47 A10 1o gray ('99) 2.50 *2.50*
48 A10 2o pale brn ('99) 2.50 *1.75*
49 A10 3o orange yel 1.75 .25
50 A10 5o dp green ('98) 6.00 .25
b. Booklet pane of 6 *800.00*
51 A10 10o carmine ('98) 12.00 .25
b. Booklet pane of 6 *1,100.*
d. 10o rose ('94) 250.00 2.50
e. Imperf *4,000.*
52 A10 15o brown ('08) 50.00 12.00
53 A10 20o dp ultra 24.00 .25
b. Booklet pane of 6
54 A10 25o red vio ('01) 55.00 3.00
55 A10 30o sl gray ('07) 45.00 3.50
56 A10 35o dk bl grn ('98) 11.00 8.50
57 A10 50o maroon ('94) 50.00 2.50
58 A10 60o dk blue ('00) 60.00 13.00
Nos. 47-58 (12) 319.75 47.75

Two dies exist of 3, 10 and 20o.

See Nos. 74-95, 162-166, 187-191, 193, 307-309, 325-326, 416-419, 606, 709-714, 960-968, 1141-1145.

For overprints and surcharge see Nos. 99, 207-211, 220-224, 226, 329.

1893-98 Wmk. 160 *Perf. 13½x12½*

47a A10 1o gray ('95) 15.00 *30.00*
49a A10 3o orange ('95) 30.00 6.00
50a A10 5o green 42.50 6.00
51a A10 10o carmine ('96) 27.50 1.50
c. 10o rose ('95) 75.00 1.75
53a A10 20o dull ultra ('95) 110.00 4.25
54a A10 25o red violet ('98) 90.00 30.00
56a A10 35o dark blue green ('95) 90.00 30.00
57a A10 50o maroon ('97) 400.00 25.00
Nos. 47a-57a (8) 805.00 132.75

Two dies exist of each except 25 and 35o.

No. 12 Surcharged in Green, Blue or Carmine

1905 Unwmk. *Perf. 14½x13½*

59 A4 1k on 2s org (G) 42.50 35.00
60 A4 1.50k on 2s org (Bl) 75.00 95.00
61 A4 2k on 2s org (C) 85.00 100.00
Nos. 59-61 (3) 202.50 230.00

Used values are for stamps canceled after 1910. Stamps used before that sell for twice as much.

Nos. 19 and 21 Surcharged in Black

1906-08 Wmk. 160 *Perf. 14½x13½*

62 A5 15o on 4s lilac ('08) 4.50 5.50
a. 15o on 4s violet ('08) 11.00 13.00
63 A5 30o on 7s red brn 7.50 11.00
a. Inverted overprint *9,000.*

Used values are for stamps canceled after 1914. Stamps used before that sell for twice as much.

King Haakon VII — A11

Die A

Die B

Die C

Die A — Background of ruled lines. The coils at the sides are ornamented with fine cross-lines and small dots. Stamps 20¼mm high.
Die B — Background of ruled lines. The coils are ornamented with large white dots and dashes. Stamps 21¼mm high.
Die C — Solid background. The coils are without ornamental marks. Stamps 20¾mm high.

Die A

1907 Typo. *Perf. 14½x13½*
64 A11 1k yellow grn 45.00 35.00
65 A11 1.50k ultra 85.00 85.00
66 A11 2k rose 130.00 130.00
Nos. 64-66 (3) 260.00 250.00

Used values are for stamps postmarked 1910-14. Stamps postmarked before that sell for twice as much. Stamps postmarked after 1914 sell for one-half the values listed. See note after No. 180.

1909-10 Die B
67 A11 1k green 175.00 130.00
68 A11 1.50k ultra 210.00 *425.00*
69 A11 2k rose 150.00 9.00
Nos. 67-69 (3) 535.00 *564.00*

Used values for Nos. 67-68 are for stamps canceled through 1914.

1911-18 Die C
70 A11 1k light green .75 .25
a. 1k dark green 85.00 4.00
71 A11 1.50k ultra 1.75 1.50
72 A11 2k rose ('15) 2.50 1.50
73 A11 5k dk violet ('18) 5.00 6.00
Nos. 70-73 (4) 10.00 9.25
Set, never hinged 32.50

See note following No. 180.

Post Horn Type Redrawn

Original

Redrawn

In the redrawn stamps the white ring of the post horn is continuous instead of being broken by a spot of color below the crown. On the 3 and 30 ore the top of the figure "3" in the oval band is rounded instead of flattened.

1910-29 *Perf. 14½x13½*
74 A10 1o pale olive .60 *.75*
75 A10 2o pale brown .75 *.60*
76 A10 3o orange .75 *.25*
77 A10 5o green 4.50 .25
a. Booklet pane of 6 150.00
Complete booklet, 4 #77a 2,500.
78 A10 5o magenta ('22) .75 .25
79 A10 7o green ('29) .75 .25
80 A10 10o car rose 5.00 .25
a. Booklet pane of 6 80.00
Complete booklet, 2 #80a 400.00
81 A10 10o green ('22) 6.00 .85
82 A10 12o purple ('17) 1.00 1.75
83 A10 15o brown 5.00 .35
a. Booklet pane of 6 12.50
Complete booklet, 2 #83a 50.00
84 A10 15o indigo ('20) 5.00 .25
85 A10 20o deep ultra 6.00 .25
a. Booklet pane of 6 300.00
Complete booklet, 2 #85a *3,000.*
86 A10 20o ol grn ('21) 6.00 .25
87 A10 25o red lilac 45.00 .35
88 A10 25o car rose ('22) 5.50 .95
89 A10 30o slate gray 8.50 .50
90 A10 30o lt blue ('27) 7.50 8.00
91 A10 35o dk olive ('20) 8.50 .35
92 A10 40o ol grn ('17) 6.00 .75
93 A10 40o dp ultra ('22) 24.00 .30
94 A10 50o claret 18.00 .35
95 A10 60o deep blue 24.00 .50
Nos. 74-95 (22) 189.10 18.35
Set, never hinged 750.00

Constitutional Assembly of 1814 — A12

1914, May 10 Engr. *Perf. 13½*
96 A12 5o green .75 .75
97 A12 10o car rose 1.75 .75
98 A12 20o deep blue 9.00 9.50
Nos. 96-98 (3) 11.50 11.00
Set, never hinged 72.50

Norway's Constitution of May 17, 1814.

No. 87 Surcharged

1922, Mar. 1 *Perf. 14½x13½*
99 A10 5o on 25o red lilac .50 *.75*
Never hinged 1.50

Lion Rampant — A13

"NORGE" in Roman capitals, Line below "Ore"

1922-24 Typo. *Perf. 14½x13½*
100 A13 10o dp grn ('24) 9.00 .85
101 A13 20o dp vio 13.00 .25
102 A13 25o scarlet ('24) 25.00 .75
103 A13 45o blue ('24) 1.25 1.50
Nos. 100-103 (4) 48.25 3.35
Set, never hinged 190.00

For surcharge see No. 129.

Polar Bear and Airplane — A14

1925, Apr. 1
104 A14 2o yellow brn 2.25 *3.50*
105 A14 3o orange 4.50 *5.50*
106 A14 5o magenta 11.00 *18.00*
107 A14 10o yellow grn 15.00 *32.50*
108 A14 15o dark blue 15.00 *30.00*
109 A14 20o plum 21.00 *35.00*
110 A14 25o scarlet 5.00 *7.00*
Nos. 104-110 (7) 73.75 131.50
Set, never hinged 150.00

Issued to help finance Roald Amundsen's attempted flight to the North Pole.

A15

1925, Aug. 19
111 A15 10o yellow green 7.00 *15.00*
112 A15 15o indigo 5.00 *6.50*
113 A15 20o plum 7.00 *2.50*
114 A15 45o dark blue 6.00 *7.00*
Nos. 111-114 (4) 25.00 31.00
Set, never hinged 80.00

Annexation of Spitsbergen (Svalbard).
For surcharge see No. 130.

A16

"NORGE" in Sans-serif Capitals, No Line below "Ore"

1926-34 Wmk. 160
Size: 16x19½mm
115 A16 10o yel grn .60 .25
116 A16 14o dp org ('29) 1.50 3.00
117 A16 15o olive brown .60 .25
118 A16 20o plum 22.50 .60
119 A16 20o scar ('27) .60 .25
a. Booklet pane of 6 65.00
Complete booklet, 2 #119a 300.00
120 A16 25o red 10.00 3.00
121 A16 25o org brn ('27) 1.00 .25
122 A16 30o dull bl ('28) 1.00 .25
123 A16 35o ol brn ('27) 70.00 .25
124 A16 35o red vio ('34) 2.00 .25
125 A16 40o dull blue 5.00 1.50
126 A16 40o slate ('27) 2.00 .25
127 A16 50o claret ('27) 2.00 .25
128 A16 60o Prus bl ('27) 2.00 .25
Nos. 115-128 (14) 120.80 10.60
Set, never hinged 650.00

See Nos. 167-176, 192, 194-202A. For overprints and surcharges see Nos. 131, 212-219, 225, 227-234, 302-303.

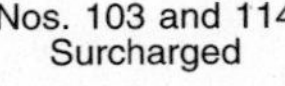

Nos. 103 and 114 Surcharged

1927, June 13
129 A13 30o on 45o blue 11.00 3.00
130 A15 30o on 45o dk blue 4.00 10.00
Set, never hinged 45.00

No. 120 Surcharged

1928
131 A16 20o on 25o red 1.75 2.50
Never hinged 12.00

See Nos. 302-303.

Henrik Ibsen — A17

1928, Mar. 20 Litho.
132 A17 10o yellow grn 6.00 3.00
133 A17 15o chnt brown 3.50 4.25
134 A17 20o carmine 3.00 .75
135 A17 30o dp ultra 4.25 4.25
Nos. 132-135 (4) 16.75 12.25
Set, never hinged 70.00

Ibsen (1828-1906), dramatist.

Postage Due Stamps of 1889-1923 Overprinted

a

b

1929, Jan.
136 D1 (a) 1o gray .50 *1.25*
137 D1 (a) 4o lilac rose .50 .75
138 D1 (a) 10o green 2.25 *5.00*
139 D1 (b) 15o brown 3.00 *6.50*
140 D1 (b) 20o dull vio 1.25 .75
141 D1 (b) 40o deep ultra 2.50 1.00
142 D1 (b) 50o maroon 8.50 9.50
143 D1 (a) 100o orange yel 3.50 *3.50*
144 D1 (b) 200o dk violet 5.00 4.25
Nos. 136-144 (9) 27.00 32.50
Set, never hinged 65.00

Niels Henrik Abel — A18

1929, Apr. 6 Litho. *Perf. 14½x13½*
145 A18 10o green 3.25 1.00
146 A18 15o red brown 3.25 1.75
147 A18 20o rose red 1.00 .50
148 A18 30o deep ultra 3.25 3.00
Nos. 145-148 (4) 10.75 6.25
Set, never hinged 45.00

Abel (1802-1829), mathematician.

No. 12 Surcharged

Perf. 14½x13½
1929, July 1 Unwmk.
149 A4 14o on 2s orange 3.50 *6.00*
Never hinged 6.00

Saint Olaf A19

Trondheim Cathedral A20

Death of Olaf in Battle of Stiklestad — A21

Typo.; Litho. (15o)
Perf. 14½x13½
1930, Apr. 1 Wmk. 160
150 A19 10o yellow grn 11.00 .60
151 A20 15o brn & blk 1.40 .85
152 A19 20o scarlet 1.00 .50

Engr.
Perf. 13½
153 A21 30o deep blue 3.50 5.00
Nos. 150-153 (4) 16.90 6.95
Set, never hinged 75.00

King Olaf Haraldsson (995-1030), patron saint of Norway.

Björnson — A22

1932, Dec. 8 *Perf. 14½x13½*
154 A22 10o yellow grn 9.00 .75
155 A22 15o black brn 1.50 1.50
156 A22 20o rose red 1.00 .50
157 A22 30o ultra 3.00 *3.00*
Nos. 154-157 (4) 14.50 5.75
Set, never hinged 50.00

Björnstjerne Björnson (1832-1910), novelist, poet and dramatist.

Holberg — A23

1934, Nov. 23
158 A23 10o yellow grn 2.00 .85
159 A23 15o brown .65 1.25
160 A23 20o rose red 11.00 .50
161 A23 30o ultra 3.00 3.50
Nos. 158-161 (4) 16.65 6.10
Set, never hinged 70.00

Ludvig Holberg (1684-1754), Danish man of letters.

Types of 1893-1900, 1926-34 Second Redrawing
Perf. 13x13½
1937 Wmk. 160 Photo.
Size: 17x21mm
162 A10 1o olive .70 2.00
163 A10 2o yellow brn .60 1.50
164 A10 3o deep orange 1.75 *4.00*
165 A10 5o rose lilac .50 .50
166 A10 7o brt green .50 .50
167 A16 10o brt green .50 .25
Complete booklet, 2 panes of 6 #167 675.00
168 A16 14o dp orange 3.00 5.00
169 A16 15o olive bis 1.25 .25
170 A16 20o scarlet 1.00 .25
Complete booklet, 2 panes of 6 #170 1,250.
Complete booklet, panes of 6 ea of #165, 167, 170 500.00
171 A16 25o dk org brn 5.00 .55
172 A16 30o ultra 2.75 .75
173 A16 35o brt vio 2.00 .50
174 A16 40o dk slate grn 3.00 .50
175 A16 50o deep claret 3.00 .75
176 A16 60o Prussian bl 1.50 .50
Nos. 162-176 (15) 27.05 17.80
Set, never hinged 110.00

Nos. 162 to 166 have a solid background inside oval. Nos. 74, 75, 76, 78, 79 have background of vertical lines.

King Haakon VII — A24

1937-38

177	A24	1k dark green	.25	.50
178	A24	1.50k sapphire ('38)	1.00	4.00
179	A24	2k rose red ('38)	.75	2.50
180	A24	5k dl vio ('38)	6.00	*10.00*
		Nos. 177-180 (4)	8.00	17.00
		Set, never hinged	20.00	

Nos. 64-66, 67-69, 70-73, 177-180 and B11-B14 were demonitized and banned on Sept. 30, 1940. Nos. 267, B19, B32-B34 and B38-B41 were demonetized on May 15, 1945. All of these stamps became valid again Sept. 1, 1981. Nos. 64-66, 67-69 and 70-73 rarely were used after 1981, and values represent stamps used in the earlier period. Values for Nos. B11-B14 used are for stamps used in the earlier period, and used examples in the later period are worth the same as mint stamps. Values for the other stamps used are for examples used in the later period, and stamps with dated cancellations prior to May 15, 1945 sell for more. False cancellations exist.

Reindeer A25

Borgund Church A26

Jolster in Sunnfiord — A27

Perf. 13x13½, 13½x13

1938, Apr. 20 Wmk. 160

181	A25	15o olive brn	1.00	1.25
182	A26	20o copper red	4.50	.55
183	A27	30o brt ultra	4.00	2.50
		Nos. 181-183 (3)	9.50	4.30
		Set, never hinged	30.00	

1939, Jan. 16 Unwmk.

184	A25	15o olive brn	.50	.75
185	A26	20o copper red	.50	.25
186	A27	30o brt ultra	.50	.75
		Nos. 184-186 (3)	1.50	1.75
		Set, never hinged	3.00	

Types of 1937

Perf. 13x13½

1940-49 Unwmk. Photo.

Size: 17x21mm

187	A10	1o olive grn ('41)	.25	.25
188	A10	2o yel brn ('41)	.25	.25
189	A10	3o dp org ('41)	.25	.25
190	A10	5o rose lilac ('41)	.25	.25
191	A10	7o brt green ('41)	.25	.25
192	A16	10o brt green	.25	.25
		Complete booklet, 2 panes of 6 #192	50.00	
193	A10	12o brt vio	.50	2.00
194	A16	14o dp org ('41)	1.00	4.00
195	A16	15o olive bister	.50	.35
196	A16	20o red	.25	.25
		Complete booklet, 2 panes of 6 #196	60.00	
		Complete booklet, pane of 6 ea of #190, 192, 196	200.00	
		Complete booklet, pane of 10 ea of #190, 192, 196	125.00	
197	A16	25o dk org brn	1.25	.25
197A	A16	25o scarlet ('46)	.25	.25
		Complete booklet, pane of 10 ea of #190, 192, 197A	110.00	
		Complete booklet, pane of 10 ea of #192, 195, 197A	100.00	
198	A16	30o brt ultra ('41)	1.75	.40
198A	A16	30o gray ('49)	4.00	.25
199	A16	35o brt vio ('41)	1.75	.25
200	A16	40o dk sl grn ('41)	1.00	.25
200A	A16	40o dp ultra ('46)	2.50	.45
201	A16	50o dp claret ('41)	1.20	.25
201A	A16	55o dp org ('46)	10.00	.45
202	A16	60o Prus bl ('41)	1.25	.25
202A	A16	80o dk org brn ('46)	10.00	.45
		Nos. 187-202A (21)	38.70	11.60
		Set, never hinged	150.00	

Lion Rampant — A28

1940 Unwmk. Photo. *Perf. 13x13½*

203	A28	1k brt green	1.00	.25
204	A28	1½k deep blue	1.50	.30
205	A28	2k bright red	2.50	1.25
206	A28	5k dull purple	3.50	*6.00*
		Nos. 203-206 (4)	8.50	7.80
		Set, never hinged	30.00	

For overprints see Nos. 235-238.

Stamps of 1937-41, Types A10, A16, A28, Overprinted in Black

1941 Wmk. 160 *Perf. 13x13½*

207	A10	1o olive	.50	*8.00*
208	A10	2o yellow brn	.50	*12.00*
209	A10	3o orange	1.75	*25.00*
210	A10	5o rose lilac	.50	*2.50*
211	A10	7o brt green	.50	*6.00*
212	A16	10o brt green	6.00	*40.00*
213	A16	14o dp orange	1.00	*22.50*
214	A16	15o olive bis	.50	*1.25*
215	A16	30o ultra	1.25	*4.50*
216	A16	35o brt violet	1.00	*1.00*
217	A16	40o dk slate grn	7.50	*11.00*
218	A16	50o dp claret	200.00	*600.00*
		Never hinged	500.00	
219	A16	60o Prus blue	.85	*2.50*
		Nos. 207-217,219 (12)	21.85	*136.25*
		Set, never hinged	55.00	

The "V" overprint exists on Nos. 170-171, but these were not regularly issued.

Unwmk.

220	A10	1o olive	.25	*6.00*
221	A10	2o yellow brn	.25	*10.00*
222	A10	3o deep orange	.25	*6.50*
223	A10	5o rose lilac	.35	.65
224	A10	7o brt green	1.00	*8.50*
225	A16	10o brt green	.25	.25
226	A10	12o brt violet	.75	*20.00*
227	A16	15o olive bis	1.40	*18.00*
228	A16	20o red	.25	.25
a.		Inverted overprint	1,100.	1,500.
229	A16	25o dk orange brn	.50	.50
230	A16	30o brt ultra	.75	*5.00*
231	A16	35o brt violet	1.00	1.00
232	A16	40o dk slate grn	.70	.90
233	A16	50o dp claret	1.00	*3.50*
234	A16	60o Prus blue	3.00	1.75
235	A28	1k brt green	.75	1.00
236	A28	1½k dp blue	3.00	*18.00*
237	A28	2k bright red	9.00	*60.00*
238	A28	5k dull purple	18.00	*150.00*

Lion Rampant with "V" — A29

Coil Stamp

239	A29	10o brt green	1.00	*15.00*
		Nos. 220-239 (20)	43.45	*326.80*
		Set, never hinged	110.00	

No. 239 has a white "V" incorporated into design, rather than an overprint. Nos. 207-239 were demonitized March 29, 1944. Used values are for stamps with postmarks dated prior to March 29, 1944. Forged cancellations exist.

Dream of Queen Ragnhild A30

Snorri Sturluson A32

Einar Tambarskjelve in Fight at Svolder — A31

Designs: 30o, King Olaf sailing in wedding procession to Landmerket. 50o, Syipdag's sons and followers going to Hall of Seven Kings. 60o, Before Battle of Stiklestad.

1941 *Perf. 13½x13, 13x13½*

240	A30	10o bright green	.25	.25
241	A31	15o olive brown	.25	.75
242	A32	20o dark red	.50	.25
243	A31	30o blue	.85	*2.50*
244	A31	50o dull violet	.75	*1.75*
245	A31	60o Prus blue	1.10	2.25
		Nos. 240-245 (6)	3.70	7.75
		Set, never hinged	15.00	

700th anniversary of the death of Snorri Sturluson, writer and historian. Issued: 10o, 30o, 60o, 9/23; others, 10/23.

University of Oslo — A36

1941, Sept. 2 *Perf. 13x13½*

246	A36	1k dk olive grn	30.00	65.00
		Never hinged	65.00	

Centenary of cornerstone laying of University of Oslo building.

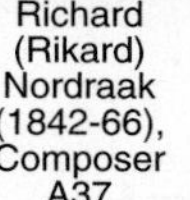

Richard (Rikard) Nordraak (1842-66), Composer A37

"Broad Sails Go over the North Sea" A38

View of Coast and Lines of National Anthem — A39

1942, June 12 *Perf. 13*

247	A37	10o dp green	1.40	*3.00*
248	A38	15o dp brown	1.20	*3.00*
249	A37	20o rose red	1.20	*3.50*
250	A39	30o sapphire	1.20	*3.00*
		Nos. 247-250 (4)	5.00	12.50
		Set, never hinged	12.00	

Johan Herman Wessel (1742-1785), Author — A40

1942, Oct. 6

251	A40	15o dull brown	.25	.50
252	A40	20o henna	.25	.50
		Set, never hinged	1.00	

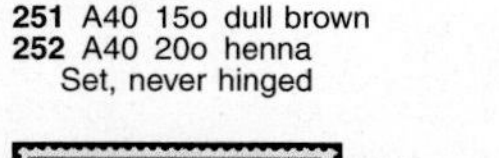

Designs of 1942 and 1855 Stamps of Norway — A41

1942, Oct. 12

253	A41	20o henna	.25	1.75
254	A41	30o sapphire	.35	2.75
		Set, never hinged	1.25	

European Postal Congress at Vienna, October, 1942.

Nos. 253-254, B24-B27, B31 and B35-B37 were demonitized May 15, 1945. Used values are for stamps with postmarks dated prior to May 15, 1945. Forged cancellations exist.

Edvard Grieg (1843-1907), Composer — A42

1943, June 15

255	A42	10o deep green	.25	*.35*
256	A42	20o henna	.25	*.35*
257	A42	40o grnsh black	.25	*.50*
258	A42	60o dk grnsh blue	.25	*.50*
		Nos. 255-258 (4)	1.00	1.70
		Set, never hinged	1.90	

Destroyer Sleipner — A43

5o, 10o, "Sleipner." 7o, 30o, Convoy under midnight sun. 15o, Plane and pilot. 20o, "We will win." 40o, Ski troops. 60o, King Haakon VII.

1943-45 Unwmk. Engr. *Perf. 12½*

259	A43	5o rose vio ('45)	.25	.25
260	A43	7o grnsh blk ('45)	.25	.50
261	A43	10o dk blue grn	.25	.25
262	A43	15o dk olive grn	.50	*1.75*
263	A43	20o rose red	.25	.25
264	A43	30o dp ultra	.60	*2.00*
265	A43	40o olive black	.60	*1.75*
266	A43	60o dark blue	.60	*1.75*
		Nos. 259-266 (8)	3.30	*8.50*
		Set, never hinged	8.50	

Nos. 261-266 were used for correspondence carried on Norwegian ships until after the liberation of Norway, when they became regular postage stamps.

Nos. 261-266 exist with overprint "London 17-5-43" and serial number. Value for set, unused, $700; canceled $1,100.

Gran's Plane and Map of His North Sea Flight Route — A49

1944, July 30 *Perf. 13*

267	A49	40o dk grnsh blue	.25	.50
		Never hinged	.75	

20th anniv. of the 1st flight over the North Sea, made by Tryggve Gran on July 30, 1914.

Value for used stamp postmarked before May 15, 1945, $6. See note following No. 180.

New National Arms of 1943 — A50

1945, Feb. 15 Typo. *Perf. 13*

268	A50	1½k dark blue	1.25	.60
		Never hinged	4.00	

Henrik Wergeland — A51

1945, July 12 Photo.

269	A51	10o dk olive green	.25	*.35*
270	A51	15o dark brown	.50	1.25
271	A51	20o dark red	.25	.30
		Nos. 269-271 (3)	1.00	1.90
		Set, never hinged	1.50	

Wergeland, poet & playwright, death cent.

Lion Rampant — A52

1945, Dec. 19

272	A52	10o dk olive green	.50	.50
273	A52	20o red	.50	.50
		Set, never hinged	3.00	

Norwegian Folklore Museum, 50th anniv.

Pilot and Mechanic — A53

1946, Mar. 22 Engr. *Perf. 12*
274 A53 15o brown rose .40 *1.50*
Never hinged .85

Issued in honor of Little Norway, training center in Canada for Norwegian pilots.

Catalogue values for unused stamps in this section, from this point to the end of the section, are for Never Hinged items.

King Haakon VII — A54

1946, June 7 Photo. *Perf. 13*
275 A54 1k bright green 2.75 .25
276 A54 1½k Prus blue 7.00 .25
277 A54 2k henna brown 45.00 .25
278 A54 5k violet 35.00 .50
Nos. 275-278 (4) 89.75 1.25

Hannibal Sehested — A55

Designs: 10o, Letter carrier, 1700. 15o, Adm. Peter W. Tordenskjold. 25o, Christian Magnus Falsen. 30o, Cleng Peerson and "Restaurationen." 40o, Post ship "Constitution." 45o, First Norwegian locomotive. 50o, Sven Foyn and whaler. 55o, Fridtjof Nansen and Roald Amundsen. 60o, Coronation of King Haakon VII and Queen Maud, 1906. 80o, Return of King Haakon, June 7, 1945.

1947, Apr. 15 Photo. *Perf. 13*
279 A55 5o red lilac .70 .25
280 A55 10o green .70 .25
281 A55 15o brown 1.25 .25
282 A55 25o orange red 1.00 .25
283 A55 30o gray 2.25 .25
284 A55 40o blue 5.00 .25
285 A55 45o violet 2.50 .75
286 A55 50o orange brn 4.75 .35
287 A55 55o orange 6.50 .35
288 A55 60o slate gray 7.00 2.00
289 A55 80o dk brown 6.50 .35
Nos. 279-289 (11) 38.15 5.30

Establishment of the Norwegian Post Office, 300th anniv.

Petter Dass — A66

1947, July 1 Unwmk.
290 A66 25o bright red 1.50 1.25

300th birth anniv. of Petter Dass, poet.

King Haakon VII — A67

1947, Aug. 2
291 A67 25o orange red .80 .80

75th birthday of King Haakon.

Axel Heiberg — A68

1948, June 15
292 A68 25o deep carmine 1.00 .50
293 A68 80o dp red brown 2.50 .30

50th anniv. of the Norwegian Society of Forestry; birth cent. of Axel Heiberg, its founder.

Alexander L. Kielland — A69

1949, May 9
295 A69 25o rose brown 1.50 .50
296 A69 40o greenish blue 1.90 .75
297 A69 80o orange brown 2.50 1.00
Nos. 295-297 (3) 5.90 2.25

Birth cent. of Alexander L. Kielland, author.

Symbols of UPU Members A70

Stylized Pigeons and Globe A71

Symbolical of the UPU — A72

1949, Oct. 8 *Perf. 13*
299 A70 10o dk green & blk .50 .60
300 A71 25o scarlet .70 .50
301 A72 40o dull blue .70 .50
Nos. 299-301 (3) 1.90 1.60

75th anniv. of the formation of the UPU.

Nos. 196 and 200A Surcharged with New Value and Bar in Black

1949 *Perf. 13x13½*
302 A16 25o on 20o red .75 .25
303 A16 45o on 40o dp ultra 3.00 .65

King Harald Haardraade and Oslo City Hall — A73

1950, May 15 Photo. *Perf. 13*
304 A73 15o green .90 .90
305 A73 25o red .90 .50
306 A73 45o ultramarine .90 .90
Nos. 304-306 (3) 2.70 2.30

900th anniversary of Oslo.

Redrawn Post Horn Type of 1937

1950-51 Photo. *Perf. 13x13½*
Size: 17x21mm
307 A10 10o grnsh gray 1.00 .25
Complete booklet, pane of 10 #307 250.00
308 A10 15o dark green 2.50 .50
309 A10 20o chnt brn ('51) 5.00 3.00
Nos. 307-309 (3) 8.50 3.75

King Haakon VII — A74

1950-51 Photo. *Perf. 13x13½*
310 A74 25o dk red ('50) .90 .25
Complete booklet, pane of 10 ea of #307, 308, 310 85.00
311 A74 30o gray 9.00 .75
312 A74 35o red brn 18.00 .35
313 A74 45o brt blue 1.75 2.50
314 A74 50o olive brn 5.00 .25
315 A74 55o orange 2.25 1.25
316 A74 60o gray blue 15.00 .25
317 A74 80o chnt brn 3.00 .35
Nos. 310-317 (8) 54.90 5.95

See Nos. 322-324, 345-352. For surcharge see No. 321.

Arne Garborg — A75

1951, Jan. 25 *Perf. 13*
318 A75 25o red 1.00 .50
319 A75 45o dull blue 3.75 4.00
320 A75 80o brown 3.75 2.00
Nos. 318-320 (3) 8.50 6.50

Birth cent. of Arne Garborg, poet.

No. 310 Surcharged with New Value in Black

1951 *Perf. 13x13½*
321 A74 30o on 25o dk red .90 .30

Haakon Type of 1950-51

1951-52 Photo.
322 A74 25o gray 20.00 .25
323 A74 30o dk red ('52) .90 .25
Complete booklet, pane of 10 ea of #307, 308, 323 225.00
Complete booklet, pane of 10 ea of #307, 325, 323 110.00
324 A74 55o blue ('52) 2.00 .40
Nos. 322-324 (3) 22.90 .90

Redrawn Post Horn Type of 1937

1952, June 3 *Perf. 13x13½*
325 A10 15o org brn .70 .25
326 A10 20o dark green .70 .25

King Haakon VII — A76

1952, Aug. 3 Unwmk. *Perf. 13*
327 A76 30o red .50 .50
328 A76 55o deep blue 1.50 1.50

80th birthday of King Haakon VII.

No. 308 Surcharged with New Value

1952, Nov. 18 *Perf. 13x13½*
329 A10 20o on 15o dk grn .70 .25

Medieval Sculpture, Nidaros Cathedral — A77

1953, July 15 *Perf. 13*
330 A77 30o henna brn 1.40 .75

800th anniv. of the creation of the Norwegian Archbishopric of Nidaros.

Train of 1854 and Horse-drawn Sled — A78

Designs: 30o, Diesel train. 55o, Engineer.

1954, Apr. 30 Photo.
331 A78 20o green 1.10 .50
332 A78 30o red 1.25 .35
333 A78 55o ultra 1.75 1.25
Nos. 331-333 (3) 4.10 2.10

Inauguration of the first Norwegian railway, cent.

Carsten T. Nielsen — A79

Designs: 30o, Government radio towers. 55o, Lineman and telegraph poles in snow.

1954, Dec. 10
334 A79 20o ol grn & blk .55 .50
335 A79 30o brt red .55 .35
336 A79 55o blue 1.40 1.10
Nos. 334-336 (3) 2.50 1.95

Centenary (in 1955) of the inauguration of the first Norwegian public telegraph line.

Norway No. 1 — A80

Stamp Reproductions: 30o, Post horn type A5. 55o, Lion type A13.

1955, Jan. 3 *Perf. 13*
337 A80 20o dp grn & gray bl .45 .45
338 A80 30o red & carmine .40 .40
339 A80 55o gray bl & dp bl .75 .50
Nos. 337-339 (3) 1.60 1.35

Centenary of Norway's first postage stamp.

Nos. 337-339 Overprinted in Black

1955, June 4
340 A80 20o dp grn & gray bl 12.50 12.50
341 A80 30o red & carmine 12.50 12.50
342 A80 55o gray bl & dp bl 12.50 12.50
Nos. 340-342 (3) 37.50 37.50

Norway Philatelic Exhibition, Oslo, 1955. Sold at exhibition post office for face value plus 1kr admission fee.

King Haakon VII and Queen Maud in Coronation Robes — A81

1955, Nov. 25 Photo. *Perf. 13*
343 A81 30o rose red .40 .40
344 A81 55o ultra .75 .75

Haakon's 50th anniv. as King of Norway.

Haakon Type of 1950-51

1955-57 Unwmk. *Perf. 13x13½*
345 A74 25o dk grn ('56) 1.20 .25
346 A74 35o brn red ('56) 4.75 .25
Complete booklet, pane of 10 ea of #307, 325, 346 100.00
347 A74 40o pale pur 2.00 .25
Complete booklet, pane of 10 ea of #307, 325, 347 80.00
348 A74 50o bister ('57) 4.75 .25
349 A74 65o ultra ('56) 1.20 .40
350 A74 70o brn ol ('56) 20.00 .25
351 A74 75o mar ('57) 2.75 .25
352 A74 90o dp org 1.60 .25
Nos. 345-352 (8) 38.25 2.15

Northern Countries Issue

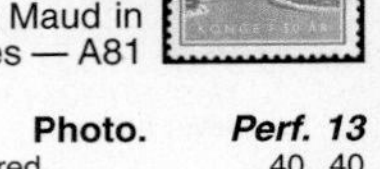

Whooper Swans — A81a

1956, Oct. 30 Engr. *Perf. 12½*
353 A81a 35o rose red .70 .60
354 A81a 65o ultra .70 .70

Close bonds connecting the northern countries: Denmark, Finland, Iceland, Norway and Sweden.

Jan Mayen Island A82

Map of Spitsbergen A83

Design: 65o, Map of South Pole with Queen Maud Land.

Perf. 12½x13, 13x12½

1957, July 1 Photo. Unwmk.
355 A82 25o slate green .70 .60
356 A83 35o dk red & gray .70 .40
357 A83 65o dk grn & bl .70 .60
Nos. 355-357 (3) 2.10 1.60

Intl. Geophysical Year, 1957-58.

King Haakon VII — A84

1957, Aug. 3 ***Perf. 13***
358 A84 35o dark red .60 .40
359 A84 65o ultra 1.20 1.20

85th birthday of King Haakon VII.

King Olav V — A85

1958-60 Photo. ***Perf. 13x13½***
360 A85 25o emerald 1.10 .25
Complete booklet, pane of 4 of #360 125.00
361 A85 30o purple ('59) 2.00 .25
361A A85 35o brown car ('60) .95 .25
362 A85 40o dark red .95 .25
Complete booklet, pane of 10 of ea of #307, 325, 362 100.00
363 A85 45o scarlet 1.40 .25
Complete booklet, pane of 10 of #363 65.00
Complete booklet, pane of 10 ea of #307, 325, 363 85.00
364 A85 50o bister ('59) 6.00 .25
365 A85 55o dk gray ('59) 1.75 .75
366 A85 65o blue 2.00 .40
367 A85 80o org brn ('60) 11.00 .85
368 A85 85o olive brn ('59) 2.00 .25
369 A85 90o orange ('59) 1.50 .25
Nos. 360-369 (11) 30.65 4.00

See Nos. 408-412.

King Olav V — A86

1959, Jan. 12
370 A86 1k green 1.50 .25
371 A86 1.50k dark blue 4.00 .25
372 A86 2k crimson 4.00 .25
373 A86 5k lilac 50.00 .25
374 A86 10k dp orange 7.50 .25
Nos. 370-374 (5) 67.00 1.25

See Phosphorescence note following No. 430.

Asbjörn Kloster — A87

1959, Feb. 2
375 A87 45o violet brown .50 .35

Centenary of the founding of the Norwegian Temperance Movement; Asbjörn Kloster, its founder.

Agricultural Society Medal — A88

1959, May 26
376 A88 45o red & ocher .60 .60
377 A88 90o blue & gray 2.00 2.00

150th anniversary of the Royal Agricultural Society of Norway.

Sower — A89

Design: 90o, Grain, vert.

1959, Oct. 1 Photo. ***Perf. 13***
378 A89 45o ocher & blk .75 .60
379 A89 90o blue & blk 1.50 1.50

Agricultural College of Norway, cent.

Society Seal — A90

1960, Feb. 26 Unwmk.
380 A90 45o carmine .55 .50
381 A90 90o dark blue 1.60 1.60

Bicentenary of the Royal Norwegian Society of Sciences, Trondheim.

Viking Ship — A91

25o, Caravel & fish. 45o, Sailing ship & nautical knot. 55o, Freighter & oil derricks. 90o, Passenger ship & Statue of Liberty.

1960, Aug. 27 ***Perf. 12½x13***
382 A91 20o gray & blk 1.60 1.40
383 A91 25o yel grn & blk 1.00 1.00
384 A91 45o ver & blk 1.00 .40
385 A91 55o ocher & blk 2.75 2.75
386 A91 90o Prus bl & blk 3.25 2.25
Nos. 382-386 (5) 9.60 7.80

Norwegian shipping industry.

Common Design Types pictured following the introduction.

Europa Issue
Common Design Type

1960, Sept. 19 ***Perf. 13***
Size: 27x21mm
387 CD3 90o blue 1.00 .80

DC-8 Airliner — A91a

1961, Feb. 24 Photo. ***Perf. 13***
388 A91a 90o dark blue .80 .80

Scandinavian Airlines System, SAS, 10th anniv.

Javelin Thrower — A92

1961, Mar. 15
389 A92 20o shown 1.10 1.00
390 A92 25o Skater 1.00 .90
391 A92 45o Ski jumper .75 .40
392 A92 90o Sailboat 1.25 1.25
Nos. 389-392 (4) 4.10 3.55

Norwegian Sports Federation centenary.

Haakonshallen A93

1961, May 25 ***Perf. 12½x13***
393 A93 45o maroon & gray .70 .50
394 A93 1k gray green & gray 1.00 .40

700th anniv. of Haakonshallen, castle in Bergen.

Domus Media, Oslo University — A94

1961, Sept. 2 Photo. ***Perf. 12½x13***
395 A94 45o dark red .70 .50
396 A94 1.50k Prus blue 1.00 .40

150th anniversary of Oslo University.

Fridtjof Nansen — A95

1961, Oct. 10 ***Perf. 13***
397 A95 45o orange red & gray .80 .40
398 A95 90o chlky blue & gray 1.50 1.50

Birth centenary of Fridtjof Nansen, explorer.

Roald Amundsen — A96

Design: 90o, Explorers and tent at Pole.

1961, Nov. 10 Unwmk. ***Perf. 13***
399 A96 45o dl red brn & gray 1.00 .60
400 A96 90o dk & lt blue 1.75 1.75

50th anniversary of Roald Amundsen's arrival at the South Pole.

Frederic Passy, Henri Dunant — A97

1961, Dec. 9 Photo.
401 A97 45o henna brown .50 .50
402 A97 1k yellow green 1.25 .50

Winners of the first Nobel Peace prize. Frederic Passy, a founder of the Interparliamentary Union, and Henri Dunant, founder of the International Red Cross.

Vilhelm Bjerknes — A98

1962, Mar. 14 ***Perf. 13***
403 A98 45o dk red & gray .50 .40
404 A98 1.50k dk blue & gray 1.00 .50

Vilhelm Bjerknes (1862-1951), physicist, mathematician, meteorologist, etc.

German Rumpler Taube over Oslo Fjord — A99

1962, June 1 Photo.
405 A99 1.50k dl bl & blk 3.50 .70

50th anniversary of Norwegian aviation.

Fir Branch and Cone — A100

1962, June 15
406 A100 45o salmon & blk .60 .60
407 A100 1k pale grn & blk 6.00 .40

State Forest Administration, centenary.

Olav Type of 1958-60

1962 Unwmk. ***Perf. 13x13½***
408 A85 25o slate grn 1.25 .25
Complete booklet, pane of 4 of #408 125.00
Complete booklet, pane of 10 ea of #190, 307, 408 35.00
409 A85 35o emerald 5.00 .25
410 A85 40o gray 3.50 1.75
411 A85 50o scarlet 8.00 .25
Complete booklet, pane of 10 of #411 175.00
412 A85 60o violet 5.50 .50
Nos. 408-412 (5) 23.25 3.00

Europa Issue
Common Design Type

1962, Sept. 17 Photo. ***Perf. 13***
Size: 37x21mm
414 CD5 50o dp rose & maroon .55 .50
415 CD5 90o blue & dk blue 1.20 1.20

Post Horn Type of 1893-1908 Redrawn and

Rock Carvings A101

Boatswain's Knot A102

Designs: 30o, 55o, 85o, Rye and fish. 65o, 80o, Stave church and northern lights.

1962-63 Engr. ***Perf. 13x13½***
416 A10 5o rose cl .25 .25
417 A10 10o slate .25 .25
Complete booklet, pane of 10 of #417 40.00
418 A10 15o orange brn .25 .25
419 A10 20o green .25 .25
Complete booklet, pane of 4 ea of #416, 419 20.00
420 A101 25o gray grn ('63) 1.25 .25
Complete booklet, pane of 4 of #420 20.00
Complete booklet, pane of 10 ea of #416, 417, 420 45.00
421 A101 30o olive brn ('63) 4.00 4.00
422 A102 35o brt green ('63) .30 .25
423 A101 40o lake ('63) 3.00 .25
424 A102 50o vermilion 4.25 .25
Complete booklet, pane of 10 of #424 90.00
425 A101 55o orange brn ('63) .45 .45
426 A102 60o dk grnsh gray ('63) 12.50 .25
427 A102 65o dk blue ('63) 3.00 .35
Complete booklet, pane of 10 of #427 100.00
428 A102 80o rose lake ('63) 2.25 2.25
429 A101 85o sepia ('63) .45 .25
430 A101 90o blue ('63) .30 .25
Nos. 416-430 (15) 32.75 9.80

Nos. 416-419 have been redrawn and are similar to 1910-29 issue, with vertical lines inside oval and horizontal lines in oval frame. See Nos. 462-470, 608-615.

Phosphorescence
Nos. 370-372, 416-419, 423, 425, 428, 430, 462, 466, O65-O68, O75, O78-O82, O83-O84 and O88 have been issued on both ordinary and phosphorescent paper.

Camilla Collett (1813-1895), Author — A103

1963, Jan. 23 Photo. ***Perf. 13***
431 A103 50o red brn & tan .60 .40
432 A103 90o slate & gray 1.40 1.25

Girl in Boat Loaded with Grain A104

Still Life A105

1963, Mar. 21 Unwmk. ***Perf. 13***
433 A104 25o yellow brown .50 .40
434 A104 35o dark green .75 .75
435 A105 50o dark red .75 .50
436 A105 90o dark blue 1.40 1.10
Nos. 433-436 (4) 3.40 2.75

FAO "Freedom from Hunger" campaign.

River Boat — A106

Design: 90o, Northern sailboat.

1963, May 20 Unwmk. *Perf. 13*
437 A106 50o brown red 1.00 1.00
438 A106 90o blue 3.00 3.00

Tercentenary of regular postal service between Northern and Southern Norway.

Ivar Aasen — A107

1963, Aug. 5 Photo.
439 A107 50o dk red & gray .60 .40
440 A107 90o dk blue & gray 1.75 1.75

150th birth anniv. of Ivar Aasen, poet and philologist.

Europa Issue
Common Design Type
1963, Sept. 14 Unwmk. *Perf. 13*
Size: 27x21½mm
441 CD6 50o dull rose & org .60 .40
442 CD6 90o blue & yel grn 2.00 2.00

Patterned Fabric — A108

1963, Sept. 24
443 A108 25o olive & ol grn .75 .75
444 A108 35o Prus bl & dk bl 1.40 1.40
445 A108 50o dk car rose & plum .60 .60
Nos. 443-445 (3) 2.75 2.75

Norwegian textile industry, 150th anniv.

"Loneliness" A109

Paintings by Edvard Munch (1863-1944): 25o, Self-portrait, vert. 35o, "Fertility." 90o, "Girls on Bridge," vert.

1963, Dec. 12 Litho. *Perf. 13*
446 A109 25o black .40 .40
447 A109 35o dark green .40 .40
448 A109 50o deep claret .60 .40
449 A109 90o gray bl & dk bl 1.00 1.00
Nos. 446-449 (4) 2.40 2.20

Eilert Sundt — A110

50o, Beehive, Workers' Society emblem.

1964, Feb. 17 Photo.
450 A110 25o dark green .60 .60
451 A110 50o dk red brown .60 .25

Centenary of the Oslo Workers' Society.

Cato M. Guldberg and Peter Waage by Stinius Fredriksen — A111

1964, Mar. 11 Unwmk. *Perf. 13*
452 A111 35o olive green .70 .70
453 A111 55o bister 1.50 1.50

Centenary of the presentation of the Law of Mass Action (chemistry) by Professors Cato M. Guldberg and Peter Waage in the Oslo Scientific Society.

Eidsvoll Building — A112

Design: 90o, Storting (Parliament House).

1964, May 11 Photo.
454 A112 50o hn brn & blk 1.00 .50
455 A112 90o Prus bl & dk bl 2.25 2.00

150th anniv. of Norway's constitution.

Church and Ships in Harbor — A113

1964, Aug. 17 *Perf. 13*
456 A113 25o dk sl grn & buff .60 .60
457 A113 90o dk bl & gray 2.00 2.00

Centenary of the Norwegian Seamen's Mission, which operates 32 stations around the world.

Europa Issue
Common Design Type
1964, Sept. 14 Photo. *Perf. 13*
458 CD7 90o dark blue 3.50 3.50

Herman Anker and Olaus Arvesen — A114

1964, Oct. 31 Litho. Unwmk.
459 A114 50o rose .80 .50
460 A114 90o blue 2.50 2.50

Centenary of the founding of Norwegian schools of higher education (Folk High Schools).

Types of Regular Issue, 1962-63

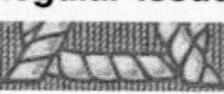
Type I

Type II

Two types of 60o:
I — Four twists across bottom of knot.
II — Five twists.

Designs: 30o, 45o, Rye and fish. 40o, 100o, Rock carvings. 50o, 60o, 65o, 70o, Boatswain's knot.

1964-70 Engr. *Perf. 13x13½*
462 A101 30o dull green .40 .25
463 A101 40o lt bl grn ('68) .30 .25
464 A101 45o lt yel grn ('68) .60 .60
465 A102 50o indigo ('68) .25 .25
466 A102 60o brick red, II ('75) 1.50 .50
a. Type I 1.25 .30
Complete booklet, pane of 10 of #466a 80.00
467 A102 65o lake ('68) .50 .25
Complete booklet, pane of 10 of #467 35.00
468 A102 70o brown ('70) .25 .25
Complete booklet, pane of 10 of #468 30.00
469 A101 100o violet bl ('70) .60 .25
Complete booklet, pane of 4 ea of #416, 419, 469 8.00
Nos. 462-469 (8) 4.40 2.60

See Phosphorescence note following #430.

Coil Stamp
1965 *Perf. 13½ Horiz.*
470 A101 30o dull green 3.50 3.50

Telephone Dial and Waves — A115

Design: 90o, Television mast and antenna.

1965, Apr. 1 Engr. *Perf. 13*
471 A115 60o redsh brown .60 .40
472 A115 90o slate 1.60 1.60

ITU, centenary.

Mountain Scene — A116

Design: 90o, Coastal view.

1965, June 4 Unwmk. *Perf. 13*
473 A116 60o brn blk & car .80 .60
474 A116 90o slate bl & car 3.50 3.50

Centenary of the Norwegian Red Cross.

Europa Issue
Common Design Type
1965, Sept. 25 Photo. *Perf. 13*
Size: 27x21mm
475 CD8 60o brick red .90 .40
476 CD8 90o blue 1.50 1.50

St. Sunniva and Buildings of Bergen — A117

90o, St. Sunniva and stylized view of Bergen.

1965, Oct. 25 *Perf. 13*
477 A117 30o dk green & blk .50 .40
478 A117 90o blue & blk, horiz. 1.75 1.75

Bicentenary of Bergen's philharmonic society "Harmonien."

Rondane Mountains by Harold Sohlberg — A118

1965, Nov. 29 Photo. *Perf. 13*
484 A118 1.50k dark blue 2.50 .30

Rock Carving of Skier, Rodoy Island, c. 2000 B.C. — A120

Designs: 55o, Ski jumper. 60o, Cross country skier. 90o, Holmenkollen ski jump, vert.

1966, Feb. 8 Engr. *Perf. 13*
486 A120 40o sepia 1.40 1.20
487 A120 55o dull green 1.60 1.60
488 A120 60o dull red .80 .40
489 A120 90o blue 1.50 1.50
Nos. 486-489 (4) 5.30 4.70

World Ski Championships, Oslo, Feb. 17-27.

Open Bible and Chrismon — A121

1966, May 20 Photo. *Perf. 13*
490 A121 60o dull red .60 .40
491 A121 90o slate blue 1.40 1.40

150th anniv. of the Norwegian Bible Society.

Engine-turned Bank Note Design A122

Bank of Norway A123

1966, June 14 Engr.
492 A122 30o green .70 .70
493 A123 60o dk carmine rose .50 .30

150th anniversary of Bank of Norway.

Johan Sverdrup — A124

1966, July 30 Photo. *Perf. 13*
494 A124 30o green .45 .45
495 A124 60o rose lake .45 .40

Johan Sverdrup (1816-92), Prime Minister of Norway (1884-89).

Canceled to Order
The Norwegian philatelic agency began in 1966 to sell commemorative and definitive issues canceled to order at face value.

Europa Issue
Common Design Type
1966, Sept. 26 Engr. *Perf. 13*
Size: 21x27mm
496 CD9 60o dark carmine .60 .40
497 CD9 90o blue gray 1.75 1.75

Nitrogen Molecule in Test Tube — A125

Design: 55o, Wheat and laboratory bottle.

1966, Oct. 29 Photo. *Perf. 13x12½*
498 A125 40o bl & dp bl 1.50 1.50
499 A125 55o red, org & lil rose 2.00 2.00

Centenary of the birth of Kristian Birkeland (1867-1917), and of Sam Eyde (1866-1940), who together developed the production of nitrates.

EFTA Emblem — A126

1967, Jan. 16 Engr. *Perf. 13*
500 A126 60o rose red .50 .35
501 A126 90o dark blue 2.00 2.00

European Free Trade Association. Tariffs were abolished Dec. 31, 1966, among EFTA members: Austria, Denmark, Finland, Great Britain, Norway, Portugal, Sweden, Switzerland.

Sabers, Owl and Oak Leaves — A127

1967, Feb. 16 Engr. *Perf. 13*
502 A127 60o chocolate .80 .80
503 A127 90o black 3.00 3.00

Higher military training in Norway, 150th anniv.

Europa Issue
Common Design Type
1967, May 2 Photo. *Perf. 13*
Size: 21x27mm
504 CD10 60o magenta & plum .60 .40
505 CD10 90o bl & dk vio bl 1.40 1.40

Johanne Dybwad, by Per Ung — A128

1967, Aug. 2 Photo. *Perf. 13*
506 A128 40o slate blue .50 .45
507 A128 60o dk carmine rose .50 .40

Johanne Dybwad (1867-1950), actress.

Missionary L.O. Skrefsrud A129

Ebenezer Church, Benagaria, Santal A130

1967, Sept. 26 Engr. *Perf. 13*

508 A129 60o red brown .55 .45
509 A130 90o blue gray 1.25 1.25

Norwegian Santal (India) mission, cent.

Mountaineers A131

Designs: 60o, Mountain view. 90o, Glitretind mountain peak.

1968, Jan. 22 Engr. *Perf. 13*

510 A131 40o sepia 1.25 1.25
511 A131 60o brown red .75 .30
512 A131 90o slate blue 1.25 1.25
Nos. 510-512 (3) 3.25 2.80

Centenary of the Norwegian Mountain Touring Association.

Two Smiths — A132

1968, Mar. 30 Photo. *Perf. 12½x13*

513 A132 65o dk car rose & brn .45 .25
514 A132 90o blue & brown 1.20 1.20

Issued to honor Norwegian craftsmen.

A. O. Vinje — A133

1968, May 21 Engr. *Perf. 13*

515 A133 50o sepia .60 .50
516 A133 65o maroon .50 .30

Aasmund Olafsson Vinje (1818-1870), poet, journalist and language reformer.

Cross and Heart — A134

1968, Sept. 16 Photo.

517 A134 40o brt grn & brn red 2.25 2.25
518 A134 65o brn red & vio bl .50 .25

Centenary of the Norwegian Lutheran Home Mission Society.

Cathinka Guldberg — A135

1968, Oct. 31 Engr. *Perf. 13*

519 A135 50o bright blue .50 .45
520 A135 65o dull red .50 .25

Nursing profession; centenary of Deaconess House in Oslo. Cathinka Guldberg was a pioneer of Norwegian nursing and the first deaconess.

Klas P. Arnoldson and Fredrik Bajer — A136

1968, Dec. 10 Engr. *Perf. 13*

521 A136 65o red brown .50 .30
522 A136 90o dark blue 1.50 1.50

60th anniv. of the awarding of the Nobel Peace prize to Klas P. Arnoldson (1844-1916), Swedish writer and statesman, and to Fredrik Bajer (1837-1922), Danish writer and statesman.

Nordic Cooperation Issue

Five Ancient Ships — A136a

1969, Feb. 28 Engr. *Perf. 13*

523 A136a 65o red .35 .30
524 A136a 90o blue 1.40 1.40

50th anniv. of the Nordic Society and centenary of postal cooperation among the northern countries. The design is taken from a coin found on the site of Birka, an ancient Swedish town.

See Demark Nos. 454-455, Finland No. 481, Iceland Nos. 404-405 and Sweden Nos. 808-810.

Ornament from Urnes Stave Church A137

Traena Island A138

1969 Engr. *Perf. 13*

526 A137 1.15k sepia 1.00 .45
529 A138 3.50k bluish blk 1.60 .25

Issue dates: 1.15k, Jan. 23, 3.50k, June 18.

Plane, Train, Ship and Bus — A139

Child Crossing Street — A140

1969, Mar. 24 Photo. *Perf. 13*

531 A139 50o green 1.00 1.00
532 A140 65o slate grn & dk red .50 .25

No. 531 for the centenary of the publication of "Rutebok of Norway" (Communications of Norway); No. 532 publicizes traffic safety.

Europa Issue
Common Design Type

1969, Apr. 28 Size: 37x21mm

533 CD12 65o dk red & gray .60 .35
534 CD12 90o chalky bl & gray 1.60 1.60

Johan Hjort — A141

Design: 90o, different emblem.

1969, May 30 Engr. *Perf. 13*

535 A141 40o brn & bl 1.00 1.00
536 A141 90o bl & grn 1.75 1.75

Zoologist and oceanographer (1869-1948).

King Olav V — A142

1969-83 Engr. *Perf. 13*

537 A142 1k lt ol grn ('70) .60 .25
538 A142 1.50k dk blue ('70) .70 .25
539 A142 2k dk red ('70) .75 .25
540 A142 5k vio bl ('70) 2.00 .25
541 A142 10k org brn ('70) 5.00 .25
542 A142 20k brown 9.00 .25
543 A142 50k dk ol grn ('83) 16.00 1.50
Nos. 537-543 (7) 34.05 3.00

Man, Woman and Child, by Vigeland — A143

65o, Mother and Child, by Gustav Vigeland.

1969, Sept. 8 Photo. *Perf. 13*

545 A143 65o car rose & blk .50 .35
546 A143 90o blue & black 1.25 1.25

Gustav Vigeland (1869-1943), sculptor.

People — A144

1969, Oct. 10

547 A144 65o Punched card .50 .35
548 A144 90o shown 1.25 1.25

1st Norwegian census, 200th anniv.

Queen Maud — A145

1969, Nov. 26 Engr. *Perf. 13*

549 A145 65o dk carmine .50 .35
550 A145 90o violet blue 1.25 1.25

Queen Maud (1869-1938), wife of King Haakon VII.

Pulsatilla Vernalis — A146

European Nature Conservation Year: 40o, Wolf. 70o, Voringsfossen (waterfall). 100o, White-tailed sea eagle, horiz.

1970, Apr. 10 Photo. *Perf. 13*

551 A146 40o sep & pale bl 1.25 1.25
552 A146 60o lt brn & gray 2.50 2.50
553 A146 70o pale bl & brn 1.25 .60
554 A146 100o pale bl & brn 1.75 1.75
Nos. 551-554 (4) 6.75 6.10

"V" for Victory — A147

Design: 100o, Convoy, horiz.

Perf. 13x12½, 12½x13

1970, May 8 Photo.

555 A147 70o red & lilac 2.00 .60
556 A147 100o vio bl & brt grn 2.00 1.75

Norway's liberation from the Germans, 25th anniv.

"Citizens" — A148

Designs: 70o, "The City and the Mountains." 100o, "Ships."

1970, June 23 Engr. *Perf. 13*

557 A148 40o green 1.75 1.25
558 A148 70o rose claret 2.50 .40
559 A148 100o violet blue 2.00 2.00
Nos. 557-559 (3) 6.25 3.65

City of Bergen, 900th anniversary.

Olive Wreath and Hands Upholding Globe — A149

1970, Sept. 15 Engr. *Perf. 13*

560 A149 70o dk car rose 2.50 .50
561 A149 100o steel blue 1.50 1.50

25th anniversary of the United Nations.

Georg Ossian Sars (1837-1927) — A150

Portraits: 50o, Hans Strom (1726-1797). 70o, Johan Ernst Gunnerus (1718-1773). 100o, Michael Sars (1805-1869).

1970, Oct. 15 Engr. *Perf. 13*

562 A150 40o brown 1.25 1.25
563 A150 50o dull purple 1.25 .90
564 A150 70o brown red 1.25 .50
565 A150 100o bright blue 1.25 1.25
Nos. 562-565 (4) 5.00 3.90

Issued to honor Norwegian zoologists.

Central School of Gymnastics, Oslo, Cent. — A151

50o, Ball game, vert. 70o, Leapfrog.

1970, Nov. 17 Photo. *Perf. 13*

566 A151 50o dk blue, brn .80 .40
567 A151 70o red, brn, blk 1.00 .30

Seal of Tonsberg — A152

1971, Jan. 20 Photo. *Perf. 13*

568 A152 70o dark red .85 .30
569 A152 100o blue black 1.25 1.25

City of Tonsberg, 1,100th anniversary.

Parliament A153

1971, Feb. 23

570 A153 70o red brn & lil .60 .30
571 A153 100o dk bl & sl grn 1.25 1.25

Centenary of annual sessions of Norwegian Parliament.

Hand, Heart and Eye — A154

1971, Mar. 26 Photo. *Perf. 13*

572 A154 50o emerald & blk .60 .50
573 A154 70o scarlet & blk .60 .30

Joint northern campaign for the benefit of refugees.

"Haugianerne" by Adolph Tiedemand A155

1971, Apr. 27 Photo. Perf. 13

574 A155 60o dark gray .65 .65
575 A155 70o brown .50 .30

Hans Nielsen Hauge (1771-1824), church reformer.

Worshippers Coming to Church — A156

Design: 70o, Building first church, vert.

1971, May 21

576 A156 70o black & dk red .40 .35
577 A156 1k black & blue 1.60 1.60

900th anniversary of the Bishopric of Oslo.

Roald Amundsen, Antarctic Treaty Emblem — A157

1971, June 23 Engr. Perf. 13

578 A157 100o blue & org red 3.50 2.50

Antarctic Treaty pledging peaceful uses of and scientific cooperation in Antarctica, 10th anniv.

The Farmer and the Woman — A158

Designs: 50o, The Preacher and the King, horiz. 70o, The Troll and the Girl. Illustrations for legends and folk tales by Erik Werenskiold.

1971, Nov. 17 Photo. Perf. 13

579 A158 40o olive & blk .80 .50
580 A158 50o blue & blk .80 .30
581 A158 70o magenta & blk .50 .25
Nos. 579-581 (3) 2.10 1.05

Engine Turning — A159

1972, Apr. 10 Photo. Perf. 13

582 A159 80o red & gold .60 .30
583 A159 1.20k ultra & gold 1.25 1.25

Norwegian Savings Bank sesquicentennial.

Norway #18 — A160

Engr. & Photo.

1972, May 6 Perf. 12

584 A160 80o shown 1.25 .30
585 A160 1k Norway #17 1.25 .50
a. Souvenir sheet of 2, #584-585 6.00 7.50

Centenary of the post horn stamps. No. 585a sold for 2.50k.

Dragon's Head, Oseberg Viking Ship — A161

Ancient Artifacts: 50o, Horseman from Stone of Alstad. 60o, Horseman, wood carving, stave church, Hemsedal. 1.20k, Sword hilt, found at Lodingen.

1972, June 7 Engr. Perf. 13

586 A161 50o yellow grn .60 .60
587 A161 60o brown 1.40 1.40
588 A161 80o dull red 1.40 .45
589 A161 1.20k ultra 1.60 1.60
Nos. 586-589 (4) 5.00 4.05

1,100th anniversary of unification.

King Haakon VII (1872-1957) — A162

1972, Aug. 3 Engr. Perf. 13

590 A162 80o brown orange 2.75 .35
591 A162 1.20k Prussian bl 1.75 1.60

"Joy" — A163

Design: 1.20k, "Solidarity."

1972, Aug. 15 Photo. Perf. 13x13½

592 A163 80o brt magenta .75 .30
593 A163 1.20k Prussian blue 1.25 1.25

2nd Intl. Youth Stamp Exhib., INTERJUNEX 72, Kristiansand, Aug. 25-Sept. 3.

Nos. 592-593 Overprinted "INTERJUNEX 72"

1972, Aug. 25

594 A163 80o brt magenta 2.50 2.50
595 A163 1.20k Prussian blue 2.50 2.50

Opening of INTERJUNEX 72. Sold at exhibition only together with 3k entrance ticket.

"Fram." — A164

Polar Exploration Ships: 60o, "Maud." 1.20k, "Gjoa."

1972, Sept. 20 Perf. 13½x13

596 A164 60o olive & green 1.40 1.00
597 A164 80o red & black 2.50 .35
598 A164 1.20k blue & red brn 2.10 1.60
Nos. 596-598 (3) 6.00 2.95

"Little Man" — A165

Illustrations for folk tales by Theodor Kittelsen (1857-1914): 60o, The Troll who wondered how old he was. 80o, The princess riding the polar bear.

1972, Nov. 15 Litho. Perf. 13½x13

599 A165 50o green & blk .85 .25
600 A165 60o blue & blk 1.00 .75
601 A165 80o pink & blk .85 .25
Nos. 599-601 (3) 2.70 1.25

Dr. Armauer G. Hansen and Leprosy Bacillus Drawing — A166

Design: 1.40k, Dr. Hansen and leprosy bacillus, microscopic view.

1973, Feb. 28 Engr. Perf. 13x13½

602 A166 1k henna brn & bl .50 .25
603 A166 1.40k dk bl & dp org 1.25 1.25

Centenary of the discovery of the Hansen bacillus, the cause of leprosy.

Europa Issue
Common Design Type

1973, Apr. 30 Photo. Perf. 12½x13
Size: 37x20mm

604 CD16 1k red, org & lil *2.50 .30*
605 CD16 1.40k dk grn, grn & bl *1.50 1.50*

Types of 1893 and 1962-63

Designs: 75o, 85o, Rye and fish. 80o, 140o, Stave church. 100o, 110o, 120o, 125o, Rock carvings.

1972-75 Engr. Perf. 13x13½

606 A10 25o ultra ('74) .25 .25
Complete booklet, pane of 4 of #606 2.00
608 A101 75o green ('73) .30 .25
609 A102 80o red brown .40 .35
Complete booklet, pane of 10 of #609 50.00
610 A101 85o bister ('74) .30 .25
611 A101 100o red ('73) .75 .25
Complete booklet, pane of 10 of #611 40.00
612 A101 110o rose car ('74) .50 .25
613 A101 120o gray blue .60 .50
614 A101 125o red ('75) .75 .25
Complete booklet, pane of 10 of #614 17.50
615 A102 140o dk blue ('73) .60 .40
Nos. 606-615 (9) 4.45 2.75

Nordic Cooperation Issue

Nordic House, Reykjavik — A167

1973, June 26 Engr. Perf. 12½

617 A167 1k multi 1.00 .40
618 A167 1.40k multi 1.25 1.25

A century of postal cooperation among Denmark, Finland, Iceland, Norway and Sweden; Nordic Postal Conference, Reykjavik, Iceland.

King Olav V — A168

1973, July 2 Engr. Perf. 13

619 A168 1k car & org brn 1.25 .30
620 A168 1.40k blue & org brn 1.25 1.25

70th birthday of King Olav V.

Jacob Aall — A169

1973, Aug. 22 Engr. Perf. 13

621 A169 1k deep claret .60 .30
622 A169 1.40k dk blue gray 1.25 1.25

Jacob Aall (1773-1844), mill owner and industrial pioneer.

Blade Decoration — A170

Handicraft from Lapland: 1k, Textile pattern. 1.40k, Decoration made of tin.

1973, Oct. 9 Photo. Perf. 13x12½

623 A170 75o blk brn & buff .60 .50
624 A170 1k dp car & buff 1.00 .30
625 A170 1.40k blk & dl bl 1.25 1.25
Nos. 623-625 (3) 2.85 2.05

Viola Biflora — A171

70o, Veronica Fruticans. 1k, Phyllodoce corrulea.

1973, Nov. 15 Litho. Perf. 13

626 A171 65o shown .60 .50
627 A171 70o multicolored .60 .60
628 A171 1k multicolored .60 .30
Nos. 626-628 (3) 1.80 1.40

See Nos. 754-756, 770-771.

Surveyor in Northern Norway, 1907 — A172

1.40k, South Norway Mountains map, 1851.

1973, Dec. 14 Engr. Perf. 13

629 A172 1k red orange .60 .30
630 A172 1.40k slate blue 1.25 1.25

Geographical Survey of Norway, bicent.

Lindesnes — A173

Design: 1.40k, North Cape.

1974, Apr. 25 Photo. Perf. 13

631 A173 1k olive 1.00 .50
632 A173 1.40k dark blue 2.50 2.50

Ferry in Hardanger Fjord, by A. Tidemand and H. Gude — A174

Classical Norwegian paintings: 1.40k, Stugunoset from Filefjell, by Johan Christian Dahl.

1974, May 21 Litho. Perf. 13

633 A174 1k multi .65 .30
634 A174 1.40k multi 1.10 1.10

Gulating Law Manuscript, 1325 A175

King Magnus VI Lagaböter A176

1974, June 21 Engr.

635 A175 1k red & brn .65 .30
636 A176 1.40k ultra & brn 1.40 1.40

700th anniv. of the National Code given by King Magnus VI Lagaböter (1238-80).

Saw Blade and Pines — A177

Design: 1k, Cog wheel and guard.

1974, Aug. 12 Photo. Perf. 13

637 A177 85o grn, ol & dk grn 2.00 2.00
638 A177 1k org, plum & dk red 1.25 .40

Safe working conditions.

J.H.L. Vogt — A178

Geologists: 85o, V. M. Goldschmidt. 1k, Theodor Kjerulf. 1.40k, Waldemar C. Brogger.

1974, Sept. 4 Engr. Perf. 13

639 A178 65o olive & red brn .40 .30
640 A178 85o mag & red brn 1.75 1.75
641 A178 1k org & red brn .75 .25
642 A178 1.40k blue & red brn 1.25 1.25
Nos. 639-642 (4) 4.15 3.55

"Man's Work," Famous Buildings — A179

Design: 1.40k, "Men, our brethren," people of various races.

1974, Oct. 9 Photo. *Perf. 13*
643 A179 1k green & brn .65 .30
644 A179 1.40k brn & grnsh bl 1.25 1.25

Centenary of Universal Postal Union.

Horseback Rider A180

Flowers A181

1974, Nov. 15 Litho. *Perf. 13*
645 A180 85o multicolored .50 .50
646 A181 1k multicolored .50 .25

Norwegian folk art, rose paintings from furniture decorations.

Woman Skier, c. 1900 — A182

1975, Jan. 15 Litho. *Perf. 13*
647 A182 1k shown .75 .30
648 A182 1.40k Telemark turn 1.00 1.00

"Norway, homeland of skiing."

Women — A183

Design: Detail from wrought iron gates of Vigeland Park, Oslo.

1975, Mar. 7 Litho. *Perf. 13*
649 A183 1.25k brt rose lil & dk bl .65 .25
650 A183 1.40k bl & dk bl 1.00 1.00

International Women's Year.

Nusfjord Fishing Harbor — A184

1.25k, Street in Stavanger. 1.40k, View of Roros.

1975, Apr. 17 Litho. *Perf. 13*
651 A184 1k yellow green .95 .60
652 A184 1.25k dull red .65 .25
653 A184 1.40k blue 1.00 1.00
Nos. 651-653 (3) 2.60 1.85

European Architectural Heritage Year.

Norwegian Krone, 1875 — A185

Ole Jacob Broch — A186

1975, May 20 Engr. *Perf. 13*
654 A185 1.25k dark carmine .90 .25
655 A186 1.40k blue 1.00 1.00

Centenary of Monetary Convention of Norway, Sweden and Denmark (1.25k); and of Intl. Meter Convention, Paris, 1875. Ole Jacob Broch (1818-1889) was first director of Intl. Bureau of Weights and Measures.

Scouting in Summer — A187

Design: 1.40k, Scouting in winter (skiers).

1975, June 19 Litho. *Perf. 13*
656 A187 1.25k multicolored .90 .30
657 A187 1.40k multicolored 1.25 1.25

Nordjamb 75, 14th Boy Scout Jamboree, Lillehammer, July 29-Aug. 7.

Sod Hut and Settlers — A188

Cleng Peerson and Letter from America, 1874 — A189

1975, July 4 Engr.
658 A188 1.25k red brown .85 .25
659 A189 1.40k bluish blk 1.10 1.10

Sesquicentennial of Norwegian emigration to America.

Templet, Tempelfjord, Spitsbergen A190

Miners Leaving Coal Pit A191

Design: 1.40k, Polar bear.

1975, Aug. 14 Engr. *Perf. 13*
660 A190 1k olive black .90 .50
661 A191 1.25k maroon .90 .25
662 A191 1.40k Prus blue 1.90 1.90
Nos. 660-662 (3) 3.70 2.65

50th anniversary of union of Spitsbergen (Svalbard) with Norway.

Microphone with Ear Phones A192

Radio Tower and Houses A193

Designs after children's drawings.

1975, Oct. 9 Litho. *Perf. 13*
663 A192 1.25k multi .60 .25
664 A193 1.40k multi .80 .80

50 years of broadcasting in Norway.

Annunciation A194

Nativity A195

Painted vault of stave church of Al, 13th cent: 1k, Visitation. 1.40k, Adoration of the Kings.

1975, Nov. 14
665 A194 80o red & multi .40 .30
666 A194 1k red & multi .50 .50
667 A195 1.25k red & multi .60 .25
668 A195 1.40k red & multi .90 .80
Nos. 665-668 (4) 2.40 1.85

Sigurd and Regin — A196

1976, Jan. 20 Engr. *Perf. 13*
669 A196 7.50k brown 3.25 .25

Norwegian folk tale, Sigurd the Dragon-killer. Design from portal of Hylestad stave church, 13th century.

Halling, Hallingdal Dance — A197

Folk Dances: 1k, Springar, Hordaland region. 1.25k, Gangar, Setesdal.

1976, Feb. 25 Litho. *Perf. 13*
670 A197 80o black & multi .80 .50
671 A197 1k black & multi .80 .30
672 A197 1.25k black & multi .60 .25
Nos. 670-672 (3) 2.20 1.05

Silver Sugar Shaker, Stavanger, c. 1770 — A198

1.40k, Goblet, Nostetangen glass, c. 1770.

1976, Mar. 25 Engr. *Perf. 13*
673 A198 1.25k multicolored .60 .30
674 A198 1.40k multicolored .80 .80

Oslo Museum of Applied Art, centenary.

Ceramic Bowl Shaped Like Bishop's Mitre — A199

Europa: 1.40k, Plate and CEPT emblem. Both designs after faience works from Herrebo Potteries, c. 1760.

1976, May 3 Litho. *Perf. 13*
675 A199 1.25k rose mag & brn *.60 .40*
676 A199 1.40k brt bl & vio bl *.85 .85*

The Pulpit, Lyse Fjord A200

Gulleplet (Peak), Sogne Fjord A201

Perf. 13 on 3 Sides

1976, May 20 Litho.
677 A200 1k multi .60 .25
a. Booklet pane of 10 6.50
Complete booklet, #677a 7.50
678 A201 1.25k multi 1.00 .25
a. Booklet pane of 10 10.00
Complete booklet, #678a 12.00

Nos. 677-678 issued only in booklets.

Graph Paper, Old and New Subjects — A202

Design: 2k, Graph of national product.

1976, July 1 Engr. *Perf. 13*
679 A202 1.25k red brown .50 .25
680 A202 2k dark blue .90 .35

Central Bureau of Statistics, centenary.

Olav Duun on Dun Mountain — A203

1976, Sept. 10 Engr. *Perf. 13*
681 A203 1.25k multi .50 .25
682 A203 1.40k multi .80 .80

Olav Duun (1876-1939), novelist.

"Birches" by Th. Fearnley (1802-1842) A204

Design: 1.40k, "Gamle Furutraer" (trees), by L. Hertervig (1830-1902).

1976, Oct. 8 Litho. *Perf. 13*
683 A204 1.25k multi .55 .30
684 A204 1.40k multi 1.00 1.00

"April" A205

"May" A206

Baldishol Tapestry A207

80o, 1k, Details from 13th cent. Baldishol tapestry, found in Baldishol stave church.

1976, Nov. 5 Litho. *Perf. 13*
685 A205 80o multi .40 .30
686 A206 1k multi .50 .30
687 A207 1.25k multi .60 .25
Nos. 685-687 (3) 1.50 .85

Five Water Lilies — A208

Photo. & Engr.

1977, Feb. 2 *Perf. 12½*
688 A208 1.25k multi .75 .30
689 A208 1.40k multi .75 .75

Nordic countries cooperation for protection of the environment and 25th Session of Nordic Council, Helsinki, Feb. 19.

Akershus Castle, Oslo — A209

Steinviksholm Fort, Asen Fjord — A210

Torungen Lighthouses, Arendal — A211

1977, Feb. 24 Engr. *Perf. 13*
690 A209 1.25k red .50 .25
Complete booklet pane of 10 #690 6.00
Complete booklet pane of 8 #690 8.50
691 A210 1.30k olive brown .60 .25
692 A211 1.80k blue .75 .30
Nos. 690-692 (3) 1.85 .80

See Nos. 715-724, 772-774.

Europa Issue

Hamnoy, Lofoten, Fishing Village A212

Huldre Falls, Loen A213

Perf. 13 on 3 Sides

1977, May 2 **Litho.**

693 A212 1.25k multi 1.00 .25
a. Booklet pane of 10 10.00
Complete booklet, #693a 12.00
694 A213 1.80k multi .75 .75
a. Booklet pane of 10 8.00
Complete booklet, #694a 9.00

Nos. 693-694 issued only in booklets.

Norwegian Trees — A214

1977, June 1 **Engr.** ***Perf. 13***

695 A214 1k Spruce .50 .30
696 A214 1.25k Fir .75 .30
697 A214 1.80k Birch .90 .90
Nos. 695-697 (3) 2.15 1.50

"Constitutionen," Norway's 1st Steamship, at Arendal — A215

Designs: 1.25k, "Vesteraalen" off Bodo, 1893. 1.30k, "Kong Haakon," 1904 and "Dronningen," 1893, off Stavanger. 1.80k, "Nordstjernen" and "Harald Jarl" at pier, 1970.

1977, June 22

698 A215 1k brown .50 .25
699 A215 1.25k red .80 .25
700 A215 1.30k green 1.50 1.50
701 A215 1.80k blue 1.00 .90
Nos. 698-701 (4) 3.80 2.90

Norwegian ships serving coastal routes.

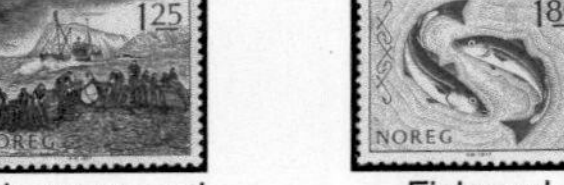

Fishermen and Boats A216

Fish and Fishhooks A217

1977, Sept. 22 **Engr.** ***Perf. 13***

702 A216 1.25k buff, lt brn & dk brn .80 .25
703 A217 1.80k lt bl, bl & dk bl .90 .90

Men, by Halfdan Egedius — A218

Landscape, by August Cappelen — A219

1977, Oct. 7 **Litho.** ***Perf. 13***

704 A218 1.25k multi .45 .25
705 A219 1.80k multi 1.00 1.00

Norwegian classical painting.

David with the Bells — A220

Christmas: 1k, Singing Friars. 1.25k, Virgin and Child, horiz. Designs from Bible of Bishop Aslak Bolt, 13th century.

1977, Nov. 10 **Litho.** ***Perf. 13***

Size: 21x27mm

706 A220 80o multi .40 .30
707 A220 1k multi .50 .25

Size: 34x27mm

708 A220 1.25k multi .50 .25
Nos. 706-708 (3) 1.40 .80

Post Horn Type of 1893 and Scenic Types of 1977

Designs: 1k, Austrat Manor, 1650. 1.10k, Trondenes Chruch, early 13th Cent. 1.40k, Ruins of Hamar Cathedral, 12th Cent. 1.75k, Seamen's Hall, Stavern, 1926, vert. 2k, Tofte Estate, Dovre, 16-17th cent., vert. 2.25k, Oscarhall, Oslofijord, 1847, vert. 2.50k, Log house, Breiland, 1785. 2.75k, Damsgard Building, Lakesvag, 1770. 3k, Selje Monastery, 11th cent. 3.50k, Lighthouse, Lindesnes, 1655.

Perf. 13x13½, 13½x13

1978-83 **Engr.**

709 A10 40o olive .25 .25
710 A10 50o dull purple .25 .25
711 A10 60o vermilion .25 .25
712 A10 70o orange .40 .30
713 A10 80o red brown .40 .35
714 A10 90o brown .40 .40
715 A209 1k green .40 .25
Complete booklet, pane of 4 ea #416, 419, 715 12.00
716 A209 1.10k rose mag .50 .25
717 A209 1.40k dark purple .60 .25
718 A211 1.75k green ('82) .60 .25
719 A211 2k brown red ('82) .60 .25
720 A211 2.25k dp vio ('82) .80 .35
721 A209 2.50k brn red ('83) .80 .25
722 A209 2.75k dp mag ('82) 1.25 1.00
723 A209 3k dk bl ('82) .80 .25
724 A209 3.50k dp vio ('83) 1.25 .30
Nos. 709-724 (16) 9.55 5.20

See Nos. 772-774.

Peer Gynt, and Reindeer by Per Krogh A222

Henrik Ibsen, by Erik Werenskiold, 1895 A223

1978, Mar. 10 **Litho.** ***Perf. 13***

725 A222 1.25k buff & blk .50 .25
726 A223 1.80k multicolored 1.00 .90

Ibsen (1828-1906), poet and dramatist.

Heddal Stave Church, c. 1250 — A224

Europa: 1.80k, Borgund stave church.

1978, May 2 **Engr.** ***Perf. 13***

727 A224 1.25k redsh brn & org 1.00 .25
728 A224 1.80k sl grn & bl 1.25 1.25

Lenangstindene and Jaegervasstindene A225

1.25k, Gaustatoppen, mountain, Telemark.

Perf. 13 on 3 Sides

1978, June 1 **Litho.**

729 A225 1k multi .60 .25
a. Booklet pane of 10 6.50
Complete booklet, #729a 8.00
730 A225 1.25k multi .90 .25
a. Booklet pane of 10 9.00
Complete booklet, #730a 10.00

Nos. 729-730 issued only in booklets.

Olav V Sailing — A226

Design: 1.80k, King Olav delivering royal address in Parliament, vert.

1978, June 30 **Engr.** ***Perf. 13***

731 A226 1.25k red brown .80 .25
732 A226 1.80k violet blue 1.00 .70

75th birthday of King Olav V.

Norway No. 107 — A227

Stamps: b, #108. c, #109. d, #110. e, #111. f, #112. g, #113. h, #114.

Perf. 13 on 3 Sides

1978, Sept. 19 **Litho.**

733 Booklet pane of 8 8.00 8.00
a.-h. A227 1.25k, any single 1.00 1.00
Complete booklet, #733 8.00

NORWEX '80 Philatelic Exhibition, Oslo, June 13-22, 1980. Booklet sold for 15k; the additional 5k went for financing the exhibition.

Willow Pipe Player — A228

Musical Instruments: 1.25k, Norwegian violin. 1.80k, Norwegian zither. 7.50k, Ram's horn.

1978, Oct. 6 **Engr.** ***Perf. 13***

734 A228 1k deep green .35 .25
735 A228 1.25k dk rose car .55 .25
736 A228 1.80k dk violet blue .90 .75
737 A228 7.50k gray 4.00 .25
Nos. 734-737 (4) 5.80 1.50

Wooden Doll, 1830 — A229

Christmas: 1k, Toy town 1896-97. 1.25k, Wooden horse from Torpo in Hallingdal.

1978, Nov. 10 **Litho.**

738 A229 80o multi .40 .25
739 A229 1k multi .50 .25
740 A229 1.25k multi .50 .25
Nos. 738-740 (3) 1.40 .75

Ski Jump, Huseby Hill, c. 1900 — A230

1.25k, Crown Prince Olav, Holmenkollen ski jump competition, 1922. 1.80k, Cross-country race, Holmenkollen, 1976.

1979, Mar. 2 **Engr.** ***Perf. 13***

741 A230 1k green .60 .35
742 A230 1.25k red .60 .25
743 A230 1.80k blue 1.00 .90
Nos. 741-743 (3) 2.20 1.50

Huseby Hills and Holmenkollen ski competitions, centenary.

Girl, by Mathias Stoltenberg — A231

1.80k, Boy, by H. C. F. Hosenfelder.

1979, Apr. 26 **Litho.** ***Perf. 13***

744 A231 1.25k multi .50 .25
745 A231 1.80k multi .80 .80

International Year of the Child.

Road to Briksdal Glacier — A232

1.25k, Boat on Skjernoysund, near Mandal.

1979, June 13 ***Perf. 13 on 3 Sides***

746 A232 1k multi .60 .25
a. Booklet pane of 10 6.00
Complete booklet, #746a 7.00
747 A232 1.25k multi .75 .25
a. Booklet pane of 10 7.50
Complete booklet, #747a 9.00

Nos. 746-747 issued only in booklets.

Johan Falkberget, by Harald Dal — A233

1.80k, "Ann-Magritt and the Hovi Bullock" (by Falkberget), monument by Kristofer Leirdal.

1979, Sept. 4 **Engr.** ***Perf. 13***

748 A233 1.25k deep claret .50 .25
749 A233 1.80k Prus blue .90 .90

Johan Falkberget (1879-1967), novelist.

Kylling Bridge, Verma, 1923 — A234

Norwegian Engineering: 2k, Vessingsjo Dam, Nea, 1960. 10k, Stratfjord A, oil drilling platform in North Sea.

1979, Oct. 5

750 A234 1.25k black & brown .50 .25
751 A234 2k dk blue & blue .80 .25
752 A234 10k brown & bister 4.00 .45
Nos. 750-752 (3) 5.30 .95

Souvenir Sheet

Dornier Wal over Polar Map — A235

Arctic Aviation and Polar Maps: 2k, Dirigible Norge. 2.80k, Loening air yacht amphibian. 4k, Reidar Viking DC-7C.

1979, Oct. 5 **Litho.** ***Perf. 13***

753 Sheet of 4 5.50 5.00
a. A235 1.25k multi 1.25 1.25
b. A235 2k multi 1.25 1.25
c. A235 2.80k multi 1.25 1.25
d. A235 4k multi 1.25 1.25

Norwex '80 Intl. Phil. Exhib., Oslo, June 13-22, 1980. No. 753 sold for 15k.

Mountain Flower Type of 1973

80o, Ranunculus glacialis. 1k, Potentilla crantzii. 1.25k, Saxiflora oppositifolia.

1979, Nov. 22 **Litho.** ***Perf. 13½***

754 A171 80o multicolored .40 .25
755 A171 1k multicolored .40 .25
756 A171 1.25k multicolored .50 .25
Nos. 754-756 (3) 1.30 .75

Norwegian Christian Youth Assn. Centenary A237

180o, Emblems and doves.

1980, Feb. 26 **Litho.** ***Perf. 13***

757 A237 100o shown .50 .25
758 A237 180o multicolored .80 .80

Oyster Catcher — A238

Perf. 13 on 3 Sides

1980, Apr. 18 **Litho.**

759 A238 100o shown .35 .25
760 A238 100o Mallard .35 .25
a. Bklt. pane, 5 #759, 5 #760 4.00
Complete booklet, #760a 5.00
761 A238 125o Dipper .55 .25
762 A238 125o Great tit .55 .25
a. Bklt. pane, 5 #761, 5 #762 5.50
Complete booklet, #762a 6.00
Nos. 759-762 (4) 1.80 1.00

Nos. 759-762 issued in booklets only.
See Nos. 775-778, 800-801, 821-822.

Dish Antenna, Old Phone — A239

National Telephone Service Centenary: 1.80k, Erecting telephone pole.

1980, May 9 Litho. Perf. 13½

763	A239 1.25k multi	.50	.25
764	A239 1.80k multi	.80	.80

Souvenir Sheet

NORWEX '80 Stamp Exhibition — A240

1980, June 13

765	A240 Sheet of 4	5.00	5.00
a.	1.25k Paddle Steamer "Bergen"	1.25	1.25
b.	2k Train, 1900	1.25	1.25
c.	2.80k Bus, 1940	1.25	1.25
d.	4k Boeing 737	1.25	1.25

NORWEX '80 Stamp Exhibition, Oslo, June 13-22. Sold for 15k.

Nordic Cooperation Issue

Vulcan as an Armourer, by Henrich Bech, 1761 — A241

Henrich Bech Cast Iron Stove Ornament: 1.80k, Hercules at a Burning Altar, 1769.

1980, Sept. 9 Engr. Perf. 13

766	A241 1.25k dk vio brn	.50	.25
767	A241 1.80k dark blue	.80	.80

Self-Portrait, by Christian Skredsvig (1854-1924) A242

Paintings: 1.25k, Fire, by Nikolai Astrup.

1980, Nov. 14 Litho. Perf. 13½x13

768	A242 1.25k multi	.50	.25
769	A242 1.80k multi	1.00	.80

Mountain Flower Type of 1973

1980, Nov. 14 Perf. 13

770	A171 80o Sorbus aucuparia	.40	.25
771	A171 1k Rosa canina	.40	.25

Scenic Type of 1977

1.50k, Stavanger Cathedral, 13th cent. 1.70k, Rosenkrantz Tower, Bergen, 13th-16th cent. 2.20k, Church of Tromsdalen (Arctic Cathedral), 1965.

Perf. 13x13½, 13½x13

1981, Feb. 26 Engr.

772	A211 1.50k brown red	.60	.25
773	A211 1.70k olive green	.80	.60
774	A209 2.20k dark blue	1.00	.60
	Nos. 772-774 (3)	2.40	1.45

Bird Type of 1980

Perf. 13 on 3 Sides

1981, Feb. 26 Litho.

775	A238 1.30k Anser erythropus	.50	.50
776	A238 1.30k Peregrine falcon	.50	.50
a.	Booklet pane of 10 (5 each)	5.50	
	Complete booklet, #776a	6.50	
777	A238 1.50k Black guillemot	.65	.25
778	A238 1.50k Puffin	.65	.25
a.	Booklet pane of 10 (5 each)	6.50	
	Complete booklet, #778a	7.50	
	Nos. 775-778 (4)	2.30	1.50

Nos. 775-778 issued in booklets. See Nos. 800-801, 821-822.

Nat'l Milk Producers Assn. Centenary — A244

1981, Mar. 24 Litho. Perf. 13x13½

779	A244 1.10k Cow	.50	.35
780	A244 1.50k Goat	.60	.25

A245

Europa: 1.50k, The Mermaid, painted dish, Hol. 2.20k, The Proposal, painted box, Nes.

1981, May 4 Litho. Perf. 13

781	A245 1.50k multi	.75	.25
782	A245 2.20k multi	1.00	.75

A246

Designs: 1.30k, Weighing anchor. 1.50k, Climbing rigging, vert. 2.20k, Training Ship Christian Radich.

1981, May 4 Engr.

783	A246 1.30k dk olive grn	.60	.35
784	A246 1.50k orange red	.60	.25
785	A246 2.20k dark blue	1.00	.75
	Nos. 783-785 (3)	2.20	1.35

Paddle Steamer Skibladner, 1856, Mjosa Lake — A247

Lake Transportation: 1.30k, Victoria, 1882, Bandak Channel. 1.50k, Faemund II, 1905, Fermund Lake. 2.30k, Storegut, 1956, Tinnsjo Lake.

1981, June 11 Engr. Perf. 13

786	A247 1.10k dark brown	.60	.25
787	A247 1.30k green	.75	.50
788	A247 1.50k red	.75	.25
789	A247 2.30k dark blue	1.00	.50
	Nos. 786-789 (4)	3.10	1.50

Group Walking Arm in Arm — A248

1981, Aug. 25 Engr.

790	A248 1.50k shown	.60	.25
791	A248 2.20k Group, diff.	.90	.90

Intl. Year of the Disabled.

Paintings — A249

1.50k, Interior in Blue, by Harriet Backer (1845-1932). 1.70k, Peat Moor on Jaeren, by Kitty Lange Kielland (1843-1914).

1981, Oct. 9 Litho. Perf. 13

792	A249 1.50k multi	.60	.25
793	A249 1.70k multi	.75	.75

Tapestries — A250

1.10k, One of the Three Kings, Skjak, 1625. 1.30k, Adoration of the Infant Christ, tapestry, Skjak, 1625. 1.50k, The Marriage in Cana, Storen, 18th cent.

1981, Nov. 25 Litho. Perf. 13½

794	A250 1.10k multi	.40	.25
795	A250 1.30k multi	.50	.35

Size: 29x37mm

796	A250 1.50k multi	.55	.25
	Nos. 794-796 (3)	1.45	.85

1921 Nobel Prize Winners — A251

5k, Christian L. Lange (1869-1938) and Hjalmar Branting (1860-1925).

1981, Nov. 25 Engr. Perf. 13

797	A251 5k black	2.25	.25

World Skiing Championship, Oslo — A252

1982, Feb. 16 Perf. 13½

798	A252 2k Poles	.65	.25
799	A252 3k Skis	.90	.50

Bird Type of 1980

Perf. 13 on 3 Sides

1982, Apr. 1 Litho.

Booklet Stamps

800	A238 2k Blue-throat	.75	.25
801	A238 2k Robin	.75	.25
a.	Bklt. pane, 5 each #800-801	7.50	
	Complete booklet, #801a	8.50	

Fight Against Tuberculosis — A253

1982, Apr. 1 Perf. 13

802	A253 2k Nurse	.50	.25
803	A253 3k Microscope	.90	.85

Mouth Harp — A254

1982, May 3 Engr. Perf. 13

804	A254 15k sepia	6.00	.35

Europa 1982 — A255

2k, Haakon VII, 1905. 3k, Prince Olav, King Haakon VII, 1945.

1982, May 3

805	A255 2k brown red	1.75	.25
806	A255 3k indigo	1.50	.60

Girls from Telemark, by Erik Werenskiold (1855-1938) A256

Design: 2k, Tone Veli at the Fence, by Henrik Sorensen (1882-1962), vert.

1982, June 23 Litho. Perf. 13

807	A256 1.75k multi	.60	.50
808	A256 2k multi	.60	.25

Consecration Ceremony, Nidaros Cathedral, Trondheim — A257

1982, Sept. 2 Engr. Perf. 13x13½

809	A257 3k blue	1.75	1.00

Reign of King Olav, 25th anniv.

Sigrid Undset (1882-1949), Writer, by A.C. Svarstad — A258

Painting: 1.75k, Bjornstjerne Bjornson (1832-1910), writer, by Erik Werenskiold, horiz.

1982, Oct. 1 Litho. Perf. 13

810	A258 1.75k multi	.75	.35
811	A258 2k multi	.75	.25

A souvenir sheet containing Nos. 810-811 was prepared by the Norwegian Philatelic Association.

Graphical Union of Norway Centenary — A259

1982, Oct. 1

812	A259 2k "A"	.65	.25
813	A259 3k Type	1.00	.60

Fridtjof Nansen — A260

1982, Nov. 15 Engr. Perf. 13½x13

814	A260 3k dark blue	1.50	.60

Fridtjof Nansen (1861-1930) polar explorer, 1922 Nobel Peace Prize winner.

Christmas — A261

Painting: Christmas Tradition, by Adolf Tidemand (1814-1876).

Perf. 13 on 3 Sides

1982, Nov. 15 Litho.

815	A261 1.75k multi	.50	.25
a.	Booklet pane of 10	6.00	
	Complete booklet, #815a	6.75	

Farm Dog — A262

1983, Feb. 16 Litho. Perf. 13x13½

816	A262 2k shown	1.00	.50
817	A262 2.50k Elk hound	1.25	.25
818	A262 3.50k Hunting dog	.75	1.00
	Nos. 816-818 (3)	3.00	1.75

Nordic Cooperation Issue — A263

1983, Mar. 24 Litho. *Perf. 13*

819 A263 2.50k Mountains .90 .25
820 A263 3.50k Fjord 1.25 .80

Bird Type of 1980

1983, Apr. 14 *Perf. 13 on 3 Sides*

821 A238 2.50k Goose 1.10 .25
822 A238 2.50k Little auk 1.10 .25
a. Bklt. pane, 5 each #821-822 11.00
Complete booklet, #822a 12.00

Nos. 821-822 issued only in booklets.

Europa — A264

Designs: 2.50k, Edvard Grieg (1843-1907), composer and his Piano Concerto in A-minor. 3.50k, Niels Henrik Abel (1802-1829), mathematician, by Gustav Vigeland, vert.

1983, May 3 Engr. *Perf. 13*

823 A264 2.50k red orange 1.75 .25
824 A264 3.50k dk bl & grn 1.75 .75

World Communications Year — A265

Symbolic arrow designs.

1983, May 3 Litho.

825 A265 2.50k multi .90 .25
826 A265 3.50k multi 1.25 .75

80th Birthday of King Olav V, July 2 — A266

1983, June 22 Engr. *Perf. 13x13½*

827 A266 5k green 2.50 .40

Jonas Lie (1833-1908), Writer — A267

1983, Oct. 7 Engr. *Perf. 13½x13*

828 A267 2.50k red 1.00 .25

Northern Ships — A268

1983, Oct. 7 Litho.

829 A268 2k Nordlandsfemboring 1.00 .50
830 A268 3k Nordlandsjekt 1.50 .75

Christmas 1983 — A269

Paintings: 2k, The Sleigh Ride by Axel Ender (1853-1920). 2.50k, The Guests are Arriving by Gustav Wenzel (1859-1927).

Perf. 13 on 3 sides

1983, Nov. 17 Litho.

831 A269 2k multi 1.00 .25
a. Booklet pane of 10 10.00
Complete booklet, #831a 11.00
832 A269 2.50k multi 1.00 .25
a. Booklet pane of 10 10.00
Complete booklet, #832a 11.00

Postal Services — A270

1984, Feb. 24 Litho. *Perf. 13½x13*

833 A270 2k Counter service 1.00 .40
834 A270 2.50k Sorting 1.10 .25
835 A270 3.50k Delivery 1.50 .60
Nos. 833-835 (3) 3.60 1.25

Freshwater Fishing — A271

1984, Apr. 10 Engr. *Perf. 13*

836 A271 2.50k shown 1.00 .25
837 A271 3k Salmon fishing 1.00 .50
838 A271 3.50k Ocean fishing 1.50 .50
Nos. 836-838 (3) 3.50 1.25

Christopher Hansteen (1784-1873), Astronomer — A272

3.50k, Magnetic meridians, parallels, horiz.

1984, Apr. 10

839 A272 3.50k multicolored 1.40 .50
840 A272 5k multicolored 2.00 .40

Europa (1959-84) — A273

1984, June 4 Litho. *Perf. 13*

841 A273 2.50k multi 1.50 .25
842 A273 3.50k multi 1.60 .80

Produce, Spices — A274

1984, June 4 *Perf. 13*

843 A274 2k shown .80 .40
844 A274 2.50k Flowers .90 .25

Horticultural Society centenary.

A275

1984, June 4

845 A275 2.50k Worker bees .85 .25
846 A275 2.50k Rooster .85 .25

Centenaries: Beekeeping Society (No. 845); Poultry-breeding Society (No. 846).

A276

1984, Oct. 5 Engr. *Perf. 13*

847 A276 2.50k lake 1.10 .25

Ludvig Holberg (1684-1754), writer, by J.M. Bernigeroth.

A277

1984, Oct. 5 Litho. & Engr.

848 A277 2.50k Children reading .75 .25
849 A277 3.50k First edition 1.00 .50

Norwegian Weekly Press sesquicentennial.

A278

Illustrations from Children's Stories by Thorbjorn Egner: No. 850, Karius & Baktus. No. 851, Tree Shrew. No. 852, Cardamom Rovers. No. 853, Chief Constable Bastian.

Perf. 13½x13 on 3 sides

1984, Nov. 15 Litho.

Booklet Stamps

850 A278 2k multi 1.75 .50
851 A278 2k multi 1.75 .50
a. Bklt. pane, 5 each #850-851 17.50
Complete booklet, #851a 24.00
852 A278 2.50k multi 1.75 .25
853 A278 2.50k multi 1.75 .25
a. Bklt. pane, 5 each #852-853 22.50
Complete booklet, #853a 25.00
Nos. 850-853 (4) 7.00 1.50

Parliament Centenary A279

7.50k, Sverdrup Govt. parliament, 1884.

1984, Nov. 15 Engr. *Perf. 13½x13*

854 A279 7.50k multicolored 4.00 1.00

Antarctic Mountains — A280

2.50k, The Saw Blade. 3.50k, The Chopping Block.

1985, Apr. 18 Litho. *Perf. 13*

855 A280 2.50k multi 1.50 .25
856 A280 3.50k multi 2.00 .80

Liberation from the German Occupation Forces, 40th Anniv. — A281

1985, May 8 Engr. *Perf. 13x13½*

857 A281 3.50k dk bl & red 1.75 .60

Norwegian Artillery — A282

Anniv.: 3k, Norwegian Artillery, 300th. 4k, Artillery Officers Training School, 200th.

1985, May 22 Litho. *Perf. 13½x13*

858 A282 3k multi 1.50 .80
859 A282 4k multi 2.00 .50

Kongsten Fort, 300th Anniv. — A283

1985, May 22

860 A283 2.50k multi 1.50 .25

Europa — A284

Designs: 2.50k, Torgeir Augundsson (1801-1872), fiddler. 3.50k, Ole Bull (1810-1880), composer, violinist.

1985, June 19 Engr.

861 A284 2.50k brown lake 1.75 .25
862 A284 3.50k dark blue 2.00 .60

Intl. Youth Year — A285

Stone and bronze sculptures: 2k, Boy and Girl, detail, Vigeland Museum, Oslo. 3.50k, Fountain, detail, Vigeland Park, Oslo.

1985, June 19 Litho.

863 A285 2k multi 1.00 .40
864 A285 3.50k multi 1.60 .90

Electrification of Norway, Cent. — A286

2.50k, Glomfjord Dam penstock. 4k, Linemen.

1985, Sept. 6 Engr. *Perf. 13½x13*

865 A286 2.50k dp car & scar 1.00 .25
866 A286 4k ultra & bl grn 1.75 .40

Public Libraries, 200th Anniv. — A287

Designs; 2.50k, Carl Deichman (1705-1780), Public Libraries System founder. 10k, Modern library interior, horiz.

1985, Oct. 4

867 A287 2.50k hn brn & yel brn 1.25 .25
868 A287 10k dark green 5.00 .60

Ship Navigation — A288

2.50k, Dredger Berghavn, 1980. 5k, Sextant and chart, 1791.

Lithographed & Engraved

1985, Nov. 14 *Perf. 13x13½*

869 A288 2.50k multicolored 1.00 .25
870 A288 5k multicolored 2.50 .50

Port Authorities, 250th anniv., Hydrographic Services, bicent.

Christmas Wreath A289

Bullfinches A290

Booklet Stamps

Perf. 13½ on 3 Sides

1985, Nov. 14 Litho.

871 A289 2k multi 2.00 .25
a. Booklet pane of 10 20.00
Complete booklet, #871a 22.50
872 A290 2.50k multi 2.00 .25
a. Booklet pane of 10 20.00
Complete booklet, #872a 22.50

World Biathlon Championships, Feb. 18-23 — A290a

3.50k, Shooting upright.

1986, Feb. 18 *Perf. 13x13½*

873 A290a 2.50k shown 1.00 .25
874 A291 3.50k multicolored 1.50 1.00

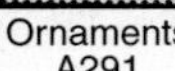
Ornaments
A291

Fauna
A292

Litho. & Engr.

1986-90 *Perf. 13½x13*

875 A291 2.10k Sun 1.00 .25
876 A291 2.30k Fish 1.00 .25
877 A292 2.60k Fox 1.10 .25
878 A291 2.70k Flowers, wheat 1.25 .25
879 A292 2.90k Capercaillie 1.50 .25
880 A292 3k Ermine 1.40 .25
881 A292 3.20k Mute swan 1.40 .25
882 A292 3.80k Reindeer 2.00 .25
883 A291 4k Stars 1.50 .30
883A A292 4k Squirrel 1.75 .25
883B A292 4.50k Beaver 1.75 .25
Nos. 875-883B (11) 15.65 2.80

Issued: 2.10k, #883, 2/18/86; 2.30k, 2.70k, 2/12/87; 2.90k, 3.80k, 2/18/88; 2.60k, 3k, #883A, 2/20/89; 3.20k, 4.50k, 2/23/90.

See Nos. 958-959.

Mushrooms — A293

No. 884, Cantharellus tubaeformis. No. 885, Rozites caperata. No. 886, Lepista nuda. No. 887, Lactarius deterrimus. No. 888, Cantharellus cibarius. No. 889, Suillus luteus.

Booklet Stamps

Perf. 13½x13 on 3 Sides

1987-89 **Litho.**

884 A293 2.70k multi 1.25 .25
885 A293 2.70k multi 1.25 .25
a. Bklt. pane, 5 #884, 5 #885 12.50
Complete booklet, #885a 15.00
886 A293 2.90k multi 1.25 .25
887 A293 2.90k multi 1.25 .25
a. Bklt. pane, 5 #886, 5 #887 12.50
Complete booklet, #887a 15.00
888 A293 3k multi 1.25 .25
889 A293 3k multi 1.25 .25
a. Bklt. pane, 5 #888, 5 #889 12.50
Complete booklet, #889a 16.00
Nos. 884-889 (6) 7.50 1.50

Issued: 2.70k, 5/8; 2.90k, 4/26/88; 3k, 2/20/89.

Natl. Federation of Craftsmen, Cent. — A294

1986, Apr. 11 **Engr.**

890 A294 2.50k Stone cutter 1.00 .25
891 A294 7k Carpenter 3.50 .80

Europa — A295

1986, Apr. 11 **Litho.** *Perf. 13*

892 A295 2.50k Bird, industry 1.25 .40
893 A295 3.50k Acid rain 1.75 1.25

Nordic Cooperation Issue — A296

Sister towns.

1986, May 27 *Perf. 13½x13*

894 A296 2.50k Moss 1.25 .25
895 A296 4k Alesund 1.75 .50

Famous Men — A297

Designs: 2.10k, Hans Poulson Egede (1686-1758), missionary, and map of Norway and Greenland. 2.50k, Herman Wildenvey (1886-1959), poet, and poem carved in Seaman's Commemoration Hall, Stavern. 3k, Tore Orjasaeter (1886-1968), poet, and antique cupboard, Skjak. 4k, Engebret Soot, engineer, and canal lock, Orje.

Engr., Litho. & Engr. (#897)

1986, Oct. 17 *Perf. 13x13½*

896 A297 2.10k multi .90 .90
897 A297 2.50k multi 1.00 .25
898 A297 3k multi 1.25 .50
899 A297 4k multi 1.50 .50
Nos. 896-899 (4) 4.65 2.15

Christmas — A298

Stained glass windows by Gabriel Kielland, Nidaros Cathedral, Trondheim: 2.10k, Olav Kyrre Founding The Diocese in Nidaros. 2.50k, The King and the Peasant at Sul.

Perf. 13½ on 3 Sides

1986, Nov. 26 **Litho.**

Booklet Stamps

900 A298 2.10k multi 1.50 .40
a. Booklet pane of 10 17.50
Complete booklet, #900a 20.00
901 A298 2.50k multi 1.50 .25
a. Booklet pane of 10 17.50
Complete booklet, #901a 20.00

Intl. Peace Year — A299

Lithographed & Engraved

1986, Nov. 26 *Perf. 13½x13*

902 A299 15k brt grn, org & lt bl 8.00 .75

A300

1987, Feb. 12 **Litho.** *Perf. 13½*

903 A300 3.50k red, yel & dk bl 1.75 .80
904 A300 4.50k bl, yel & grn 2.00 .50

Europa — A301

Modern architecture: 2.70k, Wood. 4.50k, Glass and stone.

1987, Apr. 3 **Litho.** *Perf. 13½x13*

905 A301 2.70k multi 1.25 .25
906 A301 4.50k multi 2.50 .75

A302

1987, Apr. 3 **Engr.** *Perf. 13x13½*

907 A302 12k dark green 6.00 .55

Odelsting (Norwegian Assembly) voting on Law Administering Local Councils, 150th anniv.

Miniature Sheet

Red Crescent-Red Cross Rehabilitation Center, Mogadishu, Somalia — A303

1987, May 8 **Litho.** *Perf. 13½x13*

908 A303 4.50k multi 2.50 2.00

See Somalia Nos. 576-577.

Sandvig Collection, Maihaugen Open-air Museum — A305

2.70k, Bjornstad Farm, Vaga. 3.50k, Horse and Rider, by Christen E. Listad.

1987, June 10 **Engr.** *Perf. 13x13½*

911 A305 2.70k multi .90 .25
912 A305 3.50k multi 1.60 .80

Churchyard, Inspiration for Valen's Churchyard by the Sea
A306

Fartein Valen (1887-1952), Composer
A306a

Perf. 13x13½, 13½x13

1987, Aug. 25 **Engr.**

913 A306 2.30k emer grn & dark blue .90 .90
914 A306a 4.50k dark brown 1.75 .40

Tempest at Sea, by Christian Krogh (1852-1925)
A307

Painting: 5k, The Farm, by Gerhard Munthe (1849-1929).

1987, Oct. 9 **Litho.** *Perf. 13½x13*

915 A307 2.70k multi 1.25 .25
916 A307 5k multi 2.50 .50

Norwegian Horse Breeds — A308

Litho. & Engr.

1987, Nov. 12 *Perf. 13x13½*

917 A308 2.30k Dales 1.25 1.00
918 A308 2.70k Fjord 1.25 .25
919 A308 4.50k Nordland 2.10 .60
Nos. 917-919 (3) 4.60 1.85

Christmas — A309

2.30k, Children making tree ornaments. 2.70k, Baking gingersnaps.

Booklet Stamps

Perf. 13½x13 on 3 sides

1987, Nov. 12 **Litho.**

920 A309 2.30k multi 1.40 .40
a. Booklet pane of 10 14.00
Complete booklet, #920a 16.00
921 A309 2.70k multi 1.25 .25
a. Booklet pane of 10 12.50
Complete booklet, #921a 16.00

Salvation Army in Norway, Cent. — A310

4.80k, Othilie Tonning, early Salvation Army worker in Norway.

1988, Feb. 18 *Perf. 13½*

922 A310 2.90k multi 1.25 .25
923 A310 4.80k multi 2.25 .90

European North-South Solidarity Campaign
A311

1988, Apr. 26 *Perf. 13x13½*

924 A311 25k multi 10.00 1.00

Defense Forces Activities — A312

Defense Forces, 300th anniv.: 2.50k, Fortress construction. 2.90k, Army Signal Corps on duty. 4.60k, Pontoon bridge under construction, Corps of Engineers.

1988, Apr. 26 **Engr.**

925 A312 2.50k dark green 1.00 .40
926 A312 2.90k carmine lake 1.25 .25
927 A312 4.60k dark blue 2.00 .60
Nos. 925-927 (3) 4.25 1.25

Europa — A313

Transport: 2.90k, *Prinds Gustav* passing Lofoten Isls., 1st passenger steamer in northern Norway, sesquicent. 3.80k, Heroybrua Bridge, between Leinoy and Blankholm, 1976.

Litho. & Engr.

1988, July 1 *Perf. 13x13½*

928 A313 2.90k multi 2.00 .25
929 A313 3.80k multi 2.25 1.50

85th Birthday of King Olav V -- A314

Designs: No. 930, Portrait, c. 1988. No. 931a, Arrival in 1905 after Norway declared independence from Sweden. No. 931b, Olav in snowstorm at Holmenkollen.

1988, July 1 **Litho.** *Perf. 13½x13*

930 A314 2.90k multi 1.50 1.00

Souvenir Sheet

931 Sheet of 3 5.00 5.00
a. A314 2.90k org red, black & ultra 1.50 1.50
b. A314 2.90k multi 1.25 .25
c. A314 2.90k like No. 930, no date 1.50 1.50

Reign of King Christian IV (1577-1648), 400th Anniv. — A315

Designs: 10k, Reverse of a rixdaler struck in Christiania (Oslo), 1628, and excerpt of a mining decree issued by Christian IV.

Litho. & Engr.

1988, Oct. 7 *Perf. 13½x13*

932 A315 2.50k black & buff 1.50 .25
933 A315 10k multi 5.00 .50

Miniature Sheet

Handball — A316

Ball sports: b, Soccer. c, Basketball. d, Volleyball.

1988, Oct. 7 Litho. *Perf. 13½x13*
934 Sheet of 4 10.00 10.00
a.-d. A316 2.90k any single 2.00 2.00

Stamp Day. No. 934 sold for 15k.

Christmas — A317

Ludvig, a cartoon character created by Kjell Aukrust: No. 935, With ski pole. No. 936, Reading letter.

Perf. 13½x13 on 3 sides
1988, Nov. 15 Litho.
Booklet Stamps
935 A317 2.90k multi 1.50 .25
936 A317 2.90k multi 1.50 .25
a. Bklt. pane, 5 #935, 5 #936 15.00
Complete booklet, #936a 17.00

World Cross-Country Running Championships, Stavanger, Mar. 19 — A318

1989, Feb. 20 Litho. *Perf. 13x13½*
937 A318 5k multi 2.00 .30

Port City Bicentennials — A319

Litho. & Engr.
1989, Apr. 20 *Perf. 13½x13*
938 A319 3k Vardo 1.25 .25
939 A319 4k Hammerfest 2.00 .80

Nordic Cooperation Issue — A320

Folk costumes.

1989, Apr. 20 Litho. *Perf. 13x13½*
940 A320 3k Setesdal (woman) 1.25 .25
941 A320 4k Kautokeino (man) 2.00 .80

Europa 1989 — A321

Children's games: 3.70k, Building snowman. 5k, Cat's cradle.

1989, June 7 Litho. *Perf. 13x13½*
942 A321 3.70k multi 1.75 .75
943 A321 5k multi 2.50 .90

Public Primary Schools, 250th Anniv. — A322

3k, Child learning to write.

Litho. & Engr.
1989, June 7 *Perf. 13½x13*
944 A322 2.60k shown 1.25 .60

Engr.
945 A322 3k multi 1.25 .25

Souvenir Sheet

Winter Olympic Gold Medalists from Norway — A323

Portraits: a, Bjoerg Eva Jensen, women's 3000-meter speed skating, 1980. b, Eirik Kvalfoss, 10k biathlon, 1984. c, Tom Sandberg, combined cross-country and ski jumping, 1984. d, Women's Nordic ski team, 20k relay, 1984.

1989, Oct. 6 Litho. *Perf. 13½x13*
946 Sheet of 4 7.50 7.50
a.-d. 4k any single 1.75 1.75

Sold for 20k to benefit Olympic sports promotion.
See Nos. 984, 997, 1021, 1035.

Souvenir Sheet

Impression of the Countryside, 1982, by Jakob Weidemann — A324

1989, Oct. 6
947 A324 Sheet of 4 8.50 8.50
a.-d. 3k any single 2.00 2.00

Stamp Day. Sold for 15k to benefit philatelic promotion.

Writers — A325

3k, Arnulf Overland (1889-1968), poet. 25k, Hanna Winsnes (1789-1872), author.

Litho. & Engr.
1989, Nov. 24 *Perf. 13x13½*
948 A325 3k dk red & brt bl 1.25 .25
949 A325 25k multicolored 11.00 1.00

Manors — A326

1989, Nov. 24 Engr. *Perf. 13*
950 A326 3k Manor at Larvik 1.25 .25
951 A326 3k Rosendal Barony 1.25 .25

Christmas Decorations — A327

Perf. 13 on 3 sides
1989, Nov. 24 Litho.
Booklet Stamps
952 A327 3k Star 1.25 .25
953 A327 3k Round ornament 1.25 .25
a. Bklt. pane of 10, 5 #952, 5 #953 12.50
Complete booklet, #953a 15.00

Winter City Events, Tromso — A328

1990, Feb. 23 Litho. *Perf. 13½*
954 A328 5k multicolored 2.25 .35

Fauna Type of 1988 and

Scenes of Norway — A329

Designs: 4k, Cable cars. 4.50k, Goat Mountain. 5.50k, Top of the World outpost.

1991-94 Litho. *Perf. 13*
955 A329 4k multicolored 2.00 .60
956 A329 4.50k multicolored 2.50 .60
957 A329 5.50k multicolored 2.50 .50

Litho. & Engr.
958 A292 5.50k Lynx 2.50 .25
959 A292 6.40k Owl 2.50 .40
Nos. 955-959 (5) 12.00 2.35

Issued: #958-959, 2/21/91; #955-957, 4/19/94.

Posthorn Type of 1893
1991-92 Engr. *Perf. 12½x13*
960 A10 1k orange & black .50 .25
961 A10 2k emerald & lake .60 .25
962 A10 3k blue & green 1.00 .25
963 A10 4k org & henna brn 1.20 .25
964 A10 5k green & dark blue 1.40 .25
965 A10 6k grn & red vio 1.75 .60
966 A10 7k red brn & bl 2.00 .60
967 A10 8k red vio & bl grn 2.50 .35
968 A10 9k ultra & red brn 3.00 .50
Nos. 960-968 (9) 13.95 3.30

Issued: 1k-5k, 11/23/92; others, 11/22/91.

Orchids — A332

No. 970, Dactylorhiza fuchsii. No. 971, Epipactis atrorubens. No. 972, Cypripedium calceolus. No. 973, Ophrys insectifera.

Perf. 13½x13 on 3 Sides
1990-92 Litho. Booklet Stamps
970 A332 3.20k multi 1.25 .25
971 A332 3.20k multi 1.25 .25
a. Bklt. pane, 5 #970, 5 #971 12.50
Complete booklet, #971a 14.00
972 A332 3.30k multi 1.25 .25
973 A332 3.30k multi 1.25 .25
a. Bklt. pane, 5 each #972-973 13.00
Complete booklet, #973a 17.50
Nos. 970-973 (4) 5.00 1.00

Issued: #970-971, 2/23; #972-973, 2/21/92.

A334

German Invasion of Norway, 50th Anniv.: 3.20k, King Haakon VII's monogram, merchant navy, air force, Norwegian Home Guard and cannon Moses. 4k, Recapture of Narvik, May 28, 1940, by the Polish, British, Norwegian and French forces.

1990, Apr. 9 Litho. *Perf. 13x13½*
975 A334 3.20k shown 2.10 .25
976 A334 4k multicolored 2.50 .50

Souvenir Sheet

A335

Stamps on stamps: b, Norway #1.

1990, Apr. 9 *Perf. 13½x13*
977 Sheet of 2 9.00 9.00
a.-b. A335 5k any single 3.00 3.00

Penny Black, 150th anniv. Sold for 15k.

A336

1990, June 14 Litho. & Engr.
978 A336 3.20k Portrait 1.75 .25
979 A336 5k Coat of arms 2.10 .50

Tordenskiold (Peter Wessel, 1690-1720), naval hero.

A337

Europa: Post offices.

1990, June 14 Litho. *Perf. 13x13½*
980 A337 3.20k Trondheim 1.75 .25
981 A337 4k Longyearbyen 2.25 .80

A338

2.70k, Svendsen. 15k, Monument by Fredriksen.

1990, Oct. 5 Litho. & Engr. *Perf. 13*
982 A338 2.70k multicolored 1.40 .60
983 A338 15k multicolored 7.00 .60

Johan Severin Svendsen (1840-1911), composer.

Winter Olympic Type of 1989
Souvenir Sheet

Gold medal winners: a, Thorleif Haug, skier, 1924. b, Sonja Henie, figure skater, 1928, 1932, 1936. c, Ivar Ballangrud, speed skater, 1928, 1936. d, Hjalmar Andersen, speed skater, 1952.

1990, Oct. 5 Litho. *Perf. 13½x13*
984 Sheet of 4 8.50 8.50
a.-d. A323 4k any single 1.90 1.90

Sold for 20k to benefit Olympic sports promotion.

A339

Litho & Engr.
1990, Nov. 23 *Perf. 13*
985 A339 30k bl, brn & car rose 15.00 1.00

Lars Olof Jonathan Soderblom (1866-1931), 1930 Nobel Peace Prize winner.

A340

Christmas (Children's drawings): No. 987, Church, stars, and Christmas tree.

Perf. 13 on 3 sides
1990, Nov. 23 Litho.
986 A340 3.20k multicolored 1.25 .25
987 A340 3.20k multicolored 1.25 .25
a. Bklt. pane, 5 each #986-987 12.50
Complete booklet, #987a 15.00

Ship Building Industry — A341

1991, Feb. 21 Litho. *Perf. 13½x13*

988 A341 5k multicolored 2.50 .85

Europa — A342

3.20k, ERS-1. 4k, Andoya rocket range.

1991, Apr. 16 Litho. *Perf. 13*

989 A342 3.20k multi 1.75 .40
990 A342 4k multi 2.50 .75

City of Christiansand, 350th Anniv. — A343

Litho. & Engr.

1991, Apr. 16 *Perf. 13*

991 A343 3.20k Early view 1.50 .25
992 A343 5.50k Modern view 2.50 .40

Lifeboat Service, Cent. — A344

Designs: 3.20k, Rescue boat, Skomvaer III, horiz. 27k, Sailboat Colin Archer.

Litho & Engr.

1991, June 7 *Perf. 13*

993 A344 3.20k multicolored 1.75 .25
994 A344 27k multicolored 12.00 1.50

Tourism — A345

Designs: 3.20k, Fountain, Vigeland Park. 4k, Globe, North Cape.

1991, June 7 Litho. *Perf. 13½x13*

995 A345 3.20k multicolored 1.75 .25
996 A345 4k multicolored 3.00 1.50

Winter Olympic Type of 1989

Souvenir Sheet

Gold medal winners: a, Birger Ruud, ski jumping. b, Johan Grottumsbraten, cross country skiing. c, Knut Johannesen, speed skating. d, Magnar Solberg, biathlon.

1991, Oct. 11 Litho. *Perf. 13½x13*

997 Sheet of 4 8.50 8.50
a.-d. A323 4k any single 1.75 1.75

Sold for 20k to benefit Olympic sports promotion.

A346

Natl. Stamp Day: a, Hands engraving. b, Magnifying glass above hands. c, View of hands through magnifying glass. d, Printed label being removed from plate.

1991, Oct. 11 *Perf. 13x13½*

Souvenir Sheet

998 Sheet of 4 9.00 9.00
a. A346 2.70k multicolored 1.75 1.75
b. A346 3.20k multicolored 1.75 1.75
c. A346 4k multicolored 1.75 1.75
d. A346 5k multicolored 1.75 1.75

Sold for 20k.

A347

Christmas: No. 1000, People with lantern.

Perf. 13½x13 on 3 Sides

1991, Nov. 22 Litho.

Booklet Stamps

999 A347 3.20k multicolored 1.25 .25
1000 A347 3.20k multicolored 1.25 .25
a. Bklt. pane, 5 each #999-1000 12.50
Complete booklet, #1000a 14.00

Queen Sonja A348

King Harald A349

A349a

Perf. 13x13½, 12½x13½ (6.50k)

1992-2002 Litho. & Engr.

1004 A348 2.80k multi 1.40 .25
1005 A348 3k multi 1.25 .25
1007 A349 3.30k multi 1.75 .25
1008 A349 3.50k multi 1.40 .25
1009 A349 4.50k carmine 1.75 .40
1011 A349 5.50k multi 2.00 .30
1012 A349 5.60k multi 2.50 .25
1014 A349 6.50k green 1.75 .70
1015 A349 6.60k multi 3.00 .40
1016 A349 7.50k violet 2.75 2.00
1016A A349 8.50k brown 3.00 2.00

Perf. 13½x13

1017 A349a 10k dark grn 3.00 .25
a. Perf. 13½x13¾ 3.00 .75
1019 A349a 20k deep vio 6.00 .50
b. Perf. 13½x13¾ 8.00 1.20
1019A A349a 30k dark blue 9.00 .50
1020 A349a 50k olive black 15.00 1.75
a. Perf. 13½x13¾ 15.00 2.50
Nos. 1004-1020 (15) 55.55 10.05

Issued: 2.80k, 3.30k, 5.60k, 6.60k, 2/21/92; 50k, 6/12/92; 3k, 3.50k, 5.50k, 2/23/93; 10k, 20k, 6/17/93; 6.50k, 2/12/94; 30k, 11/18/94; 4.50k, 7.50k, 8.50k, 11/24/95; Nos. 1019b, 1020a, Dec. 2001. No. 1017a, 2002.

Winter Olympic Type of 1989

Souvenir Sheet

Gold Medal winners: a, Hallgeir Brenden, cross-country skiing. b, Arnfinn Bergmann, ski jumping. c, Stein Eriksen, giant slalom. d, Simon Slattvik, Nordic combined.

1992, Feb. 21 Litho. *Perf. 13½x13*

1021 Sheet of 4 8.50 8.50
a.-d. A323 4k any single 1.75 1.75

Sold for 20k to benefit Olympic sports promotion.

Expo '92, Seville — A350

Designs: 3.30k, Norwegian pavilion, ship. 5.20k, Mountains, boat and fish.

1992, Apr. 20 Litho. *Perf. 13x13½*

1022 A350 3.30k multicolored 1.25 .25
1023 A350 5.20k multicolored 2.00 .50

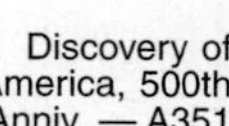

Discovery of America, 500th Anniv. — A351

Europa: 3.30k, Sailing ship Restauration at sea, 1825. 4,20k, Stavangerfjord in New York Harbor, 1918.

Litho. & Engr.

1992, Apr. 21 *Perf. 13x13½*

1024 A351 3.30k multicolored 1.90 .25
1025 A351 4.20k multicolored 2.50 .80

Kristiansund, 250th Anniv. — A352

Litho. & Engr.

1992, June 12 *Perf. 13*

1026 A352 3.30k brn, bl & blk 1.50 .25
1027 A352 3.30k View of Molde 1.50 .25

Molde, 250th anniv. (#1027).

Souvenir Sheet

Glass A353

Stamp Day: a, Decorated vase. b, Carafe with gold design. c, Cut glass salad bowl. d, Decorated cup.

1992, Oct. 9 Litho. *Perf. 13x13½*

1028 A353 Sheet of 4 10.00 10.00
a. 2.80k multicolored 2.00 2.00
b. 3.30k multicolored 2.00 2.00
c. 4.20k multicolored 2.00 2.00
d. 5.20k multicolored 2.00 2.00

No. 1028 sold for 20k.

A354

Designs: 3.30k, Flags, buildings in Lillehammer. 4.20k, Flag.

1992, Oct. 9 Litho. *Perf. 13x13½*

1029 A354 3.30k multicolored 1.40 .25
1030 A354 4.20k multicolored 1.90 .75

1994 Winter Olympics, Lillehammer.
See Nos. 1047-1048, 1053-1058.

A355

Christmas: No. 1031, Elves in front of mailbox. No. 1032, One elf holding other on shoulders to mail letters.

Perf. 13 on 3 Sides

1992, Nov. 23 Litho.

Booklet Stamps

1031 A355 3.30k multicolored .90 .25
1032 A355 3.30k multicolored .90 .25
b. Booklet pane, 5 each #1031-1032 12.00
Complete booklet, #1032b 15.00

Butterflies — A356

Designs: No. 1033, Anthocharis cardamines. No. 1034, Aglais urticae.

Perf. 13½x13 on 3 Sides

1993, Feb. 23 Litho.

Booklet Stamps

1033 A356 3.50k multicolored 1.00 .25
1034 A356 3.50k multicolored 1.00 .25
b. Booklet pane, 5 each #1033-1034 12.50
Complete booklet, #1034b 15.00

See Nos. 1051-1052.

Winter Olympic Type of 1989

Souvenir Sheet

1992 Gold Medal winners: a, Finn Christian Jagge, slalom. b, Bjorn Daehlie, cross-country skiing. c, Geir Karlstad, speed skating. d, Vegard Ulvang, cross-country skiing.

1993, Feb. 23 *Perf. 13½x13*

1035 Sheet of 4 8.50 8.50
a.-d. A323 4.50k any single 1.75 1.75

No. 1035 sold for 22k to benefit Olympic sports promotion.

Norden — A357

1993, Apr. 23 Litho. *Perf. 13½x13*

1036 A357 4k Canoe on lake 2.00 .40
1037 A357 4.50k River rafting 2.25 .50

Edvard Grieg — A358

Litho. & Engr.

1993, Apr. 23 *Perf. 13x13½*

1038 A358 3.50k Portrait 1.50 .25
1039 A358 5.50k Landscape 2.25 .50

1993 World Championships in Norway — A359

1993, June 17 Litho. *Perf. 13½x13*

1040 A359 3.50k Team handball 1.50 .25
1041 A359 5.50k Cycling 2.50 .50

Hurtigruten Shipping Line, Cent. — A360

3.50k, Richard With, ship. 4.50k, Ship, officers.

Litho. & Engr.

1993, June 17 *Perf. 12½x13*

1042 A360 3.50k multicolored 1.75 .25
1043 A360 4.50k multicolored 2.25 .75

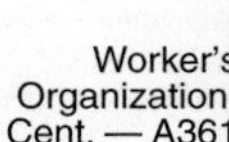

Worker's Organization, Cent. — A361

1993, Sept. 24 Engr. *Perf. 13x13½*

1044 A361 3.50k Johan Castberg 1.75 .25
1045 A361 12k Betzy Kjelsberg 5.00 .50

Souvenir Sheet

Carvings A362

Stamp Day: a, Spiral leaf scroll. b, Interlocking scroll. c, "1754" surrounded by scroll. d, Face with scroll above.

1993, Sept. 24 Litho. *Perf. 13½x13*

No.	Type	Description	Unused	Used
1046	A362	Sheet of 4, #a.-d.	10.00	10.00
a.		3k multicolored	1.75	1.75
b.		3.50k multicolored	1.75	1.75
c.		4.50k multicolored	1.75	1.75
d.		5.50k multicolored	1.75	1.75

No. 1046 sold for 21k.

See No. 1069.

1994 Winter Olympic Type of 1992

#1047, Flags, cross country skiier. #1048, Flags, buildings in Lillehammer.

1993, Nov. 27 Litho. *Perf. 13x13½*

No.	Type	Description	Unused	Used
1047	A354	3.50k multicolored	1.10	.25
1048	A354	3.50k multicolored	1.10	.25
a.		Pair, #1047-1048	2.50	2.50

No. 1048a has a continuous design.

Christmas — A363

Designs: No. 1049, Store Mangen Chapel. No. 1050, Church of Stamnes, Sandnes.

Perf. 13½x13 on 3 Sides

1993, Nov. 27 Booklet Stamps

No.	Type	Description	Unused	Used
1049	A363	3.50k shown	1.00	.25
1050	A363	3.50k multicolored	1.00	.25
b.		Booklet pane, 5 each #1049-1050	10.00	
		Complete booklet, #1050b	12.50	

Butterfly Type of 1993

No. 1051, Colias hecla. No. 1052, Clossiana freija.

Perf. 13½x13 on 3 Sides

1994, Feb. 12 Litho.

Booklet Stamps

No.	Type	Description	Unused	Used
1051	A356	3.50k multi	1.10	.25
1052	A356	3.50k multi	1.10	.25
b.		Booklet pane, 5 each #1051-1052	12.50	
		Complete booklet, #1052b	15.00	

1994 Winter Olympic Type of 1992

Designs: No. 1053, Stylized Norwegian flag, Olympic rings UR. No. 1054, Stylized Norwegian flag, Olympic rings, UL. No. 1055, Olympic rings, buildings in Lillehammer. No. 1056, Olympic rings, ski jump. 4.50k, Flags of Norway, Belgium, Greece, Switzerland, Sweden, Germany, United Kingdom. 5.50k, Flags of Australia, New Zealand, Brazil, Canada, US, Japan, Mexico, South Korea.

1994, Feb. 12 *Perf. 13x13½*

No.	Type	Description	Unused	Used
1053	A354	3.50k multicolored	1.25	.25
1054	A354	3.50k multicolored	1.25	.25
1055	A354	3.50k multicolored	1.25	.25
1056	A354	3.50k multicolored	1.25	.25
a.		Block of 4, #1053-1056	6.00	6.00
1057	A354	4.50k multicolored	1.75	.50
1058	A354	5.50k multicolored	2.10	.40
		Nos. 1053-1058 (6)	8.85	1.90

1994 Paralympics — A365

1994, Mar. 10 Litho. *Perf. 13*

No.	Type	Description	Unused	Used
1059	A365	4.50k Skier	1.75	.60
1060	A365	5.50k Skier, diff.	1.50	.50

Tromso Charter, Bicent. — A366

Litho. & Engr.

1994, Apr. 19 *Perf. 13*

No.	Type	Description	Unused	Used
1061	A366	3.50k Royal seal	1.50	.25
1062	A366	4.50k Cathedral	2.00	.60

Norwegian Folk Museum, Cent. — A367

Designs: 3k, Log buildings, Osterdal Valley. 3.50k, Sled, 1750.

Litho. & Engr.

1994, June 14 *Perf. 12½x13*

No.	Type	Description	Unused	Used
1063	A367	3k multicolored	1.25	.40
1064	A367	3.50k multicolored	1.50	.25

Research in Norway — A368

Abstract designs with various formulas, microchips, glass flasks.

1994, June 14 Litho.

No.	Type	Description	Unused	Used
1065	A368	4k multicolored	1.50	.50
1066	A368	4.50k multicolored	2.00	.50

Electric Tram Lines, Cent. — A369

3.50k, Early tram, map. 12k, Modern tram, map.

Litho. & Engr.

1994, Sept. 23 *Perf. 13x13½*

No.	Type	Description	Unused	Used
1067	A369	3.50k multi	1.50	.25
1068	A369	12k multi	5.00	.50

Stamp Day Type of 1993

Ornamental broaches: a, Gold, embossed designs. b, Silver, embossed designs. c, Silver, circular designs. d, Gold, jeweled center.

1994, Sept. 23 Litho. *Perf. 13½x13*

No.	Type	Description	Unused	Used
1069		Sheet of 4, #a.-d.	9.00	9.00
a.	A362	3k multicolored	1.75	1.75
b.	A362	3.50k multicolored	1.75	1.75
c.	A362	4.50k multicolored	1.75	1.75
d.	A362	5.50k multicolored	1.75	1.75

No. 1069 sold for 21k.

Christmas — A370

Perf. 13½x13 on 3 Sides

1994, Nov. 18 Litho.

Booklet Stamps

No.	Type	Description	Unused	Used
1070	A370	3.50k Sled	1.25	.25
1071	A370	3.50k Kick sled	1.25	.25
a.		Booklet pane, 5 each	12.50	
		Complete booklet, #1071a	13.50	

Berries — A371

No. 1086, Vaccinium vitis. No. 1087, Vaccinium uliginosum. No. 1088, Fragaria vesca. No. 1089, Rubus chamaemorus.

Booklet Stamps

1995-96 Litho. *Perf. 13½x13*

No.	Type	Description	Unused	Used
1086	A371	3.50k multi	1.10	.25
1087	A371	3.50k multi	1.10	.25
a.		Bklt. pane, 4 ea #1086-1087	9.00	
		Complete booklet, #1087a	11.00	
1088	A371	3.50k multi	1.10	.25
1089	A371	3.50k multi	1.10	.25
a.		Bklt. pane, 4 ea #1088-1089	9.00	
		Complete booklet, #1089a	11.00	
		Nos. 1086-1089 (4)	4.40	1.00

Issued: #1086-1087, 2/23/95; #1088-1089, 2/22/96.

A372

Apothecary Shops, 400th Anniv.: 3.50k, Swan Pharmacy, Bergen. 25k, Apothecary's tools.

Litho. & Engr.

1995, Feb. 23 *Perf. 13½x13*

No.	Type	Description	Unused	Used
1090	A372	3.50k multicolored	1.75	.25
1091	A372	25k multicolored	11.00	1.00

Tourism — A373

4k, Skudeneshavn Harbor. 4.50k, Torghatten mountain, Helgeland coastline.

1995, May 8 Litho. *Perf. 13½x13*

Booklet Stamps

No.	Type	Description	Unused	Used
1092	A373	4k multicolored	1.25	.40
a.		Booklet pane of 8	10.00	
		Complete booklet, #1092a	12.00	
1093	A373	4.50k multicolored	1.25	.40
a.		Booklet pane of 8	12.00	
		Complete booklet, #1093a	14.00	

Christianity in Norway — A374

3.50k, Old Moster Church, c. 1100. 15k, Slettebakken Church, Bergen, 1970.

Litho. & Engr.

1995, May 8 *Perf. 13x13½*

No.	Type	Description	Unused	Used
1094	A374	3.50k multicolored	1.75	.25
1095	A374	15k multicolored	6.00	.60

End of World War II, 50th Anniv. — A375

Designs: 3.50k, German commander saluting Terje Rollem in 1945, German forces marching down Karl Johans Gate from Royal Palace, 1940. 4.50k, King Haakon VII, Crown Prince leaving Norway in 1940, King saluting upon return in 1945. 5.50k, Children waving Norwegian flags, 1945.

1995, May 8 Litho. *Perf. 13½x13*

No.	Type	Description	Unused	Used
1096	A375	3.50k multicolored	1.75	.25
1097	A375	4.50k multicolored	2.25	.50
1098	A375	5.50k multicolored	2.50	.40
		Nos. 1096-1098 (3)	6.50	1.15

Kirsten Flagstad (1895-1962), Opera Singer — A376

Design: 5.50k, In Lohengrin.

1995, June 26 Litho. *Perf. 13*

No.	Type	Description	Unused	Used
1099	A376	3.50k multicolored	1.75	.25
1100	A376	5.50k multicolored	2.50	.40

Conciliation Boards, Bicent. — A377

Designs: 7k, Three-man board between two people facing away from each other. 12k, Seated board member, two people talking to each other.

1995, June 26 *Perf. 13½*

No.	Type	Description	Unused	Used
1101	A377	7k multicolored	2.75	.40
1102	A377	12k multicolored	4.75	.50

UN, 50th Anniv. — A378

UN emblem and: 3.50k, Trygve Lie, Secretary General 1946-53. 5.50k, Woman drinking from clean water supply.

Litho. & Engr.

1995, Sept. 22 *Perf. 13*

No.	Type	Description	Unused	Used
1103	A378	3.50k multicolored	1.75	.25
1104	A378	5.50k multicolored	2.50	.40

Norway Post, 350th Anniv. — A379

No. 1105, Signature, portrait of Hannibal Sehested, letter post, 1647. No. 1106, Wax seal, registered letters, 1745. No. 1107, Christiania, etc. postmarks. No. 1108, Funds transfer, coins, canceled envelopes, 1883. No. 1109, "Norske Intelligenz-Seddeler," first newspaper, newspapers, magazines, 1660. No. 1110, Postmarks, label, parcel post, 1827. No. 1111, No. 1, Type A5, stamps, 1855. No. 1112, Savings book stamps, bank services, 1950.

Booklet Stamps

1995, Sept. 22 Litho.

No.	Type	Description	Unused	Used
1105	A379	3.50k multicolored	1.25	.30
1106	A379	3.50k multicolored	1.25	.30
1107	A379	3.50k multicolored	1.25	.30
1108	A379	3.50k multicolored	1.25	.30
1109	A379	3.50k multicolored	1.25	.30
1110	A379	3.50k multicolored	1.25	.30
1111	A379	3.50k multicolored	1.25	.30
a.		Missing gray stamp at LR	*12.50*	5.00
1112	A379	3.50k multicolored	1.25	.30
a.		Booklet pane, #1105-1112	12.50	18.00
		Complete booklet, #1112a	15.00	
b.		Booklet pane, #1105-1110, #1111a, 1112	25.00	25.00
		Complete booklet, #1112b	27.50	

Christmas — A380

Booklet Stamps

Perf. 13 on 3 Sides

1995, Nov. 24 Litho.

No.	Type	Description	Unused	Used
1113	A380	3.50k Knitted cap	1.10	.25
1114	A380	3.50k Knitted mitten	1.10	.25
a.		Bklt. pane, 4 ea #1113-1114	9.00	
		Complete booklet, #1114a	11.00	

Svalbard Islands — A381

1996, Feb. 22 Litho. *Perf. 13*

No.	Type	Description	Unused	Used
1115	A381	10k Advent Bay	4.25	.50
1116	A381	20k Polar bear	9.00	.75

Olympic Games, Cent. — A382

Children's drawings: 3.50k, Cross country skier. 5.50k, Runner.

1996, Apr. 18 Litho. *Perf. 13½*

No.	Type	Description	Unused	Used
1117	A382	3.50k multicolored	1.75	.25
1118	A382	5.50k multicolored	2.50	.40

Tourism — A383

4k, Besseggen. 4.50k, Urnes Stave Church. 5.50k, Alta Rock Carvings.

1996, Apr. 18 *Perf. 13 on 3 Sides*
1119 A383 4k multi 1.00 .60
a. Booklet pane of 8 8.00
Complete booklet, #1119a 10.00
1120 A383 4.50k multi 1.25 .50
a. Booklet pane of 8 10.00
Complete booklet, #1120a 12.00
1121 A383 5.50k multi 1.50 .60
a. Booklet pane of 8 12.00
Complete booklet, #1121a 14.00
Nos. 1119-1121 (3) 3.75 1.70

See Nos. 1155-1157.

Railway Centennials A384

Litho. & Engr.
1996, June 19 *Perf. 13*
1122 A384 3k Urskog-Holand 1.25 .40
1123 A384 4.50k Setesdal 1.75 .75

The Troll Offshore Gasfield — A385

3.50k, Size of Troll platform compared to Eiffel Tower. 25k, Troll platform, map of gas pipelines.

1996, June 19 **Litho.**
1124 A385 3.50k multicolored 1.50 .25
1125 A385 25k multicolored 9.00 1.00

Norway Post, 350th Anniv. — A386

#1126, Postal courier on skis. #1127, Fjord boat, SS "Framnaes," 1920's. #1128, Mail truck, Oslo, 1920's. #1129, Early airmail service. #1130, Unloading mail, East Railroad Station, Oslo, 1950's. #1131, Using bicycle for rural mail delivery, 1970's. #1132, Customer, mail clerk, Elverum post office. #1133, Computer, globe, E-mail service.

Booklet Stamps
1996, Sept. 20 **Litho.** *Perf. 13*
1126 A386 3.50k multicolored 1.00 .60
1127 A386 3.50k multicolored 1.00 .60
1128 A386 3.50k multicolored 1.00 .60
1129 A386 3.50k multicolored 1.00 .60
1130 A386 3.50k multicolored 1.00 .60
1131 A386 3.50k multicolored 1.00 .60
1132 A386 3.50k multicolored 1.00 .60
1133 A386 3.50k multicolored 1.00 .60
a. Booklet pane, #1126-1133 10.00 10.00
Complete booklet, #1133a 11.00

Motion Pictures, Cent. — A387

Film strips showing: 3.50k, Leif Juster, Sean Connery, Liv Ullmann, The Olsen Gang Films, Il Temp Gigante. 5.50k, Wenche Foss, Jack Fjeldstad, Marilyn Monroe, murder, blood, shooting. 7k, Charlie Chaplin, Ottar Gladvedt, Laurel & Hardy, Marlene Dietrich.

1996, Sept. 20
1134 A387 3.50k multicolored 1.40 .25
1135 A387 5.50k multicolored 1.75 .40
1136 A387 7k multicolored 2.75 .40
Nos. 1134-1136 (3) 5.90 1.05

A388

Christmas (Embroidered motif from Norwegian folk costume): Denomination at UL (#1137), UR (#1138).

Perf. 13 on 3 Sides
1996, Nov. 21 **Litho.**
1137 A388 3.50k multicolored 1.10 .25
1138 A388 3.50k multicolored 1.10 .25
a. Bklt. pane, 4 ea #1137-1138 9.00
Complete booklet, #1138a 10.00

A389

Amalie Skram (1846-1905), Novelist: 3.50k, Portrait. 15k, Scene from performance of Skram's "People of Hellemyr."

1996, Nov. 21 **Engr.**
1139 A389 3.50k claret 1.50 .35
1140 A389 15k claret & dk blue 6.00 1.25

Posthorn Type of 1893 Redrawn
1997, Jan. 2 **Litho.** *Perf. 13x13½*
Color of Oval
1141 A10 10o red .25 .25
1142 A10 20o blue .25 .25
a. Perf. 13¾x13¼ .40 .40
1143 A10 30o orange .25 .25
1144 A10 40o gray .25 .25
1145 A10 50o bl grn, bl grn numeral .25 .25
Nos. 1141-1145 (5) 1.25 1.25

Numerous design differences exist in the vertical shading lines, the size and shading of the posthorn, and in the corner wings.
See No. 1282A for stamp similar to No. 1145 but with blue numeral.
Issued: No. 1142a, Dec. 2000.

Insects — A390

1997, Jan. 2 *Perf. 13 on 3 Sides*
1146 A390 3.70k Bumblebee 1.10 .25
1147 A390 3.70k Ladybug 1.10 .25
a. Bklt. pane, 4 ea #1146-1147 9.00
Complete booklet 10.00

See Nos. 1180-1181.

Flowers — A391

3.20k, Red clover. 3.70k, Coltsfoot. 4.30k, Lily of the Valley. 5k, Harebell. 6k, Oxeye daisy.

1997, Jan. 2 *Perf. 13*
1148 A391 3.20k multi 1.25 .40
1149 A391 3.70k multi 1.40 .25
1150 A391 4.30k multi 1.75 .40
1151 A391 5k multi 1.75 .40
1152 A391 6k multi 2.10 .40
Nos. 1148-1152 (5) 8.25 1.85

See #1182-1187, 1210-1212, 1244-1247.

World Nordic Skiing Championships, Trondheim — A392

3.70k, Ski jumping. 5k, Cross-country skiing.

1997, Feb. 20
1153 A392 3.70k multi 1.50 .40
1154 A392 5k multi 2.00 .60

Tourism Type of 1996

4.30k, Roros. 5k, Faerder Lighthouse. 6k, Nusfjord.

Perf. 13 on 3 Sides
1997, Apr. 16 **Litho.**
Booklet Stamps
1155 A383 4.30k multi 1.50 .75
a. Booklet pane of 8 12.00
Complete booklet, #1155a 14.00
1156 A383 5k multi 1.75 .60
a. Booklet pane of 8 14.00
Complete booklet, #1156a 16.00
1157 A383 6k multi 2.00 .60
a. Booklet pane of 8 16.00
Complete booklet #1157a 18.00

King Harald, Queen Sonja, 60th Birthdays — A393

No. 1159, King Harald, vert.

1997, Apr. 16 **Litho.** *Perf. 13*
1158 A393 3.70k shown 1.50 .25
1159 A393 3.70k multi 1.50 .25

Norway Post, 350th Anniv. — A394

Post-World War II development: No. 1160, Tools for construction, 1945. No. 1161, Kon-Tiki Expedition, 1947. No. 1162, Environmental protection, establishing national parks, 1962. No. 1163, Welfare, help for the elderly, 1967. No. 1164, Off-shore oil drilling, 1969. No. 1165, Grete Waitz, marathon winner, 1983. No. 1166, Askoy Bridge, 1992. No. 1167, Winter Olympic Games, Lillehammer, 1994.

1997, Apr. 16 **Booklet Stamps**
1160 A394 3.70k multicolored 1.10 .60
1161 A394 3.70k multicolored 1.10 .60
1162 A394 3.70k multicolored 1.10 .60
1163 A394 3.70k multicolored 1.10 .60
1164 A394 3.70k multicolored 1.10 .60
1165 A394 3.70k multicolored 1.10 .60
1166 A394 3.70k multicolored 1.10 .60
1167 A394 3.70k multicolored 1.10 .60
a. Booklet pane, #1160-1167 12.00 12.00
Complete booklet, #1167a 14.00 14.00

City of Trondheim, Millenium — A395

Stylized designs: 3.70k, New Trondheim. 12k, Ships entering harbor, King, early settlements in Old Nidaros.

1997, June 6 **Litho.** *Perf. 13½x13*
1168 A395 3.70k multicolored 1.50 .40
1169 A395 12k multicolored 5.00 .80

Einar Gerhardsen (1897-1987), Prime Minister — A396

Caricatures: 3.70k, In front on government buildings. 25k, Scenes of Norway.

1997, June 6 *Perf. 13½*
1170 A396 3.70k multicolored 1.50 .40
1171 A396 25k multicolored 11.00 1.25

Junior Stamp Club — A397

Topics found on stamps: No. 1172, Insect, butterfly (silhouette of person's face), cartoon character, fish, flag, hand holding pen, heart, tiger, horn, boy with dog, globe. No. 1173, Flag, hand holding pen, tree, butterfly (silhouette of person's face), ladybug, cartoon character, antique postal vehicle, soccer ball, stylized bird, man on bicycle, lighthouse.

1997, Sept. 29 **Litho.** *Perf. 13*
1172 A397 3.70k multicolored 1.50 .40
1173 A397 3.70k multicolored 1.50 .40

Harald Saeverud (1897-1992), Composer — A398

15k, Tarjei Vesaas (1897-1970), writer.

Litho. & Engr.
1997, Sept. 19 *Perf. 13½x13*
1174 A398 10k blue 4.25 .80
1175 A398 15k green 6.50 1.50

Petter Dass (1647-1706), Poet, Priest — A399

Designs: 3.20k, Dass standing in rowboat, verse. 3.70k, Dass, church on island of Alsten.

Litho. & Engr.
1997, Nov. 26 *Perf. 13*
1176 A399 3.20k multicolored 1.25 .75
1177 A399 3.70k multicolored 1.50 .40

Christmas — A400

Various designs from Norwegian calendar stick, medieval forerunner of modern day calendar.

Serpentine Die Cut 13½ on 3 Sides
1997, Nov. 26 **Litho.**
Self-Adhesive
Booklet Stamps
1178 A400 3.70k yellow & multi 1.10 .25
1179 A400 3.70k blue & multi 1.10 .25
a. Bklt. pane, 2 ea #1178-1179 5.00
Complete booklet, 2 #1179a 10.00

Insect Type of 1997
1998, Jan. 2 *Perf. 13½ on 3 Sides*
Booklet Stamps
1180 A390 3.80k Dragonfly 1.25 .25
1181 A390 3.80k Grasshopper 1.25 .25
a. Bklt. pane, 4 ea #1180-1181 10.00
Complete booklet, #1181a 12.00

Flower Type of 1997

3.40k, Marsh marigold. 3.80k, Wild pansy. 4.50k, White clover. 5.50k, Hepatica. 7.50k, Pale pasqueflower. 13k, Purple saxifrage.

1998, Jan. 2 **Litho.** *Perf. 13*
1182 A391 3.40k multi 1.00 .50
1183 A391 3.80k multi 1.25 .25
1184 A391 4.50k multi 1.50 .40
1185 A391 5.50k multi 1.75 .45
1186 A391 7.50k multi 2.25 .45
1187 A391 13k multi 4.00 .55
Nos. 1182-1187 (6) 11.75 2.60

Valentine's Day — A401

1998, Feb. 9 *Die Cut Perf. 14x13*
Self-Adhesive
1188 A401 3.80k multicolored 1.00 .50

No. 1188 was issued in sheets of 3 + 4 labels.

A402

Coastal Shipping: 3.80k, Mail boat, SS Hornelen. 4.50k, Catamaran, Kommandoren.

Litho. & Engr.
1998, Apr. 20 *Perf. 13x13½*
1189 A402 3.80k dark bl & grn 1.50 .30
1190 A402 4.50k bl & dark grn 2.00 1.00

A403

Tourism: 3.80k, Holmenkollen ski jump, Oslo. 4.50k, Fisherman, city of Alesund. 5.50k, Summit of Hamaroyskaftet Mountain.

Perf. 13 on 3 Sides

1998, Apr. 20 **Litho.**

1191 A403 3.80k multicolored 1.25 .35
a. Booklet pane of 8 10.00
Complete booklet, #1191a 10.00
1192 A403 4.50k multicolored 1.50 1.00
a. Booklet pane of 8 12.00
Complete booklet, #1192a 12.00
1193 A403 5.50k multicolored 1.75 .75
a. Booklet pane of 8 14.00
Complete booklet, #1193a 14.00
Nos. 1191-1193 (3) 4.50 2.10

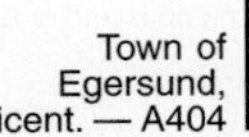

Town of Egersund, Bicent. — A404

Designs: 3.80k, Port, herring boats. 6k, Pottery, white stoneware.

Litho. & Engr.

1998, Apr. 20 ***Perf. 13***

1194 A404 3.80k dk blue & pink 1.25 .30
1195 A404 6k mag & dp bl 2.00 .60

Minerals — A405

1998, June 18 **Litho.** ***Perf. 13***

1196 A405 3.40k Silver 1.00 .70
1197 A405 5.20k Cobaltite 2.00 .75

Contemporary Art — A406

Designs: 6k, "Water Rider," painting by Frans Widerberg. 7.50k, "Red Moon," tapestry by Synnove Anker Aurdal. 13k, "King Haakon VII," sculpture by Nils Aas.

1998, June 18

1198 A406 6k multicolored 2.00 .40
1199 A406 7.50k multicolored 2.25 .80
1200 A406 13k multicolored 4.50 1.25
Nos. 1198-1200 (3) 8.75 2.45

Children's Games — A407

1998, Sept. 18 **Litho.** ***Perf. 13***

1201 A407 3.80k Hopscotch 1.10 .40
1202 A407 5.50k Pitching coins 1.75 .80

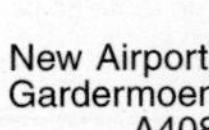

New Airport, Gardermoen A408

1998, Sept. 18 ***Perf. 13½***

1203 A408 3.80k DC-3 1.50 .50
1204 A408 6k Boeing 737 2.25 .75
1205 A408 24k New airport 9.00 1.50
Nos. 1203-1205 (3) 12.75 2.75

The Royal Palace — A409

1998, Nov. 20 **Engr.** ***Perf. 13x13½***

1206 A409 3.40k Royal Guard 1.25 .75
1207 A409 3.80k Facade 1.40 .75

Christmas — A410

Serpentine Die Cut 14x13 on 3 Sides

1998, Nov. 20 **Photo.**

Self-Adhesive

Booklet Stamps

1208 A410 3.80k red & multi 1.25 .30
1209 A410 3.80k blue & multi 1.25 .30
a. Bklt. pane, 2 ea #1208-1209 5.00
Complete booklet, 2 #1209a 10.00

Flower Type of 1997

3.60k, Red campion. 4k, Wood anemone. 7k, Yellow wood violet.

1999, Jan. 2 **Litho.** ***Perf. 13***

1210 A391 3.60k multi 1.25 .40
1211 A391 4k multi 1.50 .25
1212 A391 7k multi 2.50 .40
Nos. 1210-1212 (3) 5.25 1.05

Norwegian Inventions — A411

Designs: 3.60k, Cheese slicer, by Thor Bjorklund. 4k, Paper clip, by Johan Vaaler.

Die Cut Perf. 13

1999, Jan. 2 **Photo.**

Self-Adhesive

1213 A411 3.60k blue & black 1.00 .40
1214 A411 4k red & gray 1.40 .25

See No. 1260.

Salmon A412

Cod A413

Die Cut Perf. 14x13

1999, Jan. 2 **Litho. & Photo.**

Self-Adhesive

Booklet Stamps

1215 A412 4k multicolored 1.25 .25
1216 A413 4k multicolored 1.25 .25
a. Bklt. pane, 2 ea #1215-1216 5.00
Complete booklet, 2 #1216a 10.00

St. Valentine's Day — A414

1999, Feb. 14 **Litho.** ***Perf. 13x13½***

1217 A414 4k multicolored 1.50 .40

A415

Litho. & Engr.

1999, Apr. 12 ***Perf. 13***

1218 A415 4k multicolored 1.40 .40

Norwegian Confederation of Trade Unions, Cent.

A416

Tourism: 4k, Swans on lake. 5k, Hamar Cathedral. 6k, Man in traditional attire.

1999, Apr. 12 **Litho.** ***Perf. 13***

Booklet Stamps

1219 A416 4k multicolored 1.25 .40
a. Booklet pane of 8 10.00
Complete booklet, #1219a 10.00
1220 A416 5k multicolored 1.25 .50
a. Booklet pane of 8 12.50
Complete booklet, #1220a 12.50
1221 A416 6k multicolored 1.75 .75
a. Booklet pane of 8 15.00
Complete booklet, #1221a 15.00

Ice Hockey World Championships A417

Designs: 4k, Poland vs Norway, 1998 Class B Championships. 7k, Sweden vs Switzerland, 1998 Class A Championships.

1999, Apr. 12 ***Perf. 13½***

1222 A417 4k multicolored 1.25 .40
1223 A417 7k multicolored 2.25 .75

Millennium Stamps — A418

Events from 1000-1899: 4k, Family leaving Sejestad Station, emigration period, 1800's. 6k, Statue of St. Olav (995-1030), Christian III Bible, 1550, Christianization period. 14k, King Christian IV speciedaler, miners, union period, 1380-1814. 26k, Textile factory, paper mill on Aker River, Oslo, 1850's, industrialization period.

Litho. & Engr.

1999, June 11 ***Perf. 12¾x13***

1224 A418 4k multicolored 1.40 .50
1225 A418 6k multicolored 2.00 .75
1226 A418 14k multicolored 4.75 1.25
1227 A418 26k multicolored 8.00 1.75
Nos. 1224-1227 (4) 16.15 4.25

Pictures of Everyday Life — A419

No. 1228, Carriage on ferry. No. 1229, Men with hammers. No. 1230, Pumping gasoline. No. 1231, Milking cow. No. 1232, Rakers. No. 1233, Skier. No. 1234, Boat captain. No. 1235, Soccer player.

1999, Sept. 9 **Litho.** ***Perf. 13***

1228 A419 4k multicolored 1.50 .50
1229 A419 4k multicolored 1.50 .50
1230 A419 4k multicolored 1.50 .50
1231 A419 4k multicolored 1.50 .50
1232 A419 4k multicolored 1.50 .50
1233 A419 4k multicolored 1.50 .50
1234 A419 4k multicolored 1.50 .50
1235 A419 4k multicolored 1.50 .50
a. Souv. sheet of 8, #1228-1235 12.50 12.50

Children's Games — A420

1999, Sept. 9 **Litho.** ***Perf. 13¼***

1236 A420 4k Skateboarder 1.25 .50
1237 A420 6k Roller skater 2.00 .75

National Theater, Cent. — A421

Designs: 3.60k, Scene from "An Ideal Husband." 4k, Scene from "Peer Gynt."

1999, Nov. 19 **Engr.** ***Perf. 12¾x13¼***

1238 A421 3.60k claret & org yel 1.50 1.50
1239 A421 4k dk bl & royal bl 1.25 .50

Christmas — A422

Designs: No. 1240, Mother, children at door. No. 1241, Mother, children at window.

Die Cut Perf. 14x13 on 3 sides

1999, Nov. 19 **Litho.**

Self-Adhesive

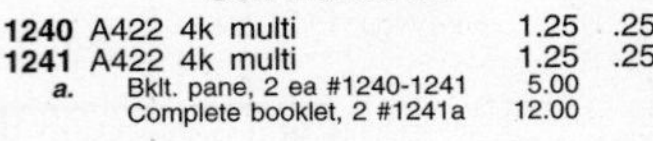

1240 A422 4k multi 1.25 .25
1241 A422 4k multi 1.25 .25
a. Bklt. pane, 2 ea #1240-1241 5.00
Complete booklet, 2 #1241a 12.00

Millennium — A423

Winners of photo competition: No. 1242, "Winter Night." No. 1243, "Sunset."

Die Cut Perf. 13¼x13

1999, Dec. 31 **Litho. & Photo.**

Self-Adhesive

1242 A423 4k multi 1.40 .50
1243 A423 4k multi 1.40 .50
a. Bklt. pane of 2, #1242-1243 4.00
Complete booklet, #1243a 5.00
b. Bklt. pane, 2 ea #1242-1243 7.50
Complete booklet, 2 #1243b 15.00

One complete booklet containing No. 1243a was given free to each Norwegian household in January 2000.

Flower Type of 1997

Designs: 5.40k, Oeder's lousewort. 8k, White water lily. 14k, Globe flower. 25k, Melancholy thistle.

2000, Feb. 9 **Litho.** ***Perf. 12¾x13¼***

1244 A391 5.40k multi 1.75 .60
1245 A391 8k multi 2.50 .75
1246 A391 14k multi 4.25 1.00
1247 A391 25k multi 8.00 1.25
Nos. 1244-1247 (4) 16.50 3.60

Love — A424

2000, Feb. 9 ***Perf. 13x13¼***

1248 A424 4k multi 1.25 .40

Oslo, 1000th Anniv. — A425

4k, Angry Child sculpture, Frogner Park. 6k, Statue of King Christian IV, by C. L. Jacobsen. 8k, Oslo City Hall. 27k, Oslo Stock Exchange.

2000, Apr. 7 **Litho.** ***Perf. 13¼***

1249 A425 4k multi 1.25 .40
1250 A425 6k multi 1.75 .75
1251 A425 8k multi 2.50 .80
1252 A426 27k multi 8.00 1.50
Nos. 1249-1252 (4) 13.50 3.45

Fauna — A426

2000, Apr. 7 ***Perf. 13¼ on 3 sides***

Booklet Stamps

1253 A426 5k Golden eagle 1.40 .75
a. Booklet pane of 8 12.00
Booklet, #1253a 12.50
1254 A426 6k Elk 1.75 .75
a. Booklet pane of 8 14.00
Booklet, #1254a 15.00
1255 A426 7k Whale 2.00 1.00
a. Booklet pane of 8 16.00
Complete booklet, #1255a 17.00
Nos. 1253-1255 (3) 5.15 2.50

Expo 2000, Hanover — A427

Artwork of Marianne Heske: 4.20k, The Quiet Room. 6.30k, Power and Energy.

2000, June 1 ***Perf. 13¼***

1256 A427 4.20k multi 1.75 .75
1257 A427 6.30k multi 2.40 .65

Royal Norwegian Military Academy, 250th Anniv. — A428

Litho. & Engr.

2000, June 2 ***Perf. 13x13¼***

1258 A428 3.60k 1750 Cadets 1.25 .80
1259 A428 8k 2000 Cadets 2.50 1.00

Inventions Type of 1999

4.20k, Aerosol container, by Erik Rotheim.

Die Cut Perf. 12¾

2000, June 2 **Photo.**

Self-Adhesive

1260 A411 4.20k green & black 1.25 .25

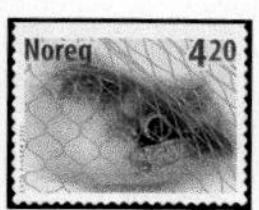

Mackerel A429

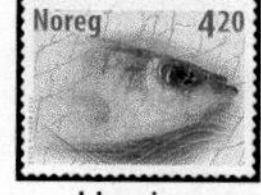

Herring A430

Die Cut Perf. 14x13 on 3 sides

2000, June 2 **Photo. & Litho.**

Self-Adhesive

Booklet Stamps

1261 A429 4.20k multi 1.25 .25
1262 A430 4.20k multi 1.25 .25
a. Booklet pane, 2 each #1261-1262 5.00
Complete booklet, 2#1262a 10.00

A431

Litho. & Engr.

2000, Sept. 15 ***Perf. 13¼x13***

1263 A431 5k multi 1.75 .75

Lars Levi Laestadius (1800-61), botanist.

A432

Intl. Museum of Children's Art, Oslo: 4.20k, Astronaut, by May-Therese Vorland. 6.30k, Rocket, by Jann Fredrik Ronning.

Perf. 13¼x13¾

2000, Sept. 15 **Litho.**

1264 A432 4.20k multi 1.25 .40
1265 A432 6.30k multi 1.75 .60

Skien, 1000th Anniv. — A433

Designs: 4.20k, Monument to loggers. 15k, Skien Church.

2000, Sept. 15 ***Perf. 13¼x13***

1266 A433 4.20k multi 1.25 .75
1267 A433 15k multi 4.75 1.25

Church Altar Pieces — A434

3.60k, Hamaroy Church. 4.20k, Ski Church.

2000, Nov. 17 **Litho.** ***Perf. 13x13¼***

1268 A434 3.60k multi 1.25 1.25
1269 A434 4.20k multi 1.25 .60

Comic Strips — A435

Designs: No. 1270, Nils og Blamman, by Sigurd Winsnes and Ivar Mauritz-Hansen. No. 1271, Nr. 91 Stomperud, by Ernst Garvin and Torbjorn Wen.

Die Cut Perf. 14x13 on 3 sides

2000, Nov. 17 **Photo. & Litho.**

Booklet Stamps

Self-Adhesive

1270 A435 4.20k multi 1.25 .25
1271 A435 4.20k multi 1.25 .25
a. Booklet pane, 2 each #1270-1271 5.00
Complete booklet, 2 #1271a 14.00

Rose Varieties — A436

Designs: No. 1272, Sekel (green denomination). No. 1273, Namdal (brown denomination).

Die Cut Perf.13¼ on 3 sides

2001, Jan. 2 **Photo.**

Booklet Stamps

Self-Adhesive

1272 A436 4.50k multi 1.25 .25
1273 A436 4.50k multi 1.25 .25
a. Booklet pane, 2 each #1272-1273 5.00
Complete booklet, 2 #1273a 10.00

See Nos. 1303-1304.

Crafts — A437

Designs: 4k, Mat of bound birch roots. 4.50k, Birch bark basket. 7k, Embroidered bunad.

2001, Jan. 2 ***Die Cut Perf. 12¾***

Coil Stamps

Self-Adhesive

1274 A437 4k multi 1.25 .30
1275 A437 4.50k multi 1.50 .25
1276 A437 7k multi 2.25 .50
Nos. 1274-1276 (3) 5.00 1.05

See Nos. 1305-1307, 1354.

Actors and Actresses — A438

Designs: 4k, Aase Bye (1904-91). 4.50k, Per Aabel (1902-99). 5.50k, Alfred Maurstad (1896-1967). 7k, Lillebil Ibsen (1899-1989). 8k, Tore Segelcke (1901-79).

2001, Jan. 2 **Litho.** ***Perf. 14x12¾***

1277 A438 4k brn & blk 1.25 .75
1278 A438 4.50k bl & blk 1.50 .40
1279 A438 5.50k gold & blk 1.75 .75
1280 A438 7k pur & blk 2.10 .80
1281 A438 8k bl gray & blk 2.50 1.00
Nos. 1277-1281 (5) 9.10 3.70

Ties That Bind, by Magne Furuholmen A439

2001, Feb. 7 **Litho.** ***Perf. 14¾x14***

1282 A439 4.50k multi 1.50 .40

Redrawn Posthorn — A439a

2001-06 **Litho.** ***Perf. 13¾x13¼***

Color of Oval

1282A A439a 50o green, blue denomination .25 .25
1283 A439a 1k green .50 .25
a. Horiz. rows of dots between vert. lines .50 .25
1284 A439a 2k Prus blue .60 .40
a. Horiz. rows of dots between vert. lines .60 .40
1285 A439a 3k blue 1.00 .60
1287 A439a 5k purple 1.50 .60
a. Horiz. rows of dots between vert. lines 1.50 .25
1288 A439a 6k purple 1.75 .50
1289 A439a 7k brown 2.25 .70
1291 A439a 9k orange brn 2.75 .90
a. Horiz. rows of dots between vert. lines 2.75 .90
Nos. 1282A-1291 (8) 10.60 4.20

Numerous design differences exist between types A10 and A439a in the vertical shading lines, the size and shading of the posthorn and in the corner wings.

No. 1282A has no dots between vertical lines. Dots between vertical lines on Nos. 1283-1284, 1287-1288 and 1291 are arranged diagonally. Nos. 1285 and 1289 have horizontal rows of dots between vertical lines.

Issued: Nos.1283, 1284, 6k, 2/7/01; 50o, 3/01; 5k, 9k, 2/11/02; Nos. 1283a, 1284a, 1291a, 2003; 3k, 7k, 4/15/05; No. 1287a, 2006.

See No. 1145 for green 50o stamp with green denomination. See Nos. 1628-1630, 1661, 1690, 1723-1724, 1749-1752, 1783, 1802B, 1822-1824, 1872, 1911, 1945, 1947.

School Bands, Cent. — A440

Designs: 4.50k, Tuba player. 9k, Drum majorette.

2001, Apr. 20 **Litho.** ***Perf. 14¾x14***

1292 A440 4.50k multi 1.40 .50
1293 A440 9k multi 3.00 1.50

Adventure Sports — A441

Designs: 4.50k, Kayaking. 7k, Rock climbing.

Serpentine Die Cut 14x13 on 3 Sides

2001, Apr. 20 **Photo. & Litho.**

Booklet Stamps

Self-Adhesive

1294 A441 4.50k multi 1.75 .50
a. Booklet of 8 15.00
1295 A441 7k multi 2.50 .75
a. Booklet of 8 20.00

Norwegian Architecture A442

Designs: 5.50k, Bank of Norway, Oslo, by Christian Heinrich Grosch. 8.50k, Ivar Aasen Center, Orsta, by Sverre Fehn.

2001, June 22 **Litho.** ***Perf. 14¾x14***

1296 A442 5.50k multi 1.75 .75
1297 A442 8.50k multi 3.00 1.00

Actors and Actresses — A443

Designs: 5k, Lalla Carlsen (1889-1967). 5.50k, Leif Juster (1910-95). 7k, Kari Diesen (1914-87). 9k, Arvid Nilssen (1913-76). 10k, Einar Rose (1898-1979).

2001, June 22 ***Perf. 13x14***

1298 A443 5k multi 1.40 1.00
1299 A443 5.50k multi 1.50 .60
1300 A443 7k multi 2.00 1.00
1301 A443 9k multi 2.50 2.50
1302 A443 10k multi 2.75 1.50
Nos. 1298-1302 (5) 10.15 6.60

Rose Type of 2001

Die Cut Perf. 13¼x13 on 3 Sides

2001, June 22 **Photo. & Litho.**

Booklet Stamps

Self-Adhesive

1303 A436 5.50k Red roses 1.75 .30
1304 A436 5.50k Pink roses 1.75 .30
a. Booklet pane, 2 each #1303-1304 7.00
Booklet, 2 #1304a 16.00

Nos. 1303-1304 are impregnated with a rose scent.

Roses on No. 1303 have white centers. Compare with Illustration A460.

Crafts Type of 2001

Designs: 5k, Carved bird-shaped drinking vessel. 5.50k, Doll with crocheted clothing. 8.50k, Knitted cap.

Die Cut Perf. 14½

2001, June 22 **Photo.**

Coil Stamps

Self-Adhesive

1305 A437 5k multi 2.50 2.50
1306 A437 5.50k multi 2.50 2.50
1307 A437 8.50k multi 4.25 4.25
Nos. 1305-1307 (3) 9.25 9.25

2001, June 22 **Photo.**

Coil Stamps

Self-Adhesive

1305a Die cut perf. 12¾ 1.75 .30
1306a Die cut perf. 12¾ 1.75 .30
1307a Die cut perf. 12¾ 3.00 .30

Nobel Peace Prize, Cent. — A444

Designs: No. 1308, 1991 winner Aung San Suu Kyi. No. 1309, 1993 winner Nelson Mandela. No. 1310, Alfred Nobel. No. 1311, 1901 winner Henri Dunant. No. 1312, 1922 winner Fridjof Nansen. No. 1313, 1990 winner, Mikhail S. Gorbachev. No. 1314, 1964 winner, Dr. Martin Luther King, Jr. No. 1315, 1992 winner Dr. Rigoberta Menchú Tum.

Perf. 13¼x13¾

2001, Sept. 14 **Litho. & Engr.**

1308 A444 5.50k multi 1.75 .75
1309 A444 5.50k multi 1.75 .75
a. Vert. pair, #1308-1309 3.50 3.00
1310 A444 7k multi 2.50 1.25
a. Souvenir sheet of 1 3.50 2.75
1311 A444 7k multi 2.50 1.25
a. Vert. pair, #1310-1311 5.00 4.50
1312 A444 9k multi 2.75 1.50
1313 A444 9k multi 2.75 1.50
a. Vert. pair, #1312-1313 5.50 5.00
1314 A444 10k multi 3.00 2.00
1315 A444 10k multi 3.00 2.00
a. Vert. pair, #1314-1315 6.00 5.00
Nos. 1308-1315 (8) 20.00 11.00

Pets — A445

2001, Sept. 14 **Litho.** ***Perf. 14x13¼***

1316 A445 5.50k Kittens 1.75 .50
1317 A445 7.50k Goat 2.10 1.25

Aurora Borealis — A446

2001, Nov. 15

1318 A446 5k Trees 1.50 1.25
1319 A446 5.50k Reindeer 1.75 1.00

Christmas — A447

Gingerbread: No. 1320, Man. No. 1321, House.

Serp. Die Cut 14x13 on 3 Sides

2001, Nov. 15 Photo. & Litho.

Booklet Stamps

Self-Adhesive

1320 A447 5.50k multi 1.50 .30
1321 A447 5.50k multi 1.50 .30
a. Booklet pane, 2 each #1320-1321 6.00
Complete booklet, 2 #1321a 12.00

Actors and Actresses — A448

Designs: 5k, Tordis Maurstad (1901-97). 5.50k, Rolf Just Nilsen (1931-81). 7k, Lars Tvinde (1886-1973). 9k, Henry Gleditsch (1902-42). 10k, Norma Balean (1907-89).

2002, Feb. 11 Litho. *Perf. 13x14*

Background Color

1322 A448 5k rose lilac 1.40 1.25
1323 A448 5.50k lilac 1.40 .60
1324 A448 7k beige 2.00 .80
1325 A448 9k light green 2.50 2.50
1326 A448 10k dull rose 2.75 1.75
Nos. 1322-1326 (5) 10.05 6.90

Contemporary Sculpture — A449

Designs: 7.50k, Monument to Whaling, by Sivert Donali. 8.50k, Throw, by Kare Groven.

2002, Apr. 12 Litho. *Perf. 13¼x13¾*

1327 A449 7.50k multi 2.00 .80
1328 A449 8.50k multi 2.50 1.25

Fairy Tales
A450 A451

Designs: No. 1329, Askeladden and the Good Helpers, by Ivo Caprino. No. 1330, Giant Troll on Karl Johan, by Theodor Kittelsen.

Serpentine Die Cut 13x14 on 3 Sides

2002, Apr. 12 Photo. & Litho.

Booklet Stamps

Self-Adhesive

1329 A450 5.50k multi 1.50 .25
a. Booklet pane of 4 6.00
Booklet, 2 #1329a 12.00
1330 A451 9k multi 2.50 1.25
a. Booklet pane of 4 10.00
Booklet, 2 #1330a 20.00

Norwegian Soccer Association, Cent. — A452

No. 1331: a, Boys playing soccer. b, Referee pointing, player. c, Girls playing soccer. d, Boy kicking ball.

2002, Apr. 12 *Die Cut Perf.*

Self-Adhesive

1331 Booklet pane of 4 6.00
a.-d. A452 5.50k Any single 1.60 .70
Booklet, 2 #1331 12.50

The margins of the two panes in the booklet differ.

Niels Henrik Abel (1802-29), Mathematician A453

Designs: 5.50k, Abel, formula and curves. 22k, Formula, front page of book by Abel, curve.

Perf. 13¼x13¾

2002, June 5 Litho. & Engr.

1332 A453 5.50k multi 1.50 1.50
1333 A453 22k multi 6.00 3.00

For overprints, see No. 1346-1347.

City Charter Anniversaries A454

Designs: No. 1334, Holmestrand, 250th anniv. No. 1335, Kongsberg, 200th anniv.

2002, June 5 Litho.

1334 A454 5.50k multi 1.50 .60
1335 A454 5.50k multi 1.50 .60

Authors — A455

Designs: 11k, Johan Collett Muller Borgen (1902-79). 20k, Nordahl Grieg (1902-43).

2002, June 5 *Perf. 14¼x14*

1336 A455 11k multi 3.00 2.00
1337 A455 20k multi 5.50 3.00

Europa — A456

Designs: 5.50k, Clown juggling balls. 8.50k, Elephant, monkey on rocking horse.

2002, Sept. 20 *Perf. 14x14¾*

1338 A456 5.50k multi 1.75 .75
1339 A456 8.50k multi 2.50 1.25

Great Moments in Norwegian Soccer — A457

Players involved in: 5k, Victory against Germany in 1936 Olympics. No. 1341, Victory against Brazil in 1998 World Cup tournament. No. 1342, Victory of women's team against US in 2000 Olympics. 7k, Victory against Sweden, 1960. 9k, Victory against England, 1981. 10k, Rosenborg's victory against Milan, in Champions League tournament, 1996.

2002, Sept. 20 *Perf. 13¼x13¾*

1340 A457 5k multi 1.60 .70
1341 A457 5.50k multi 1.75 .70
1342 A457 5.50k multi 1.75 .70
1343 A457 7k multi 2.00 1.25
1344 A457 9k multi 2.50 1.25
1345 A457 10k multi 2.60 1.40
a. Souvenir sheet, #1340-1345 + 6 labels 12.50 12.50
Nos. 1340-1345 (6) 12.20 6.00

Norwegian Soccer Association, cent.

Nos. 1332-1333 Overprinted

Perf. 13¼x13¾

2002, Oct. 10 Litho. & Engr.

1346 A453 5.50k multi 2.50 2.50
1347 A453 22k multi 10.00 10.00

Pastor Magnus B. Landstad (1802-80), Hymn Writer and Folk Song Collector — A458

Designs: 5k, Landstad on horse, front page of 1853 book of folk songs. 5.50k, Church's hymn board, front page of 1870 hymn book, portrait of Landstad.

2002, Nov. 20

1348 A458 5k multi 1.50 1.00
1349 A458 5.50k multi 1.75 .75

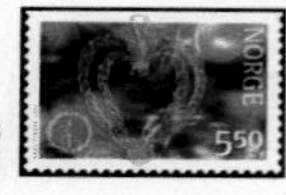

Christmas Ornaments — A459

Die Cut Perf. 13½x13 on 3 Sides

2002, Nov. 20 Photo.

Booklet Stamps

Self-Adhesive

1350 A459 5.50k Hearts 1.50 .30
1351 A459 5.50k Star 1.50 .30
a. Booklet pane, 2 each #1350-1351 6.00
Booklet, 2 #1351a 12.00

Rose Type of 2001 and

Grand Prix Rose — A460

Design: No. 1353, Champagne roses (light yellow).

Die Cut Perf. 13¼x13 on 3 Sides

2003, Feb. 10 Photo. & Litho.

Booklet Stamps

Self-Adhseive

1352 A460 5.50k multi 2.00 .25
1353 A436 5.50k multi 2.00 .25
a. Booklet pane, 2 each #1352-1353 8.00
Booklet, 2 #1353a 16.00

Roses on No. 1303 have white centers, while those on No. 1352 do not.

Crafts Type of 2001

2003, Feb. 10 *Die Cut Perf. 12¾*

Self-Adhesive

1354 A437 5.50k Duodji knife handle 1.75 .25

No. 1354 was printed in sheets and coils.

Graphic Arts — A461

Designs: 5k, Nordmandens Krone, by Kaare Espolin Johnson. 8.50k, Bla Hester, by Else Hagen. 9k, Dirigent og Solist, by Niclas Gulbrandsen. 11k, Olympia, by Svein Strand. 22k, Still Life XVII, by Rigmor Hansen.

Perf. 13¼x12¾

2003, Feb. 10 Litho.

1355 A461 5k multi 1.40 1.00
1356 A461 8.50k multi 2.75 1.50
1357 A461 9k multi 2.75 1.75
1358 A461 11k multi 3.25 1.50
1359 A461 22k multi 6.00 2.00
a. Perf. 14x12¾ 6.00 2.25
Nos. 1355-1359 (5) 16.15 7.75

St. Valentine's Day — A462

Inscriptions beneath scratch-off heart: b, Elsker deg! c, Jusen kyss! d, Glad i dag! e, Klem fra meg! f, Du er snill! g, Min beste venn! h, Yndlings-bror. i, Yndlings-soster. j, Verdens beste far. k, Verdens beste mor.

2003, Feb. 10 *Perf. 14¾x14*

1360 Sheet of 10 18.00 18.00
a. A462 5.50k Any single, unscrached 1.75 1.00
b.-k. A462 5.50k Any single, scratched .65

Unused value for No. 1360a is for stamp with attached selvage. Inscriptions are shown in selvage next to each stamp.

Fairy Tale Illustrations by Theodor Kittelsen (1857-1914)
A463 A464

Serpentine Die Cut 13x14 on 3 Sides

2003, May 22 Photo. & Litho.

Booklet Stamps

Self-Adhesive

1361 A463 5.50k Forest troll 1.40 .45
a. Booklet pane of 4 7.00
Complete booklet, 2 #1361a 14.00

Serpentine Die Cut 14x13 on 3 Sides

1362 A464 9k Water sprite 2.50 1.25
a. Booklet pane of 4 10.00
Complete booklet, 2 #1362a 20.00

Bergen Intl. Music Festival, 50th Anniv. — A465

Musical score and: 5.50k, Violinist. 10k, Children.

2003, May 22 Litho. *Perf. 13¼x14*

1363 A465 5.50k multi 1.75 1.00
1364 A465 10k multi 3.00 2.00

Public Health Service, 400th Anniv. — A466

Designs: 5.50k, Heart transplant operation. 7k, Infant welfare clinic.

2003, May 22

1365 A466 5.50k multi 1.75 1.00
1366 A466 7k multi 2.10 1.75

Norwegian Refugee Council, 50th Anniv. — A467

Designs: 5.50k, Child with bread. 10k, Line of refugees.

2003, June 20

1367 A467 5.50k multi 1.75 1.00
1368 A467 10k multi 3.00 1.10

King Olav V (1903-91) — A468

Designs: 5.50k, As child, with parents. 8.50k, With Crown Princess Märtha. 11k, In uniform.

Litho. & Engr.

2003, June 20 *Perf. 14x13¼*

1369 A468 5.50k multi 1.75 1.00
1370 A468 8.50k multi 2.50 1.50
1371 A468 11k multi 3.00 2.00
a. Souvenir sheet, #1369-1371 11.00 11.00
Nos. 1369-1371 (3) 7.25 4.50

Norwegian Nobel Laureates A469

Designs: 11k, Bjornsterne Bjornson, Literature, 1903. 22k, Lars Onsager, Chemistry, 1968.

Perf. 13¼x13¾

2003, Sept. 19 Litho. & Engr.

1372 A469 11k multi 3.50 1.75
1373 A469 22k multi 6.75 2.50

See nos. 1414-1415.

Europa — A470

Poster art: 8.50k, Dagbladet newspaper poster, by Per Krohg. 9k, Travel poster, by Knut Yran. 10k, 1985 North of Norway Music Festival poster, by Willibald Storn.

2003, Sept. 19 Litho. *Perf. 13¾*

1374 A470 8.50k multi 2.50 1.75
1375 A470 9k multi 2.60 1.75
1376 A470 10k multi 3.00 1.75
Nos. 1374-1376 (3) 8.10 5.25

Special Occasions — A471

Designs: No. 1377, Baby, children's names. No. 1378, Children, birthday cake, toys. No. 1379, Man and woman at party, musical notes. No. 1380, Hands, Cupid. No. 1381, Lily.

Die Cut Perf. 13x13½

2003, Sept. 19 Photo.

Self-Adhesive

1377 A471 5.50k multi 1.75 1.00
1378 A471 5.50k multi 1.75 1.00
1379 A471 5.50k multi 1.75 1.00
1380 A471 5.50k multi 1.75 1.00
1381 A471 5.50k multi 1.75 1.00
Nos. 1377-1381 (5) 8.75 5.00

Graphic Arts — A472

Designs: 5k, Winter Landscape, woodcut by Terje Grostad. 5.50k, Goatherd and Goats, by Rolf Nesch.

Perf. 13¾x12¾

2003, Nov. 21 Litho.

1382 A472 5k multi 1.60 1.00
1383 A472 5.50k multi 1.75 1.00

Christmas — A473

Serpentine Die Cut 13¼x13 on 3 Sides

2003, Nov. 21 Photo.

Booklet Stamps

Self-Adhesive

1384 A473 5.50k Santa Claus 1.40 .30
1385 A473 5.50k Gift 1.40 .30
a. Booklet pane, 2 each #1384-1385 6.00
Complete booklet, 2 #1385a 12.00

Paintings — A474

Designs: 6k, Idyll, by Christian Skredsvig. 9.50k, Stetind in Fog, by Peder Balke. 10.50k, Worker's Protest, by Reidar Aulie.

2004, Jan. 2 Litho. *Perf. 13x14*

1386 A474 6k multi 1.75 .85
1387 A474 9.50k multi 2.75 1.75
1388 A474 10.50k multi 3.00 2.00
Nos. 1386-1388 (3) 7.50 4.60

Marine Life — A475

Designs: 5.50k, Periphylla periphylla. 6k, Anarhichas lupus. 9k, Sepiola atlantica.

Die Cut Perf. 15½x14¼

2004, Jan. 2 Photo.

Self-Adhesive

1389 A475 5.50k multi 1.75 .30
1390 A475 6k multi 2.00 .25
1391 A475 9k multi 2.60 .50
Nos. 1389-1391 (3) 6.35 1.05

See Nos. 1440-1441.

"Person to Person" — A476

Stylized: No. 1392, Man and woman. No. 1393, Globe.

Serpentine Die Cut 13¼x13 on 3 Sides

2004, Jan. 2 Photo. & Litho.

Self-Adhesive

Booklet Stamps

1392 A476 6k multi 1.75 .25
1393 A476 6k multi 1.75 .25
a. Booklet pane, 2 each #1392-1393 7.00
Complete booklet, 2 #1393a 14.00

Sunflower Heart — A477

2004, Feb. 6 Litho. *Perf. 14x13¼*

1394 A477 6k multi 1.75 .75

Printed in sheets of 6 stamps and 3 labels.

Europa — A478

Designs: 6k, Bicyclist in Moskenes. 7.50k, Kayaker on Oslo Fjord. 9.50k, Hikers crossing Stygge Glacier.

Die Cut Perf. 13½x13 on 3 Sides

2004, Mar. 26 Photo. & Litho.

Self-Adhesive

Booklet Stamps

1395 A478 6k multi 1.75 .50
a. Booklet pane of 4 7.00
Complete booklet, 2 #1395a 14.00
1396 A478 7.50k multi 2.10 1.00
a. Booklet pane of 4 8.50
Complete booklet, 2 #1396a 17.00
1397 A478 9.50k multi 2.75 1.25
a. Booklet pane of 4 11.00
Complete booklet, 2 #1397a 22.00
Nos. 1395-1397 (3) 6.60 2.75

Otto Sverdrup (1854-1930), Arctic Explorer — A479

Litho. & Engr.

2004, Mar. 26 *Perf. 13¼*

1398 A479 6k shown 2.00 1.25
1399 A479 9.50k Ship "Fram" 2.75 2.10
a. Souvenir sheet, #1398-1399 + label 7.50 7.50

See Canada Nos. 2026-2027, Greenland No. 426.

Norse Mythology — A480

Designs: 7.50k, Njord, god of wind, sea and fire and ship. 10.50k, Nanna, wife of Balder, Balder's horse, ship.

Perf. 14¼x13¾

2004, Mar. 26 Litho.

1400 A480 7.50k multi 2.50 1.75
1401 A480 10.50k multi 3.00 2.25
a. Souvenir sheet, #1400-1401 7.50 6.00

Souvenir Sheet

Birth of Princess Ingrid Alexandra — A481

2004, Apr. 17 *Perf. 13¾*

1402 A481 6k multi 2.50 2.50

King Haakon IV Haakonson (1204-63) — A482

Designs: 12k, Silhouette of King Haakon IV Haakonson, bows of Viking ships. 22k, Sword and Haakon's Hall, Bergen.

2004, June 18 *Perf. 14¼x14¾*

1403 A482 12k multi 3.50 1.90
1404 A482 22k multi 9.00 2.50

Railways in Norway, 150th Anniv. — A483

Designs: 6k, Koppang Station. 7.50k, Dovre Station. 9.50k, Locomotive, Kylling Bridge. 10.50k, Airport Express train.

2004, June 18 *Perf. 13¼*

1405 A483 6k multi 1.75 .65
1406 A483 7.50k multi 2.10 1.50
1407 A483 9.50k multi 2.90 1.75
1408 A483 10.50k multi 3.25 2.25
Nos. 1405-1408 (4) 10.00 6.15

A484

Children's Stamps — A485

2004, Sept. 17 *Perf. 13¼x14*

1409 A484 6k multi 1.75 .75
1410 A485 9k multi 3.00 1.50

Oseberg Excavations, Cent. A486

Designs: 7.50k, Archaeologists uncovering ship's stern, excavated containers. 9.50k, Textile fragment, ceremonial sleigh. 12k, Bed and rattle.

Litho. & Engr.

2004, Sept. 17 *Perf. 13x13¼*

1411 A486 7.50k multi 2.25 1.75
1412 A486 9.50k multi 2.60 1.75
1413 A486 12k multi 3.50 1.75
Nos. 1411-1413 (3) 8.35 5.25

Norwegian Nobel Laureates Type of 2003

Designs: 5.50k, Odd Hassel, Chemistry, 1969. 6k, Christian Lous Lange, Peace, 1921.

Perf. 13¼x13¾

2004, Nov. 19 Litho. & Engr.

1414 A469 5.50k multi 1.40 1.40
1415 A469 6k multi 1.75 1.00

Christmas — A487

Winning art in UNICEF children's stamp design contest: No. 1416, Children and sun, by Hanne Soteland. No. 1417, Child on woman's lap, by Synne Amalie Lund Kallak.

Serpentine Die Cut 13x13¼ on 3 Sides

2004, Nov. 19 Photo. & Litho.

Self-Adhesive

Booklet Stamps

1416 A487 6k multi 1.75 .30
1417 A487 6k multi 1.75 .30
a. Booklet pane, 2 each #1416-1417 7.00
Complete booklet, 2 #1417a 14.00

Illustrations From "The Three Princesses in the Blue Hill," by Erik Werenskiold (1855-1936) — A488

Designs: 7.50k, Princesses and guard. 9.50k, Baby in cradle.

2005, Jan. 7 Litho. *Perf. 14¼x14*

1418 A488 7.50k multi 2.00 1.25
1419 A488 9.50k multi 2.60 2.00

St. Valentine's Day — A489

2005, Feb. 4 *Perf. 13¼x13¾*

1420 A489 6k red & silver 1.75 .90

Church City Missions, 150th Anniv. — A490

Designs: 5.50k, Soup kitchen. 6k, Ministers administering communion.

2005, Feb. 4 *Perf. 13¾x14¼*

1421 A490 5.50k multi 1.75 1.25
1422 A490 6k multi 2.00 1.00

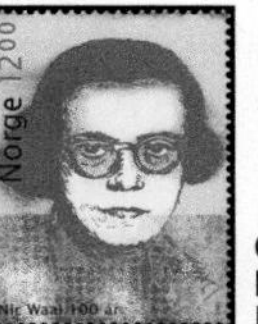

Children's Mental Health Pioneers — A491

Designs: 12k, Nic Waal (1905-60), first Norwegian child psychiatrist. 22k, Aase Gruda

Skard (1905-85), first Norwegian child psychologist.

2005, Feb. 4 ***Perf. 14¼x14¾***

1423 A491 12k multi 3.25 2.00
1424 A491 22k multi 6.50 2.00

A492

Children's Drawings of Norway in 2105 — A493

2005, Apr. 15 Litho. *Perf. 14x12¾*

1425 A492 6k multi 1.75 1.00
1426 A493 7.50k multi 2.25 1.50

Tourism — A494

Designs: 6k, Geiranger Fjord. 9.50k, Kjofossen Waterfall, Flam. 10.50k, Polar bear, Svalbard.

Die Cut Perf. 13x13¼ on 3 Sides

2005, Apr. 15 Photo. & Litho.

Booklet Stamps

Self-Adhesive

1427 A494 6k multi 1.75 .30
a. Booklet pane of 4 7.00
Complete booklet, 2 #1427a 14.00
1428 A494 9.50k multi 3.00 1.50
a. Booklet pane of 4 12.00
Complete booklet, 2 #1428a 24.00
1429 A494 10.50k multi 3.25 1.75
a. Booklet pane of 4 13.00
Complete booklet, 2 #1429a 26.00
Nos. 1427-1429 (3) 8.00 3.55

Dissolution of Union with Sweden, Cent. — A495

Designs: 6k, Norwegian Prime Minister Christian Michelsen, Norwegian negotiators and signatures. 7.50k, King Haakon VII, ships.

Perf. 12½x12¾

2005, May 27 Litho. & Engr.

1430 A495 6k multi 1.75 1.00
1431 A495 7.50k multi 2.25 1.25
a. Souvenir sheet, #1430-1431 4.00 4.00

See Sweden No. 2514.

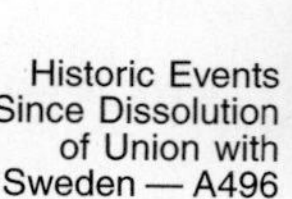

Historic Events Since Dissolution of Union with Sweden — A496

Designs: No. 1432, King Haakon VII taking oath of allegiance, 1905. No. 1433, Crown Prince Olav celebrating end of World War II, 1945. No. 1434, King Olav V at inauguration of Norwegian television broadcasting, 1960. No. 1435, Prime Minister Trygve Bratteli opening Ekofisk oil field, 1971. No. 1436, Victory of Norwegian World Cup soccer team over Brazil, 1998.

2005, June 7 Litho. *Perf. 13¾*

1432 A496 6k multi 1.75 1.00
1433 A496 6k multi 1.75 1.00
1434 A496 6k multi 1.75 1.00
1435 A496 6k multi 1.75 1.00
1436 A496 9k multi 2.75 1.50
Nos. 1432-1436 (5) 9.75 5.50

Tall Ships — A497

Designs: 6k, Christian Radich. 9.50k, Sorlandet. 10.50k, Statsraad Lehmkuhl.

2005, June 7 ***Perf. 13¾x13½***

1437 A497 6k multi 1.75 1.00
1438 A497 9.50k multi 2.75 1.75
1439 A497 10.50k multi 3.00 2.40
Nos. 1437-1439 (3) 7.50 5.15

Marine Life Type of 2004

Designs: B, Orcinus orca. A, Urticina eques.

Die Cut Perf. 15½x14¼

2005, Sept. 1 Photo.

Self-Adhesive

1440 A475 B multi 1.75 .30
1441 A475 A multi 2.00 .30

No. 1440 sold for 5.50k and No. 1441 sold for 6k on day of issue.

Lighthouses — A498

Designs: No. 1442, Jomfruland (white lighthouse). No. 1443, Tranoy (red and white lighthouse).

Die Cut Perf. 13¼x13 on 3 Sides

2005, Sept. 1 Photo. & Litho.

Self-Adhesive

Booklet Stamps

1442 A498 A multi 2.00 .30
1443 A498 A multi 2.00 .30
a. Booklet pane, 2 each #1442-1443 8.00
Complete booklet, 2 #1443a 16.00

Nos. 1442-1443 each sold for 6k on day of issue.

Europa — A499

2005, Sept. 16 Litho. *Perf. 14¾x14*

1444 A499 9.50k Fish 2.75 1.75
1445 A499 10.50k Table 3.00 1.75

Norwegian Telegraph Service, 150th Anniv. — A500

Designs: 6k, Telegraph key and poles. 10.50k, Woman and symbols of modern communication.

Perf. 13½x13¾

2005, Sept. 16 Litho. & Engr.

1446 A500 6k multi 2.00 1.40
1447 A500 10.50k multi 3.00 2.00

Geological Society of Norway, Cent. — A501

Designs: 5.50k, Thortveitite and feldspar. 6k, Oil rig, ship, map of Norway, microfossil and stylized rock layers.

2005, Sept. 16 Litho. *Perf. 13¾*

1448 A501 5.50k multi 1.75 1.40
1449 A501 6k multi 2.00 1.25

Norwegian Postage Stamps, 150th Anniv. — A502

Designs: A, Eye, vignette and spandrels of Norway #1. 12k, Norway #1, woman writing letter.

Litho., Engr. & Silk Screened

2005, Nov. 17 ***Perf. 14x14¼***

1450 A502 A multi 2.00 1.00

Souvenir Sheet

1451 Sheet, #1450, 1451a 5.50 5.50
a. A502 12k multi 3.50 3.50

No. 1450 sold for 6k on day of issue.

Royal House, Cent. A503

Designs: No. 1452, Norwegian Prime Minister greeting King Haakon VII and Crown Prince Olav, 1905. No. 1453, Royal coat of arms, King Haakon VII, Queen Maud and Crown Prince Olav, 1945, King Harald V, Crown Prince Haakon, and Princess Ingrid Alexandra, 2004.

2005, Nov. 18 Litho. *Perf. 14x13½*

1452 A503 6k multi 2.00 1.00
1453 A503 6k multi 2.00 1.00

Christmas — A504

Designs: No. 1454, Gingerbread Christmas tree. No. 1455, Oranges studded with cloves on bed of nuts.

Serpentine Die Cut 13x13¼ on 3 Sides

2005, Nov. 19 Photo. & Litho.

Booklet Stamps

Self-Adhesive

1454 A504 A multi 1.75 .30
1455 A504 A multi 1.75 .30
a. Booklet pane, 2 each #1454-1455 7.00
Complete booklet, 2, #1455a 14.00

Nos. 1454-1455 each sold for 6k on day of issue and are impregnated with a cinnamon scent.

Norwegian Language Society, Cent. — A505

2006, Feb. 3 Litho. *Perf. 13¼x13¾*

1456 A505 6k multi 1.75 1.40

St. Valentine's Day — A506

2006, Feb. 3 ***Perf. 13¾x14¼***

1457 A506 A multi 1.75 1.00

Sold for 6k on day of issue.

2006 Winter Olympics, Turin — A507

Designs: 6k, Kari Traa, freestyle skier. 22k, Ole Einar Bjorndalen, biathlon.

2006, Feb. 3 ***Perf. 14¼x14¾***

1458 A507 6k multi 2.00 1.00
1459 A507 22k multi 7.25 2.00

Norwegian Lifesaving Society, Cent. — A508

Designs: 10k, Lifeguard carrying man. 10.50k, Child swimming.

2006, Feb. 24 ***Perf. 13¾***

1460 A508 10k multi 3.00 2.50
1461 A508 10.50k multi 3.00 2.75

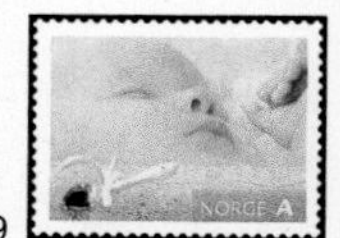

Greetings — A509

Designs: No. 1462, Baby and spoon. No. 1463, Birthday cake. No. 1464, Heart and wedding rings. No. 1465, Flower.

2006, Feb. 24 ***Die Cut Perf. 13¼***

Self-Adhesive

1462 A509 A multi 2.00 1.00
1463 A509 A multi 2.00 1.00
1464 A509 A multi 2.00 1.00
1465 A509 A multi 2.00 1.00
Nos. 1462-1465 (4) 8.00 4.00

Each stamp sold for 6k on day of issue. Each stamp was issued on a white paper backing with surrounding selvage and in coils on a translucent paper backing without surrounding selvage.

Polycera Quadrilineata A510

Die Cut Perf. 15½x14½

2006, Mar. 29 Photo.

Coil Stamp

1466 A510 10k multi 3.00 .50

Wildlife — A511

6.50k, Lynx. 8.50k, Capercaillie. 10k, Golden eagle. 10.50k, Arctic fox. 13k, Arctic hare.

2006, Mar. 29 Litho. *Perf. 13¼x14*

1467 A511 6.50k multi 2.00 .50
1468 A511 8.50k multi 2.00 2.00
1469 A511 10k multi 3.00 2.00
1470 A511 10.50k multi 3.00 2.50
1471 A511 13k multi 3.50 2.50
Nos. 1467-1471 (5) 13.50 9.50

See Nos. 1498-1499, 1531-1533, 1565-1567, 1600-1602, 1636-1637, 1726C-1728, 1756, 1763, 1825.

Souvenir Sheet

Norse Mythology — A512

No. 1472: a, Design on Sami shaman's drum. b, Carved door post from Hylestad Stave Church depicting dragon and dragon slayer.

2006, Mar. 29 ***Perf. 14x14¼***

1472 A512 Sheet of 2 7.50 8.00
a. A multi 2.75 2.75
b. 10.50k multi 3.25 3.25

No. 1472a sold for 6k on day of issue.

Norwegian Arctic Expeditions, Cent. — A513

Designs: 6.50k, Gunnar Isachsen and assistant surveying terrain. 8.50k, Coal cable car terminal, Store Norske Spitzbergen mines. 22k, Longyearbyen.

Litho. & Engr.

2006, June 9 ***Perf. 13½x14***

1473 A513 6.50k multi 2.25 .75

1474 A513 8.50k multi 2.75 2.00

Litho.

1475 A513 22k multi 4.25 4.25

a. Souvenir sheet, #1473-1475 10.00 10.00

Nos. 1473-1475 (3) 9.25 7.00

Tourism — A514

Designs: No. 1476, Paddle steamer Skibladner. No. 1477, Maihaugen Museum, Lillehammer. No. 1478, Kirkeporten natural arch. No. 1479, North Cape. No. 1480, Bryggen UNESCO World Heritage Site. No. 1481, Storeseisundet Bridge on Atlantic Road.

Die Cut Perf. 13¼x13½

2006, June 9 **Photo.**

Self-Adhesive

Booklet Stamps

1476 A514 6.50k multi 2.00 .50

1477 A514 6.50k multi 2.00 .50

a. Booklet pane, 5 each #1476-1477 20.00

1478 A514 8.50k multi 2.50 2.00

1479 A514 8.50k multi 2.50 2.00

a. Booklet pane, 5 each #1478-1479 25.00

1480 A514 10.50k multi 3.00 2.50

1481 A514 10.50k multi 3.00 2.50

a. Booklet pane, 5 each #1480-1481 30.00

Nos. 1476-1481 (6) 15.00 10.00

Consumer Cooperatives, Cent. — A515

2006, June 9 **Litho.** ***Perf. 13½x14***

1482 A515 6.50k multi 2.00 1.00

Personalized Stamp — A516

Serpentine Die Cut 11¾ Syncopated

2006, Aug. 22 **Self-Adhesive**

1483 A516 A multi 2.00 2.00

No. 1483 sold for 6.50k on the day of issue. The image shown is the generic image sold at face value. Stamps could be personalized, presumably for an extra fee.

Marine Life — A517

Designs: B, Strongylocentrotus droebachiensis. A, Labrus bimaculatus.

Die Cut Perf. 15½x14½

2006, Sept. 15 **Photo.**

Self-Adhesive

Coil Stamps

1484 A517 B multi 1.75 .50

1485 A517 A multi 2.00 .30

On day of issue, No. 1484 sold for 6k; No. 1485 for 6.50k.

King's Guard, 150th Anniv. — A518

Designs: 6.50k, King's Guard in dress uniforms. 13k, In field uniforms, with helicopter.

2006, Sept. 15 **Litho.** ***Perf. 14x13¼***

1486 A518 6.50k multi 2.00 1.25

1487 A518 13k multi 3.50 3.00

a. Souvenir sheet, #1486-1487 7.00 7.00

Europa — A519

Designs: 8.50k, Five children. 13k, Three children playing soccer.

2006, Nov. 17 ***Perf. 13¾***

1488 A519 8.50k multi 2.50 2.00

1489 A519 13k multi 3.50 3.00

Christmas — A520

Designs: No. 1490, Children and Christmas tree. No. 1491, Child and snowman.

Die Cut Perf. 13¼x13½

2006, Nov. 17 **Photo. & Litho.**

Self-Adhesive

Booklet Stamps

1490 A520 A multi 2.00 .50

1491 A520 A multi 2.00 .50

a. Booklet pane, 5 each #1490-1491 20.00

On day of issue each stamp sold for 6.50k.

Personalized Stamp — A521

Serpentine Die Cut 11¾ Syncopated

2006, Nov. 17 **Litho.**

Self-Adhesive

1492 A521 A multi 2.00 2.00

No. 1492 sold for 6.50k on the day of issue. The image shown is the generic image sold at face value. Stamps could be personalized, presumably for an extra fee.

St. Valentine's Day — A522

2007, Feb. 6 **Litho.** ***Perf. 13¼***

1493 A522 A multi 2.00 1.50

Sold for 6.50k on day of issue. Values are for stamps with surrounding selvage.

Winter Rally Race Cars — A523

Designs: No. 1494, Petter Solberg's Subaru Impreza. No. 1495, Henning Solberg's Peugeot 307. No. 1496, Thomas Schie's Ford Focus.

Litho. With Foil Application

2007, Feb. 6 ***Perf. 13¼x13¾***

1494 A523 A Innland multi 2.00 1.50

1495 A523 A Europa multi 2.50 2.25

1496 A523 A Verden multi 3.00 3.00

a. Souvenir sheet, #1494-1496 7.50 7.50

Nos. 1494-1496 (3) 7.50 6.75

On day of issue, No. 1494 sold for 6.50k; No. 1495, for 8.50k; No. 1496, for 10.50k.

King Harald V, 70th Birthday — A524

Perf. 13¾x13¼

2007, Feb. 21 **Litho.**

1497 A524 6.50k multi 2.00 1.50

Wildlife Type of 2006

2007, Feb. 21 ***Perf. 13¼x13¾***

1498 A511 12k Hedgehog 3.50 1.75

1499 A511 22k Red squirrel 6.50 2.50

Souvenir Sheet

Intl. Polar Year A526

No. 1500: a, Ice core, oceanographic equipment. b, K/V Svalbard, dish antenna.

2007, Feb. 21

1500 A526 Sheet of 2 7.50 7.50

a. 10.50k multi 3.00 3.00

b. 13k multi 4.00 4.00

Porsgrunn, Bicent. A527

2007, Apr. 27

1501 A527 A Innland multi 2.00 1.50

Sold for 7k on day of issue.

Illustrations by Theodor Kittelsen (1857-1914) — A528

Designs: No. 1502, An Attack (grasshoppers, mosquito, flower). No. 1503, Premature Delivery (frogs, hatched bird).

2007, Apr. 27 ***Perf. 14x13½***

1502 A528 A Europa multi 2.75 2.00

1503 A528 A Verden multi 3.25 2.75

On day of issue, No. 1502 sold for 9k; No. 1503, for 11k.

Skydivers A529

Cyclists A530

Buildings, Roros A531

Bridge, Fredrikstad A532

Pilot House, Portor — A533

Reine Harbor — A534

Die Cut Perf. 13¼x13¾

2007, Apr. 27

Self-Adhesive

Booklet Stamps

1504 A529 A Innland multi 2.00 .50

1505 A530 A Innland multi 2.00 .50

a. Booklet pane, 5 each #1504-1505 20.00

1506 A531 A Europa multi 2.75 1.00

1507 A532 A Europa multi 2.75 1.00

a. Booklet pane, 5 each #1506-1507 27.50

1508 A533 A Verden multi 3.25 1.00

1509 A534 A Verden multi 3.25 1.00

a. Booklet pane, 5 each #1508-1509 32.50

Nos. 1504-1509 (6) 16.00 5.00

On day of issue, Nos. 1504-1505 each sold for 7k; Nos. 1506-1507 each sold for 9k; Nos. 1508-1509 each sold for 11k.

Marine Life — A535

Designs: No. 1510, Pandalus montagui. No. 1511, Homarus gammarus. No. 1512, Cancer pagurus. No. 1513, Galathea strigosa. 11k, Scomber scombrus.

2007 ***Die Cut Perf. 15½x14½***

Self-Adhesive

Coil Stamps

1510 A535 A Innland multi 2.00 .50

1511 A535 A Innland multi 2.00 .50

1512 A535 A Innland multi 2.00 .50

1513 A535 A Innland multi 2.00 .50

a. Horiz. strip of 4, #1510-1513 8.50

1514 A535 11k multi 2.75 .90

Nos. 1510-1514 (5) 10.75 2.90

Issued; Nos. 1510-1513, 9/21; No. 1514, 5/2. On day of issue, Nos. 1510-1513 each sold for 7k.

Europa — A536

Designs: 9k, Scouts, knots. 11k, Hitch diagrams, camp gateway.

Perf. 13¼x13¾

2007, May 11 **Litho. & Engr.**

1515 A536 9k multi 2.75 2.00

1516 A536 11k multi 3.00 2.50

Scouting, cent.

Building Anniversaries A537

Designs: 14k, Church of Our Lady, Trondheim, 800th anniv. 23k, Vardohus Fortress, 700th anniv.

2007, May 11

1517 A537 14k multi 3.25 3.00

1518 A537 23k multi 6.50 5.00

Riksmaal Society, Cent. — A538

2007, June 15 **Litho.**

1519 A538 7k multi 2.00 1.25

Personalized Stamp — A539

Serpentine Die Cut 11½ Syncopated

2007, June 15

1520 A539 A Innland multi 2.00 2.00

No. 1520 sold for 7k on day of issue. The image shown is the generic image sold at face value. Stamps could be personalized, presumably for an extra fee.

Ona Lighthouse, Romsdal A540

Tungeneset Lighthouse, Ersfjorden A541

Die Cut Perf. 13¼x13¾

2007, June 15

1521 A540 A Innland multi 2.00 .50
1522 A541 A Innland multi 2.00 .50
a. Booklet pane, 5 each #1521-1522 20.00

Nos. 1521-1522 each sold for 7k on day of issue.

Haldis Moren Vesaas (1907-95), Poet — A542

Litho. With Foil Application

2007, Sept. 21 ***Perf. 14x13½***

1523 A542 23k multi 7.00 3.00

Mining Academy, Kongsberg, 250th Anniv. — A543

Norwegian Academy of Science and Letters, 150th Anniv. — A544

Perf. 13¼x13¾

2007, Nov. 23 **Litho. & Engr.**

1524 A543 14k multi 4.00 2.25
1525 A544 14k multi 4.00 2.25

Personalized Stamp — A545

Booklet Stamp

Serpentine Die Cut 10¼ Syncopated

2007, Nov. 23 **Self-Adhesive**

1526 A545 A Innland multi 2.25 1.00
a. Booklet pane of 8 18.00

No. 1526 sold for 7k on day of issue. The image shown is the generic image sold at face value. Stamps could be personalized, presumably for an extra fee.

Christmas Star — A546

Adoration of the Magi — A547

Die Cut Perf. 13¼x13¾

2007, Nov. 23 **Photo.**

Self-Adhesive

Booklet Stamps

1527 A546 A Innland multi 2.25 .50
1528 A547 A Innland multi 2.25 .50
a. Booklet pane, 5 each #1527-1528 22.50

On day of issue, Nos. 1527-1528 each sold for 7k.

A548

St. Valentine's Day — A549

2008, Feb. 8 **Litho.** ***Perf. 13¼x13¾***

1529 A548 A Innland multi 1.75 .75
1530 A549 A Europa multi 2.60 1.25

On day of issue, Nos. 1529-1530 sold for 7k and 9k, respectively.

Wildlife Type of 2006

2008, Feb. 21

1531 A511 11k Elk 3.25 1.25
1532 A511 14k Bear 4.25 2.25
1533 A511 23k Wolf 7.00 3.00
Nos. 1531-1533 (3) 14.50 6.50

Thorleif Haug, 1924 Olympic Cross-country Skiing Gold Medalist — A551

Espen Bredesen, 1994 Olympic Ski Jumping Gold Medalist — A552

Children Skiing — A553

Kjetil André Aamodt, 1992, 2002, and 2006 Olympic Alpine Skiing Gold Medalist — A554

Die Cut Perf. 15½x14½

2008, Mar. 14 **Photo.**

Coil Stamps

Self-Adhesive

1534 A551 A Innland multi 2.10 .70
1535 A552 A Innland multi 2.10 .70
1536 A553 A Innland multi 2.10 .70
1537 A554 A Innland multi 2.10 .70
a. Horiz. strip of 4, #1534-1537 8.50 4.00

On day of issue, Nos. 1534-1537 each sold for 7k. Norwegian Ski Federation, cent.

Souvenir Sheet

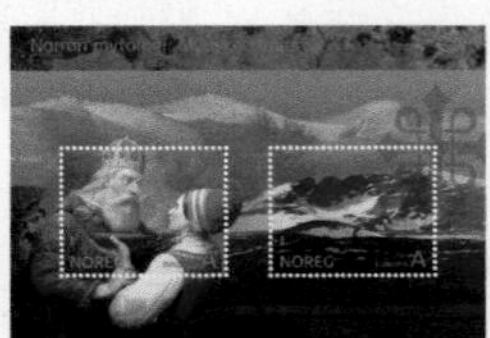

Norse Mythology — A555

No. 1538: a, Harald Fairhair meeting Snofrid. b, Snohetta Mountain.

2008, Mar. 27 **Litho.** ***Perf. 14x14¼***

1538 A555 Sheet of 2 5.00 5.00
a. A Innland multi 2.10 2.10
b. A Europa multi 2.40 2.40

On day of issue, No. 1538a sold for 7k, and No. 1538b sold for 9k.

Opera House, Oslo — A556

Litho. With Foil Application

2008, Apr. 12 ***Perf. 14x13½***

1539 A556 A Innland multi 2.10 .95

Sold for 7k on day of issue.

Famous Men — A557

Designs: No. 1540, Frederik Stang (1808-84), Interior Minister. No. 1541, Henrik Wergeland (1808-45), lyricist.

Perf. 13¼x13¾

2008, Apr. 12 **Litho. & Engr.**

1540 A557 A Innland multi 4.25 2.10
1541 A557 A Innland multi 4.25 2.10

On day of issue, Nos. 1540-1541 each sold for 7k.

Oslo Harbor — A558

Divers, Sculpture, by Ola Enstad, Oslo — A559

The Blade, Sunnmore Alps — A560

Kjerag Boulder — A561

Sailboat and Lyngor Lighthouse A562

Lyngor A563

Die Cut Perf. 13¼x13¾

2008, Apr. 12 **Photo.**

Booklet Stamps

Self-Adhesive

1542 A558 A Innland multi 2.10 .70
1543 A559 A Innland multi 2.10 .70
a. Booklet pane of 10, 5 each #1542-1543 21.00
1544 A560 A Europa multi 2.75 1.40
1545 A561 A Europa multi 2.75 1.40
a. Booklet pane of 10, 5 each #1544-1545 27.50
1546 A562 A Varden multi 3.25 1.75
1547 A563 A Varden multi 3.25 1.75
a. Booklet pane of 10, 5 each #1546-1547 32.50
Nos. 1542-1547 (6) 16.20 7.70

On day of issue, Nos. 1542-1543 each sold for 7k; Nos. 1544-1545, for 9k; Nos. 1546-1547, for 11k.

Stavanger, 2008 European Cultural Capital A564

Designs: 7k, Dancer in a Cultural Landscape, photograph by Marcel Lelienhof. 14k, Swords in Rock, sculpture by Fritz Roed. 23k, Scene from musical, The Thousandth Heart, vert.

Perf. 14x13½, 13½x14

2008, June 6 **Litho.**

1548 A564 7k multi 2.10 .95
1549 A564 14k multi 4.00 1.90
1550 A564 23k multi 7.00 2.60
a. Souvenir sheet, #1548-1550 15.00 15.00
Nos. 1548-1550 (3) 13.10 5.45

No. 1550a issue 10/23. Nordia 2008 Philatelic Exhibition, Stavenger (#1550a).

Transportation Centenaries A565

Designs: 7k, SS Boroysund. 9k, SS Oster. 25k, Automobile used on first bus route. 30k, Train on Thamshavn electric railroad line.

Perf. 13¼x13¾

2008, June 6 **Litho. & Engr.**

1551 A565 7k ocher & green 2.10 .95
1552 A565 9k rose pink & blue 2.75 1.40
1553 A565 25k lt bl & brown 7.25 3.00
1554 A565 30k pur & green 9.00 4.25
Nos. 1551-1554 (4) 21.10 9.60

2008 Summer Olympics, Beijing — A566

Designs: 9k, Andreas Thorkildsen, javelin thrower. 23k, Women's handball player, Gro Hammerseng.

2008, Aug. 8 **Litho.** ***Perf. 14¾x14¼***

1555 A566 9k multi 2.75 1.75
1556 A566 23k multi 6.75 3.00

Personalized Stamp — A567

No. 1558: a, Like No. 1557, but with line of post horns running through middle of top line of "E" in "Norge." b, "Bring."

Serpentine Die Cut 11¾ Syncopated

2008, Sept. 5 **Litho.**

Self-Adhesive

1557 A567 A Innland multi 2.10 2.10

Souvenir Sheet

1558 Sheet of 2 32.50
a. A567 A Innland red & gray 16.00 16.00
b. A567 A Innland green & gray 16.00 16.00

No. 1557 sold for 7k on day of issue. The image shown is the generic image sold at face value. Stamps could be personalized for an extra fee.

No. 1557 has line of post horn running through the right side of the top line of the "E" in "Norge."

About 375,000 examples of No. 1558 were distributed free of charge by Norway Post to the general public at post offices throughout Norway and through their agents abroad in a campaign to promote the sale of personalized stamps. The sheet was never offered for sale by Norway Post or their agents. Nos. 1558a and 1558b each had a franking value of 7k, and could not be personalized.

Art — A568

Designs: No. 1559, In the Forecourt of the Revolution, by Arne Ekeland. No. 1560, Svalbard Motif, by Kare Tveter. No. 1561, Composition in Red, by Inger Sitter. No. 1562, From Sagorsk, c. 1985, by Terje Bergstad.

Die Cut Perf. 15½x14½

2008, Oct. 24 **Photo.**

Coil Stamps

Self-Adhesive

1559 A568 A Innland multi 2.10 .70
1560 A568 A Innland multi 2.10 .70
1561 A568 A Innland multi 2.10 .70
1562 A568 A Innland multi 2.10 .70
a. Horiz. strip of 4, #1559-1562 8.50 8.50
Nos. 1559-1562 (4) 8.40 2.80

On day of issue, Nos. 1559-1562 each sold for 7k.

Gnomes, Amperhaugen Farm, Stor-Elvdal A569

Gnome, Nordre Lien Farm, Stor-Elvdal A570

Booklet Stamps

Die Cut Perf. 13¼x13¾

2008, Nov. 17 **Self-Adhesive**

1563 A569 A Innland multi 2.10 .50
1564 A570 A Innland multi 2.10 .50
a. Booklet pane of 10, 5 each #1563-1564 21.00

Christmas. On day of issue, Nos. 1563-1564 each sold for 7k.

Wildlife Type of 2006

2009, Jan. 2 **Litho.** ***Perf. 13¼x13¾***

1565 A511 11.50k Roe deer 3.50 1.25
1566 A511 15.50k Reindeer 4.50 2.50
1567 A511 25k Willow grouse 7.25 3.50
Nos. 1565-1567 (3) 15.25 7.25

Art — A572

Designs: B, Summer Night, a Tribute to E. M., by Kjell Nupen. 12k, Light at Whitsuntide, by Irma Salo Jaeger.

Die Cut Perf. 15½x14½

2009, Jan. 2 **Photo.**

Coil Stamps

Self-Adhesive

1568 A572 B Innland multi 1.75 .75
1569 A572 12k multi 3.50 1.00

No. 1568 sold for 7.50k on day of issue.

Souvenir Sheet

Global Warming A573

No. 1570: a, Warm globe. b, Globe with melting ice at meridians.

Litho. (#1570a), Litho and Embossed (#1570b)

2009, Feb. 20 ***Perf. 13½***

1570 A573 Sheet of 2 5.00 5.00
a.-b. 8k Either single 2.50 2.50

Personalized Stamp — A574

Serpentine Die Cut 10x10¼ Syncopated

2009, Mar. 2 **Litho.**

Booklet Stamp

Self-Adhesive

1571 A574 A Innland gray 1.75 .95
a. Booklet pane of 8 17.00

No. 1571 sold for 8k on day of issue. The image shown is the generic image sold at face value. Stamps could be personalized for an extra fee.

National Anthem by Bjornestjerne Bjornson, 150th Anniv. A575

Litho. & Engr.

2009, Apr. 17 ***Perf. 13½x14***

1572 A575 12k multi 3.50 2.10

Bergen Line Train in Mountains A576

Bergen Line Train Leaving Tunnel A577

Stotta Fjord A578

Rocky Shore, Revtangen A579

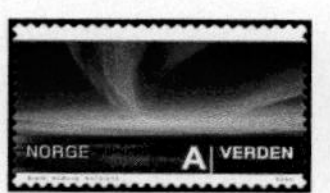

Aurora Borealis — A580

Pot Rock, Vagsoy — A581

Die Cut Perf. 13¼x13½

2009, Apr. 17 **Photo.**

Booklet Stamps

Self-Adhesive

1573 A576 A Innland multi 2.10 .95
1574 A577 A Innland multi 2.10 .95
a. Booklet pane of 10, 5 each #1573-1574 21.00
1575 A578 A Europa multi 2.60 1.25
1576 A579 A Europa multi 2.60 1.25
a. Booklet pane of 10, 5 each #1575-1576 26.00
1577 A580 A Verden multi 3.25 1.75
1578 A581 A Verden multi 3.25 1.75
a. Booklet pane of 10, 5 each #1577-1578 32.50
Nos. 1573-1578 (6) 15.90 7.90

On day of issue, Nos. 1573-1574 each sold for 8k, Nos. 1575-1576 each sold for 10k, and Nos. 1577-1578 each sold for 12k.

Royal Norwegian Society for Development, Bicent. A582

Perf. 13¼x13¾

2009, June 12 **Litho.**

1579 A582 12k multi 3.50 2.10

Submarine Branch of Norwegian Navy, Cent. — A583

Designs: 14.50k, The Kobben. 15.50k, Ula Class submarine.

Litho. & Engr.

2009, June 12 ***Perf. 13¼x14***

1580 A583 14.50k multi 4.25 2.50
1581 A583 15.50k multi 4.50 2.60

Norwegian Year of Cultural Heritage — A584

Designs: No. 1582, Kurér radio, 1950. No. 1583, Telephone booth, 1932.

Die Cut Perf. 15½x14½

2009, June 12 **Litho.**

Coil Stamps

Self-Adhesive

1582 A584 A Innland multi 2.10 .95
1583 A584 A Innland multi 2.10 .95
a. Horiz. pair, #1582-1583 4.25 4.25

On day of issue, Nos. 1582-1583 each sold for 8k.

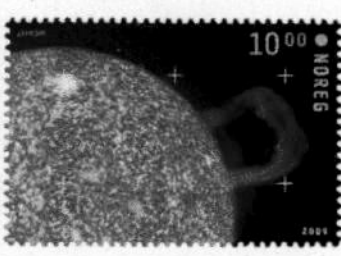

Europa — A585

Designs: 10k, Solar explosion. 12k, Moon.

2009, June 12 ***Perf. 14¼x13¾***

1584 A585 10k multi 3.00 2.50
1585 A585 12k multi 3.50 3.00
a. Souvenir sheet of 2, #1584-1585 6.50 6.50

Intl. Year of Astronomy.

Knut Hamsun (1859-1952), 1920 Nobel Literature Laureate — A586

Litho. & Engr.

2009, Aug. 4 ***Perf. 14¼***

1586 A586 25k multi 7.25 4.25

Rock 'n' Roll Pioneers — A587

Designs: No. 1587, Per "Elvis" Granberg (1941-80). No. 1588, Roald Stensby. No. 1589, Rocke-Pelle (Per Hartvig) (1938-80). No. 1590, Jan Rohde (1942-2005).

Die Cut Perf. 15½x14½

2009. Aug. 21 **Photo.**

Coil Stamps

Self-Adhesive

1587 A587 A Innland multi 2.10 .95
1588 A587 A Innland multi 2.10 .95
1589 A587 A Innland multi 2.10 .95
1590 A587 A Innland multi 2.10 .95
a. Horiz. strip of 4, #1587-1590 8.50 8.50

On day of issue, Nos. 1587-1590 each sold for 8k.

Norwegian Shipowners' Association, Cent. — A588

Perf. 13¾x13¼

2009, Sept. 15 **Litho.**

1591 A588 15.50k multi 4.50 2.75

Norwegian Association of the Blind, Cent. — A589

Litho. & Embossed

2009, Oct. 8 ***Perf. 13¼x14***

1592 A589 8k red 2.10 .95

Sculptures — A590

Designs: No. 1593, Woman on a Man's Lap, by Gustav Vigeland. No. 1594, Crow, by Nils Aas. No. 1595, Birds in Flight, by Arnold Haukeland. No. 1596, Granite Head Lying on its Side, by Kristian Blystad.

Die Cut Perf. 15½x14½

2009, Nov. 16 **Photo.**

Coil Stamps

Self-Adhesive

1593 A590 A Innland multi 2.10 .95
1594 A590 A Innland multi 2.10 .95
1595 A590 A Innland multi 2.10 .95
1596 A590 A Innland multi 2.10 .95
a. Horiz. strip of 4, #1593-1596 8.50 4.25
Nos. 1593-1596 (4) 8.40 3.80

Nos. 1593-1596 each sold for 8k on day of issue.

Christmas — A591

Text and: No. 1597, Apple and snowflakes. No. 1598, Stars.

Die Cut Perf. 13¼x13¾

2009, Nov. 16 **Photo.**

Booklet Stamps

Self-Adhesive

1597 A591 A Innland multi 2.10 .95
1598 A591 A Innland multi 2.10 .95
a. Booklet pane of 10, 5 each #1597-1598 21.00

Nos. 1597-1598 each sold for 8k on day of issue.

Man Drinking, Sculpture bu Per Palle Storm — A592

Die Cut Perf. 15½x14½

2010, Jan. 2 **Litho.**

Coil Stamp

Self-Adhesive

1599 A592 13k multi 3.50 2.10

Wildlife Type of 2006

2010, Jan. 2 ***Perf. 13¼x13¾***

1600 A511 15k European otter 4.50 2.50
1601 A511 16k Lemming 4.75 2.50
1602 A511 26k Wolverine 7.25 3.75
Nos. 1600-1602 (3) 16.50 8.75

Famous Men — A595

Designs: No. 1603, Peter Andreas Munch (1810-63), historian, and illuminated text. No. 1604, Ole Bull (1810-80), violinist.

2010, Feb. 5 ***Die Cut Perf. 15½x14½***

Coil Stamps

Self-Adhesive

1603 A595 A Innland multi 2.10 .95
1604 A595 A Innland multi 2.10 .95
a. Horiz. pair, #1603-1604 4.25 2.50

On day of issue, Nos. 1603-1604 each sold for 8.50k.

Souvenir Sheet

Dried Cod A596

Perf. 13¼x13¾

2010, Mar. 24 Litho.

1605 A596 A Europa multi 3.25 3.25

No. 1605 sold for 11k on day of issue.

Personalized Stamp — A597

Serpentine Die Cut 10x10¼ Syncopated

2010, Apr. 16 Self-Adhesive

1606 A597 A Europa gray 3.25 3.25

No. 1606 sold for 11k on day of issue. The image shown is the generic image sold at face value. Stamps could be personalized for an additional fee.

Valdresflya Road — A598

Gamle Strynefjellsvegen Road — A599

Sognefjellet Road — A600

Trollstigen Road — A601

Helgelandskysten Nord Road — A602

Lofoten National Tourist Road — A603

Booklet Stamps

Die Cut Perf. 13¼x13½

2010, Apr. 16 Self-Adhesive

1607 A598 A Innland multi 2.10 .95
1608 A599 A Innland multi 2.10 .95
a. Booklet pane of 10, 5 each #1607-1608 21.00
1609 A600 A Europa multi 2.60 1.25
1610 A601 A Europa multi 2.60 1.25
a. Booklet pane of 10, 5 each #1609-1610 26.00
1611 A602 A Verda multi 3.25 1.75
1612 A603 A Verda multi 3.25 1.75
a. Booklet pane of 10, 5 each #1611-1612 32.50
Nos. 1607-1612 (6) 15.90 7.90

On day of issue, Nos. 1607-1608 each sold for 8.50k, Nos. 1609-1610 each sold for 11k, and Nos. 1611-1612 each sold for 13k.

Norwegian Eurovision Song Contest Contestants A604

Designs: No. 1613, Bobbysocks, 1985 winner. No. 1614, Secret Garden, 1995 winner. No. 1615, Alexander Rybak, 2009 winner. No. 1616, Jahn Teigen, 1978 finalist.

Coil Stamps

Die Cut Perf. 15½x14½

2010, May 18 Self-Adhesive

1613 A604 A Innland multi 2.10 .95
1614 A604 A Innland multi 2.10 .95
1615 A604 A Innland multi 2.10 .95
1616 A604 A Innland multi 2.10 .95
a. Horiz. strip of 4, #1613-1616 8.50 4.50
Nos. 1613-1616 (4) 8.40 3.80

On day of issue, Nos. 1613-1616 each sold for 8.50k.

Molde Jazz Festival, 50th Anniv. A605

2010, June 18 ***Perf. 13¼x13¾***

1617 A605 13k gray & blue 4.00 2.10

Norwegian National Health Association, Cent. — A606

2010, June 18 Litho. & Engr.

1618 A606 26k multi 8.00 4.25

A607

A608

A609

Television in Norway, 50th Anniv. — A610

Designs: Nos. 1619a, 1620, Children's television characters Bjornen Teodor, Kometkameratene, Pompel & Pilt, Titten Tei. No. 1621, Comedy stars Trond Kirkvag, Robert Stoltenberg, Rolv Wesenlund and Trond-Viggo Torgersen. Nos. 1619b, 1622, Erik Diesen, Dan Borge Akero, Ivar Dyrhaug and Anne Grosvold. No. 1623, Arne Scheie, Ingrid Espelid Hovig, Erik Bye and Ragnhild Saelthun Fjortoft.

2010, Aug. 20 Litho. ***Perf. 13¼x13***

1619 Sheet of 2 5.00 5.00
a. A607 A Innland multi 2.25 2.25
b. A609 A Innland multi 2.25 2.25

Coil Stamps

Self-Adhesive

Die Cut Perf. 15½x14½

1620 A607 A Innland multi 2.10 .95
1621 A608 A Innland multi 2.10 .95
1622 A609 A Innland multi 2.10 .95
1623 A610 A Innland multi 2.10 .95
a. Horiz. strip of 4, #1620-1623 8.50 4.50
Nos. 1620-1623 (4) 8.40 3.80

On day of issue, Nos. 1619a-1619b, 1620-1623 each sold for 8.50k.

Norwegian Press Association, Norwegian Media Businesses Association, Cent. — A611

2010, Sept. 15 ***Perf. 13¼x13¾***

1624 A611 11k multi 3.50 1.75

Norwegian Seafarers' Union, Cent. — A612

2010, Sept. 15 ***Perf. 13¾x13¼***

1625 A612 16k multi 4.50 2.50

Norwegian University of Technology and Science, Cent. — A613

Royal Norwegian Society of Science and Letters, 250th Anniv. A614

Perf. 13¼x13¾

2010, Sept. 15 Litho. & Engr.

1626 A613 8.50k multi 2.10 .95
1627 A614 13k multi 3.50 1.75

Redrawn Posthorn Type of 2001-06

Perf. 13¾x13¼

2010, Nov. 15 Litho.

Color of Oval

1628 A439a 4k blue 1.25 .60
1629 A439a 8k brown 2.50 .95
1630 A439a 30k dull violet 8.50 1.75
Nos. 1628-1630 (3) 12.25 3.30

No. 1630 has a silver frame. See No. 1802B for self-adhesive example of No. 1628.

A615

Europa — A616

Illustrations from children's books by Anne-Cath. Vestly (1920-2008): A Innland, Marte and Grandma and Grandma and Morten. A Europa, The House in the Woods — A New Home.

Litho. With Foil Application

2010, Nov. 15 ***Perf. 13¼***

1631 A615 A Innland multi 2.10 .95
1632 A616 A Europa multi 2.75 1.40

On day of issue, No. 1631 sold for 8.50k and No. 1632 sold for 11k.

Christmas — A617

Designs from embroidered Christmas tablecloth: No. 1633, Straw billy goat. No. 1634, Candlesticks and mistletoe.

Die Cut Perf. 13¼x13¾

2010, Nov. 15 Litho.

Booklet Stamps

Self-Adhesive

1633 A617 A Innland multi 2.10 .95
1634 A617 A Innland multi 2.10 .95
a. Booklet pane of 10, 5 each #1633-1634 21.00

On day of issue, Nos. 1633-1634 each sold for 8.50k.

Norwegian Sports Confederation, 150th Anniv. — A618

Die Cut Perf. 15½x15

2011, Jan. 3 Coil Stamp Litho.

Self-Adhesive

1635 A618 14k multi 4.00 2.50

Wildlife Type of 2006

2011, Jan. 3 Litho. ***Perf. 13¼x13¾***

1636 A511 17k Polar bear 4.75 2.40
a. Perf. 14¼x13¾ 9.50 5.00
1637 A511 27k Musk ox 7.25 3.00

2011 World Nordic Skiing Championships, Oslo — A619

Designs: 9k, Holmenkollen ski jump. 12k, Skiers, Holmenkollen Ski Stadium.

2011, Feb. 23 ***Perf. 13½x13¼***

1638 A619 9k multi 2.75 1.40
1639 A619 12k multi 3.50 2.00
a. Souvenir sheet of 2, #1638-1639 6.50 6.50

Fridtjof Nansen (1861-1930), Explorer and Statesman A620

2011, Apr. 15 Litho. ***Perf. 14x13¼***

1640 A620 12k multi 3.50 2.10

Amnesty International, 50th Anniv. — A621

Perf. 14¼x14½

2011, Apr. 15 Litho. & Engr.

1641 A621 A Innland multi 2.10 .95

No. 1641 sold for 9k on day of issue.

Roald Amundsen Expedition to South Pole, Cent. A622

Designs: 14k, Amundsen (1872-1928), men on expedition, Norwegian flag. 17k, Polar ship Fram and sled dogs.

2011, Apr. 15 Litho. ***Perf. 14x13¼***

1642 A622 14k multi 4.00 2.50
1643 A622 17k multi 5.00 3.00

Buildings — A623

Designs: No. 1644, Global Seed Vault, Svalbard. No. 1645, Visitor's Center, Borgund. No. 1646, Preikestolen Mountain Lodge, Lysefjorden.

Booklet Stamps

Die Cut Perf. 13¼x13½

2011, Apr. 15 Self-Adhesive

1644 A623 A Innland multi 2.10 .95
a. Booklet pane of 10 21.00
1645 A623 A Europa multi 2.75 1.40
a. Booklet pane of 10 27.50
1646 A623 A Verden multi 3.25 1.75
a. Booklet pane of 10 32.50
Nos. 1644-1646 (3) 8.10 4.10

On day of issue, Nos. 1644-1646 sold for 9k, 12k and 14k, respectively.

Drammen, Bicent. A624

2011, May 20 ***Perf. 14x13¼***

1647 A624 9k multi 2.75 1.40

Fire and Rescue Services, 150th Anniv. — A625

Designs: 9k, Firemen and fire truck from Sagene Fire Station, Oslo. 27k, Firemen training.

2011, June 3 *Perf. 13¼x13¾*

1648 A625 9k multi 2.75 1.40
1649 A625 27k multi 8.00 4.50

Europa A626

Designs: 12k, Logging, Bjornsasen. 14k, Forest, Farrisvannet.

2011, June 10 **Litho.**

1650 A626 12k multi 3.50 2.10
1651 A626 14k multi 4.00 2.50

Intl. Year of Forests.

University of Oslo, Bicent. A627

2011, Sept. 2 **Litho. & Engr.**

1652 A627 9k ver & brn 2.75 1.40

Comic Strip Art — A628

Designs: 9k, Bird in nest, by John Arne Saeteroy. 14k, Hold Brillan (man opening envelope), by Cristopher Nielsen. 17k, Nemi (women with index finger and pinkie raised), by Lise Myhre. 20k, Pondus (soccer player), by Frode Overli.

2011, Sept. 16 **Litho.**

1653 A628 9k multi 2.75 1.40
1654 A628 14k multi 4.00 2.50
1655 A628 17k multi 4.75 2.50
1656 A628 20k multi 6.50 3.50
Nos. 1653-1656 (4) 18.00 9.90

Female Singers — A629

Designs: No. 1657, Wenche Myhre. No. 1658, Inger Lise Rypdal. No. 1659, Mari Boine. No. 1660, Sissel Kyrkjebo.

Coil Stamps

Die Cut Perf. 15½x14½

2011, Sept. 16 **Self-Adhesive**

1657 A629 A Innland multi 2.10 .95
1658 A629 A Innland multi 2.10 .95
1659 A629 A Innland multi 2.10 .95
1660 A629 A Innland multi 2.10 .95
a. Horiz. coil strip of 4, #1657-1660 8.50 5.00
Nos. 1657-1660 (4) 8.40 3.80

On day of issue, Nos. 1657-1660 each sold for 9k.

Redrawn Posthorn Type of 2001-06

Perf. 13¾x13¼

2011, Nov. 11 **Litho.**

Color of Oval

1661 A439a 50k blue gray 15.00 4.00

No. 1661 has a silver frame. See No. 1751 for similar self-adhesive stamp.

Christmas — A630

Designs: No. 1662, Boy holding letter. No. 1663, Girl holding gifts.

Die Cut Perf. 13½x13¼

2011, Nov. 11 **Litho.**

Self-Adhesive

1662 A630 A Innland multi 2.10 .95
1663 A630 A Innland multi 2.10 .95
a. Horiz. pair, #1662-1663, on tan backing paper 4.50
b. Booklet pane of 10, 5 each #1662-1663 21.00

On day of issue, Nos. 1662-1663 each sold for 9k. On No. 1663b, Nos. 1662 and 1663 are arranged in vertical pairs.

Personalized Stamp — A631

Serpentine Die Cut 10x10¼ Syncopated

2012, Feb. 21 **Self-Adhesive**

1664 A631 A Innland multi 2.10 1.25

No. 1664 sold for 9.50k on day of issue. The image shown is the generic image sold at face value. Stamps could be personalized for an additional fee.

75th Birthdays of King and Queen — A632

Designs: 9.50k, Queen Sonja. 13k, King Harald V.

Perf. 14¼x14½

2012, Feb. 21 **Litho. & Engr.**

1665 A632 9.50k multi 2.75 1.25
1666 A632 13k multi 3.75 2.50

A booklet containing booklet panes of 2 No. 1665, 2 No. 1666 and 1 each of Nos. 1665-1666 sold for 99k. Value $30.

Griffin From Roof Of National Gallery Oslo, Sculpture by Lars Utne A633

Branntomt, by Hakon Stenstadvold A634

Die Cut Perf. 15½x14½

2012, Feb. 21 **Litho.**

Coil Stamps
Self-Adhesive

1667 A633 B Innland multi 1.75 .95
1668 A634 14k multi 4.00 2.50

No. 1667 sold for 9k on day of issue. An etiquette alternates with No. 1667 on rolls produced for sale to the public. On later printings, the etiquette is not present on the rolls.

Souvenir Sheet

Rescue Helicopter — A635

2012, Mar. 21 *Perf. 14x13½*

1669 A635 A Europa multi 3.50 3.50

No. 1669 sold for 13k on day of issue.

Famous People — A636

Designs: No. 1670, Sonja Henie (1912-69), figure skater. No. 1671, Close-up of Henie. No. 1672, Thorbjorn Egner (1912-90), writer of children's books. No. 1673, Egner's illustration of Kardemomme Town.

Coil Stamps

Die Cut Perf. 15½x14½

2012, Apr. 13 **Self-Adhesive**

1670 A636 A Innland multi 2.25 .95
1671 A636 A Innland multi 2.25 .95
1672 A636 A Innland multi 2.25 .95
1673 A636 A Innland multi 2.25 .95
a. Horiz. strip of 4, #1670-1673 9.00
Nos. 1670-1673 (4) 9.00 3.80

On day of issue, Nos. 1670-1673 each sold for 9.50k. No. 1673a was made available with stamps on the strip in a different order and having a different distance between stamps.

Nidaros Cathedral, Trondheim A637

Abbey Ruins, Selja Island A638

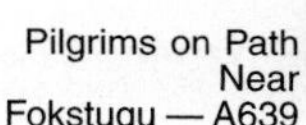

Pilgrims on Path Near Fokstugu — A639

Die Cut Perf. 13¼x13½

2012, Apr. 13 **Self-Adhesive**

1674 A637 A Innland multi 2.25 1.00
a. Booklet pane of 10 on white backing paper 22.50
1675 A638 A Europa multi 3.25 1.60
a. Booklet pane of 10 on white backing paper 32.50
1676 A639 A Verden multi 4.00 2.25
a. Booklet pane of 10 on white backing paper 40.00
Nos. 1674-1676 (3) 9.50 4.85

Europa. On day of issue Nos. 1674-1676 each sold for 9.50k, 13k and 15k, respectively. Values for unused examples of Nos. 1674-1676 are for copies either on white backing paper (from booklet panes) or tan backing paper (single stamps).

Norwegian Aviation, Cent. — A640

Designs: 14k, Start (Rumpler Taube), first airplane of Navy Air Service. 15k, Douglas DC-3 Dakota. 27k, Glider.

2012, May 18 **Litho.** *Perf. 13¼*

1677 A640 14k multi 4.00 2.50
1678 A640 15k multi 4.75 2.50
1679 A640 27k multi 8.00 4.50
a. Souvenir sheet of 3, #1677-1679 17.00 17.00
Nos. 1677-1679 (3) 16.75 9.50

Hadeland Glassworks, 250th Anniv. A641

Perf. 13¼x13¾

2012, June 15 **Litho. & Engr.**

1680 A641 13k multi 3.75 1.75

Kavringen Lighthouse A642

Medfjordbaen Lighthouse A643

Die Cut Perf. 13½x13¼

2012, June 15 **Litho.**

Self-Adhesive

1681 A642 A Innland multi 2.25 1.00
1682 A643 A Innland multi 2.25 1.00
a. Horiz. pair, #1681-1682, on tan backing paper 4.50
b. Booklet pane of 10, 5 each #1681-1682 22.50

On day of issue, Nos. 1681-1682 each sold for 9.50k. On No. 1682b, Nos. 1681 and 1682 are arranged in vertical pairs.

Norwegian Nurses Organization, Cent. — A644

2012, Sept. 14 *Perf. 13¼x13¾*

1683 A644 13k multi 3.75 1.75

Famous Men — A645

Designs: 14k, Knud Knudsen (1812-95), linguist. 15k, Peter Christen Asbjornsen (1812-85) and Jorgen Moe (1813-82), collectors of Norwegian folklore.

2012, Sept. 14 *Perf. 14x13¼*

1684 A645 14k multi 2.50 1.25
1685 A645 15k multi 2.50 1.25

Popular Musicians — A646

Designs: No. 1686, Sondre Lerche. No. 1687, Ole Paus. No. 1688, Age Aleksandersen. No. 1689, Morten Abel.

Coil Stamps

Die Cut Perf. 15½x14½

2012, Sept. 14 **Self-Adhesive**

1686 A646 A Innland multi 2.50 1.25
1687 A646 A Innland multi 2.50 1.25
1688 A646 A Innland multi 2.50 1.25
1689 A646 A Innland multi 2.50 1.25
a. Horiz. strip of 4, #1686-1689 10.00
Nos. 1686-1689 (4) 10.00 5.00

Redrawn Posthorn Type of 2001-06

Perf. 13¾x13¼

2012, Nov. 12 **Litho.**

Color of Oval

1690 A439a 40k gray 12.00 2.50

No. 1690 has a silver frame. See No. 1824 for similar self-adhesive stamp.

Ruins of Hamar Cathedral A647

2012, Nov. 12 **Litho.**

1691 A647 15k multi 5.00 2.25

Directorate for Cultural Heritage, cent.

Santa Claus and Carpenter Andersen A648

Mrs. Claus and Children A649

Die Cut Perf. 13¼x13¾

2012, Nov. 12 Self-Adhesive

1692 A648 A Innland multi 2.50 1.25
1693 A649 A Innland multi 2.50 1.25
a. Booklet pane of 10, 5 each #1692-1693, on white backing paper 25.00

Nos. 1692-1693 each sold for 9.50k on day of issue. Horizontal pairs of Nos. 1692-1693 are on white backing paper, which are from No. 1693a, and a tan backing paper, which were prepared for philatelic sale. The stamps on the tan backing paper were only made available as pairs, and were not available in coil rolls.

Fashion — A650

Fashion designs by: No. 1694, Nina Skarras. No. 1695, Camilla Bruerberg.

2013, Jan. 2 ***Die Cut Perf. 15½x14½***

Coil Stamps
Self-Adhesive

1694 A650 15k multi 5.00 2.50
1695 A650 15k multi 5.00 2.50
a. Horiz. pair, #1694-1695 10.00

Paintings by Edvard Munch (1863-1944) A651

Details from: 13k, Self-Portrait in Front of the House Wall, 1926. 15k, The Sick Child, 1898. 17k, Madonna, 1895. No. 1699, The Scream, 1893.
No. 1700, The Sun, 1911.

2013, Feb. 15 ***Perf. 14x13¼***

1696 A651 13k multi 4.00 2.50
a. Booklet pane of 1 8.50 —
1697 A651 15k multi 5.00 2.75
a. Booklet pane of 1 8.50 —
1698 A651 17k multi 5.50 3.50
a. Booklet pane of 1 8.50 —
1699 A651 20k multi 6.00 4.25
a. Booklet pane of 1 8.50 —
Nos. 1696-1699 (4) 20.50 13.00

Souvenir Sheet

1700 A651 20k multi 7.00 7.00
a. Booklet pane of 1 8.50 —
Complete booklet, #1696a, 1697a, 1698a, 1699a, 1700a 42.50

Complete booklet sold for 139k.

Statue of King Karl Johan, by Brynjulv Bergslien — A652

Perf. 14¼x14½

2013, Apr. 19 Litho. & Engr.

1701 A652 30k multi 10.50 7.00

King Karl Johan (1763-1844).

Ice Climber, Jostedal Glacier — A653

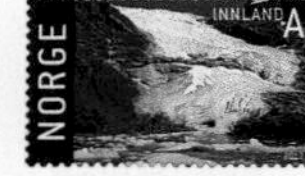
Boya Glacier — A654

Hikers at Gaustatoppen A655

Hikers at Gaustatoppen A656

Rafters, Sjoa River — A657

Riverboarder, Sjoa River — A658

Die Cut Perf. 13¼x13½

2013, Apr. 19 Litho.

Booklet Stamps
Self-Adhesive

1702 A653 A Innland multi 2.50 1.25
1703 A654 A Innland multi 2.50 1.25
a. Booklet pane of 10, 5 each #1702-1703 25.00
1704 A655 A Europa multi 3.00 1.50
1705 A656 A Europa multi 3.00 1.50
a. Booklet pane of 10, 5 each #1704-1705 30.00
1706 A657 A Verden multi 4.00 2.50
1707 A658 A Verden multi 4.00 2.50
a. Booklet pane of 10, 5 each #1706-1707 40.00
Nos. 1702-1707 (6) 26.00 26.00

On day of issue, Nos. 1702-1703 each sold for 9.50k, Nos. 1704-1705 each sold for 13k, and Nos. 1706-1707 each sold for 15k.

Norwegian Student Society, 200th Anniv. — A659

2013, June 10 Litho. ***Perf. 13¼***

1708 A659 17k multi 5.25 3.00

Europa A660

Postal vehicles: 13k, 1932 Harley-Davidson motorcycles and sidecars. 15k, Ford electric vans.

2013, June 10 Litho. ***Perf. 14x13½***

1709 A660 13k multi 4.25 2.50
1710 A660 15k multi 4.75 2.75

Crown Prince Haakon A661

Crown Princess Mette-Marit A662

Crown Prince Haakon, Crown Princess Mette-Marit and Their Children A663

King Harald V, Crown Prince Haakon, Princess Ingrid Alexandra A664

Die Cut Perf. 15½x14½

2013, June 10 Litho.

Coil Stamps
Self-Adhesive

1711 A661 A Innland multi 2.50 1.25
1712 A662 A Innland multi 2.50 1.25
1713 A663 A Innland multi 2.50 1.25
1714 A664 A Innland multi 2.50 1.25
a. Horiz. strip of 4, #1711-1714 10.00
Nos. 1711-1714 (4) 10.00 5.00

Fortieth birthdays of Crown Prince Haakon and Crown Princess Mette-Marit. On day of issue, Nos. 1711-1714 each sold for 9.50k.

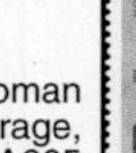

Woman Suffrage, Cent. — A665

Designs: 17k, Camilla Collett (1813-95), feminist writer, front page of *Amtmandens Dottre.* 30k, Anna Rogstad (1854-1938), first female in Parliament, Parliament Building.

Perf. 13¼x13¾

2013, Sept. 9 Litho. & Engr.

1715 A665 17k multi 4.25 2.50
1716 A665 30k multi 9.00 4.25

National Language Year — A666

Designs: No. 1717, Lasse Kolstad (1922-2012), actor. No. 1718, Ivar Aasen (1813-96), writer and lexicographer.

Die Cut Perf. 15½x14½

2013, Sept. 9 Litho.

Coil Stamps
Self-Adhesive

1717 A666 A Innland multi 2.50 1.25
1718 A666 A Innland multi 2.50 1.25
a. Horiz. pair, #1717-1718 5.00

Nos. 1717-1718 each sold for 9.50k on day of issue.

Rock Bands — A667

Designs: No. 1719, The Pussycats. No. 1720, DumDum Boys. No. 1721, Turbonegro. No. 1722, DeLillos.

Die Cut Perf. 15½x14½

2013, Oct. 4 Litho.

Coil Stamps
Self-Adhesive

1719 A667 A Innland multi 2.50 1.25
1720 A667 A Innland multi 2.50 1.25
1721 A667 A Innland multi 2.50 1.25
1722 A667 A Innland multi 2.50 1.25
a. Horiz. strip of 4, #1719-1722 10.00
Nos. 1719-1722 (4) 10.00 5.00

Nos. 1719-1722 each sold for 9.50k on day of issue.

Redrawn Posthorn Type of 2001-06

Perf. 13¾x13¼

2013, Nov. 11 Litho.

Color of Oval

1723 A439a 10k brown 3.00 1.25
1724 A439a 20k brown 5.50 1.50

See No. 1872 for self-adhesive example of No. 1723.

Solan Gundersen A668

Nabonissen House A669

Die Cut Perf. 13½x13¼

2013, Nov. 11 Litho.

Self-Adhesive

1725 A668 A Innland multi 2.50 1.25
1726 A669 A Innland multi 2.50 1.25
a. Horiz. pair, #1725-1726, on tan backing paper 5.00
b. Bookleet pane of 10, 5 each #1725-1726, on white backing paper 25.00

Christmas. Nos. 1725-1726 each sold for 9.50k on day of issue.

Wildlife Type of 2006

2014 Litho. ***Perf. 14¼x13¾***

Self-Adhesive

1726C A511 16k Lemming 4.00 2.00
1727 A511 19k Red deer 5.00 1.75
1728 A511 35k Badger 9.00 2.75
Nos. 1726C-1728 (3) 18.00 6.50

Issued: Nos 1727-1728, 1/2; 1726C, 1/22.

Norwegian Church Abroad, 150th Anniv. — A670

Die Cut Perf. 14½x15½

2014, Jan. 2 Litho.

Coil Stamp
Self-Adhesive

1729 A670 15k multi 4.00 1.75

Marit Bjorgen — A671

Tora Berger — A672

Petter Northug A673

Aksel Lund Svindal — A674

Die Cut Perf. 13¼x13½

2014, Feb. 7 Litho.

Coil Stamps
Self-Adhesive

1730 A671 A Innland multi 2.50 1.25
1731 A672 A Innland multi 2.50 1.25
1732 A673 A Innland multi 2.50 1.25
1733 A674 A Innland multi 2.50 1.25
a. Horiz. strip of 4, #1730-1733 10.00
Nos. 1730-1733 (4) 10.00 5.00

2014 Winter Olympics, Sochi, Russia. Nos. 1730-1733 each sold for 10k on day of issue.

Souvenir Sheet

Supply Ship MS Normand Arctic A675

2014, Mar. 17 Litho. ***Perf. 14x13¼***

1734 A675 A Europe multi 3.50 3.50

No. 1734 sold for 13k on day of issue.

Viking Buckle, Longhouse and Woman in Viking Costume Sewing — A676

Viking Helmet, Actors Recreating Viking Fight — A677

Draken Harald Harfagre, Dragon Figurehead — A678

Die Cut Perf. 13¼x13½

2014, Apr. 28 Litho.

Self-Adhesive

1735 A676 A Innland multi	2.50	1.25
a. Booklet pane of 10	25.00	
1736 A677 A Europa multi	3.50	1.75
a. Booklet pane of 10	35.00	
1737 A678 A Verda multi	4.00	2.50
a. Booklet pane of 10	40.00	
Nos. 1735-1737 (3)	10.00	5.50

On day of issue, No. 1735 sold for 10k; No. 1736, for 13k; No. 1737, for 16k. Nos. 1735-1737 are on brownish translucent paper (single stamps for sale to collectors) and white translucent paper (stamps in booklet panes).

Thor Heyerdahl (1914-2002), Ethnographer A679

Kon-Tiki A680

Easter Island Moai — A681

Ra II — A682

2014, Apr. 28 Litho. *Perf. 13¾x14*

Booklet Stamps

1737B A679 A Innland multi	5.50	5.50
f. Booklet pane of 1	5.50	—
1737C A680 A Innland multi	5.50	5.50
g. Booklet pane of 1	5.50	—
1737D A681 A Innland multi	5.50	5.50
h. Booklet pane of 1	5.50	—
1737E A682 A Innland multi	5.50	5.50
i. Booklet pane of 1	5.50	—
j. Booklet pane of 4, #1737B-1737E	22.00	—
Complete booklet, #1737Bf, 1737Cg, 1737Dh, 1737Ei, 1737Ej	44.00	
Nos. 1737B-1737E (4)	22.00	22.00

Coil Stamps

Self-Adhesive

Die Cut Perf. 13x13½

1738 A679 A Innland multi	2.75	2.75
1739 A680 A Innland multi	2.75	2.75
1740 A681 A Innland multi	2.75	2.75
1741 A682 A Innland multi	2.75	2.75
a. Horiz. strip of 4, #1738-1741	11.00	
Nos. 1738-1741 (4)	11.00	11.00

Nos. 1737B-1737E each had a franking value of 10k on day of issue. Complete booklet sold for 139k. Nos. 1738-1741 each sold for 10k on day of issue.

Norwegian Constitution, 200th Anniv. A683

Designs: 13k, Constituent Assembly meeting at Eidsvoll, 1814. 16k, Prince Christian Frederik and 1814 Constitution. 19k, Lion statue at Parliament, May 17 parade. 30k, Hands forming heart, 1814 Constitution.

Litho. & Engr.

2014, May 16 *Perf. 14x13¼*

1742 A683 13k multi	3.50	1.75
1743 A683 16k multi	4.00	2.25
1744 A683 19k multi	5.00	2.75
1745 A683 30k multi	9.00	4.00
Nos. 1742-1745 (4)	21.50	10.75

See No. B71.

Personalized Stamp — A684

Serpentine Die Cut 10¼x10 Syncopated

2014, May 16 Litho.

Self-Adhesive

1746 A684 A Verden multi 3.75 2.00

No. 1746 sold for 16k on day of issue. The image shown, depicting the Aurora Borealis, is the generic image sold at face value. Stamps could be personalized for an additional fee.

Alf Proysen (1914-70), Writer, and Radio — A685

Mrs. Pepperpot and Mouse — A686

Die Cut Perf. 15½x14½

2014, June 13 Coil Stamps Litho.

Self-Adhesive

1747 A685 A Innland multi	2.75	2.00
1748 A686 A Innland multi	2.75	2.00
a. Horiz. pair, #1747-1748	5.50	

Nos. 1747-1748 each sold for 10k on day of issue.

Redrawn Posthorn Type of 2001-06

2014-15 Litho. *Perf. 13¾x13¼*

Self-Adhesive

Color of Oval

1749 A439a 1k green	.55	
a. Die cut perf. 13¾x13¼	.30	.30
1750 A439a 5k purple	1.60	
a. Die cut perf. 13¾x13¼	1.25	1.25
1751 A439a 50k blue gray	16.00	
a. Die cut perf. 13¾x13¼	11.00	11.00
1752 A439a 70k gray grn	22.00	5.50
Nos. 1749-1752 (4)	40.15	

Issued: No. 1749, 1/7/15; No. 1749a, 11/19/18; No. 1750, 9/9; No. 1750a, 4/5/18; No. 1751, 7/17/14; No. 1751a, 11/15/21; No. 1752, 9/12. Used examples of Nos. 1749-1751 off the backing paper are identical to used examples of Nos. 1283, 1287 and 1661, respectively. Nos. 1749-1751 have ragged-ended perforation tips, while Nos. 1749a, 1750a and 1751a have clean-cut straight perforation tips.

Norwegian Chess Federation, Cent. — A687

Litho. & Engr.

2014, Aug. 1 *Perf. 13¼*

1753 A687 15k multi 5.00 2.75

Solvguttene Boys' Choir — A688

Characters From Production of *Putti Plutti Pott* — A689

Die Cut Perf. 13¼x13½

2014, Nov. 10 Litho.

Self-Adhesive

1754 A688 A Innland multi	2.50	1.25
1755 A689 A Innland multi	2.50	1.25
a. Horiz. pair, #1754-1755, on tan backing paper	5.00	
b. Booklet pane of 10, 5 each #1754-1755	25.00	

Christmas. Nos. 1754-1755 both sold for 10k on day of issue.

Wildlife Type of 2006

Design: 31k, Eurasian eagle owl.

2015, Jan. 2 Litho. *Perf. 14¼x13¾*

Self-Adhesive

1756 A511 31k multicolored 8.25 3.50

Birds — A690

Designs: No. 1757, Cyanistes caeruleus. No. 1758, Lophophanes cristatus.

Die Cut Perf. 15½x14½

2015, Jan. 2 Litho. Coil Stamps

Self-Adhesive

1757 A690 16k multi	4.25	1.75
1758 A690 16k multi	4.25	1.75
a. Horiz. pair, #1757-1758	8.50	

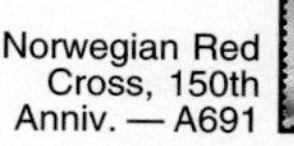

Norwegian Red Cross, 150th Anniv. — A691

Designs: No. 1759, Rescue team members in snow. No. 1760, Visitor service representative meeting with elderly woman. No. 1761, Emergency aid worker with Philippine children. No. 1762, Attempt to create world's largest human cross, 2010.

Die Cut Perf. 15½x14½

2015, Feb. 20 Litho.

Coil Stamps

Self-Adhesive

1759 A691 A Innland multi	2.50	1.25
1760 A691 A Innland multi	2.50	1.25
1761 A691 A Innland multi	2.50	1.25
1762 A691 A Innland multi	2.50	1.25
a. Horiz. strip of 4, #1759-1762	10.00	
Nos. 1759-1762 (4)	10.00	5.00

On day of issue, Nos. 1759-1762 each sold for 10.50k.

Wildlife Type of 2006

2015, Mar. 4 Litho. *Perf. 14¼x13¾*

Self-Adhesive

1763 A511 14k Bear 3.75 2.25

Halden, 350th Anniv. — A692

Litho. & Engr.

2015, Apr. 10 *Perf. 14½*

1764 A692 20k multi 6.00 2.00

Photographs by Anders Beer Wilse (1865-1949) A693

Design: A Innland, Street View of Oslo, 1924. 14k, Kyrkja Mountain, 1933. 16k, Three Large Cod, 1910. 20k, Setesdal on the Way to Church, 1934.

2015, Apr. 16 Litho. *Perf. 14x13½*

1765 A693 A Innland multi	2.50	1.25
1766 A693 14k multi	3.75	1.75
1767 A693 16k multi	4.25	2.50
Nos. 1765-1767 (3)	10.50	5.50

Souvenir Sheet

1768 A693 20k multi 6.00 6.00

No. 1765 sold for 10.50k on day of issue. No. 1768 contains one 70x30mm stamp. A booklet containing panes of 1 of each of Nos. 1765-1768 sold for 139k.

Europa — A694

Old toys: 14k, Anne dolls. 17k Tomte Ford F-100 truck and firetruck.

2015, June 5 Litho. *Perf. 14¼x14½*

1769 A694 14k multi	3.50	1.75
1770 A694 17k multi	4.25	2.50

Halfdan Kjerulf (1815-68), Composer A695

Agnar Mykle (1915-94), Writer A696

Die Cut Perf. 15½x14½

2015, June 5 Litho.

Coil Stamps

Self-Adhesive

1771 A695 A Innland multi	2.60	1.25
1772 A696 A Innland multi	2.60	1.25
a. Horiz. pair, #1771-1772	5.20	

Nos. 1771-1772 each sold for 10.50k on day of issue.

Lighthouses — A697

Designs: No. 1773, Kvitsoy Lighthouse. No. 1774, Slatteroy Lighthouse. No. 1775, Lindesnes Lighthouse. No. 1776, Kjeungskjaeret Lighthouse.

Die Cut Perf. 13¾x13¼

2015, June 5 Litho.

Self-Adhesive

1773 A697 A Europa multi	2.75	1.50
1774 A697 A Europa multi	2.75	1.50
a. Booklet pane of 10, 5 each #1773-1774	27.50	
1775 A697 A Verda multi	3.25	1.75
1776 A697 A Verda multi	3.25	1.75
a. Horiz. strip of 4, #1773-1776, on tan backing paper	12.00	
b. Booklet pane of 10, 5 each #1773-1774	27.50	
Nos. 1773-1776 (4)	12.00	6.50

On day of issue, Nos. 1773-1774 each sold for 14k and Nos. 1775-1776 each sold for 17k.

Bergen Philharmonic Orchestra, 250th Anniv. A698

2015, Aug. 20 Litho. *Perf. 14x13½*

1777 A698 31k multi 7.50 3.00

Supreme Court of Norway, 200th Anniv. A699

Litho. & Engr.

2015, Oct. 3 *Perf. 13½x14*

1778 A699 20k multi 4.75 2.40

Birds — A700

Designs: No. 1779, Somateria spectabilis. No. 1780, Somateria mollissima. No. 1781, Motacilla alba. No. 1782, Oenanthe oenanthe.

Die Cut Perf. 15½x14½

2015, Oct. 3 Litho.

Coil Stamps

Self-Adhesive

1779 A700 B Innland	1.75	1.25
1780 A700 B Innland	1.75	1.25
1781 A700 A Innland	2.10	1.25
1782 A700 A Innland	2.10	1.25
a. Horiz. strip of 4, #1779-1782	8.50	
Nos. 1779-1782 (4)	7.70	5.00

On day of issue, Nos. 1779-1780 each sold for 9.50k and Nos. 1781-1782 each sold for 10.50k.

Redrawn Posthorn Type of 2001-06
Perf. 13¾x13¼
2015, Nov. 13 Litho.
Self-Adhesive
Color of Oval
1783 A439a 60k dull bl grn 15.00 3.50

A701

Christmas — A702

Serpentine Die Cut 11
2015, Nov. 13 Litho.
Booklet Stamps
Self-Adhesive
1784 A701 A Innland 2.25 1.00
1785 A702 A Innland 2.25 1.00
a. Booklet pane of 8, 4 each #1784-1785 18.00

Reign of King Harald V, 25th Anniv. — A703

Die Cut Perf. 14½x15½
2016, Jan. 11 Coil Stamp Litho.
Self-Adhesive
1786 A703 17k multi 4.50 1.50

Youth Winter Olympic Games, Lillehammer
A704

Designs: No. 1787, Skier. No. 1788, Person on mountain top.

Die Cut Perf. 13½x13¼
2016, Jan. 11 Litho.
Self-Adhesive
1787 A704 A Innland multi 2.25 1.00
1788 A704 A Innland multi 2.25 1.00
a. Horiz. pair, #1787-1788, on tan backing paper 4.50
b. Booklet pane of 10, 5 each #1787-1788 22.50

World Biathlon Championships, Oslo — A705

Two competitors: 21k, Skiing. 33k, Shooting.

Litho. With Foil Application
2016, Feb. 19 ***Perf. 14x13½***
1789 A705 21k blue & multi 5.00 1.75
1790 A705 33k sil & multi 8.00 3.00

Cities — A706

Designs: 11k, Harbor of Grimstad, statue of fisherman by Terje Vigen. 17k, Cannons of Nyholmd Skandse, Bodo, Bishop Mathias Bonsach Krogh, city founder. 18k, Cannons near Kragero, *Winter, Kragero,* by Edvard Munch. 21k, Waterfall, Sarpsborg, statue of St. Olav by Finn Eirik Modahl.

2016, Apr. 15 Litho. ***Perf. 13½x13¾***
1791 A706 11k multi 2.75 1.25
1792 A706 17k multi 4.25 1.50
1793 A706 18k multi 4.50 1.50
1794 A706 21k multi 5.00 1.75
Nos. 1791-1794 (4) 16.50 6.00

Grimstad, 200th anniv.; Bodo, 200th anniv.; Kragero, 350th anniv.; Sarpsborg, 1000th anniv.

Nordic Food Culture — A707

Designs: No. 1795, Glazed langoustines, by Chef Espen Holmboe Bang. No. 1796, Beetroot barley risotto with Atlantic cod and kale, by Chef Freddy Storaker Bruu.

2016, Apr. 15 Litho. ***Perf. 14x13½***
1795 A707 14k multi 4.00 4.00
1796 A707 14k multi 4.00 4.00
a. Souvenir sheet of 2, #1795-1796 8.00 8.00

A708

Europa — A709

2016, May 9 Litho. ***Perf. 13½x13¾***
1797 A708 14k multi 4.00 4.00
1798 A709 18k multi 4.50 1.50

Think Green Issue.

Norwegian Meteorological Institute, 150th Anniv. — A710

Clouds and: 17k, Lightning. 33k, Tree

2016, June 10 Litho. ***Perf. 14x13½***
1799 A710 17k multi 4.25 1.50
1800 A710 33k multi 8.00 3.00

A booklet containing a pane of 1 of No. 1799 and a pane of 1 of No. 1800 sold for 149k and was printed in limited quantities.

Captain Sabertooth
A711

Julius the Chimpanzee
A712

Die Cut Perf. 14½x15½
2016, June 10 Litho.
Coil Stamps
Self-Adhesive
1801 A711 A Innland multi 2.75 1.25
1802 A712 A Innland multi 2.75 1.25
a. Horiz. pair, #1801-1802 5.50

Kristiansand Zoo, 50th anniv. Nos. 1801-1802 each sold for 11k on day of issue.

Redrawn Posthorn Type of 2001-06
2016, Sept. 1 Litho. ***Perf. 13¾x13¼***
Self-Adhesive
Color of Oval
1802B A439a 4k dp ultra 1.00

A used example of No. 1802B off the backing paper is identical to a used example of No. 1628.

Central Bank of Norway, 200th Anniv.
A713

Designs: 21k, 1819 Speciedaler coin, various banknotes. 50k, Bank headquarters, Oslo.

Litho. & Engr.
2016, Oct. 1 ***Perf. 14x13½***
1803 A713 21k multi 5.25 1.75
1804 A713 50k multi 12.50 6.25

Lighthouses — A714

Designs: No. 1805, Sandvigodden Lighthouse. No. 1806, Sklinna Lighthouse.

Die Cut Perf. 13¾x13¼
2016, Oct. 1 Litho.
Self-Adhesive
1805 A714 A Innland multi 2.75 1.25
1806 A714 A Innland multi 2.75 1.25
a. Horiz. pair on tan backing paper 5.50
b. Booklet pane of 10, 5 each #1805-1806 27.50

Nos. 1805-1806 each sold for 11k on day of issue.

Famous Men — A715

Designs: 20k, Tor Jonsson (1916-51), writer. 30k, Johan Sverdrup (1816-92), Prime Minister.

Perf. 14¼x14½
2016, Nov. 11 Litho. & Engr.
1807 A715 20k multi 4.75 1.90
1808 A715 30k multi 12.00 6.00

A716

Christmas — A717

Die Cut Perf. 13¼x13½
2016, Nov. 11 Litho.
Self-Adhesive
1809 A716 A Innland multi 2.60 1.00
1810 A717 A Innland multi 2.60 1.00
a. Horiz. pair, #1809-1810, on tan backing paper 5.20
b. Booklet pane of 10, 5 each #1809-1810 26.00

On day of issue, Nos. 1809-1810 each sold for 11k.

Falcons — A718

Designs: No. 1811, Falco columbarius. No. 1812, Falco subbuteo.

Die Cut Perf. 15½x14¼
2017, Jan. 2 Litho.
Coil Stamps
Self-Adhesive
1811 A718 20k multi 4.75 1.75
1812 A718 20k multi 4.75 1.75
a. Horiz. pair, #1811-1812 9.50

Sami Culture — A719

Sami flag and: No. 1813, Triangles (Sami Parliament). No. 1814, Elsa Laula Renberg (1877-1931), Sami politician.

Die Cut Perf. 13½
2017, Feb. 6 Litho.
Self-Adhesive
1813 A719 A Innland multi 2.75 1.00
1814 A719 A Innland multi 2.75 1.00
a. Horiz. pair, #1813-1814, on tan backing paper 5.50
b. Booklet pane of 10, 5 each #1813-1814 27.50

On day of issue, Nos. 1813-1814 each sold for 13k.

Royalty
A720

80th birthday of: 23k, Queen Sonja. 36k, King Harald V.

2017, Feb. 21 Litho. ***Perf. 13½x14***
Self-Adhesive
1815 A720 23k gold & multi 5.50 2.50
1816 A720 36k gold & multi 8.50 3.00

Viking Ship Excavated Near Tune and Drawing of Reconstructed Ship — A721

Viking Ship at Sea — A722

Die Cut Perf. 15½x14½
2017, Apr. 21 Litho.
Coil Stamps
Self-Adhesive
1817 A721 A Innland multi 2.75 1.00
1818 A722 A Innland multi 2.75 1.00
a. Horiz. pair, #1817-1818 5.50

Nos. 1817-1818 each sold for 13k on day of issue.

National Archives, 200th Anniv. — A723

2017, Apr. 21 Litho. ***Perf. 13¼***
1819 A723 36k multi 8.50 4.25

Europa
A724

Designs: 17k, Akershus Castle. 21k, Royal Palace.

2017, Apr. 21 Litho. ***Perf. 14x13¼***
1820 A724 17k multi 4.00 1.50
1821 A724 21k multi 5.00 1.75

Redrawn Posthorn Type of 2001-06
2017 Litho. ***Perf. 13¾x13¼***
Self-Adhesive
Color of Oval
1822 A439a 2k Prus blue .60
1823 A439a 3k blue —
1824 A439a 40k gray —

Issued: 2k, 11/30; 3k, 3/2; 40k, 2/7. No. 1824 has a silver frame. Used examples of Nos. 1822-1824 off the backing paper areidentical to used examples of Nos. 1284,1285, and 1690, respectively,

Wildlife Type of 2006

Perf. 14¼x13¾

2017, Mar. 29 **Litho.**

Self-Adhesive

1825 A511 11.50k Roe deer — —

Statue of King Frederik II, Frederikstad — A725

Perf. 13¾x13¼

2017, June 16 **Litho.**

1826 A725 23k multi 5.50 2.50

Frederikstad, 450th anniv.

International Cycling Union 2017 Road World Championships, Norway — A726

Designs: No. 1827, Six cyclists. No. 1828, Two cyclists, vert.

Die Cut Perf. 13¼x13½

2017, June 16 **Litho.**

Self-Adhesive

1827 A726 A Innland multi 2.75 1.00

Die Cut Perf. 13½x13¼

1828 A726 A Innland multi 2.75 1.00
- *a.* Pair, #1827-1828, on translucent paper without back printing 5.50
- *b.* Booklet pane of 10, 5 each #1827-1828 27.50

On day of issue, Nos. 1827-1828 each sold for 13k.

Famous Men — A727

Designs: 23k: Marcus Thrane (1817-90), labor union leader, red flags and union newspaper. 30k, Eilert Sundt (1817-75), sociologist, buildings, and painting by Johannes Flintoe.

Perf. 13¼x13¾

2017, June 16 **Litho. & Engr.**

1829 A727 23k multi 5.50 2.50
1830 A727 30k multi 7.25 3.75

Automobiles A728

Designs: Nos. 1831a, 1832, 1917 Mustad Giant. Nos. 1831b, 1833, 1921 Bjering. Nos. 1831c, 1834, 1956 Troll. Nos. 1831d, 1835, 1998 Think City A266.

2017, Oct. 7 **Litho.** ***Perf. 13¼x13***

Miniature Sheet

1831 Sheet of 4 13.00 13.00
- *a.-d.* A728 A Innland Any single 3.25 3.25

Coil Stamps

Self-Adhesive

Die Cut Perf. 15½x14½

1832 A728 A Innland multi 3.25 3.25
1833 A728 A Innland multi 3.25 3.25
1834 A728 A Innland multi 3.25 3.25
1835 A728 A Innland multi 3.25 3.25
- *a.* Horiz. strip of 4, #1832-1835 13.00

Nos. 1832-1835 (4) 13.00 13.00

On day of issue, Nos. 1831a-1831d, 1832-1835 each sold for 13k. A booklet containing four panes of one of Nos. 1831a-1831d sold for 169k.

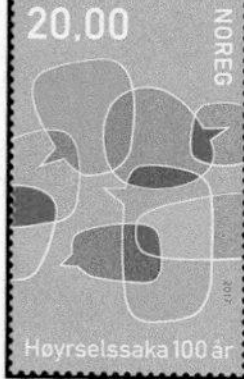

National Federation for the Deaf and Hard of Hearing, Cent. — A729

National Association of the Deaf, Cent. (in 2018) — A730

2017, Nov. 10 **Litho.** ***Perf. 13¼x14***

1836 A729 20k multi 5.00 5.00
1837 A730 20k multi 5.00 5.00

A731

Christmas — A732

Die Cut Perf. 13¼x13½

2017, Nov. 10 **Litho.**

Self-Adhesive

1838 A731 A Innland 3.25 3.25
1839 A732 A Innland 3.25 3.25
- *a.* Pair, #1838-1839, on translucent backing paper with numerals only or without printing on reverse 6.50
- *b.* Booklet pane of 10, 5 each #1838-1839 32.50

On day of issue, Nos. 1838-1839 each sold for 13k.

Birds — A733

Designs: (14k), Strix nebulosa. 21k, Bubo scandiacus. 48k, Buteo lagopus.

Die Cut Perf. 15½x14½

2018, Jan. 2 **Litho.**

Coil Stamps

Self-Adhesive

1840 A733 (14k) multi 3.50 3.50
1841 A733 21k multi 5.25 5.25
1842 A733 48k multi 12.00 12.00
- *a.* Horiz. strip of 3, #1840-1842 21.00

Nos. 1840-1842 (3) 20.75 20.75

No. 1840 is inscribed "Innland."

Wildlife of Bouvet Island — A734

Designs: 24k, Arctocephalus gazella. 38k, Pygoscelis antarcticus.

Die Cut Perf. 13½x13¼

2018, Feb. 16 **Litho.**

Self-Adhesive

1843 A734 24k multi 6.25 6.25
1844 A734 38k multi 9.75 9.75
- *a.* Pair, #1843-1844, on translucent backing paper without printing on back 16.00

Perca Fluviatilis — A735

Die Cut Perf. 13¼

2018, Apr. 20 **Litho.**

Self-Adhesive

1845 A735 18k multi 4.50 4.50

Personalized Stamps — A736

Die Cut Perf. 11½

2018, Apr. 20 **Litho.**

Self-Adhesive

Inscrbed "Innland"

1846 A736 (14k) multi 3.50 3.50

Inscribed "Europa"

1847 A736 (18k) multi 4.50 4.50

Vignette portions of Nos. 1846-1847 could be personalized for an additional fee. A generic image of twelve Instagram photographs is shown in the A736 illustration, and a generic image of twelve different Instagram photographs was used for No. 1847.

Spjelkavik School Band — A737

Kampen Marching Band — A738

Die Cut Perf. 21

2018, Apr. 20 **Litho.**

Self-Adhesive

1848 A737 (14k) multi 3.50 3.50
1849 A738 (14k) multi 3.50 3.50
- *a.* Horiz. pair on translucent paper 7.00
- *b.* Booklet pane of 10, 5 each #1848-1849 35.00

Norwegian Marching Band Association, cent.

Souvenir Sheet

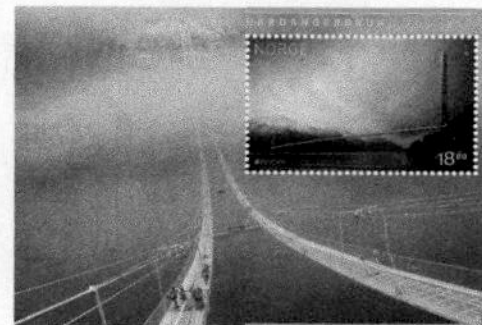

Hardanger Bridge — A739

2018, Apr. 20 **Litho.** ***Perf. 13¼***

1850 A739 18k multi 4.50 4.50

Europa.

Gunnar Sonsteby (1918-2012), Hero of World War II Resistance Against Nazis, and War Cross Medal with Three Swords A740

Perf. 13¾x13½

2018, June 15 **Litho. & Engr.**

1851 A740 24k multi 6.00 6.00

Rochette Car of Floibanen Funicular A741

Blamann Car of Floibanen Funicular A742

Die Cut Perf. 15½x14½

2018, June 15 **Litho.**

Coil Stamps

Self-Adhesive

1852 A741 (14k) multi 3.50 3.50
1853 A742 (14k) multi 3.50 3.50
- *a.* Horiz. pair, #1852-1853 7.00

Floibanen Funicular, Bergen, cent.

Kayaking in Vesteralen A743

Hikers A744

Sun Over Grahogda A745

Svartvassbu Mountain Lodge and Skier A746

Die Cut Perf. 13¼x13

2018, June 15 **Litho.**

Booklet Stamps

Self-Adhesive

1854 A743 (14k) multi 3.50 3.50
1855 A744 (14k) multi 3.50 3.50
- *a.* Booklet pane of 10, 5 each #1854-1855 35.00

1856 A745 (18k) multi 4.50 4.50
1857 A746 (18k) multi 4.50 4.50
- *a.* Booklet pane of 10, 5 each #1856-1857 45.00

Nos. 1854-1857 (4) 16.00 16.00

Norwegian Trekking Association, 150th anniv. A booklet containing perf. 13¼x12¾ water-activated gum booklet panes of one of stamps like Nos. 1854-1857 sold for 179k.

Souvenir Sheet

50th Wedding Anniversary of King Harald V and Queen Sonja — A747

Litho. & Engr.

2018, Aug. 29 ***Perf. 14¼***

1858 A747 50k multi 12.00 12.00

Norwegian Postal Codes, 50th Anniv. — A748

Litho. With Foil Application

2018, Oct. 6 ***Die Cut Perf. 13¼x13¾***

Self-Adhesive

1859 A748 24k multi 5.75 5.75

Writers — A749

Designs: 21k, André Bjerke (1918-85). 38k, Hans Borli (1918-89).

Die Cut Perf. 13¾x13¼

2018, Nov. 9 **Litho.**

Self-Adhesive

1860 A749 21k multi 5.00 5.00
1861 A749 38k multi 9.00 9.00

A750

Christmas — A751

Die Cut Perf. 21

2018, Nov. 9 **Litho.**

Booklet Stamps
Self-Adhesive

1862 A750 (14k) multi 3.25 3.25
1863 A751 (14k) multi 3.25 3.25
a. Horiz. pair, #1862-1863, on backing paper without image on reverse 6.50
b. Booklet pane of 10, 5 each #1862-1863 32.50

Oslo, 2019 European Green Capital — A752

Die Cut Perf. 14¼x15½

2019, Jan. 4 **Litho.**

Coil Stamp
Self-Adhesive

1864 A752 23k multi 5.50 5.50

Holtanna Peak, Antarctica A753

Carsten Borchgrevink (1864-1934), Antarctic Explorer A754

Die Cut Perf. 13x13½

2019, Jan. 4 **Litho.**

Self-Adhesive

1865 A753 26k multi 6.25 6.25

Die Cut Perf. 13½x13

1866 A754 42k multi 10.00 10.00
a. Horiz. pair, #1865-1866, on white backing paper —

See No. 1877A.

Discovery of Ekofisk Oil Field, 50th Anniv. — A755

Die Cut Perf. 13¼x13

2019, Feb. 15 **Litho.**

Self-Adhesive

1867 A755 (16k) multi 3.75 3.75
a. On white backing paper without bar code on back —

Cinclus Cinclus — A756

Serpentine Die Cut 12

2019, Apr. 11 **Litho.**

Self-Adhesive

1868 A756 (21k) multi + label, no perpendicular corners, on backing paper without back printing 5.00 5.00
a. multi + label, serpentine die cut 12, with 3 perpendicular corners 5.00 5.00
b. multi + label, serpentine die cut 12¼x12, with 3 perpendicular corners 5.00 5.00
c. multi + label, serpentine die cut 12, with 2 perpendicular corners 5.00 5.00
d. Booklet pane of 10, 4 each #1868a, 1868b, 2 #1868c 50.00

Europa. The perpendicular corners can be at the lower left and lower right corners of the label, because the horizontal die cutting separating the stamp from the label does not touch the die cutting on the sides of the stamps.

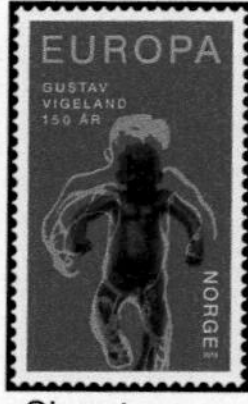
Sinnataggen A757

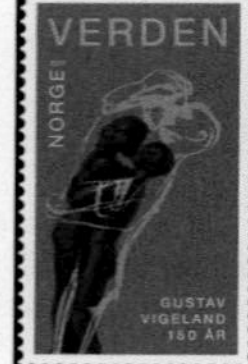
The Kiss A758

Die Cut Perf. 11¼

2019, Apr. 11 **Litho.**

Self-Adhesive

1869 A757 (21k) sil & multi 5.00 5.00
1870 A758 (24k) sil & multi 5.50 5.50

Sculptures by Gustav Vigeland (1869-1943).

Oslo Stock Exchange, 200th Anniv. — A759

Die Cut Perf. 13¼

2019, Apr. 11 **Litho.**

Self-Adhesive

1871 A759 50k multi 11.50 11.50

Redrawn Posthorn Type of 2001-06

Die Cut Perf. 13¾x13¼

2019, May 16 **Litho.**

Self-Adhesive
Color of Oval

1872 A439a 10k brown lake 2.40

A used example of No. 1872 off the backing paper is identical to a used example of No. 1723.

Egon Olsen Leaving Prison — A760

Dynamite Harry, Egon Olsen, Benny Fransen, Kjell and Valborg Jensen A761

Die Cut Perf. 13¼

2019, June 8 **Litho.**

Self-Adhesive

1873 A760 (16k) multi 3.75 3.75
1874 A761 23k multi 5.50 5.50
a. Horiz. pair, #1873-1874 on white backing paper —

Olsen Gang Movies, 50th anniv. A booklet containing two booklet panes containing one perf. 13¼ example with water-activated gum of types A760 and A761, respectively, sold for 179k.

2019 Orienteering World Cup Competition, Norway — A762

Die Cut Perf. 14¼x15½

2019, June 14 **Litho.**

Booklet Stamp
Self-Adhesive

1875 A762 (16k) multi 3.75 3.75
a. Booklet pane of 10 37.50
1875b Single on white backing paper without back printing —

Paintings by Harald Sohlberg (1869-1935) A763

Designs: 26k, Self-portrait, 1896, and Gate in Roros, 1902. 45k, Gate in Roros, 1903.

Die Cut Perf. 11¼

2019, June 14 **Litho.**

Self-Adhesive

1876 A763 26k multi 6.25 6.25
1877 A763 45k multi 10.50 10.50
b. Horiz. pair, #1876-1877 on white backing paper —

Borchgrevink Type of 2019

Souvenir Sheet

2019, Aug. 23 **Litho.** ***Perf. 14***

1877A A754 42k multi 11.00 11.00

Nordia 2019 Stamp Exhibition, Gralum. No. 1877A sold for 50k.

Bicycles — A764

Designs: No. 1878, 1933 Diamond cross-country bicycle. No. 1879, 1936 Ideal commuter bicycle. No. 1880, 1972 DBS Kombi Butterfly bicycle. No. 1881, 1975 DBS Apache bicycle.

Die Cut Perf. 15½x14¼

2019, Aug. 23 **Litho.**

Coil Stamps
Self-Adhesive
Panel Color

1878 A764 (16k) light brown 3.50 3.50
1879 A764 (16k) yellow 3.50 3.50
1880 A764 (16k) light green 3.50 3.50
1881 A764 (16k) orange 3.50 3.50
a. Horiz. strip of 4, #1878-1881 14.00
Nos. 1878-1881 (4) 14.00 14.00

Nos. 1878-1881 are each inscribed "Innland."

Pets — A765

Designs: No. 1882, Puppy. No. 1883, Kitten.

Die Cut Perf. 13¼x13½

2019, Oct. 6 **Litho.**

Booklet Stamps
Self-Adhesive

1882 A765 (16k) multi 3.50 3.50
1883 A765 (16k) multi 3.50 3.50
a. Booklet pane of 10, 5 each #1882-1883 35.00

Nos. 1882-1883 are both inscribed "Innland."

Souvenir Sheet

Queen Maud (1869-1938) — A766

Litho. & Engr.

2019, Nov. 8 ***Perf. 14x13¼***

1884 A766 16k copper & multi 3.50 3.50

Cobbler and Talking Shoe — A767

Children — A768

Die Cut Perf. 21

2019, Nov. 8 **Litho.**

Booklet Stamps
Self-Adhesive

1885 A767 (16k) multi 3.50 3.50
1886 A768 (16k) multi 3.50 3.50
a. Booklet pane of 10, 5 each #1885-1886 35.00
b. Horiz. pair, #1885-1886 on white backing paper without back printing —

Characters from Norwegian Broadcasting Corporation Christmas programs.

Personalized Stamp — A769

Die Cut Perf. 11½

2020, Feb. 21 **Litho.**

Self-Adhesive
Inscribed "Verden"

1887 A769 (32k) multi 7.00 7.00

Vignette portion of No. 1887 could be personalized for an additional fee. A generic image of twelve Instagram photographs is shown in the A769 illustration.

Jan Mayen Island — A770

Designs: 27k, Beerenberg Volcano. 45k, Meteorologist with weather balloon.

Die Cut Perf. 13x13½

2020, Feb. 21 **Litho.**

Self-Adhesive

1888 A770 27k multi 5.75 5.75
1889 A770 45k multi 9.75 9.75
a. Horiz. pair, #1888-1889 on backing paper without back printing —

Bergen, 950th Anniv. — A771

Moss, 300th Anniv. — A772

Die Cut Perf. 13¼x13¾

2020, Feb. 21 **Litho.**

Coil Stamps
Self-Adhesive

1890 A771 (24k) multi 5.25 5.25
1891 A772 (24k) multi 5.25 5.25
a. Horiz. pair, #1890-1891 10.50

Kjell Aukrust (1920-2002), Writer — A773

Anne-Cath Vestly (1920-2008), Writer — A774

Jens Bjorneboe (1920-76), Writer — A775

Die Cut Perf. 13¼

2020, Mar. 19 **Litho.**

Self-Adhesive

1892 A773 (17k) multi	3.25	3.25
1893 A774 (24k) multi	4.50	4.50
1894 A775 27k multi	5.25	5.25
a. Horiz. strip of 3, #1892-1894 on backing paper without back printing		—
Nos. 1892-1894 (3)	13.00	13.00

Souvenir Sheet

Old Post Road A776

Litho. with Foil Application

2020, Apr. 17 ***Perf. 13¼x14***

1895 A776 (26k) multi	5.00	5.00

Europa.

Ship and Orcinus Orca — A777

Die Cut Perf. 13¼x13

2020, Apr. 17 **Litho.**

Self-Adhesive

1896 A777 (26k) multi	5.00	5.00
a. On backing paper without back printing		—

End of World War II, 75th Anniv. — A778

Litho. & Engr.

2020, May 8 ***Perf. 14¼***

1897 A778 (17k) multi	3.50	3.50
a. Souvenir sheet of 1	3.50	3.50

Opening of New Edvard Munch Museum, Oslo — A779

Die Cut Perf. 13¼

2020, June 12 **Litho.**

Self-Adhesive

1898 A779 (26k) multi	5.50	5.50

Dogs — A780

Designs: No. 1899, Norwegian lundehund named Zkipper. No. 1900, Belgian Malinois named Altea. No. 1901, Whippet named Flint. No. 1902, Great Dane named Milo.

Die Cut Perf. 13¼x13½

2020, June 12 **Litho.**

Coil Stamps

Self-Adhesive

1899 A780 (17k) multi	3.50	3.50
1900 A780 (17k) multi	3.50	3.50
1901 A780 (17k) multi	3.50	3.50
1902 A780 (17k) multi	3.50	3.50
a. Horiz. coil strip of 4, #1899-1902	14.00	
Nos. 1899-1902 (4)	14.00	14.00

Fountain Model by Carl Nesjar (1920-2015) — A781

Die Cut Perf. 13¼

2020, Aug. 14 **Litho.**

Self-Adhesive

1903 A781 27k silver & multi	6.25	6.25

Medical Innovations A782 A783

Die Cut Perf. 13½

2020, Sept. 17 **Litho.**

Booklet Stamps

Self-Adhesive

1904 A782 (17k) multi	3.75	3.75
1905 A783 (17k) multi	3.75	3.75
a. Booklet pane of 10, 5 each #1904-1905	37.50	
b. Horiz. pair, #1904-1905, on backing paper without back printing		—

Nobel prize-winning brain research by May-Britt and Edvard Moser (No. 1904), Ultrasound cardiac examinations (No. 1905).

Singers Enshrined in Rockheim Hall of Fame — A784

Designs: No. 1906, Radka Toneff (1952-82). No. 1907, Halvdan Sivertsen. No. 1908, Jonas Fjeld.

Die Cut Perf. 13¼x13½

2020, Nov. 6 **Litho.**

Coil Stamps

Self-Adhesive

1906 A784 (17k) multi	4.00	4.00
1907 A784 (24k) multi	5.50	5.50
1908 A784 (24k) multi	5.50	5.50
a. Horiz. pair, #1907-1908	11.00	
Nos. 1906-1908 (3)	15.00	15.00

Nos. 1907-1908 are inscribed "Innland 50g." A booklet containing panes of one of perf. 13¼x14¼ water-activated gum versions of Nos. 1906-1908 sold for 189k.

Christmas Market in Daylight — A785

Christmas Market at Night — A786

Die Cut Perf. 13¼x13½

2020, Nov. 6 **Litho.**

Booklet Stamps

Self-Adhesive

1909 A785 (17k) multi	4.00	4.00
1910 A786 (17k) multi	4.00	4.00
a. Booklet pane of 10, 5 each #1909-1910	40.00	

Redrawn Posthorn Type of 2001-06

Die Cut Perf. 13¾x13¼

2020, Nov. 30 **Litho.**

Self-Adhesive

Color of Oval

1911 A439a 20k maroon	4.50	4.50

Peter I Island, Antarctica — A787

Designs: 27k, Scientific campsite. 45k, Aerial view of island.

Die Cut Perf. 13¼

2021, Feb. 19 **Litho.**

Self-Adhesive

1912 A787 27k multi	6.50	6.50
1913 A787 45k multi	10.50	10.50

Lillesand, 200th Anniv. — A788

Larvik, 350th Anniv. — A789

Tonsberg, 1150th Anniv. — A790

Die Cut Perf. 15¾x14½

2021, Feb. 19 **Litho.**

Coil Stamps

Self-Adhesive

1914 A788 (18k) multi	4.25	4.25
1915 A789 (24k) multi	5.75	5.75
1916 A790 (24k) multi	5.75	5.75
a. Horiz. pair, #1915-1916	11.50	
Nos. 1914-1916 (3)	15.75	15.75

Fratercula Arctica A791

Bombus Distinguendus A792

Die Cut Perf. 13¼

2021, Apr. 23 **Litho.**

Self-Adhesive

1917 A791 (27k) multi	6.50	6.50
1918 A792 (27k) multi	6.50	6.50

Norwegian endangered animals; Europa.

Train at Station A793

Train and Snow Fences A794

Die Cut Perf. 13¼

2021, Apr. 23 **Litho.**

Booklet Stamps

Self-Adhesive

1919 A793 (18k) multi	4.50	4.50
1920 A794 (18k) multi	4.50	4.50
a. Booklet pane of 10, 5 each #1919-1920	45.00	

Dovre Railway, cent. A booklet containing a booklet pane of one stamp with water-activated gum that has the design of No. 1919, and a booklet pane of one stamp with water-activated gum that has the design of No. 1920 sold for 189k.

Deer and Hunter — A795

Fish and Fisherman A796

Die Cut Perf. 13¼x13¾

2021, June 11 **Litho.**

Self-Adhesive

1921 A795 (24k) multi	5.75	5.75
1922 A796 (24k) multi	5.75	5.75

Norwegian Association of Hunters and Anglers, 150th anniv.

Piglet — A797

Calf — A798

Die Cut Perf. 13¼x13½

2021, June 11 **Litho.**

Booklet Stamps

Self-Adhesive

1923 A797 (27k) multi	6.25	6.25
1924 A798 (27k) multi	6.25	6.25
a. Booklet pane of 10, 5 each #1923-1924	62.50	

Motorcycles, Scooters and Mopeds — A799

Designs: No. 1925, 1927 Atlanta motorcycle. No. 1926, 1954 Mustad Folkescooter. No. 1927, 1964 Raufoss moped. No. 1928, 1970 Tempo Corvette 300 moped.

Die Cut Perf. 15¾x14½

2021, Oct. 2 **Litho.**

Coil Stamps

Self-Adhesive

1925 A799 (18k) multi	4.25	4.25
1926 A799 (18k) multi	4.25	4.25
1927 A799 (18k) multi	4.25	4.25
1928 A799 (18k) multi	4.25	4.25
a. Horiz. coil strip of 4, #1925-1928	17.00	
Nos. 1925-1928 (4)	17.00	17.00

John Ugelstad (1921-97), Chemical Engineer and Inventor — A800

Hugin Autonomous Underwater Vehicle A801

Rimfax Radar Imager on Mars A802

Perf. 13¾x13¼

2021, Oct. 2 **Litho. & Engr.**

Souvenir Sheet

1929 A800 45k multi	11.00	11.00

Booklet Stamps

Self-Adhesive

Litho.

Die Cut Perf. 13¾x13¼

1930 A801 (18k) multi	4.25	4.25
1931 A802 (18k) multi	4.25	4.25
a. Booklet pane of 10, 5 each #1930-1931	42.50	

Souvenir Sheet

Flag of Norway, 200th Anniv. A803

Litho. & Embossed With Foil Application

2021, Nov. 5 *Perf. 14x13¼*

1932 A803 55k multi 12.50 12.50

A804

Christmas — A805

Die Cut Perf. 13¼x13½

2021, Nov. 5 **Litho.**

Booklet Stamps

Self-Adhesive

1933 A804 (18k) multi 4.00 4.00
1934 A805 (18k) multi 4.00 4.00
a. Booklet pane of 10, 5 each #1933-1934 40.00

Roald Amundsen (1872-1928), Polar Explorer, Map of Antarctica — A806

Amundsen, Norge Airship, Map of Arctic Region — A807

Die Cut Perf. 13x13¼

2022, Jan. 3 **Litho.**

Self-Adhesive

1935 A806 (28k) multi 6.50 .50
1936 A807 46k multi 10.50 10.50
a. Horiz. pair, #1935-1936 on translucent paper without back printing 17.00

Male Postal Worker — A808

Female Postal Worker — A809

Die Cut Perf. 13¼x13½

2022, Jan. 17 **Litho.**

Self-Adhesive

1937 A808 (19k) multi 4.25 4.25
1938 A809 (19k) multi 4.25 4.25
a. Horiz. pair, #1937-1938, on translucent paper without back printing 8.50
b. Booklet pane of 10, 5 each #1937-1938 42.50

Norwegian Postal Service, 375th anniv.

Troll A810

Forest Nymph A811

Die Cut Perf. 13x13¼

2022, Apr. 22 **Litho.**

Self-Adhesive

1939 A810 (28k) multi 6.00 6.00
1940 A811 (28k) multi 6.00 6.00
a. Horiz. pair, #1939-1940, on translucent paper without back printing 12.00
b. Booklet pane of 10, 5 each #1939-1940 60.00

Europa.

85th Birthday of King Harald V A812

85th Birthday of Queen Sonja A813

King Haakon VII (1872-1957) A814

18th Birthday of Princess Ingrid Alexandra A815

Die Cut Perf. 14½x15¾

2022, Apr. 22 **Litho.**

Coil Stamps

Self-Adhesive

1941 A812 (19k) multi 4.00 4.00
1942 A813 (19k) multi 4.00 4.00
a. Vert. coil pair, #1941-1942 8.00
1943 A814 (25k) multi 5.25 5.25
1944 A815 (25k) multi 5.25 5.25
a. Vert. coil pair, #1943-1944 10.50
Nos. 1941-1944 (4) 18.50 18.50

A booklet containing four panes, each containing one perf. 12¾x13¼ water-activated gum stamp having the designs of Nos. 1941-1944 was printed in limited quantities and sold for 199k.

Redrawn Posthorn Type of 2001-06

Die Cut Perf. 13¾x13¼

2022, June 17 **Litho.**

Self-Adhesive

Color of Oval

1945 A439a 90k brown 18.00 18.00
a. On translucent paper without barcode on back 18.00

Rainbow Flag and Heart — A816

Die Cut Perf. 13¾

2022, June 17 **Litho.**

Self-Adhesive

1946 A816 (25k) multi 5.00 5.00
a. On translucent paper, without surrounding selvage 5.00

Redrawn Posthorn Type of 2001-06

Souvenir Sheet

2022, Oct. 1 **Litho.** *Perf. 13¾x13¼*

Color of Oval

1947 A439a 19k purple 3.50 3.50

Posthorn stamp design, 150th anniv. No. 1947 is dated "2022."

Souvenir Sheet

Arctic University Museum of Norway, 150th Anniv. — A817

No. 1948: a, Sailboat near shore. b, Sami with sled and reindeer.

Litho. & Engr.

2022, Oct. 1 *Perf. 14¼x14*

1948 A817 Sheet of 2 7.00 7.00
a.-b. 19k Either single 3.50 3.50

Equinor Offshore Floating Wind Generator A818

Stingray Laser Sea Lice Removal Method A819

Die Cut Perf. 13¾x13¼

2022, Oct. 1 **Litho.**

Booklet Stamps

Self-Adhesive

1949 A818 (34k) multi 6.25 6.25
1950 A819 (34k) multi 6.25 6.25
a. Booklet pane of 10, 5 each #1949-1950 62.50

Voluntarism A820

Die Cut Perf. 13¼x13½

2022, Nov. 11 **Litho.**

Coil Stamp

Self-Adhesive

1951 A820 (19k) multi 4.00 4.00

Gingerbread House Made by Elin Vatnar Nilsen A821

Gingerbread House Made by Maren Baxter A822

Gingerbread House Made by Maren Vollestad — A823

Gingerbread Man Made by Margrethe Lim — A824

Die Cut Perf. 13½

2022, Nov. 11 **Litho.**

Booklet Stamps

Self-Adhesive

1952 A821 (19k) multi 4.00 4.00
1953 A822 (19k) multi 4.00 4.00
1954 A823 (19k) multi 4.00 4.00
1955 A824 (19k) multi 4.00 4.00
a. Booklet pane of 10, 3 each # 1952, 1954, 2 each #1953, 1955 40.00
Nos. 1952-1955 (4) 16.00 16.00

Christmas.

Forlandet National Park — A825

Reindeer — A826

Die Cut Perf. 13¼

2023, Feb. 21 **Litho.**

Self-Adhesive

1956 A825 (30k) multi 5.75 5.75
1957 A826 48k multi 9.25 9.25

Svalbard Archipelago tourism.

Arendal, 300th Anniv. — A827

Risor, 300th Anniv. — A828

Die Cut Perf. 13¼x13½

2023, Feb. 21 **Litho.**

Coil Stamps

Self-Adhesive

1958 A827 (26k) multi 5.00 5.00
1959 A828 (26k) multi 5.00 5.00
a. Horiz. coil pair, #1958-1959 10.00

Aurora Borealis Over Ytresand A829

Svolvaergeita Mountain Pinnacle A830

Girl and Goats Near Skei A831

Person on Mountain Overlooking Olden A832

Hovdsundet Beach A833

Wharf Buildings, Trondheim A834

Die Cut Perf. 13¼

2023, Apr. 21 **Litho.**

Self-Adhesive

1960 A829 (20k) multi 3.75 3.75
1961 A830 (20k) multi 3.75 3.75
a. Booklet pane of 10, 5 each #1960-1961 37.50
1962 A831 (29k) multi 5.50 5.50
1963 A832 (29k) multi 5.50 5.50
a. Booklet pane of 10, 5 each #1962-1963 55.00
b. Horiz. strip of 4, #1960-1963, on translucent backing paper 18.50
1964 A833 (35k) multi 6.50 6.50
1965 A834 (35k) multi 6.50 6.50
a. Booklet pane of 10, 5 each #1964-1965 65.00
b. Horiz. pair, #1964-1965, on translucent backing paper 13.00
Nos. 1960-1965 (6) 31.50 31.50

Europa — A835

Die Cut Perf. 13¼

2023, May 9 **Litho.**

1966 A835 (29k) multi 5.25 5.25

Crown Princess Mette-Marit, 50th Birthday A836

Crown Prince Haakon, 50th Birthday A837

Die Cut Perf. 14½x15½

2023, June 14 Litho.

Coil Stamps
Self-Adhesive

1967 A836 (20k) multi 3.75 3.75
1968 A837 (20k) multi 3.75 3.75
a. Vert. coil pair, #1967-1968 7.50

Souvenir Sheet

Game Bird Takes Off, Painting by Jakob Weidemann (1923-2001) — A838

2023, June 14 Litho. *Perf. 14¼*

1969 A838 (20k) multi 3.75 3.75

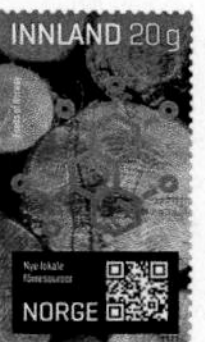

Spruce Logs for Animal Feed A839

COVID-19 Virus and Stylized Nucleotide Strand A840

Die Cut Perf. 13¾x13¼

2023, Oct. 7 Litho.

Self-Adhesive

1970 A839 (21k) multi 3.75 3.75
1971 A840 (21k) multi 3.75 3.75
a. Booklet pane of 10, 5 each #1970-1971 37.50
b. Horiz. pair, #1970-1971, on translucent backing paper 7.50

Ferries — A841

Designs: No. 1972, MF Ampere. No. 1973, Svelvik. No. 1974, MF Vaeroy. No. 1975, MS Angvik.

Die Cut Perf. 15½x14½

2023, Oct. 7 Litho.

Coil Stamps
Self-Adhesive

1972 A841 (27k) multi 5.00 5.00
1973 A841 (27k) multi 5.00 5.00
1974 A841 (27k) multi 5.00 5.00
1975 A841 (27k) multi 5.00 5.00
a. Horiz. coil strip of 4, #1972-1975 20.00
Nos. 1972-1975 (4) 20.00 20.00

A booklet containing four panes, each containing one water-activated gum stamp having the designs of Nos. 1972-1975 was printed in limited quantities and sold for 199k.

Duckling — A842

Rabbit — A843

Die Cut Perf. 13¼x13½

2023, Nov. 7 Litho.

Self-Adhesive

1976 A842 (21k) multi 4.00 4.00
1977 A843 (21k) multi 4.00 4.00
a. Booklet pane of 10, 5 each #1976-1977 40.00
b. Horiz. pair, #1976-1977, on translucent backing paper without text on back 8.00

Church, Alstahaug A844

Church, Oppdal A845

Die Cut Perf. 13¼x13½

2023, Nov. 7 Litho.

Self-Adhesive

1978 A844 (21k) multi 4.00 4.00
1979 A845 (21k) multi 4.00 4.00
a. Booklet pane of 10, 5 each #1978-1979 40.00
b. Horiz. pair, #1978-1979, on translucent backing paper without text on back 8.00

Christmas.

SEMI-POSTAL STAMPS

North Cape Issue

North Cape — SP1

Perf. 13½x14

1930, June 28 Wmk. 160 Photo.

Size: 33¼x21½mm

B1 SP1 15o + 25o blk brn 3.00 *4.25*
B2 SP1 20o + 25o car 35.00 *55.00*
B3 SP1 30o + 25o ultra 90.00 *100.00*
Nos. B1-B3 (3) 128.00 *159.25*
Set, never hinged 210.00

The surtax was given to the Tourist Association. See Nos. B9-B10, B28-B30, B54-B56, B59-B61.

Radium Hospital — SP2

1931, Apr. 1 *Perf. 14½x13½*

B4 SP2 20o + 10o carmine 10.00 7.50
Never hinged 50.00

The surtax aided the Norwegian Radium Hospital.

Fridtjof Nansen — SP3

1935, Dec. 13 *Perf. 13½*

B5 SP3 10o + 10o green 3.50 *4.75*
B6 SP3 15o + 10o red brn 9.50 *13.00*
B7 SP3 20o + 10o crimson 2.50 3.00
B8 SP3 30o + 10o brt ultra 8.50 *13.00*
Nos. B5-B8 (4) 24.00 33.75
Set, never hinged 45.00

The surtax aided the International Nansen Office for Refugees.

North Cape Type of 1930

1938, June 20 *Perf. 13x13½*

Size: 27x21mm

B9 SP1 20o + 25o brn car 1.75 *7.00*
B10 SP1 30o + 25o dp ultra 8.50 29.00
Set, never hinged 25.00

Surtax given to the Tourist Assoc.

Queen Maud — SP4

Perf. 13x13½

1939, July 24 Photo. Unwmk.

B11 SP4 10o + 5o brt grn .50 10.00
B12 SP4 15o + 5o red brn .50 10.00
B13 SP4 20o + 5o scarlet .50 7.50
B14 SP4 30o + 5o brt ultra .50 12.00
Nos. B11-B14 (4) 2.00 39.50
Set, never hinged 3.00

The surtax was used for charities.

Fridtjof Nansen — SP5

1940, Oct. 21

B15 SP5 10o + 10o dk grn 1.50 4.50
B16 SP5 15o + 10o henna brn 1.75 6.00
B17 SP5 20o + 10o dark red .60 1.50
B18 SP5 30o + 10o ultra 1.25 4.50
Nos. B15-B18 (4) 5.10 16.50
Set, never hinged 15.00

The surtax was used for war relief work.

SP6

Ancient Sailing Craft off Lofoten Islands.

1941, May 16

B19 SP6 15o + 10o deep blue 1.25 1.50
Never hinged 3.50

Haalogaland Exposition. Surtax for relief fund for families of lost fishermen.

Value for used stamp postmarked before May 15, 1945, $9.50. See note following No. 180.

Nos. 70-73, 177-180, 267, B19, B32-B34 and B38-B41 were demonetized from May 15, 1945 until Sept. 1, 1981. Used values are for stamps canceled after this period. Stamps with dated cancellations prior to May 15, 1945 sell for more. False cancellations exist.

Colin Archer and Lifeboat SP7

Lifeboat SP8

1941, July 9 *Perf. 13x13½, 13½x13*

B20 SP7 10o + 10o yel grn 1.00 2.50
B21 SP7 15o + 10o dk ol brn 1.20 3.50
B22 SP8 20o + 10o brt red .25 1.00
B23 SP8 30o + 10o ultra 2.50 8.00
Nos. B20-B23 (4) 4.95 15.00
Set, never hinged 15.00

Norwegian Lifeboat Society, 50th anniv.

Legionary, Norwegian and Finnish Flags — SP9

1941, Aug. 1 *Perf. 13½x13*

B24 SP9 20o + 80o scar ver 30.00 100.00
Never hinged 100.00

The surtax was for the Norwegian Legion.

Vidkun Quisling — SP10

1942, Feb. 1

B25 SP10 20o + 30o henna 3.00 *25.00*
Never hinged 11.00

Overprinted in Red

B26 SP10 20o + 30o henna 3.00 *30.00*
Never hinged 12.00

Inauguration of Quisling as prime minister.

Catalogue values for unused stamps in this section, from this point to the end of the section, are for Never Hinged items.

Vidkun Quisling — SP11

1942, Sept. 26 *Perf. 13*

B27 SP11 20o + 30o henna .85 *7.50*

8th annual meeting of Nasjonal Samling, Quisling's party. The surtax aided relatives of soldiers killed in action.

North Cape Type of 1930

1943, Apr. 1 Size: 27x21mm

B28 SP1 15o + 25o olive brn 1.75 2.00
B29 SP1 20o + 25o dark car 3.50 3.50
B30 SP1 30o + 25o chalky blue 3.50 3.50
Nos. B28-B30 (3) 8.75 9.00

The surtax aided the Tourist Association.

Frontier Guardsmen Emblem — SP12

1943, Aug. 2 Unwmk.

B31 SP12 20o + 30o henna .75 *9.00*

The surtax aided the Frontier Guardsmen (Norwegian Nazi Volunteers).

Fishing Village SP13

Drying Grain SP14

Barn in Winter — SP15

1943, Nov. 10

B32 SP13 10o + 10o gray green 1.75 5.00
B33 SP14 20o + 10o henna 1.75 5.00
B34 SP15 40o + 10o grnsh blk 1.75 5.00
Nos. B32-B34 (3) 5.25 15.00

The surtax was for winter relief.

Value, set postmarked before May 15, 1945, $15. See note following No. B19.

The Baroy Sinking
SP16

Sanct Svithun Aflame
SP17

Design: 20o+10o, "Irma" sinking.

1944, May 20

B35 SP16 10o + 10o gray grn 1.25 *5.00*
B36 SP17 15o + 10o dk olive 1.25 *5.00*
B37 SP16 20o + 10o henna 1.25 *5.00*
Nos. B35-B37 (3) 3.75 *15.00*

The surtax aided victims of wartime ship sinkings, and their families.

Spinning
SP19

Plowing
SP20

Tree Felling
SP21

Child Care
SP22

1944, Dec. 1

B38 SP19 5o + 10o deep mag 1.00 .50
B39 SP20 10o + 10o dark yel grn 1.00 .50
B40 SP21 15o + 10o chocolate 1.00 .50
B41 SP22 20o + 10o henna 1.00 .50
Nos. B38-B41 (4) 4.00 2.00

The surtax was for National Welfare.

Value, set postmarked before May 15, 1945, $20. See note following No. B19.

Red Cross Nurse — SP23

1945, Sept. 22

B42 SP23 20o + 10o red 1.00 *1.40*

80th anniv. of the founding of the Norwegian Red Cross. The surtax was for that institution.

For surcharge see No. B47.

Crown Prince Olav — SP24

1946, Mar. 4 **Unwmk.**

B43 SP24 10o + 10o ol grn .75 .60
B44 SP24 15o + 10o ol brn .75 .60
B45 SP24 20o + 10o dk red 1.00 .60
B46 SP24 30o + 10o brt bl 2.50 2.50
Nos. B43-B46 (4) 5.00 4.30

The surtax was for war victims.

No. B42 Surcharged in Black

1948, Dec. 1

B47 SP23 25o + 5o on 20o+10o 1.00 *1.25*

The surtax was for Red Cross relief work.

Child Picking Flowers — SP25

1950, Aug. 15 **Photo.** ***Perf. 13***

B48 SP25 25o + 5o brt red 2.00 1.40
B49 SP25 45o + 5o dp bl 7.00 7.00

The surtax was for poliomyelitis victims.

Skater
SP26

Winter Scene
SP27

Design: 30o+10o, Ski jumper.

1951, Oct. 1

B50 SP26 15o + 5o olive grn 1.90 2.50
B51 SP26 30o + 10o red 2.75 2.75
B52 SP27 55o + 20o blue 10.00 *10.00*
Nos. B50-B52 (3) 14.65 15.25

Olympic Winter Games, Oslo, 2/14-29/52.

Kneeling Woman — SP28

1953, June 1 **Photo. & Litho.**

B53 SP28 30o + 10o red & cr 2.00 2.00

The surtax was for cancer research.

North Cape Type of 1930

1953, June 15 **Photo.**

Size: 27x21mm

B54 SP1 20o + 10o green 11.50 11.50
B55 SP1 30o + 15o red 13.00 13.00
B56 SP1 55o + 25o gray blue 15.00 15.00
Nos. B54-B56 (3) 39.50 39.50

The surtax aided the Tourist Association.

Crown Princess Martha — SP29

1956, Mar. 28 ***Perf. 13***

B57 SP29 35o + 10o dark red 1.40 1.40
B58 SP29 65o + 10o dark blue 4.50 4.50

The surtax was for the Crown Princess Martha Memorial Fund.

North Cape Type of 1930

1957, May 6 **Size: 27x21mm**

B59 SP1 25o + 10o green 6.25 6.25
B60 SP1 35o + 15o red 7.50 7.50
B61 SP1 65o + 25o gray blue 3.25 2.75
Nos. B59-B61 (3) 17.00 16.50

The surtax aided the Tourist Association.

White Anemone — SP30

Design: 90o+10o, Hepatica.

1960, Jan. 12 **Litho.** ***Perf. 13***

B62 SP30 45o + 10o brt red & grn 2.75 2.75
B63 SP30 90o + 10o bl, org & grn 8.25 *8.25*

The surtax was for anti-tuberculosis work.

Mother, Child, WRY Emblem — SP31

1960, Apr. 7 **Photo.** **Unwmk.**

B64 SP31 45o + 25o rose & blk 6.00 6.00
B65 SP31 90o + 25o bl & blk 11.00 11.00

World Refugee Year, July 1, 1959-June 30, 1960. The surtax was for aid to refugees.

Severed Chain and Dove — SP32

Design: 60o+10o, Norwegian flags.

1965, May 8 **Photo.** ***Perf. 13***

B66 SP32 30o + 10o grn, blk & tan .50 .50
B67 SP32 60o + 10o red & dk bl .90 .60

20th anniversary of liberation from the Germans. The surtax was for war cripples.

Souvenir Sheet

Offshore Oil Drilling — SP33

Designs: a, Ekofisk Center. b, Treasure Scout drilling rig and Odin Viking supply vessel at Tromsoflaket, 1982. c, Statfjord C oil platform, 1984. d, Men working on deck of Neptune Nordraug.

1985, Oct. 4 **Litho.** ***Perf. 13½x13***

B68 SP33 Sheet of 4 8.00 10.00
a.-d. 2k + 1k, any single 1.75 2.50

Stamp Day 1985. Surtax for philatelic promotion.

Souvenir Sheet

Paper Industry — SP34

Paper mill: a, Wood aging containers. b, Boiling plant. c, Paper-making machine. d, Paper dryer.

1986, Oct. 17 **Litho.** ***Perf. 13½***

B69 SP34 Sheet of 4 12.50 12.50
a.-d. 2.50k + 1k, any single 3.00 3.00

Surtax for philatelic promotion. Nos. B69a-B69b and B69c-B69d printed in continuous designs.

Souvenir Sheet

Salmon Industry — SP35

Designs: a, Eggs and milt pressed out of fish by hand. b, Cultivation of eggs in tanks. c, Outdoor hatchery. d, Market.

1987, Oct. 9 **Litho.** ***Perf. 13½x13***

B70 SP35 Sheet of 4 14.00 *15.00*
a. 2.30k +50o multi 3.00 3.00
b. 2.70k +50o multi 3.00 3.00
c. 3.50k +50o multi 3.00 3.00
d. 4.50k +50o multi 3.00 3.00

Souvenir Sheet

Norwegian Constituent Assembly, 200th Anniv. — SP36

No. B71: a, Prince Christian Frederik, Constitution of 1814. b, Parliament Lion sculpture, parade.

2014, Nov. 21 **Litho.** ***Perf. 14x13¼***

B71 SP36 Sheet of 2 10.00 10.00
a. 16k multi 4.25 4.25
b. 19k multi 5.50 5.50

Nordia 2014 Stamp Exhibition, Oslo. No. B71 sold for 41k, with 6k defraying the costs of the exhibition.

AIR POST STAMPS

Airplane over Akershus Castle — AP1

Perf. 13½x14½

1927-34 **Typo.** **Wmk. 160**

C1 AP1 45o lt bl, strong frame line ('34) 4.50 *5.00*
Never hinged 22.50
a. Faint or broken frame line 15.00 8.00
Never hinged 160.00

Airplane over Akershus Castle — AP2

1937, Aug. 18 **Photo.** ***Perf. 13***

C2 AP2 45o Prussian blue 1.20 .70
Never hinged 3.50

1941, Nov. 10 **Unwmk.**

C3 AP2 45o indigo .50 .25
Never hinged 1.75

POSTAGE DUE STAMPS

Numeral of Value — D1

Inscribed "at betale"

Perf. 14½x13½

1889-1914 **Typo.** **Wmk. 160**

J1 D1 1o olive green ('15) .75 *1.75*
Never hinged 2.25
J2 D1 4o magenta ('11) 1.50 1.00
Never hinged 12.00
J3 D1 10o carmine rose ('99) 3.00 .75
Never hinged 21.00
a. 10o rose red ('89) 75.00 25.00
J4 D1 15o brown ('14) 1.50 1.25
J5 D1 20o ultra ('99) 2.50 .65
Never hinged 20.00
a. Perf. 13½x12½ ('95) 210.00 100.00
J6 D1 50o maroon ('89) 5.00 2.50
Never hinged 40.00
Nos. J1-J6 (6) 14.25 7.90

See #J7-J12. For overprint see #136-144.

1922-23 **Inscribed "a betale"**

J7 D1 4o lilac rose 5.00 11.00
Never hinged 22.50
J8 D1 10o green 2.50 2.50
Never hinged 17.50
J9 D1 20o dull violet 3.00 5.50
Never hinged 25.00
J10 D1 40o deep ultra 6.00 1.25
Never hinged 35.00
J11 D1 100o orange yel 22.50 12.50
Never hinged 130.00
J12 D1 200o dark violet 55.00 25.00
Never hinged 130.00
Nos. J7-J12 (6) 94.00 57.75

OFFICIAL STAMPS

Coat of Arms — O1

Perf. 14½x13½

1926 **Typo.** **Wmk. 160**

O1 O1 5o rose lilac .75 *1.75*
O2 O1 10o yellow green .50 .50
O3 O1 15o indigo 2.00 *4.25*
O4 O1 20o plum .50 .50

O5 O1 30o slate 3.00 *8.00*
O6 O1 40o deep blue 1.25 *2.50*
O7 O1 60o Prussian blue 3.00 *10.00*
Nos. O1-O7 (7) 11.00 *27.50*
Set, never hinged 35.00

Official Stamp of 1926 Surcharged

1929, July 1
O8 O1 2o on 5o magenta .80 *1.50*
Never hinged 1.50

Coat of Arms — O2

Perf. 14½x13½

1933-34 Litho. Wmk. 160

Size: 35x19¼mm

O9 O2 2o ocher .55 *1.60*
O10 O2 5o rose lilac 4.00 *6.25*
O11 O2 7o orange 4.00 *9.00*
O12 O2 10o green 27.50 1.10
O13 O2 15o olive .55 *1.10*
O14 O2 20o vermilion 27.50 .55
O15 O2 25o yellow brn .55 *.90*
O16 O2 30o ultra .80 *1.10*
O18 O2 40o slate 27.50 1.10
O19 O2 60o blue 16.00 1.75
O20 O2 70o olive brn 1.25 *3.50*
O21 O2 100o violet 1.75 3.00
Nos. O9-O16,O18-O21 (12) 111.95 30.95
Same, never hinged 550.00

On the lithographed stamps, the lion's left leg is shaded.

Typo.

Size: 34x18¾mm

O10a O2 5o rose lilac 1.25 3.50
O11a O2 7o orange 7.25 *22.50*
O12a O2 10o green .50 .60
O13a O2 15o olive 3.50 *18.00*
O14a O2 20o vermilion .60 .50
O17 O2 35o red violet ('34) .60 .60
O18a O2 40o slate .85 .75
O19a O2 60o blue .85 1.00
Nos. O10a-O14a,O17,O18a-O19a (8) 15.40 *47.45*
Same, never hinged 55.00

Coat of Arms — O3

1937-38 Photo. *Perf. 13½x13*
O22 O3 5o rose lilac ('38) .60 1.50
O23 O3 7o dp orange .60 3.75
O24 O3 10o brt green .25 .25
O25 O3 15o olive bister .55 1.40
O26 O3 20o carmine ('38) 1.75 4.25
O27 O3 25o red brown ('38) .75 1.00
O28 O3 30o ultra .75 1.00
O29 O3 35o red vio ('38) .75 .75
O30 O3 40o Prus grn ('38) .60 .60
O31 O3 60o Prus bl ('38) .75 1.40
O32 O3 100o dk vio ('38) 1.50 2.50
Nos. O22-O32 (11) 8.85 *18.40*
Set, never hinged 35.00

See Nos. O33-O43, O55-O56. For surcharge see No. O57.

1939-47 Unwmk.
O33 O3 5o dp red lil ('41) .25 .25
O34 O3 7o dp orange ('41) .25 *1.50*
O35 O3 10o brt green ('41) .25 .25
O36 O3 15o olive ('45) .25 .45
O37 O3 20o carmine .25 .25
O38 O3 25o red brown 3.00 *7.50*
O38A O3 25o scarlet ('46) .25 .25
O39 O3 30o ultra 2.50 3.00
O39A O3 30o dk gray ('47) .60 .60
O40 O3 35o brt lilac ('41) .75 .60
O41 O3 40o grnsh blk ('41) .55 .50
O41A O3 40o dp ultra ('46) 2.50 .50
O42 O3 60o Prus blue ('41) .50 .50
O43 O3 100o dk violet ('41) 1.00 .50
Nos. O33-O43 (14) 12.90 *16.65*
Set, never hinged 40.00

Norwegian Nazi Party Emblem — O4

1942-44
O44 O4 5o magenta .25 *2.00*
O45 O4 7o yellow org .25 *2.00*
O46 O4 10o emerald .25 .40
O47 O4 15o olive ('44) 1.50 *30.00*
O48 O4 20o bright red .25 .40
O49 O4 25o red brn ('43) 2.50 *35.00*
O50 O4 30o brt ultra ('44) 1.75 *35.00*
O51 O4 35o brt pur ('43) 1.75 *15.00*
O52 O4 40o grnsh blk ('43) .25 .50
O53 O4 60o indigo ('43) 1.50 *17.50*
O54 O4 1k blue vio ('43) 1.50 *25.00*
Nos. O44-O54 (11) 11.75 *162.80*
Set, never hinged 25.00

Type of 1937

1947, Nov. 1
O55 O3 50o deep magenta .50 1.00
O56 O3 200o orange 1.75 .50
Set, never hinged 5.00

No. O37 Surcharged in Black

1949, Mar. 15
O57 O3 25o on 20o carmine .25 .50
Never hinged .50

Norway Coat of Arms — O5

1951-52 Unwmk. Photo. *Perf. 13*
O58 O5 5o rose lilac .75 .50
O59 O5 10o dk gray .75 .25
O60 O5 15o dp org brn ('52) 1.00 .90
O61 O5 30o scarlet .35 .25
O62 O5 35o red brn ('52) 1.25 .90
O63 O5 60o blue gray .90 .25
O64 O5 100o vio bl ('52) 1.25 .75
Nos. O58-O64 (7) 6.25 3.80
Set, never hinged 15.00

Catalogue values for unused stamps in this section, from this point to the end of the section, are for Never Hinged items.

Norway Coat of Arms — O6

1955-61
O65 O6 5o rose lilac .25 .25
O66 O6 10o slate .25 .25
O67 O6 15o orange brn .50 2.50
O68 O6 20o bl grn ('57) .50 .25
O69 O6 25o emer ('59) .70 .25
O70 O6 30o scarlet 3.00 .75
O71 O6 35o brown red .55 .25
O72 O6 40o blue lilac 1.10 .25
O73 O6 45o scar ('58) 1.10 .25
O74 O6 50o gldn brn ('57) 3.00 .25
O75 O6 60o blue 12.00 .55
O76 O6 70o brn olive ('56) 5.25 1.00
O77 O6 75o maroon ('57) 20.00 13.50
O78 O6 80o org brn ('58) 6.75 1.00
O79 O6 90o org ('58) 1.00 .25
O80 O6 1k vio ('57) 1.75 .25
O81 O6 2k gray grn ('60) 3.00 .25
O82 O6 5k red lil ('61) 6.75 .65
Nos. O65-O82 (18) 67.45 22.70

See Phosphorescence note after No. 430.

1962-74 Photo.
O83 O6 30o green ('64) 2.00 .25
O84 O6 40o ol grn ('68) 2.00 .50
O85 O6 50o scarlet 2.50 .25
O86 O6 50o slate ('69) .70 .40
O87 O6 60o dk red ('64) 1.10 .25
O87A O6 60o grnsh bl ('72) 4.25 8.25
O88 O6 65o dk red ('68) 1.75 .25
O89 O6 70o dk red ('70) .50 .40
O90 O6 75o lt grn ('73) 1.25 1.25
O90A O6 80o red brn ('72) 1.25 .40
O91 O6 85o ocher ('74) .95 3.00
O92 O6 1k dp org ('73) .50 .40
O93 O6 1.10k car lake ('74) 1.00 1.25
Nos. O83-O93 (13) 19.75 16.85

Shades exist of several values of type O6. Nos O87A, O90A are on phosphored paper.

1975-82 Litho.
O94 O6 5o rose lil ('80) .40 1.75
O95 O6 10o bluish gray ('82) .70 3.50
O96 O6 15o henna brn 1.00 4.00
O97 O6 20o green ('82) 6.00 5.50
O98 O6 25o yellow grn .40 .40
O99 O6 40o ol grn ('79) 2.25 10.00
O100 O6 50o grnsh gray ('76) .50 .25
O101 O6 60o dk grnsh bl 2.25 8.00
O102 O6 70o dk red ('82) 5.50 12.50
O103 O6 80o red brn ('76) .60 .25
O104 O6 1k vio ('80) 2.50 .50
O105 O6 1.10k red ('80) 2.00 3.50
O106 O6 1.25k dull red .70 .25
O107 O6 1.30k lilac ('81) 1.75 3.00
O108 O6 1.50k red ('81) .70 .40
O109 O6 1.75k dl bl grn ('82) 1.75 1.75
O110 O6 2k dk gray grn 1.00 .25
O111 O6 2k cerise ('82) 1.40 .40
O112 O6 3k purple ('82) 1.75 .50
O113 O6 5k lt vio 30.00 3.00
O114 O6 5k blue ('77) 1.75 .25
Nos. O94-O114 (21) 64.90 59.95

In lithographed set, shield's background is dotted; on photogravure stamps it is solid color.

Official stamps invalid as of Apr. 1, 1985.

NOSSI-BE

ˌnō-sē-ˈbā

LOCATION — Island in the Indian Ocean, off the northwest coast of Madagascar
GOVT. — French Protectorate
AREA — 130 sq. mi.
POP. — 9,000 (1900 est.)
CAPITAL — Hellville

In 1896 the island was placed under the authority of the Governor-General of Madagascar and postage stamps of Madagascar were placed in use.

100 Centimes = 1 Franc

Stamps of French Colonies Surcharged in Blue

a

b

c

On the following issues the colors of the French Colonies stamps, type A9, are: 5c, green, *greenish*; 10c, black, *lavender*; 15c, blue; 20c, red, *green*; 30c, brown, *bister*; 40c, vermilion, *straw*; 75c, carmine, *rose*; 1fr, bronze green, *straw*.

1889 Unwmk. *Imperf.*
1 A8(a) 25 on 40c red, *straw* 2,600. 1,100.
a. Double surcharge 3,400.
b. Inverted surcharge 3,750. 1,600.
2 A8(b) 25c on 40c red, *straw* 3,100. 2,000.
a. Double surcharge 5,500. 2,800.
b. Inverted surcharge 5,500. 2,800.
c. Pair, "a" and "c"

Perf. 14x13½
3 A9(b) 5c on 10c 3,750. 1,450.
a. Double surcharge 3,500.
b. Inverted surcharge 5,000. 3,100.
4 A9(b) 5c on 20c 4,000. 1,600.
a. Inverted surcharge 5,000. 3,100.
5 A9(c) 5c on 10c 3,100. 1,100.
a. Inverted surcharge 5,600.
6 A9(c) 5c on 20c 3,600. 2,400.
7 A9(a) 15 on 20c 2,800. 1,100.
a. Double surcharge 2,400.
b. Inverted surcharge 4,250. 1,750.
c. 15 on 30c (error) *32,000.* *28,000.*
8 A9(a) 25 on 30c 2,800. 950.
a. Double surcharge 2,200.
b. Inverted surcharge 3,600. 1,600.
9 A9(a) 25 on 40c 2,400. 1,100.
a. Double surcharge 2,000.
b. Inverted surcharge 3,600. 1,600.

d

e

f

1890 Black Surcharge
10 A9(d) 25c on 20c 425.00 300.00
11 A9(e) 0.25 on 20c 425.00 300.00
12 A9(f) 25 on 20c 1,000. 675.00
13 A9(d) 25c on 75c 425.00 300.00
14 A9(e) 0.25 on 75c 425.00 300.00
15 A9(f) 25 on 75c 1,000. 675.00
16 A9(d) 25c on 1fr 425.00 300.00
17 A9(e) 0.25 on 1fr 425.00 300.00
18 A9(f) 25 on 1fr 1,000. 675.00

The 25c on 20c with surcharge composed of "25 c." as in "d," "N S B" as in "e," and frame as in "f" is an essay.

Surcharged or Overprinted in Black, Carmine, Vermilion or Blue

j

k

m

1893
23 A9(j) 25 on 20c (Bk) 52.50 45.00
24 A9(j) 50 on 10c (Bk) 67.50 47.50
a. Inverted surcharge 400.00 260.00
25 A9(j) 75 on 15c (Bk) 300.00 240.00
26 A9(j) 1fr on 5c (Bk) 150.00 110.00
a. Inverted surcharge 400.00 275.00
27 A9(k) 10c (C) 28.00 24.00
a. Inverted overprint 130.00 120.00
28 A9(k) 10c (V) 27.50 24.00
29 A9(k) 15c (Bk) 32.50 32.50
a. Inverted overprint 140.00 130.00
30 A9(k) 20c (Bk) 500.00 75.00
31 A9(m) 20c (Bl) 130.00 67.50
a. Inverted overprint 190.00 180.00

Counterfeits exist of surcharges and overprints of Nos. 1-31.

Navigation and Commerce — A14

1894 Typo. *Perf. 14x13½*

Name of Colony in Blue or Carmine
32 A14 1c blk, *lil bl* 1.60 1.60
33 A14 2c brn, *buff* 2.00 2.00
34 A14 4c claret, *lav* 2.75 2.00
35 A14 5c grn, *greenish* 4.00 3.25
36 A14 10c blk, *lav* 9.50 6.50
37 A14 15c blue, quadrille paper 13.50 6.50
38 A14 20c red, *grn* 9.50 6.50
39 A14 25c blk, *rose* 16.00 9.50
40 A14 30c brn, *bister* 16.00 14.50
41 A14 40c red, *straw* 22.50 16.00
42 A14 50c carmine, *rose* 22.50 16.00
43 A14 75c dp vio, *orange* 37.50 37.50
44 A14 1fr brnz grn, *straw* 27.50 27.50
Nos. 32-44 (13) 184.85 149.35

Perf. 13½x14 stamps are counterfeits.

POSTAGE DUE STAMPS

Stamps of French Colonies Surcharged in Black

n

o

1891 Unwmk. *Perf. 14x13½*
J1 A9(n) 20 on 1c blk, *lil bl* 425.00 300.00
a. Inverted surcharge 925.00 675.00
b. Surcharged vertically 1,200. *1,400.*
c. Surcharge on back 1,050. 1,050.
J2 A9(n) 30 on 2c brn, *buff* 400.00 300.00
a. Inverted surcharge 875.00 675.00
b. Surcharge on back 1,000. *1,200.*
J3 A9(n) 50 on 30c brn, *bister* 120.00 105.00
a. Inverted surcharge 925.00 675.00
b. Surcharge on back 1,050. *1,300.*
J4 A9(o) 35 on 4c cl, *lav* 450.00 325.00
a. Inverted surcharge 925.00 675.00
b. Surcharge on back 1,100. *1,300.*
c. Pair, one without surcharge

J5 A9(o) 35 on 20c red, *green* 450.00 325.00
a. Inverted surcharge 925.00 675.00
J6 A9(o) 1fr on 35c vio, *orange* 325.00 240.00
a. Inverted surcharge 925.00 625.00

p

q

r

1891
J7 A9(p) 5c on 20c 225.00 225.00
J8 A9(q) 5c on 20c 275.00 275.00
b. In se-tenant pair with #J7 725.00
J9 A9(r) 0.10c on 5c 27.50 24.00
J10 A9(p) 10c on 15c 225.00 225.00
J11 A9(q) 10c on 15c 275.00 275.00
b. In se-tenant pair with #J10 725.00
J12 A9(p) 15c on 10c 200.00 200.00
J13 A9(q) 15c on 10c 210.00 210.00
b. In se-tenant pair with #J12 725.00
J14 A9(r) 0.15c on 20c 32.50 32.50
a. 25c on 20c (error) *40,000.* *35,000.*
J15 A9(p) 25c on 5c 180.00 180.00
J16 A9(q) 25c on 5c 200.00 200.00
b. In se-tenant pair with #J15 700.00
J17 A9(r) 0.25c on 75c 650.00 575.00

Inverted Surcharge

J7a	A9(p)	5c on 20c	425.00	425.00
J8a	A9(q)	5c on 20c	425.00	425.00
J10a	A9(p)	10c on 15c	425.00	425.00
J11a	A9(q)	10c on 15c	425.00	425.00
J12a	A9(p)	15c on 10c	425.00	425.00
J13a	A9(q)	15c on 10c	425.00	425.00
J15a	A9(p)	25c on 5c	425.00	425.00
J16a	A9(q)	25c on 5c	425.00	425.00
J17a	A9(r)	0.25c on 75c	1,800.	1,500.

Stamps of Nossi-Be were superseded by those of Madagascar.
Counterfeits exist of surcharges on #J1-J17.

NYASALAND PROTECTORATE

nī-'a-sə-,land prə-'tek-t̩ə-,rət

LOCATION — In southern Africa, bordering on Lake Nyasa
GOVT. — British Protectorate
AREA — 49,000 sq. mi.
POP. — 2,950,000 (est. 1962)
CAPITAL — Zomba

For previous issues, see British Central Africa.

Nyasaland joined the Federation of Rhodesia and Nyasaland in 1953, using its stamps until 1963. As the Federation began to dissolve in 1963, Nyasaland withdrew its postal services and issued provisional stamps. On July 6, 1964, Nyasaland became the independent state of Malawi.

12 Pence = 1 Shilling
20 Shillings = 1 Pound

Catalogue values for unused stamps in this country are for Never Hinged items, beginning with Scott 68 in the regular postage section and Scott J1 in the postage due section.

A1

King Edward VII — A2

Wmk. Crown and C A (2)
1908, July 22 Typo. *Perf. 14*
Chalky Paper
1 A1 1sh black, *green* 7.00 *19.00*

Wmk. Multiple Crown and C A (3)
Ordinary Paper
2 A1 ½p green 2.00 2.25
3 A1 1p carmine 10.00 1.10

Chalky Paper
4 A1 3p violet, *yel* 2.00 *4.75*
5 A1 4p scar & blk, *yel* 2.25 *1.75*
6 A1 6p red vio & vio 7.00 *12.50*
7 A2 2sh6p car & blk, *bl* 80.00 *110.00*
8 A2 4sh black & car 120.00 *180.00*
9 A2 10sh red & grn, *grn* 225.00 *325.00*
10 A2 £1 blk & vio, *red* 650.00 *750.00*
11 A2 £10 ultra & lilac 12,000. *8,000.*
Nos. 1-10 (10) 1,105. 1,406.

A3

King George V — A4

1913-19 Ordinary Paper
12 A3 ½p green 1.75 *2.25*
13 A3 1p scarlet 8.25 1.00
a. 1p carmine 4.25 2.00
14 A3 2p gray 11.00 1.00
15 A3 2½p ultra 2.75 *9.00*

Chalky Paper
16 A3 3p violet, *yel* 8.50 4.50
a. 3p violet, *pale yel* 6.50 10.00
17 A3 4p scar & blk, *yel* 2.00 *2.50*
a. 4p scar & blk, *pale yel* 6.50 8.50
18 A3 6p red vio & dull vio 6.00 *8.50*
19 A3 1sh black, *green* 2.50 *9.00*
a. 1sh black, *emerald* 5.50 *7.00*
b. 1sh blk, *bl grn*, olive back 6.00 1.75
20 A4 2sh6p red & blk, *bl* ('18) 14.00 *30.00*
21 A4 4sh blk & red ('18) 55.00 *100.00*
22 A4 10sh red & grn, *grn* 130.00 *160.00*
23 A4 £1 blk & vio, *red* ('18) 200.00 190.00
24 A4 £10 brt ultra & slate vio ('19) *4,500.* *2,250.*
Revenue cancel 275.00
a. £10 pale ultra & dull vio ('14) 8,500.
Revenue cancel 300.00
Nos. 12-23 (12) 441.75 *517.75*

Stamps of Nyasaland Protectorate overprinted "N. F." are listed under German East Africa.

1921-30 Wmk. 4 Ordinary Paper
25 A3 ½p green 3.25 .50
26 A3 1p rose red 4.00 .50
27 A3 1½p orange 4.00 *17.50*
28 A3 2p gray 4.00 .50

Chalky Paper
29 A3 3p violet, *yel* 22.00 3.25
30 A3 4p scar & blk, *yel* 7.00 *11.00*
31 A3 6p red vio & dl vio 7.00 3.50
32 A3 1sh blk, *grn* ('30) 14.50 4.50
33 A4 2sh ultra & dl vio, *bl* 22.50 15.00
34 A4 2sh6p red & blk, *bl* ('24) 27.50 42.50
35 A4 4sh black & car 30.00 *50.00*
36 A4 5sh red & grn, *yel* ('29) 55.00 85.00
37 A4 10sh red & grn, *emer* 120.00 *120.00*
Nos. 25-37 (13) 320.75 *353.75*

George V and Leopard — A5

1934-35 Engr. *Perf. 12½*
38 A5 ½p green .75 *1.25*
39 A5 1p dark brown .75 .75
40 A5 1½p rose .90 *3.00*
41 A5 2p gray 1.25 *1.25*
42 A5 3p dark blue 3.00 2.00
43 A5 4p rose lilac ('35) 10.00 4.00
44 A5 6p dk violet 3.50 .50
45 A5 9p olive bis ('35) 10.00 *16.00*
46 A5 1sh orange & blk 24.00 *15.00*
Nos. 38-46 (9) 54.15 *43.75*

Common Design Types pictured following the introduction.

Silver Jubilee Issue
Common Design Type
1935, May 6 *Perf. 11x12*
47 CD301 1p gray blk & ultra 1.25 *2.50*
48 CD301 2p indigo & grn 1.25 2.50
49 CD301 3p ultra & brn 12.00 *22.50*
50 CD301 1sh brown vio & ind 29.00 *55.00*
Nos. 47-50 (4) 43.50 *82.50*
Set, never hinged 60.00

Coronation Issue
Common Design Type
1937, May 12 *Perf. 11x11½*
51 CD302 ½p deep green .25 .30
52 CD302 1p dark brown .40 .40
53 CD302 2p gray black .40 .60
Nos. 51-53 (3) 1.05 1.30
Set, never hinged 1.75

A6

King George VI — A7

1938-44 Engr. *Perf. 12½*
54 A6 ½p green .25 *2.00*
54A A6 ½p dk brown ('42) .25 *2.25*
55 A6 1p dark brown 2.50 *.35*
55A A6 1p green ('42) .25 *1.75*
56 A6 1½p dark carmine 5.00 *6.00*
56A A6 1½p gray ('42) .25 *5.75*
57 A6 2p gray 5.00 1.25
57A A6 2p dark car ('42) .25 *2.00*
58 A6 3p blue .60 1.00
59 A6 4p rose lilac 1.75 2.00
60 A6 6p dark violet 2.00 2.00
61 A6 9p olive bister 2.00 *5.25*
62 A6 1sh orange & blk 2.10 *3.25*
Nos. 54-62 (13) 22.20 34.85

Typo. *Perf. 14*
Chalky Paper
63 A7 2sh ultra & dl vio, *bl* 7.00 *17.50*
64 A7 2sh6p red & blk, *bl* 9.00 *24.00*
65 A7 5sh red & grn, *yel* 35.00 30.00
a. 5sh dk red & dp grn, *yel* ('44) 55.00 *140.00*
66 A7 10sh red & grn, *grn* 35.00 *70.00*

Wmk. 3
67 A7 £1 blk & vio, *red* 30.00 *52.50*
Nos. 63-67 (5) 116.00 194.00
Nos. 54-67 (18) 138.20 *228.85*
Set, never hinged 220.00

Catalogue values for unused stamps in this section, from this point to the end of the section, are for Never Hinged items.

Canoe on Lake Nyasa — A8

Soldier of King's African Rifles — A9

Tea Estate, Mlanje Mountain — A10

Map and Coat of Arms — A11

Fishing Village, Lake Nyasa — A12

Tobacco Estate — A13

Arms of Nyasaland and George VI — A14

1945, Sept. 1 Engr. *Perf. 12*
68 A8 ½p brn vio & blk .50 .25
69 A9 1p dp green & blk .25 .75
70 A10 1½p gray grn & blk .35 .45
71 A11 2p scarlet & blk 1.50 .90
72 A12 3p blue & blk .60 .30
73 A13 4p rose vio & blk 2.50 .80
74 A10 6p violet & blk 4.00 .90
75 A8 9p ol grn & blk 4.50 *3.00*
76 A11 1sh myr grn & ind 4.00 .25
77 A12 2sh dl red brn & grn 9.50 5.50
78 A13 2sh6p ultra & green 11.00 7.50
79 A14 5sh ultra & lt vio 7.50 *10.00*
80 A11 10sh green & lake 25.00 18.00
81 A14 20sh black & scar 30.00 *45.00*
Nos. 68-81 (14) 101.20 93.60

Peace Issue
Common Design Type
Perf. 13½x14
1946, Dec. 16 Wmk. 4
82 CD303 1p bright green .25 .30
83 CD303 2p red orange .30 .30

A15

1947, Oct. 20 *Perf. 12*
84 A15 1p emerald & org brn .75 .50

Silver Wedding Issue
Common Design Types
1948, Dec. 15 Photo. *Perf. 14x14½*
85 CD304 1p dark green .25 .25

Engr.; Name Typo.
Perf. 11½x11
86 CD305 10sh purple 18.00 *35.00*

UPU Issue
Common Design Types
Engr.; Name Typo. on 3p, 6p
Perf. 13½, 11x11½
1949, Nov. 21 Wmk. 4
87 CD306 1p blue green .35 .35
88 CD307 3p Prus blue 3.00 4.00
89 CD308 6p rose violet .85 1.25
90 CD309 1sh violet blue .35 1.00
Nos. 87-90 (4) 4.55 6.60

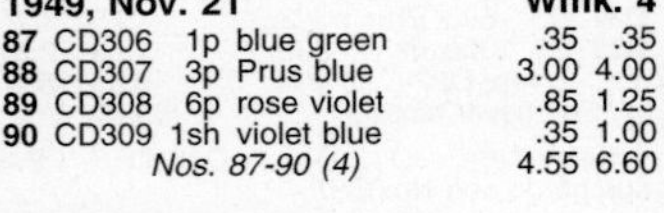

Arms of British Central Africa and Nyasaland Protectorate — A16

1951, May 15 Engr. *Perf. 11x12*
Arms in Black
91 A16 2p rose 1.25 1.25
92 A16 3p blue 1.25 1.25
93 A16 6p purple 1.50 *2.25*
94 A16 5sh deep blue 10.00 *12.00*
Nos. 91-94 (4) 14.00 *16.75*

60th anniv. of the Protectorate, originally British Central Africa.

Exhibition Seal — A17

1953, May 30 *Perf. 14x13½*
95 A17 6p purple .65 .50

Central African Rhodes Cent. Exhib.

Coronation Issue
Common Design Type

1953, June 2 *Perf. 13½x13*
96 CD312 2p orange & black .75 .75

Types of 1945-47 with Portrait of Queen Elizabeth II and

Grading Cotton — A18

1953, Sept. 1 *Perf. 12*
97 A8 ½p red brn & blk .25 *1.25*
a. Booklet pane of 4 3.75
b. Perf. 12x12½ ('54) .25 *1.25*
98 A15 1p emer & org brn .65 .25
a. Booklet pane of 4 3.75
99 A10 1½p gray grn & blk .25 *1.75*
100 A11 2p orange & blk .85 .30
a. Booklet pane of 4 4.25
b. Perf. 12x12½ ('54) .40 .30
101 A18 2½p blk & brt grn .30 *.50*
102 A13 3p scarlet & blk .30 .30
103 A12 4½p blue & blk .90 .45
104 A10 6p violet & blk 1.25 1.25
a. Booklet pane of 4 11.50
b. Perf. 12x12½ ('54) 2.00 .90
105 A8 9p olive & blk 1.25 *2.75*
106 A11 1sh myr grn & ind 3.75 .50
107 A12 2sh rose brn & grn 3.50 *3.75*
108 A13 2sh6p ultra & grn 4.25 *6.75*
109 A14 5sh Prus bl & rose lil 10.00 7.00
110 A11 10sh green & lake 11.00 *17.50*
111 A14 20sh black & scar 25.00 *32.50*
Nos. 97-111 (15) 63.50 *76.80*

Issue date: Nos. 97b, 100b, 104b, Mar. 8.

Revenue Stamps Overprinted in Black

Arms of Nyasaland — A19

Perf. 11½x12
1963, Nov. 1 **Engr.** **Unwmk.**
112 A19 ½p on 1p blue .30 .30
113 A19 1p green .30 .25
114 A19 2p rose red .30 .30
115 A19 3p dark blue .30 .25
116 A19 6p rose lake .30 .25
117 A19 9p on 1sh car rose .40 .40
118 A19 1sh purple .45 2.75
119 A19 2sh6p black 1.25 *2.00*
120 A19 5sh brown 3.00 3.50
121 A19 10sh gray olive 5.25 *8.00*
122 A19 £1 violet 5.75 *8.50*
Nos. 112-122 (11) 17.60 *26.50*

Nos. 112, 117 have 3 bars over old value.

Mother and Child — A20

Designs: 1p, Chambo fish. 2p, Zebu bull. 3p, Peanuts. 4p, Fishermen in boat. 6p, Harvesting tea. 1sh, Lumber and tropical pine branch. 1sh3p, Tobacco industry. 2sh6p, Cotton industry. 5sh, Monkey Bay, Lake Nyasa. 10sh, Afzelia tree (pod mahogany). £1, Nyala antelope, vert.

Perf. 14½
1964, Jan. 1 **Unwmk.** **Photo.**
Size: 23x19mm
123 A20 ½p lilac .25 *.35*
124 A20 1p green & blk .25 *.25*
125 A20 2p red brown .25 *.25*
126 A20 3p pale brn, brn red & grn .25 *.25*
127 A20 4p org yel & indigo .30 *.35*

Size: 41½x25mm, 25x41½mm
128 A20 6p bl pur & brt yel grn .70 *.70*
129 A20 1sh yel brn & dk grn .50 .30
130 A20 1sh3p red brn & olive 3.75 .30
131 A20 2sh6p blue & brn 3.25 .50
132 A20 5sh grn, bl, sep & yel 1.50 1.50
133 A20 10sh org brn grn & gray 2.75 *3.25*
134 A20 £1 yel & dk brn 8.00 *11.00*
Nos. 123-134 (12) 21.75 19.00

POSTAGE DUE STAMPS

Catalogue values for unused stamps in this section are for Never Hinged items.

D1

Perf. 14
1950, July 1 **Wmk. 4** **Typo.**
J1 D1 1p rose red 4.00 *32.50*
J2 D1 2p ultramarine 21.00 *32.50*
J3 D1 3p green 17.50 *8.00*
J4 D1 4p claret 30.00 *60.00*
J5 D1 6p ocher 42.50 *170.00*
Nos. J1-J5 (5) 115.00 *303.00*

NYASSA

nī-ˈa-sə

LOCATION — In the northern part of Mozambique in southeast Africa
AREA — 73,292 sq. mi.
POP. — 3,000,000 (estimated)
CAPITAL — Porto Amelia

The district formerly administered by the Nyassa Company is now a part of Mozambique.

1000 Reis = 1 Milreis
100 Centavos = 1 Escudo (1919)

Mozambique Nos. 24-35 Overprinted in Black

Perf. 11½, 12½ (Nos. 5, 7, 10, 12)
1898 **Unwmk.**
1 A3 5r yellow 3.75 3.50
2 A3 10r redsh violet 3.75 3.50
3 A3 15r chocolate 3.75 3.50
4 A3 20r gray violet 3.75 3.50
5 A3 25r blue green 3.75 3.50
6 A3 50r light blue 3.75 3.50
a. Inverted overprint 67.50
b. Perf. 12½ 12.00 7.50
7 A3 75r rose 4.75 4.25
8 A3 80r yellow grn 4.75 4.25
9 A3 100r brown, *buff* 4.75 4.25
10 A3 150r car, *rose* 14.00 13.00
11 A3 200r dk blue, *blue* 8.25 7.50
12 A3 300r dk blue, *salmon* 8.25 7.50
Nos. 1-12 (12) 67.25 61.75

Reprints of Nos. 1, 5, 8, 9, 10 and 12 have white gum and clean-cut perforation 13½. Value of No. 9, $15; others $3 each.

Same Overprint on Mozambique Issue of 1898

1898 *Perf. 11½*
13 A4 2½r gray 2.90 2.70
14 A4 5r orange 2.90 2.70
15 A4 10r light green 2.90 2.70
16 A4 15r brown 4.00 2.90
17 A4 20r gray violet 4.00 2.90
18 A4 25r sea green 4.00 2.90
19 A4 50r blue 4.00 2.90
20 A4 75r rose 4.00 3.25
21 A4 80r violet 3.75 2.75
22 A4 100r dk bl, *bl* 3.75 2.75
23 A4 150r brown, *straw* 3.75 2.75
24 A4 200r red lilac, *pnksh* 5.00 2.75
25 A4 300r dk blue, *rose* 6.00 2.75
Nos. 13-25 (13) 50.95 36.70

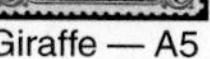

Giraffe — A5

Camels — A6

1901 **Engr.** *Perf. 14*
26 A5 2½r blk & red brn 2.60 1.20
27 A5 5r blk & violet 2.60 1.20
28 A5 10r blk & dp grn 2.60 1.20
29 A5 15r blk & org brn 2.60 1.20
30 A5 20r blk & org red 2.60 1.70
31 A5 25r blk & orange 2.60 1.70
32 A5 50r blk & dl bl 2.60 1.70
33 A6 75r blk & car lake 2.75 2.00
34 A6 80r blk & lilac 2.75 2.00
35 A6 100r blk & brn bis 3.00 2.00
36 A6 150r blk & dp org 3.25 2.25
37 A6 200r blk & grnsh bl 3.50 2.25
38 A6 300r blk & yel grn 3.50 2.25
Nos. 26-38 (13) 36.95 22.65

Nos. 26 to 38 are known with inverted centers but are believed to be purely speculative and never regularly issued. Value $100 each.
Perf 13½, 14½, 15½ & compound also exist.
For overprints and surcharges see Nos. 39-50, 63-80.

Nos. 34, 36, 38 Surcharged

1903
39 A6 65r on 80r 1.90 1.50
40 A6 115r on 150r 1.90 1.50
41 A6 130r on 300r 1.90 1.50
Nos. 39-41 (3) 5.70 4.50

Nos. 29, 31 Overprinted

1903
42 A5 15r black & org brn 1.90 1.50
43 A5 25r black & orange 1.90 1.50

Nos. 34, 36, 38 Surcharged

1903
44 A6 65r on 80r 57.50 47.50
45 A6 115r on 150r 57.50 47.50
46 A6 130r on 300r 57.50 47.50
Nos. 44-46 (3) 172.50 142.50

Nos. 29, 31 Overprinted

1903
47 A5 15r black & org brn 375.00 180.00
48 A5 25r black & orange 250.00 170.00

Forgeries exist of Nos. 44-48.

Nos. 26, 35 Surcharged

1910
49 A5 5r on 2½r 2.00 1.75
50 A6 50r on 100r 2.00 1.75
a. "50 REIS" omitted 350.00

Reprints of Nos. 49-50, made in 1921, have 2mm space between surcharge lines, instead of 1½mm. Value, each 25 cents.

Zebra
A7

Vasco da Gama's Flagship "San Gabriel"
A8

Designs: Nos. 51-53, Camels. Nos. 57-59, Giraffe and palms.

1911 **Red Overprint**
51 A7 2½r blk & dl vio 2.00 1.20
52 A7 5r black 2.00 1.20
53 A7 10r blk & gray grn 2.00 1.20
54 A7 20r blk & car lake 2.00 1.20
55 A7 25r blk & vio brn 2.00 1.20
56 A7 50r blk & dp bl 2.00 1.20
57 A8 75r blk & brn 2.00 1.20
58 A8 100r blk & brn, *grn* 2.00 1.20
59 A8 200r blk & dp grn, *sal* 2.00 1.90
60 A8 300r blk, *blue* 4.75 3.75
61 A8 400r blk & dk brn 5.50 3.75
62 A8 500r ol & vio brn 7.50 6.00
Nos. 51-62 (12) 35.75 25.00

Nos. 51-62 exist without overprint but were not issued in that condition. Value $7.50 each.
For surcharges see Nos. 81-105.

Stamps of 1901-03 Surcharged

1918 **On Nos. 26-38**
63 A5 ¼c on 2½r 250.00 180.00
64 A5 ½c on 5r 250.00 180.00
65 A5 1c on 10r 250.00 180.00
66 A5 1½c on 15r 4.00 2.25
67 A5 2c on 20r 2.75 2.25
68 A5 3½c on 25r 2.90 2.20
69 A5 5c on 50r 2.50 2.20
70 A6 7½c on 75r 2.50 2.20
71 A6 8c on 80r 2.50 2.20
72 A6 10c on 100r 2.50 2.20
73 A6 15c on 150r 4.00 4.00
74 A6 20c on 200r 4.00 4.00
75 A6 30c on 300r 6.50 5.50

On Nos. 39-41
76 A6 40c on 65r on 80r 35.00 34.00
77 A6 50c on 115r on 150r 5.00 4.25
78 A6 1e on 130r on 300r 5.50 4.25

On Nos. 42-43
79 A5 1½c on 15r 8.50 6.50
80 A5 3½c on 25r 3.25 2.20
Nos. 63-80 (18) 841.40 620.20

On Nos. 70-78 there is less space between "REPUBLICA" and the new value than on the other stamps of this issue.
On Nos. 76-78 the 1903 surcharge is canceled by a bar.
The surcharge exists inverted on #64, 66-70, 72, 76, 78-80, and double on #64, 67, 69.

Nos. 51-62 Surcharged in Black or Red

Numerals: The "1" (large or small) is thin, sharp-pointed, and has thin serifs. The "2" is italic, with the tail thin and only slightly wavy. The "3" has a flat top. The "4" is open at the top. The "7" has thin strokes.
Centavos: The letters are shaded, i.e., they are thicker in some parts than in others. The "t" has a thin cross bar ending in a downward stroke at the right. The "s" is flat at the bottom and wider than in the next group.

1921 **Lisbon Surcharges**
81 A7 ¼c on 2½r 5.00 4.00
83 A7 ½c on 5r (R) 5.00 4.00
a. ½c on 2½r (R) (error) 330.00 310.00
84 A7 1c on 10r 5.00 4.00
85 A8 1½c on 300r (R) 5.00 4.00
86 A7 2c on 20r 5.00 4.00
87 A7 2½c on 25r 5.00 4.00
88 A8 3c on 400r 5.00 4.00
a. "Republica" omitted
89 A7 5c on 50r 5.00 4.00
90 A8 7½c on 75r 5.00 4.00
91 A8 10c on 100r 5.00 4.00

92 A8 12c on 500r 5.00 4.00
93 A8 20c on 200r 5.00 4.00
Nos. 81-93 (12) 60.00 48.00

Forgeries exist of Nos. 81-93.

London Surcharges

Numerals — The "1" has the vertical stroke and serifs thicker than in the Lisbon printing. The "2" is upright and has a strong wave in the tail. The small "2" is heavily shaded. The "3" has a rounded top. The "4" is closed at the top. The "7" has thick strokes.

Centavos — The letters are heavier than in the Lisbon printing and are of even thickness throughout. The "t" has a thick cross bar with scarcely any down stroke at the end. The "s" is rounded at the bottom and narrower than in the Lisbon printing.

94 A7 ¼c on 2½r 3.75 3.50
95 A7 ½c on 5r (R) 3.75 3.50
96 A7 1c on 10r 3.75 3.50
97 A8 1½c on 300r (R) 3.75 3.50
98 A7 2c on 20r 3.75 3.50
99 A7 2½c on 25r 3.75 3.50
100 A8 3c on 400r 3.75 3.50
101 A7 5c on 50r 3.75 3.50
102 A8 7½c on 75r 3.75 3.50
103 A8 10c on 100r 3.75 3.50
104 A8 12c on 500r 3.75 3.50
105 A8 20c on 200r 3.75 3.50
Nos. 94-105 (12) 45.00 42.00

A9

Zebra and Warrior — A10

Designs: 2c-6c, Vasco da Gama. 7½c-20c, "San Gabriel." 2e-5e, Dhow and warrior.

Perf. 13½-15 & Compound

1921-23 **Engr.**

106 A9 ¼c claret 1.75 1.10
107 A9 ½c steel blue 1.75 1.10
108 A9 1c grn & blk 1.75 1.10
109 A9 1½c blk & ocher 1.75 1.10
110 A9 2c red & blk 1.75 1.10
111 A9 2½c blk & ol grn 1.75 1.10
112 A9 4c blk & org 1.75 1.10
113 A9 5c ultra & blk 1.75 1.10
114 A9 6c blk & vio 1.75 1.10
115 A9 7½c blk & blk brn 1.75 1.10
116 A9 8c blk & ol grn 1.75 1.10
117 A9 10c blk & red brn 1.75 1.10
118 A9 15c blk & carmine 1.75 1.10
119 A9 20c blk & pale bl 1.75 1.10
120 A10 30c blk & bister 1.75 1.10
121 A10 40c blk & gray bl 1.75 1.10
122 A10 50c blk & green 1.75 1.40
123 A10 1e blk & red brn 1.90 1.40
124 A10 2e red brn & blk ('23) 6.00 5.25
125 A10 5e ultra & red brn ('23) 5.50 4.00
Nos. 106-125 (20) 43.15 29.65

1921

108a A9 1c grn & blk 1.60 1.00
109a A9 1½c blk & ocher 1.60 1.00
110a A9 2c red & blk 1.60 1.00
111a A9 2½c blk & ol grn 1.60 1.00
112a A9 4c blk & org 1.60 1.00
113a A9 5c ultra & blk 1.60 1.00
114a A9 6c blk & vio 1.60 1.00
115a A9 7½c blk & blk brn 1.60 1.00
116a A9 8c blk & red brn 1.60 1.00
117a A9 10c blk & carmine 1.60 1.00
118a A9 15c blk & car 1.60 1.00
119a A9 20c blk & pale bl 1.60 1.00
120a A10 30c blk & bister 1.60 1.00
121a A10 40c blk & gray bl 1.60 1.00
122a A10 50c blk & green 1.60 1.00
123a A10 1e blk & red brn 1.60 1.00
Nos. 108a-123a (16) 25.60 16.00

POSTAGE DUE STAMPS

Giraffe D1

½c, 1c, Giraffe. 2c, 3c, Zebra. 5c, 6c, 10c, "San Gabriel." 20c, 50c, Vasco da Gama.

1924 **Unwmk.** **Engr.** ***Perf. 14***

J1 D1 ½c deep green 4.00 *3.00*
J2 D1 1c gray 4.00 *3.00*
J3 D1 2c red 4.00 *3.00*
J4 D1 3c red orange 4.00 *3.00*
J5 D1 5c dark brown 4.00 *3.00*
J6 D1 6c orange brown 4.00 *3.00*
J7 D1 10c brown violet 4.00 *3.00*
J8 D1 20c carmine 4.00 *3.00*
J9 D1 50c lilac gray 4.00 *3.00*
Nos. J1-J9 (9) 36.00 *27.00*

Used values are for c-t-o copies.

NEWSPAPER STAMP

Mozambique No. P6 Ovptd. Like Nos. 1-25 in Black

1898 **Unwmk.** ***Perf. 13½***

P1 N3 2½r brown 3.75 3.50

Reprints have white gum and clean-cut perf. 13½. Value $1.

POSTAL TAX STAMPS

Pombal Issue

Mozambique Nos. RA1-RA3 Overprinted "NYASSA" in Red

1925 **Unwmk.** ***Perf. 12½***

RA1 CD28 15c brown & blk 11.50 10.50
RA2 CD29 15c brown & blk 11.50 10.50
RA3 CD30 15c brown & blk 11.50 10.50
Nos. RA1-RA3 (3) 34.50 31.50

POSTAL TAX DUE STAMPS

Pombal Issue

Mozambique Nos. RAJ1-RAJ3 Overprinted "NYASSA" in Red

1925 **Unwmk.** ***Perf. 12½***

RAJ1 CD28 30c brown & blk 17.00 15.00
RAJ2 CD29 30c brown & blk 17.00 15.00
RAJ3 CD30 30c brown & blk 17.00 15.00
Nos. RAJ1-RAJ3 (3) 51.00 45.00

OBOCK

'ō-ˌbäk

LOCATION — A seaport in eastern Africa on the Gulf of Aden, directly opposite Aden.

Obock was the point of entrance from which French Somaliland was formed. The port was acquired by the French in 1862 but was not actively occupied until 1884 when Sagallo and Tadjoura were ceded to France. In 1888 Djibouti was made into a port and the seat of government moved from Obock to the latter city. In 1902 the name Somali Coast was adopted on the postage stamps of Djibouti, these stamps superseding the individual issues of Obock.

100 Centimes = 1 Franc

Counterfeits exist of Nos. 1-31.

Stamps of French Colonies Handstamped in Black

Nos. 1-11

Nos. 12-20

1892 **Unwmk.** ***Perf. 14x13½***

1 A9 1c blk, *lil bl* 45.00 45.00
2 A9 2c brn, *buff* 45.00 45.00
3 A9 4c claret, *lav* 450.00 *475.00*
4 A9 5c grn, *grnsh* 40.00 32.50
5 A9 10c blk, *lavender* 80.00 47.50
6 A9 15c blue 72.50 50.00
7 A9 25c blk, *rose* 110.00 80.00
8 A9 35c vio, *org* 450.00 450.00
9 A9 40c red, *straw* 400.00 *425.00*
10 A9 75c car, *rose* 450.00 *475.00*
11 A9 1fr brnz grn, *straw* 500.00 550.00
Nos. 1-11 (11) 2,643. 2,675.

No. 3 has been reprinted. On the reprints the second "O" of "OBOCK" is 4mm high instead of 3½mm. Value $32.50.

1892

12 A9 4c claret, *lav* 27.50 27.50
13 A9 5c grn, *grnsh* 27.50 27.50
14 A9 10c blk, *lavender* 27.50 27.50
15 A9 15c blue 27.50 27.50
16 A9 20c red, *grn* 47.50 45.00
17 A9 25c blk, *rose* 35.00 27.50
18 A9 40c red, *straw* 60.00 52.50
19 A9 75c car, *rose* 325.00 275.00
20 A9 1fr brnz grn, *straw* 87.50 80.00
Nos. 12-20 (9) 665.00 590.00

Exists inverted or double on all denominations.

Nos. 14, 15, 17, 20 with Additional Surcharge Handstamped in Red, Violet or Black

Nos, 21-30

No. 31

1892

21 A9 1c on 25c blk, *rose* 20.00 20.00
22 A9 2c on 10c blk, *lav* 72.50 60.00
23 A9 2c on 15c blue 22.50 20.00
24 A9 4c on 15c bl (Bk) 20.00 20.00
25 A9 4c on 25c blk, *rose* (Bk) 20.00 20.00
26 A9 5c on 25c blk, *rose* 27.50 27.50
27 A9 20c on 10c blk, *lav* 95.00 95.00
28 A9 30c on 10c blk, *lav* 120.00 110.00
29 A9 35c on 25c blk, *rose* 100.00 92.50
  a. "3" instead of "35" 950.00 950.00
30 A9 75c on 1fr brnz grn, *straw* 110.00 110.00
  b. "57" instead of "75" *8,750.* *9,250.*
  c. "55" instead of "75" *8,750.* *9,250.*
31 A9 5fr on 1fr brnz grn, *straw* (V) 775.00 700.00
Nos. 21-31 (11) 1,383. 1,275.

Exists inverted on most denominations.

Navigation and Commerce — A4

Obock in Red (1c, 5c, 15c, 25c, 75c, 1fr) or Blue

1892 **Typo.** ***Perf. 14x13½***

32 A4 1c blk, *lil bl* 2.75 2.75
33 A4 2c brn, *buff* 2.00 2.00
34 A4 4c claret, *lav* 2.75 2.75
35 A4 5c grn, *grnsh* 6.25 4.00
36 A4 10c blk, *lavender* 8.00 5.25
37 A4 15c bl, quadrille paper 19.50 11.50
38 A4 20c red, *grn* 27.50 27.50
39 A4 25c blk, *rose* 27.50 24.00
40 A4 30c brn, *bis* 24.00 20.00
41 A4 40c red, *straw* 24.00 20.00
42 A4 50c car, *rose* 28.00 24.00
43 A4 75c vio, *org* 32.50 24.00
  a. Name double 350.00 350.00
  b. Name inverted 5,500. 5,500.
44 A4 1fr brnz grn, *straw* 47.50 40.00
Nos. 32-44 (13) 252.25 207.75

Perf. 13½x14 stamps are counterfeits.

Camel and Rider — A5

Quadrille Lines Printed on Paper

1893 **Size: 32mm at base** ***Imperf.***

44A A5 2fr slate 65.00 55.00

Size: 45mm at base

45 A5 5fr red 140.00 125.00

Somali Warriors — A7

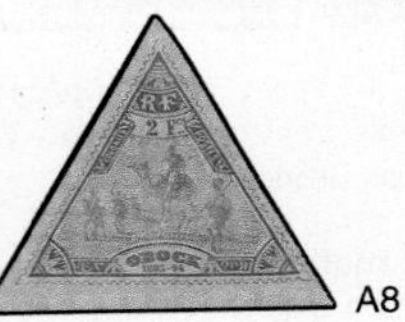
A8

1894 ***Imperf.***

Quadrille Lines Printed on Paper

46 A7 1c blk & rose 2.75 2.75
47 A7 2c vio brn & grn 2.75 2.75
48 A7 4c brn vio & org 2.75 2.75
49 A7 5c bl grn & brn 3.50 3.50
50 A7 10c blk & grn 9.50 8.00
  a. Half used as 5c on cover ('01) 350.00
51 A7 15c bl & rose 9.50 7.25
52 A7 20c brn org & mar 9.50 8.00
  a. Half used as 10c on cover ('01) 325.00
53 A7 25c blk & bl 10.50 6.50
  a. Right half used as 5c on cover ('01) 300.00
  b. Left half used as 2c on cover ('03) 300.00
54 A7 30c bis & yel grn 20.00 14.50
  a. Half used as 15c on cover ('01) 2,200.
55 A7 40c red & bl grn 17.00 13.00
56 A7 50c rose & bl 15.00 12.00
  a. Half used as 25c on cover 3,400.
57 A7 75c gray lil & org 20.00 13.00
58 A7 1fr ol grn & mar 17.00 10.50

Size: 37mm at base

60 A8 2fr vio & org 120.00 120.00

Size: 42mm at base

61 A8 5fr rose & bl 95.00 95.00

Size: 46mm at base

62 A8 10fr org & red vio 160.00 160.00
63 A8 25fr brn & bl 875.00 875.00
64 A8 50fr red vio & grn 1,000. 1,000.

Counterfeits exist of Nos. 63-64.

Stamps of Obock were replaced in 1901 by those of Somali Coast. The 5c on 75c, 5c on 25fr and 10c on 50fr of 1902 are listed under Somali Coast.

POSTAGE DUE STAMPS

Postage Due Stamps of French Colonies Handstamped Like #1-20

Nos. J1-J4

Nos. J5-J18

1892 **Unwmk.** ***Imperf.***

J1 D1 5c black *11,000.*
J2 D1 10c black 240.00 *275.00*
J3 D1 30c black 375.00 *450.00*
J4 D1 60c black 475.00 *550.00*
J5 D1 1c black 55.00 55.00
J6 D1 2c black 45.00 45.00
J7 D1 3c black 52.50 52.50
J8 D1 4c black 45.00 45.00
J9 D1 5c black 16.00 16.00
J10 D1 10c black 35.00 35.00
J11 D1 15c black 24.00 24.00
J12 D1 20c black 32.50 32.50
J13 D1 30c black 32.50 32.50
J14 D1 40c black 60.00 60.00
J15 D1 60c black 80.00 80.00
J16 D1 1fr brown 225.00 225.00
J17 D1 2fr brown 240.00 240.00
J18 D1 5fr brown 525.00 525.00
Nos. J2-J18 (17) 2,558. 2,743.

Overprint Inverted

J5a D1 1c black *200.00 200.00*
J6a D1 2c black *200.00 200.00*
J7a D1 3c black *200.00 200.00*
J8a D1 4c black *200.00 200.00*
J9a D1 5c black *200.00 200.00*
J10a D1 10c black *250.00 250.00*
J11a D1 15c black *200.00 200.00*
J15a D1 60c black *275.00 275.00*
J16a D1 1fr brown *550.00 550.00*
J17a D1 2fr brown *550.00 550.00*

Double Overprint

J5b D1 1c black *200.00 200.00*
J6b D1 2c black *200.00 200.00*
J9b D1 5c black *250.00 250.00*
J10b D1 10c black *300.00 300.00*

J11b	D1	15c black	*250.00*	*250.00*
J12b	D1	20c black	*250.00*	*250.00*
J13b	D1	30c black	*300.00*	*300.00*

These handstamped overprints may be found double on some values. Counterfeits exist of Nos. J1-J18.

No. J1 has been reprinted. The overprint on the original measures 12½x3¾mm and on the reprint 12x3¼mm. Value, $325.

OLTRE GIUBA

ˌōl-trā-ˈjü-bə

(Italian Jubaland)

LOCATION — A strip of land, 50 to 100 miles in width, west of and parallel to the Juba River in East Africa
GOVT. — Former Italian Protectorate
AREA — 33,000 sq. mi.
POP. — 12,000
CAPITAL — Kismayu

Oltre Giuba was ceded to Italy by Great Britain in 1924 and in 1926 was incorporated with Italian Somaliland. In 1936 it became part of Italian East Africa.

100 Centesimi = 1 Lira

Watermark

Wmk. 140 — Crown

Italian Stamps of 1901-26 Overprinted

On #1-15

On #16-20

1925, July 29 Wmk. 140 *Perf. 14*

1	A42	1c brown	5.50	*30.00*
a.		Inverted overprint	475.00	
2	A43	2c yel brown	4.25	*30.00*
3	A48	5c green	4.25	*12.50*
4	A48	10c claret	4.25	*12.50*
5	A48	15c slate	4.25	*17.50*
6	A50	20c brn orange	4.25	*17.50*
7	A49	25c blue	4.25	*17.50*
8	A49	30c org brown	5.50	*22.50*
9	A49	40c brown	11.00	*17.50*
10	A49	50c violet	11.00	*17.50*
11	A49	60c carmine	11.00	*22.50*
12	A46	1 l brn & green	16.00	30.00
13	A46	2 l dk grn & org	85.00	60.00
14	A46	5 l blue & rose	110.00	87.50
15	A51	10 l gray grn & red	21.00	*95.00*
		Nos. 1-15 (15)	301.50	*490.00*

1925-26

16	A49	20c green	7.00	*17.50*
17	A49	30c gray	10.00	*22.50*
18	A46	75c dk red & rose	42.50	*95.00*
19	A46	1.25 l bl & ultra	87.50	*160.00*
20	A46	2.50 l dk grn & org	120.00	*275.00*
		Nos. 16-20 (5)	267.00	*570.00*

Issue years: #18-20, 1926; others 1925.

Victor Emmanuel Issue

Italian Stamps of 1925 Overprinted

1925-26 Unwmk. *Perf. 11*

21	A78	60c brown car	1.60	*16.00*
a.		Perf. 13½	*12,000.*	
22	A78	1 l dark blue	1.60	*25.00*
a.		Perf. 13½	650.00	*2,400.*
23	A78	1.25 l dk bl ('26)	6.50	*40.00*
a.		Perf. 13½	6.50	*40.00*
		Nos. 21-23 (3)	9.70	*81.00*

Saint Francis of Assisi Issue

Italian Stamps and Type of 1926 Overprinted

1926, Apr. 12 Wmk. 140 *Perf. 14*

24	A79	20c gray green	2.50	*45.00*
25	A80	40c dark violet	2.50	*45.00*
26	A81	60c red brown	2.50	*65.00*

Overprinted in Red

Unwmk.

27	A82	1.25 l dk bl, perf. 11	2.50	*87.50*
28	A83	5 l + 2.50 l ol grn, perf. 13½	8.00	*135.00*
		Nos. 24-28 (5)	18.00	*377.50*

Map of Oltre Giuba — A1

1926, Apr. 21 Typo. Wmk. 140

29	A1	5c yellow brown	1.60	*35.00*
30	A1	20c blue green	1.60	*35.00*
31	A1	25c olive brown	1.60	*35.00*
32	A1	40c dull red	1.60	*35.00*
33	A1	60c brown violet	1.60	*35.00*
34	A1	1 l blue	1.60	*35.00*
35	A1	2 l dark green	1.60	*35.00*
		Nos. 29-35 (7)	11.20	*245.00*

Oltre Giuba was incorporated with Italian Somaliland on July 1, 1926, and stamps inscribed "Oltre Giuba" were discontinued.

SEMI-POSTAL STAMPS

Note preceding Italy semi-postals applies to No. 28.

Colonial Institute Issue

"Peace" Substituting Spade for Sword — SP1

Wmk. 140

1926, June 1 Typo. *Perf. 14*

B1	SP1	5c + 5c brown	1.20	*9.50*
B2	SP1	10c + 5c ol grn	1.20	*9.50*
B3	SP1	20c + 5c blue grn	1.20	*9.50*
B4	SP1	40c + 5c brn red	1.20	*9.50*
B5	SP1	60c + 5c orange	1.20	*9.50*
B6	SP1	1 l + 5c blue	1.20	*20.00*
		Nos. B1-B6 (6)	7.20	*67.50*

Surtax for Italian Colonial Institute.

SPECIAL DELIVERY STAMPS

Special Delivery Stamps of Italy Ovptd.

1926 Wmk. 140 *Perf. 14*

E1	SD1	70c dull red	32.50	*65.00*
E2	SD2	2.50 l blue & red	67.50	*180.00*

POSTAGE DUE STAMPS

Italian Postage Due Stamps of 1870-1903 Ovptd. Like Nos. E1-E2

1925, July 29 Wmk. 140 *Perf. 14*

J1	D3	5c buff & magenta	24.00	24.00
J2	D3	10c buff & magenta	24.00	24.00
J3	D3	20c buff & magenta	24.00	*40.00*
J4	D3	30c buff & magenta	24.00	*40.00*
J5	D3	40c buff & magenta	24.00	*45.00*
J6	D3	50c buff & magenta	32.50	*55.00*
J7	D3	60c buff & brown	32.50	*65.00*
J8	D3	1 l blue & magenta	35.00	*80.00*
J9	D3	2 l blue & magenta	175.00	*275.00*
J10	D3	5 l blue & magenta	225.00	275.00
		Nos. J1-J10 (10)	620.00	*923.00*

PARCEL POST STAMPS

These stamps were used by affixing them to the waybill so that one half remained on it following the parcel, the other half staying on the receipt given the sender. Most used halves are right halves. Complete stamps were obtainable canceled, probably to order. Both unused and used values are for complete stamps.

Italian Parcel Post Stamps of 1914-22 Overprinted

1925, July 29 Wmk. 140 *Perf. 13½*

Q1	PP2	5c brown	21.00	*45.00*
Q2	PP2	10c blue	17.50	*45.00*
Q3	PP2	20c black	17.50	*45.00*
Q4	PP2	25c red	17.50	*45.00*
Q5	PP2	50c orange	21.00	*45.00*
Q6	PP2	1 l violet	17.50	*100.00*
a.		Double overprint	550.00	
Q7	PP2	2 l green	28.00	*100.00*
Q8	PP2	3 l bister	65.00	*130.00*
Q9	PP2	4 l slate	29.00	*130.00*
Q10	PP2	10 l rose lilac	95.00	*225.00*
Q11	PP2	12 l red brown	175.00	*350.00*
Q12	PP2	15 l olive green	160.00	*350.00*
Q13	PP2	20 l brown violet	160.00	*350.00*
		Nos. Q1-Q13 (13)	824.00	1,960.

Halves Used

Q1-Q4	1.75
Q5-Q7	3.00
Q8-Q9	4.75
Q10	9.25
Q11	15.00
Q12-Q13	10.00

OMAN

ˈō-ˌmän

Muscat and Oman

LOCATION — Southeastern corner of the Arabian Peninsula
GOVT. — Sultanate
AREA — 105,000 sq. mi.
POP. — 5,110,000 (2020 est.)
CAPITAL — Muscat

Nos. 16-93, the stamps with "value only" surcharges, were used not only in Muscat, but also in Dubai (Apr. 1, 1948 - Jan. 6, 1961), Qatar (Aug. 1950 - Mar. 31, 1957), and Abu Dhabi (Mar. 30, 1963 - Mar. 29, 1964). Occasionally they were also used in Bahrain and Kuwait.

The Sultanate of Muscat and Oman changed its name to Oman in 1970.

12 Pies = 1 Anna
16 Annas = 1 Rupee
100 Naye Paise = 1 Rupee (1957)
64 Baizas = 1 Rupee (1966)
1000 Baizas = 1 Rial Saidi (1970)

Watermarks

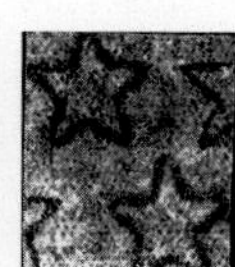

Wmk. 196 — Multiple Stars

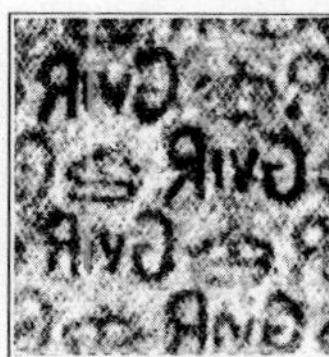

Wmk. 251 — Crown and GviR Multiple

Wmk. 259 — Crown and Large G VI R

Wmk. 298 — Tudor Crown and E 2 R Multiple

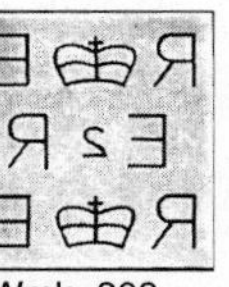

Wmk. 308 — St. Edward's Crown and E 2 R Multiple

Wmk. 322 — St. Edward's Crown Multiple

Catalogue values for all unused stamps in this country are for Never Hinged items, beginning with No. 16.

Muscat

Stamps of India 1937-43 Overprinted in Black

On Nos. 1-13 the overprint is smaller — 13x6mm.

Perf. 13½x14

1944, Nov. 20 Wmk. 196

1	A83	3p slate	.40	*8.00*
2	A83	½a rose violet	.40	*8.00*
3	A83	9p lt green	.40	*8.00*
4	A83	1a carmine rose	.40	*8.00*
5	A84	1½a dark purple	.40	*8.00*
a.		Double overprint	325.00	
6	A84	2a scarlet	.50	*8.00*
7	A84	3a violet	1.00	*8.00*
8	A84	3½a ultra	1.00	*8.00*
9	A85	4a chocolate	1.10	*8.00*
10	A85	6a pck blue	1.25	*8.00*
11	A85	8a blue violet	1.40	*8.50*
12	A85	12a car lake	1.50	*8.50*
13	A81	14a rose violet	2.75	*13.50*
14	A82	1r brown & slate	1.75	*12.50*
15	A82	2r dk brn & dk vio	5.00	*22.50*
		Nos. 1-15 (15)	19.25	*145.50*

200th anniv. of Al Busaid Dynasty.

Used values for Nos. 1-15 are for stamps canceled with contempraneous postmarks of the Indian postal administration. Examples with later British post office cancellations are worth much less.

Great Britain Nos. 258 to 263, 243, 248, 249A Surcharged

No. 16

No. 24

Perf. 14½x14

1948, Apr. 1 Wmk. 251

16	A101	½a on ½p green	3.00	*8.00*
17	A101	1a on 1p vermilion	3.25	*.30*
18	A101	1½a on 1½p lt red brn	15.00	*4.25*
19	A101	2a on 2p lt org	2.25	*3.50*
20	A101	2½a on 2½p ultra	4.25	*8.50*

21 A101 3a on 3p violet 4.00 *.25*
22 A102 6a on 6p rose lilac 4.50 *.25*
23 A103 1r on 1sh brown 5.00 *.75*

Wmk. 259 ***Perf. 14***

24 A104 2r on 2sh6p yel grn 15.00 *55.00*
Nos. 16-24 (9) 56.25 *80.80*

Silver Wedding Issue

Great Britain Nos. 267-268 Surcharged in Black

Perf. 14½x14, 14x14½

1948, Apr. 26 **Wmk. 251**

25 A109 2½a on 2½p brt ultra 3.50 *5.00*
26 A110 15r on £1 dp chlky bl 37.50 *37.50*

Three bars obliterate the original denomination on No. 26.

Olympic Games Issue

Great Britain, Nos. 271 to 274, Surcharged with New Value in Black

1948, July 29 ***Perf. 14½x14***

27 A113 2½a on 2½p brt ultra 1.00 *3.00*
28 A114 3a on 3p dp violet 1.15 *3.00*
29 A115 6a on 6p red violet 1.25 *3.50*
30 A116 1r on 1sh dk brn 3.00 *4.75*
a. Double surcharge 1,500.
Nos. 27-30 (4) 6.40 14.25

A square of dots obliterates the original denomination on Nos. 28-30.

UPU Issue

Great Britain Nos. 276 to 279 Surcharged with New Value and Square of Dots in Black

1949, Oct. 10 **Photo.**

31 A117 2½a on 2½p brt ultra 1.10 *3.00*
32 A118 3a on 3p brt violet 1.40 *4.25*
33 A119 6a on 6p red violet 1.50 *2.75*
34 A120 1r on 1sh brown 4.00 *7.50*
Nos. 31-34 (4) 8.00 17.50

Great Britain Nos. 280-286 Surcharged in Black

1951

35 A101 ½a on ½p lt org 1.00 *9.50*
36 A101 1a on 1p ultra .60 *8.00*
37 A101 1½a on 1½p green 17.00 *35.00*
38 A101 2a on 2p lt red brn .85 *9.00*
39 A101 2½a on 2½p vermilion 1.50 *16.00*
40 A102 4a on 4p ultra 1.25 *3.75*

Perf. 11x12
Wmk. 259

41 A121 2r on 2sh6p green 45.00 8.00
Nos. 35-41 (7) 67.20 *89.25*

Two types of surcharge on No. 41.

Great Britain 1952-54 Stamps Srchd. in Black and Dark Blue

1952-54 **Wmk. 298** ***Perf. 14½x14***

42 A126 ½a on ½p red org ('53) .35 *2.25*
43 A126 1a on 1p ultra ('53) .35 *2.25*
44 A126 1½a on 1½p grn ('52) .40 *2.25*
45 A126 2a on 2p red brn ('53) .50 .30
46 A127 2½a on 2½p scar ('52) .35 .30
47 A127 3a on 3p dk pur (dk bl) .50 *1.25*
48 A128 4a on 4p ultra ('53) 2.10 *4.25*
49 A129 6a on 6p lilac rose .60 .50
50 A132 12a on 1sh3p dk grn ('53) 7.75 .95
51 A131 1r on 1sh6p dk bl ('53) 3.00 .80
Nos. 42-51 (10) 15.90 15.10

Coronation Issue

Great Britain Nos. 313-316 Surcharged

1953, June 10

52 A134 2½a on 2½p scarlet 2.25 3.00
53 A135 4a on 4p brt ultra 2.25 1.25
54 A136 12a on 1sh3p dk grn 4.25 1.25
55 A137 1r on 1sh6p dk blue 5.50 1.00
Nos. 52-55 (4) 14.25 6.50

Squares of dots obliterate the original denominations on Nos. 54-55.

Great Britain Stamps of 1955-56 Surcharged

Perf. 14½x14

1955-57 **Wmk. 308** **Photo.**

56 A126 1a on 1p ultra .50 *.60*
56A A126 1½a on 1½p grn 6,000. *950.00*
57 A126 2a on 2p red brn .85 *2.00*
58 A127 2½a on 2½p scar 1.00 *3.00*
59 A127 3a on 3p dk pur 1.10 *7.50*
60 A128 4a on 4p ultra 6.50 *19.00*
61 A129 6a on 6p lilac rose 1.40 *6.50*
62 A131 1r on 1sh6p dk bl 8.00 *.50*

Engr. ***Perf. 11x12***

63 A133 2r on 2sh6p dk brown 8.00 1.50
64 A133 5r on 5sh crimson 14.00 3.50
Nos. 56,57-64 (9) 41.35 *44.10*

Surcharge on No. 63 exists in three types, on No. 64 in two types.

Issued: 2r, 9/23/55; 2a, 2½a, 6/8/56; 1r, 8/2/56; 4a, 12/9/56; 1½a, 1956; 3a, 2/3/57; 6a, 2/10/57; 5r, 3/1/57; 1a, 3/4/57.

Great Britain Nos. 317-325, 328, 332 Surcharged

1957, Apr. 1 ***Perf. 14½x14***

65 A129 1np on 5p lt brown .25 *.90*
66 A126 3np on ½p red org .35 *2.00*
67 A126 6np on 1p ultra .40 *2.25*
68 A126 9np on 1½p green .50 *1.50*
69 A126 12np on 2p red brown .55 *1.75*
70 A127 15np on 2½p scar, I .65 .50
a. Type II .55 *3.00*
71 A127 20np on 3p dk pur .40 .30
72 A128 25np on 4p ultra 1.20 *6.00*
73 A129 40np on 6p lilac rose .90 .60
74 A130 50np on 9p dp ol grn 1.75 2.50
75 A132 75np on 1sh3p dk grn 3.50 .75
Nos. 65-75 (11) 10.45 *19.05*

The arrangement of the surcharge varies on different values; there are three bars through value on No. 74.

Jubilee Jamboree Issue

Great Britain Nos. 334-336 Surcharged with New Value and Square of Dots

Perf. 14½x14

1957, Aug. 1 **Wmk. 308**

76 A138 15np on 2½p scar 1.75 1.75
77 A138 25np on 4p ultra 1.75 1.75
78 A138 75np on 1sh3p dk grn 1.75 1.75
Nos. 76-78 (3) 5.25 5.25

50th anniv. of the Boy Scout movement and the World Scout Jubilee Jamboree, Aug. 1-12.

Great Britain Stamps of 1958-60 Surcharged

Perf. 14½x14

1960-61 **Wmk. 322** **Photo.**

79 A129 1np on 5p lt brn .25 *.30*
80 A126 3np on ½p red org 1.00 *1.25*
81 A126 5np on 1p ultra 1.75 *3.00*
82 A126 6np on 1p ultra 1.25 1.00
83 A126 10np on 1½p green 1.00 *2.50*
84 A126 12np on 2p red brn 3.00 3.00
85 A127 15np on 2½p scar .50 .25
86 A127 20np on 3p dk pur .50 .25
87 A128 30np on 4½p hn brn .75 *1.10*
88 A129 40np on 6p lil rose .85 .30
89 A130 50np on 9p dp ol grn 1.50 *2.25*
90 A132 75np on 1sh3p dk grn 4.00 1.75
91 A131 1r on 1sh6p dk blue 30.00 6.50
92 A133 2r on 2sh6p dk brn 15.00 *37.50*
93 A133 5r on 5sh crim 35.00 *55.00*
Nos. 79-93 (15) 96.35 *115.95*

Issued: 15np, 4/26; 3np, 6np, 12np, 6/21; 1np, 8/8; 20np, 40np, 9/28; 5np, 10np, 30np, 50np-5r, 4/8/61.

Muscat and Oman

Crest
A1

View of Harbor
A2

Nakhal Fort — A3

BAIZAS

RUPEES

Crest and: 50b, Samail Fort. 1r, Sohar Fort. 2r, Nizwa Fort. 5r, Matrah Fort. 10r, Mirani Fort.

Perf. 14½x14 (A1), 14x14½ (A2), 14x13½ (A3)

1966, Apr. 29 **Photo.** **Unwmk.**

94 A1 3b dp claret .25 .25
95 A1 5b brown .25 .25
96 A1 10b red brown .25 .25
97 A2 15b black & violet .90 .25
98 A2 20b black & ultra 1.35 .25
99 A2 25b black & orange 2.00 .60
100 A3 30b dk blue & lil rose 2.40 .65
101 A3 50b red brn & brt grn 3.50 1.50
a. Value in "baizas" in Arabic 225.00 100.00
102 A3 1r org & dk bl 6.75 1.75
103 A3 2r grn & brn org 12.50 5.00
104 A3 5r dp car & vio 26.00 17.00
105 A3 10r dk vio & car rose 52.50 35.00
Nos. 94-105 (12) 108.65 62.75

No. 101 has value in rupees in Arabic.

See Nos. 110-121. For overprints & surcharges see Nos. 122-133C.

Mina al Fahal Harbor — A4

Designs: 25b, Oil tanks. 40b, Oil installation in the desert. 1r, View of Arabian Peninsula from Gemini IV.

Perf. 13½x13

1969, Jan. 1 **Litho.** **Unwmk.**

106 A4 20b multicolored 4.50 .90
107 A4 25b multicolored 6.25 1.35
108 A4 40b multicolored 9.00 2.00
109 A4 1r multicolored 23.00 5.00
Nos. 106-109 (4) 42.75 9.25

1st oil shipment from Muscat & Oman, July, 1967.

Types of 1966

Designs: 50b, Nakhal Fort. 75b, Samail Fort. 100b, Sohar Fort. ¼r, Nizwa Fort. ½r, Matrah Fort. 1r, Mirani Fort.

Perf. 14½x14 (A1), 14x14½ (A2), 14x13½ (A3)

1970, June 27 **Photo.** **Unwmk.**

110 A1 5b plum 1.00 .25
111 A1 10b brown 2.00 .40
112 A1 20b red brown 2.25 .45
113 A2 25b black & vio 4.00 .60
114 A2 30b black & ultra 5.00 1.00
115 A2 40b black & org 6.00 1.25
116 A3 50b dk blue & lil rose 8.00 1.50
117 A3 75b red brn & brt grn 9.50 2.00
118 A3 100b orange & dk bl 11.00 2.25
119 A3 ¼r grn & brn org 27.50 5.50
120 A3 ½r brn car & vio 52.50 17.50
121 A3 1r dk vio & car rose 95.00 30.00
Nos. 110-121 (12) 223.75 62.70

Sultanate of Oman

Nos. 110-121 Overprinted

a

b

c

Type 1

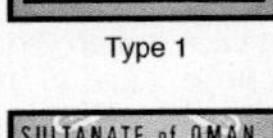

Type 2

5b, 10b 20b:

Type 1 — Lower bars 15¼mm long; letter "A" has low, thick crossbar.

Type 2 — Lower bars 14¾mm; "A" crossbar high, thin.

Perf. 14½x14, 14x14½, 14x13½

1971, Jan. 16 **Photo.** **Unwmk.**

122 A1 (a) 5b plum 11.50 .60
a. Type 2 65.00 25.00
123 A1 (a) 10b brown 32.00 17.50
a. Type 2 70.00 30.00
124 A1 (a) 20b red brown 15.00 .80
a. Type 2 75.00 30.00
125 A2 (b) 25b black & vio 2.10 .50
126 A2 (b) 30b black & ultra 3.00 .80
127 A2 (b) 40b black & org 3.75 1.00
128 A3 (c) 50b dk bl & lil rose 5.25 1.25
129 A3 (c) 75b red brn & brt grn 7.75 2.00
130 A3 (c) 100b org & dk bl 10.25 3.50
131 A3 (c) ¼r grn & brn org 25.00 8.50
132 A3 (c) ½r brn car & vio 57.50 15.00
133 A3 (c) 1r dk vio & car rose 120.00 30.00
Nos. 122-133 (12) 293.10 81.45

For surcharge see No. 133B.

No. 94 Surcharged Nos. 127, 102 Surcharged

Perf. 14½x14, 14x14½, 14½x13½

1971-72

133A A1 5b on 3b *170.00* *20.00*
133B A2 25b on 40b *180.00* *120.00*
133C A3 25b on 1r *200.00* *140.00*
Nos. 133A-133C (3) *550.00* *280.00*

No. 133C surcharge resembles type "c" with "Sultanate of Oman" omitted and bars of criss-cross lines.

No. 133A exists with inverted surchagre and in pair, one with surcharge omitted. No. 133C exists with Arabic "2" or "5" omitted.

Issued: 5b, 11/1/71; #133C, 6/6/72; #133B, 7/1/72.

Sultan Qaboos bin Said and New Buildings
A5

National Day: 40b, Sultan Qaboos and freedom symbols. 50b, Crest of Oman and health clinic. 100b, Crest of Oman, classrooms and school.

1971, July 23 Litho. *Perf. 13½x14*

134	A5	10b multicolored	3.25	.45
135	A5	40b multicolored	12.00	.90
136	A5	50b multicolored	15.00	1.50
137	A5	100b multicolored	30.00	5.00
		Nos. 134-137 (4)	60.25	7.85

Open Book — A6

1972, Jan. 3 *Perf. 14x14½*

138	A6	25b ap grn, dk bl & dk red	27.50	5.00

International Book Year, 1972.

View of Muscat, 1809 — A7

Designs: 5, 10, 20, 25b, View of Matrah, 1809. 30, 40, 50, 75b, View of Shinas, 1809.

Wmk. 314 Sideways

1972, July 23 Litho. *Perf. 14x14½*

Size: 21x17mm

139	A7	5b tan & multi	1.00	.30
140	A7	10b blue & multi	1.75	.30
141	A7	20b gray grn & multi	2.00	.30
142	A7	25b violet & multi	2.75	.30

Perf. 14½x14

Size: 25x21mm

143	A7	30b tan & multi	3.50	.35
144	A7	40b gray blue & multi	3.50	.40
145	A7	50b rose brn & multi	4.50	.50
146	A7	75b olive & multi	10.00	.90

Perf. 14

Size: 41x25mm

147	A7	100b lilac & multi	13.50	1.50
148	A7	¼r green & multi	30.00	3.00
149	A7	½r bister & multi	55.00	8.00
150	A7	1r dull bl grn & multi	85.00	17.00
		Nos. 139-150 (12)	212.50	32.85

Perf. 14x14½, 14½x14

1972-75 Wmk. 314 Upright

139a	A7	5b tan & multi ('75)	.45	.25
140a	A7	10b blue & multi ('75)	1.25	.35
141a	A7	20b gray grn & multi ('75)	2.50	.65
142a	A7	25b violet & multi ('75)	3.50	.90
143a	A7	30b tan & multi	4.75	1.20
144a	A7	40b blue & multi	7.50	1.50
145a	A7	50b rose brn & multi	8.00	1.75
146a	A7	75b olive & multi	13.50	5.00
		Nos. 139a-146a (8)	41.45	11.60

Issue dates: Nov. 17, 1972, Sept. 11, 1975.

Perf. 14x14½, 14½x14, 14

1976-82 Wmk. 373

139b	A7	5b tan & multi ('78)	.80	.60
140b	A7	10b blue & multi ('78)	1.25	.50
141b	A7	20b gray grn & multi ('82)	2.00	.55
142b	A7	25b vio & multi ('78)	2.50	.60
143b	A7	30b tan & multi	3.00	.85
144b	A7	40b blue & multi	4.00	1.25
145b	A7	50b rose brn & multi	5.00	1.40
146b	A7	75b olive & multi	8.75	1.60
147b	A7	100b lilac & multi	9.00	2.25
148a	A7	¼r grn & multi ('78)	25.00	6.50
149a	A7	½r bister & multi	35.00	11.00
150a	A7	1r dull bl grn & multi	85.00	22.50
		Nos. 139b-150a (12)	181.30	49.60

Issued: 4/12/76; 1/27/78; 3/15/82.

Ministerial Complex A8

Litho.; Date Typo.

1973, Sept. 20 Unwmk. *Perf. 13*

151	A8	25b emerald & multi	4.25	1.25
152	A8	100b brown org & multi	15.00	3.00

Opening of ministerial complex.

Nos. 151-152 exist with date omitted and hyphen omitted.

Dhows — A9

Perf. 12½x12

1973, Nov. 18 Litho. Wmk. 314

153	A9	15b shown	2.25	.55
154	A9	50b Seeb Airport	10.00	2.25
155	A9	65b Dhow and tanker	11.00	2.50
156	A9	100b Camel rider	17.50	3.00
		Nos. 153-156 (4)	40.75	8.30

National Day.

Port Qaboos A10

1974, July 30 Litho. *Perf. 13*

157	A10	100b multicolored	18.00	4.00

Opening of Port Qaboos.

Open Book, Map of Arab World — A11

100b, Hands reaching for book, vert.

1974, Sept. 8 Wmk. 314 *Perf. 14½*

158	A11	25b multicolored	4.25	.55
159	A11	100b multicolored	14.00	3.25

International Literacy Day, Sept. 8.

Sultan Qaboos, UPU and Arab Postal Union Emblems A12

1974, Oct. 29 Litho. *Perf. 13½*

160	A12	100b multicolored	5.00	2.00

Centenary of Universal Postal Union.

Arab Scribe — A13

1975, May 8 Photo. *Perf. 13x14*

161	A13	25b multicolored	12.00	3.00

Eradication of illiteracy.

New Harbor at Mina Raysoot A14

Designs: 50b, Stadium and map of Oman. 75b, Water desalination plant. 100b, Oman color television station. 150b, Satellite earth station and map. 250b, Telephone, radar, cable and map.

Perf. 14x13½

1975, Nov. 18 Litho. Wmk. 373

162	A14	30b multicolored	1.50	.65
163	A14	50b multicolored	3.00	.75
164	A14	75b multicolored	4.00	1.25
165	A14	100b multicolored	5.50	2.25
166	A14	150b multicolored	7.50	3.25
167	A14	250b multicolored	14.00	5.00
		Nos. 162-167 (6)	35.50	13.15

National Day 1975.

For surcharges see Nos. 190A, 190C.

Mother with Child, Nurse, Globe, Red Crescent, IWY Emblem A15

Design: 150b, Hand shielding mother and children, Omani flag, IWY emblem, vert.

Perf. 13½x14, 14x13½

1975, Dec. 27 Litho.

168	A15	75b citron & multi	3.75	1.25
169	A15	150b ultra & multi	6.25	2.25

International Women's Year 1975.

For surcharge see No. 190B.

Sultan Presenting Colors and Opening Seeb-Nizwa Road — A16

National Day: 40b, Paratroopers bailing out from plane and mechanized harvester. 75b, Helicopter squadron and Victory Day procession. 150b, Army building road and Salalah television station.

1976, Nov. 15 Litho. *Perf. 14½*

173	A16	25b multicolored	1.50	.50
174	A16	40b multicolored	4.00	.75
175	A16	75b multicolored	8.00	1.75
176	A16	150b multicolored	10.00	2.00
		Nos. 173-176 (4)	23.50	5.00

Great Bath at Mohenjo-Daro A17

1977, Jan. 6 Wmk. 373 *Perf. 13½*

177	A17	125b multicolored	9.00	3.50

UNESCO campaign to save Mohenjo-Daro excavations in Pakistan.

APU Emblem, Members' Flags — A18

1977, Apr. 4 Litho. *Perf. 12*

178	A18	30b emerald & multi	4.50	1.10
179	A18	75b blue & multi	8.75	3.25

Arab Postal Union, 25th anniversary.

Coffeepots — A19

Designs: 75b, Earthenware. 100b, Stone tablet, Khor Rori, 100 B.C. 150b, Jewelry.

1977, Nov. 18 Litho. *Perf. 13½*

180	A19	40b multicolored	2.00	.60
181	A19	75b multicolored	4.00	1.10
182	A19	100b multicolored	6.00	1.75
183	A19	150b multicolored	10.00	2.25
		Nos. 180-183 (4)	22.00	5.70

National Day 1977.

Forts — A20

Wmk. 373

1978, Nov. 18 Litho. *Perf. 14*

184	A20	20b Jalali	1.25	.30
185	A20	25b Nizwa	1.50	.40
186	A20	40b Rostaq	3.50	.80
187	A20	50b Sohar	4.00	.90
188	A20	75b Bahla	4.50	1.50
189	A20	100b Jibrin	7.50	2.00
		Nos. 184-189 (6)	22.25	5.90

National Day 1978.

Pilgrims, Mt. Arafat, Holy Kaaba — A21

1978, Nov. 1 Litho. *Perf. 13½*

190	A21	40b multicolored	7.25	2.75

Pilgrimage to Mecca.

Nos. 166, 169 and 167 Surcharged

Perf. 14x13½

1978, July 30 Litho. Wmk. 373

190A	A14	40b on 150b	*450.00*	*200.00*
190B	A15	50b on 150b	*475.00*	*425.00*
190C	A14	75b on 250b	*2,500.*	*700.00*
		Nos. 190A-190C (3)	*3,425.*	*1,325.*

World Map, Book, Symbols of Learning — A22

1979, Mar. 22 Litho. *Perf. 14x13½*

191	A22	40b multicolored	3.25	.60
192	A22	100b multicolored	6.25	1.50

Cultural achievements of the Arabs.

Girl on Swing, IYC Emblem — A23

1979, Oct. 28 Litho. *Perf. 14*

193	A23	40b multicolored	5.00	2.50

International Year of the Child.

Gas Plant — A24

National Day: 75b, Fisheries.

1979, Nov. 18 Photo. *Perf. 11½*

194	A24	25b multicolored	3.50	.85
195	A24	75b multicolored	9.00	2.75

Sultan on Horseback, Military Symbols A25

Design: 100b, Soldier, parachutes, tank.

1979, Dec. 11

196	A25	40b multicolored	8.50	1.75
197	A25	100b multicolored	14.00	4.00

Armed Forces Day.

Hegira (Pilgrimage Year) — A26

1980, Nov. 9 Photo. *Perf. 11½*
198 A26 50b shown 7.00 1.10
199 A26 150b Hegira emblem 11.00 3.75

Omani Women A27

75b, Bab Alkabir. 100b, Corniche Highway. 250b, Polo match.

1980, Nov. 18 Granite Paper
200 A27 75b multi 2.75 1.10
201 A27 100b multi 4.00 2.00
202 A27 250b multi 7.25 4.75
203 A27 500b shown 14.50 8.75
Nos. 200-203 (4) 28.50 16.60

10th National Day.
For surcharges see Nos. 212-213.

Sultan and Patrol Boat — A28

750b, Sultan, mounted troops.

1980, Dec. 11 Granite Paper
204 A28 150b shown 7.00 3.00
205 A28 750b multi 35.00 16.00

Armed Forces Day.
For surcharges see Nos. 210-211.

Policewoman and Children Crossing Street — A29

100b, Marching band. 150b, Mounted police on beach. ½r, Headquarters.

1981, Feb. 7 Litho. *Perf. 13½x14*
206 A29 50b shown 4.50 1.00
207 A29 100b multi 5.50 2.00
208 A29 150b multi 6.50 3.00
209 A29 ½r multi 16.50 9.50
Nos. 206-209 (4) 33.00 15.50

First National Police Day.

Nos. 204-205, 200, 203 Surcharged in Black on Silver

1981, Apr. 8 Photo. *Perf. 11½*
210 A28 20b on 150b multi 6.50 1.00
211 A28 30b on 750b multi 8.00 1.25
212 A27 50b on 75b multi 9.00 2.25
213 A27 100b on 500b multi 15.00 3.75
Nos. 210-213 (4) 38.50 8.25

Welfare of the Blind — A30

1981, Oct. 14 Photo. *Perf. 11½*
214 A30 10b multicolored 27.50 2.75

World Food Day — A31

1981, Oct. 16 Photo. *Perf. 12*
215 A31 50b multicolored 7.50 2.50

Hegira (Pilgrimage Year) — A32

1981, Oct. 25 Litho. *Perf. 14½*
216 A32 50b multicolored 8.25 3.25

11th Natl. Day — A32a

160b, Al-Razha match (sword vs. stick). 300b, Sultan, map, vert.

1981, Nov. 18 Photo. *Perf. 12*
216A A32a 160b multicolored 6.00 3.25
216B A32a 300b multicolored 10.00 5.00

Voyage of Sinbad — A33

50b, Muscat Port, 1981. 100b, Dhow Shohar. 130b, Map. 200b, Muscat Harbor, 1650.

1981, Nov. 23 Litho. *Perf. 14½x14*
217 A33 50b multicolored 2.50 1.10
218 A33 100b multicolored 5.25 3.00
219 A33 130b multicolored 6.25 4.00
220 A33 200b multicolored 8.75 5.50
a. Souvenir sheet of 4, #217-220 57.50 57.50
Nos. 217-220 (4) 22.75 13.60

Armed Forces Day — A34

1981, Dec. 11 Photo. *Perf. 11½*
221 A34 100b Sultan, planes 7.00 3.25
222 A34 400b Patrol boats 18.00 8.75

Natl. Police Day — A35

1982, Jan. 5 Litho. *Perf. 14½*
223 A35 50b Patrol launch 3.75 1.50
224 A35 100b Band, vert. 6.50 3.00

Nerium Mascatense A36

Red-legged Partridge A37

10b, Dionysia mira. 20b, Teucrium mascatense. 25b, Geranium mascatense. 30b, Cymatium boschi, horiz. 40b, Acteon eloiseae, horiz. 50b, Cypraea teulerei, horiz. 75b, Cypraea pulchra, horiz. ¼r, Hoopoe. ½r, Tahr. 1r, Arabian oryx.

1982, July 7 Photo. *Perf. 12½, 11½*
Granite Paper
225 A36 5b multicolored .35 .25
226 A36 10b multicolored .35 .25
227 A36 20b multicolored .65 .25
228 A36 25b multicolored .65 .30
229 A36 30b multicolored 1.00 .45
230 A36 40b multicolored 1.00 .55
231 A36 50b multicolored 1.25 .65
232 A36 75b multicolored, perf. 11½ 1.50 .95
233 A37 100b multicolored 5.00 1.25
234 A37 ¼r multicolored 11.50 5.75

Size: 25x38mm
235 A37 ½r multicolored 14.00 8.25
236 A37 1r multicolored 22.50 15.50
Nos. 225-236 (12) 59.75 34.40

2nd Municipalities Week (1981) A38

1982, Oct. 28 Litho. *Perf. 13½x14½*
237 A38 40b multicolored 8.50 3.00

ITU Plenipotentiaries Conference, Nairobi, Sept. — A39

1982, Nov. 6 *Perf. 14½x13½*
238 A39 100b multicolored 12.00 4.00

12th Natl. Day — A40

40b, State Consultative Council inaugural session. 100b, Oil refinery.

1982, Nov. 18 *Perf. 12*
239 A40 40b multicolored 5.00 2.00
240 A40 100b multicolored 9.50 3.50

Armed Forces Day — A41

1982, Dec. 11 *Perf. 13½x14*
241 A41 50b Soldiers 5.00 2.00
242 A41 100b Mounted band 9.50 4.00

Arab Palm Tree Day — A42

Perf. 13½x14½
1982, Sept. 19 Litho.
243 A42 40b Picking coconuts 5.50 2.25
244 A42 100b Dates 11.00 3.50

Natl. Police Day — A43

1983, Jan. 5 Litho. *Perf. 14x13½*
245 A43 50b multicolored 8.50 2.50

World Communications Year — A44

1983, May 17 *Perf. 13½x14*
246 A44 50b multicolored 6.75 2.50

Bees A45

Designs: a, Beehive. b, Bee, flower.

1983, Aug. 15 Litho. *Perf. 13½*
247 A45 Pair 22.50 22.50
a.-b. 50b any single 5.00 3.25

Hegira (Pilgrimage Year) — A46

1983, Sept. 14 Photo. *Perf. 13½*
248 A46 40b multicolored 11.50 3.25

Youth Year — A47

Perf. 12½x13½
1983, Nov. 15 Litho.
249 A47 50b multicolored 7.75 2.75

National Day 1983 — A48

50b, Sohar Copper Factory. 100b, Sultan Qaboos University.

1983, Nov. 18 Litho. *Perf. 13½x14*
250 A48 50b multicolored 5.25 2.25
251 A48 100b multicolored 9.25 4.50

Armed Forces Day — A49

1983, Dec. 11 Litho. *Perf. 13½x14*
252 A49 100b multicolored 10.00 4.00

Police Day — A50

1984, Jan. 5 Litho. *Perf. 13½x14*
253 A50 100b multicolored 11.00 3.50

7th Arabian Gulf Soccer Tournament, Muscat, Mar. 9-26 — A51

1984, Mar. 9 Litho. *Perf. 13½*
254 A51 40b Players, cup, vert. 3.75 1.60
255 A51 50b Emblem 6.25 2.50

Pilgrims at Stone-Throwing Ceremony A52

1984, Sept. 5 Litho. *Perf. 13½x14*

256	A52	50b multicolored	7.50	2.75

Pilgrimage to Mecca.

National Day 1984 — A53

130b, Mail sorting, new p.o. 160b, Map, vert.

Perf. 13½x14, 14x13½

1984, Nov. 18 Litho.

257	A53	130b multicolored	7.50	3.25
258	A53	160b multicolored	9.50	4.00

Inauguration of the new Central P.O., development of telecommunications.

16th Arab Scout Conference, Muscat — A54

No. 259, Setting-up camp. No. 260, Map reading. No. 261, Saluting natl. flag. No. 262, Scouts and girl guides.

1984, Dec. 5 Litho. *Perf. 14½*

259	A54	50b multicolored	2.25	.75
260	A54	50b multicolored	2.25	.75
a.		Pair, #259-260	9.50	9.50
261	A54	130b multicolored	7.00	2.25
262	A54	130b multicolored	7.00	2.25
a.		Pair, #261-262	22.50	22.50
		Nos. 259-262 (4)	18.50	6.00

Armed Forces Day — A55

1984, Dec. 11 *Perf. 13½x14*

263	A55	100b multicolored	11.50	4.50

Police Day — A56

1985, Jan. 5 *Perf. 14x13½*

264	A56	100b multicolored	11.50	4.00

Hegira (Pilgrimage Year) — A57

50b, Al-Khaif Mosque, Mina.

1985, Aug. 20 Litho. *Perf. 13½x14*

265	A57	50b multicolored	6.75	2.00

Intl. Youth Year — A58

50b, Emblems. 100b, Emblem, youth activities.

1985, Sept. 22 Litho. *Perf. 13½x14*

266	A58	50b multicolored	3.75	1.00
267	A58	100b multicolored	6.75	2.25

Jabrin Palace Restoration A59

1985, Sept. 22 Litho. *Perf. 13½x14*

268	A59	100b Interior	3.50	2.00
269	A59	250b Restored ceiling	8.75	5.75

Intl. Symposium on Traditional Music — A60

1985, Oct. 6 Litho. *Perf. 13½x14*

270	A60	50b multicolored	6.50	2.00

UN Child Survival Campaign A61

1985, Oct. 25 Litho. *Perf. 13½x14*

271	A61	50b multicolored	5.25	1.50

Flags, Map and Sultan Qaboos A62

50b, Supreme Council, vert.

1985, Nov. 3 Litho. *Perf. 12½*

272	A62	40b shown	3.25	1.25
273	A62	50b multi	4.25	1.50

6th Session of Arab Gulf States Supreme Council, Muscat.

Natl. Day 1985 — A63

Progress and development. 20b, Sultan Qaboos University. 50b, Date picking, plowing field. 100b, Port Qaboos Cement Factory. 200b, Post, transportation and communications. 250b, Sultan Qaboos, vert.

1985, Nov. 18

274	A63	20b multicolored	1.10	1.00
275	A63	50b multicolored	2.75	2.00
276	A63	100b multicolored	5.00	3.00
277	A63	200b multicolored	8.25	5.25
278	A63	250b multicolored	9.75	6.00
		Nos. 274-278 (5)	26.85	17.25

Armed Forces Day — A64

1985, Dec. 11 *Perf. 13½x14*

279	A64	100b multicolored	10.50	2.25

Fish and Crustaceans — A65

20b, Chaetodon collaris. 50b, Chaetodon melapterus. 100b, Chaetodon gardineri. 150b, Scomberomorus commerson. 200b, Panulirus homarus.

Perf. 11½x12, 12x11½

1985, Dec. 15 Photo.

280	A65	20b multicolored	.65	.25
281	A65	50b multicolored	1.25	.45
282	A65	100b multicolored	2.00	1.00
283	A65	150b multicolored	3.00	2.10
284	A65	200b multicolored	4.25	2.75
		Nos. 280-284 (5)	11.15	6.55

Nos. 280-282, vert.

Frankincense Trees in Oman — A66

1985, Dec. 15 Litho. *Perf. 13½x14*

285	A66	100b multicolored	1.75	1.25
286	A66	3r multicolored	47.50	32.50

Police Day — A67

50b, Camel Corps, Muscat.

1986, Jan. 5 Litho. *Perf. 13½x14*

287	A67	50b multi	6.00	1.75

Statue of Liberty, Cent. — A68

Maps and: 50b, Sultanah, voyage from Muscat to US 1840. 100b, Statue, Shabab Oman voyage from Oman to US, 1986, and fortress.

1986, July 4 *Perf. 14½*

288	A68	50b multicolored	4.75	1.75
289	A68	100b multicolored	8.00	3.00
a.		Souvenir sheet of 2, #288-289	32.50	22.50

No. 289a sold for 250b.

Pilgrimage to Mecca — A69

1986, Aug. 9

290	A69	50b Holy Kaaba	4.75	1.50

17th Arab Scout Camp — A70

1986, Aug. 20

291	A70	50b Erecting tent	3.50	1.25
292	A70	100b Surveying	5.50	2.50

Sultan Qaboos Sports Complex Inauguration A71

1986, Oct. 18 Litho. *Perf. 14½*

293	A71	100b multicolored	4.50	2.00

Intl. Peace Year — A72

1986, Oct. 24 *Perf. 13½x13*

294	A72	130b multicolored	4.25	1.75

A73

A74

Natl. Day 1986 A75

1986, Nov. 18 *Perf. 14½*

295	A73	50b mutlicolored	1.75	1.00
296	A74	100b multicolored	4.25	2.10

Perf. 13½x13

297	A75	130b multicolored	5.00	2.50
		Nos. 295-297 (3)	11.00	5.60

Police Day — A76

1987, Jan. 5 *Perf. 13½x14*

298	A76	50b multicolored	4.50	1.75

Second Arab Gulf Week for Social Work, Bahrain — A77

1987, Mar. 21 *Perf. 13½x13*

299	A77	50b multicolored	3.50	1.25

Intl. Environment Day — A78

50b, Flamingos in flight. 130b, Irrigation canal, vert.

Perf. 13½xl3, 13x13½

1987, June 5 Litho.

300	A78	50b multi	3.50	1.00
301	A78	130b multi	6.00	1.50

Pilgrimage to Mecca — A79

Stages of Pilgrimage (not in consecutive order): a, Pilgrims walking the tawaf, circling the Holy Kaaba 7 times. b, Tent City, Mina. c, Symbolic stoning of Satan. d, Pilgrims in Muzdalifah at dusk, picking up stones. e, Veneration of the prophet (pilgrims praying), Medina. f, Pilgrims wearing ihram, Pilgrim's Village, Jeddah.

1987, July 29 Litho. *Perf. 13½*

302		Strip of 6	25.00	25.00
a.-f.	A79	50b any single	1.75	1.25

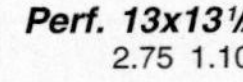

Third Municipalities Month — A80

1987, Oct. 1 ***Perf. 13x13½***
303 A80 50b multicolored 2.75 1.10

Natl. Day — A81

Designs: 50b, Marine Biology and Fisheries Center. 130b, Royal Hospital.

1987, Nov. 18 Litho. ***Perf. 13½x13***
304 A81 50b multicolored 1.25 .75
305 A81 130b multicolored 3.50 2.00

Royal Omani Amateur Radio Soc., 15th Anniv. — A82

1987, Dec. 23 Litho. ***Perf. 13½x13***
306 A82 130b multicolored 4.25 1.75

Traditional Handicrafts A83

1988, June 1 Photo. ***Perf. 12x11½***
Granite Paper
307 A83 50b Weaver 1.40 .75
308 A83 100b Potter 2.10 1.00
309 A83 150b Halwa maker 2.75 1.75
310 A83 200b Silversmith 3.25 2.25
a. Souvenir sheet of 4, #307-310 23.00 17.50
Nos. 307-310 (4) 9.50 5.75

No. 310a sold for 600b.

1988 Summer Olympics, Seoul — A84

1988, Sept. 17 Litho. ***Perf. 14½***
311 A84 100b Equestrian 1.50 .80
312 A84 100b Field hockey 1.50 .80
313 A84 100b Soccer 1.50 .80
314 A84 100b Running 1.50 .80
315 A84 100b Swimming 1.50 .80
316 A84 100b Shooting 1.50 .80
a. Block of 6, #311-316 20.00 20.00
b. Souvenir sheet of 6, #311-316 32.50 25.00

WHO, 40th Anniv. — A85

1988, Nov. 1 Litho. ***Perf. 13½***
317 A85 100b multicolored 2.00 1.50

Natl. Day, Agriculture Year — A86

1988, Nov. 18 ***Perf. 14½x13½***
318 A86 100b Tending crops 1.90 1.40
319 A86 100b Animal husbandry 1.90 1.40
a. Pair, #318-319 8.50 8.50

No. 319a has a continuous design.

Women Wearing Regional Folk Costume — A87

Designs: 200b-1r, Men wearing regional folk costumes.

1989 Photo. ***Perf. 11½x12***
Granite Paper
320 A87 30b Dhahira 1.40 .25
321 A87 40b Eastern 1.75 .40
322 A87 50b Batinah 2.00 .50
323 A87 100b Interior 4.25 .90
324 A87 130b Southern 5.25 1.75
325 A87 150b Muscat 6.25 2.00
a. Souvenir sheet of 6, #320-325 37.50 37.50
326 A87 200b Dhahira 3.25 1.40
327 A87 ¼r Eastern 3.75 1.60
328 A87 ½r Southern 7.00 2.00
329 A87 1r Muscat 14.00 3.00
a. Souvenir sheet of 4, #326-329 37.50 37.50
Nos. 320-329 (10) 48.90 13.80

No. 325a sold for 700b, No. 329a for 2r.
Issued: 30b-150b, 8/26; 200b-1r, 11/11.

National Day, Agriculture Year — A88

1989, Nov. 18 ***Perf. 12½x13***
330 A88 100b Fishing 2.00 1.00
331 A88 100b Farming 2.00 1.00
a. Pair, #330-331 5.00 4.50

Printed se-tenant in a continuous design.

10th Session of Supreme Council of the Cooperation Council for Arab Gulf States — A89

No. 332, Flags, Omani crest. No. 333, Sultan Qaboos, council emblem.

1989, Dec. 18 Litho. ***Perf. 13x12***
332 A89 50b multi 1.75 .75
333 A89 50b multi 1.75 .75
a. Pair, #332-333 4.50 4.00

No. 333a has a continuous design.

Gulf Investment Corp., 5th Anniv. (in 1989) — A90

1990, Jan. 1 Litho. ***Perf. 13x12***
334 A90 50b multicolored 2.50 1.00
335 A90 130b multicolored 3.25 1.75

Gulf Air, 40th Anniv. — A91

1990, Mar. 24 ***Perf. 13x13½***
336 A91 80b multicolored 6.00 2.00

Symposium on the Oman Ophiolite — A92

1990, Apr. 22 Photo. ***Perf. 11½***
Granite Paper
337 A92 80b shown 1.75 1.00
338 A92 150b multicolored 3.50 2.00

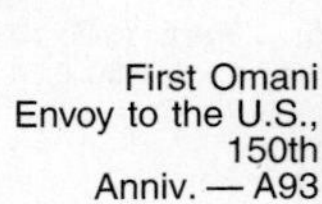

First Omani Envoy to the U.S., 150th Anniv. — A93

1990, Apr. 30 Litho. ***Perf. 13***
339 A93 200b multicolored 3.50 2.00

Sultan Qaboos Rose — A94

1990, May 5 Photo. ***Perf. 11½***
Granite Paper
340 A94 200b multicolored 3.25 2.00

20th National Day — A95

100b, Natl. Day emblem. 200b, Sultan Qaboos.

Litho. & Embossed
1990, Nov. 18 ***Perf. 12x11½***
Granite Paper
341 A95 100b gold, red & green 2.10 1.00
342 A95 200b gold, green & red 4.25 2.10
a. Souvenir sheet of 2, #341-342 12.50 12.50

No. 342a sold for 500b.

Blood Donors — A96

1991, Apr. 22 Litho. ***Perf. 13½x13***
343 A96 50b multicolored .80 .60
344 A96 200b multicolored 4.25 2.00
a. Pair, #343-344 40.00 40.00

National Day A97

1991, Nov. 18 Photo. ***Perf. 13½***
345 A97 100b shown 3.50 1.10
346 A97 200b Sultan Qaboos 5.75 2.25
a. Souvenir sheet of 2, #345-346 10.00 8.00

No. 346a sold for 400b.

Armed Forces Day — A98

1991, Dec. 11 Litho. ***Perf. 14½***
347 A98 100b multicolored 3.50 1.25

A99

1992, Jan. 29 Litho. ***Perf. 13½x14***
348 A99 100b multicolored 3.25 1.25
a. Sheet of 1, perf. 13x13½ 16.00 9.00

Inauguration of Omani-French Museum, Muscat. No. 348a sold for 300b.

A100

1992, Mar. 23 Litho. ***Perf. 14½***
349 A100 200b multicolored 4.25 1.75

World Meteorological Day.

A101

1992, June 5 Litho. ***Perf. 13x13½***
350 A101 100b multicolored 2.50 1.25

World Environment Day.

A102

1992, Sept. 26 Litho. ***Perf. 13½x14***
351 A102 70b multicolored 2.25 .75

Welfare of Handicapped Children.

Sultan Qaboos Encyclopedia of Arab Names — A103

1992, Oct. 10 ***Perf. 14½***
352 A103 100b gold & multi 2.75 1.25

National Day A104

Sultan Qaboos and emblems of: 100b, Year of Industry. 200b, Majlis As'shura.

1992, Nov. 18 Litho. ***Perf. 14x13½***
353 A104 100b multicolored 3.00 1.75
354 A104 200b multicolored 4.25 2.50

Royal Oman Police Day — A105

1993, Jan. 5 Litho. ***Perf. 13½x14***
355 A105 80b multicolored 3.00 1.10

1993 Census A106

1993, Sept. 4 Litho. ***Perf. 14x13½***
356 A106 100b multicolored 3.00 1.25

Royal Navy Day — A107

1993, Nov. 3 Litho. ***Perf. 13***
357 A107 100b multicolored 3.25 1.50

23rd National Day — A108

1993, Nov. 18 Photo. ***Perf. 12***
Granite Paper
358 A108 100b Year of Youth emblem 2.25 1.50
359 A108 200b Sultan Qaboos 3.50 2.00

Scouting A109

#360, Emblem of Scouts & Guides, Scout Headquarters. #361, Scout camp, Sultan Qaboos.

1993, Nov. 20 Litho. ***Perf. 13x13½***
360 A109 100b multicolored 1.75 1.25
361 A109 100b multicolored 1.75 1.25
a. Pair, #360-361 5.00 5.00

Scouting movement in Oman, 61st anniv. (#360). Installation of Sultan Qaboos as chief scout, 10th anniv. (#361).

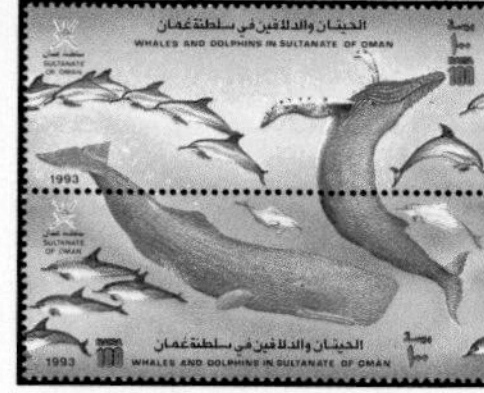

Whales and Dolphins A110

#362, Dolphins, humpback whale. #363, Dolphins, sperm whale.

1993, Dec. 8 ***Perf. 14½***
362 100b multicolored 3.75 1.75
363 100b multicolored 3.75 1.75
a. A110 Pair, #362-363 12.00 12.00
b. Souvenir sheet of 2, #362-363 45.00 45.00

No. 363a has a continuous design. No. 363b sold for 400b and has a white border surrounding the stamps.

World Day for Water — A111

1994, Mar. 22 Litho. ***Perf. 13½***
364 A111 50b multicolored 2.25 .75

Muscat Municipality, 70th Anniv. — A112

1994, Apr. 16
365 A112 50b multicolored 2.25 1.00

Intl. Olympic Committee, Cent. A113

1994, Aug. 29 Litho. ***Perf. 13½***
366 A113 100b multicolored 16.00 8.25

Al Busaid Dynasty, 250th Anniv. — A114

Natl. arms or sultan, dates: a, 1744-75. b, 1775-79. c, 1779-92. d, 1792-1804. e, 1804-7. f, Sa'id ibn Sultan, 1807-56. g, 1856-65. h, 1866-68. i, 1868-71. j, Sultan, 1871-88. k, Sultan, 1888-1913. l, Sultan Taymur ibn Faysal, 1913-32. m, Sultan Qaboos, laurel tree. n, Sultan Sa'id ibn Taymur, 1932-70. o, Sultan Qaboos, 1970-.

200b, Sultan Qaboos atop family "tree," Arabic listing of former Sultans, years in power.

Litho. & Embossed
1994, Dec. 28 ***Perf. 11½***
367 A114 50b Block of 15, #a.-o. *60.00 60.00*

Litho. & Typo.
Imperf
Size: 140x110mm
367P A114 200b gold & multi 9.50 7.50

Nos. 367f, 367j-367o contain portraits of sultans.

Open Parliament A115

1995, Jan. 7 Litho. ***Perf. 14***
Granite Paper
368 A115 50b silver & multi 2.40 1.00

24th National Day, Year of the Heritage A116

1994, Nov. 18 Litho. ***Perf. 13½***
369 A116 50b Emblem 1.00 .75
370 A116 50b Sultan Qaboos 1.00 .75
a. Pair, #369-370 8.25 8.25

ICAO, 50th Anniv. — A117

1994, Dec. 7 ***Perf. 13½x14***
371 A117 100b multicolored 6.50 3.00

Arab League, 50th Anniv. — A118

1995, Mar. 22 Litho. ***Perf. 13***
372 A118 100b multicolored 2.50 1.00

UN, 50th Anniv. — A119

1995, Sept. 2 ***Perf. 13½***
373 A119 100b multicolored 4.50 1.50

16th Session of Supreme Council of the Co-operative Council for Arab Gulf States — A120

Designs: 100b, Emblem. 200b, Flags of Arab Gulf States, map, Sultan Qaboos.

1995, Dec. 4 ***Perf. 12***
Granite Paper
374 A120 100b multicolored 3.00 1.25
375 A120 200b multicolored 4.00 1.75
a. Pair, #374-375 *34.00 22.00*

25th National Day — A121

Portraits of Sultan Qaboos: 50b, In traditional attire. 100b, In military uniform.

Litho. & Embossed
1995, Nov. 18 ***Perf. 11½***
Granite Paper
376 A121 50b multicolored 1.75 .80
377 A121 100b multicolored 3.25 1.00
a. Souvenir sheet of 2, #376-377 7.50 5.50

No. 377a sold for 300b.

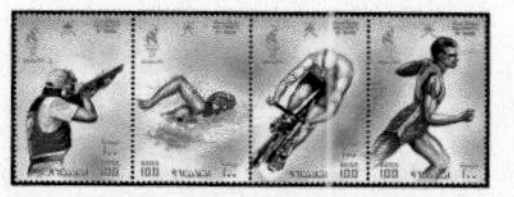

1996 Summer Olympic Games, Atlanta — A122

a, Shooting. b, Swimming. c, Cycling. d, Running.

1996, July 19 Litho. ***Perf. 14½***
378 A122 100b Strip of 4, #a.-d. 30.00 22.50

13th Arabian Gulf Cup Soccer Tournament A123

1996, Oct. 15 ***Perf. 13½***
379 A123 100b multicolored *10.00 2.50*

UN Decade Against Drug Abuse A124

1996, June 26 ***Perf. 13½x14***
380 A124 100b multicolored *45.00 25.00*

UNICEF, 50th Anniv. — A125

1996, Dec. 11 Litho. ***Perf. 14½***
381 A125 100b multicolored 2.75 1.10

26th National Day — A126

Designs: No. 382, Sultan Qaboos waving, boats in harbor. No. 383, Boats in harbor, Sultan Qaboos.

1996, Nov. 26 ***Perf. 13½***
382 50b multicolored 1.50 .90
383 50b multicolored 1.50 .90
a. A126 Pair, #382-383 4.75 4.75

No. 383a is a continuous design.

Traditional Boats A127

1996, Apr. 15 Photo. ***Perf. 13½x14***
384 A127 50b Ash'Shashah .30 .25
385 A127 100b Al-Battil .80 .60
386 A127 200b Al-Boum 1.50 1.10
387 A127 250b Al-Badan 1.90 1.40
388 A127 350b As'Sanbuq 2.75 2.00
389 A127 450b Al-Galbout 3.25 2.50
390 A127 650b Al-Baghlah 4.50 3.50
391 A127 1r Al-Ghanjah 7.75 5.50
Nos. 384-391 (8) 22.75 16.85

Souvenir Sheet
Imperf

392 A127 600b Designs of #384-391 15.00 11.00

No. 392 has simulated perfs. and individual stamps are defaced and not valid for postage.

Tourism — A128

a, Oasis fort among palm trees. b, Small waterfalls, trees. c, Highway, coastline, castle on hilltop. d, Lake, mountains. e, Ruins of ancient fort on cliff. f, Waterfall, mountain stream.

1997, Oct. 26 Litho. ***Perf. 13½x14***
393 A128 100b Block of 6, #a.-f. 13.50 13.50

27th National Day — A129

Waterfall, Sultan Qaboos wearing: No. 394, Multicolored outfit. No. 395, Wearing white outfit.

1997, Nov. 18 Litho. ***Perf. 13½***
394 100b multicolored 2.00 1.25
395 100b multicolored 2.00 1.25
a. A129 Pair, #394-395 7.00 7.00

Girl Guides in Oman, 25th Anniv. — A130

1997, Nov. 30 ***Perf. 14½***
396 A130 100b multicolored 2.75 1.50

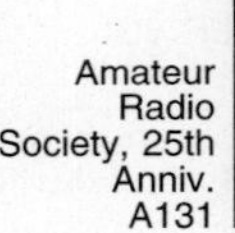
Amateur Radio Society, 25th Anniv. A131

1997, Dec. 23 ***Perf. 13½***
397 A131 100b multicolored 3.50 2.00

Al-Khanjar Assaidi — A132

1997, Mar. 22 ***Perf. 11½***
Granite Paper
398 A132 50b red & multi .85 .70
399 A132 50b green & multi .85 .70
400 A132 100b purple & multi 2.25 1.50
401 A132 200b brown & multi 3.25 2.25
Nos. 398-401 (4) 7.20 5.15

See No. 418.

Traffic Week — A133

1998, Apr. 25 ***Perf. 13½***
402 A133 100b multicolored 8.00 4.00

Tourism A134

Designs: a, Fort. b, Rocky mountainside, lake. c, City. d, Men raising swords, drummers. e, Stream running through countryside. f, Girls standing beside stream, trees.

1998, July 23 ***Perf. 13½x13***
403 A134 100b Block of 6, #a.-f. 14.00 14.00

4th Arab Gulf Countries Philatelic Exhibition, Muscat — A135

1998, Sept. 5 Litho. ***Perf. 13½***
404 A135 50b multicolored 2.00 .80

Sultan Qaboos, Recipient of Intl. Peace Award — A136

1998, Dec. 7
405 A136 500b multicolored 19.00 14.00

28th National Day A137

1998, Nov. 18 ***Perf. 12½***
406 A137 100b Sultan Qaboos 2.25 1.00
407 A137 100b Emblem, map 2.25 1.00
a. Pair, #406-407 6.50 6.50
b. Souvenir sheet, #406-407 *45.00 45.00*

Opening of Raysut Port-Salalah Container Terminal — A138

1998, Dec. 1 ***Perf. 13x13½***
408 A138 50b multicolored 5.50 2.25

World Stamp Day — A139

1998, Oct. 9 ***Perf. 13½***
409 A139 100b multicolored 2.00 1.50

Royal Air Force of Oman, 40th Anniv. A140

Perf. 13½x13¾
1999, June 20 Litho.
410 A140 100b multicolored 4.00 1.75

Butterflies — A141

Designs: a, Danaus chrysippus. b, Papilio demoleus. c, Precis orithya. d, Precis hierta.

1999, July 23 Litho. ***Perf. 13¼***
411 A141 100b Block of 4, #a.-d. *13.00 13.00*
e. Souvenir sheet of 4, #a.-d. *25.00 25.00*

See No. 421.

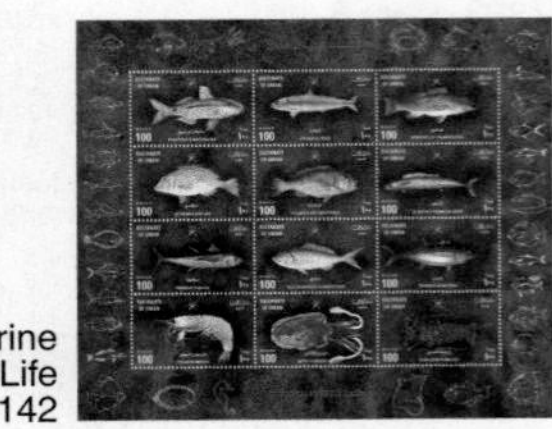
Marine Life A142

Designs: a, Parupeneus macronema. b, Etrumeus teres. c, Epinephelus chlorostigma. d, Lethrinus lentjan. e, Lutjanus erythropterus. f, Acanthocybium solandri. g, Thunnus tongol. h, Pristipomoides filamentosus. i, Thunnus albacares. j, Penaeus indicus. k, Sepia pharaonis. l, Panulirus homarus.

1999, Aug. 21 Litho. ***Perf. 13½x13***
412 A142 100b Sheet of 12, #a.-l. 21.00 21.00

Wildlife A143

Designs: a, Sand cat. b, Genet. c, Leopard. d, Sand fox. e, Caracal lynx. f, Hyena.

1999, Sept. 18 Litho. ***Perf. 13½x13***
413 100b Block of 6, #a.-f. 10.00 10.00
g. A143 Souvenir sheet, #a.-f. *35.00 35.00*

UPU, 125th Anniv. — A144

1999, Oct. 9 ***Perf. 11***
414 A144 200b multi 2.75 2.25

29th National Day A145

1999, Nov. 18 Litho. ***Perf. 13½***
415 100b Sultan in black 2.25 1.25
416 100b Sultan in white 2.25 1.25
a. A145 Pair, #415-416 6.00 6.00

Souvenir Sheet

Millennium — A146

Litho. & Embossed with Foil Application

2000, Jan. 1 ***Perf. 13¼***
417 A146 500b multi 14.00 14.00

Al-Khanjar Assaidi Type of 1997

2000, Feb. 12 Litho. ***Perf. 11½***
Granite Paper
418 A132 80b orange & multi 1.75 1.25

GCC Water Week — A147

2000, Mar. 22 Litho. ***Perf. 13¼***
419 A147 100b multi 2.00 1.10

Gulf Air, 50th Anniv. A148

2000, Mar. 24 ***Perf. 13½***
420 A148 100b multi 2.00 1.10

Butterfly Type of 1999

No. 421: a, Colotis danae. b, Anaphaeis aurota. c, Tarucus rosaceus. d, Lampides boeticus.

2000, Apr. 24 Litho. ***Perf. 13½***
421 Block of 4 12.00 12.00
a.-d. A141 100b Any single 2.50 1.25
e. Souvenir sheet, #421 *27.50 27.50*

Fish — A148a

No. 421F: g, Hippocampus kuda. h, Ostracion cubicus. i, Monocentris japonicus. j, Pterois antennata. k, Phinecanthus assasi. l, Taenura lymma.

Perf. 13½x13¾
2000, June 12 Litho.
421F A148a 100b Block of 6, #g-l 22.50 17.50
m. Souvenir sheet, #421F 24.00 17.50

2000 Summer Olympics, Sydney — A149

Designs: a, Shooting. b, Emblem of Sydney Games. c, Running. d, Swimming.

2000, Sept. 15 ***Perf. 13½x13¾***
422 A149 100b Block of 4, #a-d 10.00 10.00
e. Souvenir sheet, #422 *27.50 27.50*

Coup by Sultan Qaboos, 30th Anniv. A150

No. 423: a, Emblem, Sultan in blue hat. b, Emblem, Sultan seated. c, Emblem, Sultan in red beret. d, Emblem, Sultan in white hat. e, Emblem. f, Emblem, Sultan in black hat.

Litho. & Embossed

2000, Nov. 18 ***Perf. 13½***
423 Block of 6 12.00 12.00
a.-f. A150 100b Any single 1.75 1.25
g. Souvenir sheet, #423 15.00 15.00

Wildlife A151

No. 424: a, Arabian tahr. b, Nubian ibex. c, Arabian oryx. d, Arabian gazelle.

2000, July 23 Litho. ***Perf. 13½x13***
424 A151 100b Block of 4, #a-d 12.00 9.00
e. Souvenir sheet, #424 22.50 13.00

Souvenir Sheet

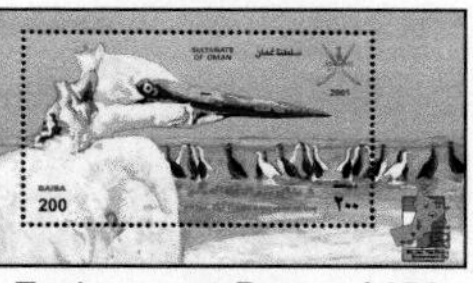

Environment Day — A152

2001, Jan. 8 Litho. ***Perf. 13¾x14¼***
425 A152 200b multi 14.00 10.00

Souvenir Sheet

Palestinian Uprising in Jerusalem — A153

Litho. & Embossed

2001, July 31 ***Perf. 13½x13***
426 A153 100b multi 19.00 19.00

Al-Khanjar A'Suri — A154

Perf. 14½x13¾

2001, Mar. 19 Litho.
427 A154 50b red & multi .75 .50
428 A154 80b yel org & multi 1.25 1.00

Size: 26x34mm

Perf. 13¼x13
429 A154 100b blue & multi 1.50 1.25
430 A154 200b multi 3.00 2.50
a. Miniature sheet, #427-430 9.00 7.50

See Nos. 474-476.

Souvenir Sheets

Jewelry A155

Litho., Typo. & Embossed

2001, Dec. 29 ***Perf. 12¾x12½***
431 A155 100b Hair plait decoration 4.75 3.00

Stamp Size: 62x27mm

Perf. 13¼x13¾
432 A155 100b Pendant 4.75 3.00

Stamp Size: 44x44mm

Perf. 12¾
433 A155 100b Necklace 4.75 3.00

Stamp Size: 38mm Diameter

Perf.
434 A155 100b Mazrad 4.75 3.00
Nos. 431-434 (4) 19.00 12.00

Supreme Council of Arab Gulf Cooperation Council States, 22nd Session — A156

Designs: 50b, Map. 100b, Sultan Qaboos.

Litho. & Typo.

2001, Dec. 30 ***Perf. 14x14¼***
435-436 A156 Set of 2 3.25 2.00

Year of Dialogue Among Civilizations — A157

2001, Oct. 9 Litho. ***Perf. 13¾x13¼***
437 A157 200b multi 13.50 9.00

Shells A157a

No. 437A: b, Nassarius coronatus. c, Epitoneum pallasii d, Cerithium caeruleum. e, Cerithidea cingulata.

2001, Dec. 26 Litho. ***Perf. 13¼***
437A A157a 100b Block of 4, #b-e 7.00 5.75

31st National Day A158

No. 438: a, Map of Oman, tree. b, Sultan Qaboos.

2001, Nov. 18 ***Perf. 13¼***
438 A158 100b Horiz. pair, #a-b 4.75 4.75

Turtles A159

No. 439: a, Olive Ridley. b, Green. c, Hawksbill. d, Loggerhead.

2002, Aug. 12 Litho. ***Perf. 13¼x13***
439 A159 100b Block of 4, #a-d 8.25 7.00
e. Souvenir sheet, #439a-439d 12.00 7.00

Sultan Qaboos Grand Mosque A160

No. 440: a, Interior view of dome and chandelier. b, Exterior view of mosque and minaret. c, Exterior view of archway. d, Interior view of corner arches.
100b, Aerial view of mosque.

Litho. With Foil Application

2002, May 25 ***Perf. 13¼***
440 A160 50b Block of 4, #a-d 6.00 4.75

Size: 120x90mm

Imperf
441 A160 100b multi 7.50 4.75

Souvenir Sheet

32nd National Day A160a

Design: 100b, Sultan Qaboos, flowers in corners.

Litho. With Foil Application

2002, Nov. 18 ***Perf. 13x13¼***
441A A160a 100b multi 5.25 3.00
441B A160a 200b shown 3.50 2.75

Birds A161

No. 442: a, Streptopelia decaocto. b, Tchagra senegala. c, Ploceus galbula. d, Hieraaetus fasciatus. e, Pycnonotus xanthopygos. f, Bubo bubo. g, Eremalauda dunni. h, Burhinus capensis. i, Prinia gracilis. j, Francolinus pondicerianus. k, Onychognathus tristramii. l, Hoplopterus indicus. m, Corvus splendens. n, Chlamydotis undulata. o, Halcyon chloris. p, Pterocles coronatus.

2002, Dec. 15 ***Perf. 13x13¼***
442 A161 50b Sheet of 16, #a-p 22.50 17.50

Early Intervention for Children With Special Needs — A161a

2002, Oct. 30 Litho. ***Perf. 13x13¼***
442Q A161a 100b multi 3.50 1.75

Booklet Stamp
Self-Adhesive

Perf. 12¾
442R A161a 100b multi 4.75 2.50
s. Booklet pane of 10 47.50 —

Muscat Festival 2003 — A162

2003, Jan. 8 ***Perf. 14½***
443 A162 100b multi 2.00 1.00

Oman - People's Republic of China Diplomatic Relations, 25th Anniv. — A163

2003, May 25 Litho. ***Perf. 12***
444 A163 70b multi 2.50 1.25

Souvenir Sheets

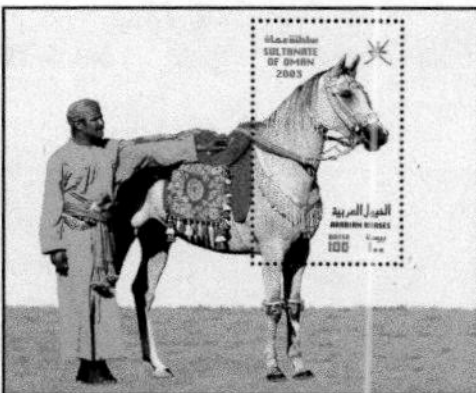

A164

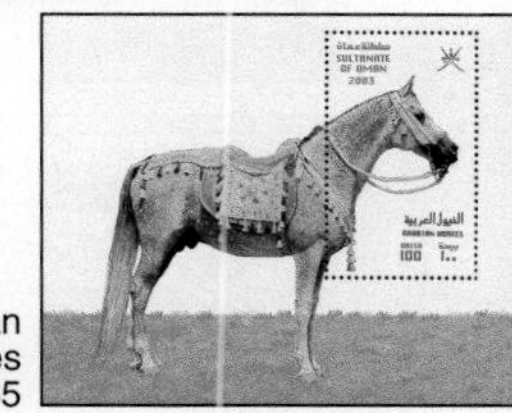

Arabian Horses A165

2003, Apr. 8 ***Perf. 13¼x12¾***
445 A164 100b shown 4.00 3.00
446 A165 100b shown 4.00 3.00
447 A165 100b White horse facing left 4.00 3.00
448 A165 100b Brown horse 4.00 3.00
Nos. 445-448 (4) 16.00 12.00

Census A166

No. 449: a, Emblem, buildings. b, Emblem, blue circle.

2003, Sept. 16 Litho. ***Perf. 13***
449 A166 50b Horiz. pair, #a-b 2.25 1.25

Intl. Day of Peace — A167

2003, Sept. 21 *Perf. 13¼x12¾*
450 A167 200b multi 2.75 2.50

Organization of the Islamic Conference A168

Litho. & Embossed
2003, Sept. 25 *Perf. 13*
451 A168 100b multi 2.00 1.50

Self-Employment and National Autonomous Development Program — A169

2003, Oct. 6 Litho. *Perf. 13¼*
Souvenir Sheet
452 A169 100b multi 2.00 2.00

Booklet Stamp
Self-Adhesive
Serpentine Die Cut 12½
453 A169 100b multi 1.90 1.10
a. Booklet pane of 4 7.75
Complete booklet, 3 #453a 23.50

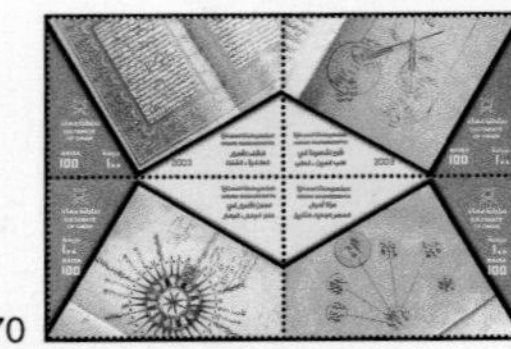

A170

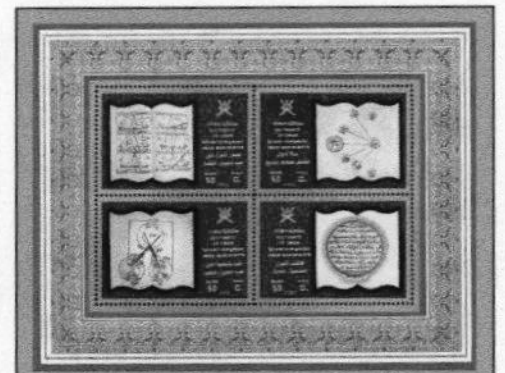

Manuscripts — A171

No. 454: a, Denomination at lower left. b, Denomination at lower right. c, Denomination at left center. d, Denomination at right center.
No. 455: a, Illustrations of ships. b, Illustration of connected circles. c, Illustration of concentric circles. d, Text in large red circle.

2003, Oct. 14 Litho. *Perf. 13½x13¼*
454 A170 100b Block of 4, #a-d 5.00 5.00

Miniature Sheet
Litho. With Foil Application
Perf. 13¼
455 A171 50b Sheet of 4, #a-d 4.75 4.00

33rd National Day A172

No. 456 — Sultan Qaboos and background color of: a, Light green. b, Light blue. c, Buff. d, Light red violet.

Litho. & Embossed
2003, Nov. 18 *Perf. 13x13¼*
456 A172 50b Block or strip of 4, #a-d 3.50 3.50

Flowers — A173

No. 457: a, Anogeissus dhofarica. b, Tecomella undulata. c, Euryops pinifolius. d, Aloe dhufarensis. e, Cleome glaucescens. f, Cassia italica. g, Cibirhiza dhofarensis. h, Ipomoea nil. i, Viola cinerea. j, Dyschoriste dalyi. k, Calotropis procera. l, Lavandula dhofarensis. m, Teucrium mascatense. n, Capparis mucronifolia. o, Geranium mascatense. p, Convolvulus arvensis.

2004, Jan. 24 Litho. *Perf. 14½*
457 Sheet of 16 11.50 11.50
a.-p. A173 50b Any single .60 .50

FIFA (Fédération Internationale de Football Association), Cent. — A174

Litho. & Embossed
2004, May 21 *Perf. 13¾*
458 A174 250b multi 4.25 3.75

Worldwide Fund for Nature (WWF) — A175

No. 459 — Arabian leopard: a, Front feet on mound. b, Pair of leopards. c, Rear feet on mound. d, Feet in depression.

2004, June 5 Litho. *Perf. 13¾x13½*
459 A175 Horiz. strip of 4 5.00 5.00
a.-d. 50b Any single .85 .75

Corals — A176

No. 460: a, Montipora. b, Porites. c, Acropora. d, Cycloseris.

2004, Aug. 1 *Perf. 13¾*
460 Horiz. strip of 4 7.00 7.00
a.-d. A176 100b Any single .90 .75

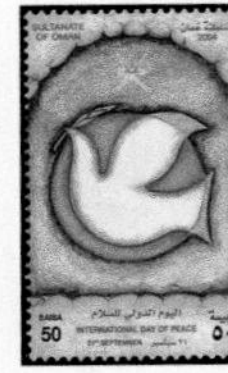

Intl. Day of Peace — A177

Designs: 50b, Dove and green circle. 100b, Doves and Earth.

2004, Sept. 21 *Perf. 13½x13¾*
461-462 A177 Set of 2 1.50 1.50

Souvenir Sheet

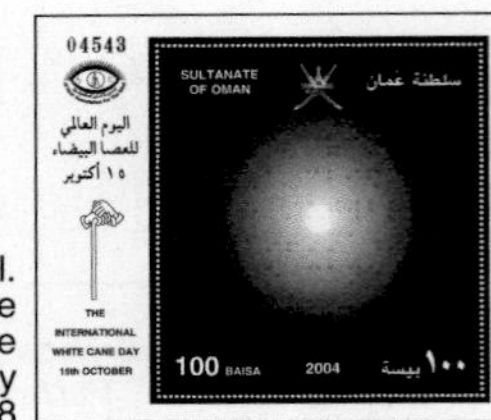

Intl. White Cane Day A178

2004 Litho. *Perf. 14x13¼*
463 A178 100b black 5.50 5.50

Braille text was applied by a thermographic process producing a shiny, raised effect.

34th National Day A179

No. 464 — Sultan Qaboos with kaffiyah in: a, Red. b, Blue green. c, Gray and white. d, Black and white.

Litho. & Embossed With Foil Application
2004, Nov. 18 *Perf. 13¾x13½*
464 A179 100b Block of 4, #a-d 3.50 3.50

Water Supply Projects A180

No. 465: a, Al Massarat. b, Ash'Sharqiyah.

2004, Dec. 1 Litho. *Perf. 14*
465 A180 50b Horiz. pair, #a-b 12.00 12.00

10th Gulf Cooperation Council Stamp Exhibition A181

2004, Dec. 4 *Perf. 13½*
466 A181 50b multi 1.75 1.75

Self-Adhesive
Booklet Stamp
Serpentine Die Cut 12½
467 A181 50b multi 1.40 1.00
a. Booklet pane of 4 5.50
Complete booklet, 3 #467a 17.00

Civil Defense A182

Designs: 50b, Civil defense workers, Omani people. 100b, Rescue workers in action.

2005, May 14 Litho. *Perf. 14*
468-469 A182 Set of 2 2.10 2.10

World Blood Donor Day — A183

2005, June 14 Litho. *Perf. 13¾x14*
470 A183 100b multi 1.50 1.50

Agricultural Census — A184

No. 471 — Census taker and: a, Herder and livestock. b, Farmer and crops.

2005, July 18 *Perf. 14x13¼*
471 A184 100b Horiz. pair, #a-b 3.25 3.25

World Summit on the Information Society, Tunis — A185

2005, Nov. 16 *Perf. 14*
472 A185 100b multi 1.75 1.75

Miniature Sheet

35th National Day A186

No. 473: a, Airplane, dish antennas. b, Helicopter, mounted soldiers. c, Sultan Qaboos. d, People in costumes. e, Military aircraft, ship, vehicle. f, Tower, highway. g, Tower, people at computers. h, Emblem of 35th National Day. i, Man at oasis. j, Petroleum facility.

Litho., Litho. & Embossed With Foil Application (#473c)
2005, Nov. 18 *Perf. 13¼x13½*
473 A186 100b Sheet of 10, #a-j 14.00 14.00

Al-Khanjar A'Suri Type of 2001
2005, Dec. 7 Litho. *Perf. 13¼x13*
Size: 26x34mm
474 A154 250b bl grn & multi 2.50 1.40
475 A154 300b red vio & multi 3.25 1.60
476 A154 400b yel brn & multi 4.25 2.10
Nos. 474-476 (3) 10.00 5.10

A187

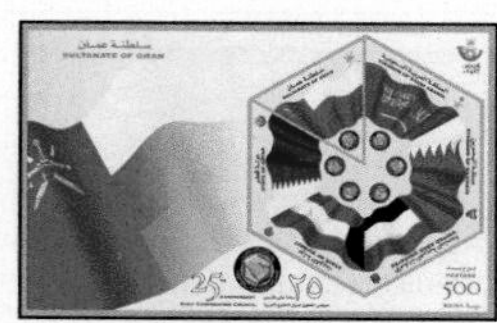

Gulf Cooperation Council, 25th Anniv. — A188

Litho. With Foil Application

2006, May 25 ***Perf. 14***

477 A187 100b multi 6.00 6.00

Imperf

Size: 165x100mm

478 A188 500b multi 24.00 24.00

See Bahrain Nos. 628-629, Kuwait Nos. 1646-1647, Qatar Nos. 1007-1008, Saudi Arabia No. 1378, and United Arab Emirates Nos. 831-832.

Souvenir Sheet

Muscat, 2006 Capital of Arab Culture A189

2006, Aug. 26 **Litho.** ***Perf. 14***

479 A189 100b multi 4.50 4.50

Tourism A190

No. 480: a, Man picking flowers, houses on mountain. b, Six men, building. c, Scuba diver, turtle on beach. d, Women with clothing on line, camels.

2006, Sept. 27 **Litho.** ***Perf. 14***

480 A190 100b Block of 4, #a-d 6.00 6.00

Oman Post Emblem A191

Text in: 100b, Blue. 250b, White.

Litho. With Foil Application

2006, Nov. 6 ***Perf. 13¾x13½***

481-482 A191 Set of 2 4.75 4.75

36th National Day — A192

2006, Nov. 18 ***Perf. 13x13½***

483 A192 100b multi 1.50 1.50

Sultan Qaboos Prize for Cultural Innovation A193

2006, Dec. 24 **Litho.** ***Perf. 13¼x13***

484 A193 250b multi 4.00 4.00

Exportation of Crude Oil, 40th Anniv. — A194

No. 485: a, Oil tanker and oil storage facility. b, Oil storage facility and oil well.

2007, July 27 **Litho.** ***Perf. 13¾***

485 A194 100b Horiz. pair, #a-b 1.75 1.75

Symposium on Agricultrual Development — A195

2007, Oct. 1 **Litho.** ***Perf. 13¾x14***

486 A195 100b multi 1.25 1.25

37th National Day — A196

2008, Nov. 18 ***Perf. 13***

487 A196 100b multi 2.25 2.25

Khasab Castle A197

No. 488: a, Exterior of castle. b, Man behind table. c, People reading. d, Men and cannons near door.

2007, Dec. 1 ***Perf. 13¼x13***

488 A197 100b Block of 4, #a-d 4.50 4.50

Scouting, Cent., and Scouting in Oman, 75th Anniv. A198

2007, Dec. 20 ***Perf. 13¾x13¼***

489 A198 250b multi 2.50 2.50

19th Arabian Gulf Cup Soccer Tournament A199

2009, Jan. 4 **Litho.** ***Perf. 12¾x13¼***

490 A199 100b multi 1.25 1.25

38th National Day — A200

Litho. & Embossed With Foil Application

2008, Nov. 18 ***Perf. 13¾***

491 A200 200b multi 2.00 2.00

Souvenir Sheet

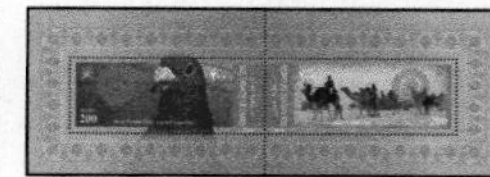

Arab Postal Day A201

No. 492 — Emblem and: a, World map, pigeon. b, Camel caravan.

Perf. 14½x13¾

2008, Dec. 21 **Litho.**

492 A201 200b Sheet of 2, #a-b 12.00 12.00

Supreme Council of Gulf Cooperation Council, 29th Session — A202

Emblem and: 100b, Flags. 300b, Rulers of Council states.

Litho. With Foil Application

2008, Dec. 29 ***Perf. 13¼x13***

493 A202 100b multi 3.00 3.00

Size: 162x81mm

Imperf

494 A202 300b multi 4.75 4.75

Jerusalem, 2009 Capital of Arab Culture A203

2009, Nov. 10 **Litho.** ***Perf. 13¾***

495 A203 250b multi 2.75 2.75

Souvenir Sheet

With White Frame Around Stamp

496 A203 250b multi *20.00 20.00*

15th Gulf Cooperation Council Stamps Exhibition, Oman — A204

No. 497: a, Part of Bahrain flag at right. b, Part of Bahrain flag at left, part of United Arab Emirates flag at right. c, Part of United Arab Emirates flag at left. d, Part of Oman flag at right. e, Part of Oman flag at left, part of Saudi Arabia flag at right. f, Part of Saudi Arabia flag at left. g, Part of Kuwait flag at right. h, Part of Kuwait flag at left, part of Qatar flag at right. i, Part of Qatar flag at left.

50b, No flag in background.

2009, Nov. 15 **Litho.** ***Perf. 13***

497 Sheet of 9 + 6 labels 14.00 14.00

a.-i. A204 200b Any single 1.40 1.40

Booklet Stamp

Self-Adhesive

Serpentine Die Cut 12¾

498 A204 50b multi .50 .50

a. Booklet pane of 12 7.50 7.50

39th National Day — A205

Litho. & Embossed

2009, Nov. 18 ***Perf. 13¼***

499 A205 200b multi 1.75 1.75

Oman, Champions of 19th Arabian Gulf Cup Soccer Tournament — A206

2009, Dec. 19 **Litho.** ***Perf. 13¼***

500 A206 200b multi 2.00 2.00

Censuses — A207

Emblem of: No. 502, 50b, Third census of Oman. No. 503, 50b, Joint Gulf Cooperation Council census.

2010, Feb. 2 **Litho.** ***Perf. 13¼***

502-503 A207 Set of 2 1.00 1.00

Arab Water Day — A209

2010, Mar. 3 **Litho.** ***Perf. 14¼***

506 A209 100b multi .90 .90

A210

Expo 2010, Shanghai — A211

2010, May 1 ***Perf. 12¾x13¼***

Souvenir Sheet

507 A210 100b multi 2.75 2.75

Self-Adhesive

Serpentine Die Cut

508 A211 50b multi .50 .50

Souvenir Sheet

Jewel of Muscat A212

2010, July 3 ***Perf. 13¾x13¼***

509 A212 100b multi 2.75 2.75

Miniature Sheet

Renaissance Day — A213

No. 510 — Sultan Qaboos in: a, Blue uniform. b, Brown uniform, red brown background. c, White uniform. d, Beige uniform. e, Brown uniform, gray brown background.

Litho. & Embossed

2010, July 23 *Perf. 13¼*
510 A213 50b Sheet of 5, #a-e 2.75 2.75

Souvenir Sheet

40th National Day A214

No. 511 — Doves and: a, 100b, Map of Oman. b, 150b, Sultan Qaboos.

2010, Oct. 18 *Perf.*
511 A214 Sheet of 2, #a-b 3.25 3.25

Traffic Safety Day A215

2010, Oct. 18 Litho. *Perf. 13¼*

Souvenir Sheet

512 A215 100b multi 2.50 2.50

Self-Adhesive

Serpentine Die Cut 13¼

513 A215 50b white & multi .75 .75

Miniature Sheet

Second Asian Beach Games, Muscat A216

No. 514: a, Handball. b, Sepak takraw (player kicking ball in air). c, Soccer player dribbling ball. d, Triathlon. e, Volleyball. f, Water polo. g, Swimming. h, Sailing. i, Jet skiing. j, Woodball (player with mallet and ball). k, Water skiing. l, Tent pegging (rider on horse). m, Kabbadi (two athletes wrestling). n, Body building.

2010, Dec. 8 Litho. *Perf. 13¼*
514 A216 50b Sheet of 14, #a-n 5.50 5.50

Miniature Sheet

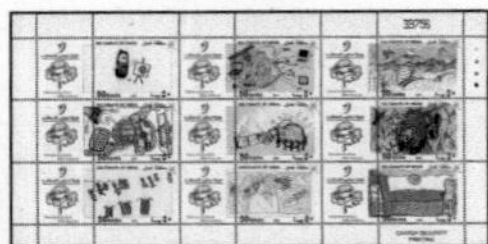

Children's Art — A217

No. 515: a, Cell phone with palette and brush painting Earth on easel. b, Satellite, satellite dish, electronic devices, scissors cutting cables. c, Car on road near buildings and mountains with satellite dishes. d, Cell phone, hand pointing at electronic options, telephone handset. e, Electronic devices, film strip, people circling Earth. f, Spider web, satellite dish, cell phones, antenna towers. g, Children and boxes with colored squares. h, Boy using cell phone. i, Flag of Oman, Sun, cell phones.

2010, Dec. 19 *Perf. 14¼x14*
515 A217 50b Sheet of 9, #a-i, + 9 labels 4.00 4.00

Sultan Qaboos University, 25th Anniv. — A218

Emblems, tower, and: 50b, Symbols of science and industry. 100b, Sultan Qaboos, horiz.

2011, Nov. 9 *Perf. 13¾x13¼*
516 A218 50b multi .50 .50

Size: 90x65mm

Imperf

517 A218 100b multi 1.00 1.00

41st National Day A219

Sultan Qaboos, Royal Opera House, Muscat, and scenes from various productions: 50b, 100b, 150b.

2011, Nov. 18
518-520 A219 Set of 3 3.50 3.50

Intl. Year of Chemistry — A220

2011, Dec. 27 *Perf. 14¼x14*
521 A220 100b multi .75 .75

Friendship With Japan, 40th Anniv. — A221

2012, May 7 *Perf. 14x13¼*
522 A221 100b multi .75 .75

Frankincense and Incense Burner — A222

2012, June 21 Litho. *Perf. 13¼x14*
523 A222 250b multi 3.00 3.00

Salalah Tourism Festival. Portions of No. 523 have a scratch-and-sniff covering with a frankincese aroma.

Miniature Sheet

Muscat, 2012 Arab Tourism Capital A223

No. 524: a, Old Muscat. b, Sultan Qaboos Grand Mosque. c, Matrah and port. d, Royal Opera House at night. e, Matrah Corniche with docked ships. f, Barr al Jissah Resort.

2012, July 23 Litho. *Perf. 14¼x14*
524 A223 50b Sheet of 6, #a-f, + 6 labels 6.00 6.00

Arab Postal Day — A224

Litho. & Embossed

2012, Aug. 3 *Perf. 13½*
525 A224 100b multi .70 .70

Sultan Qaboos Sailing Trophy — A225

Litho. & Embossed With Foil Application

2012, Nov. 3 *Perf. 14x13½*
526 A225 250b multi 1.75 1.75

42nd National Day A226

Sultan Qaboos and various ships at Oman Drydock Company: 50b, 100b, 150b.

Perf. 13½x13¼

2012, Nov. 18 Litho.
527-529 A226 Set of 3 3.75 3.75

Miniature Sheets

Arabian Horses A227

No. 530, 100b — Horse named Dorar: a, Facing right, black background. b, Facing left, outdoors. c, Head, facing right, and hindquarters, black background, vert. d, Facing left, black background. e, Standing, facing right, outdoors.

No. 531, 100b — Horse named: a, Ajlad, standing and facing right. b, Psymamon, vert. c, Ajlad, head only, vert. d, Modheeah. e, Sadeed, vert.

2012, Dec. 12 Litho. *Perf. 13¼*

Sheets of 5, #a-e

530-531 A227 Set of 2 7.00 7.00

Omani Environment Day — A228

Designs: 50b, Adenium obesum. 100b, Cistanche tubulosa. 200b, Amygdalus arabica. 250b, Aegopordon berardoides.

2013, Jan. 8 Litho. *Perf. 14*
532-535 A228 Set of 4 — —

Miniature Sheet

Omani Crafts Day A229

No. 536: a, Woven bowl and lid. b, Silver sphere on pedestal. c, Teapot, bowl and cups. d, Copper plate. e, Jewel box and string of pearls. f, Bowl with lid showing emblem of Oman. g, Carpet with tassels. h, Basket.

Litho. & Embossed

2013, Mar. 3 *Perf. 13½*
536 A229 150b Sheet of 8, #a-h, + central label — —

Diplomatic Relations Between Oman and People's Republic of China, 35th Anniv. — A230

2013, May 25 Litho. *Perf. 13*
537 A230 200b multi — —

Girl Guides 20th Arab Regional Conference — A231

2013, Aug. 24 Litho. *Perf. 14¼x14*
538 A231 100b multi .70 .70

Oman Boy Scouts 16th Intl. Youth Gathering for Cultural Exchange — A232

2013, Sept. 4 Litho. *Perf. 14¼x14*
539 A232 200b multi 1.40 1.40

A233

Omani Women's Day — A234

Litho. & Embossed

2013, Oct. 17 *Perf. 14*
540 A233 100b multi 1.25 1.25
541 A234 100b multi 1.25 1.25

Traffic Safety Day — A235

2013, Oct. 18 Litho. *Perf. 14*
542 A235 50b multi 1.00 1.00

A236

A237

Sultan Qaboos — A238

2013, Nov. 18 Litho. *Perf. 13½x13*
543 A236 200b multi 1.50 1.50
544 A237 200b multi 1.50 1.50
545 A238 200b multi 1.50 1.50
Nos. 543-545 (3) 4.50 4.50

43rd National Day. Nos. 543-545 each were printed in sheets of 4.

Sultan's Armed Forces Museum, 25th Anniv. — A239

Designs: 50b, Museum exterior. 100b, Sultan Qaboos in museum.

2013, Dec. 11 Litho. *Perf. 13½*
546-547 A239 Set of 2 1.75 1.75

Establishment of Omani Philatelic Association A240

Designs: 100b, Association emblem. 150b, Cancels and canceler. 200b, Various Oman stamps.

2014, May 21 Litho. *Perf. 13x13¼*
548-550 A240 Set of 3 3.25 3.25
550a Souvenir sheet of 3, #548-550 3.25 3.25

Salalah Festival — A241

Emblem and: 100b, People, raised hands, flag.
150b, Building, vert.

2014, July 30 Litho. *Perf. 13¼*
551 A241 100b multi .70 .70

Souvenir Sheet

Perf. 13½x13

552 A241 150b multi 1.10 1.10

No. 552 contains one 30x40mm stamp.

Muscat Festival — A242

2014, Aug. 14 Litho. *Perf. 13x13½*
553 A242 100b multi .70 .70

Souvenir Sheet

Tour of Oman Bicycle Race A243

2014, Aug. 14 Litho. *Perf. 13x13½*
554 A243 250b multi 1.75 1.75

Architectural Details From Castles and Forts — A244

No. 555: a, Jabreen Castle. b, Nizwa Fort. c, Bahla Fort. d, Al Hazm Castle.

No. 556, 250b, Like #555a. No. 557, 250b, Like #555b. No. 558, 250b, Like #555c. No. 559, 250b, Like #555d.

2014, Sept. 29 Litho. *Perf. 13½x13*
555 A244 150b Sheet of 4, #a-d 4.25 4.25

Souvenir Sheets

556-559 A244 Set of 4 7.00 7.00

44th National Day A245

No. 560 — Sultan Qaboos with background color of: a, Purple brown. b, Blue. c, Green. d, Purple.
200b, Sultan Qaboos, diff.

2014, Nov. 18 Litho. *Perf. 13½x13*
560 A245 100b Sheet of 4, #a-d 4.00 4.00

Souvenir Sheet

Litho. With Foil Application

Imperf

561 A245 200b gold & multi 2.40 2.40

Sultan Qaboos Award for Volunteer Work — A246

2014, Dec. 5 Litho. *Perf. 13¼*
562 A246 250b multi — —

Souvenir Sheets

Souq Muttrah A247

Designs: 200b, Entrance. 250b, Souq Muttrah, diff.

2014, Dec. 12 Litho. *Perf. 14x14¼*
563-564 A247 Set of 2 3.25 3.25

Miniature Sheet

Oman Post Mascot A248

No. 565 — Inscription: a, Delivery items. b, Kids corner. c, Deposit boxes. d, Post boxes.

2014, Dec. 14 Litho. *Perf. 13¼*
565 A248 100b Sheet of 4, #a-d 2.75 2.75

Wildlife A249

No. 566 — Arabian gazelles: a, 100b, One gazelle and tail of another gazelle. b, 150b, Two gazelles. c, 200b, Two gazelles, diff.
No. 567 — Butterflies: a, Papilio demoleus. b, Stone hamia varanes. c, Precis hierta. d, Belenois aurota.
No. 568 — Merops persicus facing: a, Right. b, Left.
No. 569, 150b, Ploceus galbula. No. 570, 200b, Treron waalia. No. 571, 200b, Coracias benghalensis. No. 572, 200b, Falco concolor. No. 573, 200b, Arabian owls.

Litho. & Embossed

2014, Dec. 14 *Perf. 14*
566 A249 Sheet of 3, #a-c — —
567 A249 150b Sheet of 4, #a-d 4.25 4.25
568 A249 150b Sheet of 2, #a-b 2.10 2.10

Souvenir Sheets

569-573 A249 Set of 5 6.75 6.75

Souvenir Sheets

Arabian and World Water Day A250

Designs: No. 574, 200b, Falaj Al-Khatmeen. No. 575, 200b, Falaj Dares.

2015, Mar. 3 Litho. *Perf. 14¼x14½*
574-575 A250 Set of 2 2.75 2.75

Nizwa, Capital of Islamic Culture A251

No. 576: a, Old door. b, Emblem, white backround. c, Siaal Mosque. d, Arrazha dance art. e, Emblem light brown background. f, Falaj Daris.
No. 577, 250b: a, Like #576e. b, Like #576a. c, Like #576c.
No. 578, 250b: a, Like #576d. b, Like #576b. c, Like #576f.

2015, Mar. 15 Litho. *Perf. 13¼x13*
576 A251 200b Sheet of 6, #a-f 8.50 8.50

Souvenir Sheets of 3, #a-c

577-578 A251 Set of 2 10.50 10.50

Gulf Cooperation Council Stamp Exhibition, Nizwa — A252

2015, Oct. 15 Litho. *Perf. 13½*
579 A252 200b multi — —

Nizwa, 2015 Capital of Islamic Culture.

International Telecommunication Union, 150th Anniv. — A253

2015, Nov. 30 Litho. *Perf. 14*
580 A253 100b multi — —

A254

A255

45th National Day A256

No. 581: a, 100b, 45th National Day emblem (40x40mm). b, 200b, Royal Opera House, Muscat, at night (40x40mm). c, 200b, Daytime view of Royal Opera House (40x40mm). d, 200b, Interior of Royal Opera House (40x40mm). e, 200b, Sultan Qaboos (40x70mm).
No. 582, 200b, New Salalah Airport.
250b, Sultan Qaboos and Royal Opera House at night.

Litho., Litho. With Foil Application (#582)

2015, Nov. 18 *Perf. 14*
581 A254 Sheet of 5, #a-e, + label — —

Souvenir Sheet

Size: 70x35mm

Perf. 14¼

582 A255 200b sil & multi — —

Size: 90x60mm

Imperf

583 A256 250b multi — —

Diplomatic Relations Between Oman and India, 60th Anniv. — A257

2015, Dec. 31 Litho. *Perf. 14¼*
584 A257 200b multi — —

No. 584 was printed in sheets of 6 + 3 central labels.

Souvenir Sheets

Omani Postal Service, 50th Anniv. A258

No. 585, 250b: a, Post office and mail sorters. b, Oman #105, 129, 137, horiz. c, Red pillar box.
No. 586, 250b: a, Mail trucks. b, Oman #99, horiz. c, Yellow mail box.

Litho., Sheet Margin Litho. With Foil Application

Perf. 13¼x13 (vert. stamps), 13x13¼

2016, Apr. 30 Sheets of 3, #a-c
585-586 A258 Set of 2 10.50 10.50

Arab Postal Day A259

No. 587: a, Blue background, denomination at LR. b, Green background, denomination at LL.

2016, Aug. 3 Litho. *Perf. 14*
587 A259 150b Horiz. pair, #a-b 2.10 2.10

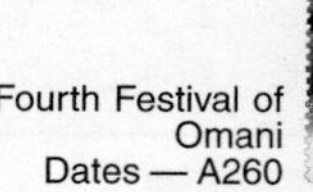

Fourth Festival of Omani Dates — A260

2016, Oct. 23 Litho. *Perf. 13*

588 A260 100b multi .70 .70

National Oncology Center A261

2016, Nov. 2 Litho. *Perf. 13*

589 A261 100b multi .70 .70

46th National Day — A262

Litho. & Embossed With Foil Application

2016, Nov. 18 *Perf. 13x13¼*

590 A262 300b multi 2.10 2.10

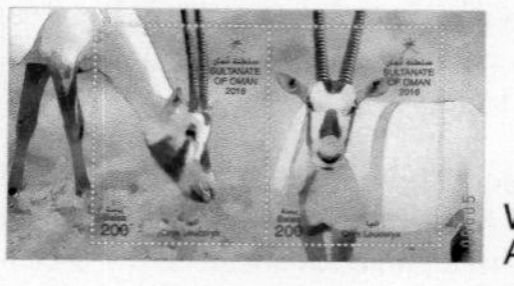

Wildlife A263

No. 591, 200b — Oryx leucoryx with: a, Head down. b, Head up.

No. 592, 200b — Bubo ascalaphus: a, Feet visible. b, Feet not visible.

No. 593, 200b: a, Neophron pecnopterus. b, Alectoris chukar.

No. 594, 200b: a, Byblia ilithyia ilithyia. b, Hypolimnas misippus.

No. 595, 400b, Paraechinus aethiopicus, horiz. No. 596, 400b, Pterocles exustus, horiz.

Litho. & Embossed

2016, Dec. 20 *Perf. 13*

Sheets of 2, #a-b

591-594 A263 Set of 4 11.50 11.50

Souvenir Sheets

595-596 A263 Set of 2 5.75 5.75

A264

A265

A266

A267

A268

A269

A270

A271

A272

Arches in Sultan Qaboos Grand Mosque — A273

2016, Dec. 21 Litho. *Perf. 13x13¼*

597	Booklet pane of 5	7.00	—
a.	A264 200b multi	1.40	1.40
b.	A265 200b multi	1.40	1.40
c.	A266 200b multi	1.40	1.40
d.	A267 200b multi	1.40	1.40
e.	A268 200b multi	1.40	1.40
	Complete booklet, #597	7.00	
598	Booklet pane of 5	7.00	—
a.	A269 200b multi	1.40	1.40
b.	A270 200b multi	1.40	1.40
c.	A271 200b multi	1.40	1.40
d.	A272 200b multi	1.40	1.40
e.	A273 200b multi	1.40	1.40
	Complete booklet, #598	7.00	

Souvenir Sheet

2nd International Military Sports Council World Cup Soccer Tournament, Muscat — A274

No. 599: a, Tournament emblem. b, Mascot.

Litho. With Foil Application

2017, Jan. 15 *Perf. 13*

599 A274 250b Sheet of 2, #a-b, + central label 3.50 3.50

Miniature Sheet

Children A275

No. 600: a, Girl with magnifying glass (56x33mm). b, Two girls (56x66mm). c, Five children reading (56x33mm). d, Two children reading (56x33mm). e, Three children playing with toys (56x33mm).

Litho. With Foil Application

2017, Apr. 3 *Perf. 13½x13¼*

600 A275 250b Sheet of 5, #a-e 8.75 8.75

Miniature Sheet

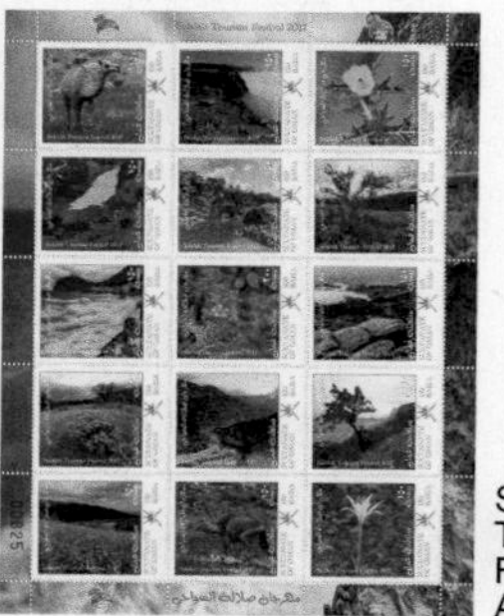

Salalah Tourism Festival A276

No. 601: a, Camel facing right. b, Clouds in canyon. c, Yellow flower. d, River and lake. e, Swimmers. f, Small tree. g, Waves hitting rocks, mountain in background. h, Pink flower. i, Waves and rocky shore. j, Flowering plants and tree, valley in background. k, Dry river bed in valley. l, Small tree, road in background. m, Field of red violet flowers. n, Camel facing left. o, White flower.

2017, July 8 Litho. *Perf. 14*

601 A276 150b Sheet of 15, #a-o 16.00 16.00

National Day A277

No. 602 — Sultan Qaboos and: a, Ships and cranes at Duqm Special Economic Zone. b, Aerial view of Duqm Special Economic Zone.

Litho. & Embossed

2017, Nov. 18 *Perf. 14¼x14*

602	Horiz. pair	3.75	3.75
a.	A277 200b multi	1.10	1.10
b.	A277 500b multi	2.60	2.60

Oman Soccer Team, Winner of 23rd Arabian Gulf Cup Tournament A278

Designs: 200b, Goaltender diving for ball. No. 604, 500b, Players, soccer ball, trophy. No. 605, 500b, Players and trophy in rowboat on shore. No. 606, 500b, Trophy, players in stadium, flag of Oman.

2018, Mar. 4 Litho. *Perf. 13*

603-606 A278 Set of 4 9.00 9.00

606a Souvenir sheet of 4, #603-606 9.00 9.00

2018 World Cup Soccer Championships, Russia — A279

2018, July 1 Litho. *Perf. 13*

607 A279 500b gold & multi 3.50 3.50

a. Miniature sheet of 5 17.50 17.50

Values for No. 607 are for stamps with surrounding selvage.

Arab Document Day — A280

Designs: 400b, Cover of *L'Univers Illustré* depicting 1875 visit to Paris of Sultan of Zanzibar. 600b, 1947 photograph of Muscat.

2018, Oct. 17 Litho. *Perf. 14¼*

608-609 A280 Set of 2 7.00 7.00

609a Souvenir sheet of 2, #608-609, perf. 13 7.00 7.00

Adolescent and Youth Health — A281

2018, Oct. 21 Litho. *Perf.*

610 A281 400b multi 2.75 2.75

a. Souvenir sheet of 4 11.00 11.00

48th National Day — A282

Designs: 200b, "48." 400b, Sultan Qaboos.

Litho. With Foil Application

2018, Nov. 18 *Perf. 13*

611-612 A282 Set of 2 4.25 4.25

612a Souvenir sheet of 2, #611-612 4.25 4.25

Airports of Oman A283

Designs: 200b, Interior of airport. 600b, Aerial view of Muscat International Airport.

2018, Dec. 5 Litho. *Perf. 13x12¾*

613-614 A283 Set of 2 5.75 5.75

614a Souvenir sheet of 2, #613-614 5.75 5.75

Shell Oman Marketing Company, 60th Anniv. — A284

Designs: 200b, Modern Shell gas station. 500b, Modern and old Shell gas stations. 600b, Shell gas station sign, children holding solar panel. 800b, Building with solar panels on roof.

Perf. 14x13x14x14

2018, Dec. 12 **Litho.**

615-618	A284 Set of 4	15.00	15.00
618a	Souvenir sheet of 4, #615-618, perf. 14	15.00	15.00

Oman's Chairmanship of the Arab Women Organization A285

Litho. With Foil Application

2018, Dec. 18 ***Perf. 13***

619	A285 200b gold & multi	1.40	1.40
a.	Souvenir sheet of 4	5.75	5.75

A286

Call of Peace from Children of the World — A287

2019, Feb. 19 **Litho.** ***Perf. 13x13¼***

620	A286 400b multi	2.75	2.75
621	A287 400b multi	2.75	2.75
a.	Souvenir sheet of 2, #620-621	5.50	5.50

Khanjars — A288

Designs: No. 622, 200b, Al Batenia or Al Sahelia khanjar. No. 623, 200b, Al Janbiya khanjar. No. 624, 500b, Al Saidia khanjar. No. 625, 500b, Al Suria khanjar. No. 626, 500b, Al Nizwania khanjar.

Litho. & Embossed

2019, Mar. 3 ***Perf. 14***

622-626	A288 Set of 5	13.50	13.50
626a	Souvenir sheet of 5, #622-626	13.50	13.50

Musical Instruments A289

Designs: No. 627, 100b, Al-Rauwah (drums). No. 628, 100b, Kasir and Rahmani (drums). No. 629, 500b, Azi (drums). No. 630, 500b, Barghum (animal horn).

2019, Mar. 4 **Litho.** ***Perf. 14***

627-630	A289 Set of 4	8.50	8.50
630a	Souvenir sheet of 4, #627-630	8.50	8.50

Tourism — A289a

Designs: No. 630B, 50b, A'Rustaq Fort. No. 630C, 200b, Musandam. No. 630D, 500b, Balad Sayt. No. 630E, 800b, Al Ayjah.

2019 **Litho.** ***Perf. 13***

630B-630E	A289a Set of 4	11.00	11.00
630Ef	Souvenir sheet of 4, #630B-630E	11.00	11.00

Turtles — A290

Designs: Nois. 631, 636a, 100b, Leatherback turtle. Nos. 632, 636b, 100b, Green turtle. Nos. 633, 636c, 100b, Hawksbill turtle. Nos. 634, 636d, 100b, Loggerhead turtle. Nos. 635, 636e, 500b, Olive ridley turtle.

2019, Sept. 29 **Litho.** ***Perf. 13¼***

Stamps With Dark Blue Frames

631-635	A290 Set of 5	6.50	6.50

Souvenir Sheet

Stamps With Marine Life in Frames

636	A290 Sheet of 5, #a-e	6.50	6.50

Oman's Message of Islam — A291

Designs: 200b, Emblem. No. 638, 250b, Emblem and the prophet's 629 letter to the people of Oman. No. 639, 250b, Emblem and map of Oman inscribed with word for "peace" in various languages. 300b, Emblem and Muslim men at entrance to mosque.

2019, Nov. 16 **Litho.** ***Perf. 14***

637-640	A291 Set of 4	7.00	7.00
640a	Souvenir sheet of 4, #637-640	7.00	7.00

49th National Day — A292

Sultan Qaboos and: 200b, Highway cloverleaf. 300b, Highway cloverleaf, horiz.

Litho. With Foil Application

2019, Nov. 18 ***Perf. 14x14¼***

641	A292 200b gold & multi	1.40	1.40
a.	Perf. 13½	1.40	1.40

Perf. 14¼x14

642	A292 300b gold & multi	2.10	2.10
a.	Perf. 13½	2.10	2.10
b.	Souvenir sheet of 2, #641a, 642a	3.50	3.50

United Nations Convention on the Rights of the Child, 30th Anniv. — A293

2019, Nov. 24 **Litho.** ***Perf. 14***

643	A293 500b multi	3.50	3.50
a.	Souvenir sheet of 1	3.50	3.50

A294

A295

A296

A297

Aflaj Irrigation Systems UNESCO World Heritage Sites — A298

2019, Dec. 30 **Litho.** ***Perf. 13¼x13***

644	A294 100b multi	.70	.70
645	A295 100b multi	.70	.70
646	A296 100b multi	.70	.70
647	A297 500b multi	3.50	3.50
648	A298 500b multi	3.50	3.50
a.	Souvenir sheet of 5, #644-648	9.25	9.25
	Nos. 644-648 (5)	9.10	9.10

Doves, Flag of the Palestinian Authority, Dome of the Rock, Jerusalem A299

2020, Feb. 9 **Litho.** ***Perf. 14¼***

649	A299 250b multi	1.75	1.75
a.	Souvenir sheet of 1, perf. 13¼	1.75	1.75

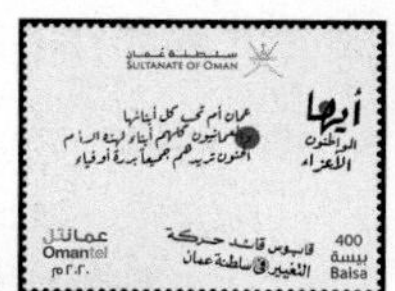

A300

A301

Achievements of Sultan Qaboos (1940-2020) A302

2020, Mar. 3 **Litho.** ***Perf. 14¼***

650	A300 400b multi	2.75	2.75
651	A301 400b multi	2.75	2.75
652	A302 400b multi	2.75	2.75
a.	Souvenir sheet of 3, #650-652, perf. 13¼	8.25	8.25

Campaign Against COVID-19 A303

2020, June 22 **Litho.** ***Perf. 14***

653	A303 500b multi	3.50	3.50
a.	Souvenir sheet of 2	7.00	7.00

Arab League, 75th Anniv. — A304

Litho. With Foil Application

2020, June 28 ***Perf. 13¼x12¾***

654	A304 500b gold & multi	3.50	3.50
a.	Souvenir sheet of 2	7.00	7.00

Oman Center for Traditional Music — A305

Designs: 100b, Drummers and dancers. 200b, Drummers and man blowing sea shell. 300b, Drummers and dancers, diff. 400b, Drummer and singer.

Litho. With Foil Application

2020, July 5 ***Perf. 13***

655-658	A305 Set of 4	7.00	7.00
658a	Souvenir sheet of 4, #655-658	7.00	7.00

Diplomatic Relations Between Oman and People's Republic of China, 40th Anniv. A306

2020, Oct. 20 **Litho.** ***Perf. 12¾x13¼***

659	A306 200b multi	1.40	1.40

A souvenir sheet containing one example of No. 659 sold for 600b.

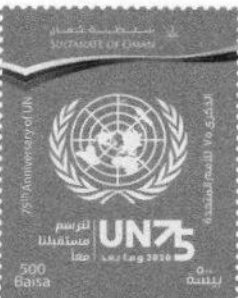

United Nations, 75th Anniv. — A307

2020, Oct. 24 **Litho.** ***Perf. 14***

660	A307 500b multi	3.50	3.50
a.	Souvenir sheet of 1	3.50	3.50

Camel Ardhah, UNESCO Intangible Cultural Heritage — A308

Litho. With Foil Application

2020, Nov. 11 ***Perf. 14***

661	Horiz. strip of 4	8.50	8.50
a.	A308 100b Camel Ardhah	.70	.70
b.	A308 200b Camel Ardhah, diff.	1.40	1.40
c.	A308 400b Camel Ardhah, diff.	2.80	2.80
d.	A308 500b Camel Hambal	3.50	3.50
e.	Souvenir sheet of 4, #661a-661d	8.50	8.50

Horse Ardhah, UNESCO Intangible Cultural Heritage — A309

No. 662: a, 100b, Two men riding horses, one standing on horse's back, inscribed "Horse Ardhah." b, 200b, Two men with arms touching riding horses, inscribed "Horse Ardhah." c, 400b, Line of mounted horses, inscribed "Horse Hambal." d, 500b, Mounted horses and mosque, inscribed "Horse Hambal."

Litho. With Foil Application

2020, Nov. 11 ***Perf. 14***

662	Horiz. strip of 4	8.50	8.50
a.	A309 100b gold & multi	.70	.70
b.	A309 200b gold & multi	1.40	1.40
c.	A309 400b gold & multi	2.75	2.75
d.	A309 500b gold & multi	3.50	3.50
e.	Souvenir sheet of 4, #662a-662d	8.50	8.50

Adventure Tourism Locations — A310

No. 663: a, Wadi Qa'sha. b, Wadi Umq Bir. c, Saab Bani Khamis. d, Wadi Bani Auf.

2020, Dec. 1 **Litho.** ***Perf. 13***

663	Horiz. strip of 4	8.50	8.50
a.	A310 100b multi	.70	.70
b.	A310 200b multi	1.40	1.40
c.	A310 400b multi	2.80	2.80
d.	A310 500b multi	3.50	3.50
e.	Souvenir sheet of 4, #663a-663d	8.50	8.50

Sultan Qaboos (1940-2020) A311

50th National Day Emblem — A312

Sultan Haitham — A313

2020, Nov. 18 Litho. *Perf. 13*

664 Horiz. strip of 3 10.50 10.50
a. A311 500b multi 3.50 3.50
b. A312 500b multi 3.50 3.50
c. A313 500b multi 3.50 3.50
d. Souvenir sheet of 3, #664a-644c 10.50 10.50

50th National Day.

Whales and Dolphins A314

No. 665: a, Blue whale. b, Arabian Sea humpback whale. c, Indian Ocean humpback dolphin. d, Spinner dolphin. e, Indo-Pacific bottlenose dolphin.

2020, Dec. 24 Litho. *Perf. 13¼*

665 Horiz. strip of 5 8.50 8.50
a.-b. A314 100b Either single .70 .70
c. A314 200b gold & multi 1.40 1.40
d. A314 300b gold & multi 2.10 2.10
e. A314 500b gold & multi 3.50 3.50
f. Souvenir sheet of 5, #665a-665e 8.50 8.50

Dar Al Hanan Children's Cancer Home, 10th Anniv. — A315

2021, Jan. 28 Litho. *Perf. 13¼x13*

666 A315 1r multi 7.00 7.00

Computer Security — A316

2021, Feb. Litho. *Perf. 13*

667 A316 500b multi 3.50 3.50
a. Souvenir sheet of 1 3.50 3.50

Al Saida School, Muscat, 80th Anniv. (in 2020) — A317

No. 668: a, School building. b, Students and teachers in classroom. c, Photograph of students and faculty. e, Students with flags.

2021, Mar. 9 Litho. *Perf. 13*

668 Horiz. strip of 4 7.00 7.00
a.-b. A317 100b Either single .70 .70
c. A317 300b multi 2.10 2.10
d. A317 500b multi 3.50 3.50
e. Souvenir sheet of 4, #668a-668d 7.00 7.00

Lizards — A318

No. 669: a, Thomas' mastigur. b, Dhofar agama. c, Carter's semaphore gecko. d, Chamaeleo arabicus.

Litho. & Embossed

2021, May 22 *Perf. 13x13¼*

669 Horiz. strip of 4 7.00 7.00
a.-d. A318 250b Any single 1.75 1.75
e. Souvenir sheet of 4, #669a-669d 7.00 7.00

Nursing and Midwifery — A319

No. 670: a, 200b, Nurse. b, 300b, Midwife and infant.
1r, Nurse, diff.

2021, May 29 Litho. *Perf. 13*

670 A319 Horiz. pair, #a-b 3.50 3.50

Size: 100x100mm

Imperf

671 A319 1r multi 7.00 7.00

Omani Wheat Harvest A320

Inscriptions: Nos. 672a, 673b, Ripe Wheat Spikes. Nos. 672b, 673a, Harvesting Wheat Crops. Nos. 672c, 673d, Omani Wheat Grains. Nos. 672d, 673c, Filtering the Wheat Crop.

No Wheat Spikes in Top and Bottom Panels on Nos. 672a-672b, 672d, Top and Bottom Panels in Orange Brown on No. 672c

2021, Aug. Litho. *Perf. 13x13¼*

672 A320 250b Block of 4, #a-d 7.00 7.00

Miniature Sheet

Wheat Spikes in Top and Bottom Panels on Nos. 673a-673c, Top and Bottom Panels in Light Brown on No. 673d

673 A320 250b Sheet of 4, #a-d 7.00 7.00

Sand Dunes — A321

No. 674 — Man and: a, Sugar Dunes, Mahut. b, Empty Quarter, Ibri.

2021, Oct. Litho. *Perf. 13*

674 A321 500b Vert. pair, #a-b 7.00 7.00
c. Souvenir sheet of 2, #674a-674b 7.00 7.00

A322

A323

A324

Corals — A325

2021, Oct. 12 Litho. *Perf. 13*

675 Block of 4 7.00 7.00
a. A322 100b multi .70 .70
b. A323 200b multi 1.40 1.40
c. A324 200b multi 1.40 1.40
d. A325 500b multi 3.50 3.50
e. Souvenir sheet of 4, #675a-675d 7.00 7.00

A326

A327

A328

Women's Costumes — A329

Litho. With Foil Application

2021, Oct. 21 *Perf. 13¼x13*

676 Block of 4 7.00 7.00
a. A326 100b gold & multi .70 .70
b. A327 200b gold & multi 1.40 1.40
c. A328 200b gold & multi 1.40 1.40
d. A329 500b gold & multi 3.50 3.50
e. Souvenir sheet of 4, #676a-676d 7.00 7.00

ICC Men's T20 Cricket World Cup Tournament, Oman and United Arab Emirates — A330

2021, Oct. 28 Litho. *Perf. 14*

677 A330 250b multi 1.75 1.75

Souvenir Sheet

677A A330 1r multi 7.00 7.00

The ICC Men's T20 Cricket World Cup Tournament was originally to be held in Australia in 2020, but was postponed until 2021 and moved to Oman and the United Arab Emirates because of the COVID-19 pandemic.

Admisssion of Oman to United Nations, 50th Anniv. — A331

2021, Nov. 14 Litho. *Perf. 13*

678 A331 500b multi 3.50 3.50

Souvenir Sheet

679 A331 5r multi 35.00 35.00

Sultan Haitham — A332

Litho. With Foil Application

2021, Nov. 27 *Perf. 14¼*

680 A332 500b gold & multi 3.50 3.50

Souvenir Sheet

Perf. 14½

681 A332 2r gold & multi 14.00 14.00

51st National Day. No. 681 contains one 44x59mm stamp.

Ahmad Bin Majid al Saadi (1421-1500), Navigator A333

Al Muhallab Bin Abi Sufra Al Azdi (632-702), General and Governor A334

Abdullah Bin Suleiman Al Harthy (1886-1940), Newspaper Publisher in Zanzibar A335

Nasser Bin Salim Al Bahlani (1273-1339), Poet A336

Al Khalil Bin Ahmad Al Farahidi (718-86), Lexicographer and Grammarian — A337

2021, Dec. 7 Litho. *Perf. 13*

682 Horiz. strip of 5 9.75 9.75
a. A333 100b multi .70 .70
b. A334 200b multi 1.40 1.40
c. A335 200b multi 1.40 1.40
d. A336 400b multi 2.75 2.75
e. A337 500b multi 3.50 3.50
f. Souvenir sheet of 5, #682a-682e 9.75 9.75

Sultan Haitham — A338

2021, Dec. Litho. *Perf. 13*

683 A338 500b cop & multi 3.50 3.50

Souvenir Sheet

Litho. With Foil Application, Sheet Margin Embossed with Foil Application

Imperf

684 A338 1r cop, gold & multi 7.00 7.00

No. 684 contains one 40x60mm stamp.

Omani Kummah (Man's Cap) Design A339

Omani Kummah Being Created A340

2021, Dec. Litho. *Perf. 13¼x13*

685 A339 1r multi 7.00 7.00
686 A340 3r multi 21.00 21.00

Opening of National Museum, 5th Anniv. A341

No. 687: a, 100b, Will of Sultan Qaboos. b, 100b, Saidi-style dagger. c, 100b, Oldest incense burner in Oman. d, 500b, Throne of Sultan Qaboos.

2022, Jan. 2 Litho. *Perf. 14¼*

687 A341 Block of 4, #a-d 5.75 5.75
e. Souvenir sheet of 4, #687a-687d 5.75 5.75

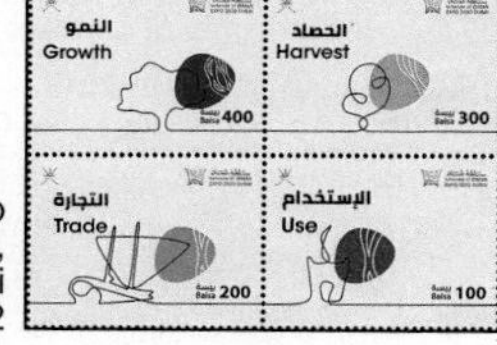

Expo 2020, Dubai A342

No. 688 — Inscription: a, 100b, Use. b, 200b, Trade. c, 300b, Harvest. d, 400b, Growth.

2022, Jan. 18 Litho. *Perf. 14*

688 A342 Block of 4, #a-d 7.00 7.00
e. Souvenir sheet of 4, #688a-688d 7.00 7.00

Expo 2020 was postponed until 2021 because of the COVID-19 pandemic.

Royal Opera House, Muscat, 10th Anniv. A343

Opera House: 200b, Interior. 300b, Exterior.

Perf. 12¾x13¼

2022, Mar. 28 Litho.

689-690 A343 Set of 2 3.50 3.50
690a Souvenir sheet of 2, #689-690, + 2 labels 3.50 3.50

Petroleum Development Oman, 85th Anniv. — A344

Designs: 50b, Boats in harbor, 1937. 150b, Oil tanker carrying first shipment of Omani oil, 1967. 200b, Oil worker at plant, 2002. 250b, 85th anniversary emblem, 2022.

2022, May 12 Litho. *Perf. 14*

691 A344 50b multi .35 .35
692 A344 150b multi 1.10 1.10
693 A344 200b multi 1.40 1.40
694 A344 250b multi 1.75 1.75
a. Block of 4, #691-694 4.75 .75
b. Souvenir sheet of 4, #691-694 4.75 4.75
Nos. 691-694 (4) 4.60 4.60

Issued in panes of 16, with each pane containing blocks of 4 of Nos. 691-694. A se-tenant block of 4 is in the center of the pane.

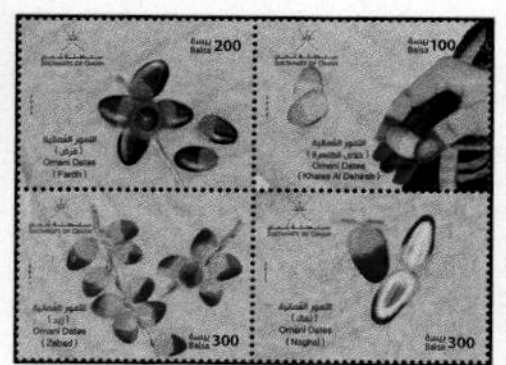

Date Varieties A345

No. 695: a, 100b, Khalas Al Dahirah dates. b, 200b, Fardh dates. c, 300b, Naghal dates. d, 300b, Zabad dates.

2022, July 21 Litho. *Perf. 14*

695 A345 Block of 4, #a-d 6.50 6.50
e. Souvenir sheet of 4, #695a-695d 6.50 6.50

Freshwater Fish — A346

No. 696: a, Awaous jayakari. b, Aphaniops kruppi. c, Cyprinion muscatense. d, Glossogobius tenuiformis.

2022, Sept. 18 Litho. *Perf. 14x13¾*

696 Horiz. strip of 4 7.00 7.00
a. A346 100b multi .70 .70
b. A346 200b multi 1.40 1.40
c. A346 300b multi 2.10 2.10
d. A346 400b multi 2.75 2.75
e. Souvenir sheet of 4, #696a-696d 7.00 7.00

House of Wonders, Stonetown, Zanzibar, Tanzania — A347

2022, Oct. 9 Litho. *Perf. 14¼*

697 A347 500b multi 3.50 3.50

See Tanzania No.

A349

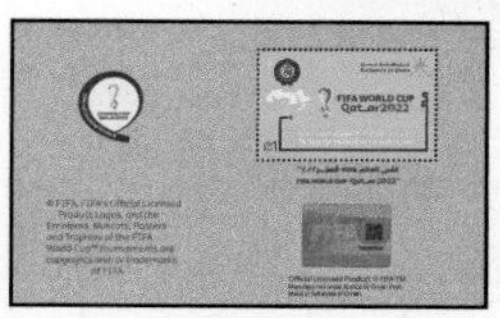

2022 World Cup Soccer Championships, Qatar — A350

2022 Litho. *Perf. 13¼x13*

700 A349 500b multi 3.50 3.50

Souvenir Sheets

701 A349 1r multi 7.00 7.00

Perf. 13¼

702 A350 1r multi 7.00 7.00

Issued: Nos. 700-701, 10/27; No. 702, 12/18.

2022 Aga Khan Awards for Architecture and Music Ceremony, Muscat — A351

No. 703: a, Royal Opera House, Muscat, as seen through archway. b, Building and four lamp posts.

2022, Oct. 31 Litho. *Perf. 13¾*

703 A351 500b Vert. pair, #a-b 7.00 7.00
c. Souvenir sheet of 2, #703a-703b 7.00 7.00

Muscat, 2022 Arab Digital Capital — A352

2022, Nov. 3 Litho. *Perf. 13¼x13½*

704 A352 500b multi 3.50 3.50

Souvenir Sheet

705 A352 1r multi 7.00 7.00

Miniature Sheet

52nd National Day A353

No. 706 — Inscriptions: a, 100b, Oman Convention and Exhibition Center (30x40mm). b, 100b, Sultan Qaboos Mosque, Sohar, (30x40mm). c, 100b, Oman Across Ages Museum (30x40mm). d, 100b, Oman Botanic Garden (30x40mm). e, 100b, Muttrah Fort (30x40mm). f, 100b, Forseeing the Future (30x40mm). g, 100b, Wakan Village (30x40mm). h, 100b, Ayn Athum (30x40mm). i, 100b, Khor Najd (30x40mm). j, 100b, Pink Lakes (30x40mm). k, 100b, Duqm Refinery, Zinat al Bihaar Ship (30x40mm). l, 100b, Barr al Hikman (30x40mm). m, 100b, Ras al Ruwais (30x40mm). n, 100b, Sohat Port and Freezone (30x40mm). o, 500b, Maidan Muttrah (and Sultan Haitham) (60x40mm).

Perf. 13¼x13 on 2, 3 or 4 Sides

2022, Nov. 18 Litho.

706 A353 Sheet of 15, #a-o 13.50 13.50

National Pavilion of the Sultanate of Oman for the 2022 Venice Biennale — A354

No. 707 — Inscriptions: a, Speed of Art. b, Reflections from Memories. c, Breathe. d, Under, Inner, Under.

2022, Dec. 26 Litho. *Perf. 13¾*

707 Horiz. strip of 4 7.00 7.00
a. A354 100b multi .70 .70
b. A354 200b multi 1.40 1.40
c. A354 300b multi 2.10 2.10
d. A354 400b multi 2.80 2.80
e. Souvenir sheet of 4, #707a-707d 7.00 7.00

Omani Armed Forces — A355

No. 708 — Inscriptions: a, Office of Chief of Staff of Sultan's Armed Forces. b, Royal Army of Oman. c, Royal Air Force of Oman. d, Royal Navy of Oman.

2022, Dec. 11 Litho. *Perf. 14*

708 Horiz. strip of 4 7.00 7.00
a. A355 200b multi 1.40 1.40
b. A355 250b multi 1.75 1.75
c. A355 250b multi 1.75 1.75
d. A355 300b multi 2.10 2.10
e. Souvenir sheet of 4, #708a-708d 7.00 7.00

A356

Gulf Cooperation Council, 40th Anniv. (in 2021) — A357

2022, Dec. 13 Litho. *Perf. 13½*

709 A356 500b multi 3.50 3.50

Souvenir Sheet

710 A357 1r multi 7.00 7.00

Oman Daily Newspaper, 50th Anniv. — A358

Perf. 13¾x13¼

2022, Dec. 14 Litho.

711 A358 500b multi 3.50 3.50

Souvenir Sheet

712 A358 1r multi 7.00 7.00

Ancient Omani Alphabet — A360

Inscriptions: No. 714, 50b, Muscat. No. 715, 50b, Khasab. No. 716, 100b, Nizwa. No. 717, 100b, Ibra. No. 718, 100b, Haima. No. 719, 200b, Sur. No. 720, 200b, Buraimi. No. 721, 400b, Rustaq. No. 722, 400b, Suhar. 1r, Salalah. 3r, Ibri.

2023, Mar. 20 Litho. *Perf. 13½x13*

714-724 A360 Set of 11 39.50 39.50
724a Sheet of 11, #714-724 39.50 39.50

SEMI-POSTAL STAMP

UNICEF Emblem, Girl with Book — SP1

Wmk. 314

1971, Dec. 25 Litho. ***Perf. 14***

B1 SP1 50b + 25b multicolored 42.50 6.50

25th anniv. of UNICEF.

OFFICIAL STAMPS

Official Stamps of India 1938-43 Overprinted in Black

Perf. 13½x14

1944, Nov. 20 **Wmk. 196**

O1	O8	3p slate	.80	*15.00*
O2	O8	½a dk rose violet	.80	*15.00*
O3	O8	9p green	.80	*15.00*
O4	O8	1a carmine rose	.80	*15.00*
O5	O8	1½a dull purple	.80	*15.00*
O6	O8	2a scarlet	.80	*15.00*
O7	O8	2½a purple	5.50	*15.00*
O8	O8	4a dark brown	2.00	*15.00*
O9	O8	8a blue violet	3.50	*17.50*
O10	A82	1r brown & slate	6.00	*27.50*
		Nos. O1-O10 (10)	21.80	*165.00*

Al Busaid Dynasty, 200th anniv. On Nos. O1-O9 the overprint is smaller — 13x6mm.

Used values for Nos. O1-O10 are for stamps canceled with contemporaneous postmarks of the Indian postal administration. Examples with the later British post office cancellations are worth much less.

ORANGE RIVER COLONY

'ăr-inj 'ri-vər 'kä-lə-nē

(Orange Free State)

LOCATION — South Africa, north of the Cape of Good Hope between the Orange and Vaal Rivers

GOVT. — A former British Crown Colony

AREA — 49,647 sq. mi.

POP. — 528,174 (1911)

CAPITAL — Bloemfontein

Orange Free State was an independent republic, 1854-1900. Orange River Colony existed from May, 1900, to June, 1910, when it united with Cape of Good Hope, Natal and the Transvaal to form the Union of South Africa.

12 Pence = 1 Shilling

Values for unused stamps are for examples with original gum as defined in the catalogue introduction. Very fine examples of Nos. 1-60c will have perforations touching the design on one or more sides due to the narrow spacing of the stamps on the plates. Stamps with perfs clear of the design on all four sides are scarce and will command higher prices.

Een = 1
Twee = 2
Drie = 3
Vier = 4

Issues of the Republic

Orange Tree — A1

1868-1900 Unwmk. Typo. ***Perf. 14***

1 A1 ½p red brown ('83) 8.25 .75
2 A1 ½p orange ('97) 3.00 .60
a. ½p yellow ('97) 3.00 .40
3 A1 1p red brown 22.50 .50
a. 1p pale brown 35.00 2.50
b. 1p deep brown 32.50 .60
4 A1 1p violet ('94) 5.00 .35
5 A1 2p violet ('83) 20.00 1.75
a. 2p pale mauve ('83-'84) 23.00 .30
6 A1 3p ultra ('83) 8.25 2.25
7 A1 4p ultra ('78) 6.50 4.50
a. 4p pale blue ('78) 26.00 5.25
8 A1 6p car rose ('90) 30.00 13.00
a. 6p rose ('71) 37.50 8.00
b. 6p pale rose ('68) 72.50 8.75
c. 6p bright carmine ('94) 18.50 2.25
9 A1 6p ultramarine ('00) 80.00
10 A1 1sh orange 65.00 1.75
a. 1sh orange buff *110.00* *7.25*
11 A1 1sh brown ('97) 32.50 1.75
12 A1 5sh green ('78) 14.00 *24.00*
Nos. 1-8,10-12 (11) 215.00 51.20

No. 8b was not placed in use without surcharge.

For surcharges see #13-53, 44j-53c, 57-60.

No. 13

No. 8a Surcharged in Four Different Types

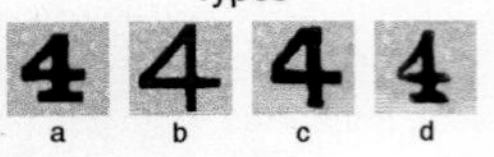

1877

13 (a) 4p on 6p rose 450.00 65.00
a. Inverted surcharge — 600.00
b. Double surcharge, one inverted ("a" + "c" inverted) *4,250.*
c. Double surcharge, one inverted ("a" inverted + "c" *6,000.*
14 (b) 4p on 6p rose 1,450. 225.00
a. Inverted surcharge — 1,250.
b. Double surcharge, one inverted ("b" and "d") —
15 (c) 4p on 6p rose 220.00 42.50
a. Inverted surcharge — 400.00
16 (d) 4p on 6p rose 325.00 50.00
a. Inverted surcharge *1,500.* 500.00
b. Double surcharge, one inverted ("d" and "c" inverted) — *4,250.*
c. Double surcharge, one inverted ("d" inverted and "c") — *6,500.*

No. 17

No. 12 Surcharged with Bar and

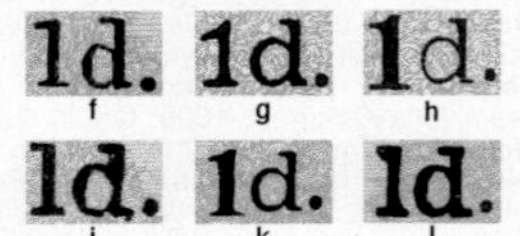

1881

First Printing

17 (f) 1p on 5sh green 120.00 32.50

Second Printing

18 (g) 1p on 5sh green 65.00 32.50
a. Inverted surcharge — *1,250.*
b. Double surcharge *1,450.*
19 (h) 1p on 5sh green 300.00 95.00
a. Inverted surcharge — *1,450.*
b. Double surcharge — *1,650.*
20 (i) 1p on 5sh green 100.00 32.50
a. Double surcharge — *1,325.*
b. Inverted surcharge *2,000.* *1,000.*
21 (k) 1p on 5sh green 600.00 275.00
a. Inverted surcharge — *2,500.*
b. Double surcharge *2,500.*

Third Printing

21C (l) 1p on 5sh green 95.00 32.50
d. Inverted surcharge *875.00*
e. Double surcharge *900.00*
Nos. 17-21C (6) 1,280. 500.00

No. 12 Surcharged

1882

22 A1 ½p on 5sh green 27.50 7.50
a. Double surcharge 575.00 400.00
b. Inverted surcharge *1,500.* *1,000.*

No. 7 Surcharged with Thin Line and

m

n

o

p

q

1882

23 (m) 3p on 4p ultra 100.00 40.00
a. Double surcharge 1,400.
24 (n) 3p on 4p ultra 100.00 20.00
a. Double surcharge 1,400.
25 (o) 3p on 4p ultra 55.00 30.00
a. Double surcharge 1,400.
26 (p) 3p on 4p ultra 275.00 80.00
a. Double surcharge 3,500.
27 (q) 3p on 4p ultra 100.00 25.00
a. Double surcharge 1,400.
Nos. 23-27 (5) 630.00 195.00

No. 6 Surcharged

1888

28 A1 2p on 3p ultra 60.00 2.25
a. Wide "2" at top 77.50 10.00
b. As No. 28, invtd. surch. 350.00
c. As No. 28a, invtd. surch. 825.00
d. Curved base on "2" *1,450.* *650.00*

Nos. 6 and 7 Surcharged

r

s

t

1890-91

29 (r) 1p on 3p ultra ('91) 9.50 1.00
a. Double surcharge 100.00 77.50
b. "1" and "d" wide apart 170.00 135.00
30 (r) 1p on 4p ultra 45.00 12.50
a. Double surcharge 170.00 135.00
b. Triple surcharge *3,250.*
31 (s) 1p on 3p ultra ('91) 27.50 3.00
a. Double surcharge 325.00 300.00
32 (s) 1p on 4p ultra 95.00 60.00
a. Double surcharge 475.00 375.00
33 (t) 1p on 4p ultra *2,500.* *675.00*

No. 6 Surcharged

1892

34 A1 2½p on 3p ultra 21.00 .80
a. Without period 92.50 55.00

No. 6 Surcharged

v

w

x

y

z

1896

35 (v) ½p on 3p ultra 8.50 12.50
a. Double surcharge "v" and "y" 15.50 15.50
36 (w) ½p on 3p ultra 14.50 3.00
a. Double surcharge "w" and "y" 15.00 11.00
37 (x) ½p on 3p ultra 14.50 2.50
38 (y) ½p on 3p ultra 9.00 5.50
a. Double surcharge 14.50 11.00
b. Triple surcharge 77.50 77.50
39 (z) ½p on 3p ultra 14.50 2.50

Surcharged as "v" but "1" with Straight Serif

40 A1 ½p on 3p ultra 15.50 *16.50*
a. Double surcharge, one type "y" 75.00 75.00

Surcharged as "z" but "1" with Straight Serif

41 A1 ½p on 3p ultra 15.50 15.50
a. Double surcharge, one type "y" 75.00 75.00
Nos. 35-41 (7) 92.00 58.00

No. 6 Surcharged

1896

42 A1 ½p on 3p ultra 1.10 .65
a. No period after "Penny" 24.00 *40.00*
b. "Peuny" 24.00 *40.00*
c. Inverted surcharge 65.00 *72.50*
d. Double surch., one inverted 200.00 *225.00*
e. Without bar 10.00
f. With additional surcharge as on Nos. 35-41 37.50
g. As "a", inverted surcharge 2,250.
h. As "b", inverted surcharge 1,750.

No. 6 Surcharged

1897

43 A1 2½p on 3p ultra 12.00 2.00
a. Roman "I" instead of "1" in "½" 185.00 100.00

Issued under British Occupation

Nos. 2-8, 8a, 10-12 Surcharged or Overprinted

Periods in "V.R.I." Level with Bottoms of Letters

1900, Mar.-Apr. Unwmk. ***Perf. 14***

44 A1 ½p on ½p org 5.00 *7.25*
a. No period after "V" 25.00 *35.00*
b. No period after "I" 175.00 175.00
c. "I" and period after "R" omitted 300.00 275.00
f. "½" omitted *210.00* *210.00*
g. Small "½" 65.00 65.00
h. Double surcharge 200.00
i. As "g," double surcharge 575.00
45 A1 1p on 1p violet 3.00 2.00
a. No period after "V" 20.00 18.50
b. "I" and period after "R" omitted 300.00 300.00
d. "1" of "1d" omitted 225.00 225.00
e. "d" omitted 425.00 425.00
f. "1d" omitted, "V.R.I." at top 475.00
45O A1 1p on 1p brown *675.00* *450.00*
y. No period after "V" *4,000.*
46 A1 2p on 2p violet 4.75 3.00
a. No period after "V" 22.00 24.00
b. No period after "R" 360.00 360.00
c. No period after "I" 360.00 360.00
47 A1 '2½' on 3p ultra 22.50 22.50
a. No period after "V" 105.00 105.00
b. Roman "I" in "½" 275.00 275.00
48 A1 3p on 3p ultra 3.25 4.75
a. No period after "V" 25.00 30.00
b. Dbl. surch. one diagonal 600.00
c. Pair, one with surcharge omitted 725.00
j. "3d" omitted 275.00 275.00
k. "V.R.I." omitted 275.00 275.00
49 A1 4p on 4p ultra 11.00 *18.50*
a. No period after "V" 72.50 *82.50*

50 A1 6p on 6p car rose 50.00 45.00
a. No period after "V" 275.00 300.00
b. "6" omitted 340.00 325.00
51 A1 6p on 6p ultra 16.00 7.50
a. No period after "V" 55.00 55.00
c. "6" omitted 95.00 *100.00*
h. "V.R.I." omitted 550.00 425.00
52 A1 1sh on 1sh brown 8.00 3.00
a. No period after "V" 55.00 35.00
c. "1" of "1s" omitted 165.00 155.00
j. "1s" omitted 225.00 220.00
k. "V.R.I." omitted 225.00 220.00
52G A1 1sh on 1sh org *4,100.* *2,750.*
53 A1 5sh on 5sh green 32.50 60.00
a. No period after "V" 300.00 *360.00*
b. "5" omitted 1,100. 1,100.

#47, 47c overprinted "V.R.I." on #43.

No. 45f ("1d" omitted) with "V.R.I." at bottom is a shift which sells for a fifth of the value of the listed item. Varieties such as "V.R.I." omitted, denomination omitted and pair, one without surcharge are also the result of shifts.

For surcharges see Nos. 57, 60.

Nos. 2, 4-12 Surcharged or Overprinted

Periods in "V.R.I." Raised Above Bottoms of Letters

1900-01

44j A1 ½p on ½p orange .35 .25
k. Mixed periods 3.25 2.25
l. Pair, one with level periods 17.50 *21.00*
m. No period after "V" 4.50 *5.00*
n. No period after "I" 45.00 45.00
o. "V" omitted 675.00
p. Small "½" 22.50 *25.00*
q. "1" for "I" in "V.R.I." 10.00
r. Thick "V" 6.00 4.00
45i A1 1p on 1p violet .35 .25
j. Mixed periods 2.75 *3.25*
k. Pair, one with level periods 27.50 *29.00*
l. No period after "V" 4.50 *9.00*
m. No period after "R" 19.00 19.00
n. No period after "I" 19.00 19.00
p. Double surcharge 130.00 120.00
q. Inverted surcharge 425.00
s. Small "1" in "1d" 120.00 120.00
t. "1" for "I" in "V.R.I." 13.00
u. Thick "V" 9.00 .40
v. As "u," invtd. "1" for "I" in "V.R.I." 30.00 30.00
w. As "u," double surcharge 400.00 400.00
z. As "u," no period after "R" 70.00 *75.00*
za. Pair, one without surchage 325.00
zb. Stamp double impression, one inverted 2,750.
46e A1 2p on 2p violet 3.75 .35
f. Mixed periods 9.00 5.50
g. Pair, one with level periods 16.00 *17.00*
h. Inverted surcharge 375.00 375.00
i. Thick "V" 16.50 15.50
j. As "i," invtd. "1" for "I" in "V.R.I." 32.50 *35.00*
47c A1 '2½' on 3p ultra 250.00 250.00
d. Thick "V" 4,250.
f. As "d," Roman "I" on "½" —
48d A1 3p on 3p ultra 2.75 .35
e. Mixed periods 12.00 12.00
f. Pair, one with level periods 26.00 *27.50*
g. Double surcharge 440.00
h. Thick "V" 12.50 *22.50*
i. As "h," invtd. "1" for "I" in "V.R.I." 72.50 *85.00*
l. Double surcharge, one diagonal 600.00
m. As "l", thick "V" *600.00*
n. As "l", mixed periods *7,500.*
o. As "n", thick "V" —
49b A1 4p on 4p ultra 3.25 *5.00*
c. Mixed periods 11.00 *16.00*
d. Pair, one with level periods 24.00 *37.50*
50c A1 6p on 6p car rose 45.00 *55.00*
d. Mixed periods 160.00 *175.00*
e. Pair, one with level periods 300.00 *350.00*
f. Thick "V" *500.00* *525.00*
51d A1 6p on 6p ultra 1.10 .45
e. Mixed periods 12.00 *13.00*
f. Pair, one with level periods 27.50 *32.50*
g. Thick "V" 25.00 37.50
i. "6d" omitted 500.00
52e A1 1sh on 1sh brown 12.00 .50
f. Mixed periods 29.00 25.00
h. Pair, one with level periods 55.00 *55.00*
i. Thick "V" 45.00 14.00
52j A1 1sh on 1sh orange *1,500.* *1,500.*
53c A1 5sh on 5sh green 11.00 *22.50*
d. Mixed periods 400.00 400.00
e. Pair, one with level periods *1,100.*
f. "5" with short flag 65.00 *77.50*
g. Thick "V" 72.50 *60.00*

Stamps with mixed periods have one or two periods level with the bottoms of letters. One stamp in each pane had all periods level. Later settings had several stamps with thick "V." Forgeries of the scarcer varieties exist.

"V.R.I." stands for Victoria Regina Imperatrix. On No. 59, "E.R.I." stands for Edward Rex Imperator.

Cape of Good Hope Stamps of 1893-98 Overprinted

1900 **Wmk. 16**

54 A15 ½p green .70 .25
a. No period after "COLONY" 14.00 *27.50*
b. Double overprint 750.00 800.00
55 A13 2½p ultramarine 9.00 2.00
a. No period after "COLONY" 82.50 82.50

Overprinted as in 1900

1902, May

56 A15 1p carmine rose 2.75 .25
a. No period after "COLONY" 27.00 *37.50*

Nos. 51d, 53c, Surcharged and No. 8b Surcharged like No. 51 but Reading "E.R.I."

Carmine or Vermilion and Black Surcharges

1902 **Unwmk.**

57 A1 4p on 6p on 6p ultra 2.25 4.50
a. Thick "V" 3.00 *11.00*
b. As "a," invtd. "1" instead of "I" 9.00 *32.50*
c. No period after "R" 42.50 *57.50*

Black Surcharge

59 A1 6p on 6p ultra 9.00 *23.00*
a. Double surcharge, one invtd. — —

Orange Surcharge

60 A1 1sh on 5sh on 5sh grn 13.00 *27.50*
a. Thick "V" 19.00 *55.00*
b. "5" with short flag 80.00 *95.00*
c. Double surcharge 1,100.
Nos. 57-60 (3) 24.25 *55.00*

"E.R.I." stands for Edward Rex Imperator.

King Edward VII — A8

"IOSTAGE" Variety

The "IOSTAGE" variety on the 4p is the result of filled in type.

1903-04 **Wmk. 2** **Typo.**

61 A8 ½p yellow green 10.00 2.50
62 A8 1p carmine 14.00 .25
63 A8 2p chocolate 12.00 2.25
64 A8 2½p ultra 9.00 2.75
65 A8 3p violet 11.50 1.50
66 A8 4p olive grn & car 42.50 9.00
67 A8 6p violet & car 9.25 2.50
68 A8 1sh bister & car 55.00 4.50
69 A8 5sh red brn & bl ('04) 175.00 35.00
Nos. 61-69 (9) 338.25 60.25

Some of the above stamps are found with the overprint "C. S. A. R." for use by the Central South African Railway.

Issue dates: 1p, Feb. 3. ½p, 2p, 2½p, 3p, 4p, 6p, 1sh, July 6. 5sh, Oct. 31.

1907-08 **Wmk. 3**

70 A8 ½p yellow green 19.00 1.60
71 A8 1p carmine 12.00 .35
72 A8 4p olive grn & car 5.00 8.25
73 A8 1sh bister & car 85.00 30.00
Nos. 70-73 (4) 121.00 40.20

The "IOSTAGE" variety on the 4p is the result of filled-in type.

Stamps of Orange River Colony were replaced by those of Union of South Africa.

MILITARY STAMP

M1

1899, Oct. 15 **Unwmk.** ***Perf. 12***

M1 M1 black, *bister yellow* 50.00 85.00

No. M1 was provided to members of the Orange Free State army on active service during the Second Boer War. Soldiers' mail carried free was required to bear either No. M1 or be signed by the sender's unit commander.

The stamps were used extensively from Oct. 1899 until the fall of Kroonstad in May 1900.

No. M1 was typeset and printed by Curling & Co., Bloemfontein, in sheets of 20 (5x4), with each row of five containing slightly different types.

Forgeries exist. The most common counterfeits either have 17 pearls, rather than 16, in the top and bottom frames, or omit the periods after "BRIEF" and "FRANKO."

PAKISTAN

'pa-ki-ˌstan

LOCATION — In southern, central Asia
GOVT. — Republic
AREA — 307,293 sq. mi.
POP. — 220,890,000 (2020 est.)
CAPITAL — Islamabad

Pakistan was formed August 14, 1947, when India was divided into the Dominions of the Union of India and Pakistan, with some princely states remaining independent. Pakistan became a republic on March 23, 1956.

Pakistan had two areas made up of all or part of several predominantly Moslem provinces in the northwest and northeast corners of pre-1947 India. West Pakistan consists of the entire provinces of Baluchistan, Sind (Scinde) and "Northwest Frontier" (now Khyber Pukhtunkhwa), and 15 districts of the Punjab. East Pakistan, consisting of the Sylhet district in Assam and 14 districts in Bengal Province, became independent as Bangladesh in December 1971.

The state of Las Bela was incorporated into Pakistan.

12 Pies = 1 Anna
16 Annas = 1 Rupee
100 Paisa = 1 Rupee (1961)

Catalogue values for all unused stamps in this country are for Never Hinged items.

Watermarks

Wmk. 274

Wmk. 351 — Crescent and Star Multiple

Stamps of India, 1937-43, Overprinted in Black

Nos. 1-12

Nos. 13-19

Perf. 13½x14

1947, Oct. 1 **Wmk. 196**

1 A83 3p slate .25 .25
2 A83 ½a rose violet .25 .25
3 A83 9p lt green .25 .25
4 A83 1a car rose .25 .25
4A A84 1a3p bister ('49) 4.75 *4.00*
5 A84 1½a dk purple 2.00 .25
6 A84 2a scarlet .25 .25
7 A84 3a violet .25 .25
8 A84 3½a ultra 1.25 *1.75*
9 A85 4a chocolate .55 .25
10 A85 6a peacock blue 1.50 1.25
11 A85 8a blue violet .65 *.65*
12 A85 12a carmine lake 2.00 .25
13 A81 14a rose violet 3.00 4.25
14 A82 1r brn & slate 8.00 1.50
a. Inverted overprint 250.00
b. Pair, one without ovpt. 950.00
15 A82 2r dk brn & dk vio 4.00 6.00
16 A82 5r dp ultra & dk grn 9.00 10.00
17 A82 10r rose car & dk vio 11.00 10.50
18 A82 15r dk grn & dk brn 90.00 *100.00*
19 A82 25r dk vio & bl vio 100.00 120.00
Nos. 1-19 (20) 239.20 262.15
Set, hinged 135.00

Provisional use of stamps of India with handstamped or printed "PAKISTAN" was authorized in 1947-49. Nos. 4A, 14a 14b exist only as provisional issues.

Used values are for postal cancels. Telegraph cancels (concentric circles) sell for much less.

Constituent Assembly Building, Karachi
A1

Crescent and Urdu Inscription
A2

Designs: 2½a, Karachi Airport entrance. 3a, Lahore Fort gateway.

Unwmk.

1948, July 9 **Engr.** ***Perf. 14***

20 A1 1½a bright ultra 1.25 *2.00*
21 A1 2½a green 1.25 .25
22 A1 3a chocolate 1.25 .30

Perf. 12

23 A2 1r red 1.25 .85
a. Perf. 14 6.00 *25.00*
Nos. 20-23 (4) 5.00 3.40

Pakistan's independence, Aug. 15, 1947.

Examples of No. 23a used on cover are unknown. Used examples of No. 23a are cto.

Scales, Star and Crescent
A3

Star and Crescent
A4

Karachi Airport Building
A5

Karachi Port Authority Building
A6

Khyber Pass — A7

2½a, 3½a, 4a, Sukkur Barrage. 1r, 2r, 5r, Salimullah Hostel.

Perf. 12½, 14 (3a, 10a), 14x13½ (2½a, 3½a, 6a, 12a)

1948-57 **Unwmk.**

24 A3 3p org red, perf. 12½ .25 .25
a. Perf. 13½ ('54) 3.75 1.00
25 A3 6p pur, perf. 12½ 1.25 .25
a. Perf. 13½ ('54) 8.00 5.00
26 A3 9p dk grn, perf. 12½ .55 .25
a. Perf. 13½ ('54) 11.50 1.75
27 A4 1a dark blue .25 .50
28 A4 1½a gray green .25 .25
29 A4 2a orange red 7.00 .70
30 A6 2½a green 9.00 *12.50*
31 A5 3a olive green 8.00 1.00
32 A6 3½a violet blue 8.50 *5.00*
33 A6 4a chocolate 1.25 .25
34 A6 6a deep blue 2.00 .55
35 A6 8a black 1.40 *1.40*
36 A5 10a red 8.00 *10.50*

37 A6 12a red 11.00 1.00

Perf. 14

38 A5 1r ultra 25.00 .25
a. Perf. 13½ ('54) 24.00 12.00
39 A5 2r dark brown 17.50 .80
a. Perf. 13½ ('54) 23.00 11.00

Perf. 13½

40 A5 5r car ('54) 23.00 2.50
a. Perf. 13½x14 17.00 .25

Perf. 13

41 A7 10r rose lilac ('51) 19.00 3.00
a. Perf. 14 22.50 *45.00*
b. Perf. 12 130.00 11.50
42 A7 15r blue green ('57) 27.50 37.50
a. Perf. 14 22.50 *110.00*
b. Perf. 12 18.00 30.00

Perf. 14

43 A7 25r purple 55.00 *150.00*
a. Perf. 13 ('54) 45.00 42.50
b. Perf. 12 42.50 *40.00*
Nos. 24-43 (20) 225.70 228.45
Set, hinged 100.00

Many compound perforations exist.
See No. 259, types A9-A11. For surcharges and overprints see Nos. 124, O14-O26, O35-O37, O41-O43A, O52, O63, O68.
Imperfs of Nos. 24-43 are from proof sheets improperly removed from the printer's archives.

"Quaid-i-Azam" (Great Leader), "Mohammed Ali Jinnah" — A8

1949, Sept. 11 Engr. *Perf. 13½x14*
44 A8 1½a brown 2.00 1.75
45 A8 3a dark green 2.00 1.00
46 A8 10a blk (*English inscriptions*) 7.50 *7.50*
Nos. 44-46 (3) 11.50 10.25

1st anniv. of the death of Mohammed Ali Jinnah (1876-1948), Moslem lawyer, president of All-India Moslem League and first Governor General of Pakistan.

Re-engraved (Crescents Reversed)

A9

A10

A11

Perf. 12½, 13½x14 (3a, 10a), 14x13½ (6a, 12a)

1949-53
47 A10 1a dk blue ('50) 3.50 .75
a. Perf. 13 ('52) 11.00 .25
48 A10 1½a gray green 3.50 .75
a. Perf. 13 ('53) 3.00 .25
49 A10 2a orange red 4.00 .25
a. Perf. 13 ('53) 6.00 .25
50 A9 3a olive green 15.00 1.00
51 A11 6a deep blue ('50) 24.00 2.00
52 A11 8a black ('50) 24.00 2.00
53 A9 10a red 27.50 3.50
54 A11 12a red ('50) 30.00 .50
Nos. 47-54 (8) 131.50 10.75

For overprints see #O27-O31, O38-O40.

Vase and Plate — A12

Star and Crescent, Plane and Hour Glass — A13

Moslem Leaf Pattern A14

Arch and Lamp of Learning A15

1951, Aug. 14 Engr. *Perf. 13*
55 A12 2½a dark red 1.90 1.25
56 A13 3a dk rose lake 1.00 .25
57 A12 3½a dp ultra (Urdu "⅓") 1.25 *8.00*
57A A12 3½a dp ultra (Urdu "3½") ('56) 5.00 6.00
58 A14 4a deep green 1.75 .25
59 A14 6a red orange 1.75 .25
60 A15 8a brown 4.50 .35
61 A15 10a purple 2.00 2.00
62 A13 12a dk slate blue 2.75 .25
Nos. 55-62 (9) 21.90 18.60

Fourth anniversary of independence.
On No. 57, the characters of the Urdu denomination at right appears as "⅓." On the reengraved No. 57A, they read "3½."
Issue date: Dec. 1956.
See Nos. 88, O32-O34.
For surcharges see Nos. 255, 257.

Scinde District Stamp and Camel Train — A16

1952, Aug. 14
63 A16 3a olive green, *citron* 1.00 .85
64 A16 12a dark brown, *salmon* 1.75 .25

5th anniv. of Pakistan's Independence and the cent. of the 1st postage stamps in the Indo-Pakistan sub-continent.

Peak K-2, Karakoram Mountains — A17

1954, Dec. 25
65 A17 2a violet .50 .30

Conquest of K-2, world's 2nd highest mountain peak, in July 1954.

Kaghan Valley A18

Gilgit Mountains A19

Tea Garden, East Pakistan — A20

Designs: 1a, Badshahi Mosque, Lahore. 1½a, Emperor Jahangir's Mausoleum, Lahore. 1r, Cotton field. 2r, River craft and jute field.

1954, Aug. 14 Engr.
66 A18 6p rose violet .25 .25
67 A19 9p blue *5.00* 3.00
68 A19 1a carmine rose .25 .25
69 A18 1½a red .25 .25
70 A20 14a dark green 5.00 .25
71 A20 1r yellow green 12.00 .25
72 A20 2r orange 3.00 .25
Nos. 66-72 (7) 25.75 4.50

Seventh anniversary of independence.
Nos. 66, 69 exist in booklet panes of 4 torn from sheets. Value of booklet, $9.
For overprints & surcharges see #77, 101, 123, 126, O44-O50, O53-O56, O60-O62, O67, O69-O71.

Karnaphuli Paper Mill, East Pakistan (Urdu "½") — A21

6a, Textile mill. 8a, Jute mill. 12a, Sui gas plant.

1955, Aug. 14 Unwmk. *Perf. 13*
73 A21 2½a dk car (Urdu "½") 1.00 *1.50*
73A A21 2½a dk car (Urdu "2½") ('56) 3.50 *1.50*
74 A21 6a dark blue 1.75 .25
75 A21 8a violet 4.00 .25
76 A21 12a car lake & org 4.00 .25
Nos. 73-76 (5) 14.25 3.75

Eighth anniversary of independence.
On No. 73, the characters of the Urdu denomination at right appear as "½." On the reengraved No. 73A, they read "2½."
Issue date: Dec. 1956.
See No. 87. For overprints and surcharges see Nos. 78, 102-103, 256, O51, O58-O59.

Nos. 69 and 76 Overprinted in Ultramarine

1955, Oct. 24
77 A18 1½a red *1.75* *4.50*
78 A21 12a car lake & org *1.75* *3.50*

UN, 10th anniv.
Beware of forgeries. Two settings exists, "United Nations," 1mm to left of normal "N" over "NI". Value set, $32.50.

Map of West Pakistan — A22

1955, Dec. 7 Unwmk. *Perf. 13½x13*
79 A22 1½a dark green 1.30 2.00
80 A22 2a dark brown 1.25 .40
81 A22 12a deep carmine 2.00 .50
Nos. 79-81 (3) 4.55 2.90

West Pakistan unification, Nov. 14, 1955.
Nos. 79-81 from the bottom (eighth) row of the sheet are 41.5mm tall instead of 40.5mm. Value, $4 each.

National Assembly — A23

1956, Mar. 23 Litho. *Perf. 13x12½*
82 A23 2a green .75 .25

Proclamation of the Republic of Pakistan, Mar. 23, 1956.

Crescent and Star — A24

1956, Aug. 14 Engr. *Perf. 13*
83 A24 2a red .60 .25

Ninth anniversary of independence.
For surcharges and overprints see Nos. 127, O57, O72-O73.

Map of East Pakistan — A25

1956, Oct. 15 *Perf. 13½x13*
84 A25 1½a dark green .60 *1.50*
85 A25 2a dark brown .60 .25
86 A25 12a deep red .60 *1.25*
Nos. 84-86 (3) 1.80 3.00

1st Session at Dacca (East Pakistan) of the National Assembly of Pakistan.
Nos. 84-86 from the bottom (eighth) row of the sheet are 1mm taller. Value, $4 each.

Redrawn Types of 1951, 1955 and

Orange Tree — A26

Perf. 13x13½, 13½x13
1957, Mar. 23 Engr.
87 A21 2½a dark carmine .25 .25
88 A12 3½a bright blue .35 .25
89 A26 10r dk green & orange .90 .25
Nos. 87-89 (3) 1.50 .75

Nos. 87-89 inscribed "Pakistan" in English, Urdu and Bengali. Denomination in English only.
Islamic Republic of Pakistan, 1st anniv.
See Nos. 95, 258, 475A. For surcharge and overprint see Nos. 159, O64.

Flag and Broken Chain — A27

1957, May 10 Litho. *Perf. 13*
90 A27 1½a green .50 .60
91 A27 12a blue 1.25 .25

Cent. of the struggle for Independence (Indian Mutiny).
Examples of Nos. 90-91 exist that are 1mm taller than other stamps from the sheet. Value, $4 each.

Industrial Plants and Roses as Symbols of Progress — A28

1957, Aug. 14 Unwmk. *Perf. 13½*
92 A28 1½a light ultra .25 .40
93 A28 4a orange vermilion .50 *1.50*
94 A28 12a red lilac .40 .50
Nos. 92-94 (3) 1.15 2.40

Tenth anniversary of independence.

Type of 1957

Design: 15r, Coconut Tree.

1958, Mar. 23 Engr. *Perf. 13½x13*
95 A26 15r rose lilac & red 2.50 1.50

Issued to commemorate the second anniversary of the Islamic Republic of Pakistan.

Verse of Iqbal Poem — A29

1958, Apr. 21 Photo. *Perf. 14½x14*
Black Inscriptions
96 A29 1½a citron .50 1.00
97 A29 2a orange brown .50 .25
98 A29 14a aqua *2.50* .25
Nos. 96-98 (3) 3.50 *1.50*

20th anniv. of the death of Mohammad Iqbal (1877-1938), Moslem poet and philosopher.

Globe and Book — A30

1958, Dec. 10 Litho. *Perf. 13*
99 A30 1½a Prus blue .25 .25
100 A30 14a dark brown .50 *.25*

10th anniv. of the signing of the Universal Declaration of Human Rights.

Nos. 66 and 75 Overprinted

1958, Dec. 28 Engr. *Perf. 13*

101 A18 6p rose violet .40 .25
102 A21 8a violet .75 .25

2nd National Boy Scout Jamboree held at Chittagong, Dec. 28-Jan. 4.

Numerous plate flaws exist for Nos. 101-102. Value: $2 each.

No. 74 Overprinted in Red

1959, Oct. 27

103 A21 6a dark blue 1.00 .25

First anniversary of the 1958 Revolution.

Red Cross — A31

Engr.; Cross Typo.

1959, Nov. 19 Unwmk. *Perf. 13*

104 A31 2a green & red .30 .25
105 A31 10a dk blue & red .60 .25

Armed Forces Emblem — A32

1960, Jan. 10 Litho. *Perf. 13*

106 A32 2a blue grn, red & ultra .50 .25
107 A32 14a ultra & red 1.00 .25

Issued for Armed Forces Day.

Map Showing Disputed Areas — A33

1960, Mar. 23 Engr. Unwmk.

108 A33 6p purple .40 .25
109 A33 2a copper red .60 .25
110 A33 8a green 1.20 .25
111 A33 1r blue 1.90 .25
Nos. 108-111 (4) 4.10 1.00

Publicizing the border dispute with India over Jammu and Kashmir, Junagarh and Manavadar.

For overprints and surcharges see Nos. 122, 125, 128, 178, O65-O66, O74-O75.

Uprooted Oak Emblem — A34

1960, Apr. 7

112 A34 2a carmine rose .30 .25
113 A34 10a green .30 *.25*

Issued to publicize World Refugee Year, July 1, 1959-June 30, 1960.

House, Field and Column (Allegory of Democratic Development) — A35

1960, Oct. 27 Photo. *Perf. 13*

114 A35 2a brown, pink & grn .25 .25
a. Green & pink omitted 27.50
115 A35 14a multicolored .50 *.25*

Revolution Day, Oct. 27, 1960.

No. 114a is easily counterfeited.

Punjab Agricultural College, Lyallpur — A36

Design: 8a, College shield.

1960, Oct. Engr. *Perf. 12½x14*

116 A36 2a rose red & gray blue .25 .25
117 A36 8a lilac & green .35 *.25*

50th anniv. of the Punjab Agricultural College, Lyallpur.

Caduceus, College Emblem — A37

1960, Nov. 16 Photo. *Perf. 13½x13*

118 A37 2a blue, yel & blk .65 .25
119 A37 14a car rose, blk & emerald 1.75 1.00

King Edward Medical College, Lahore, cent.

Map of South-East Asia and Commission Emblem — A38

1960, Dec. 5 Engr. *Perf. 13*

120 A38 14a red orange 1.00 *.25*

Conf. of the Commission on Asian and Far Eastern Affairs of the Intl. Chamber of Commerce, Karachi, Dec. 5-9.

"Kim's Gun" and Scout Badge — A39

Perf. 12½x14

1960, Dec. 24 Unwmk.

121 A39 2a dk green, car & yel .85 .25

3rd Natl. Boy Scout Jamboree, Lahore, Dec. 24-31.

No. 110 Ovptd. in Red

1961, Feb. 12

122 A33 8a green .95 1.75

10th Lahore Stamp Exhibition, Feb. 12.

New Currency

Nos. 24, 68-69, 83, 108-109 Surcharged with New Value in Paisa

1961 *Perf. 13*

123 A18 1p on 1½a red .40 .25
124 A3 2p on 3p orange red .25 .25
125 A33 3p on 6p purple .25 .25
126 A19 7p on 1a car rose .40 .25
127 A24 13p on 2a red .40 .25
128 A33 13p on 2a copper red .30 .25
Nos. 123-128 (6) 2.00 1.50

Various violet handstamped surcharges were applied to a variety of regular-issue stamps. Most of these repeat the denomination of the basic stamp and add the new value. Example: "8 Annas (50 Paisa)" on No. 75. Many errors exist from printer's waste.

For overprints see Nos. O74-O75.

Many errors exist from No. 123 onwards on stamps printed within Pakistan. These are generally printer's waste.

Khyber Pass — A40

Chota Sona Masjid Gate — A41

Design: 10p, 13p, 25p, 40p, 50p, 75p, 90p, Shalimar Gardens, Lahore.

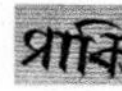

Type I

Type II

Two types of 1p, 2p and 5p:

I — First Bengali character beside "N" lacks appendage at left side of loop.

II — This character has a downward-pointing appendage at left side of loop, correcting "sh" to read "p".

On Nos. 129, 130, 132 the corrections were made individually on the plates, and each stamp may differ slightly. On No. 131a, the corrected letter is more clearly corrected, and the added appendage comes close to, almost touching, the leg of the first Bengali character.

1961-63 Engr. *Perf. 13½x14*

129 A40 1p violet (II) .50 .25
a. Type I 1.50 .25
130 A40 2p rose red (II) .50 .25
a. Type I 1.50 .25
131 A40 3p magenta .75 .25
a. Retouched plate 8.00 5.00
132 A40 5p ultra (II) 4.50 1.00
a. Type I 2.50 .25
133 A40 7p emerald .90 .25
134 A40 10p brown .25 .25
135 A40 13p blue vio .25 .25
136 A40 25p dark blue ('62) 2.75 .25
137 A40 40p dull purple ('62) .75 .25
138 A40 50p dull green ('62) .40 .25
139 A40 75p dk carmine ('62) .80 .70
140 A40 90p lt olive grn ('62) 1.00 .70

Perf. 13½x13

141 A41 1r vermilion ('63) 7.00 .25
142 A41 1.25r purple 1.00 1.75
143 A41 2r orange ('63) 5.00 .25
144 A41 5r green ('63) 6.00 3.00
Nos. 129-144 (16) 32.35 9.90

See #200-203. For surcharge and overprints see Nos. 184, O76-O82, O85-O93A.

Designs Redrawn

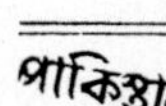

1961-62 Bengali Inscription

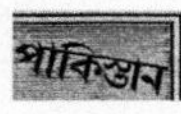

Redrawn Bengali Inscription

Bengali inscription redrawn with straight connecting line across top of characters. Shading of scenery differs, especially in Shalimar Gardens design where reflection is strengthened and trees at right are composed of horizontal lines instead of vertical lines and dots.

Designs as before; 15p, 20p, Shalimar Gardens.

1963-70 *Perf. 13½x14*

129b A40 1p violet .25 .25
130b A40 2p rose red ('64) 3.00 .25
131b A40 3p magenta ('70) 15.00 7.00
132b A40 5p ultra .25 .25
133a A40 7p emerald ('64) 7.00 3.00
134a A40 10p brown .25 .25
135a A40 13p blue violet .25 .25
135B A40 15p rose lilac ('64) .25 .25
135C A40 20p dull green ('70) .35 .25
136a A40 25p dark blue 10.00 .25
137a A40 40p dull purple ('64) .35 .25
138a A40 50p dull green ('64) .35 .25
139a A40 75p dark carmine ('64) .90 .70
140a A40 90p lt olive green ('64) 1.00 1.00
Nos. 129b-140a (14) 39.20 14.20

Many exists imperf.

For overprints see #174, O76b, O77b, O78a, O79b, O80a, O81a, O82a, O83-O84A, O85a, O86a.

Warsak Dam, Kabul River — A42

1961, July 1 Engr. *Perf. 12½x13½*

150 A42 40p black & lt ultra .70 .25

Dedication of hydroelectric Warsak Project.

Symbolic Flower A43

1961, Oct. 2 Unwmk. *Perf. 14*

151 A43 13p greenish blue .50 .25
152 A43 90p red lilac 1.20 .25

Issued for Children's Day.

Roses — A44

1961, Nov. 4 *Perf. 13½x13*

153 A44 13p deep green & ver .40 .25
154 A44 90p blue & vermilion .90 .90

Cooperative Day.

Police Crest and Traffic Policeman's Hand — A45

1961, Nov. 30 Photo. *Perf. 13x12½*

155 A45 13p dk blue, sil & blk .60 .25
156 A45 40p red, silver & blk 1.10 .25

Centenary of the police force.

"Eagle Locomotive, 1861" — A46

Design: 50pa, Diesel Engine, 1961.

1961, Dec. 31 *Perf. 13½x14*

157 A46 13p yellow, green & blk .75 .80
158 A46 50p green, blk & yellow 1.00 1.50

Centenary of Pakistan railroads.

No. 87 Surcharged in Red with New Value, Boeing 720-B Jetliner and: "FIRST JET FLIGHT KARACHI-DACCA"

1962, Feb. 6 Engr. *Perf. 13*

159 A21 13p on 2½a dk carmine 1.75 1.25

1st jet flight from Karachi to Dacca, Feb. 6, 1962.

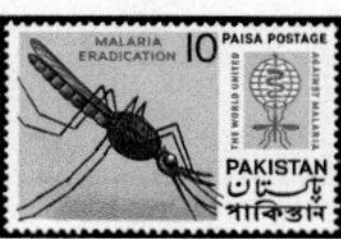

Mosquito and Malaria Eradication Emblem — A47

13p, Dagger pointing at mosquito, and emblem.

1962, Apr. 7 Photo. *Perf. 13½x14*

160 A47 10p multicolored .45 .25
161 A47 13p multicolored .45 .25

WHO drive to eradicate malaria.

Map of Pakistan and Jasmine A48

1962, June 8 Unwmk. *Perf. 12*

162 A48 40p grn, yel grn & gray 1.15 .25

Introduction of new Pakistan Constitution.

Soccer — A49

13p, Hockey & Olympic gold medal. 25p, Squash rackets & British squash rackets championship cup. 40p, Cricket & Ayub challenge cup.

1962, Aug. 14 Engr. *Perf. 12½x13½*

163 A49 7p blue & black .25 .25
164 A49 13p green & black .60 1.50
165 A49 25p lilac & black .25 .25
166 A49 40p brown org & blk 3.00 2.25
Nos. 163-166 (4) 4.10 4.25

Marble Fruit Dish and Clay Flask — A50

13p, Sporting goods. 25p, Camel skin lamp, brass jug. 40p, Wooden powder bowl, cane basket. 50p, Inlaid box, brassware.

1962, Nov. 10 *Perf. 13½x13*

167 A50 7p dark red .25 .25
168 A50 13p dark green 1.50 1.50
169 A50 25p bright purple .25 .25
170 A50 40p yellow green .25 .25
171 A50 50p dull red .25 .25
Nos. 167-171 (5) 2.50 2.50

Pakistan Intl. Industries Fair, Oct. 12-Nov. 20, publicizing Pakistan's small industries.

Children's Needs — A51

1962, Dec. 11 Photo. *Perf. 13½x14*

172 A51 13p blue, plum & blk .40 .25
173 A51 40p multicolored .40 .25

16th anniv. of UNICEF.

No. 135a Overprinted in Red: "U.N. FORCE W. IRIAN"

1963, Feb. 15 Engr. Unwmk.

174 A40 13p blue violet .25 2.00

Issued to commemorate the dispatch of Pakistani troops to West New Guinea.

Camel, Bull, Dancing Horse and Drummer — A52

1963, Mar. 13 Photo. *Perf. 12*

175 A52 13p multicolored .25 .25

National Horse and Cattle Show, 1963.

Wheat and Tractor — A53

Design: 50p, Hands and heap of rice.

1963, Mar. 21 Engr. *Perf. 12½x13½*

176 A53 13p brown orange 3.75 .25
177 A53 50p brown 5.00 .65

FAO "Freedom from Hunger" campaign.

No. 109 Surcharged with New Value and: "INTERNATIONAL/DACCA STAMP/EXHIBITION/1963"

1963, Mar. 23 *Perf. 13*

178 A33 13p on 2a copper red .60 .50

International Stamp Exhibition at Dacca.

Centenary Emblem — A54

Engr. and Typo.

1963, June 25 *Perf. 13½x12½*

179 A54 40p dark gray & red 2.50 .25

International Red Cross, cent.

Paharpur Stupa — A55

Designs: 13p, Cistern, Mohenjo-Daro, vert. 40p, Stupas, Taxila. 50pa, Stupas, Mainamati.

Perf. 12½x13½, 13½x12½

1963, Sept. 16 Engr. Unwmk.

180 A55 7p ultra .60 .25
181 A55 13p brown .60 .25
182 A55 40p carmine rose 1.10 .25
183 A55 50p dark violet 1.10 .25
Nos. 180-183 (4) 3.40 1.00

No. 131 Surcharged and Overprinted: "100 YEARS OF P.W.D. OCTOBER, 1963"

1963, Oct. 7 *Perf. 13½x14*

184 A40 13p on 3pa magenta .25 .25

Centenary of Public Works Department.

Atatürk Mausoleum, Ankara — A56

1963, Nov. 10 *Perf. 13x13½*

185 A56 50p red .50 .25

25th anniv. of the death of Kemal Atatürk, pres. of Turkey.

Globe and UNESCO Emblem — A57

1963, Dec. 10 Photo. *Perf. 13½x14*

186 A57 50p dk brn, vio blue & red .45 .25

15th anniv. of the Universal Declaration of Human Rights.

Multan Thermal Power Station — A58

1963, Dec. 25 Engr. *Perf. 12½x13½*

187 A58 13p ultra .25 .25

Issued to mark the opening of the Multan Thermal Power Station.

Type of 1961-63

Perf. 13½x13

1963-65 Engr. Wmk. 351

200 A41 1r vermilion 1.50 .25
201 A41 1.25r purple ('64) 3.00 2.00
202 A41 2r orange 1.25 .25
203 A41 5r green ('65) 7.50 .90
Nos. 200-203 (4) 13.25 3.40

For overprints see Nos. O92-O93A.

A59

13p, Temple of Thot, Dakka, and Queen Nefertari with Goddesses Hathor and Isis. 50p, Ramses II, Abu Simbel, and View of Nile.

Perf. 13x13½

1964, Mar. 30 Unwmk.

204 A59 13p brick red & turq blue .60 .25
205 A59 50p black & rose lilac 1.20 .25

UNESCO world campaign to save historic monuments in Nubia.

Pakistan Pavilion and Unisphere — A60

1.25r, Pakistan pavilion, Unisphere, vert.

Perf. 12½x14, 14x12½

1964, Apr. 22 Engr. Unwmk.

206 A60 13p ultramarine .25 .25
207 A60 1.25r dp orange & ultra .45 .25

New York World's Fair, 1964-65.

Mausoleum of Shah Abdul Latif — A61

1964, June 25 *Perf. 13½x13*

208 A61 50p magenta & ultra 1.00 .25

Bicentenary (?) of the death of Shah Abdul Latif of Bhit (1689-1752).

Examples of No. 208 exist that are 1mm taller than other stamps from the sheet. Value, $4.

Mausoleum of Jinnah — A62

Design: 15p, Mausoleum, horiz.

1964, Sept. 11 Unwmk. *Perf. 13*

209 A62 15p green 1.00 .25
210 A62 50p greenish gray 2.00 .25

16th anniv. of the death of Mohammed Ali Jinnah (1876-1948), the Quaid-i-Azam (Great Leader), founder and president of Pakistan.

Bengali Alphabet on Slate and Slab with Urdu Alphabet — A63

1964, Oct. 5 Engr.

211 A63 15p brown .25 .25

Issued for Universal Children's Day.

West Pakistan University of Engineering and Technology A64

1964, Dec. 21 *Perf. 12½x14*

212 A64 15p henna brown .25 .25

1st convocation of the West Pakistan University of Engineering & Technology, Lahore, Dec. 1964.

Eyeglasses and Book — A65

Perf. 13x13½

1965, Feb. 28 Litho. Unwmk.

213 A65 15p yellow & ultra .25 .25

Issued to publicize aid for the blind.

ITU Emblem, Telegraph Pole and Transmission Tower — A66

1965, May 17 Engr. *Perf. 12½x14*

214 A66 15p deep claret 1.90 .30

Cent. of the ITU.

ICY Emblem — A67

1965, June 26 Litho. *Perf. 13½*

215 A67 15p blue & black 1.25 .25
216 A67 50p yellow & green 1.75 .40

International Cooperation Year, 1965.

Hands Holding Book — A68

50p, Map & flags of Turkey, Iran & Pakistan.

Perf. 13½x13, 13x12½

1965, July 21 Litho. Unwmk.

Size: 46x35mm

217 A68 15p org brn, dk brn & buff .25 .25

Size: 54x30½mm

218 A68 50p multicolored 1.10 .25

1st anniv. of the signing of the Regional Cooperation for Development Pact by Turkey, Iran and Pakistan.

See Iran 1327-1328, Turkey 1648-1649.

Tanks, Army Emblem and Soldier — A69

Designs: 15p, Navy emblem, corvette No. O204 and officer. 50p, Air Force emblem, two F-104 Starfighters and pilot.

1965, Dec. 25 Litho. *Perf. 13½x13*

219 A69 7p multicolored .70 .25
220 A69 15p multicolored 1.50 .25
221 A69 50p multicolored 2.50 .30
Nos. 219-221 (3) 4.70 .80

Issued to honor the Pakistani armed forces.

Emblems of Pakistan Armed Forces — A70

1966, Feb. 13 Litho. *Perf. 13½x13*

222 A70 15p buff, grn & dk bl 1.00 .25

Issued for Armed Forces Day.

Atomic Reactor, Islamabad — A71

Unwmk.

1966, Apr. 30 Engr. *Perf. 13*
223 A71 15p black .25 .25

Pakistan's first atomic reactor.

Habib Bank Emblem — A72

Perf. 12½x13½

1966, Aug. 25 Litho. Unwmk.
224 A72 15p brown, org & dk grn .25 .25

25th anniversary of the Habib Bank.

Boy and Girl — A73

1966, Oct. 3 Litho. *Perf. 13x13½*
225 A73 15p multicolored .25 .25

Issued for Children's Day.

UNESCO Emblem — A74

1966, Nov. 24 Unwmk. *Perf. 14*
226 A74 15p multicolored 4.00 .30

20th anniv. of UNESCO.

Secretariat Buildings, Islamabad, Flag and Pres. Mohammed Ayub Khan — A75

1966, Nov. 29 Litho. *Perf. 13*
227 A75 15p multicolored .30 .25
228 A75 50p multicolored .60 .25

Publicizing the new capital, Islamabad.

Avicenna — A76

1966, Dec. 3 *Perf. 13½*
229 A76 15p sal pink & slate grn .30 .25

Issued to publicize the Health Institute.

Mohammed Ali Jinnah — A77

Design: 50p, Different frame.

Lithographed and Engraved

1966, Dec. 25 Unwmk. *Perf. 13*
230 A77 15p orange, blk & bl .25 .25
231 A77 50p lilac, blk & vio bl .35 .25

90th anniv. of the birth of Mohammed Ali Jinnah (1876-1948), 1st Governor General of Pakistan.

ITY Emblem A78

1967, Jan. 1 Litho.
232 A78 15p bis brn, blue & blk .25 .25

International Tourist Year, 1967.

Red Crescent Emblem — A79

1967, Jan. 10 Litho. *Perf. 13½*
233 A79 15p brn, brn org & red .25 .25

Tuberculosis eradication campaign.

Scout Sign and Emblem — A80

Perf. 12½x13½

1967, Jan. 29 Photo.
234 A80 15p dp plum & brn org .25 .25

4th National Pakistan Jamboree.
"Faisa" is a plate flaw, not an error. Value, unused or used, $5.

Justice Holding Scales — A81

Unwmk.

1967, Feb. 17 Litho. *Perf. 13*
235 A81 15p multicolored .25 .25

Centenary of High Court of West Pakistan.

Mohammad Iqbal — A82

1967, Apr. 21 Litho. *Perf. 13*
236 A82 15p red & brown .25 .25
237 A82 1r dk green & brn .40 .25

90th anniv. of the birth of Mohammad Iqbal (1877-1938), poet and philosopher.

Flag of Valor A83

1967, May 15 Litho. *Perf. 13*
238 A83 15p multicolored .25 .25

Flag of Valor awarded to the cities of Lahore, Sialkot and Sargodha.

Star and "20" — A84

1967, Aug. 14 Photo. Unwmk.
239 A84 15p red & slate green .25 .25

20th anniversary of independence.

Rice Plant and Globe — A85

Cotton Plant, Bale and Cloth — A86

Design: 50p, Raw jute, bale and cloth.

1967, Sept. 26 Photo. *Perf. 13x13½*
240 A85 10p dk blue & yellow .25 .25

Perf. 13

241 A86 15p orange, bl grn & yel .25 .25
242 A86 50p blue grn, brn & tan .25 .25
Nos. 240-242 (3) .75 .75

Issued to publicize major export products.

Toys — A87

1967, Oct. 2 Litho. *Perf. 13*
243 A87 15p multicolored .25 .25

Issued for International Children's Day.

Shah and Empress Farah of Iran — A88

Lithographed and Engraved

1967, Oct. 26 *Perf. 13*
244 A88 50p yellow, blue & lilac 1.50 .40

Coronation of Shah Mohammed Riza Pahlavi and Empress Farah of Iran.

"Each for all, . . ." — A89

1967, Nov. 4 Litho. *Perf. 13*
245 A89 15p multicolored .25 .25

Cooperative Day, 1967.

Mangla Dam — A90

1967, Nov. 23 Litho. *Perf. 13*
246 A90 15p multicolored .25 .25

Indus Basin Project, harnessing the Indus River for flood control and irrigation.

"Fight Against Cancer" — A91

1967, Dec. 26
247 A91 15p red & dk brown .70 .25

Issued to publicize the fight against cancer.

Human Rights Flame — A92

1968, Jan. 31 Photo. *Perf. 14x12½*
248 A92 15p Prus green & red .25 .25
249 A92 50p yellow, silver & red .25 .25

International Human Rights Year 1968.

Agricultural University and Produce — A93

1968, Mar. 28 Litho. *Perf. 13½*
250 A93 15p multicolored .25 .25

Issued to publicize the first convocation of the East Pakistan Agricultural University.

WHO Emblem — A94

1968, Apr. 7 Photo. *Perf. 13½x12½*
251 A94 15p emerald & orange .25 .25
252 A94 50p orange & dk blue .25 .25

20th anniv. of WHO. "Pais" is a plate flaw, not an error. Value $2.

Kazi Nazrul Islam — A95

Lithographed and Engraved

1968, June 25 Unwmk. *Perf. 13*
253 A95 15p dull yellow & brown .40 .25
254 A95 50p rose & brown .90 .25

Kazi Nazrul Islam, poet and composer.

Nos. 56, 61 and 74 Surcharged with New Value and Bars in Black or Red

1968, Sept. Engr. *Perf. 13*
255 A13 4p on 3a dk rose lake 1.00 *1.75*
256 A21 4p on 6a dk blue (R) 1.25 *1.75*
257 A15 60p on 10a purple (R) 1.00 .35
a. Black surcharge .35 2.00
Nos. 255-257 (3) 3.25 3.85

Types of 1948-57

1968 Wmk. 351 Engr. *Perf. 13*
258 A26 10r dk grn & org 5.00 5.50
259 A7 25r purple 8.00 13.00

Children with Hoops — A96

Unwmk.

1968, Oct. 7 Litho. *Perf. 13*
260 A96 15p buff & multi .25 .25

Issued for International Children's Day.

Symbolic of Political Reforms A97

Designs: 15p, Agricultural and industrial development. 50p, Defense. 60p, Scientific and cultural advancement.

1968, Oct. 27 Litho. *Perf. 13*
261 A97 10p multicolored .25 .40
262 A97 15p multicolored .25 .25
263 A97 50p multicolored 2.00 .35
264 A97 60p multicolored .50 1.40
Nos. 261-264 (4) 3.00 2.40

Development Decade, 1958-1968.

Chittagong Steel Mill — A98

1969, Jan. 7 Unwmk. *Perf. 13*
265 A98 15p lt gray grn, lt blue & blk .25 .25

Opening of Pakistan's first steel mill.

Family of Four — A99

1969, Jan. 14 Litho. *Perf. 13½*
266 A99 15p lt blue & plum .25 .25

Issued to publicize family planning.

Hockey Player and Medal — A100

1969, Jan. 30 Photo. *Perf. 13½*
267 A100 15p green, lt bl, blk & gold 1.00 .40
268 A100 1r grn, sal pink, blk & gold 2.50 .90

Pakistan's hockey victory at the 19th Olympic Games in Mexico.

Mirza Ghalib A101

1969, Feb. 15 Litho. *Perf. 13*
269 A101 15p blue & multi .25 .25
270 A101 50p multicolored .60 .25

Mirza Ghalib (Asad Ullab Beg Khan, 1797-1869), poet who modernized the Urdu language.

Dacca Railroad Station — A102

1969, Apr. 27 Litho. *Perf. 13*
271 A102 15p yel, grn, blk & dl bl .90 .30

Opening of the new railroad station in Kamalpur area of Dacca.

ILO Emblem and Ornamental Border — A103

1969, May 15 Litho. *Perf. 13½*
272 A103 15p brt grn & ocher .25 .25
273 A103 50p car rose & ocher .50 .25

50th anniv. of the ILO.

Lady on Balcony, Mogul Miniature, Pakistan — A104

50p, Lady Serving Wine, Safavi miniature, Iran. 1r, Sultan Suleiman Receiving Sheik Abdul Latif, 16th cent. miniature, Turkey.

1969, July 21 Litho. *Perf. 13*
274 A104 20p multicolored .25 .25
275 A104 50p multicolored .25 .25
276 A104 1r multicolored .25 .25
Nos. 274-276 (3) .75 .75

5th anniv. of the signing of the Regional Cooperation for Development Pact by Turkey, Iran and Pakistan.
See Iran 1513-1515, Turkey 1813-1815.

Eastern Refinery, Chittagong — A105

1969, Sept. 14 Photo. *Perf. 13½*
277 A105 20p yel, blk & vio bl .25 .25

Opening of the 1st oil refinery in East Pakistan.

Children Playing A106

1969, Oct. 6 *Perf. 13*
278 A106 20p blue & multi .30 .25

Issued for Universal Children's Day.

Japanese Doll, Map of Dacca-Tokyo Pearl Route — A107

1969, Nov. 1 Litho. *Perf. 13½x13*
279 A107 20p multicolored .65 .25
280 A107 50p ultra & multi .90 .30

Inauguration of the Pakistan International Airways' Dacca-Tokyo "Pearl Route."

Reflection of Light Diagram A108

1969, Nov. 4 *Perf. 13*
281 A108 20p multicolored .25 .25

Alhazen (abu-Ali al Hasan ibn-al-Haytham, 965-1039), astronomer and optician.

Vickers Vimy and London-Darwin Route over Karachi — A109

1969, Dec. 2 Photo. *Perf. 13½x13*
282 A109 50p multicolored 2.00 .40

50th anniv. of the 1st England to Australia flight.

View of EXPO '70, Sun Tower, Flags of Pakistan, Iran and Turkey — A110

1970, Feb. 15 Litho. *Perf. 13*
283 A110 50p multicolored .25 .25

Issued to publicize EXPO '70 International Exhibition, Osaka, Japan, Mar. 15-Sept. 13.

UPU Headquarters, Bern — A111

1970, May 20 Litho. *Perf. 13½x13*
284 A111 20p multicolored .25 .25
285 A111 50p multicolored .25 .25

Opening of new UPU headquarters in Bern.
A souvenir sheet of 2 exists, inscribed "U.P.U. Day 9th Oct. 1971". It contains stamps similar to Nos. 284-285, imperf. Value, $25.

UN Headquarters, New York — A112

Design: 50p, UN emblem.

1970, June 26
286 A112 20p green & multi .25 .25
287 A112 50p violet & multi .25 .25

25th anniversary of the United Nations.

Education Year Emblem and Open Book — A113

1970, July 6 Litho. *Perf. 13*
288 A113 20p blue & multi .25 .25
289 A113 50p orange & multi .25 .25

International Education Year, 1970.

Saiful Malook Lake, Pakistan — A114

Designs: 50p, Seeyo-Se-Pol Bridge, Esfahan, Iran. 1r, View, Fethiye, Turkey.

1970, July 21
290 A114 20p yellow & multi .25 .25
291 A114 50p yellow & multi .35 .25
292 A114 1r yellow & multi .40 .25
Nos. 290-292 (3) 1.00 .75

6th anniv. of the signing of the Regional Cooperation for Development Pact by Pakistan, Iran and Turkey.
See Iran 1558-1560, Turkey 1857-1859.

Asian Productivity Year Emblem — A115

1970, Aug. 18 Photo. *Perf. 12½x14*
293 A115 50p black, yel & grn .25 .25

Asian Productivity Year, 1970.

Dr. Maria Montessori — A116

1970, Aug. 31 Litho. *Perf. 13*
294 A116 20p red & multi .25 .25
295 A116 50p multicolored .25 .25

Maria Montessori (1870-1952) Italian educator and physician.

Tractor and Fertilizer Factory A117

1970, Sept. 12
296 A117 20p yel grn & brn org .25 .40

10th Regional Food and Agricultural Organization Conf. for the Near East in Islamabad.

Boy, Girl, Open Book — A118

1970, Oct. 5 Photo. *Perf. 13*
297 A118 20p multicolored .25 .25

Issued for Children's Day.

Flag and Inscription — A119

1970, Dec. 7 Litho. *Perf. 13½x13*
298 A119 20p violet & green .25 .25
299 A119 20p brt pink & green .25 .25

No. 298 inscribed "Elections for National Assembly 7th Dec. 1970," No. 299 inscribed "Elections for Provincial Assemblies 17th Dec. 1970."

Emblem and Burning of Al Aqsa Mosque A120

1970, Dec. 26 ***Perf. 13½x12½***
300 A120 20p multicolored 1.25 .25

Islamic Conference of Foreign Ministers, Karachi, Dec. 26-28.

Coastal Embankment A121

1971, Feb. 25 **Litho.** ***Perf. 13***
301 A121 20p multicolored .25 .25

Development of coastal embankments in East Pakistan.

Men of Different Races — A122

1971, Mar. 21 **Litho.** ***Perf. 13***
302 A122 20p multicolored .25 .25
303 A122 50p lilac & multi .25 .25

Intl. Year against Racial Discrimination.

Cement Factory, Daudkhel A123

1971, July 1 **Litho.** ***Perf. 13***
304 A123 20p purple, blk & brn .25 .25

20th anniversary of Colombo Plan.

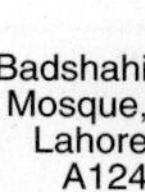

Badshahi Mosque, Lahore A124

Designs: 10pa, Mosque of Selim, Edirne, Turkey. 50pa, Religious School, of Chaharbagh, Isfahan, Iran, vert.

1971, July 21 **Litho.** ***Perf. 13***
305 A124 10p red & multi .25 .25
306 A124 20p green & multi .25 .25
307 A124 50p blue & multi .50 .30
Nos. 305-307 (3) 1.00 .80

7th anniversary of Regional Cooperation among Pakistan, Iran and Turkey.
See Iran 1599-1601, Turkey 1886-1888.

Electric Train and Boy with Toy Locomotive — A125

1971, Oct. 4 **Litho.** ***Perf. 13***
308 A125 20p slate & multi 1.50 .50

Children's Day.

Messenger and Statue of Cyrus the Great — A126

1971, Oct. 15
309 A126 10p green & multi .30 .25
310 A126 20p blue & multi .50 .30
311 A126 50p red & multi .90 .50
Nos. 309-311 (3) 1.70 1.05

2500th anniversary of the founding of the Persian Empire by Cyrus the Great.
A souvenir sheet of 3 contains stamps similar to Nos. 309-311, imperf. Value, $52.50.

Hockey Player and Cup — A127

1971, Oct. 24
312 A127 20p red & multi 2.00 .50

First World Hockey Cup, Barcelona, Spain, Oct. 15-24.

Great Bath at Mohenjo-Daro — A128

1971, Nov. 4
313 A128 20p dp org, dk brn & blk .25 .25

25th anniv. of UNESCO.

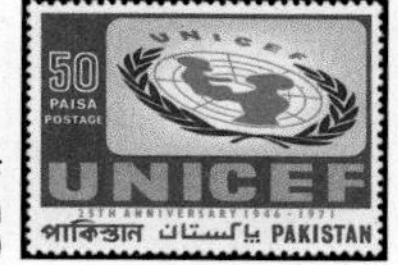
UNICEF Emblem A129

1971, Dec. 11 **Litho.** ***Perf. 13***
314 A129 50p dull bl, org & grn .25 .25

25th anniv. of UNICEF.

King Hussein and Jordan Flag — A130

1971, Dec. 25
315 A130 20p blue & multi .25 .25

50th anniversary of the Hashemite Kingdom of Jordan.

Pakistan Hockey Federation Emblem, and Cup — A131

1971, Dec. 31
316 A131 20p yellow & multi 2.75 .75

Pakistan, world hockey champions, Barcelona, Oct. 1971.

Arab Scholars — A132

1972, Jan. 15 **Litho.** ***Perf. 13½***
317 A132 20p brown, blk & blue .25 .30

International Book Year 1972.

Angels and Grand Canal, Venice A133

1972, Feb. 5 ***Perf. 13***
318 A133 20p blue & multi .35 .35

UNESCO campaign to save Venice.

ECAFE Emblem A134

1972, Mar. 28 **Litho.** ***Perf. 13***
319 A134 20p blue & multi .25 .30

Economic Commission for Asia and the Far East (ECAFE), 25th anniversary.

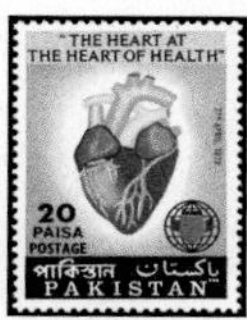
"Your Heart is your Health" — A135

1972, Apr. 7 ***Perf. 13x13½***
320 A135 20p vio blue & multi .25 .30

World Health Day 1972.

"Only One Earth" — A136

1972, June 5 **Litho.** ***Perf. 12½x14***
321 A136 20p ultra & multi .25 .30

UN Conference on Human Environment, Stockholm, June 5-16.

Young Man, by Abdur Rehman Chughtai — A137

Paintings: 10p, Fisherman, by Cevat Dereli (Turkey). 20p, Persian Woman, by Behzad.

1972, July 21 **Litho.** ***Perf. 13***
322 A137 10p multicolored .30 .25
323 A137 20p multicolored .50 .30
324 A137 50p multicolored 1.20 .60
Nos. 322-324 (3) 2.00 1.15

Regional Cooperation for Development Pact among Pakistan, Turkey and Iran, 8th anniversary.
See Iran 1647-1649, Turkey 1912-1914.

Jinnah and Independence Memorial — A138

"Land Reforms" A139

Designs: Nos. 326-329, Principal reforms. 60pa, State Bank, Islamabad, meeting-place of National Assembly, horiz.

Perf. 13 (A138), 13½x12½ (A139)
1972, Aug. 14
325 A138 10p shown .25 .25
326 A139 20p shown .25 .25
327 A139 20p Labor reforms .25 .25
328 A139 20p Education .25 .25
329 A139 20p Health care .25 .25
a. Vert. strip of 4, As #326-329 plus "labels" 1.00 1.00
330 A138 60p rose lilac & car .35 .30
Nos. 325-330 (6) 1.60 1.55

25th anniversary of independence. No. 329a contains designs of Nos. 326-329, each with a decorative label, separated by simulated perfs.

Blood Donor, Society Emblem — A140

1972, Sept. 6 **Litho.** ***Perf. 14x12½***
331 A140 20p multicolored .25 .35

Pakistan National Blood Transfusion Service.

Census Chart — A141

1972, Sept. 16 **Litho.** ***Perf. 13½***
332 A141 20p multicolored .25 .25

Centenary of population census.

Children Leaving Slum for Modern City — A142

1972, Oct. 2 **Litho.** ***Perf. 13***
333 A142 20p multicolored .25 .30

Children's Day.

Giant Book and Children A143

1972, Oct. 23
334 A143 20p purple & multi .25 .30

Education Week.

Nuclear Power Plant, Karachi — A144

1972, Nov. 28 **Litho.** ***Perf. 13***
335 A144 20p multicolored .25 .40

Pakistan's first nuclear power plant.

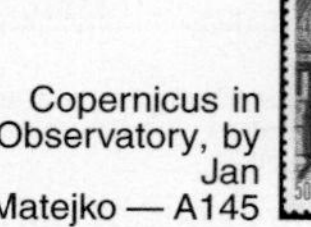

Copernicus in Observatory, by Jan Matejko — A145

1973, Feb. 19 **Litho.** ***Perf. 13***
336 A145 20p multicolored .60 .30

Dancing Girl, Public Baths, Mohenjo-Daro A146

1973, Feb. 23 ***Perf. 13½x13***
337 A146 20p multicolored .35 .30

Mohenjo-Daro excavations, 50th anniv.

Radar, Lightning, WMO Emblem — A147

1973, Mar. 23 **Litho.** ***Perf. 13***
338 A147 20p multicolored .25 .40

Cent. of intl. meteorological cooperation.

Prisoners of War — A148

1973, Apr. 18
339 A148 1.25r black & multi 1.50 *2.50*

A plea for Pakistani prisoners of war in India.

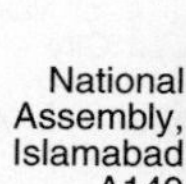

National Assembly, Islamabad A149

1973, Apr. 21 ***Perf. 12½x13½***
340 A149 20p green & multi .55 .55

Constitution Week.

State Bank and Emblem A150

1973, July 1 **Litho.** ***Perf. 13***
341 A150 20p multicolored .25 .25
342 A150 1r multicolored .30 .35

State Bank of Pakistan, 25th anniversary.

Street, Mohenjo-Daro, Pakistan — A151

Designs: 20p, Statue of man, Shahdad, Kerman, Persia, 4000 B.C. 1.25r, Head from mausoleum of King Antiochus I (69-34 B.C.), Turkey.

1973, July 21 ***Perf. 13x13½***
343 A151 20p blue & multi .25 .25
344 A151 60p emerald & multi .65 .35
345 A151 1.25r red & multi 1.00 .75
Nos. 343-345 (3) 1.90 1.35

Regional Cooperation for Development Pact among Pakistan, Turkey and Iran, 9th anniversary.

See Iran 1714-1716, Turkey 1941-1943.

Pakistani Flag and Constitution — A152

1973, Aug. 14 **Litho.** ***Perf. 13***
346 A152 20p blue & multi .25 .25

Independence Day.

Mohammed Ali Jinnah — A153

1973, Sept. 11 **Litho.** ***Perf. 13***
347 A153 20p emerald, yel & blk .25 .25

Mohammed Ali Jinnah (1876-1948), president of All-India Moslem League.

Wallago Attu — A154

Fish: 20p, Labeo rohita. 60p, Tilapia mossambica. 1r, Catla catla.

1973, Sept. 24 **Litho.** ***Perf. 13½***
348 A154 10p multicolored 1.10 1.10
349 A154 20p multicolored 1.25 1.25
350 A154 60p multicolored 1.40 1.40
351 A154 1r ultra & multi 1.40 1.40
a. Strip of 4, #348-351 6.00 6.00

Book, Torch, Child and School A155

1973, Oct. 1
352 A155 20p multicolored .25 .25

Universal Children's Day.

Sindhi Farmer and FAO Emblem A156

1973, Oct. 15 **Litho.** ***Perf. 13***
353 A156 20p multicolored .75 .35

World Food Organization, 10th anniv.

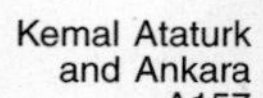

Kemal Ataturk and Ankara A157

1973, Oct. 29
354 A157 50p multicolored .75 .40

50th anniversary of Turkish Republic.

Scout Pointing to Planet and Stars — A158

Perf. 13½x12½
1973, Nov. 11 **Litho.**
355 A158 20p dull blue & multi 2.00 .50

25th anniversary of Pakistani Boy Scouts and Silver Jubilee Jamboree.

Human Rights Flame, Sheltered Home — A159

1973, Nov. 16
356 A159 20p multicolored .45 .40

25th anniversary of the Universal Declaration of Human Rights.

al-Biruni and Jhelum Observatory A160

1973, Nov. 26 **Litho.** ***Perf. 13***
357 A160 20p multicolored .50 .25
358 A160 1.25r multicolored 1.25 .50

International Congress on Millenary of abu-al-Rayhan al-Biruni, Nov. 26-Dec. 12.

Dr. A. G. Hansen — A161

1973, Dec. 29
359 A161 20p ultra & multi 1.20 .50

Centenary of the discovery by Dr. Armauer Gerhard Hansen of the Hansen bacillus, the cause of leprosy.

Family and WPY Emblem A162

1974, Jan. 1 **Litho.** ***Perf. 13***
360 A162 20p yellow & multi .30 .25
361 A162 1.25r salmon & multi .30 .40

World Population Year 1974.

Summit Emblem and Ornament A163

Emblem, Crescent and Rays A164

1974, Feb. 22 ***Perf. 14x12½, 13***
362 A163 20p multicolored .25 .25
363 A164 65p multicolored .30 .40
a. Souvenir sheet of 2 2.50 3.25

Islamic Summit Meeting. No. 363a contains two stamps similar to Nos. 362-363 with simulated perforations.

Metric Measures — A165

1974, July 1 **Litho.** ***Perf. 13***
364 A165 20p multicolored .25 .30

Introduction of metric system.

Kashan Rug, Lahore — A166

Designs: 60p, Persian rug, late 16th century. 1.25r, Anatolian rug, 15th century.

1974, July 21
365 A166 20p multicolored .25 .25
366 A166 60p multicolored .40 .50
367 A166 1.25r multicolored .75 1.00
Nos. 365-367 (3) 1.40 1.75

10th anniversary of the Regional Cooperation for Development Pact among Pakistan, Iran and Turkey.

See Iran 1806-1808, Turkey 1979-1981.

Hands Protecting Sapling — A167

1974, Aug. 9 **Litho.** ***Perf. 13***
368 A167 20p multicolored .60 .60

Arbor Day.

Torch over Map of Africa with Namibia — A168

1974, Aug. 26
369 A168 60p green & multi .55 .60

Namibia (South-West Africa) Day. See note after United Nations No. 241.

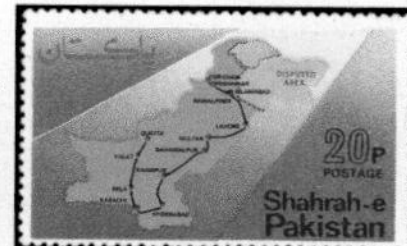

Map of Pakistan with Highways and Disputed Area — A169

1974, Sept. 23

370 A169 20p multicolored 1.25 1.00

Highway system under construction.

Child and Students — A170

1974, Oct. 7 Litho. *Perf. 13*

371 A170 20p multicolored .40 .50

Universal Children's Day.

UPU Emblem — A171

2.25r, Jet, UPU emblem, mail coach.

1974, Oct. 9 Size: 24x36mm

372 A171 20p multicolored .25 .25

Size: 29x41mm

373 A171 2.25r multicolored .55 .70

a. Souv. sheet of 2, #372-373, imperf. 2.00 2.00

Centenary of Universal Postal Union.

Liaqat Ali Khan — A172

1974, Oct. 16 Litho. *Perf. 13x13½*

374 A172 20p black & red .45 .35

Liaqat Ali Khan, Prime Minister 1947-1951.

Mohammad Allama Iqbal — A173

1974, Nov. 9 Litho. *Perf. 13*

375 A173 20p multicolored .45 .35

Mohammad Allama Iqbal (1877-1938), poet and philosopher.

Dr. Schweitzer on Ogowe River, 1915 — A174

1975, Jan. 14 Litho. *Perf. 13*

376 A174 2.25r multicolored 4.50 *4.50*

Dr. Albert Schweitzer (1875-1965), medical missionary, birth centenary.

Tourism Year 75 Emblem — A175

1975, Jan. 15

377 A175 2.25r multicolored .60 .80

South Asia Tourism Year, 1975.

Flags of Participants, Memorial and Prime Minister Bhutto A176

1975, Feb. 22 Litho. *Perf. 13*

378 A176 20p lt blue & multi .25 .25

379 A176 1r brt pink & multi 1.25 1.00

2nd Lahore Islamic Summit, Feb. 22, 1st anniv.

IWY Emblem and Woman Scientist A177

Design: 2.25r, Old woman and girl learning to read and write.

1975, June 15 Litho. *Perf. 13*

380 A177 20p multicolored .25 .25

381 A177 2.25r multicolored 1.40 1.75

International Women's Year 1975.

Globe with Dates, Arabic "X" — A178

1975, July 14 Litho. *Perf. 13*

382 A178 20p multicolored .75 .60

International Congress of Mathematical Sciences, Karachi, July 14-20.

Camel Leather Vase, Pakistan — A179

60p, Ceramic plate and RCD emblem, Iran, horiz. 1.25r, Porcelain vase, Turkey.

1975, July 21

383 A179 20p lilac & multi .30 .25

384 A179 60p violet blk & multi .60 .75

385 A179 1.25r blue & multi 1.00 1.10

Nos. 383-385 (3) 1.90 2.10

Regional Cooperation for Development Pact among Turkey, Iran and Pakistan.

See Iran 1871-1873, Turkey 2006-2008.

Sapling, Trees and Ant — A180

1975, Aug. 9 Litho. *Perf. 13x13½*

386 A180 20p multicolored .45 .45

Tree Planting Day.

Black Partridge — A181

1975, Sept. 30 Litho. *Perf. 13*

387 A181 20p blue & multi 1.50 .25

388 A181 2.25r yellow & multi 4.50 3.50

Wildlife Protection.

Universal Children's Day — A182

1975, Oct. 6

389 A182 20p multicolored .45 .50

Hazrat Amir Khusrau, Sitar and Tabla A183

1975, Oct. 24 Litho. *Perf. 14x12½*

390 A183 20p lt blue & multi .25 .50

391 A183 2.25r pink & multi 1.00 2.00

700th anniversary of Hazrat Amir Khusrau (1253-1325), musician who invented the sitar and tabla instruments.

Mohammad Iqbal — A184

1975, Nov. 9 *Perf. 13*

392 A184 20p multicolored .50 .50

Mohammad Allama Iqbal (1877-1938), poet and philosopher, birth centenary.

Wild Sheep of the Punjab — A185

1975, Dec. 31 Litho. *Perf. 13*

393 A185 20p multicolored .45 .25

394 A185 3r multicolored 2.20 1.75

Wildlife Protection. See Nos. 410-411.

Mohenjo-Daro and UNESCO Emblem — A186

View of Mohenjo-Daro excavations.

1976, Feb. 29 Litho. *Perf. 13*

395 A186 10p multicolored .70 .80

396 A186 20p multicolored .80 .90

397 A186 65p multicolored .80 .90

398 A186 3r multicolored .80 .90

399 A186 4r multicolored .90 1.00

a. Strip of 5, #395-399 4.25 4.25

UNESCO campaign to save Mohenjo-Daro excavations.

Dome and Minaret of Rauza-e-Mubarak Mausoleum — A187

1976, Mar. 3 Photo. *Perf. 13½x14*

400 A187 20p blue & multi .25 .25

401 A187 3r gray & multi .75 .70

International Congress on Seerat, the teachings of Mohammed, Mar. 3-15.

Alexander Graham Bell, 1876 Telephone and Dial — A188

1976, Mar. 10 *Perf. 13*

402 A188 3r blue & multi 1.50 2.00

Centenary of first telephone call by Alexander Graham Bell, Mar. 10, 1876.

College Emblem A189

1976, Mar. 15 Litho. *Perf. 13*

403 A189 20p multicolored .45 .45

Cent. of Natl. College of Arts, Lahore.

Peacock A190

1976, Mar. 31 Litho. *Perf. 13*

404 A190 20p lt blue & multi 1.00 .40

405 A190 3r pink & multi 4.00 3.75

Wildlife protection.

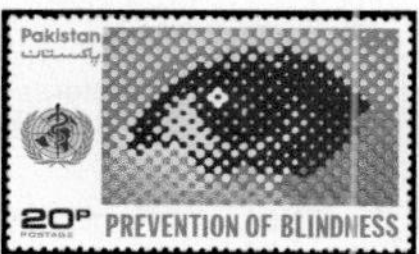

Eye and WHO Emblem A191

1976, Apr. 7

406 A191 20p multicolored 1.10 .75

World Health Day: "Foresight prevents blindness."

Mohenjo-Daro, UNESCO Emblem, Bull (from Seal) — A192

1976, May 31 **Litho.** ***Perf. 13***
407 A192 20p multicolored .45 .40

UNESCO campaign to save Mohenjo-Daro excavations.

Jefferson Memorial, US Bicentennial Emblem A193

Declaration of Independence, by John Trumbull — A194

1976, July 4 ***Perf. 13***
408 A193 90p multicolored .90 .50
Perf. 13½x13
409 A194 4r multicolored 3.25 *3.50*

American Bicentennial.

Wildlife Type of 1975

Wildlife protection: 20p, 3r, Ibex.

1976, July 12
410 A185 20p multicolored .50 .35
411 A185 3r multicolored 1.75 2.00

Mohammed Ali Jinnah A195

65p, Riza Shah Pahlavi. 90p, Kemal Ataturk.

1976, July 21 **Litho.** ***Perf. 14***
412 A195 20p multicolored .70 .50
413 A195 65p multicolored .70 .50
414 A195 90p multicolored .70 .50
a. Strip of 3, #412-414 2.50 3.25

Regional Cooperation for Development Pact among Pakistan, Turkey and Iran, 12th anniversary.

See Iran 1903-1905, Turkey 2041-2043.

Ornament A196

Jinnah and Wazir Mansion A197

Designs (Jinnah and): 40p, Sind Madressah (building). 50p, Minar Qarardad (minaret). 3r, Mausoleum.

1976, Aug. 14 **Litho.** ***Perf. 13½***
415 A196 5p multicolored .25 .25
416 A196 10p multicolored .25 .25
417 A196 15p multicolored .25 .25
418 A197 20p multicolored .25 .25
419 A197 40p multicolored .25 .25
420 A197 50p multicolored .25 .25
421 A196 1r multicolored .35 .40
422 A197 3r multicolored .50 .50
a. Block of 8, #415-422 3.50 3.50

Mohammed Ali Jinnah (1876-1948), first Governor General of Pakistan, birth centenary. Horizontal rows of types A196 and A197 alternate in sheet.

Mohenjo-Daro and UNESCO Emblem — A198

1976, Aug. 31 ***Perf. 14***
423 A198 65p multicolored .45 .50

UNESCO campaign to save Mohenjo-Daro excavations.

Racial Discrimination Emblem — A199

Perf. 12½x13½
1976, Sept. 15 **Litho.**
424 A199 65p multicolored .50 .50

Fight against racial discrimination.

Child's Head, Symbols of Health, Education and Food — A200

1976, Oct. 4 ***Perf. 13***
425 A200 20p blue & multi .65 .45

Universal Children's Day.

Verse by Allama Iqbal — A201

1976, Nov. 9 **Litho.** ***Perf. 13***
426 A201 20p multicolored .30 .30

Mohammed Allama Iqbal (1877-1938), poet and philosopher, birth centenary.

Scout Emblem, Jinnah Giving Salute — A202

1976, Nov. 20
427 A202 20p multicolored 1.10 .45

Quaid-I-Azam Centenary Jamboree, Nov. 1976.

Children Reading — A203

1976, Dec. 15 **Litho.** ***Perf. 13***
428 A203 20p multicolored .60 .30

Books for children.

Mohammed Ali Jinnah — A204

Lithographed and Embossed

1976, Dec. 25 ***Perf. 12½***
429 A204 10r gold & green 3.00 3.00

Mohammed Ali Jinnah (1876-1948), 1st Governor General of Pakistan.

An imperf presentation sheet of 1 exists. Value $100.

Farm Family and Village, Tractor, Ambulance — A205

1977, Apr. 14 **Litho.** ***Perf. 13***
430 A205 20p multicolored .45 .25

Social Welfare and Rural Development Year, 1976-77.

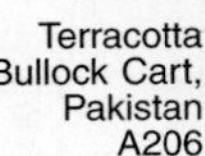

Terracotta Bullock Cart, Pakistan A206

Designs: 20p, Terra-cotta jug, Turkey. 90p, Decorated jug, Iran.

1977, July 21 **Litho.** ***Perf. 13***
431 A206 20p ultra & multi .50 .25
432 A206 65p blue green & multi .70 .35
433 A206 90p lilac & multi 1.10 1.40
Nos. 431-433 (3) 2.30 2.00

Regional Cooperation for Development Pact among Pakistan, Turkey and Iran, 13th anniversary.

See Iran 1946-1948, Turkey 2053-2055.

Trees — A207

1977, Aug. 9 **Litho.** ***Perf. 13***
434 A207 20p multicolored .25 .30

Tree planting program.

Desert — A208

1977, Sept. 5 **Litho.** ***Perf. 13***
435 A208 65p multicolored .45 .30

UN Conference on Desertification, Nairobi, Kenya, Aug. 29-Sept. 9.

"Water for the Children" — A209

1977, Oct. 3 **Litho.** ***Perf. 14x12½***
436 A209 50p multicolored .45 .40

Universal Children's Day.

Aga Khan III — A210

1977, Nov. 2 **Litho.** ***Perf. 13***
437 A210 2r multicolored .75 .75

Aga Khan III (1877-1957), spiritual ruler of Ismaeli sect, statesman, birth centenary.

Mohammad Iqbal — A211

20p, Spirit appearing to Iqbal, painting by Behzad. 65p, Iqbal looking at Jamaluddin Afghani & Saeed Halim offering prayers, by Behzad. 1.25r, Verse in Urdu. 2.25r, Verse in Persian.

1977, Nov. 9
438 A211 20p multicolored .60 .60
439 A211 65p multicolored .60 .60
440 A211 1.25r multicolored .70 .70
441 A211 2.25r multicolored .75 .75
442 A211 3r multicolored .85 .85
a. Strip of 5, #438-442 4.50 4.50

Mohammad Allama Iqbal (1877-1938), poet and philosopher, birth centenary.

Holy Kaaba, Mecca — A212

1977, Nov. 21 ***Perf. 14***
443 A212 65p green & multi .45 .30

1977 pilgrimage to Mecca.

Healthy and Sick Bodies — A213

1977, Dec. 19 **Litho.** ***Perf. 13***
444 A213 65p blue green & multi .50 .30

World Rheumatism Year.

Woman from Rawalpindi-Islamabad A214

1978, Feb. 5 Litho. *Perf. 12½x13½*

445 A214 75p multicolored .45 .25

Indonesia-Pakistan Economic and Cultural Cooperation Organization.

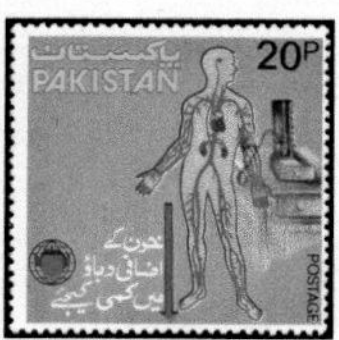

Blood Circulation and Pressure Gauge — A215

1978, Apr. 20 Litho. *Perf. 13*

446 A215 20p blue & multi .30 .25
447 A215 2r yellow & multi .90 .75

Campaign against hypertension.

Henri Dunant, Red Cross, Red Crescent — A216

1978, May 8 *Perf. 14*

448 A216 1r multicolored 1.00 .30

Henri Dunant (1828-1910), founder of Red Cross, 150th birth anniversary.

Red Roses, Pakistan — A217

90p, Pink roses, Iran. 2r, Yellow rose, Turkey.

1978, July 21 Litho. *Perf. 13½*

449 A217 20p multicolored .35 .25
450 A217 90p multicolored .50 .25
451 A217 2r multicolored .75 .35
a. Strip of 3, #449-451 2.00 2.00

Regional Cooperation for Development Pact among Turkey, Iran and Pakistan.
See Iran 1984-1986, Turkey 2094-2096.

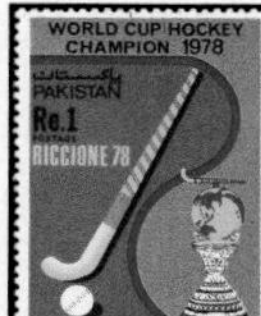

Hockey Stick and Ball, Championship Cup — A218

Fair Building, Fountain, Piazza Tourismo — A219

1978, Aug. 26 Litho. *Perf. 13*

452 A218 1r multicolored 1.40 .25
453 A219 2r multicolored .60 .30

Riccione '78, 30th International Stamp Fair, Riccione, Italy, Aug. 26-28. No. 452 also commemorates Pakistan as World Hockey Cup Champion.

Globe and Cogwheels A220

1978, Sept. 3

454 A220 75p multicolored .45 .25

UN Conference on Technical Cooperation among Developing Countries, Buenos Aires, Argentina, Sept. 1978.

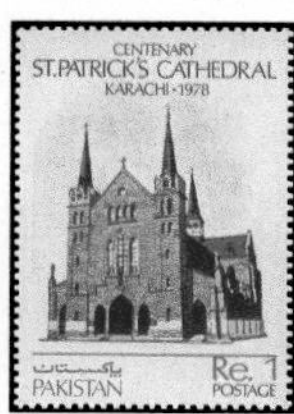

St. Patrick's Cathedral, Karachi — A221

Design: 2r, Stained-glass window.

1978, Sept. 29 Litho. *Perf. 13*

455 A221 1r multicolored .25 .25
456 A221 2r multicolored .65 .25

St. Patrick's Cathedral, Karachi, centenary.

"Four Races" — A222

1978, Nov. 20 Litho. *Perf. 13*

457 A222 1r multicolored .45 .25

Anti-Apartheid Year.

Maulana Jauhar — A223

1978, Dec. 10 Litho. *Perf. 13*

458 A223 50p multicolored .55 .25

Maulana Muhammad Ali Jauhar, writer, journalist and patriot, birth centenary.

Type of 1957 and

Qarardad Monument — A224

Tractor — A225

Tomb of Ibrahim Khan Makli — A225a

Engr.; Litho. (10p, 25p, 40p, 50p, 90p)

1978-81 *Perf. 14*

459 A224 2p dark green .25 .25
460 A224 3p black .25 .25
461 A224 5p violet blue .25 .25
462 A225 10p lt blue & blue ('79) .25 .25
463 A225 20p yel green ('79) .40 .25
464 A225 25p rose car & grn ('79) .75 .25
465 A225 40p carmine & blue .25 .25
466 A225 50p bl grn & vio ('79) .25 .25
467 A225 60p black .25 .25
468 A225 75p dull red .50 .25
469 A225 90p blue & carmine .25 .25

Perf. 13½x13

Engr. Wmk. 351

470 A225a 1r olive ('80) .25 .25
471 A225a 1.50r dp org ('79) .25 .25
472 A225a 2r car rose ('79) .25 .25
473 A225a 3r indigo ('80) .25 .25
474 A225a 4r black ('81) .25 .25
475 A225a 5r dk brn ('81) .25 .25
475A A26 15r rose lil & red ('79) 1.50 1.50
Nos. 459-475A (18) 6.65 5.75

Lithographed stamps, type A225, have bottom panel in solid color with colorless lettering and numerals 2mm high instead of 3mm.
For overprints see Nos. O94-O110.

Tornado Jet Fighter, de Havilland Rapide and Flyer A — A226

Wright Flyer A and: 1r, Phantom F4F jet fighter & Tristar airliner. 2r, Bell X15 fighter & TU-104 airliner. 2.25r, MiG fighter & Concorde.

Unwmk.

1978, Dec. 24 Litho. *Perf. 13*

476 A226 65p multicolored 1.10 1.60
477 A226 1r multicolored 1.20 1.90
478 A226 2r multicolored 1.25 2.00
479 A226 2.25r multicolored 1.25 2.00
a. Block of 4, #476-479 6.50 6.50

75th anniv. of 1st powered flight.

Koran Lighting the World and Mohammed's Tomb — A227

1979, Feb. 10 Litho. *Perf. 13*

480 A227 20p multicolored .45 .25

Mohammed's birth anniversary.

Mother and Children A228

1979, Feb. 25

481 A228 50p multicolored .75 .25

APWA Services, 30th anniversary.

Lophophorus Impejanus A229

Pheasants: 25p, Lophura leucomelana. 40p, Puccrasia macrolopha. 1r, Catreus walichii.

1979, June 17 Litho. *Perf. 13*

482 A229 20p multicolored 1.35 .60
483 A229 25p multicolored 1.35 .75
484 A229 40p multicolored 1.60 1.75
485 A229 1r multicolored 3.25 2.00
Nos. 482-485 (4) 7.55 5.10

For overprint see No. 525.

At the Well, by Allah Baksh A230

Paintings: 75p, Potters, by Kamalel Molk, Iran. 1.60r, Plowing, by Namik Ismail, Turkey.

1979, July 21 Litho. *Perf. 14x13*

486 A230 40p multicolored .25 .25
487 A230 75p multicolored .25 .25
488 A230 1.60r multicolored .25 .25
a. Strip of 3, #486-488 .90 .90

Regional Cooperation for Development Pact among Pakistan, Iran and Turkey, 15th anniversary.
See Iran 2020-2022, Turkey 2112-2114.

Guj Embroidery A231

Handicrafts: 1r, Enamel inlay brass plate. 1.50r, Baskets. 2r, Peacock, embroidered rug.

1979, Aug. 23 Litho. *Perf. 14x13*

489 A231 40p multicolored .25 .25
490 A231 1r multicolored .25 .25
491 A231 1.50r multicolored .30 .30
492 A231 2r multicolored .40 .35
a. Block of 4, #489-492 1.50 1.50

Children, IYC and SOS Emblems A232

1979, Sept. 10 Litho. *Perf. 13*

493 A232 50p multicolored .50 .30

SOS Children's Village, Lahore, opening.

Playground, IYC Emblem A233

IYC Emblem and: Children's drawings.

1979, Oct. 22 *Perf. 14x12½*

494 A233 40p multicolored .25 .25
495 A233 75p multicolored .25 .25
496 A233 1r multicolored .25 .30
497 A233 1.50r multicolored .30 .30
a. Block of 4, #494-497 1.25 1.25

Souvenir Sheet

Imperf

498 A233 2r multi, vert. 1.50 *2.10*

IYC. For overprints see #520-523.

Fight Against Cancer — A234

Unwmk.

1979, Nov. 12 Litho. *Perf. 14*

499 A234 40p multicolored .75 .70

Pakistan Customs Service Centenary — A235

1979, Dec. 10 *Perf. 13x13½*
500 A235 1r multicolored .35 .25

"1378" is a plate flaw, not an error.

Tippu Sultan Shaheed A236

15r, Syed Ahmad Khan. 25r, Altaf Hussain Hali.

1979, Mar. 23 **Wmk. 351** *Perf. 14*
501 A236 10r shown .75 1.00
502 A236 15r multicolored 1.00 1.50
503 A236 25r multicolored 1.50 2.25
a. Strip of 3, #501-503 4.00 4.00

See No. 699.

A237 A238

Ornament — A239

Perf. 12x11½, 11½x12
1980 **Unwmk.**
506 A237 10p dk grn & yel org .25 .25
507 A237 15p dk grn & apple grn .25 .25
508 A237 25p multicolored .25 .25
509 A237 35p multicolored .25 .25
510 A238 40p red & lt brown .25 .25
511 A239 50p olive & vio bl .25 .25
512 A239 80p black & yel grn .25 .30
Nos. 506-512 (7) 1.75 1.80

Issued: 25, 35, 50, 80p, 3/10; others, 1/15.
See Nos. O111-O117.

Pakistan International Airline, 25th Anniversary A240

1980, Jan. 10 **Litho.** *Perf. 13*
516 A240 1r multicolored 2.00 1.00

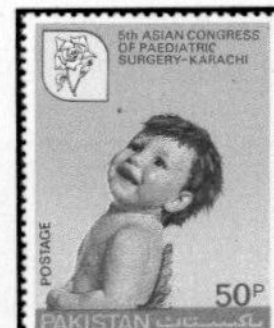

Infant, Rose — A241

1980, Feb. 16 *Perf. 13*
517 A241 50p multicolored 1.00 1.25

5th Asian Congress of Pediatric Surgery, Karachi, Feb. 16-19.

Conference Emblem — A242

1980, May 17 **Litho.** *Perf. 13*
518 A242 1r multicolored .80 .50

11th Islamic Conference of Foreign Ministers, Islamabad, May 17-21.

Lighthouse, Oil Terminal, Map Showing Karachi Harbor — A243

1980, July 15 *Perf. 13½*
519 A243 1r multicolored 2.00 1.50

Karachi Port, cent. of independent management.

Nos. 494-497 Overprinted in Red: RICCIONE 80

1980, Aug. 30 **Litho.** *Perf. 14x12½*
520 A233 40p multicolored .30 *.50*
521 A233 75p multicolored .40 *.60*
522 A233 1r multicolored .45 *.65*
523 A233 1.50r multicolored .60 *.75*
a. Block of 4, #520-523 2.00 *3.00*

RICCIONE 80 International Stamp Exhibition, Riccione, Italy, Aug. 30-Sept. 2.

Quetta Command and Staff College, 75th Anniversary — A244

1980, Sept. 18 **Litho.** *Perf. 13*
524 A244 1r multicolored .25 .40

No. 485 Overprinted: "World Tourism Conference/Manila 80"

1980, Sept. 27
525 A229 1r multicolored 1.00 .50

World Tourism Conf., Manila, Sept. 27.

Birth Centenary of Mohammed Shairani — A245

1980, Oct. 5 **Litho.** *Perf. 13*
526 A245 40p multicolored .45 .45

Aga Khan Architecture Award A246

1980, Oct. 23 **Litho.** *Perf. 13½*
527 A246 2r multicolored .60 .55

Rising Sun — A247

1981, Mar. 7 **Litho.** *Perf. 13*
Size: 30x41mm
528 A247 40p Hegira emblem .25 .40

1980, Nov. 6 **Litho.** *Perf. 13*
529 A247 40p shown .25 .25

Perf. 14
Size: 33x33mm
530 A247 2r Moslem symbols .25 .35

Perf. 13x13½
Size: 31x54mm
531 A247 3r Globe, hands holding Koran .25 .50
Nos. 528-531 (4) 1.00 1.50

Souvenir Sheet
Imperf
532 A247 4r Candles 1.00 1.00

Hegira (Pilgrimage Year).

Airmail Service, 50th Anniversary A248

Postal History: No. 533, Postal card cent. No. 534, Money order service cent.

1980-81 *Perf. 13*
533 A248 40p multi, vert. .25 .35
534 A248 40p multi, vert. .25 .35
535 A248 1r multi .75 .25
Nos. 533-535 (3) 1.25 .95

Issued: #533, 12/27; #534, 12/20; #535, 2/15/81.

Heinrich von Stephan, UPU Emblem — A249

1981, Jan. 7 *Perf. 13½*
536 A249 1r multicolored .45 .25

Von Stephan (1831-97), founder of UPU.

Conference Emblem, Afghan Refugee — A250

Conference Emblem, Flags of Participants, Men — A251

Conference Emblem, Map of Afghanistan A252

1981, Mar. 29 **Litho.** *Perf. 13*
537 A250 40p multicolored .25 .25
538 A251 40p multicolored .25 .25
539 A250 1r multicolored .50 .25
540 A251 1r multicolored .50 .25
541 A252 2r multicolored .65 .35
Nos. 537-541 (5) 2.15 1.35

Conference Emblem in Ornament A253

Conference Emblem, Flags of Participants A254

1981, Mar. 29 *Perf. 13½*
542 A253 40p multicolored .25 .25
543 A254 40p multicolored .25 .25
544 A253 85p multicolored .25 .25
545 A254 85p multicolored .25 .25
Nos. 542-545 (4) 1.00 1.00

3rd Islamic Summit Conference, Makkah al-Mukarramah, Jan. 25-28.

Kemal Ataturk (1881-1938), First President of Turkey — A255

1981, May 19 **Litho.** *Perf. 13x13½*
546 A255 1r multicolored .60 .25

Green Turtle — A256

1981, June 20 **Litho.** *Perf. 12x11½*
547 A256 40p multicolored 1.50 .75

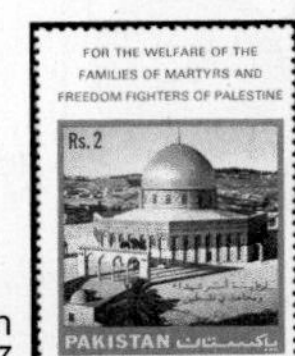

Palestinian Cooperation — A257

1981, July 25 **Litho.** *Perf. 13*
548 A257 2r multicolored .55 .25

Mountain Ranges and Peaks A258

Designs: No. 549, Malubiting West, range. No. 550, Peak. No. 551, Mt. Maramosh, range. No. 552, Mt. Maramosh, peak. No. 553, K6, range. No. 554, Peak. No. 555, K2, range. No. 556, Peak.

1981, Aug. 20 *Perf. 14x13½*
549 40p multicolored .45 .30
550 40p multicolored .45 .30
a. A258 Pair, #549-550 1.00 1.00
551 1r multicolored .65 .50
552 1r multicolored .65 .50
a. A258 Pair, #551-552 1.50 1.50
553 1.50r multicolored .80 .60
554 1.50r multicolored .80 .60
a. A258 Pair, #553-554 1.75 1.75
555 2r multicolored .80 .80
556 2r multicolored .80 .80
a. A258 Pair, #555-556 1.75 1.75
Nos. 549-556 (8) 5.40 4.40

Inauguration of Pakistan Steel Furnace No. 1, Karachi — A260

1981, Aug. 31 *Perf. 13*

557 A260 40p multicolored .25 .25
558 A260 2r multicolored .60 .75

Western Tragopan in Summer — A261

1981, Sept. 15 **Litho.** *Perf. 14*

559 A261 40p shown 2.50 .75
560 A261 2r Winter 4.75 4.00

Intl. Year of the Disabled A262

1981, Dec. 12 **Litho.** *Perf. 13*

561 A262 40p multicolored .25 .30
562 A262 2r multicolored 1.25 1.00

World Cup Championship A263

1982, Jan. 31 **Litho.** *Perf. 13½x13*

563 A263 1r Cup, flags in arc 2.00 1.00
564 A263 1r shown 2.00 1.00
a. Pair, #563-564 4.50 4.50

Nos. 563-564 were printed with a vertical strip of labels, picturing different scenes, in the middle of each sheet, allowing for pairs with label between. Value, pair with label $4.

Camel Skin Lampshade A264

1982, Feb. 20 **Litho.** *Perf. 14*

565 A264 1r shown .80 .60
566 A264 1r Hala pottery .80 .60

See Nos. 582-583.

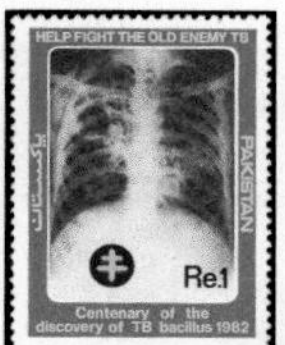

TB Bacillus Centenary — A265

1982, Mar. 24

567 A265 1r multicolored 1.50 1.25

Blind Indus Dolphin — A266

1982, Apr. 24 **Litho.** *Perf. 12x11½*

568 A266 40p Dolphin 1.50 .75
569 A266 1r Dolphin, diff. 3.50 1.50

Peaceful Uses of Outer Space A267

1982, June 7 **Litho.** *Perf. 13*

570 A267 1r multicolored 2.00 1.10

No. 570 was printed with a vertical strip of labels, picturing different space satellites, in the middle of each sheet, allowing for pairs with label between. Value, pair with label $4.

50th Anniv. of Sukkur Barrage A268

1982, July 17 **Litho.** *Perf. 13*

571 A268 1r multicolored .35 .25

For overprint see No. 574.

Independence Day — A269

1982, Aug. 14

572 A269 40p Flag .25 .25
573 A269 85p Map .50 .50

No. 571 Overprinted "RICCIONE-82/1932-1982"

1982, Aug. 28

574 A268 1r multicolored .25 .25

RICCIONE '82 Intl. Stamp Exhibition, Riccione, Italy, Aug. 28-30.

University of the Punjab Centenary — A270

1982, Oct. 14 **Litho.** *Perf. 13½*

575 A270 40p multicolored 1.20 .40

No. 575 was printed with a vertical strip of labels, picturing different university buildings, in the middle of each sheet, allowing for pairs with label between. Value, pair with label: $4.

Scouting Year — A271

1982, Dec. 23 **Litho.** *Perf. 13*

576 A271 2r Emblem .50 .35

Quetta Natural Gas Pipeline Project — A272

1983, Jan. 6 **Litho.** *Perf. 13*

577 A272 1r multicolored .35 .25

Common Peacock — A273

Designs: 50p, Common rose. 60p, Plain tiger. 1.50r, Lemon butterfly.

1983, Feb. 15 **Litho.** *Perf. 14*

578 A273 40p shown 1.25 .25
579 A273 50p multi 1.50 .25
580 A273 60p multi 1.75 .55
581 A273 1.50r multi 2.50 2.25
Nos. 578-581 (4) 7.00 3.30

Handicraft Type of 1982

Designs: No. 582, Straw mats. No. 583, Five-flower cloth design.

1983, Mar. 9

582 A264 1r multi .30 .25
583 A264 1r multi .30 .25

Opening of Aga Khan University — A274

1983, Mar. 16 *Perf. 13½*

584 A274 2r multicolored 1.25 1.00

No. 584 was printed with a vertical strip of labels, picturing different university views, in the middle of each sheet, allowing for pairs with label between. Value, pair with label $4.

Yak Caravan, Zindiharam-Darkot Pass, Hindu Kush Mountains — A275

1983, Apr. 28 **Litho.** *Perf. 13*

585 A275 1r multicolored 1.60 .50

Marsh Crocodile — A276

1983, May 19 *Perf. 13½x14*

586 A276 3r multicolored 4.00 1.60

1983, June 20 **Litho.** *Perf. 14*

Size: 50x40mm

587 A276 1r Gazelle 3.25 1.60

36th Anniv. of Independence A277

1983, Aug. 14 *Perf. 13*

588 A277 60p Star .25 .25
589 A277 4r Torch .40 .40

25th Anniv. of Indonesia-Pakistan Economic and Cultural Cooperation Org. — A278

Weavings — No. 590, Pakistani (geometric). No. 591, Indonesian (figures).

1983, Aug. 19 **Litho.** *Perf. 13*

590 A278 2r multicolored .30 .25
591 A278 2r multicolored .30 .25

Siberian Cranes A279

1983, Sept. 8 *Perf. 13½*

592 A279 3r multicolored 4.00 3.00

World Communications Year — A280

1983, Oct. 9 **Litho.** *Perf. 13*

593 A280 2r multicolored .35 .25

Size: 33x33mm

594 A280 3r Symbol, diff. .30 .25

World Food Day — A281

1983, Oct. 24 **Litho.** *Perf. 13*

595 A281 3r Livestock 1.50 1.50
596 A281 3r Fruit 1.50 1.50
597 A281 3r Grain 1.50 1.50
598 A281 3r Seafood 1.50 1.50
a. Strip of 4, #595-598 6.50 6.50

National Fertilizer Corp. — A282

1983, Oct. 24 **Litho.** *Perf. 13½*

599 A282 60p multicolored .25 .25

View of Lahore City, 1852 — A283

1983, Nov. 13 **Litho.** *Perf. 13*

600 Strip of 6 3.50 3.50
a.-f. A283 60p any single .50 .50

PAKPHILEX '83 Natl. Stamp Exhibition.

Yachting Victory in 9th Asian Games, 1982 — A284

1983, Dec. 31 Litho. *Perf. 13*
601 A284 60p OK Dinghy 1.75 1.75
602 A284 60p Enterprise 1.75 1.75

Snow Leopard A285

1984, Jan. 21 *Perf. 14*
603 A285 40p lt green & multi 2.00 1.00
604 A285 1.60r blue & multi 5.00 5.00

Jehangir Khan (b. 1963), World Squash Champion — A286

1984, Mar. 17 Litho. *Perf. 13*
605 A286 3r multicolored 2.75 1.40

Pakistan Intl. Airway China Service, 20th Anniv. — A287

1984, Apr. 29 Litho. *Perf. 13*
606 A287 3r Jet 5.75 4.50

Glass Work, Lahore Fort — A288

Various glass panels.

1984, May 31 Litho. *Perf. 13*
607 A288 1r green & multi .25 .25
608 A288 1r purple & multi .25 .25
609 A288 1r vermilion & multi .25 .25
610 A288 1r brt blue & multi .25 .25
Nos. 607-610 (4) 1.00 1.00

Forts — A289

1984-88 Litho. *Perf. 11*
613 A289 5p Kot Diji *.40* .25
614 A289 10p Rohtas *.40* .25
615 A289 15p Bala Hissar ('86) *.75* .25
616 A289 20p Attock *1.50* .25
617 A289 50p Hyderabad ('86) *1.50* .25
618 A289 60p Lahore *1.25* .25
619 A289 70p Sibi ('88) *1.50* .25
620 A289 80p Ranikot ('86) *1.50* .25
Nos. 613-620 (8) *8.80* 2.00

Issued: 5p, 11/1; 10p, 9/25; 80p, 7/1.
For overprints see Nos. O118-O124.

Shah Rukn-i-Alam Tomb, Multan A290

1984, June 26 Litho. *Perf. 13*
624 A290 60p multicolored 2.50 1.40

Aga Khan Award for Architecture.

Asia-Pacific Broadcasting Union, 20th Anniv. — A290a

1984, July 1 Litho. *Perf. 13*
625 A290a 3r multicolored .90 .50

1984 Summer Olympics, Los Angeles — A291

1984, July 31
626 A291 3r Athletics 1.35 1.00
627 A291 3r Boxing 1.35 1.00
628 A291 3r Hockey 1.35 1.00
629 A291 3r Yachting 1.35 1.00
630 A291 3r Wrestling 1.35 1.00
Nos. 626-630 (5) 6.75 5.00

Issued in sheets of 10.
A press sheet containing sheets of 10 each of Nos. 626-630 was produced for limited sales overseas. Value, $100.

Independence, 37th Anniv. — A292

1984, Aug. 14
631 A292 60p Jasmine .25 .25
632 A292 4r Lighted torch .50 .45

Intl. Trade Fair, Sept. 1-21, Karachi — A293

1984, Sept. 1
633 A293 60p multicolored .60 .30

1984 Natl. Tourism Convention, Karachi, Nov. 5-8 — A293a

Shah Jahan Mosque: a, Main dome interior. b, Tile work. c, Entrance. d, Archways. e, Dome interior, diff.

1984, Nov. 5 Litho. *Perf. 13½*
634 Strip of 5 3.00 3.00
a.-e. A293a 1r any single .50 .40

United Bank Limited, 25th Anniv. — A294

1984, Nov. 7
635 A294 60p multicolored .75 .60

UNCTAD, UN Conference on Trade and Development, 20th Anniv. — A294a

1984, Dec. 24 *Perf. 14½x14*
636 A294a 60p multicolored .85 .35

Postal Life Insurance, Cent. — A295

1984, Dec. 29 *Perf. 13½x14*
637 A295 60p multicolored .50 .25
638 A295 1r multicolored .75 .25

UNESCO World Heritage Campaign — A296

No. 639, Unicorn, rock painting. No. 640, Unicorn seal, round.

1984, Dec. 31
639 2r multicolored 1.50 .80
640 2r multicolored 1.50 .80
a. A296 Pair, #639-640 3.50 3.50

Restoration of Mohenjo-Daro.

IYY, Girl Guides 75th Anniv. — A297

1985, Jan. 5 *Perf. 13½*
641 A297 60p Emblems 3.75 1.25

Smelting — A298

Pouring Steel — A299

1985, Jan. 15 *Perf. 13*
642 A298 60p multicolored .75 .30
643 A299 1r multicolored 1.25 .40

Referendum Reinstating Pres. Zia — A300

1985, Mar. 20 Litho. *Perf. 13*
644 A300 60p Map, sunburst 1.25 .40

Minar-e-Qarardad-e-Pakistan Tower — A301

Ballot Box — A302

1985 Elections.

1985, Mar. 23
645 A301 1r multicolored .70 .25
646 A302 1r multicolored .70 .25

Mountaineering — A303

40p, Mt. Rakaposhi, Karakoram. 2r, Mt. Nangaparbat, Western Himalayas.

1985, May 27 Litho. *Perf. 14*
647 A303 40p multicolored 2.00 .75
648 A303 2r multicolored 4.25 5.50

Championship Pakistani Men's Field Hockey Team — A304

Design: 1984 Olympic gold medal, 1985 Dhaka Asia Cup, 1982 Bombay World Cup.

1985, June 5 Litho. *Perf. 13*
649 A304 1r multicolored 2.50 1.25

King Edward Medical College, Lahore, 125th Anniv. A305

1985, July 28 Litho. *Perf. 13*
650 A305 3r multicolored 2.25 .80

Natl. Independence Day — A306

Designs: No. 651a, 37th Independence Day written in English. No. 651b, In Urdu.

1985, Aug. 14
651 A306 Pair + 2 labels .75 .75
a.-b. 60p any single .35 .30

Printed in sheets of 4 stamps + 4 labels.

Sind Madressah-Tul-Islam, Karachi, Education Cent. — A307

1985, Sept. 1
652 A307 2r multicolored 2.10 .80

Mosque, Jinnah Avenue, Karachi A308

1985, Sept. 14
653 A308 1r Mosque by day 1.00 .35
654 A308 1r At night 1.00 .35

35th anniv. of the Jamia Masjid Pakistan Security Printing Corporation's miniature replica of the Badshahi Mosque, Lahore.

Lawrence College, Murree, 125th Anniv. — A309

1985, Sept. 21
655 A309 3r multicolored 2.50 .75

UN, 40th Anniv. A310

1985, Oct. 24 Litho. *Perf. 14x14½*
656 A310 1r UN building, sun .40 .25
657 A310 2r Building emblem .60 .30

10th Natl. Scouting Jamboree, Lahore, Nov. 8-15 — A311

1985, Nov. 8 *Perf. 13*
658 A311 60p multicolored 3.00 1.90

Islamabad and Capital Development Authority Emblem — A312

1985, Nov. 30 *Perf. 14½*
659 A312 3r multicolored 2.10 .50

Islamabad, capital of Pakistan, 25th anniv.

Flags and Map of SAARC Nations — A313

Flags as Flower Petals — A314

1985, Dec. 8 *Perf. 13½, 13*
660 A313 1r multicolored 2.75 3.50
661 A314 2r multicolored 1.25 1.75

SAARC, South Asian Assoc. for Regional Cooperation.

Dove and World Map — A315

1985, Dec. 14 *Perf. 13*
662 A315 60p multicolored 1.00 .60

UN Declaration on the Granting of Independence to Colonial Countries and Peoples, 25th Anniv.

Shaheen Falcon — A316

1986, Jan. 20 *Perf. 13½x14*
663 A316 1.50r multicolored 5.00 4.00

Agricultural Development Bank, 25th Anniv. — A317

1986, Feb. 18 Litho. *Perf. 13*
664 A317 60p multicolored 1.00 .40

Sadiq Egerton College, Bahawalpur, Cent. — A318

1986, Apr. 25
665 A318 1r multicolored 3.50 1.00

A319

1986, May 11 *Perf. 13½*
666 A319 1r multicolored 3.25 .85

Asian Productivity Organization, 25th anniv.

A320

1986, Aug. 14 Litho. *Perf. 14½x14*
667 A320 80p "1947-1986" 1.25 .60
668 A320 1r Urdu text, fireworks 1.25 .60

Independence Day, 39th anniv.

Intl. Literacy Day — A321

1986, Sept. 8 *Perf. 13*
669 A321 1r Teacher, students 1.50 .60

A322

1986, Oct. 28 Litho. *Perf. 13½x13*
670 A322 80p multicolored 2.50 .40

UN Child Survival Campaign.

Aitchison College, Lahore, Cent. A323

1986, Nov. 3 *Perf. 13½*
671 A323 2.50r multicolored 1.25 .60

Intl. Peace Year — A324

1986, Nov. 20 *Perf. 13*
672 A324 4r multicolored .65 .55

4th Asian Cup Table Tennis Tournament, Karachi — A325

1986, Nov. 25 *Perf. 14½*
673 A325 2r multicolored 2.50 .50

Marcopolo Sheep A326

1986, Dec. 4 Litho. *Perf. 14*
674 A326 2r multicolored 3.25 2.50

See No. 698.

Eco Philex '86 — A327

Mosques: No. 675a, Selimiye, Turkey. No. 675b, Gawhar Shad, Iran. No. 675c, Grand Mosque, Pakistan.

1986, Dec. 20 *Perf. 13*
675 Strip of 3 4.00 4.00
a.-c. A327 3r any single 1.25 1.25

St. Patrick's School, Karachi, 125th Anniv. A328

1987, Jan. 29 Litho. *Perf. 13*
676 A328 5r multicolored 3.00 1.10

Savings Bank Week A329

Birds, berries and: a, National defense. b, Education. c, Agriculture. d, Industry.

1987, Feb. 21 Litho. *Perf. 13*
677 Block of 4 + 2 labels 5.00 5.00
a.-d. A329 5r any single 1.00 .75

Parliament House Opening, Islamabad — A330

1987, Mar. 23
678 A330 3r multicolored .60 .25

Fight Against Drug Abuse — A331

1987, June 30 Litho. *Perf. 13*
679 A331 1r multicolored .60 .25

Natl. Independence, 40th Anniv. — A332

Natl. flag and: 80p, Natl. anthem, written in Urdu. 3r, Jinnah's first natl. address, the Minar-e-Qarardad-e-Pakistan and natl. coat of arms.

1987, Aug. 14 Litho. *Perf. 13*
680 A332 80p multicolored .60 .25
681 A332 3r multicolored 1.75 .75

Miniature Sheet

Air Force, 40th Anniv. A333

Aircraft: a, Tempest II. b, Hawker Fury. c, Super Marine Attacker. d, F86 Sabre. e, F104 Star Fighter. f, C130 Hercules. g, F6. h, Mirage III. i, A5. j, F16 Fighting Falcon.

1987, Sept. 7 Litho. *Perf. 13½*
682 Sheet of 10 16.00 16.00
a.-j. A333 3r any single 1.25 1.00

Tourism Convention 1987 — A334

Views along Karakoram Highway: a, Pasu Glacier. b, Apricot trees. c, Highway winding through hills. d, Khunjerab peak.

1987, Oct. 1 *Perf. 13*
683 Block of 4 2.50 2.50
a.-d. A334 1.50r any single .50 .25

Shah Abdul Latif Bhitai Mausoleum — A335

1987, Oct. 8 ***Perf. 13***
684 A335 80p multicolored .25 .25

D.J. Sind Government Science College, Karachi, Cent. — A336

1987, Nov. 7
685 A336 80p multicolored .25 .25

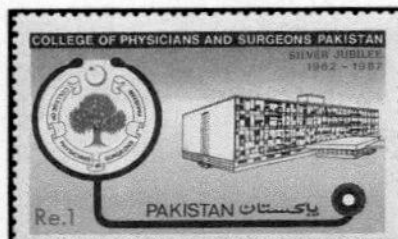

College of Physicians and Surgeons, 25th Anniv. A337

1987, Dec. 9 **Litho.** ***Perf. 13***
686 A337 1r multicolored 1.75 .60

Intl. Year of Shelter for the Homeless — A338

1987, Dec. 15
687 A338 3r multicolored .50 .35

Cathedral Church of the Resurrection, Lahore, Cent. — A339

1987, Dec. 20
688 A339 3r multicolored .50 .25

Natl. Postal Service, 40th Anniv. — A340

1987, Dec. 28
689 A340 3r multicolored .50 .25

Radio Pakistan A341

1987, Dec. 31
690 A341 80p multicolored .25 .25

A342

Design: Jamshed Nusserwanjee Mehta (1886-1952), Mayor of Karachi, member of the Sind Legislative assembly.

1988, Jan. 7
691 A342 3r multicolored .50 .35

World Leprosy Day — A343

1988, Jan. 31
692 A343 3r multicolored .75 .25

World Health Organization, 40th Anniv. A344

1988, Apr. 7 **Litho.** ***Perf. 13***
693 A344 4r multicolored .75 .30

Intl. Red Cross and Red Crescent Organizations, 125th Annivs. — A345

1988, May 8
694 A345 3r multicolored .70 .45

Independence Day, 41st Anniv. — A346

1988, Aug. 14 **Litho.** ***Perf. 13½***
695 A346 80p multicolored .35 .25
696 A346 4r multicolored .35 .35

Miniature Sheet

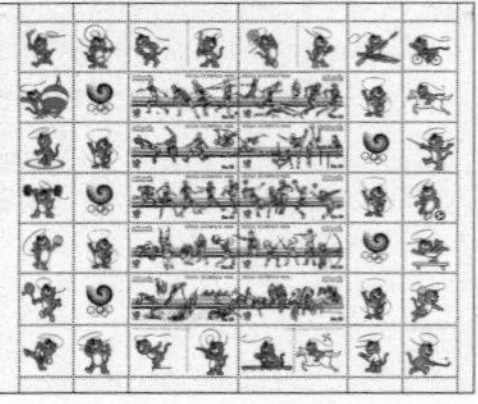

1988 Summer Olympics, Seoul — A347

Events: a, Discus, shot put, hammer throw, javelin. b, Relay, hurdles, running, walking. c, High jump, long jump, triple jump, pole vault. d, Gymnastic floor exercises, rings, parallel bars. e, Table tennis, tennis, field hockey, baseball. f, Volleyball, soccer, basketball, team handball. g, Wrestling, judo, boxing, weight lifting. h, Sport pistol, fencing, rifle shooting, archery. i, Swimming, diving, yachting, quadruple-sculling, kayaking. j, Equestrian jumping, cycling, steeplechase.

1988, Sept. 17 **Litho.** ***Perf. 13½x13***
697 A347 Sheet of 10 + 32 labels 13.00 13.00
a.-j. 10r any single 1.00 1.00

Labels contained in No. 697 picture the Seoul Games character trademark or emblem. Size of No. 697: 251x214mm.

Fauna Type of 1986

2r, Suleman markhor, vert.

1988, Oct. 29 **Litho.** ***Perf. 14***
698 A326 2r multi .85 .40

Pioneers of Freedom Type of 1979

3r, Maulana Hasrat Mohani.

1989, Jan. 23 **Litho.** **Wmk. 351**
699 A236 3r multi .45 .25

Islamia College, Peshawar, 75th Anniv. A348

1988, Dec. 22 **Unwmk.** ***Perf. 13½***
700 A348 3r multicolored .60 .25

SAARC Summit Conference, Islamabad A349

Designs: 25r, Flags, symbols of commerce. 50r, Globe, communication and transportation. 75r, Bangladesh #69, Maldive Islands #1030, Bhutan #132, Pakistan #403, Ceylon #451, India #580, Nepal #437.

1988, Dec. 29 ***Perf. 13***
701 A349 25r shown 1.75 1.50

No. 701 exists with attached label. Values: *$10* mint, *$20* used.

Size: 33x33mm
Perf. 14
702 A349 50r multicolored 4.75 3.25

Size: 52x28mm
Perf. 13½x13
703 A349 75r multicolored 3.75 *3.50*
Nos. 701-703 (3) 10.25 8.25

No. 703 exists with attached label. Value, strip of three with label $20.

Adasia '89, 16th Asian Advertising Congress, Lahore, Feb. 18-22 — A350

1989, Feb. 18 **Litho.** ***Perf. 13***
704 Strip of 3 3.50 3.25
a. A350 1r deep rose lilac & multi .95 .65
b. A350 1r green & multi .95 .65
c. A350 1r bright vermilion & multi .95 .65

Printed in sheets of 9.

Pres. Zulfikar Ali Bhutto (1928-1979), Ousted by Military Coup and Executed — A351

Portraits.

1989, Apr. 4 **Litho.** ***Perf. 13***
705 A351 1r shown .25 .25
706 A351 2r multi, diff. .40 .25

Submarine Operations, 25th Anniv. — A352

Submarines: a, *Agosta.* b, *Daphne.* c, *Fleet Snorkel.*

1989, June 1 **Litho.** ***Perf. 13½***
707 Strip of 3 4.25 4.25
a.-c. A352 1r any single 1.25 1.25

Oath of the Tennis Court, by David A353

1989, June 24 **Litho.** ***Perf. 13½***
708 A353 7r multicolored 2.25 .80

French revolution, bicent.

Archaeological Heritage — A354

Terra cotta vessels excavated in Baluchistan: a, Pirak, c. 2200 B.C. b, Nindo Damb, c. 2300 B.C. c, Mehrgarh, c. 3600 B.C. d, Nausharo, c. 2600 B.C.

1989, June 28 ***Perf. 14½x14***
709 Block of 4 1.50 1.25
a.-d. A354 1r any single .25 .25

Asia-Pacific Telecommunity, 10th Anniv. — A355

1989, July 1 ***Perf. 13½x14***
710 A355 3r multicolored .50 .25

Laying the Foundation Stone for the 1st Integrated Container Terminal, Port Qasim — A356

1989, Aug. 5 **Litho.** ***Perf. 14***
711 A356 6r Ship in berth 3.25 3.25

Mohammad Ali Jinnah — A357

Litho & Engr.
1989, Aug. 14 **Wmk. 351** ***Perf. 13***
712 A357 1r multicolored .65 .25
713 A357 1.50r multicolored .80 .25
714 A357 2r multicolored .90 .25
715 A357 3r multicolored 1.00 .30
716 A357 4r multicolored 1.50 .35
717 A357 5r multicolored 1.75 .40
Nos. 712-717 (6) 6.60 1.80

Independence Day.

Nos. 712-717 exist overprinted "NATIONAL SEMINAR ON PHILATELY MULTAN 1992." These were available only at the seminar and were not sold in post offices. Value $125. Beware of forgeries.

Abdul Latif Bhitai Memorial — A358

1989, Sept. 16 **Litho.** **Unwmk.**
718 A358 2r multicolored .60 .25

245th death and 300th birth annivs. of Shah Abdul Latif Bhitai.

World Wildlife Fund A359

Himalayan black bears and WWF emblem: a, Bear on slope, emblem UR. b, Bear on slope, emblem UL. c, Bear on top of rock, emblem UR. d, Seated bear, emblem UL.

Perf. 14x13½

1989, Oct. 7 Litho. Unwmk.

719 A359 Block of 4 4.00 4.00
a.-d. 4r, any single .75 .75

World Food Day — A360

1989, Oct. 16 ***Perf. 14x12½***

720 A360 1r multicolored .45 .30

Quilt and Bahishiti Darwaza (Heavenly Gate) A361

1989, Oct. 20 ***Perf. 13***

721 A361 3r multicolored .50 .25

800th Birth anniv. of Baba Farid.

4th SAF Games, Islamabad — A362

1989, Oct. 20

722 A362 1r multicolored .45 .40

Pakistan Television, 25th Anniv. — A363

1989, Nov. 26 Litho. ***Perf. 13½***

723 A363 3r multicolored .50 .25

SAARC Year Against Drug Abuse and Drug Trafficking — A364

1989, Dec. 8 ***Perf. 13***

724 A364 7r multicolored 2.75 .85

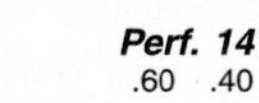

Murray College, Sialkot, Cent. — A365

1989, Dec. 18 ***Perf. 14***

725 A365 6r multicolored .60 .40

Government College, Lahore, 125th Anniv. A366

1989, Dec. 21 ***Perf. 13***

726 A366 6r multicolored .60 .50

Center on Integrated Rural Development for Asia and the Pacific (CIRDAP), 10th Anniv. — A367

1989, Dec. 31

727 A367 3r multicolored .60 .40

Organization of the Islamic Conference (OIC), 20th Anniv. A368

1990, Feb. 9 Litho. ***Perf. 13***

728 A368 1r multicolored 1.40 .50

7th World Field Hockey Cup, Lahore, Feb. 12-23 A369

1990, Feb. 12 ***Perf. 14x13½***

729 A369 2r multicolored 5.25 4.00

A370

Pakistan Resolution, 50th Anniv. — A371

Designs: a, Allama Mohammad Iqbal addressing the Allahabad Session of the All-India Muslim League and swearing-in of Liat Ali Khan as league secretary-general. b, Freedom fighter Maulana Mohammed Ali Jauhar at Muslim rally and Mohammed Ali Jinnah at microphone. c, Muslim woman holding flag and swearing-in of Mohammed Ali Jinnah as governor-general of Pakistan, Aug. 14, 1947. 7r, English and Urdu translations of the resolution, natl. flag and Minar-e-Qarardade Pakistan.

1990, Mar. 23 Litho. ***Perf. 13***

730 Strip of 3 3.00 3.00
a.-c. A370 1r any single 1.00 .75

Size: 90x45mm

Perf. 13½

731 A371 7r multicolored 2.00 2.00

Safe Motherhood South Asia Conference, Lahore A372

1990, Mar. 24 ***Perf. 13½***

732 A372 5r multicolored .75 .50

Calligraphic Painting of a Ghalib Verse, by Shakir Ali (1916-1975) — A373

1990, Apr. 19 Litho. ***Perf. 13½x13***

733 A373 1r multicolored 2.00 .65

See Nos. 757-758.

Badr-1 Satellite A374

1990, July 26 Litho. ***Perf. 13***

734 A374 3r multicolored 3.75 2.50

Pioneers of Freedom — A375

No. 735: a, Allama Mohammad Iqbal (1877-1938). b, Mohammad Ali Jinnah (1876-1948). c, Sir Syed Ahmad Khan (1817-98). d, Nawab Salimullah (1884-1915). e, Mohtarma Fatima Jinnah (1893-1967). f, Aga Khan III (1877-1957). g, Nawab Mohammad Ismail Khan (1884-1958). h, Hussain Shaheed Suhrawardy (1893-1963). i, Syed Ameer Ali (1849-1928).

No. 736: a, Nawab Bahadur Yar Jung (1905-44). b, Khawaja Nazimuddin (1894-1964). c, Maulana Obaidullah Sindhi (1872-1944). d, Sahibzada Abdul Qaiyum Khan (c. 1863-1937). e, Begum Jahanara Shah Nawaz (1896-1979). f, Sir Ghulam Hussain Hidayatullah (1879-1948). g, Qazi Mohammad Isa (1913-76). h, Sir M. Shahnawaz Khan Mamdot (1883-1942). i, Pir Shaib of Manki Sharif (1923-60).

No. 737: a, Liaquat Ali Khan (1895-1951). b, Maulvi A.K. Fazl-Ul-Haq (1873-1962). c, Allama Shabbir Ahmad Usmani (1885-1949). d, Sardar Abdur Rab Nishtar (1899-1958). e, Bi Amma (c. 1850-1924). f, Sir Abdullah Haroon (1872-1942). g, Chaudhry Rahmat Ali (1897-1951). h, Raja Sahib of Mahmudabad (1914-73). i, Hassanally Effendi (1830-1895).

No. 737J: k, Maulana Zafar Ali Khan (1873-1956). l, Maulana Mohamed Ali Jauhar (1878-1931). m, Chaudhry Khaliquzzaman (1889-1973). n, Hameed Nizami (1915-62). o, Begum Ra'ana Liaquat Ali Khan (1905-90). p, Mirza Abol Hassan Ispahani (1902-81). q, Raja Ghazanfar Ali Khan (1895-1963). r, Malik Barkat Ali (1886-1946). s, Mir Jaffer Khan Jamali (c. 1911-67).

1990-91 Litho. ***Perf. 13***

Miniature Sheets

735 Sheet of 9 4.00 3.50
a.-i. A375 1r any single .40 .25
736 Sheet of 9 4.00 3.50
a.-i. A375 1r any single .40 .25
737 Sheet of 9 4.00 3.50
a.-i. A375 1r any single .40 .25
737J Sheet of 9 ('91) 6.75 6.00
k.-s. A375 1r any single .40 .25
Nos. 735-737J (4) 18.75 16.50

Issued: #735-737, Aug. 19; #737J, 1991.

See Nos. 773, 792, 804, 859-860, 865, 875-876, 922-924.

Indonesia Pakistan Economic and Cultural Cooperation Organization, 1968-1990 A376

1990, Aug. 19

738 A376 7r multicolored 1.75 1.10

Intl. Literacy Year — A377

1990, Sept. 8

739 A377 3r multicolored 1.25 .75

A378

1990, Sept. 22

740 A378 2r multicolored 1.10 .40

Joint meeting of Royal College of Physicians, Edinburgh and College of Physicians and Surgeons, Pakistan.

World Summit for Children — A379

1990, Sept. 19

741 A379 7r multicolored .85 .50

Year of the Girl Child — A380

1990, Nov. 21 Litho. ***Perf. 13½***

742 A380 2r multicolored .75 .50

Security Papers Ltd., 25th Anniv. — A381

1990, Dec. 8 ***Perf. 13***

743 A381 3r multicolored 2.50 1.50

Intl. Civil Defense Day — A382

1991, Mar. 1 **Litho.** ***Perf. 13***
744 A382 7r multicolored 2.75 2.00

South & West Asia Postal Union A383

1991, Mar. 21
745 A383 5r multicolored 2.10 1.50

World Population Day — A384

1991, July 11
746 A384 10r multicolored 2.50 1.50

Intl. Special Olympics — A385

1991, July 19
747 A385 7r multicolored 2.10 1.50

Habib Bank Limited, 50th Anniv. — A386

1991, Aug. 25 **Litho.** ***Perf. 13***
748 A386 1r brt red & multi 1.25 .45
749 A386 5r brt green & multi 4.50 3.25

St. Joseph's Convent School, Karachi A387

1991, Sept. 8
750 A387 5r multicolored 4.25 3.00

Emperor Sher Shah Suri (c. 1472-1545) — A388

1991, Oct. 5
751 A388 5r multicolored 1.75 1.75

Souvenir Sheet
Size: 90x81mm
Imperf

752 A388 7r multicolored 2.00 2.00

Pakistani Scientific Expedition to Antarctica A389

1991, Oct. 28
753 A389 7r multicolored 3.50 2.50

Houbara Bustard — A390

1991, Nov. 4
754 A390 7r multicolored 3.00 2.00

Asian Development Bank, 25th Anniv. — A391

1991, Dec. 19 **Litho.** ***Perf. 13***
755 A391 7r multicolored 2.75 1.50

Hazrat Sultan Bahoo, 300th Death Anniv. — A392

1991, Dec. 22
756 A392 7r multicolored 2.10 1.10

Painting Type of 1990

Paintings and artists: No. 757, Village Life, by Allah Ustad Bux (1892-1978). No. 758, Miniature of Royal Procession, by Muhammad Haji Sharif (1889-1978).

1991, Dec. 24
757 A373 1r multicolored 2.25 1.25
758 A373 1r multicolored 2.25 1.25

American Express Travelers Cheques, 100th Anniv. — A393

1991, Dec. 26 ***Perf. 13½***
759 A393 7r multicolored 2.50 1.50

Muslim Commercial Bank, First Year of Private Operation A394

7r, City skyline, worker, cogwheels, computer operators.

1992, Apr. 8 **Litho.** ***Perf. 13***
760 A394 1r multicolored .25 .25
761 A394 7r multicolored 1.00 .65

Pakistan, 1992 World Cricket Champions A395

World Cricket Cup and: 2r, Pakistani player, vert. 7r, Pakistan flag, fireworks, vert.

1992, Apr. 27
762 A395 2r multicolored .75 .50
763 A395 5r multicolored 1.75 1.10
764 A395 7r multicolored 2.00 1.40
Nos. 762-764 (3) 4.50 3.00

Intl. Space Year — A396

Design: 2r, Globe, satellite.

1992, June 7 **Litho.** ***Perf. 13***
771 A396 1r multicolored .35 .25
772 A396 2r multicolored .55 .35

30th anniv. of first Pakistani rocket (#771).

Pioneers of Freedom Type of 1990

Designs: a, Syed Suleman Nadvi (1884-1953). b, Nawab Iftikhar Hussain Khan Mamdot (1906-1969). c, Maulana Muhammad Shibli Naumani (1857-1914).

1992, Aug. 14 **Litho.** ***Perf. 13***
773 A375 1r Strip of 3, #a.-c. 4.50 3.75

World Population Day — A397

1992, July 25
774 A397 6r multicolored 1.10 1.10

Medicinal Plants — A398

1992, Nov. 22 **Litho.** ***Perf. 13***
775 A398 6r multicolored 3.75 3.50

See No. 791.

Extraordinary Session of Economic Cooperation Organization Council of Ministers, Islamabad A399

1992, Nov. 28
776 A399 7r multicolored 1.40 1.00

Intl. Conference on Nutrition, Rome — A400

1992, Dec. 5 ***Perf. 14***
777 A400 7r multicolored .85 .85

Islamic Cultural Heritage — A401

1992, Dec. 14 ***Perf. 13***
778 A401 7r Alhambra, Spain .75 .60

Islamic Scouts, Islamabad — A402

1992, Aug. 23 ***Perf. 14x12½***
779 A402 6r 6th Jamboree .70 .60
780 A402 6r 4th Conference .70 .60

Government Islamia College, Lahore, Cent. A403

1992, Nov. 1 ***Perf. 13***
781 A403 3r multicolored .60 .60

Industries — A404

Designs: a, 10r, Surgical instruments. b, 15r, Leather goods. c, 25r, Sports equipment.

1992, July 5 **Litho.** ***Perf. 13½x13***
782 A404 Strip of 3, #a.-c. 5.50 5.50

World Telecommunications Day — A405

1993, May 17 **Litho.** ***Perf. 13***
783 A405 1r multicolored 1.50 .55

21st Islamic Foreign Ministers Conference — A406

1993, Apr. 25
784 A406 1r buff & multi .50 .50
785 A406 6r green & multi 2.25 1.40

A407

Traditional costumes of provinces.

1993, Mar. 10
786 A407 6r Sindh 1.50 1.00
787 A407 6r North West Frontier 1.50 1.00
788 A407 6r Baluchistan 1.50 1.00
789 A407 6r Punjab 1.50 1.00
Nos. 786-789 (4) 6.00 4.00

A408

Birds: a, Gadwall. b, Common shelduck. c, Mallard. d, Greylag goose.

The order of the birds is different on each row. Therefore the arc of the rainbow is different on each of the 4 Gadwalls, etc.

1992, Dec. 31 *Perf. 14x13*

790 A408 5r Sheet of 16 10.00 *15.00*
a.-d. Any single .60 .60
e. Horiz. strip of 4, #a-d 2.00 *3.00*

Medicinal Plants Type

1993, June 20 Litho. *Perf. 13*

791 A398 6r Fennel, chemistry equipment 3.25 1.25

Pioneers of Freedom Type of 1990

Designs: a, Rais Ghulam Mohammad Bhurgri (1878-1924). b, Mir Ahmed Yar Khan, Khan of Kalat (1902-1977). c, Mohammad Abdul Latif Pir Sahib Zakori Sharif (1914-1978).

1993, Aug. 14 Litho. *Perf. 13*

792 A375 1r Strip of 3, #a.-c. 3.50 2.50

Gordon College, Rawalpindi, Cent. — A410

1993, Sept. 1

793 A410 2r multicolored 1.50 1.00

Juniper Forests, Ziarat — A411

1993, Sept. 30

794 A411 7r multicolored 7.00 3.00

See No. 827.

World Food Day — A412

1993, Oct. 16 *Perf. 14*

795 A412 6r multicolored 1.00 1.00

A413

Wmk. 351

1993, Dec. 25 Litho. *Perf. 13½*

796 A413 1r multicolored 1.50 .55

Wazir Mansion, birthplace of Muhammad Ali Jinnah.

A414

Perf. 13x13½

1993, Oct. 28 Unwmk.

797 A414 7r multicolored 2.50 1.00

Burn Hall Institutions, 50th anniv.

South & West Asia Postal Union — A415

1993, Nov. 18 *Perf. 13*

798 A415 7r multicolored 2.00 1.00

Pakistani College of Physicians & Surgeons, Intl. Medical Congress — A416

1993, Dec. 10

799 A416 1r multicolored 1.75 .65

ILO, 75th Anniv. A417

1994, Apr. 11 Litho. *Perf. 13*

800 A417 7r multicolored 1.75 1.00

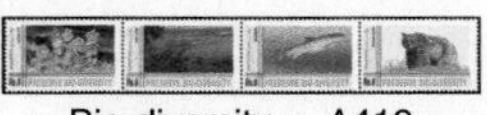

Bio-diversity — A418

a, Ratan jot, medicinal plant. b, Wetlands. c, Mahseer fish. d, Himalayan brown bear.

1994, Apr. 20 Litho. *Perf. 13½*

801 A418 6r Strip or block of 4, #a.-d. 3.50 2.00

Intl. Year of the Family — A419

1994, May 15 *Perf. 13*

802 A419 7r multicolored .75 .75

World Population Day — A420

1994, July 11 Litho. *Perf. 13*

803 A420 7r multicolored .75 .75

Pioneers of Freedom Type of 1990

Miniature Sheet of 8

Designs: a, Nawab Mohsin-Ul-Mulk (1837-1907). b, Sir Shahnawaz Bhutto (1888-1957). c, Nawab Viqar-Ul-Mulk (1841-1917). d, Pir Ilahi Bux (1890-1975). e, Sheikh Sir Abdul Qadir (1874-1950). f, Dr. Sir Ziauddin Ahmed (1878-1947). g, Jam Mir Ghulam Qadir Khan (1920-88). h, Sardar Aurangzeb Khan (1899-1953).

1994, Aug. 14 Litho. *Perf. 13*

804 A375 1r #a.-h. + label 3.25 3.25

A421

1994, Oct. 2 *Perf. 13x13½*

805 A421 2r multicolored 1.35 .45

First Intl. Festival of Islamic Artisans.

Intl. Literacy Day — A422

1994, Sept. 8

806 A422 7r multicolored .75 .75

Hyoscyamus Niger — A423

1994 *Perf. 13*

807 A423 6r multicolored 1.00 .75

Mohammad Ali Jinnah — A424

Litho. & Engr.

1994, Sept. 11 Wmk. 351 *Perf. 13*

808 A424 1r slate & multi .25 .25
809 A424 2r claret & multi .35 .25
810 A424 3r brt bl & multi .45 .25
811 A424 4r emer & multi .50 .25
812 A424 5r lake & multi .55 .25
813 A424 7r blue & multi .70 .25
814 A424 10r green & multi .55 .30
815 A424 12r orange & multi .65 .60
816 A424 15r violet & multi .70 .80
817 A424 20r rose & multi .75 1.00
818 A424 25r brown & multi .90 1.25
818A A424 28r blk & multi — —
819 A424 30r olive brn & multi 1.25 1.25
Nos. 808-819 (12) 7.60 6.70

Issued: 28r, 9/30/2011.

2nd SAARC & 12th Natl. Scout Jamboree, Quetta — A425

1994, Sept. 22 Litho.

820 A425 7r multicolored 1.25 .60

Publication of Ferdowsi's Book of Kings, 1000th Anniv. — A426

1994, Oct. 27

821 A426 1r multicolored .50 .50

Indonesia-Pakistan Economic & Cultural Cooperation Organization — A427

1994, Aug. 19

822 A427 10r Hala pottery 1.25 .60
823 A427 10r Lombok pottery 1.25 .60
a. Pair, #822-823 4.25 4.25

See Indonesia Nos. 1585-1586.

Lahore Museum, Cent. — A428

Wmk. 351

1994, Dec. 27 Litho. *Perf. 13*

824 A428 4r multicolored .60 .60

Pakistan, 1994 World Cup Field Hockey Champions A429

1994, Dec. 31

825 A429 5r multicolored .65 .40

World Tourism Organization, 20th Anniv. — A430

1995, Jan. 2

826 A430 4r multicolored .65 .30

Juniper Forests Type of 1993

1995, Feb. 14 Litho. *Perf. 13*

827 A411 1r like #794 .75 .25

Third Economic Cooperation Organization Summit, Islamabad — A431

1995, Mar. 14 Litho. *Perf. 14*

828 A431 6r multicolored .95 1.10

Khushall Khan Khatak (1613-89) — A432

1995, Feb. 28 *Perf. 13*

829 A432 7r multicolored 2.25 2.25

Earth Day — A433

Wmk. 351

1995, Apr. 20 Litho. ***Perf. 13***
830 A433 6r multicolored 1.25 .75

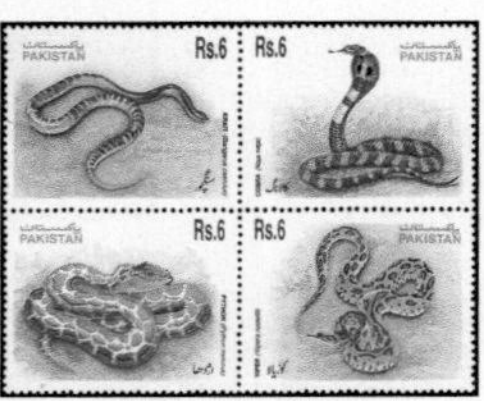
Snakes — A434

a, Krait. b, Cobra. c, Python. d, Viper.

1995, Apr. 15 Unwmk. ***Perf. 13½***
831 A434 6r Block of 4, #a.-d. 4.00 4.00

Traditional Means of Transportation A435

5r, Horse-drawn carriage.

Wmk. 351

1995, May 22 Litho. ***Perf. 13***
832 A435 5r multicolored .85 .85

Louis Pasteur (1822-95) — A436

Wmk. 351

1995, Sept. 28 Litho. ***Perf. 13***
833 A436 5r multicolored .85 .80

UN, FAO, 50th Anniv. A437

1995, Oct. 16
834 A437 1.25r multicolored .25 .25

Kinnaird College for Women, Lahore — A438

1995, Nov. 3 ***Perf. 14x13***
835 A438 1.25r multicolored .25 .25

4th World Conference on Women, Beijing — A439

Women in various activities: a, Playing golf, in armed forces, repairing technical device. b, Graduates, student, chemist, computer operator, reading gauge. c, At sewing machine, working with textiles. d, Making rugs, police woman, laborers.

1995, Sept. 15 ***Perf. 13***
836 A439 1.25r Strip of 4, #a.-d. 2.00 1.40

Presentation Convent School, Rawalpindi, Cent. — A440

Wmk. 351

1995, Sept. 8 Litho. ***Perf. 13½***
837 A440 1.25r multicolored .80 .45

A440a

Panel colors: 5p, Orange. 15p, Violet. 25p, Red. 75p, Red brown.

1995-96 Litho. Unwmk. ***Perf. 13½***
837A-837D A440a Set of 4 2.50 .60

Issued: 5p, 15p, 10/10/95; 25p, 9/28/95; 75p, 5/15/96.

Liaquat Ali Khan (1895-1951) A441

1995, Oct. 1 ***Perf. 13***
838 A441 1.25r multicolored .40 .40

1st Conference of Women Parliamentarians from Muslim Countries — A442

Designs: No. 839, Dr. Tansu Ciller, Prime Minister of Turkey. No. 840, Mohtarma Benazir Bhutto, Prime Minister of Pakistan.

1995, Aug. 1 **Unwmk.**
839 A442 5r multicolored .90 .90
840 A442 5r multicolored .90 .90
a. Pair, #839-840 2.00 *7.50*

Intl. Conference of Writers and Intellectuals A443

Wmk. 351

1995, Nov. 30 Litho. ***Perf. 14***
841 A443 1.25r multicolored .40 .40

Allama Iqbal Open University, 20th Anniv. A444

1995, Dec. 16 ***Perf. 13***
842 A444 1.25r multicolored .45 .30

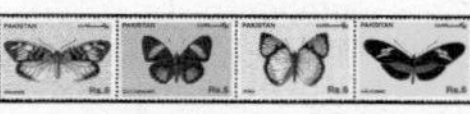
Butterflies — A445

Designs: a, Érasmie. b, Catogramme. c, Ixias. d, Héliconie.

Wmk. 351

1995, Sept. 1 Litho. ***Perf. 13½***
843 A445 6r Strip of 4, #a.-d. 3.00 2.50

Fish — A446

Designs: a, Sardinella long. b, Tilapia mossambica. c, Salmo fario. d, Labeo rohita.

1995, Sept. 1
844 A446 6r Strip of 4, #a.-d. 3.50 3.50

SAARC, 10th Anniv. — A447

1995, Dec. 8 ***Perf. 13***
845 A447 1.25r multicolored .75 .40

UN, 50th Anniv. A448

Wmk. 351

1995, Oct. 24 Litho. ***Perf. 13½***
846 A448 7r multicolored 1.25 1.25

Karachi '95, Natl. Water Sports Gala — A449

Designs: a, Man on jet ski. b, Gondola race. c, Sailboard race. d, Man water skiing.

1995, Dec. 14 ***Perf. 14x13***
847 A449 1.25r Block of 4, #a.-d. 1.50 1.50

University of Baluchistan, Quetta, 25th Anniv. — A452

Wmk. 351

1995, Dec. 31 Litho. ***Perf. 13***
850 A452 1.25r multicolored .25 .25

Zulfikar Ali Bhutto (1928-79), Politician, President — A455

Designs: 1.25r, Bhutto, flag, crowd of people, vert. 8r, like No. 855

Wmk. 351

1996, Apr. 4 Litho. ***Perf. 13***
855 A455 1.25r multicolored .75 .35
856 A455 4r shown 2.25 1.10

Size: 114x69mm

Imperf

857 A455 8r multicolored 2.50 2.50

Raja Aziz Bhatti Shaheed (1928-65) A456

Wmk. 351

1995, Sept. 5 Litho. ***Perf. 13***
858 A456 1.25r multicolored 1.25 .40

See Nos. 953, 983, 997, 1016.

Pioneers of Freedom Type of 1990

#859, Maulana Shaukat Ali (1873-1938). #860, Chaudhry Ghulam Abbas (1904-67).

1995, Aug. 14 Unwmk. ***Perf. 13***
859 A375 1r green & brown .65 .50
860 A375 1r green & brown .65 .50
a. Pair, #859-860 1.50 1.50

1996 Summer Olympic Games, Atlanta A457

Design: 25r, #861-864 without denominations, simulated perfs, Olympic rings, "100," Atlanta '96 emblem.

Wmk. 351

1996, Aug. 3 Litho. ***Perf. 13***
861 A457 5r Wrestling .60 .60
862 A457 5r Boxing .60 .60
863 A457 5r Pierre de Coubertin .60 .60
864 A457 5r Field hockey .60 .60
Nos. 861-864 (4) 2.40 2.40

Imperf

Size: 111x101mm

864A A457 25r multicolored 3.00 3.00

Pioneers of Freedom Type of 1990

Allama Abdullah Yousuf Ali (1872-1953).

Unwmk.

1996, Aug. 14 Litho. ***Perf. 13***
865 A375 1r green & brown .45 .40

Restoration of General Post Office, Lahore — A458

1996, Aug. 21 Wmk. 351 ***Perf. 14***
866 A458 5r multicolored .45 .45

Intl. Literacy Day — A459

1996, Sept. 8 Wmk. 351 ***Perf. 13***
867 A459 2r multicolored .45 .40

Yarrow — A459a

Wmk. 351

1996, Nov. 25 Litho. ***Perf. 13***
867A A459a 3r multicolored 1.75 .65

Faiz Ahmed Faiz, Poet, 86th Birthday — A460

Unwmk.

1997, Feb. 13 Litho. ***Perf. 13***
868 A460 3r multicolored .25 .25

Tamerlane (1336-1405) — A461

Unwmk.

1997, Apr. 8 Litho. *Perf. 13*
869 A461 3r multicolored .45 .40

Famous Men — A462

Designs: No. 870, Allama Mohammad Iqbal. No. 871, Jalal-Al-Din Moulana Rumi.

1997, Apr. 21 *Perf. 13½*
870 A462 3r multicolored .25 .25
871 A462 3r multicolored .25 .25

Compare with Iran 2726-2727.

Pakistani Independence, 50th Anniv. — A463

1997, Mar. 23 *Perf. 13*
872 A463 2r multicolored .45 .45

Special Summit of Organization of Islamic Countries, Islamabad.

World Population Day — A464

Unwmk.

1997, July 11 Litho. *Perf. 13*
873 A464 2r multicolored .45 .40

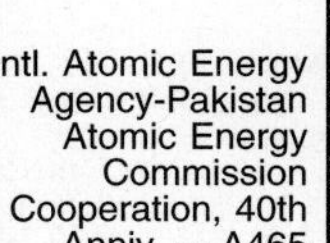

Intl. Atomic Energy Agency-Pakistan Atomic Energy Commission Cooperation, 40th Anniv. — A465

1997, July 29 *Perf. 14*
874 A465 2r multicolored .45 .40

Pioneers of Freedom Type of 1990

No. 875, Begum Salma Tassaduq Hussain (1908-95). No. 876, Mohammad Ayub Khuhro (1901-80).

1997, Aug. 14 Litho. *Perf. 13*
875 A375 1r green & brown .55 .55
876 A375 1r green & brown .55 .55

Fruits of Pakistan — A466

1997, May 8
877 A466 2r Apples .45 .45

Independence, 50th Anniv. — A467

Designs: a, Allama Mohammad Iqbal. b, Mohammad Ali Jinnah. c, Liaquat Ali Khan. d, Mohtarma Fatima Jinnah.

Block of 4 + 2 Labels

1997, Aug. 14
878 A467 3r gold & multi 2.00 .75

No. 878 exists with No. 878d unretouched. Value, $5 mint or used.

Lophophorus Impejanus — A468

Wmk. 351

1997, Oct. 29 Litho. *Perf. 13*
879 A468 2r multicolored 2.50 .90

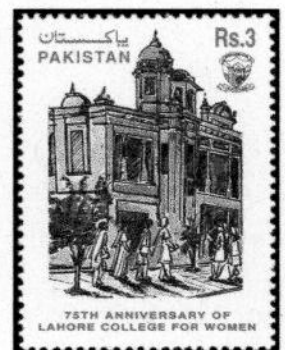

Lahore College for Women, 75th Anniv. — A469

1997, Sept. 23
880 A469 3r multicolored .40 .40

Intl. Day of the Disabled A470

Unwmk.

1997, Dec. 3 Litho. *Perf. 13*
881 A470 4r multicolored .45 .45

Protection of the Ozone Layer — A471

1997, Nov. 15
882 A471 3r multicolored 1.25 1.00

Pakistan Motorway, 50th Anniv. — A472

1997, Nov. 26 *Perf. 13½*
883 A472 10r multicolored 2.25 2.25
a. Souvenir sheet of 1 2.50 2.50

No. 883a sold for 15r.

Karachi Grammar School, 150th Anniv. — A473

1997, Dec. 30 Litho. *Perf. 13½*
884 A473 2r multicolored .50 .50

Garlic — A474

1997, Oct. 22 *Perf. 13*
885 A474 2r multicolored .70 .25

Mirza Asad Ullah Khan Ghalib (1797-1869), Poet — A475

1998, Feb. 15
886 A475 2r multicolored .40 .40

Pakistan Armed Forces, 50th Anniv. — A476

Wmk. 351

1997, Mar. 23 Litho. *Perf. 13½*
887 A476 7r multicolored .75 .75

Sir Syed Ahmad Khan (1817-98), Educator, Jurist, Author A477

1998, Mar. 27 *Perf. 14*
888 A477 7r multicolored .65 .65

27th Natl. Games, Peshawar — A478

Wmk. 351

1998, Apr. 22 Litho. *Perf. 13*
889 A478 7r multicolored .65 .65

Jimsonweed — A479

1998, Apr. 27
890 A479 2r multicolored .25 .25

Faisalabad Government College, Cent. (in 1997) — A480

1998, Aug. 14 Litho. *Perf. 13*
891 A480 5r multicolored .30 .30

Pakistan Senate, 25th Anniv. — A481

1998, Aug. 6 *Perf. 13½*
892 A481 2r green & multi .25 .25
893 A481 5r blue & multi .30 .30

Mohammed Ali Jinnah — A482

Litho. & Engr.

1998-2001 Wmk. 351 *Perf. 14*
893A A482 1r red & black *3.00 3.00*
894 A482 2r dk bl & red .25 .25
895 A482 3r slate grn & brn .25 .25
896 A482 4r dp vio blk & org .25 .25
897 A482 5r dp brn & grn .65 .65
898 A482 6r dp grn & bl grn .75 .65
899 A482 7r dp brn red & dp vio .90 .90
Nos. 894-899 (6) 3.05 2.95

Nos. 894 issued 8/14/98. No. 893A, 2001(?).

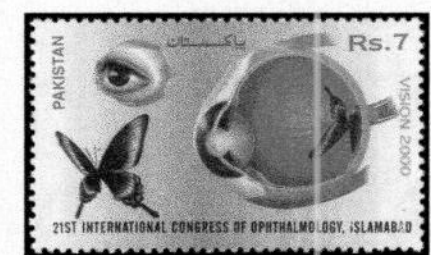

21st Intl. Congress of Ophthalmology, Islamabad — A483

Wmk. 351

1998, Sept. 11 Litho. *Perf. 13*
900 A483 7r multicolored 1.60 1.60

Syed Ahmed Shah Patrus Bukhari, Birth Cent. — A484

1998, Oct. 1
901 A484 5r multicolored .25 .25

Philately in Pakistan, 50th Anniv. — A485

Various portions of stamps inside "50," #20-23.

1998, Oct. 4
902 A485 6r multicolored .25 .25

World Food Day — A486

Wmk. 351

1998, Oct. 16 Photo. *Perf. 13*
903 A486 6r multicolored .25 .25

Mohammad Ali Jinnah (1876-1948) — A487

Wmk. 351

1998, Sept. 11 Photo. *Perf. 13½*
904 A487 15r multicolored .90 .90
a. Souvenir sheet of 1, unwmk. 1.75 1.75

No. 904a sold for 20r.

Universal Declaration of Human Rights, 50th Anniv. — A488

Perf. 13x14

1998, Dec. 10 Wmk. 351
905 A488 6r multicolored .35 .35

Better Pakistan, 2010 — A489

No. 906, Harvesting grain. No. 907, Health care. No. 908, Satellite dishes. No. 909, Airplane.

1998, Nov. 27 Unwmk.
906 A489 2r multicolored .45 .35
907 A489 2r multicolored .45 .35
908 A489 2r multicolored .45 .35
909 A489 2r multicolored .45 .35
Nos. 906-909 (4) 1.80 1.40

Dr. Abdus Salam, Scientist — A490

Unwmk.

1998, Nov. 21 Litho. *Perf. 13*
910 A490 2r multicolored .30 .30

See No. 916.

National Flag March — A491

1998, Dec. 16 Wmk. 351
911 A491 2r multicolored .25 .25

Intl. Year of the Ocean — A492

1998, Dec. 15 *Perf. 14*
912 A492 5r multicolored 1.50 1.00

UNICEF in Pakistan, 50th Anniv. — A493

a, Distributing water. b, Child holding book. c, Girl. d, Child receiving oral vaccine.

1998, Dec. 15
913 A493 2r Block of 4, #a.-d. 1.50 1.50

Kingdom of Saudi Arabia, Cent. — A494

Perf. 13½

1999, Jan. 27 Litho. Unwmk.
914 A494 2r Emblem on sand .40 .40
915 A494 15r Emblem on carpet 1.25 1.25
a. Souvenir sheet of 1 2.25 2.25

No. 915a sold for 20r.

Scientists of Pakistan Type

Dr. Salimuz Zaman Siddiqui (1897-1994).

1999, Apr. 14 *Perf. 13*
916 A490 5r multicolored .40 .40

Pakistani Nuclear Test, 1st Anniv. A495

1999, May 28 Litho. *Perf. 13*
917 A495 5r multicolored .30 .30

Completion of Data Darbar Mosque Complex — A496

1999, May 31 Litho. *Perf. 13*
918 A496 7r multicolored .25 .25

Fasting Buddha, c. 3-4 A.D. — A497

1999, July 21 Litho. *Perf. 13½x13¾*
919 A497 7r shown .80 .80
920 A497 7r Facing forward .80 .80
a. Souv. sheet of 2, #919-920 2.50 2.50

No. 920a sold for 25r. China 1999 World Philatelic Exhibition (No. 920a).

Geneva Conventions, 50th Anniv. — A498

Perf. 12¾x13¾

1999, Aug. 12 Litho.
921 A498 5r pink, black & red .60 .60

Pioneers of Freedom Type of 1990

Designs: No. 922, Chaudhry Muhammad Ali (1905-80), 1st Secretary General. No. 923, Sir Adamjee Haji Dawood (1880-1948), banker. No. 924, Maulana Abdul Hamid Badayuni (1898-1970), religious scholar.

1999, Aug. 14 Litho. *Perf. 13*
922 A375 2r green & brown .45 .45
923 A375 2r green & brown .45 .45
924 A375 2r green & brown .45 .45
Nos. 922-924 (3) 1.35 1.35

Ustad Nusrat Fateh Ali Khan (1948-97), Singer A499

1999, Aug. 16
925 A499 2r multicolored .60 .60

Islamic Development Bank, 25th Anniv. (in 2000) — A500

1999, Sept. 18
926 A500 5r multicolored .30 .30

People's Republic of China, 50th Anniv. — A501

2r, Gate of Heavenly Peace. 15r, Arms, Mao Zedong, horiz.

1999, Sept. 21
927 A501 2r multicolored .25 .25
928 A501 15r multicolored 1.00 1.00

Ninth Asian Sailing Championship — A502

No. 929: a, Enterprise class. b, 470 class. c, Optimist class. d, Laser class. e, Mistral class.

1999, Sept. 28 *Perf. 13½x13¼*
929 A502 2r Strip of 5, #a.-e. 1.25 1.25

10th Asian Optimist Sailing Championships — A502a

1999, Oct. 7 Litho. *Perf. 13¾x13½*
929F A502a 2r multi + label .60 .60

UPU, 125th Anniv. — A503

1999, Oct. 9 *Perf. 14¼*
930 A503 10r multicolored 1.00 1.00

Hakim Mohammed Said (1920-98), Physician — A504

1999, Oct. 17 Litho. *Perf. 13*
931 A504 5r multicolored .65 .65

National Bank of Pakistan, 50th Anniv. — A505

Perf. 13¼x13¾

1999, Nov. 8 Litho. Wmk. 351
932 A505 5r multi .80 .80

Shell Oil in Pakistan, Cent. — A506

Perf. 13¼x13

1999, Nov. 15 Wmk. 351
933 A506 4r multi .80 .80

Rights of the Child, 10th Anniv. — A507

Perf. 13x13¼

1999, Nov. 20 Unwmk.
934 A507 2r multi .25 .25

Allam Iqbal Open University, Islamabad A508

Designs: 2r, University crest, flasks, microphone, mortarboard, book, computer. 3r, Similar to 2r, crest in center. 5r, Crest, map, mortarboard, book.

Unwmk.

1999, Nov. 20 Litho. *Perf. 13*
935 A508 2r bl grn & multi .35 .35
936 A508 3r multi .45 .45
937 A508 5r multi 1.75 1.00
Nos. 935-937 (3) 2.55 1.80

Shabbir Hassan Khan Josh Malihabadi (1898-1982), Poet — A509

1999, Dec. 5
938 A509 5r multi .25 .25

Dr. Afzal Qadri (1912-74), Entomologist A510

1999, Dec. 6
939 A510 3r multi .25 .25

Ghulam Bari Aleeg (1907-49), Journalist — A511

1999, Dec. 10 Litho. *Perf. 13*
940 A511 5r multi .25 .25

See No. 982.

Plantain — A512

1999, Dec. 20
941 A512 5r multi .50 .50

Eid-Ul-Fitr — A513

Perf. 13¾x13½
1999, Dec. 24 Litho.
942 A513 2r green & multi .75 .75
943 A513 15r blue & multi 2.25 2.25

SOS Children's Villages of Pakistan, 25th Anniv. — A514

2000, Mar. 12 *Perf. 13*
944 A514 2r multi .50 .50

International Cycling Union, Cent. — A515

2000, Apr. 14 Litho. *Perf. 13¼*
945 A515 2r multi 1.00 1.00

Convention on Human Rights and Dignity — A516

Perf. 13¼
2000, Apr. 21 Litho. Unwmk.
946 A516 2r multi .50 .50

Edwardes College, Peshawar, Cent. A517

2000, Apr. 24 *Perf. 13½*
947 A517 2r multi .50 .50

Mahomed Ali Habib (1904-59), Banker, Philantropist A518

2000, May 15 Litho. *Perf. 13*
948 A518 2r multi .50 .50

Institute of Cost and Management Accountants, 50th Anniv. — A519

Design: 2r, Arrow. 15r, Globe.

2000, June 23 Litho. *Perf. 13*
949 A519 2r multi .30 .30
950 A519 15r multi 2.00 2.00

Ahmed E. H. Jaffer (1909-90), Politician — A520

2000, Aug. 9 Litho. *Perf. 13*
951 A520 10r multi .75 .75

Creation of Pakistan, 53rd Anniv. A521

a, No tree. b, Tree in foreground. c, Tree behind people, cart. d, Tree in distance.

2000, Aug. 14 Litho. *Perf. 13*
952 A521 5r Strip of 4, #a-d 2.50 2.50

Nishan-e-Haider Medal Type of 1995

Nishan-e-haider gallantry award winners: a, Capt. Muhammad Sarwar Shaheed (1910-48). b, Maj. Tufail Muhammad (1914-58).

2000, Sept. 6 Litho. *Perf. 13*
953 A456 5r Pair, #a-b 1.75 1.75

2000 Summer Olympics, Sydney — A523

No. 954: a, Runners. b, Field hockey. c, Weight lifting. d, Cycling.

2000, Sept. 20 *Perf. 14¼*
954 A523 4r Block of 4, #a-d 2.25 2.25

Natl. College of Arts, 125th Anniv. — A524

2000, Oct. 28
955 A524 5r multi .45 .45

Creating the Future — A525

2000, Nov. 4 *Perf. 13½x13¼*
956 A525 5r multi 1.25 1.25

Intl. Defense Exhibition and Seminar A526

2000, Nov. 14 Litho. *Perf. 13*
957 A526 7r multi .60 .60

Licorice — A527

2000, Nov. 28 Litho. *Perf. 13*
958 A527 2r multi .65 .65

Rotary Intl. Campaign Against Polio — A528

2000, Dec. 13
959 A528 2r multi .75 .75

UN High Commissioner for Refugees, 50th Anniv. — A529

2000, Dec. 14
960 A529 2r multi .45 .45

Poets — A530

Design: 2r, Hafeez Jalandhri (1900-82). 5r, Khawaja Ghulam Farid.

2001 Litho. *Perf. 13*
961 A530 2r multi .50 .50
962 A530 5r multi 1.25 1.25

Issued: 2r, 1/14. 5r, 9/25.

See No. 986.

Habib Bank AG Zurich A531

2001, Mar. 20 Litho. *Perf. 13*
963 A531 5r multi 1.25 1.25

Chashma Nuclear Power Plant — A532

2001, Mar. 29
964 A532 4r multi 1.40 1.25

9th SAF Games, Islamabad A533

Background colors: No. 965, 4r, Light blue. No. 966, 4r, Lilac.

2001, Apr. 9 *Perf. 13½x13¼*
965-966 A533 Set of 2 1.40 1.40

Pakistan-People's Rep. of China Diplomatic Relations, 50th Anniv. — A534

Designs: No. 967, Yugur and Hunza women, flags.

No. 968 — Paintings by Yao Youdou: a, Ma Gu's Birthday Offering. b, Two Pakistani Women Drawing Water.

2001, May 12 *Perf. 13*
967 A534 4r multi .25 .25
968 A534 4r Horiz. pair, #a-b 2.00 2.00

Mohammed Ali Jinnah (1876-1948) — A535

2001, Aug. 14
969 A535 4r multi .90 .90

Sindh Festival — A536

Unwmk.
2001, Sept. 22 Litho. *Perf. 13*
970 A536 4r multi .75 .75

Year of Dialogue Among Civilizations — A537

2001, Oct. 9 *Perf. 13½*
971 A537 4r multi 1.25 1.25

Turkmenistan, 10th Anniv. of Independence — A538

2001, Oct. 27 *Perf. 13*
972 A538 5r multi .90 .90

Convent of Jesus and Mary, Lahore, 125th Anniv. A539

2001, Nov. 15 **Wmk. 351**
973 A539 4r multi 1.00 1.00

Men of Letters Type of 1999

Design: 4r, Dr. Ishtiaq Husain Qureshi (1903-81), historian.

2001, Nov. 20 **Unwmk.**
974 A511 4r multi .75 .75

Birds A540

No. 975: a, Blue throat. b, Hoopoe. c, Pin-tailed sandgrouse. d, Magpie robin.

2001, Nov. 26 ***Perf. 13¼x13***
975 A540 4r Block of 4, #a-d 3.00 3.00

Pakistan — United Arab Emirates Friendship, 30th Anniv. A541

Designs: 5r, Flags, handshake, vert. 30r, Sheik Zaid bin Sultan al Nahayan, Mohammed Ali Jinnah.

2001, Dec. 2 ***Perf. 13***
976-977 A541 Set of 2 3.75 3.75

Nishtar Medical College, Multan, 50th Anniv. — A542

2001, Dec. 20
978 A542 5r multi .75 .75

Quaid Year A543

No. 979: a, Mohammed Ali Jinnah reviewing troops, 1948. b, Jinnah, soldiers, artillery gun, 1948.

No. 980, vert.: a, Jinnah taking oath as Governor General, 1947. b, Jinnah at opening ceremony of State Bank of Pakistan, 1948. c, Jinnah saluting at presentation of colors, 1948.

2001, Dec. 25 ***Perf. 13***
979 Horiz. pair .80 .80
a.-b. A543 4r Any single .25 .25

Size: 33x56mm

Perf. 13x13¼

980 Horiz. strip of 3 1.00 1.00
a.-c. A543 4r Any single .25 .25

Pakistan Ordnance Factories, 50th Anniv. — A544

2001, Dec. 28 ***Perf. 13¼x13½***
981 A544 4r multi .75 .75

Men of Letters Type of 1999

Design: 5r, Syed Imtiaz Ali Taj (1900-70), playwright.

2001, Oct. 13 ***Perf. 13***
982 A511 5r multi .60 .60

Nishan-e-Haider Type of 1995

No. 983: a, Maj. Mohammad Akram Shaheed (1938-71). b, Maj. Shabbir Sharif Shaheeb (1943-71).

2001, Sept. 6 ***Perf. 13***
983 Horiz. pair .75 .75
a.-b. A456 4r Any single .30 .30

Peppermint — A545

Design: 5r, Hyssop.

2001-02 **Litho.** **Wmk. 351** ***Perf. 13***
984 A545 4r multi 1.00 1.00
985 A545 5r multi .80 .80

Issued: 4r, 11/12/01. 5r, 2/15/02.

Poets Type of 2001

Design: Samandar Khan Samandar (1901-90).

2002, Jan. 17 **Litho.** ***Perf. 13***
986 A530 5r multi .60 .60

Pakistan — Japan Diplomatic Relations, 50th Anniv. — A546

2002, Apr. 28 **Litho.** ***Perf. 14***
987 A546 5r multi .85 .85

Pakistan - Kyrgyzstan Diplomatic Relations, 10th Anniv. — A547

2002, May 27 ***Perf. 13¾x12¾***
988 A547 5r multi .75 .75

Mangoes A548

No. 989: a, Anwar Ratol. b, Dusheri. c, Chaunsa. d, Sindhri.

2002, June 18
989 A548 4r Block of 4, #a-d 2.40 2.40

Independence, 55th Anniv. — A549

Famous people: No. 990, 4r, Noor-us-Sabah Begum (1908-78), Muslim leader and writer. No. 991, 4r, Prime Minister Ismail I. Chundrigar (1897-1960). No. 992, 4r, Habib Ibrahim Rahimtoola (1912-91), governmental minister. No. 993, 4r, Qazi Mureed Ahmed (1913-89), politician.

2002, Aug. 14 **Litho.** ***Perf. 13¼x13***
990-993 A549 Set of 4 2.40 2.40

World Summit on Sustainable Development, Johannesburg — A550

Designs: No. 994, 4r, Children, Pakistani flag, dolphin, goat. No. 995, 4r, Water droplet, mountain (33x33mm).

2002, Aug. 26 ***Perf. 13¼, 14¼ (#995)***
994-995 A550 Set of 2 1.50 1.50

Mohammad Aly Rangoonwala (1924-98), Philanthropist — A551

2002, Aug. 31 ***Perf. 13***
996 A551 4r multi .60 .60

Nishan-e-Haidar type of 1995

No. 997: a, Lance Naik Muhammad Mahfuz Shaheed (1944-71). b, Sawar Muhammad Hussain Shaheed (1949-71).

2002, Sept. 6 ***Perf. 13***
997 Horiz. pair 1.00 1.00
a.-b. A456 4r Either single .25 .25

Muhammad Iqbal Year — A552

No. 998: a, Iqbal wearing hat. b, Iqbal without hat.

Unwmk.

2002, Nov. 9 **Litho.** ***Perf. 13***
998 A552 4r Horiz. pair, #a-b 1.25 1.25

Eid ul-Fitr — A553

Perf. 13¾x14

2002, Nov. 14 **Wmk. 351**
999 A553 4r multi .75 .75

Shifa-ul-Mulk Hakim Muhammad Hassan Qarshi (1896-1974), Physician — A554

2002, Dec. 20 **Unwmk.** ***Perf. 13½***
1000 A554 4r multi 1.00 1.00

Pakistan 2003 Natl. Philatelic Exhibition, Karachi — A555

Wmk. 351

2003, Jan. 31 **Litho.** ***Perf. 13***
1001 A555 4r multi + label 1.25 1.25

Pakistan Academy of Sciences, 50th Anniv. — A556

2003, Feb. 15 **Unwmk.** ***Perf. 14¼***
1002 A556 4r multi .60 .60

North West Frontier Province, Cent. — A557

Perf. 13½x13¼

2003, Mar. 23 **Litho.** **Wmk. 351**
1003 A557 4r multi .60 .60

Pakistan Council of Scientific and Industrial Research, 50th Anniv. — A558

2003, Mar. 31 ***Perf. 14x13¾***
1004 A558 4r multi .75 .75

A. B. A. Haleem (1897-1975), Educator — A559

2003, Apr. 20 ***Perf. 13½x13¼***
1005 A559 2r multi .60 .60

Campaign Against Illegal Drugs — A560

2003, Apr. 21 ***Perf. 13***
1006 A560 2r multi 1.25 1.25

Sir Syed Memorial, Islamabad — A561

2003, Apr. 30 ***Perf. 13¼x13½***
1007 A561 2r multi .60 .60

Rosa Damascena — A562

Perf. 13¼x12¾

2003, July 14 **Unwmk.**
1008 A562 2r multi 1.00 1.00

Mohtarma Fatima Jinnah (1893-1967), Presidential Candidate in 1964 — A563

2003, July 31 **Litho.**
1009 A563 4r multi .60 .60

Famous Men — A564

Designs: No. 1010, 2r, M. A. Rahim (1919-2003), labor leader. No. 1011, 2r, Abdul Rahman (1959-2002), slain postal worker.

2003, Aug. 3 ***Perf. 12¾x13¼***
1010-1011 A564 Set of 2 1.00 1.00

Famous Men — A565

Designs: No. 1012, 2r, Moulana Abdul Sattar Khan Niazi (1915-2001), politician. No. 1013, 2r, Muhammad Yousaf Khattak (1917-91), politician. No. 1014, 2r, Moulana Muhammad Ismail Zabeeh (1913-2001), political leader and journalist.

2003, Apr. 14 ***Perf. 13¼x12¾***
1012-1014 A565 Set of 3 1.75 1.75

UN Literacy Decade, 2003-12 — A566

2003, Sept. 6
1015 A566 1r multi .60 .60

Nishan-e-Haider Type of 1995

2003, Sept. 7 ***Perf. 14***
1016 A456 2r Pilot Officer Rashid Minhas Shaheed .75 .75

Pakistan Academy of Letters, 25th Anniv. — A567

2003, Sept. 24 ***Perf. 13¼x12¾***
1017 A567 2r multi .60 .60

Karakoram Highway, 25th Anniv. — A568

Perf. 12¾x13

2003, Oct. 1 **Litho.** **Unwmk.**
1018 A568 2r multi .60 .60

Pakistan Air Force Public School, Sargodha, 50th Anniv. — A569

Perf. 13x13¼

2003, Oct. 10 **Litho.** **Wmk. 351**
1019 A569 4r multi 1.00 1.00

First Ascent of Nanga Parbat, 50th Anniv. — A570

Perf. 12¾x13

2003, Oct. 6 **Litho.** **Unwmk.**
1020 A570 2r multi 1.75 1.75

Exports — A571

No. 1021: a, Leather garments. b, Towels. c, Ready-made garments. d, Karachi Port Trust and Port Qasim. e, Fisheries. f, Yarn. g, Sporting goods. h, Fabrics. i, Furniture. j, Surgical instruments. k, Gems and jewelry. l, Leather goods. m, Information technology. n, Rice. o, Auto parts. p, Carpets. q, Marble and granite. r, Fruits. s, Cutlery. t, Engineering goods.

2003, Oct. 20 ***Perf. 13x12¾***
1021 Sheet of 20 7.50 7.50
a.-t. A571 1r Any single .35 .35

Intl. Day of the Disabled — A572

2003, Dec. 3 ***Perf. 12¾x13***
1022 A572 2r multi 1.00 1.00

World Summit on the Information Society, Geneva, Switzerland — A573

2003, Dec. 10 ***Perf. 13x12¾***
1023 A573 2r multi 1.25 1.25

Submarines — A574

Khalid Class (Agosta 90B) submarine and flag of: 1r, Pakistan Navy, vert. 2r, Pakistan.

2003, Dec. 12 ***Perf. 13x12¾, 12¾x13***
1024-1025 A574 Set of 2 3.00 3.00

Powered Flight, Cent. — A575

Designs: No. 1026, 2r, Pakistan Air Force's transition into jet age, 1956. No. 1027, 2r, Air Force in action at Siachen, 1988-90.

2003, Dec. 17 ***Perf. 12¾x13***
1026-1027 A575 Set of 2 1.75 1.75

12th South Asian Association for Regional Cooperation Summit, Islamabad — A576

2004, Jan. 4
1028 A576 4r multi .60 .60

Sadiq Public School, Bahawalpur, 50th Anniv. — A577

2004, Jan. 28 **Litho.** ***Perf. 14***
1029 A577 4r multi .60 .60

Ninth SAF Games, Islamabad — A578

No. 1030: a, Gold medal. b, Running. c, Squash (yellow and blue uniform). d, Boxing. e, Wrestling. f, Judo. g, Javelin. h, Soccer. i, Rowing. j, Shooting. k, Shot put. l, Badminton (white uniform). m, Weight lifting. n, Volleyball. o, Table tennis. p, Swimming.

2004, Mar. 29 **Litho.** ***Perf. 13x12¾***
1030 A578 2r Sheet of 16, #a-p 6.00 6.00

Pir Muhammad Karam Shah Al-Azhari (1918-98), Jurist — A579

2004, Apr. 7
1031 A579 2r multi .60 .60

Cadet College, Hasan Abdal — A580

2004, Apr. 8 ***Perf. 12¾x13***
1032 A580 4r multi .60 .60

Central Library, Bahawalpur — A581

2004, Apr. 26 **Litho.** ***Perf. 13x12¾***
1033 A581 2r multi .60 .60

Mosque, Bhong — A582

2004, May 12 ***Perf. 12¾x13***
1034 A582 4r multi .60 .60

FIFA (Fédération Internationale de Football Association), Cent. — A583

No. 1035 — FIFA centenary emblem and: a, Player. b, Blue panel at bottom. c, Player, green panel at bottom.

2004, May 21 ***Perf. 14***
1035 A583 Horiz. strip of 3 2.40 2.40
a.-c. 5r Any single .70 .70

Silk Road — A584

Designs: No. 1036, 4r, Indus River near Chilas. No. 1037, 4r, Haramosh Peak near Gilgit, vert.

2004, June 7 ***Perf. 12¾x13, 13x12¾***
1036-1037 A584 Set of 2 .75 .75

Sui Southern Gas Company, 50th Anniv. — A585

2004, July 24 **Litho.** ***Perf. 12¾x13***
1038 A585 4r multi .60 .60

First Ascent of K2, 50th Anniv. — A586

2004, July 31 ***Perf. 13x12¾***
1039 A586 5r shown .60 .60

Imperf

Size: 95x64mm

1040 A586 30r Tent, K2 2.75 2.75

2004 Summer Olympics, Athens — A587

No. 1041: a, Track. b, Boxing. c, Field hockey. d, Wrestling.

2004, Aug. 13 ***Perf. 13x12¾***
1041 A587 Horiz. strip of 4 2.40 2.40
a.-d. 5r Any single .60 .60

7 Lines of Text — A588

6½ Lines of Text — A589

6 Lines of Text — A590

6¾ Lines of Text — A591

2004, Aug. 14
1042 Horiz. strip of 4 1.50 1.50
a. A588 5r multi .30 .30
b. A589 5r multi .30 .30
c. A590 5r multi .30 .30
d. A591 5r multi .30 .30

Independence, 57th anniv.

Maulvi Abdul Haq (1870-1961), Lexicographer — A592

2004, Aug. 16
1043 A592 4r multi .60 .60

Fourth Intl. Calligraphy and Calligraphic Art Exhibitiion and Competition, Lahore — A593

2004, Oct. 1
1044 A593 5r multi .50 .50

Tropical Fish — A594

No. 1045: a, Neon tetra. b, Striped gourami. c, Black widow. d, Yellow dwarf cichlid. e, Tiger barb.

2004, Oct. 9 ***Perf. 12½***
1045 Horiz. strip of 5 2.00 2.00
a.-e. A594 2r Any single .35 .35

Japanese Economic Assistance, 50th Anniv. — A595

Designs: No. 1046, 5r, Training for handicapped. No. 1047, 5r, Polio eradication. No. 1048, 5r, Ghazi Barotha hydroelectric power project. No. 1049, 5r, Kohat Friendship Tunnel. 30r, Vignettes of Nos. 1046-1049, Friendship Tunnel.

2004, Nov. 8 Litho. ***Perf. 12¾x13***
1046-1049 A595 Set of 4 .75 .75

Imperf

1050 A595 multi 3.00 3.00

Year of Child Welfare and Rights — A596

2004, Nov. 20 ***Perf. 12½***
1051 A596 4r multi .45 .45

Allama Iqbal Open University, Islamabad, 30th Anniv. — A597

2004, Dec. 6 ***Perf. 12¾x13***
1052 A597 20r multi .65 .65

Khyber Medical College, Peshawar, 50th Anniv. — A598

2004, Dec. 30
1053 A598 5r multi .60 .60

Prof. Ahmed Ali (1910-94), Writer — A599

2005, Jan. 14 Litho. ***Perf. 13x12¾***
1054 A599 5r multi .50 .50

Pakistan — Romania Friendship — A600

Poets Mihai Eminescu and Allama Iqbal and: No. 1055, 5r, Flags of Romania and Pakistan. No. 1056, 5r, Flags, monument to Eminescu and Iqbal by Emil Ghitulescu, Islamabad.

2005, Jan. 14
1055-1056 A600 Set of 2 1.40 1.40

Saadat Hasan Manto (1912-55), Writer — A601

2005, Jan. 18 ***Perf. 13x12¾***
1057 A601 5r multi .50 .50

A602

A603

A604

Pakistan Air Force, 50th Anniv. — A605

2005, Mar. 23 Litho. ***Perf. 12¾x13***
1058 A602 5r multi .40 .40
1059 A603 5r multi .40 .40
1060 A604 5r multi .40 .40

Perf. 13x12¾

1061 A605 5r multi .40 .40
Nos. 1058-1061 (4) 1.60 1.60

Command and Staff College, Quetta, Cent. — A606

2005, Apr. 2 ***Perf. 12¾x13***
1062 A606 5r multi .50 .50

Turkish Grand National Assembly, 85th Anniv. — A607

No. 1063 — Assembly building and: a, Kemal Ataturk, Turkish flag. b, Ataturk, Mohammed Ali Jinnah, Turkish and Pakistani flags.

2005, Apr. 23 ***Perf. 14***
1063 A607 10r Horiz. pair, #a-b 2.00 2.00

Institute of Business Administration, Karachi, 50th Anniv. — A608

Various views of campus with country name at: No. 1064, 3r, Right. No. 1065, 3r, Bottom.

2005, Apr. 30 ***Perf. 12¾x13***
1064-1065 A608 Set of 2 .50 .50

Islamia High School, Quetta, 95th Anniv. — A609

2005, May 25 ***Perf. 13x12¾***
1066 A609 5r multi .40 .40

Akhtar Shairani (1905-48), Poet — A610

2005, June 30
1067 A610 5r multi .50 .50

World Summit on Information Technology, Tunis, Tunisia — A611

2005, July 15
1068 A611 5r multi 1.00 1.00

Abdul Rehman Baba (1632-1707), Poet — A612

2005, Aug. 4
1069 A612 5r multi .50 .50

Lahore Marathon — A613

2005, Sept. 10 ***Perf. 12¾x13***
1070 A613 5r multi .50 .50

Mushrooms — A614

No. 1071: a, Lepiota procera. b, Tricholoma gambosum. c, Amanita caesarea. d, Cantharellus cibarius. e, Boletus luridus. f, Morchella vulgaris. g, Amanita vaginata. h, Agaricus arvensis. i, Coprinus comatus. j, Clitocybe geotropa.

2005, Oct. 1 Litho. ***Perf. 13¼x12¾***
1071 A614 Block of 10 4.50 4.50
a.-j. 5r Any single .40 .40

Intl. Year of Sports and Physical Education A615

2005, Nov. 5 ***Perf. 14***
1072 A615 5r multi .75 .75

South Asian Association for Regional Cooperation, 20th Anniv. — A616

2005, Nov. 12 ***Perf. 13¼x12¾***
1073 A616 5r multi 1.25 1.25

Khwaja Sarwar Hasan (1902-73), Diplomat — A617

2005, Nov. 18 ***Perf. 14***
1074 A617 5r multi .40 .40

SOS Children's Villages in Pakistan, 30th Anniv. — A618

2005, Nov. 20 ***Perf. 12¾x13¼***
1075 A618 5r multi .50 .50

20th World Men's Team Squash Championships, Islamabad A619

2005, Dec. 8 Litho. ***Perf. 14***
1076 A619 5r multi .50 .50

Supreme Court, 50th Anniv. — A620

Supreme Court Building: 4r, In daylight. 15r, At night.

2006, Mar. 23
1077-1078 A620 Set of 2 1.60 1.60

Mohammed Ali Jinnah's 1948 Visit to Armored Corps Center — A621

Jinnah, soldiers and: No. 1079, 5r, Tanks. No. 1080, 5r, Flags, vert.

2006, Apr. 14
1079-1080 A621 Set of 2 .80 .80

Begum Ra'na Liaquat Ali Khan (1905-90), Diplomat — A622

2006, June 13 ***Perf. 13½***
1081 A622 4r multi .40 .40

Sri Arjun Dev Jee (1563-1606), Sikh Guru — A623

2006, June 16
1082 A623 5r multi .50 .50

Polo at Shandur Pass — A624

2006, July 1 ***Perf. 14***
1083 A624 5r multi .60 .60

Tourism A625

No. 1084: a, Hanna Lake. b, Lake Payee. c, Lake Saiful Maluk. d, Lake Dudi Pat Sar.

2006, July 20
1084 A625 5r Block of 4, #a-d 2.50 2.50

Miniature Sheet

Painters A626

No. 1085: a, Shakir Ali (1916-75). b, Anna Molka Ahmed (1917-94). c, Sadequain (1930-87). d, Ali Imam (1924-2002). e, Zubeida Agha (1922-97). f, Laila Shahzada (1926-94). g, Ahmed Parvez (1926-79). h, Bashir Mirza (1941-2000). i, Zahoorul Akhlaque (1941-99). j, Askari Mian Irani (1940-2004).

2006, Aug. 14 *Perf. 13x12¾*
1085 A626 4r Sheet of 10, #a-j 2.50 2.50

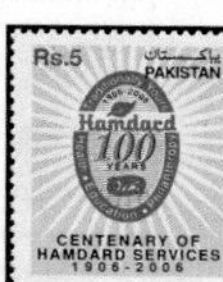

Hamdard Services, Cent. — A627

2006, Aug. 25 *Perf. 13¼x13*
1086 A627 5r multi .40 .35

Oct. 8, 2005 Earthquake, 1st Anniv. — A628

2006, Oct. 8 *Perf. 13½x13¾*
1087 A628 5r multi .60 .50

Medicinal Plants — A629

Designs: No. 1088, 5r, Aloe vera. No. 1089, 5r, Chamomile, vert.

Perf. 13½x13¼, 13¼x13½
2006, Oct. 28
1088-1089 A629 Set of 2 .80 .80

Intl. Anti-Corruption Day — A630

2006, Dec. 9 *Perf. 13*
1090 A630 5r multi .60 .60

Baltit Fort Heritage Trust, 10th Anniv. — A631

2006, Dec. 20 *Perf. 13¼*
1091 A631 15r multi 1.25 1.25

Miniature Sheet

Muslim League, Cent. A632

No. 1092: a, Mohammed Ali Jinnah's letter requesting membership in Muslim League. b, Jinnah in sherwani and cap. c, Jinnah addressing Lucknow session. d, Jinnah and wife with youth and women's wing. e, Jinnah hoisting Muslim League flag. f, Jinnah addressing Lahore session. g, Crowd, flags and ballot box. h, Jinnah addressing first Constituent Assembly.

Wmk. 351
2006, Dec. 28 **Litho.** *Perf. 13*
1092 A632 4r Sheet of 8, #a-h 2.50 2.50

Karachi Municipal Corporation Building, 75th Anniv. — A633

2007, Jan. 16 *Perf. 14¼*
1093 A633 10r multi .75 .75

Cadet College Petaro, 50th Anniv. — A634

Wmk. 351
2007, Feb. 28 **Litho.** *Perf. 14¼*
1094 A634 10r multi .60 .60

Intl. Women's Day — A635

2007, Mar. 8 *Perf. 13*
1095 A635 10r multi .60 .60

Hugh Catchpole (1907-97), Educator — A636

2007, May 26
1096 A636 10r multi .60 .60

Pakistan Post Emblem — A637

2007, June 7 *Perf. 14¼*
1097 A637 4r multi .50 .50

First Public Appearance of JF-17 Thunder Airplane A638

2007, Sept. 6 *Perf. 13*
1098 A638 5r multi .80 .80

Completion of Term of National Assembly A639

2007, Nov. 15
1099 A639 15r multi .75 .75

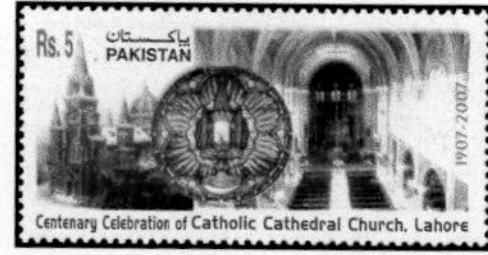

Catholic Cathedral, Lahore, Cent. — A640

2007, Nov. 19
1100 A640 5r multi .50 .50

Third Meeting of Economic Cooperation Organization Postal Authorities, Tehran (in 2006) A641

Wmk. 351
2007, Sept. 22 **Litho.** *Perf. 13*
1101 A641 10r multi *10.00 12.50*

No. 1101 was withdrawn from sale a few weeks after issuance as it is inscribed "I. R. Iran" and lacks the "Pakistan" country name. It is additionally inscribed with a denomination in Iranian currency, and dated "2006" though issued in 2007. This stamp was not valid in Iran, as Iran issued a similar stamp, No. 2917, in 2006.

Pres. Zulfikar Ali Bhutto (1928-79) and Prime Minister Benazir Bhutto (1953-2007) — A642

Wmk. 351
2008, Apr. 4 **Litho.** *Perf. 13*
1102 A642 4r multi .40 .40

Imperf
Size: 106x71mm
1103 A642 20r multi 2.00 2.00

No. 1103 contains No. 1102 with simulated perforations.

Benazir Bhutto (1953-2007), Prime Minister — A643

Designs: 4r, Head. 5r, 20r, Bhutto waving.

Wmk. 351
2008, June 21 **Litho.** *Perf. 13*
1104 A643 4r multi .40 .40

Size: 34x57mm
Perf. 13x13¼
1105 A643 5r multi .40 .40

Size: 67x99mm
Imperf
1106 A643 20r multi 1.40 1.40

No. 1106 has simulated perforations.

Oct. 8, 2005 Earthquake, 3rd Anniv. A644

2008, Oct. 8 *Perf. 13*
1107 A644 4r multi .60 .60

Selection of Benazir Bhutto for 2008 United Nations Human Rights Award — A645

Wmk. 351
2008, Dec. 10 **Litho.** *Perf. 13*
1108 A645 4r multi .40 .40

Assassination of Benazir Bhutto, 1st Anniv. — A646

2008, Dec. 27 **Wmk. 351** *Perf. 13*
1109 A646 4r multi .60 .60

Size: 98x67mm
Imperf
Unwmk.
1110 A646 20r multi 1.50 1.50

10th Economic Cooperation Organization Summit, Tehran — A647

Perf. 13¼x13½
2009, Mar. 11 **Wmk. 351**
1111 A647 5r multi 1.25 1.25

Compare with Azerbaijan 895, Iran 2981.

Natl. Environment Year — A648

Designs: No. 1112, 5r, Deodar tree. No. 1113, 5r, Jasmine flower. No. 1114, 5r, Markhor. No. 1115, 5r, Chukar.

2009, Mar. 23 *Perf. 13*
1112-1115 A648 Set of 4 1.50 1.50

Habib Public School, 50th Anniv. — A649

2009, Mar. 29
1116 A649 5r multi .35 .35

Bai Virbaiji Soparivala Parsi High School, Karachi, 150th Anniv. — A650

2009, May 23 *Perf. 13¼x13½*
1117 A650 5r multi .40 .40

Karachi Chamber of Commerce and Industry Building, 75th Anniv. A651

Wmk. 351
2009, May 30 **Litho.** *Perf. 13*
1118 A651 4r multi .40 .40

Ahmad Nadeem Qasmi (1916-2006), Writer — A652

2009, July 10
1119 A652 5r multi .40 .40

Minorities Week — A653

Wmk. 351
2009, Aug. 11 **Litho.** *Perf. 13*
1120 A653 5r multi .50 .50

Independence Day — A654

Wmk. 351
2009, Aug. 14 **Litho.** *Perf. 13*
1121 A654 5r multi .40 .40

Festival of Hazrat Musa Pak Shaheed — A655

2009, Aug. 15
1122 A655 5r multi .60 .60

"United For Peace" — A656

2009, Aug. 16 *Perf. 13½*
1123 A656 5r multi .60 .60

Diplomatic Relations Between Pakistan and the Philippines, 60th Anniv. A657

Wmk. 351
2009, Sept. 9 **Litho.** *Perf. 13*
1124 A657 5r multi 1.25 1.25

People's Republic of China, 60th Anniv. — A658

2009, Oct. 1
1125 A658 5r multi .90 .90

A659

Polio-free Pakistan A660

2009, Oct. 10
1126 A659 5r multi .40 .40
1127 A660 5r multi .40 .40

Seventh Natl. Finance Commission Award — A661

Wmk. 351
2010, Jan. 11 **Litho.** *Perf. 13*
1128 A661 8r multi .60 .60

Port of Gwardar A662

2010, Jan. 11
1129 A662 8r multi .60 .60

Navy Rifle Association 50th Anniv. Meet — A663

Wmk. 351
2010, Feb. 13 **Litho.** *Perf. 13½*
1130 A663 10r multi .60 .60

Awarding of Hilal-i-Eissar (Selflessness) Awards to Cities — A664

No. 1131 — Flag and: a, War Memorial, Nowshera. b, Islamia College, Peshawar. c, Judicial Complex, Swabi. d, Takht-e-Bahi, Mardan. e, Sugar mills, Charsadda.

2010, Feb. 22 *Perf. 13*
1131 Vert. strip of 5 1.50 1.50
a.-e. A664 5r Any single .30 .30

Overseas Investors Chamber of Commerce and Industry, 150th Anniv. — A665

2010, Apr. 7 *Perf. 13x13¼*
1132 A665 8r multi .60 .60

2010 Youth Olympics, Singapore — A666

Wmk. 351
2010, Aug. 14 **Litho.** *Perf. 13¼*
1133 A666 8r multi 1.25 1.25

Lawrence College, Murree Hills, 150th Anniv. — A667

No. 1134 — Crest of college and: a, Building and flagpoles. b, Building in brown. c, Aerial view of building. d, Building and plaza.

2010, Oct. 7 **Litho.** *Perf. 13*
1134 A667 Block of 4 + 2 central labels 1.75 1.75
a.-d. 8r Any single .30 .30

Children's Art Competition — A668

2010, Nov. 5
1135 A668 8r multi + label .60 .60

International Islamic University, Islamabad, 25th Anniv. — A669

Perf. 13x13¼
2010, Dec. 15 **Wmk. 351**
1136 A669 8r multi .60 .60

Islamabad, 50th Anniv. A670

2010, Dec. 31 *Perf. 13½*
1137 A670 5r multi 1.25 1.25

100 Million Cell Phone Subscribers of Pakistan Telecommunications Authority — A671

2011, Jan. 19 *Perf. 13x13¼*
1138 A671 8r multi 1.75 1.75

Sixth Population and Housing Census — A672

2011, Feb. 10 **Wmk. 351**
1139 A672 10r multi 1.75 1.75

Railways in Pakistan, 150th Anniv. A673

2011, May 13 **Litho.**
1140 A673 8r multi .60 .60

Diplomatic Relations Between Pakistan and People's Republic of China, 60th Anniv. — A674

No. 1141 — Flags of Pakistan and People's Republic of China and: a, Pakistan President Asif Ali Zardari and Chinese President Hu Jintao (handshake above baseline). b, Pakistan Prime Minister and Yousuf Raza Gilani and Chinese Premier Wen Jiabao (handshake touching baseline).

2011, May 21 *Perf. 13x13¼*
1141 A674 8r Horiz. pair, #a-b 2.00 2.00

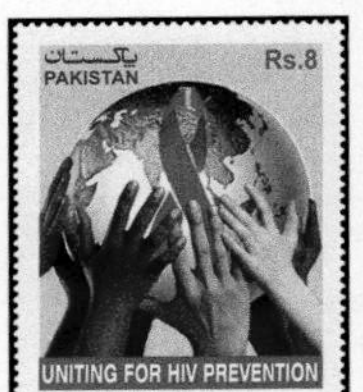

Campaign Against Human Immunodeficiency Virus — A675

Perf. 13½x13¾

2011, June 8 **Wmk. 351**
1142 A675 8r multi 1.25 1.25

Friendship Between Pakistan and Russia — A676

Perf. 13x13¼

2011, June 10 **Litho.** **Wmk. 351**
1143 A676 8r multi .60 .60

A677

A678

A679

A680

A681

A682

A683

Works From Children's Art Competition at National Stamp Exhibition, Kurrachee A684

2011, June 24 **Unwmk.** ***Perf. 13***
1144 Sheet of 8 + 2 labels 4.50 4.50
a. A677 8r multi .40 .40
b. A678 8r multi .40 .40
c. A679 8r multi .40 .40
d. A680 8r multi .40 .40
e. A681 8r multi .40 .40
f. A682 8r multi .40 .40
g. A683 8r multi .40 .40
h. A684 8r multi .40 .40

Institute of Chartered Accountants of Pakistan, 50th Anniv. — A685

Perf. 13x13¼

2011, July 1 **Wmk. 351**
1145 A685 8r multi .60 .60

Dr. Syedna Mohammed Burhannudin Saheb, Religious Leader, 100th Birthday — A686

2011, July 17
1146 A686 8r multi .60 .60

Dr. Burhanuddin Saheb was born in 1915. The centenary of his birth is based on the Islamic calendar.

Zarai Taraqiati Bank, Ltd., 50th Anniv. — A687

2011, Aug. 14 ***Perf. 13***
1147 A687 8r multi .60 .60

Frequency Allocation Board, 60th Anniv. — A688

2011, Aug. 18 ***Perf. 13x13¼***
1148 A688 8r multi .60 .60

Towers in Pakistan and Iran A689

No. 1149: a, Milad Tower, Tehran. b, Minar-e-Pakistan, Lahore.

2011, Aug. 29 ***Perf. 13***
1149 A689 8r Horiz. pair, #a-b, + flanking label 2.00 2.00

See Iran No. 3023.

Pakistan Space and Upper Atmosphere Research Commission, 50th Anniv. — A690

2011, Sept. 16 **Wmk. 351**
1150 A690 8r multi .60 .60

Karachi Gymkhana, 125th Anniv. — A691

No. 1151: a, Building with archways, tree at right. b, Building, white pole at right. c, Building, two white poles and trees in front. d, Building, shelter with awning at left.

2011, Sept. 23 ***Perf. 13x13¼***
1151 A691 8r Block of 4, #a-d 2.00 2.00

Campaign Against Breast Cancer A692

2011, Nov. 30 ***Perf. 13***
1152 A692 8r multi .60 .60

Diplomatic Relations Between Pakistan and Thailand, 60th Anniv. — A693

2011, Dec. 13 ***Perf. 13¼x13***
1153 A693 8r multi .60 .60

St. Patrick's High School, Karachi, 150th Anniv. — A694

2011, Dec. 31
1154 A694 8r multi .60 .60

100th Meeting of Federal Cabinet A695

2012, Jan. 18 ***Perf. 13x13¼***
1155 A695 8r multi .60 .60

Arfa Karim (1995-2012), World's Youngest Microsoft Certified Professional A696

2012, Feb. 2
1156 A696 8r multi .60 .60

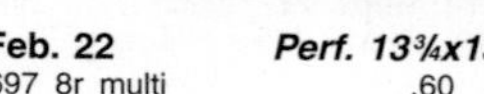

Nur Khan (1923-2011), Air Marshal A697

2012, Feb. 22 ***Perf. 13¾x13½***
1157 A697 8r multi .60 .60

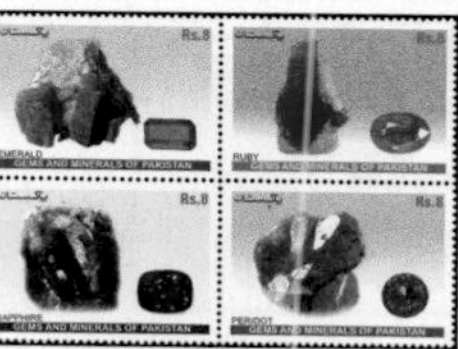

Gemstones — A698

No. 1158: a, Emerald. b, Ruby. c, Sapphire. d, Peridot.

2012, Feb. 24 ***Perf. 13***
1158 A698 8r Block of 4, #a-d 2.00 2.00

Aitchison College, Lahore, 125th Anniv. — A699

2012, Mar. 3
1159 A699 8r multi .60 .60

St. Joseph's Convent School, Karachi, 150th Anniv. A700

2012, Mar. 19 ***Perf. 13¾x13½***
1160 A700 8r multi .60 .60

Asian-Pacific Postal Union, 50th Anniv. — A701

2012, Apr. 1 **Wmk. 351** ***Perf. 13***
1161 A701 8r multi .60 .60

Government High School No. 1, Thana, Cent. — A702

2012, Apr. 15 ***Perf. 13½***
1162 A702 8r multi .60 .60

Martyr's Day — A703

2012, Apr. 30 ***Perf. 13x13¼***
1163 A703 8r multi .60 .60

State Visit of Thailand's King Bhumibol Adulyadej and Queen Sirikit to Pakistan, 50th Anniv. A704

2012, May 5 **Litho.**
1164 A704 8r multi .60 .60

Campaign Against Thalassemia A705

2012, May 8 **Wmk. 351**
1165 A705 8r multi .60 .60

World Environment Day — A706

No. 1166: a, Mountains and lake. b, Horses and riders. c, Arches at Shalimar Gardens, Lahore. d, Khyber Pass Gateway and flag.

2012, June 5 ***Perf. 13x13¼***
1166 A706 8r Block of 4, #a-d 1.50 1.50

United Nations Environment Program, 40th anniv.

Ayub Bridge, 50th Anniv. A707

2012, June 15
1167 A707 8r multi .60 .60

A708

A709

A710

A711

A712

A713

A714

Works From Children's Art Competition at 2012 National Stamp Exhibition, Kurrachee A715

2012, June 22 ***Perf. 13***
1168 Sheet of 8 + 2 labels 3.50 3.50
a. A708 8r multi .40 .40
b. A709 8r multi .40 .40
c. A710 8r multi .40 .40
d. A711 8r multi .40 .40
e. A712 8r multi .40 .40
f. A713 8r multi .40 .40
g. A714 8r multi .40 .40
h. A715 8r multi .40 .40

Eid Greetings — A716

No. 1169: a, Yellow roses, pale orange frame. b, Rink roses, yellow frame. c, White roses, light blue frame. d, Yellow roses, light green frame.

2012, Aug. 13
1169 A716 8r Block of 4, #a-d 1.50 1.50

King Edward Medical University, Lahore, 150th Anniv. — A717

2012, Aug. 28 ***Perf. 13x13¼***
1170 A717 8r multi .60 .60

Pakistan No. 23, Abdur Rahman Chughtai (1897-1975), Painter — A718

2012, Aug. 30 ***Perf. 13¼x13½***
1171 A718 10r multi .60 .60

Independence, 65th anniv.

Sialkot Chamber of Commerce and Industry, 30th Anniv. — A719

2012, Sept. 26 ***Perf. 13x13¼***
1172 A719 8r multi .60 .60

Birds in Flight A720

No. 1173: a, White storks. b, Shoveler ducks. c, Snow geese. d, Siberian cranes.

2012, Sept. 27 **Wmk. 351**
1173 A720 8r Block of 4, #a-d 1.50 1.50

A721

A722

A723

Arabian Sea Coral Reefs A724

2012, Oct. 4 **Litho.**
1174 Block of 4 2.00 2.00
a. A721 8r multi .50 .50
b. A722 8r multi .50 .50
c. A723 8r multi .50 .50
d. A724 8r multi .50 .50

Hameed Naseem (1920-98), Writer — A725

2012, Oct. 19 ***Perf. 13***
1175 A725 8r multi .60 .60

Men of Letters. See Nos. 1181-1183, 1185-1189, 1196, 1202, 1206, 1248.

University of Karachi Geography Department, 60th Anniv. — A726

2012, Nov. 19 ***Perf. 13x13¼***
1176 A726 15r multi .90 .90

National Investment Trust Limited, 50th Anniv. — A727

2012, Nov. 21 **Wmk. 351**
1177 A727 15r multi .90 .90

Muhammad Luthfullah Khan (1916-2012), Writer and Recordings Collector — A728

2012, Nov. 25 ***Perf. 13***
1178 A728 15r multi .90 .90

Publishing in Pakistan, 60th Anniv. — A729

2012, Dec. 15 ***Perf. 13½x13¼***
1179 A729 15r multi .30 .30

Commercial Operation of First Wind Farm Power Project in Pakistan — A730

2012, Dec. 24 ***Perf. 13x13¼***
1180 A730 15r multi .90 .90

Men of Letters Type of 2012

Designs: No. 1181, Syed Nasir Raza Kazmi (1925-72), poet. No. 1182, Allama Muhammad Asad (1900-92), writer. No. 1183, Qudrat Ullah Shahab (1917-86), writer.

2013
1181 A725 15r multi .60 .60
1182 A725 15r multi .60 .60
1183 A725 15r multi .60 .60
Nos. 1181-1183 (3) 1.80 1.80

Issued: No. 1181, 3/2; Nos. 1182, 1183, 3/23.

Kinnaird College, Lahore, Cent. — A732

2013, Apr. 11
1184 A732 15r multi .90 .90

Men of Letters Type of 2012

Design: No. 1185, Sufi Barkat Ali (1911-97), Muslim Sufi saint. No. 1186, Syed Zamir Jafri (1916-99), poet. No. 1187, Shafiq-ur-Rehman (1920-2000), writer. No. 1188, Mumtaz Mufti (1905-95), writer. No. 1189, Ishfaq Ahmed (1925-2004), writer.

2013
1185 A725 8r multi .60 .60
1186 A725 8r multi .60 .60
1187 A725 8r multi .60 .60
1188 A725 8r multi .60 .60
1189 A725 8r multi .60 .60
Nos. 1185-1189 (5) 3.00 3.00

Issued: No. 1185, 4/27; No. 1186, 5/29; No. 1187, 6/6; Nos. 1188-1189, 6/12.

Sir Muhammad Iqbal (1877-1938), Poet — A733

Wmk. 351
2013, Apr. 21 **Litho.** ***Perf. 13½***
1190 A733 15r multi .90 .90

Reopening of Pakistan Army Museum, Rawalpindi — A734

2013, Apr. 30 ***Perf. 13x13¼***
1191 A734 15r multi .90 .90

2013 General Elections A735

2013, May 11

1192 A735 8r multi .60 .60

Recipients of Pakistan's Highest Military Medals — A736

No. 1193: a, Capt. Karnal Sher Khan Shaheed (1970-99), Nishan-e-Haider medal. b, Havildar Lalak Jan Shaheed (1967-99), Nishan-e-Haider medal. c, Naik Saif Ali Janjua Shaheed (1922-48), Hilal-i-Kashmir medal.

Perf. 13½x13¼

2013, Apr. 30 Litho. Wmk. 351

1193 A736 Horiz. strip of 3 1.50 1.50
a.-c. 8r Any single .50 .50

Sadiq Muhammad Khan Abbasi V (1904-66), Nawab of Bahawalpur — A737

Wmk. 351

2013, May 24 Litho. *Perf. 13*

1194 A737 8r multi .60 .60

Islamia College, Peshawar, Cent. A738

2013, May 30

1195 A738 8r multi .60 .60

Men of Letters Type of 2012

Design: Ibn-e-Insha (1927-78), poet.

2013, June 15

1196 A725 8r multi .50 .50

All-Pakistan Newspaper Society, 60th Anniv. — A739

2013, June 20

1197 A739 8r multi .60 .60

Red-vented Bulbul — A740

Perf. 13½x13¼

2013, July 1 Litho. Wmk. 351

1198 A740 8r multi .60 .60

Pir Meher Ali Shah (1859-1937), Sufi Scholar — A741

Wmk. 351

2013, July 30 Litho. *Perf. 13*

1199 A741 8r multi — —

Frigate PNS Aslat — A742

Wmk. 351

2013, Sept. 3 Litho. *Perf. 13¼*

1200 A742 10r multi .60 .60

Noor Jahan (1926-2000), Singer A743

Wmk. 351

2013, Sept. 21 Litho. *Perf. 13¼*

1201 A743 8r multi .60 .60

Men of Letters Type of 2012

Design: Jon Elia (1931-2002), writer.

Wmk. 351

2013, Nov. 8 Litho. *Perf. 13*

1202 A725 8r multi .50 .50

Two Decades of Extended Cooperation with Economic Cooperation Organization A744

Perf. 13¼x13

2013, Nov. 28 Litho. Wmk. 351

1203 A744 25r multi .60 .60

Perveen Shakir (1952-94), Poet — A745

Wmk. 351

2013, Dec. 26 Litho. *Perf. 13*

1204 A745 10r multi .60 .60

Pakistan Bible Society, 150th Anniv. A746

Wmk. 351

2013, Dec. 28 Litho. *Perf. 13*

1205 A746 8r multi .60 .60

Men of Letters Type of 2012

Design: Habib Jalib (1928-93), poet.

Wmk. 351

2014, Mar. 12 Litho. *Perf. 13*

1206 A725 15r multi .50 .50

Air Commodore Muhammad Mahmood Alam (1935-2013) A747

Perf. 13¾x13½

2014, Mar. 20 Litho. Wmk. 351

1207 A747 8r multi .60 .60

Hyder M. Habib (1931-2011), Banker A748

Wmk. 351

2014, Apr. 6 Litho. *Perf. 13*

1208 A748 8r multi .60 .60

Forman Christian College, 150th Anniv. A749

Wmk. 351

2014, May 14 Litho. *Perf. 13*

1209 A749 8r multi .25 .25

Pakistan Navy Submarine Force, 50th Anniv. — A750

Wmk. 351

2014, June 1 Litho. *Perf. 13*

1210 A750 10r multi .25 .25

Frontier Constabulary, Cent. A751

Wmk. 351

2014, July 11 Litho. *Perf. 13½*

1211 A751 8r multi .25 .25

Sahiwal Cattle Conservation, Cent. — A752

Perf. 13x13¼

2014, Aug. 5 Litho. Wmk. 351

1212 A752 8r multi .25 .25

A753

Pakistan 2025 Planning Program A754

Perf. 13½x13¼

2014, Aug. 11 Litho. Wmk. 351

1213 A753 8r multi .25 .25

Perf. 13

1214 A754 10r multi .25 .25

Norman Borlaug (1914-2009), 1970 Nobel Peace Laureate A755

Perf. 13x13¼

2014, Dec. 4 Litho. Wmk. 351

1215 A755 8r multi .25 .25

Intl. Anti-Corruption Day — A756

Perf. 13x13¼

2014, Dec. 9 Litho. Wmk. 351

1216 A756 8r multi .25 .25

Gems and Minerals A757

No. 1217: a, Apatite. b, Aquamarine. c, Black tourmaline. d, Garnet. e, Epidot. f, Vesuvianite. g, Topaz. h, Sphene.

Perf. 13x13¼

2014, Dec. 11 Litho. Wmk. 351

1217 Block of 8 1.60 1.60
a.-h. A757 10r Any single .25 .25

14th National Scout Jamboree, Khairpur A758

Perf. 13x13¼

2014, Dec. 23 Litho. Wmk. 351

1218 A758 8r multi .25 .25

Artifacts of Ancient Civilizations — A759

No. 1219: a, Artifacts from Trypillia, Ukraine archaeological site, flag of Ukraine. b, Artifacts from Mohenjo-daro, Pakistan archaeological site, flag of Pakistan.

Perf. 13¼x13

2014, Dec. 25 Litho. Wmk. 351

1219 A759 20r Horiz. pair, #a-b 1.00 1.00
c. Souvenir sheet of 2, #1219a-1219b, imperf. 1.00 1.00

No. 1219c has simulated perforations and sold for 50r.

See Ukraine No. 997.

Moulana Altaf Hussain Hali (1837-1914), Poet — A760

Perf. 13x13¼

2014, Dec. 31 Litho. Wmk. 351

1220 A760 8r multi .25 .25

First 100 Megawatt Solar Plant in Pakistan — A762

Wmk. 351

2015, May 4 Litho. *Perf. 13½*
1222 A762 8r multi .25 .25

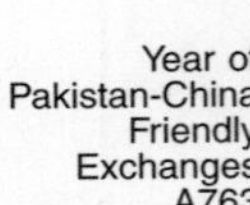

Year of Pakistan-China Friendly Exchanges A763

No. 1223: a, Flag of People's Republic of China and Pres. Xi Jinping. b, Great Wall of China. c, Karakoram Highway. d, Shalimar Garden, Pakistan. e, Flag of Pakistan and Prime Minister Nawaz Sharif.

Wmk. 351

2015, Aug. 14 Litho. *Perf. 13*
1223 Horiz. strip of 5 1.25 1.25
a.-f. A763 10r Any single .25 .25

A764

A765

A766

A767

A768

India-Pakistan War, 50th Anniv. — A769

Perf. 13x13¼

2015, Sept. 7 Litho. Wmk. 351
1224 Block of 6 1.50 1.50
a. A764 10r multi .25 .25
b. A765 10r multi .25 .25
c. A766 10r multi .25 .25
d. A767 10r multi .25 .25
e. A768 10r multi .25 .25
f. A769 10r multi .25 .25

Cadet College, Kohat, 50th Anniv. A770

Wmk. 351

2015, Oct. 10 Litho. *Perf.*
1225 A770 8r multi .25 .25

Urdu Language in Turkey, Cent. A771

Wmk. 351

2015, Oct. 12 Litho. *Perf. 13*
1226 A771 10r multi .25 .25

Restoration of Murree General Post Office A772

Wmk. 351

2015, Nov. 4 Litho. *Perf. 13*
1227 A772 8r multi .25 .25

Army Public School Massacre, 1st Anniv. — A773

Wmk. 351

2015, Dec. 16 Litho. *Perf. 13*
1228 A773 16r multi .30 .30

Reopening of Murree General Post Office — A774

Wmk. 351

2015, Dec. 29 Litho. *Perf. 13*
1229 A774 10r multi .25 .25

Safe Operation of First Pinstech Nuclear Reactor, 50th Anniv. — A775

Perf. 14 Syncopated

2016, Feb. 10 Litho. Wmk. 351
1230 A775 50r multi 1.00 1.00

Water Conservation — A776

Wmk. 351

2016, Mar. 22 Litho. *Perf. 13*
1231 A776 8r multi .25 .25

National Book Day — A777

Wmk. 351

2016, Apr. 22 Litho. *Perf. 13*
1232 A777 8r multi .25 .25

S. P Singha (1893-1948), Politician — A778

Perf. 14 Syncopated

2016, Apr. 26 Litho. Wmk. 351
1233 A778 10r multi .25 .25

Diplomatic Relations Between Pakistan and People's Republic of China, 65th Anniv. — A779

Wmk. 351

2016, May 21 Litho. *Perf. 13*
1234 A779 8r multi .25 .25

Abdul Sattar Edhi (1928-2016), Philanthropist A780

Perf. 13¼x13½

2016, Aug. 14 Litho. Wmk. 351
1235 A780 20r multi .40 .40

Souvenir Sheet

Directorate General of Training and Research Building (Old Custom House), Karachi, Cent. — A781

No. 1236 — Various views of building with: a, Country name in white at left, "100" in red at bottom. b, Country name in black at right, "100" in blue at bottom. c, Country name in black at right, "100" in magenta at bottom.

Wmk. 351

2016, Sept. 6 Litho. *Perf.*
1236 A781 8r Sheet of 3, #a-c .50 .50

Habib Bank Limited, 75th Anniv. A782

Wmk. 351

2016, Sept. 23 Litho. *Perf. 13*
1237 A782 8r multi .25 .25

National Parks of Pakistan and Belarus A783

No. 1238: a, Saiful Muluk National Park, flag and arms of Pakistan. b, Narachanski National Park, flag and arms of Belarus.

Perf. 13¼x13½

2016, Oct. 5 Litho. Wmk. 351
1238 Horiz. pair .80 .80
a.-b. A783 20r Either single .40 .40

See Belarus No. 1014.

Diplomatic Relations Between Pakistan and Singapore, 50th Anniv. — A784

No. 1239: a, Vanda Miss Joaquim orchid, Merlion's head. b, Jasmine flower, flag of Pakistan.

Wmk. 351

2016, Oct. 18 Litho. *Perf. 13*
1239 A784 8r Horiz. pair, #a-b .30 .30

See Singapore Nos. 1800-1801.

Rotary Foundation, Cent. — A785

Wmk. 351

2016, Nov. 20 Litho. *Perf. 13*
1240 A785 8r multi .25 .25

Lahore High Court, 150th Anniv. A786

Wmk. 351

2016, Nov. 26 Litho. *Perf. 13*
1241 A786 8r multi .25 .25

National Voter's Day — A787

Perf. 14 Syncopated

2016, Dec. 7 Litho. Wmk. 351
1242 A787 8r multi .25 .25

Dinshaw B. Avari (1902-88), Philanthropist A788

Wmk. 351

2016, Dec. 18 Litho. *Perf. 13*
1243 A788 8r multi .25 .25

A789

A790

A791

A792

A793

A794

A795

Works From Children's Art Competition at 2016 National Stamp Exhibition, Karachi — A796

Wmk. 351

2016, Dec. 30 Litho. *Perf. 13*

1244	Sheet of 8 + 2 labels	2.00	2.00
a.	A789 8r multi	.25	.25
b.	A790 8r multi	.25	.25
c.	A791 8r multi	.25	.25
d.	A792 8r multi	.25	.25
e.	A793 8r multi	.25	.25
f.	A794 8r multi	.25	.25
g.	A795 8r multi	.25	.25
h.	A796 8r multi	.25	.25

International Year of Sustainable Tourism for Development

No. 1245 — United Nations World Tourism Organization emblem and mountains: a, Broad Peak. b, Gasherbrum I. c, Nangaparbat. d, K2.

Perf. 13¼x13½

2017, Jan. 1 Litho. Wmk. 351

1245	Horiz. strip of 4, #a-d	1.00	1.00
a.-d.	A797 10r Any single	.25	.25

A798

13th Econonic Cooperation Organization Summit, Islamabad — A799

Perf. 14 Syncopated

2017, Mar. 6 Litho. Wmk. 351

1246 A798 8r multi .25 .25

Perf. 13

1247 A799 8r multi .25 .25

Men of Letters Type of 2012

Design: Majeed Amjad (1914-74), poet.

Wmk. 351

2017, June 29 Litho. *Perf. 13*

1248 A725 8r multi .25 .25

Partnership Between Pakistan and Asian Development Bank, 50th Anniv. — A800

Perf. 13¼x13½

2017, July 6 Litho. Wmk. 351

1249 A800 8r multi .25 .25

Maulana Mufti Mahmood (1919-80), Governmental Minister — A801

Wmk. 351

2017, Oct. 14 Litho. *Perf. 13*

1250 A801 8r multi .25 .25

Sir Syed Ahmed Khan (1817-98), Educator, Jurist, Philosopher A802

Wmk. 351

2017, Oct. 17 Litho. *Perf. 13½*

1251	A802 10r multi	.25	.25
a.	Souvenir sheet of 1, imperf.	.40	.40

No. 1251a has simulated perforations, smaller-sized reproductions of Nos. 502, 735c, 888, and sold for 20r.

Government Islamia College, Lahore, 125th Anniv. — A803

Wmk. 351

2017, Nov. 1 Litho. *Perf. 14*

1252 A803 8r multi .25 .25

Pakistan Cricket Team, Winners of 2017 ICC Champions Trophy A804

No. 1253: a, Team standing behind orange letters spelling "Champions." b, Trophy and stadium. c, Team on victory platform.

Wmk. 351

2017, Nov. 2 Litho. *Perf. 13*

1253	Horiz. strip of 3	.75	.75
a.-c.	A804 10r Any single	.25	.25
d.	Souvenir sheet of 3, #1253a-1253c, imperf.	.95	.95

No. 1253d sold for 50r and stamps have simulated perforations.

Souvenir Sheet

Diplomatic Relations Between Pakistan and Turkey, 70th Anniv. — A805

No. 1254: a, Mehmet Akif Ersoy (1873-1936), poet. b, Allama Muhammad Iqbal (1877-1938), poet.

Perf. 13¼x13½

2017, Nov. 9 Litho. Wmk. 351

1254 A805 10r Sheet of 2, #a-b .40 .40

See Turkey No. 3577.

Pakistan Air Force's No. 6 Air Transport Support Squadron, 75th Anniv. A806

Wmk. 351

2017, Dec. 1 Litho. *Perf. 13*

1255 A806 10r multi .25 .25

Souvenir Sheet

Dr. Ruth Katharina Martha Pfau (1929-2017), Nun and Physician to Lepers — A807

Wmk. 351

2017, Dec. 3 Litho. *Perf.*

1256 A807 8r brt pur, dp vio & multi .25 .25

Aga Khan IV, 60th Anniv. as Imam A808

No. 1257 — Inscriptions: a, Providing clean drinking water. b, Early childhood development. c, Aga Khan University. d, Restoration of Shahi Hammam. e, Skills development. f, Aga Khan Medical Center.

Wmk. 351

2017, Dec. 8 Litho. *Perf. 13*

1257 A808 10r Block of 6, #a-f 1.10 1.10

Green Pakistan Program A809

A810

Design: No. 1260, Foliage in background, denomination in white.

Wmk. 351

2018, Feb. 9 Litho. *Perf. 13*

1258	A809 8r multi	.25	.25
1259	A810 8r multi	.25	.25
1260	A809 8r multi	.25	.25
	Nos. 1258-1260 (3)	.75	.75

Army Burn Hall College, Abbottabad, 75th Anniv. — A811

Wmk. 351

2018, Mar. 5 Litho. *Perf. 13*

1261 A811 8r multi .25 .25

Mosques A812

No. 1262: a, Heydar Mosque, Baku, Azerbaijan, flag of Azerbaijan. b, Wazir Khan Mosque, Lahore, Pakistan, flag of Pakistan.

Wmk. 351

2018, June 9 Litho. *Perf. 13*

1262 A812 8r Pair, #a-b .30 .30

A souvenir sheet containing Nos. 1262a-1262b sold for 50r.

Joint Issue between Pakistan and Azerbaijan. See Azerbaijan No. 1215.

2018 Summit of Shanghai Cooperation Organization, Qingdao, People's Republic of China — A813

Perf. 13¼x13½

2018, June 9 Litho. Wmk. 351

1263 A813 10r multi .25 .25

Urdu Dictionary Board, 60th Anniv. A814

Wmk. 351

2018, June 14 Litho. *Perf. 13*

1264 A814 8r multi .25 .25

State Bank of Pakistan, 70th Anniv. A815

Wmk. 351

2018, July 1 Litho. *Perf. 13*

1265 A815 8r multi .25 .25

Atrocities in Indian-Occupied Kashmir — A816

No. 1266 — Inscriptions at LL: a, Use of chemical weapons. b, Half widows (sign behind woman). c, Children abuse. d, Fake encounters. e, Freedom prayer. f, Use of pellet guns. g, Half widows (woman and child). h, Human shield. i, Women harassment. j, Missing persons. k, Mass graves. l, Over 100,000 Kashmiris martyred. m, Burhan Wani (1994-2016), freedom icon. n, Bleeding Kashmir. o, Protest against killers. p, Braid chopping. q, Homeless children. r, Freedom struggle. s, Brutality. t, Tortured women.

Perf. 13x13¼

2018, July 13 Litho. Wmk. 351

1266 Sheet of 20 2.60 2.60

a.-t. A816 8r Any single .25 .25

Mama Parsi Girls Secondary School, Cent. — A817

Wmk. 351

2018, July 24 Litho. *Perf. 13*

1267 A817 8r multi .25 .25

Jamsheed Marker (1922-2018), Diplomat — A818

Wmk. 351

2018, Nov. 24 Litho. *Perf. 13*

1268 A818 8r multi .25 .25

10th International Defense Exhibition and Seminar, Karachi A819

Wmk. 351

2018, Nov. 27 Litho. *Perf. 13*

1269 A819 10r multi .25 .25

Anti-Corruption Day — A820

Wmk. 351

2018, Dec. 9 Litho. *Perf.*

1270 A820 8r multi .25 .25

Gulam Ishaq Khan Institute of Engineering Sciences and Technology, Topi, 25th Anniv. — A821

Wmk. 351

2018, Dec. 24 Litho. *Perf. 13*

1271 A821 8r multi .25 .25

Crescent Model Higher Secondary School, Lahore, 50th Anniv. A822

Wmk. 351

2018, Dec. 26 Litho. *Perf. 13*

1272 A822 8r multi .25 .25

Mirza Asadullah Khan Ghalib (1797-1869), Poet — A823

Perf. 14 Syncopated

2019, Feb. 15 Litho. Wmk. 351

1273 A823 8r multi .25 .25

Launch of PRSS-1 and PakTES-1A Satellites, 1st Anniv. A824

Wmk. 351

2019, July 9 Litho. *Perf. 13¼*

1274 A824 20r multi .25 .25

Commonwealth of Nations, 70th Anniv. — A825

Perf. 13¼x13¾

2019, Aug. 14 Litho. Wmk. 351

1275 A825 20r multi .25 .25

Commission on Science and Technology for Sustainable Development in the South, 25th Anniv. A826

Wmk. 351

2019, Oct. 4 Litho. *Perf. 13¼*

1276 A826 20r multi .25 .25

Co-operation Between Pakistan and Japan — A827

No. 1277 — Inscriptions: a, Capacity building in construction technology. b, Irrigation management system. c, Skills development & market diversification. d, Kohat Friendship Tunnel.

Wmk. 351

2019, Oct. 22 Litho. *Perf. 13*

1277 A827 20r Block of 4, #a-d, + 2 central labels 1.10 1.10

Convention on the Rights of the Child, 30th Anniv. — A828

Wmk. 351

2019, Nov. 4 Litho. *Perf. 13*

1278 A828 20r multi .25 .25

Gurdwara Janam Asthan, Nankana Sahib — A829

No. 1279: a, Orange panel at left, denomination at UL. b, Dark blue panel at right, denomination at UR.

Wmk. 351

2019, Nov. 12 Litho. *Perf. 13*

1279 Horiz. pair + central label .50 .50

a.-b. A829 20r Either single .25 .25

Sri Guru Nanak Dev Ji (1469-1539), founder of Sikhism. A souvenir sheet containing perf. 11¼x13 examples of Nos. 1279a-1279b sold for 550r.

Organization of Islamic Cooperation, 50th Anniv. — A830

Wmk. 351

2019, Dec. 30 Litho. *Perf.*

1280 A830 50r multi .65 .65

A souvenir sheet of 1 sold for 250r.

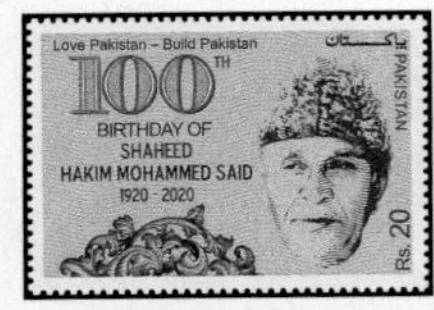

Hakim Mohammed Said (1920-98), Medical Researcher and Governor of Sindh Province A831

Wmk. 351

2020, Jan. 10 Litho. *Perf. 13*

1281 A831 20r multi .25 .25

Kashmir Solidarity Day — A832

Perf. 13¼x13

2020, Feb. 5 Litho. Wmk. 351

1282 A832 20r multi .30 .30

Presence of Afghan Refugees in Pakistan, 40th Anniv. — A833

No. 1283: a, Afghan refugees in front of building. b, Trucks and refugees. c, Refugees praying. d, Doctor examining child.

Wmk. 351

2020, Feb. 17 Litho. *Perf. 13*

1283 A833 20r Block or vert. strip of 4, #a-d 1.10 1.10

No. 1283 was printed in sheets of 16 + 4 central labels.

Mahmud Ali (1919-2006), Politician — A834

Perf. 13¼x13½

2020, Feb. 18 Litho. Wmk. 351

1284 A834 20r multi .30 .30

International Day Against Drug Abuse and Illicit Trafficking A835

Perf. 13x13¼

2020, June 26 Litho. Wmk. 351

1285 A835 20r multi .25 .25

World Population Day — A836

Perf. 13¼x13

2020, July 11 Litho. Wmk. 351

1286 A836 20r multi .25 .25

Indian Reorganization Act for Jammu and Kashmir, 1st Anniv. — A837

Perf. 13x13¼

2020, Aug. 5 Litho. Wmk. 351

1287 A837 58r multi .70 .70

Shaukat Khanum Memorial Cancer Hospital and Research Center, Lahore, 25th Anniv. — A838

Perf. 13¼x13

2020, Aug. 6 Litho. Wmk. 351

1288 A838 20r multi .25 .25

Miangul Abdul Haq Jahan Zeb (1908-87), Wali of Swat State — A839

Perf. 13¼x13

2020, Sept. 14 Litho. Wmk. 351

1289 A839 20r multi .25 .25

United Nations, 75th Anniv. A840

Perf. 13¼ Syncopated

2020, Oct. 24 Litho. Wmk. 351

1290 A840 20r multi .25 .25

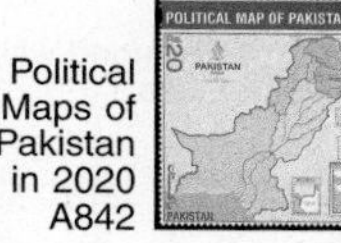

Breast Cancer Awareness Campaign — A841

Wmk. 351

2020, Nov. 11 Litho. *Perf. 13*

1291 A841 20r multi .30 .30

Political Maps of Pakistan in 2020 A842

No. 1292 — Map of Pakistan with: a, Two inset maps. b, Three inset maps, including inset map of Jammu and Kashmir disputed territory.

Wmk. 351

2020, Dec. 25 Litho. *Perf. 13¼*

1292 A842 20r Horiz. pair, #a-b .50 .50

Karnal Sher Khan Cadet College, Swabi, 10th Anniv. A843

Perf. 13¼ Syncopated

2021, Apr. 4 Litho. Wmk. 351

1293 A843 20r multi .30 .30

Gwadar Port, Pakistan A844

Zhuhai Port, People's Republic of China A845

Wmk. 351

2021, May 21 Litho. *Perf. 14*

1294 Horiz. pair .60 .60
- *a.* A844 20r multi .30 .30
- *b.* A845 20r multi .30 .30

Diplomatic relations between Pakistan and People's Republic of China, 70th anniv.

World Environment Day — A846

Perf. 13¼ Syncopated

2021, June 5 Litho. Wmk. 351

1295 A846 20r multi .30 .30

Discovery of Insulin, Cent. A847

Perf. 13¼ Syncopated

2021, June 24 Litho. Wmk. 351

1296 A847 20r multi .30 .30

State Bank Museum, Karachi, 10th Anniv. A848

Wmk. 351

2021, July 1 Litho. *Perf. 13*

1297 A848 20r multi .30 .30

NED University of Engineering and Technology, Karachi, Cent. — A849

Wmk. 351

2021, Aug. 1 Litho. *Perf. 13*

1298 A849 20r multi .30 .30

National Newspaper Readership Day — A850

Perf. 13¼ Syncopated

2021, Sept. 25 Litho. Wmk. 351

1299 A850 20r multi .30 .30

Pakistan Telecommunication Authority, 25th Anniv. — A851

Wmk. 351

2021, Sept. 30 Litho. *Perf. 13*

1300 A851 20r multi .30 .30

Inauguration of 1100-Megawatt Karachi Nuclear Power Plant Unit 2 — A852

Wmk. 351

2021, Sept. 30 Litho. *Perf. 13*

1301 A852 20r multi .30 .30

University of Engineering and Technology, Lahore, Cent. — A853

Wmk. 351

2021, Nov. 1 Litho. *Perf. 13*

1302 A853 20r multi .30 .30

Johann Wolfgang von Goethe (1749-1832) and Allama Muhammad Iqbal (1877-1938), Writers — A854

Wmk. 351

2021, Nov. 9 Litho. *Perf. 13*

1303 A854 20r multi .30 .30

Diplomatic relations between Pakistan and Germany, 70th anniv.

Sinking of Indian Navy Frigate Khukri by Pakistani Submarine Hangor, 50th Anniv. — A855

Wmk. 351

2021, Dec. 9 Litho. *Perf. 13*

1304 A855 20r multi .30 .30

Diplomatic Relations Between Pakistan and Thailand, 70th Anniv. — A856

No. 1305: a, Religious statues in Pakistan. b, Temple and religious statue in Thailand.

Wmk. 351

2021, Dec. 31 Litho. *Perf. 13*

1305 A856 20r Horiz. pair, #a-b .45 .45

Parliament House, Islamabad, and Diet Building, Tokyo — A857

Perf. 13¼x13½

2022, Jan. 1 Litho. Wmk. 351

1306 A857 20r multi .30 .30

Diplomatic relations between Pakistan and Japan, 70th anniv. (in 2021).

Diplomatic Relations Between Pakistan and Spain, 70th Anniv. (in 2021) — A858

No. 1307: a, Plaza de Cibeles, Madrid. b, Islamia College, Peshawar.

Wmk. 351

2022, Jan. 14 Litho. *Perf. 13*

1307 A858 20r Horiz. pair, #a-b .45 .45

48th Organization of Islamic Cooperation Council of Foreign Ministers Conference, Islamabad — A859

Wmk. 351

2022, Mar. 23 Litho. *Perf. 13*

1308 A859 20r multi .30 .30

Lahore College for Women, Cent. — A860

Wmk. 351

2022, May 25 Litho. *Perf. 13*

1309 A860 20r multi .30 .30

Attock Refinery Limited, Cent. A861

Wmk. 351

2022, July 25 Litho. *Perf. 13*

1310 A861 20r multi .30 .30

11th International Defense Exhibition and Seminar, Karachi — A862

Wmk. 351

2022, Aug. 14 Litho. *Perf. 13*

1311 A862 20r multi .30 .30

A863

A864

Independence, 75th Anniv. — A865

Perf. 13¼ Syncopated

2022, Aug. 14 Litho. Wmk. 351

1312 A863 20r multi .30 .30
1313 A864 20r multi .30 .30

Imperf

1314 A865 75r multi .70 .70

Pakistan Institute of International Affairs, 75th Anniv. — A866

Perf. 13¼ Syncopated

2022, Nov. 15 Litho. Wmk. 351

1315 A866 20r multi .30 .30

Parliament House, Islamabad, and Parliament House, Canberra — A867

Perf. 13¼x13½

2022, Nov. 15 Litho. Wmk. 351

1316 A867 20r multi .30 .30

Diplomatic relations between Pakistan and Australia, 75th anniv.

Ida Rieu School for the Blind and Deaf, Karachi, Cent. A868

Wmk. 351

2022, Nov. 23 Litho. *Perf. 13*

1317 A868 20r multi .30 .30

Statue of Liberty, New York and Minar-e-Pakistan, Lahore — A869

Perf. 13¼ Syncopated

2022, Dec. 27 Litho. Wmk. 351

1318 A869 20r multi .30 .30

Diplomatic relations between Pakistan and the United States, 75th anniv.

Asian-Pacific Postal Union, 60th Anniv. — A870

Wmk. 351

2022, Dec. 28 Litho. *Perf. 13½*

1319 A870 20r multi .30 .30

Allama Muhammad Iqbal (1877-1938), Writer — A871

Perf. 13¼x13¾

2022 Litho. & Engr. Wmk. 351

1320 A871 68r multi .65 .65

No. 1320 lacks 'Pakistan' inscription.

Campaign Against Violence Against Women A873

Wmk. 351

2023, Mar. 8 Litho. *Perf. 13*

1322 A873 20r multi .30 .30

International Women's Day.

SEMI-POSTAL STAMPS

Earthquake Relief — SP1

2005, Oct. 27 Litho. *Perf. 13¾x14*

B1 SP1 4r +(8.50r) multi 1.25 1.25

Printed in sheets of 8 stamps +17 labels.

Child and Man at Refugee Camp — SP2

Perf. 13x13½

2009, Aug. 1 Litho. Unwmk.

B2 SP2 5r +(7.50r) multi 2.00 2.00

Printed in sheets of eight stamps + 17 labels. Surtax for Prime Minister's Relief Fund for Swat Refugees.

OFFICIAL STAMPS

Official Stamps of India, 1939-43, Overprinted in Black

1947-49 Wmk. 196 *Perf. 13½x14*

O1 O8 3p slate 3.25 3.25
O2 O8 ½a dk rose vio .60 .25
O3 O8 9p green 5.00 4.00
O4 O8 1a carmine rose .60 .25
O4A O8 1a3p bister ('49) *15.00 42.50*
O5 O8 1½a dull purple .60 .25
O6 O8 2a scarlet .60 .90
O7 O8 2½a purple 6.25 *15.00*
O8 O8 4a dk brown 1.40 *1.50*
O9 O8 8a blue violet 2.00 *3.00*

India Nos. O100-O103 Overprinted in Black

O10 A82 1r brown & slate 1.00 *4.00*
O11 A82 2r dk brn & dk vio 17.50 14.00
O12 A82 5r dp ultra & dk grn 40.00 *67.50*
Telegraph cancel 7.50
O13 A82 10r rose car & dk vio 85.00 *170.00*
Telegraph cancel 5.00
Nos. O1-O13 (14) 178.80 326.40
Set, hinged 90.00

Regular Issue of 1948 Overprinted in Black or Carmine — a

"C" in "SERVICE" is nearly round.

Perf. 12½, 13, 13½x14, 14x13½

1948, Aug. 14 Unwmk.

O14 A3 3p orange red .25 .25
O15 A3 6p purple (C) .25 .25
O16 A3 9p dk green (C) .40 .25
O17 A4 1a dk blue (C) 3.50 .25
O18 A4 1½a gray grn (C) 3.50 .25
O19 A4 2a orange red 2.00 .25
O20 A5 3a olive green 27.50 22.50
O21 A6 4a chocolate 3.00 .25
O22 A6 8a black (C) 3.00 *10.00*
O23 A5 1r ultra 1.25 .25
O24 A5 2r dark brown 12.75 10.00
O25 A5 5r carmine 60.00 27.50
O26 A7 10r rose lil, perf. 14x13½ 25.00 *75.00*
a. Perf. 12 35.00 *80.00*
b. Perf. 13 24.00 *85.00*
Nos. O14-O26 (13) 142.40 147.00
Set, hinged 72.50

Issued: No. O26a, 10/10/51; No. O26b, 1954(?).

Nos. 47-50 and 52 Overprinted Type "a" in Black or Carmine

1949-50 *Perf. 12½, 13½x14*

O27 A10 1a dark blue (C) 7.50 .25
O28 A10 1½a gray green (C) 5.00 .25
a. Inverted ovpt. 350.00 55.00
O29 A10 2a orange red 12.50 .25
O30 A9 3a olive grn ('49) 40.00 8.00
O31 A11 8a black (C) 60.00 25.00
Nos. O27-O31 (5) 125.00 33.75

No. O32

No. O33

No. O34

Inscribed "SERVICE"

Unwmk.

1951, Aug. 14 Engr. *Perf. 13*

O32 A13 3a dark rose lake 9.25 *10.00*
O33 A14 4a deep green 2.40 .25
O34 A15 8a brown *13.00* 12.00
Nos. O32-O34 (3) 24.65 *22.25*

See Nos. 56, 58, 60.

Nos. 24-26, 47-49, 38-41 Overprinted in Black or Carmine — b

"C" in "SERVICE" is oval.

1954

O35 A3 3p orange red .25 .25
O36 A3 6p purple (C) .25 .25
O37 A3 9p dk green (C) .25 .25
O38 A10 1a dk blue (C) .25 .25
O39 A10 1½a gray grn (C) .25 .25
O40 A10 2a orange red .40 .25
O41 A5 1r ultra 9.00 7.50
O42 A5 2r dark brown 8.00 1.00
O43 A5 5r carmine 90.00 35.00
O43A A7 10r rose lilac 30.00 *90.00*
Nos. O35-O43A (10) 138.65 *135.00*

Nos. 66-72 Overprinted Type "b" in Carmine or Black

1954, Aug. 14

O44 A18 6p rose violet (C) .25 *3.50*
O45 A19 9p blue (C) 4.50 *13.50*
O46 A19 1a carmine rose .25 *2.50*
O47 A18 1½a red .25 *2.50*
O48 A20 14a dk green (C) 2.75 *14.00*
O49 A20 1r yellow grn (C) .90 .25
O50 A20 2r orange 8.00 .25
Nos. O44-O50 (7) 16.90 *36.50*

No. 75 Overprinted in Carmine Type "b" Overprint: 13x2½mm

1955, Aug. 14 Unwmk. *Perf. 13*

O51 A21 8a violet 1.75 .25

Nos. 24, 40, 66-72, 74-75, 83, 89 Overprinted in Black or Carmine — c

1957-61

O52 A3 3p org red ('58) .25 .25
O53 A18 6p rose vio (C) .25 .25
O54 A19 9p blue (C) ('58) .25 *.25*
O55 A19 1a carmine rose .25 .25
O56 A18 1½a red .25 .25
O57 A24 2a red ('58) .25 .25
O58 A21 6a dk bl (C) ('60) .25 .25
O59 A21 8a vio (C) ('58) .25 .25
O60 A20 14a dk grn (C) ('58) .90 *6.50*
O61 A20 1r yel grn (C) ('58) .90 .25
O62 A20 2r orange ('58) 7.50 .25
O63 A5 5r carmine ('58) 9.00 .25
O64 A26 10r dk grn & org (C) ('61) 6.75 *11.00*
Nos. O52-O64 (13) 27.05 20.25

For surcharges see Nos. O67-O73.

Nos. 110-111 Overprinted Type "c"

1961, Apr.

O65 A33 8a green .90 .25
O66 A33 1r blue .90 .25
a. Inverted overprint 11.00

New Currency

Nos. O52, O55-O57 Surcharged with New Value in Paisa

1961

O67 A18 1p on 1½a red .25 .25
a. Overprinted type "b" 9.00 2.00
O68 A3 2p on 3p orange red .25 .25
a. Overprinted type "b" 27.50 6.00
O69 A19 6p on 1a car rose
O70 A19 7p on 1a car rose .25 .25
a. Overprinted type "b" 27.50 *22.00*
O71 A18 9p on 1½a red
O72 A24 13p on 2a red ("PAISA") .25 .25
O73 A24 13p on 2a red ("Paisa")

Nos. O69, O71, O73 were locally overprinted at Mastung. On these stamps "paisa" is in lower case.

Forgeries of No. O69, O71 and O73 abound.

Nos. 125, 128 Overprinted Type "c"

1961

O74 A33 3p on 6p purple .25 .25
O75 A33 13p on 2a copper red .25 .25

Various violet handstamped surcharges were applied to several official stamps. Most of these repeat the denomination of the basic stamp and add the new value. Example: "4 ANNAS (25 Paisa)" on No. O33.

Nos. 129-135, 135B, 135C, 136a, 137-140a Overprinted in Carmine — d

1961-78 *Perf. 13½x14*

O76 A40 1p violet (II) 11.00 .25
a. Type I .25 .25
O77 A40 2p rose red (II) 1.25 .25
a. Type I .25 .25
O78 A40 3p magenta .25 .25
O79 A40 5p ultra (II) 9.00 .25
a. Type I .25 .25
O80 A40 7p emerald .25 .25
O81 A40 10p brown .25 .25
O82 A40 13p blue violet .25 .25
O85 A40 40p dull pur ('62) .25 .25

O86 A40 50p dull grn ('62) .25 .25
O87 A40 75p dk car ('62) .30 .25
Nos. O76-O87 (10) 23.05 2.50

1961-78 Designs Redrawn

O76b A40 1p violet (#129b) ('63) .25 .25
O77b A40 2p rose red (#130b) ('64) .25 .25
O78a A40 3p mag (#131a) ('66) 4.00 1.25
O78b A40 3p mag (#131b) 3.00 1.00
O79b A40 5p ultra (#132b) ('63) .25 .25
O80a A40 7p emerald (#133a) 45.00 16.00
O81a A40 10p brown (#134a) ('64) .25 .25
O82a A40 13p blue vio (#135a) ('63) .25 .25
O83 A40 15p rose lil (#135B; '64) .25 2.00
O84 A40 20p dl grn (#135C; '70) .25 .35
O84A A40 25p dk blue (#136a; '77) 20.00 5.00
O85a A40 40p dull purple (#137a) 27.50 12.50
O86a A40 50p dull grn (#138a) ('64) .25 .25
O87a A40 75p dark carmine (#139a) 40.00 32.50
O88 A40 90p lt ol grn (#140a; '78) 17.50 12.50
Nos. O76b-O88 (14) 156.00 83.60

Nos. 141, 143-144 Overprinted Type "c" in Black or Carmine

1963, Jan. 7 Unwmk. *Perf. 13½x13*

O89 A41 1r vermilion .40 .25
O90 A41 2r orange 1.50 .25
O91 A41 5r green (C) 4.00 9.00
Nos. O89-O91 (3) 5.90 9.50

Nos. 200, 202-203 Overprinted Type "c"

1968-? Wmk. 351 *Perf. 13½x13*

O92 A41 1r vermilion 4.50 1.00
O93 A41 2r orange 22.00 2.00
O93A A41 5r green (C) 47.50 13.00
Nos. O92-O93A (3) 74.00 16.00

Nos. 459-468, 470-475 Overprinted Type "d" in Carmine or Black

1979-84

O94 A224 2p dark green .25 *.30*
O95 A224 3p black .25 *.30*
O96 A224 5p violet blue .25 *.30*
O97 A225 10p grnsh blue .25 *.30*
O98 A225 20p yel grn ('81) .25 .25
O99 A225 25p rose car & grn ('81) .25 .25
O100 A225 40p car & bl .45 .25
O101 A225 50p bl grn & vio .25 .25
O102 A225 60p black 1.75 .25
O103 A225 75p dp orange 1.75 .25
O105 A225a 1r olive ('81) 4.00 .25
O106 A225a 1.50r dp orange .25 *.30*
O107 A225a 2r car rose .25 .25
O108 A225a 3r indigo ('81) .30 .30
O109 A225a 4r black ('84) 3.50 .50
O110 A225a 5r dk brn ('84) 3.50 .50
Nos. O94-O110 (16) 17.50 4.80

Types A237-A239 Inscribed "SERVICE POSTAGE"

No. O111

No. O115

No. O117

1980 Litho. *Perf. 12x11½, 11½x12*

O111 A237 10p dk grn & yel org 1.40 .25
O112 A237 15p dk grn & ap grn 1.40 .25
O113 A237 25p dp vio & rose car .25 *1.00*
O114 A237 35p rose pink & brt yel grn .25 *7.50*
O115 A238 40p red & lt brn 1.40 .25
O116 A239 50p olive & vio bl .25 *.60*
O117 A239 80p blk & yel grn .40 *1.50*
Nos. O111-O117 (7) 5.35 *11.35*

Issued: 10p, 15p, 40p, 1/15; others, 3/10.

Nos. 613-614, 616-620 Ovptd. "SERVICE" in Red

1984-87 Litho. *Perf. 11*

O118 A289 5p Kot Diji .25 .60
O119 A289 10p Rohtas .25 .25
O120 A289 20p Attock Fort .30 .40
O121 A289 50p Hyderabad .40 .40
O122 A289 60p Lahore ('86) .45 *.50*
O123 A289 70p Sibi .50 *.70*
O124 A289 80p Ranikot .55 *.70*
Nos. O118-O124 (7) 2.70 3.55

Issued: 10p, 9/25; 80p, 8/3/87.

No. 712 Ovptd. "SERVICE"
Litho. & Engr.

1989, Dec. 24 *Perf. 13*

O124A A357 1r multicolored *5.00 5.00*

National Assembly, Islamabad — O1

Wmk. 351

1991-99 Litho. *Perf. 13½*

O125 O1 1r green & red .25 .25
O126 O1 2r rose car & red .25 .25
O127 O1 3r ultra & red .35 .25
O128 O1 4r red brown & red .45 .25
O129 O1 5r rose lilac & red .50 .25
O130 O1 10r brown & red 1.25 .40
Nos. O125-O130 (6) 3.05 1.65

Issued: 10r, 2/6/99; others, 4/12/91.

1999 Unwmk.

O131 O1 2r rose car & red .40 .25

National Assembly Type of 1991-99
Perf. 13¼x13½

2012 ? Litho. Wmk. 351

O132 O1 8r claret & red .25 .25

BAHAWALPUR

LOCATION — A State of Pakistan.
AREA — 17,494 sq. mi.
POP. — 1,341,209 (1941)
CAPITAL — Bahawalpur

Bahawalpur was an Indian princely state located in the Punjab region of India. In anticipation of receipt of approval from the Imperial Government to operate its own postal system for ordinary mail, Bahawalpur ordered stamps from security printer Thomas De La Rue & Co. in London in 1933. After several years of persistence, records show that an agreement was finally reached with the Imperial Government to allow Bahawalpur to use its own "SERVICE" overprinted stamps on Official mail carried within the state boundaries beginning Jan.1, 1945.

Bahawalpur was autonomous from Aug. 15, 1947, until it acceded to Pakistan Oct. 3, 1947. These stamps had franking power solely within Bahawalpur.

Catalogue values for unused stamps in this country are for Never Hinged items.

On cover values are for a single example used on cover.

STAMPS OF INDIA USED IN BAHAWALPUR

Nos. A1 - A110 were produced locally using a rubber die. Stamps of India were overprinted as provisional stamps, immediately after Bahawalpur became an independent kingdom Aug. 15, 1947, pending receipt of machine-overprinted stamps from Nasik, India (Nos. 111 - 127). In most cases, fewer than 10 examples exist; in some as few as only one or two have been recorded. These stamps are found in somewhat toned condition.

Handstamped in Black on Regular Issues of India

No. A3

Perf. 13½x14, 14x13½

1947, Aug. Typo. Wmk. 196

A1 A80 9p green —
A2 A80 1a carmine —
A3 A81 12a car lake 2,000.
A4 A82 1r brn & slate 2,500.
A5 A82 2r dk brn & dk vio 5,000.
A6 A82 10r rose car & dk vio 10,000.
A7 A83 3p slate 1,000.
A8 A83 ½a rose vio 1,000.
A9 A83 9p green 1,000.
A10 A83 1a car rose 1,000.
A11 A84 1a3p yel brn 1,500.
A12 A84 2a scarlet 1,000.
A13 A84 13½a ultra 1,250.
A14 A85 4ar chocolate 1,250.
A15 A85 6a peacock bl 1,500.
A16 A85 8a blue vio 1,500.
A17 A85 12a car lake 1,500.
A18 A85 14a rose vio 2,000.
A19 A86 9p green 1,500.
A20 A86 1½a dull purple 1,500.
A21 A86 3½a ultra 2,000.
A22 A86 12a brown lake 2,500.
A23 A85 3p on 1a3p bis 1,000.

India Official Stamps Handstamped "SERVICE" Type "a" in Black

1947, Aug.

A24 A80 9p green 1,250.

"SERVICE" Type "b" Overprint

A25 A82 1r brown & slate 2,500.
A26 A82 2r dk brn & dk vio 5,000.
A27 A82 5r dp ultra & dk grn 7,500.
A28 A82 10r rose car & dk vio 10,000.
A29 O8 ½a brown 1,000.
A30 O8 ½a dk rose vio 1,000.
A31 O8 9p green 1,000.
A32 O8 1a car rose 1,000.
A33 O8 4a dk brown 1,000.
A34 O8 8a blue vio 1,000.

Regular Issues of India Handstamped in Purple

No. A41

No. A51

1947, Aug.

A35 A81 2a6p purple 2,000.
A36 A81 3a6p ultra 2,000.
A37 A81 4a dk brown 2,000.
A38 A82 1r brown & slate 2,500.
A39 A82 2r dk brn & dk vio 5,000.
A40 A82 5r dk brn & dk vio —
A41 A82 10r rose car & dk vio 10,000.
A42 A83 3p slate 1,000.
A43 A83 ½a rose vio 1,000.
A44 A83 9p green 1,000.
A45 A83 1a car rose 1,000.
A46 A84 1a3p yel brown 1,500.
A47 A84 1½a dk purple 1,000.
A48 A84 2a scarlet 1,000.
A49 A84 3½a ultra 1,250.
A50 A85 4a chocolate 1,250.
A51 A85 6a peacock bl 1,500.
A52 A85 8a blue vio 1,500.
A53 A85 12a car lake 1,500.
A54 A81 14a rose vio 2,000.
A55 A86 3½a ultra 2,000.
A56 A86 12a brn lake 2,500.
A57 A84 3p on 1a3p bis 1,000.

Official Stamps of India Handstamped "SERVICE" Type "a" in Purple

1947, Aug.

A58 A80 ½a brown 1,250.
A59 A82 1r brown & slate 2,500.
A60 A82 5r dp ultra & dk grn 7,500.
A61 A82 10r rose car & dk vio 10,000.
A62 A69 1a on 1a3p vio 2,000.
A63 O8 9p green 1,000.
A64 O9 1a car rose 1,000.
A65 O8 1a3p bister 1,000.
A66 O8 1½a dl purple 1,000.
A67 O8 2a scarlet 1,000.
A68 O8 4a dk brown 1,000.
A69 O8 8a dk brown 1,000.

Regular Issues of India Handstamped in Green

1947, Aug.

A70 A80 ½a brown —
A71 A81 2a scarlet 2,000.
A71 A81 2a scarlet 2,000.
A72 A82 10a rose car & dk vio 10,000.
A73 A83 ½a rose vio 1,000.
A74 A83 9p green 1,000.
A75 A83 1a car rose 1,000.
A76 A84 1a3p yel brn 1,500.
A77 A84 2a scarlet 1,000.
A78 A84 3½a ultra 1,250.
A79 A85 4a chocolate 1,250.
A80 A85 6a peacock bl 1,500.
A81 A85 8a blue vio 1,500.
A82 A85 12a car lake 1,500.
A83 A81 14a rose vio 2,000.
A84 A86 12a brn lake 2,500.

Regular Issues of India Handstamped "SERVICE" Type "b" in Green

1947, Aug.

A85 A82 1r brown & slate 2,500.
A86 A69 1a on 1a3p vio 2,000.
A87 O8 ½a dk rose vio 1,000.
A88 O9 1a car rose 1,000.

Regular Issues of India Handstamped "SERVICE" Type "b" in Red

1947, Aug.

A89 A81 3a yel green 2,000.
A90 A82 1r brown & slate 2,500.
A91 A82 2r dk brn & dk vio 5,000.
A92 A82 10r rose car & dk vio —
A93 A83 3p slate 1,000.
A94 A83 ½a rose vio 1,000.
A95 A83 9p green 1,000.
A96 A83 1a car rose 1,000.
A97 A84 1a3p yel brown 1,500.
A98 A84 2a scarlet 1,000.
A99 A84 3a violet 1,250.
A100 A85 4a chocolate 1,250.
A101 A85 8a bl vio 1,500.
A102 A85 12a car lake 1,500.
A103 A81 14a rose vio 2,000.
A104 A86 9p green 1,500.
A105 A86 1½a dl purple 1,500.
A106 A86 3½a ultra 2,000.
A107 A84 3p on 1a3p bis 1,000.

Official Stamps of India Handstamped "SERVICE" Type "b" in Red

1947, Aug.

A108 A82 2r dk brn & dk vio 5,000.
A109 A82 5r dp ultra & dk grn 7,000.
A110 A86 9p green 1,500.

Nos. A111-A127 were overprinted in Bombay using a metal die supplied by Thomas De La Rue & Co.

Stamps of India Machine Overprinted in Black or Red

No. A113

1947, Aug. 15

A111 A83 3p slate (R) 150.00
A112 A83 ½a rose vio 150.00
A113 A83 9p green (R) 150.00
Hinged 100.00
A114 A83 1a car rose 150.00
A115 A84 1½a dk purple (R) 150.00
Hinged 100.00

A116 A84 2a scarlet 150.00
Hinged 100.00
a. Double overprint 22,500.
A117 A84 3a violet (R) 150.00
Hinged 100.00
A118 A84 3½a ultramarine 150.00
Hinged 100.00
A119 A85 4a chocolate 150.00
Hinged 100.00
A120 A85 6a peacock bl (R) 150.00
Hinged 100.00
a. Double overprint 22,500.
A121 A85 8a blue vio (R) 150.00
Hinged 100.00
A122 A85 12a car lake 150.00
Hinged 100.00
A123 A81 14a rose vio 375.00
A124 A82 1r brown & slate 300.00
A125 A82 2r dk brn & dk vio (R) 13,000.
A126 A82 5r dp ultra & dk grn (R) 13,000.
A127 A82 10r rose car & dk vio 13,000.

Catalogue values for unused stamps in this section, from this point to the end of the section are for Never Hinged items.

Nos. 1-29 were issued after Bahawalpur acceded to Pakistan.

Amir Muhammad Bahawal Khan I Abbasi — A1

Perf. 12½x12
1947, Dec. 1 Wmk. 274 Engr.
1 A1 ½a brt car rose & blk 7.50 *25.00*

Bicentenary of the ruling family.

Nawab Sadiq Muhammad Khan V Abbasi Bahadur A2

Tombs of the Amirs A3

Mosque, Sadiq Garh — A4

Fort Dirawar — A5

Nur-Mahal Palace — A6

Palace, Sadiq Garh — A7

Nawab Sadiq Muhammad Khan V Abbasi Bahadur — A8

A9

Perf. 12½ (A2), 12x12½ (A3, A5, A6, A7), 12½x12 (A4, A8), 13x13½ (A9)
1948, Apr. 1 Engr. Wmk. 274

2	A2	3p dp blue & blk	4.00	*40.00*
3	A2	½a lake & blk	4.00	*40.00*
4	A2	9p dk green & blk	4.00	*40.00*
5	A2	1a dp car & blk	4.00	*40.00*
6	A2	1½a violet & blk	6.00	*40.00*
7	A3	2a car & dp grn	6.00	*40.00*
8	A4	4a brn & org red	6.00	*40.00*
9	A5	6a dp bl & vio brn	6.00	*40.00*
10	A6	8a brt pur & car	7.00	*40.00*
11	A7	12a dp car & dk bl grn	10.00	*70.00*
12	A8	1r chocolate & vio	10.00	*110.00*
13	A8	2r dp mag & dk grn	4.50	*200.00*
14	A8	5r purple & black	4.50	*240.00*
15	A9	10r black & car	50.00	*300.00*
		Nos. 2-15 (14)	126.00	*1,280.*

See Nos. 18-21. For overprints see Nos. O17-O24.

Soldiers of 1848 and 1948 — A10

1948, Oct. 15 Engr. *Perf. 11½*
16 A10 1½a dp car & blk 3.00 *20.00*

Centenary of the Multan Campaign.

Amir Khan V and Mohammed Ali Jinnah — A11

1948, Oct. 3 *Perf. 13x12½*
17 A11 1½a grn & car rose 3.00 *20.00*

1st anniv. of the union of Bahawalpur with Pakistan.

Types of 1948
1948 *Perf. 12x11½*

18	A8	1r orange & dp grn	1.50	*40.00*
19	A8	2r carmine & blk	1.50	*50.00*
20	A8	5r ultra & red brn	1.50	*85.00*

Perf. 13½

21	A9	10r green & red brn	1.50	*110.00*
		Nos. 18-21 (4)	6.00	*285.00*

Panjnad Weir — A12

1949, Mar. 3 *Perf. 14*

22	A12	3p shown	1.00	*20.00*
23	A12	½a Wheat	1.00	*20.00*
24	A12	9p Cotton	1.00	*20.00*
25	A12	1a Sahiwal Bull	1.00	*20.00*
		Nos. 22-25 (4)	4.00	*80.00*

25th anniv. of the acquisition of full ruling powers by Amir Khan V.

UPU Monument, Bern — A13

1949, Oct. 10 *Perf. 13*
Center in Black

26	A13	9p green	.30	*5.00*
a.		Perf. 17x17½	5.00	35.00
27	A13	1a red violet	.30	*5.00*
a.		Perf. 17x17½	5.00	35.00
28	A13	1½a brown orange	.30	*5.00*
a.		Perf. 17x17½	5.00	35.00
29	A13	2½a blue	.30	*5.00*
a.		Perf. 17x17½	5.00	35.00
		Nos. 26-29,O25-O28 (8)	2.40	*44.00*

UPU, 75th anniv. Exist perf 17½x17; value, each $3. Exist imperf.
For overprints see Nos. O25-O28.

LOCAL STAMPS

In 1924 Crown Prince Sadiq Mohammad Khan Abbasi V became ruler of Bahawalpur.The amir ordered from security printer Thomas De La Rue & Co., London, a set of seven stamps to be used on mail within Bahawalpur in an attempt to revive the State Dawk postal service. A small number of these stamps were used on mail between special post offices at Sadiqgarh Palace and other government departments. The Imperial Government refused to authorize the use of the stamps until an agreement was reached in 1945.

Crest with State Shield — L1

1933, Feb. 3 Unwmk. *Perf. 14*
1L1 L1 1a black, *grn* 25.00

Centenary of trade alliance between Bahawalpur and the British East India Company.

OFFICIAL STAMPS

Catalgoue values for unused stamps in this section, from this point to the end of the section are for Never Hinged items.

Two printings of Nos. O1-O10 exist. The first printing has brownish, streaky gum, and the second printing has clear, even gum.

Panjnad Weir — O1

Camel and Calf — O2

Antelopes — O3

Pelicans — O4

Juma Masjid Palace, Fort Derawar — O5

Temple at Pattan Munara — O6

SARKARI

SARKARK

Red Overprint
Wmk. 274
1945, Jan. 1 Engr. *Perf. 14*

O1	O1	½a brt grn & blk	40.00	*25.00*
		Hinged	25.00	
O2	O2	1a carmine & blk	7.50	*25.00*
		Hinged	5.00	
O3	O3	2a violet & blk	7.50	*25.00*
		Hinged	5.00	
O4	O4	4a olive & blk	45.00	*65.00*
		Hinged	30.00	
O5	O5	8a brown & blk	100.00	*35.00*
		Hinged	65.00	
O6	O6	1r orange & blk	115.00	*35.00*
		Hinged	75.00	
		Nos. O1-O6 (6)	315.00	*210.00*

For types overprinted, see Nos. O7-O9, O11-O13.

Two stamps exist overprinted in black on unwatermarked revenue stamps. The 1a black on green shows crest with state shield. Value, $750 never hinged, $500 hinged, $25,000 on cover. The 1a brown & black shows type O2. Value, $750 never hinged, $500 hinged, $5,000 on cover.

Camels — O7

Unwmk.
1945, Mar. 10 Engr. *Perf. 14*
Red Overprint
O7 O7 1a brown & black 300.00 *150.00*
Hinged 200.00

Black Overprint & Surcharge

1945, Mar.-May Unwmk.

O8	O5	½a on 8a lake & blk	*30.00*	*10.00*
		Hinged	20.00	
O9	O6	1½a on 1r org & blk	110.00	*16.00*
		Hinged	75.00	
O10	O1	1½a on 2r ultra & blk	400.00	15.00
		Hinged	250.00	
		Nos. O8-O10 (3)	540.00	41.00

Black Overprint

Wmk. 274
1945, June Engr. *Perf. 14*

O11	O1	½a carmine & black	5.00	*15.00*
		Hinged	3.00	
O12	O2	1a carmine & black	8.00	*17.00*
		Hinged	5.00	
O13	O3	2a orange & black	12.00	*75.00*
		Hinged	8.00	
		Nos. O11-O13 (3)	25.00	*107.00*

Nawab Sadiq Muhammad Khan V Abbasi Bahadur — O8

Unwmk.

1945, Sept. Engr. *Perf. 14*

O14 O8 3p dp blue & blk 18.00 *30.00*
Hinged 12.00
O15 O8 1½a dp violet & blk 50.00 12.00
Hinged 35.00

Flags of Allied Nations — O9

Unwmk.

1946, May 1 & Litho *Perf. 14*

O16 O9 1½a emerald & gray 15.00 *10.00*
Hinged 10.00

Victory of Allied Nations in World War II.

Nos. O17-O28 were issued after Bahawalpur acceded to Pakistan.

Stamps of 1948 Overprinted in Carmine or Black

Perf. 12½, 12½x12, 12x11½, 13½

1948 Wmk. 274

O17 A2 3p dp bl & blk (C) 1.50 *25.00*
O18 A2 1a dp carmine & blk 1.50 *25.00*
O19 A3 2a car & dp grn 1.50 *25.00*
O20 A4 4a brown & org red 1.50 *25.00*
O21 A8 1r org & dp grn (C) 1.50 *30.00*
O22 A8 2r car & blk (C) 1.50 *35.00*
O23 A8 5r ultra & red brn (C) 1.50 *75.00*
O24 A9 10r grn & red brn (C) 1.50 *75.00*
Nos. O17-O24 (8) 12.00 *315.00*

Same Ovpt. in Carmine on #26-29

1949 Center in Black *Perf. 13, 18*

O25 A13 9p green .30 *6.00*
a. Perf. 17x17½ 4.00 40.00
O26 A13 1a red violet .30 *6.00*
a. Perf. 17x17½ 4.00 40.00
O27 A13 1½a brown orange .30 *6.00*
a. Perf. 17x17½ 4.00 40.00
O28 A13 2½a blue .30 *6.00*
a. Perf. 17x17½ 4.00 40.00
Nos. O25-O28 (4) 1.20 *24.00*

75th anniv. of the UPU.
Exist imperf.

PALAU

pə-'lau

LOCATION — Group of 100 islands in the West Pacific Ocean about 1,000 miles southeast of Manila
AREA — 179 sq. mi.
POP. — 18,000 (2020 est.)
CAPITAL — Melekeok

Palau, the western section of the Caroline Islands (Micronesia), was part of the US Trust Territory of the Pacific, established in 1947. By agreement with the USPS, the republic began issuing its own stamps in 1984, with the USPS continuing to carry the mail to and from the islands.

On Jan. 10, 1986 Palau became a Federation as a Sovereign State in Compact of Free Association with the US.

100 Cents = 1 Dollar

Catalogue values for all unused stamps in this country are for Never Hinged items.

Inauguration of Postal Service — A1

1983, Mar. 10 Litho. *Perf. 14*

1 A1 20c Constitution preamble .55 .55
2 A1 20c Hunters .55 .55
3 A1 20c Fish .55 .55
4 A1 20c Preamble, diff. .55 .55
a. Block of 4, #1-4 2.75 2.75

Palau Fruit Dove — A2

1983, May 16 *Perf. 15*

5 A2 20c shown .45 .45
6 A2 20c Palau morningbird .45 .45
7 A2 20c Giant white-eye .45 .45
8 A2 20c Palau fantail .45 .45
a. Block of 4, #5-8 2.50 2.50

Sea Fan — A3

3c, Map cowrie. 5c, Jellyfish. 10c, Hawksbill turtle. 13c, Giant Clam. 20c, Parrotfish. 28c, Chambered Nautilus. 30c, Dappled sea cucumber. 37c, Sea Urchin. 50c, Starfish. $1, Squid. $2, Dugong. $5, Pink sponge.

1983-84 Litho. *Perf. 13½x14*

9 A3 1c shown .25 .25
10 A3 3c multicolored .25 .25
11 A3 5c multicolored .25 .25
12 A3 10c multicolored .25 .25
13 A3 13c multicolored .25 .25
a. Booklet pane of 10 *10.00* —
b. Bklt. pane of 10 (5 #13, 5 #14) *12.00* —
14 A3 20c multicolored .35 .35
b. Booklet pane of 10 *11.00* —
15 A3 28c multicolored .45 .45
16 A3 30c multicolored .50 .50
17 A3 37c multicolored .55 .55
18 A3 50c multicolored .80 .80
19 A3 $1 multicolored 1.60 1.60

Perf. 15x14

20 A3 $2 multicolored 4.25 4.25
21 A3 $5 multicolored 10.50 10.50
Nos. 9-21 (13) 20.25 20.25

See Nos. 75-85.

Humpback Whale, World Wildlife Emblem — A4

1983, Sept. 21 *Perf. 14*

24 A4 20c shown 1.25 1.25
25 A4 20c Blue whale 1.25 1.25
26 A4 20c Fin whale 1.25 1.25
27 A4 20c Great sperm whale 1.25 1.25
a. Block of 4, #24-27 6.50 6.50

Christmas 1983 — A5

Paintings by Charlie Gibbons, 1971 — No. 28, First Child ceremony. No. 29, Spearfishing from Red Canoe. No. 30, Traditional feast at the Bai. No. 31, Taro gardening. No. 32, Spearfishing at New Moon.

1983, Oct. Litho. *Perf. 14½*

28 A5 20c multicolored .50 .50
29 A5 20c multicolored .50 .50
30 A5 20c multicolored .50 .50
31 A5 20c multicolored .50 .50
32 A5 20c multicolored .50 .50
a. Strip of 5, #28-32 2.75 2.75

A6

Capt. Wilson's Voyage, Bicentennial — A7

No. 33, Capt. Henry Wilson. No. 34, Approaching Pelew. No. 35, Englishman's Camp on Ulong. No. 36, Prince Lee Boo. No. 37, King Abba Thulle. No. 38, Mooring in Koror. No. 39, Village scene of Pelew Islands. No. 40, Ludee.

1983, Dec. 14 *Perf. 14x15*

33 A6 20c multicolored .45 .45
34 A7 20c multicolored .45 .45
35 A7 20c multicolored .45 .45
36 A6 20c multicolored .45 .45
37 A6 20c multicolored .45 .45
38 A7 20c multicolored .45 .45
39 A7 20c multicolored .45 .45
40 A6 20c multicolored .45 .45
a. Block or strip of 8, #33-40 5.00 5.00

Local Seashells — A8

Shell paintings (dorsal and ventral) by Deborah Dudley Max.

1984, Mar. 15 Litho. *Perf. 14*

41 A8 20c Triton trumpet, d. .45 .45
42 A8 20c Horned helmet, d. .45 .45
43 A8 20c Giant clam, d. .45 .45
44 A8 20c Laciniate conch, d. .45 .45
45 A8 20c Royal cloak scallop, d. .45 .45
46 A8 20c Triton trumpet, v. .45 .45
47 A8 20c Horned helmet, v. .45 .45
48 A8 20c Giant clam, v. .45 .45
49 A8 20c Laciniate conch, v. .45 .45
50 A8 20c Royal cloak scallop, v. .45 .45
a. Block of 10, #41-50 5.50 5.50

Explorer Ships — A9

1984, June 19 Litho. *Perf. 14*

51 A9 40c Oroolong, 1783 .85 .85
52 A9 40c Duff, 1797 .85 .85
53 A9 40c Peiho, 1908 .85 .85
54 A9 40c Albatross, 1885 .85 .85
a. Block of 4, #51-54 4.25 4.25

UPU Congress.

Ausipex '84 A10

Fishing Methods: No. 55, Throw spear fishing. No. 56, Kite fishing. No. 57, Underwater spear fishing. No. 58, Net fishing.

1984, Sept. 6 Litho. *Perf. 14*

55 A10 20c multicolored .40 .40
56 A10 20c multicolored .40 .40
57 A10 20c multicolored .40 .40
58 A10 20c multicolored .40 .40
a. Block of 4, #55-58 2.25 2.25

Christmas Flowers — A11

No. 59, Mountain Apple. No. 60, Beach Morning Glory. No. 61, Turmeric. No. 62, Plumeria.

1984, Nov. 28 Litho. *Perf. 14*

59 A11 20c multicolored .40 .40
60 A11 20c multicolored .40 .40
61 A11 20c multicolored .40 .40
62 A11 20c multicolored .40 .40
a. Block of 4, #59-62 2.00 2.00

Audubon Bicentenary A12

1985, Feb. 6 Litho. *Perf. 14*

63 A12 22c Shearwater chick .85 .85
64 A12 22c Shearwater's head .85 .85
65 A12 22c Shearwater in flight .85 .85
66 A12 22c Swimming .85 .85
a. Block of 4, #63-66 4.50 4.50
Nos. 63-66,C5 (5) 4.50 4.50

Canoes and Rafts A13

1985, Mar. 27 Litho.

67 22c Cargo canoe .55 .55
68 22c War canoe .55 .55
69 22c Bamboo raft .55 .55
70 22c Racing/sailing canoe .55 .55
a. A13 Block of 4, #67-70 2.25 2.25

Marine Life Type of 1983

14c, Trumpet triton. 22c, Bumphead parrotfish. 25c, Soft coral, damsel fish. 33c, Sea anemone, clownfish. 39c, Green sea turtle. 44c, Pacific sailfish. $10, Spinner dolphins.

1985, June 11 Litho. *Perf. 14½x14*

75 A3 14c multicolored .30 .30
a. Booklet pane of 10 *8.50* —
76 A3 22c multicolored .55 .55
a. Booklet pane of 10 *10.50* —
b. Booklet pane, 5 14c, 5 22c *12.00* —
77 A3 25c multicolored .60 .60
79 A3 33c multicolored .80 .80
80 A3 39c multicolored .95 .95
81 A3 44c multicolored 1.10 1.10

Perf. 15x14

85 A3 $10 multicolored 19.00 19.00
Nos. 75-85 (7) 23.30 23.30

A14

IYY emblem and children of all nationalities joined in a circle.

1985, July 15 Litho. *Perf. 14*

86 A14 44c multicolored .85 .85
87 A14 44c multicolored .85 .85
88 A14 44c multicolored .85 .85
89 A14 44c multicolored .85 .85
a. Block of 4, #86-89 3.75 3.75

No. 89a has a continuous design.

A15

Christmas: Island mothers and children.

1985, Oct. 21 Litho. *Perf. 14*

90 A15 14c multicolored .35 .35
91 A15 22c multicolored .50 .50
92 A15 33c multicolored .80 .80
93 A15 44c multicolored 1.10 1.10
Nos. 90-93 (4) 2.75 2.75

Souvenir Sheet

Pan American Airways Martin M-130 China Clipper — A16

1985, Nov. 21 Litho. *Perf. 14*

94 A16 $1 multicolored 2.50 2.50

1st Trans-Pacific Mail Flight, Nov. 22, 1935.
See Nos. C10-C13.

Return of Halley's Comet — A17

Fictitious local sightings — No. 95, Kaeb canoe, 1758. No. 96, U.S.S. Vincennes, 1835. No. 97, S.M.S. Scharnhorst, 1910. No. 98, Yacht, 1986.

1985, Dec. 21 Litho. *Perf. 14*

95 A17 44c multicolored .80 .80
96 A17 44c multicolored .80 .80
97 A17 44c multicolored .80 .80
98 A17 44c multicolored .80 .80
a. Block of 4, #95-98 4.00 4.00

Songbirds — A18

No. 99, Mangrove flycatcher. No. 100, Cardinal honeyeater. No. 101, Blue-faced parrotfinch. No. 102, Dusky and bridled white-eyes.

1986, Feb. 24 Litho. *Perf. 14*

99 A18 44c multicolored .85 .85
100 A18 44c multicolored .85 .85
101 A18 44c multicolored .85 .85
102 A18 44c multicolored .85 .85
a. Block of 4, #99-102 4.00 4.00

World of Sea and Reef A19

Designs: a, Spear fisherman. b, Native raft. c, Sailing canoes. d, Rock islands, sailfish. e, Inter-island boat, flying fish. f, Bonefish. g, Common jack. h, Mackerel. i, Sailfish. j, Barracuda. k, Triggerfish. l, Dolphinfish. m, Spear fisherman, grouper. n, Manta ray. o, Marlin. p, Parrotfish. q, Wrasse. r, Red snapper. s, Herring. t, Dugong. u, Surgeonfish. v, Leopard ray. w, Hawksbill turtle. x, Needlefish. y, Tuna. z, Octopus. aa, Clownfish. ab, Squid. ac, Grouper. ad, Moorish idol. ae, Queen conch, starfish. af, Squirrelfish. ag, Starfish, sting ray. ah, Lion fish. ai, Angel fish. aj, Butterfly fish. ak, Spiny lobster. al, Mangrove crab. am, Tridacna. an, Moray eel.

1986, May 22 Litho. *Perf. 15x14*

103 Sheet of 40 *37.50*
a.-an. A19 14c any single .75 .50

AMERIPEX '86, Chicago, May 22-June 1
See Nos. 854, 1326.

Seashells — A20

1986, Aug. 1 Litho. *Perf. 14*

104 A20 22c Commercial trochus .55 .55
105 A20 22c Marble cone .55 .55
106 A20 22c Fluted giant clam .55 .55
107 A20 22c Bullmouth helmet .55 .55
108 A20 22c Golden cowrie .55 .55
a. Strip of 5, #104-108 3.25 3.25

See Nos. 150-154, 191-195, 212-216.

Intl. Peace Year A21

1986, Sept. 19 Litho.

109 22c Soldier's helmet .75 .75
110 22c Plane wreckage .75 .75
111 22c Woman playing guitar .75 .75
112 22c Airai vista .75 .75
a. A21 Block of 4, #109-112 3.50 3.50
Nos. 109-112,C17 (5) 4.00 4.00

Reptiles — A22

1986, Oct. 28 Litho. *Perf. 14*

113 A22 22c Gecko .65 .65
114 A22 22c Emerald tree skink .65 .65
115 A22 22c Estuarine crocodile .65 .65
116 A22 22c Leatherback turtle .65 .65
a. Block of 4, #113-116 2.75 2.75

Christmas — A23

Joy to the World, carol by Isaac Watts and Handel: No. 117, Girl playing guitar, boys, goat. No. 118, Girl carrying bouquet, boys singing. No. 119, Palauan mother and child. No. 120, Children, baskets of fruit. No. 121, Girl, fairy tern. Nos. 117-121 printed in a continuous design.

1986, Nov. 26 Litho.

117 A23 22c multicolored .40 .40
118 A23 22c multicolored .40 .40
119 A23 22c multicolored .40 .40
120 A23 22c multicolored .40 .40
121 A23 22c multicolored .40 .40
a. Strip of 5, #117-121 2.50 2.50

Butterflies — A23a

No. 121B, Tangadik, soursop. No. 121C, Dira amartal, sweet orange. No. 121D, Ilhuochel, swamp cabbage. No. 121E, Bauosech, fig.

1987, Jan. 5 Litho. *Perf. 14*

121B A23a 44c multicolored 1.00 .90
121C A23a 44c multicolored 1.00 .90
121D A23a 44c multicolored 1.00 .90
121E A23a 44c multicolored 1.00 .90
f. Block of 4, #121B-121E 4.50 4.50

See Nos. 183-186.

Fruit Bats A24

1987, Feb. 23 Litho.

122 44c In flight .85 .85
123 44c Hanging .85 .85
124 44c Eating .85 .85
125 44c Head .85 .85
a. A24 Block of 4, #122-125 4.00 4.00

Indigenous Flowers — A25

1c, Ixora casei. 3c, Lumnitzera littorea. 5c, Sonneratia alba. 10c, Tristellateria australasiae. 14c, Bikkia palauensis. 15c, Limnophila aromatica. 22c, Bruguiera gymnorhiza. 25c, Fagraea ksid. 36c, Ophiorrhiza palauensis. 39c, Cerbera manghas. 44c, Sandera indica. 45c, Maesa canfieldiae. 50c, Dolichandrone spathacea. $1, Barringtonia racemosa. $2, Nepenthes mirabilis. $5, Dendrobium palawense. $10, Bouquet.

1987-88 Litho. *Perf. 14*

126 A25 1c multicolored .25 .25
127 A25 3c multicolored .25 .25
128 A25 5c multicolored .25 .25
129 A25 10c multicolored .25 .25
130 A25 14c multicolored .25 .25
a. Booklet pane of 10 4.00 —
131 A25 15c multi ('88) .25 .25
a. Booklet pane of 10 ('88) 3.25 —
132 A25 22c multicolored .40 .40
a. Booklet pane of 10 6.50 —
b. Booklet pane, 5 each 14c, 22c 6.50 —
133 A25 25c multi ('88) .50 .50
a. Booklet pane of 10 ('88) 5.00 —
b. Booklet pane, 5 each 15c, 25c ('88) 5.00 —
134 A25 36c multi ('88) .65 .65
135 A25 39c multicolored .70 .70
136 A25 44c multicolored .85 .85
137 A25 45c multi ('88) .90 .90
138 A25 50c multicolored 1.00 1.00
139 A25 $1 multicolored 2.00 2.00
140 A25 $2 multicolored 4.25 4.00
141 A25 $5 multicolored 10.00 9.50

Size: 49x28mm

142 A25 $10 multi ('88) 17.00 16.00
Nos. 126-142 (17) 39.75 38.00

Issued: 3/12; $10, 3/17; 15c, 25c, 36c, 45c, 7/1; #131a, 133a-133b, 7/5.

CAPEX '87 — A26

1987, June 15 Litho. *Perf. 14*

146 22c Babeldaob Is. .50 .50
147 22c Floating Garden Isls. .50 .50
148 22c Rock Is. .50 .50
149 22c Koror .50 .50
a. A26 Block of 4, #146-149 2.25 2.25

Seashells Type of 1986

1987, Aug. 25 Litho. *Perf. 14*

150 A20 22c Black-striped triton .55 .55
151 A20 22c Tapestry turban .55 .55
152 A20 22c Adusta murex .55 .55
153 A20 22c Little fox miter .55 .55
154 A20 22c Cardinal miter .55 .55
a. Strip of 5, #150-154 3.00 3.00

US Constitution Bicentennial — A27

Excerpts from Articles of the Palau and US Constitutions and Seals: No. 155, Art. VIII, Sec. 1, Palau. No. 156, Presidential seals. No. 157, Art. II, Sec. 1, US. No. 158, Art. IX, Sec. 1, Palau. No. 159, Legislative seals. No. 160, Art. I, Sec. 1, US. No. 161, Art X, Sec. 1, Palau. No. 162, Supreme Court seals. No. 163, Art. III, Sec. 1, US.

1987, Sept. 17 Litho. *Perf. 14*

155 A27 14c multicolored .25 .25
156 A27 14c multicolored .25 .25
157 A27 14c multicolored .25 .25
a. Triptych + label, #155-157 .80 .80
158 A27 22c multicolored .40 .40
159 A27 22c multicolored .40 .40
160 A27 22c multicolored .40 .40
a. Triptych + label, #158-160 1.50 1.50
161 A27 44c multicolored .75 .75
162 A27 44c multicolored .75 .75
163 A27 44c multicolored .75 .75
a. Triptych + label, #161-163 3.00 3.00
Nos. 155-163 (9) 4.20 4.20

Nos. 156, 159 and 162 are each 28x42mm. Labels picture national flags.

Japanese Links to Palau — A28

Japanese stamps, period cancellations and installations: 14c, No. 257 and 1937 Datsun sedan used as mobile post office, near Ngerchelechuus Mountain. 22c, No. 347 and phosphate mine at Angaur. 33c, No. B1 and Japan Airways DC-2 over stone monuments at Badrulchau. 44c, No. 201 and Japanese post office, Koror. $1, Aviator's Grave, Japanese Cemetary, Peleliu, vert.

1987, Oct. 16 Litho. *Perf. 14x13½*

164 A28 14c multicolored .30 .30
165 A28 22c multicolored .45 .45
166 A28 33c multicolored .65 .65
167 A28 44c multicolored .85 .85
Nos. 164-167 (4) 2.25 2.25

Souvenir Sheet

Perf. 13½x14

168 A28 $1 multicolored 2.25 2.25

Christmas — A30

Verses from carol "I Saw Three Ships," Biblical characters, landscape and Palauans in outrigger canoes.

1987, Nov. 24 Litho. *Perf. 14*

173 A30 22c I saw... .50 .50
174 A30 22c And what was... .50 .50
175 A30 22c 'Twas Joseph... .50 .50
176 A30 22c Saint Michael... .50 .50
177 A30 22c And all the bells... .50 .50
a. Strip of 5, #173-177 3.00 3.00

Symbiotic Marine Species — A31

#178, Snapping shrimp, goby. #179, Mauve vase sponge, sponge crab. #180, Pope's damselfish, cleaner wrasse. #181, Clown anemone fish, sea anemone. #182, Four-color nudibranch, banded coral shrimp.

1987, Dec. 15

178	A31	22c	multicolored	.55	.55
179	A31	22c	multicolored	.55	.55
180	A31	22c	multicolored	.55	.55
181	A31	22c	multicolored	.55	.55
182	A31	22c	multicolored	.55	.55
a.			Strip of 5, #178-182	3.25	3.25

Butterflies and Flowers Type of 1987

Designs: No. 183, Dannaus plexippus, Tournefotia argentia. No. 184, Papilio machaon, Citrus reticulata. No. 185, Captopsilia, Crataeva speciosa. No. 186, Colias philodice, Crataeva speciosa.

1988, Jan. 25

183	A23a	44c	multicolored	.75	.75
184	A23a	44c	multicolored	.75	.75
185	A23a	44c	multicolored	.75	.75
186	A23a	44c	multicolored	.75	.75
a.			Block of 4, #183-186	3.50	3.50

Ground-dwelling Birds — A32

1988, Feb. 29 Litho. *Perf. 14*

187	A32	44c	Whimbrel	.75	.75
188	A32	44c	Yellow bittern	.75	.75
189	A32	44c	Rufous night-heron	.75	.75
190	A32	44c	Banded rail	.75	.75
a.			Block of 4, #187-190	3.50	3.50

Seashells Type of 1986

1988, May 11 Litho. *Perf. 14*

191	A20	25c	Striped engina	.55	.55
192	A20	25c	Ivory cone	.55	.55
193	A20	25c	Plaited miter	.55	.55
194	A20	25c	Episcopal miter	.55	.55
195	A20	25c	Isabelle cowrie	.55	.55
a.			Strip of 5, #191-195	4.00	4.00

Souvenir Sheet

Postal Independence, 5th Anniv. — A33

FINLANDIA '88: a, Kaep (pre-European outrigger sailboat). b, Spanish colonial cruiser. c, German colonial cruiser SMS Cormoran, c. 1885. d, Japanese mailbox, WWII machine gun, Koror Museum. e, US Trust Territory ship, Malakal Harbor. f, Koror post office.

1988, June 8 Litho. *Perf. 14*

196	A33		Sheet of 6	3.00	3.00
a.-f.			25c multicolored	.45	.45

Souvenir Sheet

US Possessions Phil. Soc., 10th Anniv. — A34

PRAGA '88: a, "Collect Palau Stamps," original artwork for No. 196f and head of a man. b, Soc. emblem. c, Nos. 1-4. d, China Clipper original artwork and covers. e, Man and boy studying covers. f, Girl at show cancel booth.

1988, Aug. 26 Litho. *Perf. 14*

197	A34		Sheet of 6	5.00	5.00
a.-f.			45c any single	.80	.80

Christmas — A35

Hark! The Herald Angels Sing: No. 198, Angels playing the violin, singing and sitting. No. 199, 3 angels and 3 children. No. 200, Nativity. No. 201, 2 angels, birds. No. 202, 3 children and 2 angels playing horns. Se-tenant in a continuous design.

1988, Nov. 7 Litho. *Perf. 14*

198	A35	25c	multicolored	.50	.50
199	A35	25c	multicolored	.50	.50
200	A35	25c	multicolored	.50	.50
201	A35	25c	multicolored	.50	.50
202	A35	25c	multicolored	.50	.50
a.			Strip of 5, #199-202 + 5 labels	2.75	2.75

Printed in sheets containing 3 strips + 5 labels.

Miniature Sheet

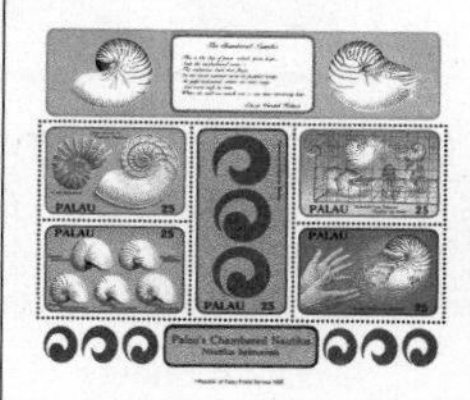

Chambered Nautilus — A36

Designs: a, Fossil and cross section. b, Palauan *bai* symbols for the nautilus. c, Specimens trapped for scientific study. d, *Nautilus belauensis, pompilius, macromphalus, stenomphalus* and *scrobiculatus.* e, Release of a tagged nautilus.

1988, Dec. 23 Litho. *Perf. 14*

203	A36		Sheet of 5	3.00	3.00
a.-e.			25c multicolored	.60	.60

Endangered Birds of Palau — A37

No. 204, Nicobar pigeon. No. 205, Ground dove. No. 206, Micronesian megapode. No. 207, Owl.

1989, Feb. 9 Litho. *Perf. 14*

204	A37	45c	multicolored	.85	.85
205	A37	45c	multicolored	.85	.85
206	A37	45c	multicolored	.85	.85
207	A37	45c	multicolored	.85	.85
a.			Block of 4, #204-207	4.00	4.00

Exotic Mushrooms A38

1989, Mar. 16 Litho. *Perf. 14*

208	A38	45c	Gilled auricularia	.90	.80
209	A38	45c	Rock mushroom	.90	.80
210	A38	45c	Polyporous	.90	.80
211	A38	45c	Veiled stinkhorn	.90	.80
a.			Block of 4, #208-211	4.00	4.00

Seashells Type of 1986

No. 212, Robin redbreast triton. No. 213, Hebrew cone. No. 214, Tadpole triton. No. 215, Lettered cone. No. 216, Rugose miter.

1989, Apr. 12 Litho. *Perf. 14x14½*

212	A20	25c	multicolored	.55	.55
213	A20	25c	multicolored	.55	.55
214	A20	25c	multicolored	.55	.55
215	A20	25c	multicolored	.55	.55
216	A20	25c	multicolored	.55	.55
a.			Strip of 5, #212-216	3.25	3.25

Souvenir Sheet

A Little Bird, Amidst Chrysanthemums, 1830s, by Hiroshige (1797-1858) — A39

1989, May 17 Litho. *Perf. 14*

217	A39	$1	multicolored	2.25	2.25

Hirohito (1901-1989) and enthronement of Akihito as emperor of Japan.

Miniature Sheet

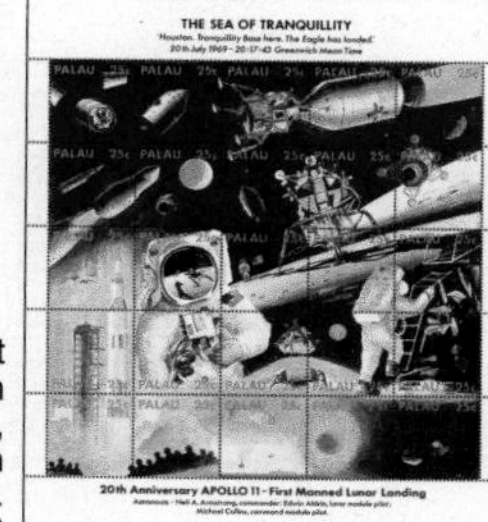

First Moon Landing, 20th Anniv. A40

Apollo 11 mission: a, Third stage jettison. b, Lunar spacecraft. c, Module transposition *(Eagle).* d, *Columbia* module transposition (command module). e, *Columbia* module transposition (service module). f, Third stage burn. g, Vehicle entering orbit, Moon. h, *Columbia* and *Eagle.* i, *Eagle* on the Moon. j, *Eagle* in space. k, Three birds, Saturn V third stage, lunar spacecraft and escape tower. l, Astronaut's protective visor, pure oxygen system. m, Astronaut, American flag. n, Footsteps on lunar plain Sea of Tranquillity, pure oxygen system. o, Armstrong descending from *Eagle.* p, Mobile launch tower, Saturn V second stage. q, Space suit remote control unit and oxygen hoses. r, *Eagle* lift-off from Moon. s, Armstrong's first step on the Moon. t, Armstrong descending ladder, module transposition *(Eagle* and *Columbia).* u, Launch tower, spectators and Saturn V engines achieving thrust. v, Spectators, clouds of backwash. w, Parachute splashdown, U.S. Navy recovery ship and helicopter. x, Command module reentry. y, Jettison of service module prior to reentry.

1989, July 20 Litho. *Perf. 14*

218	A40		Sheet of 25	12.00	12.00
a.-y.			25c any single	.45	.45

Buzz Aldrin Photographed on the Moon by Neil Armstrong — A41

1989, July 20 *Perf. 13½x14*

219	A41	$2.40	multicolored	4.75	4.75

First Moon landing 20th anniv.

Literacy A42

Imaginary characters and children reading: a, Youth astronaut. b, Boy riding dolphin. c, Cheshire cat in palm tree. d, Mother Goose. e, New York Yankee at bat. f, Girl reading. g, Boy reading. h, Mother reading to child. i, Girl holding flower and listening to story. j, Boy dressed in baseball uniform. Printed se-tenant in a continuous design.

1989, Oct. 13 Litho. *Perf. 14*

220	A42		Block of 10	4.75	4.75
a.-j.			25c any single	.40	.40

No. 220 printed in sheets containing two blocks of ten with strip of 5 labels between. Inscribed labels contain book, butterflies and "Give Them / Books / Give Them / Wings." Value, sheet $15.

Miniature Sheet

Stilt Mangrove Fauna — A43

World Stamp Expo '89: a, Bridled tern. b, Sulphur butterfly. c, Mangrove flycatcher. d, Collared kingfisher. e, Fruit bat. f, Estuarine crocodile. g, Rufous night-heron. h, Stilt mangrove. i, Bird's nest fern. j, Beach hibiscus tree. k, Common eggfly. l, Dog-faced watersnake. m, Jingle shell. n, Palau bark cricket. o, Periwinkle, mangrove oyster. p, Jellyfish. q, Striped mullet. r, Mussels, sea anemones, algae. s, Cardinalfish. t, Snapper.

1989, Nov. 20 Litho. *Perf. 14½*

221	A43		Block of 20	12.00	12.00
a.-t.			25c any single	.55	.55

Christmas — A44

Whence Comes this Rush of Wings? a carol: No. 222, Dusky tern, Audubon's shearwater, angels, island. No. 223, Fruit pigeon, angel. No. 224, Madonna and Child, ground pigeons, fairy terns, rails, sandpipers. No. 225, Angel, blue-headed green finch, red flycatcher, honeyeater. No. 226, Angel, blackheaded gulls. Printed se-tenant in a continuous design.

1989, Dec. 18 Litho. *Perf. 14*

222	A44	25c	multicolored	.55	.55
223	A44	25c	multicolored	.55	.55
224	A44	25c	multicolored	.55	.55
225	A44	25c	multicolored	.55	.55
226	A44	25c	multicolored	.55	.55
a.			Strip of 5, #222-226	3.25	3.25

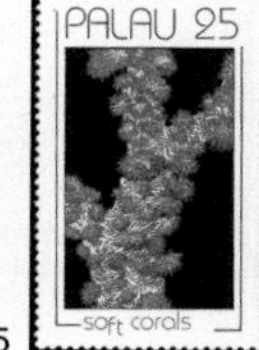

Soft Coral — A45

1990, Jan. 3

227	A45	25c	Pink coral	.50	.50
228	A45	25c	Pink & violet coral	.50	.50
229	A45	25c	Yellow coral	.50	.50
230	A45	25c	Red coral	.50	.50
a.			Block of 4, #227-230	3.00	3.00

Birds of the Forest — A46

1990, Mar. 16

231 A46 45c Siberian rubythroat .85 .85
232 A46 45c Palau bush-warbler .85 .85
233 A46 45c Micronesian starling .85 .85
234 A46 45c Cicadabird .85 .85
a. Block of 4, #231-234 4.00 4.00

Miniature Sheet

State Visit of Prince Lee Boo of Palau to England, 1784 — A47

Prince Lee Boo, Capt. Henry Wilson and: a, HMS *Victory* docked at Portsmouth. b, St. James's Palace, London. c, Rotherhithe Docks, London. d, Capt. Wilson's residence, Devon. e, Lunardi's Grand English Air Balloon. f, St. Paul's and the Thames. g, Lee Boo's tomb, St. Mary's Churchyard, Rotherhithe. h, St. Mary's Church. i, Memorial tablet, St. Mary's Church.

1990, May 6 Litho. *Perf. 14*

235 A47 Sheet of 9 4.50 4.50
a.-i. 25c any single .45 .45

Stamp World London '90.

Souvenir Sheet

Penny Black, 150th Anniv. A48

1990, May 6

236 A48 $1 Great Britain #1 2.00 2.00

Orchids — A49

No. 237, Corymborkis veratrifolia. No. 238, Malaxis setipes. No. 239, Dipodium freycinetianum. No. 240, Bulbophyllum micronesiacum. No. 241, Vanda teres and hookeriana.

1990, June 7 *Perf. 14*

237 A49 45c multicolored .90 .90
238 A49 45c multicolored .90 .90
239 A49 45c multicolored .90 .90
240 A49 45c multicolored .90 .90
241 A49 45c multicolored .90 .90
a. Strip of 5, #237-241 5.00 5.00

Butterflies and Flowers — A50

No. 242, Wedelia strigulosa. No. 243, Erthrina variegata. No. 244, Clerodendrum inerme. No. 245, Vigna marina.

1990, July 6 Litho. *Perf. 14*

242 A50 45c multicolored .85 .85
243 A50 45c multicolored .85 .85
244 A50 45c multicolored .85 .85
245 A50 45c multicolored .85 .85
a. Block of 4, #242-245 3.75 3.75

Miniature Sheet

Fairy Tern, Lesser Golden Plover, Sanderling — A51

Lagoon life: b, Bidekill fisherman. c, Sailing yacht, insular halfbeaks. d, Palauan kaeps. e, White-tailed tropicbird. f, Spotted eagle ray. g, Great barracuda. h, Reef needlefish. i, Reef blacktip shark. j, Hawksbill turtle. k, Octopus. l, Batfish. m, Lionfish. n, Snowflake moray. o, Porcupine fish, sixfeeler threadfins. p, Blue sea star, regal angelfish, cleaner wrasse. q, Clown triggerfish. r, Spotted garden eel and orange fish. s, Blue-lined sea bream, blue-green chromis, sapphire damselfish. t, Orangespine unicornfish, white-tipped soldierfish. u, Slatepencil sea urchin, leopard sea cucumber. v, Partridge tun shell. w, Mandarinfish. x, Tiger cowrie. y, Feather star-fish, orange-fin anemonefish.

1990, Aug. 10 Litho. *Perf. 15x14½*

246 A51 25c Sheet of 25, #a.-y. 12.50 12.50

Nos. 246a-246y inscribed on reverse.

Pacifica A52

1990, Aug. 24 Litho. *Perf. 14*

247 45c Mailship, 1890 1.50 1.50
248 45c US #803 on cover, fork-lift, plane 1.50 1.50
a. A52 Pair, #247-248 3.25 3.25

Christmas — A53

Christmas

Here We Come A-Caroling: No. 250, Girl with music, poinsettias, doves. No. 251, Boys playing guitar, flute. No. 252, Family. No. 253, Three girls singing.

1990, Nov. 28

249 A53 25c multicolored .50 .40
250 A53 25c multicolored .50 .40
251 A53 25c multicolored .50 .40
252 A53 25c multicolored .50 .40
253 A53 25c multicolored .50 .40
a. Strip of 5, #249-253 3.00 3.00

US Forces in Palau, 1944 — A54

Designs: No. 254, B-24s over Peleliu. No. 255, LCI launching rockets. No. 256, First Marine Division launching offensive. No. 257, Soldier, children. No. 258, USS *Peleliu.*

1990, Dec. 7

254 A54 45c multicolored 1.00 .85
255 A54 45c multicolored 1.00 .85
256 A54 45c multicolored 1.00 .85
257 A54 45c multicolored 1.00 .85
a. Block of 4, #254-257 4.25 4.25

Souvenir Sheet

Perf. 14x13½

258 A54 $1 multicolored 2.50 2.50

No. 258 contains one 51x38mm stamp.

See No. 339 for No. 258 with added inscription.

Coral A55

1991, Mar. 4 Litho. *Perf. 14*

259 30c Staghorn .65 .65
260 30c Velvet Leather .65 .65
261 30c Van Gogh's Cypress .65 .65
262 30c Violet Lace .65 .65
a. A55 Block of 4, #259-262 3.25 3.25

Miniature Sheet

Angaur, The Phosphate Island — A56

Designs: a, Virgin Mary Statue, Nkulangelul Point. b, Angaur kaep, German colonial post-mark. c, Swordfish, Caroline Islands No. 13. d, Phosphate mine locomotive. e, Copra ship off Lighthouse Hill. f, Dolphins. g, Estuarine crocodile. h, Workers cycling to phosphate plant. i, Ship loading phosphate. j, Hammerhead shark, German overseer. k, Marshall Islands No. 15. l, SMS Scharnhorst. m, SMS Emden. n, Crab-eating macaque monkey. o, Great sperm whale. p, HMAS Sydney.

1991, Mar. 14

263 A56 30c Sheet of 16, #a.-p. 10.00 10.00

Nos. 263b-263c, 263f-263g, 263j-263k, 263n-263o printed in continuous design showing map of island.

Birds — A57

1c, Palau bush-warbler. 4c, Common moorhen. 6c, Banded rail. 19c, Palau fantail. 20c, Mangrove flycatcher. 23c, Purple swamphen. 29c, Palau fruit dove. 35c, Great crested tern. 40c, Pacific reef heron. 45c, Micronesian pigeon. 50c, Great frigatebird. 52c, Little pied cormorant. 75c, Jungle night jar. 95c, Cattle egret. $1.34, Great sulphur-crested cockatoo. $2, Blue-faced parrotfinch. $5, Eclectus parrot. $10, Palau bush warbler.

Perf. 14½x15, 13x13½

1991-92 Litho.

266 A57 1c multicolored .25 .25
267 A57 4c multicolored .25 .25
268 A57 6c multicolored .25 .25
269 A57 19c multicolored .35 .30
b. Booklet pane, 10 #269 3.50 —
Complete booklet, #269b 3.75
270 A57 20c multicolored .40 .30
271 A57 23c multicolored .45 .35
272 A57 29c multicolored .55 .45
a. Booklet pane, 5 each #269, #272 5.00 —
Complete booklet, #272a 5.25
b. Booklet pane, 10 #272 4.50 —
Complete booklet, #272b 4.50
273 A57 35c multicolored .70 .55
274 A57 40c multicolored .80 .60
275 A57 45c multicolored .90 .70
276 A57 50c multicolored 1.00 .80
277 A57 52c multicolored 1.00 .90
278 A57 75c multicolored 1.50 1.25
279 A57 95c multicolored 2.00 1.50
280 A57 $1.34 multicolored 2.25 2.00
281 A57 $2 multicolored 3.25 3.00
282 A57 $5 multicolored 8.00 7.75

Size: 52x30mm

283 A57 $10 multicolored 16.00 15.00
Nos. 266-283 (18) 39.90 36.20

The 1, 6, 20, 52, 75c, $10 are perf. 14½x15.

Issued: 1, 6, 20, 52, 75c, $5, 4/6/92; $10, 9/10/92; #269b, 272a, 272b, 8/23/91; others, 4/18/91.

Miniature Sheet

Christianity in Palau, Cent. — A58

Designs: a, Pope Leo XIII, 1891. b, Ibedul Ilengelekei, High Chief of Koror, 1871-1911. c, Fr. Marino de la Hoz, Br. Emilio Villar, Fr. Elias Fernandez. d, Fr. Edwin G. McManus (1908-1969), compiler of Palauan-English dictionary. e, Sacred Heart Church, Koror. f, Pope John Paul II.

1991, Apr. 28 *Perf. 14½*

288 A58 29c Sheet of 6, #a.-f. 3.50 3.50

Miniature Sheet

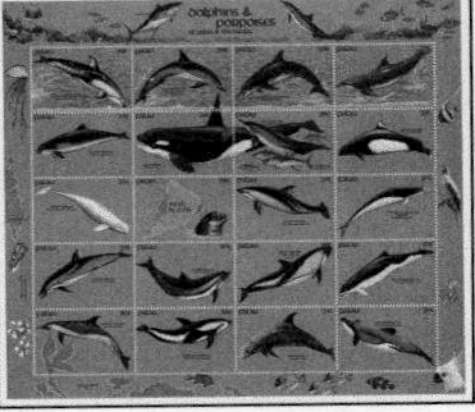

Marine Life A59

Designs: a, Pacific white-sided dolphin. b, Common dolphin. c, Rough-toothed dolphin. d, Bottlenose dolphin. e, Harbor porpoise. f, Killer whale. g, Spinner dolphin, yellowfin tuna. h, Dall's porpoise. i, Finless porpoise. j, Map of Palau, dolphin. k, Dusky dolphin. l, Southern right-whale dolphin. m, Striped dolphin. n, Fraser's dolphin. o, Peale's dolphin. p, Spectacled porpoise. q, Spotted dolphin. r, Hourglass dolphin. s, Risso's dolphin. t, Hector's dolphin.

1991, May 24 Litho. *Perf. 14*

289 A59 29c Sheet of 20, #a.-t. 13.50 13.50

Miniature Sheet

Operations Desert Shield / Desert Storm — A60

Designs: a, F-4G Wild Weasel fighter. b, F-117A Stealth fighter. c, AH-64A Apache helicopter. d, TOW missle launcher on M998 HMMWV. e, Pres. Bush. f, M2 Bradley fighting vehicle. g, Aircraft carrier USS Ranger. h, Corvette fast patrol boat. i, Battleship Wisconsin.

No. 291, Fairy tern, yellow ribbon.

1991, July 2 Litho. *Perf. 14*

290 A60 20c Sheet of 9, #a.-i. 3.75 3.75

Size: 38x51mm

291 A60 $2.90 multicolored 5.25 5.25

Souvenir Sheet

292 A60 $2.90 like #291 5.75 5.75

No. 291 has a white border around design. No. 292 printed in continuous design.

Republic of Palau, 10th Anniv. — A61

Designs: a, Palauan bai. b, Palauan bai interior, denomination UL. c, Same, denomination UR. d, Demi-god Chedechuul. e, Spider, denomination at UL. f, Money bird facing right. g, Money bird facing left. h, Spider, denomination at UR.

1991, July 9 *Perf. 14½*

293 A61 29c Sheet of 8, #a.-h. 5.00 5.00

See No. C21.

Miniature Sheet

Giant Clams — A62

Designs: a, Tridacna squamosa, Hippopus hippopus, Hippopus porcellanus, and Tridacna derasa. b, Tridacna gigas. c, Hatchery and tank culture. d, Diver, bottom-based clam nursery. e, Micronesian Mariculture Demonstration Center.

1991, Sept. 17 Litho. *Perf. 14*
294 A62 50c Sheet of 5, #a.-e. 5.00 5.00

No. 294e is 109x17mm and imperf on 3 sides, perf 14 at top.

Miniature Sheet

Japanese Heritage in Palau — A63

Designs: No. 295: a, Marine research. b, Traditional arts, carving story boards. c, Agricultural training. d, Archaeological research. e, Training in architecture and building. f, Air transportation. $1, Map, cancel from Japanese post office at Parao.

1991, Nov. 19
295 A63 29c Sheet of 6, #a.-f. 3.50 3.50

Souvenir Sheet

296 A63 $1 multicolored 3.00 3.00

Phila Nippon '91.

Miniature Sheet

Peace Corps in Palau, 25th Anniv. — A64

Children's drawings: No. 297a, Flag, doves, children, and islands. b, Airplane, people being greeted. c, Red Cross instruction. d, Fishing industry. e, Agricultural training. f, Classroom instruction.

1991, Dec. 6 Litho. *Perf. 13½*
297 A64 29c Sheet of 6, #a.-f. 3.75 3.75

Christmas — A65

Silent Night: No. 298: a, Silent night, holy night. b, All is calm, all is bright. c, Round yon virgin, mother and Child. d, Holy Infant, so tender and mild. e, Sleep in heavenly peace.

1991, Nov. 14 *Perf. 14*
298 A65 29c Strip of 5, #a.-e. 2.75 2.75

Miniature Sheet

World War II in the Pacific — A66

Designs: No. 299a, Pearl Harbor attack begins. b, Battleship Nevada gets under way. c, USS Shaw explodes. d, Japanese aircraft carrier Akagi sunk. e, USS Wasp sunk off Guadalcanal. f, Battle of the Philippine Sea. g, US landing craft approach Saipan. h, US 1st Cavalry on Leyte. i, Battle of Bloody Nose Ridge, Peleliu. j, US troops land on Iwo Jima.

1991, Dec. 6 *Perf. 14½x15*
299 A66 29c Sheet of 10, #a.-j. 8.50 8.50

See No. C22.

A67

Butterflies: a, Troides criton. b, Alcides zodiaca. c, Papillio poboroi. d, Vindula arsinoe.

1992, Jan. 20 Litho. *Perf. 14*
300 A67 50c Block of 4, #a.-d. 4.00 4.00

A68

Shells: a, Common hairy triton. b, Eglantine cowrie. c, Sulcate swamp cerith. d, Black-spined murex. e, Black-mouth moon.

1992, Mar. 11
301 A68 29c Strip of 5, #a.-e. 3.00 3.00

Miniature Sheet

Age of Discovery — A69

Designs: a, Columbus. b, Magellan. c, Drake. d, Wind as shown on old maps.
Maps and: e, Compass rose. f, Dolphin, Drake's ship Golden Hinde. g, Corn, Santa Maria. h, Fish. i, Betel palm, cloves and black pepper. j, Victoria, shearwater and great crested tern. k, White-tailed tropicbird, bicolor parrotfish, pineapple and potatoes. l, Compass. m, Sea monster. n, Paddles and astrolabe. o, Parallel ruler, dividers and Inca gold treasures. p, Back staff.
Portraits: q, Wind, diff. r, Vespucci. s, Pizarro. t, Balboa.

1992, May 25 Litho. *Perf. 14*
302 A69 29c Sheet of 20, #a.-t. 12.00 12.00

Miniature Sheet

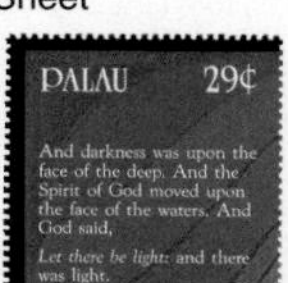

Biblical Creation of the World — A70

Designs: a, "And darkness was..." b, Sun's rays. c, Water, sun's rays. d, "...and it was good." e, "Let there be a..." f, Land forming. g, Water and land. h, "...and it was so." i, "Let the waters..." j, Tree branches. k, Shoreline. l, Shoreline, flowers, tree. m, "Let there be lights..." n, Comet, moon. o, Mountains. p, Sun, hillside. q, "Let the waters..." r, Birds. s, Fish, killer whale. t, Fish. u, "Let the earth..." v, Woman, man. w, Animals. x, "...and it was very good."

1992, June 5 *Perf. 14½*
303 A70 29c Sheet of 24, #a.-x. 14.00 14.00

Nos. 303a-303d, 303e-303h, 303i-303l, 303m-303p, 303q-303t, 303u-303x are blocks of 4.

Souvenir Sheets

1992 Summer Olympics, Barcelona — A71

1992, July 10 *Perf. 14*
304 A71 50c Dawn Fraser 1.00 1.00
305 A71 50c Olga Korbut 1.00 1.00
306 A71 50c Bob Beamon 1.00 1.00
307 A71 50c Carl Lewis 1.00 1.00
308 A71 50c Dick Fosbury 1.00 1.00
309 A71 50c Greg Louganis 1.00 1.00
Nos. 304-309 (6) 6.00 6.00

Miniature Sheet

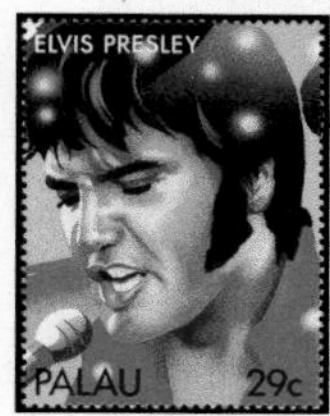

Elvis Presley — A72

Various portraits.

1992, Aug. 17 *Perf. 13½x14*
310 A72 29c Sheet of 9, #a.-i. 7.00 7.00

See No. 350.

Christmas — A73

The Friendly Beasts carol depicting animals in Nativity Scene: No. 312a, "Thus Every Beast." b, "By Some Good Spell." c, "In The Stable Dark Was Glad to Tell." d, "Of The Gift He Gave Emanuel." e, "The Gift He Gave Emanuel."

1992, Oct. 1 Litho. *Perf. 14*
312 A73 29c Strip of 5, #a.-e. 3.00 3.00

Fauna — A74

Designs: a, Dugong. b, Masked booby. c, Macaque. d, New Guinean crocodile.

1993, July 9 Litho. *Perf. 14*
313 A74 50c Block of 4, #a.-d. 4.00 4.00

Seafood — A75

Designs: a, Giant crab. b, Scarlet shrimp. c, Smooth nylon shrimp. d, Armed nylon shrimp.

1993, July 22
314 A75 29c Block of 4, #a.-d. 2.25 2.25

Sharks A76

Designs: a, Oceanic whitetip. b, Great hammerhead. c, Leopard. d, Reef black-tip.

1993, Aug. 11 Litho. *Perf. 14½*
315 A76 50c Block of 4, #a.-d. 4.00 4.00

Miniature Sheet

World War II in the Pacific — A77

Actions in 1943: a, US takes Guadalcanal, Feb. b, Hospital ship Tranquility supports action. c, New Guineans join Allies in battle. d, US landings in New Georgia, June. e, USS California participates in every naval landing. f, Dauntless dive bombers over Wake Island, Oct. 6. g, US flamethrowers on Tarawa, Nov. h, US landings on Makin, Nov. i, B-25s bomb Simpson Harbor, Rabaul, Oct. 23. j, B-24s over Kwajalein, Dec. 8.

1993, Sept. 23 Litho. *Perf. 14½x15*
316 A77 29c Sheet of 10, #a.-j. + label 8.00 8.00

See Nos. 325-326.

Christmas — A78

Christmas carol, "We Wish You a Merry Christmas," with Palauan customs: a, Girl, goat. b, Goats, children holding leis, prow of canoe. c, Santa Claus. d, Children singing. e, Family with fruit, fish.

1993, Oct. 22 Litho. *Perf. 14*
317 A78 29c Strip of 5, #a.-e. 3.00 3.00

Miniature Sheet

Prehistoric and Legendary Sea Creatures — A79

1993, Nov. 26 Litho. *Perf. 14*
318 A79 29c Sheet of 25, #a.-y. 14.00 14.00

Miniature Sheet

Intl. Year of Indigenous People — A80

Paintings, by Charlie Gibbons: No. 319: a, After Child-birth Ceremony. b, Village in Early Palau.
Storyboard carving, by Ngiraibuuch: $2.90, Quarrying of Stone Money, vert.

1993, Dec. 8 ***Perf. 14x13½***
319 A80 29c Sheet, 2 ea #a.-b. 2.25 2.25

Souvenir Sheet
Perf. 13½x14
320 A80 $2.90 multicolored 6.00 6.00

Miniature Sheet

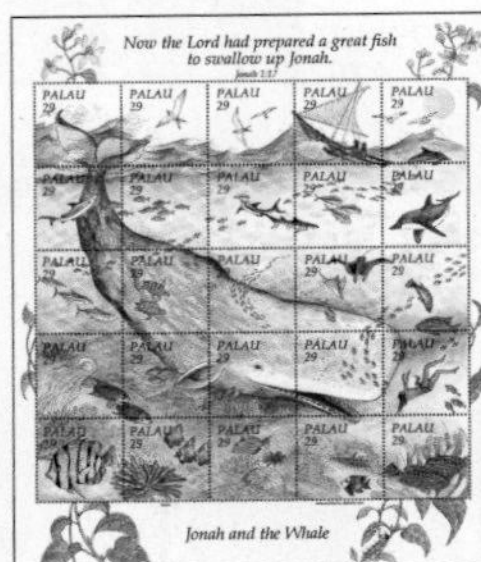

Jonah and the Whale A81

1993, Dec. 28 **Litho.** ***Perf. 14***
321 A81 29c Sheet of 25, #a.-y. 14.50 14.50

Hong Kong '94 — A82

Rays: a, Manta (b). b, Spotted eagle (a). c, Coachwhip (d). d, Black spotted.

1994, Feb. 18 **Litho.** ***Perf. 14***
322 A82 40c Block of 4, #a.-d. 3.00 3.00

Estuarine Crocodile — A83

Designs: a, With mouth open. b, Hatchling. c, Crawling on river bottom. d, Swimming.

1994, Mar. 14
323 A83 20c Block of 4, #a.-d. 3.50 3.50
World Wildlife Fund.

Large Seabirds — A84

a, Red-footed booby. b, Great frigatebird. c, Brown booby. d, Little pied cormorant.

1994, Apr. 22 **Litho.** ***Perf. 14***
324 A84 50c Block of 4, #a.-d. 4.00 4.00

World War II Type of 1993
Miniature Sheets

Action in the Pacific, 1944: No. 325: a, US Marines capture Kwajalien, Feb. 1-7. b, Japanese enemy base at Truk destroyed, Feb. 17-18. c, SS-284 Tullibee participates in Operation Desecrate, March. d, US troops take Saipan, June 15-July 9. e, Great Marianas Turkey Shoot, June 19-20. f, Guam liberated, July-Aug. g, US troops take Peleliu, Sept. 15-Oct. 14. h, Angaur secured in fighting, Sept. 17-22. i, Gen. Douglas MacArthur returns to Philippines, Oct. 20. j, US Army Memorial, Palau, Nov. 27.
D-Day, Allied Invasion of Normandy, June 6, 1944: No. 326: a, C-47 transport aircraft dropping Allied paratroopers. b, Allied warships attack beach fortifications. c, Commandos attack from landing craft. d, Tanks land. e, Sherman flail tank beats path through minefields. f, Allied aircraft attack enemy reinforcements. g, Gliders deliver troops behind enemy lines. h, Pegasus Bridge, first French house liberated. i, Allied forces move inland to form bridgehead. j, View of beach at end of D-Day.

1994, May **Sheets of 10** ***Perf. 14½***
325 A77 29c #a.-j. + label 8.50 8.50
326 A77 50c #a.-j. + label 12.00 12.00

Pierre de Coubertin (1863-1937) A85

Winter Olympic medalists: No. 328, Anne-Marie Moser, vert. No. 329, James Craig. No. 330, Katarina Witt. No. 331, Eric Heiden, vert. No. 332, Nancy Kerrigan. $2, Dan Jansen.

1994, July 20 **Litho.** ***Perf. 14***
327 A85 29c multicolored .70 .70

Souvenir Sheets
328 A85 50c multicolored 1.00 1.00
329 A85 50c multicolored 1.00 1.00
330 A85 $1 multicolored 2.00 2.00
331 A85 $1 multicolored 2.00 2.00
332 A85 $1 multicolored 2.00 2.00
333 A85 $2 multicolored 4.00 4.00
Intl. Olympic Committee, cent.

Miniature Sheets

PHILAKOREA '94 — A86

Wildlife carrying letters: No. 334: a, Sailfin goby. b, Sharpnose puffer. c, Lightning butterflyfish. d, Clown anemonefish. e, Parrotfish. f, Batfish. g, Clown triggerfish. h, twinspot wrasse.
No. 335a, Palau fruit bat. b, Crocodile. c, Dugong. d, Banded sea snake. e, Bottle-nosed dophin. f, Hawksbill turtle. g, Octopus. h, Manta ray.
No. 336: a, Palau fantail. b, Banded crake. c, Island swiftlet. d, Micronesian kingfisher. e. Red-footed booby. f, Great frigatebird. g, Palau owl. h, Palau fruit dove.

1994, Aug. 16 **Litho.** ***Perf. 14***
334 A86 29c Sheet of 8, #a.-h. 6.00 6.00
335 A86 40c Sheet of 8, #a.-h. 8.00 8.00
336 A86 50c Sheet of 8, #a.-h. 10.00 10.00
No. 336 is airmail.

Miniature Sheet

First Manned Moon Landing, 25th Anniv. A87

Various scenes from Apollo moon missions.

1994, July 20
337 A87 29c Sheet of 20, #a.-t. 12.00 12.00

Independence Day — A88

#338: b, Natl. seal. c, Pres. Kuniwo Nakamura, Palau, US Pres. Clinton. d, Palau, US flags. e, Musical notes of natl. anthem.

1994, Oct. 1 ***Perf. 14***
338 A88 29c Strip of 5, #a.-e. 2.75 2.75
No. 338c is 57x42mm.

No. 258 with added text "50th ANNIVERSARY / INVASION OF PELELIU / SEPTEMBER 15, 1944"

1994 **Litho.** ***Perf. 14X13½***
339 A54 $1 multicolored 2.50 2.50

Miniature Sheet

Disney Characters Visit Palau — A89

No. 340: a, Mickey, Minnie arriving. b, Goofy finding way to hotel. c, Donald enjoying beach. d, Minnie, Daisy learning the Ngloik. e, Minnie, Mickey sailing to Natural Bridge. f, Scrooge finding money in Babeldaob jungle. g, Goofy, Napoleon Wrasse. h, Minnie, Clam Garden. i, Grandma Duck weaving basket.
No. 341, Mickey exploring underwater shipwreck. No. 342, Donald visiting Airai Bai on Babeldaob. No. 343, Pluto, Mickey in boat, vert.

1994, Oct. 14 ***Perf. 13½x14***
340 A89 29c Sheet of 9, #a.-i. 6.00 6.00

Souvenir Sheets
341-342 A89 $1 each 3.00 3.00
Perf. 14x13½
343 A89 $2.90 multicolored 7.75 7.75

Miniature Sheet

Intl. Year of the Family — A90

Story of Tebruchel: a, With mother as infant. b, Father. c, As young man. d, Wife-to-be. e, Bringing home fish. f, Pregnant wife. g, Elderly mother. h, Elderly father. i, With first born. j, Wife seated. k, Caring for mother. l, Father, wife and baby.

1994, Nov. 1 **Litho.** ***Perf. 14***
344 A90 20c Sheet of 12, #a.-l. 4.75 4.75

Christmas — A91

O Little Town of Bethlehem: a, Magi, cherubs. b, Angel, shepherds, sheep. c, Angels, nativity. d, Angels hovering over town, shepherd, sheep. e, Cherubs, doves.

1994, Nov. 23 **Litho.** ***Perf. 14***
345 A91 29c Strip of 5, #a-e 3.00 3.00

No. 345 is a continuous design and is printed in sheets containing three strips. The bottom strip is printed with se-tenant labels.

Miniature Sheets

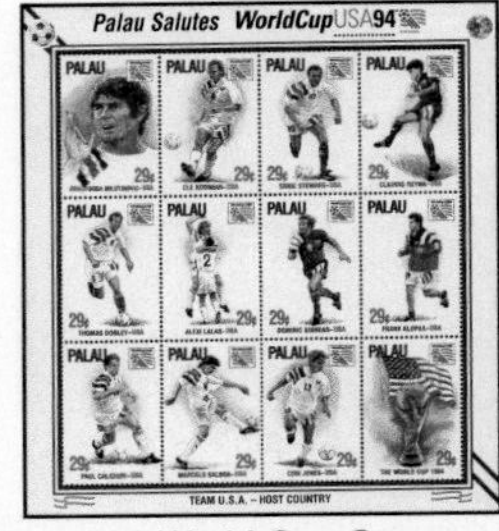

1994 World Cup Soccer Championships, US — A92

US coach, players: No. 346: a, Bora Milutinovic. b, Cle Kooiman. c, Ernie Stewart. d, Claudio Reyna. e, Thomas Dooley. f, Alexi Lalas. g, Dominic Kinnear. h, Frank Klopas. i, Paul Caligiuri. j, Marcelo Balboa. k, Cobi Jones. l, US flag, World Cup trohpy.
US players: No. 347a, Tony Meola. b, John Doyle. c, Eric Wynalda. d, Roy Wegerle. e, Fernando Clavijo. f, Hugo Perez. g, John Harkes. h, Mike Lapper. i, Mike Sorber. j, Brad Friedel. k, Tab Ramos. l, Joe-Max Moore.
No. 348: a, Babeto, Brazil. b, Romario, Brazil. c, Franco Baresi, Italy. d, Roberto Baggio, Italy. e, Andoni Zubizarreta, Spain. f, Oleg Salenko, Russia. g, Gheorghe Hagi, Romania. h, Dennis Bergkamp, Netherlands. i, Hristo Stoichkov, Bulgaria. j, Tomas Brolin, Sweden. k, Lothar Matthaus, Germany. l, Arrigo Sacchi, Italy, Carlos Alberto Parreira, Brazil, flags of Italy & Brazil, World Cup trophy.

1994, Dec. 23
346 A92 29c Sheet of 12, #a.-l. 6.25 6.25
347 A92 29c Sheet of 12, #a.-l. 6.25 6.25
348 A92 50c Sheet of 12, #a.-l. 10.50 10.50

Elvis Presley Type of 1992
Miniature Sheet

Various portraits.

1995, Feb. 28 **Litho.** ***Perf. 14***
350 A72 32c Sheet of 9, #a.-i. 6.25 6.25

Fish — A93

1c, Cube trunkfish. 2c, Lionfish. 3c, Long-jawed squirrelfish. 4c, Longnose filefish. 5c, Ornate butterflyfish. 10c, Yellow seahorse. 20c, Magenta dottyback. 32c, Reef lizardfish. 50c, Multibarred goatfish. 55c, Barred blenny. $1, Fingerprint sharpnose puffer. $2, Longnose hawkfish. $3, Mandarinfish. $5, Blue surgeonfish. $10, Coral grouper.

1995, Apr. 3 **Litho.** ***Perf. 14½***
351 A93 1c multicolored .25 .25
352 A93 2c multicolored .25 .25
353 A93 3c multicolored .25 .25
354 A93 4c multicolored .25 .25
355 A93 5c multicolored .25 .25
356 A93 10c multicolored .25 .25
357 A93 20c multicolored .35 .30
358 A93 32c multicolored .50 .45
359 A93 50c multicolored .85 .70
360 A93 55c multicolored 1.00 .75
361 A93 $1 multicolored 1.75 1.50
362 A93 $2 multicolored 3.50 3.00
363 A93 $3 multicolored 5.00 4.50
364 A93 $5 multicolored 8.50 7.75

Size: 48x30mm
365 A93 $10 multicolored 17.50 16.00
Nos. 351-365 (15) 40.45 36.45

Booklet Stamps
Size: 18x21mm
Perf. 14x14½ Syncopated
366 A93 20c multicolored .40 .40
a. Booklet pane of 10 3.75
Complete booklet, #366a 4.00
367 A93 32c multicolored .60 .60
a. Booklet pane of 10 6.00
Complete booklet, #367a 6.25
b. Booklet pane, 5 ea #366, 367 5.25
Complete booklet, #367b 5.50

Miniature Sheet

Lost Fleet of the Rock Islands — A94

Underwater scenes, silhouettes of Japanese ships sunk during Operation Desecrate, 1944: a, Unyu Maru 2. b, Wakatake. c, Teshio Maru. d, Raizan Maru. e, Chuyo Maru. f, Shinsei Maru. g, Urakami Maru. h, Ose Maru. i, Iro. j, Shosei Maru. k, Patrol boat 31. l, Kibi Maru. m, Amatsu Maru. n, Gozan Maru. o, Matuei Maru. p, Nagisan Maru. q, Akashi. r, Kamikazi Maru.

1995, Mar. 30 Litho. *Perf. 14*
368 A94 32c Sheet of 18, #a.-r. 12.00 12.00

Miniature Sheet

Flying Dinosaurs — A95

Designs: a, Pteranodon sternbergi. b, Pteranodon ingens (a, c). c, Pterodoctyls (b). d, Dorygnathus (e). e, Dimorphodon (f). f, Nyctosaurus (e, c). g, Pterodactylus kochi. h, Ornithodesmus (g, i). i, Diatryma (l). j, Archaeopteryx. k, Campylognathoides (l). l, Gallodactylus. m, Batrachognathus (j). n, Scaphognathus (j, k, m, o). o, Peteinosaurus (l). p, Ichthyorinis. q, Ctenochasma (m, p, r). r, Rhamphorhynchus (n, o, q).

1995 Litho. *Perf. 14*
369 A95 32c Sheet of 18, #a.-r. 12.00 12.00

Earth Day, 25th anniv.

Miniature Sheet

Research & Experimental Jet Aircraft — A96

Designs: a, Fairey Delta 2. b, B-70 "Valkyrie." c, Douglas X-3 "Stilletto." d, Northrop/NASA HL-10. e, Bell XS-1. f, Tupolev Tu-144. g, Bell X-1. h, Boulton Paul P.111. i, EWR VJ 101C. j, Handley Page HP-115. k, Rolls Royce TMR "Flying Bedstead." l, North American X-15.
$2, BAC/Aerospatiale Concorde SST.

1995 Litho. *Perf. 14*
370 A96 50c Sheet of 12, #a.-l. 12.00 12.00

Souvenir Sheet

371 A96 $2 multicolored 3.75 3.75

No. 370 is airmail. No. 371 contains one 85x29mm stamp.

Miniature Sheet

Submersibles A97

Designs: a, Scuba gear. b, Cousteau diving saucer. c, Jim suit. d, Beaver IV. e, Ben Franklin. f, USS Nautilus. g, Deep Rover. h, Beebe Bathysphere. i, Deep Star IV. j, DSRV. k, Aluminaut. l. Nautile. m, Cyana. n, FNRS Bathyscaphe. o, Alvin. p, Mir 1. q, Archimede. r, Trieste.

1995, July 21 Litho. *Perf. 14*
372 A97 32c Sheet of 18, #a.-r. 12.00 12.00

Singapore '95 — A98

Designs: a, Dolphins, diver snorkeling, marine life. b, Turtle, diver, seabirds above. c, Fish, coral, crab. d, Coral, fish, diff.

1995, Aug. 15 Litho. *Perf. 13½*
373 A98 32c Block of 4, #a.-d. 2.50 2.50

No. 373 is a continuous design and was issued in sheets of 24 stamps.

UN, FAO, 50th Anniv. — A99

Designs: No. 374a, Outline of soldier's helmet, dove, peace. b, Outline of flame, Hedul Gibbons, human rights. c, Books, education. d, Outline of tractor, bananas, agriculture.
No. 375, Palau flag, bird, UN emblem. No. 376, Water being put on plants, UN emblem, vert.

1995, Sept. 15 Litho. *Perf. 14*
374 A99 60c Block of 4, #a.-d. 4.75 4.75

Souvenir Sheets

375 A99 $2 multicolored 4.00 4.00
376 A99 $2 multicolored 4.00 4.00

Independence, 1st Anniv. — A100

Palau flag and: a, Fruit doves. b, Rock Islands. c, Map of islands. d, Orchid, hibiscus. 32c, Marine life.

1995, Sept. 15 *Perf. 14½*
377 A100 20c Block of 4, #a.-d. 1.50 1.50
378 A100 32c multicolored .65 .65

No. 377 was issued in sheets of 16 stamps. See US No. 2999.

Miniature Sheets

A101

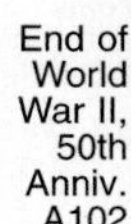

End of World War II, 50th Anniv. A102

Paintings by Wm. F. Draper: No. 379a, Preparing Tin-Fish. b, Hellcats Take-off into Palau's Rising Sun. c, Dauntless Dive Bombers over Malakai Harbor. d, Planes Return from Palau. e, Communion Before Battle. f, The Landing. g, First Task Ashore. h, Fire Fighters Save Flak-torn Pilot.
Paintings by Tom Lea: No. 379i, Young Marine Headed for Peleliu. j, Peleliu. k, Last Rites. l, The Thousand-Yard Stare.
Portraits by Albert Murray, vert.: No. 380a, Adm. Chester W. Nimitz. b, Adm. William F. Halsey. c, Adm. Raymond A. Spruance. d, Vice Adm. Marc A. Mitscher. e, Gen. Holland M. Smith, USMC.
$3, Nose art of B-29 Bock's Car.

1995, Oct. 18 *Perf. 14x13½*
379 A101 32c Sheet of 12, #a.-l 7.75 7.75

Perf. 13½x14

380 A101 60c Sheet of 5, #a.-e. 7.50 7.50

Souvenir Sheet

Perf. 14

381 A102 $3 multicolored 6.00 6.00

Christmas — A103

Native version of "We Three Kings of Orient Are:" a, Angel, animals. b, Two wise men. c, Joseph, Mary, Jesus in manger. d, Wise man, shepherd, animals. e, Girl with fruit, goat, shepherd.

1995, Oct. 31 Litho. *Perf. 14*
382 A103 32c Strip of 5, #a.-e. 3.00 3.00

No. 382 is a continuous design and was issued in sheets of 15 stamps + 5 labels se-tenant with bottom row of sheet.

Miniature Sheet

Life Cycle of the Sea Turtle A104

Small turtles, arrows representing routes during life cycle and: a, Large turtle. b, Upper half of turtle shell platter, Palau map. c, Rooster in tree, island scene. d, Native woman. e, Lower half of turtle shell platter, Palau map, island couple. f, Fossil, palm trees, native house

1995, Nov. 15 Litho. *Perf. 14*
383 A104 32c Sheet of 12, 2 each, #a.-f. 9.50 9.50

John Lennon (1940-80) — A105

1995, Dec. 8 Litho. *Perf. 14*
384 A105 32c multicolored 1.10 1.10

No. 384 was issued in sheets of 16.

Miniature Sheet

New Year 1996 (Year of the Rat) — A106

Stylized rats in parade: No. 385: a, One carrying flag, one playing horn. b, Three playing musical instruments. c, Two playing instruments. d, Family in front of house.
Mirror images, diff. colors: No. 386: a, Like #385c-385d. b, Like #385a-385b.

1996, Feb. 2 Litho. *Perf. 14*
385 A106 10c Strip of 4, #a.-d. 1.75 1.75

Miniature Sheet

386 A106 60c Sheet of 2, #a.-b. 2.25 2.25

No. 385 was issued in sheets of 2 + 4 labels like No. 386. Nos. 386a-386b are airmail and are each 56x43mm.

UNICEF, 50th Anniv. — A107

Three different children from Palau in traditional costumes, child in middle wearing: a, Red flowerd dress. b, Pink dress. c, Blue shorts. d, Red headpiece and shorts.

1996, Mar. 12 Litho. *Perf. 14*
387 A107 32c Block of 4, #a.-d. 2.50 2.50

No. 387 was issued in sheets of 4.

Marine Life A108

Letter spelling "Palau," and: a, "P," fairy basslet, vermiculate parrotfish. b, "A," yellow cardinalfish. c, "L," Marten's butterflyfish. d, "A," starry moray, slate pencil sea urchin. e, "U," cleaner wrasse, coral grouper.

1996, Mar. 29 Litho. *Perf. 14*
388 A108 32c Strip of 5, #a.-e. 3.00 3.00

No. 388 was issued in miniature sheets of 3.
China '96, Intl. Stamp Exhibition, Beijing.

Capex '96 — A109

Circumnavigators of the earth: No. 389: a, Ferdinand Magellan, ship Victoria. b, Charles Wilkes, ship Vincennes. c, Joshua Slocum, oyster boat Spray. d, Ben Carlin, amphibious vehicle Half-Safe. e, Edward L. Beach, submarine USS Triton. f, Naomi James, yacht Express Crusader. g, Sir Ranulf Fiennes, polar vehicle. h, Rick Hansen, wheel chair. i, Robin Knox-Johnson, catamaran Enza New Zealand.
No. 390: a, Lowell Smith, Douglas World Cruisers. b, Ernst Lehmann, Graf Zeppelin. c, Wiley Post, Lockheed Vega Winnie Mae. d, Yuri Gagarin, spacecraft Vostok I. e, Jerrie Mock, Cessna 180 Spirit of Columbus. f, Ross Perot, Jr., Bell Longranger III, Spirit of Texas. g, Brooke Knapp, Gulfstream III, The American Dream. h, Jeana Yeager, Dick Rutan, airplane Voyager. i, Fred Lasby, piper Commanche.
Each $3: No. 391, Bob Martin, Mark Sullivan, Troy Bradley, Odyssey Gondola. No. 392, Sir Francis Chichester, yacht Gipsy Moth IV.

1996, May 3 Litho. *Perf. 14*
389 A109 32c Sheet of 9, #a.-i. 5.50 5.50
390 A109 60c Sheet of 9, #a.-i. 11.00 11.00

Souvenir Sheets

391-392 A109 Set of 2 12.00 12.00

No. 390 is airmail.

Miniature Sheet

Disney Sweethearts A110

1c, like #393a. 2c, #393c. 3c, #393d. 4c, like #393e. 5c, #393f. 6c, #393h.

#393: a, Simba, Nala, Timon. b, Bernard, Bianca, Mr. Chairman. c, Georgette, Tito, Oliver. d, Duchess, O'Malley, Marie. e, Bianca, Jake, Polly. f, Tod, Vixey, Copper. g, Robin Hood, Maiden Marian, Alan-a-Dale. h, Thumper, Flower, their sweethearts. i, Pongo, Perdita, puppies.
Each $2: #394, Lady, vert. #395, Bambi, Faline.

1996, May 30 Litho. *Perf. 14x13½*
392A-392F A110 Set of 6 1.00 1.00

Sheet of 9

393 A110 60c #a.-i. 13.50 13.50

Souvenir Sheets

Perf. 13½x14, 14x13½

394-395 A110 Set of 2 9.50 9.50

Jerusalem, 3000th Anniv. — A111

Biblical illustrations of the Old Testament appearing in "In Our Image," by Guy Rowe (1894-1969): a, Creation. b, Adam and Eve. c, Noah and his Wife. d, Abraham. e, Jacob's Blessing. f, Jacob Becomes Israel. g, Joseph and his Brethren. h, Moses and the Burning Bush. i, Moses and the Tablets. j, Balaam. k, Joshua. l, Gideon. m, Jephthah. n, Samson. o, Ruth and Naomi. p, Saul Anointed. q, Saul Denounced. r, David and Jonathan. s, David and Nathan. t, David Mourns. u, Solomon Praying. v, Solomon Judging. w, Elijah. x, Elisha. y, Job. z, Isaiah. aa, Jeremiah. ab, Ezekiel. ac, Nebuchadnezzar's Dream. ad, Amos.

1996, June 15 Litho. *Perf. 14*

396 A111 20c Sheet of 30, #a.-ad. 12.00 12.00

For overprint see No. 461.

1996 Summer Olympics, Atlanta — A112

No. 397, Fanny Blankers Koen, gold medalist, 1948, vert. No. 398, Bob Mathias, gold medalist, 1948, 1952, vert. No. 399, Torchbearer entering Wembley Stadium, 1948. No. 400, Olympic flag, flags of Palau and U.K. before entrance to Stadium, Olympia, Greece.

Athletes: No. 401: a, Hakeem Olajuwan, US. b, Pat McCormick, US. c, Jim Thorpe, US. d, Jesse Owens, US. e, Tatyana Gutsu, Unified Team. f, Michael Jordan, US. g, Fu Mingxia, China. h, Robert Zmelik, Czechoslovakia. i, Ivan Pedroso, Cuba. j, Nadia Comaneci, Romania. k, Jackie Joyner-Kersee, US. l, Michael Johnson, US. m, Kristin Otto, E. Germany. n, Vitali Scherbo, Unified Team. o, Johnny Weissmuller, US. p, Babe Didrikson, US. q, Eddie Tolan, US. r, Krisztina Egerszegi, Hungary. s, Sawao Kato, Japan. t, Alexander Popov, Unified Team.

1996, June 17 Litho. *Perf. 14*

397 A112 40c multicolored .90 .90
398 A112 40c multicolored .90 .90
a. Pair, #397-398 2.00 2.00
399 A112 60c multicolored 1.40 1.40
400 A112 60c multicolored 1.40 1.40
a. Pair, #399-400 3.00 3.00
401 A112 32c Sheet of 20, #a.-t. 13.00 13.00

Nos. 398a, 400a were each issued in sheets of 20 stamps. No. 401 is a continuous design.

Birds Over Palau Lagoon A113

Designs: a, Lakkotsiang, female. b, Maladaob. c, Belochel (g). d, Lakkotsiang, male. e, Sechosech. f, Mechadelbedaoch (j). g, Laib. h, Cheloteachel. i, Deroech. j, Kerkirs. k, Dudek. l, Lakkotsiang. m, Bedaoch. n, Bedebedchaki. o, Sechou (gray Pacific reef-heron) (p). p, Kekereiderariik. q, Sechou (white Pacific reef-heron). r, Ochaieu. s, Oltirakladial. t, Omechederiibabad.

1996, July 10

402 A113 50c Sheet of 20, #a.-t. 20.00 20.00

Aircraft A114

Stealth, surveillance, and electronic warfare: No. 403: a, Lockheed U-2. b, General Dynamics EF-111A. c, Lockheed YF-12A. d, Lockheed SR-71. e, Teledyne-Ryan-Tiere II Plus. f, Lockheed XST. g, Lockhood ER-2. h, Lockheed F-117A Nighthawk. i, Lockheed EC-130E. j, Ryan Firebee. k, Lockheed Martin/Boeing "Darkstar." l, Boeing E-3A Sentry.

No. 404: a, Northrop XB-35. b, Leduc O.21. c, Convair Model 118. d, Blohm Und Voss BV 141. e, Vought V-173. f, McDonnell XF-85 Goblin. g, North American F-82B Twin Mustang. h, Lockheed XFV-1. i, Northrop XP-79B. j, Saunders Roe SR/A1. k, Caspian Sea Monster. l, Grumman X-29.

No. 405, Northrop B-2A Stealth Bomber. No. 406, Martin Marietta X-24B.

1996, Sept. 9 Litho. *Perf. 14*

403 A114 40c Sheet of 12, #a.-l. 10.00 10.00
404 A114 60c Sheet of 12, #a.-l. 15.00 15.00

Souvenir Sheets

405 A114 $3 multicolored 6.50 6.50
406 A114 $3 multicolored 6.50 6.50

No. 404 is airmail. No. 406 contains one 85x28mm stamp.

Independence, 2nd Anniv. — A115

Paintings, by Koh Sekiguchi: No. 407, "In the Blue Shade of Trees-Palau (Kirie). No. 408 "The Birth of a New Nation (Kirie).

1996, Oct. 1 Litho. *Perf. 14½*

407 20c multicolored .40 .40
408 20c multicolored .40 .40
a. A115 Pair, #407-408 .80 .80

#408a issued in sheets of 16 stamps.

Christmas — A116

Christmas trees: a, Pandanus. b, Mangrove. c, Norfolk Island pine. d, Papaya. e, Casuarina.

1996, Oct. 8 *Perf. 14*

409 A116 32c Strip of 5, #a.-e. 3.25 3.25

No. 409 was issued in sheets of 3.

Voyage to Mars A117

No. 410: a, Viking 1 (US) in Mars orbit. b, Mars Lander fires de-orbit engines. c, Viking 1 symbol (top). d, Viking 1 symbol (bottom). e, Martian moon phobos. f, Mariner 9 in Mars orbit. g, Viking lander enters Martian atmosphere. h, Parachute deploys for Mars landing, heat shield jettisons. i, Proposed manned mission to Mars, 21st cent., US-Russian spacecraft (top). j, US-Russian spacecraft (bottom). k, Lander descent engines fire for Mars landing. l, Viking 1 lands on Mars, July 20, 1976.

Each $3: No. 411, NASA Mars rover. No. 412, NASA water probe on Mars. Illustration reduced.

1996, Nov. 8 Litho. *Perf. 14x14½*

410 A117 32c Sheet of 12, #a.-l. 7.75 7.75

Souvenir Sheets

411-412 A117 Set of 2 12.00 12.00

No. 411 contains one 38x30mm stamp.

Souvenir Sheet

New Year 1997 (Year of the Ox) A117a

1997, Jan. 2 Litho. *Perf. 14*

412A A117a $2 multicolored 4.25 4.25

Souvenir Sheet

South Pacific Commission, 50th Anniv. — A118

1997, Feb. 6 Litho. *Perf. 14*

413 A118 $1 multicolored 2.00 2.00

Hong Kong '97 — A119

Flowers: 1c, Pemphis acidula. 2c, Sea lettuce. 3c, Tropical almond. 4c, Guettarda. 5c, Pacific coral bean. $3, Sea hibiscus.

No. 420: a, Black mangrove. b, Cordia. c, Lantern tree. d, Palau rock-island flower.

No. 421: a, Fish-poison tree. b, Indian mulberry. c, Pacific poison-apple. d, Ailanthus.

1997, Feb. 12 *Perf. 14½, 13½ (#419)*

414-419 A119 Set of 6 7.00 7.00
420 A119 32c Block of 4, #a.-d. 2.50 2.50
421 A119 50c Block of 4, #a.-d. 4.00 4.00

Size of No. 419 is 73x48mm.

Nos. 420-421 were each issued in sheets of 16 stamps.

Bicent. of the Parachute A120

Uses of parachute: No. 422: a, Apollo 15 Command Module landing safely. b, "Caterpillar Club" flyer ejecting safely over land. c. Skydiving team formation. d, Parasailing. e, Military parachute demonstration teams. f, Parachute behind dragster. g, Dropping cargo from C-130 aircraft. h, "Goldfish Club" flyer ejecting safely at sea.

No. 423: a, Demonstrating parachute control. b, A.J. Gernerin, first successful parachute descent, 1797. c, Slowing down world land-speed record breaking cars. d, Dropping spies behind enemy lines. e, C-130E demonstrating "LAPES." f, Parachutes used to slow down high performance aircraft. g, ARD parachutes. g, US Army parachutist flying Parafoil.

Each $2: No. 424 Training tower at Ft. Benning, Georgia. No. 425, "Funny Car" safety chute.

Perf. 14½x14, 14x14½

1997, Mar. 13 Litho.

422 A120 32c Sheet of 8, #a.-h. 5.25 5.25
423 A120 60c Sheet of 8, #a.-h. 9.75 9.75

Souvenir Sheets

Perf. 14

424-425 A120 Set of 2 10.00 10.00

Nos. 422a-423a, 422b-423b, 422g-423g, 422h-423h are 20x48mm. No. 424 contains one 28x85mm, No. 425 one 57x42mm stamps.

No. 423 is airmail.

Postage Stamp Mega-Event, NYC, Mar. 1997 (#422-423).

Native Birds A121

a, Gray duck, banana tree. b, Red junglefowl, calamondin. c, Nicobar pigeon, fruited parinari tree. d, Cardinal honeyeater, wax apple tree. e, Yellow bittern, purple swamphen, giant taro, taro. f, Eclectus parrot, pangi football fruit tree. g, Micronesian pigeon, Rambutan. h, Micronesian starling, mango tree. i, Fruit bat, breadfruit tree. j, Collared kingfisher, coconut palm. k, Palau fruit dove, sweet orange tree. l, Chestnut mannikin, soursop tree.

1997, Mar. 27 Litho. *Perf. 13½x14*

426 A121 20c Sheet of 12, #a.-l. 5.00 5.00

UNESCO, 50th Anniv. A122

Sites in Japan, vert: Nos. 427: a, c-h, Himeji-jo. b, Kyoto.

Sites in Germany: Nos. 428: a-b, Augustusburg Castle. c, Falkenlust Castle. d, Roman ruins, Trier. e, Historic house, Trier.

Each $2: No. 429, Forest, Shirakami-Sanchi, Japan. No. 430, Yakushima, Japan.

Perf. 13½x14, 14x13½

1997, Apr. 7 Litho.

Sheets of 8 or 5 + Label

427 A122 32c #a.-h. 5.50 5.50
428 A122 60c #a.-e. 6.25 6.25

Souvenir Sheets

429-430 A122 Set of 2 8.75 8.75

A123

Paintings by Hiroshige (1797-1858): No. 431: a, Swallows and Peach Blossoms under a Full Moon. b, A Parrot on a Flowering

Branch. c, Crane and Rising Sun. d, Cock, Umbrella, and Morning Glories. e, A Titmouse Hanging Head Downward on a Camellia Branch.

Each $2: No. 432, Falcon on a Pine Tree with the Rising Sun. No. 433, Kingfisher and Iris.

1997, June 2 Litho. *Perf. 14*

431 A123 32c Sheet of 5, #a.-e. 4.00 4.00

Souvenir Sheets

432-433 A123 Set of 2 8.25 8.25

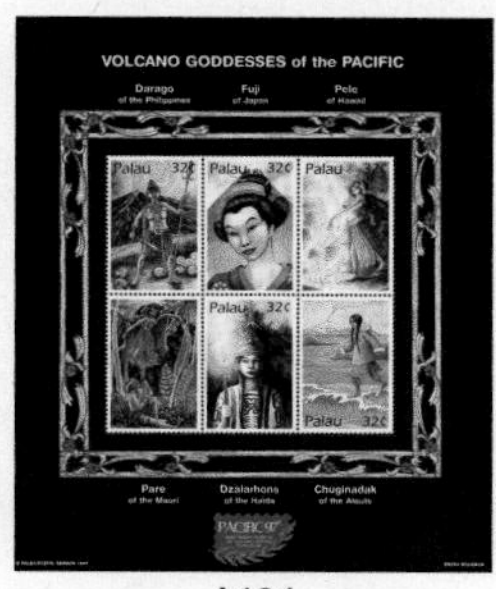

A124

Volcano Goddesses of the Pacific: a, Darago, Philippines. b, Fuji, Japan. c, Pele, Hawaii. d, Pare, Maori. e, Dzalarhons, Haida. f, Chuginadak, Aleuts.

1997 Litho. *Perf. 14*

434 A124 32c Sheet of 6, #a.-f. 4.50 4.50

PACIFIC 97.

Independence, 3rd Anniv. — A125

1997, Oct. 1 Litho. *Perf. 14*

435 A125 32c multicolored .65 .65

No. 435 was issued in sheets of 12.

Oceanographic Research — A126

Ships: No. 436: a, Albatross. b, Mabahiss. c, Atlantis II. d, Xarifa. e, Meteor. f, Egabras III. g, Discoverer. h, Kaiyo. i, Ocean Defender.

Each $2: No. 437, Jacques-Yves Cousteau (1910-97). No. 438, Cousteau, diff., vert. No. 439, Pete Seeger, vert.

1997, Oct. 1 *Perf. 14x14½, 14½x14*

436 A126 32c Sheet of 9, #a.-i. 6.00 6.00

Souvenir Sheets

437-439 A126 Set of 3 13.00 13.00

Diana, Princess of Wales (1961-97) — A127

1997, Nov. 26 Litho. *Perf. 14*

440 A127 60c multicolored 1.25 1.25

No. 440 was issued in sheets of 6.

Disney's "Let's Read" A128

Various Disney characters: 1c, like #447i. 2c, like #447d. 3c, like #447c. 4c, like #447f. 5c, #447b. 10c, like #447h.

No. 447: a, "Exercise your right to read." b, "Reading is the ultimate luxury." c, "Share your knowledge." d, "Start them Young." e, "Reading is fundamental." f, "The insatiable reader." g, "Reading time is anytime." h, "Real men read." i, "I can read by myself."

No. 448, Daisy, "The library is for everyone," vert. No. 449, Mickey, "Books are magical."

1997, Oct. 21 *Perf. 14x13½, 13½x14*

441-446 A128 Set of 6 1.00 1.00

Sheet of 9

447 A128 32c #a.-i. 5.75 5.75

Souvenir Sheets

448 A128 $2 multicolored 4.50 4.50

449 A128 $3 multicolored 6.50 6.50

Christmas — A129

Children singing Christmas carol, "Some Children See Him:" No. 450: a, Girl, boy in striped shirt. b, Boy, girl in pigtails. c, Girl, boy, Madonna and Child. d, Girl, two children. e, Boy, girl with long black hair.

1997, Oct. 28 *Perf. 14*

450 A129 32c Strip of 5, #a.-e. 3.25 3.25

No. 450 was issued in sheets of 3 strips, bottom strip printed se-tenant with 5 labels containing lyrics.

Souvenir Sheets

New Year 1998 (Year of the Tiger) A130

Chinese toys in shape of tiger: No. 451, White background. No. 452, Green background.

1998, Jan. 2 Litho. *Perf. 14*

451 A130 50c multicolored 1.25 1.25

452 A130 50c multicolored 1.25 1.25

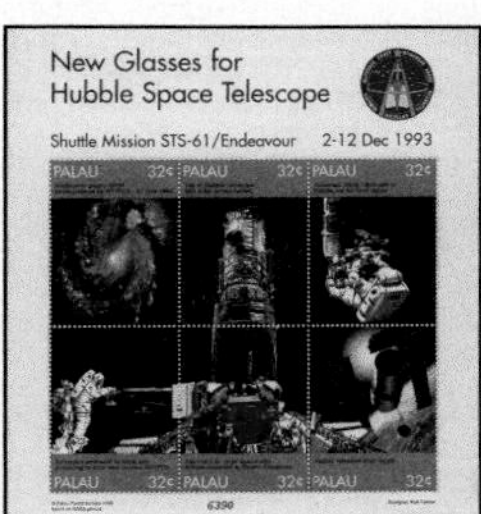

Repair of Hubble Space Telescope — A131

No. 453: a, Photograph of nucleus of galaxy M100. b, Top of Hubble telescope with solar arrays folded. c, Astronaut riding robot arm. d, Astronaut anchored to robot arm. e, Astronaut in cargo space with Hubble mounted to shuttle Endeavor. f, Hubble released after repair.

Each $2: No. 454, Hubble cutaway, based on NASA schematic drawing. No. 455, Edwin Hubble (1889-1953), astronomer who proved existence of star systems beyond Milky Way. No. 456, Hubble Mission STS-82/Discovery.

1998, Mar. 9 Litho. *Perf. 14*

453 A131 32c Sheet of 6, #a.-f. 4.00 4.00

Souvenir Sheets

454-456 A131 Set of 3 12.50 12.50

Mother Teresa (1910-97) — A132

Various portraits.

1998, Mar. 12 Litho. *Perf. 14*

457 A132 60c Sheet of 4, #a.-d. 5.00 5.00

Deep Sea Robots — A133

No. 458: a, Ladybird ROV. b, Slocum Glider. c, Hornet. d, Scorpio. e, Odyssey AUV. f, Jamstec Survey System Launcher. g, Scarab. h, USN Torpedo Finder/Salvager. i, Jamstec Survey System Vehicle. j, Cetus Tether. k, Deep Sea ROV. l, ABE. m, OBSS. n, RCV 225G Swimming Eyeball. o, Japanese UROV. p, Benthos RPV. q, CURV. r, Smartie.

Each $2: No. 459, Jason Jr. inspecting Titanic. No. 460, Dolphin 3K.

1998, Apr. 21

458 A133 32c Sheet of 18, #a.-r. 12.00 12.00

Souvenir Sheets

459-460 A133 Set of 2 8.50 8.50

UNESCO Intl. Year of the Ocean.

No. 396 Ovptd. in Silver

1998, May 13 Litho. *Perf. 14*

461 A111 20c Sheet of 30, #a.-ad. 12.00 12.00

No. 461 is overprinted in sheet margin, "ISRAEL 98 — WORLD STAMP EXHIBITION / TEL AVIV 13-21 MAY 1998." Location of overprint varies.

Legend of Orachel — A134

#462: a, Bai (hut), people. b, Bai, lake. c, Bai, lake, person in canoe. d, Bird on branch over lake. e, Men rowing in canoe. f, Canoe, head of snake. g, Alligator under water. h, Fish, shark. i, Turtle, body of snake. j, Underwater bai, "gods". k, Snails, fish, Orachel swimming. l, Orachel's feet, coral, fish.

1998, May 29 Litho. *Perf. 14*

462 A134 40c Sheet of 12, #a.-l. 9.50 9.50

1998 World Cup Soccer Championships, France — A135

Players, color of shirt — #463: a, Yellow, black & red. b, Blue, white & red. c, Green & white. d, White, red & blue. e, Green & white (black shorts). f, White, red & black. g, Blue & yellow. h, Red & white.

$3, Pele.

1998, June 5

463 A135 50c Sheet of 8, #a.-h. 8.00 8.00

Souvenir Sheet

464 A135 $3 multicolored 6.00 6.00

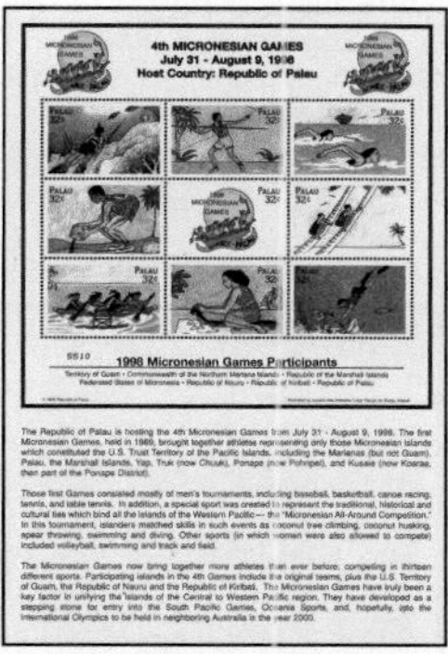

4th Micronesian Games, Palau — A136

Designs: a, Spear fishing. b, Spear throwing. c, Swimming. d, Pouring milk from coconut. e, Logo of games. f, Climbing coconut trees. g, Canoeing. h, Husking coconut. i, Deep sea diving.

1998, July 31 Litho. *Perf. 14*

465 A136 32c Sheet of 9, #a.-i. 5.75 5.75

Rudolph The Red-Nosed Reindeer — A137

Christmas: a, Rudolph, two reindeer, girl. b, Two reindeer, girl holding flowers. c, Girl, two reindeer, boy. d, Two reindeer, girl smiling. e, Santa, children, Christmas gifts.

1998, Sept. 15 Litho. *Perf. 14*

466 A137 32c Strip of 5, #a.-e. 3.25 3.25

No. 466 is a continuous design and was issued in sheets of 15 stamps.

Disney/Pixar's "A Bug's Life" — A138

No. 467: a, Dot. b, Heimlich, Francis, Slim. c, Hopper. d, Princess Atta.

No. 468: Various scenes with Flik, Princess Atta.

No. 469, horiz.: a, Circus bugs. b, Slim, Francis, Heimlich. c, Manny. d, Francis.

No. 470: a, Slim, Flik. b, Heimlich, Slim, Francis performing.c, Manny, Flik. d, Gypsy, Manny, Rosie.

Each $2: No. 471, Gypsy. No. 472, Princess Atta, Flik, horiz. No. 473, Slim, Francis, Heimlich, horiz. No. 474, Francis, Slim, Flik, Heimlich, horiz.

Perf. 13½x14, 14x13½

1998, Dec. 1 Litho. Sheets of 4

467 A138 20c #a.-d. 1.75 1.75
468 A138 32c #a.-d. 2.75 2.75
469 A138 50c #a.-d. 4.25 4.25
470 A138 60c #a.-d. 5.25 5.25

Souvenir Sheets

471-474 A138 Set of 4 18.00 18.00

Nos. 473-474 each contain one 76x51mm stamp.

John Glenn's Return to Space — A139

No. 475, Various photos of Project Mercury, Friendship 7 mission, 1962, each 60c.
No. 476, Various photos of Discovery Space Shuttle mission, 1998, each 60c.
Each $2: No. 477, Portrait, 1962. No. 478, Portrait, 1998.

1999, Jan. 7 Litho. *Perf. 14*
Sheets of 8, #a-h

475-476 A139 Set of 2 19.00 19.00

Souvenir Sheets

477-478 A139 Set of 2 8.50 8.50

Nos. 477-478 each contain one 28x42mm stamp.

Environmentalists — A140

a, Rachel Carson. b, J.N. "Ding" Darling, US Duck stamp #RW1. c, David Brower. d, Jacques Cousteau. e, Roger Tory Peterson. f, Prince Philip. g, Joseph Wood Krutch. h, Aldo Leopold. i, Dian Fossey. j, US Vice-President Al Gore. k, David Attenborough. l, Paul McCready. m, Sting (Gordon Sumner). n, Paul Winter. o, Ian MacHarg. p, Denis Hayes.

1999, Feb. 1 Litho. *Perf. 14½*

479 A140 33c Sheet of 16, #a.-p. 10.50 10.50

No. 479i shows Dian Fossey's name misspelled "Diane."

MIR Space Station A141

No. 480: a, Soyuz Spacecraft, Science Module. b, Specktr Science Module. c, Space Shuttle, Spacelab Module. d, Kvant 2, Scientific and Air Lock Module. e, Kristall Technological Module. f, Space Shutle, Docking Module.
Each $2: No. 481, Astronaut Charles Precout, Cosmonaut Talgat Musabayev. No. 482, Cosmonaut Valeri Poliakov. No. 483, US Mission Specialist Shannon W. Lucid, Cosmonaut Yuri Y. Usachov. No. 484, Cosmonaut Anatoly Solovyov.

1999, Feb. 18 Litho. *Perf. 14*

480 A141 33c Sheet of 6, #a.-f. 3.75 3.75

Souvenir Sheets

481-484 A141 Set of 4 16.00 16.00

Personalities — A142

1c, Haruo Remiliik. 2c, Lazarus Salil. 20c, Charlie W. Gibbons. 22c, Adm. Raymond A. Spruance. 33c, Kuniwo Nakamura. 50c, Adm. William F. Halsey. 55c, Col. Lewis "Chesty" Puller. 60c, Franklin D. Roosevelt. 77c, Harry S Truman. $3.20, Jimmy Carter.

1999, Mar. 4 *Perf. 14x15*

485	A142	1c green	.25	.25
486	A142	2c purple	.25	.25
487	A142	20c violet	.40	.40
488	A142	22c bister	.45	.45
489	A142	33c red brown	.65	.65
490	A142	50c brown	1.00	1.00
491	A142	55c blue green	1.10	1.10
492	A142	60c orange	1.25	1.25
493	A142	77c yellow brown	1.50	1.50
494	A142	$3.20 red violet	6.50	6.50
		Nos. 485-494 (10)	13.35	13.35

Nos. 485, 492 exist dated 2001.

Australia '99 World Stamp Expo A143

Endangered species — #495: a, Leatherback turtle. b, Kemp's ridley turtle. c, Green turtle. d, Marine iguana. e, Table mountain ghost frog. f, Spiny turtle. g, Hewitt's ghost frog. h, Geometric tortoise. i, Limestone salamander. j, Desert rain frog. k, Cape plantanna. l, Long-toed tree frog.
Each $2: No. 496, Marine crocodile. No. 497, Hawksbill turtle.

1999, Mar. 19 Litho. *Perf. 13*

495 A143 33c Sheet of 12, #a.-l. 8.00 8.00

Souvenir Sheets

496-497 A143 Set of 2 8.00 8.00

IBRA '99, Nuremburg — A144

No. 498, Leipzig-Dresden Railway, Caroline Islands Type A4. No. 499, Gölsdorf 4-8-0, Caroline Islands #8, 10.
$2, Caroline Islands #1.

1999, Apr. 27 Litho. *Perf. 14*

498-499 A144 55c Set of 2 2.25 2.25

Souvenir Sheet

500 A144 $2 multicolored 4.00 4.00

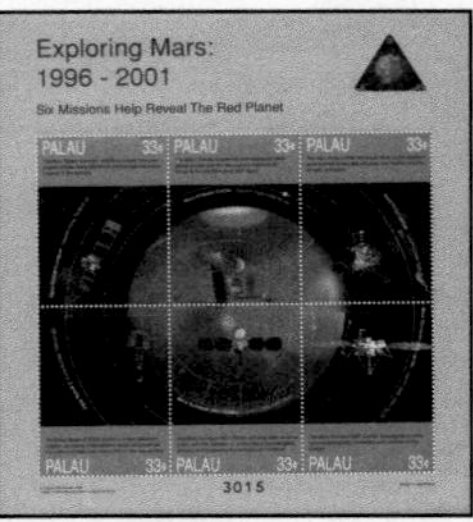

Exploration of Mars — A145

No. 501: a, Mars Global Surveyor. b, Mars Climate Orbiter. c, Mars Polar Lander. d, Deep Space 2. e, Mars Surveyor 2001 Orbiter. f, Mars Surveyor 2001 Lander.
Each $2: No. 502, Mars Global Surveyor. No. 503, Mars Climate Orbiter. No. 504, Mars Polar Lander. No. 505, Mars Surveyor 2001 Lander.

1999, May 10 Litho. *Perf. 14*

501 A145 33c Sheet of 6, #a.-f. 4.00 4.00

Souvenir Sheets

502-505 A145 Set of 4 16.00 16.00

Nos. 502-505 each contain one 38x50mm stamp.
See Nos. 507-511.

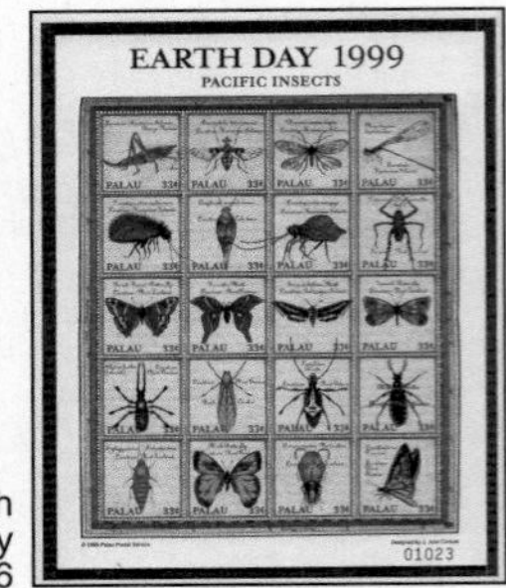

Earth Day A146

Pacific insects: a, Banza Natida. b, Drosophila heteroneura. c, Nesomicromus vagus. d, Megalagrian leptodemus. e, Pseudopsectra cookearum. f, Ampheida neacaledonia. g, Pseudopsectra swezeyi. h, Deinacrida heteracantha. i, Beech forest butterfly. j, Hercules moth. k, Striped sphinx moth. l, Tussock butterfly. m. Elytrocheilus. n, Bush cricket. o, Longhorn beetle. p, Abathrus bicolor. q, Stylagymnusa subantartica. r, Moth butterfly. s, Paraconosoma naviculare. t, Ornithoptera priamus.

1999, May 24

506 A146 33c Sheet of 20, #a.-t. 13.50 13.50

Space Type

International Space Station — #507: a, Launch 1R. b, Launch 14A. c, Launch 8A. d, Launch 1J. e, Launch 1E. f, Launch 16A.
Each $2: No. 508, Intl. Space Station. No. 509, Cmdr. Bob Cabana, Cosmonaut Sergei Krikalev. No. 510, Crew of Flight 2R, horiz. No. 511, X-38 Crew Return Vehicle, horiz.

1999, June 12 Litho. *Perf. 14*

507 A145 33c Sheet of 6, #a.-f. 4.00 4.00

Souvenir Sheets

508-511 A145 Set of 4 16.00 16.00

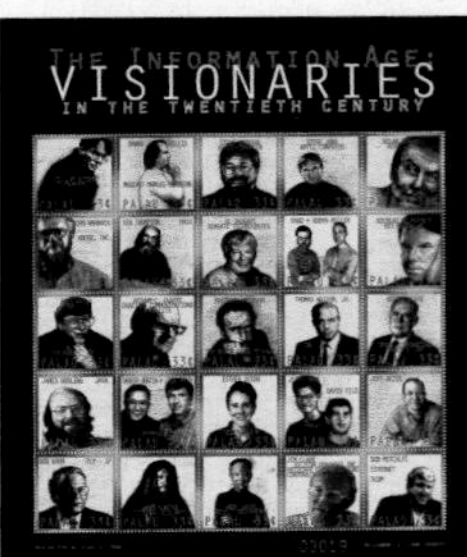

20th Century Visionaries — A147

Designs: a, William Gibson, "Cyberspace." b, Danny Hillis, Massively Parallel Processing. c, Steve Wozniak, Apple Computer. d, Steve Jobs, Apple Computer. e, Nolan Bushnell, Atari, Inc. f, John Warnock, Adobe, Inc. g, Ken Thompson, Unix. h, Al Shugart, Seagate Technologies. i, Rand & Robyn Miller, "MYST." j, Nicolas Negroponte, MIT Media Lab. k, Bill Gates, Microsoft, Inc. l, Arthur C. Clarke, Orbiting Communications Satellite. m, Marshall Mcluhan, "The Medium is the Message." n, Thomas Watson, Jr., IBM. o, Gordon Moore, Intel Corporation, "Moore's Law." p, James Gosling, Java. q, Sabeer Bhatia & Jack Smith, Hotmail.com. r, Esther Dyson, "Release 2.0." s, Jerry Yang, David Filo, Yahoo! t, Jeff Bezos, Amazon.com. u, Bob Kahn, TCP-IP. v, Jaron Lanter, "Virtual Reality." w, Andy Grove, Intel Corporation. x, Jim Clark, Silicon Graphics, Inc., Netscape Communications Corp. y, Bob Metcalfe, Ethernet, 3com.

1999, June 30 Litho. *Perf. 14*

512 A147 33c Sheet of 25, #a.-y. 17.00 17.00

Paintings by Hokusai (1760-1849) — A148

No. 513, each 33c: a, Women Divers. b, Bull and Parasol. c, Drawings of Women (partially nude). d, Drawings of Women (seated, facing forward). e, Japanese spaniel. f, Porters in Landscape.
No. 514, each 33c: a, Bacchanalian Revelry. b, Bacchanalian Revelry (two seated back to back). c, Drawings of Women (crawling). d, Drawings of Women (facing backward). e, Ox-Herd. f, Ox-Herd (man on bridge).
Each $2: No. 515, Mount Fuji in a Thunderstorm, vert. No. 516, At Swan Lake in Shinano.

1999, July 20 *Perf. 14x13¾*
Sheets of 6, #a-f

513-514 A148 Set of 2 8.00 8.00

Souvenir Sheets

515-516 A148 Set of 2 8.00 8.00

Apollo 11, 30th Anniv. A149

No. 517: a, Lift-off, jettison of stages. b, Earth, moon, capsule. c, Astronaut on lunar module ladder. d, Lift-off. e, Planting flag on moon. f, Astronauts Collins, Armstrong and Aldrin.
Each $2: No. 518, Rocket on launch pad. No. 519, Astronaut on ladder, earth. No. 520, Lunar module above moon. No. 521, Capsule in ocean.

1999, July 20 Litho. *Perf. 13½x14*

517 A149 33c Sheet of 6, #a.-f. 4.00 4.00

Souvenir Sheets

518-521 A149 Set of 4 16.00 16.00

Queen Mother (b. 1900) — A150

No. 522: a, In Australia, 1958. b, In 1960. c, In 1970. d, In 1987.
$2, Holding book, 1947.

Gold Frames

1999, Aug. 4 *Perf. 14*

522 A150 60c Sheet of 4, #a.-d., + label 4.75 4.75

Souvenir Sheet
Perf. 13¾

523 A150 $2 black 4.00 4.00

No. 523 contains one 38x51mm stamp.
See Nos. 636-637.

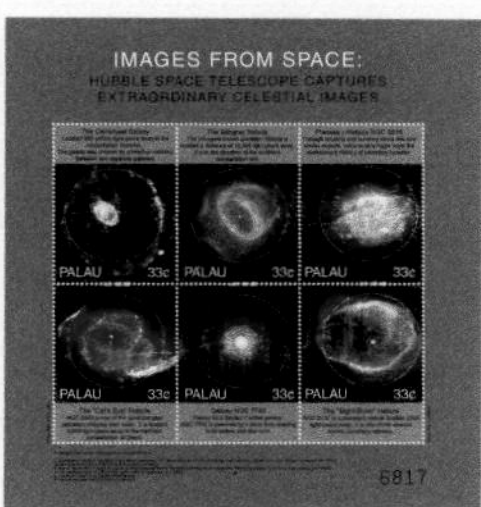

Hubble Space Telescope Images — A151

No. 524: a, Cartwheel Galaxy. b, Stingray Nebula. c, NGC 3918. d, Cat's Eye Nebula (NGC 6543). e, NGC 7742. f, Eight-burst Nebula (NGC 3132).

Each $2: No. 525, Eta Carinae. No. 526, Planetary nebula M2-9. No. 527, Supernova 1987-A. No. 528, Infrared aurora of Saturn.

1999, Oct. 15 Litho. *Perf. 13¾*

524 A151 33c Sheet of 6, #a.-f. 4.00 4.00

Souvenir Sheets

525-528 A151 Set of 4 16.00 16.00

Christmas — A152

Birds and: a, Cows, chickens. b, Donkey, geese, rabbit. c, Infant, cat, lambs. d, Goats, geese. e, Donkey, rooster.

1999, Nov. 15 *Perf. 14*

529 A152 20c Strip of 5, #a.-e. 2.00 2.00

Love for Dogs — A153

No. 530: a, Keep safe. b, Show affection. c, A place of one's own. d, Communicate. e, Good food. f, Annual checkup. g, Teach rules. h, Exercise & play. i, Let him help. j, Unconditional love.

Each $2: No. 531, Pleasure of your company. No. 532, Love is a gentle thing.

1999, Nov. 23 Litho. *Perf. 14*

530 A153 33c Sheet of 10, #a.-j. 6.75 6.75

Souvenir Sheets

531-532 A153 Set of 2 8.00 8.00

Futuristic Space Probes — A154

Text starting with — No. 533: a, Deep space probes like. . . b, This piggy-back. . . c, Deep space telescope. . . d, Mission planning. . . e, In accordance. . . f, Utilizing onboard. . .

Each $2: No. 534, This secondary. . . No. 535, Deep space probes are an integral. . . No. 536, Deep space probes are our. . . , horiz. No. 537, With the. . . , horiz.

2000, Jan. 18 Litho. *Perf. 13¾*

533 A154 55c Sheet of 6, #a.-f. 6.00 6.00

Souvenir Sheets

534-537 A154 Set of 4 16.00 16.00

Millennium — A155

Highlights of 1800-50 — No. 538, each 20c: a, Brazilian Indians. b, Haiti slave revolt. c, Napoleon becomes Emperor of France. d, Shaka Zulu. e, "Frankenstein" written. f, Simon Bolivar. g, Photography invented. h, First water purification works built. i, First all-steam railway. j, Michael Faraday discovers electromagnetism. k, First use of anesthesia. l, Samuel Morse completes first telegraph line. m, Women's rights convention in Seneca Falls, NY. n, Birth of Karl Marx. o, Revolution in German Confederation. p, Charles Darwin's voyages on the "Beagle" (60x40mm). q, Beijing, China.

Highlights of 1980-89 — No. 539, each 20c; a, Lech Walesa organizes Polish shipyard workers. b, Voyager I photographs Saturn. c, Ronald Reagan elected US president. d, Identification of AIDS virus. e, Wedding of Prince Charles and Lady Diana Spencer. f, Compact discs go into production. g, Bhopal, India gas disaster. h, I. M. Pei's Pyramid entrance to the Louvre opens. i, Mikhail Gorbachev becomes leader of Soviet Union. j, Chernobyl nuclear disaster. k, Explosion of Space Shuttle "Challenger." l, Klaus Barbie convicted of crimes against humanity. m, Life of author Salman Rushdie threatened by Moslems. n, Benazir Bhutto becomes first woman prime minister of a Moslem state. o, Tiananmen Square revolt. p, Berlin Wall falls (60x40mm). q, World Wide Web.

2000, Feb. 2 Litho. *Perf. 12¾x12½*

Sheets of 17, #a.-q.

538-539 A155 Set of 2 14.00 14.00

Misspellings and historical inaccuracies abound on Nos. 538-539.

See No. 584.

New Year 2000 (Year of the Dragon) A156

2000, Feb. 5 *Perf. 13¾*

540 A156 $2 multi 4.00 4.00

US Presidents — A157

2000, Mar. 1 Litho. *Perf. 13½x13¼*

541 A157 $1 Bill Clinton 2.00 2.00
542 A157 $2 Ronald Reagan 4.00 4.00
543 A157 $3 Gerald Ford 6.00 6.00
544 A157 $5 George Bush 10.00 10.00

Size: 40x24mm

Perf. 14¾x14

545 A157 $11.75 Kennedy 22.50 22.50
Nos. 541-545 (5) 44.50 44.50

20th Century Discoveries About Prehistoric Life — A158

Designs: a, Australopithecines. b, Australopithecine skull. c, Homo habilis. d, Hand axe. e, Homo habilis skull. f, Lucy, Australopithecine skeleton. g, Archaic Homo sapiens skull. h, Diapithicine skull. i, Homo erectus. j, Wood hut. k, Australopithecine ethopsis skull. l, Dawn of mankind. m, Homo sapiens skull. n, Taung baby's skull. o, Homo erectus skull. p, Louis Leakey (1903-72), paleontologist. q, Neanderthal skull. r, Neandertahal. s, Evolution of the foot. t, Raymond Dart (1893-1988), paleontologist.

2000, Mar. 15 *Perf. 14¼*

546 A158 20c Sheet of 20, #a.-t. 8.00 8.00

Misspellings and historical inaccuracies are found on Nos. 546g, 546m, 546p, 546t and perhaps others.

2000 Summer Olympics, Sydney — A159

Designs: a, Charlotte Cooper, tennis player at 1924 Olympics. b, Women's shot put. c, Helsinki Stadium, site of 1952 Olympics. d, Ancient Greek athletes.

2000, Mar. 31 *Perf. 14*

547 A159 33c Sheet of 4, #a.-d. 2.75 2.75

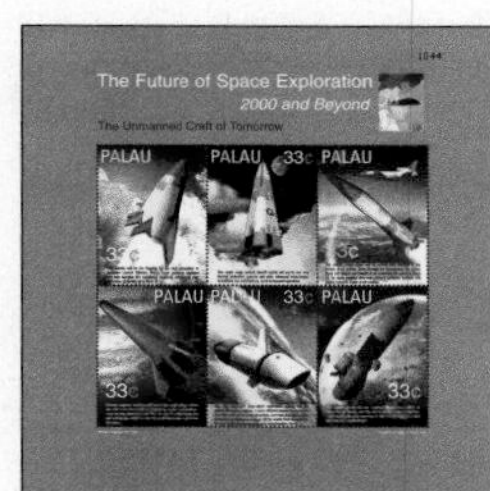

Future of Space Exploration — A160

Text starting with — No. 548: a, This vehicle will be. . . b, This single stage. . . c, This robotic rocket. . . d, Dynamic. . . e, This fully. . . f, This launch vehicle. . .

Each $2: No. 549, Increasingly, space travel. . . No. 550, Designed with projects. . ., horiz. No. 551, Design is currently. . ., horiz. No. 552, Inevitably, the future. . ., horiz.

2000, Apr. 10 *Perf. 13¾*

548 A160 33c Sheet of 6, #a.-f. 4.00 4.00

Souvneir Sheets

549-552 A160 Set of 4 16.00 16.00

Birds — A161

No. 553: a, Slatey-legged crake. b, Micronesian kingfisher. c, Little pied cormorant. d, Pacific reed egret. e, Nicobar pigeon. f, Rufous night heron.

No. 554: a, Palau ground dove. b, Palau scops owl. c, Mangrove flycatcher. d, Palau bush warbler. e, Palau fantail. f, Morningbird.

Each $2: No. 555, Palau fruit dove, horiz. No. 556, Palau white-eye, horiz.

2000, Apr. 14 Litho. *Perf. 14¼*

553 A161 20c Sheet of 6, #a.-f. 2.40 2.40
554 A161 33c Sheet of 6, #a.-f. 4.00 4.00

Souvenir Sheets

555-556 A161 Set of 2 8.00 8.00

Visionaries of the 20th Century — A162

a, Booker T. Washington. b, Buckminster Fuller. c, Marie Curie. d, Walt Disney. e, F. D. Roosevelt. f, Henry Ford. g, Betty Friedan. h, Sigmund Freud. i, Mohandas Gandhi. j, Mikhail Gorbachev. k, Stephen Hawking. l, Martin Luther King, Jr. m, Toni Morrison. n, Georgia O'Keeffe. o, Rosa Parks. p, Carl Sagan. q, Jonas Salk. r, Sally Ride. s, Nikola Tesla. t, Wilbur and Orville Wright.

2000, Apr. 28 Litho. *Perf. 14¼x14½*

557 A162 33c Sheet of 20, #a.-t. 13.50 13.50

20th Century Science and Medicine Advances — A163

No. 558, each 33c: a, James D. Watson, 1962 Nobel laureate. b, Har Gobind Khorana and Robert Holley, 1968 Nobel laureates. c, Hamilton O. Smith and Werner Arber, 1978 Nobel laureates. d, Extraction fo DNA from cells. e, Richard J. Roberts, 1993 Nobel laureate.

No. 559, each 33c: a, Francis Crick, 1962 Nobel laureate. b, Marshall W. Nirenberg, 1968 Nobel laureate. c, Daniel Nathans, 1978 Nobel laureate. d, Harold E. Varmus and J. Michael Bishop, 1989 Nobel laureates. e, Phillip A. Sharp, 1993 Nobel laureate.

No. 560, each 33c: a, Maurice H. F. Wilkins, 1962 Nobel laureate. b, DNA strand. c, Frederick Sanger and Walter Gilbert, 1980 Nobel laureates. d, Kary B. Mullis, 1993 Nobel laureate. e, Two DNA strands.

No. 561, each 33c: a, Four sheep, test tube. b, Two DNA strands, diagram of DNA fragments. c, Paul Berg, 1980 Nobel laureate. d, Michael Smith, 1993 Nobel laureate. e, Deer, DNA strands.

Each $2: #562, Deer. #563, Dolly, 1st cloned sheep.

Illustration reduced.

2000, May 10 *Perf. 13¾*

Sheets of 5, #a.-e.

558-561 A163 Set of 4 14.00 14.00

Souvenir Sheets

562-563 A163 Set of 2 8.00 8.00

Nos. 562-563 each contain one 38x50mm stamp.

Marine Life A164

No. 564, each 33c: a, Prawn. b, Deep sea angler. c, Rooster fish. d, Grenadier. e, Platyberix opalescens. f, Lantern fish.

No. 565, each 33c: a, Emperor angelfish. b, Nautilus. c, Moorish idol. d, Sea horse. e, Clown triggerfish. f, Clown fish.

Each $2: No. 566, Giant squid. No. 567, Manta ray.

2000, May 10 Litho. *Perf. 14*

Sheets of 6, #a-f

564-565 A164 Set of 2 8.00 8.00

Souvenir Sheets

566-567 A164 Set of 2 8.00 8.00

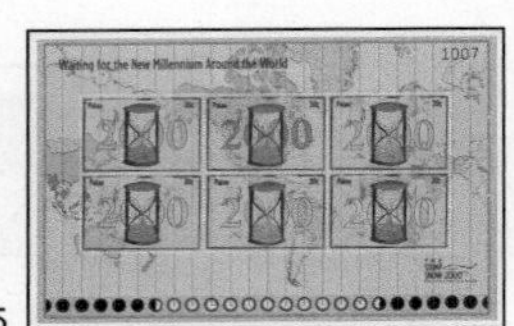

A165

Millennium — A165a

No. 568, horiz. — "2000," hourglass, and map of: a, North Pacific area. b, U.S. and Canada. c, Europe. d, South Pacific. e, South America. f, Southern Africa.

No. 569 — Clock face and: a, Sky. b, Building. c, Cove and lighthouse. d, Barn. e, Forest. f, Desert.

2000, May 25 *Perf. 13¾*

568 A165 20c Sheet of 6, #a-f 2.40 2.40
569 A165a 55c Sheet of 6, #a-f 6.75 6.75

The Stamp Show 2000, London.

New and Recovering Species — A166

No. 570, each 33c: a, Aleutian Canada goose. b, Western gray kangaroo. c, Palau scops owl. d, Jocotoco antpitta. e, Orchid. f, Red lechwe.

No. 571, each 33c: a, Bald eagle. b, Small-whorled pogonia. c, Arctic peregrine falcon. d, Golden lion tamarin. e, American alligator. f, Brown pelican.

Each $2: No. 572, Leopard. No. 573, Lahontan cutthroat trout, horiz.

2000, June 20 *Perf. 14*

Sheets of 6, #a-f

570-571 A166 Set of 2 8.00 8.00

Souvenir Sheets

572-573 A166 Set of 2 8.00 8.00

Dinosaurs — A167

No. 574: a, Rhamphorhynchus. b, Ceratosaurus. c, Apatosaurus. d, Stegosaurus. e, Archaeopteryx. f, Allosaurus.

No. 575: a, Parasaurolophus. b, Pteranodon. c, Tyrannosaurus. d, Triceratops. e, Ankylosaurus. f, Velociraptor.

Each $2: No. 576, Jurassic era view. No. 577, Cretaceous era view.

2000, June 20

574 A167 20c Sheet of 6, #a-f 2.40 2.40
575 A167 33c Sheet of 6, #a-f 4.00 4.00

Souvenir Sheets

576-577 A167 Set of 2 8.00 8.00

Queen Mother, 100th Birthday A168

No. 578, 55c: a, With King George VI. b, Wearing brown hat.

No. 579, 55c: a, Wearing green hat. b, Wearing white hat.

2000, Sept. 1 Litho. *Perf. 14*

Sheets of 4, 2 each #a-b

578-579 A168 Set of 2 9.00 9.00

Souvenir Sheet

580 A168 $2 Wearing yellow hat 4.00 4.00

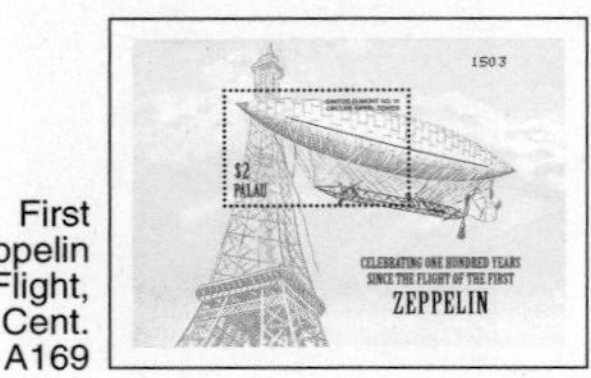

First Zeppelin Flight, Cent. A169

No. 581: a, Le Jaune. b, Forlanini's Leonardo da Vinci. c, Baldwin's airship. d, Astra-Torres I. e, Parseval PL VII. f, Lebaudy's Liberte.

No. 582, $2, Santos-Dumont No. VI. No. 583, $2, Santos-Dumont Baladeuse No. 9.

2000, Sept. 1

581 A169 55c Sheet of 6, #a-f 6.75 6.75

Souvenir Sheets

582-583 A169 Set of 2 8.00 8.00

Millennium Type of 2000

Sheet of 17

Undersea History and Exploration: a, Viking diver. b, Arab diver Issa. c, Salvage diver. d, Diver. e, Diving bell. f, Turtle. g, Siebe helmet. h, C.S.S. Hunley. i, Argonaut. j, Photosphere. k, Helmet diver. l, Bathysphere. m, Coelacanth. n, WWII charioteers. o, Trieste. p, Alvin visits geothermal vents (60x40mm). q, Jim suit.

2000, Oct. 16 *Perf. 12¾x12½*

584 A155 33c #a-q + label 13.00 13.00

Photomosaic of Pope John Paul II — A170

Various photos with religious themes.

2000, Dec. 1 *Perf. 13¾*

585 A170 50c Sheet of 8, #a-h 8.00 8.00

Souvenir Sheets

New Year 2001 (Year of the Snake) A171

Snake color: #586, Black. #587, Red.

2000, Dec. 1 *Perf. 14¼*

586-587 A171 60c Set of 2 2.40 2.40

Pacific Ocean Marine Life A172

No. 588: a, Scalloped hammerhead shark. b, Whitetip reef shark. c, Moon jellyfish. d, Lionfish. e, Seahorse. f, Spotted eagle ray.

2000 *Perf. 14½x14¼*

588 A172 55c Sheet of 6, #a-f 6.75 6.75

Atlantic Ocean Fish A173

No. 589, horiz.: a, Reef bass. b, White shark. c, Sharptail eel. d, Sailfish. e, Southern stingray. f, Ocean triggerfish.

#590, Short bigeye. #591, Gafftopsail catfish.

2000 *Perf. 13¾*

589 A173 20c Sheet of 6, #a-f 2.40 2.40

Souvenir Sheets

590-591 A173 $2 Set of 2 8.00 8.00

Pacific Arts Festival A174

No. 592: a, Dancers, by S. Adelbai. b, Story Board Art, by D. Inabo. c, Traditional Money, by M. Takeshi. d, Clay Lamp and Bowl, by W. Watanabe. e, Meeting House, by Pasqual Tiakl. f, Outrigger Canoe, by S. Adelbai. g, Weaver, by M. Vitarelli. h, Rock Island Scene, by W. Marcil. i, Contemporary Music, by J. Imetuker.

2000, Nov. 1 Litho. *Perf. 14¼*

592 A174 33c Sheet of 9, #a-i 6.00 6.00

National Museum, 45th Anniv. A175

No. 593: a, Klilt, turtle shell bracelet. b, Sculpture by H. Hijikata. c, Turtle shell women's money. d, Cherecheroi, by T. Suzuki. e, Money jar, by B. Sylvester. f, Prince Lebu by Ichikawa. g, Beach at Lild, by H. Hijikata. h, Traditional mask. i, Taro platter, by T. Rebluud. j, Meresebang, by Ichikawa. k, Wood sculpture, by B. Sylvester. l, Birth Ceremony, by I. Kishigawa.

2000, Nov. 1 *Perf. 14x14¾*

593 A175 33c Sheet of 12, #a-l 8.00 8.00

Butterflies A176

Designs: No. 594, 33c, Indian red admiral. No. 595, 33c, Fiery jewel. No. 596, 33c, Checkered swallowtail. No. 597, 33c, Yamfly.

No. 598, 33c: a, Large green-banded blue. b, Union Jack. c, Broad-bordered grass yellow. d, Striped blue crow. e, Red lacewing. f, Palmfly.

No. 599, 33c: a, Cairn's birdwing. b, Meadow argus. c, Orange albatross. d, Glass-wing. e, Beak. f, Great eggfly.

No. 600, $2, Clipper. No. 601, $2, Blue triangle.

2000, Dec. 15 *Perf. 14*

594-597 A176 Set of 4 2.75 2.75

Sheets of 6, #a-f

598-599 A176 Set of 2 8.00 8.00

Souvenir Sheets

600-601 A176 Set of 2 8.00 8.00

Flora and Fauna A177

No. 602, 33c: a, Giant spiral ginger. b, Good luck plant. c, Ti tree, coconuts. d, Butterfly. e, Saltwater crocodile. f, Orchid.

No. 603, 33c: a, Little kingfisher. b, Mangrove snake. c, Bats, breadfruit. d, Giant tree frog. e, Giant centipede. f, Crab-eating macaque.

No. 604, $2, Soft coral, surgeonfish. No. 605, $2, Land crab, vert.

2000, Dec. 29 ***Perf. 14x14¼, 14¼x14***

Sheets of 6, #a-f

602-603 A177 Set of 2 8.00 8.00

Souvenir Sheets

604-605 A177 Set of 2 8.00 8.00

Personalities Type of 1999

Designs: 11c, Lazarus Salil. 70c, Gen. Douglas MacArthur. 80c, Adm. Chester W. Nimitz. $12.25, John F. Kennedy.

2001 **Litho.** ***Perf. 14x14¾***

606 A142 11c purple .25 .25
607 A142 70c lilac 1.40 1.40
608 A142 80c green 1.60 1.60
609 A142 $12.25 red 25.00 25.00
Nos. 606-609 (4) 28.25 28.25

Issued: Nos. 607-609, 6/10.

Phila Nippon '01, Japan A178

No. 610, 60c: a, Ono no Komachi Washing the Copybook, by Kiyomitsu Torii. b, Woman Playing Samisen and Woman Reading al Letter, by School of Matabei Iwasa. c, The Actor Danjura Ichikawa V as a Samurai in a Wrestling Arena Striking a Pose on a Go Board, by Shunsho Katsukawa. d, Gentleman Entertained by Courtesans, by Kiyonaga Torii. e, Geisha at a Teahouse in Shinagawa, by Kiyonaga Torii.

No. 611, 60c: a, Preparing Sashimi, by Utamaro. b, Ichimatsu Sanogawa I as Sogo no Goro and Kikugoro Onoe as Kyo no Jiro in Umewakana Futaba Soga, by Toyonobu Ishikawa. c, Courtesan Adjusting Her Comb, by Dohan Kaigetsudo. d, The Actor Tomijuro Nakamura I in a Female Role Dancing, by Shunsho Katsukawa. e, Woman with Poem Card and Writing Brush, by Gakutei Yashima.

No. 612, Six panels of screen, Kitano Shrine in Kyoto, by unknown artist.

No. 613, $2, Raiko Attacks a Demon Kite, by Hokkei Totoya. No. 614, $2, Beauty Writing a Letter, by Doshin Kaigetsudo. No. 615, $2, Fireworks at Ikenohata, by Kiyochika Kobayashi.

2001, Aug. 13 **Litho.** ***Perf. 14***

Sheets of 5, #a-e

610-611 A178 Set of 2 12.00 12.00
612 A178 60c Sheet of 6, #a-f 7.25 7.25

Souvenir Sheets

613-615 A178 Set of 3 12.00 12.00

Moths — A179

Designs: 20c, Veined tiger moth. 21c, Basker moth. 80c, White-lined sphinx moth. $1, Isabella tiger moth.

No. 620, 34c: a, Cinnabar moth. b, Beautiful tiger moth. c, Great tiger moth. d, Provence burnet moth. e, Jersey tiger moth. f, Ornate moth.

No. 621, 70c: a, Hoop pine moth. b, King's bee hawk moth. c, Banded bagnest moth. d, Io moth. e, Tau emperor moth. f, Lime hawkmoth.

No. 622, $2, Spanish moon moth. No. 623, $2, Owl moth.

2001, Oct. 15 **Litho.** ***Perf. 14***

616-619 A179 Set of 4 4.50 4.50

Sheets of 6, #a-f

620-621 A179 Set of 2 12.50 12.50

Souvenir Sheets

622-623 A179 Set of 2 8.00 8.00

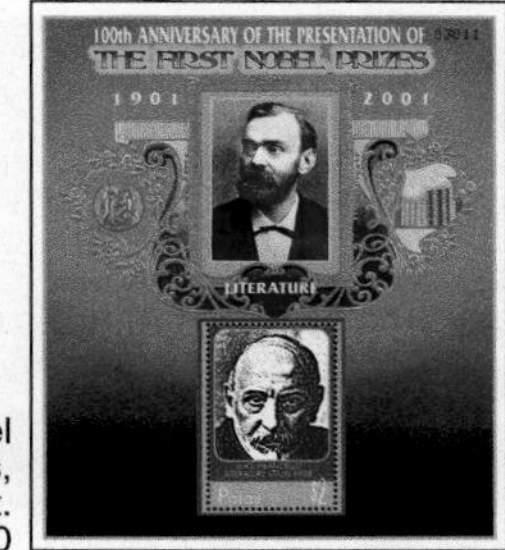

Nobel Prizes, Cent. A180

Literature laureates — No. 624, 34c: a, Ivo Andric, 1961. b, Eyvind Johnson, 1974. c, Salvatore Quasimodo, 1959. d, Mikhail Sholokhov, 1965. e, Pablo Neruda, 1971. f, Saul Bellow, 1976.

No. 625, 70c: a, Boris Pasternak, 1958. b, Francois Mauriac, 1952. c, Frans Eemil Sillanpää, 1939. d, Roger Martin du Gard, 1937. e, Pearl Buck, 1938. f, André Gide, 1947.

No. 626, 80c: a, Karl Gjellerup, 1917. b, Anatole France, 1921. c, Sinclair Lewis, 1930. d, Jacinto Benavente, 1922. e, John Galsworthy, 1932. f, Erik. A. Karlfeldt, 1931.

No. 627, $2, Luigi Pirandello, 1934. No. 628, $2, Bertrand Russell, 1950. No. 629, Harry Martinson, 1974.

2001, Oct. 30 **Sheets of 6, #a-f**

624-626 A180 Set of 3 22.50 22.50

Souvenir Sheets

627-629 A180 Set of 3 12.00 12.00

2002 World Cup Soccer Championships, Japan and Korea — A181

No. 630, 34c — World Cup posters from: a, 1950. b, 1954. c, 1958. d, 1962. e, 1966. f, 1970.

No. 631, 80c — World Cup posters from: a, 1978. b, 1982. c, 1986. d, 1990. e, 1994. f, 1998.

No. 632, $2, World Cup poster, 1930. No. 633, $2, Head and globe from World Cup trophy.

2001, Nov. 29 ***Perf. 13¾x14¼***

Sheets of 6, #a-f

630-631 A181 Set of 2 14.00 14.00

Souvenir Sheets

Perf. 14½x14¼

632-633 A181 Set of 2 8.00 8.00

Christmas — A182

Denominations: 20c, 34c.

2001, Nov. 29 ***Perf. 14***

634-635 A182 Set of 2 1.10 1.10

Queen Mother Type of 1999 Redrawn

No. 636: a, In Australia, 1958. b, In 1960. c, In 1970. d, In 1987.

$2, Holding book, 1947.

2001, Dec. 13 ***Perf. 14***

Yellow Orange Frames

636 A150 60c Sheet of 4, #a-d, + label 4.75 4.75

Souvenir Sheet

Perf. 13¾

637 A150 $2 black 4.00 4.00

Queen Mother's 101st birthday. No. 637 contains one 38x51mm stamp that is slightly darker than that found on No. 523. Sheet margins of Nos. 636-637 lack embossing and gold arms and frames found on Nos. 522-523.

Pasturing Horses, by Han Kan — A183

2001, Dec. 17 ***Perf. 14x14¾***

638 A183 60c multi 1.25 1.25

New Year 2002 (Year of the Horse). Printed in sheets of 4.

Birds A184

No. 639, 55c: a, Yellow-faced myna. b, Red-bellied pitta. c, Red-bearded bee-eater. d, Superb fruit dove. e, Coppersmith barbet. f, Diard's trogon.

No. 640, 60c: a, Spectacled monarch. b, Banded pitta. c, Rufous-backed kingfisher. d, Scarlet robin. e, Golden whistler. f, Jewel babbler.

No. 641, $2, Paradise flycatcher. No. 642, $2, Common kingfisher.

2001, Dec. 26 ***Perf. 14***

Sheets of 6, #a-f

639-640 A184 Set of 2 14.00 14.00

Souvenir Sheets

Perf. 14¾

641-642 A184 Set of 2 8.00 8.00

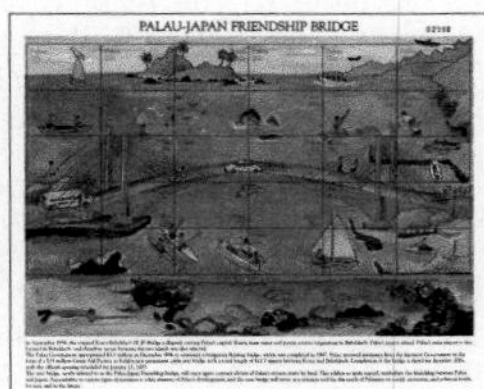

Opening of Palau-Japan Frendship Bridge — A185

No. 643, 20c; No. 644, 34c: a, Bird on orange rock. b, Island, one palm tree. c, Island, three palm trees. d, Rocks, boat prow. e, Boat, bat. f, Cove, foliage. g, Red boat with two people. h, Buoy, birds. i, Birds, dolphin's tail. j, Dolphins. k, Person on raft. l, Two people standing in water. m, Person with fishing pole in water. n, Bridge tower. o, Bicyclist, taxi. p, Front of taxi. q, People walking on bridge, bridge tower. r, Truck, boat. s, School bus. t, Base of bridge tower. u, Birds under bridge, oar. v, Birds under bridge. w, Base of bridge tower, tip of sail. x, Motorcyclist. y, Birds on black rock. z, Kayakers. aa, Kayak, boat. ab, Boat, sailboat. ac, Sailboat, jetty. ad, Jetski.

2002, Jan. 11 ***Perf. 13***

Sheets of 30, #a-ad

643-644 A185 Set of 2 32.50 32.50

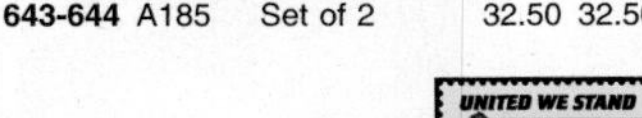

United We Stand — A186

2002, Jan. 24 ***Perf. 14***

645 A186 $1 multi 2.00 2.00

Reign of Queen Elizabeth II, 50th Anniv. A187

No. 646: a, In uniform. b, Wearing flowered hat. c, Prince Philip. d, Wearing tiara.

$2, Wearing white dress.

2002, Feb. 6 ***Perf. 14¼***

646 A187 80c Sheet of 4, #a-d 6.50 6.50

Souvenir Sheet

647 A187 $2 multi 4.00 4.00

Birds — A188

Designs: 1c, Gray-backed white-eye. 2c, Great frigatebird. 3c, Eclectus parrot. 4c, Red-footed booby. 5c Cattle egret. 10c, Cardinal honeyeater. 11c, Blue-faced parrot-finch. 15c, Rufous fantail. 20c, White-faced storm petrel. 21c, Willie wagtail. 23c, Black-headed gull. 50c, Sanderling. 57c, White-tailed tropicbird. 70c, Rainbow lorikeet. 80c, Moorhen. $1, Buff-banded rail. $2, Beach thick-knee. $3, Common tern. $3.50, Ruddy turnstone. $3.95, White-collared kingfisher. $5, Sulphur-crested cockatoo. $10, Barn swallow.

2002, Feb. 20 ***Perf. 14¼***

648 A188 1c multi .25 .25
649 A188 2c multi .25 .25
650 A188 3c multi .25 .25
651 A188 4c multi .25 .25
652 A188 5c multi .25 .25
653 A188 10c multi .25 .25
654 A188 11c multi .25 .25
655 A188 15c multi .30 .30
656 A188 20c multi .40 .40
657 A188 21c multi .40 .40
658 A188 23c multi .45 .45
659 A188 50c multi 1.00 1.00
660 A188 57c multi 1.10 1.10
661 A188 70c multi 1.40 1.40
662 A188 80c multi 1.60 1.60
663 A188 $1 multi 2.00 2.00
664 A188 $2 multi 4.00 4.00
665 A188 $3 multi 6.00 6.00
666 A188 $3.50 multi 7.00 7.00
667 A188 $3.95 multi 8.00 8.00
668 A188 $5 multi 10.00 10.00
669 A188 $10 multi 20.00 20.00
Nos. 648-669 (22) 65.40 65.40

Flowers — A189

Designs: 20c, Euanthe sanderiana. 34c, Ophiorrhiza palauensis. No. 672, 60c, Cerbera manghas. 80c, Mendinilla pterocaula.

No. 674, 60c: a, Bruguiera gymnorhiza. b, Samadera indiccal. c, Maesa canfieldiae. d, Lumnitzera litorea. e, Dolichandrone palawense. f, Limnophila aromatica (red and white orchids).

No. 675, 60c: a, Sonneratia alba. b, Barringtonia racemosa. c, Ixora casei. d, Tristellateia australasiae. e, Nepenthes mirabilis. f, Limnophila aromatica (pink flowers).

No. 676, $2, Fagraea ksid. No. 677, $2, Cerbera manghas, horiz.

2002, Mar. 4 ***Perf. 14***

670-673 A189 Set of 4 4.00 4.00

Sheets of 6, #a-f

674-675 A189 Set of 2 14.50 14.50

Souvenir Sheets

676-677 A189 Set of 2 8.00 8.00

2002 Winter Olympics, Salt Lake City — A190

Skier with: No. 678, $1, Blue pants. No. 679, $1, Yellow pants.

2002, Mar. 18 ***Perf. 14¼***

678-679 A190 Set of 2 4.00 4.00
679a Souvenir sheet, #678-679 4.00 4.00

A191

Cats and Dogs — A191a

No. 680, 50c, horiz.: a, Himalayan. b, Norwegian forest cat. c, Havana. d, Exotic shorthair. e, Persian. f, Maine coon cat.

No. 681, 50c, horiz.: a, Great Dane. b, Whippet. c, Bedlington terrier. d, Golden retriever. e, Papillon. f, Doberman pinscher.

No. 682, $2, British shorthair. No. 683, $2, Shetland sheepdog.

2002, Mar. 18 Litho. ***Perf. 14***

Sheets of 6, #a-f

680-681 A191 Set of 2 12.00 12.00

Souvenir Sheets

682-683 A191a Set of 2 8.00 8.00

Intl. Year of Mountains — A192

No. 684: a, Mt. Fuji, Japan. b, Mt. Everest, Nepal and China. c, Mt. Owen, US. d, Mt. Huascarán, Peru.

$2, Mt. Eiger, Switzerland.

2002, June 17 Litho. ***Perf. 14***

684 A192 80c Sheet of 4, #a-d 6.50 6.50

Souvenir Sheet

685 A192 $2 multi 4.00 4.00

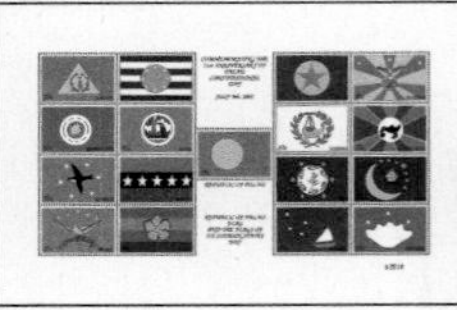

Flags of Palau and its States A193

No. 686: a, Palau (no inscription). b, Kayangel. c, Ngarchelong. d, Ngaraard. e, Ngardmau. f, Ngaremlengui. g, Ngiwal. h, Ngatpang. i, Melekeor. j, Ngchesar. k, Aimeliik. l, Airai. m, Koror. n, Peleliu. o, Angaur. p, Sonsorol. q, Hatohobei.

2002, July 9

686 A193 37c Sheet of 17, #a-q 13.00 13.00

All stamps on No. 686 lack country name.

Winter Olympics Type of 2002 Redrawn with White Olympic Rings

Skier with: No. 687, $1, Blue pants. No. 688, $1, Yellow pants.

2002, July 29 ***Perf. 13½***

687-688 A190 Set of 2 4.00 4.00
688a Souvenir sheet, #687-688 4.00 4.00

Intl. Year of Ecotourism — A194

No. 689: a, Divers, angelfish facing right. b, Ray. c, Sea cucumber. d, Emperor angelfish facing left. e, Sea turtle. f, Nautilus.

$2, Person in canoe.

2002, Apr. 26 ***Perf. 14½x14¼***

689 A194 60c Sheet of 6, #a-f 7.25 7.25

Souvenir Sheet

690 A194 $2 multi 4.00 4.00

Japanese Art — A195

No. 691, vert. (38x50mm): a, The Actor Shuka Bando as Courtesan Shiraito, by Kunisada Utagawa. b, The Actor Danjuro Ichikawa VII as Sugawara no Michizane, by Kunisada Utagawa. c, The Actor Sojuro Sawamura III as Yuranosuke Oboshi, by Toyokuni Utagawa. d, The Actor Nizaemon Kataoka VII as Shihei Fujiwara, by Toyokuni Utagawa. e, Bust Portrait of the Actor Noshio Nakamura II, by Kunimasa Utagawa. f, The Actor Gon-Nosuke Kawarazaki as Daroku, by Kunichika Toyohara.

No. 692, 80c, vert. (27x88mm): a, Bush Clover Branch and Sweetfish, by Kuniyoshi Utagawa. b, Catfish, by Kuniyoshi Utagawa. c, Scene at Takanawa, by Eisen Keisai. d, Ochanomizu, by Keisai.

No. 693, 80c (50x38mm): a, Gaslight Hall, by Kiyochika Kobayashi. b, Cherry Blossoms at Night at Shin Yoshiwara, by Yasuji Inoue. c, Night Rain at Oyama, by Toyokuni Utagawa II. d, Kintai Bridge, by Keisai.

No. 694, $2, Okane, a Strong Woman of Omi, by Kuniyoshi Utagawa. No. 695, $2, Scene on the Banks of the Oumaya River, by Kuniyoshi Utagawa.

Perf. 14¼, 13½ (#692)

2002, Sept. 23

691 A195 60c Sheet of 6, #a-f 7.25 7.25

Sheets of 4, #a-d

692-693 A195 Set of 2 13.00 13.00

Size: 105x85mm

Imperf

694-695 A195 Set of 2 8.00 8.00

Popeye A196

No. 696, vert.: a, Wimpy. b, Swee'Pea. c, Popeye. d, Fish. e, Jeep. f, Brutus.

$2, Popeye golfing.

2002, Oct. 7 ***Perf. 14***

696 A196 60c Sheet of 6, #a-f 7.25 7.25

Souvenir Sheet

697 A196 $2 multi 4.00 4.00

Elvis Presley (1935-77) — A197

No. 698: a, On horse. b, Holding guitar, wearing white jacket, no hat. c, Wearing black hat. d, With guitar with two necks. e, Holding guitar, wearing colored jacket, no hat. f, Wearing shirt.

2002, Oct. 23

698 A197 37c Sheet of 6, #a-f 4.75 4.75

Christmas A198

Designs: 23c, Presentation of Jesus in the Temple, by Perugino, vert. 37c, Madonna and Child Enthroned Between Angels and Saints, by Domenico Ghirlandaio, vert. 60c, Maesta, by Simone Martini, vert. 80c, Sacred Conversation, by Giovanni Bellini. $1, Nativity, by Ghirlandaio.

$2, Sacred Conversation (detail), by Bellini.

2002, Nov. 5

699-703 A198 Set of 5 6.00 6.00

Souvenir Sheet

704 A198 $2 multi 4.00 4.00

The painting shown on No. 704 does not appear to be a detail of the painting shown on No. 702.

Teddy Bears, Cent. A199

No. 705: a, Accountant bear. b, Computer programmer bear. c, Businesswoman bear. d, Lawyer bear.

2002, Nov. 19

705 A199 60c Sheet of 4, #a-d 5.00 5.00

Queen Mother Elizabeth (1900-2002) — A200

No. 706: a, Holding bouquet. b, Wearing blue blouse and pearls. c, Wearing purple hat. d, Wearing tiara.

$2, Wearing flowered hat.

2002, Dec. 30

706 A200 80c Sheet of 4, #a-d 6.50 6.50

Souvenir Sheet

707 A200 $2 multi 4.00 4.00

20th World Scout Jamboree, Thailand (in 2002) — A201

No. 708, horiz.: a, Scout climbing rocks. b, Scout emblem, knife. c, Branches lashed together with rope. d, Cub scout (wearing cap). e, Knot. f, Boy scout (without cap).

$2 Lord Robert Baden-Powell.

2003, Jan. 13 ***Perf. 14***

708 A201 60c Sheet of 6, #a-f 7.25 7.25

Souvenir Sheet

709 A201 $2 multi 4.00 4.00

Shells A202

No. 710: a, Leafy murex. b, Trumpet triton. c, Giant tun. d, Queen conch. e, Spotted tun. f, Emperor helmet.

$2, Angular triton.

2003, Jan. 13

710 A202 60c Sheet of 6, #a-f 7.25 7.25

Souvenir Sheet

711 A202 $2 multi 4.00 4.00

New Year 2003 (Year of the Ram) — A203

No. 712: a, Ram facing right. b, Ram facing forward. c, Ram facing left.

2003, Jan. 27 ***Perf. 14¼x13¾***

712 A203 37c Vert. strip of 3, #a-c 2.25 2.25
Sheet of 2 strips 4.50

No. 712 printed in sheets of 2 strips with slightly different backgrounds.

Pres. John F. Kennedy (1917-63) — A204

No. 713: a, Wearing cap. b, Facing left. c, Facing right. d, Holding ship's wheel.

2003, Feb. 10 ***Perf. 14***
713 A204 80c Sheet of 4, #a-d 6.50 6.50

Bird Type of 2002 With Unserifed Numerals

Designs: 26c, Golden whistler. 37c, Pale white-eye.

2003, Mar. 1 ***Perf. 14¼x13¾***
714 A188 26c multi .55 .55
715 A188 37c multi .75 .75

Astronauts Killed in Space Shuttle Columbia Accident — A205

No. 716: a, Mission Specialist 1 David M. Brown. b, Commander Rick D. Husband. c, Mission Specialist 4 Laurel Blair Salton Clark. d, Mission Specialist 4 Kalpana Chawla. e, Payload Commander Michael P. Anderson. f, Pilot William C. McCool. g, Payload Specialist 4 Ilan Ramon.

2003, Apr. 7 ***Perf. 13¼***
716 A205 37c Sheet of 7, #a-g 5.25 5.25

Orchids A206

No. 717: a, Phalaenopsis grex. b, Cattleya loddigesii. c, Phalaenopsis joline. d, Dendrobium. e, Laelia anceps. f, Cymbidium Stanley Fouracre.
$2, Vanda rothschildiana.

2003, Jan. 13 **Litho.** ***Perf. 14***
717 A206 60c Sheet of 6, #a-f 7.25 7.25

Souvenir Sheet

718 A206 $2 multi 4.00 4.00

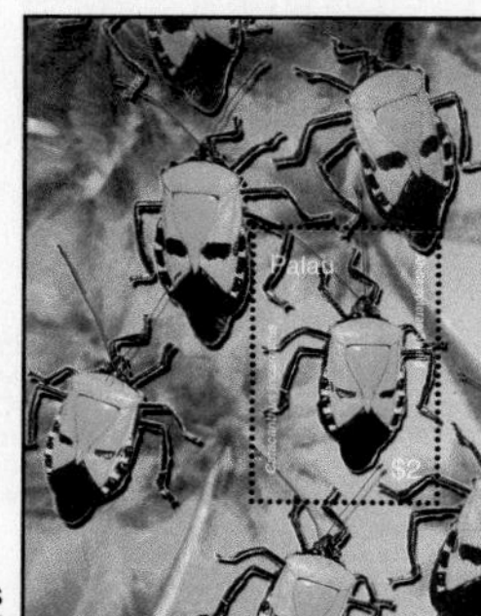

Insects A207

No. 719: a, Giant water bug. b, Weevil. c, Blister beetle. d, Bess beetle. e, Metallic stag beetle. f, Violin beetle.
$2, Aheteropteran shield.

2003, Jan. 13
719 A207 60c Sheet of 6, #a-f 7.25 7.25

Souvenir Sheet

720 A207 $2 multi 4.00 4.00

First Non-stop Solo Transatlantic Flight, 75th Anniv. — A208

No. 721: a, Charles Lindbergh, Donald Hall and Spirit of St. Louis. b, Spirit of St. Louis, Apr. 28, 1927. c, Spirit of St. Louis towed from Curtiss Field, May 20, 1927. d, Spirit of St. Louis takes off, May 20, 1927. e, Arrival in Paris, May 21, 1927. f, New York ticker tape parade.

2003, Feb. 10
721 A208 60c Sheet of 6, #a-f 7.25 7.25

Pres. Ronald Reagan A209

Reagan with: a, Orange bandana. b, Red shirt. c, Blue shirt, head at left. d, Blue shirt, head at right.

2003, Feb. 10
722 A209 80c Sheet of 4, #a-d 6.50 6.50

Princess Diana (1961-97) — A210

Diana and clothing worn in: a, India. b, Canada. c, Egypt. d, Italy.

2003, Feb. 10
723 A210 80c Sheet of 4, #a-d 6.50 6.50

Coronation of Queen Elizabeth II, 50th Anniv. — A211

No. 724 — Queen with: a, Tiara. b, Pink dress. c, Hat.
$2, Tiara, diff.

2003, May 13
724 A211 $1 Sheet of 3, #a-c 6.00 6.00

Souvenir Sheet

725 A211 $2 multi 4.00 4.00

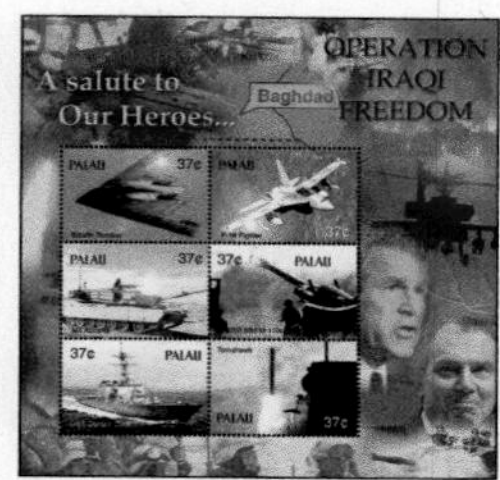

Operation Iraqi Freedom — A212

No. 726: a, Stealth bomber. b, F-18 fighter. c, MT Abrams tank. d, 203mm M-110s. e, USS Donald Cook. f, Tomahawk missile.

2003, May 14
726 A212 37c Sheet of 6, #a-f 4.50 4.50

Prince William, 21st Birthday A213

No. 727 — William: a, In yellow green shirt. b, As infant. c, In black sweater.
$2, As infant with Princess Diana.

2003, June 21
727 A213 $1 Sheet of 3, #a-c 6.00 6.00

Souvenir Sheet

728 A213 $2 multi 4.00 4.00

Tour de France Bicycle Race, Cent. A214

No. 729: a, Henri Pelissier, 1923. b, Ottavio Bottecchia, 1924. c, Bottecchia, 1925. d, Lucien Buysse, 1926.
$2, Philippe Thys, 1920.

2003, Aug. 23 ***Perf. 13¼***
729 A214 60c Sheet of 4, #a-d 5.00 5.00

Souvenir Sheet

730 A214 $2 multi 4.00 4.00

Powered Flight, Cent. A215

No. 731: a, Fokker 70. b, Boeing 747-217B. c, Curtiss T-32 Condor. d, Vickers Viscount Type 761. e, Wright Flyer III. f, Avro Ten Achilles.
$2, Wright Flyer III, diff.

2003, Aug. 25 ***Perf. 14***
731 A215 55c Sheet of 6, #a-f 6.75 6.75

Souvenir Sheet

732 A215 $2 multi 4.00 4.00

Paintings by James McNeill Whistler A216

Designs: 37c, Blue and Silver: Trouville. 55c, The Last of Old Westminster. 60c, Wapping. $1, Cremorne Gardens, No. 2.
No. 737, vert.: a, Arrangement in Flesh Color and Black, Portrait of Theodore Duret. b, Arrangement in White and Black. c, Harmony in Pink and Gray, Portrait of Lady Meux. d, Arrangement in Black and Gold, Comte Robert de Montesquiou-Fezensac.
$2, Arrangement in Gray and Black No. 1, Portrait of Painter's Mother, vert.

Perf. 14¼, 13¼ (#737)
2003, Sept. 22
733-736 A216 Set of 4 5.25 5.25
737 A216 80c Sheet of 4, #a-d 6.50 6.50

Souvenir Sheet

738 A216 $2 multi 4.00 4.00

No. 737 contains four 35x71mm stamps.

Circus Performers — A217

No. 739, 80c — Clowns: a, Apes. b, Mo Life. c, Gigi. d, "Buttons" McBride.
No. 740, 80c: a, Dogs. b, Olena Yaknenko. c, Mountain High. d, Chinese Circus.

2003, Sept. 29 ***Perf. 14***

Sheets of 4, #a-d

739-740 A217 Set of 2 13.00 13.00

Christmas — A218

Designs: 37c, Madonna della Melagrana, by Botticelli. 60c, Madonna del Magnificat, by Botticelli. 80c, Madonna and Child with the Saints and the Angels, by Andrea del Sarto. $1, La Madonna del Roseto, by Botticelli.
$2, Madonna and Child with the Angels and Saints, by Domenico Ghirlandaio.

2003, Dec. 1 ***Perf. 14¼***
741-744 A218 Set of 4 5.75 5.75

Souvenir Sheet

745 A218 $2 multi 4.00 4.00

Sea Turtles A219

No. 746: a, Mating. b, Laying eggs at night. c, Hatching. d, Turtles going to sea. e, Growing up at sea. f, Returning to lay eggs.
$2, Head of sea turtle.

2004, Feb. 6 ***Perf. 14***
746 A219 60c Sheet of 6, #a-f 7.25 7.25

Souvenir Sheet

747 A219 $2 multi 4.00 4.00

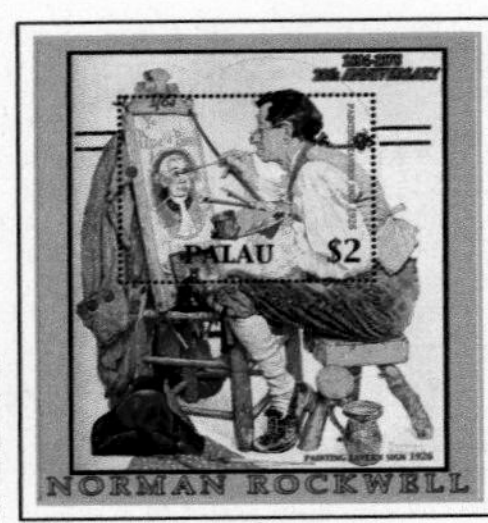

Paintings by Norman Rockwell A220

No. 748, vert.: a, The Connoisseur. b, Artist Facing a Blank Canvas (Deadline). c, Art Critic. d, Stained Glass Artistry.
$2, Painting Tavern Sign.

2004, Feb. 6 Litho. *Perf. 14¼*
748 A220 80c Sheet of 4, #a-d 6.50 6.50

Souvenir Sheet

749 A220 $2 multi 4.00 4.00

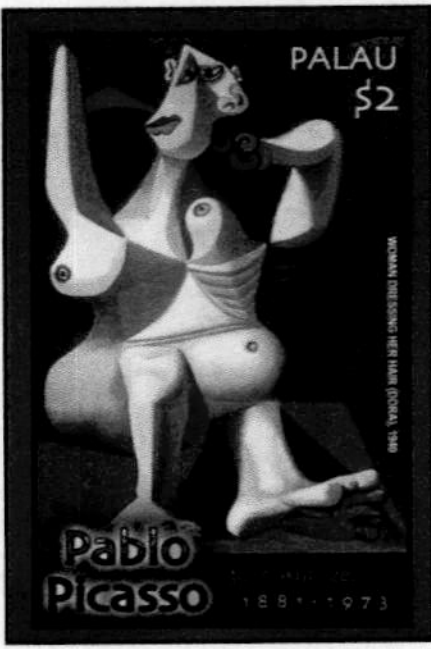

Paintings by Pablo Picasso A221

No. 750: a, Dora Maar. b, The Yellow Sweater (Dora). c, Woman in Green (Dora). d, Woman in an Armchair (Dora).
$2, Woman Dressing Her Hair (Dora).

2004, Feb. 16 Litho. *Perf. 14¼*
750 A221 80c Sheet of 4, #a-d 6.50 6.50

Imperf

751 A221 $2 multi 4.00 4.00
No. 750 contains four 37x50mm stamps.

Paintings in the Hermitage, St. Petersburg, Russia — A222

Designs: 37c, Antonia Zarate, by Francisco de Goya. 55c, Portrait of a Lady, by Antonio Correggio. 80c, Portrait of Count Olivarez, by Diego Velázquez. $1, Portrait of a Young Man With a Lace Collar, by Rembrandt.
$2, Family Portrait, by Anthony Van Dyck.

2004, Feb. 16 Litho. *Perf. 14¼*
752-755 A222 Set of 4 5.50 5.50

Size: 62x81mm

Imperf

756 A222 $2 multi 4.00 4.00

Marine Life A223

No. 757: a, Coral hind. b, Sea octopus. c, Manta ray. d, Dugong. e, Marine crab. f, Grouper.
$2, Gray reef shark.

2004, Feb. 16 *Perf. 14¼*
757 A223 55c Sheet of 6, #a-f 6.75 6.75

Souvenir Sheet

758 A223 $2 multi 4.00 4.00

Minerals A224

No. 759: a, Phosphate. b, Antimony. c, Limonite. d, Calcopyrite. e, Bauxite. f, Manganite.
$2, Gold.

2004, Feb. 16
759 A224 55c Sheet of 6, #a-f 6.75 6.75

Souvenir Sheet

760 A224 $2 multi 4.00 4.00

New Year 2004 (Year of the Monkey) — A225

Green Bamboo and a White Ape, by Ren Yu: 50c, Detail. $1, Entire painting.

2004, Mar. 9 *Perf. 13¼*
761 A225 50c multi 1.00 1.00

Souvenir Sheet

Perf. 13½x13¼

762 A225 $1 multi 2.00 2.00
No. 761 printed in sheets of 4. No. 762 contains one 27x83mm stamp.

Ninth Festival of Pacific Arts A226

No. 763, 26c: a, Oraschel, by M. Takeshi. b, Flute, by Sim Adelbai. c, Rur, by W. Watanabe. d, Bamboo Raft, by P. Tiakl. e, Story Telling, by K. Murret. f, Yek, by A. Imetuker. g, Canoe House, by W. Marsil. h, Carving Axe, by Watanabe. i, Weaving, by Marsil. j, Dancing Props, by Adelbai.
No. 764, 37c: a, Ongall, by Tiakl. b, Bai, by S. Weers. c, Taro Plant, by S. Smaserui. d, Toluk, by Watanabe. e, Medicinal Plants, by Smaserui. f, War Canoe, by Takeshi. g, Painting, by Adelbai. h, Pounding Taro, by Imetuker. h, Llengel, by Takeshi. i, Spear Technique, by Imetuker.

2004, Apr. 13 *Perf. 13*

Sheets of 10, #a-j

763-764 A226 Set of 2 13.00 13.00

Marine Life A227

No. 765, 26c: a, Cuttlefish. b, Long fin bannerfish. c, Red sponge, Medusa worm. d, Risbecia tryoni. e, Emperor angelfish. f, Chromodoris coi.
No. 766, 37c: a, Spotted eagle ray. b, Jellyfish. c, Nautilus. d, Gray reef shark. e, Tunicates. f, Manta ray.
No. 767, $2, Pink anemonefish. No. 768, $2, Dusky anemonefish.

2004, May 20 *Perf. 14*

Sheets of 6, #a-f

765-766 A227 Set of 2 7.75 7.75

Souvenir Sheets

767-768 A227 Set of 2 8.00 8.00
No. 765 contains six labels.

Intl. Year of Peace A228

No. 769, vert.: a, Mahatma Gandhi. b, Nelson Mandela. c, Dr. Martin Luther King, Jr.
$2, Dove.

2004, May 24 *Perf. 13½x13¼*
769 A228 $3 Sheet of 3, #a-c 18.00 18.00

Souvenir Sheet

Perf. 13¼x13½

770 A228 $2 multi 4.00 4.00

2004 Summer Olympics, Athens A229

Designs: 37c, Athletes. 55c, Gold medals, Atlanta, 1996. 80c, Johannes Edström, Intl. Olympic Committee President, 1942-52, vert. $1, Women's soccer, Atlanta, 1996.

2004, June 18 *Perf. 14¼*
771-774 A229 Set of 4 5.50 5.50

Election of Pope John Paul, 25th Anniv. (in 2003) A230

Pope John Paul II: a, With Mehmet Agca, 1983. b, Visiting Poland, 2002. c, At concert in Ischia, Italy, 2002. d, With Patriarch Zakka, 2003.

2004, June 18
775 A230 80c Sheet of 4, #a-d 6.50 6.50

Souvenir Sheet

Deng Xiaoping (1904-97) Chinese Leader — A231

2004, June 18
776 A231 $2 multi 4.00 4.00

D-Day, 60th Anniv. A232

No. 777: a, LCA 1377. b, Landing Craft, Infantry. c, LCVP. d, U-309. e, HMS Begonia. f, HMS Roberts.
$2, LSTs.

2004, June 18
777 A232 50c Sheet of 6, #a-f 6.00 6.00

Souvenir Sheet

778 A232 $2 multi 4.00 4.00

European Soccer Championships, Portugal — A233

No. 779, vert.: a, Rinus Michels. b, Rinat Dasaev. c, Marco Van Basten. d, Olympiastadion.
$2, 1988 Netherlands team.

2004, June 18
779 A233 80c Sheet of 4, #a-d 6.50 6.50

Souvenir Sheet

780 A233 $2 multi 4.00 4.00
No. 779 contains four 28x42mm stamps.

Babe Ruth (1895-1948), Baseball Player — A234

Ruth and: No. 781, 37c, Signed baseball. No. 782, 37c, World Series 100th anniversary emblem.

2004, Sept. 3 *Perf. 13½x13¼*
781-782 A234 Set of 2 1.50 1.50
Nos. 781-782 each printed in sheets of 8.

Trains, Bicent. A235

No. 783: a, ATSF 315. b, Amtrak 464. c, Railway N52. d, SD 70 MAC Diesel-electric locomotive. No. 784, 50c: a, CS SO2002. b, P 36 N0032. c, SW-600. d, Gambier LNV 9703 4-4-0 NG.
No. 785, $2, CN5700 locomotive. No. 786, $2, Eurostar.

2004, Sept. 27 *Perf. 13¼x13½*
783 A235 26c Sheet of 4, #a-d 2.10 2.10
784 A235 50c Sheet of 4, #a-d 4.00 4.00

Souvenir Sheet

785 A235 $2 multi 4.00 4.00
786 A235 $2 multi 4.00 4.00

Butterflies, Reptiles, Amphibians and Birds — A236

No. 787, 80c — Butterflies: a, Cethosia hypsea. b, Cethosia myrina. c, Charaxes durnfordi. d, Charaxes nitebis.
No. 788, 80c — Reptiles: a, Bull snake. b, Garter snake. c, Yellow-lipped sea snake. d, Yellow-bellied sea snake.
No. 789, 80c, vert. — Birds: a, Blue-faced parrot finch. b, Mangrove flycatcher. c, Palau swiftlet. d, Bridled white-eye.
No. 790, $2, Charaxes nitebis, diff. No. 791, $2, Glass frog. No. 792, $2, Dusky white-eye, vert.

2004, Oct. 13 Litho. *Perf. 14*

Sheets of 4, #a-d

787-789 A236 Set of 3 19.50 19.50

Souvenir Sheets

790-792 A236 Set of 3 12.00 12.00

Dinosaurs — A237

No. 793, 26c, vert.: a, Kritosaurus. b, Triceratops. c, Hypselosaurus. d, Yingshanosaurus.
No. 794, 80c: a, Hadrosaurus. b, Pterodaustro. c, Agilisaurus. d, Amargasaurus.
No. 795, 80c, vert.: a, Corythosaurus. b, Dryosaurus. c, Euoplocephalus. d, Compsognathus.
No. 796, $2, Ornithomimus. No. 797, $2, Archaeopteryx. No. 798, $2, Deinonychus, vert.

2004, Oct. 13 Sheets of 4, #a-d

793-795 A237 Set of 3 15.00 15.00

Souvenir Sheets

796-798 A237 Set of 3 12.00 12.00

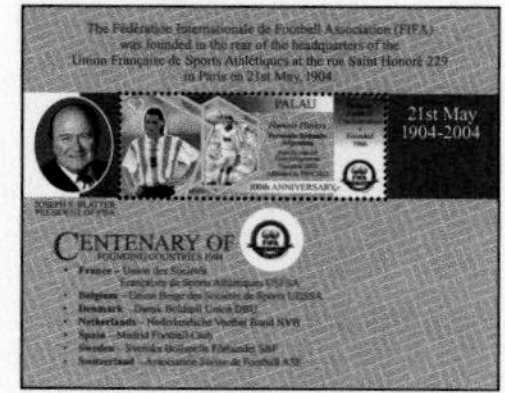

FIFA (Fédération Internationale de Football Association), Cent. — A238

No. 799: a, Diego Maradona. b, David Seaman. c, Andreas Brehme. d, Paul Ince.
$2, Fernando Redondo.

2004, Oct. 27 *Perf. 12¾x12½*

799 A238 80c Sheet of 4, #a-d 6.50 6.50

Souvenir Sheet

800 A238 $2 multi 4.00 4.00

National Basketball Association Players — A239

Designs: No. 801, 26c, Chris Bosh, Toronto Raptors. No. 802, 26c, Tim Duncan, San Antonio Spurs. No. 803, 26c, Kevin Garnett, Minnesota Timberwolves.

2004, Nov. 3 *Perf. 14*

801-803 A239 Set of 3 1.60 1.60

Each stamp printed in sheets of 12.

Christmas A240

Paintings of Madonna and Child by: 37c, Quentin Metsys. 60c, Adolphe William Bouguereau. 80c, William Dyce. $1, Carlo Crivelli.
$2, Peter Paul Rubens, vert.

2004, Dec. 23 *Perf. 14¼*

804-807 A240 Set of 4 5.75 5.75

Souvenir Sheet

808 A240 $2 multi 4.00 4.00

Miniature Sheet

Palau — Republic of China Diplomatic Relations, 5th Anniv. — A241

No. 809: a, Agricultural products. b, Republic of China Navy ship. c, Ngarachamayong Cultural Center. d, Palau National Museum.

2004, Dec. 29 *Perf. 14*

809 A241 80c Sheet of 4, #a-d 6.50 6.50

Souvenir Sheet

New Year 2005 (Year of the Rooster) A242

No. 810: a, Rooster facing right, tail feathers at LL. b, Rooster facing left, tail feathers at LR. c, Rooster facing right, no tail feathers at LL. d, Rooster facing left, no tail feathers at LR.

2005, Jan. 26 Litho. *Perf. 12½*

810 A242 50c Sheet of 4, #a-d 4.00 4.00

Souvenir Sheet

Rotary International, Cent. — A243

No. 811: a, Rotary International emblem. b, Rotary Centennial bell. c, Flags of Rotary International, US, Great Britain, Canada, Germany, China and Italy. d, James Wheeler Davidson.

2005, Apr. 4 *Perf. 14*

811 A243 80c Sheet of 4, #a-d 6.50 6.50

Friedrich von Schiller (1759-1805), Writer — A244

No. 812 — Schiller facing: a, Right (sepia tone). b, Right (color). c, Left (sepia tone).
$2, Facing left, diff.

2005, Apr. 4

812 A244 $1 Sheet of 3, #a-c 6.00 6.00

Souvenir Sheet

813 A244 $2 multi 4.00 4.00

Hans Christian Andersen (1805-75), Author — A245

No. 814, vert. — Book covers: a, Hans Christian Andersen Fairy Tales. b, Hans Christian Andersen's The Ugly Duckling. c, Tales of Hans Christian Andersen.
$2, The Little Match Girl.

2005, Apr. 4

814 A245 $1 Sheet of 3, #a-c 6.00 6.00

Souvenir Sheet

815 A245 $2 multi 4.00 4.00

Battle of Trafalgar, Bicent. A246

Various ships in battle: 37c, 55c, 80c, $1.
$2, Admiral Horatio Nelson Wounded During Battle of Trafalgar.

2005, Apr. 4 *Perf. 14¼*

816-819 A246 Set of 4 5.50 5.50

Souvenir Sheet

820 A246 $2 multi 4.00 4.00

End of World War II, 60th Anniv. A247

No. 821, 80c — Dambuster Raid: a, Pilots review routes prior to mission. b, Dambuster crew. c, Ground crews prepare Lancaster bomber. d, Bomber over Möhne Dam.
No. 822, 80c — Battle of Kursk: a, Russian tanks move forward. b, Tank commanders review maps. c, Russian and German armor clash. d, Destroyed German tank.
No. 823, $2, Squadron 617 leader Guy Gibson and "Highball Bouncing Bomb." No. 824, $2, Russian troops converge on destroyed German tank.

2005, May 9 *Perf. 13½*

Sheets of 4, #a-d

821-822 A247 Set of 2 13.00 13.00

Souvenir Sheets

823-824 A247 Set of 2 8.00 8.00

Jules Verne (1828-1905), Writer — A248

No. 825, horiz.: a, 20,000 Leagues Under the Sea. b, Mysterious Island. c, Journey to the Center of the Earth.
$2, Around the World in 80 Days.

2005, June 7 *Perf. 12¾*

825 A248 $1 Sheet of 3, #a-c 6.00 6.00

Souvenir Sheet

826 A248 $2 multi 4.00 4.00

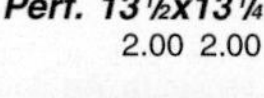

Pope John Paul II (1920-2005) — A249

2005, June 27 *Perf. 13½x13¼*

827 A249 $1 multi 2.00 2.00

A250

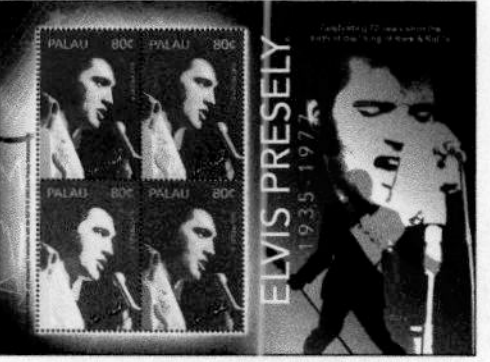

Elvis Presley (1935-77) — A251

No. 829 — Color of Presley: a, Blue. b, Green. c, Yellow. d, Orange.

2005, July 2 *Perf. 14*

828 A250 80c multi 1.60 1.60

829 A251 80c Sheet of 4, #a-d 6.50 6.50

No. 828 printed in sheets of 4.

Trains Type of 2004

No. 830: a, Birney N62 Interurban. b, C62-2-103103. c, WR MO 2007. d, Atchison, Topeka & Santa Fe locomotive 314.
$2, Royal Hudson #2860, vert.

2005 ***Perf. 13¼x13½***
830 A235 80c Sheet of 4, #a-d 6.50 6.50

Souvenir Sheet
Perf. 13½x13¼
831 A235 $2 multi 4.00 4.00

V-J Day, 60th Anniv. A252

No. 832, vert.: a, Audie Murphy. b, John F. Kennedy. c, Fleet Admiral Chester W. Nimitz. d, Marines recapture Guam from the Japanese.
$2, Sailors going home.

2005, June 7 **Litho.** ***Perf. 12¾***
832 A252 80c Sheet of 4, #a-d 6.50 6.50

Souvenir Sheet
833 A252 $2 multi 4.00 4.00

Miniature Sheet

Expo 2005, Aichi, Japan A253

No. 834: a, Seagulls. b, The cosmos. c, Koala. d, Childbirth.

2005, June 27 ***Perf. 12***
834 A253 80c Sheet of 4, #a-d 6.50 6.50

Sailing A254

No. 835: a, Tepukei. b, Tainui. c, Palauan canoe. d, Yap outrigger.
$2, Kon-Tiki.

2005, June 27 ***Perf. 12¾***
835 A254 80c Sheet of 4, #a-d 6.50 6.50

Souvenir Sheet
836 A254 $2 multi 4.00 4.00

World Cup Soccer Championships, 75th Anniv. — A255

No. 837, $1 — Scene from final match of: a, 1954. b, 1966. c, 1974.
No. 838, $1: a, Scene from 2002 final match. b, Lothar Matthias. c, Gerd Muller.
No. 839, $2, Sepp Herberger. No. 840, $2, Franz Beckenbauer.

2005, July 19 ***Perf. 12***
Sheets of 3, #a-c
837-838 A255 Set of 2 12.00 12.00

Souvenir Sheets
839 A255 $2 multi 4.00 4.00
Perf. 12¾
840 A255 $2 multi 4.00 4.00

No. 840 contains one 42x28mm stamp.

Vatican City No. 61 — A256

2005, Aug. 9 ***Perf. 13x13¼***
841 A256 37c multi .75 .75

Printed in sheets of 12.

Miniature Sheet

Taipei 2005 Intl. Stamp Exhibition — A257

No. 842: a, Wildeve rose. b, Graham Thomas rose. c, Crocus rose. d, Tes of the d'Urbervilles rose.

2005, Aug. 19 ***Perf. 14***
842 A257 80c Sheet of 4, #a-d 6.50 6.50

Miniature Sheet

Items from National Museum A258

No. 843: a, Decorated bowl, light yellow background. b, Potsherds, dull rose background. c, Sculpture with three people, blue background. d, Model of native house, light yellow background. e, Lidded container with strings. f, Cannon. g, Drawing of man on ship. h, Drawing of native craftwork. i, Bird-shaped figurine. j, Decorated bowl, pink background.

2005, Sept. 30
843 A258 37c Sheet of 10, #a-j 7.50 7.50

Pope Benedict XVI — A259

2005, Nov. 21 ***Perf. 13¾x13½***
844 A259 80c multi 1.60 1.60

Printed in sheets of 4.

Christmas — A260

Paintings: 37c, Madonna and Child, by Daniel Seghers. 60c, Madonna and Child, by Raphael. 80c, The Rest on the Flight to Egypt, by Gerard David. $1, Granducci Madonna, by Raphael.
$2, Madonna and Child, by Bartolome Esteban Murillo.

2005, Dec. 21 ***Perf. 14***
845-848 A260 Set of 4 5.75 5.75

Souvenir Sheet
849 A260 $2 multi 4.00 4.00

New Year 2006 (Year of the Dog) — A261

2006, Jan. 3 ***Perf. 13¼***
850 A261 50c multi 1.00 1.00

Printed in sheets of 4.

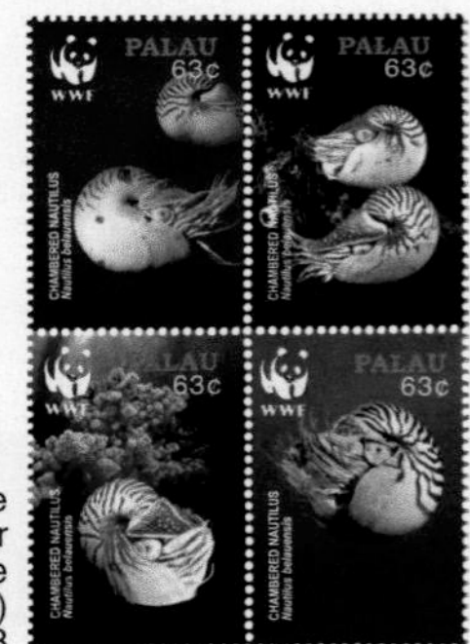

Birds — A262

Designs: 24c, Black oystercatcher. 39c, Great blue heron, vert.

2006, Feb. 21 **Litho.** ***Perf. 12***
851 A262 24c multi .50 .50
852 A262 39c multi .80 .80

Worldwide Fund for Nature (WWF) A263

No. 853 — Chambered nautilus: a, Two facing right. b, Two facing left. c, One, near coral. d, One, no coral.

2006, Feb. 21 ***Perf. 12¾***
853 A263 63c Block of 4, #a-d 5.25 5.25
e. Sheet, 2 each #853a-853d 10.50 10.50

World of Sea and Reef Type of 1986 Redrawn

Miniature Sheet

No. 854: a, Spear fisherman. b, Native raft. c, Sailing canoes. d, Rock islands, sailfish. e, Inter-island boat, flying fish. f, Bonefish. g, Common jack. h, Mackerel. i, Sailfish. j, Barracuda. k, Triggerfish. l, Dolphinfish. m, Spear fisherman, grouper. n, Manta ray. o, Marlin. p, Parrotfish. q, Wrasse. r, Red snapper. s, Herring. t, Dugong. u, Surgeonfish. v, Leopard ray. w, Hawksbill turtle. x, Needlefish. y, Tuna. z, Octopus. aa, Clownfish, ab, Squid. ac, Grouper. ad, Moorish idol. ae, Queen conch. af, Squirrelfish. ag, Starfish, sting ray. ah, Lionfish. ai, Angelfish. aj, Butterflyfish. ak, Spiny lobster. al, Mangrove crab, am, Tridacna. an, Moray eel.

2006, May 29 **Litho.** ***Perf. 13***
854 Sheet of 40 14.50 14.50
a.-an. A19 18c Any single .35 .35

Washington 2006 World Philatelic Exhibition.

Souvenir Sheet

Wolfgang Amadeus Mozart (1756-91), Composer — A264

2006, June 23 ***Perf. 12¾***
855 A264 $2 multi 4.00 4.00

Queen Elizabeth II, 80th Birthday A265

No. 856 — Queen wearing crown or tiara with background color of: a, Tan. b, Red. c, Blue. d, Lilac.
$2, Sepia photograph.

2006, June 23 ***Perf. 14¼***
856 A265 84c Sheet of 4, #a-d 6.75 6.75

Souvenir Sheet
857 A265 $2 multi 4.00 4.00

Rembrandt (1606-69), Painter — A266

No. 858: a, Old Man in a Fur Hat. b, Head of a Man. c, An Old Man in a Cap. d, Portrait of an Old Man.
$2, Saskia With a Veil.

2006, June 23 ***Perf. 13¼***
858 A266 $1 Sheet of 4, #a-d 8.00 8.00

Size: 70x100mm
Imperf
859 A266 $2 multi 4.00 4.00

No. 858 contains four 38x50mm stamps.

A267

Space Achievements — A268

No. 860 — Inscription, "International Space Station": a, At left. b, At UR, in white. c, At LL. d, AT UR, in black.

No. 861, 75c — Viking 1: a, Viking orbiting Mars. b, Simulation of Viking on Mars. c, Viking probe. d, Solar panels. e, Picture from Viking on Mars, parts of spacecraft at right. f, Picture from Viking on Mars, large rock at right.

No. 862, 75c, vert. — First flight of Space Shuttle Columbia: a, Shuttle on launch pad. b, Half of shuttle, denomination at UL. c, Half of shuttle, denomination at UR. d, Mission emblem. e, Astronaut Robert Crippen. f, Commander John Young.

No. 863, $2, Sputnik 1. No. 864, $2, Apollo 11. No. 865, $2, Space Shuttle Columbia lift-ing off.

2006, July 10 ***Perf. 14¼***
860 A267 $1 Sheet of 4, #a-d 8.00 8.00

Sheets of 6, #a-f

861-862 A267 Set of 2 18.00 18.00

Souvenir Sheets

863-865 A268 Set of 3 12.00 12.00

Souvenir Sheet

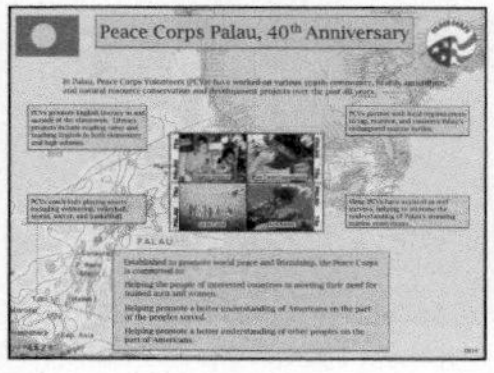

Peace Corps, 40th Anniv. A269

No. 867: a, English literacy. b, Sea turtle conservation. c, Swim camp. d, Reef survey.

2006, Nov. 6 Litho. ***Perf. 14x14¾***
867 A269 75c Sheet of 4, #a-d 6.00 6.00

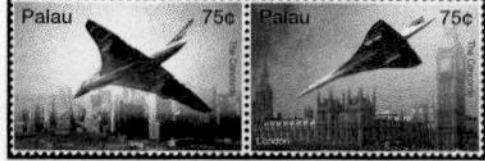

Concorde — A270

No. 868, 75c: a, Concorde over New York City. b, Concorde over London.
No. 869, 75c: a, Wheel. b, Nose.

2006, Dec. 20 ***Perf. 13¼x13½***

Pairs, #a-b

868-869 A270 Set of 2 6.00 6.00

Souvenir Sheet

Christmas — A271

No. 870 — Tree ornaments: a, Soldier. b, Santa Claus. c, Elf holding gift. d, Mice in sleigh.

2006 ***Perf. 13¼***
870 A271 84c Sheet of 4, #a-d 6.75 6.75

New Year 2007 (Year of the Pig) — A272

2007, Jan. 3 Litho. ***Perf. 13¼***
871 A272 75c multi 1.50 1.50

Printed in sheets of 4.

Souvenir Sheet

Marilyn Monroe (1926-62), Actress — A273

Various drawings.

2007, Feb. 15
872 A273 84c Sheet of 4, #a-d 6.75 6.75

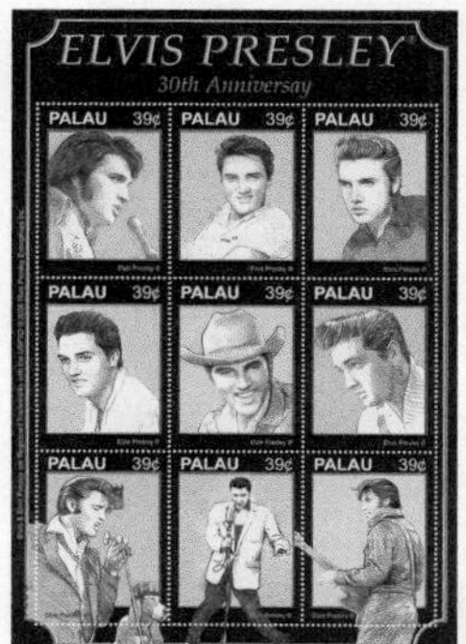

A274

Elvis Presley (1935-77) — A275

No. 873 — Presley with: a, Microphone. b, Shirt with design on pocket. c, Dark shirt. d, White shirt. e, Hat. f, Sweater. g, Dog. h, Jacket and microphone. i, Guitar.

No. 874 — Presley with or without guitar and background color of: a, Yellow. b, Red violet. c, Pale green. d, Red. e, Pale blue. f, Orange.

2007, Feb. 15 ***Perf. 13¼***
873 A274 39c Sheet of 9, #a-i 7.25 7.25

Perf. 14¼

874 A275 75c Sheet of 6, #a-f 9.00 9.00

Scouting, Cent. A276

No. 875, horiz. — Dove, Scouting flag, globe featuring Europe and frame color of: a, Purple. b, Bright pink. c, Green and blue.
$2, Lord Robert Baden-Powell.

2007, Feb. 15 ***Perf. 13¼***
875 A276 $1 Sheet of 3, #a-c 6.00 6.00

Souvenir Sheet

876 A276 $2 multi 4.00 4.00

Mushrooms — A277

No. 877, vert.: a, Entoloma hochstetteri. b, Aseroe rubra. c, Omphalotus nidiformis. d, Amanita sp.
$2, Aseroe rubra, diff.

2007, Feb. 15 ***Perf. 14¼x14***
877 A277 $1 Sheet of 4, #a-d 8.00 8.00

Souvenir Sheet

Perf. 14x14¼

878 A277 $2 multi 4.00 4.00

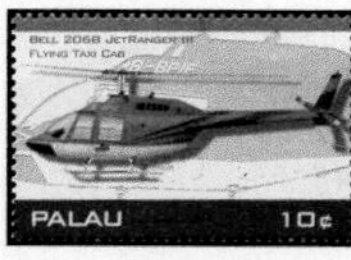

Helicopters, Cent. — A278

Designs: 10c, Bell 206B JetRanger III. 19c, McDonnell Douglas MD500D. 20c, McDonnell Douglas AH-64A Apache. 22c, Aérospatiale AS 332 Super Puma. 75c, Aérospatiale AS 355F-1 Twin Squirrel. 84c, MBB Eurocopter BO 105DBS/4. $1, Sikorsky MH-53J Pave Low III.
$2, Boeing Helicopters 234LR Chinook.

2007, Feb. 26 ***Perf. 14x14¼***
879-885 A278 Set of 7 6.75 6.75

Souvenir Sheet

886 A278 $2 multi 4.00 4.00

Souvenir Sheet

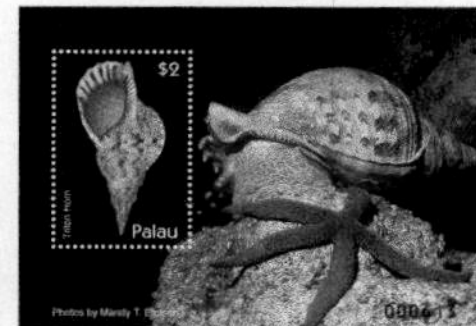

Triton Horn Shell A279

2007, Mar. 1 ***Perf. 13¼***
887 A279 $2 multi 4.00 4.00

Miniature Sheets

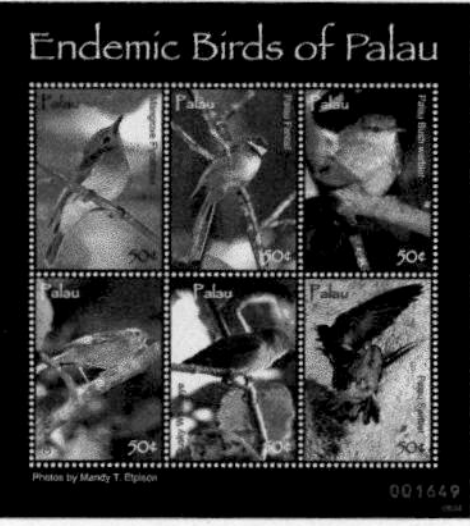

Birds A280

No. 888, 50c: a, Mangrove flycatcher. b, Palau fantail. c, Palau bush warbler. d, Giant white-eye. e, Dusky white-eye. f, Palau swiftlet.

No. 889, 50c: a, Palau owl. b, Palau fruit dove. c, Palau ground dove. d, Morning bird. e, Palau megapode. f, Rusty-capped kingfisher.

2007, Mar. 1 Litho.

Sheets of 6, #a-f

888-889 A280 Set of 2 12.00 12.00

Wedding of Queen Elizabeth II and Prince Philip, 60th Anniv. — A281

No. 890 — Photograph from: a, July 1947. b, November 1947.

2007, May 1
890 A281 60c Pair, #a-b 2.40 2.40

Printed in sheets containing three of each stamp.

Souvenir Sheet

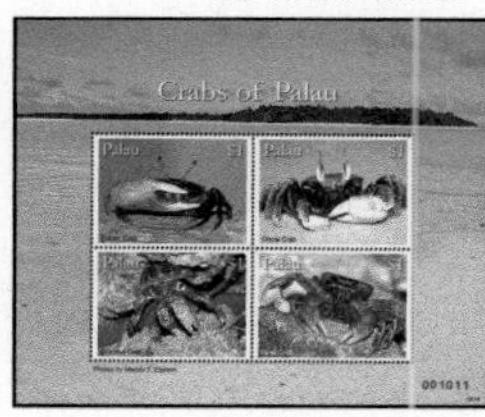

Crabs A282

No. 891: a, Fiddler crab. b, Ghost crab. c, Coconut crab. d, Land crab.

2007, May 16
891 A282 $1 Sheet of 4, #a-d 8.00 8.00

Flowers A283

No. 892: a, Plumeria. b, Streptosolen jamesonii. c, Heliconia pseudoaemygdiana. d, Mananita.
$2, Spider lily.

2007, May 16 ***Perf. 13¼***
892 A283 $1 Sheet of 4, #a-d 8.00 8.00

Souvenir Sheet

893 A283 $2 multi 4.00 4.00

Pope Benedict XVI — A284

2007, June 20
894 A284 41c multi .85 .85

Printed in sheets of 8.

Princess Diana (1961-97) — A285

No. 895 — Diana with: a, Earring at right, white dress. b, Choker. c, Earring at right. d, Earring at left, country name in white.
$2, Wearing veiled hat.

2007, June 20
895 A285 90c Sheet of 4, #a-d 7.25 7.25

Souvenir Sheet

896 A285 $2 multi 4.00 4.00

Butterflies — A286

Designs: 2c, Troides amphrysus. 3c, Paraeronia boebera. 4c, Delias catisa. 5c, Chilasa clytia. 11c, Ornithoptera goliath. 15c, Graphium delesserii. 20c, Euploea sp. 23c, Papilio euchenor. 26c, Ornithoptera tithonus. 41c, Hypolimnas misippus. 45c, Delias meeki. 50c, Papilio ulysses autolycus. 75c, Ornithoptera croesus. 90c, Trogonoptera brookiana. $1, Idea lynceus. $2, Parantica weiskei. $3, Graphium weiskei. $4, Ornithoptera goliath titan. $5, Attacus lorquini. $10, Delias henningia voconia.

2007, July 5 *Perf. 12½x13½*

No.	Design	Value	Color	Unused	Used
897	A286	2c	multi	.25	.25
898	A286	3c	multi	.25	.25
899	A286	4c	multi	.25	.25
900	A286	5c	multi	.25	.25
901	A286	11c	multi	.25	.25
902	A286	15c	multi	.30	.30
903	A286	20c	multi	.40	.40
904	A286	23c	multi	.50	.50
905	A286	26c	multi	.55	.55
906	A286	41c	multi	.85	.85
907	A286	45c	multi	.90	.90
908	A286	50c	multi	1.00	1.00
909	A286	75c	multi	1.50	1.50
910	A286	90c	multi	1.90	1.90
911	A286	$1	multi	2.00	2.00
912	A286	$2	multi	4.00	4.00
913	A286	$3	multi	6.00	6.00
914	A286	$4	multi	8.00	8.00
915	A286	$5	multi	10.00	10.00
916	A286	$10	multi	20.00	20.00
	Nos. 897-916 (20)			59.15	59.15

Miniature Sheet

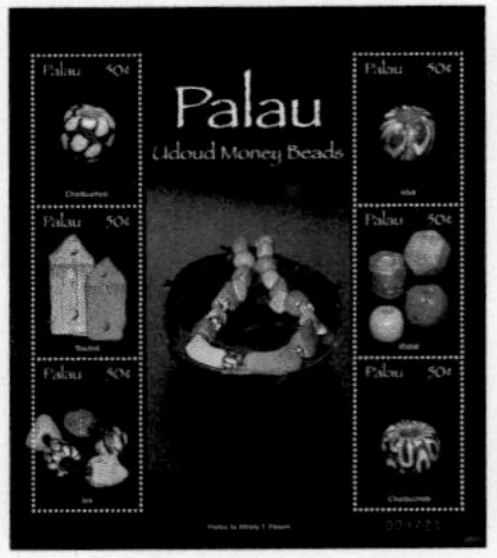

Udoud Money Beads A287

No. 917: a, Black and white Chelbucheb. b, Kluk. c, Bachel. d, Kldait. e, Iek. f, Green and white Chelbucheb.

2007, Mar. 1 **Litho.** *Perf. 13¼*
917 A287 50c Sheet of 6, #a-f 6.00 6.00

Miniature Sheet

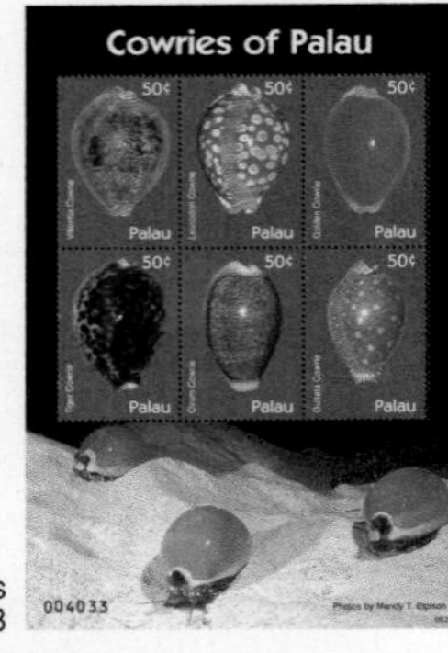

Cowries A288

No. 918: a, Valentia cowrie. b, Leucodon cowrie. c, Golden cowrie. d, Tiger cowrie. e, Ovum cowrie. f, Guttata cowrie.

2007, Mar. 1
918 A288 50c Sheet of 6, #a-f 6.00 6.00

Miniature Sheet

Children and Wildlife A289

No. 919: a, Praying mantis. b, Boy holding lobster. c, Boy holding bat. d, Dolphins.

2007, Mar. 1
919 A289 75c Sheet of 4, #a-d, + 4 labels 6.00 6.00

Birds of Southeast Asia — A290

No. 920: a, Red-billed leiothrix. b, Unidentified bird. c, Wahne's parotia. d, White-bellied yuhina.
$2, Wilson's bird-of-paradise.

2007, May 16
920 A290 80c Sheet of 4, #a-d 6.50 6.50

Souvenir Sheet

921 A290 $2 multi 4.00 4.00

Tropical Fish A291

No. 922: a, Boxfish. b, Copperband butterflyfish. c, Long-nosed hawkfish. d, Emperor angelfish.
$2, Firefish.

2007, May 16
922 A291 80c Sheet of 4, #a-d 6.50 6.50

Souvenir Sheet

923 A291 $2 multi 4.00 4.00

Miniature Sheet

Intl. Holocaust Remembrance Day — A292

No. 924 — United Nations diplomats and delegates: a, Eduardo J. Sevilla Somoza, Nicaragua. b, Aminu Bashir Wali, Nigeria. c, Stuart Beck, Palau. d, Ricardo Alberto Arias, Panama. e, Robert G. Aisi, Papua New Guinea. f, Eladio Loizaga, Paraguay. g, Jorge Voto-Bernales, Peru. h, Ban-Ki Moon, United Nations Secretary General.

2007, Nov. 20
924 A292 50c Sheet of 8, #a-h 8.00 8.00

Christmas — A293

Color of ornament: 22c, Red. 26c, Green. 41c, Blue. 90c, Yellow brown.

2007, Nov. 20 **Litho.** *Perf. 12*
925-928 A293 Set of 4 3.75 3.75

32nd America's Cup Yacht Races — A294

Various yachts.

2007, Dec. 13 *Perf. 13¼*

No.			Unused	Used
929	Strip of 4		8.50	8.50
a.	A294 26c multi		.50	.50
b.	A294 80c multi		1.60	1.60
c.	A294 $1.14 multi		2.40	2.40
d.	A294 $2 multi		4.00	4.00

New Year 2008 (Year of the Rat) — A295

2008, Jan. 2 *Perf. 12*
930 A295 50c multi 1.00 1.00

Printed in sheets of 4.

Miniature Sheet

Pres. John F. Kennedy (1917-63) — A296

No. 931: a, Crowd, Kennedy campaign poster. b, Kennedy shaking hands with crowd. c, Kennedy at lectern. d, Kennedy behind microphones, with hands showing.

2008, Jan. 2 *Perf. 14¼*
931 A296 90c Sheet of 4, #a-d 7.25 7.25

2008 Summer Olympics, Beijing — A297

No. 932 — Items and athletes from 1908 London Olympics: a, Fencing poster. b, Program cover. c, Wyndham Halswelle, track gold medalist. d, Dorando Pietri, marathon runner.

2008, Jan. 8
932 A297 50c Sheet of 4, #a-d 4.00 4.00

Taiwan Tourist Attractions — A298

No. 933: a, National Taiwan Democracy Memorial Hall. b, Chinese ornamental garden, Taipei. c, Taipei skyline. d, Eastern coast of Taiwan.
$2, Illuminated temple, Southern Taiwan.

2008, Apr. 11 *Perf. 11½*
933 A298 50c Sheet of 4, #a-d 4.00 4.00

Souvenir Sheet

Perf. 13¼

934 A298 $2 multi 4.00 4.00

2008 Taipei Intl. Stamp Exhibition. No. 933 contains four 40x30mm stamps.

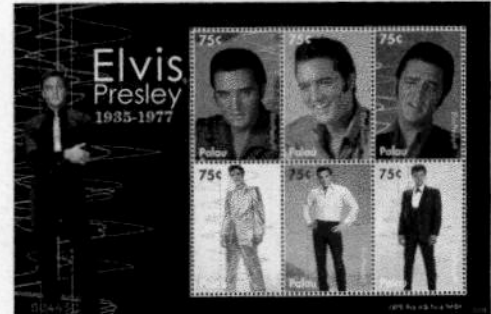

2008 World Stamp Championships, Israel — A299

2008, May 14 *Imperf.*
935 A299 $3 multi 6.00 6.00

Miniature Sheet

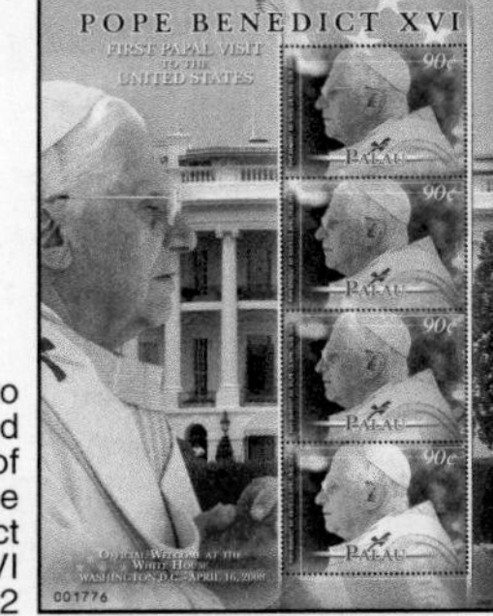

Sir Edmund Hillary (1919-2008), Mountaineer — A300

No. 936: a, Hillary and Prince Charles. b, Hillary. c, Hillary and Nepal Prime Minister Lokendra Bahadur Chand. d, Hillary with bird on shoulder.

2008, May 28 *Perf. 13¼*
936 A300 90c Sheet of 4, #a-d 7.25 7.25

Miniature Sheet

Elvis Presley (1935-77) — A301

No. 301 — Presley wearing: a, Gray shirt. b, Green shirt. c, Red shirt. d, Gold suit. e, White shirt, no jacket. f, White shirt, black suit.

2008, June 12
937 A301 75c Sheet of 6, #a-f 9.00 9.00

Miniature Sheet

Visit to United States of Pope Benedict XVI A302

No. 938 — Pope Benedict XVI and US flag faintly in background: a, Part of flag star on Pope's head (no frame line above denomination). b, Red stripe under "au" of "Palau." c, Red stripe under "P" of Palau. d, Red stripe under entire country name.

2008, July 28
938 A302 90c Sheet of 4, #a-d 7.25 7.25

Miniature Sheets

Muhammad Ali, Boxer — A303

No. 939 — Ali: a, In suit, clenching fist. b, Behind microphones, with both arms raised, with hands around his right forearm. c, Behind microphones, with towel around neck. d, Behind microphones, scratching head. e, Behind microphones, raising arms, with crowd. f, With hand of Howard Cosell on shoulder.

No. 940 — Ali: a, Pointing up, wearing short-sleeved shirt. b, Pointing to left, wearing suit. c, Making fist, in robe. d, Pointing to right, wearing suit.

2008, Sept. 22 ***Perf. 11½x12***

939 A303 75c Sheet of 6, #a-f 9.00 9.00

Perf. 13¼

940 A303 94c Sheet of 4, #a-d 7.50 7.50

No. 940 contains four 50x37mm stamps.

Miniature Sheets

Space Exploration, 50th Anniv. (in 2007) — A304

No. 941, 75c — Mir Space Station: a, With black background. b, With Earth at bottom. c, Technical drawing. d, Above clouds. e, With Space Shuttle Atlantis. f, Against starry background.

No. 942, 75c: a, Pres. John F. Kennedy. b, Apollo 11 Command Module. c, Apollo 11 Lunar Module, Earth and Moon. d, Lunar Module and Moon. e, Kennedy, Astronaut John Glenn and Friendship 7 capsule. f, Edwin "Buzz" Aldrin on Moon.

No. 943, 94c: a, Technical drawing of R-7 launch vehicle. b, Sputnik 1, antennae at right. c, Technical drawing of Sputnik 1. d, Sputnik 1, antennae at left.

No. 944, 94c: a, Yuri Gagarin, first man in space, wearing medals. b, Technical drawing of Vostok rocket. c, Technical drawing of Vostok 1. d, Gagarin in space helmet.

2008, Sept. 22 ***Perf. 13¼***

Sheets of 6, #a-f

941-942 A304 Set of 2 18.00 18.00

Sheets of 4, #a-d

943-944 A304 Set of 2 15.00 15.00

Miniature Sheets

Star Trek The Next Generation — A305

No. 945: a, Capt. Jean-Luc Picard. b, Lt. Commander Data. c, Commander William T. Riker. d, Counselor Deanna Troi. e, Lt. Commander Geordi La Forge. f, Lieutenant Worf.

No. 946: a, Wesley Crusher. b, Worf. c, Picard. d, Dr. Beverly Crusher.

2008, Dec. 4 ***Perf. 11½***

945 A305 75c Sheet of 6, #a-f 9.00 9.00

Perf. 13¼

946 A305 94c Sheet of 4, #a-d 7.50 7.50

No. 946 contains four 37x50mm stamps.

Christmas — A306

Designs: 22c, Angel holding candle. 26c, Angel with violin. 42c, Angel and conifer wreath. 94c, Angel in light display.

2008, Dec. 11 Litho. ***Perf. 14x14¾***

947-950 A306 Set of 4 3.75 3.75

Inauguration of US Pres. Barack Obama — A307

No. 951, horiz. — Pres. Obama: a, Holding microphone. b, Smiling, denomination at LL. c, Smiling, denomination at UL. d, With index finger raised.

$2, Head of Pres. Obama.

2009, Jan. 20 ***Perf. 11½x11¼***

951 A307 94c Sheet of 4, #a-d 7.75 7.75

Souvenir Sheet

952 A307 $2 multi 4.00 4.00

No. 951 contains four 40x30mm stamps.

New Year 2009 (Year of the Ox) A308

No. 953 — Ox and Chinese characters in diamond in: a, Black. b, White.

2009, Jan. 26 ***Perf. 12***

953 A308 94c Horiz. pair, #a-b 4.00 4.00

Printed in sheets containing two pairs.

Miniature Sheet

Teenage Mutant Ninja Turtles, 25th Anniv. A309

No. 954: a, Donatello. b, Raphael. c, Michelangelo. d, Leonardo.

2009, Feb. 25 ***Perf. 13¼***

954 A309 94c Sheet of 4, #a-d 7.75 7.75

Miniature Sheets

A310

Michael Jackson (1958-2009), Singer — A311

No. 955 — Background color: a, Red (Jackson with mouth open). b, Green. c, Blue. d, Red (Jackson with mouth closed).

No. 956 — Jackson dancing with denomination at: a, 28c, Right. b, 28c, Left. c, 75c, Right. d, 75c, Left.

2009, Sept. 3 ***Perf. 12x11½***

955 A310 44c Sheet of 4, #a-d 3.75 3.75

956 A311 Sheet of 4, #a-d 4.25 4.25

Miniature Sheet

Palau Pacific Resort, 25th Anniv. A312

No. 957: a, Four beach umbrellas, shadow of palm trees. b, Palm trees near beach under cloudy skies. c, Resort at night. d, Lounge chairs on beach. e, Swimming pool. f, Palm tree, two beach umbrellas.

2009, Oct. 5 ***Perf. 11½***

957 A312 26c Sheet of 6, #a-f 3.25 3.25

Dolphins — A313

Designs: 28c, Spinner dolphin. 44c, Hourglass dolphin. 98c, Costero. $1.05, Risso's dolphin.

No. 962: a, Heaviside's dolphin. b, Chilean dolphin. c, Dusky dolphin. d, Commerson's dolphin. e, Fraser's dolphin. f, Striped dolphin.

2009, Oct. 13 ***Perf. 14¾x14***

958-961 A313 Set of 4 5.50 5.50

962 A313 75c Sheet of 6, #a-f 9.00 9.00

Shells — A314

Designs: 28c, Morula musiva. 44c, Littoraria articulata. 98c, Architectonica perdix. $1.05, Scalptia crossei.

No. 967: a, Pugilina cochlidium. b, Epitonium scalare. c, Ellobium tornatelliforme. d, Polinices sebae. e, Cyclophorus siamensis. f, Acrosterigma maculosum.

2009, Oct. 13

963-966 A314 Set of 4 5.50 5.50

967 A314 75c Sheet of 6, #a-f 9.00 9.00

A315

Cats A316

No. 968: a, Devon Rex cream lynx point sirex. b, Ocicat chocolate. c, Asian chocolate smoke. d, Burmilla lilac shaded. e, Egyptian Mau bronze. f, Himalayan blue tortie point.

No. 969: a, Turkish Van and fireplace. b, Tiffany. c, Turkish Van, diff. d, Birman seal lynx point.

No. 970, $2, Golden Persian. No. 971, $2, Red silver tabby.

2009, Oct. 13 ***Perf. 14***

968 A315 75c Sheet of 6, #a-f 9.00 9.00

969 A315 94c Sheet of 4, #a-d 7.75 7.75

Souvenir Sheets

970-971 A316 Set of 2 8.00 8.00

Miniature Sheet

Fish A317

No. 972: a, Two-spot snappers. b, Goggle-eye. c, Bluestreak cardinalfish. d, Bluefin trevally. e, Rainbow runners. f, Fire goby.

2009, Oct. 13 ***Perf. 11½x11¼***

972 A317 75c Sheet of 6, #a-f 9.00 9.00

Miniature Sheet

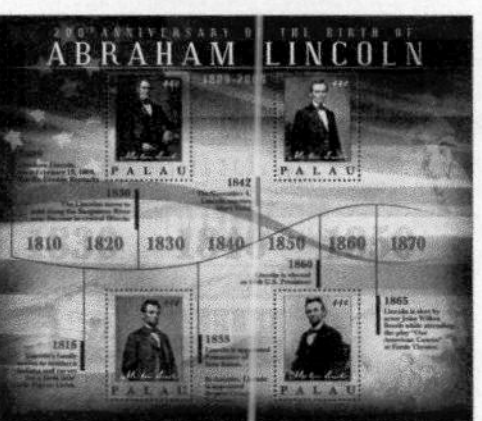

Pres. Abraham Lincoln (1809-65) — A318

No. 973 — Photographs of Lincoln: a, Hands showing, denomination in white. b, Hands not showing, denomination in white. c, Hands not showing, denomination in black. d, Hand showing, denomination in black.

2009, Oct. 13 ***Perf. 11¼x11½***

973 A318 44c Sheet of 4, #a-d 3.75 3.75

Souvenir Sheet

Visit of Pope Benedict XVI to Yad Vashem Holocaust Memorial, Israel — A319

No. 974 — Pope Benedict XVI: a, 98c, Looking at flame (30x40mm). b, $2, Praying in front of flowers (60x40mm).

2009, Oct. 13
974 A319 Sheet of 3, #974b, 2 #974a 8.00 8.00

Souvenir Sheets

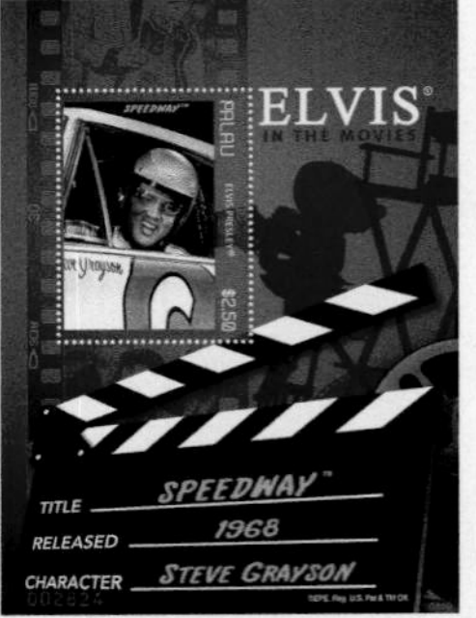

A320

A321

SPEEDWAY

A322

ELVIS PRESLEY "SPEEDWAY"

Elvis Presley (1935-77) — A323

2009, Oct. 13 *Perf. 13¼*
975 A320 $2.50 multi 5.00 5.00
976 A321 $2.50 multi 5.00 5.00
977 A322 $2.50 multi 5.00 5.00
978 A323 $2.50 multi 5.00 5.00
Nos. 975-978 (4) 20.00 20.00

A324

Fish — A325

Designs: 1c, Giant trevally. 2c, Pink anemonefish. 3c, Gray reef shark. 4c, Leaf fish. 5c, Scissor-tailed fusiliers. 26c, Helfrich's dartfish. 44c, Bigscale soldierfish. $1, Peach anthias. $2, Spotted eagle ray. $3, African pompano. $4, Harlequin grouper. $5, Pyramid butterflyfish. $10, Longnose hawkfish.

2009, Oct. 13 Litho. *Perf. 11¾x12¼*
979 A324 1c multi .25 .25
980 A324 2c multi .25 .25
981 A324 3c multi .25 .25
982 A324 4c multi .25 .25
983 A324 5c multi .25 .25
984 A325 26c multi .55 .55
985 A324 44c multi .90 .90
986 A324 $1 multi 2.00 2.00
987 A324 $2 multi 4.00 4.00
988 A324 $3 multi 6.00 6.00
989 A324 $4 multi 8.00 8.00
990 A324 $5 multi 10.00 10.00
991 A324 $10 multi 20.00 20.00
Nos. 979-991 (13) 52.70 52.70

Worldwide Fund for Nature (WWF) — A326

No. 992 — Red lionfish: a, Two fish. b, One fish facing forward, brown background. c, One fish facing right. d, One fish facing forward, blue background.

2009, Nov. 9 Litho. *Perf. 13¼*
992 A326 53c Block of 4, #a-d 4.25 4.25
a. Sheet of 8, 2 each #992a-992d 8.50 8.50

Miniature Sheet

First Man on the Moon, 40th Anniv. A327

No. 993: a, Lunar Module before landing. b, Lunar Module ascent stage. c, Command module. d, Mission patch and plaque left on Moon.

2009, Dec. 10 *Perf. 12x11½*
993 A327 98c Sheet of 4, #a-d 8.00 8.00

Intl. Year of Astronomy.

Christmas — A328

Designs: 26c, Christmas ornaments and stocking on coral. 44c, Wreath and "Merry Christmas." 98c, Gingerbread house with flag of Palau. $2, Wreath and bell.

2009, Dec. 10 *Perf. 14¼x14¾*
994-997 A328 Set of 4 7.50 7.50

Miniature Sheet

Charles Darwin (1809-82), Naturalist — A329

No. 998: a, HMS Beagle. b, Captain Robert Fitzroy. c, Sextant of HMS Beagle. d, Diagram of HMS Beagle. e, Darwin. f, Darwin's report on the zoology of the voyage of the HMS Beagle.

2010, Mar. 2 *Perf. 13¼*
998 A329 75c Sheet of 6, #a-f 9.00 9.00

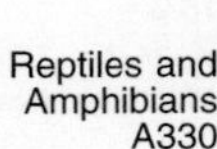

Reptiles and Amphibians A330

Designs: 26c, Bufo marinus. 44c, Chelonia mydas. 98c, Lepidodactylus lugubris. $1.05, Varanus olivaceus.

No. 1003: a, Northern forest dragon. b, Common house gecko. c, Hawksbill turtle. d, Indopacific tree gecko. e, Amboina box turtle. f, Flying dragon.

2010, Mar. 2 *Perf. 12*
999-1002 A330 Set of 4 5.50 5.50
1003 A330 75c Sheet of 6, #a-f 9.00 9.00

Pope John Paul II (1920-2005) — A331

2010, Apr. 22 *Perf. 12x11½*
1004 A331 75c multi 1.50 1.50

Printed in sheets of 4. Compare with type A451.

Miniature Sheet

Pres. Abraham Lincoln (1809-65) — A332

No. 1005 — Lincoln: a, Without beard. b, With beard, no cowlick on forehead. c, With beard, cowlick on forehead, point of shirt above "M." d, With beard, cowlick on forehead, point of shirt above "LIN."

2010, Apr. 22 *Perf. 11½*
1005 A332 75c Sheet of 4, #a-d 6.00 6.00

Miniature Sheet

Elvis Presley (1935-77) — A333

No. 1005 — Presley: a, Facing backwards. b, Wearing sequined suit. c, With hand and microphone cord at left. d, Wearing suit with bordered lapels.

2010, Apr. 22 *Perf. 11½*
1006 A333 75c Sheet of 4, #a-d 6.00 6.00

Girl Guides, Cent. A334

No. 1007, horiz.: a, Two Girl Guides in blue uniforms. b, Two Girl Guides, one wearing cap. c, Girl Guide playing bongo drum. d, Four Girl Guides.

$2.50, Girl Guide in green uniform.

2010, June 9 *Perf. 11½x12*
1007 A334 94c Sheet of 4, #a-d 7.75 7.75

Souvenir Sheet
Perf. 11½

1008 A334 $2.50 multi 5.00 5.00

Souvenir Sheet

Governmental Buildings — A335

No. 1009: a, Executive Building. b, OEK Congress. c, Judiciary Building.

2010, July 1 *Perf. 13½*
1009 A335 $1 Sheet of 3, #a-c 6.00 6.00

Princess Diana (1961-97) — A336

No. 1010 — Princess Diana wearing: a, Tiara. b, Blue violet gown.

2010, Sept. 8 *Perf. 12x11½*
1010 A336 75c Pair, #a-b 3.00 3.00

Printed in sheets containing two pairs.

Miniature Sheet

Mother Teresa (1910-97), Humanitarian — A337

No. 1011 — Mother Teresa and: a, Blue sky behind name and country name. b, Blue sky behind country name, cloud behind name. c, Cloud behind country name, blue sky partly behind name. d, Blue sky partly behind country name, cloud behind name.

2010, Sept. 8 *Perf. 11½*
1011 A337 94c Sheet of 4, #a-d 7.75 7.75

Henri Dunant (1828-1910), Founder of Red Cross — A338

No. 1012 Dunant and: a, Frédèric Passy. b, Czar Nicholas II, c, Henri Dufour. d, Bertha von Suttner.
$2.50, Obverse and reverse of Nobel medal.

2010, Sept. 8 ***Perf. 11½x12***
1012 A338 94c Sheet of 4, #a-d 7.75 7.75

Souvenir Sheet
Perf. 11½
1013 A338 $2.50 multi 5.00 5.00

Paintings by Sandro Botticelli (1445-1510) — A339

No. 1014, vert.: a, Madonna and Child. b, Nastagio Degli Onesti. c, Calumny of Apelles. d, Primavera.
$2.50, Orazione Nell'Orto.

2010, Sept. 8 ***Perf. 12x11½***
1014 A339 94c Sheet of 4, #a-d 7.75 7.75

Souvenir Sheet
Perf. 11½
1015 A339 $2.50 multi 5.00 5.00

Souvenir Sheet

Issuance of the Penny Black, 170th Anniv. A340

No. 1016: a, Penny Black (Great Britain #1). b, Palau #2.

2010, Sept. 8 ***Perf. 13¼***
1016 A340 $2 Sheet of 2, #a-b 8.00 8.00

Christmas — A341

Paintings: 26c, Adoration of the Magi, by Leonardo da Vinci. 44c, Adoration of the Shepherds, by Carlo Crivelli. 98c, Adoration of the Magi, by Hieronymus Bosch. $2, Adoration of the Magi, by Albrecht Altdorfer.

2010, Sept. 8 ***Perf. 11½***
1017-1020 A341 Set of 4 7.50 7.50

Miniature Sheets

2010 World Cup Soccer Championships, South Africa — A342

No. 1021, 61c: a, Gabriel Heinze. b, Philipp Lahm. c, Javier Mascherano. d, Mesut Dezil. e, Angel Di Maria. f, Lukas Podolski.
No. 1022, 61c: a, Antolin Alcaraz. b, Cesc Fabregas. c, Dario Veron. d, Carlos Puyol. e, Victor Caceres. f, Xabi Alonso.

2010, Dec. 16 ***Perf. 12***

Sheets of 6, #a-f
1021-1022 A342 Set of 2 15.00 15.00

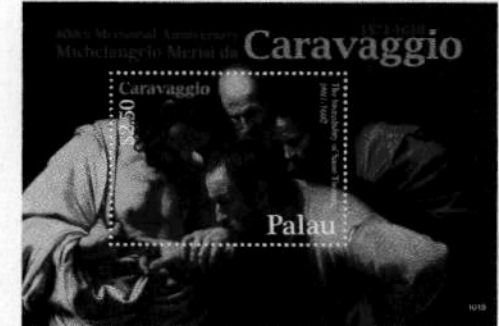

Paintings by Michelangelo Merisi da Caravaggio (1571-1610) — A343

No. 1023: a, Supper at Emmaus. b, Ecce Homo. c, Omnia Vincit Amor. d, Flagellazione di Cristo.
$2.50, The Incredulity of Saint Thomas.

2010, Dec. 16 ***Perf. 12***
1023 A343 94c Sheet of 4, #a-d 7.75 7.75

Souvenir Sheet
Perf. 12½
1024 A343 $2.50 multi 5.00 5.00

No. 1023 contains four 40x30mm stamps.

Pope Benedict XVI — A344

2010, Dec. 16 ***Perf. 12***
1025 A344 75c multi 1.50 1.50

Printed in sheets of 4 with slight color differences in the background.

Miniature Sheets

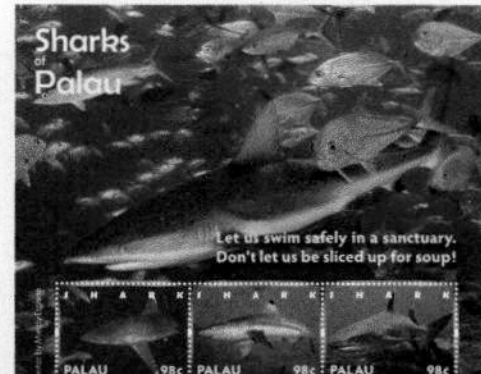

Sharks A346

Sea Turtles A347

Dugongs A348

No. 1027 — Shark with dorsal fin: a, Touching "R" in "Shark." b, Between "A" and "R" in "Shark." c, Touching "A" in "Shark."
No. 1028 — Sea turtle: a, Swimming left. b, At ocean floor. c, Swimming right.
No. 1029: a, Dugong at water's surface. b, Two dugongs. c, Dugong and fish.

Perf. 13 Syncopated

2010, Dec. 21 **Litho.**

1027	A346 98c	Sheet of 3, #a-c	6.00	6.00
1028	A347 98c	Sheet of 3, #a-c	6.00	6.00
1029	A348 98c	Sheet of 3, #a-c	6.00	6.00
		Nos. 1027-1029 (3)	18.00	18.00

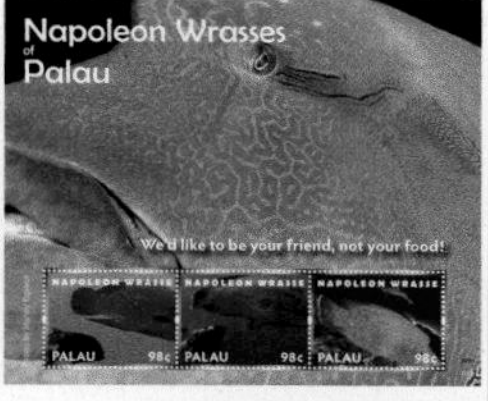

The top sheet, containing poorly cropped stamp images, was received by Palau postal officials but was never put on sale in Palau. The bottom sheet was sold by dealers, but was never received by Palau postal officials.

Miniature Sheet

Pres. Abraham Lincoln (1809-65) — A349

Various photographs of Lincoln.

2011, Mar. 11 ***Perf. 12***
1030 A349 75c Sheet of 4, #a-d 6.00 6.00

Miniature Sheet

Inauguration of Pres. John F. Kennedy, 50th Anniv. — A350

No. 1031 — Kennedy: a, Behind microphone. b, At inauguration. c, In rocking chair. d, Shaking person's hand.

2011, Mar. 11
1031 A350 75c Sheet of 4, #a-d 6.00 6.00

Miniature Sheet

Pres. Barack Obama's Visit to the United Nations A351

No. 1032 — Pres. Obama and: a, US flag. b, Kyrgyzstan Pres. Rosa Otunbaeva. c, Philippines Pres. Benigno Aquino III. d, United Nations flags.

2011, Mar. 11 ***Perf. 13 Syncopated***
1032 A351 75c Sheet of 4, #a-d 6.00 6.00

Indipex 2011 Intl. Philatelic Exhibition, New Delhi — A352

No. 1033: a, Bhagat Singh (1907-31), nationalist. b, Lal Bahadur Shastri (1904-66), Prime Minister. c, Subhas Chandra Bose (1897-1945), politician. d, Dr. Rajendra Prasad (1884-1963), politician. e, Jawaharlal Nehru (1889-1964), Prime Minister. f, Sardar Patel (1875-1950), Deputy Prime Minister.
$2.50, Mohandas K. Gandhi (1869-1948), independence leader.

2011, Mar. 11 ***Perf. 12***
1033 A352 50c Sheet of 6, #a-f 6.00 6.00

Souvenir Sheet
Perf. 13 Syncopated
1034 A352 $2.50 multi 5.00 5.00

Whales A353

No. 1035: a, Blainville's beaked whale. b, Shepherd's beaked whale. c, Cuvier's beaked whale. d, Baird's beaked whale. e, Stejneger's beaked whale. f, Ginkgo-toothed beaked whale.
$2.50, Pygmy sperm whale.

2011, Mar. 11 ***Perf. 13 Syncopated***
1035 A353 75c Sheet of 6, #a-f 9.00 9.00

Souvenir Sheet
1036 A353 $2.50 multi 5.00 5.00

Visit to Spain of Pope Benedict XVI A354

No. 1037: a, Pope Benedict XVI, Prince Felipe and Princess Letizia of Spain. b, Santiago de Compostela Cathedral. c, Pope Benedict XVI celebrating mass. d, King Juan Carlos and Queen Sofia of Spain.
$2.50, Pope Benedict XVI and Sagrada Familia Basilica, Barcelona, vert.

2011, Mar. 11 **Litho.**

1037 A354 94c Sheet of 4, #a-d 7.75 7.75

Souvenir Sheet

1038 A354 $2.50 multi 5.00 5.00

Miniature Sheet

Pres. Ronald Reagan (1911-2004) — A355

No. 1039: a, Pres. Reagan at podium. b, Pres. Reagan with wife, Nancy. c, Pres. Reagan. d, Pres. Reagan with Soviet Union General Secretary Mikhail Gorbachev.

2011, Apr. 5 ***Perf. 13 Syncopated***

1039 A355 98c Sheet of 4, #a-d 8.00 8.00

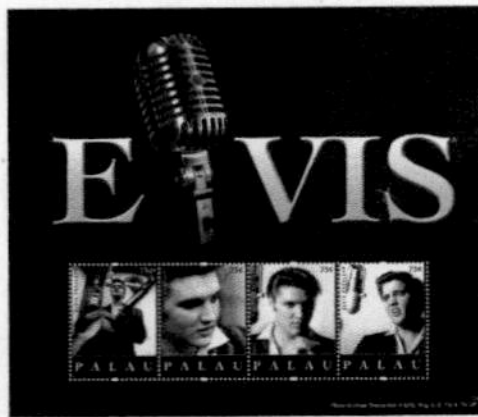

A356

A357

A358

A359

A360

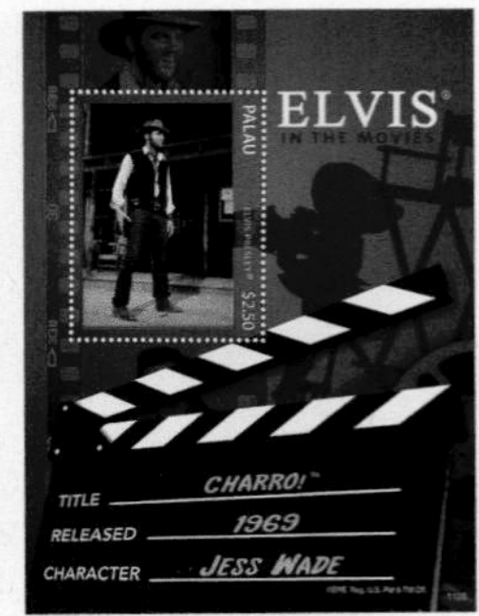

Elvis Presley (1935-77) — A361

No. 1040: a, Presley with guitar, two microphones. b, Presley facing right. c, Presley with closed mouth, microphone at left. d, Presley singing, microphone at left.

No. 1041 — Presley: a, With hand on ear. b, Microphone at left. c, Microphone at right, denomination in white. d, Microphone at right, denomination in black.

2011 ***Perf. 13 Syncopated***

1040 A356 75c Sheet of 4, #a-d 6.00 6.00
1041 A357 75c Sheet of 4, #a-d 6.00 6.00

Souvenir Sheets

Perf. 12¾

1042 A358 $2.50 multi 5.00 5.00
1043 A359 $2.50 multi 5.00 5.00
1044 A360 $2.50 multi 5.00 5.00
1045 A361 $2.50 multi 5.00 5.00
Nos. 1042-1045 (4) 20.00 20.00

Issued: Nos. 1040-1041, 7/14; Nos. 1042-1045, 4/5.

Beatification of Pope John Paul II — A362

No. 1046 — Pope John Paul II: a, With Queen Elizabeth II. b, Greeting crowd. c, Wearing miter. d, Holding paper.

$2.50, Wearing miter, priests in background.

2011, May 25 ***Perf. 13 Syncopated***

1046 A362 75c Sheet of 4, #a-d 6.00 6.00

Souvenir Sheet

Perf. 12¾

1047 A362 $2.50 multi 5.00 5.00

No. 1047 contains one 38x51mm stamp.

Wedding of Prince William and Catherine Middleton — A363

Designs: 98c, Couple.

No. 1049, $2, Prince William. No. 1050, $2, Catherine Middleton.

2011, June 17 ***Perf. 12x12½***

1048 A363 98c multi 2.00 2.00

Souvenir Sheets

Perf. 13½

1049-1050 A363 Set of 2 8.00 8.00

Nos. 1049-1050 each contain one 51x32mm triangular stamp.

Miniature Sheets

A364

Princess Diana (1961-97) — A365

No. 1051 — Princess Diana wearing: a, Black lace dress and choker on black ribbon. b, White dress. c, Pink hat. d, Black dress, no choker.

No. 1052 — Princess Diana wearing: a, Earring. b, Plaid jacket. c, Red Cross uniform. d, Black hat with veil.

2011, July 6 ***Perf. 13 Syncopated***

1051 A364 75c Sheet of 4, #a-d 6.00 6.00
1052 A365 75c Sheet of 4, #a-d 6.00 6.00

Taro Festival — A366

No. 1053 — Taro plant and inscription: a, Dung er a terrekaki. b, Renged. c, Meuarch. d, Okelang. e, Metengal e ngas. f, Kirang. g, Rriu. h, Ngerbachel. i, Saikerei. j, Oiremech. k, Terebkul. l, Esuuch. m, Dungersuul. n, Ngesuas. o, Kerdeu. p, Terrekaki. q, Ngiroilang. r, Dilisior. s, Brak. t, Ulechem. u, Homusted. v, Besechel. w, Ungildil. x, Urungel. y, Ngatmadei. z, Dois. aa, Bsachel. ab, Ochab. ac, Kirang (redil). ad, Ngeruuch.

2011, July 8 ***Perf. 12¾x13***

1053 Sheet of 30 18.00 18.00
a.-ad. A366 29c Any single .60 .60

Souvenir Sheet

Haruo I. Remeliik (1933-85), First President of Palau — A367

2011, July 8 ***Perf. 13¼***

1054 A367 $2 multi 4.00 4.00

Birds A368

No. 1055, 98c: a, Black-headed gull. b, Red-tailed tropicbird. c, Intermediate egret. d, Yellow bittern.

No., 1056, 98c, vert.: a, Cattle egret. b, Red-footed booby. c, Australian pelican. d, Little pied cormorant.

No. 1057, $2, Greater crested tern. No. 1058, $2, Brown noddy, vert.

2011, July 14 ***Perf. 13 Syncopated***

Sheets of 4, #a-d

1055-1056 A368 Set of 2 16.00 16.00

Souvenir Sheets

1057-1058 A368 Set of 2 8.00 8.00

Pres. Abraham Lincoln (1809-65) — A369

No. 1059 — Details from First Reading of the Emancipation Proclamation of President Lincoln, by Francis Bicknell Carpenter: a, Treasury Secretary Salmon P. Chase, Secretary of War Edwin M. Stanton. b, Lincoln. c, Secretary of the Navy Gideon Welles. d, Postmaster General Montgomery Blair, Interior Secretary, Caleb B. Smith, Secretary of State William H. Seward. e, Attorney General Edward Bates.

$2.50, Photograph of Lincoln.

2011, July 27 ***Perf. 11½x11¾***

1059 A369 60c Sheet of 5, #a-d 6.00 6.00

Souvenir Sheet

Perf. 12x12½

1060 A369 $2.50 multi 5.00 5.00

No. 1060 contains one 30x80mm stamp.

Miniature Sheet

Peace Corps, 50th Anniv. A370

No. 1061 — Peace Corps emblem and: a, Students and volunteer painting. b, Palauan host family and volunteers walking. c, Volunteer and teachers work on Internet project. d, Volunteers working in community garden.

2011, Aug. 2 ***Perf. 13x13¼***

1061 A370 50c Sheet of 4, #a-d 4.00 4.00

Sept. 11, 2001 Terrorist Attacks, 10th Anniv. A371

No. 1062 — Firefighters, soldiers, U.S. flag and: a, Firefighter on rubble pile. b, Flags and flowers. c, Person looking at candlelight tribute. d, Tribute in light.

$2.50, World Trade Center and U.S flag.

2011, Sept. 11 ***Perf. 12***

1062 A371 75c Sheet of 4, #a-d 6.00 6.00

Souvenir Sheet

Perf. 12¾

1063 A371 $2.50 multi 5.00 5.00

No. 1063 contains one 38x51mm stamp.

Miniature Sheets

A372

Women's World Cup Soccer Championships, Germany — A373

No. 1064: a, Nahomi Kawasumi. b, Japanese team members lifting trophy, "Team Japan" in black. c, Members of Japanese team. d, Yuki Nagasato.

No. 1065: a, Japan coach Norio Sasaki. b, Japanese team members lifting trophy, "Team Japan" in white. c, U.S. team. d, U.S. coach Pia Sundhage.

2011, Sept. 21 ***Perf. 12x12½***

1064 A372 98c Sheet of 4, #a-d 8.00 8.00
1065 A373 98c Sheet of 4, #a-d 8.00 8.00

Pres. Barack Obama, 50th Birthday A374

No. 1066 — Pres. Obama, White House, and one-quarter of Presidential Seal at: a, LR. b, LL. c, UR. d, UL.

$2.50, Pres. Obama.

2011, Oct. 26 ***Perf. 13 Syncopated***

1066 A374 98c Sheet of 4, #a-d 8.00 8.00

Souvenir Sheet

1067 A374 $2.50 multi 5.00 5.00

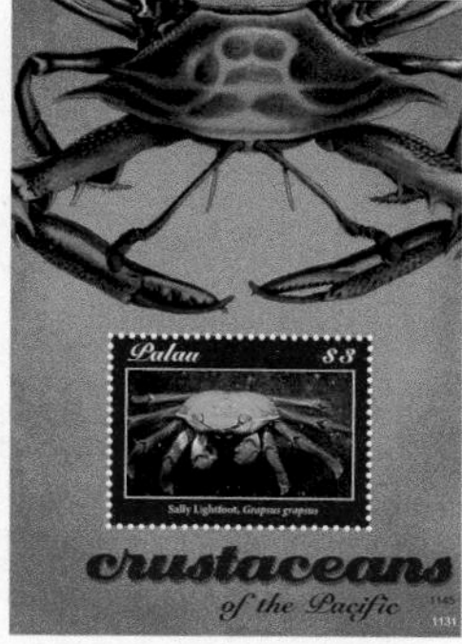

Crustaceans — A375

No. 1068, $1.25, vert.: a, Calcinus elegans. b, Dardanus pedunculatus. c, Odontodactylus scyllarus. d, Dardanus megistos.

No. 1069, $1.25, vert.: a, Birgus latro. b, Goneplax rhomboides. c, Bellia picta. d, Etisus dentatus.

No. 1070, $3, Grapsus grapsus. No. 1071, $3, Zebra mantis shrimp, vert.

2011, Oct. 26 ***Perf. 12***

Sheets of 4, #a-d

1068-1069 A375 Set of 2 20.00 20.00

Souvenir Sheets

1070-1071 A375 Set of 2 12.00 12.00

No. 1071 contains one 30x50mm stamp.

Marine Life A376

No. 1072: a, Gray reef shark. b, Blue-spotted ray. c, Red lionfish. d, Feather duster worm. e, Regal tang, Yellow tang.

No. 1073: a, Pfeffer's flamboyant cuttlefish. b, Striped surgeonfish. c, Spiny sea urchin.

No. 1074, Box jellyfish, vert. No. 1075, Sawtooth barracuda.

2011, Nov. 29 ***Perf. 11½x12***

1072 A376 75c Sheet of 5, #a-e 7.50 7.50

Perf. 12½x12

1073 A376 $1 Sheet of 3, #a-c 6.00 6.00

Souvenir Sheets

Perf. 13½

1074 A376 $2.50 multi 5.00 5.00

Perf.

1075 A376 $2.50 multi 5.00 5.00

No. 1074 contains one 38x51mm stamp. No. 1075 contains one 35mm diameter stamp.

Christmas — A377

Paintings: 22c, Landscape with the Flight into Egypt, by Annibale Carracci. 44c, Madonna and Saints, by Giovanni Bellini. 98c, Merode Altarpiece, by Robert Campin. $4.25, The Annunciation, by Matthias Grünewald.

2012, Jan. 2 ***Perf. 14***

1076-1079 A377 Set of 4 12.00 12.00

Lizards A378

No. 1080, 98c: a, Snake-eyed skink. b, Solomon Islands skink. c, Vanuatu gecko. d, White-bellied skink.

No. 1081, 98c: a, Emerald tree skink. b, Common dwarf gecko. c, Mourning gecko. d, Moth skink.

No. 1082, $2.50, White-line gecko. No. 1083, $2.50, Mangrove monitor.

2012, Jan. 2 ***Perf. 13 Syncopated***

Sheets of 4, #a-d

1080-1081 A378 Set of 2 16.00 16.00

Souvenir Sheets

1082-1083 A378 Set of 2 10.00 10.00

Miniature Sheet

Japan-Palau Friendship Bridge, 10th Anniv. — A379

No. 1084: a, Side view of bridge, tower at left. b, Side view of bridge, tower at right. c, Aerial view of bridge, approach at bottom. d, Aerial view of bridge with road connecting other islands in distance.

2012, Jan. 11 ***Perf. 12***

1084 A379 50c Sheet of 4, #a-d 4.00 4.00

Painting of the Sistine Chapel Ceiling by Michelangelo, 500th Anniv. — A380

No. 1085, horiz.: a, Downfall of Adam and Eve. b, The Ignudi. c, The Prophet Jonah.

$3.50, The Persian Sibyl.

2012, Jan. 24 ***Perf. 12***

1085 A380 $1.25 Sheet of 3, #a-c 7.50 7.50

Souvenir Sheet

1086 A380 $3.50 multi 7.00 7.00

Nos. 1085 and 1086 are erroneously inscribed "700th Anniversary."

Sinking of the Titanic, Cent. A381

No. 1087: a, Titanic at sea. b, Lifeboat. c, Man walking on deck. d, People reading newspapers reporting on the sinking.

$3, Titanic, diff.

2012, Jan. 25 ***Perf. 13 Syncopated***

1087 A381 $1 Sheet of 4, #a-d 8.00 8.00

Souvenir Sheet

1088 A381 $3 multi 6.00 6.00

Disappearance of Amelia Earhart, 75th Anniv. — A382

No. 1089 — Earhart: a, Standing in front of airplane without helmet, hands visible. b, Wearing helmet and goggles. c, Standing in front of airplane without helmet, hands not visible. d, Standing in airplane cockpit without helmet.

No. 1090 — Earhart in helmet and goggles, airplane diagram, and text, "Amelia Earhart" in: a, White. b, Black.

2012, Feb. 6 ***Perf. 13½***

1089 A382 $1.25 Sheet of 4, #a-d 10.00 10.00

Souvenir Sheet

Perf. 12x12½

1090 A382 $1.25 Sheet of 2, #a-b 5.00 5.00

Miniature Sheet

2012 Summer Olympics, London — A383

No. 1091: a, Tennis. b, Swimming. c, Weight lifting. d, Basketball.

2012, Mar. 26 ***Perf. 13¼x13***

1091 A383 80c Sheet of 4, #a-d 6.50 6.50

Cherry Trees in Bloom and Washington Monument — A384

No. 1092, horiz. — Blossoms of flowering trees: a, Washington hawthorn. b, Flowering dogwood. c, Callery pear. d, Crabapple. e, Magnolia. f, Eastern redbud.

2012, Mar. 26 ***Perf. 12***

1092 A384 $1 Sheet of 6, #a-f 12.00 12.00

Souvenir Sheet

1093 A384 $3.50 shown 7.00 7.00

Miniature Sheets

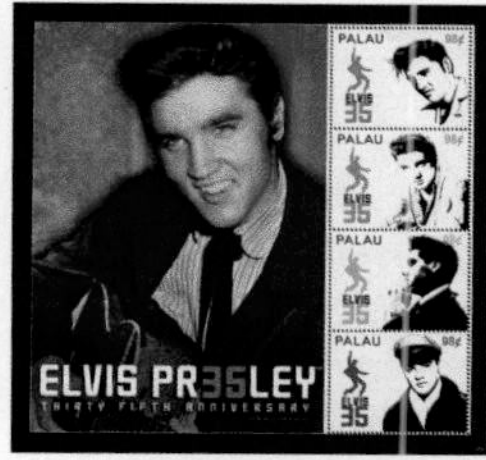

A385

Elvis Presley (1935-77) — A386

No. 1094 — Color of "35" and silhouette: a, Red violet. b, Green. c, Yellow. d, Violet.

No. 1095 — Presley wearing: a, Red jacket, white shirt. b, Tan shirt. c, Red jacket, black shirt. d, Gray jacket, white shirt.

2012, Apr. 11 ***Perf. 12½***

1094 A385 98c Sheet of 4, #a-d 8.00 8.00
1095 A386 98c Sheet of 4, #a-d 8.00 8.00

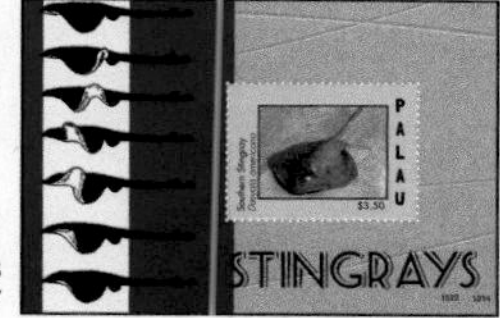

Stingrays A387

No. 1096: a, Spotted eagle ray. b, Pacific electric ray. c, Blue-spotted stingray. d, Blotched fantail ray.

$3.50, Southern stingray.

2012, May 7 ***Perf. 12***

1096 A387 $1.25 Sheet of 4, #a-d 10.00 10.00

Souvenir Sheet

1097 A387 $3.50 multi 7.00 7.00

Souvenir Sheets

Elvis Presley (1935-77) — A388

Designs: No. 1098, $3.50, Presley on *Love Me Tender* record cover. No. 1099, $3.50, Presley on *Jailhouse Rock* album cover. No. 1100, $3.50, Presley on *Blue Hawaii* album cover. No. 1101, $3.50, Presley on *Just Tell Her Jim Said Hello/She's Not You* record cover. No. 1102, $3.50, Presley on *G.I. Blues* record cover.

2012, May 14 ***Perf. 12½***

1098-1102 A388 Set of 5 35.00 35.00

Miniature Sheet

Characters From *Peter Pan,* by Sir James M. Barrie (1860-1937) — A389

No. 1103: a, Peter Pan. b, Tiger Lily. c, Captain Hook. d, Wendy Darling.

2012, June 7 *Perf. 12*

1103 A389 $1.25 Sheet of 4, #a-d 10.00 10.00

Miniature Sheet

Televised Tour of the White House, 50th Anniv. A390

No. 1104: a, Jacqueline Kennedy, chandelier. b, Jacqueline Kennedy, table and chairs. c, Pres. John F. Kennedy, picture frame. d, Pres. Kennedy, White House.

2012, Aug. 28 **Litho.**

1104 A390 $1.25 Sheet of 4, #a-d 10.00 10.00

Pope Benedict XVI, 85th Birthday A391

No. 1105 — Pope Benedict wearing: a, Miter. b, Zucchetto.

2012, Aug. 28 *Perf. 14*

1105 A391 $1.25 Horiz. pair, #a-b 5.00 5.00

Printed in sheets containing two pairs.

Miniature Sheets

End of Apollo Moon Missions, 40th Anniv. A392

No. 1106, $1.25: a, Apollo 9. b, Apollo 7. c, Apollo 15. d, Apollo 12.

No. 1107, $1.25: a, Apollo 14. b, Apollo 17. c, Apollo 8. d, Apollo 11.

2012, Aug. 28 *Perf. 13 Syncopated*

Sheets of 4, #a-d

1106-1107 A392 Set of 2 20.00 20.00

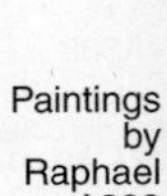

Paintings by Raphael A393

No. 1108: a, Giuliano de' Medici. b, Saint Sebastian. c, Portrait of Julius II. d, Bindo Altoviti.

$3, St. Catherine of Alexandria.

2012, Sept. 5 *Perf. 12½*

1108 A393 $1 Sheet of 4, #a-d 8.00 8.00

Souvenir Sheet

1109 A393 $3 multi 6.00 6.00

Dog Breeds A394

No. 1110: a, Akita. b, Cane Corso. c, Collie. d, Rottweiler.

$3.50, Golden retriever.

2012, Sept. 5 *Perf. 13¾*

1110 A394 $1.25 Sheet of 4, #a-d 10.00 10.00

Souvenir Sheet

1111 A394 $3.50 multi 7.00 7.00

Souvenir Sheets

Famous Speeches — A395

Orators of famous speeches: No. 1112, $3.50, Pres. Theodore Roosevelt. No. 1113, $3.50, Mahatma Gandhi. No. 1114, $3.50, Pres. John F. Kennedy. No. 1115, $3.50, Dr. Martin Luther King, Jr.

2012, Sept. 5 *Perf. 12½*

1112-1115 A395 Set of 4 28.00 28.00

Carnivorous Plants — A396

No. 1116: a, Pale butterwort. b, Corkscrew plant. c, Alice sundew. d, Zigzag bladderwort.

$3.50, King sundew, vert.

2012, Nov. 28 *Perf. 13¾*

1116 A396 $1.20 Sheet of 4, #a-d 9.75 9.75

Souvenir Sheet

Perf. 12½

1117 A396 $3.50 multi 7.00 7.00

No. 1117 contains one 38x51mm stamp.

Christmas — A397

Paintings by Albrecht Dürer: No. 1118, 29c, Madonna and Child. No. 1119, 29c, The Flight to Egypt. No. 1120, 45c, The Virgin and Child with St. Anne. No. 1121, 45c, Virgin and Child Holding a Half-eaten Pear. No. 1122, $1.05, Mother of Sorrows. No. 1123, $1.05, The Virgin Mary in Prayer.

$3.50, Jesus Boy with a Globe.

2012, Dec. 24 *Perf. 12½*

1118-1123 A397 Set of 6 7.25 7.25

Souvenir Sheet

1124 A397 $3.50 multi 7.00 7.00

The Hindenburg — A398

Designs: $1.20, Hindenburg. $3.50, Hindenburg, Chrysler Building, Eiffel Tower, Empire State Building, 40 Wall Street Building, vert.

2012, Dec. 31 *Perf. 12*

1125 A398 $1.20 multi 2.40 2.40

Souvenir Sheet

Perf. 12½

1126 A398 $3.50 multi 7.00 7.00

No. 1125 was printed in sheets of 4. No. 1126 contains one 38x51mm stamp.

World Radio Day A399

No. 1127: a, Microphone. b, Antenna and waves. c, Table radio. d, Radio waves, diagram of ear canals.

$3.50, Solar system, radio wave, horiz.

2013, Jan. 2 **Litho.** *Perf. 13¾*

1127 A399 $1.20 Sheet of 4, #a-d 9.75 9.75

Souvenir Sheet

Perf. 12½

1128 A399 $3.50 multi 7.00 7.00

No. 1128 contains one 51x38mm stamp.

Paintings by Paul Signac (1863-1935) — A400

No. 1129: a, L'Orage (The Storm). b, The Pine, Saint Tropez. c, Portrait of Félix Fénéon.

$3.50, Femmes au Puits (Women at the Well).

2013, Jan. 8 **Litho.** *Perf. 12½*

1129 A400 $1.50 Sheet of 3, #a-c 9.00 9.00

Souvenir Sheet

1130 A400 $3.50 multi 7.00 7.00

Reign of Queen Elizabeth II, 60th Anniv. (in 2012) A401

No. 1131 — Queen Elizabeth II: a, With Prince Philip. b, With dog. c, Waving. d, With Prince Charles.

$3.50, Queen Elizabeth II, vert.

2013, Jan. 8 **Litho.** *Perf. 13¾*

1131 A401 $1.20 Sheet of 4, #a-d 9.75 9.75

Souvenir Sheet

Perf. 12½

1132 A401 $3.50 multi 7.00 7.00

No. 1132 contains one 38x51mm stamp.

Shells A402

No. 1133: a, Conus gloriamaris. b, Hydatina albocincta. c, Marginella strigata. d, Conus betulinus.

$3.50, Tellina pharaonis, horiz.

2013, Mar. 20 **Litho.** *Perf. 12*

1133 A402 $1.20 Sheet of 4, #a-d 9.75 9.75

Souvenir Sheet

1134 A402 $3.50 multi 7.00 7.00

Cat Breeds A403

Cat Depictions From Other Cultures — A404

No. 1135, $1.20: a, Russian Blue. b, Turkish Angora. c, Norwegian forest cat. d, Siamese.

No. 1136, $1.20: a, Siberian. b, Oriental shorthair. c, Japanese bobtail. d, Chartreux.

No. 1137, $3.50, Egyptian goddess Bastet. No. 1138, $3.50, Japanese Maneki-neko figurine.

2013, Mar. 20 **Litho.** *Perf. 12*

Sheets of 4, #a-d

1135-1136 A403 Set of 2 19.50 19.50

Souvenir Sheets

Perf. 13¾

1137-1138 A404 Set of 2 14.00 14.00

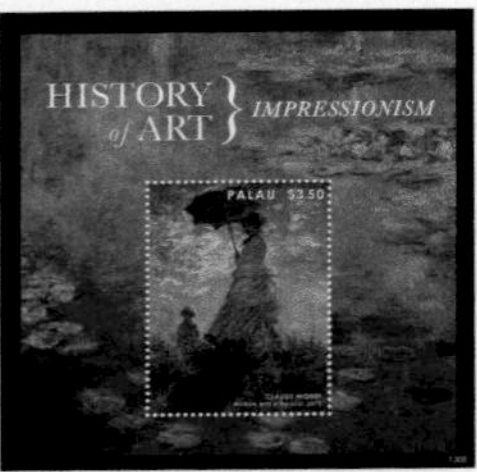

History of Art A405

No. 1139, $1.50: a, Sunset at Ivry, by Armand Guillaumin. b, Landscape with Big Trees, by Camille Pissarro. c, A Box at the Theater, by Pierre-Auguste Renoir.

No. 1140, $1.50: a, Sunshine in the Blue Room, by Anna Ancher. b, Woman Washing Her Feet in a Brook, by Pissarro. c, Woman in the Bath, by Edgar Degas.

No. 1141, $3.50, Woman with a Parasol, by Claude Monet. No. 1142, $3.50, The Star, by Edgar Degas.

2013, Apr. 4 **Litho.** *Perf. 12½*

Sheets of 3, #a-c

1139-1140 A405 Set of 2 18.00 18.00

Souvenir Sheets

1141-1142 A405 Set of 2 14.00 14.00

Grand Central Terminal, New York City, Cent. A406

No. 1143: a, Ticket window, c. 1945. b, Commuters in station, c. 1941. c, Terminal exterior, c. 1920. d, Light shining through windows, c. 1930. e, Terminal under construction, c. 1907. f, Mercury Clock, c. 1988.

$3.50, Terminal exterior, horiz.

2013, Apr. 29 Litho. *Perf. 13¾*
1143 A406 $1 Sheet of 6, #a-f 12.00 12.00

Souvenir Sheet
Perf. 12½

1144 A406 $3.50 multi 7.00 7.00

No. 1144 contains one 51x38mm stamp.

A407

Pres. John F. Kennedy (1917-63) — A408

No. 1145 — Black-and-white images of Pres. Kennedy: a, Facing right, flag in background. b, Facing left, flag in background. c, With people in background. d, With door in background.

No. 1146 — Color images of Pres. Kennedy: a, Facing right, with woman's head in background. b, With black background. c, With tie pattern visible. d, Facing right, with indistinguishable light reflections in background.

No. 1147, $3.50, Pres. Kennedy, country name at LL in blue panel. No. 1148, $3.50, Pres. Kennedy pointing, country name at UL in blue panel.

Perf. 13 Syncopated
2013, Apr. 29 Litho.
1145 A407 $1.20 Sheet of 4, #a-d 9.75 9.75
1146 A408 $1.20 Sheet of 4, #a-d 9.75 9.75

Souvenir Sheets

1147-1148 A408 Set of 2 14.00 14.00

Election of Pope Francis A409

No. 1150 — Pope Francis: a, Waving to crowd below (orange background). b, Addressing crowd from balcony of St. Peter's Basilica (with cardinals). c, Behind microphone, addressing crowd, with assistant holding Bible. d, Waving to crowd (shadow and wall in background).
$3.50, Pope Francis, diff.

2013, June 3 Litho. *Perf. 12*
1149 A409 $1.20 Sheet of 4, #a-d 9.75 9.75

Souvenir Sheet
Perf. 12½

1150 A409 $3.50 multi 7.00 7.00

No. 1150 contains one 38x51mm stamp.

Lady Margaret Thatcher (1925-2013), British Prime Minister — A410

No. 1151 — Thatcher: a, Wearing black dress. b, With Pres. George H. W. Bush. c, Wearing gray striped dress. d, Wearing black dresss with whtie dots.
$3.50, Thatcher in doorway of bus.

2013, June 3 Litho. *Perf. 12*
1151 A410 $1.25 Sheet of 4, #a-d 10.00 10.00

Souvenir Sheet
Perf. 12½

1152 A410 $3.50 multi 7.00 7.00

No. 1152 conatins one 38x51mm stamp.

Henry Ford (1863-1947), Automobile Manufacturer — A411

No. 1153: a, Ford and first car. b, Assembly line. c, Parked Model T autombiles. d, Ford and Model T.
$3.50, Ford, vert.

2013, June 25 Litho. *Perf. 12*
1153 A411 $1.20 Sheet of 4, #a-d 9.75 9.75

Souvenir Sheet

1154 A411 $3.50 multi 7.00 7.00

Tropical Fish A412

No. 1155, $1.20: a, Australasian snapper. b, Tomato clownfish. c, Pennant coralfish. d, Yellow watchman goby.

No. 1156, $1.20: a, Pink-spotted shirmp goby. b, Ocellated dragonet. c, Common warehou. d, Gray moray.

No. 1157, $3.50, Blue-eyed triplefin. No. 1158, $3.50, Barred mudskipper.

2013, June 25 Litho. *Perf. 12*
Sheets of 4, #a-d
1155-1156 A412 Set of 2 19.50 19.50

Souvenir Sheets

1157-1158 A412 Set of 2 14.00 14.00

Thailand 2013 World Stamp Exhibition, Bangkok — A413

No. 1159: a, Mondop Staircases. b, Floating market. c, Asian elephants. d, Buddhist temple.
$3.50, Sedge hats.

2013, July 7 Litho. *Perf. 12*
1159 A413 $1.20 Sheet of 4, #a-d 9.75 9.75

Souvenir Sheet

1160 A413 $3.50 multi 7.00 7.00

Butterflies — A414

No. 1161, horiz.: a, Tailed jay swallowtail. b, Old world swallowtail. c, Common albatross. d, Australian lurcher.
$3.50, Macleay's swallowtail.

2013, Sept. 17 Litho. *Perf. 12*
1161 A414 $1.20 Sheet of 4, #a-d 9.75 9.75

Souvenir Sheet

1162 A414 $3.50 multi 7.00 7.00

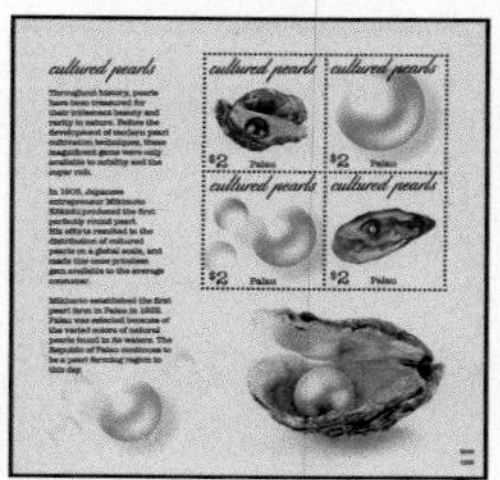

Cultured Pearls A415

No. 1163: a, Large brown pearl in oyster shell, upper shell. b, Large white pearl. c, Three pearls. d, Small pearl in oyster shell.
$4, Pearl, tan background.

2013, Sept. 17 Litho. *Perf. 13¾*
1163 A415 $2 Sheet of 4, #a-d 16.00 16.00

Souvenir Sheet

1164 A415 $4 multi 8.00 8.00

Birth of Prince George of Cambridge — A416

No. 1165: a, Duchess of Cambridge holding Prince George. b, Prince George, close-up. c, Prince Charles, Princess Diana, Prince William. d, Duke and Duchess of Cambridge with Prince George.
$3.50, Duke and Duchess of Cambridge with Prince George, diff.

2013, Sept. 17 Litho. *Perf. 14*
1165 A416 $1.20 Sheet of 4, #a-d 9.75 9.75

Souvenir Sheet
Perf. 12

1166 A416 $3.50 multi 7.00 7.00

No. 1166 contains one 30x50mm stamp.

Miniature Sheets

Photographs by Kevin Davidson — A417

No. 1167: a, Oxypora coral, country name at UL, reading across. b, Coral dweller cobie, country name at UL, reading across. c, Bannerfish. d, Mushroom Rock Island, country name at UL, reading across. e, Medusa worm on red sponge. f, Eagle ray, decimal point of denomination to right of ray, wing of ray just touching vertical line of first "1" in denomination.

No. 1168: a, Baby green turtles. b, Mandarin fish, country name at UL, reading across. c, Eagle ray, decimal point of denomination on ray. d, Pink anemone fish, country name at UL, reading across. e, Head of fish (incorrectly inscribed "Medusa worm on red sponge"). f, Masked angelfish.

No. 1169: a, Harlequin sweetlips. b, Nautilus. c, Eagle Ray, decimal point of denomination to right of ray, wing of ran not touching vertical line of first "1" in denomination. d, Red sea fan. e, Soft coral crab.

No. 1170: a, Oxypora coral, country name at left, reading up. b, Coral dweller cobie, country name at left, reading up. c, Pink anemone fish, country name at left, reading up. d, Mushroom Rock Island, country name at left, reading up. e, Mandarin fish, country name at left, reading up. f, Longnose hawkfish.

No. 1171, vert.: a, Three jellyfish. b, Starfish on red coral fan, country name at UL, reading across. c, Jellyfish and diver. d, Oxypora coral, country name at UL, reading across. e, Seahorse. f, Lionfish.

No. 1172, vert.: a, Coconut climber. b, Pink anemone fish, country name at UL, reading across. c, Cup coral, country name at UL, reading across. d, Humphead wrasse, e, Shark.

No. 1173, vert.: a, Cup coral, country name at UL, reading up. b, Manta ray. c, Rock Island. d, Red seahorse. e, Pink anemone fish, country name at UL, reading up. f, Starfish on red coral fan, country name at UL, reading up.

2013, Oct. 1 Litho. *Perf. 12*
1167 A417 $1.10 Sheet of 6, #a-f 13.50 13.50
1168 A417 $1.10 Sheet of 6, #a-f 13.50 13.50
1169 A417 $1.10 Sheet of 6, #a-e, 1168f 13.50 13.50
1170 A417 $1.10 Sheet of 6, #a-f 13.50 13.50
1171 A417 $1.10 Sheet of 6, #a-f 13.50 13.50
1172 A417 $1.10 Sheet of 6, #a-e, 1171d 13.50 13.50
1173 A417 $1.10 Sheet of 6, #a-f 13.50 13.50
Nos. 1167-1173 (7) 94.50 94.50

Souvenir Sheet

Elvis Presley (1935-77) — A418

Litho., Margin Embossed With Foil Application
2013, Oct. 1 *Imperf.*
1174 A418 $10 multi 20.00 20.00

Coronation of Queen Elizabeth II, 60th Anniv. — A419

No. 1175 — Queen Elizabeth II: a, With Prince Philip. b, Wearing pink hat. c, Wearing white hat. d, Alone, wearing sash and tiara.
$3.50, Queen Elizabeth II in coach, vert.

2013, Oct. 7 Litho. *Perf. 14*
1175 A419 $1.20 Sheet of 4, #a-d 9.75 9.75

Souvenir Sheet

1176 A419 $3.50 multi 7.00 7.00

World Water Day — A420

Designs: $1.20, Water droplets. $3.50, Water droplet, vert.

2013, Nov. 18 Litho. *Perf. 13¾*

1177 A420 $1.20 multi 2.40 2.40

Souvenir Sheet

Perf. 12½

1178 A420 $3.50 multi 7.00 7.00

No. 1177 was printed in sheets of 4. No. 1178 contains one 38x51mm stamp.

Christmas — A421

Paintings: 29c, Madonna Worshipping the Child and an Angel, by Biagio D'Antonio Tucci. 44c, Nativity, by unknown artist. $1.05, The Annunciation, by Simone Martini. $3.50, Virgin and Child, by Gentile da Fabriano.

2013, Dec. 2 Litho. *Perf. 12½*

1179-1182 A421 Set of 4 11.00 11.00

A422

Nelson Mandela (1918-2013), President of South Africa — A423

No. 1183: a, Mandela and wife, Winnie, waving. b, Mandela as young man wearing traditional collar. c, Mandela in crowd, laughing.

No. 1184 — Mandela: a, wearing black and gray shirt. b, Wearing suit and tie, building in background. c, Holding microphone stand. d, Seated. e, Behind microphone, pointing. f, With raised fist.

No. 1185, $3.50, Mandela holding ballot, wearing shirt with pens in pocket, vert. No. 1186, $3.50, Mandela with arm raised, wearing patterned shirt, vert.

2013, Dec. 15 Litho. *Perf. 13¾*

1183 A422 $1.20 Vert. strip of 3, #a-c 7.25 7.25

1184 A423 $1.20 Sheet of 6, #a-f 14.50 14.50

Souvenir Sheets

Perf. 12½

1185-1186 A423 Set of 2 14.00 14.00

No. 1183 was printed in sheet of 6 stamps containing two each of Nos. 1183a-1183c. Nos. 1185-1186 each contain on 38x51mm stamp.

Orchids A424

No. 1187: Various Phalaenopsis orchids, as shown.

$3.50, Lady's slipper, horiz.

2013, Dec. 18 Litho. *Perf. 13¾*

1187 A424 $1 Sheet of 6, #a-f 12.00 12.00

Souvenir Sheet

Perf. 12½

1188 A424 $3.50 multi 7.00 7.00

No. 1188 contains one 51x38mm stamp.

Chess in Art A425

No. 1189: a, Etude of the Life of the Russian Tsars, by Vyacheslav Schwarz (players, table with green tablecloth). b, Scene from the Court of King Christian VII, by Kristian Zahrtmann (woman and man playing). c, The Chess Players, by Giulio Rosati (players on bench). d, The Chess Game, by Charles Bargue (woman and cardinal playing).

$3.50, Proposal, by Knut Ekwall, vert.

2013, Dec. 23 Litho. *Perf. 12½*

1189 A425 $1.20 Sheet of 4, #a-d 9.75 9.75

Souvenir Sheet

1190 A425 $3.50 multi 7.00 7.00

Modern Art A426

No. 1191, $1.50 — Paintings: a, Ajax, by John Steuart Curry. b, Landscape, by Diego Rivera. c, Red Tree, by Marsden Hartley.

No. 1192, $1.50 — Photographs: a, Power Farming Displaces Tenants, by Dorothea Lange. b, Toward Los Angeles, California, by Lange. c, Power House Mechanic Working on Steam Pump, by Lewis Hine.

No. 1193, $3.50, Red Cavalry, by Kazimir Malevich. No. 1194, $3.50, The Alarm Clock, by Rivera.

2014, Jan. 2 Litho. *Perf. 12½*

Sheets of 3, #a-c

1191-1192 A426 Set of 2 18.00 18.00

Souvenir Sheets

1193-1194 A426 Set of 2 14.00 14.00

Shells A427

No. 1195, $1.75: a, Chicoreus palma-rosae. b, Phalium glaucum. c, Conus generalis (blue background at top). d, Conus episcopus.

No. 1196, $1.75: a, Conus generalis (purple background at top). b, Harpa articularis. c, Strombus minimus. d, Strombus gibberulus.

No. 1197, $3.50: a, Chicoreus ramosus. b, Murex troscheli.

No. 1198, $3.50: a, Charonia tritonis. b, Syrinx aruanus.

2014, Feb. 26 Litho. *Perf. 12*

Sheets of 4, #a-d

1195-1196 A427 Set of 2 28.00 28.00

Souvenir Sheets of 2, #a-b

Perf. 12½

1197-1198 A427 Set of 2 28.00 28.00

Nos. 1197-1198 each contain two 38x51mm stamps.

Caroline Kennedy, United States Ambassador to Japan — A428

No. 1199 — Caroline Kennedy: a, Greeting Japanese students. b, With parents and brother. c, As young woman at graduation ceremony. d, As child, with father.

$4, Caroline Kennedy, vert.

2014, Mar. 5 Litho. *Perf. 13¾*

1199 A428 $1.50 Sheet of 4, #a-d 12.00 12.00

Souvenir Sheet

Perf. 12½

1200 A428 $4 multi 8.00 8.00

No. 1200 contains one 38x51mm stamp.

Miniature Sheets

Winter Sports A429

No. 1201: a, Ice hockey. b, Speed skating. c, Bobsled. d, Figure skating.

No. 1202, horiz.: a, Freestyle skiing. b, Nordic combined skiing. c, Curling. d, Luge. f, Skeleton. g, Bobsled, diff.

2014, Mar. 5 Litho. *Perf. 12½*

1201 A429 $1.20 Sheet of 4, #a-d 9.75 9.75

Perf. 14

1202 A429 $1.20 Sheet of 6, #a-f 14.50 14.50

No. 1202 contains six 40x30mm stamps.

Pope Francis A430

No. 1203, $1.20: a, Pres. Horacio Cartes of Paraguay. b, Pope Francis (painting in backgound). c, Pres. Cartes and Pope Francis (painting in background). d, Pres. Cartes and Pope Francis (painting and table in background).

No. 1204, $1.20: a, Pres. Denis Sassou Nguesso of Congo Republic. b, Pope Francis (book shelves in background). c, Pres. Sassou Nguesso and Pope Francis (painting and chairs in background). d, Pres. Sassou Nguesso and Pope Francis (corner of room in background).

No. 1205, $2: a, Pope Francis hugging person. b, Pope Francis patting child's head.

No. 1206, $2: a, Pope Francis looking upwards. b, Pope Francis with hands together.

2014, Mar. 10 Litho. *Perf. 12½*

Sheets of 4, #a-d

1203-1204 A430 Set of 2 19.50 19.50

Souvenir Sheets of 2, #a-b

Perf. 12

1205-1206 A430 Set of 2 16.00 16.00

Nos. 1205-1206 each contain two 30x40mm stamps.

World War I, Cent. A431

No. 1207, $2.50: a, London Scottish Regiment drill. b, British Army recruits in training. c, New recruits with officers, London. d, British Army volunteers, Aldershot.

No. 1208, $2.50: a, Bergmann MP18 machine gun, Germany. b, Carl Gustav Mauser M96, Sweden. c, Browning 1917 A1 machine gun, Belgium. d, Fedorov Avtomat rifle, Russia.

No. 1209, $2: a, Herbert Henry Asquith, British Prime Minister. b, Winston Churcill, First Lord of the Admiralty.

No. 1210, $2: a, Luger P08, Germany. b, Model 1892 revolver, France.

2014, Apr. 23 Litho. *Perf. 14*

Sheets of 4, #a-d

1207-1208 A431 Set of 2 40.00 40.00

Souvenir Sheets of 2, #a-b

Perf. 12½

1209-1210 A431 Set of 2 16.00 16.00

Nos. 1209-1210 each contain two 51x38mm stamps.

Miniature Sheet

South Korean Stamps A432

No. 1211: a, South Korea #936 (1975 stamp). b, South Korea #1398 (1985 stamp). c, South Korea #1635 (1991 stamp). d, South Korea #704 (1970 stamp). e, South Korea #948 (1975 stamp). f, Never-used stamp of 1884. g, South Korea #861 (1973 stamp). h, South Korea #300 (1959 stamp).

2014, May 12 Litho. *Perf. 12*

1211 A432 $1 Sheet of 8, #a-h 16.00 16.00

Philakorea 2014 World Stamp Exhibition, Seoul.

Reptiles A433

No. 1212, $3.50: a, Frilled lizard. b, Fiji crested iguana. c, Knob-tailed gecko. d, Tuatara.
No. 1213, $3.50: a, Eastern brown snake (35x35mm). b, Children's python (35x35mm). c, Copperhead (35x70mm). d, Red-bellied black snake (35x35mm).
No. 1214, $3.50, Green sea turtle. No. 1215, $3.50, Saltwater crocodile.

Perf. 12½, 13¾ (#1213)

2014, July 1 Litho.

Sheets of 4, #a-d

1212-1213 A433 Set of 2 56.00 56.00

Souvenir Sheets

1214-1215 A433 Set of 2 14.00 14.00

Miniature Sheets

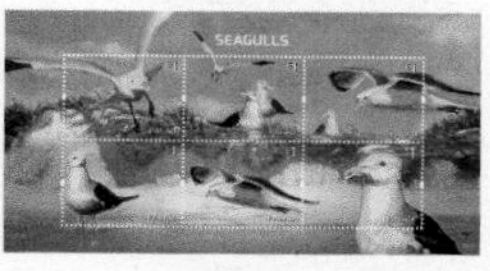

A434

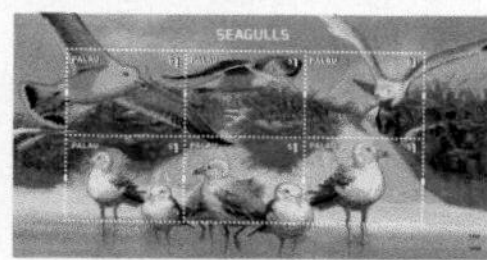

Seagulls A435

Various depictions of seagulls, as shown.

Perf. 13 Syncopated

2014, July 21 Litho.

1216 A434 $1 Sheet of 6, #a-f 12.00 12.00
1217 A435 $1 Sheet of 6, #a-f 12.00 12.00

Prince George of Cambridge — A436

No. 1218: a, Duke and Duchess of Cambridge, Prince George. b, Prince George. c, Duchess of Cambridge and Prince George.
No. 1219: a, Duke of Cambridge and Prince George. b, Prince George, diff.
No. 1220, $4, Prince George facing left, horiz. No. 1221, $4, Prince George facing right, horiz.

2014, July 21 Litho. *Perf. 14*

1218 A436 75c Horiz. strip of 3, #a-c 4.50 4.50
1219 A436 $1 Pair, #a-b 4.00 4.00

Souvenir Sheets

1220-1221 A436 Set of 2 16.00 16.00

No. 1218 was printed in sheets of 8 stamps containing 4 #1218b and 2 each #1218a and 1218c. No. 1219 was printed in sheets containing 3 pairs.

Miniature Sheet

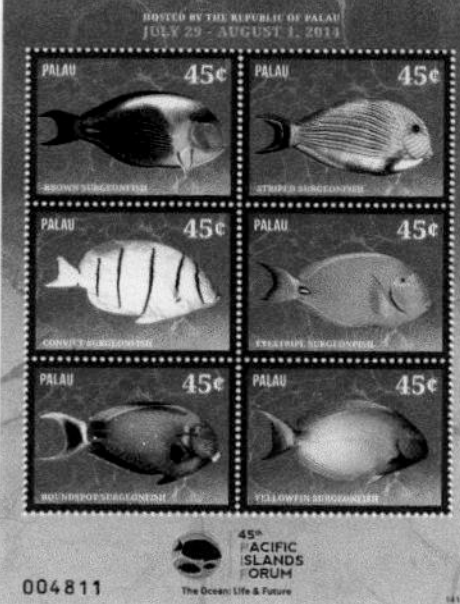

Fish A437

No. 1222: a, Brown surgeonfish. b, Striped surgeonfish. c, Convict surgeonfish. d, Eyestripe surgeonfish. e, Roundspot surgeonfish. f, Yellowfin surgeonfish.

2014, July 30 Litho. *Perf. 12½x13¼*

1222 A437 45c Sheet of 6, #a-f 5.50 5.50

45th Pacific Islands Forum, Palau.

Illustrations for *Alice's Adventures in Wonderland,* by Sir John Tenniel (1820-1914) — A438

No. 1223, $1.75: a, Alice, Flamingo and Duchess (club in panel). b, Playing Cards painting rose bush (diamond in panel). c, Fish delivers letter to frog (heart in panel). d, Alice and the Queen of Hearts (spade in panel).
No. 1224, $1.75: a, Alice at tea party (club in panel). b, Alice and flowers (diamond in panel). c, Alice holding bottle (heart in panel). d, Alice and playing cards (spade in panel).
No. 1225, $2.50: a, King of Hearts (club in panel). b, Queen of Hearts (heart in panel).
No. 1226, $2.50: a, Knave of Hearts (spade in panel). b, Birds in powdered wigs (diamond in panel).

2014, July 31 Litho. *Perf. 12½*

Sheets of 4, #a-d

1223-1224 A438 Set of 2 28.00 28.00

Souvenir Sheets of 2, #a-b

1225-1226 A438 Set of 2 20.00 20.00

Tourist Attractions in Russia — A439

No. 1227: a, Uzon Caldera. b, Mt. Elbrus. c, Trans-Siberian Railway.
No. 1228, vert.: a, Peter and Paul Cathedral, St. Petersburg. b, St. Sophia Cathedral, Vologda.

2014, Aug. 14 Litho. *Perf. 12*

1227 A439 $1.50 Sheet of 3, #a-c 9.00 9.00

Souvenir Sheet

1228 A439 $2 Sheet of 2, #a-b 8.00 8.00

Owls A440

No. 1229: a, Buffy fish owl. b, Barking owl. c, Tasmanian spotted owl. d, Indian scops owl. $3, Ural owl. $4, Short-eared owl.

2014, Aug. 14 Litho. *Perf. 12*

1229 A440 $1 Sheet of 4, #a-d 8.00 8.00

Souvenir Sheets

1230 A440 $3 multi 6.00 6.00
1231 A440 $4 multi 8.00 8.00

Marine Life — A441

Designs: 2c, Damselfish. 3c, Green sea turtle. 5c, Mailed butterflyfish. 10c, Ornate butterflyfish. 15c, Queen triggerfish. 20c, Reef manta ray. 75c, Yellow boxfish. $1, Palau nautilus.

2014, Aug. 27 Litho. *Perf. 13¾*

1232 A441 2c multi .25 .25
1233 A441 3c multi .25 .25
1234 A441 5c multi .25 .25
1235 A441 10c multi .25 .25
1236 A441 15c multi .30 .30
1237 A441 20c multi .40 .40
1238 A441 75c multi 1.50 1.50
1239 A441 $1 multi 2.00 2.00
Nos. 1232-1239 (8) 5.20 5.20

Trains A442

No. 1240: a, Golden Arrow. b, Orient Express. c. Royal Scot. d, Super Chief. $3.50, 20th Century Limited.

2014, Sept. 3 Litho. *Perf. 12*

1240 A442 $1.20 Sheet of 4, #a-d 9.75 9.75

Souvenir Sheet

1241 A442 $3.50 multi 7.00 7.00

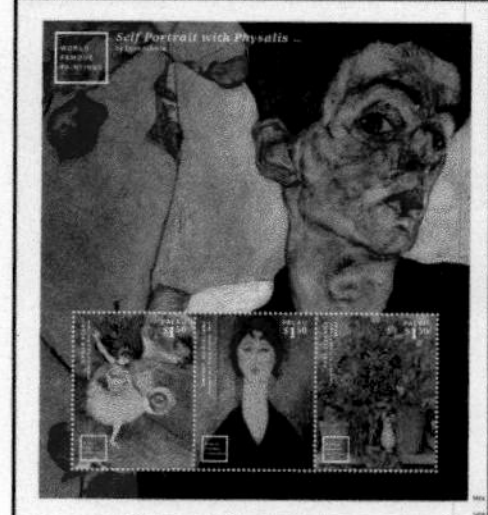
Paintings A443

No. 1242, $1.50: a, Dancer Taking a Bow, by Edgar Degas. b, Portrait of a Young Woman, by Amedeo Modigliani. c, Terracotta Pots and Flowers, by Paul Cézanne.
No. 1243, $1.50: a, The Ballet Class, by Degas. b, Anxiety, by Edvard Munch. c, The Child's Bath, by Mary Cassatt.
No. 1244, $4, In the Kitchen, by Carl Larsson. No. 1245, $4, Farewell, by August Macke.

2014, Sept. 3 Litho. *Perf. 12½*

Sheets of 3, #a-c

1242-1243 A443 Set of 2 18.00 18.00

Size: 100x100mm

Imperf

1244-1245 A443 Set of 2 16.00 16.00

Frogs and Toads A444

No. 1246, $1.20: a, Rough-backed forest frog. b, Common tree frog. c, Luzon frog. d, Wrinkled ground frog.
No. 1247, $1.20: a, Taylor's wrinkled ground frog. b, Woodworth's wart frog. c, Pygmy forest frog. d, Kalinga narrowmouth toad.
No. 1248, $4, Luzon fanged frog. No. 1249, $4, Harlequin tree frog.

Perf. 14, 12 (#1249)

2014, Sept. 15 Litho.

Sheets of 4, #a-d

1246-1247 A444 Set of 2 19.50 19.50

Souvenir Sheets

1248-1249 A444 Set of 2 16.00 16.00

Miniature Sheets

Characters From *Downton Abbey* Television Series — A445

No. 1250, $1.20: a, Dowager Countess of Grantham. b, Earl of Grantham. c, Countess of Grantham. d, Lady Mary Crawley. e, Lady Edith Crawley.
No. 1251, $1.20: a, Thomas Barrow. b, Mr. Carson. c, Mrs. Hughes. d, Mrs. Patmore. e, Daisy Mason.

2014, Nov. 11 Litho. *Perf. 14*

Sheets of 5, #a-e

1250-1251 A445 Set of 2 24.00 24.00

Christmas — A446

Paintings and details of paintings by Raphael: 34c, The Adoration of the Magi. 49c, The Adoration of the Magi, diff. $1.50, Ansidei Madonna. $3.50, Colonna Madonna.

2014, Nov. 24 Litho. *Perf. 12½*

1252-1255 A446 Set of 4 12.00 12.00

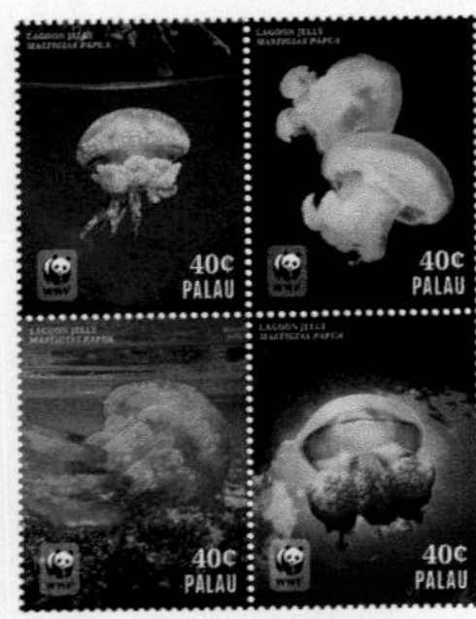

Worldwide Fund for Nature (WWF) — A447

Nos. 1256 and 1257 — Lagoon jellyfish: a, Near water's surface. b, Two jellyfish. c, Above seafloor. d, In sea cave.

2014, Dec. 1 Litho. *Perf. 14*

1256 A447 40c Block or horiz. strip of 4, #a-d 3.25 3.25
1257 A447 90c Block or horiz. strip of 4, #a-d 7.25 7.25

Pope Benedict XVI A448

No. 1258 — Pope Benedict XVI: a, Wearing red vestments. b, Swinging censer. c, Close-up. d, Standing in front of bushes.
$4, Pope Benedict XVI in green vestments.

2014, Dec. 16 Litho. *Perf. 14*

1258 A448 $1.20 Sheet of 4, #a-d 9.75 9.75

Souvenir Sheet

1259 A448 $4 multi 8.00 8.00

Dinosaurs — A449

No. 1260, $1.20: a, Nigersaurus. b, Iguanodon. c, Agustinia. d, Doliosauriscus.
No. 1261, $1.20: a, Ankylosaurus. b, Giganotosaurus. c, Diplodocus. d, Tyrannosaurus.
No. 1262, $4, Stegosaurus. No. 1263, $4, Gigantspinosaurus.

2014, Dec. 22 Litho. *Perf. 12*
Sheets of 4, #a-d

1260-1261 A449 Set of 2 19.50 19.50

Souvenir Sheets

1262-1263 A449 Set of 2 16.00 16.00

No. 1261 contains four 50x30mm stamps.

Bubble Tea A450

No. 1264 — Cup of tea with straw and inscription of: a, Pineapple. b, Taro. c, Strawberry. d, Mango. e, Avocado. f, Blueberry.
$4, Cup of tea with lid and straw.

2015, Jan. 5 Litho. *Perf. 13¾*

1264 A450 $1.20 Sheet of 6, #a-f 14.50 14.50

Souvenir Sheet
Perf. 12

1265 A450 $4 multi 8.00 8.00

No. 1265 contains one 30x40mm stamp. Asian International Stamp Exhibition, 30th Anniv.

Pope John Paul II (1920-2005) — A451

2015, Feb. 2 Litho. *Perf. 12*

1266 A451 75c multi 1.50 1.50

Printed in sheets of 4. Compare with type A331.

Camouflage of World War I — A452

No. 1267: a, Dreadnought Battleship. b, USS Leviathan. c, HMS Kildangan. d, Sopwith Camel airplane. e, British dummy tank.
$4, Soldier in tree-climbing camouflage.

2015, Feb. 2 Litho. *Perf. 14*

1267 A452 $1.20 Sheet of 5, #a-e 12.00 12.00

Souvenir Sheet
Perf. 13¾

1268 A452 $4 multi 8.00 8.00

No. 1268 contains one 35x35mm stamp.

UNESCO World Heritage Sites — A453

No. 1269: a, Great Barrier Reef, Australia. b, Prambanan Temple Compounds, Indonesia. c, Rice Terraces of the Philippine Cordilleras, Philippines. d, Kinabalu Park, Malaysia. e, Komodo National Park, Indonesia.
$4, Rock Islands Southern Lagoon, Palau.

2015, Mar. 9 Litho. *Perf. 14*

1269 A453 $1.20 Sheet of 5, #a-e 12.00 12.00

Souvenir Sheet
Perf. 13¾

1270 A453 $4 multi 8.00 8.00

No. 1270 contains one 70x35mm stamp.

Ships Involved in the 1940 Evacuation of Dunkirk — A454

No. 1271, 45c: a, Minnehaha, b, Cygnet. c, Rapid. d, Skylark. e, Wanda. f, Marchioness. g, Jovial. h, Fedalma II. i, Jane Hannah MacDonald. j, Massey Shaw. k, Mimosa. l, Aberdonia. m, Reda. n, Blue Bird. o, Dorian. p, White Heathe.
No. 1272, 45c: a, Cachalot. b, Fervant. c, Omega. d, Greater London. e, Jane Holland. f, Lucy Lavers. g, Tom Tit. h, Cyril and Lillian Bishop. i, Latona. j, Endeavour. k, Polly. l, Tigris. m, Eothen. n, Lazy Days. o, Wairakei II. p, Matoya.

2015, May 25 Litho. *Perf. 14*
Sheets of 16, #a-p, + Label

1271-1272 A454 Set of 2 29.00 29.00

Queen Elizabeth II, Longest-Reigning British Monarch — A455

No. 1273 — Queen Elizabeth II wearing: a, Dark green dress, light green hat and gloves. b, Pink dress and hat, black gloves. c, Green coat. b, Dark blue dress. c, White gown and tiara. d, Lilac dress.
$4, Queen Elizabeth II in white and blue dress with blue buttons and matching hat.

2015, May 25 Litho. *Perf. 14*

1273 A455 $1.20 Sheet of 6, #a-f 14.50 14.50

Souvenir Sheet
Perf. 12

1274 A455 $4 multi 8.00 8.00

Battle of Britain, 75th Anniv. A456

No. 1275: a, Hawker Hurricane. b, Prime Minister Winston Churchill inspects bomb damage in London. c, British soldier guards a German fighter plane. d, Pilots push a Spitfire onto a runway. e, Spitfires patrol a coastline. f, Ground crew replenishes Hurricane aircraft ammunition.
$4, Churchill and Queen Elizabeth inspect damage to Buckingham Palace.

2015, June 1 Litho. *Perf. 12*

1275 A456 65c Sheet of 6, #a-f 8.00 8.00

Souvenir Sheet

1276 A456 $4 multi 8.00 8.00

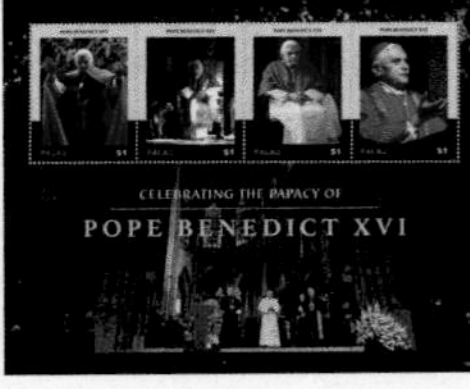

Pope Benedict XVI A457

No. 1277 — Pope Benedict XVI: a, With arms raised. b, Seated next to bishop. c, Seated alone. d, With hand outstretched.
$3.50, Pope Benedict XVI wearing large crucifix.

2015, June 8 Litho. *Perf. 12½*

1277 A457 $1 Sheet of 4, #a-d 8.00 8.00

Souvenir Sheet

1278 A457 $3.50 multi 7.00 7.00

Birds A458

No. 1279: a, Eclectus parrot (30x40mm). b, Brahminy kite (60x40mm). c, Whiskered tern (30x40mm). d, Black-winged stilt (30x40mm). e, Collared kingfisher (60x40mm). f, Black kite (30x40mm).
$4, Sulphur-crested cockatoo, horiz.

2015, June 15 Litho. *Perf. 12*

1279 A458 65c Sheet of 6, #a-f 8.00 8.00

Souvenir Sheet

1280 A458 $4 multi 8.00 8.00

No. 1280 contains one 40x30mm stamp.

Birth of Princess Charlotte of Cambridge — A459

No. 1281: a, Duke of Cambridge and Prince George. b, Princess Diana and Prince William. c, Duchess of Cambridge and Prince George. d, Duke and Duchess of Cambridge, Princess Charlotte.
$4, Duchess of Cambridge holding Princess Charlotte.

2015, July 13 Litho. *Perf. 12*

1281 A459 $1.20 Sheet of 4, #a-d 9.75 9.75

Souvenir Sheet

1282 A459 $4 multi 8.00 8.00

Visit of Pope Francis to Washington, D.C. — A460

No. 1283 — Pope Francis: a, Smiling, denomination at UR. b, Facing right, denomination at UL. c, Waving, hand at right, denomination at UR. d, Smiling, denomination at UL. e, Waving, hand at left, denomination at UR. f, Waving, hand at left, denomination at UL.
$4, Pope Francis with Pres. Barack Obama and wife, Michelle.

2015, Nov. 25 Litho. *Perf. 14*

1283 A460 65c Sheet of 6, #a-f 8.00 8.00

Souvenir Sheet

1284 A460 $4 multi 8.00 8.00

No. 1284 contains one 80x30mm stamp.

Pres. Dwight D. Eisenhower (1890-1969) — A461

No. 1285 — Pres. Eisenhower: a, Wearing golf cap. b, With three men on golf course. c, Giving "V" for victory sign. d, Holding baseball. e, Waving to crowd from train. f, Wearing military uniform, standing in car.
$4, Pres. Eisenhower with wife, Mamie, horiz.

2015, Dec. 7 Litho. *Perf. 14*

1285 A461 65c Sheet of 6, #a-f 8.00 8.00

Souvenir Sheet

Perf. 12½

1286 A461 $4 multi 8.00 8.00

No. 1286 contains one 51x38mm stamp.

Sir Winston Churchill (1874-1965), British Prime Minister — A462

No. 1287 — Churchill: a, Smoking cigar. b, Aiming submachine gun. c, With Pres. Franklin D. Roosevelt. d, Giving "V" for Victory sign.
$4, Churchill speaking in front of picture of Abraham Lincoln, horiz.

2015, Dec. 7 Litho. *Perf. 12½*

1287 A462 $1.20 Sheet of 4, #a-d 9.75 9.75

Souvenir Sheet

1288 A462 $4 multi 8.00 8.00

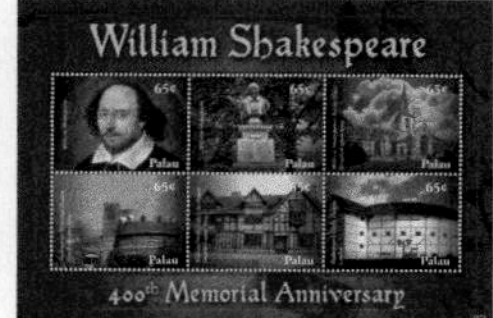

William Shakespeare (1564-1616), Writer — A463

No. 1289: a, Portrait of Shakespeare. b, Statue of Shakespeare. c, Shakespeare's burial place, Stratford-upon-Avon, Great Britain. d, Shakespeare Memorial Theater, Stratford-upon-Avon. e, Shakespeare's birthplace, Stratford-upon-Avon. f, Globe Theater, London.
$4, Shakespeare's first folio, 1623, vert.

2015, Dec. 7 Litho. *Perf. 14*

1289 A463 65c Sheet of 6, #a-f 8.00 8.00

Souvenir Sheet

Perf. 12

1290 A463 $4 multi 8.00 8.00

No. 1290 contains one 30x50mm stamp.

Christmas — A464

Paintings by Bartolomé Esteban Murillo: 34c, The Annunciation. 49c, Virgin and Child in Glory. $1, Madonna and Child. $2, Virgin with Child.

2015, Dec. 7 Litho. *Perf. 12½*

1291-1294 A464 Set of 4 7.75 7.75

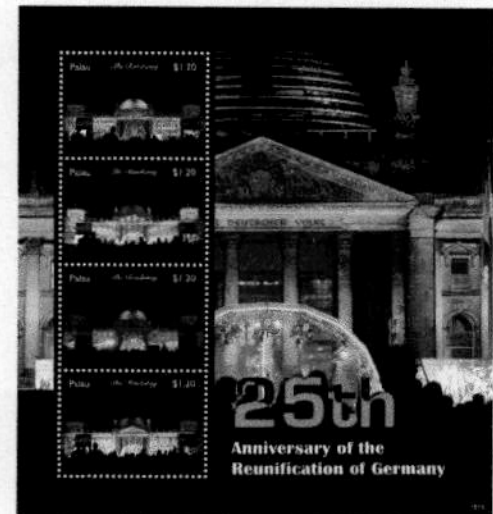

German Reunification, 25th Anniv. — A465

No. 1295 — Reichstag Building, Berlin: a, Side towers in red light. b, Side towers in yellow light. c, Side towers in purple light, statues near dome not visible. d, Side towers in purple light, statues near dome in blue light.
$4, Reichstag Building with columns in red and white light, vert.

2015, Dec. 17 Litho. *Perf. 12*

1295 A465 $1.20 Sheet of 4, #a-d 9.75 9.75

Souvenir Sheet

Perf. 12½

1296 A465 $4 multi 8.00 8.00

No. 1296 contains one 38x51mm stamp.

Spacecraft from *Star Trek Deep Space Nine* — A466

No. 1297: a, U.S.S. Defiant, denomination at UR. b, Deep Space 9. c, U.S.S. Defiant, denomination at UL. d, Runabout. e, Cardassian Galor Class. f, Bajoran Solar Sail.
$4, U.S.S. Defiant, diff.

2015, Dec. 31 Litho. *Perf. 12*

1297 A466 65c Sheet of 6, #a-f 8.00 8.00

Souvenir Sheet

Perf. 14

1298 A466 $4 multi 8.00 8.00

No. 1298 contains one 80x30mm stamp.

Mollusks A467

No. 1299: a, Palau nautilus, tentacles at left. b, Chambered nautilus, tentacles at left. c, Palau nautilus, tentacles at right. d, Chambered nautilus, tentacles at right.
$4, Palau nautilus, vert.

2015, Dec. 31 Litho. *Perf. 14*

1299 A467 $1.20 Sheet of 4, #a-d 9.75 9.75

Souvenir Sheet

Perf. 12

1300 A467 $4 multi 8.00 8.00

Coral Reef Snakes A468

No. 1301: a, Turtle-headed sea snake, name in white at top. b, Turtle-headed sea snake, name in black at bottom. c, Yellow-lipped sea krait, snake's body extending to right. d, Yellow-lipped sea krait, snake's body extending to left. e, Yellow-lipped sea krait and orange rock. f, Yellow-lipped sea krait, snake's body going through coral.
$4, Head of Yellow-lipped sea krait, horiz.

2015, Dec. 31 Litho. *Perf.*

1301 A468 65c Sheet of 6, #a-f 8.00 8.00

Souvenir Sheet

1302 A468 $4 multi 8.00 8.00

No. 1302 contains one 44x33mm oval stamp.

World War II Submarines — A469

No. 1303: a, USS Archerfish. b, USS Gar. c, USS Blackfish. d, USS Tullibee, e, USS Seawolf. f, USS Darter.
$4, USS Seal.

2015, Dec. 31 Litho. *Perf. 12*

1303 A469 65c Sheet of 6, #a-f 8.00 8.00

Souvenir Sheet

Perf. 14

1304 A469 $4 multi 8.00 8.00

No. 1304 contains one 80x30mm stamp.

Flora A470

No. 1305: a, Screw pine. b, Coral tree flowers. c, Bayhops. d, Breadfruit. e, Coconut palm. f, Beach naupaka.
$4, Mangrove flowers.

2016, Feb. 2 Litho. *Perf.*

1305 A470 65c Sheet of 6, #a-f 8.00 8.00

Souvenir Sheet

1306 A470 $4 multi 8.00 8.00

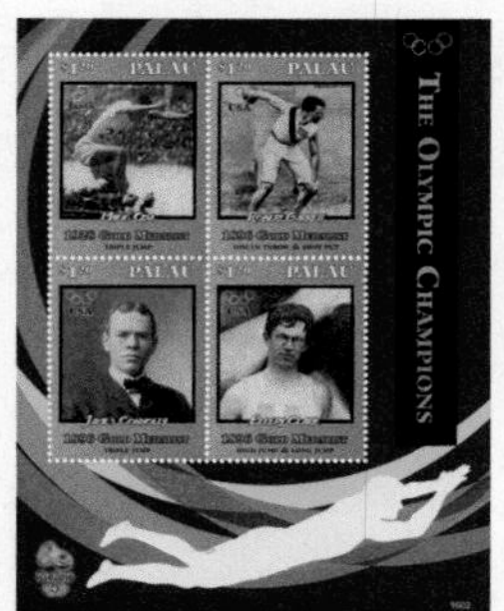

2016 Summer Olympics, Rio de Janeiro — A471

No. 1307 — Gold medalists: a, Mikio Oda, 1928 triple jump, Japan. b, Robert Garrett, 1896 discus and shot put, United States. c, James Connolly, 1896 triple jump, United States. d, Ellery Clark, 1896 high jump and long jump, United States.
$4, Yoshiyuki Tsuruta, 1928 200-meter breaststroke, Japan.

2016, Mar. 8 Litho. *Perf. 14*

1307 A471 $1.20 Sheet of 4, #a-d 9.75 9.75

Souvenir Sheet

Perf. 12½

1308 A471 $4 multi 8.00 8.00

No. 1308 contains one 38x51mm stamp.

1888 Paintings of the Roulin Family by Vincent van Gogh (1853-90) — A472

No. 1309: a, Portrait of the Postman Joseph Roulin (Nov.-Dec.). b, Portrait of Madame Augustine Roulin. c, Portrait of Madame Augustine Roulin and Baby Marcelle. d, Young Man with a Cap (Armand Roulin). e, The Schoolboy with Uniform Cap (Camille Roulin). f, Portait of Marcelle Roulin.
$4, Portrait of the Postman Joseph Roulin (April).

2016, Mar. 8 Litho. *Perf. 14*

1309 A472 65c Sheet of 6, #a-f 8.00 8.00

Souvenir Sheet

Perf. 12½

1310 A472 $4 multi 8.00 8.00

No. 1310 contains one 38x51mm stamp.

A473

Jimi Hendrix (1942-70), Rock Guitarist — A474

No. 1311 — Various photographs of Hendrix with frame color of: a, Magenta. b, Purple. c, Green. d, Greenish blue. e, Red orange. f, Yellow.
No. 1312 — Various photographs of Hendrix with frame color of: a, Red orange. b, Greenish blue. c, Yellow. d, Green. e, Magenta. f, Purple.
$4, Hendrix, greenish blue frame, vert.

2016, Mar. 8 Litho. *Perf.*

1311 A473 65c Sheet of 6, #a-f 8.00 8.00
1312 A474 65c Sheet of 6, #a-f 8.00 8.00

Souvenir Sheet

Perf. 12½

1313 A474 $4 multi 8.00 8.00

No. 1313 contains one 38x51mm stamp.

Souvenir Sheets

Elvis Presley (1935-77) — A475

Presley: No. 1314, $4, Donating blood to the Red Cross. No. 1315, $4, At recording session, vert. No. 1316, $4, At 1975 Tornado Victim Benefit Concert, vert. No. 1317, $4, Enjoying a moment of Army downtime, vert.

2016, Mar. 8 Litho. *Perf. 14*
1314-1317 A475 Set of 4 32.00 32.00

Queen Elizabeth II, 90th Birthday A476

No. 1318 — Queen Elizabeth II: a, Waving, b, Wearing deep violet hat. c, Wearing pale yellow hat.
$5, Queen Elizabeth II wearing blue dress.

2016, Apr. 1 Litho. *Perf. 12½*
1318 A476 $1.50 Sheet of 3, #a-c 9.00 9.00

Souvenir Sheet

1319 A476 $5 multi 10.00 10.00

World Stamp Show 2016, New York A477

No. 1320: a, Gapstow Bridge, Central Park. b, Statue of Liberty. c, Grand Central Terminal. d, Manhattan Bridge.
$3, New York City skyline, horiz.

2016, Apr. 19 Litho. *Perf. 12*
1320 A477 $1.25 Sheet of 4, #a-d 10.00 10.00

Souvenir Sheet
Perf. 14

1321 A477 $3 multi 6.00 6.00

No. 1321 contains one 160x60mm stamp.

Nancy Reagan (1921-2016), First Lady — A478

No. 1322 — Mrs. Reagan with: a, Pres. Ronald Reagan, Queen Elizabeth II and Prince Philip. b, Queen Elizabeth II. c, Princess Diana. d, Pres. Reagan, Pope John Paul II. e, British Prime Minister Margaret Thatcher. f, Pres. Reagan, Japanese Prime Minister Yasuhiro Nakasone and his wife, Tsutako.

No. 1323 — Mrs. Reagan with: a, Pres. Reagan, Vice-President George H.W. Bush and his wife, Barbara. b, Pres. George W. Bush and his wife, Laura. c, First ladies Rosalynn Carter, Barbara Bush, Betty Ford and Hillary Clinton. d, Pres. Barack Obama.

No. 1324, Mrs. Reagan as actress with picture having: a, White background. b, Black background.
$5, Mrs. Reagan seated, vert.

2016, Apr. 19 Litho. *Perf. 14*
1322 A478 $1 Sheet of 6, #a-f 12.00 12.00
1323 A478 $1.20 Sheet of 4, #a-d 9.75 9.75

Souvenir Sheets
Perf. 13¾

1324 A478 $2.50 Sheet of 2, #a-b 10.00 10.00

Perf. 12

1325 A478 $5 multi 10.00 10.00

No. 1324 contains two 50x50mm diamond-shaped stamps.

World of Sea and Reef Type of 1986 Redrawn

Miniature Sheet

No. 1326: a, Spear fisherman. b, Native raft. c, Sailing canoes. d, Rock islands, sailfish. e, Inter-island boat, flying fish. f, Bonefish. g, Common jack. h, Mackerel. i, Sailfish. j, Barracuda. k, Triggerfish. l, Dolphinfish. m, Spear fisherman, grouper. n, Manta ray. o, Marlin. p, Parrotfish. q, Wrasse. r, Red snapper. s, Herring. t, Dugong. u, Surgeonfish. v, Leopard ray. w, Hawksbill turtle. x, Needlefish. y, Tuna. z, Octopus. aa, Clownfish. ab, Squid. ac, Grouper. ad, Moorish idol. ae, Queen conch, starfish. af, Squirrelfish. ag, Starfish, sting ray. ah, Lionfish. ai, Angelfish. aj, Butterflyfish. ak, Spiny lobster. al, Mangrove crab. am, Tridacna. an, Moray eel.

2016, May 18 Litho. *Perf. 13¼*
1326 Sheet of 40 38.00 38.00
a.-an. A19 47c Any single .95 .95

World Stamp Show 2016, New York. No. 1326 contains forty 26x21mm stamps.

Characters From *Star Trek* Television Series — A479

No. 1327: a, Capt. James T. Kirk. b, Mr. Spock. c, Scotty. d, Sulu. e, Dr. McCoy. f, Uhura.
$3, Kirk, Spock, McCoy, Uhura and Sulu.

2016, Aug. 15 Litho. *Perf. 14*
1327 A479 $1 Sheet of 6, #a-f 12.00 12.00

Souvenir Sheet
Perf. 12

1328 A479 $3 multi 6.00 6.00

No. 1328 contains one 40x60mm stamp.

Birds A480

No. 1329: a, Dusky white-eye. b, Palau flycatcher. c, Palau fantail. d, Giant white-eye.
$5, Palau fruit dove, vert.

2016, Sept. 22 Litho. *Perf. 12½*
1329 A480 $1.50 Sheet of 4, #a-d 12.00 12.00

Souvenir Sheet

1330 A480 $5 multi 10.00 10.00

Ngardmau Waterfall — A481

No. 1331 — Waterfall with: a, White frame at left, top and bottom. b, White frame at right, top and bottom. c, Orange frame at left, top and bottom. d, Orange frame at right, top and bottom.
$5, Waterfall, diff.

2016, Sept. 22 Litho. *Perf. 12*
1331 A481 $1.50 Sheet of 4, #a-d 12.00 12.00

Souvenir Sheet

1332 A481 $5 multi 10.00 10.00

Visit of Pres. Barack Obama to the United Kingdom A482

No. 1333: a, Pres. Obama, flags in background. b, British Prime Minister David Cameron, flags in background. c, Pres. Obama waving, open airplane door in background. d, Pres. Obama waving. e, Pres. Obama shaking hands with Cameron. f, Pres. Obama and Cameron, fence in background.

No. 1334: a, Pres. Obama shaking hands with Queen Elizabeth II (40x30mm). b, Queen Elizabeth II, Pres. Obama and his wife, Michelle (40x30mm). c, The Obamas with Prince Harry, Duke and Duchess of Cambridge (80x30mm).

No. 1335: a, Pres. Obama seated. b, Cameron seated.

2016, Sept. 22 Litho. *Perf. 14*
1333 A482 $1 Sheet of 6, #a-f 12.00 12.00
1334 A482 $2 Sheet of 3, #a-c 12.00 12.00

Souvenir Sheet
Perf. 12

1335 A482 $2.50 Sheet of 2, #a-b 10.00 10.00

William Shakespeare (1564-1616), Writer — A483

No. 1336: a, 1873 engraving depicting scene from *As You Like It.* b, Line from *As You Like It.* c, Line from *Twelfth Night.* d, 1873 engraving depicting scene from *Twelfth Night.* e, 1873 engraving depicting scene from *King Richard II.* f, Line from *King Richard II.*

No. 1337 — 1870 engravings depicting scenes from: a, *Hamlet.* b, *The Winter's Tale.* c, *A Midsummer Night's Dream.* d, *Twelfth Night.*
$5, Shakespeare, vert.

2016, Sept. 30 Litho. *Perf. 14*
1336 A483 $1 Sheet of 6, #a-f 12.00 12.00

Perf. 12½

1337 A483 $1.50 Sheet of 4, #a-d 12.00 12.00

Souvenir Sheet
Perf.

1338 A483 $5 multi 10.00 10.00

No. 1337 contains four 51x38mm stamps. No. 1338 contains one 33x43mm oval stamp.

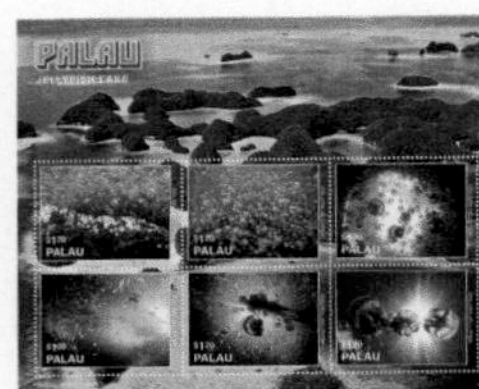

A484

A485

A486

Tourism A487

No. 1339, $1.20: Various photographs of golden jellyfish in Jellyfish lake, as shown.

No. 1340, $1.20 — Giant clams: a, True giant clam. b, Bear claw giant clam. c, China giant clam. d, Smooth giant clam. e, Elongated giant clam. f, Fluted giant clam.

No. 1341, $1.25 — Abais: a, Koror Abai. b, Melekeok Abai. c, Aimeliik Abai. d, Airai Abai.

No. 1342, $1.50 — Rock Islands landscapes: a, Tutkalrenguis. b, Milky Way. c, Akasi Island. d, Arc Island.

No. 1343, $1.75 — Rays: a, Manta ray. b, Manta ray and diver. c, Devil ray. d, Two Manta rays.

No. 1344, $1.75 — Underwater World War II airplane wreckage: a, Jake float plane wing and engine. b, Jake float plane fuselage. c, Jake float plane propeller. d, Zero plane.

No. 1345, $1.50 — Protected species: a, Gray reef shark. b, Hawksbill turtle. c, Napolleon wrasse.

No. 1346, $1.75 — Crabs: a, Hermit crab. b, Land crab. c, Coconut crab.

2016, Oct. 1 Litho. *Perf. 12½*

Sheets of 6, #a-f

1339-1340 A484 Set of 2 29.00 29.00

Sheets of 4, #a-d
Perf. 14

1341-1342 A485 Set of 2 22.00 22.00
1343-1344 A486 Set of 2 28.00 28.00

Sheets of 3, #a-c

1345-1346 A487 Set of 2 19.50 19.50

Attack on Pearl Harbor, 75th Anniv. A488

No. 1347: a, Sailor. b, U. S. Coast Guard poster. c, These Colors Won't Run poster. d, Avenge Pearl Harbor poster. e, American flag at half-staff. f, Remember Pearl Harbor recruitment poster.

No. 1348, horiz.: a, USS West Virginia. b, USS Arizona.

2016, Dec. 30 Litho. *Perf. 14*

1347 A488 $1.35 Sheet of 6, #a-f 16.50 16.50

Souvenir Sheet

Perf. 12

1348 A488 $3 Sheet of 2, #a-b 12.00 12.00

No. 1348 contains two 64x32mm triangular stamps.

Fish A489

No. 1349: a, Orange-striped wrasse. b, Palauan deepwater cardinalfish. c, Aurora anthias. d, Dabra goby. e, Bullseye pygmy goby. f, Needlespine coral goby.

No. 1350: a, Giant pygmy goby. b, Deep blue chromis.

2016, Dec. 30 Litho. *Perf. 12*

1349 A489 $1 Sheet of 6, #a-f 12.00 12.00

Souvenir Sheet

1350 A489 $2.50 Sheet of 2, #a-b 10.00 10.00

Miniature Sheet

2016 Summer Olympics, Rio de Janeiro — A490

No. 1351 — Photographs of Palauan Olympic Team: a, 50c, Shawn Dingilius Wallace (30x40mm). b, 50c, Dirngulbau Ub Misech (30x40mm). c, 50c, Florian Temengil (30x40mm). d, 50c, Rodman Teltull (30x40mm). e, 50c, Marina Toribiong (30x40mm). f, $1, Olympic team following Palauan flagbearer (90x40mm). g, $1, Palauan athletes and Olympic rings (60x40mm).

2016, Dec. 20 Litho. *Perf. 14*

1351 A490 Sheet of 7, #a-g 9.00 9.00

Miniature Sheet

2016 Festival of the Pacific Arts A491

No. 1352: a, 50c, Man and woman (30x40mm). b, 50c, Man and woman, large pole in background (30x40mm). c, 50c, Man dancing with spears (30x40mm). d, 50c, Man standing (30x40mm). e, 50c, Man kneeling, holding shell (30x40mm). f, 50c, Woman facing right (30x40mm). g, 50c, Women dancing (30x40mm). h, 50c, Two women, one with greenish blue skirt (30x40mm). i, $1, Festival participants in front of building (120x40mm). j, $1, Four women (60x40mm). k, $1, Male dancers holding spears (60x40mm).

2016, Dec. 30 Litho. *Perf. 14*

1352 A491 Sheet of 11, #a-k 14.00 14.00

Legends of the Wild West A492

No. 1353: a, Bat Masterson. b, Annie Oakley. c, Kit Carson. d, Wild Bill Hickok. e, John Frémont. f, Wyatt Earp.

$5, Buffalo Bill Cody.

Perf. 13¼x12½

2017, Feb. 28 Litho.

1353 A492 $1 Sheet of 6, #a-f 12.00 12.00

Souvenir Sheet

Perf. 13¼

1354 A492 $5 multi 10.00 10.00

No. 1354 contains one 38x51mm stamp.

Miniature Sheets

A493

Princess Diana (1961-97) — A494

No. 1355 — Photograph of Princess Diana and flag of: a, $1, Saudi Arabia (30x40mm). b, $1, Hong Kong (30x40mm). c, $1, Italy (30x40mm). d, $1, Pakistan (30x40mm). e, $1, Egypt (30x40mm). f, $1, Nepal (30x40mm). g, $1.50, India (60x40mm).

No. 1356 — Princess Diana wearing: a, Black dress and pearl necklace. b, Purple dress. c, Black dress, no necklace. d, Yellow jacket.

2017, Apr. 14 Litho. *Perf. 14*

1355 A493 Sheet of 7, #a-g 15.00 15.00

Perf.

1356 A494 $1.80 Sheet of 4, #a-d 14.50 14.50

Miniature Sheets

A495

Pres. John F. Kennedy (1917-63) — A496

No. 1357 — Pres. John F. Kennedy: a, As baby. b, As young boy, holding dog. c, In Navy uniform. d, On sailboat with wife, Jacqueline. e, With wife and children. f, Seated at desk.

No. 1358 — Pres. Kennedy with: a, His father, mother and siblings. b, Mother, Rose and sister, Eunice. c, Brother Joe, Jr., sisters Kathleen and Rosemary. d, Brothers Robert and Edward.

2017, Apr. 14 Litho. *Perf. 14*

1357 A495 $1.35 Sheet of 6, #a-f 16.50 16.50

Perf. 12

1358 A496 $1.60 Sheet of 4, #a-d 13.00 13.00

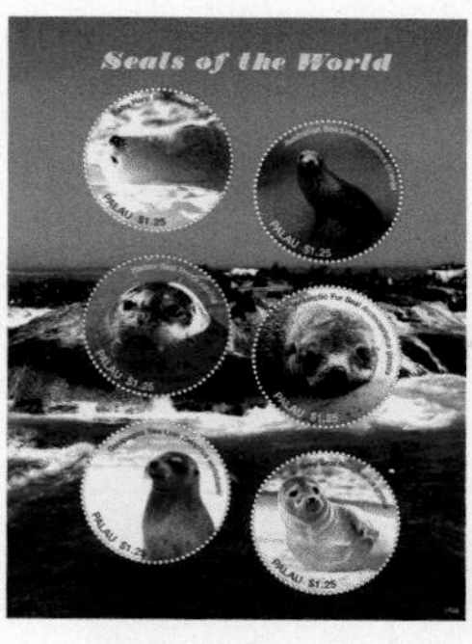

Seals A497

No. 1359: a, Baby harp seal. b, Australian sea lion. c, Harbor seal. d, Antarctic fur seal. e, Galapagos sea lion. f, Grey seal.

$4.50, New Zealand fur seal.

2017, May 5 Litho. *Perf.*

1359 A497 $1.25 Sheet of 6, #a-f 15.00 15.00

Souvenir Sheet

1360 A497 $4.50 multi 9.00 9.00

Animals A498

No. 1361: a, Waxy monkey frog. b, Persian leopard. c, Alexandrine parakeet. d, Yellow-bellied slider.

$4, Golden lion tamarin, vert.

2017, May 15 Litho. *Perf. 12½x12¾*

1361 A498 $2 Sheet of 4, #a-d 16.00 16.00

Souvenir Sheet

1362 A498 $4 multi 8.00 8.00

Paintings by Gustav Klimt (1862-1918) — A499

No. 1363: a, Portrait of Hermine Gallia. b, Portrait of Helene Klimt. c, Portrait of Serena Lederer. d, Margaret Stonborough-Wittgenstein.

$4, Adele Bloch-Bauer I (not named on stamp).

2017, Oct. 19 Litho. *Perf. 12*

1363 A499 $1.60 Sheet of 4, #a-d 13.00 13.00

Souvenir Sheet

Perf. 12½

1364 A499 $4 multi 8.00 8.00

No. 1364 contains one 38x51mm stamp.

Souvenir Sheets

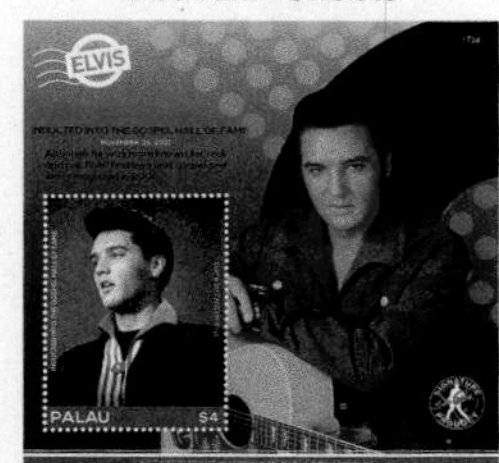

Elvis Presley (1935-77) — A500

Inscriptions: No. 1365, $4, Inducted into the Gospel Hall of Fame. No. 1366, $4, Joins Country Music Hall of Fame. No. 1367, $4, Receives W. C. Handy Award. No. 1368, $4, Inducted into the Rock 'n' Roll Hall of Fame.

2017, Oct. 26 Litho. *Perf. 12½*

1365-1368 A500 Set of 4 32.00 32.00

Miniature Sheet

Palau Community Action Agency, 50th Anniv. — A501

No. 1369 — Inscriptions: a, Agriculture. b, Apprentice Program. c, History. d, Small Business. e, Care for Environment. f, Fishing Industry. g, Pre-school Head Start. h, Health Screening. i, Nutrition Healthy Food. j, Play to Learn. k, Education. l, Local Produce Market. m, Local Medicine. n, Tourism & Community. o, Youth Programs.

2017, Nov. 10 Litho. *Perf. 11*

1369 A501 50c Sheet of 15, #a-o 15.00 15.00

Birds A502

No. 1370: a, 50c, Red bird-of-paradise. b, 50c, Northern cardinal. c, $1.50, European robin. d, $1.50, Bali myna. e, $2, Sulphur-crested cockatoo. f, $2.50, Bluethroat.

No. 1371: a, $1.25, Atlantic puffin. b, $2.25, Lilac-breasted roller. c, $3.25, Nicobar pigeon.

2018, Jan. 24 Litho. *Perf. 14*

1370 A502 Sheet of 6, #a-f 17.00 17.00

Souvenir Sheet

Perf. 12

1371 A502 Sheet of 3, #a-c 13.50 13.50

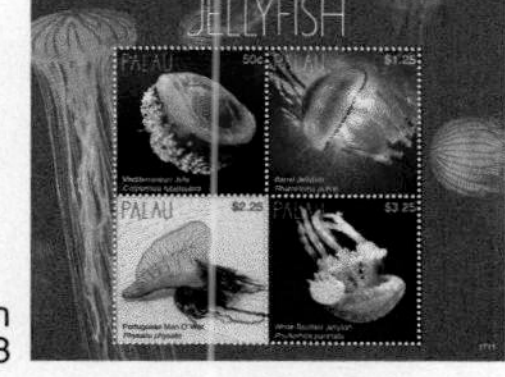

Jellyfish A503

No. 1372: a, 50c, Mediterranean jelly. b, $1.25, Barrel jellyfish. c, $2.25, Portuguese man o' war. d, $3.25, White-spotted jellyfish.

No. 1373, vert.: a, Lion's mane jellyfish. b, Mediterranean jelly, turquoise blue background.

2018, Jan. 24 Litho. *Perf. 13¾*

1372 A503 Sheet of 4, #a-d 14.50 14.50

Souvenir Sheet

Perf. 12¾x12½

1373 A503 $3 Sheet of 2, #a-b 12.00 12.00

No. 1373 contains two 38x51mm stamps.

Underwater Landscapes — A504

No. 1374: a, 50c, Bora Bora, Pacific Ocean. b, $1.25, Japan, Pacific Ocean. c, $2.25, Iceland, Atlantic Ocean. d, $3.25, Indonesia, Indian Ocean.
No. 1375: a, Palau, Pacific Ocean. b, Maldives, Indian Ocean.

2018, Jan. 24 Litho. *Perf. 14*
1374 A504 Sheet of 4, #a-d 14.50 14.50

Souvenir Sheet
Perf. 12½

1375 A504 $3 Sheet of 2, #a-b 12.00 12.00

No. 1375 contains two 51x38mm stamps.

Visit of Pres. Donald Trump to Japan A505

No. 1376: a, First Lady Melania Trump. b, Pres. Donald Trump. c, Japanese Prime Minister Shinzo Abe. d, Akie Abe.
$4, Abe and Pres. Trump, horiz.

2018, Jan. 24 Litho. *Perf. 12*
1376 A505 $1.60 Sheet of 4, #a-d 13.00 13.00

Souvenir Sheet
Perf. 12¾

1377 A505 $4 multi 8.00 8.00

No. 1376 contains one 51x38mm stamp.

Souvenir Sheet

Engagement of Prince Harry and Meghan Markle — A506

No. 1378 — Couple and background of: a, Grass. b, Brick wall.

2018, Jan. 31 Litho. *Perf. 12*
1378 A506 $3 Sheet of 2, #a-b 12.00 12.00

Miniature Sheet

Seahorses — A507

No. 1379: a, 50c, Big belly seahorse. b, 75c, Leafy seadragon. c, $1, Weedy seadragon. d, $1.25, Zebra seahorse. e, $1.50, Yellow seahorse. f, $1.75, Pygmy seahorse.

2018, Feb. 1 Litho. *Perf. 13¾*
1379 A507 Sheet of 6, #a-f 13.50 13.50

Miniature Sheet

Elvis Presley (1935-77) — A508

No. 1380 — Presley: a, Holding microphone, both hands visible. b, Wearing vest and red shirt. c, Playing guitar. d, Holding microphone, one hand visible.

2018, June 5 Litho. *Perf. 14*
1380 A508 $2 Sheet of 4, #a-d 16.00 16.00

Souvenir Sheet

Marine Life Preservation — A509

No. 1381: a, Carcharhinus melanopterus. b, Chelonia mydas.

2018, June 26 Litho. *Perf. 12*
1381 A509 $1.50 Sheet of 2, #a-b 6.00 6.00

Palau Fruit Dove — A510

2018, July 5 Litho. *Perf. 14*
1382 A510 $2 multi 4.00 4.00

Printed in sheets of 4.

Palau Nautilus A511

No. 1383: a, Two nautiluses, one facing right, other facing left. b, Nautilus facing left. c, Two nautiluses facing left. d, Nautilus facing right.
No. 1384: a, Nautilus facing right. b, Nautilus facing left.

2018, July 5 Litho. *Perf. 12*
1383 A511 $2 Sheet of 4, #a-d 16.00 16.00

Souvenir Sheet

1384 A511 $3 Sheet of 2, #a-b 12.00 12.00

Miniature Sheet

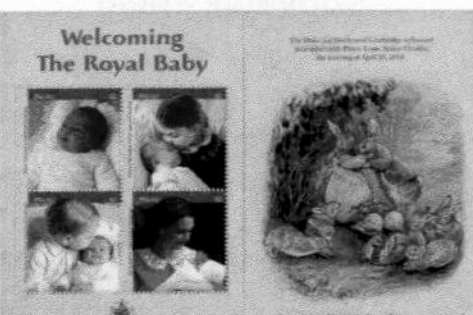

Birth of Prince Louis of Cambridge — A512

No. 1385: a, Prince Louis. b, Princess Charlotte and Prince Louis. c, Princes George and Louis. d, Duchess of Cambridge and Prince Louis.

2018, July 13 Litho. *Perf. 13¾*
1385 A512 $2 Sheet of 4, #a-d 16.00 16.00

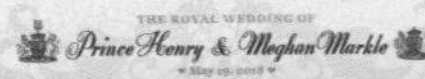

Wedding of Prince Harry and Meghan Markle A513

No. 1386: a, $1, Bride (30x40mm). b, $1, Groom (30x40mm). c, $2, Couple (30x40mm). d, $4, Couple riding in carriage (90x40mm).
No. 1387, $4, Couple standing.

2018, July 13 Litho. *Perf. 14*
1386 A513 Sheet of 4, #a-d 16.00 16.00

Souvenir Sheet
Perf. 12

1387 A513 $4 multi 8.00 8.00

No. 1387 contains one 30x50mm stamp.

Miniature Sheet

Summit Meeting of U. S. Pres. Donald Trump and North Korean Supreme Leader Kim Jong Un A514

No. 1388: a, Pres. Trump holding signed document. b, Trump and Kim shaking hands. c, Kim. d, Trump and Kim standing apart. e, Signed document. f, Trump touching Kim's shoulder.

2018, July 30 Litho. *Perf. 14*
1388 A514 $1 Sheet of 6, #a-f 12.00 12.00

First Man on the Moon, 50th Anniv. (in 2019) A515

No. 1389: a, 50c, Crew of Apollo 11. b, 75c, Footprint on moon. c, $1, Lunar Module on moon. d, $1.25, Astronaut Edwin E. Aldrin, Jr. saluting flag. e, $1.50, Aldrin on Moon. f, $1.75, Earthrise.
$4, Launch of Apollo 11, vert.

2018, Aug. 30 Litho. *Perf. 12*
1389 A515 Sheet of 6, #a-f 13.50 13.50

Souvenir Sheet
Perf. 14

1390 A515 $4 multi 8.00 8.00

No. 1390 contains one 30x80mm stamp.

Miniature Sheet

Visit of Pres. Donald Trump to Helsinki, Finland A516

No. 1391: a, $1, Pres. Trump and Russian Pres. Vladimir Putin shaking hands. b, $2, Trump and Putin standing. c, $3, Trump and Finland Pres. Sauli Niinistö. d, $4, Trump, Niinistö and their wives.

2018, Nov. 9 Litho. *Perf. 12*
1391 A516 Sheet of 4, #a-d 20.00 20.00

Miniature Sheet

Sea Turtles A517

No. 1392: a, 50c, Green sea turtle. b, 75c, Green sea turtle, diff. c, $1, Hawksbill sea turtle. d, $1.25, Hawksbill sea turtle, diff. e, $1.50, Loggerhead sea turtle. f, $1.75, Loggerhead sea turtle, diff.

2018, Nov. 9 Litho. *Perf. 14*
1392 A517 Sheet of 6, #a-f 13.50 13.50

Giant Clams A518

No. 1393 — Various photographs of clams: a, $1. b, $1.50. c, $2. d, $2.50.
$4, Giant clam, vert.

2018, Nov. 9 Litho. *Perf. 14*
1393 A518 Sheet of 4, #a-d 14.00 14.00

Souvenir Sheet
Perf. 12½

1394 A518 $4 multi 8.00 8.00

No. 1394 contains one 38x51mm stamp.

Miniature Sheet

Frangipani Flowers — A519

No. 1395: a, Bunch of flowers with white petals. b, Bunch of flowers with pink petals. c, Single flower with pink petals. d, Two flowers with white petals.

2018, Nov. 30 Litho. *Perf.*
1395 A519 $2 Sheet of 4, #a-d 16.00 16.00

Whales A520

No. 1396: a, 75c, Beluga whale. b, $1, Blue whale. c, $1.25, Humpback whale. d, $1.50, Minke whale. e, $1.75, Killer whale. f, $2, Sperm whale.

No. 1397, vert. — Killer whale and: a, Cubes. b, Sphere.

2018, Nov. 30 Litho. *Perf. 14*

1396 A520 Sheet of 6, #a-f 16.50 16.50

Souvenir Sheet

Perf. 12½

1397 A520 $3 Sheet of 2, #a-b 12.00 12.00

No. 1397 contains two 38x51mm stamps.

Sea Birds A521

No. 1398: a, 25c, Sooty tern. b, 50c, Black-billed plover. c, $1, Bulwer's petrel. d, $1.50, Whiskered tern. e, $2, Pacific golden plover. f, $2.50, Common tern.

No. 1399: a, $1, Brown noddy. b, $2, Dunlin. c, $3, Ruddy turnstone.

2018, Dec. 10 Litho. *Perf. 14*

1398 A521 Sheet of 6, #a-f 15.50 15.50

Souvenir Sheet

1399 A521 Sheet of 3, #a-c 12.00 12.00

Dolphins A522

No. 1400: a, $1, Spinner dolphin. b, $2, Pantropical spotted dolphin. c, $3, Atlantic spotted dolphins. d, $4, Striped dolphin.

No. 1401, Common bottlenose dolphin.

2018, Dec. 10 Litho. *Perf. 14*

1400 A522 Sheet of 4, #a-d 20.00 20.00

Souvenir Sheet

Perf. 12½

1401 A522 $4 multi 8.00 8.00

No. 1401 contains one 51x38mm stamp.

Nicobar Pigeons A523

No. 1402 — Various photographs of Nicobar pigeons: a, $1. b, $1.50. c, $2. d, $2.50.

No. 1403, horiz. — Various photographs of Nicobar pigeons: a, $3. b, $3.50.

2018, Dec. 19 Litho. *Perf. 14*

1402 A523 Sheet of 4, #a-d 14.00 14.00

Souvenir Sheet

1403 A523 Sheet of 2, #a-b 13.00 13.00

A524

Birds A525

No. 1404: a, 25c, Nutmeg mannikin. b, 50c, Slaty-legged crake. c, 75c, Red-legged crake. d, $1, Western yellow wagtail. e, $1.50, Nocobar pigeon. f, $2, Palau flycatcher.

No. 1405: a, 50c, Buff-banded rail. b, $1, Micronesian myzomela. c, $2, Micronesian myzomela, diff. d, $3, Buff-banded rail, diff. $4, Citrine white-eye.

2018, Dec. 19 Litho. *Perf. 14*

1404 A524 Sheet of 6, #a-f 12.00 12.00

1405 A525 Sheet of 4, #a-d 13.00 13.00

Souvenir Sheet

Perf. 12½

1406 A525 $4 multi 8.00 8.00

No. 1406 contains one 51x38mm stamp.

Miniature Sheet

Space Shuttle Columbia Disaster, 15th Anniv. — A527

No. 1409: a, Mission specialist David M. Brown (1956-2003). b, Mission specialist Ilan Ramon (1954-2003). c, Mission specialist Kalpana Chawla (1962-2003). d, Lift-off of Space Shuttle Columbia. e, Commander Rick D. Husband (1957-2003). f, Insignia of Shuttle mission STS-107. g, Mission specialist Laurel Clark (1961-2003). h, Payload commander Michael B. Anderson (1959-2003). i, Pilot William C. McCool (1961-2003).

2018, Dec. 25 Litho. *Perf. 14*

1409 A527 $1 Sheet of 9, #a-i 18.00 18.00

Sharks A528

No. 1410: a, 50c, Bull shark, country name in purple. b, 50c, Bull shark, country name in orange. c, $1, Tiger shark, country name in purple. d, $1, Tiger shark, country name in orange. e, $2, Whale shark, country name in purple. f, $2, Whale shark, country name in orange.

$4, Great white shark.

2018, Dec. 25 Litho. *Perf. 14*

1410 A528 Sheet of 6, #a-f 14.00 14.00

Souvenir Sheet

Perf. 12½

1411 A528 $4 multi 8.00 8.00

No. 1411 contains one 51x38mm stamp.

Miniature Sheets

Waterfowl — A529

No. 1412: a, 50c, Two Eurasian teal. b, 75c, One Eurasian teal. c, $1, Eurasian wigeons. d, $1.25, Eurasian wigeons, diff. e, $1.50, Mallard in flight. f, $1.75, Mallard on water.

No. 1413: a, 50c, Northern pintail facing right. b, 75c, Northern pintail facing left. c, $1, Northern shoveler in flight. d, $1.25, Northern shoveler standing. e, $1.50, Tufted duck facing left. f, $1.75, Tufted duck facing right.

2018, Dec. 27 Litho. *Perf. 14*

Sheets of 6, #a-f

1412-1413 A529 Set of 2 27.00 27.00

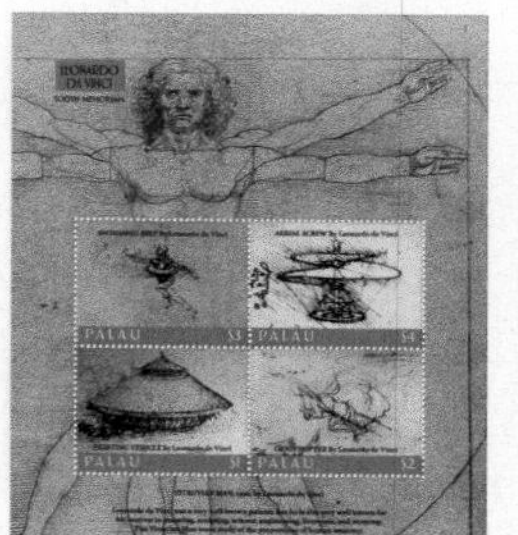
Drawings by Leonardo da Vinci (1452-1519), Sculptor and Painter — A530

No. 1414 — Drawing of: a, $1, Fighting vehicle. b, $2, Ornithopter. c, $3, Aerial screw. d, $4, Swimming belt.

$5, Self-portrait, Vitruvian Man, and Town Plan of Imola.

2018, Dec. 27 Litho. *Perf. 14*

1414 A530 Sheet of 4, #a-d 20.00 20.00

Size: 130x80mm

Imperf

1415 A530 $5 multi 10.00 10.00

Souvenir Sheets

Elvis Presley (1935-77) — A531

Inscriptions: No. 1416, $5, Elvis installs Graceland's music gates. No. 1417, $5, What have you got? No. 1418, $5, Elvis rides "Bear" at Graceland, vert. No. 1419, $5, A hard day of basic training, vert.

2018, Dec. 27 Litho. *Perf. 14*

1416-1419 A531 Set of 4 40.00 40.00

Protanguila Palau — A532

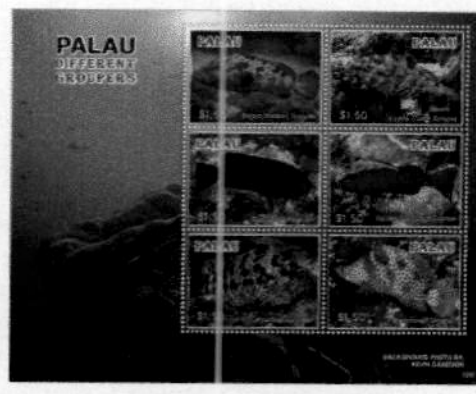
Groupers A533

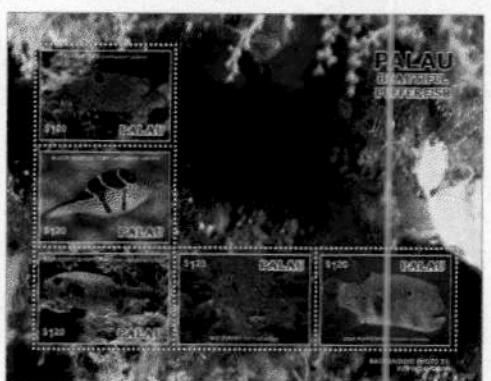
Pufferfish A534

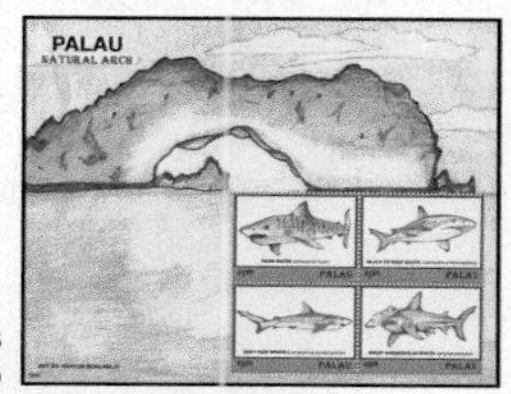
Sharks A535

Sharks A536

Manta Ray A537

Golden Jellyfish A538

No. 1420 — Background color: a, Black. b, Blue violet.

No. 1421: a, Brown marbled grouper. b, Honey comb grouper. c, Red mouth grouper. d, Square tail coral grouper. e, Camouflage grouper. f, Barramundi grouper.

No. 1422: a, Papuan toby. b, Black-saddled toby. c, Blue-spotted puffer. d, Map puffer. e, Star pufferfish.

No. 1423: a, Tiger shark. b, Black-tip reef shark. c, Gray reef shark. d, Great hammerhead shark.

No. 1424: a, Black-tip reef sharks. b, Gray reef shark, facing left, and other marine life. c, Gray reef shark, facing left, dark background. d, Gray reef shark, facing right, and fish.

2019, Jan. 1 Litho. *Perf. 14*

1420 A532 $1.95 Pair, #a-b 8.00 8.00

Miniature Sheets

1421 A533 $1.50 Sheet of 6, #a-f 18.00 18.00

1422 A534 $1.20 Sheet of 5, #a-e 12.00 12.00

1423 A535 $1.20 Sheet of 4, #a-d 9.75 9.75

1424 A536 $1.20 Sheet of 4, #a-d 9.75 9.75

Nos. 1421-1424 (4) 49.50 49.50

Souvenir Sheets

Perf. 12½

1425 A537 $4 multi 8.00 8.00

1426 A538 $4 multi 8.00 8.00

No. 1420 was printed in sheets containing two each Nos. 1420a-1420b.

Strawberry Hermit Crab — A539

No. 1427: a, $1, Crab facing forward. b, $1, Crab facing right. c, $2, Crab, diff. d, $4, Crab, diff.
$5, Crab, diff.

2019, Apr. 21 Litho. *Perf. 13¾*

1427 A539 Sheet of 4, #a-d 16.00 16.00

Souvenir Sheet

1428 A539 $5 multi 10.00 10.00

A540

Mimic Octopus A541

Nos. 1429 and 1430 — Various depictions of Mimic octopus: a, $1. b, $2. c, $3.
$5, Mimic octopus, horiz.

2019, May 1 Litho. *Perf. 12*

1429 A540 Sheet of 3, #a-c 12.00 12.00

1430 A541 Sheet of 3, #a-c 12.00 12.00

Souvenir Sheet

Perf. 14

1431 A541 $5 multi 10.00 10.00

No. 1431 contains one 80x30mm stamp.

Clearfin Lionfish A542

No. 1432: Various depictions of Clearfin lionfish, as shown.
$5, Clearfin lionfish, vert.

2019, May 6 Litho. *Perf. 13¾*

1432 A542 $2 Sheet of 4, #a-d 16.00 16.00

Souvenir Sheet

Perf. 12½

1433 A542 $5 multi 10.00 10.00

No. 1433 contains one 38x51mm stamp.

Miniature Sheet

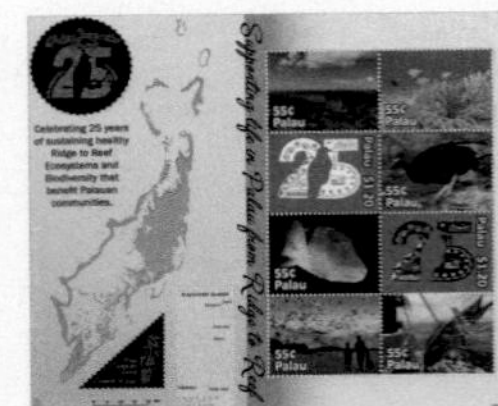

Palau Conservation Society, 25th Anniv. — A543

No. 1434: a, 55c, Aerial view of lagoon. b, 55c, Fish and coral. c, 55c, Bird. d, 55c, Grouper. e, 55c, Children on beach, flock of birds. f, 55c, Fishing boat and caught fish. g, $1.20, Bird, "25" in white. h, $1.20, Bird, "25" in black.

2019, June 14 Litho. *Perf. 12*

1434 A543 Sheet of 8, #a-h 11.50 11.50

Miniature Sheet

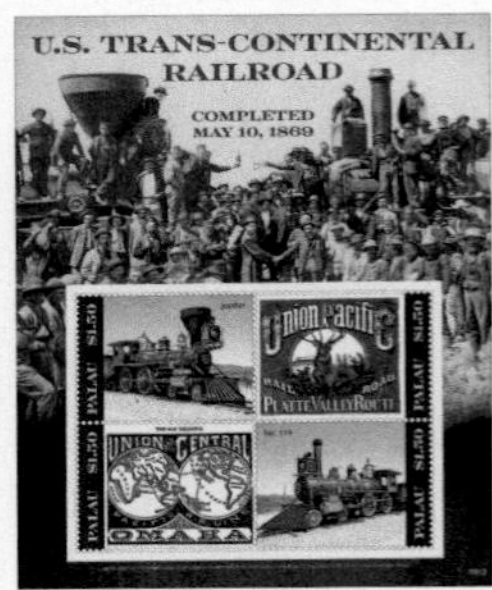

U.S. Transcontinental Railroad, 150th Anniv. — A544

No. 1435: a, Jupiter locomotive. b, Union Pacific Railroad emblem. c, Union and Central Pacific Railroad emblem. d, Locomotive No. 119.

2019, July 2 Litho. *Perf. 14*

1435 A544 $1.50 Sheet of 4, #a-d 12.00 12.00

Miniature Sheet

Abdication of Japanese Emperor Akihito — A545

No. 1436: a, $1, Emperor Akihito. b, $1, Emperor Akihito and Empress Michiko. c, $3, U.S. President Barack Obama and Emperor Akihito. d, $3, Emperor Akihito and Queen Elizabeth II.

2019, July 2 Litho. *Perf. 14*

1436 A545 Sheet of 4, #a-d 16.00 16.00

Miniature Sheet

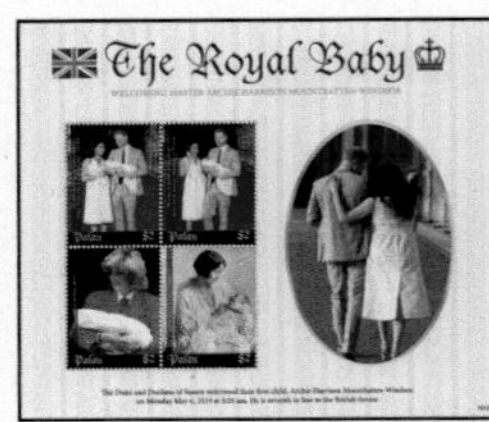

Birth of Archie Mountbatten-Windsor — A546

No. 1437: a, Duke and Duchess of Sussex, with son, Archie. b, As "a," Duchess waving hand. c, Princess Diana holding infant Prince Harry. d, Queen Mother holding infant Princess Elizabeth.

2019, July 11 Litho. *Perf. 14*

1437 A546 $2 Sheet of 4, #a-d 16.00 16.00

Long-tailed Macaque — A547

Emblem of 2019 Singpex International Stamp Exhibition and: a, $1, Macaque eating. b, $1, Macaque's head. c, $2, Adult macaque and juvenile. d, $2, Macaque looking left.
$5, Emblem and macaque, diff.

2019, July 31 Litho. *Perf. 14*

1438 A547 Sheet of 4, #a-d 12.00 12.00

Souvenir Sheet

Perf. 12½

1439 A547 $5 multi 10.00 10.00

No. 1439 contains one 38x51mm stamp.

Miniature Sheet

Mohandas K. Gandhi (1869-1948), Indian Nationalist Leader — A548

No. 1440: a, 50c, Drawing of Gandhi. b, $1.50, Photograph of Gandhi. c, $2.50, Drawing of Gandhi, diff. d, $3.50, Photograph of Gandhi, diff.

2019, Oct. 11 Litho. *Perf. 14*

1440 A548 Sheet of 4, #a-d 16.00 16.00

Dorje Chang Buddha III, Religious Leader — A549

2019, Dec. 8 Litho. *Perf. 13x13½*

1441 A549 $1 multi 2.00 2.00

Maroon Clownfish — A550

No. 1442 — Various photographs of clownfish and sea anemones: a, $1. b, $2. c, $3.

No. 1443, vert. — Various photographs of clownfish and sea anemones: a, $3. b, $4.

2019, Dec. 27 Litho. *Perf. 12*

1442 A550 Sheet of 3, #a-c 12.00 12.00

Souvenir Sheet

Perf. 14

1443 A550 Sheet of 2, #a-b 14.00 14.00

No. 1443 contains two 30x40mm stamps.

Jellyfish A551

No. 1444: a, $1, Lion's mane jellyfish. b, $1.50, Lion's mane jellyfish, diff. c, $2, Moon jellyfish. d, $2.50, Moon jellyfish, diff.
$5, White spotted jellyfish.

2019, Dec. 27 Litho. *Perf. 12*

1444 A551 Sheet of 4, #a-d 14.00 14.00

Souvenir Sheet

Perf. 13¾

1445 A551 $5 multi 10.00 10.00

No. 1445 contains one 35x35mm stamp.

Miniature Sheet

Diplomatic Relations Between Palau and Japan, 25th Anniv. — A552

No. 1446: a, Itabori. b, Japan-Palau Friendship Bridge. c, Palau International Coral Reef Center. d, Judo. e, Belau Eco Glass. f, Future Palauan Olympians in training.

2019, Dec. 28 Litho. *Perf. 14*

1446 A552 $1 Sheet of 6, #a-f 12.00 12.00

Miniature Sheets

A553

Butterflies — A554

No. 1447: a, $1, Cabbage white butterfly, purple flowers. b, $1.50, Zebra longwing butterfly, pink flowers. c, $2, Red admiral butterfly, yellow flower. d, $2.50, Pipevine swallowtail butterfly, red flowers.

No. 1448: a, $1, Cabbage white butterfly, green backgroun. b, $1.50, Zebra longwing butterfly, yellow flower. c, $2, Red admiral butterfly, pink flowers. d, $5, Pipevine swallowtail butterfly, light purple flowers.

2020, June 15 Litho. *Perf. 14*

1447 A553 Sheet of 4, #a-d 14.00 14.00

1448 A554 Sheet of 4, #a-d 19.00 19.00

Fruits and Vegetables — A555

No. 1449: a, Heart-shaped tray of various fruits and vegetables. b, Avocado. c, Dragon-fruit. d, Vegetables and shopping bag.

No. 1450: a, Pineapple, orange background (40x30mm). b, Pineapple, yellow background (30x40mm).

2020, June 15 Litho. *Perf. 13¾*

1449 A555 $2 Sheet of 4, #a-d 16.00 16.00

Souvenir Sheet

Perf. 14

1450 A555 $3 Sheet of 2, #a-b 12.00 12.00

Miniature Sheet

Medical Workers During the COVID-19 Pandemic — A556

No. 1451: a, Military corpsman wearing cap and protective face mask. b, Technician wearing two proetective face masks, yellow gown and gloves. c, Globe and group of medical workers wearing protective clothing and masks. d, Two medical workers wearing protective face masks, hands with thumbs up.

2020, Aug. 7 Litho. *Perf. 12*

1451 A556 $2 Sheet of 4, #a-d 16.00 16.00

Paintings by Raphael (1483-1520) — A557

No. 1452: a, Portrait of Agnolo Doni, 1506. b, Portrait of Pietro Bembo, 1506. c, La Donna Gravida, 1506. d, Portrait of a Cardinal, 1510. $4, La Donna Velata, 1515.

2020, Aug. 7 Litho. *Perf. 14*

1452 A557 $1.60 Sheet of 4, #a-d 13.00 13.00

Souvenir Sheet

Perf. 12½

1453 A557 $4 multi 8.00 8.00

No. 1453 contains one 38x51mm stamp.

Souvenir Sheets

Elvis Presley (1935-77) — A558

Inscriptions: No. 1454, $8, Graceland becomes a historic landmark. No. 1455, $8, "I wish." No. 1456, $8, "Rhythm is something you either have or don't." No. 1457, $8, "I've been so lucky," horiz.

2020, Aug. 7 Litho. *Perf. 14*

1454-1457 A558 Set of 4 64.00 64.00

Westward Expansion of Settlers in the United States — A559

No. 1458: a, Independence Rock, Oregon Trail, Wyoming. b, Fort Osage, Santa Fe Trail, Missouri. c, Journey's End Monument, Santa Fe National Historic Trail. d, Oregon Trail (Campfire), painting by Albert Bierstadt (1830-1902). e, Wagon train, Santa Fe Trail. f, Zero Milestone, Old Spanish Trail.

$8, Fort Union, Santa Fe Trail, New Mexico.

2020, Sept. 4 Litho. *Perf. 14*

1458 A559 $1.50 Sheet of 6, #a-f 18.00 18.00

Souvenir Sheet

Perf. 12½

1459 A559 $8 multi 16.00 16.00

No. 1459 contains one 51x38mm stamp.

Mohandas K. Gandhi (1869-1948), Indian Nationalist Leader — A560

2020, Nov. 30 Litho. *Perf. 14*

1460 A560 25c multi .50 .50

Miniature Sheet

World War II Victory in Europe (V-E Day), 75th Anniv. A561

No. 1461: a, Gen. Charles de Gaulle (1890-1970), and flag of France. b, Gen. Dwight D. Eisenhower (1890-1969), and flag of the United States. c, Winston Churchill (1874-1965), Prime Minister of Great Britain, flag of Great Britain. d, Harry S. Truman (1884-1972), 33rd President, flag of the United States. e, Churchill and the British royal family. f, Field Marshal Bernard Montgomery (1887-1976), flag of Great Britain.

2020, Nov. 30 Litho. *Perf. 14¼x14*

1461 A561 $1.60 Sheet of 6, #a-f 19.50 19.50

A562

Rabbits A563

No. 1462: a, Brown rabbit, no grass. b, Brown rabbit on grass. c, White rabbit with ears up. d, White rabbit with ears down.

No. 1463: a, Two rabbits. b, One rabbit.

Perf. 13¼x13¾

2020, Nov. 30 Litho.

1462 A562 $2 Sheet of 4, #a-d 16.00 16.00

Souvenir Sheet

Perf. 13¾x13¼

1463 A563 $3 Sheet of 2, #a-b 12.00 12.00

A564

Sea Turtles A565

No. 1464: a, Turtle swimming forward. b, Turtle swimming to right. c, Turtle swimming to left. d, Turtle's head.

No. 1465: a, Turtle swiming to right, diff. b, Turtle swimming to left, diff.

Perf. 13¾x13¼

2020, Nov. 30 Litho.

1464 A564 $2 Sheet of 4, #a-d 16.00 16.00

Souvenir Sheet

1465 A565 $3 Sheet of 2, #a-b 12.00 12.00

A566

Meeting of U.S. Pres. Donald Trump and North Korean Supreme Leader Kim Jong-un A567

No. 1466: a, Kim and Trump shaking hands at Demilitarized Zone border. b, Kim, Trump and North Koreans. c, Kim watching Trump cross border at Demilitarized Zone. d, Kim and Trump seated.

No. 1467: a, Trump and South Korean Pres. Moon Jae-in. b, Trump and Kim standing in front of Demilitarized Zone building. c, Presidents Trump and Moon shaking hands with soldiers. d, Trump writing on brick wall.

Perf. 14¼x13¾

2020, Nov. 30 Litho.

1466 A566 $2 Sheet of 4, #a-d 16.00 16.00

1467 A567 $2 Sheet of 4, #a-d 16.00 16.00

SEMI-POSTAL STAMPS

Olympic Sports — SP1

No. B1, Baseball glove, player. No. B2, Running shoe, athlete. No. B3, Goggles, swimmer. No. B4, Gold medal, diver.

1988, Aug. 8 Litho. *Perf. 14*

B1 SP1 25c +5c multi .50 .50

B2 SP1 25c +5c multi .50 .50

a. Pair, #B1-B2 1.25 1.25

B3 SP1 45c +5c multi 1.25 1.25

B4 SP1 45c +5c multi 1.25 1.25

a. Pair, #B3-B4 2.75 2.75

AIR POST STAMPS

White-tailed Tropicbird AP1

1984, June 12 Litho. *Perf. 14*

C1 AP1 40c shown .75 .75

C2 AP1 40c Fairy tern .75 .75

C3 AP1 40c Black noddy .75 .75

C4 AP1 40c Black-naped tern .75 .75

a. Block of 4, #C1-C4 3.50 3.50

Audubon Type of 1985

1985, Feb. 6 Litho. *Perf. 14*

C5 A12 44c Audubon's Shear-water 1.10 1.10

Palau-Germany Political, Economic & Cultural Exchange Cent. — AP2

Germany Nos. 40, 65, Caroline Islands Nos. 19, 13 and: No. C6, German flag-raising at Palau, 1885. No. C7, Early German trading post in Angaur. No. C8, Abai architecture recorded by Prof. & Frau Kramer, 1908-1910. No. C9, S.M.S. Cormoran.

1985, Sept. 19 Litho. *Perf. 14x13½*

C6 AP2 44c multicolored .95 .95

C7 AP2 44c multicolored .95 .95

C8 AP2 44c multicolored .95 .95

C9 AP2 44c multicolored .95 .95

a. Block of 4, #C6-C9 4.50 4.50

Trans-Pacific Airmail Anniv. Type of 1985

Aircraft: No. C10, 1951 Trans-Ocean Airways PBY-5A Catalina Amphibian. No. C11, 1968 Air Micronesia DC-6B Super Cloudmaster. No. C12, 1960 Trust Territory Airline SA-16 Albatross. No. C13, 1967 Pan American Douglas DC-4.

1985, Nov. 21 Litho. *Perf. 14*

C10 A16 44c multicolored .85 .85

C11 A16 44c multicolored .85 .85

C12 A16 44c multicolored .85 .85

C13 A16 44c multicolored .85 .85

a. Block of 4, #C10-C13 3.75 3.75

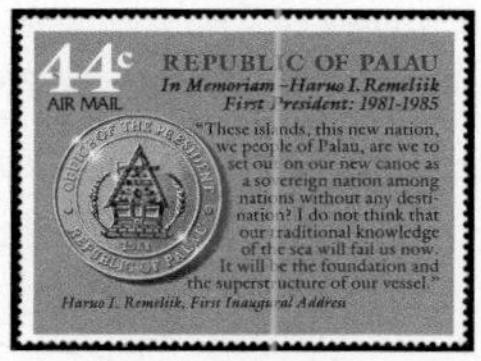

Haruo I. Remeliik (1933-1985), 1st President — AP3

Designs: No. C14, Presidential seal, excerpt from 1st inaugural address. No. C15, War canoe, address excerpt, diff. No. C16, Remeliik, US Pres. Reagan, excerpt from Reagan's speech, Pacific Basin Conference, Guam, 1984.

1986, June 30 Litho. *Perf. 14*

C14 AP3 44c multicolored 1.10 1.10

C15 AP3 44c multicolored 1.10 1.10

C16 AP3 44c multicolored 1.10 1.10

a. Strip of 3, #C14-C16 3.75 3.75

Intl. Peace Year, Statue of Liberty Cent. — AP4

1986, Sept. 19 Litho.

C17 AP4 44c multicolored 1.00 1.00

Aircraft — AP5

36c, Cessna 207 Skywagon. 39c, Embraer EMB-110 Bandeirante. 45c, Boeing 727.

1989, May 17 Litho. *Perf. 14x14½*

C18 AP5 36c multicolored .65 .65
a. Booklet pane of 10 7.00 —
C19 AP5 39c multicolored .85 .85
a. Booklet pane of 10 7.50 —
C20 AP5 45c multicolored 1.00 1.00
a. Booklet pane of 10 8.25 —
b. Booklet pane, 5 each 36c, 45c 8.50 —
Nos. C18-C20 (3) 2.50 2.50

Palauan Bai Type

1991, July 9 Litho. *Die Cut*
Self-Adhesive

C21 A61 50c like #293a 1.50 1.50

World War II in the Pacific Type
Miniature Sheet

Aircraft: No. C22: a, Grumman TBF Avenger, US Navy. b, Curtiss P-40C, Chinese Air Force "Flying Tigers." c, Mitsubishi A6M Zero-Sen, Japan. d, Hawker Hurricane, Royal Air Force. e, Consolidated PBY Catalina, Royal Netherlands Indies Air Force. f, Curtiss Hawk 75, Netherlands Indies. g, Boeing B-17E, US Army Air Force. h, Brewster Buffalo, Royal Australian Air Force. i, Supermarine Walrus, Royal Navy. j, Curtiss P-40E, Royal New Zealand Air Force.

1992, Sept. 10 Litho. *Perf. 14½x15*

C22 A66 50c Sheet of 10, #a.-j. 11.00 11.00

Birds AP6

a, Palau swiftlet. b, Barn swallow. c, Jungle nightjar. d, White-breasted woodswallow.

1994, Mar. 24 Litho. *Perf. 14*

C23 AP6 50c Block of 4, #a.-d. 4.00 4.00

No. C23 is printed in sheets of 16 stamps.

PALESTINE

'pa-lə-ˌstin

LOCATION — Western Asia bordering on the Mediterranean Sea
GOVT. — Former British Mandate
AREA — 10,429 sq. mi.
POP. — 1,605,816 (estimated)
CAPITAL — Jerusalem

Formerly a part of Turkey, Palestine was occupied by the Egyptian Expeditionary Forces of the British Army in World War I and was mandated to Great Britain in 1923. Mandate ended May 14, 1948.

10 Milliemes = 1 Piaster
1000 Milliemes = 1 Egyptian Pound
1000 Mils = 1 Palestine Pound (1928)

Jordan stamps overprinted with "Palestine" in English and Arabic are listed under Jordan.

Watermark

Wmk. 33

Issued under British Military Occupation

For use in Palestine, Transjordan, Lebanon, Syria and in parts of Cilicia and northeastern Egypt

A1

Wmk. Crown and "GvR" (33)

1918, Feb. 10 Litho. *Rouletted 20*

1 A1 1pi deep blue 190.00 105.00
2 A1 1pi ultra 2.50 2.50

Nos. 2 & 1 Surcharged in Black

1918, Feb. 16

3 A1 5m on 1pi ultra 8.50 4.25
a. 5m on 1pi gray blue 110.00 *600.00*

Nos. 1 and 3a were issued without gum. No. 3a is on paper with a surface sheen.

1918 Typo. *Perf. 15x14*

4 A1 1m dark brown .35 *.45*
5 A1 2m blue green .35 *.50*
6 A1 3m light brown .50 .40
7 A1 4m scarlet .40 *.45*
8 A1 5m orange .75 .35
9 A1 1pi indigo .50 .30
10 A1 2pi olive green 3.50 1.00
11 A1 5pi plum 3.75 2.50
12 A1 9pi bister 12.50 7.50
13 A1 10pi ultramarine 12.50 4.50
14 A1 20pi gray 18.50 *20.00*
Nos. 4-14 (11) 53.60 37.95

Many shades exist.
Nos. 4-11 exist with rough perforation.
Issued: 1m, 2m, 4m, 2pi, 5pi, 7/16; 5m, 9/25; 1pi, 11/9; 3m, 9pi, 10pi, 12/17; 20pi, 12/27.
Nos. 4-11 with overprint "O. P. D. A." (Ottoman Public Debt Administration) or "H.J.Z." (Hejaz-Jemen Railway) are revenue stamps; they exist postally used.
For overprints on stamps and types see #15-62 & Jordan #1-63, 73-90, 92-102, 130-144, J12-J23.

Issued under British Administration
Overprinted at Jerusalem

Stamps and Type of 1918 Overprinted in Black or Silver

1920, Sept. 1 Wmk. 33 *Perf. 15x14*
Arabic Overprint 8mm long

15 A1 1m dark brown 10.00 2.25
16 A1 2m bl grn, perf 14 4.50 1.75
d. Perf 15x14 14.00 6.00
17 A1 3m lt brown 18.50 8.50
d. Perf 14 140.00 70.00
e. Inverted overprint 550.00 *700.00*
18 A1 4m scarlet 5.25 1.75
19 A1 5m org, perf 14 8.00 .75
e. Perf 15x14 27.50 10.00
20 A1 1pi indigo (S) 5.75 1.25
21 A1 2pi olive green 7.00 2.50
22 A1 5pi plum 27.50 *30.00*
23 A1 9pi bister 15.00 *23.00*
24 A1 10pi ultra 13.00 *19.50*
25 A1 20pi gray 35.00 *50.00*
Nos. 15-25 (11) 149.50 141.25

Forgeries exist of No. 17e.

Similar Ovpt., with Arabic Line 10mm Long, Arabic "S" and "T" Joined, ".." at Left Extends Above Other Letters

1920-21 *Perf. 15x14*

15a A1 1m dark brown 2.75 1.20
e. Perf. 14 875.00 975.00
g. As "a," invtd. ovpt. 450.00
16a A1 2m blue green 12.00 4.50
e. "PALESTINE" omitted *2,500.* *1,500.*
f. Perf. 14 6.00 6.00
17a A1 3m light brown 4.25 1.20
18a A1 4m scarlet 6.25 1.60
b. Perf. 14 95.00 125.00
19a A1 5m orange 4.50 .90
f. Perf. 14 12.00 1.25
20a A1 1pi indigo, perf. 14 (S) ('21) 67.50 2.00
d. Perf. 15x14 575.00 40.00
21a A1 2pi olive green ('21) 90.00 42.50
22a A1 5pi plum ('21) 52.50 11.00
d. Perf. 14 225.00 *525.00*
Nos. 15a-22a (8) 239.75 64.90

This overprint often looks grayish to grayish black. In the English line the letters are frequently uneven and damaged.

Similar Ovpt., with Arabic Line 10mm Long, Arabic "S" and "T" Separated and 6mm Between English and Hebrew Lines

1920, Dec. 6

15b A1 1m dk brn, perf 14 62.50 37.50
17b A1 3m lt brn, perf 15x14 60.00 37.50
19b A1 5m orange, perf 14 475.00 37.50
d. Perf. 15x14 *16,000.* *13,750.*
Nos. 15b-19b (3) 597.50 112.50

Overprinted as Before, 7½mm Between English and Hebrew Lines, ".." at Left Even With Other Letters

1921 *Perf. 15x14*

15c A1 1m dark brown 21.00 4.00
f. 1m dull brown, perf 14 *2,300.*
16c A1 2m blue green 32.50 6.25
17c A1 3m light brown 47.50 3.50
18c A1 4m scarlet 50.00 4.00
19c A1 5m orange 82.50 1.10
20c A1 1pi indigo (S) 32.50 1.60
21c A1 2pi olive green 26.50 7.00
22c A1 5pi plum 29.00 9.25
23c A1 9pi bister 75.00 *125.00*
24c A1 10pi ultra 90.00 16.00
25c A1 20pi pale gray 135.00 75.00
d. Perf. 14 *13,750.* *2,900.*
Nos. 15c-25c (11) 621.50 *252.70*

Overprinted at London

Stamps of 1918 Overprinted

1921 *Perf. 15x14*

37 A1 1m dark brown 2.25 .35
38 A1 2m blue green 3.25 .35
39 A1 3m light brown 3.50 .35
40 A1 4m scarlet 4.00 .70
41 A1 5m orange 3.75 .35
42 A1 1pi bright blue 3.00 .40
43 A1 2pi olive green 5.00 .45
44 A1 5pi plum 12.50 5.75
45 A1 9pi bister 26.00 16.00
46 A1 10pi ultra 29.00 *675.00*
47 A1 20pi gray 85.00 *1,600.*
Nos. 37-47 (11) 140.00
Nos. 37-45 (9) 24.70

The 2nd character from left on bottom line that looks like quotation marks consists of long thin lines.
Deformed or damaged letters exist in all three lines of the overprint.

Similar Overprint on Type of 1921

1922 Wmk. 4 *Perf. 14*

48 A1 1m dark brown 2.50 .35
a. Inverted overprint — *13,750.*
b. Double overprint 260.00 500.00
49 A1 2m yellow 3.25 .35
50 A1 3m Prus blue 3.50 .25
51 A1 4m rose 3.50 .25
52 A1 5m orange 2.75 .35
53 A1 6m blue green 3.00 .35
54 A1 7m yellow brown 3.00 .35
55 A1 8m red 3.00 .35
56 A1 1pi gray 3.50 .35
57 A1 13m ultra 4.00 .25
58 A1 2pi olive green 4.00 .40
a. Inverted overprint 350.00 *575.00*
b. 2pi yellow bister *140.00* *7.50*
59 A1 5pi plum 6.25 1.40
a. Perf. 15x14 67.50 7.50

Perf. 15x14

60 A1 9pi bister 10.00 10.00
a. Perf. 14 1,150. 275.00
61 A1 10pi light blue 8.50 4.25
a. Perf. 14 95.00 17.50
62 A1 20pi violet 12.50 6.25
a. Perf. 14 225.00 125.00
Nos. 48-62 (15) 73.25 25.50

The 2nd character from left on bottom line that looks like quotation marks consists of short thick lines.
The "E. F. F." for "E. E. F." on No. 61 is caused by damaged type.

Rachel's Tomb A3

Mosque of Omar (Dome of the Rock) A4

Citadel at Jerusalem A5

Tiberias and Sea of Galilee A6

1927-42 Typo. *Perf. 13½x14½*

63 A3 2m Prus blue 2.75 .25
64 A3 3m yellow green 1.75 .25
65 A4 4m rose red 9.00 1.60
66 A4 4m violet brn ('32) 3.25 .25
67 A5 5m brown org 4.25 .25
c. Perf. 14½x14 (coil stamp) ('36) 16.00 *21.00*
68 A4 6m deep green 1.50 .25
69 A5 7m deep red 12.00 .70
70 A5 7m dk violet ('32) 1.00 .25
71 A4 8m yellow brown 18.50 7.00
72 A4 8m scarlet ('32) 1.50 .25
73 A3 10m deep gray 2.25 .25
a. Perf. 14½x14 (coil stamp) ('38) 23.50 *27.50*
74 A4 13m ultra 17.50 .40
75 A4 13m olive bister ('32) 3.75 .25
76 A4 15m ultra ('32) 5.75 .25
77 A5 20m olive green 2.50 .25

Perf. 14

78 A6 50m brown purple 3.50 .40
79 A6 90m bister 87.50 *60.00*
80 A6 100m bright blue 2.60 .80
81 A6 200m dk violet 9.25 5.75
82 A6 250m dp brown ('42) 7.50 3.50
83 A6 500m red ('42) 9.00 3.50
84 A6 £1 gray black ('42) 13.00 4.00
Nos. 63-84 (22) 219.60 90.40

Issued: 3m, #74, 6/1; 2m, 5m, 6m, 10m, #65, 69, 71, 77-81, 8/14; #70, 72, 6/1/32; #75, 15m, 8/1/32; #66, 11/1/32; #82-84, 1/15/42.

POSTAGE DUE STAMPS

D1

1923 Unwmk. Typo. *Perf. 11*

J1 D1 1m bister brown 27.50 *40.00*
b. Horiz. pair, imperf. btwn. 1,300. *750.00*
J2 D1 2m green 22.50 11.50
J3 D1 4m red 12.00 *13.50*
J4 D1 8m violet 8.50 *8.50*
b. Horiz. pair, imperf. btwn. *2,300.*
J5 D1 13m dark blue 7.50 *8.50*
a. Horiz. pair, imperf. btwn. 1,200.
Nos. J1-J5 (5) 78.00 *82.00*

Imperfs. of 1m, 2m, 8m, are from proof sheets.
Values for Nos. J1-J5 are for fine centered copies.

D2

1924, Dec. 1 Wmk. 4

J6 D2 1m brown 1.10 2.00
J7 D2 2m yellow 4.00 1.75
J8 D2 4m green 2.00 1.50
J9 D2 8m red 3.00 1.00
J10 D2 13m ultramarine 3.50 2.50
J11 D2 5pi violet 15.00 1.75
Nos. J6-J11 (6) 28.60 10.50

D3

1928-45 *Perf. 14*

J12	D3 1m lt brown	2.75	1.00
a.	Perf. 15x14 ('45)	42.50	80.00
J13	D3 2m yellow	3.75	.70
J14	D3 4m green	4.25	1.60
a.	4m bluish grn, perf. 15x14 ('45)	75.00	120.00
J15	D3 6m brown org ('33)	19.00	5.00
J16	D3 8m red	2.75	2.00
J17	D3 10m light gray	2.00	.70
J18	D3 13m ultra	4.50	3.00
J19	D3 20m olive green	4.50	1.25
J20	D3 50m violet	5.00	2.50
	Nos. J12-J20 (9)	48.50	17.75

The Hebrew word for "mil" appears below the numeral on all values but the 1m.

Issued: 6m, Oct. 1933; others, Feb. 1, 1928.

PALESTINIAN AUTHORITY

'pa-lə-ˌs-ti-nē-ən 'o-thōr-itē

LOCATION — Areas of the West Bank and the Gaza Strip.

AREA — 2,410 sq. mi.

POP. — 2,825,000 (2000 est.)

1000 Fils (Mils) = 5 Israeli Shekels

1000 Fils = 1 Jordanian Dinar (Jan. 1, 1998)

Catalogue values for all unused stamps in this country are for Never Hinged items.

Hisham Palace, Jericho — A1

5m, 10m, 20m, Hisham Palace. 30m, 40m, 50m, 75m, Mosque, Jerusalem. 125, 150m, 250m, 300m, 500m, Flag. 1000m, Dome of the Rock.

1994 **Litho.** *Perf. 14*

1	A1 5m multicolored	.25	.25
2	A1 10m multicolored	.25	.25
3	A1 20m multicolored	.25	.25
4	A1 30m multicolored	.25	.25
5	A1 40m multicolored	.25	.25
6	A1 50m multicolored	.30	.30
7	A1 75m multicolored	.35	.35
8	A1 125m multicolored	.60	.60
9	A1 150m multicolored	.90	.90
10	A1 250m multicolored	1.25	1.25
11	A1 300m multicolored	1.75	1.75

Size: 51x29mm

12	A1 500m multicolored	2.50	2.50
13	A1 1000m multicolored	4.00	4.00
	Nos. 1-13 (13)	12.90	12.90

Issued: 125m-500m, 8/15; others, 9/1.

Nos. 1-13 Surcharged "FILS" in English and Arabic in Black or Silver and with Black Bars Obliterating "Mils"

1995, Apr. 10 **Litho.** *Perf. 14*

14	A1 5f multicolored	.25	.25
15	A1 10f multicolored	.25	.25
16	A1 20f multicolored	.25	.25
17	A1 30f multicolored (S)	.25	.25
18	A1 40f multicolored (S)	.25	.25
19	A1 50f multicolored (S)	.30	.30
20	A1 75f multicolored (S)	.35	.35
21	A1 125f multicolored	.50	.50
22	A1 150f multicolored	.65	.65
23	A1 250f multicolored	1.10	1.10
24	A1 300f multicolored	1.40	1.40

Size: 51x29mm

25	A1 500f multicolored	2.25	2.25
26	A1 1000f multicolored	4.00	4.00
	Nos. 14-26 (13)	11.80	11.80

Palestine No. 63 — A2

350f, Palestine #67. 500f, Palestine #72.

1995, May 17 **Litho.** *Perf. 14*

27	A2 150f multicolored	1.00	1.00
28	A2 350f multicolored	1.60	1.60
29	A2 500f multicolored	2.00	2.00
	Nos. 27-29 (3)	4.60	4.60

Traditional Costumes — A3

Women wearing various costumes.

1995, May 31

30	A3 250f multicolored	.90	.90
31	A3 300f multicolored	1.00	1.00
32	A3 550f multicolored	2.00	2.00
33	A3 900f multicolored	3.00	3.00
	Nos. 30-33 (4)	6.90	6.90

Christmas — A4

Designs: 10f, Ancient view of Bethlehem. 20f, Modern view of Bethlehem. 50f, Entrance to grotto, Church of the Nativity. 100f, Yasser Arafat, Pope John Paul II. 1000f, Star of the Nativity, Church of the Nativity, Bethlehem.

10f, 20f, 100f, 1000f are horiz.

1995, Dec. 18

34	A4 10f multicolored	.25	.25
35	A4 20f multicolored	.25	.25
36	A4 50f multicolored	.25	.25
37	A4 100f multicolored	.60	.60
38	A4 1000f multicolored	5.00	5.00
	Nos. 34-38 (5)	6.35	6.35

Pres. Yasser Arafat — A5

1996, Mar. 20

39	A5 10f red vio & bluish blk	.25	.25
40	A5 20f yellow & bluish black	.25	.25
41	A5 50f blue & bluish black	.25	.25
42	A5 100f apple grn & bluish blk	.50	.50
43	A5 1000f org & bluish blk	4.25	4.25
	Nos. 39-43 (5)	5.50	5.50

1996 Intl. Philatelic Exhibitions A6

Exhibition, site: 20f, CHINA '96, Summer Palace, Beijing. 50f, ISTANBUL '96, Hagia Sofia. 100f, ESSEN '96, Villa Hugel. 1000f, CAPEX '96, Toronto skyline.

1996, May 18

44	A6 20f multicolored	.25	.25
45	A6 50f multicolored	.30	.30
46	A6 100f multicolored	.45	.45
47	A6 1000f multicolored	4.50	4.50
a.	Sheet, 2 each #44-47 + 2 labels	13.00	
	Nos. 44-47 (4)	5.50	5.50

Souvenir Sheet

1st Palestinian Parliamentary & Presidential Elections — A7

1996, May 20

48	A7 1250f multicolored	5.50	5.50

1996 Summer Olympic Games, Atlanta — A8

Designs: 30f, Boxing. 40f, Medal, 1896. 50f, Runners. 150f, Olympic flame. 1000f, Palestinian Olympic Committee emblem.

1996, July 19 *Perf. 13½*

49	A8 30f multicolored	.25	.25
50	A8 40f multicolored	.25	.25
51	A8 50f multicolored	.35	.35
52	A8 150f multicolored	.70	.70
a.	Sheet of 3, #49, 51-52	5.50	5.50
53	A8 1000f multicolored	4.25	4.25
	Nos. 49-53 (5)	5.80	5.80

Flowers — A9

1996, Nov. 22

54	A9 10f Poppy	.25	.25
55	A9 25f Hibiscus	.25	.25
56	A9 100f Thyme	.50	.50
57	A9 150f Lemon	.70	.70
58	A9 750f Orange	3.00	3.00
	Nos. 54-58 (5)	4.70	4.70

Souvenir Sheet

59	A9 1000f Olive	4.50	4.50

Souvenir Sheet

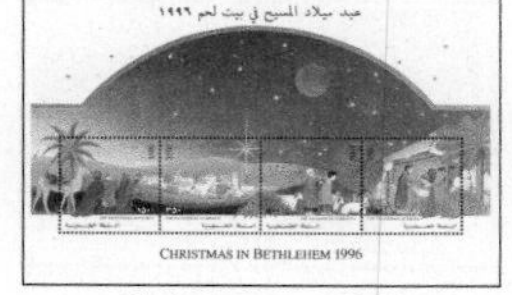

Christmas — A10

a, 150f, Magi. b, 350f, View of Bethlehem. c, 500f, Shepherds, sheep. d, 750f, Nativity scene.

1996, Dec. 14 *Perf. 14*

60	A10 Sheet of 4, #a.-d.	6.50	6.50

Birds — A11

1997, May 29

61	A11 25f Great tit	.30	.30
62	A11 75f Blue rock thrush	.40	.40
63	A11 150f Golden oriole	.85	.85
64	A11 350f Hoopoe	2.00	2.00
65	A11 600f Peregrine falcon	2.75	2.75
	Nos. 61-65 (5)	6.30	6.30

Historic Views A12

1997, June 19

66	A12 350f Gaza, 1839	1.50	1.50
67	A12 600f Hebron, 1839	2.50	2.50

Souvenir Sheet

Return of Hong Kong to China A13

1997, July 1

68	A13 225f multicolored	2.40	2.40

Friends of Palestine A14

#69, Portraits of Yasser Arafat, Hans-Jürgen Wischnewski. #70, Wischnewski shaking hands with Arafat. #71, Mother Teresa. #72, Mother Teresa with Arafat.

1997 **Litho.** *Perf. 14*

69	A14 600f multicolored	1.75	1.75
70	A14 600f multicolored	1.75	1.75
a.	Pair, #69-70	4.50	4.50
71	A14 600f multicolored	2.00	2.00
72	A14 600f multicolored	2.00	2.00
a.	Pair, #71-72	4.75	4.75
	Nos. 69-72 (4)	7.50	7.50

#70a, 72a were issued in sheets of 4 stamps.

Issued: #69-70, 7/24; #71-72, 12/17.

Christmas — A15

1997, Nov. 28

73	A15 350f multicolored	1.25	1.25
74	A15 700f multicolored	2.25	2.25
a.	Pair, #73-74	3.75	3.75

Mosaics from Floor of Byzantine Church, Jabalia-Gaza — A16

50f, Rabbit, palm tree. 125f, Goat, rabbit, dog. 200f, Basket, fruit tree, jar. 400f, Lion.

1998, June 22 **Litho.** *Perf. 13½*

75	A16 50f multicolored	.30	.30
76	A16 125f multicolored	.90	.60
77	A16 200f multicolored	1.25	1.00
78	A16 400f multicolored	2.75	1.75
	Nos. 75-78 (4)	5.20	3.65

Souvenir Sheet

Baal A17

1998, June 15 *Perf. 14*

79	A17 600f multicolored	2.75	2.75

Medicinal Plants — A18

1998, Sept. 30 Litho. *Perf. 14*

80	A18	40f Urginea maritima	.25	.25
81	A18	80f Silybum marianum	.30	.30
82	A18	500f Foeniculum vulgare	1.50	1.50
83	A18	800f Inula viscosa	3.00	3.00
		Nos. 80-83 (4)	5.05	5.05

Raptors — A19

1998, Nov. 12 Litho. *Perf. 14*

84	A19	20f Bonelli's eagle	.25	.25
85	A19	60f Hobby	.30	.30
86	A19	340f Verreaux's eagle	1.75	1.75
87	A19	600f Bateleur	2.75	2.75
88	A19	900f Buzzard	3.75	3.75
		Nos. 84-88 (5)	8.80	8.80

Souvenir Sheet

Granting of Additional Rights to Palestinian Authority's Observer to UN — A20

1998, Nov. 12

89 A20 700f multicolored 3.00 3.00

Butterflies — A21

Designs: a, 100f, Papilio alexanor. b, 200f, Danaus chrysippus. c, 300f, Gonepteryx cleopatra. d, 400f, Melanargia titea.

1998, Dec. 3

90 A21 Sheet of 4, #a.-d. 4.50 4.50

Souvenir Sheet

Christmas, Bethlehem 2000 — A22

1998, Dec. 3

91 A22 1000f multicolored 4.25 4.25

Souvenir Sheet

Signing of Middle East Peace Agreement, Wye River Conference, Oct. 23, 1998 — A23

Palestinian Pres. Yasser Arafat and US Pres. Bill Clinton.

1999 Litho. *Perf. 14*

92 A23 900f multicolored 3.75 3.75

New Airport, Gaza — A24

Designs: 80f, Control tower, vert. 300f, Airplane. 700f, Terminal building.

1999

93	A24	80f multicolored	.25	.25
94	A24	300f multicolored	.90	.90
95	A24	700f multicolored	2.50	2.50
		Nos. 93-95 (3)	3.65	3.65

Intl. Philatelic Exhibitions & UPU, 125th Anniv. — A25

a, 20f, Buildings, China 1999. b, 260f, Buildings, Germany, IBRA '99. c. 80f, High-rise buildings, Australia '99. d, 340f, Eiffel Tower, Philex France '99. e, 400f, Aerial view of countryside, denomination LR, UPU, 125th anniv. f, 400f, like #96e, denomination LL.

1999

96 A25 Block of 6, #a.-f. 6.75 6.75

Hebron — A26

a, 400f, Lettering in gold. b, 500f, Lettering in white.

1999, Aug. 20 Litho. *Perf. 14*

97 A26 Pair, #a.-b. 4.00 4.00

Arabian Horses — A27

a, 25f. b, 75f. c, 150f. d, 350f. e, 800f.

1999, Apr. 27

98 A27 Strip of 5, #a.-e. 5.50 5.50

Souvenir Sheet

Palestinian Sunbird — A28

1999 Litho. *Perf. 13¾*

99 A28 750f multi 3.50 3.50

A29

Christmas, Bethlehem 2000 — A30

Giotto Paintings (Type A30): 200f, 280f, 2000f, The Nativity. 380f, 460f, The Adoration of the Magi. 560f, The Flight into Egypt. Inscription colors: Nos. 108a, 110a, Black. Nos. 109a, 111a, White. No. 112a, Yellow. Nos. 108b-112b have silver inscriptions and frames. No. 113, country name at lower left. No. 113A, country name at upper right, denomination at lower left.

1999, Dec. 8 Litho. *Perf. 13¼x13*

Background Color

100	A29	60f black	.35	.35
101	A29	80f light blue	.35	.35
102	A29	100f dark gray	.45	.45
103	A29	280f lilac rose	1.15	1.15
104	A29	300f green	1.20	1.20
105	A29	400f red violet	1.75	1.75
106	A29	500f dark red	2.00	2.00
107	A29	560f light gray	2.40	2.40

Perf. 13¼

108	A30	200f Pair, #a.-b	*3.25*	*3.25*
109	A30	280f Pair, #a.-b.	*3.50*	*3.50*
110	A30	380f Pair, #a.-b.	*4.25*	*4.25*
111	A30	460f Pair, #a.-b.	*5.50*	*5.50*
112	A30	560f Pair, #a.-b.	*8.75*	*8.75*

Litho. & Embossed Foil Application

113	A30	2000f multi	6.50	6.50
113A	A30	2000f multi, booklet pane of 1	9.00	9.00
		Nos. 100-113 (14)	*41.40*	*41.40*

Nos. 108-112 each printed in sheets of 10 containing 9 "a" +1 "b." No. 113 printed in sheets of 4. Nos. 108a-112a also exist in sheets of 10.

Issued: No. 113A, 2000.

For surcharges, see Nos. 345-346.

Easter A31

Designs: 150f, Last Supper, by Giotto, white inscriptions. 200f, Last Supper, yellow inscriptions. 300f, Lamentation, by Giotto, white inscriptions. 350f, Lamentation, yellow inscriptions. 650f, Crucifix, by Giotto, orange frame.

No. 119, 2000f, Crucifix, gold frame, denomination and country name in orange. No. 119A, 2000f, denomination and country name in white.

2000 Litho. *Perf. 13¼*

114-118 A31 Set of 5 5.50 5.50

Souvenir Sheet

Litho. & Embossed Foil Application

119	A31	2000f multi	7.00	7.00
119A	A31	2000f multi, booklet pane of 1	11.00	

See Nos. 140-144.

Christmas A32

Madonna of the Star by Fra Angelico.

Litho. & Embossed Foil Application

2000 *Perf. 13¼*

120	A32	2000f Miniature sheet of 1	8.50	8.50
	a.	Booklet pane of 1	10.50	10.50
		Complete booklet, #113A, 119A, 120a	31.00	

See Nos. 134-139.

Holy Land Visit of Pope John Paul II — A33

Designs: 500f, Pope, Yasser Arafat holding hands. 600f, Pope with miter. 750f, Pope touching Arafat's shoulder. 800f, Pope, creche. 1000f, Pope, back of Arafat's head.

2000 Litho. *Perf. 13¾*

121-125 A33 Set of 5 12.00 12.00

Intl. Children's Year — A34

Designs: 50f, Landscape. 100f, Children. 350f, Domed buildings. 400f, Family.

2000

126-129 A34 Set of 4 3.25 3.25

Pres. Arafat's Visit to Germany — A35

Arafat and: 200f, German Chancellor Gerhard Schröder. 300f, German President Johannes Rau.

2000 *Perf. 14x14¼*

130-131 A35 Set of 2 2.75 2.75

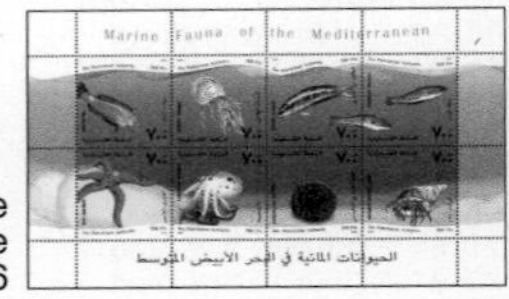

Marine Life A36

No. 132: a, Parrotfish. b, Mauve stinger. c, Ornate wrasse. d, Rainbow wrasse. e, Red starfish. f, Common octopus. g, Purple sea urchin. h, Striated hermit crab.

2000 Litho. *Perf. 13¾*

132 A36 700f Sheet of 8, #a-h 16.50 16.50

Souvenir Sheet

Blue Madonna A37

2000 ***Perf. 14x13¾***
133 A37 950f multi 3.25 3.25

Christmas Type of 2000

Designs: No. 134, 100f, No. 138, 500f, Nativity, by Gentile da Fabriano, horiz. No. 135, 150f, Adoration of the Magi, by Fabriano, horiz. No. 136, 250f, Immaculate Conception, by Fabriano, horiz. No. 137, 350f, No. 139, 1000f, Like #120.

2000 **Litho.** ***Perf. 13¼***
134-139 A32 Set of 6 7.75 7.75

Easter Type of 2000

Designs: 150f, Christ Carrying Cross, by Fra Angelico, blue inscriptions. 200f, Christ Carrying Cross, white inscriptions. 300f, Removal of Christ from Cross, by Fra Angelico, yellow inscriptions. 350f, Removal of Christ from the Cross, white inscriptions.
2000f, Crucifix, by Giotto, vert.

2001 **Litho.** ***Perf. 13¼***
140-143 A31 Set of 4 6.50 6.50

Souvenir Sheet
Litho. & Embossed

144 A31 2000f gold & multi 16.50 16.50

A38

Palestinian Authority flag and flag of various organizations: 50f, 100f, 200f, 500f.

2001 **Litho.** ***Perf. 13¾***
145-148 A38 Set of 4 3.25 3.25

Souvenir Sheet

Art by Ibrahim Hazimeh A39

No. 149: a, 350f, Jerusalem After Rain. b, 550f, Mysticism. c, 850f, Ramallah. d, 900f, Remembrance.

2001 ***Perf. 14x13¾***
149 A39 Sheet of 4, #a-d 12.00 12.00

Worldwide Fund for Nature (WWF) — A40

No. 150 — Houbara bustard, WWF emblem at: a, 350f, UR. b, 350f, LR. c, 750f, UL. d, 750f, LL.

2001 **Litho.** ***Perf. 13¾x14***
150 A40 Block of 4, #a-d 11.50 11.50

Graf Zeppelin Over Holy Land — A41

Zeppelin and: 200f, Map of voyage. 600f, Hills.

2001 ***Perf. 13¾***
151-152 A41 Set of 2 3.25 3.25

Legends — A42

Designs: 300f, Man with magic lamp, buildings. 450f, Eagle, snake, gemstones, man. 650f, Man and woman on flying horse. 800f, Man hiding behind tree.

2001 ***Perf. 13¾x14***
153-156 A42 Set of 4 9.00 9.00

Souvenir Sheet

Peace for Bethlehem — A43

2001 ***Perf. 14x13¾***
157 A43 950f multi 6.50 6.50

City Views — A44

Designs: 450f, Jerusalem. 650f, El-Eizariya. 850f, Nablus.

2002 **Litho.** ***Perf. 13¾***
158-160 A44 Set of 3 7.25 7.25

Women's Traditional Clothing — A44a

Various costumes: 50f, 100f, 500f.

2002, June **Litho.** ***Perf. 14***
160A-160C A44a Set of 3 17.50 17.50

Souvenir Sheet

Christmas — A45

2002, Dec. 20 ***Perf. 14¼x14***
161 A45 1000f multi 16.50 16.50

Succulent Plants — A46

Designs: 550f, Prickly pear. 600f, Big-horned euphorbia. 750f, Century plant.

2003, May 10 **Litho.** ***Perf. 13¾x14***
162-164 A46 Set of 3 8.00 8.00
164a Souvenir sheet, #162-164 8.00 8.00

Trees — A47

Designs: 300f, Olive tree. 700f, Blessing tree.

2003, July 12
165-166 A47 Set of 2 8.50 8.50

Universities A48

Designs: 250f, Al-Azhar University, Gaza. 650f, Hebron University, Hebron. 800f, Arab American University, Jenin.

2003, July 19
167-169 A48 Set of 3 7.75 7.75

Handicrafts — A49

Designs: 150f, Glass necklaces. 200f, Headdress. 450f, Embroidery. 500f, Costume embroidery. 950f, Head veil.

2003, Oct. 11 **Litho.** ***Perf. 13¾***
170-174 A49 Set of 5 11.00 11.00

French President Jacques Chirac — A50

No. 175 — Chirac and: a, 200f, Yasser Arafat, French flag. b, 450f, Palestinian flag.

2004 **Litho.** ***Perf. 14***
175 A50 Pair, #a-b 5.25 5.25

Printed in sheets containing two each of Nos. 175a-175b

Souvenir Sheet

Worship of the Virgin Mary A51

2004
176 A51 1000f multi 5.25 5.25

Souvenir Sheet

Arab League, 60th Anniv. A52

2005 **Litho.** ***Perf. 13¾***
177 A52 750f multi *30.00 30.00*

Mahmoud Darwish (1941-2008), Poet — A53

Denominations: 150f, 250f, 350f, 400f.

2008, July 29 **Litho.** ***Perf. 13***
178-181 A53 Set of 4 9.00 9.00

A54 Jericho, 10,000th Anniv. — A55

2010, Dec. 26 ***Perf. 13¼x13***

Background Color

182 A54 50f white .40 .40
183 A55 150f pink 1.25 1.25
184 A54 350f gray 2.75 2.75
185 A55 1000f light green 7.75 7.75
Nos. 182-185 (4) 12.15 12.15

Christmas — A56

Color of panel above denomination: 100f, Red. 150f, Purple. 250f, Green. 500f, Blue.

2010, Dec. 26
186-189 A56 Set of 4 7.50 7.50

Souvenir Sheet

Arab Postal Day A57

No. 190 — Emblem and: a, 350f, Camel caravan. b, 500f, Pigeon and map.

Litho. With Foil Application

2011, Mar. 17 ***Perf. 13¾x13¼***
190 A57 Sheet of 2, #a-b 9.50 9.50

Ramadan — A58

Designs: 50f, Dome of the Rock, crescent, arches, flag. 100f, Lantern, arabesque, flag. 250f, Lantern, crescent, arabesque, arch, flag. 500f, Dome of the Rock, crescent, flag.
No. 195, 1000f, Dome of the Rock, lantern, crescent. No. 196, 1000f, Flag, crescent, Arabic text.

2011, Aug. 1 **Litho.** ***Perf. 13x13¼***
191-194 A58 Set of 4 8.25 8.25

Souvenir Sheets

Perf. 13¼x14¼

195-196 A58 Set of 2 16.00 16.00

Nos. 195 and 196 each contain one 45x35mm stamp.

Yasser Arafat (1929-2004), President of the Palestinian Authority — A59

Various photographs of Arafat: 50f, 100f, 150f, 5000f.

2012, June 6 Litho. *Perf. 14¼*

197-200 A59 Set of 4 21.00 21.00

A booklet containing five 250f, three 500f, three 750f, and four 1000f stamps, each depicting Arafat, sold for 20,000f.

Souvenir Sheet

Soccer Ball and Flag of Palestinian Authority — A60

2012, June 6 Litho. *Perf. 13*

201 A60 1000f multi 4.25 4.25

Recognition by FIFA of first home soccer match of Palestinian Authority team, 4th anniv. Compare with type A68.

Miniature Sheet

Governmental Ministries — A61

No. 202 — Ministry of: a, Transport. b, Public Works and Housing. c, Telecommunication and Information Technology. d, Finance. e, Interior.

2012, June 6 Litho. *Perf. 13¼*

202 A61 300f Sheet of 5, #a-e 7.25 7.25

Miniature Sheet

Fruit A62

No. 203: a, 150f, Grapes. b, 300f, Oranges. c, 350f, Bananas. d, 450f, Dates.

2012, June 6 Litho. *Perf. 14*

203 A62 Sheet of 8, 2 each #a-d 12.00 12.00

The two examples of Nos. 203a-203d on the sheet have different frames, being placed in different areas on the marginal illustration depicting trees.

Arab Postal Day — A63

Denominations: 150f, 250f, 350f, 1000f, 5000f.

2012, Aug. 3 Litho. *Perf. 13¼*

204-208 A63 Set of 5 25.00 25.00

Christmas — A64

Various depictions of Christmas trees: 20f, 250f, 600f.

1000f, Man praying.

2012, Dec. 24 Litho. *Perf. 14*

209-211 A64 Set of 3 7.25 7.25

Souvenir Sheet

212 A64 1000f multi 9.00 9.00

For surcharge, see No. 347.

Intl. Day of Civil Defense — A65

Designs: 200f, Firemen in smoke. 250f, Firemen and fire truck. 500f, Firemen spraying water on building, ladder truck.

1000f, Firemen and fire truck, diff.

2013 Litho. *Perf. 14*

213-215 A65 Set of 3 4.50 4.50

Souvenir Sheet

216 A65 1000f multi 5.00 5.00

Flora and Fauna — A66

Designs: 20f, White flower. 100f, Caracal. 200f, Bird. 480f, Poppies. 720f, Turtle. 1080f, Nubian ibex.

No. 223, 1000f, Daisies, horiz. No. 224, 1000f, Eagle, horiz.

2013, June 3 Litho. *Perf. 14*

217-222 A66 Set of 6 13.50 13.50

Souvenir Sheets

223-224 A66 Set of 2 13.50 13.50

For surcharge, see No. 348.

Police — A67

Designs: 100f, Policeman directing traffic. 200f, Policemen inspecting plants. 250f, Policemen with pick and hoe.

500f, Policeman assisting elderly woman, vert.

2013 Litho. *Perf. 14*

225-227 A67 Set of 3 3.25 3.25

Souvenir Sheet

228 A67 500f multi 3.00 3.00

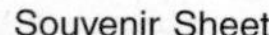

Souvenir Sheet

Soccer Ball and Flag of Palestinian Authority — A68

2013 Litho. *Perf. 13*

229 A68 1000f multi 9.00 9.00

Recognition by FIFA of first home soccer match of Palestinian Authority team, 5th anniv. Compare with type A60.

UNESCO Recognition of State of Palestine — A69

Dove, text, UNESCO emblem and panel color of: 100f, Green. 200f, Red brown. 420f, Black.

1000f, Dove, text and UNESCO emblem on Palestinian Authority flag, vert.

2013, Oct. 31 Litho. *Perf. 14*

230-232 A69 Set of 3 4.25 4.25

Souvenir Sheet

233 A69 1000f multi 5.75 5.75

Abdel Rahim Mahmoud (1913-48), Poet — A70

Background color: 80f, Apple green. 200f, Yellow orange. 500f, Gray.

1800f, Turquoise green background.

2013, July 13 Litho. *Perf. 14*

234-236 A70 Set of 3 4.50 4.50

Souvenir Sheet

237 A70 1800f multi 10.00 10.00

Declaration of State of Palestine, 1st Anniv. — A71

No. 238: a, Folk dancers. b, Musical score. c, Woman and olive tree. d, Dove, Al-Aqsa Mosqu, Church of the Holy Sepulchre. e, Sunbird and anemone flowers.

1000f, Dove, Pres. Mahmoud Abbas speaking at United Nations.

2013, Nov. 29 Litho. *Perf. 13¼*

238 A71 200f Sheet of 5, #a-e 5.75 5.75

Souvenir Sheet

239 A71 1000f multi 5.75 5.75

International Anti-Corruption Day — A72

Designs: 200f, Stop sign. 360f, Man refusing bribe. 420f, Money and gavel on balance. 720f, Hand.

1000f, "No" symbol over hand accepting bribe, horiz.

2013, Dec. 9 Litho. *Perf. 14*

240-243 A72 Set of 4 7.75 7.75

Souvenir Sheet

244 A72 1000f multi 5.75 5.75

Souvenir Sheet

Mosques A73

No. 245: a, Al-Aqsa Mosque, Jerusalem (one minaret). b, Sultan Ahmed Mosque, Istanbul (six minarets).

2014, Apr. Litho. *Perf. 13½x13¾*

245 A73 1000f Sheet of 2, #a-b 11.00 11.00

Joint issue between Palestine Authority and Turkey.

See Turkey No. 3371.

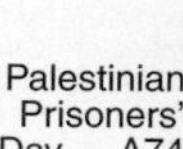

Palestinian Prisoners' Day — A74

Designs: 200f, Dove, chained hands, barbed wire. 360f, Prisoner holding prison bars. 600f, Blindfolded prisoner, barbed wire.

1200f, Maysara Abu Hamdiya (1948-2013), jailed Palestinian Liberation Organization fighter.

2014, Apr. 17 Litho. *Perf. 14*

246-248 A74 Set of 3 6.50 6.50

Souvenir Sheet

249 A74 1200f multi 6.75 6.75

Palestinian Scouts, Cent. (in 2012) — A75

Emblem with panel color of: 120f, Red. 480f, Yellow. 720f, Green.

1500f, Scouting trefoil.

2014, May 7 Litho. *Perf. 14*

250-252 A75 Set of 3 7.00 7.00

Souvenir Sheet

253 A75 1500f multi 8.00 8.00

Popular Resistence — A76

Designs: 60f, Bab Al-Shams. 920f, Tents, flag of Palestinian Authority.

1500f, Tent, flag of Palestinian Authority, horiz.

2014, May 15 Litho. *Perf. 14*

254-255 A76 Set of 2 5.25 5.25

Souvenir Sheet

256 A76 1500f multi 8.00 8.00

Visit of Pope Francis — A77

Pope Francis, Pres. Mahmoud Abbas, and Ecumenical Patriarch of Constantinople Bartholomew I and: 250f, People near doorway of Church of the Nativity, Jerusalem. 480f, Stylized key.

1500f, Pope Francis, Abbas, Patriarch Bartholomew I and Church of the Nativity, Jerusalem.

2014, May 25 Litho. *Perf. 14*
257-258 A77 Set of 2 4.00 4.00

Souvenir Sheet

259 A77 1500f multi 8.00 8.00

Euromed Postal Emblem and Mediterranean Sea — A78

2014, July 9 Litho. *Perf. 12¾x13¼*
260 A78 500f multi 3.00 3.00

Souvenir Sheet

Arab Lawyers Union, 70th Anniv. A79

2014, Aug. 12 Litho. *Perf. 14*
261 A79 1200f multi 6.25 6.25

A80

A81

National Reading Campaign — A82

2014, Oct. 22 Litho. *Perf. 14*
262 A80 200f multi 1.00 1.00
263 A81 250f multi 1.25 1.25

Souvenir Sheet

264 A82 1000f multi 5.00 5.00

International Year of Solidarity With the Palestinian People — A83

Palestinians and flag with background color of: 200f, Buff. 420f, Rose lilac.
1800f, Palestinians, flag and houses of worship.

2014, Nov. 29 Litho. *Perf. 14*
265-266 A83 Set of 2 3.00 3.00

Souvenir Sheet

267 A83 1800f multi 8.75 8.75

International Women's Day — A84

Images of various women: 250f, 600f.
1500f, Woman holding tree.

2015, Mar. 8 Litho. *Perf. 14*
268-269 A84 Set of 2 4.50 4.50

Souvenir Sheet

270 A84 1500f multi 7.75 7.75

Miniature Sheet

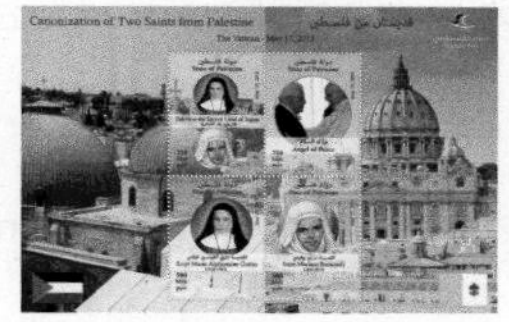

Canonization of Saints — A85

No. 271: a, 500f, St. Marie Alphonsine Gattas (1843-1927). b, 500f, St. Mariam Baouardy (1846-78). c, 750f, Both saints. d, 750f, Pope Francis and Pres. Mahmoud Abbas.

2015, May 17 Litho. *Perf. 14*
271 A85 Sheet of 4, #a-d *33.00 33.00*

Euromed Postal Emblem and Fishing Boat — A86

2015, July 9 Litho. *Perf. 14*
272 A86 500f multi 2.60 2.60

Jerusalem, Permanent Capital of Arab Culture — A87

Emblem and panel color of: 100f, Olive green. 200f, Red orange. 500f, Lilac.
1000f, Emblem and Jerusalem buildings.

2015, Oct. 2 Litho. *Perf. 14*
273-275 A87 Set of 3 4.25 4.25

Souvenir Sheet

276 A87 1000f multi 5.25 5.25

Figs and Olives — A88

Designs: 480f, Figs, green and black olives. 920f, Fig leaf and olive branch.
1200f, Olives on tree and figs.

2015, Oct. 10 Litho. *Perf. 14*
277-278 A88 Set of 2 7.25 7.25

Souvenir Sheet

279 A88 1200f multi 6.25 6.25

Islamic New Year — A89

Designs: 200f, Camel caravan in desert. 420f, Camels, mosque, Holy Ka'aba.
1500f, Camel, spider web, bird, palm tree.

2015, Nov. 15 Litho. *Perf. 14*
280-281 A89 Set of 2 3.25 3.25

Souvenir Sheet

282 A89 1500f multi 7.75 7.75

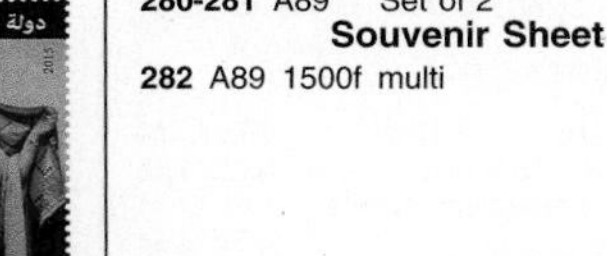

Speeches by Palestinian Leaders at United Nations — A90

No. 283: a, 2012 speech by Pres. Mahmoud Abbas. b, 1974 speech by Yasser Arafat.
1500f, Like No. 283b.

2015, Nov. 29 Litho. *Perf. 14*
283 A90 750f Sheet of 2, #a-b 7.75 7.75

Souvenir Sheet

284 A90 1500f multi 7.75 7.75

Grotto of the Nativity — A91

Serpentine Die Cut 14x15
2016, Mar. 27 Litho.

Self-Adhesive

285 A91 250f multi 1.40 1.40
a. Dated "2018" 1.40 1.40

International Workers' Day — A92

Designs: 250f, Man holding large claw hammer. 920f, Man, pliers, mallet, wrench.
1500f, Man, crane, mortared bricks.

2016, May 1 Litho. *Perf. 14*
286-287 A92 Set of 2 6.00 6.00

Souvenir Sheet

288 A92 1500f multi 7.75 7.75

Fish — A93

No. 289: a, Gray mullet. b, Red mullet. c, Grouper. d, Malabar grouper. e, Sea bass. f, Meagre. g, Sardine. h, Mackerel. i, Blue runner. j, Albacore tuna.

2016, July 3 Litho. *Perf. 12¾x13¼*
289 Sheet of 10 26.00 26.00
a.-j. A93 500f Any single 2.60 2.60

Solomon's Pools — A94

Various photographs of pools: 250f, 420f.
1500f, Pool at night, vert.

2016, Aug. 8 Litho. *Perf. 14*
290-291 A94 Set of 2 3.50 3.50

Souvenir Sheet

292 A94 1500f multi 7.75 7.75

Water Rights A95

No. 293: a, "No water no life." b, "Water is a human right."
No. 294, vert.: a, "Our water is our right." b, "Water for development."
1200f, "Water is life," vert.

2016, Aug. 8 Litho. *Perf. 14*
293 A95 420f Horiz. pair, #a-b 4.50 4.50
294 A95 800f Vert. pair, #a-b 8.25 8.25

Souvenir Sheet

295 A95 1200f multi 6.25 6.25

Arab Postal Day A96

No. 296: a, 10f, Green background, denomination at LL. b, 480f, Blue background, denomination at LR.

2016, Oct. 17 Litho. *Perf. 14*
296 A96 Horiz. pair, #a-b 2.60 2.60

Flag Day — A97

Designs: 250f, Palestinian Authority flag at United Nations Headquarters. 420f, Woman, flag and tree.
1800f, Dove carrying flag over Jerusalem.

Litho. With Foil Application
2016, Sept. 30 *Perf. 14*
297-298 A97 Set of 2 3.50 3.50

Souvenir Sheet

299 A97 1800f multi 9.25 9.25

Olive Tree — A98

2016, Nov. 15 Litho. *Perf. 14*

Background Color

300 A98 200f pale orange 1.00 1.00
301 A98 1400f pale green 7.00 7.00
302 A98 4500f white 22.00 22.00
Nos. 300-302 (3) 30.00 30.00

A99

Arabic Calligraphy Day — A100

Calligraphic designs with background color of: 250f, Dark brown. 420f, Grayish green.
No. 305: a, Calligraphic design with four dots at bottom, floral embellishment at UL and LL. b, Calligraphic design, diff. c, As "a," floral embellishment at UR and LR.

2016, Dec. 18 Litho. *Perf. 13x13¼*
303-304 A99 Set of 2 3.25 3.25

Souvenir Sheet
Perf. 14

305 A100 600f Sheet of 3, #a-c 9.00 9.00

Fadwa Touqan (1917-2003), Poet — A101

Denominations: 150f, 500f.
1800f, Touqan, diff.

2017, Mar. 1 Litho. *Perf. 14*
306-307 A101 Set of 2 3.50 3.50

Souvenir Sheet

308 A101 1800f multi 9.75 9.75

Faqqu'a Iris — A102

2017, Apr. 5 Litho. *Perf. 14*
309 A102 500f shown 2.75 2.75

Souvenir Sheet

310 A102 1500f Irises 8.50 8.50

Miniature Sheet

Stones A103

No. 311: a, 100f, Jerusalem stone. b, 200f, Nablus stone. c, 300f, Jenin stone. d, 400f, Ramallah stone. e, 500f, Hebron stone. f, 600f, Tulkarm stone. g, 700f, Bethlehem stone. h, 800f, Qalqilya stone.

2017, June 1 Litho. *Perf. 14*
311 A103 Sheet of 8, #a-h 20.00 20.00

Miniature Sheet

Dead Sea A104

No. 312: a, 150f, No shoreline. b, 280f, Shoreline at UL and LL. c, 420f, Shoreline at top. d, 950f, Shoreline at top and left.

2017, July 17 Litho. *Perf. 14*
312 A104 Sheet of 4, #a-d 10.00 10.00

Dates — A105

Designs: 150f, Medjool dates. 200f, Berhi dates. 500f, Hayani dates.
1500f, Date palms.

2017, Aug. 25 Litho. *Perf. 14*
313-315 A105 Set of 3 4.75 4.75

Souvenir Sheet

316 A105 1500f multi 8.50 8.50

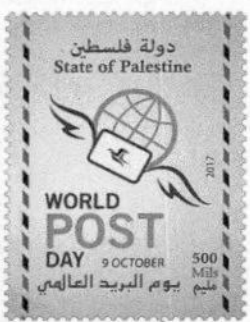

World Post Day — A106

2017, Oct. 9 Litho. *Perf. 14*
317 A106 500f multi 2.75 2.75

Teachers' Day — A107

Teacher pointing to map, with background color of: 200f, Light blue. 400f, Red brown.
1500f, Buff.

2017, Dec. 14 Litho. *Perf. 14*
318-319 A107 Set of 2 3.50 3.50

Souvenir Sheet

320 A107 1500f multi 8.50 8.50

Palestine Postage Stamps, Cent. (in 2018) — A109

Designs: 500f, Palestine #1. 1000f, Part of sheet of Palestine #1.

2019, Jan. 15 Litho. *Perf. 14*
322 A109 500f dark blue 2.75 2.75

Souvenir Sheet

323 A109 1000f dark blue 10.00 10.00

Archbishop Hilarion Capucci (1922-2017) — A110

Background color: 400f, Blue. 480f, Brown.
1500f, Capucci, diff.

2019, Jan. 15 Litho. *Perf. 14*
324-325 A110 Set of 2 5.00 5.00

Souvenir Sheet

326 A110 1500f multi 8.50 8.50

Miniature Sheet

1937 Palestine Banknotes — A111

No. 327: a, 150f, 500-mils note. b, 250f, 1-pound note. c, 350f, 5-pound note. d, 450f, 10-pound note. e, 550f, 50-pound note. f, 650f, 100-pound note.

2019, Jan. 15 Litho. *Perf. 14*
327 A111 Sheet of 6, #a-f 13.50 13.50

Miniature Sheet

1927 Coins of Palestine A112

No. 328: a, 100f, 1-mil coin. b, 200f, 2-mil coin. c, 300f, 5-mil coin. d, 400f, 10-mil coin. e, 500f, 20-mil coin. f, 600f, 50-mil coin. g, 700f, 100-mil coin.

2019, Jan. 15 Litho. *Perf. 14*
328 A112 Sheet of 7, #a-g, + label 15.50 15.50

A113

An-Najah National University, Nablus, Cent. — A114

Emblem with: 200f, One circle. 420f, Two circles.

2019, Jan. 15 Litho. *Perf. 14*
329-330 A113 Set of 2 3.50 3.50

Imperf

331 A114 1200f multi 6.75 6.75

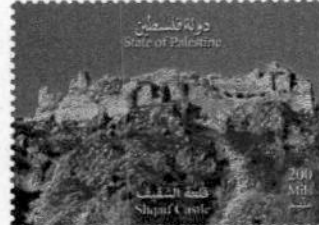

Shqaif (Beaufort) Castle. Lebanon — A115

Yassir Arafat and Others at Shqaif (Beaufort) Castle. Lebanon — A116

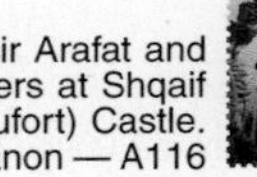

Design: 2000f, Shqaif (Beaufort) Castle, diff.

2019, Jan. 15 Litho. *Perf. 14*
332 A115 200f multi 1.10 1.10
333 A116 400f multi 2.25 2.25

Size: 106x71mm

Imperf

334 A115 2000f multi 11.00 11.00

Souvenir Sheet

Al Khan Al Ahmar A117

No. 335: a, Palestinian Authority flag on rock. b, Backhoe destroying house.

2019, Jan. 15 Litho. *Perf. 14*
335 A117 1000f Sheet of 2, #a-b 11.00 11.00

Souvenir Sheet

Pres. Mahmoud Abbas at Opening Ceremony for Palestinian Authority Embassy in Vatican City — A118

2019, Jan. 15 Litho. *Perf. 14*
336 A118 2000f Sheet of 2, #a-b 11.00 11.00

World Telecommunications Day — A119

Designs: 250f, Globe, musical notes, telephone handset, cameras, envelope, information and wi-fi symbols. 350f, Globe in envelope, world map.
1500f, Various symbols.

2019, Jan. 15 Litho. *Perf. 14*
337-338 A119 Set of 2 3.25 3.25

Souvenir Sheet

339 A119 1500f multi 8.25 8.25

Dated 2018.

Diplomatic Relations Between the Palestinian Authority and People's Republic of China, 20th Anniv. (in 2018) — A120

No. 340: a, Palestinian Authority President Mahmoud Abbas and People's Republic of China President Xi Jinping, flags of Palestinian Authority and People's Republic of China. b, Flags of Palestinian Authority and People's Republic of China.
2000f, Abbas, Xi and flags, vert.

2019, Aug. 8 Litho. *Perf. 12*
340 A120 1000f Horiz. pair, #a-b 11.50 11.50
c. Souvenir sheet of 2, #340a-340b 11.50 11.50

Souvenir Sheet
On Plastic
Without Gum

341 A120 2000f gold & multi 13.50 13.50

No. 341 contains one 50x76mm stamp.

A121

A122

Palestinian Authority's 2019 Chairmanship of Group of 77 — A123

No. 342 — Group of 77 emblem, Palestinian Authority flag and: a, Anemone flower. b, Dove. c, Palestinian sunbird. d, Olive tree. e, Palestinian gazelle.

Litho. With Foil Application

2019, Aug. 8 *Perf. 14¼*
342 A121 300f Sheet of 5, #a-e 8.50 8.50

Souvenir Sheets

Perf. 14x13

343 A122 1500f gold & multi 8.50 8.50
344 A123 1500f gold & multi 8.50 8.50

No. 104 Surcharged

No. 110a Surcharged

No. 209 Surcharged

No. 217 Surcharged

Methods and Perfs. As Before

2020, Nov. 18

345	A29 250m on 300f #104	—	—
346	A30 250m on 380f #110a	—	—
347	A64 250m on 60f #209	—	—
348	A66 250m on 20f #217	—	—

Al-Aqsa Mosque, Jerusalem — A124

2021, Oct. 12 Litho. *Perf. 14*

Background Color

349	A124 100m red brown	—	—
350	A124 1000m blue green	—	—

Souvenir Sheet

351	A124 1200m blue, horiz.	—	—

United Nations, 75th Anniv. — A125

2021 Litho. *Perf. 10*

Background Color

352	A125 400m white	—	—

Souvenir Sheet

354	A125 1500m orange	—	—

An additional stamp was issued in this set. The editors would like to examine any example of it.

Souvenir Sheet

Mohandas K. Gandhi (1869-1948) Indian Nationalist Leader — A126

2021 Litho. *Perf. 10*

355	A126 1500m multi	—	—

Souvenir Sheet

Famous Men A127

No. 356: a, Emile Touma (1919-85), newspaper publisher. b, Dr. Haider Abdel Shafi (1919-2007), physician and leader of Palestinian delegation to 1991 Madrid Peace Conference.

2021 Litho. *Perf. 10*

356	A127 750m Sheet of 2, #a-b	—	—

Bethlehem, 2020 Capital of Arab Culture — A128

2021 Litho. *Perf. 10*

357	A128 250m multi	—	—
358	A128 420m multi	—	—

SEMI-POSTAL STAMPS

Souvenir Sheet

Gaza-Jericho Peace Agreement — SP1

1994, Oct. 7 Litho. *Perf. 14*

B1	SP1 750m +250m multi	6.50	6.50

For surcharge see No. B3.

Souvenir Sheet

Arab League, 50th Anniv. SP2

Painting: View of Palestine, by Ibrahim Hazimeh.

1995, Mar. 22 *Perf. 13½*

B2	SP2 750f +250f multi	3.50	3.50

No. B1 Surcharged "FILS" in English & Arabic and with Added Text at Left and Right

1995, Apr. 10 Litho. *Perf. 14*

B3	SP1 750f +250f multi	6.50	6.50

Honoring 1994 Nobel Peace Prize winners Arafat, Rabin and Peres.

International Day of Persons With Disabilities — SP3

2015, Dec. 3 Litho. *Perf. 14*

B4	SP3 100f +100f multi	1.10	1.10

OFFICIAL STAMPS

Natl. Arms — O1

1994, Aug. 15 Litho. *Perf. 14*

O1	O1 50m yellow	.25	.25
O2	O1 100m green blue	.45	.45
O3	O1 125m blue	.65	.65
O4	O1 200m orange	.90	.90
O5	O1 250m olive	1.25	1.25
O6	O1 400m maroon	1.75	1.75
	Nos. O1-O6 (6)	5.25	5.25

Nos. O1-O6 could also be used by the general public, and non-official-use covers are known.

PANAMA

ˈpa-nə-ˌmä

LOCATION — Central America between Costa Rica and Colombia
GOVT. — Republic
AREA — 30,134 sq. mi.
POP. — 4,320,000 (2020 est.)
CAPITAL — Panama

Formerly a department of the Republic of Colombia, Panama gained its independence in 1903. Dividing the country at its center is the Panama Canal.

100 Centavos = 1 Peso
100 Centesimos = 1 Balboa (1904)

Catalogue values for unused stamps in this country are for Never Hinged items, beginning with Scott 350 in the regular postage section, Scott C82 in the airpost section, Scott CB1 in the airpost semi-postal section, and Scott RA21 in the postal tax section.

Watermarks

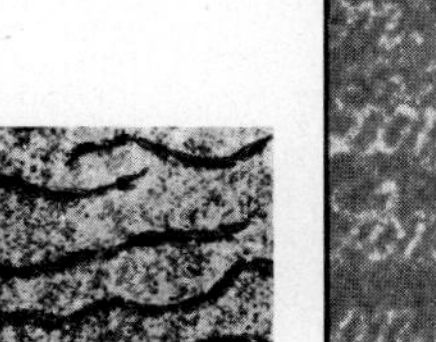

Wmk. 229 — Wavy Lines

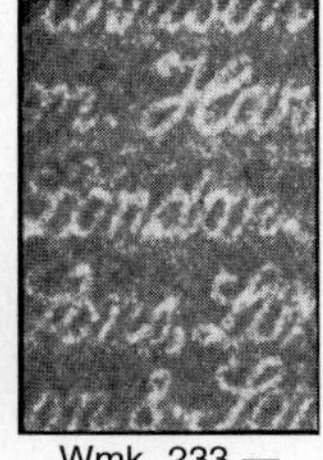

Wmk. 233 — "Harrison & Sons, London." in Script

Wmk. 311 — Star and RP Multiple

Wmk. 334 — Rectangles

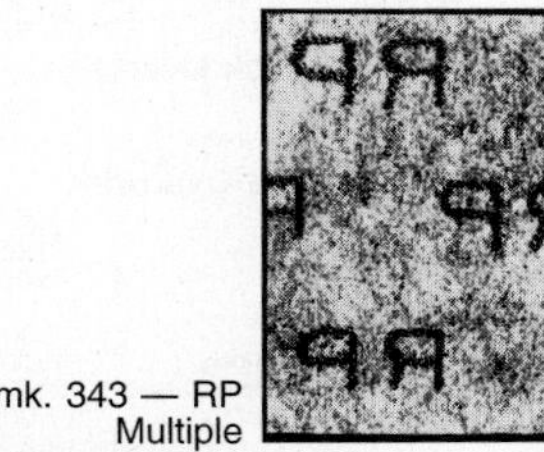

Wmk. 343 — RP Multiple

Wmk. 365 — Argentine Arms, Casa de Moneda de la Nacion & RA Multiple

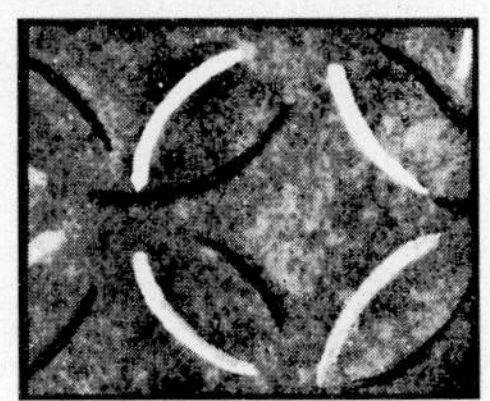

Wmk. 377 — Interlocking Circles

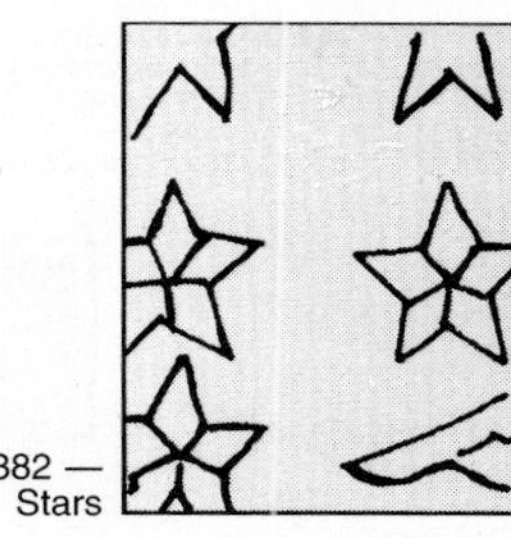

Wmk. 382 — Stars

Wmk. 382 may be a sheet watermark. It includes stars, wings with sun in middle and "Panama R de P."

Issues of the Sovereign State of Panama Under Colombian Dominion

Valid only for domestic mail.

Coat of Arms
A1 A2

1878 Unwmk. Litho. *Imperf.*

Thin Wove Paper

1	A1 5c gray green	25.00	30.00
a.	5c yellow green	25.00	30.00
2	A1 10c blue	60.00	60.00
3	A1 20c rose red	40.00	32.50
	Nos. 1-3 (3)	125.00	122.50

Very Thin Wove Paper

4	A2 50c buff	*1,500.*	

All values of this issue are known rouletted unofficially.

Medium Thick Paper

5	A1 5c blue green	25.00	30.00
6	A1 10c blue	65.00	70.00
7	A2 50c orange	13.00	
	Nos. 5-7 (3)	103.00	100.00

Nos. 5-7 were printed before Nos. 1-4, according to Panamanian archives.

Values for used Nos. 1-5 are for handstamped postal cancellations.

These stamps have been reprinted in a number of shades, on thin to moderately thick, white or yellowish paper. They are without gum or with white, crackly gum. All values have been reprinted from new stones made from retouched dies. The marks of retouching are plainly to be seen in the sea and clouds. On the original 10c the shield in the upper left corner has two blank sections; on the reprints the design of this shield is completed. The impression of these reprints is frequently blurred.

Reprints of the 50c are rare. Beware of remainders of the 50c offered as reprints.

Issues of Colombia for use in the Department of Panama

Issued because of the use of different currency.

Map of Panama — A3

1887-88 *Perf. 13½*

8	A3 1c black, *green*	.90	.80
9	A3 2c black, *pink* ('88)	1.60	1.25
a.	2c black, *salmon*	1.60	1.60
10	A3 5c black, *blue*	.90	.35
11	A3 10c black, *yellow*	.90	.40
a.	Imperf., pair		
12	A3 20c black, *lilac*	1.00	.50
13	A3 50c brown ('88)	2.00	1.00
a.	Imperf.		
	Nos. 8-13 (6)	7.30	4.30

See No. 14. For surcharges and overprints see Nos. 24-30, 107-108, 115-116, 137-138.

1892 Pelure Paper

14	A3 50c brown	2.50	1.10

The stamps of this issue have been reprinted on papers of slightly different colors from those of the originals.

These are: 1c yellow green, 2c deep rose, 5c bright blue, 10c straw, 20c violet.

The 50c is printed from a very worn stone, in a lighter brown than the originals. The series includes a 10c on lilac paper.

All these stamps are to be found perforated, imperforate, imperforate horizontally or imperforate vertically. At the same time that they were made, impressions were struck upon a variety of glazed and surface-colored papers.

Map of Panama — A4

Wove Paper

1892-96 **Engr.** ***Perf. 12***

15 A4 1c green .25 .25
16 A4 2c rose .40 .25
17 A4 5c blue 1.50 .50
18 A4 10c orange .35 .25
19 A4 20c violet ('95) .50 .35
20 A4 50c bister brn ('96) .50 .40
21 A4 1p lake ('96) 6.50 4.00
Nos. 15-21 (7) 10.00 6.00

In 1903 Nos. 15-21 were used in Cauca and three other southern Colombia towns. Stamps canceled in these towns are worth much more.

For surcharges and overprints see Nos. 22-23, 51-106, 109-114, 129-136, 139, 151-161, 181-184, F12-F15, H4-H5.

Nos. 16, 12-14 Surcharged

a

b

c

d

e

f

g

1894 **Black Surcharge**

22 (a) 1c on 2c rose .50 .40
a. Inverted surcharge 2.50 2.50
b. Double surcharge
23 (b) 1c on 2c rose .40 .50
a. "CCNTAVO" 5.00 5.00
b. Inverted surcharge 5.00 5.00
c. Double surcharge

Red Surcharge

24 (c) 5c on 20c black, *lil* 2.50 1.50
a. Inverted surcharge 12.50 12.50
b. Double surcharge
c. Without "HABILITADO"
25 (d) 5c on 20c black, *lil* 3.50 3.00
a. "CCNTAVOS" 7.50 7.50
b. Inverted surcharge 12.50 12.50
c. Double surcharge
d. Without "HABILITADO"
26 (e) 5c on 20c black, *lil* 6.00 5.00
a. Inverted surcharge 12.50 12.50
b. Double surcharge
27 (f) 10c on 50c brown 3.00 3.00
a. "1894" omitted
b. Inverted surcharge
c. "CCNTAVOS" 15.00
28 (g) 10c on 50c brown 12.50 12.50
a. "CCNTAVOS" 32.50
b. Inverted surcharge

Pelure Paper

29 (f) 10c on 50c brown 4.00 3.00
a. "1894" omitted 7.50
b. Inverted surcharge 12.50 12.50
c. Double surcharge
30 (g) 10c on 50c brown 10.00 10.00
a. "CCNTAVOS"
b. Without "HABILITADO"
c. Inverted surcharge 25.00 25.00
d. Double surcharge
Nos. 22-30 (9) 42.40 38.90

There are several settings of these surcharges. Usually the surcharge is about 15½mm high, but in one setting, it is only 13mm. All the types are to be found with a comma after "CENTAVOS." Nos. 24, 25, 26, 29 and 30 exist with the surcharge printed sideways. Nos. 23, 24 and 29 may be found with an inverted "A" instead of "V" in "CENTAVOS." There are also varieties caused by dropped or broken letters.

Issues of the Republic Issued in the City of Panama

Stamps of 1892-96 Overprinted

1903, Nov. 16 **Rose Handstamp**

51 A4 1c green 2.00 1.50
52 A4 2c rose 2.00 3.00
53 A4 5c blue 2.00 1.25
54 A4 10c yellow 2.00 2.00
55 A4 20c violet 4.00 3.50
56 A4 50c bister brn 10.00 7.00
57 A4 1p lake 50.00 40.00
Nos. 51-57 (7) 72.00 58.25

Blue Black Handstamp

58 A4 1c green 2.00 1.25
59 A4 2c rose 1.00 1.00
60 A4 5c blue 7.00 6.00
61 A4 10c yellow 5.00 3.50
62 A4 20c violet 10.00 7.50
63 A4 50c bister brn 10.00 7.50
64 A4 1p lake 50.00 42.50
Nos. 58-64 (7) 85.00 69.25

The stamps of this issue are to be found with the handstamp placed horizontally, vertically or diagonally; inverted; double; double, one inverted; double, both inverted; in pairs, one without handstamp; etc.

This handstamp is known in brown rose on the 1, 5, 20 and 50c, in purple on the 1, 2, 50c and 1p, and in magenta on the 5, 10, 20 and 50c.

Reprints were made in rose, black and other colors when the handstamp was nearly worn out, so that the "R" of "REPUBLICA" appears to be shorter than usual, and the bottom part of "LI" has been broken off. The "P" of "PANAMA" leans to the left and the tops of "NA" are broken. Many of these varieties are found inverted, double, etc.

Overprinted

Bar in Similar Color to Stamp

1903, Dec. 3 **Black Overprint**

65 A4 2c rose 2.50 2.50
a. "PANAMA" 15mm long 3.50
b. Violet bar 5.00
66 A4 5c blue 100.00 100.00
a. "PANAMA" 15mm long 100.00
67 A4 10c orange 2.50 2.50
a. "PANAMA" 15mm long 6.00 6.00
b. Horizontal overprint 17.50

Gray Black Overprint

68 A4 2c rose 2.00 2.00
a. "PANAMA" 15mm long 2.50

Carmine Overprint

69 A4 5c blue 2.50 2.50
a. "PANAMA" 15mm long 3.50
b. Bar only 75.00 75.00
c. Double overprint
70 A4 20c violet 7.50 6.50
a. "PANAMA" 15mm long 10.00
b. Double overprint, one in black 150.00
Nos. 65,67-70 (5) 17.00 16.00

This overprint was set up to cover fifty stamps. "PANAMA" is normally 13mm long and 1¾mm high but, in two rows in each sheet, it measures 15 to 16mm.

This word may be found with one or more of the letters taller than usual; with one, two or three inverted "V's" instead of "A's"; with an inverted "Y" instead of "A"; an inverted "N"; an "A" with accent; and a fancy "P."

Owing to misplaced impressions, stamps exist with "PANAMA" once only, twice on one side, or three times.

Overprinted in Red

1903, Dec.

71 A4 1c green .75 .60
a. "PANAMA" 15mm long 1.25
b. "PANAMA" reading down 3.00 .75
c. "PANAMA" reading up and down 3.00
d. Double overprint 8.00
72 A4 2c rose .50 .40
a. "PANAMA" 15mm long 1.00
b. "PANAMA" reading down .75 .50
c. "PANAMA" reading up and down 4.00
d. Double overprint 8.00 8.00
73 A4 20c violet 1.50 1.00
a. "PANAMA" 15mm long 2.25
b. "PANAMA" reading down
c. "PANAMA" reading up and down 8.00 8.00
d. Double overprint 18.00 18.00
74 A4 50c bister brn 3.00 2.50
a. "PANAMA" 15mm long 5.00
b. "PANAMA" reading up and down 12.00 12.00
c. Double overprint 6.00 6.00
75 A4 1p lake 6.00 4.50
a. "PANAMA" 15mm long 6.25
b. "PANAMA" reading up and down 15.00 15.00
c. Double overprint 15.00
d. Inverted overprint 25.00
Nos. 71-75 (5) 11.75 9.00

This setting appears to be a re-arrangement (or two very similar re-arrangements) of the previous overprint. The overprint covers fifty stamps. "PANAMA" usually reads upward but sheets of the 1, 2 and 20c exist with the word reading upward on one half the sheet and downward on the other half.

In one re-arrangement one stamp in fifty has the word reading in both directions. Nearly all the varieties of the previous overprint are repeated in this setting excepting the inverted "Y" and fancy "P." There are also additional varieties of large letters and "PANAMA" occasionally has an "A" missing or inverted. There are misplaced impressions, as the previous setting.

Overprinted in Red

1904-05

76 A4 1c green .25 .25
a. Both words reading up 1.50
b. Both words reading down 2.75
c. Double overprint 20.00
d. Pair, one without overprint 15.00
e. "PANAAM" 20.00
f. Inverted "M" in "PANAMA" 5.00
77 A4 2c rose .25 .25
a. Both words reading up 2.50
b. Both words reading down 2.50
c. Double overprint 10.00
d. Double overprint, one inverted 14.00
e. Inverted "M" in "PANAMA" 5.00
78 A4 5c blue .30 .25
a. Both words reading up 3.00 .30
b. Both words reading down 4.25
c. Inverted overprint 15.00
d. "PANAAM" 25.00
e. "PANANA" 8.00
f. "PAMANA" 5.00
g. Inverted "M" in "PANAMA" 7.50
h. Double overprint 20.00
79 A4 10c orange .30 .25
a. Both words reading up 5.00
b. Both words reading down 5.00
c. Double overprint 25.00
d. Inverted overprint 6.75 6.75
e. "PANAMA" 8.00
f. Inverted "M" in "PANAMA" 15.00
g. Red brown overprint 7.50 3.50
80 A4 20c violet 2.00 1.00
a. Both words reading up 5.00 5.00
b. Both words reading down 10.00
81 A4 50c bister brn 2.00 1.60
a. Both words reading up 10.50
b. Both words reading down 10.00
c. Double overprint
82 A4 1p lake 5.00 5.00
a. Both words reading up 12.50 12.50
b. Both words reading down 12.50
c. Double overprint
d. Double overprint, one inverted 20.00
e. Inverted "M" in "PANAMA" 45.00
Nos. 76-82 (7) 10.10 8.60

This overprint is also set up to cover fifty stamps. One stamp in each fifty has "PANAMA" reading upward at both sides. Another has the word reading downward at both sides, a third has an inverted "V" in place of the last "A" and a fourth has a small thick "N." In a resetting all these varieties are corrected except the inverted "V." There are misplaced overprints as before.

Later printings show other varieties and have the bar 2½mm instead of 2mm wide. The colors of the various printings of Nos. 76-82 range from carmine to almost pink.

Experts consider the black overprint on the 50c to be speculative.

The 20c violet and 50c bister brown exist with bar 2½mm wide, including the error "PAMANA," but are not known to have been issued. Some examples have been canceled "to oblige."

Issued in Colon

Handstamped in Magenta or Violet

1903-04 **On Stamps of 1892-96**

101 A4 1c green .75 .75
102 A4 2c rose .75 .75
103 A4 5c blue 1.00 1.00
104 A4 10c yellow 3.50 3.00
105 A4 20c violet 8.00 6.50
106 A4 1p lake 80.00 70.00

On Stamps of 1887-92

Ordinary Wove Paper

107 A3 50c brown 25.00 20.00
Nos. 101-107 (7) 119.00 102.00

Pelure Paper

108 A3 50c brown 70.00

Handstamped in Magenta, Violet or Red

On Stamps of 1892-96

109 A4 1c green 5.50 5.00
110 A4 2c rose 5.50 5.00
111 A4 5c blue 5.50 5.00
112 A4 10c orange 8.25 7.00
113 A4 20c violet 12.00 9.00
114 A4 1p lake 70.00 60.00

On Stamps of 1887-92

Ordinary Wove Paper

115 A3 50c brown 35.00 25.00
Nos. 109-115 (7) 141.75 116.00

Pelure Paper

116 A3 50c brown 50.00 37.50

The first note after No. 64 applies also to Nos. 101-116.

The handstamps on Nos. 109-116 have been counterfeited.

Stamps with this overprint were a private speculation. They exist on cover. The overprint was to be used on postal cards.

Overprinted On Stamps Of 1892-96

On Stamps of 1892-96

Carmine Overprint

129 A4 1c green .40 .40
a. Inverted overprint 6.00
b. Double overprint 2.25
c. Double overprint, one inverted 6.00
130 A4 5c blue .50 .50

Brown Overprint

131 A4 1c green 12.00
a. Double overprint, one inverted

Black Overprint

132 A4 1c green 60.00 30.00
a. Vertical overprint 42.50
b. Inverted overprint 42.50
c. Double overprint, one inverted 42.50
133 A4 2c rose .50 .50
a. Inverted overprint
134 A4 10c orange .50 .50
a. Inverted overprint 4.00
b. Double overprint 16.00 16.00
c. Double overprint, one inverted 6.00
135 A4 20c violet .50 .50
a. Inverted overprint 4.00
b. Double overprint 5.50
136 A4 1p lake 16.00 14.00

On Stamps of 1887-88

Blue Overprint

Ordinary Wove Paper

137 A3 50c brown 3.00 3.00

Pelure Paper

138 A3 50c brown 3.00 3.00
a. Double overprint 14.00

This overprint is set up to cover fifty stamps. In each fifty there are four stamps without accent on the last "a" of "Panama," one with accent on the "a" of "Republica" and one with a thick, upright "i."

Overprinted in Carmine

On Stamp of 1892-96

139	A4	20c violet	*200.00*	
a.		Double overprint		

Unknown with genuine cancels.

Issued in Bocas del Toro

Stamps of 1892-96 Overprinted Handstamped in Violet

1903-04

151	A4	1c green	20.00	14.00
152	A4	2c rose	20.00	14.00
153	A4	5c blue	25.00	16.00
154	A4	10c yellow	15.00	8.25
155	A4	20c violet	50.00	30.00
156	A4	50c bister brn	100.00	55.00
157	A4	1p lake	140.00	110.00
		Nos. 151-157 (7)	370.00	247.25

The handstamp is known double and inverted. Counterfeits exist.

Handstamped in Violet

158	A4	1c green	*100.00*	
159	A4	2c rose	*70.00*	
160	A4	5c blue	*80.00*	
161	A4	10c yellow	*100.00*	
		Nos. 158-161 (4)	*350.00*	

This handstamp was applied to these 4 stamps only by favor, experts state. Counterfeits are numerous. The 1p exists only as a counterfeit.

General Issues

A5

1905, Feb. 4 **Engr.** ***Perf. 12***

179	A5	1c green	.60	.40
180	A5	2c rose	.80	.50

Panama's Declaration of Independence from the Colombian Republic, Nov. 3, 1903.

Surcharged in Vermilion on Stamps of 1892-96 Issue

1906

181	A4	1c on 20c violet	.25	.25
a.		"Panrma"	6.00	6.00
b.		"Pnnama"	5.00	5.00
c.		"Pauama"	5.00	5.00
d.		Inverted surcharge	4.00	4.00
e.		Double surcharge	8.00	8.00
f.		Double surcharge, one inverted		

Stamps of 1892-96 Surcharged in Vermilion

182	A4	2c on 50c bister brn	.25	.25
a.		3rd "A" of "PANAMA" inverted	5.00	5.00
b.		Both "PANAMA" reading down	4.00	4.00
c.		Double surcharge	50.00	50.00
d.		Inverted surcharge	2.50	2.50

The 2c on 20c violet was never issued to the public. All examples are inverted. Value, 75c.

Carmine Surcharge

183	A4	5c on 1p lake	.60	.40
a.		Both "PANAMA" reading down	6.00	6.00
b.		"5" omitted		
c.		Double surcharge	75.00	75.00
d.		Inverted surcharge		
e.		3rd "A" of "PANAMA" inverted	10.00	10.00

On Stamp of 1903-04, No. 75

184	A4	5c on 1p lake	.60	.40
a.		"PANAMA" 15mm long		
b.		"PANAMA" reading up and down	10.00	10.00
c.		Both "PANAMA" reading down	25.00	25.00
d.		Inverted surcharge		
e.		Double surcharge	10.00	10.00
f.		3rd "A" of "PANAMA" inverted		
		Nos. 181-184 (4)	1.70	1.30

National Flag
A6

Vasco Núñez de Balboa
A7

Fernández de Córdoba
A8

Coat of Arms
A9

Justo Arosemena
A10

Manuel J. Hurtado
A11

José de Obaldía
A12

Tomás Herrera
A13

José de Fábrega — A14

1906-07 **Engr.** ***Perf. 11½***

185	A6	½c orange & multi	.70	.35
186	A7	1c dk green & blk ('07)	.70	.35
187	A8	2c scarlet & blk	1.00	.35
188	A9	2½c red orange	1.00	.35
189	A10	5c blue & black	1.75	.35
a.		5c ultramarine & black	2.00	.50
190	A11	8c purple & blk	1.50	.65
191	A12	10c violet & blk	1.50	.50
192	A13	25c brown & blk	3.50	1.10
193	A14	50c black	9.00	3.50
		Nos. 185-193 (9)	20.65	7.50

Inverted centers exist of Nos. 185-187, 189, 189a, 190-193, Value, each $25. Nos. 185-193 exist imperf.

For surcharge see No. F29.

Issued: Nos. 185, 188-193, 11/20; No. 187, 9/1.

Map
A17

Balboa
A18

Córdoba
A19

Arms
A20

Arosemena
A21

Obaldía
A23

1909-16 ***Perf. 12***

195	A17	½c org ('11)	1.00	.30
196	A17	½c rose ('15)	.70	.60
197	A18	1c dk grn & blk	1.00	.50
a.		Inverted center	7,500.	7,500.
b.		Booklet pane of 6 ('16)	*160.00*	
		Complete booklet, 4 #197b		—
198	A19	2c ver & blk	1.00	.30
a.		Booklet pane of 6	*160.00*	
199	A20	2½c red orange	1.50	.30
200	A21	5c blue & blk	2.00	.30
a.		Booklet pane of 6 ('16)	*350.00*	
201	A23	10c violet & blk	3.75	1.10
		Complete booklet, panes of 6 (3x2) of #195 (3), 197 (3), 199 (2), 200, 201 ('11)		—
		Nos. 195-201 (7)	10.95	3.40

Value for No. 197a used is for an off-center example with faults.

The panes contained in the booklet listed following No. 201 are marginal blocks of 6 (3x2), without gum, stapled within the booklet cover, with advertising paper interleaving. The complete booklet was sold for B1.50.

Nos. 197b and 198a are gummed panes of 6 (2x3), imperf on outside edges.

For overprints and surcharges see #H23, I4-I7.

Balboa Sighting Pacific Ocean, His Dog "Leoncico" at His Feet — A24

1913, Sept. 1

202	A24	2½c dk grn & yel grn	1.75	.65

400th anniv. of Balboa's discovery of the Pacific Ocean.

Panama-Pacific Exposition Issue

Chorrera Falls — A25

Map of Panama Canal — A26

Balboa Taking Possession of the Pacific — A27

Ruins of Cathedral of Old Panama — A28

Palace of Arts — A29

Gatun Locks — A30

Culebra Cut — A31

Santo Domingo Monastery's Flat Arch — A32

1915, Mar. 1 ***Perf. 12***

204	A25	½c ol grn & blk	.40	.30
205	A26	1c dk grn & blk	.95	.30
206	A27	2c car & blk	.75	.30
a.		2c ver & blk ('16)	.75	.40
208	A28	2½c scarlet & blk	.95	.35
209	A29	3c violet & blk	1.60	.55
210	A30	5c blue & blk	2.10	.35
a.		Center inverted	1,500.	650.00
211	A31	10c orange & blk	2.10	.70
212	A32	20c brown & blk	10.50	3.25
a.		Center inverted	300.00	—
		Nos. 204-212 (8)	19.35	6.10

For surcharges and overprints see Nos. 217, 233, E1-E2.

Manuel J. Hurtado — A33

1916

213	A33	8c violet & blk	9.00	4.25

For surcharge see No. F30.

S. S. Panama in Culebra Cut Aug. 11, 1914 — A34

S. S. Panama in Culebra Cut Aug. 11, 1914 — A35

S. S. Cristobal in Gatun Lock — A36

1918, Aug. 23

214	A34	12c purple & blk	15.00	5.75
215	A35	15c brt blue & blk	10.00	3.50
216	A36	24c yellow brn & blk	15.00	3.50
		Nos. 214-216 (3)	40.00	12.75

No. 208 Surcharged in Dark Blue

1919, Aug. 15

217	A28	2c on 2½c scar & blk	.40	.40
a.		Inverted surcharge	11.00	5.00
b.		Double surcharge	15.00	6.00

City of Panama, 400th anniversary.

Dry Dock at Balboa — A38

Ship in Pedro Miguel Lock — A39

1920, Sept. 1 **Engr.**

218	A38	50c orange & blk	30.00	22.50
219	A39	1b dk violet & blk	40.00	27.50

For overprint and surcharge see Nos. C6, C37.

Arms of Panama City
A40

José Vallarino
A41

"Land Gate"
A42

Simón Bolivar
A43

Statue of Cervantes
A44

Bolívar's Tribute
A45

Carlos de Ycaza
A46

Municipal Building in 1821 and 1921
A47

Statue of Balboa
A48

Villa de Los Santos Church
A49

Herrera
A50

Fábrega
A51

1921, Nov.

220 A40 ½c orange .80 .25
221 A41 1c green 1.00 .25
222 A42 2c carmine 1.25 .25
223 A43 2½c red 2.75 1.10
224 A44 3c dull violet 2.75 1.10
225 A45 5c blue 2.75 .35
226 A46 8c olive green 10.00 3.50
227 A47 10c violet 6.75 1.50
228 A48 15c lt blue 8.00 2.00
229 A49 20c olive brown 14.50 3.50
230 A50 24c black brown 14.50 4.25
231 A51 50c black 25.00 8.00
Nos. 220-231 (12) 90.05 26.05

Centenary of independence.
For overprints and surcharges see Nos. 264, 275-276, 299, 304, 308-310, C35.

Hurtado — A52

1921, Nov. 28

232 A52 2c dark green .65 .65

Manuel José Hurtado (1821-1887), president and folklore writer.
For overprints see Nos. 258, 301.

No. 208 Surcharged in Black

1923

233 A28 2c on 2½c scar & blk .45 .45
a. "1923" omitted 4.00
b. Bar over "CENTESIMOS" 4.00
c. Inverted surcharge 4.00
d. Double surcharge 4.00
e. Pair, one without surcharge 4.00

Two stamps in each sheet have a bar above "CENTESIMOS" (No. 233b).

Arms — A53

1924, May **Engr.**

234 A53 ½c orange .25 .25
235 A53 1c dark green .25 .25
236 A53 2c carmine .25 .25
237 A53 5c dark blue .45 .25
238 A53 10c dark violet .60 .25
239 A53 12c olive green .75 .40
240 A53 15c ultra .95 .40
241 A53 24c yellow brown 1.90 .60
242 A53 50c orange 4.50 1.10
243 A53 1b black 6.75 2.50
Nos. 234-243 (10) 16.65 6.25

For overprints & surcharges see Nos. 277, 321A, 331-338, 352, C19-C20, C68, RA5, RA10-RA22.

Bolívar
A54

Statue of Bolívar
A55

Bolívar Hall — A56

1926, June 10 ***Perf. 12½***

244 A54 ½c orange .55 .25
245 A54 1c dark green .55 .25
246 A54 2c scarlet .70 .30
247 A54 4c gray .90 .35
248 A54 5c dark blue 1.40 .50
249 A55 8c lilac 2.25 .80
250 A55 10c dull violet 1.60 .80
251 A55 12c olive green 2.50 1.00
252 A55 15c ultra 3.25 1.25
253 A55 20c brown 6.75 1.60
254 A56 24c black violet 8.00 2.00
255 A56 50c black 13.50 5.00
Nos. 244-255 (12) 41.95 14.10

Bolivar Congress centennial.
For surcharges and overprints see Nos. 259-263, 266-267, 274, 298, 300, 302-303, 305-307, C33-C34, C36, C38-C39.

Lindbergh's Airplane, "The Spirit of St. Louis" — A57

Lindbergh's Airplane and Map of Panama — A58

1928, Jan. 9 **Typo.** ***Rouletted 7***

256 A57 2c dk red & blk, *salmon* .40 .40
257 A58 5c dk blue, *grn* .60 .40

Visit of Colonel Charles A. Lindbergh to Central America by airplane.
No. 256 has black overprint.

No. 232 Overprinted in Red

1928, Nov. 1 ***Perf. 12***

258 A52 2c dark green .40 .40

25th anniversary of the Republic.

No. 247 Surcharged in Black

1930, Dec. 17 ***Perf. 12½, 13***

259 A54 1c on 4c gray .40 .40

Centenary of the death of Simón Bolívar, the Liberator.

Nos. 244-246 Overprinted in Red or Blue

1932 ***Perf. 12½***

260 A54 ½c orange (R) .40 .40
261 A54 1c dark green (R) .40 .40
a. Double overprint 18.00
262 A54 2c scarlet (Bl) .40 .40

No. 252 Surcharged in Red

263 A55 10c on 15c ultra 1.00 .50
a. Double surcharge 55.00
Nos. 260-263 (4) 2.20 1.70

No. 220 Overprinted as in 1932 in Black

1933, May 25 ***Perf. 12***

Overprint 19mm Long

264 A40 ½c orange .40 .40
a. Overprint 17mm long 50.00 —

Dr. Manuel Amador Guerrero — A60

1933, June 30 **Engr.** ***Perf. 12½***

265 A60 2c dark red .50 .25

Centenary of the birth of Dr. Manuel Amador Guerrero, founder of the Republic of Panama and its first President.

No. 251 Surcharged in Red

1933

266 A55 10c on 12c olive grn 1.25 .65

No. 253 Overprinted in Red

267 A55 20c brown 2.25 1.75

José Domingo de Obaldía
A61

Quotation from Emerson
A63

National Institute — A64

Designs: 2c, Eusebio A. Morales. 12c, Justo A. Facio. 15c, Pablo Arosemena.

1934, July 24 **Engr.** ***Perf. 14***

268 A61 1c dark green 1.00 .50
269 A61 2c scarlet 1.00 .45
270 A63 5c dark blue 1.25 .80
271 A64 10c brown 3.25 1.50
272 A61 12c yellow green 6.50 2.00
273 A61 15c Prus blue 8.50 2.50
Nos. 268-273 (6) 21.50 7.75
Set, never hinged 32.50

25th anniv. of the Natl. Institute.

Nos. 248, 227 Overprinted in Black or Red

1935-36 ***Perf. 12½, 12***

274 A54 5c dark blue .90 .30
275 A47 10c violet (R) ('36) 1.25 .60

No. 225 Surcharged in Red

1936, Sept. 19 ***Perf. 11½***

276 A45 1c on 5c blue .40 .40
a. Lines of surcharge 1½mm btwn. 6.50

No. 241 Surcharged in Blue

1936, Sept. 24 ***Perf. 12***

277 A53 2c on 24c yellow brn .60 .50
a. Double surcharge 20.00

Centenary of the birth of Pablo Arosemena, president of Panama in 1910-12. See Nos. C19-C20.

Panama Cathedral — A67

Designs: ½c, Ruins of Custom House, Portobelo. 1c, Panama Tree. 2c, "La Pollera." 5c, Simon Bolivar. 10c, Cathedral Tower Ruins. Old Panama. 15c, Francisco Garcia y Santos, 20c, Madden Dam, Panama Canal. 25c, Columbus. 50c, Gaillard Cut. 1b, Panama Cathedral.

1936, Dec. 1 **Engr.** ***Perf. 11½***

278 A67 ½c yellow org .55 .25
279 A67 1c blue green .55 .25
280 A67 2c carmine rose .55 .25
281 A67 5c blue .80 .50
282 A67 10c dk violet 1.75 .75
283 A67 15c turq blue 1.75 .75
284 A67 20c red 2.00 1.50
285 A67 25c black brn 3.50 2.00
286 A67 50c orange 7.75 5.00
287 A67 1b black 18.00 12.00
Nos. 278-287,C21-C26 (16) 62.70 40.00
Set, never hinged 95.00

4th Postal Congress of the Americas and Spain.

Stamps of 1936 Overprinted in Red or Blue

1937, Mar. 9

288 A67 ½c yellow org (R) .35 .30
a. Inverted overprint 25.00 25.00
289 A67 1c blue green (R) .45 .25
290 A67 2c car rose (Bl) .45 .25
291 A67 5c blue (R) .70 .25
292 A67 10c dk vio (R) 1.10 .35
293 A67 15c turq bl (R) 5.25 3.25
294 A67 20c red (Bl) 2.00 1.25
295 A67 25c black brn (R) 2.75 1.25
296 A67 50c orange (Bl) 9.00 6.00
297 A67 1b black (R) 14.50 10.00
Nos. 288-297,C27-C32 (16) 84.60 54.15
Set, never hinged 135.00

Stamps of 1921-26 Overprinted in Red or Blue

1937, July ***Perf. 12, 12½***

298 A54 ½c orange (R) 1.10 .80
a. Inverted overprint 30.00
299 A41 1c green (R) .35 .25
a. Inverted overprint 30.00
300 A54 1c dk green (R) .35 .25
301 A52 2c dk green (R) .45 .35
302 A54 2c scarlet (Bl) .55 .35

Stamps of 1921-26 Surcharged in Red

No.	Type	Description	Unused	Used
303	A54	2c on 4c gray	.70	.45
304	A46	2c on 8c ol grn	.70	.60
305	A55	2c on 8c lilac	.70	.45
306	A55	2c on 10c dl vio	.70	.50
307	A55	2c on 12c ol grn	.70	.45
308	A48	2c on 15c lt blue	.70	.60
309	A50	2c on 24c blk brn	.70	.75
310	A51	2c on 50c black	.70	.35
		Nos. 298-310 (13)	8.40	6.15
		Set, never hinged	12.50	

Ricardo Arango A77

Juan A. Guizado A78

La Concordia Fire — A79

Modern Fire Fighting Equipment A80

Firemen's Monument A81

David H. Brandon — A82

Perf. 14x14½, 14½x14

1937, Nov. 25 Photo. Wmk. 233

No.	Type	Description	Unused	Used
311	A77	½c orange red	2.10	.35
312	A78	1c green	2.10	.35
313	A79	2c red	2.10	.25
314	A80	5c brt blue	4.00	.50
315	A81	10c purple	7.25	1.25
316	A82	12c yellow grn	11.50	2.00
		Nos. 311-316,C40-C42 (9)	49.30	7.05
		Set, never hinged	66.00	

50th anniversary of the Fire Department.

Old Panama Cathedral Tower and Statue of Liberty Enlightening the World, Flags of Panama and US — A83

Engr. & Litho.

1938, Dec. 7 Unwmk. *Perf. 12½*

Center in Black; Flags in Red and Ultramarine

No.	Type	Description	Unused	Used
317	A83	1c deep green	.35	.25
318	A83	2c carmine	.55	.25
319	A83	5c blue	.80	.30
320	A83	12c olive	1.40	.75
321	A83	15c brt ultra	1.75	1.25
		Nos. 317-321,C49-C53 (10)	22.45	15.35
		Set, never hinged	33.75	

150th anniv. of the US Constitution.

No. 236 Overprinted in Black

1938, June 5 *Perf. 12*

No.	Type	Description	Unused	Used
321A	A53	2c carmine	.45	.40
		ever hinged	.70	
b.		Inverted overprint	22.50	
		Nos. 321A,C53A-C53B (3)	1.25	1.20

Opening of the Normal School at Santiago, Veraguas Province, June 5, 1938.

Gatun Lake — A84

Designs: 1c, Pedro Miguel Locks. 2c, Allegory. 5c, Culebra Cut. 10c, Ferryboat. 12c, Aerial View of Canal. 15c, Gen. William C. Gorgas. 50c, Dr. Manuel A. Guerrero. 1b, Woodrow Wilson.

1939, Aug. 15 Engr. *Perf. 12½*

No.	Type	Description	Unused	Used
322	A84	½c yellow	.35	.25
323	A84	1c dp blue grn	.55	.25
324	A84	2c dull rose	.65	.25
325	A84	5c dull blue	1.00	.25
326	A84	10c dk violet	1.10	.35
327	A84	12c olive green	1.10	.50
328	A84	15c ultra	1.10	.80
329	A84	50c orange	2.75	1.60
330	A84	1b dk brown	5.75	3.00
		Nos. 322-330,C54-C61 (17)	34.35	14.45
		Set, never hinged	51.50	

25th anniversary of the opening of the Panama Canal. For surcharges see Nos. C64, G2.

Stamps of 1924 Overprinted in Black or Red

1941, Jan. 2 *Perf. 12*

No.	Type	Description	Unused	Used
331	A53	½c orange	.35	.25
332	A53	1c dk grn (R)	.35	.30
333	A53	2c carmine	.35	.25
334	A53	5c dk bl (R)	.55	.30
335	A53	10c dk vio (R)	.80	.50
336	A53	15c ultra (R)	1.75	.65
337	A53	50c dp org	6.25	3.50
338	A53	1b blk (R)	14.50	6.00
		Nos. 331-338,C67-C71 (13)	49.90	31.25

New Panama constitution, effective 1/241.

Black Overprint

1942, Feb. 19 Engr.

No.	Type	Description	Unused	Used
339	A93	10c purple	1.40	1.00

Surcharged with New Value

No.	Type	Description	Unused	Used
340	A93	2c on 5c dk bl	1.75	.50
		Nos. 339-340,C72 (3)	7.15	4.00

Flags of Panama and Costa Rica — A94

Engraved and Lithographed

1942, April 25

No.	Type	Description	Unused	Used
341	A94	2c rose red, dk bl & dp rose	.30	.40

1st anniv. of the settlement of the Costa Rica-Panama border dispute. See No. C73.

National Emblems A95

Farm Girl in Work Dress A96

Cart Laden with Sugar Cane (Inscribed "ACARRERO DE CAÑA") — A97

Balboa Taking Possession of the Pacific — A98

Golden Altar of San José — A99

San Blas Indian Woman and Child A101

Santo Tomas Hospital A100

Modern Highway — A102

Engr.; Flag on ½c Litho.

1942, May 11

No.	Type	Description	Unused	Used
342	A95	½c dl vio, bl & car	.25	.25
343	A96	1c dk green	.25	.25
344	A97	2c vermilion	.25	.25
345	A98	5c dp bl & blk	.25	.25
346	A99	10c car rose & org	.65	.25
347	A100	15c lt bl & blk	1.00	.50
348	A101	50c org red & ol blk	2.50	1.00
349	A102	1b black	3.50	1.00
		Nos. 342-349 (8)	8.65	3.75

See Nos. 357, 365, 376-377, 380, 395, 409.

For surcharges and overprints see Nos. 366-370, 373-375, 378-379, 381, 387-388, 396, C129-C130, RA23.

Catalogue values for unused stamps in this section, from this point to the end of the section, are for Never Hinged items.

Flag of Panama A103

Arms of Panama A104

Engraved; Flag on 2c Lithographed

1947, Apr. 7 Unwmk. *Perf. 12½*

No.	Type	Description	Unused	Used
350	A103	2c car, bl & red	.80	.40
351	A104	5c deep blue	.80	.40

Natl. Constitutional Assembly of 1945, 2nd anniv.

No. 241 Surcharged in Black

1947, Oct. 29 *Perf. 12*

No.	Type	Description	Unused	Used
352	A53	50c on 24c yel brn	3.75	1.50
a.		"Habiiltada"	2.25	2.25

Nos. C6C, C75, C74 and C87 Surcharged in Black or Carmine

No.	Type	Description	Unused	Used
353	AP5	½c on 8c gray blk	.45	.25
a.		"B/.0.0½ CORREOS" (transposed)	3.00	3.00
354	AP34	½c on 8c dk ol brn & blk (C)	.45	.25
355	AP34	1c on 7c rose car	.45	.25
356	AP42	2c on 8c vio	.45	.25
		Nos. 352-356 (5)	5.55	2.50

Flag Type of 1942

1948 Engr. and Litho.

No.	Type	Description	Unused	Used
357	A95	½c car, org, bl & dp car	.80	.40

Monument to Firemen of Colon — A105

American-La France Fire Engine — A106

20c, Firemen & hose cart. 25c, New Central Fire Station, Colon. 50c, Maximino Walker. 1b, J. J. A. Ducruet.

1948, June 10 Engr.

Center in Black

No.	Type	Description	Unused	Used
358	A105	5c dp car	.80	.35
359	A106	10c orange	1.10	.35
360	A106	20c gray bl	2.10	.50
361	A106	25c chocolate	2.10	.90
362	A105	50c purple	4.00	.90
363	A105	1b dp grn	6.00	2.00
		Nos. 358-363 (6)	16.10	5.00

50th anniversary of the founding of the Colon Fire Department.

For overprint see No. C125.

Cervantes — A107

1948, Nov. 15 Unwmk. *Perf. 12½*

No.	Type	Description	Unused	Used
364	A107	2c car & blk	1.25	.40
		Nos. 364,C105-C106 (3)	3.75	1.20

Miguel de Cervantes Saavedra, novelist, playwright and poet, 400th birth anniv.

Oxcart Type of 1942 Redrawn

Inscribed: "ACARREO DE CANA"

1948 *Perf. 12*

No.	Type	Description	Unused	Used
365	A97	2c vermilion	1.10	.40

No. 365 Surcharged or Overprinted in Black

1949, May 26

No.	Type	Description	Unused	Used
366	A97	1c on 2c ver	.45	.25
367	A97	2c vermilion	.45	.25
a.		Inverted overprint	10.00	5.00
		Nos. 366-367,C108-C111 (6)	6.90	3.90

Incorporation of Chiriqui Province, cent.

Stamps and Types of 1942-48 Issues Overprinted in Black or Red

1949, Sept. 9 Engr.

No.	Type	Description	Unused	Used
368	A96	1c dk green	.35	.25
369	A97	2c ver (#365)	.90	.25
370	A98	5c blue (R)	1.30	.25
		Nos. 368-370,C114-C118 (8)	12.45	4.55

75th anniv. of the UPU.

Overprint on No. 368 is slightly different and smaller, 15½x12mm.

Francisco Javier de Luna — A108

1949, Dec. 7 *Perf. 12½*

371 A108 2c car & blk .65 .40

200th anniversary of the founding of the University of San Javier. See No. C119.

Dr. Carlos J. Finlay — A109

1950, Jan. 12 **Unwmk.** *Perf. 12*

372 A109 2c car & gray blk .75 .25

Issued to honor Dr. Carlos J. Finlay (1833-1915), Cuban physician and biologist who found that a mosquito transmitted yellow fever. See No. C120.

Nos. 343, 357 and 345, Overprinted or Surcharged in Carmine or Black

1950, Aug. 17

373 A96 1c dk green .45 .25

374 A95 2c on ½c car, org, bl & dp car (Bk) .45 .25

375 A98 5c dp bl & blk .50 .25

Nos. 373-375,C121-C125 (8) 10.75 3.75

Gen. José de San Martin, death cent.
The overprint is in four lines on No. 375.

Types of 1942

1950, Oct. 13 **Engr.**

376 A97 2c ver & blk .80 .40

377 A98 5c blue .80 .40

No. 376 is inscribed "ACARREO DE CANA."

Nos. 376 and 377 Overprinted in Green or Carmine

1951, Sept. 26

378 A97 2c ver & blk (G) .50 .40
- *a.* Inverted overprint 20.00 20.00
- *b.* First line omitted, second line repeated 20.00 20.00

379 A98 5c blue (C) 1.20 .40
- *a.* Inverted overprint 20.00 20.00

St. Jean-Baptiste de la Salle, 500th birth anniv.

Altar Type of 1942

1952 **Engr.** *Perf. 12*

380 A99 10c pur & org 1.25 .40

No. 357 Surcharged in Black

1952, Oct. 29

381 A95 1c on ½c multi .80 .40

Queen Isabella I and Arms — A110

1952, Oct. 20 **Engr.** *Perf. 12½*

Center in Black

382 A110 1c green .65 .40

383 A110 2c carmine .65 .40

384 A110 5c dk bl .65 .40

385 A110 10c purple .90 .40

Nos. 382-385,C131-C136 (10) 20.50 7.55

Queen Isabella I of Spain. 500th birth anniv.

No. 380 and Type of 1942 Srchd. "B/ .0.01 1953" in Black or Carmine

1953 *Perf. 12*

387 A99 1c on 10c pur & org .80 .40

388 A100 1c on 15c black (C) .80 .40

Issued: No. 387, 4/22; No. 388, 9/4.
A similar surcharge on No. 346 was privately applied.

A111 A112

2c, Baptism of the Flag. 5c, Manuel Amador Guerrero & Senora de Amador. 12c, Santos Jorge A. & Jeronimo de la Ossa. 20c, Revolutionary Junta. 50c, Old city hall. 1b, Natl. coinage.

1953, Nov. 2 **Engr.** *Perf. 12*

389 A111 2c purple .55 .25

390 A112 5c red orange .65 .25

391 A112 12c dp red vio 1.50 .25

392 A112 20c slate gray 2.75 .25

393 A111 50c org yel 4.00 .60

394 A112 1b blue 7.25 1.25

Nos. 389-394 (6) 16.70 2.85

Founding of the Republic of Panama, 50th anniv.
See #C140-C145. For surcharge see #413.

Farm Girl Type of 1942

1954 **Unwmk.** *Perf. 12*

395 A96 1c dp car rose .80 .40

Surcharged in Black

396 A96 3c on 1c dp car rose .80 .40

Issued: No. 395, 4/21; No. 396, 6/21.

Monument to Gen. Tomas Herrera — A113

1954, Dec. 4 **Litho.** *Perf. 12½*

397 A113 3c purple .35 .25

Nos. 397,C148-C149 (3) 5.85 2.75

Gen. Tomas Herrera, death cent.

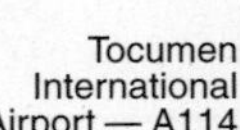

Tocumen International Airport — A114

1955, Apr. 16

398 A114 ½c org brn .95 .40

For surcharges see Nos. 411-412.

General Remon Cantera, 1908-1955 — A115

1955, June 1

399 A115 3c lilac rose & blk .80 .40

See No. C153.

Victor de la Guardia y Ayala and Miguel Chiari — A116

1955, Sept. 12

400 A116 5c violet .85 .40

Centenary of province of Coclé.

Ferdinand de Lesseps A117

First Excavation of Panama Canal A118

Design: 50c, Theodore Roosevelt.

1955, Nov. 22

401 A117 3c rose brn, *rose* .65 .25

402 A118 25c vio bl, *lt bl* 2.75 1.40

403 A117 50c vio, *lt vio* 3.50 1.50

Nos. 401-403,C155-C156 (5) 13.85 5.90

Ferdinand de Lesseps, 150th birth anniv., French promoter connected with building of Panama Canal. 75th anniv. of the 1st French excavations.
Imperfs exist, but were not sold at any post office.

St. Pius I — A118a

Pope Pius XII — A118b

Designs: Heads of Pope Pius's. 2c, St. Pius I (140-155). 3c, Pius II (1458-1464). 4c, Pius III (1503). 5c, Pius IV (1559-1565). 6c, Pius V (1566-1572). 10c, Pius VI (1775-1799). 20c, Pius VII (1800-1823). 25c, Pius VIII (1829-1830). 50c, Pius IX (1846-1878). 75c, Pius X (1903-1914), 1b, Pius XI (1922-1939). 2b, Pius XII (1939-1958).

Unwmk.

1956, July 2 **Litho.** *Perf. 12*

403A A118a 2c bright gr 3.50 3.50

403B A118a 3c red 4.00 4.00

403C A118a 4c brnsh red 6.25 6.25

403D A118a 5c lil pur 8.00 8.00

403E A118a 6c gray bl 5.75 5.75

403F A118a 10c blue 6.75 6.75

403G A118a 20c green 8.00 8.00

403H A118a 25c org red 9.25 9.25

403I A118a 50c brown 12.50 12.50

403J A118a 75c org 13.00 13.00

403K A118a 1b yellow 13.00 13.00

403L A118b 2b purple 13.00 13.00

Nos. 403A-403L (12) 103.00 103.00

Because of the speculative creation of the Popes issue, Nos. 403A-403L were sold in Panama and valid for postage for a period limited to six months from the issue date. The remainder were then removed from sale and destroyed.

Arms of Panama City — A119

Perf. 12½

1956, Aug. 17 **Litho.** **Unwmk.**

404 A119 3c green .40 .40

Sixth Inter-American Congress of Municipalities, Panama City, Aug. 14-19, 1956.
For souvenir sheet see C182a.

Carlos A. Mendoza — A120

1956, Oct. 31 **Wmk. 311**

405 A120 10c rose red & dp grn .65 .40

Pres. Carlos A. Mendoza, birth cent.

National Archives — A121

1956, Nov. 27

406 A121 15c shown 1.00 .35

407 A121 25c Pres. Belisario Porras 1.40 .40

Nos. 406-407,C183-C184 (4) 3.45 1.55

Centenary of the birth of Pres. Belisario Porras. For surcharge see No. 446.

Pan-American Highway, Panama — A122

1957, Aug. 1

408 A122 3c gray green .35 .25

Nos. 408,C185-C187 (4) 4.80 3.30

7th Pan-American Highway Congress.

Hospital Type of 1942

Unwmk.

1957, Aug. 17 **Engr.** *Perf. 12*

409 A100 15c black .75 .40

Manuel Espinosa Batista — A123

Wmk. 311

1957, Sept. 12 **Litho.** *Perf. 12½*

410 A123 5c grn & ultra .65 .40

Centenary of the birth of Manuel Espinosa B., independence leader.

No. 398 Surcharged "1957" and New Value in Violet or Black

1957, Dec. 21 **Unwmk.**

411 A114 1c on ½c org brn (V) .65 .40

412 A114 3c on ½c org brn .65 .40

No. 391 Surcharged "1958," New Value and Dots

1958, June 6 **Engr.** *Perf. 12*

413 A112 3c on 12c dp red vio .65 .40

Flags of 21 American Nations — A124

Center yellow & black; flags in national colors

Perf. 12½

1958, Aug. 12 Litho. Unwmk.

414 A124 1c lt gray .40 .25
415 A124 2c brt yel grn .40 .25
416 A124 3c red org .40 .25
417 A124 7c vio bl .40 .25
Nos. 414-417,C203-C206 (8) 6.65 3.70

Organization of American States, 10th anniv.

Brazilian Pavilion, Brussels Fair — A125

3c, Argentina. 5c, Venezuela. 10c, Great Britain.

1958, Sept. 8 Wmk. 311

418 A125 1c org yel & emer .40 .25
419 A125 3c lt bl & olive .40 .25
420 A125 5c lt brn & slate .40 .25
421 A125 10c aqua & redsh brn .40 .25
Nos. 418-421,C207-C209 (7) 5.70 3.30

World's Fair, Brussels, Apr. 17-Oct. 19.

Pope Pius XII as Young Man — A126

Wmk. 311

1959, Jan. 21 Litho. *Perf. 12½*

422 A126 3c orange brown .40 .25
Nos. 422,C210-C212 (4) 3.30 1.55

Pope Pius XII, 1876-1958. See #C212a.

UN Headquarters Building — A127

Design: 15c, Humanity looking into sun.

1959, Apr. 14 Wmk. 311

423 A127 3c maroon & olive .35 .25
424 A127 15c orange & emer .35 .25
Nos. 423-424,C213-C217 (7) 5.10 3.30

10th anniv. (in 1958) of the signing of the Universal Declaration of Human Rights.
For overprints see Nos. 425-426, C219-C221.

Nos. 423-424 Overprinted in Dark Blue

1959, May 16

425 A127 3c maroon & olive .40 .25
426 A127 15c orange & emer .55 .25
Nos. 425-426,C218-C221 (6) 5.65 3.15

Issued to commemorate the 8th Reunion of the Economic Commission for Latin America.

Eusebio A. Morales A128

National Institute A129

Wmk. 311

1959, Aug. 5 Litho. *Perf. 12½*

427 A128 3c shown .50 .40
428 A128 13c Abel Bravo .80 .40
429 A129 21c shown 1.20 .40
Nos. 427-429,C222-C223 (5) 3.40 2.00

50th anniversary, National Institute.

Soccer — A130

1959, Oct. 26

430 A130 1c shown .30 .25
431 A130 3c Swimming .45 .25
432 A130 20c Hurdling 2.10 .80
Nos. 430-432,C224-C226 (6) 7.65 3.05

3rd Pan American Games, Chicago, 8/27-9/7/59.
For overprint and surcharge see #C289, C349.

Fencing — A131

Wmk. 343

1960, Sept. 23 Litho. *Perf. 12½*

433 A131 3c shown .35 .25
434 A131 5c Soccer .60 .25
Nos. 433-434,C234-C237 (6) 6.30 2.55

17th Olympic Games, Rome, 8/25-9/11.
For surcharges & overprints see #C249-C250, C254, C266-C270, C290, C298, C350, RA40.

Agricultural Products and Cattle — A132

1961, Mar. 3 Wmk. 311 *Perf. 12½*

435 A132 3c blue green .65 .40

Issued to publicize the second agricultural and livestock census, Apr. 16, 1961.

Children's Hospital — A133

1961, May 2

436 A133 3c greenish blue .55 .40
Nos. 436,C245-C247 (4) 2.60 1.60

25th anniv. of the Lions Club of Panama. See #C245-C247.

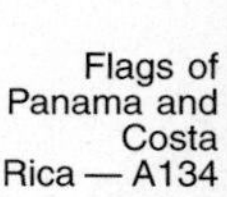

Flags of Panama and Costa Rica — A134

1961, Oct. 2 Wmk. 343 *Perf. 12½*

437 A134 3c car & bl .65 .40

Meeting of Presidents Mario Echandi of Costa Rica and Roberto F. Chiari of Panama at Paso Canoa, Apr. 21, 1961. See No. C251.

Arms of Colon — A135

1962, Feb. 28 Litho. Wmk. 311

438 A135 3c car, yel & vio bl .40 .40

3rd Central American Municipal Assembly, Colon, May 13-17. See No. C255.

Mercury and Cogwheel — A136

1962, Mar. 16 Wmk. 343

439 A136 3c red orange .70 .40

First industrial and commercial census.

Social Security Hospital — A137

1962, June 1 *Perf. 12½*

440 A137 3c vermilion & gray .65 .40

Opening of the Social Security Hospital.
For surcharge see No. 445.

San Francisco de la Montana Church, Veraguas A138

Ruins of Old Panama Cathedral (1519-1671) A139

Designs: 3c, David Cathedral. 5c, Natá Church. 10c, Don Bosco Church. 15c, Church of the Virgin of Carmen. 20c, Colon Cathedral. 25c, Greek Orthodox Temple. 50c, Cathedral of Panama. 1b, Protestant Church of Colon.

1960-64 Litho. Wmk. 343

Buildings in Black

441 A138 1c red & bl .35 .25
441A A139 2c red & yel .35 .25
441B A138 3c vio & yel .35 .25
441C A139 5c rose & lt grn .35 .25
441D A139 10c grn & yel .35 .25
441E A139 10c red & bl ('64) .35 .25
441F A139 15c ultra & lt grn .50 .25
441G A139 20c red & pink .75 .25
441H A138 25c grn & pink .90 .45
441I A139 50c ultra & pink 1.50 .60
441J A138 1b lilac & yel 3.75 1.60
Nos. 441-441J (11) 9.50 4.65

Freedom of religion in Panama.
Issued: #441E, 6/4/64; others, 7/29/60.
See #C256-C265; souvenir sheet #C264a.
For surcharges and overprints see Nos. 445A, 451, 467, C288, C296-C297, C299.

Bridge of the Americas during Construction A140

1962, Oct. 12 *Perf. 12½*

442 A140 3c carmine & gray .65 .40

Opening of the Bridge of the Americas (Thatcher Ferry Bridge), Oct. 12, 1962. See No. C273. For surcharge see No. 445B.

Fire Brigade Exercises, Inauguration of Aqueduct, 1906 A141

Portraits of Fire Brigade Officials: 3c, Lt. Col. Luis Carlos Endara P., Col. Raul Arango N. and Major Ernesto Arosemena A. 5c, Guillermo Patterson Jr., David F. de Castro, Pres. T. Gabriel Duque, Telmo Rugliancich and Tomas Leblanc.

1963, Jan. 22 Wmk. 311 *Perf. 12½*

443 A141 1c emer & blk .65 .40
443A A141 3c vio bl & blk .65 .40
444 A141 5c mag & blk 1.25 .40
Nos. 443-444,C279-C281 (6) 6.50 2.40

75th anniversary (in 1962) of the Panamanian Fire Brigade.
For surcharge see No. 445C.

Nos. 440, 441A, 442, 443A and 407 Surcharged in Black or Red

1963 Wmk. 343 *Perf. 12½*

445 A137 4c on 3c ver & gray .75 .40
445A A138 4c on 3c vio & yel .75 .40
445B A140 4c on 3c car & gray .75 .40

Wmk. 311

445C A141 4c on 3c vio bl & blk .75 .40
446 A121 10c on 25c dk car rose & bluish blk (R) 1.00 .40
Nos. 445-446 (5) 4.00 2.00

Issued: Nos. 445-445C, 8/30; No. 446, 10/9.

1964 Winter Olympics, Innsbruck — 141a

Perf. 14x13½, 13½x14 (#447A, 447C)

1963, Dec. 20 Litho.

447 A141a ½c Mountains .35 .25
447A A141a 1c Speed skating .35 .25
447B A141a 3c like No. 447 .75 .25
447C A141a 4c like No. 447A .85 .25
447D A141a 5c Slalom skiing 1.10 .25
447E A141a 15c like No. 447D 2.00 .60
447F A141a 21c like No. 447D 3.75 1.00
447G A141a 31c like No. 447D 5.50 1.50
h. Souv. sheet of 2, #447F-447G, perf. 13½x14 19.00 10.00
Nos. 447-447G (8) 14.65 4.35

#447D-447G are airmail. #447Gh exists imperf., with background colors switched. Value, $17.50.

Pres. Francisco J. Orlich, Costa Rica — A142

Flags and Presidents: 2c, Luis A. Somoza, Nicaragua. 3c, Dr. Ramon Villeda M., Honduras. 4c, Roberto F. Chiari, Panama.

Perf. 12½x12

1963, Dec. 18 Litho. Unwmk.

Portrait in Slate Green

448 A142 1c lt grn, red & ultra .50 .25
448A A142 2c lt bl, red & ultra .50 .25
448B A142 3c pale pink, red & ultra .50 .25
448C A142 4c rose, red & ultra .50 .25
Nos. 448-448C,C292-C294 (7) 6.45 2.70

Meeting of Central American Presidents with Pres. John F. Kennedy, San José, Mar. 18-20, 1963.

Vasco Nuñez de Balboa — A143

1964, Jan. 22 Photo. *Perf. 13*

449 A143 4c green, *pale rose* .80 .40

450th anniv. of Balboa's discovery of the Pacific Ocean. See No. C295.

No. C231 Surcharged "Correos B/.0.10" in Red

Wmk. 311

1964, Feb. 25 Litho. *Perf. 12½*

450 AP74 10c on 21c lt bl .80 .40

Type of 1962 Overprinted in Red

1964, Oct. 20 Wmk. 343

451 A138 1b red, bl & blk 3.00 2.50

1964 Summer Olympics, Tokyo A144

1964, Mar. 4 *Perf. 13½x14*

452 A144 ½c shown .35 .25
452A A144 1c Torch bearer .35 .25

Perf. 14x13½

452B A144 5c Olympic stadium .65 .25
452C A144 10c like No. 452B 1.00 .30
452D A144 21c like No. 452B 2.40 .60
452E A144 50c like No. 452B 4.75 1.25
f. Souv. sheet of 1, perf. 13½x14 18.00 16.00
Nos. 452-452E (6) 9.50 2.90

Nos. 452B-452E are airmail. No. 452Ef exists imperf. with different colors. Value, $18.

Space Conquest A145

½c, Projected Apollo spacecraft. 1c, Gemini, Agena spacecraft. 5c, Astronaut Walter M. Schirra. 10c, Astronaut L. Gordon Cooper. 21c, Schirra's Mercury capsule. 50c, Cooper's Mercury capsule.

1964, Apr. 24 *Perf. 14x14x13½*

453 A145 ½c bl grn & multi .35 .25
453A A145 1c dk blue & multi .35 .25
453B A145 5c yel bis & multi .45 .35
453C A145 10c lil rose & multi .75 .45
453D A145 21c blue & multi 1.75 1.00
453E A145 50c violet & multi 7.75 5.00
f. Souvenir sheet of 1 23.50 20.00
Nos. 453-453E (6) 11.40 7.30

Nos. 453B-453E are airmail. No. 453Ef exists imperf. with different colors. Value, $23.50.

Aquatic Sports — A146

Perf. 14x13½, 13½x14

1964, Jun3. 17

454 A146 ½c Water skiing .35 .25
454A A146 1c Skin diving .35 .25
454B A146 5c Fishing .45 .25
454C A146 10c Sailing, vert. 2.25 .50
454D A146 21c Hydroplane racing 4.25 1.00
454E A146 31c Water polo 5.25 1.25
f. Souvenir sheet of 1 21.00 20.00
Nos. 454-454E (6) 12.90 3.50

Nos. 454B-454E are airmail.
Nos. 454-454Ef exist imperf in different colors. Value imperf, Nos. 454-454E $22. Value imperf, No. 454Ef $21.

Eleanor Roosevelt — A147

Perf. 12x12½

1964, Oct. 9 Litho. Unwmk.

455 A147 4c car & blk, *grnsh* .70 .25

Issued to honor Eleanor Roosevelt (1884-1962). See Nos. C330-C330a.

Canceled to Order
Canceled sets of new issues have been sold by the government. Postally used examples are worth more.

1964 Winter Olympics, Innsbruck A147a

Olympic medals and winners: ½c, Women's slalom. 1c, Men's 500-meter speed skating. 2c, Four-man bobsled. 3c, Women's figure skating. 4c, Ski jumping. 5c, 15km cross country skiing. 6c, 50km cross country skiing. 7c, Women's 3000-meter speed skating. 10c, Men's figure skating. 21c, Two-man bobsled. 31c, Men's downhill skiing.

Litho. & Embossed

Perf. 13½x14

1964, Oct. 14 Unwmk.

456 A147a ½c bl grn & multi .35 .25
456A A147a 1c dk bl & multi .35 .25
456B A147a 2c brn vio & multi .35 .25
456C A147a 3c lil rose & multi .65 .25
456D A147a 4c brn lake & multi 1.00 .25
456E A147a 5c brt vio & multi .75 .30
456F A147a 6c grn bl & multi 1.00 .40
456G A147a 7c dp vio & multi 1.60 .65
456H A147a 10c emer grn & multi 2.50 1.00
456I A147a 21c ver & multi 3.00 1.10
456J A147a 31c ultra & multi 5.25 2.00
k. Souv. sheet of 3, #456H-456J 19.00 16.00
Nos. 456-456J (11) 16.80 6.70

Nos. 456E-456J are airmail.
No. 456Jk exists imperf. Value $19.
See Nos. 458-458J.

Satellites A147b

Designs: ½c, Telstar 1. 1c, Transit 2A. 5c, OSO 1 Solar Observatory. 10c, Tiros 2 weather satellite. 21c, Weather station. 50c, Syncom 3.

1964, Dec. 21 *Perf. 14x14x13½*

457 A147b ½c ver & multi .75 .25
457A A147b 1c vio & multi .75 .25
457B A147b 5c lil rose & multi .75 .40
457C A147b 10c blue & multi 1.00 .25
457D A147b 21c bl grn & multi 2.80 1.25
457E A147b 50c green & multi 4.40 1.75
f. Souvenir sheet of 1 22.00 16.00
Nos. 457-457E (6) 10.45 4.15

Nos. 457B-457E are airmail. No. 457Ef exists imperf in different colors. Value, $22.
For overprints see Nos. 489-489b.

1964 Olympic Medals Type

Summer Olympic Medals and Winners: ½c, Parallel bars. 1c, Dragon-class sailing. 2c, Individual show jumping. 3c, Two-man kayak. 4c, Team road race cycling. 5c, Individual dressage. 6c, Women's 800-meter run. 7c, 3000-meter steeplechase. 10c, Men's floor exercises. 21c, Decathlon. 31c, Men's 100-meter freestyle swimming.

Litho. & Embossed

1964, Dec. 28 *Perf. 13½x14*

458 A147a ½c org & multi .45 .25
458A A147a 1c plum & multi .45 .25
458B A147a 2c bl grn & multi .45 .25
458C A147a 3c red brn & multi .45 .25
458D A147a 4c lilac rose & multi .55 .25
458E A147a 5c dull grn & multi 1.00 .25
458F A147a 6c blue & multi 1.20 .25
458G A147a 7c dk vio & multi 1.40 .30
458H A147a 10c ver & multi 2.10 .40
458I A147a 21c dl vio & multi 3.25 .65
458J A147a 31c dk bl grn & multi 6.00 1.00
k. Souv. sheet of 3, #458H-458J 25.00 17.50
Nos. 458-458J (11) 17.30 4.10

#458E-458J are airmail. #458Jk exists imperf. Value, $25.

John F. Kennedy & Cape Kennedy A147c

Designs: 1c, Launching of Titan II rocket, Gemini capsule. 2c, Apollo lunar module. 3c, Proposed Apollo command and service modules. 5c, Gemini capsule atop Titan II rocket. 6c, Soviet cosmonauts Komarov, Yegorov, Feoktistov. 11c, Ranger VII. 31c, Lunar surface.

1965, Feb. 25 Litho. *Perf. 14*

459 A147c ½c vio bl & multi .75 .25
459A A147c 1c blue & multi .75 .25
459B A147c 2c plum & multi .75 .25
459C A147c 3c ol grn & multi 1.00 .30
459D A147c 5c lilac rose & multi 1.00 .40
459E A147c 10c dull grn & multi 1.75 .70
459F A147c 11c brt vio & multi 2.90 1.10
459G A147c 31c grn & multi 5.25 2.00
h. Souvenir sheet of 1 22.00 20.00
Nos. 459-459G (8) 14.15 5.25

Nos. 459D-459G are airmail. Nos. 459-459Gh exists imperf. in different colors. Values: set, $24; souvenir sheet, $22. For overprints see Nos. 491-491b.

Atomic Power for Peace A147d

Designs: ½c, Nuclear powered submarine *Nautilus*. 1c, Nuclear powered ship *Savannah*. 4c, First nuclear reactor, Calderhall, England. 6c, Nuclear powered icebreaker *Lenin*. 10c, Nuclear powered observatory. 21c, Nuclear powered space vehicle.

1965, May 12

460 A147d ½c blue & multi
460A A147d 1c grn & multi
460B A147d 4c red & multi
460C A147d 6c dl bl grn & multi
460D A147d 10c blue grn & multi
460E A147d 21c dk vio & multi
f. Souv. sheet of 2, #460D-460E 13.00 12.50
Set, #460-460E 9.75 3.50

Nos. 460C-460E are airmail.
Nos. 460-460Ef exists imperf in different colors. Value imperf, Nos. 460-460E $15. Value imperf, No. 460Ef $13.

John F. Kennedy Memorial — A147e

Kennedy and: ½c, PT109. 1c, Space capsule. 10c, UN emblem. 21c, Winston Churchill. 31c, Rocket launch at Cape Kennedy.

1965, Aug. 23 *Perf. 13½x13*

461 A147e ½c multicolored
461A A147e 1c multicolored
461B A147e 10c + 5c, multi
461C A147e 21c + 10c, multi
461D A147e 31c + 15c, multi
e. Souv. sheet of 2, #461A, 461D, perf. 12½x12 21.00 20.00
Set, #461-461D 9.50 1.50

Nos. 461B-461D are airmail semipostal.
Nos. 461-461De exist imperf in different colors. Value $21.
For overprints see Nos. C367A-C367B.

Keel-billed Toucan — A148

Song Birds: 2c, Scarlet macaw. 3c, Red-crowned woodpecker. 4c, Blue-gray tanager, horiz.

1965, Oct. 27 Unwmk. *Perf. 14*

462 A148 1c brt pink & multi .40 .40
462A A148 2c multicolored .40 .40
462B A148 3c brt vio & multi 1.40 .40
462C A148 4c org yel & multi 1.40 .40
Nos. 462-462C,C337-C338 (6) 9.10 2.40

Snapper A149

1965, Dec. 7 Litho.

463 A149 1c shown .65 .40
463A A149 2c Dorado .65 .40
Nos. 463-463A,C339-C342 (6) 7.60 2.40

Pope Paul VI, Visit to UN — A149a

Designs: ½c, Pope on Balcony of St. Peters, Vatican City. 1c, Pope Addressing UN General Assembly. 5c, Arms of Vatican City, Panama, UN emblem. 10c, Lyndon Johnson, Pope Paul VI, Francis Cardinal Spellman. 21c, Ecumenical Council, Vatican II. 31c, Earlybird satellite.

1966 Apr. 4 ***Perf. 12x12½***

464 A149a ½c multicolored
464A A149a 1c multicolored
464B A149a 5c multicolored
464C A149a 10c multicolored
464D A149a 21c multicolored
464E A149a 31c multicolored
f. Souv. sheet of 2, #464B, 464E, perf. 13x13½ 22.00 20.00
Set, #464-464E 11.00 3.00

Nos. 464B-464E are airmail. No. 464Ef exists imperf. with different margin color. Value $22.

For overprints see Nos. 490-490B.

Famous Men — A149b

Designs: ½c, William Shakespeare. 10c, Dante Alighieri. 31c, Richard Wagner.

1966, May 26 ***Perf. 14***

465 A149b ½c multicolored
465A A149b 10c multicolored
465B A149b 31c multicolored
c. Souv. sheet of 2, #465A-465B, perf. 13½x14 19.00 15.00
Set, #465-465B 8.25 3.25

Nos. 465A-465B are airmail. No. 465Bc exists imperf. with different margin color. Value $19.

Works by Famous Artists — A149c

Paintings: ½c, Elizabeth Tucher by Durer. 10c, Madonna of the Rocky Grotto by Da Vinci. 31c, La Belle Jardiniere by Raphael.

1966, May 26

466 A149c ½c multicolored
466A A149c 10c multicolored
466B A149c 31c multicolored
c. Souv. sheet of 2, #466-466B 15.00 15.00
Set, #466-466B 8.50 2.25

Nos. 466A-466B are airmail.

No. 466Bc exists imperf. with different margin color. Value $30.

No. 441H Surcharged

1966, June 27 Wmk. 343 ***Perf. 12½***

467 A138 13c on 25c grn & pink .90 .40

The "25c" has not been obliterated.

A149d

No. 468A, Uruguay, 1930, 1950. No. 468B, Italy, 1934, 1938. No. 468C, Brazil, 1958, 1962. No. 468D, Germany, 1954. No. 468E, Great Britain.

1966, July 11 ***Perf. 14***

468 A149d ½c multi
468A A149d .005b multi
468B A149d 10c multi
468C A149d 10c multi
468D A149d 21c multi
468E A149d 21c multi
f. Souv. sheet of 2, #468B, 468D 16.00 15.00
g. Souv. sheet of 2, #468, 468E, imperf. 13.00 11.00
Set, #468-465E 9.00 2.25

World Cup Soccer Championships, Great Britain. Nos. 468B-468E are airmail.

Nos. 468-468E exist imperf in different colors. Value, $27.50.

A149e

Italian Contributions to Space Research: ½c, Launch of Scout rocket, San Marco satellite. 1c, San Marco in orbit, horiz. 5c, Italian scientists, rocket. 10c, Arms of Panama, Italy, horiz. 21c, San Marco boosted into orbit, horiz.

Perf. 12x12½, 12½x12

1966, Aug. 12

469 A149e ½c multicolored
469A A149e 1c multicolored
469B A149e 5c multicolored
469C A149e 10c multicolored
469D A149e 21c multicolored
e. Souv. sheet of 2, #469C-469D, imperf. 17.00 15.00
Set, #469-469D 9.75 4.00

Nos. 469B-469D are airmail.

Nos. 469-469D exist imperf in different colors. Value: set, $27.

Nos. 468-468g Ovptd.

1966, Nov. 21 ***Perf. 14***

470 A149d ½c on #468
470A A149d .005b on #468A
470B A149d 10c on #468B
470C A149d 10c on #468C
470D A149d 21c on #468D
470E A149d 21c on #468E
f. on #468Ef 30.00 30.00
g. on #468Eg, imperf. 30.00 30.00
Set, #470-470E 16.50 3.75

Nos. 470B-470E are airmail.

Nos. 470-470E exist imperf in different colors. Value: set, $27.50.

A149f

Religious Paintings — A149g

Paintings: ½c, Coronation of Mary. 1c, Holy Family with Angel. 2c, Adoration of the Magi. 3c, Madonna and Child. No. 471D, The Annunciation. No. 471E, The Nativity. No. 471Fh, Madonna and Child.

1966, Oct. 24 ***Perf. 11***

Size of No. 471D: 32x34mm

471 A149f ½c Velazquez
471A A149f 1c Saraceni
471B A149g 2c Durer
471C A149f 3c Orazio
471D A149g 21c Rubens
471E A149f 21c Boticelli

Souvenir Sheet

Perf. 14

471F Sheet of 2
g. A149f 21c like No. 471E, black inscriptions 12.50 11.00
h. A149f 31c Mignard 18.00 18.00
Set, #471-471E 12.00 1.25

Nos. 471D-471F are airmail.

Nos. 471-471F exist imperf in different colors. Value imperf, Nos. 471-471E $12. Value imperf, No. 471F $17.50.

Sir Winston Churchill, British Satellites A149h

Churchill and: 10c, Blue Streak, NATO emblem. 31c, Europa 1, rocket engine.

1966, Nov. 25 ***Perf. 12x12½***

472 A149h ½c shown
472A A149h 10c org & multi
472B A149h 31c dk bl & multi
c. Souv. sheet of 2, #472A-472B, perf. 13½x14 13.00 11.50
Set, #472-472B 7.25 2.00

Nos. 472A-472B are airmail.

No. 472Bc exists imperf in different colors. Value $15.

For overprints see Nos. 492-492B.

John F. Kennedy, 3rd Death Anniv. A149i

10c, Kennedy, UN building. 31c, Kennedy, satellites & map.

1966, Nov. 25 ***Perf. 14***

473 A149i ½c shown
473A A149i 10c multi
473B A149i 31c multi
c. Souv. sheet of 2, #473A-473B 19.00 18.00
Set, #473-473B 7.25 2.00

Nos. 473A-473B are airmail.

No. 473Bc exists imperf in different colors. Value $19.

Jules Verne (1828-1905), French Space Explorations A149j

Designs: ½c, Earth, A-1 satellite. 1c, Verne, submarine. 5c, Earth, FR-1 satellite. 10c, Verne, telescope. 21c, Verne, capsule heading toward Moon. 31c, D-1 satellite over Earth.

1966, Dec. 28 ***Perf. 13½x14***

474 A149j ½c bl & multi
474A A149j 1c bl grn & multi
474B A149j 5c ultra & multi
474C A149j 10c lil, blk & red
474D A149j 21c vio & multi
f. Souv. sheet of 2, #474C, 474D, imperf. 14.00 12.50
474E A149j 31c dl bl & multi
g. Souvenir sheet of 1 17.50 15.00
Set, #474-474E 11.50 2.00

Nos. 474B-474E are airmail.

Nos. 474-474Eg exist imperf in different colors. Value imperf. Nos. 474-474E $22.50. Value imperf, No. 474Eg $17.50.

Hen and Chicks — A150

Domestic Animals: 3c, Rooster. 5c, Pig, horiz. 8c, Cow, horiz.

1967, Feb. 3 Unwmk. ***Perf. 14***

475 A150 1c multi .40 .40
475A A150 3c multi .40 .40
475B A150 5c multi .40 .40
475C A150 8c multi .40 .40
Nos. 475-475C,C353-C356 (8) 13.60 3.20

Easter — A150a

Paintings: ½c, Christ at Calvary, by Giambattista Tiepolo. 1c, The Crucifixion, by Rubens. 5c, Pieta, by Sarto, horiz. 10c, Body of Christ, by Raphael Santi. 21c, The Arisen Christ, by Multscher. No. 476E, Christ Ascending into Heaven, by Grunewald. No. 476F, Christ on the Cross, by Van der Weyden. No. 476G, Madonna and Child, by Rubens.

1967, Mar. 13 ***Perf. 14x13½, 13½x14***

476 A150a ½c multi
476A A150a 1c multi
476B A150a 5c multi
476C A150a 10c multi
476D A150a 21c multi
476E A150a 31c multi
Set, #476-476E 10.50 3.00

Souvenir Sheets

Perf. 12½x12x12½x13½

476F A150a 31c multi 22.00 20.00

Imperf

476G A150a 31c multi 22.00 20.00

Nos. 476B-476G are airmail.

1968 Summer Olympics, Mexico City A150b

Indian Ruins at: ½c, Teotihuacan. 1c, Tajin. 5c, Xochicalco. 10c, Monte Alban. 21c, Palenque. 31c, Chichen Itza.

1967, Apr. 18 ***Perf. 12x12½***

477 A150b ½c plum & multi
477A A150b 1c red lil & multi
477B A150b 5c blue & multi
477C A150b 10c ver & multi
477D A150b 21c grn bl & multi
477E A150b 31c grn & multi
Set, #477-477E 11.00 3.00

Souvenir Sheet

Perf. 12x12½x14x12½

477F A150a 31c multi 20.00 18.00

Nos. 477B-477E are airmail.

New World Anhinga — A151

Birds: 1c, Quetzals. 3c, Turquoise-browed motmot. 4c, Double-collared aracari, horiz. 5c, Macaw. 13c, Belted kingfisher. 50c, Hummingbird.

1967, July 20 ***Perf. 14***

478 A151 ½c lt bl & multi 1.20 .60
478A A151 1c lt gray & multi 1.20 .60
478B A151 3c pink & multi 1.40 .60
478C A151 4c lt grn & multi 1.75 .60
478D A151 5c buff & multi 2.10 .60
478E A151 13c yel & multi 8.25 2.00
Nos. 478-478E (6) 15.90 5.00

Souvenir Sheet

Perf. 14½

478F	A151	50c Sheet of 1	23.00	17.50

No. 478A exists imperf. with blue background. Value $32.

Works of Famous Artists — A151a

Paintings: No. 479, Maiden in the Doorway, by Rembrandt. No. 479A, Blueboy, by Gainsborough. No. 479B, The Promise of Louis XIII, by Ingres. No. 479C, St. George and the Dragon, by Raphael. No. 479D, The Blacksmith's Shop, by Velazquez, horiz. No. 479E, St. Hieronymus, by Durer. Nos. 479F-479K, Self-portraits.

Perf. 14x13½, 13½x14

1967, Aug. 23

479	A151a	5c multi		
479A	A151a	5c multi		
479B	A151a	5c multi		
479C	A151a	21c multi		
479D	A151a	21c multi		
479E	A151a	21c multi		
	Set, #479-479E		8.75	2.00

Souvenir Sheets

Various Compound Perfs.

479F	A151a	21c Gainsborough	17.00	8.00
479G	A151a	21c Rembrandt	17.00	8.00
479H	A151a	21c Ingres	17.00	8.00
479I	A151a	21c Raphael	17.00	8.00
479J	A151a	21c Velazquez	17.00	8.00
479K	A151a	21c Durer	17.00	8.00
	Nos. 479F-479K (6)		102.00	48.00

Nos. 479C-479K are airmail.

Red Deer, by Franz Marc — A152

Animal Paintings by Franz Marc: 3c, Tiger, vert. 5c, Monkeys. 8c, Blue Fox.

1967, Sept. 1 *Perf. 14*

480	A152	1c multicolored	.65	.40
480A	A152	3c multicolored	.65	.40
480B	A152	5c multicolored	.65	.40
480C	A152	8c multicolored	.65	.40
	Nos. 480-480C,C357-C360 (8)		14.00	3.20

Paintings by Goya — A152a

Designs: 2c, The Water Carrier. 3c, Count Floridablanca. 4c, Senora Francisca Sebasa y Garcia. 5c, St. Bernard and St. Robert. 8c, Self-portrait. 10c, Dona Isabel Cobos de Porcel. 13c, Clothed Maja, horiz. 21c, Don Manuel Osoria de Zuniga as a child. 50c, Cardinal Luis of Bourbon and Villabriga.

1967, Oct. 17 *Perf. 14x13½, 13½x14*

481	A152a	2c multicolored		
481A	A152a	3c multicolored		
481B	A152a	4c multicolored		
481C	A152a	5c multicolored		
481D	A152a	8c multicolored		
481E	A152a	10c multicolored		
481F	A152a	13c multi, horiz.		
481G	A152a	21c multicolored		
	Set, #481-481G		13.00	3.20

Souvenir Sheet

481H	A152a	50c multicolored	22.00	20.00

Nos. 481C-481H are airmail.

Life of Christ — A152b

Paintings: No. 482, The Holy Family, by Michaelangelo. No. 482A, Christ Washing Feet, by Brown. 3c, Christ's Charge to Peter, by Rubens. 4c, Christ and the Money Changers in the Temple, by El Greco, horiz. No. 482D, Christ's Entry into Jerusalem, by Van Dyck, horiz. No. 482E, The Last Supper, by de Juanes.

No. 482Fl, Pastoral Adoration. No. 482Fm, The Holy Family. No. 482Gn, Christ with Mary and Martha. No. 482Go, Flight from Egypt. No. 482Hp, St. Thomas. No. 482Hq, The Tempest. No. 482Ir, The Transfiguration. No. 482Is, The Crucification.

No. 482J, The Baptism of Christ, by Guido Reni. No. 482K, Christ at the Sea of Galilee, by Tintoretto, horiz.

1968, Jan. 10 *Perf. 14x13½x13½x14*

482	A152b	1c multi		
482A	A152b	1c multi		
482B	A152b	3c multi		
482C	A152b	4c multi		
482D	A152b	21c multi		
482E	A152b	21c multi		
	Set, #482-482E		10.00	3.00

Souvenir Sheets

Various Perfs.

482F		Sheet of 2	19.00	16.00
l.	A152b	1c Schongauer		
m.	A152b	21c Raphael		
482G		Sheet of 2	19.00	16.00
n.	A152b	3c Tintoretto		
o.	A152b	21c Caravaggio		
482H		Sheet of 2	19.00	16.00
p.	A152b	21c Anonymous, 12th cent.		
q.	A152b	31c multicolored		
482I		Sheet of 2	19.00	16.00
r.	A152b	21c Raphael		
s.	A152b	31c Montanez		
482J	A152b	22c Sheet of 1	19.00	16.00
482K	A152b	24c Sheet of 1	19.00	16.00

Nos. 482C-482K are airmail.
Nos. 482J-482K also exist imperf.

Butterflies A152c

½c, Apodemia albinus. 1c, Caligo ilioneus, vert. 3c, Meso semia tenera. 4c, Pamphila epictetus. 5c, Entheus peleus. 13c, Tmetoglene drymo.

50c, Thymele chalco, vert.

1968, Feb. 23 *Perf. 14*

483	A152c	½c multi		
483A	A152c	1c multi		
483B	A152c	3c multi		
483C	A152c	4c multi		
483D	A152c	5c multi		
483E	A152c	13c multi		
	Set, #483-483E		24.50	5.00

Souvenir Sheet

Perf. 14½

483F	A152c	50c multi	50.00	15.00

Nos. 483D-483F are airmail.
No. 483F exists imperf with pink margin. Value $50.

10th Winter Olympics, Grenoble A152d

½c, Emblem, vert. 1c, Ski jumper. 5c, Skier. 10c, Mountain climber. 21c, Speed skater. 31c, Two-man bobsled.

1968, Feb. 2 *Perf. 14x13½, 13½x14*

484	A152d	½c multi		
484A	A152d	1c multi		
484B	A152d	5c multi		
484C	A152d	10c multi		
484D	A152d	21c multi		
484E	A152d	31c multi		
	Set, #484-484E		10.00	1.50

Souvenir Sheets

Perf. 14

484F		Sheet of 2	18.00	15.00
h.	A152d	10c Emblem, snowflake		
i.	A152d	31c Figure skater		
484G		Sheet of 2	18.00	15.00
j.	A152d	31c Biathlon		
k.	A152d	10c Skier on ski lift		

Nos. 484B-484G are airmail.

Sailing Ships A152e

Paintings by: ½c, Gamiero, vert. 1c, Lebreton. 3c, Anonymous Japanese. 4c, Le Roi. 5c, Van de Velde. 13c, Duncan. 50c, Anonymous Portuguese, vert.

1968, May 7 *Perf. 14*

485	A152e	½c multicolored		
485A	A152e	1c multicolored		
485B	A152e	3c multicolored		
485C	A152e	4c multicolored		
485D	A152e	5c multicolored		
485E	A152e	13c multicolored		
	Set, #485-485E		11.00	5.00

Souvenir Sheet

Perf. 14½

485F	A152e	50c multicolored	10.00	9.00

Nos. 485D-485E are airmail. No. 485F exists imperf. with light blue margin. Value $10.

Tropical Fish — A152f

½c, Balistipus undulatus. 1c, Holacanthus ciliaris. 3c, Chaetodon ephippium. 4c, Epinephelus elongatus. 5c, Anisotremus virginicus. 13c, Balistoides conspicillum.

50c, Raja texana, vert.

1968, June 26 *Perf. 14*

486	A152f	½c multi		
486A	A152f	1c multi		
486B	A152f	3c multi		
486C	A152f	4c multi		
486D	A152f	5c multi		
486E	A152f	13c multi		
	Set, #486-486E		9.75	2.00

Souvenir Sheet

Perf. 14½

486F	A152f	50c multi	25.00	9.00

Nos. 486D-486F are airmail. No. 486F exists imperf. with pink margin. Value $25 .

Olympic Medals and Winners, Grenoble A152g

Olympic Medals and Winners: 1c, Men's giant slalom. 2c, Women's downhill. 3c, Women's figure skating. 4c, 5000-meter speed skating. 5c, 10,000-meter speed skating. 6c, Women's slalom. 8c, Women's 1000-meter speed skating. 13c, Women's 1500-meter speed skating. 30c, Two-man bobsled. 70c, Nordic combined.

Litho. & Embossed

1968, July 30 *Perf. 13½x14*

487	A152g	1c pink & multi		
487A	A152g	2c vio & multi		
487B	A152g	3c grn & multi		
487C	A152g	4c plum & multi		
487D	A152g	5c red brn & multi		
487E	A152g	6c brt vio & multi		
487F	A152g	8c Prus bl & multi		
487G	A152g	13c bl & multi		
487H	A152g	30c rose lil & multi		
	Set, #487-487H		11.25	3.60

Souvenir Sheet

487I	A152g	70c red & multi	19.00	18.00

Nos. 487G-487H are airmail.

Miniature Sheet

Music — A152h

Paintings of Musicians, Instruments: 5c, Mandolin, by de la Hyre. 10c, Lute, by Caravaggio. 15c, Flute, by ter Brugghen. 20c, Chamber ensemble, by Tourmer. 25c, Violin, by Caravaggio. 30c, Piano, by Vermeer. 40c, Harp, by Memling.

1968, Sept. 11 **Litho.** *Perf. 13½x14*

488	A152h	Sheet of 6	13.00	2.40
a.		5c multicolored		
b.		10c multicolored		
c.		15c multicolored		
d.		20c multicolored		
e.		25c multicolored		
f.		30c multicolored		

Souvenir Sheet

Perf. 14

488A	A152h	40c multicolored	19.00	18.00

Nos. 457, 457E Ovptd. in Black

1968, Oct. 17

489	A147b	½c on No. 457	11.50	.75
489A	A147b	50c on No. 457E	11.50	.75
b.		Souv. sheet of 1, on No. 457Ef	*22.50*	*22.50*

Nos. 489-489A exist with gold overprint. Value: set, $100. Overprint differs on No. 489Ab.

Nos. 464, 464D & 464Ef Ovptd. in Black or Gold

1968, Oct. 18 *Perf. 12x12½*

490	A149a	½c on No. 464	7.25	
490A	A149a	21c on No. 464D	7.25	

Souvenir Sheet

Perf. 13x13½

490B		on No. 464Ef (G)	*27.50*	*27.50*

Nos. 490A-490B are airmail. No. 490B exists imperf. with different colored border. Value same as No. 490B. Overprint differs on No. 490B.

Nos. 459, 459G-459Gh Ovptd. in Black

1968, Oct. 21 ***Perf. 14***

491 A147c ½c on No. 459 7.50
491A A147c 31c on No. 459G 7.50
b. on souv. sheet, No. 459Gh 22.00 19.00

Nos. 491A-491Ab are airmail.

Nos. 491-491A exist overprinted in gold, and imperf., overprinted in gold. No. 491Ab exists imperf in different colors and black or gold overprints. Values, black $9, gold $105.

Nos. 472-472A, 472Bc Overprinted in Black or Gold

1968, Oct. 22 ***Perf. 12x12½***

492 A149h ½c (#472) 11.00
492A A149h 10c (#472A) 11.00

Souvenir Sheet

Perf. 13½x14

492B on No. 472Bc 13.50 13.50

Nos. 492A-492B are airmail.

Nos. 492-492A with gold overprint, value $105. No. 492B exists imperf in different colors.

Hunting on Horseback
A152i

Paintings and Tapestries: 1c, Koller. 3c, Courbet. 5c, Tischbein, the Elder. 10c, Gobelin, vert. 13c, Oudry. 30c, Rubens.

1968, Oct. 29 ***Perf. 14***

493 A152i 1c multicolored
493A A152i 3c multicolored
493B A152i 5c multicolored
493C A152i 10c multicolored
493D A152i 13c multicolored
493E A152i 30c multicolored
Set, #493-493E 8.75 4.00

Nos. 493D-493E are airmail.

Miniature Sheet

Famous Race Horses — A152j

Horse Paintings: a, 5c, Lexington, by Edward Troye. b, 10c, American Eclipse, by Alvan Fisher. c, 15c, Plenipotentiary, by Abraham Cooper. d, 20c, Gimcrack, by George Stubbs. e, 25c, Flying Childers, by James Seymour. f, 30c, Eclipse, by Stubbs.

1968, Dec. 18 ***Perf. 13½x14***

494 A152j Sheet of 6, #a.-f. 17.50 12.50

1968 Summer Olympics, Mexico City — A152k

Mexican art: 1c, Watermelons, by Diego Rivera. 2c, Women, by Jose Clemente Orozco. 3c, Flower Seller, by Miguel Covarrubias, vert. 4c, Nutall Codex, vert. 5c, Mayan statue, vert. 6c, Face sculpture, vert. 8c, Seated figure, vert. 13c. Ceramic angel, vert. 30c, Christ, by David Alfaro Siqueiros. 70c, Symbols of Summer Olympic events.

1968, Dec. 23 ***Perf. 13½x14, 14x13½***

495 A152k 1c multicolored
495A A152k 2c multicolored
495B A152k 3c multicolored
495C A152k 4c multicolored
495D A152k 5c multicolored
495E A152k 6c multicolored
495F A152k 8c multicolored
495G A152k 13c multicolored
495H A152k 30c multicolored
Set, #495-495H 15.00 3.60

Souvenir Sheet

Perf. 14

495I A152k 70c multicolored 16.00 16.00

Nos. 495G-495H are airmail.

First Visit of Pope Paul VI to Latin America — A152l

Paintings: 1c, Madonna and Child, by Raphael. 2c, Madonna and Child, by Ferruzzi. 3c, Madonna and Child, by Bellini. 4c, The Annunciation, 17th cent. 5c, Madonna and Child, by Van Dyck. 6c, Madonna and Child, by Albani. 7c, Adoration of the Magi, by Master of the Viennese Schottenaltar. 8c, Adoration of the Magi, by Van Dyck. 10c, Holy Family, 16th cent.

50c, Madonna and Child, angel, by Del Sarto.

1969, Aug. 5 ***Perf. 14***

496 A152l 1c multi
496A A152l 2c multi
496B A152l 3c multi
496C A152l 4c multi
496D A152l 5c multi
496E A152l 6c multi
496F A152l 7c multi
496G A152l 8c multi
496H A152l 10c multi
Set, #496-496H 14.00 3.60

Souvenir Sheet

Perf. 14½

496I A152l 50c multi 15.00 7.50

Nos. 496E-496I are airmail.

Map of Americas and People — A153

5c, Map of Panama, People and Houses, horiz.

1969, Aug. 14 **Photo.** **Wmk. 350**

500 A153 5c violet blue .70 .40
501 A153 10c bright rose lilac .90 .40

Issued to publicize the 1970 census.

Cogwheel
A154

1969, Aug. 14

502 A154 13c yel & dk bl gray .65 .40

50th anniv. of Rotary Intl. of Panama.

Cornucopia and Map of Panama — A155

Perf. 14½x15

1969, Oct. 10 **Litho.** **Unwmk.**

503 A155 10c lt bl & multi .65 .40

1st anniv. of the October 11 Revolution.

Map of Panama and Ruins
A156

Natá Church
A157

Designs: 5c, Farmer, wife and mule. 13c, Hotel Continental. 20c, Church of the Virgin of Carmen. 21c, Gold altar, San José Church. 25c, Del Rey bridge. 30c, Dr. Justo Arosemena monument. 34c, Cathedral of Panama. 38c, Municipal Palace. 40c, French Plaza. 50c, Thatcher Ferry Bridge (Bridge of the Americas). 59c, National Theater.

Perf. 14½x15, 15x14½

1969-70 **Litho.** **Unwmk.**

504 A156 3c org & blk .40 .25
505 A156 5c lt bl grn ('70) .40 .25
506 A157 8c dl brn ('70) .40 .25
507 A156 13c emer & blk .55 .25
508 A157 20c vio brn ('70) .80 .25
509 A157 21c yellow ('70) .80 .40
510 A156 25c lt bl grn ('70) 1.00 .25
511 A157 30c black ('70) 1.25 .40
512 A156 34c org brn ('70) 1.50 .50
513 A156 38c brt bl ('70) 1.50 .40
514 A156 40c org yel ('70) 2.00 .60
515 A156 50c brt rose lil & blk 2.10 .70
516 A156 59c brt rose lil ('70) 3.00 .90
Nos. 504-516 (13) 15.70 5.40

Issued: Nos. 504, 507, 515, 10/10/69. Others, 1/28/70.

For surcharges see Nos. 541, 543, 545-547, RA78-RA80.

Stadium and Discus Thrower
A158

Flor del Espiritu Santo — A159

Wmk. 365

1970, Jan. 6 **Litho.** ***Perf. 13½***

517 A158 1c ultra & multi .45 .25
518 A158 2c ultra & multi .45 .25
519 A158 3c ultra & multi .45 .25
520 A158 5c ultra & multi .45 .25
521 A158 10c ultra & multi .60 .25
522 A158 13c ultra & multi .65 .25
523 A159 13c pink & multi .80 .25
524 A158 25c ultra & multi 1.60 .50
525 A158 30c ultra & multi 2.00 .75
Nos. 517-525,C368-C369 (11) 11.95 4.05

11th Central American and Caribbean Games, Feb. 28-Mar. 14.

Office of Comptroller General, 1970 — A160

Designs: 5c, Alejandro Tapia and Martin Sosa, first Comptrollers, 1931-34, horiz. 8c, Comptroller's emblem. 13c, Office of Comptroller General, 1955-70, horiz.

1971, Feb. 25 **Litho.** **Wmk. 365**

526 A160 3c yel & multi .80 .40
527 A160 5c brn, buff & gold .80 .40
528 A160 8c gold & multi .80 .40
529 A160 13c blk & multi .80 .40
Nos. 526-529 (4) 3.20 1.60

Comptroller General's Office, 40th anniv.

Indian Alligator Design — A161

1971, Aug. 18 **Wmk. 343** ***Perf. 13½***

530 A161 8c multicolored 1.25 .40

SENAPI (Servicio Nacional de Artesania y Pequeñas Industrias), 5th anniv.

Education Year Emblem, Map of Panama — A162

1971, Aug. 19 **Litho.**

531 A162 1b multicolored 4.00 2.50

International Education Year, 1970.

For surcharge see No. 542.

Congress Emblem
A163

1972, Aug. 25

532 A163 25c multicolored 1.50 .60

9th Inter-American Conference of Saving and Loan Associations, Panama City, Jan. 23-29, 1971.

UPU Headquarters, Bern — A164

Design: 30c, UPU Monument, Bern, vert.

1971, Dec. 14 **Wmk. 343**

533 A164 8c multicolored .85 .40
534 A164 30c multicolored 2.60 .60

Inauguration of Universal Postal Union Headquarters, Bern, Switzerland.

For surcharge see No. RA77.

Cow, Pig and Produce
A165

1971, Dec. 15

535 A165 3c yel, brn & blk .80 .40

3rd agricultural census.

Map of Panama and "4-S" Emblem
A166

1971, Dec. 16

536 A166 2c multicolored .80 .40

Rural youth 4-S program.

UNICEF Emblem, Children A167

Wmk. 365

1972, Sept. 12 Litho. ***Perf. 13½***

537 A167 1c yel & multi		.45	.25
Nos. 537,C390-C392 (4)		4.05	1.30

25th anniv. (in 1971) of UNICEF. See No. C392a.

Tropical Fruits — A168

1972, Sept. 13

538 A168 1c shown	.50	.25
539 A168 2c Isla de Noche	.50	.25
540 A168 3c Carnival float, vert.	.50	.25
Nos. 538-540,C393-C395 (6)	7.00	1.70

Tourist publicity.
For surcharges see Nos. RA75-RA76.

Nos. 516, 531 and 511 Surcharged in Red

Perf. 14½x15, 15x14½, 13½
Wmk. 343, Unwmkd.

1973, Mar. 15

541 A156 8c on 59c brt rose lil	.85	.25
542 A162 10c on 1b multi	.85	.25
543 A157 13c on 30c blk	.85	.25
Nos. 541-543,C402 (4)	3.55	1.05

UN Security Council Meeting, Panama City, Mar. 15-21. Surcharges differ in size and are adjusted to fit shape of stamp.

José Daniel Crespo, Educator — A169

Wmk. 365

1973, June 20 Litho. ***Perf. 13½***

544 A169 3c lt bl & multi	.55	.25
Nos. 544,C403-C413 (12)	18.90	4.35

For overprints and surcharges see Nos. C414-C416, C418-C421, RA81-RA82, RA84.

Nos. 511-512 and 509 Surcharged in Red

Perf. 15x14½, 14½x15

1974, Nov. 11 **Unwmk.**

545 A157 5c on 30c blk	.80	.25
546 A156 10c on 34c org brn	.80	.25
547 A157 13c on 21c yel	.80	.25
Nos. 545-547,C417-C421 (8)	6.40	2.00

Surcharge vertical on No. 546.

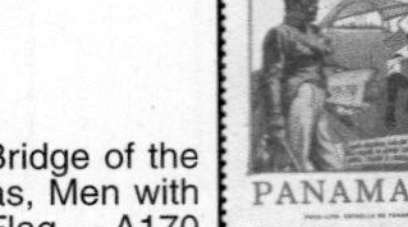

Bolivar, Bridge of the Americas, Men with Flag — A170

Perf. 12½

1976, Mar. 30 Litho. Unwmk.

548 A170 6c multicolored	.45	.25
Nos. 548,C426-C428 (4)	4.95	1.40

150th anniversary of Congress of Panama.

Evibacus Princeps — A171

Marine life: 3c, Ptitosarcus sinuosus, vert. 4c, Acanthaster planci. 7c, Starfish. 1b, Mithrax spinossimus.

Perf. 12½x13, 13x12½

1976, May 6 Litho. Wmk. 377

549 A171 2c multi	.95	.25
550 A171 3c multi	.95	.25
551 A171 4c multi	.95	.25
552 A171 7c multi	.95	.25
Nos. 549-552,C429-C430 (6)	9.45	2.15

Souvenir Sheet

Imperf

553 A171 1b multi	7.25

Bolivar from Bolivar Monument A172

Bolivar and Argentine Flag — A173

Stamps of design A172 show details of Bolivar Monument, Panama City; design A173 shows head of Bolivar and flags of Latin American countries.

Perf. 13½

1976, June 22 Unwmk. Litho.

554 A172 20c shown	1.40	1.00
555 A173 20c shown	1.40	1.00
556 A173 20c Bolivia	1.40	1.00
557 A173 20c Brazil	1.40	1.00
558 A173 20c Chile	1.40	1.00
559 A172 20c Battle scene	1.40	1.00
560 A173 20c Colombia	1.40	1.00
561 A173 20c Costa Rica	1.40	1.00
562 A173 20c Cuba	1.40	1.00
563 A173 20c Ecuador	1.40	1.00
564 A173 20c El Salvador	1.40	1.00
565 A173 20c Guatemala	1.40	1.00
566 A173 20c Guyana	1.40	1.00
567 A173 20c Haiti	1.40	1.00
568 A172 20c Assembly	1.40	1.00
569 A172 20c Liberated people	1.40	1.00
570 A173 20c Honduras	1.40	1.00
571 A173 20c Jamaica	1.40	1.00
572 A173 20c Mexico	1.40	1.00
573 A173 20c Nicaragua	1.40	1.00
574 A173 20c Panama	1.40	1.00
575 A173 20c Paraguay	1.40	1.00
576 A173 20c Peru	1.40	1.00
577 A173 20c Dominican Rep.	1.40	1.00
578 A172 20c Bolivar and flag bearer	1.40	1.00
579 A173 20c Surinam	1.40	1.00
580 A173 20c Trinidad-Tobago	1.40	1.00
581 A173 20c Uruguay	1.40	1.00
582 A173 20c Venezuela	1.40	1.00
583 A172 20c Indian delegation	1.40	1.00
a. Sheet of 30, #554-583	42.00	36.00
Nos. 554-583 (30)	42.00	30.00

Souvenir Sheet

584 Sheet of 3	8.25	8.25
a. A172 30c Bolivar and flag bearer	1.40	1.40
b. A172 30c Monument, top	1.40	1.40
c. A172 40c Inscription tablet	1.75	1.75

Amphictyonic Congress of Panama, sesquicentennial. No. 584 comes perf. and imperf. Values the same.

Nos. 554-583 amd 584 were overprinted to honor the 1980 Olympics. The overprinted sets were issued Nov. 27, 1980.

Nicanor Villalaz, Designer of Coat of Arms — A174

National Lottery Building, Panama City — A175

1976, Nov. 12 Litho. ***Perf. 12½***

585 A174 5c dk blue	1.00	.40
586 A175 6c multicolored	1.00	.40

Contadora Island — A176

1976, Dec. 29 ***Perf. 12½***

587 A176 3c multicolored	.75	.40

Pres. Carter and Gen. Omar Torrijos Signing Panama Canal Treaties A177

Design: 23c, like No. 588. Design includes Alejandro Orfila, Secretary General of OAS.

1978, Jan. 3 Litho. ***Perf. 12***

Size: 90x40mm

588 A177 50c Strip of 3	9.75	9.75
a. 3c multicolored	.25	.25
b. 40c multicolored	1.00	1.00
c. 50c multicolored	1.25	*1.25*

Perf. 14

Size: 36x26mm

589 A177 23c multicolored	.75	.40

Signing of Panama Canal Treaties, Washington, DC, Sept. 7, 1977.

Pres. Carter and Gen. Torrijos Signing Treaties A178

1978, Nov. 13 Litho. ***Perf. 12***

590 A178 Strip of 3	9.00	8.00
a. 5c multi (30x40mm)	.40	.40
b. 35c multi (30x40mm)	1.10	.45
c. 41c multi (45x40mm)	1.10	.50

Size: 36x26mm

591 A178 3c Treaty signing	.40	.40

Signing of Panama Canal Treaties ratification documents, Panama City, Panama, June 6, 1978.

World Commerce Zone, Colon — A179

1978, Nov. 13 Litho. ***Perf. 12***

592 A179 6c multicolored	.80	.40

Free Zone of Colon, 30th anniversary.

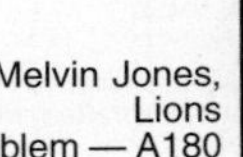

Melvin Jones, Lions Emblem — A180

1978, Nov. 13

593 A180 50c multicolored	1.75	1.25

Birth centenary of Melvin Jones, founder of Lions International.

Torrijos with Children, Ship, Flag — A181

"75," Coat of Arms — A182

Rotary Emblem, "75" — A183

Gen. Torrijos and Pres. Carter, Flags, Ship — A184

UPU Emblem, Globe — A185

Boy and Girl Inside Heart — A186

1979, Oct. 1 Litho. ***Perf. 14***

594 A181 3c multicolored	1.10	.25
595 A182 6c multicolored	1.10	.25
596 A183 17c multicolored	1.10	.30
597 A184 23c multicolored	1.75	.25
598 A185 35c multicolored	2.25	.60
599 A186 50c multicolored	3.75	.50
Nos. 594-599 (6)	11.05	2.15

Return of Canal Zone to Panama, Oct. 1 (3c, 23c); Natl. Bank, 75th anniv.; Rotary Intl., 75th anniv.; 18th UPU Cong., Rio, Sept.-Oct., 1979; Intl. Year of the Child.

Colon Station, St. Charles Hotel, Engraving A187

Postal Headquarters, Balboa, Inauguration A188

Return of Canal Zone to Panama, Oct. 1, 1979 — A189

Census of the Americas — A190

Panamanian Tourist and Convention Center Opening — A191

Inter-American Development Bank, 25th Anniversary A192

Canal Centenary A193

Olympic Stadium, Moscow '80 Emblem — A194

1980, May 21 Litho. *Perf. 12*

600	A187	1c rose violet	.75	.40
601	A188	3c multicolored	.75	.40
602	A189	6c multicolored	.75	.40
603	A190	17c multicolored	.75	.40
604	A191	23c multicolored	.90	.40
605	A192	35c multicolored	1.50	.50
606	A193	41c pale rose & blk	1.80	.75
607	A194	50c multicolored	1.90	1.25
		Nos. 600-607 (8)	9.10	4.50

Transpanamanian Railroad, 130th anniv. (1c); 22nd Summer Olympic Games, Moscow, July 19-Aug. 3 (50c).

La Salle Congregation, 75th Anniv. (1979) — A195

1981, May 15 Litho. *Perf. 12*

608 A195 17c multicolored 1.10 .40

Louis Braille — A196

1981, May 15

609 A196 23c multicolored 1.40 .40

Intl. Year of the Disabled.

Bull's Blood A197

6c, Lory, vert. 41c, Hummingbird, vert. 50c, Toucan.

1981, June 26 Litho. *Perf. 12*

610	A197	3c shown	1.20	.45
611	A197	6c multicolored	1.20	.45
612	A197	41c multicolored	5.00	.90
613	A197	50c multicolored	6.25	.75
		Nos. 610-613 (4)	13.65	2.55

Apparition of the Virgin to St. Catherine Laboure, 150th Anniv. — A198

1981, June 26 Litho. *Perf. 12*

614 A198 35c multicolored 1.50 .40

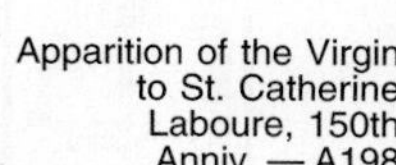

Gen. Torrijos and Bayano Dam — A199

Wmk. 311

1982, Mar. 22 Litho. *Perf. 10½*

615 A199 17c multicolored .85 .40

78th Anniv. of Independence Soldiers Institute — A200

1981, Mar. 17 Litho. *Perf. 10½*

616 A200 3c multicolored .85 .40

First Death Anniv. of Gen. Omar Torrijos Herrera — A201

5c, Aerial view. 6c, Army camp. 50c, Felipillo Engineering Works.

1982, May 14 Litho. *Perf. 10½*

617	A201	5c multicolored	.40	.25
618	A201	6c multicolored	.40	.25
619	A201	50c multicolored	1.60	.40
		Nos. 617-619,C433-C434 (5)	6.25	1.70

Ricardo J. Alfaro (1882-1977), Statesman — A202

1982, Aug. 18 Wmk. 382

620 A202 3c multicolored .50 .25

See Nos. C436-C437.

1982 World Cup — A203

1982, Dec. 27 Litho. *Perf. 10½*

621 A203 50c Italian team 2.25 .50

See Nos. C438-C440.

Expo Comer '83, Panama Intl. Commerce Exposition, Jan. 12-16 — A204

Wmk. 382

1983, Jan. 12 Litho. *Perf. 10½*

622 A204 17c multicolored 1.20 .40

Visit of Pope John Paul II — A205

Various portraits of the Pope. 35c airmail.

Perf. 12x11

1983, Mar. 1 Litho. Wmk. 382

623	A205	6c multicolored	1.20	.65
624	A205	17c multicolored	1.20	.65
625	A205	35c multicolored	2.75	.65
		Nos. 623-625 (3)	5.15	1.95

Bank Emblem — A206

1983, Mar. 18

626 A206 50c multicolored 1.75 .40

24th Council Meeting of Inter-American Development Bank, Mar. 21-23.

Simon Bolivar (1783-1830) — A207

1983, July 25 Litho. *Perf. 12*

627 A207 50c multicolored 2.50 .50

Souvenir Sheet

Imperf

628 A207 1b like 50c 4.25 1.25

World Communications Year — A208

1983, Oct. 9 Litho. *Perf. 14*

629	A208	30c UPAE emblem	1.10	.25
630	A208	40c WCY emblem	1.40	.35
631	A208	50c UPU emblem	1.75	.45
632	A208	60c Dove in flight	2.40	.55
		Nos. 629-632 (4)	6.65	1.60

Souvenir Sheet

Imperf

633 A208 1b multicolored 5.50 2.75

No. 633 contains designs of Nos. 629-632 without denominations.

Freedom of Worship — A209

3c, Panama Mosque. 5c, Bahai Temple. 6c, St. Francis Church. 17c, Kol Shearit Israel Synagogue.

1983, Oct. 21 Litho. *Perf. 11½*

634	A209	3c multicolored	1.60	.25
635	A209	5c multicolored	1.60	.25
636	A209	6c multicolored	1.60	.25
637	A209	17c multicolored	4.50	.25
		Nos. 634-637 (4)	9.30	1.00

No. 637 incorrectly inscribed.

Ricardo Miro (1883-1940), Poet — A210

Famous Men: 3c, Richard Newman (1883-1946), educator. 5c, Cristobal Rodriguez (1883-1943), politician. 6c, Alcibiades Arosemena (1883-1958), industrialist and financier. 35c, Cirilo Martinez (1883-1924), linguist.

1983, Nov. 8 Litho. *Perf. 14*

638	A210	1c multicolored	.50	.25
639	A210	3c multicolored	.50	.25
640	A210	5c multicolored	.50	.25
641	A210	6c multicolored	.50	.25
642	A210	35c multicolored	2.50	.35
		Nos. 638-642 (5)	4.50	1.35

The Prophet, by Alfredo Sinclair — A211

#643, Village House, by Juan Manuel Cedeno. #644, Large Nude, by Manuel Chong Neto. 3c, On Another Occasion, by Spiros Vamvas. 6c, Punta Chame Landscape, by Guillermo Trujillo. 28c, Neon Light, by Alfredo Sinclair. 41c, Highland Girls, by Al Sprague. 1b, Bright Morning, by Ignacio Mallol Pibernat. Nos. 643-647, 650 horiz.

1983, Dec. 12 *Perf. 12*

643	A211	1c multicolored	.45	.35
644	A211	1c multicolored	.45	.35
645	A211	3c multicolored	.45	.35
646	A211	6c multicolored	.45	.35
647	A211	28c multicolored	1.40	.85
648	A211	35c multicolored	1.75	1.10
649	A211	41c multicolored	2.00	1.30
650	A211	1b multicolored	5.50	4.00
		Nos. 643-650 (8)	12.45	8.65

Double Cup, Indian Period — A212

Pottery: 40c, Raised dish, Tonosi period. 50c, Jug with face, Canazas period, vert. 60c, Bowl, Conte, vert.

1984, Jan. 16 Litho. *Perf. 12*

651	A212	30c multicolored	1.40	1.10
652	A212	40c multicolored	1.60	1.40
653	A212	50c multicolored	2.10	1.90
654	A212	60c multicolored	2.50	2.25
		Nos. 651-654 (4)	7.60	6.65

Souvenir Sheet

Imperf

655 A212 1b like 30c 7.00 7.00

Pre-Olympics A213

1984, Mar. 15 Litho. *Perf. 14*

656	A213	19c Baseball	2.35	.40
657	A213	19c Basketball, vert.	2.35	.40
658	A213	19c Boxing	2.35	.40
659	A213	19c Swimming, vert.	2.35	.40
		Nos. 656-659 (4)	9.40	1.60

Roberto Duran — A214

1984, June 14 Litho. *Perf. 14*

660 A214 26c multicolored 2.50 .40

1st Panamanian to hold 3 boxing championships.

1984 Olympic Games A214a

1984, July, 12 Litho. *Perf. 14*

660A A214a 6c Shooting .55 .40
660B A214a 30c Weight lifting 1.60 .40
660C A214a 37c Wrestling 1.75 .40
660D A214a 1b Long jump 5.50 1.50
Nos. 660A-660D (4) 9.40 2.70

Souvenir Sheet

660E A214a 1b Running 5.25 5.00

Nos. 660B-660D are airmail. No. 660E contains one 45x45x64mm stamp.

Paintings — A215

Paintings by Panamanian artists: 1c, Woman Thinking, by Manuel Chong Neto. 3c, The Child, by Alfredo Sinclair. 6c, A Day in the Life of Rumalda, by Brooke Alfaro. 30c, Highlands People, by Al Sprague. 37c, Intermission during the Dance, by Roberto Sprague. 44c, Punta Chame Forest, by Guillermo Trujillo. 50c, The Blue Plaza, by Juan Manuel Cedeno. 1b, Ira, by Spiros Vamvas.

1984, Sept. 17 Litho. *Perf. 14*

661 A215 1c multi .40 .40
662 A215 3c multi, horiz. .40 .40
663 A215 6c multi, horiz. .40 .40
664 A215 30c multi 1.30 .40
665 A215 37c multi, horiz. 1.50 .40
666 A215 44c multi, horiz. 1.78 .50
667 A215 50c multi, horiz. 2.25 .55
668 A215 1b multi, horiz. 4.50 1.50
Nos. 661-668 (8) 12.53 4.55

Postal Sovereignty A216

19c, Gen. Torrijos, canal.

1984, Oct. 1 Litho. *Perf. 12*

669 A216 19c multicolored 1.40 .30

Fauna — A217

3c, Manatee. 30c, Gato negro. 44c, Tigrillo congo. 50c, Puerco de monte.
1b, Perezoso de tres dedos, vert.

1984, Dec. 5 Engr. *Perf. 14*

670 A217 3c black .40 .40
671 A217 30c black 2.25 .50
672 A217 44c black 3.25 .75
673 A217 50c black 3.50 .90
Nos. 670-673 (4) 9.40 2.55

Souvenir Sheet

674 A217 1b black 8.00 5.00

Nos. 671-673 are airmail.

Coins — A218

Perf. 11x12

1985, Jan. 17 Litho. Wmk. 353

675 A218 3c 1935 1c .40 .40
676 A218 3c 1904 10c .40 .40
677 A218 6c 1916 5c .40 .40
678 A218 30c 1904 50c 1.90 .50
679 A218 37c 1962 half-balboa 2.40 .60
680 A218 44c 1953 balboa 3.00 .70
Nos. 675-680 (6) 8.50 3.00

Nos. 678-680 are airmail.

Contadora Type of 1985

Souvenir Sheet

Perf. 13½x13

1985, Oct. 1 Litho. Unwmk.

680A AP108 1b Dove, flags, map 8.75 8.00

Cargo Ship in Lock — A219

1985, Oct. 16 *Perf. 14*

681 A219 19c multicolored 1.60 .40

Panama Canal, 70th anniv. (1984).

UN 40th Anniv. — A220

1986, Jan. 17 Litho. *Perf. 14*

682 A220 23c multicolored 1.25 .40

Intl. Youth Year — A221

1986, Jan. 17

683 A221 30c multicolored 1.50 .40

Waiting Her Turn, by Al Sprague (b.1938) — A222

Oil paintings: 5c, Aerobics, by Guillermo Trujillo (b. 1927). 19c, Cardboard House, by Eduardo Augustine (b. 1954). 30c, Door to the Homeland, by Juan Manuel Cedeno (b. 1914). 36c, Supper for Three, by Brooke Alfaro (b. 1949). 42c, Tenderness, by Alfredo Sinclair (b. 1915). 50c, Woman and Character, by Manuel Chong Neto (b. 1927). 60c, Calla lillies, by Maigualida de Diaz (b. 1950).

1986, Jan. 21

684 A222 3c multicolored .35 .35
685 A222 5c multicolored .35 .35
686 A222 19c multicolored 1.10 .40
687 A222 30c multicolored 1.75 .50
688 A222 36c multicolored 2.00 .55
689 A222 42c multicolored 2.40 .65
690 A222 50c multicolored 3.00 .80
691 A222 60c multicolored 3.75 1.00
Nos. 684-691 (8) 14.70 4.60

Miss Universe Pageant — A223

1986, July 7 Litho. *Perf. 12*

692 A223 23c Atlapa Center 1.00 .40
693 A223 60c Emblem, vert. 2.90 .80

Halley's Comet — A224

30c, Old Panama Cathedral tower, vert.

1986, Oct. 30 Litho. *Perf. 13½*

694 A224 23c multicolored 1.50 .40
695 A224 30c multicolored 2.10 .40

Size: 75x86mm

Imperf

695A A224 1b multicolored 8.50

A225

1986 World Cup Soccer Championships, Mexico — Illustrations from Soccer History, by Sandoval and Meron: 23c, Argentina, winner. 30c, Fed. Rep. of Germany, 2nd. 37c, Argentina, Germany.
1b, Argentina, two players one with black shorts, one with blue shorts.

1986, Oct. 30

696 A225 23c multicolored 1.30 .40
697 A225 30c multicolored 1.50 .40
698 A225 37c multicolored 1.90 .60
Nos. 696-698 (3) 4.70 1.40

Souvenir Sheet

698A A225 1b multicolored 4.50

A226

1986, Nov. 21

699 A226 20c shown 1.40 .40
700 A226 23c Montage of events 1.50 .35

15th Central American and Caribbean Games, Dominican Republic.

Christmas — A227

1986, Dec. 18 Litho.

701 A227 23c shown 1.25 .40
702 A227 36c Green tree 2.00 .50
703 A227 42c Silver tree 2.25 .55
Nos. 701-703 (3) 5.50 1.45

Intl. Peace Year — A228

1986, Dec. 30 *Perf. 13½*

704 A228 8c multicolored .50 .40
705 A228 19c multicolored 1.40 .40

Tropical Carnival, Feb.-Mar. — A229

20c, Diablito Sucio mask. 35c, Sun.

1987, Jan. 27 Litho. *Perf. 13½*

706 A229 20c multi .90 .40
707 A229 35c multi 2.00 .50

Size: 74x84mm

Imperf

708 A229 1b like 35c 4.50 1.50
Nos. 706-708 (3) 7.40 2.40

1st Panamanian Eye Bank — A230

1987, Feb. 17 Litho. *Perf. 14*

709 A230 37c multicolored 2.75 .75

Panama Lions Club, 50th Anniv. (in 1985). Dated 1986.

Flowering Plants — A231

Birds — A232

3c, Brownea macrophylla. 5c, Thraupis episcopus. 8c, Solandra grandiflora. 15c, Tyrannus melancholicus. 19c, Barleria micans. 23c, Pelecanus occidentalis. 30c, Cordia dentata. 36c, Columba cayennensis.

1987, Mar. 5

710 A231 3c multicolored .50 .40
711 A232 5c multicolored .50 .40
712 A231 8c multicolored .50 .40
713 A232 15c multicolored 1.10 .40
714 A231 19c multicolored 1.50 .40
715 A232 23c multicolored 1.60 .40
716 A231 30c multicolored 2.25 .45
717 A232 36c multicolored 3.00 .55
Nos. 710-717 (8) 10.95 3.40

Dated 1986.

Monument and Octavio Mendez Pereira, Founder — A233

1987, Mar. 26 Litho. *Perf. 14*

718 A233 19c multicolored 1.10 .40

University of Panama, 50th anniv. (in 1985). Stamp dated "1986."

UNFAO, 40th Anniv. (in 1985) — A234

1987, Apr. 9 *Perf. 13½*

719 A234 10c blk, pale ol & yel org .40 .40
720 A234 45c blk, dk grn & yel grn 2.40 .70

Natl. Theater, 75th Anniv. — A235

Baroque composers: 19c, Schutz (1585-1672). 37c, Bach. 60c, Handel. Nos. 721, 723-724 vert.

1987, Apr. 28 *Perf. 14*

721 A235 19c multicolored .90 .40
722 A235 30c shown 1.30 .50
723 A235 37c multicolored 1.50 .60
724 A235 60c multicolored 2.50 1.00
Nos. 721-724 (4) 6.20 2.50

A236

1987, May 13 Litho. *Perf. 14*
725 A236 23c multicolored 1.25 .45

Inter-American Development Bank, 25th anniv.

Panama Fire Brigade, Cent. — A237

25c, Fire wagon, 1887, and modern ladder truck. 35c, Fireman carrying victim.

1987, Nov. 28 Litho. *Perf. 14*
726 A237 25c multicolored 2.50 .40
727 A237 35c multicolored 3.50 .60

A238

1987, Dec. 11
728 A238 15c Wrestling, horiz. 1.10 .40
729 A238 23c Tennis 1.60 .40
730 A238 30c Swimming, horiz. 2.10 .50
731 A238 41c Basketball 2.90 .70
732 A238 60c Cycling 4.50 1.00
Nos. 728-732 (5) 12.20 3.00

Souvenir Sheet

733 A238 1b Weight lifting 4.25 4.00

10th Pan American Games, Indianapolis.
For surcharges see Nos. 813, 817.

A239

Christmas (Religious paintings): 22c, Adoration of the Magi, by Albrecht Nentz (d. 1479). 35c, Virgin Adored by Angels, by Matthias Grunewald (d. 1528). 37c, The Virgin and Child, by Konrad Witz (c. 1400-1445).

1987, Dec. 17
734 A239 22c multicolored 1.00 .35
735 A239 35c multicolored 1.60 .60
736 A239 37c multicolored 1.90 .60
Nos. 734-736 (3) 4.50 1.55

Intl. Year of Shelter for the Homeless A240

45c, by A. Sinclair. 50c, Woman, boy, girl, shack, housing in perspective by A. Pulido.

1987, Dec. 29 *Perf. 14*
737 A240 45c multicolored 1.75 .75
738 A240 50c multicolored 2.25 .80

For surcharge see No. 814.

Reforestation Campaign — A241

1988, Jan. 14 Litho. *Perf. 14½x14*
739 A241 35c dull grn & yel grn 2.00 .55
740 A241 40c red & pink 2.25 .70
741 A241 45c brn & lemon 2.50 .75
Nos. 739-741 (3) 6.75 2.00

Dated 1987. For surcharge see No. 816.

Say No to Drugs — A242

1988, Jan. 14
742 A242 10c org lil rose .55 .40
743 A242 17c yel grn & lil rose 1.30 .40
744 A242 25c pink & sky blue 2.10 .40
Nos. 742-744 (3) 3.95 1.20

Child Survival Campaign A243

20c, Breast-feeding. 31c, Universal immunization. 45c, Growth and development, vert.

1988, Feb. 29 Litho. *Perf. 14*
745 A243 20c multicolored .90 .40
746 A243 31c multicolored 1.60 .60
747 A243 45c multicolored 2.50 .90
Nos. 745-747 (3) 5.00 1.90

For surcharge see No. 816A.

Fish — A244

7c, Myripristis jacobus. 35c, Pomacanthus paru. 60c, Holocanthus tricolor. 1b, Equetus punctatus.

1988, Mar. 14
748 A244 7c multicolored .40 .40
749 A244 35c multicolored 1.40 .60
750 A244 60c multicolored 2.50 1.00
751 A244 1b multicolored 4.50 1.60
Nos. 748-751 (4) 8.80 3.60

The 7c actually shows the Holocanthus tricolor, the 60c the Myripristis jacobus.
For surcharge see No. 819.

Girl Guides, 75th Anniv. — A245

1988, Apr. 14
752 A245 35c multicolored 1.60 .60

Christmas — A246

Paintings: 17c, *Virgin and Gift-givers.* 45c, *Virgin of the Rosary and St. Dominic.*

1988, Dec. 29 Litho. *Perf. 12*
753 A246 17c multicolored 1.00 .40
754 A246 45c multicolored 2.10 .75

See No. C446.

St. John Bosco (1815-1888) — A247

1989, Jan. 31
755 A247 10c Portrait .50 .40
756 A247 20c Minor Basilica 1.50 .40

1988 Summer Olympics, Seoul — A248

Athletes and medals.

1989, Mar. 17 Litho. *Perf. 12*
757 A248 17c Running .70 .40
758 A248 25c Wrestling 1.10 .40
759 A248 60c Weight lifting 2.75 1.00
Nos. 757-759 (3) 4.55 1.80

Souvenir Sheet

760 A248 1b Swimming, vert. 4.75 3.75

See No. C447.

A249

1b, Emergency and rescue services.

1989, Apr. 12 Litho. *Perf. 12*
761 A249 40c red, blk & blue 1.50 .75
762 A249 1b multicolored 4.00 1.75

Intl. Red Cross and Red Crescent organizations, 125th annivs.

America Issue: Pre-Columbian Artifacts — A250

20c, Monolith of Barriles. 35c, Vessel.

1989, Oct. 12 Litho. *Perf. 12*
767 A250 20c multi 1.75 .50
768 A250 35c multi 3.25 1.25

French Revolution, Bicent. — A251

1989, Nov. 14 *Perf. 13½*
769 A251 25c multicolored 1.40 .50
Nos. 769,C450-C451 (3) 6.40 2.00

Christmas A252

17c, Holy family in Panamanian costume. 35c, Creche. 45c, Holy family, gift givers.

1989, Dec. 1
770 A252 17c multicolored 1.00 .40
771 A252 35c multicolored 2.25 .65
772 A252 45c multicolored 2.50 .85
Nos. 770-772 (3) 5.75 1.90

Rogelio Sinán (b. 1902), Writer — A253

1990, July 3
773 A253 23c brown & blue 1.40 .45

A254

1990, Nov. 20 Litho. *Perf. 13½*
774 A254 25c blue & black 1.40 .45
775 A254 35c Experiment 1.75 .60
776 A254 45c Beakers, test tubes, books 2.25 .75
Nos. 774-776 (3) 5.40 1.80

Dr. Guillermo Patterson, Jr., chemist.

Fruits — A255

20c, Byrsonima crassifolia. 35c, Bactris gasipaes. 40c, Anacardium occidentale.

1990, May 18 *Perf. 13½*
777 A255 20c multicolored .90 .40
778 A255 35c multicolored 1.60 .60
779 A255 40c multicolored 2.10 .70
Nos. 777-779 (3) 4.60 1.70

Tortoises — A256

35c, Pseudemys scripta. 45c, Lepidochelys olivacea. 60c, Geochelone carbonaria.

1990, Sept. 11
780 A256 35c multicolored 1.60 .60
781 A256 45c multicolored 2.10 .75
782 A256 60c multicolored 3.50 1.00
Nos. 780-782 (3) 7.20 2.35

For surcharges see Nos. 815, 818.

Native American — A257

1990, Oct. 12
783 A257 20c shown 1.80 .40
784 A257 35c Native, vert. 2.75 .85

Discovery of Isthmus of Panama, 490th Anniv. A258

1991, Nov. 19 Litho. *Perf. 12*
785 A258 35c multicolored 2.25 1.25

St. Ignatius of Loyola, 500th Birth Anniv. — A259

No. 786, St. Ignatius of Loyola.
No. 786B: c, St. Ignatius' seal over map of Panama (horiz.); d, 5c stamp, Panama Scott No. C119 in black (horiz.).

1991, Nov. 29
786 A259 20c multicolored 1.40 .40
a. Tete beche pair 2.25 1.25

Souvenir Sheet

786B Sheet of 2, #a.-b. — —
c. A259 25c multi — —
d. A259 25c multi — —

Society of Jesus, 450th anniv.

Christmas A260

1991, Dec. 2

787 A260 35c Luke 2:14 1.40 .65
788 A260 35c Nativity scene 1.40 .65
a. Pair, #787-788 3.25 2.50

Social Security Administration, 50th Anniv. — A261

Design: No. 790, Dr. Arnulfo Arias Madrid (1901-1988), Constitution of Panama, 1941.

1991, Feb. 20 Litho. *Perf. 12*

789 A261 10c multicolored .85 .40
790 A261 10c multicolored .85 .40

Women's citizenship rights, 50th anniv. (No. 790).

Epiphany A262

1992, Feb. 5 Litho. *Perf. 12*

791 A262 10c multicolored 1.00 .40
a. Tete beche pair 2.00 .80

New Life Housing Project A263

1992, Feb. 17

792 A263 5c multicolored 1.00 .40
a. Tete beche pair 2.00 .80

Border Treaty Between Panama and Costa Rica, 50th Anniv. A264

a, 20c, Hands clasped. b, 40c, Map. c, 50c, Pres. Rafael A. Calderon, Costa Rica, Pres. Arnulfo Arias Madrid, Panama.

1992, Feb. 20

793 A264 Strip of 3, #a.-c. 5.00 3.25

Causes of Hole in Ozone Layer — A265

1992, Feb. 24

794 A265 40c multicolored 2.25 .70
a. Tete beche pair 5.00 4.00

Expocomer '92, Intl. Commercial Exposition A266

1992, Mar. 11

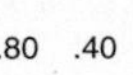

795 A266 10c multicolored .80 .40

A267

Margot Fonteyn (1919-91), ballerina: a, 35c, Wearing dress. b, 45c, In costume.

1992, Mar. 13

796 A267 Pair, #a.-b. 8.50 4.50

A268

1992, June 22 Litho. *Perf. 12*

797 A268 10c multicolored 1.00 .40
a. Tete beche pair 2.00 .75

Maria Olimpia de Obaldia (1891-1985), poet.

1992 Summer Olympics, Barcelona A269

1992, June 22 Litho. *Perf. 12*

798 A269 10c multicolored 1.00 .40
a. Tete-beche pair 2.00 .75

Zion Baptist Church, Bocas del Toro, 1892 A270

1992, Oct. 1 Litho. *Perf. 12*

799 A270 20c multicolored 1.10 .40
a. Tete beche pair 2.25 1.50

Baptist Church in Panama, Cent.

Discovery of America, 500th Anniv. — A271

a, 20c, Columbus' fleet. b, 35c, Coming ashore.

1992, Oct. 12

800 A271 Pair, #a.-b. 4.00 3.00

Endangered Wildlife — A272

a, 5c, Agouti paca. b, 10c, Harpia harpyja. c, 15c, Felis onca. d, 20c, Iguana iguana.

1992, Sept. 23

801 A272 Strip of 4, #a.-d. 8.25 6.25

Expo '92, Seville — A273

1992, Dec. 21 Litho. *Perf. 12*

802 A273 10c multicolored 1.00 .40
a. Tete beche pair 2.00 .75

Worker's Health Year — A274

1992, Dec. 21

803 A274 15c multicolored 1.00 .40
a. Tete beche pair 2.25 1.50

Unification of Europe — A275

1992, Dec. 21 Litho. *Perf. 12*

804 A275 10c multi + label 1.25 .40

Christmas — A276

a, 20c, Angel announcing birth of Christ. b, 35c, Mary and Joseph approaching city gate.

1992, Dec. 21

805 A276 Pair, #a.-b. 2.75 1.75

Evangelism in America, 500th Anniv. (in 1992) A277

1993, Apr. 13 Litho. *Perf. 12*

806 A277 10c multicolored 1.00 .40
a. Tete beche pair 2.25 1.50

Natl. Day for the Disabled — A278

1993, May 10

807 A278 5c multicolored 1.00 .40
a. Tete beche pair 2.25 1.80

Dr. Jose de la Cruz Herrera (1876-1961), Humanitarian — A279

1993, May 26

808 A279 5c multicolored 1.00 .40
a. Tete beche pair 2.25 1.80

1992 Intl. Conference on Nutrition, Rome A280

1993, June 22 Litho. *Perf. 12*

809 A280 10c multicolored 1.00 .40
a. Tete beche pair 2.25 .75

Columbus' Exploration of the Isthmus of Panama, 490th Anniv. A281

1994, June 2 Litho. *Perf. 12*

810 A281 50c multicolored 2.40 .95
a. Tete beche pair + 2 labels 5.50 3.50

Dated 1993.

Greek Community in Panama, 50th Anniv. — A282

Designs: 20c, Greek influences in Panama, Panamanian flag, vert. No. 812a, Parthenon. No. 812b, Greek Orthodox Church.

1995, Feb. 16 Litho. *Perf. 12*

811 A282 20c multicolored 1.10 .40

Souvenir Sheet

812 A282 75c Sheet of 2, #a.-b. 5.00 2.50

Nos. 729, 731, 737, 741, 747, 750, 781-782 Surcharged

1995 *Perfs., Etc. as Before*

813 A238 20c on 23c #729 .95 .40
814 A240 25c on 45c #737 1.30 .50
815 A256 30c on 45c #781 1.60 .65
816 A241 35c on 45c #741 1.75 .75
816A A243 35c on 45c No. 747 2.00 .85
817 A238 40c on 41c #731 2.25 .90
818 A256 50c on 60c #782 3.75 1.25
819 A244 1b on 60c No. 750 6.25 2.50
Nos. 813-819 (8) 19.85 7.80

Issued: #816A, 819, 5/3; Others, 4/6.

First Settlement of Panama, 475th Anniv. (in 1994) — A283

Designs: 15c, Horse and wagon crossing bridge. 20c, Arms of first Panama City, vert. 25c, Model of an original cathedral. 35c, Ruins of cathedral, vert.

1996, Oct. 11 Litho. *Perf. 14*

820 A283 15c beige, blk & brn .75 .40
821 A283 20c multicolored 1.00 .40
822 A283 25c beige, blk & brn 1.25 .45
823 A283 35c beige, blk & brn 2.00 .70
Nos. 820-823 (4) 5.00 1.95

Endangered Species — A284

1996, Oct. 18 Litho. *Perf. 14*

824 A284 20c Tinamus major 1.75 .60

Mammals A285

a, Nasua narica. b, Tamandua mexicana. c, Cyclopes didactylus. d, Felis concolor.

1996, Oct. 18

825 A285 25c Block of 4, #a.-d. 6.75 4.75

A286

1996, Oct. 22 Litho. *Perf. 14*
826 A286 40c multicolored 1.50 .75

Kiwanis Clubs of Panama, 25th anniv. (in 1993.)

A287

1996, Oct. 15
827 A287 5b multicolored 17.50 9.50

Rotary Clubs of Panama, 75th anniv. (in 1994).

UN, 50th anniv. (in 1995) — A288

1996, Oct. 21
828 A288 45c multicolored 2.00 .85

A289

Design: Ferdinand de Lesseps (1805-94), builder of Suez Canal.

1996, Oct. 21
829 A289 35c multicolored 1.75 .70

Andrés Bello Covenant, 25th Anniv. (in 1995) — A290

1996, Oct. 23
830 A290 35c multicolored 1.75 .70

Chinese Presence in Panama — A291

1996, June 10 *Perf. 14½*
831 A291 60c multicolored 2.75 1.10

Litho.

Imperf

Size: 80x68mm

Patterns depicting four seasons: 1.50b, Invierno, Primavera, Verano, Otono.

832 A291 1.50b multicolored 22.00 22.00

Radiology, Cent. (in 1995) — A292

1996, Oct. 24 Litho. *Perf. 14*
833 A292 1b multicolored 3.75 1.90

University of Panama, 60th Anniv. — A293

1996, Oct. 14
834 A293 40c multicolored 1.90 .75

Christmas — A295

1996, Oct. 24 Litho. *Perf. 14*
836 A295 35c multicolored 1.75 .70

Mail Train — A296

1996, Dec. 10 Litho. *Perf. 14*
837 A296 30c multicolored 2.50 .60

America issue.

Universal Congress of the Panama Canal — A297

No. 838: a, Pedro Miguel Locks. b, Miraflores Double Locks.
1.50b, Gatún Locks.

1997, Sept. 9 Litho. *Perf. 14½x14*
838 A297 45c Pair, #a.-b. 4.00 2.75

Imperf

839 A297 1.50b multicolored 5.50 5.00

Perforated portion of No. 839 is 76x31mm.

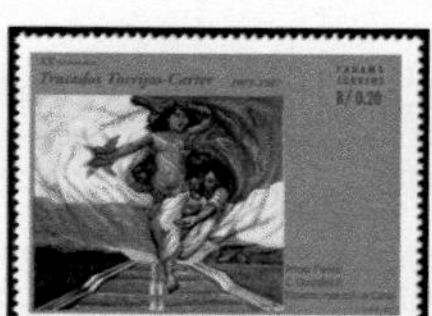

Torrijos-Carter Panama Canal Treaties, 20th Anniv. — A298

Designs: 20c, Painting, "Panama, More Than a Canal," by C. Gonzalez P. 30c, "Curtain of Our Flag," by A. Siever M., vert. 45c, "Huellas Perpetuas," by R. Marinez R. 50c, 1.50b, #588.

1997, Sept. 9 *Perf. 14*
840 A298 20c multicolored 1.10 .50
841 A298 30c multicolored 1.50 .75
842 A298 45c multicolored 2.00 1.10
843 A298 50c multicolored 2.40 1.25
Nos. 840-843 (4) 7.00 3.60

Imperf

844 A298 1.50b multicolored 5.50 5.00

Perforated portion of No. 844 is 114x50mm.

India's Independence, 50th Anniv. — A299

1997, Oct. 2 *Perf. 14x14½*
845 A299 50c Mahatma Gandhi 4.25 1.25

Crocodylus Acutus — A300

World Wildlife Fund: a, Heading right. b, Looking left. c, One in distance, one up close. d, With mouth wide open.

1997, Nov. 18 *Perf. 14½x14*
846 A300 25c Block of 4, #a.-d. 7.50 5.00

Christmas — A301

1997, Nov. 18 Litho. *Perf. 14x14½*
847 A301 35c multicolored 2.25 .70

Colon Fire Brigade, Cent. — A302

1997, Nov. 21 Litho. *Perf. 14½x14*
848 A302 20c multicolored 1.20 .50

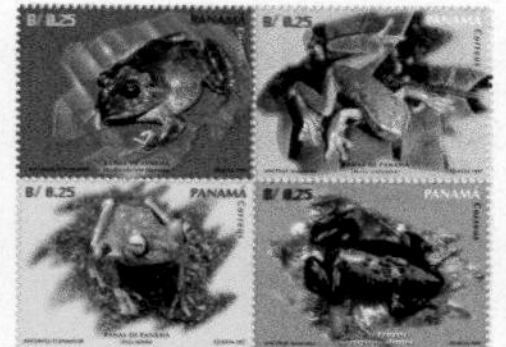

Frogs — A303

Designs: a, Eleutherodactylus biporcatus. b, Hyla colymba. c, Hyla rufitela. d, Nelsonphryne aterrima.

1997, Nov. 21
849 A303 25c Block of 4, #a.-d. 5.25 3.25

National Costumes A304

1997, Nov. 25
850 A304 20c multicolored 1.50 .75

America issue.

Colon Chamber of Commerce, Agriculture and Industry, 85th Anniv. — A305

1997, Nov. 27 *Perf. 14x14½*
851 A305 1b multicolored 3.75 2.50

Justo Arosemena, Lawyer, Politician, Death Cent. (in 1996) — A306

1997, Nov. 27
852 A306 40c multicolored 1.90 1.00

Panamanian Aviation Co., 50th Anniv. — A307

Designs: a, Douglas DC-3. b, Martin-404. c, Avro HS-748. d, Electra L-168. e, Boeing B727-100. f, Boeing B737-200 Advanced.

1997, Dec. 3 *Perf. 14½x14*
853 A307 35c Block of 6, #a.-f. 10.00 7.00

Jerusalem, 3000th Anniv. — A308

20c, Jewish people at the Wailing Wall. 25c, Christians being led in worship at Church of the Holy Sepulchre. 60c, Muslims at the Dome of the Rock.

1997, Dec. 29 *Perf. 14x14½*
854 A308 20c multicolored 1.95 .50
855 A308 25c multicolored 1.30 .65
856 A308 60c multicolored 2.75 1.50
Nos. 854-856 (3) 6.00 2.65

Imperf

857 A308 1.50b like #854-856 5.50 4.75

Perforated portion of No. 857 is 90x40mm.

Tourism — A309

10c, Old center of town, Panama City. 20c, Soberania Park. 25c, Panama Canal. 35c, Panama Bay. 40c, Fort St. Jerónimo. 45c, Rafting on Chagres River. 60c, Beach, Kuna Yala Region.

Perf. 14x14½, 14½x14

1998, July 7 Litho.
858 A309 10c multi, vert .40 .40
859 A309 20c multi, vert .95 .40
860 A309 25c multi 1.20 .50
861 A309 35c multi 1.60 .70
862 A309 40c multi 1.80 .80
863 A309 45c multi 2.25 .90
864 A309 60c multi 2.90 1.25
Nos. 858-864 (7) 11.10 4.95

Organization of American States (OAS), 50th Anniv. — A310

1998, Apr. 30 *Perf. 14½x14*
865 A310 40c multicolored 1.75 .80

Colón Free Trade Zone, 50th Anniv. — A311

Perf. 14x14½

1998, Feb. 2 Litho. Unwmk.
866 A311 15c multi 1.20 .40

Protection of the Harpy Eagle — A312

Contest-winning art by students: a, Luis Mellilo. b, Jorvisis Jiménez. c, Samuel Castro. d, Jorge Ramos.

1998, Jan. 20
867 A312 20c Block of 4, #a.-d. 6.50 4.50

Universal Declaration of Human Rights, 50th Anniv. — A313

1998, Feb. 10
868 A313 15c multi 1.20 .40

Panamanian Assoc. of Business Executives, 40th Anniv. — A314

1998, Jan. 28 ***Perf. 14½x14***
869 A314 50c multi 2.75 1.00

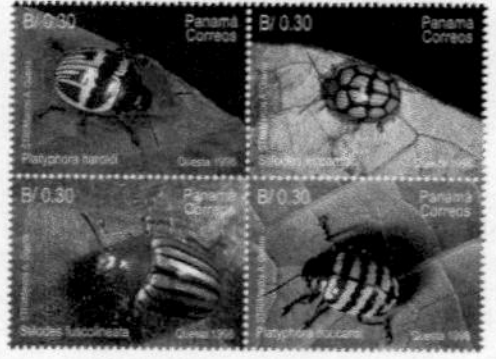

Beetles — A315

Designs: a, Platyphora haroldi. b, Stilodes leoparda. c, Stilodes fuscolineata. d, Platyphora boucardi.

1998, Feb. 10
870 A315 30c Block of 4, #a.-d. 8.75 6.75

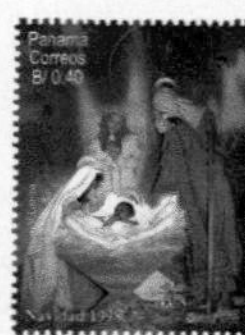

Christmas — A316

1998, Jan. 14 Litho. ***Perf. 14x14½***
871 A316 40c multi 1.90 .80

Panama Pavilion, Expo '98, Lisbon — A317

1998, Jan. 14 Litho. ***Perf. 14½x14***
872 A317 45c multi 2.10 .90

Panama Canal, 85th Anniv. (in 1999) A318

No. 873: a, Canal builders and crane on train trestle. b, Partially built structures, construction equipment.

2000, Sept. 7 Litho. ***Perf. 14½x14***
873 A318 40c Pair, #a-b 5.00 4.00

Souvenir Sheet

874 A318 1.50b Valley 8.00 7.25

No. 874 contains one label.

Reversion of Panama Canal to Panama (in 1999) — A319

Various ships. Denominations: 20c, 35c, 40c, 45c.

2000, Sept. 7 ***Perf. 14½x14***
875-878 A319 Set of 4 8.25 3.50

Pres. Arnulfo Arias Madrid (1901-88) — A320

No. 879: a, 20c, Arias as medical doctor, with people. b, 20c, Arias giving speech, holding glasses.
No. 880, a, 30c, Arias in 1941, 1951 and 1969, Panamanian flag. b, 30c, Arias giving speech, crowd.

2001, Aug. 14 Litho. ***Perf. 13x13½***
Horiz. pairs, #a-b
879-880 A320 Set of 2 6.00 4.50

Christmas — A321

2001, Dec. 4 Litho. ***Perf. 14x14½***
881 A321 35c multi 1.25 .70

Dated 1999.

Holy Year (in 2000) — A322

2001, Dec. 4 ***Perf. 14½x14***
882 A322 20c multi 1.40 .50

Dated 2000.

18th UPAEP Congress (in 2000) — A323

2001, Dec. 4
883 A323 5b multi 23.00 17.50

Dated 2000.

Dreaming of the Future — A324

Children's art by: No. 884, 20c, I. Guerra. No. 885, 20c, D. Ortega.
No. 886, horiz.: a, J. Aguilar P. b, S. Sittón.

2001, Dec. 4 ***Perf. 14x14½***
884-885 A324 Set of 2 3.75 2.75

Souvenir Sheet
Perf. 14½x14

886 A324 75c Sheet of 2, #a-b 7.75 6.75

Dated 2000.

Architecture of the 1990s — A325

Designs: No. 887, 35c, Los Delfines Condominium, by Edwin Brown. No. 888, 35c, Banco General Tower, by Carlos Medina.
No. 889, horiz.: a, Building with round sides, by Ricardo Moreno. b, Building with three peaked roofs, by Moreno.

2001, Dec. 4 ***Perf. 14x14½***
887-888 A325 Set of 2 4.25 3.50

Souvenir Sheet
Perf. 14½x14

889 A325 75c Sheet of 2, #a-b 7.75 7.00

Dated 2000.

Orchids — A326

Designs: No. 890, 35c, Cattleya dowiana. No. 891, 35c, Psychopsis krameriana.
No. 892: a, Peristeria clata. b, Miltoniopsis roezlii.

2001, Dec. 4 ***Perf. 14½x14***
890-891 A326 Set of 2 8.50 5.00

Souvenir Sheet

892 A326 75c Sheet of 2, #a-b 10.50 10.00

Dated 2000.

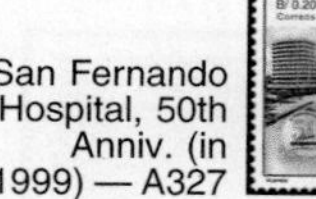
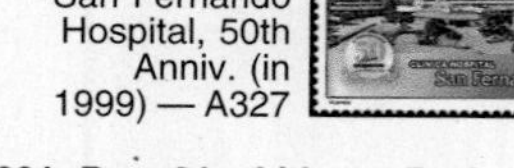

San Fernando Hospital, 50th Anniv. (in 1999) — A327

2001, Dec. 21 Litho. ***Perf. 14½x14***
893 A327 20c multi 1.30 .80

Dated 2000.

Pres. Mireya Moscoso — A328

2002, Mar. 25
894 A328 35c multi 2.10 1.00

Dated 2000.

Independence From Spain, 180th Anniv. — A329

Details from mural by Roberto Lewis: No. 895, 15c, "180" at L. No. 896, 15c, "180" at R.

2002, Apr. 30 ***Perf. 13¼x13***
895-896 A329 Set of 2 2.25 .85

Dated 2001.

Discovery of the Isthmus, 500th Anniv. — A330

Designs: 50c, Natives, ship. 5b, Native, European, crucifix, ships.

2002, Apr. 30 ***Perf. 13x13¼***
897-898 A330 Set of 2 21.00 15.00

Dated 2001. No. 898 is airmail.

America Issue — UNESCO World Heritage — A331

No. 899, 15c: a, Castle of San Lorenzo. b, Salón Bolivar, Panama City.
No. 900, 1.50b, horiz.: a, Cathedral, Panama City. b, Portobelo Fortifications.

2002, May 30 ***Perf. 13¼x13, 13x13¼***
Horiz. Pairs, #a-b
899-900 A331 Set of 2 16.00 10.00

Dated 2001. No. 900 is airmail.

Murals by Roberto Lewis in Palacio de las Garzas — A332

No. 901: a, Heron, flagbearer and natives. b, Battle with natives. c, Woman, horse, men. d, Heron, woman in dress, woman picking fruit.

2002, June 19 ***Perf. 13x13¼***
901 Horiz. strip of 4 3.50 2.00
a.-d. A332 5c Any single .75 .25

Dated 2001.

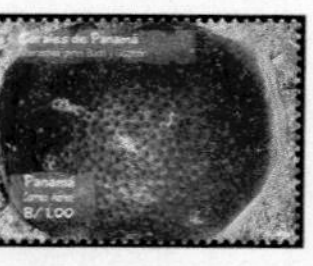

Corals — A333

No. 902: a, Montastraea annularis. b, Pavona chiriquiensis.
1b, Siderastrea glynni. 2b, Pociliopora.

2002, June 28
902 A333 10c Horiz. pair, #a-b .80 .50
903 A333 1b multi 4.50 3.00
904 A333 2b multi 9.00 6.00
Nos. 902-904 (3) 14.30 9.50

Dated 2001. Nos. 903-904 are airmail.

Butterflies and Caterpillars A334

Designs: No. 905, 10c, Ophioderes materna. No. 906, 10c, Rhuda focula. 1b, Morpho peleides. 2b, Tarchon felderi.

2002, June 28 Litho. ***Perf. 13x13¼***
905-908 A334 Set of 4 25.00 10.00

Dated 2001. Nos. 907-908 are airmail.

Christmas 2002 — A335

2003, June 16 Litho. *Perf. 14*

909 A335 15c multi 5.50 2.50

Dated 2002.

America Issue — Youth, Education and Literacy — A336

2003, June 23

910 A336 45c multi 1.90 1.00

Dated 2002.

Clara González de Behringer, First Female Lawyer in Panama — A337

2003, July 10 *Perf. 13½x13*

911 A337 30c multi 1.50 .80

Dated 2002.

Colón, 150th Anniv. (in 2002) — A338

2003, July 17

912 A338 15c multi 1.00 .50

Dated 2002.

Luis C. Russell (b. 1902), Jazz Musician — A339

2003, Aug. 6 *Perf. 14*

913 A339 10c multi 2.50 1.50

Dated 2002.

Artwork in the National Theater — A340

Designs: No. 914, 5c, Statue of Erato (holding lyre). No. 915, 5c, Statue of Melpomene (holding mask). 50c, Decoration on front of theater box, horiz. 60c, Theater facade and painting, horiz.

Perf. 13½x13, 14 (50c), 13x13½ (60c)

2003, Aug. 12

914-917 A340 Set of 4 7.00 3.50

Dated 2002. Nos. 916-917 are airmail.

St. Josemaría Escrivá de Balaguer (1902-75) — A341

2003, Aug. 13 *Perf. 14*

918 A341 10c multi 1.10 .40

Dated 2002.

Republic of Panama, Cent. — A342

Designs: 5c, National arms. 10c, First national flag. No. 921a, Manuel Amador Guerrero, first president. No. 921b, Pres. Mireya Moscoso. 25c, Declaration of Independence. No. 923a, Sterculia apetala. No. 923b, Peristeria elata. 35c, Revolutionary junta. 45c, Flag, Constitution of 1904, Constituent Delegates.

2003, Nov. 26 *Perf. 12*

919	A342	5c multi	.60	.40
920	A342	10c multi	.70	.40
921	A342	15c Horiz. pair, #a-b	1.75	.95
922	A342	25c multi	1.75	.80
923	A342	30c Horiz. pair, #a-b	3.75	2.10
924	A342	35c multi	2.25	1.10
925	A342	45c multi	2.90	1.40
		Nos. 919-925 (7)	13.70	7.15

Nos. 924-925 are airmail.

Republic of Panama, Cent. Type of 2003 Redrawn

2003, Nov. 26 Litho. *Perf. 12*

925A	Souvenir booklet	16.00	
b.	Booklet pane, #f-g	.85	—
c.	Booklet pane, #h-i	1.75	—
d.	Booklet pane, #j, m	3.75	—
e.	Booklet pane, #k-l	3.75	—
f.	A342 5c Similar to #919	.40	.25
g.	A342 10c Similar to #920	.40	.25
h.	A342 15c Similar to #921a	.85	.30
i.	A342 15c Similar to #921b	.85	.30
j.	A342 25c Similar to #922	1.75	.50
k.	A342 30c Similar to #923a	1.75	.60
l.	A342 30c Similar to #923b	1.75	.60
m.	A342 35c Similar to #924	1.75	.70

The text "1903 — Centenario de lar República de Panamá - 2003" is inscribed across the se-tenant pair stamps in each booklet pane. Other differences in text are also on each of Nos. 925Af-925Am.

Christmas A343

2003, Nov. 28

926 A343 10c multi 5.50 2.75

Panama, 2003 Iberoamerican Cultural Capital — A344

2003, Dec. 4

927 A344 5c multi 1.00 .25

For surcharges, see Nos. 945-948.

Pres. Mireya Moscoso — A345

2004, Aug. 10 Litho. *Perf. 14½x14*

928 A345 35c multi 2.10 1.60

Compare with Type A328. Dated 2000.

A346

Publication of Don Quixote, by Miguel de Cervantes, 400th Anniv. (in 2005).

2007, Apr. 23 Litho. *Perf. 12*

929 A346 45c multi 1.80 1.40

St. Augustine High School, Panama, 50th Anniv. — A347

2007, May 7

930 A347 35c multi 5.50 4.50

A348

A349

A350

Worldwide Fund for Nature (WWF) — A351

2007, June 27

931	Horiz. strip of 4	5.25	5.25
a.	A348 20c multi	.90	.90
b.	A349 20c multi	.90	.90
c.	A350 20c multi	.90	.90
d.	A351 20c multi	.90	.90

Popes A352

No. 932: a, Pope John Paul II (1920-2005). b, Pope Benedict XVI.

Imperf. x Perf. 12 on 1 Side

2007, June 29

932 A352 50c Horiz. pair, #a-b 4.25 3.50

Tourism A353

2007, July 10 *Perf. 12*

933 A353 5c multi 1.00 .40

See Nos. 936-941.

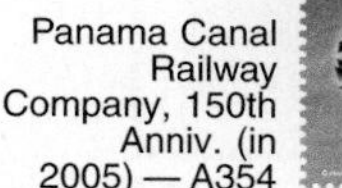

Panama Canal Railway Company, 150th Anniv. (in 2005) — A354

Designs: 20c, Emblem, Diesel and steam trains. 30c, Emblem, Diesel and steam trains, Diesel train in foreground.

2007, Nov. 27 Litho. *Perf. 12*

934-935 A354 Set of 2 2.25 1.50

Tourism Type of 2007

Designs: 15c, Devil's mask. 20c, Chorrera Waterfalls, vert. 25c, Sarigua National Park. 35c, Pottery from Barilles archaeological site. 45c, San Fernando Fort, Portobelo. 60c, Colonial era buildings, vert.

2008, Feb. 27 Litho. *Perf. 12*

936-941 A353 Set of 6 9.00 4.00

Dated 2007.

Carter-Torrijos Panama Canal Treaty, 30th Anniv. — A355

2008, Nov. 11 Litho. *Perf. 14*

942 A355 35c multi 1.75 1.10

Souvenir Sheet

Various Airplanes of Copa Airlines A356

2010, July 30 *Perf. 14 on 3 Sides*

943 A356 1b multi 4.00 3.00

Copa Airlines, 60th anniv.

Miniature Sheet

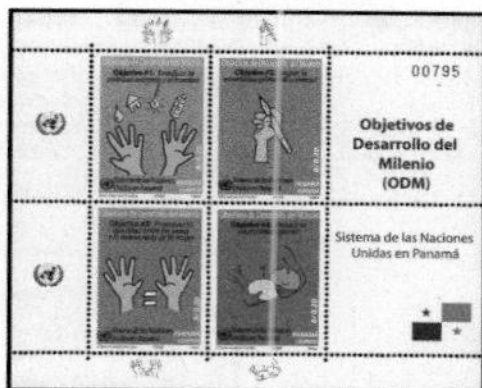

United Nations Millennium Objectives — A357

No. 944: a, Objective #1, Eradication of extreme poverty and hunger. b, Objective #2, Universal primary education. c, Objective #3, Promotion of equality of the sexes and women's rights. d, Objective #4, Reduction of infant mortality.

2010, Aug. 18 *Perf. 14*

944 A357 20c Sheet of 4, #a-d 4.50 3.00

Dated 2008.

No. 927 Surcharged in Black or Blue

No. 945

No. 946

No. 947

No. 948

Methods and Perfs. As Before

2014

945 A344 10c on 5c #927 (Bl) 1.00 .40
946 A344 20c on 5c #927 (Bl) 1.60 .40
947 A344 25c on 5c #927 (Bl) 2.00 .50
948 A344 35c on 5c #927 2.75 .70
Nos. 945-948 (4) 7.35 2.00

Issued: No. 945, 7/7; No. 946, 6/18; No. 947, 8/24; No. 948, 6/2.

Nos. 873, 902, 923 Surcharged in Black or Silver

No. 949a

No. 949b

No. 950a

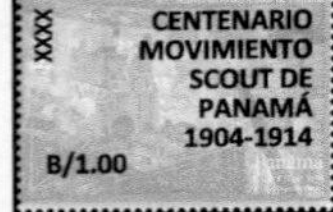

No. 950b

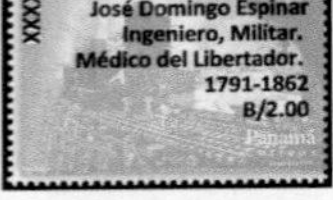

No. 951a

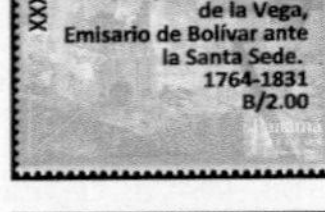

No. 951b

No. 952a

No. 952b

No. 953a

No. 953b

Methods and Perfs As Before

2015, Dec. 1

949 Horiz. pair (S) 8.00 8.00
a. A342 1b on 30c #923a (S) 4.00 4.00
b. A342 1b on 30c #923b (S) 4.00 4.00
950 Horiz. pair 12.00 12.00
a. A318 1b on 40c #873a 6.00 6.00
b. A318 1b on 40c #873b 6.00 6.00
951 Horiz. pair 16.00 16.00
a. A318 2b on 40c #873a 8.00 8.00
b. A318 2b on 40c #873b 8.00 8.00
952 Horiz. pair (S) 32.00 40.00
a. A342 4b on 30c #923a (S) 16.00 16.00
b. A342 4b on 30c #923b (S) 16.00 16.00
953 Horiz. pair (S) 40.00 40.00
a. A333 5b on 10c #902a (S) 20.00 20.00
b. A333 5b on 10c #902b (S) 20.00 20.00
Nos. 949-953 (5) 108.00 116.00

Tourism — A358

Designs: 20c, San Francisco de la Montaña Church, Veraguas Province. 25c, Centennial Bridge over Panama Canal. 35c, Presidential Palace, Panama City. 60c, Building, Mi Pueblito Afroantilliano Complex, Cerro Ancón. 1b, Beach, Guna Yala Province. 4b, Cinta Costera 1, Panama City. 10b, Royal Customs House, San Felipe Portobelo.

2016, Nov. 29 **Litho.** ***Perf. 13x13¼***
954-960 A358 Set of 7 44.00 40.00

National Library, 75th Anniv. A359

2018, July 11 **Litho.** ***Perf. 11½***
961 A359 35c multi 1.30 .70

Winning Items by Estefania Zevallos L. in 2010 National Pollera Contest — A360

Designs: 30c, Pollera. 40c, Earrings & necklace, horiz. 50c, Hairpins, butterfly broch. 60c, Jewelry, diff., horiz.

2018, July 22 **Litho.** ***Perf. 11½***
962-965 A360 Set of 4 6.50 3.75

A361

Justo Arosemena Quesada (1817-96), Pro-Independence Politician — A361a

Paintings of Arosemena with his name and "1817-2017": No. 966, Above and below painting. No. 967, Above painting.
1.50b, Arosemena, diff.

2018, Aug. 1 **Litho.** ***Perf. 11½***
966 A361 35c multicolored 1.30 .70
967 A361a 35c multicolored 1.30 .70

Size: 120x59mm

Imperf

968 A361 1.50b multi 4.50 3.00

Panamanian Red Cross, Cent. (in 2017) — A362

2018, Aug. 8 **Litho.** ***Perf. 11½***
969 A362 35c multi 1.30 .70

Lions Clubs International, Cent. (in 2017) — A363

2018, Aug. 16 **Litho.** ***Perf. 11½***
970 A363 5b multi 13.00 12.50

Widening of the Panama Canal A364

Designs: 1b, Canal at night. 2b, Cocolí Locks. 3b, Agua Clara Locks. 4b, Container ship in canal.
No. 975: a, Ship and tugboat in Cocolí Locks. b, Ship in Agua Clara Locks.

2018, Aug. 20 **Litho.** ***Perf. 11½***
971-974 A364 Set of 4 27.00 20.00

Souvenir Sheet

975 A364 75c Sheet of 2, #a-b 4.75 3.00

No. 975 contains two 40x30mm stamps.

Demetrio H. Brid Municipal Palace A365

Designs: 20c, Shown. 25c, Brid and other members of the 1903 Municipal Council of the District of Panama. 35c, Brid and Gallery of Rulers.
$1.50, Brid (1859-1917), leader of Municipal Council, independence movement leader, and first de facto President of Panama, vert.

2018, Sept. 19 **Litho.** ***Perf. 11½***
976-978 A365 Set of 3 3.50 1.60

Size: 88x124mm

Imperf

979 A365 1.50b multi 4.75 3.00

Firefighters of Panama, 130th Anniv. (in 2017) A366

2018, Sept. 27 **Litho.** ***Perf. 11½***
980 A366 5c multi .85 .25

Republican Band, 150th Anniv. (in 2017) A367

2018, Oct. 16 **Litho.** ***Perf. 11½***
981 A367 35c multi 1.30 .70

Artifacts From Gran Coclé Archaelogical Site — A368

Designs: 20c, Seahorse-shaped pendant. 35c, Warrior and birds pendant. 45c, Two-headed idol, horiz.
No. 985, 75c: a, Like 20c, with frame line. b, Like 35c, with frame line.

2018, Oct.23 **Litho.** ***Perf. 11½***
982-984 A368 Set of 3 4.00 2.00

Souvenir Sheet

985 A368 75c Sheet of 2, #a-b 4.50 3.00

No. 985 contains two 32x40mm stamps.

National Symbols and People Connected With Them A369

Designs: 10c, National flag. 20c, Manuel E. Amador (1869-1952), designer of flag, vert. 25c, María Ossa de Amador (1855-1948), creator of first flag, vert. 30c, National coat of arms, vert. 35c, Nicanor Villaláz (1855-1932), creator of coat of arms, vert. 45c Max Lemm (1868-1939), artist for coat of arms, vert. 50c, National anthem, vert. 60c, Santos Jorge (1870-1941), composer of national anthem, vert. 75c, Jerónimo Ossa (1847-1907), lyricist of national anthem, vert.

2018, Nov. 14 **Litho.** ***Perf. 11½***
986-994 A369 Set of 9 12.50 7.00

Nos. 986-992 has text in black, Nos. 993-994 has text in red.

Flag of Panama and Ernestina Sucre Tapia (1892-1982), Writer of Flag Pledge — A370

2019, June 7 **Litho.** ***Perf. 14¼***
995 A370 5c multi .85 .25

Flag and pledge of Panama, 60th anniv.

Postal Service of the Republic of Panama, 115th Anniv. — A371

Designs: 5b, Modern forms of telecommunication. 10b, Old and modern post offices.

Perf. 13¼ Syncopated

2019, June 7 **Litho.**
996-997 A371 Set of 2 30.00 30.00

Popes and Their Coats of Arms — A372

Designs: No. 998, 25c, Pope John Paul II (1920-2005). No. 999, 25c, Pope Benedict XVI. No. 1000, 25c, Pope Francis.

2019, June 7 Litho. *Perf. 14¼*
998-1000 A372 Set of 3 3.50 1.50

Basilicas A373

Designs: No. 1001, 25c, Minor Basilica of Jesús Nazareno de Atalaya. No. 1002, 25c, Santiago Apóstol Minor Basilica, Natá fr los Caballeros. 35c, Don Bosco Minor Basilica, Panama. 45c, Santa María Cathedral Basilica, Panama.

2019, June 7 Litho. *Perf. 14¼*
1001-1004 A373 Set of 4 5.25 2.60

World Youth Day, Panama — A374

Designs: 20c, Cross, crowd and icon. 25c, Youth carrying cross. 35c, Stylized city skyline and crowd. 45c, Santa María la Antigua, patron saint of Panama.

2019, June 7 Litho. *Perf. 14¼*
1005 A374 20c multi .80 .40
a. Booklet pane of 6 5.00 —
1006 A374 25c multi 1.00 .50
a. Booklet pane of 6 6.00 —
1007 A374 35c multi 1.50 .70
a. Booklet pane of 6 9.00 —
1008 A374 45c multi 1.80 .90
a. Booklet pane of 6 11.00
Complete booklet, #1005a, 1006a, 1007a, 1008a 31.00
b. Souvenir sheet of 4, #1005-1008 6.00 6.00
Nos. 1005-1008 (4) 5.10 2.50

Complete booklet sold for 10b. No. 1008b sold for 1.50b.

Fruit and Nuts — A375

Designs: Nos. 1009, 1016, Annona muricata. Nos. 1010, 1017, Hylocereus triangularis and Hylocereus ocamposis. Nos. 1011, 1018, Anacardium occidentale. Nos. 1012, 1019, Inga feuillei. Nos. 1013, 1020, Acronomia aculeata. Nos. 1014, 1021, Mammea americana. Nos. 1015, 1022, Carica papaya.

2019, June 7 Litho. *Perf. 13¼*
1009 A375 25c multi .75 .50
a. Booklet pane of 6 6.25 —
1010 A375 25c multi .75 .50
a. Booklet pane of 6 6.25 —
1011 A375 25c multi .75 .50
a. Booklet pane of 6 6.25 —
1012 A375 25c multi .75 .50
a. Booklet pane of 6 6.25 —
1013 A375 25c multi .75 .50
a. Booklet pane of 6 6.25 —
1014 A375 25c multi .75 .50
a. Booklet pane of 6 6.25 —
1015 A375 25c multi .75 .50
a. Booklet pane of 6 6.25 —
Complete booklet, #1009a, 1010a, 1011a, 1012a, 1013a, 1014a, 1015a 42.00
1016 A375 1b multi 3.00 2.00
1017 A375 2b multi 6.00 4.00
1018 A375 3b multi 9.00 6.00
1019 A375 4b multi 12.00 8.00
1020 A375 5b multi 14.00 10.00
1021 A375 10b multi 30.00 20.00
1022 A375 15b multi 45.00 30.00
Nos. 1009-1022 (14) 124.25 83.50

Complete booklet sold for 15b.

Old Quarter, Panama, 500th Anniv. — A376

Designs: No. 1023, 20c, Santo Domingo Convent. No, 1024, 20c, Concepción Convent. No. 1025, 20c, Cathedral Tower. No. 1026, 20c, Ruins of Jesuit Church. No. 1027, 20c, King's Bridge (Puente del Rey).

Litho. & Thermography With Grit Embedded

2019, June 18 *Perf. 14¼*
1023-1027 A376 Set of 5 5.00 2.00

University of Panama School of Law and Political Science, Cent. — A377

2019, June 20 Litho. *Perf. 14¼*
1028 A377 20c multi 1.00 .40

Panama City, 2019 Iberoamerican Capital of Culture — A378

2019, June 24 Litho. *Perf. 14¼*
1029 A378 25c multi 1.10 .50

Panama Soccer Team at 2018 World Cup Soccer Championships, Russia — A379

Photograph of team members at: 20c, Nizhny Novgorod. 35c, Nizhny Novgorod, diff. 45c, Sochi. 60c, Saransk.
No. 1034, 75c: a, Like 45c. b, Like 60c.

2019, June 27 Litho. *Perf. 14¼*
1030-1033 A379 Set of 4 6.00 3.25

Souvenir Sheet

1034 A379 75c Sheet of 2, #a-b 4.75 3.00

Pres. Belisario Porras (1856-1942), Leading People — A380

Maria "Pantalones" Carter (1929-2013), Community Activist — A381

Cultural Diversity A382

People in Parque Norte — A383

Litho. & Thermography With Grit Embedded

2019, June 27 *Perf. 14¼*
1035 A380 25c multi .80 .50
a. Booklet pane of 6 8.00 5.50
1036 A381 25c multi .80 .50
a. Booklet pane of 6 8.00 5.50
1037 A382 25c multi .80 .50
a. Booklet pane of 6 8.00 5.50
1038 A383 25c multi .80 .50
a. Booklet pane of 6 8.00 5.50
Complete booklet, #1035a, 1036a, 1037a, 1038a 27.50
1039 A380 1b multi 3.25 2.00
1040 A381 2b multi 5.25 4.00
1041 A382 3b multi 9.25 6.00
1042 A383 4b multi 11.50 8.00
Nos. 1035-1042 (8) 32.45 22.00

Panama City, 500th anniv. Complete booklet sold for 10b.

AIR POST STAMPS

Special Delivery Stamp No. E3 Srchd. in Dark Blue

1929, Feb. 8 Unwmk. *Perf. 12½*
C1 SD1 25c on 10c org 1.00 .80
a. Inverted surcharge 22.50 22.50

Nos. E3-E4 Overprinted in Blue

1929, May 22
C2 SD1 10c orange .50 .50
a. Inverted overprint 20.00 17.50
b. Double overprint 20.00 17.50

Some specialists claim the red overprint is a proof impression.

With Additional Surcharge of New Value

C3 SD1 15c on 10c org .50 .50
C4 SD1 25c on 20c dk brn 1.10 1.00
a. Double surcharge 20.00 20.00
Nos. C2-C4 (3) 2.10 2.00

No. E3 Surcharged in Blue

1930, Jan. 25
C5 SD1 5c on 10c org .50 .50

No. 219 Overprinted in Red

1930, Feb. 28 *Perf. 12*
C6 A39 1b dk vio & blk 16.00 12.50

AP5

1930-41 Engr. *Perf. 12*
C6A AP5 5c blue ('41) .35 .35
C6B AP5 7c rose car ('41) .35 .35
C6C AP5 8c gray blk ('41) .35 .35
C7 AP5 15c dp grn .35 .35
C8 AP5 20c rose .35 .35
C9 AP5 25c deep blue .65 .65
Nos. C6A-C9 (6) 2.40 2.40

Issued: Nos. C7-C9, 1/20; Nos. C6A-C6C, 7/1/41. See No. C112.
For surcharges and overprints see Nos. 353, C16-C16A, C53B, C69, C82-C83, C109, C122, C124.

Airplane over Map of Panama — AP6

1930, Aug. 4 *Perf. 12½*
C10 AP6 5c ultra .25 .25
C11 AP6 10c orange .30 .25
C12 AP6 30c dp vio 5.50 4.00
C13 AP6 50c dp red 1.50 .50
C14 AP6 1b black 5.50 4.00
Nos. C10-C14 (5) 13.05 9.00

For surcharge and overprints see Nos. C53A, C70-C71, C115.

Amphibian — AP7

1931, Nov. 28 Typo.
Without Gum
C15 AP7 5c deep blue .80 1.00
a. 5c gray blue .80 1.00
b. Horiz. pair, imperf. btwn. 50.00

For the start of regular airmail service between Panama City and the western provinces, but valid only on Nov. 28-29 on mail carried by hydroplane "3 Noviembre."
Many sheets have a papermaker's watermark "DOLPHIN BOND" in double-lined capitals.

No. C9 Surcharged in Red 19mm long

1932, Dec. 14 *Perf. 12*
C16 AP5 20c on 25c dp bl 6.25 .70

Surcharge 17mm long

C16A AP5 20c on 25c dp bl 200.00 2.50

Special Delivery Stamp No. E4 Overprinted in Red or Black

1934 *Perf. 12½*
C17 SD1 20c dk brn 10.00 .50
C17A SD1 20c dk brn (Bk) 100.00 55.00

Issued: No. C17, 7/31.

Surcharged In Black

1935, June
C18 SD1 10c on 20c dk brn .80 .50

Same Surcharge with Small "10"

C18A SD1 10c on 20c dk brn 40.00 5.00
b. Horiz. pair, imperf. vert. 100.00

Nos. 234 and 242 Surcharged in Blue

1936, Sept. 24
C19 A53 5c on ½c org 400.00 250.00
C20 A53 5c on 50c org 1.00 .80
a. Double surcharge 60.00 60.00

Centenary of the birth of President Pablo Arosemena.
It is claimed that No. C19 was not regularly issued. Counterfeits of No. C19 exist.

Urracá Monument AP8

Palace of Justice AP9

10c, Human Genius Uniting the Oceans. 20c, Panama City. 30c, Balboa Monument. 50c, Pedro Miguel Locks.

1936, Dec. 1 Engr. *Perf. 12*
C21 AP8 5c blue .65 .40
C22 AP9 10c yel org .85 .60
C23 AP9 20c red 3.00 1.50
C24 AP9 30c dk vio 3.50 2.50
C25 AP9 50c car rose 8.00 5.75
C26 AP9 1b black 9.50 6.00
Nos. C21-C26 (6) 25.50 16.75

4th Postal Congress of the Americas and Spain.

Nos. C21-C26 Overprinted in Red or Blue

1937, Mar. 9

C27	AP8	5c blue (R)	.55	.30
a.		Inverted overprint	50.00	
C28	AP9	10c yel org (Bl)	.75	.45
C29	AP9	20c red (Bl)	1.75	1.00
a.		Double overprint	50.00	
C30	AP8	30c dk vio (R)	4.50	3.25
C31	AP8	50c car rose (Bl)	18.00	13.00
a.		Double overprint	175.00	
C32	AP9	1b black (R)	22.50	13.00
		Nos. C27-C32 (6)	48.05	31.00

Regular Stamps of 1921-26 Surcharged in Red

1937, June 30 ***Perf. 12, 12½***

C33	A55	5c on 15c ultra	.75	.75
C34	A55	5c on 20c brn	.75	.75
C35	A47	10c on 10c vio	1.75	1.50

Regular Stamps of 1920-26 Surcharged in Red

C36	A56	5c on 24c blk vio	.75	.75
C37	A39	5c on 1b dk vio & blk	.75	.50
C38	A56	10c on 50c blk	2.25	2.00
a.		Inverted surcharge	30.00	

No. 248 Overprinted in Red

C39	A54	5c dark blue	.75	.75
a.		Double overprint	18.00	
		Nos. C33-C39 (7)	7.75	7.00

Fire Dept. Badge AP14

Florencio Arosemena AP15

José Gabriel Duque — AP16

Perf. 14x14½

1937, Nov. 25 **Photo.** **Wmk. 233**

C40	AP14	5c blue	4.50	.60
C41	AP15	10c orange	6.75	1.00
C42	AP16	20c crimson	9.00	.75
		Nos. C40-C42 (3)	20.25	2.35

50th anniversary of the Fire Department.

Basketball AP17

Baseball AP18

1938, Feb. 12 ***Perf. 14x14½, 14½x14***

C43	AP17	1c shown	2.25	.25
C44	AP18	2c shown	2.25	.25
C45	AP18	7c Swimming	3.00	.25
C46	AP18	8c Boxing	3.00	.25
C47	AP17	15c Soccer	5.00	1.25
a.		Souv. sheet of 5, #C43-C47	18.00	18.00
b.		As "a," No. C43 omitted	*3,500.*	
		Nos. C43-C47 (5)	15.50	2.25
		Set, never hinged	23.25	

4th Central American Caribbean Games.

US Constitution Type

Engr. & Litho.

1938, Dec. 7 **Unwmk.** ***Perf. 12½***

Center in Black, Flags in Red and Ultramarine

C49	A83	7c gray	.35	.25
C50	A83	8c brt ultra	.55	.35
C51	A83	15c red brn	.70	.45
C52	A83	50c orange	8.00	5.75
C53	A83	1b black	8.00	5.75
		Nos. C49-C53 (5)	17.60	12.55

Nos. C12 and C7 Surcharged in Red

1938, June 5 ***Perf. 12½, 12***

C53A	AP6	7c on 30c dp vio	.40	.40
c.		Double surcharge	27.50	
d.		Inverted surcharge	27.50	
C53B	AP5	8c on 15c dp grn	.40	.40
e.		Inverted surcharge	22.50	

Opening of the Normal School at Santiago, Veraguas Province, June 5, 1938. The 8c surcharge has no bars.

Belisario Porras — AP23

Designs: 2c, William Howard Taft. 5c, Pedro J. Sosa. 10c, Lucien Bonaparte Wise. 15c, Armando Reclus. 20c, Gen. George W. Goethals. 50c, Ferdinand de Lesseps. 1b, Theodore Roosevelt.

1939, Aug. 15 **Engr.**

C54	AP23	1c dl rose	.40	.25
C55	AP23	2c dp bl grn	.40	.25
C56	AP23	5c indigo	.65	.25
C57	AP23	10c dk vio	.70	.25
C58	AP23	15c ultra	1.60	.35
C59	AP23	20c rose pink	4.00	1.40
C60	AP23	50c dk brn	5.00	.70
C61	AP23	1b black	7.25	3.75
		Nos. C54-C61 (8)	20.00	7.00

Opening of Panama Canal, 25th anniv.

For surcharges see Nos. C63, C65, G1, G3.

Flags of the 21 American Republics — AP31

1940, Apr. 15 **Unwmk.**

C62	AP31	15c blue	.40	.40

Pan American Union, 50th anniversary.

For surcharge see No. C66.

Stamps of 1939-40 Surcharged in Black

a

b

c

d

1940, Aug. 12

C63	AP23 (a)	5c on 15c lt ultra	.40	.40
a.		"7 AEREO 7" on 15c	60.00	60.00
C64	A84 (b)	7c on 15c ultra	.40	.40
C65	AP23 (c)	7c on 20c rose pink	.40	.40
C66	AP31 (d)	8c on 15c blue	.40	.40
		Nos. C63-C66 (4)	1.60	1.60

Stamps of 1924-30 Overprinted in Black or Red

e

f

g

1941, Jan. 2 ***Perf. 12½, 12***

C67	SD1 (e)	7c on 10c org	1.00	1.00
C68	A53 (f)	15c on 24c yel brn (R)	2.50	2.50
C69	AP5 (g)	20c rose	2.00	2.00
C70	AP6 (g)	50c deep red	6.00	4.00
C71	AP6 (g)	1b black (R)	13.50	10.00
		Nos. C67-C71 (5)	25.00	19.50

New constitution of Panama which became effective Jan. 2, 1941.

Liberty — AP32

Black Overprint

1942, Feb. 19 **Engr.** ***Perf. 12***

C72	AP32	20c chestnut brn	4.00	2.50

Costa Rica - Panama Type

Engr. & Litho.

1942, Apr. 25 **Unwmk.**

C73	A94	15c dp grn, dk bl & dp rose	.70	.40

Swordfish AP34

J. D. Arosemena Normal School AP35

Designs: 8c, Gate of Glory, Portobello. 15c, Taboga Island, Balboa Harbor. 50c, Firehouse. 1b, Gold animal figure.

1942, May 11 **Engr.** ***Perf. 12***

C74	AP34	7c rose carmine	.90	.25
C75	AP34	8c dk ol brn & blk	.25	.25
C76	AP34	15c dark violet	.45	.25
C77	AP35	20c red brown	.65	.25
C78	AP34	50c olive green	1.10	.40
C79	AP34	1b blk & org yel	2.75	.80
		Nos. C74-C79 (6)	6.10	2.20

See Nos. C96-C99, C113, C126. For surcharges and overprints see Nos. 354-355, C84-C86, C108, C110-C111, C114, C116, C118, C121, C123, C127-C128, C137.

Alejandro Meléndez G. — AP40

Design: 5b, Ernesto T. Lefevre.

1943, Dec. 15

C80	AP40	3b dk olive gray	6.00	4.75
C81	AP40	5b dark blue	9.00	7.50

For overprint & surcharge see #C117, C128A.

Catalogue values for unused stamps in this section, from this point to the end of the section, are for Never Hinged items.

Nos. C6C and C7 Surcharged in Carmine

1947, Mar. 8 ***Perf. 12***

C82	AP5	5c on 8c gray blk	.65	.40
a.		Double overprint	25.00	22.50
C83	AP5	10c on 15c dp grn	1.40	.40

Nos. C74 to C76 Surcharged in Black or Carmine

C84	AP34	5c on 7c rose car (Bk)	.65	.40
a.		Double surcharge		*500.00*
b.		Pair, one without surcharge	75.00	
C85	AP34	5c on 8c dk ol brn & blk	.65	.40
C86	AP34	10c on 15c dk vio	.65	.40
a.		Double surcharge	30.00	30.00
		Nos. C82-C86 (5)	4.00	2.00

National Theater — AP42

1947, Apr. 7 **Engr.** **Unwmk.**

C87	AP42	8c violet	.90	.40

Natl. Constitutional Assembly of 1945, 2nd anniv.

For surcharge see No. 356.

Manuel Amador Guerrero — AP43

Manuel Espinosa B. — AP44

5c, José Agustin Arango. 10c, Federico Boyd. 15c, Ricardo Arias. 50c, Carlos Constantino Arosemena. 1b, Nicanor de Obarrio. 2b, Tomas Arias.

1948, Feb. 20 ***Perf. 12½***

Center in Black

C88	AP43	3c blue	.55	.25
C89	AP43	5c brown	.55	.25
C90	AP43	10c orange	.55	.25
C91	AP43	15c deep claret	.55	.25
C92	AP44	20c deep carmine	.95	.55
C93	AP44	50c dark gray	1.75	.80
C94	AP44	1b green	5.50	2.50
C95	AP44	2b yellow	12.00	6.00
		Nos. C88-C95 (8)	22.40	10.85

Members of the Revolutionary Junta of 1903.

Types of 1942

1948, June 14 ***Perf. 12***

C96	AP34	2c carmine	1.10	.25
C97	AP34	15c olive gray	.55	.25
C98	AP35	20c green	.55	.25
C99	AP34	50c rose carmine	8.75	3.00
		Nos. C96-C99 (4)	10.95	3.75

Franklin D. Roosevelt and Juan D. Arosemena
AP45

Four Freedoms
AP46

Monument to F. D. Roosevelt
AP47

Map showing Boyd-Roosevelt Trans-Isthmian Highway
AP48

Franklin D. Roosevelt — AP49

1948, Sept. 15 *Perf. 12½*
C100 AP45 5c dp car & blk .45 .25
C101 AP46 10c yellow org .60 .30
C102 AP47 20c dull green .75 .35
C103 AP48 50c dp ultra & blk 1.20 .60
C104 AP49 1b gray black 3.00 1.25
Nos. C100-C104 (5) 6.00 2.75

Franklin Delano Roosevelt (1882-1945).
For surcharges see Nos. RA28-RA29.

Monument to Cervantes
AP50

10c, Don Quixote attacking windmill.

1948, Nov. 15
C105 AP50 5c dk blue & blk .90 .40
C106 AP50 10c purple & blk 1.60 .40

400th anniv. of the birth of Miguel de Cervantes Saavedra, novelist, playwright and poet.

No. C106 Ovptd. in Carmine

1949, Jan. 18
C107 AP50 10c purple & blk 1.10 .40
a. Inverted overprint 52.50

José Gabriel Duque (1849-1918), newspaper publisher and philanthropist.

Nos. C96, C6A, C97 and C99 Overprinted in Black or Red

h

i

1949, May 26
C108 AP34(h) 2c carmine .45 .25
a. Double overprint 7.50 7.00
b. Inverted surcharge 20.00 20.00
c. On No. C74 (error) 70.00
C109 AP5(i) 5c blue (R) .45 .25
C110 AP34(h) 15c ol gray (R) 1.10 .65
C111 AP34(h) 50c rose car 4.00 2.25
Nos. C108-C111 (4) 6.00 3.40

Centenary of the incorporation of Chiriqui Province.

Types of 1930-42

Design: 10c, Gate of Glory, Portobelo.

1949, Aug. 3 *Perf. 12*
C112 AP5 5c orange .80 .40
C113 AP34 10c dk blue & blk .80 .40

For surcharge see No. C137.

Stamps of 1943-49 Overprinted or Surcharged in Black, Green or Red

1949, Sept. 9
C114 AP34 2c carmine .35 .25
a. Inverted overprint 24.00
b. Double overprint 32.50
c. Double overprint, one inverted 37.50 35.00
C115 AP5 5c orange (G) 1.60 .35
a. Inverted overprint 12.50
b. Double overprint 30.00 30.00
c. Double ovpt., one inverted 30.00 30.00
C116 AP34 10c dk bl & blk (R) 1.60 .40
C117 AP40 25c on 3b dk ol gray (R) 2.10 .70
C118 AP34 50c rose carmine 4.25 2.10
Nos. C114-C118 (5) 9.90 3.80

75th anniv. of the UPU.
No. C115 has small overprint, 15½x12mm, like No. 368. Overprint on Nos. C114, C116 and C118 as illustrated. Surcharge on No. C117 is arranged vertically, 29x18mm.

University of San Javier — AP51

1949, Dec. 7 **Engr.** *Perf. 12½*
C119 AP51 5c dk blue & blk .90 .40

See note after No. 371.

Mosquito — AP52

1950, Jan. 12 *Perf. 12*
C120 AP52 5c dp ultra & gray blk 2.25 .65

See note after No. 372.

Nos. C96, C112, C113 and C9 Overprinted in Black or Carmine (5 or 4 lines)

1950, Aug. 17 **Unwmk.**
C121 AP34 2c carmine .90 .25
C122 AP5 5c orange 1.10 .35
C123 AP34 10c dk bl & blk (C) 1.10 .40
C124 AP5 25c deep blue (C) 1.25 .75

Same on No. 362, Overprinted "AEREO"

C125 A105 50c pur & blk (C) 5.00 1.25
Nos. C121-C125 (5) 9.35 3.00

Gen. José de San Martin, death cent.

Firehouse Type of 1942

1950, Oct. 30 **Engr.**
C126 AP34 50c deep blue 4.00 1.00

Nos. C113 and C81 Surcharged in Carmine or Orange

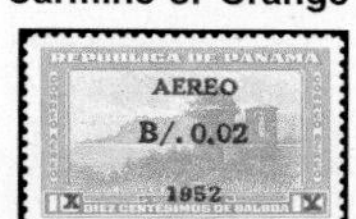

1952, Feb. 20
C127 AP34 2c on 10c .50 .25
a. Pair, one without surch. 375.00
C128 AP34 5c on 10c (O) .50 .25
b. Pair, one without surch. 375.00
C128A AP40 1b on 5b 29.00 20.00

The surcharge on No. C128A is arranged to fit stamp, with four bars covering value panel at bottom, instead of crosses.

Nos. 376 and 380 Srchd. "AEREO 1952" and New Value in Carmine or Black

1952, Aug. 1
C129 A97 5c on 2c ver & blk (C) .50 .25
a. Inverted surcharge 32.50
C130 A99 25c on 10c pur & org 1.75 1.00

Isabella Type of Regular Issue

Perf. 12½

1952, Oct. 20 **Unwmk.** **Engr.**

Center in Black

C131 A110 4c red orange .65 .40
C132 A110 5c olive green .65 .40
C133 A110 10c orange .85 .40
C134 A110 25c gray blue 2.25 .40
C135 A110 50c chocolate 3.25 .85
C136 A110 1b black 10.00 3.50
Nos. C131-C136 (6) 17.65 5.95

Queen Isabella I of Spain, 500th birth anniv.

No. C113 Surcharged "5 1953" in Carmine

1953, Apr. 22 *Perf. 12*
C137 AP34 5c on 10c dk bl & blk .85 .40

Masthead of La Estrella — AP54

1953, July 15
C138 AP54 5c rose carmine .50 .40
C139 AP54 10c blue 1.10 .40

Panama's 1st newspaper, La Estrella de Panama, cent.
For surcharges see Nos. C146-C147.

Act of Independence
AP55

Senora de Remon and Pres. José A. Remon Cantera
AP56

Designs: 7c, Pollera. 25c, National flower. 50c, Marcos A. Salazar, Esteban Huertas and Domingo Diaz A. 1b, Dancers.

1953, Nov. 2
C140 AP55 2c deep ultra .55 .25
C141 AP56 5c deep green .55 .25
C142 AP56 7c gray .65 .25
C143 AP56 25c black 4.00 .65
C144 AP56 50c dark brown 2.75 .75
C145 AP56 1b red orange 7.25 1.50
Nos. C140-C145 (6) 15.75 3.65

Founding of republic, 50th anniversary.
For overprints see Nos. C227-C229.

Nos. C138-C139 Surcharged with New Value in Black or Red

1953-54
C146 AP54 1c on 5c rose car ('54) .80 .40
C147 AP54 1c on 10c blue (R) .80 .40

Gen. Herrera at Conference Table — AP57

Design: 1b, Gen. Herrera leading troops.

1954, Dec. 4 **Litho.** *Perf. 12½*
C148 AP57 6c deep green .50 .25
C149 AP57 1b scarlet & blk 5.00 2.25

Death of Gen. Tomas Herrera, cent.
For surcharge see No. C198.

Rotary Emblem and Map — AP58

1955, Feb. 23
C150 AP58 6c rose violet .35 .25
C151 AP58 21c red .90 .35
C152 AP58 1b black 6.50 2.50
a. 1b violet black 7.00 3.75
Nos. C150-C152 (3) 7.75 3.10

Rotary International, 50th anniv.
For surcharge see No. C154.

Cantera Type

1955, June 1
C153 A115 6c rose vio & blk .80 .40

Issued in tribute to Pres. José Antonio Remon Cantera, 1908-1955.
For surcharge see No. C188.

No. C151 Surcharged

1955, Dec. 7
C154 AP58 15c on 21c red .90 .40

Pedro J. Sosa
AP60

First Barge Going through Canal and de Lesseps
AP61

Perf. 12½

1955, Nov. 22 **Unwmk.** **Litho.**
C155 AP60 5c grn, *lt grn* .45 .25
C156 AP61 1b red lilac & blk 6.50 2.50

150th anniversary of the birth of Ferdinand de Lesseps. Imperforates exist.

Pres. Dwight D. Eisenhower
AP62

Statue of Bolivar
AP63

Bolivar Hall — AP64

Portraits-Presidents: C158, Pedro Aramburu, Argentina. C159, Dr. Victor Paz Estenssoro, Bolivia. C160, Dr. Juscelino Kubitschek O., Brazil. C161, Gen. Carlos Ibanez del Campo, Chile. C162, Gen. Gustavo Rojas Pinilla, Colombia. C163, Jose Figueres, Costa Rica. C164, Gen. Fulgencio Batista y Zaldivar, Cuba. C165, Gen. Hector B. Trujillo Molina, Dominican Rep. C166, José Maria Velasco Ibarra, Ecuador. C167, Col. Carlos Castillo Armas, Guatemala. C168, Gen. Paul E. Magloire, Haiti. C169, Julio Lozano Diaz, Honduras. C170, Adolfo Ruiz Cortines, Mexico. C171, Gen. Anastasio Somoza, Nicaragua. C172, Ricardo Arias Espinosa, Panama. C173, Gen. Alfredo Stroessner, Paraguay. C174, Gen. Manuel Odria, Peru. C175, Col. Oscar Osorio, El Salvador. C176, Dr. Alberto F. Zubiria, Uruguay. C177, Gen. Marcos Perez Jimenez, Venezuela. 1b, Simon Bolivar.

1956, July 18
C157 AP62 6c rose car & vio bl .75 .30
C158 AP62 6c brt grnsh bl & blk .75 .30
C159 AP62 6c bister & blk .75 .30
C160 AP62 6c emerald & blk .75 .30
C161 AP62 6c lt grn & brn .75 .30
C162 AP62 6c yellow & grn .75 .30
C163 AP62 6c brt vio & grn .75 .30
C164 AP62 6c dl pur & vio bl .75 .30
C165 AP62 6c red lil & sl grn .75 .30
C166 AP62 6c citron & vio bl .75 .30

C167 AP62 6c ap grn & brn .75 .30
C168 AP62 6c brn & vio bl .75 .30
C169 AP62 6c brt car & grn .75 .30
C170 AP62 6c red & brn .75 .30
C171 AP62 6c lt bl & grn .75 .30
C172 AP62 6c vio bl & grn .75 .30
C173 AP62 6c orange & blk .75 .30
C174 AP62 6c bluish gray & brn .75 .30
C175 AP62 6c sal rose & blk .75 .30
C176 AP62 6c dk grn & vio bl .75 .30
C177 AP62 6c dk org brn & dk grn .75 .30
C178 AP63 20c dk bluish gray 1.90 .65
C179 AP64 50c green 3.00 1.10
C180 AP63 1b brown 8.50 2.00
Nos. C157-C180 (24) 29.15 10.05

Pan-American Conf., Panama City, July 21-22, 1956, and 130th anniv. of the 1st Pan-American Conf. Imperforates exist.

Ruins of First Town Council Building — AP65

Design: 50c, City Hall, Panama City.

1956, Aug. 17
C181 AP65 25c red 1.00 .40
C182 AP65 50c black 2.00 .90
a. Souv. sheet of 3, #404, C181-C182, imperf. 2.75 2.40

6th Inter-American Congress of Municipalities, Panama City, Aug. 14-19, 1956.
No. C182a sold for 85c.
For overprint see No. C187a.

Monument AP66

St. Thomas Hospital AP67

1956, Nov. 27 **Wmk. 311**
C183 AP66 5c green .40 .40
C184 AP67 15c dk carmine .65 .40

Centenary of the birth of Pres. Belisario Porras.

Highway Construction — AP68

20c, Road through jungle, Darien project. 1b, Map of Americas showing Pan-American Highway.

Wmk. 311
1957, Aug. 1 **Litho.** ***Perf. 12½***
C185 AP68 10c black .35 .25
C186 AP68 20c lt blue & blk .85 .55
C187 AP68 1b green 3.25 2.25
a. AP65 Souvenir sheet of 3, unwmkd. 16.00 16.00
Nos. C185-C187 (3) 4.45 3.05

7th Pan-American Highway Congress.
No. C187a is No. C182a overprinted in black: "VII degree CONGRESSO INTER-AMERICANO DE CARRETERAS 1957."

No. C153 Surcharged "1957" and New Value

1957, Aug. 13 **Unwmk.**
C188 A115 10c on 6c rose vio & blk .80 .40

Remon Polyclinic AP69

Customs House, Portobelo AP70

Buildings: #C191, Portobelo Castle. #C192, San Jeronimo Castle. #C193, Remon Hippodrome. #C194, Legislature. #C195, Interior & Treasury Department. #C196, El Panama Hotel. #C197, San Lorenzo Castle.

Wmk. 311
1957, Nov. 1 **Litho.** ***Perf. 12½***
Design in Black
C189 AP69 10c lt blue .45 .25
C190 AP70 10c lilac .45 .25
C191 AP70 10c gray .45 .25
C192 AP70 10c lilac rose .45 .25
C193 AP70 10c ultra .45 .25
C194 AP70 10c brown ol .45 .25
C195 AP70 10c orange yel .45 .25
C196 AP70 10c yellow grn .45 .25
C197 AP70 1b red 4.75 1.60
Nos. C189-C197 (9) 8.35 3.60

No. C148 Surcharged in Red

1958, Feb. 11 **Unwmk.**
C198 AP57 5c on 6c dp grn .80 .40

United Nations Emblem AP71

Flags of Panama and UN AP72

1958, Mar. 5 **Litho.** **Wmk. 311**
C199 AP71 10c brt green .40 .25
C200 AP71 21c lt ultra .65 .25
C201 AP71 50c orange 1.60 .85
C202 AP72 1b gray, ultra & car 3.25 1.60
a. Souv. sheet of 4, #C199-C202, imperf. 7.00 5.25
Nos. C199-C202 (4) 5.90 2.95

10th anniv. of the UN (in 1955).
The sheet also exists with the 10c and 50c omitted.

OAS Type of Regular Issue, 1958

Designs: 10c, 1b, Flags of 21 American Nations. 50c, Headquarters in Washington.

1958, Aug. 12 **Unwmk.** ***Perf. 12½***
Center yellow and black; flags in national colors
C203 A124 5c lt blue .40 .25
C204 A124 10c carmine rose .40 .25
C205 A124 50c gray 1.00 .60
C206 A124 1b black 3.25 1.60
Nos. C203-C206 (4) 5.05 2.70

Type of Regular Issue

Pavilions: 15c, Vatican City. 50c, United States. 1b, Belgium.

1958, Sept. 8 **Wmk. 311** ***Perf. 12½***
C207 A125 15c gray & lt vio .40 .25
C208 A125 50c dk gray & org brn 1.10 .65
C209 A125 1b brt vio & bluish grn 2.60 1.40
a. Souv. sheet of 7, #418-421, C207-C209 8.75 5.25
Nos. C207-C209 (3) 4.10 2.30

No. C209a sold for 2b.

Pope Type of Regular Issue

Portraits of Pius XII: 5c, As cardinal. 30c, Wearing papal tiara. 50c, Enthroned.

1959, Jan. 21 **Litho.** **Wmk. 311**
C210 A126 5c violet .40 .25
C211 A126 30c lilac rose 1.00 .40
C212 A126 50c bluish gray 1.50 .65
a. Souv. sheet of 4, #422, C210-C212, imperf. 4.25 2.25
Nos. C210-C212 (3) 2.90 1.30

#C212a is watermarked sideways and sold for 1b. The sheet also exists with 30c omitted. #C212a with C.E.P.A.L. overprint is listed as #C221a.

Human Rights Issue Type

Designs: 5c, Humanity looking into sun. 10c, 20c, Torch and UN emblem. 50c, UN Flag. 1b, UN Headquarters building.

1959, Apr. 14 ***Perf. 12½***
C213 A127 5c emerald & bl .35 .25
C214 A127 10c gray & org brn .35 .25
C215 A127 20c brown & gray .35 .25
C216 A127 50c green & ultra 1.10 .65
C217 A127 1b red & blue 2.25 1.40
Nos. C213-C217 (5) 4.40 2.80

Nos. C213-C215, C212a Overprinted and C216 Surcharged in Red or Dark Blue

1959, May 16
C218 A127 5c emer & bl (R) .40 .25
C219 A127 10c gray & org brn (Bl) .40 .25
C220 A127 20c brown & gray (R) .65 .25
C221 A127 1b on 50c grn & ultra (R) 3.25 1.90
a. Souvenir sheet of 4 9.00 7.00
Nos. C218-C221 (4) 4.70 2.65

8th Reunion of the Economic Commission for Latin America.
This overprint also exists on Nos. C216-C217. These were disavowed by Panama's postmaster general.
No. C221a is No. C212a with two-line black overprint at top of sheet: "8a. REUNION DE LA C.E.P.A.L. MAYO 1959."

Type of Regular Issue, 1959

Portraits: 5c, Justo A. Facio, Rector. 10c, Ernesto de la Guardia, Jr., Pres. of Panama.

Wmk. 311
1959, Aug. 5 **Litho.** ***Perf. 12½***
C222 A128 5c black .50 .40
C223 A128 10c black .40 .40

Type of Regular Issue, 1959

1959, Oct. 26 **Wmk. 311** ***Perf. 12½***
C224 A130 5c Boxing .45 .25
C225 A130 10c Baseball .85 .25
C226 A130 50c Basketball 3.50 1.25
Nos. C224-C226 (3) 4.80 1.75

For surcharge see No. C349.

Nos. C143-C145 Overprinted in Vermilion, Red or Black

Unwmk.
1960, Feb. 6 **Engr.** ***Perf. 12***
C227 AP56 25c black (V) 1.20 .25
C228 AP56 50c dk brown (R) 1.75 .40
C229 AP56 1b red orange 2.75 1.25
Nos. C227-C229 (3) 5.70 1.90

World Refugee Year, July 1, 1959-June 30, 1960.
The revenues from the sale of Nos. C227-C229 went to the United Nations Refugee Fund.

Administration Building, National University — AP74

Designs: 21c, Humanities building. 25c, Medical school. 30c, Dr. Octavio Mendez Pereria first rector of University.

Wmk. 311
1960, Mar. 23 **Litho.** ***Perf. 12½***
C230 AP74 10c brt green .45 .40
C231 AP74 21c lt blue 1.00 .40
C232 AP74 25c ultra 1.40 .40
C233 AP74 30c black 1.75 .40
Nos. C230-C233 (4) 4.60 1.60

National University, 25th anniv.
For surcharges see Nos. 450, C248, C253, C287, C291.

Olympic Games Type

5c, Basketball. 10c, Bicycling, horiz. 25c, Javelin thrower. 50c, Athlete with Olympic torch.

1960, Sept. 22 **Wmk. 343** ***Perf. 12½***
C234 A131 5c orange & red .35 .25
C235 A131 10c ocher & blk .75 .25
C236 A131 25c lt bl & dk bl 1.50 .55
C237 A131 50c brown & blk 2.75 1.00
a. Souv. sheet of 2, #C236-C237 5.50 4.50
Nos. C234-C237 (4) 5.35 2.05

For surcharges see Nos. C249-C250, C254, C266-C270, C290, C350, RA40.

Citizens' Silhouettes AP75

10c, Heads and map of Central America.

1960, Oct. 4 **Litho.** **Wmk. 229**
C238 AP75 5c black .80 .40
C239 AP75 10c brown .80 .40

6th census of population and the 2nd census of dwellings (No. C238), Dec. 11, 1960, and the All America Census, 1960 (No. C239).

Boeing 707 Jet Liner — AP76

1960, Dec. 1 **Wmk. 343** ***Perf. 12½***
C240 AP76 5c lt grnsh blue .65 .40
C241 AP76 10c emerald .65 .40
C242 AP76 20c red brown 1.25 .40
Nos. C240-C242 (3) 2.55 1.20

1st jet service to Panama. For surcharge see No. RA41.

Souvenir Sheet

UN Emblem AP77

Wmk. 311
1961, Mar. 7 **Litho.** ***Imperf.***
C243 AP77 80c blk & car rose 2.75 2.50

15th anniv. (in 1960) of the UN.
Counterfeits without control number exist.

No. C243 Overprinted in Blue with Large Uprooted Oak Emblem and "Ano de los Refugiados"

1961, June 2
C244 AP77 80c blk & car rose 3.25 3.00

World Refugee Year, July 1, 1959-June 30, 1960.

Lions International Type

Designs: 5c, Helen Keller School for the Blind. 10c, Children's summer camp. 21c, Arms of Panama and Lions emblem.

1961, May 2 Wmk. 311 *Perf. 12½*

C245 A133 5c black .55 .40
C246 A133 10c emerald .55 .40
C247 A133 21c ultra, yel & red .95 .40
Nos. C245-C247 (3) 2.05 1.20

For overprints see Nos. C284-C286.

Nos. C230 and C236 Surcharged in Black or Red

1961 Wmk. 311 (1c); Wmk. 343

C248 AP74 1c on 10c .35 .25
C249 A131 1b on 25c (Bk) 2.75 2.00
C250 A131 1b on 25c (R) 2.90 2.00
Nos. C248-C250 (3) 6.00 4.25

Issued: Nos. C248-C249, 7/6; No. C250, 9/5.

Pres. Roberto F. Chiari and Pres. Mario Echandi — AP78

Wmk. 343

1961, Oct. 2 Litho. *Perf. 12½*

C251 AP78 1b black & gold 3.25 1.60

Meeting of the Presidents of Panama and Costa Rica at Paso Canoa, Apr. 21, 1961.

Dag Hammarskjold — AP79

1961, Dec. 27 *Perf. 12½*

C252 AP79 10c black .80 .40

Dag Hammarskjold, UN Secretary General, 1953-61.

No. C230 Surcharged

1962, Feb. 21 Wmk. 311

C253 AP74 15c on 10c brt grn .80 .40

No. C236 Surcharged

Wmk. 343

C254 A131 1b on 25c 3.25 1.25

City Hall, Colon — AP80

1962, Feb. 28 Litho. Wmk. 311

C255 AP80 5c vio bl & blk .90 .40

Issued to publicize the third Central American Municipal Assembly, Colon, May 13-17.

Church Type of Regular Issue, 1962

Designs: 5c, Church of Christ the King. 7c, Church of San Miguel. 8c, Church of the Sanctuary. 10c, Saints Church. 15c, Church of St. Ann. 21c, Canal Zone Synagogue (Now used as USO Center). 25c, Panama Synagogue. 30c, Church of St. Francis. 50c, Protestant Church, Canal Zone. 1b, Catholic Church, Canal Zone.

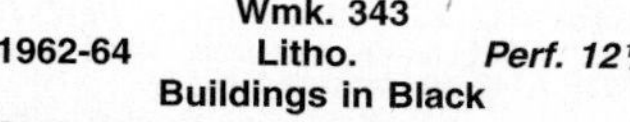

Wmk. 343

1962-64 Litho. *Perf. 12½*

Buildings in Black

C256 A138 5c purple & buff .45 .25
C257 A138 7c lil rose & brt pink .45 .25
C258 A139 8c purple & bl .45 .25
C259 A139 10c lilac & sal .45 .25
C259A A139 10c grn & dl red brn ('64) .45 .25
C260 A139 15c red & buff .65 .25
C261 A138 21c brown & blue .95 .40
C262 A138 25c blue & pink 1.20 .35
C263 A139 30c lil rose & bl 1.30 .40
C264 A138 50c lilac & lt grn 1.90 .65
a. Souv. sheet of 4, #441H-441I, C262, C264, imperf. 7.75 5.75
C265 A139 1b bl & sal 4.00 1.40
Nos. C256-C265 (11) 12.25 4.70

Freedom of religion in Panama. Issue dates: #C259A, 6/4/64; others, 7/20/62.

For overprints and surcharges see Nos. C288, C296-C297, C299.

Nos. C234, C236 Overprinted & Surcharged in Black, Green, Orange or Red

1962, July 27 Wmk. 343 *Perf. 12½*

C266 A131 5c org & red .45 .25
C267 A131 10c on 25c (G) 1.10 .35
C268 A131 15c on 25c (O) 1.40 .45
C269 A131 20c on 25c (R) 1.50 .50
C270 A131 25c lt bl & dk bl 1.75 .55
Nos. C266-C270 (5) 6.20 2.10

Ninth Central American and Caribbean Games, Kingston, Jamaica, Aug. 11-25.

Nos. CB1-CB2 Surcharged

1962, May 3 Wmk. 311

C271 SPAP1 10c on 5c + 5c 1.75 .75
C272 SPAP1 20c on 10c + 10c 2.75 1.50

Type of Regular Issue, 1962

Design: 10c, Canal bridge completed.

1962, Oct. 12 Wmk. 343

C273 A140 10c blue & blk .65 .40

John H. Glenn, "Friendship 7" Capsule — AP81

Designs: 10c, "Friendship 7" capsule and globe, horiz. 31c, Capsule in space, horiz. 50c, Glenn with space helmet.

1962, Oct. 19 Wmk. 311 *Perf. 12½*

C274 AP81 5c rose red .40 .25
C275 AP81 10c yellow .55 .25
C276 AP81 31c blue 2.25 .80
C277 AP81 50c emerald 2.75 1.00
a. Souv. sheet of 4, #C274-C277, imperf. 6.50 6.50
Nos. C274-C277 (4) 5.95 2.30

1st orbital flight of US astronaut Lt. Col. John H. Glenn, Jr., Feb. 20, 1962. No. C277a sold for 1b.

For surcharges see Nos. C290A-C290D, C367, CB4-CB7.

UPAE Emblem — AP82

1963, Jan. 8 Litho. Wmk. 343

C278 AP82 10c multi .85 .40

50th anniversary of the founding of the Postal Union of the Americas and Spain, UPAE.

Type of Regular Issue

10c, Fire Engine "China", Plaza de Santa Ana. 15c, 14th Street team. 21c, Fire Brigade emblem.

1963, Jan. 22 Wmk. 311 *Perf. 12½*

C279 A141 10c orange & blk .85 .40
C280 A141 15c lilac & blk 1.00 .40
C281 A141 21c gold, red & ultra 2.10 .40
Nos. C279-C281 (3) 3.95 1.20

"FAO" and Wheat Emblem — AP83

1963, Mar. 21 Litho.

C282 AP83 10c green & red .80 .40
C283 AP83 15c ultra & red 1.00 .40

FAO "Freedom from Hunger" campaign.

No. C245 Ovptd. in Yellow, Orange or Green

1963, Apr. 18 Wmk. 311 *Perf. 12½*

C284 A133 5c black (Y) 1.15 .25
C285 A133 5c black (O) 1.15 .25
C286 A133 5c black (G) 1.15 .25
Nos. C284-C286 (3) 3.45 .75

22nd Central American Lions Congress, Panama, Apr. 18-21.

No. C230 Surcharged

1963, June 11

C287 AP74 4c on 10c brt grn .80 .40

Nos. 445 and 432 Overprinted Vertically

1963 Wmk. 343 *Perf. 12½*

C288 A139 10c green, yel & blk .80 .40

Wmk. 311

C289 A130 20c emerald & red brn 1.15 .40

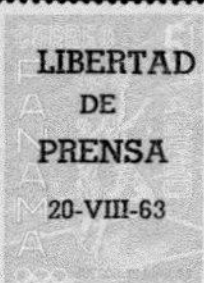

No. C234 Overprinted

1963, Aug. 20 Wmk. 343

C290 A131 5c orange & red .80 .40

Freedom of Press Day, Aug. 20, 1963.

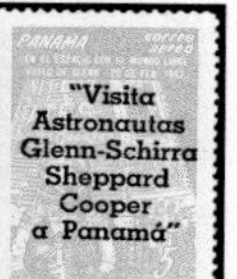

Nos. C274, C277a Overprinted or Surcharged — a

No. C274 Surcharged in Black — b

Wmk. 311

1963, Aug. 22 Litho. *Perf. 12½*

C290A AP81(a) 5c on #C274 3.50
C290B AP81(a) 10c on 5c #C274 7.50
C290C AP81(b) 10c on 5c #C274 9.25

Souvenir Sheet

Imperf.

C290D AP81(a) Sheet of 4, #C277a 54.00

Overprint on No. C290D has names in capital letters and covers all four stamps.

No. C232 Surcharged in Red

1963, Oct. 9 Wmk. 311 *Perf. 12½*

C291 AP74 10c on 25c ultra .80 .40

Type of Regular Issue, 1963

Flags and Presidents: 5c, Julio A. Rivera, El Salvador. 10c, Miguel Ydigoras F., Guatemala. 21c, John F. Kennedy, US.

Perf. 12½x12

1963, Dec. 18 Litho. Unwmk.

Portrait in Slate Green

C292 A142 5c yel, red & ultra .70 .25
C293 A142 10c bl, red & ultra 1.00 .35
C294 A142 21c org yel, red & ultra 2.75 1.10
Nos. C292-C294 (3) 4.45 1.70

Balboa Type of Regular Issue, 1964

1964, Jan. 22 Photo. *Perf. 13*

C295 A143 10c dk vio, *pale pink* .80 .40

No. C261 Srchd. in Red

1964 Wmk. 343 Litho. *Perf. 12½*

C296 A138 50c on 21c brn, bl & blk 1.50 .70

Type of 1962 Overprinted

C297 A139 1b emer, yel & blk 2.50 2.25

Issued. No. C296, 2/25; No. C297, 2/20.

Nos. 434 and 444 Surcharged

1964 Wmk. 343 *Perf. 12½*

C298 A131 10c on 5c bl grn & emer .80 .40
C299 A139 10c on 5c rose, lt grn & blk .80 .40

Issued: No. C298, 4/6; No. C299, 3/30.

St. Patrick's Cathedral, New York — AP84

Cathedrals: #C301, St. Stephen's, Vienna. #C302, St. Sofia's, Sofia. #C303, Notre Dame, Paris. #C304, Cologne. #C305, St. Paul's, London. #C306, Metropolitan, Athens. #C307, St. Elizabeth's, Kosice, Czechoslovakia (inscr. Kassa, Hungary). #C308, New Delhi. #C309, Milan. #C310, Guadalupe Basilica. #C311, New Church, Delft, Netherlands. #C312, Lima. #C313, St. John's Poland. #C314, Lisbon. #C315, St. Basil's, Moscow. #C316, Toledo. #C317, Stockholm. #C318, Basel. #C319, St. George's Patriarchal Church, Istanbul. 1b, Panama City. 2b, St. Peter's Basilica, Rome.

Unwmk.

1964, Feb. 17 Engr. *Perf. 12*

Center in Black

C300 AP84 21c olive 1.75 .90
C301 AP84 21c chocolate 1.75 .90
C302 AP84 21c aqua 1.75 .90
C303 AP84 21c red brown 1.75 .90
C304 AP84 21c magenta 1.75 .90
C305 AP84 21c red 1.75 .90
C306 AP84 21c orange red 1.75 .90
C307 AP84 21c blue 1.75 .90
C308 AP84 21c brown 1.75 .90
C309 AP84 21c green 1.75 .90
C310 AP84 21c violet bl 1.75 .90
C311 AP84 21c dk slate grn 1.75 .90
C312 AP84 21c violet 1.75 .90
C313 AP84 21c black 1.75 .90
C314 AP84 21c emerald 1.75 .90
C315 AP84 21c dp violet 1.75 .90
C316 AP84 21c olive grn 1.75 .90
C317 AP84 21c carmine rose 1.75 .90
C318 AP84 21c Prus green 1.75 .90
C319 AP84 21c dark brown 1.75 .90
C320 AP84 1b dark blue 9.00 5.00
C321 AP84 2b yellow green 17.50 9.00
a. Souv. sheet of 6 18.00 15.00
Nos. C300-C321 (22) 61.50 32.00

Vatican II, the 21st Ecumenical Council of the Roman Catholic Church.

No. C321a contains 6 imperf. stamps similar to Nos. C300, C303, C305, C315, C320 and C321. Size: 198x138mm. Sold for 3.85b.

For overprints, see Nos. C329C-C329i.

World's Fair, New York — AP84a

5c, 10c, 15c, Various pavilions. 21c, Unisphere.

1964, Sept. 14 Wmk. 311 *Perf. 12½*

C322 AP84a 5c yellow & blk
C323 AP84a 10c red & blk
C324 AP84a 15c green & blk
C325 AP84a 21c ultra & blk
Set, #C322-C325 9.25 3.00

Souvenir Sheet

Perf. 12

C326 AP84a 21c ultra & blk 12.50 6.00

No. C326 contains one 49x35mm stamp. Exists imperf. Value, same as No. C326.

AP84b

Hammarskjold Memorial, UN Day: No. C327, C329a, Dag Hammarskjold. No. C328, C329b, UN emblem.

Perf. 13½x14

1964, Sept. 1 Unwmk.

C327 AP84b 21c black & blue 1.50 .60
C328 AP84b 21c black & blue 1.50 .60

Souvenir Sheet

Imperf

C329 Sheet of 2 7.75 6.75
a.-b. AP84b 21c blk & grn, any single 1.25 1.25

Nos. C327-C328 exist imperf in black and green. Value $5.

Nos. C300//C321a Overprinted "1964"

1964, Sept. 28

C329C AP84 21c olive (#C300) 1.30 .75
C329D AP84 21c red (#C305) 1.30 .75
C329E AP84 21c grn (#C309) 1.30 .75
C329F AP84 21c dk brn (#C319) 1.30 .75
C329G AP84 1b dk blue (#C320) 5.00 3.25
C329H AP84 2b yel grn (#C321) 11.00 7.50
i. Souv. sheet of 6 (#C321a) 80.00 80.00
Nos. C329C-C329H (6) 21.20 13.75

Vatican II, the 21st Ecumenical Council of the Roman Catholic Church, Third Period.

On No. C329i, the original dates are obliterated by a bar, with "1964" and papal arms overprinted below.

The overprint is olive bister on the stamps, yellow on the souvenir sheet. The overprint also exists in yellow gold on the same six stamps and in olive bister on the souvenir sheet. Values: set, $400; souvenir sheet $325.

Roosevelt Type of Regular Issue

Perf. 12x12½

1964, Oct. 9 Litho. Unwmk.

C330 A147 20c grn & blk, *buff* .95 .40
a. Souv. sheet of 2, #455, C330, imperf. 1.50 1.00

AP84c

1964, Sept. 1 *Perf. 13½x14*

C331 AP84c 21c shown 2.50 2.00
C332 AP84c 21c Papal coat of arms 2.50 2.00
a. Souv. sheet of 2, #C331-C332 9.75 5.00

Pope John XXIII (1881-1963). Nos. C331-C332 exist imperf in different colors. Value $20.

Galileo, 400th Birth Anniv. AP84d

21c, Galileo, studies of gravity.

1965, May 12 *Perf. 14*

C333 AP84d 10c blue & multi 5.75 .75
C334 AP84d 21c green & multi 5.75 .75
a. Souv. sheet of 2, #C333-C334 30.00 30.00

Nos. C333-C334a exist imperf in different colors. Value, $11.

Alfred Nobel (1833-1896), Founder of Nobel Prize — AP84e

10c, Peace Medal, rev. 21c, Peace Medal, obv.

1965, May 12 Litho. & Embossed

C335 AP84e 10c multi 2.75 .75
C336 AP84e 21c multi 2.75 .75
a. Souv. sheet of 2, #C335-C336 23.50 23.50

Nos. C335-C336a exist imperf in different colors. Value: $5, set; $23.50, souvenir sheet.

Bird Type of Regular Issue, 1965

Song Birds: 5c, Common troupial, horiz. 10c, Crimson-backed tanager, horiz.

1965, Oct. 27 Unwmk. *Perf. 14*

C337 A148 5c dp org & multi 2.00 .40
C338 A148 10c brt blue & multi 3.50 .40
a. Souv. sheet of 6, #462-462C, C337-C338 24.00 24.00

No. C338a exists imperf. Value, $24.

Fish Type of Regular Issue

Designs: 8c, Shrimp. 12c, Hammerhead. 13c, Atlantic sailfish. 25c, Seahorse, vert.

1965, Dec. 7 Litho.

C339 A149 8c multi .90 .40
C340 A149 12c multi 1.30 .40
C341 A149 13c multi 1.10 .40
C342 A149 25c multi 3.00 .40
a. Souv. sheet of 3, #C340-C342 16.00 16.00
Nos. C339-C342 (4) 6.30 1.60

English Daisy and Emblem AP85

Junior Chamber of Commerce Emblem and: #C344, Hibiscus. #C345, Orchid. #C346, Water lily. #C347, Gladiolus. #C348, Flor del Espiritu Santo.

1966, Mar. 16

C343 AP85 30c brt pink & multi 1.30 .35
C344 AP85 30c salmon & multi 1.30 .35
C345 AP85 30c pale yel & multi 1.30 .35
C346 AP85 40c lt grn & multi 1.80 .35
C347 AP85 40c blue & multi 1.80 .35
C348 AP85 40c pink & multi 1.80 .35
a. Souv. sheet of 2, #C345, C347 30.00 15.00
b. Souv. sheet of 2, #C347, C348 30.00 15.00
Nos. C343-C348 (6) 9.30 2.10

50th anniv. of the Junior Chamber of Commerce. A souvenir sheet containing Nos. C344 and C348, and one containing Nos. C345 and C347, exist.

Nos. C224 and C236 Surcharged

1966, June 27 Wmk. 311 *Perf. 12½*

C349 A130 3c on 5c blk & red brn .80 .40

Wmk. 343

C350 A131 13c on 25c lt & dk bl .80 .40

The old denominations are not obliterated on Nos. C349-C350.

ITU Cent. — AP85a

1966, Aug. 12 *Perf. 13½x14*

C351 AP85a 31c multicolored 5.00 4.75

Souvenir Sheet

Perf. 14

C352 AP85a 31c multicolored 18.00 18.00

No. C352 exists imperf. with blue green background. Value $15.

Animal Type of Regular Issue, 1967

Domestic Animals: 10c, Pekingese dog. 13c, Zebu, horiz. 30c, Cat. 40c, Horse, horiz.

1967, Feb. 3 Unwmk. *Perf. 14*

C353 A150 10c multi 1.60 .40
C354 A150 13c multi 2.40 .40
C355 A150 30c multi 3.50 .40
C356 A150 40c multi 4.50 .40
Nos. C353-C356 (4) 12.00 1.60

Nos. C353 and C355 exist with changed colors in imperforate souvenir sheets of 1.

Young Hare, by Durer — AP86

10c, St. Jerome and the Lion, by Albrecht Durer. 20c, Lady with the Ermine, by Leonardo Da Vinci. 30c, The Hunt, by Delacroix, horiz.

1967, Sept. 1

C357 AP86 10c black, buff & car 1.40 .40
C358 AP86 13c lt yellow & multi 2.25 .40
C359 AP86 20c multicolored 3.00 .40
C360 AP86 30c multicolored 4.75 .40
Nos. C357-C360 (4) 11.40 1.60

Panama-Mexico Friendship AP86a

Designs: 1b, Pres. Gustavo Diaz Ordaz of Mexico and Pres. Marco A. Robles of Panama, horiz.

1968, Jan. 20 *Perf. 14*

C361 AP86a 50c shown 2.25 .60
C361A AP86a 1b multi 4.75 1.10
b. Souv. sheet of 2, #C361-C361A, imperf. 8.25 8.25

For overprints see Nos. C364-C364B.

Souvenir Sheet

Olympic Equestrian Events — AP86b

1968, Oct. 29 *Imperf.*

C362 AP86b Sheet of 2 50.00 40.00
a. 8c Dressage 1.50 1.00
b. 30c Show jumping 5.00 3.50

Intl. Human Rights Year AP86c

1968, Dec. 18 *Perf. 14*

C363 AP86c 40c multicolored 11.50 7.50
a. Miniature sheet of 1 42.00 42.00

Nos. C361-C361b Ovptd. in Red or Black

1969, Jan. 31

C364 AP86a 50c on #C361 (R) 6.75 1.50
C364A AP86a 1b on #C361A (B) 6.75 1.50

Souvenir Sheet

C364B on #C361b (R) 11.75 11.75

Intl. Philatelic and Numismatic Expo.

Overprint larger on No. C364A, larger and in different arrangement on No. C364B.

Intl. Space Exploration AP86d

Designs: a, France, Diadem I. b, Italy, San Marco II. c, Great Britain, UK 3. d, US, Saturn V/Apollo 7. e, US, Surveyor 7. f, Europe/US, Esro 2.

1969, Mar. 14

C365	Sheet of 6	22.50	18.00
a.	AP86d 5c multicolored	.50	.25
b.	AP86d 10c multicolored	1.00	.40
c.	AP86d 15c multicolored	1.50	.50
d.	AP86d 20c multicolored	2.00	.75
e.	AP86d 25c multicolored	3.00	1.00
f.	AP86d 30c multicolored	4.00	1.25

Satellite Transmission of Summer Olympics, Mexico, 1968 AP86e

1969, Mar. 14 ***Perf. 14½***

C366	AP86e 1b multi	11.00	1.00
a.	Miniature sheet of 1	27.00	2.00

Nos. CB4, 461B & 461C Surcharged

1969, Apr. 5 ***Perf. 13½x13***

C367	AP81	5c on 5c+5c	4.00	.50
C367A	A147e	5c on 10c+5c	4.00	.50
C367B	A147e	10c on 21c+10c	4.00	.50

Games Type of Regular Issue and

San Blas Indian Girl — AP87

Design: 13c, Bridge of the Americas.

1970, Jan. 6 **Litho.** ***Perf. 13½***

C368	A158 13c multi	2.00	.30
C369	AP87 30c multi	2.50	.75
a.	"AEREO" omitted	*50.00*	*50.00*

See notes after No. 525.

Juan D. Arosemena and Arosemena Stadium AP88

Designs: 2c, 3c, 5c, like 1c. No. C374, Basketball. No. C375, New Panama Gymnasium. No. C376, Revolution Stadium. No. C377, Panamanian man and woman in Stadium. 30c, Stadium, eternal flame, arms of Mexico, Puerto Rico and Cuba.

1970, Oct. 7 **Wmk. 365** ***Perf. 13½***

C370	AP88	1c pink & multi	.45	.25
C371	AP88	2c pink & multi	.60	.25
C372	AP88	3c pink & multi	.60	.25
C373	AP88	5c pink & multi	.60	.25
C374	AP88	13c lt blue & multi	1.00	.25
C375	AP88	13c lilac & multi	1.00	.25
C376	AP88	13c yellow & multi	1.00	.25
C377	AP88	13c pink & multi	1.00	.25
C378	AP88	30c yellow & multi	3.00	.50
a.		Souv. sheet of 1, imperf.	3.50	3.50
		Nos. C370-C378 (9)	9.25	2.50

11th Central American and Caribbean Games, Feb. 28-Mar. 14.

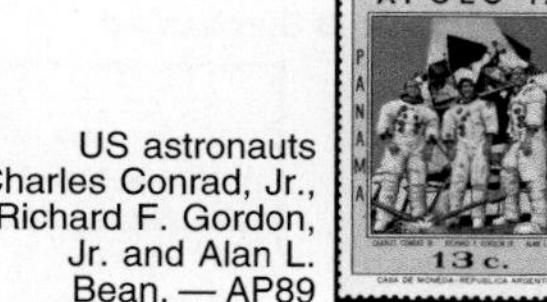

US astronauts Charles Conrad, Jr., Richard F. Gordon, Jr. and Alan L. Bean. — AP89

No. C379, Astronaut on Moon.

1971, Aug. 20 **Wmk. 343** ***Perf. 13½***

C379	AP89 13c gold & multi	1.00	.50
C380	AP89 13c lt green & multi	1.00	.50

Man's first landing on the moon, Apollo 11, July 20, 1969 (No. C379) and Apollo 12 moon mission, Nov. 14-24, 1969.

EXPO '70 Emblem and Pavilion — AP90

1971, Aug. 24 **Litho.**

C381	AP90 10c pink & multi	1.00	.40

EXPO '70 International Exposition, Osaka, Japan, Mar. 15-Sept. 13.

Flag of Panama AP91

Design: 13c, Map of Panama superimposed on Western Hemisphere, and tourist year emblem.

1971, Dec. 11 **Wmk. 343**

C382	AP91 5c multi	.95	.45
C383	AP91 13c multi	.95	.45

Proclamation of 1972 as Tourist Year of the Americas.

Mahatma Gandhi — AP92

1971, Dec. 17

C384	AP92 10c black & multi	*60.00*	*25.00*

Centenary of the birth of Mohandas K. Gandhi (1869-1948), leader in India's fight for independence.

Central American Independence Issue

Flags of Central American States — AP92a

1971, Dec. 20

C385	AP92a 13c multi	.85	.40

160th anniv. of Central America independence.

AP93

1971, Dec. 21

C386	AP93 8c Panama #4	.80	.40

2nd National Philatelic and Numismatic Exposition, 1970.

AP94

1972, Sept. 7 **Wmk. 365**

C387	AP94 40c Natá Church	1.25	.80

450th anniversary of the founding of Natá. For surcharges see Nos. C402, RA85.

Telecommunications Emblem — AP95

1972, Sept. 8

C388	AP95 13c lt bl, dp bl & blk	1.00	.40

3rd World Telecommunications Day (in 1971).

Apollo 14 — AP96

1972, Sept. 11

C389	AP96 13c tan & multi	1.30	.50

Apollo 14 US moon mission, 1/1-2/9/71.

Shoeshine Boy Counting Coins — AP97

1972, Sept. 12

C390	AP97	5c shown	.55	.25
C391	AP97	8c Mother & Child	.55	.25
C392	AP97	50c UNICEF emblem	2.50	.55
a.		Souv. sheet of 1, imperf.	4.75	2.50
		Nos. C390-C392 (3)	3.60	1.05

25th anniv. (in 1971) of the UNICEF.

San Blas Cloth, Cuna Indians — AP98

8c, Beaded necklace, Guaymi Indians. 25c, View of Portobelo.

1972, Sept. 13

C393	AP98	5c multicolored	.50	.25
C394	AP98	8c multicolored	.50	.25
C395	AP98	25c multicolored	4.50	.45
a.		Souv. sheet of 2, #C393, C395, imperf.	5.00	3.50
		Nos. C393-C395 (3)	5.50	.95

Tourist publicity.
For surcharges see Nos. C417, RA83.

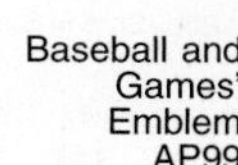

Baseball and Games' Emblem AP99

Games' Emblem and: 10c, Basketball, vert. 13c, Torch, vert. 25c, Boxing. 50c, Map and flag of Panama, Bolivar. 1b, Medals.

Perf. 12½

1973, Feb. 10 **Litho.** **Unwmk.**

C396	AP99	8c rose red & yel	.40	.30
C397	AP99	10c black & ultra	.40	.30
C398	AP99	13c blue & multi	.70	.70
C399	AP99	25c blk, yel grn & red	1.20	.75
C400	AP99	50c green & multi	2.60	1.75
C401	AP99	1b multicolored	5.50	2.75
		Nos. C396-C401 (6)	10.80	6.55

7th Bolivar Games, Panama City, 2/17-3/3.

No. C387 Surcharged in Red Similar to No. 542

1973, Mar. 15 **Wmk. 365** ***Perf. 13½***

C402	AP94 13c on 40c multi	1.00	.30

UN Security Council Meeting, Panama City, Mar. 15-21.

Portrait Type of Regular Issue 1973

Designs: 5c, Isabel Herrera Obaldia, educator. 8c, Nicolas Victoria Jaén, educator. 10c, Forest Scene, by Roberto Lewis. No. C406, Portrait of a Lady, by Manuel E. Amador. No. C407, Ricardo Miró, poet. 20c, Portrait, by Isaac Benitez. 21c, Manuel Amador Guerrero, statesman. 25c, Belisario Porras, statesman. 30c, Juan Demostenes Arosemena, statesman. 34c, Octavio Mendez Pereira, writer. 38c, Ricardo J. Alfaro, writer.

1973, June 20 **Litho.** ***Perf. 13½***

C403	A169	5c pink & multi	.55	.25
C404	A169	8c pink & multi	.55	.25
C405	A169	10c gray & multi	.80	.25
C406	A169	13c pink & multi	1.40	.25
C407	A169	13c pink & multi	1.40	.25
C408	A169	20c blue & multi	1.50	.40
C409	A169	21c yellow & multi	1.60	.40
C410	A169	25c pink & multi	1.90	.40
C411	A169	30c gray & multi	2.25	.45
C412	A169	34c lt blue & multi	2.40	.60
C413	A169	38c lt blue & multi	4.00	.60
		Nos. C403-C413 (11)	18.35	4.10

Famous Panamanians.
For overprints and surcharges see Nos. C414-C416, C418-C421.

Nos. C403, C410, and C412 Overprinted in Black or Red

1973, Sept. 14 **Litho.** ***Perf. 13½***

C414	A169	5c pink & multi	.45	.25
C415	A169	25c pink & multi	1.50	.45
C416	A169	34c bl & multi (R)	1.75	.75
		Nos. C414-C416 (3)	3.70	1.45

50th anniversary of the Isabel Herrera Obaldia Professional School.

Nos. C395, C408, C413, C412 and C409 Surcharged in Red

1974, Nov. 11 **Litho.** ***Perf. 13½***

C417	AP98	1c on 25c multi	.80	.25
C418	A169	3c on 20c multi	.80	.25
C419	A169	8c on 38c multi	.80	.25
C420	A169	10c on 34c multi	.80	.25
C421	A169	13c on 21c multi	.80	.25
		Nos. C417-C421 (5)	4.00	1.25

Women's Hands, Panama Map, UN and IWY Emblems — AP100

Perf. 12½

1975, May 6 Litho. Unwmk.

C422 AP100 17c blue & multi 1.10 .40
 a. Souv. sheet, typo., imperf., no gum 2.50 2.00

International Women's Year 1975.

Victoria Sugar Plant, Sugar Cane, Map of Veraguas Province — AP101

Designs: 17c, Bayano electrification project and map of Panama, horiz. 33c, Tocumen International Airport and map, horiz.

1975, Oct. 9 Litho. *Perf. 12½*

C423 AP101 17c bl, buff & blk .85 .35
C424 AP101 27c ultra & yel grn 1.20 .45
C425 AP101 33c bl & multi 1.30 .45
 Nos. C423-C425 (3) 3.35 1.25

Oct. 11, 1968, Revolution, 7th anniv.

Bolivar Statue and Flags — AP102

Bolivar Hall, Panama City — AP103

Design: 41c, Bolivar with flag of Panama, ruins of Old Panama City.

1976, Mar.

C426 AP102 23c multi 1.00 .25
C427 AP103 35c multi 1.75 .30
C428 AP102 41c multi 1.75 .60
 Nos. C426-C428 (3) 4.50 1.15

150th anniversary of Congress of Panama. Issued: 23c, Mar. 5; others Mar. 30.

Marine Life Type of 1976

Marine life: 17c, Diodon hystrix, vert. 27c, Pocillopora damicornis.

Perf. 13x12½, 12½x13

1976, May 6 Litho. Wmk. 377

C429 A171 17c multi 2.40 .50
C430 A171 27c multi 3.25 .65

Cerro Colorado AP104

1976, Nov. 12 Litho. *Perf. 12½*

C431 AP104 23c multi 1.00 .40

Cerro Colorado copper mines, Chiriqui Province.

Gen. Omar Torrijos Herrera (1929-1981) — AP105

1982, Feb. 13 Litho. *Perf. 10½*

C432 AP105 23c multi 1.30 .40

Torrijos Type of 1982

35c, Security Council reunion, 1973. 41c, Torrijos Airport.

Wmk. 311

1982, May 14 Litho. *Perf. 10½*

C433 A201 35c multicolored 1.60 .30
C434 A201 41c multicolored 2.25 .50

Souvenir Sheet

Imperf

C435 A201 23c like #C432 4.50 3.00

No. C435 sold for 1b.

Alfaro Type of 1982

Photos by Luiz Gutierrez Cruz.

1982, Aug. 18 Wmk. 382

C436 A202 17c multi 1.30 .25
C437 A202 23c multi 1.50 .25

World Cup Type of 1982

1982, Dec. 27 Litho. *Perf. 10½*

C438 A203 23c Map 1.10 .25
C439 A203 35c Pele, vert. 1.60 .30
C440 A203 41c Cup, vert. 2.00 .40
 Nos. C438-C440 (3) 4.70 .95

1b imperf. souvenir sheet exists in design of 23c; black control number. Size; 85x75mm. Value $13.50.

Nicolas A. Solano (1882-1943), Tuberculosis Researcher — AP106

Wmk. 382 (Stars)

1983, Feb. 8 Litho. *Perf. 10½*

C441 AP106 23c brown 1.20 .40

World Food Day — AP107

1984, Oct. 16 Litho. *Perf. 12*

C442 AP107 30c Hand grasping fork 1.75 .50

Contadora Group for Peace — AP108

1985, Oct. 1 Litho. *Perf. 14*

C443 AP108 10c multi 1.75 .30
C444 AP108 20c multi 2.10 .35
C445 AP108 30c multi 3.00 .50
 Nos. C443-C445 (3) 6.85 1.15

See No. 680A.

Christmas Type of 1988

1988, Dec. 29 Litho. *Perf. 12*

C446 A246 35c St. Joseph and the Infant 1.60 .40

Olympics Type of 1989

1989, Mar. 17 Litho. *Perf. 12*

C447 A248 35c Boxing 1.60 .40

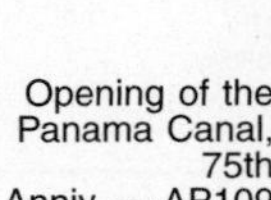

Opening of the Panama Canal, 75th Anniv. — AP109

35c, Ancon in lock, 1914. 60c, Ship in lock, 1989.

1989, Sept. 29 Litho. *Perf. 13½*

C448 AP109 35c multicolored 1.60 .65
C449 AP109 60c multicolored 2.50 1.10

Revolution Type of 1989

1989, Nov. 14 Litho.

C450 A251 35c Storming of the Bastille 2.25 .65
C451 A251 45c Anniv. emblem 2.75 .85

French revolution, bicent.

Christmas 2001 — AP110

Designs: 60c, Man, woman, drums. 1b, Guitar, drum, candle. 2b, Pots, potted plant.

2002, Apr. 30 Litho. *Perf. 13x13¼*

C452-C454 AP110 Set of 3 16.00 15.00

Dated 2001.

La Salle Schools in Panama, Cent. (in 2002) — AP111

2003, May 15 Litho. *Perf. 13x13½*

C455 AP111 5b multi 16.00 10.00

Dated 2002.

Natá, 480th Anniv. (in 2002) — AP112

2003, May 20

C456 AP112 1b multi 3.75 2.00

Dated 2002.

Trains — AP113

Designs: 40c, Colón locomotive. 50c, Panama Railroad, vert.

Perf. 13x13½, 14 (50c)

2003, July 17

C457-C458 AP113 Set of 2 5.00 2.50

Dated 2002.

Santa María de Belén, 500th Anniv. — AP114

2003, July 31 *Perf. 14*

C459 AP114 1.50b multi 5.50 3.00

Dated 2002.

Fourth Voyage of Christopher Columbus, 500th Anniv. (in 2002) — AP115

2003, July 31 *Perf. 13x13½*

C460 AP115 2b multi 7.25 4.00

Dated 2002.

Kuna Indians — AP116

Designs: No. C461, 50c, Village, people in canoe, woman. No. C462, 50c, Man and woman, vert. No. C463, 60c, Woman sewing. No. C464, 60c, Dancers.
1.50b, Fish.

Perf. 14 (#C461), 13½x13 (#C462), 13x13½

2003, Aug. 13

C461-C464 AP116 Set of 4 9.00 5.00

Souvenir Sheet

Perf. 13½x14

C465 AP116 1.50b multi 8.00 5.75

Dated 2002. No. C465 contains one 50x45mm stamp.

Medicine in Panama AP117

Designs: No. C466, 50c, Santo Tomás de Villanueva Hospital, 300th anniv. No. C467, 50c, Gorgas Memorial Institute of Tropical and Preventative Medicine, 75th anniv.

2003 *Perf. 12*

C466-C467 AP117 Set of 2 4.25 3.25

Issued: No. C466, 12/17; No. C467, 11/17.

Jewelry — AP118

Designs: 45c, Necklaces. 60c, Brooches.

2003, Nov. 24

C468-C469 AP118 Set of 2 4.25 3.25

For surcharges, see Nos. C474-C475.

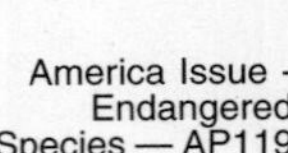

America Issue - Endangered Species — AP119

2003, Nov. 26

C470 AP119 2b multi 7.00 6.50

La Estrella de Panama Newspaper, 150th Anniv. — AP120

2003, Dec. 3

C471 AP120 40c multi 1.75 1.40

Scouting, Cent. — AP121

2010, Sept. 3 Litho. *Perf. 14*

C472 AP121 20c multi 1.10 .60

Printed in sheets of 4.

Salesian Order in Panama, Cent. — AP122

2010, Aug. 27

C473 AP122 20c multi 1.10 .80

No. C468 Surcharged

No. C474

No. C475

Methods and Perfs. As Before

2014

C474 AP118 15c on 45c #C468 1.10 .30
C475 AP118 30c on 45c #C468 2.40 .60

Issued: No. C474, 6/25; No. C475, 6/11.

Ships AP123

No. C476: a, MSC Oscar. b, Carnival Horizon. c, Drive Green. d, Ship of COSCO fleet. e, Ship of EMAS fleet. f, Navios Coral.

2019, June 19 Litho. *Perf. 14¼*

C476 AP123 35c Block of 6, #a-f 7.00 4.25

Panamanian ship registry, 102nd anniv.

AIR POST SEMI-POSTAL STAMPS

Catalogue values for unused stamps in this section are for Never Hinged items.

"The World Against Malaria" — SPAP1

Wmk. 311

1961, Dec. 20 Litho. *Perf. 12½*

CB1 SPAP1 5c + 5c car rose 1.00 .50
CB2 SPAP1 10c + 10c vio bl 1.00 .50
CB3 SPAP1 15c + 15c dk grn 1.00 .50
Nos. CB1-CB3 (3) 3.00 1.50

WHO drive to eradicate malaria.
For surcharges see Nos. C271-C272.

Nos. C274-C276 Surcharged in Red

Wmk. 311

1963, Mar. 4 Litho. *Perf. 12½*

CB4 AP81 5c +5c on #C274 1.50 .75
CB5 AP81 10c +10c on #C275 3.00 1.50
CB6 AP81 15c +31c on #C276 3.00 1.50

Surcharge on No. CB4 differs to fit stamp. See No. CB7.

No. CB4 Surcharged in Black

1963, Aug. 22

CB7 AP81 10c on 5c+5c 7.00 5.00

Intl. Red. Cross cent.

SPECIAL DELIVERY STAMPS

Nos. 211-212 Overprinted in Red

1926 Unwmk. *Perf. 12*

E1 A31 10c org & blk 7.50 3.25
  a. "EXRPESO" 40.00
E2 A32 20c brn & blk 10.00 3.25
  a. "EXRPESO" 40.00
  b. Double overprint 35.00 35.00

Bicycle Messenger — SD1

1929, Feb. 8 Engr. *Perf. 12½*

E3 SD1 10c orange 1.25 1.00
E4 SD1 20c dk brn 4.75 2.50

For surcharges and overprints see Nos. C1-C5, C17-C18A, C67.

REGISTRATION STAMPS

Issued under Colombian Dominion

R1

1888 Unwmk. Engr. *Perf. 13½*

F1 R1 10c black, *gray* 8.00 5.25

Imperforate and part-perforate examples without gum and those on surface-colored paper are reprints.

Magenta, Violet or Blue Black Handstamped Overprint

1898 *Perf. 12*

F2 A4 10c orange 7.00 6.50

The handstamp on No. F2 was also used as a postmark.

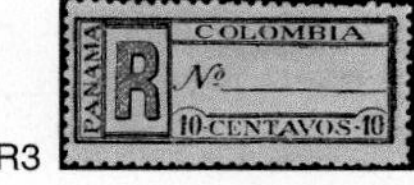

R3

1900 Litho. *Perf. 11*

F3 R3 10c blk, *lt bl* 4.00 3.50

1901

F4 R3 10c brown red 30.00 20.00

R4

1902 Blue Black Surcharge

F5 R4 20c on 10c brn red 20.00 16.00

Issues of the Republic Issued in the City of Panama

Registration Stamps of Colombia Handstamped in Violet, Blue Black or Rose

1903-04 *Imperf.*

F6 R9 20c red brn, *bl* 45.00 42.50
F7 R9 20c blue, *blue* (R) 45.00 42.50

For surcharges and overprints see Nos. F8-F11, F16-F26.

Reprints exist of Nos. F6 and F7; see note after No. 64.

With Additional Surcharge in Rose

F8 R9 10c on 20c red brn, *bl* 60.00 55.00
  b. "10" in blue black 60.00 55.00
F9 R9 10c on 20c bl, *bl* 60.00 45.00

Handstamped in Rose

F10 R9 10c on 20c red brn, *bl* 60.00 55.00
F11 R9 10c on 20c blue, *blue* 45.00 42.50

Issued in Colon

Regular Issues Handstamped "R/COLON" in Circle (as on F2) Together with Other Overprints and Surcharges

Handstamped

1903-04 *Perf. 12*

F12 A4 10c orange 3.00 2.50

Handstamped

F13 A4 10c orange 22.50

Overprinted in Red

F14 A4 10c orange 3.00 2.50

Overprinted in Black

F15 A4 10c orange 7.50 5.00

The handstamps on Nos. F12 to F15 are in magenta, violet or red; various combinations of these colors are to be found. They are struck in various positions, including double, inverted, one handstamp omitted, etc.

Colombia No. F13 Handstamped Like No. F12 in Violet

Imperf

F16 R9 20c red brn, *bl* 60.00 55.00

Overprinted Like No. F15 in Black

F17 R9 20c red brn, *bl* 6.00 5.75

No. F17 Surcharged in Manuscript

F18 R9 10c on 20c red brn, *bl* 60.00 55.00

No. F17 Surcharged in Purple **10**

F19 R9 10c on 20c 82.50 80.00

No. F17 Surcharged in Violet

F20 R9 10c on 20c 82.50 80.00

The varieties of the overprint which are described after No. 138 are also to be found on the Registration and Acknowledgment of Receipt stamps. It is probable that Nos. F17 to F20 inclusive owe their existence more to speculation than to postal necessity.

Issued in Bocas del Toro

Colombia Nos. F17 and F13 Handstamped in Violet

1903-04

F21 R9 20c blue, *blue* 125.00 125.00
F22 R9 20c red brn, *bl* 125.00 125.00

No. F21 Surcharged in Manuscript in Violet or Red

F23 R9 10c on 20c bl, *bl* 150.00 140.00

Colombia Nos. F13, F17 Handstamped in Violet

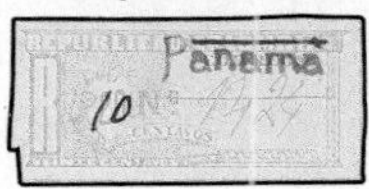

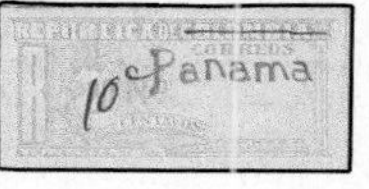

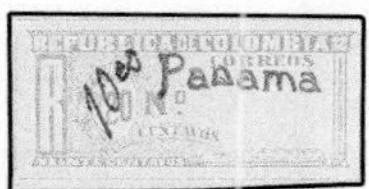

Surcharged in Manuscript "10", "10c", "10cs" in Red

F25 R9 10c on 20c red brn, *bl* 70.00 65.00
F26 R9 10c on 20c bl, *bl* 55.00 50.00
Nos. F21-F26 (5) 525.00 505.00

No. F25 without surcharge is bogus, according to leading experts.

General Issue

R5

1904, Aug. 1 Engr. *Perf. 12*

F27 R5 10c green 1.00 .50

Nos. 190 and 213 Surcharged in Red

#F29

#F29b

#F30

1916-17

F29 A11 5c on 8c pur & blk 3.00 2.25
  a. "5" inverted 75.00
  b. Large, round "5" 50.00
  c. Inverted surcharge 12.50 11.00
  d. Tête bêche surcharge
  e. Pair, one without surcharge 10.00
F30 A33 5c on 8c vio & blk 3.50 .80
  a. Inverted surcharge 13.00 8.25
  b. Tête bêche surcharge
  c. Double surcharge 60.00

Issued: No. F29, 1/1/16; No. F30, 1/28/17.

Stamps similar to No. F30, overprinted in green were unauthorized.

INSURED LETTER STAMPS

Stamps of 1939 Surcharged in Black

1942, Nov. 14 Unwmk. *Perf. 12½*

G1	AP23	5c on 1b blk	.75	.50
G2	A84	10c on 1b dk brn	1.25	.80
G3	AP23	25c on 50c dk brn	3.00	2.00
		Nos. G1-G3 (3)	5.00	3.30

ACKNOWLEDGMENT OF RECEIPT STAMPS

Issued under Colombian Dominion

Experts consider this handstamp- "A.R. / COLON / COLOMBIA"-to be a cancellation or a marking intended for a letter to receive special handling. It was applied at Colon to various stamps in 1897-1904 in different colored inks for philatelic sale. It exists on cover, usually with the bottom line removed by masking the handstamp.

Nos. 17-18 Handstamped in Rose

1902

H4	A4	5c blue	5.00	5.00
H5	A4	10c yellow	10.00	10.00

This handstamp was also used as a postmark.

Issues of the Republic Issued in the City of Panama

Colombia No. H3 Handstamped in Rose

1903-04 Unwmk. *Imperf.*

H9	AR2	10c blue, *blue*	10.00	8.00

Reprints exist of No. H9, see note after No. 64.

No. H9 Surcharged

H10	AR2	5c on 10c bl, *bl*	10.00	5.00

Colombia No. H3 Handstamped in Rose

H11	AR2	10c blue, *blue*	17.50	14.00

Issued in Colon

Handstamped in Magenta or Violet

Imperf

H17	AR2	10c blue, *blue*	15.00	15.00

Handstamped

H18	AR2	10c blue, *blue*	82.50	70.00

Overprinted in Black

H19	AR2	10c blue, *blue*	11.00	8.00

No. H19 Surcharged in Manuscript

H20	AR2	10c on 5c on 10c	100.00	82.50

Issued in Bocas del Toro

Colombia No. H3 Handstamped in Violet and Surcharged in Manuscript in Red Like Nos. F25-F26

1904

H21	AR2	5c on 10c blue, *blue*		

No. H21, unused, without surcharge is bogus.

General Issue

AR3

1904, Aug. 1 Engr. *Perf. 12*

H22	AR3	5c blue	1.00	.80

No. 199 Overprinted in Violet

1916, Jan. 1

H23	A20	2½c red orange	1.00	.80
a.		"R.A." for "A.R."	50.00	
b.		Double overprint	8.00	
c.		Inverted overprint	8.00	

LATE FEE STAMPS

Issues of the Republic Issued in the City of Panama

Colombia No. I4 Handstamped in Rose or Blue Black

LF3

REPUBLICA DE PANAMA

1903-04 Unwmk. *Imperf.*

I1	LF3	5c pur, *rose*	12.50	9.00
I2	LF3	5c pur, *rose* (Bl Blk)	17.50	12.50

Reprints exist of #I1-I2; see note after #64.

General Issue

LF4

1904 Engr. *Perf. 12*

I3	LF4	2½c lake	1.00	.65

No. 199 Overprinted with Typewriter

1910, Aug. 12

I4	A20	2½c red orange	125.00	100.00

Used only on Aug. 12-13.
Counterfeits abound.

Handstamped

1910

I5	A20	2½c red orange	60.00	50.00

Counterfeits abound.

No. 195 Surcharged in Green

1917, Jan. 1

I6	A17	1c on ½c orange	.80	.80
a.		"UN CENTESIMO" inverted	50.00	
b.		Double surcharge	12.50	
c.		Inverted surcharge	10.00	10.00

No. 196 Surcharged in Green

1921

I7	A17	1c on ½c rose	25.00	20.00

POSTAGE DUE STAMPS

San Lorenzo Castle Gate, Mouth of Chagres River
D1

Statue of Columbus
D2

Pedro J. Sosa — D4

Design: 4c, Capitol, Panama City.

Unwmk.

1915, Mar. 25 Engr. *Perf. 12*

J1	D1	1c olive brown	3.50	.75
J2	D2	2c olive brown	5.25	.65
J3	D1	4c olive brown	7.25	1.25
J4	D4	10c olive brown	5.25	1.75
		Nos. J1-J4 (4)	21.25	4.40

Type D1 was intended to show a gate of San Lorenzo Castle, Chagres, and is so inscribed.

D5

1930, Dec. 30 *Perf. 12½*

J5	D5	1c emerald	1.00	.60
J6	D5	2c dark red	1.00	.60
J7	D5	4c dark blue	1.60	.80
J8	D5	10c violet	1.60	.80
		Nos. J5-J8 (4)	5.20	2.80

POSTAL TAX STAMPS

Pierre and Marie Curie — PT1

Unwmk.

1939, June 15 Engr. *Perf. 12*

RA1	PT1	1c rose carmine	.65	.40
RA2	PT1	1c green	.65	.40
RA3	PT1	1c orange	.65	.40
RA4	PT1	1c blue	.65	.40
		Nos. RA1-RA4 (4)	2.60	1.60
		Set, never hinged	3.90	

See Nos. RA6-RA18, RA24-RA27, RA30.

Stamp of 1924 Overprinted in Black

1940, Dec. 20

RA5	A53	1c dark green	1.40	.75
		Never hinged	2.40	

1941, Jan. 30 Inscribed 1940

RA6	PT1	1c rose carmine	.65	.40
RA7	PT1	1c green	.65	.40
RA8	PT1	1c orange	.65	.40
RA9	PT1	1c blue	.65	.40
		Nos. RA6-RA9 (4)	2.60	1.60
		Set, never hinged	3.90	

1942 Inscribed 1942

RA10	PT1	1c violet	.40	.40
		Never hinged	.65	

1943 Inscribed 1943

RA11	PT1	1c rose carmine	.40	.40
RA12	PT1	1c green	.40	.40
RA13	PT1	1c orange	.40	.40
RA14	PT1	1c blue	.40	.40
		Nos. RA11-RA14 (4)	1.60	1.60
		Set, never hinged	2.60	

1945 Inscribed 1945

RA15	PT1	1c rose carmine	.90	.40
RA16	PT1	1c green	.90	.40
RA17	PT1	1c orange	.90	.40
RA18	PT1	1c blue	.90	.40
		Nos. RA15-RA18 (4)	3.60	1.60
		Set, never hinged	5.40	

Nos. 234 and 235 Surcharged in Black or Red

1946 Unwmk. *Perf. 12*

RA19	A53	1c on ½c orange	.60	.40
RA20	A53	1c on 1c dk grn (R)	.60	.40
		Set, never hinged	2.00	

Catalogue values for unused stamps in this section, from this point to the end of the section, are for Never Hinged items.

Nos. 239 and 241 Surcharged in Black

1947, Apr. 7

RA21	A53	1c on 12c ol grn	1.50	.40
RA22	A53	1c on 24c yel brn	1.50	.40

Surcharged in Red on No. 342

RA23 A95 1c on ½c dl vio, bl & car 1.50 .40

Type of 1939
Inscribed 1947

1947, July 21

RA24 PT1 1c rose carmine 1.75 .40
RA25 PT1 1c green 1.75 .40
RA26 PT1 1c orange 1.75 .40
RA27 PT1 1c blue 1.75 .40
Nos. RA24-RA27 (4) 7.00 1.60

Nos. C100 and C101 Surcharged in Black

a

b

1949, Feb. 16 Unwmk. *Perf. 12½*

RA28 AP45 (a) 1c on 5c 1.10 .40
a. Inverted surcharge 15.00
RA29 AP46 (b) 1c on 10c yel org 1.10 .40
a. Inverted surcharge —

Type of 1939

1949 Inscribed 1949 *Perf. 12*

RA30 PT1 1c brown 2.50 .40

The tax from the sale of Nos. RA1-RA30 was used for the control of cancer.

Juan D. Arosemena Stadium PT2

Torch Emblem PT3

No. RA33, Adan Gordon Olympic Swimming Pool.

1951 Unwmk. Engr. *Perf. 12½*

RA31 PT2 1c carmine & blk 2.10 .40
RA32 PT3 1c dk bl & blk 2.10 .40
RA33 PT2 1c grn & blk 2.10 .40
Nos. RA31-RA33 (3) 6.30 1.20

Issued: No. RA31, 2/21; No. RA32, 7/12; No. RA33, 12/13.

Discobolus — PT4

No. RA34, Turners' emblem.

1952

RA34 PT3 1c org & blk 2.10 .40
RA35 PT4 1c pur & blk 2.10 .40

Issued: No. RA34, 4/18; No. RA35, 9/10.

The tax from the sale of Nos. RA31-RA35 was used to promote physical education.

Boys Doing Farm Work — PT5

Wmk. 311

1958, Jan. 24 Litho. *Perf. 12½*
Size: 35x24mm

RA36 PT5 1c rose red & gray .80 .40

Type of 1958
Inscribed 1959

1959 Size: 35x24mm

RA37 PT5 1c gray & emerald .80 .40
RA38 PT5 1c vio bl & gray .80 .40

Issued: No. RA37, 4/8; No. RA38, 9/28.

Type of 1958
Inscribed 1960
Wmk. 334

1960, July 20 Litho. *Perf. 13½*
Size: 32x23mm

RA39 PT5 1c carmine & gray .80 .40

Nos. C235 and C241 Surcharged in Black or Red

1961, May 24 Wmk. 343 *Perf. 12½*

RA40 A131 1c on 10c ocher & blk .80 .40
RA41 AP76 1c on 10c emer (R) .80 .40

Girl at Sewing Machine — PT6

Wmk. 343

1961, Nov. 24 Litho. *Perf. 12½*

RA42 PT6 1c brt vio .80 .40
RA43 PT6 1c rose lilac .80 .40
RA44 PT6 1c yellow .80 .40
RA45 PT6 1c blue .80 .40
RA46 PT6 1c emerald .80 .40
Nos. RA42-RA46 (5) 4.00 2.00

1961, Dec. 1

Design: Boy with hand saw.

RA47 PT6 1c red lilac .80 .40
RA48 PT6 1c rose .80 .40
RA49 PT6 1c orange .80 .40
RA50 PT6 1c blue .80 .40
RA51 PT6 1c gray .80 .40
Nos. RA47-RA51 (5) 4.00 2.00

Boy Scout — PT7

Designs: Nos. RA57-RA61, Girl Scout.

1964, Feb. 7 Wmk. 343

RA52 PT7 1c olive .80 .40
RA53 PT7 1c gray .80 .40
RA54 PT7 1c lilac .80 .40
RA55 PT7 1c carmine rose .80 .40
RA56 PT7 1c blue .80 .40
RA57 PT7 1c bluish green .80 .40
RA58 PT7 1c violet .80 .40
RA59 PT7 1c orange .80 .40
RA60 PT7 1c yellow .80 .40
RA61 PT7 1c brn org .80 .40
Nos. RA52-RA61 (10) 8.00 4.00

The tax from Nos. RA36-RA61 was for youth rehabilitation.

Map of Panama, Flags — PT8

1973, Jan. 22 Unwmk.

RA62 PT8 1c black .80 .40

7th Bolivar Sports Games, Feb. 17-Mar. 3, 1973. The tax was for a new post office in Panama City.

Post Office — PT9

Designs: No. RA63, Farm Cooperative. No. RA64, 5b silver coin. No. RA65, Victoriano Lorenzo. No. RA66, RA69, Cacique Urraca. No. RA67, RA70, Post Office.

1973-75

RA63 PT9 1c brt yel grn & ver .95 .40
RA64 PT9 1c gray & red .95 .40
RA65 PT9 1c ocher & red .95 .40
RA66 PT9 1c org & red .95 .40
RA67 PT9 1c bl & red .95 .40
RA68 PT9 1c blue ('74) .95 .40
RA69 PT9 1c orange ('74) .95 .40
RA70 PT9 1c vermilion ('75) .95 .40
Nos. RA63-RA70 (8) 7.60 3.20

Issued: No. RA63, 3/19; No. RA64, 6/4; No. RA65, 6/6; No. RA66, 8/16; No. RA67, 8/17; Nos. RA68-RA69, 4/9/74; No. RA70, 11/24/75.

The tax was for a new post office in Panama City.

Stamps of 1969-1973 Surcharged in Violet Blue, Yellow, Black or Carmine

1975, Sept. 3

RA75 A168 1c on 1c (#538; VB) .95 .40
RA76 A168 1c on 2c (#539; Y) .95 .40
RA77 A164 1c on 30c (#534; B) .95 .40
RA78 A157 1c on 30c (#511; B) .95 .40
RA79 A156 1c on 40c (#514; B) .95 .40
RA80 A156 1c on 50c (#515; B) .95 .40
RA81 A169 1c on 20c (#C408; C) .95 .40
RA82 A169 1c on 25c (#C410; B) .95 .40
RA83 AP98 1c on 25c (#C395; B) .95 .40
RA84 A169 1c on 30c (#C411; B) .95 .40
RA85 AP94 1c on 40c (#C387; C) .95 .40
Nos. RA75-RA85 (11) 10.45 4.40

The tax was for a new post office in Panama City. Surcharge vertical, reading down on No. RA75 and up on Nos. RA76, RA78 and RA83. Nos. RA75-RA85 were obligatory on all mail.

PT10

No. RA86, Boys. No. RA87, Boy and chicks. RA88, Working in fields. RA89, Boys feeding piglet.

1980, Dec. 3 Litho. *Perf. 12*

RA86 PT10 2c multi .80 .40
RA87 PT10 2c multi .80 .40
RA88 PT10 2c multi .80 .40
RA89 PT10 2c multi .80 .40
a. Souv. sheet of 4, #RA86-RA89 13.00
b. Block of 4, #RA86-RA89 3.20

Tax was for Children's Village (Christmas 1980). #RA89a sold for 1b.

PT11

1981, Nov. 1 Litho. *Perf. 12*

RA90 PT11 2c Boy, pony .80 .40
RA91 PT11 2c Nativity .80 .40
RA92 PT11 2c Tree .80 .40
RA93 PT11 2c Church .80 .40
a. Block of 4, #RA90-RA93 3.20

Souvenir Sheet

RA94 Sheet of 4 14.00
a.-d. PT11 2c, Children's drawings

Tax was for Children's Village. No. RA94 sold for 5b.

PT12

1982, Nov. 1 Litho. *Perf. 13½x12½*

RA95 PT12 2c Carpentry .80 .40
RA96 PT12 2c Beekeeping .80 .40
a. Pair, #RA95-RA96 1.60
RA97 PT12 2c Pig farming, vert. .80 .40
RA98 PT12 2c Gardening, vert. .80 .40
a. Pair, #RA97-RA98 1.60

Tax was for Children's Village (Christmas 1982).

Two imperf souvenir sheets solf for 2B each. Value, each $17.

Children's Drawings — PT13

No. RA99, Annunciation. No. RA100, Bethlehem and Star. No. RA101, Church and Houses. No. RA102, Flight into Egypt.

1983, Nov. 1 Litho. *Perf. 14½*

RA99 PT13 2c multicolored .80 .40
RA100 PT13 2c multicolored .80 .40
RA101 PT13 2c multicolored .80 .40
RA102 PT13 2c multicolored .80 .40
Nos. RA99-RA102 (4) 3.20 1.60

Nos. RA100-RA102 are vert.

Souvenir sheets exist showing undenominated designs of Nos. RA99, RA101 and Nos. RA100, RA102 respectively. They sold for 2b each. Value $10.50 each.

Boy — PT14

1984, Nov. 1 Litho. *Perf. 12x12½*

RA103 PT14 2c White-collared shirt .80 .40
RA104 PT14 2c T-shirt .80 .40
RA105 PT14 2c Checked shirt .80 .40
RA106 PT14 2c Scout uniform .80 .40
a. Block of 4, #RA103-RA106 3.20

Tax was for Children's Village. An imperf. souvenir sheet sold for 2b, with designs similar to Nos. RA103-RA106, exists. Value $11.

Christmas 1985 — PT15

Inscriptions: No. RA107, "Ciudad del Nino es . . . mi vida." No. RA108, "Feliz Navidad." No. RA109, "Feliz Ano Nuevo." No. RA110, "Gracias."

1985, Dec. 10 Litho. *Perf. 13½x13*

RA107 PT15 2c multi .80 .40
RA108 PT15 2c multi .80 .40
RA109 PT15 2c multi .80 .40
RA110 PT15 2c multi .80 .40
a. Block of 4, #RA107-RA110 3.20

Tax for Children's Village. A souvenir sheet, perf. and imperf., sold for 2b, with designs of Nos. RA107-RA110. Value, each $14.

Children's Village, 20th Anniv. — PT16

Inscriptions and Embera, Cuna, Embera and Guaymies tribal folk figures: No. RA111, "1966-1986." No. RA112, "Ciudad del Nino es . . . mi vida." No. RA113, "20 anos de fundacion." No. RA114, "Gracias."

1986, Nov. 1 Litho. *Perf. 13½*

RA111 PT16 2c multi .90 .40
RA112 PT16 2c multi .90 .40
RA113 PT16 2c multi .90 .40
RA114 PT16 2c multi .90 .40
Nos. RA111-RA114 (4) 3.60 1.60

Nos. RA111-RA114 obligatory on all mail through Nov., Dec. and Jan.; tax for Children's Village. Printed se-tenant. Sheets of 4 exist perf. and imperf. Sold for 2b. Sheet exists, perf and imperf, with one 58x68mm 2b stamp showing similar characters. Value $8.50 each.

PAPUA NEW GUINEA

ˈpa-pyə-wə ˈnü ˈgi-nē

LOCATION — Eastern half of island of New Guinea, north of Australia
GOVT. — Independent state in British Commonwealth.
AREA — 185,136 sq. mi.
POP. — 8,950,000 (2020 est.)
CAPITAL — Port Moresby

In 1884 a British Protectorate was proclaimed over this part of the island, called "British New Guinea." In 1905 the administration was transferred to Australia and in 1906 the name was changed to Territory of Papua.

In 1949 the administration of Papua and New Guinea was unified, as the 1952 issue indicates. In 1972 the name was changed to Papua New Guinea. In 1973 came self-government, followed by independence on September 16, 1975.

Issues of 1925-39 for the mandated Territory of New Guinea are listed under New Guinea.

12 Pence = 1 Shilling
20 Shillings = 1 Pound
100 Cents = 1 Dollar (1966)
100 Toea = 1 Kina (1975)

Catalogue values for unused stamps in this country are for Never Hinged items, beginning with Scott 122 in the regular postage section and Scott J1 in the postage due section.

Watermarks

Wmk. 13 — Crown and Double-Lined A

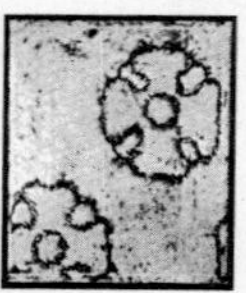

Wmk. 47 — Multiple Rosette

Wmk. 74 — Crown and Single-Lined A Sideways

Wmk. 228 — Small Crown and C of A Multiple

Wmk. 387

British New Guinea

Lakatoi — A1

Wmk. 47

1901, July 1 Engr. *Perf. 14*

Center in Black

No.	Type	Denomination	Unused	Used
1	A1	½p yellow green	24.00	6.00
2	A1	1p carmine	13.50	5.50
3	A1	2p violet	13.50	7.50
4	A1	2½p ultra	40.00	12.00
5	A1	4p black brown	45.00	40.00
6	A1	6p dark green	65.00	40.00
7	A1	1sh orange	65.00	*75.00*
8	A1	2sh6p brown ('05)	700.00	*700.00*
		Nos. 1-8 (8)	966.00	*886.00*

The paper varies in thickness and the watermark is found in two positions, with the greater width of the rosette either horizontal or vertical.

For stamps inscribed "Papua New Guinea" see Nos. 1024-1029.

For overprints see Nos. 11-26.

Papua

Stamps of British New Guinea, Overprinted

Large Overprint

1906, Nov. 8 Wmk. 47 *Perf. 14*

Center in Black

No.	Type	Denomination	Unused	Used
11	A1	½p yellow green	12.00	*25.00*
12	A1	1p carmine	20.00	*22.50*
13	A1	2p violet	19.00	5.00
14	A1	2½p ultra	12.00	*18.00*
15	A1	4p black brown	250.00	160.00
16	A1	6p dark green	50.00	*50.00*
17	A1	1sh orange	30.00	*50.00*
18	A1	2sh6p brown	200.00	*225.00*
		Nos. 11-18 (8)	593.00	*555.50*

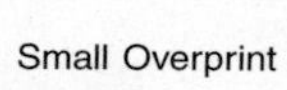

Small Overprint

1907 Center in Black

No.	Type	Denomination	Unused	Used
19	A1	½p yel grn	24.00	*29.00*
a.		Double overprint	3,500.	
20	A1	1p carmine	12.00	*7.50*
a.		Vertical overprint, up	8,250.	4,500.
21	A1	2p violet	8.00	4.00
a.		Double overprint	4,250.	
22	A1	2½p ultra	21.00	*24.00*
a.		Double overprint		
23	A1	4p blk brn	50.00	*70.00*
24	A1	6p dk grn	50.00	*55.00*
a.		Double overprint	7,000.	*13,000.*
25	A1	1sh orange	55.00	*60.00*
a.		Double overprint	*21,000.*	*14,000.*
26	A1	2sh6p brown	60.00	*75.00*
b.		Vert. ovpt., down	*8,500.*	
d.		Double horiz. ovpt.		4,500.
		Nos. 19-26 (8)	280.00	*324.50*

A2

Small "PAPUA"

Perf. 11, 12½

1907-08 Litho. Wmk. 13

Center in Black

No.	Type	Denomination	Unused	Used
28	A2	1p carmine ('08)	7.50	*5.75*
29	A2	2p violet ('08)	27.50	8.00
30	A2	2½p ultra ('08)	17.50	*9.00*
31	A2	4p black brown	9.00	*9.00*
32	A2	6p dk green ('08)	17.50	*18.50*
33	A2	1sh orange ('08)	57.50	*25.00*
		Nos. 28-33 (6)	136.50	*75.25*

Perf. 12½

No.	Type	Denomination	Unused	Used
30a	A2	2½p	180.00	*190.00*
31a	A2	4p	13.00	*13.00*
33a	A2	1sh	77.50	*100.00*
		Nos. 30a-33a (3)	270.50	*303.00*

1909-10 Wmk. Sideways

Center in Black

No.	Type	Denomination	Unused	Used
34	A2	½p yellow green	5.50	*6.50*
a.		Perf. 11x12½	*5,500.*	*5,500.*
b.		Perf. 11	3.00	*3.50*
35	A2	1p carmine	10.00	*14.00*
a.		Perf. 11	11.00	9.25
36	A2	2p violet ('10)	10.00	*15.00*
a.		Perf. 11x12½	1,700.	
b.		Perf. 11	27.50	*10.50*
37	A2	2½p ultra ('10)	7.00	*26.00*
a.		Perf. 12½	13.00	*45.00*
38	A2	4p black brn ('10)	6.50	*12.00*
a.		Perf. 11x12½	*16,000.*	
39	A2	6p dark green	12.50	22.50
a.		Perf. 12½	5,500.	*14,000.*
40	A2	1sh orange ('10)	25.00	*65.00*
a.		Perf. 11	65.00	*85.00*
		Nos. 34-40 (7)	76.50	*161.00*

One stamp in each sheet has a white line across the upper part of the picture which is termed the "rift in the clouds."

Large "PAPUA"

2sh6p:

Type I — The numerals are thin and irregular. The body of the "6" encloses a large spot of color. The dividing stroke is thick and uneven.

Type II — The numerals are thick and well formed. The "6" encloses a narrow oval of color. The dividing stroke is thin and sharp.

1910 Wmk. 13

Center in Black

No.	Type	Denomination	Unused	Used
41	A2	½p yellow green	6.00	*14.00*
42	A2	1p carmine	15.00	16.00
43	A2	2p violet	7.50	*8.00*
44	A2	2½p blue violet	13.00	*22.50*
45	A2	4p black brown	13.50	*14.00*
46	A2	6p dark green	11.00	*13.00*
47	A2	1sh orange	14.00	*22.50*
48	A2	2sh6p brown, type II	77.50	*75.00*
a.		Type I	60.00	*60.00*
		Nos. 41-48 (8)	157.50	*185.00*

Wmk. Sideways

No.	Type	Denomination	Unused	Used
49	A2	2sh6p choc, type I	85.00	*100.00*

1911 Typo. Wmk. 74 *Perf. 12½*

No.	Type	Denomination	Unused	Used
50	A2	½p yellow green	1.25	*4.00*
51	A2	1p lt red	2.25	1.25
52	A2	2p lt violet	4.00	1.25
53	A2	2½p ultra	6.75	*11.00*
54	A2	4p olive green	3.50	*14.00*
55	A2	6p orange brown	5.00	*6.50*
56	A2	1sh yellow	14.00	*20.00*
57	A2	2sh6p rose	46.00	*50.00*
		Nos. 50-57 (8)	82.75	*108.00*

For surcharges see Nos. 74-79.

1915, June *Perf. 14*

No.	Type	Denomination	Unused	Used
59	A2	1p light red	22.50	3.00

A3

1916-31

No.	Type	Denomination	Unused	Used
60	A3	½p pale yel grn & myr grn ('19)	1.00	1.50
61	A3	1p rose red & blk	2.50	1.50
62	A3	1½p yel brn & gray bl ('25)	2.50	1.00
63	A3	2p red vio & vio brn ('19)	2.75	1.25
64	A3	2p red brn & vio brn ('31)	3.25	1.25
a.		2p cop red & vio brn ('31)	29.00	2.25
65	A3	2½p ultra & dk grn ('19)	5.75	*15.00*
66	A3	3p emerald & blk	4.75	3.00
a.		3p dp bl grn & blk	5.75	9.25
67	A3	4p org & lt brn ('19)	4.00	7.00
68	A3	5p ol brn & sl ('31)	5.50	*18.00*
69	A3	6p vio & dl vio ('23)	5.50	*11.00*
70	A3	1sh ol grn & dk brn ('19)	7.00	*9.00*
71	A3	2sh6p rose & red brn ('19)	27.50	*47.50*
72	A3	5sh dp grn & blk	55.00	*60.00*
73	A3	10sh gray bl & grn ('25)	175.00	*200.00*
		Nos. 60-73 (14)	302.00	*377.00*

Type A3 is a redrawing of type A2. The lines of the picture have been strengthened, making it much darker, especially the sky and water.

See Nos. 92-93. For surcharges & overprints see Nos. 88-91, O1-O10.

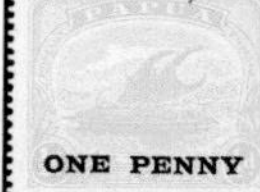

Stamps of 1911 Surcharged

1917 *Perf. 12½*

No.	Type	Denomination	Unused	Used
74	A2	1p on ½p yellow grn	1.75	*1.90*
75	A2	1p on 2p lt violet	14.50	*17.50*
76	A2	1p on 2½p ultra	1.50	*4.50*
77	A2	1p on 4p olive green	2.10	*5.25*
78	A2	1p on 6p org brn	10.00	*24.50*
79	A2	1p on 2sh6p rose	4.00	*7.00*
		Nos. 74-79 (6)	33.85	*60.65*

No. 62 Surcharged

1931, Jan. 1 *Perf. 14*

No.	Type	Denomination	Unused	Used
88	A3	2p on 1½p yellow brn & gray blue	1.50	*2.25*

Nos. 70, 71 and 72 Surcharged in Black

1931

No.	Type	Denomination	Unused	Used
89	A3	5p on 1sh #70	1.75	*3.00*
90	A3	9p on 2sh6p #71	7.50	*12.00*
91	A3	1sh3p on 5sh #72	7.50	*14.00*
		Nos. 89-91 (3)	16.75	*29.00*

Type of 1916 Issue

1932 Wmk. 228 *Perf. 11*

No.	Type	Denomination	Unused	Used
92	A3	9p dp violet & gray	9.50	*37.50*
93	A3	1sh3p pale bluish grn & grayish vio	14.50	*37.50*

For overprints see Nos. O11-O12.

Motuan Girl — A5

Bird of Paradise and Boar's Tusk — A6

Mother and Child A7

Papuan Motherhood A8

Dubu (Ceremonial Platform) A9

Fire Maker A10

Designs: 1p, Steve, son of Oala. 1½p, Tree houses. 3p, Papuan dandy. 5p, Masked dancer. 9p, Shooting fish. 1sh3p, Lakatoi. 2sh, Delta art. 2sh6p, Pottery making. 5sh, Sgt.-Major Simoi. £1, Delta house.

Unwmk.

1932, Nov. 14 Engr. *Perf. 11*

No.	Type	Denomination	Unused	Used
94	A5	½p orange & blk	4.50	4.00
95	A5	1p yel grn & blk	4.00	.70
96	A5	1½p red brn & blk	4.50	*9.25*
97	A6	2p light red	12.50	.35
98	A5	3p blue & blk	4.25	*7.50*
99	A7	4p olive green	12.00	11.00
100	A5	5p grnsh sl & blk	7.00	3.50

101 A8 6p bister brown 8.50 *6.25*
102 A5 9p lilac & blk 11.50 *24.00*
103 A9 1sh bluish gray 10.00 *10.00*
104 A5 1sh3p brown & blk 19.00 *29.00*
105 A5 2sh bluish slate & blk 18.00 *26.00*
106 A5 2sh6p rose lilac & blk 29.00 *42.50*
107 A5 5sh olive & blk 70.00 60.00
108 A10 10sh gray lilac 150.00 120.00
109 A5 £1 lt gray & black 275.00 180.00
Nos. 94-109 (16) 639.75 *534.05*

For overprints see Nos. 114-117.

Hoisting Union Jack at Port Moresby — A21

H. M. S. "Nelson" at Port Moresby — A22

1934, Nov. 6

110 A21 1p dull green 3.00 *3.50*
111 A22 2p red brown 2.75 *3.00*
112 A21 3p blue 3.00 *3.00*
113 A22 5p violet brown 12.00 *22.50*
Nos. 110-113 (4) 20.75 *32.00*
Set, never hinged 27.50

Declaration of British Protection, 50th anniv.

Silver Jubilee Issue

Stamps of 1932 Issue Overprinted in Black

a

b

1935, July 9 **Glazed Paper**

114 A5(a) 1p yellow grn & blk 1.20 *4.00*
115 A6(b) 2p light red 3.50 *5.50*
116 A5(a) 3p lt blue & blk 2.25 *4.00*
117 A5(a) 5p grnsh slate & blk 2.25 *4.00*
Nos. 114-117 (4) 9.20 *17.50*
Set, never hinged 16.50

25th anniv. of the reign of George V.

Coronation Issue

King George VI — A22a

Unwmk.

1937, May 14 **Engr.** ***Perf. 11***

118 A22a 1p green .40 .25
119 A22a 2p salmon rose .40 *1.50*
120 A22a 3p blue .40 *1.50*
121 A22a 5p brown violet .40 *2.00*
Nos. 118-121 (4) 1.60 *5.25*
Set, never hinged 2.50

Catalogue values for unused stamps in this section, from this point to the end of the section, are for Never Hinged items.

Papua and New Guinea

Tree-climbing Kangaroo A23

Kiriwina Chief's House A24

Copra Making — A25

Designs: 1p, Buka head-dress. 2p, Youth. 2½p, Bird of paradise. 3p, Policeman. 3½p, Chimbu headdress. 7½p, Kiriwina yam house. 1sh, Trading canoe. 1sh6p, Rubber tapping. 2sh, Shields and spears. 2sh6p, Plumed shepherd. 10sh, Map. £1, Spearing fish.

Unwmk.

1952, Oct. 30 **Engr.** ***Perf. 14***

122 A23 ½p green .30 .25
123 A23 1p chocolate .25 .25
124 A23 2p deep ultra .75 .25
125 A23 2½p orange 3.50 .60
126 A23 3p dark green .85 .25
127 A23 3½p dk carmine .85 .25
128 A24 6½p vio brown 2.25 .25
129 A24 7½p dp ultra 5.00 2.50
130 A25 9p chocolate 4.75 .75
131 A25 1sh yellow green 3.50 .25
132 A24 1sh6p dark green 8.50 1.50
133 A24 2sh deep blue 7.50 .25
134 A25 2sh6p dk red brown 7.00 .75
135 A25 10sh gray black 50.00 16.00
136 A24 £1 chocolate 65.00 20.00
Nos. 122-136 (15) 160.00 44.10
Set, hinged 85.00

See #139-141. For surcharges & overprints see #137-138, 147, J1-J3, J5-J6.

Nos. 125 Surcharged

Nos. 131 Surcharged

1957, Jan. 29 ***Perf. 14***

137 A23 4p on 2½p orange .85 .30
138 A25 7p on 1sh yellow green 1.75 .40

Type of 1952 and

Klinki Plymill — A26

Designs: 3½p, Chimbu headdress. 4p, 5p, Cacao. 8p, Klinki Plymill. 1sh7p, Cattle. 2sh5p, Cattle. 5sh, Coffee, vert.

1958-60 **Engr.** ***Perf. 14***

139 A23 3½p black 7.00 2.00
140 A23 4p vermilion 1.25 .25
141 A23 5p green ('60) 1.50 .25
142 A26 7p gray green 11.00 .25
143 A26 8p dk ultra ('60) 2.50 2.00
144 A26 1sh7p red brown 30.00 16.00
145 A26 2sh5p vermilion ('60) 6.00 2.50
146 A26 5sh gray olive & brn red 11.00 2.10
Nos. 139-146 (8) 70.25 25.35

Issued: June 2, 1958, Nov. 10, 1960.
For surcharge see No. J4.

No. 122 Surcharged

1959, Dec. 1

147 A23 5p on ½p green 1.00 .25

Council Chamber and Frangipani Flowers — A27

1961, Apr. 10 **Photo.** ***Perf. 14½x14***

148 A27 5p green & yellow .90 .35
149 A27 2sh3p grn & salmon 9.00 4.00

Reconstitution of the Legislative Council.

Woman's Head A28

Red-plumed Bird of Paradise A29

Port Moresby Harbor — A30

Constable Ragas Amis Matia, Port Moresby — A32

View of Rabaul, by Samuel Terarup Cham A33

Woman Dancer A31

Elizabeth II — A34

Designs: 3p, Man's head. 6p, Golden opossum. 2sh, Male dancer with drum. 2sh3p, Piaggio transport plane landing at Tapini.

Perf. 14 (A28, A31, A32), 11½ (A29, A33), 14x13½ (A30), 14½ (A34)

1961-63 **Engr.** **Unwmk.**

153 A28 1p dk carmine .70 .25
154 A28 3p bluish black .45 .25

Photo.

155 A29 5p lt brn, red brn, blk & yel .50 .25
156 A29 6p gray, ocher & slate .75 1.25

Engr.

157 A30 8p green .30 .25
158 A31 1sh gray green 4.75 .90
159 A31 2sh rose lake 1.50 .45
160 A30 2sh3p dark blue .90 .40
161 A32 3sh green 2.25 2.00

Photo.

162 A33 10sh multicolored 16.50 13.00
163 A34 £1 brt grn, blk & gold 9.00 8.50
Nos. 153-163 (11) 37.60 27.50

The 5p and 6p are on granite paper.
Issued: 3sh, 9/5/62; 10sh, 2/13/63: 5p, 6p, 3/27/63; 8p, 2sh3p, 5/8/63; £1, 7/3/63; others, 7/26/61.

Malaria Eradication Emblem — A35

1962, Apr. 7 **Litho.** ***Perf. 14***

164 A35 5p lt blue & maroon 1.15 .50
165 A35 1sh lt brown & red 2.10 .75
166 A35 2sh yellow green & blk 2.50 *3.25*
Nos. 164-166 (3) 5.75 4.50

WHO drive to eradicate malaria.

Map of Australia and South Pacific — A36

1962, July 9 **Engr.** **Unwmk.**

167 A36 5p dk red & lt grn 1.75 .30
168 A36 1sh6p dk violet & yel 2.75 1.00
169 A36 2sh6p green & lt blue 2.75 2.25
Nos. 167-169 (3) 7.25 3.55

5th So. Pacific Conf., Pago Pago, July 1962.

High Jump — A37

1962, Oct. 24 **Photo.** ***Perf. 11½***

Size: 26x21mm

Granite Paper

171 A37 5p shown .50 .30
172 A37 5p Javelin .50 .30

Size: 32½x22½mm

173 A37 2sh3p runners 2.50 2.00
Nos. 171-173 (3) 3.50 2.60

British Empire and Commonwealth Games, Perth, Australia, Nov. 22-Dec. 1.
Nos. 171 and 172 printed in alternating horizontal rows in sheet.

Red Cross Centenary Emblem — A38

1963, May 1 ***Perf. 13½***

174 A38 5p blue grn, gray & red .55 .25

Games Emblem — A38a

1963, Aug. 14 **Engr.** ***Perf. 13½x14***

176 A38a 5p olive bister .25 .25
177 A38a 1sh green .75 .50

So. Pacific Games, Suva, Aug. 29-Sept. 7.

Top of Wooden Shield — A39

Various Carved Heads.

Perf. 11½

1964, Feb. 5 **Unwmk.** **Photo.**

Granite Paper

178 A39 11p multicolored .60 .25
179 A39 2sh5p multicolored .65 *1.75*
180 A39 2sh6p multicolored .75 .25
181 A39 5sh multicolored .90 .25
Nos. 178-181 (4) 2.90 2.50

Casting Ballot — A40

1964, Mar. 4 **Unwmk.** ***Perf. 11½***

Granite Paper

182 A40 5p dk brn & pale brn .25 .25
183 A40 2sh3p dk brn & lt bl .80 .50

First Common Roll elections.

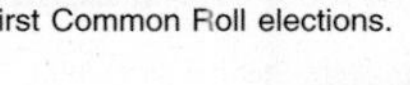

Territorial Health Services — A41

Designs: 5p, Patients at health center clinic. 8p, Dentist and school child patient. 1sh,

Nurse holding infant. 1sh2p, Medical student using microscope.

1964, Aug. 5 Engr. *Perf. 14*

184 A41 5p violet .25 .25
185 A41 8p green .25 .25
186 A41 1sh deep ultra .25 .25
187 A41 1sh2p rose brown .40 .40
Nos. 184-187 (4) 1.15 1.15

A42

Designs: 1p, Striped gardener bower birds. 3p, New Guinea regent bower birds. 5p, Blue birds of paradise. 6p, Lawes six-wired birds of paradise. 8p, Sickle-billed birds of paradise. 1sh, Emperor birds of paradise. 2sh, Brown sickle-billed bird of paradise. 2sh3p, Lesser bird of paradise. 3sh, Magnificent bird of paradise. 5sh, Twelve-wired bird of paradise. 10sh, Magnificent rifle birds.

Birds in Natural Colors
Size: 21x26mm

1964-65 Unwmk. Photo. *Perf. 11½*

188 A42 1p brt cit & dk brn .55 .25
189 A42 3p gray & dk brn .65 .25
190 A42 5p sal pink & blk .70 .25
191 A42 6p pale grn & sep 1.05 .25
192 A42 8p pale lil & dk brn 1.50 .35

Size: 25x36mm

193 A42 1sh salmon & blk 1.50 .25
194 A42 2sh blue & dk brn 1.05 .40
195 A42 2sh3p lt grn & dk brn 1.05 1.10
196 A42 3sh yel & dk brn 1.05 *1.50*
197 A42 5sh lt ultra & dk brn 11.00 2.25
198 A42 10sh gray & dk blue 4.75 *11.00*
Nos. 188-198 (11) 24.85 17.85

Issued: 6p, 8p, 1sh, 10sh, 10/28/64; others, 1/20/65.

Carved Crocodile's Head — A43

Designs: Wood carvings from Sepik River Region used as ship's prows and as objects of religious veneration.

1965, Mar. 24 Photo. *Perf. 11½*

199 A43 4p multicolored .60 .25
200 A43 1sh2p gray brn, bister & dk brn 1.75 1.75
201 A43 1sh6p lil, dk brn & buff .60 .25
202 A43 4sh bl, dk vio & mar .90 .55
Nos. 199-202 (4) 3.85 2.80

"Simpson and His Donkey" by Wallace Anderson — A43a

1965, Apr. 14 *Perf. 13½x13*

203 A43a 2sh3p brt grn, sep & blk .80 .50

ANZAC issue. See note after Australia No. 387.

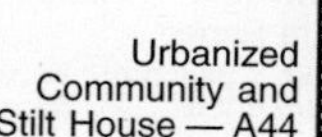

Urbanized Community and Stilt House — A44

Design: 1sh, Stilt house at left.

1965, July 7 Photo. *Perf. 11½*

204 A44 6p multicolored .25 .25
205 A44 1sh multicolored .25 .25

6th South Pacific Conf., Lae, July, 1965.

UN Emblem, Mother and Child — A45

UN Emblem and: 1sh, Globe and orbit, vert. 2sh, Four globes in orbit, vert.

1965, Oct. 13 Unwmk. *Perf. 11½*

206 A45 6p brown, grnsh bl & dp bl .25 .25
207 A45 1sh dull pur, blue & org .25 .25
208 A45 2sh dp blue, pale grn & grn .25 .25
Nos. 206-208 (3) .75 .75

20th anniversary of the United Nations.

New Guinea Birdwing — A46

Butterflies: 1c, Blue emperor, vert. 3c, White-banded map butterfly, vert. 4c, Mountain swallowtail, vert. 5c, Port Moresby terinos, vert. 12c, Blue crow. 15c, Euchenor butterfly. 20c, White-spotted parthenos. 25c, Orange Jezebel. 50c, New Guinea emperor. $1, Blue-spotted leaf-wing. $2, Paradise birdwing.

1966 Photo. *Perf. 11½*
Granite Paper

209 A46 1c sal, blk & aqua .40 *1.00*
210 A46 3c gray grn, brn & org .40 *1.00*
211 A46 4c multicolored .40 *1.00*
212 A46 5c multicolored .45 .25
213 A46 10c multicolored .55 .30
214 A46 12c salmon & multi 3.75 2.25
215 A46 15c pale vio, dk brn & buff 1.75 .80
216 A46 20c yel bister, dk brn & yel org .65 .25
217 A46 25c gray, blk & yel 1.40 1.25
218 A46 50c multicolored 11.00 2.00
219 A46 $1 pale blue, dk brn & dp org 3.50 2.75
220 A46 $2 multicolored 6.25 *10.00*
Nos. 209-220 (12) 30.50 *22.85*

In 1967 Courvoisier made new plates for the $1 and $2. Stamps from these plates show many minor differences and slight variations in shade.

Issued: 12c, 10/10; others, 2/14.

Molala Harai and Paiva Streamer — A47

Myths of Elema People: 7c, Marai, the fisherman. 30c, Meavea Kivovia and the Black Cockatoo. 60c, Toivita Tapaivita (symbolic face decorations).

1966, June 8 Photo. *Perf. 11½*
Granite Paper

221 A47 2c black & carmine .35 .25
222 A47 7c blue, blk & yel .35 .35
223 A47 30c blk, yel grn & car .40 .25
224 A47 60c blk, org & car .90 .60
Nos. 221-224 (4) 2.00 1.45

Discus — A48

1966, Aug. 31 *Perf. 11½*
Granite Paper

225 A48 5c shown .25 .25
226 A48 10c Soccer .30 .25
227 A48 20c Tennis .40 .35
Nos. 225-227 (3) .95 .85

Second South Pacific Games, Noumea, New Caledonia, Dec. 8-18.

d'Albertis' Creeper — A49

Flowers: 10c, Tecomanthe dendrophila. 20c, Rhododendron macgregoriae. 60c, Rhododendron konori.

1966, Dec. 7 Photo. *Perf. 11½*

228 A49 5c multicolored .30 .25
229 A49 10c multicolored .30 .25
230 A49 20c multicolored .65 .25
231 A49 60c multicolored 1.75 1.50
Nos. 228-231 (4) 3.00 2.25

Book and Pen ("Fine Arts") — A50

3c, "Surveying," transit, view finder, pencil. 4c, "Civil Engineering," buildings, compass. 5c, "Science," test tubes, chemical formula. 20c, "Justice," Justitia, scales.

1967, Feb. 8 Photo. *Perf. 12½x12*

232 A50 1c orange & multi .25 .25
233 A50 3c blue & multi .25 .25
234 A50 4c brown & multi .25 .25
235 A50 5c green & multi .25 .25
236 A50 20c pink & multi .25 .25
Nos. 232-236 (5) 1.25 1.25

Issued to publicize the development of the University of Papua and New Guinea and the Institute of Higher Technical Education.

Leaf Beetle — A51

Beetles: 10c, Eupholus schoenherri. 20c, Sphingnotus albertisi. 25c, Cyphogastra albertisi.

1967, Apr. 12 Unwmk. *Perf. 11½*

237 A51 5c blue & multi .40 .25
238 A51 10c lt green & multi .55 .25
239 A51 20c rose & multi .85 .35
240 A51 25c yellow & multi 1.20 .45
Nos. 237-240 (4) 3.00 1.30

Hydroelectric Power — A52

Designs: 10c, Pyrethrum (Chrysanthemum cinerariaefolium). 20c, Tea. 25c, like 5c.

1967, June 28 Photo. *Perf. 12x12½*

241 A52 5c multicolored .25 .25
242 A52 10c multicolored .25 .25
243 A52 20c multicolored .35 .25
244 A52 25c multicolored .35 .25
Nos. 241-244 (4) 1.20 1.00

Completion of part of the Laloki River Hydroelectric Works near Port Moresby, and the Hydrological Decade (UNESCO), 1965-74.

Battle of Milne Bay — A53

Designs: 5c, Soldiers on Kokoda Trail, vert. 20c, The coast watchers. 50c, Battle of the Coral Sea.

1967, Aug. 30 Unwmk. *Perf. 11½*

245 A53 2c multicolored .25 *.45*
246 A53 5c multicolored .25 .25
247 A53 20c multicolored .35 .25
248 A53 50c multicolored .90 .75
Nos. 245-248 (4) 1.75 1.70

25th anniv. of the battles in the Pacific, which stopped the Japanese from occupying Papua and New Guinea.

Pesquet's Parrot — A54

Parrots: 5c, Fairy lory. 20c, Dusk-orange lory. 25c, Edward's fig parrot.

1967, Nov. 29 Photo. *Perf. 12*

249 A54 5c multicolored .60 .25
250 A54 7c multicolored .75 .90
251 A54 20c multicolored 1.15 .25
252 A54 25c multicolored 1.40 .25
Nos. 249-252 (4) 3.90 1.65

Chimbu District Headdress — A55

Headdress from: 10c, Southern Highlands District, horiz. 20c, Western Highlands District, horiz. 60c, Chimbu District (different from 5c).

Perf. 12x12½, 12½x12

1968, Feb. 21 Photo. Unwmk.

253 A55 5c multi .25 .25
254 A55 10c multi .35 .25
255 A55 20c multi .35 .25
256 A55 60c multi 1.10 .80
Nos. 253-256 (4) 2.05 1.55

Frogs — A56

1968, Apr. 24 Photo. *Perf. 11½*

257 A56 5c Tree .60 .45
258 A56 10c Tree, diff. .60 .25
259 A56 15c Swamp .60 .25
260 A56 20c Tree, diff. .80 .55
Nos. 257-260 (4) 2.60 1.50

Human Rights Flame and Headdress — A57

Symbolic Designs: 10c, Human Rights Flame surrounded by the world. 20c, 25c, "Universal Suffrage" in 2 abstract designs.

1968, June 26 Litho. *Perf. 14x13*

261 A57 5c black & multi .30 .25
262 A57 10c black & multi .30 .25
263 A57 20c black & multi .35 .30
264 A57 25c black & multi .35 .30
Nos. 261-264 (4) 1.30 1.10

Issued for Human Rights Year, 1968, and to publicize free elections.

Sea Shells — A58

Designs: 1c, Ovula ovum. 3c, Strombus sinuatus. 4c, Conus litoglyphus. 5c, Conus marmoreus. 7c, Mitra mitra. 10c, Cymbiola rutila ruckeri. 12c, Phalium areola. 15c, Lambis scorpius. 20c, Tridacna squamosa. 25c, Lioconcha castrensis. 30c, Murex ramosus. 40c, Nautilus pompilius. 60c, Charonia tritonis. $1, Papustyla pulcherrima. $2, Conus gloriamaris, vert.

1968-69 Photo. *Perf. 12½x12*
Granite Paper
Size: 30x22½mm

265 A58 1c multicolored .25 .25
266 A58 3c multicolored .40 *1.40*
267 A58 4c multicolored .25 *1.40*
268 A58 5c multicolored .35 .25
269 A58 7c multicolored .45 .25
270 A58 10c multicolored .60 .25
271 A58 12c multicolored 1.75 *2.25*
272 A58 15c multicolored 1.80 *1.25*
273 A58 20c multicolored 1.00 .25

Size: 30x25mm
Perf. 11

274 A58 25c multicolored 1.00 *1.75*
275 A58 30c multicolored 1.00 *1.10*
276 A58 40c multicolored 1.10 *1.40*
277 A58 60c multicolored 1.00 .60
278 A58 $1 multicolored 1.60 1.00

Size: 25x30mm
Perf. 12x12½

279 A58 $2 multicolored 12.00 4.50
Nos. 265-279 (15) 24.55 17.90

Issued: 5c, 20c, 25c, 30c, 60c, 8/28/68; 3c, 10c, 15c, 40c, $1, 10/30/68; others, 1/29/69.

Legend of Tito-Iko — A59

Myths of Elema People: No. 281, 5c inscribed "Iko." No. 282, 10c inscribed "Luvuapo." No. 283, 10c inscribed "Miro."

Nos. 280, 282: Perf. 12½x13½xRoul. 9xPerf. 13½

Nos. 281, 283: Roul. 9 x Perf. 13½x12½x13½

1969, Apr. 9 Litho. Unwmk.

280		5c black, yellow & red	.25	.25
281		5c black, yellow & red	.25	.25
a.	A59	Vert. pair, #280-281	.55	*.90*
282		10c black, gray & red	.25	.25
283		10c black, gray & red	.25	.25
a.		Vert. pair, #282-283	.60	*.90*
		Nos. 280-283 (4)	1.00	1.00

Nos. 281a, 283a have continuous designs, rouletted between.

Fireball Class Sailboat, Port Moresby Harbor — A60

Designs: 10c, Games' swimming pool, Boroko, horiz. 20c, Main Games area, Konedobu, horiz.

Perf. 14x14½, 14½x14

1969, June 25 Engr.

284	A60	5c black	.25	.25
285	A60	10c bright violet	.25	.25
286	A60	20c green	.40	.30
		Nos. 284-286 (3)	.90	.80

3rd S. Pacific Games, Port Moresby, Aug. 13-23.

Dendrobium Ostrinoglossum — A61

Orchids: 10c, Dendrobium lawesii. 20c, Dendrobium pseudofrigidum. 30c, Dendrobium conanthum.

1969, Aug. 27 Photo. *Perf. 11½*
Granite Paper

287	A61	5c multicolored	.70	.25
288	A61	10c multicolored	.80	.50
289	A61	20c multicolored	1.00	.80
290	A61	30c multicolored	1.10	.85
		Nos. 287-290 (4)	3.60	2.40

Issued to publicize the 6th World Orchid Conference, Sydney, Australia, Sept. 1969.

Potter — A62

1969, Sept. 24 Photo. *Perf. 11½*
Granite Paper

291	A62	5c multicolored	.35	.25

50th anniv. of the ILO.

Bird of Paradise — A63

Coil Stamps

1969-71 *Perf. 14½ Horiz.*

291A	A63	2c red, dp blue & blk	.35	*.50*
292	A63	5c orange & emerald	.35	.25

Issue dates: 5c, Sept. 24, 2c, Apr. 1, 1971.

Seed Pod Rattle (Tareko) — A64

Musical Instruments: 10c, Hand drum (garamut). 25c, Pan pipes (iviliko). 30c, Hourglass drum (kundu).

1969, Oct. 29 Photo. *Perf. 12½*

293	A64	5c multicolored	.25	.25
294	A64	10c multicolored	.25	.25
295	A64	25c multicolored	.40	.35
296	A64	30c multicolored	.80	.40
		Nos. 293-296 (4)	1.70	1.25

Prehistoric Ambum Stone and Skull — A65

Designs: 10c, Masawa canoe of the Kula Circuit. 25c, Map of Papua and New Guinea made by Luis Valez de Torres, 1606. 30c, H.M.S. Basilisk, 1873.

1970, Feb. 11 Photo. *Perf. 12½*

297	A65	5c violet brown & multi	.25	.25
298	A65	10c ocher & multi	.25	.25
299	A65	25c org brn & multi	.50	.35
300	A65	30c olive green & multi	1.10	.40
		Nos. 297-300 (4)	2.10	1.25

King of Saxony Bird of Paradise — A66

Birds of Paradise: 10c, King. 15c, Augusta Victoria. 25c, Multi-crested.

1970, May 13 Photo. *Perf. 11½*

301	A66	5c tan & multi	.90	.25
302	A66	10c multicolored	1.10	.60
303	A66	15c lt blue & multi	1.50	1.00
304	A66	25c multicolored	2.25	.75
		Nos. 301-304 (4)	5.75	2.60

Canceled to Order

Starting in 1970 or earlier, the Philatelic Bureau at Port Moresby began to sell new issues canceled to order at face value.

Douglas DC-3 and Matupi Volcano — A67

Aircraft: No. 305, DC-6B and Mt. Wilhelm. No. 306, Lockheed Mark II Electra and Mt. Yule. No. 307, Boeing 727 and Mt. Giluwe. No. 308, Fokker F27 Friendship and Manam Island Volcano. 30c, Boeing 707 and Hombom's Bluff.

1970, July 8 Photo. *Perf. 14½x14*

305	A67	5c "TAA" on tail	.30	.25
306	A67	5c Striped tail	.30	.25
307	A67	5c "T" on tail	.30	.25
308	A67	5c Red tail	.30	.25
a.		Block of 4, #305-308	1.60	*2.00*
309	A67	25c multicolored	.75	.40
310	A67	30c multicolored	.75	.55
		Nos. 305-310 (6)	2.70	1.95

Development of air service during the last 25 years between Australia and New Guinea.

Nicolaus N. de Miklouho-Maclay, Explorer, and Mask — A68

Designs: 10c, Bronislaw Kaspar Malinowski, anthropologist, and hut. 15c, Count Tommaso Salvadori, ornithologist, and cassowary. 20c, Friedrich R. Schlechter, botanist, and orchid.

1970, Aug. 19 Photo. *Perf. 11½*

311	A68	5c brown, blk & lilac	.25	.25
312	A68	10c multicolored	.25	.25
313	A68	15c dull lilac & multi	.80	.35
314	A68	20c slate & multi	.80	.35
		Nos. 311-314 (4)	2.10	1.20

42nd Cong. of the Australian and New Zealand Assoc. for the Advancement of Science, Port Moresby, Aug. 17-21.

Wogeo Island Food Bowl — A69

National Handicraft: 10c, Lime pot. 15c, Aibom sago storage pot. 30c, Manus Island bowl, horiz.

1970, Oct. 28 Photo. *Perf. 12½*

315	A69	5c multicolored	.30	.25
316	A69	10c multicolored	.40	.25
317	A69	15c multicolored	.40	.25
318	A69	30c multicolored	.60	.50
		Nos. 315-318 (4)	1.70	1.25

Eastern Highlands Round House — A70

Local Architecture: 7c, Milne Bay house. 10c, Purari Delta house. 40c, Sepik or Men's Spirit House.

1971, Jan. 27 Photo. *Perf. 11½*

319	A70	5c dark olive & multi	.30	.25
320	A70	7c Prus blue & multi	.35	*.60*
321	A70	10c deep org & multi	.35	.25
322	A70	40c brown & multi	.80	.75
		Nos. 319-322 (4)	1.80	1.85

Spotted Cuscus — A71

Animals: 10c, Brown and white striped possum. 15c, Feather-tailed possum. 25c, Spiny anteater, horiz. 30c, Good-fellow's tree-climbing kangaroo, horiz.

1971, Mar. 31 Photo. *Perf. 11½*

323	A71	5c blue green & multi	.50	.25
324	A71	10c multicolored	.55	.25
325	A71	15c multicolored	.85	.90
326	A71	25c dull yellow & multi	1.20	.90
327	A71	30c olive & multi	1.20	.60
		Nos. 323-327 (5)	4.30	2.90

Basketball — A72

1971, June 9 Litho. *Perf. 14*

328	A72	7c shown	.35	.25
329	A72	14c Yachting	.50	.25
330	A72	21c Boxing	.50	.30
331	A72	28c Field events	.50	.45
		Nos. 328-331 (4)	1.85	1.25

Fourth South Pacific Games, Papeete, French Polynesia, Sept. 8-19.

Bartering Fish for Coconuts and Taro — A73

Primary industries: 9c, Man stacking yams and taro. 14c, Market scene. 30c, Farm couple tending yams.

1971, Aug. 18 Photo. *Perf. 11½*

332	A73	7c multicolored	.30	.25
333	A73	9c multicolored	.40	.25
334	A73	14c multicolored	.55	.25
335	A73	30c multicolored	.75	.50
		Nos. 332-335 (4)	2.00	1.25

Siaa Dancer — A74

Designs: 9c, Urasena masked dancer. 20c, Two Siassi masked dancers, horiz. 28c, Three Siaa dancers, horiz.

1971, Oct. 27 Photo. *Perf. 11½*

336	A74	7c orange & multi	.30	.25
337	A74	9c yel green & multi	.30	.25
338	A74	20c bister & multi	.80	.80
339	A74	28c multicolored	1.00	.95
		Nos. 336-339 (4)	2.40	2.25

Papua New Guinea and Australia Arms — A75

#341, Papua New Guinea & Australia flags.

1972, Jan. 26 *Perf. 12½x12*

340	A75	7c gray blue, org & blk	.30	.30
341	A75	7c gray blue, blk, red & yel	.30	.30
a.		Pair, #340-341	.75	.75

Constitutional development for the 1972 House of Assembly elections.

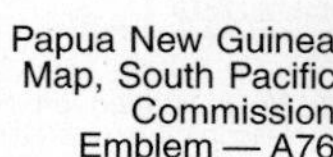

Papua New Guinea Map, South Pacific Commission Emblem — A76

#343, Man's head, So. Pacific Commission flag.

1972, Jan. 26

342	A76	15c brt green & multi	.55	.40
343	A76	15c brt green & multi	.55	.40
a.		Pair, #342-343	1.50	1.50

South Pacific Commission, 25th anniv.

Pitted-shelled Turtle — A77

Designs: 14c, Angle-headed agamid. 21c, Green python. 30c, Water monitor.

1972, Mar. 15 Photo. *Perf. 11½*

344	A77	7c multicolored	.40	.25
345	A77	14c car rose & multi	1.10	1.10
346	A77	21c yellow & multi	1.10	1.25
347	A77	30c yel green & multi	1.40	1.10
		Nos. 344-347 (4)	4.00	3.70

Curtiss Seagull MF 6 and Ship — A78

14c, De Havilland 37 & porters from gold fields. 20c, Junkers G 31 & heavy machinery. 25c, Junkers F 13 & Lutheran mission church.

1972, June 7 Granite Paper

348	A78	7c dp yellow & multi	.25	.25
349	A78	14c dp orange & multi	.65	1.10
350	A78	20c olive & multi	1.10	1.10
351	A78	25c multicolored	1.25	1.10
		Nos. 348-351 (4)	3.25	3.55

50th anniv. of aviation in Papua New Guinea.

National Day Unity Emblem — A79

Designs: 10c, Unity emblem and kundu (drum). 30c, Unity emblem and conch.

1972, Aug. 16 *Perf. 12x12½*

No.	Type	Description	Unused	Used
352	A79	7c violet blue & multi	.30	.25
353	A79	10c orange & multi	.40	.30
354	A79	30c vermilion & multi	.60	.55
		Nos. 352-354 (3)	1.30	1.10

National Day, Sept. 15, 1972.

Rev. Copland King — A80

Pioneering Missionaries: No. 356, Pastor Ruatoka. No. 357, Bishop Stanislaus Henry Verjus. No. 358, Rev. Dr. Johannes Flierl.

1972, Oct. 25 **Photo.** *Perf. 11½*

No.	Type	Description	Unused	Used
355	A80	7c dark blue & multi	.40	.40
356	A80	7c dark red & multi	.40	.40
357	A80	7c dark green & multi	.40	.40
358	A80	7c dark olive bister & multi	.40	.40
		Nos. 355-358 (4)	1.60	1.60

Christmas 1972.

A81

Designs: No. 359, Relay station on Mt. Tomavatur. No. 360, Helicopter approaching Mt. Kerigomna. No. 361, Sattelburg. No. 362, Wideru. 9c, Teleprinter. 30c, Map of network.

1973, Jan. 24 **Photo.** *Perf. 12½*

No.	Type	Description	Unused	Used
359		7c multi	.35	.25
360		7c multi	.35	.25
361		7c multi	.35	.25
362		7c multi	.35	.25
a.		A81 Block of 4, #359-362	1.50	1.50
		Complete booklet, 3 each #359, 361, 2 each #360, 362	13.00	
363	A81	9c multi	.40	.25
364	A81	30c multi	1.40	.85
		Nos. 359-364 (6)	3.20	2.10

Telecommunications development 1968-1972. No. 362a has a unifying frame.

Queen Carol's Bird of Paradise — A82

Birds of Paradise: 14c, Goldie's. 21c, Ribbon-tailed astrapia. 28c, Princess Stephanie's.

1973, Mar. 30 **Photo.** *Perf. 11½*

Size: 22½x38mm

No.	Type	Description	Unused	Used
365	A82	7c citron & multi	.90	.45
366	A82	14c dull green & multi	2.25	1.25

Size: 17x48mm

No.	Type	Description	Unused	Used
367	A82	21c lemon & multi	2.75	1.75
368	A82	28c lt blue & multi	3.50	2.50
		Nos. 365-368 (4)	9.40	5.95

Wood Carver, Milne Bay — A83

Designs: 3c, Wig makers, Southern Highlands. 5c, Bagana Volcano, Bougainville. 6c, Pig Exchange, Western Highlands. 7c, Coastal village, Central District. 8c, Arawe mother, West New Britain. 9c, Fire dancers, East New Britain. 10c, Tifalmin hunter, West Sepik District. 14c, Crocodile hunters, Western District. 15c, Mt. Elimbari, Chimbu. 20c, Canoe racing, Manus District. 21c, Making sago, Gulf District. 25c, Council House, East Sepik. 28c, Menyamya bowmen, Morobe. 30c, Shark snaring, New Ireland. 40c, Fishing canoes, Madang. 60c, Women making tapa cloth, Northern District. $1, Asaro mudmen, Eastern Highlands. $2, Sing festival, Enga District.

1973-74 **Photo.** *Perf. 11½*

Granite Paper

No.	Type	Description	Unused	Used
369	A83	1c multicolored	.25	.25
370	A83	3c multi ('74)	.35	.25
371	A83	5c multicolored	.65	.25
372	A83	6c multi ('74)	.90	*2.00*
373	A83	7c multicolored	.30	.25
374	A83	8c multi ('74)	.35	.30
375	A83	9c multicolored	.40	.25
376	A83	10c multi ('74)	.60	.25
377	A83	14c multicolored	.45	*.90*
378	A83	15c multicolored	.65	.35
379	A83	20c multi ('74)	.90	.45
380	A83	21c multicolored	.50	*1.25*
381	A83	25c multicolored	.50	*.60*
382	A83	28c multicolored	.50	*1.25*
383	A83	30c multicolored	.60	.60
385	A83	40c multicolored	.50	.50
386	A83	60c multi ('74)	.60	.75
387	A83	$1 multi ('74)	.75	1.50
388	A83	$2 multi ('74)	3.00	*6.50*
		Nos. 369-383,385-388 (19)	12.75	18.45

Issued: 1c, 7c, 9c, 15c, 25c, 40c, 6/13; 5c, 14c, 21c, 28c, 30c, Aug.; 3c, 8c, 10c, 20c, 60c, $1, 1/23/74.

Papua New Guinea No. 7 — A84

1c, Ger. New Guinea #1-2. 6c, Ger. New Guinea #17. 7c, New Britain #43. 25c, New Guinea #1. 30c, Papua New Guinea #108.

Litho. (1c, 7c); Litho. & Engr. (others)

1973, Oct. 24 *Perf. 13½x14*

Size: 54x31mm

No.	Type	Description	Unused	Used
389	A84	1c gold, brn, grn & blk	.30	.25
390	A84	6c silver, blue & indigo	.35	.25
391	A84	7c gold, red, blk & buff	.35	.25

Perf. 14x14½

Size: 45x38mm

No.	Type	Description	Unused	Used
392	A84	9c gold, org, blk & brn	.45	.35
393	A84	25c gold & orange	.75	*.90*
394	A84	30c silver & dp lilac	.80	*1.00*
		Nos. 389-394 (6)	3.00	3.00

75th anniv. of stamps in Papua New Guinea.

Masks — A85

1973, Dec. 5 **Photo.** *Perf. 12½*

Granite Paper

No.	Type	Description	Unused	Used
395	A85	7c multicolored	.35	.25
396	A85	10c violet blue & multi	.65	.65

Self-government.

Queen Elizabeth II — A86

1974, Feb. 22 **Photo.** *Perf. 14x14½*

No.	Type	Description	Unused	Used
397	A86	7c dp carmine & multi	.35	.25
398	A86	30c vio blue & multi	.90	.90

Visit of Queen Elizabeth II and the Royal Family, Feb. 22-27.

Wreathed Hornbill — A87

Size of No. 400, 32½x48mm.

Perf. 12, 11½ (10c)

1974, June 12 **Photo.**

Granite Paper

No.	Type	Description	Unused	Used
399	A87	7c shown	1.50	.75
400	A87	10c Great cassowary	2.50	*3.25*
401	A87	30c Kapul eagle	5.50	*7.50*
		Nos. 399-401 (3)	9.50	*11.50*

Dendrobium Bracteosum — A88

Orchids: 10c, Dendrobium anosmum. 20c, Dendrobium smillieae. 30c, Dendrobium insigne.

1974, Nov. 20 **Photo.** *Perf. 11½*

Granite Paper

No.	Type	Description	Unused	Used
402	A88	7c dark green & multi	.95	.25
403	A88	10c dark blue & multi	.75	.60
404	A88	20c bister & multi	1.25	1.25
405	A88	30c green & multi	1.60	1.60
		Nos. 402-405 (4)	4.55	3.70

Motu Lakatoi — A89

Traditional Canoes: 10c, Tami two-master morobe. 25c, Aramia racing canoe. 30c, Buka Island canoe.

1975, Feb. 26 **Photo.** *Perf. 11½*

Granite Paper

No.	Type	Description	Unused	Used
406	A89	7c multicolored	.30	.25
407	A89	10c orange & multi	.50	.50
408	A89	25c apple green & multi	.90	*2.50*
409	A89	30c citron & multi	1.00	*1.25*
		Nos. 406-409 (4)	2.70	4.50

Paradise Birdwing Butterfly, 1t Coin — A90

Ornate Butterfly Cod on 2t and Plateless Turtle on 5t — A91

New coinage: 10t, Cuscus on 10t. 20t, Cassowary on 20t. 1k, River crocodiles on 1k coin with center hole; obverse and reverse of 1k.

Perf. 11, 11½ (A91)

1975, Apr. 21 **Photo.**

Granite Paper

No.	Type	Description	Unused	Used
410	A90	1t green & multi	.25	.25
411	A91	7t brown & multi	.35	.35
412	A90	10t violet blue & multi	.35	.35
413	A90	20t carmine & multi	.70	.70
414	A91	1k dull blue & multi	2.00	*2.75*
		Nos. 410-414 (5)	3.65	4.40

Ornithoptera Alexandrae — A92

Birdwing Butterflies: 10t, O. victoriae regis. 30t, O. allottei. 40t, O. chimaera.

1975, June 11 **Photo.** *Perf. 11½*

Granite Paper

No.	Type	Description	Unused	Used
415	A92	7t multicolored	.40	.25
416	A92	10t multicolored	.45	.45
417	A92	30t multicolored	1.40	1.40
418	A92	40t multicolored	1.75	*3.25*
		Nos. 415-418 (4)	4.00	5.35

Boxing and Games' Emblem — A93

1975, Aug. 2 **Photo.** *Perf. 11½*

Granite Paper

No.	Type	Description	Unused	Used
419	A93	7t shown	.35	.25
420	A93	20t Track and field	.60	.45
421	A93	25t Basketball	.65	.60
422	A93	30t Swimming	.70	*.75*
		Nos. 419-422 (4)	2.30	2.05

5th South Pacific Games, Guam, Aug. 1-10.

Map of South East Asia and Flag of PNG — A94

Design: 30t, Map of South East Asia and Papua New Guinea coat of arms.

1975, Sept. 10 **Photo.** *Perf. 11½*

Granite Paper

No.	Type	Description	Unused	Used
423	A94	7t red & multi	.25	.25
424	A94	30t blue & multi	.60	.60
a.		Souvenir sheet of 2, #423-424	1.40	1.40

Papua New Guinea independence, Sept. 16, 1975.

M. V. Bulolo — A95

Ships of the 1930's: 15t, M.V. Macdhui. 25t, M.V. Malaita. 60t, S.S. Montoro.

1976, Jan. 21 **Photo.** *Perf. 11½*

Granite Paper

No.	Type	Description	Unused	Used
425	A95	7t multicolored	.25	.25
426	A95	15t multicolored	.30	.30
427	A95	25t multicolored	.60	.50
428	A95	60t multicolored	1.40	*2.25*
		Nos. 425-428 (4)	2.55	3.30

Rorovana Carvings — A96

Bougainville Art: 20t, Upe hats. 25t, Kapkaps (tortoise shell ornaments). 30t, Carved canoe paddles.

1976, Mar. 17 **Photo.** *Perf. 11½*

Granite Paper

No.	Type	Description	Unused	Used
429	A96	7t multicolored	.30	.25
430	A96	20t blue & multi	.50	.45
431	A96	25t dp orange & multi	.60	*1.10*
432	A96	30t multicolored	.75	.75
		Nos. 429-432 (4)	2.15	2.55

Houses — A97

1976, June 9 **Photo.** *Perf. 11½*

Granite Paper

No.	Type	Description	Unused	Used
433	A97	7t Rabaul	.25	.25
434	A97	15t Aramia	.30	.25
435	A97	30t Telefomin	.60	.60
436	A97	40t Tapini	.60	*1.25*
		Nos. 433-436 (4)	1.75	2.35

Boy Scouts and Scout Emblem — A98

De Havilland Sea Plane, Map of Pacific — A99

Designs: 15t, Sea Scouts on outrigger canoe, Scout emblem. 60t, Plane on water.

1976, Aug. 18 Photo. *Perf. 11½*
Granite Paper

437 A98 7t multicolored .30 .25
438 A99 10t lilac & multi .30 .25
439 A98 15t multicolored .40 .40
440 A99 60t multicolored 1.00 *2.00*
Nos. 437-440 (4) 2.00 2.90

50th anniversaries: Papua New Guinea Boy Scouts; 1st flight from Australia.

Father Ross and Mt. Hagen — A100

1976, Oct. 28 Photo. *Perf. 11½*
Granite Paper

441 A100 7t multicolored .50 .25

Rev. Father William Ross (1896-1973), American missionary in New Guinea.

Clouded Rainbow Fish — A101

Tropical Fish: 15t, Imperial angelfish. 30t, Freckled rock cod. 40t, Threadfin butterflyfish.

1976, Oct. 28 Granite Paper

442 A101 5t multicolored .25 .25
443 A101 15t multicolored .70 .50
444 A101 30t multicolored 1.40 .80
445 A101 40t multicolored 1.90 1.90
Nos. 442-445 (4) 4.25 3.45

Kundiawa Man A102

Mekeo Headdress A103

Headdresses: 5t, Masked dancer, East Sepik Province. 10t, Dancer, Koiari area. 15t, Hanuabada woman. 20t, Young woman, Orokaiva. 25t, Haus Tambaran dancer, East Sepik Province. 30t, Asaro Valley man. 35t, Garaina man, Morobe. 40t, Waghi Valley man. 50t, Trobriand dancer, Milne Bay. 1k, Wasara.

Sizes: 25x30mm (1, 5, 20t), 26x26mm (10, 15, 25, 30, 50t), 23x38mm (35, 40t)

Perf. 12 (15, 25, 30t), 11½ (others)

1977-78 Photo.

446 A102 1t multicolored .25 .25
447 A102 5t multicolored .25 .25
448 A102 10t multicolored .30 .25
449 A102 15t multicolored .30 .25
450 A102 20t multicolored .55 .25
451 A102 25t multicolored .35 .30
452 A102 30t multicolored .40 .40
453 A102 35t multicolored .65 .50
454 A102 40t multicolored .60 .30
455 A102 50t multicolored .85 *.90*

Litho.

Perf. 14½x14

Size: 28x35½mm

456 A102 1k multicolored 1.25 *1.75*

Perf. 14½x15

Size: 33x23mm

457 A103 2k multicolored 1.75 *3.25*
Nos. 446-457 (12) 7.50 8.65

Issued: #456-457, 1/12/77; #448, 450, 453, 455, 6/7/78; others, 3/29/78.

Elizabeth II and P.N.G. Arms — A104

Designs: 7t, Queen and P.N.G. flag. 35t, Queen and map of P.N.G.

1977, Mar. 16 Photo. *Perf. 15x14*

462 A104 7t multicolored .35 .25
a. Silver omitted *500.00*
463 A104 15t multicolored .40 .40
464 A104 35t multicolored .70 *.90*
Nos. 462-464 (3) 1.45 1.55

25th anniv. of the reign of Elizabeth II.

Whitebreasted Ground Dove — A105

Protected Birds: 7t, Victoria crowned pigeon. 15t, Pheasant pigeon. 30t, Orange-fronted fruit dove. 50t, Banded imperial pigeon.

1977, June 8 Photo. *Perf. 11½*
Granite Paper

465 A105 5t multicolored .55 .25
466 A105 7t multicolored .55 .25
467 A105 15t multicolored .90 .85
468 A105 30t multicolored 1.00 1.25
469 A105 50t multicolored 1.50 *3.00*
Nos. 465-469 (5) 4.50 *5.60*

Girl Guides and Gold Badge — A106

Designs (Girl Guides): 15t, Mapping and blue badge. 30t, Doing laundry in brook and red badge. 35t, Wearing grass skirts, cooking and green badge.

1977, Aug. 10 Litho. *Perf. 14½*

470 A106 7t multicolored .25 .25
471 A106 15t multicolored .30 .25
472 A106 30t multicolored .60 .60
473 A106 35t multicolored .60 .60
Nos. 470-473 (4) 1.75 1.70

Papua New Guinea Girl Guides, 50th anniv.

Legend of Kari Marupi — A107

Myths of Elema People: 20t, Savoripi Clan. 30t, Oa-Laea. 35t, Oa-Iriarapo.

1977, Oct. 19 Litho. *Perf. 13½*

474 A107 7t black & multi .25 .25
475 A107 20t black & multi .50 .35
476 A107 30t black & multi .65 .65
477 A107 35t black & multi .65 .65
Nos. 474-477 (4) 2.05 1.90

Blue-tailed Skink — A108

Lizards: 15t, Green tree skink. 35t, Crocodile skink. 40t, New Guinea blue-tongued skink.

1978, Jan. 25 Photo. *Perf. 11½*
Granite Paper

478 A108 10t blue & multi .30 .25
479 A108 15t lilac & multi .40 .25
480 A108 35t olive & multi .60 *.75*
481 A108 40t orange & multi .85 .85
Nos. 478-481 (4) 2.15 2.10

Roboastra Arika — A109

Sea Slugs: 15t, Chromodoris fidelis. 35t, Flabellina macassarana. 40t, Chromodoris trimarginata.

1978, Aug. 29 Photo. *Perf. 11½*

482 A109 10t multicolored .30 .25
483 A109 15t multicolored .40 .40
484 A109 35t multicolored .65 .65
485 A109 40t multicolored .90 *1.15*
Nos. 482-485 (4) 2.25 2.45

Mandated New Guinea Constabulary A110

Constabulary and Badge: 10t, Royal Papua New Guinea. 20t, Armed British New Guinea. 25t, German New Guinea police. 30t, Royal Papua and New Guinea.

1978, Oct. 26 Photo. *Perf. 14½x14*

486 A110 10t multicolored .25 .25
487 A110 15t multicolored .35 .35
488 A110 20t multicolored .40 .40
489 A110 25t multicolored .45 .45
490 A110 30t multicolored .55 .55
Nos. 486-490 (5) 2.00 2.00

Ocarina, Chimbu Province — A111

Musical Instruments: 20t, Musical bow, New Britain, horiz. 28t, Launut, New Ireland. 35t, Nose flute, New Hanover, horiz.

Perf. 14½x14, 14x14½

1979, Jan. 24 Litho.

491 A111 7t multicolored .30 .25
492 A111 20t multicolored .40 .30
493 A111 28t multicolored .60 .60
494 A111 35t multicolored .70 .70
Nos. 491-494 (4) 2.00 1.85

Prow and Paddle, East New Britain — A112

Canoe Prows and Paddles: 21t, Sepik war canoe. 25t, Trobriand Islands. 40t, Milne Bay.

1979, Mar. 28 Litho. *Perf. 14½*

495 A112 14t multicolored .30 .25
496 A112 21t multicolored .40 .25
497 A112 25t multicolored .55 .55
498 A112 40t multicolored .70 .70
Nos. 495-498 (4) 1.95 1.75

Belt of Shell Disks — A113

Traditional Currency: 15t, Tusk chest ornament. 25t, Shell armband. 35t, Shell necklace.

1979, June 6 Litho. *Perf. 12½x12*

499 A113 7t multicolored .25 .25
500 A113 15t multicolored .35 .30
501 A113 25t multicolored .55 .55
502 A113 35t multicolored .65 .65
Nos. 499-502 (4) 1.80 1.75

Oenetus — A114

Moths: 15t, Celerina vulgaris. 20t, Alcidis aurora, vert. 25t, Phyllodes conspicillator. 30t, Nyctalemon patroclus, vert.

1979, Aug. 29 Photo. *Perf. 11½*

503 A114 7t multicolored .25 .25
504 A114 15t multicolored .40 .35
505 A114 20t multicolored .45 .45
506 A114 25t multicolored .50 *.75*
507 A114 30t multicolored .65 *.90*
Nos. 503-507 (5) 2.25 2.70

Baby in String Bag Scale — A115

IYC (Emblem and): 7t, Mother nursing baby. 30t, Boy playing with dog and ball. 60t, Girl in classroom.

1979, Oct. 24 Litho. *Perf. 14x13½*

508 A115 7t multicolored .30 .25
509 A115 15t multicolored .35 .25
510 A115 30t multicolored .45 .45
511 A115 60t multicolored .80 .80
Nos. 508-511 (4) 1.90 1.75

Mail Sorting, Mail Truck — A116

UPU Membership: 25t, Wartime mail delivery. 35t, UPU monument, airport and city. 40t, Hand canceling, letter carrier.

1980, Jan. 23 Litho. *Perf. 13½x14*

512 A116 7t multicolored .30 .25
513 A116 25t multicolored .40 .30
514 A116 35t multicolored .50 .50
515 A116 40t multicolored .65 .65
Nos. 512-515 (4) 1.85 1.70

Male Dancer, Betrothal Ceremony — A117

Third South Pacific Arts Festival, Port Moresby (Minj Betrothal Ceremony Mural): a, One dancer, orange and yellow. b, Two dancers, red, yellow & blk. c, Two dancers side by side, orange, black. d, Two dancers, one in front of the other one. e, One dancer, yellow and red.

No. 516 has continuous design.

1980, Mar. 26 Photo. *Perf. 11½*
Granite Paper

516 A117 Strip of 5 1.75 *2.00*
a.-e. 20t any single .30 .30

National Census A118

1980, June 4 Litho. *Perf. 14*

517 A118 7t shown .25 .25
518 A118 15t Population symbol .25 .25
519 A118 40t P. N. G. map .55 .55
520 A118 50t Faces .75 .75
Nos. 517-520 (4) 1.80 1.80

Blood Transfusion, Donor's Badge — A119

15t, Donating blood. 30t, Map of donation centers. 60t, Blood components and types.

1980, Aug. 27 Litho. *Perf. 14½*

521 A119 7t shown .25 .25
522 A119 15t multicolored .25 .25
523 A119 30t multicolored .50 .50
524 A119 60t multicolored .85 .85
Nos. 521-524 (4) 1.85 1.85

Dugong — A120

30t, Native spotted cat, vert. 35t, Tube-nosed bat, vert. 45t, Raffray's bandicoot.

1980, Oct. 29 Photo. *Perf. 11½*

525 A120 7t shown .25 .25
526 A120 30t multicolored .60 .60
527 A120 35t multicolored .70 .70
528 A120 45t multicolored .95 .95
Nos. 525-528 (4) 2.50 2.50

Beach Kingfisher — A121

7t, Forest kingfisher. 20t, Sacred kingfisher. 25t, White-tailed paradise kingfisher. 60t, Blue-winged kookaburra.

1981, Jan. 21 Photo. *Perf. 12*

Granite Paper

529 A121 3t shown .30 *.60*
530 A121 7t multicolored .30 .25
531 A121 20t multicolored .45 .45

Size: 26x45½mm

532 A121 25t multicolored .55 .55

Size: 26x36mm

533 A121 60t multicolored 1.40 *2.75*
Nos. 529-533 (5) 3.00 4.60

Mask — A122

Coil Stamps

Perf. 14½ Horiz.

1981, Jan. 21 Photo.

534 A122 2t shown .25 .25
535 A122 5t Hibiscus .25 .25

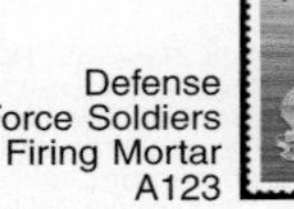

Defense Force Soldiers Firing Mortar A123

15t, DC-3 military plane. 40t, Patrol boat Eitape. 50t, Medics treating civilians.

1981, Mar. 25 Photo. *Perf. 13½x14*

536 A123 7t shown .25 .25
537 A123 15t multicolored .30 .25
538 A123 40t multicolored .65 .65
539 A123 50t multicolored .80 .80
Nos. 536-539 (4) 2.00 1.95

For surcharge see No. 615.

Missionary Aviation Fellowship Plane — A124

Planes of Missionary Organizations: 15t, Holy Ghost Society. 20t, Summer Institute of Linguistics. 30t, Lutheran Mission. 35t, Seventh Day Adventist.

1981, June 17 Litho. *Perf. 14*

540 A124 10t multicolored .25 .25
541 A124 15t multicolored .30 .25
542 A124 20t multicolored .40 .30
543 A124 30t multicolored .50 .50
544 A124 35t multicolored .60 .60
Nos. 540-544 (5) 2.05 1.90

Scoop Net Fishing — A125

1981, Aug. 26

545 A125 10t shown .25 .25
546 A125 15t Kite fishing .30 .30
547 A125 30t Rod fishing .55 .55
548 A125 60t Scissor net fishing 1.00 1.00
Nos. 545-548 (4) 2.10 2.10

Forcartia Buhleri — A126

15t, Naninia citrina. 20t, Papuina adonis, papuina hermione. 30t, Papustyla hindei, papustyla novaepommeraniae. 40t, Rhynchotrochus strabo.

1981, Oct. 28 Photo. *Perf. 12*

Granite Paper

549 A126 5t multicolored .25 .25
550 A126 15t multicolored .30 .30
551 A126 20t multicolored .40 .40
552 A126 30t multicolored .55 .55
553 A126 40t multicolored .70 .70
Nos. 549-553 (5) 2.20 2.20

75th Anniv. of Boy Scouts — A127

15t, Lord Baden-Powell, flag raising. 25t, Leader, campfire. 35t, Scout, hut building. 50t, Percy Chatterton, first aid.

1982, Jan. 20 Photo. *Perf. 11½*

Granite Paper

554 A127 15t multicolored .25 .25
555 A127 25t multicolored .40 .40
556 A127 35t multicolored .55 .55
557 A127 50t multicolored .80 .80
Nos. 554-557 (4) 2.00 2.00

Wanigela Pottery — A128

10t, Boiken, East Sepik. 20t, Gumalu, Madang. 50t, Ramu Valley, Madang.

1982, Mar. 24 Litho. *Perf. 14*

Size: 29x29mm

558 A128 10t multicolored .25 .25
559 A128 20t multicolored .40 .40

Perf. 14½

Size: 36x23mm

560 A128 40t shown .65 .65
561 A128 50t multicolored .80 .80
Nos. 558-561 (4) 2.10 2.10

Nutrition — A129

1982, May 5 Litho. *Perf. 14½x14*

562 A129 10t Mother, child .25 .25
563 A129 15t Protein .35 .35
564 A129 30t Fruits, vegetables .65 .65
565 A129 40t Carbohydrates .85 .85
Nos. 562-565 (4) 2.10 2.10

Coral — A130

1t, Stony Coral (Stylophora). 5t, Finger Coral (Acropora humilis). 15t, Lace Coral (Distichopora). 1k, Pulse Coral (Xenia).

1982, July 21 Photo. *Perf. 11½*

Granite Paper

566 A130 1t Stylophora sp. .35 .25
567 A130 5t Acropora humilis .35 .25
568 A130 15t Distichopora sp. .75 .40
569 A130 1k Xenia sp. 3.75 2.75
Nos. 566-569 (4) 5.20 3.65

See Nos. 575-579, 588-591, 614.

Centenary of Catholic Church in Papua New Guinea — A131

a, Ship and Men, one dog. b, Men and three dogs. c, Men and tree.

1982, Sept. 15 Photo. *Perf. 11½*

570 A131 Strip of 3 1.00 1.00
a.-c. 10t any single .30 .30

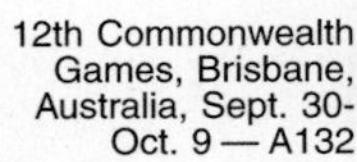

12th Commonwealth Games, Brisbane, Australia, Sept. 30-Oct. 9 — A132

1982, Oct. 6 Litho. *Perf. 14½*

571 A132 10t Running .25 .25
572 A132 15t Boxing .25 .25
573 A132 45t Shooting .80 .80
574 A132 50t Lawn bowling .90 .90
Nos. 571-574 (4) 2.20 2.20

Coral Type of 1982

3t, Cup Coral (Dendrophyllia). 10t, Carnation Tree Coral (Dendronephthya), orange coral, gray background. 30t, Carnation Tree Coral (Dendronephthya), red coral, blue green background. 40t, Black Coral (Antipathes). 3k, Lace Coral (Distichopora).

1983, Jan. 12 Photo. *Perf. 11½*

Granite Paper

575 A130 3t multi .70 *1.25*
576 A130 10t multi .90 .90
577 A130 30t multi 1.40 .90
578 A130 40t multi 1.50 1.50
579 A130 3k multi 6.50 6.50
Nos. 575-579 (5) 11.00 11.05

Nos. 575-579 vert.

Commonwealth Day — A133

10t, Flag, arms. 15t, Youth, recreation. 20t, Technical assistance. 50t, Export assistance.

1983, Mar. 9 Litho. *Perf. 14*

580 A133 10t multi .25 .25
581 A133 15t multi .25 .25
582 A133 20t multi .40 .40
583 A133 50t multi .90 .90
Nos. 580-583 (4) 1.80 1.80

World Communications Year — A134

10t, Mail transport. 25t, Writing & receiving letter. 30t, Telephone calls. 60t, Family reunion.

1983, Sept. 7 Litho. *Perf. 14*

584 A134 10t multi .30 .25
585 A134 25t multi .50 .40
586 A134 30t multi .55 .45
587 A134 60t multi 1.00 1.00
Nos. 584-587 (4) 2.35 2.10

Coral Type of 1982

20t, Bamboo Coral (Isis). 25t, Small Polyp Stony Coral (Acropora). 35t, Elegant Hydrocoral (Stylaster elegans). 45t, Cup Coral (Turbinaria).

1983, Nov. 9 Photo. *Perf. 11½*

Granite Paper

588 A130 20t multi 1.10 .70
589 A130 25t multi .90 .90
590 A130 35t multi 1.60 1.40
591 A130 45t multi 2.50 1.75
Nos. 588-591 (4) 6.10 4.75

Nos. 588-591 vert.

Turtles — A135

5t, Chelonia depressa. 10t, Chelonia mydas. 15t, Eretkmochelys imbricata. 20t, Lepidochelys olivacea. 25t, Caretta caretta. 40t, Dermochelys coriacea.

1984, Feb. 8 Photo.

Granite Paper

592 A135 5t multicolored .25 .25
593 A135 10t multicolored .30 .30
594 A135 15t multicolored .50 .50
595 A135 20t multicolored .65 .60
596 A135 25t multicolored 1.00 1.00
597 A135 40t multicolored 1.10 1.10
Nos. 592-597 (6) 3.80 3.75

Papua-Australia Airmail Service, 50th Anniv. — A136

Mail planes — 20t, Avro X VH-UXX. 25t, DH86B VH-UYU Carmania. 40t, Westland Widgeon. 60t, Consolidated Catalina NC777.

1984, May 9 Litho. *Perf. 14½x14*

598 A136 20t multicolored .45 .45
599 A136 25t multicolored .55 .55
600 A136 40t multicolored .90 .90
601 A136 60t multicolored 1.25 1.25
Nos. 598-601 (4) 3.15 3.15

Parliament House Opening A137

1984, Aug. 7 Litho. *Perf. 13½x14*

602 A137 10t multicolored .40 .40

Bird of Paradise — A138

1984, Aug. 7 Photo. *Perf. 11½*

Granite Paper

603 A138 5k multicolored 10.00 10.00

Ceremonial Shield — A139

1984, Sept. 21

604 A139 10t Central Province .25 .25
605 A139 20t West New Britain .55 .55
606 A139 30t Madang .85 .85
607 A139 50t East Sepik .90 *2.50*
Nos. 604-607 (4) 2.55 4.15

See Nos. 677-680.

British New Guinea Proclamation Centenary — A140

1984, Nov. 6 Litho. *Perf. 14½x14*

608 A140 Pair .50 *.90*
a. 10t Nelson, Port Moresby, 1884 .25 *.45*
b. 10t Port Moresby, 1984 .25 *.45*
609 A140 Pair 2.50 *3.25*
a. 45t Rabaul, 1984 1.10 *1.60*
b. 45t Elizabeth, Rabaul, 1884 1.10 *1.60*

Chimbu Gorge — A142

10t, Fergusson Island, vert. 25t, Sepik River, vert. 60t, Dali Beach, Vanimo.

1985, Feb. 6 Photo. *Perf. 11½*
610 A142 10t multicolored .25 .25
611 A142 25t multicolored .65 .65
612 A142 40t shown 1.05 1.05
613 A142 60t multicolored 1.75 1.75
Nos. 610-613 (4) 3.70 3.70

Coral Type of 1982

12t, Carnation Tree Coral (Dendronephthya), orange coral, blue green background, vert.

1985, May 29 Photo. *Perf. 11½*
614 A130 12t multicolored 4.50 4.50

For surcharge see No. 686.

No. 536 Surcharged

1985, Apr. 1 Litho. *Perf. 13½x14*
615 A123 12t on 7t multi .70 *1.00*
a. Inverted surcharge —

Ritual Structures — A143

Designs: 15t, Dubu platform, Central Province. 20t, Tamuniai house, West New Britain. 30t, Yam tower, Trobriand Island. 60t, Huli grave, Tari.

1985, May 1 *Perf. 13x13½*
616 A143 15t multicolored .45 .45
617 A143 20t multicolored .65 .65
618 A143 30t multicolored .90 .90
619 A143 60t multicolored 1.40 1.40
Nos. 616-619 (4) 3.40 3.40

A set of four with designs similar to Nos. 616-619 and without the "t" in the denomination was prepared but not officially issued. A small number of sets found their way into the marketplace. Value, set $200.

Indigenous Birds of Prey — A144

1985, Aug. 26 *Perf. 14x14½*
620 12t Accipiter brachyurus .75 .75
621 12t In flight .75 .75
a. A144 Pair, #620-621 1.75 1.75
622 30t Megatriorchis doriae 1.25 1.25
623 30t In Flight 1.25 1.25
a. A144 Pair, #622-623 3.00 3.00
624 60t Henicopernis longicauda 2.50 2.50
625 60t In flight 2.50 2.50
a. A144 Pair, #624-625 6.00 6.00
Nos. 620-625 (6) 9.00 9.00

Flag and Gable of Parliament House, Port Moresby — A145

1985, Sept. 11 *Perf. 14½x15*
626 A145 12t multicolored .60 .60

Post Office Centenary — A146

Designs: 12t, No. 631a, 1901 Postal card, aerogramme, spectacles and inkwell. 30t, No. 631b, Queensland Type A15, No. 628. 40t, No. 631c, Plane and news clipping, 1885. 60t, No. 631d, 1892 German canceler, 1985 first day cancel.

1985, Oct. 9 *Perf. 14½x14*
627 A146 12t multicolored .60 .60
628 A146 30t multicolored 1.60 1.60
629 A146 40t multicolored 2.25 2.25
630 A146 60t multicolored 2.75 2.75
Nos. 627-630 (4) 7.20 7.20

Souvenir Sheet

631 Sheet of 4 8.00 8.00
a. A146 12t multicolored .80 .80
b. A146 30t multicolored 1.40 1.40
c. A146 40t multicolored 1.75 1.75
d. A146 60t multicolored 3.00 3.00

Nombowai Cave Carved Funerary Totems — A147

12t, Bird Rulowlaw, headman. 30t, Barn owl Raus, headman. 60t, Melerawuk. 80t, Cockerel, woman.

1985, Nov. 13 *Perf. 11½*
632 A147 12t multicolored .60 .30
633 A147 30t multicolored 1.25 .70
634 A147 60t multicolored 2.00 *2.25*
635 A147 80t multicolored 2.50 *3.75*
Nos. 632-635 (4) 6.35 7.00

Conch Shells — A148

15t, Cypraea valentia. 35t, Oliva buelowi. 45t, Oliva parkinsoni. 70t, Cypraea aurantium.

1986, Feb. 12 *Perf. 11½*
636 A148 15t multicolored .70 .45
637 A148 35t multicolored 1.75 1.50
638 A148 45t multicolored 2.00 2.00
639 A148 70t multicolored 2.75 *4.25*
Nos. 636-639 (4) 7.20 8.20

Common Design Types pictured following the introduction.

Queen Elizabeth II 60th Birthday
Common Design Type

Designs: 15t, In ATS officer's uniform, 1945. 35t, Silver wedding anniv. portrait by Patrick Lichfield, Balmoral, 1972. 50t, Inspecting troops, Port Moresby, 1982. 60t, Banquet aboard Britannia, state tour, 1982. 70t, Visiting Crown Agents' offices, 1983.

Perf. 14½
1986, Apr. 21 Litho. Unwmk.
640 CD337 15t scar, blk & sil .30 .30
641 CD337 35t ultra & multi .65 .65
642 CD337 50t green & multi .90 .90
643 CD337 60t violet & multi 1.00 1.00
644 CD337 70t rose vio & multi 1.25 1.25
Nos. 640-644 (5) 4.10 4.10

AMERIPEX '86 A149

Small birds — 15t, Pitta erythrogaster. 35t, Melanocharis striativentris. 45t, Rhipidura rufifrons. 70t, Poecilodryas placens, vert.

1986, May 22 Photo. *Perf. 12½*
Granite Paper
645 A149 15t multicolored 1.10 .70
646 A149 35t multicolored 2.25 1.60
647 A149 45t multicolored 2.50 2.10
648 A149 70t multicolored 3.75 *4.50*
Nos. 645-648 (4) 9.60 8.90

Lutheran Church, Cent. — A150

15t, Monk, minister. 70t, Churches from 1886, 1986.

1986, July 7 Litho. *Perf. 14x15*
649 A150 15t multicolored .60 .55
650 A150 70t multicolored 2.75 2.75

Indigenous Orchids — A151

15t, Dendrobium vexillarius. 35t, Dendrobium lineale. 45t, Dendrobium johnsoniae. 70t, Dendrobium cuthbertsonii.

1986, Aug. 4 Litho. *Perf. 14*
651 A151 15t multicolored 1.10 .75
652 A151 35t multicolored 2.25 1.60
653 A151 45t multicolored 2.50 2.10
654 A151 70t multicolored 3.25 *5.00*
Nos. 651-654 (4) 9.10 9.45

Folk Dancers — A152

1986, Nov. 12 Litho. *Perf. 14*
655 A152 15t Maprik .95 .65
656 A152 35t Kiriwina 1.75 1.50
657 A152 45t Kundiawa 2.00 1.90
658 A152 70t Fasu 3.50 *4.50*
Nos. 655-658 (4) 8.20 8.55

Fish — A153

17t, White-cap anemonefish. 30t, Black anemonefish. 35t, Tomato clownfish. 70t, Spine-cheek anemonefish.

Unwmk.
1987, Apr. 15 Litho. *Perf. 15*
659 A153 17t multicolored 1.00 .35
660 A153 30t multicolored 1.50 1.75
661 A153 35t multicolored 2.00 1.40
662 A153 70t multicolored 3.00 *4.50*
Nos. 659-662 (4) 7.50 8.00

For surcharges see Nos. 720, 823, 868.

Ships — A154

1t, La Boudeuse, 1768. 5t, Roebuck, 1700. 10t, Swallow, 1767. 15t, Fly, 1845. 17t, like No. 666. 20t, Rattlesnake, 1849. 30t, Vitiaz, 1871. 35t, San Pedrico, Zabre, 1606. 40t, L'Astrolabe, 1827. 45t, Neva, 1876. 60t, Caravel of Jorge De Meneses, 1526. 70t, Eendracht, 1616. 1k, Blanche, 1872. 2k, Merrie England, 1889. 3k, Samoa, 1884.

1987-88 Photo. Unwmk. *Perf. 11½*
Granite Paper
663 A154 1t multicolored .55 *1.25*
664 A154 5t multicolored 1.10 *1.50*
665 A154 10t multicolored 1.40 1.40
666 A154 15t multicolored 2.00 1.25
667 A154 17t multicolored 2.00 .75
668 A154 20t multicolored 2.00 1.00
669 A154 30t multicolored 2.00 2.00
670 A154 35t multicolored .75 *.90*
671 A154 40t multicolored 2.25 2.25
672 A154 45t multicolored .90 .90
673 A154 60t multicolored 2.75 *3.25*
674 A154 70t multicolored 2.25 2.25
675 A154 1k multicolored 2.75 2.75
676 A154 2k multicolored 4.25 4.25
676A A154 3k multicolored 5.25 *7.00*
Nos. 663-676A (15) 32.20 32.70

Issued: 5, 35, 45, 70t, 2k, 6/15/87; 15, 20, 40, 60t, 2/17/88; 17t, 1k, 3/1/88; 1, 10, 30t, 3k, 11/16/88.

See Nos. 960-963. For surcharge see No. 824.

Shield Type of 1984

War shields — 15t, Elema shield, Gulf Province, c. 1880. 35t, East Sepik Province. 45t, Simbai region, Madang Province. 70t, Telefomin region, West Sepik.

Perf. 11½x12
1987, Aug. 19 Photo. Unwmk.
677 A139 15t multicolored .30 .30
678 A139 35t multicolored .65 .65
679 A139 45t multicolored .80 .80
680 A139 70t multicolored 1.25 1.25
Nos. 677-680 (4) 3.00 3.00

Starfish — A156

17t, Protoreaster nodosus. 35t, Gomophia egeriae. 45t, Choriaster granulatus. 70t, Neoferdina ocellata.

1987, Sept. 30 Litho. *Perf. 14*
682 A156 17t multicolored .75 .40
683 A156 35t multicolored 1.50 .90
684 A156 45t multicolored 1.75 1.10
685 A156 70t multicolored 2.25 *3.50*
Nos. 682-685 (4) 6.25 5.90

No. 614 Surcharged

1987, Sept. 23 Photo. *Perf. 11½*
Granite Paper
686 A130 15t on 12t multi 1.60 1.25

Aircraft — A157

Designs: 15t, Cessna Stationair 6, Rabaraba Airstrip. 35t, Britten-Norman Islander over Hombrum Bluff. 45t, DHC Twin Otter over the Highlands. 70t, Fokker F28 over Madang.

Unwmk.
1987, Nov. 11 Litho. *Perf. 14*
687 A157 15t multicolored 1.25 .45
688 A157 35t multicolored 1.75 1.00
689 A157 45t multicolored 2.00 1.25
690 A157 70t multicolored 3.00 *5.25*
Nos. 687-690 (4) 8.00 7.95

Royal Papua New Guinea Police Force, Cent. — A158

Historic and modern aspects of the force: 17t, Motorcycle constable and pre-independence officer wearing a lap-lap. 35t, Sir William McGregor, Armed Native Constabulary founder, 1890, and recruit. 45t, Badges. 70t, Albert Hahl, German official credited with founding the island's police movement in 1888, and badge, early officer.

Perf. 14x15
1988, June 15 Litho. Unwmk.
691 A158 17t multicolored .60 .45
692 A158 35t multicolored 1.10 .85
693 A158 45t multicolored 1.40 1.10
694 A158 70t multicolored 2.00 2.00
Nos. 691-694 (4) 5.10 4.40

Sydney Opera House and a Lakatoi (ship) A159

Fireworks and Globes — A160

1988, July 30 Litho. *Perf. 13½*

695 A159 35t multicolored .85 .85
696 A160 Pair 1.90 1.90
a.-b. 35t any single .85 .85
c. Souvenir sheet of 2, #a.-b. 2.60 2.60

SYDPEX '88, Australia (No. 695); Australia bicentennial (No. 696).

World Wildlife Fund — A161

Metamorphosis of a Queen Alexandra's birdwing butterfly — 5t, Courtship. 17t, Ovipositioning and larvae, vert. 25t, Emergence from pupa, vert. 35t, Adult male on leaf.

1988, Sept. 19 *Perf. 14½*

697 A161 5t multicolored *2.50* *2.00*
698 A161 17t multicolored *3.75* *1.25*
699 A161 25t multicolored *4.25* *3.50*
700 A161 35t multicolored *5.50* *4.50*
Nos. 697-700 (4) *16.00* *11.25*

1988 Summer Olympics, Seoul — A162

1988, Sept. 19 Litho. *Perf. 13½*

701 A162 17t Running .75 .75
702 A162 45t Weight lifting 1.50 1.50

Rhododendrons A163

Wmk. 387

1989, Jan. 25 Litho. *Perf. 14*

703 A163 3t R. zoelleri .25 .25
704 A163 20t R. cruttwellii .65 .65
705 A163 60t R. superbum 1.60 1.60
706 A163 70t R. christianae 2.00 2.00
Nos. 703-706 (4) 4.50 4.50

Intl. Letter Writing Week — A164

1989, Mar. 22 *Perf. 14½*

707 A164 20t Writing letter .40 .40
708 A164 35t Mailing letter .70 .60
709 A164 60t Stamping letter 1.15 1.15
710 A164 70t Reading letter 1.35 1.35
Nos. 707-710 (4) 3.60 3.50

Thatched Dwellings A165

20t, Buka Is., 1880s. 35t, Koiari tree houses. 60t, Lauan, New Ireland, 1890s. 70t, Basilaki, Milne Bay Province, 1930s.

1989, May 17 Wmk. 387 *Perf. 15*

711 A165 20t multicolored .45 .40
712 A165 35t multicolored .95 .75
713 A165 60t multicolored 1.50 1.50
714 A165 70t multicolored 1.75 1.75
Nos. 711-714 (4) 4.65 4.40

Small Birds — A166

No. 715, Oreocharis arfaki female, shown. No. 716, Male. No. 717, Ifrita kowaldi. No. 718, Poecilodryas albonotata. No. 719, Sericornis nouhuysi.

1989, July 12 Unwmk. *Perf. 14½*

715 A166 20t multicolored 1.40 1.40
716 A166 20t multicolored 1.40 1.40
a. Pair, #715-716 3.25 3.25
717 A166 35t multicolored 1.90 1.40
718 A166 45t multicolored 1.90 1.60
719 A166 70t multicolored 2.50 2.50
Nos. 715-719 (5) 9.10 8.30

No. 659 Surcharged

1989, July 12 Unwmk. *Perf. 15*

720 A153 20t on 17t multi .90 .90
a. Double surcharge 180.00

Traditional Dance — A167

Designs: 20t, Motumotu, Gulf Province. 35t, Baining, East New Britain Province. 60t, Vailala River, Gulf Province. 70t, Timbunke, East Sepik Province.

Perf. 14x14½

1989, Sept. 6 Litho. Wmk. 387

721 A167 20t multicolored .70 .65
722 A167 35t multicolored 1.25 1.10
723 A167 60t multicolored 2.40 2.40
724 A167 70t multicolored 2.75 2.75
Nos. 721-724 (4) 7.10 6.90

For surcharge see No. 860.

Christmas A168

Designs: 20t, Hibiscus, church and symbol from a gulf gope board, Kavaumai. 35t, Rhododendron, madonna and child, and mask, Murik Lakes region. 60t, D'Albertis creeper, candle, and shield from Oksapmin, West Sepik highlands. 70t, Pacific frangipani, peace dove and flute mask from Chungrebu, a Rao village in Ramu.

Perf. 14x14½

1989, Nov. 8 Litho. Unwmk.

725 A168 20t multicolored .55 .50
726 A168 35t multicolored .85 .85
727 A168 60t multicolored 1.60 1.60
728 A168 70t multicolored 1.75 1.75
Nos. 725-728 (4) 4.75 4.70

Waterfalls — A169

Unwmk.

1990, Feb. 1 Litho. *Perf. 14*

729 A169 20t Guni Falls .75 .55
730 A169 35t Rouna Falls 1.10 .90
731 A169 60t Ambua Falls 2.10 2.10
732 A169 70t Wawoi Falls 2.40 2.40
Nos. 729-732 (4) 6.35 5.95

For surcharges see Nos. 866, 870.

Natl. Census — A170

20t, Three youths, form. 70t, Man, woman, child, form.

1990, May 2 *Perf. 14½x15*

733 A170 20t multicolored .60 .60
734 A170 70t multicolored 2.50 2.50

For surcharge see No. 869.

Gogodala Dance Masks — A171

1990, July 11 Litho. *Perf. 13½*

735 A171 20t shown 1.25 .50
736 A171 35t multi, diff. 1.75 .90
737 A171 60t multi, diff. 2.75 *3.75*
738 A171 70t multi, diff. 3.00 *3.75*
Nos. 735-738 (4) 8.75 8.90

For surcharges see Nos. 867, 871.

Waitangi Treaty, 150th Anniv. — A172

Designs: 20t, Dwarf Cassowary, Great Spotted Kiwi. No. 740, Double Wattled Cassowary, Brown Kiwi. No. 741, Sepik mask and Maori carving.

1990, Aug. 24 Litho. *Perf. 14½*

739 A172 20t multicolored 1.25 .90
740 A172 35t multicolored 1.75 .90
741 A172 35t multicolored 2.25 1.40
Nos. 739-741 (3) 5.25 3.20

No. 741 for World Stamp Exhibition, New Zealand 1990.
For surcharges see Nos. 862-863.

Birds — A173

20t, Whimbrel. 35t, Sharp-tailed sandpiper. 60t, Ruddy turnstone. 70t, Terek sandpiper.

1990, Sept. 26 Litho. *Perf. 14*

742 A173 20t multi 1.25 .70
743 A173 35t multi 1.90 1.10
744 A173 60t multi 3.00 *3.75*
745 A173 70t multi 3.75 *3.75*
Nos. 742-745 (4) 9.90 9.30

Musical Instruments — A174

1990, Oct. 31 Litho. *Perf. 13*

746 A174 20t Jew's harp .90 .75
747 A174 35t Musical bow 1.40 1.25
748 A174 60t Wantoat drum 2.75 2.75
749 A174 70t Gogodala rattle 3.00 3.00
Nos. 746-749 (4) 8.05 7.75

For surcharge see No. 861.

Snail Shells — A174a

Designs: 21t, Rhynchotrochus weigmani. 40t, Forcartia globula, Canefriula azonata. 50t, Planispira deaniana. 80t, Papuina chancel, Papuina xanthocheila.

1991, Mar. 6 Litho. *Perf. 14x14½*

750 A174a 21t multicolored 1.00 .65
751 A174a 40t multicolored 1.60 1.10
752 A174a 50t multicolored 2.25 2.25
753 A174a 80t multicolored 3.25 3.25
Nos. 750-753 (4) 8.10 7.25

For surcharge see No. 864.

A175

A176

1t, Ptiloris magnificus. 5t, Loria loriae. 10t, Cnemophilus macgregorii. 20t, Parotia wahnesi. 21t, Manucodia chalybata. 30t, Paradisaea decora. 40t, Loboparadisea sericea. 45t, Cicinnurus regius. 50t, Paradigalla brevicauda. 60t, Parotia carolae. 90t, Paradisaea guilielmi. 1k, Diphyllodes magnificus. 2k, Lophorina superba. 5k, Phonygammus keraudrenii. 10k, Paradisaea minor.

1991-94 Litho. *Perf. 14½*

755 A175 1t multicolored .25 .25
756 A175 5t multicolored .25 .25
757 A175 10t multicolored .25 .25
758 A175 20t multicolored .45 .45
759 A175 21t multicolored .50 .50
a. Dated "MAY 1992" —
760 A175 30t multicolored .70 .70
761 A175 40t multicolored .90 .90
762 A175 45t multicolored 2.25 1.10
763 A175 50t multicolored 1.25 1.25
764 A175 60t multicolored 3.75 1.40
765 A175 90t multicolored 3.75 2.10
766 A175 1k multicolored 2.25 2.25
767 A175 2k multicolored 4.10 4.50
a. Strip of 4, #761, 763, 766-767 + label 9.00 9.00
768 A175 5k multicolored 10.00 10.00

Perf. 13

769 A176 10k multicolored 20.00 20.00
Nos. 755-769 (15) 50.65 45.90

No. 767a for Hong Kong '94 and sold for 4k.
Stamps in No. 767a do not have "1992 BIRD OF PARADISE" at bottom of design.
Issued: 21t, 45t, 60t, 90t, 3/25/92; 5t, 40t, 50t, 1k, 2k, 9/2/92; 1t, 10t, 20t, 30t, 5k, 1993; 10k, 5/1/91; No. 767a, 2/18/94.
For surcharges see #878A, 878C.

Large T — A176a

1993 Litho. *Perf. 14½*

770A A176a 21T like #759 1.50 .75
770B A176a 45T like #762 3.00 1.60
770C A176a 60T like #764 3.50 3.50
770D A176a 90T like #765 4.25 4.25
Nos. 770A-770D (4) 12.25 10.10

Originally scheduled for release on Feb. 19, 1992, #770A-770D were withdrawn when the denomination was found to have an upper case "T." Corrected versions with a lower case "T" are #759, 762, 764-765. A quantity of the original stamps appeared in the market and to prevent speculation in these items, the Postal Administration of Papua New Guinea released the stamps with the upper case "T."
For surcharges see #878B, 878D.

1991 South Pacific Games — A177

1991, June 26 Litho. *Perf. 13*

771 A177 21t Cricket 2.50 .80
772 A177 40t Running 2.10 1.60
773 A177 50t Baseball 2.50 2.50
774 A177 80t Rugby 4.75 4.75
Nos. 771-774 (4) 11.85 9.65

Anglican Church in Papua New Guinea, Cent. — A178

Churches: 21t, Cathedral of St. Peter & St. Paul, Dogura. 40t, Kaieta Shrine, Anglican landing site. 80t, First thatched chapel, modawa tree.

1991, Aug. 7 Litho. *Perf. 14½*

775 A178 21t multicolored 1.00 .70
776 A178 40t multicolored 2.00 2.00
777 A178 80t multicolored 3.00 *3.50*
Nos. 775-777 (3) 6.00 6.20

Traditional Headdresses — A179

Designs: 21t, Rambutso, Manus Province. 40t, Marawaka, Eastern Highlands. 50t, Tufi, Oro Province. 80t, Sina Sina, Simbu Province.

1991, Oct. 16 Litho. *Perf. 13*

778 A179 21t multicolored .95 .60
779 A179 40t multicolored 1.75 1.75
780 A179 50t multicolored 2.00 2.00
781 A179 80t multicolored 2.75 *4.25*
Nos. 778-781 (4) 7.45 8.60

Discovery of America, 500th Anniv. — A180

1992, Apr. 15 Litho. *Perf. 14*

782 A180 21t Nina .70 .50
783 A180 45t Pinta 1.75 1.10
784 A180 60t Santa Maria 2.10 2.10
785 A180 90t Columbus, ships 3.00 *3.50*
a. Souvenir sheet of 2, #784-785 7.00 7.00
Nos. 782-785 (4) 7.55 7.20

World Columbian Stamp Expo '92, Chicago. Issue date: No. 785a, June 3.

A181

Papuan Gulf Artifacts: 21t, Canoe prow shield, Bamu. 45t. Skull rack, Kerewa. 60t, Ancestral figure, Era River. 90t, Gope (spirit) board, Urama.

1992, June 3 Litho. *Perf. 14*

786 A181 21t multicolored .75 .55
787 A181 45t multicolored 1.50 1.25
788 A181 60t multicolored 1.75 1.60
789 A181 90t multicolored 2.75 2.75
Nos. 786-789 (4) 6.75 6.15

A182

Soldiers from: 21t, Papuan Infantry Battalion. 45t, Australian Militia. 60t, Japanese Nankai Force. 90t, US Army.

1992, July 22 Litho. *Perf. 14*

790 A182 21t multicolored .95 .60
791 A182 45t multicolored 1.75 1.25
792 A182 60t multicolored 2.50 2.10
793 A182 90t multicolored 3.25 3.25
Nos. 790-793 (4) 8.45 7.20

World War II, 50th anniv.

Flowering Trees — A183

21t, Hibiscus tiliaceus. 45t, Castanospermum australe. 60t, Cordia subcordata. 90t, Acacia auriculiformis.

1992, Oct. 28 Litho. *Perf. 14*

794 A183 21t multicolored 1.00 .60
795 A183 45t multicolored 1.90 1.25
796 A183 60t multicolored 3.25 2.40
797 A183 90t multicolored 4.00 4.00
Nos. 794-797 (4) 10.15 8.25

Mammals — A184

21t, Myoictis melas. 45t, Microperoryctes longicauda. 60t, Mallomys rothschildi. 90t, Pseudocheirus forbesi.

1993, Apr. 7 Litho. *Perf. 14*

798 A184 21t multicolored .70 .50
799 A184 45t multicolored 1.30 1.20
800 A184 60t multicolored 1.90 1.90
801 A184 90t multicolored 2.60 2.60
Nos. 798-801 (4) 6.50 6.20

Small Birds — A185

21t, Clytomyias insignis. 45t, Pitta superba. 60t, Rhagologus leucostigma. 90t, Toxorhamphus poliopterus.

1993, June 9 Litho. *Perf. 14*

802 A185 21t multicolored .85 .50
803 A185 45t multicolored 1.40 1.10
804 A185 60t multicolored 2.00 2.00
805 A185 90t multicolored 2.75 2.75
Nos. 802-805 (4) 7.00 6.35

Nos. 802-805 Redrawn with Taipei '93 emblem in Blue and Yellow

1993, Aug. 13 Litho. *Perf. 14*

806 A185 21t multicolored 1.10 .45
807 A185 45t multicolored 2.10 1.15
808 A185 60t multicolored 2.40 2.40
809 A185 90t multicolored 2.75 *4.50*
Nos. 806-809 (4) 8.35 8.50

Freshwater Fish — A186

Designs: 21t, Iriatherina werneri. 45t, Tateurndina ocellicauda. 60t, Melanotaenia affinis. 90t, Pseudomugil connieae.

1993, Sept. 29 Litho. *Perf. 14x14½*

810 A186 21t multicolored 1.10 .70
811 A186 45t multicolored 2.10 1.40
812 A186 60t multicolored 2.50 2.50
813 A186 90t multicolored 3.50 3.50
Nos. 810-813 (4) 9.20 8.10

For surcharges see Nos. 876-878.

Air Niugini, 20th Anniv. — A187

1993, Oct. 27 *Perf. 14*

814 A187 21t DC3 1.10 .65
815 A187 45t F27 2.50 1.25
816 A187 60t Dash 7 3.00 3.00
817 A187 90t Airbus A310-300 3.25 *4.50*
Nos. 814-817 (4) 9.85 9.40

Souvenir Sheet

Paradisaea Rudolphi — A188

1993, Sept. 29 Litho. *Perf. 14*

818 A188 2k multicolored 11.00 11.00

Bangkok '93.

Huon Tree Kangaroo — A189

21t, Domesticated joey. 45t, Adult male. 60t, Female, joey in pouch. 90t, Adolescent.

1994, Jan. 19 Litho. *Perf. 14½*

819 A189 21t multicolored .75 .65
820 A189 45t multicolored 1.60 1.25
821 A189 60t multicolored 2.25 2.25
822 A189 90t multicolored 3.25 *3.75*
Nos. 819-822 (4) 7.85 7.90

No. 661 Surcharged

No. 671 Surcharged

Perfs. and Printing Methods as Before

1994, Mar. 23

823 A153 21t on 35t multi *15.00* .80
824 A154 1.20k on 40t multi *4.50* 1.75

No. 824 exists with double surcharge. Other varieties may exist.

Artifacts — A190

Designs: 1t, Hagen ceremonial axe, Western Highlands. 2t, Telefomin war shield, West Sepik. 20t, Head mask, Gulf of Papua. 21t, Kanganaman stool, East Sepik. 45t, Trobriand lime gourd, Milne Bay. 60t, Yuat River flute stopper, East Sepik. 90t, Tami island dish, Morobe. 1k, Kundu drum, Ramu River estuary. 5k, Gogodala dance mask, Western Province. 10k, Malanggan mask, New Ireland.

1994-95 Litho. *Perf. 14½*

825 A190 1t multicolored .25 .25
826 A190 2t multicolored .25 .25
828 A190 20t multicolored .35 .35
829 A190 21t multicolored .35 .35
833 A190 45t multicolored .80 .80
835 A190 60t multicolored 1.10 1.10
836 A190 90t multicolored 1.65 1.65
837 A190 1k multicolored 5.00 3.00
839 A190 5k multicolored 9.00 9.00
840 A190 10k multicolored 15.00 15.00
Nos. 825-840 (10) 33.75 31.75

Issued: 21, 45, 60, 90t, 3/23; 1, 2, 20t, 5k, 6/29/94; 1k, 10k, 4/12/95.

Classic Cars — A191

1994, May 11 Litho. *Perf. 14*

841 A191 21t Model T Ford .80 .65
842 A191 45t Chevrolet 490 1.50 1.15
843 A191 60t Baby Austin 2.25 2.25
844 A191 90t Willys Jeep 3.00 3.00
Nos. 841-844 (4) 7.55 7.05

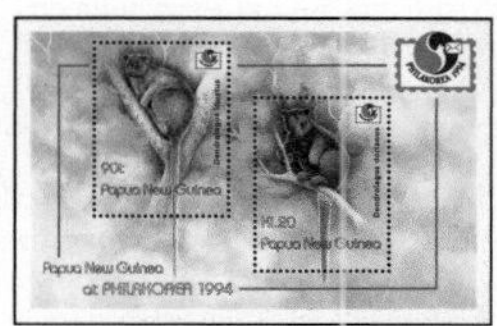
PHILAKOREA '94 — A192

Tree kangaroos: 90t, Dendrolagus inustus. 1.20k, Dendrolagus dorianus.

1994, Aug. 10 Litho. *Perf. 14*

845 A192 Sheet of 2, #a.-b. 8.50 8.50

Moths — A193

Designs: 21t, Daphnis hypothous pallescens. 45t, Tanaorhinus unipuncta. 60t, Neodiphthera sciron. 90t, Parotis maginata.

1994, Oct. 26 Litho. *Perf. 14*

846 A193 21t multicolored .60 .50
847 A193 45t multicolored 1.50 1.00
848 A193 60t multicolored 1.75 1.75
849 A193 90t multicolored 3.00 3.00
Nos. 846-849 (4) 6.85 6.25

Beatification of Peter To Rot — A194

No. 850, Peter To Rot. No. 851, Pope John Paul II.

1995, Jan. 11 Litho. *Perf. 14*

850 A194 21t multi .80 .80
851 A194 1k on 90t multi 4.50 4.50
a. Pair, #850-851 + label 6.50 6.50

No. 851 was not issued without surcharge. For surcharge see No. 1008.

Tourism — A195

#852, Cruising. #853, Handicrafts. #854, Jet. #855, Resorts. #856, Trekking adventure. #857, White-water rafting. #858, Boat, diver. #859, Divers, sunken plane.

1995, Jan. 11

852 A195 21t multicolored .80 .80
853 A195 21t multicolored .80 .80
a. Pair, #852-853 2.25 2.25
854 A195 50t on 45t multi 2.00 2.00
855 A195 50t on 45t multi 2.00 2.00
a. Pair, #854-855 5.00 5.00
856 A195 65t on 60t multi 2.60 2.60
a. "65t" omitted 35.00
857 A195 65t on 60t multi 2.60 2.60
a. Pair, #856-857 6.00 6.00
858 A195 1k on 90t multi 4.00 4.00
859 A195 1k on 90t multi 4.00 4.00
a. Pair, #858-859 9.25 9.25
Nos. 852-859 (8) 18.80 18.80

Nos. 854-859 were not issued without surcharge.

Nos. 662, 722, 730, 732, 734, 736, 738, 740-741, 747, 753, 762, 765, 770B, 770D Surcharged

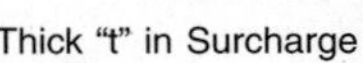
Thick "t" in Surcharge

1994 ***Perfs., Etc. as Before***

860 A167 5t on 35t #722 *5.75* 1.00
861 A174 5t on 35t #747 *27.50* *17.50*
862 A172 10t on 35t #740 *24.00* *16.00*
863 A172 10t on 35t #741 *17.50* *6.50*
864 A174a 21t on 80t #753 *75.00* *3.50*
866 A169 50t on 35t #730 *35.00* *17.50*
867 A171 50t on 35t #736 *80.00* *50.00*
a. Inverted surcharge *625.00*
868 A153 65t on 70t #662 4.00 1.75
869 A170 65t on 70t #734 4.00 1.75
870 A169 1k on 70t #732 *20.00* *6.50*
871 A171 1k on 70t #738 27.50 2.50
Nos. 860-871 (11) *320.25* *124.50*

Size, style and location of surcharge varies.

No. 861 exists in pair, one without surcharge. Other varieties exist.

Issued: #862, 8/23/94; #864, 8/28/94; #861, 863, 864, 10/3/94; #860, 871, 10/6/94; #866-868, 869-870, 11/28/94.

Mushrooms — A196

25t, Lentinus umbrinus. 50t, Amanita hemibapha. 65t, Boletellus emodensis. 1k, Ramaria zippellii.

1995, June 21 **Litho.** ***Perf. 14***

872 A196 25t multicolored .80 .60
Complete booklet, 10 #872 15.00
873 A196 50t multicolored 1.50 1.50
Complete booklet, 10 #873 22.50
874 A196 65t multicolored 1.90 1.90
875 A196 1k multicolored 3.00 3.00
Nos. 872-875 (4) 7.20 7.00

1996 **Litho.** ***Perf. 12***

875A A196 25t like #872 2.25 2.25

No. 875A has a taller vignette, a smaller typeface for the description, denomination, and country name and does not have a date inscription like #872.

Nos. 876-878 Surcharged Thick "t"

Nos. 878A-878D Surcharged Thin "t"

Thin "t" in Srch.

See illustration above #860.

1995 **Litho.** ***Perf. 14x14½***

876 A186 21t on 45t #811 *1.25* .35
877 A186 21t on 60t #812 *3.50* 1.75
878 A186 21t on 90t #813 *1.25* .70
878A A175 21t on 45t #762 *12.00* .70
878B A176a 21t on 45T #770B *35.00* 1.75
878C A175 21t on 90t #765 *12.00* .70
878D A176a 21t on 90T #770D *35.00* 1.75
Nos. 876-878D (7) *100.00* 7.70

Nos. 878A-878D exist with thick surcharge. This printing of 3200 each does not seem to have seen much, if any, public sale. Value, $10 to $150 each.

Nos. 878A, 878C dated 1993. Nos. 878B, 878D dated 1992. Nos. 878A, 878C exist dated 1992.

Issued: Nos. 876-878, 6/20; Nos. 878A-878B, 5/16; No. 878C, 3/27; No. 878D, 4/25.

Independence, 20th Anniv. — A197

Designs: 50t, 1k, "20" emblem.

1995, Aug. 30 ***Perf. 14***

879 A197 21t multi .65 .65
880 A197 50t multi 1.40 1.40
881 A197 1k multi 2.75 2.75
Nos. 879-881 (3) 4.80 4.80

Souvenir Sheet

Singapore '95 — A198

Orchids: a, 21t, Dendrobium rigidifolium. b, 45t, Dendrobium convolutum. c, 60t, Dendrobium spectabile. d, 90t, Dendrobium tapiniense.

1995, Aug. 30 **Litho.** ***Perf. 14***

882 A198 Sheet of 4, #a.-d. 6.00 6.00

No. 882 sold for 3k.

Souvenir Sheet

New Year 1995 (Year of the Boar) A199

1995, Sept. 14

883 A199 3k multicolored 7.25 7.25

Beijing '95.

Eruption of Rabaul Volcano, 1st Anniv. — A200

1995, Sept. 19

884 A200 2k multicolored 4.75 4.75

Crabs — A201

1995, Oct. 25 **Litho.** ***Perf. 14***

885 A201 21t Zosimus aeneus .70 .55
886 A201 50t Cardisoma carnifex 1.25 1.25
887 A201 65t Uca tetragonon 1.75 1.75
888 A201 1k Eriphia sebana 2.40 2.40
Nos. 885-888 (4) 6.10 5.95

For surcharge see #939B.

Parrots — A202

Designs: 25t, Psittrichas fulgidas. 50t, Trichoglossus haemotodus. 65t, Alisterus chloropterus. 1k, Aprosmictus erythropterus.

1996, Jan. 17 **Litho.** ***Perf. 12***

889 A202 25t multicolored 1.75 .60
890 A202 50t multicolored 2.50 1.05
891 A202 65t multicolored 3.00 2.25
892 A202 1k multicolored 3.75 3.75
Nos. 889-892 (4) 11.00 7.65

Beetles — A203

Designs: 25t, Lagriomorpha indigacea. 50t, Eupholus geoffroyi. 65t, Promechus pulcher. 1k, Callistola pulchra.

1996, Mar. 20 **Litho.** ***Perf. 12***

893 A203 25t multicolored .65 .65
894 A203 50t multicolored 1.30 1.30
895 A203 65t multicolored 1.70 1.70
896 A203 1k multicolored 2.60 2.60
Nos. 893-896 (4) 6.25 6.25

Souvenir Sheet

Zhongshan Memorial Hall, Guangzhou, China — A204

1996, Apr. 22 **Litho.** ***Perf. 14***

897 A204 70t multicolored 2.50 2.50

CHINA '96, 9th Asian Intl. Philatelic Exhibition.

1996 Summer Olympics, Atlanta — A205

1996, July 24 **Litho.** ***Perf. 12***

898 A205 25t Shooting .45 .45
899 A205 50t Track .85 .85
900 A205 65t Weight lifting 1.60 1.60
901 A205 1k Boxing 2.25 2.25
Nos. 898-901 (4) 5.15 5.15

Olymphilex '96.

Radio, Cent. — A206

25t, Air traffic control. 50t, Commercial broadcasting. 65t, Gerehu earth station. 1k, 1st transmission in Papua New Guinea.

1996, Sept. 11 **Litho.** ***Perf. 12***

902 A206 25t multicolored .40 .40
903 A206 50t multicolored .85 .85
904 A206 65t multicolored 1.10 1.10
905 A206 1k multicolored 1.60 1.60
Nos. 902-905 (4) 3.95 3.95

Souvenir Sheet

Taipei '96, 10th Asian Intl. Philatelic Exhibition — A207

a, Dr. Sun Yat-sen (1866-1925). b, Dr. John Guise (1914-91).

1996, Oct. 16 **Litho.** ***Perf. 14***

906 A207 65t Sheet of 2, #a.-b. 4.50 4.50

Flowers — A208

Designs: 1t, Hibiscus rosa-sinensis. 5t, Bougainvillea spectabilis. 65t, Plumeria rubra. 1k, Mucuna novo-guineensis.

1996, Nov. 27 **Litho.** ***Perf. 14***

907 A208 1t multicolored .40 .25
908 A208 5t multicolored .40 .25
909 A208 65t multicolored 1.25 1.25
910 A208 1k multicolored 1.90 1.90
Nos. 907-910 (4) 3.95 3.65

Souvenir Sheet

Oxen and Natl. Flag A209

1997, Feb. 3 **Litho.** ***Perf. 14***

911 A209 1.50k multicolored 3.75 3.75

Hong Kong '97.

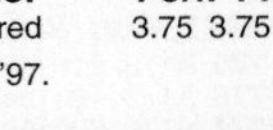

Boat Prows — A210

1997, Mar. 19 **Litho.** ***Perf. 14½x14***

912 A210 25t Gogodala .35 .35
913 A210 50t East New Britain .75 .75
914 A210 65t Trobriand Island 1.10 1.10
915 A210 1k Walomo 1.60 1.60
Nos. 912-915 (4) 3.80 3.80

Queen Elizabeth II and Prince Philip, 50th Wedding Anniv. — A211

#916, Princess Anne, polo players. #917, Queen up close. #918, Prince in riding attire. #919, Queen, another person riding horses. #920, Grandsons riding horses, Prince waving. #921, Queen waving, riding pony.

2k, Queen, Prince riding in open carriage.

1997, June 25 **Litho.** ***Perf. 13½***

916 A211 25t multicolored .45 .45
917 A211 25t multicolored .45 .45
a. Pair, #916-917 1.10 1.10
918 A211 50t multicolored .90 .90
919 A211 50t multicolored .90 .90
a. Pair, #918-919 2.25 2.25
920 A211 1k multicolored 1.60 1.60
921 A211 1k multicolored 1.60 1.60
a. Pair, #920-921 3.75 3.75
Nos. 916-921 (6) 5.90 5.90

Souvenir Sheet

922 A211 2k multicolored 3.75 3.75

Souvenir Sheet

Air Niugini, First Flight, Port Moresby-Osaka — A212

1997, July 19 **Litho.** ***Perf. 12***

923 A212 3k multicolored 5.75 5.75

1997 Pacific Year of Coral Reef — A213

Designs: 25t, Pocillopora woodjonesi. 50t, Subergorgia mollis. 65t, Oxypora glabra. 1k, Turbinaria reinformis.

1997, Aug. 27 **Litho.** ***Perf. 12***

924 A213 25t multicolored .45 .45
925 A213 50t multicolored .90 .90
926 A213 65t multicolored 1.40 1.40
927 A213 1k multicolored 1.75 1.75
Nos. 924-927 (4) 4.50 4.50

Flowers — A214

Designs: 10t, Thunbergia fragrans. 20t, Caesalpinia pulcherrima. 25t, Hoya. 30t, Heliconia. 50t, Amomum goliathensis.

1997, Nov. 26 Litho. *Perf. 12*

928 A214 10t multicolored .60 .40
929 A214 20t multicolored .80 .70
930 A214 25t multicolored 1.00 .90
931 A214 30t multicolored 1.25 1.25
932 A214 50t multicolored 1.75 1.40
Nos. 928-932 (5) 5.40 4.65

Birds — A215

Designs: 25t, Tyto tenebricosa. 50t, Aepypodius arfakianus. 65t, Accipiter poliocephalus. 1k, Zonerodius heliosylus.

1998, Jan. 28 Litho. *Perf. 12*

933 A215 25t multicolored 1.40 .75
934 A215 50t multicolored 1.75 1.40
935 A215 65t multicolored 2.75 2.75
936 A215 1k multicolored 3.75 3.75
Nos. 933-936 (4) 9.65 8.65

Diana, Princess of Wales (1961-97)
Common Design Type

Designs: a, In beige colored dress. b, In violet dress with lace collar. c, Wearing plaid jacket. d, Holding flowers.

1998, Apr. 29 Litho. *Perf. 14½x14*

937 CD355 1k Sheet of 4, #a.-d. 6.25 6.25

No. 937 sold for 4k + 50t with surtax from international sales being donated to the Princess Diana Memorial fund and surtax from national sales being donated to designated local charity.

Mother Teresa (1910-97) — A216

1998, Apr. 29 *Perf. 14½*

938 A216 65t With child 1.25 1.25
939 A216 1k shown 1.90 1.90
a. Pair, #938-939 4.00 4.00

No. 887 Surcharged

1998, May 28 Litho. *Perf. 14*

939B A201 25t on 65t multi 1.10 1.10

Moths — A217

25t, Daphnis hypothous pallescens. 50t, Theretra polistratus. 65t, Psilogramma casurina. 1k, Meganoton hyloicoides.

1998, June 17 Litho. *Perf. 14*

940 A217 25t multicolored .55 .55
941 A217 50t multicolored .90 .90
942 A217 65t multicolored 1.25 1.25
943 A217 1k multicolored 1.75 1.75
Nos. 940-943 (4) 4.45 4.45

A218

First Orchid Spectacular '98: 25t, Coelogyne fragrans. 50t, Den. cuthbertsonii. 65t, Den. vexillarius. 1k, Den. finisterrae.

1998, Sept. 15 Litho. *Perf. 14*

944 A218 25t multicolored .60 .60
945 A218 50t multicolored 1.00 1.00
946 A218 65t multicolored 1.40 1.40
947 A218 1k multicolored 2.00 2.00
Nos. 944-947 (4) 5.00 5.00

A219

Sea Kayaking World Cup, Manus Island: 25t, Couple in kayak. 50t, Competitor running through Loniu Caves. 65t, Man standing in boat with sail, man seated in kayak. 1k, Competitor in kayak, bird of paradise silhouette.

1998, Oct. 5 Litho. *Perf. 14*

948 A219 25t multicolored .60 .60
949 A219 50t multicolored 1.00 1.00
950 A219 65t multicolored 1.40 1.40
951 A219 1k multicolored 2.00 2.00
Nos. 948-951 (4) 5.00 5.00

1998 Commonwealth Games, Kuala Lumpur — A220

1998, Sept. 30 Litho. *Perf. 14*

952 A220 25t Weight lifting .40 .40
953 A220 50t Lawn bowls .70 .70
954 A220 65t Rugby .95 .95
955 A220 1k Squash 1.25 1.25
Nos. 952-955 (4) 3.30 3.30

Christmas A221

Designs: 25t, Infant in manger. 50t, Mother breastfeeding infant. 65t, "Wise men" in traditional masks, headdresses looking at infant. 1k, Map of Papua New Guinea.

1998, Nov. 18 Litho. *Perf. 14*

956 A221 25t multicolored .35 .35
957 A221 50t multicolored .70 .70
958 A221 65t multicolored .95 .95
959 A221 1k multicolored 1.40 1.40
Nos. 956-959 (4) 3.40 3.40

Australia '99, World Stamp Expo — A222

Ships: 25t, "Boudeuse," 1768. 50t, "Neva," 1876. 65t, "Merrir England," 1889. 1k, "Samoa," 1884.

#964: a, 5t, Rattlesnake, 1849. b, 10t, Swallow, 1767. c, 15t, Roebeck, 1700. d, 20t, Blanche, 1872. e, 30t, Vitiaz, 1871. f, 40t, San Pedrico and Eabre, 1606. g, 60t, Jorge de Menesis, 1526. h, 1.20k, L'Astrolabe, 1827.

1999, Mar. 17

960 A222 25t multicolored .30 .30
961 A222 50t multicolored .65 .65
962 A222 65t multicolored 1.05 1.05
963 A222 1k multicolored 1.25 1.25
Nos. 960-963 (4) 3.25 3.25

Sheet of 8

964 A222 #a.-h. 5.75 5.75

No. 964a is incorrectly inscribed "Simpson Blanche '1872."

IBRA '99, World Philatelic Exhibition, Nuremberg — A223

Exhibition emblem and: a, German New Guinea #17. b, German New Guinea #1, #2.

1999 Litho. *Perf. 14*

965 A223 1k Pair, #a.-b. 3.00 3.00

Millennium A224

Map and: 25t, Stopwatch, computer keyboard. 50t, Concentric circles. 65t, Internet page, computer user. 1k, Computers, satellite dish.

1999 Litho. *Perf. 12¾*

966 A224 25t multicolored .50 .25
967 A224 50t multicolored .70 .40
968 A224 65t multicolored 1.25 .90
969 A224 1k multicolored 1.75 1.75
Nos. 966-969 (4) 4.20 3.30

For surcharge see No. 1010.

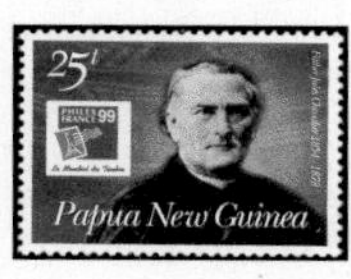

PhilexFrance '99 — A225

Frenchmen with historical ties to Papua New Guinea: 25t, Father Jules Chevalier. 50t, Bishop Alain-Marie. 65t, Chevalier D'Entrecasteaux. 1k, Count de Bougainville.

1999, Mar. 2 Litho. *Perf. 12¾*

970 A225 25t multicolored .30 .25
971 A225 50t multicolored .55 .55
972 A225 65t multicolored .85 .85
973 A225 1k multicolored 1.25 *1.40*
Nos. 970-973 (4) 2.95 3.05

For surcharge see No. 1011.

Hiri Moale Festival — A226

Designs: 25t, Clay pots, native. 50t, Hanenamo, native. 65t, Lakatoi, native. #977, 1k, Sorcerer, native.

No. 978: a, Sorcerer. b, Clay pots. c, Lakatoi.

1999, Sept. 8 *Perf. 12¾*

974 A226 25t multicolored .35 .30
975 A226 50t multicolored .55 .55
976 A226 65t multicolored .85 .85
977 A226 1k multicolored 1.25 1.25
Nos. 974-977 (4) 3.00 2.95

Souvenir Sheet

978 A226 1k Sheet of 3, #a.-c. 3.75 3.75

For surcharge see No. 1012.

Souvenir Sheet

Year of the Rabbit (in 1999) A227

Color of rabbit: a, Gray. b, Tan. c, White. d, Pink.

2000, Apr. 21 Litho. *Perf. 12¾*

979 A227 65t Sheet of 4, #a-d 3.75 3.75

Queen Mother, 100th Birthday — A228

Various photos. Color of frame: 25t, Yellow. 50t, Lilac. 65t, Green. 1k, Dull orange.

2000, Aug. 4 *Perf. 14*

980-983 A228 Set of 4 3.50 3.50

Shells — A229

Designs: 25t, Turbo petholatus. 50t, Charonia tritonis. 65t, Cassis cornuta. 1k, Ovula ovum.

2000, Feb. 23 Litho. *Perf. 14*

984-987 A229 Set of 4 3.75 3.75

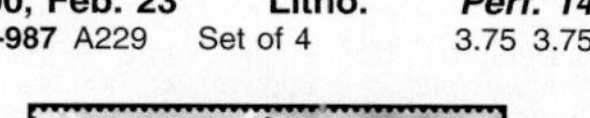

Independence, 25th Anniv. — A230

Designs: 25t, Shell. 50t, Bird of Paradise. 65t, Ring. 1k, Coat of arms.

2000, June 21 *Perf. 14*
Stamps with se-tenant label

988-991 A230 Set of 4 3.75 3.75
991a Souvenir sheet, #988-991, no labels 3.75 3.75

Strips with two stamps alternating with two different labels exist for Nos. 989 and 990.

2000 Summer Olympics, Sydney — A231

Designs: 25t, Running. 50t, Swimming. 65t, Boxing. 1k, Weight lifting.

2000, July 12

992-995 A231 Set of 4 3.75 3.75

For surcharge see No. 1009.

Souvenir Sheet

Olymphilex 2000, Sydney — A232

2000, July 12 *Perf. 14¼*

996 A232 3k multi 4.00 4.00

Sold for 3.50k.

Birds — A233

Designs: 35t, Comb-crested jacana. 70t, Masked lapwing. 90t, White ibis. 1.40k, Black-tailed godwit.

2001, Mar. 21 Litho. *Perf. 14*
997-1000 A233 Set of 4 5.00 5.00

Mission Aviation Fellowship, 50th Anniv. in Papua New Guinea A234

Designs: 35t, Cessna 170, pig, bird, Bibles. 70t, Harry Hartwig (1916-51), Auster Autocar. 90t, Pilot and Cessna 260. 1.40k, Twin Otter and plane mechanics.

2001, Oct. 17 *Perf. 13¼x13¾*
1001-1004 A234 Set of 4 4.50 4.50

A235

Designs: 10t, Flags, world map. 50t, Dragon, bird of paradise. 2k, Tien An Men Square, Papua New Guinea Parliament Building.

2001, Oct. 12 Litho. *Perf. 12*
1005-1007 A235 Set of 3 5.25 5.25

Papua New Guinea and People's Republic of China Diplomatic Relations, 25th Anniv.

Nos. 850, 968, 972, 976 and 992 Srchd.

Methods and Perfs As Before
2001, Dec. 1

1008 A194 50t on 21t #850 2.50 1.25
a. Horiz. pair, 1008, 851 + central label 6.00 4.00
1009 A231 50t on 25t #992 1.00 .50
a. Obliterator present, missing new denomination —
1010 A224 50t on 65t #968 1.00 .50
1011 A225 2.65k on 65t #972 4.00 4.00
1012 A226 2.65k on 65t #976 4.00 4.00
Nos. 1008-1012 (5) 12.50 10.25

Provincial Flags — A236

2001, Dec. 12 Litho. *Perf. 14*

1013 A236 10t Enga .45 .25
1014 A236 15t Simbu .45 .25
1015 A236 20t Manus .45 .25
1016 A236 50t Central 1.10 .40
1017 A236 2k New Ireland 3.50 2.25
1018 A236 5k Sandaun 4.75 4.75
Nos. 1013-1018 (6) 10.70 8.15

For surcharge see No. 1113.

Reign Of Queen Elizabeth II, 50th Anniv. Issue
Common Design Type

Designs: Nos. 1019, 1023a, 1.25k, Princess Elizabeth with Queen Mother and Princess Margaret, 1941. Nos. 1020, 1023b, 1.45k, Wearing tiara, 1975. Nos. 1021, 1023c, 2k, With Princes Philip and Charles, 1951. Nos. 1022, 1023d, 2.65k, Wearing red hat. No. 1023e, 5k, 1955 portrait by Annigoni (38x50mm).

Perf. 14¼x14½, 13¾ (#1023e)
2002, Feb. 6 Litho. Wmk. 373
With Gold Frames

1019 CD360 1.25k multicolored 1.20 1.20
1020 CD360 1.45k multicolored 1.40 1.40
1021 CD360 2k multicolored 1.90 1.90
1022 CD360 2.65k multicolored 2.50 2.50
Nos. 1019-1022 (4) 7.00 7.00

Souvenir Sheet
Without Gold Frames

1023 CD360 Sheet of 5, #a-e 7.50 7.50

Lakatoi Type of 1901 Inscribed "Papua New Guinea"

Frame colors: 5t, Red. 15t, Brown violet. 20t, Light blue. 1.25k, Brown. 1.45k, Green. 10k, Orange.

Perf. 14½x14
2002, June 5 Litho. Unwmk.
Center in Brown Black

1024-1029 A1 Set of 6 14.00 14.00
1029a Souvenir sheet, #1024-1029 16.00 16.00

British New Guinea stamps, cent. (in 2001).

Orchids — A237

Designs: 5t, Cadetia taylori. 30t, Dendrobium anosmum. 45t, Dendrobium bigibbum. 1.25k, Dendrobium cuthbertsonii. 1.45k, Sprianthes sinensis. 2.65k, Thelymitra carnea.
No. 1036, horiz.: a, Dendrobium bracteosum. b, Calochilus campestris. c, Anastomus oscitans. d, Thelymitra carnea, diff. e, Dendrobium macrophyllum. f, Dendrobium johnsoniae.
7k, Bulbophyllum graveolens, horiz.

2002, Aug. 28 *Perf. 14*
1030-1035 A237 Set of 6 8.00 8.00
1036 A237 2k Sheet of 6, #a-f 11.50 11.50

Souvenir Sheet

1037 A237 7k multi 9.00 9.00

Protected Butterflies A238

Designs: No. 1038, 50t, Ornithoptera chimaera. No. 1039, 50t, Ornithoptera goliath. 1.25k, Ornithoptera meridionalis. 1.45k, Ornithoptera paradisea. 2.65k, Ornithoptera victoriae. 5k, Ornithoptera alexandrae.

2002, Oct. 16
1038-1043 A238 Set of 6 15.00 15.00

Queen Mother Elizabeth (1900-2002) — A239

No. 1044, horiz.: a, With Queen Elizabeth II (28x23mm). b, With Elizabeth and two other women (28x23mm). c, With pearl necklace visible at left (26x29mm). d, Color photograph (40x29mm). e, With pearl necklace visible at right (26x29mm). f, With man in top hat at right (28x23mm). g, With King George VI (28x23mm).
No. 1045, blue shading in UR of stamps : a, 3k, As child. b, 3k, Wearing black hat.
No. 1046, blue shading in UL of stamps: a, 3k, Wearing white hat. b, 3k, Wearing hat and brooch.

Perf. 13¼x14¼ (#1044d), Compound x 14¼ (#1044c, 1044e) 13¼x10¾
2002
1044 A239 2k Sheet of 7, #a-g 14.00 14.00

Souvenir Sheets
Perf. 14¾

1045-1046 A239 Set of 2 14.00 14.00

A240

United We Stand — A241

2002, Nov. 20 Litho. *Perf. 14*
1047 A240 50t multi 1.25 1.25
1048 A241 50t multi 1.25 1.25

No. 1048 was printed in sheets of 4.

Intl. Year of Mountains A242

Designs: 50t, Mt. Wilhelm, Papua New Guinea. 1.25k, Matterhorn, Switzerland. 1.45k, Mt. Fuji, Japan. 2.65k, Massif des Aravis, France.

2002, Nov. 20
1049-1052 A242 Set of 4 6.25 6.25

Clay Pots — A243

Designs: 65t, Sago storage pot. 1k, Smoking pot. 1.50k, Water jar. 2.50k, Water jar, diff. 4k, Ridge pot.

2003, Jan. 22
1053-1057 A243 Set of 5 9.00 9.00

20th World Scout Jamboree, Thailand — A244

Designs: 50t, Group of scouts. 1.25k, Two scouts seated. 1.45k, Scouts on tower. 2.65k, Two scouts standing.

2003, Feb. 12
1058-1061 A244 Set of 4 8.00 8.00

A245

Various portraits of Queen Elizabeth II with background colors of: No. 1062, 65t, Purple. No. 1063, 65t, Olive green. 1.50k, Dark blue. No. 1065, 2k, Red. 2.50k, Dull green. 4k, Orange.
No. 1068, 2k — Yellow orange background with Queen: a, Without hat. b, Wearing crown and sash. c, Wearing hat with blue flowers. d, Wearing tiara. e, Wearing red dress. f, Wearing black hat.
8k, Wearing black robe, gray green background.

2003, Apr. 30 Litho. *Perf. 14*
1062-1067 A245 Set of 6 9.50 9.50
1068 A245 2k Sheet of 6, #a-f 10.00 10.00

Souvenir Sheet

1069 A245 8k multi 7.00 7.00

Coronation of Queen Elizabeth, 50th anniv.

A246

Prince William: No. 1070, 65t, Wearing colored sports shirt. No. 1071, 65t, Wearing white shirt. 1.50k, As child. No. 1073, 2k, Wearing suit and tie, gray green background. 2.50k, Wearing plaid shirt. 4k, On polo pony.
No. 1076, 2k — Lilac background: a, As toddler. b, Wearing sunglasses. c, Wearing suit and tie (full face). d, Wearing suit and tie (profile). e, Wearing deep blue shirt. f, Wearing yellow shirt with black collar.
8k, Wearing suit and tie, gray green background, diff.

2003, June 18
1070-1075 A246 Set of 6 8.25 8.25
1076 A246 2k Sheet of 6, #a-f 9.25 9.25

Souvenir Sheet

1077 A246 8k multi 6.75 6.75

Prince William, 21st birthday.

Coastal Villages — A247

Designs: No. 1078, 65t, Gabagaba. No. 1079, 65t, Wanigela (Koki). 1.50k, Tubuserea. 2k, Hanuabada. 2.50k, Barakau. 4k, Porebada.

2003, July 24
1078-1083 A247 Set of 6 9.25 9.25

For surcharges see Nos. 1114-1115.

Powered Flight, Cent. — A248

Designs: 65t, Orville Wright circles plane over Fort Myer, Va., 1908. 1.50k, Orville Wright pilots "Baby Grand" Belmont, 1910. No. 1086, 2.50k, Wilbur Wright holding anemometer, Pau, France, 1909. 4k, Wilbur Wright pilots Model A, Pau, France, 1909.
No. 1088, 2.50k — 1903 photos from Kitty Hawk: a, Untried airplane outside hangar. b, Rollout of airplane from hangar. c, Preparing airplane for takeoff. d, Airplane takes off.
10k, Airplane takes off, diff.

2003, Aug. 27
1084-1087 A248 Set of 4 8.00 8.00
1088 A248 Sheet of 4, #a-d 9.00 9.00

Souvenir Sheet

1089 A248 10k multi 9.00 9.00

Worldwide Fund for Nature (WWF) — A249

Tree kangaroos: Nos. 1090a, 1091a, Dendrolagus inustus. Nos. 1090b, 1091b, Dendrolagus matschiei. Nos. 1090c, 1091c, Dendrolagus dorianus. Nos. 1090d, 1091d, Dendrolagus goodfellowi.

2003, Oct. 15 *Perf. 14½x14¾*
With White Frames

1090 Horiz. strip of 4 8.00 8.00
a. A249 65t multi .75 .75
b. A249 1.50k multi 1.40 1.40
c. A249 2.50k multi 2.25 2.25
d. A249 4k multi 3.25 3.25

Without White Frames

1091 Sheet, 2 each #a-d 14.00 14.00
a. A249 65t multi .65 .65
b. A249 1.50k multi 1.25 1.25
c. A249 2.50k multi 2.00 2.00
d. A249 4k multi 2.75 2.75

Endangered Dolphins — A250

Designs: No. 1092, 65t, Humpback dolphin. No. 1093, 65t, Bottlenose dolphins. No. 1094, 1.50k, Bottlenose dolphin, with frame line. 2k, Irrawaddy dolphin. 2.50k, Humpback dolphin and fishermen. 4k, Irrawaddy dolphin and diver.

No. 1098, 1.50k: a, Humpback dolphin and sailboat. b, Bottlenose dolphin, without frame line. c, Bottlenose dolphins, diff. d, Irrawaddy dolphin and diver, diff. e, Irrawady dolphin, diff. f, Humpback dolphin underwater.

2003, Nov. 19 ***Perf. 13½***

1092-1097 A250 Set of 6 10.00 10.00
1098 A250 1.50k Sheet of 6, #a-f 8.00 8.00

For surcharges see Nos. 1116-1117.

Freshwater Fish — A251

Designs: No. 1099, 70t, Lake Wanam rainbowfish. No. 1100, 70t, Kokoda mogurnda. 1k, Sepik grunter. 2.70k, Papuan black bass. 4.60k, Lake Tebera rainbowfish. 20k, Wichmann's mouth almighty.

2004, Jan. 30 ***Perf. 14¼***

1099-1104 A251 Set of 6 25.00 25.00
Complete booklet, 10 #1099 6.00
Complete booklet, 10 #1100 6.00

For surcharges see Nos. 1154-1155.

Dinosaurs A252

Designs: 70t, Ankylosaurus. 1k, Oviraptor. 2k, Tyrannosaurus. 2.65k, Gigantosaurus. 2.70k, Centrosaurus. 4.60k, Carcharodontosaurus.

No. 1111: a, Edmontonia. b, Struthiomimus. c, Psittacosaurus. d, Gastonia. e, Shunosaurus. f, Iguanodon.

7k, Afrovenator.

2004, Feb. 25 ***Perf. 14***

1105-1110 A252 Set of 6 11.50 11.50
1111 A252 1.50k Sheet of 6, #a-f 8.75 8.75

Souvenir Sheet

1112 A252 7k multi 6.25 6.25

Nos. 1015, 1078, 1079, 1092 and 1093 Surcharged

a

b

Methods and Perfs As Before

2004

1113 A236(a) 5t on 20t #1015 .75 .75
1114 A247(b) 70t on 65t #1078 1.50 1.50
1115 A247(b) 70t on 65t #1079 1.75 1.75
1116 A250(a) 70t on 65t #1092 1.75 1.75
1117 A250(a) 70t on 65t #1093 1.50 1.50
Nos. 1113-1117 (5) 7.25 7.25

Issued: Nos. 1114-1115, 1/20; others, 6/2.

Orchids — A253

Designs: 70t, Phalaenopsis amabilis. 1k, Phaius tankervilleae. No. 1120, 2k, Bulbophyllum macranthum. 2.65k, Dendrobium rhodostictum. 2.70k, Diplocaulobium ridleyanum. 4.60k, Spathoglottis papuana.

No. 1124, 2k: a, Dendrobium cruttwellii. b, Dendrobium coeloglossum. c, Dendrobium alaticaulinum. d, Dendrobium obtusisepalum. e, Dendrobium johnsoniae. f, Dendrobium insigne.

7k, Dendrobium biggibum.

2004, May 19 **Litho.** ***Perf. 14***

1118-1123 A253 Set of 6 13.50 13.50
1124 A253 2k Sheet of 6, #a-f 12.50 12.50

Souvenir Sheet

1125 A253 7k multi 7.75 7.75

Headdresses A254

Province of headdress: No. 1126, 70t, Simbu. No. 1127, 70t, East Sepik. 2.65k, Southern Highlands. 2.70k, Western Highlands. 4.60k, Eastern Highlands. 5k, Central.

2004, June 2

1126-1131 A254 Set of 6 14.00 14.00
Complete booklet, 10 #1126 7.50
Complete booklet, 10 #1127 7.50

For surcharges see Nos. 1156-1157.

2004 Summer Olympics, Athens A255

Designs: 70t, Swimming. 2.65k, Weight lifting, vert. 2.70k, Torch race, vert. 4.60k, Poster for 1952 Helsinki Olympics, vert.

2004, Aug. 11 ***Perf. 13¼***

1132-1135 A255 Set of 4 10.50 10.50

National Soccer Team A256

Various players in action: 70t, 2.65k, 2.70k, 4.60k.

2004, Sept. 8 ***Perf. 14¼***

1136-1139 A256 Set of 4 13.00 13.00

FIFA (Fédération Internationale de Football Association), Cent. — A257

No. 1140: a, Bruno Conti. b, Oliver Kahn. c, Mario Kempes. d, Bobby Moore.

10k, Bobby Robson.

2004, Sept. 8 ***Perf. 13¼x13½***

1140 A257 2.50k Sheet of 4, #a-d 11.50 11.50

Souvenir Sheet

1141 A257 10k multi 10.00 10.00

Provincial Flags — A258

Province: No. 1142, 70t, East New Britain. No. 1143, 70t, Madang. 2.65k, Eastern Highlands. 2.70k, Morobe. 4.60k, Milne Bay. 10k, East Sepik.

2004, Oct. 20 ***Perf. 14***

1142-1147 A258 Set of 6 20.00 20.00

Shells — A259

Designs: No. 1148, 70t, Phalium areola. No. 1149, 70t, Conus auratus. 2.65k, Oliva miniacea. 2.70k, Lambis chiragra. 4.60k, Conus suratensis. 10k, Architectonica perspectiva.

2004, Nov. 17

1148-1153 A259 Set of 6 17.50 17.50

For surcharges see Nos. 1223-1224.

Nos. 1099, 1100, 1126, 1127 Surcharged

Methods and Perfs as Before

2005, Jan. 3

1154 A251 75t on 70t #1099 1.10 1.10
1155 A251 75t on 70t #1100 1.10 1.10
1156 A254 75t on 70t #1126 1.10 1.10
1157 A254 75t on 70t #1127 1.10 1.10
Nos. 1154-1157 (4) 4.40 4.40

Birds — A260

Designs: 5t, Little egret. No. 1159, 75t, White-faced heron. No. 1160, 75t, Nankeen night heron. 3k, Crested tern. 3.10k, Bar-tailed godwit. 5.20k, Little pied heron.

2005, Jan. 26 **Litho.** ***Perf. 14***

1158-1163 A260 Set of 6 10.00 10.00

Rotary International, Cent. — A261

Designs: 75t, Mobilizing communities in the fight against HIV and AIDS. 3k, Barefoot child, PolioPlus and Rotary centennial emblems. 3.10k, Co-founders of first Rotary Club. 5.20k, Chicago skyline.

No. 1168, vert.: a, Silvester Schiele (1870-1945), first Rotary President. b, Paul Harris, founder. c, Children.

10k, Emblem and globe, vert.

2005, Feb. 23 **Litho.** ***Perf. 14***

1164-1167 A261 Set of 4 9.00 9.00
1168 A261 4k Sheet of 3, #a-c 9.00 9.00

Souvenir Sheet

1169 A261 10k multi 7.25 7.25

Frangipani Varieties A262

Designs: No. 1170, 75t, Evergreen. No. 1171, 75t, Lady in Pink. 1k, Carmine Flush. 3k, Cultivar acutifolia. 3.10k, American Beauty. 5.20k, Golden Kiss.

2005, Apr. 6 ***Perf. 12¾***

1170-1175 A262 Set of 6 10.50 10.50

Mushrooms — A263

Designs: No. 1176, 75t, Gymnopilus spectabilis. No. 1177, 75t, Melanogaster ambiguus. 3.10k, Microporus xanthopus. 5.20k, Psilocybe subcubensis.

No. 1180: a, Amanita muscaria. b, Amanita rubescens. c, Suillus luteus. d, Stropharia cubensis. e, Aseroes rubra. f, Psilocybe aucklandii.

10k, Mycena pura.

2005, May 18

1176-1179 A263 Set of 4 7.50 7.50
1180 A263 2k Sheet of 6, #a-f 9.25 9.25

Souvenir Sheet

1181 A263 10k multi 7.25 7.25

Beetles — A264

Designs: No. 1182, 75t, Promechus pulcher. No. 1183, 75t, Callistola pulchra. 1k, Lagriomorpha indigacea. 3k, Hellerhinus papuanus. 3.10k, Aphorina australis. 5.20k, Bothricara pulchella.

2005, June 29 ***Perf. 14***

1182-1187 A264 Set of 6 9.50 9.50

Souvenir Sheet

Pope John Paul II (1920-2005) — A265

No. 1188 — Denomination and country name in: a, Blue. b, Green. c, Orange. d, Red violet.

2005, Aug. 10 **Litho.** ***Perf. 12¾***

1188 A265 2k Sheet of 4, #a-d 6.25 6.25

Provincial Flags — A266

Province: No. 1189, 75t, Gulf. No. 1190, 75t, Southern Highlands. 1k, North Solomons. 3k, Oro. 3.10k, Western Highlands. 5.20k, Western.

2005, Sept. 21 ***Perf. 14***

1189-1194 A266 Set of 6 10.00 10.00

Cats and Dogs — A267

Designs: No. 1195, 75t, Somali Rudy cat. No. 1196, 75t, Balinese Seal Lynx Point cat. 3k, Sphynx Brown Mackerel Tabby and White cat. 3.10k, Korat Blue cat. 5.20k, Bengal Brown Spotted Tabby cat.

No. 1200: a, Yorkshire terrier. b, Basenji. c, Neapolitan mastiff. d, Poodle.

10k, Boston terrier, horiz.

2005, Nov. 2 ***Perf. 12¾***

1195-1199 A267 Set of 5 10.00 10.00
1200 A267 2.50k Sheet of 4, #a-d 8.00 8.00

Souvenir Sheet

1201 A267 10k multi 8.00 8.00

Summer Institute of Languages in Papua New Guinea, 50th Anniv. — A268

Designs: No. 1202, 80t, Postal services. No. 1203, 80t, Literacy. 1k, Jim Dean, first director. 3.20k, Tokples preschools. 3.25k, Aviation. 5.35k, Community development.

2006, Jan. 4 Litho. *Perf. 13¼*
1202-1207 A268 Set of 6 16.00 16.00

Miniature Sheets

Queen Elizabeth II, 80th Birthday A269

No. 1208, 2.50k: a, Wearing polka dot dress. b, Engraving in brown from Canadian bank note. c, Engraving in blue from banknote. d, With Queen Mother.

No. 1209: a, 80t, With Pres. Bill Clinton. b, 3.20k, Dancing with Pres. Gerald Ford. c, 3.25k, With Pres. Ronald Reagan. d, 5.35k, With Pres. George W. Bush.

2006, Feb. 22 Litho. *Perf. 13½*
Sheets of 4, #a-d
1208-1209 A269 Set of 2 17.00 17.00

Contemporary Art — A270

Designs: 5t, Shown. No. 1211, 80t, One head. No. 1212, 80t, Two heads. 3.20k, Man wearing headdress. 3.25k, Man and woman. 5.35k, Man with beads and man with painted face.

2006, Apr. 12 *Perf. 13¼x13½*
1210-1215 A270 Set of 6 10.50 10.50

Miniature Sheet

2006 World Cup Soccer Championships, Germany — A271

No. 1216 — Player and uniform from: a, 80t, England. b, 3.20k, Germany. c, 3.25k, Argentina. d, 5.35k, Australia.

2006, May 17 *Perf. 12*
1216 A271 Sheet of 4, #a-d 9.50 9.50

Salvation Army in Papua New Guinea, 50th Anniv. — A272

Designs: 5t, Salvation Army emblem. 80t, Emblem, flags of Papua New Guinea and Salvation Army Papua New Guinea Territory. 1k, Lt. Ian Cutmore and Senior Major Keith Baker. 3.20k, Colonels, Andrew and Julie Kalai. 3.25k, Kei Geno. 5.35k, Lt. Dorothy Elphick holding baby.

2006, June 14 *Perf. 13¼*
1217-1222 A272 Set of 6 10.00 10.00

Nos. 1148-1149 Surcharged

2006, July 5 Litho. *Perf. 14*
1223 A259 80t on 70t #1148 .80 .80
1224 A259 80t on 70t #1149 .80 .80

Butterflies A273

Designs: 80t, Delias iltis. 3.20k, Ornithoptera paradisea. 3.25k, Taenaris catops. 5.35k, Papilio ulysses autolycus.

2006, Aug. 30 *Perf. 13¼*
1225-1228 A273 Set of 4 10.50 10.50

Snakes — A274

Designs: 5t, Black whip snake. 80t, Papuan taipan. 2k, Smooth-scaled death adder. 3.20k, Papuan black snake. 3.25k, New Guinea small-eyed snake. 5.35k, Eastern brown snake.

2006, Sept. 13 *Perf. 14¼x14*
1229-1234 A274 Set of 6 11.50 11.50

A275

Elvis Presley (1935-77) — A276

Designs: 80t, Wearing white jacket and pants. 3.20k, Wearing red shirt. 3.25k, Wearing white jacket and black bow tie. 5.35k, With guitar.

No. 1239 — Record covers: a, 80t, 50,000 Elvis Fans Can't Be Wrong. b, 3.20k, Elvis Country. c, 3.25k, His Hand in Mine. d, 5.35k, King Creole.

10k, Holding teddy bears.

Perf. 13½, 13¼ (#1239)
2006, Nov. 15 Litho.
1235-1238 A275 Set of 4 9.50 9.50
1239 A276 Sheet of 4, #a-d 9.00 9.00

Souvenir Sheet
1240 A275 10k multi 8.25 8.25

Tropical Fruits — A277

Designs: 5t, Mangos. No. 1242, 85t, Watermelons. No. 1243, 85t, Pineapples. No. 1244, 3.35t, Guavas. No. 1245, 3.35t, Pawpaws (papaya). 5.35t, Lemons.

2007, Jan. 2 *Perf. 14x14¼*
1241-1246 A277 Set of 6 9.50 9.50

Endangered Turtles — A278

Designs: 10t, Hawksbill turtle. 35t, Flatback turtle. No. 1249, 85t, Loggerhead turtle. No. 1250, 3k, Leatherback turtle (blue violet panel). No. 1251, 3.35k, Green turtle (emerald panel). No. 1252, 5.35k, Olive Ridley turtle (tan panel).

No. 1253: a, 85t, Flatback turtle, diff. b, 3k, Leatherback turtle, diff. (olive green panel). c, 3.35k, Green turtle, diff. (olive green panel). d, 5.35k, Olive Ridley turtle, diff. (emerald panel).

2007, Mar. 23 Litho. *Perf. 13¼*
1247-1252 A278 Set of 6 13.00 13.00

Souvenir Sheet
1253 A278 Sheet of 4, #a-d 13.00 13.00

Scouting, Cent. — A279

Designs: 10t, Scouts standing at attention. 85t, Scouts carrying flag. 3.35k, Scouts and leaders at campsite. 5.35k, Scouts and leader.

10k, Lord Robert Baden-Powell, vert.

2007, May 23 Litho. *Perf. 14x14¼*
1254-1257 A279 Set of 4 8.00 8.00
1257a Souvenir sheet, #1254-1257 6.25 6.25

Souvenir Sheet
1257B A279 10k multi 6.50 6.50

Law, Justice, Health and Education A280

Inscriptions: 5t, "A Just, Safe & Secure Society for All." 30t, "Prosperity Through self-reliance." 85t, "HIV/AIDS." 3k, "Crime Reduction." 3.35k, "Infant Care & Child Immunization." 5.35k, "Minimizing Illiteracy."

2007, July 25 *Perf. 13¼*
1258-1263 A280 Set of 6 8.25 8.25

A281

A282

A283

A284

A285

A286

A287

A288

A289

A290

A291

Orchids A292

2007, Aug. 3 Litho. *Perf. 14*

1264	Sheet of 12 +12 labels	13.50	13.50
a.	A281 1k multi + label	1.10	1.10
b.	A282 1k multi + label	1.10	1.10
c.	A283 1k multi + label	1.10	1.10
d.	A284 1k multi + label	1.10	1.10
e.	A285 1k multi + label	1.10	1.10
f.	A286 1k multi + label	1.10	1.10
g.	A287 1k multi + label	1.10	1.10
h.	A288 1k multi + label	1.10	1.10
i.	A289 1k multi + label	1.10	1.10
j.	A290 1k multi + label	1.10	1.10
k.	A291 1k multi + label	1.10	1.10
l.	A292 1k multi + label	1.10	1.10

Labels could not be personalized.

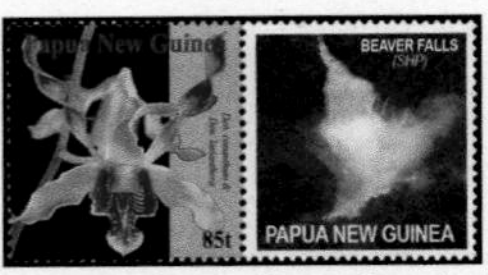

Dendrobium Conanthum, Dendrobium Lasianthera — A293

Dendrobium Conanthum — A294

Dendrobium Lasianthera "May River Red" — A295

Dendrobium Wulaiense — A296

2007, Aug. 21 Litho. *Perf. 14*

1265 A293 85t multi + label .60 .60
1266 A294 3k multi + label 2.10 2.10
1267 A295 3.35k multi + label 2.40 2.40
1268 A296 5.35k multi + label 3.75 3.75
Nos. 1265-1268 (4) 8.85 8.85

Nos. 1265-1268 were each issued in sheets of 20 + 20 labels. The labels illustrated are generic labels. Labels could be personalized for an additional fee.

Rotary International in Papua New Guinea, 50th Anniv. — A297

Inscriptions: 85t, Rotary's humanitarian service. 3.35k, Rotary against malaria. 5k, Rotary clubs in Papua New Guinea. 5.35k, Donations in kind.

2007, Sept. 5 Litho. *Perf. 13¼*

1269-1272 A297 Set of 4 9.50 9.50
1272a Souvenir sheet, #1269-1272 9.50 9.50

A298

Wedding of Queen Elizabeth II and Prince Philip, 60th Anniv. — A299

No. 1273: a, Couple, pink background. b, Queen, pink background. c, Queen, lilac background. d, Couple, lilac background. e, Couple, pale yellow background. f, Queen, pale yellow background.

2007, Oct. 31 Litho. *Perf. 14*

1273 A298 2k Sheet of 6, #a-f 8.00 8.00

Souvenir Sheet

1274 A299 10k multi 7.00 7.00

A300

Princess Diana (1961-97) — A301

No. 1275 — Photographs of Diana from: a, 85t, 1965. b, 2.45k, 1971. c, 3.35k, 1981. d, 5.35k, 1983.

2007, Oct. 31

1275 A300 Sheet of 4, #a-d 8.00 8.00

Souvenir Sheet

1276 A301 10k multi 6.75 6.75

St. John Ambulance in Papua New Guinea, 50th Anniv. — A302

Inscriptions: 5t, St. John Health Service. 20t, St. John Blood Service. 85t, St. John Blind Service. 1k, St. John Ambulance Service. 3.35k, St. John Volunteer Service. 5.35k, Order of St. John.

2007, Nov. 30 *Perf. 14¼*

1277-1282 A302 Set of 6 7.75 7.75
1282a Miniature sheet, #1277-1282 7.75 7.75

Contemporary Art — A303

Designs: 5t, Oro Gagara. 30t, Western Province tribesman. 85t, Sorcerer. 3k, Hewa wigman. 3.35k, Pigs Into Python Legend. 5.35k, Tolai masks.

2007, Dec. 12

1283-1288 A303 Set of 6 9.25 9.25
1288a Miniature sheet, #1283-1288 9.25 9.25

Protected Birds — A304

Designs: 10t, Papuan hornbill. 50t, Osprey. 85t, New Guinea harpy eagle. 3k, Victoria crowned pigeon.

No. 1293: a, 1k, Palm cockatoo. b, 5.35k, Great white egret.

10k, Like #1293a.

2008, Jan. 25 Litho. *Perf. 14x14¼*

1289-1292 A304 Set of 4 4.00 4.00
1293 A304 Sheet of 6, #1289-1292, 1293a, 1293b 9.00 9.00

Souvenir Sheet

1294 A304 10k multi 8.50 8.50

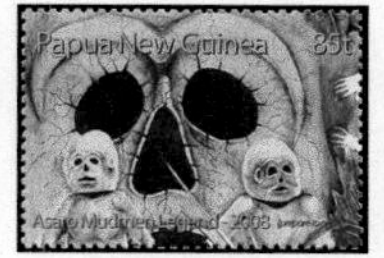

Asaro Mudmen Legend — A305

Designs: 85t, Two Mudmen, large skull. 3k, Three Mudmen scouting for enemies in forest. 3.35k, Mudmen attacking enemies. 5.35k, Retreat of enemies.

10k, Similar to 85t.

2008, Feb. 27 *Perf. 13¼*

1295-1298 A305 Set of 4 9.25 9.25
1298a Miniature sheet, #1295-1298 9.25 9.25

Souvenir Sheet

1299 A305 10k multi 8.00 8.00

Marine Life — A306

Designs: No. 1300, 85t, Leather coral. No. 1301, 3k, Kunei's chromodoris. No. 1302, 3.35k, Scorpion spider snail. No. 1303, 5.35k, Veined sponge.

No. 1304: a, 85t, Radiant sea urchin. b, 3k, Varicose. c, 3.35k, Sea squirt. d, 5.35k, Heffernan's sea star.

10k, White grape coral.

2008, Mar. 21 *Perf. 14x14¼*

1300-1303 A306 Set of 4 13.00 13.00
1304 A306 Sheet of 4, #a-d 16.00 16.00

Souvenir Sheet

1305 A306 10k multi 11.00 11.00

Miniature Sheet

2008 Summer Olympics, Beijing — A307

No. 1306: a, Weight lifting. b, Diving. c, Hurdles. d, Boxing.

2008, Apr. 16 *Perf. 12¾*

1306 A307 1.40k Sheet of 4, #a-d 4.50 4.50

Papua New Guinea Partnership With European Union, 30th Anniv. — A308

Flags of Papua New Guinea and European Union, bird of paradise, circle of stars and background color of: Nos. 1307, 1311a, 85t, Gray. Nos. 1308, 1311b, 3k, Yellow. Nos. 1309, 1311c, 3.35k, Rose pink. Nos. 1310, 1311d, 5.35k, Light blue.

10k, Gray, without blue panel at bottom.

2008, May 9 *Perf. 13x13¼*

Stamps With Blue Panel With Bold White Drawings

1307-1310 A308 Set of 4 9.50 9.50

Stamps With Blue Panel With Faint White Drawings

1311 A308 Sheet of 4, #a-d 9.50 9.50

Souvenir Sheet

1312 A308 10k multi 8.00 8.00

Art by Timothy Akis (1944-84) — A309

Designs: No. 1313, 85t, Long Hair. No. 1314, 3k, Alone. No. 1315, 3.35k, Woman with Cassowary and Child. No. 1316, 5.35k, Man Shooting Cassowary.

No. 1317: a, 85t, Five Men in Their Gardens (top half). b, 3k, The Crocodile Woman and Two Headed Man (top half). c, 3.35k, As "a," bottom half. d, 5.35k, As "b," bottom half.

10k, Flying Fox.

2008, June 25 Litho. *Perf. 14¼x14*

1313-1316 A309 Set of 4 9.25 9.25
1317 A309 Sheet of 4, #a-d 9.25 9.25

Souvenir Sheet

1318 A309 10k multi 7.25 7.25

Headdresses — A310

Headdresses of: No. 1319, 85t, Central Province (person showing shoulder). No. 1320, 3k, Western Highlands Province. No. 1321, 3.35k, Oro Province. No. 1322, 5.35k, Western Highlands Province, diff.

No. 1323: a, 85t, Central Province (headdress with yellow side tassels). b, 3k, Central Province, diff. c, 3.35k, Southern Highlands Province, diff. d, 5.35k, Oro Province, diff.

10k, Central Province, diff.

2008, July 31

1319-1322 A310 Set of 4 9.75 9.75
1323 A310 Sheet of 4, #a-d 9.75 9.75

Souvenir Sheet

1324 A310 10k multi 7.75 7.75

Marilyn Monroe (1926-62), Actress — A311

No. 1325, horiz. — Various photographs of Monroe: a, 85t. b, 3k. c, 3.35k. d, 5.35k

10k, Monroe in automobile.

2008, Aug. 6 Litho. *Perf. 13¼*

1325 A311 Sheet of 4, #a-d 9.00 9.00

Souvenir Sheet

1326 A311 10k multi 7.00 7.00

Birds of Paradise — A312

Designs: No. 1327, 85t, Paradisaea guilielmi. No. 1328, 3k, Parotia lawesi. No. 1329, 3.35k, Epimachus meyeri. No. 1330, 5.35k, Diphyllodes magnificus.

No. 1331: a, 85t, Astrapia stephaniae. b, 3k, Cnemophilus macgregorii. c, 3.35k, Pteridophora alberti. d, 5.35k, Astrapia meyeri.

10k, Cicinnurus regius.

2008, Sept. 3 Litho. *Perf. 14¼x14*

1327-1330 A312 Set of 4 10.00 10.00
1331 A312 Sheet of 4, #a-d 11.00 11.00

Souvenir Sheet

1332 A312 10k multi 8.00 8.00

For surcharge, see No. 1734C.

Gold Mining — A313

Designs: No. 1333, 85t, Tunnel drilling. No. 1334, 3k, Logistics. No. 1335, 3.35k, Refinery. No. 1336, 5.35k, Gold bars.

No. 1337: a, 85t, Open pit mining. b, 3k, Conveyor belt. c, 3.35k, Plant site. d, 5.35k, Refinery.

10k, Gold bar.

2008, Oct. 31 *Perf. 14¼*
1333-1336 A313 Set of 4 9.50 9.50
1337 A313 Sheet of 4, #a-d 9.50 9.50

Souvenir Sheet

1338 A313 10k multi 7.75 7.75

World AIDS Day — A314

Red ribbon and inscription: 5t, HIV and the workplace. 10t, Voluntary counseling and testing. 50t, Role of men and women. Nos. 1342, 1348a, 85t, Education. 1k, 10k, Eradicating stigma and discrimination. 2k, Living with the virus. Nos. 1345, 1348b, 3k, Care, support and the role of family. Nos. 1346, 1348c, 3.70k, Building leadership. Nos. 1347, 1348d, 6k, Health and nutrition.

2008, Dec. 1 **Litho.** *Perf. 14¼*
1339-1347 A314 Set of 9 14.00 14.00
1348 A314 Sheet of 4, #a-d 13.00 13.00

Souvenir Sheet

1349 A314 10k multi 8.75 8.75

No. 1348 contains four 42x28 stamps; No. 1349 contains one 42x28mm stamp.

Christmas A315

Designs: No. 1350, 85t, Holy Family. No. 1351, 3k, Santa Claus on reindeer. No. 1352, 3.35k, Book and candle. No. 1353, 5.35k, Bell and book.

No. 1354: a, 85t, Journey to Bethlehem. b, 3k, Silent night. c, 3.35k, Behold that star. d, 5.35k, Three wise men.

10k, Gift and map of Papua New Guinea.

2008, Dec. 3 *Perf. 14¼*
1350-1353 A315 Set of 4 9.50 9.50
1354 A315 Sheet of 4, #a-d 9.50 9.50

Souvenir Sheet

1355 A315 10k multi 7.75 7.75

Plants — A316

Designs: No. 1356, 85t, Bixa. No. 1357, 3k, Perfume tree. No. 1358, 3.70k, Beach kalofilum. No. 1359, 6k, Macaranga.

No. 1360: a, 85t, Native frangipani. b, 3k, Ten cent flower. c, 3.70k, Beach terminali. d, 6k, Red beech.

10k, Beach convolvulus (morning glory).

2009, Jan. 14 *Perf. 14¼*
1356-1359 A316 Set of 4 9.75 9.75
1360 A316 Sheet of 4, #a-d 9.75 9.75

Souvenir Sheet

1361 A316 10k multi 7.50 7.50

For surcharges, see Nos. 1732K, 1732V, 1732W.

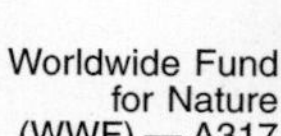

Worldwide Fund for Nature (WWF) — A317

Designs: No. 1362, 85t, Albericus siegfriedi. No. 1363, 3k, Cophixalus nubicola. No. 1364, 3.70k, Nyctimystes pulcher. No. 1365, 6k, Sphenophryne cornuta.

No. 1366: a, 85t, Litoria sauroni. b, 3k, Litoria prora. c, 3.70k, Litoria multiplica. d, 6k, Litoria pronimia.

10k, Oreophryne sp.

2009, Feb. 18 **Litho.** *Perf. 13¼*
1362-1365 A317 Set of 4 10.00 10.00
1366 A317 Sheet of 4, #a-d 10.00 10.00

Souvenir Sheet

1367 A317 10k multi 7.50 7.50

Art by David Lasisi A318

Designs: No. 1368, 85t, Chota. No. 1369, 3k, Stability. No. 1370, 3.70k, Taumimir. No. 1371, 6k, The Moieties.

No. 1372: a, 85t, Like a Log Being Adrifted. b, 3k, Lasisi. c, 3.70k, Lupa. d, 6k, In Memory of Marker Craftsman.

10k, Trapped by Cobweb of Stinging Pain.

2008, Mar. 11 *Perf. 13½*
1368-1371 A318 Set of 4 9.25 9.25
1372 A318 Sheet of 4, #a-d 9.25 9.25

Souvenir Sheet

1373 A318 10k multi 7.00 7.00

A319

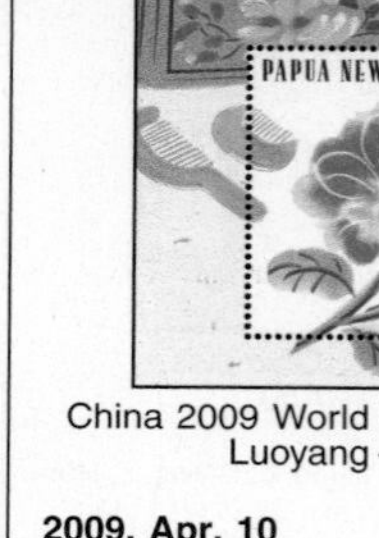

China 2009 World Stamp Exhibition, Luoyang — A320

2009, Apr. 10 *Perf. 12¾x12½*
1374 A319 1k multi .90 .90

Souvenir Sheet

1375 A320 6k multi 4.75 4.75

Chinese Antiquities — A321

Designs: Nos. 1376, 1382a, 5t, Vessel with design of deities, animals and masks. Nos. 1377, 1382b, 10t, Evening in the Peach and Plum Garden, by Li Bai. Nos. 1378, 1382c, 85t, Reliquary with Buddhist figures. Nos. 1379, 1382d, 3k, Brick relief figure. Nos. 1380, 1382e, 3.70k, Round tray with scroll designs. Nos. 1381, 1382f, 6k, Plate in the shape of two peach halves with design of two foxes.

2009, Apr. 10 *Perf. 14¼x14¾*

With Inscription "World Stamp Exhibition / China 2009" At Left

1376-1381 A321 Set of 6 9.25 9.25

Stamps Without Inscription "World Stamp Exhibition / China 2009" At Left

1382 A321 Sheet of 6, #a-f 9.25 9.25

Assets of Coral Triangle — A322

Designs: No. 1383, 85t, Fish. No. 1384, 3k, Marine turtle (blue green frame). No. 1385, 3.70k, Mangroves. No. 1386, 6k, Coral reefs.

No. 1387: a, 85t, Dolphins. b, 3k, Marine turtle (no frame). c, 3.70k, Reef fish. d, 6k, Killer whale.

10k, Grouper.

2009, May 22 **Litho.** *Perf. 14½x14¼*
1383-1386 A322 Set of 4 10.00 10.00
1387 A322 Sheet of 4, #a-d 10.00 10.00

Souvenir Sheet

1388 A322 10k multi 7.50 7.50

Kokoda Trail — A323

Designs: No. 1389, 85t, Guides assisting a trekker. No. 1390, 3k, Crossing Vabuyavi River. No. 1391, 3.70k, Waterfall near Abuari. No. 1392, 6k, Crossing Lake Myola 1.

No. 1393: a, 85t, Crossing Emune River. b, 3k, Entering Imita Ridge. c, 3.70k, Crossing Alo Creek. d, 6k, Templeton's Crossing No. 2.

10k, Golden Staircase, Imita Ridge.

2009, June 23 *Perf. 14¼*
1389-1392 A323 Set of 4 10.50 10.50
1393 A323 Sheet of 4, #a-d 10.50 10.50

Souvenir Sheet

1394 A323 10k multi 7.50 7.50

Bats — A324

Designs: No. 1395, 85t, Black-bellied bat. No. 1396, 3k, Least blossom bat. No. 1397, 3.70k, Sanborn's broad-nosed bat. No. 1398, 6k, Mantled mastiff bat.

No. 1399: a, 85t, Trident leaf-nosed bat. b, 3k, Flower-faced bat. c, 3.70k, Eastern horseshoe bat. d, 6k, Greater tube-nosed bat.

10k, Bougainville's fruit bat.

2009, July 15
1395-1398 A324 Set of 4 10.50 10.50
1399 A324 Sheet of 4, #a-d 10.50 10.50

Souvenir Sheet

1400 A324 10k multi 7.75 7.75

For surcharge, see No. 1732I.

Intl. Day of Non-violence — A325

Doves and: No. 1401, 85t, Abraham Lincoln. No. 1402, 3k, Princess Diana. No. 1403, 3.70k, Nelson Mandela. No. 1404, 6k, Barack Obama.

No. 1405: a, 85t, Obama. b, 3k, Dr. Martin Luther King, Jr. c, 3.70k, Mohandas K. Gandhi. d, 6k, Princess Diana.

10k, Obama, diff.

2009, Aug. 6 *Perf. 13¼*
1401-1404 A325 Set of 4 10.50 10.50
1405 A325 Sheet of 4, #a-d 10.50 10.50

Souvenir Sheet

1406 A325 10k multi 7.50 7.50

No. 1406 contains one 38x51mm stamp.

Volcanoes A326

Designs: No. 1407, 85t, Mount Vulcan. No. 1408, 3k, Mount Tavurvur. No. 1409, 3.70k, Mount Bagana. No. 1410, 6k, Manam Island.

No. 1411: a, 85t, Mount Tavurvur, diff. b, 3k, Manam Island, diff. c, 3.70k, Mount Tavurvur, diff. d, 6k, Mount Ulawun.

10k, Mount Tavurvur, diff.

2009, Sept. 9 *Perf. 14¼*
1407-1410 A326 Set of 4 10.00 10.00
1411 A326 Sheet of 4, #a-d 10.00 10.00

Souvenir Sheet

1412 A326 10k multi 7.50 7.50

Palm Oil Production A327

Designs: No. 1413, 85t, Oil palm fruitlets. No. 1414, 3k, Oil palm nursery. No. 1415, 3.70k, Oil palm bunches. No. 1416, 6k, Fruit collection.

No. 1417: a, 85t, Irrigation. b, 3k, Oil palm bunches. c, 3.70k, Loose fruits. d, 6k, Mill.

10k, Oil palm fruitlets in hand.

2009, Oct. 7 **Litho.** *Perf. 14¼*
1413-1416 A327 Set of 4 10.00 10.00
1417 A327 Sheet of 4, #a-d 10.00 10.00

Souvenir Sheet

1418 A327 10k multi 7.50 7.50

For surcharge, see No. 1732P.

Canoes A328

Canoe from: No. 1419, 85t, Mortlock Island. No. 1420, 3k, Manus Province. No. 1421, 3.70k, Bilbil. No. 1422, 6k, Central Province.

No. 1423: a, 85t, Kimbe. b, 3k, Vuvulu Island. c, 3.70k, Suau Island. d, 6k, Mailu.

10k, Gogodala.

2009, Nov. 4 **Litho.** *Perf. 12¾*
1419-1422 A328 Set of 4 10.00 10.00
1423 A328 Sheet of 4, #a-d 10.00 10.00

Souvenir Sheet

1424 A328 10k multi 7.25 7.25

Traditional Dances A329

Designs: No. 1425, 1k, Engagement dance, Western Highlands Province. No. 1426, 3k, Bride price dance, Central Province. No. 1427, 4.65k, Engagement dance, Manus Province. No. 1428, 6.30k, Trobriand love dance, Milne Bay Province.

No. 1429: a, 1k, Courtship dance, Chimbu Province. b, 3k, Engagement dance, Enga Province. c, 4.65k, Engagement Dance, Central Province. d, 6.30k, Womanhood dance, Central Province.

10k, Trobriand love dance, Milne Bay Province, diff.

2009, Dec. 2 *Perf. 14¼*
1425-1428 A329 Set of 4 11.00 11.00
1429 A329 Sheet of 4, #a-d 11.00 11.00

Souvenir Sheet

1430 A329 10k multi 7.25 7.25

Pioneer Art — A330

Paintings by Jakupa Ako: No. 1431, 1k, Fish Man. No. 1432, 3k, Story Board. No. 1433, 4.65k, Hunting Trip. No. 1434, 6.30k, Warrior.

No. 1435: a, 1k, Bird Art. b, 3k, Bird Eating. c, 4.65k, Bird Nest. d, 6.30k, Marsupial.

10k, Spirit Mask.

2010, Jan. 1 *Perf. 14¼*
1431-1434 A330 Set of 4 10.50 10.50

1435 A330 Sheet of 4, #a-d 10.50 10.50

Souvenir Sheet

1436 A330 10k multi 7.25 7.25

Beche-de-Mer Industry — A331

Edible sea cucumbers: No. 1437, 1k, Chalkfish. No. 1438, 3k, Elephant trunk fish. No. 1439, 4.65k, Curryfish. No. 1440, 6.30k, Tigerfish.

No. 1441: a, 1k, Surf redfish. b, 3k, Lollyfish. c, 4.65k, Brown sandfish. d, 6.30k, Sandfish.

10k, Pinkfish.

2010, Feb. 8 Litho. *Perf. 14x14¼*

1437-1440 A331 Set of 4 11.00 11.00
1441 A331 Sheet of 4, #a-d 11.00 11.00

Souvenir Sheet

1442 A331 10k multi 7.50 7.50

For surcharge, see No. 1732M.

Carteret Atoll — A332

Designs: No. 1443, 1k, Huene Island divided. No. 1444, 3k, Upsurge of water through man-made barriers. No. 1445, 4.65k, Salt water intrusion No. 1446, 6.30k, Tree killed by salt water.

No. 1447: a, 1k, Dwindling island. b, 3k, Tree killed by salt water, diff. c, 4.65k, Storm surge and erosion. d, 6.30k, Man-made barriers.

10k, Divided atolls.

2010, Mar. 18

1443-1446 A332 Set of 4 11.00 11.00
1447 A332 Sheet of 4, #a-d 11.00 11.00

Souvenir Sheet

1448 A332 10k multi 7.50 7.50

Girl Guides, Cent. — A333

Designs: No. 1449, 1k, Guides learning cooking for badge work, 1970. No. 1450, 3k, Guide creating a wash bowl for badge work. No. 1451, 4.65k, Trainer teaching knot tying. No. 1452, 6.30k, Brownies displaying badge work.

No. 1453: a, 1k, Lady Kala Olewale, Second Papua New Guinea Chief Commissioner. b, 3k, Lady Christian Chartterton, founder of Papua New Guinea Girl Guides. c, 4.65k, Princess Anne visiting Papua New Guinea Girl Guides. d, 6.30k, Enny Moaitz, First Papua New Guinea Chief Commissioner.

10k, Lady Olave Baden-Powell.

2010, Apr. 10 Litho. *Perf. 14x14¼*

1449-1452 A333 Set of 4 11.00 11.00
1453 A333 Sheet of 4, #a-d 11.00 11.00

Souvenir Sheet

1454 A333 10k multi 7.50 7.50

For surcharges, see Nos. 1732O, 1732R.

Kokoda Campaigns, 68th Anniv. — A334

No. 1455: a, Soldiers in battle. b, Injured Australian soldier, Papuan natives. c, Tourists at Kokoda.

No. 1456: a, Veterans at Kokoda Campaign Memorial, Isurava. b, Veterans of Kokoda Campaign, Papuan houses.

2010, Apr. 20 Litho. *Perf. 14¾x14*

1455 A334 Horiz. strip of 3 2.40 2.40
a.-c. 1k Any single .80 .80
1456 A334 Horiz. pair 7.50 7.50
a.-b. 4.65k Either single 3.75 3.75
c. Souvenir sheet, #1455a-1455c, 1456a-1456b 10.00 10.00

See Australia Nos. 3244-3252.

National Population and Housing Census — A335

Inscriptions: No. 1457, 1k, Young and old. No. 1458, 1k, Youths. No. 1459, 3k, Infants. No. 1460, 3k, Villagers.

No. 1461: a, 1k, School kids. b, 1k, Elderly men. c, 3k, Elderly women. d, 3k, All walks of life.

2010, May 3 *Perf. 14x14¼*

1457-1460 A335 Set of 4 6.00 6.00
1461 A335 Sheet of 4, #a-d 6.00 6.00

For surcharge, see No. 1732Q.

Expo 2010, Shanghai — A336

Designs: 1k, Summer Palace, Wenchang Tower. No. 1463, 3k, Dancer, Shanghai Intl. Culture and Art Festival. 4.65k, Oriental Pearl Tower, Pudong, Shanghai. 6.30k, Male Chinese acrobatic performers.

No. 1466: a, 5t, Like 1k. b, 10t, Like #1463. c, 85t, Like 4.65k. d, 3k, Female Chinese acrobatic performers. e, 3.70k, Like 6.30k. f, 6k, Ancient Chinese building.

10k, Tower, Suzhou.

2010, May 21 *Perf. 11¼x11½*

1462-1465 A336 Set of 4 11.00 11.00
1466 A336 Sheet of 6, #a-f 10.00 10.00

Souvenir Sheet

1467 A336 10k multi 9.00 9.00

Sport Fishing A337

Inscriptions: No. 1468, 1k, Female angler. No. 1469, 3k, Team effort. No. 1470, 4.65k, 25kg Sailfish. No. 1471, 6.30k, 10kg Barramundi.

No. 1472: a, 1k, Game fishing boat. b, 3k, Male angler. c, 4.65k, 14kg Wahoo. d, 6.30k, 11kg Barramundi.

10k, Irene Robinson's world record catch blue fin trevally (92.6kg) on a 4kg line.

2010, June 11 *Perf. 13½*

1468-1471 A337 Set of 4 11.00 11.00
1472 A337 Sheet of 4, #a-d 11.00 11.00

Souvenir Sheet

1473 A337 10k multi 7.25 7.25

Coffee — A338

Designs: 15t, Coffee tree with cherries. No. 1475, 1k, Budding beans. No. 1476, 4.65k, Green coffee cherries. No. 1477, 6.30k, Red coffee cherries.

No. 1478: a, 1k, Man harvesting cherries. b, 3k, Fermentation. c, 4.65k, Drying parchment. d, 6.30k, Man holding green coffee beans.

10k, Green and red coffee cherries.

2010, July 7 Litho. *Perf. 14¼*

1474-1477 A338 Set of 4 9.00 9.00
1478 A338 Sheet of 4, #a-d 11.00 11.00

Souvenir Sheet

1479 A338 10k multi 7.25 7.25

Bowerbirds — A339

Designs: 5t, Macgregor's gardener bowerbird. No. 1481, 1k, Flame bowerbird. No. 1482, 4.65k, Archbold's bowerbird. No. 1483, 6.30k, Adelbert regent bowerbird.

No. 1484: a, 1k, Pair of Flame bowerbirds. b, 3k, Yellow-fronted gardener bowerbird. c, 4.65k, Vogelkop gardener bowerbird. d, 6.30k, Lauterbach's bowerbird.

10k, Head of Flame bowerbird.

2010, Aug. 4

1480-1483 A339 Set of 4 8.75 8.75
1484 A339 Sheet of 4, #a-d 11.00 11.00

Souvenir Sheet

1485 A339 10k multi 7.25 7.25

2010 Commonwealth Games, Delhi — A340

Designs: No. 1486, 1k, Rugby sevens. No. 1487, 3k, Boxing. No. 1488, 4.65k, Netball. No. 1489, 6.30k, Hurdles.

No. 1490: a, 1k, Weight lifting. b, 3k, Swimming. c, 4.65k, Lawn bowling. d, 6.30k, Sprinting.

10k, Tennis.

2010, Sept. 3 *Perf. 13½*

1486-1489 A340 Set of 4 11.00 11.00
1490 A340 Sheet of 4, #a-d 11.00 11.00

Souvenir Sheet

1491 A340 10k multi 7.25 7.25

Orchids — A341

Designs: No. 1492, 1k, Dendrobium lasianthera May River Red. No. 1493, 3k, Dendrobium violaceoflavens J.J. Smith. No. 1494, 4.65k, Dendrobium mirbelianum var. Vanimo. No. 1495, 6.30k, Dendrobium helix.

No. 1496: a, 1k, Dendrobium nindii W. Hill. b, 3k, Dendrobium sp. off. D. gouldii Reichb. f. c, 4.65k, Dendrobium gouldii Reichb. f. var. Bougainville White. d, 6.30k, Dendrobium discolor var. pink Bensbach.

10k, Dendrobium lasianthera var. Sepik Blue.

2010, Sept. 28 *Perf. 14¼*

1492-1495 A341 Set of 4 11.00 11.00
1496 A341 Sheet of 4, #a-d 11.00 11.00

Souvenir Sheet

1497 A341 10k multi 7.25 7.25

For surcharge, see No. 1732L.

Mother Teresa (1910-97) — A342

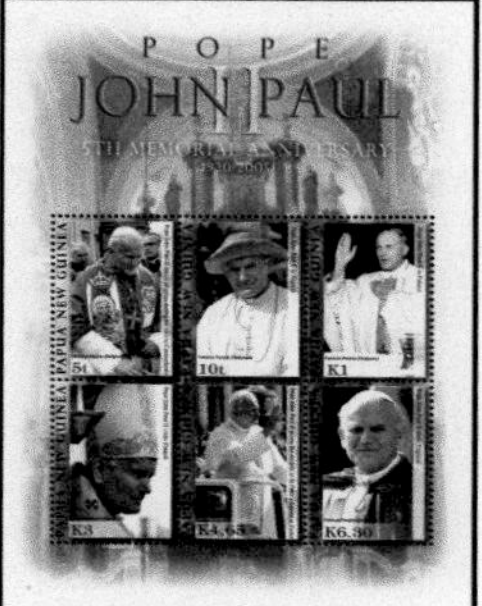

Pope John Paul II (1920-2005) — A343

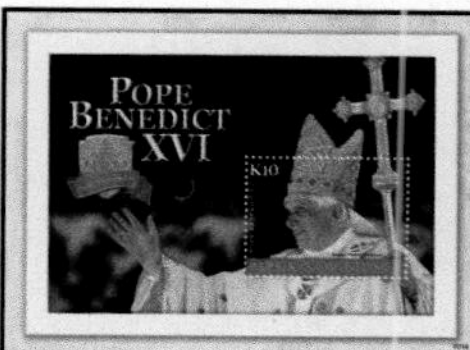

Pope Benedict XVI A344

Photographs of Mother Teresa from: 1k, 1997. 3k, 1971. 4.65k, 1983. 6.30k, 1984.

No. 1502 — Photographs of Pope John Paul II: a, 5t, Meeting with pilgrims at Czestochowa. b, 10t, In Nigeria. c, 1k, In Poland, as young man (without miter). d, 3k, In Poland (wearing miter). e, 4.65k, Greeting crowds in St. Peter's Square. f, 6.30k, In England.

2010, Oct. 13 *Perf. 12*

1498-1501 A342 Set of 4 11.00 11.00
1502 A343 Sheet of 6, #a-f 11.00 11.00

Souvenir Sheet

1503 A344 10k multi 7.25 7.25

Spiders — A345

Designs: No. 1504, 1k, Nephila pilipes. No. 1505, 3k, Argiope aemula. No. 1506, 4.65k, Gasterocantha (blue violet color at UL). No. 1507, 6.30k, Cyrtophora moluccensis.

No. 1508: a, 1k, Leucauge celebesiana. b, 3k, Holconia. c, 4.65k, Gasterocantha (red background color at UL). d, 6.30k, Ocrisiona.

10k, Nephila pilipes, diff.

2010, Nov. 3 Litho. *Perf. 14½*

1504-1507 A345 Set of 4 11.00 11.00
1508 A345 Sheet of 4, #a-d 11.00 11.00

Souvenir Sheet

1509 A345 10k multi 7.25 7.25

War Dances — A346

Designs: 50t, Warrior with bow and arrow, Western Highlands Province. 1.05k, Simbu warrior with spear, Chimbu Province. 5k, Warrior with spear and shield, Western Highlands Province. 7k, Mudman with bow and arrow, Eastern Highlands Province.

10k, Tasman Island knife dancer, North Solomons Province.

2010, Dec. 1 Litho. *Perf. 14¼x14*

1510-1513 A346 Set of 4 10.00 10.00

Souvenir Sheet

1514 A346 10k multi 7.25 7.25

Monitor Lizards — A347

Designs: No. 1515, 1.05k, Emerald tree monitor. No. 1516, 5k, Papuan argus monitor. No. 1517, 5k, Papuan monitor. 7k, Blue-tailed monitor.

No. 1519: a, 1.05k, Blue-tailed monitor, diff. b, 2k, Spotted tree monitor. c, 5k, Mangrove monitor. d, 5k, Peach-throat monitor.

No. 1520, Papuan argus monitor with tongue extended.

2011, Jan. 5 Litho. *Perf. 14x14¼*

1515-1518 A347 Set of 4 13.00 13.00
1519 A347 Sheet of 4, #a-d 10.00 10.00

Souvenir Sheet

1520 A347 5k multi 3.75 3.75

Chinese Zodiac Animals — A348

Designs: No. 1521, 5t, Dragon. No. 1522, 50t, Tiger. No. 1523, 1.05k, Horse. 2k, Monkey. No. 1525, 5k, Snake. No. 1526, 5k, Dog.
No. 1527: a, 5t, Ox. b, 50t, Rooster. c, 55t, Sheep. d, 1.05k, Rat. e, 5k, Boar. f, 7k, Rabbit.

2011, Feb. 8 ***Perf. 13 Syncopated***

1521-1526 A348 Set of 6 10.50 10.50
1527 A348 Sheet of 6 #a-f 10.50 10.50

Paintings by Mathias Kauage (1944-2003) A349

Designs: No. 1528, 1.05k, Pailet Draivim Balus (Pilot Flying an Airplane). No. 1529, 5k, Fes Misineri (First Missionary). No. 1530, 5k, Pailet i Trein Long Draivim Balus (Trainee Pilot at Training). No. 1531, 7k, Eia Bas (Airbus).
No. 1532 — Details from Eia Bas Bilong Eiu Gini (Air New Guinea's Airbus): a, 1.05k, Wing at top. b, 5k, Bird at top. c, 5k, Wing at bottom. 7k, Rear wheel.
10k, Barasut Man (Parachute Man).

2011, Mar. 18 **Litho.** ***Perf. 13¼***

1528-1531 A349 Set of 4 14.50 14.50
1532 A349 Sheet of 4, #a-d 14.50 14.50

Souvenir Sheet

1533 A349 10k multi 8.00 8.00

Fish — A350

Designs: No. 1534, 1.05k, Cephalopholis miniata. No. 1535, 1.05k, Cromileptes altivelis. 5k, Plectropomus areolatus. 7k, Epinephelus lanceolatus.
10k, Epinephelus polyphekadion.

2011, Apr. 6 ***Perf. 14¼***

1534-1537 A350 Set of 4 11.50 11.50

Souvenir Sheet

1538 A350 10k multi 8.00 8.00

American Civil War, 150th Anniv. — A351

Designs: 1k, Pres. Abraham Lincoln, text "With malice toward none, with charity for all." No. 1540, 1.05k, Lincoln, text "Of the people, by the people, for the people." No. 1541, 5k, Slave and banner. No. 1542, 7k, Lincoln, Confederate States Pres. Jefferson Davis, US and Confederate flags, eagle, banner.
No. 1543: a, 5t, The Peacemakers, painting by George P. A. Healy. b, 50t, Battle of Fort Sumter. c, 55t, Lincoln and his Cabinet. d, 1.05k, Lincoln, Generals Ulysses S. Grant and Robert E. Lee. e, 5k, Lincoln, slave, text "If slavery is not wrong, nothing is wrong." f, 7k, Battle of Gettysburg.
10k, Lincoln, text "A house divided cannot stand."

2011, Apr. 20 ***Perf. 12***

1539-1542 A351 Set of 4 11.50 11.50

13 Syncopated

1543 A351 Sheet of 6, #a-f 11.50 11.50

Souvenir Sheet

1544 A351 10k multi 7.50 7.50

Butterflies A352

Designs: No. 1545, 1.05k, Orange birdwing. No. 1546, 1.05k, Green birdwing. 5k, Blue birdwing. 7k, Goliath birdwing.
10k, Pair of Queen Alexandra's birdwings.

2011, May 3 **Litho.** ***Perf. 14x14¼***

1545-1548 A352 Set of 4 12.00 12.00

Souvenir Sheet

1549 A352 10k multi 8.50 8.50

Pineapples A353

Pineapple slices and: No. 1550, 1.05k, African Queen pineapples sliced. No. 1551, 1.05k, African Queen and Hawaiian pineapples sliced. No. 1552, 5k, One Hawaiian and Two African Queen pineapples, one basket. No. 1553, 7k, One Hawaiian and two African Queen pineapples, two baskets.
No. 1554 — Popular pineapple varieties found in Papua New Guinea: a, 10t. b, 2k. c, 5k. d, 7k.
10k, African pineapple species cut.

2011, May 25 ***Perf. 14x14¼***

1550-1553 A353 Set of 4 12.00 12.00
1554 A353 Sheet of 4, #a-d 12.00 12.00

Souvenir Sheet

1555 A353 10k multi 8.25 8.25

Nos. 1550-1555 are impregnated with a pineapple scent.

Urban Safety and Crime Prevention — A354

Designs: 5t, National Capital District Commission emblem. No. 1557, 1.05k, No guns emblem. No. 1558, 5k, Meri SEIF Ples emblem. No. 1559, 7k, UN-Habitat certificate of recognition.
No. 1560: a, 1.05k, Shelter for women and children. b, 1.05k, Krismas SEIF Kempan members. c, 5k, Meri SEIF Ples members. d, 7k, Port Moresby Chamber of Commerce and Industry emblem.
10k, National Capital District Commission emblem, diff.

2011, June 15 ***Perf. 14¼x14***

1556-1559 A354 Set of 4 11.50 11.50
1560 A354 Sheet of 4, #a-d 12.00 12.00

Souvenir Sheet

1561 A354 10k multi 8.75 8.75

For surcharge, see No. 1732J.

Cacao Production A355

Designs: 5t, Harvesting cocoa pods. No. 1563, 1.05k, Breaking cocoa pod. No. 1564, 5k, Drying cocoa. No. 1565, 7k, Exporting cocoa bags.
No. 1566: a, 1.05k, Cocoa seedling. b, 1.05k, Cocoa flower. c, 5k, Pruning cocoa treas. d, 7k, Cocoa pods.
10k, Exporting cocoa bags, diff.

2011, July 7 ***Perf. 14x14¼***

1562-1565 A355 Set of 4 11.50 11.50
1566 A355 Sheet of 4, #a-d 12.00 12.00

Souvenir Sheet

1567 A355 10k multi 8.75 8.75

Tattoos — A356

Designs: No. 1568, 1.05k, Face tattoo from Tufi. No. 1569, 1.05k, Face tattoo from Nondugl-Banz. No. 1570, 5k, Face tattoo from Asaro. No. 1571, 7k, Face tattoo from Kudjip.
No. 1572: a, 1.05k, Arm tattoo from Kairuku. b, 1.05k, Chest tattoo from Gumine. c, 5k, Leg tattoo from South Whagi. d, 7k, Minei tribe arm tattoo, Manus.
10k, Face tattoo from Tufi, diff.

2011, Aug. 4 ***Perf. 14¼x14***

1568-1571 A356 Set of 4 13.00 13.00
1572 A356 Sheet of 4, #a-d 13.00 13.00

Souvenir Sheet

1573 A356 10k multi 9.00 9.00

Southern Cassowaries — A357

Designs: No. 1574, 1.05k, Two newly-weaned chicks feeding. No. 1575, 1.05k, One weaned chick feeding. No. 1576, 5k, Adult feeding. No. 1577, 7k, Heads of two adults.
No. 1578: a, 1.05k, Head and shoulder of adult. b, 1.05k, Back rump of adult. c, 5k, Full view of chick. d, 7k, Legs of adult.
10k, Cassowary in natural habitat.

2011, Aug. 25

1574-1577 A357 Set of 4 13.00 13.00
1578 A357 Sheet of 4, #a-d 13.00 13.00

Souvenir Sheet

1579 A357 10k multi 9.25 9.25

Waterfalls A358

Designs: No. 1580, 1.05k, Kesesoru Falls. No. 1581, 1.05k, Mageni Falls aerial view. No. 1582, 5k, Mageni Falls outlet. No. 1583, 7k, Waghi Falls.
No. 1584: a, 1.05k, Sogeri Falls. b, 1.05k, Beaver Falls. c, 5k, Wawoi Falls. d, 7k, Remote Island Falls.
10k, Ambua Falls.

2011, Sept. 22 ***Perf. 14x14¼***

1580-1583 A358 Set of 4 13.00 13.00
1584 A358 Sheet of 4, #a-d 13.00 13.00

Souvenir Sheet

1585 A358 10k multi 9.25 9.25

Wedding of Prince William and Catherine Middleton A359

Badge of the House of Windsor and: No. 1586, 1.05k, Catherine Middleton (at right). No. 1587, 1.05k, Middleton and sister, Pippa. No. 1588, 5k, Prince William. No. 1589, 7k, Couple.
No. 1590 — Badge of the House of Windsor and: a, 1.05k, Middleton (at left). b, 1.05k, Couple waving. c, 5k, Couple holding hands. d, 7k, Prince William, diff.
10k, Couple and badge of the House of Windsor.

2011, Oct. 19 ***Perf. 12, 14 (#1590)***

1586-1589 A359 Set of 4 13.50 13.50
1590 A359 Sheet of 4, #a-d 13.50 13.50

Souvenir Sheet

1591 A359 10k multi 9.50 9.50

World War II Relics — A360

Designs: No. 1592, 1.05k, American B-17E 41-2446. No. 1593, 1.05k, Japanese Ki-21 Sally. No. 1594, 5k, American P-38F 12647-S. No. 1595, 7k, American B17E 41-9234.
No. 1596: a, 1.05k, Japanese 95 Ha Go tank. b, 1.05k, Australian Hudson A16-91. c, 5k, New Zealand PV-1 Ventura NZ4613 Tail 13. d, 7k, Japanese 120mm dual purpose gun.
10k, American B-17F "Black Jack."

2011, Nov. 16 ***Perf. 13¼***

1592-1595 A360 Set of 4 13.50 13.50
1596 A360 Sheet of 4, #a-d 13.50 13.50

Souvenir Sheet

1597 A360 10k multi 9.50 9.50

Victory Dancers — A361

Designs: No. 1598, 1.05k, Kiriwina woman. No. 1599, 1.05k, Oro man. No. 1600, 5k, Kandep woman. No. 1601, 7k, Siasi man.
No. 1602: a, 1.05k, Kerowagi man. b, 1.05k, Tolai man. c, 5k, Rigo man. d, 7k, Huli man.
10k, Baining fire dancer.

2011, Dec. 1 ***Perf. 14¼x14***

1598-1601 A361 Set of 4 13.50 13.50
1602 A361 Sheet of 4, #a-d 13.50 13.50

Souvenir Sheet

1603 A361 10k multi 9.50 9.50

For surcharge, see No. 1732S.

Fish — A362

Designs: No. 1604, 1.20k, Emperor angelfish. No. 1605, 1.20k, Yellow-mask angelfish. No. 1606, 6k, Meyer's butterflyfish. No. 1607, 8k, Barrier Reef anemonefish.
No. 1608: a, 1.20k, Clown anemonefish. b, 1.20k, Clown triggerfish. c, 6k, Clark's anemonefish. d, 8k, Spotfin lionfish.
10k, Bearded scorpionfish.

2012, Jan. 5 ***Perf. 14x14¼***

1604-1607 A362 Set of 4 15.50 15.50
1608 A362 Sheet of 4, #a-d 15.50 15.50

Souvenir Sheet

1609 A362 10k multi 9.25 9.25

A363

A364

A365

A366

Paintings by Philip Yobale (1968-2009) — A367

Designs: No. 1610, Fish Berserk. No. 1611, Facing Faces. No. 1612, Regiana Bird of Paradise and Its Four Captors. No. 1613, Face Without Eye.
No. 1614 — Untitled works with: a, 1.20k, Faces. b, 1.20k, Head with headband. c, 6k, Eye at UL. d, 8k, Mask at UR.
10k, On-looking Eyes.

2012, Feb. 22 ***Perf. 14¼x14***

1610 A363 1.20k multi 1.10 1.10
1611 A364 1.20k multi 1.10 1.10
1612 A365 6k multi 5.75 5.75
1613 A366 8k multi 7.50 7.50
Nos. 1610-1613 (4) 15.45 15.45
1614 A367 Sheet of 4, #a-d 15.50 15.50

Souvenir Sheet

1615 A367 10k multi 9.50 9.50

Blessed Peter To Rot (1912-45), Christian Martyr — A368

Designs: No. 1616, 1.20k, Beatification ceremony, 1995. No. 1617, 1.20k, To Rot baptizing child. No. 1618, 6k, Beatification ceremony, diff. No. 1619, 8k, To Rot giving holy communion.

No. 1620: a, 1.20k, To Rot in Taliligap Catechist School. b, 1.20k, To Rot officiating a marriage. c, 6k, To Rot leading worship and devotion. d, 8k, Murder of To Rot in cell in Japanese concentration camp.

10k, Statue of To Rot.

2012, Mar. 14 ***Perf. 14x14¼***

1616-1619 A368 Set of 4 16.50 16.50

Perf. 14

1620 A368 Sheet of 4, #a-d 16.50 16.50

Souvenir Sheet

1621 A368 10k multi 10.00 10.00

Traditional Clay Cooking Pots — A369

Cooking pots from: No. 1622, 1.20k, Central Province. No. 1623, 1.20k, Madang Province. No. 1624, 6k, Autonomous Region of Bougainville. No. 1625, 8k, East Sepik Province.

No. 1626: a, 1.20k, Milne Bay Province (brown pot). b, 1.20k, Milne Bay Province (black pot). c, 6k, East Sepik Province, diff. d, 8k, Manus Province.

10k, West Sepik Province.

2012, Apr. 11 ***Perf. 14x14¼***

1622-1625 A369 Set of 4 15.50 15.50

Perf. 14

1626 A369 Sheet of 4, #a-d 15.50 15.50

Souvenir Sheet

1627 A369 10k multi 9.50 9.50

For surcharges, see Nos. 1732A, 1732B, 1734D, 1734E.

Marsupials A370

Designs: No. 1628, 1.20k, Common gray cuscus. No. 1629, 1.20k, Common spotted cuscus. No. 1630, 6k, Black spotted cuscus. No. 1631, 8k, Woodlark cuscus.

No. 1632: a, 1.20k, Sugar glider. b, 1.20k, Feather-tail possum. c, 6k, Striped possum. d, 8k, Northern glider.

10k, Common spotted cuscus, diff.

2012, May 7 ***Perf. 13¼***

1628-1631 A370 Set of 4 15.50 15.50

1632 A370 Sheet of 4, #a-d 15.50 15.50

Souvenir Sheet

1633 A370 10k multi 9.50 9.50

For surcharges, see Nos. 1732C, 1732D, 1734A, 1734B.

Sports Legends A371

Designs: No. 1634, 1.20k, Iamo Launa, track and field. No. 1635, 1.20k, Martin Beni, boxer. No. 1636, 6k, Stanley Nandex, kick boxer. No. 1637, 8k, Will Genia, rugby player.

No. 1638: a, 1.20k, Tau John, track. b, 1.20k, Iwila Jacobs, weight lifter. c, 6k, Takale Tuna, track. d, 8k, John Aba, boxer.

10k, Genia, diff.

2012, June 18

1634-1637 A371 Set of 4 15.50 15.50

1638 A371 Sheet of 4, #a-d 15.50 15.50

Souvenir Sheet

1639 A371 10k multi 9.50 9.50

For surcharge, see No. 1732E.

Orchids — A372

Designs: No. 1640, 1.20k, Dendrobium macrophyllum. No. 1641, 1.20k, Dendrobium williamsianum. No. 1642, 6k, Pink Dendrobium bracteosum. No. 1643, 8k, Phalaenopsis amabilis.

No. 1644: a, 1.20k, White Dendrobium bracteosum. b, 1.20k, Dendrobium bifalce. c, 6k, Dendrobium strepsiceros. d, 8k, Vanda hindsii.

10k, Dendrobium spectabile.

2012, July 2 ***Perf. 14x14¼***

1640-1643 A372 Set of 4 15.50 15.50

Perf. 14

1644 A372 Sheet of 4, #a-d 15.50 15.50

Souvenir Sheet

1645 A372 10k multi 9.50 9.50

For surcharges, see Nos. 1732F, 1732G, 1734F, 1734G.

2012 Summer Olympics, London — A373

No. 1646: a, 50t, Weight lifting. b, 55t, Swimming. c, 1k, Relay race.

5k, Boxing.

2012, July 27 ***Perf. 12***

1646 A373 Sheet of 3, #a-c 2.00 2.00

Souvenir Sheet

1647 A373 5k multi 4.75 4.75

New Year 2012 (Year of the Snake) — A374

Flags of Papua New Guinea and People's Republic of China and snake with background color of: No. 1648, 1.20k, Pink. No. 1649, 1.20k, Blue. No. 1650, 6k, Yellow orange. No. 1651, 8k, Green.

No. 1652: a, 1.20k, Green. b, 1.20k, Yellow orange. c, 6k, Pink. d, 8k, Blue.

10k, Yellow.

2012, Aug. 1 ***Perf. 14, 12 (#1652)***

1648-1651 A374 Set of 4 15.50 15.50

1652 A374 Sheet of 4, #a-d 15.50 15.50

Souvenir Sheet

1653 A374 10k multi 9.50 9.50

Traditional Costumes — A375

Designs: No. 1654, 1.20k, Man from Telefomin, Sandaun Province. No. 1655, 1.20k, Woman from Pomio, East New Britain Province. No. 1656, 6k, Women from Hanuabada, National Capital District. No. 1657, 8k, Woman and child from Duna, Southern Highlands Province.

No. 1658: a, 1.20k, Bride from Mendi, Southern Highlands Province. b, 1.20k, Woman from Tari, Southern Highlands Province. c, 6k, Family from Trobriand Islands, Milne Bay Province. d, 8k, Women from Mukawa, Milne Bay Province.

10k, Woman from Popondetta, Oro Province.

2012, Sept. 5 ***Perf. 14¼***

1654-1657 A375 Set of 4 15.50 15.50

1658 A375 Sheet of 4, #a-d 15.50 15.50

Souvenir Sheet

1659 A375 10k multi 9.50 9.50

For surcharges, see Nos. 1732H, 1734H, 1734I.

Reign of Queen Elizabeth II, 60th Anniv. — A376

Profile of Queen Elizabeth II, Diamond Jubilee emblem, and: 25t, Duchess of Cornwall and Prince of Wales. 50t, Prince of Wales. 1k, Prince of Wales, Duchess of Cornwall, Queen Elizabeth II and Prince Philip. 1.25k, Prince of Wales with sword. 6k, Queen Elizabeth II and Prince of Wales. 8k, Queen Elizabeth II and Prince Philip.

10k, Queen Elizabeth II, vert.

2012, Nov. 4 ***Perf. 14¼***

1660-1665 A376 Set of 6 16.50 16.50

Souvenir Sheet

1666 A376 10k multi 9.75 9.75

Public Transportation A377

Designs: No. 1667, 1.30k, Passenger truck. No. 1668, 1.30k, Banana boat. No. 1669, 6k, Remote service airplane. No. 1670, 8.70k, Trading canoe.

No. 1671: a, 1.30k, Taxi. b, 1.30k, Passenger bus. c, 6k, Domestic and international airplane. d, 8k, Ship.

10k, Dugout canoe.

2013, Jan. 2 ***Perf. 13¾x13¼***

1667-1670 A377 Set of 4 17.00 17.00

1671 A377 Sheet of 4, #a-d 17.00 17.00

Souvenir Sheet

1672 A377 10k multi 9.75 9.75

Sculptures by Gigmai Kundun — A378

Designs: No. 1673, 1.30k, Hiri Trade Canoe (Lakatoi). No. 1674, 1.30k, Kundu Slit Gong. No. 1675, 6k, Hiri Moale Queen. No. 1676, 8.70k, Bird of Paradise.

No. 1677: a, 1.30k, Follow the Leader. b, 1.30k, Walking Together. c, 6k, Relieving Education Burden. d, 8k, Inherited Believe System.

10k, Indo-Pacific Lionfish (Pterois).

2013, Feb. 20 ***Perf. 12***

1673-1676 A378 Set of 4 16.50 16.50

1677 A378 Sheet of 4, #a-d 16.50 16.50

Souvenir Sheet

1678 A378 10k multi 9.50 9.50

In 2012, Papua New Guinea postal officials permitted customers who wished to purchase personalized stamps to work with them in designing the stamps and labels, instead of only providing the image for the attached label, as had been done with previous personalized stamp issues. Some of the items produced by customers are known to lack the country name on the stamp and label. These stamps are known to have a number of different denominations. Beyond Nos. 1264-1268, Papua New Guinea postal officials have not provided any information on other personalizable stamps that are available to any customer.

Pres. John F. Kennedy (1917-63) — A379

Designs: No. 1679, 1.30k, Pres. Kennedy seated. No. 1680, 1.30k, Pres. Kennedy, wife, Jacqueline, and Vice-president Lyndon B. Johnson. No. 1681, 6k, Pres. Kennedy in limousine. No. 1682, 8.70k, Honor guard holding flag over Pres. Kennedy's casket.

No. 1683: a, 1.30k, Pres. Kennedy and flag. b, 1.30k, Pres. Kennedy and wife at Love Field, Dallas, Texas. c, 6k, Flag-draped coffin of Pres. Kennedy. d, 8.70k, Johnson being sworn in as President.

10k, Pres. Kennedy, vert.

2013, Mar. 13 **Litho.** ***Perf. 14***

1679-1682 A379 Set of 4 16.00 16.00

1683 A379 Sheet of 4, #a-d 16.00 16.00

Souvenir Sheet

Perf. 12

1684 A379 10k multi 9.25 9.25

Root Crops — A380

Designs: No. 1685, 1.30k, Cassava. No. 1686, 1.30k, Chinese taro. No. 1687, 6k, Sweet potatoes. No. 1688, 8.70k, Taro.

No. 1689: a, 1.30k, Five-leaflet yam. b, 1.30k, Lesser yam. c, 6k, Greater yam. d, 8.70k, Nummularia yam.

10k, Queensland arrowroot.

2013, Apr. 10 **Litho.** ***Perf. 12***

1685-1688 A380 Set of 4 16.00 16.00

1689 A380 Sheet of 4, #a-d 16.00 16.00

Souvenir Sheet

1690 A380 10k multi 9.25 9.25

Orchids — A381

Designs: No. 1691, 1.30k, Dendrobium gouldii. No. 1692, 1.30k, Dendrobium lineale. No. 1693, 6k, Dendrobium mirbelianum. No. 1694, 8.70k, Dendrobium sp. aff. D. cochilodes.

No. 1695: a, 1.30k, Dendrobium sp. aff. D. gouldii. b, 1.30k, Dendrobium sp. aff. D. conanthum. c, 6k, Dendrobium lineale, diff. d, 8.70k, Dendrobium carronii.

10k, Dendrobium mussauense.

2013, May 24 **Litho.** ***Perf. 12***

1691-1694 A381 Set of 4 15.50 15.50

1695 A381 Sheet of 4, #a-d 15.50 15.50

Souvenir Sheet

1696 A381 10k multi 9.00 9.00

Spacecraft and Space Stations — A382

Designs: No. 1697, 1.30k, Skylab. No. 1698, 1.30k, Salyut 6 Space Station. No. 1699, 6k, Spacehab. No. 1700, 8.70k, Mir Space Station.

No. 1701: a, 1.30k, Skylab, diff. b, 1.30k, Salyut 6 Space Station, diff. c, 6k, Space shuttle re-entering atmosphere. d, 8.70k, Mir Space Station, diff.

10k, Space shuttle as seen from International Space Station window.

2013, July 15 **Litho.** ***Perf. 14***

1697-1700 A382 Set of 4 15.50 15.50

Perf. 12

1701 A382 Sheet of 4, #a-d 15.50 15.50

Souvenir Sheet

1702 A382 10k multi 9.00 9.00

Launch of the International Space Station, 15th anniv.

Woven Baskets — A383

Designs: No. 1703, 1.30k, Common "Tolai" carry basket, East New Britain Province. No. 1704, 1.30k, Pepeni (yam basket), Kitava Island, Milne Bay Province. No. 1705, 6k, Carry basket, Milne Bay Province. No. 1706, 8.70k, Carry baskets, Ialibu, Southern Highlands Province.

No. 1707: a, 1.30k, Common Sepik basket, East Sepik Province. b, 1.30k, Carry basket, Milne Bay Province, diff. c, 6k, Carry basket, Gulf Province. d, 8.70k, Manus carry basket, Manus Province.

10k, Temporary palm leaf basket, Coastal and Island Provinces.

2013, Aug. 9 Litho. *Perf. 12*

1703-1706 A383 Set of 4 15.00 15.00
1707 A383 Sheet of 4, #a-d 15.00 15.00

Souvenir Sheet

1708 A383 10k multi 8.75 8.75

Coconuts — A384

Designs: 4k, Green coconuts. No. 1710, 6k, Coconut husking. No. 1711, 8.70k, Coconut juice. 12k, Coconut meat.

No. 1713: a, 1k, Dry coconut. b, 1.30k, Inner shell. c, 6k, Meat. d, 8.70k, Apple.

10k, Inner shell.

2013, Aug. 21 Litho. *Perf. 12*

1709-1712 A384 Set of 4 25.00 25.00
1713 A384 Sheet of 4, #a-d 14.00 14.00

Souvenir Sheet

1714 A384 10k multi 8.25 8.25

Birth of Prince George of Cambridge — A385

Designs (inscribed "22nd of July 2013" at top: No. 1715, 1.30k, Duke and Duchess of Cambridge, Prince George. No. 1716, 1.30k, Duke of Cambridge, Prince George. No. 1717, 6k, Duchess of Cambridge, Prince George. No. 1718, 8.70k, Duke and Duchess of Cambridge, Prince George, diff.

No. 1719 (stamps without "22nd of July 2013" inscription at top): a, 1.30k, Like #1715. b, 1.30k, Like #1716. c, 6k, Like #1717. d, 8.70k, Like #1718.

10k, Prince George in arms of Duchess of Cambridge.

Perf. 13¼x12½

2013, Sept. 11 Litho.

1715-1718 A385 Set of 4 14.00 14.00

Perf. 12x12½

1719 A385 Sheet of 4, #a-d 14.00 14.00

Souvenir Sheet

1720 A385 10k multi 8.25 8.25

Cooking Methods — A386

Designs: No. 1721, 1.30k, Boiling. No. 1722, 1.30k, Drying. No. 1723, 6k, Drying, diff. No. 1724, 8.70k, Roasting.

No. 1725: a, 1.30k, Dug out mumu pit. b, 1.30k, Stones being heated in mumu pit. c, 6k, Food placed in mumu pit. d, 8.70k, Covered mumu pit.

10k, Hot stones steaming in pot.

2013, Nov. 6 Litho. *Perf. 12*

1721-1724 A386 Set of 4 13.50 13.50
1725 A386 Sheet of 4, #a-d 13.50 13.50

Souvenir Sheet

1726 A386 10k multi 7.75 7.75

New Year 2014 (Year of the Horse) — A387

Various horses with background colors of: No. 1727, 1.70k, Grayish lilac. No. 1728, 1.70k, Tan. No. 1729, 6k, Red. No. 1730, 8.70k, Blue violet.

No. 1731 — Various horses with background colors of: a, 1.30k, Violet. b, 1.30k, Olive bister. c, 6k, Grayish lilac. d, 8.70k, Blue green.

10k, Horse with greenish gray background.

2014, Jan. 2 Litho. *Perf. 12*

1727-1730 A387 Set of 4 14.50 14.50
1731 A387 Sheet of 4, #a-d 14.00 14.00

Souvenir Sheet

1732 A387 10k multi 8.00 8.00

For surcharges, see Nos. 1733-1734.

Nos. 1358, 1395, 1416, 1440, 1451, 1452, 1460, 1494, 1495, 1512, 1557, 1601, 1622, 1623, 1628, 1629, 1634, 1640, 1641, 1654, 1655 Surcharged in Black or Black and Red

Serifed "K"

Sans-serif "K"

Methods and Perfs. As Before

2014, Jan.

Serifed "K" Surcharges

1732A A369 1.30k on 1.20k #1622 —
1732B A369 1.30k on 1.20k #1623 — —
1732C A370 1.30k on 1.20k #1628 — —
1732D A370 1.30k on 1.20k #1629 —
1732E A371 1.30k on 1.20k #1634 — —
1732F A372 1.30k on 1.20k #1640 (Bk&R) — —
1732G A372 1.30k on 1.20k #1641 — —

Sans-serif "K" Surcharges

1732H A375 1.30k on 1.20k #1654 —
1732I A324 15k on 85t #1395 — —
1732J A354 15k on 1.05k #1557 — —
1732K A316 15k on 3.70k #1358 —
1732L A341 25k on 4.65k #1494 — —
1732M A331 25k on 6.30k #1440 — —
1732N A341 25k on 6.30k #1495 — —
1732O A333 40k on 4.65k #1451 — —
1732P A327 40k on 6k #1416 — —
1732Q A335 90k on 3k #1460 — —
1732R A333 90k on 6.30k #1452 — —
1732S A361 90k on 7k #1601 — —

Obliterators and sizes of surcharges vary. Nos. 1732A, 1732B, 1732C, 1732G have horizontal single straigjht-line obliterators and Nos. 1732D, 1732F, 1732H has a rectangular obliterator. Compare these stamps with Nos. 1734A, 1734B, 1734D-1734G, which have slanted single straight-line obliterators.

Nos. 1512, 1601 With Sans-Serif Surcharge Like No. 1732H

Methods and Perfs As Before

2014

1732T A346 25k on 5k #1512 — —
1732U A361 90k on 7k #1601 — —

Nos. 1356, 1358 With Sans-Serif Surcharge Like No. 1732H

Methods and Perfs. As Before

2014

1732V A316 40k on 3.70k #1358 — —
1732W A316 45k on 85t #1356 — —

No. 1641 With Serifed Surcharge in Black and Red

2014 Method and Perf. As Before

1732X A372 1.30k on 1.20k #1641 (Bk&R) —

No. 1655 With Sans-Serif Surcharge

2014 Method and Perf. As Before

Rectangular Obliterator

1732Y A375 1.30k on 1.20k #1655 —

Compare with No. 1734H, which has a slanted, single-line obliterator.

Nos. 1727-1728 Surcharged in Black and Red

2014, Feb. 12 Litho. *Perf. 12*

1733 A387 5k on 1.70k #1727 4.50 4.50
1734 A387 5k on 1.70k #1728 4.50 4.50

Nos. 1327, 1622-1623, 1628-1629, 1640-1641, 1654-1655 Surcharged With Slanted Single-Line Obliterator

Methods and Perfs. As Before

2014

Serifed "K" Surcharges

1734A A370 1.30k on 1.20k #1628 — —
1734B A370 1.30k on 1.20k #1629 — —

Sans-serif "K" Surcharges

1734C A312 1.30k on 85t #1327 — —
1734D A369 1.30k on 1.20k #1622 — —
1734E A369 1.30k on 1.20k #1623 — —
1734F A372 1.30k on 1.20k #1640 — —
1734G A372 1.30k on 1.20k #1641 — —
1734H A375 1.30k on 1.20k #1654 — —
1734I A375 1.30k on 1.20k #1655 — —

Nelson Mandela (1918-2013), President of South Africa — A388

Various photographs of Mandela (stamps with white frames): No. 1735, 1.30k. No. 1736, 3k. No. 1737, 6k. No. 1738, 8k.

No. 1739 — Various photographs of Mandela (stamps with green frames): a, 1.30k. b, 3k. c, 6k. d, 8k.

10k, Mandela, diff. (stamp without frame).

2014, Mar. 31 Litho. *Perf. 12*

1735-1738 A388 Set of 4 13.50 13.50
1739 A388 Sheet of 4, #a-d 13.50 13.50

Souvenir Sheet

1740 A388 10k multi 7.25 7.25

Spirit of Hela Liquified Natural Gas Tanker — A389

Various photographs of Spirit of Hela with side panel color of: 1.30k, Pale green, 3k, Beige. 6k, Light blue green. 8k, Lilac.

10k, Spirit of Hela, light blue panel.

2014, Apr. 7 Litho. *Perf. 13½*

1741-1744 A389 Set of 4 13.00 13.00
1744a Souvenir sheet of 4, #1741-1744 13.00 13.00

Souvenir Sheet

1745 A389 10k multi 7.25 7.25

World War I, Cent. — A390

Designs: No. 1746, 1.30k, Russian soldier. No. 1747, 5k, American bugler. No. 1748, 6k, French airplanes. No. 1749, 8k, German observation balloon.

No. 1750: a, 1.30k, French lancers. b, 5k, British Army. c, 6k, American National Guard. 8k, French battleship.

10k, British soldier.

2014, Apr. 24 Litho. *Perf. 13¼x12½*

1746-1749 A390 Set of 4 14.50 14.50

Perf. 12x12½

1750 A390 Sheet of 4, #a-d 14.50 14.50

Souvenir Sheet

1751 A390 10k multi 7.25 7.25

Pope Francis — A391

Coat of arms of Pope Francis and various photographs with frame color of: No. 1752, 1.30k, Red violet. No. 1753, 5k, Green. No. 1754, 6k, Blue. No. 1755, 8k, Vermilion.

No. 1756 — Coat of arms of Pope Francis and photographs with bister frame: a, 1.30k, Photo like #1753. b, 5k, Photo like #1754. c, 6k, Photo like #1755. d, 8k, Photo like #1752

10k, Pope Francis, coat of arms.

2014, July 28 Litho. *Perf. 13¼x12½*

1752-1755 A391 Set of 4 16.00 16.00

Perf. 12x12½

1756 A391 Sheet of 4, #a-d 16.00 16.00

Souvenir Sheet

1757 A391 10k multi 8.00 8.00

Artifacts — A392

Designs: No. 1758, 1.30k, Trobriand Islands lime pot. No. 1759, 5k, Manus Island bowl. No. 1760, 6k, Wogeo Island food bowl. No. 1761, 8k, Sepik Region pan pipes.

No. 1762, horiz. — Various Sepik River canoe prows: a, 1.30k. b, 5k. c, 6k. d, 8k.

10k, Kiriwina lime pot.

Perf. 13¼x13¾, 13¾x13¼ (#1762)

2014, Aug. 28 Litho.

1758-1761 A392 Set of 4 16.50 16.50
1762 A392 Sheet of 4, #a-d 16.50 16.50

Souvenir Sheet

1763 A392 10k multi 8.25 8.25

Bank of Papua New Guinea, 40th Anniv. — A393

Bank building, 40th anniv. emblem and bank governors: No. 1764, 1.30k, Loi M. Bakani. No. 1765, 4k, Sir Mekere Morauta. No. 1766, 6k, Sir Henry ToRobert. No. 1767, 8k, Sir Wilson Kamit.

No. 1768 — 40th anniv. emblem and: a, 1.30k, Bank building, bank governor John Vulupindi. b, 4k, Bank building, bank governor Koiari Tarata. c, 6k, Bank building. d, 8k, Bank building, bank governor Morea Vele.

10k, 40th anniv. emblem, native costume, vert.

Litho. With Foil Application

2014, Sept. 15 ***Perf. 13¾x13¼***

1764-1767 A393 Set of 4 15.50 15.50
1768 A393 Sheet of 4, #a-d 15.50 15.50

Souvenir Sheet

Perf. 13¼x13¾

1769 A393 10k multi 8.00 8.00

A394

A395

A396

New Year 2015 (Year of the Ram) — A397

No. 1774: a, 1.35k, Ram in circle. b, 1.35k, Ram in rectangle. c, 6.20k, Ram on pot. d, 8.95, Ram in circle, flowers at top.

10k, Ram and Chinese characters.

2015, Jan. 5 Litho. ***Perf. 13¼x12½***

1770 A394 1.35k multi 1.00 1.00
1771 A395 1.35k multi 1.00 1.00
1772 A396 6.20k multi 4.75 4.75
1773 A397 8.95k multi 6.75 6.75
Nos. 1770-1773 (4) 13.50 13.50

Miniature Sheet

1774 A397 Sheet of 4, #a-d 13.50 13.50

Souvenir Sheet

1775 A397 10k multi 7.75 7.75

Traditional Paintings A398

Designs: No. 1776, 1.35k, Arawe Mother and Child. No. 1777, 1.35k, Motuan Village Totem Pole. No. 1778, 6.20k, Baining Fire Dancers. No. 1779, 8.95k, Crocodile Hunters.

No. 1780: a, 1.35k, Mount Elimbari. b, 1.35k, Wig Makers. c, 6.20k, Tifalmin Hunter. d, 8.95k, Wood Carver.

10k, Like No. 1777.

2015, Mar. 9 Litho. ***Perf. 14½x14***

1776-1779 A398 Set of 4 13.50 13.50
1780 A398 Sheet of 4, #a-d 13.50 13.50

Souvenir Sheet

1781 A398 10k multi 7.50 7.50

Christian Leaders' Training College, 50th Anniv. A399

Designs: No. 1782, 1.35k, College founder Dr. Gilbert J. McArthur and student leader, Jezreel Flora. No. 1783, 1.35k, Students of 1967. No. 1784, 6.20k, Graduates. No. 1785, 8.95k, Aerial view of Banz Campus.

No. 1786: a, 1.35k, Banz Campus, 1965. b, 1.35k, Banz Campus, 2015. c, 6.20k, Port Moresby Campus. d, 8.95k, Lae Campus.

10k, Graduation ceremony.

Litho. With Foil Application

2015, Mar. 30 ***Perf. 14½x14***

1782-1785 A399 Set of 4 13.50 13.50
1786 A399 Sheet of 4, #a-d 13.50 13.50

Souvenir Sheet

1787 A399 10k multi 7.50 7.50

Traditional Headdresses A400

Headdress from: No. 1788, 1.35k, Central Province. No. 1789, 1.35k, Eastern Highlands Province. 6.20k, Central Province, diff. 8.95k, East Sepik Province.

10k, Headdress from Simbu Province.

2015, June 22 Litho. ***Perf. 14¼x14***

1788-1791 A400 Set of 4 13.00 13.00
1791a Souvenir sheet of 4, #1788-1791 13.00 13.00

Souvenir Sheet

1792 A400 10k multi 7.25 7.25

2015 Pacific Games, Port Moresby A401

Emblem, mascot and: No. 1793, 1.35k, Dika Toua, weight lifting. No. 1794, 1.35k, Toea Wisil, running. No. 1795, 6.20k, Ryan Pini, swimming. No. 1796, 8.95k, Jack Biyufa, body building.

No. 1797: a, 1.35k, Abigail Tere Apisah, tennis. b, 1.35k, Betty Burua, running. c, 6.20k, Linda Pulsan, powerlifting. d, 8.95k, Steven Kari, weight lifting.

10k, Emblem and mascot.

2015, June 22 Litho. ***Perf. 14¼x14***

1793-1796 A401 Set of 4 13.00 13.00
1797 A401 Sheet of 4, #a-d 13.00 13.00

Souvenir Sheet

1798 A401 10k multi 7.25 7.25

Queen Elizabeth II, Longest Reigning British Monarch — A402

Designs: No. 1799, 1.35k, Princesses Elizabeth and Margaret as children. No. 1800, 1.35k, Color photograph of Queen Elizabeth II. 6.20k, Queen Elizabeth II wearing crown. 8.95k, Queen Elizabeth II and Prince Philip.

10k, Queen Elizabeth II wearing crown, diff.

2015, July 6 Litho. ***Perf. 14***

1799-1802 A402 Set of 4 13.00 13.00
1802a Souvenir sheet of 4, #1799-1802, perf. 12 13.00 13.00

Souvenir Sheet

Perf. 12

1803 A402 10k multi 7.25 7.25

Birth of Princess Charlotte of Cambridge — A403

Designs: No. 1804, 1.35k, Princess Charlotte in arms of Duchess of Cambridge. No. 1805, 1.35k, Duke and Duchess of Cambridge, Princess Charlotte. 6.20k, Duke and Duchess of Cambridge, Princess Charlotte, diff. 8.95k, Duke and Duchess of Cambridge, Princess Charlotte, diff.

10k, Duchess of Cambridge holding Princess Charlotte.

2015, Aug. 3 Litho. ***Perf. 14***

1804-1807 A403 Set of 4 13.00 13.00
1807a Souvenir sheet of 4, #1804-1807 13.00 13.00

Souvenir Sheet

1808 A403 10k multi 7.25 7.25

Singapore 2015 Intl. Stamp Exhibition — A404

Designs: No. 1809, 3.75k, Bird of paradise. No. 1810, 3.75k, Merlion.

No. 1811: a, Bird of paradise. b, Merlion.

2015, Aug. 14 Litho. ***Perf. 12***

1809-1810 A404 Set of 2 5.25 5.25

Embossed With Foil Application, Litho. Sheet Margin

Souvenir Sheet

1811 A404 20k Sheet of 2, #a-b 28.00 28.00

Nos. 1809-1810 were each printed in sheets of 4.

University of Papua New Guinea, 50th Anniv. — A405

Designs: No. 1812, 1.35k, Cockatoo sculpture. No. 1813, 1.35k, University Chapel. 6.20k, Michael Somare Library. 8.95k, Graduation day.

10k, Sir John Gunther (1910-84), first university vice-chancellor.

2015, Oct. 19 Litho. ***Perf. 14x14¼***

1812-1815 A405 Set of 4 12.50 12.50
1815a Souvenir sheet of 4, #1812-1815 12.50 12.50

Souvenir Sheet

1816 A405 10k multi 6.75 6.75

Papuan Hornbills — A406

Designs: No. 1817, 1.45k, Two hornbills in flight, orange pink background. No. 1818, 6.60k, Hornbill, lilac background. No. 1819, 15k, Two hornbills on perches, light green background. No. 1820, 25k, Two hornbills in flight, gray background.

No. 1821 — Stamps with pink background: a, 1.45k, Like #1817. b, 6.60k, Like #1818. c, 15k, Like #1819. d, 25k, Like #1820.

10k, Two hornbills on perches, light green background.

2016, Jan. 4 Litho. ***Perf. 12***

1817-1820 A406 Set of 4 32.00 32.00
1821 A406 Sheet of 4, #a-d 32.00 32.00

Souvenir Sheet

1822 A406 10k multi 6.75 6.75

New Year 2016 (Year of the Monkey) — A407

Monkey: No. 1823, 1.45k, Walking to left, green and orange background. No. 1824, 1.45k, Leaping with one arm raised, yellow and purple background. No. 1825, 3.30k, Sitting, purple and red background. No. 1826, 6.60k, Leaping with both arms raised, blue and green background.

No. 1827 — Orange and purple background, monkey: a, 1.45k, Running to right. b, 1.45k, Holding peach. c, 3.30k, Sitting. d, 6.60k, Walking to left.

10k, Monkey leaping with one arm raised.

2016, Mar. 30 Litho. ***Perf. 13½***

1823-1826 A407 Set of 4 8.50 8.50
1827 A407 Sheet of 4, #a-d 8.50 8.50

Souvenir Sheet

1828 A407 10k multi 6.50 6.50

No. 1827 contains four 30x40mm stamps.

Coins and Banknotes A408

Bank of Papua New Guinea Governor Loi M. Bakani, standard and colored 2015 Pacific Games coins, and: No. 1829, 1.45k, Detail of 10-kina Pacific Games banknote at UR, denomination in bright purple. No. 1830, 1.45k, Detail of 20-kina Pacific Games banknote at UR, denomination in violet. No. 1831, 3.30k, Detail of standard 2015 Pacific Games coin at UR, denomination in brown purple. No. 1832, 6.60k, Detail of colored 2015 Pacific Games coin at UR, denomination in deep green.

No. 1833 — Bakani, standard and colored 2015 Pacific Games coin, detail of 2015 Independence Anniversary banknote, red denomination, and at upper right: a, 1.45k, Butterfly. b, 1.45k, Opossum. c, 3.30k, Cassowary. d, 6.60k, Turtle.

No. 1834, 5k — Bakani, standard and colored 2015 Pacific Games coin, detail of 2015 Independence Anniversary banknote, red denomination, and at upper right: a, Turtle. b, Cassowary.

2016, May 19 Litho. ***Perf. 13¾x13¼***

1829-1832 A408 Set of 4 8.25 8.25
1833 A408 Sheet of 4, #a-d 8.25 8.25

Souvenir Sheet

1834 A408 5k Sheet of 2, #a-b 6.50 6.50

A409

A410

A411

Traditional Salt Making of Keri Tribe — A412

No. 1839 — Two men with: a, 1.45k, One holding hatchet, one pouring water. b, 2k, One holding sticks, one pointing at salt block. c, 4k, One holding water containers, one pouring water on salt block. d, 6.60k, One pointing at other, salt block and flowers on fabric.

10k, Man holding salt block.

2016, Oct. 28 Litho. *Perf. 14½x14*

1835 A409 1.45k multi .95 .95
1836 A410 2k multi 1.25 1.25
1837 A411 4k multi 2.50 2.50
1838 A412 6.60k multi 4.25 4.25
Nos. 1835-1838 (4) 8.95 8.95

Miniature Sheet

1839 A412 Sheet of 4, #a-d 9.00 9.00

Souvenir Sheet

1840 A412 10k multi 6.50 6.50

Tunas — A413

Designs: No. 1841, 1.45k, Yellowfin tuna. No. 1842, 2k, Bluefin tuna. No. 1843, 5k, Skipjack tuna. No. 1844, 6.60k, Albacore tuna.

No. 1845: a, 1.45k, Like #1842. b, 2k, Like #1844. c, 5k, Like #1841. d, 6.60k, Like #1843.

10k, Bluefin tuna, diff.

2016, Oct. 29 Litho. *Perf. 14x14¼*

1841-1844 A413 Set of 4 9.50 9.50
1845 A413 Sheet of 4, #a-d 9.50 9.50

Souvenir Sheet

1846 A413 10k multi 6.50 6.50

For surcharges, see Nos. 1994-1996.

Worldwide Fund for Nature (WWF) — A414

No. 1847 — Various photographs of pig-nosed turtle with denomination in: a, 1.45k, Green. b, 3.80k, Yellow, c, 3.80k, Green. d, 6.60k, Green.

2016, Nov. 4 Litho. *Perf. 14*

1847 A414 Block or horiz. strip of 4, #a-d 10.00 10.00
e. Miniature sheet of 8, 2 each #1847a-1847d 20.00 20.00

Women's Under-20 World Cup Soccer Championships, Papua New Guinea — A415

Emblem, mascot and: 75t, Woman kicking ball. 1.50k, Goaltender reaching for ball. 3.40k, Flags and woman kicking ball. 5k, Athletic shoes and ball.

10k, Two women chasing ball.

2016, Dec. 23 Litho. *Perf. 12*

1848-1851 A415 Set of 4 6.75 6.75
1851a Souvenir sheet of 4, #1848-1851 6.75 6.75

Souvenir Sheet

1852 A415 10k multi 6.50 6.50

New Year 2017 (Year of the Rooster) — A416

Rooster facing: No. 1853, 1.50k, Right, both feet on ground. No. 1854, 2k, Left, one leg raised. No. 1855, 3.40k, Right, one leg raised. No. 1856, 6.80k, Left, both feet on ground.

No. 1857 — Two roosters: a, 1.50k. b, 2k, c, 3.40k. d, 6.80k.

13k, Two roosters, diff.

2017, June 23 Litho. *Perf. 12*

1853-1856 A416 Set of 4 8.75 8.75
1857 A416 Sheet of 4, #a-d 8.75 8.75

Souvenir Sheet

1858 A416 13k multi 8.25 8.25

No. 1857 contains four 30x40mm stamps. No. 1858 contains one 30x60mm stamp.

Faces of People From Southern Region — A417

Designs: No. 1859, 1.50k, Michael Hota, Motuan. No. 1860, 3.40k, Ruthie Masihada, Trobriand Islander. No. 1861, 5k, Madlyn Hera, Kairukuan. No. 1862, 6.80k, Rosemary Patrick, Motuan.

No. 1863: a, 1.50k, Hota, diff. b, 3.40k, Masihada, diff. c, 5k, Hera, diff. d, 6.80k, Patrick, diff.

13k, Pamela Lougaha, Tufian.

2017, June 26 Litho. *Perf. 12*

1859-1862 A417 Set of 4 10.50 10.50
1863 A417 Sheet of 4, #a-d 10.50 10.50

Souvenir Sheet

1864 A417 13k multi 8.25 8.25

No. 1863 contains four 30x40mm stamps.

A418

Princess Diana (1961-97) — A419

No. 1865 — Princess Diana wearing: a, Tiara. b, White hat.

No. 1866 — Princess Diana wearing a, Dark green hat. b, White hat, diff.

2017, June 28 Litho. *Perf. 14*

1865 A418 5k Pair, #a-b 6.25 6.25
1866 A419 8k Horiz. pair, #a-b 10.00 10.00

No. 1865 was printed in sheets containing three each of Nos. 1865a-1865b. No. 1866 was printed in sheets containing two pairs.

Shells — A420

Designs: No. 1867, 75t, Tulip shells used for necklace. No. 1868, 1.50k, Conch shell used for communication. No. 1869, 3.40k, Cypraeidae shells used for traditional attire. No. 1870, 6.80k, Nassarius shells used for currency.

No. 1871: a, 75t, Man blowing into conch shell. b, 1.50k, Traditional costume made of Cypraeidae shells. c, 3.40k, Nassarius shell ring. d, 6.80k, Necklace made of shells.

13k, Papustyla pulcherrima used in Manus Province emblem.

2017, Aug. 17 Litho. *Perf. 14*

1867-1870 A420 Set of 4 7.75 7.75
1871 A420 Sheet of 4, #a-d 7.75 7.75

Souvenir Sheet

1872 A420 13k multi 8.25 8.25

New Year 2018 (Year of the Dog) — A421

No. 1873: a, Chinese character for "dog." b, Dog.

18k, Dog, horiz.

2017, Aug. 18 Litho. *Perf. 14*

1873 A421 5k Pair, #a-b 6.25 6.25

Souvenir Sheet

1874 A421 18k multi 11.50 11.50

Birds — A422

Designs: No. 1875, 75t, Slaty-mantled goshawk. No. 1876, 1.50k, New Britain goshawk. No. 1877, 3.40k, Brown-collared brush turkey. No. 1878, 6.80k, Black honey buzzard.

No. 1879: a, 75t, Little eagle. b, 1.50k, Black-billed brush turkey. c, 3.40k, Magnificent ground pigeon. d, 6.80k, Collared sparrowhawk.

13k, Raggiana bird of paradise.

2017, Aug. 24 Litho. *Perf. 14*

1875-1878 A422 Set of 4 7.75 7.75
1879 A422 Sheet of 4, #a-d 7.75 7.75

Souvenir Sheet

1880 A422 13k multi 8.25 8.25

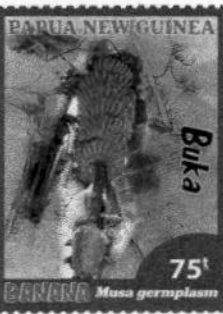

Bananas — A423

Designs: No. 1881, 75t, Buka. No. 1882, 1.50k, Goum. No. 1883, 3.40k, Itonia. No. 1884, 6.80k, Arawa.

No. 1885: a, 75t, Baby banana. b, 1.50k, Duma. c, 3.40k, Bubun. d, 6.80k, Abaus.

13k, Kalapua.

Perf. 13¼x13½

2017, Aug. 28 Litho.

1881-1884 A423 Set of 4 7.75 7.75
1885 A423 Sheet of 4, #a-d 7.75 7.75

Souvenir Sheet

1886 A423 13k multi 8.25 8.25

Protestant Reformation, 500th Anniv. — A424

Martin Luther (1483-1546), Refomation 500th anniv. emblem, and emblem of Evangelical Lutheran Church of Papua New Guinea, and: No. 1887, 1.50k, Stained-glass window. No. 1888, 2k, Painting. No. 1889, 5k, Luther nailing 95 Theses on church door. No. 1890, 6.80k, Luther.

No. 1891, vert. — Head of Luther in: a, 1.50k, Bister. b, 2k, Dull ultramarine. c, 5k, Olive gray. d, 6.80k, Dull blue.

13k, Luther and Papua New Guinea church.

2017, Oct. 25 Litho. *Perf. 13¼x13½*

1887-1890 A424 Set of 4 9.50 9.50
1891 A424 Sheet of 4, #a-d 9.50 9.50

Souvenir Sheet

1892 A424 13k multi 8.25 8.25

No. 1891 contains four 30x40mm stamps.

Christmas — A425

Inscriptions: No. 1893, 75t, Hailareva soa (natives and hut). No. 1894, 1.50k, Bolmahogu wai (woman and infant). No. 1895, 3.40k, Abona lukara na kinakava (candles). No. 1896, 6.80k, Tamwasawasi towatanawa (natives carrying baskets).

No. 1897: a, 75t, Awogu amozin orande (Nativity scene). b, 1.50k, Lang nahpwen (natives carrying baskets). c, 3.40k, Abona lukara na kinakava (infant Jesus). d, 6.80k, Numan enem (three men wearing headdresses).

13k, Shondha gavo andha (Santa Claus).

Perf. 13¼x13½

2017, Nov. 11 Litho.

1893-1896 A425 Set of 4 7.75 7.75

Perf. 13½x13¼

1897 A425 Sheet of 4, #a-d 7.75 7.75

Souvenir Sheet

1898 A425 13k multi 8.25 8.25

No. 1897 contains four 40x30mm stamps. No. 1898 contains one 40x30mm stamp.

Battle of Kokoda, 75th Anniv. — A426

Designs: No. 1899, 75t, Soldier assisting wounded soldier. No. 1900, 1.50k, Four Papuan natives carrying wounded soldier. No. 1901, 3.40k, Papuan soldiers. No. 1902, 6.80k, Papuan native assisting wounded soldier.

No. 1903, horiz.: a, 75t, Soldier assisting wounded soldier, Papuan natives carrying medical supplies. b, 1.50k, Soldiers on hike. c, 3.40k, Eleven Papuan natives carrying wounded soldier. d, 6.80k, Papuan natives carrying medical supplies.

13k, Veterans embracing.

Perf. 13¼x13½, 13½x13¼ (#1903)

2017, Nov. 18 Litho.

1899-1902 A426 Set of 4 7.75 7.75
1903 A426 Sheet of 4, #a-d 7.75 7.75

Souvenir Sheet

1904 A426 13k multi 8.25 8.25

Papua New Guinea's Chairmanship of Asia-Pacific Economic Cooperation Area — A427

Inscription at left: 75t, People. 1.50k, Planet. No. 1907, 3.40k, Peace. No. 1908, 3.40k, Prosperity. No. 1909, 6.80k, Partnership. No. 1910, 6.80k, APEC.
No. 1911: a, 75t, Woman and child. b, 1.50k, Building and flags. c, 3.40k, Airplane, ship and dump truck. d, 6.80k, People and workers.
No. 1912, 20k, Map with lines leading to Papua New Guinea. No. 1913, 20k, Emblem of Papua New Guinea.

Perf. 13¼x13½, 13½x13¼ (#1911)
2017, Dec. 4 Litho.
1905-1910 A427 Set of 6 14.00 14.00
1911 A427 Sheet of 4, #a-d 7.75 7.75
Souvenir Sheets
1912-1913 A427 Set of 2 25.00 25.00

No. 1911 contains four 40x30mm stamps.
For surcharges, see Nos. 1997-2000.

Birds — A428

Designs: No. 1914, 1.50k, Peacock. No. 1914A, 6.80k, 1915a, 10k, Bird of paradise.

Perf. 14 Syncopated
2017, Dec. 30 Litho.
1914-1914A A428 Set of 2 5.25 5.25
Souvenir Sheet
1915 A428 Sheet of 2, #1914, 1915a 7.25 7.25
a. 10k multi 6.25 6.25

See India Nos. 2984-2985.

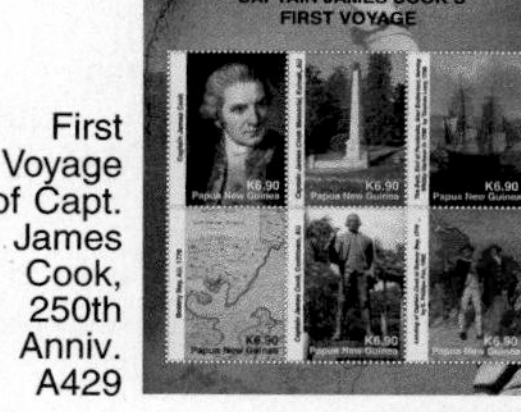

First Voyage of Capt. James Cook, 250th Anniv. A429

No. 1916: a, Capt. James Cook (1728-79). b, Captain Cook Memorial, Kurnell, New South Wales, Australia. c, The Bark, Earl of Pembroke, Later Endeavour, Leaving Whitby Harbor in 1768, by Thomas Luny. d, Map of Botany Bay, 1770. e, Statue of Captain Cook, Cooktown, Queensland, Australia. f, Landing of Captain Cook at Botany Bay, 1770, by E. Phillips Fox.
20k, Map of first voyage, horiz.

2018, Feb. 15 Litho. *Perf. 14*
1916 A429 6.90k Sheet of 6, #a-f 26.00 26.00
Souvenir Sheet
1917 A429 20k multi 12.50 12.50

Drawings by Joseph Bayagau — A430

Designs: No. 1918, 20t, Kundu Drummer, Momase. No. 1919, 1.60k, Bamboo Harp, Highlands. No. 1920, 5k, Bougainville Panpiper, New Guinea Islands. No. 1921, 6.90k, Mekea Dancer, Southern.
No. 1922: a, 20t, Ging Hunting, Highlands. b, 1.60k, Oxokaiven Dancer, Southern. c, 5k, Headdress, New Guinea Islands. d, 6.90k, Morobe Meri, Momase.
13k, Baby Bilas, Momase.

Perf. 13¼x13½
2018, Mar. 24 Litho.
1918-1921 A430 Set of 4 8.50 8.50
1922 A430 Sheet of 4, #a-d 8.50 8.50
Souvenir Sheet
1923 A430 13k multi 8.00 8.00

Birdpex 8 Philatelic Exhibition, Mondorf-les-Bains, Luxembourg — A431

Designs: No. 1924, 1.60k, Red-billed brush turkey. 2.50k, Meyer's goshawk. 3.45k, Gurney's eagle. No. 1927, 10k, Dusky scrubfowl.
No. 1928: a, 1.60k, Head of Dusky scrubfowl. b, 8k, Leg of Dusky scrubfowl. c, 10k, Eggs of Dusky scrubfowl.
No. 1929: a, 8k, Chestnut-shouldered goshawk facing left. b, 8k, Chestnut-shouldered goshawk facing right.

2018, Apr. 16 Litho. *Perf. 13¼x13½*
1924-1927 A431 Set of 4 11.00 11.00
1928 A431 Sheet of 3, #a-c 12.00 12.00
Souvenir Sheet
1929 A431 8k Sheet of 2, #a-b 9.75 9.75

Activities of the European Union in Papua New Guinea, 40th Anniv. — A432

Inscriptions: No. 1930, 80t, Supporting access to clean water for rural communities. No. 1931, 1.60k, Support to promoting sustainable fisheries. No. 1932, 3.45k, Supporting the National WaSH Policy: Water tanks to remote islands. No. 1933, 6.90k, Supporting the National WaSH Policy: Water tanks to remote highlands.
No. 1934: a, 80t, Support to promoting children's rights. b, 1.60k, Support to teachers' training college infrastructure development. c, 3.45k, Support to producing Braille materials for children. d, 6.90k, Support to rural teacher training.
13k, Signing of the Lomé Convention.

2018, May 14 Litho. *Perf. 13¼x13½*
1930-1933 A432 Set of 4 8.00 8.00
1934 A432 Sheet of 4, #a-d 8.00 8.00
Souvenir Sheet
1935 A432 13k multi 8.00 8.00

Coffee Processing A433

Designs: No. 1936, 1.60k, Hand sorting. 3.45k, Roasting. 5k, Grinding. No. 1939, 6.90k, Packaging.
No. 1940: a, 1.60k, Picking coffee berries. b, 3.40k, Drying beans. c, 5k, Packing coffee beans. d, 6.90k, Export.
16k, Cup of coffee and coffee beans.

Perf. 13½x13¼, 14¼ (#1940)
2018, May 21 Litho.
1936-1939 A433 Set of 4 10.50 10.50
1940 A433 Sheet of 4, #a-d 10.50 10.50
Souvenir Sheet
1941 A433 16k multi 10.00 10.00

No. 1940 contains four 45x30mm triangular stamps. Nos. 1936-1941 are impregnated with a coffee scent.

Faces of Papua New Guineans — A434

Designs: Nos. 1942, 1946a, 1.60k, Esther Kelege, Autonomous Region of Bougainville. Nos. 1943, 1946b, 3k, Lydia Gitaria, East New Britain. Nos. 1944, 1946c, 5k, Margaret Talereng, New Ireland. Nos. 1945, 1946d, 6.90k, Sophie Mengai, Manus.
No. 1947: a, Jonathan Telek, West New Britain. b, Michelangelo Telek, West New Britain.

2018, May 21 Litho. *Perf. 12*
1942-1945 A434 Set of 4 10.50 10.50
1946 A434 Sheet of 4, #a-d 10.50 10.50
Souvenir Sheet
1947 A434 6.50k Sheet of 2, #a-b 8.00 8.00

No. 1946 contains four 30x40mm stamps. No. 1947 contains two 30x40mm stamps.

Miniature Sheet

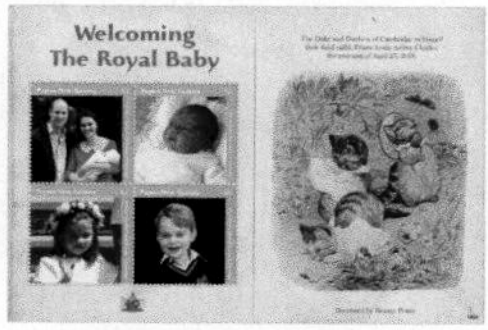

Birth of Prince Louis of Cambridge — A435

No. 1948: a, Prince Louis with parents, Duke and Duchess of Cambridge. b, Prince Louis. c, Princess Charlotte of Cambridge. d, Prince George of Cambridge.

2018, June 11 Litho. *Perf. 13¾*
1948 A435 8k Sheet of 4, #a-d 20.00 20.00

Coronation of Queen Elizabeth II, 65th Anniv. — A436

No. 1949 — Black-and-white images of Queen Elizabeth II: a, Seated in coach. b, Receiving scepter. c, Seated on throne holding scepters. d, Waving.
20k, Color photograph.

2018, June 11 Litho. *Perf. 14*
1949 A436 8k Sheet of 4, #a-d 20.00 20.00
Souvenir Sheet
Perf. 12
1950 A436 20k multi 12.50 12.50

No. 1950 contains one 30x50mm stamp.

Wedding of Prince Harry and Meghan Markle A437

No. 1951 — Couple: a, Facing left. b, Facing forward. c, Kissing. d, In car, waving.
20k, Couple holding hands, Princess Diana with infant Prince Harry, horiz..

2018, June 11 Litho. *Perf. 13¾*
1951 A437 8k Sheet of 4, #a-d 20.00 20.00
Souvenir Sheet
Perf. 12½
1952 A437 20k multi 12.50 12.50

No. 1952 contains one 102x38mm stamp.

United Church in Papua New Guinea, 50th Anniv. A438

Designs: No. 1953, 1.60k, Arua Daera, first Papuan Christian, facing right. 2k, Rev. Jack Sharp. 5k, Rev. Leslie Boseto. No. 1956, 6.90k, Rev. George Brown.
No. 1957: a, 80t, Macfarlane Samuel, missionary. b, 1.60k, Daera, facing forward. c, 3.45k, The Act of Union. d, 6.90k, James Chalmers, missionary.
20k, First church in Port Moresby.

Perf. 13¼x13½
2018, June 18 Litho.
1953-1956 A438 Set of 4 9.50 9.50
1957 A438 Sheet of 4, #a-d 8.00 8.00
Souvenir Sheet
1958 A438 20k multi 12.50 12.50

New Year 2019 (Year of the Pig) A439

Chinese Zodiac Animals A440

No. 1959: a, Black pig in foreground. b, Red pig in foreground.
No. 1960: a, Rat. b, Ox. c, Tiger. d, Rabbit. e, Dragon. f, Snake. g, Horse. h, Goat. i, Monkey. j, Rooster. k, Dog. l, Pig.

2019, Feb. 18 Litho. *Perf. 12*
1959 A439 8k Pair, #a-b 9.50 9.50
Perf. 14
1960 A440 1k Sheet of 12, #a-l 7.25 7.25

No. 1959 was printed in sheets containing two each of Nos. 1959a-1959b.

Team Sports — A441

Designs: 1.60k, Women's rugby. 3k, Women's basketball. 5k, Men's cricket. 6.90k, Men's rugby.
No. 1965: a, Men's soccer. b, Men's basketball. c, Women's soccer. d, Men's field hockey.
20k, Men's rugby, diff.

Perf. 14x14½, 13¼x13¾ (No. 1965)

2019, Mar. 15 Litho.

1961-1964 A441 Set of 4 9.75 9.75
1965 A441 2k Sheet of 4, #a-d 4.75 4.75

Souvenir Sheet

1966 A441 20k multi 12.00 12.00

No. 1965 contains four 30x40mm stamps.

First Man on the Moon, 50th Anniv. A442

No. 1967: a, Astronaut on Moon. b, Astronaut's foot and footprint on Moon. c, Lunar Module above Moon. d, Astronaut carrying equipment on Moon.
20k, Rocket on launch pad.

2019, July 31 Litho. *Perf. 14*

1967 A442 5.50k Sheet of 4, #a-d 13.00 13.00

Souvenir Sheet

1968 A442 20k multi 12.00 12.00

No. 1968 contains one 30x80mm stamp.

Reef Fish A443

Designs: 1.60k, Tailspot lizardfish. 2k, Scorpionfish. 5k, Juvenile Sweetlips. 6.90k, Pink anemonefish.
No. 1973: a, Lionfish. b, Parrotfish. c, Coral trout. d, Black saddled puffer.
20k, Anemonefish.

Perf. 13½, 14½ (No. 1973)

2019, Sept. 25 Litho.

1969-1972 A443 Set of 4 9.25 9.25
1973 A443 4k Sheet of 4, #a-d 9.50 9.50

Souvenir Sheet

1974 A443 20k multi 12.00 12.00

No. 1973 contains four 40x28mm stamps. No. 1974 contains one 40x30mm stamp.

Fruits and Vegetables — A444

Designs: No. 1975, 1.60k, Yams. No. 1976, 3.45k, Potatoes. No. 1977, 5k, Taro. No. 1978, 6.90k, Sweet potatoes.
No. 1979: a, 1.60k, Bananas. b, 3.45k, Avocados. c, 5k, Cucumbers. d, 6.90k, Tomatoes.
20k, Broccoli.

Perf. 13½, 14x14½ (No. 1979)

2019, Sept. 26 Litho.

1975-1978 A444 Set of 4 10.00 10.00
1979 A444 Sheet of 4, #a-d 10.00 10.00

Souvenir Sheet

1980 A444 20k multi 12.00 12.00

No. 1979 contains four 40x28mm stamps.

Paintings by Laben Sakale John — A445

Various unnamed paintings depicting people: 1.60k, 3k, 5k, 6.90k.
No. 1985: a, Mother and child. b, Child. c, Native facing right. d, Mask.
20k, Face.

2019, Sept. 30 Litho. *Perf. 13½*

1981-1984 A445 Set of 4 9.75 9.75
1985 A445 8k Sheet of 4, #a-d 19.00 19.00

Souvenir Sheet

1986 A445 20k multi 12.00 12.00

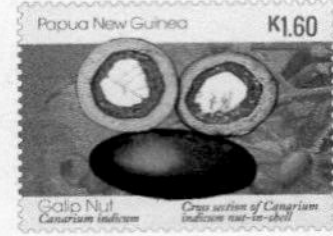

A446

Galip Nuts A447

Designs: 1.60k, Cross-section of nut in shell. 2k, Immature nuts on tree. 5k, Matured nuts ready to be collected. No. 1990, 6.90k, Kernels of nuts at market.
No. 1991 — Various drawings of fresh nut kernels, as shown.
20k, Man cracking nut kernels.

2019, Oct. 1 Litho. *Perf. 13½*

1987-1990 A446 Set of 4 9.25 9.25
1991 A447 6.90k Sheet of 4, #a-d 16.50 16.50

Souvenir Sheet

1992 A446 20k multi 12.00 12.00

Dorje Chang Buddha III, Religious Leader — A448

2019, Dec. 21 Litho. *Perf. 13x13½*

1993 A448 5k multi 3.00 3.00

Nos. 1841-1842 Surcharged in Red and Black

Methods and Perfs. As Before

2020, Mar. 6

1994 A413 1.60k on 2k #1842 .95 .95
a. Red obliterator bar omitted — —
b. New denomination omitted, red obliterator bar doubled, one inverted — —
c. Inverted surcharge — —
1995 A413 5k on 1.45k #1841 3.00 3.00
1996 A413 6.90k on 1.45k #1841 4.00 4.00
a. Red obliterator bar omitted — —
b. New denomination omitted — —
Nos. 1994-1996 (3) 7.95 7.95

Nos. 1907-1910 Surcharged in Red and Black

Methods and Perfs. As Before

2020, Mar. 7

1997 A427 1.60k on 6.80k #1909 .95 .95
a. New denomination omitted — —
1998 A427 1.60k on 6.80k #1910 .95 .95
1999 A427 5k on 3.40k #1907 3.00 3.00
2000 A427 6.90k on 3.40k #1908 4.00 4.00
Nos. 1997-2000 (4) 8.90 8.90

Breadfruit — A449

Designs: 1.60k, Male and female flowers. 2.50k, Female flower. 3.45k, Fruit starting. 10k, Matured fruit.
No. 2005: a, Flower. b, Sprouting fruit. c, Leaf. d, Fruit.
20k, Matured fruit, diff.

2020, May 27 Litho. *Perf. 12*

2001-2004 A449 Set of 4 10.50 10.50
2005 A449 5k Sheet of 4, #a-d 11.50 11.50

Souvenir Sheet

2006 A449 20k multi 11.50 11.50

Post-Courier Daily Newspaper, 50th Anniv. — A450

Designs: 1.60k, Front page of newspaper. 3.45k, Luke Sela, founding editor. 5k, Printing press. 6.90k, Front page of Papua New Guinea Independence Day newspaper.
No. 2011, horiz.: a, Man reading newspaper. b, Delivery of newspaper bundles. c, Newsroom. d, Newspapers coming out of press.
20k, Newspaper being printed on press.

Perf. 13½x13¼, 13¼x13½ (#2011)

2020, June 30 Litho.

2007-2010 A450 Set of 4 9.75 9.75
2011 A450 5k Sheet of 4, #a-d 11.50 11.50

Souvenir Sheet

2012 A450 20k multi 11.50 11.50

String Bags — A451

Various string bags with denomination color of: No. 2013, 1.60k, Dark green. No. 2014, 1.60k, Lilac. No. 2015, 6.90k, Blue. No. 2016, 6.90k, Brown.
20k, Brown.

2021 Litho. *Perf. 12*

2013-2016 A451 Set of 4 11.50 11.50
2016a Souvenir sheet of 4, #2013-2016 11.50 11.50

Souvenir Sheet

2017 A451 20k multi 11.50 11.50

Nos. 2013-2017 and 2016a were scheduled to be issued July 25, 2020, but because of the COVID-19 pandemic, the stamps were not delivered to Papua New Guinea until early 2021.

Saltwater Crocodiles A452

Various depictions of saltwater crocodiles with denomination having Roman lettering and numbers: 1.60k, 5k, 6.90k, 20k.
No. 2022, 20k, Like No. 2021, with denomination having italic lettering and numbers.

2021 Litho. *Perf. 12*

2018-2021 A452 Set of 4 19.00 19.00
2021a Souvenir sheet of 4, #2018-2021 19.00 19.00

Souvenir Sheet

2022 A452 20k multi 11.50 11.50

Nos. 2018-2022 and 2021a were scheduled to be issued July 28, 2020, but because of the COVID-19 pandemic, the stamps were not delivered to Papua New Guinea until early 2021.

Mission Aviation Fellowship, 70th Anniv. — A453

Inscriptions: No. 2023, 1.60k, Investing in education for remote schools. No. 2024, 1.60k, Life saving medevac flights. No. 2025, 6.90k, Taking the Gospel to the communities. No. 2026, 6.90k, Facilitating community development.
No. 2027: a, 1.60k, Training the next generation. b, 1.60k, Encouraging the local church. c, 6.90k, Delivering life-saving medical supplies. d, 6.90k, Responding to disaster.
20k, Fellowship members standing around airplane.

2021, June 30 Litho. *Perf. 13¼*

2023-2026 A453 Set of 4 9.75 9.75
2027 A453 Sheet of 4, #a-d 9.75 9.75

Souvenir Sheet

2028 A453 20k multi 11.50 11.50

Birds of Paradise — A454

Designs: No. 2029, 1k, Huon astrapia. No. 2030, 1.50k, Curl-crested manucode. No. 2031, 2.30k, Long-tailed paradigalla. No. 2032, 2.50k, Jobi manucode. No. 2033, 2.50k, Glossy-mantled manucode. No. 2034, 2.50k, Pale-billed sicklebill. No. 2035, 2.50k, Splendid astrapia. No. 2036, 3.30k, MacGregor's honeyeater. No. 2037, 5k, Greater bird of paradise. No. 2038, 6.90k, Arfak astrapia.
No. 2039: a, 5k, Like #2032. b, 5k, Like #2033. c, 5k, Like #2034. d, 5k, Like #2035. e, 5k, Long-tailed paradigalla, diff. f, 5k, MacGregor's honeyeater, diff.
20k, Like #2037.

Perf. 12, 13¼ (No. 2039)

2021, Aug. 31 Litho.

2029-2038 A454 Set of 10 17.50 17.50
2039 A454 Sheet of 6, #a-f 17.50 17.50

Souvenir Sheet

2040 A454 20k multi 11.50 11.50

No. 2039 contains six 20x30mm stamps.

Reign of Queen Elizabeth II (1926-2022), 70th Anniv. — A456

Photographs of Queen Elizabeth II taken in: No. 2047, 15k, 1936. No. 2048, 15k, 1953. No. 2049, 15k, 1975. No. 2050, 15k, 2006. No. 2051, 15k, 2021.

2022, Sept. 19 Litho. *Perf. 13½*

2047-2051 A456 Set of 5 43.00 43.00
2050a Souvenir sheet of 4, #2047-2050 34.50 34.50
2051a Souvenir sheet of 1, #2051 8.75 8.75

Insects — A457

Designs: No. 2052, 15k, Blue dasher dragonfly. No. 2053, 15k, Ladybug. No. 2054, 15k, Honey Bee. No. 2055, 15k, Eastern Tiger Swallowtail. No. 2056, 15k, Lubber grasshopper.

2022, Nov. 8 Litho. *Perf. 14*

2052-2056	A457	Set of 5	43.00	43.00
2055a		Souvenir sheet of 4, #2052-2055	34.50	34.50
2056a		Souvenir sheet of 1, #2056	8.75	8.75

Queen Elizabeth II (1926-2022) — A458

A459

Queen Elizabeth II: No. 2057, 1.60k, With King Charles III. No. 2058, 5k, With Prince William. No. 2059, 6.90k, Wearing Girls of Great Britain and Ireland tiara.

No. 2060: a, Like #2057. b, Like #2059.

No. 2061— Queen Elizabeth II: a, Holding flowers, waving. b, Smiling, black-and-white photograph. c, With Prince Philip, color photograph. d, With Prince Phillip and family. e, Handing Prince Philip a polo trophy, black-and-white photograph. f, Wearing blue hat.

2022, Nov. 29 Litho. *Perf. 13¾*

2057-2059	A458	Set of 3	7.75	7.75
2060	A458	Sheet of 3, #2058, 2060a, 2060b	8.75	8.75

Souvenir Sheet

Perf. 14

2061	A459	14.96k Sheet of 6, #a-f	51.00	51.00

Princess Diana (1961-97) — A460

Princess Diana wearing: No. 2062, 15k, Hat with brim. No. 2063, 15k, Headscarf. No. 2064, 15k, Tiara. No. 2065, 15k, White and gold jacket. No. 2066, 15k, Purple and white hat.

2022, Nov. 30 Litho. *Perf. 13¾*

2062-2066	A460	Set of 5	43.00	43.00
2065a		Souvenir sheet of 4, #2062-2065	34.50	34.50
2066a		Souvenir sheet of 1, #2066	8.75	8.75

AIR POST STAMPS

Regular Issue of 1916 Overprinted

1929 Wmk. 74 *Perf. 14*

C1	A3 3p blue grn & dk gray	3.50	*20.00*
b.	Vert. pair, one without ovpt.	*6,000.*	
c.	Horiz. pair, one without ovpt.	*6,500.*	
d.	3p blue grn & sepia blk	57.50	*75.00*
e.	Overprint on back, vert.	*5,000.*	

No. C1 exists on white and on yellowish paper, No. C1d on yellowish paper only.

Regular Issues of 1916-23 Overprinted in Red

1930, Sept. 15 Wmk. 74

C2	A3 3p blue grn & blk	2.00	*11.00*
a.	Yellowish paper	3,800.	*5,600.*
b.	Double overprint	1,500.	
C3	A3 6p violet & dull vio	8.00	*12.00*
a.	Yellowish paper	5.00	*15.00*
C4	A3 1sh ol grn & ol brn	6.00	*17.50*
a.	Inverted overprint	*15,500.*	
b.	Yellowish paper	10.00	26.00
	Nos. C2-C4 (3)	16.00	*40.50*

Port Moresby — AP1

Unwmk.

1938, Sept. 6 Engr. *Perf. 11*

C5	AP1	2p carmine	2.75	3.50
C6	AP1	3p ultra	2.75	2.50
C7	AP1	5p dark green	2.75	*3.75*
C8	AP1	8p red brown	6.50	*24.00*
C9	AP1	1sh violet	17.50	27.50
		Nos. C5-C9 (5)	32.25	*61.25*
		Set, never hinged	65.00	

Papua as a British possession, 50th anniv.

Papuans Poling Rafts — AP2

1939-41

C10	AP2	2p carmine	3.00	*8.50*
C11	AP2	3p ultra	3.00	*14.00*
C12	AP2	5p dark green	3.00	2.50
C13	AP2	8p red brown	7.50	6.00
C14	AP2	1sh violet	9.00	*10.00*
C15	AP2	1sh6p lt olive ('41)	27.50	*42.50*
		Nos. C10-C15 (6)	53.00	*83.50*
		Set, never hinged	90.00	

POSTAGE DUE STAMPS

Catalogue values for unused stamps in this section are for Never Hinged items.

Nos. 128, 122, 129, 139 and 125 Surcharged in Black, Blue, Red or Orange

1960 Unwmk. Engr. *Perf. 14*

J1	A24	1p on 6½p	7.00	*7.00*
J2	A23	3p on ½p (Bl)	8.25	5.00
a.		Double surcharge	700.00	
J3	A24	6p on 7½p (R)	25.00	12.00
a.		Double surcharge	700.00	
J4	A23	1sh3p on 3½p (O)	9.50	*7.50*
J5	A23	3sh on 2½p	25.00	15.00
		Nos. J1-J5 (5)	74.75	46.50

No. 129 Surcharged in Red

J6	A24	6p on 7½p	1,100.	775.
a.		Double surcharge	4,000.	2,200.

Surcharge forgeries exist.

D1

Perf. 13½x14

1960, June 2 Litho. Wmk. 228

J7	D1	1p orange	.50	.75
J8	D1	3p ocher	.55	.55
J9	D1	6p light ultra	.55	.35
J10	D1	9p vermilion	.55	1.25
J11	D1	1sh emerald	.55	.30
J12	D1	1sh3p bright violet	.80	1.40
J13	D1	1sh6p light blue	4.00	4.50
J14	D1	3sh yellow	3.50	.70
		Nos. J7-J14 (8)	11.00	9.80

OFFICIAL STAMPS

Nos. 60-63, 66-71, 92-93 Overprinted

1931 Wmk. 74 *Perf. 14½*

O1	A3	½p #60	3.00	*5.50*
O2	A3	1p #61	7.00	*15.00*
O3	A3	1½p #62	2.00	*14.00*
O4	A3	2p #63	7.00	*16.00*
O5	A3	3p #66	3.00	*25.00*
O6	A3	4p #67	3.25	*21.00*
O7	A3	5p #68	7.00	*42.50*
O8	A3	6p #69	5.00	*9.75*
O9	A3	1sh #70	10.00	*35.00*
O10	A3	2sh6p #71	47.50	*97.50*

1932 Wmk. 228 *Perf. 11½*

O11	A3	9p #92	37.50	*55.00*
O12	A3	1sh3p #93	37.50	*55.00*
		Nos. O1-O12 (12)	169.75	*391.25*

PARAGUAY

'par-ə-ˌgwī

LOCATION — South America, bounded by Bolivia, Brazil and Argentina
GOVT. — Republic
AREA — 157,042 sq. mi.
POP. — 7,130,000 (2020 est.)
CAPITAL — Asuncion

10 Reales = 100 Centavos = 1 Peso
100 Centimos = 1 Guarani (1944)

Catalogue values for unused stamps in this country are for Never Hinged items, beginning with Scott 430 in the regular postage section, Scott B11 in the semi-postal section, and Scott C154 in the airpost section.

Watermarks

Wmk. 319 — Stars and R P Multiple

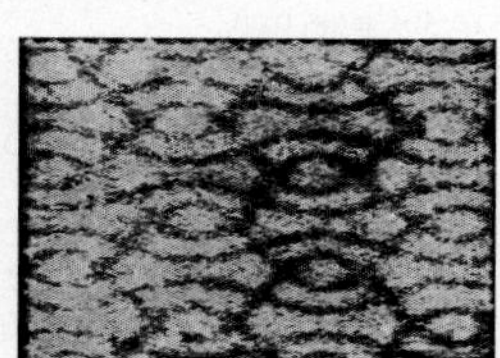

Wmk. 320 — Interlacing Lines

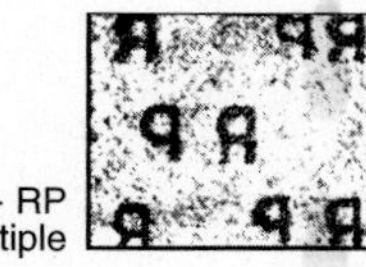

Wmk. 347 — RP Multiple

Vigilant Lion Supporting Liberty Cap

A1 A2

A3

1870, Aug. Unwmk. Litho. *Imperf.*

1	A1	1r rose	6.50	*10.00*
2	A2	2r blue	120.00	*150.00*
3	A3	3r black	230.00	*250.00*
		Nos. 1-3 (3)	356.50	*410.00*

Counterfeits of 2r in blue and other colors are on thicker paper than originals. They show a colored dot in upper part of "S" of "DOS" in upper right corner.

For surcharges see Nos. 4-9, 19.

Handstamp Surcharged

1878 Black Surcharge

4	A1	5c on 1r rose	100.	*120.*
5	A2	5c on 2r blue	450.	400.
5E	A3	5c on 3r black	550.	550.
		Nos. 4-5E (3)	1,100.	1,070.

Blue Surcharge

5F	A1	5c on 1r rose	100.	*120.*
5H	A2	5c on 2r blue	*1,200.*	*1,200.*
6	A3	5c on 3r black	675.	650.
		Nos. 5F-6 (3)	*1,975.*	*1,970.*

The surcharge may be found inverted, double, sideways and omitted.

Remainders of Nos. 4 and 5F were placed on sale at Post Offices during 1892. Covers dated 1892 are worth about $7,500.

The originals are surcharged in dull black or dull blue. The reprints are in intense black and bright blue. The reprint surcharges are over-inked and show numerous breaks in the handstamp.

Handstamp Surcharged

Black Surcharge

7	A2	5c on 2r blue	450.00	375.00
8	A3	5c on 3r black	575.00	550.00

Blue Surcharge

9	A3	5c on 3r black	550.00	550.00
a.		Dbl. surch., large & small "5"		—
		Nos. 7-9 (3)	1,575.	1,475.

The surcharge on Nos. 7, 8 and 9 is usually placed sideways. It may be found double or inverted on Nos. 8 and 9.

Nos. 4 to 9 have been extensively counterfeited.

Two examples recorded of No. 9a, one without gum, the other with full but disturbed original gum.

A4

1879 Litho. *Perf. 12½*

Thin Paper

10	A4	5r orange	.80
11	A4	10r red brown	.90
a.		Imperf.	
b.		Horiz. pair, imperf. vert.	60.00

Nos. 10 and 11 were never placed in use.

For surcharges see Nos. 17-18.

A4a

1879-81 Thin Paper
12 A4a 5c orange brown 2.50 2.50
13 A4a 10c blue grn ('81) 3.50 3.50
a. Imperf., pair 10.00 *12.00*

Reprints of Nos. 10-13 are imperf., perf. 11½, 12, 12½ or 14. They have yellowish gum and the 10c is deep green.

A5

A6

A7

1881, Aug. Litho. *Perf. 11½-13½*
14 A5 1c blue .80 .80
a. Imperf., pair —
b. Horiz. pair, imperf. btwn. —
15 A6 2c rose red .80 .70
a. 2c dull orange red 1.00 .90
b. Imperf., pair —
c. Horiz. pair, imperf. vert. 25.00 25.00
d. Vert. pair, imperf. horiz. 25.00 25.00
16 A7 4c brown .80 *.70*
a. Imperf., pair —
b. Horiz. pair, imperf. vert. 25.00 25.00
c. Vert. pair, imperf. horiz. 25.00 25.00

No. 11 Handstamped Surcharge in Black or Gray

1881, July *Perf. 12½*
17 A4 1c on 10c blue grn 16.00 15.00
18 A4 2c on 10c blue grn 16.00 15.00

Gray handstamps sell for 10 times more than black as many specialists consider the black to be reprints.

No. 1 Handstamped Surcharge in Black

1884, May 8 *Imperf.*
19 A1 1c on 1r rose 10.00 8.00

The surcharges on Nos. 17-19 exist double, inverted and in pairs with one omitted. Counterfeits exist.

Seal of the Treasury — A11

1884, Aug. 3 Litho. *Perf. 12½*
20 A11 1c green 1.00 .80
21 A11 2c rose pink, thin paper 1.00 .80

Perf. 11½
22 A11 5c pale blue, yellowish paper 1.00 .80
Nos. 20-22 (3) 3.00 2.40

There are two types of each value differing mostly in the shape of the numerals. In addition, there are numerous small flaws in the lithographic transfers.

For overprints see Nos. O1, O8, O15.

Imperf., Pairs
20a A11 1c green 12.50
21a A11 2c rose red 16.00
22a A11 5c blue 16.00
Nos. 20a-22a (3) 44.50

Seal of the Treasury — A12

Perf. 11½, 11½x12, 12½x11½
1887 Typo.
23 A12 1c green .30 .25
24 A12 2c rose .30 .25
25 A12 5c blue .50 .35
26 A12 7c brown .90 .50
27 A12 10c lilac .60 .35
28 A12 15c orange .60 .35
29 A12 20c pink .60 .35
Nos. 23-29 (7) 3.80 2.40

See #42-45. For surcharges & overprints see #46, 49-50, 71-72, 167-170A, O20-O41, O49.

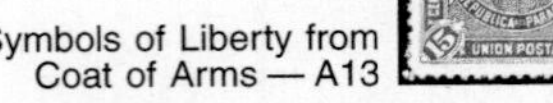
Symbols of Liberty from Coat of Arms — A13

1889, Feb. Litho. *Perf. 11½*
30 A13 15c red violet 2.50 2.00
a. Imperf., pair 10.00 8.00

For overprints see Nos. O16-O19.

Overprint Handstamped in Violet

1892, Oct. 12 *Perf. 12x12½*
31 A15 10c violet blue 10.00 5.00

Discovery of America by Columbus, 400th anniversary. Overprint reads: "1492 / 12 DE OCTUBRE / 1892." Sold only on day of issue.

Cirilo A. Rivarola — A15

Designs: 2c, Salvador Jovellanos. 4c, Juan B. Gil. 5c, Higinio Uriarte. 10c, Cándido Bareiro. 14c, Gen. Bernardino Caballero. 20c, Gen. Patricio Escobar. 30c, Juan G. González.

1892-96 Litho. *Perf. 12x12½*
32 A15 1c gray (centavos) .25 .25
33 A15 1c gray (centavo) ('96) .25 .25
34 A15 2c green .25 .25
a. Chalky paper ('96) .25 .25
35 A15 4c carmine .25 .25
a. Chalky paper ('96) .25 .25
36 A15 5c violet ('93) .25 .25
a. Chalky paper ('96) .25 .25
37 A15 10c vio bl (punched) ('93) .25 .25
Unpunched ('96) 5.00
38 A15 10c dull blue ('96) .25 .25
39 A15 14c yellow brown .75 .50
40 A15 20c red ('93) 1.25 .50
41 A15 30c light green 2.00 .80
Nos. 32-41 (10) 5.75 3.55

The 10c violet blue (No. 37) was, until 1896, issued punched with a circular hole in order to prevent it being fraudulently overprinted as No. 31.

Nos. 33 and 38 are on chalky paper.

For surcharge see No. 70.

Seal Type of 1887

1892 Typo.
42 A12 40c slate blue 3.00 1.25
43 A12 60c yellow 1.50 .50
44 A12 80c light blue 1.40 .50
45 A12 1p olive green 1.40 .50
Nos. 42-45 (4) 7.30 2.75

For surcharges see Nos. 71-72.

No. 26 Surcharged in Black

1895, Aug. 1 *Perf. 11½x12*
46 A12 5c on 7c brown .75 .75

Telegraph Stamps Surcharged

1896, Apr. Engr. *Perf. 11½*
Denomination in Black
47 5c on 2c brown & gray .90 .60
a. Inverted surcharge 10.00 10.00
48 5c on 4c yellow & gray .90 .60
a. Inverted surcharge 7.50 7.50

Nos. 28, 42 Surcharged

1898-99 Typo.
49 A12 10c on 15c org ('99) .75 .45
a. Inverted surcharge 17.50 17.50
b. Double surcharge 11.00 11.00
50 A12 10c on 40c slate bl .35 .25

Surcharge on No. 49 has small "c."

Telegraph Stamps Surcharged

1900, May 14 Engr. *Perf. 11½*
50A 5c on 30c grn, gray & blk 2.75 1.50
50B 10c on 50c dl vio, gray & blk 6.00 3.75

The basic telegraph stamps are like those used for Nos. 47-48, but the surcharges on Nos. 50A-50B consist of "5 5" and "10 10" above a blackout rectangle covering the engraved denominations.

A 40c red, bluish gray and black telegraph stamp (basic type of A24) was used provisionally in August, 1900, for postage. Value, postally used, $5.

Seal of the Treasury — A25

1900, Sept. Engr. *Perf. 11½, 12*
51 A25 2c gray .40 .30
52 A25 3c orange brown .40 .30
53 A25 5c dark green .40 .30
54 A25 8c dark brown .40 .30
55 A25 10c carmine rose 1.00 .30
56 A25 24c deep blue 1.20 .30
Nos. 51-56 (6) 3.80 1.80

See Nos. 57-67. For surcharges see Nos. 69, 74, 76, 156-157.

Small Figures

1901, Apr. Litho. *Perf. 11½*
57 A25 2c rose .25 .25
58 A25 5c violet brown .25 .25
59 A25 40c blue .85 .40
Nos. 57-59 (3) 1.35 .90

1901-02 Larger Figures
60 A25 1c gray green ('02) .30 .30
61 A25 2c gray .30 .30
a. Half used as 1c on cover 10.00
62 A25 4c pale blue .30 .30
63 A25 5c violet .30 .30
64 A25 8c gray brown ('02) .30 .30
65 A25 10c rose red ('02) .75 .30
66 A25 28c orange ('02) 1.50 .30
67 A25 40c blue .75 .30
Nos. 60-67 (8) 4.50 2.40

For surcharges see Nos. 74, 76.

J. B. Egusquiza — A26

Chalky Paper

1901, Sept. 24 Typo. *Perf. 12x12½*
68 A26 1p slate .30 .30

For surcharge see No. 73.

No. 56 Surcharged in Red

1902, Aug.
69 A25 20c on 24c dp blue .50 .40
a. Inverted surcharge 6.25

Counterfeit surcharges exist.

Nos. 39, 43-44 Surcharged

1902, Dec. 22 *Perf. 12x12½*
70 A15 1c on 14c yellow brn .30 .30
a. No period after "cent" .90 .75
b. Comma after "cent" .65 .50
c. Accent over "Un" .65 .50

1903 *Perf. 11½*
71 A12 5c on 60c yellow .35 .30
72 A12 5c on 80c lt blue .30 .30

Nos. 68, 64, 66 Surcharged

No. 73

No. 74

No. 76

1902-03 *Perf. 12*
73 A26 1c on 1p slate ('03) .40 .40
a. No period after "cent" 4.00 3.00

Perf. 11½
74 A25 5c on 8c gray brown .50 .40
a. No period after "cent" 1.75 1.50
b. Double surcharge 7.00 6.00
76 A25 5c on 28c orange .50 .40
a. No period after "cent" 1.75 1.50
b. Comma after "cent" .80 .60
Nos. 73-76 (3) 1.40 1.20

The surcharge on Nos. 73 and 74 is found reading both upward and downward.

Sentinel Lion with Right Paw Ready to Strike for "Peace and Justice" — A32

Perf. 11½
1903, Feb. 28 Litho. Unwmk.
77 A32 1c gray .30 .30
78 A32 2c blue green .45 .30
79 A32 5c blue .60 .30
80 A32 10c orange brown .75 .30
81 A32 20c carmine .75 .30
82 A32 30c deep blue .90 .30
83 A32 60c purple 2.10 1.00
Nos. 77-83 (7) 5.85 2.80

For surcharges and overprints see Nos. 139-140, 166, O50-O56.

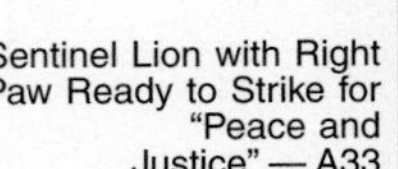
Sentinel Lion with Right Paw Ready to Strike for "Peace and Justice" — A33

1903, Sept.
84 A33 1c yellow green .30 .30
85 A33 2c red orange .30 .30
86 A33 5c dark blue .45 .30
87 A33 10c purple .45 .30
88 A33 20c dark green 5.00 .45
89 A33 30c ultramarine 1.50 .30
90 A33 60c ocher 1.75 .75
Nos. 84-90 (7) 9.75 2.70

Nos. 84-90 exist imperf. Value for pairs, $3 each for 1c-20c, $4 for 30c, $5 for 60c.

The three-line overprint "Gobierno provisorio Ago. 1904" is fraudulent.

Sentinel Lion at Rest — A35

Perf. 11½, 12, 11½x12

1905-10 Engr.

Dated "1904"

91 A35 1c orange .30 .25
92 A35 1c vermilion ('07) .30 .25
93 A35 1c grnsh bl ('07) .30 .25
94 A35 2c vermilion ('06) .30 .25
95 A35 2c olive grn ('07) 60.00
96 A35 2c car rose ('08) .45 .25
97 A35 5c dark blue .30 .25
98 A35 5c slate blue ('06) .30 .25
99 A35 5c yellow ('06) .30 .25
100 A35 10c bister ('06) .30 .25
101 A35 10c emerald ('07) .30 .25
102 A35 10c dp ultra ('08) .30 .25
103 A35 20c violet ('06) .45 .25
104 A35 20c bister ('07) .45 .25
105 A35 20c apple grn ('07) .45 .25
106 A35 30c turq bl ('06) .65 .25
107 A35 30c blue gray ('07) .65 .25
108 A35 30c dull lilac ('08) .90 .25
109 A35 60c chocolate ('07) .60 .25
110 A35 60c org brn ('07) 5.25 1.60
111 A35 60c salmon pink ('10) 5.25 1.60
Nos. 91-111 (21) 78.10
Nos. 91-94,96-111 (20) 18.10 7.70

All but Nos. 92 and 104 exist imperf. Value for pair, $10 each, except No. 95 at $35.00 and Nos. 109-111 at $15.00 each pair.

For surcharges and overprints see Nos. 129-130, 146-155, 174-190, 266.

Sentinel Lion at Rest — A36

1904, Aug. Litho. *Perf. 11½*

112 A36 10c light blue .50 .40
a. Imperf., pair 6.00

No. 112 Surcharged in Black

1904, Dec.

113 A36 30c on 10c light blue .80 .50

Peace between a successful revolutionary party and the government previously in power.

Governmental Palace, Asunción — A37

Dated "1904"

Center in Black

1906-10 Engr. *Perf. 11½, 12*

114 A37 1p bright rose 2.50 1.50
115 A37 1p brown org ('07) 1.00 .50
116 A37 1p ol gray ('07) 1.00 .50
117 A37 2p turquoise ('07) .50 .40
118 A37 2p lake ('09) .50 .40
119 A37 2p brn org ('10) .60 .40
120 A37 5p red ('07) 1.50 1.00
121 A37 5p ol grn ('10) 1.50 1.00
122 A37 5p dull bl ('10) 1.50 1.00
123 A37 10p brown org ('07) 1.40 1.00
124 A37 10p dp blue ('10) 1.40 1.00
125 A37 10p choc ('10) 1.50 1.00
126 A37 20p olive grn ('07) 3.50 3.25
127 A37 20p violet ('10) 3.50 3.25
128 A37 20p yellow ('10) 3.50 3.25
Nos. 114-128 (15) 25.40 19.45

Nos. 94 and 95 Surcharged

1907

129 A35 5c on 2c vermilion .45 .30
a. "5" omitted 1.50 1.50
b. Inverted surcharge 5.25 5.25
c. Double surcharge
d. Double surcharge, one inverted 1.50 1.50
e. Double surcharge, both invtd. 9.00 9.00
130 A35 5c on 2c olive grn .60 .30
a. "5" omitted 1.50 1.50
b. Inverted surcharge 3.25 3.25
c. Double surcharge 3.00 3.00
d. Bar omitted 3.00 3.00

Official Stamps of 1906-08 Surcharged

1908

131 O17 5c on 10c bister .45 .30
a. Double surcharge 4.50 4.50
132 O17 5c on 10c violet .45 .30
a. Inverted surcharge 3.50 3.50
133 O17 5c on 20c emerald .45 .30
134 O17 5c on 20c violet .45 .30
a. Inverted surcharge 4.75 4.75
135 O17 5c on 30c slate bl 1.50 1.00
136 O17 5c on 30c turq bl 1.50 1.00
a. Inverted surcharge
b. Double surcharge 9.00 9.00
137 O17 5c on 60c choc .45 .30
a. Double surcharge 9.00 9.00
138 O17 5c on 60c red brown .90 .30
a. Inverted surcharge 1.60 1.60
Nos. 131-138 (8) 6.15 3.80

Same Surcharge on Official Stamps of 1903

139 A32 5c on 30c dp blue 3.75 3.25
140 A32 5c on 60c purple 1.50 .90
a. Double surcharge 7.50 7.50

Official Stamps of 1906-08 Overprinted

141 O17 5c deep blue .40 .40
a. Inverted overprint 3.00 3.00
b. Bar omitted 9.00 9.00
c. Double overprint 4.00 4.00
142 O17 5c slate blue .50 .40
a. Inverted overprint 4.00 4.00
b. Double overprint 3.50 3.50
c. Bar omitted 9.00 9.00
143 O17 5c greenish blue .40 .40
a. Inverted overprint 2.50 2.50
b. Bar omitted 7.50 7.50
144 O18 1p brown org & blk .50 .50
a. Double overprint 2.00 2.00
b. Double overprint, one inverted 11.00 11.00
c. Triple overprint, two inverted 4.50 4.50
145 O18 1p brt rose & blk .90 .70
a. Bar omitted
Nos. 141-145 (5) 2.70 2.40

Regular Issues of 1906-08 Surcharged

1908

146 A35 5c on 1c grnsh bl .30 .30
a. Inverted surcharge 1.50 1.50
b. Double surcharge 2.25 2.25
c. "5" omitted 2.25 2.25
147 A35 5c on 2c car rose .30 .30
a. Inverted surcharge 2.50 2.50
b. "5" omitted 3.00 3.00
c. Double surcharge 5.25 5.25
d. Double surcharge, one invtd.
148 A35 5c on 60c org brn .30 .30
a. Inverted surcharge 3.75 3.75
b. "5" omitted 1.50 1.50
149 A35 5c on 60c sal pink .30 .30
a. Double surcharge 2.50 2.50
b. Double surcharge, one invtd. 5.25 5.25
150 A35 5c on 60c choc .30 .30
a. Inverted surcharge 7.50 7.50
151 A35 20c on 1c grnsh bl .30 .30
a. Inverted surcharge 5.00 5.00
152 A35 20c on 2c ver 9.00 7.50
153 A35 20c on 2c car rose 5.25 4.50
a. Inverted surcharge 19.00
154 A35 20c on 30c dl lil .30 .30
a. Inverted surcharge 2.25 2.25
b. Double surcharge
155 A35 20c on 30c turq bl 2.25 2.25
Nos. 146-155 (10) 18.60 16.35

Same Surcharge on Regular Issue of 1901-02

156 A25 5c on 28c org 2.25 2.25
157 A25 5c on 40c dk bl .75 .45
a. Inverted surcharge 6.00 6.00

Same Surcharge on Official Stamps of 1908

158 O17 5c on 10c emer .40 .40
a. Double surcharge 14.00
159 O17 5c on 10c red lil .40 .40
a. Double surcharge 4.00 4.00
b. "5" omitted 3.00 3.00
160 O17 5c on 20c bis .80 .60
a. Double surcharge 2.50 2.50
161 O17 5c on 20c sal pink .80 .60
a. "5" omitted 3.50 3.50
162 O17 5c on 30c bl gray .40 .40
163 O17 5c on 30c yel .40 .40
a. "5" omitted 3.00 3.00
b. Inverted surcharge 2.50 2.50
164 O17 5c on 60c org brn .40 .40
a. Double surcharge 12.00 12.00
165 O17 5c on 60c dp ultra .40 .40
a. Inverted surcharge 5.00 5.00
b. "5" omitted 3.00
Nos. 158-165 (8) 4.00 3.60

Same Surcharge on No. O52

166 A32 20c on 5c blue 2.50 2.00
a. Inverted surcharge 9.50 9.50

Stamp of 1887 Surcharged

1908 On Stamp of 1887

167 A12 20c on 2c car 6.50 3.00
a. Inverted surcharge 22.50

On Official Stamps of 1892

168 A12 5c on 15c org 10.00 5.25
169 A12 5c on 20c pink 120.00 95.00
170 A12 5c on 50c gray 52.50 37.50
170A A12 20c on 5c blue 4.50 3.75
b. Inverted surcharge 25.00 25.00
Nos. 167-170A (5) 193.50 144.50

Nos. 151, 152, 153, 155, 167, 170A, while duly authorized, all appear to have been sold to a single individual, and although they paid postage, it is doubtful whether they can be considered as ever having been placed on sale to the public.

Nos. O82-O84 Surcharged (Date in Red)

1908-09

171 O18 1c on 1p brt rose & blk .50 .50
172 O18 1c on 1p lake & blk .50 .50
173 O18 1c on 1p brn org & blk ('09) 5.00 5.00
Nos. 171-173 (3) 6.00 6.00

Varieties of surcharge on Nos. 171-173 include: "CETTAVO"; date omitted, double or inverted; third line double or omitted.

Types of 1905-1910 Overprinted

1908, Mar. 5 *Perf. 11½*

174 A35 1c emerald .30 .30
175 A35 5c yellow .30 .30
176 A35 10c lilac brown .30 .30
177 A35 20c yellow orange .30 .30
178 A35 30c red .40 .30
179 A35 60c magenta .30 .30
180 A37 1p light blue .30 .30
Nos. 174-180 (7) 2.20 2.10

Overprinted

1909, Sept.

181 A35 1c blue gray .40 .40
182 A35 1c scarlet .40 .40
183 A35 5c dark green .40 .40
184 A35 5c deep orange .40 .40
185 A35 10c rose .40 .40
186 A35 10c bister brown .40 .40
187 A35 20c yellow .40 .40
188 A35 20c violet .40 .40
189 A35 30c orange brown .60 .40
190 A35 30c dull blue .60 .40
Nos. 181-190 (10) 4.40 4.00

Counterfeits exist.

Coat of Arms above Numeral of Value — A38

1910-21 Litho. *Perf. 11½*

191 A38 1c brown .50 .30
192 A38 5c bright violet .50 .30
a. Pair, imperf. between 2.00 2.00
193 A38 5c blue grn ('19) .50 .30
194 A38 5c lt blue ('21) .50 .30
195 A38 10c yellow green .50 .30
196 A38 10c dp vio ('19) .50 .30
197 A38 10c red ('21) .50 .30
198 A38 20c red .50 .30
199 A38 50c car rose .50 .30
200 A38 75c deep blue .50 .30
a. Diag. half perforated ('11) .40 .25
Nos. 191-200 (10) 5.00 3.00

Nos. 191-200 exist imperforate.

No. 200a was authorized for use as 20c.

For surcharges see Nos. 208, 241, 261, 265.

"The Republic" — A39

1911 Engr.

201 A39 1c olive grn & blk .30 .30
202 A39 2c dk blue & blk .45 .30
203 A39 5c carmine & indigo .45 .30
204 A39 10c dp blue & brn .45 .30
205 A39 20c olive grn & ind .60 .30
206 A39 50c lilac & indigo .75 .30
207 A39 75c ol grn & red lil .75 .30
Nos. 201-207 (7) 3.75 2.10

Centenary of National Independence.

The 1c, 2c, 10c and 50c exist imperf. Value for pairs, $2.25 each.

No. 199 Surcharged

1912

208 A38 20c on 50c car rose .30 .30
a. Inverted surcharge 2.00 2.00
b. Double surcharge 2.00 2.00
c. Bar omitted 2.50 2.50

National Coat of Arms — A40

1913 Engr. *Perf. 11½*

209 A40 1c gray .30 .30
210 A40 2c orange .30 .30
211 A40 5c lilac .30 .30
212 A40 10c green .30 .30
213 A40 20c dull red .30 .30
214 A40 40c rose .30 .30
215 A40 75c deep blue .30 .30
216 A40 80c yellow .30 .30
217 A40 1p light blue .45 .30
218 A40 1.25p pale blue .45 .30
219 A40 3p greenish blue .45 .30
Nos. 209-219 (11) 3.75 3.30

For surcharges see Nos. 225, 230-231, 237, 242, 253, 262-263, L3-L4.

Nos. J7-J10 Overprinted

1918

220 D2 5c yellow brown .30 .30
221 D2 10c yellow brown .30 .30
222 D2 20c yellow brown .30 .30
223 D2 40c yellow brown .30 .30

Nos. J10 and 214 Surcharged

224 D2 5c on 40c yellow brn .30 .30
225 A40 30c on 40c rose .30 .30
Nos. 220-225 (6) 1.80 1.80

Nos. 220-225 exist with surcharge inverted, double and double with one inverted.

The surcharge "Habilitado-1918-5 cents 5" on the 1c gray official stamps of 1914, is bogus.

No. J11 Overprinted

1920

229 D2 1p yellow brown .30 .30
a. Inverted overprint .65 .65
e. As "g," "AABILITADO" .75 .75
f. As "g," "1929" for "1920" .75 .75
g. Overprint lines 8mm apart .25 .25

Nos. 216 and 219 Surcharged

230 A40 50c on 80c yellow .30 .30
231 A40 1.75p on 3p grnsh bl .75 .65

Same Surcharge on No. J12

232 D2 1p on 1.50p yel brn .30 .30
Nos. 229-232 (4) 1.65 1.55

Nos. 229-232 exist with various surcharge errors, including inverted, double, double inverted and double with one inverted. Those that were issued are listed.

Parliament Building — A41

1920 **Litho.** ***Perf. 11½***

233 A41 50c red & black .35 .30
a. "CORRLOS" 5.00 5.00
234 A41 1p lt blue & blk 1.00 .45
235 A41 1.75p dk blue & blk .30 .30
236 A41 3p orange & blk 1.50 .30
Nos. 233-236 (4) 3.15 1.35

50th anniv. of the Constitution.

All values exist imperforate and Nos. 233, 235 and 236 with center inverted. It is doubtful that any of these varieties were regularly issued.

No. 215 Surcharged

1920

237 A40 50c on 75c deep blue .60 .40

Nos. 200, 215 Surcharged

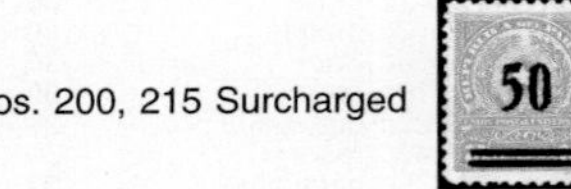

1921

241 A38 50c on 75c deep blue .40 .40
242 A40 50c on 75c deep blue .40 .40

A42

1922, Feb. 8 **Litho.** ***Perf. 11½***

243 A42 50c car & dk blue .40 .40
a. Imperf. pair 5.00
b. Center inverted 25.00 25.00
244 A42 1p dk blue & brn .40 .40
a. Imperf. pair 5.00
b. Center inverted 30.00 30.00
c. As "b," imperf. pair 110.00

For overprints see Nos. L1-L2.

Rendezvous of Conspirators A43

1922-23

245 A43 1p deep blue .40 .40
246 A43 1p scar & dk bl ('23) .40 .40
247 A43 1p red vio & gray ('23) .40 .40
248 A43 1p org & gray ('23) .40 .40
249 A43 5p dark violet 1.20 .40
250 A43 5p dk bl & org brn ('23) 1.20 .40
251 A43 5p dl red & lt bl ('23) 1.20 .40
252 A43 5p emer & blk ('23) 1.20 .40
Nos. 245-252 (8) 6.40 3.20

National Independence.

No. 218 Surcharged "Habilitado en $1:-1924" in Red

1924

253 A40 1p on 1.25p pale blue .40 .40

This stamp was for use in Asunción. Nos. L3 to L5 were for use in the interior, as is indicated by the "C" in the surcharge.

Map of Paraguay — A44

1924 **Litho.** ***Perf. 11½***

254 A44 1p dark blue .40 .40
255 A44 2p carmine rose .40 .40
256 A44 4p light blue .40 .40
a. Perf. 12 .80 .40
Nos. 254-256 (3) 1.20 1.20

#254-256 exist imperf. Value $3 each pair.

For surcharges and overprint see Nos. 267, C5, C15-C16, C54-C55, L7.

Gen. José E. Díaz — A45

1925-26 ***Perf. 11½, 12***

257 A45 50c red .30 .30
258 A45 1p dark blue .30 .30
259 A45 1p emerald ('26) .30 .30
Nos. 257-259 (3) .90 .90

#257-258 exist imperf. Value $1 each pair.

For overprints see Nos. L6, L8, L10.

Columbus — A46

1925 ***Perf. 11½***

260 A46 1p blue .50 .40
a. Imperf., pair 10.00

For overprint see No. L9.

Nos. 194, 214-215, J12 Surcharged in Black or Red

1926

261 A38 1c on 5c lt blue .30 .30
262 A40 7c on 40c rose .30 .30
263 A40 15c on 75c dp bl (R) .30 .30
264 D2 1.50p on 1.50p yel brn .30 .30
Nos. 261-264 (4) 1.20 1.20

Nos. 194, 179 and 256 Surcharged "Habilitado" and New Values

1927

265 A38 2c on 5c lt blue .30 .30
266 A35 50c on 60c magenta .30 .30
a. Inverted surcharge 2.00
267 A44 1.50p on 4p lt blue .30 .30

Official Stamp of 1914 Surcharged "Habilitado" and New Value

268 O19 50c on 75c dp bl .30 .30
Nos. 265-268 (4) 1.20 1.20

National Emblem A47

Pedro Juan Caballero A48

Map of Paraguay A49

Fulgencio Yegros A50

Ignacio Iturbe A51

Oratory of the Virgin, Asunción A52

Perf. 12, 11, 11½, 11x12

1927-38 **Typo.**

269 A47 1c lt red ('31) .25 .25
270 A47 2c org red ('30) .25 .25
271 A47 7c lilac .25 .25
272 A47 7c emerald ('29) .25 .25
273 A47 10c gray grn ('28) .25 .25
a. 10c light green ('31) .25 .25
274 A47 10c lil rose ('30) .25 .25
275 A47 10c light bl ('35) .25 .25
276 A47 20c dull bl ('28) .25 .25
277 A47 20c lil brn ('30) .25 .25
278 A47 20c lt vio ('31) .25 .25
279 A47 20c rose ('35) .25 .25
280 A47 50c ultramarine .25 .25
281 A47 50c dl red ('28) .25 .25
282 A47 50c orange ('30) .25 .25
283 A47 50c gray ('31) .25 .25
284 A47 50c brn vio ('34) .25 .25
285 A47 50c rose ('36) .25 .25
286 A47 70c ultra ('28) .25 .25
287 A48 1p emerald .25 .25
288 A48 1p org red ('30) .25 .25
289 A48 1p brn org ('34) .25 .25
290 A49 1.50p brown .25 .25
291 A49 1.50p lilac ('28) .25 .25
292 A49 1.50p rose red ('32) .25 .25
293 A50 2.50p bister .25 .25
294 A51 3p gray .25 .25
295 A51 3p rose red ('36) .25 .25
296 A51 3p brt vio ('36) .25 .25
297 A52 5p chocolate .25 .25
298 A52 5p violet ('36) .25 .25
299 A52 5p pale org ('38) .25 .25
300 A49 20p red ('29) 7.00 5.50
301 A49 20p emerald ('29) 7.00 5.50
302 A49 20p vio brn ('29) 7.00 5.50
Nos. 269-302 (34) 28.75 24.25

No. 281 is also known perf. 10½x11½.

Papermaker's watermarks are sometimes found on No. 271 ("GLORIA BOND" in double-lined circle) and No. 280 ("Extra Vencedor Bond" or "ADBANCE/M M C").

For surcharges and overprints see Nos. 312, C4, C6, C13-C14, C17-C18, C25-C32, C34-C35, L11-L30, O94-O96, O98.

Arms of Juan de Salazar de Espinosa — A53

1928, Aug. 15 ***Perf. 12***

303 A53 10p violet brown 3.00 2.00

Juan de Salazar de Espinosa, founder of Asunción.

A papermaker's watermark ("INDIAN BOND EXTRA STRONG S.&C") is sometimes found on Nos 303, 305-307.

Columbus — A54

1928 **Litho.**

304 A54 10p ultra 2.40 1.50
305 A54 10p vermilion 2.40 1.50
306 A54 10p deep red 2.40 1.50
Nos. 304-306 (3) 7.20 4.50

For surcharge and overprint see Nos. C33, L37.

President Rutherford B. Hayes of US and Villa Occidental A55

1928, Nov. 20 ***Perf. 12***

307 A55 10p gray brown 10.00 3.50
308 A55 10p red brown 10.00 3.50

50th anniv. of the Hayes' Chaco decision.

Portraits of Archbishop Bogarin — A56

1930, Aug. 15

309 A56 1.50p lake 2.00 1.50
310 A56 1.50p turq blue 2.00 1.50
311 A56 1.50p dull vio 2.00 1.50
Nos. 309-311 (3) 6.00 4.50

Archbishop Juan Sinforiano Bogarin, first archbishop of Paraguay.

For overprints see Nos. 321-322.

No. 272 Surcharged

1930

312 A47 5c on 7c emer .25 .25

A57

1930-39 **Typo.** ***Perf. 11½, 12***

313 A57 10p brown *5.00 2.00*
314 A57 10p brn red, *bl* ('31) *5.00 2.00*
315 A57 10p dk bl, *pink* ('32) *5.00 2.00*
316 A57 10p gray brn ('36) *4.00 2.00*
317 A57 10p gray ('37) *4.00 1.75*
318 A57 10p blue ('39) *2.00 1.25*
Nos. 313-318 (6) *25.00 11.00*

1st Paraguayan postage stamp, 60th anniv.

For overprint see No. L31.

Gunboat "Humaitá" A58

1931 ***Perf. 12***

319 A58 1.50p purple .80 .50
Nos. 319,C39-C53 (16) 50.60 18.05

Constitution, 60th anniv.

For overprint see No. L33.

View of San Bernardino A59

1931, Aug.

320 A59 1p light green .50 .40

Founding of San Bernardino, 50th anniv.

For overprint see No. L32.

Nos. 309-310 Overprinted in Blue or Red

1931, Dec. 31
321 A56 1.50p lake (Bl) 3.00 3.00
322 A56 1.50p turq blue (R) 3.00 3.00

Map of the Gran Chaco — A60

1932-35 Typo. *Perf. 12*
323 A60 1.50p deep violet 5.00 .40
324 A60 1.50p rose ('35) 5.00 .40

For overprints see Nos. L34-L36, O97.

Nos. C74-C78 Surcharged

1933 Litho.
325 AP18 50c on 4p ultra 1.75 .40
326 AP18 1p on 8p red 3.25 .80
327 AP18 1.50p on 12p bl grn 3.25 .80
328 AP18 2p on 16p dk vio 3.25 .80
329 AP18 5p on 20p org brn 8.00 1.75
Nos. 325-329 (5) 19.50 4.55

Flag of the Race Issue

Flag with Three Crosses: Caravels of Columbus — A61

1933, Oct. 10 Litho. *Perf. 11*
330 A61 10c multicolored .50 .50
331 A61 20c multicolored .75 .75
332 A61 50c multicolored .75 .75
333 A61 1p multicolored .75 .75
334 A61 1.50p multicolored .75 .75
335 A61 2p multicolored .90 .90
336 A61 5p multicolored 1.40 1.40
337 A61 10p multicolored 1.75 .75
Nos. 330-337 (8) 7.55 6.55

441st anniv. of the sailing of Christopher Columbus from the port of Palos, Aug. 3, 1492, on his first voyage to the New World.

Nos. 332, 334 and 335 exist with Maltese crosses omitted.

Monstrance — A62

1937, Aug. Unwmk. *Perf. 11½*
338 A62 1p dk blue, yel & red .40 .40
339 A62 3p dk blue, yel & red .40 .40
340 A62 10p dk blue, yel & red .40 .40
Nos. 338-340 (3) 1.20 1.20

1st Natl. Eucharistic Congress, Asuncion.

Arms of Asunción — A63

1937, Aug.
341 A63 50c violet & buff .60 .40
342 A63 1p bis & lt grn .60 .40
343 A63 3p red & lt bl .60 .40
344 A63 10p car rose & buff .60 .40
345 A63 20p blue & drab .60 .40
Nos. 341-345 (5) 3.00 2.00

Founding of Asuncion, 400th anniv.

Oratory of the Virgin, Asunción — A64

1938-39 Typo. *Perf. 11, 12*
346 A64 5p olive green 1.50 .40
347 A64 5p pale rose ('39) 1.50 .40
348 A64 11p violet brown 2.00 .50
Nos. 346-348 (3) 5.00 1.30

Founding of Asuncion, 400th anniv.

Carlos Antonio Lopez — A65

José Eduvigis Diaz — A66

1939 *Perf. 12*
349 A65 2p lt ultra & pale brn .90 .60
350 A66 2p lt ultra & brn .90 .60

Reburial of ashes of Pres. Carlos Antonio Lopez (1790-1862) and Gen. José Eduvigis Diaz in the National Pantheon, Asuncion.

Pres. Patricio Escobar and Ramon Zubizarreta — A67

Design: 5p, Pres. Bernardino Caballero and Senator José S. Decoud.

1939-40 Litho. *Perf. 11½*
Heads in Black
351 A67 50c dull org ('40) .60 .60
352 A67 1p lt violet ('40) .60 .60
353 A67 2p red brown ('40) .60 .60
354 A67 5p lt ultra .75 .60
Nos. 351-354,C122-C123,O99-O104 (12) 34.45 26.20

Founding of the University of Asuncion, 50th anniv.

Varieties of this issue include inverted heads (50c, 1p, 2p); doubled heads; Caballero and Decoud heads in 50c frame: imperforates and part-perforates. Examples with inverted heads were not officially issued.

Coats of Arms — A69

Flags of Paraguay, United States — A70

Designs: 1p, Pres. Baldomir, flags of Paraguay, Uruguay. 2p, Pres. Benavides, flags of Paraguay, Peru. 5p, Pres. Alessandri, flags of Paraguay, Chile. 6p, Pres. Vargas, flags of Paraguay, Brazil. 10p, Pres. Ortiz, flags of Paraguay, Argentina.

1939 Engr.; Flags Litho. *Perf. 12*
Flags in National Colors
355 A69 50c violet blue .30 .30
356 A70 1p olive .30 .30
357 A70 2p blue green .30 .30
358 A70 3p sepia .35 .35
359 A70 5p orange .30 .30
360 A70 6p dull violet .75 .60
361 A70 10p bister brn .60 .35
Nos. 355-361,C113-C121 (16) 42.45 28.25

First Buenos Aires Peace Conference.

For overprint and surcharge, see Nos.387-390, B10 in the Scott *Standard Postage Stamp Catalogue*.

Coats of Arms of New York and Asunción — A76

1939, Nov. 30
362 A76 5p scarlet .55 .55
363 A76 10p deep blue .85 .80
364 A76 11p dk blue grn .85 1.20
365 A76 22p olive blk 1.40 1.60
Nos. 362-365,C124-C126 (7) 33.65 31.15

New York World's Fair.

Paraguayan Soldier A77

Paraguayan Woman A78

Cowboys A79

Plowing A80

View of Paraguay River — A81

Oxcart — A82

Pasture — A83

Pirareta Falls — A84

1940, Jan. 1 Photo. *Perf. 12½*
366 A77 50c deep orange .40 .25
367 A78 1p brt red violet .40 .25
368 A79 3p bright green .40 .25
369 A80 5p chestnut .40 .25
370 A81 10p magenta .40 .25
371 A82 20p violet 1.00 .30
372 A83 50p cobalt blue 2.00 .45
373 A84 100p black 4.00 1.40
Nos. 366-373 (8) 9.00 3.40

Second Buenos Aires Peace Conference.
For surcharge see No. 386.

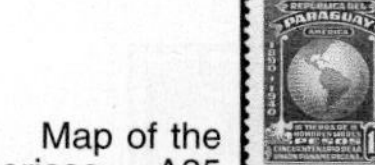
Map of the Americas — A85

1940, May Engr. *Perf. 12*
374 A85 50c red orange .30 .25
375 A85 1p green .30 .25
376 A85 5p dark blue .50 .25
377 A85 10p brown 1.00 .50
Nos. 374-377,C127-C130 (8) 12.20 9.20

Pan American Union, 50th anniversary.

Reproduction of Type A1 — A86

Sir Rowland Hill — A87

Designs: 6p, Type A2. 10p, Type A3.

1940, Aug. 15 Photo. *Perf. 13½*
378 A86 1p aqua & brt red vio .50 .25
379 A87 5p dp yel grn & red brn .65 .30
380 A86 6p org brn & ultra 1.50 .65
381 A86 10p ver & black 1.50 1.00
Nos. 378-381 (4) 4.15 2.20

Postage stamp centenary.

Dr. José Francia A90 A91

1940, Sept. 20 Engr. *Perf. 12*
382 A90 50c carmine rose .30 .30
383 A91 50c plum .30 .30
384 A90 1p bright green .30 .30
385 A91 5p deep blue .30 .30
Nos. 382-385 (4) 1.20 1.20

Centenary of the death of Dr. Jose Francia (1766-1840), dictator of Paraguay, 1814-1840.

No. 366 Surcharged in Black

1940, Sept. 7 *Perf. 12½*
386 A77 5p on 50c dp org .40 .30

In honor of Pres. Jose F. Estigarribia who died in a plane crash Sept. 7, 1940.

No. 360 Overprinted in Black

1941, Aug. *Perf. 12*
387 A70 6p multi .40 .40
Never hinged .65

Visit to Paraguay of Pres. Vargas of Brazil.

Nos. C113-C115 Overprinted in Blue or Red

1942, Jan. 17 *Perf. 12½*
388 A69 1p multi (Bl) .30 .30
389 A69 3p multi (R) .30 .30
390 A70 5p multi (R) .30 .30
Nos. 388-390 (3) .90 .90
Set, never hinged 1.65

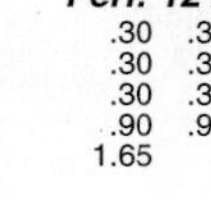

Coat of Arms — A92

1942-43 Litho. ***Perf. 11, 12, 11x12***

391 A92 1p light green .50 .30
392 A92 1p orange ('43) .50 .30
393 A92 7p light blue .50 .30
394 A92 7p yel brn ('43) .50 .30
Nos. 391-394 (4) 2.00 1.20
Set, never hinged 3.00

Values are for examples perforated 11. Stamps perforated 12 and 11x12 are worth more. Nos. 391-394 exist imperf.

The Indian Francisco A93

Domingo Martinez de Irala and His Vision A94

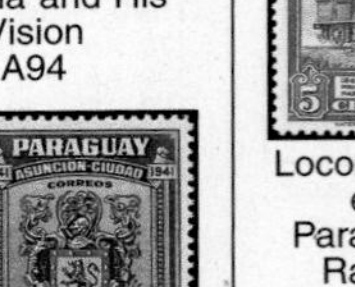
Arms of Irala — A95

1942, Aug. 15 Engr. ***Perf. 12***

395 A93 2p green 1.10 .50
396 A94 5p rose 1.10 .50
397 A95 7p sapphire 1.10 .50
Nos. 395-397,C131-C133 (6) 13.80 8.60
Set, never hinged 16.00

400th anniversary of Asuncion.

Pres. Higinio Morinigo, Scenes of Industry & Agriculture — A96

1943, Aug. 15 **Unwmk.**

398 A96 7p blue .30 .30

For surcharges see Nos. 404, 428.

Christopher Columbus — A97

1943, Aug. 15

399 A97 50c violet .30 .30
400 A97 1p gray brn .30 .30
401 A97 5p dark grn .50 .30
402 A97 7p brt ultra .30 .30
Nos. 399-402 (4) 1.40 1.20
Set, never hinged 2.75

Discovery of America, 450th anniv.
For surcharges see Nos. 405, 429.

No. 296 Surcharged in Black

1944 ***Perf. 12, 11, 11½, 11x12***

403 A51 1c on 3p brt vio .50 .30
Never hinged .75

Nos. 398 and 402 Surcharged in Red

1944 ***Perf. 12***

404 A96 5c on 7p blue .50 .30
405 A97 5c on 7p brt ultra .50 .30
Nos. 404-405 (2) 1.00 .60

Set, never hinged 1.50

Imperforates
Starting with No. 406, many Paraguayan stamps exist imperf.

Primitive Postal Service among Indians — A98

Ruins of Humaitá Church — A99

Locomotive of early Paraguayan Railroad A100

Marshal Francisco S. Lopez A101

Early Merchant Ship A102

Port of Asunción A103

Birthplace of Paraguay's Liberation A104

Monument to Heroes of Itororó A105

1944-45 Unwmk. Engr. ***Perf. 12½***

406 A98 1c black .25 .25
407 A99 2c copper brn ('45) .25 .25
408 A100 5c light olive .70 .25
409 A101 7c light blue ('45) .30 .25
410 A102 10c green ('45) .35 .25
411 A103 15c dark blue ('45) .35 .30
412 A104 50c black brown .45 .40
413 A105 1g dk rose car ('45) 1.30 1.00
Nos. 406-413 (8) 3.95 2.95
Nos. 406-413,C134-C146 (21) 26.55 14.50
Set, never hinged 40.00

See #435, 437, 439, 441, C158-C162.
For surcharges see #414, 427.

No. 409 Surcharged in Red

1945

414 A101 5c on 7c light blue .50 .30

Handshake, Map and Flags of Paraguay and Panama — A106

Designs: 3c, Venezuela Flag. 5c, Colombia Flag. 2g, Peru Flag.

Engr.; Flags Litho. in Natl. Colors

1945, Aug. 15 Unwmk. ***Perf. 12½***

415 A106 1c dark green .25 .25
416 A106 3c lake .25 .25
417 A106 5c blue blk .25 .25
418 A106 2g brown 1.10 .75
Nos. 415-418,C147-C153 (11) 21.40 21.05
Set, never hinged 32.00

Goodwill visits of Pres. Higinio Morinigo during 1943.

Nos. B6 to B9 Surcharged in Black

1945 Engr. ***Perf. 12***

419 SP4 2c on 7p + 3p red brn 1.90 1.90
420 SP4 2c on 7p + 3p purple 1.90 1.90
421 SP4 2c on 7p + 3p car rose 1.90 1.90
422 SP4 2c on 7p + 3p saph 1.90 1.90
423 SP4 5c on 7p + 3p red brn 1.90 1.90
424 SP4 5c on 7p + 3p purple 1.90 1.90
425 SP4 5c on 7p + 3p car rose 1.90 1.90
426 SP4 5c on 7p + 3p saph 1.90 1.90
Nos. 419-426 (8) 15.20 15.20
Set, never hinged 17.00

Similar Surcharge in Red on Nos. 409, 398 and 402

Perf. 12½, 12

427 A101 5c on 7c lt blue .40 .40
428 A96 5c on 7p blue .40 .40
429 A97 5c on 7p brt ultra .40 .40
Nos. 427-429 (3) 1.20 1.20
Set, never hinged 1.95

Nos. 427-429 exist with black surcharge.

Catalogue values for unused stamps in this section, from this point to the end of the section, are for Never Hinged items.

Coat of Arms ("U.P.U." at bottom) — A110

1946 Litho. ***Perf. 11, 12***

430 A110 5c gray .65 .30

See Nos. 459-463, 478-480, 498-506, 525-536, 646-658.
For overprints see Nos. 464-466.

Nos. B6 to B9 Surcharged "1946" and New Value in Black

1946 ***Perf. 12***

431 SP4 5c on 7p + 3p red brn 6.25 1.50
432 SP4 5c on 7p + 3p purple 6.25 1.50
433 SP4 5c on 7p + 3p car rose 6.25 1.50
434 SP4 5c on 7p + 3p saph 6.25 1.50
Nos. 431-434 (4) 25.00 6.00

Types of 1944-45 and

First Telegraph in South America A111

Monument to Antequera A112

Colonial Jesuit Altar — A113

1946, Sept. 21 Engr. ***Perf. 12½***

435 A102 1c rose car .60 .40
436 A111 2c purple .60 .40
437 A98 5c ultra .60 .40
438 A112 10c org yel .60 .40
439 A105 15c brn olive .60 .40
440 A113 50c deep grn 1.00 .40
441 A104 1g brt ultra 1.90 .80
Nos. 435-441 (7) 5.90 3.20

See Nos. C135-C138, C143, C172.

Marshal Francisco Solano Lopez — A114

1947, May 15 ***Perf. 12***

442 A114 1c purple .35 .25
443 A114 2c org red .35 .25
444 A114 5c green .35 .25
445 A114 15c ultra .35 .25
446 A114 50c dark grn 1.20 .65
Nos. 442-446,C163-C167 (10) 13.50 10.70

Juan Sinforiano Bogarin, Archbishop of Asunción A115

Archbishopric Coat of Arms A116

Projected Monument of the Sacred Heart of Jesus A117

Vision of Projected Monument A118

1948, Jan. 6 Engr. ***Perf. 12½***

447 A115 2c dark blue .45 .25
448 A116 5c deep car .45 .25
449 A117 10c gray blk .45 .25
450 A118 15c green .80 .25
Nos. 447-450,C168-C175 (12) 21.70 10.00

Archbishopric of Asunción, 50th anniv.
See Nos. C168-C171, C173-C175.

"Political Enlightenment" — A119

1948, Sept. 11 **Engr. & Litho.**

451 A119 5c car red .35 .30
452 A119 15c red org .35 .30
Nos. 451-452,C176-C177 (4) 10.50 9.50

Issued to honor the Barefeet, a political group.
See Nos. C176-C177.

C. A. Lopez, J. N. Gonzalez and Freighter Paraguari — A120

Centers in Carmine, Black, Ultramarine and Blue

1949 **Litho.**

453 A120 2c orange .55 .25
454 A120 5c blue vio .55 .25
455 A120 10c black .55 .25
456 A120 15c violet .55 .25
457 A120 50c blue grn .55 .25
458 A120 1g dull vio brn .55 .25
Nos. 453-458 (6) 3.30 1.50

Paraguay's merchant fleet centenary.

Arms Type of 1946

1950 Unwmk. ***Perf. 10***

459 A110 5c red .70 .30
460 A110 10c blue .70 .30
461 A110 50c rose lilac 1.00 .30
462 A110 1g pale violet 1.00 .30

1951 — Coarse Impression

No.	Type	Value	Description	Unused	Used
463	A110	30c	green	1.00	.30
			Nos. 459-463 (5)	4.40	1.50

Nos. 459, 460 and 463 Overprinted in Various Colors

1951, Apr. 18

No.	Type	Value	Description	Unused	Used
464	A110	5c	red (Bk), block	1.50	1.00
465	A110	10c	blue (R), block	3.00	2.00
466	A110	30c	green (V), block	4.50	3.00
			Nos. 464-466 (3)	9.00	6.00

1st Economic Cong. of Paraguay, 4/18/51.

Columbus Lighthouse A121

1952, Feb. 11 — Perf. 10

No.	Type	Value	Description	Unused	Used
467	A121	2c	org brn	.95	.25
468	A121	5c	light ultra	.95	.25
469	A121	10c	rose	.95	.25
470	A121	15c	light blue	.95	.25
471	A121	20c	lilac	.95	.25
472	A121	50c	orange	.95	.25
473	A121	1g	bluish grn	.95	.25
			Nos. 467-473 (7)	6.65	1.75

Silvio Pettirossi, Aviator — A122

1954, Mar. — Litho. — Perf. 10

No.	Type	Value	Description	Unused	Used
474	A122	5c	blue	.80	.25
475	A122	20c	rose pink	.80	.25
476	A122	50c	vio brn	.80	.25
477	A122	60c	lt vio	.80	.25
			Nos. 474-477,C201-C204 (8)	6.40	2.00

Arms Type of 1946

1954 — Perf. 11

No.	Type	Value	Description	Unused	Used
478	A110	10c	vermilion	2.50	.25

Perf. 10

No.	Type	Value	Description	Unused	Used
478A	A110	10c	ver, redrawn	.75	.25
479	A110	10g	orange	5.00	2.00
480	A110	50g	vio brn	9.50	7.00
			Nos. 478-480 (4)	17.75	9.50

No. 478A measures 20½x24mm, has 5 frame lines at left and 6 at right. No. 478 measures 20x24½mm, has 6 frame lines at left and 5 at right.

Three National Heroes A123

1954, Aug. 15 — Litho. — Perf. 10

No.	Type	Value	Description	Unused	Used
481	A123	5c	light vio	.30	.25
482	A123	20c	light blue	.30	.25
483	A123	50c	rose pink	.30	.25
484	A123	1g	org brn	.30	.25
485	A123	2g	blue grn	.40	.25
			Nos. 481-485,C216-C220 (10)	19.75	10.10

Marshal Francisco S. Lopez, Pres. Carlos A. Lopez and Gen. Bernardino Caballero.

Pres. Alfredo Stroessner and Pres. Juan D. Peron — A124

Photo. & Litho.

1955, Apr. — Wmk. 90 — Perf. 13x13½

No.	Type	Value	Description	Unused	Used
486	A124	5c	multicolored	.40	.25
487	A124	10c	multicolored	.40	.25
488	A124	50c	multicolored	.40	.25
489	A124	1.30g	multicolored	.40	.25
490	A124	2.20g	multicolored	.55	.25
			Nos. 486-490,C221-C224 (9)	5.95	4.45

Visit of Pres. Juan D. Peron of Argentina.

Jesuit Ruins, Trinidad Belfry A125

Santa Maria Cornice A126

Jesuit Ruins: 20c, Corridor at Trinidad. 2.50g, Tower of Santa Rosa. 5g, San Cosme gate. 15g, Church of Jesus. 25g, Niche at Trinidad.

Perf. 12½x12, 12x12½

1955, June 19 — Engr. — Unwmk.

No.	Type	Value	Description	Unused	Used
491	A125	5c	org yel	.60	.30
492	A125	20c	olive bister	.60	.30
493	A126	50c	lt red brn	.60	.30
494	A126	2.50g	olive	.60	.30
495	A125	5g	yel brn	.60	.30
496	A125	15g	blue grn	.60	.30
497	A126	25g	deep grn	1.40	.30
			Nos. 491-497,C225-C232 (15)	10.85	4.15

25th anniv. of the priesthood of Monsignor Rodriguez.

For surcharges see Nos. 545-551.

Arms Type of 1946

Perf. 10, 11 (No. 500)

1956-58 — Litho. — Unwmk.

No.	Type	Value	Description	Unused	Used
498	A110	5c	brown ('57)	1.00	.50
499	A110	30c	red brn ('57)	2.00	.50
500	A110	45c	gray olive	3.00	.50
500A	A110	90c	lt vio bl	5.00	.75
501	A110	2g	ocher	5.00	.25
502	A110	2.20g	lil rose	2.00	.25
503	A110	3g	ol bis ('58)	3.00	.25
503A	A110	4.20g	emer ('57)	6.00	.25
504	A110	5g	ver ('57)	10.00	5.00
505	A110	10g	lt grn ('57)	10.00	5.00
506	A110	20g	blue ('57)	10.00	5.00
			Nos. 498-506 (11)	57.00	18.25

No. 500A exists with four-line, carmine overprint: "DIA N. UNIDAS 24 Octubre 1945-1956". It was not regularly issued and no decree authorizing it is known.

Soldiers, Angel and Asuncion Cathedral — A127

Nos. 513-519, Soldier & nurse in medallion & flags.

Perf. 13½

1957, June 12 — Photo. — Unwmk.

Granite Paper

Flags in Red and Blue

No.	Type	Value	Description	Unused	Used
508	A127	5c	bl grn	.55	.25
509	A127	10c	carmine	.55	.25
510	A127	15c	ultra	.55	.25
511	A127	20c	dp claret	.55	.25
512	A127	25c	gray blk	.55	.25
513	A127	30c	lt blue	.55	.25
514	A127	40c	gray blk	.55	.25
515	A127	50c	dark car	.55	.25
516	A127	1g	bluish grn	.55	.25
517	A127	1.30g	ultra	.55	.25
518	A127	1.50g	dp claret	.55	.25
519	A127	2g	brt grn	.55	.25
			Nos. 508-519 (12)	6.60	3.00

Heroes of the Chaco war. See #C233-C245.

Statue of St. Ignatius (Guarani Carving) A128

Blessed Roque Gonzales and St. Ignatius A129

A129a

1.50g, St. Ignatius and San Ignacio Monastery.

Wmk. 319

1958, Mar. 15 — Litho. — Perf. 11

No.	Type	Value	Description	Unused	Used
520	A128	50c	dk red brn	1.00	*1.25*
521	A129	50c	lt bl grn	1.00	*1.25*
522	A129a	1.50g	brt vio	1.00	*1.25*
523	A128	3g	light bl	1.00	.50
524	A129	6.25g	rose car	1.00	.25
			Nos. 520-524 (5)	5.00	4.50

St. Ignatius of Loyola (1491-1556).

See Nos. 935-942.

On designs A129a text under Paraguay is different from those of design A185b (Nos. 939-942).

Arms Type of 1946

1958-64 — Litho. — Perf. 10, 11

No.	Type	Value	Description	Unused	Used
525	A110	45c	gray olive	2.40	1.40
526	A110	50c	rose vio	1.50	1.40
527	A110	70c	lt brn ('59)	2.40	1.40
527A	A110	90c	vio blue	2.40	1.40
528	A110	1g	violet	1.50	.70
529	A110	1.50g	lilac ('59)	1.75	1.40
529A	A110	2g	bister ('64)	6.00	4.00
530	A110	3g	ol bis ('59)	6.00	4.00
531	A110	4.50g	lt ultra ('59)	2.40	2.75
531A	A110	5g	rose red ('59)	1.25	1.40
531B	A110	10g	bl grn ('59)	2.40	1.40
532	A110	12.45g	yel green	3.50	4.00
533	A110	15g	dl orange	12.00	2.75
534	A110	30g	citron	3.50	2.75
535	A110	50g	brown red	2.40	1.40
536	A110	100g	gray vio	3.50	2.75
			Nos. 525-536 (16)	54.90	34.90

Pres. Alfredo Stroessner — A130

Wmk. 320

1958, Aug. 15 — Litho. — Perf. 13½

Center in Slate

No.	Type	Value	Description	Unused	Used
537	A130	10c	sal pink	.35	*.30*
538	A130	15c	violet	.35	*.30*
539	A130	25c	yel grn	.35	*.30*
540	A130	30c	light fawn	.35	*.30*
541	A130	50c	rose car	.45	.30
542	A130	75c	light ultra	.45	.30
543	A130	5g	lt bl grn	.65	.50
544	A130	10g	brown	1.25	.50
			Nos. 537-544,C246-C251 (14)	27.35	17.80

Re-election of President General Alfredo Stroessner.

Nos. 491-497 Srchd. in Red

Perf. 12½x12, 12x12½

1959, May 14 — Engr. — Unwmk.

No.	Type	Value	Description	Unused	Used
545	A125	1.50g	on 5c org yel	.30	*.50*
546	A125	1.50g	on 20c ol bis	.30	*.50*
547	A126	1.50g	on 50c lt red brn	.30	*.50*
548	A126	3g	on 2.50g ol	.30	*.50*
549	A125	6.25g	on 5g yel brn	.30	*.50*
550	A125	20g	on 15g bl grn	.85	*.80*
551	A126	30g	on 25g dp grn	1.25	*1.00*
			Nos. 545-551,C252-C259 (15)	19.15	12.30

The surcharge is made to fit the stamps. Counterfeits of surcharge exist.

Goalkeeper Catching Soccer Ball — A131

1960, Mar. 18 — Photo. — Perf. 12½

No.	Type	Value	Description	Unused	Used
556	A131	30c	brt red & bl grn	.50	.30
557	A131	50c	plum & dk bl	.50	.30
558	A131	75c	ol grn & org	.50	.30
559	A131	1.50g	dk vio & bl grn	.50	.30
			Nos. 556-559,C262-C264 (7)	4.50	2.25

Olympic Games of 1960.

WRY Emblem — A132

1960, Apr. 7 — Litho. — Perf. 11

No.	Type	Value	Description	Unused	Used
560	A132	25c	sal & yel grn	.75	.25
561	A132	50c	lt yel grn & red org	.75	.25
562	A132	70c	lt brn & lil rose	.90	.25
563	A132	1.50g	lt bl & ultra	.90	.25
564	A132	3g	gray & bis brn	1.75	.45
			Nos. 560-564,C265-C268 (9)	12.00	4.75

World Refugee Year, July 1, 1959-June 30, 1960 (1st issue).

UN Emblem and Dove — A133

UN Declaration of Human Rights: 3g, Hand holding scales. 6g, Hands breaking chains. 20g, Flame.

1960, Apr. 21 — Perf. 12½x13

No.	Type	Value	Description	Unused	Used
565	A133	1g	dk car & bl	.50	.25
566	A133	3g	lt blue & org	.50	.25
567	A133	6g	gray grn & sal	.65	.25
568	A133	20g	ver & yel	.90	.25
			Nos. 565-568,C269-C271 (7)	4.75	2.20

Miniature sheets exist, perf. and imperf., containing one each of Nos. 565-568, all printed in purple and orange. Values: perf. $5; imperf. $15.

Flags of UN and Paraguay and UN Emblem — A134

Perf. 13x13½

1960, Oct. 24 — Photo. — Unwmk.

No.	Type	Value	Description	Unused	Used
569	A134	30c	lt bl, red & bl	.50	.30
570	A134	75c	yel, red & bl	.50	.30
571	A134	90c	pale lil, red & bl	.50	.30
			Nos. 569-571,C272-C273 (5)	2.90	1.50

15th anniversary of the United Nations.

International Bridge, Arms of Brazil, Paraguay — A135

1961, Jan. 26 — Litho. — Perf. 14

No.	Type	Value	Description	Unused	Used
572	A135	15c	green	.65	.50
573	A135	30c	dull blue	.65	.50
574	A135	50c	orange	.65	.50
575	A135	75c	vio blue	.65	.50
576	A135	1g	violet	.65	.50
			Nos. 572-576,C274-C277 (9)	8.75	6.75

Inauguration of the International Bridge between Paraguay and Brazil.

Truck Carrying Logs — A136

90c, 2g, Logs on river barge. 1g, 5g, Radio tower.

Unwmk.

1961, Apr. 10 Photo. *Perf. 13*

577 A136 25c yel grn & rose car .30 .25
578 A136 90c blue & yel .30 .25
579 A136 1g car rose & org .30 .25
580 A136 2g ol grn & sal .30 .25
581 A136 5g lilac & emer .30 .25
Nos. 577-581,C278-C281 (9) 5.80 3.70

Paraguay's progress, "Paraguay en Marcha."

P. J. Caballero, José G. R. Francia, F. Yegros, Revolutionary Leaders — A137

1961, May 16 Litho. *Perf. 14½*

582 A137 30c green .55 .25
583 A137 50c lil rose .55 .25
584 A137 90c violet .55 .25
585 A137 1.50g Prus bl .55 .25
586 A137 3g olive bis .55 .25
587 A137 4g ultra .55 .25
588 A137 5g brown .55 .25
Nos. 582-588,C282-C287 (13) 13.25 7.90

150th anniv. of Independence (1st issue).

"Chaco Peace" — A138

1961, June 12 *Perf. 14x14½*

589 A138 25c vermilion .50 .40
590 A138 30c green .50 .40
591 A138 50c red brn .50 .40
592 A138 1g bright vio .50 .40
593 A138 2g dk bl gray .50 .40
Nos. 589-593,C288-C290 (8) 9.90 7.10

Chaco Peace; 150th anniv. of Independence (2nd issue).

Puma — A139

1961, Aug. 16 Unwmk. *Perf. 14*

594 A139 75c dull vio 1.10 1.00
595 A139 1.50g brown 1.10 1.00
596 A139 4.50g green 1.10 1.00
597 A139 10g Prus blue 1.10 1.00
Nos. 594-597,C291-C293 (7) 16.90 13.00

150th anniv. of Independence (3rd issue).

University Seal — A140

1961, Sept. 18 *Perf. 14x14½*

598 A140 15c ultra .50 .30
599 A140 25c dk red .50 .30
600 A140 75c bl grn .50 .30
601 A140 1g orange .50 .30
Nos. 598-601,C294-C296 (7) 5.20 2.80

Founding of the Catholic University in Asuncion; 150th anniv. of Independence (4th issue).

Hotel Guarani — A141

1961, Oct. 14 Litho. *Perf. 15*

602 A141 50c slate bl .55 *1.00*
603 A141 1g green .55 *1.00*
604 A141 4.50g lilac .55 *1.00*
Nos. 602-604,C297-C300 (7) 12.65 10.25

Opening of the Hotel Guarani; 150th anniv. of Independence (5th issue).

Tennis Racket and Balls in Flag Colors — A142

1961, Oct. 16 Litho. *Perf. 11*

605 A142 35c multi .80 .25
606 A142 75c multi .80 .25
607 A142 1.50g multi .80 .25
608 A142 2.25g multi .80 .25
609 A142 4g multi .80 .25
Nos. 605-609 (5) 4.00 1.25

28th South American Tennis Championships, Asuncion, Oct. 15-23 (1st issue). Some specialists question the status of this issue. See Nos. C301-C303.

Imperforates exist in changed colors as well as two imperf. souvenir sheets with stamps in changed colors. Values: stamps, set $27; souvenir sheets, pair $40.

Alan B. Shepard, First US Astronaut — A143

18.15g, 36g, 50g, Shepard, Saturn, horiz.

1961, Dec. 22 Litho. *Perf. 11*

610 A143 10c blue & brown .30 .25
611 A143 25c blue & car rose .30 .25
612 A143 50c blue & yel org .30 .25
613 A143 75c blue & green .30 .25
614 A143 18.15g green & blue *11.00 6.50*
615 A143 36g org & blue *11.00 6.50*
616 A143 50g car rose & blue *14.50 9.75*
a. Souvenir sheet of 1 40.00
Nos. 610-616 (7) 37.70 23.75

Nos. 614-616a are airmail.

Also exist imperf in different colors. Value, set $36, souvenir sheet $210.

Uprooted Oak Emblem — A145

1961, Dec. 30 Unwmk. *Perf. 11*

619 A145 10c ultra & lt bl .35 .25
620 A145 25c maroon & org .35 .25
621 A145 50c car rose & pink .35 .25
622 A145 75c dk bl & yel grn .35 .25
Nos. 619-622 (4) 1.40 1.00

World Refugee Year, 1959-60 (2nd issue). Imperforates in changed colors and souvenir sheets exist. Values: imperf. set of 7, $5; souvenir sheet, perf. or imperf., each $15. Some specialists question the status of this issue.

See Nos. C307-C309.

Europa — A146

Design: 20g, 50g, Dove.

1961, Dec. 31

623 A146 50c multicolored .40 .35
624 A146 75c multicolored .40 .35
625 A146 1g multicolored .40 .35
626 A146 1.50g multicolored .40 .35
627 A146 4.50g multicolored 1.00 .75
a. Souvenir sheet of 5, #623-627 21.00
628 A146 20g multicolored 22.00
629 A146 50g multicolored 25.00
a. Souvenir sheet of 1 90.00
Nos. 623-629 (7) 49.60 2.15

Nos. 628-629 are airmail.

Imperforates in changed colors exist. Values: set, $67.50; souvenir sheets, pair, $100.

Tennis Player — A147

1962, Jan. 5 *Perf. 15x14½*

630 A147 35c Prussian bl .70 .25
631 A147 75c dark vio .70 .25
632 A147 1.50g red brn .70 .25
633 A147 2.25g emerald .70 .25
634 A147 4g carmine 2.40 .25
635 A147 12.45g red lil 2.40 .25
636 A147 20g bl grn 2.40 .40
637 A147 50g org brn 2.40 .65
Nos. 630-637 (8) 12.40 2.55

28th South American Tennis Championships, 1961 (2nd issue) and the 150th anniv. of Independence (6th issue).

Nos. 634-637 are airmail.

Scout Bugler — A148

Lord Baden-Powell — A148a

1962, Feb. 6 *Perf. 11*

Olive Green Center

638 A148 10c dp magenta .30 .25
639 A148 20c red orange .30 .25
640 A148 25c dk brown .30 .25
641 A148 30c emerald .30 .25
642 A148 50c indigo .30 .25
643 A148a 12.45g car rose & bl 1.90 .85
644 A148a 36g car rose & emer 5.25 2.40
645 A148a 50g car rose & org yel 7.25 3.25
Nos. 638-645 (8) 15.90 7.75

Issued to honor the Boy Scouts. Imperfs in changed colors exist and imperf souvenir sheets exist. Value, set $24, souvenir sheet $95. Some specialists question the status of this issue.

Nos. 643-645 are airmail.

Arms Type of 1946

1962-68 Litho. Wmk. 347

646 A110 50c steel bl ('63) 3.00 *2.00*
647 A110 70c dull lil ('63) 3.00 *2.00*
648 A110 1.50g violet ('63) 3.00 *1.00*
649 A110 3g dp bl ('68) 5.00 *2.00*
650 A110 4.50g redsh brn ('67) 5.00 *1.00*
651 A110 5g lilac ('64) 5.00 *2.00*
652 A110 10g car rose ('63) 10.00 *3.00*
653 A110 12.45g ultra 7.00 *3.00*
654 A110 15.45g org ver 10.00 *2.00*
655 A110 18.15g lilac 10.00 *2.00*
656 A110 20g lt brn ('63) 10.00 *2.00*
657 A110 50g dl red brn ('67) 10.00 *3.00*
658 A110 100g bl gray ('63) 3.00 *2.00*
Nos. 646-658 (13) 84.00 *27.00*

Map and Laurel Branch — A149

Design: 20g, 50g, Hands holding globe.

Perf. 14x14½

1962, Apr. 14 Unwmk.

659 A149 50c ocher .50 .30
660 A149 75c vio blue .50 .30
661 A149 1g purple .50 .30
662 A149 1.50g brt grn .50 .30
663 A149 4.50g vermilion .50 .30
664 A149 20g lil rose .50 .30
665 A149 50g orange 1.50 .90
Nos. 659-665 (7) 4.50 2.70

Day of the Americas; 150th anniv. of Independence (7th issue).

Nos. 664-665 are airmail.

UN Emblem — A150

Design: #670-673, UN Headquarters, NYC.

1962, Apr. 23 *Perf. 15*

666 A150 50c bister brn .45 .25
667 A150 75c dp claret .45 .25
668 A150 1g Prussian bl .45 .25
669 A150 2g orange brn 2.40 .25
670 A150 12.45g dl vio 2.40 .35
671 A150 18.15g ol grn 2.40 .65
672 A150 23.40g brn red 2.40 .95
673 A150 30g carmine 2.40 1.10
Nos. 666-673 (8) 13.35 4.05

UN; Independence, 150th anniv. (8th issue).

Nos. 670-673 are airmail.

Malaria Eradication Emblem and Mosquito — A151

Design: 75c, 1g, 1.50g, Microscope, anopheles mosquito and eggs. 3g, 4g, Malaria eradication emblem. 12.45g, 18.15g, 36g, Mosquito, UN emblem and microscope.

Perf. 14x13½

1962, May 23 Wmk. 346

674 A151 30c pink, ultra & blk .45 .30
675 A151 50c bis, grn & blk .45 .30
676 A151 75c rose red, blk & bis .45 .30
677 A151 1g brt grn, blk & bis .45 .30
678 A151 1.50g dl red brn, blk & bis .45 .30
679 A151 3g bl, red & blk .45 .30
680 A151 4g grn, red & blk .45 .30
681 A151 12.45g ol bis, grn & blk .45 .30
682 A151 18.15g rose lil, red & blk .90 .45
683 A151 36g rose red, vio bl & blk 2.25 1.10
Nos. 674-683 (10) 6.75 3.95

WHO drive to eradicate malaria.

Imperforates exist in changed colors. Value, $12.50. Also, two souvenir sheets exist, one containing one copy of No. 683, the other an imperf 36g in blue, red & black. Value, each $21.

Some specialists question the status of this issue.

Nos. 679-683 are airmail.

Stadium
A152

Soccer Players and Globe
A152a

Perf. 13½x14

1962, July 28 Litho. Wmk. 346

No.	Type	Value	Color	Unused	Used
684	A152	15c	yel & dk brn	.30	.25
685	A152	25c	brt grn & dk brn	.30	.25
686	A152	30c	lt vio & dk brn	.30	.25
687	A152	40c	dl org & dk brn	.30	.25
688	A152	50c	brt yel grn & dk brn	.30	.25
689	A152a	12.45g	brt rose, blk & vio	1.00	.35
690	A152a	18.15g	lt red brn, blk & vio	1.40	.45
691	A152a	36g	gray grn, blk & brn	3.25	.80
			Nos. 684-691 (8)	7.15	2.85

World Soccer Championships, Chile, May 30-June 17.

Imperfs exist. Value $11. A souvenir sheet containing one No. 691 exists, both perforated and imperf. Value, $25 and $60, respectively.

Some specialists question the status of this issue.

Nos. 689-691 are airmail.

Freighter
A153

Ship's Wheel
A153a

Designs: Various merchantmen. 44g, Like 12.45g with diagonal colorless band in background.

Perf. 14½x15

1962, July 31 Unwmk.

No.	Type	Value	Color	Unused	Used
692	A153	30c	bister brn	.30	.25
693	A153	90c	slate bl	.30	.25
694	A153	1.50g	brown red	.30	.25
695	A153	2g	green	.30	.25
696	A153	4.20g	vio blue	.35	.25

Perf. 15x14½

No.	Type	Value	Color	Unused	Used
697	A153a	12.45g	dk red	5.75	.25
698	A153a	44g	blue	5.75	.35
			Nos. 692-698 (7)	13.05	1.85

Issued to honor the merchant marine.

Nos. 697-698 are airmail.

Friendship 7 over South America
A154

Lt. Col. John H. Glenn, Jr., Lt. Cmdr. Scott Carpenter
A154a

Perf. 13½x14

1962, Sept. 4 Litho. Wmk. 346

No.	Type	Value	Color	Unused	Used
699	A154	15c	dk bl & bis	1.25	.45
700	A154	25c	vio brn & bis	1.25	.45
701	A154	30c	dk sl grn & bis	1.25	.45
702	A154	40c	dk gray & bis	1.25	.45
703	A154	50c	dk vio & bis	1.25	.45
704	A154a	12.45g	car lake & gray	1.25	.45
705	A154a	18.15g	red lil & gray	1.25	.45
706	A154a	36g	dl cl & gray	1.25	.80
			Nos. 699-706 (8)	10.00	3.95

U.S. manned space flights. A souvenir sheet containing one No. 706 exists. Value $20.

Imperfs in changed colors exist. Values: set, $18; souvenir sheet $60. Some specialists question the status of this issue.

Nos. 704-706 are airmail.

Discus Thrower — A155

Olympic flame &: 12.45g, Melbourne, 1956. 18.15g, Rome, 1960. 36g, Tokyo, 1964.

1962, Oct. 1 Litho.

No.	Type	Value	Color	Unused	Used
707	A155	15c	blk & yel	1.50	.25
708	A155	25c	blk & lt grn	1.50	.25
709	A155	30c	blk & pink	1.50	.25
710	A155	40c	blk & pale vio	1.50	.25
711	A155	50c	blk & lt bl	1.50	.25
712	A155	12.45g	brt grn, lt grn & choc	1.75	.75
713	A155	18.15g	ol brn, yel & choc	1.75	.75
714	A155	36g	rose red, pink & choc	3.00	1.00
			Nos. 707-714 (8)	14.00	3.75

Olympic Games from Amsterdam 1928 to Tokyo 1964. Each stamp is inscribed with date and place of various Olympic Games. A souvenir sheet containing one No. 714 exists. Value $12.

Imperfs in changed colors exist. Values: set, $27.50; souvenir sheet $125.

Some specialists question the status of this issue.

Nos. 712-714 are airmail.

Peace Dove and Cross — A156

Dove Symbolizing Holy Ghost — A156a

Perf. 14½

1962, Oct. 11 Litho. Unwmk.

No.	Type	Value	Color	Unused	Used
715	A156	50c	olive	.30	.25
716	A156	70c	dark blue	.30	.25
717	A156	1.50g	bister	.30	.25
718	A156	2g	violet	.30	.25
719	A156	3g	brick red	.30	.25
720	A156a	5g	vio bl	1.40	.25
721	A156a	10g	brt grn	1.40	.25
722	A156a	12.45g	lake	1.40	.25
723	A156a	18.15g	orange	1.40	.30
724	A156a	23.40g	violet	1.40	.40
725	A156a	36g	rose red	1.40	.50
			Nos. 715-725 (11)	9.90	3.20

Vatican II, the 21st Ecumenical Council of the Roman Catholic Church, which opened Oct. 11, 1962.

Nos. 720-725 are airmail.

Europa — A157

1962, Dec. 17 Perf. 11

No.	Type	Value	Color	Unused	Used
726	A157	4g	yel, red & brn	.65	.50
727	A157	36g	multi, diff.	12.50	3.00
a.			Souvenir sheet of 2, #726-727	*25.00*	
			Nos. 726-727 (2)	13.15	3.50

No. 727 is airmail.

Exist imperf. in changed colors. Values: set, $45; souvenir sheet, $70.

Solar System — A158

12.45g, 36g, 50g, Inner planets, Jupiter & rocket.

Perf. 14x13½

1962, Dec. 17 Wmk. 346

No.	Type	Value	Color	Unused	Used
728	A158	10c	org & purple	.50	.35
729	A158	20c	org & brn vio	.50	.35
730	A158	25c	org & dk vio	.50	.35
731	A158	30c	org & ultra	.50	.35
732	A158	50c	org & dull green	.50	.35
733	A158	12.45g	org & brown	3.25	1.25
734	A158	36g	org & blue	6.25	2.00
735	A158	50g	org & green	12.50	4.25
a.			Souvenir sheet of 1	17.50	
			Nos. 728-735 (8)	24.50	9.25

Nos. 733-735 are airmail.

Exist imperf. in changed colors. Values: set, $25; souvenir sheet, $80.

The following stamps exist imperf. in different colors: Nos. 736-743a, 744-751a, 752-759a, 760-766a, 775-782a, 783-790a, 791-798a, 799-805a, 806-813a, 814-821a, 828-835a, 836-843, 841a, 850-857a, 858-865a, 871-878, 876a, 887-894a, 895-902, 900a, 903-910a, 911-918a, 919-926a, 927-934a, 943-950a, 951-958a, 959-966a, 978-985a, 986-993a, 994-1001a, 1002-1003, 1003d, 1004-1007a, 1051-1059, B12-B19.

Pierre de Coubertin (1836-1937), Founder of Modern Olympic Games — A159

Summer Olympic Games sites and: 15c, Athens, 1896. 25c, Paris, 1900. 30c, St. Louis, 1904. 40c, London, 1908. 50c, Stockholm, 1912. 12.45g, No games, 1916. 18.15g, Antwerp, 1920. 36g, Paris, 1924.

12.45g, 18.15g, 36g, Torch bearer & stadium.

Perf. 14x13½

1963, Feb. 16 Wmk. 346

No.	Type	Value	Color	Unused	Used
736	A159	15c	multicolored	.35	.25
737	A159	25c	multicolored	.35	.25
738	A159	30c	multicolored	.35	.25
739	A159	40c	multicolored	.35	.25
740	A159	50c	multicolored	.35	.25
741	A159	12.45g	multicolored	4.00	3.50
742	A159	18.15g	multicolored	4.00	3.50
743	A159	36g	multicolored	5.00	4.50
a.			Souvenir sheet of 1	35.00	
			Nos. 736-743 (8)	14.75	12.75

Nos. 741-743a are airmail.

Exist imperf. in changed colors. Values: set, $32; souvenir sheet $120.

Walter M. Schirra, US Astronaut — A160

Design: 12.45g, 36g, 50g, Schirra.

1963, Mar. 16 Perf. 13½x14

No.	Type	Value	Color	Unused	Used
744	A160	10c	brn org & blk	.35	.25
745	A160	20c	car & blk	.35	.25
746	A160	25c	lake & blk	.35	.25
747	A160	30c	ver & blk	.35	.25
748	A160	50c	mag & blk	.35	.25
749	A160	12.45g	bl blk & lake	4.50	4.25
750	A160	36g	dl gray vio & lake	4.50	4.25
751	A160	50g	dk grn bl & lake	5.75	5.25
a.			Souvenir sheet of 1	15.00	
			Nos. 744-751 (8)	16.50	15.00

Nos. 749-751a are airmail.

Exist imperf. in changed colors. Values: set, $27; souvenir sheet, $125.

Winter Olympics — A161

Games sites and: 10c, Chamonix, 1924. 20c, St. Moritz, 1928. 25c, Lake Placid, 1932. 30c, St. Moritz, 1948. 12.45g, Oslo, 1952. 36g, Cortina d'Ampezzo, 1956. 50g, Squaw Valley, 1960.

12.45g, 36g, 50g, Snowflake.

1963, May 16 Perf. 14x13½

No.	Type	Value	Color	Unused	Used
752	A161	10c	multicolored	.35	.25
753	A161	20c	multicolored	.35	.25
754	A161	25c	multicolored	.35	.25
755	A161	30c	multicolored	.35	.25
756	A161	50c	multicolored	.35	.25
757	A161	12.45g	multicolored	4.75	3.75
758	A161	36g	multicolored	4.75	3.75
759	A161	50g	multicolored	5.75	4.50
a.			Souvenir sheet of 1	25.00	25.00
			Nos. 752-759 (8)	17.00	13.25

Nos. 757-759a are airmail.

Exist imperf. in changed colors. Values: set, $29.50; souvenir sheet, $175.

Freedom from Hunger — A162

1963, May 31 Perf. 13½x14, 14x13½

No.	Type	Value	Color	Unused	Used
760	A162	10c	yel grn & brn	.35	.25
761	A162	25c	lt bl & brn	.35	.25
762	A162	50c	lt grn bl & brn	.35	.25
763	A162	75c	lt lil & brn	.35	.25
764	A162	18.15g	yel org & brn	5.50	1.75
765	A162	36g	lt bl grn & brn	5.50	1.75
766	A162	50g	bis & brn	5.50	1.75
a.			Souvenir sheet of 1	18.00	
			Nos. 760-766 (7)	17.90	6.25

Nos. 760-763 are vert. Nos. 764-766a are airmail.

Exist imperf. in changed colors. Values: set, $19; souvenir sheet, $24.

Pres. Alfredo Stroessner — A163

1963, Aug. 6 Wmk. 347 Perf. 11

No.	Type	Value	Color	Unused	Used
767	A163	50c	ol gray & sep	1.10	*2.50*
768	A163	75c	buff & sepia	1.10	*2.50*
769	A163	1.50g	lt lil & sep	1.10	*2.50*
770	A163	3g	emer & sepia	1.10	1.00
771	A163	12.45g	pink & claret	5.50	1.00
772	A163	18.15g	pink & grn	5.50	1.00
773	A163	36g	pink & vio	5.50	1.00
			Nos. 767-773 (7)	20.90	11.50

Third presidential term of Alfredo Stroessner. A 36g imperf. souvenir sheet exists. Value, $20.

Nos. 771-773 are airmail.

Souvenir Sheet

Dag Hammarskjold, UN Secretary General — A164

1963, Aug. 21 Unwmk. *Imperf.*

No.	Type	Value	Description	Unused	Used
774	A164	2g	Sheet of 2	26.00	26.00

Project Mercury Flight of L. Gordon Cooper — A165

12.45g, 18.15g, 50g, L. Gordon Cooper, vert.

Perf. 14x13½, 13½x14

1963, Aug. 23 Litho. Wmk. 346

No.	Type	Value	Color	Unused	Used
775	A165	15c	brn & orange	.35	.25
776	A165	25c	brn & blue	.35	.25
777	A165	30c	brn & violet	.35	.25
778	A165	40c	brn & green	.35	.25
779	A165	50c	brn & red vio	.35	.25
780	A165	12.45g	brn & bl grn	4.00	2.50
781	A165	18.15g	brn & blue	4.00	2.50
782	A165	50g	brn & pink	4.00	2.50
a.			Souvenir sheet of 1	25.00	
			Nos. 775-782 (8)	13.75	8.75

Nos. 780-782 are airmail.

Exist imperf. in changed colors. Values: set, $24; souvenir sheet, $32.

1964 Winter Olympics, Innsbruck — A166

Design: 12.45g, 18.15g, 50g, Innsbruck Games emblem, vert.

Perf. 14x13½, 13½x14

1963, Oct. 28 **Unwmk.**

783 A166 15c choc & red .35 .25
784 A166 25c gray grn & red .35 .25
785 A166 30c plum & red .35 .25
786 A166 40c sl grn & red .35 .25
787 A166 50c dp bl & red .35 .25
788 A166 12.45g sep & red 4.25 1.75
789 A166 18.15g grn bl & red 4.25 1.75
790 A166 50g tan & red 4.25 1.75
a. Souvenir sheet of 1 20.00
Nos. 783-790 (8) 14.50 6.50

Nos. 788-790 are airmail.
Exist imperf. in changed colors. Values: set, $26; souvenir sheet, $26.

1964 Summer Olympics, Tokyo — A167

12.45g, 18.15g, 50g, Tokyo games emblem.

1964, Jan. 8 ***Perf. 13½x14***

791 A167 15c blue & red .35 .25
792 A167 25c org & red .35 .25
793 A167 30c tan & red .35 .25
794 A167 40c vio brn & red .35 .25
795 A167 50c grn bl & red .35 .25
796 A167 12.45g vio & red 2.50 1.60
797 A167 18.15g brn & red 2.50 1.60
798 A167 50g grn bl & red 2.50 1.60
a. Souvenir sheet of 1 30.00
Nos. 791-798 (8) 9.25 6.05

Nos. 796-798 are airmail.
Exist imperf. in changed colors. Values: set, $22; souvenir sheet, $42.50.

Intl. Red Cross, Cent. — A168

Designs: 10c, Helicopter. 25c, Space ambulance. 30c, Red Cross symbol, vert. 50c, Clara Barton, founder of American Red Cross, vert. 18.15g, Jean Henri Dunant, founder of Intl. Red Cross, vert. 36g, Red Cross space hospital, space ambulance. 50g, Plane, ship, ambulance, vert.

1964, Feb. 4 ***Perf. 14x13½, 13½x14***

799 A168 10c vio brn & red .30 .25
800 A168 25c bl grn & red .30 .25
801 A168 30c dk bl & red .30 .25
802 A168 50c ol blk & red .30 .25
803 A168 18.15g choc, red, & pink 1.90 .80
804 A168 36g grn bl & red 2.75 1.10
805 A168 50g vio & red 4.25 2.00
a. Souvenir sheet of 1 15.00 11.00
Nos. 799-805 (7) 10.10 4.90

Nos. 803-805 are airmail.
Exist imperf. in changed colors. Values: set, $52; souvenir sheet, $21.

Space Research — A169

15c, 25c, 30c, Gemini spacecraft rendezvous with Agena rocket. 40c, 50c, Future Apollo and Lunar Modules, vert. 12.45g, 18.15g, 50g, Telstar communications satellite, Olympic rings, vert.

1964, Mar. 11

806 A169 15c vio & tan .35 .25
807 A169 25c grn & tan .35 .25
808 A169 30c bl & tan .35 .25
809 A169 40c brt bl & red .35 .25
810 A169 50c sl grn & red .35 .25
811 A169 12.45g dk bl & tan 3.50 2.00
812 A169 18.15g dk grn bl & tan 3.50 2.00
813 A169 50g dp vio & tan 3.50 2.00
a. Souvenir sheet of 1 15.00 13.00
Nos. 806-813 (8) 12.25 7.25

1964 Summer Olympic Games, Tokyo (Nos. 811-813a). Nos. 811-813a are airmail.
Exist imperf. in changed colors. Values: set, $27; souvenir sheet, $18.

Rockets and Satellites — A170

15c, 25c, Apollo command module mockup. 30c, Tiros 7 weather satellite, vert. 40c, 50c, Ranger 6. 12.45g, 18.15g, 50g, Saturn I lift-off, vert.

1964, Apr. 25

814 A170 15c brn & tan .35 .25
815 A170 25c vio & tan .35 .25
816 A170 30c Prus bl & lake .35 .25
817 A170 40c ver & tan .35 .25
818 A170 50c ultra & tan .35 .25
819 A170 12.45g grn bl & choc 1.90 .85
820 A170 18.15g bl & choc 3.00 1.60
821 A170 50g lil rose & choc 4.75 2.50
a. Souvenir sheet of 1 13.00
Nos. 814-821 (8) 11.40 6.20

Nos. 819-821a are airmail.
Exist imperf. in changed colors. Values: set, $29; souvenir sheet, $18.

Popes Paul VI, John XXIII and St. Peter's, Rome — A171

Design: 12.45g, 18.15g, 36g, Asuncion Cathedral, Popes Paul VI and John XXIII.

1964, May 23 **Wmk. 347**

822 A171 1.50g claret & org .30 .25
823 A171 3g claret & dk grn .30 .25
824 A171 4g claret & bister .30 .25
825 A171 12.45g sl grn & lem 1.25 1.00
826 A171 18.15g pur & lem 1.25 1.00
827 A171 36g vio bl & lem 2.50 2.00
Nos. 822-827 (6) 5.90 4.75

National holiday of St. Maria Auxiliadora (Our Lady of Perpetual Help).
Nos. 825-827 are airmail.

United Nations — A172

Designs: 15c, John F. Kennedy. 25c, 12.45g, Pope Paul VI and Patriarch Atenagoras. 30c, Eleanor Roosevelt, Chairman of UN Commission on Human Rights. 40c, Relay, Syncom and Telstar satellites. 50c, Echo 2 satellite. 18.15g, U Thant, UN Sec. Gen. 50g, Rocket, flags of Europe, vert.

Perf. 14x13½, 14 (15c, 25c, 12.45g)

1964, July 30 **Unwmk.**

Size: 35x35mm (#830, 834), 40x29mm (#831-832, 835)

828 A172 15c blk & brn .30 .25
829 A172 25c blk, bl & red .30 .25
830 A172 30c blk & ver .30 .25
831 A172 40c dk bl & sep .30 .25
832 A172 50c vio & car .30 .25
833 A172 12.45g blk, grn & red 1.20 .75
834 A172 18.15g blk & grn 1.20 .75

Perf. 13½x14

835 A172 50g multicolored 2.50 1.75
a. Souvenir sheet of 1 32.50
Nos. 828-835 (8) 6.40 4.50

Nos. 833-835a are airmail.
Exist imperf. in changed colors. Values: set, $17.50; souvenir sheet, $35.

Space Achievements — A173

Designs: 10c, 30c, Ranger 7, Moon, vert. 15c, 12.45+6g, Wernher von Braun looking through periscope, vert. 20c, 20+10g, John F. Kennedy, rockets, vert. 40c, 18.15+9g, Rockets, von Braun.

1964, Sept. 12 ***Perf. 12½x12***

836 A173 10c bl & blk .30 .25
837 A173 15c yel grn & brt pink .30 .25
838 A173 20c yel org & bl .30 .25
839 A173 30c mag & blk .30 .25
840 A173 40c yel org, bl & blk .30 .25
841 A173 12.45g +6g red & bl 2.90 1.60
a. Souvenir sheet of 2, #840-841 24.00
842 A173 18.15g +9g grn bl, brn & blk 2.90 1.60
843 A173 20g +10g red & bl 4.00 2.40
Nos. 836-843 (8) 11.30 6.85

Nos. 841-843 are airmail.
Exist imperf. in changed colors. Values: set, $24.50; souvenir sheet, $40.

Coats of Arms of Paraguay and France — A174

Designs: 3g, 12.45g, 36g, Presidents Stroessner and de Gaulle. 18.15g, Coats of Arms of Paraguay and France.

1964, Oct. 6 **Wmk. 347**

844 A174 1.50g brown .55 .30
845 A174 3g ultramarine .55 .30
846 A174 4g gray .55 .30
847 A174 12.45g lilac .65 .40
848 A174 18.15g bl grn 1.00 .60
849 A174 36g magenta 4.00 1.75
Nos. 844-849 (6) 7.30 3.65

Visit of Pres. Charles de Gaulle of France.
Nos. 847-849 are airmail.

Boy Scout Jamborees A175

Boy Scout Emblem — A175a

Designs: 10c, Argentina, 1961. 15c, Peru, canceled. 20c, Chile, 1959. 30c, Brazil, 1954. 50c, Uruguay, 1957. 12.45g, Brazil, 1960. 18.15g, Venezuela, 1964. 36g, Brazil, 1963.
15c, 18.15g, Lord Robert Baden-Powell (1857-1941), Boy Scouts founder.

1965, Jan. 15 **Unwmk.** ***Perf. 14***

850 A175 10c multicolored .30 .25
851 A175 15c multicolored .30 .25
852 A175a 20c multicolored .30 .25
853 A175a 30c multicolored .30 .25
854 A175 50c multicolored .30 .25
855 A175a 12.45g multicolored 1.90 1.50
856 A175 18.15g multicolored 2.00 1.40
857 A175 36g multicolored 3.75 2.50
a. Souvenir sheet of 1, perf. 12x12½ 25.00
Nos. 850-857 (8) 9.15 6.65

Nos. 855-857a are airmail.
Exist imperf. in changed colors. Values: set, $27; souvenir sheet, $85.

A176

Olympic and Paraguayan Medals: 25c, John F. Kennedy. 30c, Medal of Peace and Justice, reverse. 40c, Gens. Stroessner and DeGaulle, profiles. 50c, 18.15g, DeGaulle and Stroessner, in uniform. 12.45g, Medal of Peace and Justice, obverse.

Litho. & Embossed

1965, Mar. 30 ***Perf. 13½x13***

Background Color

858 A176 15c dull turq grn .30 .25
859 A176 25c pink .30 .30
860 A176 30c dull pale grn .30 .30

Perf. 12½x12

861 A176 40c dull pale org .30 .30
862 A176 50c grnsh gray .30 .30
863 A176 12.45g multicolored 2.75 1.50
864 A176 18.15g multicolored 3.50 1.75
865 A176 50g multicolored 5.25 1.75
a. Souv. sheet of 1, perf. 13½x13 35.00
Nos. 858-865 (8) 13.00 6.45

Nos. 863-865a are airmail. Medal on Nos. 858-862 is gold foil.
Exist imperf. in changed colors. Values: set, $22; souvenir sheet, $60.

Overprinted in Black — A177

Design: Map of Americas.

1965, Apr. 26 **Wmk. 347** ***Perf. 11***

866 A177 1.50g dull grn .60 .40
867 A177 3g car red .60 .40
868 A177 4g dark blue .60 .40
869 A177 12.45g brn & blk .60 .40
870 A177 36g brt lil & blk 1.50 .70
Nos. 866-870 (5) 3.90 2.30

Centenary of National Epic. Not issued without overprint.
Nos. 869-870 are airmail.

Scientists — A178

Unwmk.

1965, June 5 **Litho.** ***Perf. 14***

871 A178 10c Newton .30 .25
872 A178 15c Copernicus .30 .25
873 A178 20c Galileo .30 .25
874 A178 30c like #871 .30 .25
875 A178 40c Einstein .30 .25
876 A178 12.45g +6g like #873 1.50 .50
a. Souvenir sheet of 2, #875-876 21.00
877 A178 18.15g +9g like #875 2.25 1.00
878 A178 20g +10g like #872 2.50 1.50
Nos. 871-878 (8) 7.75 4.25

Nos. 876-878 are airmail.
Exist imperf. in changed colors. Values: set, $22; souvenir sheet, $21.

Cattleya Warscewiczii A179

Ceibo Tree A179a

1965, June 28 Unwmk. *Perf. 14½*

No.	Type	Denom.	Color	Unused	Used
879	A179	20c	purple	.30	.25
880	A179	30c	blue	.30	.25
881	A179	90c	bright mag	.30	.25
882	A179	1.50g	green	.30	.25
883	A179a	3g	brn red	1.60	.90
884	A179a	4g	green	2.10	.90
885	A179	4.50g	orange	2.10	.90
886	A179a	66g	brn org	4.25	1.40
			Nos. 879-886 (8)	11.25	5.10

150th anniv. of Independence (1811-1961).
Nos. 883-884, 886 are airmail.

John F. Kennedy and Winston Churchill A180

Designs: 15c, Kennedy, PT 109. 25c, Kennedy family. 30c, 12.45g, Churchill, Parliament building. 40c, Kennedy, Alliance for Progress emblem. 50c, 18.15g, Kennedy, rocket launch at Cape Canaveral. 50g, John Glenn, Kennedy, Lyndon Johnson examining Friendship 7.

1965, Sept. 4 *Perf. 12x12½*

No.	Type	Denom.	Color	Unused	Used
887	A180	15c	bl & brn	.30	.25
888	A180	25c	red & brn	.30	.25
889	A180	30c	vio & blk	.30	.25
890	A180	40c	org & sep	.30	.25
891	A180	50c	bl grn & sep	.30	.25
892	A180	12.45g	yel & blk	1.75	.75
893	A180	18.15g	car & blk	2.50	1.20
894	A180	50g	grn & blk	4.25	1.75
a.			Souvenir sheet of 1	21.00	
			Nos. 887-894 (8)	10.00	4.95

Nos. 892-894a are airmail.
Exist imperf. in changed colors. Values: set, $17; souvenir sheet, $21.

ITU, Cent. A181

Satellites: 10c, 40c, Ranger 7 transmitting to Earth. 15c, 20g+10g, Syncom, Olympic rings. 20c, 18.15g+9g, Early Bird. 30c, 12.45g+6g, Relay, Syncom, Telstar, Echo 2.

1965, Sept. 30

No.	Type	Denom.	Color	Unused	Used
895	A181	10c	dull bl & sep	.30	.25
896	A181	15c	lilac & sepia	.30	.25
897	A181	20c	ol grn & sep	.30	.25
898	A181	30c	blue & sepia	.30	.25
899	A181	40c	grn & sep	.30	.25
900	A181	12.45g	+6g ver & sep	1.50	.50
a.			Souvenir sheet of 2, #899-900	23.00	
901	A181	18.15g	+9g org & sep	2.25	.75
902	A181	20g	+10g vio & sep	3.75	1.25
			Nos. 895-902 (8)	9.00	3.75

Nos. 900-902 are airmail.
Exist imperf. in changed colors. Values: set, $19.50; souvenir sheet, $29.

Pope Paul VI, Visit to UN — A182

Designs: 10c, 50c, Pope Paul VI, U Thant, A. Fanfani. 15c, 12.45g, Pope Paul VI, Lyndon B. Johnson. 20c, 36g, Early Bird satellite, globe, papal arms. 30c, 18.15g, Pope Paul VI, Unisphere.

1965, Nov. 19

No.	Type	Denom.	Color	Unused	Used
903	A182	10c	multicolored	.30	.25
904	A182	15c	multicolored	.30	.25
905	A182	20c	multicolored	.30	.25
906	A182	30c	multicolored	.30	.25
907	A182	50c	multicolored	.30	.25
908	A182	12.45g	multicolored	1.00	.50
909	A182	18.15g	multicolored	1.75	1.25
910	A182	36g	multicolored	3.50	1.75
a.			Souvenir sheet of 1	23.00	
			Nos. 903-910 (8)	7.75	4.75

Nos. 908-910a are airmail.
Exist imperf. in changed colors. Values: set, $27; souvenir sheet, $34.

Astronauts and Space Exploration A183

15c, 50g, Edward White walking in space, 6/3/65. 25c, 18.15g, Gemini 7 & 8 docking, 12/16-18/65. 30c, Virgil I. Grissom, John W. Young, 3/23/65. 40c, 50c, Edward White, James McDivitt, 6/3/65. 12.45g, Photographs of lunar surface.

1966, Feb. 19 *Perf. 14*

No.	Type	Denom.	Color	Unused	Used
911	A183	15c	multicolored	.30	.25
912	A183	25c	multicolored	.30	.25
913	A183	30c	multicolored	.30	.25
914	A183	40c	multicolored	.30	.25
915	A183	50c	multicolored	.30	.25
916	A183	12.45g	multicolored	1.40	1.10
917	A183	18.15g	multicolored	2.40	1.90
918	A183	50g	multicolored	4.25	3.25
a.			Souvenir sheet of 1	45.00	
			Nos. 911-918 (8)	9.55	7.50

Nos. 916-918a are airmail.
Exist imperf. in changed colors. Values: set, $14; souvenir sheet, $33.

Events of 1965 A184

10c, Meeting of Pope Paul VI & Cardinal Spellman, 10/4/65. 15c, Intl. Phil. Exposition, Vienna. 20c, OAS, 75th anniv. 30c, 36g, Intl. Quiet Sun Year, 1964-65. 50c, 18.15g, Saturn rockets at NY World's Fair. 12.45g, UN Intl. Cooperation Year.

1966, Mar. 9

No.	Type	Denom.	Color	Unused	Used
919	A184	10c	multicolored	.30	.25
920	A184	15c	multicolored	.30	.25
921	A184	20c	multicolored	.30	.25
922	A184	30c	multicolored	.30	.25
923	A184	50c	multicolored	.30	.25
924	A184	12.45g	multicolored	1.40	.75
925	A184	18.15g	multicolored	2.40	1.50
926	A184	36g	multicolored	4.75	1.25
a.			Souvenir sheet of 1	25.00	
			Nos. 919-926 (8)	10.05	4.75

Nos. 924-926a are airmail.
Exist imperf. in changed colors. Values: set, $27; souvenir sheet, $32.50.

1968 Summer Olympics, Mexico City — A185

15c, God of Death. 20c, Aztec calendar stone. 50c, Zapotec deity.

Perf. 12½x12 (Nos. 927, 929, 931, 933), 13½x13

1966, Apr. 1

No.	Type	Denom.	Color	Unused	Used
927	A185	10c	shown	.30	.25
928	A185	15c	multi	.30	.25
929	A185	20c	multi	.30	.25
930	A185	30c	like No. 928	.30	.25
931	A185	50c	multi	.30	.25
932	A185	12.45g	like No. 931	1.75	.75
933	A185	18.15g	like No. 927	2.75	1.25
934	A185	36g	like No. 929	6.00	3.00
a.			Souvenir sheet of 1	17.50	
			Nos. 927-934 (8)	12.00	6.25

Nos. 932-934a are airmail.
Exist imperf. in changed colors. Values: set, $17; souvenir sheet, $37.50.

A185a

St. Ignatius and San Ignacio Monastery A185b

1966, Apr. 20 Wmk. 347 *Perf. 11*

No.	Type	Denom.	Color	Unused	Used
935	A185a	15c	ultramarine	1.40	.50
936	A185a	25c	ultramarine	1.40	.50
937	A185a	75c	ultramarine	1.40	.50
938	A185a	90c	ultramarine	1.40	.50
939	A185b	3g	brown	1.40	.50
940	A185b	12.45g	sepia	1.40	.50
941	A185b	18.15g	sepia	1.40	.50
942	A185b	23.40g	sepia	1.40	.50
			Nos. 935-942 (8)	11.20	4.00

350th anniv. of the founding of San Ignacio Guazu Monastery.
Nos. 939-942 are airmail.
On designs A185b text under Paraguay is different from that of design A129a (No. 522)

A186

A186a

German Contributors in Space Research — A186b

Designs: 10c, 36g, Paraguay #835, C97, Germany #C40. 15c, 50c, 18.15g, 3rd stage of Europa 1 rocket. 20c, 12.45g, Hermann Oberth, jet propulsion engineer. 30c, Reinhold K. Tiling, builder of 1st German rocket, 1931, vert.

Perf. 12x12½ (Nos. 943, 950), 12½x12 (Nos. 945, 947, 949), 13½x13

1966, May 16 Unwmk.

No.	Type	Denom.	Color	Unused	Used
943	A186	10c	multicolored	.30	.25
944	A186a	15c	multicolored	.30	.25
945	A186b	20c	multicolored	.30	.25
946	A186b	30c	multicolored	.30	.25
947	A186a	50c	multicolored	.30	.25
948	A186b	12.45g	multicolored	1.90	.50
949	A186a	18.15g	multicolored	2.40	1.00
950	A186	36g	multicolored	4.50	2.25
a.			Souvenir sheet of 1, perf. 12x13½x13x13½	30.00	
			Nos. 943-950 (8)	10.30	5.00

Nos. 948-950a are airmail.
Exist imperf. in changed colors. Values: set, $27; souvenir sheet, $47.

Writers A187

1966, June 11 *Perf. 12x12½*

No.	Type	Denom.	Color	Unused	Used
951	A187	10c	Dante	.30	.25
952	A187	15c	Moliere	.30	.25
953	A187	20c	Goethe	.30	.25
954	A187	30c	Shakespeare	.30	.25
955	A187	50c	like #952	.30	.25
956	A187	12.45g	like #953	2.40	1.50
957	A187	18.15g	like #954	2.75	1.50
958	A187	36g	like #951	4.50	1.50
a.			Souvenir sheet of 1, perf. 13½x14	15.00	
			Nos. 951-958 (8)	11.15	5.75

Nos. 956-958a are airmail.
Exist imperf. in changed colors. Values: set, $14; souvenir sheet, $22.

Italian Contributors in Space Research A188

10c, 36g, Italian satellite, San Marco 1. 15c, 18.15g, Drafting machine, Leonardo Da Vinci. 20c, 12.45g, Map, Italo Balbo (1896-1940), aviator. 30c, 50c, Floating launch & control facility, satellite.

1966, July 11

No.	Type	Denom.	Color	Unused	Used
959	A188	10c	multicolored	.30	.25
960	A188	15c	multicolored	.30	.25
961	A188	20c	multicolored	.30	.25
962	A188	30c	multicolored	.30	.25
963	A188	50c	multicolored	.30	.25
964	A188	12.45g	multicolored	1.75	.50
965	A188	18.15g	multicolored	3.00	.50
966	A188	36g	multicolored	5.50	3.00
a.			Souvenir sheet of 1, perf. 13x13½	15.00	
			Nos. 959-966 (8)	11.75	5.25

Nos. 964-966a are airmail.
Exist imperf. in changed colors. Values: set, $14; souvenir sheet, $24.

Rubén Dario A189

"Paraguay de Fuego" by Dario A189a

1966, July 16 Wmk. 347

No.	Type	Denom.	Color	Unused	Used
967	A189	50c	ultramarine	.65	.40
968	A189	70c	bister brn	.65	.40
969	A189	1.50g	rose car	.65	.40
970	A189	3g	violet	.65	.40
971	A189	4g	greenish bl	.65	.40
972	A189	5g	black	.65	.40
973	A189a	12.45g	blue	1.90	.40
974	A189a	18.15g	red lil	1.90	.40
975	A189a	23.40g	org brn	1.90	.40
976	A189a	36g	brt grn	1.90	.90
977	A189a	50g	rose car	1.90	1.20
			Nos. 967-977 (11)	13.40	5.70

50th death anniv. of Ruben Dario (pen name of Felix Rubén Garcia Sarmiento, 1867-1916), Nicaraguan poet, newspaper correspondent and diplomat.
Nos. 973-977 are airmail.

Space Missions A190

10c, Gemini 8. 15c, Gemini 9. 20c, Surveyor 1 on moon. 30c, Gemini 10.

1966, Aug. 25 Unwmk.

No.	Type	Denom.	Color	Unused	Used
978	A190	10c	multi	.30	.25
979	A190	15c	multi	.30	.25
980	A190	20c	multi	.30	.25
981	A190	30c	multi	.30	.25
982	A190	50c	like #981	.30	.25
983	A190	12.45g	like #980	3.25	1.25
984	A190	18.15g	like #979	3.25	1.25
985	A190	36g	like #978	19.00	6.00
a.			Souvenir sheet of 1, perf. 13x13½	22.00	
			Nos. 978-985 (8)	27.00	9.75

Nos. 983-985a are airmail.
Exist imperf. in changed colors. Values: set, $37; souvenir sheet, $30.

1968 Winter Olympics, Grenoble A191

1966, Sept. 30 ***Perf. 14***

986 A191 10c Figure skating .30 .25
987 A191 15c Downhill skiing .30 .25
988 A191 20c Speed skating .30 .25
989 A191 30c 2-man luge .30 .25
990 A191 50c like #989 .30 .25
991 A191 12.45g like #988 1.40 .50
992 A191 18.15g like #987 1.75 .50
993 A191 36g like #986 3.25 2.50
a. Souvenir sheet of 1 15.00
Nos. 986-993 (8) 7.90 4.75

Nos. 987, 992, World Skiing Championships, Portillo, Chile, 1966. Nos. 991-993a are airmail.

Exist imperf. in changed colors. Values: set, $15; souvenir sheet, $30.

Pres. John F. Kennedy, 3rd Death Anniv. A192

10c, Echo 1 & 2. 15c, Telstar 1 & 2. 20c, Relay 1 & 2. 30c, Syncom 1, 2 & 3, Early Bird.

Perf. 12x12½, 13½x14 (#997-998, 1001)

1966, Nov. 7

994 A192 10c multi .30 .25
995 A192 15c multi .30 .25
996 A192 20c multi .30 .25
997 A192 30c multi .30 .25
998 A192 50c like #997 .30 .25
999 A192 12.45g like #996 1.50 .50
1000 A192 18.15g like #995 1.75 .50
1001 A192 36g like #994 6.00 3.50
a. Souvenir sheet of 1, perf. 13x14x13½x14 22.00
Nos. 994-1001 (8) 10.75 5.75

Nos. 999-1001a are airmail.

Exist imperf. in changed colors. Values: set, $23; souvenir sheet, $25.

Paintings — A193

Portraits of women by: No. 1002a, 10c, De Largilliere. b, 15c, Rubens. c, 20c, Titian. d, 30c, Hans Holbein. e, 50c, Sanchez Coello.

Paintings: No. 1003a, 12.45g, Mars and Venus with United by Love by Veronese. b, 18.15g, Allegory of Prudence, Peace and Abundance by Vouet. c, 36g, Madonna and Child by Andres Montegna.

1966, Dec. 10 ***Perf. 14x13½***

1002 A193 Strip of 5, #a.-e. 1.75 1.25
1003 A193 Strip of 3, #a.-c. 6.00 4.50
d. Souvenir sheet of 1, #1003c 23.00
Nos. 1002-1003 (2) 7.75 5.75

Nos. 1003a-1003d are airmail. No. 1003d has green pattern in border and is perf. 12½x12.

Exist imperf. in changed colors. Values: set, $17; souvenir sheet, $23.

Holy Week Paintings — A194

Life of Christ by: No. 1004a, 10c, Raphael. b, 15c, Rubens. c, 20c, Da Ponte. d, 30c, El Greco. e, 50c, Murillo, horiz.

12.45g, G. Reni. 18.15g, Tintoretto. 36g, Da Vinci, horiz.

1967, Feb. 28 ***Perf. 14x13½, 13½x14***

1004 A194 Strip of 5, #a.-e. 2.50 1.25
1005 A194 12.45g multicolored 1.10 .50
1006 A194 18.15g multicolored 1.10 .50
1007 A194 36g multicolored 13.50 5.00
a. Souvenir sheet of 1 16.00
Nos. 1004-1007 (4) 18.20 7.25

Nos. 1005-1007a are airmail. No. 1007a has salmon pattern in border and contains one 60x40mm, perf. 14 stamp.

Exist imperf. in changed colors. Values: set, $17; souvenir sheet, $16.

Birth of Christ by Barocci — A195

16th Cent. Paintings: 12.45g, Madonna and Child by Caravaggio. 18.15g, Mary of the Holy Family (detail) by El Greco. 36g, Assumption of the Virgin by Vasco Fernandes.

1967, Mar. 10 ***Perf. 14½***

1008 A195 10c lt bl & multi .30 .25
1009 A195 15c lt grn & multi .30 .25
1010 A195 20c lt brn & multi .30 .25
1011 A195 30c lil & multi .30 .25
1012 A195 50c pink & multi .30 .25
1013 A195 12.45g lt bl grn & multi .60 .50
1014 A195 18.15g brt pink & multi .60 .50
1015 A195 36g lt vio & multi 7.50 4.00
a. Souv. sheet of 1, sep & multi 23.00
Nos. 1008-1015 (8) 10.20 6.25

Nos. 1013-1015a are airmail.

Exist imperf. with changed borders. Values: set, $17; souvenir sheet, $23.

Globe and Lions Emblem A196

Medical Laboratory "Health" A196a

Designs: 1.50g, 3g, Melvin Jones. 4g, 5g, Lions' Headquarters, Chicago. 12.45g, 18.15g, Library "Education."

1967, May 9 **Litho.** **Wmk. 347**

1016 A196 50c light vio 1.10 .50
1017 A196 70c blue 1.10 .50
1018 A196 1.50g ultra 1.10 .50
1019 A196 3g brown 1.10 .50
1020 A196 4g Prus grn 1.10 .50
1021 A196 5g ol gray 2.25 .50
1022 A196a 12.45g dk brn 2.25 .50
1023 A196a 18.15g violet 2.25 .50
1024 A196a 23.40g rose cl 2.25 .50
1025 A196a 36g Prus blue 2.25 .50
1026 A196a 50g rose car 2.25 .50
Nos. 1016-1026 (11) 19.00 5.50

50th anniversary of Lions International. Nos. 1022-1026 are airmail.

Vase of Flowers by Chardin — A197

Still Life Paintings by: No. 1027b, 15c, Fontanesi, horiz. c, 20c, Cezanne. d, 30c, Van Gogh. e, 50c, Renoir.

Paintings: 12.45g, Cha-U-Kao at the Moulin Rouge by Toulouse-Lautrec. 18.15g, Gabrielle with Jean Renoir by Renoir. 36g, Patience Escalier, Shepherd of Provence by Van Gogh.

1967, May 16 ***Perf. 12½x12***

1027 A197 Strip of 5, #a.-e. 1.60 1.25
1028 A197 12.45g multicolored .65 .50
1029 A197 18.15g multicolored .65 .50
1030 A197 36g multicolored 5.25 4.00
a. Souvenir sheet of 1, perf. 14x12x14x13½ 22.00
Nos. 1027-1030 (4) 8.15 6.25

Nos. 1028-1030a are airmail. No. 1030a has a green pattern in border.

Exist imperf. with changed borders. Values: set, $17; souvenir sheet, $25.

Famous Paintings A198

10c, Jan Steen. 15c, Frans Hals, vert. 20c, Jordaens. 25c, Rembrandt. 30c, de Marees, vert. 50c, Quentin, vert. 12.45g, Nicolaes Maes, vert. 18.15g, Vigee-Lebrun, vert. 36g, Rubens, vert.

50g, G. B. Tiepolo.

1967, July 16 ***Perf. 12x12½***

1031 A198 10c multicolored .30 .25

Perf. 14x13½, 13½x14

1032 A198 15c multicolored .30 .25
1033 A198 20c multicolored .30 .25
1034 A198 25c multicolored .30 .25
1035 A198 30c multicolored .30 .25
1036 A198 50c multicolored .30 .25
1037 A198 12.45g multicolored .75 .50
1038 A198 18.15g multicolored .75 .50
1039 A198 36g multicolored 7.50 4.00
Nos. 1031-1039 (9) 10.80 6.50

Souvenir Sheet

Perf. 12x12½

1040 A198 50g multicolored 11.00

Nos. 1037-1039 are airmail. An imperf. souvenir sheet of 3, Nos. 1037-1039 exists with dark green pattern in border. Value $16.

John F. Kennedy, 50th Birth Anniv. — A199

Kennedy and: 10c, Recovery of Alan Shepard's capsule, Lyndon Johnson, Mrs. Kennedy. 15c, John Glenn. 20c, Mr. and Mrs. M. Scott Carpenter. 25c, Rocket 2nd stage, Wernher Von Braun. 30c, Cape Canaveral, Walter Schirra. 50c, Syncom 2 satellite, horiz. 12.45g, Launch of Atlas rocket. 18.15g, Theorized lunar landing, horiz. 36g, Portrait of Kennedy by Torres. 50g, Apollo lift-off, horiz.

Perf. 14x13½, 13½x14

1967, Aug. 19

1041 A199 10c multicolored .30 .25
1042 A199 15c multicolored .30 .25
1043 A199 20c multicolored .30 .25
1044 A199 25c multicolored .30 .25
1045 A199 30c multicolored .30 .25
1046 A199 50c multicolored .30 .25
1047 A199 12.45g multicolored 1.75 .75
1048 A199 18.15g multicolored 2.50 1.00
1049 A199 36g multicolored 9.00 4.00
Nos. 1041-1049 (9) 15.05 7.25

Souvenir Sheet

1050 A199 50g multicolored 22.50

Nos. 1047-1050 are airmail. An imperf. souvenir sheet of 3 containing Nos. 1047-1049 exists with violet border. Value $32.50.

Sculptures A200

10c, Head of athlete. 15c, Myron's Discobolus. 20c, Apollo of Belvedere. 25c, Artemis. 30c, Venus De Milo. 50c, Winged Victory of Samothrace. 12.45g, Laocoon Group. 18.15g, Moses. 50g, Pieta.

1967, Oct. 16 ***Perf. 14x13½***

1051 A200 10c multicolored .30 .25
1052 A200 15c multicolored .30 .25
1053 A200 20c multicolored .30 .25
1054 A200 25c multicolored .30 .25
1055 A200 30c multicolored .30 .25
1056 A200 50c multicolored .30 .25
1057 A200 12.45g multicolored 1.40 .40
1058 A200 18.15g multicolored 2.00 .40
1059 A200 50g multicolored 9.00 3.00
Nos. 1051-1059 (9) 14.20 5.30

Nos. 1057-1059 are airmail.

Exist imperf. in changed colors. Value, set $19.

Mexican Art — A201

Designs: 10c, Bowl, Veracruz. 15c, Knobbed vessel, Colima. 20c, Mixtec jaguar pitcher. 25c, Head, Veracruz. 30c, Statue of seated woman, Teotihuacan. 50c, Vessel depicting a woman, Aztec. 12.45g, Mixtec bowl, horiz. 18.15g, Three-legged vessel, Teotihuacan, horiz. 36g, Golden mask, Teotihuacan, horiz. 50g, The Culture of the Totonac by Diego Rivera, 1950, horiz.

1967, Nov. 29 ***Perf. 14x13½***

1060 A201 10c multicolored .30 .25
1061 A201 15c multicolored .30 .25
1062 A201 20c multicolored .30 .25
1063 A201 25c multicolored .30 .25
1064 A201 30c multicolored .30 .25
1065 A201 50c multicolored .30 .25

Perf. 13½x14

1066 A201 12.45g multicolored 2.50 .60
1067 A201 18.15g multicolored 3.00 .60
1068 A201 36g multicolored 15.00 6.00
Nos. 1060-1068 (9) 22.30 8.70

Souvenir Sheet

Perf. 14

1069 A201 50g multicolored 21.00

1968 Summer Olympics, Mexico City (#1065-1069).

Nos. 1066-1069 are airmail. An imperf. souvenir sheet of 3 containing #1066-1068 exists with green pattern in border. Value $34.

Paintings of the Madonna and Child — A202

1968, Jan. 27 ***Perf. 14x13½,13½x14***

1070 A202 10c Bellini .30 .25
1071 A202 15c Raphael .30 .25
1072 A202 20c Corregio .30 .25
1073 A202 25c Luini .30 .25
1074 A202 30c Bronzino .30 .25
1075 A202 50c Van Dyck .30 .25
1076 A202 12.45g Vignon, horiz. .75 .40
1077 A202 18.15g de Ribera .75 .40
1078 A202 36g Botticelli 10.00 3.00
Nos. 1070-1078 (9) 13.30 5.30

Nos. 1076-1078 are airmail and also exist as imperf. souvenir sheet of 3 with olive brown pattern in border. Value $37.50.

Paintings of Winter Scenes A203

1968 Winter Olympics Emblem — A204

10c, Pissarro. 15c, Utrillo, vert. 20c, Monet. 25c, Breitner, vert. 30c, Sisley. 50c, Brueghel, vert. 12.45g, Avercampe, vert. 18.15g, Brueghel, diff. 36g, P. Limbourg & brothers, vert.

1968, Apr. 23 ***Perf. 13½x14, 14x13½***

1079 A203 10c multi .30 .25
1080 A203 15c multi .30 .25
1081 A203 20c multi .30 .25
1082 A203 25c multi .30 .25
1083 A203 30c multi .30 .25
1084 A203 50c multi .30 .25
1085 A203 12.45g multi 1.20 .40
1086 A203 18.15g multi 1.75 .40
1087 A203 36g multi 5.00 2.00
Nos. 1079-1087 (9) 9.75 4.30

Souvenir Sheet

1088 Sheet of 2 30.00
a. A204 50g multicolored

Nos. 1087-1088, 1088a are airmail. No. 1088 contains #1088a and #1087 with red pattern.

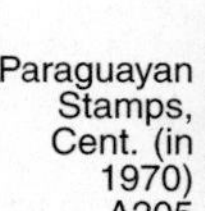

Paraguayan Stamps, Cent. (in 1970) A205

Perf. 13½x14, 14x13½

1968, June 3 **Litho.**

1089 A205 10c #1, 4 .30 .25
1090 A205 15c #C21, 310, vert. .30 .25
1091 A205 20c #203, C140 .30 .25
1092 A205 25c #C72, C61, vert. .30 .25
1093 A205 30c #638, 711 .30 .25
1094 A205 50c #406, C38, vert. .30 .25
1095 A205 12.45g #B2, B7 1.20 .45
1096 A205 18.15g #C10, C11, vert. 1.20 .45
1097 A205 36g #828, C76, 616 12.00 4.50
Nos. 1089-1097 (9) 16.20 6.90

Souvenir Sheet

Perf. 14

1098 Sheet of 2 42.00 25.00
a. A205 50g #929 & #379

Nos. 1095-1098a are airmail. No. 1098 contains No. 1098a and No. 1097 with light brown pattern in border.

Paintings — A206

#1099-1106, paintings of children. #1107-1108, paintings of sailboats at sea.

1968, July 9 ***Perf. 14x13½, 13½x14***

1099 A206 10c Russell .30 .25
1100 A206 15c Velazquez .30 .25
1101 A206 20c Romney .30 .25
1102 A206 25c Lawrence .30 .25
1103 A206 30c Caravaggio .30 .25
1104 A206 50c Gentileschi .30 .25
1105 A206 12.45g Renoir .85 .45
1106 A206 18.15g Copley .85 .45
1107 A206 36g Sessions, horiz. 8.25 3.00
Nos. 1099-1107 (9) 11.75 5.40

Souvenir Sheet

Perf. 14

1108 Sheet of 2 50.00 50.00
a. A206 50g Currier & Ives, horiz.

1968 Summer Olympics, Mexico City (Nos. 1107-1108).
Nos. 1106-1108a are airmail. No. 1108 contains No. 1108a and No. 1107 with a red pattern in border.

A207

WHO Emblem — A207a

1968, Aug. 12 **Wmk. 347** ***Perf. 11***

1109 A207 3g bluish grn .65 .40
1110 A207 4g brt pink .65 .40
1111 A207 5g bister brn .65 .40
1112 A207 10g violet .65 .40
1113 A207a 36g blk brn 2.50 .40
1114 A207a 50g rose claret 2.50 .50
1115 A207a 100g brt bl 2.50 1.20
Nos. 1109-1115 (7) 10.10 3.70

WHO, 20th anniv.; cent. of the natl. epic. Nos. 1113-1115 are airmail.

39th Intl. Eucharistic Congress — A208

Paintings of life of Christ by various artists (except No. 1125a).

Perf. 14x13½

1968, Sept. 25 **Litho.** **Unwmk.**

1116 A208 10c Caravaggio .30 .25
1117 A208 15c El Greco .30 .25
1118 A208 20c Del Sarto .30 .25
1119 A208 25c Van der Weyden .30 .25
1120 A208 30c De Patinier .30 .25
1121 A208 50c Plockhorst .30 .25
1122 A208 12.45g Bronzino .90 .40
1123 A208 18.15g Raphael .90 .40
1124 A208 36g Correggio 9.50 3.00
Nos. 1116-1124 (9) 13.10 5.30

Souvenir Sheet

Perf. 14

1125 Sheet of 2 23.00
a. A208 36g Pope Paul VI
b. A208 50g Tiepolo

Pope Paul VI's visit to South America (No. 1125). Nos. 1122-1125b are airmail.

Events of 1968 — A209

Designs: 10c, Mexican 25p Olympic coin. 15c, Rentry of Echo 1 satellite. 20c, Visit of Pope Paul VI to Fatima, Portugal. 25c, Dr. Christian Barnard, 1st heart transplant. 30c, Martin Luther King, assasination. 50c, Pres. Alfredo Stroessner laying wreath at grave of Pres. Kennedy, vert. 12.45g, Pres. Stroessner, Pres. Lyndon B. Johnson. 18.15g, John F. Kennedy, Abraham Lincoln, Robert Kennedy. 50g, Summer Olympics, Mexico City, satellite transmissions, vert.

1968, Dec. 21 ***Perf. 13½x14, 14x13½***

1126 A209 10c multicolored .30 .25
1127 A209 15c multicolored .30 .25
1128 A209 20c multicolored .30 .25
1129 A209 25c multicolored .30 .25
1130 A209 30c multicolored .30 .25
1131 A209 50c multicolored .30 .25
1132 A209 12.45g multicolored 1.25 .40
1133 A209 18.15g multicolored 1.75 .40
1134 A209 50g multicolored 9.00 3.00
Nos. 1126-1134 (9) 13.80 5.30

Nos. 1132-1134 are airmail. Set exists imperf. in sheets of 3 in changed colors. Value, set of 3 sheets $63.

1968 Summer Olympics, Mexico City — A210

Olympic Stadium — A210a

Gold Medal Winners: 10c, Felipe Munoz, Mexico, 200-meter breast stroke. 15c, Daniel Rebillard, France, 4000-meter cycling. 20c, David Hemery, England, 400-meter hurdles. 25c, Bob Seagren, US, pole vault. 30c, Francisco Rodriguez, Venezuela, light flyweight boxing. 50c, Bjorn Ferm, Sweden, modern pentathlon. 12.45g, Klaus Dibiasi, Italy, platform diving. 50g, Ingrid Becker, West Germany, fencing, women's pentathlon.

1969, Feb. 13 ***Perf. 14x13½***

1135 A210 10c multicolored .30 .25
1136 A210 15c multicolored .30 .25
1137 A210 20c multicolored .30 .25
1138 A210 25c multicolored .30 .25
1139 A210 30c multicolored .30 .25
1140 A210 50c multicolored .30 .25
1141 A210 12.45g multicolored .90 .30
1142 A210a 18.15g multicolored 1.25 .40
1143 A210 50g multicolored 7.00 3.00
Nos. 1135-1143 (9) 10.95 5.20

Nos. 1141-1143 are airmail. Set exists imperf. in sheets of 3 in changed colors. Value, set of 3 sheets $35.

Space Missions A211

Designs: 10c, Apollo 7, John F. Kennedy. 15c, Apollo 8, Kennedy. 20c, Apollo 8, Kennedy, diff. 25c, Study of solar flares, ITU emblem. 30c, Canary Bird satellite. 50c, ESRO satellite. 12.45g, Wernher von Braun, rocket launch. 18.15g, Global satellite coverage, ITU emblem. 50g, Otto Lilienthal, Graf Zeppelin, Hermann Oberth, evolution of flight.

1969, Mar. 10 ***Perf. 13½x14***

1144 A211 10c multicolored .30 .25
1145 A211 15c multicolored .30 .25
1146 A211 20c multicolored .30 .25
1147 A211 25c multicolored .30 .25
1148 A211 30c multicolored .30 .25
1149 A211 50c multicolored .30 .25
1150 A211 12.45g multicolored 1.10 .40
1151 A211 18.15g multicolored 1.75 .40
1152 A211 50g multicolored 6.00 2.00
Nos. 1144-1152 (9) 10.65 4.30

Nos. 1150-1152 are airmail. Set exists imperf. in sheets of 3 in changed colors. Value, set of 3 sheets $100.

"World United in Peace" — A212

1969, June 28 **Wmk. 347** ***Perf. 11***

1153 A212 50c rose .70 .50
1154 A212 70c ultra .70 .50
1155 A212 1.50g light brn .70 .50
1156 A212 3g lil rose .70 .50
1157 A212 4g emerald 1.00 .50
1158 A212 5g violet 1.25 .50
1159 A212 10g brt lilac 3.50 .50
Nos. 1153-1159 (7) 8.55 3.50

Peace Week.

Birds A213

Designs: 10c, Pteroglossus viridis. 15c, Phytotoma rutila. 20c, Porphyrula martinica. 25c, Oxyrunchus cristatus. 30c, Spizaetus ornatus. 50c, Phoenicopterus ruber. 75c, Amazona ochrocephala. 12.45g, Ara ararauna, Ara macao. 18.15g, Colibri coruscans.

Perf. 13½x14, 14x13½

1969, July 9 **Unwmk.**

1160 A213 10c multicolored 1.20 .25
1161 A213 15c multicolored 1.20 .25
1162 A213 20c multicolored 1.20 .25
1163 A213 25c multicolored 1.20 .25
1164 A213 30c multicolored 1.20 .25
1165 A213 50c multicolored 1.20 .25
1166 A213 75c multicolored 1.20 .25
1167 A213 12.45g multicolored 3.50 .50
1168 A213 18.15g multicolored 8.50 1.00
Nos. 1160-1168 (9) 20.40 3.25

Nos. 1167-1168 are airmail. Nos. 1161, 1164-1168 are vert.

Fauna A214

1969, July 9

1169 A214 10c Porcupine .35 .25
1170 A214 15c Lemur, vert. .35 .25
1171 A214 20c 3-toed sloth, vert. .35 .25
1172 A214 25c Puma .35 .25
1173 A214 30c Alligator .35 .25
1174 A214 50c Jaguar .35 .25
1175 A214 75c Anteater .35 .25
1176 A214 12.45g Tapir 1.25 .25
1177 A214 18.15g Capybara 3.50 1.00
Nos. 1169-1177 (9) 7.20 3.00

Nos. 1176-1177 are airmail.

Olympic Soccer Champions, 1900-1968 A215

Designs: 10c, Great Britain, Paris, 1900. 15c, Canada, St. Louis, 1904. 20c, Great Britain, London, 1908 and Stockholm, 1912. 25c, Belgium, Antwerp, 1920. 30c, Uruguay, Paris, 1924 and Amsterdam, 1928. 50c, Italy, Berlin, 1936. 75c, Sweden, London, 1948; USSR, Melbourne, 1956. 12.45g, Yugoslavia, Rome, 1960. 18.15g, Hungary, Helsinki, 1952, Tokyo, 1964 and Mexico, 1968.

No. 1187, Soccer ball, Mexico 1968 emblem. No. 1188, Soccer player and ball.

1969, Nov. 26 ***Perf. 14***

1178 A215 10c multicolored .30 .25
1179 A215 15c multicolored .30 .25
1180 A215 20c multicolored .30 .25
1181 A215 25c multicolored .30 .25
1182 A215 30c multicolored .30 .25
1183 A215 50c multicolored .30 .25
1184 A215 75c multicolored .30 .25
1185 A215 12.45g multicolored .85 .40
1186 A215 18.15g multicolored 8.50 2.50
Nos. 1178-1186 (9) 11.45 4.65

Souvenir Sheet

1187 A215 23.40g multicolored 12.00 12.00
1188 A215 23.40g multi 20.00 20.00

Nos. 1185-1188 are airmail. No. 1187 contains one 49x60mm stamp. No. 1188 contains one 50x61mm stamp.

A216

World Cup or South American Soccer Champions: 10c, Paraguay, 1953. 15c, Uruguay, 1930. 20c, Italy, 1934. 25c, Italy, 1938. 30c, Uruguay, 1950. 50c, Germany, 1954, horiz. 75c, Brazil, 1958. 12.45g, Brazil, 1962. 18.15g, England, 1966. No. 1198, Trophy. No. 1199, Soccer player, satellite.

1969, Nov. 26 *Perf. 14*

1189 A216 10c multicolored .30 .25
1190 A216 15c multicolored .30 .25
1191 A216 20c multicolored .30 .25
1192 A216 25c multicolored .30 .25
1193 A216 30c multicolored .30 .25
1194 A216 50c multicolored .35 .25
1195 A216 75c multicolored .55 .25
1196 A216 12.45g multicolored 2.50 .25
1197 A216 18.15g multicolored 5.75 1.50
Nos. 1189-1197 (9) 10.65 3.50

Souvenir Sheets

Perf. 13½, Imperf(#1199)

1198 A216 23.40g multicolored 50.00 50.00
1199 A216 23.40g multicolored 25.00 25.00

Nos. 1196-1199 are airmail. No. 1198 contains one 50x60mm stamp. No. 1199 contains one 45x57mm stamp.

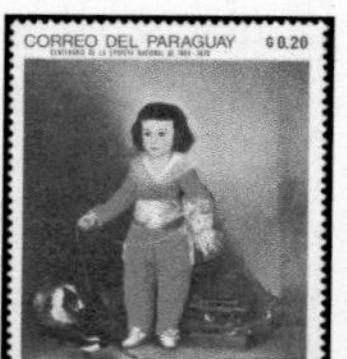

Paintings by Francisco de Goya (1746-1828) A217

Designs: 10c, Miguel de Lardibazal. 15c, Francisca Sabasa y Gracia. 20c, Don Manuel Osorio. 25c, Young Women with a Letter. 30c, The Water Carrier. 50c, Truth, Time and History. 75c, The Forge. 12.45g, The Spell. 18.15g, Duke of Wellington on Horseback. 23.40g, "La Maja Desnuda."

1969, Nov. 29 **Litho.** *Perf. 14x13½*

1200 A217 10c multicolored .30 .25
1201 A217 15c multicolored .30 .25
1202 A217 20c multicolored .30 .25
1203 A217 25c multicolored .30 .25
1204 A217 30c multicolored .30 .25
1205 A217 50c multicolored .30 .25
1206 A217 75c multicolored .45 .25
1207 A217 12.45g multicolored 3.25 .60
1208 A217 18.15g multicolored 6.75 1.25
Nos. 1200-1208 (9) 12.25 3.60

Souvenir Sheet

Perf. 14

1209 A217 23.40g multicolored 28.50 28.50

Nos. 1207-1209 are airmail.

Christmas A218

Various paintings of The Nativity or Madonna and Child: 10c, Master Bertram. 15c, Procaccini. 20c, Di Crediti. 25c, De Flemalle. 30c, Correggio. 50c, Borgianni. 75c, Botticelli. 12.45g, El Greco. 18.15g, De Morales.

23.40g, Isenheimer Altar.

1969, Nov. 29 *Perf. 14x13½*

1210 A218 10c multi .30 .25
1211 A218 15c multi .30 .25
1212 A218 20c multi .30 .25
1213 A218 25c multi .30 .25
1214 A218 30c multi .30 .25
1215 A218 50c multi .30 .25
1216 A218 75c multi .30 .25
1217 A218 12.45g multi 3.50 .60
1218 A218 18.15g multi 6.00 1.50
Nos. 1210-1218 (9) 11.60 3.85

Souvenir Sheet

Perf. 13½

1219 A218 23.40g multi 23.00 23.00

Nos. 1217-1219 are airmail.

Souvenir Sheet

European Space Program — A219

No. 1220, ESRO 1B. No. 1221, Ernst Stuhlinger.

1969, Nov. 29 **Litho.** *Perf. 14*

1220 A219 23.40g multi 21.00 21.00

Imperf

1221 A219 23.40g multi 25.00 25.00

Francisco Solano — A220

1970, Mar. 1 **Wmk. 347** *Perf. 11*

1222 A220 1g bis brn 1.25 1.00
1223 A220 2g violet 1.25 1.00
1224 A220 3g brt pink 1.25 .50
1225 A220 4g rose claret 1.25 1.00
1226 A220 5g blue 1.25 1.00
1227 A220 10g bright grn 1.25 .75
1228 A220 15g lt Prus bl 1.25 *2.00*
1229 A220 20g org brn 1.25 *2.00*
1230 A220 30g gray grn 1.25 1.00
1231 A220 40g gray brn 1.25 3.00
Nos. 1222-1231 (10) 12.50 13.25

Marshal Francisco Solano Lopez (1827-1870), President of Paraguay. Nos. 1228-1231 are airmail.

1st Moon Landing, Apollo 11 — A221

Designs: 10c, Wernher von Braun, lift-off. 15c, Eagle and Columbia in lunar orbit. 20c, Deployment of lunar module. 25c, Landing on Moon. 30c, First steps on lunar surface. 50c, Gathering lunar soil. 75c, Lift-off from Moon. 12.45g, Rendevouz of Eagle and Columbia. 18.15g, Pres. Kennedy, von Braun, splashdown. No. 1241, Gold medal of Armstrong, Aldrin and Collins. No. 1242, Moon landing medal, Kennedy, von Braun. No. 1243, Apollo 12 astronauts Charles Conrad and Alan Bean on moon, and Dr. Kurt Debus.

1970, Mar. 11 **Unwmk.** *Perf. 14*

1232 A221 10c multicolored .30 .25
1233 A221 15c multicolored .30 .25
1234 A221 20c multicolored .30 .25
1235 A221 25c multicolored .30 .25
1236 A221 30c multicolored .30 .25
1237 A221 50c multicolored .30 .25
1238 A221 75c multicolored .30 .25
1239 A221 12.45g multicolored 4.50 .60
1240 A221 18.15g multicolored 10.00 1.25
Nos. 1232-1240 (9) 16.60 3.60

Souvenir Sheets

1241 A221 23.40g multicolored 16.00 12.00

Imperf

1242 A221 23.40g multicolored 35.00 30.00
1243 A221 23.40g multicolored 21.00 16.00

Nos. 1239-1243 are airmail. Nos. 1241-1242 contain one 50x60mm stamp, No. 1243 one 60x50mm stamp.

Easter A222

Designs: 10c, 15c, 20c, 25c, 30c, 50c, 75c, Stations of the Cross. 12.45g, Christ appears to soldiers, vert. 18.15g, Christ appears to disciples, vert. 23.40g, The sad Madonna, vert.

1970, Mar. 11

1244 A222 10c multicolored .30 .25
1245 A222 15c multicolored .30 .25
1246 A222 20c multicolored .30 .25
1247 A222 25c multicolored .30 .25
1248 A222 30c multicolored .30 .25
1249 A222 50c multicolored .30 .25
1250 A222 75c multicolored .55 .25
1251 A222 12.45g multicolored 2.25 .50
1252 A222 18.15g multicolored 6.00 1.50
Nos. 1244-1252 (9) 10.60 3.75

Souvenir Sheet

Perf. 13½

1253 A222 23.40g multicolored 10.50

Nos. 1251-1253 are airmail. No. 1253 contains one 50x60mm stamp.

Paraguay No. 2 — A223

Designs (First Issue of Paraguay): 2g, 10g, #1. 3g, #3. 5g, #2. 15g, #3. 30g, #2. 36g, #1.

1970, Aug. 15 **Litho.** **Wmk. 347**

1254 A223 1g car rose 1.20 1.00
1255 A223 2g ultra 1.20 1.00
1256 A223 3g org brn 1.20 1.00
1257 A223 5g violet 1.20 1.00
1258 A223 10g lilac 1.20 1.00
1259 A223 15g vio brn 2.40 2.00
1260 A223 30g dp grn 2.40 2.00
1261 A223 36g brt pink 2.40 2.00
Nos. 1254-1261 (8) 13.20 11.00

Centenary of stamps of Paraguay. #1259-1261 are airmail.

1972 Summer Olympics, Munich — A224

No. 1262: a, 10c, Discus. b, 15c, Cycling. c, 20c, Men's hurdles. d, 25c, Fencing. e, 30c, Swimming, horiz.

50c, Shotput. 75c, Sailing. 12.45, Women's hurdles, horiz. 18.15g, Equestrian, horiz. No. 1267, Flags, Olympic coins. No. 1268, Frauenkirche Church, Munich. No. 1269, Olympic Village, Munich, horiz.

1970, Sept. 28 **Unwmk.** *Perf. 14*

1262 A224 Strip of 5, #a.-e. 1.75 1.25
1263 A224 50c multicolored .30 .25
1264 A224 75c multicolored .45 .25
1265 A224 12.45g multicolored 2.25 .45
1266 A224 18.15g multicolored 5.50 1.25
Nos. 1262-1266 (5) 10.25 3.45

Souvenir Sheets

Perf. 13½

1267 A224 23.40g multicolored 27.00

Imperf

1268 A224 23.40g multicolored 62.00
1269 A224 23.40g multicolored 24.00 24.00

Nos. 1265-1269 are airmail. Nos. 1267-1269 each contain one 50x60mm stamp.

Paintings, Pinakothek, Munich, 1972 — A225

Nudes by: No. 1270a, 10c, Cranach. b, 15c, Baldung. c, 20c, Tintoretto. d, 25c, Rubens. e, 30c, Boucher, horiz. 50c, Baldung, diff. 75c, Cranach, diff.

12.45g, Self-portrait, Durer. 18.15g, Alterpiece, Altdorfer. 23.40g, Madonna and Child.

1970, Sept. 28 *Perf. 14*

1270 A225 Strip of 5, #a.-e. 1.50 1.25
1271 A225 50c multicolored .65 .25
1272 A225 75c multicolored .65 .25
1273 A225 12.45g multicolored 3.25 .50
1274 A225 18.15g multicolored 4.50 1.50
Nos. 1270-1274 (5) 10.55 3.75

Souvenir Sheet

Perf. 13½

1275 A225 23.40g multicolored 27.50 27.50

Nos. 1273-1275 are airmail. No. 1275 contains one 50x60mm stamp.

Apollo Space Program A226

No. 1276: a, 10c, Ignition, Saturn 5. b, 15c, Apollo 1 mission emblem, vert. c, 20c, Apollo 7, Oct. 1968. d, 25c, Apollo 8, Dec. 1968. e, 30c, Apollo 9, Mar. 1969.

50c, Apollo 10, May 1969. 75c, Apollo 11, July 1969. 12.45g, Apollo 12, Nov. 1969. 18.15g, Apollo 13, Apr. 1970. No. 1281, Lunar landing sites. No. 1282, Wernher von Braun, rockets. No. 1283, James A. Lovell, John L. Swigert, Fred W. Haise.

1970, Oct. 19 *Perf. 14*

1276 A226 Strip of 5, #a.-e. 1.50 1.25
1277 A226 50c multicolored .40 .25
1278 A226 75c multicolored .40 .25
1279 A226 12.45g multicolored 2.00 .50
1280 A226 18.15g multicolored 7.00 1.50
Nos. 1276-1280 (5) 11.30 3.75

Souvenir Sheets

Perf. 13½

1281 A226 23.40g multicolored 10.00

Imperf

1282 A226 23.40g multicolored 65.00
1283 A226 23.40g multicolored 30.00

Nos. 1279-1283 are airmail. Nos. 1281-1283 each contain one 60x50mm stamp.

1970, Oct. 19 *Perf. 14*

Future Space Projects: No. 1284a, 10c, Space station, 2000. b, 15c, Lunar station, vert. c, 20c, Space transport. d, 25c, Lunar rover. e, 30c, Skylab.

50c, Space station, 1971. 75c, Lunar vehicle. 12.45g, Lunar vehicle, diff., vert. 18.15g, Vehicle rising above lunar surface. 23.40g, Moon stations, transport.

1284 A226 Strip of 5, #a.-e. 1.50 1.25
1285 A226 50c multicolored .40 .25
1286 A226 75c multicolored .40 .25
1287 A226 12.45g multicolored 2.25 .50
1288 A226 18.15g multicolored 3.75 1.00
Nos. 1284-1288 (5) 8.30 3.25

Souvenir Sheet

Perf. 13½

1289 A226 23.40g multicolored 16.50 16.50

Nos. 1287-1289 are airmail. No. 1289 contains one 50x60mm stamp. For overprints see Nos. 2288-2290, C653.

EXPO '70, Osaka, Japan — A228

Paintings from National Museum, Tokyo: No. 1288a, 10c, Buddha. b, 15c, Fire, people. c, 20c, Demon, Ogata Korin. d, 25c, Japanese play, Hishikawa Moronobu. e, 30c, Birds.

50c, Woman, Utamaro. 75c, Samurai, Wantabe Kazan. 12.45c, Women Beneath Tree, Kano Hideroi. 18.15g, Courtesans, Torrii Kiyonaga. 50g, View of Mt. Fuji, Hokusai, horiz. No. 1296, Courtesan, Kaigetsudo Ando. No. 1297, Emblem of Expo '70. No. 1298, Emblem of 1972 Winter Olympics, Sapporo.

1970, Nov. 26 Litho. *Perf. 14*

1290 A228 Strip of 5, #a.-e. 1.50 1.25
1291 A228 50c multicolored .50 .25
1292 A228 75c multicolored .50 .25
1293 A228 12.45g multicolored 1.00 .50
1294 A228 18.15g multicolored 1.75 .60
1295 A228 50g multicolored 7.50 1.50
Nos. 1290-1295 (6) 12.75 4.35

Souvenir Sheets

Perf. 13½

1296 A228 20g multicolored 12.00
1297 A228 20g multicolored 18.00
1298 A228 20g multicolored 42.50

Nos. 1293-1298 are airmail. Nos. 1296-1298 each contain one 50x60mm stamp.

Flower Paintings — A229

Artists: No. 1299a, 10c, Von Jawlensky. b, 15c, Purrmann. c, 20c, De Vlaminck. d, 25c, Monet. e, 30c, Renoir.

50c, Van Gogh. 75, Cezanne. 12.45g, Van Huysum. 18.15g, Ruysch. 50g, Walscappelle. 20g, Bosschaert.

1970, Nov. 26 *Perf. 14*

1299 A229 Strip of 5, #a.-e. 1.50 1.25
1300 A229 50c multicolored .50 .25
1301 A229 75c multicolored .50 .25
1302 A229 12.45g multicolored 2.00 .40
1303 A229 18.15g multicolored 2.75 .40
1304 A229 50g multicolored 5.50 1.00
Nos. 1299-1304 (6) 12.75 3.55

Souvenir Sheet

Perf. 13½

1305 A229 20g multicolored 17.50 17.50

Nos. 1302-1305 are airmail. No. 1305 contains one 50x60mm stamp.

Paintings from The Prado, Madrid A230

Nudes by: No. 1306a, 10c, Titian. b, 15c, Velazquez. c, 20c, Van Dyck. d, 25c, Tintoretto. e, 30c, Rubens.

50c, Venus and Sleeping Adonis, Veronese. 75c, Adam and Eve, Titian. 12.45g, The Holy Family, Goya. 18.15g, Shepherd Boy, Murillo. 50g, The Holy Family, El Greco.

1970, Dec. 16 *Perf. 14*

1306 A230 Strip of 5, #a.-e. 1.50 1.25
1307 A230 50c multicolored .60 .25
1308 A230 75c multicolored .60 .25
1309 A230 12.45g multicolored 1.50 .25
1310 A230 18.15g multicolored 1.50 .25
1311 A230 50g multicolored 7.00 1.50
Nos. 1306-1311 (6) 12.70 3.75

Nos. 1309-1311 are airmail. Nos. 1307-1311 are vert.

1970, Dec. 16

Paintings by Albrecht Durer (1471-1528): No. 1312a, 10c, Adam and Eve. b, 15c, St. Jerome in the Wilderness. c, 20c, St. Eustachius and George. d, 25c, Piper and drummer. e, 30c, Lucretia's Suicide.

50c, Oswald Krel. 75c, Stag Beetle. 12.45g, Paul and Mark. 18.15g, Lot's Flight. 50g, Nativity.

1312 A230 Strip of 5, #a.-e. 1.50 1.25
1313 A230 50c multicolored .45 .25
1314 A230 75c multicolored .45 .25
1315 A230 12.45g multicolored 1.00 .40
1316 A230 18.15g multicolored 2.25 .40
1317 A230 50g multicolored 6.50 1.25
Nos. 1312-1317 (6) 12.15 3.80

Nos. 1315-1317 are airmail. See No. 1273.

Christmas A232

Paintings: No. 1318a, 10c, The Annunciation, Van der Weyden. b, 15c, The Madonna, Zeitblom. c, 20c, The Nativity, Von Soest. d, 25c, Adoration of the Magi, Mayno. e, 30c, Adoration of the Magi, Da Fabriano.

50c, Flight From Egypt, Masters of Martyrdom. 75c, Presentation of Christ, Memling. 12.45g, The Holy Family, Poussin, horiz. 18.15g, The Holy Family, Rubens. 20g, Adoration of the Magi, Giorgione, horiz. 50g, Madonna and Child, Batoni.

1971, Mar. 23

1318 A232 Strip of 5, #a.-e. 1.50 1.25
1319 A232 50c multicolored .35 .25
1320 A232 75c multicolored .35 .25
1321 A232 12.45g multicolored .90 .40
1322 A232 18.15g multicolored 2.25 .40
1323 A232 50g multicolored 5.25 1.25
Nos. 1318-1323 (6) 10.60 3.80

Souvenir Sheet

Perf. 13½

1324 A232 20g multicolored 26.00 25.00

Nos. 1321-1324 are airmail. No. 1324 contains one 60x50mm stamp.

1972 Summer Olympics, Munich — A233

Olympic decathlon gold medalists: No. 1325a, 10c, Hugo Wieslander, Stockholm 1912. b, 15c, Helge Lovland, Antwerp 1920. c, 20c, Harold M. Osborn, Paris 1924. d, 25c, Paavo Yrjola, Amsterdam 1928. e, 30c, James Bausch, Los Angeles 1932.

50c, Glenn Morris, Berlin 1936. 75c, Bob Mathias, London 1948, Helsinki 1952. 12.45g, Milton Campbell, Melbourne 1956. 18.15g, Rafer Johnson, Rome 1960. 50g, Willi Holdorf, Tokyo 1964. No. 1331, Bill Toomey, Mexico City 1968.

No. 1332, Pole vaulter, Munich, 1972.

1971, Mar. 23 *Perf. 14*

1325 A233 Strip of 5, #a.-e. 1.50 1.25
1326 A233 50c multicolored .45 .25
1327 A233 75c multicolored .45 .25
1328 A233 12.45g multicolored 1.00 .40
1329 A233 18.15g multicolored 2.50 .40
1330 A233 50g multicolored 6.25 1.25
Nos. 1325-1330 (6) 12.15 3.80

Souvenir Sheets

Perf. 13½

1331 A233 20g multicolored 20.00 15.00
1332 A233 20g multicolored 20.00 15.00

Nos. 1328-1332 are airmail. Nos. 1331-1332 each contain one 50x60mm stamp.

Art — A234

Paintings by: No. 1333a, 10c, Van Dyck. b, 15c, Titian. c, 20c, Van Dyck, diff. d, 25c, Walter. e, 30c, Orsi.

50c, 17th cent. Japanese artist, horiz. 75c, David. 12.45g, Huguet. 18.15g, Perugino. 20g, Van Eyck. 50g, Witz.

1971, Mar. 26 *Perf. 14*

1333 A234 Strip of 5, #a.-e. 1.50 1.25
1334 A234 50c multicolored .45 .25
1335 A234 75c multicolored .45 .25
1336 A234 12.45g multicolored 1.40 .40
1337 A234 18.15g multicolored 2.50 .40
1338 A234 50g multicolored 6.00 1.25
Nos. 1333-1338 (6) 12.30 3.80

Souvenir Sheet

Perf. 13½

1339 A234 20g multicolored 26.00 25.00

Nos. 1336-1339 are airmail. No. 1339 contains one 50x60mm stamp.

Paintings from the Louvre, Paris

Portraits of women by: No. 1340a, 10c, De la Tour. b, 15c, Boucher. c, 20c, Delacroix. d, 25c, 16th cent. French artist. e, 30c, Ingres.

50c, Ingres, horiz. 75c, Watteau, horiz. 12.45g, 2nd cent. artist. 18.15g, Renoir. 20g, Mona Lisa, Da Vinci. 50g, Liberty Guiding the People, Delacroix.

1971, Mar. 26 *Perf. 14*

1340 A234 Strip of 5, #a.-e. 1.50 1.25
1341 A234 50c multicolored .60 .25
1342 A234 75c multicolored .60 .25
1343 A234 12.45g multicolored 1.75 .40
1344 A234 18.15g multicolored 2.25 .40
1345 A234 50g multicolored 5.50 1.00
Nos. 1340-1345 (6) 12.20 3.55

Souvenir Sheet

Perf. 13½

1346 A234 20g multicolored 21.00 20.00

Nos. 1343-1346 are airmail. No. 1346 contains one 50x60mm stamp.

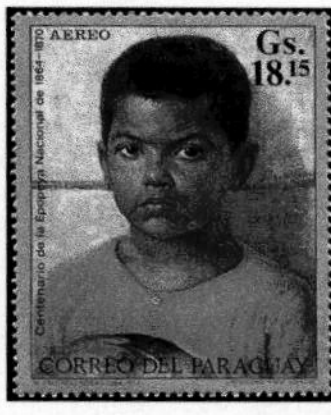

Paintings — A236

Artist: No. 1347a, 10c, Botticelli. b, 15c, Titian. c, 20c, Raphael. d, 25c, Pellegrini. e, 30c, Caracci.

50c, Titian, horiz. 75c, Ricci, horiz. 12.45g, Courtines. 18.15g, Rodas. 50g, Murillo.

1971, Mar. 29 *Perf. 14*

1347 A236 Strip of 5, #a.-e. 1.50 1.25
1348 A236 50c multicolored .50 .25
1349 A236 75c multicolored .50 .25
1350 A236 12.45g multicolored 1.75 .40
1351 A236 18.15g multicolored 2.75 .40
1352 A236 50g multicolored 6.50 1.00
Nos. 1347-1352 (6) 13.50 3.55

Nos. 1350-1352 are airmail.

Hunting Scenes A237

Different Paintings by: No. 1353a, 10c, Gozzoli, vert. b, 15c, Velazquez, vert. c, 20c, Brun. d, 25c, Fontainebleau School, 1550, vert. e, 30c, Uccello, vert.

50c, P. De Vos. 75c, Vernet. 12.45g, 18.15g, 50g, Alken & Sutherland. No. 1359, Paul & Derveaux. No. 1360, Degas.

1971, Mar. 29

1353 A237 Strip of 5, #a.-e. 1.50 1.25
1354 A237 50c multicolored .50 .25
1355 A237 75c multicolored .50 .25
1356 A237 12.45g multicolored 1.50 .40
1357 A237 18.15g multicolored 1.90 .40
1358 A237 50g multicolored 6.75 1.00
Nos. 1353-1358 (6) 12.65 3.55

Souvenir Sheets

Perf. 13½

1359 A237 20g multicolored 18.00 17.00
1360 A237 20g multicolored 18.00 17.00

Nos. 1356-1360 are airmail. Nos. 1359-1360 each contain one 60x50mm stamp.

Philatokyo '71 — A238

Designs: Nos. 1361a-1361e, 10c, 15c, 20c, 25c, 30c, Different flowers, Gukei. 50c, Birds, Lu Chi. 75c, Flowers, Sakai Hoitsu. 12.45g, Man and Woman, Utamaro. 18.15g, Tea Ceremony, from Tea museum. 50g, Bathers, Utamaro. No. 1367, Woman, Kamakura Period. No. 1368, Japan #1, #821, #904, #1023.

1971, Apr. 7 *Perf. 14*

1361 A238 Strip of 5, #a.-e. 2.50 1.25
1362 A238 50c multicolored .55 .25
1363 A238 75c multicolored .55 .25
1364 A238 12.45g multicolored 1.75 .40
1365 A238 18.15g multicolored 1.75 .40
1366 A238 50g multicolored 8.00 1.00
Nos. 1361-1366 (6) 15.10 3.55

Souvenir Sheets

Perf. 13½

1367 A238 20g multicolored 15.00 15.00
1368 A238 20g multicolored 17.00 17.00

Nos. 1364-1368 are airmail. Nos. 1367-1368 each contain one 50x60mm stamp.

See Nos. 1375-1376.

1972 Winter Olympics, Sapporo — A239

Paintings of women by: No. 1369a, 10c, Harunobu. b, 15c, Hosoda. c, 20c, Harunobu, diff. d, 25c, Uemura Shoen. e, 30c, Ketao.

50c, Three Women, Torii. 75c, Old Man, Kakizahi. 12.45g, 2-man bobsled. 18.15g, Ice sculptures, horiz. 50g, Mt. Fuji, Hokusai, horiz. No. 1375, Skier, horiz. No. 1376, Sapporo Olympic emblems.

1971, Apr. *Perf. 14*

1369 A239 Strip of 5, #a.-e. 1.50 1.25
1370 A239 50c multicolored .50 .25
1371 A239 75c multicolored .50 .25
1372 A239 12.45g multicolored 1.40 .40
1373 A239 18.15g multicolored 2.75 .40
1374 A239 50g multicolored 7.25 1.00
Nos. 1369-1374 (6) 13.90 3.55

Souvenir Sheets

Perf. 14½

1375 A239 20g multicolored 37.50 37.50

Perf. 13½

1376 A239 20g multicolored 22.50 22.50

Nos. 1372-1376 are airmail. No. 1375 contains one 35x25mm stamp with PhilaTokyo 71 emblem. No. 1376 contains one 50x60mm stamp.

For Japanese painting stamps with white border and Winter Olympics emblem see #1409-1410.

UNESCO and Paraguay Emblems, Globe, Teacher and Pupil — A240

Wmk. 347

1971, May 18 Litho. ***Perf. 11***

1377 A240 3g ultra 1.10 1.00
1378 A240 5g lilac 1.10 1.00
1379 A240 10g emerald 1.10 1.00
1380 A240 20g claret 2.25 2.00
1381 A240 25g brt pink 2.25 2.00
1382 A240 30g brown 2.25 2.00
1383 A240 50g gray olive 2.25 2.00
Nos. 1377-1383 (7) 12.30 11.00

International Education Year.
Nos. 1380-1383 are airmail.

Paintings, Berlin-Dahlem Museum — A241

Artists: 10c, Caravaggio. No. 1385: a, 15c, b, 20c, Di Cosimo. 25c, Cranach. 30c, Veneziano. 50g, Holbein. 75c, Baldung. 12.45g, Cranach, diff. 18.15g, Durer. 50g, Schongauer.

1971, Dec. 24 Unwmk. ***Perf. 14***

1384 A241 10c multicolored .30 .25
1385 A241 Pair, #a.-b. .30 .25
1386 A241 25c multicolored .30 .25
1387 A241 30c multicolored .30 .25
1388 A241 50c multicolored .30 .25
1389 A241 75c multicolored .30 .25
1390 A241 12.45g multicolored 1.90 .40
1391 A241 18.15g multicolored 1.90 .40
1392 A241 50g multicolored 7.25 1.00
Nos. 1384-1392 (9) 12.85 3.30

Nos. 1390-1392 are airmail. No. 1385 has continuous design.

Napoleon I, 150th Death Anniv. — A242

Paintings: No. 1393a, 10c, Desiree Clary, Gerin. b, 15c, Josephine de Beauharnais, Gros. c, 20c, Maria Luisa, Gerard. d, 25c, Juliette Recamier, Gerard. e, 30c, Maria Walewska, Gerard.
50c, Victoria Kraus, unknown artist, horiz. 75c, Napoleon on Horseback, Chabord. 12.45g, Trafalgar, A. Mayer, horiz. 18.15g, Napoleon Leading Army, Gautherot, horiz. 50g, Napoleon's tomb.

1971, Dec. 24

1393 A242 Strip of 5, #a.-e. 1.50 1.25
1394 A242 50c multicolored .30 .25
1395 A242 75c multicolored .30 .25
1396 A242 12.45g multicolored 1.75 .40
1397 A242 18.15g multicolored 2.00 .40
1398 A242 50g multicolored 7.50 1.00
Nos. 1393-1398 (6) 13.35 3.55

Nos. 1396-1398 are airmail.

Locomotives A243

Designs: No. 1399a, 10c, Trevithick, Great Britain, 1804. b, 15c, Blenkinsops, 1812. c, 20c, G. Stephenson #1, 1825. d, 25c, Marc Seguin, France, 1829. e, 30c, "Adler," Germany, 1835.
50c, Sampierdarena #1, Italy, 1854. 75c, Paraguay #1, 1861. 12.45g, "Munich," Germany, 1841. 18.15g, US, 1875. 20g, Japanese locomotives, 1872-1972. 50g, Mikado D-50, Japan, 1923.

1972, Jan. 6

1399 A243 Strip of 5, #a.-e. 1.50 1.25
1400 A243 50c multicolored .30 .25
1401 A243 75c multicolored .30 .25
1402 A243 12.45g multicolored 2.25 .40
1403 A243 18.15g multicolored 2.25 .40
1404 A243 50g multicolored 8.00 .90
Nos. 1399-1404 (6) 14.60 3.45

Souvenir Sheet

Perf. 13½

1405 A243 20g multicolored 62.50 60.00

Nos. 1402-1405 are airmail. No. 1405 contains one 60x50mm stamp.
See Nos. 1476-1480.

1972 Winter Olympics, Sapporo A244

Designs: Nos. 1406a, 10c, Hockey player. b, 15c, Jean-Claude Killy. c, 20c, Gaby Seyfert. d, 25c, 4-Man bobsled. e, 30c, Luge.
50c, Ski jumping, horiz. 75c, Slalom skiing, horiz. 12.45g, Painting, Kuniyoshi. 18.15g, Winter Scene, Hiroshige, horiz. 50g, Ski lift, man in traditional dress.

1972, Jan. 6 ***Perf. 14***

1406 A244 Strip of 5, #a.-e. 1.60 1.25
1407 A244 50c multicolored .30 .25
1408 A244 75c multicolored .30 .25
1409 A244 12.45g multicolored 1.60 .40
1410 A244 18.15g multicolored 1.60 .40
1411 A244 50g multicolored 6.00 1.25
Nos. 1406-1411 (6) 11.40 3.80

Souvenir Sheet

Perf. 13½

1412 A244 20g Skier 17.50 17.50
1413 A244 20g Flags 25.00 25.00

Nos. 1409-1413 are airmail. Nos. 1412-1413 each contain one 50x60mm stamp. For overprint see Nos. 2295-2297. For Winter Olympic stamps with gold border, see Nos. 1372-1373.

UNICEF, 25th Anniv. (in 1971) — A245

1972, Jan. 24 **Granite Paper**

1414 A245 1g red brn 1.20 1.00
1415 A245 2g ultra 1.20 1.00
1416 A245 3g lil rose 1.20 1.00
1417 A245 4g violet 1.20 1.00
1418 A245 5g emerald 1.20 1.00
1419 A245 10g claret 2.40 *3.00*
1420 A245 20g brt bl 2.40 *3.00*
1421 A245 25g lt ol 2.40 *3.00*
1422 A245 30g dk brn 2.40 *3.00*
Nos. 1414-1422 (9) 15.60 17.00

Nos. 1420-1422 are airmail.

Race Cars — A246

No. 1423: a, 10c, Ferrari. b, 15c, B.R.M. c, 20c, Brabham. d, 25c, March. e, 30c, Honda.
50c, Matra-Simca MS 650. 75c, Porsche. 12.45g, Maserati-8 CTF, 1938. 18.15g, Bugatti 35B, 1929. 20g, Lotus 72 Ford. 50g, Mercedes, 1924.

1972, Mar. 20 Unwmk. ***Perf. 14***

1423 A246 Strip of 5, #a.-e. 1.50 1.25
1424 A246 50c multicolored .50 .25
1425 A246 75c multicolored .50 .25
1426 A246 12.45g multicolored 2.00 .45
1427 A246 18.15g multicolored 2.00 .45
1428 A246 50g multicolored 7.50 5.25
Nos. 1423-1428 (6) 14.00 7.90

Souvenir Sheet

Perf. 13½

1429 A246 20g multicolored 28.00

Nos. 1426-1429 are airmail. No. 1429 contains one 60x50mm stamp.

Sailing Ships A247

Paintings: No. 1430a, 10c, Holbein. b, 15c, Nagasaki print. c, 20c, Intrepid, Roux. d, 25c, Portuguese ship, unknown artist. e, 30c, Mount Vernon, US, 1798, Corne.
50c, Van Eertvelt, vert. 75c, Santa Maria, Van Eertvelt, vert. 12.45g, Royal Prince, 1679, Van Beecq. 18.15g, Van Bree. 50g, Book of Arms, 1497, vert.

1972, Mar. 29 ***Perf. 14***

1430 A247 Strip of 5, #a.-e. 1.50 1.25
1431 A247 50c multicolored .50 .25
1432 A247 75c multicolored .65 .25
1433 A247 12.45g multicolored 1.75 .35
1434 A247 18.15g multicolored 2.50 .40
1435 A247 50g multicolored 5.50 .75
Nos. 1430-1435 (6) 12.40 3.25

Nos. 1433-1435 are airmail.

Paintings in Vienna Museum — A248

Nudes by: No. 1436a, 10c, Rubens. b, 15c, Bellini. c, 20c, Carracci. d, 25c, Cagnacci. e, 30c, Spranger.
50c, Mandolin Player, Strozzi. 75c, Woman in Red Hat, Cranach the elder. 12.45g, Adam and Eve, Coxcie. 18.15g, Legionary on Horseback, Poussin. 50g, Madonna and Child, Bronzino.

1972, May 22

1436 A248 Strip of 5, #a.-e. 1.50 1.25
1437 A248 50c multicolored .50 .25
1438 A248 75c multicolored .50 .25
1439 A248 12.45g multicolored 1.75 .40
1440 A248 18.15g multicolored 1.75 .40
1441 A248 50g multicolored 6.50 1.25
Nos. 1436-1441 (6) 12.50 3.80

Nos. 1439-1441 are airmail.

Paintings in Asuncion Museum — A249

No. 1442: a, 10c, Man in Straw Hat, Holden Jara. b, 15c, Portrait, Tintoretto. c, 20c, Indians, Holden Jara. d, 25c, Nude, Bouchard. e, 30c, Italian School.
50c, Reclining Nude, Berisso, horiz. 75c, Carracci, horiz. 12.45g, Reclining Nude, Schiaffino, horiz. 18.15g, Reclining Nude, Lostow, horiz. 50g, Madonna and Child, 17th cent. Italian School.

1972, May 22

1442 A249 Strip of 5, #a.-e. 1.50 1.25
1443 A249 50c multicolored .45 .25
1444 A249 75c multicolored .45 .25
1445 A249 12.45g multicolored 1.50 .40
1446 A249 18.15g multicolored 1.50 .40
1447 A249 50g multicolored 5.25 1.25
Nos. 1442-1447 (6) 10.65 3.80

Nos. 1445-1447 are airmail.

Presidential Summit — A250

No. 1448: a, 10c, Map of South America. b, 15c, Brazil natl. arms. c, 20c, Argentina natl. arms. d, 25c, Bolivia natl. arms. e, 30c, Paraguay natl. arms.
50c, Pres. Emilio Garrastazu, Brazil. 75c, Pres. Alejandro Lanusse, Argentina. 12.45g, Pres. Hugo Banzer Suarez, Bolivia. 18.15, Pres. Stroessner, Paraguay, horiz. 23.40g, Flags.

1972, Nov. 18

1448 A250 Strip of 5, #a.-e. 1.50 1.25
1449 A250 50c multicolored .35 .25
1450 A250 75c multicolored .35 .25
1451 A250 12.45g multicolored 2.00 .25
1452 A250 18.15g multicolored 2.75 .30
Nos. 1448-1452 (5) 6.95 2.30

Souvenir Sheet

Perf. 13½

1453 A250 23.40g multicolored 10.50

Nos. 1451-1453 are airmail. No. 1453 contains one 50x60mm stamp. For overprint see No. 2144.

Pres. Stroessner's Visit to Japan — A251

No. 1454: a, 10c, Departure of first Japanese mission to US & Europe, 1871. b, 15c, First railroad, Tokyo-Yokahama, 1872. c, 20c, Samurai. d, 25c, Geishas. e, 30c, Cranes, Hiroshige.
50c, Honda race car. 75c, Pres. Stroessner, Emperor Hirohito, Mt. Fuji, bullet train, horiz. 12.45g, Rocket. 18.15g, Stroessner, Hirohito, horiz. No. 1459, Mounted samurai, Masanobu, 1740. No. 1460, Hirohito's speech, state dinner, horiz. No. 1461, Delegations at Tokyo airport, horiz.

1972, Nov. 18 ***Perf. 14***

1454 A251 Strip of 5, #a.-e. 1.50 1.25
1455 A251 50c multicolored .50 .25
1456 A251 75c multicolored .50 .25
1457 A251 12.45g multicolored 4.50 2.00
1458 A251 18.15g multicolored 5.50 2.50
Nos. 1454-1458 (5) 12.50 6.25

Souvenir Sheets

Perf. 13½

1459 A251 23.40g multicolored 18.00 18.00
1460 A251 23.40g multicolored 18.00 18.00

Imperf

1461 A251 23.40g multicolored 18.00 18.00

Nos. 1457-1461 are airmail. Nos. 1459-1460 each contain one 50x60mm stamp. No. 1461 contains one 85x42mm stamp with simulated perforations. For overprints see Nos. 2192-2194, 2267.

Wildlife — A252

Paintings — #1462: a, 10c, Cranes, Botke. b, 15c, Tiger, Utamaro. c, 20c, Horses, Arenys. d, 25c, Pheasant, Dietzsch. e, 30c, Monkey, Brueghel, the Elder. All vert.
50c, Deer, Marc. 75c, Crab, Durer. 12.45g, Rooster, Jakuchu, vert. 18.15g, Swan, Asselyn.

1972, Nov. 18 ***Perf. 14***

1462 A252 Strip of 5, #a.-e. 1.50 1.25
1463 A252 50c multicolored .30 .25
1464 A252 75c multicolored .30 .25
1465 A252 12.45g multicolored 4.50 .75
1466 A252 18.15g multicolored 5.50 1.00
Nos. 1462-1466 (5) 12.10 3.50

Nos. 1465-1466 are airmail.

Acaray Dam — A253

Designs: 2g, Francisco Solano Lopez monument. 3g, Friendship Bridge. 5g, Tebicuary River Bridge. 10g, Hotel Guarani. 20g, Bus and car on highway. 25g, Hospital of Institute for Social Service. 50g, "Presidente Stroessner" of state merchant marine. 100g, "Electra C" of Paraguayan airlines.

Perf. 13½x13

1972, Nov. 16 **Wmk. 347**

Granite Paper

1467 A253 1g sepia 2.25 1.00
1468 A253 2g brown 2.25 1.00
1469 A253 3g brt ultra 2.25 1.00
1470 A253 5g brt pink 2.25 1.00
1471 A253 10g dl grn 3.25 2.00
1472 A253 20g rose car 3.25 2.00
1473 A253 25g gray 3.25 2.00
1474 A253 50g violet 3.25 2.00
1475 A253 100g brt lil 3.25 2.00
Nos. 1467-1475 (9) 25.25 14.00

Tourism Year of the Americas.
Nos. 1472-1475 are airmail.

Locomotives Type

No. 1476: a, 10c, Stephenson's Rocket, 1829. b, 15c, First Swiss railroad, 1847. c, 20c, 1st Spanish locomotive, 1848. d, 25c, Norris, US, 1850. e, 30c, Ansaldo, Italy, 1859.
50c, Badenia, Germany, 1863. 75c, 1st Japanese locomotive, 1895. 12.45g, P.L.M., France, 1924. 18.15g, Stephenson's Northumbrian.

1972, Nov. 25 **Unwmk.** ***Perf. 14***

1476 A243 Strip of 5, #a.-e. 1.50 1.25
1477 A243 50c multicolored .30 .25
1478 A243 75c multicolored .30 .25
1479 A243 12.45g multicolored 4.25 .40
1480 A243 18.15g multicolored 6.00 1.00
Nos. 1476-1480 (5) 12.35 3.15

Nos. 1479-1480 are airmail.

South American Wildlife A254

No. 1481: a, 10c, Tetradactyla. b, 15c, Nasua socialis. c, 20c, Priodontes giganteus. d, 25c, Blastocerus dichotomus. e, 30c, Felis pardalis.
50c, Aotes, vert. 75c, Rhea americana. 12.45g, Desmodus rotundus. 18.15g, Urocyon cinereo-argenteus.

1972, Nov. 25

1481 A254 Strip of 5, #a.-e. 1.50 1.25
1482 A254 50c multicolored .40 .25
1483 A254 75c multicolored .40 .25
1484 A254 12.45g multicolored 4.50 .75
1485 A254 18.15g multicolored 6.00 1.25
Nos. 1481-1485 (5) 12.80 3.75

Nos. 1484-1485 are airmail.

OAS Emblem — A255

Perf. 13x13½

1973 **Litho.** **Wmk. 347**

Granite Paper

1486 A255 1g multi 1.10 1.00
1487 A255 2g multi 1.10 1.00
1488 A255 3g multi 1.10 1.00
1489 A255 4g multi 1.10 1.00
1490 A255 5g multi 1.10 1.00
1491 A255 10g multi 1.10 1.00
1492 A255 20g multi 2.25 1.00
1493 A255 25g multi 2.25 1.00
1494 A255 50g multi 3.25 1.00
1495 A255 100g multi 5.50 1.00
Nos. 1486-1495 (10) 19.85 10.00

Org. of American States, 25th anniv.
Nos. 1492-1495 are airmail.

Paintings in Florence Museum — A256

Artists: No. 1496: a, 10c, Cranach, the Elder. b, 15c, Caravaggio. c, 20c, Fiorentino. d, 25c, Di Credi. e, 30c, Liss. f, 50c, Da Vinci. g, 75c, Botticelli.
No. 1497: a, 5g, Titian, horiz. b, 10g, Del Piombo, horiz. c, 20g, Di Michelino, horiz.

1973, Mar. 13 **Unwmk.** ***Perf. 14***

1496 A256 Strip of 7, #a.-g. 3.50 1.00
1497 A256 Strip of 3, #a.-c. 8.00 2.50
Nos. 1496-1497 (2) 11.50 3.50

No. 1497 is airmail.

Butterflies A257

#1498: a, 10c, Catagramma patazza. b, 15c, Agrias narcissus. c, 20c, Papilio zagreus. d, 25c, Heliconius chestertoni. e, 30c, Metamorphadido. f, 50c, Catagramma astarte. g, 75c, Papilio brasiliensis.
No. 1499a, 5g, Agrias sardanapalus. b, 10g, Callithea saphhira. c, 20g, Jemadia hospita.

1973, Mar. 13

1498 A257 Strip of 7, #a.-g. 4.00 1.00
1499 A257 Strip of 3, #a.-c. 13.50 3.50
Nos. 1498-1499 (2) 17.50 4.50

No. 1499 is airmail.

Cats — A258

Faces of Cats: No. 1500: a, 10c, b, 15c. c, 20c, d, 25c, e, 30c. f, 50c. g, 75c.
No. 1501a, 5g, Cat under rose bush, by Desportes. b, 10g, Two cats, by Marc, horiz. c, 20g, Man with cat, by Rousseau.

1973, June 29

1500 A258 Strip of 7, #a.-g. 3.50 1.00
1501 A258 Strip of 3, #a.-c. 14.00 3.50
Nos. 1500-1501 (2) 17.50 4.50

No. 1500 is airmail. For other cat designs, see type A287.

Flemish Paintings — A259

Nudes by: No. 1502: a, 10c, Spranger. b, 15c, Jordaens. c, 20c, de Clerck. d, 25c, Spranger, diff. e, 30c, Goltzius. f, 50c, Rubens. g, 75c, Vase of flowers, J. Brueghel.
No. 1503a, 5g, Nude, de Clerck, horiz. b, 10g, Woman with mandolin, de Vos. c, 20g, Men, horses, Rubens, horiz.

1973, June 29 **Litho.** ***Perf. 14***

1502 A259 Strip of 7, #a.-g. 3.50 1.00
1503 A259 Strip of 3, #a.-c. 9.00 3.00
Nos. 1502-1503 (2) 12.50 4.00

No. 1503 is airmail.

Hand Holding Letter — A260

Wmk. 347

1973, July 10 **Litho.** ***Perf. 11***

1504 A260 2g lil rose & blk 5.00 1.50

No. 1504 was issued originally as a nonobligatory stamp to benefit mailmen, but its status was changed to regular postage.

EXPOPAR 73, Paraguayan Industrial Exhib. — A261

1973, Aug. 11 ***Perf. 13x13½***

Granite Paper

1505 A261 1g org brn 2.25 2.00
1506 A261 2g vermilion 2.25 2.00
1507 A261 3g blue 2.25 2.00
1508 A261 4g emerald 2.25 2.00
1509 A261 5g lilac 2.25 2.00
1510 A261 20g lilac rose 8.00 3.00
1511 A261 25g rose claret 8.00 3.00
Nos. 1505-1511 (7) 27.25 16.00

Nos. 1510-1511 are airmail.

1974 World Cup Soccer Championships, Munich — A262

No. 1512: a, 10c, Uruguay vs. Paraguay. b, 15c, Crerand, England and Eusebio, Portugal. c, 20c, Bobby Charlton, England. d, 25c, Franz Beckenbauer, Germany. e, 30c, Erler, Germany and McNab, England. f, 50c, Pele, Brazil and Willi Schulz, Germany. g, 75c, Arsenio Erico, Paraguay.
5g, Brian Labone, Gerd Mueller, Bobby Moore. No. 1514a, 10g, Luigi Riva, Italy. No. 1514b, 20g, World Cup medals. No. 1515, World Cup trophy. 25g, Player scoring goal.

1973 **Litho.** **Unwmk.** ***Perf. 14***

1512 A262 Strip of 7, #a.-g. 2.00 1.00
1513 A262 5g multicolored 9.50 1.50
1514 A262 Pair, #a.-b. 4.25 1.00
Nos. 1512-1514 (3) 15.75 3.50

Souvenir Sheets

Perf. 13½

1515 A262 25g multicolored 62.00 62.00
1516 A262 25g multicolored 22.50 22.50

Nos. 1513-1516 are airmail. Issue dates: Nos. 1512-1514, 1516, Oct. 8. No. 1515, June 29. For overprint see No. 2131.

Paintings — A263

Details from paintings, artist: No. 1517a, 10c, Lion of St. Mark, Carpaccio. b, 15c, Venus and Mars, Pittoni. c, 20c, Rape of Europa, Veronese. d, 25c, Susannah and the Elders, Tintoretto. e, 30c, Euphrosyne, Amigoni. f, 50c, Allegory of Moderation, Veronese. g, 75c, Ariadne, Tintoretto.
5g, Pallas and Mars, Tintoretto. No. 1519a, 10g, Portrait of Woman in Fur Hat, G.D. Tiepolo. b, 20g, Dialectic of Industry, Veronese.

1973, Oct. 8 ***Perf. 14***

1517 A263 Strip of 7, #a.-g. 2.00 1.00
1518 A263 5g multicolored 4.00 .75
1519 A263 Pair, #a.-b. 4.75 1.25
Nos. 1517-1519 (3) 10.75 3.00

Nos. 1518-1519 are airmail.

Birds — A264

No. 1520: a, 10c, Tersina viridis. b, 15c, Pipile cumanensis. c, 20c, Pyrocephalus rubinus. d, 25c, Andigena laminirostris. e, 30c, Xipholena punicea. f, 50c, Tangara chilensis. g, 75, Polytmus guainumbi.
5g, Onychorhynchus mexicanus, vert. No. 1522a, 10g, Rhinocrypta lanceolata, vert. b, 20g, Trogon collaris, vert. 25g, Colibri florisuga mellivora, vert.

1973, Nov. 14

1520 A264 Strip of 7, #a.-g. 2.00 1.10
1521 A264 5g multicolored 6.00 1.50
1522 A264 Pair, #a.-b. 4.00 .50
Nos. 1520-1522 (3) 12.00 3.10

Souvenir Sheet

Perf. 13½

1523 A264 25g multicolored 32.50 32.50

Nos. 1521-1523 are airmail. No. 1523 contains one 50x60mm stamp.

Space Exploration A265

No. 1524a, 10c, Apollo 11. b, 15c, Apollo 12. c, 20c, Apollo 13. d, 25c, Apollo 14. e, 30c, Apollo 15. f, 50c, Apollo 16. g, 75c, Apollo 17.
5g, Skylab. No. 1526a, 10g, Space shuttle. b, 20g, Apollo-Soyuz mission. No. 1527, Pioneer 11, Jupiter. No. 1528, Pioneer 10, Jupiter, vert.

1973, Nov. 14 ***Perf. 14***

1524 A265 Strip of 7, #a.-g. 2.00 1.10
1525 A265 5g multicolored 4.50 1.50
1526 A265 Pair, #a.-b. 2.00 1.00
Nos. 1524-1526 (3) 8.50 3.60

Souvenir Sheet

Perf. 14½

1527 A265 25g multicolored 30.00 20.00

Perf. 13½

1528 A265 25g multicolored 26.00 15.00

Nos. 1525-1528 are airmail. No. 1527 contains on 35x25mm stamp, No. 1528 one 50x60mm stamp.

Souvenir Sheet

Women of Avignon, Pablo Picasso A266

1973, Nov. 14 ***Perf. 13½***

1529 A266 25g multicolored 25.00 25.00

Traditional Costumes A267

No. 1530: a, 25c, Indian girl. b, 50c, Bottle dance costume. c, 75c, Dancer balancing vase on head. d, 1g, Dancer with flowers. e, 1.50g, Weavers. f, 1.75g, Man, woman in dance costumes. g, 2.25g, Musicians in folk dress, horiz.

1973, Dec. 30 ***Perf. 14***

1530 A267 Strip of 7, #a.-g. 7.75 5.00

Flowers — A268

Designs: No. 1531a, 10c Passion flower. b, 20c, Dahlia. c, 25c, Bird of paradise. d, 30c, Freesia. e, 40c, Anthurium. f, 50c, Water lily. g, 75c, Orchid.

1973, Dec. 31

1531 A268 Strip of 7, #a.-g. 9.75 5.00

Roses — A269

Designs: No. 1532a, 10c, Hybrid perpetual. b, 15c, Tea scented. c, 20c, Japanese rose. d, 25c, Bouquet of roses and flowers. e, 30c, Rose of Provence. f, 50c, Hundred petals rose. g, 75c, Bouquet of roses, dragonfly.

1974, Feb. 2

1532 A269 Strip of 7, #a.-g. 10.00 3.00

Paintings in Gulbenkian Museum — A270

Designs and artists: No. 1533a, 10c, Cupid and Three Graces, Boucher. b, 15c, Bath of Venus, Burne-Jones. c, 20c, Mirror of Venus, Burne-Jones. d, 25c, Two Women, Natoire. e, 30c, Fighting Cockerels, de Vos. f, 50c, Portrait of a Young Girl, Bugiardini. g, 75c, Madonna and Child, J. Gossaert.

5g, Outing on Beach at Enoshima, Utamaro. No. 1535: a, 10g, Woman with Harp, Lowrence. b, 20g, Centaurs Embracing, Rubens.

1974, Feb. 4

1533 A270 Strip of 7, #a.-g. 2.00 1.10
1534 A270 5g multicolored 3.50 1.75
1535 A270 Pair, #a.-b. 5.25 3.50
Nos. 1533-1535 (3) 10.75 6.35

Nos. 1534-1535 are airmail.

UPU Cent. A271

Horse-drawn mail coaches: No. 1536a, 10c, London. b, 15c, France. c, 20c, England. d, 25c, Bavaria. e, 30c, Painting by C.C. Henderson. f, 50c, Austria, vert. g, 75c, Zurich, vert.

5g, Hot air balloon, Apollo spacecraft, airplane, Graf Zeppelin. No. 1538a, 10g, Steam locomotive. b, 20g, Ocean liner, sailing ship. No. 1539, Airship, balloon. No. 1540, Mail coach crossing river.

1974, Mar. 20 ***Perf. 14***

1536 A271 Strip of 7, #a.-g. 2.00 1.25
1537 A271 5g multicolored 1.75 .65
1538 A271 Pair, #a.-b. 7.00 3.50
Nos. 1536-1538 (3) 10.75 5.40

Souvenir Sheets

Perf. 14½

1539 A271 15g multicolored 26.00 26.00

Perf. 13½

1540 A271 15g multicolored 26.00 26.00

Nos. 1537-1540 are airmail. No. 1539 contains one 50x35mm stamp, No. 1540 one 60x50mm stamp. Nos. 1539-1540 each include a 5g surtax for a monument to Francisco Solano Lopez. For overprint see No. 2127.

Paintings — A272

Details from works, artist: No. 1541a, 10c, Adam and Eve, Mabuse. b, 15c, Portrait, Piero di Cosimo. c, 20c, Bathsheba in her Bath, Cornelisz. d, 25c, Toilet of Venus, Boucher. e, 30c, The Bathers, Renoir. f, 50c, Lot and his Daughters, Dix. g, 75c, Bouquet of Flowers, van Kessel.

5g, King's Pet Horse, Seele. No. 1543a, 10g, Woman with Paintbrushes, Batoni. b, 20g, Three Musicians, Flemish master.

1974, Mar. 20

1541 A272 Strip of 7, #a.-g. 1.60 1.25
1542 A272 5g multicolored 2.00 .40
1543 A272 Pair, #a.-b. 12.50 3.00
Nos. 1541-1543 (3) 16.10 4.65

Nos. 1542-1543 are airmail.

Sailing Ships A272a

Designs: No. 1544a, 5c, Ship, map. b, 10c, English ship. c, 15c, Dutch ship. d, 20c, Whaling ships. e, 25c, Spanish ship. f, 35c, USS Constitution. g, 40c, English frigate. h, 50c, "Fanny," 1832.

1974, Sept. 13 ***Perf. 14½***

1544 A272a Strip of 8, #a.-h. 7.00 1.00

Strip price includes a 50c surtax.

Paintings in Borghese Gallery, Rome — A273

Details from works and artists: No. 1545a, 5c, Portrait, Romano. b, 10c, Boy Carrying Fruit, Caravaggio. c, 15c, A Sybil, Domenichino. d, 20c, Nude, Titian. e, 25c, The Danae, Correggio. f, 35c, Nude, Savoldo. g, 40c, Nude, da Vinci. h, 50c, Nude, Rubens. 15g, Christ Child, Piero di Cosimo.

1975, Jan. 15 ***Perf. 14***

1545 A273 Strip of 8, #a.-h. 5.50 1.50

Souvenir Sheet

Perf. 14½

1546 A273 15g multicolored 17.50 10.00

No. 1546 is airmail and price includes a 5g surtax used for a monument to Francisco Solano Lopez.

Christmas A274

Paintings, artists: No. 1547a, 5c, The Annunciation, della Robbia. b, 10c, The Nativity, G. David. c, 15c, Madonna and Child, Memling. d, 20c, Adoration of the Shepherds, Giorgione. e, 25c, Adoration of the Magi, French school, 1400. f, Madonna and Child with Saints, 35c, Pulzone. g, 40c, Madonna and Child, van Orley. h, 50c, Flight From Egypt, Pacher.

15g, Adoration of the Magi, Raphael.

1975, Jan. 17 ***Perf. 14***

1547 A274 Strip of 8, #a.-h. 5.00 1.50

Souvenir Sheet

Perf. 14½

1548 A274 15g multicolored 10.00 5.00

No. 1548 is airmail and price includes a 5g surtax for a monument to Francisco Solano Lopez.

"U.P.U.," Pantheon, Carrier Pigeon, Globe — A275

1975, Feb. **Wmk. 347** ***Perf. 13½x13***

1549 A275 1g blk & lilac .30 .25
1550 A275 2g blk & rose red .30 .25
1551 A275 3g blk & ultra .30 .25
1552 A275 5g blk & blue .30 .25
1553 A275 10g blk & lil rose .70 .25
1554 A275 20g blk & brn 2.10 .25
1555 A275 25g blk & emer 2.10 .25
Nos. 1549-1555 (7) 6.10 1.75

Centenary of Universal Postal Union. Nos. 1554-1555 are airmail.

Paintings in National Gallery, London — A276

Details from paintings, artist: 5c, The Rokeby Venus, Velazquez, horiz. 10c, The Range of Love, Watteau. 15c, Venus (The School of Love), Correggio. 20c, Mrs. Sarah Siddons, Gainsborough. 25c, Cupid Complaining to Venus, L. Cranach the Elder. 35c, Portrait, Lotto. 40c, Nude, Rembrandt. 50c, Origin of the Milky Way, Tintoretto. 15g, Rider and Hounds, Pisanello.

1975, Apr. 25 **Unwmk.** ***Perf. 14***

1556 A276 5c multicolored .70 .25
1557 A276 10c multicolored .85 .25
1558 A276 15c multicolored 1.10 .25
1559 A276 20c multicolored 1.25 .25
1560 A276 25c multicolored 1.40 .25
1561 A276 35c multicolored 1.75 .25
1562 A276 40c multicolored 2.00 .25
1563 A276 50c multicolored 2.25 .25
Nos. 1556-1563 (8) 11.30 2.00

Souvenir Sheet

Perf. 13½

1564 A276 15g multicolored 15.00 15.00

No. 1564 is airmail, contains one 50x60mm stamp and price includes a 5g surtax for a monument to Francisco Solano Lopez.

Dogs — A277

1975, June 7 ***Perf. 14***

1565 A277 5c Boxer .75 .25
1566 A277 10c Poodle .75 .25
1567 A277 15c Basset hound .75 .25
1568 A277 20c Collie .75 .25
1569 A277 25c Chihuahua 1.00 .25
1570 A277 35c German shepherd 1.50 .25
1571 A277 40c Pekinese 1.60 .25
1572 A277 50c Chow 2.10 .25
Nos. 1565-1572 (8) 9.20 2.00

Souvenir Sheet

Perf. 13½

1573 A277 15g Fox hound, horse 21.00 12.00

No. 1573 is airmail, contains one 39x57mm stamp and price includes a 5g surtax for a monument to Francisco Solano Lopez.

South American Fauna A278

Designs: No. 1574a, 5c, Piranha (Pirana). b, 10c, Anaconda. c, 15c, Turtle (Tortuga). d, 20c, Iguana. e, 25c, Mono, vert. f, 35c, Mara. g, 40c, Marmota, vert. h, 50c, Peccary.

1975, Aug. 20 **Litho.** ***Perf. 14***

1574 A278 Strip of 8, #a.-h. 7.00 1.50

Souvenir Sheet

Perf. 13½

1575 A278 15g Aguara guazu 10.00 7.50

No. 1575 is airmail, contains one 60x50mm stamp, and price includes a 5g surtax for a monument to Francisco Solano Lopez.

For overprints see Nos. 2197.

Michelangelo (1475-1564), Italian Sculptor and Painter — A279

No. 1583: Statues, a, 5c, David. b, 10c, Aurora.

Paintings, c, 15c, Original Sin. d, 20c, The Banishment. e, 25c, The Deluge. f, 35c, Eve. g, 40c, Mary with Jesus and John. h, 50c, Judgement Day.

4g, Adam Receiving Life from God, horiz. No. 1585a, 5g, Libyan Sybil. b, 10g, Delphic Sybil. No. 1586, God Creating the Heaven and the Earth, horiz. No. 1587, The Holy Family.

1975, Aug. 23 **Litho.** ***Perf. 14***

1583 A279 Strip of 8, #a.-h. 2.00 1.50
1584 A279 4g multicolored 7.50 2.75
1585 A279 Pair, #a.-b. 1.90 .75

Souvenir Sheets

Perf. 12

1586 A279 15g multicolored 29.00 15.00

Perf. 13½

1587 A279 15g multicolored 18.00 15.00

Nos. 1586-1587 sold for 20g with surtax for a monument to Francisco Solano Lopez. Nos. 1584-1587 are airmail.

Winter Olympics, Innsbruck, 1976 — A280

No. 1596, Luge. No. 1599, 4-Man bobsled.

No. 1597a, 2g, Slalom skier. b, 3g, Cross country skier. c, 4g, Pair figure skating. d, 5g, Hockey.

No. 1598a, 10g, Speed skater. b, 15g, Downhill skier.

No. 1600, Ski jumper. No. 1601, Woman figure skater.

1975, Aug. 27 Litho. *Perf. 14*

1596 A280 1g multi .30 .25
1597 A280 Strip of 4, #a.-d. 3.25 1.00
1598 A280 Pair, #a.-b. 4.00 .80
1599 A280 20g multi 5.00 1.50
Nos. 1596-1599 (4) 12.55 3.55

Souvenir Sheet

Perf. 13½

1600 A280 25g multi 35.00 35.00
1601 A280 25g multi 22.50 22.50

Nos. 1596, 1598-1601 are horiz. Nos. 1598-1601 are airmail. Nos. 1600-1601 each contain one 60x50mm stamp.

Summer Olympics, Montreal, 1976 — A281

No. 1606: a, 1g, Weightlifting. b, 2g, Kayak. c, 3g, Hildegard Flack, 800 meter run. d, 4g, Lasse Viren, 5,000 meter run.

No. 1607: a, 5g, Dieter Kottysch, boxing. b, 10g, Lynne Evans, archery. c, 15g, Akinori Nakayama, balance rings. 20g, Heide Rosendahl, broad jump. No. 1609, Decathlon. No. 1610, Liselott Linsenhoff, dressage, horiz.

1975, Aug. 28 *Perf. 14*

1606 A281 Strip of 4, #a.-d. 1.00 .80
1607 A281 Strip of 3, #a.-c. 4.25 1.00
1608 A281 20g multicolored 5.25 1.50
Nos. 1606-1608 (3) 10.50 3.30

Souvenir Sheets

Perf. 14½

1609 A281 25g multicolored 32.00 30.00
1610 A281 25g multicolored 32.00 30.00

Nos. 1607b-1610 are airmail.

US, Bicent. A282

Ships: 5c, Sachem, vert. 10c, Reprisal, Lexington. 15c, Wasp. 20c, Mosquito, Spy. 25c, Providence, vert. 35c, Yankee Hero, Milford. 40c, Cabot, vert. 50c, Hornet, vert.
15g, Montgomery.

Unwmk.

1975, Oct. 20 Litho. *Perf. 14*

1616 A282 5c multicolored .55 .25
1617 A282 10c multicolored .80 .25
1618 A282 15c multicolored .80 .25
1619 A282 20c multicolored 1.10 .25
1620 A282 25c multicolored 1.10 .25
1621 A282 35c multicolored 1.00 .25
1622 A282 40c multicolored 1.10 .25
1623 A282 50c multicolored 1.60 .30
Nos. 1616-1623 (8) 8.05 2.05

Souvenir Sheet

1624 A282 15g multicolored 23.50 22.50

No. 1624 is airmail and contains one 50x70mm stamp.

US, Bicent. A283

Details from paintings, artists: No. 1625a, 5c, The Collector, Kahill. b, 10c, Morning Interlude, Brackman, vert. c, 15c, White Cloud, Catlin, vert. d, 20c, Man From Kentucky, Benton, vert. e, 25c, The Emigrants, Remington. f, 35c, Spirit of '76, Willard, vert. g, John Paul Jones capturing Serapis, unknown artist. h, 50c, Declaration of Independence, Trumbull. 15g, George Washington, Stuart and Thomas Jefferson, Peale.

1975, Nov. 20 *Perf. 14*

1625 A283 Strip of 8, #a.-h. 8.00 1.50

Souvenir Sheet

Perf. 13½

1625A A283 15g multicolored 30.00 30.00

No. 1625A is airmail, contains one 60x50mm stamp and price includes a 5g surtax for a monument to Francisco Solano Lopez.

Institute of Higher Education A284

Perf. 13½x13

1976, Mar. 16 Litho. Wmk. 347

1626 A284 5g vio, blk & red 1.25 .50
1627 A284 10g ultra, blk & red 2.25 1.50
1628 A284 30g brn, blk & red 2.25 1.50
Nos. 1626-1628 (3) 5.75 3.50

Inauguration of Institute of Higher Education, Sept. 23, 1974.
No. 1628 is airmail.

Rotary Intl., 70th Anniv. — A285

1976, Mar. 16 *Perf. 13x13½*

1629 A285 3g blk, bl & citron 1.10 .75
1630 A285 4g car, bl & citron 1.10 .75
1631 A285 25g emer, bl & lemon 3.50 2.00
Nos. 1629-1631 (3) 5.70 3.50

No. 1631 is airmail.

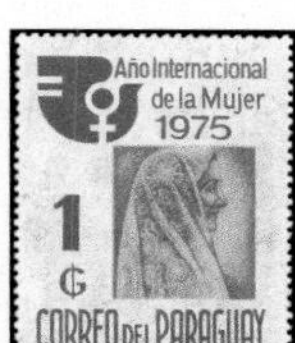

IWY Emblem, Woman's Head — A286

1976, Mar. 16

1632 A286 1g ultra & brn 1.10 .75
1633 A286 2g car & brn 1.10 .75
1634 A286 20g grn & brn 3.50 2.00
Nos. 1632-1634 (3) 5.70 3.50

Intl Women's Year (1975).
No. 1634 is airmail.

Cats — A287

Various cats: No. 1635a, 5c. b, 10c. c, 15c. d, 20c. e, 25c. f, 35c. g, 40c. h, 50c. 15g.

1976, Apr. 2 Unwmk. *Perf. 14*

1635 A287 Strip of 8, #a.-h. 12.00 1.00

Souvenir Sheet

Perf. 13½

1636 A287 15g multicolored 42.00 12.00

No. 1636 is airmail, contains one 50x60mm stamp and price includes a 5g surtax for a monument to Francisco Solano Lopez.

See Nos. 2132-2133, 2201-2202, 2274-2275. For overprint see No. 2212.

Railroads, 150th Anniv. (in 1975) A288

Locomotives: 1g, Planet, England, 1830. 2g, Koloss, Austria, 1844. 3g, Tarasque, France, 1846. 4g, Lawrence, Canada, 1853. 5g, Carlsruhe, Germany, 1854. 10g, Great Sagua, US, 1856. 15g, Berga, Spain. 20g, Encarnacion, Paraguay. 25g, English locomotive, 1825.

1976, Apr. 2 *Perf. 13x13½*

1637 A288 1g multicolored .30 .25
1638 A288 2g multicolored .30 .25
1639 A288 3g multicolored .30 .25
1640 A288 4g multicolored .30 .25
1641 A288 5g multicolored .30 .25
1642 A288 10g multicolored 4.00 .40
1643 A288 15g multicolored 6.50 .60
1644 A288 20g multicolored 8.00 1.00
Nos. 1637-1644 (8) 20.00 3.25

Souvenir Sheet

1645 A288 25g multicolored 52.50 52.50

Nos. 1642-1645 are airmail. No. 1645 contains one 40x27mm stamp.

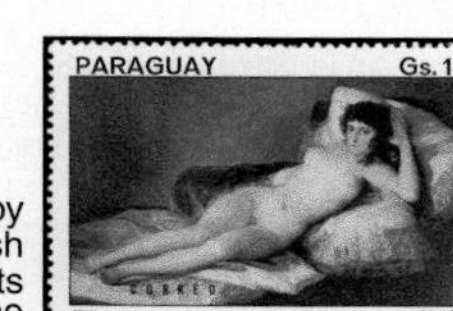

Painting by Spanish Artists A289

Paintings: 1g, The Naked Maja by Goya. 2g, Nude by J. de Torres. 3g, Nude holding oranges by de Torres, vert. 4g, Woman playing piano by Z. Velazquez, vert. 5g, Knight on white horse by Esquivel, vert. 10g, The Shepherd by Murillo, vert. 15g, The Immaculate Conception by Antolinez, vert. 20g, Nude by Zuloaga. 25g, Prince Baltasar Carlos on Horseback by D. Velasquez.

1976, Apr. 2 *Perf. 13x13½,13½x13*

1646 A289 1g multicolored .30 .25
1647 A289 2g multicolored .30 .25
1648 A289 3g multicolored .30 .25
1649 A289 4g multicolored .30 .25
1650 A289 5g multicolored .90 .25
1651 A289 10g multicolored 2.25 .40
1652 A289 15g multicolored 3.25 .50
1653 A289 20g multicolored 4.50 .60
Nos. 1646-1653 (8) 12.10 2.75

Souvenir Sheet

1654 A289 25g multicolored 9.50 5.00

Nos. 1651-1654 are airmail. No. 1654 contains one 58x82mm stamp.

Butterflies A290

No. 1655: a, 5c, Prepona praeneste. b, 10c, Prepona proschion. c, 15c, Pereute leucodrosime. d, 20c, Agrias amydon. e, 25c, Morpho aegea gynandromorphe. f, 35c, Pseudatteria leopardina. g, 40c, Morpho helena. h, 50c, Morpho hecuba.

1976, May 12 Unwmk. *Perf. 14*

1655 A290 Strip of 8, #a.-h. 9.50 1.50

Farm Animals A291

1976, June 15

1656 A291 1g Rooster, vert. .75 .25
1657 A291 2g Hen, vert. 1.10 .25
1658 A291 3g Turkey, vert. 1.10 .25
1659 A291 4g Sow 1.25 .25
1660 A291 5g Donkeys 1.50 .25
1661 A291 10g Brahma cattle 1.75 .35
1662 A291 15g Holstein cow 2.00 .35
1663 A291 20g Horse 2.50 .50
Nos. 1656-1663 (8) 11.95 2.45

Nos. 1661-1663 are airmail.

US and US Post Office, Bicent. A292

Designs: 1g, Pony Express rider. 2g, Stagecoach. 3g, Steam locomotive, vert. 4g, American steamship, Savannah. 5g, Curtiss Jenny biplane. 10g, Mail bus. 15g, Mail car, rocket train. 20g, First official missile mail, vert. No. 1672, First flight cover, official missile mail. No. 1673, US #C76 tied to cover by moon landing cancel.

1976, June 18

1664 A292 1g multicolored .50 .25
1665 A292 2g multicolored .70 .25
1666 A292 3g multicolored .80 .25
1667 A292 4g multicolored 1.00 .25
1668 A292 5g multicolored 1.25 .25
1669 A292 10g multicolored 1.75 .50
1670 A292 15g multicolored 3.25 .70
1671 A292 20g multicolored 5.00 1.00
Nos. 1664-1671 (8) 14.25 3.45

Souvenir Sheets

Perf. 14½

1672 A292 25g multicolored 24.00 24.00
1673 A292 25g multicolored 24.00 24.00

Nos. 1669-1673 are airmail and each contain one 50x40mm stamp.

Mythological Characters A293

Details from paintings, artists: No. 1674a, 1g, Jupiter, Ingres. b, 2g, Saturn, Rubens. c, 3g, Neptune, Tiepolo. d, 4g, Uranus and Aphrodite, Medina, horiz. e, 5g, Pluto and Prosperpine, Giordano, horiz. f, 10g, Venus, Ingres. g, 15g, Mercury, de la Hyre. No. 1675, Mars and Venus, Veronese.
25g, Viking Orbiter descending to Mars, horiz.

1976, July 18 *Perf. 14*

1674 A293 Strip of 7, #a.-g. 7.25 3.25
1675 A293 20g multicolored 4.00 1.60
Nos. 1674-1675 (2) 11.25 4.85

Souvenir Sheet

Perf. 14½

1676 A293 25g multicolored 52.00 52.00

Nos. 1674f-1674g, 1675-1676 are airmail.

Sailing Ships A294

Paintings: No. 1677a, 1g, Venice frigate of the Spanish Armada, vert. b, 2g, Swedish war ship, Vasa, 1628, vert. c, 3g, Spanish galleon being attacked by pirates by Puget. d, 4g, Combat by Dawson. e, 5g, European boat in Japan, vert. f, 10g, Elizabeth Grange in Liverpool by Walters. g, 15g, Prussen, 1903, by Holst. 20g, Grand Duchess Elizabeth, 1902, by Bohrdt.

1976, July 15 *Perf. 14*

1677 A294 Strip of 7, #a.-g. 9.00 2.50
1678 A294 20g multicolored 5.00 .50
Nos. 1677-1678 (2) 14.00 3.00

Nos. 1677f-1678 are airmail.

German Sailing Ships A295

Ship, artist: 1g, Bunte Kuh, 1402, Zeeden. 2g, Arms of Hamburg, 1667, Wichman, vert. 3g, Kaiser Leopold, 1667, Wichman, vert. 4g, Deutschland, 1848, Pollack, vert. 5g, Humboldt, 1851, Fedeler. 10g, Borussia, 1855, Seitz. 15g, Gorch Fock, 1958, Stroh, vert. 20g, Grand Duchess Elizabeth, 1902, Bohrdt. 25g, SS Pamir, Zeytline, vert.

Unwmk.

1976, Aug. 20 Litho. *Perf. 14*

1685	A295	1g multicolored	.55	.25
1686	A295	2g multicolored	.80	.25
1687	A295	3g multicolored	1.00	.25
1688	A295	4g multicolored	1.25	.25
1689	A295	5g multicolored	1.40	.30
1690	A295	10g multicolored	1.60	.45
1691	A295	15g multicolored	2.90	.80
1692	A295	20g multicolored	3.50	1.00
		Nos. 1685-1692 (8)	13.00	3.55

Souvenir Sheet

Perf. 14½

1693	A295	25g multicolored	21.00	21.00

Intl. German Naval Exposition, Hamburg; NORDPOSTA '76 (No. 1693). Nos. 1690-1693 are airmail.

US Bicentennial A296

Western Paintings by: No. 1694a, 1g, E. C. Ward. b, 2g, William Robinson Leigh. c, 3g, A. J. Miller. d, 4g, Charles Russell. e, 5g, Frederic Remington. f, 10g, Remington, horiz. g, 15g, Carl Bodmer.

No. 1695, A. J. Miller. No. 1696, US #1, 2, 245, C76.

Unwmk.

1976, Sept. 9 Litho. *Perf. 14*

1694	A296	Strip of 7, #a.-g.	11.00	2.00
1695	A296	20g multicolored	6.00	1.00
		Nos. 1694-1695 (2)	17.00	3.00

Souvenir Sheet

Perf. 13x13½

1696	A296	25g multicolored	47.50	47.50

Nos. 1694f-1694g, 1695-1696 are airmail. No. 1696 contains one 65x55mm stamp.

1976 Summer Olympics, Montreal — A297

Gold Medal Winners: No. 1703a, 1g, Nadia Comaneci, Romania, gymnastics, vert. b, 2g, Kornelia Ender, East Germany, swimming. c, 3g, Luann Ryan, US, archery, vert. d, 4g, Jennifer Chandler, US, diving. e, 5g, Shirley Babashoff, US, swimming. f, 10g, Christine Stuckelberger, Switzerland, equestrian. g, 15g, Japan, volleyball, vert.

20g, Annegret Richter, W. Germany, running, vert. No. 1705, Bruce Jenner, US, decathlon. No. 1706, Alwin Schockemohle, equestrian. No. 1707, Medals list, vert.

Unwmk.

1976, Dec. 18 Litho. *Perf. 14*

1703	A297	Strip of 7, #a.-g.	7.00	2.00
1704	A297	20g multicolored	3.00	.75
		Nos. 1703-1704 (2)	10.00	2.75

Souvenir Sheets

Perf. 14½

1705	A297	25g multicolored	37.50	37.50
1706	A297	25g multicolored	37.50	37.50
1707	A297	25g multicolored	37.50	37.50

Nos. 1703f-1703g, 1705-1707 are airmail. Nos. 1705-1706 each contain one 50x40mm stamp. No. 1707 contains one 50x70mm stamp.

Titian, 500th Birth Anniv. — A298

Details from paintings: No. 1708a, 1g, Venus and Adonis. b, 2g, Diana and Callisto. c, 3g, Perseus and Andromeda. d, 4g, Venus of the Mirror. e, 5g, Venus Sleeping, horiz. f, 10g, Bacchanal, horiz. g, 15g, Venus, Cupid and the Lute Player, horiz. 20g, Venus and the Organist, horiz.

1976, Dec. 18 *Perf. 14*

1708	A298	Strip of 7, #a.-g.	12.00	3.50
1709	A298	20g multicolored	4.00	1.50
		Nos. 1708-1709 (2)	16.00	5.00

No. 1708f-1708g, 1709 are airmail.

Peter Paul Rubens, 400th Birth Anniv. — A299

Paintings: No. 1710a, 1g, Adam and Eve. b, 2g, Tiger and Lion Hunt. c, 3g, Bathsheba Receiving David's Letter. d, 4g, Susanna in the Bath. e, 5g, Perseus and Andromeda. f, 10g, Andromeda Chained to the Rock. g, 15g, Shivering Venus. 20g, St. George Slaying the Dragon. 25g, Birth of the Milky Way, horiz.

1977, Feb. 18

1710	A299	Strip of 7, #a.-g.	8.00	3.25
1711	A299	20g multicolored	4.00	1.75
		Nos. 1710-1711 (2)	12.00	5.00

Souvenir Sheet

Perf. 14½

1712	A299	25g multicolored	57.50	35.00

Nos. 1710f-1710g, 1711-1712 are airmail.

US, Bicent. A300

Space exploration: No. 1713a, 1g, John Glenn, Mercury 7. b, 2g, Pres. Kennedy, Apollo 11. c, 3g, Wernher von Braun, Apollo 17. d, 4g, Mercury, Venus, Mariner 10. e, 5g, Jupiter, Saturn, Pioneer 10/11. f, 10g, Viking, Mars. g, 15g, Viking A on Mars. 20g, Viking B on Mars. No. 1715, Future space projects on Mars, vert. No. 1716, Future land rover on Mars.

1976, Mar. 3 *Perf. 14*

1713	A300	Strip of 7, #a.-g.	6.50	2.50
1714	A300	20g multicolored	3.50	1.50
		Nos. 1713-1714 (2)	10.00	4.00

Souvenir Sheets

Perf. 13½

1715	A300	25g multicolored	35.00	35.00
1716	A300	25g multicolored	35.00	35.00

Nos. 1713f-1713g, 1714-1716 are airmail. No. 1715 contains one 50x60mm stamp, No. 1716 one 60x50mm stamp.

Olympic History — A301

Designs: 1g, Spiridon Louis, marathon 1896, Athens, Pierre de Coubertin. 2g, Giuseppe Delfino, fencing 1960, Rome, Pope John XXIII. 3g, Jean Claude Killy, skiing 1968, Grenoble, Charles de Gaulle. 4g, Ricardo Delgado, boxing 1968, Mexico City, G. Diaz Ordaz. 5g, Hayata, gymnastics 1964, Tokyo, Emperor Hirohito. 10g, Klaus Wolfermann, javelin 1972, Munich, Avery Brundage. 15g, Michel Vaillancourt, equestrian 1976, Montreal, Queen Elizabeth II. 20g, Franz Klammer, skiing 1976, Innsbruck, Austrian national arms.

25g, Emblems of 1896 Athens games and 1976 Montreal games.

1977, June 7 *Perf. 14*

1717	A301	1g multicolored	.30	.25
1718	A301	2g multicolored	.30	.25
1719	A301	3g multicolored	.50	.25
1720	A301	4g multicolored	.80	.25
1721	A301	5g multicolored	1.00	.40
1722	A301	10g multicolored	1.25	.50
1723	A301	15g multicolored	1.60	.50
1724	A301	20g multicolored	2.60	1.00
		Nos. 1717-1724 (8)	8.35	3.40

Souvenir Sheet

Perf. 13½

1725	A301	25g multicolored	32.00	22.50

Nos. 1722-1725 are airmail. No. 1725 contains one 49x60mm stamp.

LUPOSTA '77, Intl. Stamp Exhibition, Berlin — A302

Graf Zeppelin 1st South America flight and: 1g, German girls in traditional costumes. 2g, Bull fighter, Seville. 3g, Dancer, Rio de Janeiro. 4g, Gaucho breaking bronco, Uruguay. 5g, Like #1530b. 10g, Argentinian gaucho. 15g, Ceremonial indian costume, Bolivia. 20g, Indian on horse, US.

No. 1734, Zeppelin over sailing ship. No. 1735, Ferdinand Von Zeppelin, zeppelin over Berlin, horiz.

1977, June 9 *Perf. 14*

1726	A302	1g multicolored	.60	.25
1727	A302	2g multicolored	.60	.25
1728	A302	3g multicolored	.70	.25
1729	A302	4g multicolored	1.20	.25
1730	A302	5g multicolored	1.50	.30
1731	A302	10g multicolored	1.90	.40
1732	A302	15g multicolored	2.40	.45
1733	A302	20g multicolored	4.00	.75
		Nos. 1726-1733 (8)	12.90	2.90

Souvenir Sheets

Perf. 13½

1734	A302	25g multicolored	62.50	62.50
1735	A302	25g multicolored	22.50	22.50

#1731-1735 are airmail. #1734 contains one 49x60mm stamp, #1735 one 60x49mm stamp.

Mburucuya Flowers — A303

Weaver with Spider Web Lace — A304

Designs: 1g, Ostrich feather panel. 2g, Black palms. 20g, Rose tabebuia. 25g, Woman holding ceramic pot.

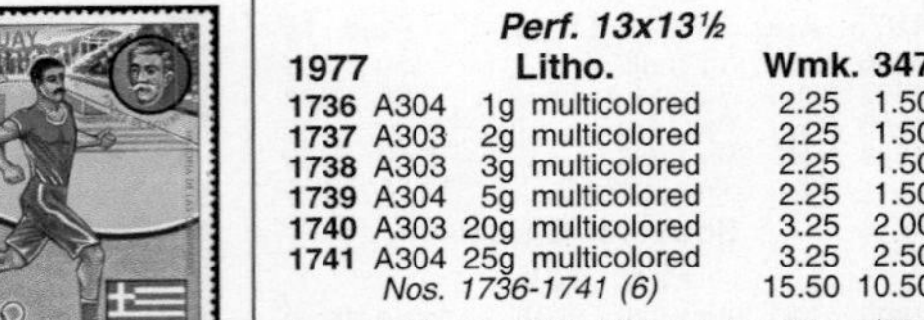

Perf. 13x13½

1977 Litho. Wmk. 347

1736	A304	1g multicolored	2.25	1.50
1737	A303	2g multicolored	2.25	1.50
1738	A303	3g multicolored	2.25	1.50
1739	A304	5g multicolored	2.25	1.50
1740	A303	20g multicolored	3.25	2.00
1741	A304	25g multicolored	3.25	2.50
		Nos. 1736-1741 (6)	15.50	10.50

Issued: 2g, 3g, 20g, 4/25; 1g, 5g, 25g, 6/27.

Nos. 1740-1741 are airmail.

Aviation History A305

Designs: No. 1742a, 1g, Orville and Wilbur Wright, Wright Flyer, 1903. b, 2g, Alberto Santos-Dumont, Canard, 1906. c, 3g, Louis Bleriot, Bleriot 11, 1909. d, 4g, Otto Lilienthal, Glider, 1891. e, 5g, Igor Sikorsky, Avion le Grande, 1913. f, 10g, Juan de la Cierva, Autogiro. g, 15g, Silvio Pettirossi, Deperdussin acrobatic plane. No. 1743, Concorde jet. No. 1744, Lindbergh, Spirit of St. Louis, Statue of Liberty, Eiffel Tower. No. 1745, Design of flying machine by da Vinci.

1977, July 18 Unwmk. *Perf. 14*

1742	A305	Strip of 7, #a.-g.	7.50	2.50
1743	A305	20g multicolored	4.00	1.50
		Nos. 1742-1743 (2)	11.50	4.00

Souvenir Sheet

Perf. 14½

1744	A305	25g multicolored	35.00	35.00
1745	A305	25g multicolored	37.50	37.50

Nos. 1742f-1745 are airmail. No. 1745 contains one label.

Francisco Solano Lopez — A306

Perf. 13x13½

1977, July 24 Litho. Wmk. 347

1752	A306	10g brown	1.50	*2.00*
1753	A306	50g dk vio	3.25	1.50
1754	A306	100g green	5.50	3.00
		Nos. 1752-1754 (3)	10.25	6.50

Marshal Francisco Solano Lopez (1827-1870), President of Paraguay.

Nos. 1753-1754 are airmail.

Paintings A307

Paintings by: No. 1755a, 1g, Gabrielle Rainer Istvanffy. b, 2g, L. C. Hoffmeister. c, 3g, Frans Floris. d, 4g, Gerard de Lairesse. e, 5g, David Teniers I. f, 10g, Jacopo Zucchi. g, 15g, Pierre Paul Prudhon. 20g, Francois Boucher. 25g, Ingres. 5g-25g vert.

1977, July 25 *Perf. 14*

1755	A307	Strip of 7, #a.-g.	9.25	3.50
1756	A307	20g multicolored	3.25	1.50
		Nos. 1755-1756 (2)	12.50	5.00

Souvenir Sheet

Perf. 14½

1757	A307	25g multicolored	27.50	27.50

Nos. 1755f-1757 are airmail.

German Sailing Ships A308

Designs: No. 1764a, 1g, De Beurs van Amsterdam. b, 2g, Katharina von Blankenese. c, 3g, Cuxhaven. d, 4g, Rhein. e, 5g, Churprinz and Marian. f, 10g, Bark of Bremen, vert. g, 15g, Elbe II, vert. 20g, Karacke. 25g, Admiral Karpeanger.

Unwmk.

1977, Aug. 27 Litho. *Perf. 14*

1764	A308	Strip of 7, #a.-g.	4.50	3.00
1765	A308	20g multicolored	6.50	2.00
		Nos. 1764-1765 (2)	11.00	5.00

Souvenir Sheet

Perf. 13½

1766	A308	25g multicolored	15.50	15.50

Nos. 1764f-1766 are airmail. No. 1766 contains one 40x30mm stamp.

Nobel Laureates for Literature A309

Authors and scenes from books: No. 1773a, 1g, John Steinbeck, Grapes of Wrath, vert. b, 2g, Ernest Hemingway, Death in the Afternoon. c, 3g, Pearl S. Buck, The Good Earth, vert. d, 4g, George Bernard Shaw, Pygmalion, vert. e, 5g, Maurice Maeterlinck, Joan of Arc, vert. f, 10g, Rudyard Kipling, The Jungle Book. g, 15g, Henryk Sienkiewicz, Quo Vadis. 20g, C. Theodor Mommsen, History of Rome. 25g, Nobel prize medal.

1977, Sept. 5 *Perf. 14*

1773	A309	Strip of 7, #a.-g.	6.50	2.50
1774	A309	20g multicolored	3.50	1.50
		Nos. 1773-1774 (2)	10.00	4.00

Souvenir Sheet

Perf. 14½

1775	A309	25g multicolored	48.50	48.50

Nos. 1773f-1775 are airmail.

1978 World Cup Soccer Championships, Argentina — A310

Posters and World Cup Champions: No. 1782a, 1g, Uruguay, 1930. b, 2g, Italy, 1934. c, 3g, Italy, 1938. d, 4g, Uruguay, 1950. e, 5g, Germany, 1954. f, 10g, Soccer player by Fritz Genkinger. g, 15g, Soccer player, orange shirt by Genkinger.

No. 1783a, 1g, Brazil, 1958. b, 2g, Brazil, 1962. c, 3g, England, 1966. d, 4g, Brazil, 1970. e, 5g, Germany, 1974. f, 10g, Player #4 by Genkinger. g, 15g, Player #1 by Genkinger, horiz.

No. 1784, World Cup Trophy. No. 1785, German players, Argentina '78. No. 1786, The Loser, by Genkinger. No. 1787, The Defender, (player #11) by Genkinger.

1977, Oct. 28 Unwmk. *Perf. 14*

1782	A310	Strip of 7, #a.-g.	7.75	2.25
1783	A310	Strip of 7, #a.-g.	7.50	2.25
1784	A310	20g multicolored	2.25	.65
1785	A310	20g multicolored	2.50	.65
		Nos. 1782-1785 (4)	20.00	5.80

Souvenir Sheets

Perf. 14½

1786	A310	25g red & multi	40.00	40.00
1787	A310	25g black & multi	40.00	40.00

Nos. 1782f-1782g, 1783f-1783g, 1784-1787 are airmail.

Peter Paul Rubens, 400th Birth Anniv. — A312

Details from paintings: No. 1788a, 1g, Rubens and Isabella Brant under Honeysuckle Bower. b, 2g, Judgment of Paris. c, 3g, Union of Earth and Water. d, 4g, Daughters of Kekrops Discovering Erichthonius. e, 5g, Holy Family with the Lamb. f, 10c, Adoration of the Magi. g, 15c, Philip II on Horseback.

20g, Education of Marie de Medici, horiz. 25g, Triumph of Eucharist Over False Gods.

1978, Jan. 19 Unwmk. *Perf. 14*

1788	A312	Strip of 7, #a.-g.	9.00	2.50
1789	A312	20g multicolored	5.00	1.40
		Nos. 1788-1789 (2)	14.00	3.90

Souvenir Sheet

Perf. 14½

1790	A312	25g multi, gold	25.00	25.00
1790A	A312	25g multi, silver	37.00	37.00

Nos. 1788f-1788g, 1789-1790 are airmail. No. 1790 contains one 50x70mm stamp and exists inscribed in gold or silver.

1978 World Chess Championships, Argentina — A313

Paintings of chess players: No. 1791a, 1g, De Cremone. b, 2g, L. van Leyden. c, 3g, H. Muehlich. d, 4g, Arabian artist. e, 5g, Benjamin Franklin playing chess, E. H. May. f, 10g, G. Cruikshank. g, 15g, 17th cent. tapestry. 20g, Napoleon playing chess on St. Helena. 25g, Illustration from chess book, Shah Name.

1978, Jan. 23 *Perf. 14*

1791	A313	Strip of 7, #a.-g.	28.00	9.50
1792	A313	20g multicolored	14.00	4.50
		Nos. 1791-1792 (2)	42.00	14.00

Souvenir Sheet

Perf. 14½

1793	A313	25g multicolored	47.00	47.00

Nos. 1791f-1791g, 1792-1793 are airmail. No. 1793 contains one 50x40mm stamp.

Jacob Jordaens, 300th Death Anniv. — A314

Paintings: No. 1794a, 3g, Satyr and the Nymphs. b, 4g, Satyr with Peasant. c, 5g, Allegory of Fertility. d, 6g, Upbringing of Jupiter. e, 7g, Holy Family. f, 8g, Adoration of the Shepherds. g, 20g, Jordaens with his family. 10g, Meleagro with Atalanta, horiz. No. 1796, Feast for a King, horiz. No. 1797, Holy Family with Shepherds.

1978, Jan. 25 *Perf. 14*

1794	A314	Strip of 7, #a.-g.	12.00	2.75
1795	A314	10g multicolored	2.75	.75
1796	A314	25g multicolored	5.50	1.40
		Nos. 1794-1796 (3)	20.25	4.90

Souvenir Sheet

Perf. 14½

1797	A314	25g multicolored	15.00	15.00

Nos. 1795-1797 are airmail. No. 1797 contains one 50x70mm stamp.

Albrecht Durer, 450th Death Anniv. — A315

Monograms and details from paintings: No. 1804a, 3g, Temptation of the Idler. b, 4g, Adam and Eve. c, 5g, Satyr Family. d, 6g, Eve. e, 7g, Adam. f, 8g, Portrait of a Young Man. g, 20g, Squirrels and Acorn. 10g, Madonna and Child. No. 1806, Brotherhood of the Rosary (Lute-playing Angel). No. 1807, Soldier on Horseback with a Lance.

1978, Mar. 10 *Perf. 14*

1804	A315	Strip of 7, #a.-g.	7.25	2.25
1805	A315	10g multicolored	2.50	.50
1806	A315	25g multicolored	4.50	1.20
		Nos. 1804-1806 (3)	14.25	3.95

Souvenir Sheet

Perf. 13½

1807	A315	25g blk, buff & sil	47.50	47.50

Nos. 1805-1807 are airmail. No. 1807 contains one 30x40mm stamp.

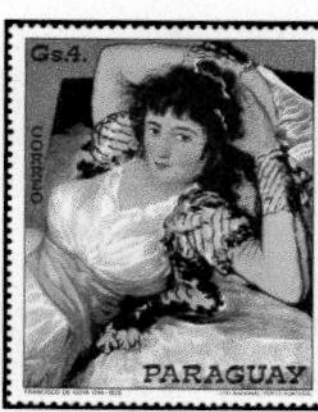

Francisco de Goya, 150th Death Anniv. — A316

Paintings: No. 1814a, 3g, Allegory of the Town of Madrid. b, 4g, The Clothed Maja. c, 5g, The Parasol. d, 6g, Dona Isabel Cobos de Porcel. e, 7g, The Drinker. f, 8g, The 2nd of May 1908. g, 20g, General Jose Palafox on Horseback. 10g, Savages Murdering a Woman. 25g, The Naked Maja, horiz.

1978, May 11 *Perf. 14*

1814	A316	Strip of 7, #a.-g.	7.50	1.25
1815	A316	10g multicolored	1.90	.85
1816	A316	25g multicolored	3.00	1.90
		Nos. 1814-1816 (3)	12.40	4.00

Nos. 1815-1816 are airmail.

Future Space Projects A317

Various futuristic space vehicles and imaginary creatures: No. 1817a, 3g. b, 4g. c, 5g. d, 6g. e, 7g. f, 8g. g, 20g.

1978, May 16

1817	A317	Strip of 7, #a.-g.	7.50	2.25
1818	A317	10g multicolored	1.50	.50
1819	A317	25g multi, diff.	4.50	1.00
		Nos. 1817-1819 (3)	13.50	3.75

Nos. 1818-1819 are airmail.

Racing Cars — A318

No. 1820: a, 3g, Tyrell Formula I. b, 4g, Lotus Formula 1, 1978. c, 5g, McLaren Formula 1. d, 6g, Brabham Alfa Romeo Formula 1. e, 7g, Renault Turbo Formula 1. f, 8g, Wolf Formula 1. g, 20g, Porsche 935. 10g, Bugatti. 25g, Mercedes Benz W196, Stirling Moss, driver. No. 1823, Ferrari 312T.

1978, June 28 *Perf. 14*

1820	A318	Strip of 7, #a.-g.	7.50	1.90
1821	A318	10g multicolored	1.20	.25
1822	A318	25g multicolored	2.90	.80
		Nos. 1820-1822 (3)	11.60	2.95

Souvenir Sheet

Perf. 14½

1823	A318	25g multicolored	26.00	26.00

Nos. 1821-1823 are airmail. No. 1823 contains one 50x35mm stamp.

Paintings by Peter Paul Rubens — A319

3g, Holy Family with a Basket. 4g, Amor Cutting a Bow. 5g, Adam & Eve in Paradise. 6g, Crown of Fruit, horiz. 7g, Kidnapping of Ganymede. 8g, The Hunting of Crocodile & Hippopotamus. 10g, The Reception of Marie de Medici at Marseilles. 20g, Two Satyrs. 25g, Felicity of the Regency.

1978, June 30 *Perf. 14*

1824	A319	3g multicolored	.40	.25
1825	A319	4g multicolored	.70	.25
1826	A319	5g multicolored	.90	.25
1827	A319	6g multicolored	.95	.25
1828	A319	7g multicolored	1.20	.30
1829	A319	8g multicolored	1.40	.40
1830	A319	10g multicolored	3.25	.80
1831	A319	20g multicolored	4.75	1.10
1832	A319	25g multicolored	6.50	1.60
		Nos. 1824-1832 (9)	20.05	5.20

Nos. 1830, 1832 are airmail.

National College A320

Perf. 13½x13

1978 Litho. Wmk. 347

1833	A320	3g claret	2.25	2.00
1834	A320	4g violet blue	2.25	2.00
1835	A320	5g lilac	2.25	2.00
1836	A320	20g brown	2.25	2.00
1837	A320	25g violet black	3.25	2.00
1838	A320	30g bright green	3.25	2.00
		Nos. 1833-1838 (6)	15.50	12.00

Centenary of National College in Asuncion.

Nos. 1836-1838 are airmail.

José Estigarribia, Bugler, Flag of Paraguay — A321

1978 Litho. *Perf. 13x13½*

1839	A321	3g multi	3.25	2.00
1840	A321	5g multi	3.25	2.00
1841	A321	10g multi	3.25	2.00
1842	A321	20g multi	5.25	3.00
1843	A321	25g multi	5.25	3.00
1844	A321	30g multi	5.25	3.00
		Nos. 1839-1844 (6)	25.50	15.00

Induction of Jose Felix Estigarribia (1888-1940), general and president of Paraguay, into Salon de Bronce (National Heroes' Hall of Fame).

Nos. 1842-1844 are airmail.

Queen Elizabeth II Coronation, 25th Anniv. — A322

Flowers and: 3g, Barbados #234. 4g, Tristan da Cunha #13. 5g, Bahamas #157. 6g, Seychelles #172. 7g, Solomon Islands #88. 8g, Cayman Islands #150. 10g, New Hebrides #77. 20g, St. Lucia #156. 25g, St. Helena #139.

No. 1854, Solomon Islands #368a-368c, Gilbert Islands #312a-312c. No. 1855, Great Britain #313-316.

1978, July 25 Unwmk. *Perf. 14*

1845	A322	3g multicolored	.40	.25
1846	A322	4g multicolored	.80	.25
1847	A322	5g multicolored	.90	.25
1848	A322	6g multicolored	.95	.25
1849	A322	7g multicolored	1.20	.30
1850	A322	8g multicolored	1.40	.40
1851	A322	10g multicolored	3.25	.80
1852	A322	20g multicolored	4.75	1.20
1853	A322	25g multicolored	6.50	1.60
		Nos. 1845-1853 (9)	20.15	5.30

Souvenir Sheets

Perf. 13½

1854 A322 25g multicolored 62.50 62.50
1855 A322 25g multicolored 62.50 62.50

Nos. 1851, 1853-1855 are airmail. Nos. 1854-1855 each contain one 60x40mm stamp.

Intl. Philatelic Exhibitions A323

Various paintings, ship, nudes, etc. for: No. 1856a, 3g, Nordposta '78. b, 4g, Riccione '78. c, 5g, Uruguay '79. d, 6g, ESSEN '78. e, 7g, ESPAMER '79. f, 8g, London '80. g, 20g, PRAGA '78. 10g, EUROPA '78. No. 1858, Eurphila '78.

No. 1859, Francisco de Pinedo, map of his flight.

1978, July 19 *Perf. 14*

1856 A323 Strip of 7, #a.-g. 9.00 1.25
1857 A323 10g multicolored 2.10 .40
1858 A323 25g multicolored 3.25 .70
Nos. 1856-1858 (3) 14.35 2.35

Souvenir Sheet

Perf. 13½x13

1859 A323 25g multicolored 30.00 30.00

No. 1859 for Riccione '78 and Eurphila '78 and contains one 54x34mm stamp. Nos. 1857-1859 are airmail. Nos. 1856b-1858 are vert.

Intl. Year of the Child — A324

Grimm's Snow White and the Seven Dwarfs: No. 1866a, 3g, Queen pricking her finger. b, 4g, Queen and mirror. c, 5g, Man with dagger, Snow White. d, 6g, Snow White in forest. e, 7g, Snow White asleep, seven dwarfs. f, 8g, Snow White dancing with dwarfs. g, 20g, Snow White being offered apple. 10g, Snow White in repose. 25g, Snow White, Prince Charming on horseback.

1978, Oct. 26

1866 A324 Strip of 7, #a.-g. 7.50 2.25
1867 A324 10g multicolored 1.75 .50
1868 A324 25g multicolored 4.25 1.00
Nos. 1866-1868 (3) 13.50 3.75

Nos. 1867-1868 are airmail.
See Nos. 1893-1896, 1916-1919.

Mounted South American Soldiers — A325

No. 1869a, 3g, Gen. Jose Felix Bogado (1771-1829). b, 4g, Colonel, First Volunteer Regiment, 1806. c, 5g, Colonel wearing dress uniform, 1860. d, 6g, Soldier, 1864-1870. e, 7g, Dragoon, 1865. f, 8g, Lancer. g, 20g, Soldier, 1865. 10g, Gen. Bernardo O'Higgins, 200th birth anniv. 25g, Jose de San Martin, 200th birth anniv.

1978, Oct. 31

1869 A325 Strip of 7, #a.-g. 8.75 1.75
1870 A325 10g multicolored 1.50 .25
1871 A325 25g multicolored 4.25 .45
Nos. 1869-1871 (3) 14.50 2.45

Nos. 1870-1871 are airmail.

1978 World Cup Soccer Championships, Argentina — A326

Soccer Players: No. 1872a, 3g, Paraguay, vert. b, 4g, Austria, Sweden. c, 5g, Argentina, Poland. d, 6g, Italy, Brazil. e, 7g, Netherlands, Austria. f, 8g, Scotland, Peru. g, 20g, Germany, Italy. 10g, Argentina, Holland. 25g, Germany, Tunisia.

No. 1875, Stadium.

1979, Jan. 9 *Perf. 14*

1872 A326 Strip of 7, #a.-g. 9.25 2.00
1873 A326 10g multicolored 1.25 .25
1874 A326 25g multicolored 3.75 .50
Nos. 1872-1874 (3) 14.25 2.75

Souvenir Sheet

Perf. 13½

1875 A326 25g multicolored 52.50 52.50

Nos. 1873-1875 are airmail. No. 1875 contains one 60x40mm stamp.

For overprint see No. C610.

Christmas A327

Paintings of the Nativity and Madonna and Child by: No. 1876a, 3g, Giorgione, horiz. b, 4g, Titian. c, 5g, Titian, diff. d, 6g, Raphael. e, 7g, Schongauer. f, 8g, Muratti. g, 20g, Van Oost. 10g, Memling. No. 1878, Rubens.

No. 1879, Madonna and Child Surrounded by a Garland and Boy Angels, Rubens.

1979, Jan. 10 **Litho.** *Perf. 14*

1876 A327 Strip of 7, #a.-g. 7.75 2.25
1877 A327 10g multicolored 1.50 .35
1878 A327 25g multicolored 3.25 .90
Nos. 1876-1878 (3) 12.50 3.50

Souvenir Sheet

Photo. & Engr.

Perf. 12

1879 A327 25g multicolored 87.50 87.50

Nos. 1877-1879 are airmail.

First Powered Flight, 75th Anniv. (in 1978) A328

Airplanes: No. 1880a, 3g, Eole, C. Ader, 1890. b, 4g, Flyer III, Wright Brothers. c, 5g, Voisin, Henri Farman, 1908. d, 6g, Curtiss, Eugene Ely, 1910. e, 7g, Etrich-Taube A11. f, 8g, Fokker EIII. g, 20g, Albatros C, 1915. 10g, Boeing 747 carrying space shuttle. No. 1882, Boeing 707. No. 1883, Zeppelin flight commemorative cancels.

1979, Apr. 24 **Litho.** *Perf. 14*

1880 A328 Strip of 7, #a.-g. 7.00 1.40
1881 A328 10g multicolored 1.00 .25
1882 A328 25g multicolored 2.50 .50
Nos. 1880-1882 (3) 10.50 2.15

Souvenir Sheet

Perf. 14½

1883 A328 25g blue & black 72.50 72.50

Nos. 1881-1883 are airmail. Nos. 1880-1883 incorrectly commemorate 75th anniv. of ICAO. No. 1883 contains one 50x40mm stamp.

Albrecht Durer, 450th Death Anniv. (in 1978) — A329

Paintings: No. 1884a, 3g, Virgin with the Dove. b, 4g, Virgin Praying. c, 5g, Mater Dolorosa. d, 6g, Virgin with a Carnation. e, 7g, Madonna and Sleeping Child. f, 8g, Virgin Before the Archway. g, 20g, Flight Into Egypt. No. 1885, Madonna of the Haller family. No. 1886, Virgin with a Pear.

No. 1887, Lamentation Over the Dead Christ for Albrecht Glimm. No. 1888, Space station, horiz., with Northern Hemisphere of Celestial Globe in margin.

1979, Apr. 28 *Perf. 14*

1884 A329 Strip of 7, #a.-g. 6.75 2.25
1885 A329 10g multicolored 1.50 .75
1886 A329 25g multicolored 4.50 1.50
Nos. 1884-1886 (3) 12.75 4.50

Souvenir Sheets

Perf. 13½

1887 A329 25g multicolored 36.00 36.00
1888 A329 25g multicolored 25.00 25.00

Intl. Year of the Child (#1885-1886).

Nos. 1885-1886, 1888 are airmail. No. 1887 contains one 30x40mm stamp, No. 1888 one 40x30mm stamp.

Sir Rowland Hill, Death Cent. A330

Hill and: No. 1889a, 3g, Newfoundland #C1, vert. b, 4g, France #C14. c, 5g, Spain #B106. d, 6g, Similar to Ecuador #C2, vert. e, 7g, US #C3a. f, 8g, Gelber Hund inverted overprint, vert. g, 20g, Switzerland #C20a.

10g, Privately issued Zeppelin stamp. No. 1891, Paraguay #C82, #C96, vert. No. 1892, Italy #C49. No. 1892A, France #C3-C4.

1979, June 11 *Perf. 14*

1889 A330 Strip of 7, #a.-g. 7.50 2.25
1890 A330 10g multicolored 2.00 .75
1891 A330 25g multicolored 5.75 2.00
Nos. 1889-1891 (3) 15.25 5.00

Souvenir Sheet

Perf. 13½x13

1892 A330 25g multicolored 32.00 32.00

Perf. 14½

1892A A330 25g multicolored 21.00 21.00

Issue dates: No. 1892A, Aug. 28. Others, June 11. Nos. 1890-1892A are airmail.

Grimm's Fairy Tales Type of 1978

Cinderella: No. 1893a, 3g, Two stepsisters watch Cinderella cleaning. b, 4g, Cinderella, father, stepsisters. c, 5g, Cinderella with birds while working. d, 6g, Finding dress. e, 7g, Going to ball. f, 8g, Dancing with prince. g, 20g, Losing slipper leaving ball.

10g, Prince Charming trying slipper on Cinderella's foot. No. 1895, Couple riding to castle. No. 1896, Couple entering ballroom.

1979, June 24 *Perf. 14*

1893 A324 Strip of 7, #a.-g. 7.50 2.25
1894 A324 10g multicolored 1.75 .55
1895 A324 25g multicolored 5.00 1.20
Nos. 1893-1895 (3) 14.25 4.00

Souvenir Sheet

Perf. 13½

1896 A324 25g multicolored 25.00 25.00

Intl. Year of the Child.

Congress Emblem — A331

1979, Aug. **Litho.** *Perf. 13x13½*

1897 A331 10g red, blue & black 5.25 2.00
1898 A331 50g red, blue & black 5.25 2.00

22nd Latin-American Tourism Congress, Asuncion. No. 1898 is airmail.

1980 Winter Olympics, Lake Placid A332

#1899: a, 3g, Monica Scheftschik, luge. b, 4g, E. Deufl, Austria, downhill skiing. c, 5g, G. Thoeni, Italy, slalom skiing. d, 6g, Canada Two-man bobsled. e, 7g, Germany vs. Finland, ice hockey. f, 8g, Hoenl, Russia, ski jump. g, 20g, Dianne De Leeuw, Netherlands, figure skating, vert.

10g, Hanni Wenzel, Liechtenstein, slalom skiing. No. 1901, Frommelt, Liechtenstein, slalom skiing, vert. No. 1902, Kulakova, Russia, cross country skier. No. 1903, Dorothy Hamill, US, figure skating, vert. No. 1904, Brigitte Totschnig, skier.

1979 **Unwmk.** *Perf. 14*

1899 A332 Strip of 7, #a.-g. 6.50 2.75
1900 A332 10g multicolored 1.50 .75
1901 A332 25g multicolored 4.25 1.50
Nos. 1899-1901 (3) 12.25 5.00

Souvenir Sheets

Perf. 13½

1902 A332 25g multicolored 21.00 21.00
1903 A332 25g multicolored 22.50 22.50
1904 A332 25g multicolored 62.50 62.50

#1900-1904 are airmail. #1902-1903 each contain one 40x30mm stamp, #1904, one 25x36mm stamp.

Issued: #1899-1902, 8/22; #1903, 6/11; #1904, 4/24.

Sailing Ships A333

No. 1905: a, 3g, Caravel, vert. b, 4g, Warship. c, 5g, Warship, by Jan van Beeck. d, 6g, H.M.S. Britannia, vert. e, 7g, Salamis, vert. f, 8g, Ariel, vert. g, 20g, Warship, by Robert Salmon.

1979, Aug. 28 *Perf. 14*

1905 A333 Strip of 7, #a.-g. 8.00 2.50
1906 A333 10g Lisette 1.25 .30
1907 A333 25g Holstein, vert. 3.50 .70
Nos. 1905-1907 (3) 12.75 3.50

Nos. 1906-1907 are airmail.

Intl. Year of the Child — A334

Various kittens: No. 1908a, 3g. b, 4g. c, 5g. d, 6g. e, 7g. f, 8g. g, 20g.

1979, Nov. 29 *Perf. 14*

1908 A334 Strip of 7, #a.-g. 6.50 2.00
1909 A334 10g multicolored 2.50 .30
1910 A334 25g multicolored 2.25 2.75
Nos. 1908-1910 (3) 11.25 5.05

Nos. 1909-1910 are airmail.

Grimm's Fairy Tales Type of 1978

Little Red Riding Hood: No. 1916a, 3g, Leaving with basket. b, 4g, Meets wolf. c, 5g, Picks flowers. d, 6g, Wolf puts on Granny's gown. e, 7g, Wolf in bed. f, 8g, Hunter arrives. g, 20g, Saved by the hunter.

10g, Hunter enters house. No. 1918, Hunter leaves. No. 1919, Overall scene.

1979, Dec. 4 *Perf. 14*
1916 A324 Strip of 7, #a.-g. 6.25 4.25
1917 A324 10g multicolored 1.50 1.00
1918 A324 25g multicolored 4.25 2.25
Nos. 1916-1918 (3) 12.00 7.50

Souvenir Sheet
Perf. 14½
1919 A324 25g multicolored 25.00 25.00

Intl. Year of the Child. No. 1919 contains one 50x70mm stamp.

Greek Athletes — A335

Paintings on Greek vases: No. 1926a, 3g, 3 runners. b, 4g, 2 runners. c, 5g, Throwing contest. d, 6g, Discus. e, 7g, Wrestlers. f, 8g, Wrestlers, diff. g, 20g, 2 runners, diff.
10g, Horse and rider, horiz. 25g, 4 warriors with shields, horiz.

1979, Dec. 20 *Perf. 14*
1926 A335 Strip of 7, #a.-g. 9.00 5.00
1927 A335 10g multicolored 1.75 .75
1928 A335 25g multicolored 3.50 1.75
Nos. 1926-1928 (3) 14.25 7.50

Nos. 1927-1928 are airmail.

Electric Trains A336

No. 1929: a, 3g, First electric locomotive, Siemens, 1879, vert. b, 4g, Switzerland, 1897. c, 5g, Model E71 28, Germany. d, 6g, Mountain train, Switzerland. e, 7g, Electric locomotive used in Benelux countries. f, 8g, Locomotive "Rheinpfeil," Germany. g, 20g, Model BB-9004, France.
10g, 200-Km/hour train, Germany. 25g, Japanese bullet train.

1979, Dec. 24 **Litho.** *Perf. 14*
1929 A336 Strip of 7, #a.-g. 8.00 2.40
1930 A336 10g multicolored 4.75 1.30
1931 A336 25g multicolored 5.25 1.30
Nos. 1929-1931 (3) 18.00 5.00

Nos. 1930-1931 are airmail.

Sir Rowland Hill, Death Cent. A337

Hill and: No. 1938a, 3g, Spad S XIII, 1917-18. b, 4g, P-51 D Mustang, 1944-45. c, 5g, Mitsubishi A6M6c Zero-Sen, 1944. d, 6g, Depperdussin float plane, 1913. e, 7g, Savoia Marchetti SM 7911, 1936. f, 8g, Messerschmitt Me 262B, 1942-45. g, 20g, Nieuport 24bis, 1917-18.
10g, Zeppelin LZ 104-/l59, 1917. No. 1940, Fokker Dr-1 Caza, 1917. No. 1941, Vickers Supermarine "Spitfire" Mk.IX, 1942-45.

1980, Apr. 8 *Perf. 14*
1938 A337 Strip of 7, #a.-g. 6.75 2.00
1939 A337 10g multicolored 1.25 .55
1940 A337 25g multicolored 2.25 1.10
Nos. 1938-1940 (3) 12.25 3.65

Souvenir Sheet
Perf. 13½
1941 A337 25g multicolored 35.00 30.00

Incorrectly commemorates 75th anniv. of ICAO. Nos. 1939-1941 are airmail. No. 1941 contains one 37x27mm stamp.

Sir Rowland Hill, Paraguayan Stamps — A338

Hill and: No. 1948a, 3g, #1. b, 4g, #5. c, 5g, #6. d, 6g, #379. e, 7g, #381. f, 8g, #C384. g, 20g, #C389.
10g, #C83, horiz. No. 1950, #C92, horiz. No. 1951, #C54, horiz. No. 1952, #C1, horiz.

1980, Apr. 14 **Litho.** *Perf. 14*
1948 A338 Strip of 7, #a.-g. 9.75 2.75
1949 A338 10g multicolored 2.00 .65
1950 A338 25g multicolored 4.50 1.60
Nos. 1948-1950 (3) 16.25 5.00

Souvenir Sheets
Perf. 14½
1951 A338 25g multicolored 35.00 32.50
1952 A338 25g multicolored 35.00 32.50

#1949-1952 are airmail. #1951 contains one 50x40mm stamp. #1952 one 50x35mm stamp.

1980 Winter Olympics, Lake Placid — A339

No. 1953: a, 3g, Thomas Wassberg, Sweden, cross country skiing. b, 4g, Scharer & Benz, Switzerland, 2-man bobsled. c, 5g, Annemarie Moser-Proll, Austria, women's downhill skiing. d, 6g, Hockey team, US. e, 7g, Leonhard Stock, Austria, men's downhill skiing. f, 8g, Anton (Toni) Innauer, Austria, ski jump. g, 20g, Christa Kinshofer, Germany, slalom skiing.
10g, Ingemar Stenmark, slalom, Sweden. No. 1955, Robin Cousins, figure skating, Great Britain. No. 1956, Eric Heiden, speed skating, US, horiz.

1980, June 4 *Perf. 14*
1953 A339 Strip of 7, #a.-g. 7.75 3.50
1954 A339 10g multi, horiz. 1.60 .70
1955 A339 25g multi, horiz. 5.50 2.75
Nos. 1953-1955 (3) 14.85 6.95

Souvenir Sheet
Perf. 13½
1956 A339 25g multicolored 26.00 25.00

Nos. 1954-1956 are airmail. No. 1956 contains one 60x49mm stamp.

Composers and Paintings of Young Ballerinas A340

Paintings of ballerinas by Cydney or Degas and: No. 1957a, 3g, Gioacchino Rossini. b, 4g, Johann Strauss, the younger. c, 5g, Debussy. d, 6g, Beethoven. e, 7g, Chopin. f, 8g, Richard Wagner. g, 20g, Johann Sebastian Bach, horiz. 10g, Robert Stoltz. 25g, Verdi.

1980, July 1 *Perf. 14*
1957 A340 Strip of 7, #a.-g. 7.75 2.50
1958 A340 10g multicolored 1.75 .60
1959 A340 25g multicolored 5.25 1.40
Nos. 1957-1959 (3) 14.75 4.50

Birth and death dates are incorrectly inscribed on 4g, 8g, 10g. No. 1957f is incorrectly inscribed "Adolph" Wagner. Nos. 1958-1959 are airmail. For overprints see Nos. 1998-1999.

Pilar City Bicentennial A341

Perf. 13½x13
1980, July 17 **Litho.** **Wmk. 347**
1966 A341 5g multi 5.25 2.00
1967 A341 25g multi 5.25 2.00

No. 1967 is airmail.

Christmas, Intl. Year of the Child — A342

No. 1968: a, 3g, Christmas tree. b, 4g, Santa filling stockings. c, 5g, Nativity scene. d, 6g, Adoration of the Magi. e, 7g, Three children, presents. f, 8g, Children, dove, fruit. g, 20g, Children playing with toys. 10g, Madonna and Child, horiz. No. 1970, Children blowing bubbles, horiz. No. 1971, Five children, horiz.

1980, Aug. 4 **Unwmk.** *Perf. 14*
1968 A342 Strip of 7, #a.-g. 9.00 5.00
1969 A342 10g multicolored 1.40 .90
1970 A342 25g multicolored 2.50 1.40
Nos. 1968-1970 (3) 12.90 7.30

Souvenir Sheet
1971 A342 25g multicolored 26.00 25.00

Nos. 1969-1970 are airmail.

Ships A343

Emblems and ships: No. 1972a, 3g, ESPAMER '80, Spanish Armada. b, 4g, NORWEX '80, Viking longboat. c, 5g, RICCIONE '80, Battle of Lepanto. d, 6g, ESSEN '80, Great Harry of Cruickshank. e, 7g, US Bicentennial, Mount Vernon. f, 8g, LONDON '80, H.M.S. Victory. g, 20g, ESSEN '80, Hamburg III, vert. 10g, ESSEN '80, Gorch Fock. 25g, vert. PHILATOKYO '81, Nippon Maru, horiz.

1980, Sept. 15 *Perf. 14*
1972 A343 Strip of 7, #a.-g. 6.25 2.25
1973 A343 10g multicolored 1.50 .55
1974 A343 25g multicolored 4.50 1.40
Nos. 1972-1974 (3) 12.25 4.20

Nos. 1973-1974 are airmail. For overprint see No. 2278.

Souvenir Sheet

King Juan Carlos A344

1980, Sept. 19 *Perf. 14½*
1975 A344 25g multicolored 22.00 21.00

Paraguay Airlines Boeing 707 Service Inauguration A345

Perf. 13½x13
1980, Sept. 17 **Litho.** **Wmk. 347**
1976 A345 20g multi 2.75 1.50
1977 A345 100g multi 2.75 1.50

No. 1977 is airmail.

A346

World Cup Soccer Championships, Spain — A346a

Various soccer players, winning country: No. 1978a, 3g, Uruguay 1930, 1950. b, 4g, Italy 1934, 1938. c, 5g, Germany 1954, 1974. d, 6g, Brazil 1958, 1962, 1970. e, 7g, England, 1966. f, 8g, Argentina, 1978. g, 20g, Espana '82 emblem.
10g, World Cup trophy, flags. 25g, Soccer player from Uruguay.

1980, Dec. 10 **Unwmk.** *Perf. 14*
1978 A346 Strip of 7, #a.-g. 7.00 1.75
1979 A346 10g multicolored 2.10 .50
1980 A346 25g multicolored 7.25 1.75
Nos. 1978-1980 (3) 16.35 4.00

Souvenir Sheet
Perf. 14½
1981 A346a 25g Sheet of 1 + 2 labels 26.00 25.00

Nos. 1979-1981 are airmail.

1980 World Chess Championships, Mexico — A347

Illustrations from The Book of Chess: No. 1982a, 3g, Two men, chess board. b, 4g, Circular chess board, players. c, 5g, Four-person chess match. d, 6g, King Alfonso X of Castile and Leon. e, 7g, Two players, chess board, horiz. f, 8g, Two veiled women, chess board, horiz. g, 20g, Two women in robes, chess board, horiz.
10g, Crusader knights, chess board, horiz. 25g, Three players, chess board, horiz.

1980, Dec. 15 **Litho.** *Perf. 14*
1982 A347 Strip of 7, #a.-g. 11.00 2.50
1983 A347 10g multicolored 2.00 .35
1984 A347 25g multicolored 2.25 .70
Nos. 1982-1984 (3) 15.25 3.55

Nos. 1983-1984 are airmail.
See Nos. C506-C510. Compare with illustration AP199.

1980 Winter Olympics, Lake Placid — A348

Olympic scenes, gold medalists: No. 1985a, 25c, Lighting Olympic flame. b, 50c, Hockey team, US. c, 1g, Eric Heiden, US, speed skating. d, 2g, Robin Cousins, Great Britain, figure skating. e, 3g, Thomas Wassberg, Sweden, cross country skiing. f, 4g, Annie Borckinck, Netherlands, speed skating. g, 5g, Gold, silver, and bronze medals.

No. 1986, Irene Epple, silver medal, slalom, Germany. 10g, Ingemar Stenmark, slalom, giant slalom, Sweden. 30g, Annemarie Moser-Proll, downhill, Austria. 25g, Baron Pierre de Coubertin.

1981, Feb. 4 Litho. *Perf. 14*

1985	A348	Strip of 7, #a.-g.	4.50	1.90
1986	A348	5g multicolored	1.20	.35
1987	A348	10g multicolored	1.60	.50
1988	A348	30g multicolored	4.50	1.00
		Nos. 1985-1988 (4)	11.80	3.75

Souvenir Sheet

Perf. 13½

1988A	A348	25g multicolored	21.00	20.00

No. 1985 exists in strips of 4 and 3. Nos. 1986-1988A are airmail. No. 1988A contains one 30x40mm stamp.

Locomotives A349

No. 1989, 25c, Electric model 242, Germany. b, 50c, Electric, London-Midlands-Lancashire, England. c, 1g, Electric, Switzerland. d, 2g, Diesel-electric, Montreal-Vancouver, Canada. e, 3g, Electric, Austria. f, 4g, Electric inter-urban, Lyons-St. Etienne, France, vert. g, 5g, First steam locomotive in Paraguay.

No. 1990, 5g, Steam locomotive, Japan. No. 1991, 10g, Stephenson's steam engine, 1830 England. No. 1992, 30g, Stephenson's Rocket, 1829, England, vert.

No. 1993, 25g, Crocodile locomotive, Switzerland.

1981, Feb. 9 Litho. *Perf. 14*

1989	A349	Strip of 7, #a.-g.	4.50	1.10
1990	A349	5g multicolored	2.25	.35
1991	A349	10g multicolored	3.75	.65
1992	A349	30g multicolored	12.00	2.00
		Nos. 1989-1992 (4)	22.50	4.10

Souvenir Sheet

Perf. 13½x13

1993	A349	25g multicolored	37.50	35.00

Electric railroads, cent. (#1989a-1989f), steam-powered railway service, 150th anniv. (#1989g, 1990-1991), Liverpool-Manchester Railway, 150th anniv. (#1992). Swiss Railways, 75th anniv. (#1993).

Nos. 1990-1993 are airmail. No. 1993 contains one 54x34mm stamp.

Intl. Year of the Child — A350

Portraits of children with assorted flowers: No. 1994a, 10g. b, 25g. c, 50g. d, 100g. e, 200g. f, 300g. g, 400g.

1981, Apr. 13 Litho. *Perf. 14*

1994	A350	Strip of 7, #a.-g.	20.50	8.25
1995	A350	75g multicolored	2.50	.70
1996	A350	500g multicolored	10.50	4.00
1997	A350	1000g multicolored	19.50	8.00
		Nos. 1994-1997 (4)	53.00	20.95

Nos. 1995-1997 are airmail.

Nos. 1957b and 1958 Overprinted in Red

1981, May 22

1998	A340	4g on #1957b	1.25	.60
1999	A340	10g on #1958	2.25	1.00

No. 1999 is airmail.

The following stamps were issued in sheets of 8 with 1 label: Nos. 2001, 2013, 2037, 2044, 2047, 2055, 2140.

The following stamp was issued in sheets of 10 with 2 labels: No. 1994a.

The following stamps were issued in sheets of 6 with 3 labels: Nos. 2017, 2029, 2035, 2104, 2145.

The following stamps were issued in sheets of 3 with 6 labels: 2079, 2143.

The following stamps were issued in sheets of 5 with 4 labels: Nos. 2050-2051, 2057, 2059, 2061, 2067, 2069, 2077, 2082, 2089, 2092, 2107, 2117, 2120, 2121, 2123, 2125, 2129, 2135, 2138, 2142, 2146, 2148, 2151, 2160, 2163, 2165, 2169, 2172, 2176, 2179, 2182, 2190, 2196, 2202, 2204, 2214, 2222, 2224, 2232, 2244, 2246, 2248, 2261, 2263, 2265, 2269, 2271, 2273, 2275, 2277.

The following stamps were issued in sheets of 4 with 5 labels: Nos. 2307, 2310, 2313, 2316, 2324, 2329.

Royal Wedding of Prince Charles and Lady Diana Spencer A351

Prince Charles, sailing ships: No. 2000a, 25c, Royal George. b, 50c, Great Britain. c, 1g, Taeping. d, 2g, Star of India. e, 3g, Torrens. f, 4g, Loch Etive. No. 2001, Medway.

No. 2002, Charles, flags, and Concorde. 10g, Flags, flowers, Diana, Charles. 25g, Charles, Diana, flowers, vert. 30g, Coats of arms, flags.

1981, June 27

2000	A351	Strip of 6, #a.-f.	5.00	1.40
2001	A351	5g multicolored	1.60	.35
2002	A351	5g multicolored	1.00	.45
2003	A351	10g multicolored	3.25	.75
2004	A351	30g multicolored	5.50	2.25
		Nos. 2000-2004 (5)	16.35	5.20

Souvenir Sheet

Perf. 13½

2005	A351	25g multicolored	26.00	25.00

Nos. 2002-2005 are airmail. No. 2005 contains one 50x60mm stamp. For overprint see No. 2253.

No. 2005 has an orange margin. It also exists with gray margin. Same value.

Traditional Costumes and Itaipu Dam — A352

Women in various traditional costumes: a, 10g. b, 25g. c, 50g. d, 100g. e, 200g. f, 300g. g, 400g, President Stroessner, Itaipu Dam.

1981, June 30 *Perf. 14*

2006	A352	Strip of 7, #a.-g.	27.00	8.00

For overprints see No. 2281.

UPU Membership Centenary A353

1981, Aug. 18 Litho. *Perf. 13½x13*

2007	A353	5g rose lake & blk	2.25	1.00
2008	A353	10g lil & blk	2.25	1.00
2009	A353	20g grn & blk	2.25	1.00
2010	A353	25g lt red brn & blk	2.25	1.00
2011	A353	50g bl & blk	3.25	2.00
		Nos. 2007-2011 (5)	12.25	6.00

Peter Paul Rubens, Paintings — A354

Details from paintings: No. 2012: a, 25c, Madonna Surrounded by Saints. b, 50c, Judgment of Paris. c, 1g, Duke of Buckingham Conducted to the Temple of Virtus. d, 2g, Minerva Protecting Peace from Mars. e, 3g, Henry IV Receiving the Portrait of Marie de Medici. f, 4g, Triumph of Juliers. 5g, Madonna and Child Reigning Among Saints (Cherubs).

1981, July 9 Litho. *Perf. 14*

2012	A354	Strip of 6, #a.-f.	5.25	.75
2013	A354	5g multicolored	1.50	.25
		Nos. 2012-2013 (2)	6.75	1.00

Jean Auguste-Dominique Ingres (1780-1867), Painter — A355

Details from paintings: No. 2014: a, 25c, c, 1g, d, 2g, f, 4g, The Turkish Bath. b, 50c, The Source. e, 3g, Oedipus and the Sphinx. g, 5g, Half-figure of a Bather.

1981, Oct. 13

2014	A355	Strip of 7, #a.-g.	6.75	1.50

A horiz. strip of 5 containing Nos. 2014a-2014e exists.

No. 2014f and 2014g exist in sheet of 8 (four each) plus label.

For overprints see No. 2045.

Pablo Picasso, Birth Cent. A356

Designs: No. 2015: a, 25c, Women Running on the Beach. b, 50c, Family on the Beach.

No. 2016: a, 1g, Still-life. b, 2g, Bullfighter. c, 3g, Children Drawing. d, 4g, Seated Woman. 5g, Paul as Clown.

1981, Oct. 19

2015	A356	Pair, #a.-b.	.90	.50
2016	A356	Strip of 4, #a.-d.	8.75	1.50
2017	A356	5g multicolored	2.10	.40
		Nos. 2015-2017 (3)	11.75	2.40

Nos. 2015-2016 Ovptd. in Silver

1981, Oct. 22

2018	A356	on #2015a-2015b	1.00	.50
2019	A356	on #2016a-2016d	4.50	1.00
		Nos. 2018-2019 (2)	5.50	1.50

Philatelia '81, Frankfurt.

Nos. 2015-2016 Ovptd. in Gold

1981, Oct. 25

2020	A356	on #2015a-2015b	1.00	.50
2021	A356	on #2016a-2016d	4.50	1.00
		Nos. 2020-2021 (2)	5.50	1.50

Espamer '81 Philatelic Exhibition.

Royal Wedding of Prince Charles and Lady Diana — A357

Designs: No. 2022a-2022c, 25c, 50c, 1g, Diana, Charles, flowers. d, 2g, Couple. e, 3g, Couple leaving church. f, 4g, Couple, Queen Elizabeth II waving from balcony. 2022G, 5g, Diana. No. 2023, Wedding party, horiz. 10g, Riding in royal coach, horiz. 30g, Yeomen of the guard, horiz.

1981, Dec. 4 Litho. *Perf. 14*

2022	A357	Strip of 6, #a.-f.	2.40	1.50
2022G	A357	5g multicolored	.40	.25
2023	A357	5g multicolored	3.50	.70
2024	A357	10g multicolored	6.75	1.40
2025	A357	30g multicolored	24.00	4.50
		Nos. 2022-2025 (5)	37.05	8.35

Souvenir Sheets

Perf. 14½

2026	A357	25g like #2022d	40.00	37.50
2027	A357	25g Wedding portrait	40.00	37.50

No. 2022g exists in sheets of 8 plus label. Nos. 2023-2027 are airmail. Nos. 2026-2027 contain one each 50x70mm stamp.

Christmas A358

Designs: No. 2028a, 25c, Jack-in-the-box. b, 50c, Jesus and angel. c, 1g, Santa, angels. d, 2g, Angels lighting candle. e, 3g, Christmas plant. f, 4g, Nativity scene. 5g, Children singing by Christmas tree.

1981, Dec. 17 *Perf. 14*

2028	A358	Strip of 6, #a.-f.	5.00	1.00

Size: 28x45mm

Perf. 13½

2029	A358	5g multicolored	2.75	.55

Intl. Year of the Child (Nos. 2028-2029). For overprints see No. 2042.

Intl. Year of the Child — A359

Story of Puss 'n Boots: No. 2030a, 25c, Boy, Puss. b, 50c, Puss, rabbits.

1g, Puss, king. 2g, Prince, princess, king. 3g, Giant ogre, Puss. 4g, Puss chasing mouse. 5g, Princess, prince, Puss.

1982, Apr. 16 Litho. *Perf. 14*

2030	A359	Pair, #a.-b.	.70	.50
2031	A359	1g multicolored	.35	.25
2032	A359	2g multicolored	.70	.25
2033	A359	3g multicolored	1.00	.25
2034	A359	4g multicolored	1.60	.25
2035	A359	5g multicolored	6.50	1.50
		Nos. 2030-2035 (6)	10.85	3.00

Nos. 2031-2034 printed se-tenant with label.

Scouting, 75th Anniv. and Lord Baden-Powell, 125th Birth Anniv. — A360

No. 2036: a, 25c, Tetradactyla, Scout hand salute. b, 50c, Nandu (rhea), Cub Scout and trefoil. c, 1g, Peccary, Wolf's head totem. d, 2g, Coatimundi, emblem on buckle. e, 3g, Mara, Scouting's Intl. Communications emblem. f, 4g, Deer, boy scout.

No. 2037, Aotes, Den mother, Cub Scout. No. 2038, Ocelot, scouts cooking. 10g, Collie, boy scout. 30g, Armadillo, two scouts planting tree. 25g, Lord Robert Baden-Powell, founder of Boy Scouts.

1982, Apr. 21

2036	A360	Strip of 6, #a.-f.	2.75	1.00
2037	A360	5g multicolored	2.25	.40
2038	A360	5g multicolored	2.25	.40
2039	A360	10g multicolored	3.25	.45
2040	A360	30g multicolored	4.00	.40
		Nos. 2036-2040 (5)	14.50	2.65

Souvenir Sheet

Perf. 14½

2041	A360	25g multicolored	33.00	32.00

Nos. 2038-2041 are airmail. For overprint see No. 2140.

No. 2028 Overprinted with ESSEN 82 Emblem

1982, Apr. 28 *Perf. 14*

2042	A358	on #2028a-2028f	4.00	2.50

Essen '82 Intl. Philatelic Exhibition.

Cats and Kittens A361

Various cats or kittens: No. 2043a, 25c. b, 50c. c, 1g. d, 2g. e, 3g. f, 4g.

1982, June 7 *Perf. 14*

2043	A361	Strip of 6, #a.-f.	5.00	1.00
2044	A361	5g multi, vert.	1.75	.35
		Nos. 2043-2044 (2)	6.75	1.35

For overprints see Nos. 2054-2055.

Nos. 2014a-2014e Ovptd. PHILEXFRANCE 82 Emblem ans "PARIS 11-21.6.82" in Blue

1982, June 11

2045	A355	Strip of 5, #a.-e.	4.75	1.00

Philexfrance '82 Intl. Philatelic Exhibition. Size of overprint varies.

World Cup Soccer Championships, Spain — A362

Designs: 2046a, 25c, Brazilian team. b, 50c, Chilean team. c, 1g, Honduran team. d, 2g, Peruvian team. e, 3g, Salvadoran team. f, 4g, Globe as soccer ball, flags of Latin American finalists. No. 2047, Ball of flags. No. 2048, Austrian team. No. 2049, Players from Brazil, Austria. No. 2050, Spanish team. No. 2051, Two players from Argentina, Brazil, vert. No. 2052, W. German team. No. 2053, Players from Argentina, Brazil. No. 2053A, World Cup trophy, world map on soccer balls. No. 2053B, Players from W. Germany, Mexico, vert.

1982 Litho. *Perf. 14*

2046	A362	Strip of 6, #a.-f.	3.75	1.25
2047	A362	5g multicolored	.35	.25
2048	A362	5g multicolored	1.95	1.40
2049	A362	5g multicolored	3.25	1.00
2050	A362	10g multicolored	.90	.25
2051	A362	10g multicolored	.50	.50
2052	A362	30g multicolored	2.25	.25
2053	A362	30g multicolored	.25	.25
		Nos. 2046-2053 (8)	13.20	5.15

Souvenir Sheets

Perf. 14½

2053A	A362	25g multicolored	18.00	17.00
2053B	A362	25g multicolored	18.00	17.00

Issued: #2049, 2051, 2053, 2053A, 4/19; others, 6/13.

Nos. 2047 exists in sheets of 8 plus label. Nos. 2048-2053B are airmail.

For overprints see Nos. 2086, 2286, C593.

Nos. 2043-2044 Overprinted in Silver With PHILATECIA 82 and Intl. Year of the Child Emblems

1982, Sept. 12 *Perf. 14*

2054	A361	Strip of 5, #a.-e.	5.50	1.25
2055	A361	5g on #2044	2.25	.40
		Nos. 2054-2055 (2)	7.75	1.65

Philatelia '82, Hanover, Germany and Intl. Year of the Child.

Raphael, 500th Birth Anniv. — A363

Details from paintings: No. 2056a, 25c, Adam and Eve (The Fall). b, 50c, Creation of Eve. c, 1g, Portrait of a Young Woman (La Fornarina). d, 2g The Three Graces. e, 3g, f, 4g, Cupid and the Three Graces. 5g. Leda and the Swan.

1982, Sept. 27

2056	A363	Strip of 6, #a.-f.	6.75	1.50
2057	A363	5g multicolored	5.00	1.00
		Nos. 2056-2057 (2)	11.75	2.50

Nos. 2056e-2056f have continuous design.

Christmas A364

Entire works or details from paintings by Raphael: No. 2058a, 25c, The Belvedere Madonna. b, 50c, The Ansidei Madonna. c, 1g, La Belle Jardiniere. d, 2g, The Aldobrandini (Garvagh) Madonna. e, 3g, Madonna of the Goldfinch. f, 4g, The Alba Madonna. No. 2059, Madonna of the Grand Duke. No. 2060, Madonna of the Linen Window. 10g, The Alba Madonna, diff. 25g, The Holy Family with St. Elizabeth and the Infant St. John and Two Angels. 30g, The Canigiani Holy Family.

1982 *Perf. 14, 13x13½ (#2061)*

2058	A364	Strip of 6, #a.-f.	6.00	2.50
2059	A364	5g multicolored	2.40	.90
2060	A364	5g multicolored	5.50	1.75
2061	A364	10g multicolored	2.50	.90
2062	A364	30g multicolored	1.25	.40
		Nos. 2058-2062 (5)	17.65	6.45

Souvenir Sheet

Perf. 14½

2063	A364	25g multicolored	19.00	17.50

Issued: #2058-2059, 9/30; others, 12/17.

Nos. 2058a-2058f and 2059 exist perf. 13. Nos. 2060-2063 are airmail and have silver lettering. For overprint see No. 2087.

Life of Christ, by Albrecht Durer — A365

Details from paintings: No. 2064a, 25c, The Flight into Egypt. b, 50c, Christ Among the Doctors. c, 1g, Christ Carrying the Cross. d, 2g, Nailing of Christ to the Cross. e, 3g, Christ on the Cross. f, 4g, Lamentation Over the Dead Christ. 5g, The Circumcision of Christ.

1982, Dec. 14 *Perf. 14*

2064	A365	Strip of 6, #a.-f.	7.50	2.75

Perf. 13x13½

2065	A365	5g multicolored	4.00	.75
		Nos. 2064-2065 (2)	11.50	3.50

For overprint see No. 2094.

South American Locomotives A366

Locomotives from: No. 2066a, 25c, Argentina. b, 50c, Uruguay. c, 1g, Ecuador. d, 2g, Bolivia. e, 3g, Peru. f, 4g, Brazil. 5g, Paraguay.

1983, Jan. 17 Litho. *Perf. 14*

2066	A366	Strip of 6, #a.-f.	3.75	1.00
2067	A366	5g multicolored	3.00	.75
		Nos. 2066-2067 (2)	6.75	1.75

For overprint see No. 2093.

Race Cars — A367

No. 2068: a, 25c, ATS-Ford D 06. b, 50c, Ferrari 126 C 2. c, 1g, Brabham-BMW BT 50. d, 2g, Renault RE 30 B. e, 3g, Porsche 956. f, 4g, Talbot-Ligier-Matra JS 19. 5g, Mercedes Benz C-111.

1983, Jan. 19 *Perf. 14*

2068	A367	Strip of 6, #a.-f.	5.25	1.60

Perf. 13½x13

2069	A367	5g multicolored	2.50	.90
		Nos. 2068-2069 (2)	7.75	2.50

For overprint see No. 2118.

Itaipua Dam, Pres. Stroessner A368

1983, Jan. 22 Litho. Wmk. 347

2070	A368	3g multi	2.25	1.00
2071	A368	5g multi	2.25	1.00
2072	A368	10g multi	2.25	1.00
2073	A368	20g multi	2.25	1.00
2074	A368	25g multi	2.25	1.00
2075	A368	50g multi	2.25	1.00
		Nos. 2070-2075 (6)	13.50	6.00

25th anniv. of Stroessner City.
Nos. 2073-2075 airmail.

1984 Winter Olympics, Sarajevo A369

Ice skaters: No. 2076a, 25c, Marika Kilius, Hans-Jurgens Baumler, Germany, 1964. b, 50c, Tai Babilonia, Randy Gardner, US, 1976. c, 1g, Anett Poetzsch, E. Germany, 1980, vert. d, 2g, Tina Riegel, Andreas Nischwitz, Germany, 1980, vert. e, Dagmar Lurz, Germany, 1980, vert. f, 4g, Trixi Schuba, Austria, 1972, vert. 5g, Peggy Fleming, US, 1968, vert.

Perf. 13½x13, 13x13½

1983, Feb. 23 Unwmk.

2076	A369	Strip of 6, #a.-f.	3.25	1.00
2077	A369	5g multicolored	5.00	.75
		Nos. 2076-2077 (2)	8.25	1.75

For overprints see Nos. 2177, 2266.

Pope John Paul II — A370

#2078: a, 25c, Virgin of Caacupe. b, 50c, Cathedral of Caacupe. c, 1g, Cathedral of Asuncion. d, 2g, Pope holding crucifix. e, 3g, Our Lady of the Assumption. f, 4g, Pope giving blessing. 5g, Pope with hands clasped. 25g, Madonna & child.

1983, June 11 Litho. *Perf. 14*

2078	A370	Strip of 6, #a.-f.	6.75	2.00
2079	A370	5g multicolored	3.25	.80
		Nos. 2078-2079 (2)	10.00	2.80

Souvenir Sheet

Perf. 14½

2080	A370	25g multicolored	18.50	14.00

No. 2080 is airmail. For overprint see No. 2143.

Antique Automobiles A371

No. 2081: a, 25c, Bordino Steamcoach, 1854. b, 50c, Panhard & Levassor, 1892. c, 1g, Benz Velo, 1894. d, 2g, Peugeot-Daimler, 1894. e, 3g, 1st car with patented Lutzmann system, 1898. f, 4g, Benz Victory, 1891-92. No. 2082, Ceirano 5CV. No. 2083, Mercedes Simplex PS 32 Turismo, 1902. 10g, Stae Electric, 1909. 25g, Benz Velocipede, 1885. 30g, Rolls Royce Silver Ghost, 1913.

1983, July 18 *Perf. 14*

2081	A371	Strip of 6, #a.-f.	3.00	1.25
2082	A371	5g multicolored	1.90	.40
2083	A371	5g multicolored	7.00	1.10
2084	A371	10g multicolored	1.25	.25
2085	A371	30g multicolored	2.75	.25
		Nos. 2081-2085 (5)	15.90	3.25

Souvenir Sheet

Perf. 14½

2085A	A371	25g Sheet of 1 + label	21.00	20.00

Nos. 2083-2085A are airmail.

No. 2046 Ovptd. in Red, No. 2058 Ovptd. in Black with "52o CONGRESO F.I.P." and Brasiliana 83 Emblem

1983, July 27 *Perf. 14*

2086	A362	Strip of 6, #a.-f.	6.50	5.00
2087	A364	Strip of 6, #a.-f.	6.50	5.00

Brasiliana '83, Rio de Janeiro and 52nd FIP Congress. No. 2087 exists perf. 13.

Aircraft Carriers A372

Carriers and airplanes: No. 2088a, 25c, 25 de Mayo, A-4Q Sky Hawk, Argentina. b, 50c, Minas Gerais, Brazil. c, 1g, Akagi, A6M3 Zero, Japan. d, 2g, Guiseppe Miraglia, Italy. e, 3g, Enterprise, S-3A Viking, US. f, 4g, Dedalo, AV-8A Matador, Spain. No. 2089, 5g, Schwabenland, Dornier DO-18, Germany.

No aircraft on Nos. 2088b, 2088d.

25g, US astronauts Donn Eisele, Walter Schirra & Walt Cunningham, Earth & Apollo 7.

1983, Aug. 29 *Perf. 14*

2088	A372	Strip of 6, #a.-f.	5.50	1.50
2089	A372	5g multicolored	2.50	.75
		Nos. 2088-2089 (2)	8.00	2.25

Souvenir Sheet

Perf. 13½

2090	A372	25g multicolored	22.00	21.00

No. 2090 is airmail and contains one 55x45mm stamp.

Birds — A373

#2091: a, 25c, Pulsatrix perspicillata. b, 50c, Ortalis ruficauda. c, 1g, Chloroceryle amazona. d, 2g, Trogon violaceus. e, 3g, Pezites militaris. f, 4g, Bucco capensis. 5g, Cyanerpes cyaneus.

1983, Oct. 22 *Perf. 14*

2091	A373	Strip of 6, #a.-f.	5.50	1.00

Perf. 13

2092	A373	5g multicolored	2.25	.40
		Nos. 2091-2092 (2)	7.75	1.40

No. 2066 Ovptd. for PHILATELICA 83 in Silver

1983, Oct. 28

2093	A366	Strip of 6, #a.-f.	6.75	2.00

Philatelia '83, Dusseldorf, Germany.

No. 2064 Overprinted in Silver for EXFIVIA - 83

1983, Nov. 5

2094	A365	Strip of 6, #a.-f.	7.50	2.00

Exfivia '83 Philatelic Exhibition, La Paz, Bolivia.

Re-election of President Stroessner A374

10g, Passion flower, vert. 25g, Miltonia phalaenopsis, vert. 50g, Natl. arms, Chaco soldier. 75g, Acaray hydroelectric dam. 100g, Itaipu hydroelectric dam. 200g, Pres. Alfredo Stroessner, vert.

1983, Nov. 24 *Perf. 14*

2095	A374	10g multicolored	.50	.30
2096	A374	25g multicolored	.80	.30
2097	A374	50g multicolored	1.60	.30
2098	A374	75g multicolored	1.25	.30

Perf. 13

2099	A374	100g multicolored	1.75	.30
2100	A374	200g multicolored	3.50	1.00
		Nos. 2095-2100 (6)	9.40	2.50

Nos. 2099-2100 are airmail. No. 2096 exists perf 13. For overprint see No. C577.

Montgolfier Brothers' 1st Flight, Bicent. A375

No. 2101: a, 25c, Santos-Dumont's Biplane, 1906. b, 50c, Airship. c, 1g, Paulhan's biplane over Juvisy. d, 2g, Zeppelin LZ-3, 1907. e, 3g, Biplane of Henri Farman. f, 4g, Graf Zeppelin over Friedrichshafen. 5g, Lebaudy's dirigible. 25g, Detail of painting, Great Week of Aviation at Betheny, 1910.

1984, Jan. 7 *Perf. 13*

2101	A375	Strip of 6, #a.-f.	3.00	1.25

Perf. 14

2104	A375	5g multicolored	5.25	.75
		Nos. 2101-2104 (2)	8.25	2.00

Souvenir Sheet

Perf. 13½

2105	A375	25g multicolored	22.00	21.00

No. 2105 is airmail and contains one 75x55mm stamp. For overprint see No. 2145.

Dogs — A376

#2106: a, 25c, German Shepherd. b, 50c, Great Dane, vert. c, 1g, Poodle, vert. d, 2g, Saint Bernard. e, 3g, Greyhound. f, 4g, Dachshund. 5g, Boxer.

1984, Jan. 11 **Litho.** *Perf. 14*

2106	A376	Strip of 6, #a.-f.	4.50	2.10
2107	A376	5g multicolored	2.25	.90
		Nos. 2106-2107 (2)	6.75	3.00

See nos. 2181-2182.

Animals, Anniversaries A377

1984, Jan. 24 *Perf. 13*

2108	A377	10g Puma	.45	.30
2109	A377	25g Alligator	1.20	.30
2110	A377	50g Jaguar	2.25	.45
2111	A377	75g Peccary	3.50	.70
2112	A377	100g Simon Bolivar, vert.	5.25	1.10
2113	A377	200g Girl scout, vert.	10.00	3.25
		Nos. 2108-2113 (6)	22.65	6.10

Simon Bolivar, birth bicent. and Girl Scouts of Paraguay, 76th anniv.

Nos. 2112-2113 are airmail.

Christmas — A378

Designs: No. 2114a, 25c, Pope John Paul II. b, 50c, Christmas tree. c, 1g, Children. d, 2g, Nativity Scene. e, 3g, Three Kings. f, 4g, Madonna and Child. No. 2115, Madonna and Child by Raphael.

1984, Mar. 23 *Perf. 13x13½*

2114	A378	Strip of 6, #a.-f.	8.75	1.50
2115	A378	5g multicolored	4.00	1.00
		Nos. 2114-2115 (2)	12.75	2.50

Troubadour Knights — A379

Illustrations of medieval miniatures: No. 2116a, 25c, Ulrich von Liechtenstein. b, 50c, Ulrich von Gutenberg. c, 1g, Der Putter. d, 2g, Walther von Metz. e, 3g, Hartman von Aue. f, 4g, Lutok von Seuen. 5g, Werner von Teufen.

1984, Mar. 27 *Perf. 14*

2116	A379	Strip of 6, #a.-f.	5.50	1.25

Perf. 13

2117	A379	5g multicolored	3.25	.75
		Nos. 2116-2117 (2)	8.75	2.00

For overprint see No. 2121.

No. 2068 Ovptd. in Silver with ESSEN 84 Emblem

1984, May 10

2118	A367	Strip of 6, #a.-f.	5.50	1.25

Essen '84 Intl. Philatelic Exhibition.

Endangered Animals A380

#2119: a, 25c, Priodontes giganteus. b, 50c, Catagonus wagneri. c, 1g, Felis pardalis. d, 2g, Chrysocyon brachyurus. e, 3g, Burmeisteria retusa. f, 4g, Myrmecophaga tridactyla. 5g, Caiman crocodilus.

1984, June 16 *Perf. 14*

2119	A380	Strip of 6, #a.-f.	6.25	3.25

Perf. 13

2120	A380	5g multicolored	3.00	.75
		Nos. 2119-2120 (2)	9.25	4.00

A canceled-to-order perf. 13 strip of seven stamps containing Nos. 2119a-2119g and 2120 exists. For overprint see No. 2129.

No. 2117 Ovptd. in Silver with Emblems, etc., for U.P.U. 19th World Congress, Hamburg

1984, June 19 *Perf. 13*

2121	A379	5g on #2117	2.75	2.00

UPU Congress, Hamburg '84 — A381

Sailing ships: No. 2122a, 25c, Admiral of Hamburg. b, 50c, Neptune. c, 1g, Archimedes. d, 2g, Passat. e, 3g, Finkenwerder cutter off Heligoland. f, 4g, Four-masted ship. 5g, Deutschland.

1984, June 19 *Perf. 13*

2122	A381	Strip of 6, #a.-f.	5.75	1.50
2123	A381	5g multicolored	2.25	.50
		Nos. 2122-2123 (2)	8.00	2.00

For overprints see Nos. 2146, 2279-2280.

British Locomotives A382

No. 2124: a, 25c, Pegasus 097, 1868. b, 50c, Pegasus 097, diff. c, 1g, Cornwall, 1847. d, 2g, Cornwall, 1847, diff. e, 3g, Patrick Stirling #1, 1870. f, 4g, Patrick Stirling #1, 1870, diff. 5g, Stepney Brighton Terrier, 1872.

1984, June 20 *Perf. 14*

2124	A382	Strip of 6, #a.-f.	7.50	1.50

Perf. 13

2125	A382	5g multicolored	3.25	.50
		Nos. 2124-2125 (2)	10.75	2.00

No. C486 Overprinted in Blue on Silver with UN emblem and "40o Aniversario de la / Fundacion de las / Naciones Unidas 26.6.1944"

1984, Aug. 1 **Litho.** *Perf. 14½*

2126	AP161	25g on No. C486	21.00	20.00

No. 1536 Ovptd. in Orange (#a.-d.) or Silver (#e.-g.)

and

A383

1984, Aug. 21 *Perf. 14*

2127	A271	Strip of 7, #a.-g.	9.25	1.75

Souvenir Sheet

Perf. 14½

2128	A383	25g multicolored	14.50	14.00

Ausipex '84 Intl. Philatelic Exhibition, Melbourne, Australia. No. 2128 is airmail.

Nos. 2120 and C551 Ovptd. in Black and Red

1984 *Perf. 13*

2129	A380	5g on #2120	2.90	2.00

Perf. 14

2130	AP178	30g on #C551	4.25	4.00

Issued: #2129, Sept. 20; #2130, Aug. 30.

No. 2130 is airmail.

No. 1512 Ovptd. "VFB STUTTGART CAMPEON NACIONAL DE FUTBOL DE ALEMANIA 1984" and Emblem

1984, Sept. 5 ***Perf. 14***
2131 A262 Strip of 7, #a.-g. 4.75 3.00

VFB Stuttgart, 1984 German Soccer Champions.

Cat Type of 1976

Various cats: No. 2132: a, 25c. b, 50c. c, 1g. d, 2g. e, 3g. f, 4g.

1984, Sept. 10 ***Perf. 13x13½***
2132 A287 Strip of 6, #a.-f. 4.25 3.25
2133 A287 5g multicolored 3.50 1.75
Nos. 2132-2133 (2) 7.75 5.00

1984 Summer Olympics, Los Angeles A384

Gold medalists: No. 2134a, 25c Michael Gross, W. Germany, swimming. b, 50c, Peter Vidmar, US, gymnastics. c, 1g, Fredy Schmidtke, W. Germany, cycling. d, 2g, Philippe Boisse, France, fencing. e, 3g, Ulrike Meyfarth, W. Germany, women's high jump. f, 4g, Games emblem. 5g, Mary Lou Retton, US, women's all-around gymnastics, vert. 30g, Rolf Milser, W. Germany, weight lifting, vert.

1985, Jan. 16 **Litho.** ***Perf. 13***
2134 A384 Strip of 6, #a.-f. 3.50 1.90
2135 A384 5g multicolored 5.25 1.10
Nos. 2134-2135 (2) 8.75 3.00

Souvenir Sheet

Perf. 13½

2136 A384 30g multicolored 17.50 15.00

No. 2136 is airmail and contains one 50x60mm stamp. For overprints see Nos. 2174, 2199, 2200. Compare with type A399.

Mushrooms A385

#2137: a, 25c, Boletus luteus. b, 50c, Agaricus campester. c, 1g, Pholiota spectabilis. d, 2g, Tricholoma terreum. e, 3g, Laccaria laccata. f, 4g, Amanita phalloides. 5g, Scleroderma verrucosum.

1985, Jan. 19 ***Perf. 14***
2137 A385 Strip of 6, #a.-f. 10.00 3.00
2138 A385 5g multicolored 9.00 3.00
Nos. 2137-2138 (2) 19.00 6.00

See Nos. 2166-2167.

World Wildlife Fund — A386

Endangered or extinct species: No. 2139a, 25c, Capybara. b, 50c, Mono titi, vert. c, 1g, Rana cornuda adornada. d, 2g, Priodontes giganteus, digging. e, 3g, Priodontes giganteus, by water. f, 4g, Myrmecophaga tridactyla. g, 5g, Myrmecophaga tridactyla, with young.

1985, Mar. 13 ***Perf. 14***
2139 A386 Strip of 7, #a.-g. 50.00 5.00

See No. 2252.

No. 2037 Ovptd. in Red with ISRAPHIL Emblem

1985, Apr. 10
2140 A360 5g on No. 2037 2.50 2.00

Israel '85 Intl. Philatelic Exhibition.

John James Audubon, Birth Bicent. — A387

Birds: No. 2141a, 25c, Piranga flava. b, 50c, Polyborus plancus. c, 1g, Chiroxiphia caudata. d, 2g, Xolmis irupero. e, 3g, Phloeoceastes leucopogon. f, 4g, Thraupis bonariensis. 5g, Parula pitiayumi, horiz.

1985, Apr. 18 ***Perf. 13***
2141 A387 Strip of 6, #a.-f. 6.50 1.25
2142 A387 5g multicolored 3.00 .50
Nos. 2141-2142 (2) 9.50 1.75

No. 2079 Ovptd. in Silver with Italia '85 Emblem

1985, May 20 ***Perf. 14***
2143 A370 5g on #2079 6.50 2.00

Italia '85 Intl. Philatelic Exhibition.

No. 1448e Ovptd. in Red on Silver

1985, June 12
2144 A250 30c on #1448e 2.40 1.25

No. 2104 Ovptd. in Silver and Blue with LUPO 85 Congress Emblem

1985, July 5
2145 A375 5g on No. 2104 1.25 .50

LUPO '85, Lucerne, Switzerland.

No. 2123 Ovptd. in Silver and Blue with MOPHILA 85 Emblem and "HAMBURGO 11-12. 9. 85"

1985, July 5 ***Perf. 13***
2146 A381 5g on #2123 1.25 .50

Mophila '85 Intl. Philatelic Exhibition, Hamburg.

Intl. Youth Year — A388

Scenes from Tom Sawyer and Huckleberry Finn: No. 2147a, 25c, Mississippi riverboat. b, 50c, Finn. c, 1g, Finn and friends by campfire. d, 2g, Finn and Joe, sinking riverboat. e, 3g, Finn, friends, riverboat. f, 4g, Cemetery. 5g, Finn, Sawyer. 25g, Raft, riverboat.

1985, Aug. 5 ***Perf. 13½x13***
2147 A388 Strip of 6, #a.-f. 4.50 1.50
2148 A388 5g multicolored 3.75 .75
Nos. 2147-2148 (2) 8.25 2.25

Souvenir Sheet

Perf. 14½

2149 A388 25g multicolored 18.00 17.00

No. 2149 is airmail. For overprint see No. C612.

German Railroads, 150th Anniv. A389

Locomotives: No. 2150a, 25c, T3, 1883. b, 50c, T18, 1912. c, 1g, T16, 1914. d, 2g, #01 118, Historic Trains Society, Frankfurt. e, 3g, #05 001 Express, Nuremberg Transit Museum. f, 4g, #10 002 Express, 1957. 5g, Der Adler, 1835.

25g, Painting of 1st German Train, Dec. 7, 1835.

1985, Aug. 8 ***Perf. 14***
2150 A389 Strip of 6, #a.-f. 5.75 1.90

Perf. 13

2151 A389 5g multicolored 2.25 .60
Nos. 2150-2151 (2) 8.00 2.50

Souvenir Sheet

Perf. 13½

2152 A389 25g multicolored 32.00 30.00

No. 2152 is airmail and contains one 75x53mm stamp. For overprint see No. 2165.

Development Projects A390

Pres. Stroessner and: 10g, Soldier, map, vert. 25g, Model of Yaci Reta Hydroelectric Project. 50g, Itaipu Dam. 75g, Merchantman Lago Ipoa. 100g, 1975 Coin, vert. 200g, Asuncion Intl. Airport.

1985, Sept. 17 **Litho.** ***Perf. 13***
2153 A390 10g multicolored .50 .35
2154 A390 25g multicolored .50 .35
2155 A390 50g multicolored 1.00 .35
2156 A390 75g multicolored 1.50 .35
2157 A390 100g multicolored 2.00 .35
2158 A390 200g multicolored 4.00 .75
Nos. 2153-2158 (6) 9.50 2.50

Chaco Peace Agreement, 50th Anniv. (#2153, 2157). Nos. 2157-2158 are airmail. For overprints see Nos. 2254-2259.

Nudes by Peter Paul Rubens — A391

Details from paintings: No. 2159a, 25c, b, 50c, Venus in the Forge of Vulcan. c, 1g, Cimon and Iphigenia, horiz. d, 2g, The Horrors of War. e, 3g, Apotheosis of Henry IV and the Proclamation of the Regency. f, 4g, The Reception of Marie de Medici at Marseilles. 5g, Union of Earth and Water.

25g, Nature Attended by the Three Graces.

1985, Oct. 18 ***Perf. 14***
2159 A391 Strip of 6, #a.-f. 9.50 1.50

Perf. 13x13½

2160 A391 5g multicolored 4.25 .50
Nos. 2159-2160 (2) 13.75 2.00

Souvenir Sheet

Perf. 14

2161 A391 25g multicolored 26.00 25.00

No. 2161 is airmail.

1986, Jan. 16 ***Perf. 14***

Nudes by Titian: details from paintings. No. 2162a, 25c, Venus, an Organist, Cupid and a Little Dog. b, 50c, Diana and Acteon. c, 1g, Diana and Actaeon. d, 2g, Danae. e, 3g, Nymph and a Shepherd. f, 4g, Venus of Urbino. 5g, Cupid Blindfolded by Venus, vert.

25g, Diana and Callisto, vert.

2162 A391 Strip of 6, #a.-f. 8.25 2.00

Perf. 13

2163 A391 5g multicolored 3.50 1.00
Nos. 2162-2163 (2) 11.75 3.00

Souvenir Sheet

Perf. 13½

2164 A391 25g multicolored 26.00 25.00

No. 2164 is airmail and contains one 50x60mm stamp.

Nos. 2150 Ovptd. in Red

1986, Feb. 25 ***Perf. 14***
2165 A389 Strip of 6, #a.-f. 6.75 2.00

Essen '86 Intl. Philatelic Exhibition.

Mushrooms Type of 1985

Designs: No. 2166a, 25g, Lepiota procera. b, 50c, Tricholoma albo-brunneum. c, 1g, Clavaria. d, 2g, Volvaria. e, 3g, Licoperdon perlatum. f, 4g, Dictyophora duplicata. 5g, Polyporus rubrum.

1986, Mar. 17 ***Perf. 14***
2166 A385 Strip of 6, #a.-f. 7.25 1.50

Perf. 13

2167 A385 5g multicolored 3.00 .50
Nos. 2166-2167 (2) 10.25 2.00

Automobile, Cent. A393

No. 2168: a, 25c, Wolseley, 1904. b, 50c, Peugeot, 1892. c, 1g, Panhard, 1895. d, 2g, Cadillac, 1903. e, 3g, Fiat, 1902. f, 4g, Stanley Steamer, 1898. 5g, Carl Benz Velocipede, 1885. 25g, Carl Benz (1844-1929), automotive engineer.

1986, Apr. 28 **Litho.** ***Perf. 13½x13***
2168 A393 Strip of 6, #a.-f. 4.00 1.50
2169 A393 5g multicolored 4.75 1.25
Nos. 2168-2169 (2) 8.75 2.75

Souvenir Sheet

Perf. 13½

2170 A393 25g multicolored 17.50 17.00

No. 2170 is airmail and contains one 30x40mm stamp.

World Cup Soccer Championships, Mexico City — A394

Various match scenes, Paraguay vs.: No. 2171a, 25c, b, 50c, US, 1930. c, 1g, d, 2g, Belgium, 1930. e, 3g, Bolivia, 1985. f, 4g, Brazil, 1985.

5g, Natl. Team, 1986. 25g, Player, vert.

1986, Mar. 12 ***Perf. 13½x13***
2171 A394 Strip of 6, #a.-f. 4.00 1.50
2172 A394 5g multicolored 4.75 1.00
Nos. 2171-2172 (2) 8.75 2.50

Souvenir Sheet

Perf. 14½

2173 A394 25g multicolored 20.00 19.00

No. 2173 is airmail. For overprints see Nos. 2283, 2287.

No. 2135 Ovptd. in Silver "JUEGOS / PANAMERICANOS / INDIANAPOLIS / 1987"

1986, June 9 ***Perf. 13***
2174 A384 5g on No. 2135 3.75 2.00

1987 Pan American Games, Indianapolis.

Maybach Automobiles A395

#2175: a, 25c, W-6, 1930-36. b, 50c, SW-38 convertible. c, 1g, SW-38 hardtop, 1938. d, 2g, W-6/DSG, 1933. e, 3g, Zeppelin DS-8, 1931. f, 4g, Zeppelin DS-8, 1936. 5g, Zeppelin DS-8 aerodynamic cabriolet, 1936.

1986, June 19 ***Perf. 13½x13***

2175	A395	Strip of 6, #a.-f.	3.50	1.25
2176	A395	5g multicolored	6.25	1.25
		Nos. 2175-2176 (2)	9.75	2.50

No. 2077 Overprinted in Bright Blue with Olympic Rings and "CALGARY 1988"

1986, July 9 ***Perf. 13***
2177 A369 5g on #2077 2.75 1.25

1988 Winter Olympics, Calgary.

Statue of Liberty, Cent. A396

Passenger liners: No. 2178a, 25c, City of Paris, England, 1867. b, 50c, Mauretania, England. c, 1g, Normandie, France, 1932. d, 2g, Queen Mary, England, 1938. e, 3g, Kaiser Wilhelm the Great II, Germany, 1897. f, 4g, United States, US, 1952. 5g, Bremen, Germany, 1928. 25g, Sailing ship Gorch Fock, Germany, 1976, vert.

1986, July 25 ***Perf. 13***

2178	A396	Strip of 6, #a.-f.	7.00	1.50
2179	A396	5g multicolored	7.00	.60
		Nos. 2178-2179 (2)	14.00	2.10

Souvenir Sheet

Perf. 14½

2180 A396 25g multicolored 16.00 15.00

No. 2180 is airmail and contains one 50x70mm stamp.

Dog Type of 1984

#2181: a, 25c, German shepherd. b, 50c, Icelandic shepherd. c, 1g, Collie. d, 2g, Boxer. e, 3g, Scottish terrier. f, 4g, Welsh springer spaniel. 5g, Painting of Labrador retriever by Ellen Krebs, vert.

1986, Aug. 28 ***Perf. 13x13½***
2181 A376 Strip of 6, #a.-f. 5.75 2.00

Perf. 13½x13

2182	A376	5g multicolored	3.50	1.00
		Nos. 2181-2182 (2)	9.25	3.00

Paraguay Official Stamps, Cent. — A397

#2183-2185, #O1. #2186-2188, #O4.

1986, Aug. 28 **Litho.** ***Perf. 13x13½***

2183	A397	5g multi	1.75	1.50
2184	A397	15g multi	1.75	1.50
2185	A397	40g multi	1.75	1.50
2186	A397	65g multi	1.75	1.50
2187	A397	100g multi	1.75	1.50
2188	A397	150g multi	1.75	1.50
		Nos. 2183-2188 (6)	10.50	9.00

Nos. 2186-2188 are airmail.

Tennis Players — A398

Designs: No. 2189a, Victor Pecci, Paraguay. b, 50c, Jimmy Connors, US. c, 1g, Gabriela Sabatini, Argentina. d, 2g, Boris Becker, W. Germany. e, 3g, Claudia Kohde, E. Germany. f, 4g, Sweden, 1985 Davis Cup team champions, horiz. 5g, Steffi Graf, W. Germany. 25g, 1986 Wimbledon champions Martina Navratilova and Boris Becker, horiz.

Perf. 13x13½, 13½x13

1986, Sept. 17 **Unwmk.**

2189	A398	Strip of 6, #a.-f.	4.50	1.25
2190	A398	5g multicolored	2.25	.50
		Nos. 2189-2190 (2)	6.75	1.75

Souvenir Sheet

Perf. 13½

2191 A398 25g multicolored 15.00 15.00

No. 2191 is airmail and contains one 75x55mm stamp. For overprints see No. 2229.

Nos. 1454-1456 Ovptd. in Red or Silver (#2192c, 2192d): "Homenage a la visita de Sus Altezas Imperiales los Principees Hitachi --28.9-3.10.86"

1986, Sept. 28 ***Perf. 14***

2192	A251	Strip of 5, #a.-e.	4.00	1.50
2193	A251	50c on #1455	1.60	.75
2194	A251	75c on #1456	1.60	1.00
		Nos. 2192-2194 (3)	7.20	3.25

1988 Summer Olympics, Seoul — A399

Athletes, 1984 Olympic medalists: No. 2195a, 25c, Runner. b, 50c, Boxer. c, 1g, Joaquim Cruz, Brazil, 800-meter run. d, 2g, Mary Lou Retton, US, individual all-around gymnastics. e, 3g, Carlos Lopes, Portugal, marathon. f, 4g, Fredy Schmidtke, W. Germany, 1000-meter cycling, horiz. 5g, Joe Fargis, US, equestrian, horiz.

1986, Oct. 29 ***Perf. 13x13½,13½x13***

2195	A399	Strip of 6, #a.-f.	7.50	1.25
2196	A399	5g multicolored	10.75	1.75
		Nos. 2195-2196 (2)	18.25	3.00

For overprints see Nos. 2227-2228, 2230.

Nos. 1574c-1574g Ovptd. in Silver, Ship Type of 1983 Ovptd. in Red

1987, Mar. 20 **Litho.** ***Perf. 14***

2197	A278	Strip of 5, #a.-e.	5.50	3.00
2198	AP176	10g multicolored	2.50	1.50
		Nos. 2197-2198 (2)	8.00	4.50

500th Anniv. of the discovery of America and the 12th Spanish-American Stamp & Coin Show, Madrid.

Olympics Type of 1985 Overprinted in Silver with Olympic Rings and 500th Anniv. of the Discovery of America Emblems and "BARCELONA 92 / Sede de las Olimpiadas en el ano del 500o Aniversario del Descubrimiento de America"

Designs like Nos. 2134a-2134f.

1987, Apr. 24 ***Perf. 14***
2199 A384 Strip of 6, #a.-f. 9.50 8.00

1992 Summer Olympics, Barcelona and discovery of America, 500th anniv. in 1992.

No. 2135 Overprinted in Silver "ROMA / OLYMPHILEX" / Olympic Rings / "SEOUL / CALGARY / 1988"

1987, Apr. 30 ***Perf. 13***
2200 A384 5g on No. 2135 3.50 2.50

Olymphilex '87 Intl. Philatelic Exhibition, Rome.

Cat Type of 1976

Various cats and kittens: No. 2201: a, 1g. b, 2g. c, 3g. d, 5g. 60g, Black cat.

1987, May 22 ***Perf. 13x13½***

2201	A287	Strip of 4, #a.-d.	3.75	.75
2202	A287	60g multicolored	2.50	.95
		Nos. 2201-2202 (2)	6.25	1.70

No. 2202 also exists perf. 14. For overprint see No. 2212.

No. 2203: a, 1g, The Four Corners of the World, horiz. b, 2g, Jupiter and Calisto. c, 3g, Susanna and the Elders. d, 5g, Marriage of Henry IV and Marie de Medici in Lyon.

60g, The Last Judgment. 100g, The Holy Family with St. Elizabeth and John the Baptist. No. 2205A, War and Peace.

1987 **Litho.** ***Perf. 13x13½, 13½x13***

2203	A400	Strip of 4, #a.-d.	4.00	1.00
2204	A400	60g multicolored	5.75	1.50
		Nos. 2203-2204 (2)	9.75	2.50

Souvenir Sheets

2205	A400	100g multicolored	18.00	17.00
2205A	A400	100g multicolored	18.00	17.00

Christmas 1986 (#2205).

Issued: #2204, May 25; #2205, May 26.

Nos. 2205-2205A are airmail and contain one 54x68mm stamp.

MUESTRA

Some illustrated stamps show the word "MUESTRA" ("SPECIMEN"). This overprint is not on the actual stamps. The editors would like to borrow examples without the overprint so that replacement illustrations can be made.

Places and Events A401

10g, ACEPAR Industrial Plant. 25g, Franciscan monk, native, vert. 50g, Yaguaron Church altar, vert. 75g, Founding of Asuncion, 450th anniv. 100g, Paraguay Airlines passenger jet. 200g, Pres. Stoessner, vert.

1987, June 2 **Litho.** ***Perf. 13***

2206	A401	10g multicolored	1.75	.25
2207	A401	25g multicolored	1.75	.25
2208	A401	50g multicolored	1.75	.25
2209	A401	75g multicolored	3.75	.25
2210	A401	100g multicolored	5.75	.30
2211	A401	200g multicolored	7.50	.50
		Nos. 2206-2211 (6)	22.25	1.80

Nos. 2210-2211 are airmail. For overprints see Nos. 2225-2226, C685, C722.

No. 2201 Ovptd. in Blue

1987, June 12 ***Perf. 13x13½***
2212 A287 Strip of 4, #a.-d. 3.25 3.25

Discovery of America, 500th Anniv. (in 1992) A402

Discovery of America anniv. emblem and ships: No. 2213a, 1g, Spanish galleon, 17th cent. b, 2g, Victoria, 1st to circumnavigate the globe, 1519-22. c, 3g, San Hermenegildo. d, 5g, San Martin, c.1582. 60g, Santa Maria, c.1492, vert.

1987, Sept. 9 ***Perf. 14***
2213 A402 Strip of 4, #a.-d. 8.25 1.50

Perf. 13x13½

2214	A402	60g multicolored	3.00	1.60
		Nos. 2213-2214 (2)	11.25	3.10

Colorado Party, Cent. — A403

Bernardino Caballero (founder), President Stroessner and: 5g, 10g, 25g, Three-lane highway. 150g, 170g, 200g, Power lines.

Perf. 13½x13

1987, Sept. 11 **Wmk. 347**

2215	A403	5g multi	3.25	2.00
2216	A403	10g multi	3.25	2.00
2217	A403	25g multi	3.25	2.00
2218	A403	150g multi	3.25	2.00
2219	A403	170g multi	3.25	2.00
2220	A403	200g multi	3.25	2.00
		Nos. 2215-2220 (6)	19.50	12.00

Nos. 2218-2220 are airmail.

Berlin, 750th Anniv. A404

Berlin Stamps and Coins: No. 2221: a, 1g, #9NB145. b, 2g, #9NB154. c, 3g, #9N57, vert. d, 5g, #9N170, vert. 60g, 1987 Commemorative coin, vert.

Perf. 13½x13, 13½x13

1987, Sept. 12 **Unwmk.**

2221 A404 Strip of 4, #a.-d. 7.25 2.00
2222 A404 60g multicolored 4.00 3.00
Nos. 2221-2222 (2) 11.25 5.00

For overprints see Nos. 2239, 2294.

Race Cars — A405

No. 2223: a, 1g, Audi Sport Quattro. b, 2g, Lancia Delta S 4. c, 3g, Fiat 131. d, 5g, Porsche 911 4x4. 60g, Lancia Rally.

1987, Sept. 27 ***Perf. 13***

2223 A405 Strip of 4, #a.-d. 2.60 1.00

Perf. 14

2224 A405 60g multicolored 2.60 1.00
Nos. 2223-2224 (2) 5.20 2.00

Nos. 2209-2210 Ovptd. in Blue

1987, Sept. 30 ***Perf. 13***

2225 A401 75g on #2209 .90 .70
2226 A401 100g on #2210 1.10 .80
Nos. 2225-2226 (2) 2.00 1.50

EXFIVIA '87 Intl. Philatelic Exhibition, LaPaz, Bolivia. No. 2226 is airmail. No. 2225 surcharge is in dark blue; and No. 2226 surcharge is bright blue.

Nos. 2195d-2195f, 2196 Overprinted in Black or Silver

1987, Oct. 1 ***Perf. 13½x13***

2227 A399 Strip of 3, #a.-c. 7.00 3.00
2228 A399 5g on No. 2196 (S) 3.75 3.00
Nos. 2227-2228 (2) 10.75 6.00

Olymphilex '87 Intl. Phil. Exhib., Seoul.

No. 2189 Ovptd. with Emblem and "PHILATELIA '87," etc.

1987, Oct. 15 ***Perf. 13x13½, 13½x13***

2229 A398 Strip of 6, #a.-f. 5.75 4.25

PHILATELIA '87 Intl. Phil. Exhib., Cologne. Size and configuration of overprint varies.

Nos. 2195a-2195b Ovptd. in Bright Blue for EXFILNA '87 and BARCELONA 92

1987, Oct. 24 ***Perf. 13x13½***

2230 A399 Pair, #a.-b. 4.75 4.00

Exfilna '87 Intl. Philatelic Exhibition.

Ship Paintings — A406

No. 2231: a, 1g, San Juan Nepomuceno. b, 2g, San Eugenio. c, 3g, San Telmo. d, 5g, San Carlos. 60g, Spanish galleon, 16th cent. 100g, One of Columbus' ships.

1987 **Litho.** ***Perf. 14***

2231 A406 Strip of 4, #a.-d. 8.00 2.50

Perf. 13x13½

2232 A406 60g multicolored 3.25 1.50
Nos. 2231-2232 (2) 11.25 4.00

Souvenir Sheet

Perf. 13½

2233 A406 100g multicolored 18.00 17.00

Discovery of America, 500th anniv. in 1992 (#2233). Issue dates: Nos. 2231-2232, Dec. 10. No. 2233, Dec. 12.

No. 2233 is airmail and contains one 54x75mm stamp.

1988 Winter Olympics, Calgary A407

#2237: a, 5g, Joel Gaspoz. b, 60g, Peter Mueller.

1987, Dec. 31 ***Perf. 14***

2234 A407 1g Maria Walliser 3.75 1.25
2235 A407 2g Erika Hess 3.75 1.25
2236 A407 3g Pirmin Zurbriggen 3.75 1.25
Nos. 2234-2236 (3) 11.25 3.75

Miniature Sheet

Perf. 13½x13

2237 A407 Sheet of 4 each #2237a, 2237b+label 42.50 40.00

Souvenir Sheet

Perf. 14½

2238 A407 100g Walliser, Zurbriggen 17.50 16.50

No. 2238 is airmail. For overprints see Nos. 2240-2242.

No. 2221 Ovptd. in Silver "AEROPEX 88 / ADELAIDE"

1988, Jan. 29 ***Perf. 13***

2239 A404 Strip of 4, #a.-d. 9.00 5.00

Aeropex '88, Adelaide, Australia.

Nos. 2234-2236 Ovptd. in Gold with Olympic Rings and "OLYMPEX / CALGARY 1988"

1988, Feb. 13 ***Perf. 14***

2240 A407 1g on #2234 1.20 .75
2241 A407 2g on #2235 2.40 1.50
2242 A407 3g on #2236 3.25 2.00
Nos. 2240-2242 (3) 6.85 4.25

Olympex '88, Calgary. Size and configuration of overprint varies.

1988 Summer Olympics, Seoul A408

Equestrians: No. 2243a, 1g, Josef Neckermann, W. Germany, on Venetia. b, 2g, Henri Chammartin, Switzerland. c, 3g, Christine Stueckelberger, Switzerland, on Granat. d, 5g, Liselott Linsenhoff, W. Germany, on Piaff. 60g, Hans-Guenter Winkler, W. Germany.

1988, Mar. 7 ***Perf. 13***

2243 A408 Strip of 4, #a.-d. 6.25 2.00

Perf. 13½x13

2244 A408 60g multicolored 3.00 2.00
Nos. 2243-2244 (2) 9.25 4.00

For overprint see No. 2291.

Berlin, 750th Anniv. — A409

Paintings: No. 2245a, 1g, Virgin and Child, by Jan Gossaert. b, 2g, Virgin and Child, by Rubens. c, 3g, Virgin and Child, by Hans Memling. d, 5g, Madonna, by Albrecht Durer. 60g, Adoration of the Shepherds, by Martin Schongauer.

1988, Apr. 8 ***Perf. 13***

2245 A409 Strip of 4, #a.-d. 7.25 2.00
2246 A409 60g multicolored 4.00 3.00
Nos. 2245-2246 (2) 11.25 5.00

Christmas 1987. See Nos. C727-C731.

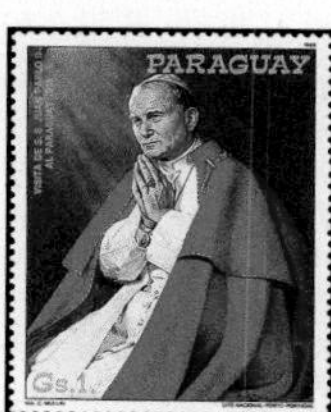

Visit of Pope John Paul II — A410

Religious art: No. 2247a, 1g, Pope John Paul II, hands clasped. b, 2g, Statue of the Virgin. c, 3g, Czestochowa Madonna. d, 5g, Our Lady of Caacupe. Nos. 2247a-2247d are vert.

1988, Apr. 11 ***Perf. 13***

2247 A410 Strip of 4, #a.-d. 6.00 1.00
2248 A410 60g multicolored 3.50 1.00
Nos. 2247-2248 (2) 9.50 2.00

Visit of Pope John Paul II — A411

Rosette window and crucifix.

1988, May 5 **Litho.** ***Perf. 13x13½***

2249 A411 10g blue & blk 2.25 .75
2250 A411 20g blue & blk 2.25 .75
2251 A411 50g blue & blk 2.25 .75
Nos. 2249-2251 (3) 6.75 2.25

World Wildlife Fund Type of 1985

Endangered Animals: No. 2252a, 1g, like #2139g. b, 2g, like #2139f. c, 3g, like #2139d. d, 5g, like #2139e.

1988, June 14 **Unwmk.** ***Perf. 14***

2252 A386 Strip of 4, #a.-d. 37.50 6.00

Nos. 2252a-2252d have denomination and border in blue.

Nos. 2000a-2000d Ovptd. in Gold with Emblem and "Bicentenario de / AUSTRALIA / 1788-1988"

1988, June 17

2253 A351 Strip of 4, #a.-d. 6.00 6.00

Australia, bicent.

Types of 1985 Overprinted in 2 or 4 Lines in Gold "NUEVO PERIODO PRESIDENCIAL CONSTITUCIONAL 1988-1993"

1988, Aug. 12 ***Perf. 14***

2254 A390 10g like #2153 .55 .55
2255 A390 25g like #2154 .55 .55
2256 A390 50g like #2155 .90 .90
2257 A390 75g like #2156 1.75 1.75
2258 A390 100g like #2157 2.10 2.10
2259 A390 200g like #2158 3.50 3.50
Nos. 2254-2259 (6) 9.35 9.35

Pres. Stroessner's new term in office. Nos. 2258-2259 are airmail.

Olympic Tennis, Seoul — A412

Designs: No. 2260a, 1g, Steffi Graf, W. Germany. b, 2g, Olympic gold medal, horiz. c, 3g, Boris Becker, W. Germany. d, 5g, Emilio Sanchez, Spain. 60g, Steffi Graf, diff.

1988, Aug. 16 ***Perf. 13***

2260 A412 Strip of 4, #a.-d. 13.00 3.25
2261 A412 60g multicolored 3.25 2.50
Nos. 2260-2261 (2) 16.25 5.75

1992 Summer Olympics, Barcelona A413

Olympic medalists from Spain: No. 2262a, 1g, Ricardo Zamora, soccer, Antwerp, 1920, vert. b, 2g, Equestrian team, Amsterdam, 1928. c, 3g, Angel Leon, shooting, Helsinki, 1952. d, 5g, Kayak team, Montreal, 1976. 60g, Francisco Fernandez Ochoa, slalom, Sapporo, 1972, vert. 100g, Olympic Stadium, Barcelona, vert.

1989, Jan. 5 ***Perf. 14***

2262 A413 Strip of 4, #a.-d. 8.00 3.25

Perf. 13

2263 A413 60g multicolored 2.25 1.25
Nos. 2262-2263 (2) 10.25 4.50

Souvenir Sheet

Perf. 13½

2264 A413 100g multicolored 17.50 17.00

Discovery of America 500th anniv. (in 1992). No. 2264 is airmail and contains one 50x60mm stamp. For overprint see No. 2293.

Columbus Space Station — A414

1989, Jan. 7 Litho. *Perf. 13x13½*

2265 A414 60g multicolored 4.25 2.00

Discovery of America 500th anniv. (in 1992). Printed in sheets of 4 + 5 labels.

No. 2076 Overprinted in Silver, Red and Blue with Olympic Rings, "1992" and Emblem

1989, Jan. 10 *Perf. 13½x13, 13x13½*

2266 A369 Strip of 6, #a.-f. 8.75 8.75

1992 Winter Olympics, Albertville. Location and configuration of overprint varies.

No. 1454 Ovptd. in Silver "HOMENAJE AL EMPERADOR HIROITO DE JAPON 29.IV,1901-6.1.1989"

1989, Feb. 8 *Perf. 14*

2267 A251 Strip of 5, #a.-e. 4.75 4.75

Death of Emperor Hirohito of Japan.

Formula 1 Drivers, Race Cars — A415

No. 2268: a, 1g, Stirling Moss, Mercedes W196. b, 2g, Emerson Fittipaldi, Lotus. c, 3g, Nelson Piquet, Lotus. d, 5g, Niki Lauda, Ferrari 312 B. 60g, Juan Manuel Fangio, Maserati 250F.

1989, Mar. 6 *Perf. 13*

2268 A415 Strip of 4, #a.-d. 8.75 2.50
2269 A415 60g multicolored 3.50 3.00
Nos. 2268-2269 (2) 12.25 5.50

No. 2269 was printed in sheets of 5 + 4 labels.

Paintings by Titian — A416

No. 2270: a, 1g, Bacchus and Ariadne (Bacchus). b, 2g, Bacchus and Ariadne (tutelary spirit). c, 3g, Death of Actaeon. d, 5g, Portrait of a Young Woman with a Fur Cape. 60g, Concert in a Field. 100g, Holy Family with Donor.

1989, Apr. 17 *Perf. 13x13½*

2270 A416 Strip of 4, #a.-d. 9.00 1.75
2271 A416 60g multicolored 4.25 .75
Nos. 2270-2271 (2) 13.25 2.50

Souvenir Sheet

Perf. 13½

2271A A416 100g multicolored 19.00 18.00

No. 2271A is airmail and contains one 60x49mm stamp. Issue date: May 27.

1994 Winter Olympics, Lillehammer A417

Athletes: No. 2272a, 1g, Torbjorn Lokken, 1987 Nordic combined world champion. b, 2g, Atle Skardal, skier, Norway. c, 3g, Geir Karlstad, Norway, world 10,000-meter speed skating champion, 1987. d, 5g, Franck Piccard, France, 1988 Olympic medalist, skiing. 60g, Roger Ruud, ski jumper, Norway.

1989, May 23 *Perf. 13½x13*

2272 A417 Strip of 4, #a.-d. 13.00 4.25
2273 A417 60g multicolored 5.75 3.75
Nos. 2272-2273 (2) 18.75 8.00

Cat Type of 1976

Various cats: #2274a, 1g. b, 2g. c, 3g. d, 5g.

1989, May 25 *Perf. 13*

2274 A287 Strip of 4, #a.-d. 10.00 2.00
2275 A287 60g Siamese 3.75 2.00
Nos. 2274-2275 (2) 13.75 4.00

Federal Republic of Germany, 40th Anniv. A418

Famous men and automobiles: No. 2276a, 1g, Konrad Adenauer, chancellor, 1949-1963, Mercedes. b, 2g, Ludwig Erhard, chancellor, 1963-1966, Volkswagen Beetle. c, 3g, Felix Wankel, engine designer, 1963 NSU Spider. d, 5g, Franz Josef Strauss, President of Bavarian Cabinet, BMW 502. 60g, Pres. Richard von Weizsacker and Dr. Josef Neckermann.

1989, May 27 *Perf. 13½x13*

2276 A418 Strip of 4, #a.-d. 9.50 2.50
2277 A418 60g multicolored 3.75 3.00
Nos. 2276-2277 (2) 13.25 5.50

For overprints see No. 2369.

Ship Type of 1980 Overprinted with Discovery of America, 500th Anniv. Emblem in Red on Silver

1989, May 29 *Perf. 14½*

Miniature Sheet

2278 A343 Sheet of 7+label, like #1972 40.00 37.50

Discovery of America 500th anniv. (in 1992).

No. 2122a Overprinted with Hamburg Emblem and Nos. 2122b-2122f, 2123 Ovptd. with Diff. Emblem in Red on Silver

1989, May 30 Litho. *Perf. 13½x13*

2279 A381 Strip of 6, #a.-f. 21.00 21.00
2280 A381 5g on #2123 6.25 6.25
Nos. 2279-2280 (2) 27.25 27.25

City of Hamburg, 800th anniv.

Nos. 2006a-2006b Ovptd. "BRASILIANA / 89"

1989, July 5 *Perf. 14*

2281 A352 Pair, #a.-b. 4.50 2.00

No. 2171 Overprinted in Metallic Red and Silver with FIFA and Italia 90 Emblems and "PARAGUAY PARTICIPO EN 13 CAMPEONATOS MUNDIALES"

1989, Sept. 14 Litho. *Perf. 13½x13*

2283 A394 Strip of 6, #a.-f. 5.50 5.50

Size and configuration of overprint varies.

Nos. C738, C753 Ovptd. in metallic red with Italia '90 emblem & "SUDAMERICA-GRUPO 2 / PARAGUAY-COLOMBIA / PARAGUAY-ECUADOR / COLOMBIA-PARAGUAY / ECUADOR-PARAGUAY" and in metallic red on silver with FIFA emblem

1989, Sept. 14 Litho. *Perf. 13*

2284 AP228 25g on #C738 9.00 4.00
2285 AP232 25g on #C753 9.00 4.00
Nos. 2284-2285 (2) 18.00 8.00

Nos. 2046, 2172 Overprinted in Metallic Red on Silver at top: "PARAGUAY CLASIFICADO EN 1930, 1950, 1958 Y 1986" and Emblems or "ITALIA '90". Overprinted Silver on stamps and Blue on Silver on side margins

1989, Sept. 15 Litho. *Perf. 14*

2286 A362 Strip of 6, #a.-f. 17.00 5.00

Perf. 13½x13

2287 A394 5g multicolored 5.75 3.25
Nos. 2286-2287 (2) 22.75 8.25

1990 World Cup Soccer Championships, Italy. Location and size of overprint varies.

Nos. 1284-1286 Ovptd. in Gold "...BIEN ESTUVIMOS EN LA LUNA AHORA NECESITAMOS LOS MEDIOS PARA LLEGAR A LOS PLANETAS" Wernher von Braun's Signature and UN and Space Emblems

1989, Sept. 16 *Perf. 14*

2288 A226 Strip of 5, #a.-e. 6.25 6.25
2289 A226 50c multicolored 3.00 3.00
2290 A226 75c multicolored 4.50 4.50
Nos. 2288-2290 (3) 13.75 13.75

Location, size and configuration of overprint varies.

Nos. 2243, C764 Overprinted in Silver or Gold with Emblem and "ATENAS 100 ANOS DE LOS JUEGOS OLIMPICOS 1896-1996"

1989, Sept. 18 *Perf. 13*

2291 A408 Strip of 4, #a.-d. 5.75 5.75
2292 AP233 25g on #C764 (G) 11.00 11.00
Nos. 2291-2292 (2) 16.75 16.75

1992 Summer Olympics Barcelona, Spain. Size and location of overprint varies.

Nos. 2262a-2262d Ovptd. in Silver with Heads of Steffi Graf or Boris Becker and: "WIMBLEDON 1988 / SEUL 1988 / WIMBLEDON 1989 / EL TENIS NUEVAMENTE EN / LAS OLIMPIADAS 1988-1992" or Similar

1989, Sept. 19 *Perf. 14*

2293 A413 Strip of 4, #a.-d. 14.50 8.00

Addition of tennis as an Olympic sport in 1992. Size and configuration of overprint varies.

No. 2221 Ovptd. in Gold and Blue "PRIMER AEROPUERTO PARA / /COHETES, BERLIN 1930 OBERTH, / NEBEL, RITTER, VON BRAUN" space emblem and "PROF. DR. HERMANN / OBERTH 95o ANIV. / NACIMIENTO 25.6.1989"

Perf. 13½x13, 13x13½

1989, Sept. 20

2294 A404 Strip of 4, #a.-d. 19.00 6.00

Dr. Hermann Oberth, rocket scientist, 95th birth anniv. Overprint size, etc, varies.

Nos. 1406-1408 Ovptd. in Metallic Red and Silver with Emblems and "OLIMPIADAS / DE INVIERNO / ALBERTVILLE 1992" in 2 or 3 Lines

1989, Sept. 21 *Perf. 14*

2295 A244 Strip of 5, #a.-e. 10.00 3.00
2296 A244 50c multicolored 4.75 2.50
2297 A244 75c multicolored 7.00 4.00
Nos. 2295-2297 (3) 21.75 9.50

1992 Winter Olympics, Albertville. Size and configuration of overprint varies.

Nos. 2251, C724 Overprinted

Perf. 13½, 13½x13

1989, Oct. 9 **Litho.** **Wmk. 347**

2298 A411 50g on #2251 10.00 7.50
2299 AP226 120g on #C724 10.00 8.00

Parafil '89, Paraguay-Argentina philatelic exhibition.

Birds Facing Extinction A419

50g, Ara chloroptera. 100g, Mergus octosetaceus. 300g, Rhea americana. 500g, Ramphastos toco. 1000g, Crax fasciolata. 2000g, Ara ararauna.

Perf. 13½x13

1989, Dec. 19 **Litho.** **Wmk. 347**

2300 A419 50g multicolored .60 .30
2301 A419 100g multicolored .60 .30
2302 A419 300g multicolored 1.50 .75
2303 A419 500g multicolored 2.40 1.20
2304 A419 1000g multicolored 4.50 2.25
2305 A419 2000g multicolored 8.50 4.25
Nos. 2300-2305 (6) 18.10 9.05

Nos. 2302-2305 airmail. Nos. 2300 & 2305 vert. Frames and typestyles vary greatly. Watermark on 50g, 100g, 300g is 8mm high.

1992 Summer Olympics, Barcelona — A420

Athletes: No. 2306a, 1g, A. Fichtel and S. Bau, W. Germany, foils, 1988. b, 2g, Spanish basketball team, 1984. c, 3g, Jackie Joyner-Kersee, heptathalon and long jump, 1988, horiz. d, 5g, L. Beerbaum, W. Germany, show jumping, team, 1988. 60g, W. Brinkmann, W. Germany, show jumping, team, 1988. 100g, Emilio Sanchez, tennis.

Unwmk.

1989, Dec. 26 **Litho.** *Perf. 14*

2306 A420 Strip of 4, #a.-d. 7.00 2.00

Perf. 13

2307 A420 60g multicolored 7.50 3.50
Nos. 2306-2307 (2) 14.50 5.50

Souvenir Sheet

Perf. 13½

2308 A420 100g multicolored 20.00 15.00

No. 2308 is airmail and contains one 47x57mm stamp.

World Cup Soccer Championships, Italy — A421

1986 World Cup soccer players in various positions: No. 2309a, 1g, England vs. Paraguay. b, 2g, Spain vs. Denmark. c, 3g, France vs. Italy. d, 5g, Germany vs. Morocco. 60g, Mexico vs. Paraguay. 100g, Germany vs. Argentina.

1989, Dec. 29 *Perf. 14*

2309 A421 Strip of 4, #a.-d. 9.25 2.50

Perf. 13½

2310 A421 60g multicolored 6.00 2.50
Nos. 2309-2310 (2) 15.25 5.00

Souvenir Sheet

Perf. 14½

2311 A421 100g multicolored 21.50 12.50

No. 2311 is airmail and contains one 40x50mm stamp.

For overprints see Nos. 2355-2356.

1992 Summer Olympics, Barcelona — A422

Barcelona '92, proposed Athens '96 emblems and: No. 2312a, 1g, Greece #128. b, 2g, Greece #126, vert. c, 3g, Greece #127, vert. d, 5g, Greece #123, vert. 60g, Paraguay #736. 100g, Horse and rider, vert.

1990, Jan. 4 *Perf. 13½x13, 13x13½*

2312 A422 Strip of 4, #a.-d. 6.25 2.00
2313 A422 60g multicolored 12.00 4.00
Nos. 2312-2313 (2) 18.25 6.00

Souvenir Sheet

Perf. 13½

2314 A422 100g multicolored 21.00 17.50

No. 2314 is airmail and contains one 50x60mm stamp and exists with either white or yellow border, same value. Stamps inscribed 1989.

For overprints see No. 2357.

Swiss Confederation, 700th Anniv. — A423

No. 2315: a, 3g, Monument to William Tell. b, 5g, Manship Globe, UN Headquarters, Geneva.

60g, 15th cent. messenger, Bern.

No. 2317, 1st Swiss steam locomotive, horiz. No. 2318, Jean Henri Dunant, founder of the Red Cross, horiz.

1990, Jan. 25 *Perf. 14*

2315 A423 Pair, #a.-b. 8.50 2.00

Perf. 13

2316 A423 60g multicolored 7.50 3.50
Nos. 2315-2316 (2) 16.00 5.50

Souvenir Sheets

Perf. 14½

2317 A423 100g multicolored 26.00 25.00
2318 A423 100g multicolored 26.00 25.00

Nos. 2317-2318 are airmail. For overprints see Nos. 2352-2354.

Wood Carving — A424

Discovery of America, 500th anniv. emblem &: #2319: a, 1g, 1st cathechism in Guarani. b, 2g, shown. #2319 has continuous design.

1990, Jan. 26 *Perf. 14*

2319 A424 Pair, #a.-b. + label 6.25 1.40

Organization of American States, Cent. — A425

Designs: 50g, Letter showing "100 OEA" design on green background, horiz. 200g, Map of Paraguay.

Perf. 13½x13

1990, Feb. 9 **Litho.** **Wmk. 347**

2320 A425 50g multicolored .60 .30
2321 A425 100g multicolored .90 .35
2322 A425 200g multicolored 1.80 .65
Nos. 2320-2322 (3) 3.30 1.30

1992 Winter Olympics, Albertville A426

Calgary 1988 skiers: No. 2323a, 1g, Alberto Tomba, Italy, slalom and giant slalom. b, 2g, Vreni Schneider, Switzerland, women's slalom and giant slalom, vert. c, 3g, Luc Alphand, France, skier, vert. d, 5g, Matti Nykaenen, Finland, ski-jumping.

60g, Marina Kiehl, W. Germany, women's downhill. 100g, Frank Piccard, France, super giant slalom.

1990, Mar. 7 **Unwmk.** *Perf. 14*

2323 A426 Strip of 4, #a.-d. 6.50 2.50

Perf. 13

2324 A426 60g multicolored 2.75 2.50
Nos. 2323-2324 (2) 9.25 5.00

Souvenir Sheet

Perf. 14½

2325 A426 100g multicolored 21.50 21.50

No. 2325 is airmail, contains one 40x50mm stamp and exists with either white or yellow border.

Pre-Columbian Art, Customs — A427

UPAE Emblem and: 150g, Pre-Columbian basket. 500g, Aboriginal ceremony.

1990, Mar. 8 **Wmk. 347** *Perf. 13*

2326 A427 150g multicolored 1.75 1.10
2327 A427 500g multicolored 4.00 2.25

No. 2327 is airmail.

For overprints see Nos. 2345-2346.

First Postage Stamp, 150th Anniv. — A428

Penny Black, Mail Transportation 500th anniv. emblem and: No. 2328a, 1g, Penny Black on cover. b, 2g, Mauritius #1-2 on cover. c, 3g, Baden #4b on cover. d, 5g, Roman States #4 on cover. 60g, Paraguay #C38 and four #C54 on cover.

1990, Mar. 12 **Unwmk.** *Perf. 14*

2328 A428 Strip of 4, #a.-d. 7.00 5.00

Perf. 13½x13

2329 A428 60g multicolored 3.00 2.00

Postal Union of the Americas and Spain (UPAE) — A429

1990, July 2 *Perf. 13x13½*

2330 A429 200g Map, flags 1.00 .45
2331 A429 250g Paraguay #1 1.25 .50
2332 A429 350g FDC of #2326-2327, horiz. 2.90 .65
Nos. 2330-2332 (3) 5.15 1.60

National University, Cent. (in 1989) — A430

1990, Sept. 8

2333 A430 300g Future site 1.50 1.00
2334 A430 400g Present site 2.00 1.25
2335 A430 600g Old site 3.00 2.00
Nos. 2333-2335 (3) 6.50 4.25

Franciscan Churches A431

Perf. 13½x13

1990, Sept. 25 **Litho.** **Wmk. 347**

2336 A431 50g Guarambare .40 .30
2337 A431 100g Yaguaron .65 .35
2338 A431 200g Ita 1.25 .65
Nos. 2336-2338 (3) 2.30 1.30

For overprints see Nos. 2366-2368.

Democracy in Paraguay A432

Designs: 100g, State and Catholic Church, vert. 200g, Human rights, vert. 300g, Freedom of the Press, vert. 500g, Return of the exiles. 3000g, People and democracy.

Perf. 13½x13, 13x13½

1990, Oct. 5 **Litho.** **Wmk. 347**

2339 A432 50g multicolored .45 .30
2340 A432 100g multicolored .45 .30
2341 A432 200g multicolored .95 .50
2342 A432 300g multicolored 1.40 .80
2343 A432 500g multicolored 17.50 1.40
2344 A432 3000g multicolored 12.50 7.50
Nos. 2339-2344 (6) 33.25 10.80

Nos. 2343-2344 are airmail.

Nos. 2326-2327 Overprinted in Magenta

1990 **Litho.** **Wmk. 347** *Perf. 13*

2345 A427 150g multicolored 5.00 .60
2346 A427 500g multicolored 15.00 1.90

No. 2346 is airmail.

UN Development Program, 40th Anniv. — A433

Designs: 50m, Human Rights, sculpture by Hugo Pistilli. 100m, United Nations, sculpture by Hermann Guggiari. 150m, Miguel de Cervantes Literature Award, won by Augusto Roa Bastos.

1990, Oct. 26
2347 A433 50g lilac & multi .60 .30
2348 A433 100g gray & multi .90 .35
2349 A433 150g green & multi 1.40 .60
Nos. 2347-2349 (3) 2.90 1.25

America A434

50g, Paraguay River banks. 250g, Chaco land.

Perf. 13½x13
1990, Oct. 31 **Wmk. 347**
2350 A434 50g multicolored 20.00 5.00
2351 A434 250g multicolored 40.00 10.00

No. 2351 is airmail.

Nos. 2315-2316, 2318 Ovptd. in Metallic Red and Silver

Unwmk.
1991, Apr. 2 **Litho.** ***Perf. 14***
2352 A423 Pair, #a.-b. 5.75 4.00
Perf. 13
2353 A423 60g on #2316 5.00 3.50
Nos. 2352-2353 (2) 10.75 7.50

Souvenir Sheet
Perf. 14½
2354 A423 100g on #2318 25.00 25.00

Swiss Confederation, 700th anniv. and Red Cross, 125th anniv. No. 2354 is airmail. No. 2352 exists perf. 13. Location of overprint varies.

Nos. 2309-2310 Ovptd. in Silver

1991, Apr. 4 ***Perf. 14***
2355 A421 Strip of 4, #a.-d. 8.25 6.25
Perf. 13x13½
2356 A421 60g on #2310 5.00 3.75
Nos. 2355-2356 (2) 13.25 10.00

1994 World Cup Soccer Championships. Location of overprint varies.

Nos. 2312, C822, C766 Ovptd. in Silver

1991, Apr. 4 ***Perf. 13***
2357 A422 Strip of 4, #a.-d. 7.50 5.00
2358 AP246 25g on #C822 5.00 3.00
Perf. 13x13½
2359 AP233 30g on #C766 6.50 4.00

Participation of reunified Germany in 1992 Summer Olympics. Nos. 2358-2359 are airmail. Location of overprint varies.

Professors — A435

Designs: 50g, Julio Manuel Morales, gynecologist. 100g, Carlos Gatti, clinician. 200g, Gustavo Gonzalez, geologist. 300g, Juan Max Boettner, physician and musician. 350g, Juan Boggino, pathologist. 500g, Andres Barbero, physician, founder of Paraguayan Red Cross.

Perf. 13x13½
1991, Apr. 5 **Wmk. 347**
2360 A435 50g multicolored .60 .30
2361 A435 100g multicolored .60 .30
2362 A435 200g multicolored 1.25 .50
2363 A435 300g multicolored 2.00 .80
2364 A435 350g multicolored 2.00 .90
2365 A435 500g multicolored 3.25 1.40
Nos. 2360-2365 (6) 9.70 4.20

Nos. 2364-2365 are airmail.

Nos. 2336-2338 Ovptd. in Black and Red

1991 **Wmk. 347** ***Perf. 13½x13***
2366 A431 50g on #2336 .65 .50
2367 A431 100g on #2337 .85 .60
2368 A431 200g on #2338 1.25 .90
Nos. 2366-2368 (3) 2.75 2.00

Espamer '91 Philatelic Exhibition.

Nos. 2276a-2276b Ovptd. in Silver

Nos. 2276c-2276d Ovptd. in Silver

1991 **Unwmk.** ***Perf. 13***
2369 A418 Strip of 4, #a.-d. 11.25 5.00

Writers and Muscians A436

Designs: 50g, Ruy Diaz de Guzman, historian. 100g, Maria Talavera, war correspondent, vert. 150g, Augusto Roa Bastos, writer, vert. 200g, Jose Asuncion Flores, composer, vert. 250g, Felix Perez Cardozo, harpist. 300g, Juan Carlos Moreno Gonzalez, composer.

Perf. 13½x13,13x13½
1991, Aug. 27 **Litho.** **Wmk. 347**
2373 A436 50g multicolored .40 .30
2374 A436 100g multicolored .45 .35
2375 A436 150g multicolored .80 .50
2376 A436 200g multicolored 1.00 .65
2377 A436 250g multicolored 1.25 .80
2378 A436 300g multicolored 1.50 1.00
Nos. 2373-2378 (6) 5.40 3.60

Nos. 2376-2378 are airmail.

America — A437

100g, War of Tavare. 300g, Arrival of Spanish explorer Domingo Martinez de Irala in Paraguay.

Perf. 13x13½
1991, Oct. 9 **Litho.** **Wmk. 347**
2379 A437 100g multicolored 1.75 .35
2380 A437 300g multicolored 2.00 .90

No. 2380 is airmail.

Paintings — A438

Designs: 50g, Compass of Life, by Alfredo Moraes. 100g, The Lighted Alley, by Michael Burt. 150g, Earring, by Lucy Yegros. 200g, Migrant Workers, by Hugo Bogado Barrios. 250g, Passengers Without a Ship, by Bernardo Ismachoviez. 300g, Native Guarani, by Lotte Schulz.

Perf. 13x13½
1991, Nov. 12 **Litho.** **Wmk. 347**
2381 A438 50g multicolored .55 .30
2382 A438 100g multicolored .65 .35
2383 A438 150g multicolored 1.10 .50
2384 A438 200g multicolored 1.40 .65
2385 A438 250g multicolored 1.60 .80
2386 A438 300g multicolored 2.00 1.00
Nos. 2381-2386 (6) 7.30 3.60

Nos. 2384-2386 are airmail.

Endangered Species A439

Perf. 13x13½, 13½x13
1992, Jan. 28 **Litho.** **Wmk. 347**
2387 A439 50g Catagonus wagneri, vert. 1.20 .30
2388 A439 100g Felis pardalis 1.40 .35
2389 A439 150g Tapirus terrestri 2.40 .50
2390 A439 200g Chrysocyon brachyurus 3.00 .65
Nos. 2387-2390 (4) 8.00 1.80

Tile Designs of Christianized Indians — A440

Perf. 13x13½
1992, Mar. 2 **Litho.** **Wmk. 347**
2391 A440 50g Geometric .50 .30
2392 A440 100g Church .50 .30
2393 A440 150g Missionary ship .75 .35
2394 A440 200g Plant 1.10 .50
Nos. 2391-2394 (4) 2.85 1.45

Discovery of America, 500th anniv.

Leprosy Society of Paraguay, 60th Anniv. — A441

Designs: 50g, Society emblem, Malcolm L. Norment, founder. 250g, Gerhard Henrik Armauer Hansen (1841-1912), discoverer of leprosy bacillus.

Perf. 13x13½
1992, Apr. 28 **Litho.** **Wmk. 347**
2395 A441 50g multicolored .75 .30
2396 A441 250g multicolored 2.25 .80

Earth Summit, Rio de Janeiro — A442

Earth Summit emblem, St. Francis of Assisi, and: 50g, Hands holding symbols of clean environment. 100g, Butterfly, industrial pollution. 250g, Globe, calls for environmental protection.

1992, June 9
2397 A442 50g multicolored .65 .30
2398 A442 100g multicolored .75 .35
2399 A442 250g multicolored 1.75 .80
Nos. 2397-2399 (3) 3.15 1.45

For overprints see Nos. 2422-2424.

Natl. Census A443

1992. July 30 ***Perf. 13½x13, 13x13½***
2400 A443 50g Economic activity .40 .30
2401 A443 200g Houses, vert. .85 .65
2402 A443 250g Population, vert. 1.20 .80
2403 A443 300g Education 1.50 1.00
Nos. 2400-2403 (4) 3.95 2.75

1992 Summer Olympics, Barcelona A444

1992, Sept. 1 ***Perf. 13x13½, 13½x13***
2404 A444 50g Soccer, vert. .45 .30
2405 A444 100g Tennis, vert. .50 .35
2406 A444 150g Running, vert. .85 .50
2407 A444 200g Swimming 1.10 .60
2408 A444 250g Judo, vert. 1.25 .80
2409 A444 350g Fencing 1.75 1.10
Nos. 2404-2409 (6) 5.90 3.65

Evangelism in Paraguay, 500th Anniv. — A445

Designs: 50g, Friar Luis Bolanos. 100g, Friar Juan de San Bernardo. 150g, San Roque Gonzalez de Santa Cruz. 200g, Father Amancio Gonzalez. 250g, Monsignor Juan Sinforiano Bogarin, vert.

Rough Perf. 13½x13, 13x13½
1992, Oct. 9 **Unwmk.**
2410 A445 50g multicolored .70 .30
2411 A445 100g multicolored .70 .35
2412 A445 150g multicolored 1.40 .50
2413 A445 200g multicolored 1.75 .65
2414 A445 250g multicolored 2.10 .80
Nos. 2410-2414 (5) 6.65 2.60

For overprints see Nos. 2419-2421.

America A446

Designs: 150g, Columbus, fleet arriving in New World. 350g, Columbus, vert.

Rough Perf. 13½x13, 13x13½

1992, Oct. 12

2415	A446	150g multicolored	1.25	.50
2416	A446	350g multicolored	1.75	1.10

No. 2416 is airmail.

Ovptd. "PARAFIL 92" in Blue

1992, Nov. 9

2417	A446	150g multicolored	4.25	4.25
2418	A446	350g multicolored	6.25	6.25

No. 2418 is airmail.

Nos. 2410-2412 Ovptd. in Green

1992, Nov. 6 ***Rough Perf. 13½x13***

2419	A445	50g multicolored	5.00	5.00
2420	A445	100g multicolored	6.00	6.00
2421	A445	150g multicolored	10.00	10.00
		Nos. 2419-2421 (3)	21.00	21.00

Nos. 2397-2399 Ovptd. in Blue

Perf. 13x13½

1992, Oct. 24 **Wmk. 347**

2422	A442	50g multicolored	2.00	2.00
2423	A442	100g multicolored	2.50	2.50
2424	A442	250g multicolored	6.25	6.25
		Nos. 2422-2424 (3)	10.75	10.75

Inter-American Institute for Cooperation in Agriculture, 50th Anniv. — A447

Designs: 50g, Field workers. 100g, Test tubes, cattle in pasture. 200g, Hands holding flower. 250g, Cows, corn, city.

Perf. 13x13½

1992, Nov. 27 **Unwmk.**

2425	A447	50g multicolored	.65	.30
2426	A447	100g multicolored	.75	.35
2427	A447	200g multicolored	1.25	.75
2428	A447	250g multicolored	1.60	.90
		Nos. 2425-2428 (4)	4.25	2.30

For overprints see Nos. 2461-2462.

Notary College of Paraguay, Cent. — A448

Designs: 50g, Yolanda Bado de Artecona. 100g, Jose Ramon Silva. 150g, Abelardo Brugada Valpy. 200g, Tomas Varela. 250g, Jose Livio Lezcano. 300g, Francisco I. Fernandez.

1992, Nov. 29 ***Rough Perf. 13½x13***

2429	A448	50g multicolored	.40	.30
2430	A448	100g multicolored	.50	.35
2431	A448	150g multicolored	.80	.60
2432	A448	200g multicolored	1.00	.75
2433	A448	250g multicolored	1.25	.90
2434	A448	300g multicolored	1.50	1.00
		Nos. 2429-2434 (6)	5.45	3.90

Opening of Lopez Palace, Cent. — A449

Paintings of palace by: 50g, Michael Burt. 100g, Esperanza Gill. 200g, Emili Aparici. 250g, Hugo Bogado Barrios, vert.

1993, Mar. 9 ***Perf. 13½x13, 13x13½***

2435	A449	50g multicolored	.55	.30
2436	A449	100g multicolored	.65	.35
2437	A449	200g multicolored	1.40	.75
2438	A449	250g multicolored	1.60	.90
		Nos. 2435-2438 (4)	4.20	2.30

For overprints see Nos. 2453-2456.

Treaty of Asuncion, 1st Anniv. — A450

Rough Perf. 13x13½

1993, Mar. 10 **Wmk. 347**

2439	A450	50g Flags, map	.75	.30
2440	A450	350g Flags, globe	1.75	1.25

Santa Isabel Leprosy Assoc., 50th Anniv. — A451

Various flowers.

Perf. 13x13½

1993, May 24 **Unwmk.**

2441	A451	50g multicolored	.40	.30
2442	A451	200g multicolored	1.00	.75
2443	A451	250g multicolored	1.20	.90
2444	A451	350g multicolored	1.60	1.25
		Nos. 2441-2444 (4)	4.20	3.20

Goethe College, Cent. — A452

Designs: 50g, Goethe, by Johann Heinrich Lips, inscription. 100g, Goethe (close-up), by Johann Heinrich Wilhelm Tischbein.

1993, June 18

2445	A452	50g multicolored	.45	.30
2446	A452	200g multicolored	1.10	.75

For overprints see Nos. 2451-2452.

World Friendship Crusade, 35th Anniv. — A453

Designs: 50g, Stylized globe. 100g, Map, Dr. Ramon Artemio Bracho. 200g, Children. 250g, Two people embracing.

1993, July 1

2447	A453	50g multicolored	.55	.30
2448	A453	100g multicolored	.55	.35
2449	A453	200g multicolored	1.10	.75
2450	A453	250g multicolored	1.40	.90
		Nos. 2447-2450 (4)	3.60	2.30

For overprint see No. 2486.

Nos. 2445-2446 Ovptd. "BRASILIANA 93"

1993, July 12

2451	A452	50g multicolored	2.75	2.75
2452	A452	200g multicolored	7.75	7.75

Nos. 2435-2438 Ovptd.

Perf. 13½x13, 13x13½

1993, Aug. 13

2453	A449	50g multicolored	1.25	1.25
2454	A449	100g multicolored	1.75	1.75
2455	A449	200g multicolored	3.50	3.50
2456	A449	250g multicolored	4.50	4.50
		Nos. 2453-2456 (4)	11.00	11.00

Size of overprint varies.

Church of the Incarnation, Cent. — A454

Design: 50g, Side view of church, vert.

Unwmk.

1993, Oct. 8 **Litho.** ***Perf. 13***

2457	A454	50g multicolored	.40	.30
2458	A454	350g multicolored	1.60	.60

Endangered Animals A455

America: 50g, Myrmecophaga tridactyla. 250g, Speothos venaticus.

1993, Oct. 27

2459	A455	50g multicolored	2.75	.60
2460	A455	250g multicolored	1.75	.75

No. 2459 is airmail.

Nos. 2426-2427 Ovptd.

1993, Nov. 16 ***Perf. 13x13½***

2461	A447	100g multicolored	3.50	3.50
2462	A447	200g multicolored	7.00	7.00

Christmas — A456

1993, Nov. 24

2463	A456	50g shown	.40	.30
2464	A456	250g Stars, wise men	1.10	.30

Scouting in Paraguay, 80th Anniv. — A457

50g, Girl scouts watching scout instuctor. 100g, Boy scouts learning crafts. 200g, Lord Robert Baden-Powell. 250g, Girl scout with flag.

1993, Dec. 30

2465	A457	50g multicolored	.45	.30
2466	A457	100g multicolored	.45	.30
2467	A457	200g multicolored	.90	.30
2468	A457	250g multicolored	1.20	.50
		Nos. 2465-2468 (4)	3.00	1.40

First Lawyers to Graduate from Natl. University of Ascuncion, Cent. — A458

50g, Cecilio Baez. 100g, Benigno Riquelme, vert. 250g, Emeterio Gonzalez. 500g, J. Gaspar Villamayor.

1994, Apr. 8 ***Perf. 13***

2469	A458	50g multicolored	.55	.30
2470	A458	100g multicolored	.70	.30
2471	A458	250g multicolored	.85	.45
2472	A458	500g multicolored	1.40	.75
		Nos. 2469-2472 (4)	3.50	1.80

Phoenix Sports Corporation, 50th Anniv. — A459

Designs: 50g, Basketball player, vert. 200g, Soccer players, vert. 250g, Pedro Andrias Garcia Arias, founder, tennis player.

1994, May 20 **Litho.** ***Perf. 13***

2473	A459	50g multicolored	.50	.30
2474	A459	200g multicolored	.55	.35
2475	A459	250g multicolored	.85	.45
		Nos. 2473-2475 (3)	1.90	1.10

1994 World Cup Soccer Championships, U.S. — A460

Various soccer plays.

1994, June 2

2476	A460	250g multicolored	.60	.45
2477	A460	500g multicolored	1.25	.75
2478	A460	1000g multicolored	2.10	1.50
		Nos. 2476-2478 (3)	3.95	2.70

For overprints see Nos. 2483-2485.

Intl. Olympic Committee, Cent. — A461

350g, Runner. 400g, Lighting Olympic flame.

Unwmk.

1994, June 23 **Litho.** ***Perf. 13***

2479	A461	350g multicolored	.85	.60
2480	A461	400g multicolored	.90	.65

World Congress on Physical Education, Asuncion A462

Designs: 1000g, Stylized family running to break finish line, vert.

Perf. 13½x13, 13x13½

1994, July 19 **Litho.**

2481 A462 200g multicolored .70 .45
2482 A462 1000g multicolored 3.25 2.25

Nos. 2476-2478 Ovptd.

1994, Aug. 2 *Perf. 13*

2483 A460 250g multicolored 1.50 1.50
2484 A460 500g multicolored 3.00 3.00
2485 A460 1000g multicolored 6.25 6.25
Nos. 2483-2485 (3) 10.75 10.75

No. 2448 Ovptd.

1994, Aug. 3 *Perf. 13x13½*

2486 A453 100g multicolored 10.25 10.25

Agustin Pio Barrios Mangore (1885-1944), Musician — A463

250g, In tuxedo. 500g, In traditional costume.

1994, Aug. 5 *Perf. 13x13½*

2487 A463 250g multi .75 .50
2488 A463 500g multi 1.60 1.00

Paraguayan Police, 151st Anniv. — A464

50g, 1913 Guardsman on horseback. 250g, Pedro Nolasco Fernandez, 1st capital police chief; Carlos Bernadino Cacabelos, 1st commissioner.

1994, Aug. 26 *Perf. 13x13½*

2489 A464 50g multicolored .45 .30
2490 A464 250g multicolored 1.00 .60

For overprint see Nos. 2569-2570.

Parafil '94 — A465

Birds: 100g, Ciconia maquari. 150g, Paroaria capitata. 400g, Chloroceryle americana, vert. 500g, Jabiru mycteria, vert.

1994, Sept. 9 *Perf. 13*

2491 A465 100g multicolored .60 .30
2492 A465 150g multicolored .85 .40
2493 A465 400g multicolored 2.25 .90
2494 A465 500g multicolored 3.25 1.10
Nos. 2491-2494 (4) 6.95 2.70

Solar Eclipse — A466

Designs: 50g, Eclipse, Copernicus. 200g, Sundial, Johannes Kepler.

Unwmk.

1994, Sept. 23 **Litho.** *Perf. 13*

2495 A466 50g multicolored .45 .30
2496 A466 200g multicolored .95 .45

America Issue — A467

100g, Derelict locomotive. 1000g, Motorcycle.

1994, Oct. 11 *Perf. 13½*

2497 A467 100g multicolored .60 .45
2498 A467 1000g multicolored 5.00 3.00

Intl. Year of the Family — A468

1994, Oct. 25 *Perf. 13x13½*

2499 A468 50g Mother, child .60 .30
2500 A468 250g Family faces 1.10 .60

Christmas A469

Ceramic figures: 150g, Nativity. 700g, Joseph, infant Jesus, Mary, vert.

1994, Nov. 4 *Perf. 13½*

2501 A469 150g multicolored .55 .35
2502 A469 700g multicolored 2.50 1.60

Paraguayan Red Cross, 75th Anniv. — A470

Black Red Cross — A470a

Designs: 150g, Boy Scouts, Jean-Henri Dunant. 700g, Soldiers, paramedics, Dr. Andres Barbero.

1994, Nov. 25 *Perf. 13½x13*

2503 A470 150g multi .70 .45
2503A A470a 500g multi 200.00
2504 A470 700g multi 3.40 2.40

When it was discovered that No. 2503A contained a black cross instead of a red cross it was withdrawn.

San Jose College, 90th Anniv. — A471

Pope John Paul II and: 200g, Eternal flame. 250g, College entrance.

1994, Dec. 4

2505 A471 200g multicolored .85 .45
2506 A471 250g multicolored 1.00 .60

Louis Pasteur (1822-95) — A472

1995, Mar. 24 **Litho.** *Perf. 13½*

2507 A472 1000g multicolored 3.25 2.10

Fight Against AIDS — A473

1995, May 4

2508 A473 500g Faces 1.75 .75
2509 A473 1000g shown 3.25 1.50

FAO, 50th Anniv. — A474

1995, June 23

2510 A474 950g Bread, pitcher 2.10 1.50
2511 A474 2000g Watermelon 5.00 3.00

Fifth Neotropical Ornithological Congress A475

100g, Parula pitiayumi. 200g, Chirroxiphia caudata. 600g, Icterus icterus. 1000g, Carduelis magellanica.

1995, July 6

2512 A475 100g multicolored .70 .45
2513 A475 200g multicolored .90 .45
2514 A475 600g multicolored 3.00 1.20
2515 A475 1000g multicolored 3.50 2.10
Nos. 2512-2515 (4) 8.10 4.20

Fifth Intl. Symposium on Municipalities, Ecology & Tourism — A476

Designs: 1150g, Rio Monday rapids. 1300g, Aregua Railroad Station.

1995, Aug. 4 **Litho.** *Perf. 13½*

2516 A476 1150g multicolored 2.10 1.25
2517 A476 1300g multicolored 2.40 1.40

Volleyball, Cent. — A477

600g, Ball, net. 1000g, Hands, ball, net.

1995, Sept. 28

2518 A477 300g shown .65 .30
2519 A477 600g multi 1.40 .60
2520 A477 1000g multi 1.95 1.00
Nos. 2518-2520 (3) 4.00 1.90

America Issue — A478

Preserve the environment: 950g, Macizo Monument, Achay. 2000g, Tinfunique Reserve, Chaco, vert.

1995, Oct. 12

2521 A478 950g multicolored 3.25 1.00
2522 A478 2000g multicolored 5.25 2.10

UN, 50th Anniv. — A479

Designs: 200g, Flags above olive branch. 3000g, UN emblem, stick figures.

1995, Oct. 20

2523 A479 200g multicolored .35 .30
2524 A479 3000g multicolored 5.00 3.00

Christmas — A480

1995, Nov. 7

2525 A480 200g shown .60 .30
2526 A480 1000g Nativity 2.40 1.00

Jose Marti (1853-95) A481

Designs: 200g, Hedychium coronarium, Marti, vert. 1000g, Hedychium coronarium, map & flag of Cuba, Marti.

1995, Dec. 19 **Litho.** *Perf. 13½*

2527 A481 200g multicolored .75 .30
2528 A481 1000g multicolored 2.75 1.10

Lion's Clubs of South America & the Caribbean, 25th Anniv. — A482

1996, Jan. 11

2529 A482 200g Railway station .50 .30
2530 A482 1000g Viola House 2.10 1.10

Orchids A483

Designs: 100g, Cattleya nobilior. 200g, Oncidium varicosum. 1000g, Oncidium jonesianum, vert. 1150g, Sophronitis cernua.

Perf. 13½x13, 13x13½

1996, Apr. 22 **Litho.**

2531	A483	100g	multicolored	.60	.45
2532	A483	200g	multicolored	.60	.45
2533	A483	1000g	multicolored	2.60	1.20
2534	A483	1150g	multicolored	2.90	1.40
		Nos. 2531-2534 (4)		6.70	3.50

1996 Summer Olympic Games, Atlanta — A484

1996, June 6 ***Perf. 13½x13***

2535	A484	500g	Diving	1.25	.45
2536	A484	1000g	Running	2.25	.90

Founding of Society of Salesian Fathers in Paraguay, Cent. — A485

Pope John Paul II, St. John Bosco (1815-88), and: 200g, Men, boys from Salesian Order, natl. flag. 300g, Madonna and Child, vert. 1000g, Map of Paraguay, man following light.

1996, July 22 ***Perf. 13½x13, 13x13½***

2537	A485	200g	multicolored	.50	.30
2538	A485	300g	multicolored	.65	.30
2539	A485	1000g	multicolored	2.10	.90
		Nos. 2537-2539 (3)		3.25	1.50

UNICEF, 50th Anniv. — A486

Children's paintings: 1000g, Outdoor scene, by S. Báez, 1300g, Four groups of children, by C. Pérez.

1996, Sept. 27 ***Perf. 13½x13***

2540	A486	1000g	multicolored	2.50	.90
2541	A486	1300g	multicolored	2.75	1.25

Visit of Pope John Paul II to Caacupe, Site of Apparition of the Virgin — A487

Design: 200g, Pope John Paul II, church, Virgin of Caacupe, vert.

1996, Oct. 4 ***Perf. 13x13½, 13½x13***

2542	A487	200g	multicolored	.50	.35
2543	A487	1300g	multicolored	3.00	1.50

Traditional Costumes — A488

America issue: 500g, Woman in costume. 1000g, Woman, man, in costumes.

1996, Oct. 11 ***Perf. 13x13½***

2544	A488	500g	multicolored	1.50	.45
2545	A488	1000g	multicolored	3.25	.90

UN Year for Eradication of Poverty — A489

1996, Oct. 17 ***Perf. 13½x13, 13x13½***

2546	A489	1000g	Food products	1.75	.90
2547	A489	1150g	Boy, fruit, vert.	2.10	1.10

Christmas — A490

Madonna and Child, by: 200g, Koki Ruíz. 1000g, Hernán Miranda.

1996, Nov. 7 ***Perf. 13x13½***

2548	A490	200g	multicolored	.90	.30
2549	A490	1000g	multicolored	2.10	.90

Butterflies — A491

Designs: 200g, Eryphanis automedon. 500g, Dryadula phaetusa. 1000g, Vanessa myrinna. 1150g, Heliconius ethilla.

1997, Mar. 5 **Litho.** ***Perf. 13x13½***

2550	A491	200g	multicolored	.65	.30
2551	A491	500g	multicolored	1.90	.45
2552	A491	1000g	multicolored	3.25	.80
2553	A491	1150g	multicolored	4.00	.95
		Nos. 2550-2553 (4)		9.80	2.50

Official Buildings A492

200g, 1st Legistlature. 1000g, Postal Headquarters.

1997, May 5 ***Perf. 13½x13***

2554	A492	200g	multicolored	.90	.30
2555	A492	1000g	multicolored	2.10	.90

1997, Year of Jesus Christ — A493

1000g, Crucifix, Pope John Paul II.

1997, June 10 ***Perf. 13x13½***

2556	A493	1000g	multi	2.25	.75

11th Summit of the Rio Group Chiefs of State, Asunción A494

1997, Aug. 23 ***Perf. 13½x13***

2557	A494	1000g	multicolored	2.25	1.00

Environmental and Climate Change A495

Flowers: 300g, Opunita elata. 500g, Bromelia balansae, 1000g, Monvillea kroenlaini.

Perf. 13½x13, 13x13½

1997, Aug. 25

2558	A495	300g	multi	.75	.30
2559	A495	500g	multi, vert.	1.00	.50
2560	A495	1000g	multi	2.10	1.00
		Nos. 2558-2560 (3)		3.85	1.80

1st Philatelic Exposition of MERCOSUR Countries, Chile and Bolivia — A496

Fauna: 200g, Felis tigrina. 1000g, Alouatta caraya, vert. 1150g, Agouti paca.

Perf. 13½x13, 13x13½

1997, Aug. 29

2561	A496	200g	multicolored	.60	.25
2562	A496	1000g	multicolored	2.25	1.00
2563	A496	1150g	multicolored	2.75	1.10
		Nos. 2561-2563 (3)		5.60	2.35

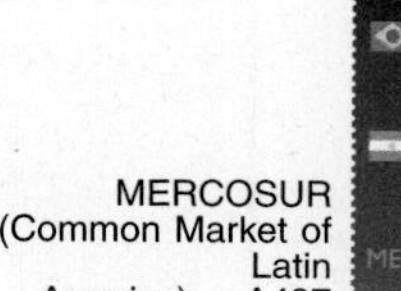

MERCOSUR (Common Market of Latin America) — A497

1997, Sept. 26 ***Perf. 13x13½***

2564	A497	1000g	multicolored	2.25	.90

See Argentina #1975, Bolivia #1019, Brazil #2646, Urugray #1681.

America Issue — A498

Life of a postman: 1000g, Postman, letters going around the world, vert. 1150g, Window with six panes showing weather conditions, different roads, postman.

1997, Oct. 10 ***Perf. 13x13½, 13½x13***

2565	A498	1000g	multicolored	2.75	1.00
2566	A498	1150g	multicolored	2.75	1.25

Natl. Council on Sports, 50th Anniv. — A499

200g, Neri Kennedy throwing javelin. 1000g, Ramón Milciades Giménez Gaona throwing discus.

1997, Oct. 16 ***Perf. 13x13½***

2567	A499	200g	multicolored	.60	.30
2568	A499	1000g	multicolored	2.40	1.10

Nos. 2489-2490 Ovptd. in Red

1997, Nov. 14

2569	A464	50g	multicolored	2.75	.45
2570	A464	250g	multicolored	7.75	2.00

Christmas — A500

Paintings of Madonna and Child: 200g, By Olga Blinder. 1000g, By Hermán Miranda.

1997, Nov. 17

2571	A500	200g	multicolored	.60	.30
2572	A500	1000g	multicolored	2.40	1.00

UN Fund for Children of the World with AIDS — A501

Children's paintings: 500g, Boy. 1000g, Girl.

1997, Dec. 5

2573	A501	500g	multicolored	1.25	.45
2574	A501	1000g	multicolored	2.00	.90

Rotary Club of Asunción, 70th Anniv. — A502

1997, Dec. 11

2575	A502	1150g	multicolored	2.25	1.00

1998 World Cup Soccer Championships, France — A503

200g, Julio César Romero, vert. 500g, Carlos Gamarra, vert. 1000g, 1998 Paraguayan team.

1998, Jan. 22 **Litho.** ***Perf. 13***

2576	A503	200g	multicolored	.35	.25
2577	A503	500g	multicolored	1.10	.45
2578	A503	1000g	multicolored	2.25	.90
		Nos. 2576-2578 (3)		3.70	1.60

Fish — A504

Designs: 200g, Tetrogonopterus argenteus. 300g, Pseudoplatystoma coruscans. 500g, Salminus brasiliensis. 1000g, Acestrorhynchus altus.

1998, Apr. 17 Litho. *Perf. 13½*
2579 A504 200g multicolored .80 .30
2580 A504 300g multicolored 1.00 .30
2581 A504 500g multicolored 1.50 .45
2582 A504 1000g multicolored 3.25 .90
Nos. 2579-2582 (4) 6.55 1.95

Contemporary Paintings A505

200g, Hands, geometric shape, by Carlos Colombino. 300g, Mother nursing infant, by Félix Toranzos. 400g, Flowers, by Edith Giménez. 1000g, Woman lifting tray of food, by Ricardo Migliorisi.

1998, June 5
2583 A505 200g multi, vert. .40 .25
2584 A505 300g multi, vert. .80 .30
2585 A505 400g multi, vert. .90 .30
2586 A505 1000g multi 2.10 .75
Nos. 2583-2586 (4) 4.20 1.60

Mushrooms — A506

400g, Boletus edulis. 600g, Macrolepiota procera. 1000g, Geastrum triplex.

1998, June 26
2587 A506 400g multicolored .90 .30
2588 A506 600g multicolored 1.20 .50
2589 A506 1000g multicolored 2.10 .90
Nos. 2587-2589 (3) 4.20 1.70

Organization of American States (OAS), 50th Anniv. — A507

Designs: 500g, Home of Carlos A. López, botantical and zoological gardens, Asunción. 1000g, Palmerola Villa, Areguá.

1998, July 16
2590 A507 500g multicolored 1.10 .40
2591 A507 1000g multicolored 2.40 .90

Episcopacy of Hernando de Trejo y Sanabria, 400th Anniv. — A508

Pope John Paul II and: 400g, Sacrarium doors, Caazapá Church, vert. 1700g, Statue of St. Francis of Assisi, Atyrá Church.

Perf. 13x13½, 13½x13
1998, Sept. 5 Litho.
2592 A508 400g multi 1.25 .40
2593 A508 1700g multi 3.25 1.75

Ruins of Jesuit Mission Church — A509

1998, Sept. 16 Litho. *Perf. 13½x13*
2594 A509 5000g multicolored 8.25 5.00

Flowers — A510

Designs: 100g, Acacia caven. 600g, Cordia trichotoma. 1900g, Glandularia sp.

1998, Sept. 16 Litho. *Perf. 13x13½*
2595 A510 100g multi .40 .25
2596 A510 600g multi 1.60 .50
2597 A510 1900g multi 3.50 1.75
Nos. 2595-2597 (3) 5.50 2.50

America Issue — A511

Famous women and buildings: 1600g, Serafina Davalos (1883-1957), first woman lawyer, National College building. 1700g, Adela Speratti (1865-1902), director of Normal School.

1998, Oct. 12 Litho. *Perf. 13½x13*
2598 A511 1600g multi 3.50 1.50
2599 A511 1700g multi 4.50 1.75

Universal Declaration of Human Rights, 50th Anniv. — A512

Artwork by: 500g, Carlos Colombino. 1000g, Jose Filártiga.

1998, Oct. 23 *Perf. 13x13½*
2600 A512 500g multi 1.10 .50
2601 A512 1000g multi 2.25 1.00

Christmas Creche Figures — A513

Perf. 13½x13, 13x13½
1998, Sept. 16 Litho.
2602 A513 300g shown 2.00 .25
2603 A513 1600g Stable, vert. 6.50 1.75

Reptiles A514

Designs: 100g, Micrurus frontalis. 300g, Ameiva ameiva. 1600g, Geochelone carbonaria. 1700g, Caiman yacare.

1999, May 13 Litho. *Perf. 13½x13*
2604-2607 A514 Set of 4 10.00 4.00

Paintings A515

Paintings by: 500g, Ignacio Nuñez Soler. 1600g, Modesto Delgado Rodas. 1700g, Jaime Bestard.

1999, June 23 Litho. *Perf. 13½x13*
2608 A515 500g multi .75 .40
2609 A515 1600g multi 2.25 1.40
2610 A515 1700g multi 2.75 1.40
Nos. 2608-2610 (3) 5.75 3.20

America Soccer Cup — A516

Designs: 300g, Carlos Humberto Paredes, vert. 500g, South American Soccer Confederation Building, Luque. 1900g, Feliciano Cáceres Stadium, Luque.

Perf. 13x13½, 13½x13
1999, June 24
2611 A516 300g multi .50 .25
2612 A516 500g multi .85 .35
2613 A516 1900g multi 3.25 1.50
Nos. 2611-2613 (3) 4.60 2.10

SOS Children's Villages, 50th Anniv. — A517

1999, July 16 *Perf. 13½x13, 13x13½*
2614 A517 1700g Toucan 2.75 1.10
2615 A517 1900g Toucan, vert. 3.75 1.40

Protests of Assassination of Vice-President Luis Maria Argaña — A518

Designs: 100g, Protest at Governmental Palace. 500g, Argaña, vert. 1500g, Protest at National Congress.

1999, Aug. 26
2616 A518 100g multi .30 .25
2617 A518 500g multi .90 .40
2618 A518 1500g multi 2.40 1.25
Nos. 2616-2618 (3) 3.60 1.90

Medicinal Plants — A519

Designs: 600g, Cochlospermum regium. 700g, Borago officinalis. 1700g, Passiflora cincinnata.

1999, Sept. 8 *Perf. 13x13½*
2619 A519 600g multi .90 .35
2620 A519 700g multi .90 .45
2621 A519 1700g multi 2.50 1.00
Nos. 2619-2621 (3) 4.30 1.80

America Issue, A New Millennium Without Arms — A520

Various artworks by Ricardo Migliorisi.

Perf. 13½x13, 13x13½
1999, Oct. 12 Litho.
2622 A520 1500g multi 2.25 1.10
2623 A520 3000g multi, vert. 3.75 2.25

Intl. Year of the Elderly — A521

Artwork by: 1000g, Olga Blinder. 1900g, Maria de los Reyes Omella Herrero, vert.

Perf. 13½x13, 13x13½
1999, Oct. 20 Litho.
2624-2625 A521 Set of 2 4.00 2.00

Christmas — A522

Artwork by: 300g, Manuel Viedma. 1600g, Federico Ordiñana.

1999, Nov. 11 Litho. *Perf. 13x13½*
2626 A522 300g multi 1.00 .25
2627 A522 1600g multi 2.50 1.00

City of Pedro Juan Caballero, Cent. — A523

Flowers: 1000g, Tabebuia impetiginosa. 1600g, Tabebuia pulcherrima, vert.

Perf. 13½x13, 13x13½
1999, Dec. 1 Litho.
2628 A523 1000g multi 1.50 .70
2629 A523 1600g multi 2.00 1.00

Inter-American Development Bank, 40th Anniv. — A524

Designs: 600g, Oratory of Our Lady of Asuncion and Pantheon of Heroes, Asuncion. 700g, Governmental Palace.

1999, Dec. 6 *Perf. 13½x13*
2630 A524 600g multi 1.25 .35
2631 A524 700g multi 1.50 .45

Intl. Women's Day — A525

Carmen Casco de Lara Castro and sculpture: 400g, Conjunction, by Domingo Rivarola. 2000g, Violation, by Gustavo Beckelmann.

2000, Apr. 7 Litho. *Perf. 13x13½*
2632-2633 A525 Set of 2 3.50 3.00

Expo 2000, Hanover A526

Designs: 500g, Yacyreta Dam and deer. 2500g, Itaipú Dam, tapir.

2000, May 5 *Perf. 13½x13*
2634-2635 A526 Set of 2 4.50 3.50

Salesians in Paraguay, Cent. — A527

Madonna and Child, Pope John Paul II and: 600g, Salesians, vert. 2000g, College building.

Perf. 13x13½, 13½x13

2000, May 19 **Litho.**
2636-2637 A527 Set of 2 3.50 3.00

2000 Summer Olympics, Sydney — A528

Designs: 2500g, Soccer, vert. 3000g, Runner Francisco Rojas Soto.

2000, July 28 ***Perf. 13x13½, 13½x13***
2638-2639 A528 Set of 2 8.00 7.50

Rights of the Child — A529

Designs: 1500g, Child between hands, vert. 1700g, Handprints.

Perf. 13x13½, 13½x13

2000, Aug. 16
2640-2641 A529 Set of 2 5.00 4.50

Fire Fighters A530

Designs: 100g, Fire fighters, white truck, vert. 200g, Fire fighter in old uniform, emblem, vert. 1500g, Fire fighters at fire. 1600g, Fire fighters, yellow truck.

Perf. 13x13½, 13½x13

2000, Sept. 28
2642-2645 A530 Set of 4 6.00 4.50

Roads and Flowers A531

Designs: 500g, Paved road between San Bernardino and Altos, Rosa banksiae. 3000g, Gaspar Rodriguez de Francia Highway, Calliandra brevicaulis.

2000, Oct. 5 **Litho.** ***Perf. 13½x13¼***
2646-2647 A531 Set of 2 5.50 5.00

America Issue, Fight Against AIDS — A532

Designs: 1500g, Signs with arrows. 2500g, Tic-tac-toe game.

2000, Oct. 19 ***Perf. 13x13½***
2648-2649 A532 Set of 2 6.00 5.50

Intl. Year of Culture and Peace — A533

Sculptures by: 500g, Hugo Pistilli. 2000g, Herman Guggiari.

2000, Oct. 27 **Litho.** ***Perf. 13¼x13½***
2650-2651 A533 Set of 2 3.75 3.25

Christmas — A534

Designs: 100g, Holy Family, sculpture by Hugo Pistilli. 500g, Poem by José Luis Appleyard. 2000g, Creche figures, horiz.

Perf. 13x13½, 13½x13

2000, Nov. 17 **Litho.**
2652-2654 A534 Set of 3 4.25 3.50

Artisan's Crafts — A535

Designs: 200g, Campesina Woman, by Behage. 1500g, Cattle horns, by Quintin Velazquez, horiz. 2000g, Silver filigree orchid, by Quirino Torres.

Perf. 13¼x13½, 13½x13¼

2000, Nov. 28 **Litho.**
2655-2657 A535 Set of 3 6.00 5.25

Guarania Music, 75th Anniv. — A536

Designs: 100g, José Asunción Flores (1904-72), composer. 1500g, Violin. 2500g, Trombone.

2000, Dec. 20 ***Perf. 13¼x13½***
2658-2660 A536 Set of 3 5.50 5.00

Signing of Asunción Treaty, 10th Anniv. — A537

Designs: 500g, Delegates signing treaty. 2500g, Map of South America with signatory nations colored, vert.

Perf. 13½x13¼, 13¼x13½

2001, June 20
2661-2662 A537 Set of 2 4.00 3.50

Cacti — A538

Designs: 2000g, Opuntia sp. 2500g, Cereus stenogonus.

2001, June 29 ***Perf. 13¼x13½***
2663-2664 A538 Set of 2 6.50 6.00

Second Paz del Chaco Philatelic Exhibition.

Under 20 Soccer Championships, Argentina A539

Designs: 2000g, Players. 2500g, Players, diff., vert.

Perf. 13½x13¼, 13¼x13½

2001, June 29
2665-2666 A539 Set of 2 6.50 6.00

Cattle — A540

Designs: 200g, Holando-Argentino. 500g, Nelore. 1500g, Pampa Chaqueño.

2001, July 20 ***Perf. 13½x13¼***
2667-2669 A540 Set of 3 4.25 3.50

Engravings A541

Woodcuts by: No. 2670, 500g, Josefina Plá. No. 2671, 500g, Leonor Cecotto, vert. 1500g, Jacinto Rivero. 2000g, Livio Abramo.

Perf. 13½x13¼, 13¼x13½

2001, Aug. 28
2670-2673 A541 Set of 4 7.00 6.00

Mythological Heavens of the Guarani A542

Designs: 100g, Eichu (Pleiades). 600g, Mborevi Rape (Milky Way). 1600g, Jagua Ho'u Jasy (lunar eclipse).

2001, Sept. 24 ***Perf. 13½x13¼***
2674-2676 A542 Set of 3 4.00 3.25

America Issue — UNESCO World Heritage Sites — A543

No. 2677: a, 500g, St. Ignatius of Loyola, Jesuit Mission Ruins, Trinidad. b, 2000g, Jesuit Mission Ruins.

2001, Oct. 9 ***Perf. 13¼x13½***
2677 A543 Horiz. pair, #a-b, + 2 flanking labels 4.50 3.50

World Teachers' Day — A544

Designs: 200g, Children studying, school blackboard, J. Inocencio Lezcano (1889-1935), educator. 1600g, Symbols of education, Ramón I. Cardozo (1876-1943), educator.

2001, Oct. 9 ***Perf. 13½x13¼***
2678-2679 A544 Set of 2 3.00 2.50

Year of Dialogue Among Civilizations — A545

2001, Oct. 23 ***Perf. 13¼x13½***
2680 A545 3000g multi + 2 flanking labels 30.00 30.00

Christmas A546

Nativity scenes by: 700g, Gladys and Maria de Feliciangeli. 4000g, Mercedes Servin.

2001, Nov. 29 ***Perf. 13½x13¼***
2681-2682 A546 Set of 2 5.50 5.00

No to Terrorism A547

Designs: 700g, Statue of Liberty, World Trade Center, vert. 5000g, Flags of Paraguay and U.S., chain becoming doves.

Perf. 13¼x13½, 13½x13¼

2001, Dec. 19 **Litho.**
2683-2684 A547 Set of 2 9.00 8.50

Passiflora Caerulea — A548

2001, Dec. 21 ***Perf. 13¼x13½***
2685 A548 4000g multi 4.75 4.00

Paraguayan, Bolivian, and Argentinian Scout Jamboree, Boquerón Province — A549

2002, Jan. 24
2686 A549 6000g multi 9.75 9.50

El Mbiguá Social Club, Asunción, Cent. — A550

2002, May 3 ***Perf. 13½x13¼***
2687 A550 700g multi 1.40 1.10

Juan de Salazar Spanish Cultural Center, 25th Anniv. — A551

Jesuit wood carvings, 18th cent.: 2500g, Pieta. 5000g, St. Michael Archangel.

2002, May 7 ***Perf. 13¼x13½***
2688-2689 A551 Set of 2 16.50 11.00

2002 World Cup Soccer Championships, Japan and Korea — A552

Designs: 3000g, Paraguay team. 5000g, Players in action, vert.

Perf. 13½x13¼, 13¼x13½

2002, May 18
2690-2691 A552 Set of 2 16.50 12.00

For overprint see No. 2705.

Arrival of Mennonites in Paraguay, 75th Anniv. — A553

Cross, plow, Menno Simons (1496-1561), Religious Leader, and: 2000g, Mennonite Church, Filadelfia. 4000g, Mennonite Church, Loma Plata.

2002, June 25 ***Perf. 13½x13¼***
2692-2693 A553 Set of 2 8.25 7.50

Horses — A554

Designs: 700g, Criollo. 1000g, Cuarto de Milla (quarterhorse). 6000g, Arabian.

2002, July 12
2694-2696 A554 Set of 3 10.25 9.50

Olimpia Soccer Team, Cent. A555

2002, July 24
2697 A555 700g multi + 2 flanking labels 2.25 2.00

Pan-American Health Organization, Cent. — A556

Medicinal plants: 4000g, Stevia rebaudiana bertoni. 5000g, Ilex paraguayensis.

2002, Sept. 16 ***Perf. 13¼x13½***
2698-2699 A556 Set of 2 13.50 13.00

International Forum on Postal Service Modernization and Reform — A557

Forum emblem and statues by Serafin Marsal: 1000g, Campesina. 4000g, Quygua-vera.

2002, Sept. 30 ***Perf. 13½x13¼***
2700-2701 A557 Set of 2 7.50 7.00

Paraguay — Republic of China Diplomatic Relations, 45th Anniv. — A558

2002, Oct. 10 ***Perf. 13¼x13½***
2702 A558 4000g multi + 2 flanking labels 6.75 6.00

America Issue — Youth, Education and Literacy — A559

Designs: 3000g, Classroom. 6000g, Children playing.

2002, Oct. 12 ***Perf. 13½x13¼***
2703-2704 A559 Set of 2 12.50 12.00

No. 2690 Overprinted

2002
2705 A552 3000g on #2690 10.25 10.25

Christmas — A560

Various creche figures: a, 1000g. b, 4000g. c, 700g.

2002, Dec. 2 **Litho.** ***Perf. 13¼***
2706 A560 Horiz. strip of 3, #a-c 8.00 7.00

Church, Areguá — A561

2002, Dec. 18
2707 A561 4000g multi 5.50 4.50

District of San Antonio, Cent. — A562

2003, Apr. 21 **Litho.** ***Perf. 13¼***
2708 A562 700g multi 1.10 .85

Josefina Plá (1903-99), Artist — A563

Designs: 700g, Plate. 6000g, Carving.

2003, May 30 **Litho.** ***Perf. 13¼***
2709-2710 A563 Set of 2 5.75 5.00

Parrots — A564

Designs: 1000g, Amazona aestiva. 2000g, Myiopsitta monachus. 4000g, Aratinga leucophtalmus.

2003, June 9
2711-2713 A564 Set of 3 7.25 6.50

Paraguay Philatelic Center, 90th anniv. (#2711), Paz del Chaco Bi-national Philatelic Exhibition (#2712), PARAFIL Bi-national Philatelic Exhibition (#2713).

Legislative Palace — A565

2003, June 24 ***Perf. 13½x13¼***
2714 A565 4000g multi + label 4.50 3.50

Printed in sheets of 12 stamps and 18 labels.

Pontificate of Pope John Paul II, 25th Anniv. — A566

2003, June 27 ***Perf. 13¼***
2715 A566 6000g multi + label 6.25 6.25

Farm Animals A567

Designs: 1000g, Pig. 3000g, Sheep. 8000g, Goat.

2003, July 18
2716-2718 A567 Set of 3 9.25 8.50

Foods — A568

Designs: 700g, Peanuts, honey and nougat. 2000g, Sopa Paraguaya. 3000g, Chipá.

2003, July 25
2719-2721 A568 Set of 3 6.75 5.50

Folk Artists — A569

Designs: 700g, Julio Correa (1890-1953), playwright. 1000g, Emiliano Rivarola Fernández (1894-1949), singer. 2000g, Manuel Ortiz Guerrero (1894-1933), poet.

2003, Sept. 12
2722-2724 A569 Set of 3 5.00 4.00

Dances — A570

Designs: 700g, Golondriana. 3000g, Polka. 4000g, Galopera.

2003, Sept. 23
2725-2727 A570 Set of 3 8.50 7.50

Guaraní Soccer Team, Cent. A571

2003, Oct. 9
2728 A571 700g multi + label 1.10 .85

Native Clothing — A572

Designs: 4000g, Sixty-strip poncho, Para'i. 5000g, Shirt, Ao Poí.

2003, Oct. 22
2729-2730 A572 Set of 2 8.75 7.50

Christmas — A573

Designs: 700g, Journey to Egypt. 1000g, Adoration of the Shepherds. 4000g, Nativity.

2003, Nov. 12
2731-2733 A573 Set of 3 6.00 5.00

Indoor Soccer World Cup Championships, Paraguay — A574

No. 2734 — Various players: a, 4000g. b, 5000g.

2003, Nov. 14
2734 A574 Horiz. pair, #a-b 8.00 6.50

Printed in sheets with two columns of five pairs separated by a column of labels.

No. 2734 Overprinted "PARAGUAY / CAMPEON MUNDIAL" in Silver

No. 2734C: d, On #2734a. e, On #2734b.

2003 **Litho.** ***Perf. 13¼***
2734C A574 Horiz. pair, #d-e 12.50 12.50

America Issue - Flowers — A575

Designs: 1000g, Cordia bordasii. No. 2736, 5000g, Bulnesia sarmientoi. No. 2737, 5000g, Chorisia insignis.

2003, Nov. 26
2735-2737 A575 Set of 3 13.50 10.00

For overprints see Nos. 2797-2798.

Comics by Robin Wood — A576

Designs: 1000g, Anahí. 3000g, Nippur de Lagash. 5000g, Dago.

2004, May 24 Litho. *Perf. 13¼*
2738-2740 A576 Set of 3 7.75 7.00

National Soccer Team, Cent. A577

2004, June 25
2741 A577 700g multi + label 1.10 .85

San José College, Cent. — A578

2004, July 2 Litho. *Perf. 13¼*
2742 A578 700g multi 1.10 .85

Pablo Neruda (1904-73), Poet — A579

2004, July 6 Litho. *Perf. 13¼*
2743 A579 5000g multi 4.50 3.50

World of the Guaranís A580

Designs: 700g, Monday Waterfalls. 6000g, Entrance to Ciudad de Tobati.

2004, July 7
2744-2745 A580 Set of 2 4.75 4.00

Nos. 2744 and 2745 were issued in sheets of 15 stamps and 10 labels.

Independence House — A581

Dr. Carlos Pussineri and: 700g, Mural by José Laterza Parodi. 5000g, Independence House.

2004, Aug. 13 Litho. *Perf. 13¼*
2746-2747 A581 Set of 2 4.75 4.00

José Asunción Flores (1904-72), Composer — A582

2004, Aug. 24 Litho. *Perf. 13¼*
2748 A582 5000g multi 4.50 3.50

Museo del Barro, 25th Anniv. — A583

Designs: 2000g, Painting by Enrique Careaga. 3000g, Anthropomorphic jug, vert. 4000g, Christ of the Column, vert.

2004, Aug. 26
2749-2751 A583 Set of 3 8.25 7.00

For overprint see No. 2799.

Paraguayan Railroads, 150th Anniv. — A584

Designs: 2000g, Locomotive No. 151, Camello. 3000g, Locomotive No. 104, El Coqueto, horiz.
6000g, Locomotiove No. 10, Sapucai, horiz.

2004, Sept. 22 *Perf. 13¼*
2752-2753 A584 Set of 2 7.50 6.00

Souvenir Sheet
Rouletted 5¼

2754 A584 6000g multi 5.25 5.00

No. 2754 contains one 50x40mm stamp.

America Issue — Environmental Protection A585

Designs: No. 2755, Procnias nudicollis. No. 2756, Ceratophrys cranwelli.

2004, Oct. 11 Litho. *Perf. 13¼*
2755 A585 6000g multi 7.50 6.00

Souvenir Sheet
Rouletted 5¼

2756 A585 6000g multi 5.25 5.00

Water Conservation A586

Designs: 3000g, Felis pardalis, storks, telephone poles. 4000g, Myrmecophaga tridactyla, Hydrochoerus hydrochaeris, Chauna torquata.

2004, Oct. 22
2757-2758 A586 Set of 2 7.50 7.00

Crops — A587

Designs: 2000g, Corn. 4000g, Cotton. 6000g, Soybeans.

2004, Oct. 22 Litho. *Perf. 13¼*
2759-2761 A587 Set of 3 9.25 8.00

Christmas A588

Paintings by Ricardo Migliorisi: 3000g, Madonna and Child. 5000g, Angel, vert.

2004, Nov. 12
2762-2763 A588 Set of 2 6.50 5.50

Latin American Parliament, 40th Anniv. — A589

2004, Nov. 16
2764 A589 4000g multi + label 3.00 2.50

For overprint, see No. 3006.

Itaipú Dam, 30th Anniv. — A590

Designs: 4000g, Dam and spillway. 5000g, Aerial view of dam, vert.

2004, Dec. 10 Litho. *Perf. 13¼*
2765-2766 A590 Set of 2 7.25 6.00

Rotary International, Cent. — A591

Jesuit Mission ruins, Trinidad: 3000g, Building ruins. 4000g, Religious statue, vert.

2005, Feb. 23 Litho. *Perf. 13¼*
2767-2768 A591 Set of 2 4.50 4.50

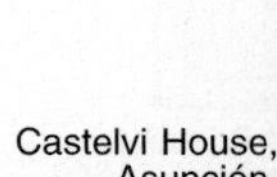

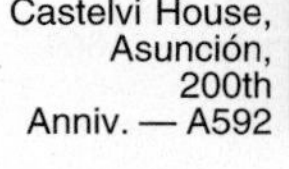

Castelvi House, Asunción, 200th Anniv. — A592

2005, Mar. 14
2769 A592 5000g multi 3.00 3.00

Herminio Giménez (1905-91), Conductor A593

2005, Apr. 22
2770 A593 700g multi .50 .50

Cabildo Cultural Center, Asunción, 1st Anniv. — A594

2005, May 19
2771 A594 1000g multi .70 .70

Fernheim Colony, 75th Anniv. — A595

Designs: 5000g, Pioneer's Monument. 6000g, Cross, cactus, oxcart.

2005, June 15 *Perf. 13¼*
2772 A595 5000g multi 3.50 3.50

Souvenir Sheet
Rouletted 5¼

2773 A595 6000g multi 3.50 3.50

Libertad Soccer Team, Cent. A596

Illustration reduced.

2005, July 20 *Perf. 13¼*
2774 A596 700g multi + label .50 .50

Publication of Don Quixote, 400th Anniv. — A597

2005, July 26
2775 A597 8000g multi 5.00 5.00

Writers — A598

Designs: 3000g, Herib Campos Cervera (1905-53), poet. 5000g, Gabriel Casaccia (1907-80), novelist.

2005, July 27
2776-2777 A598 Set of 2 5.00 5.00

Pope John Paul II (1920-2005) A599

2005, Aug. 18
2778 A599 2000g multi 2.00 2.00

Truth and Justice — A600

2005, Aug. 23
2779 A600 8000g multi 4.50 4.50

America Issue, Fight Against Poverty — A601

Designs: 5000g, Women selling vegetables. 6000g, Cobbler.

2005, Aug. 31
2780-2781 A601 Set of 2 6.50 6.50

Dogs and Cats — A602

Designs: No. 2782, 2000g, Samoyed. No. 2783, 2000g, Three European cats. No. 2784, 3000g, Doberman pinscher. No. 2785, 3000g, White European cat.

2005, Oct. 7
2782-2785 A602 Set of 4 8.50 7.50

Anthropologists A603

Designs: 1000g, Branislava Susnik, bracelet. 2000g, Miguel Chase-Sardi, poncho. 8000g, León Cadogan, basket.

2005, Oct. 26
2786-2788 A603 Set of 3 8.25 7.25

Intl. Year of Sports and Physical Education A604

Designs: 5000g, Lucy Aguero throwing hammer and javelin. 6000g, Golfer Carlos Franco.

2005, Nov. 9 ***Perf. 13¼***
2789 A604 5000g multi 4.50 3.50

Souvenir Sheet

Rouletted 5¼

2790 A604 6000g multi 5.00 5.00

Christmas — A605

Designs: 700g, Angels, people celebrating Christmas, rooftops. 5000g, Nativity scene.

2005, Nov. 22 ***Perf. 13¼***
2791-2792 A605 Set of 2 5.50 4.50

Yacyreta Dam — A606

Various views of dam: 3000g, 5000g.

2005, Nov. 28
2793-2794 A606 Set of 2 5.25 4.75

Ministry of Defense, 150th Anniv. — A607

Designs: 700g, Monument to the Residents, by Javier Báez Rolón. 1000g, Defense Ministry Building, Marshal Francisco Solano López.

2005, Dec. 21
2795-2796 A607 Set of 2 2.00 1.50

Nos. 2736-2737 Overprinted

2005, Dec. 28 ***Perf. 13¼***
2797 A575 5000g On #2736 5.25 5.25
2798 A575 5000g On #2737 5.25 5.25

No. 2751 Overprinted

2005, Dec. 28 ***Perf. 13¼***
2799 A583 4000g On #2751 5.25 5.25

Paraguay — Germany Chamber of Commerce and Industry, 50th Anniv. — A608

2006, Mar. 14
2800 A608 8000g multi 5.50 5.00

2006 World Cup Soccer Championships, Germany — A609

Emblem and: 3000g, Paraguayan team. 5000g, World Cup.

2006, May 17 **Litho.** ***Perf. 13¼***
2801-2802 A609 Set of 2 7.00 6.00

French Alliance of Asuncion, 50th Anniv. — A610

2006, June 20
2803 A610 8000g multi + label 6.50 5.50

Cervantes Club, 50th Anniv. — A611

2006, June 27
2804 A611 700g multi 1.30 1.00

Paraguayan Soccer Association, Cent. — A612

2006, Aug. 1
2805 A612 1000g multi 1.90 1.50

National Commerce School, Cent. — A613

2006, Sept. 7
2806 A613 700g multi 1.90 1.50

Japanese Emigration to Paraguay, 70th Anniv. — A614

Flags of Paraguay and Japan and butterflies: 1000g, Junonia evarete. 2000g, Anartia jatrophae. 3000g, Agraulis vanillae. 6000g, Danaus plexippus.

2006, Sept. 8 ***Perf. 13¼***
2807-2809 A614 Set of 3 6.00 5.00

Souvenir Sheet

Rouletted 5¼

2810 A614 6000g multi 5.25 5.25

No. 2810 contains one 50x40mm stamp.

OPEC Intl. Development Fund, 30th Anniv. — A615

2006, Sept. 18 ***Perf. 13¼***
2811 A615 8000g multi 5.50 5.00

Tuparenda Shrine, 25th Anniv. — A616

2006, Oct. 9
2812 A616 700g multi 1.30 1.00

America Issue, Energy Conservation A617

Designs: 5000g, Windmills. 6000g, Solar collector.

2006, Oct. 11
2813-2814 A617 Set of 2 7.60 6.50

Agronomy and Veterinary Medicine Faculties of Asuncion National University, 50th Anniv. — A618

Designs: No. 2815, 4000g, Symbols of agronomy. No. 2816, 4000g, Livestock.

2006, Oct. 20
2815-2816 A618 Set of 2 6.25 5.00

South American Soccer Confederation, 90th Anniv. — A619

2006, Nov. 6
2817 A619 8000g multi 5.40 5.00

Musical Instruments A620

Designs: 5000g, Harp. 6000g, Guitar.

2006, Nov. 10
2818-2819 A620 Set of 2 7.60 6.50

Christmas — A621

Designs: 4000g, Our Lady of Asuncion Cathedral. 6000g, Holy Trinity Church, horiz.

2006, Nov. 17
2820-2821 A621 Set of 2 8.00 6.00

First Lieutenant Adolfo Rojas Silva (1906-27), Military Hero — A622

Designs: 4000g, Rojas Silva and hut. 6000g, Rojas Silva, vert.

2007, Feb. 27 **Litho.**
2822-2823 A622 Set of 2 7.00 6.50

B'nai B'rith of Paraguay, 50th Anniv. — A623

2007, Mar. 29 ***Perf. 13¼***
2824 A623 8000g multi 5.50 5.00

Junior Chamber International Conference, Asuncion A624

2007, Apr. 18
2825 A624 8000g multi 5.50 5.00

World Tobacco-Free Day — A625

Emblem and: 5000g, Person wearing gas mask. 6000g, Map of Paraguay with umbrella, vert.

2007, May 30
2826-2827 A625 Set of 2 7.50 6.50

Arlequin Theater, Asuncion, 25th Anniv. — A626

2007, June 11
2828 A626 700g multi 1.30 .60

Paz del Chaco 07 Philatelic Exhibition, Asuncion A627

Exhibition emblem and: 700g, Felis pardalis. 8000g, Chaco War postman riding cow.

2007, June 11
2829-2830 A627 Set of 2 6.00 5.00

Diplomatic Relations Between Paraguay and South Korea, 45th Anniv. — A628

Flags of Paraguay and South Korea and: 1000g, Open horse-drawn wagon. 2000g, Covered horse-drawn carriage. 3000g, Ox cart, vert.
6000g, Mugungfa flower.

2007, June 15 ***Perf. 13¼***
2831-2833 A628 Set of 3 4.50 3.50

Souvenir Sheet

Rouletted 7¼

2834 A628 6000g multi 6.25 5.00

No. 2834 contains one 50x40mm stamp.

Friendship Between Paraguay and Republic of China, 50th Anniv. — A628a

2007, July 8 ***Perf. 13¼***
2834A A628a 7000g multi + 2 flanking labels 6.25 4.25

Diplomatic Relations Between Paraguay and Indonesia, 25th Anniv. — A629

2007, July 9
2835 A629 11,000g multi 7.25 6.50

Official Veterinary Service, 40th Anniv. — A630

Designs: 5000g, Prize-winning cow. 7000g, Veterinarian inspecting cow, cattle herd, prize-winning cow, horiz.

2007, June 11
2836-2837 A630 Set of 2 8.25 7.00

Peace Corps in Paraguay, 40th Anniv. — A631

2007, Sept. 19
2838 A631 7000g multi 4.50 4.50

Scouting, Cent. — A632

Designs: 700g, Scouts near campfire. 6000g, Lord Robert Baden-Powell, female Scouts.

2007, Oct. 11
2839-2840 A632 Set of 2 5.00 4.00

Institute of Fine Arts, 50th Anniv. — A633

Designs: 4000g, Pendants, by Engelberto Giménez Legal. 8000g, Sculpture by Hugo Pistilli, vert.

2007, Nov. 20
2841-2842 A633 Set of 2 8.25 7.00

Gabriel Casaccia Bibolini (1907-80), Writer — A634

2007, Nov. 23
2843 A634 8000g multi 5.25 5.00

Marco Aguayo Foundation, 15th Anniv. — A635

Designs: 1000g, Dr. Marco Aguayo (1956-92), red ribbon. 8000g, Red ribbon and geometrical design.

2007, Dec. 11
2844-2845 A635 Set of 2 6.25 5.50

Dr. Nicolas Leoz Stadium A636

2007, Oct. 22
2846 A636 700g multi 1.30 1.00

Gen. Martin T. McMahon (1838-1906), US Minister to Paraguay — A637

2007, Sept. 19
2847 A637 700g multi 4.75 .50

Intl. Day of Deserts and Desertification (in 2006) — A638

2007, Nov. 28
2848 A638 7000g multi 4.75 4.00

Parks and Reserves A639

Designs: 3000g, Nú Guazú Park, Luque. 6000g, Monkey.

2007, Nov. 27 ***Perf. 13¼***
2849 A639 3000g multi 2.25 1.90

Souvenir Sheet

Rouletted 7¼

2850 A639 6000g multi 4.25 4.00

No. 2850 contains one 50x40mm stamp.

America Issue, Education for All — A640

Teachers and school children in class: 5000g, 6000g.

2007, Sept. 3 ***Perf. 13¼***
2851-2852 A640 Set of 2 7.50 6.50

Architecture — A641

Designs: 6000g, Nautilus Building, by Genaro Pindú. 7000g, Museo del Barro, by Carlos Colombino.

2007, Sept. 3
2853-2854 A641 Set of 2 8.75 8.00

Christmas A642

Designs: 700g, Coconut flower. 8000g, Creche figures.

2007, Nov. 29 **Litho.** ***Perf. 13¼***
2855-2856 A642 Set of 2 6.25 5.00

Paraguayan Atheneum, 125th Anniv. — A643

2008, July 28
2857 A643 700g multi .85 .60

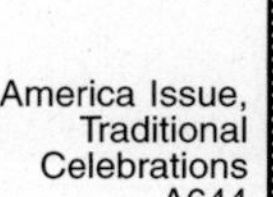

America Issue, Traditional Celebrations A644

2008, July 30
2858 A644 11,000g multi 7.75 7.50

Nasta Publicity Agency, 40th Anniv. — A645

Designs: 700g, Flower. 5000g, Flower, vert.

2008, Apr. 1
2859-2860 A645 Set of 2 4.00 3.50

Scouting in Paraguay, 70th Anniv. — A646

Designs: 3000g, Three scouts, tent. 4000g, Scout troop.

2008, Oct. 11
2861-2862 A646 Set of 2 5.25 4.75

Asuncion Rotary Club, 80th Anniv. — A647

Rotary International emblem and: 2000g, Stylized gearwheels. 8000g, Forest path, horiz.

2008, Apr. 4
2863-2864 A647 Set of 2 7.00 6.50

Birds — A648

Designs: 5000g, Coryphospingus cucullatus. 6000g, Pitangus sulphuratus.

2008, July 28
2865-2866 A648 Set of 2 8.00 7.50

Christmas — A649

Paintings: 700g, Madonna and Child, by unknown artist. 5000g, Madonna and Child, by José Laterza Parodi.

2008, Oct. 9
2867-2868 A649 Set of 2 4.50 4.00

Carter-Torrijos Treaty, 30th Anniv. (in 2007) — A650

Designs: 700g, Signing ceremony. 7000g, Panamanian General Omar Torrijos, U.S. President Jimmy Carter, ship in Panama Canal.

2008, Aug. 5
2869-2870 A650 Set of 2 5.50 5.00

City of Coronel Oviedo, 250th Anniv. — A651

Cotton boll and: 3000g, Cathedral. 7000g, Road.

2008, Oct. 28
2871-2872 A651 Set of 2 7.50 7.00

Arbitration Decision of Pres. Rutherford B. Hayes in Chaco Land Dispute in Favor of Paraguay, 130th Anniv. — A652

2008, Nov. 10 Litho. *Perf. 13¼*
2873 A652 1000g multi 1.00 .75

SOS Children's Village, Asuncion, 25th Anniv. — A653

SOS Children's Village emblem and: 2000g, Children and flower. 7000g, Red, white and blue ribbon.

2008, Nov. 18 Litho. *Perf. 13¼*
2874-2875 A653 Set of 2 7.00 6.50

Year of the Harp — A654

2008, Oct. 20 *Perf. 13¼x13½*
2876 A654 5000g multi 3.75 3.50

Schoenstatt Movement in Paraguay, 50th Anniv. — A655

2009, Oct. 18 *Perf. 13¼*
2877 A655 3000g multi 2.10 1.90

Christmas — A656

Designs: 800g, Our Lady of Caacupé. 5000g, Our Lady of Asunción.

2009, Dec. 1
2878-2879 A656 Set of 2 4.25 3.75

Dr. José Segundo Decoud (1848-1909), Politician and Journalist A657

2009, Dec. 3
2880 A657 7000g multi 5.25 5.00

Exports A658

Designs: 2000g, Nelore cow. 5000g, Stevia rebaudiana.

2009, Dec. 18
2881-2882 A658 Set of 2 5.00 4.50

Arsenio Erico (1915-77), Soccer Player — A659

Erico: 700g, Kicking soccer ball. 1000g, Holding four soccer balls, vert.

2009, Dec. 22
2883-2884 A659 Set of 2 1.75 1.20

Ceryle Torquata A660

2009
2885 A660 7000g multi 4.00 3.00

Charles Darwin (1809-82), naturalist. Printed in sheets of 15 + 10 labels.

Diplomatic Relations Between Paraguay and Russia, Cent. — A661

2009
2886 A661 7000g multi 4.00 3.00

Printed in sheets of 15 + 10 labels.

America Issue, Children's Games — A662

Children: 4000g, Spinning top. 7000g, Playing marbles, horiz.

2010, Jan. 2
2887-2888 A662 Set of 2 8.00 7.50

Independence, Bicent. — A663

Designs: 700g, Governor's House. 2000g, Painting by Jaime Bestard.

2010, Feb. 23
2889-2890 A663 Set of 2 2.60 2.10

Astronomy Aided By Telescopes, 400th Anniv. — A664

2010, Mar. 3
2891 A664 2500g multi 2.10 1.90

Printed in sheets of 15 + 10 labels.

2010 World Cup Soccer Championships, South Africa — A665

Designs: 700g, Paraguayan players. 6000g, Team, crowd holding Paraguayan flags.

2010, July 2 Litho. *Perf. 13¼*
2892 A665 700g multi + label 2.25 2.00
2893 A665 6000g multi 2.25 2.00

America Issue — A666

National symbols: 5000g, National anthem. 6000g, Flag and emblems, horiz.

2010, Oct. 9 Litho. *Perf. 13¼*
2894-2895 A666 Set of 2 7.50 7.00

Christmas A667

Designs: 700g, Magi following Star of Bethlehem. 6000g, Nativity, vert. 11,000g, Journey to Bethlehem.

2010, Nov. 19
2896-2898 A667 Set of 3 12.50 11.50

Road Safety Day — A668

2010
2899 A668 700g multi .85 .60

Famous Paraguayan Buildings A669

Designs: 700g, Venancio López Palace. 2000g, Residencia Patri.

2010, Dec. 17
2900-2901 A669 Set of 2 2.25 1.75

2010 Youth Olymmpics, Singapore A670

Emblem and: 2000g, Diego Galeano Harrison, tennis player. 5000g, Paraguayan athletes.

2010, Dec. 31
2902-2903 A670 Set of 2 5.50 5.00

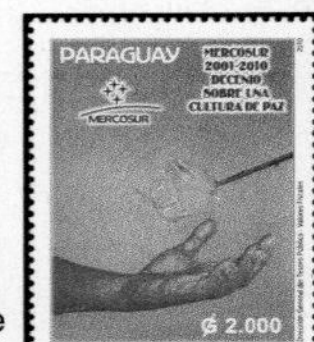
Decade for Culture of Peace — A671

Designs: 2000g, Hand below rose. 6000g, Hand holding rose.

2010, Dec. 31
2904-2905 A671 Set of 2 5.75 5.25

Postal Union of the Americas, Spain and Portugal (UPAEP), Cent. — A672

Designs: 6000g, Map of South and Central America, Spain and Portugal with flags. 11,000g, Building and flags, horiz.

2011, Mar. 18
2906-2907 A672 Set of 2 11.50 11.00

Dated 2010.

National Development Bank, 50th Anniv. — A673

2011, Apr. 12 *Perf. 13¼*
2908 A673 700g multi + label .85 .60

Republic of China, Cent. A674

No. 2909: a, National Pantheon of Heroes, Paraguay. b, Pantheon of the Martyrs of the National Revolution, Taiwan.

2011, Apr. 24 **Litho.**

2909 A674 6000g Horiz. pair, #a-b, + central label 9.00 8.50

Asunción Buildings — A675

No. 2910: a, Asunción, Cathedral. b, Train station. c, Governmental Palace. d, Municipal Theater. e, Town Hall (Cabildo).
11,000g, Independence House, horiz.

2011, May 6 ***Perf. 13¼***

2910 Horiz. strip of 5 + flanking label 4.75 3.50
a.-e. A675 1000g Any single .80 .80

Souvenir Sheet

Rouletted

2911 A675 11,000g multi 8.00 7.75

Marie Curie (1867-1934), Chemist and Physicist — A676

2011, May 9 ***Perf. 13¼***

2912 A676 2000g multi + label 2.00 1.75

Intl. Year of Chemistry.

Campaign Against Violence Towards Women — A677

2011, Apr. 29 **Litho.** ***Perf. 13¼***

2913 A677 700g multi + label .85 .60

Souvenir Sheet

Beatification of Pope John Paul II — A678

2011, May 9 **Litho.** ***Rouletted 1¼***

2914 A678 10,000g multi 8.00 7.25

Masons in Paraguay, 140th Anniv. — A679

2011, May 25 **Litho.** ***Perf. 13¼***

2915 A679 11,000g multi + label 8.25 8.00

Intl. Friendship Day — A680

2011, Nov. 8 **Litho.** ***Perf. 13¼***

2916 A680 700g multi + label .85 .60

Radio Cáritas, 75th Anniv. A681

2011, Nov. 21 **Litho.** ***Perf. 13¼***

2917 A681 700g multi + label .80 .55

San José Academy, Cent. — A682

2011, Nov. 29 **Litho.** ***Perf. 13¼***

2918 A682 700g multi + label .80 .55

America Issue A683

No. 2919: a, 5000g, Red mailbox. b, 6000g, Green mailbox.

2011, Dec. 13 **Litho.** ***Perf. 13¼***

2919 A683 Horiz. pair, #a-b 8.75 8.25

Campaign Against AIDS, 30th Anniv. — A684

2011, Dec. 13 **Litho.** ***Perf. 13¼***

2920 A684 1000g multi + label 1.10 .85

Intl. Year of Forests — A685

Designs: 5000g, Animals and forest. 6000g, Trees and map of North and South America.

2011, Dec. 13 **Litho.** ***Perf. 13¼***

2921 A685 5000g multi 4.25 4.00

Souvenir Sheet

Rouletted 4

2922 A685 6000g multi 5.00 4.75

Actors and Actresses — A686

Designs: 2000g, Map of Paraguay, Perlita Fernández (1951-2002), César Alvarez Blanco (1927-2003), Máxima Lugo (1925-91), José Olitte (1937-2000). 6000g, Edda de los Rios (1942-2007).

2011, Dec. 13 **Litho.** ***Perf. 13¼***

2923 A686 2000g multi + label 1.90 1.60

Souvenir Sheet

Rouletted 5

2924 A686 6000g multi 5.00 4.75

A687

Christmas — A688

Designs: 700g, Star of Bethlehem and Magi. 5000g, Star of Bethlehem and manger. 11,000g, Holy Family and lambs.

2011, Dec. 13 **Litho.** ***Perf. 13¼***

2925 A687 700g multi .55 .50
2926 A687 5000g multi 3.75 3.25
2927 A688 11,000g multi 7.50 6.50
Nos. 2925-2927 (3) 11.80 10.25

Campaign Against Terrorism — A689

No. 2928 — Handprint in: a, 2000g, Black. b, 5000g, White.

2011, Dec. 30 **Litho.** ***Perf. 13¼***

2928 A689 Horiz. pair, #a-b 6.00 5.50

A690

2011 Copa America Soccer Tournament, Argentina A691

2011, Dec. 30 **Litho.** ***Perf. 13¼***

2929 A690 700g multi + label .60 .55
2930 A691 6000g multi 5.25 4.75

José Luis Chilavert, Soccer Player, Estaban Casarino, Squash Player, Olegario Farrés, Shooter, Juan Carlos Giménez, Boxer — A692

Benjamin Hockin Brusquetti, Swimmer — A693

2011, Dec. 30 **Litho.** ***Perf. 13¼***

2931 A692 700g multi + label .80 .55

Souvenir Sheet

Rouletted 5x6

2932 A693 6000g multi 5.00 4.75

Miniature Sheet

Expo 2012, Yeosu, South Korea A694

No. 2933, 2000g — Expo 2012 emblem and: a, Small waterfall in Ybycuí National Park. b, Karapa Waterfall. c, Large waterfall in Ybycuí National Park. d, Monday Waterfall. e, Cristal Waterfall.

2012, May 28 **Litho.** ***Perf. 13¼***

2933 A694 2000g Sheet of 5, #a-e, + 25 labels 9.50 7.75

Souvenir Sheet

National Police Band, Cent. A695

2012, June 1 **Litho.** ***Rouletted 5***

2934 A695 7000g multi 5.75 5.50

Myths and Legends A696

No. 2935 — Guarani monsters: a, Teju Jagua. b, Moñai. c, Jasy Jatere. d, Luisón. e, Kurupi. f, Ao Ao. g, Mbói Tui.
7000p, Kerana, horiz.

2012, June 7 **Litho.** ***Perf. 13¼***

2935 A696 1000g Sheet of 7, #a-g, + 23 labels 7.25 5.50

Souvenir Sheet

Rouletted 5

2936 A696 7000g multi 5.75 5.50

America Issue.

Souvenir Sheets

Korean and Paraguayan Dancers — A697

Paraguayan Dancers — A698

Korean Dancers A699

2012, June 26 Litho. *Rouletted 5*

2937 A697 2000g multi	2.00	1.75
2938 A698 2000g multi	2.00	1.75
2939 A699 2000g multi	2.00	1.75
Nos. 2937-2939 (3)	6.00	5.25

Diplomatic relations between Paraguay and South Korea, 50th anniv.

Authentic Radical Liberal Party, 125th Anniv. A700

Party flag and: 2000g, Anodorhynchus hyacinthinus. 16,000g, Morpho peleides.

2012, July 14 Litho. *Perf. 13¼*
Stamp + Label

2940-2941 A700 Set of 2	14.50	14.00

2012 Summer Olympics, London — A701

No. 2942 — Paraguayan flag, emblem of Paraguayan Olympic Committee and: a, Judo. b, Javelin. c, Running. d, Tennis. e, Table tennis. f, Rowing and swimming.
No. 2943, 4000g, Paraguayan flag, emblem of Paraguayan Olympic Committee, Marcelo Aguirre, table tennis player, and Benjamin Hockin Busquetti, swimmer. No. 2944, 4000g, Paraguayan flag, emblem of Paraguayan Olympic Committee and various athletes.

2012, Aug. 9 Litho. *Perf. 13¼*

2942 Horiz. strip of 6	7.00	5.50
a.-f. A701 1000g Any single	1.00	.90

Souvenir Sheets
Rouletted 5

2943-2944 A701 Set of 2	8.00	7.50

Paraguayan Academy of History, 75th Anniv. — A702

No. 2945 — Academy emblem, building and: a, Ruy Díaz de Guzmán (c. 1558-1692), conquistador and historian. b, Dr. Manuel Domínguez (1868-1935), Vice-President of Paraguay and writer. c, Dr. Fulgencio R. Moreno (1872-1933), historian. d, Dr. Efraím Cardozo (1906-73), historian. e, Dr. Rafael E. Velázquez (1926-94), historian.

2012, Aug. 10 Litho. *Perf. 13¼*

2945 Horiz. strip of 5	6.75	5.50
a.-e. A702 1400g Any single	1.25	1.10

Souvenir Sheet

Asunción, 475th Anniv. — A703

2012, Aug. 14 Litho. *Rouletted 5*

2946 A703 10,000g multi	7.25	7.00

Souvenir Sheet

Locomotive — A704

2012, Aug. 14 Litho. *Rouletted 5*

2947 A704 8000g multi	6.25	6.00

Carlos Antonio López (1792-1862), first President of Paraguay.

National University of Asunción Economic Sciences Faculty, 75th Anniv. — A705

2012, Aug. 22 Litho. *Perf. 13¼*

2948 A705 1400g multi	1.40	1.10

Technical Planning Ministry, 50th Anniv. A706

2012, Sept. 17 Litho. *Perf. 13¼*

2949 A706 8000g multi + label	6.25	6.00

Cerro Porteño Basketball Team — A707

Cerro Porteño Soccer Team A708

2012, Oct. 1 Litho. *Perf. 13¼*

2950 A707 1000g multi	.80	.80
2951 A708 6000g multi + label	4.75	4.25

Cerro Porteño Sports Club, cent.

Independence of Slovakia, 20th Anniv. — A709

2012, Nov. 13 Litho. *Perf. 13¼*

2952 A709 11,000g multi + label	8.50	8.25

No. 2952 was printed in sheets of 10 stamps + 15 labels.

First National Eucharistic Congress, 75th Anniv. — A710

2012, Nov. 19 Litho. *Perf. 13¼*

2953 A710 3000g multi + label	2.50	2.25

Ardea Alba A711

2012, Nov. 20 Litho. *Perf. 13¼*

2954 A711 1400g multi + label	1.30	1.10

Completion of new dam near Encarnacion. No. 2954 was printed in sheets containing 10 stamps + 15 labels.

Radio Nanduti, 50th Anniv. A712

2012, Nov. 29 Litho. *Perf. 13¼*

2955 A712 1400g multi + label	1.30	1.10

United Nations Environmental Program, 40th Anniv. — A713

Designs: 3000g, Butorides striatus. 16,000g, Platalea ajaja.

2012, Dec. 18 Litho. *Perf. 13¼*

2956 A713 3000g multi	2.50	2.25

Souvenir Sheet
Rouletted 5

2957 A713 16,000g multi	12.50	12.00

Christmas A714

No. 2958 — Various creche figures: a, 1000g. b, 5000g. c, 11,000g.

2012, Dec. 18 Litho. *Perf. 13¼*

2958 A714 Vert. strip of 3, #a-c	13.75	13.00

National Library, 125th Anniv. — A715

2012, Dec. 27 Litho. *Perf. 13¼*

2959 A715 1400g multi	1.30	1.10

Alternative Energy Sources — A716

No. 2960: a, Wind energy (wind turbines). b, Solar energy (solar collector). c, Biodiesel (jatropha tree). d, Biomass (hay roll). e, Biodiesel (corn).
3000g, Biodiesel (sunflower), horiz.

2012, Dec. 27 Litho. *Perf. 13¼*

2960 Horiz. strip of 5	7.25	6.00
a.-e. A716 1500g Any single	1.30	1.20

Souvenir Sheet
Rouletted 5

2961 A716 3000g multi	2.50	2.25

First Tramway in Paraguay, Cent. — A717

No. 2962: a, Van following tram. b, Motorcyclist and tram.
7000p, Line 5 tram, vert.

2013, Aug. 19 Litho. *Perf. 13¼*

2962 Horiz. pair + central label	3.00	1.90
a.-b. A717 2000g Either single	1.25	.95

Souvenir Sheet
Rouletted 5

2963 A717 7000g multi	4.75	3.25

Paraguayan-Japanese Center, Asuncion — A718

No. 2964: a, Building exterior and flags. b, Cherry blossoms.

2013, Aug. 19 Litho. *Perf. 13¼*

2964 Horiz. pair + central label	9.25	8.75
a. A718 1400g multi	1.00	1.00
b. A718 11,000g multi	7.75	7.75

Birds — A719

No. 2965: a, Dendrocygna viduata. b, Amazona aestiva. c, Chlorostilbon aureoventris. d, Jabiru mycteria. e, Zenaida auriculata. f, Athene cunicularia. g, Aramides ypecaha. h, Dendrocygna autumnalis. i, Caracara plancus. j, Vanellus chilensis.

2013, Aug. 19 Litho. *Perf. 13¼*

2965 Block of 10	17.50	15.00
a.-j. A719 2000g Any single	1.75	1.50

Mammals A720

No. 2966: a, Lycalopex gymnocercus. b, Myrmecophaga tridactyla. c, Cebus apella paraguayanus. d, Tayassu pecari. e, Nasua nasua.
6000g, Panthera onca, vert.

2013, Aug. 19 Litho. *Perf. 13¼*

2966 Horiz. strip of 5 11.25 10.00
a.-e. A720 3000g Any single 2.25 2.00

Souvenir Sheet

Rouletted 5

2967 A720 6000g multi 4.50 4.50

Scouting in Paraguay, Cent. — A721

No. 2968: a, Group of Scouts. b, Scouts running.

2013, Aug. 23 Litho. *Perf. 13¼*

2968 Horiz. pair + central label 10.00 9.50
a. A721 5000g multi 3.75 3.75
b. A721 8000g multi 5.75 5.75

Rubio Nú Soccer Team, Cent. — A722

Designs: 1400g, Six palyers celebrating. 6000g, Team photograph.

2013, Aug. 24 Litho. *Perf. 13¼*

2969-2970 A722 Set of 2 6.00 5.50

Flowers — A723

No. 2971 — Inscriptions at LL: a, Azahar. b, Aguape. c, Agosto Poty. d, Chivato Poty. e, Santa Lucia. f, Ceibo.

No. 2972, 10,000g, Samu'u (yellow flower), horiz. No. 2973, 10,000g, Mburucuja (blue flower), horiz.

2013, Sept. 17 Litho. *Perf. 13¼*

2971 Horiz. strip of 6 22.50 21.00
a.-f. A723 5000g Any single 3.50 3.50

Souvenir Sheets

Rouletted 5

2972-2973 A723 Set of 2 17.00 16.00

Agustín Barboza (1913-98), Musician — A724

Barboza: 1400g, Holding neck of guitar. 4000g, Playing guitar.

2013, Oct. 9 Litho. *Perf. 13¼*

2974-2975 A724 Set of 2 4.50 4.00

Campaign Against Discrimination A725

Paintings by Juan de Dios Valdez depicting: 5000g, Old man. 10,000g, Old woman.

2013, Oct. 9 Litho. *Perf. 13¼*

2976 A725 5000g multi 3.75 3.50

Souvenir Sheet

Rouletted 5

2977 A725 10,000g multi 7.25 7.00

America Issue.

Republic of Paraguay, 200th Anniv. — A726

200th Anniv. emblem and: 1000g, Map of Asuncion, 1809. 8000g, Consuls Fulgencio Yegros (1780-1821) and Dr. José Gaspar de Francia (1766-1840), vert.

2013, Oct. 12 Litho. *Perf. 13¼*

2978 A726 1000g multi + label 1.00 .75

Souvenir Sheet

Rouletted 5

2979 A726 8000g multi 6.00 5.75

National Pantheon of Heroes and Oratory of Our Lady of Asuncion, 150th Anniv. — A727

Design: 6000g Building's dome and flags, horiz.

2013, Nov. 1 Litho. *Perf. 13¼*

2980 A727 11,000g multi 8.25 8.00

Souvenir Sheet

Rouletted 5

2981 A727 6000p multi 4.25 2.75

Paraguayan Atheneum, 130th Anniv. — A728

2013, Dec. 5 Litho. *Perf. 13¼*

2982 A728 1400g multi 1.25 1.00

Philatelic Center of Paraguay, Cent. — A729

2013, Dec. 6 Litho. *Perf. 13¼*

2983 A729 1400g multi 1.25 1.00

Christmas — A730

Designs: 3000g, Virgin Mary and St. Joseph. 8000g, Holy Family creche figurines. 16,000g, Creche figurines, horiz.

2013, Dec. 6 Litho. *Perf. 13¼*

2984-2986 A730 Set of 3 20.00 19.00

Paraguayan postal officials declared as "illegal" two blocks of nine stamps and two souvenir sheets of four dated 2013 and inscribed "Winter War."

Encarnación, 400th Anniv. (in 2015) — A731

Designs: 3000g, Mirador San José, Virgin of Itacuá. 11,000g, Woman in Carnaval costume, vert.

2014, Feb. 6 Litho. *Perf. 13¼*

2987 A731 3000g multi 2.40 2.10

Souvenir Sheet

Rouletted 5

2988 A731 11,000g multi 8.25 8.00

Asuncion Tennis Club, Cent. — A732

2014, Mar. 4 Litho. *Perf. 13¼*

2989 A732 1400g multi 1.25 1.00

Villeta, 300th Anniv. A733

2014, Mar. 5 Litho. *Perf. 13¼*

2990 A733 1400g multi + label 1.25 1.00

Campaign Against Violence Towards Women — A734

2014, Mar. 7 Litho. *Perf. 13¼*

2991 A734 700g multi .75 .50

Vice-President Domingo F. Sánchez National College, 50th Anniv. — A735

2014, Mar. 28 Litho. *Perf. 13¼*

2992 A735 1400g multi 1.25 1.00

Jorge Castro, Singer — A736

Castro: 1400g, On horse. 5000g, With orchestra.

2014, Apr. 25 Litho. *Perf. 13¼*

2993 A736 1400g multi 2.00 1.00

Souvenir Sheet

Rouletted 5

2994 A736 5000g multi 6.50 4.50

Cabildo Cultural Center, Asuncion, 10th Anniv. — A737

2014, May 13 Litho. *Perf. 13¼*

2995 A737 1400g multi 1.25 1.00

Itaipu Dam and Speothos Venaticus A738

2014, May 20 Litho. *Perf. 13¼*

2996 A738 16,000g multi 11.25 11.00

Itaipu Binacional, 40th anniv.

44th General Assembly of the Organization of American States, Asuncion — A739

2014, June 5 Litho. *Perf. 13¼*

2997 A739 5000g multi + label 3.75 3.50

Pope Francis and Map of South America A740

2014, June 27 Litho. *Perf. 13¼*

2998 A740 9000g multi 6.50 6.00

Gen. José Gervasio Artigas (1764-1850), National Hero of Uruguay — A741

2014, July 18 Litho. *Perf. 13¼*

2999 A741 4000g multi + label 3.00 2.75

Salvador Cabañas and Emblem of 12 de Octubre Soccer Team A742

2014, Aug. 8 Litho. *Perf. 13¼*

3000 A742 1400g multi + label 1.25 1.00

12 de Octubre Soccer Team, cent.

Apostolic Movement of Schoenstatt, Cent. — A743

2014, Oct. 6 Litho. *Perf. 13¼*

3001 A743 3000g multi + label 2.40 2.00

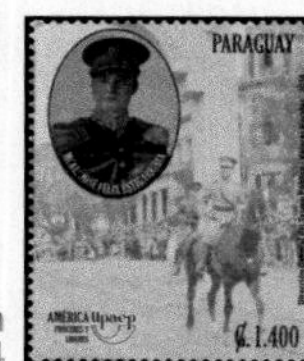

Paraguayan Presidents — A744

Designs: 1400g, José Félix Estigarribia (1888-1940). 4000g, Bernardino Caballero (1839-1912)

2014, Oct. 9 Litho. *Perf. 13¼*

3002-3003 A744 Set of 2 4.25 3.75

America issue.

Telecommunications in Paraguay, 150th Anniv. — A745

2014, Oct. 9 Litho. *Perf. 13¼*
3004 A745 9000g multi + label 6.40 6.00

Asuncion Zoo and Botanical Gardens, Cent. — A746

No. 3005: a, Ara ararauna. b, Rhea americana.

2014, Oct. 15 Litho. *Perf. 13¼*
3005 Horiz. pair + central label 9.50 9.00
a. A746 3000g multi 2.00 2.00
b. A746 10,000g multi 7.00 7.00

No. 2764 Overprinted

Method and Perf. As Before
2014, Oct. 16
3006 A589 4000g multi + label 3.00 2.75

Latin American Parliament, 50th anniv.

Asuncion, Green Capital — A747

2014, Nov. 6 Litho. *Perf. 13¼*
3007 A747 1400g multi + label 1.25 1.00

Carlos Miguel Jiménez (1914-70), Musician — A748

2014, Nov. 10 Litho. *Perf. 13¼*
3008 A748 2000g black + label 2.25 1.75

Silvio Pettirossi (1887-1916), Aviator — A749

No. 3009: a, Pettirossi, airplane inverted in flight, note written by Pettirossi. b, Pettirossi in airplace cockpit.

2014, Nov. 17 Litho. *Perf. 13¼*
3009 Horiz. pair + central label 10.50 8.00
a. A749 2500g multi 2.00 1.75
b. A749 9000g multi 7.00 6.25

Spanish Academy, 300th Anniv. — A750

Designs: No. 3010, Flowers. No. 3011, Emblem of Paraguayan Spanish Language Academy.

2014, Nov. 21 Litho. *Perf. 13¼*
3010 A750 11,000g multi 8.25 8.00

Souvenir Sheet
Rouletted 5
3011 A750 11,000g multi 8.25 8.00

Christmas — A751

Designs: 1400g, Star, pottery, angel. 5000g, Star, pottery, melons, grapes.

2014, Dec. 5 Litho. *Perf. 13¼*
3012-3013 A751 Set of 2 5.00 4.50

Campaign Against Discrimination A752

Designs: 1000g, Three empty chairs of different heights. 10,000g, Handicapped child with other children.

2015, Jan. 7 Litho. *Perf. 13¼*
3014-3015 A752 Set of 2 9.00 7.50

Dated 2014.

Visit of United Nations Secretary General Ban Ki-moon — A753

2015, Feb. 25 Litho. *Perf. 13¼*
3016 A753 10,000g multi + label 7.25 7.00

Encarnación, 400th Anniv. — A754

No. 3017: a, Municipal Building, horse-drawn carriage. b, San Roque González de Santa Cruz Basilica, St. Roque González de Santa Cruz (1576-1628).

2015, Mar. 25 Litho. *Perf. 13¼*
3017 Horiz. pair + central label 7.75 6.00
a. A754 1000g multi .75 .50
b. A754 10,000g multi 6.00 5.50

Lorenzo Prieto, Record-Setting Bicyclist — A755

2015, Apr. 24 Litho. *Perf. 13¼*
3018 A755 2000g multi + label 1.60 1.40

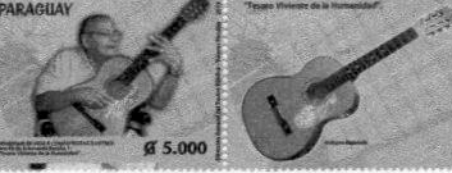

Efrén Echeverría, Guitarist — A756

2015, Apr. 24 Litho. *Perf. 13¼*
3019 A756 5000g multi + label 3.50 3.25

Secretary of Social Action, 20th Anniv. — A757

2015, May 7 Litho. *Perf. 13¼*
3020 A757 10,000g multi + label 6.75 5.50

Instruments of the Recycled Orchestra of Catuera A758

2015, May 25 Litho. *Perf. 13¼*
3021 A758 5000g Trumpet 4.50 2.75

Souvenir Sheet
Rouletted 5
3022 A758 2000g Saxophone, vert. 2.00 .80

Santa Teresa de Jesus College, Cent. A759

2015, May 25 Litho. *Perf. 13¼*
3023 A759 13,000g multi + label 8.75 7.25

Animals A760

No. 3024: a, 1000g, Azara's night monkey (ka'i pyhare). b, 1400g, Geoffroy's cat (gato montés). c, 3000g, Capybara (carpincho).
No. 3025, 3000g, Blue-fronted Amazons (loro hablador).

2015, June 12 Litho. *Perf. 13¼*
3024 A760 Block of 3, #a-c, + label 4.25 3.00

Souvenir Sheet
Rouletted 5
3025 A760 3000g multi 2.60 2.40

Junior Chamber International in Paraguay, cent.

Francisco Lopez Military Academy, Cent. — A761

2015, June 18 Litho. *Perf. 13¼*
3026 A761 10,000g multi + label 6.75 4.00

Visit of Pope Francis to Paraguay A762

Designs: 5000g, Pope Francis, map and flag of Paraguay.
6000g, Pope Francis, church.

2015, July 6 Litho. *Perf. 13¼*
3027 A762 5000g multi + label 3.50 2.75

Souvenir Sheet
Rouletted 8
3028 A762 6000g multi 4.25 3.50

See Nos. 3032-3033.

St. John Bosco (1815-88) — A763

2015, Aug. 12 Litho. *Perf. 13¼*
3029 A763 2000g multi + label 1.60 1.40

Postal Headquarters — A764

No. 3030 — Postal Headquarters in: a, 5000g, Guatemala (denomination at left). b, 10,000g, Paraguay (denomination at right).

2015, Aug. 13 Litho. *Perf. 13¼*
3030 A764 Horiz. pair, #a-b 9.50 6.50

See Guatemala No. 708.

Luis Alberto del Paraná (1926-74) and Los Paraguayos, Musical Group — A765

No. 3031: a, 2000g, Three band members. b, 5000g, Del Paraná.

2015, Sept. 15 Litho. *Perf. 13¼*
3031 A765 Horiz. pair, #a-b, + flanking label 4.75 4.25

Visit of Pope Francis Type of 2015
2015, Oct. 27 Litho. *Perf. 13¼*
Stamp + Label
3032 A762 6000g Like #3027 3.25 2.25

Souvenir Sheet
Rouletted 8
3033 A762 5000g Like #3028 4.00 3.50

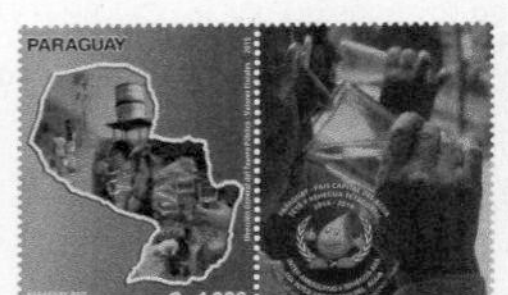

Paraguay, Land of Water — A766

2015, Nov. 4 Litho. *Perf. 13¼*
3034 A766 4000g multi + label 2.60 2.25

Campaign Against Human Trafficking — A767

No. 3035: a, 5000g, Woman bound in ropes. b, 11,000g, Silhouettes of two people.

2015, Nov. 9 Litho. *Perf. 13¼*
3035 A767 Horiz. pair, #a-b 10.00 9.00

America Issue.

Children's Drawing of Farm — A768

2015, Nov. 20 Litho. *Perf. 13¼*
3036 A768 2500g multi + label 1.75 1.50

Miniature Sheet

Tourism Ambassadors of Paraguay — A769

No. 3037: a, Roque Santa Cruz, soccer player. b, Ismael Ledesma playing harp. c, Daiana Ferreira, guitarist. d, Luis Szarán, orchestra conductor. e, Arnaldo André, actor.

2015, Dec. 3 Litho. *Perf. 13¼*
3037 A769 2000g Sheet of 5, #a-e, + 7 labels 7.25 6.00

Souvenir Sheet

Christmas — A770

No. 3038 — Altar of Corn, by Koki Ruiz, and: a, 2000g, Pope Francis at pulpit. b, 12,000g, Statue of Madonna and Child.

2015, Dec. 3 Litho. *Perf. 13¼*
3038 A770 Sheet of 2, #a-b, + 2 labels 9.00 8.00

Canonization of St. Emilie de Villeneuve (1811-54) — A771

2016, May 26 Litho. *Perf. 13¼*
3039 A771 2500g multi + label 1.60 1.25

Campaign Against Child Abuse and Sexual Violence — A772

2016, May 31 Litho. *Perf. 13¼*
3040 A772 9000g multi + label 5.00 4.00

Souvenir Sheet

Japanese Immigration to Paraguay, 80th Anniv. — A773

2016, May 31 Litho. *Perf. 13¼*
3041 A773 9000g multi + 3 labels 5.00 4.00

College of Accounting, Cent. — A774

2016, June 10 Litho. *Perf. 13¼*
3042 A774 1400g multi + label 1.10 .85

International Day of Responsible Gambling — A775

2016, June 15 Litho. *Perf. 13¼*
3043 A775 2500g multi 1.75 1.50

Diplomatic Relations Between Paraguay and Israel — A776

No. 3044 — Flags of Paraguay and Israel and: a, 6000g, Bare-throated bellbird. b, 10,000g, Hoopoes.

2016, June 20 Litho. *Perf. 13¼*
3044 A776 Horiz. pair, #a-b 10.00 9.00

Hotel Guarani, Asuncion — A777

2016, June 27 Litho. *Perf. 13¼*
3045 A777 10,000g multi 6.25 5.50

Employment of Prisoners A778

2016, June 27 Litho. *Perf. 13¼*
3046 Horiz. pair + central label 8.25 7.50
a. A778 3000g Embroiderer 1.50 1.40
b. A778 10,000g Polisher 5.00 4.00

Miniature Sheet

Tourism Ambassadors — A779

No. 3047: a, Nelson Sanabria, racer in Dakar Rally. b, Chiara D'Odorico, pianist. c, Koki Ruiz, artist. d, José Mongelos, opera singer.

2016, June 27 Litho. *Perf. 13¼*
3047 A779 2000g Sheet of 4, #a-d, + 6 labels 10.00 9.00

Demetrio Ortiz (1916-75), Musician — A780

2016, June 30 Litho. *Perf. 13¼*
3048 A780 10,000g multi + label 6.25 5.50

Social Security Week A781

2016, July 20 Litho. *Perf. 13¼*
3049 A781 2000g multi + label 1.50 1.25

Paraguayan Customs Broker Center, 90th Anniv. — A782

2016, July 28 Litho. *Perf. 13¼*
3050 A782 1400g multi + label 1.10 .75

Souvenir Sheet

Paraguayan Olympic Committee Emblem — A783

2016, July 29 Litho. *Rouletted 8*
3051 A783 4000g multi 3.00 2.40

Famous People — A784

No. 3052: a, Doña Máxima Lugo (1925-91), actress. b, Pedro Sosa Melgarejo (Carlos Sosa) (1926-89), composer.

2016, Aug. 22 Litho. *Perf. 13¼*
3052 Horiz. pair + central label 3.00 2.50
a. A784 1400g multi 1.00 .75
b. A784 3000g multi 1.75 1.50

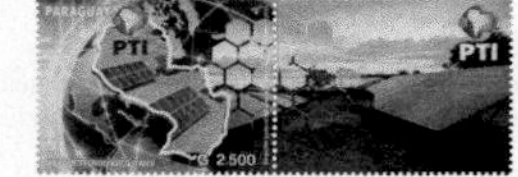

Itaipú Technological Park — A785

2016, Nov. 28 Litho. *Perf. 13¼*
3053 A785 2500g multi + label 1.75 1.30

Christmas — A786

No. 3054: a, 3000g, Flight into Egypt. b, 10,000g, Nativity.

2016, Dec. 1 Litho. *Perf. 13¼*
3054 A786 Horiz. pair, #a-b, + central label 8.25 7.00

Paraguayan Industrial Union, Cent. — A787

2016, Dec. 6 Litho. *Perf. 13¼*
3055 A787 9000g multi 5.50 5.00

Miniature Sheet

39th Dakar Rally A788

No. 3056: a, 1400g, Wheels of rally vehicle. b, 2000g, Vehicle number and visor of driver. c, 2500g, Nelson Sanabria on vehicle. d, 3000g, Map of Paraguayan portion of rally, flag of Paraguay.

2016, Dec. 13 Litho. *Perf. 13¼*
3056 A788 Sheet of 4, #a-d, + 12 labels 6.25 5.00

Souvenir Sheet

Annual Meeting of Governors of the Interamerican Development Bank, Paraguay — A789

No. 3057: a, 1400g, Palacio Alegre, Asunción. b, 2000g, Grain field. c, 3000g, Paraguayan coins and banknotes.

2017, Mar. 13 Litho. *Perf. 13¼*
3057 A789 Sheet of 3, #a-c, + label 4.75 3.50

Miniature Sheet

Flowers and Butterflies — A790

No. 3058: a, 700g, Cereus forbesii. b, 700g, Harrisia bonplandii. c, 1000g, Agraulis vanillae. d, 1400g, Male Euryades duponcheli. e, 2000g, Female Euryades duponcheli. f, 2500g, Echinopsis rhodotricha.

2017, Mar. 28 Litho. *Perf. 13¼*
3058 A790 Sheet of 6, #a-f, + 2 labels 6.50 5.00

Mother's Day — A791

No. 3059: a, 1400g, Family in archway. b, 2000g, Family making meal.

2017, May 15 Litho. *Perf. 13¼*

3059 A791 Pair, #a-b 2.60 2.00

Miniature Sheet

Russian Immigrants to Paraguay — A792

No. 3060: a, 1000g, First Russian immigrants. b, 1400g, Sergio Bobrovsky and Sergio Conradi. c, 2000g, Tala Ern de Retivoff and Agripina Voitenko. d, 2500g, Nicolás Ern and Stephan Vysokolan. e, 3000g, Oreliev de Serebriakoff and Boris Kassianoff. f, 5000g, Dr. Arturo Weiss and Dr. Constantino Gramatchicoff. g, 6000g, Gen. Juan Belaieff and Paraguayans.

2017, June 5 Litho. *Perf. 13¼*

3060 A792 Sheet of 7, #a-g, + 9 labels 14.50 12.00

Pres. Horacio Cartes and Patriarch Kirill of Moscow A793

Chamaemelum Nobile — A794

2017, June 8 Litho. *Perf. 13¼*

3061 Horiz. pair + central label 9.25 8.50
a. A793 6000g multi 4.50 4.00
b. A794 9000g multi 4.50 4.00

Visit of Patriarch Kirill to Paraguay.

Souvenir Sheet

Augusto Roa Bastos (1917-2005), Writer — A795

2017, June 13 Litho. *Perf. 13¼*

3062 A795 13,000g multi + 3 labels 8.25 7.50

Peace Corps in Paraguay, 50th Anniv. — A796

2017, June 19 Litho. *Perf. 13¼*

3063 A796 10,000g multi + label 6.50 5.50

Institute of Fine Arts, 60th Anniv. A797

2017, July 5 Litho. *Perf. 13¼*

3064 A797 5000g multi + label 3.25 2.50

Diplomatic Relations Between Paraguay and Republic of China, 60th Anniv. — A798

No. 3065: a, 1000g, Presidential Palace, Taipei, Republic of China. b, 3000g, López Presidential Palace, Asunción.

2017, July 12 Litho. *Perf. 13¼*

3065 Horiz. pair + central label 3.00 2.50
a. A798 1000g multi .70 .40
b. A798 3000g multi 3.25 1.75

Souvenir Sheet

Asunción, 480th Anniv. — A799

2017, Aug. 11 Litho. *Perf. 13¼*

3066 A799 1400g multi + 3 labels 1.00 .65

Souvenir Sheet

Quemil Yambay, Guitarist A800

2017, Aug. 22 Litho. *Perf. 13¼*

3067 A800 5000g multi + 3 labels 3.25 2.75

Souvenir Sheet

National Radio of Paraguay, 75th Anniv. — A801

2017, Aug. 30 Litho. *Perf. 13¼*

3068 A801 1400g multi + 3 labels 1.10 .75

Flower and Cactus — A802

Hummingbird and Cactus Flower — A803

2017, Sept. 29 Litho. *Perf. 13¼*

3069 Horiz. pair + central label 2.90 2.00
a. A802 1000g multi .65 .40
b. A803 3000g multi 2.00 1.50

National Secretary of Youth.

International Year of Sustainable Tourism for Development — A804

Designs: 2500g, Jesuit Mission of Santísima Trinidad UNESCO World Heritage Site. 3000p, Ypacaraí Lake.

2017, Oct. 9 Litho. *Perf. 13¼*

3070 A804 2500g multi + label 1.75 1.25

Souvenir Sheet

Rouletted 5

3071 A804 3000g multi 2.00 1.75

Souvenir Sheet

Laguna Salada A805

2017, Oct. 9 Litho. *Perf. 13¼*

3072 A805 4000g multi + 3 labels 2.75 2.40

America issue.

Souvenir Sheet

Paraguay Central Railway, 160th Anniv. (in 2021) A806

No. 3073: a, 5000g, Locomotive and Central Station, Asunción. b, 8000g, Locomotive and line of people.

2017, Oct. 26 Litho. *Perf. 13¼*

3073 A806 Sheet of 2, #a-b, + 2 labels 8.25 7.50

Souvenir Sheet

Flowers A807

2017, Nov. 6 Litho. *Perf. 13¼*

3074 A807 5000g multi + 3 labels 3.50 3.50

Atyra, model of sustainable city.

Alberto de Luque (1938-2020), Musician — A808

2017, Nov. 20 Litho. *Perf. 13¼*

3075 A808 1400g multi + label 1.10 .85

Souvenir Sheet

Municipal Theater, Asunción, 128th Anniv. — A809

2017, Nov. 28 Litho. *Perf. 13¼*

3076 A809 5000g multi + 3 labels 3.50 3.00

Souvenir Sheet

Christmas — A810

2017, Dec. 11 Litho. *Perf. 13¼*

3077 A810 9000g multi + 3 labels 5.50 4.50

Consumer and User Protection Secretariat, 20th Anniv. — A811

2018, Mar. 16 Litho. *Perf. 13¼*

3078 A811 2000g multi 1.40 1.20

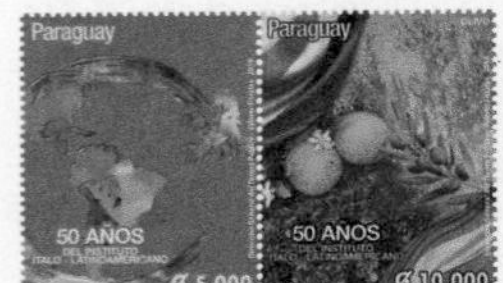

Italo-Latin American Institute, 50th Anniv. — A812

No. 3079: a, 5000g, Distorted globe. b, 10,000g, Oranges, olives, flags of Paraguay and Italy.

2018, Mar. 26 Litho. *Perf. 13¼*

3079 A812 Horiz. pair, #a-b 9.50 9.00

Marie Curie (1867-1934), Chemist and Physicist, and Emblem of National University of Asunción — A813

2018, May 8 Litho. *Perf. 13¼*

3080 A813 10,000g multi + label 6.25 6.00

Chemistry faculty of National University, 80th Anniv. Printed in sheets of 2 + 2 labels.

Passage of Law 5777 to end Violence Against Women A814

2018, May 11 Litho. *Perf. 13¼*

3081 A814 8000g multi 5.00 4.75

Souvenir Sheet

Hats A815

2018, May 29 Litho. *Rouletted 5*
3082 A815 3000g multi 2.10 1.80

ZP12 Radio Station, Pilar, 55th anniv.

Souvenir Sheet

Locomotives — A816

No. 3083: a, 4000g, Model of Sapucai locomotive. b, 10,000g, Baldwin steam locomotive.

2018, June 13 Litho. *Perf. 13¼*
3083 A816 Sheet of 2, #a-b, + 2 labels 9.25 8.25

Joint Issue between Paraguay & Ecuador. See Ecuador No. 2207.

Souvenir Sheet

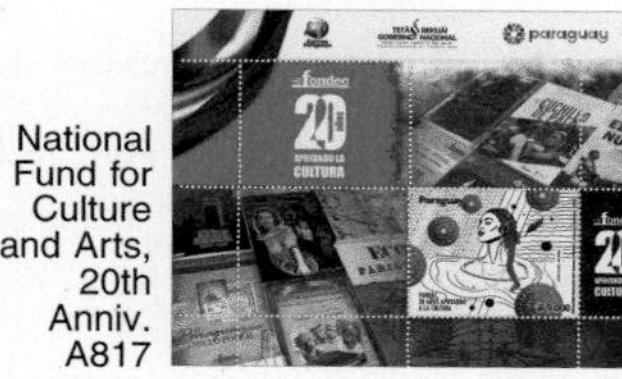

National Fund for Culture and Arts, 20th Anniv. A817

2018, July 6 Litho. *Perf. 13¼*
3084 A817 9000g multi + 3 labels 5.50 5.25

Souvenir Sheet

Beatification of María Guggiari Echeverría (1925-59) — A818

2018, July 9 Litho. *Perf. 13¼*
3085 A818 11,000g multi + 3 labels 6.75 6.50

National Youth Tourism Program — A819

Designs: 1400g, Youths wearing helmets. 2000g, Youth Tourism emblem, horiz.

2018, Aug. 6 Litho. *Perf. 13¼*
3086 A819 1400g multi 1.10 .90

Souvenir Sheet
Rouletted 7x8

3087 A819 2000g multi 1.50 1.25

Nasta Advertising Agency, 50th Anniv. — A820

50th anniversary emblem and: 2000g, Buildings.
5000g, Woman, motorcycle and buildings.

2018, Aug. 14 Litho. *Perf. 13¼*
3088 A820 2000g multi 1.40 1.20

Souvenir Sheet
Rouletted 5

3089 A820 5000g multi 3.75 3.50

Souvenir Sheet

Rafael Rojas Doria (1931-2018) and César Alvarez Blanco (1927-2003), Comedians — A821

2018, Sept. 14 Litho. *Perf. 13¼*
3090 A821 13,000g multi + 3 labels 8.00 7.75

Miniature Sheet

Birds of the Chaco A822

No. 3091: a, 2000g, Gallito de collar (olive-crowned crescentchest). b, 2500g, Hornerito copetón (crested hornero). c, 3000g, Durmili (Caatinga puffbird). d, 3500g, Fueguero rojo (hepatic tanager). e, 4000g, Surucuá aurora (blue-crowned trogon).

2018, Sept. 21 Litho. *Perf. 13¼*
3091 A822 Sheet of 5, #a-e, + label 10.00 9.00

America Issue A823

No. 3092: a, 1400g, Mestizo dog. b, 2500g, Dalmatian.
9000g, Shih tzu.

2018, Oct. 9 Litho. *Perf. 13¼*
3092 A823 Horiz. pair, #a-b 2.75 2.25

Souvenir Sheet
Rouletted 7x8

3093 A823 9000g multi 5.50 5.25

Meeting of the Postal Union of the Americas, Spain and Portugal Advisory and Executive Council — A824

No. 3094 — Flags of member nations and: a, 5000g, Patri Palace (Post Office), Asunción, and map of Paraguay. b, 10,000g, Patri Palace.

2018, Nov. 19 Litho. *Perf. 13¼*
3094 A824 Horiz. pair, #a-b 8.25 7.75

America issue.

Diplomatic Relations Between Paraguay and Peru, 160th Anniv. — A825

No. 3095: a, 6000g, Benigno López Palace (Paraguayan Ministry of Foreign Affairs), Asunción. b, 10,000g, Torre Tagle Palace (Peruvian Ministry of Foreign Affairs), Lima, Peru.

2018, Nov. 30 Litho. *Perf. 13¼*
3095 A825 Horiz. pair, #a-b 10.00 9.50

Organization of American States, 70th Anniv. — A826

2018, Dec. 7 Litho. *Perf. 13¼*
3096 A826 10,000g multi 6.25 6.00

Christmas — A827

No. 3097: a, 2000g, Paper cutting, poinsettia, candle in lantern. b, 2500g, Nativitiy scene in lantern, Christmas ornaments.

2018, Dec. 7 Litho. *Perf. 13¼*
3097 A827 Horiz. pair, #a-b 3.25 2.75

Map of Airline Flights Leaving Paragauay and Emblems of International and Paraguayan Civil Aviation Organizations — A828

2018, Dec. 10 Litho. *Perf. 13¼*
3098 A828 4000g multi + label 4.00 3.75

Souvenir Sheet

International Day of Disabled Persons — A829

No. 3099: a, 6000g, Brain in head. b, 7000g, Stylized person in wheelchair.

2018, Dec. 10 Litho. *Perf. 13¼*
3099 A829 Sheet of 2, #a-b, + 2 labels 8.25 7.75

First Paraguay Postage Stamp, 150th Anniv. — A830

2018, Dec. 27 Litho. *Perf. 13¼*
3100 A830 200g multi .60 .35

Souvenir Sheet

Volunteer Firefighter Corps of Paraguay, 40th Anniv. — A831

No. 3101: a, 1500g, Yellow fire truck. b, 2500g, Orange fire trucks.

2019, Feb. 22 Litho. *Perf. 13¼*
3101 A831 Sheet of 2, #a-b, + 2 labels 3.25 2.75

Souvenir Sheet

International Labor Organization, Cent. — A832

No. 3102: a, 5000g, Woman working in factory. b, 10,000g, Construction workers.

2019, May 22 Litho. *Perf. 13¼*
3102 A832 Sheet of 2, #a-b, + 2 labels 10.50 10.00

Souvenir Sheet

Isla Po'i Social Welfare Institute Clinic, Asuncion, 75th Anniv. — A833

2019, May 31 Litho. *Perf. 13¼*
3103 A833 2200g multi + 3 labels 1.75 1.50

Souvenir Sheet

Mohandas K. Gandhi (1869-1948), Indian Nationalist Leader — A834

2019, July 10 Litho. *Rouletted 5*
3104 A834 10,000g multi 7.00 6.50

Horses — A835

Various horses: 1000g, 2500g, 9000g.

2019, July 15 Litho. *Perf. 13¼*
3105-3107 A835 Set of 3 9.50 8.75

Cultural Center of the Republic, Asuncion
A836

2019, Aug. 14 Litho. *Perf. 13¼*
3108 A836 5000g multi + label 3.25 3.00

Souvenir Sheet

General Bernardino Caballero (1839-1912), Ninth President of Paraguay — A837

2019, Sept. 11 Litho. *Rouletted 5*
3109 A837 1000g multi .85 .60

Express Mail Service, 20th Anniv. — A838

2019, Sept. 20 Litho. *Perf. 13¼*
3110 A838 16,000g multi 9.00 8.75

Tree Flowers — A839

Designs: 800g, Ceiba chodatii. 4000g, Flamboyant. 8000g, Cocos nucifera.

2019, Sept. 20 Litho. *Perf. 13¼*
3111-3113 A839 Set of 3 7.75 7.00

Miniature Sheet

America Issue
A840

No. 3114 — Traditional Paraguayan dishes: a, 1000g, Vorí vorí (soup with dumplings). b, 3000g, Sopa Paraguaya (corn bread). c, 6000g, Empanadas de mandioca (meat and cassava empanadas). d, 10,000g, Chipa almidón (cassava bread).

2019, Oct. 9 Litho. *Perf. 13¼*
3114 A840 Sheet of 4, #a-d 12.00 11.00

Miniature Sheet

Reconstruction of Paraguay After Paraguayan War — A841

No. 3115: a, 1000g, Handwritten document. b, 1400g, Picture postcard depicting Port of Asunción. c, 2200g, Picture postcard depicting Palacio de López and flag. d, 5000g, Picture postcard depicting Palacio de López.

2019, Oct. 21 Litho. *Perf. 13¼*
3115 A841 Sheet of 4, #a-d 6.25 5.25

World Hemophilia Day — A842

2019, Nov. 28 Litho. *Perf. 13¼*
3116 A842 1400g multi 1.00 .80

Cayo Sila Godoy (1919-2014), Guitarist — A843

2019, Dec. 2 Litho. *Perf. 13¼*
3117 A843 2200g dark gray — —

Art by Edith Jiménez (1918-2004)
A844

2019, Dec. 2 Litho. *Perf. 13¼*
3118 A844 4000g multi 2.30 2.00

Christmas — A845

No. 3119: a, 1000g, Holy Family. b, 10,000g, Child looking at bird.

2019, Dec. 11 Litho. *Perf. 13¼*
3119 A845 Horiz. pair, #a-b 6.25 5.75

Souvenir Sheet

First Paraguay-Argentina Airmail Flight, Cent. — A846

2019, Dec. 16 Litho. *Perf. 13¼*
3120 A846 2500g multi + 3 labels 1.60 1.40

Executive Branch Human Rights Network, 10th Anniv. — A847

No. 3121 — Peace dove with inscription in: a, Guarani. b, Spanish.

2019, Dec. 18 Litho. *Perf. 13¼*
3121 A847 1400g Vert. pair, #a-b 2.00 1.50

Souvenir Sheet

Diplomatic Relations Between Paraguay and Japan, Cent. — A848

No. 3122 — Flags of Paraguay and Japan and: a, Cherry tree in bloom. b, Cherry blossom.

2019, Dec. 18 Litho. *Perf. 13¼*
3122 A848 10,000g Sheet of 2, #a-b, + 2 labels 11.50 11.00

Souvenir Sheet

International Year of Indigenous Languages — A849

2019, Dec. 23 Litho. *Perf. 13¼*
3123 A849 1400g multi + 3 labels 1.00 .80

Souvenir Sheet

Paraguayan Red Cross, Cent. — A850

No. 3124: a, 2200g, Air ambulance. b, 2500g, Red Cross ambulances and drivers.

2019, Dec. 27 Litho. *Perf. 13¼*
3124 A850 Sheet of 2, #a-b, + 2 labels 3.00 2.50

Promotion of Breastfeeding by Itapúa Department — A851

2020, Feb. 27 Litho. *Perf. 13¼*
3125 A851 2400g multi + label 1.60 1.40

Souvenir Sheet

Secretary of National Emergencies, 15th Anniv. — A852

2020, June 10 Litho. *Perf. 13¼*
3126 A852 1500g multi + 3 labels 1.20 .95

Souvenir Sheet

First Paraguayan Stamps, 150th Anniv. — A853

No. 3127: a, 2200g, Paraguay #1. b, 4000g, Paraguay #2. c, 10,000g, Paraguay #3.

2020, Oct. 9 Litho. *Perf. 13¼*
3127 A853 Sheet of 3, #a-c, + label 10.50 9.50

Souvenir Sheet

Asunción Architecture — A854

No. 3128: a, 4000g, Villa Arcallana. b, 6000g, Central Bank of Paraguay.

2020, Oct. 9 Litho. *Perf. 13¼*
3128 A854 Sheet of 2, #a-b, + 2 labels 6.50 6.00

America issue.

Souvenir Sheet

Superior Tribunal of Electoral Justice, 25th Anniv.
A855

2020, Oct. 13 Litho. *Perf. 13¼*
3129 A855 5000g multi + 3 labels 3.25 3.00

Souvenir Sheet

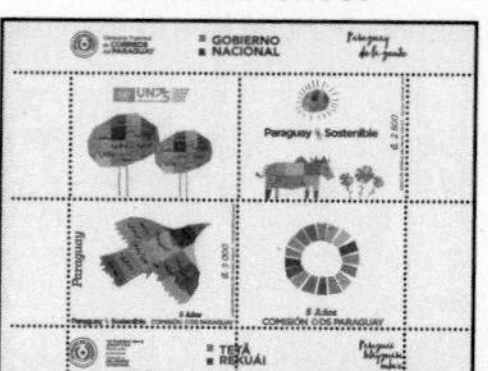

Sustainable Paraguay — A856

No. 3130: a, 2500g, Sun, cow, and flowers. b, 3000g, Bird.

2020, Oct. 23 Litho. *Perf. 13¼*
3130 A856 Sheet of 2, #a-b, + 2 labels 3.75 3.25

Paraguayan Sustainable Development Goals Commission, 5th anniv. and United Nations, 75th anniv.

Souvenir Sheet

Paraguayan Olympic Committee, 50th Anniv. — A857

2020, Oct. 30 Litho. *Rouletted 7x8*
3131 A857 3000g multi 2.00 1.75

Latin American Integration Association, 40th Anniv. — A858

2020, Dec. 2 Litho. *Perf. 13¼*
3132 A858 2500g multi + label 1.80 1.50

Christmas — A859

2020, Dec. 2 Litho. *Perf. 13¼*
3133 A859 5500g multi + label 3.50 3.25

Battle of Acosta Nu, 150th Anniv. (in 2019) A860

2020, Dec. 17 Litho. *Perf. 13¼*
3134 A860 3000g multi + label 2.00 1.75

Founding of Scientific Society of Paraguay by Andrés Barbero (1877-1951), Cent. — A861

2021, Jan. 9 Litho. *Perf. 13¼*
3135 A861 2400g multi 1.60 1.40

María Elena Sachero, Actress A862

2021, June 30 Litho. *Perf. 13¼*
3136 A862 2500g multi + label 1.75 1.50

Independence of Peru, 200th Anniv. — A863

2021, July 15 Litho. *Perf. 13¼*
3137 A863 1500g multi + label 1.25 1.00

Souvenir Sheet

Monsignor Lasagna Salesian School, 125th Anniv. — A864

2021, July 23 Litho. *Perf. 13¼*
3138 A864 1900g multi + 3 labels 1.30 1.10

Souvenir Sheet

National Development Bank, 60th Anniv. — A865

2021, Sept. 13 Litho. *Perf. 13¼*
3139 A865 2000g multi + 3 labels — —

Terere Drink, UNESCO Intangible World Heritage Item — A866

2021, Sept. 15 Litho. *Perf. 13¼*
3140 A866 10,000g multi 6.50 6.00

Souvenir Sheet

Tourism A867

No. 3141: a, 2200g, Boats on Cerrito Beach. b, 2400g, Victoria cruziana a Piquete Cué.

2021, Oct. 12 Litho. *Perf. 13¼*
3141 A867 Sheet of 3, #a-b, + 2 labels 3.25 2.75

America issue.

Souvenir Sheet

Luqueño Sports Club, Cent. A868

2021, Oct. 13 Litho. *Perf. 13¼*
3142 A868 3000g multi + 3 labels — —

Asunción Classical and Modern Municipal Ballet Company, 50th Anniv. — A869

2021, Nov. 17 Litho. *Perf. 13¼*
3143 A869 2000g multi + label 1.50 1.25

Souvenir Sheet

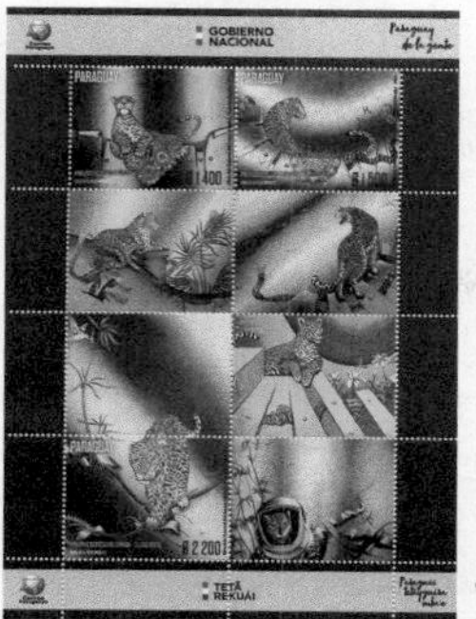

Jaguars A870

No. 3144 — Various depictions of jaguars with denomination of: a, 1400g. b, 1500g. c, 2200g.

2021, Nov. 22 Litho. *Perf. 13¼*
3144 A870 Sheet of 3, #a-c, + 5 labels 4.00 3.25

Maneco Galeano (1945-80), Musician and Journalist — A871

2021, Nov. 26 Litho. *Perf. 13¼*
3145 A871 1000g multi .95 .70

Painting by Modesto Delgado Rodas (1886-1963) — A872

2021, Dec. 14 Litho. *Perf. 13¼*
3146 A872 2200g multi 1.60 1.40

Christmas — A873

2021, Dec. 17 Litho. *Perf. 13¼*
3147 A873 16,000g multi + label 9.50 9.25

Souvenir Sheet

Bluecrown Passionflower, National Flower of Paraguay — A874

2021, Dec. 20 Litho. *Perf. 13¼*
3148 A874 2500g multi + 3 labels 1.95 1.60

Mercosur (Southern Common Market), 30th anniv.

Supreme Council of the Ancient and Accepted Scottish Rite Masons in Paraguay, 150th Anniv. — A875

2021, Dec. 21 Litho. *Perf. 13¼*
3149 A875 4000g multi 3.00 2.50

Radio Caritas, 85th Anniv. — A876

2021, Dec. 28 Litho. *Perf. 13¼*
3150 A876 2200g multi 1.95 1.60

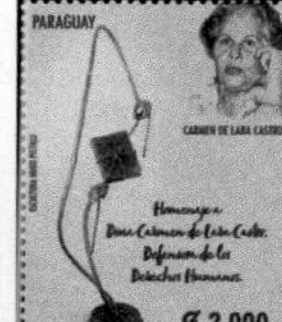

Carmen de Lara Castro (1918-93), Politician and Human Rights Advocate — A877

2022, Mar. 4 Litho. *Perf. 13¼*
3151 A877 2000g multi *1.40 1.10*

Dated 2021.

Souvenir Sheet

2020 Summer Olympics, Tokyo — A878

No. 3152 — Paraguayan athletes: a, 10,000g, Alejandra Alonso. b, 11,000g, Aguamarina Espinola, Verónica Cepede.

2022, Mar. 30 Litho. *Perf. 13¼*
3152 A878 Sheet of 2, #a-b, + 2 labels 12.00 11.50

The 2020 Summer Olympics was postponed until 2021 because of the COVID-19 pandemic. Dated 2021.

Melissa Nair Tillner Galeano, Paraguayan Paralympian A879

Rodrigo Fabian Hermosa Ayala, Paraguayan Paralympian A880

2022, Mar. 30 Litho. *Perf. 13¼*
3153 Horiz. pair + central label 2.75 2.25
a. A879 1500g multi .90 .75
b. A880 2500g multi 1.50 1.20

2020 Summer Paralympics, Tokyo. The 2020 Summer Paralympics was postponed until 2021 because of the COVID-19 pandemic. Dated 2021.

Souvenir Sheet

Club Centro de Balderrama, Luque, 112th Anniv. — A881

2022, Apr. 22 Litho. *Perf. 13¼*
3154 A881 3000g multi + 3 labels 2.00 1.75

Souvenir Sheet

Campaign Against COVID-19 — A882

2022, June 21 Litho. *Rouletted 5*
3155 A882 4000g multi + 3 labels *2.50 2.25*

Diplomatic Relations Between Paraguay and South Korea, 60th Anniv. — A883

2022, June 28 Litho. *Perf. 13¼*
3156 A883 3000g multi + label *2.00 1.75*

20th World Conference of Supreme Councils, Asuncion — A884

2022, July 27 Litho. *Perf. 13¼*
3157 A884 5500g multi 3.25 3.60

Jacinto Herrera (1919-69), Actor — A885

2022, Aug. 25 Litho. *Perf. 13¼*
3158 A885 10,000g black 5.75 5.50

SEMI-POSTAL STAMPS

Red Cross Nurse — SP1

Unwmk.

1930, July 22 Typo. *Perf. 12*
B1 SP1 1.50p + 50c gray violet 2.00 1.20
B2 SP1 1.50p + 50c deep rose 2.00 1.20
B3 SP1 1.50p + 50c dark blue 2.00 1.20
Nos. B1-B3 (3) 6.00 3.60
Set, never hinged 9.00

The surtax was for the benefit of the Red Cross Society of Paraguay.

College of Agriculture SP2

1930
B4 SP2 1.50p + 50c blue, *pale pink* .60 .50

Surtax for the Agricultural Institute.

The sheet of No. B4 has a papermaker's watermark: "Vencedor Bond."

A 1.50p+50c red on pale yellow was prepared but not regularly issued. Value, 40 cents hinged; 65 cents never hinged.

Red Cross Headquarters — SP3

1932
B5 SP3 50c + 50c rose .60 .60

Our Lady of Asunción — SP4

1941 Engr.
B6 SP4 7p + 3p red brown .40 .35
B7 SP4 7p + 3p purple .40 .35
B8 SP4 7p + 3p carmine rose .40 .35
B9 SP4 7p + 3p sapphire .40 .35
Nos. B6-B9 (4) 1.60 1.40

For surcharges see Nos. 419-426, 431-434.

No. 361 Surcharged in Black

1944
B10 A70 10c on 10p multicolored .70 .50

The surtax was for the victims of the San Juan earthquake in Argentina.

Catalogue values for unused stamps in this section, from this point to the end of the section, are for Never Hinged items.

No. C169 Surcharged in Carmine "AYUDA AL ECUADOR 5 + 5"

1949 Unwmk. *Perf. 12½*
B11 A117 5c + 5c on 30c dk blue .55 .30

Surtax for the victims of the Ecuador earthquake.

38th Intl. Eucharistic Congress, Bombay SP5

Various coins and coat of arms.

Litho. & Engr.

1964, Dec. 11 *Perf. 12x12½*
B12 SP5 20g +10g multi 6.75 6.50
B13 SP5 30g +15g multi 6.75 6.50
B14 SP5 50g +25g multi 6.75 6.50
B15 SP5 100g +50g multi 6.75 6.50
a. Souvenir sheet of 4, #B12-B15 130.00 100.00
Nos. B12-B15 (4) 27.00 26.00

Buildings and Coats of Arms of Popes John XXIII & Paul VI — SP6

#B16, Dome of St. Peters. #B17, Site of Saint Peter's tomb. #B18, Saint Peter's Plaza. #B19,Taj Mahal.

1964, Dec. 12
B16 SP6 20g +10g multi 6.75 6.50
B17 SP6 30g +15g multi 6.75 6.50
B18 SP6 50g +25g multi 6.75 6.50
B19 SP6 100g +50g multi 6.75 6.50
a. Souvenir sheet of 4, #B16-B19 145.00 140.00
Nos. B16-B19 (4) 27.00 26.00

AIR POST STAMPS

Official Stamps of 1913 Surcharged

1929, Jan. 1 Unwmk. *Perf. 11½*
C1 O19 2.85p on 5c lilac 2.25 1.50
C2 O19 5.65p on 10c grn 1.25 1.50
C3 O19 11.30p on 50c rose 2.00 1.25
Nos. C1-C3 (3) 5.50 4.25

Counterfeits of surcharge exist.

Regular Issues of 1924-27 Surcharged

1929, Feb. 26 *Perf. 12*
C4 A51 3.40p on 3p gray 4.50 4.00
a. Surch. "Correo / en $3.40 / Habilitado / Aereo" 60.00
b. Double surcharge 8.75
c. "Aéro" instead of "Aéreo"
C5 A44 6.80p on 4p lt bl 4.50 3.25
a. Surch. "Correo / Aereo / en $6.80 / Habilitado" 8.75
C6 A52 17p on 5p choc 4.50 3.25
a. Surch. "Correo / Habilitado / Habilitado / en 17p" 4.50
b. Double surcharge 25.00 25.00
Nos. C4-C6 (3) 13.50 10.50

Wings — AP1

Pigeon with Letter — AP2

Airplanes AP3

1929-31 Typo. *Perf. 12*
C7 AP1 2.85p gray green 1.75 1.25
a. Imperf., pair 37.50
C8 AP1 2.85p turq grn ('31) .50 .50
C9 AP2 5.65p brown 2.00 1.25
C10 AP2 5.65p scar ('31) 1.00 .50
C11 AP3 11.30p chocolate 1.75 1.25
a. Imperf., pair 37.50
C12 AP3 11.30p dp blue ('31) .50 .50
Nos. C7-C12 (6) 7.50 5.25

Sheets of these stamps sometimes show portions of a papermaker's watermark "Indian Bond C. Extra Strong."

Excellent counterfeits are plentiful.

Regular Issues of 1924-28 Surcharged in Black or Red

1929 *Perf. 11½, 12*
C13 A47 95c on 7c lilac .35 .30
C14 A47 1.90p on 20c dull bl .35 .30
C15 A44 3.40p on 4p lt bl (R) .40 .30
a. Double surcharge 3.00
C16 A44 4.75p on 4p lt bl (R) .95 .75
a. Double surcharge 3.00
C17 A51 6.80p on 3p gray 1.00 .90
a. Double surcharge 4.50
C18 A52 17p on 5p choc 3.00 3.00
a. Horiz. pair, imperf. between 37.50
Nos. C13-C18 (6) 6.05 5.55
Set, never hinged 9.00

Six stamps in the sheet of No. C17 have the "$" and numerals thinner and narrower than the normal type.

Airplane and Arms AP4

Cathedral of Asunción AP5

Airplane and Globe — AP6

1930 *Perf. 12*
C19 AP4 95c dp red, *pink* 1.50 .90
C20 AP4 95c dk bl, *blue* 1.50 .90
C21 AP5 1.90p lt red, *pink* 1.50 .90
C22 AP5 1.90p violet, *blue* 1.50 .90
C23 AP6 6.80p blk, *lt bl* 1.50 .90
C24 AP6 6.80p green, *pink* 1.50 .90
Nos. C19-C24 (6) 9.00 5.40
Set, never hinged 13.50

Sheets of Nos. C19-C24 have a papermaker's watermark: "Extra Vencedor Bond."

Counterfeits exist.

Stamps and Types of 1927-28 Overprinted in Red

1930
C25 A47 10c olive green .60 .40
a. Double overprint 6.00
C26 A47 20c dull blue .60 .40
a. "CORREO CORREO" instead of "CORREO AEREO" 5.00
b. "AEREO AEREO" instead of "CORREO AEREO" 5.00
C27 A48 1p emerald 1.40 1.40
C28 A51 3p gray 1.40 1.40
Nos. C25-C28 (4) 4.00 3.60
Set, never hinged 6.00

Counterfeits of Nos. C26a and C26b exist.

Nos. 273, 282, 286, 288, 300, 302, 305 Surcharged in Red or Black

#C29-C30, C32

#C31

#C33

#C34-C35

1930 Red or Black Surcharge

C29 A47 5c on 10c gray grn (R) .50 .50
a. "AEREO" omitted 30.00
C30 A47 5c on 70c ultra (R) .50 .50
a. Vert. pair, imperf. between 40.00
C31 A48 20c on 1p org red .60 .50
a. "CORREO" double 6.00 6.00
b. "AEREO" double 6.00 6.00
C32 A47 40c on 50c org (R) .60 .50
a. "AEREO" omitted 9.00 9.00
b. "CORREO" double 6.00 6.00
c. "AEREO" double 6.00 6.00
C33 A54 6p on 10p red 2.50 2.00
C34 A49 10p on 20p red 10.00 10.00
C35 A49 10p on 20p vio brn 10.00 10.00
Nos. C29-C35 (7) 24.70 24.00
Set, never hinged 37.00

Declaration of Independence AP11

1930, May 14 Typo.

C36 AP11 2.85p dark blue .70 .50
C37 AP11 3.40p dark green .70 .40
C38 AP11 4.75p deep lake .70 .40
Nos. C36-C38 (3) 2.10 1.30
Set, never hinged 3.15

Natl. Independence Day, May 14, 1811.

Gunboat Type

Gunboat "Paraguay."

1931-39 *Perf. 11½, 12*

C39 A58 1p claret 1.20 .60
C40 A58 1p dk blue ('36) 1.20 .60
C41 A58 2p orange 1.20 .60
C42 A58 2p dk brn ('36) 1.20 .60
C43 A58 3p turq green 1.50 .75
C44 A58 3p lt ultra ('36) 1.75 .75
C45 A58 3p brt rose ('39) 1.20 .60
C46 A58 6p dk green 2.40 .90
C47 A58 6p violet ('36) 2.75 .90
C48 A58 6p dull bl ('39) 2.40 .75
C49 A58 10p vermilion 6.00 1.75
C50 A58 10p bluish grn ('35) 9.00 3.00
C51 A58 10p yel brn ('36) 6.50 2.25
C52 A58 10p dk blue ('36) 5.50 1.50
C53 A58 10p lt pink ('39) 6.00 2.00
Nos. C39-C53 (15) 49.80 17.55

1st constitution of Paraguay as a Republic and the arrival of the "Paraguay" and "Humaita."

Counterfeits of #C39-C53 are plentiful.

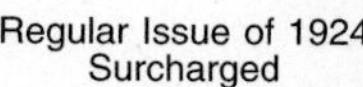

Regular Issue of 1924 Surcharged

1931, Aug. 22

C54 A44 3p on 4p lt bl 16.00 16.00

Overprinted

C55 A44 4p lt blue 16.00 16.00
Set, #C54-C55, never hinged 50.00

On Nos. C54-C55 the Zeppelin is handstamped. The rest of the surcharge or overprint is typographed.

War Memorial AP13

Orange Tree and Yerba Mate AP14

Yerba Mate — AP15

Palms — AP16

Eagle — AP17

1931-36 Litho.

C56 AP13 5c lt blue .25 .40
a. Horiz. pair, imperf. btwn. 6.25
C57 AP13 5c dp grn ('33) .25 .40
C58 AP13 5c lt red ('33) .30 .40
C59 AP13 5c violet ('35) .25 .40
C60 AP14 10c dp violet .25 .40
C61 AP14 10c brn lake ('33) .25 .40
C62 AP14 10c yel brn ('33) .25 .40
C63 AP14 10c ultra ('35) .25 .40
a. Imperf., pair 5.50
C64 AP15 20c red .25 .40
C65 AP15 20c dl blue ('33) .30 .40
C66 AP15 20c emer ('33) .25 .40
C67 AP15 20c yel brn ('35) .25 .40
a. Imperf., pair 4.00
C68 AP16 40c dp green .25 .40
C69 AP16 40c slate bl ('35) .25 .40
C70 AP16 40c red ('36) .30 .40
C71 AP17 80c dull blue .25 .40
C72 AP17 80c dl grn ('33) .55 .40
C73 AP17 80c scar ('33) .30 .40
Nos. C56-C73 (18) 5.00 7.20
Set, never hinged 9.50

Airship "Graf Zeppelin" AP18

1932, Apr. Litho.

C74 AP18 4p ultra 3.75 3.75
a. Imperf., pair 35.00
C75 AP18 8p red 6.25 5.00
C76 AP18 12p blue grn 5.00 5.00
C77 AP18 16p redsh pur 8.75 6.25
C78 AP18 20p orange brn 8.75 6.25
Nos. C74-C78 (5) 32.50 26.25

For surcharges see Nos. 325-329.

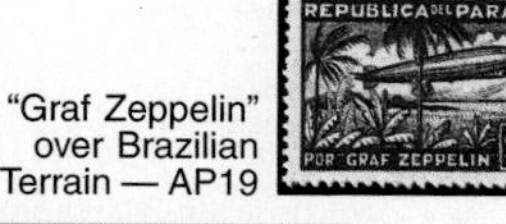

"Graf Zeppelin" over Brazilian Terrain — AP19

"Graf Zeppelin" over Atlantic AP20

1933, May 5

C79 AP19 4.50p dp blue 4.00 3.00
C80 AP19 9p dp rose 7.00 5.00
a. Horiz. pair, imperf. between 150.00
C81 AP19 13.50p blue grn 8.00 6.00
C82 AP20 22.50p bis brn 18.00 14.00
C83 AP20 45p dull vio 24.00 24.00
Nos. C79-C83 (5) 61.00 52.00

Excellent counterfeits are plentiful.
For overprints see Nos. C88-C97.

Posts and Telegraph Building, Asunción AP21

1934-37 *Perf. 11½*

C84 AP21 33.75p ultra 6.00 5.25
C85 AP21 33.75p car ('35) 6.00 5.25
a. 33.75p rose ('37) 5.25 4.50
C86 AP21 33.75p emerald ('36) 7.50 6.00
C87 AP21 33.75p bis brn ('36) 2.25 2.25
Nos. C84-C87 (4) 21.75 18.75

Excellent counterfeits exist.
For surcharge see No. C107.

Nos. C79-C83 Overprinted in Black

1934, May 26

C88 AP19 4.50p deep bl 3.75 2.25
C89 AP19 9p dp rose 4.75 3.00
C90 AP19 13.50p blue grn 13.00 7.50
C91 AP20 22.50p bis brn 11.00 6.00
C92 AP20 45p dull vio 17.00 10.50
Nos. C88-C92 (5) 49.50 29.25

Types of 1933 Issue Overprinted in Black

1935

C93 AP19 4.50p rose red 6.50 6.50
C94 AP19 9p lt green 8.25 8.25
C95 AP19 13.50p brown 17.50 17.50
C96 AP20 22.50p violet 14.00 14.00
C97 AP20 45p blue 40.00 40.00
Nos. C93-C97 (5) 86.25 86.25

Tobacco Plant AP22

1935-39 Typo.

C98 AP22 17p lt brown 12.50 12.50
C99 AP22 17p carmine 21.00 21.00
C100 AP22 17p dark blue 15.00 15.00
C101 AP22 17p pale yel grn ('39) 8.00 8.00
Nos. C98-C101 (4) 56.50 56.50

Excellent counterfeits are plentiful.

Church of Incarnation — AP23

1935-38

C102 AP23 102p carmine 7.50 5.00
C103 AP23 102p blue 7.50 5.00
C103A AP23 102p indigo ('36) 4.50 4.50
C104 AP23 102p yellow brn 5.50 4.75
a. Imperf., pair 30.00
C105 AP23 102p violet ('37) 2.50 2.50
C106 AP23 102p brn org ('38) 2.25 2.25
Nos. C102-C106 (6) 29.75 24.00

Excellent counterfeits are plentiful.
For surcharges see Nos. C108-C109.

Types of 1934-35 Surcharged in Red

1937, Aug. 1

C107 AP21 24p on 33.75p sl bl 1.00 .70
C108 AP23 65p on 102p ol bis 2.50 1.75
C109 AP23 84p on 102p bl grn 2.50 1.50
Nos. C107-C109 (3) 6.00 3.95
Set, never hinged 9.00

Plane over Asunción — AP24

1939, Aug. 3 Typo. *Perf. 10½, 11½*

C110 AP24 3.40p yel green 1.00 .65
C111 AP24 3.40p orange brn .60 .50
C112 AP24 3.40p indigo .60 .50
Nos. C110-C112 (3) 2.20 1.65
Set, never hinged 3.30

Buenos Aires Peace Conference Type and

Map of Paraguay with New Chaco Boundary — AP28

Designs: 1p, Flags of Paraguay and Bolivia. 3p, Coats of Arms. 5p, Pres. Ortiz of Argentina, flags of Paraguay, Argentina. 10p, Pres. Vargas, Brazil. 30p, Pres. Alessandri, Chile. 50p, US Eagle and Shield. 100p, Pres. Benavides, Peru. 200p, Pres. Baldomir, Uruguay.

Engr.; Flags Litho.

1939, Nov. *Perf. 12½*

Flags in National Colors

C113 A69 1p red brown .65 .60
C114 A69 3p dark blue .65 .60
C115 A70 5p olive blk .65 .60
C116 A70 10p violet .65 .60
C117 A70 30p orange .65 .60
C118 A70 50p black brn 1.00 .60
C119 A70 100p brt green 1.30 .90
C120 A70 200p green 6.00 3.75
C121 AP28 500p black 28.00 17.50
Nos. C113-C121 (9) 39.55 25.75
Set, never hinged 59.00

For overprints see Nos. 388-390.

University of Asuncion Type

Pres. Bernardino Caballero and Senator José S. Decoud.

1939, Sept. Litho. *Perf. 12*

C122 A67 28p rose & blk 10.00 10.00
C123 A67 90p yel grn & blk 12.00 12.00

Map with Asunción to New York Air Route — AP35

1939, Nov. 30 Engr.

C124 AP35 30p brown 8.00 6.00
C125 AP35 80p orange 9.50 9.00
C126 AP35 90p purple 12.50 12.00
Nos. C124-C126 (3) 30.00 27.00

New York World's Fair.

Pan American Union Type

1940, May *Perf. 12*

C127 A85 20p rose car .60 .60
C128 A85 70p violet bl 1.25 .60
C129 A85 100p Prus grn 1.50 1.50
C130 A85 500p dk violet 6.75 5.25
Nos. C127-C130 (4) 10.10 7.95

Asuncion 400th Anniv. Type

1942, Aug. 15

C131 A93 20p deep plum .90 .50
C132 A94 70p fawn 2.60 1.60
C133 A95 500p olive gray 7.00 5.00
Nos. C131-C133 (3) 10.50 7.10

Imperforates

Starting with No. C134, many Paraguayan air mail stamps exist imperforate.

Port of Asunción — AP40

First Telegraph in South America — AP41

Early Merchant Ship AP42

Birthplace of Paraguay's Liberation AP43

Monument to Antequera AP44

Locomotive of First Paraguayan Railroad AP45

Monument to Heroes of Itororó AP46

Primitive Postal Service among Indians AP48

Government House — AP47

Colonial Jesuit Altar — AP49

Ruins of Humaitá Church AP50

Oratory of the Virgin AP51

Marshal Francisco S. Lopez — AP52

1944-45 Unwmk. *Perf. 12½*

C134	AP40	1c blue	.45	.25
C135	AP41	2c green	.45	.25
C136	AP42	3c brown vio	.45	.25
C137	AP43	5c brt bl grn	.45	.25
C138	AP44	10c dk violet	.45	.25
C139	AP45	20c dk brown	.45	.25
C140	AP46	30c lt blue	.45	.25
C141	AP47	40c olive	.45	.25
C142	AP48	70c brown red	.55	.30
C143	AP49	1g orange yel	1.60	.60
C144	AP50	2g copper brn	2.10	.90
C145	AP51	5g black brn	4.25	2.75
C146	AP52	10g indigo	10.50	5.00
		Nos. C134-C146 (13)	22.60	11.55

See Nos. C158-C162. For surcharges see Nos. C154-C157.

Flags Type

20c, Ecuador. 40c, Bolivia. 70c, Mexico. 1g, Chile. 2g, Brazil. 5g, Argentina. 10g, US.

Engr.; Flags Litho. in Natl. Colors

1945, Aug. 15

C147	A106	20c orange	.60	.60
C148	A106	40c olive	.60	.60
C149	A106	70c lake	.60	.60
C150	A106	1g slate bl	1.00	1.00
C151	A106	2g blue vio	1.50	1.50

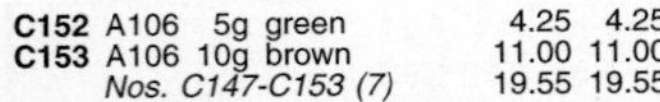

C152	A106	5g green	4.25	4.25
C153	A106	10g brown	11.00	11.00
		Nos. C147-C153 (7)	19.55	19.55

Sizes: Nos. C147-C151, 30x26mm; 5g, 32x28mm; 10g, 33x30mm.

Catalogue values for unused stamps in this section, from this point to the end of the section, are for Never Hinged items.

Nos. C139-C142 Srchd. in Black

1946 Engr. *Perf. 12½*

C154	AP45	5c on 20c dk brn	1.00	.80
C155	AP46	5c on 30c lt blue	1.00	.80
C156	AP47	5c on 40c olive	1.00	.80
C157	AP48	5c on 70c brn red	1.00	.80
		Nos. C154-C157 (4)	4.00	3.20

Types of 1944-45

1946, Sept. 21 Engr.

C158	AP50	10c dp car	.45	.40
C159	AP40	20c emerald	.45	.40
C160	AP47	1g brown org	.80	.70
C161	AP52	5g purple	2.25	2.00
C162	AP51	10g rose car	12.50	10.00
		Nos. C158-C162 (5)	16.45	13.50

Marshal Francisco Solano Lopez Type

1947, May. 15 *Perf. 12*

C163	A114	32c car lake	.35	.30
C164	A114	64c orange brn	.55	.45
C165	A114	1g Prus green	1.10	.90
C166	A114	5g Prus grn & brn vio	2.90	2.40
C167	A114	10g dk car rose & dk yel grn	6.00	5.00
		Nos. C163-C167 (5)	10.90	9.05

Archbishopric of Asunción Types

1948, Jan. 6 Unwmk. *Perf. 12½*

Size: 25½x31mm

C168	A116	20c gray blk	.45	.25
C169	A117	30c dark blue	.45	.25
C170	A118	40c lilac	.80	.35
C171	A115	70c orange red	1.00	.45
C172	A112	1g brown red	1.00	.45
C173	A118	2g red	2.10	1.25

Size: 25½x34mm

C174	A115	5g brt car & dk bl	5.25	2.25
C175	A116	10g dk grn & brn	8.50	3.75
		Nos. C168-C175 (8)	19.55	9.00

For surcharges see Nos. B11, C178.

Type of Regular Issue of 1948 Inscribed "AEREO"

1948, Sept. 11 Engr. & Litho.

C176	A119	69c dk grn	1.80	1.40
C177	A119	5g dk blue	8.00	7.50

The Barefeet, a political group.

No. C171 Surcharged in Black

1949, June 29

C178	A115	5c on 70c org red	.55	.30

Archbishop Juan Sinforiano Bogarin (1863-1949).

Symbols of UPU — AP65

1950, Sept. 4 Engr. *Perf. 13½x13*

C179	AP65	20c green & violet	.70	.25
C180	AP65	30c rose vio & brn	1.00	.40
C181	AP65	50c gray & green	1.40	.50
C182	AP65	1g blue & brown	1.75	.65
C183	AP65	5g rose & black	4.00	1.00
		Nos. C179-C183 (5)	8.85	2.80

UPU, 75th anniv. (in 1949).

Franklin D. Roosevelt — AP66

Engr.; Flags Litho.

1950, Oct. 2 *Perf. 12½*

Flags in Carmine & Violet Blue

C184	AP66	20c red	.50	.35
C185	AP66	30c black	.50	.35
C186	AP66	50c claret	.50	.35
C187	AP66	1g dk gray grn	.65	.35
C188	AP66	5g deep blue	.85	.40
		Nos. C184-C188 (5)	3.00	1.80

Franklin D. Roosevelt (1882-1945).

Urn Containing Remains of Columbus AP67

1952, Feb. 11 Litho. *Perf. 10*

C189	AP67	10c ultra	.65	.30
C190	AP67	20c green	.65	.30
C191	AP67	30c lilac	.65	.30
C192	AP67	40c rose	.65	.30
C193	AP67	50c bister brn	.65	.30
C194	AP67	1g blue	.65	.30
C195	AP67	2g orange	.65	.30
C196	AP67	5g red brown	.95	.30
		Nos. C189-C196 (8)	5.50	2.40

Queen Isabella I — AP68

1952, Oct. 12

C197	AP68	1g vio blue	.40	.35
C198	AP68	2g chocolate	.40	.35
C199	AP68	5g dull green	1.00	.75
C200	AP68	10g lilac rose	2.10	1.50
		Nos. C197-C200 (4)	3.90	2.95

500th birth anniv. of Queen Isabella I of Spain (in 1951).

Pettirossi Type

1954, Mar.

C201	A122	40c brown	.80	.25
C202	A122	55c green	.80	.25
C203	A122	80c ultra	.80	.25
C204	A122	1.30g gray blue	.80	.25
		Nos. C201-C204 (4)	3.20	1.00

Church of San Roque — AP70

1954, June 20 Engr. *Perf. 12x13*

C205	AP70	20c carmine	.45	.40
C206	AP70	30c brown vio	.45	.40
C207	AP70	50c ultra	.45	.40
C208	AP70	1g red brn & bl grn	.50	.40
C209	AP70	1g red brn & lil rose	.50	.40
C210	AP70	1g red brn & blk	.50	.40
C211	AP70	1g red brn & org	.50	.40
a.		Min. sheet of 4, #C208-C211, perf. 12x12½	15.00	12.00
C212	AP70	5g dk red brn & vio	1.00	.50
C213	AP70	5g dk red brn & ol grn	1.00	.50
C214	AP70	5g dk red brn & org yel	1.00	.50
C215	AP70	5g dk red brn & yel org	1.00	.50
a.		Min. sheet of 4, #C212-C215, perf. 12x12½	15.00	12.00
		Nos. C205-C215 (11)	7.35	4.80

Centenary (in 1953) of the establishment of the Church of San Roque, Asuncion.

Nos. C211a and C215a issued without gum.

Heroes Type

Unwmk.

1954, Aug. 15 Litho. *Perf. 10*

C216	A123	5g violet	.55	.25
C217	A123	10g olive green	1.10	.40
C218	A123	20g gray brown	2.00	.70
C219	A123	50g vermilion	3.00	1.75
C220	A123	100g blue	11.50	5.75
		Nos. C216-C220 (5)	18.15	8.85

Peron Visit Type

Photo. & Litho.

1955, Apr. Wmk. 90 *Perf. 13x13½*

Frames & Flags in Blue & Carmine

C221	A124	60c ol grn & cream	.95	.80
C222	A124	2g bl grn & cream	.95	.80
C223	A124	3g brn org & cream	.95	.80
C224	A124	4.10g brt rose pink & cr	.95	.80
		Nos. C221-C224 (4)	3.80	3.20

Monsignor Rodriguez Type

Jesuit Ruins: 3g, Corridor at Trinidad. 6g, Tower of Santa Rosa. 10g, San Cosme gate. 20g, Church of Jesus. 30g, Niche at Trinidad. 50g, Sacristy at Trinidad.

Perf. 12½x12, 12x12½

1955, June 19 Engr. Unwmk.

C225	A125	2g aqua	.60	.25
C226	A125	3g olive grn	.60	.25
C227	A126	4g lt blue grn	.60	.25
C228	A126	6g brown	.60	.25
C229	A125	10g rose	.60	.25
C230	A125	20g brown ol	.60	.25
C231	A126	30g dk green	1.00	.25
C232	A126	50g dp aqua	1.25	.30
		Nos. C225-C232 (8)	5.85	2.05

For surcharges see Nos. C252-C259.

Soldier and Flags AP75

"Republic" and Soldier AP76

1957, June 12 Photo. *Perf. 13½*

Granite Paper

Flags in Red and Blue

C233	AP75	10c ultra	.45	.30
C234	AP75	15c dp claret	.45	.30
C235	AP75	20c red	.45	.30
C236	AP75	25c light blue	.45	.30
C237	AP75	50c bluish grn	.45	.30
C238	AP75	1g rose car	.55	.30
C239	AP76	1.30g dp claret	.55	.30
C240	AP76	1.50p light blue	.55	.30
C241	AP76	2g emerald	.55	.30
C242	AP76	4.10g red	.55	.30
C243	AP76	5g gray black	.55	.30
C244	AP76	10g bluish grn	.65	.30
C245	AP76	25g ultra	.55	.30
		Nos. C233-C245 (13)	6.75	3.90

Heroes of the Chaco war.

Stroessner Type of Regular Issue

1958, Aug. 16 Litho. Wmk. 320

Center in Slate

C246	A130	12g rose lilac	1.10	1.00
C247	A130	18g orange	1.40	1.00
C248	A130	23g orange brn	1.40	1.00
C249	A130	36g emerald	2.75	2.00
C250	A130	50g citron	5.50	4.00
C251	A130	65g gray	11.00	6.00
		Nos. C246-C251 (6)	23.15	15.00

Re-election of Pres. General Alfredo Stroessner.

Nos. C225-C232 Surcharged like #545-551 in Red

Perf. 12½x12, 12x12½

1959, May 26 Engr. Unwmk.

C252	A125	4g on 2g aqua	.60	*1.00*
C253	A125	12.45g on 3g ol grn	.60	.50
C254	A126	18.15g on 6g brown	.85	.50
C255	A125	23.40g on 10g rose	1.00	.50
C256	A125	34.80g on 20g brn ol	1.25	1.00
C257	A126	36g on 4g lt bl grn	2.50	1.00
C258	A126	43.95g on 30g dk grn	2.50	1.00
C259	A126	100g on 50g deep aqua	6.25	2.50
		Nos. C252-C259 (8)	15.55	8.00

The surcharge is made to fit the stamps. Counterfeits of surcharge exist.

UN Emblem — AP77

Unwmk.

1959, Aug. 27 Typo. *Perf. 11*

C260 AP77 5g ocher & ultra 1.25 1.00

Visit of Dag Hammarskjold, Secretary General of the UN, Aug. 27-29.

Map and UN Emblem — AP78

1959, Oct. 24 Litho. *Perf. 10*

C261 AP78 12.45g blue & salmon .75 .50

United Nations Day, Oct. 24, 1959.

Olympic Games Type of Regular Issue

Design: Basketball.

1960, Mar. 18 Photo. *Perf. 12½*

C262 A131 12.45g red & dk bl .50 .30
C263 A131 18.15g lilac & gray ol .50 .30
C264 A131 36g bl grn & rose car 1.50 .45
Nos. C262-C264 (3) 2.50 1.05

The Paraguayan Philatelic Agency reported as spurious the imperf. souvenir sheet reproducing one of No. C264. Value, $10.50

Uprooted Oak Emblem — AP79

1960, Apr. 7 Litho. *Perf. 11*

C265 AP79 4g green & pink .85 .40
C266 AP79 12.45g bl & yel grn 1.50 .65
C267 AP79 18.15g car & ocher 2.10 .75
C268 AP79 23.40g red org & bl 2.50 1.50
Nos. C265-C268 (4) 6.95 3.30

World Refugee Year, July 1, 1959-June 30, 1960 (1st issue).

Human Rights Type of Regular Issue, 1960

Designs: 40g, UN Emblem. 60g, Hands holding scales. 100g, Flame.

1960, Apr. 21 *Perf. 12½x13*

C269 A133 40g dk ultra & red .30 .25
C270 A133 60g grnsh bl & org .50 .30
C271 A133 100g dk ultra & red 1.40 .65
Nos. C269-C271 (3) 2.20 1.20

An imperf. miniature sheet exists, containing one each of Nos. C269-C271, all printed in green and vermilion. Value, $16.

UN Type of Regular Issue

Perf. 13x13½

1960, Oct. 24 Photo. Unwmk.

C272 A134 3g orange, red & bl .70 .30
C273 A134 4g pale grn, red & bl .70 .30

International Bridge, Paraguay-Brazil AP80

1961, Jan. 26 Litho. *Perf. 14*

C274 AP80 3g carmine .65 .50
C275 AP80 12.45g brown lake 1.00 .75
C276 AP80 18.15g Prus grn 1.25 1.00
C277 AP80 36g dk blue 2.60 2.00
a. Souv. sheet of 4, #C274-C277, imperf. 16.00 15.00
Nos. C274-C277 (4) 5.50 4.25

Inauguration of the International Bridge between Paraguay and Brazil.

"Paraguay en Marcha" Type of 1961

12.45g, Truck carrying logs. 18.15g, Logs on river barge. 22g, Radio tower. 36g, Jet plane.

1961, Apr. 10 Photo. *Perf. 13*

C278 A136 12.45g yel & vio bl .65 .35
C279 A136 18.15g pur & ocher .90 .50
C280 A136 22g ultra & ocher 1.00 .60
C281 A136 36g brt grn & yel 1.75 1.00
Nos. C278-C281 (4) 4.30 2.45

Declaration of Independence AP81

1961, May 16 Litho. *Perf. 14½*

C282 AP81 12.45g dl red brn .80 .40
C283 AP81 18.15g dk blue .90 .60
C284 AP81 23.40g green 1.25 .90
C285 AP81 30g lilac 1.60 1.00
C286 AP81 36g rose 2.10 1.50
C287 AP81 44g olive 2.75 1.75
Nos. C282-C287 (6) 9.40 6.15

150th anniv. of Independence (1st issue).

"Paraguay" and Clasped Hands — AP82

1961, June 12 *Perf. 14x14½*

C288 AP82 3g vio blue .75 .50
C289 AP82 4g rose claret .90 .60
C290 AP82 100g gray green 5.75 4.00
Nos. C288-C290 (3) 7.40 5.10

Chaco Peace; 150th anniv. of Independence (2nd issue).

South American Tapir — AP83

1961, Aug. 16 Unwmk. *Perf. 14*

C291 AP83 12.45g claret 3.25 2.00
C292 AP83 18.15g ultra 3.25 2.50
C293 AP83 34.80g red brown 6.00 4.50
Nos. C291-C293 (3) 12.50 9.00

150th anniv. of Independence (3rd issue).

Catholic University Type of 1961

1961, Sept. 18 *Perf. 14x14½*

C294 A140 3g bister brn .80 .40
C295 A140 12.45g lilac rose .80 .40
C296 A140 36g blue 1.60 .80
Nos. C294-C296 (3) 3.20 1.60

Hotel Guarani Type of 1961

Design: Hotel Guarani, different view.

1961, Oct. 14 Litho. *Perf. 15*

C297 A141 3g dull red brn 2.00 1.75
C298 A141 4g ultra 2.00 1.75
C299 A141 18.15g orange 2.25 1.75
C300 A141 36g rose car 4.75 2.00
Nos. C297-C300 (4) 11.00 7.25

Tennis Type

1961, Oct. 16 Unwmk. *Perf. 11*

C301 A142 12.45g multi 2.10 .65
C302 A142 20g multi 4.00 1.25
C303 A142 50g multi 10.00 3.00
Nos. C301-C303 (3) 16.10 4.90

Some specialists question the status of this issue.

Two imperf. souvenir sheets exist containing four 12.45g stamps each in a different color with simulated perforations and black marginal inscription.

WRY Type

Design: Oak emblem rooted in ground, wavy-lined frame.

1961, Dec. 30

C307 A145 18.15g brn & red .75 .50
C308 A145 36g car & emer 3.50 1.25
C309 A145 50g emer & org 4.50 1.60
Nos. C307-C309 (3) 8.75 3.35

Imperforates in changed colors and souvenir sheets exist. Some specialists question the status of this issue.

Pres. Alfredo Stroessner and Prince Philip — AP84

1962, Mar. 9 Litho.

Portraits in Ultramarine

C310 AP84 12.45g grn & buff 3.25 2.50
C311 AP84 18.15g red & pink 3.25 2.50
C312 AP84 36g brn & yel 3.25 2.50
Nos. C310-C312 (3) 9.75 7.50

Visit of Prince Philip, Duke of Edinburgh, perf. and imperf. souvenir sheets exist. Values: each $5.

Illustrations AP85-AP89, AP92-AP94, AP96-AP97, AP99-AP105, AP107-AP110, AP113-AP115, AP117, AP123, AP127a, AP132-AP133, AP136, AP138, AP140, AP142, AP144-AP145, AP149-AP150, AP152-AP153, AP156, AP158-AP159, AP165, AP167, AP171, AP180, AP183-AP184, AP187, AP196, AP202, AP205, AP208, AP211, AP221-AP222, AP224-AP225, AP229, AP234-AP235, AP237 and AP240 are reduced.

Souvenir Sheet

Abraham Lincoln (1809-1865), 16th President of U.S. — AP85

1963, Aug. 21 Litho. *Imperf.*

C313 AP85 36g gray & vio brn 10.50 10.00

Souvenir Sheet

1960 Summer Olympics, Rome — AP86

1963, Aug. 21 Litho. & Engr.

C314 AP86 50g lt bl, vio brn & sep 77.50 75.00

Souvenir Sheet

Cattleya Cigas AP87

1963, Aug. 21 Litho.

C315 AP87 66g multicolored 65.00 60.00

Souvenir Sheet

Pres. Alfredo Stroessner — AP88

1964, Nov. 3

C316 AP88 36g multicolored 9.50 9.00

Souvenir Sheet

Saturn V Rocket, Pres. John F. Kennedy AP89

1968, Jan. 27 *Perf. 14*

C317 AP89 50g multicolored 21.00 20.00

Pres. Kennedy, 4th death anniv. (in 1967).

Torch, Book, Houses — AP90

1969, June 28 Wmk. 347 *Perf. 11*

C318 AP90 36g blue 2.25 1.00
C319 AP90 50g bister brn 4.25 2.00
C320 AP90 100g rose car 6.25 3.00
Nos. C318-C320 (3) 12.75 6.00

National drive for teachers' homes.

Souvenir Sheets

U.S. Space Program AP91

John F. Kennedy, Wernher von Braun, moon and: No. C321, Apollo 11 en route to moon. No. C322, Saturn V lift-off. No. C323, Apollo 9. No. C324, Apollo 10.

1969, July 9 ***Perf. 14***

C321 AP91 23.40g multi 28.50 28.00
C322 AP91 23.40g multi 23.00 22.50

Imperf

C323 AP91 23.40g multi 34.00 33.00
C324 AP91 23.40g multi 43.00 42.00

Nos. C323-C324 each contain one 56x46mm stamp.

Souvenir Sheets

Events and Anniversaries — AP92

#C325, Apollo 14. #C326, Dwight D. Eisenhower, 1st death anniv. #C327, Napoleon Bonaparte, birth bicent. #C328, Brazil, winners of Jules Rimet World Cup Soccer Trophy.

1970, Dec. 16 ***Perf. 13½***

C325 AP92 20g multicolored 32.00 30.00
C326 AP92 20g multicolored 22.50 22.00
C327 AP92 20g multicolored 23.50 23.00
C328 AP92 20g multicolored 21.00 20.00
Nos. C325-C328 (4) 99.00 95.00

Souvenir Sheets

Paraguayan Postage Stamps, Cent. — AP93

No. C329, Marshal Francisco Solano Lopez, Pres. Alfredo Stroessner, Paraguay #1. No. C330, #3, 1014, 1242. No. C331, #1243, C8, C74.

1971, Mar. 23

C329 AP93 20g multicolored 17.00 16.00
C330 AP93 20g multicolored 45.00 42.50
C331 AP93 20g multicolored 36.00 35.00
Nos. C329-C331 (3) 98.00 93.50

Issued: #C329, 3/23; #C330-C331, 3/29.

Souvenir Sheets

Emblems of Apollo Space Missions AP94

Designs: No. C332, Apollo 7, 8, 9, & 10. No. C333, Apollo 11, 12, 13, & 14.

1971, Mar. 26

C332 AP94 20g multicolored 20.00 19.00
C333 AP94 20g multicolored 20.00 19.00

Souvenir Sheet

Charles de Gaulle AP95

1971, Dec. 24 ***Perf. 14***

C334 AP95 20g multicolored 27.50 27.00

Souvenir Sheet

Taras Shevchenko (1814-1861), Ukrainian Poet — AP96

1971, Dec. 24 ***Perf. 13½***

C335 AP96 20g multicolored 16.50 16.00

Souvenir Sheets

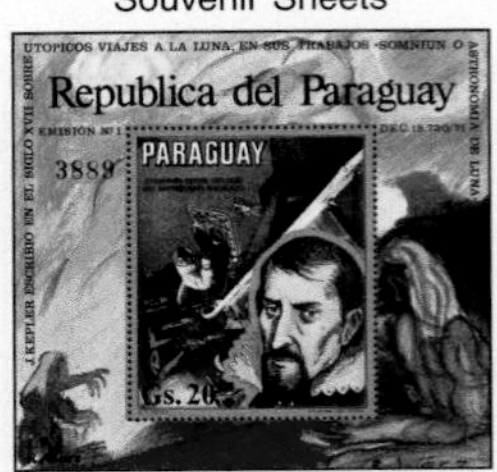

Johannes Kepler (1571-1630), German Astronomer — AP97

Kepler and: No. C336, Apollo lunar module over moon. No. C337, Astronaut walking in space.

1971, Dec. 24

C336 AP97 20g multicolored 21.00 20.00
C337 AP97 20g multicolored 21.00 20.00

Souvenir Sheet

10 years of U.S. Space Program AP98

1972, Jan. 6 ***Perf. 13½***

C338 AP98 20g multicolored 29.00 28.00

Souvenir Sheet

Apollo 16 Moon Mission AP99

1972, Mar. 29 **Litho.** ***Perf. 13½***

C339 AP99 20g multicolored 23.00 22.50

Souvenir Sheets

History of the Olympics AP100

Designs: No. C340, Pierre de Coubertin (1863-1937), founder of modern Olympics. No. C341, Skier, Garmisch-Partenkirchen, 1936. No. C342, Olympic flame, Sapporo, 1972. No. C343, French, Olympic flags. No. C344, Javelin thrower, Paris, 1924. No. C345, Equestrian event.

1972, Mar. 29 ***Perf. 14½***

C340 AP100 20g multicolored 27.50 27.00
C341 AP100 20g multicolored 27.50 27.00
C342 AP100 20g multicolored 27.50 27.00
C343 AP100 20g multicolored 27.50 27.00
C344 AP100 20g multicolored 27.50 27.00
C345 AP100 20g multicolored 27.50 27.00
Nos. C340-C345 (6) 165.00 162.00

Souvenir Sheet

Medal Totals, 1972 Winter Olympics, Sapporo — AP101

1972, Nov. 18 ***Perf. 13½***

C346 AP101 23.40g multi 23.00 22.50

Souvenir Sheets

French Contributions to Aviation and Space Exploration — AP102

Georges Pompidou, Charles de Gaulle and: No. C347, Concorde. No. C348, Satellite D2A, Mirage G 8 jets.

1972, Nov. 25

C347 AP102 23.40g multi 62.00 60.00
C348 AP102 23.40g multi 60.00 57.50

Souvenir Sheets

Summer Olympic Gold Medals, 1896-1972 — AP103

No. C349, 9 medals, 1896-1932, vert. No. C350, 8 medals, 1936-1972.

1972, Nov. 25

C349 AP103 23.40g multi 22.00 21.00
C350 AP103 23.40g multi 22.00 21.00

Souvenir Sheet

Adoration of the Shepherds by Murillo — AP104

1972, Nov. 25

C351 AP104 23.40g multi 35.00 34.00

Christmas.

Souvenir Sheet

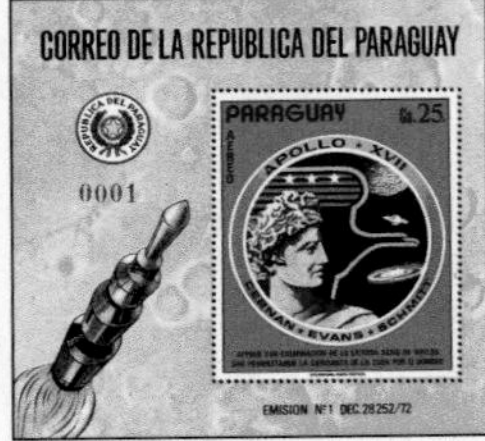

Apollo 17 Moon Mission AP105

1973, Mar. 13

C352 AP105 25g multicolored 56.00 54.00

Souvenir Sheet

Medal Totals, 1972 Summer Olympics, Munich — AP106

1973, Mar. 15 ***Perf. 13½***

C353 AP106 25g multicolored 31.00 30.00

Souvenir Sheets

The Holy Family by Peter Paul Rubens AP107

Design: No. C355, In the Forest at Pierrefonds by Alfred de Dreux.

1973, Mar. 15

C354 AP107 25g multicolored 42.00 40.00
C355 AP107 25g multicolored 19.50 19.00

Souvenir Sheet

German Championship Soccer Team F.C. Bayern, Bavaria #2 — AP108

1973, June 29 ***Imperf.***

C356 AP108 25g multicolored 19.00 18.00

IBRA '73 Intl. Philatelic Exhibition, Munich,

Souvenir Sheet

Copernicus, 500th Birth Anniv. and Space Exploration — AP109

#C357, Lunar surface, Apollo 11. #C358, Copernicus, position of Earth at soltices and equinoxes, vert. #C359, Skylab space laboratory.

1973, June 29 *Perf. 13½*

C357 AP109 25g multicolored 31.00 30.00
C358 AP109 25g multicolored 31.00 30.00
C359 AP109 25g multicolored 26.00 25.00
Nos. C357-C359 (3) 88.00 85.00

Souvenir Sheets

Exploration of Mars — AP110

1973, Oct. 8

C360 AP110 25g Mariner 9 26.00 25.00
C361 AP110 25g Viking probe, horiz. 39.00 37.50

Pres. Stroessner's Visit to Europe and Morocco AP111

Designs: No. C362a, 5g, Arms of Paraguay, Spain, Canary Islands. b, 10g, Gen. Franco, Stroessner, vert. c, 25g, Arms of Paraguay, Germany. d, 50g, Stroessner, Giovanni Leone, Italy, vert. No. C363, Itaipu Dam between Paraguay and Brazil.

1973, Dec. 30 *Perf. 14*

C362 AP111 Strip of 4, #a.-d. 2.75 2.00
C363 AP111 150g multicolored 3.50 3.00
Nos. C362-C363 (2) 6.25 5.00

Souvenir Sheet

Imperf

C364 AP111 100g Country flags 15.00 15.00

No. C364 contains one 60x50mm stamp. See Nos. C375-C376.

1974 World Cup Soccer Championships, Munich — AP112

Abstract paintings of soccer players: No. C366a, 10g, Player seated on globe. b, 20g, Player as viewed from under foot. No. C367, Player kicking ball. No. C368, Goalie catching ball, horiz.

1974, Jan. 31 *Perf. 14*

C365 AP112 5g shown 13.00 10.00
C366 AP112 Pair, #a.-b. 2.75 5.00
Nos. C365-C366 (2) 15.75 15.00

Souvenir Sheets

Perf. 13½

C367 AP112 25g multicolored 15.00 15.00
C368 AP112 25g multicolored 15.00 15.00

Nos. C367-C368 each contain one 50x60mm stamp.

Souvenir Sheets

Tourism Year AP113

Design: No. C370, Painting, Birth of Christ by Louis le Nain (1593-1648), horiz.

1974, Feb. 4 *Perf. 13½*

C369 AP113 25g multicolored 17.50 17.00
C370 AP113 25g multicolored 10.50 10.00

Christmas (No. C370).

Souvenir Sheets

Events and Anniversaries — AP114

No. C371, Rocket lift-off. No. C372, Solar system, horiz. No. C373, Skylab 2 astronauts, horiz. No. C374, Olympic Flame.

1974, Mar. 20

C371 AP114 25g multicolored 25.00 24.00
C372 AP114 25g multicolored 29.00 28.00
C373 AP114 25g multicolored 19.50 19.00
C374 AP114 25g multicolored 22.00 21.00
Nos. C371-C374 (4) 95.50 92.00

UPU centennial (#C371-C372). 1976 Olympic Games (#C374).

President Stroessner Type of 1973

100g, Stroessner, Georges Pompidou. 200g, Stroessner and Pope Paul VI.

1974, Apr. 25 *Perf. 14*

C375 AP111 100g multicolored 2.25 2.00

Souvenir Sheet

Perf. 13½

C376 AP111 200g multicolored 5.25 5.00

No. C376 contains one 60x50mm stamp.

Souvenir Sheet

Lufthansa Airlines Intercontinental Routes, 40th Anniv. — AP115

1974, July 13 *Perf. 13½*

C377 AP115 15g multicolored 19.00 18.00

No. C377 face value was 15g plus 5g extra for a monument to Francisco Solano Lopez.

Souvenir Sheet

Hermann Oberth, 80th Anniv. of Birth AP115a

1974, July 13 **Litho.** *Perf. 13½*

C378 AP115a 15g multi 58.00 55.00

No. C378 face value was 15g plus 5g extra for a monument to Francisco Solano Lopez.

1974 World Cup Soccer Championships, West Germany — AP116

1974, July 13 *Perf. 14*

C379 AP116 4g Goalie 13.50 6.75
C380 AP116 5g Soccer ball 3.25 1.50
C381 AP116 10g shown 4.75 2.00
Nos. C379-C381 (3) 21.50 10.25

Souvenir Sheet

Perf. 13½

C382 AP116 15g Soccer ball, diff. 23.00 22.50

No. C382 contains one 53x46mm stamp. No. C382 face value was 15g plus 5g extra for a monument for Francisco Solano Lopez.

Souvenir Sheet

First Balloon Flight over English Channel AP117

1974, Sept. 13 ***Imperf.***

C383 AP117 15g multicolored 33.00 32.50

No. C383 face value was 15g plus 5g extra for a monument for Francisco Solano Lopez.

Anniversaries and Events — AP118

Designs: 4g, US #C76 on covers that went to Moon. No. C385a, 5g, Pres. Pinochet of Chile. No. C385b, 10g, Pres. Stroessner's visit to South Africa. No. C386, Mariner 10 over Mercury, horiz.

1974, Dec. 2 *Perf. 14*

C384 AP118 4g multicolored 9.00 8.50
C385 AP118 Pair #a.-b. 3.00 2.75
Nos. C384-C385 (2) 12.00 11.25

Souvenir Sheets

Perf. 13½

C386 AP118 15g multicolored 20.50 20.00

Nos. C386 contains one 60x50mm stamp. Face value was 15g plus 5g extra for a monument to Francisco Solano Lopez. Compare No. C386 with No. C392.

Anniversaries and Events — AP119

Designs: 4g, UPU, cent. 5g, 17th Congress, UPU, Lausanne. 10g, Intl. Philatelic Exposition, Montevideo, Uruguay. No. C392, Mariner 10 orbiting Mercury, horiz. No. C393, Figure skater, horiz. No. C394, Innsbruck Olympic emblem.

1974, Dec. 7 *Perf. 14*

C389 AP119 4g multicolored 7.00 6.00
C390 AP119 5g multicolored 2.50 2.25
C391 AP119 10g multicolored 2.50 2.25
Nos. C389-C391 (3) 12.00 10.50

Souvenir Sheets

Perf. 13½

C392 AP119 15g bl & multi 25.00 24.00
C393 AP119 15g multicolored 22.00 21.00
C394 AP119 15g multicolored 22.00 21.00

UPU centennial (#C389). Nos. C392-C394 each contain one 60x50mm stamp and face value was 15g plus 5g extra for a monument to Francisco Solano Lopez.

German World Cup Soccer Champions AP120

4g, Holding World Cup trophy, vert. 5g, Team on field. 10g, Argentina '78 emblem, vert.

No. C398, Players holding trophy, vert. No. C399, Hemispheres, emblems of 1974 and 1978 World Cup championships.

1974, Dec. 20 *Perf. 14*

C395 AP120 4g multicolored 6.25 4.00
C396 AP120 5g multicolored .95 .45
C397 AP120 10g multicolored 1.90 .45
Nos. C395-C397 (3) 9.10 4.90

Souvenir Sheets

Perf. 13½

C398 AP120 15g multicolored 34.00 33.00
C399 AP120 15g multicolored 34.00 33.00

No. C398 contains one 50x60mm stamp, and No. C399 contains one 60x50mm stamp. Face value of each sheet was 15g plus 5g extra for a monument to Francisco Solano Lopez.

Souvenir Sheet

Apollo-Soyuz — AP121

1974, Dec. 20 *Perf. 13½*

C400 AP121 15g multicolored 34.00 33.00

Expo '75 — AP122

4g, Ryukyumurasaki. 5g, Hibiscus, horiz. 10g, Ancient sailing ship, horiz.
15g, Expo emblem, vert.

1975, Feb. 24 ***Perf. 14***

C401 AP122 4g multicolored 7.25 2.50
C402 AP122 5g multicolored 1.80 .40
C403 AP122 10g multicolored 3.50 .40
Nos. C401-C403 (3) 12.55 3.30

Souvenir Sheet

Perf. 14½

C404 AP122 15g multicolored 15.00 14.00

No. C404 face value was 15g plus 5g extra for a monument to Francisco Solano Lopez.

Souvenir Sheets

Anniversaries and Events — AP123

Designs: No. C405, Dr. Kurt Debus, space scientist, 65th birth anniv. No. C406, 1976 Summer Olympics, Montreal, horiz.

1975, Feb. 24 ***Perf. 13½***

C405 AP123 15g multicolored 19.00 18.00
C406 AP123 15g multicolored 24.00 23.00

Nos. C405-C406 face value was 15g plus 5g extra for a monument to Francisco Solano Lopez.

GEOS Satellite — AP124

No. C408a, 5g, ESPANA 75. b, 10g, Mother and Child, Murillo.

No. C409, Spain #1139, 1838, C167, charity stamp. No. C410, Zeppelin, plane, satellites. No. C411, Jupiter.

1975, Aug. 21 ***Perf. 14***

C407 AP124 4g shown 3.25 2.10
C408 AP124 Pair, #1.-b. 2.50 .55
Nos. C407-C408 (2) 5.75 2.65

Souvenir Sheet

Perf. 13½

C409 AP124 15g multicolored 42.00 40.00
C410 AP124 15g multicolored 65.00 62.00

Perf. 14½

C411 AP124 15g multicolored 23.00 22.00

Nos. C409-C411 face value was 15g plus 5g extra for a monument to Francisco Solano Lopez.

Size of stamps: No. C409, 45x55mm; C410, 55x45mm; C411, 32x22mm.

Souvenir Sheets

Anniversaries and Events — AP125

#C413, UN emblem, Intl. Women's Year, vert. #C414, Helios space satellite.

1975, Aug. 26 ***Perf. 13½***

C413 AP125 15g multicolored 15.00 15.00
C414 AP125 15g multicolored 15.00 15.00

Nos. C413-C414 face value was 15g plus 5g extra for a monument to Francisco Solano Lopez.

Anniversaries and Events AP125a

Designs: 4g, First Zeppelin flight, 75th anniv. 5g, Emblem of 1978 World Cup Soccer Championships, Argentina, vert. 10g, Emblem of Nordposta 75, statue.

1975, Oct. 13 **Litho.** ***Perf. 14***

C415-C417 AP125a Set of 3 6.75 3.50

Souvenir Sheets

Anniversaries and Events — AP126

No. C418, Zeppelin, boats. No. C419, Soccer, Intelsat IV, vert. No. C420, Viking Mars landing.

1975, Oct. 13 ***Perf. 13½***

C418 AP126 15g multicolored 25.00 24.00
C419 AP126 15g multicolored 21.00 20.00
C420 AP126 15g multicolored 21.00 20.00
Nos. C418-C420 (3) 67.00 64.00

Nos. C418-C420 face value was 15g plus 5g extra for a monument to Francisco Solano Lopez.

United States, Bicent. AP127

#C421: a, 4g, Lunar rover. b, 5g, Ford Elite, 1975. c, 10g, Ford, 1896. No. C422, Airplanes and spacecraft. No. C423, Arms of Paraguay & US.

1975, Nov. 28 **Litho.** ***Perf. 14***

C421 AP127 Strip of 3, #a.-c. 10.75 6.00

Souvenir Sheets

Perf. 13½

C422 AP127 15g multicolored 35.00 33.00
C423 AP127 15g multicolored 27.50 26.00

Nos. C422-C423 each contain one 60x50mm stamp and face value was 15g plus 5g surtax for a monument to Francisco Solano Lopez.

Souvenir Sheet

La Musique by Francois Boucher AP127a

1975, Nov. 28 ***Perf. 13½***

C424 AP127a 15g multicolored 17.50 17.00

No. C424 face value was 15g plus 5g extra for a monument to Francisco Solano Lopez.

Anniversaries and Events AP128

Designs: 4g, Flight of Concorde jet. 5g, JU 52/3M, Lufthansa Airlines, 50th anniv. 10g, EXFILMO '75 and ESPAMER '75. No. C428, Concorde, diff. No. C429, Dr. Albert Schweitzer, missionary and Konrad Adenauer, German statesman. No. C430, Ferdinand Porsche, auto designer, birth cent., vert.

1975, Dec. 20 ***Perf. 14***

C425 AP128 4g multicolored 5.50 3.50
C426 AP128 5g multicolored .55 .55
C427 AP128 10g multicolored .55 .55
Nos. C425-C427 (3) 6.60 4.60

Souvenir Sheets

Perf. 13½

C428 AP128 15g multicolored 31.00 30.00
C429 AP128 15g multicolored 15.00 12.00
C430 AP128 15g multicolored 82.00 80.00

Nos. C428-C430 face value was 15g plus 5g extra for a monument to Francisco Solano Lopez. No. C428 contains one 54x34mm stamp, No. C429 one 60x50mm stamp, No. C430 one 30x40mm stamp.

Anniversaries and Events AP129

Details: 4g, The Transfiguration by Raphael, vert. 5g, Nativity by Del Mayno. 10g, Nativity by Vignon. No. C434, Detail from Adoration of the Shepherds by Ghirlandaio. No. C435, Austria, 1000th anniv., Leopold I, natl. arms, vert. No. C436, Sepp Herberger and Helmut Schon, coaches for German soccer team.

1976, Feb. 2 **Litho.** ***Perf. 14***

C431 AP129 4g multicolored 4.50 2.25
C432 AP129 5g multicolored .90 .45
C433 AP129 10g multicolored .90 .45
Nos. C431-C433 (3) 6.30 3.15

Souvenir Sheets

Perf. 13½

C434 AP129 15g multicolored 10.50 10.00
C435 AP129 15g multicolored 52.50 50.00

Perf. 13½x13

C436 AP129 15g multicolored 105.00 100.00

Nos. C434-C436 face value was 15g plus 5g extra for a monument to Francisco Solano Lopez. No. C434 contains one 40x30mm stamp, No. C435 one 30x40mm stamp, No. C436 one 54x34mm stamp.

Souvenir Sheet

Apollo-Soyuz — AP130

1976, Apr. 2 ***Perf. 13½x13***

C437 AP130 25g multicolored 23.50 22.50

Souvenir Sheet

Lufthansa, 50th Anniv. — AP131

1976, Apr. 7 ***Perf. 13½x13***

C438 AP131 25g multicolored 20.00 18.00

Souvenir Sheet

Interphil '76 AP132

1976, May 12 ***Perf. 13½***

C439 AP132 15g multicolored 16.00 15.00

No. C439 face value was 15g plus 5g extra for a monument to Francisco Solano Lopez.

Souvenir Sheets

Anniversaries and Events — AP133

Designs: No. C440, Alexander Graham Bell, telephone cent. No. C441, Gold, silver, and bronze medals, 1976 Winter Olympics, Innsbruck. No. C442, Gold medalist Rosi Mittermaier, downhill and slalom, vert. No. C443, Viking probe on Mars. No. C444, UN Postal Administration, 25th anniv. and UPU, cent., vert. No. C445, Prof. Hermanm Oberth, Wernher von Braun. No. C446, Madonna and Child by Durer, vert.

1976 ***Perf. 13½***

C440 AP133 25g multi 42.00 40.00
C441 AP133 25g multi 23.50 22.50
C442 AP133 25g multi 180.00 175.00

Perf. 14½

C443 AP133 25g multi 34.00 32.50
C444 AP133 25g multi 55.00 52.50
C445 AP133 25g multi 95.00 90.00
C446 AP133 25g multi 84.00 80.00
Nos. C440-C446 (7) 513.50 492.50

No. C442 contains one 35x54mm stamp, No. C443 one 46x36mm stamp, No. C444 one 25x35mm stamp.

Issued: #C440-C441, 6/15; #C443, 7/8; #C442, C444, 7/15; #C445, 8/20; #C446, 9/9.

Souvenir Sheet

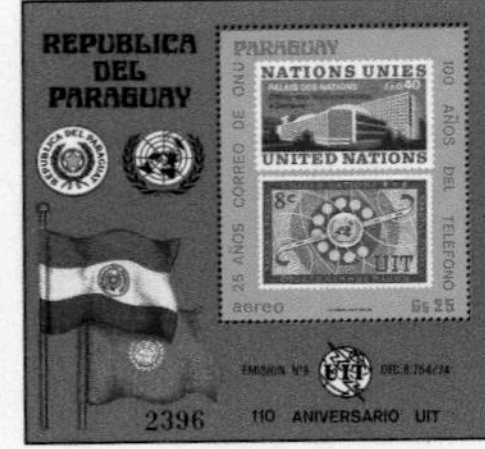

UN Offices in Geneva #22, UN #42 AP136

1976, Dec. 18 ***Perf. 13½***

C447 AP136 25g multicolored 18.00 17.50

UN Postal Administration, 25th anniv. and telephone, cent.

Souvenir Sheet

Ludwig van Beethoven (1770-1827) — AP137

1977, Feb. 28 **Litho.** ***Perf. 14¼***

C448 AP137 25g multi 16.50 16.00

Souvenir Sheet

Alfred Nobel, 80th Death Anniv. and First Nobel Prize, 75th Anniv. AP138

1977, June 7 *Perf. 13½*
C449 AP138 25g multicolored 42.00 40.00

Souvenir Sheet

Coronation of Queen Elizabeth II, 25th Anniv. — AP139

1977, July 25 *Perf. 14½*
C450 AP139 25g multicolored 31.00 30.00

Souvenir Sheet

Uruguay '77 Intl. Philatelic Exhibition — AP140

1977, Aug. 27 Litho. *Perf. 13½*
C451 AP140 25g multicolored 18.50 18.00

Souvenir Sheets

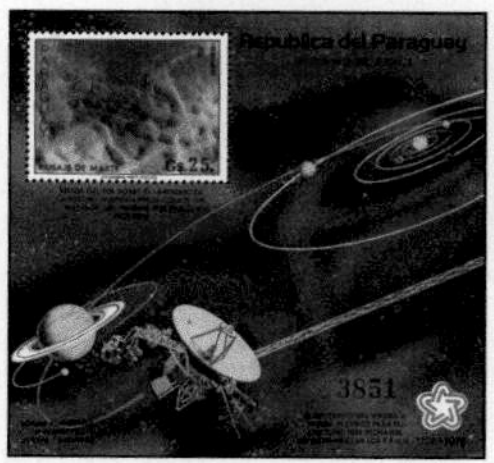

Exploration of Mars — AP141

No. C452, Martian craters. No. C453, Wernher von Braun. No. C454, Projected Martian lander.

1977, Sept. 5 *Perf. 13½*
C452 AP141 25g multicolored 47.50 45.00

Perf. 14¼x14½

1977, Nov. 28 **Litho.**
C453 AP141 25g multicolored 67.50 60.00

1977, Oct. 28 Litho. *Perf. 13½*
C454 AP141 25g multicolored 82.50 80.00

Souvenir Sheet

Sepp Herberger, German Soccer Team Coach — AP142

1978, Jan. 23 Litho. *Perf. 13½*
C455 AP142 25g multicolored 47.50 45.00

Souvenir Sheet

Austria #B331, Canada #681, US #716, Russia #B66 AP143

1978, Mar. 10 Litho. *Perf. 14½*
C456 AP143 25g multicolored 35.00 34.00

Inner perforations are simulated.

Souvenir Sheet

Alfred Nobel AP144

1978, Mar. 15 Litho. *Perf. 13½*
C457 AP144 25g multicolored 44.00 42.50

Souvenir Sheets

Anniversaries and Events — AP145

Designs: No. C458, Queen Elizabeth II wearing St. Edward's Crown, holding orb and scepter. No. C459, Queen Elizabeth II presenting World Cup Trophy to English team captain. No. C460, Flags of nations participating in 1978 World Cup Soccer Championships. No. C461, Soccer action. No. C462, Argentina, 1978 World Cup Champions.

1978 *Perf. 14½, 13½ (#C461)*
C458 AP145 25g multi 32.00 30.00
C459 AP145 25g multi 32.00 30.00
C460 AP145 25g multi 40.00 37.50
C461 AP145 25g multi 32.00 30.00
C462 AP145 25g multi 32.00 30.00
Nos. C458-C462 (5) 168.00 157.50

Coronation of Queen Elizabeth II, 25th Anniv. (#C458-C459). 1978 World Cup Soccer Championships, Argentina (#C460-C462).

No. C460 contains one 70x50mm stamp, No. C461 one 39x57mm stamp.

Issued: #C458, 5/11; #C459-C460, 5/16; #C461, 6/30; #C462, 10/26.

Souvenir Sheet

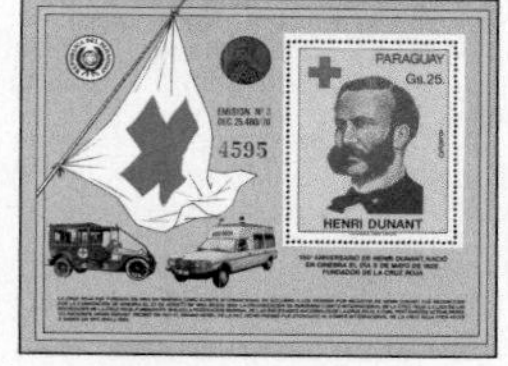

Jean-Henri Dunant, 150th Birth Anniv. — AP146

1978, June 28 *Perf. 14½*
C463 AP146 25g multicolored 28.00 27.00

Souvenir Sheet

Capt. James Cook, 250th Birth Anniv. AP147

1978, July 19 *Perf. 13½*
C464 AP147 25g multicolored 26.00 25.00

Discovery of Hawaii, Death of Capt. Cook, bicentennial; Hawaii Statehood, 20th anniv.

Aregua Satellite Communication Station — AP148

Coat of Arms AP148a

Pres. Alfredo Stroessner — AP148b

1978, Aug. 15 Litho. *Perf. 14*
C465 AP148 75g multi 3.25 1.25
C466 AP148a 500g multi 13.00 8.00
C467 AP148b 1000g multi 24.00 16.00
Nos. C465-C467 (3) 40.25 25.25

Souvenir Sheet

Adoration of the Magi by Albrecht Durer — AP149

1978, Oct. 31 *Perf. 13½*
C468 AP149 25g multicolored 15.00 15.00

Souvenir Sheet

Prof. Hermann Oberth, 85th Birth Anniv. AP150

1979, Aug. 28 *Perf. 14½*
C469 AP150 25g multicolored 42.00 40.00

Souvenir Sheet

World Cup Soccer Championships — AP151

1979, Nov. 29
C470 AP151 25g multicolored 34.00 30.00

Souvenir Sheet

Helicopters — AP152

1979, Nov. 29 Litho. *Perf. 13½*
C471 AP152 25g multicolored 26.00 25.00

Souvenir Sheet

1980 Summer Olympics, Moscow — AP153

1979, Dec. 20 *Perf. 14½*
C472 AP153 25g Two-man canoe 32.00 35.00

Souvenir Sheet

1982 World Cup Soccer Championships, Spain — AP154

1979, Dec. 24 Litho. *Perf. 13x13½*
C473 AP154 25g Sheet of 1 + label 32.00 30.00

Souvenir Sheet

Maybach DS-8 "Zeppelin" — AP155

1980, Apr. 8 *Perf. 14½*
C474 AP155 25g multicolored 52.00 50.00

Wilhelm Maybach, 50th death anniv. Karl Maybach, 100th birth anniv.

Souvenir Sheet

Rotary Intl., 75th Anniv. AP156

1980, July 1 **Litho.** ***Perf. 14½***
C475 AP156 25g multicolored 40.00 37.50

Apollo 11 Type of 1970

Souvenir Sheet

Design: 1st steps on lunar surface.

1980, July 30 ***Perf. 13½***
Size: 36x26mm
C476 A221 25g multicolored 23.00 22.00

Souvenir Sheet

Virgin Surrounded by Animals by Albrecht Durer — AP158

Photo. & Engr.

1980, Sept. 24 ***Perf. 12***
C477 AP158 25g multi 180.00 175.00

Souvenir Sheet

1980 Olympic Games AP159

1980, Dec. 15 **Litho.** ***Perf. 14***
C478 AP159 25g multi 32.00 30.00

Metropolitan Seminary Centenary AP160

1981, Mar. 26 **Litho.** **Wmk. 347**

C479	AP160	5g ultra	1.75	1.25
C480	AP160	10g red brn	1.75	1.25
C481	AP160	25g green	1.75	1.25
C482	AP160	50g gray	3.25	1.25
		Nos. C479-C482 (4)	8.50	5.00

Anniversaries and Events — AP161

5g, George Washington, 250th birth anniv. (in 1982). 10g, Queen Mother Elizabeth, 80th birthday (in 1980). 30g, Phila Tokyo '81.

No. C486, Emperor Hirohito, 80th birthday. No. C487, Washington Crossing the Delaware.

1981, July 10 **Unwmk.** ***Perf. 14***

C483	AP161	5g multicolored	7.50	2.25
C484	AP161	10g multicolored	1.40	.45
C485	AP161	30g multicolored	1.75	.55
		Nos. C483-C485 (3)	10.65	3.25

Souvenir Sheets

Perf. 14½

C486	AP161	25g multicolored	18.00	17.50
C487	AP161	25g multicolored	28.00	27.00

No. C484 issued in sheets of 8 plus label. For overprints see Nos. 2126, C590-C591, C611.

First Space Shuttle Mission AP162

Pres. Ronald Reagan and: 5g, Columbia in Earth orbit. 10g, Astronauts John Young and Robert Crippen. 30g, Columbia landing.

George Washington and: No. C491, Columbia re-entering atmosphere. No. C492, Columbia inverted above Earth.

1981, Oct. 9 ***Perf. 14***

C488	AP162	5g multicolored	10.50	3.25
C489	AP162	10g multicolored	2.00	.80
C490	AP162	30g multicolored	3.25	1.00
		Nos. C488-C490 (3)	15.75	5.05

Souvenir Sheets

Perf. 13½

C491	AP162	25g multicolored	23.00	20.00
C492	AP162	25g multicolored	23.00	20.00

Nos. C491-C492 each contain one 60x50mm stamp. Inauguration of Pres. Reagan, George Washington, 250th birth anniv. (in 1982) (#C491-C492).

World Cup Soccer, Spain, 1982 — AP163

1981, Oct. 15 ***Perf. 14***

Color of Shirts

C493	AP163	5g yellow, green	4.75	2.00
C494	AP163	10g blue, white	1.25	.50
C495	AP163	30g white & blk, org	.75	.30
		Nos. C493-C495 (3)	6.75	2.80

Souvenir Sheet

Perf. 14½

C496 AP163 25g Goalie 21.00 20.00

No. C494 exists in sheets of 5 plus 4 labels.

Christmas AP164

Paintings: 5g, Virgin with the Child by Stefan Lochner. 10g, Our Lady of Caacupe. 25g, Altar of the Virgin by Albrecht Durer. 30g, Virgin and Child by Matthias Grunewald.

1981, Dec. 21 ***Perf. 14***

C497	AP164	5g multicolored	1.60	.50
C498	AP164	10g multicolored	3.25	1.00
C499	AP164	30g multicolored	8.75	2.50
		Nos. C497-C499 (3)	13.60	4.00

Souvenir Sheet

Perf. 13½

C500 AP164 25g multicolored 25.00

No. C500 contains one 54x75mm stamp.

Souvenir Sheet

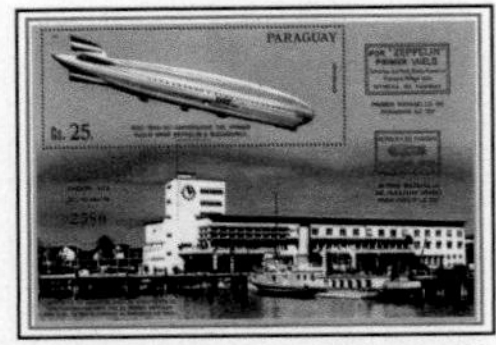

Graf Zeppelin's First Flight to South America, 50th Anniv. — AP165

1981, Dec. 28 ***Perf. 14½***
C501 AP165 25g multicolored 37.00 35.00

Mother Maria Mazzarello (1837-1881), Co-Founder of Daughters of Mary — AP166

Perf. 13x13½

1981, Dec. 30 **Litho.** **Wmk. 347**

C502	AP166	20g blk & grn	1.25	1.00
C503	AP166	25g blk & red brn	1.25	1.00
C504	AP166	50g blk & gray vio	1.25	1.00
		Nos. C502-C504 (3)	3.75	3.00

Souvenir Sheet

The Magus (Dr. Faust) by Rembrandt — AP167

Litho. & Typo.

1982, Apr. 23 **Unwmk.** ***Perf. 14½***
C505 AP167 25g blk, buff & gold 26.00 24.00

Johann Wolfgang von Goethe, 150th death anniv.

The following stamps were issued 4 each in sheets of 8 with 1 label: Nos. C590-C591, C669-C670, C677-C678, C682-C683, C690-C691, C699-C700, C718-C719, C747-C748.

The following stamps were issued in sheets of 4 with 5 labels: Nos. C765-C766, C774, C779-C780, C785, C803, C813, C818, C823.

The following stamps were issued in sheets of 3 with 6 labels: Nos. C739, C754.

The following stamps were issued in sheets of 5 with 4 labels: Nos. C507, C512, C515, C519, C524, C529, C535, C539, C542, C548, C550, C559, C569, C572, C579, C582, C585, C588, C596, C598, C615, C622, C626, C634, C642, C647, C650, C656, C705, C711, C731, C791, C798, C808.

The following stamp was issued in sheets of 7 with 2 labels: No. C660.

World Chess Championships Type of 1980

Illustrations from The Book of Chess: 5g, The Game of the Virgins. 10g, Two gothic ladies. 30g, Chess game at apothecary shop.

No. C509, Christians and Jews preparing to play in garden. No. C510, Indian prince introducing chess to Persia.

1982, June 10 **Litho.** ***Perf. 14***

C506	A347	5g multicolored	7.00	2.25
C507	A347	10g multicolored	3.25	1.10
C508	A347	30g multicolored	1.60	.50
		Nos. C506-C508 (3)	11.85	3.85

Souvenir Sheets

Perf. 13½

C509 A347 25g multicolored 15.00 15.00

Perf. 14½

C510 A347 25g multicolored 21.00 20.00

No. C509 contains one 50x60mm stamp, No. C510 one 50x70mm stamp. For overprint see No. C665.

Italy, Winners of 1982 World Cup Soccer Championships AP168

Players: 5g, Klaus Fischer, Germany. 10g, Altobelli holding World Cup Trophy. 25g, Forster, Altobelli, horiz. 30g, Fischer, Gordillo.

1982, Oct. 20 ***Perf. 14***

C511	AP168	5g multicolored	7.75	1.60
C512	AP168	10g multicolored	2.25	.65
C513	AP168	30g multicolored	1.10	.35
		Nos. C511-C513 (3)	11.10	2.60

Souvenir Sheet

C513A AP168 25g multicolored 17.50 16.00

Christmas AP169

Paintings by Peter Paul Rubens: 5g, The Massacre of the Innocents. 10g, The Nativity, vert. 25g, The Madonna Adored by Four Penitents and Saints. 30g, The Flight to Egypt.

1982, Oct. 23

C514	AP169	5g multicolored	7.00	1.50
C515	AP169	10g multicolored	3.25	1.00
C516	AP169	30g multicolored	1.60	.35
		Nos. C514-C516 (3)	11.85	2.85

Souvenir Sheet

Perf. 14½

C517 AP169 25g multicolored 18.00 16.00

No. C517 contains one 50x70mm stamp.

The Sampling Officials of the Draper's Guild by Rembrandt AP170

Details from Rembrandt Paintings: 10g, Self portrait, vert. 25g, Night Watch, vert. 30g, Self portrait, diff., vert.

1983, Jan. 21 ***Perf. 14, 13 (10g)***

C518	AP170	5g multicolored	5.50	1.75
C519	AP170	10g multicolored	2.60	.80
C520	AP170	30g multicolored	1.50	.35
		Nos. C518-C520 (3)	9.60	2.90

Souvenir Sheet

Perf. 13½

C521 AP170 25g multicolored 15.00 15.00

No. C521 contains one 50x60mm stamp.

Souvenir Sheet

1982 World Cup Soccer Championships, Spain — AP171

1983, Jan. 21 ***Perf. 13½***
C522 AP171 25g Fuji blimp 20.00 18.00

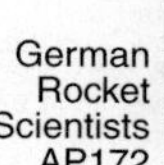

German Rocket Scientists AP172

Designs: 5g, Dr. Walter R. Dornberger, V2 rocket ascending. 10g, Nebel, Ritter, Oberth, Riedel, and Von Braun examining rocket mock-up. 30g, Dr. A. F. Staats, Cyrus B research rocket.

No. C526, Dr. Eugen Sanger, rocket design. No. C527, Fritz Von Opel, Opel-Sander rocket plane. No. C528, Friedrich Schmiedl, first rocket used for mail delivery.

1983 ***Perf. 14***

C523 AP172 5g multicolored 6.00 1.75
C524 AP172 10g multicolored 2.50 .85
C525 AP172 30g multicolored 1.20 .35
Nos. C523-C525 (3) 9.70 2.95

Souvenir Sheets

Perf. 14½

C526 AP172 25g multicolored 57.50 55.00
C527 AP172 25g multicolored 42.00 40.00
C528 AP172 25g multicolored 67.50 65.00

Issued: No. C528, Apr. 13; others, Jan. 24.

First Manned Flight, 200th Anniv. — AP173

Balloons: 5g, Montgolfier brothers, 1783. 10g, Baron von Lutgendorf's, 1786. 30g, Adorne's, 1784.

No. C532, Montgolfier brothers, diff. No. C533, Profiles of Montgolfier Brothers. No. C534, Bicentennial emblem, nova.

1983 ***Perf. 14, 13 (10g)***

C529 AP173 5g multicolored 4.75 2.90
C530 AP173 10g multicolored 3.00 1.50
C531 AP173 30g multicolored 1.90 .45
Nos. C529-C531 (3) 9.65 4.85

Souvenir Sheets

Perf. 13½

C532 AP173 25g multicolored 21.00 20.00
C533 AP173 25g multicolored 21.00 20.00
C534 AP173 25g multicolored 27.00 26.00

Nos. C532-C533 each contain one 50x60mm stamp, No. C534 one 30x40mm stamp.

Issued: #C529-C533, 2/25; #C534, 10/19.

1984 Summer Olympics, Los Angeles — AP174

1932 Gold medalists: 5g, Wilson Charles, US, 100-meter dash. 10g, Ellen Preis, Austria, fencing. 25g, Rudolf Ismayr, Germany, weight lifting. 30g, John Anderson, US, discus.

1983, June 13 ***Perf. 14***

C535 AP174 5g multicolored 1.75 .45
C536 AP174 10g multicolored 2.75 .60
C537 AP174 30g multicolored 7.25 .80
Nos. C535-C537 (3) 11.75 1.85

Souvenir Sheet

Perf. 14½

C538 AP174 25g Sheet of 1 + label 25.00 22.50

No. C535 incorrectly credits Charles with gold medal.

Flowers — AP175

1983, Aug. 31 ***Perf. 14***

C539 AP175 5g Episcia reptans 4.25 .85
C540 AP175 10g Lilium 2.10 .55
C541 AP175 30g Heliconia 4.25 .55
Nos. C539-C541 (3) 10.60 1.95

Intl. Maritime Organization, 25th Anniv. — AP176

5g, Brigantine Undine. 10g, Training ship Sofia, 1881, horiz. 30g, Training ship Stein, 1879.

No. C545, Santa Maria. No. C546, Santa Maria and Telstar communications satellite.

Perf. 14, 13½x13 (10g)

1983, Oct. 24 **Litho.**

C542 AP176 5g multicolored 4.25 .75
C543 AP176 10g multicolored 2.25 .55
C544 AP176 30g multicolored 2.60 .35
Nos. C542-C544 (3) 9.10 1.65

Souvenir Sheets

Perf. 14½

C545 AP176 25g multicolored 21.00 15.00

Perf. 13½

C546 AP176 25g multicolored 21.00 15.00

No. C546 contains one 90x57mm stamp. Discovery of America, 490th Anniv. (in 1982) (#C545-C546). For overprint see No. 2198.

Space Achievements — AP177

Designs: 5g, Space shuttle Challenger. 10g, Pioneer 10, vert. 30g, Herschel's telescope, Cerro Tololo Obervatory, Chile, vert.

1984, Jan. 9 ***Perf. 14***

C547 AP177 5g multicolored 3.50 .90
C548 AP177 10g multicolored 3.50 .90
C549 AP177 30g multicolored 1.25 .35
Nos. C547-C549 (3) 8.25 2.15

Summer Olympics, Los Angeles — AP178

5g, 400-meter hurdles. 10g, Small bore rifle, horiz. 25g, Equestrian, Christine Stuckleberger. 30g, 100-meter dash.

1984, Jan. ***Perf. 14***

C550 AP178 5g multicolored 4.75 .80
C551 AP178 10g multicolored 4.75 .55
C552 AP178 30g multicolored 2.10 .25
Nos. C550-C552 (3) 11.60 1.60

Souvenir Sheet

Perf. 14½

C553 AP178 25g multicolored 35.00 30.00

For overprint see No. 2130.

1984 Winter Olympics, Sarajevo AP179

No. C554, Steve Podborski, downhill. No. C555, Olympic Flag. No. C556, Gaetan Boucher, speed skating.

Perf. 14, 13x13½ (10g)

1984, Mar. 24

C554 AP179 5g multicolored 5.00 3.00
C555 AP179 10g multicolored 3.25 2.25
C556 AP179 30g multicolored 4.00 .75
Nos. C554-C556 (3) 12.25 6.00

No. C555 printed se-tenant with label.

Souvenir Sheets

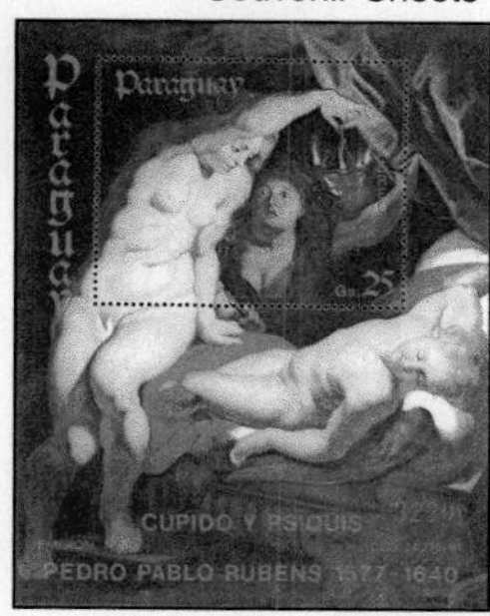

Cupid and Psyche by Peter Paul Rubens AP180

Design: No. C558, Satyr and Maenad (copy of Rubens' Bacchanal) by Jean-Antoine Watteau (1684-1721).

1984, Mar. 26 ***Perf. 13½***

C557 AP180 25g multicolored 18.00 16.00
C558 AP180 25g multicolored 27.50 25.00

No. C558 contains one 78x57mm stamp.

1982, 1986 World Cup Soccer Championships, Spain, Mexico City — AP181

Soccer players: 5g, Tardelli, Breitner. 10g, Zamora, Stielke. 30g, Walter Schachner, player on ground.

No. C562, Player from Paraguay. No. C563, World Cup Trophy, Spanish, Mexican characters, horiz.

1984, Mar. 29 ***Perf. 14, 13 (10g)***

C559 AP181 5g multicolored 4.75 2.75
C560 AP181 10g multicolored 3.00 2.75
C561 AP181 30g multicolored 3.00 .50
Nos. C559-C561 (3) 10.75 6.00

Souvenir Sheets

Perf. 14½

C562 AP181 25g multicolored 20.00 18.00
C563 AP181 25g multicolored 20.00 18.00

Souvenir Sheet

ESPANA '84 AP182

1984, Mar. 31

C564 AP182 25g multicolored 32.50 27.50

No. C564 has one stamp and a label.

Souvenir Sheets

ESPANA '84 AP183

No. C565, Holy Family of the Lamb by Raphael. No. C566, Adoration of the Magi by Rubens.

1984, Apr. 16 ***Perf. 13½***

C565 AP183 25g multicolored 25.00 20.00
C566 AP183 25g multicolored 21.00 18.00

Souvenir Sheet

19th UPU Congress — AP184

1984, June 9

C567 AP184 25g multicolored 15.00 12.00

Intl. Chess Federation, 60th Anniv. — AP185

10g, Woman holding chess piece. 30g, Bishop, knight.

Perf. 14, 13x13½ (10g)

1984, June 18

C568 AP185 5g shown 4.00 1.20
C569 AP185 10g multicolored 3.25 .80
C570 AP185 30g multicolored 2.50 .25
Nos. C568-C570 (3) 9.75 2.25

First Europe to South America Airmail Flight by Lufthansa, 50th Anniv. AP186

Designs: 5g, Lockheed Superconstellation. 10g, Dornier Wal. 30g, Boeing 707.

Perf. 14, 13½x13 (10g)

1984, June 22

C571	AP186	5g multicolored	4.50	.75
C572	AP186	10g multicolored	1.50	.30
C573	AP186	30g multicolored	1.75	.25
		Nos. C571-C573 (3)	7.75	1.30

For overprint see No. C592.

Souvenir Sheets

First Moon Landing, 15th Anniv. AP187

No. C574, Apollo 11 lunar module. No. C575, Prof. Hermann Oberth.

1984, June 23 ***Perf. 14½***

C574	AP187	25g multicolored	47.00	35.00
C575	AP187	25g multicolored	47.00	35.00

Hermann Oberth, 90th Birthday (#C575).

Souvenir Sheet

The Holy Family with John the Baptist AP188

Photo. & Engr.

1984, Aug. 3 ***Perf. 14***

C576	AP188	20g multicolored	67.50	55.00

Raphael, 500th birth anniv. (in 1983).

No. 2099 Overprinted ANIVERSARIO GOBIERNO CONSTRUCTIVO Y DE LA PAZ DEL PRESIDENTE CONSTITUCIONAL GRAL. DE EJERCITO ALFREDO STROESSNER 15 / 8 / 1964 in Red

1984, Aug. 15 **Litho.** ***Perf. 13***

C577	A374	100g on No. 2099	3.50	3.25

1984 Winter Olympics, Sarajevo AP189

Gold medalists: 5g, Max Julen, giant slalom, Switzerland. 10g, Hans Stanggassinger, Franz Wembacher, luge, West Germany. 30g, Peter Angerer, biathlon, Germany.

Perf. 14, 13½x13 (10g)

1984, Sept. 12 **Litho.**

C578	AP189	5g multicolored	5.00	1.50
C579	AP189	10g multicolored	6.50	2.25
C580	AP189	30g multicolored	2.60	1.25
		Nos. C578-C580 (3)	14.10	5.00

For overprint see No. C596.

Motorcycles, Cent. AP190

5g, Reitwagen, Daimler-Maybach, 1885. 10g, BMW, 1980. 30g, Opel, 1930.

1984, Nov. 9 ***Perf. 14, 13½x13 (10g)***

C581	AP190	5g multicolored	4.25	1.90
C582	AP190	10g multicolored	3.25	2.25
C583	AP190	30g multicolored	1.75	.85
		Nos. C581-C583 (3)	9.25	5.00

Christmas AP191

10g, Girl playing guitar. 30g, Girl, candle, basket.

1985, Jan. 18 ***Perf. 13***

C584	AP191	5g shown	2.90	1.10
C585	AP191	10g multicolored	1.60	.75
C586	AP191	30g multicolored	1.25	.65
		Nos. C584-C586 (3)	5.75	2.50

1986 World Cup Soccer Championships, Mexico — AP192

Various soccer players.

1985, Jan. 21 ***Perf. 13x13½, 13½x13***

Color of Shirt

C587	AP192	5g red & white	2.90	1.60
C588	AP192	10g white & black, horiz.	1.90	.80
C589	AP192	30g blue	1.90	.50
		Nos. C587-C589 (3)	6.70	2.90

No. C484 Ovptd. in Silver

No. C590, INTERPEX / 1985. No. C591, STAMPEX / 1985.

1985, Feb. 6 ***Perf. 14***

C590	AP161	10g multicolored	2.25	1.00
C591	AP161	10g multicolored	2.25	1.00

No. C572 Ovptd. in Vermilion

1985, Feb. 16 ***Perf. 13½x13***

C592	AP186	10g on No. C572	4.25	1.50

No. 2053A Ovptd. "FINAL / ALEMANIA 1 : 3 ITALIA"

1985, Mar. 7 ***Perf. 14½***

C593	A362	25g multicolored	21.00	21.00

Souvenir Sheets

Rotary Intl., 80th Anniv. AP193

Designs: No. C594, Paul Harris, founder of Rotary Intl. No. C595, Rotary Intl. Headquarters, Evanston, IL, horiz.

1985, Mar. 11

C594	AP193	25g multicolored	57.50	50.00
C595	AP193	25g multicolored	57.50	50.00

No. C579 Ovptd. "OLYMPHILEX 85" in Black and Olympic Rings in Silver

1985, Mar. 18 ***Perf. 13½x13***

C596	AP189	10g on No. C579	4.25	2.00

Music Year — AP194

Designs: 5g, Agustin Barrios (1885-1944), musician, vert. 10g, Johann Sebastian Bach, composer, score. 30g, Folk musicians.

Perf. 14, 13½x13 (10g)

1985, Apr. 16

C597	AP194	5g multicolored	4.00	1.25
C598	AP194	10g multicolored	2.25	1.20
C599	AP194	30g multicolored	2.50	1.00
		Nos. C597-C599 (3)	8.75	3.45

1st Paraguayan Locomotive, 1861 AP195

Transrapid 06, Germany — AP195a

30g, TGV, France.

1985, Apr. 20 ***Perf. 14***

C600	AP195	5g shown	10.00	3.50
a.		Horiz. Pair	40.00	*40.00*
C601	AP195a	10g multi	2.75	.75
C602	AP195a	30g multi	2.75	.75
		Nos. C600-C602 (3)	15.50	5.00

Souvenir Sheet

Visit of Pope John Paul II to South America AP196

1985, Apr. 22 **Litho.** ***Perf. 13½***

C603	AP196	25g silver & multi	21.00	21.00

No. C603 also exists with gold inscriptions.

Inter-American Development Bank, 25th Anniv. — AP197

1985, Apr. 25 **Litho.** **Wmk. 347**

C604	AP197	3g dl red brn, org & yel	1.25	1.00
C605	AP197	5g vio, org & yel	1.25	1.00
C606	AP197	10g rose vio, org & yel	1.25	1.00
C607	AP197	50g sep, org & yel	1.25	1.00
C608	AP197	65g bl, org & yel	1.25	1.00
C609	AP197	95g pale bl grn, org & yel	1.25	1.00
		Nos. C604-C609 (6)	7.50	6.00

No. 1875 Ovptd. in Black

1985, May 24 **Unwmk.** ***Perf. 13½***

C610	A326	25g on No. 1875	12.00	12.00

No. C485 Ovptd. in Dark Blue with Emblem and: "Expo '85/TSUKUBA"

1985, July 5 ***Perf. 14***

C611	AP161	30g on No. C485	4.25	2.25

No. 2149 Overprinted in Dark Blue

1985, Aug. 5 ***Perf. 14½***

C612	A388	25g on No. 2149	18.00	18.00

Jean-Henri Dunant, Founder of Red Cross, 75th Death Anniv. AP198

Dunant and: 5g, Enclosed ambulance. 10g, Nobel Peace Prize, Red Cross emblem. 30g, Open ambulance with passengers.

1985, Aug. 6 ***Perf. 13***

C614	AP198	5g multicolored	9.00	2.25
C615	AP198	10g multicolored	8.50	2.25
C616	AP198	30g multicolored	3.50	1.00
		Nos. C614-C616 (3)	21.00	5.50

World Chess Congress, Austria AP199

5g, The Turk, copper engraving, Book of Chess by Racknitz, 1789. 10g, King seated, playing chess, Book of Chess, 14th cent. 25g, Margrave Otto von Brandenburg playing chess with his wife, Great Manuscript of Heidelberg Songs, 13th cent. 30g, Three men playing chess, Book of Chess, 14th cent.

1985, Aug. 9 **Litho.** ***Perf. 13***

C617	AP199	5g multicolored	8.00	3.75
C618	AP199	10g multicolored	1.90	.85
C619	AP199	30g multicolored	1.90	.85
		Nos. C617-C619 (3)	11.80	5.45

Souvenir Sheet

Perf. 13½

C620	AP199	25g multicolored	30.00	30.00

No. C620 contains one 60x50mm stamp.

Discovery of America 500th Anniv. — AP200

Explorers, ships: 5g, Marco Polo and ship. 10g, Vicente Yanez Pinzon, Nina, horiz. 25g, Christopher Columbus, Santa Maria. 30g, James Cook, Endeavor.

Perf. 14, 13½x13 (10g)

1985, Oct. 19 **Litho.**

C621 AP200 5g multicolored 5.00 1.20
C622 AP200 10g multicolored 1.75 .90
C623 AP200 30g multicolored 2.50 .90
Nos. C621-C623 (3) 9.25 3.00

Souvenir Sheet

Perf. 14½

C624 AP200 25g multicolored 26.00 26.00

Year of Cook's death is incorrect on No. C623. For overprint see No. C756.

ITALIA '85 — AP201

Nudes (details): 5g, La Fortuna, by Guido Reni, vert. 10g, The Triumph of Galatea, by Raphael. 30g, Sleeping Venus, by Il Giorgione.
25g, The Birth of Venus, by Botticelli, vert.

1985, Dec. 3 ***Perf. 14***

C625 AP201 5g multicolored 6.25 1.75
C626 AP201 10g multicolored 2.75 .60
C627 AP201 30g multicolored 2.40 .50
Nos. C625-C627 (3) 11.40 2.85

Souvenir Sheet

Perf. 13½

C628 AP201 25g multicolored 47.00 47.00

No. C628 contains one 49x60mm stamp.

Souvenir Sheet

Maimonides, Philosopher, 850th Birth Anniv. — AP202

1985, Dec. 31 ***Perf. 13½***

C629 AP202 25g multicolored 37.00 37.00

UN, 40th Anniv. — AP203

1986, Feb. 27 **Wmk. 392**

C630 AP203 5g bl & sepia 1.25 1.25
C631 AP203 10g bl & gray 1.25 1.25
C632 AP203 50g bl & grysh brn 1.25 1.25
Nos. C630-C632 (3) 3.75 3.75

For overprint see No. C726.

AMERIPEX '86 — AP204

Discovery of America 500th anniv. emblem and: 5g, Spain #424. 10g, US #233. 25g, Spain #426, horiz. 30g, Spain #421.

Perf. 14, 13½x13 (10g)

1986, Mar. 19 **Unwmk.**

C633 AP204 5g multicolored 8.00 2.90
C634 AP204 10g multicolored 3.25 1.10
C635 AP204 30g multicolored 2.90 1.00
Nos. C633-C635 (3) 14.15 5.00

Souvenir Sheet

Perf. 13½

C636 AP204 25g multicolored 20.00 *20.00*

No. C636 contains one 60x40mm stamp. For overprint see No. C755.

Souvenir Sheet

1984 Olympic Gold Medalist, Dr. Reiner Klimke on Ahlerich AP205

1986, Mar. 20 ***Perf. 14½***

C637 AP205 25g multicolored 27.00 27.00

Tennis Players — AP206

Designs: 5g, Martina Navratilova, US. 10g, Boris Becker, W. Germany. 30g, Victor Pecci, Paraguay.

1986, Mar. 26 ***Perf. 14, 13 (10g)***

C638 AP206 5g multicolored 8.00 2.00
C639 AP206 10g multicolored 4.00 1.00
C640 AP206 30g multicolored 1.00 .50
Nos. C638-C640 (3) 13.00 3.50

Nos. C638-C640 exist with red inscriptions, perf. 13. Same Values. For overprints see Nos. C672-C673.

Halley's Comet AP207

5g, Bayeux Tapestry, c. 1066, showing comet. 10g, Edmond Halley, comet. 25g, Comet, Giotto probe. 30g, Rocket lifting off, Giotto probe, vert.

Perf. 14, 13½x13 (10g)

1986, Apr. 30

C641 AP207 5g multicolored 6.00 2.00
C642 AP207 10g multicolored 3.75 1.10
C643 AP207 30g multicolored 2.75 .65
Nos. C641-C643 (3) 12.50 3.75

Souvenir Sheet

Perf. 14½

C644 AP207 25g multicolored 30.00 30.00

Souvenir Sheet

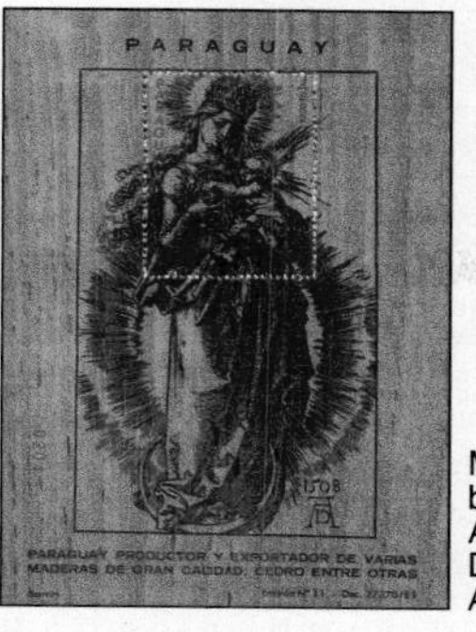

Madonna by Albrecht Durer AP208

1986, June 4 **Typo.** ***Rough Perf. 11***

Self-Adhesive

C645 AP208 25g black & red 32.00 30.00

No. C645 was printed on cedar.

Locomotives AP209

5g, #3038. 10g, Canadian Pacific A1E, 1887. 30g, 1D1 #483, 1925.

1986, June 23 **Litho.** ***Perf. 13***

C646 AP209 5g multi 3.25 1.00
C647 AP209 10g multi 2.25 1.00
C648 AP209 30g multi 3.25 1.00
Nos. C646-C648 (3) 8.75 3.00

1986 World Cup Soccer Championships — AP210

Paraguay vs.: 5g, Colombia. 10g, Chile. 30g, Chile, diff.
25g, Paraguay Natl. team.

Perf. 13, 13½x13 (10g)

1986, June 24

C649 AP210 5g multicolored 3.50 1.00
C650 AP210 10g multicolored 2.25 1.00
C651 AP210 30g multicolored 3.75 .90
Nos. C649-C651 (3) 9.50 2.90

Souvenir Sheet

Perf. 14½

C652 AP210 25g multicolored 15.00 15.00

No. C652 contains one 81x75mm stamp. For overprints see Nos. C693-C695.

No. 1289 Ovptd. in Silver on Dark Blue with Mercury Capsule and "MERCURY / 5-V-1961 / 25 Anos Primer / Astronauta / Americano / Alan B. Shepard / 1986"

1986, July 11 ***Perf. 13½***

C653 A226 23.40g on No. 1289 25.00 25.00

Souvenir Sheet

Trajectory Diagram of Halley's Comet, Giotto Probe — AP211

1986, July 28

C654 AP211 25g multicolored 30.00 30.00

German Railroads, 150th Anniv. AP212

5g, VT 10 501DB, 1954. 10g, 1st Electric, 1879. 30g, Hydraulic diesel, class 218.
25g, Christening of the 1st German Train, 1835, by E. Schilling & B. Goldschmitt.

1986, Sept. 1 ***Perf. 13½x13***

C655 AP212 5g multicolored 5.75 1.50
C656 AP212 10g multicolored 2.25 .50
C657 AP212 30g multicolored 2.75 2.00
Nos. C655-C657 (3) 10.75 4.00

Souvenir Sheet

Perf. 13½

C658 AP212 25g multicolored 20.00 20.00

No. C658 contains one 54x75mm stamp.

Intl. Peace Year — AP213

Details from The Consequences of War by Rubens: 5g, Two women. 10g, Woman nursing child. 30g, Two men.

1986, Oct. 27 ***Perf. 13***

C659 AP213 5g multicolored 7.50 1.90
C660 AP213 10g multicolored 4.00 2.75
C661 AP213 30g multicolored 2.25 .40
Nos. C659-C661 (3) 13.75 5.05

Japanese Emigrants in Paraguay, 50th Anniv. AP214

5g, La Colemna Vineyard. 10g, Cherry, lapacho flowers. 20g, Integration monument, vert.

1986, Nov. 6 ***Perf. 13½x13, 13x13½***

C662 AP214 5g multicolored 2.25 2.25
C663 AP214 10g multicolored 2.25 2.25
C664 AP214 20g multicolored 2.25 2.25
Nos. C662-C664 (3) 6.75 6.75

No. C507 Ovptd. in Silver "XXVII-DUBAI / Olimpiada de / Ajedrez - 1986"

1986, Dec. 30 **Unwmk.** ***Perf. 14***

C665 A347 10g on No. C507 6.75 3.50

1986 World Cup Soccer Championships, Mexico — AP214a

Match scenes — 5g, England vs. Paraguay. 10g, Larios catching ball. 20g, Trejo, Ferreira. 25g, Torales, Flores, Romero. 30g, Mendoza. 100g, Romero.

1987, Feb. 19 ***Perf. 14***

C666 AP214a 5g multicolored .95 .30
C667 AP214a 10g multicolored 7.00 1.75
C668 AP214a 20g multicolored 2.00 .50

Perf. 13½x13

C669 AP214a 25g multicolored 1.90 1.50
C670 AP214a 30g multicolored 2.40 1.75
Nos. C666-C670 (5) 14.25 5.80

Souvenir Sheet

Perf. 14½

C671 AP214a 100g multi 15.00 13.00

Nos. C669-C670 are horiz. No. C671 contains one 40x50mm stamp.

Nos. C639-C640 Ovptd. in Silver including Olympic Rings and "NUEVAMENTE EL / TENIS EN LAS / OLYMPIADAS 1988 / SEOUL / COREA"

1987, Apr. 15 *Perf. 13*

C672	AP206 10g on No. C639		*4.75*	*3.00*
C673	AP206 30g on No. C640		*4.75*	*3.00*

Automobiles AP215

5g, Mercedes 300 SEL 6.3. 10g, Jaguar Mk II 3.8. 20g, BMW 635 CSI. 25g, Alfa Romeo GTA. 30g, BMW 1800 Tisa.

1987, May 29 **Litho.** *Perf. 13½*

C674	AP215	5g multicolored	.80	.35
C675	AP215	10g multicolored	6.00	1.75
C676	AP215	20g multicolored	1.50	.50
C677	AP215	25g multicolored	2.00	1.75
C678	AP215	30g multicolored	2.00	1.75
	Nos. C674-C678 (5)		12.30	6.10

1988 Winter Olympics, Calgary AP216

Gold medalists or Olympic competitors: 5g, Michela Figini, Switzerland, downhill, 1984, vert. 10g, Hanni Wenzel, Liechtenstein, slalom and giant slalom, 1980. 20g, 4-Man bobsled, Switzerland, 1956, 1972. 25g, Markus Wasmeier, downhill. 30g, Ingemar Stenmark, Sweden, slalom and giant slalom, 1980. 100g, Pirmin Zurbriggen, Switzerland, vert. (downhill, 1988).

1987, Sept. 10 *Perf. 14*

C679	AP216	5g multicolored	1.10	.35
C680	AP216	10g multicolored	6.75	1.60
C681	AP216	20g multicolored	2.25	.50

Perf. 13½x13

C682	AP216	25g multicolored	2.10	1.25
C683	AP216	30g multicolored	2.50	1.60
	Nos. C679-C683 (5)		14.70	5.30

Souvenir Sheet

Perf. 13½

C684	AP216	100g multicolored	20.00	20.00

No. C684 contains one 45x57mm stamp.

Nos. 2211 and C467 Ovptd. in Red on Silver "11.IX.1887 - 1987 / Centenario de la fundacion de / la A.N.R. (Partido Colarado) / Bernardino Caballero Fundador / General de Ejercito / D. Alfredo Stroessner Continuador"

1987, Sept. 11 *Perf. 13, 14*

C685	A401	200g on No. 2211	.70	.70
C686	AP148	1000g on No. C467	3.75	3.75
	Nos. C685-C686 (2)		4.45	4.45

1988 Summer Olympics, Seoul AP217

Medalists and competitors: 5g, Sabine Everts, West Germany, javelin. 10g, Carl Lewis, US, 100 and 200-meter run, 1984. 20g, Darrell Pace, US, archery, 1976, 1984. 25g, Juergen Hingsen, West Germany, decathlon, 1984. 30g, Claudia Losch, West Germany, shot put, 1984. 100g, Fredy Schmidtke, West Germany, cycling, 1984.

1987, Sept. 22 *Perf. 14*

C687	AP217	5g multi	1.00	.40
C688	AP217	10g multi, vert.	4.00	.60
C689	AP217	20g multi	2.40	.50

Perf. 13½x13

C690	AP217	25g multi, vert.	2.25	2.25
C691	AP217	30g multi, vert.	2.25	2.25
	Nos. C687-C691 (5)		11.90	6.00

Souvenir Sheet

Perf. 14½

C692	AP217	100g multi, vert.	22.50	22.50

Nos. C650-C652 Ovptd. in Violet or Blue (#C694) with Soccer Ball and "ZURICH 10.VI.87 / Lanzamiento ITALIA '90 / Italia 3 - Argentina 1"

Perf. 13½x13, 13

1987, Oct. 19 **Litho.**

C693	AP210	10g on No. C650	3.00	3.00
C694	AP210	30g on No. C651	4.00	4.00
	Nos. C693-C694 (2)		7.00	7.00

Souvenir Sheet

Perf. 14½

C695	AP210	25g on No. C652	21.00	21.00

Paintings by Rubens — AP218

Details from: 5g, The Virtuous Hero Crowned. 10g, The Brazen Serpent, 1635. 20g, Judith with the Head of Holofernes, 1617. 25g, Assembly of the Gods of Olympus. 30g, Venus, Cupid, Bacchus and Ceres.

1987, Dec. 14 *Perf. 13*

C696	AP218	5g multicolored	1.25	.35
C697	AP218	10g multicolored	7.00	2.10
C698	AP218	20g multicolored	2.25	.50

Perf. 13x13½

C699	AP218	25g multicolored	1.75	1.40
C700	AP218	30g multicolored	2.00	1.60
	Nos. C696-C700 (5)		14.25	5.95

Christmas AP219

Details from paintings: 5g, Virgin and Child with St. Joseph and St. John the Baptist, anonymous. 10g, Madonna and Child under the Veil with St. Joseph and St. John, by Marco da Siena. 20g, Sacred Conversation with the Donors, by Titian. 25g, The Brotherhood of the Rosary, by Durer. 30g, Madonna with Standing Child, by Rubens. 100g, Madonna and Child, engraving by Albrecht Durer.

1987 **Litho.** *Perf. 14*

C701	AP219	5g multicolored	.65	.35
C702	AP219	10g multicolored	2.25	.75
C703	AP219	20g multicolored	1.25	.35
C704	AP219	25g multicolored	1.90	.55

Perf. 13x13½

C705	AP219	30g multicolored	3.25	2.75
	Nos. C701-C705 (5)		9.30	4.75

Souvenir Sheet

Perf. 14½

C706	AP219	100g multi	32.00	30.00

Issued: #C701-C705, 12/16; #C706, 12/17.

Austrian Railways, Sesquicentennial — AP220

Locomotives: 5g, Steam #3669, 1899. 10g, Steam #GZ 44074. 20g, Steam, diff. 25g, Diesel-electric. 30g, Austria No. 1067. 100g, Steam, vert.

1988, Jan. 2 *Perf. 14*

C707	AP220	5g multicolored	1.10	.35
C708	AP220	10g multicolored	4.90	1.10
C709	AP220	20g multicolored	1.50	.40
C710	AP220	25g multicolored	2.60	.50

Perf. 13½x13

C711	AP220	30g multicolored	4.00	2.75
	Nos. C707-C711 (5)		14.10	5.10

Souvenir Sheet

Perf. 13½

C712	AP220	100g multicolored	32.00	30.00

No. C712 contains one 50x60mm stamp.

Souvenir Sheet

Christmas — AP221

1988, Jan. 4 *Perf. 13½*

C713	AP221	100g Madonna, by Rubens	26.00	25.00

Souvenir Sheet

1988 Summer Olympics, Seoul — AP222

1988, Jan. 18 *Perf. 14½*

C714	AP222	100g gold & multi	18.00	17.00

Exists with silver lettering and frame. Same value.

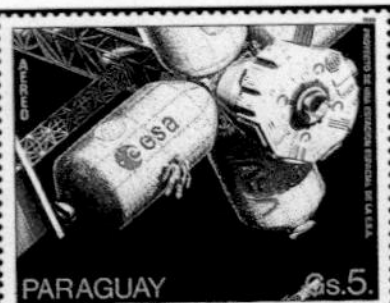

Colonization of Space AP223

5g, NASA-ESA space station. 10g, Europspace module Columbus docked at space station. 20g, NASA space sation. 25g, Ring section of space station, vert. 30g, Space station living quarters in central core, vert.

1988, Mar. 9 **Litho.** *Perf. 13½x13*

C715	AP223	5g multicolored	1.25	.35
C716	AP223	10g multicolored	6.00	1.10
C717	AP223	20g multicolored	2.25	.45

Perf. 13x13½

C718	AP223	25g multicolored	3.25	1.00
C719	AP223	30g multicolored	5.25	3.50
	Nos. C715-C719 (5)		18.00	6.40

Souvenir Sheet

Berlin, 750th Anniv. AP224

1988, Mar. 10 **Litho.** *Perf. 14½*

C720	AP224	100g multicolored	25.00	25.00

LUPOSTA '87.

Souvenir Sheet

Apollo 15 Launch, 1971 AP225

1988, Apr. 12

C721	AP225	100g multicolored	25.00	25.00

No. 2210 Ovptd. in Metallic Red

1988, Apr. 28 *Perf. 13*

C722	A401	100g on No. 2210	3.50	3.00

Caacupe Basilica and Pope John Paul II — AP226

Perf. 13½x13

1988, May 5 **Litho.** **Wmk. 347**

C723	AP226	100g multi	2.25	2.25
C724	AP226	120g multi	2.25	2.25
C725	AP226	150g multi	2.25	2.25
	Nos. C723-C725 (3)		6.75	6.75

Visit of Pope John Paul II.

No. C631 Overprinted

Perf. 13x13½

1988, June 15 **Wmk. 392**
C726 AP203 10g blue & gray 5.25 2.00

Paraguay Philatelic Center, 75th Anniv.

Berlin, 750th Anniv. Paintings Type of 1988

5g, Venus and Cupid, 1742, by Francois Boucher. 10g, Perseus Liberates Andromeda, 1662, by Rubens. 20g, Venus and the Organist by Titian. 25g, Leda and the Swan by Correggio. 30g, St. Cecilia by Rubens.

1988, June 15 **Unwmk.** ***Perf. 13***
C727 A409 5g multi, horiz. *.50* *.35*
C728 A409 10g multi, horiz. *1.10* *.50*
C729 A409 20g multi, horiz. *1.50* *.75*
C730 A409 25g multi, horiz. *2.25* *1.00*

Perf. 13x13½
C731 A409 30g multicolored *3.50* *3.50*
Nos. C727-C731 (5) 8.85 6.10

Founding of "New Germany" and 1st Cultivation of Herbal Tea, Cent. — AP227

90g, Cauldron, vert. 105g, Farm workers carrying crop.

Perf. 13x13½, 13½x13

1988, June 18 **Litho.** **Wmk. 347**
C732 AP227 90g multi 3.25 2.50
C733 AP227 105g multi 3.25 2.50
C734 AP227 120g like 105g 3.25 2.50
Nos. C732-C734 (3) 9.75 7.50

1990 World Cup Soccer Championships, Italy — AP228

5g, Machine slogan cancel from Montevideo, May 21, 1930. 10g, Italy #324, vert. 20g, France #349. 25g, Brazil #696, vert. 30g, Paraguayan commemorative cancel for ITALIA 1990.

1988, Aug. 1 **Unwmk.** ***Perf. 13***
C735 AP228 5g multicolored 1.75 .35
C736 AP228 10g multicolored 5.25 1.20
C737 AP228 20g multicolored 2.10 .65
C738 AP228 25g multicolored 2.75 1.25

Perf. 13½x13
C739 AP228 30g multicolored 3.25 1.60
Nos. C735-C739 (5) 15.10 5.05

For overprint see No. 2284.

Souvenir Sheet

Count Ferdinand von Zeppelin, Airship Designer, Birth Sesquicentennial — AP229

1988, Aug. 3 ***Perf. 14½***
C740 AP229 100g multicolored 26.00 24.00

Government Palace and Pres. Stroessner AP230

Wmk. 347

1988, Aug. 5 **Litho.** ***Perf. 13½***
C741 AP230 200g multi 1.10 .55
C742 AP230 500g multi 2.50 1.50
C743 AP230 1000g multi 4.50 3.00
Nos. C741-C743 (3) 8.10 5.05

Pres. Stroessner's new term in office, 1988-1993. Size of letters in watermark on 200g, 1000g: 5mm. On 500g, 10mm.

1988 Winter Olympics, Calgary AP231

Gold medalists: 5g, Hubert Strolz, Austria, Alpine combined. 10g, Alberto Tomba, Italy, giant slalom and slalom. 20g, Franck Piccard, France, super giant slalom. 25g, Thomas Muller, Hans-Peter Pohl and Hubert Schwarz, Federal Republic of Germany, Nordic combined team, vert. 30g, Vreni Schneider, Switzerland, giant slalom and slalom, vert. 100g, Marina Kiehl, Federal Republic of Germany, downhill, vert.

Perf. 13½x13

1988, Sept. 2 **Unwmk.**
C744 AP231 5g multicolored 1.20 .35
C745 AP231 10g multicolored 3.50 1.20
C746 AP231 20g multicolored 2.25 .65

Perf. 13x13½
C747 AP231 25g multicolored 2.00 1.30
C748 AP231 30g multicolored 2.25 1.50
Nos. C744-C748 (5) 11.20 5.00

Souvenir Sheet

Perf. 14½
C749 AP231 100g multicolored 21.00 19.00

1990 World Cup Soccer Championships, Italy — AP232

Designs: 5g, Mexico #C350. 10g, Germany #1146. 20g, Argentina #1147, vert. 25g, Spain #2211. 30g, Italy #1742.

1988, Oct. 4 ***Perf. 13***
C750 AP232 5g multicolored .85 .35
C751 AP232 10g multicolored 3.75 1.40
C752 AP232 20g multicolored 1.40 .50
C753 AP232 25g multicolored 2.10 .95

Perf. 14
C754 AP232 30g multicolored 2.40 1.90
Nos. C750-C754 (5) 10.50 5.10

For overprint see No. 2285.

No. C635 Ovptd. in Metallic Red

1988, Nov. 25 ***Perf. 14***
C755 AP204 30g on No. C635 4.25 4.00

No. C623 Ovptd. in Gold

1988, Nov. 25 ***Perf. 14***
C756 AP200 30g on No. C623 4.75 3.50

1988 Summer Olympics, Seoul AP233

Gold medalists: No. C757, Nicole Uphoff, individual dressage. No. C758, Anja Fichtel, Sabine Bau, Zita Funkenhauser, Anette Kluge and Christine Weber, team foil. No. C759, Silvia Sperber, smallbore standard rifle. No. C760, Mathias Baumann, Claus Erhorn, Thies Kaspareit and Ralph Ehrenbrink, equestrian team 3-day event. No. C761, Anja Fichtel, individual foil, vert. No. C762, Franke Sloothaak, Ludger Beerbaum, Wolfgang Brinkmann and Dirk Hafemeister, equestrian team jumping. No. C763, Arnd Schmitt, individual epee, vert. No. C764, Jose Luis Doreste, Finn class yachting. No. C765, Steffi Graf, tennis. No. C766, Michael Gross, 200-meter butterfly, vert. No. C767, West Germany, coxed eights. No. C768, Nicole Uphoff, Monica Theodorescu, Ann Kathrin Linsenhoff and Reiner Klimke, team dressage.

1989 ***Perf. 13***
C757 AP233 5g multicolored .95 .35
C758 AP233 5g multicolored .95 .35
C759 AP233 10g multicolored 4.50 .35
C760 AP233 10g multicolored 4.50 .35
C761 AP233 20g multicolored 1.60 .60
C762 AP233 20g multicolored 1.60 .40
C763 AP233 25g multicolored 2.50 .75
C764 AP233 25g multicolored 2.50 1.75

Perf. 13½x13
C765 AP233 30g multicolored 4.50 4.50
C766 AP233 30g multicolored 4.50 4.50
Nos. C757-C766 (10) 28.10 13.90

Souvenir Sheets

Perf. 14½
C767 AP233 100g multicolored 20.00 18.00
C768 AP233 100g multicolored 20.00 18.00

Nos. C767-C768 each contain one 80x50mm stamp.

Issue dates: Nos. C757, C759, C761, C763, C765, and C767, Mar. 3. Others, Mar. 20.

For overprints see Nos. 2292, 2359.

Souvenir Sheet

Intl. Red Cross, 125th Anniv. (in 1988) AP234

1989, Apr. 17 **Litho.** ***Perf. 13½***
C769 AP234 100g #803 in changed colors 18.00 16.00

No. C769 has perforated label picturing Nobel medal.

Olympics Type of 1989

1988 Winter Olympic medalists or competitors: 5g, Pirmin Zurbriggen, Peter Mueller, Switzerland, and Franck Piccard, France, Alpine skiing. 10g, Sigrid Wolf, Austria, super giant slalom, vert. 20g, Czechoslovakia vs. West Germany, hockey, vert. 25g, Piccard, skiing, vert. 30g, Piccard, wearing medal, vert.

1989, Apr. 17 ***Perf. 13½x13***
C770 AP233 5g multicolored 1.10 .35

Perf. 13x13½
C771 AP233 10g multicolored 2.25 .80
C772 AP233 20g multicolored 1.75 .55
C773 AP233 25g multicolored 2.00 .70
C774 AP233 30g multicolored 3.75 3.75
Nos. C770-C774 (5) 10.85 6.15

Souvenir Sheet

1990 World Cup Soccer Championships, Italy — AP235

1989, Apr. 21 ***Perf. 14½***
C775 AP235 100g Sheet of 1 + label 19.00 17.00

1st Moon Landing, 20th Anniv. AP236

Designs: 5g, Wernher von Braun, Apollo 11 launch, vert. 10g, Michael Collins, lunar module on moon. 20g, Neil Armstrong, astronaut on lunar module ladder, vert. 25g, Buzz Aldrin, solar wind experiment, vert. 30g, Kurt Debus, splashdown of Columbia command module, vert.

1989, May 24 ***Perf. 13***
C776 AP236 5g multicolored .75 .35
C777 AP236 10g multicolored 5.25 1.75
C778 AP236 20g multicolored 3.25 1.00
C779 AP236 25g multicolored 1.90 1.60
C780 AP236 30g multicolored 2.10 1.75
Nos. C776-C780 (5) 13.25 6.45

Souvenir Sheet

Luis Alberto del Parana and the Paraguayans — AP237

1989, May 25 ***Perf. 14½***
C780A AP237 100g multi 33.00 30.00

A clear plastic phonograph record is affixed to the souvenir sheet.

Hamburg, 800th Anniv. AP238

Hamburg anniv. emblem, SAIL '89 emblem, and: 5g, Galleon and Icarus, woodcut by Pieter Brueghel. 10g, Windjammer, vert. 20g, Bark in full sail. 25g, Old Hamburg by A.E. Schliecker, vert. 30g, Commemorative coin issued by Federal Republic of Germany. 100g, Hamburg, 13th cent. illuminated manuscript, vert.

1989, May 26 ***Perf. 13½x13, 13x13½***
C781 AP238 5g multicolored 1.00 .35
C782 AP238 10g multicolored 4.50 1.40
C783 AP238 20g multicolored 1.50 .50
C784 AP238 25g multicolored 2.10 .60
C785 AP238 30g multicolored 4.00 3.50
Nos. C781-C785 (5) 13.10 6.35

Souvenir Sheet

Perf. 14½
C786 AP238 100g multicolored 20.00 20.00

No. C786 contains one 40x50mm stamp.

French Revolution, Bicent. AP239

Details from paintings: 5g, Esther Adorns Herself for her Presentation to King Ahasuerus, by Theodore Chasseriau, vert. 10g, Olympia, by Manet, vert. 20g, The Drunker Erigone with a Panther, by Louis A. Reisener. 25g, Anniv. emblem and natl. coats of arms. 30g, Liberty Leading the People, by Delacroix, vert. 100g, The Education of Maria de Medici, by Rubens, vert.

1989, May 27 ***Perf. 13x13½, 13½x13***
C787 AP239 5g multicolored 1.10 .35
C788 AP239 10g multicolored 5.00 1.60
C789 AP239 20g multicolored 1.75 .50

C790 AP239 25g multicolored 2.25 .60
C791 AP239 30g multicolored 3.50 3.00
Nos. C787-C791 (5) 13.60 6.05

Souvenir Sheet

Perf. 14½

C792 AP239 100g multicolored 22.50 20.00

Souvenir Sheet

Railway Zeppelin, 1931 AP240

1989, May 27 Litho. *Perf. 13½*

C793 AP240 100g multicolored 18.50 18.00

Jupiter and Calisto by Rubens — AP241

Details from paintings by Rubens: 10g, Boreas Abducting Oreithyia (1619-20). 20g, Fortuna (1625). 25g, Mars with Venus and Cupid (1625). 30g, Virgin with Child (1620).

1989, Dec. 27 Litho. *Perf. 14*

C794 AP241 5g multicolored 1.10 .35
C795 AP241 10g multicolored 1.75 .35
C796 AP241 20g multicolored 3.75 .55
C797 AP241 25g multicolored 5.00 1.00

Perf. 13

C798 AP241 30g multicolored 4.50 2.75
Nos. C794-C798 (5) 16.10 5.00

Death of Rubens, 350th anniversary.

Penny Black, 150th Anniv. — AP242

Penny Black, 500 years of postal services emblem, Stamp World '90 emblem and: 5g, Brazil #1. 10g, British Guiana #2. 20g, Chile #1. 25g, Uruguay #1. 30g, Paraguay #1.

1989, Dec. 30 *Perf. 14*

C799 AP242 5g multicolored .60 .35
C800 AP242 10g multicolored 1.20 .35
C801 AP242 20g multicolored 2.40 .55
C802 AP242 25g multicolored 3.00 .75

Perf. 13

C803 AP242 30g multicolored 4.00 3.00
Nos. C799-C803 (5) 11.20 5.00

Animals — AP243

Designs: 5g, Martucha. 10g, Mara. 20g, Lobo de crin. 25g, Rana cornuda tintorera, horiz. 30g, Jaguar, horiz. Inscribed 1989.

1990, Jan. 8 *Perf. 13x13½, 13½x13*

C804 AP243 5g multicolored 1.10 .35
C805 AP243 10g multicolored 2.40 .75
C806 AP243 20g multicolored 3.00 .95
C807 AP243 25g multicolored 4.00 1.40
C808 AP243 30g multicolored 4.00 2.60
Nos. C804-C808 (5) 14.50 6.05

Columbus' Fleet — AP244

Discovery of America 500th anniversary emblem and: 10g, Olympic rings, stylized basketball player, horiz. 20g, Medieval nave, Expo '92 emblem. 25g, Four-masted barkentine, Expo '92 emblem, horiz. 30g, Similar to Spain Scott 2571, Expo '92 emblem.

1990, Jan. 27 *Perf. 14*

C809 AP244 5g multicolored 1.00 .35
C810 AP244 10g multicolored 2.00 .50
C811 AP244 20g multicolored 2.25 .60
C812 AP244 25g multicolored 2.60 .80

Perf. 13½x13

C813 AP244 30g multicolored 3.25 2.60
Nos. C809-C813 (5) 11.10 4.85

Postal Transportation, 500th Anniv. — AP245

500th Anniv. Emblem and: 5g, 10g, 20g, 25g, Penny Black and various post coaches, 10g, vert. 30g, Post coach.

1990, Mar. 9 *Perf. 13½x13, 13x13½*

C814 AP245 5g multicolored .70 .35
C815 AP245 10g multicolored 1.25 .45
C816 AP245 20g multicolored 2.75 .85
C817 AP245 25g multicolored 3.50 1.00
C818 AP245 30g multicolored 5.00 4.00
Nos. C814-C818 (5) 13.20 6.65

Fort and City of Arco by Durer AP246

Paintings by Albrecht Durer, postal transportation 500th anniversary emblem and: 10g, Trent Castle. 20g, North Innsbruck. 25g, Fort yard of Innsbruck, vert. 30g, Virgin of the Animals. No. C824, Madonna and Child, vert. No. C825, Postrider, vert.

1990, Mar. 14 *Perf. 14*

C819 AP246 5g multicolored .70 .35
C820 AP246 10g multicolored 1.30 .40
C821 AP246 20g multicolored 2.90 .80
C822 AP246 25g multicolored 4.00 1.25

Perf. 13

C823 AP246 30g multicolored 5.25 4.50
Nos. C819-C823 (5) 14.15 7.30

Souvenir Sheets

Perf. 14½

C824 AP246 100g multicolored 25.00 22.00
C825 AP246 100g multicolored 26.00 24.00

Nos. C824-C825 each contain one 40x50mm stamp.

For overprint see No. 2358.

AP247

Wmk. 347

1986-88? Photo. *Perf. 11*

C826 AP247 40g red lilac 1.40 .85
C827 AP247 60g brt grn ('88) 2.10 1.25

POSTAGE DUE STAMPS

D1

1904 Unwmk. Litho. *Perf. 11½*

J1 D1 2c green 1.00 *2.00*
J2 D1 4c green 1.00 *2.00*
J3 D1 10c green 1.00 *2.00*
J4 D1 20c green 1.00 *2.00*
Nos. J1-J4 (4) 4.00 8.00

D2

1913 Engr.

J5 D2 1c yellow brown 1.00 1.00
J6 D2 2c yellow brown 1.00 1.00
J7 D2 5c yellow brown 1.00 1.00
J8 D2 10c yellow brown 1.00 1.00
J9 D2 20c yellow brown 1.00 1.00
J10 D2 40c yellow brown 1.00 1.00
J11 D2 1p yellow brown 1.00 1.00
J12 D2 1.50p yellow brown 1.00 1.00
Nos. J5-J12 (8) 8.00 8.00

For overprints and surcharges see Nos. 220-224, 229, 232, 264, L5.

INTERIOR OFFICE ISSUES

The "C" signifies "Campana" (rural). These stamps were sold by Postal Agents in country districts, who received a commission on their sales. These stamps were available for postage in the interior but not in Asunción or abroad.

Nos. 243-244 Overprinted in Red

1922

L1 A42 50c car & dk bl .50 .50
L2 A42 1p dk bl & brn .50 .50

The overprint on Nos. L2 exists double or inverted. Counterfeits exist. Double or inverted overprints on No. L1 and all overprints in black are counterfeit.

Nos. 215, 218, J12 Surcharged

1924

L3 A40 50c on 75c deep bl .60 .60
L4 A40 1p on 1.25p pale bl .60 .60
L5 D2 1p on 1.50p yel brn .60 .60
Nos. L3-L5 (3) 1.80 1.80

Nos. L3-L4 exist imperf.

Nos. 254, 257-260 Overprinted in Black or Red

1924-26

L6 A45 50c red ('25) 1.00 1.00
L7 A44 1p dk blue (R) 1.00 1.00
L8 A45 1p dk bl (R) ('25) 1.00 1.00
L9 A46 1p blue (R) ('25) 1.00 1.00
L10 A45 1p emerald ('26) 2.00 .75
Nos. L6-L10 (5) 6.00 4.75

Nos. L6, L8-L9 exist imperf. Value $2.50 each pair.

Same Overprint on Stamps and Type of 1927-36 in Red or Black

1927-39

L11 A47 50c ultra (R) .50 .50
L12 A47 50c dl red ('28) .50 .50
L13 A47 50c orange ('29) .50 .50
L14 A47 50c lt bl ('30) .50 .50
L15 A47 50c gray (R) ('31) .50 .50
L16 A47 50c bluish grn (R) ('33) .50 .50
L17 A47 50c vio (R) ('34) .50 .50
L18 A48 1p emerald .50 .50
L19 A48 1p org red ('29) .50 .50
L20 A48 1p lil brn ('31) .50 .50
L21 A48 1p dk bl (R) ('33) .50 .50
L22 A48 1p brt vio (R) ('35) .50 .50
L23 A49 1.50p brown .50 .50
a. Double overprint 3.00
L24 A49 1.50p lilac ('28) .50 .50
L25 A49 1.50p dull bl (R) .50 .50
L26 A50 2.50p bister ('28) .50 .50
L27 A50 2.50p vio (R) ('36) .50 .50
L28 A51 3p gray (R) .50 .50
L29 A51 3p rose red ('39) .50 .50
L30 A52 5p vio (R) ('36) .50 .50
L31 A57 10p gray brn (R) ('36) 5.00 3.00
Nos. L11-L31 (21) 15.00 13.00

Types of 1931-35 and No. 305 Overprinted in Black or Red

1931-36

L32 A59 1p light red 2.00 1.00
L33 A58 1.50p dp bl (R) 1.00 .75
L34 A60 1.50p bis brn ('32) 2.00 1.00
L35 A60 1.50p grn (R) ('34) 2.00 1.00
L36 A60 1.50p bl (R) ('36) 2.00 1.00
L37 A54 10p vermilion 8.00 2.50
Nos. L32-L37 (6) 17.00 7.25

OFFICIAL STAMPS

O1 O2

O3 O4

O5 O6

O7

Unwmk.

1886, Aug. 20 Litho. *Imperf.*

O1 O1 1c orange 7.00 7.00
O2 O2 2c violet 7.00 7.00
O3 O3 5c red 7.00 7.00
O4 O4 7c green 7.00 7.00
O5 O5 10c brown 7.00 7.00
O6 O6 15c slate blue 7.00 7.00
a. Wavy lines on face of stamp
b. "OFICIAL" omitted 1.25
O7 O7 20c claret 7.00 7.00
Nos. O1-O7 (7) 49.00 49.00

Nos. O1 to O7 have the date and various control marks and letters printed on the back of each stamp in blue and black.

The overprints exist inverted on all values.

Nos. O1 to O7 have been reprinted from new stones made from slightly retouched dies.

Types of 1886 With Overprint

1886 ***Perf. 11½***

O8 O1 1c dark green 1.50 1.50
O9 O2 2c scarlet 1.50 1.50
O10 O3 5c dull blue 1.50 1.50
O11 O4 7c orange 1.50 1.50
O12 O5 10c lake 1.50 1.50
O13 O6 15c brown 1.50 1.50
O14 O7 20c blue 1.50 1.50
Nos. O8-O14 (7) 10.50 10.50

The overprint exists inverted on all values. Value, each $1.50.

No. 20 Overprinted

1886, Sept. 1

O15 A11 1c dark green 6.00 6.00

Types of 1889 Regular Issue Surcharged

Handstamped Surcharge in Black

1889 ***Imperf.***

O16 A13 3c on 15c violet 3.75 2.75
O17 A13 5c on 15c red brn 3.75 2.25

Perf. 11½

O18 A13 1c on 15c maroon 4.00 2.25
O19 A13 2c on 15c maroon 4.00 2.25
Nos. O16-O19 (4) 15.50 9.50

Counterfeits of Nos. O16-O19 abound.

Regular Issue of 1887 Handstamp Overprinted in Violet

Perf. 11½-12½ & Compounds

1890 **Typo.**

O20 A12 1c green .75 .30
O21 A12 2c rose red .75 .30
O22 A12 5c blue .75 .30
O23 A12 7c brown 10.00 8.00
O24 A12 10c lilac .75 .35
O25 A12 15c orange 1.75 .45
O26 A12 20c pink 1.90 .45
Nos. O20-O26 (7) 16.65 10.15

Nos. O20-O26 exist with double overprint and all but the 20c with inverted overprint.

Nos. O20-O22, O24-O26 exist with blue overprint. The status is questioned. Value, set $15.

Stamps and Type of 1887 Regular Issue Overprinted in Black

1892

O33 A12 1c green .30 .30
O34 A12 2c rose red .30 .30
O35 A12 5c blue .30 .30
O36 A12 7c brown 4.00 1.75
O37 A12 10c lilac 1.25 .55
O38 A12 15c orange .35 .30
O39 A12 20c pink .65 .35
O40 A12 50c gray .75 .35
Nos. O33-O40 (8) 7.90 4.20

No. 26 Overprinted

1893

O41 A12 7c brown 20.00 20.00

Counterfeits of No. O41 exist.

O16

1901, Feb. **Engr.** ***Perf. 11½, 12½***

O42 O16 1c dull blue .75 .50
O43 O16 2c rose red .75 .50
O44 O16 4c dark brown .75 .50
O45 O16 5c dark green .75 .50
O46 O16 8c orange brn .75 .50
O47 O16 10c car rose 2.50 1.00
O48 O16 20c deep blue 2.50 1.00
Nos. O42-O48 (7) 8.75 4.50

A 12c deep green, type O16, was prepared but not issued.

No. 45 Overprinted

1902 ***Perf. 12x12½***

O49 A12 1p olive grn 2.00 2.00
a. Inverted overprint 10.00

Counterfeits of No. O49a exist.

Regular Issue of 1903 Overprinted

1903 ***Perf. 11½***

O50 A32 1c gray .90 .60
O51 A32 2c blue green .90 .60
O52 A32 5c blue .90 .60
O53 A32 10c orange brn .90 .60
O54 A32 20c carmine .90 .60
O55 A32 30c deep blue .90 .60
O56 A32 60c purple .90 .60
Nos. O50-O56 (7) 6.30 4.20

O17

1905-08 **Engr.** ***Perf. 11½, 12***

O57 O17 1c gray grn .50 .30
O58 O17 1c ol grn ('05) .90 .30
O59 O17 1c brn org ('06) .80 .30
O60 O17 1c ver ('08) .50 .30
O61 O17 2c brown org .35 .30
O62 O17 2c gray grn ('05) .35 .30
O63 O17 2c red ('06) 2.00 .75
O64 O17 2c gray ('08) 1.00 .50
O65 O17 5c deep bl ('06) .50 .35
O66 O17 5c gray bl ('08) 4.00 2.00
O67 O17 5c grnsh bl ('08) 2.00 1.50
O68 O17 10c violet ('06) .35 .50
O69 O17 20c violet ('08) 2.00 1.25
Nos. O57-O69 (13) 15.25 8.65

O18

1908

O70 O17 10c bister 10.50
O71 O17 10c emerald 10.50
O72 O17 10c red lilac 13.50
O73 O17 20c bister 9.00
O74 O17 20c salmon pink 10.50
O75 O17 20c green 10.50
O76 O17 30c turquoise bl 10.50
O77 O17 30c blue gray 10.50
O78 O17 30c yellow 4.50
O79 O17 60c chocolate 12.00
O80 O17 60c orange brn 15.00
O81 O17 60c deep ultra 12.00
O82 O18 1p brt rose & blk 72.50
O83 O18 1p lake & blk 72.50
O84 O18 1p brn org & blk 75.00
Nos. O70-O84 (15) 349.00

Nos. O70-O84 were not issued, but were surcharged or overprinted for use as regular postage stamps. See Nos. 131-138, 141-145, 158-165, 171-173.

O19

1913 ***Perf. 11½***

O85 O19 1c gray .30 .35
O86 O19 2c orange .30 .35
O87 O19 5c lilac .30 .35
O88 O19 10c green .30 .35
O89 O19 20c dull red .30 .35
O90 O19 50c rose .30 .35
O91 O19 75c deep blue .30 .35
O92 O19 1p dull blue 1.00 .50
O93 O19 2p yellow 1.00 .50
Nos. O85-O93 (9) 4.10 3.45

For surcharges see Nos. 268, C1-C3.

Type of Regular Issue of 1927-38 Overprinted in Red

1935

O94 A47 10c light ultra .40 .30
O95 A47 50c violet .40 .30
O96 A48 1p orange .40 .30
O97 A60 1.50p green .40 .30
O98 A50 2.50p violet .40 .30
Nos. O94-O98 (5) 2.00 1.50

Overprint is diagonal on 1.50p.

University of Asunción Type

1940 **Litho.** ***Perf. 12***

O99 A67 50c red brn & blk 1.65 .30
O100 A67 1p rose pink & blk 1.65 .30
O101 A67 2p lt bl grn & blk 1.65 .30
O102 A67 5p ultra & blk 1.65 .30
O103 A67 10p lt vio & blk 1.65 .30
O104 A67 50p dp org & blk 1.65 .30
Nos. O99-O104 (6) 9.90 1.80

PENRHYN ISLAND

pen-ˈrin ˈī-lənd

(Tongareva)

AREA — 3 sq. mi.
POP. — 395 (1926)

Stamps of Cook Islands were used in Penrhyn from 1932 until 1973.

12 Pence = 1 Shilling

Catalogue values for unused stamps in this country are for Never Hinged items, beginning with Scott 35 in the regular postage section, Scott B1 in the semi-postal section and Scott O1 in the officials section.

Watermarks

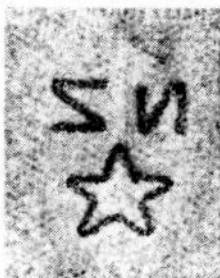
Wmk. 61 — N Z and Star Close Together

Wmk. 63 — Double-lined N Z and Star

On watermark 61 the margins of the sheets are watermarked "NEW ZEALAND POSTAGE" and parts of the double-lined letters of these words are frequently found on the stamps. It occasionally happens that a stamp shows no watermark whatever.

Stamps of New Zealand Surcharged in Carmine, Vermilion, Brown or Blue

½ pence

1 pence

2½ pence

1902 **Wmk. 63** ***Perf. 14***

1 A18 ½p green (C) 1.00 *14.00*
a. No period after "ISLAND" 175.00 *325.00*
2 A35 1p carmine (Br) 3.00 *27.50*
a. Perf. 11 1,000. *1,200.*
b. Perf. 11x14 1,200. *1,400.*

Wmk. 61 ***Perf. 14***

5 A18 ½p green (V) 4.75 *12.50*
a. No period after "ISLAND" 180.00 *375.00*
6 A35 1p carmine (Bl) 1.25 *9.50*
a. No period after "ISLAND" 60.00 *170.00*
b. Perf. 11x14 15,000. *8,500.*

Unwmk. ***Perf. 11***

8 A22 2½p blue (C) 17.50 17.50
a. "½" and "PENI" 2mm apart 30.00 *35.00*
9 A22 2½p blue (V) 14.50 10.00
a. "½" and "PENI" 2mm apart 42.00 *91.00*
Nos. 1-9 (6) 42.00 *91.00*

Stamps with compound perfs. also exist perf. 11 or 14 on one or more sides.

d

e

f

1903 **Wmk. 61**

10 A23(d) 3p yel brn (Bl) 11.00 *42.50*
11 A26(e) 6p rose (Bl) 16.00 *50.00*
12 A29(f) 1sh org red (Bl) 62.50 *67.50*
a. 1sh bright red (Bl) 47.50 *47.50*
b. 1sh brown red (Bl) 65.00 *65.00*
Nos. 10-12 (3) 89.50 *160.00*

1914-15 ***Perf. 14, 14x14½***

13 A41(a) ½p yel grn (C) .90 *12.00*
a. No period after "ISLAND" 25.00 *110.00*
b. No period after "PENI" 110.00 *350.00*
14 A41(a) ½p yel grn (V) ('15) .90 *9.25*
a. No period after "ISLAND" 11.50 *70.00*
b. No period after "PENI" 55.00 *190.00*
15 A41(e) 6p car rose (Bl) 25.00 *82.50*
16 A41(f) 1sh ver (Bl) 50.00 *110.00*
Nos. 13-16 (4) 76.80 *213.75*

New Zealand Stamps of 1915-19 Overprinted in Red or Dark Blue

Perf. 14x13½, 14x14½

1917-20 **Typo.**

17 A43 ½p yel grn (R) ('20) 1.00 *2.25*
18 A47 1½p gray black (R) 7.00 *27.50*
19 A47 1½p brn org (R) ('19) 1.00 *27.50*
20 A43 3p choc (Bl) ('19) 4.75 *47.50*

Engr.

21 A44 2½p dull bl (R) ('20) 2.00 *11.00*
22 A45 3p vio brn (Bl) ('18) 9.00 *70.00*
23 A45 6p car rose (Bl) ('18) 5.00 *21.00*
24 A45 1sh vermilion (Bl) 14.00 *40.00*
Nos. 17-24 (8) 43.75 *246.75*

Landing of Capt. Cook
A10

Avarua Waterfront
A11

Capt. James Cook A12

Coconut Palm A13

Arorangi Village, Rarotonga A14

Avarua Harbor A15

1920 Unwmk. *Perf. 14*

25	A10 ½p emerald & blk		1.25	*22.50*
a.	Center inverted		1,000.	
26	A11 1p red & black		1.50	*17.00*
a.	Center inverted		1,000.	
27	A12 1½p violet & blk		6.00	*18.00*
28	A13 3p red org & blk		2.25	*17.50*
29	A14 6p dk brn & red brn		3.00	*20.00*
30	A15 1sh dull bl & blk		12.00	*30.00*
	Nos. 25-30 (6)		26.00	*125.00*

Rarotongan Chief (Te Po) — A16

1927 Engr. Wmk. 61

31 A16 2½p blue & red brn 19.00 *50.00*

Types of 1920 Issue

1928-29

33 A10 ½p yellow grn & blk 6.50 *25.00*
34 A11 1p carmine rose & blk 6.50 *25.00*

PENRHYN

Northern Cook Islands

POP. — 606 (1996).

The Northern Cook Islands include six besides Penrhyn that are inhabited: Nassau, Palmerston (Avarua), Manihiki (Humphrey), Rakahanga (Reirson), Pukapuka (Danger) and Suwarrow (Anchorage).

100 Cents = 1 Dollar

Catalogue values for unused stamps in this section are for Never Hinged items.

Cook Islands Nos. 200-201, 203, 205-208, 211-212, 215-217 Overprinted

1973 Photo. Unwmk. *Perf. 14x13½*

35	A34 1c gold & multi	.25	.25
36	A34 2c gold & multi	.25	.25
37	A34 3c gold & multi	.25	.25
38	A34 4c gold & multi	.25	.25
a.	Overprinted on #204	38.00	38.00
39	A34 5c gold & multi	.25	.25
40	A34 6c gold & multi	.25	.35
41	A34 8c gold & multi	.25	.45
42	A34 15c gold & multi	.35	.60
43	A34 20c gold & multi	1.25	1.00
44	A34 50c gold & multi	.90	2.00
45	A35 $1 gold & multi	.90	2.25
46	A35 $2 gold & multi	.90	4.50
	Nos. 35-46 (12)	6.05	12.40

Nos. 45-46 are overprinted "Penrhyn" only. Overprint exists with broken "E" or "O."

Issued with and without fluorescent security underprinting.

Issued: #35-45, Oct. 24; #46, Nov. 14.

Cook Islands Nos. 369-371 Overprinted in Silver: "PENRHYN / NORTHERN"

1973, Nov. 14 Photo. *Perf. 14*

47	A60 25c Princess Anne	.35	.25
48	A60 30c Mark Phillips	.35	.25
49	A60 50c Princess and Mark Phillips	.35	.25
	Nos. 47-49 (3)	1.05	.75

Wedding of Princess Anne and Capt. Mark Phillips.

Fluorescence

Starting with No. 50, stamps carry a "fluorescent security underprinting" in a multiple pattern combining a sailing ship, "Penrhyn Northern Cook Islands" and stars.

Ostracion — A17

Aerial View of Penrhyn Atoll A18

Designs: ½c-$1, Various fish of Penrhyn. $5, Map showing Penrhyn's location.

1974-75 Photo. *Perf. 13½x14*

50	A17 ½c multicolored	.25	.25
51	A17 1c multicolored	.25	.25
52	A17 2c multicolored	.25	.25
53	A17 3c multicolored	.25	.25
54	A17 4c multicolored	.25	.25
55	A17 5c multicolored	.25	.25
56	A17 8c multicolored	.25	.25
57	A17 10c multicolored	.25	.25
58	A17 20c multicolored	.75	.40
59	A17 25c multicolored	.80	.45
60	A17 60c multicolored	2.00	1.10
61	A17 $1 multicolored	3.25	1.75
62	A18 $2 multicolored	6.50	*10.00*
63	A18 $5 multicolored	8.50	3.50
	Nos. 50-63 (14)	23.80	19.20

Issued: $2, 2/12/75; $5, 3/12/75; others 8/15/74.

For surcharges and overprints see Nos. 72, 352-353, O1-O12.

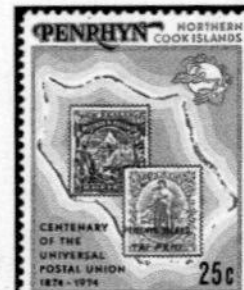

Map of Penrhyn and Nos. 1-2 — A19

UPU, cent.: 50c, UPU emblem, map of Penrhyn and Nos. 27-28.

1974, Sept. 27 *Perf. 13*

64 A19 25c violet & multi .30 .30
65 A19 50c slate grn & multi .60 .60

Adoration of the Kings, by Memling A20

Christmas: 10c, Adoration of the Shepherds, by Hugo van der Goes. 25c, Adoration of the Kings, by Rubens. 30c, Holy Family, by Orazio Borgianni.

1974, Oct. 30

66	A20 5c multicolored	.25	.25
67	A20 10c multicolored	.25	.25
68	A20 25c multicolored	.30	.30
69	A20 30c multicolored	.40	.40
	Nos. 66-69 (4)	1.20	1.20

Churchill Giving "V" Sign — A21

1974, Nov. 30 Photo.

70 A21 30c shown .35 *.80*
71 A21 50c Portrait .45 *.90*

Winston Churchill (1874-1965).

No. 63 Overprinted

1975, July 24 *Perf. 13½x13*

72 A18 $5 multicolored 2.25 2.75

Safe splashdown of Apollo space capsule.

Madonna, by Dirk Bouts — A22

Madonna Paintings: 15c, by Leonardo da Vinci. 35c, by Raphael.

1975, Nov. 21 Photo. *Perf. 14½x13*

73	A22 7c gold & multi	.45	.25
74	A22 15c gold & multi	.75	.30
75	A22 35c gold & multi	1.10	.45
	Nos. 73-75 (3)	2.30	1.00

Christmas 1975.

Pietà, by Michelangelo — A23

1976, Mar. 19 Photo. *Perf. 14x13*

76	A23 15c gold & dark brown	.25	.25
77	A23 20c gold & deep purple	.40	.30
78	A23 35c gold & dark green	.55	.35
a.	Souvenir sheet of 3, #76-78	1.60	1.60
	Nos. 76-78 (3)	1.20	.90

Easter and for the 500th birth anniv. of Michelangelo Buonarroti (1475-1564), Italian sculptor, painter and architect.

The Spirit of '76, by Archibald M. Willard A24

No. 79, Washington Crossing the Delaware, by Emmanuel Leutze.

1976, May 20 Photo. *Perf. 13½*

79	A24 Strip of 3	1.00	1.00
a.	30c Boatsman	.30	.30
b.	30c Washington	.30	.30
c.	30c Men in boat	.30	.30
80	A24 Strip of 3	2.00	2.00
a.	50c Drummer boy	.50	.50
b.	50c Old drummer	.50	.50
c.	50c Fifer	.50	.50
d.	Souvenir sheet, #79-80	3.25	3.25

American Bicentennial. Nos. 79-80 printed in sheets of 15, 5 strips of 3 and 3-part corner labels.

For overprint see No. O13.

Running — A25

Montreal Olympic Games Emblem and: 30c, Long jump. 75c, Javelin.

1976, July 9 Photo. *Perf. 13½*

81	A25 25c multicolored	.30	.25
82	A25 30c multicolored	.35	.30
83	A25 75c multicolored	.75	.50
a.	Souvenir sheet of 3, #81-83, perf. 14½x13½	1.40	1.40
	Nos. 81-83 (3)	1.40	1.05

21st Olympic Games, Montreal, Canada, July 17-Aug. 1. Nos. 81-83 printed in sheets of 6 (2x3).

Flight into Egypt, by Dürer — A26

Etchings by Albrecht Dürer: 15c, Adoration of the Shepherds. 35c, Adoration of the Kings.

1976, Oct. 20 Photo. *Perf. 13x13½*

84	A26 7c silver & dk brown	.25	.25
85	A26 15c silver & slate grn	.25	.25
86	A26 35c silver & purple	.45	.35
	Nos. 84-86 (3)	.95	.85

Christmas. Nos. 84-86 printed in sheets of 8 (2x4) with decorative border.

Elizabeth II and Westminster Abbey — A27

$1, Elizabeth II & Prince Philip. $2, Elizabeth II.

1977, Mar. 24 Photo. *Perf. 13½x13*

87	A27 50c silver & multi	.25	.25
88	A27 $1 silver & multi	.30	.30
89	A27 $2 silver & multi	.45	.45
a.	Souvenir sheet of 3, #87-89	1.25	1.25
	Nos. 87-89 (3)	1.00	1.00

25th anniversary of reign of Queen Elizabeth II. Nos. 87-89 issued in sheets of 4.

For overprints see Nos. O14-O15.

Annunciation — A28

Designs: 15c, Announcement to Shepherds. 35c, Nativity. Designs from "The Bible in Images," by Julius Schnorr von Carolsfeld (1794-1872).

1977, Sept. 23 Photo. *Perf. 13½*

90	A28 7c multicolored	.25	.25
91	A28 15c multicolored	.65	.65
92	A28 35c multicolored	1.10	1.10
	Nos. 90-92 (3)	2.00	2.00

Christmas. Issued in sheets of 6.

A29

No. 93a, Red Sickle-bill (I'wii). No. 93b, Chief's Feather Cloak. No. 94a, Crimson creeper (apapane). No. 94b, Feathered head of Hawaiian god. No. 95a, Hawaiian gallinule (alae). No. 95b, Chief's regalia: feather cape, staff (kahili) and helmet. No. 96a, Yellow-tufted

bee-eater (o'o). No. 96b, Scarlet feathered image (head).
Birds are extinct; their feathers were used for artifacts shown.

1978, Jan. 19 Photo. *Perf. 12½x13*

93 A29 20c Pair, #a.-b. 1.40 .70
94 A29 30c Pair, #a.-b. 1.75 .90
95 A29 35c Pair, #a.-b. 1.90 1.00
96 A29 75c Pair, #a.-b. 3.00 1.60
c. Souv. sheet, #93a, 94a, 95a, 96a 4.25 4.25
d. Souv. sheet, #93b, 94b, 95b, 96b 4.25 4.25
Nos. 93-96 (4) 8.05 4.20

Bicentenary of Capt. Cook's arrival in Hawaii. Printed in sheets of 8 (4x2).

A31

Rubens' Paintings: 10c, St. Veronica by Rubens. 15c, Crucifixion. 35c, Descent from the Cross.

1978, Mar. 10 Photo. *Perf. 13½x13*
Size: 25x36mm

101 A31 10c multicolored .25 .25
102 A31 15c multicolored .25 .25
103 A31 35c multicolored .50 .50
a. Souvenir sheet of 3 1.10 1.10
Nos. 101-103 (3) 1.00 1.00

Easter and 400th birth anniv. of Peter Paul Rubens (1577-1640). Nos. 101-103 issued in sheets of 6. No. 103a contains one each of Nos. 101-103 (27x36mm).

Miniature Sheet

A32

1978, May 24 Photo. *Perf. 13*

104 A32 Sheet of 6 1.75 1.75
a. 90c Arms of United Kingdom .35 .25
b. 90c shown .35 .25
c. 90c Arms of New Zealand .35 .25
d. Souvenir sheet of 3, #104a-104c 1.40 1.40

25th anniv. of coronation of Elizabeth II.
No. 104 contains 2 horizontal se-tenant strips of Nos. 104a-104c, separated by horizontal gutter showing coronation.

A33

Paintings by Dürer: 30c, Virgin and Child. 35c, Virgin and Child with St. Anne.

1978, Nov. 29 Photo. *Perf. 14x13½*

105 A33 30c multicolored .70 .60
106 A33 35c multicolored .75 .65
a. Souvenir sheet of 2, #105-106 1.45 1.25

Christmas and 450th death anniv. of Albrecht Dürer (1471-1528), German painter. Nos. 105-106 issued in sheets of 6.

A34

#107a, Penrhyn #64-65. #107b, Rowland Hill, Penny Black. #108a, Penrhyn #104b. #108b, Hill portrait.

1979, Sept. 26 Photo. *Perf. 14*

107 A34 75c Pair, #a.-b. 1.00 1.00
108 A34 90c Pair, #a.-b. 1.25 1.25
c. Souvenir sheet of 4, #107-108 2.25 2.25

Sir Rowland Hill (1795-1879), originator of penny postage. Issued in sheets of 8.

Max and Moritz, IYC Emblem — A35

IYC: Scenes from Max and Moritz, by Wilhelm Busch (1832-1908).

1979, Nov. 20 Photo. *Perf. 13x12½*

111 Sheet of 4 1.00
a. A35 12c shown .25
b. A35 12c Looking down chimney .25
c. A35 12c With stolen chickens .25
d. A35 12c Woman and dog, empty pan .25
112 Sheet of 4 1.00
a. A35 15c Sawing bridge .25
b. A35 15c Man falling into water .25
c. A35 15c Broken bridge .25
d. A35 15c Running away .25
113 Sheet of 4 1.00
a. A35 20c Baker .25
b. A35 20c Sneaking into bakery .25
c. A35 20c Falling into dough .25
d. A35 20c Baked into breads .25
Nos. 111-113 (3) 3.00

Sheets come with full labels at top and bottom showing text from stories or trimmed with text removed. Values of 3 sheets with full labels $11.

A36

Easter (15th Century Prayerbook Illustrations): 12c, Jesus Carrying the Cross. 20c, Crucifixion, by William Vreland. 35c, Descent from the Cross.

1980, Mar. 28 Photo. *Perf. 13x13½*

114 A36 12c multicolored .25 .25
115 A36 20c multicolored .25 .25
116 A36 35c multicolored .40 .40
a. Souvenir sheet of 3, #114-116 .75 .75
Nos. 114-116 (3) .90 .90

See Nos. B4-B6.

A37

1980, Sept. 17 Photo. *Perf. 13*

117 A37 $1 multicolored 1.20 1.20

Souvenir Sheet

118 A37 $2.50 multicolored 2.00 2.00

Queen Mother Elizabeth, 80th birthday.

A38

Platform diving: #119a, Falk Hoffman, DDR. #119b, Martina Jaschke.
Archery: #120a, Tomi Polkolainen. #120b, Kete Losaberidse.
Soccer: #121a, Czechoslovakia, gold. #121b, DDR, silver.
Running: #122a, Barbel Wockel. #122b, Pietro Mennea.

1980, Nov. 14 Photo. *Perf. 13½*

119 A38 10c Pair, #a.-b. .25 .25
120 A38 20c Pair, #a.-b. .45 .45
121 A38 30c Pair, #a.-b. .70 .70
122 A38 50c Pair, #a.-b. 1.10 1.10
Nos. 119-122 (4) 2.50 2.50

Souvenir Sheet

123 A38 Sheet of 8 2.50 2.50

22nd Summer Olympic Games, Moscow, July 19-Aug. 3.
No. 123 contains #119-122 with gold borders and white lettering at top and bottom.

A39

Christmas (15th Century Virgin and Child Paintings by): 20c, Virgin and Child, by Luis Dalmau. 35c, Serra brothers. 50c, Master of the Porciuncula.

1980, Dec. 5 Photo. *Perf. 13*

127 A39 20c multicolored .25 .25
128 A39 35c multicolored .30 .30
129 A39 50c multicolored .45 .45
a. Souvenir sheet of 3, #127-129 2.25 2.25
Nos. 127-129 (3) 1.00 1.00

See Nos. B7-B9.

A40

A41

Cutty Sark, 1869 — A42

#160a, 165a, Amatasi. #160b, 165b, Ndrua. #160c, 165c, Waka. #160d, 165d, Tongiaki. #161a, 166a, Va'a teu'ua. #161b, 166b, Victoria, 1500. #161c, 166c, Golden Hinde, 1560. #161d, 166d, Boudeuse, 1760. #162a, 167a, Bounty, 1787. #162b, 167b, Astrolabe, 1811. #162c, 167c, Star of India, 1861. #162d, 167d, Great Rep., 1853. #163a, 168a, Balcutha, 1886. #163b, 168b, Coonatto, 1863. #163c, 168c, Antiope, 1866. #163d, 168d, Teaping, 1863. #164a, 169a, Preussen, 1902. #164b, 169b, Pamir, 1921. #164c, 169c, Cap Hornier, 1910. #164d, 169d, Patriarch, 1869.

1981 Photo. *Perf. 14*

160 A40 1c Block of 4, #a.-d. .30 .30
161 A40 3c Block of 4, #a.-d. .50 .50
162 A40 4c Block of 4, #a.-d. .65 .65
163 A40 6c Block of 4, #a.-d. 1.00 1.00
164 A40 10c Block of 4, #a.-d. 1.25 1.25

Perf. 13½x14½

165 A41 15c Block of 4, #a.-d. 1.40 1.40
166 A41 20c Block of 4, #a.-d. 1.60 1.60
167 A41 30c Block of 4, #a.-d. 2.75 2.75
168 A41 50c Block of 4, #a.-d. 4.50 4.50
169 A41 $1 Block of 4, #a.-d. 11.00 11.00

Perf. 13½

170 A42 $2 shown 5.00 5.00
171 A42 $4 Mermerus, 1872 10.00 10.00
172 A42 $6 Resolution, Discovery, 1776 17.00 17.00
Nos. 160-172 (13) 56.95 56.95

Issued: 1c-10c, Feb. 16; 15c-50c, Mar. 16; $1, May 15; $2, $4, June 26; $6, Sept. 21.
For surcharges and overprints see Nos. 241-243, 251, 254, 395, O35, O37, O39.

Christ with Crown of Thorns, by Titian — A44

Easter: 30c, Jesus at the Grove, by Paolo Veronese. 50c, Pieta, by Van Dyck.

1981, Apr. 5 *Perf. 14*

173 A44 30c multicolored .40 .30
174 A44 40c multicolored .60 .45
175 A44 50c multicolored .75 .60
a. Souv. sheet, #173-175, perf 13½ 3.00 3.00
Nos. 173-175 (3) 1.75 1.35

See Nos. B10-B12.

A45

Designs: Portraits of Prince Charles.

1981, July 10 Photo. *Perf. 14*

176 A45 40c multicolored .25 .25
177 A45 50c multicolored .25 .25
178 A45 60c multicolored .25 .25
179 A45 70c multicolored .30 .30
180 A45 80c multicolored .35 .35
a. Souv. sheet of 5, #176-180+label 2.00 2.00
Nos. 176-180 (5) 1.40 1.40

Royal wedding. Nos. 176-180 each issued in sheets of 5 plus label showing couple.
For overprints and surcharges see Nos. 195-199, 244-245, 248, 299-300, B13-B18.

1982 World Cup Soccer — A46

Shirts: No. 181: a, Red. b, Striped. c, Blue. No. 182: a, Blue. b, Red. c, Striped. No. 183: a, Orange. b, Purple. c, Black.

1981, Dec. 7 Photo. *Perf. 13*

181 A46 15c Strip of 3, #a.-c. 1.00 1.00
182 A46 35c Strip of 3, #a.-c. 1.75 1.75
183 A46 50c Strip of 3, #a.-c. 2.75 2.75
Nos. 181-183 (3) 5.50 5.50

See No. B19.

Christmas — A47

Dürer Engravings: 30c, Virgin on a Crescent, 1508. 40c, Virgin at the Fence, 1503. 50c, Holy Virgin and Child, 1505.

1981, Dec. 15 Photo. *Perf. 13x13½*

184 A47 30c multicolored .75 .75
185 A47 40c multicolored 1.25 1.25
186 A47 50c multicolored 1.50 1.50
a. Souvenir sheet of 3 3.25 3.25
Nos. 184-186 (3) 3.50 3.50

Souvenir Sheets
Perf. 14x13½

187 A47 70c + 5c like #184 1.10 1.10
188 A47 70c + 5c like #185 1.10 1.10
189 A47 70c + 5c like #186 1.10 1.10

No. 186a contains Nos. 184-186 each with 2c surcharge. Nos. 187-189 each contain one 25x40mm stamp. Surtaxes were for childrens' charities.

21st Birthday of Princess Diana — A48

Designs: Portraits of Diana.

1982, July 1 Photo. *Perf. 14*

190	A48	30c multicolored	.65	.65
191	A48	50c multicolored	.85	.85
192	A48	70c multicolored	1.05	1.05
193	A48	80c multicolored	1.25	1.25
194	A48	$1.40 multicolored	2.75	2.75
a.		Souv. sheet, #190-194 + label	6.50	6.50
		Nos. 190-194 (5)	6.55	6.55

For new inscriptions, overprints and surcharges, see Nos. 200-204, 246-247, 249-250, 301-302.

Nos. 176-180a Overprinted

1982, July 30

195	A45	40c multicolored	.40	.40
196	A45	50c multicolored	.55	.55
197	A45	60c multicolored	.60	.60
198	A45	70c multicolored	.70	.70
199	A45	80c multicolored	.75	.75
a.		Souv. sheet, #195-199 + label	5.50	5.50
		Nos. 195-199 (5)	3.00	3.00

Nos. 190-194a Inscribed in Silver

1982 Photo. *Perf. 14*

200	A48	30c Pair, #a.-b.	.70	.70
201	A48	50c Pair, #a.-b.	.90	.90
202	A48	70c Pair, #a.-b.	1.60	1.60
203	A48	80c Pair, #a.-b.	1.75	1.75
204	A48	$1.40 Pair, #a.-b.	3.00	3.00
c.		Souv. sheet, #200a, 201a, 202a, 203a, 204a + label	6.00	6.00
		Nos. 200-204 (5)	7.95	7.95

Miniature sheets of each denomination were issued containing 2 "21 JUNE 1982...," 3 "COMMEMORATING...," and a label. Value, set of 5 sheets, $21.

Se-tenant pairs come with or without label.

For surcharges see Nos. 247, 250, 253.

A49

Christmas — Virgin and Child Paintings: 35c, Joos Van Cleve (1485-1540). 48c, Filippino Lippi (1457-1504). 60c, Cima Da Conegliano (1459-1517).

1982, Dec. 10 Photo. *Perf. 14*

205	A49	35c multicolored	.50	.50
206	A49	48c multicolored	.70	.70
207	A49	60c multicolored	.80	.80
a.		Souvenir sheet of 3	3.00	3.00
		Nos. 205-207 (3)	2.00	2.00

Souvenir Sheets

208	A49	70c + 5c like 35c	1.60	1.60
209	A49	70c + 5c like 48c	1.60	1.60
210	A49	70c + 5c like 60c	1.60	1.60

Nos. 205-207 were printed in sheets of five plus label. No. 207a contains Nos. 205-207 each with 2c surcharge. Nos. 208-210 each contain one stamp, perf. 13½. Surtaxes were for childrens' charities.

A50

#a, Red coral. #b, Aerial view. #c, Eleanor Roosevelt, grass skirt. #d, Map.

1983, Mar. 14 *Perf. 13½x13*

211	A50	60c Block of 4, #a.-d.	2.25	2.25

Commonwealth day.

For surcharges see No. O27-O30.

Scouting Year — A51

Emblem and various tropical flowers.

1983, Apr. 5 *Perf. 13½x14½*

215	A51	36c multicolored	1.75	.75
216	A51	48c multicolored	2.25	1.00
217	A51	60c multicolored	2.50	1.25
		Nos. 215-217 (3)	6.50	3.00

Souvenir Sheet

218	A51	$2 multicolored	3.50	3.50

Nos. 215-218 Overprinted: "XV / WORLD JAMBOREE / CANADA / 1983"

1983, July 8 Photo. *Perf. 13½x14½*

219	A51	36c multicolored	1.60	.65
220	A51	48c multicolored	2.10	1.25
221	A51	60c multicolored	2.50	1.25
		Nos. 219-221 (3)	6.20	3.15

Souvenir Sheet

222	A51	$2 multicolored	3.50	3.50

15th World Boy Scout Jamboree.

Save the Whales Campaign — A52

Various whale hunting scenes.

1983, July 29 Photo. *Perf. 13*

223	A52	8c multicolored	.80	.70
224	A52	15c multicolored	1.20	1.00
225	A52	35c multicolored	2.40	1.40
226	A52	60c multicolored	3.75	2.00
227	A52	$1 multicolored	5.75	2.75
		Nos. 223-227 (5)	13.90	7.85

World Communications Year — A53

Designs: Cable laying Vessels.

1983, Sept. Photo. *Perf. 13*

228	A53	36c multicolored	1.00	.50
229	A53	48c multicolored	1.25	.70
230	A53	60c multicolored	1.50	.90
		Nos. 228-230 (3)	3.75	2.10

Souvenir Sheet

231		Sheet of 3	2.75	2.75
a.		A53 36c + 3c like No. 228	.65	.65
b.		A53 48c + 3c like No. 229	.85	.85
c.		A53 60c + 3c like No. 230	1.00	1.00

Surtax was for local charities.

Nos. 164, 166-167, 170, 172, 178-180, 192-194, 202-204 Surcharged

Blocks of 4, #a.-d. (#241-243) Pairs, #a.-b. (#247, 250, 253)

Perf. 14, 13½x14½, 13½

1983 Photo.

241	A40	18c on 10c #164	3.50	3.25
242	A41	36c on 20c #166	4.25	4.00
243	A41	36c on 30c #167	4.25	4.00
244	A45	48c on 60c multi	1.05	1.00
245	A45	72c on 70c multi	1.50	1.40
246	A48	72c on 70c #192	1.50	1.40
247	A48	72c on 70c #202	3.50	3.00
248	A45	96c on 80c multi	3.00	1.75
249	A48	96c on 80c #193	3.25	1.75
250	A48	96c on 80c #203	4.00	3.25
251	A42	$1.20 on $2 multi	4.25	2.50
252	A48	$1.20 on $1.40 #194	3.50	2.50
253	A48	$1.20 on $1.40 #204	6.00	4.00
254	A42	$5.60 on $6 multi	18.00	12.25
		Nos. 241-254 (14)	61.55	46.05

Issued: #241-243, 245, 251, Sept. 26; #244, 246, 249, 252, 254, Oct. 28; others Dec. 1.

First Manned Balloon Flight, 200th Anniv. — A54

Designs: 36c, Airship, Sir George Cayley (1773-1857). 48c, Man-powered airship, Dupuy de Lome (1818-1885). 60c, Brazilian Aviation Pioneer, Alberto Santos Dumont (1873-1932). 96c, Practical Airship, Paul Lebaudy (1858-1937). $1.32, L-Z 127 Graf Zeppelin.

1983, Oct. 31 Litho. *Perf. 13*

255	A54	36c multicolored	.75	.75
256	A54	48c multicolored	1.10	1.10
257	A54	60c multicolored	1.30	1.30
258	A54	96c multicolored	1.70	1.70
259	A54	$1.32 multicolored	2.60	2.60
a.		Souvenir sheet of 5, #255-259	7.50	7.50
		Nos. 255-259 (5)	7.45	7.45

Nos. 255-259 se-tenant with labels. Sheets of 5 for each value exist.

Nos. 255-259 are misspelled "ISLANS." For correcting overprints see Nos. 287-291.

Christmas — A55

Raphael Paintings: 36c, Madonna in the Meadow. 42c, Tempi Madonna. 48c, Small Cowper Madonna. 60c, Madonna Della Tenda.

1983, Nov. 30 Photo. *Perf. 13x13½*

260	A55	36c multicolored	.75	.45
261	A55	42c multicolored	1.00	.55
262	A55	48c multicolored	1.25	.60
263	A55	60c multicolored	1.50	.80
a.		Souvenir sheet of 4	4.50	4.50
		Nos. 260-263 (4)	4.50	2.40

Souvenir Sheets

Perf. 13½

264	A55	75c + 5c like #260	1.20	1.20
265	A55	75c + 5c like #261	1.20	1.20
266	A55	75c + 5c like #262	1.20	1.20
267	A55	75c + 5c like #263	1.20	1.20

No. 263a contains Nos. 260-263 each with 3c surcharge. Nos. 264-267 each contain one 29x41mm stamp. Issued Dec. 28. Surtaxes were for children's charities.

Waka Canoe — A56

4c, Amatasi fishing boat. 5c, Ndrua canoe. 8c, Tongiaki canoe. 10c, Victoria, 1500. 18c, Golden Hind, 1560. 20c, Boudeuse, 1760. 30c, Bounty, 1787. 36c, Astrolabe, 1811. 48c, Great Republic, 1853. 50c, Star of India, 1861. 60c, Coonatto, 1863. 72c, Antiope, 1866. 80c, Balcutha, 1886. 96c, Cap Hornier, 1910. $1.20, Pamir, 1921. $3, Mermerus, 1872. $5, Cutty Sark, 1869. $9.60, Resolution, Discovery.

1984 Photo. *Perf. 14½*

268	A56	2c multicolored	.25	.25
269	A56	4c multicolored	.25	.25
270	A56	5c multicolored	.25	.25
271	A56	8c multicolored	.25	.25
272	A56	10c multicolored	.25	.25
273	A56	18c multicolored	.75	.45
274	A56	20c multicolored	.50	.50
275	A56	30c multicolored	1.00	.70
276	A56	36c multicolored	.40	.90
277	A56	48c multicolored	1.20	1.20
278	A56	50c multicolored	1.30	1.30
279	A56	60c multicolored	1.40	1.40
280	A56	72c multicolored	1.80	1.80
281	A56	80c multicolored	2.00	2.00
282	A56	96c multicolored	2.60	2.60
283	A56	$1.20 multicolored	1.30	1.30

Perf. 13

Size: 42x34mm

284	A56	$3 multicolored	5.00	5.00
285	A56	$5 multicolored	8.00	8.00
286	A56	$9.60 multicolored	16.00	16.00
		Nos. 268-286 (19)	44.50	44.40

Issue dates: Nos. 268-277, Feb. 8. Nos. 278-283, Mar. 23. Nos. 284-286 June 15.

For overprints and surcharges see Nos. O16-O26, O31-O34, O36, O38, O40.

Nos. 255-259a Overprinted

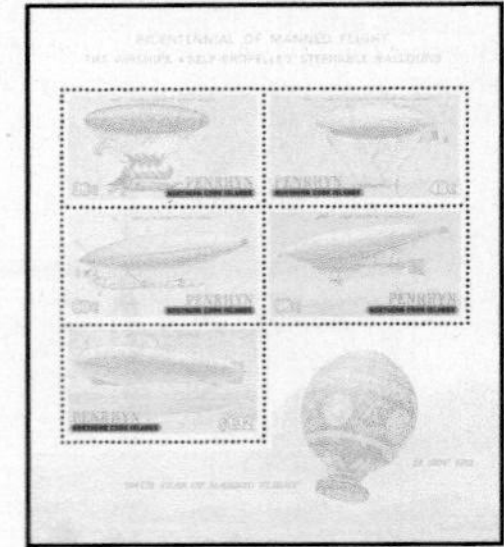

1984 Litho. *Perf. 13*

287	A54	36c multicolored	.80	.80
288	A54	48c multicolored	1.00	1.00
289	A54	60c multicolored	1.30	1.30
290	A54	96c multicolored	2.10	2.10
291	A54	$1.32 multicolored	2.75	2.75
a.		Souvenir sheet of 5, #287-291	7.50	*8.75*
		Nos. 287-291 (5)	7.95	7.95

1984 Los Angeles Summer Olympic Games — A57

35c, Olympic flag. 60c, Torch, flags. $1.80, Classic runners, Memorial Coliseum.

1984, July 20 Photo. *Perf. 13½x13*

292	A57	35c multicolored	.45	.45
293	A57	60c multicolored	.80	.80
294	A57	$1.80 multicolored	2.00	2.00
		Nos. 292-294 (3)	3.25	3.25

Souvenir Sheet

295		Sheet of 3 + label	3.00	3.00
a.		A57 35c + 5c like #292	.35	.35
b.		A57 60c + 5c like #293	.50	.50
c.		A57 $1.80 + 5c like #294	1.75	1.75

Surtax for amateur sports.

AUSIPEX '84 — A57a

60c, Nos. 161c, 107b, 180, 104b. $1.20, Map of South Pacific.

1984, Sept. 20

296	A57a	60c multicolored	.85	.85
297	A57a	$1.20 multicolored	1.75	1.75

Souvenir Sheet

298 Sheet of 2 3.00 3.00
a. A57a 96c like #296 1.50 1.50
b. A57a 96c like #297 1.50 1.50

For surcharge see No. 345.

Nos. 176-177, 190-191 Ovptd. "Birth of/Prince Henry/15 Sept. 1984" and Surcharged in Black or Gold

1984, Oct. 18 ***Perf. 14***
299 A45 $2 on 40c 1.60 1.60
300 A45 $2 on 50c 1.60 1.60
301 A48 $2 on 30c 1.60 1.60
302 A48 $2 on 50c 1.60 1.60
Nos. 299-302 (4) 6.40 6.40

Nos. 209-302 printed in sheets of 5 plus one label each picturing a portrait of the royal couple or an heraldic griffin.

Christmas 1984 — A58

Paintings: 36c, Virgin and Child, by Giovanni Bellini. 48c, Virgin and Child, by Lorenzo di Credi. 60c, Virgin and Child, by Palma, the Older. 96c, Virgin and Child, by Raphael.

1984, Nov. 15 Photo. ***Perf. 13x13½***
303 A58 36c multicolored .55 .55
304 A58 48c multicolored .90 .90
305 A58 60c multicolored 1.00 1.00
306 A58 96c multicolored 1.75 1.75
a. Souvenir sheet of 4 4.25 4.25
Nos. 303-306 (4) 4.20 4.20

Souvenir Sheets

307 A58 96c + 10c like #303 1.60 1.60
308 A58 96c + 10c like #304 1.60 1.60
309 A58 96c + 10c like #305 1.60 1.60
310 A58 96c + 10c like #306 1.60 1.60

No. 306a contains Nos. 303-306, each with 5c surcharge. Nos. 307-310 issued Dec. 10. Surtax for children's charities.

Audubon Bicentenary A59

20c, Harlequin duck. 55c, Sage grouse. 65c, Solitary sandpiper. 75c, Red-backed sandpiper.

1985, Apr. 9 Photo. ***Perf. 13***
311 A59 20c multi 1.50 1.50
312 A59 55c multi 4.00 4.00
313 A59 65c multi 4.75 4.75
314 A59 75c multi 5.25 5.25
Nos. 311-314 (4) 15.50 15.50

Souvenir Sheets

Perf. 13½x13
315 A59 95c Like #311 3.00 2.00
316 A59 95c Like #312 3.00 2.00
317 A59 95c Like #313 3.00 2.00
318 A59 95c Like #314 3.00 2.00

For surcharges see Nos. 391-394.

Queen Mother, 85th Birthday — A60

75c, Photograph, 1921. 95c, New mother, 1926. $1.20, Coronation day, 1937. $2.80, 70th birthday.
$5, Portrait, c. 1980.

1985, June 24 Photo. ***Perf. 13x13½***
319 A60 75c multicolored .55 *.65*
320 A60 95c multicolored .70 *.80*
321 A60 $1.20 multicolored 1.00 *1.00*
322 A60 $2.80 multicolored 2.25 *2.50*
a. Souvenir sheet of 4, #319-322 15.00 15.00
Nos. 319-322 (4) 4.50 *4.95*

Souvenir Sheet

323 A60 $5 multicolored 3.75 3.75

No. 322a issued on 8/4/86, for 86th birthday.

Intl. Youth Year — A61

Grimm Brothers' fairy tales: 75c, House in the Wood. 95c, Snow White and Rose Red. $1.15, Goose Girl.

1985, Sept. 10 ***Perf. 13x13½***
324 A61 75c multicolored 2.25 2.25
325 A61 95c multicolored 3.25 3.25
326 A61 $1.15 multicolored 4.50 4.50
Nos. 324-326 (3) 10.00 10.00

Christmas 1985 — A62

Paintings (details) by Murillo: 75c, No. 330a, The Annunciation. $1.15, No. 330b, Adoration of the Shepherds. $1.80, No. 330c, The Holy Family.

1985, Nov. 25 Photo. ***Perf. 14***
327 A62 75c multicolored 1.50 1.50
328 A62 $1.15 multicolored 2.25 2.25
329 A62 $1.80 multicolored 3.75 3.75
Nos. 327-329 (3) 7.50 7.50

Souvenir Sheets

Perf. 13½
330 Sheet of 3 4.25 4.25
a.-c. A62 95c any single 1.30 1.30
331 A62 $1.20 like #327 1.75 1.75
332 A62 $1.45 like #328 2.00 2.00
333 A62 $2.75 like #329 3.25 3.25

Halley's Comet — A63

Fire and Ice, by Camille Rendal. Nos. 334-335 se-tenant in continuous design.

1986, Feb. 4 ***Perf. 13½x13***
334 A63 $1.50 Comet head 3.50 3.50
335 A63 $1.50 Comet tail 3.50 3.50
a. Pair, #334-335 7.00 7.00

Size: 109x43mm

Imperf
336 A63 $3 multicolored 6.00 6.00
Nos. 334-336 (3) 13.00 13.00

Elizabeth II, 60th Birthday — A64

1986, Apr. 21 ***Perf. 14***
337 A64 95c Age 3 1.25 1.25
338 A64 $1.45 Wearing crown 1.60 1.60

Size: 60x34mm

Perf. 13½x13
339 A64 $2.50 Both portraits 2.75 2.75
Nos. 337-339 (3) 5.60 5.60

A65

Statue of Liberty, Cent.: 95c, Statue, scaffolding. $1.75 Removing copper facade. $3, Restored statue on Liberty Island.

1986, June 27 Photo. ***Perf. 13½***
340 A65 95c multicolored .85 .85
341 A65 $1.75 multicolored 1.75 1.75
342 A65 $3 multicolored 3.00 3.00
Nos. 340-342 (3) 5.60 5.60

A66

1986, July 23 ***Perf. 13x13½***
343 A66 $2.50 Portraits 3.00 3.00
344 A66 $3.50 Profiles 3.75 3.75

Wedding of Prince Andrew and Sarah Ferguson. Nos. 343-344 each printed in sheets of 4 plus 2 center decorative labels.

No. 298 Surcharged with Gold Circle, Bar, New Value in Black and Exhibition Emblem in Gold and Black

1986, Aug. 4
345 Sheet of 2 8.75 8.75
a. A57a $2 on 96c #298a 4.25 4.25
b. A57a $2 on 96c #298b 4.25 4.25

STAMPEX '86, Adelaide, Aug. 4-10.

Christmas — A67

Engravings by Rembrandt: 65c, No. 349a, Adoration of the Shepherds. $1.75, No. 349b, Virgin and Child. $2.50, No. 349c, The Holy Family.

1986, Nov. 20 Litho. ***Perf. 13x13½***
346 A67 65c multicolored 2.50 2.50
347 A67 $1.75 multicolored 3.50 3.50
348 A67 $2.50 multicolored 5.00 5.00
Nos. 346-348 (3) 11.00 11.00

Souvenir Sheet

Perf. 13½x13
349 Sheet of 3 13.00 13.00
a.-c. A67 $1.50 any single 4.00 4.00

Corrected inscription is black on silver.
For surcharges see Nos. B20-B23.

Souvenir Sheets

Statue of Liberty, Cent. — A68

Photographs: No. 350a, Workmen, crown. No. 350b, Ellis Is., aerial view. No. 350c, Immigration building, Ellis Is. No. 350d, Buildings, opposite side of Ellis Is. No. 350e, Workmen inside torch structure. No. 351a, Liberty's head and torch. No. 351b, Torch. No. 351c, Workmen on scaffold. No. 351d, Statue, full figure. No. 351e, Workmen beside statue. Nos. 351a-351e vert.

1987, Apr. 15 Litho. ***Perf. 14***
350 A68 Sheet of 5 + label 5.75 5.75
a.-e. 65c any single 1.05 1.05
351 A68 Sheet of 5 + label 5.75 5.75
a.-e. 65c any single 1.05 1.05

Nos. 62-63 Ovptd. "Fortieth Royal Wedding / Anniversary 1947-87" in Lilac Rose

1987, Nov. 20 Photo. ***Perf. 13½x14***
352 A18 $2 multicolored 2.00 2.00
353 A18 $5 multicolored 5.50 5.50

Christmas — A69

Paintings (details) by Raphael: 95c, No. 357a, The Garvagh Madonna, the National Gallery, London. $1.60, No. 357b, The Alba Madonna, the National Gallery of Art, Washington. $2.25, No. 357c, $4.80, The Madonna of the Fish, Prado Museum, Madrid.

1987, Dec. 11 Photo. ***Perf. 13½***
354 A69 95c multicolored 2.40 2.40
355 A69 $1.60 multicolored 3.00 3.00
356 A69 $2.25 multicolored 4.75 4.75
Nos. 354-356 (3) 10.15 10.15

Souvenir Sheets

357 Sheet of 3 + label 16.00 16.00
a.-c. A69 $1.15 any single 4.75 4.75
358 A69 $4.80 multicolored 16.00 16.00

No. 358 contains one 31x39mm stamp.

1988 Summer Olympics, Seoul — A70

Events and: 55c, $1.25, Seoul Games emblem. 95c, Obverse of a $50 silver coin issued in 1987 to commemorate the participation of Cook Islands athletes in the Olympics for the 1st time. $1.50, Coin reverse.

Perf. 13½x13, 13x13½
1988, July 29 Photo.
359 A70 55c Running 1.10 1.10
360 A70 95c High jump, vert. 2.20 2.20
361 A70 $1.25 Shot put 2.50 2.50
362 A70 $1.50 Tennis, vert. 4.00 4.00
Nos. 359-362 (4) 9.80 9.80

Souvenir Sheet

363 Sheet of 2 9.00 9.00
a. A70 $2.50 like 95c 4.25 4.25
b. A70 $2.50 like $1.50 4.25 4.25

Nos. 359-363 Ovptd. for Olympic Gold Medalists

a. "CARL LEWIS / UNITED STATES / 100 METERS"
b. "LOUISE RITTER / UNITED STATES / HIGH JUMP"
c. "ULF TIMMERMANN / EAST GERMANY / SHOT-PUT"
d. "STEFFI GRAF / WEST GERMANY / WOMEN'S TENNIS"
e. "JACKIE / JOYNER-KERSEE / United States / Heptathlon"
f. "STEFFI GRAF / West Germany / Women's Tennis / MILOSLAV MECIR / Czechoslovakia / Men's Tennis"

Perf. 13½x13, 13x13½
1988, Oct. 14 Photo.
364 A70(a) 55c on No. 359 1.20 1.20
365 A70(b) 95c on No. 360 2.40 2.40
366 A70(c) $1.25 on No. 361 2.75 2.75
367 A70(d) $1.50 on No. 362 4.50 4.50
Nos. 364-367 (4) 10.85 10.85

Souvenir Sheet

368 Sheet of 2 9.00 9.00
a. A70(e) $2.50 on No. 363a 4.25 4.25
b. A70(f) $2.50 on No. 363b 4.25 4.25

Christmas — A71

Virgin and Child paintings by Titian.

1988, Nov. 9 ***Perf. 13x13½***
369 A71 70c multicolored 1.40 1.40
370 A71 85c multi, diff. 1.75 1.75
371 A71 95c multi, diff. 2.25 2.25
372 A71 $1.25 multi, diff. 2.50 2.50
Nos. 369-372 (4) 7.90 7.90

Souvenir Sheet
Perf. 13

373 A71 $6.40 multi, diff. 9.00 9.00

No. 373 contains one diamond-shaped stamp, size: 55x55mm.

1st Moon Landing, 20th Anniv. — A72

Apollo 11 mission emblem, US flag and: 55c, First step on the Moon. 75c, Astronaut carrying equipment. 95c, Conducting experiment. $1.25, Crew members Armstrong, Collins and Aldrin. $1.75, Armstrong and Aldrin aboard lunar module.

1989, July 24 Photo. *Perf. 14*
374-378 A72 Set of 5 12.00 12.00

Christmas — A73

Details from *The Nativity*, by Albrecht Durer, 1498, center panel of the Paumgartner altarpiece: 55c, Madonna. 70c, Christ child, cherubs. 85c, Joseph. $1.25, Attendants. $6.40, Entire painting.

1989, Nov. 17 Photo. *Perf. 13x13½*
379-382 A73 Set of 4 6.00 6.00

Souvenir Sheet

383 A73 $6.40 multicolored 9.50 9.50

No. 383 contains one 31x50mm stamp.

Queen Mother, 90th Birthday A74

1990, July 24 Photo. *Perf. 13½*
384 A74 $2.25 multicolored 3.25 3.25

Souvenir Sheet

385 A74 $7.50 multicolored 16.00 16.00

Christmas — A75

Paintings: 55c, Adoration of the Magi by Veronese. 70c, Virgin and Child by Quentin Metsys. 85c, Virgin and Child Jesus by Van Der Goes. $1.50, Adoration of the Kings by Jan Gossaert. $6.40, Virgin and Child with Saints Francis, John the Baptist, Zenobius and Lucy by Domenico Veneziano.

1990, Nov. 26 Litho. *Perf. 14*
386-389 A75 Set of 4 9.00 9.00

Souvenir Sheet

390 A75 $6.40 multicolored 10.50 10.50

Nos. 311-314 Surcharged in Red or Black

1990, Dec. 5 Photo. *Perf. 13*
391 A59 $1.50 on 20c (R) 2.75 2.75
392 A59 $1.50 on 55c 2.75 2.75
393 A59 $1.50 on 65c 2.75 2.75
394 A59 $1.50 on 75c (R) 2.75 2.75
Nos. 391-394 (4) 11.00 11.00

Birdpex '90, 20th Intl. Ornithological Cong., New Zealand. Surcharge appears in various locations.

No. 172 Overprinted "COMMEMORATING 65th BIRTHDAY OF H.M. QUEEN ELIZABETH II"

1991, Apr. 22 Photo. *Perf. 13½*
395 A42 $6 multicolored 13.00 13.00

Christmas — A76

Paintings: 55c, Virgin and Child with Saints, by Gerard David. 85c, The Nativity, by Tintoretto. $1.15, Mystic Nativity, by Botticelli. $1.85, Adoration of the Shepherds, by Murillo. $6.40, Madonna of the Chair, by Raphael.

1991, Nov. 11 Litho. *Perf. 14*
396-399 A76 Set of 4 9.00 9.00

Souvenir Sheet

400 A76 $6.40 multicolored 15.00 15.00

1992 Summer Olympics, Barcelona A77

1992, July 27 Litho. *Perf. 14*
401 A77 75c Runners 2.25 2.25
402 A77 95c Boxing 2.60 2.60
403 A77 $1.15 Swimming 3.00 3.00
404 A77 $1.50 Wrestling 3.25 3.25
Nos. 401-404 (4) 11.10 11.10

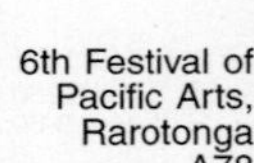

6th Festival of Pacific Arts, Rarotonga A78

Festival poster and: $1.15, Marquesan canoe. $1.75, Statue of Tangaroa. $1.95, Manihiki canoe.

1992, Oct. 16 Litho. *Perf. 14x15*
405 A78 $1.15 multicolored 2.50 2.50
406 A78 $1.75 multicolored 3.00 3.00
407 A78 $1.95 multicolored 3.50 3.50
Nos. 405-407 (3) 9.00 9.00

For overprints see Nos. 455-457.

Overprinted "ROYAL VISIT"

1992, Oct. 16
408 A78 $1.15 on #405 3.00 3.00
409 A78 $1.75 on #406 3.75 3.75
410 A78 $1.95 on #407 4.25 4.25
Nos. 408-410 (3) 11.00 11.00

Christmas — A79

Paintings by Ambrogio Bergognone: 55c, $6.40, Virgin with Child and Saints. 85c, Virgin on Throne. $1.05, Virgin on Carpet. $1.85, Virgin of the Milk.

1992, Nov. 18 Litho. *Perf. 13½*
411-414 A79 Set of 4 8.25 8.25

Souvenir Sheet

415 A79 $6.40 multicolored 11.00 11.00

No. 415 contains one 38x48mm stamp.

Discovery of America, 500th Anniv. — A80

Designs: $1.15, Vicente Yanez Pinzon, Nina. $1.35, Martin Alonso Pinzon, Pinta. $1.75, Columbus, Santa Maria.

1992, Dec. 4 *Perf. 15x14*
416 A80 $1.15 multicolored 2.75 2.75
417 A80 $1.35 multicolored 3.00 3.00
418 A80 $1.75 multicolored 4.25 4.25
Nos. 416-418 (3) 10.00 10.00

Coronation of Queen Elizabeth II, 40th Anniv. — A81

1993, June 4 Litho. *Perf. 14x14½*
419 A81 $6 multicolored 9.50 9.50

Marine Life — A82

Marine Life — A82a

5c, Helmet shell. 10c, Daisy coral. 15c, Hydroid coral. 20c, Feather star. 25c, Sea star. 30c, Nudibranch. 50c, Smooth sea star. 70c, Black pearl oyster. 80c, Pyjama nudibranch. 85c, Prickly sea cucumber. 90c, Organ pipe coral. $1, Aeolid nudibranch. $2, Textile cone shell.

1993-98 Litho. *Perf. 14*
420 A82 5c multi .25 .25
421 A82 10c multi .25 .25
422 A82 15c multi .25 .25
423 A82 20c multi .25 .25
424 A82 25c multi .30 .30
425 A82 30c multi .35 .35
426 A82 50c multi .55 .55
427 A82 70c multi .85 .80
428 A82 80c multi .95 .90
429 A82 85c multi 1.05 .95
430 A82 90c multi 1.05 1.00
431 A82 $1 multi 1.25 1.10
432 A82 $2 multi 3.50 2.25
433 A82a $3 pink & multi 5.00 3.25
434 A82a $5 lilac & multi 8.50 5.50

Perf. 14x13½

435 A82a $8 blue & multi 12.00 11.00
435A A82a $10 grn & multi 13.00 12.00
Nos. 420-435A (17) 49.35 40.95

For overprints see #O41-O53.

Issued: 80c, 85c, 90c, $1, $2, 12/3/93; $3, $5, 11/21/94; $8, 11/17/97; $10, 10/1/98; others, 10/18/93.

Christmas — A83

Details from Virgin on Throne with Child, by Cosimo Tura: 55c, Madonna and Child. 85c, Musicians. $1.05, Musicians, diff. $1.95, Woman. $4.50, Entire painting.

1993, Nov. 2 Litho. *Perf. 14*
436 A83 55c multicolored 1.40 1.40
437 A83 85c multicolored 2.10 2.10
438 A83 $1.05 multicolored 2.50 2.50
439 A83 $1.95 multicolored 3.75 3.75

Size: 32x47mm
Perf. 13½

440 A83 $4.50 multicolored 6.25 6.25
Nos. 436-440 (5) 16.00 16.00

First Manned Moon Landing, 25th Anniv. — A84

1994, July 20 Litho. *Perf. 14*
441 A84 $3.25 multicolored 10.00 10.00

Christmas — A85

Details or entire paintings: No. 442a, Virgin and Child with Saints Paul & Jerome, by Vivarini. b, The Virgin and Child with St. John, by B. Luini. c, The Virgin and Child with Saints Jerome & Dominic, by F. Lippi. d, Adoration of Shepherds, by Murillo.

No. 443a, Adoration of the Kings, by Reni. b, Madonna & Child with the Infant Baptist, by Raphael. c, Adoration of the Kings, by Reni, diff. d, Virgin and Child, by Bergognone.

1994, Nov. 30 Litho. *Perf. 14*
442 A85 90c Block of 4, #a.-d. 5.75 5.75
443 A85 $1 Block of 4, #a.-d. 6.25 6.25

End of World War II, 50th Anniv. A86

Designs: a, Battleships on fire, Pearl Harbor, Dec. 7, 1941. b, B-29 bomber Enola Gay, A-bomb cloud, Aug. 1945.

1995, Sept. 4 Litho. *Perf. 13*
444 A86 $3.75 Pair, #a.-b. 22.00 22.00

Queen Mother, 95th Birthday — A87

1995, Sept. 14 Litho. *Perf. 13½*
445 A87 $4.50 multicolored 12.00 12.00

No. 445 was issued in sheets of 4.

UN, 50th Anniv. A88

1995, Oct. 20 Litho. *Perf. 13½*
446 A88 $4 multicolored 5.75 5.75

No. 446 was issued in sheets of 4.

1995, Year of the Sea Turtle — A89

No. 447: a, Loggerhead. b, Hawksbill.
No. 448: a, Olive ridley. b, Green.

1995, Dec. 7 Litho. *Perf. 13½*

447 A89 $1.15 Pair, #a.-b. 4.75 4.75
448 A89 $1.65 Pair, #a.-b. 7.25 7.25

Queen Elizabeth II, 70th Birthday — A90

1996, June 20 Litho. *Perf. 14*

449 A90 $4.25 multicolored 7.50 7.50

No. 449 was issued in sheets of 4.

1996 Summer Olympic Games, Atlanta — A91

1996, July 12 Litho. *Perf. 14*

450 A91 $5 multicolored 9.50 9.50

Queen Elizabeth II and Prince Philip, 50th Wedding Anniv. — A92

1997, Nov. 20 Litho. *Perf. 14*

451 A92 $3 multicolored 4.50 4.50

Souvenir Sheet

452 A92 $4 multicolored 5.50 5.50

No. 452 is a continuous design.

Diana, Princess of Wales (1961-97) — A93

1998, May 7 Litho. *Perf. 14*

453 A93 $1.50 multicolored 3.00 3.00

Souvenir Sheet

454 A93 $3.75 like #453 6.00 6.00

No. 453 was issued in sheets of 5 + label. For surcharge see #B24.

Nos. 405-407 Ovptd. "KIA ORANA / THIRD MILLENNIUM"

Methods and Perfs as before

1999, Dec. 31

455 A78 $1.15 multi 1.30 1.30
456 A78 $1.75 multi 2.10 2.10
457 A78 $1.95 multi 2.60 2.60
Nos. 455-457 (3) 6.00 6.00

Queen Mother, 100th Birthday A94

No. 458: a, With King George VI. b, With Princess Elizabeth. c, With King George VI, Princesses Elizabeth and Margaret. d, With Princesses.

2000, Oct. 20 Litho. *Perf. 14*

458 A94 $2.50 Sheet of 4, #a-d 12.00 12.00

Souvenir Sheet

459 A94 $10 Portrait 12.00 12.00

2000 Summer Olympics, Sydney — A95

No. 460, horiz.: a, Ancient javelin. b, Javelin. c, Ancient discus. d, Discus.

2000, Dec. 14

460 A95 $2.75 Sheet of 4, #a-d 12.00 12.00

Souvenir Sheet

461 A95 $3.50 Torch relay 5.00 5.00

Worldwide Fund for Nature (WWF) — A96

Various photos of ocean sunfish: 80c, 90c, $1.15, $1.95.

2003, Feb. 24

462-465 A96 Set of 4 7.00 7.00

Each printed in sheets of 4.

United We Stand — A97

2003, Sept. 30

466 A97 $1.50 multicolored 1.75 1.75

Printed in sheets of 4.

Pope John Paul II (1920-2005) — A98

2005, Nov. 11

467 A98 $1.45 multicolored 2.75 2.75

Printed in sheets of 5 + label.

Worldwide Fund for Nature (WWF) — A99

Pacific reef egret: 80c, Male and female. 90c, Bird at water's edge. $1.15, Bird in flight. $1.95, Adult and chicks.

2008, Oct. 16 *Perf. 13½*

468-471 A99 Set of 4 5.75 5.75

Nos. 468-471 each were printed in sheets of 4.

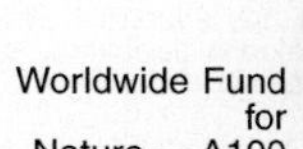

Worldwide Fund for Nature — A100

Striped dolphin: 80c, Breaching. 90c Pair underwater. $1.10, Breaching, diff. $1.20, Pod breaching.

2010, Dec. 9 *Perf. 14*

472-475 A100 Set of 4 6.00 6.00

Nos. 472-475 each were printed in sheets of 4.

A101

Engagement of Prince William and Catherine Middleton — A102

Designs: Nos. 476, 479a, 481, Prince. Nos. 477, 479b, 482, Middleton.

No. 478: a, Prince in military uniform. b, Prince playing polo. c, Middleton, fence. d, Prince, man and woman in background. e, Middleton, woman in background. f, Couple, Prince at left. g, Middleton with black hat. h, Prince. i, Couple, Middleton at left. j, Hands of couple, engagement ring.

$8.10, Couple, Prince in uniform at left.

2011, Jan. 14 *Perf. 14*

476 A101 $2 multi 3.25 3.25
477 A101 $2 multi 3.25 3.25

Miniature Sheets

478 A102 50c Sheet of 10, #a-j 7.75 7.75

Perf. 13¾x13½

479 A101 $2 Sheet of 2, #a-b 6.25 6.25

Souvenir Sheets

Perf. 14¼

480 A101 $8.10 multi 12.50 12.50
481 A101 $11 multi 17.00 17.00
482 A101 $11 multi 17.00 17.00
Nos. 480-482 (3) 46.50 46.50

No. 479 contains two 28x44mm stamps. Nos. 480-482 each contain one 38x50mm stamp.

A103

Peonies A104

2011, Apr. 8 Litho. *Perf. 13¼*

483 A103 $1.10 multi 1.75 1.75

Souvenir Sheet

Perf. 14¾x14

484 A104 $7.20 multi 11.50 11.50

Miniature Sheets

Pearl Industry A105

No. 485 — Inscription "Pinctada Margaritifera" and: a, 80c, Buildings near shore. b, 90c, Pearls. c, $1.10, Diver at surface holding string of oysters. d, $1.20, Diver tending string of oysters underwater.

No. 486 — Inscription "Pearl Industry" and: a, 20c, Shark. b, 30c, Diver at surface. c, 50c, Pearls, diff. d, $1, Pearl in tongs. e, $2, Pearl oysters.

2011, May 5 *Perf. 13¾*

485 A105 Sheet of 4, #a-d 6.50 6.50
486 A105 Sheet of 5, #a-e 6.50 6.50

Tourism — A106

Designs: 10c, Birds flying over ocean. 20c, Ray. 30c, Buildings on shore. 40c, Rocky coastline. 50c, Road in forest. 60c, Sharks. 70c, Aerial view of island. 80c, Clouds over ocean. 90c, Palm trees near shore. $1, Sharks, diff. $1.10, Saab 340 airplane, aerial view of island. $1.20, Pearls. $1.50, Sea turtle. $2, Aerial view of island, diff. $3, Sun and clouds above island.

2011, May 6 *Perf. 14*

487 A106 10c multi .25 .25
488 A106 20c multi .35 .35
489 A106 30c multi .50 .50
490 A106 40c multi .65 .65
491 A106 50c multi .80 .80
492 A106 60c multi .95 .95
493 A106 70c multi 1.10 1.10
494 A106 80c multi 1.25 1.25
495 A106 90c multi 1.50 1.50
496 A106 $1 multi 1.60 1.60
497 A106 $1.10 multi 1.75 1.75
498 A106 $1.20 multi 1.90 1.90
499 A106 $1.50 multi 2.40 2.40
500 A106 $2 multi 3.25 3.25
501 A106 $3 multi 4.75 4.75
a. Miniature sheet of 15, #487-501 23.00 23.00
Nos. 487-501 (15) 23.00 23.00

Souvenir Sheet

Wedding of Prince William and Catherine Middleton — A107

No. 502 — Couple in wedding procession: a, $1. b, $1.20.

2011, July 15 *Perf. 15x14¼*

502 A107 Sheet of 2, #a-b 3.75 3.75

Christmas — A108

No. 503: a, Partridge in a pear tree. b, Two turtle doves. c, Three French hens. d, Four calling birds.

2011, Dec. 24 *Perf. 13¼*

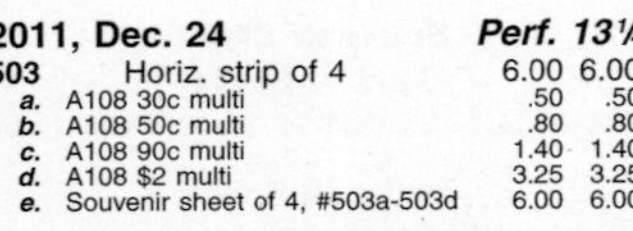

503	Horiz. strip of 4	6.00	6.00
a.	A108 30c multi	.50	.50
b.	A108 50c multi	.80	.80
c.	A108 90c multi	1.40	1.40
d.	A108 $2 multi	3.25	3.25
e.	Souvenir sheet of 4, #503a-503d	6.00	6.00

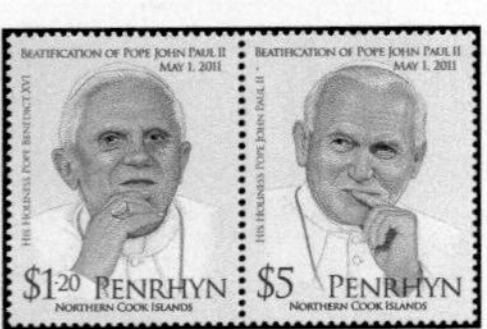

Beatification of Pope John Paul II — A109

No. 504: a, $1.20, Pope Benedict XVI. b, $5, Pope John Paul II.

2012, Jan. 10 *Perf. 13¾*

504 A109	Horiz. pair, #a-b	10.50	10.50

Christ Taking Leave of His Mother, by Correggio A110

Deposition, by Correggio A111

The Martyrdom of Four Saints, by Correggio A112

Mystic Marriage of St. Catherine and St. Sebastian, by Correggio A113

Nativity, by Correggio, c. 1510 — A114

The Nativity of Christ, by Correggio, c. 1529-30 — A115

Perf. 14¾x14¼

2012, Nov. 16 **Litho.**

Stamps With White Frames

505	Horiz. pair	2.80	2.80
a.	A110 80c multi	1.40	1.40
b.	A111 80c multi	1.40	1.40
506	Horiz. pair	3.00	3.00
a.	A112 90c multi	1.50	1.50
b.	A113 90c multi	1.50	1.50
507	Horiz. pair	10.00	10.00
a.	A114 $3 multi	5.00	5.00
b.	A115 $3 multi	5.00	5.00
	Nos. 505-507 (3)	15.80	15.80

Miniature Sheet

Stamps With Colored Frames

508	Sheet of 6	16.00	16.00
a.	A110 80c multi	1.40	1.40
b.	A111 80c multi	1.40	1.40
c.	A112 90c multi	1.50	1.50
d.	A113 90c multi	1.50	1.50
e.	A114 $3 multi	5.00	5.00
f.	A115 $3 multi	5.00	5.00

Fish A116

Nos. 509 and 512: a, 80c, Myripristis hexagonia. b, 90c, Scarus psittacus. c, $1.10, Zanclus cornutus. d, $1.20, Acanthurus guttatus.

Nos. 510 and 513: a, $2, Pygoplites diacanthus. b, $2.25, Chaetodon flavirostris. c, $4, Pseudanthias pleurotaenia. d, $5, Chaetodon ornatissimus.

Nos. 511 and 514: a, $6, Chaetodon melanotus. b, $8, Gymnothorax rueppellii. c, $10, Synchiropus ocellatus. d, $20, Kyphosus sandwichensis.

2012, Nov. 27 **Litho.** *Perf. 14*

Stamps With White Frames

509 A116	Block of 4, #a-d	6.75	6.75
510 A116	Block of 4, #a-d	22.00	22.00
511 A116	Block of 4, #a-d	72.50	72.50
	Nos. 509-511 (3)	101.25	101.25

Stamps Without White Frames

512 A116	Sheet of 4, #a-d	6.75	6.75
513 A116	Sheet of 4, #a-d	22.00	22.00
514 A116	Sheet of 4, #a-d	72.50	72.50
e.	Sheet of 12, #512a-512d, 513a-513d, 514a-514d	102.00	102.00
	Nos. 512-514 (3)	101.25	101.25

Personalizable Stamp — A117

A117a

A117b

2012, Dec. 21 **Litho.** *Perf. 14x14¾*

515 A117 $4 multi		6.75	6.75
a.	A117a 50c multi	.70	.70
b.	A117b $1 multi	1.40	1.40

Christmas (#515a, 515b). Issued: Nos. 515a, 515b, 12/16/19. Nos. 515a-515b have the same frame as the personalizable stamp No. 515, but have different denominations. The editors do not know if 50c and $1 stamps having these frames were made available to the public that may have different personalized images other than the images shown above placed in the vignette area. The editors also do not know if there are stamps of type A117 that are available in denominations other than 50c, $1, or $4.

Miniature Sheet

New Year 2013 (Year of the Snake) A118

No. 516 — Various snakes with background color of: a, Blue. b, Bright rose. c, Green. d, Yellow.

Perf. 14¾x14¼

2013, Feb. 21 **Litho.**

516 A118 $1.20	Sheet of 4, #a-d	8.00	8.00

Souvenir Sheet

Duchess of Cambridge — A119

No. 517 — Various photographs of pregnant Duchess of Cambridge: a, $1.30. b, $1.50. c, $1.70.

2013, Aug. 1 **Litho.** *Perf. 13¾x13½*

517 A119	Sheet of 3, #a-c	7.25	7.25

Birth of Prince George of Cambridge.

Souvenir Sheet

China International Collection Expo 2013, Beijing — A120

No. 518: a, $1.50, Painting by Paul Gauguin. b, $1.70, Beijing Exhibition Center.

2013, Sept. 26 **Litho.** *Perf. 12*

518 A120	Sheet of 2, #a-b	5.50	5.50

Pres. John F. Kennedy (1917-63) — A121

Designs: $2, Photograph of Kennedy. $3, Photograph of Kennedy and crowd, quote from Kennedy.

2013, Nov. 8 **Litho.** *Perf. 14x14¼*

519-520 A121	Set of 2	8.25	8.25

Fish — A122

Designs: 30c, Chaetodon ornatissimus. 50c, Kyphosus pacificus. $1, Acanthurus guttatus. $1.30, Chaetodon flavirostris. $1.50, Myripristis murdjan. $1.70, Pygoplites diacanthus. $2.40, Zanclus cornutus. $2.50, Scarus psittacus. $3, Rhinomuraena quaesita. $4.50, Synchiropus ocellatus. $7.50, Gymnothorax rueppelliae. $12.90, Hoplolatilus starcki.

2013, Nov. 11 **Litho.** *Perf. 14*

Stamps With White Frames

521 A122	30c	multi	.50	.50
522 A122	50c	multi	.85	.85
523 A122	$1	multi	1.75	1.75
524 A122	$1.30	multi	2.25	2.25
525 A122	$1.50	multi	2.50	2.50
526 A122	$1.70	multi	2.75	2.75
527 A122	$2.40	multi	4.00	4.00
528 A122	$2.50	multi	4.25	4.25
529 A122	$3	multi	5.00	5.00
530 A122	$4.50	multi	7.50	7.50
531 A122	$7.50	multi	12.50	12.50
532 A122	$12.90	multi	21.50	21.50
	Nos. 521-532 (12)		65.35	65.35

Stamps Without White Frames

533	Sheet of 12	66.00	66.00
a.	A122 30c multi	.50	.50
b.	A122 50c multi	.85	.85
c.	A122 $1 multi	1.75	1.75
d.	A122 $1.30 multi	2.25	2.25
e.	A122 $1.50 multi	2.50	2.50
f.	A122 $1.70 multi	2.75	2.75
g.	A122 $2.40 multi	4.00	4.00
h.	A122 $2.50 multi	4.25	4.25
i.	A122 $3 multi	5.00	5.00
j.	A122 $4.50 multi	7.50	7.50
k.	A122 $7.50 multi	12.50	12.50
l.	A122 $12.90 multi	21.50	21.50

Christmas — A123

Paintings by: $1, Peter Paul Rubens. $1.30, Albrecht Dürer.

No. 536 — Paintings by: a, $2, Sandro Botticelli. b, $2.40, William Brassey Hole. c, $2.60, Gerard van Honthorst.

2013, Nov. 18 **Litho.** *Perf. 13¼*

534-535 A123	Set of 2	3.75	3.75

Souvenir Sheet

536 A123	Sheet of 3, #a-c	11.50	11.50

Miniature Sheet

New Year 2014 (Year of the Horse) A124

No. 537 — Background color: a, $1, Yellow. b, $1.30, Red. c, $1.50, Blue. d, $1.70, Green.

2014, Jan. 10 **Litho.** *Perf. 13¾*

537 A124	Sheet of 4, #a-d	9.00	9.00

Easter A125

No. 538 — Religious paintings by: a, 50c, Peter Paul Rubens. b, $1, Lambert Lombard. c, $1.30, Titian. d, $1.50, Paolo Veronese. e, $1.70, Raphael.

$9.50, Painting by Dirck Bouts.

2014, Apr. 9 **Litho.** *Perf. 13¼*

538 A125	Sheet of 5, #a-e, + label	10.50	10.50

Souvenir Sheet

539 A125 $9.50 multi		16.50	16.50

Worldwide Fund for Nature (WWF) — A126

Pacific green turtle: Nos. 540, 544a, $1, On beach. Nos. 541, 544b, $1.70, Swimming. Nos. 542, 544c, $2, Swimming, diff. Nos. 543, 544d, $2.40, Pair on seafloor.

$7.50, Turtle swimming, diff.

Perf. 14¾x14¼

2014, Nov. 28 **Litho.**

Stamps With White Frames

540-543 A126	Set of 4	11.50	11.50

Stamps Without White Frames

544 A126	Strip of 4, #a-d	11.50	11.50

Souvenir Sheet

545 A126 $7.50 multi		12.00	12.00

Souvenir Sheet

Christmas — A127

No. 546 — Religious paintings by: a, Antonio da Correggio. b, Piero della Francesca. c, Sandro Botticelli.

Perf. 14¾x14¼

2014, Dec. 14 **Litho.**

546 A127 $1.50 Sheet of 3, #a-c 7.00 7.00

Souvenir Sheet

New Year 2015 (Year of the Sheep) A128

No. 547: a, $3.80, Red sheep. b, $4.10, Green sheep.

2015, Jan. 5 **Litho.** ***Perf. 13½***

547 A128 Sheet of 2, #a-b 12.50 12.50

Miniature Sheet

Easter A129

No. 548 — Details from religious paintings by: a, Peter Paul Rubens. b, Edouard Manet. c, Carl Heinrich Bloch. d, Jacopo Tintoretto.

2015, Mar. 31 **Litho.** ***Perf. 14***

548 A129 $2 Sheet of 4, #a-d 12.50 12.50

Souvenir Sheet

Birth of Princess Charlotte of Cambridge — A130

No. 549: a, Duke and Duchess of Cambridge, Princess Charlotte. b, Duke of Cambridge holding Prince George.

Perf. 14¾x14¼

2015, June 23 **Litho.**

549 A130 $4.50 Sheet of 2, #a-b 12.00 12.00

New Year 2016 (Year of the Monkey) — A131

Monkey with: $2.60, Both arms raised. $3, One arm raised.

No. 552 — Monkey with: a, $3.80, Both arms raised. b, $4.10, One arm raised.

2015, Sept. 25 **Litho.** ***Perf. 13¼***

550-551 A131 Set of 2 7.50 7.50

Souvenir Sheet

552 A131 Sheet of 2, #a-b 10.50 10.50

No. 552 contains two 50x50mm diamond-shaped stamps.

Miniature Sheet

Queen Elizabeth II, Longest-Reigning British Monarch — A132

No. 553 — Various photographs of Queen Elizabeth II: a, $1.30. b, $1.50. c, $1.70. d, $2.

2015, Nov. 20 **Litho.** ***Perf. 14***

553 A132 Sheet of 4, #a-d 8.75 8.75

Souvenir Sheet

Christmas — A133

No. 554 — Nativity, by Gerard David (details): a, Virgin Mary. b, Infant Jesus and animals. c, St. Joseph.

2015, Dec. 9 **Litho.** ***Perf. 13¼***

554 A133 $1 Sheet of 3, #a-c 4.25 4.25

Souvenir Sheet

Queen Elizabeth II, 90th Birthday A134

No. 555 — Queen Elizabeth II wearing: a, Gown. b, Hat and coat.

2016, May 10 **Litho.** ***Perf. 13¼***

555 A134 $3 Sheet of 2, #a-b 8.25 8.25

Marae Moana Marine Park — A135

Designs: 30c, Blue whale. 50c, Brown booby. 80c, Gray reef shark. $1, Emblem of Marae Moana Marine Park. $1.10, Humphead wrasse. $1.30, Scalloped hammerhead shark. $1.50, Hawksbill turtle. $1.70 False killer whale. $2, Brown noddy. $2.40, Blue shark. $2.50, Shortfin mako shark.

2016, May 27 **Litho.** ***Perf. 14x14¾***

556	A135	30c multi	.45	.45
557	A135	50c multi	.80	.80
558	A135	80c multi	1.20	1.20
559	A135	$1 multi	1.55	1.55
560	A135	$1.10 multi	1.65	1.65
561	A135	$1.30 multi	1.90	1.90
562	A135	$1.50 multi	2.30	2.30
563	A135	$1.70 multi	2.65	2.65
564	A135	$2 multi	3.00	3.00
565	A135	$2.40 multi	3.50	3.50
566	A135	$2.50 multi	3.75	3.75
		Nos. 556-566 (11)	22.75	22.75

New Year 2017 (Year of the Rooster) — A136

Rooster facing: $2.30, Right. $4.50, Left.

2016, Aug. 10 **Litho.** ***Perf. 13¼***

567-568 A136 Set of 2 11.00 11.00

568a Souvenir sheet of 2, #567-568 11.00 11.00

Christmas — A137

No. 569 — Stained-glass windows depicting: a, 50c, Madonna and Child, farm animals. b, 50c, Madonna and Child. c, $1, Madonna and Child. d, $1, Nativity with farm animals.

2016, Dec. 19 **Litho.** ***Perf. 13¼***

569 A137 Block of 4, #a-d 4.25 4.25

Miniature Sheet

First Contact of Explorers with Penrhyn Islanders, 200th Anniv. — A138

No. 570: a, $1, Aerial view of Penrhyn Island (36x36mm). b, $2, Otto von Kotzebue (1787-1846), explorer (36x36mm). c, $3, Map of Kotzebue's route (36x29mm). d, $4, Kotzebue's ship, Rurick (36x29mm).

2016, Dec. 28 **Litho.** ***Perf. 13¼***

570 A138 Sheet of 4, #a-d 14.00 14.00

Miniature Sheet

Easter A139

No. 571 — Paintings of the Resurrection of Jesus by: a, Caravaggio. b, Mikhail Vasilyevich Nesterov. c, Rembrandt. d, Tintoretto.

2017, Apr. 12 **Litho.** ***Perf. 13***

571 A139 $1 Sheet of 4, #a-d 5.75 5.75

Miniature Sheet

Pres. John F. Kennedy (1917-63) — A140

No. 572: a, $1, Pres. Kennedy and wife, Jacqueline at ceremony awarding medal to Alan B. Shepard, Jr. b, $1, Pres. Kennedy giving address at Rice University. c, $2.50, Nuclear weapon test on Bikini Atoll and radioactivity symbol. d, $2.50, Pres. Kennedy speaking after signing Nuclear Test Ban Treaty.

2017, July 3 **Litho.** ***Perf. 13***

572 A140 Sheet of 4, #a-d 10.50 10.50

Miniature Sheet

Reign of Queen Elizabeth II, 65th Anniv. A141

No. 573 — Queen Elizabeth II: a, Wearing coat with fur collar. b, Wearing tiara. c, Wearing maroon hat. d, Standing with military officer.

2017, July 17 **Litho.** ***Perf. 13***

573 A141 $2.50 Sheet of 4, #a-d 15.00 15.00

New Year 2018 (Year of the Dog) — A142

Dog facing: $3, Right. $3.80, Left.

2017, Nov. 1 **Litho.** ***Perf. 13¼***

574-575 A142 Set of 2 10.00 10.00

575a Souvenir sheet of 2, #574-575 10.00 10.00

Worldwide Fund for Nature (WWF) — A143

Photographs of Bennett's butterflyfish: Nos. 576, 580a, $1, With three other fish. Nos. 577, 580b, $1.70, Nose facing UL corner. Nos. 578, 580c, $2, Nose facing LR corner. Nos. 579, 580d, $2.40, facing left.

2017, Nov. 6 **Litho.** ***Perf. 13x13¼***

Stamps With White Frames

576-579 A143 Set of 4 10.75 10.75

Stamps Without White Frames

580 A143 Block or horiz. strip of 4, #a-d 10.75 10.75

No. 580 was printed in sheets containing two each of Nos. 580a-580d.

Christmas — A144

No. 581: a, $1, Seahorse. b, $1, Sailboat. c, $2.40, Bird. d, $2.40, Shell.

2017, Dec. 5 Litho. *Perf. 12½*
581 A144 Block of 4, #a-d 9.75 9.75

Miniature Sheet

Easter A145

No. 582: a, $1, Church and palm tree. b, $1, Flowers. c, $2.40, Palm trees and Easter eggs. d, $2.40, Crosses, butterflies, shell, starfish.

2018, Mar. 19 Litho. *Perf. 12½*
582 A145 Sheet of 4, #a-d 10.00 10.00

Birdpex 2018 Philatelic Exhibition, Mondorf-les-Bains, Luxembourg — A146

No. 583: a, Marbled godwit. b, Temminck's stint. c, Wilson's phalarope. d, Common sandpiper.

2018, May 4 Litho. *Perf. 13¼x13*
583 A146 $1.50 Block of 4, #a-d 8.50 8.50

Wedding of Prince Harry and Meghan Markle A147

No. 584: a, Bride walking down aisle. b, Princes Harry and William.
$8, Bride and groom in coach.

2018, Aug. 2 Litho. *Perf. 13*
584 A147 $4.80 Sheet of 2, #a-b 12.50 12.50

Souvenir Sheet
585 A147 $8 multi 10.50 10.50

New Year 2019 (Year of the Pig) — A148

Designs: $3, Pig. $3.80, Pig, diff.

2018, Dec. 10 Litho. *Perf. 13¼*
586-587 A148 Set of 2 9.25 9.25

Birds — A149

Designs: Nos. 588, 600a, Secretarybirds. Nos. 589, 600b, White-tailed eagle. Nos. 590, 600c, European honey buzzard. Nos. 591, 600d, Black-shouldered kite. Nos. 592, 600e, Swallow-tailed kite. Nos. 593, 600f, Osprey. Nos. 594, 600g, Snail kite. Nos. 595, 600h, Pallas's sea eagle. Nos. 596, 600i, Steller's sea eagles. Nos. 597, 600j, Bald eagle. Nos. 598, 600k, Yellow-billed kite. Nos. 599, 600l, Bearded vulture.

2018, Dec. 20 Litho. *Perf. 12¾*
Stamps With White Frames
588 A149 20c multi .25 .25
589 A149 30c multi .40 .40
590 A149 40c multi .55 .55
591 A149 50c multi .65 .65
592 A149 $1 multi 1.40 1.40
593 A149 $2 multi 2.75 2.75
a. Souvenir sheet of 6, #588-593 7.00 7.00
594 A149 $2.40 multi 3.25 3.25
595 A149 $2.60 multi 3.50 3.50
596 A149 $4.50 multi 6.00 6.00
597 A149 $5 multi 6.75 6.75
598 A149 $7.50 multi 10.00 10.00
599 A149 $10 multi 13.50 13.50
a. Souvenir sheet of 6, #594-599 45.00 45.00
Nos. 588-599 (12) 49.00 49.00

Stamps Without White Frame
600 Sheet of 12 50.00 50.00
a. A149 20c multi .25 .25
b. A149 30c multi .40 .40
c. A149 40c multi .55 .55
d. A149 50c multi .65 .65
e. A149 $1 multi 1.40 1.40
f. A149 $2 multi 2.75 2.75
g. A149 $2.40 multi 3.25 3.25
h. A149 $2.60 multi 3.50 3.50
i. A149 $4.50 multi 6.00 6.00
j. A149 $5 multi 6.75 6.75
k. A149 $7.50 multi 10.00 10.00
l. A149 $7.50 multi 13.50 13.50

Stamps from Nos. 593a and 599a have white frames on 1 or 2 sides. See Nos. 603-607, 608-612, 623-627, 628-632, 653-659.

New Year 2020 (Year of the Rat) — A150

Designs: $3, Rat. $3.80, Rat, diff.

2019, Oct. 11 Litho. *Perf. 13¼*
601-602 A150 Set of 2 8.75 8.75

Birds Type of 2018

Designs: Nos. 603, 607a, Military macaw. Nos. 604, 607b, Blue-throated macaw. Nos. 605, 607c, Scarlet macaws. Nos. 606, 607d, Chestnut-fronted macaw.

2019, Oct. 11 Litho. *Perf. 12¾*
Stamps With White Frames
603 A149 $5.50 multi 7.25 7.25
604 A149 $6.70 multi 8.75 8.75
605 A149 $22.40 multi 29.00 29.00
606 A149 $29.90 multi 38.50 38.50
Nos. 603-606 (4) 83.50 83.50

Stamps Without White Frames Size:48x40mm
Perf. 13½x13
607 Block or vert. strip of 4 83.50 83.50
a. A149 $5.50 multi 7.25 7.25
b. A149 $6.70 multi 8.75 8.75
c. A149 $22.40 multi 29.00 29.00
d. A149 $29.90 multi 38.50 38.50
e. Souvenir sheet of 4, #607a-607d 83.50 83.50

Stamps on No. 607e have white frames on two sides.

Birds Type of 2018

Designs: Nos. 608, 612a, Mississippi kite. Nos. 609, 612b, Snowy owl. Nos. 610, 612c, Black kite. Nos. 611, 612d, African goshawk.

2019, Nov. 15 Litho. *Perf. 12¾*
Stamps With White Frames
608 A149 $2.50 multi 3.25 3.25
609 A149 $3 multi 3.75 3.75
610 A149 $4 multi 5.25 5.25
611 A149 $6 multi 7.75 7.75
Nos. 608-611 (4) 20.00 20.00

Stamps Without White Frames Size:48x40mm
Perf. 13½x13
612 Block or vert. strip of 4 20.00 20.00
a. A149 $2.50 multi 3.25 3.25
b. A149 $3 multi 3.75 3.75
c. A149 $4 multi 5.25 5.25
d. A149 $6 multi 7.75 7.75
e. Souvenir sheet of 4, #612a-612d 20.00 20.00

Stamps on No. 612e have white frames on two sides.

Butterflies A151

Designs: Nos. 613, 621a, 50c, Large marble butterfly. Nos. 614, 621b, $1, Luzon peacock swallowtail butterfly. Nos. 615, 621c, $5, Blue morpho butterfly. Nos. 616, 621d, $7, Banded Orange butterfly. Nos. 617, 622a, $10, Question mark butterfly. Nos. 618, 622b, $20, Glasswinged butterfly. Nos 619, 622c, $30, Common buckeye butterfly. Nos. 620, 622d, $34.70, Ceylon rose butterfly.

2020, Jan. 15 Litho. *Perf. 13*
Stamps With White Frames
613 A151 50c multi .65 .65
614 A151 $1 multi 1.30 1.30
615 A151 $5 multi 6.50 6.50
616 A151 $7 multi 9.00 9.00
617 A151 $10 multi 13.00 13.00
618 A151 $20 multi 26.00 26.00
619 A151 $30 multi 39.00 39.00
620 A151 $34.70 multi 45.00 45.00
Nos. 613-620 (8) 140.45 140.45

Stamps Without White Frames Stamp Size: 48x40mm
Perf. 13¼x13
621 A151 Block or vert. strip of 4, #a-d 17.50 17.50
e. Souvenir sheet of 4, #621a-621d 17.50 17.50
622 A151 Block or vert. strip of 4, #a-d 125.00 125.00
e. Souvenir sheet of 4, #622a-622d 125.00 125.00

Nos. 621a-621d and 622a-622d were printed in sheets of 8 containing two of each stamp. Stamps on Nos. 621e and 622e have white frames on two adjacent sides.

Nos. 621d-621e have wrong inscription of "Ceylon Rose Butterfly."

Birds Type of 2018

Designs: Nos. 623, 627a, $2.50, Brown sicklebill. Nos. 624, 627b, $3, Twelve-wired bird-of-paradise. Nos. 625, 627c, $4, Lesser bird-of-paradise. Nos. 626, 627d, $6, Magnificent bird-of-paradise.

2020, May 8 Litho. *Perf. 13*
Stamps With White Frames
623 A149 $2.50 multi 3.25 3.25
624 A149 $3 multi 3.75 3.75
625 A149 $4 multi 5.00 5.00
626 A149 $6 multi 7.50 7.50
Nos. 623-626 (4) 19.50 19.50

Stamps Without White Frames Stamp Size: 48x40mm
Perf. 13¼x13
627 A149 Block or vert. strip of 4, #a-d 19.50 19.50
e. Souvenir sheet of 4, #627a-627d 19.50 19.50

Nos. 627a-627d were printed in sheets of 8 containing two of each stamp. Stamps on No. 627e have white frames on two adjacent sides.

Birds Type of 2018

Designs: Nos. 628, 632a, $5.50, American flamingos. Nos. 629, 632b, $6.70, Chilean flamingo. Nos. 630, 632c, $22.40, Greater flamingo. Nos. 631, 632d, $29.90, Andean flamingo.

2020, May 20 Litho. *Perf. 13*
Stamps With White Frames
628 A149 $5.50 multi 7.00 7.00
629 A149 $6.70 multi 8.50 8.50
630 A149 $22.40 multi 28.00 28.00
631 A149 $29.90 multi 37.50 37.50
Nos. 628-631 (4) 81.00 81.00

Stamps Without White Frames Stamp Size: 48x40mm
Perf. 13¼x13
632 A149 Block or vert. strip of 4, #a-d 81.00 81.00
e. Souvenir sheet of 4, #632a-632d 81.00 81.00

Nos. 632a-632d were printed in sheets of 8 containing two of each stamp. Stamps on No. 632e have white frames on two adjacent sides.

Whales and Dolphins — A152

Designs: Nos. 633, 641a, 50c, Blue whale. Nos. 634, 641b, $1, Long-beaked common dolphin. Nos. 635, 641c, $5, Spinner dolphins. Nos. 636, 641d, $7, Sperm whale. Nos. 637, 642a, $10, Striped dolphin. Nos. 638, 642b, $20, Killer whale. Nos. 639, 642c, $30, Atlantic spotted dolphin. Nos. 640, 642d, $34.70, Humpback whale.

2020, June 15 Litho. *Perf. 13*
Stamps With White Frames
633 A152 50c multi .65 .65
634 A152 $1 multi 1.30 1.30
635 A152 $5 multi 6.50 6.50
636 A152 $7 multi 9.00 9.00
637 A152 $10 multi 13.00 13.00
638 A152 $20 multi 26.00 26.00
639 A152 $30 multi 39.00 39.00
640 A152 $34.70 multi 45.00 45.00
Nos. 633-640 (8) 140.45 140.45

Stamps Without White Frames Stamp Size: 48x40mm
Perf. 13¼x13
641 A152 Block or vert. strip of 4, #a-d 17.50 17.50
e. Souvenir sheet of 4, #641a-641d 17.50 17.50
642 A152 Block or vert. strip of 4, #a-d 125.00 125.00
e. Souvenir sheet of 4, #642a-642d 125.00 125.00

Nos. 641a-641d and 642a-642d were printed in sheets of 8 containing two of each stamp. Stamps on Nos. 641e and 642e have white frames on two adjacent sides.

Souvenir Sheet

New Year 2021 (Year of the Ox) A153

2021, Apr. 7 Litho. *Perf. 13¼x13*
643 A153 $5 multi 7.25 7.25

Spaceflight of Freedom 7, 60th Anniv. — A154

No. 644: a, Diagram showing trajectory and descent of Freedom 7. b, Launch of Freedom 7.

$3, Helicopter over Freedom 7 capsule in ocean, horiz. $4, Helicopter recovering Freedom 7 pilot Alan B. Shepard, Jr., horiz.

2021, May 5 Litho. *Perf. 13*
644 A154 $1.30 Pair, #a-b 3.75 3.75

Souvenir Sheets

Perf. 13¼x13

645 A154 $3 multi 4.50 4.50
646 A154 $4 multi 5.75 5.75

Nos. 645 and 646 each contain one 48x40mm stamp.

Miniature Sheets

Smithsonian Institution Programs and Museums — A155

No. 647: a, African mask. b, Airplane cockpit. c, Illustration of Parisian fashions of 1914. d, Advertisement illustration for John A. Salzer Seed Company. e, Tractor and barn. f, Compass rose.

No. 648, horiz.: a, Animal skull. b, Photograph taken by Chandra X-ray Observatory. c, Heads of two flamingos. d, Butterfly on flower. e, Volcano. f, Flower.

2021, May 5 Litho. *Perf. 13*

647 A155 20c Sheet of 6, #a-f 1.75 1.75
648 A155 40c Sheet of 6, #a-f 3.50 3.50

Souvenir Sheet

New Year 2022 (Year of the Tiger) A156

2022, Feb. 23 Litho. *Perf. 13x13¼*

649 A156 $6.70 multi 9.00 9.00

Miniature Sheet

Reign of Queen Elizabeth II, 70th Anniv. A157

No. 650 — Queen Elizabeth II (1926-2022): a, Wearing yellow jacket, seated with Prince Philip. b, Wearing crown entering ceremony with Prince Philip. c, Wearing white hat. d, With dignitaries and military officers. e, Wearing tiara, standing near microphones. f, Seated in coach with Prince Philip.

2022, June 20 Litho. *Perf. 13*

650 A157 $3 Sheet of 6, #a-f 22.50 22.50

For overprints, see No. 652.

Souvenir Sheet

White Fronted Terns A158

2022, Aug. 18 Litho. *Perf. 13¼x13*

651 A158 $8.50 multi 10.50 10.50

2022 Birdpex Philatelic Exhibition, Gmunden, Austria

No. 650 With "IN LOVING MEMORY / 1926-2022" Overprinted on Each Stamp

Designs as before.

2022, Sept. 19 Litho. *Perf. 13*

652 A157 $3 Sheet of 6, #a-f 20.50 20.50

Birds Type of 2018

Various photographs of Striated heron: $5, On rock. $17.50, On tree. $20, Standing amidst water lilies. $25, Standing in stream.
Nos. 658-659 are vert.

2023, Aug. 16 Litho. *Perf. 13¼x13*

Stamps With White Frames
Size: 48x40mm

653 A149 $5 multi 6.00 6.00
654 A149 $17.50 multi 20.50 20.50
655 A149 $20 multi 23.50 23.50
656 A149 $25 multi 29.50 29.50
Nos. 653-656 (4) 79.50 79.50

Stamps Without White Frames

657 Block or vert. strip of 4 80.00 80.00
a. A149 $5 multi 6.00 6.00
b. A149 $17.50 multi 20.50 20.50
c. A149 $20 multi 23.50 23.50
d. A149 $25 multi 29.50 29.50
e. Souvenir sheet of 1 #657b 20.50 20.50
f. Souvenir sheet of 1 #657c 23.50 23.50

Souvenir Sheets

Perf. 13x13¼

658 A149 $5 multi 6.00 6.00
659 A149 $25 multi 29.50 29.50

SEMI-POSTAL STAMPS

Catalogue values for unused stamps in this section are for Never Hinged items.

Easter Type of 1978

Souvenir Sheets

Rubens Paintings: No. B1, like #101. No. B2, like #102. No. B3, like #103.

1978, Apr. 17 Photo. *Perf. 13½x13*

B1 A31 60c + 5c multi .50 .50
B2 A31 60c + 5c multi .50 .50
B3 A31 60c + 5c multi .50 .50
Nos. B1-B3 (3) 1.50 1.50

Surtax was for school children.

Easter Type of 1980

Souvenir Sheets

1980, Mar. 28 Photo. *Perf. 13x13½*

B4 A36 70c + 5c like #114 .45 .45
B5 A36 70c + 5c like #115 .45 .45
B6 A36 70c + 5c like #116 .45 .45
Nos. B4-B6 (3) 1.35 1.35

Surtax was for local charities.

Christmas Type of 1980

Souvenir Sheets

1980, Dec. 5 Photo. *Perf. 13*

B7 A39 70c + 5c like #127 1.00 1.00
B8 A39 70c + 5c like #128 1.00 1.00
B9 A39 70c + 5c like #129 1.00 1.00
Nos. B7-B9 (3) 3.00 3.00

Surtax was for local charities.

Easter Type of 1981

Souvenir Sheets

1981, Apr. 5 Photo. *Perf. 13½*

B10 A44 70c + 5c like #173 1.00 1.00
B11 A44 70c + 5c like #174 1.00 1.00
B12 A44 70c + 5c like #175 1.00 1.00
Nos. B10-B12 (3) 3.00 3.00

Surtax was for local charities.

Nos. 176-180a Surcharged

1981, Nov. 30 Photo. *Perf. 14*

B13 A45 40c + 5c like #176 .25 .25
B14 A45 50c + 5c like #177 .25 .25
B15 A45 60c + 5c like #178 .25 .25
B16 A45 70c + 5c like #179 .30 .30
B17 A45 80c + 5c like #180 .30 .30
Nos. B13-B17 (5) 1.35 1.35

Souvenir Sheet

B18 Sheet of 5 1.50 1.50
a. A45 40c + 10c like #176 .25 .25
b. A45 50c + 10c like #177 .25 .25
c. A45 60c + 10c like #178 .25 .25
d. A45 70c + 10c like #179 .25 .25
e. A45 80c + 10c like #180 .25 .25

Intl. Year of the Disabled. Surtax was for the disabled.

Soccer Type of 1981

1981, Dec. 7 *Perf. 13*

B19 A46 Sheet of 9 5.75 4.75

No. B19 contains Nos. 181-183. Surtax was for local sports.

Nos. 346-349 Surcharged ".SOUTH PACIFIC PAPAL VISIT . 21 TO 24 NOVEMBER 1986" in Metallic Blue

1986, Nov. 24 Litho. *Perf. 13x13½*

B20 A67 65c + 10c multi 4.50 4.50
B21 A67 $1.75 + 10c multi 6.50 6.50
B22 A67 $2.50 + 10c multi 8.00 8.00
Nos. B20-B22 (3) 19.00 19.00

Souvenir Sheet

Perf. 13½x13

B23 Sheet of 3 23.00 23.00
a.-c. A67 $1.50 + 10c on #349a-349c 7.00 7.00

No. B23 inscribed "COMMEMORATING FIRST PAPAL VISIT TO SOUTH PACIFIC / VISIT OF POPE JOHN PAUL II . NOVEMBER 1986."

No. 454 Surcharged "CHILDREN'S CHARITIES" in Silver

Souvenir Sheet

1998, Nov. 19 Litho. *Perf. 14*

B24 A93 $3.75 +$1 multi 6.00 6.00

OFFICIAL STAMPS

Catalogue values for unused stamps in this section are for Never Hinged items.

Nos. 51-60, 80, 88-89 Overprinted or Surcharged in Black, Silver or Gold

Perf. 13½x14, 13½, 13½x13

1978, Nov. 14 Photo.

O1 A17 1c multi .25 .25
O2 A17 2c multi .25 .25
O3 A17 3c multi .30 .25
O4 A17 4c multi .30 .25
O5 A17 5c multi .40 .25
O6 A17 8c multi .45 .25
O7 A17 10c multi .50 .25
O8 A17 15c on 60c multi .55 .35
O9 A17 18c on 60c multi .60 .35
O10 A17 20c multi .60 .35
O11 A17 25c multi (S) .65 .40
O12 A17 30c on 60c multi .70 .60
O13 A24 Strip of 3, multi 4.25 2.75
a. 50c, No. 80a (G) 1.25 .80
b. 50c, No. 80b (G) 1.25 .80
c. 50c, No. 80c (G) 1.25 .80
O14 A27 $1 multi (S) 2.75 .65
O15 A27 $2 multi (G) 5.25 .70
Nos. O1-O15 (15) 17.80 7.90

Overprint on No. O14 diagonal.

Nos. 268-276, 278, 277, 211-214, 280, 282, 281, 283, 170, 284, 171, 285, 172, 286 Surcharged with Bar and New Value or Ovptd. "O.H.M.S." in Silver or Metallic Red

1985-87 Photo. *Perfs. as before*

O16 A56 2c multi .25 .25
O17 A56 4c multi .25 .25
O18 A56 5c multi .25 .25
O19 A56 8c multi .25 .25
O20 A56 10c multi .25 .25
O21 A56 18c multi .25 .25
O22 A56 20c multi .25 .25
O23 A56 30c multi .25 .25
O24 A56 40c on 36c .35 .35
O25 A56 50c multi .40 .40
O26 A56 55c on 48c .45 .45
O27 A50 65c on 60c #211a .55 .55
O28 A50 65c on 60c #211b .55 .55
O29 A50 65c on 60c #211c .55 .55
O30 A50 65c on 60c #211d .55 .55
O31 A56 75c on 72c 1.05 .65
O32 A56 75c on 96c 1.05 .65
O33 A56 80c multi 1.05 .65
O34 A56 $1.20 multi 1.25 .85
O35 A42 $2 multi (R) 1.75 1.25
O36 A56 $3 multi 3.50 2.10
O37 A42 $4 multi (R) 4.00 3.50
O38 A56 $5 multi 6.50 4.00
O39 A42 $6 multi (R) 9.25 6.50
O40 A56 $9.60 multi 12.00 10.00
Nos. O16-O40 (25) 46.80 35.55

Issued: Nos. O16-O30, 8/15; Nos. O31-O37, 4/29/86; Nos. O38-O40, 11/2/87.

Nos. 420-432 Ovptd. in Silver

1998 Litho. *Perf. 14*

O41 A82 5c multicolored .30 .30
O42 A82 10c multicolored .30 .30
O43 A82 15c multicolored .30 .30
O44 A82 20c multicolored .30 .30
O45 A82 25c multicolored .30 .30
O46 A82 30c multicolored .40 .40
O47 A82 50c multicolored .55 .55
O48 A82 70c multicolored .70 .70
O49 A82 80c multicolored .95 .95
O50 A82 85c multicolored 1.10 1.10
O51 A82 90c multicolored 1.20 1.20
O52 A82 $1 multicolored 1.30 1.30
O53 A82 $2 multicolored 4.00 4.00
Nos. O41-O53 (13) 11.70 11.70

Nos. O41-O52 were not sold unused to local customers.

Issued: $2, 9/30; others, 7/20.

PERU

pə-'rü

LOCATION — West coast of South America
GOVT. — Republic
AREA — 496,093 sq. mi.
POP. — 32,970,000 (2020 est.)
CAPITAL — Lima

8 Reales = 1 Peso (1857)
100 Centimos = 8 Dineros = 4 Pesetas = 1 Peso (1858)
100 Centavos = 1 Sol (1874)
100 Centimos = 1 Inti (1985)
100 Centimos = 1 Sol (1991)

Catalogue values for unused stamps in this country are for Never Hinged items, beginning with Scott 426 in the regular postage section, Scott B1 in the semi-postal section, Scott C78 in the airpost section, Scott CB1 in the airpost semi-postal section, and Scott RA31 in the postal tax section.

Watermark

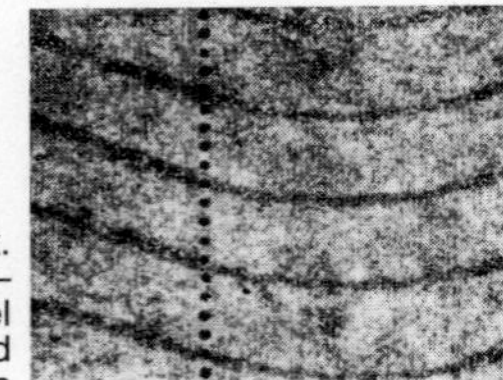

Wmk. 346 — Parallel Curved Lines

ISSUES OF THE REPUBLIC

Sail and Steamship — A1

Design: 2r, Ship sails eastward.

Unwmk.

1857, Dec. 1 Engr. *Imperf.*

1	A1 1r blue, *blue*		1,700.	2,250.
2	A1 2r brn red, *blue*		1,900.	3,000.

The Pacific Steam Navigation Co. gave a quantity of these stamps to the Peruvian government so that a trial of prepayment of postage by stamps might be made.

Stamps of 1 and 2 reales, printed in various colors on white paper, laid and wove, were prepared for the Pacific Steam Navigation Co. but never put in use. Value $50 each on wove paper, $400 each on laid paper.

Coat of Arms
A2 A3

A4

Wavy Lines in Spandrels

1858, Mar. 1 Litho.

3	A2 1d deep blue		275.00	47.50
4	A3 1p rose red		1,100.	160.00
5	A4 ½ peso rose red		*6,500.*	*4,750.*
6	A4 ½ peso buff		*2,750.*	375.00
a.	½ peso orange yellow		*2,750.*	375.00

A5

A6

Large Letters

1858, Dec. Double-lined Frame

7	A5 1d slate blue	450.00	45.00
8	A6 1p red	450.00	65.00

A7

A8

1860-61

Zigzag Lines in Spandrels

9	A7 1d blue	175.00	10.50
a.	1d Prussian blue	175.00	20.00
b.	Cornucopia on white ground	375.00	80.00
c.	Zigzag lines broken at angles	225.00	22.50
10	A8 1p rose	450.00	42.50
a.	1p brick red	450.00	42.50
b.	Cornucopia on white ground	450.00	42.50

Retouched, 10 lines instead of 9 in left label

11	A8 1p rose	250.00	27.50
a.	Pelure paper	425.00	32.50
	Nos. 9-11 (3)	875.00	80.50

A9

A10

1862-63 Embossed

12	A9 1d red	14.50	4.50
a.	Arms embossed sideways	550.00	150.00
b.	Thick paper	120.00	37.50
c.	Diag. half used on cover		350.00
13	A10 1p brown ('63)	120.00	37.50
a.	Diag. half used on cover		1,000.

Counterfeits of Nos. 13 and 15 exist.

A11

1868-72

14	A11 1d green	19.00	3.75
a.	Arms embossed inverted	*2,250.*	*1,200.*
b.	Diag. half used on cover		*2,000.*
15	A10 1p orange ('72)	150.00	55.00
a.	Diag. half used on cover		*1,100.*

Nos. 12-15, 19 and 20 were printed in horizontal strips. Stamps may be found printed on two strips of paper where the strips were joined by overlapping.

Llamas — A12

A13

A14

1866-67 Engr. *Perf. 12*

16	A12 5c green	10.50	.95
17	A13 10c vermilion	15.00	2.25
18	A14 20c brown	35.00	7.00
a.	Diagonal half used on cover		675.00
	Nos. 16-18 (3)	60.50	10.20

See Nos. 109, 111, 113.

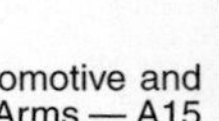

Locomotive and Arms — A15

1871, Apr. Embossed *Imperf.*

19	A15 5c scarlet	125.00	42.50
a.	5c pale red	125.00	42.50

20th anniv. of the first railway in South America, linking Lima and Callao.

The so-called varieties "ALLAO" and "CALLA" are due to over-inking.

Llama — A16

1873, Mar. *Rouletted Horiz.*

20	A16 2c dk ultra	50.00	*325.00*

Counterfeits are plentiful.

Sun God of the Incas — A17

Coat of Arms
A18 A19

A20

A21

A22 A23

Embossed with Grill

1874-84 Engr. *Perf. 12*

21	A17 1c orange ('79)	.90	.65
22	A18 2c dk violet	1.25	.95
23	A19 5c blue ('77)	1.40	.45
24	A19 5c ultra ('79)	13.00	3.25
25	A20 10c green ('76)	.45	.30
a.	Imperf., pair	35.00	
26	A20 10c slate ('84)	2.00	.45
a.	Diag. half used as 5c on cover		—
27	A21 20c brown red	3.50	1.10
28	A22 50c green	15.00	4.25
29	A23 1s rose	2.40	2.40
	Nos. 21-29 (9)	39.90	13.80

No. 25a lacks the grill.

No. 26 with overprint "DE OFICIO" is said to have been used to frank mail of Gen. A. A. Caceres during the civil war against Gen. Miguel Iglesias, provisional president. Experts question its status.

1880

30	A17 1c green	2.50
31	A18 2c rose	2.50

Nos. 30 and 31 were prepared for use but not issued without overprint.

See Nos. 104-108, 110, 112, 114-115.

For overprints see Nos. 32-103, 116-128, J32-J33, O2-O22, N11-N23, 1N1-1N9, 3N11-3N20, 5N1, 6N1-6N2, 7N1-7N2, 8N7, 8N10-8N11, 9N1-9N3, 10N3-10N8, 10N10-10N11, 11N1-11N5, 12N1-12N3, 13N1, 14N1-14N16, 15N5-15N8, 15N13-15N18, 16N1-16N22.

Stamps of 1874-80 Overprinted in Red, Blue or Black

1880, Jan. 5

32	A17 1c green (R)	.90	.65
a.	Inverted overprint	10.00	10.00
b.	Double overprint	13.50	13.50
33	A18 2c rose (Bl)	1.75	1.10
a.	Inverted overprint	10.00	10.00
b.	Double overprint	14.00	12.00
34	A18 2c rose (Bk)	75.00	60.00
a.	Inverted overprint		
b.	Double overprint		
35	A19 5c ultra (R)	3.50	1.75
a.	Inverted overprint	10.00	10.00
b.	Double overprint	14.00	14.00
36	A22 50c green (R)	45.00	27.50
a.	Inverted overprint	45.00	45.00
b.	Double overprint	55.00	55.00
37	A23 1s rose (Bl)	70.00	50.00
a.	Inverted overprint	110.00	110.00
b.	Double overprint	110.00	110.00
	Nos. 32-37 (6)	196.15	141.00

Stamps of 1874-80 Overprinted in Red or Blue

1881, Jan. 28

38	A17 1c green (R)	1.25	.95
a.	Inverted overprint	8.25	8.25
b.	Double overprint	14.00	14.00
39	A18 2c rose (Bl)	24.00	15.00
a.	Inverted overprint	17.50	15.00
b.	Double overprint	25.00	20.00
40	A19 5c ultra (R)	2.75	1.25
a.	Inverted overprint	14.00	14.00
b.	Double overprint	20.00	20.00
41	A22 50c green (R)	750.00	425.00
a.	Inverted overprint	850.00	
42	A23 1s rose (Bl)	140.00	90.00
a.	Inverted overprint	175.00	

Reprints of Nos. 38 to 42 were made in 1884. In the overprint the word "PLATA" is 3mm high instead of 2½mm. The cross bars of the letters "A" of that word are set higher than on the original stamps. The 5c is printed in blue instead of ultramarine.

For stamps of 1874-80 overprinted with Chilean arms or small UPU "horseshoe," see Nos. N11-N23.

Stamps of 1874-79 Handstamped in Black or Blue

1883

65	A17 1c orange (Bk)	1.25	1.10
66	A17 1c orange (Bl)	50.00	50.00
68	A19 5c ultra (Bk)	25.00	12.00
69	A20 10c green (Bk)	1.25	1.10
70	A20 10c green (Bl)	10.00	10.00
71	A22 50c green (Bk)	10.00	4.25
73	A23 1s rose (Bk)	10.00	8.00
	Nos. 65-73 (7)	107.50	86.45
	Nos. 65,68-73 (6)	57.50	36.45

This overprint is found in 11 types.

The 1c green, 2c dark violet and 20c brown red, overprinted with triangle, are fancy varieties made for sale to collectors and never placed in regular use.

Overprinted Triangle and "Union Postal Universal Peru" in Oval

1883

77	A22 50c grn (R & Bk)	210.00	110.00
78	A23 1s rose (Bl & Bk)	250.00	160.00

The 1c green, 2c rose and 5c ultramarine, over printed with triangle and "U. P. U. Peru" oval, were never placed in regular use.

Overprinted Triangle and "Union Postal Universal Lima" in Oval

1883

79	A17 1c grn (R & Bl)	70.00	70.00
80	A17 1c grn (R & Bk)	7.00	7.00
a.	Oval overprint inverted		
b.	Double overprint of oval		
81	A18 2c rose (Bl & Bk)	7.00	7.00
82	A19 5c ultra (R & Bk)	15.00	10.00
83	A19 5c ultra (R & Bl)	25.00	10.00
84	A22 50c grn (R & Bk)	250.00	150.00
85	A23 1s rose (Bl & Bk)	275.00	275.00
	Nos. 79-85 (7)	649.00	529.00

Some authorities question the status of No. 79.

Nos. 80, 81, 84, and 85 were reprinted in 1884. They have the second type of oval overprint with "PLATA" 3mm high.

Overprinted Triangle and

86	A17 1c grn (Bk & Bk)	1.75	1.25
a.	Horseshoe inverted	10.00	
87	A17 1c grn (Bl & Bk)	5.00	3.50
88	A18 2c ver (Bk & Bk)	1.75	1.25
89	A19 5c bl (Bk & Bk)	5.00	1.60
90	A19 5c bl (Bl & Bk)	12.00	10.50
91	A19 5c bl (R & Bk)	*1,500.*	*1,100.*

Overprinted Horseshoe Alone

1883, Oct. 23

95	A17 1c green	2.25	2.25
96	A18 2c vermilion	6.50	*6.50*
a.	Double overprint		
97	A19 5c blue	3.50	3.50
98	A19 5c ultra	20.00	15.00
99	A22 50c rose	57.50	57.50
100	A23 1s ultra	75.00	22.50
	Nos. 95-100 (6)	164.75	107.25

The 2c dark violet (A18) overprinted with the above design in red and triangle in black also the 1c green (A17) overprinted with the same combination plus the horseshoe in black, are fancy varieties made for sale to collectors.

No. 23 Overprinted in Black

1884, Apr. 28

103 A19 5c blue .65 .40
a. Double overprint 5.00 5.00

Stamps of 1c and 2c with the above overprint, also with the above and "U. P. U. LIMA" oval in blue or "CORREOS LIMA" in a double-lined circle in red, were made to sell to collectors and were never placed in use.

Without Overprint or Grill

1886-95

104 A17 1c dull violet .90 .30
105 A17 1c vermilion ('95) .65 .30
106 A18 2c green 1.25 .30
107 A18 2c dp ultra ('95) .55 .30
108 A19 5c orange 1.00 .45
109 A12 5c claret ('95) 2.25 .85
110 A20 10c slate .65 .30
111 A13 10c orange ('95) 1.00 .55
112 A21 20c blue 8.75 1.10
113 A14 20c dp ultra ('95) 10.50 2.25
114 A22 50c red 2.75 1.10
115 A23 1s brown 2.25 .85
Nos. 104-115 (12) 32.50 8.65

Overprinted Horseshoe in Black and Triangle in Rose Red

1889

116 A17 1c green .75 .75
a. Horseshoe inverted 7.50

Nos. 30 and 25 Overprinted "Union Postal Universal Lima" in Oval in Red

1889, Sept. 1

117 A17 1c green 5.00 1.60
117A A20 10c green 5.00 2.00

The overprint on Nos. 117 and 117A is of the second type with "PLATA" 3mm high.

Stamps of 1874-80 Overprinted in Black

Pres. Remigio Morales Bermúdez

1894, Oct. 23

118 A17 1c orange 1.00 .65
a. Inverted overprint 7.00 7.00
b. Double overprint 7.00 7.00
119 A17 1c green .65 .55
a. Inverted overprint 3.50 3.50
b. Dbl. inverted ovpt. 5.00 5.00
120 A18 2c violet .65 .55
a. Diagonal half used as 1c
b. Inverted overprint 7.00 7.00
c. Double overprint 7.00 7.00
121 A18 2c rose .65 .55
a. Double overprint 7.00 7.00
b. Inverted overprint 9.75 7.00
122 A19 5c blue 4.50 2.75
122A A19 5c ultra 7.25 3.50
b. Inverted overprint 10.00 10.00
123 A20 10c green .65 .55
a. Inverted overprint 7.00 7.00
124 A22 50c green 2.40 2.00
a. Inverted overprint 10.00 10.00
Nos. 118-124 (8) 17.75 11.10

Same, with Additional Ovpt. of Horseshoe

125 A18 2c vermilion .55 .45
a. Head inverted 2.50 2.50
b. Head double 5.00 5.00

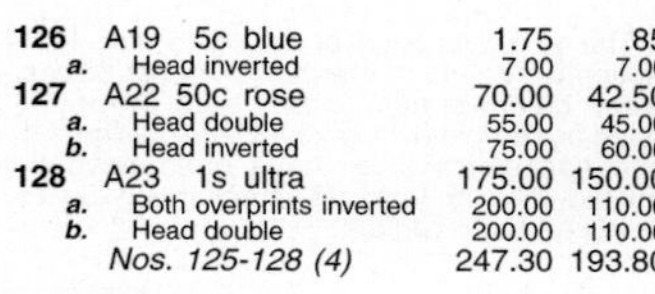

126 A19 5c blue 1.75 .85
a. Head inverted 7.00 7.00
127 A22 50c rose 70.00 42.50
a. Head double 55.00 45.00
b. Head inverted 75.00 60.00
128 A23 1s ultra 175.00 150.00
a. Both overprints inverted 200.00 110.00
b. Head double 200.00 110.00
Nos. 125-128 (4) 247.30 193.80

A23a

Vermilion Surcharge

1895 ***Perf. 11½***

129 A23a 5c on 5c grn 18.00 13.00
130 A23a 10c on 10c ver 13.00 10.00
131 A23a 20c on 20c brn 14.00 10.00
132 A23a 50c on 50c ultra 18.00 13.00
133 A23a 1s on 1s red brn 18.00 13.00
Nos. 129-133 (5) 81.00 59.00

Nos 129-133 were used only in Tumbes. The basic stamps were prepared by revolutionaries in northern Peru.

A23b

"Liberty" — A23c

1895, Sept. 8 **Engr.**

134 A23b 1c gray violet 1.90 1.10
135 A23b 2c green 1.90 1.10
136 A23b 5c yellow 1.90 1.10
137 A23b 10c ultra 1.90 1.10
138 A23c 20c orange 1.90 1.25
139 A23c 50c dark blue 10.00 7.00
140 A23c 1s car lake 55.00 35.00
Nos. 134-140 (7) 74.50 47.65

Success of the revolution against the government of General Caceres and of the election of President Pierola.

Manco Capac, Founder of Inca Dynasty A24

Francisco Pizarro Conqueror of the Inca Empire A25

General José de La Mar — A26

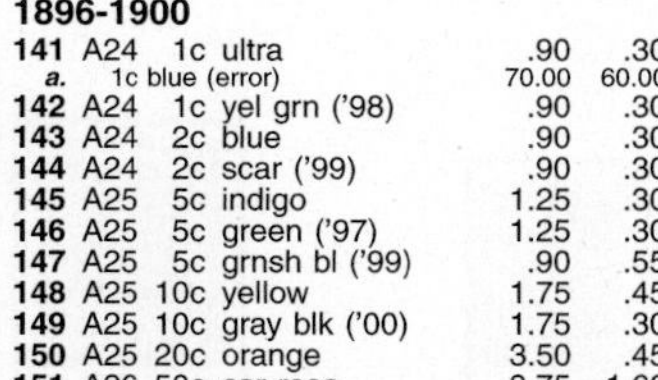

1896-1900

141 A24 1c ultra .90 .30
a. 1c blue (error) 70.00 60.00
142 A24 1c yel grn ('98) .90 .30
143 A24 2c blue .90 .30
144 A24 2c scar ('99) .90 .30
145 A25 5c indigo 1.25 .30
146 A25 5c green ('97) 1.25 .30
147 A25 5c grnsh bl ('99) .90 .55
148 A25 10c yellow 1.75 .45
149 A25 10c gray blk ('00) 1.75 .30
150 A25 20c orange 3.50 .45
151 A26 50c car rose 8.75 1.60
152 A26 1s orange red 13.00 1.60
153 A26 2s claret 3.50 1.25
Nos. 141-153 (13) 39.25 8.00

The 5c in black is a chemical changeling.

For surcharges and overprints see Nos. 187-188, E1, O23-O26.

Paucartambo Bridge — A27

Post and Telegraph Building, Lima — A28

Pres. Nicolás de Piérola — A29

1897, Dec. 31

154 A27 1c dp ultra 1.25 .60
155 A28 2c brown 1.25 .40
156 A29 5c bright rose 1.75 .60
Nos. 154-156 (3) 4.25 1.60

Opening of new P.O. in Lima.

No. J1 Overprinted in Black

1897, Nov. 8

157 D1 1c bister .90 .75
a. Inverted overprint 4.50 4.50
b. Double overprint 17.50 17.50

A31

1899

158 A31 5s orange red 2.75 2.75
159 A31 10s blue green 850.00 600.00

For surcharge see No. J36.

Pres. Eduardo de Romaña — A32

1900 **Frame Litho., Center Engr.**

160 A32 22c yel grn & blk 13.00 1.40

Admiral Miguel L. Grau — A33

2c, Col. Francisco Bolognesi. 5c, Pres. Romaña.

1901, Jan.

161 A33 1c green & blk 3.25 .75
162 A33 2c red & black 3.25 .75
163 A33 5c dull vio & blk 3.25 .75
Nos. 161-163 (3) 9.75 2.25

Advent of 20th century.

A34

1902 **Engr.**

164 A34 22c green .55 .30

Municipal Hygiene Institute Lima — A35

1905

165 A35 12c dp blue & blk 5.00 .50

For surcharges see Nos. 166-167, 186, 189.

Same Surcharged in Red or Violet

1907

166 A35 1c on 12c (R) .35 .30
a. Inverted surcharge 8.00 8.00
b. Double surcharge 8.00 8.00
167 A35 2c on 12c (V) .65 .45
a. Double surcharge 8.00 8.00
b. Inverted surcharge 8.00 8.00

Monument of Bolognesi A36

Admiral Grau A37

Llama A38

Statue of Bolivar A39

City Hall, Lima, formerly an Exhibition Building — A40

School of Medicine, Lima — A41

Post and Telegraph Building, Lima — A42

Grandstand at Santa Beatrix Race Track — A43

Columbus Monument — A44

1907

168	A36	1c yel grn & blk	.55	.30
169	A37	2c red & violet	.55	.30
170	A38	4c olive green	9.25	1.25
171	A39	5c blue & blk	1.00	.30
172	A40	10c red brn & blk	1.75	.45
173	A41	20c dk grn & blk	40.00	.75
174	A42	50c black	40.00	1.60
175	A43	1s purple & grn	200.00	3.75
176	A44	2s dp bl & blk	200.00	160.00
		Nos. 168-176 (9)	493.10	168.70

For surcharges and overprint see #190-195, E2.

Manco Capac A45

Columbus A46

Pizarro A47

San Martin A48

Bolívar A49

La Mar A50

Ramón Castilla A51

Grau A52

Bolognesi — A53

1909

177	A45	1c gray	.35	.25
178	A46	2c green	.35	.25
179	A47	4c vermilion	.45	.30
180	A48	5c violet	.35	.25
181	A49	10c deep blue	.75	.30
182	A50	12c pale blue	1.75	.30
183	A51	20c brown red	1.90	.45
184	A52	50c yellow	8.25	.55
185	A53	1s brn red & blk	17.00	.65
		Nos. 177-185 (9)	31.15	3.30

See types A54, A78-A80, A81-A89.
For surcharges and overprint see Nos. 196-200, 208, E3.

No. 165 Surcharged in Red

1913, Jan.

186	A35	8c on 12c dp bl & blk	.90	.35

Stamps of 1899-1908 Surcharged in Red

a

b

c

1915 **On Nos. 142, 149**

187	A24(a)	1c on 1c	27.50	22.50
a.		Inverted surcharge	32.50	37.50
188	A25(a)	1c on 10c	1.75	1.25
a.		Inverted surcharge	4.50	4.50
		On No. 165		
189	A35(c)	2c on 12c	.45	.30
a.		Inverted surcharge	7.75	7.75
		On Nos. 168-170, 172-174		
190	A36(a)	1c on 1c	1.10	1.10
a.		Inverted surcharge	3.50	3.50
191	A37(a)	1c on 2c	1.75	1.60
a.		Inverted surcharge	4.50	4.50
192	A38(b)	1c on 4c	3.25	2.75
a.		Inverted surcharge	10.50	10.50
193	A40(b)	1c on 10c	1.75	1.25
a.		Inverted surcharge	3.75	3.75
193C	A40(c)	2c on 10c	175.00	125.00
b.		Inverted surcharge	175.00	
194	A41(c)	2c on 20c	22.50	21.00
a.		Inverted surcharge	45.00	45.00
195	A42(c)	2c on 50c	3.25	3.25
a.		Inverted surcharge	13.00	13.00
		Nos. 187-195 (10)	238.30	180.00

Nos. 182-184, 179, 185 Surcharged in Red, Green or Violet

d

e

f

1916

196	A50(d)	1c on 12c (R)	.35	.25
a.		Double surcharge	5.00	5.00
b.		Green surcharge	7.50	7.50
197	A51(d)	1c on 20c (G)	.35	.25
198	A52(d)	1c on 50c (G)	.35	.25
a.		Inverted surcharge	5.00	5.00
199	A47(e)	2c on 4c (V)	.35	.25
a.		Green surcharge	1.60	1.25
200	A53(f)	10c on 1s (G)	1.10	.75
a.		"VALF"	10.50	10.50
		Nos. 196-200 (5)	2.50	1.75

Official Stamps of 1909-14 Ovptd. or Srchd. in Green or Red

g

h

1916

201	O1(g)	1c red (G)	.25	.25
202	O1(h)	2c on 50c ol grn (R)	.35	.25
203	O1(g)	10c bis brn (G)	.35	.25

Postage Due Stamps of 1909 Surcharged in Violet-Black

204	D7	2c on 1c brown	.75	.75
205	D7	2c on 5c brown	.25	.25
206	D7	2c on 10c brown	.25	.25
207	D7	2c on 50c brown	.25	.25
		Nos. 201-207 (7)	2.45	2.25

Many examples of Nos. 187 to 207 have a number of pin holes. It is stated that these holes were made at the time the surcharges were printed.

The varieties listed of the 1915 and 1916 issues were sold to the public at post offices. Many other varieties which were previously listed are now known to have been delivered to one speculator or to have been privately printed by him from the surcharging plates which he had acquired.

No. 179 Surcharged in Black

1917

208	A47	1c on 4c ver	.55	.55
a.		Double surcharge	8.25	8.25
b.		Inverted surcharge	8.25	8.25

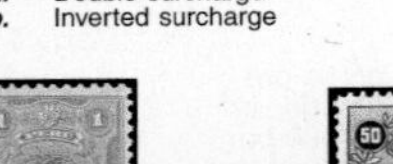

San Martin A54

Columbus at Salamanca A62

Funeral of Atahualpa — A63

Battle of Arica, "Arica, the Last Cartridge" — A64

Designs: 2c, Bolívar. 4c, José Gálvez. 5c, Manuel Pardo. 8c, Grau. 10c, Bolognesi. 12c, Castilla. 20c, General Cáceres.

1918 **Centers in Black** **Engr.**

209	A54	1c orange	.35	.25
210	A54	2c green	.35	.25
211	A54	4c lake	.45	.30
212	A54	5c dp ultra	.45	.30
213	A54	8c red brn	1.25	.45
214	A54	10c grnsh bl	.55	.30
215	A54	12c dl vio	1.75	.30
216	A54	20c ol grn	2.10	.30
217	A62	50c vio brn	8.25	.55
218	A63	1s greenish bl	21.00	.75
219	A64	2s deep ultra	35.00	1.10
		Nos. 209-219 (11)	71.50	4.85

For surcharges see Nos. 232-233, 255-256.

Augusto B. Leguía — A65

1919, Dec. **Litho.**

220	A65	5c bl & blk	.35	.30
a.		Imperf.	.35	.35
b.		Center inverted	15.00	15.00
221	A65	5c brn & blk	.35	.30
a.		Imperf.	.35	.35
b.		Center inverted	15.00	15.00

Constitution of 1919.

San Martín A66

Thomas Cochrane A70

Oath of Independence A69

Designs: 2c, Field Marshal Arenales. 4c, Field Marshal Las Heras. 10c, Martin Jorge Guisse. 12c, Vidal. 20c, Leguia. 50c, San Martin monument. 1s, San Martin and Leguia.

1921, July 28 **Engr.; 7c Litho.**

222	A66	1c ol brn & red brn	.45	.25
a.		Center inverted	600.00	600.00
223	A66	2c green	.55	.30
224	A66	4c car rose	1.90	.90
225	A69	5c ol brn	.60	.25
226	A70	7c violet	1.90	.65
227	A66	10c ultra	1.90	.65
228	A66	12c blk & slate	4.50	.90
229	A66	20c car & gray blk	4.50	1.10
230	A66	50c vio brn & dl vio	13.00	3.75
231	A69	1s car rose & yel grn	19.00	8.00
		Nos. 222-231 (10)	48.30	16.75

Centenary of Independence.

Nos. 213, 212 Surcharged in Black or Red Brown

1923-24

232	A54	5c on 8c No. 213	.75	.55
233	A54	4c on 5c (RB) ('24)	.55	.25
a.		Inverted surcharge	5.00	5.00
b.		Double surcharge, one inverted	6.00	6.00

A78

A79

Simón Bolívar — A80

Perf. 14, 14x14½, 14½, 13½

1924 **Engr.; Photo. (4c, 5c)**

234	A78	2c olive grn	.40	.25
235	A79	4c yellow grn	.65	.25
236	A79	5c black	2.25	.25
237	A80	10c carmine	.80	.25
238	A78	20c ultra	2.25	.30
239	A78	50c dull violet	5.50	1.10
240	A78	1s yellow brn	13.00	4.25
241	A78	2s dull blue	35.00	18.00
		Nos. 234-241 (8)	59.85	24.65

Centenary of the Battle of Ayacucho which ended Spanish power in South America.
No. 237 exists imperf.

José Tejada Rivadeneyra A81

Mariano Melgar A82

Iturregui A83

Leguía A84

José de La Mar A85

Monument of José Olaya A86

Statue of María Bellido A87

De Saco A88

José Leguía — A89

1924-29 **Engr.** ***Perf. 12***

Size: 18½x23mm

No.	Type	Description	Unused	Used
242	A81	2c olive gray	.35	.25
243	A82	4c dk grn	.35	.25
244	A83	8c black	3.25	3.25
245	A84	10c org red	.35	.25
245A	A85	15c dp bl ('28)	1.00	.30
246	A86	20c blue	1.75	.30
247	A86	20c yel ('29)	2.75	.30
248	A87	50c violet	8.25	.45
249	A88	1s bis brn	15.00	1.60
250	A89	2s ultra	40.00	8.00
		Nos. 242-250 (10)	73.05	14.95

See Nos. 258, 260, 276-282.

For surcharges and overprint see Nos. 251-253, 257-260, 262, 268-271, C1.

No. 246 Surcharged in Red

a

b

1925

No.	Type	Description	Unused	Used
251	A86(a)	2c on 20c blue	*550.00*	*550.00*
252	A86(b)	2c on 20c blue	1.75	1.10
a.		Inverted surcharge	50.00	50.00
b.		Double surch., one inverted	50.00	50.00

No. 245 Overprinted

1925

No.	Type	Description	Unused	Used
253	A84	10c org red	1.75	1.75
a.		Inverted overprint	21.00	21.00

This stamp was for exclusive use on letters from the plebiscite provinces of Tacna and Arica, and posted on the Peruvian transport "Ucayali" anchored in the port of Arica.

No. 213 Surcharged

a

b

1929

No.	Type	Description	Unused	Used
255	A54(a)	2c on 8c	1.25	1.25
256	A54(b)	2c on 8c	1.25	1.25

No. 247 Surcharged

No.	Type	Description	Unused	Used
257	A86	15c on 20c yellow	1.25	1.25
a.		Inverted surcharge	13.00	13.00
		Nos. 255-257 (3)	3.75	3.75

Types of 1924
Coil Stamps

1929 ***Perf. 14 Horizontally***

No.	Type	Description	Unused	Used
258	A81	2c olive gray	65.00	40.00
260	A84	10c orange red	70.00	37.50

Postal Tax Stamp of 1928 Overprinted

1930 ***Perf. 12***

No.	Type	Description	Unused	Used
261	PT6	2c dark violet	.55	.55
a.		Inverted overprint	3.25	3.25

No. 247 Surcharged

No.	Type	Description	Unused	Used
262	A86	2c on 20c yellow	.55	.55

Air Post Stamp of 1928 Surcharged

No.	Type	Description	Unused	Used
263	AP1	2c on 50c dk grn	.55	.55
a.		"Habitada"	2.10	2.10

Coat of Arms — A91

Lima Cathedral — A92

10c, Children's Hospital. 50c, Madonna & Child.

Perf. 12x11½, 11½x12

1930, July 5 **Litho.**

No.	Type	Description	Unused	Used
264	A91	2c green	1.75	.95
265	A92	5c scarlet	3.75	2.10
266	A92	10c dark blue	2.25	1.60
267	A91	50c bister brown	30.00	19.00
		Nos. 264-267 (4)	37.75	23.65

6th Pan American Congress for Child Welfare. By error the stamps are inscribed "Seventh Congress."

Type of 1924 Overprinted in Black, Green or Blue

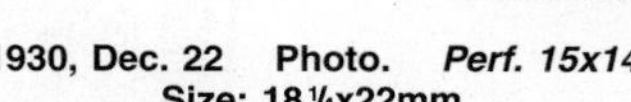

1930, Dec. 22 **Photo.** ***Perf. 15x14***

Size: 18¼x22mm

No.	Type	Description	Unused	Used
268	A84	10c orange red (Bk)	1.00	.80
a.		Inverted overprint	14.00	14.00
b.		Without overprint	8.50	8.50
c.		Double surcharge	7.00	7.00

Same with Additional Surcharge of Numerals in Each Corner

No.	Type	Description	Unused	Used
269	A84	2c on 10c org red (G)	.35	.25
a.		Inverted surcharge	17.00	
270	A84	4c on 10c org red (G)	.35	.25
a.		Double surcharge	12.50	12.50

Engr.

Perf. 12

Size: 19x23½mm

No.	Type	Description	Unused	Used
271	A84	15c on 10c org red (Bl)	.35	.25
a.		Inverted surcharge	14.00	14.00
b.		Double surcharge	14.00	14.00
		Nos. 268-271 (4)	2.05	1.55

Bolívar — A95

1930, Dec. 16 **Litho.**

No.	Type	Description	Unused	Used
272	A95	2c buff	.55	.55
273	A95	4c red	.90	.75
274	A95	10c blue green	.45	.30
275	A95	15c slate gray	.90	.90
		Nos. 272-275 (4)	2.80	2.50

Death cent. of General Simón Bolivar.

For surcharges see Nos. RA14-RA16.

Types of 1924-29 Issues

Size: 18x22mm

1931 **Photo.** ***Perf. 15x14***

No.	Type	Description	Unused	Used
276	A81	2c olive green	.45	.30
277	A82	4c dark green	.45	.30
279	A85	15c deep blue	1.25	.30
280	A86	20c yellow	2.10	.30
281	A87	50c violet	2.10	.45
282	A88	1s olive brown	3.25	.55
		Nos. 276-282 (6)	9.60	2.20

Pizarro — A96

Old Stone Bridge, Lima A97

1931, July 28 **Litho.** ***Perf. 11***

No.	Type	Description	Unused	Used
283	A96	2c slate blue	2.10	1.75
284	A96	4c deep brown	2.10	1.75
285	A96	15c dark green	2.10	1.75
286	A97	10c rose red	2.10	1.75
287	A97	10c mag & lt grn	2.10	1.75
288	A97	15c yel & bl gray	2.10	1.75
289	A97	15c dk slate & red	2.10	1.75
		Nos. 283-289 (7)	14.70	12.25

1st Peruvian Phil. Exhib., Lima, July, 1931.

Manco Capac A99

Oil Refinery A100

Sugar Cane Field A102

Picking Cotton A103

Guano Deposits A104

Mining A105

Llamas — A106

1931-32 ***Perf. 11, 11x11½***

No.	Type	Description	Unused	Used
292	A99	2c olive black	.35	.25
293	A100	4c dark green	.65	.30
295	A102	10c red orange	1.75	.25
a.		Vertical pair, imperf. between	30.00	
296	A103	15c turq blue	2.00	.30
297	A104	20c yellow	8.25	.30
298	A105	50c gray lilac	8.25	.30
299	A106	1s brown olive	20.00	1.40
		Nos. 292-299 (7)	41.25	3.10

Arms of Piura — A107

1932, July 28 ***Perf. 11½x12***

No.	Type	Description	Unused	Used
300	A107	10c dark blue	8.25	8.00
301	A107	15c deep violet	8.25	8.00
		Nos. 300-301,C3 (3)	42.50	38.50

400th anniv. of the founding of the city of Piura. On sale one day. Counterfeits exist. See No. C7.

Parakas A108

Chimu A109

Inca — A110

1932, Oct. 15 ***Perf. 11½, 12, 11½x12***

No.	Type	Description	Unused	Used
302	A108	10c dk vio	.35	.25
303	A109	15c brn red	.65	.30
304	A110	50c dk brn	1.50	.30
		Nos. 302-304 (3)	2.50	.85

4th cent. of the Spanish conquest of Peru.

Arequipa and El Misti A111

President Luis M. Sánchez Cerro A112

Monument to Simón Bolívar at Lima — A115

1932-34 **Photo.** ***Perf. 13½***

No.	Type	Description	Unused	Used
305	A111	2c black	.25	.25
306	A111	2c blue blk	.25	.25
307	A111	2c grn ('34)	.25	.25
308	A111	4c dk brn	.25	.25
309	A111	4c org ('34)	.25	.25
310	A112	10c vermilion	27.50	16.00
311	A115	15c ultra	.60	.25
312	A115	15c mag ('34)	.60	.25
313	A115	20c red brn	1.25	.25
314	A115	20c vio ('34)	1.25	.25
315	A115	50c dk grn ('33)	1.25	.25
316	A115	1s dp org	11.00	1.60
317	A115	1s org brn	12.00	1.10
		Nos. 305-317 (13)	56.70	21.20

For overprint see No. RA24.

Statue of Liberty — A116

1934

No.	Type	Description	Unused	Used
318	A116	10c rose	.75	.30

Pizarro A117

The Inca A119

Coronation of Huascar — A118

1934-35 ***Perf. 13***

No.	Type	Description	Unused	Used
319	A117	10c crimson	.40	.25
320	A117	15c ultra	1.10	.25
321	A118	20c deep bl ('35)	2.00	.25
322	A118	50c dp red brn	1.60	.25
323	A119	1s dark vio	11.00	1.10
		Nos. 319-323 (5)	16.10	2.10

For surcharges and overprint see Nos. 354-355, J54, O32.

Pizarro and the Thirteen — A120

Belle of Lima — A122

Francisco Pizarro — A123

4c, Lima Cathedral. 1s, Veiled woman of Lima.

1935, Jan. 18				*Perf. 13½*	
324	A120	2c	brown	.55	.30
325	A120	4c	violet	.60	.45
326	A122	10c	rose red	.60	.30
327	A123	15c	ultra	1.10	.75
328	A120	20c	slate gray	2.25	.95
329	A122	50c	olive grn	3.25	1.90
330	A122	1s	Prus bl	6.00	3.75
331	A123	2s	org brn	14.50	10.00
	Nos. 324-331,C6-C12 (15)			91.05	60.50

Founding of Lima, 4th cent.

View of Ica — A125

Grapes A127

Lake Huacachina, Health Resort A126

Cotton Boll — A128

Zuniga y Velazco and Philip IV — A129

Supreme God of the Nazcas — A130

Engr.; Photo. (10c)

1935, Jan. 17				*Perf. 12½*	
332	A125	4c	gray blue	.45	1.25
333	A126	5c	dark car	.45	1.25
334	A127	10c	magenta	6.50	3.25
335	A126	20c	green	2.25	2.25
336	A128	35c	dark car	11.00	8.00
337	A129	50c	org & brn	7.75	7.00
338	A130	1s	pur & red	22.50	17.00
	Nos. 332-338 (7)			50.90	40.00

Founding of the City of Ica, 300th anniv.

Pizarro and the Thirteen — A131

1935-36	Photo.			*Perf. 13½*	
339	A131	2c	dp claret	.35	.35
340	A131	4c	bl grn ('36)	.35	.35

For surcharge and overprints see Nos. 353, J53, RA25-RA26.

"San Cristóbal," First Peruvian Warship A132

Naval College at Punta A133

Independence Square, Callao — A134

Aerial View of Callao — A135

Plan of Walls of Callao in 1746 — A137

Grand Marshal José de La Mar — A138

Packetboat "Sacramento" A139

Viceroy José Antonio Manso de Velasco A140

Fort Maipú — A141

Plan of Fort Real Felipe — A142

Design: 15c, Docks and Custom House.

1936, Aug. 27	Photo.			*Perf. 12½*	
341	A132	2c	black	.75	.30
342	A133	4c	bl grn	.75	.30
343	A134	5c	yel brn	.75	.30
344	A135	10c	bl gray	.75	.30
345	A135	15c	green	.75	.30
346	A137	20c	dk brn	1.00	.30
347	A138	50c	purple	1.90	.55
348	A139	1s	olive grn	12.00	1.75
			Engr.		
349	A140	2s	violet	20.00	9.00
350	A141	5s	carmine	27.50	19.00
351	A142	10s	red org & brn	65.00	55.00
	Nos. 341-351,C13 (12)			134.40	88.85

Province of Callao founding, cent.

Nos. 340, 321 and 323 Surcharged in Black

1936				*Perf. 13½, 13*	
353	A131	2c on 4c	bl grn	.35	.30
a.		"0.20" for "0.02"		4.25	4.25
354	A118	10c on 20c	dp bl	.35	.30
a.		Double surcharge		4.25	4.25
b.		Inverted surcharge		4.25	4.25
355	A119	10c on 1s	dk vio	.55	.55
	Nos. 353-355 (3)			1.25	1.15

Many varieties of the surcharge are found on these stamps: no period after "S," no period after "Cts," period after "2," "S" omitted, various broken letters, etc.

The surcharge on No. 355 is horizontal.

Peruvian Cormorants (Guano Deposits) A143

Oil Well at Talara A144

Avenue of the Republic, Lima — A146

San Marcos University at Lima — A148

Post Office, Lima — A149

Viceroy Manuel de Amat y Junyent — A150

Designs: 10c, "El Chasqui" (Inca Courier). 20c, Municipal Palace and Museum of Natural History. 5s, Joseph A. de Pando y Riva. 10s, Dr. José Dávila Condemarin.

1936-37	Photo.			*Perf. 12½*	
356	A143	2c	lt brn	.75	.30
357	A143	2c	grn ('37)	1.00	.30
358	A144	4c	blk brn	.75	.30
359	A144	4c	int blk ('37)	.45	.30
360	A143	10c	crimson	.45	.30
361	A143	10c	ver ('37)	.35	.30
362	A146	15c	ultra	.90	.30
363	A146	15c	brt bl ('37)	.45	.30
364	A146	20c	black	.90	.30
365	A146	20c	blk brn ('37)	.35	.30
366	A148	50c	org yel	3.25	.85
367	A148	50c	dk gray vio ('37)	1.00	.30
368	A149	1s	brn vio	6.50	1.10
369	A149	1s	ultra ('37)	1.90	.30
			Engr.		
370	A150	2s	ultra	13.00	2.75
371	A150	2s	dk vio ('37)	4.50	.85
372	A150	5s	slate bl	13.00	2.75
373	A150	10s	dk vio & brn	75.00	37.50
	Nos. 356-373 (18)			124.50	49.40

No. 370 Surcharged in Black

1937					
374	A150	1s on 2s	ultra	3.25	3.25

Children's Holiday Center, Ancón A153

Chavin Pottery A154

Highway Map of Peru — A155

Archaeological Museum, Lima — A156

Industrial Bank of Peru A157

Worker's Houses, Lima A158

Toribio de Luzuriaga A159

Historic Fig Tree A160

Idol from Temple of Chavin A161

Mt. Huascarán A162

Imprint: "Waterlow & Sons Limited, Londres"

1938, July 1	Photo.			*Perf. 12½, 13*	
375	A153	2c	emerald	.25	.25
376	A154	4c	org brn	.25	.25
377	A155	10c	scarlet	.35	.25
378	A156	15c	ultra	.40	.25
379	A157	20c	magenta	.25	.25
380	A158	50c	greenish blue	.50	.25
381	A159	1s	dp claret	1.60	.25
382	A160	2s	green	6.50	.25
			Engr.		
383	A161	5s	dl vio & brn	13.00	.75
384	A162	10s	blk & ultra	27.50	1.25
	Nos. 375-384 (10)			50.60	4.00

See Nos. 410-418, 426-433, 438-441.

For surcharges see Nos. 388, 406, 419, 445-446A, 456, 758.

Palace Square — A163

Lima Coat of Arms — A164

Government Palace — A165

1938, Dec. 9 **Photo.** ***Perf. 12½***
385 A163 10c slate green .65 .45

Engraved and Lithographed

386 A164 15c blk, gold, red & bl 1.10 .55

Photo.

387 A165 1s olive 2.75 1.60
Nos. 385-387,C62-C64 (6) 9.30 5.90

8th Pan-American Conf., Lima, Dec. 1938.

No. 377 Surcharged in Black

1940 ***Perf. 13***
388 A155 5c on 10c scarlet .35 .35
a. Inverted surcharge

National Radio Station — A166

Black Overprint

1941 **Litho.** ***Perf. 12***
389 A166 50c dull yel 3.25 .25
390 A166 1s violet 3.25 .30
391 A166 2s dl gray grn 5.25 .85
392 A166 5s fawn 30.00 8.50
393 A166 10s rose vio 45.00 7.00
Nos. 389-393 (5) 86.75 16.90

Gonzalo Pizarro and Orellana A167

Francisco de Orellana A168

Francisco Pizarro A169

Map of South America with Amazon as Spaniards Knew It in 1542 A170

Gonzalo Pizarro A171

Discovery of the Amazon River A172

1943, Feb. ***Perf. 12½***
394 A167 2c crimson .35 .35
395 A168 4c slate .35 .35
396 A169 10c org brn .35 .35
397 A170 15c vio blue .65 .40
398 A171 20c yel olive .35 .35
399 A172 25c dull org 3.00 .60
400 A168 30c dp magenta .45 .40
401 A170 50c blue grn .55 .50
402 A167 70c violet 2.75 1.60
403 A171 80c lt bl 2.75 1.60
404 A172 1s cocoa brn 5.50 1.10
405 A169 5s intense blk 11.00 5.75
Nos. 394-405 (12) 28.05 13.35

400th anniv. of the discovery of the Amazon River by Francisco de Orellana in 1542.

No. 377 Surcharged in Black

1943 ***Perf. 13***
406 A155 10c on 10c scar .40 .40

Samuel Finley Breese Morse — A173

1944 ***Perf. 12½***
407 A173 15c light blue .40 .40
408 A173 30c olive gray 1.00 .40

Centenary of invention of the telegraph.

Types of 1938

Imprint: "Columbian Bank Note Co."

1945-47 **Litho.** ***Perf. 12½***
410 A153 2c green .25 .25
411 A154 4c org brn ('46) .25 .25
412 A156 15c ultra .25 .25
413 A157 20c magenta 2.40 .25
414 A158 50c grnsh bl .25 .25
415 A159 1s vio brn .25 .25
416 A160 2s dl grn 1.00 .25
417 A161 5s dl vio & brn 6.00 .50
418 A162 10s blk & ultra ('47) 7.50 .75
Nos. 410-418 (9) 18.15 3.00

No. 415 Surcharged in Black

1946
419 A159 20c on 1s vio brn .50 .30
a. Surcharge reading down 8.25 8.25

A174

A175

A176

A177

A178

Black Overprint

Perf. 12½

1947, Apr. 15 **Litho.** **Unwmk.**
420 A174 15c blk & car .30 .25
421 A175 1s olive brn .60 .35
422 A176 1.35s yel grn .60 .45
423 A177 3s Prus blue 1.10 .75
424 A178 5s dull grn 2.25 1.60
Nos. 420-424 (5) 4.85 3.40

1st National Tourism Congress, Lima. The basic stamps were prepared, but not issued, for the 5th Pan American Highway Congress of 1944.

Catalogue values for unused stamps in this section, from this point to the end of the section, are for Never Hinged items.

Types of 1938

Imprint: "Waterlow & Sons Limited, Londres."

Perf. 13x13½, 13½x13

1949-51 **Photo.**
426 A154 4c chocolate .40 .25
427 A156 15c aquamarine .40 .25
428 A157 20c blue vio .40 .25
429 A158 50c red brn .50 .25
430 A159 1s blk brn 1.10 .30
431 A160 2s ultra 2.25 .30

Engr.

Perf. 12½

432 A161 5s ultra & red brn ('50) 2.60 .65
433 A162 10s dk bl grn & blk ('51) 7.00 1.25
Nos. 426-433 (8) 14.65 3.50

Monument to Admiral Miguel L. Grau — A179

1949, June 6 ***Perf. 12½***
434 A179 10c ultra & bl grn .85 .40

Types of 1938

Imprint: "Inst. de Grav. Paris."

1951 ***Perf. 12½x12, 12x12½***
438 A156 15c peacock grn .60 .45
439 A157 20c violet .60 .45
440 A158 50c org brn .60 .45
441 A159 1s dark brn 2.00 .40
Nos. 438-441 (4) 3.80 1.75

Nos. 375 and 438 Surcharged in Black

1951-52 ***Perf. 12½, 12½x12***
445 A153 1c on 2c .85 .40
446 A156 10c on 15c .85 .40
446A A156 10c on 15c ('52) .85 .40
Nos. 445-446A (3) 2.55 1.20

On No. 446A "Sl. 0.10" is in smaller type measuring 11½mm. See No. 456.

Nos. 445-446A exist with surcharge double.

Water Promenade A180

Post Boy A181

Designs: 4c, 50c, 1s, 2s, Various buildings, Lima. 20c, Post Office Street, Lima. 5s, Lake Llangamuco, Ancachs. 10s, Ruins of Machu-Picchu.

Black Overprint: "V Congreso Panamericano de Carreteras 1951"

1951, Oct. 13 **Unwmk.** ***Perf. 12***
447 A180 2c dk grn .40 .25
448 A180 4c brt red .40 .25
449 A181 15c gray .40 .25
450 A181 20c ol brn .40 .25
451 A180 50c dp plum .60 .25
452 A180 1s blue .80 .30
453 A180 2s deep blue 1.30 .30
454 A180 5s brn lake 3.00 2.10
455 A181 10s chocolate 5.50 2.10
Nos. 447-455 (9) 12.80 6.05

5th Pan-American Congress of Highways, 1951.

No. 438 Surcharged in Black

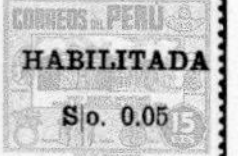

1952 **Unwmk.** ***Perf. 12½x12***
456 A156 5c on 15c pck grn .85 .40

Engineering School A182

Vicuña A183

Contour Farming, Cuzco — A184

Designs: 2c, Tourist Hotel, Tacna. 5c, Fishing boat and principal fish. 10c, Matarani. 15c, Locomotive No. 80 and coaches. 30c, Ministry of Public Health and Social Assistance. 1s, Paramonga fortress. 2s, Monument to Native Farmer.

Imprint: "Thomas De La Rue & Co. Ltd."

Perf. 13, 12 (A184)

1952-53 **Litho.** **Unwmk.**
457 A182 2c red lil ('53) .45 .40
458 A182 5c green .45 .40
459 A182 10c yel grn ('53) .45 .40
460 A182 15c gray ('53) .45 .40
461 A183 20c red brn ('53) 1.25 .40
462 A182 25c rose red .45 .40
463 A182 30c indigo ('53) .45 .40
464 A184 50c green ('53) 1.50 .40
465 A184 1s brown 1.10 .40
466 A184 2s Prus grn ('53) 2.25 .40
Nos. 457-466 (10) 8.80 4.00

See Nos. 468-478, 483-488, 497-501, C184-C185, C209.

For surcharges see Nos. C434, C437, C440-C441, C454, C494.

Gen. Marcos Perez Jimenez — A185

1956, July 25 **Engr.** ***Perf. 13½x13***
467 A185 25c brown .85 .40

Visit of Gen. Marcos Perez Jimenez, Pres. of Venezuela, June 1955.

Types of 1952-53

Imprint: "Thomas De La Rue & Co. Ltd."

Designs as before.

1957-59 **Litho.** ***Perf. 13, 12***
468 A182 15c brown ('59) 1.00 .40
469 A182 25c green ('59) 1.00 .40
470 A182 30c brown red .55 .40
471 A184 50c dull pur .85 .40
472 A184 1s lt vio bl .95 .40
473 A184 2s gray ('58) 1.60 .40
Nos. 468-473 (6) 5.95 2.40

Types of 1952-53

Imprint: "Joh. Enschedé en Zonen-Holland"

Designs as before.

Perf. 12½x13½, 13½x12½, 14x13

1960 **Litho.** **Unwmk.**
474 A183 20c lt red brn .40 .40
475 A182 30c lilac rose .40 .40
476 A184 50c rose vio .75 .40
477 A184 1s lt vio bl 1.30 .40
478 A184 2s gray 1.90 .40
Nos. 474-478 (5) 4.75 2.00

#475 measures 33x22mm, #470 32x22½mm.

Symbols of the Eucharist — A186

1960, Aug. 10 Photo. *Perf. 11½*

479 A186 50c Cross and "JHS" .50 .40
480 A186 1s shown 1.30 .50

Nos. 479-480 were intended for voluntary use to help finance the 6th National Eucharistic Congress at Piura, Aug. 25-28, 1960. Authorized for payment of postage on day of issue only, Aug. 10, but through misunderstanding within the Peruvian postal service they were accepted for payment of postage by some post offices until late in December. Reauthorized for postal use, they were again sold and used, starting in July, 1962. See Nos. RA37-RA38.

Trumpeting Angels — A187

1961, Dec. 20 Litho. *Perf. 10½*

481 A187 20c bright blue 1.00 .40

Christmas. Valid for postage for one day, Dec. 20. Used thereafter as a voluntary seal to benefit a fund for postal employees.

Centenary Cedar, Main Square, Pomabamba A188

Unwmk.

1962, Sept. 7 Engr. *Perf. 13*

482 A188 1s red & green 1.00 .40

Cent. (in 1961) of Pomabamba province.

Types of 1952-53

Designs: 20c, Vicuña. 30c, Port of Matarani. 40c, Gunboat. 50c, Contour farming. 60c, Tourist hotel, Tacna. 1s, Paramonga, Inca fortress.

Imprint: "Thomas De La Rue & Co. Ltd."

Perf. 13x13½, 13½x13, 12 (A184)

1962, Nov. 19 Litho. Wmk. 346

483 A183 20c rose claret .50 .40
484 A182 30c dark blue .50 .40
485 AP49 40c orange .50 .40
486 A184 50c lt bluish grn .50 .40
487 A182 60c grnsh blk 1.25 .40
488 A184 1s rose 2.00 .40
Nos. 483-488 (6) 5.25 2.40

Wheat Emblem and Symbol of Agriculture, Industry — A189

1963, July 23 Unwmk. *Perf. 12½*

489 A189 1s red org & ocher .50 .40

FAO "Freedom from Hunger" campaign. See No. C190.

Alliance for Progress Emblem — A190

1964, June 22 Litho. *Perf. 12x12½*

490 A190 40c multi .40 .40
Nos. 490,C192-C193 (3) 2.40 1.40

Alliance for Progress. See note after US No. 1234.

Pacific Fair Emblem — A191

1965, Oct. 30 Litho. *Perf. 12x12½*

491 A191 1.50s multi .65 .40
492 A191 2.50s multi .65 .40
493 A191 3.50s multi 1.40 .40
Nos. 491-493 (3) 2.70 1.20

4th Intl. Pacific Fair, Lima, Oct. 30-Nov. 14.

Santa Claus and Letter — A192

1965, Nov. 2 *Perf. 11*

494 A192 20c red & blk .45 .35
495 A192 50c grn & blk .80 .35
496 A192 1s bl & blk 1.75 .55
Nos. 494-496 (3) 3.00 1.25

Christmas. Valid for postage for one day, Nov. 2. Used Nov. 3, 1965-Jan. 31, 1966, as voluntary seals for the benefit of a fund for postal employees. See #522-524. For surcharges see #641-643.

Types of 1952-62

20c, Vicufia. 30c, Port of Matarani. 40c, Gunboat. 50c, Contour farming. 1s, Paramonga, Inca fortress.

Imprint: "I.N.A."

Perf. 12, 13½x14 (A184)

1966, Aug. 8 Litho. Unwmk.

497 A183 20c brn red .85 .40
498 A182 30c dk bl .85 .40
499 AP49 40c orange .85 .40
500 A184 50c gray grn .85 .40
501 A184 1s rose .85 .40
Nos. 497-501 (5) 4.25 2.00

Postal Tax Stamps Nos. RA40, RA43 Surcharged

a

b

Perf. 14x14½, 12½x12

1966, May 9 Litho.

501A PT11 (a) 10c on 2c lt brn .85 .40
501B PT14 (b) 10c on 3c lt car .85 .40

Map of Peru, Cordillera Central and Pelton Wheel — A193

1966, Nov. 24 Photo. *Perf. 13½x14*

502 A193 70c bl, blk & vio bl .70 .40

Opening of the Huinco Hydroelectric Center. See No. C205.

Inca Window and Sun — A194

Perf. 13½x14

1967, Apr. 18 Photo. Unwmk.

503 A194 90c dp lil rose, blk & gold .70 .40

6-year building program. See No. C212.

Pacific Fair Emblem — A195

1967, Oct. 9 Photo. *Perf. 12*

504 A195 1s gold, dk grn & blk .70 .40

5th Intl. Pacific Fair, Lima, Oct. 27-Nov. 12. See No. C216.

Gold Alligator, Mochica Culture — A196

Designs (gold sculptures of the pre-Inca Yunca tribes): 2.60s, Bird, vert. 3.60s, Lizard. 4.60s, Bird, vert. 5.60s, Jaguar.

Sculptures in Gold Yellow and Brown

1968, Aug. 16 Photo. *Perf. 12*

505 A196 1.90s dp magenta 1.75 .45
506 A196 2.60s black 2.50 .55
507 A196 3.60s dp magenta 3.00 .65
508 A196 4.60s black 3.50 .65
509 A196 5.60s dp magenta 5.50 .95
Nos. 505-509 (5) 16.25 3.25

See Nos. B1-B5. For surcharge see No. 685.

Indian and Wheat — A197

Designs: 3s, 4s, Farmer digging in field.

Black Surcharge

1969, Mar. 3 Litho. *Perf. 11*

510 A197 2.50s on 90c brn & yel .50 .40
511 A197 3s on 90c lil & brn .80 .40
512 A197 4s on 90c rose & grn 1.10 .40
Nos. 510-512,C232-C233 (5) 4.80 2.00

Agrarian Reform Law.
#510-512 were not issued without surcharge.

Flag, Worker Holding Oil Rig and Map — A198

1969, Apr. 9 Litho. *Perf. 12*

513 A198 2.50s multi .65 .40
514 A198 3s gray & multi .65 .40
515 A198 4s lil & multi 1.10 .40
516 A198 5.50s lt bl & multi 1.80 .40
Nos. 513-516 (4) 4.20 1.60

Nationalization of the Brea Parinas oilfields, Oct. 9, 1968.

Kon Tiki Raft. Globe and Jet — A199

1969, June 17 Litho. *Perf. 11*

517 A199 2.50s dp bl & multi 1.10 .35
Nos. 517,C238-C241 (5) 5.45 2.35

1st Peruvian Airlines (APSA) flight to Europe.

Capt. José A. Quiñones Gonzales (1914-41), Military Aviator A200

1969, July 23 Litho. *Perf. 11*

518 A200 20s red & multi 3.25 1.25

See No. C243.

Freed Andean Farmer — A201

1969, Aug. 28 Litho. *Perf. 11*

519 A201 2.50s dk bl, lt bl & red .55 .40
Nos. 519,C246-C247 (3) 2.50 1.20

Enactment of the Agrarian Reform Law of June 24, 1969.

Adm. Miguel Grau — A202

1969, Oct. 8 Litho. *Perf. 11*

520 A202 50s dk bl & multi 6.00 3.25

Issued for Navy Day.

Flags and "6" — A203

1969, Nov. 14

521 A203 2.50s gray & multi 1.00 .40
Nos. 521,C251-C252 (3) 3.05 1.20

6th Intl. Pacific Trade Fair, Lima, Nov. 14-30.

Santa Claus Type of 1965

Design: Santa Claus and letter inscribed "FELIZ NAVIDAD Y PROSPERO AÑO NUEVO."

1969, Dec. 1 Litho. *Perf. 11*

522 A192 20c red & blk .85 .40
523 A192 20c org & blk .85 .40
524 A192 20c brn & blk .85 .40
Nos. 522-524 (3) 2.55 1.20

Christmas. Valid for postage for one day, Dec. 1, 1969. Used after that date as postal tax stamps.

Gen. Francisco Bolognesi and Soldier — A204

1969, Dec. 9

525 A204 1.20s lt ultra, blk & gold .70 .40

Army Day, Dec. 9. See No. C253.

Puma-shaped Jug, Vicus Culture — A205

1970, Feb. 23 Litho. *Perf. 11*

526 A205 2.50s buff, blk & brn 1.00 .40
Nos. 526,C281-C284 (5) 10.10 3.15

Ministry of Transport and Communications A206

1970, Apr. 1 Litho. *Perf. 11*

527	A206	40c	org & gray	.85	.40
528	A206	40c	gray & lt gray	.85	.40
529	A206	40c	brick red & gray	.85	.40
530	A206	40c	brt pink & gray	.85	.40
531	A206	40c	org brn & gray	.85	.40
			Nos. 527-531 (5)	4.25	2.00

Ministry of Transport and Communications, 1st anniv.

Anchovy — A207

Fish: No. 533, Pacific hake.

1970, Apr. 30 Litho. *Perf. 11*

532	A207	2.50s	vio bl & multi	2.00	.30
533	A207	2.50s	vio bl & multi	2.00	.30
a.			Strip of 5, #532-533, C285-C287	12.50	11.00

Composite Head; Soldier and Farmer — A208

1970, June 24 Litho. *Perf. 11*

534	A208	2.50s	gold & multi	.95	.45
			Nos. 534,C290-C291 (3)	3.80	1.25

"United people and army building a new Peru."

Cadets, Chorrillos College, and Arms — A209

Coat of Arms and: No. 536, Cadets of La Punta Naval College. No. 537, Cadets of Las Palmas Air Force College.

1970, July 27 Litho. *Perf. 11*

535	A209	2.50s	blk & multi	1.25	.40
536	A209	2.50s	blk & multi	1.25	.40
537	A209	2.50s	blk & multi	1.25	.40
a.			Strip of 3, #535-537	6.50	5.50

Peru's military colleges.

Courtyard, Puruchuco Fortress, Lima — A210

1970, Aug. 6

538	A210	2.50s	multi	1.20	.25
			Nos. 538,C294-C297 (5)	9.85	2.20

Issued for tourist publicity.

Nativity, Cuzco School — A211

Christmas paintings: 1.50s, Adoration of the Kings, Cuzco School. 1.80s, Adoration of the Shepherds, Peruvian School.

1970, Dec. 23 Litho. *Perf. 11*

539	A211	1.20s	multi	.85	.40
540	A211	1.50s	multi	.85	.40
541	A211	1.80s	multi	.90	.40
			Nos. 539-541 (3)	2.60	1.20

St. Rosa of Lima — A212

1971, Apr. 12 Litho. *Perf. 11*

542	A212	2.50s	multi	.85	.40

300th anniv. of the canonization of St. Rosa of Lima (1586-1617), first saint born in the Americas.

Tiahuanacoide Cloth — A213

Design: 2.50s, Chancay cloth.

1971, Apr. 19

543	A213	1.20s	bl & multi	.50	.40
544	A213	2.50s	yel & multi	.90	.40
			Nos. 543-544,C306-C308 (5)	7.15	2.35

Nazca Sculpture, 5th Century, and Seriolella — A214

1971, June 7 Litho. *Perf. 11*

545	A214	1.50s	multi	.80	.40
			Nos. 545,C309-C312 (5)	7.50	2.85

Publicity for 200-mile zone of sovereignty of the high seas.

Mateo Garcia Pumacahua A215

#547, Mariano Melgar. #548, Micaela Bastidas. #549, Jose Faustino Sanchez Carrion. #550, Francisco Antonio de Zela. #551, Jose Baquijano y Carrillo. #552, Martin Jorge Guise.

1971

546	A215	1.20s	ver & blk	.65	.40
547	A215	1.20s	gray & multi	.65	.40
548	A215	1.50s	dk bl & multi	.65	.40
549	A215	2s	dk bl & multi	.65	.40
550	A215	2.50s	ultra & multi	.90	.40
551	A215	2.50s	gray & multi	.90	.40
552	A215	2.50s	dk bl & multi	.90	.40
			Nos. 546-552,C313-C325 (20)	21.55	8.30

150th anniv. of independence, and to honor the heroes of the struggle for independence.

Issue dates: Nos. 546, 550, May 10; Nos. 547, 551, July 5; Nos. 548-549, 552, July 27.

Gongora Portentosa — A216

Designs: Various Peruvian orchids.

1971, Sept. 27 *Perf. 13½x13*

553	A216	1.50s	pink & multi	2.10	.40
554	A216	2s	pink & multi	2.75	.40
555	A216	2.50s	pink & multi	2.75	.40
556	A216	3s	pink & multi	3.00	.40
557	A216	3.50s	pink & multi	3.00	.40
			Nos. 553-557 (5)	13.60	2.00

"Progress of Liberation," by Teodoro Nuñez Ureta — A217

3.50s, Detail from painting by Nuñez Ureta.

1971, Nov. 4 *Perf. 13x13½*

558	A217	1.20s	multi	.40	.40
559	A217	3.50s	multi	.65	.40
			Nos. 558-559,C331 (3)	8.55	3.05

2nd Ministerial meeting of the "Group of 77."

Plaza de Armas, Lima, 1843 — A218

3.50s, Plaza de Armas, Lima, 1971.

1971, Nov. 6

560	A218	3s	pale grn & blk	1.15	.40
561	A218	3.50s	lt brick red & blk	1.15	.40

3rd Annual Intl. Stamp Exhibition, EXFILIMA '71, Lima, Nov. 6-14.

Army Coat of Arms — A219

1971, Dec. 9 Litho. *Perf. 13½x13*

562	A219	8.50s	multi	1.75	.55

Sesquicentennial of Peruvian Army.

Flight into Egypt — A220

Old Stone Sculptures of Huamanga: 2.50s, Three Kings. 3s, Nativity.

1971, Dec. 18 *Perf. 13x13½*

563	A220	1.80s	multi	.65	.40
564	A220	2.50s	multi	1.00	.40
565	A220	3s	gray & multi	1.60	.40
			Nos. 563-565 (3)	3.25	1.20

Christmas. See Nos. 597-599.

Fisherman, by J. M. Ugarte Elespuru — A221

Paintings by Peruvian Workers: 4s, Threshing Grain in Cajamarca, by Camilo Blas. 6s, Huanca Highlanders, by José Sabogal.

1971, Dec. 30 *Perf. 13½x13*

566	A221	3.50s	blk & multi	1.40	.40
567	A221	4s	blk & multi	1.40	.40
568	A221	6s	blk & multi	2.40	.40
			Nos. 566-568 (3)	5.20	1.20

To publicize the revolution and change of order.

Gold Statuette, Chimu, c. 1500 — A222

Ancient Jewelry: 4s, Gold drummer, Chimu. 4.50s, Quartz figurine, Lambayeque culture, 5th century. 5.40s, Gold necklace and pendant, Mochiqua, 4th century. 6s, Gold insect, Lambayeque culture, 14th century.

1972, Jan. 31 Litho. *Perf. 13½x13*

569	A222	3.90s	red, blk & ocher	.80	.40
570	A222	4s	red, blk & ocher	.80	.40
571	A222	4.50s	brt bl, blk & ocher	1.60	.40
572	A222	5.40s	red, blk & ocher	1.60	.40
573	A222	6s	red, blk & ocher	2.75	.40
			Nos. 569-573 (5)	7.55	2.00

Popeye Catalufa — A223

Fish: 1.50s, Guadara. 2.50s, Jack mackerel.

1972, Mar. 20 *Perf. 13x13½*

574	A223	1.20s	lt bl & multi	.90	.40
575	A223	1.50s	lt bl & multi	.90	.40
576	A223	2.50s	lt bl & multi	2.00	.40
			Nos. 574-576,C333-C334 (5)	9.30	2.70

Seated Warrior, Mochica — A224

Painted pottery jugs of Mochica culture, 5th cent.: 1.50s, Helmeted head. 2s, Kneeling deer. 2.50s, Helmeted head. 3s, Kneeling warrior.

1972, May 8 *Perf. 13½x13*

Emerald Background

577	A224	1.20s	multi	.85	.40
578	A224	1.50s	multi	1.00	.40
579	A224	2s	multi	1.75	.40
580	A224	2.50s	multi	1.75	.40
581	A224	3s	multi	2.60	.40
			Nos. 577-581 (5)	7.95	2.00

"Bringing in the Harvest" (July) — A225

Monthly woodcuts from Calendario Incaico.

1972-73 Litho. *Perf. 13½x13*

Black Vignette & Inscriptions

582	A225	2.50s	red brn *(July)*	2.40	.40
583	A225	3s	grn *(Aug.)*	2.40	.40
584	A225	2.50s	rose *(Sept.)*	2.40	.40
585	A225	3s	lt bl *(Oct.)*	2.40	.40
586	A225	2.50s	org *(Nov.)*	2.40	.40
587	A225	3s	lil *(Dec.)*	2.40	.40
588	A225	2.50s	brn *(Jan.)* ('73)	2.40	.40
589	A225	3s	pale grn *(Feb.)* ('73)	2.40	.40
590	A225	2.50s	bl *(Mar.)* ('73)	2.40	.40
591	A225	3s	org *(Apr.)* ('73)	2.40	.40
592	A225	2.50s	lil rose *(May)* ('73)	2.40	.40
593	A225	3s	yel & blk *(June)* ('73)	2.40	.40
			Nos. 582-593 (12)	28.80	4.80

400th anniv. of publication of the Calendario Incaico by Felipe Guaman Poma de Ayala.

Family Tilling Field — A226

Sovereignty of the Sea (Inca Frieze) — A227

Oil Derricks — A228

Perf. 13½x13, 13x13½

1972, Oct. 31 **Litho.**

594 A226 2s multi .90 .40
595 A227 2.50s multi .90 .40
596 A228 3s gray & multi .90 .40
Nos. 594-596 (3) 2.70 1.20

4th anniversaries of land reforms and the nationalization of the oil industry and 15th anniv. of the claim to a 200-mile zone of sovereignty of the sea.

Christmas Type of 1971

Sculptures from Huamanga, 17-18th cent.: 1.50s, Holy Family, wood, vert. 2s, Holy Family with lambs, stone. 2.50s, Holy Family in stable, stone, vert.

1972, Nov. 30

597 A220 1.50s buff & multi .85 .40
598 A220 2s buff & multi .85 .40
599 A220 2.50s buff & multi .85 .40
Nos. 597-599 (3) 2.55 1.20

Morning Glory — A228a

2.50s, Amaryllis. 3s, Liabum excelsum. 3.50s, Bletia (orchid). 5s, Cantua buxifolia.

1972, Dec. 29 **Litho.** ***Perf. 13***

600 A228a 1.50s shown 1.10 .40
601 A228a 2.50s multi 1.25 .40
602 A228a 3s multi 1.80 .40
603 A228a 3.50s multi 2.10 .40
604 A228a 5s multi 3.50 .55
Nos. 600-604 (5) 9.75 2.15

Mayor on Horseback, by Fierro — A229

Paintings by Francisco Pancho Fierro (1803-1879): 2s, Man and Woman, 1830. 2.50s, Padre Abregu Riding Mule. 3.50s, Dancing Couple. 4.50s, Bullfighter Estevan Arredondo on Horseback.

1973, Aug. 13 **Litho.** ***Perf. 13***

605 A229 1.50s salmon & multi .50 .40
606 A229 2s salmon & multi .80 .40
607 A229 2.50s salmon & multi 1.10 .40
608 A229 3.50s salmon & multi 1.75 .40
609 A229 4.50s salmon & multi 2.00 .60
Nos. 605-609 (5) 6.15 2.20

Presentation in the Temple — A230

Christmas Paintings of the Cuzqueña School: 2s, Holy Family, vert. 2.50s, Adoration of the Kings.

Perf. 13x13½, 13½x13

1973, Nov. 30 **Litho.**

610 A230 1.50s multi .45 .40
611 A230 2s multi .90 .40
612 A230 2.50s multi 1.00 .40
Nos. 610-612 (3) 2.35 1.20

Peru No. 20 — A231

1974, Mar. 1 **Litho.** ***Perf. 13***

613 A231 6s brnsh gray & dk bl 1.40 .40

Peruvian Philatelic Assoc., 25th anniv.

Non-ferrous Smelting Plant, La Oroya — A232

Colombia Bridge, San Martin — A233

Designs: 8s, 10s, Different views, Santiago Antunez Dam, Tayacaja.

1974 **Litho.** ***Perf. 13x13½***

614 A232 1.50s blue .45 .35
615 A233 2s multi .45 .35
616 A232 3s rose claret .95 .35
617 A232 4.50s green 1.60 .50
618 A233 8s multi 1.90 .60
619 A233 10s multi 1.90 .60
Nos. 614-619 (6) 7.25 2.75

"Peru Determines its Destiny."
Issued: 2s, 8s, 10s, 7/1; 1.50s, 3s, 4.50s, 12/6.

Battle of Junin, by Felix Yañez — A234

2s, 3s, Battle of Ayacucho, by Felix Yañez.

1974 **Litho.** ***Perf. 13x13½***

620 A234 1.50s multi .45 .40
621 A234 2s multi .45 .40
622 A234 2.50s multi .60 .40
623 A234 3s multi .60 .40
Nos. 620-623,C400-C404 (9) 10.40 3.85

Sesquicentennial of the Battles of Junin and Ayacucho.
Issued: 1.50s, 2.50s, Aug. 6; 2s, 3s, Oct. 9.

Indian Madonna — A235

1974, Dec. 20 **Litho.** ***Perf. 13½x13***

624 A235 1.50s multi .60 .40

Christmas. See No. C417.

Maria Parado de Bellido A236

International Women's Year Emblem A237

IWY Emblem, Peruvian Colors and: 2s, Micaela Bastidas. 2.50s, Juana Alarco de Dammert.

Perf. 13x13½, 13½x13

1975, Sept. 8 **Litho.**

625 A236 1.50s bl grn, red & blk .55 .40
626 A237 2s blk & red .75 .40
627 A236 2.50s pink, blk & red .75 .40
628 A237 3s red, blk & ultra 1.40 .40
Nos. 625-628 (4) 3.45 1.60

International Women's Year.

St. Juan Macias — A238

1975, Nov. 14 ***Perf. 13½x13***

629 A238 5s blk & multi 1.00 .40

Canonization of Juan Macias in 1975.

Louis Braille — A239

1976, Mar. 2 **Litho.** ***Perf. 13x13½***

630 A239 4.50s gray, red & blk 1.00 .45

Sesquicentennial of the invention of Braille system of writing for the blind by Louis Braille (1809-1852).

Peruvian Flag — A240

1976, Aug. 29 **Litho.** ***Perf. 13x13½***

631 A240 5s gray, blk & red .85 .40

Revolutionary Government, phase II, 1st anniv.

St. Francis, by El Greco — A241

1976, Dec. 9 **Litho.** ***Perf. 13½x13***

632 A241 5s gold, buff & brn 1.25 .40

St. Francis of Assisi, 750th death anniv.

Indian Mother — A242

1976, Dec. 23

633 A242 4s multi 1.10 .40

Christmas.

Chasqui Messenger — A243

1977 **Litho.** ***Perf. 13½x13***

634 A243 6s grnsh bl & blk .75 .25
635 A243 8s red & blk .75 .25
636 A243 10s ultra & blk .95 .50
637 A243 12s lt grn & blk .95 .50
Nos. 634-637,C465-C467 (7) 12.05 4.10

For surcharge see No. C502.

"X" over Flags — A244

1977, Nov. 25 **Litho.** ***Perf. 13½x13***

638 A244 10s multi .85 .60

10th Intl. Pacific Fair, Lima, Nov. 16-27.

Republican Guard Badge — A245

1977, Dec. 1

639 A245 12s multi 1.00 .40

58th anniversary of Republican Guard.

Indian Nativity — A246

1977, Dec. 23

640 A246 8s multi .85 .40

Christmas. See No. C484.

Nos. 495, 494, 496 Surcharged with New Value and Bar in Red, Dark Blue or Black: "FRANQUEO / 10.00 / RD-0161-77"

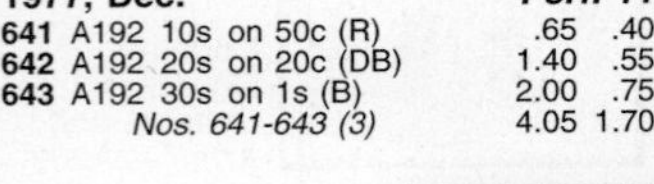

1977, Dec. ***Perf. 11***

641 A192 10s on 50c (R) .65 .40
642 A192 20s on 20c (DB) 1.40 .55
643 A192 30s on 1s (B) 2.00 .75
Nos. 641-643 (3) 4.05 1.70

Inca Head — A247

1978 **Litho.** ***Perf. 13½x13***

644 A247 6s bright green .35 .35
645 A247 10s red .35 .35
646 A247 16s red brown .65 .35
Nos. 644-646,C486-C489 (7) 10.15 4.55

For surcharges see Nos. C498-C499, C501.

Flags of Germany, Argentina, Austria, Brazil — A248

Argentina '78 Emblem and Flags of Participants: No. 648, 652, Hungary, Iran, Italy, Mexico. No. 649, 653, Scotland, Spain, France, Netherlands. No. 650, 654, Peru, Poland, Sweden and Tunisia. No. 651, like No. 647.

1978 **Litho.** ***Perf. 13x13½***

647 A248 10s blue & multi 1.25 .40
648 A248 10s blue & multi 1.25 .40
649 A248 10s blue & multi 1.25 .40
650 A248 10s blue & multi 1.25 .40
a. Block of 4, #647-650 7.00 5.00
651 A248 16s blue & multi 1.25 .40
652 A248 16s blue & multi 1.25 .40

653 A248 16s blue & multi 1.25 .40
654 A248 16s blue & multi 1.25 .40
a. Block of 4, #651-654 7.00 5.00
Nos. 647-654 (8) 10.00 3.20

11th World Soccer Cup Championship, Argentina, June 1-25.
Issued: #647-650, 6/28; #651-654, 12/4.

Thomas Faucett, Planes of 1928, 1978 — A249

1978, Oct. 19 Litho. *Perf. 13*
655 A249 40s multicolored 1.50 .50

Faucett Aviation, 50th anniversary.

Nazca Bowl, Huaco — A250

1978-79 Litho. *Perf. 13x13½*
656 A250 16s violet bl ('79) .65 .35
657 A250 20s green ('79) .65 .35
658 A250 25s lt green ('79) .80 .55
659 A250 35s rose red ('79) 1.40 .30
660 A250 45s dk brown 1.60 .55
661 A250 50s black 1.90 .65
662 A250 55s car rose ('79) 1.90 .65
663 A250 70s lilac rose ('79) 2.25 1.10
664 A250 75s blue 2.60 1.00
665 A250 80s salmon ('79) 2.60 1.00
667 A250 200s brt vio ('79) 6.50 3.25
Nos. 656-667 (11) 22.85 9.75

For surcharges see Nos. 715, 731.

Peruvian Nativity — A252

1978, Dec. 28 Litho. *Perf. 13½x13*
672 A252 16s multicolored 1.10 .50

Ministry of Education, Lima — A253

1979, Jan. 4
673 A253 16s multicolored .95 .40

National Education Program.

Nos. RA40, B1-B5 and 509 Surcharged in Various Colors

a

b

c

1978, July-Aug.
674 PT11(a) 2s on 2c (O) *.25* .25
675 PT11(b) 3s on 2c (Bk) *.25* .25
676 PT11(a) 4s on 2c (G) *.25* .25
677 PT11(a) 5s on 2c (V) *.25* .25
678 PT11(b) 6s on 2c (DBl) *.25* .25
679 SP1 20s on 1.90s + 90c (G) *1.25* 1.25
680 SP1 30s on 2.60s + 1.30s (Bl) *1.25* 1.25
681 PT11(c) 35s on 2c (C) *1.60* 1.60
682 PT11(c) 50s on 2c (LtBl) *5.50* 5.50
683 SP1 55s on 3.60s + 1.80s (VBl) *1.75* 1.75
684 SP1 65s on 4.60s + 2.30s (Go) *1.75* 1.75
685 A196 80s on 5.60s (VBl) *1.40* 1.40
686 SP1 85s on 20s + 10s (Bk) *2.75* 2.75
Nos. 674-686 (13) *18.50* 18.50

Surcharge on Nos. 679-680, 683-684, 686 includes heavy bar over old denomination.

Battle of Iquique — A254

Heroes' Crypt — A255

Col. Francisco Bolognesi — A256

War of the Pacific: No. 688, Col. Jose J. Inclan. No. 689, Corvette Union running Arica blockade. No. 690, Battle of Angamos, Aguirre, Miguel Grau (1838-1879), Perre. No. 690A, Lt. Col. Pedro Ruiz Gallo. 85s, Marshal Andres A. Caceres. No. 692, Naval Battle of Angamos. No. 693, Battle of Tarapaca. 115s, Adm. Miguel Grau. No. 697, Col. Bolognesi's Reply, by Angeles de la Cruz. No. 698, Col. Alfonso Ugarte on horseback.

Perf. 13½x13, 13x13½

1979-80 Litho.
687 A254 14s multicolored .50 .50
688 A256 25s multicolored .85 .45
689 A254 25s multicolored 1.30 .75
690 A254 25s multicolored 1.30 .75
690A A256 25s multi ('80) .65 .55
691 A256 85s multicolored 1.30 1.00
692 A254 100s multicolored 1.40 1.00
693 A254 100s multicolored 1.50 1.00
694 A256 115s multicolored 2.90 2.25
695 A255 200s multicolored 16.00 *7.00*
696 A256 200s multicolored 2.90 2.25
697 A254 200s multicolored 2.95 2.25
698 A254 200s multicolored 3.75 2.25
Nos. 687-698 (13) 37.30 22.00

For surcharges see Nos. 713, 732.

Peruvian Red Cross, Cent. — A257

1979, May 4 *Perf. 13x13½*
699 A257 16s multicolored .95 .40

Billiard Balls — A258

1979, June 4 *Perf. 13½x13*
700 A258 34s multicolored 1.00 .40

For surcharge see No. 714.

Arms of Cuzco — A259

1979, June 24
701 A259 50s multicolored 1.75 .60

Inca Sun Festival, Cuzco.

Peru Colors, Tacna Monument — A260

1979, Aug. 28 Litho. *Perf. 13½x13*
702 A260 16s multicolored 1.00 .40

Return of Tacna Province to Peru, 50th anniv.

For surcharge see No. 712.

Telecom 79 — A261

1979, Sept. 20
703 A261 15s multicolored .85 .40

3rd World Telecommunications Exhibition, Geneva, Sept. 20-26.

Caduceus — A262

1979, Nov. 13
704 A262 25s multicolored 1.00 .40

Stomatology Academy of Peru, 50th anniv.; 4th Intl. Congress.

World Map, "11," Fair Emblem — A263

1979, Nov. 24
705 A263 55s multicolored 1.10 .50

11th Pacific Intl. Trade Fair, Lima, 11/14-25.

Gold Jewelry — A264

1979, Dec. 19 *Perf. 13½x13*
706 A264 85s multicolored 3.25 1.25

Larco Herrera Archaeological Museum.

Christmas A265

1979, Dec. 27 Litho. *Perf. 13x13½*
707 A265 25s multicolored 1.00 .55

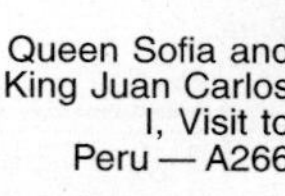

Queen Sofia and King Juan Carlos I, Visit to Peru — A266

1979, Feb. 7 Litho. *Perf. 13x13½*
708 A266 75s multicolored 1.40 .50

No. RA40 Surcharged in Black, Green or Blue

No. 709

No. 710

No. 711

1979, Oct. 8
709 PT11 7s on 2c brown .90 .40
710 PT11 9s on 2c brown (G) .90 .40
711 PT11 15s on 2c brown (B) .90 .40
Nos. 709-711 (3) 2.70 1.20

Nos. 702, 687, 700, 663 Surcharged

Perf. 13½x13, 13x13½

1980, Apr. 14 Litho.
712 A260 20s on 16s multi .70 .40
713 A254 25s on 14s multi .80 .40
714 A258 65s on 34s multi 1.50 .70
715 A250 80s on 70s lilac rose 2.25 .50
Nos. 712-715,C501-C502 (6) 7.20 2.95

Liberty Holding Arms of Peru — A267

Civic duties: 15s, Respect the Constitution. 20s, Honor country. 25s, Vote. 30s, Military service. 35s, Pay taxes. 45s, Contribute to national progress. 50s, Respect rights.

1980 Litho.
716 A267 15s greenish blue .60 .40
717 A267 20s salmon pink .60 .40
718 A267 25s ultra .60 .40
719 A267 30s lilac rose .60 .40
720 A267 35s black 1.00 .45
721 A267 45s light blue green 1.10 .60
722 A267 50s brown 2.00 .60
Nos. 716-722 (7) 6.50 3.25

Chimu Cult Cup — A268

1980, July 9 Litho.
723 A268 35s multicolored 2.00 .80

Map of Peru and Liberty A269

Return to Civilian Government A270

Perf. 13½x13, 13x13½

1980, Sept. 9 Litho.
724 A269 25s multicolored .90 .60
725 A270 35s multicolored 1.30 .60

For surcharge see No. 730.

Machu Picchu — A271

1980, Nov. 10 Litho. ***Perf. 13x13½***

726 A271 25s multicolored 2.50 2.00

World Tourism Conf., Manila, Sept. 27.

Tupac Amaru Rebellion Bicent. — A272

1980, Dec. 22 Litho. ***Perf. 13½x13***

727 A272 25s multicolored .95 .40

Christmas A273

1980, Dec. 31 Litho. ***Perf. 13***

728 A273 15s multicolored 1.10 .55

150th Death Anniv. of Simon Bolivar (in 1980) — A274

1981, Jan. 28 Litho. ***Perf. 13½x13***

729 A274 40s multicolored 1.00 .40

Nos. 725, 667, 694 Surcharged

1981 Litho. ***Perf. 13x13½***

730 A270 25s on 35s multi .50 .40
731 A250 85s on 200s brt violet 1.60 .80
732 A256 100s on 115s multi 2.40 .95
Nos. 730-732 (3) 4.50 2.15

Return to Constitutional Government, July 28, 1980 — A275

1981, Mar. 26 Litho. ***Perf. 13½x13***

733 A275 25s multicolored 1.10 .40

For surcharges see Nos. 736-737, 737C.

Tupac Amaru and Micaela Bastidas, Bronze Sculptures, by Miguel Baca-Rossi A276

1981, May 18 Litho. ***Perf. 13x13½***

734 A276 60s multicolored 1.20 .60

Rebellion of Tupac Amaru and Micaela Bastidas, bicentenary.

Nos. 733, RA41 and Voluntary Postal Tax Stamps of 1965 Surcharged in Black, Dull Brown or Lake and

Cross, Unleavened Bread, Wheat A276a

Chalice, Host A276b

Perf. 13½x13, Rouletted 11 (#735, 737B), 11½ (#737A)

1981 Litho., Photo. (#737A-737B)

735 PT17 40s on 10c #RA41 .50 .35
736 A275 40s on 25s #733 1.60 .55
737 A275 130s on 25s #733 (DB) 1.60 .55
737A A276a 140s on 50c brn, yel & red .95 .40
737B A276b 140s on 1s multi .95 .40
737C A275 140s on 25s #733 (L) 1.60 .55
Nos. 735-737C (6) 7.20 2.80

Issued: #735, Apr. 12; #736, 737, 737C, Apr. 6; #737A, Apr. 15; #737B, Apr. 28.

Carved Stone Head, Pallasca Tribe — A277

#739, 742, 749 Pottery vase, Inca, vert. #740, Head, diff., vert. #743, 749A-749B, Huaco idol (fish), Nazca. 100s, Pallasca, vert. 140s, Puma.

Perf. 13½x13, 13x13½

1981-82 Litho.

738 A277 30s dp rose lilac .70 .60
739 A277 40s orange ('82) .80 .30
740 A277 40s ultra .80 .30
742 A277 80s brown ('82) 2.50 1.50
743 A277 80s red ('82) 2.50 1.40
745 A277 100s lilac rose 2.10 1.50
748 A277 140s lt blue grn 3.00 2.10
749 A277 180s green ('82) 5.50 3.75
749A A277 240s grnsh blue ('82) 3.25 2.10
749B A277 280s violet ('82) 4.50 2.75
Nos. 738-749B (10) 25.65 16.30

For surcharges see #789, 798-799, 1026.

A278

1981, May 31 ***Perf. 13½x13***

750 A278 130s multicolored 1.40 .90

Postal and Philatelic Museum, 50th anniv.

A279

1981, Oct. 7 Litho. ***Perf. 13½x13***

751 A279 30s purple & gray .90 .40

1979 Constitution Assembly President Victor Raul Haya de la Torre.

Inca Messenger, by Guaman Poma (1526-1613) — A280

1981 Litho. ***Perf. 12***

752 A280 30s lilac & blk 1.50 1.00
753 A280 40s vermilion & blk 1.20 2.00
754 A280 130s brt yel grn & blk 3.00 2.00
755 A280 140s brt blue & blk 3.00 2.50
756 A280 200s yel brn & blk 5.50 4.50
Nos. 752-756 (5) 14.20 12.00

Christmas. Issue dates: 30s, 40s, 200s, Dec. 21; others, Dec. 31.

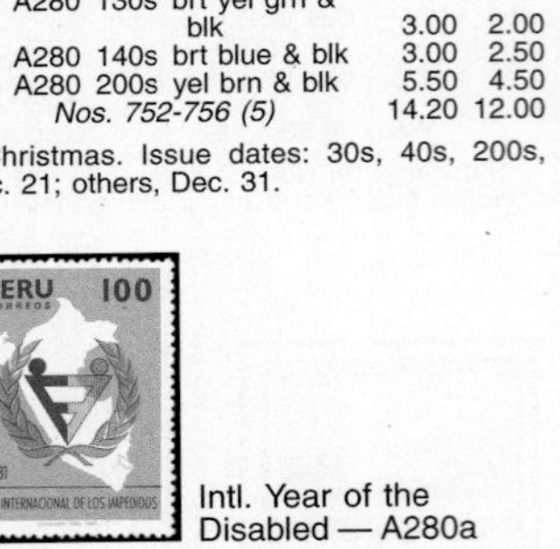

Intl. Year of the Disabled — A280a

1981 Litho. ***Perf. 13½x13***

756A A280a 100s multicolored 1.75 .85

Nos. 377, C130, C143, J56, O33, RA36, RA39, RA40, RA42, RA43 Surcharged in Brown, Black, Orange, Red, Green or Blue

1982

757 PT11 10s on 2c (#RA40, Br) 1.20 .40
758 A155 10s on 10c (#377) .90 .40
758A AP60 40s on 1.25s (#C143) .90 .40
758B PT15 70s on 5c (#RA36, R) 1.20 .40
759 D7 80s on 10c (#J56) .90 .40
760 O1 80s on 10c (#O33) .90 .40
761 PT14 80s on 3c (#RA43, O) .90 .40
762 PT17 100s on 10c (#RA42, R) 1.20 .40
763 AP57 100s on 2.20s (#C130, R) 1.50 .50
764 PT14 150s on 3c (#RA39, G) 1.75 .60
765 PT14 180s on 3c (#RA43, R) 1.75 .60
766 PT14 200s on 3c (#RA43, Bl) 2.10 .70
767 AP60 240s on 1.25s (#C143, R) 3.50 1.25
768 PT15 280s on 5c (#RA36) 3.25 1.10
Nos. 757-768 (14) 21.95 7.95

Nos. 758A, 763, 767 airmail. Nos. 759 and 760 surcharged "Habilitado / Franq. Postal / 80 Soles".

Jorge Basadre (1903-1980), Historian A281

Julio C. Tello (1882-1947), Archaeologist A282

Perf. 13½x13, 13x13½

1982, Oct. 13 Litho.

769 A281 100s pale green & blk .70 .40
770 A282 200s lt green & dk bl 1.50 .55

9th Women's World Volleyball Championship, Sept. 12-26 — A283

1982, Oct. 18 ***Perf. 12***

771 A283 80s black & red .85 .40

For surcharge see No. 791.

Rights of the Disabled — A284

1982, Oct. 22

772 A284 200s blue & red 1.40 .70

Brena Campaign Centenary A285

70s, Andres Caceres medallion.

1982, Oct. 26 ***Perf. 13x13½***

773 A285 70s multi .85 .40

For surcharge see No. 790.

1982 World Cup — A286

1982, Nov. 2 ***Perf. 12***

774 A286 80s multicolored 1.25 .40

For surcharge see No. 800.

16th Intl. Congress of Latin Notaries, Lima, June — A287

1982, Nov. 6

775 A287 500s Emblem 1.75 .85

Handicrafts Year — A288

1982, Nov. 24 ***Perf. 13x13½***

776 A288 200s Clay bull figurine 1.10 .40

Christmas — A289

1982 ***Perf. 13½x13***

777 A289 280s Holy Family 1.20 .70

For surcharge see No. 797.

Pedro Vilcapaza — A290

1982, Dec. 2 ***Perf. 13½x13***

778 A290 240s black & lt brn 1.10 .50

Death centenary of Indian leader against Spanish during Andes Rebellion.

For surcharges see Nos. 792.

Jose Davila Condemarin (1799-1882), Minister of Posts (1849-76) — A291

1982, Dec. 10 *Perf. 13x13½*
779 A291 150s blue & blk .90 .40

10th Anniv. of Intl. Potato Study Center, Lima — A292

1982, Dec. 27 *Perf. 13x13½*
780 A292 240s multicolored 1.10 .45

For surcharge see No. 793.

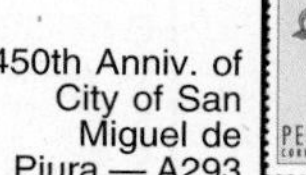

450th Anniv. of City of San Miguel de Piura — A293

1982, Dec. 31 *Perf. 13x13½*
781 A293 280s Arms 1.40 .65

For surcharge see No. 795.

TB Bacillus Centenary A294

1983, Jan. 18 *Perf. 12*
782 A294 240s Microscope, slide 1.20 .70

For surcharge see No. 794.

St. Teresa of Jesus of Avila (1515-1582), by Jose Espinoza de los Monteros, 1682 — A295

1983, Mar. 1
783 A295 100s multicolored .85 .40

10th Anniv. of State Security Service — A296

1983, Mar. 8
784 A296 100s blue & orange .85 .40

Horseman's Ornamental Silver Shoe, 19th Cent. — A297

1983, Mar. 18
785 A297 250s multicolored 1.10 .55

30th Anniv. of Santiago Declaration — A298

1983, Mar. 25
786 A298 280s Map 1.50 .60

For surcharge see No. 796.

25th Anniv. of Lima-Bogota Airmail Service — A299

1983, Apr. 8
787 A299 150s Jet 1.10 .50

75th Anniv. of Lima and Callao State Lotteries — A300

1983, Apr. 26
788 A300 100s multicolored .85 .40

Nos. 739, 773, 771, 778, 780, 782, 781, 786, 777, 749, 774 Srchd. in Black or Green

1983			**Litho.**	
789	A277	100s on 40s orange	1.75	.35
790	A285	100s on 70s multi	1.75	.35
791	A283	100s on 80s blk & red	1.75	.35
792	A290	100s on 240s multi	1.75	.35
793	A292	100s on 240s multi	1.75	.35
794	A294	100s on 240s ol grn	1.75	.35
795	A293	150s on 280s multi (G)	2.10	.65
796	A298	150s on 280s multi	2.10	.65
797	A289	200s on 280s multi	3.25	.75
798	A277	300s on 180s green	5.00	1.25
799	A277	400s on 180s green	6.25	1.60
800	A286	500s on 80s multi	1.75	1.60
		Nos. 789-800 (12)	30.95	8.60

Military Ships — A301

150s, Cruiser Almirante Grau, 1907. 350s, Submarine Ferre, 1913.

1983, May 2 *Perf. 12*
801 A301 150s multicolored 1.25 .75
802 A301 350s multicolored 2.50 2.25

Simon Bolivar Birth Bicentenary — A302

1983, Dec. 13 **Litho.** *Perf. 14*
803 A302 100s black & lt bl 1.25 .80

Christmas — A303

1983, Dec. 16
804 A303 100s Virgin and Child 1.60 1.10

25th Anniv. of Intl. Pacific Fair — A304

1983
805 A304 350s multicolored 1.40 .75

World Communications Year (in 1983) — A305

1984, Jan. 27 **Litho.** *Perf. 14*
806 A305 700s multicolored 3.25 1.75

Col. Leoncio Prado (1853-83) — A306

1984, Feb. 3 **Litho.** *Perf. 14*
807 A306 150s ol & ol brn 1.25 .60

Postal Building A307

Pottery A308

Shipbuilding and Repair — A309

Arms of City of Callao — A310

Peruvian Flora — A311

Peruvian Fauna — A312

50s, Ministry of Posts, Lima. 100s, Water jar. 150s, Llama. 200s, Painted vase. 300s, Mixed cargo ship. 400s, Arms of Cajamarca. 500s, Arms of Ayacucho. 700s, Canna edulis ker. 1000s, Lagothrix flavicauda.

1984		**Litho.**		*Perf. 14*
808	A307	50s multi	.45	.45
809	A308	100s multi	1.10	.45
810	A308	150s multi	1.10	.45
811	A308	200s multi	1.10	.45
812	A309	250s shown	1.10	.45
813	A309	300s multi	1.70	1.00
814	A310	350s shown	.90	.80
815	A310	400s multi	2.10	1.00
816	A310	500s multi	2.75	1.00
817	A311	700s multi	1.70	1.20
818	A312	1000s multi	3.25	3.00
		Nos. 808-818 (11)	17.25	10.25

Issued: 50s, 8/29; 100s-200s, 5/9; 250s-300s, 2/22; 350s, 4/23; 400s, 6/21; 500s, 6/22; 700s, 9/12; 1000s, 7/3.
See Nos. 844-853, 880-885.

A313

Designs: 50s, Hipolito Unanue (1758-1833). 200s, Ricardo Palma (1833-1919), Writer.

1984 **Litho.** *Perf. 14*
819 A313 50s dull green 1.15 .50
820 A313 200s purple 1.15 .50

Issue dates: 50s, Nov. 14; 200s, Mar. 20.
See No. 828.

1984 Summer Olympics — A315

1984, Mar. 30
821 A315 500s Shooting 1.40 .50
822 A315 750s Hurdles 2.00 .85

Independence Declaration Act — A316

1984, July 18 **Litho.** *Perf. 14*
823 A316 350s Signing document 1.25 .40

Admiral Grau — A317

Naval Battle A318

1984, Oct. 8 **Litho.** *Perf. 12½*
824 Block of 4 7.00 6.00
a. A317 600s Knight of the Seas, by Pablo Muniz 1.40 1.25
b. A318 600s Battle of Angamos 1.40 1.25
c. A317 600s Congressional seat 1.40 1.25
d. A318 600s Battle of Iquique 1.40 1.25

Admiral Miguel Grau, 150th birth anniv.

Peruvian Naval Vessels — A319

250s, Destroyer Almirante Guise, 1934. 400s, Gunboat America, 1905.

1984, Dec. **Litho.** *Perf. 14*
825 A319 250s multicolored 1.75 .80
826 A319 400s multicolored 1.75 .80

Christmas A320

1984, Dec. 11 **Litho.** *Perf. 13x13½*
827 A320 1000s multi 2.00 .75

Famous Peruvians Type of 1984

1984, Dec. 14 Litho. *Perf. 14*
828 A313 100s brown lake 1.00 .50

Victor Andres Belaunde (1883-1967), Pres. of UN General Assembly, 1959-60.

450th Anniv., Founding of Cuzco — A322

1984, Dec. 20 Litho. *Perf. 13½x13*
829 A322 1000s Street scene 1.50 .75

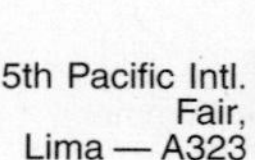

15th Pacific Intl. Fair, Lima — A323

1984, Dec. 28 Litho. *Perf. 13x13½*
830 A323 1000s Llama 1.50 .75

450th Anniv., Lima — A324

The Foundation of Lima, by Francisco Gamarra

1985, Jan. 17 Litho. *Perf. 13½x13*
831 A324 1500s multicolored 3.50 2.10

Visit of Pope John Paul II — A325

1985, Jan. 31 Litho. *Perf. 13½x13*
832 A325 2000s Portrait 3.00 2.25

Microwave Tower — A326

1985, Feb. 28 Litho. *Perf. 13½x13*
833 A326 1100s multi 1.75 .45

ENTEL Peru, Natl. Telecommunications Org., 15th anniv.

Jose Carlos Mariategui (1894-1924), Author — A327

Designs: 500s, Francisco Garcia Calderon (1832-1905), president. No. 838, Oscar Miro Quesada (1884-1981), jurist. No. 839, Cesar Vallejo (1892-1938), author. No. 840, Jose Santos Chocano (1875-1934), poet.

1985-86 Photo. *Perf. 13½x13*

836	A327	500s lt olive grn	1.10	.50
837	A327	800s dull red	1.10	.50
838	A327	800s dk olive grn	1.10	.50
839	A327	800s Prus blue ('86)	1.10	.50
840	A327	800s dk red brn ('86)	1.10	.50
		Nos. 836-840 (5)	5.50	2.50

See Nos. 901-905.

American Air Forces Cooperation System, 25th Anniv. — A328

1985, Apr. 16
842 A328 400s Member flags, emblem 1.10 .50

Jose A. Quinones Gonzales (1914-1941), Air Force Captain — A329

1985, Apr. 22 *Perf. 13x13½*
843 A329 1000s Portrait, bomber 1.60 .45

Types of 1984

Design: 200s, Entrance arch and arcade, Central PO admin. building, vert. No. 845, Spotted Robles Moqo bisque vase, Pacheco, Ica. No. 846, Huaura bisque cat. No. 847, Robles Moqo bisque llama head. No. 848, Huancavelica city arms. No. 849, Huanuco city arms. No. 850, Puno city arms. No. 851, Llama wool industry. No. 852, Hymenocallis amancaes. No. 853, Penguins, Antarctic landscape.

1985-86 Litho. *Perf. 13½x13*

844	A307	200s slate blue	.60	.60
845	A308	500s bister brn	.35	.30
846	A308	500s dull yellow brn	.35	.30
847	A308	500s black brn	.35	.30
848	A310	700s brt org yel	.80	.70
849	A310	700s brt bl ('86)	.80	.70
850	A310	900s brown ('86)	1.10	.70
851	A309	1100s multicolored	.80	.50
852	A311	1100s multicolored	.80	.50
853	A312	1500s multicolored	1.10	.60
		Nos. 844-853 (10)	7.05	5.20

Natl. Aerospace Institute Emblem, Globe — A330

1985, May 24 *Perf. 13x13½*
858 A330 900s ultra 1.20 .60

14th Inter-American Air Defense Day.

Founding of Constitution City — A333

1985, July Litho. *Perf. 13½x13*
859 A333 300s Map, flag, crucifix 1.20 .60

Natl. Radio Society, 55th Anniv. — A334

1985, July 24 *Perf. 13x13½*
860 A334 1300s bl & brt org 1.60 .60

San Francisco Convent Church — A335

1985, Oct. 12 *Perf. 13½x13*
861 A335 1300s multicolored 1.60 .60

Doctrina Christiana Frontispiece, 1585, Lima — A336

1985, Oct. 23
862 A336 300s pale buff & blk 1.75 .70

1st printed book in South America, 400th anniv.

Intl. Civil Aviation Org., 40th Anniv. — A337

1100s, 1920 Curtis Jenny.

1985, Oct. 31 *Perf. 13x13½*
863 A337 1100s multicolored 1.60 .80

Christmas — A338

2.50i, Virgin and child, 17th cent.

1985, Dec. 30 Litho. *Perf. 13½x13*
864 A338 2.50i multi 1.75 .50

Postman, Child — A338a

1985, Dec. 30 Litho. *Perf. 13½x13*
864A A338a 2.50i multi 1.50 .40

Christmas charity for children's and postal workers' funds.

Founding of Trujillo, 450th Anniv. — A339

1986, Mar. 5 Litho. *Perf. 13½x13*
865 A339 3i City arms 1.50 .85

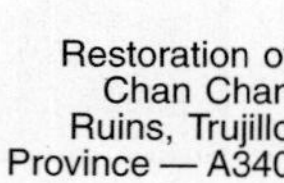

Restoration of Chan Chan Ruins, Trujillo Province — A340

1986, Apr. 5 Litho. *Perf. 13x13½*
866 A340 50c Bas-relief 1.60 .50

Saint Rose of Lima, Birth Quadricent. — A341

1986, Apr. 30 Litho. *Perf. 13½x13*
867 A341 7i multicolored 3.00 1.25

16th Intl. Pacific Fair — A342

1i, Natl. products symbols.

1986, May 20
868 A342 1i multicolored 1.20 .50

Intl. Youth Year — A343

1986, May 23 *Perf. 13x13½*
869 A343 3.50i multicolored 1.30 .50

A344

1986, June 27 Litho. *Perf. 13½x13*
870 A344 50c brown 1.00 .45

Pedro Vilcapaza (1740-81), independence hero.

UN, 40th Anniv. — A345

1986, Aug. 8 Litho. *Perf. 13x13½*
871 A345 3.50i multi 1.60 .75

A346

1986, Aug. 11 *Perf. 13½x13*
872 A346 50c grysh brown 1.00 .40

Fernando and Justo Albujar Fayaque, Manuel Guarniz Lopez, natl. heroes.

Peruvian Navy — A347

1986, Aug. 19 *Perf. 13x13½*

873	A347	1.50i R-1, 1926	.95	.65
874	A347	2.50i Abtao, 1954	2.10	1.00

Flora and Fauna Type of 1984

No. 880, Tropaeolum majus. No. 881, Datura candida. No. 884, Canis ludus. No. 885, Penelope albipennis.

1986 Litho. *Perf. 13½x13*

880	A311	80c multicolored	.75	.45
881	A311	80c multicolored	.75	.45
884	A312	2i multicolored	1.75	1.00
885	A312	2i multicolored	2.00	1.10
		Nos. 880-885 (4)	5.25	3.00

Canchis Province Folk Costumes — A348

1986, Aug. 26 Litho. ***Perf. 13½x13***
890 A348 3i multicolored 1.75 .75

Tourism Day — A349

1986, Aug. 29 ***Perf. 13x13½***
891 A349 4i Sacsayhuaman 2.10 1.00

1986, Oct. 12 Litho. ***Perf. 13x13½***
891A A349 4i Intihuatana, Cuzco 2.50 1.75

Interamerican Development Bank, 25th Anniv. — A350

1986, Sept. 4
892 A350 1i multicolored .95 .45

Beatification of Sr. Ana de Los Angeles — A351

6i, Sr. Ana, Pope John Paul II.

1986, Sept. 15
893 A351 6i multicolored 3.50 2.00

Jorge Chavez (1887-1910), Aviator, and Bleriot XI 1M — A352

1986, Sept. 23 ***Perf. 13½x13***
894 A352 5i multicolored 2.00 1.00

Chavez's flight over the Alps, 75th anniv.

VAN '86 — A353

1986, Sept. 26
895 A353 50c light blue .95 .45

Ministry of Health vaccination campaign, Sept. 27-28, Oct. 25-26, Nov. 22-23.

Natl. Journalism Day — A354

1986, Oct. 1
896 A354 1.50i multi 1.00 .50

Peruvian Navy — A355

No. 897, Brigantine Gamarra, 1848. No. 898, Monitor Manco Capac, 1880.

1986, Oct. 7 Litho. ***Perf. 13x13½***
897 A355 1i multicolored 1.25 .70
898 A355 1i multicolored 1.25 .70

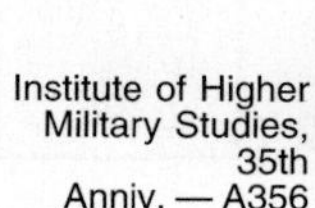

Institute of Higher Military Studies, 35th Anniv. — A356

1986, Oct. 31 Litho. ***Perf. 13x13½***
899 A356 1i multicolored 1.00 .40

Boy, Girl — A357

1986, Nov. 3 ***Perf. 13½x13***
900 A357 2.50i red, brn & blk 1.25 .50

Christmas charity for children and postal workers' funds.

Famous Peruvians Type of 1985

No. 901, Daniel A .Carrión. No. 902, José Gálvez Barrenechea. No. 904, José de la Riva Agüero. No. 905, Raúl Porras Barrenechea.

1986-87
901 A327 50c blackish brown .90 .40
902 A327 50c red brown .90 .40
904 A327 80c brown 1.10 .45
905 A327 80c orange brown .90 .40
Nos. 901-905 (4) 3.80 1.65

Issued: No. 901, 5/16/86; No. 902, 11/19/86; No. 904, 10/22/87; No. 905, 11/9/87.

Christmas — A358

1986, Dec. 3
908 A358 5i St. Joseph and Child 2.50 1.40

SENATI, 25th Anniv. — A359

1986, Dec. 19 ***Perf. 13½x13***
909 A359 4i multicolored 1.60 .75

Shipibo Tribal Costumes — A360

1987, Apr. 24 Litho. ***Perf. 13½x13***
910 A360 3i multicolored 1.50 .75

World Food Day — A361

1987, May 26
911 A361 50c multicolored 1.25 .40

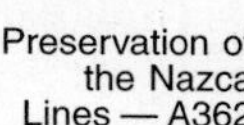

Preservation of the Nazca Lines — A362

Design: Nazca Lines and Dr. Maria Reiche (b. 1903), archaeologist.

1987, June 13 Litho. ***Perf. 13x13½***
912 A362 8i multicolored 3.50 2.00

A363

1987, July 15 Litho. ***Perf. 13½x13***
913 A363 50c violet 1.00 .35

Mariano Santos (1850-1900), "The Hero of Tarapaca," 1879, Chilean war. Dated 1986.

A364

1987, July 19 ***Perf. 13x13½***
914 A364 3i multicolored 1.60 .60

Natl. Horse Club, 50th anniv. Dated 1986.

A365

1987, Aug 13 ***Perf. 13½x13***
915 A365 2i multicolored 1.25 .65

Gen. Felipe Santiago Salaverry (1806-1836), revolution leader. Dated 1986.

Colca's Canyon — A366

1987, Sept. 8 Litho. ***Perf. 13½x13***
916 A366 6i multicolored 1.50 .70

10th Natl. Philatelic Exposition, Arequipa. Dated 1986.

AMIFIL '87 — A367

1987, Sept. 10
917 A367 1i Nos. 1-2 .95 .45

Dated 1986.

Jose Maria Arguedas (b. 1911), Anthropologist, Author — A368

1987, Sept. 19
918 A368 50c brown .95 .45

Arequipa Chamber of Commerce & Industry — A369

1987, Sept. 23 ***Perf. 13x13½***
919 A369 2i multicolored 1.25 .40

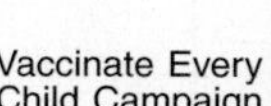

Vaccinate Every Child Campaign A370

1987, Sept. 30 Litho. ***Perf. 13x13½***
920 A370 50c brown purple .95 .45

Argentina, Winner of the 1986 World Cup Soccer Championships A371

1987, Nov. 18
921 A371 4i multicolored 1.40 .90

Restoration of Chan Chan Ruins, Trujillo Province — A372

Chimu culture (11th-15th cent.) bas-relief.

1987, Nov. 27
922 A372 50c multicolored 1.60 1.10

See No. 936.

Halley's Comet — A373

4i, Comet, Giotto satellite.

1987, Dec. 7
923 A373 4i multicolored 2.00 1.10

Jorge Chavez Dartnell (1887-1910), Aviator — A374

1987, Dec. 15 ***Perf. 13½x13***
924 A374 2i yel bis, claret brn & gold 1.10 .50

Founding of Lima, 450th Anniv. (in 1985) — A375

1987, Dec. 18 Litho. ***Perf. 13½x13***
925 A375 2.50i Osambela Palace 1.10 .50

Dated 1985.

Discovery of the Ruins at Machu Picchu, 75th Anniv. (in 1986) — A376

1987, Dec. ***Perf. 13x13½***

926 A376 9i multicolored 3.75 2.00

Dated 1986.

St. Francis's Church, Cajamarca A377

1988, Jan. 23 Litho. ***Perf. 13x13½***

927 A377 2i multicolored 1.00 .30

Cultural Heritage. Dated 1986.

Participation of Peruvian Athletes in the Olympics, 50th Anniv. — A378

Design: Athletes on parade, poster publicizing the 1936 Berlin Games.

1988, Mar. 1 Litho. ***Perf. 13½x13***

928 A378 1.50i multicolored 1.25 .40

Dated 1986.

Ministry of Education, 150th Anniv. — A379

1988, Mar. 10 ***Perf. 13x13½***

929 A379 1i multicolored 1.20 .70

Coronation of the Virgin of the Evangelization by Pope John Paul II — A380

1988, Mar. 14 Litho. ***Perf. 13x13½***

930 A380 10i multicolored 1.75 .60

Dated 1986.

Rotary Intl. Involvement in Anti-Polio Campaign A381

1988, Mar. 16

931 A381 2i org, gold & dark blue 1.00 .55

Postman, Cathedral — A382

1988, Apr. 29 Litho. ***Perf. 13½x13***

932 A382 9i brt blue 1.50 .75

Christmas charity for children and postal workers' funds.

Meeting of 8 Latin-American Presidents, Acapulco, 1st Anniv. — A383

1988, May 4 ***Perf. 13x13½***

933 A383 9i multicolored 1.75 .75

St. John Bosco (1815-1888), Educator — A384

1988, June 1 ***Perf. 13½x13***

934 A384 5i multicolored .95 .45

1st Peruvian Scientific Expedition to the Antarctic — A385

7i, Ship Humboldt, globe.

1988, June 2 ***Perf. 13x13½***

935 A385 7i multicolored 1.20 .70

Restoration of Chan-Chan Ruins, Trujillo Province — A386

1988, June 7

936 A386 4i Bas-relief 1.00 .50

Cesar Vallejo (1892-1938), Poet — A387

1988, June 15 ***Perf. 13½x13***

937 A387 25i buff, blk & brn 1.75 1.25

Journalists' Fund — A388

1988, July 12 Litho. ***Perf. 13½x13***

938 A388 4i buff & deep ultra .95 .45

Type A44 — A389

1988, Sept. 1 Litho. ***Perf. 13½x13***

939 A389 20i blk, lt pink & ultra 1.00 .50

EXFILIMA '88, discovery of America 500th anniv.

17th Intl. Pacific Fair — A390

1988, Sept. 6 ***Perf. 13x13½***

940 A390 4i multicolored 1.50 1.00

Painting by Jose Sabogal (1888-1956) A391

1988, Sept. 7

941 A391 12i multicolored .95 .45

Peru Kennel Club Emblem, Dogs — A392

1988, Sept. 9 ***Perf. 13½x13***

942 A392 20i multicolored 2.10 1.25

CANINE '88 Intl. Dog Show, Lima.

Alfonso de Silva (1902-1934), Composer, and Score to Esplendido de Flores — A393

1988, Sept. 27 Litho. ***Perf. 13x13½***

943 A393 20i multicolored 1.20 .45

2nd State Visit of Pope John Paul II — A394

1988, Oct. 10 ***Perf. 13½x13***

944 A394 50i multicolored 1.25 .75

1988 Summer Olympics, Seoul — A395

1988, Nov. 10 Litho. ***Perf. 13½x13***

945 A395 25i Women's volleyball 1.50 .45

Women's Volleyball Championships (1982) — A396

Surcharged in Red

1988, Nov. 16 ***Perf. 12***

946 A396 95i on 300s multi 1.90 1.40

No. 946 not issued without overprint.

Christmas charity for children's and postal workers' funds.

Chavin Culture Ceramic Vase — A397

Surcharged in Henna or Black

1988 Litho. ***Perf. 12***

947 A397 40i on 100s red brn 2.00 1.50

948 A397 80i on 10s blk 3.75 2.25

Nos. 947-948 not issued without surcharge. Issue dates: 40i, Dec. 15. 80i, Dec. 22.

Rain Forest Border Highway — A398

Surcharged in Black

1989, Jan. 27 Litho. ***Perf. 12***

949 A398 70i on 80s multi 1.10 .60

Not issued without surcharge.

Codex of the Indian Kings, 1681 — A399

Surcharged in Olive Brown

1989, Feb. 10

950 A399 230i on 300s multi 1.75 1.25

Not issued without surcharge.

Credit Bank of Peru, Cent. — A400

500i, Huari Culture weaving.

1989, Apr. 9 Litho. ***Perf. 13x13½***

951 A400 500i multicolored 2.00 1.50

Postal Services A401

1989, Apr. 20 ***Perf. 13***

952 A401 50i SESPO, vert. .80 .40

953 A401 100i CAN 1.20 .40

El Comercio, 150th Anniv. — A402

1989, May 15

954 A402 600i multicolored 1.50 .50

Garcilaso de la Vega (1539-1616), Historian Called "The Inca" — A403

1989, July 11 Litho. ***Perf. 12½***

955 A403 300i multicolored 1.10 .40

Express Mail Service — A404

1989, July 12

956 A404 100i dark red, org & dark blue 1.10 .40

Federation Emblem and Roca — A405

1989, Aug. 29 **Litho.** ***Perf. 13***

957 A405 100i multicolored .95 .45

Luis Loli Roca (1925-1988), founder of the Federation of Peruvian Newspaper Publishers.

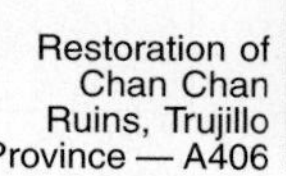

Restoration of Chan Chan Ruins, Trujillo Province — A406

Chimu culture (11th-15th cent.) bas-relief.

1989, Sept. 17 ***Perf. 12½***

958 A406 400i multicolored 3.00 2.50

Geographical Society of Lima, Cent. — A407

1989, Sept. 18 ***Perf. 13***

959 A407 600i Early map of So. America 3.00 2.50

Founders of Independence Soc. — A408

1989, Sept. 28 **Litho.** ***Perf. 12½***

960 A408 300i multicolored 1.00 .60

3rd Meeting of the Presidential Consultation and Planning Board — A409

1989, Oct. 12 ***Perf. 13***

961 A409 1300i Huacachina Lake 3.00 2.50

For surcharge see No. 1027.

Children Mailing Letters — A410

1989, Nov. 29 **Litho.** ***Perf. 12½***

962 A410 1200i multicolored 1.10 .65

Christmas charity for children's and postal workers' funds.

Cacti — A411

No. 963, Loxanthocereus acanthurus. No. 964, Corryocactus huincoensis. No. 965, Haageocereus clavispinus. No. 966, Trichocereus pervianus. No. 967, Matucana cereoides.

1989, Dec. 21 **Litho.** ***Perf. 13***

963 A411 500i multicolored 1.50 .45
964 A411 500i multicolored 1.50 .45
965 A411 500i multicolored 1.50 .45
966 A411 500i multicolored 1.50 .45
967 A411 500i multicolored 1.50 .45
Nos. 963-967 (5) 7.50 2.25

Nos. 965-967 vert. For surcharges see Nos. 1028-1031

America Issue — A412

UPAE emblem and pre-Columbian medicine jars.

1989, Dec. 28 ***Perf. 12½***

968 A412 5000i shown 8.50 5.00
969 A412 5000i multi, diff. 8.50 5.00

Belen Church, Cajamarca A413

1990, Feb. 1 **Litho.** ***Perf. 12½***

970 A413 600i multicolored 2.10 .40

Historic patrimony of Cajamarca and culture of the Americas.

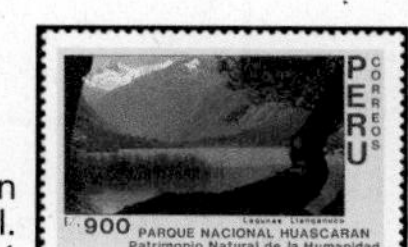

Huascaran Natl. Park — A414

No. 971, Llanganuco Lagoons. No. 972, Mountain climber, Andes, vert. No. 973, Alpamayo mountain. No. 974, Puya raimondi, vert. No. 975, Condor and Quenual. No. 976, El Huascaran.

1990, Feb. 4 ***Perf. 13***

971 A414 900i multicolored 1.00 .70
972 A414 900i multicolored 1.00 .70
973 A414 1000i multicolored 1.10 .70
974 A414 1000i multicolored 1.10 .70
975 A414 1100i multicolored 1.40 .70
976 A414 1100i multicolored 1.40 .70
Nos. 971-976 (6) 7.00 4.20

Pope and Icon of the Virgin — A415

1990, Feb. 6 ***Perf. 12½***

977 A415 1250i multicolored 1.75 1.25

Visit of Pope John Paul II. For surcharge see No. 1039.

Butterflies A416

No. 978, Amydon. No. 979, Agrias beata, female. No. 980, Sardanapalus, male. No. 981, Sardanapalus, female. No. 982, Agrias beata, male.

1990, Feb. 11 ***Perf. 13***

978 A416 1000i multi 3.25 .75
979 A416 1000i multi 3.25 .75
980 A416 1000i multi 3.25 .75
981 A416 1000i multi 3.25 .75
982 A416 1000i multi 3.25 .75
Nos. 978-982 (5) 16.25 3.75

For surcharges see Nos. 1033-1037.

A417

Victor Raul Haya de La Torre and Seat of Government.

1990, Feb. 24 ***Perf. 12½***

983 A417 2100i multicolored 1.40 .90

Return to constitutional government, 10th anniv.

A418

1990, May 24 **Litho.** ***Perf. 12½***

984 A418 300i multicolored 1.10 .60

Peruvian Philatelic Assoc., 40th anniv. Dated 1989. For surcharge see No. 1038.

Prenfil '88 — A419

1990, May 29

985 A419 300i multicolored .85 .40

World Exposition of Stamp & Literature Printers, Buenos Aires. Dated 1989. For surcharge see No. 1032.

French Revolution, Bicentennial — A420

#986, Liberty. #987, Storming the Bastille. #988, Lafayette celebrating the Republic. #989, Rousseau & symbols of the Revolution.

1990, June 5

986 A420 2000i multicolored 1.75 .75
987 A420 2000i multicolored 1.75 .75
988 A420 2000i multicolored 1.75 .75
989 A420 2000i shown 1.75 .75
a. Strip of 4, #986-989 + label 7.50 7.50

Dated 1989.

Arequipa, 450th Anniv. — A421

1990, Aug. 15 **Litho.** ***Perf. 13***

990 A421 50,000i multi 1.40 .90

Lighthouse A422

Design: 230,000i, Hospital ship Morona.

Surcharged in Black

1990, Sept. 19 ***Perf. 12½***

991 A422 110,000i on 200i blue 1.75 1.75
992 A422 230,000i on 400i blue 3.75 3.25

Not issued without surcharge. No. 991 exists with albino surcharge.

A423

110,000i, Torch bearer. 280,000i, Shooting. 290,000i, Running, horiz. 300,000i, Soccer. 560,000i, Swimming, horiz. 580,000i, Equestrian. 600,000i, Sailing. 620,000i, Tennis.

1990-91 **Litho.** ***Perf. 13***

993 A423 110,000i multi 1.30 .50
994 A423 280,000i multi 2.75 1.10
995 A423 290,000i multi 2.75 1.10
996 A423 300,000i multi 2.90 1.25
997 A423 560,000i multi 4.00 1.75
998 A423 580,000i multi 4.50 2.00
999 A423 600,000i multi 4.75 2.00
1000 A423 620,000i multi 4.75 2.00
Nos. 993-1000 (8) 27.70 11.70

4th South American Games, Lima. Issue dates: #993-996, Oct. 19. #997-1000, Feb. 5, 1991.

A424

1990, Nov. 22 **Litho.** ***Die Cut***

Self-Adhesive

1001 A424 250,000i No. 1 3.00 1.25
1002 A424 350,000i No. 2 4.00 1.75

Pacific Steam Navigation Co., 150th anniv.

Postal Workers' Christmas Fund — A425

1990, Dec. 7 **Litho.** ***Perf. 12½***

1003 A425 310,000i multi 3.50 3.25

A426

Design: Maria Jesus Castaneda de Pardo, First Woman President of Peruvian Red Cross.

1991, May 15 **Litho.** ***Perf. 12½***

1004 A426 .15im on 2500i red & blk 1.90 1.60

Dated 1990. Not issued without surcharge.

2nd Peruvian Scientific Expedition to Antarctica A427

.40im, Penguins, man. .45im, Peruvian research station, skua. .50im, Whale, map, research station.

1991, June 20

1005 A427 .40im on 50,000i 3.75 1.60
1006 A427 .45im on 80,000i 4.00 1.75
1007 A427 .50im on 100,000i 5.00 2.10
Nos. 1005-1007 (3) 12.75 5.45

Not issued without surcharge.

A428

St. Anthony Natl. Univ., Cuzco, 300th Anniv.: 10c, Siphoonandra ellipitica. 20c, Don Manuel de Mollinedo y Angulo, founder. 1s, University coat of arms.

1991, Sept. 26 Litho. *Perf. 13½x13*

1008 A428 10c multicolored .50 .40
1009 A428 20c multicolored 1.00 .80
1010 A428 1s multicolored 4.75 4.50
Nos. 1008-1010 (3) 6.25 5.70

A429

Paintings: No. 1011, Madonna and child. No. 1012, Madonna with lambs and angels.

1991, Dec. 3 Litho. *Perf. 13½x13*

1011 A429 70c multicolored 4.00 3.75
1012 A429 70c multicolored 4.00 3.75

Postal Workers' Christmas fund.

America Issue — A430

No. 1013, Mangrove swamp. No. 1014, Gera waterfall, vert.

1991, Dec. 23 *Perf. 13*

1013 A430 .50im multi 3.50 3.25
1014 A430 .50im multi 3.50 3.25

Dated 1990.

Sir Rowland Hill and Penny Black — A431

1992, Jan. 15 Litho. *Perf. 13*

1015 A431 .40im gray, blk & bl 2.25 2.00

Penny Black, 150th anniv. (in 1990).

A432

1992, Jan. 28

1016 A432 .30im multicolored 1.60 .85

Our Lady of Guadalupe College, 150th anniv. (in 1990)

Entre Nous Society, 80th Anniv. — A433

1992, Jan. 30 *Perf. 13½x13*

1017 A433 10c multicolored .85 .60

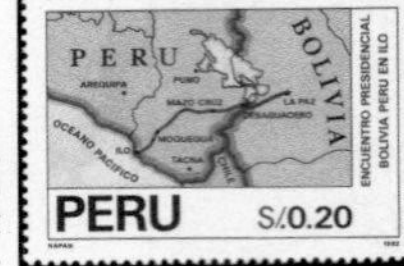
Peru-Bolivia Port Access Agreement A434

1992, Feb. 25 Litho. *Perf. 12½*

1018 A434 20c multicolored 1.30 .75

Restoration of Chan-Chan Ruins — A435

1992, Mar. 17

1019 A435 .15im multicolored 1.75 1.50

Dated 1990.

Antonio Raimondi, Naturalist and Publisher, Death Cent. — A436

1992, Mar. 31

1020 A436 .30im multicolored 1.90 1.60

Dated 1990.

Newspaper "Diario de Lima", Bicent. (in 1990) — A437

1992, May 22 Litho. *Perf. 13*

1021 A437 .35im pale yel & black 1.60 1.40

Dated 1990.

Mariano Melgar (1790-1815), Poet — A438

1992, Aug. 5 Litho. *Perf. 12½x13*

1022 A438 60c multicolored 2.75 2.50

8 Reales, 1568, First Peruvian Coinage — A439

1992, Aug. 7 *Perf. 13x12½*

1023 A439 70c multicolored 2.50 2.25

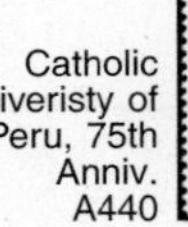
Catholic University of Peru, 75th Anniv. A440

1992, Aug. 18 *Perf. 12½*

1024 A440 90c black & tan 3.25 3.00

Pan-American Health Organization, 90th Anniv. — A441

1992, Dec. 2 Litho. *Die Cut*
Self-Adhesive

1025 A441 3s multicolored 7.50 7.25

Nos. 749, 961 Surcharged

Perf. 13½x13, 13

1992, Nov. 18 Litho.

1026 A277 50c on 180s #749 1.50 1.00
1027 A409 1s on 1300i #961 3.50 2.25

Nos. 963, 965-967, 977-982, & 984-985 Surcharged

Perfs. as Before

1992, Dec. 24 Litho.

1028 A411 40c on 500i #963 10.00 10.00
1029 A411 40c on 500i #965 10.00 10.00
1030 A411 40c on 500i #966 10.00 10.00
1031 A411 40c on 500i #967 10.00 10.00
1032 A419 50c on 300i #985 10.00 10.00
1033 A416 50c on 1000i #978 10.00 10.00
1034 A416 50c on 1000i #979 10.00 10.00
1035 A416 50c on 1000i #980 10.00 10.00
1036 A416 50c on 1000i #981 14.00 10.00
1037 A416 50c on 1000i #982 14.00 10.00
1038 A418 1s on 300i #984 21.00 10.00
1039 A415 1s on 1250i #977 21.00 10.00
Nos. 1028-1039 (12) 150.00 120.00

Virgin with a Spindle, by Urbina — A442

1993, Feb. 10 Litho. *Die Cut*
Self-Adhesive

1040 A442 80c multicolored 3.00 2.75

Sican Culture — A443

Various artifacts.

1993, Feb. 10 Self-Adhesive

1041 A443 2s multicolored 5.00 4.75
1042 A443 5s multi, vert. 11.00 10.75

Evangelization in Peru, 500th Anniv. — A444

1993, Feb. 12 Self-Adhesive

1043 A444 1s multicolored 3.50 2.75

Fruit Sellers, by Angel Chavez A445

Dancers, by Monica Rojas A446

1993, Feb. 12 Self-Adhesive

1044 A445 1.50s multicolored 4.50 2.00
1045 A446 1.50s multicolored 4.50 2.00

Statue of Madonna and Child — A447

1993, Feb. 24 Litho. *Die Cut*
Self-Adhesive

1046 A447 70c multicolored 2.40 2.10

Salesian Brothers in Peru, cent. (in 1991).

America Issue A448

UPAEP: No. 1047a, 90c, Francisco Pizarro, sailing ship. b, 1s, Sailing ship, map of north-west coast of South America.

1993, Mar. 19 *Perf. 12½*

1047 A448 Pair, #a.-b. 6.00 4.50

Sipan Gold Head A449

1993, Apr. 1

1048 A449 50c multicolored 10.75 10.50

Beatification of Josemaria Escriva, 1st Anniv. — A450

1993, July 7 Litho. *Die Cut*
Self-Adhesive

1049 A450 30c multicolored 1.50 1.25

Peru-Japan Treaty of Peace and Trade, 120th Anniv. — A451

Designs: 1.50s, Flowers. 1.70s, Peruvian, Japanese children, mountains.

1993, Aug. 21 **Litho.** ***Perf. 11***

1050 A451 1.50s multicolored 3.75 2.00
1051 A451 1.70s multicolored 4.00 3.25

Sea Lions — A452

1993, Sept. 20 **Litho.** ***Perf. 11***

1052 A452 90c shown 2.50 1.50
1053 A452 1s Parrot, vert. 3.00 2.00

Amifil '93 (#1052). Brasiliana '93 (#1053).

A453

1993, Nov. 9 **Litho.** ***Die Cut***
Self-Adhesive

1054 A453 50c olive brown 2.50 2.00

Honorio Delgado, Physician and Author, Birth Cent. (in 1992).

A454

1993, Nov. 12 **Self-Adhesive**

1055 A454 80c orange brown 3.25 2.50

Rosalia De LaValle De Morales Macedo, Social Reformer, Birth Cent.

A455

Sculptures depicting Peruvian ethnic groups.

1993, Nov. 22 **Self-Adhesive**

1056 A455 2s Quechua 10.00 10.00
1057 A455 3.50s Orejon 13.00 12.50

Intl. Pacific Fair, Lima — A456

1993, Nov. 25 **Litho.** ***Perf. 11***

1058 A456 1.50s multicolored 6.00 5.75

Christmas — A457

Design: 1s, Madonna of Loreto.

1993, Nov. 30 ***Perf. 11***

1059 A457 1s multicolored 3.50 3.25

Cultural Artifacts — A458

2.50s, Sican artifacts. 4s, Sican mask. 10s, Chancay ceramic statue, vert. 20s, Chancay textile.

Self-Adhesive

1993, Nov. 30 ***Die Cut***

1060 A458 2.50s multicolored 12.50 9.00
1061 A458 4s multicolored 15.00 12.50
1062 A458 10s multicolored 35.00 20.00
1063 A458 20s multicolored 75.00 72.50
Nos. 1060-1063 (4) 137.50 114.00

See Nos. 1079-1082.

Prevention of AIDS — A459

1993, Dec. 1 **Litho.** ***Perf. 11***

1064 A459 1.50s multicolored 4.75 4.50

A460

1994, Mar. 4 **Litho.** ***Die Cut***
Self-Adhesive

1065 A460 1s multicolored 3.00 2.75

Natl. Council on Science and Technology (Concytec), 25th Anniv. Dated 1993.

A461

20c, 30c, 40c, 50c, Bridge of Huaman Poma de Ayala.

1994 **Self-Adhesive**

1066 A461 20c blue 1.00 .75
1067 A461 40c orange 2.25 1.50
1068 A461 50c purple 2.75 2.00
Nos. 1066-1068 (3) 6.00 4.25

Litho.
Perf. 12x11

1073 A461 30c brown 1.25 1.10
1074 A461 40c black 2.25 1.75
1075 A461 50c vermilion 2.75 2.00
Nos. 1073-1075 (3) 6.25 4.85

Issued: Nos. 1066-1068, 3/11/94; Nos. 1073-1075, 5/13/94.

Cultural Artifacts Type of 1993

No. 1079, Engraved silver container, vert. No. 1080, Engraved medallion. No. 1081, Carved bull, Pucara. No. 1082, Plate with fish designs.

1994, Mar. 25 **Self-Adhesive**

1079 A458 1.50s multicolored 4.00 4.00
1080 A458 1.50s multicolored 4.00 4.00
1081 A458 3s multicolored 8.00 7.50
1082 A458 3s multicolored 8.00 7.50
Nos. 1079-1082 (4) 24.00 23.00

Dated 1993.

Sipan Artifacts — A464

3s, Peanut-shaped beads. 5s, Mask, vert.

1994, May 19 **Litho.** ***Perf. 11***

1083 A464 3s multi 9.50 7.50
1084 A464 5s multi 15.00 10.00

El Brujo Archaeological Site, Trujillo — A465

1994, Nov. 3 **Litho.** ***Perf. 14***

1085 A465 70c multicolored 2.25 2.00

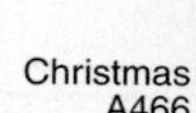

Christmas A466

Ceramic figures: 1.80s, Christ child. 2s, Nativity scene. Dated 1994.

1995, Mar. 17 **Litho.** ***Perf. 13x13½***

1086 A466 1.80s multicolored 4.50 3.50
1087 A466 2s multicolored 4.75 4.00

1994 World Cup Soccer Championships, U.S. — A467

1995, Mar. 20 ***Perf. 13½x13***

1088 A467 60c shown 1.50 1.00
1089 A467 4.80s Mascot, flags 10.50 6.50

Dated 1994.

Ministry of Transportation, 25th Anniv. — A468

1995, Mar. 22 ***Perf. 13x13½***

1090 A468 20c multicolored 1.00 .75

Dated 1994.

Cultural Artifacts — A469

Mochican art: 40c, Pitcher with figures beneath blanket. 80c, Jeweled medallion. 90c, Figure holding severed head.

1995, Mar. 27 ***Perf. 14***

1091 A469 40c multicolored 1.40 1.30
1092 A469 80c multicolored 2.50 2.00
1093 A469 90c multicolored 2.75 2.60
Nos. 1091-1093 (3) 6.65 5.90

Dated 1994.

Juan Parra del Riego, Birth Cent. — A470

No. 1095, Jose Carlos Mariategui, birth cent.

1995, Mar. 28 ***Perf. 14***

1094 A470 90c multicolored 3.50 2.50

Perf. 13½x13

1095 A470 90c multicolored 3.50 2.50

Dated 1994.

Las Carmelitas Monastery, 350th Anniv. — A471

1995, Mar. 31 **Litho.** ***Perf. 13***

1096 A471 70c multicolored 2.50 1.50

Dated 1994.

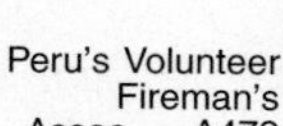

Peru's Volunteer Fireman's Assoc. — A472

Fire trucks: 50c, Early steam ladder. 90c, Modern aerial ladder.

1995, Apr. 12 ***Perf. 14***

1097 A472 50c multicolored 2.00 1.25
1098 A472 90c multicolored 3.00 2.00

Dated 1994.

Musical Instruments — A473

1995, Apr. 10 **Litho.** ***Perf. 13½x13***

1099 A473 20c Cello 1.00 .50
1100 A473 40c Drum 1.75 1.00

Union Club, Fountain, Plaza of Arms — A474

Design: 1s, Santo Domingo Convent, Lima.

1995, Apr. 19 **Litho.** ***Perf. 14***

1101 A474 90c multicolored 4.75 4.50
1102 A474 1s multicolored 4.75 4.50

Cultural history of Lima.

Ethnic Groups — A475

1995, Apr. 26 ***Perf. 13½x13***

1103 A475 1s Bora girl 3.25 3.00
1104 A475 1.80s Aguaruna man 5.25 5.00

World Food Program, 30th Anniv. — A476

1995, May 3 ***Perf. 13x13½***

1105 A476 1.80s multicolored 5.25 5.00

Solanum Ambosinum — A477

Design: 2s, Mochica ceramic representation of papa flower.

1995, May 8 ***Perf. 13½x13***

1106 A477 1.80s multicolored 5.00 4.00
1107 A477 2s multicolored 6.00 4.00

Reed Boat, Lake Titicaca — A478

1995, May 12

1108 A478 2s multicolored 6.00 5.75

Fauna — A479

1s, American owl, vert. 1.80s, Jaguar.

1995, May 18 ***Perf. 13½x13, 13x13½***

1109	A479	1s multi	3.50	3.00
1110	A479	1.80s multi	5.00	5.00

Andes Development Corporation, 25th Anniv. — A480

1995, Aug. 29 **Litho.** ***Perf. 14***

1111	A480	5s multicolored	13.00	12.00

World Tourism Day — A481

1995, Sept. 27 ***Perf. 13x13½***

1112	A481	5.40s multicolored	18.00	17.50

Dated 1994.

World Post Day — A482

1.80s, Antique mail box.

1995, Oct. 9 ***Perf. 14***

1113	A482	1.80s multi	5.00	4.75

Dated 1994.

America Issue — A483

1.50s, Landing of Columbus. 1.70s, Guanaco, vert. 1.80s, Early mail cart. 2s, Postal trucks.

Perf. 13½x14, 14x13½ (#1115)

1995, Oct. 12

1114	A483	1.50s multi	4.00	3.75
1115	A483	1.70s multi	4.50	4.25
1116	A483	1.80s multi	4.50	4.25
1117	A483	2s multi	5.00	4.75
		Nos. 1114-1117 (4)	18.00	17.00

No. 1116-1117 are dated 1994.

UN, 50th Anniv. — A484

Design: 90c, Peruvian delegates, 1945.

1995, Oct. 28 ***Perf. 14***

1118	A484	90c multicolored	2.75	2.50

Entries, Lima Cathedrals — A485

Designs: 30c, St. Apolonia. 70c, St. Louis, side entry to St. Francis.

1995, Oct. 20

1119	A485	30c multicolored	1.25	1.00
1120	A485	70c multicolored	2.25	2.00

Dated 1994.

Artifacts from Art Museums — A486

Carvings and sculptures: No. 1121, St. James on horseback, 19th cent. No. 1122, Church. 40c, Woman on pedestal. 50c, Archangel.

1995, Oct. 31 ***Perf. 14½x14***

1121	A486	20c multicolored	.95	.90
1122	A486	20c multicolored	.95	.90
1123	A486	40c multicolored	1.80	1.25
1124	A486	50c multicolored	2.50	2.10
		Nos. 1121-1124 (4)	6.20	5.15

Dated 1994.

Scouting A487

Designs: a, 80c, Lady Olave Baden-Powell. b, 1s, Lord Robert Baden-Powell.

1995, Nov. 9 **Litho.** ***Perf. 13½x13***

1125	A487	Pair, #a.-b.	5.00	4.50

Dated 1994.

Folk Dances — A488

1,80s, Festejo. 2s, Marinera limeña, horiz.

1995, Nov. 16 ***Perf. 14***

1126	A488	1.80s multicolored	4.25	3.75
1127	A488	2s multicolored	5.00	4.50

Dated 1994.

Biodiversity — A489

50c, Manu Natl. Park. 90c, Anolis punctatus, horiz.

1995, Nov. 23

1128	A489	50c multicolored	4.00	4.00
1129	A489	90c multicolored	8.00	7.50

Dated 1994.

Electricity for Development — A490

20c, Toma de Huinco. 40c, Antacoto Lake.

1995, Nov. 27

1130	A490	20c multicolored	.75	.60
1131	A490	40c multicolored	1.60	1.25

Dated 1994.

Peruvian Saints — A491

90c, St. Toribio de Mogrovejo. 1s, St. Francisco Solano.

1995, Dec. 4

1132	A491	90c multicolored	2.25	2.00
1133	A491	1s multicolored	2.75	2.50

Dated 1994.

FAO, 50th Anniv. — A492

1996, Apr. 24 **Litho.** ***Perf. 14***

1134	A492	60c multicolored	1.75	1.25

Christmas 1995 — A493

Local crafts: 30c, Nativity scene with folding panels, vert. 70c, Carved statues of three Magi.

1996, May 2

1135	A493	30c multicolored	1.00	.75
1136	A493	70c multicolored	2.25	1.75

America Issue — A494

Designs: 30c, Rock formations of Lachay. 70c, Coastal black crocodile.

1996, May 9

1137	A494	30c multicolored	2.00	1.75
1138	A494	70c multicolored	2.75	2.50

Intl. Pacific Fair — A495

1996, May 16

1139	A495	60c multicolored	1.75	1.50

1992 Summer Olympic Games, Barcelona — A496

a, 40c Shooting. b, 40c Tennis. c, 60c Swimming. d, 60c Weight lifting.

1996, June 10 **Litho.** ***Perf. 12½***

1140	A496	Block of 4, #a.-d.	7.00	6.00

Dated 1992.

For surcharges see #1220-1223.

Expo '92, Seville — A497

1996, June 17

1141	A497	1.50s multicolored	6.25	6.00

Dated 1992.

Cesar Vallejo (1892-1938), Writer — A498

1996, June 25

1142	A498	50c black & gray	2.10	1.90

Dated 1992.

Lima, City of Culture A499

1996, July 1

1143	A499	30c brown & tan	1.25	1.00

Dated 1992.

For surcharge see No. 1219.

Kon-Tiki Expedition, 50th Anniv. — A500

1997, Apr. 28 **Litho.** ***Perf. 12½***

1144	A500	3.30s multicolored	6.25	6.00

Beginning with No. 1145, most stamps have colored lines printed on the back creating a granite paper effect.

UNICEF, 50th Anniv. (in 1996) — A501

1997, Aug. 7 **Litho.** ***Perf. 13½x14***

1145	A501	1.80s multicolored	4.00	3.75

Mochica Pottery — A502

Designs: 20c, Owl. 30c, Ornamental container. 50c, Goose jar. 1s, Two monkeys on jar. 1.30s, Duck pitcher. 1.50s, Cat pitcher.

1997, Aug. 18 **Litho.** ***Perf. 14½***

1146	A502	20c green	.70	.65
1147	A502	30c lilac	1.20	1.10
1148	A502	50c black	1.75	1.60
1149	A502	1s red brown	3.50	3.25
1150	A502	1.30s red	5.00	4.50
1151	A502	1.50s brown	5.75	5.25
		Nos. 1146-1151 (6)	17.90	16.35

See Nos. 1179-1183, 1211-1214.

1996 Summer Olympics, Atlanta — A503

a, Shooting. b, Gymnastics. c, Boxing. d, Soccer.

1997, Aug. 25 ***Perf. 14x13½***

1152 A503 2.70s Strip of 4, #a.-d. 21.00 20.00

College of Biology, 25th Anniv. — A504

1997, Aug. 26

1153 A504 5s multicolored 9.25 9.00

Scouting, 90th Anniv. — A505

1997, Aug. 29

1154 A505 6.80s multicolored 12.25 12.00

8th Intl. Conference Against Corruption, Lima — A506

1997, Sept. 7 ***Perf. 13½x14***

1155 A506 2.70s multicolored 4.00 3.75

Montreal Protocol on Substances that Deplete Ozone Layer, 10th Anniv. — A507

1997, Sept. 16 ***Perf. 14x13½***

1156 A507 6.80s multicolored 14.00 13.50

Lord of Sipan Artifacts — A508

Designs: 2.70s, Animal figure with large hands, feet. 3.30s, Medallion with warrior figure, vert.

10s, Tomb of Lord of Sipan, vert.

1997, Sept. 22 **Litho.** ***Perf. 13½x14***

1157 A508 2.70s multicolored 5.50 5.25
1158 A508 3.30s multicolored 7.00 6.75

Souvenir Sheet

1159 A508 10s multicolored 18.50 18.00

Peruvian Indians — A509

1997, Oct. 12 **Litho.** ***Perf. 14x13½***

1160 A509 2.70s Man 6.00 5.75
1161 A509 2.70s Woman 6.00 5.75

America Issue. Nos. 1160-1161 are dated 1996.

Heinrich von Stephan (1831-97) — A510

1997, Oct. 9

1162 A510 10s multicolored 19.50 19.00

America Issue — A511

No. 1163, Early post carrier. No. 1164, Modern letter carrier.

1997, Oct. 12

1163 A511 2.70s multicolored 6.75 6.50
1164 A511 2.70s multicolored 6.75 6.50

13th Bolivar Games — A512

a, Tennis. b, Soccer. c, Basketball. d, Shot put.

1997, Oct. 17 **Litho.** ***Perf. 14x13½***

1165 A512 2.70s Block of 4, #a.-d. 24.50 23.50

Marshal Ramon Castilla (1797-1867) — A513

1997, Oct. 17

1166 A513 1.80s multicolored 4.50 4.25

Treaty of Tlatelolco Banning Nuclear Weapons in Latin America, 30th Anniv. — A514

1997, Nov. 3

1167 A514 20s multicolored 38.00 37.50

Manu Natl. Park — A515

Birds: a, Kingfisher. b, Woodpecker. c, Crossbill. d, Eagle. e, Jabiru. f, Owl.

1997, Oct. 24 **Sheet of 6**

1168 A515 3.30s #a.-f. + label 41.50 40.00

8th Peruvian Antarctic Scientific Expedition — A516

1997, Nov. 10

1169 A516 6s multicolored 13.00 12.50

Christmas — A517

1997, Nov. 26

1170 A517 2.70s multicolored 5.50 5.25

Hipolito Unanue Agreement, 25th Anniv. — A518

1997, Dec. 18 **Litho.** ***Perf. 14x13½***

1171 A518 1s multicolored 2.50 2.25

Souvenir Sheet

Peruvian Gold Libra, Cent. A519

1997, Dec. 18

1172 A519 10s multicolored 26.50 26.00

Dept. of Post and Telegraph, Cent. — A520

1997, Dec. 31

1173 A520 1s multicolored 2.25 2.00

Organization of American States (OAS), 50th Anniv. — A521

1998, Apr. 30 **Litho.** ***Perf. 14x13½***

1174 A521 2.70s multicolored 5.75 5.50

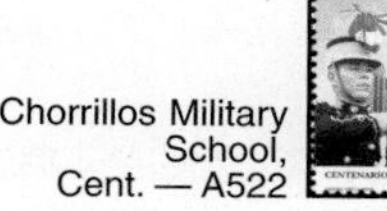

Chorrillos Military School, Cent. — A522

1998, Apr. 29 ***Perf. 13½x14***

1175 A522 2.70s multicolored 5.75 5.50

Tourism — A523

1998, June 22 **Litho.** ***Perf. 14x13½***

1176 A523 5s multicolored 9.50 9.25

Peruvian Horse — A524

1998, June 5

1177 A524 2.70s pale vio & vio 6.25 6.00

1998 World Cup Soccer Championships, France — A525

a, 2.70s, Goalie. b, 3.30s, Two players.
10s, Player kicking ball.

1998, June 26

1178 A525 Pair, #a.-b. 11.00 10.50

Souvenir Sheet

Perf. 13½x14

1178C A525 10s multicolored 19.00 18.50

Mochica Pottery Type of 1997

1s, like #1149. 1.30s, like #1146. 1.50s, like #1151. 2.70s, like #1148. 3.30s, like #1150.

1998, June 19 **Litho.** ***Perf. 14½***

1179 A502 1s slate 3.25 3.00
1180 A502 1.30s violet 4.00 3.75
1181 A502 1.50s pale blue 5.25 5.00
1182 A502 2.70s bister 9.25 9.00
1183 A502 3.30s black brown 9.75 9.50
Nos. 1179-1183 (5) 31.50 30.25

Aero Peru, 25th Anniv. — A526

1.50s, Cuzco Cathedral. 2.70s, Airplane.

1998, May 22 ***Perf. 13½x14***

1184 A526 1.50s multicolored 3.25 3.00
1185 A526 2.70s multicolored 5.75 5.50

Restoration of the Cathedral of Lima, Cent. — A527

1998, June 15 ***Perf. 14x13½***

1186 A527 2.70s multicolored 5.50 5.25

Inca Rulers — A528

No. 1187, Lloque Yupanqui. No. 1188, Sinchi Roca. No. 1189, Manco Capac.

1998, July 17 Litho. *Perf. 14x13½*

1187 A528 2.70s multicolored 7.50 7.00
1188 A528 2.70s multicolored 7.50 7.00
1189 A528 9.70s multicolored 24.00 23.00
Nos. 1187-1189 (3) 39.00 37.00

See Nos. 1225-1228.

Intl. Year of the Ocean — A529

1998, Aug. 8 *Perf. 13½x14*

1190 A529 6.80s multicolored 13.50 13.25

Natl. Symphony Orchestra, 60th Anniv. — A530

1998, Aug. 11 *Perf. 14x13½*

1191 A530 2.70s multicolored 5.50 5.25

Mother Teresa (1910-97) — A531

1998, Sept. 5

1192 A531 2.70s multicolored 6.50 6.25

Peruvian Children's Foundation — A532

1998, Sept. 17

1193 A532 8.80s multicolored 16.50 16.00

Souvenir Sheet

Heroes of the Cenepa River A533

1998, June 5

1194 A533 10s multicolored 19.00 18.50

Souvenir Sheet

Princess De Ampato A534

1998, Sept. 8

1195 A534 10s multicolored 19.00 18.50

Fauna of Manu Natl. Park — A535

1998, Sept. 27 Litho. *Perf. 14x13½*

1196 A535 1.50s multicolored 4.00 3.75

America Issue — A536

1998, Oct. 12

1197 A536 2.70s Chabuca 5.50 5.25

Stamp Day — A537

1998, Oct. 9

1198 A537 6.80s No. 3 11.50 11.25

Frogs — A538

No. 1199: a, Agalychnis craspedopus. b, Ceratophrys cornuta. c, Epipedobates macero. d, Phyllomedusa vaillanti. e, Dendrobates biolat. f, Hemiphractus proboscideus.

1998, Oct. 23 Litho. *Perf. 14x13½*

1199 A538 3.30s Block of 6, #a.-f. + label *35.00 34.00*

Christmas A539

1998, Nov. 16 *Perf. 13½x14*

1200 A539 3.30s multicolored 4.25 4.00

Universal Declaration of Human Rights, 50th Anniv. — A540

1998, Dec. 10 Litho. *Perf. 13½x14*

1201 A540 5s multicolored 5.50 5.25

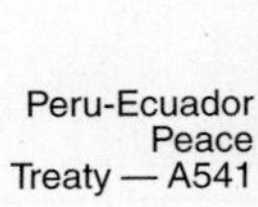

Peru-Ecuador Peace Treaty — A541

1998, Nov. 26 Litho. *Perf. 13½x14*

1202 A541 2.70s multicolored 4.25 4.00

Brasilia '98.

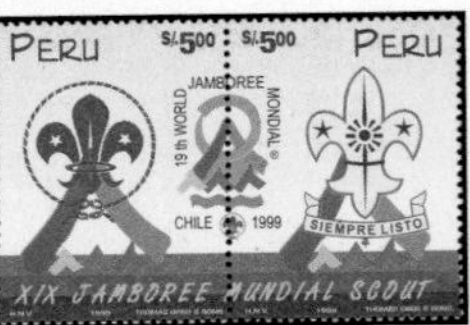

19th World Scout Jamboree, Chile — A542

Designs: a, Scouting emblem, stylized tents. b, Emblem, tents, "SIEMPRE LISTO."

1999, Jan. 5 Litho. *Perf. 14x13½*

1203 A542 5s Pair, #a.-b. 12.00 11.50

Peruvian Philatelic Assoc., 50th Anniv. — A543

1999, Jan. 10

1204 A543 2.70s No. 19 3.25 3.00

Paintings by Pancho Fierro (1809-79) — A544

Designs: 2.70s, Once Upon Time in a Shaded Grove. 3.30s, Sound of the Devil.

1999, Jan. 16

1205 A544 2.70s multicolored 4.00 3.50
1206 A544 3.30s multicolored 5.00 4.50

Regional Dance — A545

1999, Feb. 10 Litho. *Perf. 14x13½*

1207 A545 3.30s multicolored 3.75 3.50

CENDAF, 25th Anniv. — A546

1999, Mar. 1 *Perf. 13½x14*

1208 A546 1.80s multicolored 2.40 2.10

Ernest Malinowski (1818-99), Central Railroad — A547

1999, Mar. 3

1209 A547 5s multicolored 5.50 5.25

Peruvian Foundation for Children's Heart Disease — A548

1999, Mar. 6

1210 A548 2.70s multicolored 3.25 3.00

Mochica Pottery Type of 1997

Designs: 1s, like #1151. 1.50s, like #1148. 1.80s, like #1146. 2s, like #1150.

1999, Feb. 16 Litho. *Perf. 14½*

1211 A502 1s lake 1.10 .95
1212 A502 1.50s dark blue blk 2.25 2.00
1213 A502 1.80s brown 2.50 2.25
1214 A502 2s orange 2.75 2.50
Nos. 1211-1214 (4) 8.60 7.70

Fauna of the Peruvian Rain Forest — A549

1999, Apr. 23 *Perf. 14x13½*

1215 A549 5s multicolored 6.00 5.75

Souvenir Sheet

Fauna of Manu Natl. Park A550

1999, Apr. 23 *Perf. 13½x14*

1216 A550 10s multicolored 13.75 13.25

Milpo Mining Co., 50th Anniv. — A551

1999, Apr. 6 *Perf. 13½x14*

1217 A551 1.50s multicolored 2.10 1.90

See note after No. 1145.

Japanese Immigration to Peru, Cent. — A552

1999, Apr. 3 *Perf. 14x13½*

1218 A552 6.80s multicolored 7.50 7.25

Nos. 1140, 1143 Surcharged in Black, Brown, Dark Blue, Red or Green

1999 Litho. *Perf. 12½*

1219 A499 2.40s on 30c (Br) multi 2.75 2.50

Blocks of 4

1220 A496 1s on each value, #a.-d. 4.75 4.25
1221 A496 1.50s on each value, #a.-d. 6.50 6.00
1222 A496 2.70s on each value, #a.-d. 13.00 12.00
1223 A496 3.30s on each value, #a.-d. 15.00 14.00

Size and location of surcharge varies.

Antarctic Treaty, 40th Anniv. — A553

1999, May 24 ***Perf. 13½x14***

1224 A553 6.80s multicolored 9.00 8.75

Inca Rulers Type of 1998

No. 1225, Capac Yupanqui. No. 1226, Yahuar Huaca. No. 1227, Inca Roca. No. 1228, Maita Capac.

1999, June 24 Litho. ***Perf. 14x13½***

1225 A528 3.30s multi 3.75 3.50
1226 A528 3.30s multi 3.75 3.50
1227 A528 3.30s multi 3.75 3.50
1228 A528 3.30s multi 3.75 3.50
Nos. 1225-1228 (4) 15.00 14.00

Souvenir Sheet

Nazca Lines A554

1999, June 8

1229 A554 10s multicolored 11.00 10.50

Margin shows Maria Reiche (1903-98), expert in Nazca Lines.

Minerals — A555

Designs: 2.70s, Galena. 3.30s, Scheelite. 5s, Virgotrigonia peterseni.

1999, July 3 ***Perf. 13½x14***

1230 A555 2.70s multicolored 2.90 2.75
1231 A555 3.30s multicolored 3.75 3.50
1232 A555 5s multicolored 5.75 5.50
Nos. 1230-1232 (3) 12.40 11.75

See Nos. 1339-1341.

Virgin of Carmen — A556

1999, July 16 ***Perf. 14x13½***

1233 A556 3.30s multicolored 5.00 4.75

Santa Catalina Monastery, Arequipa — A557

1999, Aug. 15 Litho. ***Perf. 14x13½***

1234 A557 2.70s multicolored 3.25 3.00

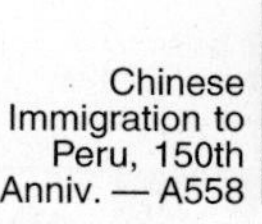

Chinese Immigration to Peru, 150th Anniv. — A558

1999 Litho. ***Perf. 13½x14***

1235 A558 1.50s red & black 3.25 3.00

Peruvian Medical Society, 25th Anniv. — A559

1999 Litho. ***Perf. 14x13½***

1236 A559 1.50s multicolored 2.10 1.90

UPU, 125th Anniv. — A560

1999, Oct. 9 Litho. ***Perf. 13½x14***

1237 A560 3.30s multicolored 3.75 3.50

America Issue

A New Millennium Without Arms — A561

2.70s, Earth, sunflower, vert.

1999, Oct. 12 ***Perf. 14x13½, 13½x14***

1238 A561 2.70s multi 2.75 2.50
1239 A561 3.30s shown 4.00 3.75

Señor de los Milagros Religious Procession — A562

1999, Oct. 18 ***Perf. 14x13½***

1240 A562 1s Incense burner 1.50 1.25
1241 A562 1.50s Procession 2.00 1.75

Inter-American Development Bank, 40th Anniv. — A563

1999, Oct. 22 ***Perf. 13½x14***

1242 A563 1.50s multicolored 2.00 1.75

Butterflies — A564

Designs: a, Pterourus zagreus chrysomelus. b, Asterope buckleyi. c, Parides chabrias. d, Mimoides pausanias. e, Nessaea obrina. f, Pterourus zagreus zagreus.

Block of 6 + Label

1999, Oct. 23 ***Perf. 14x13½***

1243 A564 3.30s #a.-f. 25.00 23.50

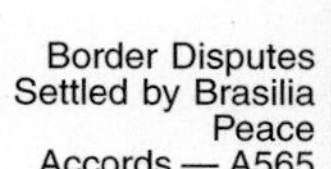

Border Disputes Settled by Brasilia Peace Accords — A565

Maps of regions from: No. 1244, Cusumasa Bumbuiza to Yaupi Santiago. No. 1245, Lagatococha to Güeppi, vert. No. 1246, Cunhuime Sur to 20 de Noviembre, vert.

1999, Oct. 26 ***Perf. 13½x14, 14x13½***

1244 A565 1s multicolored 1.50 1.25
1245 A565 1s multicolored 1.50 1.25
1246 A565 1s multicolored 1.50 1.25
Nos. 1244-1246 (3) 4.50 3.75

See Nos. 1282-1286.

Peruvian Postal Services, 5th Anniv. — A566

1999, Nov. 22 ***Perf. 14x13½***

1247 A566 2.70s multicolored 3.25 3.00

Christmas — A567

1999, Dec. 1 Litho. ***Perf. 14x13½***

1248 A567 2.70s multicolored 4.25 4.00

Ricardo Bentín Mujica (1899-1979), Businessman A568

1999, Dec. 29 Litho. ***Perf. 13½x14***

1249 A568 2.70s multicolored 3.25 3.00

Souvenir Sheet

Millennium — A569

2000, Jan. 1

1250 A569 10s multicolored 12.00 11.50

Ricardo Cillóniz Oberti, Businessman — A570

2000, Jan. 17 ***Perf. 14x13½***

1251 A570 1.50s multicolored 2.00 1.75

Printed se-tenant with label.

Alpaca Wool Industry A571

a, Alpacas at right. b, Alpacas at left.

2000, Jan. 27 Litho. ***Perf. 14x13½***

1252 A571 1.50s Pair, #a.-b. 4.25 3.75

Nuclear Energy Institute — A572

2000, Feb. 4

1253 A572 4s multicolored 4.50 4.25

Retamas S.A. Gold Mine A573

Miner, mine and buildings: a, Text in white. b, Text in blue violet.

2000, Feb. 7

1254 A573 1s Pair, #a.-b. 3.00 2.50

Comptroller General, 70th Anniv. — A574

2000, Feb. 28 ***Perf. 13½x14***

1255 A574 3.30s multicolored 3.75 3.50

Emilio Guimoye, Field of Flowers — A575

2000, Mar. 19 Litho. ***Perf. 13½x14***

Granite Paper

1256 A575 1.50s multicolored 2.25 2.00

1999 Natl. Scholastic Games — A576

2000, May 3 ***Perf. 14x13½***

Granite Paper

1257 A576 1.80s multi + label 2.75 2.50

Machu Picchu — A577

2000, July 20 ***Perf. 13½x14***

Granite Paper

1258 A577 1.30s multicolored 2.50 2.25

Campaign Against Domestic Violence — A578

2000, Aug. 22 Litho. ***Perf. 13½x14***

Granite Paper

1259 A578 3.80s multicolored 5.00 4.75

Holy Year 2000 — A579

2000, Aug. 23 **Granite Paper**

1260 A579 3.20s multicolored 4.00 3.75

Children's Drawing Contest Winners — A580

Designs: No. 1261, 3.20s, Lake Yarinacocha, by Mari Trini Ramos Vargas. No. 1262, 3.20s, Ahuashiyacu Falls, by Susan Hidalgo Bacalla, vert. 3.80s, Arequipa Countryside, by Anibal Lajo Yañez.

Perf. 13½x14, 14x13½

2000, Aug. 25 **Granite Paper**

1261-1263 A580 Set of 3 13.50 12.75

"Millennium Assembly" of UN General Assembly — A581

2000, Aug. 28 ***Perf. 13½x14***

Granite Paper

1264 A581 3.20s multi 4.00 3.75

Gen. José de San Martín (1777-1850) A582

2000, Sept. 1 **Granite Paper**

1265 A582 3.80s multi 4.50 4.25

Ormeño Bus Co., 30th Anniv. A583

No. 1266: a, 1s, Bus and map of South America. b, 2.70s, Bus and map of North America.

2000, Sept. 3 ***Perf. 14x13½***

Granite Paper

1266 A583 Pair, #a-b 6.00 5.50

Intl. Cycling Union, Cent. — A584

2000, Sept. 11 ***Perf. 13½x14***

Granite Paper

1267 A584 3.20s multi 4.50 4.25

World Meteorological Organization, 50th Anniv. — A585

2000, Sept. 13 **Granite Paper**

1268 A585 1.50s multi 2.25 2.00

Lizards of Manu Natl. Park A586

No. 1269: a, Tropidurus plica. b, Ameiva ameiva. c, Mabouya bistriata. d, Neusticurus ecpleopus. e, Anolis fuscoauratus. f, Enyalioides palpebralis.

2000, Sept. 15 ***Perf. 14x13½***

Granite Paper

1269 A586 3.80s Block of 6, #a-f 29.50 28.00

Matucana Madisoniorum A587

2000, Sept. 18 ***Perf. 13½x14***

Granite Paper

1270 A587 3.80s multi 5.00 4.75

Carlos Noriega, First Peruvian Astronaut — A588

2000, Sept. 20 **Granite Paper**

1271 A588 3.80s multi 5.00 4.75

Toribio Rodríguez de Mendoza (1750-1825), Theologian — A589

2000, Sept. 21 ***Perf. 14x13½***

Granite Paper

1272 A589 3.20s multi 4.50 4.25

Ucayali Province, Cent. — A590

2000, Sept. 25 ***Perf. 13½x14***

Granite Paper

1273 A590 3.20s multi 4.50 4.25

Pisco Wine — A591

2000, Sept. 27 **Granite Paper**

1274 A591 3.80s multi 5.00 4.75

Latin American Integration Association, 20th Anniv. — A592

2000, Sept. 29 ***Perf. 14x13½***

Granite Paper

1275 A592 10.20s multi 13.50 13.00

Peruvian Journalists Federation, 50th Anniv. — A593

2000, Sept. 30 **Granite Paper**

1276 A593 1.50s multi 2.60 2.40

Sexi Petrified Forest — A594

2000, Oct. 3 ***Perf. 13½x14***

Granite Paper

1277 A594 1.50s multi 2.75 2.50

America Issue, Campaign Against AIDS — A595

2000, Oct. 12 **Granite Paper**

1278 A595 3.80s multi 5.50 5.25

Supreme Court — A596

2000, Oct. 16 **Granite Paper**

1279 A596 1.50s multi 2.25 2.00

Salvation Army in Peru, 90th Anniv. — A597

2000, Nov. 3 ***Perf. 14x13½***

Granite Paper

1280 A597 1.50s multi 2.60 2.40

Peruvian Cancer League's Fight Against Cancer, 50th Anniv. — A598

2000, Nov. 9 ***Perf. 13½x14***

Granite Paper

1281 A598 1.50s multi 2.50 2.25

Border Map Type of 1999

Flags and maps of border separating Peru and: 1.10s, Chile, vert. 1.50s, Brazil, vert. 2.10s, Colombia. 3.20s, Ecuador. 3.80s, Bolivia, vert.

Perf. 14x13½, 13½x14

2000, Nov. 27 **Granite Paper**

1282-1286 A565 Set of 5 17.00 15.50

Railroads in Peru, 150th Anniv. — A599

2000, Nov. 27 ***Perf. 13½x14***

Granite Paper

1287 A599 1.50s multi 2.25 2.00

Luis Alberto Sanchez (1900-94), Politician — A600

2000, Nov. 27 ***Perf. 14x13½***

Granite Paper

1288 A600 3.20s multi 4.50 4.25

National Congress — A601

2000, Dec. 7 ***Perf. 13½x14***

Granite Paper

1289 A601 3.80s multi 5.00 4.75

Caretas Magazine, 50th Anniv. — A602

2000, Dec. 15 **Granite Paper**

1290 A602 3.20s multi 4.50 4.25

Cacti — A603

Designs: 1.10s, Haageocereus acranthus, vert. 1.50s, Cleistocactus xylorhizus, vert. No. 1293, 2.10s, Mila caespitosa, vert. No. 1294, 2.10s, Haageocereus setosus, vert. 3.20s, Opuntia pachypus. 3.80s, Haageocereus tenuis.

Perf. 13½x13¾, 13¾x13½

2001, Aug. 24 **Litho.**

1291-1296 A603 Set of 6 26.50 25.00

San Marcos University, 450th Anniv. — A604

2001, Sept. 4 ***Perf. 13½x13¾***

1297 A604 1.50s multi 3.25 2.90

Alianza Lima Soccer Team, Cent. A605

No. 1298: a, Players. b, Players, ball.

2001, Sept. 6

1298 A605 3.20s Horiz. pair, #a-b 12.00 11.50

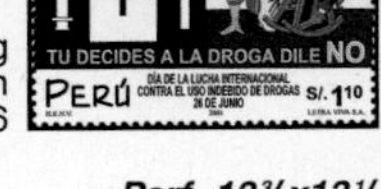

Anti-Drug Campaign A606

2001, Sept. 7 ***Perf. 13¾x13½***

1299 A606 1.10s multi 2.00 1.75

Gen. Roque Sáenz Peña (1851-1914), Pres. of Argentina A607

2001, Sept. 7
1300 A607 3.80s multi 7.25 7.00

Lurín River Valley — A608

2001, Sept. 10
1301 A608 1.10s multi 2.40 2.10

Amphipoda Hyalella — A609

2001, Sept. 10
1302 A609 1.80s multi 4.25 4.00

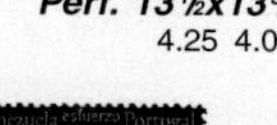

Postal and Philatelic Museum, 70th Anniv. — A610

2001, Oct. 9 ***Perf. 13½x13¾***
1303 A610 3.20s multi 4.25 4.00

9th Iberoamerican Summit of Heads of State — A611

Country names and: a, 1.10s, Rectangle. b, 2.70s, Angled line.

2002, Mar. 6 Litho. ***Perf. 14x13½***
1304 A611 Horiz. pair, #a-b 7.75 7.25
Dated 2001.

Peru — Costa Rica Diplomatic Relations, 150th Anniv. — A612

Flags, handshake and: a, 1.10s, Ruins. b, 2.70s, Grassland.

2002, Mar. 12
1305 A612 Horiz. pair, #a-b 7.75 7.25
Dated 2001.

World Conference Against Racism, Durban, South Africa — A613

2002, Mar. 13 ***Perf. 13½x14***
1306 A613 3.80s multi 7.25 7.00
Dated 2001.

Intl. Day of Indigenous People — A614

2002, Mar. 13 ***Perf. 14x13½***
1307 A614 5.80s multi 7.25 7.00
Dated 2001.

Intl. Organization for Migration, 50th Anniv. — A615

2002, Apr. 2
1308 A615 3.80s multi 7.25 7.00
Dated 2001.

Pan-American Health Organization, Cent. — A616

2002, Apr. 8 ***Perf. 13½x14***
1309 A616 3.20s multi 6.25 6.00
Dated 2001.

La Molina Agricultural University, Cent. — A617

Arms and: a, 1.10s, Sepia photograph of building. b, 2.70s, Color photograph of building.

2002, Apr. 16 ***Perf. 14x13½***
1310 A617 Horiz. pair, #a-b 8.50 8.00
Dated 2001.

Pisco Distilling — A618

Designs: 3.20s, Alembics. 3.80s, Jugs.
10s, La Fiesta de la Chicha y el Pisco, by José Sabogal.

2002, Apr. 18 ***Perf. 13½x14***
1311-1312 A618 Set of 2 15.50 15.00

Souvenir Sheet

1313 A618 10s multi 15.00 15.00
Dated 2001.

Orchids — A619

Designs: 1.50s, Stanhopea sp. 3.20s, Chloraea pavoni. 3.80s, Psychopsis sp.

2002, Apr. 30 ***Perf. 14x13½***
1314-1316 A619 Set of 3 16.50 16.00
Dated 2001.

Flowers of Tuber Plants — A620

Designs: 1.10s, Solanum stenotomum. 1.50s, Ipomoea batatas. 2.10s, Ipomoea purpurea.

2002, May 7 ***Perf. 13½x14***
1317-1319 A620 Set of 3 9.75 9.00

America Issue — UNESCO World Heritage Sites — A621

Balconies of Lima buildings: 2.70s, Palacio de Osambela. 5.80s, Palacio de Torre Tagle.

2002, May 14 Litho. ***Perf. 14x13½***
1320-1321 A621 Set of 2 11.00 10.50
Dated 2001.

Year of Dialogue Among Civilizations — A622

Designs: 1.50s, Flower. 1.80s, shown.

2002, May 16
1322-1323 A622 Set of 2 6.00 5.50
Dated 2001.

Paracas National Reserve — A623

Designs: 1.10s, Sula dactilatra, vert. 1.50s, Sula variegata. 3.20s, Haematopus palliatus. 3.80s, Grapsus grapsus.

2002, May 21 ***Perf. 14x13½, 13½x14***
1324-1327 A623 Set of 4 13.00 12.00
Dated 2001.

Souvenir Sheet

Endangered Animals — A624

2002, May 22 ***Perf. 13½x14***
1328 A624 8s multi 13.00 12.50
Dated 2001.

Scouting in Peru, 90th Anniv. A625

No. 1329: a, Lord Robert Baden-Powell. b, Juan Luis Rospigliosi.
10.20s, First Peruvian Scouts.

2002, June 4 ***Perf. 14x13½***
1329 A625 3.20s Horiz. pair, #a-b 8.50 8.00

Souvenir Sheet

1330 A625 10.20s multi 18.50 18.00
Dated 2001.

Folk Dances — A626

Designs: 2.10s, Zamacueca. 2.70s, Alcatraz.

2002, June 4
1331-1332 A626 Set of 2 9.25 8.75
Dated 2001.

International Express Service — A627

2002, June 10 ***Perf. 13½x14***
1333 A627 20s multi 23.50 23.00
Dated 2001.

Inca Rulers — A628

Designs: 1.50s, Viracocha. 2.70s, Pachacutec. 3.20s, Inca Yupanqui. 3.80s, Tupac Inca Yupanqui.

2002, June 24 Litho. ***Perf. 14x13½***
1334-1337 A628 Set of 4 15.50 14.50
Dated 2001.

Primates A629

No. 1338: a, Aotus nancymaea. b, Pithecia irrorata. c, Pithecia aequatorialis. d, Cebus albifrons. e, Saimiri boliviensis. f, Aotus vociferans.

2002, June 25
1338 A629 3.80s Block of 6, #a-f 32.50 32.00
Dated 2001.

Minerals Type of 1999

Designs: 1.80s, Chalcopyrite. No. 1340, 3.20s, Sphalerite. No. 1341, 3.20s, Pyrargyrite.

2002, July 3 ***Perf. 13½x14***
1339-1341 A555 Set of 3 14.75 14.00
Dated 2001.

Pre-Columbian Artifacts — A630

Designs: 1.50s, Crab-like man, Sipán. 3.20s, Warrior, Sicán. 3.80s, Gold breastplate, Kuntur Wasi, horiz.

10.20s, Pinchudo, Gran Pajatén, horiz.

2002, July 3 ***Perf. 14x13½, 13½x14***
1342-1344 A630 Set of 3 14.75 14.00

Souvenir Sheet

1345 A630 10.20s multi 17.00 16.50

Dated 2001.

Admiral Miguel Grau — A631

2002, July 23 ***Perf. 13½x14***
1346 A631 3.80s multi 7.25 7.00

Dated 2001.

Peruvian — Spanish Business Meeting — A632

2002, Aug. 7
1347 A632 3.80s multi 5.00 4.75

Dated 2001.

National Fisheries Society, 50th Anniv. — A633

Perf. 13½x13¾

2002, Nov. 12 **Litho.**
1348 A633 3.20s multi 4.25 4.00
a. Tete beche pair 8.50 8.00

Alexander von Humboldt's Visit to Peru, Bicent. — A634

2002, Nov. 20 ***Perf. 13¾x13½***
1349 A634 3.20s multi + label 4.25 4.00
a. Tete beche strip, 2 #1349 +2 central labels 8.50 8.00

Peru - Bolivia Integration for Development A635

2002, Nov. 29 ***Perf. 13½x14***
1350 A635 3.20s multi 4.25 4.00

Natl. Commission on Andean and Amazonian Peoples — A636

2002, Dec. 12
1351 A636 1.50s multi 2.25 2.00

Hydrography and Navigation Dept., Cent. — A637

2003, June 13 **Litho.** ***Perf. 14x13½***
1352 A637 1.10s multi 2.00 1.75

Manuela Ramos Movement, 25th Anniv. — A638

2003, July 1
1353 A638 3.80s multi 4.50 4.25

Radioprogramas del Peru Network, 40th Anniv. — A639

2003, Oct. 1 **Litho.** ***Perf. 13½x14***
1354 A639 4s multi 4.75 4.50

Pres. Fernando Belaunde Terry (1912-2002) — A640

2003, Oct. 7 ***Perf. 14x13½***
1355 A640 1.60s multi 2.25 2.00

Canonization of St. Josemaría Escrivá de Balaguer — A641

2003, Oct. 11 ***Perf. 13½x14***
1356 A641 1.20s multi 2.10 1.90

Sister Teresa de la Cruz Candamo (1875-1953), Founder of Canonesas de la Cruz — A642

2003, Nov. 3
1357 A642 4s multi 5.00 4.75

Treaty of Friendship, Commerce and Navigation Between Peru and Italy, 150th Anniv. — A643

No. 1358: a, Maps of Peru and Western Hemisphere. b, Map of Italy and Eastern Hemisphere.

2003, Nov. 13 ***Perf. 14x13½***
1358 A643 2s Horiz. pair, #a-b 5.25 4.75

UNESCO Associated Schools Project Network, 50th Anniv. — A645

2003, Nov. ***Perf. 13½x14***
1360 A645 1.20s multi 2.00 1.75

Water Snake Bilingual Education Project — A644

No. 1359: a, Head of snake, project emblem. b, Tail of snake, children's drawing.

2003, Nov. 28
1359 A644 2s Horiz. pair, #a-b 7.50 7.00

America Issue - Fauna A646

No. 1361: a, Four Rupicola peruviana and butterfly. b, One Rupicola peruviana.

2003, Dec. 1 ***Perf. 14x13½***
1361 A646 2s Horiz. pair, #a-b 5.50 5.00

Peru — Panama Diplomatic Relations, Cent. — A647

2003, Dec. 12
1362 A647 4r multi 7.25 7.00

Powered Flight, Cent. A648

2003, Dec. 17 ***Perf. 13½x14***
1363 A648 4.80s multi + label 6.00 5.50

Cajón — A649

2003, Dec. 18
1364 A649 4.80s multi 5.50 5.25

Chess — A650

2004, Jan. 5
1365 A650 1.20s multi 2.00 1.75

Dated 2003.

National Rehabilitation Institute — A651

2004, Jan. 5
1366 A651 1.20s multi 2.60 2.40

Dated 2003.

School and Labor Integration "Year of the Rights of Persons with Disabilities."

Swimming — A652

2004, Jan. 5 ***Perf. 14x13½***
1367 A652 1.20s multi 1.50 1.25

Dated 2003.

National Civil Defense System, 30th Anniv. (in 2002) — A653

2004, Jan. 14
1368 A653 4.80s multi 5.25 5.00

Dated 2002.

Christmas 2003 — A654

2004, Jan. 14 ***Perf. 13½x14***
1369 A654 4.80s multi 4.25 4.00

Dated 2002.

Cebiche — A655

2004, Jan. 14
1370 A655 4.80s multi 7.75 7.50

Dated 2003.

Viceroys A656

No. 1371: a, 1.20s, Antonio de Mendoza (1495-1552). b, 1.20s, Andres Hurtado de Mendoza (1500-61). c, 1.20s, Diego Lopez de Zúñiga y Velasco (d. 1564). d, 4.80s, Blasco Nuñez de Vela (d. 1546).

2004, Jan. 14 ***Perf. 14x13½***
1371 A656 Block of 4, #a-d 10.00 9.00

Dated 2003.

Minerals — A657

Designs: 1.20s, Orpiment. 4.80s, Rhodochrosite.

2004, Jan. 21 ***Perf. 13½x14***
1372-1373 A657 Set of 2 5.75 5.25

Dated 2002.

Peruvian Saints — A658

Designs: No. 1374, 4.80s, St. Rose of Lima (1586-1617). No. 1375, 4.80s, St. Martin de Porres (1579-1639), vert.

2004, Jan. 21 ***Perf. 13½x14, 14x13½***
1374-1375 A658 Set of 2 8.00 7.50

Dated 2002.

Orchids — A659

Designs: 1.20s, Chaubardia heteroclita, vert. 2.20s, Cochleanther amazonica, vert. 4.80s, Sobralia sp.

2004, Jan. 21 ***Perf. 14x13½, 13½x14***
1376-1378 A659 Set of 3 10.25 9.50

Dated 2002.

Jorge Basadre (1903-80), Historian — A660

2004, Jan. 30 **Engr.** ***Perf. 14x13½***
1379 A660 4.80s blue 4.50 4.25

Dated 2003.

Trains — A661

Designs: 1.20s, Locomotive and train station. 4.80s, Train on Galeras Bridge.

2004, Jan. 30 **Litho.** ***Perf. 13½x14***
1380-1381 A661 Set of 2 8.50 8.00

Dated 2002.

Endangered Species — A662

Designs: No. 1382, 1.80s, Londra felina. No. 1383, 1.80s, Ara couloni, vert.

2004, Jan. 30 ***Perf. 13½x14, 14x13½***
1382-1383 A662 Set of 2 4.75 4.25

Dated 2002.

Fire Fighting — A663

Designs: No. 1384, 2.20s, Firefighters with hose. No. 1385, 2.20s, Fire truck.

2004, Jan. 30 ***Perf. 13½x14***
1384-1385 A663 Set of 2 9.00 8.50

Dated 2002.

Incan Emperors — A664

Designs: No. 1386, 1.20s, Huáscar (d. 1533). No. 1387, 1.20s, Atahualpa (d. 1533). 4.80s, Huayna Cápac (d. 1525).

2004, Jan. 30 ***Perf. 14x13½***
1386-1388 A664 Set of 3 7.50 6.75

Dated 2002.

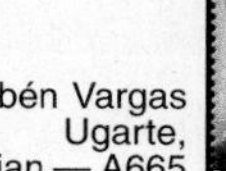

Rubén Vargas Ugarte, Historian — A665

2004, Feb. 4 ***Perf. 13½x14***
1389 A665 4.80s multi 4.50 4.25

Dated 2002.

2002 World Cup Soccer Championships, Japan and Korea — A666

2004, Feb. 4
1390 A666 4.80s multi 4.50 4.25

Dated 2002.

National Stadium, 50th Anniv. (in 2002) — A667

2004, Feb. 4
1391 A667 4.80s multi 4.50 4.25

Dated 2002.

National Day of Biological Diversity, May 22, 2002 — A668

2004, Feb. 4
1392 A668 4.80s multi 4.50 4.25

Dated 2002.

World Population Day — A669

2004, Feb. 4
1393 A669 4.80s multi 4.50 4.25

Dated 2002.

José Jiménez Borja (1901-82), Writer — A670

2004, Feb. 4 ***Perf. 14x13½***
1394 A670 4.80s multi 4.50 4.25

Dated 2002.

Cacti — A671

Designs: No. 1395, 1.20s, Eriosyce islayensis. No. 1395, 1.20s, Matucana haynei. 4.80s, Pigmaeocereus bylesianus.

2004, Feb. 4
1395-1397 A671 Set of 3 12.75 12.00

Dated 2002.

Antarctic Fauna — A672

Designs: No. 1398, 1.80s, Leucocarbo atriceps. No. 1399, 1.80s, Pygosceles papua, vert. No. 1400, 1.80s, Asteroidea sp., vert.

2004, Feb. 4 ***Perf. 13½x14, 14x13½***
1398-1400 A672 Set of 3 7.50 6.75

Dated 2002.

Pisco Sour — A673

2004, Feb. 10 ***Perf. 13½x14***
1401 A673 4.80s multi 4.75 4.50

Daniel Alcides Carrión (1857-1885), Medical Martyr — A674

2004, Feb. 19 **Litho.** ***Perf. 14x13½***
1402 A674 4.80s multi 4.75 4.50

Dated 2002.

Souvenir Sheet

Foundation of Jauja, by Wenceslao Hinostroza — A675

2004, Feb. 20 ***Perf. 13½x14***
1403 A675 7s multi 6.50 6.25

Dated 2002.

Animals — A676

2004, Feb. 23 ***Perf. 14x14½***
1404 A676 20c Alpaca .90 .70
1405 A676 30c Vicuna .90 .70
1406 A676 40c Guanaco 1.10 .90
1407 A676 50c Llama 1.40 1.10
Nos. 1404-1407 (4) 4.30 3.40

Dated 2002.

Vipers A677

No. 1408: a, Bothrops roedingeri. b, Micrurus lemniscatus. c, Bothrops atrox. d, Bothrops microphtalmus. e, Micrurus surinamensis. f, Bothrops barnetti.

2004, Feb. 23 ***Perf. 14x13½***
1408 A677 1.80s Block of 6, #a-f, + label 13.00 11.50

Dated 2003.

Souvenir Sheet

Intl. Year of Mountains (in 2002) — A678

2004, Feb. 23 ***Perf. 13½x14***
1409 A678 7s multi 6.50 6.25

Dated 2002.

Royal Tombs of Sipán Museum — A679

2004, Feb. 24
1410 A679 4.80s multi 6.25 6.00

Dated 2003.

Lighthouses — A680

No. 1411: a, Punta Capones Lighthouse. b, Chincha Islands Lighthouse.

2004, Feb. 26 ***Perf. 14x13½***
1411 A680 2s Horiz. pair, #a-b 11.50 11.00

Dated 2003.

Volunteer Firefighters of Peru, 130th Anniv. — A681

2004, Mar. 2
1412 A681 4.80s multi 9.50 9.25

Miniature Sheet

Fish A682

No. 1413: a, Trachurus murphyi. b, Mugil cephalus. c, Engraulis ringens. d, Odontesthes regia regia. e, Merluccius gayi peruanus.

2004, Mar. 3 ***Perf. 13½x14***
1413 A682 1.60s Sheet of 5, #a-e 13.75 12.50

Dated 2002.

Souvenir Sheet

Arequipa Department — A683

No. 1414: a, Cathedral tower. b, Misti Volcano, horiz.

Perf. 14x13½, 13½x14 (#1414b)

2004, Mar. 18

1414 A683 4s Sheet of 2, #a-b 7.50 7.00

Dated 2002.

Machu Picchu A684

No. 1415: a, 1.20s, Sundial. b, 1.20s, Temple of the Three Windows. c, 1.20s, Waterfall, Huayna Picchu. d, 4.80s, Aerial view of Machu Picchu.

2004, Mar. 20 *Perf. 14x13½*

1415 A684 Block of 4, #a-d 10.50 9.50

Dated 2003.

Medicinal Plants — A685

Designs: No. 1416, 4.80s, Uncaria tomentosa. No. 1417, 4.80s, Myrciaria dubia. No. 1418, 4.80s, Lepidium meyenii.

2004, Mar. 26 *Perf. 13½x14*

1416-1418 A685 Set of 3 11.75 11.00

Annual Assembly of Governors of the Inter-American Development Bank — A686

2004, Mar. 29

1419 A686 4.80s multi 4.75 4.50

Dogs A687

No. 1420: a, Italian Volpino. b, Peruvian hairless dog. c, Beauceron. d, Italian Spinone.

2004, Apr. 2 *Perf. 14x13½*

1420 A687 4.80s Block of 4, #a-d 17.00 16.00

Dated 2003.

Dances — A688

Designs: No. 1421, 1.20s, Huaylash. No. 1422, 1.20s, Huayno.

2004

1421-1422 A688 Set of 2 3.25 2.75

Issued: No. 1421, 4/16; No. 1422, 5/28. Dated 2003.

Preparation for "El Niño" — A689

2004, Apr. 21 *Perf. 13½x14*

1423 A689 4.80s multi 4.75 4.50

Dated 2002.

Tourism — A690

Designs: No. 1424, 4.80s, Lake Paca, Jauja. No. 1425, 4.80s, Ballestas Islands, Ica, vert. No. 1426, 4.80s, Inca Baths, Cajamarca, vert. No. 1427, 4.80s, Huanchaco, Trujillo, vert.

2004 *Perf. 13½x14, 14x13½*

1424-1427 A690 Set of 4 28.00 27.00

Issued: No. 1424, 4/22; No. 1425, 4/29; No. 1426, 5/6; No. 1427, 6/10. Dated 2002 (#1425-1427) or 2003 (#1424).

Santiago Apostol Temple, Puno — A691

2004, July 2 *Perf. 13½x14*

1428 A691 1.80s multi 2.25 2.00

Dated 2003.

America Issue — Youth, Education and Literacy — A692

Designs: 1.20s, Children, stylized flower. 4.80s, Computer operator, horiz.

2004, July 5 *Perf. 14x13½, 13½x14*

1429-1430 A692 Set of 2 6.00 5.50

Dated 2002 (#1429) or 2003 (#1430).

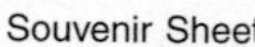

Souvenir Sheet

2004 Copa America Soccer Tournament, Peru — A693

2004, July 9 *Perf. 14x14½*

1431 A693 5s multi 7.75 7.50

Horses A694

No. 1432: a, 1.20s, White horse. b, 1.20s, Black horse, rider with raised hand. c, 1.20s, Black horse, rider with white poncho. d, 4.80s, Horse's head.

2004, Aug. 6 *Perf. 14x13½*

1432 A694 Block of 4, #a-d, + label 8.50 7.50

Dated 2002.

Miniature Sheet

Worldwide Fund for Nature (WWF) — A695

No. 1433 — Pteronura brasiliensis: a, 30c. Looking. b, 50c, With mouth open. c, 1.50s, Eating. d, 1.50s, Sleeping.

2004, Oct. 15 **Litho.**

1433 A695 Sheet of 4, #a-d 8.00 7.00

America Issue — Environmental Protection A696

2004, Oct. 25 *Perf. 13½x14*

1434 A696 4.50s multi 5.00 4.75

Railroads — A697

Designs: 5s, Modern train on bridge, 1870 train on bridge. 10s, Train on Infiernillo Bridge, horiz.

2004, Oct. 29 *Perf. 14x13½*

1435 A697 5s multi 5.00 4.75

Souvenir Sheet

Perf. 13½x14

1436 A697 10s multi 9.50 9.25

Peruvian Song Day, 60th Anniv. — A698

2004, Oct. 31 *Perf. 13½x14*

1437 A698 5s multi 5.00 4.75

FIFA (Fédération Internationale de Football Association), Cent. — A699

2004, Nov. 2

1438 A699 5s multi 5.00 4.75

Election of Pope John Paul II, 25th Anniv. (in 2003) — A700

2004, Nov. 2

1439 A700 5s multi 5.00 4.75

Canonization of Mother Teresa — A701

2004, Nov. 2 *Perf. 14x13½*

1440 A701 5s multi 5.00 4.75

Miniature Sheet

Musicians — A702

No. 1441: a, Juan Diego Flórez. b, Susana Baca. c, Gianmarco. d, Eva Ayllón, horiz. e, Libido, horiz.

Perf. 14x13½, 14x14x13½x14 (#1441d, 1441e)

2004, Nov. 12

1441 A702 2s Sheet of 5, #a-e 11.00 9.75

Flora Tristan Women's Center, 25th Anniv. — A703

2004, Nov. 9 **Litho.** *Perf. 14*

1442 A703 5s multi 5.00 4.75

Exporter's Day — A704

2004, Nov. 9

1443 A704 5s multi 5.00 4.75

Latin American Parliament, 40th Anniv. — A705

No. 1444: a, Parliament emblem. b, Andrés Townsend Escurra, first President of Latin American Parliament, and flags.

2004, Nov. 16 *Perf. 13½x14*

1444 A705 2.50s Horiz. pair, #a-b 5.50 5.00

Lima Bar Association, 200th Anniv. — A706

2004, Nov. 17
1445 A706 5s multi 5.00 4.75

Serpost, 10th Anniv. — A707

2004, Nov. 22
1446 A707 5s multi 5.00 4.75

Jungle River Fauna — A708

Designs: 2s, Serrasalmus. 4.50s, Pontoporia blainvillei. 5s, Arapaima gigas, vert.

Perf. 13½x14, 14x13½

2004, Nov. 30
1447-1449 A708 Set of 3 11.25 10.50

Christmas — A709

2004, Dec. 2 ***Perf. 14x13½***
1450 A709 5s multi 5.75 5.00

Antarctica — A710

Designs: 1.50s, Machu Picchu Scientific Base, King George Island. 2s, Megaptera novaeangliae, horiz. 4.50s, Orcinus orca, horiz.

2004, Dec. 3 ***Perf. 14x13½, 13½x14***
1451-1453 A710 Set of 3 9.75 9.00

Prehistoric Animals — A711

No. 1454: a, 1.80s, Drawings of Smilodon neogaeus and Toxodon platensis Owen. 3.20s, Fossils, depiction of body of Toxodon platensis.

2004, Dec. 6 ***Perf. 14x13½***
1454 A711 Horiz. pair, #a-b 5.00 4.75

Mochica Ceramics — A712

Various ceramic pieces with background colors of: No. 1455, 4.50s, Dark blue. No. 1456, 4.50s, Red violet. 5s, Blue, horiz.

2004, Dec. 6 ***Perf. 14x14½, 14½x14***
1455-1457 A712 Set of 3 14.25 14.00

Third Meeting of South American Presidents — A713

2004, Dec. 8 ***Perf. 14x13½***
1458 A713 5s multi 5.00 4.75

Lima Museum of Art, 50th Anniv. — A714

2004, Dec. 9 **Litho.**
1459 A714 5s multi 5.00 4.75

Battles, 180th Anniv. A715

No. 1460: a, 1.80s, Map and scene of Battle of Ayacucho. b, 3.20s, Map and scene of Battle of Junín.

2004, Dec. 9
1460 A715 Horiz. pair, #a-b 5.50 5.00

Lighthouses — A716

No. 1461: a, Pijuayal Lighthouse, Amazon River. b, Suana Lighhouse, Lake Titicaca.

2004, Dec. 10
1461 A716 4.50s Horiz. pair, #a-b 9.00 8.50

Souvenir Sheet

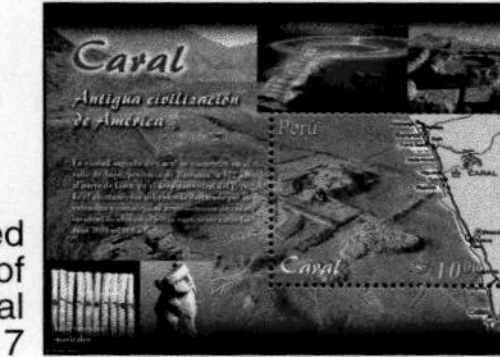

Sacred City of Caral A717

2004, Dec. 15 ***Perf. 13½x14***
1462 A717 10s multi 10.50 10.00

Parque de las Leyendes, 40th Anniv. — A718

No. 1463: a, Cantua buxifolia. b, Puma concolor.

2005, Jan. 14 ***Perf. 14x13½***
1463 A718 5s Horiz. pair, #a-b 9.50 9.00

Dated 2004.

Championship Trophies Won By Cienciano Soccer Team — A719

2005, Jan. 22
1464 A719 5s multi 4.75 4.00

Dated 2004.

Stomatology Academy of Peru, 75th Anniv. — A720

2005, Jan. 24
1465 A720 5s multi 4.75 4.50

Dated 2004.

National Health Crusade A721

2005, Feb. 2 ***Perf. 14***
1466 A721 2s multi + label 2.25 2.00

Dated 2004.

Houses of Worship — A722

Designs: 4.50s, San Cristóbal Church, Huamanga. 5s, Huancayo Cathedral.

2005, Feb. 7 **Litho.** ***Perf. 13½x14***
1467-1468 A722 Set of 2 11.00 10.50

Abolition of Slavery, 150th Anniv. — A723

2005, Feb. 25 **Engr.**
1469 A723 5s claret 4.75 4.50

Armed Forces A724

No. 1470: a, 1.80s, Army tank. b, 1.80s, Navy submarine. c, 1.80s, Air Force Mirage jets. d, 3.20s, Air Force Sukhoi jet. e, 3.20s, Army soldiers. f, 3.20s, Navy frigate.

2005, Feb. 28 **Litho.**
1470 A724 Block of 6, #a-f, + label 15.50 14.00

Fruit — A725

Designs: No. 1471, 4.50s, Eugenia stipitata. No. 1472, 4.50s, Mauritia flexuosa. 5s, Solanum sessiflorum dunal, vert.

2005, Mar. 4 ***Perf. 13½x14, 14x13½***
1471-1473 A725 Set of 3 13.25 12.50

Opera Singer Luis Alva Talledo, Founder of Prolirica — A726

2005, Mar. 10 ***Perf. 13½x14***
1474 A726 1.50s multi 1.75 1.50

Allpahuayo Reserve Wildlife — A727

No. 1475: a, Hormiguero norteño de cola castaña. b, Tiranuelo de Mishana. c, Rana arboricola. d, Sacha runa.

2005, Mar. 21 ***Perf. 14x13½***
1475 A727 4.50s Block of 4, #a-d, + label 17.00 16.00

Paintings A728

No. 1476 — Unidentified paintings by: a, Pancho Fierro. b, Ignacio Moreno. c, Daniel Hernández. d, Camilo Blas. e, Ricardo Grau. f, Fernando de Szyszlo.

2005, Apr. 4
1476 A728 2s Block of 6, #a-f, + label 14.00 12.50

Science of Antonio Raimondo — A729

No. 1477: a, 1.80s, Sculptures, Chavín de Huántar. b, 3.20s, Bird and bat. c, 4.50s, Stanophea. d, 5s, Fossil of N. C. Roemoceras Subplanum Hyatt.

2005, Apr. 18
1477 A729 Block of 4, #a-d, + label 14.00 13.00

Souvenir Sheet

Penelope Albipennis — A730

2005, May 2

1478 A730 10s multi 9.00 8.75

Architecture — A731

Designs: a, 4.50s, Government Palace. b, 4.50s, Italian Art Museum. c, 5s, Larco Mar. d, 5s, Mega Plaza.

2005, May 18 ***Perf. 13½x14***

1479 A731 Block of 4, #a-d, + label 19.00 18.00

Postal Money Orders — A732

2005, May 30

1480 A732 5s multi 5.75 5.50

Pope John Paul II (1920-2005) A733

2005, Nov. 24 Litho. ***Perf. 13½***

1481 A733 1.80s multi 2.60 2.40

Souvenir Sheet

Europa Stamps, 50th Anniv. (in 2006) A734

No. 1482: a, Mochica headdress and Spain #1526. b, Chimú ceremonial jewelry and Spain #941. c, Mochica earrings and Spain #1567. d, Mochica headdress and Spain #1607.

2005, Nov. 24 Litho. ***Perf. 14***

1482 A734 2s Sheet of 4, #a-d 10.00 9.00

Miniature Sheet

Naval Victories A735

No. 1483: a, Battle of Punta Malpelo. b, Battle of Callao. c, Sinking of the Covadonga. d, Battle of Abtao. e, Battle of Iquique. f, Battle of Pedrera.

2005, Dec. 21 Litho. ***Perf. 13½x14***

1483 A735 2s Sheet of 6, #a-f 11.50 10.00

Medical College of Peru, 35th Anniv. — A736

2005, Dec. 29

1484 A736 5.50s multi 5.50 5.25

Christmas 2005 — A737

2006, Jan. 9

1485 A737 5.50s multi 4.50 4.25

Dated 2005.

Eighth Cultural Patrimony Colloquium, Cuzco — A738

2006, Jan. 9 ***Perf. 14x13½***

1486 A738 5.50s multi 4.50 4.25

Dated 2005.

Sister Ana de los Angeles Monteagudo (1602-86) A739

2006, Jan. 10 ***Perf. 13½x14***

1487 A739 5.50s multi 5.25 5.00

Dated 2005.

Publication of Don Quixote, 400th Anniv. (in 2005) — A740

2006, Jan. 11

1488 A740 5s multi 4.75 4.50

Dated 2005.

Pope Benedict XVI A741

No. 1489: a, Profile. b, With arms raised.

2006, Jan. 11 ***Perf. 14x13½***

1489 A741 2.50s Horiz. pair, #a-b 5.75 5.25

Dated 2005.

Rotary International, Cent. (in 2005) — A742

2006, Jan. 13 ***Perf. 13½x14***

1490 A742 5.50s multi 5.50 5.25

Dated 2005.

America Issue, Fight Against Poverty — A743

2006, Jan. 16 ***Perf. 14x13½***

1491 A743 5.50s multi 5.25 5.00

Dated 2005.

Natl. Academy of History, Cent. (in 2005) — A744

2006, Jan. 20 ***Perf. 13½x14***

1492 A744 5.50s multi 5.50 5.25

Dated 2005.

St. Peter's Church, Lima A745

No. 1493: a, Exterior. b, Interior.

2006, Jan. 20 ***Perf. 14x13½***

1493 A745 2.50s Horiz. pair, #a-b 5.50 5.00

Dated 2005.

Volcanoes — A746

No. 1494: a, Pichupichu. b, Chachani. c, Misti.

2006, Jan. 20

1494 A746 Horiz. strip of 3 8.00 7.25

a.-c. 2.50s Any single 2.25 1.75

Dated 2005.

YMCA in Peru, 85th Anniv. (in 2005) — A747

2006, Jan. 23 **Litho.**

1495 A747 5.50s multi 5.50 5.25

Dated 2005.

Dr. Julio C. Tello (1880-1947), Anthropologist and Archaeologist A748

2006, Jan. 26 ***Perf. 13½x14***

1496 A748 5s multi 5.25 5.00

Dated 2005.

Cáritas, 50th Anniv. (in 2005) — A749

2006, Jan. 28

1497 A749 5.50s multi 5.25 5.00

Dated 2005.

Comptroller General, 75th Anniv. (in 2005) — A750

2006, Feb. 6 ***Perf. 14x13½***

1498 A750 5.50s multi 5.50 5.25

Dated 2005.

Creation of Cajamarca Department, 150th Anniv. (in 2005) — A751

2006, Feb. 11 ***Perf. 13½x14***

1499 A751 6s multi 5.50 5.25

Dated 2005.

Traditional Foods — A752

No. 1500: a, Chupe de camarones. b, Juane. c, Arroz con pato (duck and rice). d, Rocoto relleno.

2006, Feb. 16

1500 A752 2s Block of 4, #a-d, + label 9.25 8.25

Dated 2005.

Butterflies — A753

No. 1501: a, Heliconius sara. b, Morpho achilles. c, Dryas iulia. d, Caligo eurilochus.

2006, Feb. 17

1501 A753 2s Block of 4, #a-d, + label 10.00 9.00

Dated 2005.

12th Panamerican Scout Jamboree, Argentina — A754

No. 1502: a, Scout in foreground. b, Flag in foreground.

2006, Feb. 20 ***Perf. 14x13½***

1502 A754 2s Horiz. pair, #a-b 4.50 4.00

Dated 2005.

Pre-Columbian Cultures — A755

Artifacts of: No. 1503, 6s, Paracas culture, c. 500. No. 1504, 6s, Chavin culture, c. 1200.

2006, Feb. 22 ***Perf. 13½x14***
1503-1504 A755 Set of 2 11.50 11.00

Dated 2005.

See also Nos. 1602-1603, 1648-1649, 1700-1701, 1740-1741, 1774-1775.

Legend of the Ayar Brothers, Incan Creation Myth — A756

2006, Feb. 24
1505 A756 6s multi 5.25 5.00

Dated 2005.

National Symbols — A757

No. 1506: a, Flag. b, Coat of arms. c, National anthem.

2006, Feb. 27 ***Perf. 14x13½***
1506 A757 Horiz. strip of 3 6.50 5.75
a.-c. 2s Any single 1.60 1.40

Dated 2005.

Fruit — A758

Designs: No. 1507, 6s, Pouteria lucuma. No. 1508, 6s, Annona cherimola.

2006, Mar. 1 ***Perf. 13½x14***
1507-1508 A758 Set of 2 12.00 11.50

Dated 2005.

Peru to Brazil Interoceanic Highway — A759

2006, Mar. 3
1509 A759 6s multi 5.25 5.00

Dated 2005.

Writers — A760

Designs: No. 1510, 6s, Mario Vargas Llosa. No. 1511, 6s, Alfredo Bryce Echenique.

2006, Mar. 28 **Engr.** ***Perf. 14x13½***
1510-1511 A760 Set of 2 11.00 10.50

Dated 2005.

Health Ministry, 70th Anniv. (in 2005) — A761

2006, Apr. 7 **Litho.** ***Perf. 13½x14***
1512 A761 6s multi 5.25 5.25

Dated 2005.

Latin American Integration Association, 25th Anniv. (in 2005) — A762

2006, Apr. 7
1513 A762 6s multi 6.25 6.00

Dated 2005.

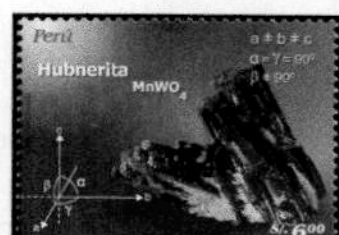

Hubnerite — A763

2006, Apr. 28
1514 A763 6s multi 6.50 6.25

Compare with type A657.

Purple Corn Chicha Beverage — A764

2006, Apr. 28
1515 A764 6s multi 5.50 5.25

Fauna of Lake Titicaca A765

No. 1516: a, Orestias spp. b, Plegadis ridgwayi. c, Phoenicoparrus andinus. d, Telmatobius culeus.

2006, May 2 ***Perf. 14x13½***
1516 A765 5.50s Block of 4, #a-d, + label 20.00 19.00

Parrots A766

No. 1517: a, Pionopsitta barrabandi. b, Tovit huetii. c, Pionites melanocephala. d, Ara severa. e, Amazona festiva. f, Ara ararauna.

2006, May 5
1517 A766 5.50s Block of 6, #a-f, + label 34.00 32.50

Viceroys of Peru A767

No. 1518: a, Francisco de Toledo (1515-82). b, Martín Enríquez de Almansa (c. 1525-83). c, Fernando Torres y Portugal. d, García Hurtado de Mendoza (1535-1609).

2006, May 8
1518 A767 5.50s Block of 4, #a-d, + label 20.00 19.00

See Nos. 1569, 1575, 1622, 1681, 1737, 1776, 1858. Compare with type A1063.

Souvenir Sheet

Lighthouses — A768

No. 1519: a, Isla Lobos de Tierra Lighthouse. b, Isla Blanca Lighthouse.

2006, May 10
1519 A768 6s Sheet of 2, #a-b 10.50 10.00

Birds — A769

Designs: No. 1520, 6s, Perlita de Iquitos. No. 1521, 6s, Tortolita moteada (turtledove). No. 1522, 6s, Ganse Andino (Andean geese), vert.

2006, May 15 ***Perf. 13½x14, 14x13½***
1520-1522 A769 Set of 3 18.25 17.50

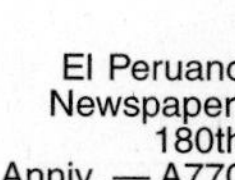

El Peruano Newspaper, 180th Anniv. — A770

2006, May 16 ***Perf. 13½x14***
1523 A770 6s multi 6.25 6.00

Surfing A771

No. 1524: a, Surfers on waves. b, Sofía Mulanovich, 2004 Surfing World Champion.

2006, May 16 ***Perf. 14x13½***
1524 A771 5.50s Horiz. pair, #a-b 10.00 9.50

Souvenir Sheet

Lima-Callao Railway, 150th Anniv. — A772

2006, May 16 ***Perf. 13½x14***
1525 A772 6s multi 5.50 5.25

Miniature Sheet

Tourism A773

No. 1526: a, Chan Chan. b, Sipán man. c, Ventanas de Otuzco. d, Kuelap Fort. e, Río Abiseo Natl. Park. f, Pacaya Samiria.

2006, May 17
1526 A773 5.50s Sheet of 6, #a-f 31.50 30.00

Miniature Sheet

Visit of Pope John Paul II to Peru, 20th Anniv. A774

No. 1527 — Pope in: a, Lima. b, Arequipa. c, Ayacucho. d, Cuzco. e, Piura. f, Trujillo. g, Iquitos. h, Callao.

2006, May 19
1527 A774 2s Sheet of 8, #a-h 17.00 15.00

Peruvian Air Force A775

No. 1528: a, Air Force emblem. b, Airplanes and pilot.

2006, May 22
1528 A775 6s Horiz. pair, #a-b 11.00 10.50

Carnival Participants — A776

Participants in carnivals from: No. 1529, 6s, Cajamarca. No. 1530, 6s, Arequipa. No. 1531, 6s, Puno.

2006, May 22 ***Perf. 14x13½***
1529-1531 A776 Set of 3 17.50 16.75

Precursors of Independence — A777

No. 1532: a, Micaela Bastidas. b, Plaza Mayor, Cuzco.

2006, May 31
1532 A777 2s Horiz. pair, #a-b 4.50 4.00

Intl. Year of Deserts and Desertification A778

2006, Dec. 22 Litho. ***Perf. 13½x14***
1533 A778 2s multi 2.25 2.00

Christmas A779

2006, Dec. 22
1534 A779 2s multi 2.25 2.00

Wolfgang Amadeus Mozart (1756-91), Composer A780

2006, Dec. 22
1535 A780 5.50s multi 5.25 5.00

2006 World Cup Soccer Championships, Germany — A781

2006, Dec. 22 ***Perf. 14x13½***
1536 A781 8.50s multi 9.25 9.00

Christopher Columbus (1451-1506), Explorer — A782

2006, Dec. 27 ***Perf. 13½x14***
1537 A782 6s multi 5.50 5.25

First International Philatelic Exhibition in Peru, 75th Anniv. — A783

Litho. With Foil Application
2006, Dec. 29 ***Perf. 13½x14***
1538 A783 8.50s #286 7.75 7.50

America Issue, Energy Conservation — A784

No. 1539: a, 3s, Solar panels. b, 5.50s, Natural gas.

2006, Dec. 29 Litho. ***Perf. 14x13½***
1539 A784 Horiz. pair, #a-b 8.50 8.00

Diplomatic Relations Between Peru and People's Republic of China, 35th Anniv. — A785

No. 1540: a, Giant panda. b, Guanaco. c, Machu Picchu. d, Great Wall of China.

2006, Dec. 29
1540 A785 2s Block of 4, #a-d, + label 8.75 7.75

"The Pirates of Callao," First Peruvian 3-D Animated Film — A786

Parrot and: No. 1541, 2s, Boy with sword. No. 1542, 2s, Captain with sword.

Litho. With Foil Application
2007, Jan. 5 ***Perf. 13½x14***
1541-1542 A786 Set of 2 4.50 4.00
Dated 2006.

Peruvian Art — A787

Designs: No. 1543, 2.20s, Sculpture of horse by Victor Delfin. No. 1544, 2.20s, Painting by Fernando de Szyszlo.

2007, Jan. 9 Litho.
1543-1544 A787 Set of 2 4.75 4.25
Dated 2006.

Souvenir Sheet

Purussaurus Fossil — A788

Litho. (Foil Application on Sheet Margin)
2007, Jan. 16
1545 A788 8.50s multi 7.75 7.50
Dated 2006.

Flutes — A789

Designs: No. 1546, 5.50s, Antara. No. 1547, 5.50s, Quena. No. 1548, 5.50s, Zampoña.

2007, Jan. 23 Litho.
1546-1548 A789 Set of 3 15.25 14.50
Dated 2006.

St. Toribio de Mogrovejo (1538-1606), Founder of First Seminary in Americas — A790

2007, Jan. 27 Engr. ***Perf. 14x13½***
1549 A790 2s chocolate 2.25 2.00
Dated 2006.

Miniature Sheet

Religious Festivals A791

No. 1550: a, Señor de los Milagros. b, Virgen de las Mercedes. c, Virgen de la Candelaria. d, Señor de Muruhuay.

2007, Jan. 30 Litho.
1550 A791 5.50s Sheet of 4, #a-d 21.00 20.00
Dated 2006.

Peruvian Film, "Dragones Destino de Fuego" — A792

Designs: No. 1551, 2s, Flying dragons. No. 1552, 2s, Head of dragon.

Litho. With Foil Application
2007, Feb. 5
1551-1552 A792 Set of 2 4.50 4.00
Dated 2006.

National Board of Elections, 75th Anniv. (in 2006) — A793

2007, Feb. 13 Engr.
1553 A793 2.20s brown 2.25 2.00
Dated 2006.

Desserts — A794

No. 1554: a, Suspiro de limeña. b, Picarones. c, Mazamorra morada.

2007, Mar. 12 Litho. ***Perf. 13½x14***
1554 A794 Horiz. strip of 3 7.75 7.00
a.-c. 2.50s Any single 1.90 1.75
Dated 2006.

Dogs A795

No. 1555: a, Perro sin pelo (hairless dog). b, Dachshund. c, Samoyed. d, Siberian husky.

2007, Mar. 26 Litho. ***Perf. 13½x14***
1555 A795 6s Block of 4, #a-d, + label 22.00 21.00
Dated 2006.

Miniature Sheet

Architecture of the Viceregal Era in Lima — A796

No. 1556: a, St. Augustine Church. b, Sacristy of St. Francis. c, St. Apollonia Gate. d, Metropolitan Cathedral

2007, Apr. 2 Litho. ***Perf. 14x13½***
1556 A796 5.50s Sheet of 4, #a-d 21.00 20.00
Dated 2006.

Incan Temples — A797

Designs: No. 1557, 6s, Tambo Colorado, Ica. No. 1558, 6s, Pachacamac, Lima. No. 1559, 6s, Tambo Machay, Cusco.

2007, Apr. 23 Litho. ***Perf. 13½x14***
1557-1559 A797 Set of 3 16.75 16.00
Dated 2006.

Felipe Pinglo Alva (1899-1936), Composer — A798

No. 1560: a, Photographs of Pinglo Alva and buildings. b, Guitar, photograph of Pinglo Alva.

2007, May 7 ***Perf. 14x13½***
1560 A798 3s Horiz. pair, #a-b 5.75 5.25
Dated 2006.

Pre-Columbian Cultures — A799

Artifacts and maps of: No. 1561, 6s, Vicús culture, 500 B.C. No. 1562, 6s, Salinar culture, 200 B.C.

2007, May 21 ***Perf. 13½x14***
1561-1562 A799 Set of 2 11.00 10.50

Dated 2006.

Dances and Costumes — A800

No. 1563: a, Danza de los Negritos. b, Danza de las Tijeras. c, Danza Cápac Colla. d, Danza La Diablada.

2007, June 4 ***Perf. 14x13½***
1563 A800 2.50s Block of 4, #a-d, + label 10.50 9.50

Dated 2006.

Exports — A801

Designs: No. 1564, 6s, Alpaca yarn. No. 1565, 6s, Mangos. No. 1566, 6s, Asparagus.

2007, June 18 ***Perf. 13½x14***
1564-1566 A801 Set of 3 16.75 16.00

Dated 2006.

Adventure Sports — A802

No. 1567: a, Rafting. b, Cycling. c, Rock climbing.

2007, July 2
1567 A802 Horiz. strip of 3 16.75 16.00
a.-c. 6s Any single 4.00 4.00

Dated 2006.

Miniature Sheet

First Peruvian Congress, 185th Anniv. — A803

No. 1568: a, Exposition Palace. b, Painting of Francisco González Gamarra. c, Tribunal of the Inquisition Building. d, Statue of Simón Bolívar. e, Legislative Palace at night. f, Pasos Perdidos Hall. g, Stained-glass window. h, Legislative Palace sculpture.

Litho., Foil Application on Margin and Label

2007, July 12 ***Perf. 14x13½***
1568 A803 2.50s Sheet of 8, #a-h, + central label 21.00 19.00

Viceroys Type of 2006

No. 1569: a, Luis de Velasco (c. 1534-1617). b, Gaspar de Zuniga y Acevedo (1560-1606). c, Juan de Mendoza y Luna (1571-1628). d, Francisco de Borja y Aragon (1581-1658).

2007, July 16 **Litho.**
1569 A767 6s Block of 4, #a-d, + label 21.00 20.00

Giuseppe Garibaldi (1807-82), Italian Leader — A804

2007, July 26 ***Perf. 13½x14***
1570 A804 6s multi 5.50 5.25

Scouting, Cent. A805

No. 1571: a, Scouting emblem, pictures of Scouts. b, Lord Robert Baden-Powell blowing kudu horn, flags.

2007, July 30 ***Perf. 14x13½***
1571 A805 3s Horiz. pair, #a-b 6.00 5.50

Endangered Animals — A806

No. 1572: a, 3s, Oncifelis colocolo. b, 3s, Lontra felina. c, 6s, Harpia harpyja. d, 6s, Odocoileus virginianus.

2007, July 30 ***Perf. 13½x14***
1572 A806 Block of 4, #a-d, + label 17.00 16.00

Medicinal Plants — A807

No. 1573: a, Bixa orellana. b, Cestrum auriculatum. c, Brugmansia suaveolens. d, Anacardium occidentale. e, Caesalpinia spinosa. f, Croton lechleri.

2007, Aug. 6 **Litho.**
1573 A807 2.50s Block of 6, #a-f, + label 15.50 14.00

Raul Maria Pereira, Architect, and Postal Headquarters, Lima — A808

2007, Aug. 10
1574 A808 2s multi 2.25 2.00

See Portugal No. 2940.

Viceroys Type of 2006

No. 1575: a, Diego Fernández de Cordoba (1578-1630). b, Luis Jerónimo de Cabrera (1589-1647). c, Pedro de Toledo y Leiva (c. 1585-1654). d, Garcia Sarmiento de Sotomayor (c. 1595-1659).

2007, Aug. 20 ***Perf. 14x13½***
1575 A767 6s Block of 4, #a-d, + label 22.00 21.00

Souvenir Sheet

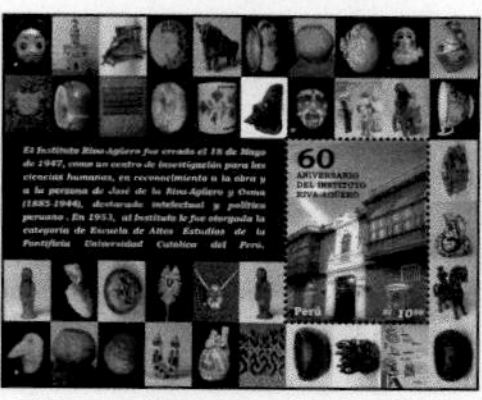

Riva-Agüero Institute, 60th Anniv. — A809

2007, Sept. 10
1576 A809 10.50s multi 9.25 9.00

Peruvian National Police Band, Cent. (in 2006) — A810

Band: 2s, On steps of building. 8.50s, In parade.

2007, Sept. 15 ***Perf. 13½x14***
1577-1578 A810 Set of 2 9.75 9.25

Birds — A811

Designs: No. 1579, 5.50s, Coeraba flaveola. No. 1580, 5.50s, Mimus longicaudatus. No. 1581, 5.50s, Pyrocephalus rubinus. No. 1582, 5.50s, Sarcoramphus papa.

Litho. With Foil Application

2007, Sept. 15
1579-1582 A811 Set of 4 21.00 20.00

Grand Masonic Lodge of Peru, 125th Anniv. — A812

2007, Sept. 17 **Litho.** ***Perf. 14x13½***
1583 A812 6.50s multi 6.00 5.75

Souvenir Sheet

Joint Command of the Armed Forces, 50th Anniv. — A813

2007, Sept. 24 ***Perf. 13½x14***
1584 A813 14s multi 12.50 12.00

Children's Art — A814

Winning pictures in children's art contest: No. 1585, 2s, River Scene, by Juana Chuquipiondo Mesía. No. 1586, 2s, Crane on Stump, by Rubén Saavedra Cobeñas, vert.

Perf. 13½x14, 14x13½

2007, Sept. 28
1585-1586 A814 Set of 2 5.00 4.50

Miniature Sheet

Automobiles — A815

No. 1587: a, 1935 Auburn Speedster 851 SC. b, 1903 Clément Brass Phaeton 9 CV. c, 1926 Dodge Special Pickup truck. d, 1928 Stutz BB Sedan Convertible Victoria. e, 1936 Pierce Arrow 1603 Touring D 700.

2007, Sept. 28 ***Perf. 13½x14***
1587 A815 3s Sheet of 5, #a-e 15.25 14.00

Santa Clara Monastery, Cusco, 450th Anniv. — A816

2007, Oct. 1 ***Perf. 14x13½***
1588 A816 5.50s multi 5.25 5.00

Cats A817

No. 1589: a, Angora. b, Persian. c, Bengal. d, Siamese.

2007, Oct. 1 **Litho.**
1589 A817 6s Block of 4, #a-d, + label 22.00 21.00

Miniature Sheet

Insects A818

No. 1590: a, Macrodontia cervicornis. b, Dynastes hercules. c, Titanus giganteus. d, Megasoma sp.

2007, Oct. 1 ***Perf. 13½x14***
1590 A818 5.50s Sheet of 4, #a-d 19.50 18.50

First Peruvian Nautical Academy, 350th Anniv. — A819

2007, Oct. 8
1591 A819 5.50s multi 5.25 5.00

America Issue, Education for All — A820

Designs: No. 1592, 5.50s, Two boys reading. No. 1593, 5.50s, Two girls reading.

2007, Oct. 9 ***Perf. 14x13½***
1592-1593 A820 Set of 2 10.25 9.75

Daniel Alcides Carrión (1857-85), Describer of Carrion's Disease — A821

2007, Oct. 13 Engr. ***Perf. 13½x14***
1594 A821 3s brown 3.00 2.75

Miniature Sheet

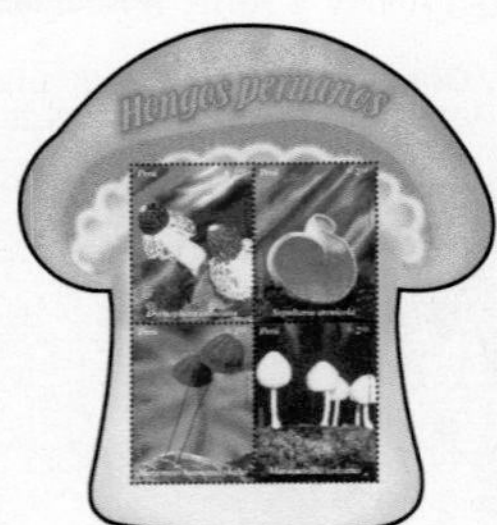

Mushrooms — A822

No. 1595: a, Dyctiophora indusiata. b, Sepultaria arenicola. c, Marasmius haematocephalus. d, Marasmiellus volvatus.

Litho., Foil Application in Margin
2007, Oct. 15 ***Perf. 14x13½***
1595 A822 2.50s Sheet of 4, #a-d 10.50 9.50

Peru No. 18 Volunteer Fire Brigade, Cent. A823

No. 1596 — Fire trucks: a, 1908 Merry Weather. b, 1969 Mack.

2007, Nov. 4 Litho. ***Perf. 13½x14***
1596 A823 3s Horiz. pair, #a-b 6.00 5.50

Víctor Raúl Haya de la Torre (1895-1979), Politician — A824

2007, Aug. 16 Engr. ***Perf. 14x13½***
1597 A824 3s claret 3.00 2.75

Souvenir Sheet

Megatherium Fossils — A825

2007, Sept. 28 **Litho.**
1598 A825 10s multi 9.00 8.75

Miniature Sheet

Bush Dog A826

No. 1599: a, 2s, Two dogs. b, 2s, One dog. c, 5.50s, One dog, facing right. d, 5.50s, One dog, facing left.

2007, Oct. 19 ***Perf. 13½x14***
1599 A826 Sheet of 4, #a-d 14.50 13.50

Souvenir Sheet

Real Felipe Fort, Callao A827

2007, Oct. 29
1600 A827 6s multi 5.50 5.25

Familia Serrana, by Camilo Blas (1910-85) — A828

2007, Nov. 5 ***Perf. 14x13½***
1601 A828 6s multi 5.50 5.25

Pre-Columbian Cultures Type of 2006

Artifacts of: 6s, Nasca culture, A.D. 600. 7s, Mochica culture, 700 B.C.-A.D. 200.

2007, Nov. 12 ***Perf. 13½x14***
1602-1603 A755 Set of 2 12.00 11.50

Souvenir Sheet

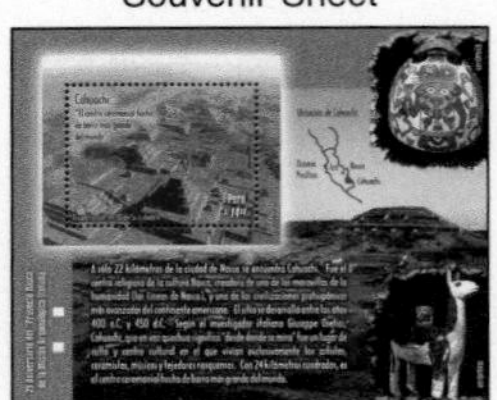

Cahuachi Archaeological Site — A829

2007, Nov. 12
1604 A829 14.50s multi 13.00 12.50

Founders of Independence Society, 150th Anniv. — A830

2007, Dec. 1
1605 A830 6s multi 5.50 5.25

Christmas — A831

2007, Dec. 1 ***Perf. 14x13½***
1606 A831 6.50s multi 6.00 5.75

First Peruvian Postage Stamps, 150th Anniv. A832

No. 1607: a, Peru #1. b, Peru #2.

2007, Dec. 1
1607 A832 2.50s Horiz. pair, #a-b 5.25 4.75

Altars in Lima Churches — A833

Altar from: 6s, Carmelite Church. 8.50s, Lima Cathedral.

2007, Dec. 1
1608-1609 A833 Set of 2 13.00 12.50

Asia-Pacific Economic Cooperation Forum — A834

2007, Dec. 3
1610 A834 6s multi 5.50 5.25

Roots — A835

Designs: No. 1611, 6s, Smallanthus sonchifolius. No. 1612, 6s, Manihot esculenta.

2007, Dec. 17
1611-1612 A835 Set of 2 11.00 10.50

Launch of First Peruvian Rocket, 1st Anniv. A836

No. 1613 — Emblem of National Space Commission and: a, Pedro Paulet Mostajo (1874-1945), aeronautical pioneer and Paulet I rocket in flight. b, Paulet I rocket on launch pad and civil ensign.

Litho., Litho. With Foil Application (#1613b)
2007, Dec. 27 ***Perf. 13½x14***
1613 A836 3s Horiz. pair, #a-b 6.00 5.50

Souvenir Sheet

First Peruvian Scientific Expedition to the Antarctic, 20th Anniv. — A837

No. 1614: a, Ship "Humboldt." b, Expedition members, horiz.

Perf. 13½x14, 14x13½ (#1614b)
Litho. With Foil Application
2008, Feb. 22
1614 A837 10s Sheet of 2, #a-b 18.00 17.50

Arms Stamps of 1858, 150th Anniv. — A838

Designs: No. 1615, 5.50s, Peru #3. No. 1616, 5.50s, Peru #4. No. 1617, 5.50s, Peru #6.

2008, Mar. 10 Litho. ***Perf. 14x13½***
1615-1617 A838 Set of 3 15.75 15.00

Santa Rosa de Santa María Monastery, 300th Anniv. — A839

2008, June 3 ***Perf. 13½x14***
1618 A839 5.50s multi 5.25 5.00

Lima Philharmonic Society, Cent. — A840

No. 1619 — Emblem and: a, Violin. b, Musicians.

2008, June 8 ***Perf. 14x13½***
1619 A840 3s Horiz. pair, #a-b 6.00 5.50

Lima General Cemetery, Bicent. — A841

Designs: No. 1620, 6.50s, Statue of angel and cross. No. 1621, 6.50s, Statue of praying woman, vert.

Perf. 13½x14, 14x13½
2008, June 17
1620-1621 A841 Set of 2 12.00 11.50

Viceroys Type of 2006

No. 1622: a, Luis Enríquez de Guzmán (c. 1605-61). b, Diego de Benavides y de la Cueva (1607-66). c, Pedro Antonio Fernandez de Castro (1634-72). d, Baltasar de la Cueva Enríquez (1626-86).

2008, June 24 ***Perf. 14x13½***
1622 A767 6s Block of 4, #a-d, + label 22.00 21.00

ExportaFacil Package Service — A842

2008, June 24
1623 A842 10s multi 9.00 8.75

America Issue A843

No. 1624: a, Inti Raymi (Festival of the Sun), Cuzco. b, Grape Harvest Festival, Ica.

2008, June 24 ***Perf. 13½x14***
1624 A843 6.50s Horiz. pair, #a-b 12.00 11.50

Latin American, Caribbean and European Union Heads of State Summit, Lima — A844

2008, July 1 ***Perf. 14x13½***
1625 A844 6.50s red & black 6.00 5.75

2008 Summer Olympics, Beijing — A845

No. 1626 — Olympic mascots and places in Peru: a, Beibei, Máncora. b, Jingjing, Lima Cathedral. c, Yingying, Machu Picchu. d, Nini, Tambopata.

2008, July 1 ***Perf. 13½x14***
1626 A845 1.40s Block of 4, #a-d, + label 6.75 5.75

Latin American and European Parliamentary Summit, Lima — A846

2008, July 2
1627 A846 6.50s multi 6.00 5.75

Aurelio Miró Quesada Sosa (1907-98), Lawyer and Writer — A847

2008, July 3
1628 A847 2.50s multi 2.60 2.40

National Literacy Program — A848

2008, July 4
1629 A848 2.50s multi 2.60 2.40

Exports Type of 2007

Designs: No. 1630, 5.50s, Olives (aceituna). No. 1631, 5.50s, Cotton (algodón). No. 1632, 5.50s, Avocados (palta).

2008, July 8
1630-1632 A801 Set of 3 15.00 14.50

Miniature Sheet

River Fish A849

No. 1633: a, Phractocephalus hemioliopterus. b, Mylossoma duriventre. c, Piaractus braphypomus. d, Ageneiosus ucayalensis. e, Brycon melanopterus.

2008, July 18
1633 A849 3s Sheet of 5, #a-e 15.00 14.00

A850

A851

A852

Judgment Day Paintings, Lima Cathedral A853

2008, Aug. 5

1634	A850 6.50s multi		6.00	5.75
1635	A851 6.50s multi		6.00	5.75
1636	A852 6.50s multi		6.00	5.75
1637	A853 6.50s multi		6.00	5.75
	Nos. 1634-1637 (4)		24.00	23.00

A854

Design: Edwin Vásquez Cam (1922-93), First Peruvian Olympic Gold medalist.

2008, Aug. 6
1638 A854 6s multi 5.25 5.00

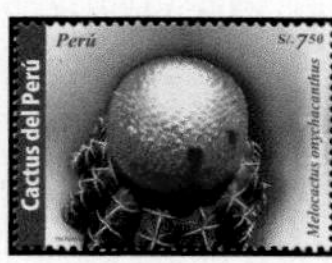
Cacti — A855

Designs: No. 1639, 7.50s, Melocactus onychacanthus. No. 1640, 7.50s, Matucana oreodoxa. No. 1641, 7.50s, Espostoa mirabilis.

2008, Aug. 13
1639-1641 A855 Set of 3 21.00 20.00

Dr. Javier Arias Stella, Pathologist — A856

2008, Aug. 22 ***Perf. 14x13½***
1642 A856 2s multi 2.25 2.00

Miniature Sheet

Seven Wonders of the Modern World A857

No. 1643: a, 2.50s, Petra, Jordan. b, 2.50s, Machu Picchu, Peru. c, 2.50s, Great Wall of China. d, 2.50s, Statue of Christ the Redeemer, Brazil. e, 7.50s, Chichén Itzá, Mexico. f, 10s, Roman Colosseum, Italy. g, 10.50s, Taj Mahal, India.

2008, July 7 Litho. ***Perf. 13½x14***
1643 A857 Sheet of 7, #a-g 36.00 34.00

Intl. Year of the Potato — A858

Litho. With Foil Application

2008, Sept. 3
1644 A858 5.50s multi 5.25 5.00

Orchids — A859

Designs: No. 1645, 7s, Cattleya rex. No. 1646, 7s, Cattleya máxima.

2008, Sept. 3 Litho. ***Perf. 14x13½***
1645-1646 A859 Set of 2 13.00 12.50

Souvenir Sheet

Crypt of the Heroes, Cent. A860

2008, Sept. 8
1647 A860 10.50s multi 9.25 9.00

Pre-Columbian Cultures Type of 2006

Artifacts of: 2s, Tiahuanaco culture, 100 B.C.-A.D. 1200. 6s, Recuay culture, A.D. 1-600.

2008, Sept. 10 ***Perf. 13½x14***
1648-1649 A755 Set of 2 7.75 7.25

Performing Arts Productions — A861

Designs: No. 1650, 6.50s, Play *Na Catita*. No. 1651, 6.50s, Ballet *Huatyacuri*.

Litho. with Foil Application

2008, Sept. 21 ***Perf. 14x13½***
1650-1651 A861 Set of 2 12.00 11.50

Nos. 1650-1651 exist imperf.

National University of Trujillo Medical School, 50th Anniv. — A862

2008, Oct. 3 **Litho.**
1652 A862 6s multi 5.50 5.25

Miniature Sheet

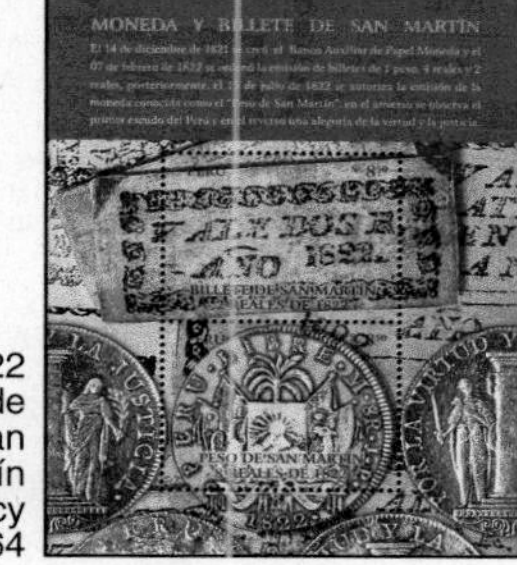
Spiders A863

No. 1653: a, Micrathena sp. b, Lycosinae sp. c, Salticidae. d, Aglaoctenus castaneus.

2008, Oct. 3 ***Perf. 13½x14***
1653 A863 2s Sheet of 4, #a-d 8.75 7.75

Souvenir Sheet

1822 José de San Martín Currency A864

No. 1654: a, 2-real note. b, 1-peso coin.

Litho. & Engr. (Foil Application in Margin)

2008, Oct. 13
1654 A864 8.50s Sheet of 2, #a-b 15.50 15.00

Souvenir Sheet

Choquequirao Ruins — A865

2008, Oct. 21 Litho. ***Perf. 14x13½***
1655 A865 10.50s multi 9.25 9.00

Museum of the Inquisition and Congress, Lima, 40th Anniv. — A866

No. 1656: a, Museum building (old National Senate Building). b, Inquisitors.

2008, Oct. 28
1656 A866 6s Horiz. pair, #a-b 11.00 10.50

Traffic Policeman and Road Signs — A867

2008, Oct. 29 *Perf. 13½x14*
1657 A867 6.50s multi 6.00 5.75

Campaign for obeying traffic signs.
No. 1657 exists imperf.

Edgardo Rebagliati National Hospital, 50th Anniv. — A868

2008, Nov. 3
1658 A868 2s multi 2.25 2.00

Paracas Mantles A869

No. 1659: a, Unbordered mantle with white and illustrated squares. b, Fringed mantle with hexagons in design. c, Fringed mantle with black squares. d, Mantle with illustrated border.

2008, Nov. 5 *Perf. 14x13½*
1659 A869 6s Block of 4 #a-d, + label 22.00 21.00

Xenoglaux Loweryi — A870

2008, Nov. 19 *Perf. 13½x14*
1660 A870 7.50s multi 6.75 6.50

Campaign Against Drug Abuse — A871

Winning art in children's stamp design contest depicting: No. 1661, 2s, Boys and Hand, by Diego Gutierrez. No. 1662, 2s, Crossed bones and marijuana leaves, by Carolina Luna Polo, vert.

Perf. 13½x14, 14x13½

2008, Nov. 21
1661-1662 A871 Set of 2 4.50 4.00

Christmas A872

2008, Dec. 1 *Perf. 13½x14*
1663 A872 8.50s multi 7.75 7.50

Free Trade Agreement Between Peru and United States, 1st Anniv. — A873

2008, Dec. 4
1664 A873 6s multi 5.75 5.50

Jerónimo de Loayza Gonzáles (1498-1575), First Archbishop of Lima — A874

2008, Dec. 10
1665 A874 2s multi 2.25 2.00

Souvenir Sheet

Inca God Wiracocha — A875

No. 1666 — Wiracocha: a, Breathing. b, With arm extended. c, Walking.

2008, Dec. 10
1666 A875 2.50s Sheet of 3, #a-c 7.75 7.00

Miniature Sheet

Intl. Polar Year A876

No. 1667: a, Iceberg. b, Raising of Peruvian flag. c, Map of Antarctica, International Polar Year emblem. d, Quelcayya Glacier, Peru.

2009, Jan. 15
1667 A876 2.20s Sheet of 4, #a-d 9.50 8.50

College of Administrators, 30th Anniv. — A877

2009, Feb. 11 **Litho.** *Perf. 13½x14*
1668 A877 6.50s multi 6.00 5.75

Intl. Heliophysical Year — A878

Litho. With Foil Application

2009, Mar. 9 *Perf. 14x13½*
1669 A878 5.50s multi 5.50 5.25

Intl. Heliophysical Year was in 2007-08. The Intl. Year of Astronomy was in 2009.

Lighthouses — A879

Designs: No. 1670, 6.50s, La Marina Lighthouse. No. 1671, 6.50s, Muelle Dársena Lighthouse and boat.

2009, Mar. 9 **Litho.**
1670-1671 A879 Set of 2 12.00 11.50

A880

Sunflowers A881

2009, Mar. 13 *Perf. 13½x14*
1672 A880 2.50s multi 2.60 2.40
1673 A881 2.50s multi 2.60 2.40

Honesty A882

Punctuality A883

2009, Mar. 16 *Perf. 13½x14*
1674 A882 6.50s multi 6.00 5.75

Perf. 14x13½

1675 A883 6.50s multi 6.00 5.75

Intl. Meteorology Day — A884

2009, Mar. 23 *Perf. 14x13½*
1676 A884 2s multi 2.25 2.00

Canyons A885

No. 1677: a, Colca Canyon. b, Cotahuasi Canyon. c, Pato Canyon.

2009, Mar. 23
1677 A885 2s Horiz. strip of 3, #a-c, + label 6.50 5.75

Parachuting — A886

No. 1678 — Skydivers with denomination in: a, UL. b, LR.

2009, Mar. 31 *Perf. 13½x14*
1678 A886 7s Horiz. pair, #a-b 13.00 12.50

New Year 2009 (Year of the Ox) A887

No. 1679 — Ring of Zodiac animals and: a, Rider on ox. b, Head of ox.

2009, Apr. 8 **Litho.**
1679 A887 2.50s Horiz. pair, #a-b 5.25 4.75

Earth Day — A888

2009, Apr. 22
1680 A888 5.50s multi 5.25 5.00

Viceroys Type of 2006

No. 1681: a, Melchor de Liñán y Cisneros (1629-1708). b, Melchor de Navarra y Rocafull (1626-91). c, Melchor Portocarrero Lasso de la Vega (1636-1705). d, Manuel de Oms y de Santa Pau (1651-1710).

2009, Apr. 23 *Perf. 14x13½*
1681 A767 6s Block of 4 #a-d, + label 22.00 21.00

National University of Central Peru, Huancayo, 50th Anniv. — A889

2009, Apr. 30
1682 A889 2s multi 2.25 2.60

Royal Commentaries of the Incas, 400th Anniv. — A890

Designs: No. 1683, 2s, Royal Commentaries of the Incas, book, by Garcellaso de la Vega. No. 1684, 2s, De la Vega (1539-1616), historian.

2009, Apr. 30
1683-1684 A890 Set of 2 4.50 4.00

America Issue, Children's Games — A891

Designs: No. 1685, 10.50s, Boy flying kite. No. 1686, 10.50s, Children playing ronda.

2009, Apr. 30 **Litho.**
1685-1686 A891 Set of 2 18.50 18.00

Endangered Animals — A892

No. 1687: a, Blastocerus dichotomus. b, Pelecanoides garnotii. c, Podocnemis expansa. d, Crax unicornis.

2009, May 4 *Perf. 13½x14*
1687 A892 7.50s Block of 4, #a-d, + label 27.00 26.00

Souvenir Sheet

"Libertad Parada" Coin A893

No. 1688: a, Obverse (arms). b, Reverse (Liberty), vert.

Perf. 13½x14 (#1688a), 14x13½ (#1688b)

2009, May 8

1688 A893 3s Sheet of 2, #a-b 5.75 5.25

Folk Art — A894

Designs: No. 1689, 6.50s, Retable, Ayacucho (Retablo Ayacuchano). No. 1690, 6.50s, Native clothing, Cusco (Muñequería Cusqueña). No. 1691, 6.50s, Decorated bull, Pucará (Torito de Pucará).

2009, May 11 ***Perf. 14x13½***

1689-1691 A894 Set of 3 17.75 17.00

Crustaceans — A895

No. 1692: a, Farfantepenaeus californiensis. b, Sicyonia aliaffnis. c, Ucides occidentalis. d, Palinurus elephas.

2009, May 15 ***Perf. 13½x14***

1692 A895 10s Block of 4, #a-d, + label 36.00 35.00

Souvenir Sheet

Peruvian Hairless Dog A896

2009, May 15 ***Perf. 14x13½***

1693 A896 7s multi 6.50 6.25

Santiago de Surco Municipality, 80th Anniv. — A897

2009, May 21 **Litho.**

1694 A897 5.50s multi 5.25 5.00

Submarines A898

No. 1695: a, BAP Pisagua. b, BAP Arica.

2009, May 22 ***Perf. 13½x14***

1695 A898 2.50s Vert. pair, #a-b 5.25 4.75

Cuzco as UNESCO World Heritage Site, 25th Anniv. (in 2008) — A899

Litho. With Foil Application

2009, May 24

1696 A899 2.50s multi 2.60 2.40

Odontological College of Peru, 45th Anniv. — A900

2009, May 29 **Litho.**

1697 A900 2s multi 2.25 2.00

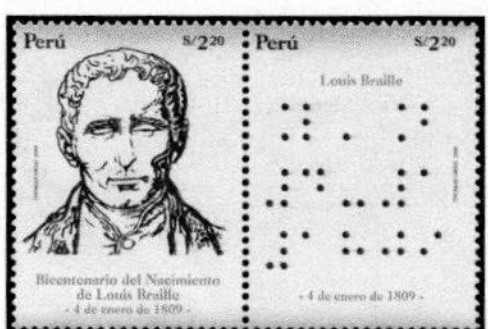

Campaign Against Rabies — A901

2009, June 25 Litho. ***Perf. 13½x14***

1698 A901 5.50s multi 5.25 5.00

Louis Braille (1809-52), Educator of the Blind — A902

No. 1699: a, Braille. b, Braille text.

Litho. & Engr.

2009, June 30 ***Perf. 14x13½***

1699 A902 2.20s Horiz. pair, #a-b 4.75 4.25

Pre-Columbian Cultures Type of 2006

Designs: No. 1700, 2s, Huari culture, 550-900. No. 1701, 2s, Chimú culture, 1000-1400.

2009, July 3 Litho. ***Perf. 13½x14***

1700-1701 A755 Set of 2 4.50 4.00

Ciro Alegría (1909-67), Journalist and Politician — A903

2009, July 8 ***Perf. 14x13½***

1702 A903 2.50s multi 2.60 2.40

Peruvian Tourist Attractions A904

Designs: No. 1703, 2.50s, Amazon River, Loretio Region. No. 1704, 2.50s, Boat on Lake Titicaca, Puno Region. No. 1705, 7.50s, Cumbemayo Archaeological Site, Cajamarca Region.

2009 ***Perf. 13½x14***

1703-1705 A904 Set of 3 11.75 11.00

Issued: Nos. 1703-1704, 7/17; No. 1705, 7/10.

Peruvian Philatelic Association, 60th Anniv. — A905

2009, July 21 ***Perf. 14x13½***

1706 A905 2s multi 2.25 2.00

Víctor Raúl Haya de la Torre (1895-1975), Politician — A906

2009, Aug. 2 Litho. ***Perf. 13½x14***

1707 A906 2s multi 2.25 2.00

Miniature Sheet

Peruvian Cuisine A907

No. 1708: a, Tacacho con cecina. b, Ocopa. c, Cebiche de conchas negras. d, Picante de papa con cuy frito. e, Frejoles con cabrito.

2009, Aug. 3

1708 A907 3s Sheet of 5, #a-e 15.25 14.00

Miniature Sheet

Incan Roads A908

No. 1709: a, 6s, Inca Bridge, Qeswachaka. b, 6s, Inca Road, Wanacaure. c, 6s, Escalerayoc Sector, Lima. d, 7.50s, Quebrada Huarautambo, Pasco.

2009, Aug. 6

1709 A908 Sheet of 4, #a-d 23.50 22.50

Exports Type of 2007

Designs: No. 1710, 2.50s, Guinea pig. No. 1711, 2.50s, Coffee.

2009, Aug. 19

1710-1711 A801 Set of 2 5.25 4.75

Souvenir Sheet

Baguatherium Jaureguii Fossil — A909

2009, Aug. 26 ***Perf. 14x13½***

1712 A909 7s multi 6.50 6.25

Miniature Sheet

Mollusks A910

No. 1713: a, Megalobulimus popelairianus. b, Megalobulimus capillaceus. c, Scutalus versicolor. d, Scutalus proteus.

2009, Aug. 31 ***Perf. 13½x14***

1713 A910 6.50s Sheet of 4, #a-d 24.00 23.00

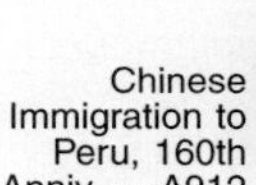

Free Trade Treaty Between Peru and People's Republic of China — A911

2009, Sept. 10 Litho. ***Perf. 13½x14***

1714 A911 7.50s multi 6.75 6.50

Chinese Immigration to Peru, 160th Anniv. — A912

2009, Oct. 12

1715 A912 8.50s multi 7.75 7.50

Natl. Museum of Archaeology, Anthropology and History of Peru — A913

2009, Oct. 13 ***Perf. 14x13½***

1716 A913 5.50s multi 5.25 5.00

Miniature Sheet

Birds A914

No. 1717: a, Actitis macularia. b, Glaucidium brasilianum. c, Numenius phaeopus. d, Egretta caerulea.

2009, Nov. 9 ***Perf. 13½x14***

1717 A914 6s Sheet of 4, #a-d 22.00 21.00

Luciano Pavarotti (1935-2007), Singer — A915

2009, Nov. 12
1718 A915 10.50s multi 9.25 9.00

Children's Art — A916

Winning art in children's environmental protection stamp design contest: No. 1719, 2s, Orchid, parrot and hand, by Ahmed Lonia Heredia Pérez. No. 1720, 2s, Children, flora and fauna, by Scarie Estefany Rojas Reátegui.

2009, Nov. 22 ***Perf. 14x13½***
1719-1720 A916 Set of 2 4.50 4.00

Christmas A917

2009, Nov. 30 ***Perf. 13½x14***
1721 A917 2.20s multi 2.40 2.10

Souvenir Sheet

Kuélap Archaeological Site — A918

No. 1722: a, Decorated enclosures (Recintos decorados). b, Principal entrance (Entrada principal). c, Decorated stone walls (Decoración parietal petrea).

2010, June 7 Litho. ***Perf. 14x13½***
1722 A918 3s Sheet of 3, #a-c 9.00 8.75

Central Station for Lima Metropolitan Bus Line — A919

No. 1723: a, Road over tunnel. b, Bus.

2010, June 22 ***Perf. 13½x14***
1723 A919 2.20s Horiz. pair, #a-b 5.00 4.50

Javier Pérez de Cuéllar, Fifth Secretary-General of the United Nations, 90th Birthday — A920

2010, Aug. 9
1724 A920 50c multi 1.00 .75

St. Francis Solano (1549-1610) — A921

2010, Aug. 12 ***Perf. 14x13½***
1725 A921 40c multi .90 .65

Gustavo Pons Muzzo (1916-2008), Historian — A922

2010, Aug. 12
1726 A922 50c multi 1.00 .75

Archdiocese of Arequipa, 400th Anniv. — A923

2010, Aug. 12 ***Perf. 13½x14***
1727 A923 2s multi 2.25 2.00

Dogs A924

No. 1728: a, Samoyed. b, Siberian husky.

2010, Aug. 12 ***Perf. 14x13½***
1728 A924 30c Horiz. pair, #a-b 1.60 1.10

Rebeca Carrión Cachot, Archaeologist, 50th Anniv. of Death — A925

2010, Aug. 13 **Litho.**
1729 A925 40c multi 1.00 .75

Afro-Peruvian Culture Day — A926

No, 1730: a, Musical instruments. b, National Afro-Peruvian Museum, Lima.

2010, Aug. 13 ***Perf. 13½x14***
1730 A926 10c Horiz. pair, #a-b 1.75 1.20

Miniature Sheet

2010 World Cup Soccer Championships, South Africa — A927

No. 1731: a, Mascot. b, Emblem. c, World Cup trophy. d, Soccer player and ball.

2010, Aug. 13 ***Perf. 14x13½***
1731 A927 10s Sheet of 4, #a-d 37.00 36.00

Tourist Sites in Lima — A928

Designs: No. 1732, 3s, Magic Fountains. No. 1733, 3s, Lake, Huascar Park.

2010, Aug. 21
1732-1733 A928 Set of 2 6.50 6.00

Souvenir Sheet

"Seated Liberty" Coin A929

2010, Aug. 21 ***Perf. 14x13½***
1734 A929 3s multi 3.25 3.00

Mushrooms — A930

No. 1735: a, Suillus luteus. b, Pleurotus cornucopiae.

2010, Aug. 24 **Litho.**
1735 A930 6s Horiz. pair, #a-b 11.50 11.00

New Year 2010 (Year of the Tiger) — A931

No. 1736: a, Tiger at left. b, Tiger at right.

2010, Aug. 26 ***Perf. 13½x14***
1736 A931 20c Vert. pair, #a-b 1.75 1.20

Viceroys Type of 2006

No. 1737: a, Diego Ladrón de Guevara Orozco y Calderon (1641-1718). b, Carmine Nicolao Caracciolo (1671-1726). c, Diego Morcillo Rubio de Auñón (1642-1730). d, José de Armendariz (1670-1740).

2010, Sept. 1 ***Perf. 14x13½***
1737 A767 3s Block of 4, #a-d, + label 13.00 12.00

Jorge Chavez (1887-1910), Pilot — A932

Litho. & Engr.

2010, Sept. 3 ***Perf. 13½x14***
1738 A932 2s multi 2.25 2.00

Centenary of Chavez's flight over Alps, after which he crash-landed and later died.

Souvenir Sheet

Stone Heads of the Chavin Culture A933

2010, Sept. 3 Litho. ***Perf. 14x13½***
1739 A933 10s multi 9.50 9.25

Pre-Columbian Cultures Type of 2006

Artifacts of: No. 1740, 50c, Chincha culture, c. 1000. No. 1741, 50c, Chancay culture, c. 1000.

2010, Sept. 7 ***Perf. 13½x14***
1740-1741 A755 Set of 2 1.90 1.40

Volunteer Fire Brigades in Peru, 150th Anniv. A934

No. 1742: a, 1860 Merryweather fire carriage. b, Pierce Contender fire truck.

2010, Sept. 9
1742 A934 6s Horiz. pair, #a-b 11.50 11.00

Club Alianza Lima Soccer Team — A935

2010, Sept. 10
1743 A935 3s multi 3.25 3.00

Miniature Sheet

Orchids A936

No. 1744: a, Anguloa virginalis. b, Masdevallia pernix. c, Stanhopea marizaiana. d, Telipogon campoverdei.

2010, Sept. 16 **Litho.**
1744 A936 3s Sheet of 4, #a-d 13.00 12.00

Colegio Nacional Iquitos Soccer Team — A937

2010, Sept. 17
1745 A937 3s multi 3.25 3.00

Frédéric Chopin (1810-49), Composer A938

2010, Sept. 21 **Litho. & Engr.**
1746 A938 3s multi 3.25 3.00

Windsurfing A939

Litho. With Foil Application

2010, Sept. 21
1747 A939 3s multi 3.25 3.00

Souvenir Sheet

Thalassocnus Littoralis — A940

2010, Sept. 21 **Litho.**
1748 A940 10s multi 9.50 9.25

Melgar Soccer Team — A941

2010, Sept. 24
1749 A941 3s multi 3.25 3.00

America Issue, National Symbols — A942

Peruvian: No. 1750, 5s, Arms. No. 1751, 5s, Flag.

2010, Oct. 5 ***Perf. 14x13½***
1750-1751 A942 Set of 2 10.00 9.50

Ollantaytambo Archaeological Site — A943

2010, Oct. 29 ***Perf. 13½x14***
1752 A943 5s multi 5.00 4.75

Christmas A944

2010, Nov. 2
1753 A944 10s multi 9.50 9.25

Children's Art — A945

Winning art in children's art contest by: No. 1754, 2s, Jimena P. Vega Gonzáles, 1st place. No. 1755, 2s, Bettina Paz Pinto, 2nd place.

2010, Nov. 22 ***Perf. 14x13½***
1754-1755 A945 Set of 2 4.50 4.00

Folk Art — A946

Designs: No. 1756, 2s, Virgin of Pino, statue by Antonio Olave Palomino. No. 1757, 2s, San Marcos, retable by Jesús Urbano Rojas. No. 1758, 2s, Procession of St. Peter, carving by Fidel Barrientos Bustos.

2010, Nov. 25 **Litho.**
1756-1758 A946 Set of 3 7.00 6.25

Ninth Lions International Forum of Latin America and the Caribbean, Lima — A947

2011, Jan. 15
1759 A947 7.80s multi 7.75 7.50

José María Arguedas (1911-69), Writer — A948

2011, Jan. 31 ***Perf. 13½x14***
1760 A948 6.60s multi 6.50 6.25

Postal Union of the Americas, Spain and Portugal (UPAEP), Cent. — A949

2011, Mar. 23
1761 A949 2s multi 2.40 2.10

Transportation Infrastructure A950

Designs: 5s, Southern Pier, Port of Callao. 5.20s, Southern Interoceanic Highway.

2011, May 16 **Litho.**
1762-1763 A950 Set of 2 10.50 10.00

Scouting in Peru, Cent. — A951

Peruvian and Scouting flags and: No. 1764, 6.40s, Boy Scout. No. 1765, 6.40s, Girl Scout.

2011, May 25 ***Perf. 14x13½***
1764-1765 A951 Set of 2 13.00 12.50

Jicamarca Radio Observatory, 50th Anniv. — A952

2011, June 7 ***Perf. 13½x14***
1766 A952 6.60s multi 6.50 6.25

Awarding of 2010 Nobel Prize for Literature to Mario Vargas Llosa — A953

2011, June 8 ***Perf. 14x13½***
1767 A953 7.80s multi 7.75 7.50

Peruvian Submarine Force, Cent. — A954

No. 1768 — Emblem of Submarine Force, various submarines with denomination at: a, UR. b, UL.

2011, June 9 ***Perf. 13½x14***
1768 A954 7.20s Horiz. pair, #a-b 14.50 14.00

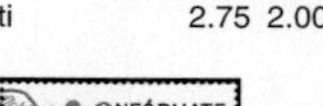
Javier Pulgar Vidal (1911-2003), Geographer — A955

2011, June 13 ***Perf. 14x13½***
1769 A955 2.40s multi 2.75 2.00

Campaign Against HIV and AIDS — A956

No. 1770 — Text, AIDS ribbon and: a, Man. b, Woman.

2011, June 13 ***Perf. 13½x14***
1770 A956 5.50s Horiz. pair, #a-b 11.50 11.00

First Call for Peruvian Independence by Francisco Antonio de Zela y Arizaga, Bicent. — A957

No. 1771: a, Painting of Zela. b, Statue of Zela.

2011, June 20 **Litho.**
1771 A957 7.20s Horiz. pair, #a-b 14.50 14.00

Amazonia National University of Peru, 50th Anniv. — A958

2011, June 23 ***Perf. 14x13½***
1772 A958 2.70s multi 9.00 8.75

National Theater, Lima — A959

2011, June 23 ***Perf. 13½x14***
1773 A959 5s multi 5.25 5.00

Pre-Columbian Cultures Type of 2006

Artifacts of: No. 1774, 6.40s, Chachapoya culture, 700-1500. No. 1775, 6.40s, Inca culture, 1400-1572.

2011, June 24 ***Perf. 13½x14***
1774-1775 A755 Set of 2 13.00 12.50

Viceroys Type of 2006

No. 1776: a, José Antonio de Mendoza Caamano y Sotomayor (1667-1746). b, José Antonio Manso de Velasco (1688-1767). c, Manuel de Amat y Junyent (1707-82). d, Manuel Guirior (1708-88).

2011, July 1 ***Perf. 14x13½***
1776 A767 7.80s Block of 4, #a-d, + label 31.00 30.00

Motocross Racing — A960

2011, July 5 **Litho.**
1777 A960 7.80s multi 7.75 7.50

Dances — A961

Designs: No. 1778, 9s, Tijeras (scissors) dance. No. 1779, 9s, Huaconada.

2011, July 5 ***Perf. 13½x14***
1778-1779 A961 Set of 2 17.50 17.00

Year of the Rabbit — A962

No. 1780: a, Rabbit. b, Chinese character for "rabbit."

2011, July 5 ***Perf. 14x13½***
1780 A962 5.50s Horiz. pair, #a-b 11.50 11.00

Souvenir Sheet

Discovery of Machu Picchu, Cent. — A963

2011, July 5
1781 A963 7.80s multi 7.75 7.50

Electric Trains A964

No. 1782: a, One train. b, Two trains.

2011, July 16 **Litho.**
1782 A964 5.50s Horiz. pair, #a-b 11.50 11.00

Maxillaria Pyhalae — A965

2011, July 19
1783 A965 10.50s multi 10.25 10.00

Governmental Palace and Presidents of Peru — A966

No. 1784: a, Government Palace, 18th cent. b, Marshal José de La Mar (1778-1830). c, Gen. Agustín Gamarra (1785-1841). d, Gen. Luis José de Orbegoso (1795-1847). e, Gen. Felipe Santiago Salaverry (1805-36). f, Marshal Andrés de Santa Cruz (1792-1865). g, Manuel Menéndez (1793-1847). h, Gen. Juan Crisóstomo Torrico (1808-75). i, Justo Figuerola (1771-1854). j, Government Palace, 20th cent. k, Gen. Manuel Ignacio de Vivanco (1806-73). l, Gen. Ramón Castilla (1797-1867). m, Gen. José Rufino Echenique (1808-87). n, Gen. Miguel de San Roman (1802-63). o, Gen. Juan Antonio Pezet (1809-79). p, Gen. Mariano Ignacio Prado (1826-1901). q, Col. José Balta (1814-72). r, Manuel Pardo y Lavalle (1834-78). s, Gen. Luis La Puerta (1811-96). t, Nicolás de Piérola (1839-1913). u, Francisco García Calderón (1834-1905). v, Admiral Lizardo Montero (1832-1905). w, Gen. Miguel Iglesias (1830-1909). x, Gold Room, Government Palace. y, Grand Hall, Government Palace. z, Flag and arms of Peru, Government Palace. aa, Túpac Amaru Room, Government Palace. ab, Gen. Andrés A. Cáceres (1836-1923). ac, Col. Remigio Morales Bermúdez (1836-94). ad, Eduardo López de Romaña (1847-1912). ae, Manuel Candamo (1841-1904). af, José Pardo Barreda (1864-1947). ag, Augusto B. Leguía (1863-1932). ah, Guillermo Billinghurst (1851-1915). ai, Gen. Oscar R. Benavides (1876-1945). aj, Lieutenant Colonel Luis M. Sánchez Cerro (1889-1933). ak, Manuel Prado y Ugarteche (1889-1967). al, José Luis Bustamente y Rivero (1894-1989). am, Gen. Manuel A. Odría (1897-1974). an, Gen. Ricardo Pérez Godoy (1905-82). ao, Honor Guard, Government Palace. ap, Gen. Nicolás Lindley (1908-95). aq, Fernando Belaunde Terry (1912-2002). ar, Gen. Juan Velasco Alvarado (1910-77). as, Gen. Francisco Morales Bermúdez. at, Alan García Pérez. au, Alberto Fujimori. av, Valentín Paniagua (1936-2006). aw, Alejandro Toledo Manrique. ax, Government Palace, 21st cent.

2011, July 25 ***Perf. 14x13½***
1784 A966 Sheet of 50 130.00 120.00
a.-ax. 2.40s Any single 2.40 1.90

Intl. Year of Chemistry — A967

2011, Aug. 1 **Litho.**
1785 A967 7.20s multi 7.25 7.00

Children's Art — A968

Winning art in children's prevention of natural disasters stamp design contest: 20c, Overturned boat, hand, tornado, dead fish and flooded house, by Carlos Renato Huaynasi Calcina. 2.40s, Children at school, by Sherley Breshley Suclupe Calderon.

2011, Aug. 18 ***Perf. 13½x14***
1786-1787 A968 Set of 2 3.25 3.00

National Archives, 150th Anniv. — A969

2011, Aug. 19
1788 A969 5.80s multi 5.75 5.00

Miniature Sheet

Peruvian Cuisine A970

No. 1789: a, Lomo Saltado (beef with onions, tomatoes, rice and fried potatoes). b, Ají de Gallina (creamed chicken with chili peppers). c, Tiradito de Pescado (raw fish in spicy sauce). d, Chicharrón (fried pork rinds).

2011, Aug. 25
1789 A970 7.80s Sheet of 4, #a-d 31.00 30.00

Statue of St. Sebastian, Patron Saint of Chepén — A971

2011, Aug. 30 ***Perf. 14x13½***
1790 A971 2s multi 2.40 2.10

Clorinda Matto de Turner (1852-1909), Writer — A972

2011, Sept. 9 ***Perf. 13½x14***
1791 A972 3.60s multi 3.75 3.50

1838 South Peru Gold 8-Escudo Coin — A973

No. 1792: a, Reverse. b, Obverse.

2011, Sept. 12 ***Perf. 14x13½***
1792 A973 5.80s Horiz. pair, #a-b 11.50 11.00

Cayetano Heredia University, 50th Anniv. — A974

2011, Sept. 22 ***Perf. 13½x14***
1793 A974 3.60s multi 3.75 3.50

First Airplane Flight in Peru by Juan Bielovucic Cavalie, Cent. — A975

2011, Sept. 23 **Litho. & Engr.**
1794 A975 7.20p multi 7.25 7.00

Miniature Sheet

Primates A976

No. 1795: a, Lagothrix flavicauda. b, Callicebus oenanthe. c, Aotus miconax. d, Cacajao calvus.

2011, Oct. 10 **Litho.** ***Perf. 14x13½***
1795 A976 7.80s Sheet of 4, #a-d 31.00 30.00

Cultivation of Cotton in Peru, 700th Anniv. — A977

Gossypium barbadense with panel at bottom in: No. 1796, 8.50s, Blue. No. 1797, 8.50s, Red brown.

2011, Oc. 11 ***Perf. 13½x14***
1796-1797 A977 Set of 2 16.50 16.00

Souvenir Sheet

Fossils of Livyatan Melvillei A978

Litho. (With Foil Application in Sheet Margin)

2011, Oct. 17 ***Perf. 14x13½***
1798 A978 10s multi 9.75 9.00

Franz Liszt (1811-86), Composer — A979

Litho. & Engr.

2011, Oct. 22 ***Perf. 14x13½***
1799 A979 5.80s multi 5.75 5.50

Endangered Birds — A980

Designs: No. 1800, 10s, Loddigesia mirabilis. No. 1801, 10s, Cinclodes palliatus.

2011, Oct. 28 **Litho.** ***Perf. 13½x14***
1800-1801 A980 Set of 2 19.50 19.00

Christmas A981

2011, Nov. 1
1802 A981 5.50s multi 5.50 5.25

America Issue — A982

Designs: No. 1803, 10s, Lion's head mailbox. No. 1804, 10s, Red rectangular mailbox.

2011, Nov. 2 ***Perf. 14x13½***
1803-1804 A982 Set of 2 19.50 19.00

Martín Chambi (1891-1973), Photographer — A983

2011, Nov. 4
1805 A983 5.20s multi 5.25 5.00

Peruvian Coffee — A984

2011, Nov. 10 ***Perf. 13½x14***
1806 A984 6.60s multi 6.50 6.25

Summit of South American and Arab Countries — A985

2011, Dec. 2 ***Perf. 14x13½***
1807 A985 8.40s multi 8.25 8.00

Diplomatic Relations Between Peru and Australia, 50th Anniv. — A986

No. 1808: a, Sloth (oso perezoso). b, Koala.

2013, Mar. 1
1808 A986 3.30s Horiz. pair, #a-b 7.25 6.75

Diplomatic Relations Between Peru and India, 50th Anniv. — A987

No. 1809: a, Machu Picchu, Peru. b, Taj Mahal, India.

2013, Mar. 19
1809 A987 3.60s Horiz. pair, #a-b 7.75 7.25

Diplomatic Relations Between Peru and South Korea, 50th Anniv. — A988

No. 1810: a, 2.50s, Machu Picchu, Peru. b, 3s, Seongsan Ilchulbong, South Korea.

2013, Apr. 1 ***Perf. 13½x14***
1810 A988 Horiz. pair, #a-b 6.25 5.75

See South Korea No. 2399.

Service and Maintenance for Peru Air Force, 80th Anniv. — A989

2013, June 13 Litho. ***Perf. 14x13½***
1811 A989 5.50s multi 5.25 5.00

World Record Black Marlin Catch, 60th Anniv. — A990

Designs: No. 1812, 2.50s, Alfred C. Glassell, Jr. and 1,560-pound black marlin. No. 1813, 2.50s, Fishing boat "Miss Texas," horiz.

Perf. 14x13½, 13½x14
2013, Aug. 2 Litho.
Stamps + Label
1812-1813 A990 Set of 2 5.25 4.75

New Year 2013 (Year of the Dragon) A991

No. 1814: a, Chinese Zodiac wheel and Chinese character for "dragon." b, Dragon figurine.

2013, Aug. 15 Litho. ***Perf. 14x13½***
1814 A991 6s Horiz. pair, #a-b 12.50 12.00

Diplomatic Relations Between Peru and Japan, 140th Anniv. — A992

No. 1815: a, Machu Picchu, Peru. b, Kinkaku-ji, Japan.

2013, Aug. 21 Litho. ***Perf. 14x13½***
1815 A992 6s Horiz. pair, #a-b 13.00 12.00

Santa Teresa Convent, Arequipa — A993

2013, Aug. 23 Litho. ***Perf. 14x13½***
1816 A993 6s multi 6.00 5.75

Anthropomorphic Monoliths, Ancash Archaeological Park and Museum — A994

2013, Aug. 28 Litho. ***Perf. 13½***
1817 A994 6s multi 6.00 5.75

Benavidesite A995

2013, Aug. 29 Litho. ***Perf. 13½x14***
1818 A995 8s multi 7.75 7.50

Federico Villareal National University, 50th Anniv. — A996

2013, Sept. 5 ***Perf. 13½x14***
1819 A996 4s multi 4.25 4.00

Souvenir Sheet

Inkayacu Paracasensis and Its Fossilized Remains — A997

Litho. (With Foil Application in Sheet Margin)
2013, Sept. 12 ***Perf. 14x13½***
1820 A997 10s multi 9.50 9.25

Diocese of Cuzco, 475th Anniv. — A998

2013, Sept. 13 Litho. ***Perf. 14x13½***
1821 A998 4s multi 4.25 4.00

Intl. Year of Quinoa — A999

2013, Sept. 27 Litho. ***Perf. 13½x14***
1822 A999 5.50s multi 5.50 5.25

Souvenir Sheet

Santo Domingo Convent and Qorikancha Incan Temple, Cuzco — A1000

2013, Sept. 27 Litho. ***Perf. 14x13½***
1823 A1000 10s multi 9.50 9.25

Souvenir Sheet

Temples of the Sun and Moon Archaeological Sites — A1001

2013, Sept. 27 Litho. ***Perf. 13½x14***
1824 A1001 10s multi 9.50 9.25

Souvenir Sheet

Five-Peseta Coin of Peru From 1880 — A1002

No. 1825: a, Reverse (head of Ceres). b, Obverse (coat of arms).

2013, Oct. 1 Litho. ***Perf. 14x13½***
1825 A1002 5s Sheet of 2, #a-b 11.50 11.00

Souvenir Sheet

1863 Centavo Coins A1003

No. 1826 — Reverse of: a, One-centavo coin. b, Two-centavo coin.

2013, Oct. 1 Litho. ***Perf. 14x13½***
1826 A1003 6s Sheet of 2, #a-b 11.50 11.00

Museum of Natural History, Lima, 95th Anniv. — A1004

2013, Oct. 4 Litho. ***Perf. 14x13½***
1827 A1004 4s multi 4.25 4.00

Souvenir Sheet

Chahuaytiri Rock Paintings — A1005

2013, Oct. 11 Litho. ***Perf. 14x13½***
1828 A1005 10s multi 9.50 9.25

Souvenir Sheet

Canaanimys Maquiensis and Its Fossilized Remains — A1006

Litho. (With Foil Application in Sheet Margin)
2013, Oct. 12 ***Perf. 14x13½***
1829 A1006 10s multi 9.75 9.50

Miniature Sheet

Eagles A1007

No. 1830: a, Harpia harpyja. b, Morphus guianensis. c, Spizaetus ornatus. d, Spizaetus isidori.

Litho. (With Foil Application in Sheet Margin)
2013, Oct. 14 ***Perf. 14x13½***
1830 A1007 3s Sheet of 4, #a-d 13.00 12.00

Miniature Sheet

Butterflies — A1008

No. 1831: a, Hypanartia splendida. b, Isanthrene flavizonata. c, Protesilaus glaucolaus. d, Histioea peruana.

2013, Oct. 24 Litho. ***Perf. 13½x14***
1831 A1008 4s Sheet of 4, #a-d 16.50 16.00

Miniature Sheet

Hummingbirds — A1009

No. 1832: a, Heliangelus regalis. b, Myrtis fanny. c, Taphrolesbia griseiventris. d, Rhodopis vesper.

2013, Oct. 31 Litho. ***Perf. 13½x14***
1832 A1009 5s Sheet of 4, #a-d 20.00 19.00

Canonization of St. Martin de Porres, 50th Anniv. (in 2012) — A1010

2013, Nov. 4 Litho. ***Perf. 13½x14***
1833 A1010 4s multi 4.25 4.00

Diplomatic Relations Between Peru and Russia, 45th Anniv. — A1011

No. 1834: a, Machu Picchu, Peru. b, Kizhi Pogost, Russia.

2013, Nov. 4 Litho. ***Perf. 13½x14***
1834 A1011 6s Horiz. pair, #a-b 12.50 12.00

America Issue A1012

No. 1835: a, Animals and corn stalk from Myth of the Garden of Gold. b, Sun God from Myth of the Garden of Gold. c, Eyes of 14 people, face paint above 5th eye on top row. d, Eyes of 14 people, face paint below 3rd and 4th eyes on bottom row.

2013, Nov. 4 Litho. ***Perf. 13½x14***
1835 A1012 4s Block of 4, #a-d, + label 17.00 16.00

Souvenir Sheet

Boat Dock on Amazon River A1013

2013, Nov. 11 Litho. ***Perf. 13½x14***
1836 A1013 8s multi 7.75 7.50

Miniature Sheet

Election of Pope Francis A1014

No. 1837: a, Pope Francis, hands not visible. b, Pope Francis, hand visible. c, St. Peter's Square. d, Pope Benedict XVI.

2013, Nov. 13 Litho. ***Perf. 14x13½***
1837 A1014 6s Sheet of 4, #a-d 23.50 22.50

Souvenir Sheet

Walls Built by the Incas, Cuzco A1015

2013, Nov. 13 Litho. ***Perf. 14x13½***
1838 A1015 10s multi 9.50 9.25

A1016

Winning Designs in 6th Children's Art Contest — A1017

2013, Dec. 2 Litho. ***Perf. 13½x14***
1839 A1016 4s multi 4.00 3.75

Perf. 14x13½
1840 A1017 4s multi 4.00 3.75

A1018

Winning Designs in 7th Children's Art Contest — A1019

2013, Dec. 6 Litho. ***Perf. 13½x14***
1841 A1018 4s multi 3.75 3.50
1842 A1019 4s multi 3.75 3.50

Resolution of Ecuador-Peru Border Dispute, 15th Anniv. — A1020

2014, Jan. 30 Litho. ***Perf. 14x13½***
1843 A1020 8s multi 8.00 7.75

Commercial Accords Between Peru, Colombia and the European Union — A1021

2014, Feb. 28 Litho. ***Perf. 14x13½***
1844 A1021 9.50s multi 9.50 9.25

A1022

Design: Captain José Abelardo Quiñones Gonzales (1914-41), military hero.

2014, Apr. 8 Litho. ***Perf. 13½x14***
1845 A1022 3.80s multi 4.25 4.00

Miguel Grau Seminario (1834-79), Admiral — A1023

2014, July 23 Litho. ***Perf. 14x13½***
1846 A1023 6s multi 5.50 5.25

Peruvian Institute of the Sea, 50th Anniv. — A1024

2014, Sept. 5 Litho. ***Perf. 13½x14***
1847 A1024 3.80s multi 3.75 3.50

Caballito de Totoro (Traditional Reed Watercraft) — A1025

2014, Sept. 17 Litho. ***Perf. 14x13½***
1848 A1025 7s multi 6.50 6.25

Tambomachay Temple Archaeological Site — A1026

2014, Sept. 19 Litho. ***Perf. 14x13½***
1849 A1026 6s multi 5.50 5.25

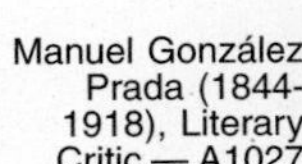

Manuel González Prada (1844-1918), Literary Critic — A1027

2014, Sept. 22 Litho. ***Perf. 13½x14***
1850 A1027 7s multi 6.50 6.25

Kotosh Temple Archaeological Site — A1028

2014, Sept. 24 Litho. ***Perf. 14x13½***
1851 A1028 6s multi 5.50 5.25

2014 Canonization of Popes — A1029

Designs: No. 1852, 7s, Pope John XXIII. No. 1853, 7s, Pope John Paul II.

2014, Sept. 26 Litho. ***Perf. 14x13½***
1852-1853 A1029 Set of 2 15.50 15.00

Musical Instruments A1030

Designs: No. 1854, 6s, Botella silbadora. No. 1855, 6s, Antara (pan flute).

2014, Sept. 30 Litho. ***Perf. 13½x14***
1854-1855 A1030 Set of 2 11.00 10.50

Souvenir Sheet

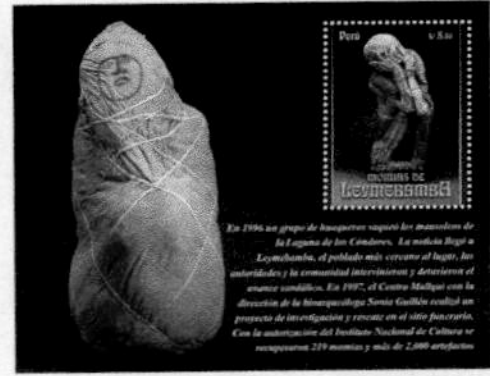

Leymebamba Mummy — A1031

2014, Sept. 30 Litho. ***Perf. 14x13½***
1856 A1031 8s multi 7.25 7.00

William Shakespeare (1564-1616), Writer — A1032

2014, Oct. 3 Litho. ***Perf. 14x13½***
1857 A1032 6s multi 5.50 5.25

Viceroys Type of 2006

No. 1858: a, Agustín de Jáuregui y Aldecoa (1711-84). b, Teodoro de Croix (1730-92). c, Francisco Gil de Taboada y Lemus (1736-1809). d, Ambrosio O'Higgins (1720-1801).

2014, Oct. 7 Litho. ***Perf. 14x13½***
1858 A767 6.50s Block of 4, #a-d, + label 24.00 23.00

Souvenir Sheet

Forensic Facial Reconstruction of the Priestess of Chornancap — A1033

2014, Oct. 13 Litho. ***Perf. 14x13½***
1859 A1033 8s multi 7.25 7.00

Dances — A1034

Designs: No. 1860, 8s, La Wuallata. No. 1861, 8s, Carnaval Cusqueño.

2014, Oct. 17 Litho. *Perf. 13½x14*
1860-1861 A1034 Set of 2 17.50 17.00

Miniature Sheet

Birds
A1035

No. 1862: a, Crotophaga sulcirostris. b, Xenospingus concolor. c, Burhinus superciliaris. d, Glaucidium peruanum.

2014, Oct. 17 Litho. *Perf. 13½x14*
1862 A1035 9s Sheet of 4, #a-d 33.50 32.50

Miniature Sheet

Trees
A1036

No. 1863: a, Swietenia macrophylla. b, Cedrela fissilis. c, Ceiba pentandra. d, Prosopis pallida.

2014, Oct. 20 Litho. *Perf. 14x13½*
1863 A1036 9.50s Sheet of 4, #a-d 33.50 32.50

Iquitos, 150th Anniv. — A1037

2014, Oct. 23 Litho. *Perf. 13½x14*
1864 A1037 6s multi 5.50 5.25

Barranco District, 140th Anniv. — A1038

2014, Oct. 26 Litho. *Perf. 14x13½*
1865 A1038 7s multi 5.50 5.25

Miniature Sheet

Mammals — A1039

No. 1866: a, Panthera onca. b, Dinomys branickii. c, Tapirus pinchaque. d, Leopardus jacobitus.

2014, Nov. 3 Litho. *Perf. 14x13½*
1866 A1039 11s Sheet of 4, #a-d 35.00 34.00

The inscription on No. 1866d is incorrect. The stamp shows Leopardus colocolo.

Souvenir Sheet

Sycorax Peruensis Preserved in Amber — A1040

Litho. (With Foil Application in Sheet Margin)

2014, Nov. 5 *Perf. 14x13½*
1867 A1040 8s multi 8.25 8.00

Minerals — A1041

Designs: 6s, Quartz (Cuarzo). 8s, Jasper (Jaspe).

2014, Nov. 10 Litho. *Perf. 13½x14*
1868-1869 A1041 Set of 2 13.00 12.50

Christmas — A1042

2014, Nov. 14 Litho. *Perf. 14x13½*
1870 A1042 6s multi 5.50 5.25

Parque de las Leyendas Zoo, 50th Anniv. — A1043

No. 1871: a, Cebuella pygmaea. b, Ateles belzebuth.

2014, Nov. 17 Litho. *Perf. 14x13½*
1871 A1043 9.50s Horiz. pair, #a-b 17.00 16.50

Serpost (Peruvian Postal Service), 20th Anniv. — A1044

2014, Nov. 22 Litho. *Perf. 13½x14*
1872 A1044 6s multi 5.50 5.25

Miniature Sheet

2014 World Cup Soccer Championships, Brazil — A1045

No. 1873: a, Mascot Fuleco. b, Emblem. c, Soccer player and ball. d, World Cup Trophy.

2014, Nov. 28 Litho. *Perf. 13½x14*
1873 A1045 3.80s Sheet of 4, #a-d 15.00 14.00

Pancho Fierro (1807-79), Painter — A1046

No. 1874 — Paintings: a, El Soldado y la Rabona. b, Fraile de la Buena Muerte. c, El Notario Público. d, La Hermana de la Caridad.

2014, Dec. 1 Litho. *Perf. 14x13½*
1874 A1046 10s Sheet of 4, #a-d 36.00 35.00

Famous Men — A1047

Designs: No. 1875, 9s, Mariano Melgar (1790-1815), poet. No. 1876, 9s, José Olaya Balandra (1782-1823), hero in War of Independence.

2014, Dec. 3 Litho. *Perf. 14x13½*
1875-1876 A1047 Set of 2 16.50 16.00

America Issue.

Chinese Zodiac Animals A1048

No. 1877: a, Snake. b, Horse.

2014, Dec. 5 Litho. *Perf. 14x13½*
1877 A1048 6.50s Horiz. pair, #a-b 12.00 11.50

Souvenir Sheet

1898 Gold Libra Coin A1049

No. 1878: a, Obverse (Anverso). b, Reverse (Reverso).

2014, Dec. 9 Litho. *Perf. 14x13½*
1878 A1049 10s multi 18.00 17.50

Battle of Ayacucho, 190th Anniv. — A1050

2014, Dec. 9 Litho. *Perf. 13½x14*
1879 A1050 7s multi 6.50 6.25

Archbiship Loayza National Hospital, 90th Anniv. — A1051

2014, Dec. 10 Litho. *Perf. 13½x14*
1880 A1051 3.80s multi 3.75 3.50

Miniature Sheet

Carriages -- A1052

No. 1881: a, Front view of covered carriage. b, Open-air carriage with red seats. c, Side view of covered carriage. d, Open-air carriage with white seats.

2014, Dec. 15 Litho. *Perf. 13½x14*
1881 A1052 11s Sheet of 4, #a-d 35.00 34.00

2016 Asia-Pacific Economic Cooperation Meetings, Peru — A1053

2016, Nov. 17 Litho. *Perf. 14x13½*
1882 A1053 10s multi 11.25 11.00

Diplomatic Relations Between Peru and People's Republic of China, 45th Anniv. — A1054

No. 1883 — Flags of Peru and People's Republic of China and: a, Machu Picchu. b, Temple of Heaven, Beijing.

2016, Nov. 17 Litho. *Perf. 14x13½*
1883 A1054 4s Horiz. pair, #a-b 7.75 7.25

Diplomatic Relations Between Peru and Malaysia, 30th Anniv. — A1055

No. 1884 — Flags of Peru and Malaysia, handshake and: a, Mt. Kinabalu, Malaysia. b, Machu Picchu.

2016, Nov. 17 Litho. *Perf. 14x13½*
1884 A1055 9s Horiz. pair, #a-b 15.00 14.50

Christmas — A1056

2016, Nov. 17 Litho. *Perf. 14x13½*
1885 A1056 6.50s multi 5.50 5.25

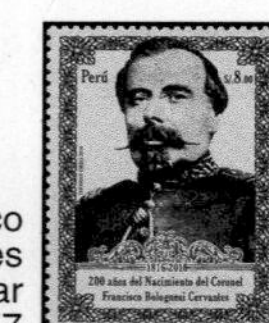

Colonel Francisco Bolognesi Cervantes (1816-80), Hero in War of the Pacific — A1057

2016, Dec. 19 Litho. *Perf. 14x13½*
1886 A1057 8s multi 3.75 3.50

Cajamarca, 30th Anniv. on Organization of American States Cultural and Historical Heritage List — A1058

No. 1887: a, Cerro Santa Apolonia. b, Santa Catalina Cathedral.

2016, Dec. 21 Litho. *Perf. 13½x14*
1887 A1058 3s Horiz. pair, #a-b 6.00 5.50

Banco de la Nación, 50th Anniv. — A1059

2016, Dec. 22 Litho. *Perf. 13½x14*
1888 A1059 10s multi 8.50 8.25

Dr. Carlos Monge Medrano (1884-1970), Founder of National Institute of Andean Biology — A1060

2016, Dec. 23 Litho. *Perf. 13½x14*
1889 A1060 10s multi 8.25 8.00

National Institute of Andean Biology, 85th anniv.

Office of the National Prosecutor, 35th Anniv. — A1061

2016, Dec. 26 Litho. *Perf. 14x13½*
1890 A1061 10s multi 8.50 8.25

World Autism Awareness Day — A1062

2016, Dec. 28 Litho. *Perf. 13½x14*
1891 A1062 10s multi 11.25 11.00

Viceroys of Peru — A1063

Designs: No. 1892, 5s, Gabriel de Avilés y del Fierro (c. 1735-1810). No. 1893, 5s, José Fernando de Abascal y Sousa (1743-1821). No. 1894, 5s, Joaquín de la Pezuela (1761-1830). No. 1895, 5s, José de la Serna e Hinojosa (1770-1832).

2017, Jan. 2 Litho. *Perf. 14x13½*
1892-1895 A1063 Set of 4 18.50 17.50

Dated 2016. Compare with type A767.

Pre-Hispanic Musical Instruments A1064

Designs: No. 1896, 6.50s, Huayllaquepa de Punkurí. No. 1897, 6.50s, Antara de Caña de Caral.

2017, Jan. 4 Litho. *Perf. 13½x14*
1896-1897 A1064 Set of 2 11.50 11.00

Dated 2016.

Dominican Order, 800th Anniv. (in 2016) — A1065

2017, Jan. 6 Litho. *Perf. 14x13½*
1898 A1065 10s multi 8.50 8.25

Dated 2016.

Flora — A1066

Designs: No. 1899, 4s, Rhizophora mangle. No. 1900, 4s, Azorella compacta. No. 1901, 4s, Cinchona pubescens. No. 1902, 4s, Puya raimondii.

2017, Jan. 6 Litho. *Perf. 13½x14*
1899-1902 A1066 Set of 4 14.50 13.50

Dated 2016.

Pelagornis and Its Fossilized Remains — A1067

2017, Jan. 10 Litho. *Perf. 13½x14*
1903 A1067 10s multi 8.50 8.25

Dated 2016.

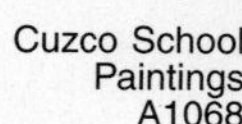

Cuzco School Paintings A1068

Designs: No. 1904, 6.50s, San Cristobal. No. 1905, 6.50s, Patrón Santiago. No. 1906, 6.50s, Paso de las Ordenes Religiosas. No. 1907, 6.50s, El Obispo Mollinedo Llevando la Custodia.

2017, Jan. 12 Litho. *Perf. 13½x14*
1904-1907 A1068 Set of 4 23.00 22.00

Dated 2016.

1879 20-Centavo Coin — A1069

Designs: No. 1908, 10s, Obverse (anverso). No. 1909, 10s, Reverse (reverso).

2017, Jan. 16 Litho. *Perf. 14x13½*
1908-1909 A1069 Set of 2 17.50 17.00

National Institute of Health, 120th Anniv. (in 2016) — A1070

2017, Jan. 17 Litho. *Perf. 13½x14*
1910 A1070 10s multi 8.50 8.25

Dated 2016.

Chess A1071

No. 1911: a, Black bishop (alfil). b, White pawn (peón).

2017, Jan. 19 Litho. *Perf. 14x13½*
1911 A1071 4s Horiz. pair, #a-b 7.75 7.25

Dated 2016.

Campaign Against Human Trafficking A1072

Designs: No. 1912, 9s, Photographs of people in blue heart. No. 1913, 9s, Raised hands and map, vert.

Perf. 13½x14, 14x13½
2017, Jan. 23 Litho.
1912-1913 A1072 Set of 2 15.50 15.00

America Issue. Dated 2016.

Pisco Sour Drink, Cent. (in 2016) A1073

No. 1914: a, Pisco Sour in glass, Pisco Sour bottle. b, Grapes and glass of Pisco Sour.

2017, Jan. 26 Litho. *Perf. 14x13½*
1914 A1073 9s Horiz. pair, #a-b 15.50 15.00

Dated 2016.

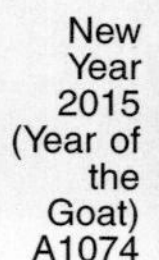

New Year 2015 (Year of the Goat) A1074

No. 1915: a, Ring of Chinese Zodiac animals, Chinese character for "goat." b, Goat.

2017, Jan. 27 Litho. *Perf. 14x13½*
1915 A1074 6.50s Horiz. pair, #a-b 11.00 10.50

Dated 2016.

New Year 2016 (Year of the Monkey) A1075

No. 1916: a, Monkeys. b, Ring of Chinese Zodiac animals, Chinese character for "monkey."

2017, Jan. 27 Litho. *Perf. 14x13½*
1916 A1075 6.50s Horiz. pair, #a-b 12.00 11.50

Dated 2016.

Fish — A1076

Designs: No. 1917, 6.50s, Piaractus brachypomus. No. 1918, 6.50s, Anisotremus interruptus. No. 1919, 6.50s, Lebiasina bimaculata. No. 1920, 6.50s, Panaque schaeferi.

2017, Feb. 1 Litho. *Perf. 13½x14*
1917-1920 A1076 Set of 4 23.00 22.00

Dated 2016.

Poisonous Frogs — A1077

Designs: No. 1921, 8s, Excidobates mysteriosus. No. 1922, 8s, Ameerega parvula. No. 1923, 8s, Ranitomeya fantastica. No. 1924, 8s, Ameerega pongoensis.

2017, Feb. 6 Litho. *Perf. 13½x14*
1921-1924 A1077 Set of 4 28.00 27.00

Dated 2016.

Peruvian-Chinese Food — A1078

Flags of People's Republic of China and Peru and: No. 1925, 3s, Sopa wantan (wonton soup). No. 1926, 3s, Arroz chaufa (rice). No. 1927, 3s, Chi Jau Cuy (guinea pig). No. 1928, 3s, Tallarín Saltado Taipa (noodles and vegetables).

2017, Feb. 8 Litho. *Perf. 13½x14*
1925-1928 A1078 Set of 4 12.00 11.00

Dated 2016.

Independence of Peru, 200th Anniv. (in 2021) — A1079

No. 1929 — Heroes: a, Juan José Crespo (1747-1812), leader of Huánuco Rebellion. b, Francisco de Zela (1768-1819), leader of Tacna Revolution. c, Mateo Pumacahua (1740-1815), leader of Cuzco Rebellion.

2017, Feb. 10 Litho. *Perf. 14x13½*
1929 A1079 3s Horiz. strip of 3, #a-c 8.50 7.75

Dated 2016.

Awajún Man — A1080

2017, Feb. 13 Litho. *Perf. 14x13½*
1930 A1080 5s multi 4.50 4.25

Dated 2016.

Vultur Gryphus A1081

Podocnemis Unifilis A1082

2017, June Litho. *Perf. 14x13½*
1931 A1081 5s multi 4.50 4.25
Perf. 13½x14
1932 A1082 5s multi 4.50 4.25
Dated 2016.

National Institute for the Defense of Competition and Protection of Intellectual Property (INDECOPI), 25th Anniv. — A1083

2017, Nov. 21 Litho. *Perf. 13x13¼*
1933 A1083 6.50s multi 5.75 5.50

Miniature Sheet

Visit to Peru of Pope Francis in 2018 A1084

No. 1934 — Pope Francis: a, In map of Peru. b, Waving, bright green panel, arms of Puerto Maldonado. c, Waving, blue panel, arms of Trujillo. d, Touching child, orange panel, arms of Lima.

2017, Nov. 29 Litho. *Perf. 13¼x13*
1934 A1084 4s Sheet of 4, #a-d 15.00 14.00

Apparition of the Virgin Mary at Fatima, Portugal, Cent. (in 2017) — A1085

2018, Jan. 5 Litho. *Perf. 13x13¼*
1935 A1085 3s multi 3.00 2.75
Dated 2017.

Holy Cross of Motupe — A1086

2018, Jan. 8 Litho. *Perf. 13¼x13*
1936 A1086 6.50s multi 5.75 5.50
Christmas. Dated 2017.

St. Rose of Lima (1586-1617) — A1087

No. 1937: a, Religious statue, roses. b, St. Rose of Lima, drawing of Lima.

2018, Jan. 10 Litho. *Perf. 13x13¼*
1937 A1087 6.50s Horiz. pair, #a-b 11.50 11.00
Dated 2017.

Pontifical Catholic University of Peru, Cent. (in 2017) — A1088

No. 1938: a, Star. b, Ship.

2018, Jan. 10 Litho. *Perf. 13¼x13*
1938 A1088 4s Horiz. pair, #a-b 7.50 7.00
Dated 2017.

Lima Central Post Office, 120th Anniv. — A1089

2018, Jan. 11 Litho. *Perf. 13x13¼*
1939 A1089 2s multi 2.25 2.00
Dated 2017.

International Decade for People of African Descent — A1090

2018, Jan. 12 Litho. *Perf. 13¼x13*
1940 A1090 2s multi 2.25 2.00
Dated 2017.

Pampa Galeras-Bárbara D'Achille National Reserve, 50th Anniv. — A1091

2018, Jan. 13 Litho. *Perf. 13x13¼*
1941 A1091 2s multi 2.25 2.00
Dated 2017.

Winning Art in "Healthy Sentiments and Values" Stamp Design Contest — A1092

2018, Jan. 13 Litho. *Perf. 13x13¼*
1942 A1092 2s multi 2.25 2.00
America issue. Dated 2017.

Inti Raymi Festival, 50th Anniv. (in 2017) — A1093

2018, Jan. 15 Litho. *Perf. 13¼x13*
1943 A1093 3s multi 3.00 2.75
Dated 2017.

Souvenir Sheet

International Year of Sustainable Tourism for Development — A1094

No. 1944: a, Amazilia viridicauda. b, Pipreola pulchra.

2018, Jan. 15 Litho. *Perf. 13¼x13*
1944 A1094 8s Sheet of 2, #a-b 14.00 13.00
Dated 2017.

A1095

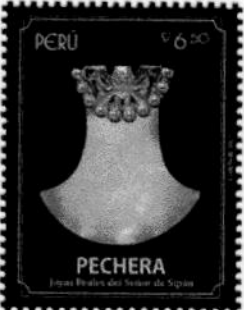
Sipán Royal Jewelry — A1096

2018, Jan. 16 Litho. *Perf. 13x13¼*
1945 A1095 6.50s multi 5.75 5.50
Perf. 13¼x13
1946 A1096 6.50s multi 5.75 5.50
Dated 2017.

Miniature Sheet

Ancash Tourism A1097

No. 1947: a, Sechin Archaeological Site, Casma. b, Jancapampa, Pomabamba. c, Hatun Machay, Recuay. d, Yayno Archaeological Site, Pomabamba.

2018, Jan. 18 Litho. *Perf. 13x13¼*
1947 A1097 3s Sheet of 4, #a-d 12.00 11.00
Dated 2017.

Steatornis Caripensis A1098

Hippocamelus Antisensis A1099

2018, Jan. 19 Litho. *Perf. 13x13¼*
1948 A1098 9s multi 7.75 7.50
Perf. 13¼x13
1949 A1099 9s multi 7.75 7.50
Dated 2017.

Souvenir Sheet

Insects A1100

No. 1950: a, Sicophion yana. b, Ancognatha corcuerai.

2018, Jan. 22 Litho. *Perf. 13¼x13*
1950 A1100 9s Sheet of 2, #a-b 15.50 15.00
Dated 2017.

Miniature Sheet

Cuzco School Paintings A1101

No. 1951: a, Virgen de Belén. b, La Ultima Cena. c, San Sebastián. d, Procesión de San Pedro.

2018, Jan. 26 Litho. *Perf. 13x13¼*
1951 A1101 6.50s Sheet of 4, #a-d 23.50 22.50
Dated 2017.

Souvenir Sheet

Minerals A1102

No. 1952: a, Plata (silver). b, Oro (gold).

2018, Jan. 29 Litho. *Perf. 13x13¼*
1952 A1102 10s Sheet of 2, #a-b 17.50 17.00
Dated 2017.

Outdoor Activities in Apurímac Region — A1103

No. 1953: a, Cyclist on Cerro Quisapata. b, Kayaker on Rio Pachachaca.

2018, Jan. 31 Litho. *Perf. 13x13¼*
1953 A1103 10s Horiz. pair, #a-b 17.50 17.00
Dated 2017.

Great Cave, Huayna Picchu A1104

No. 1954: a, Corner of wall. b, Three doorways.

2018, Feb. 2 Litho. *Perf. 13x13¼*
1954 A1104 10s Horiz. pair, #a-b 17.50 17.00
Dated 2017.

America Issue — A1105

Holy Week decorations in: No. 1955, 10s, Ayacucho. No. 1956, 10s, Tarma.

2018, Feb. 5 Litho. *Perf. 13x13¼*
1955-1956 A1105 Set of 2 17.50 17.00

Dated 2017.

Souvenir Sheet

Friendship Between Peru and Dominican Republic — A1106

No. 1957: a, Ramón Castilla y Marquesado (1797-1867), 20th President of Peru, and flag of Peru. b, Gregorio Luperón (1839-97), 20th President of Dominican Republic, flag of Dominican Republic.

2018, Feb. 7 Litho. *Perf. 13x13¼*
1957 A1106 10s Sheet of 2, #a-b 17.50 17.00

Dated 2017. See Dominican Republic No. 1626.

New Year 2017 (Year of the Rooster) A1107

No. 1958: a, Rooster and ring of Chinese zodiac animals. b, Two roosters.

2018, Feb. 9 Litho. *Perf. 13¼x13*
1958 A1107 10s Horiz. pair, #a-b 17.50 17.00

Dated 2017.

Independence of Peru, 200th Anniv. (in 2021) — A1108

No. 1959: a, Crossing of the Andes, 1817. b, First Peruvian coat of arms. c, Battle of Ayacucho, 1824.

2018, Feb. 12 Litho. *Perf. 13x13¼*
1959 Horiz. strip of 3 26.00 25.00
a.-c. A1108 10s Any single 8.00 7.00

Dated 2017.

Miniature Sheet

Fish A1109

No. 1960: a, Manta birostris. b, Sphyrna zygaena. c, Hippocampus ingens. d, Strongylura exilis.

2018, Feb. 12 Litho. *Perf. 13x13¼*
1960 A1109 3s Sheet of 4, #a-d 12.00 11.00

Dated 2017.

Souvenir Sheet

Peruvian Gastronomy — A1110

No. 1961: a, Puca picante. b, Sopa menestrón. c, Cebiche de paiche con camu camu.

2018, Feb. 14 Litho. *Perf. 13x13¼*
1961 A1110 10s Sheet of 3, #a-c 26.00 25.00

Dated 2017.

Epidendrum Nocturnum A1111

2018, Feb. 16 Litho. *Perf. 13x13¼*
1962 A1111 5s multi 4.75 4.50

Dated 2017.

Traditional Dances — A1112

Designs: No. 1963, 10s, Shacshas dancers. No. 1964, 10s, Pallas dancers, vert.

Perf. 13x13¼, 13¼x13
2018, Feb. 19 Litho.
1963-1964 A1112 Set of 2 17.50 17.00

Dated 2017.

Pedro Pablo Kuczynski Godard, 66th President of Peru — A1113

2018, Feb. 20 Litho. *Perf. 13¼x13*
1965 A1113 6s multi 5.50 5.25

Dated 2017.

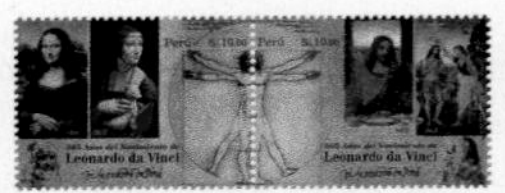

Leonardo da Vinci (1452-1519), Painter — A1114

No. 1966 — Half of Vitruvian Man and: a, Mona Lisa, and Lady with an Ermine. b, The Last Supper, and The Baptism of Christ.

2018, Feb. 20 Litho. *Perf. 13x13¼*
1966 A1114 10s Horiz. pair, #a-b 17.50 17.00

Dated 2017.

Cacao Pods A1115

Cochineal A1116

2018, Feb. 20 Litho. *Perf. 13x13¼*
1967 A1115 10s multi 8.75 8.50

Perf. 13¼x13
1968 A1116 10s multi 8.75 8.50

Peruvian exports. Dated 2017.

2018 World Cup Soccer Championships, Russia — A1117

Peruvian National Soccer Team A1118

No. 1969: a, 3s, Zabivaka, 2018 World Cup mascot. b, 3s, World Cup. c, 3.50s, Emblem of 2018 World Cup. d, 3.50s, Soccer player kicking ball.

No. 1970: a, Emblem of national soccer team. b, Team members, goaltender in yellow shirt at right. c, Team members, goaltender in blue and black shirt at right. d, Players in huddle.

2018, May 22 Litho. *Perf. 13¼x13*
1969 A1117 Sheet of 4, #a-d 18.50 17.50

Perf. 13x13¼
1970 A1118 6.50s Sheet of 4, #a-d 31.00 30.00

Nos. 1969-1970 were sold together for 50s, or individually for 20s and 35s, respectively.

10th World Potato Congress, Cusco — A1119

No. 1971: a, Hands holding potato and potato plant, Machu Picchu. b, Machu Picchu.

2018, May 23 Litho. *Perf. 13x13¼*
1971 A1119 4s Horiz. pair, #a-b 7.50 7.00

Pres. Ollanta Moisés Humala Tasso — A1120

2018, June 21 Litho. *Perf. 13¼x13*
1972 A1120 10s multi 8.50 8.25

Dated 2017.

Ernest Malinowski (1818-99), Builder of Ferrocarril Central Andino — A1121

No. 1973: a, Malinowski. b, Train and bridge of Ferrocarril Central Andino.

2019, Jan. 28 Litho. *Perf. 13¼x13*
1973 A1121 6.50s Horiz. pair, #a-b 11.50 11.00

Dated 2018.

National School of Fine Arts, Lima, Cent. (in 2018) A1122

No. 1974 — Half of building, with "1918-2018" at: a, LL. b, LR.

2019, Jan. 31 Litho. *Perf. 13¼x13*
1974 A1122 5s Horiz. pair, #a-b 9.00 8.50

Dated 2018.

Television Broadcasting in Peru, 60th Anniv. (in 2018) — A1123

2019, Feb. 4 Litho. *Perf. 13¼x13*
1975 A1123 5s multi 4.50 4.25

Dated 2018.

Lima Regional Office of the International Civil Aviation Organization, 70th Anniv. — A1124

2019, Feb. 8 Litho. *Perf. 13x13¼*
1976 A1124 7s multi 5.90 5.60

Dated 2018.

Natural History Museum, Lima, Cent. (in 2018) — A1125

2019, Feb. 11 Litho. *Perf. 13x13¼*
1977 A1125 6s multi 5.25 5.00

Dated 2018.

Yoshitaro Amano (1898-1982), Founder of Amano Textile Museum — A1126

2019, Feb. 15 Litho. *Perf. 13x13¼*
1978 A1126 6.50s multi 5.75 5.50

Dated 2018.

Domesticated Animals — A1127

Designs: No. 1979, 6.50s, Dog. No. 1980, 6.50s, Cat.

2019, Feb. 18 Litho. *Perf. 13x13¼*
1979-1980 A1127 Set of 2 11.50 11.00

America issue. Dated 2018.

New Year 2018 (Year of the Dog) A1128

No. 1981: a, Dog and ring of Chinese zodiac animals. b, Two dogs.

2019, Feb. 22 Litho. *Perf. 13¼x13*
1981 A1128 6s Horiz. pair, #a-b 10.50 10.00

Dated 2018.

2018 Visit of Pope Francis to Peru — A1129

2019, Feb. 25 Litho. *Perf. 13x13¼*
1982 A1129 5s multi 4.50 4.25

Dated 2018.

2019 Pan American Games, Lima — A1130

No. 1983: a, Runners on track. b, Mascot.

2019, Feb. 28 Litho. *Perf. 13¼x13*
1983 A1130 6.50s Horiz. pair, #a-b 11.50 11.00

Dated 2018.

Independence of Peru, 200th Anniv. (in 2021) — A1131

No. 1984 — Paintings depicting: a, José, Vicente, and Mariano Angulo, leaders of 1814 Cuzco Rebellion. b, Manco Inca (1516-44), leader of 1536 rebellion against Spaniards.

2019, Mar. 1 Litho. *Perf. 13¼x13*
1984 A1131 6.50s Horiz. pair, #a-b 11.50 11.00

Dated 2018.

Christmas 2018 — A1132

2019, Mar. 4 Litho. *Perf. 13¼x13*
1985 A1132 6.50s multi 5.75 5.00

Dated 2018.

Souvenir Sheet

Ministry of Transport and Communications, 50th Anniv. — A1133

2020, Jan. 2 Litho. *Perf. 13x13¼*
1986 A1133 1.20s multi 1.60 1.40

Souvenir Sheet

Serpost (Peruvian Postal Service), 25th Anniv. (in 2019) — A1134

2020, Jan. 2 Litho. *Perf. 13x13¼*
1987 A1134 3.60s multi 3.60 3.25

Dated 2019.

Christmas 2019 — A1135

2020, Jan. 3 Litho. *Perf. 13¼x13*
1988 A1135 3.60s multi 3.60 3.25

Dated 2019.

Rupicola Peruvianus A1136

Vultur Gryphus A1137

Cantua Buxifolia A1138

Phragmipedium Kovachii A1139

Chavín Culture Stone Head A1140

Machu Picchu A1141

Perf. 14x13½, 13½x14 (#1992, 1994)
2020, Jan. 13 Litho.

1989	A1136	1.20s multi	1.10	1.10
1990	A1137	2.60s multi	2.50	2.50
1991	A1138	3.60s multi	3.60	3.50
1992	A1139	4s multi	3.90	3.75
1993	A1140	10s multi	9.50	9.40
1994	A1141	20s multi	19.00	18.75
	Nos. 1989-1994 (6)		39.60	39.00

Dated 2019.

Souvenir Sheet

National University of San Marcos Museum of Archaeology and Anthropology, Cent. (in 2019) — A1142

2020, Jan. 27 Litho. *Perf. 13x13¼*
1995 A1142 10s multi 9.75 9.40

Dated 2019.

Souvenir Sheet

Japanese Emigration to Peru, 120th Anniv. (in 2019) — A1143

2020, Jan. 29 Litho. *Perf. 13x13¼*
1996 A1143 7.60s multi 7.50 7.25

Dated 2019.

Souvenir Sheet

Leonardo da Vinci (1452-1519), Painter and Sculptor — A1144

2020, Jan. 30 Litho. *Perf. 13¼x13*
1997 A1144 4s multi 4.00 3.75

Dated 2019.

Express Mail Service, 20th Anniv. (in 2019) — A1145

2020, Feb. 3 Litho. *Perf. 13*
1998 A1145 2.60s multi 2.75 2.50

Dated 2019.

International Year of Indigenous Languages — A1146

2020, Feb. 6 Litho. *Perf. 13¼x13*
1999 A1146 2.60s multi 2.75 2.50

Dated 2019.

Souvenir Sheet

Mohandas K. Gandhi (1869-1948), Indian Nationalist Leader — A1147

2020, Feb. 7 Litho. *Perf. 13¼x13*
2000 A1147 10s multi 9.75 9.40

Dated 2019.

Day of Latin American Integration — A1148

2020, Feb. 17 Litho. *Perf. 13¼x13*
2001 A1148 1.20s multi 1.40 1.10

Dated 2019.

Souvenir Sheet

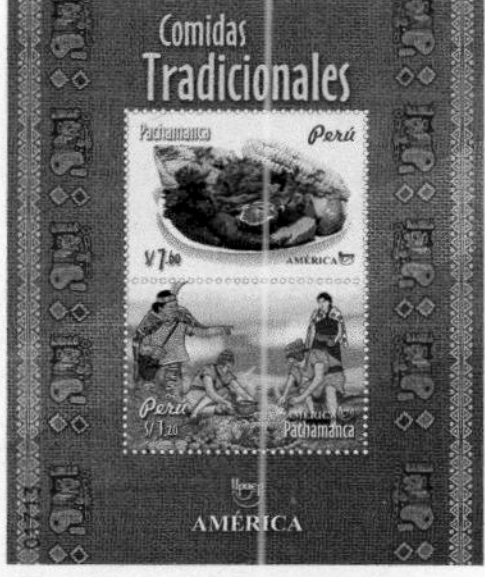

Traditional Foods — A1149

No. 2002: a, 1.20s, People preparing Pachamanca. b, 7.60s, Plate of Pachamanca.

2020, Feb. 26 Litho. *Perf. 13x13¼*
2002 A1149 Sheet of 2, #a-b 9.00 8.50

America issue.

Souvenir Sheet

New Year 2019 (Year of the Pig) A1150

2020, Feb. 24 Litho. *Perf. 13¼x13*
2003 A1150 10s multi 9.75 9.40

Dated 2019.

Peruvian Patriots A1151

No. 2004: a, José Manuel Valdés (1767-1843), physician. b, Matiaza Rimachi, heroine of 1821 Battle of Higos Urco. c, Ventura Ccalamaqui, Huamanga woman who exhorted troops to fight Spanish forces in 1814. d, Francisco Antonio de Zela y Arizaga (1768-1819), leader of 1810 Rebellion of Tacna.

2020, Feb. 28 Litho. *Perf. 13½*
2004 A1151 3.60s Block of 4, #a-d, + label 14.50 13.50

Souvenir Sheet

Historic Center of Moquegua — A1152

No. 2005: a, House of Ten Windows. b, Ornamental fountain.

2020, Mar. 6 Litho. *Perf. 13x13¼*
2005 A1152 3.60s Sheet of 2, #a-b 8.25 6.75

Souvenir Sheet

Machu Picchu Antarctic Scientific Station, 30th Anniv. (in 2019) A1153

2020, Apr. 17 Litho. *Perf. 13x13¼*
2006 A1153 1.20s multi 1.60 1.40

Dated 2019.

Javier Pérez de Cuéllar (1920-2020), Peruvian Prime Minister and United Nations Secretary-General A1154

2021, July 2 Litho. *Perf. 14¼x13½*
2007 A1154 3.60s multi 2.90 2.60

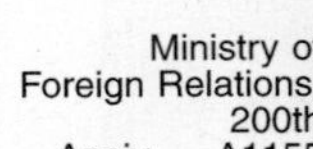

Ministry of Foreign Relations, 200th Anniv. — A1155

2021, July 2 Litho. *Perf. 13½x14¼*
2008 A1155 4s multi 3.00 2.90

Peruvian Navy, 200th Anniv. — A1156

2021, July 6 Litho. *Perf. 14¼x13½*
2009 A1156 4s multi 3.00 2.90

Brüning National Archaeological Museum, Lambayeque, Cent. — A1157

2021, July 9 Litho. *Perf. 13½x14¼*
2010 A1157 3.60s multi 2.90 2.60

Development Finance Corporation, 50th Anniv. — A1158

2021, July 12 Litho. *Perf. 13½x14¼*
2011 A1158 2.60s multi 2.10 1.90

Masonic Participation in Peruvian Independence Movement A1159

2021, July 15 Litho. *Perf. 13½x14¼*
2012 A1159 2.60s multi 2.10 1.90

National Library, 200th Anniv. — A1160

2021, July 16 Litho. *Perf. 14¼x13½*
2013 A1160 4s multi 3.00 2.90

A1161

Famous Peruvians — A1162

No. 2014: a, 1.20s, Túpac Amaru II (1738-81), leader of Inca rebellion against Spanish rulers. b, 1.20s, Micaela Bastidas (1744-81), wife of Túpac Amaru II and rebellion leader. c, 3.60s, Juan Santos Atahualpa (c. 1710-c. 1756), leader of Asháninka rebellion against Spanish rulers. d, 3.60s, Tomasa Tito Condemayta (1729-81), leader in Túpac Amaru II rebellion.

No. 2105: a, 1.20s, Mariano Melgar Valdivieso (1790-1815), poet and soldier in Peruvian War of Independence. b, 1.20s, María Andrea Parado de Bellido (1777-1822), executed spy for Peruvian forces. c, 3.60s, José Faustino Sánchez Carrión (1787-1825), pro-independence politician. d, José Olaya Balandra (1789-1823), executed emissary.

2021, July 21 Litho. *Perf. 14¼x13½*
2014 A1161 Block of 4, #a-d, + label 7.75 7.00
2015 A1162 Block of 4, #a-d, + label 7.75 7.00

History of the Peruvian Coat of Arms — A1163

No. 2016: a, Third coat of arms, 1950. b, First coat of arms, 1821. c, Second coat of arms, 1825.

2021, July 23 Litho. *Perf. 14¼x13½*
2016 Horiz. strip of 3 8.00 7.75
a. A1163 2.60s multi 1.50 1.40
b. A1163 3.60s multi 2.60 2.40
c. A1163 4s multi 3.00 2.50

Miniature Sheet

History of the Flag of Peru A1164

No. 2017: a, 1.20s, Third flag, 1822. b, 2.60s, Fourth flag, 1825. c, 3.60s, Second flag, 1822. d, 3.60s, Current flag, 1950, vert. e, 4s, First flag, 1820.

Perf. 13½x14¼, 14¼x13½
2021, July 23 Litho.
2017 A1164 Sheet of 5, #a-e 12.00 10.75

Landing of Troops of José de San Martín at Paracas, 1820 — A1165

2021, July 30 Litho. *Perf. 13½x14¼*
2018 A1165 7.60s multi 5.75 5.50

Souvenir Sheet

Casa Rosell-Ríos, Lima — A1166

No. 2019: a, 4s, Building wing. b, 7.60s, Central dome and pillars.

2021, Aug. 2 Litho. *Perf. 14¼x13½*
2019 A1166 Sheet of 2, #a-b 8.90 8.40

America issue.

Souvenir Sheet

Stevedore Sculpture, Lima, by Constantin Meunier (1831-1905) — A1167

2021, Aug. 5 Litho. *Perf. 14¼x13½*
2020 A1167 3.60s multi 2.60 2.40

Souvenir Sheet

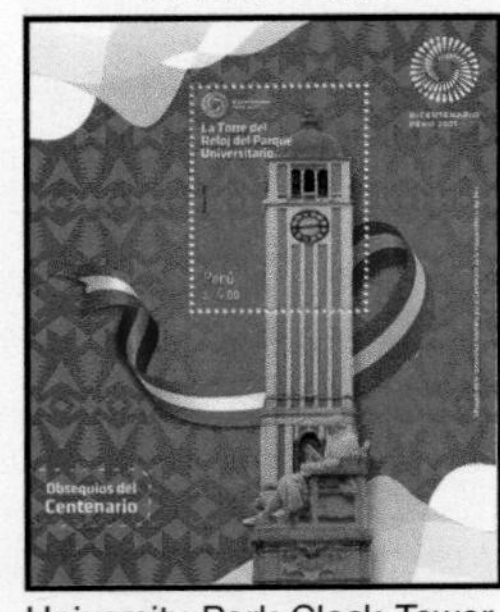

University Park Clock Tower, Lima — A1168

2021, Aug. 9 Litho. *Perf. 14¼x13½*
2021 A1168 4s multi 3.10 2.90

Battle of Pasco, 1820 — A1169

Perf. 13½x14¼
2021, Aug. 13 Litho.
2022 A1169 7.60s multi 5.75 5.50

Peruvian Army, 200th Anniv. — A1170

Perf. 14¼x13½
2021, Aug. 16 Litho.
2023 A1170 4s multi 3.10 2.90

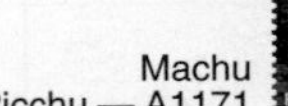

Machu Picchu — A1171

Vinicunca A1172

2021 Litho. *Perf. 13½x14¼*
2024 A1171 4s multi 3.00 2.90
2025 A1172 7.60s multi 5.90 2.90

America issue. Issued: 4s, 8/19; 7.60s, 8/26.

Souvenir Sheet

Manco Cápac Monument, Lima — A1173

2021, Aug. 30 Litho. ***Perf. 14x13½***
2026 A1173 3.60s multi 2.60 2.40

Chabuca Granda (1920-83), Singer — A1174

2021, Sept. 2 Litho. ***Perf. 14¼x13½***
2027 A1174 7.60s multi 5.75 5.50

Souvenir Sheet

New Year 2020 (Year of the Rat) A1175

2021, Sept. 6 Litho. ***Perf. 14¼x13½***
2028 A1175 7.60s multi 5.75 5.50

Dated 2020.

Campaign Against COVID-19 Pandemic — A1176

2021, Sept. 9 Litho. ***Perf. 14¼x13½***
2029 A1176 4s multi 3.10 2.90

Souvenir Sheet

Moorish Arch, Lima A1177

Perf. 14¼x13½
2021, Sept. 13 Litho.
2030 A1177 3.60s multi 2.60 2.40

Souvenir Sheet

Museum of Italian Art, Lima A1178

Perf. 14¼x13½
2021, Sept. 15 Litho.
2031 A1178 4s multi 3.10 2.90

Souvenir Sheet

Ornamental Fountain, Exhibition Park, Lima — A1179

Perf. 14¼x13½
2021, Sept. 17 Litho.
2032 A1179 4s multi 3.10 2.90

1820 Declaration in Huaura by Gen. José de San Martín of Peruvian Independence A1180

2021, Sept. 20 Litho. ***Perf. 13½x14***
2033 A1180 7.60s multi 5.75 5.50

Souvenir Sheet

Fountain of the Three Figures, Lima A1181

2021, Sept. 23 Litho. ***Perf. 14x13½***
2034 A1181 3.60s multi 2.60 2.40

Souvenir Sheet

Statue of Marshal Antonio José de Sucre, Lima A1182

2021, Sept. 27 Litho. ***Perf. 14x13½***
2035 A1182 4s multi 3.10 2.90

Souvenir Sheet

Statue of Liberty, Plazuela de la Recoleta, Lima — A1183

2021, Sept. 30 Litho. ***Perf. 14x13½***
2036 A1183 3.60s multi 2.60 2.40

Souvenir Sheet

Old National Stadium, Lima A1184

2021, Oct. 4 Litho. ***Perf. 14x13½***
2037 A1184 4s multi 3.10 2.90

Souvenir Sheet

Independence of India, 75th Anniv. — A1185

2022, Aug. 26 Litho. ***Perf. 13½x14***
2038 A1185 1.20s multi 1.00 .80

Female Parliamentarians — A1186

No. 2039: a, 1.20s, Irene Silva Linares de Santolalla (1902-92), first woman elected to Peruvian Senate. b, 1.20s, Alicia Blanco Montesinos de Salinas (1919-?), deputy for Junín region. c, 2.60s, Manuela Candelaria Billinghurst López (1919-67), deputy for Lima. d, 2.60s, María Mercedes Colina Lozano de Goluzzo (1921-2012), deputy for La Libertad.

2022, Sept. 14 Litho. ***Perf. 14x13½***
2039 A1186 Block of 4, #a-d, + label 5.75 4.75

Souvenir Sheet

First Constitutional Congress of Peru, 200th Anniv. — A1187

2022, Sept. 14 Litho. ***Perf. 14x13½***
2040 A1187 4s multi 3.10 2.90

Souvenir Sheet

María Auxiliadora Basilica, Lima, Cent. — A1188

2022, Sept. 28 Litho. ***Perf. 14x13½***
2041 A1188 7.60s multi 5.00 4.75

Yma Sumac (1922-2008), Singer and Actress — A1189

2022, Sept. 30 Litho. ***Perf. 14x13½***
2042 A1189 7.60s multi 5.00 4.75

Diplomatic Relations Between Peru and Guatemala, 165th Anniv. — A1190

No. 2043: a, Flag of Peru, Sacsayhuamán Archaeological Site. b, Flag of Guatemala, Tikal Temple.

2022 Litho. ***Perf. 14x13½***
2043 A1190 1.20s Horiz. pair, #a-b 2.00 1.50

Campaign for Immunization Against COVID-19 — A1191

2022 Litho. ***Perf. 14x13½***
2044 A1191 1.20s multi 1.00 .80

Souvenir Sheet

Santo Domingo Convent, Lima A1192

2022, Oct. 21 Litho. ***Perf. 14x13½***
2045 A1192 4s multi 2.75 2.50

Souvenir Sheet

Ships A1193

No. 2046: a, Yavarí, 1870. b, Cahuapanas, 1894. c, Yapurá, 1872.

2022, Oct. 26 Litho. ***Perf. 13½x14***
2046 A1193 2.60s Sheet of 3, #a-c, + label 5.75 4.90

Souvenir Sheet

Rescue of the Survivors of the Esmeralda in the 1879 Battle of Iquique — A1194

2022, Oct. 26 Litho. ***Perf. 13½x14***
2047 A1194 7.60s multi 5.00 4.75

Souvenir Sheet

Las Palmas Air Base, Lima, Cent. A1195

2022, Oct. 28 Litho. ***Perf. 13½x14***
2048 A1195 7.60s multi 5.00 4.75

Souvenir Sheet

Kon-Tiki Expedition of Thor Heyerdahl (1914-2002), 75th Anniv. — A1196

2022, Nov. 2 Litho. ***Perf. 13½x14***
2049 A1196 7.60s multi 5.00 4.75

Souvenir Sheet

Discovery of Cerro Sechín Temple, 85th Anniv. — A1197

2022, Nov. 4 Litho. ***Perf. 14x13½***
2050 A1197 7.60s multi 5.00 4.75

Taquile Island Man Knitting — A1198

Weaver, Cajamarca A1199

2022, Nov. 11 Litho. ***Perf. 13½x14***
2051 A1198 4s multi 2.75 2.50
2052 A1199 4s multi 2.75 2.50

America issue.

Souvenir Sheet

Plesiosaur and Its Fossilized Bone — A1200

2022, Nov. 14 Litho. ***Perf. 14x13½***
2053 A1200 7.60s multi 5.00 4.75

Flora and Fauna — A1201

Designs: No. 2054, 4s, Eretmochelys imbricata. No. 2055, 4s, Phytotoma raimondii. No. 2056, 4s, Polylepis racemosa. No. 2057, 4s, Gentianella alborosea.

2022 Litho. ***Perf. 13½x14***
2054-2057 A1201 Set of 4 11.00 10.00

Issued: Nos. 2054-2055, 11/15; Nos. 2056-2057, 11/18.

National Society of Fisheries, 70th Anniv. — A1202

2022, Nov. 15 Litho. ***Perf. 13½x14***
2058 A1202 2.60s multi 1.90 1.60

Abraham Valdelomar (1888-1919), Writer — A1203

2022, Nov. 17 Litho. ***Perf. 14x13½***
2059 A1203 4s multi 2.75 2.50

Souvenir Sheet

1615 Chronicle of Spanish Mistreatment of Andean Natives by Felipe Guaman Poma de Ayala (c. 1534-c. 1616) — A1204

2022, Nov. 23 Litho. ***Perf. 14x13½***
2060 A1204 7.60s multi 5.00 4.75

St. Jean-Baptiste de La Salle (1651-1719) — A1205

2022, Nov. 24 Litho. ***Perf. 14x13½***
2061 A1205 4s multi 2.75 2.50

De La Salle Brothers in Peru, cent.

Lithium — A1206

2022, Nov. 25 Litho. ***Perf. 14x13½***
2062 A1206 4s multi 2.75 2.50

Diplomatic Relations Between Peru and Colombia, 200th Anniv. — A1207

No. 2063: a, Flag of Peru, Moray Archaeological Site. b, Flag of Colombia, Caño Cristales River.

2022, Nov. 30 Litho. ***Perf. 13½x14***
2063 A1207 1.20s Horiz. pair, #a-b 2.00 1.50

Independence Advocates — A1208

No. 2064: a, Francisco Xavier de Luna Pizarro (1780-1855), priest and politician. b, Toribio de Luzuriaga y Mejía (1782-1842), first Grand Marshal of Peru. c, María Valdizán (c. 1760-1821), landowner executed for housing independence leaders. d, Brígida Silva de Ochoa (1776-c. 1840), intermediary between free and imprisoned independence activists.

2022, Dec. 6 Litho. ***Perf. 14x13½***
2064 A1208 2.60s Block of 4, #a-d, + flanking label 5.50 5.50

Souvenir Sheet

Nazca Lines A1209

2022, Dec. 9 Litho. ***Perf. 14x13½***
2065 A1209 4s multi 2.75 2.50

Mochica Culture Huaco Portrait Pot — A1210

2022, Dec. 14 Litho. ***Perf. 14x13½***
2066 A1210 4s multi 2.75 2.50

Christmas — A1211

2022 Litho. ***Perf. 14x13½***
2067 A1211 2.60s multi 1.90 1.60

SEMI-POSTAL STAMPS

Catalogue values for unused stamps in this section are for Never Hinged items.

Gold Funerary Mask — SP1

Designs: 2.60s+1.30s, Ceremonial knife, vert. 3.60s+1.80s, Ceremonial vessel. 4.60s+2.30s, Goblet with precious stones, vert. 20s+10s, Earplug.

Perf. 12x12½, 12½x12

1966, Aug. 16 Photo. Unwmk.

B1	SP1	1.90s + 90c multi	1.20	1.00
B2	SP1	2.60s + 1.30s multi	1.30	1.20
B3	SP1	3.60s + 1.80s multi	2.25	1.90
B4	SP1	4.60s + 2.30s multi	3.00	2.40
B5	SP1	20s + 10s multi	11.00	10.00
		Nos. B1-B5 (5)	18.75	16.50

The designs show gold objects of the 12th-13th centuries Chimu culture. The surtax was for tourist publicity.

For surcharges see Nos. 679-680, 683-684, 686.

AIR POST STAMPS

No. 248 Overprinted in Black

1927, Dec. 10 Unwmk. *Perf. 12*

C1	A87 50c violet		50.00	26.00
a.	Inverted overprint		500.00	—

Two types of overprint: first printing, dull black ink; second printing, shiny black ink. Values are the same. No. C1a occurs in the first printing.

Counterfeits exist.

President Augusto Bernardino Leguía — AP1

1928, Jan. 12 Engr.

C2	AP1 50c dark green	1.10	.55

For surcharge see No. 263.

Coat of Arms of Piura Type

1932, July 28 Litho.

C3	A107 50c scarlet	26.00	22.50

Counterfeits exist.

Airplane in Flight — AP3

1934, Feb. Engr. *Perf. 12½*

C4	AP3 2s blue	6.50	.60
C5	AP3 5s brown	15.00	1.25

For surcharges see Nos. C14-C15.

Funeral of Atahualpa AP4

Palace of Torre-Tagle AP7

Designs: 35c, Mt. San Cristobal. 50c, Avenue of Barefoot Friars. 10s, Pizarro and the Thirteen.

1935, Jan. 18 Photo. *Perf. 13½*

C6	AP4	5c emerald	.35	.25
C7	AP4	35c brown	.45	.45
C8	AP4	50c orange yel	.90	.75
C9	AP4	1s plum	1.75	1.25
C10	AP7	2s red orange	2.75	2.40
C11	AP4	5s dp claret	11.00	7.00
C12	AP4	10s dk blue	45.00	30.00
		Nos. C6-C12 (7)	62.20	42.10

4th centenary of founding of Lima.

Nos. C6-C12 overprinted "Radio Nacional" are revenue stamps.

"La Callao," First Locomotive in South America — AP9

1936, Aug. 27 *Perf. 12½*

C13	AP9 35c gray black	3.25	1.75

Founding of the Province of Callao, cent.

Nos. C4-C5 Surcharged "Habilitado" and New Value, like Nos. 353-355

1936, Nov. 4

C14	AP3 5c on 2s blue	.55	.30
C15	AP3 25c on 5s brown	1.10	.55
a.	Double surcharge	14.00	14.00
b.	No period btwn. "O" & "25 Cts"	1.60	1.60
c.	Inverted surcharge	21.00	

There are many broken letters in this setting.

Mines of Peru — AP10

Jorge Chávez — AP14

Aerial View of Peruvian Coast AP16

View of the "Sierra" AP17

St. Rosa of Lima — AP22

Designs: 5c, La Mar Park, Lima. 15c, Mail Steamer "Inca" on Lake Titicaca. 20c, Native Queña (flute) Player and Llama. 30c, Ram at Model Farm, Puno. 1s, Train in Mountains. 1.50s, Jorge Chavez Aviation School. 2s, Transport Plane. 5s, Aerial View of Virgin Forests.

1936-37 Photo. *Perf. 12½*

C16	AP10	5c	brt green	.35	.25
C17	AP10	5c	emer ('37)	.35	.25
C18	AP10	15c	lt ultra	.55	.25
C19	AP10	15c	blue ('37)	.35	.25
C20	AP10	20c	gray blk	1.50	.25
C21	AP10	20c	pale ol grn ('37)	1.00	.30
C22	AP14	25c	mag ('37)	.45	.25
C23	AP10	30c	henna brn	4.75	1.10
C24	AP10	30c	dk ol brn ('37)	1.50	.25
C25	AP14	35c	brown	2.75	2.25
C26	AP10	50c	yellow	.45	.30
C27	AP10	50c	brn vio ('37)	.65	.25
C28	AP16	70c	Prus grn	5.50	5.00
C29	AP16	70c	pck grn ('37)	1.00	.85
C30	AP17	80c	brn blk	6.50	5.00
C31	AP17	80c	ol blk ('37)	1.25	.55
C32	AP10	1s	ultra	4.75	.45
C33	AP10	1s	red brn ('37)	2.40	.30
C34	AP14	1.50s	red brn	7.75	6.00
C35	AP14	1.50s	org yel ('37)	4.75	.45
			Engr.		
C36	AP10	2s	deep blue	13.00	7.75
C37	AP10	2s	yel grn ('37)	9.25	.80
C38	AP16	5s	green	17.00	3.75
C39	AP22	10s	car & brn	125.00	110.00
			Nos. C16-C39 (24)	212.80	146.85

Nos. C23, C25, C28, C30, C36 Surcharged in Black or Red

1936, June 26

C40	AP10 15c on 30c hn brn	.65	.45
C41	AP14 15c on 35c brown	.65	.45
C42	AP16 15c on 70c Prus grn	4.50	3.50
C43	AP17 25c on 80c brn blk (R)	4.50	3.50
C44	AP10 1s on 2s dp bl	7.75	6.50
	Nos. C40-C44 (5)	18.05	14.40

Surcharge on No. C43 is vertical, reading down.

First Flight in Peru, 1911 AP23

Jorge Chávez AP24

Airport of Limatambo at Lima — AP25

Map of Aviation Lines from Peru — AP26

Designs: 10c, Juan Bielovucic (1889-?) flying over Lima race course, Jan. 14, 1911. 15c, Jorge Chavez-Dartnell (1887-1910), French-born Peruvian aviator who flew from Brixen to Domodossola in the Alps and died of plane-crash injuries.

1937, Sept. 15 Engr. *Perf. 12*

C45	AP23 10c violet	.65	.25
C46	AP24 15c dk green	.90	.25
C47	AP25 25c gray brn	.65	.25
C48	AP26 1s black	3.00	2.10
	Nos. C45-C48 (4)	5.20	2.85

Inter-American Technical Conference of Aviation, Sept. 1937.

Government Restaurant at Callao AP27

Monument on the Plains of Junin AP28

Rear Admiral Manuel Villar AP29

View of Tarma AP30

Dam, Ica River AP31

View of Iquitos AP32

Highway and Railroad Passing AP33

Mountain Road AP34

Plaza San Martín, Lima — AP35

National Radio of Peru — AP36

Stele from Chavin Temple AP37

Ministry of Public Works, Lima AP38

Crypt of the Heroes, Lima — AP39

Imprint: "Waterlow & Sons Limited, Londres."

1938, July 1 Photo. *Perf. 12½, 13*

C49	AP27	5c	violet brn	.25	.25
C50	AP28	15c	dk brown	.25	.25
C51	AP29	20c	dp magenta	.55	.30
C52	AP30	25c	dp green	.25	.25
C53	AP31	30c	orange	.25	.25
C54	AP32	50c	green	.45	.30
C55	AP33	70c	slate bl	.65	.30
C56	AP34	80c	olive	1.25	.30
C57	AP35	1s	slate grn	10.00	4.25
C58	AP36	1.50s	purple	2.25	.30
			Engr.		
C59	AP37	2s	ind & org brn	3.75	.95
C60	AP38	5s	brown	18.00	1.75
C61	AP39	10s	ol grn & ind	70.00	37.50
			Nos. C49-C61 (13)	107.90	46.95

See Nos. C73-C75, C89-C93, C103.

For surcharges see Nos. C65, C76-C77, C82-C88, C108.

Torre-Tagle Palace AP40

National Congress Building AP41

Manuel Ferreyros, José Gregorio Paz Soldán and Antonio Arenas — AP42

1938, Dec. 9 Photo. *Perf. 12½*

C62	AP40 25c brt ultra	.90	.65
C63	AP41 1.50s brown vio	2.40	1.90
C64	AP42 2s black	1.50	.75
	Nos. C62-C64 (3)	4.80	3.30

8th Pan-American Conference at Lima.

No. C52 Surcharged in Black

1942 *Perf. 13*

C65	AP30 15c on 25c dp grn	1.75	.40

Types of 1938
Imprint: "Columbian Bank Note Co."

1945-46 Unwmk. Litho. *Perf. 12½*

C73	AP27 5c violet brown	.40	.40
C74	AP31 30c orange	.40	.40
C75	AP36 1.50s purple ('46)	.40	.40
	Nos. C73-C75 (3)	1.20	1.20

Nos. C73 and C54 Overprinted in Black

1947, Sept. 25 *Perf. 12½, 13*

C76	AP27 5c violet brown	.40	.40
C77	AP32 50c green	.40	.40

1st Peru Intl. Airways flight from Lima to New York City, Sept. 27-28, 1947.

Catalogue values for unused stamps in this section, from this point to the end of the section, are for Never Hinged items.

Peru-Great Britain Air Route — AP43

Designs: 5s, Discus thrower. 10s, Rifleman.

1948, July 29 Photo. *Perf. 12½*

C78 AP43 1s blue 4.00 2.75

Basketball Players — AP44

Carmine Overprint, "AEREO"

C79 AP44 2s red brown 5.50 3.50
C80 AP44 5s yellow green 9.75 5.75
C81 AP44 10s yellow 11.50 7.00
a. Souv. sheet, #C78-C81, perf 13 55.00 52.50
Nos. C78-C81 (4) 30.75 19.00

Peru's participation in the 1948 Olympic Games held at Wembley, England, during July and August. Postally valid for four days, July 29-Aug. 1, 1948. Proceeds went to the Olympic Committee.

A surtax of 2 soles on No. C81a was for the Children's Hospital.

Remainders of Nos. C78-C81 and C81a were overprinted "Melbourne 1956" and placed on sale Nov. 19, 1956, at all post offices as "voluntary stamps" with no postal validity. Clerks were permitted to postmark them to please collectors, and proceeds were to help pay the cost of sending Peruvian athletes to Australia. On April 14, 1957, postal authorities declared these stamps valid for one day, April 15, 1957. The overprint was applied to 10,000 sets and 21,000 souvenir sheets. Value, set, $24.50; sheet, $19.

No. C55 Surcharged in Red

1948, Dec. *Perf. 13*

C82 AP33 10c on 70c slate blue .85 .40
C83 AP33 20c on 70c slate blue .85 .40
C84 AP33 55c on 70c slate blue .85 .40
Nos. C82-C84 (3) 2.55 1.20

Nos. C52, C55 and C56 Surcharged in Black

1949, Mar. 25

C85 AP30 5c on 25c dp grn .45 .30
C86 AP30 10c on 25c dp grn .45 .30
C87 AP33 15c on 70c slate bl .65 .30
C88 AP34 30c on 80c olive 2.40 .65
Nos. C85-C88 (4) 3.95 1.55

The surcharge reads up, on No. C87.

Types of 1938

Imprint: "Waterlow & Sons Limited, Londres."

Perf. 13x13½, 13½x13

1949-50 Photo.

C89 AP27 5c olive bister .45 .30
C90 AP31 30c red .45 .30
C91 AP33 70c blue .80 .30
C92 AP34 80c cerise 2.40 .45
C93 AP36 1.50s vio brn ('50) 1.60 .55
Nos. C89-C93 (5) 5.70 1.90

Overprinted "U. P. U. 1874-1949" in Red or Black

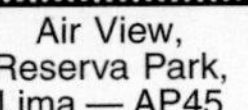

Air View, Reserva Park, Lima — AP45

Flags of the Americas and Spain — AP46

Designs: 30c, National flag. 55c, Huancayo Hotel. 95c, Blanca-Ancash Cordillera. 1.50s, Arequipa Hotel. 2s, Coal chute and dock, Chimbote. 5s, Town hall, Miraflores. 10s, Hall of National Congress, Lima.

1951, Apr. 2 Engr. *Perf. 12*

C94 AP45 5c blue grn .35 .25
C95 AP45 30c black & car .35 .25
a. Inverted overprint

C96 AP45 55c yel grn (Bk) .35 .25
C97 AP45 95c dk green .35 .25
C98 AP45 1.50s dp car (Bk) .45 .30
C99 AP45 2s deep blue .45 .30
C100 AP45 5s rose car (Bk) 5.00 3.25
C101 AP45 10s purple 6.25 4.50
C102 AP46 20s dk brn & ultra 10.50 7.00
Nos. C94-C102 (9) 24.05 16.35

UPU, 75th anniv. (in 1949).

Nos. C94-C102 exist without overprint, but were not regularly issued. Value, set, $225.

Type of 1938

Imprint: "Inst. de Grav. Paris."

1951, May Engr. *Perf. 12½x12*

C103 AP27 5c olive bister .80 .40

Type of 1938 Surcharged in Black

1951

C108 AP31 25c on 30c rose red .80 .40

Thomas de San Martin y Contreras and Jerónimo de Aliaga y Ramirez AP47

San Marcos University AP48

Designs: 50c, Church and convent of Santo Domingo. 1.20s, P. de Peralta Barnuevo, T. de San Martin y Contreras and J. Baquijano y Carrillo de Cordova. 2s, T. Rodriguez de Mendoza, J. Hipolito Unanue y Pavon and J. Cayetano Heredia y Garcia. 5s, Arms of the University, 1571 and 1735.

Perf. 11½x12½

1951, Dec. 10 Litho.

C109 AP47 30c gray .65 .45
C110 AP48 40c ultra .65 .45
C111 AP48 50c car rose .65 .45
C112 AP47 1.20s emerald .65 .45
C113 AP47 2s slate 2.10 .45
C114 AP47 5s multicolored 4.50 .45
Nos. C109-C114 (6) 9.20 2.70

400th anniv. of the founding of San Marcos University.

River Gunboat Marañon AP49

Peruvian Cormorants AP50

National Airport, Lima — AP51

Tobacco Plant — AP52

Manco Capac Monument AP54

Garcilaso de la Vega AP53

Designs: 1.50s, Housing Unit No. 3. 2.20s, Inca Solar Observatory.

Imprint: "Thomas De La Rue & Co. Ltd."

1953-60 Unwmk. *Perf. 13, 12*

C115 AP49 40c yellow grn .35 .25
a. 40c blue green ('57) .35 .25
C116 AP50 75c dk brown 2.00 .30
C116A AP50 80c pale brn red ('60) .90 .25
C117 AP51 1.25s blue .45 .25
C118 AP49 1.50s cerise .65 .30
C119 AP51 2.20s dk blue 3.00 .45
C120 AP52 3s brown 2.60 .65
C121 AP53 5s bister 2.00 .30
C122 AP54 10s dull vio brn 5.00 .85
Nos. C115-C122 (9) 16.95 3.60

See #C158-C162, C182-C183, C186-C189, C210-C211.

For surcharges see #C420-C422, C429-C433, C435-C436, C438, C442-C443, C445-C450, C455, C471-C474, C476, C478-C479, C495.

Queen Isabella I — AP55

Fleet of Columbus AP56

Perf. 12½x11½, 11½x12½

1953, June 18 Engr. Unwmk.

C123 AP55 40c dp carmine .35 .25
C124 AP56 1.25s emerald 1.00 .25
C125 AP55 2.15s dp plum 1.75 .60
C126 AP56 2.20s black 2.40 .65
Nos. C123-C126 (4) 5.50 1.75

500th birth anniv. (in 1951) of Queen Isabella I of Spain.

For surcharge see No. C475.

Arms of Lima and Bordeaux AP57

Designs: 50c, Eiffel Tower and Cathedral of Lima. 1.25s, Admiral Dupetit-Thouars and frigate "La Victorieuse." 2.20s, Presidents Coty and Prado and exposition hall.

1957, Sept. 16 *Perf. 13*

C127 AP57 40c claret, grn & ultra .45 .25
C128 AP57 50c grn, blk & hn brn .45 .25
C129 AP57 1.25s bl, ind & dk grn 1.10 .45
C130 AP57 2.20s bluish blk, bl & red brn 1.90 .90
Nos. C127-C130 (4) 3.90 1.85

French Exposition, Lima, Sept. 15-Oct. 1.

For surcharges see Nos. 763, C503-C505.

Pre-Stamp Postal Markings — AP58

10c, 1r Stamp of 1857. 15c, 2r Stamp of 1857. 25c, 1d Stamp of 1860. 30c, 1p Stamp of 1858. 40c, ½p Stamp of 1858. 1.25s, José Davila Condemarin. 2.20s, Ramon Castilla. 5s, Pres. Manuel Prado. 10s, Shield of Lima containing stamps.

Perf. 12½x13

1957, Dec. 1 Engr. Unwmk.

C131 AP58 5c silver & blk .35 .25
C132 AP58 10c lil rose & bl .35 .25
C133 AP58 15c grn & red brn .35 .25
C134 AP58 25c org yel & bl .35 .25
C135 AP58 30c vio brn & org brn .35 .25
C136 AP58 40c black & bis .35 .25
C137 AP58 1.25s dk bl & dk brn 1.20 .55
C138 AP58 2.20s red & sl bl 1.70 .75
C139 AP58 5s lil rose & mar 3.50 1.50
C140 AP58 10s ol grn & lil 6.50 2.50
Nos. C131-C140 (10) 15.00 6.80

Centenary of Peruvian postage stamps. No. C140 issued to publicize the Peruvian Centenary Phil. Exhib. (PEREX).

Carlos Paz Soldan AP59

Port of Callao and Pres. Manuel Prado AP60

Design: 1s, Ramon Castilla.

Perf. 14x13½, 13½x14

1958, Apr. 7 Litho. Wmk. 116

C141 AP59 40c brn & pale rose .50 .40
C142 AP59 1s grn & lt grn .70 .40
C143 AP60 1.25s dull pur & ind 1.50 .40
Nos. C141-C143 (3) 2.70 1.20

Centenary of the telegraph connection between Lima and Callao and the centenary of the political province of Callao.

For surcharges see Nos. 758A, 767.

Flags of France and Peru — AP61

Cathedral of Lima and Lady — AP62

1.50s, Horseback rider & mall in Lima. 2.50s, Map of Peru showing national products.

Perf. 12½x13, 13x12½

1958, May 20 Engr. Unwmk.

C144 AP61 50c dl vio, bl & car .50 .40
C145 AP62 65c multi .50 .40
C146 AP62 1.50s bl, brn vio & ol 1.00 .40
C147 AP61 2.50s sl grn, grnsh bl & claret 1.50 .40
Nos. C144-C147 (4) 3.50 1.60

Peruvian Exhib. in Paris, May 20-July 10.

Bro. Martin de Porres Velasquez — AP63

First Royal School of Medicine (Now Ministry of Government and Police) — AP64

Designs: 1.20s, Daniel Alcides Carrion Garcia. 1.50s, Jose Hipolito Unanue Pavon.

Perf. 13x13½, 13½x13

1958, July 24 Litho. Unwmk.

C148 AP63 60c multi .55 .30
C149 AP63 1.20s multi .55 .30
C150 AP63 1.50s multi .55 .30
C151 AP64 2.20s black 2.00 .70
Nos. C148-C151 (4) 3.65 1.60

Daniel A. Carrion (1857-85), medical martyr.

Gen. Ignacio Alvarez Thomas — AP65

1958, Nov. 13 ***Perf. 13x12½***

C152 AP65 1.10s brn lake, bis & ver .55 .30
C153 AP65 1.20s blk, bis & ver 1.30 .55

General Thomas (1787-1857), fighter for South American independence.

"Justice" and Emblem — AP66

1958, Nov. 13
Star in Blue and Olive Bister

C154 AP66 80c emerald .80 .40
C155 AP66 1.10s red orange .80 .40
C156 AP66 1.20s ultra .80 .40
C157 AP66 1.50s lilac rose .80 .40
Nos. C154-C157 (4) 3.20 1.60

Lima Bar Assoc., 150th anniv.

Types of 1953-57

Designs: 80c, Peruvian cormorants. 3.80s, Inca Solar Observatory.

Imprint: "Joh. Enschedé en Zonen-Holland"

Perf. 12½x14, 14x13, 13x14

1959, Dec. 9 **Unwmk.**

C158 AP50 80c brown red .45 .25
C159 AP52 3s lt green 1.40 .45
C160 AP51 3.80s orange 3.00 .55
C161 AP53 5s brown 1.40 .55
C162 AP54 10s orange ver 3.00 .65
Nos. C158-C162 (5) 9.25 2.45

WRY Emblem, Dove, Rainbow and Farmer — AP67

1960, Apr. 7 **Litho.** ***Perf. 14x13***

C163 AP67 80c multi 1.00 .55
C164 AP67 4.30s multi 1.50 1.00
a. Souv. sheet of 2, #C163-C164, imperf. 15.50 15.00

World Refugee Year, 7/1/59-6/30/60.
No. C164a sold for 15s.

Peruvian Cormorant Over Ocean — AP68

1960, May 30 ***Perf. 14x13½***

C165 AP68 1s multi 4.25 1.75

Intl. Pacific Fair, Lima, 1959.

Lima Coin of 1659 — AP69

1961, Jan. 19 **Unwmk.** ***Perf. 13x14***

C166 AP69 1s org brn & gray 1.00 .45
C167 AP69 2s Prus bl & gray 1.00 .45

1st National Numismatic Exposition, Lima, 1959; 300th anniv. of the first dated coin (1659) minted at Lima.

The Earth — AP70

1961, Mar. 8 **Litho.** ***Perf. 13½x14***

C168 AP70 1s multicolored 1.90 .65

International Geophysical Year.

Frigate Amazonas — AP71

1961, Mar. 8 **Engr.** ***Perf. 13½***

C169 AP71 50c brown & grn .60 .40
C170 AP71 80c dl vio & red org .75 .40
C171 AP71 1s green & sepia 1.40 .40
Nos. C169-C171 (3) 2.75 1.20

Centenary (in 1958) of the trip around the world by the Peruvian frigate Amazonas.

Machu Picchu Sheet

A souvenir sheet was issued Sept. 11, 1961, to commemorate the 50th anniversary of the discovery of the ruins of Machu Picchu, ancient Inca city in the Andes, by Hiram Bingham. It contains two bi-colored imperf. airmail stamps, 5s and 10s, lithographed in a single design picturing the mountaintop ruins. The sheet was valid for one day and was sold in a restricted manner. Value $22.

Olympic Torch, Laurel and Globe — AP72

1961, Dec. 13 **Unwmk.** ***Perf. 13***

C172 AP72 5s gray & ultra 1.20 .60
C173 AP72 10s gray & car 3.20 1.25
a. Souv. sheet of 2, #C172-C173, imperf. 5.00 4.50

17th Olympic Games, Rome, 8/25-9/11/60.

Fair Emblem and Llama — AP73

1962, Jan. **Litho.** ***Perf. 10½x11***

C174 AP73 1s multi .85 .40

2nd International Pacific Fair, Lima, 1961.

Map Showing Disputed Border, Peru-Ecuador — AP74

1962, May 25 ***Perf. 10½***
Gray Background

C175 AP74 1.30s blk, red & car rose .65 .25
C176 AP74 1.50s blk, red & emer .65 .25
C177 AP74 2.50s blk, red & dk bl 1.50 .70
Nos. C175-C177 (3) 2.80 1.20

Settlement of the border dispute with Ecuador by the Protocol of Rio de Janeiro, 20th anniv.

Cahuide and Cuauhtémoc — AP75

2s, Tupac Amaru (Jose G. Condorcanqui) & Miguel Hidalgo. 3s, Pres. Manuel Prado & Pres. Adolfo Lopez Mateos of Mexico.

1962, May 25 **Engr.** ***Perf. 13***

C178 AP75 1s dk car rose, red & brt grn .50 .30
C179 AP75 2s grn, red & brt grn .95 .35
C180 AP75 3s brn, red & brt grn 1.50 .55
Nos. C178-C180 (3) 2.95 1.20

Exhibition of Peruvian art treasures in Mexico.

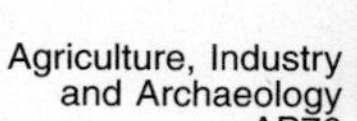

Agriculture, Industry and Archaeology — AP76

1962, Sept. 7 **Litho.** ***Perf. 14x13½***

C181 AP76 1s black & gray .85 .40

Cent. (in 1961) of Pallasca Ancash province.

Types of 1953-60

1.30s, Guanayes. 1.50s, Housing Unit No. 3. 1.80s, Locomotive No. 80 (like #460). 2s, Monument to Native Farmer. 3s, Tobacco plant. 4.30s, Inca Solar Observatory. 5s, Garcilaso de la Vega. 10s, Inca Monument.

Imprint: "Thomas De La Rue & Co. Ltd."

1962-63 **Wmk. 346** **Litho.** ***Perf. 13***

C182 AP50 1.30s pale yellow 1.00 .25
C183 AP49 1.50s claret 1.00 .25
C184 A182 1.80s dark blue 1.00 .25

Perf. 12

C185 A184 2s emerald ('63) 1.00 .25
C186 AP52 3s lilac rose .90 .25
C187 AP51 4.30s orange 1.90 .45
C188 AP53 5s citron 1.90 .75

Perf. 13½x14

C189 AP54 10s vio bl ('63) 3.75 .90
Nos. C182-C189 (8) 12.45 3.35

For surcharges see Nos. C429, C432, C446, C449, C473.

Freedom from Hunger Type

1963, July 23 **Unwmk.** ***Perf. 12½***

C190 A189 4.30s lt grn & ocher 2.00 1.10

Jorge Chávez and Wing — AP77

1964, Feb. 20 **Engr.** ***Perf. 13***

C191 AP77 5s org brn, dk brn & bl 1.30 .45

1st crossing of the Alps by air (Sept. 23, 1910) by the Peruvian aviator Jorge Chávez, 50th anniv.

Alliance for Progress Type

Design: 1.30s, Same, horizontal.

Perf. 12½x12, 12x12½

1964, June 22 **Litho.**

C192 A190 1.30s multi .50 .40
C193 A190 3s multi 1.50 .60

Fair Poster — AP78

1965, Jan. 15 **Unwmk.** ***Perf. 14½***

C194 AP78 1s multi .80 .40

3rd International Pacific Fair, Lima 1963.

Basket, Globe, Pennant — AP79

1965, Apr. 19 ***Perf. 12x12½***

C195 AP79 1.30s violet & red 1.00 .60
C196 AP79 4.30s bis brn & red 2.50 1.40

4th Women's Intl. Basketball Championship.
For surcharge see No. C493.

St. Martin de Porres — AP80

Designs: 1.80s, St. Martin's miracle: dog, cat and mouse feeding from same dish. 4.30s, St. Martin with cherubim in Heaven.

1965, Oct. 29 **Litho.** ***Perf. 11***

C197 AP80 1.30s gray & multi .70 .25
C198 AP80 1.80s gray & multi .90 .25
C199 AP80 4.30s gray & multi 1.90 .95
Nos. C197-C199 (3) 3.50 1.45

Canonization of St. Martin de Porres Velasquez (1579-1639), on May 6, 1962.
For surcharges see Nos. C439, C496 and footnote below No. RA57.

Victory Monument, Lima, and Battle Scene — AP81

Designs: 3.60s, Monument and Callao Fortress. 4.60s, Monument and José Galvez.

1966, May 2 **Photo.** ***Perf. 14x13½***

C200 AP81 1.90s multicolored 1.00 .50
C201 AP81 3.60s brn, yel & bis 1.10 .75
C202 AP81 4.60s multicolored 2.00 1.00
Nos. C200-C202 (3) 4.10 2.25

Centenary of Peru's naval victory over the Spanish Armada at Callao, May, 1866.

Civil Guard Emblem — AP82

1.90s, Various activities of Civil Guard.

1966, Aug. 30 **Photo.** ***Perf. 13½x14***

C203 AP82 90c multicolored .50 .40
C204 AP82 1.90s dp lil rose, gold & blk 1.30 .40

Centenary of the Civil Guard.

Hydroelectric Center Type

1966, Nov. 24 **Photo.** ***Perf. 13½x14***

C205 A193 1.90s lil, blk & vio bl 1.00 .40

Sun Symbol, Ancient Carving — AP83

Designs: 3.60s, Map of Peru and spiral, horiz. 4.60s, Globe with map of Peru.

Perf. 14x13½, 13½x14

1967, Feb. 16 **Litho.**

C206 AP83 2.60s red org & blk .90 .25
C207 AP83 3.60s dp blue & blk 1.10 .45
C208 AP83 4.60s tan & multi 1.50 .55
Nos. C206-C208 (3) 3.50 1.25

Photography exhibition "Peru Before the World" which opened simultaneously in Lima,

Madrid, Santiago de Chile and Washington, Sept. 27, 1966.
For surcharges see #C444, C470, C492.

Types of 1953-60

2.60s, Monument to Native Farmer. 3.60s, Tobacco plant. 4.60s, Inca Solar Observatory.

Imprint: "I.N.A."

1967, Jan. ***Perf. 13½x14, 14x13½***

C209	A184	2.60s brt green	1.40	.30
C210	AP52	3.60s lilac rose	1.85	.45
C211	AP51	4.60s orange	2.00	.90
		Nos. C209-C211 (3)	5.25	1.65

For surcharges see Nos. C433, C436-C438, C440-C442, C445, C447-C450, C454-C455, C471-C472, C474, C476, C478.

Window and Sun Type of Regular Issue

1967, Apr. 18 Photo. ***Perf. 13½x14***

C212	A194	1.90s yel brn, blk & gold	1.10	.40

St. Rosa of Lima by Angelino Medoro — AP84

St. Rosa Painted by: 2.60s, Carlo Maratta. 3.60s, Cuzquena School, 17th century.

1967, Aug. 30 Photo. ***Perf. 13½***

Black, Gold & Multi

C213	AP84	1.90s	.95	.30
C214	AP84	2.60s	1.75	.35
C215	AP84	3.60s	1.80	.75
		Nos. C213-C215 (3)	4.50	1.40

350th death anniv. of St. Rosa of Lima.
For surcharge see No. C477.

Fair Type of Regular Issue

1967, Oct. 27 Photo. ***Perf. 12***

C216	A195	1s gold, brt red lil & blk	.90	.40

Lions Emblem — AP85

1967, Dec. 29 Litho. ***Perf. 14x13½***

C217	AP85	1.60s brt bl & vio bl, *grysh*	.95	.40

50th anniversary of Lions International.

Decorated Jug, Nazca Culture — AP86

Painted pottery jugs of pre-Inca Nazca culture: 2.60s, Falcon. 3.60s, Round jug decorated with grain-eating bird. 4.60s, Two-headed snake. 5.60s, Marine bird.

1968, June 4 Photo. ***Perf. 12***

C218	AP86	1.90s multi	.95	.30
C219	AP86	2.60s multi	1.00	.35
C220	AP86	3.60s black & multi	1.00	.35
C221	AP86	4.60s brown & multi	1.60	.55
C222	AP86	5.60s gray & multi	3.50	1.10
		Nos. C218-C222 (5)	8.05	2.65

For surcharges see #C451-C453, C497, C500.

Antarqui, Inca Messenger — AP87

Design: 5.60s, Alpaca and jet liner.

1968, Sept. 2 Litho. ***Perf. 12***

C223	AP87	3.60s multi	.95	.45
C224	AP87	5.60s red, blk & brn	1.30	.65

12th anniv. of Peruvian Airlines (APSA).
For surcharges see Nos. C480-C482.

Human Rights Flame — AP88

1968, Sept. 5 Photo. ***Perf. 14x13½***

C225	AP88	6.50s brn, red & grn	1.00	.40

International Human Rights Year.

Discobolus and Mexico Olympics Emblem — AP89

1968, Oct. 19 Photo. ***Perf. 13½***

C226	AP89	2.30s yel, brn & dk bl	.60	.25
C227	AP89	3.50s yel grn, sl bl & red	.60	.25
C228	AP89	5s brt pink, blk & ultra	.60	.30
C229	AP89	6.50s lt bl, mag & brn	1.25	.40
C230	AP89	8s lil, ultra & car	1.25	.40
C231	AP89	9s org, vio & grn	1.25	.40
		Nos. C226-C231 (6)	5.55	2.00

19th Olympic Games, Mexico City, 10/12-27.

Hand, Corn and Field — AP90

1969, Mar. 3 Litho. ***Perf. 11***

C232	AP90	5.50s on 1.90s grn & yel	1.10	.40
C233	AP90	6.50s on 1.90s bl, grn & yel	1.30	.40

Agrarian Reform Law. Not issued without surcharge.

Peruvian Silver 8-reales Coin, 1568 — AP91

1969, Mar. 17 Litho. ***Perf. 12***

C234	AP91	5s yellow, gray & blk	1.00	.45
C235	AP91	5s bl grn, gray & blk	1.00	.45

400th anniv. of the first Peruvian coinage.

Ramon Castilla Monument — AP92

Design: 10s, Pres. Ramon Castilla.

1969, May 30 Photo. ***Perf. 13½***

Size: 27x40mm

C236	AP92	5s emerald & indigo	.90	.30

Perf. 12

Size: 21x37mm

C237	AP92	10s plum & brn	1.95	.65

Ramon Castilla (1797-1867), president of Peru (1845-1851 and 1855-1862), on the occasion of the unveiling of the monument in Lima.

Airline Type of Regular Issue

1969, June 17 Litho. ***Perf. 11***

C238	A199	3s org & multi	.85	.50
C239	A199	4s multi	1.00	.50
C240	A199	5.50s ver & multi	1.25	.50
C241	A199	6.50s vio & multi	1.25	.50
		Nos. C238-C241 (4)	4.35	2.00

First Peruvian Airlines (APSA) flight to Europe.

Radar Antenna, Satellite and Earth AP93

1969, July 14 Litho. ***Perf. 11***

C242	AP93	20s multi	2.75	1.10
a.		Souv. sheet	4.00	3.50

Opening of the Lurin satellite earth station near Lima.
No. C242a contains one imperf. stamp with simulated perforations similar to No. C242.

Gonzales Type of Regular Issue inscribed "AEREO"

1969, July 23 Litho. ***Perf. 11***

C243	A200	20s red & multi	3.25	1.25

WHO Emblem — AP94

1969, Aug. 14 Photo. ***Perf. 12***

C244	AP94	5s gray, red brn, gold & blk	.80	.40
C245	AP94	6.50s dl org, gray bl, gold & blk	1.00	.40

WHO, 20th anniv.

Agrarian Reform Type of Regular Issue

1969, Aug. 28 Litho. ***Perf. 11***

C246	A201	3s lil & blk	.70	.40
C247	A201	4s brn & buff	1.25	.40

Garcilaso de la Vega — AP95

Designs: 2.40s, De la Vega's coat of arms. 3.50s, Title page of "Commemtarios Reales que tratan del origen de los Yncas," Lisbon, 1609.

1969, Sept. 18 Litho. ***Perf. 12x12½***

C248	AP95	2.40s emer, sil & blk	.70	.30
C249	AP95	3.50s ultra, buff & blk	.75	.30
C250	AP95	5s sil, yel, blk & brn	1.20	.30
a.		Souv. sheet of 3, #C248-C250, imperf.	3.25	2.50
		Nos. C248-C250 (3)	2.65	.90

Garcilaso de la Vega, called "Inca" (1539-1616), historian of Peru.

Fair Type of Regular Issue, 1969

1969, Nov. 14 Litho. ***Perf. 11***

C251	A203	3s bis & multi	.55	.40
C252	A203	4s multi	1.50	.40

Bolognesi Type of Regular Issue

1969, Dec. 9 Litho. ***Perf. 11***

C253	A204	50s lt brn, blk & gold	4.75	1.90

Arms of Amazonas AP96

1970, Jan. 6 Litho. ***Perf. 11***

C254	AP96	10s multi	1.75	1.00

ILO Emblem — AP97

1970, Jan. 16

C278	AP97	3s dk vio bl & lt ultra	1.10	.30

ILO, 50th anniv.

Motherhood and UNICEF Emblem — AP98

1970, Jan. 16 Photo. ***Perf. 13½x14***

C279	AP98	5s yel, gray & blk	.85	.40
C280	AP98	6.50s brt pink, gray & blk	1.25	.40

Vicus Culture Type of Regular Issue

Ceramics of Vicus Culture, 6th-8th Centuries: 3s, Squatting warrior. 4s, Jug. 5.50s, Twin jugs. 6.50s, Woman and jug.

1970, Feb. 23 Litho. ***Perf. 11***

C281	A205	3s buff, blk & brn	1.30	.40
C282	A205	4s buff, blk & brn	1.30	.40
C283	A205	5.50s buff, blk & brn	2.75	.85
C284	A205	6.50s buff, blk & brn	3.75	1.10
a.		Vert. strip, #526, C281-C284	11.00	11.00
		Nos. C281-C284 (4)	9.10	2.75

Fish Type of Regular Issue

1970, Apr. 30 Litho. ***Perf. 11***

C285	A207	3s Swordfish	3.00	1.40
C286	A207	3s Yellowfin tuna	3.00	1.40
C287	A207	5.50s Wolf fish	3.00	2.10
		Nos. C285-C287 (3)	9.00	4.90

Telephone — AP99

1970, June 12 Litho. ***Perf. 11***

C288	AP99	5s multi	.85	.25
C289	AP99	10s multi	1.75	.55

Nationalization of the Peruvian telephone system, Mar. 25, 1970.

Soldier-Farmer Type of Regular Issue

1970, June 24 Litho. ***Perf. 11***

C290	A208	3s gold & multi	.95	.40
C291	A208	5.50s gold & multi	1.90	.40

UN Headquarters, NY — AP100

1970 June 26

C292	AP100	3s vio bl & lt bl	.85	.40

25th anniversary of United Nations.

Rotary Club Emblem AP101

1970, July 18
C293 AP101 10s blk, red & gold 1.75 .80

Rotary Club of Lima, 50th anniversary.

Tourist Type of Regular Issue

3s, Ruins of Sun Fortress, Trujillo. 4s, Sacsayhuaman Arch, Cuzco. 5.50s, Arch & Lake Titicaca, Puno. 10s, Machu Picchu, Cuzco.

1970, Aug. 6 Litho. *Perf. 11*

C294	A210	3s multi	1.30	.40
C295	A210	4s multi, vert.	1.60	.40
C296	A210	5.50s multi, vert.	2.50	.40
C297	A210	10s multi, vert.	3.25	.75
a.		Souvenir sheet of 5	8.75	7.50
		Nos. C294-C297 (4)	8.65	1.95

No. C297a contains 5 imperf. stamps similar to Nos. 538, C294-C297 with simulated perforations.

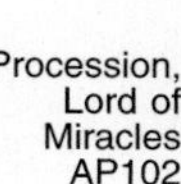

Procession, Lord of Miracles AP102

4s, Cockfight, by T. Nuñez Ureta. 5.50s, Altar of Church of the Nazarene, vert. 6.50s, Procession, by J. Vinatea Reinoso. 8s, Procession, by José Sabogal, vert.

1970, Nov. 30 Litho. *Perf. 11*

C298	AP102	3s blk & multi	.55	.35
C299	AP102	4s blk & multi	.55	.35
C300	AP102	5.50s blk & multi	1.10	.40
C301	AP102	6.50s blk & multi	1.25	.50
C302	AP102	8s blk & multi	1.90	.60
		Nos. C298-C302 (5)	5.35	2.20

October Festival in Lima.

"Tight Embrace" (from ancient monolith) AP103

1971, Feb. 8 Litho. *Perf. 11*

C303	AP103	4s ol gray, yel & red	1.00	.40
C304	AP103	5.50s dk bl, pink & red	1.00	.40
C305	AP103	6.50s sl, buff & red	1.00	.40
		Nos. C303-C305 (3)	3.00	1.20

Issued to express Peru's gratitude to the world for aid after the Ancash earthquake, May 31, 1970.

Textile Type of Regular Issue

Designs: 3s, Chancay tapestry, vert. 4s, Chancay lace. 5.50s, Paracas cloth, vert.

1971, Apr. 19 Litho. *Perf. 11*

C306	A213	3s multi	1.75	.50
C307	A213	4s grn & multi	1.75	.50
C308	A213	5.50s multi	2.25	.55
		Nos. C306-C308 (3)	5.75	1.55

Fish Type of Regular Issue

Fish Sculptures and Fish: 3.50s, Chimu Inca culture, 14th century and Chilean sardine. 4s, Mochica culture, 5th century, and engraulis ringens. 5.50s, Chimu culture, 13th century, and merluccios peruanos. 8.50s, Nazca culture, 3rd century, and brevoortis maculatachilcae.

1971, June 7 Litho. *Perf. 11*

C309	A214	3.50s multi	1.00	.40
C310	A214	4s multi	1.20	.40
C311	A214	5.50s multi	1.75	.55
C312	A214	8.50s multi	2.75	1.10
		Nos. C309-C312 (4)	6.70	2.45

Independence Type of 1971

Paintings: No. C313, Toribio Rodriguez de Mendoza. No. C314, José de la Riva Aguero. No. C315, Francisco Vidal. 3.50s, José de San Martin. No. C317, Juan P. Viscardo y Guzman. No. C318, Hipolito Unanue. 4.50s, Liberation Monument, Paracas. No. C320, José G. Condorcanqui-Tupac Amaru. No. C321, Francisco J. de Luna Pizarro. 6s, March of the Numancia Battalion, horiz. 7.50s, Peace Tower, monument for Alvarez de Arenales, horiz. 9s, Liberators' Monument, Lima, horiz. 10s, Independence Proclamation in Lima, horiz.

1971 Litho. *Perf. 11*

C313	A215	3s brt mag & blk	.65	.40
C314	A215	3s gray & multi	.65	.40
C315	A215	3s dk bl & multi	.65	.40
C316	A215	3.50s dk bl & multi	.90	.40
C317	A215	4s emer & blk	.90	.40
C318	A215	4s gray & multi	.90	.40
C319	A215	4.50s dk bl & multi	.90	.40
C320	A215	5.50s brn & blk	1.40	.40
C321	A215	5.50s gray & multi	1.40	.40
C322	A215	6s dk bl & multi	1.60	.40
C323	A215	7.50s dk bl & multi	2.10	.50
C324	A215	9s dk bl & multi	2.10	.50
C325	A215	10s dk bl & multi	2.10	.50
		Nos. C313-C325 (13)	16.25	5.50

150th anniversary of independence, and to honor the heroes of the struggle for independence. Sizes: 6s, 10s, 45x35mm, 7.50s, 9s, 41x39mm. Others 31x49mm.

Issued: #C313, C317, C320, 5/10; #C314, C318, C321, 7/5; others 7/27.

Ricardo Palma — AP104

1971, Aug. 27 *Perf. 13*
C326 AP104 7.50s ol bis & blk 1.60 .55

Sesquicentennial of National Library. Ricardo Palma (1884-1912) was a writer and director of the library.

Weight Lifter — AP105

1971, Sept. 15
C327 AP105 7.50s brt bl & blk 1.60 .55

25th World Weight Lifting Championships, Lima.

Flag, Family, Soldier's Head — AP106

1971, Oct. 4

C328	AP106	7.50s blk, lt bl & red	1.40	.40
a.		Souv. sheet of 1, imperf.	3.00	2.75

3rd anniv. of the revolution of the armed forces.

"Sacramento" AP107

1971, Oct. 8
C329 AP107 7.50s lt bl & dk bl 1.60 .55

Sesquicentennial of Peruvian Navy.

Peruvian Order of the Sun — AP108

1971, Oct. 8
C330 AP108 7.50s multi 1.25 .80

Sequicentennial of the Peruvian Order of the Sun.

Liberation Type of Regular Issue

Design: 50s, Detail from painting "Progress and Liberation," by Teodoro Nuñez Ureta.

1971, Nov. 4 Litho. *Perf. 13x13½*
C331 A217 50s multi 7.50 2.25

2nd Ministerial meeting of the "Group of 77."

Fair Emblem — AP109

1971, Nov. 12 *Perf. 13*
C332 AP109 4.50s multi 1.00 .40

7th Pacific International Trade Fair.

Fish Type of Regular Issue

3s, Pontinus furcirhinus dubius. 5.50s, Hogfish.

1972, Mar. 20 Litho. *Perf. 13x13½*

C333	A223	3s lt bl & multi	2.00	.75
C334	A223	5.50s lt bl & multi	3.50	.75

Teacher and Children, by Teodoro Nuñez Ureta — AP110

1972, Apr. 10 Litho. *Perf. 13x13½*
C335 AP110 6.50s multi 1.10 .40

Enactment of Education Reform Law.

White-tailed Trogon — AP111

2.50s, Amazonian umbrella bird. 3s, Peruvian cock-of-the-rock. 6.50s, Cuvier's toucan. 8.50s, Blue-crowned motmot.

1972, June 19 Litho. *Perf. 13½x13*

C336	AP111	2s multi	2.60	1.75
C337	AP111	2.50s multi	2.60	1.75
C338	AP111	3s multi	3.00	1.75
C339	AP111	6.50s multi	5.50	1.75
C340	AP111	8.50s multi	8.50	1.75
		Nos. C336-C340 (5)	22.20	8.75

Quipu and Map of Americas — AP112

1972, Aug. 21
C341 AP112 5s blk & multi 1.50 .50

4th Interamerican Philatelic Exhibition, EXFILBRA, Rio de Janeiro, Aug. 26-Sept. 2.

Inca Runner, Olympic Rings — AP113

1972, Aug. 28
C342 AP113 8s buff & multi 1.60 .55

20th Olympic Games, Munich, 8/26-9/11.

Woman of Catacaos, Piura — AP114

Regional Costumes: 2s, Tupe (Yauyos) woman of Lima. 4s, Indian with bow and arrow, from Conibo, Loreto. 4.50s, Man with calabash, Cajamarca. 5s, Moche woman, Trujillo. 6.50s, Man and woman of Ocongate, Cuzco. 8s, Chucupana woman, Ayacucho. 8.50s, Cotuncha woman, Junin. 10s, Woman of Puno dancing "Pandilla."

1972-73 Design AP114

C343	2s blk & multi	.55	.45
C344	3.50s blk & multi	1.75	.70
C345	4s blk & multi	2.00	.80
C346	4.50s blk & multi	1.10	.90
C346A	5s blk & multi	1.10	.90
C347	6.50s blk & multi	3.00	1.10
C347A	8s blk & multi	2.25	1.40
C347B	8.50s blk & multi	2.25	1.50
C348	10s blk & multi	2.25	1.75
	Nos. C343-C348 (9)	16.25	9.50

Issued: 3.50s, 4s, 6.50s, 9/29/72; 2s, 4.50s, 10s, 4/30/73; 5s, 8s, 8.50s, 10/15/73.
See Nos. C414-C415.

Funerary Tower, Sillustani, Puno — AP115

Archaeological Monuments: 1.50s, Stone of the 12 angles, Cuzco. 3.50s, Ruins of Chavin, Ancash. 5s, Wall and gate, Chavin, Ancash. 8s, Ruins of Machu Picchu.

Perf. 13½x13, 13x13½
1972, Oct. 16 Litho.

C349	AP115	1.50s multi	.70	.25
C350	AP115	3.50s multi, horiz.	1.10	.25
C351	AP115	4s multi	1.10	.25
C352	AP115	5s multi, horiz.	1.75	.40
C353	AP115	8s multi, horiz.	2.75	.55
		Nos. C349-C353 (5)	7.40	1.70

AP116

Inca ponchos, various textile designs.

1973, Jan. 29 Litho. *Perf. 13½x13*

C354	AP116	2s multi	.90	.50
C355	AP116	3.50s multi	1.20	.50
C356	AP116	4s multi	1.20	.50
C357	AP116	5s multi	1.20	.55
C358	AP116	8s multi	3.00	.55
		Nos. C354-C358 (5)	7.50	2.60

AP117

Antique Jewelry: 1.50s, Goblets and Ring, Mochica, 10th cent. 2.50s, Golden hands and arms, Lambayeque, 12th cent. 4s, Gold male statuette, Mochica, 8th ceny. 5s, Two gold brooches, Nazca, 8th cent. 8s, Flayed puma, Mochica, 8th cent.

1973, Mar. 19 Litho. *Perf. 13½x13*

C359	AP117	1.50s multi	1.40	.80
C360	AP117	2.50s multi	1.40	.80
C361	AP117	4s multi	1.40	.80
C362	AP117	5s multi	1.80	1.25
C363	AP117	8s multi	3.75	.80
		Nos. C359-C363 (5)	9.75	4.45

Andean Condor — AP118

Protected Animals: 5s, Vicuña. 8s, Spectacled bear.

1973, Apr. 16 Litho. *Perf. 13½x13*

C364	AP118	4s blk & multi	.85	.25
C365	AP118	5s blk & multi	1.10	.40
C366	AP118	8s blk & multi	2.40	.70
		Nos. C364-C366 (3)	4.35	1.35

See Nos. C372-C376, C411-C412.

Indian Guide, by José Sabogal — AP119

Peruvian Paintings: 8.50s, Portrait of a Lady, by Daniel Hernandez. 20s, Man Holding Figurine, by Francisco Laso.

1973, May 7 Litho. *Perf. 13½x13*

C367	AP119	1.50s multi	.60	.40
C368	AP119	8.50s multi	1.10	.60
C369	AP119	20s multi	3.50	1.10
		Nos. C367-C369 (3)	5.20	2.10

Basket and World Map — AP120

1973, May 26 *Perf. 13x13½*

C370	AP120	5s green	.90	.30
C371	AP120	20s lil rose	3.25	1.00

1st International Basketball Festival.

Darwin's Rhea — AP121

3.50s, Giant otter. 6s, Greater flamingo. 8.50s, Bush dog, horiz. 10s, Chinchilla, horiz.

1973, Sept. 3 Litho. *Perf. 13½x13*

C372	AP121	2.50s shown	2.00	1.00
C373	AP121	3.50s multi	3.25	1.25
C374	AP121	6s multi	4.00	1.25
C375	AP121	8.50s multi	4.00	1.75
C376	AP121	10s multi	5.00	2.50
		Nos. C372-C376 (5)	18.25	7.75

Protected animals.

Orchid — AP122

Designs: Various orchids.

1973, Sept. 27

C377	AP122	1.50s blk & multi	1.50	.75
C378	AP122	2.50s blk & multi	2.60	.75
C379	AP122	3s blk & multi	3.00	.75
C380	AP122	3.50s blk & multi	3.25	.75
C381	AP122	8s blk & multi	7.25	.75
		Nos. C377-C381 (5)	17.60	3.75

Pacific Fair Emblem — AP123

1973, Nov. 14 Litho. *Perf. 13½x13*

C382	AP123	8s blk, red & gray	1.60	.45

8th International Pacific Fair, Lima.

Cargo Ship ILO — AP124

Designs: 2.50s, Boats of Pescaperu fishing organization. 8s, Jet and seagull.

1973, Dec. 14 Litho. *Perf. 13*

C383	AP124	1.50s multi	.45	.25
C384	AP124	2.50s multi	.70	.30
C385	AP124	8s multi	2.25	.30
		Nos. C383-C385 (3)	3.40	.85

Issued to promote government enterprises.

Lima Monument AP125

1973, Nov. 27 *Perf. 13*

C386	AP125	8.50s red & multi	1.60	.40

50th anniversary of Air Force Academy. Monument honors Jorge Chavez, Peruvian aviator.

Bridge at Yananacu, by Enrique Camino Brant — AP126

Paintings: 10s, Peruvian Birds, by Teodoro Nuñez Ureta, vert. 50s, Boats of Totora, by Jorge Vinatea Reinoso.

1973, Dec. 28 *Perf. 13x13½, 13½x13*

C387	AP126	8s multi	1.30	.30
C388	AP126	10s multi	2.00	.65
C389	AP126	50s multi	9.25	3.25
		Nos. C387-C389 (3)	12.55	4.20

Moral House, Arequipa AP127

2.50s, El Misti Mountain, Arequipa. 5s, Puya Raymondi (cacti), vert. 6s, Huascaran Mountain. 8s, Lake Querococha. Views on 5s, 6s, 8s are views in White Cordilleras Range, Ancash Province.

1974, Feb. 11

C390	AP127	1.50s multi	.35	.25
C391	AP127	2.50s multi	.80	.25
C392	AP127	5s multi	1.10	.25
C393	AP127	6s multi	1.70	.25
C394	AP127	8s multi	2.75	.65
		Nos. C390-C394 (5)	6.70	1.65

San Jeronimo's, Cuzco — AP128

Churches of Peru: 3.50s, Cajamarca Cathedral. 5s, San Pedro's, Zepita-Puno, horiz. 6s, Cuzco Cathedral. 8.50s, Santo Domingo, Cuzco.

1974, May 6

C395	AP128	1.50s multi	1.00	.30
C396	AP128	3.50s multi	1.00	.30
C397	AP128	5s multi	1.75	.30
C398	AP128	6s multi	1.75	.40
C399	AP128	8.50s multi	2.90	.50
		Nos. C395-C399 (5)	8.40	1.80

Surrender at Ayacucho, by Daniel Hernandez AP129

Designs: 6s, Battle of Junin, by Felix Yañex. 7.50s, Battle of Ayachucho, by Felix Yañez.

1974 Litho. *Perf. 13x13½*

C400	AP129	3.50s multi	.95	.40
C401	AP129	6s multi	1.60	.40
C402	AP129	7.50s multi	1.60	.40
C403	AP129	8.50s multi	1.90	.40
C404	AP129	10s multi	2.25	.65
		Nos. C400-C404 (5)	8.30	2.25

Sesquicentennial of the Battles of Junin and Ayacucho and of the surrender at Ayacucho. Issued: 7.50s, 8/6; 6s, 10/9; others, 12/9.

Chavin Stone, Ancash — AP130

Machu Picchu, Cuzco — AP131

#C407, C409, Different bas-reliefs from Chavin Stone. #C408, Baths of Tampumacchay, Cuzco. #C410, Ruins of Kencco, Cuzco.

1974, Mar. 25 *Perf. 13½x13, 13x13½*

C405	AP130	3s multi	1.40	.25
C406	AP131	3s multi	1.00	.25
C407	AP130	5s multi	2.75	.65
C408	AP131	5s multi	1.10	.25
C409	AP130	10s multi	2.75	.65
C410	AP131	10s multi	2.40	.25
		Nos. C405-C410 (6)	11.40	2.30

Cacajao Rubicundus — AP132

1974, Oct. 21 *Perf. 13½x13*

C411	AP132	8s multi	1.50	.45
C412	AP132	20s multi	3.25	1.10

Protected animals.

Inca Gold Mask — AP133

1974, Nov. 8 *Perf. 13x13½*

C413	AP133	8s yel & multi	2.40	.80

8th World Mining Congress, Lima.

Chalan, Horseman's Cloak — AP134

1974, Nov. 11 Litho. *Perf. 13½x13*

C414	AP134	5s multi	.90	.25
C415	AP134	8.50s multi	1.75	.55

See Nos. C343-C348.

Pedro Paulet and Aerial Torpedo — AP135

1974, Nov. 28 Litho. *Perf. 13½x13*

C416	AP135	8s bl & vio	1.25	.40

UPU, cent. Pedro Paulet, inventor of the mail-carrying aerial torpedo.

Christmas Type of 1974

Design: 6.50s, Indian Nativity scene.

1974, Dec. 20 *Perf. 13½x13*

C417	A235	6.50s multi	1.00	.40

Andean Village, Map of South American West Coast — AP136

1974, Dec. 30

C418	AP136	6.50s multi	1.10	.40

Meeting of Communications Ministers of Andean Pact countries.

Map of Peru, Modern Buildings, UN Emblem — AP137

1975, Mar. 12 Litho. *Perf. 13½x13*

C419	AP137	6s blk, gray & red	1.00	.45

2nd United Nations Industrial Development Organization Conference, Lima.

Nos. C187, C211 and C160 Surcharged with New Value and Heavy Bar in Dark Blue

Wmk. 346

1975, April Litho. *Perf. 12*

C420	AP51	2s on 4.30s org	.85	.25

Perf. 13½x14, 13x14

Unwmk.

C421	AP51	2.50s on 4.60s org	1.00	.25
C422	AP51	5s on 3.80s org	1.25	.40
		Nos. C420-C422 (3)	3.10	.90

World Map and Peruvian Colors — AP138

1975, Aug. 25 Litho. *Perf. 13x13½*

C423	AP138	6.50s lt bl, vio bl & red	1.60	.30

Conference of Foreign Ministers of Nonaligned Countries.

Map of Peru and Flight Route — AP139

1975, Oct. 23 Litho. *Perf. 13x13½*

C424	AP139	8s red, pink & blk	1.50	.30

AeroPeru's first flights: Lima-Rio de Janeiro, Lima-Los Angeles.

Fair Poster — AP140

1975, Nov. 21 Litho. *Perf. 13½x13*

C425 AP140 6s blk, bis & red 1.25 .30

9th International Pacific Fair, Lima, 1975.

Col. Francisco Bolognesi — AP141

1975, Dec. 23 Litho. *Perf. 13½x13*

C426 AP141 20s multi 3.25 1.10

160th birth anniv. of Col. Bolognesi.

Indian Mother and Child — AP142

1976, Feb. 23 Litho. *Perf. 13½x13*

C427 AP142 6s gray & multi 1.25 .30

Christmas 1975.

Inca Messenger, UPAE Emblem — AP143

1976, Mar. 19 Litho. *Perf. 13½x13*

C428 AP143 5s red, blk & tan 1.25 .30

11th Congress of the Postal Union of the Americas and Spain, UPAE.

Nos. C187, C211, C160, C209, C210 Surcharged in Dark Blue or Violet Blue (No Bar)

1976 **As Before**

C429	AP51	2s on 4.30s org	.35	.25
C430	AP51	3.50s on 4.60s org	.35	.25
C431	AP51	4.50s on 3.80s org	.35	.25
C432	AP51	5s on 4.30s org	.55	.25
C433	AP51	6s on 4.60s org	.85	.25
C434	A184	10s on 2.60s brt grn	1.00	.40
C435	AP52	50s on 3.60s lil rose (VB)	5.75	3.00
		Nos. C429-C435 (7)	9.20	4.65

Stamps of 1962-67 Surcharged with New Value and Heavy Bar in Black, Red, Green, Dark Blue or Orange

1976-77 **As Before**

C436	AP52	1.50s on 3.60s (Bk) #C210	.45	.25
C437	A184	2s on 2.60s (R) #C209 ('77)	.45	.25
C438	AP52	2s on 3.60s (G) #C210	.45	.25
C439	AP80	2s on 4.30s (Bk) #C199	.45	.25
C440	A184	3s on 2.60s (Bk) #C209 ('77)	.45	.25
C441	A184	4s on 2.60s (DBl) #C209	.65	.30
C442	AP52	4s on 3.60s (DBl) #C210 ('77)	.65	.30
C443	AP51	5s on 4.30s (R) #C187	.95	.30
C444	AP83	6s on 4.60s (Bk) #C208 ('77)	.95	.30
C445	AP51	6s on 4.60s (DBl) #C211 ('77)	.95	.30
C446	AP51	7s on 4.30s (Bk) #C187 ('77)	.65	.30
C447	AP52	7.50s on 3.60s (DBl) #C210	1.00	.40
C448	AP52	8s on 3.60s (O) #C210	1.40	.30
C449	AP51	10s on 4.30s (Bk) #C187 ('77)	.75	.30
C450	AP51	10s on 4.60s (DBl) #C211	1.40	.30
C451	AP86	24s on 3.60s (Bk) #C220 ('77)	3.75	.95
C452	AP86	28s on 4.60s (Bk) #C221 ('77)	3.25	1.10
C453	AP86	32s on 5.60s (Bk) #C222 ('77)	3.25	1.10
C454	A184	50s on 2.60s (O) #C209 ('77)	9.00	1.75
C455	AP52	50s on 3.60s (G) #C210	5.25	2.25
		Nos. C436-C455 (20)	36.10	11.50

AP144

Map of Tacna and Tarata Provinces.

1976, Aug. 28 Litho. *Perf. 13½x13*

C456 AP144 10s multi 1.25 .30

Re-incorporation of Tacna Province into Peru, 47th anniversary.

AP145

Investigative Police badge.

1976, Sept. 15 Litho. *Perf. 13½x13*

C457 AP145 20s multi 1.75 .70

Investigative Police of Peru, 54th anniv.

Declaration of Bogota — AP146

1976, Sept. 22

C458 AP146 10s multi 1.25 .40

Declaration of Bogota for cooperation and world peace, 10th anniversary.

AP147

Pal Losonczi and map of Hungary.

1976, Nov. 2 Litho. *Perf. 13½x13*

C459 AP147 7s ultra & blk 1.25 .40

Visit of Pres. Pal Losonczi of Hungary, Oct. 1976.

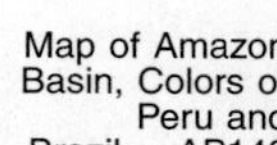

Map of Amazon Basin, Colors of Peru and Brazil — AP148

1976, Dec. 16 Litho. *Perf. 13*

C460 AP148 10s bl & multi 1.25 .40

Visit of Gen. Ernesto Geisel, president of Brazil, Nov. 5, 1976.

Liberation Monument, Lima — AP149

1977, Mar. 9 Litho. *Perf. 13x13½*

C461 AP149 20s red buff & blk 2.10 .65

Army Day.

Map of Peru and Venezuela, South America — AP150

1977, Mar. 14

C462 AP150 12s buff & multi 1.60 .55

Meeting of Pres. Francisco Morales Bermudez Cerrutti of Peru and Pres. Carlos Andres Perez of Venezuela, Dec. 1976.

Electronic Tree — AP151

1977, May 30 Litho. *Perf. 13½x13*

C463 AP151 20s gray, red & blk 2.60 .75

World Telecommunications Day.

Map of Peru, Refinery, Tanker — AP152

1977, July 13 Litho. *Perf. 13½x13*

C464 AP152 14s multi 1.25 .45

Development of Bayovar oil complex.

Messenger Type of 1977

1977 Litho. *Perf. 13½x13*

C465	A243	24s mag & blk	2.40	.75
C466	A243	28s bl & blk	3.75	.75
C467	A243	32s rose brn & blk	2.50	1.10
		Nos. C465-C467 (3)	8.65	2.60

For surcharge see No. C502.

Arms of Arequipa — AP153

1977, Sept. 3 Litho. *Perf. 13½x13*

C468 AP153 10s multi .85 .30

Gold of Peru Exhibition, Arequipa 1977.

Gen. Jorge Rafael Videla — AP154

1977, Oct. 8 Litho. *Perf. 13½x13*

C469 AP154 36s multi 1.60 .40

Visit of Jorge Rafael Videla, president of Argentina.

Stamps of 1953-67 Surcharged with New Value and Heavy Bar in Black, Dark Blue or Green

1977 **As Before**

C470	AP83	2s on 3.60s #C207	.45	.25
C471	AP51	2s on 4.60s (DB) #C211	.45	.25
C472	AP51	4s on 4.60s (DB) #C211	.65	.25
C473	AP51	5s on 4.30s #C187	.75	.40
C474	AP52	5s on 3.60s #C210	.45	.25
C475	AP55	10s on 2.15s #C125	1.00	.30
C476	AP52	10s on 3.60s (DB) #C210	1.75	.45
C477	AP84	10s on 3.60s #C215	1.60	.45
C478	AP52	20s on 3.60s (DB) #C210	1.60	.55
C479	AP51	100s on 3.80s (G) #C160	7.00	3.00
		Nos. C470-C479 (10)	15.70	6.15

Nos. C223-C224 Surcharged with New Value, Heavy Bars and: "FRANQUEO"

1977 Litho. *Perf. 12*

C480	AP87	6s on 3.60s multi	1.50	.65
C481	AP87	8s on 3.60s multi	1.90	.90
C482	AP87	10s on 5.60s multi	1.90	1.00
		Nos. C480-C482 (3)	5.30	2.55

Adm. Miguel Grau — AP155

1977, Dec. 15 Litho. *Perf. 13½x13*

C483 AP155 28s multi 1.25 .45

Navy Day. Miguel Grau (1838-1879), Peruvian naval commander.

Christmas Type of 1977

1977, Dec. 23

C484 A246 20s Indian Nativity 1.30 .40

Andrés Bello, Flag and Map of Participants AP156

1978, Jan. 12 Litho. *Perf. 13*

C485 AP156 30s multi 1.10 .35

8th Meeting of Education Ministers honoring Andrés Bello, Lima.

Inca Type of 1978

1978 Litho. *Perf. 13½x13*

C486	A247	24s dp rose lil	.95	.45
C487	A247	30s salmon	1.10	.45
C488	A247	65s brt bl	2.75	1.00
C489	A247	95s dk bl	4.00	1.60
		Nos. C486-C489 (4)	8.80	3.50

For surcharge see No. C501.

Antenna, ITU Emblem — AP157

1978, July 3 Litho. *Perf. 13x13½*

C490 AP157 50s gray & multi	1.75	1.25

10th World Telecommunications Day.

San Martin, Flag Colors of Peru and Argentina — AP158

1978, Sept. 4 Litho. *Perf. 13½x13*

C491 AP158 30s multi	1.25	.75

Gen. José de San Martin (1778-1850), soldier and statesman, protector of Peru.

Stamps of 1965-67 Surcharged "Habilitado / R.D. No. O118" and New Value in Red, Green, Violet Blue or Black

1978 Litho.

C492 AP83 34s on 4.60s multi (R) #C208	*1.10*	*.40*
C493 AP79 40s on 4.30s multi (G) #C196	*1.25*	*.50*
C494 A184 70s on 2.60s brt grn (VB) #C209	*2.25*	*.85*
C495 AP52 110s on 3.60s lil rose (Bk) #C210	*4.50*	*1.10*
C496 AP80 265s on 4.30s gray & multi (Bk) #C199	*8.00*	*3.25*
Nos. C492-C496 (5)	*17.10*	*6.10*

Stamps and Type of 1968-78 Surcharged in Violet Blue, Black or Red

1978 Litho.

C497 AP86 25s on 4.60s (VB) #C221	*1.10*	*.50*
C498 A247 45s on 28s dk grn (Bk)	*2.25*	*.55*
C499 A247 75s on 28s dk grn (R)	*3.50*	*1.10*
C500 AP86 105s on 5.60s (R) #C222	*5.00*	*1.75*
Nos. C497-C500 (4)	*11.85*	*3.90*

Nos. C498-C499 not issued without surcharge.

Nos. C486, C467 Surcharged

1980, Apr. 14 Litho. *Perf. 13½x13*

C501 A247 35s on 24s dp rose lil	.95	.45
C502 A243 45s on 32s rose brn & blk	1.00	.50

No. C130 Surcharged in Black

1981, Nov. Engr. *Perf. 13*

C503 AP57 30s on 2.20s multi	1.00	.45
C504 AP57 40s on 2.20s multi	1.00	.40

No. C130 Surcharged and Overprinted in Green: "12 Feria / Internacional / del / Pacifico 1981"

1981, Nov. 30

C505 AP57 140s on 2.20s multi	2.50	1.25

12th Intl. Pacific Fair.

AIR POST SEMI-POSTAL STAMPS

Catalogue values for unused stamps in this section are for Never Hinged items.

Chavin Griffin — SPAP1

1.50s+1s, Bird. 3s+2.50s, Cat. 4.30s+3s, Mythological figure, vert. 6s+ 4s, Chavin god, vert.

Perf. 12½x12, 12x12½

1963, Apr. 18 Litho. Wmk. 346

Design in Gray and Brown

CB1 SPAP1 1s + 50c sal pink	.45	.35
CB2 SPAP1 1.50s + 1s blue	.75	.55
CB3 SPAP1 3s + 2.50s lt grn	1.20	.85
CB4 SPAP1 4.30s + 3s green	2.40	1.60
CB5 SPAP1 6s + 4s citron	3.00	2.00
Nos. CB1-CB5 (5)	7.80	5.35

The designs are from ceramics found by archaeological excavations of the 14th century Chavin culture. The surtax was for the excavations fund.

Henri Dunant and Centenary Emblem — SPAP2

Perf. 12½x12

1964, Jan. 29 Unwmk.

CB6 SPAP2 1.30s + 70c multi	.90	.55
CB7 SPAP2 4.30s + 1.70s multi	1.75	1.10

Centenary of International Red Cross.

SPECIAL DELIVERY STAMPS

No. 149 Overprinted in Black

1908 Unwmk. *Perf. 12*

E1 A25 10c gray black	25.00	19.00

No. 172 Overprinted in Violet

1909

E2 A40 10c red brn & blk	40.00	22.50

No. 181 Handstamped in Violet

1910

E3 A49 10c deep blue	24.00	20.00

Two handstamps were used to make No. E2. Impressions from them measure 22½x6½mm and 24x6½mm.

Counterfeits exist of Nos. E1-3.

POSTAGE DUE STAMPS

Coat of Arms — D1

Steamship and Llama
D2 D3

D4

D5

With Grill

1874-79 Unwmk. Engr. *Perf. 12*

J1 D1 1c bister ('79)	.45	.30
J2 D2 5c vermilion	.55	.30
J3 D3 10c orange	.65	.30
J4 D4 20c blue	1.10	.55
J5 D5 50c brown	17.00	6.50
Nos. J1-J5 (5)	19.75	7.95

A 2c green exists, but was not regularly issued.

For overprints and surcharges see Nos. 157, J6-J31, J37-J38, 8N14-8N15, 14N18.

1902-07 Without Grill

J1a D1 1c bister	.35
J2a D2 5c vermilion	.55
J3a D3 10c orange	.55
J4a D4 20c blue	.65
Nos. J1a-J4a (4)	2.10

Nos. J1-J5 Overprinted in Blue or Red

1881 "PLATA" 2½mm High

J6 D1 1c bis (Bl)	6.00	5.00
J7 D2 5c ver (Bl)	12.00	11.00
a. Double overprint		
b. Inverted overprint	24.00	24.00
J8 D3 10c org (Bl)	12.00	11.00
a. Inverted overprint	24.00	24.00
J9 D4 20c bl (R)	45.00	32.50
J10 D5 50c brn (Bl)	100.00	90.00
Nos. J6-J10 (5)	175.00	149.50

In the reprints of this overprint "PLATA" is 3mm high instead of 2½mm. Besides being struck in the regular colors it was also applied to the 1, 5, 10 and 50c in red and the 20c in blue.

Overprinted in Red

1881

J11 D1 1c bister	9.00	9.00
J12 D2 5c vermilion	11.00	10.00
J13 D3 10c orange	13.00	13.00
J14 D4 20c blue	55.00	37.50
J15 D5 50c brown	125.00	125.00
Nos. J11-J15 (5)	213.00	194.50

Originals of Nos. J11 to J15 are overprinted in brick-red, oily ink; reprints in thicker, bright red ink. The 5c exists with reprinted overprint in blue.

Overprinted "Union Postal Universal Lima Plata" in Oval in first named color and Triangle in second named color

1883

J16 D1 1c bis (Bl & Bk)	9.00	6.50
J17 D1 1c bis (Bk & Bl)	13.00	13.00
J18 D2 5c ver (Bl & Bk)	13.00	13.00
J19 D3 10c org (Bl & Bk)	13.00	13.00
J20 D4 20c bl (R & Bk)	*850.00*	*850.00*
J21 D5 50c brn (Bl & Bk)	60.00	60.00

Reprints of Nos. J16 to J21 have the oval overprint with "PLATA" 3mm. high. The 1c also exists with the oval overprint in red.

Overprinted in Black

1884

J22 D1 1c bister	.90	.90
J23 D2 5c vermilion	.90	.90
J24 D3 10c orange	.90	.90
J25 D4 20c blue	1.90	.90
J26 D5 50c brown	5.50	1.75
Nos. J22-J26 (5)	10.10	5.35

The triangular overprint is found in 11 types.

Overprinted "Lima Correos" in Circle in Red and Triangle in Black

1884

J27 D1 1c bister	42.50	42.50

Reprints of No. J27 have the overprint in bright red. At the time they were made the overprint was also printed on the 5, 10, 20 and 50c Postage Due stamps.

Postage Due stamps overprinted with Sun and "CORREOS LIMA" (as shown above No. 103), alone or in combination with the "U. P. U. LIMA" oval or "LIMA CORREOS" in double-lined circle, are fancy varieties made to sell to collectors and never placed in use.

Overprinted

1896-97

J28 D1 1c bister	.65	.55
a. Double overprint		
J29 D2 5c vermilion	.75	.45
a. Double overprint		
b. Inverted overprint		
J30 D3 10c orange	1.00	.65
a. Inverted overprint		
J31 D4 20c blue	1.25	.85
a. Double overprint		
J32 A22 50c red ('97)	1.25	.85
J33 A23 1s brown ('97)	1.90	1.25
a. Double overprint		
b. Inverted overprint		
Nos. J28-J33 (6)	6.80	4.60

Liberty — D6

1899 Engr.

J34 D6 5s yel grn	1.90	*10.50*
J35 D6 10s dl vio	1,700.	1,700.

For surcharge see No. J39.

No. J36

No. J37

1902 On No. 159

J36 A31 5c on 10s bl grn	1.90	1.50
a. Double surcharge	20.00	20.00

On No. J4

J37 D4 1c on 20c blue	1.10	.75
a. "DEFICIT" omitted	15.00	3.50
b. "DEFICIT" double	15.00	3.50
c. "UN CENTAVO" double	15.00	3.50
d. "UN CENTAVO" omitted	18.00	10.00

Surcharged Vertically

J38 D4 5c on 20c blue	2.75	1.75

No. J35 Surcharged Diagonally

J39 D6 1c on 10s dull vio	.75	.75
Nos. J36-J39 (4)	6.50	4.75

D7

1909 Engr. *Perf. 12*

No.	Type	Description	Unused	Used
J40	D7	1c red brown	.90	.30
J41	D7	5c red brown	.90	.30
J42	D7	10c red brown	1.10	.45
J43	D7	50c red brown	1.75	.45
		Nos. J40-J43 (4)	4.65	1.50

1921 Size: 18¼x22mm

No.	Type	Description	Unused	Used
J44	D7	1c violet brown	.45	.30
J45	D7	2c violet brown	.45	.30
J46	D7	5c violet brown	.65	.30
J47	D7	10c violet brown	.90	.45
J48	D7	50c violet brown	2.75	1.25
J49	D7	1s violet brown	13.00	5.25
J50	D7	2s violet brown	22.50	6.50
		Nos. J44-J50 (7)	40.70	14.35

Nos. J49 and J50 have the circle at the center replaced by a shield containing "S/.", in addition to the numeral.

In 1929 during a shortage of regular postage stamps, some of the Postage Due stamps of 1921 were used instead.

See Nos. J50A-J52, J55-J56. For surcharges see Nos. 204-207, 757.

Type of 1909-22

Size: 18¾x23mm

No.	Type	Description	Unused	Used
J50A	D7	2c violet brown	1.25	.30
J50B	D7	10c violet brown	1.75	.45

Type of 1909-22 Issues

1932 Photo. *Perf. 14½x14*

No.	Type	Description	Unused	Used
J51	D7	2c violet brown	1.25	.45
J52	D7	10c violet brown	1.25	.45

Regular Stamps of 1934-35 Overprinted in Black

1935 *Perf. 13*

No.	Type	Description	Unused	Used
J53	A131	2c deep claret	1.25	.50
J54	A117	10c crimson	1.25	.50

Type of 1909-32

Size: 19x23mm

Imprint: "Waterlow & Sons, Limited, Londres."

1936 Engr. *Perf. 12½*

No.	Type	Description	Unused	Used
J55	D7	2c light brown	.45	.45
J56	D7	10c gray green	.90	.90

OFFICIAL STAMPS

Regular Issue of 1886 Overprinted in Red

1890, Feb. 2

No.	Type	Description	Unused	Used
O2	A17	1c dl vio	2.40	2.40
a.		Double overprint	14.00	14.00
O3	A18	2c green	2.40	2.40
a.		Double overprint		
b.		Inverted overprint	14.00	14.00
O4	A19	5c orange	3.50	2.75
a.		Inverted overprint	14.00	14.00
b.		Double overprint	14.00	14.00
O5	A20	10c slate	2.00	1.25
a.		Double overprint	14.00	14.00
b.		Inverted overprint	14.00	14.00
O6	A21	20c blue	5.50	3.50
a.		Double overprint	14.00	14.00
b.		Inverted overprint	14.00	14.00
O7	A22	50c red	7.25	3.25
a.		Inverted overprint	20.00	
b.		Double overprint		
O8	A23	1s brown	9.00	8.00
a.		Double overprint	27.50	27.50
b.		Inverted overprint	27.50	27.50
		Nos. O2-O8 (7)	32.05	23.55

Nos. 118-124 (Bermudez Ovpt.) Overprinted Type "a" in Red

1894, Oct.

No.	Type	Description	Unused	Used
O9	A17	1c green	2.40	2.40
a.		"Gobierno" and head invtd.	11.00	9.25
b.		Dbl. ovpt. of "Gobierno"		
O10	A17	1c orange	40.00	32.50
O11	A18	2c rose	2.40	2.40
a.		Overprinted head inverted	17.00	17.00
b.		Both overprints inverted		
O12	A18	2c violet	2.40	2.40
a.		"Gobierno" double		
O13	A19	5c ultra	40.00	32.50
a.		Both overprints inverted		
O14	A19	5c blue	19.00	16.00
O15	A20	10c green	6.00	6.00
O16	A22	50c green	9.00	9.00
		Nos. O9-O16 (8)	121.20	103.20

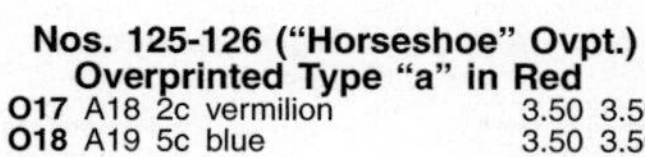

Nos. 125-126 ("Horseshoe" Ovpt.) Overprinted Type "a" in Red

No.	Type	Description	Unused	Used
O17	A18	2c vermilion	3.50	3.50
O18	A19	5c blue	3.50	3.50

Nos. 105, 107, 109, 113 Overprinted Type "a" in Red

1895, May

No.	Type	Description	Unused	Used
O19	A17	1c vermilion	13.00	13.00
O20	A18	2c dp ultra	13.00	13.00
O21	A12	5c claret	11.00	11.00
O22	A14	20c dp ultra	11.00	11.00
		Nos. O19-O22 (4)	48.00	48.00

Nos. O2-O22 have been extensively counterfeited.

Nos. 141, 148, 149, 151 Overprinted in Black

1896-1901

No.	Type	Description	Unused	Used
O23	A24	1c ultra	.35	.30
O24	A25	10c yellow	1.00	.50
a.		Double overprint	22.50	
O25	A25	10c gray blk ('01)	.35	.30
O26	A26	50c brt rose	5.00	5.00
		Nos. O23-O26 (4)	6.70	6.10

O1

1909-14 Engr. *Perf. 12*

Size: 18½x22mm

No.	Type	Description	Unused	Used
O27	O1	1c red	.55	.30
a.		1c brown red	.55	.30
O28	O1	1c orange ('14)	.90	.65
O29	O1	10c bis brn ('14)	.35	.30
a.		10c violet brown	.90	.45
O30	O1	50c ol grn ('14)	1.25	.65
a.		50c blue green	2.00	.65

Size: 18¾x23½mm

No.	Type	Description	Unused	Used
O30B	O1	10c vio brn	.90	.30
		Nos. O27-O30B (5)	3.95	2.20

See Nos. O31, O33-O34. For overprints and surcharge see Nos. 201-203, 760.

1933 Photo. *Perf. 15x14*

No.	Type	Description	Unused	Used
O31	O1	10c violet brown	1.25	.45

No. 319 Overprinted in Black

1935 Unwmk. *Perf. 13*

No.	Type	Description	Unused	Used
O32	A117	10c crimson	.35	.25

Type of 1909-33

Imprint: "Waterlow & Sons, Limited, Londres."

1936 Engr. *Perf. 12½*

Size: 19x23mm

No.	Type	Description	Unused	Used
O33	O1	10c light brown	.25	.25
O34	O1	50c gray green	.65	.65

PARCEL POST STAMPS

PP1

PP2

PP3

1897 Typeset Unwmk. *Perf. 12*

No.	Type	Description	Unused	Used
Q1	PP1	1c dull lilac	4.00	3.50
Q2	PP2	2c bister	5.50	3.75
a.		2c olive	5.50	3.75
b.		2c yellow	5.50	3.75
c.		Laid paper	65.00	65.00
Q3	PP3	5c dk bl	19.00	10.50
a.		Tête bêche pair	*375.00*	
Q4	PP3	10c vio brn	24.00	18.00
Q5	PP3	20c rose red	29.00	22.50
Q6	PP3	50c bl grn	85.00	75.00
		Nos. Q1-Q6 (6)	166.50	133.25

Surcharged in Black

1903-04

No.	Type	Description	Unused	Used
Q7	PP3	1c on 20c rose red	12.00	10.00
Q8	PP3	1c on 50c bl grn	12.00	10.00
Q9	PP3	5c on 10c vio brn	80.00	65.00
a.		Inverted surcharge	125.00	110.00
b.		Double surcharge		
		Nos. Q7-Q9 (3)	104.00	85.00

POSTAL TAX STAMPS

Plebiscite Issues

These stamps were not used in Tacna and Arica (which were under Chilean occupation) but were used in Peru to pay a supplementary tax on letters, etc.

It was intended that the money derived from the sale of these stamps should be used to help defray the expenses of the plebiscite.

Morro Arica — PT1

Adm. Grau and Col. Bolognesi Reviewing Troops PT2

Bolognesi Monument PT3

1925-26 Unwmk. Litho. *Perf. 12*

No.	Type	Description	Unused	Used
RA1	PT1	5c dp bl	2.75	.75
RA2	PT1	5c rose red	1.40	.55
RA3	PT1	5c yel grn	1.25	.55
RA4	PT2	10c brown	5.50	*22.50*
RA5	PT3	50c bl grn	35.00	17.00
		Nos. RA1-RA5 (5)	45.90	41.35

PT4

1926

No.	Type	Description	Unused	Used
RA6	PT4	2c orange	1.10	.30

PT5

1927-28

No.	Type	Description	Unused	Used
RA7	PT5	2c dp org	1.10	.30
RA8	PT5	2c red brn	1.10	.30
RA9	PT5	2c dk bl	1.10	.30
RA10	PT5	2c gray vio	1.10	.30
RA11	PT5	2c bl grn ('28)	1.10	.30
RA12	PT5	20c red	5.50	1.75
		Nos. RA7-RA12 (6)	11.00	3.25

PT6

1928 Engr.

No.	Type	Description	Unused	Used
RA13	PT6	2c dk vio	.55	.25

The use of the Plebiscite stamps was discontinued July 26, 1929, after the settlement of the Tacna-Arica controversy with Chile.

For overprint see No. 261.

Unemployment Fund Issues

These stamps were required in addition to the ordinary postage, on every letter or piece of postal matter. The money obtained by their sale was to assist the unemployed.

Nos. 273-275 Surcharged

1931

No.	Type	Description	Unused	Used
RA14	A95	2c on 4c red	1.75	.75
a.		Inverted surcharge	4.25	4.25
RA15	A95	2c on 10c bl grn	.75	.75
a.		Inverted surcharge	4.25	4.25
RA16	A95	2c on 15c sl gray	.75	.75
a.		Inverted surcharge	4.25	4.25
		Nos. RA14-RA16 (3)	3.25	2.25

"Labor" — PT7

Two types of Nos. RA17-RA18:
I — Imprint 15mm.
II — Imprint 13¾mm.

Perf. 12x11½, 11½x12

1931-32 Litho.

No.	Type	Description	Unused	Used
RA17	PT7	2c emer (I)	.30	.25
a.		Type II	.30	
RA18	PT7	2c rose car (I) ('32)	.30	.25
a.		Type II	.30	

Blacksmith — PT8

1932-34

No.	Type	Description	Unused	Used
RA19	PT8	2c dp gray	.25	.25
RA20	PT8	2c pur ('34)	.35	.25

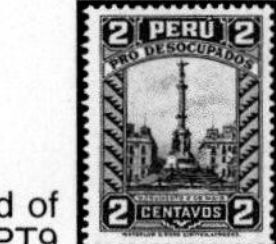

Monument of 2nd of May — PT9

Perf. 13, 13½, 13x13½

1933-35 Photo.

No.	Type	Description	Unused	Used
RA21	PT9	2c bl vio	.30	.25
RA22	PT9	2c org ('34)	.30	.25
RA23	PT9	2c brn vio ('35)	.30	.25
		Nos. RA21-RA23 (3)	.90	.75

For overprint see No. RA27.

No. 307 Overprinted in Black

1934 *Perf. 13½*

No.	Type	Description	Unused	Used
RA24	A111	2c green	.30	.25
a.		Inverted overprint	2.25	2.00

No. 339 Overprinted in Black

1935

RA25 A131 2c deep claret .30 .25

No. 339 Overprinted Type "a" in Black

1936 Unwmk. *Perf. 13½*

RA26 A131 2c deep claret .30 .25

No. RA23 Overprinted in Black

1936 *Perf. 13x13½*

RA27 PT9 2c brn vio .30 .25
- *a.* Double overprint 3.50
- *b.* Overprint reading down 3.50
- *c.* Overprint double, reading down 3.50

St. Rosa of Lima — PT10

1937 Engr. *Perf. 12*

RA28 PT10 2c car rose .30 .25

Nos. RA27 and RA28 represented a tax to help erect a church.

"Protection" by John Q. A. Ward — PT11

Imprint: "American Bank Note Company"

1938 Litho.

RA29 PT11 2c red brown .35 .25

The tax was to help the unemployed. See Nos. RA30, RA34, RA40.

Type of 1938 Redrawn

Imprint: "Columbian Bank Note Company."

1943 *Perf. 12½*

RA30 PT11 2c dl claret brn .40 .40

See note above #RA14. See #RA29, #RA34, RA40.

Catalogue values for unused stamps in this section, from this point to the end of the section, are for Never Hinged items.

PT12 PT13

Black Surcharge

1949 *Perf. 12½, 12*

RA31 PT12 3c on 4c vio bl 1.40 .40

RA32 PT13 3c on 10c blue .140 .40

The tax was for an education fund.

Symbolical of Education — PT14

1950 Typo. *Perf. 14*

Size: 16½x21mm

RA33 PT14 3c dp car .60 .40

See Nos. RA35, RA39, RA43

For surcharges see Nos. 501B, 761, 764-766, RA45-RA48, RA58.

Type of 1938

Imprint: "Thomas De La Rue & Co. Ltd."

1951 Litho.

RA34 PT11 2c lt redsh brn .60 .40

See Nos. RA29, RA30, RA40.

Type of 1950

Imprint: "Thomas De La Rue & Company, Limited."

1952 Unwmk. *Perf. 14, 13*

Size: 16½x21½mm

RA35 PT14 3c brn car .60 .40

Emblem of Congress — PT15

1954 *Rouletted 13*

RA36 PT15 5c bl & red .60 .40

The tax was to help finance the National Marian Eucharistic Congress.

For surcharges see Nos. 758B, 768.

Piura Arms and Congress Emblem — PT16

1960 Litho. *Perf. 10½*

RA37 PT16 10c ultra, red, grn & yel .60 .40
- *a.* Green ribbon inverted

RA38 PT16 10c ultra & red .60 .40

Nos. RA37-RA38 were used to help finance the 6th National Eucharistic Congress, Piura, Aug. 25-28. Obligatory on all domestic mail until Dec. 31, 1960. Both stamps exist imperf.

Type of 1950

Imprint: "Bundesdruckerei Berlin"

1961 Size: 17½x22½mm *Perf. 14*

RA39 PT14 3c dp car .60 .40

Type of 1938

Imprint: "Harrison and Sons Ltd"

1962, Apr. Litho. *Perf. 14x14½*

RA40 PT11 2c lt brn .60 .40

See Nos. RA29, RA30, RA34. For surcharges see Nos. 501A, 674-678, 681-682, 709-711, 757.

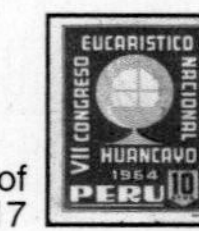

Symbol of Eucharist — PT17

1962, May 8 *Rouletted 11*

RA41 PT17 10c bl & org .60 .40

Issued to raise funds for the Seventh National Eucharistic Congress, Huancayo, 1964. Obligatory on all domestic mail.

See No. RA42. For surcharges and overprint see Nos. 735, 762, RA44.

1962 Imprint: "Iberia"

RA42 PT17 10c bl & org .60 .40

Type of 1950

Imprint: "Thomas de La Rue"

Size: 18x22mm

1965, Apr. Litho. *Perf. 12½x12*

RA43 PT14 3c light carmine .60 .40

Type of 1962 Overprinted in Red

Imprint: "Iberia"

1966, July 2 Litho. *Pin Perf.*

RA44 PT17 10c vio & org .60 .40

No. RA43 Surcharged in Green or Black

b

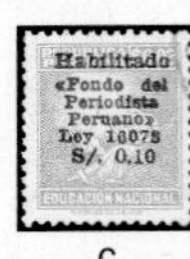

c

d

1966-67 *Perf. 12½x12*

RA45 PT14 (b) 10c on 3c (G) 1.50 .40

RA46 PT14 (c) 10c on 3c (Bk) 1.50 .40

RA47 PT14 (c) 10c on 3c (G) .45 .40

RA48 PT14 (d) 10c on 3c (G) .45 .40

Nos. RA45-RA48 (4) 3.90 1.60

The surtax of Nos. RA44-RA48 was for the Peruvian Journalists' Fund.

Pen Made of Newspaper — PT18

1967, Dec. Litho. *Perf. 11*

RA49 PT18 10c dk red & blk .65 .40

The surtax was for the Peruvian Journalists' fund.

For surcharges see Nos. RA56-RA57.

Temple at Chan-Chan — PT19

Designs: No. RA51, Side view of temple. Nos. RA52-RA55, Various stone bas-reliefs from Chan-Chan.

1967, Dec. 27

RA50 PT19 20c bl & multi .65 .40

RA51 PT19 20c lil rose & multi .65 .40

RA52 PT19 20c brt bl & blk .65 .40

RA53 PT19 20c emer & blk .65 .40

RA54 PT19 20c sep & blk .65 .40

RA55 PT19 20c lil rose & blk .65 .40

Nos. RA50-RA55 (6) 3.90 2.40

The surtax was for the excavations at Chan-Chan, northern coast of Peru. (Mochica-Chimu pre-Inca period).

Type of 1967 Surcharged in Red: "VEINTE / CENTAVOS / R.S. 16-8-68"

Designs: No. RA56, Handshake. No. RA57, Globe and pen.

1968, Oct. Litho. *Perf. 11*

RA56 PT18 20c on 50c multi 1.25 1.25

RA57 PT18 20c on 1s multi 1.25 1.25

Nos. RA56-RA57 without surcharge were not obligatory tax stamps.

No. C199 surcharged "PRO NAVIDAD/ Veinte Centavos/R.S. 5-11-68" was not a compulsory postal tax stamp.

No. RA43 Srchd. Similar to Type "c"

1968, Oct. *Perf. 12½x12*

RA58 PT14 20c on 3c lt car .65 .40

Surcharge lacks quotation marks and 4th line reads: Ley 17050.

OCCUPATION STAMPS

Issued under Chilean Occupation

Stamps formerly listed as Nos. N1-N10 are regular issues of Chile canceled in Peru.

Stamps of Peru, 1874-80, Overprinted in Red, Blue or Black

1881-82 *Perf. 12*

N11 A17 1c org (Bl) .50 1.00
- *a.* Inverted overprint

N12 A18 2c dk vio (Bk) .50 4.00
- *a.* Inverted overprint 16.50
- *b.* Double overprint 22.50

N13 A18 2c rose (Bk) 1.60 *18.00*
- *a.* Inverted overprint

N14 A19 5c bl (R) 55.00 62.50
- *a.* Inverted overprint

N15 A19 5c ultra (R) 90.00 100.00

N16 A20 10c grn (R) .50 *1.60*
- *a.* Inverted overprint 6.50 6.50
- *b.* Double overprint 12.00 12.00

N17 A21 20c brn red (Bl) 80.00 125.00

Nos. N11-N17 (7) 228.10 312.10

Reprints of No. N17 have the overprint in bright blue; on the originals it is in dull ultramarine. Nos. N11 and N12 exist with reprinted overprint in red or yellow. There are numerous counterfeits with the overprint in both correct and fancy colors.

Same, with Additional Overprint in Black

1882

N19 A17 1c grn (R) .50 .80
- *a.* Arms inverted 8.25 10.00
- *b.* Arms double 5.50 6.50
- *c.* Horseshoe inverted 12.00 13.50

N20 A19 5c bl (R) .80 .80
- *a.* Arms inverted 13.50 15.00
- *b.* Arms double 13.50 15.00

N21 A22 50c rose (Bk) 1.60 2.00
- *a.* Arms inverted 10.00

N22 A22 50c rose (Bl) 1.60 2.75

N23 A23 1s ultra (R) 3.25 4.50
- *a.* Arms inverted 13.50
- *b.* Horseshoe inverted 16.50
- *c.* Arms and horseshoe inverted 20.00
- *d.* Arms double 13.50

Nos. N19-N23 (5) 7.75 10.85

PROVISIONAL ISSUES

Stamps Issued in Various Cities of Peru during the Chilean Occupation of Lima and Callao

During the Chilean-Peruvian War which took place in 1879 to 1882, the Chilean forces occupied the two largest cities in Peru, Lima & Callao. As these cities were the source of supply of postage stamps, Peruvians in other sections of the country were left without stamps and were forced to the expedient of making provisional issues from whatever material was at hand. Many of these were former canceling devices made over for this purpose. Counterfeits exist of many of the overprinted stamps.

ANCACHS

(See Note under "Provisional Issues")

Regular Issue of Peru, Overprinted in Manuscript in Black

1884 Unwmk. *Perf. 12*

1N1 A19 5c blue 57.50 55.00

Regular Issues of Peru, Overprinted in Black

1N2 A19 5c blue 18.00 16.50

Regular Issues of Peru, Overprinted in Black

1N3 A19 5c blue 90.00 82.50

1N4 A20 10c green 55.00 40.00

1N5 A20 10c slate 55.00 35.00

Same, with Additional Overprint "FRANCA"

1N6 A20 10c green 82.50 42.50

Overprinted

1N7 A19 5c blue 30.00 30.00
1N8 A20 10c green 30.00 30.00

Same, with Additional Overprint "FRANCA"

1N9 A20 10c green

A1

Revenue Stamp of Peru, 1878-79, Ovptd. in Black "CORREO FISCAL" and/or "FRANCA"

1N10 A1 10c yellow 37.50 37.50

APURIMAC

(See Note under "Provisional Issues")

Provisional Issue of Arequipa Overprinted in Black

Overprint Covers Two Stamps

1885 **Unwmk.** ***Imperf.***
2N1 A6 10c gray 100.00 90.00

Some experts question the status of No. 2N1.

AREQUIPA

(See Note under "Provisional Issues")

Coat of Arms
A1 A2

Overprint ("PROVISIONAL 1881-1882") in Black

1881, Jan. **Unwmk.** ***Imperf.***
3N1 A1 10c blue 3.50 4.50
a. 10c ultramarine 3.50 5.00
b. Double overprint 12.00 13.50
c. Overprinted on back of stamp 8.25 10.00
3N2 A2 25c rose 3.50 6.00
a. "2" in upper left corner invtd. 8.25
b. "Cevtavos" 8.25 10.00
c. Double overprint 12.00 13.50

The overprint also exists on 5s yellow. Value, $100.

The overprints "1883" in large figures or "Habilitado 1883" are fraudulent.

For overprints see Nos. 3N3, 4N1, 8N1, 10N1, 15N1-15N3.

With Additional Overprint Handstamped in Red

1881, Feb.
3N3 A1 10c blue 3.50 3.50
a. 10c ultramarine 13.50 11.50

A4

1883 **Litho.**
3N7 A4 10c dull rose 3.50 5.00
a. 10c vermilion 3.50 5.00

Overprinted in Blue like No. 3N3

3N9 A4 10c vermilion 5.00 4.00
a. 10c dull rose 5.00 4.00

See No. 3N10. For overprints see Nos. 8N2, 8N9, 10N2, 15N4.

Reprints of No. 3N9 are in different colors from the originals, orange, bright red, etc. They are printed in sheets of 20 instead of 25.

Redrawn

3N10 A4 10c brick red (Bl) 160.00

The redrawn stamp has small triangles without arabesques in the lower spandrels. The palm branch at left of the shield and other parts of the design have been redrawn.

Same Overprint in Black, Violet or Magenta On Regular Issues of Peru

1884 **Embossed with Grill** ***Perf. 12***
3N11 A17 1c org (Bk, V or M) 6.50 6.50
3N12 A18 2c dk vio (Bk) 6.50 6.50
3N13 A19 5c bl (Bk, V or M) 2.00 1.40
a. 5c ultramarine (Bk or M) 8.25 6.50
3N15 A20 10c sl (Bk) 3.50 2.50
3N16 A21 20c brn red (Bk, V or M) 25.00 25.00
3N18 A22 50c grn (Bk or V) 25.00 25.00
3N20 A23 1s rose (Bk or V) 35.00 35.00
Nos. 3N11-3N20 (7) 103.50 101.90

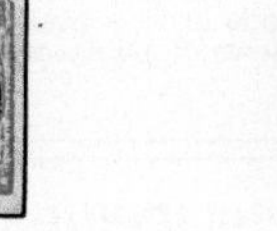

A5 A6

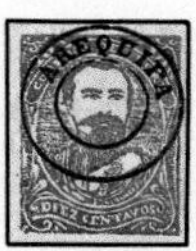

Rear Admiral M. L. Grau
A7

Col. Francisco Bolognesi
A8

Same Overprint as on Previous Issues

1885 ***Imperf.***
3N22 A5 5c olive (Bk) 5.25 5.25
3N23 A6 10c gray (Bk) 5.25 4.75
3N25 A7 5c blue (Bk) 5.25 4.75
3N26 A8 10c olive (Bk) 5.25 3.25
Nos. 3N22-3N26 (4) 21.00 18.00

For overprints see Nos. 2N1, 8N5-8N6, 8N12-8N13, 10N9, 10N12, 15N10-15N12.

These stamps have been reprinted without overprint; they exist however with forged overprint. Originals are on thicker paper with distinct mesh, reprints on paper without mesh.

Without Overprint

3N22a A5 5c olive 5.25 5.25
3N23a A6 10c gray 4.00 3.25
3N25a A7 5c blue 4.00 3.25
3N26a A8 10c olive 4.00 3.25
Nos. 3N22a-3N26a (4) 17.25 15.00

AYACUCHO

(See Note under "Provisional Issues")

Provisional Issue of Arequipa Overprinted in Black

1881 **Unwmk.** ***Imperf.***
4N1 A1 10c blue 150.00 125.00
a. 10c ultramarine 150.00 125.00

CHACHAPOYAS

(See Note under "Provisional Issues")

Regular Issue of Peru Overprinted in Black

1884 **Unwmk.** ***Perf. 12***
5N1 A19 5c ultra 190.00 160.00

CHALA

(See Note under "Provisional Issues")

Regular Issues of Peru Overprinted in Black

1884 **Unwmk.** ***Perf. 12***
6N1 A19 5c blue 25.00 13.00
6N2 A20 10c slate 35.00 16.00

CHICLAYO

(See Note under "Provisional Issues")

Regular Issue of Peru Overprinted in Black

1884 **Unwmk.** ***Perf. 12***
7N1 A19 5c blue 29.00 18.00

Same, Overprinted **FRANCA**

7N2 A19 5c blue 65.00 37.50

CUZCO

(See Note under "Provisional Issues")

Provisional Issues of Arequipa Overprinted in Black

1881-85 **Unwmk.** ***Imperf.***
8N1 A1 10c blue 125.00 110.00
8N2 A4 10c red 125.00 110.00

Overprinted "CUZCO" in an oval of dots

8N5 A5 5c olive 200.00 175.00
8N6 A6 10c gray 200.00 175.00

Regular Issue of Peru Overprinted in Black "CUZCO" in a Circle

Perf. 12

8N7 A19 5c blue 50.00 50.00

Provisional Issues of Arequipa Overprinted in Black

1883 ***Imperf.***
8N9 A4 10c red 18.00 18.00

Same Overprint in Black on Regular Issues of Peru

1884 ***Perf. 12***
8N10 A19 5c blue 27.50 18.00
8N11 A20 10c slate 29.00 18.00

Same Overprint in Black on Provisional Issues of Arequipa

Imperf

8N12 A5 5c olive 27.50 27.50
8N13 A6 10c gray 8.00 8.00

Postage Due Stamps of Peru Surcharged in Black

Perf. 12

8N14 D1 10c on 1c bis 200.00 175.00
8N15 D3 10c on 10c org 200.00 175.00

HUACHO

(See Note under "Provisional Issues")

Regular Issues of Peru Overprinted in Black

1884 **Unwmk.** ***Perf. 12***
9N1 A19 5c blue 16.00 16.00
9N2 A20 10c green 13.00 13.00
9N3 A20 10c slate 27.50 27.50
Nos. 9N1-9N3 (3) 56.50 56.50

MOQUEGUA

(See Note under "Provisional Issues")

Provisional Issues of Arequipa Overprinted in Violet

Overprint 27mm wide.

1881-83 **Unwmk.** ***Imperf.***
10N1 A1 10c blue 75.00 70.00
10N2 A4 10c red ('83) 75.00 70.00

Same Overprint on Regular Issues of Peru in Violet

1884 ***Perf. 12***
10N3 A17 1c orange 75.00 70.00
10N4 A19 5c blue 55.00 35.00

Red Overprint

10N5 A19 5c blue 65.00 55.00

Same Overprint in Violet on Provisional Issues of Peru of 1880

Perf. 12

10N6 A17 1c grn (R) 12.00 9.75
10N7 A18 2c rose (Bl) 15.00 15.00
10N8 A19 5c bl (R) 30.00 30.00

Same Overprint in Violet on Provisional Issue of Arequipa

1885 ***Imperf.***
10N9 A6 10c gray 85.00 42.50

Regular Issues of Peru Overprinted in Violet

Perf. 12

10N10 A19 5c blue 200.00 125.00
10N11 A20 10c slate 85.00 42.50

Same Overprint in Violet on Provisional Issue of Arequipa

Imperf

10N12 A6 10c gray 125.00 110.00

PAITA

(See Note under "Provisional Issues")

Regular Issues of Peru Overprinted

Black Overprint

1884 Unwmk. *Perf. 12*

11N1 A19 5c blue 40.00 40.00
a. 5c ultramarine 40.00 40.00
11N2 A20 10c green 27.50 27.50
11N3 A20 10c slate 40.00 40.00

Red Overprint

11N4 A19 5c blue 40.00 40.00

Overprint lacks ornaments on #11N4-11N5.

Violet Overprint Letters 5½mm High

11N5 A19 5c ultra 40.00 40.00
a. 5c blue 40.00

PASCO

(See Note under "Provisional Issues")

Regular Issues of Peru Overprinted in Magenta or Black

1884 Unwmk. *Perf. 12*

12N1 A19 5c blue (M) 27.50 12.50
a. 5c ultramarine (M) 45.00 22.50
12N2 A20 10c green (Bk) 65.00 55.00
12N3 A20 10c slate (Bk) 125.00 90.00
Nos. 12N1-12N3 (3) 217.50 157.50

PISCO

(See Note under "Provisional Issues")

Regular Issue of Peru Overprinted in Black

1884 Unwmk. *Perf. 12*

13N1 A19 5c blue 350.00 275.00

PIURA

(See Note under "Provisional Issues")

Regular Issues of Peru Overprinted in Black

1884 Unwmk. *Perf. 12*

14N1 A19 5c blue 21.00 21.00
a. 5c ultramarine 45.00 30.00
14N2 A21 20c brn red 150.00 150.00
14N3 A22 50c green 350.00 350.00

Same Overprint in Black on Provisional Issues of Peru of 1881

14N4 A17 1c grn (R) 35.00 35.00
14N5 A18 2c rose (Bl) 55.00 55.00
14N6 A19 5c ultra (R) 70.00 70.00

Regular Issues of Peru Overprinted in Violet, Black or Blue PIURA

14N7 A19 5c bl (V) 27.50 25.00
a. 5c ultramarine (V) 27.50 25.00
b. 5c ultramarine (Bk) 27.50 25.00
14N8 A21 20c brn red (Bk) 150.00 150.00
14N9 A21 20c brn red (Bl) 150.00 150.00

Same Overprint in Black on Provisional Issues of Peru of 1881

14N10 A17 1c grn (R) 35.00 35.00
14N11 A19 5c bl (R) 42.50 42.50
a. 5c ultramarine (R) 70.00 70.00

Regular Issues of Peru Overprinted in Black

14N13 A19 5c blue 10.00 6.50
14N14 A21 20c brn red 150.00 150.00

Regular Issues of Peru Overprinted in Black

14N15 A19 5c ultra 110.00 100.00
14N16 A21 20c brn red 250.00 225.00

Same Overprint on Postage Due Stamp of Peru

14N18 D3 10c orange 125.00 125.00

PUNO

(See Note under "Provisional Issues")

Provisional Issue of Arequipa Overprinted in Violet or Blue

Diameter of outer circle 20½mm, PUNO 11½mm wide, M 3½mm wide.
Other types of this overprint are fraudulent.

1882-83 Unwmk. *Imperf.*

15N1 A1 10c blue (V) 30.00 30.00
a. 10c ultramarine (V) 35.00 35.00
15N3 A2 25c red (V) 45.00 35.00
15N4 A4 10c dl rose (Bl) 29.00 29.00
a. 10c vermilion (Bl) 29.00 29.00

The overprint also exists on 5s yellow of Arequipa.

Same Overprint in Magenta on Regular Issues of Peru

1884 *Perf. 12*

15N5 A17 1c orange 19.00 15.00
15N6 A18 2c violet 65.00 65.00
15N7 A19 5c blue 10.00 10.00

Violet Overprint

15N8 A19 5c blue 10.00 10.00
a. 5c ultramarine 20.00 20.00

Same Overprint in Black on Provisional Issues of Arequipa

1885 *Imperf.*

15N10 A5 5c olive 16.00 13.50
15N11 A6 10c gray 10.00 10.00
15N12 A8 10c olive 19.00 19.00

Regular Issues of Peru Overprinted in Magenta

1884 *Perf. 12*

15N13 A17 1c orange 21.00 21.00
15N14 A18 2c violet 24.00 21.00
15N15 A19 5c blue 10.00 10.00
a. 5c ultramarine 20.00 20.00
15N16 A20 10c green 29.00 22.50
15N17 A21 20c brn red 150.00 150.00
15N18 A22 50c green

YCA

(See Note under "Provisional Issues")

Regular Issues of Peru Overprinted in Violet

1884 Unwmk. *Perf. 12*

16N1 A17 1c orange 70.00 70.00
16N3 A19 5c blue 22.50 18.00

Black Overprint

16N5 A19 5c blue 19.00 9.00

Magenta Overprint

16N6 A19 5c blue 19.00 9.00
16N7 A20 10c slate 55.00 55.00

Regular Issues of Peru Overprinted in Black

16N12 A19 5c blue 275.00 225.00
16N13 A21 20c brown 350.00 275.00

Regular Issues of Peru Overprinted in Carmine

16N14 A19 5c blue 275.00 225.00
16N15 A20 10c slate 350.00 275.00

Same, with Additional Overprint

16N21 A19 5c blue 275.00 275.00
16N22 A21 20c brn red 475.00 450.00

Various other stamps exist with the overprints "YCA" and "YCA VAPOR" but they are not known to have been issued. Some of them were made to fill a dealer's order and others are reprints or merely cancellations.

PHILIPPINES

ˌfi-lə-ˈpēnz

LOCATION — Group of about 7,100 islands and islets in the Malay Archipelago, north of Borneo, in the North Pacific Ocean
GOVT. — Republic
AREA — 115,830 sq. mi.
POP. — 109,580,000 (2020 est.)
CAPITAL — Manila

The islands were ceded to the United States by Spain in 1898. On November 15, 1935, they were given their independence, subject to a transition period. The Japanese occupation from 1942 to early 1945 delayed independence until July 4, 1946. On that date the Commonwealth became the Republic of the Philippines.

20 Cuartos = 1 Real
100 Centavos de Peso = 1 Peso (1864)
100 Centimos de Escudo = 1 Escudo (1871)
100 Centimos de Peseta = 1 Peseta (1872)
1000 Milesimas de Peso = 100 Centimos or Centavos = 1 Peso (1878)
100 Cents = 1 Dollar (1899)
100 Centavos = 1 Peso (1906)
100 Centavos (Sentimos) = 1 Peso (Piso) (1946)

Catalogue values for unused stamps in this country are for Never Hinged items, beginning with Scott 500 in the regular postage section, Scott B1 in the semi-postal section, Scott C64 in the air post section, Scott E11 in the special delivery section, Scott J23 in the postage due section, and Scott O50 in the officials section.

Watermarks

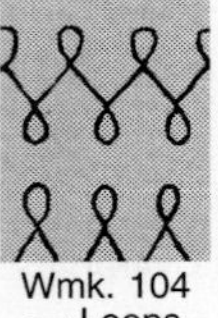

Wmk. 104 — Loops

Wmk. 257 — Curved Wavy Lines

Watermark 104: loops from different watermark rows may or may not be directly opposite each other.

Wmk. 190PI — Single-lined PIPS

Wmk. 191PI — Double-lined PIPS

Watermark 191 has double-lined USPS.

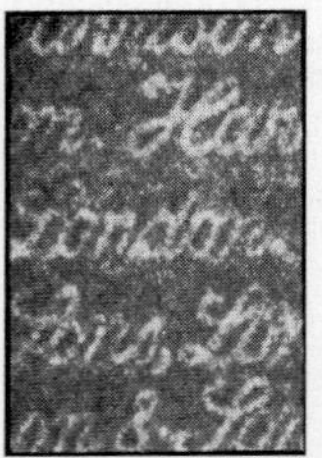

Wmk. 233 — "Harrison & Sons, London." in Script

Wmk. 372 — "RPKK" Multiple

Watermark 372 comes in two types: Type I - 24mm high Type II - 19mm high
Type II was printed by the Japanese on white paper with white gum.

Wmk. 385

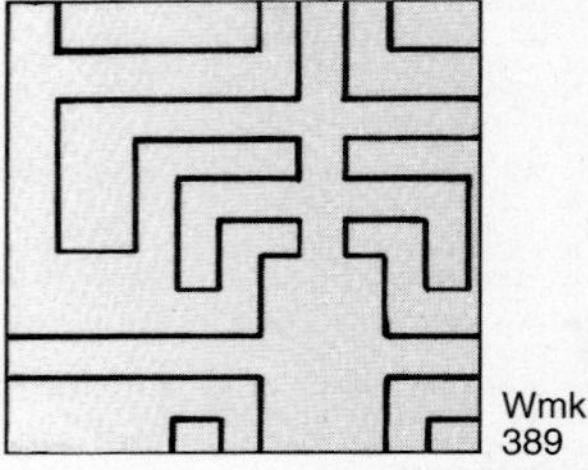

Wmk. 389

Wmk. 391 — Natl. Crest, Rising Sun and Eagle, with inscr. "REPUBLIKA / NG / PILIPINAS," "KAWANIHAN / NG / KOREO"

Issued under Spanish Dominion

The stamps of Philippine Islands punched with a round hole were used on telegraph receipts or had been withdrawn from use and punched to indicate that they were no longer available for postage. In this condition they sell for less, as compared to postally used copies.

Many color varieties exist of Nos. 1-88. Only major varieties are listed.

Queen Isabella II
A1 A2

1854 Unwmk. Engr. *Imperf.*

No.	Type	Description	Unused	Used
1	A1	5c orange	4,000.	350.
2	A1	10c carmine	700.	250.
a.		10c pale rose	800.	350.
4	A2	1r blue	1,000.	300.
a.		1r slate blue	800.	300.
5	A2	2r slate green	1,000.	250.

Forty plate varieties of each value. Many color varieties exist.

A 10c black exists. This is a proof or an unissued trial color. Value about $8,000.

For overprints see Nos. 24A-25A.

A3

1855 Litho.

No.	Type	Description	Unused	Used
6	A3	5c pale red	1,800.	500.

Four varieties.

A3a

Redrawn

No.	Type	Description	Unused	Used
7	A3a	5c vermilion	*8,000.*	*1,000.*

In the redrawn stamp the inner circle is smaller and is not broken by the labels at top and bottom. Only one variety.

Queen Isabella II — A4

Blue Paper

1856 Typo. Wmk. 104

No.	Type	Description	Unused	Used
8	A4	1r green	75.00	*75.00*
9	A4	2r carmine	375.00	200.00

Nos. 8 and 9 used can be distinguished from Cuba Nos. 2 and 3 only by the cancellations.

For overprints, see Nos. 26-27.

Queen Isabella II — A5

Dot After "CORREOS"

1859, Jan. 1 Litho. Unwmk.

No.	Type	Description	Unused	Used
10	A5	5c vermilion	15.00	8.00
a.		5c scarlet	24.00	12.00
b.		5c orange	32.50	17.50
11	A5	10c lilac rose	17.00	*35.00*

Four varieties of each value, repeated in the sheet.

For overprint see No. 28.

Dot after CORREOS
A6 A7

1861-62

No.	Type	Description	Unused	Used
12	A6	5c vermilion	40.00	40.00
13	A7	5c dull red ('62)	190.00	95.00

No. 12, one variety only, repeated in the sheet.

For overprint see No. 29.

Colon after CORREOS — A8

A8a

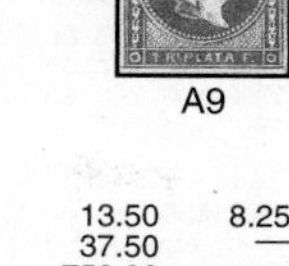

A9

1863

No.	Type	Description	Unused	Used
14	A8	5c vermilion	13.50	8.25
15	A8	10c carmine	37.50	—
16	A8	1r violet	750.00	—
17	A8	2r blue	600.00	—
18	A8a	1r gray grn	600.00	140.00
20	A9	1r green	200.00	60.00
		Nos. 14-20 (6)	2,201.	208.25

No. 18 has "CORREOS" 10½mm long, the point of the bust is rounded and is about 1mm from the circle which contains 94 pearls.

No. 20 has "CORREOS" 11mm long, and the bust ends in a sharp point which nearly touches the circle of 76 pearls. Authorized use of Nos. 15-17 is questionable.

For overprints see Nos. 30-34.

A10

1864 Typo.

No.	Type	Description	Unused	Used
21	A10	3⅛c blk, *yellow*	4.75	2.00
22	A10	6 2/8c grn, *rose*	6.75	2.00
23	A10	12 4/8c blue, *sal*	9.00	1.75
24	A10	25c red, *buff*	12.00	3.75
		Nos. 21-24 (4)	32.50	9.50

For overprints see Nos. 35-38.

Preceding Issues Handstamped

1868-74

No.	Type	Description	Unused	Used
24A	A1	5c orange ('74)	*8,000.*	*9,000.*
25	A2	1r sl bl ('74)	*2,000.*	*1,050.*
25A	A2	2r grn ('74)	*7,000.*	*7,000.*
26	A4	1r grn, *bl* ('72)	180.00	80.00
27	A4	2r car, *bl* ('72)	290.00	225.00
27A	A5	5c vermilion ('72)	*8,000.*	*10,000.*
28	A5	10c rose ('74)	80.00	35.00
29	A7	5c dull red ('73)	250.00	175.00
30	A8	5c ver ('72)	115.00	35.00
30A	A8	10c car ('70)	*6,000.*	—
31	A8	1r vio ('70)	900.00	600.00
32	A8	2r bl ('72)	500.00	425.00
33	A8a	1r gray grn ('70)	175.00	85.00
34	A9	1r grn ('70)	50.00	30.00
35	A10	3⅛c blk, *yellow*	9.50	4.75
36	A10	6 2/8c grn, *rose*	9.50	4.75
37	A10	12 4/8c bl, *salmon*	27.50	12.00
38	A10	25c red, *buff*	29.00	15.00

Reprints exist of #24A-38. These have crisp, sharp letters and usually have a broken first "A" of "HABILITADO."

Imperforates

Imperforates of designs A11-A16 probably are from proof or trial sheets.

"Spain" — A11

1871 Typo. *Perf. 14*

No.	Type	Description	Unused	Used
39	A11	5c blue	95.00	9.25
40	A11	10c deep green	15.00	6.00
41	A11	20c brown	110.00	50.00
42	A11	40c rose	190.00	60.00
		Nos. 39-42 (4)	410.00	125.25

King Amadeo — A12

1872

No.	Type	Description	Unused	Used
43	A12	12c rose	20.00	5.50
44	A12	16c blue	190.00	37.50
45	A12	25c gray lilac	13.50	5.50
46	A12	62c violet	40.00	9.75
47	A12	1p25c yellow brn	85.00	42.50
		Nos. 43-47 (5)	348.50	100.75

A 12c in deep blue and a 62c in rose exist but were not issued. Value $30 each.

"Peace" — A13

1874

No.	Type	Description	Unused	Used
48	A13	12c gray lilac	22.50	5.50
49	A13	25c ultra	8.25	4.00
50	A13	62c rose	65.00	5.50
51	A13	1p25c brown	300.00	82.50
		Nos. 48-51 (4)	395.75	97.50

King Alfonso XII — A14

1875-77

No.	Type	Description	Unused	Used
52	A14	2c rose	3.50	.95
53	A14	2c dk blue ('77)	260.00	100.00
54	A14	6c orange ('77)	14.00	*16.00*
55	A14	10c blue ('77)	4.50	1.50
56	A14	12c lilac ('76	4.50	1.50
57	A14	20c vio brn ('76	20.00	5.00
58	A14	25c dp green ('76	25.00	5.00
		Nos. 52-58 (7)	331.50	129.95

Imperforates of type A14 are from proof or trial sheets.

Nos. 52, 63 Handstamp Surcharged in Black or Blue

1877-79

No.	Type	Description	Unused	Used
59	A14	12c on 2c rose (Bk)	85.00	22.50
a.		Surcharge inverted	*400.00*	*375.00*
b.		Surcharge double	*400.00*	*350.00*
60	A16	12c on 25m blk (Bk) ('79)	105.00	47.50
a.		Surcharge inverted	*875.00*	*600.00*
61	A16	12c on 25m blk (Bl) ('79)	300.00	150.00
		Nos. 59-61 (3)	490.00	220.00

Forgeries of Nos. 59-61 exist.

A16

1878-79 Typo.

No.	Type	Description	Unused	Used
62	A16	25m black	3.50	.45
63	A16	25m green ('79)	67.50	*50.00*
64	A16	50m dull lilac	34.00	10.00
65	A16	0.0625 (62½m) gray	65.00	10.00
66	A16	100m car ('79)	110.00	37.50
67	A16	100m yel grn ('79)	10.00	2.75
68	A16	125m blue	6.00	.50
69	A16	200m rose ('79)	37.50	5.75
70	A16	200m vio rose ('79)	350.00	—
71	A16	250m bister ('79)	13.00	2.75
		Nos. 62-71 (10)	696.50	*119.70*

Imperforates of type A16 are from proof or trial sheets.

For surcharges see Nos. 60-61, 72-75.

Stamps of 1878-79 Surcharged

a b

1879

No.	Type	Description	Unused	Used
72	A16 (a)	2c on 25m grn	55.00	11.00
b.		Inverted surcharge	425.00	325.00
73	A16 (a)	8c on 100m car	52.50	6.50
a.		"COREROS"	150.00	80.00
b.		Surcharge double	400.00	—
74	A16 (b)	2c on 25m grn	400.00	57.50
75	A16 (b)	8c on 100m car	400.00	57.50
		Nos. 72-75 (4)	907.50	132.50

A19

Original state: The medallion is surrounded by a heavy line of color of nearly even thickness, touching the line below "Filipinas"; the opening in the hair above the temple is narrow and pointed.

1st retouch: The line around the medallion is thin, except at the upper right, and does not touch the horizontal line above it; the opening in the hair is slightly wider and rounded; the lock of hair above the forehead is shaped like a broad "V" and ends in a point; there is a faint white line below it, which is not found on the original. The shape of the hair and the width of the white line vary.

2nd retouch: The lock of hair is less pointed; the white line is much broader.

1880-86 Typo.

No.	Type	Description	Unused	Used
76	A19	2c carmine	.90	*.80*
77	A19	2½c brown	8.00	1.90
78	A19	2 4/8c ultra ('82)	1.25	2.25
79	A19	2 4/8c ultra, 1st retouch ('83)	.90	1.90
80	A19	2 4/8c ultra, 2nd retouch ('86)	10.50	4.25
81	A19	5c gray blue ('82)	.90	*1.90*
82	A19	6 2/8c dp grn ('82)	7.00	*18.00*
83	A19	8c yellow brn	15.00	6.25
84	A19	10c green	350.00	500.00
85	A19	10c brn lil ('82)	3.75	*4.25*
86	A19	12 4/8c brt rose ('82)	1.90	1.90
87	A19	20c bis brn ('82)	3.50	1.75
88	A19	25c dk brn ('82)	4.75	1.90
		Nos. 76-88 (13)	408.35	547.05

See #137-139. For surcharges see #89-108, 110-111.

Surcharges exist double or inverted on many of the Nos. 89-136. Several different surcharge types exist

Many bogus surcharges exist on the 1881-97 issues, prepared using the original surcharge handstamps in various colors on the same or different stamps after the end of the Spanish period. These bogus stamps include the previously listed Nos. 184 and 186, and the previously footnoted reprints. Many more bogus surcharged issues exist.

Stamps and Type of 1880-86 Handstamp Surcharged in Black, Green or Red

c

d

e f

Design A19

1881-88 Black Surcharge

No.	Type	Description	Unused	Used
89	(c)	2c on 2½c	4.25	2.25
91	(f)	10c on 2 4/8c (#80) ('87)	6.25	2.10
92	(d)	20c on 8c brn ('83)	10.00	3.25
93	(d)	1r on 2c ('83)	140.00	*140.00*
94	(d)	2r on 2 4/8c (#78; '83)	6.25	2.10
a.		On No. 79	60.00	*60.00*
b.		On No. 80	75.00	*75.00*

Most used examples of No. 93 are hole punched. Postally used examples are rare.

Green Surcharge

No.	Type	Description	Unused	Used
95	(e)	8c on 2c ('83)	11.00	2.25
95A	(d+e)	8c on 1r on 2c ('83)	250.00	150.00
96	(d)	10c on 2c ('83)	5.50	2.25
97	(d)	1r on 2c ('83)	140.00	140.00
98	(d)	1r on 5c gray bl ('83)	8.00	3.25
99	(d)	1r on 8c brn ('83)	10.00	3.25

Red Surcharge

No.	Type	Description	Unused	Used
100	(f)	1c on 2 4/8c (#79; '87)	1.25	*2.00*
101	(f)	1c on 2 4/8c (#80; '87)	3.50	3.00
102	(d)	16c on 2 4/8c (#78; '83)	10.00	4.00

103 (d) 1r on 2c ('83) 6.25 3.25
On cover 550.00
104 (d) 1r on 5c bl gray ('83) 12.00 6.00

Handstamp Surcharged in Magenta

g

h

1887
105 A19 (g) 8c on 2⅝c (#79) 1.25 .90
106 A19 (g) 8c on 2⅝c (#80) 2.75 2.00

1888
107 A19 (h) 2⅝c on 1c gray grn 1.75 1.00
108 A19 (h) 2⅝c on 5c bl gray 1.90 1.50
109 N1 (h) 2⅝c on ⅛c grn 1.90 1.40
110 A19 (h) 2⅝c on 50m bis 1.90 .80
111 A19 (h) 2⅝c on 10c grn 1.75 .65
Nos. 107-111 (5) 9.20 5.35

No. 109 is surcharged on a newspaper stamp of 1886-89 and has the inscriptions shown on cut N1.

On Revenue Stamps

R1

R2

R3(d)

Handstamp Surcharged in Black, Yellow, Green, Red, Blue or Magenta

j

k

m

1881-88 **Black Surcharge**
112 R1(c) 2c on 10c bis 50.00 40.00
113 R1(j) 2⅝c on 10c bis 12.00 1.75
114 R1(j) 2⅝c on 2r bl 200.00 140.00
115 R1(j) 8c on 10c bis *550.00* *5,000.*
116 R1(j) 8c on 2r bl 8.50 2.10
118 R1(d) 1r on 12⅝c gray bl ('83) 7.75 3.75
119 R1(d) 1r on 10c bis ('82) 11.50 4.00

Yellow Surcharge
120 R2(e) 2c on 200m grn ('82) 6.25 *8.00*
121 R1(d) 16c on 2r bl ('83) 6.00 *7.00*

Green Surcharge
122 R1(d) 1r on 10c bis ('83) 11.50 4.00

Red Surcharge
123 R1(d+e) 2r on 8c on 2r blue 65.00 45.00
a. On 8c on 2r blue (d+d) 100.00 80.00
124 R1(d) 1r on 12⅝c gray bl ('83) 16.50 13.00
125 R1(k) 6⅝c on 12⅝c gray bl ('85) 5.00 *24.00*
126 R3(d) 1r on 10p bis ('83) 95.00 45.00
127 R1(m) 1r green 350.00 *700.00*
127A R1(m) 2r blue 900.00 *1,150.*
127B R1(d) 1r on 1r grn ('83) 700.00 *800.00*
128 R2(d) 1r on 1p grn ('83) 150.00 65.00
129 R2(d) 1r on 200m grn ('83) 600.00 *800.00*
129A R1(d) 2r on 2r blue *900.00* *900.00*

The surcharge on No. 129A is pale red.

Blue Surcharge
129B R1(m) 10c bister ('81) *900.00* —

Magenta Surcharge
130 R2(h) 2⅝c on 200m grn ('88) 4.25 3.75
131 R2(h) 2⅝c on 20c brn ('88) 20.00 10.00

On Telegraph Stamps

T1

T2

Surcharged in Red, or Black

1883-88
132 T1(d) 2r on 250m ultra (R) 7.75 3.00
133 T1(d) 20c on 250m ultra *750.00* 375.00
134 T1(d) 2r on 250m ultra 10.00 4.75
135 T1(d) 1r on 20c on 250m ultra (R & Bk) 15.00 8.00

Magenta Surcharge
136 T2(h) 2⅝c on 1c bis ('88) .95 *3.00*

Most, if not all, used stamps of No. 133 are hole-punched. Used value is for examples with hole punches.

Type of 1880-86 Redrawn

1887-89
137 A19 50m bister .50 *6.00*
138 A19 1c gray grn ('88) .50 *5.00*
a. 1c yellow green ('89) .70 *10.00*
139 A19 6c yel brn ('88) 8.00 *47.50*
Nos. 137-139 (3) 9.00 *58.50*

King Alfonso XIII — A36

1890-97 **Typo.**
140 A36 1c violet ('92) 1.00 .75
141 A36 1c rose ('94) 17.50 *40.00*
142 A36 1c bl grn ('96) 2.25 1.00
143 A36 1c claret ('97) 16.00 16.00
144 A36 2c claret ('94) .25 .25
145 A36 2c violet ('92) .25 .25
146 A36 2c dk brn ('94) .25 *3.50*
147 A36 2c ultra ('96) .35 .35
148 A36 2c gray brn ('96) .85 *2.25*
149 A36 2⅝c dull blue .55 .30
150 A36 2⅝c ol gray ('92) .30 *1.40*
151 A36 5c dark blue .50 *1.40*
152 A36 5c slate green .85 *1.40*
153 A36 5c green ('92) .80 .55
155 A36 5c vio brn ('96) 7.50 3.25
156 A36 5c blue grn ('96) 6.00 3.00
157 A36 6c brown vio ('92) .30 *1.40*
158 A36 6c red orange ('94) .95 *4.00*
159 A36 6c car rose ('96) 4.75 *7.00*
160 A36 8c yellow grn .30 .30
161 A36 8c ultra ('92) .75 .30
162 A36 8c red brn ('94) .85 .30
163 A36 10c blue grn 1.75 1.25
164 A36 10c pale cl ('91) 1.60 .40
165 A36 10c claret ('94) .75 .40
166 A36 10c yel brn ('96) .85 .30
167 A36 12⅝c yellow grn .30 .25
168 A36 12⅝c org ('92) .85 *1.25*
169 A36 15c red brn ('92) .85 .30
170 A36 15c rose ('94) 2.10 .75
171 A36 15c bl grn ('96) 2.60 2.10
172 A36 20c pale vermilion 30.00 *40.00*
174 A36 20c gray brn ('92) 2.75 .45
175 A36 20c dk vio ('94) 15.00 8.00
176 A36 20c org ('96) 4.50 2.25
177 A36 25c brown 9.50 2.00
178 A36 25c dull bl ('91) 2.50 1.50
179 A36 40c dk vio ('97) 13.50 *35.00*
180 A36 80c claret ('97) 30.00 60.00
Nos. 140-180 (39) 182.50 245.15

Many of Nos. 140-180 exist imperf and in different colors. These are considered to be proofs. Only major varieties are listed. Color varieties of most issues exist.

Stamps of Previous Issues Handstamp Surcharged in Blue, Red, Black or Violet

1897 **Blue Surcharge**
181 A36 5c on 5c green 2.00 *5.00*
182 A36 15c on 15c red brn 5.50 3.00
183 A36 20c on 20c gray brn 12.00 *12.00*

Red Surcharge
185 A36 5c on 5c green 4.50 4.75

Black Surcharge
187 A36 5c on 5c green 100.00 *300.00*
188 A36 15c on 15c rose 5.50 3.00
189 A36 20c on 20c dk vio 35.00 35.00
190 A36 20c on 25c brown 25.00 *40.00*

Violet Surcharge
191 A36 15c on 15c rose *15.00* *30.00*
Nos. 181-191 (9) 204.50 432.75

Inverted, double and other variations of this surcharge exist.

The 5c on 5c blue gray (#81a) was released during US Administration. The surcharge is a mixture of red and black inks.

Impressions in violet black are believed to be reprints. The following varieties are known: 5c on 2⅝c olive gray, 5c on 5c blue green, 5c on 25c brown, 15c on 15c rose, 15c on 15c red brown, 15c on 25c brown, 20c on 20c gray brown, 20c on 20c dark violet, 20c on 25c brown. Value: each $40. These surcharges are to be found double, inverted, etc.

King Alfonso XIII — A39

1898 **Typo.**
192 A39 1m orange brown .25 *1.25*
193 A39 2m orange brown .25 *1.75*
194 A39 3m orange brown .25 *1.75*
195 A39 4m orange brown 10.00 *40.00*
196 A39 5m orange brown .25 *2.75*
197 A39 1c black violet .25 .60
198 A39 2c dk bl grn .25 .60
199 A39 3c dk brown .25 .60
200 A39 4c orange 20.00 *40.00*
201 A39 5c car rose .25 .60
202 A39 6c dk blue 1.15 *1.75*
203 A39 8c gray brown .60 .35
204 A39 10c vermilion 2.75 1.25
205 A39 15c dull ol grn 2.25 1.10
206 A39 20c maroon 2.50 1.60
207 A39 40c violet 1.25 *1.75*
208 A39 60c black 6.00 4.00
209 A39 80c red brown 8.00 7.00
210 A39 1p yellow green 20.00 *10.00*
211 A39 2p slate blue 40.00 *12.00*
Nos. 192-211 (20) 116.50 *130.70*

Nos. 192-211 exist imperf. Value, set $2,000.

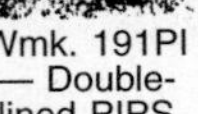
Wmk. 191PI — Double-lined PIPS

Wmk. 190PI — Single-lined PIPS

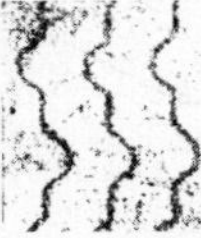
Wmk. 257 — Curved Wavy Lines

Issued under U.S. Administration

Regular Issues of the United States Overprinted in Black

1899-1901 **Unwmk.** ***Perf. 12***

On U.S. Stamp No. 260
212 A96 50c orange 300. 225.
Never hinged 775.

On U.S. Stamps Nos. 279, 279B, 279Bd, 279Bj, 279Bf, 279Bc, 268, 281, 282C, 283, 284, 275, 275a

Regular Issues of the United States Overprinted in Black

Wmk. Double-lined USPS (191)
213 A87 1c yellow green 3.50 .60
Never hinged 10.00
a. Inverted overprint *77,500.*
214 A88 2c red, type IV 1.75 .60
Never hinged 4.25
a. 2c orange red, type IV, ('01) 1.75 .60
Never hinged 4.25
b. Bklt. pane of 6, red, type IV ('00) 200.00 *300.00*
Never hinged 450.00
c. 2c reddish carmine, type IV 2.50 1.00
Never hinged 6.00
d. 2c rose carmine, type IV 3.00 1.10
Never hinged 7.25
215 A89 3c purple 9.00 1.25
Never hinged 21.50
216 A91 5c blue 9.00 1.00
Never hinged 21.50
a. Inverted overprint *6,500.*

No. 216a is valued in the grade of fine.

217 A94 10c brown, type I 35.00 4.00
Never hinged 80.00
217A A94 10c org brn, type II 110.00 27.50
Never hinged 275.00

No. 217A was overprinted on U.S. No. 283a, vertical watermark. The watermark on No. 217 is horizontal.

218 A95 15c olive green 40.00 8.00
Never hinged 95.00
219 A96 50c orange 125.00 37.50
Never hinged 300.00
a. 50c red orange 250.00 55.00
Never hinged 600.00
Nos. 213-219 (8) 333.25 80.45

Regular Issue

U.S. Stamps Nos. 280b, 282 and 272 Overprinted in Black

1901, Aug. 30
220 A90 4c orange brown 35.00 5.00
Never hinged 80.00
221 A92 6c lake 40.00 7.00
Never hinged 95.00
222 A93 8c purple brown 40.00 7.50
Never hinged 95.00
Nos. 220-222 (3) 115.00 19.50

Same Overprint in Red On U.S. Stamps Nos. 276, 276A, 277a and 278
223 A97 $1 black, type I 300.00 200.00
Never hinged 1,000.
223A A97 $1 black, type II 1,500. 750.00
Never hinged 5,000.
224 A98 $2 dark blue 350.00 325.00
Never hinged 1,150.
225 A99 $5 dark green 500.00 *900.00*
Never hinged 1,600.

U.S. Stamps Nos. 300-310 and Shades Overprinted in Black

Regular Issue

1903-04
226 A115 1c blue green 7.00 .40
Never hinged 15.50
227 A116 2c carmine 9.00 1.10
Never hinged 20.00
228 A117 3c bright violet 67.50 12.50
Never hinged 150.00
229 A118 4c brown 80.00 22.50
Never hinged 175.00
a. 4c orange brown 80.00 20.00
Never hinged 175.00
230 A119 5c blue 17.50 1.00
Never hinged 40.00
231 A120 6c brnsh lake 85.00 22.50
Never hinged 190.00
232 A121 8c violet black 50.00 15.00
Never hinged 125.00
233 A122 10c pale red brn 35.00 2.25
Never hinged 80.00
a. 10c red brown 35.00 3.00
Never hinged 80.00
b. Pair, one without overprint *1,500.*
234 A123 13c purple black 35.00 17.50
Never hinged 80.00
a. 13c brown violet 35.00 17.50
Never hinged 80.00
235 A124 15c olive green 60.00 15.00
Never hinged 135.00
236 A125 50c orange 125.00 35.00
Never hinged 275.00
Nos. 226-236 (11) 571.00 144.75
Set, never hinged 1,285.

Same Overprint in Red On U.S. Stamps Nos. 311, 312 and 313
237 A126 $1 black 300.00 200.00
Never hinged 800.00
238 A127 $2 dark blue 550.00 *800.00*
Never hinged 1,500.
239 A128 $5 dark green 800.00 *2,750.*
Never hinged 2,000.

Same Overprint in Black On U.S. Stamp Nos. 319 and 319c
240 A129 2c carmine 8.00 2.25
Never hinged 17.50
a. Booklet pane of 6 *1,500.*
b. 2c scarlet 8.00 2.75
Never hinged 19.00
c. As "b," booklet pane of 6 —

José Rizal
A40

Arms of City of Manila
A41

Designs: 4c, McKinley. 6c, Ferdinand Magellan. 8c, Miguel Lopez de Legaspi. 10c, Gen. Henry W. Lawton. 12c, Lincoln. 16c, Adm. William T. Sampson. 20c, Washington. 26c, Francisco Carriedo. 30c, Franklin. 2p-10p, Arms of City of Manila.

Wmk. Double-lined PIPS (191PI)

1906, Sept. 8 *Perf. 12*

241 A40 2c deep green .40 .25
Never hinged 1.00
a. 2c yellow green ('10) .60 .25
Never hinged 1.50
b. Booklet pane of 6 750.00 800.00
Never hinged 1,500.
242 A40 4c carmine .50 .25
Never hinged 1.25
a. 4c carmine lake ('10) 1.00 .25
Never hinged 2.50
b. Booklet pane of 6 650.00 700.00
Never hinged 1,250.
243 A40 6c violet 2.50 .25
Never hinged 6.25
244 A40 8c brown 4.50 .90
Never hinged 11.00
245 A40 10c blue 3.50 .30
Never hinged 8.75
a. 10c dark blue 3.50 .30
Never hinged 8.75
246 A40 12c brown lake 9.00 2.50
Never hinged 22.50
247 A40 16c violet black 6.00 .35
Never hinged 15.00
248 A40 20c org brn 7.00 .35
Never hinged 17.50
249 A40 26c vio brn 11.00 3.00
Never hinged 27.50
250 A40 30c olive green 6.50 1.75
Never hinged 16.00
251 A41 1p orange 55.00 17.50
Never hinged 130.00
252 A41 2p black 50.00 1.75
Never hinged 130.00
253 A41 4p dark blue 160.00 20.00
Never hinged 375.00
254 A41 10p dark green 225.00 80.00
Never hinged 575.00
Nos. 241-254 (14) 540.90 129.15
Set, never hinged 1,316.

1909-13 **Change of Colors**

255 A40 12c red orange 11.00 3.00
Never hinged 27.50
256 A40 16c olive green 6.00 .75
Never hinged 15.00
257 A40 20c yellow 9.00 1.25
Never hinged 22.50
258 A40 26c blue green 3.50 1.25
Never hinged 8.75
259 A40 30c ultramarine 13.00 3.50
Never hinged 32.50
260 A41 1p pale violet 45.00 5.00
Never hinged 110.00
260A A41 2p vio brn ('13) 100.00 12.00
Never hinged 250.00
Nos. 255-260A (7) 187.50 26.75
Set, never hinged 466.25

Wmk. Single-lined PIPS (190PI)

1911

261 A40 2c green .75 .25
Never hinged 1.80
a. Booklet pane of 6 800.00 900.00
Never hinged 1,400.
262 A40 4c carmine lake 3.00 .25
Never hinged 6.75
a. 4c carmine — —
b. Booklet pane of 6 600.00 700.00
Never hinged 1,100.
263 A40 6c deep violet 3.00 .25
Never hinged 6.75
264 A40 8c brown 9.50 .50
Never hinged 21.50
265 A40 10c blue 4.00 .25
Never hinged 9.00
266 A40 12c orange 4.00 .45
Never hinged 9.00
267 A40 16c olive green 4.50 .40
Never hinged 10.00
a. 16c pale olive green 4.50 .50
Never hinged 10.00
268 A40 20c yellow 3.50 .25
Never hinged 7.75
a. 20c orange 4.00 .30
Never hinged 9.00
269 A40 26c blue green 6.00 .30
Never hinged 13.50
270 A40 30c ultramarine 6.00 .50
Never hinged 13.50
271 A41 1p pale violet 27.50 .60
Never hinged 62.50
272 A41 2p violet brown 45.00 1.00
Never hinged 100.00
273 A41 4p deep blue 550.00 110.00
Never hinged 1,100.
274 A41 10p deep green 200.00 30.00
Never hinged 400.00
Nos. 261-274 (14) 866.75 145.00
Set, never hinged 1,862.

1914

275 A40 30c gray 12.00 .50
Never hinged 27.50

1914 *Perf. 10*

276 A40 2c green 3.00 .25
Never hinged 7.00
a. Booklet pane of 6 600.00 800.00
Never hinged 1,250.
277 A40 4c carmine 4.00 .30
Never hinged 9.00
a. Booklet pane of 6 600.00
Never hinged 1,300.
278 A40 6c light violet 45.00 9.50
Never hinged 100.00
a. 6c deep violet 50.00 6.25
Never hinged 110.00
279 A40 8c brown 55.00 10.50
Never hinged 125.00
280 A40 10c dark blue 30.00 .25
Never hinged 67.50
281 A40 16c olive green 100.00 5.00
Never hinged 225.00
282 A40 20c orange 40.00 1.00
Never hinged 85.00
283 A40 30c gray 60.00 4.50
Never hinged 130.00
284 A41 1p pale violet 150.00 3.75
Never hinged 350.00
Nos. 276-284 (9) 487.00 35.05
Set, never hinged 1,020.

Wmk. Single-lined PIPS (190PI)

1918 *Perf. 11*

285 A40 2c green 21.00 4.25
Never hinged 40.00
a. Booklet pane of 6 600.00 800.00
Never hinged 1,100.
286 A40 4c carmine 26.00 6.00
Never hinged 55.00
a. Booklet pane of 6 1,350. 2,000.
287 A40 6c deep violet 40.00 6.00
Never hinged 90.00
287A A40 8c light brown 220.00 25.00
Never hinged 400.00
288 A40 10c dark blue 60.00 3.00
Never hinged 140.00
289 A40 16c olive green 110.00 10.00
Never hinged 250.00
289A A40 20c orange 175.00 12.00
Never hinged 400.00
289C A40 30c gray 95.00 18.00
Never hinged 215.00
289D A41 1p pale violet 100.00 25.00
Never hinged 225.00
Nos. 285-289D (9) 847.00 109.25
Set, never hinged 1,815.

1917 **Unwmk.** *Perf. 11*

290 A40 2c yellow green .25 .25
Never hinged .55
Never hinged 140.00
a. 2c dark green .30 .25
Never hinged .65
b. Vert. pair, imperf. horiz. 2,750.
c. Horiz. pair, imperf. between 1,500. —
d. Vertical pair, imperf. btwn. 1,750. 1,000.
e. Booklet pane of 6 27.50 30.00
Never hinged 60.00
291 A40 4c carmine .30 .25
Never hinged .65
a. 4c light rose .30 .25
Never hinged .65
b. Booklet pane of 6 20.00 22.50
Never hinged 35.00
292 A40 6c deep violet .35 .25
Never hinged .70
a. 6c lilac .40 .25
Never hinged .80
b. 6c red violet .40 .25
Never hinged .70
c. Booklet pane of 6 550.00 800.00
Never hinged 900.00
293 A40 8c yellow brown .30 .25
Never hinged .50
a. 8c orange brown .30 .25
Never hinged .50
294 A40 10c deep blue .30 .25
Never hinged .65
295 A40 12c red orange .35 .25
Never hinged .75
296 A40 16c light olive green 65.00 .25
Never hinged 130.00
a. 16c olive bister 65.00 .50
Never hinged 130.00
297 A40 20c orange yellow .35 .25
Never hinged .75
298 A40 26c green .50 .45
Never hinged 1.10
a. 26c blue green .60 .25
Never hinged 1.35
299 A40 30c gray .55 .25
Never hinged 1.35
300 A41 1p pale violet 40.00 2.00
Never hinged 90.00
a. 1p red lilac 40.00 2.50
Never hinged 90.00
b. 1p pale rose lilac 40.00 1.10
Never hinged 90.00
301 A41 2p violet brown 35.00 1.00
Never hinged 77.50
302 A41 4p blue 32.50 .50
Never hinged 72.50
a. 4p dark blue 35.00 .55
Never hinged 77.50
Nos. 290-302 (13) 175.75 6.20
Set, never hinged 377.00

1923-26

Design: 16c, Adm. George Dewey.

303 A40 16c olive bister 1.00 .25
Never hinged 2.25
a. 16c olive green 1.25 .25
Never hinged 2.75
304 A41 10p dp grn ('26) 50.00 20.00
Never hinged 110.00

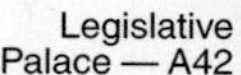

Legislative Palace — A42

1926, Dec. 20 *Perf. 12*

319 A42 2c green & black .50 .25
Never hinged 1.25
a. Horiz. pair, imperf. between 275.00 —
b. Vert. pair, imperf. between 375.00
320 A42 4c car & blk .55 .40
Never hinged 1.20
a. Horiz. pair, imperf. between 350.00 —
b. Vert. pair, imperf. between 400.00
321 A42 16c ol grn & blk 1.00 .65
Never hinged 2.25
a. Horiz. pair, imperf. between 250.00 —
b. Vert. pair, imperf. between 425.00 —
c. Double impression of center 675.00
322 A42 18c lt brn & blk 1.10 .50
Never hinged 2.50
a. Double impression of center 850.00
b. Vertical pair, imperf. between 475.00
323 A42 20c orange & black 2.00 1.00
Never hinged 4.50
a. 20c orange & brown 600.00 —
b. As No. 323, imperf., pair 575.00 575.00
c. As "a," imperf., pair 1,750. —
d. Vert. pair, imperf. between 500.00
324 A42 24c gray & black 1.00 .55
Never hinged 2.25
a. Vert. pair, imperf. between 500.00
325 A42 1p rose lil & blk 47.50 50.00
Never hinged 70.00
a. Vert. pair, imperf. between 500.00
Nos. 319-325 (7) 53.65 53.35
Set, never hinged 83.95

Opening of the Legislative Palace.
No. 322a is valued in the grade of fine.
For overprints, see Nos. O1-O4.

Rizal Type of 1906
Coil Stamp

1928 *Perf. 11 Vertically*

326 A40 2c green 7.50 12.50
Never hinged 19.00

Types of 1906-1923

1925-31 *Imperf.*

340 A40 2c yel green ('31) .50 .50
Never hinged .90
a. 2c green ('25) .80 .75
Never hinged 1.80
341 A40 4c car rose ('31) .50 1.00
Never hinged 1.00
a. 4c carmine ('25) 1.20 1.00
Never hinged 2.75
342 A40 6c violet ('31) 3.00 3.75
Never hinged 5.00
a. 6c deep violet ('25) 12.00 8.00
Never hinged 26.00
343 A40 8c brown ('31) 2.00 5.00
Never hinged 4.00
a. 8c yellow brown ('25) 13.00 8.00
Never hinged 26.00
344 A40 10c blue ('31) 5.00 7.50
Never hinged 12.00
a. 10c deep blue ('25) 45.00 20.00
Never hinged 100.00
345 A40 12c dp orange ('31) 8.00 10.00
Never hinged 15.00
a. 12c red orange ('25) 60.00 35.00
Never hinged 135.00
346 A40 16c olive green 6.00 7.50
Never hinged 11.00
a. 16c bister green ('25) 42.50 18.00
Never hinged 100.00
347 A40 20c dp yel org ('31) 5.00 7.50
Never hinged 11.00
a. 20c yellow orange ('25) 45.00 20.00
Never hinged 100.00
348 A40 26c green ('31) 6.00 9.00
Never hinged 11.00
a. 26c blue green ('25) 45.00 25.00
Never hinged 110.00
349 A40 30c light gray ('31) 8.00 10.00
Never hinged 16.00
a. 30c gray ('25) 45.00 25.00
Never hinged 110.00
350 A41 1p light violet ('31) 10.00 15.00
Never hinged 20.00
a. 1p violet ('25) 200.00 100.00
Never hinged 425.00
351 A41 2p brn vio ('31) 30.00 45.00
Never hinged 80.00
a. 2p violet brown ('25) 400.00 400.00
Never hinged 675.00
352 A41 4p blue ('31) 80.00 90.00
Never hinged 150.00
a. 4p deep blue ('25) 2,200. 1,100.
Never hinged 3,500.
353 A41 10p green ('31) 175.00 225.00
Never hinged 300.00
a. 10p deep green ('25) 2,750. 2,950.
Never hinged 4,250.
Nos. 340-353 (14) 339.00 436.75
Set, never hinged 636.90
Nos. 340a-353a (14) 5,860. 4,711.

Nos. 340a-353a were the original post office issue. These were reprinted twice in 1931 for sale to collectors (Nos. 340-353).

Mount Mayon, Luzon — A43

Post Office, Manila — A44

Pier No. 7, Manila Bay
A45

(See footnote)
A46

Rice Planting — A47

Rice Terraces — A48

Baguio Zigzag — A49

1932, May 3 *Perf. 11*

354 A43 2c yellow green .75 .30
Never hinged 1.25
355 A44 4c rose carmine .75 .30
Never hinged 1.25
356 A45 12c orange .90 .75
Never hinged 1.30
357 A46 18c red orange 45.00 15.00
Never hinged 72.50
358 A47 20c yellow 1.00 .75
Never hinged 1.60
359 A48 24c deep violet 1.60 1.00
Never hinged 2.75
360 A49 32c olive brown 1.60 1.00
Never hinged 2.75
Nos. 354-360 (7) 51.60 19.10
Set, never hinged 83.40

The 18c vignette was intended to show Pagsanjan Falls in Laguna, central Luzon, and is so labeled. Through error the stamp pictures Vernal Falls in Yosemite National Park, California.

For overprints see #C29-C35, C47-C51, C63.

Nos. 302, 302a Surcharged in Orange or Red

1932

368 A41 1p on 4p blue (O) 6.00 1.00
Never hinged 9.75
a. 1p on 4p dark blue (O) 6.00 1.00
Never hinged 9.25
P# block of 10, Impt. 140.00
Never hinged 175.00
369 A41 2p on 4p dark blue (R) 9.00 1.50
Never hinged 15.00
P# block of 10, Impt. 160.00
Never hinged 200.00
a. 2p on 4p blue (R) 9.00 1.00
Never hinged 15.00

Far Eastern Championship

Issued in commemoration of the Tenth Far Eastern Championship Games.

Baseball Players — A50

Tennis Player — A51

Basketball Players — A52

1934, Apr. 14 ***Perf. 11½***

380 A50 2c yellow brown 1.50 .80
Never hinged 2.25
381 A51 6c ultramarine .25 .25
Never hinged .30
a. Vertical pair, imperf. between 700.00
Never hinged 1,100.
382 A52 16c violet brown .50 .50
Never hinged .75
a. Vert. pair, imperf. horiz. 950.00
Never hinged 1,500.
Nos. 380-382 (3) 2.25 1.55
Set, never hinged 3.30

José Rizal A53

Woman and Carabao A54

La Filipina A55

Pearl Fishing A56

Fort Santiago — A57

Salt Spring — A58

Magellan's Landing, 1521 A59

"Juan de la Cruz" A60

Rice Terraces — A61

"Blood Compact," 1565 — A62

Barasoain Church, Malolos — A63

Battle of Manila Bay, 1898 — A64

Montalban Gorge A65

George Washington A66

1935, Feb. 15 ***Perf. 11***

383 A53 2c rose .25 .25
Never hinged .25
384 A54 4c yellow green .25 .25
Never hinged .25
385 A55 6c dark brown .25 .25
Never hinged .35
386 A56 8c violet .25 .25
Never hinged .35
387 A57 10c rose carmine .30 .25
Never hinged .45
388 A58 12c black .35 .25
Never hinged .50
389 A59 16c dark blue .35 .25
Never hinged .55
390 A60 20c light olive green .35 .25
Never hinged .45
391 A61 26c indigo .40 .40
Never hinged .60
392 A62 30c orange red .40 .40
Never hinged .60
393 A63 1p red org & blk 2.00 1.25
Never hinged 3.00
394 A64 2p bis brn & blk 12.00 2.00
Never hinged 16.00
395 A65 4p blue & black 12.00 4.00
Never hinged 16.00
396 A66 5p green & black 25.00 5.00
Never hinged 50.00
Nos. 383-396 (14) 54.15 15.05
Set, never hinged 74.45

For overprints & surcharges see Nos. 411-424, 433-446, 449, 463-466, 468, 472-474, 478-484, 485-494, C52-C53, O15-O36, O38, O40-O43, N2-N9, N28, NO2-NO6.

Issues of the Commonwealth

Issued to commemorate the inauguration of the Philippine Commonwealth, Nov. 15, 1935.

The Temples of Human Progress A67

1935, Nov. 15

397 A67 2c carmine rose .25 .25
Never hinged .35
398 A67 6c deep violet .25 .25
Never hinged .35
399 A67 16c blue .25 .25
Never hinged .40
400 A67 36c yellow green .40 .30
Never hinged .65
401 A67 50c brown .70 .55
Never hinged 1.00
Nos. 397-401 (5) 1.85 1.60
Set, never hinged 2.75

Jose Rizal Issue

75th anniversary of the birth of Jose Rizal (1861-1896), national hero of the Filipinos.

Jose Rizal — A68

1936, June 19 ***Perf. 12***

402 A68 2c yellow brown .25 .25
Never hinged .25
403 A68 6c slate blue .25 .25
Never hinged .25
a. Imperf. vertically, pair 1,000.
Never hinged 1,500.
404 A68 36c red brown .50 .70
Never hinged .75
Nos. 402-404 (3) 1.00 1.20
Set, never hinged 1.25

Commonwealth Anniversary Issue

Issued in commemoration of the first anniversary of the Commonwealth.

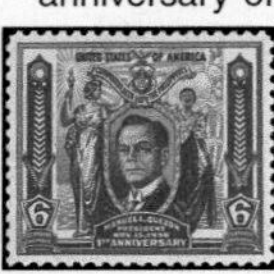

President Manuel L. Quezon — A69

1936, Nov. 15 ***Perf. 11***

408 A69 2c orange brown .25 .25
Never hinged .30
409 A69 6c yellow green .25 .25
Never hinged .30
410 A69 12c ultramarine .25 .25
Never hinged .30
Nos. 408-410 (3) .75 .75
Set, never hinged .90

Stamps of 1935 Overprinted in Black

a

b

1936-37

411 A53(a) 2c rose .25 .25
Never hinged .25
a. Bklt. pane of 6 ('37) 2.50 2.00
Never hinged 4.00
b. Hyphen omitted 125.00 100.00
412 A54(b) 4c yel grn ('37) .45 4.00
Never hinged .70
P# block of 6 35.00
Never hinged 45.00
413 A55(a) 6c dark brown .25 .25
Never hinged .25
414 A56(b) 8c violet ('37) .25 .25
Never hinged .35
415 A57(b) 10c rose carmine .25 .25
Never hinged .25
a. "COMMONWEALT" 20.00 —
Never hinged 30.00
416 A58(b) 12c black ('37) .25 .25
Never hinged .30
417 A59(b) 16c dark blue .25 .25
Never hinged .40
418 A60(a) 20c lt ol grn ('37) .90 .40
Never hinged 1.50
419 A61(b) 26c indigo ('37) .80 .35
Never hinged 1.40
420 A62(b) 30c orange red .45 .25
Never hinged .75
421 A63(b) 1p red org & blk .90 .25
Never hinged 1.50
422 A64(b) 2p bis brn & blk ('37) 12.50 4.00
Never hinged 21.00
423 A65(b) 4p bl & blk ('37) 45.00 8.00
Never hinged 72.50
424 A66(b) 5p grn & blk ('37) 12.50 25.00
Never hinged 21.00
Nos. 411-424 (14) 75.00 43.75
Set, never hinged 122.15

Eucharistic Congress Issue

Issued to commemorate the 33rd International Eucharistic Congress held at Manila, Feb. 3-7, 1937.

Map of Philippines — A70

1937, Feb. 3

425 A70 2c yellow green .25 .25
Never hinged .25
426 A70 6c light brown .25 .25
Never hinged .25
427 A70 12c sapphire .25 .25
Never hinged .25
428 A70 20c deep orange .30 .25
Never hinged .50
429 A70 36c deep violet .55 .40
Never hinged .80
430 A70 50c carmine .70 .35
Never hinged 1.10
Nos. 425-430 (6) 2.30 1.75
Set, never hinged 3.15

Arms of Manila — A71

1937, Aug. 27

431 A71 10p gray 5.00 2.00
Never hinged 7.25
P# block of 6 67.50
Never hinged 85.00
432 A71 20p henna brown 4.00 1.40
Never hinged 6.50

Stamps of 1935 Overprinted in Black

a

b

1938-40

433 A53(a) 2c rose ('39) .25 .25
Never hinged .25
P# block of 6 8.00
Never hinged 10.00
a. Booklet pane of 6 3.50 3.50
Never hinged 5.50
b. As "a," lower left-hand stamp overprinted "WEALTH COMMON-" 2,000.
Never hinged 3,250.
c. Hyphen omitted 100.00 50.00
434 A54(b) 4c yel grn ('40) 3.00 30.00
Never hinged 4.75
P# block of 6 35.00
Never hinged 45.00
435 A55(a) 6c dk brn ('39) .25 .25
Never hinged .40
a. 6c golden brown .25 .25
Never hinged .40
P# block of 6 5.50
Never hinged 7.00
436 A56(b) 8c violet ('39) .25 1.75
Never hinged .25
P# block of 6 8.00
Never hinged 10.00
a. "COMMONWEALT" (LR 31) 90.00
Never hinged 140.00
437 A57(b) 10c rose car ('39) .25 .25
Never hinged .25
P# block of 6 8.00
Never hinged 10.00
a. "COMMONWEALT" (LR 31) 65.00 —
Never hinged 100.00
438 A58(b) 12c black ('40) .25 1.00
Never hinged .25
P# block of 6 8.00
Never hinged 10.00
439 A59(b) 16c dark blue .25 .25
Never hinged .25
P# block of 6 16.00
Never hinged 20.00
440 A60(a) 20c lt ol grn ('39) .25 .25
Never hinged .25
P# block of 6 12.00
Never hinged 15.00
441 A61(b) 26c indigo ('40) 1.00 2.50
Never hinged 1.50
P# block of 6 16.00
Never hinged 20.00
442 A62(b) 30c org red ('39) 3.00 .70
Never hinged 5.00
P# block of 6 22.50
Never hinged 35.00
443 A63(b) 1p red org & blk .60 .25
Never hinged 1.00
444 A64(b) 2p bis brn & blk ('39) 10.00 1.00
Never hinged 15.00
P# block of 4 87.50
Never hinged 110.00
445 A65(b) 4p bl & blk ('40) 150.00 250.00
Never hinged 325.00
446 A66(b) 5p grn & blk ('40) 20.00 8.00
Never hinged 35.00
P# block of 4 200.00
Never hinged 250.00
Nos. 433-446 (14) 189.35 296.45
Set, never hinged 414.15

Overprint "b" measures 18½x1¾mm.

No. 433b occurs in booklet pane, No. 433a, position 5; all examples are straight-edged, left and bottom.

First Foreign Trade Week Issue
Nos. 384, 298a and 432 Surcharged in Red, Violet or Black

a

b

c

1939, July 5

449 A54(a) 2c on 4c yel grn (R) .25 .25
Never hinged .35
450 A40(b) 6c on 26c blue grn (V) .25 .50
Never hinged .35
a. 6c on 26c green 3.00 1.00
Never hinged 5.00
451 A71(c) 50c on 20p henna brn (Bk) 1.25 1.00
Never hinged 2.00 5.00
Nos. 449-451 (3) 1.75 1.75
Set, never hinged 2.70

Commonwealth 4th Anniversary Issue (#452-460)

Triumphal Arch — A72

1939, Nov. 15

452 A72 2c yellow green .25 .25
Never hinged .25
453 A72 6c carmine .25 .25
Never hinged .25
454 A72 12c bright blue .25 .25
Never hinged .25
Nos. 452-454 (3) .75 .75
Set, never hinged .75

For overprints see Nos. 469, 476.

Malacañan Palace — A73

1939, Nov. 15
455 A73 2c green .25 .25
Never hinged .25
456 A73 6c orange .25 .25
Never hinged .25
457 A73 12c carmine .25 .25
Never hinged .25
Nos. 455-457 (3) .75 .75
Set, never hinged .75

For overprint, see No. 470.

Pres. Quezon Taking Oath of Office — A74

1940, Feb. 8
458 A74 2c dark orange .25 .25
Never hinged .25
459 A74 6c dark green .25 .25
Never hinged .25
460 A74 12c purple .25 .25
Never hinged .30
Nos. 458-460 (3) .75 .75
Set, never hinged .80

For overprints, see Nos. 471, 477.

José Rizal — A75

ROTARY PRESS PRINTING

1941, Apr. 14 ***Perf. 11x10½***
Size: 19x22½mm
461 A75 2c apple green .25 *.50*
Never hinged .25

FLAT PLATE PRINTING

1941, Nov. 14 ***Perf. 11***
Size: 18¾x22¼mm
462 A75 2c pale apple green 1.00 —
Never hinged 1.25
a. Booklet pane of 6 6.00 —
Never hinged 7.50

No. 461 was issued only in sheets. No. 462 was issued only in booklet panes on Nov. 14, 1941, just before the war, and only a few used stamps and covers exist. All examples have one or two straight edges. Mint booklets reappeared after the war. In August 1942, the booklet pane was reprinted in a darker shade (apple green). However, the apple green panes were available only to U.S. collectors during the war years, so no war-period used stamps from the Philippines exist. Value of apple green booklet pane, never hinged, $6.

For type A75 overprinted, see Nos. 464, O37, O39, N1 and NO1.

Philippine Stamps of 1935-41, Handstamped in Violet

1944 ***Perf. 11, 11x10½***
463 A53 2c rose (On 411) *1,250.* *650.00*
a. Booklet pane of 6 *12,500.*
463B A53 2c rose (On 433) *2,000.* *1,750.*
464 A75 2c apple grn (On 461) 12.50 10.00
Never hinged 22.50
a. Pair, one without ovpt. — —
465 A54 4c yel grn (On 384) 47.50 *50.00*
Never hinged 80.00
466 A55 6c dk brn (On 385) *3,250.* *2,000.*
467 A69 6c yel grn (On 409) 300.00 *150.00*
Never hinged *525.00*
468 A55 6c dk brn (On 413) *4,000.* *825.00*
469 A72 6c car (On 453) *350.00* *125.00*
470 A73 6c org (On 456) *1,750.* *725.00*
471 A74 6c dk grn (On 459) *500.00* *225.00*
472 A56 8c vio (On 436) 17.50 *30.00*
Never hinged 30.00
473 A57 10c car rose (On 415) *350.00* *150.00*
474 A57 10c car rose (On 437) *275.00* *200.00*
Never hinged *475.00*
475 A69 12c ultra (On 410) *1,100.* *400.00*
476 A72 12c brt bl (On 454) *7,000.* *2,500.*
477 A74 12c pur (On 460) *500.00* *275.00*
478 A59 16c dk bl (On 389) *3,000.* —
479 A59 16c dk bl (On 417) *1,500.* *1,000.*
480 A59 16c dk bl (On 439) *500.00* *200.00*
481 A60 20c lt ol grn (On 440) 140.00 35.00
Never hinged 230.00
482 A62 30c org red (On 420) *450.00* *1,500.*
483 A62 30c org red (On 442) *800.00* *375.00*
484 A63 1p red org & blk (On 443) *6,250.* *4,500.*

Nos. 463-484 are valued in the grade of fine to very fine.

No. 463 comes only from the booklet pane. All examples have one or two straight edges.

Types of 1935-37 Overprinted

a

b

Nos. 431-432 Overprinted in Black — c

1945 ***Perf. 11***
485 A53(a) 2c rose .25 .25
Never hinged .25
486 A54(b) 4c yellow green .25 .25
Never hinged .25
487 A55(a) 6c golden brown .25 .25
Never hinged .25
488 A56(b) 8c violet .25 .25
Never hinged .25
489 A57(b) 10c rose carmine .25 .25
Never hinged .25
490 A58(b) 12c black .25 .25
Never hinged .25
491 A59(b) 16c dark blue .25 .25
Never hinged .30
492 A60(a) 20c lt olive green .30 .25
Never hinged .40
493 A62(b) 30c orange red .50 .35
Never hinged .75
494 A63(b) 1p red org & blk 1.10 .25
Never hinged 1.60
495 A71(c) 10p gray 55.00 13.50
Never hinged 90.00
496 A71(c) 20p henna brown 50.00 15.00
Never hinged 75.00
Nos. 485-496 (12) 108.65 31.10
Set, never hinged 169.55

José Rizal — A76

1946, May 28 ***Perf. 11x10½***
497 A76 2c sepia .25 .25
Never hinged .25

For overprints see Nos. 503, O44.

Catalogue values for unused stamps in this section, from this point to the end of the section, are for Never Hinged items.

Later issues, released by the Philippine Republic on July 4, 1946, and thereafter, are listed in Scott's Standard Postage Stamp Catalogue, Vol. 5A.

Republic

Philippine Girl Holding Flag of the Republic — A77

Unwmk.
1946, July 4 **Engr.** ***Perf. 11***
500 A77 2c carmine .50 .25
501 A77 6c green .60 .25
502 A77 12c blue 1.50 .40
Nos. 500-502 (3) 2.60 .90

Philippine independence, July 4, 1946.

No. 497 Overprinted in Brown

1946, Dec. 30 ***Perf. 11x10½***
503 A76 2c sepia .50 .30

50th anniv. of the execution of José Rizal.

Rizal Monument A78

Bonifacio Monument A79

Jones Bridge A80

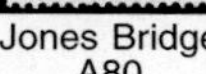
Santa Lucia Gate A81

Mayon Volcano A82

Avenue of Palms A83

1947 **Engr.** ***Perf. 12***
504 A78 4c black brown .60 .25
505 A79 10c red orange .60 .25
506 A80 12c deep blue .60 .25
507 A81 16c slate gray 3.50 .70
508 A82 20c red brown 3.50 .25
509 A83 50c dull green 4.00 .50
510 A83 1p violet 3.50 .50
Nos. 504-510 (7) 16.30 2.70

Issued: Nos. 505 & 508, 3/23; Nos. 506-07, 509, 6/19; Nos. 504 & 510, 8/1.

For surcharges see Nos. 613-614, 809. For overprints see Nos. 609, O50-O52, O54-O55.

Manuel L. Quezon — A84

1947, May 1 **Typo.**
511 A84 1c green .60 .30
a. Vert. pair, imperf. between 50.00

See No. 515.

Pres. Manuel A. Roxas Taking Oath of Office — A85

1947, July 4 **Unwmk.** ***Perf. 12½***
512 A85 4c carmine rose .60 .25
513 A85 6c dk green .90 .45
514 A85 16c purple 1.50 .85
Nos. 512-514 (3) 3.00 1.55

First anniversary of republic.

Quezon Type
Souvenir Sheet

1947, Nov. 28 ***Imperf.***
515 Sheet of 4 1.75 1.25
a. A84 1c bright green .30 .30

United Nations Emblem — A87

1947, Nov. 24 ***Perf. 12½***
516 A87 4c dk car & pink 2.75 1.40
a. Imperf. 5.50 3.75
517 A87 6c pur & pale vio 2.75 1.40
a. Imperf. 5.50 3.75
518 A87 12c dp bl & pale bl 4.00 2.50
a. Imperf. 6.00 4.00
Nos. 516-518 (3) 9.50 5.30
Nos. 516a-518a (3) 17.50 11.25

Conference of the Economic Commission in Asia and the Far East, held at Baguio.

Gen. Douglas MacArthur — A88

1948, Feb. 3 **Engr.** ***Perf. 12***
519 A88 4c purple 1.20 .60
520 A88 6c rose car 1.60 .60
521 A88 16c brt ultra 2.00 .80
Nos. 519-521 (3) 4.80 2.00

Threshing Rice — A89

1948, Feb. 23 **Typo.** ***Perf. 12½***
522 A89 2c grn & pale yel grn 1.50 .60
523 A89 6c brown & cream 2.50 .60
524 A89 18c dp bl & pale bl 4.00 1.80
Nos. 522-524 (3) 8.00 3.00

Conf. of the FAO held at Baguio. Nos. 522 and 524 exist imperf. Value, set $125.

See No. C67.

Manuel A. Roxas — A90

1948, July 15 **Engr.** ***Perf. 12***
525 A90 2c black .30 .30
526 A90 4c black .45 .30

Issued in tribute to President Manuel A. Roxas who died April 15, 1948.

José Rizal — A91

1948, June 19 **Unwmk.**
527 A91 2c bright green .40 .30
a. Booklet pane of 6 ('44) 6.00 4.00

For surcharges see Nos. 550, O56. For overprint see No. O53.

Scout Saluting — A92

1948, Oct. 31 **Typo.** ***Imperf.***
528 A92 2c chocolate & green 1.25 .55
a. Perf. 11½ 1.75 1.40
529 A92 4c chocolate & pink 2.00 .70
a. Perf. 11½ 2.50 2.00

Boy Scouts of the Philippines, 25th anniv. Nos. 528 and 529 exist part perforate.

Sampaguita, National Flower — A93

1948, Dec. 8 ***Perf. 12½***
530 A93 3c blk, pale grn & grn .75 .30

UPU Monument, Bern — A94

Unwmk.

1949, Oct. 9	**Engr.**	***Perf. 12***	
531 A94	4c green	1.00	.25
532 A94	6c dull violet	.75	.25
533 A94	18c blue gray	.75	.40
	Nos. 531-533 (3)	2.50	.90

Souvenir Sheet

Imperf

534	Sheet of 3	3.50	2.50
a.	A94 4c green	.80	.40
b.	A94 6c dull violet	.80	.40
c.	A94 18c blue	.80	.60

75th anniv. of the UPU.

In 1960 an unofficial, 3-line overprint ("President D. D. Eisenhower /Visit to the Philippines/June 14-16, 1960") was privately applied to No. 534.

For surcharge & overprint see #806, 901.

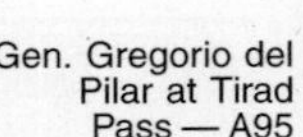

Gen. Gregorio del Pilar at Tirad Pass — A95

1949, Dec. 2		***Perf. 12***	
535 A95	2c red brown	.50	.25
536 A95	4c green	.70	.25

50th anniversary of the death of Gen. Gregorio P. del Pilar and fifty-two of his men at Tirad Pass.

Globe — A96

1950, Mar. 1			
537 A96	2c purple	.50	.25
538 A96	6c dk green	.60	.25
539 A96	18c dp blue	.70	.25
	Nos. 537-539,C68-C69 (5)	6.60	2.10

5th World Cong. of the Junior Chamber of Commerce, Manila, Mar. 1-8, 1950.

For surcharge see No. 825.

Red Lauan Tree — A97

1950, Apr. 14			
540 A97	2c green	.70	.25
541 A97	4c purple	.80	.25

50th anniversary of the Bureau of Forestry.

F. D. Roosevelt with his Stamps — A98

1950, May 22			
542 A98	4c dark brown	1.70	.25
543 A98	6c carmine rose	.90	.45
544 A98	18c blue	.90	.70
	Nos. 542-544 (3)	3.50	1.40

Honoring Franklin D. Roosevelt and for the 25th anniv. of the Philatelic Association of the Philippines. See No. C70.

Lions Club Emblem — A99

1950, June 4		**Engr.**	
545 A99	2c orange	1.40	.30
546 A99	4c violet	1.40	.35
	Nos. 545-546,C71-C72 (4)	8.30	1.95

Convention of the Lions Club, Manila, June 1950.

Pres. Elpidio Quirino Taking Oath — A100

1950, July 4	**Unwmk.**	***Perf. 12***	
547 A100	2c car rose	.40	.25
548 A100	4c magenta	.40	.25
549 A100	6c blue green	.60	.25
	Nos. 547-549 (3)	1.40	.75

Republic of the Philippines, 4th anniv.

No. 527 Surcharged in Black

1950, Sept. 20			
550 A91	1c on 2c bright green	.60	.30

Dove over Globe — A101

1950, Oct. 23			
551 A101	5c green	1.00	.25
552 A101	6c rose carmine	.70	.25
553 A101	18c ultra	.70	.40
	Nos. 551-553 (3)	2.40	.90

Baguio Conference of 1950.

For surcharge see No. 828.

Headman of Barangay Inspecting Harvest — A102

1951, Mar. 31	**Litho.**	***Perf. 12½***	
554 A102	5c dull green	1.00	.25
555 A102	6c red brown	.70	.25
556 A102	18c violet blue	.70	.40
	Nos. 554-556 (3)	2.40	.90

The government's Peace Fund campaign.

Imperf., Pairs

554a A102	5c dull green	4.00	2.00
555a A102	6c red brown	2.00	1.00
556a A102	18c violet blue	1.50	1.00
	Nos. 554a-556a (3)	7.50	4.00

Arms of Manila A103

Arms of Cebu A104

Arms of Zamboanga A105

Arms of Iloilo A106

Various Frames

1951	**Engr.**	***Perf. 12***	
557 A103	5c purple	1.70	.25
558 A103	6c gray	1.20	.25
559 A103	18c bright ultra	.80	.50

Various Frames

560 A104	5c crimson rose	1.70	.25
561 A104	6c bister brown	.70	.25
562 A104	18c violet	1.40	.50

Various Frames

563 A105	5c blue green	1.70	.25
564 A105	6c red brown	1.40	.25
565 A105	18c light blue	1.40	.50

Various Frames

566 A106	5c bright green	1.70	.25
567 A106	6c violet	1.40	.25
568 A106	18c deep blue	1.40	.50
	Nos. 557-568 (12)	16.50	4.00

Issued: A103, 2/3; A104, 4/27; A105, 6/19; A106, 8/26.

For surcharges see Nos. 634-636.

UN Emblem and Girl Holding Flag — A107

1951, Oct. 24	**Unwmk.**	***Perf. 11½***	
569 A107	5c red	2.00	.30
570 A107	6c blue green	1.25	.30
571 A107	18c violet blue	1.25	.50
	Nos. 569-571 (3)	4.50	1.10

United Nations Day, Oct. 24, 1951.

Liberty Holding Declaration of Human Rights — A108

1951, Dec. 10		***Perf. 12***	
572 A108	5c green	2.00	.25
573 A108	6c red orange	1.25	.35
574 A108	18c ultra	1.25	.50
	Nos. 572-574 (3)	4.50	1.10

Universal Declaration of Human Rights.

Students and Department Seal — A109

1952, Jan. 31			
575 A109	5c orange red	.90	.35

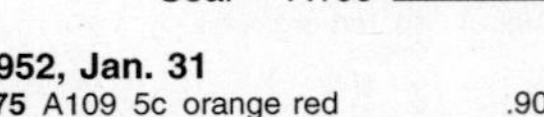

50th anniversary (in 1951) of the Philippine Educational System.

Milkfish and Map — A111

1952, Oct. 23		***Perf. 12½***	
578 A111	5c orange brown	2.00	.45
a.	Vert. pair, imperf. between	65.00	
b.	Horiz. pair, imperf. between	65.00	
579 A111	6c deep blue	1.00	.45
a.	Vert. pair, imperf. horiz.	80.00	

4th Indo-Pacific Fisheries Council Meeting, Quezon City, Oct. 23-Nov. 7, 1952.

Nos. 578-579 exist imperf. Value, set $60.

Maria Clara — A112

1952, Nov. 16			
580 A112	5c deep blue	1.40	.30
581 A112	6c brown	1.00	.40
	Nos. 580-581,C73 (3)	4.90	1.70

1st Pan-Asian Philatelic Exhibition, PANAPEX, Manila, Nov. 16-22.

Nos. 580-81 exist imperf. Value, set $75.

Wright Park, Baguio City — A113

1952, Dec. 15		***Perf. 12***	
582 A113	5c red orange	1.75	.45
583 A113	6c dp blue green	1.25	.55

3rd Lions District Convention, Baguio City.

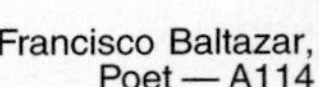

Francisco Baltazar, Poet — A114

1953, Mar. 27			
584 A114	5c citron	1.00	.30

National Language Week.

"Gateway to the East" — A115

1953, Apr. 30			
585 A115	5c turq green	.70	.25
586 A115	6c vermilion	.60	.30

Philippines International Fair.

Presidents Quirino and Sukarno — A116

1953, Oct. 5		**Engr. & Litho.**	
587 A116	5c multicolored	.80	.35
588 A116	6c multicolored	.45	.35

2nd anniversary of the visit of Indonesia's President Sukarno.

Marcelo H. del Pilar — A117

1c, Manuel L. Quezon. 2c, José Abad Santos (diff. frame). 3c, Apolinario Mabini (diff. frame). 10c, Father José Burgos. 20c, Lapu-Lapu. 25c, Gen. Antonio Luna. 50c, Cayetano Arellano. 60c, Andres Bonifacio. 2p, Graciano L. Jaena.

Perf. 12, 12½, 13, 14x13½

1952-60		**Engr.**	
589 A117	1c red brn ('53)	.30	.25
590 A117	2c gray ('60)	.30	.25
591 A117	3c brick red ('59)	.30	.25
592 A117	5c crim rose	.30	.25
595 A117	10c ultra ('55)	.60	.25
597 A117	20c car lake ('55)	1.00	.25
598 A117	25c yel grn ('58)	1.50	.30
599 A117	50c org ver ('59)	1.80	.35
600 A117	60c car rose ('58)	2.00	.60
601 A117	2p violet	6.00	1.25
	Nos. 589-601 (10)	14.10	4.00

For overprints & surcharges see #608, 626, 641-642, 647, 830, 871, 875-877, O57-O61.

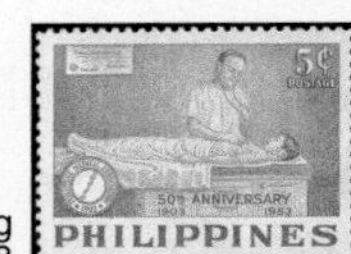

Doctor Examining Boy — A118

1953, Dec. 16			
603 A118	5c lilac rose	1.00	.25
604 A118	6c ultra	.80	.35

50th anniversary of the founding of the Philippine Medical Association.

First Philippine Stamps, Magellan's Landing and Manila Scene — A119

Stamp of 1854 in Orange

1954, Apr. 25 *Perf. 13*
605 A119 5c purple 1.00 .35
606 A119 18c deep blue 2.25 1.20
607 A119 30c green 5.25 2.80
Nos. 605-607,C74-C76 (6) 30.50 12.60

Centenary of Philippine postage stamps.
For surcharge see No. 829.

Nos. 592 and 509 Overprinted or Surcharged in Black

1954, Apr. 23 *Perf. 12*
608 A117 5c crimson rose 2.50 1.00
609 A83 18c on 50c dull grn 3.00 1.75

1st National Boy Scout Jamboree, Quezon City, April 23-30, 1954.
The surcharge on No. 609 is reduced to fit the size of the stamp.

Discus Thrower and Games Emblem — A120

1954, May 31 *Perf. 13*
610 A120 5c shown 4.00 .80
611 A120 18c Swimmer 1.75 .70
612 A120 30c Boxers 3.25 1.50
Nos. 610-612 (3) 9.00 3.00

2nd Asian Games, Manila, May 1-9.

Nos. 505 and 508 Surcharged in Blue

1954, Sept. 6 *Perf. 12*
613 A79 5c on 10c red org 1.00 .45
614 A82 18c on 20c red brn 1.00 .55

Manila Conference, 1954.
The surcharge is arranged to obliterate the original denomination.

Allegory of Independence — A121

1954, Nov. 30 *Perf. 13*
615 A121 5c dark carmine 1.20 .25
616 A121 18c deep blue 1.00 .45

56th anniversary of the declaration of the first Philippine Independence.
For surcharge see No. 826.

"Immaculate Conception," by Murillo — A122

1954, Dec. 30 *Perf. 12*
617 A122 5c blue .80 .25

Issued to mark the end of the Marian Year.

Mayon Volcano, Moro Vinta and Rotary Emblem — A123

1955, Feb. 23 **Engr.** *Perf. 13*
618 A123 5c dull blue .75 .25
619 A123 18c dk car rose 1.65 .75
Nos. 618-619,C77 (3) 5.40 2.25

Rotary Intl., 50th anniv. For surcharge see #827.

Allegory of Labor — A124

1955, May 26 *Perf. 13x12½*
620 A124 5c brown 1.75 .70

Issued in connection with the Labor-Management Congress, Manila, May 26-28, 1955.

Pres. Ramon Magsaysay — A125

1955, July 4 *Perf. 12½*
621 A125 5c blue .60 .25
622 A125 20c red 1.80 .50
623 A125 30c green 2.00 .50
Nos. 621-623 (3) 4.40 1.25

9th anniversary of the Republic.

Village Well — A126

1956, Mar. 16 *Perf. 12½x13½*
624 A126 5c violet 1.00 .30
625 A126 20c dull green 1.50 .50

Issued to publicize the drive for improved health conditions in rural areas.

No. 592 Overprinted

1956, Aug. 1 **Unwmk.** *Perf. 12*
626 A117 5c crimson rose .80 .40

5th Annual Conf. of the World Confederation of Organizations of the Teaching Profession, Manila, Aug. 1-8, 1956.

Nurse and Disaster Victims — A127

Engraved; Cross Lithographed in Red

1956, Aug. 30
627 A127 5c violet .50 .30
628 A127 20c gray brown 1.50 .60

50 years of Red Cross Service in the Philippines.

Monument to US Landing, Leyte — A128

1956, Oct. 20 **Litho.** *Perf. 12½*
629 A128 5c carmine rose .80 .30
a. Imperf, pair ('57) 5.00 3.00

Landing of US forces under Gen. Douglas MacArthur on Leyte, Oct. 20, 1944.
Issue date: No. 629a, Feb. 16.

Santo Tomas University — A129

1956, Nov. 13 **Photo.** *Perf. 11½*
630 A129 5c brown car & choc .75 .40
631 A129 60c lilac & red brn 4.25 1.80

Statue of Christ by Rizal — A130

1956, Nov. 28 **Engr.** *Perf. 12*
632 A130 5c gray olive .60 .25
633 A130 20c rose carmine 1.50 .65

2nd Natl. Eucharistic Cong., Manila, Nov. 28-Dec. 2, and for the centenary of the Feast of the Sacred Heart.

Nos. 561, 564 and 567 Surcharged with New Value in Blue or Black

1956, Dec. 7 **Unwmk.** *Perf. 12*
634 A104 5c on 6c bis brn (Bl) .70 .25
635 A105 5c on 6c red brn (Bl) .70 .25
636 A106 5c on 6c vio (Bk) .70 .25
Nos. 634-636 (3) 2.10 .75

Girl Scout, Emblem and Tents — A131

1957, Jan. 19 **Litho.** *Perf. 12½*
637 A131 5c dark blue 1.00 .60
a. Imperf, pair 7.00 6.00

Centenary of the Scout movement and for the Girl Scout World Jamboree, Quezon City, Jan. 19-Feb. 2, 1957.
Exmaples of Nos. 637 and 637a (No. 48 in sheet) exist with heavy black rectangular handstamps obliterating erroneous date at left, denomination and cloverleaf emblem.

Pres. Ramon Magsaysay (1907-57) — A132

1957, Aug. 31 **Engr.** *Perf. 12*
638 A132 5c black .40 .25

"Spoliarium" by Juan Luna — A133

1957, Oct. 23 *Perf. 14x14½*
639 A133 5c rose carmine .50 .30

Centenary of the birth of Juan Luna, painter.

Sergio Osmena and First National Assembly A134

1957, Oct. 16 *Perf. 12½x13½*
640 A134 5c blue green .50 .30

1st Philippine Assembly and honoring Sergio Osmeña, Speaker of the Assembly.

Nos. 595 and 597 Surcharged in Carmine or Black

1957, Dec. 30 *Perf. 14x13½*
641 A117 5c on 10c ultra (C) .80 .30
642 A117 10c on 20c car lake 1.00 .40

Inauguration of Carlos P. Garcia as president and Diosdado Macapagal as vice-president, Dec. 30.

University of the Philippines A135

1958, June 18 **Engr.** *Perf. 13½x13*
643 A135 5c dk carmine rose .60 .25

50th anniversary of the founding of the University of the Philippines.

Pres. Carlos P. Garcia — A136

1958, July 4 **Photo.** *Perf. 11½*
Granite Paper
644 A136 5c multicolored .35 .25
645 A136 20c multicolored .65 .30

12th anniversary of Philippine Republic.

Manila Cathedral A137

1958, Dec. 8 **Engr.** *Perf. 13x13½*
646 A137 5c multicolored .45 .25
a. Perf 12 3.00 2.00

Issued to commemorate the inauguration of the rebuilt Manila Cathedral, Dec. 8, 1958.

No. 592 Surcharged

1959, Jan. 11 *Perf. 12*
647 A117 1c on 5c crim rose .35 .25

Nos. B4-B5 Surcharged with New Values and Bars

1959, Feb. 3 *Perf. 13*
648 SP4 1c on 2c + 2c red .35 .25
649 SP5 6c on 4c + 4c vio .45 .25

14th anniversary of the liberation of Manila from the Japanese forces.

Philippine Flag — A138

1959, Feb. 8 Unwmk. *Perf. 13*

650 A138 6c dp ultra, yel & dp car .35 .25
651 A138 20c dp car, yel & dp ultra .65 .35

Seal of Bulacan Province — A139

1959, Jan. 21 Engr. *Perf. 13*

652 A139 6c lt yellow grn .35 .25
653 A139 20c rose red .65 .30

60th anniversary of the Malolos constitution.

1959, Apr. 15

Design: 6c, 25c, Seal of Capiz Province and portrait of Pres. Roxas.

654 A139 6c lt brown .35 .25
655 A139 25c purple .65 .35

Pres. Manuel A. Roxas, 11th death anniv. For surcharge see No. 848.

Seal of Bacolod City — A140

1959, Oct. 1

656 A140 6c blue green .35 .25
657 A140 10c rose lilac .65 .35

Nos. 658-803 were reserved for the rest of a projected series showing seals and coats of arms of provinces and cities.

Camp John Hay Amphitheater, Baguio — A141

1959, Sept. 1 *Perf. 13½*

804 A141 6c bright green .35 .25
a. Perf 12 2.00 1.50
805 A141 25c rose red .65 .35

50th anniversary of the city of Baguio.

No. 533 Surcharged in Red

1959, Oct. 24 *Perf. 12*

806 A94 6c on 18c blue .60 .25

Issued for United Nations Day, Oct. 24.

Maria Cristina Falls — A142

1959, Nov. 18 Photo. *Perf. 13½*

807 A142 6c vio & dp yel grn .35 .25
a. Perf 12 2.00 1.10
808 A142 30c green & brown .90 .35
a. Perf 12 6.25 4.75

No. 504 Surcharged with New Value and Bars

1959, Dec. 1 Engr. *Perf. 12*

809 A78 1c on 4c blk brn .40 .30

Manila Atheneum Emblem A143

1959, Dec. 10 *Perf. 13½*

810 A143 6c ultra .40 .25
a. Perf 12 1.50 1.25
811 A143 30c rose red .80 .35
a. Perf 12 20.00 8.00

Centenary of the Manila Atheneum (Ateneo de Manila), a school, and to mark a century of progress in education.

Manuel Quezon A144

José Rizal A145

1959-60 Engr. *Perf. 13*

812 A144 1c olive gray ('60) .30 .25

Perf. 14x12

813 A145 6c gray blue .40 .25

Issued: No. 812, 11/15/60; No. 813, 12/30/59. For overprint see No. O62.

A146

Perf. 12½x13½

1960, Feb. 8 Unwmk. Photo.

814 A146 6c brown & gold .65 .30

25th anniversary of the Philippine Constitution. See No. C82.

Site of Manila Pact — A147

1960, Mar. 26 Engr. *Perf. 12½*

815 A147 6c emerald .55 .25
816 A147 25c orange .55 .35

5th anniversary (in 1959) of the Congress of the Philippines establishing the South-East Asia Treaty Organization (SEATO).
First Day Covers Issued 9/8/59.
For overprints see Nos. 841-842.

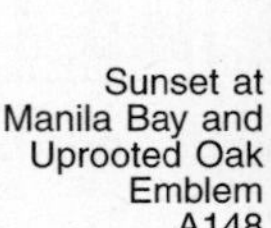

Sunset at Manila Bay and Uprooted Oak Emblem A148

1960, Apr. 7 Photo. *Perf. 13½*

817 A148 6c multicolored .35 .25
818 A148 25c multicolored .85 .35

World Refugee Year, 7/1/59-6/30/60.

A149

1960, July 29 *Perf. 13½*

819 A149 5c lt grn, red & gold .50 .25
820 A149 6c bl, red & gold .50 .30

Philippine Tuberculosis Society, 50th anniv.

Basketball A150

1960, Nov. 30 *Perf. 13x13½*

821 A150 6c shown .50 .30
822 A150 10c Runner .70 .25
Nos. 821-822,C85-C86 (4) 3.70 1.75

17th Olympic Games, Rome, 8/25-9/11.

Presidents Eisenhower and Garcia and Presidential Seals — A151

1960, Dec. 30 *Perf. 13½*

823 A151 6c multi .40 .25
824 A151 20c ultra, red & yel .60 .30

Visit of Pres. Dwight D. Eisenhower to the Philippines, June 14, 1960.

Nos. 539, 616, 619, 553, 606 and 598 Surcharged with New Values and Bars in Red or Black

1960-61 Engr. *Perf. 12, 13, 12½*

825 A96 1c on 18c dp bl (R) .30 .25
826 A121 5c on 18c dp bl (R) .75 .30
827 A123 5c on 18c dp car rose .75 .30
828 A101 10c on 18c ultra (R) .75 .30
829 A119 10c on 18c dp bl & org (R) .75 .30
830 A117 20c on 25c yel grn ('61) .75 .30
Nos. 825-830 (6) 4.05 1.75

On No. 830, no bars are overprinted, the surcharge "20 20" serving to cancel the old denomination.
Issued: Nos. 825, 827, 829, 7/4/60; Nos. 826, 828, 9/15/60; No. 830, 2/16/61.

Mercury and Globe A152

1961, Jan. 23 Photo. *Perf. 13½*

831 A152 6c red brn, bl, blk & gold .80 .25

Manila Postal Conf., Jan. 10-23. See #C87.

Nos. B10, B11 and B11a Surcharged "2nd National Boy Scout Jamboree Pasonanca Park" and New Value in Black or Red

1961, May 2 Engr. *Perf. 13*

Yellow Paper

832 SP8 10c on 6c + 4c car .50 .25
833 SP8 30c on 25c + 5c bl (R) .85 .45
a. Tete beche, *wht* (10c on 6c + 4c & 30c on 25c + 5c) (Bk) 1.80 *1.80*

Second National Boy Scout Jamboree, Pasonanca Park, Zamboanga City.

De la Salle College, Manila — A153

1961, June 16 Photo. *Perf. 11½*

834 A153 6c multi .40 .25
835 A153 10c multi .40 .25

De la Salle College, Manila, 50th anniv.

José Rizal as Student A154

6c, Rizal & birthplace at Calamba, Laguna. 10c, Rizal & parents. 20c, Rizal with Juan Luna & F. R. Hidalgo in Madrid. 30c, Rizal's execution.

1961 Unwmk. *Perf. 13½*

836 A154 5c multi .50 .30
837 A154 6c multi .50 .30
838 A154 10c grn & red brn .60 .35
839 A154 20c brn red & grnsh bl .70 .35
840 A154 30c vio, lil & org brn 1.00 .50
Nos. 836-840 (5) 3.30 1.80

Centenary of the birth of José Rizal.
Issued: Nos. 836-839, 1/19; No. 840 12/30.

Nos. 815-816 Overprinted

1961, July 4 Engr. *Perf. 12½*

841 A147 6c emerald .40 .25
842 A147 25c orange .50 .35

15th anniversary of the Republic.

Colombo Plan Emblem and Globe Showing Member Countries — A155

1961, Oct. 8 Photo. *Perf. 13x11½*

843 A155 5c multi .35 .25
844 A155 6c multi .35 .25

7th anniversary of the admission of the Philippines to the Colombo Plan.

Government Clerk — A156

1961, Dec. 9 Unwmk. *Perf. 12½*

845 A156 6c vio, bl & red .35 .25
846 A156 10c gray bl & red .60 .30

Honoring Philippine government employees.

No. C83 Surcharged

1961, Nov. 30 Engr. *Perf. 14x14½*

847 AP11 6c on 10c car .55 .30

Philippine Amateur Athletic Fed., 50th anniv.

No. 655 Surcharged with New Value and: "MACAPAGAL-PELAEZ INAUGURATION DEC. 30, 1961"

1961, Dec. 30 *Perf. 12½*

848 A139 6c on 25c pur .45 .30

Inauguration of Pres. Diosdado Macapagal and Vice-Pres. Emanuel Pelaez.

No. B8 Surcharged

1962, Jan. 23 Photo. *Perf. 13½x13*

849 SP7 6c on 5c grn & red .50 .30
a. Perf. 12 15.00 5.00

Vanda Orchids A157

Orchids: 6c, White mariposa. 10c, Sander's dendrobe. 20c, Sanggumay.

1962, Mar. 9 Photo. *Perf. 13½x14*
Dark Blue Background

850 5c rose, grn & yel .70 .30
851 6c grn & yel .70 .30
852 10c grn, car & brn .70 .30
853 20c lil, brn & grn .70 .30
a. A157 Block of 4, #850-853 3.00 2.50
b. As "a," imperf. 5.00 4.00

Apolinario Mabini — A158

Portraits: 1s, Manuel L. Quezon. 5s, Marcelo H. del Pilar. No. 857, José Rizal. No. 857A, Rizal (wearing shirt). 10s, Father José Burgos. 20s, Lapu-Lapu. 30s, Rajah Soliman. 50s, Cayetano Arellano. 70s, Sergio Osmena. No. 863, Emilio Jacinto. No. 864, José M. Panganiban.

Perf. 13½; 14 (1s); 13x12 (#857, 10s)
1962-69 Engr. Unwmk.

854 A158 1s org brn ('63) .30 .25
855 A158 3s rose red .30 .25
856 A158 5s car rose ('63) .30 .25
857 A158 6s dk red brn .30 .25
857A A158 6s pck bl ('64) .30 .25
858 A158 10s brt pur ('63) .35 .25
859 A158 20s Prus bl ('63) .45 .25
860 A158 30s vermilion 1.00 .30
861 A158 50s vio ('63) 1.50 .35
862 A158 70s brt bl ('63) 1.80 .40
863 A158 1p grn ('63) 4.00 .50
864 A158 1p dp org ('69) 3.00 .50
Nos. 854-864 (12) 13.60 3.80

Issued: Nos. 854, 856, 9/23/63; No. 855, 5/13/62; No. 857, 6/19/62; No. 857A, 6/19/64; No. 858, 3/24/63; No. 859, 10/20/63; No. 860, 11/30/62; No. 861, 5/1/63; No. 862, 12/10/63; No. 863, 1/23/63; No. 864, 2/1/69.

For surcharges & overprints see #873-874, 946, 969, 1054, 1119, 1209, O63-O69.

Pres. Macapagal Taking Oath of Office — A159

1962, June 12 Photo. *Perf. 13½*
Vignette Multicolored

865 A159 6s blue .35 .25
866 A159 10s green .35 .25
867 A159 30s violet .50 .30
Nos. 865-867 (3) 1.20 .80

Swearing in of President Diosdado Macapagal, Dec. 30, 1961.

Volcano in Lake Taal and Malaria Eradication Emblem — A160

1962, Oct. 24 Unwmk. *Perf. 11½*
Granite Paper

868 A160 6s multi .35 .25
869 A160 10s multi .35 .25
870 A160 70s multi 1.90 .75
Nos. 868-870 (3) 2.60 1.25

Issued on UN Day for the WHO drive to eradicate malaria.

No. 598 Surcharged in Red

1962, Nov. 15 Engr. *Perf. 12*

871 A117 20s on 25c yel grn .60 .25

Issued to commemorate the bicentennial of the Diego Silang revolt in Ilocos Province.

No. B6 Overprinted with Sideways Chevron Obliterating Surtax

1962, Dec. 23 *Perf. 12*

872 SP6 5c on 5c + 1c dp bl .60 .30

Nos. 855, 857 Surcharged with New Value and Old Value Obliterated

1963 *Perf. 13½*

873 A158 1s on 3s rose red .30 .25

Perf. 13x12

874 A158 5s on 6s dk red brn .30 .25
a. Inverted overprint 20.00
b. Double overprint 15.00

Issued: No. 873, 3/12/63; No. 874, 2/19/63.

No. 601 Surcharged

1963, June 12 *Perf. 12*

875 A117 6s on 2p vio .40 .30
876 A117 20s on 2p vio .60 .40
877 A117 70s on 2p vio 1.00 .60
Nos. 875-877 (3) 2.00 1.30

Diego Silang Bicentennial Art and Philatelic Exhibition, ARPHEX, Manila, May 28-June 30.

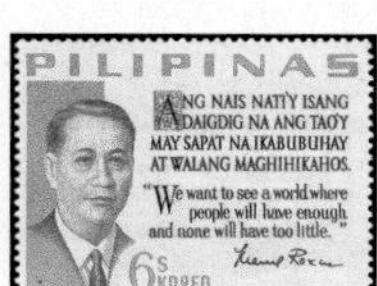

Pres. Manuel Roxas — A161

1963-73 Engr. *Perf. 13½*

878 A161 6s brt bl & blk, *bluish* .50 .25
879 A161 30s brn & blk, *brownish* 1.00 .30

Pres. Ramon Magsaysay

880 A161 6s lil & blk .50 .25
881 A161 30s yel grn & blk .100 .30

Pres. Elpidio Quirino

882 A161 6s grn & blk ('65) .50 .25
883 A161 30s rose lil & blk ('65) 1.00 .30

Gen. (Pres.) Emilio Aguinaldo

883A A161 6s dp cl & blk ('66) .50 .25
883B A161 30s bl & blk ('66) 1.00 .30

Pres. José P. Laurel

883C A161 6s red brn & blk ('66) .55 .25
883D A161 30s bl & blk ('66) 1.00 .30

Pres. Manuel L. Quezon

883E A161 10s bl gray & blk ('67) .55 .25
883F A161 30s vio & blk ('67) 1.00 .30

Pres. Sergio Osmeña

883G A161 10s rose lil & blk ('70) .55 .25
883H A161 40s grn & blk ('70) 1.00 .30

Pres. Carlos P. Garcia

883I A161 10s buff & blk ('73) .60 .25
883J A161 30s pink & blk ('73) 1.10 .30
Nos. 878-883J (16) 11.45 4.40

Nos. 878-883J honor former presidents.

Issued: Nos. 878-879, 7/4/63; Nos. 880-881, 12/30/63; Nos. 882-883, 2/28/65; Nos. 883A-883B, 2/6/66; Nos. 883C-883D, 11/6/66; Nos. 883E-883F, 11/16/67; Nos. 883G-883H, 6/12/70; Nos. 883I-883J, 2/22/73.

For surcharges see Nos. 984-985, 1120, 1146, 1160-1161.

Globe, Flags of Thailand, Korea, China, Philippines — A162

1963, Aug. 26 Photo. *Perf. 13½x13*

884 A162 6s dk grn & multi .35 .25
885 A162 20s dk grn & multi .55 .30

Asian-Oceanic Postal Union, 1st anniv.

For surcharge see No. 1078.

Red Cross Centenary Emblem — A163

1963, Sept. 1 *Perf. 11½*

886 A163 5s lt vio, gray & red .35 .25
887 A163 6s ultra, gray & red .35 .25
888 A163 20s grn, gray & red .50 .30
Nos. 886-888 (3) 1.20 .80

Centenary of the International Red Cross.

Bamboo Dance A164

Folk Dances: 6s, Dance with oil lamps. 10s, Duck dance. 20s, Princess Gandingan's rock dance.

1963, Sept. 15 Unwmk. *Perf. 14*

889 5s multi .50 .30
890 6s multi .50 .30
891 10s multi .50 .30
892 20s multi .50 .30
a. A164 Block of 4, #889-892 3.00 1.80

For surcharges and overprints see #1043-1046.

Pres. Macapagal and Filipino Family A165

1963, Sept. 28 *Perf. 14*

893 A165 5s bl & multi .35 .25
894 A165 6s yel & multi .35 .25
895 A165 20s lil & multi .55 .30
Nos. 893-895 (3) 1.25 .80

Issued to publicize Pres. Macapagal's 5-year Socioeconomic Program.

For surcharge see No. 1181.

Presidents Lopez Mateos and Macapagal A166

1963, Sept. 28 Photo. *Perf. 13½*

896 A166 6s multi .35 .25
897 A166 30s multi .60 .30

Visit of Pres. Adolfo Lopez Mateos of Mexico to the Philippines.

For surcharge see No. 1166.

Andres Bonifacio — A167

1963, Nov. 30 Unwmk. *Perf. 12*

898 A167 5s gold, brn, gray & red .35 .25
899 A167 6s sil, brn, gray & red .55 .25
900 A167 25s brnz, brn, gray & red .75 .35
Nos. 898-900 (3) 1.65 .85

Centenary of the birth of Andres Bonifacio, national hero and poet.

For surcharges see Nos. 1147, 1162.

No. 534 Overprinted: "UN ADOPTION/DECLARATION OF HUMAN RIGHTS/15TH ANNIVERSARY DEC. 10, 1963"

1963, Dec. 10 Engr. *Imperf.*
Souvenir Sheet

901 A94 Sheet of 3 4.00 3.00

15th anniv. of the Universal Declaration of Human Rights.

Woman holding Sheaf of Rice — A168

1963, Dec. 20 Photo. *Perf. 13½x13*

902 A168 6s brn & multi .40 .25
Nos. 902,C88-C89 (3) 1.90 .95

FAO "Freedom from Hunger" campaign.

Bamboo Organ — A169

1964, May 4 *Perf. 13½*

903 A169 5s multi .35 .25
904 A169 6s multi .35 .25
905 A169 20s multi .50 .30
Nos. 903-905 (3) 1.20 .80

The bamboo organ in the Church of Las Pinas, Rizal, was built by Father Diego Cera, 1816-1822.

For surcharge see No. 1055.

Apolinario Mabini — A170

Wmk. 233

1964, July 23 Photo. *Perf. 14½*

906 A170 6s pur & gold .40 .25
907 A170 10s red brn & gold .40 .25
908 A170 30s brt grn & gold .60 .30
Nos. 906-908 (3) 1.40 .80

Apolinario Mabini (1864-1903), national hero and a leader of the 1898 revolution.

For surcharge see No. 1056.

Flags Surrounding SEATO Emblem — A171

Unwmk.

1964, Sept. 8 Photo. *Perf. 13*

Flags and Emblem Multicolored

909 A171 6s dk bl & yel .35 .25
910 A171 10s dp grn & yel .45 .25
911 A171 25s dk brn & yel .60 .30
Nos. 909-911 (3) 1.40 .80

10th anniversary of the South-East Asia Treaty Organization (SEATO).
For surcharge see No. 1121.

Pres. Macapagal Signing Code — A172

1964, Dec. 21 Wmk. 233 *Perf. 14½*

912 A172 3s multi .40 .25
913 A172 6s multi .45 .25
Nos. 912-913,C90 (3) 1.55 .80

Signing of the Agricultural Land Reform Code. For surcharges see Nos. 970, 1234.

Basketball — A173

Sport: 10s, Women's relay race. 20s, Hurdling. 30s, Soccer.

1964, Dec. 28 *Perf. 14½x14*

915 A173 6s lt bl, dk brn & gold .35 .30
916 A173 10s gold, pink & dk brn .35 .30
b. Gold omitted
917 A173 20s gold, dk brn & yel .70 .35
918 A173 30s emer, dk brn & gold 1.00 .40
Nos. 915-918 (4) 2.40 1.35

18th Olympic Games, Tokyo, Oct. 10-25.
For overprints and surcharge see Nos. 962-965, 1079.

1965, Mar. 22 Imperf., Pairs

915a A173 6s 1.50 1.25
916a A173 10s 1.50 1.25
917a A173 20s 3.00 1.75
918a A173 30s 3.00 1.75
Nos. 915a-918a (4) 9.00 6.00

Presidents Lubke and Macapagal and Coats of Arms — A174

1965, Apr. 19 Unwmk. *Perf. 13½*

919 A174 6s ol grn & multi .35 .25
920 A174 10s multi .40 .25
921 A174 25s dp bl & multi .50 .30
Nos. 919-921 (3) 1.25 .80

Visit of Pres. Heinrich Lubke of Germany, Nov. 18-23, 1964.
For surcharge see No. 1167.

Emblems of Manila Observatory and Weather Bureau — A175

1965, May 22 Photo. *Perf. 13½*

922 A175 6s lt ultra & multi .35 .25
923 A175 20s lt vio & multi .40 .25
924 A175 50s bl grn & multi .65 .40
Nos. 922-924 (3) 1.40 .90

Issued to commemorate the centenary of the Meteorological Service in the Philippines.
For surcharge see No. 1069.

Pres. John F. Kennedy (1917-63) — A176

Perf. 14½x14

1965, May 29 Wmk. 233

Center Multicolored

925 A176 6s gray .35 .25
926 A176 10s brt vio .40 .25
927 A176 30s ultra .65 .30
Nos. 925-927 (3) 1.40 .80

Nos. 925-927 exist with ultramarine of tie omitted. No. 926 exist with red on face omitted. Value, $100. No. 927 exist with yellow on face omitted. Value, $100.
Nos. 925 and 927 exist imperf. Value, set $100.
For surcharges see Nos. 1148, 1210.

King and Queen of Thailand, Pres. and Mrs. Macapagal
A177

Perf. 12½x13

1965, June 12 Unwmk.

928 A177 2s brt bl & multi .50 .35
929 A177 6s bis & multi .60 .40
930 A177 30s red & multi 1.00 .50
Nos. 928-930 (3) 2.10 1.25

Visit of King Bhumibol Adulyadej and Queen Sirikit of Thailand, July 1963.
For surcharge see No. 1122.

Princess Beatrix and Evangelina Macapagal
A178

Perf. 13x12½

1965, July 4 Photo. Unwmk.

931 A178 2s bl & multi .35 .25
932 A178 6s blk & multi .40 .25
933 A178 10s multi .50 .25
Nos. 931-933 (3) 1.25 .75

Visit of Princess Beatrix of the Netherlands, Nov. 21-23, 1962.
For surcharge see No. 1188.

Map of Philippines, Cross and Legaspi-Urdaneta Monument — A179

Design: 3s, Cross and Rosary held before map of Philippines.

1965, Oct. 4 Unwmk. *Perf. 13*

934 A179 3s multi .35 .25
935 A179 6s multi .40 .25
Nos. 934-935,C91-C92 (4) 3.45 1.50

400th anniv. of the Christianization of the Philippines. See souvenir sheet No. C92a. For overprint see No. C108.

Presidents Sukarno and Macapagal and Prime Minister Tunku Abdul Rahman — A180

1965, Nov. 25 *Perf. 13*

936 A180 6s multi .35 .25
937 A180 10s multi .45 .25
938 A180 25s multi .70 .30
Nos. 936-938 (3) 1.50 .80

Signing of the Manila Accord (Mapilindo) by Malaya, Philippines and Indonesia.
For surcharge see No. 1182.

Bicyclists and Globe — A181

1965, Dec. 5 *Perf. 13½*

939 A181 6s multi .35 .25
940 A181 10s multi .45 .25
941 A181 25s multi .65 .30
Nos. 939-941 (3) 1.45 .80

Second Asian Cycling Championship, Philippines, Nov. 28-Dec. 5.

Nos. B21-B22 Surcharged

1965, Dec. 30 Engr. *Perf. 13*

942 SP12 10s on 6s + 4s .50 .35
943 SP12 30s on 30s + 5s .75 .45

Inauguration of President Ferdinand Marcos and Vice-President Fernando Lopez.

Antonio Regidor — A182

1966, Jan. 21 *Perf. 12x11*

944 A182 6s blue .40 .25
945 A182 30s brown .50 .25

Dr. Antonio Regidor, Sec. of the High Court of Manila and Pres. of Public Instruction.
For surcharges see Nos. 1110-1111.

No. 857A Overprinted in Red

1966, May 1 Engr. *Perf. 13½*

946 A158 6s peacock blue .35 .25

Anti-smuggling drive.
Exists with black overprint. Value, $35.
Exists with overprint inverted, double, double inverted and double with one inverted.
For surcharge see No. 1209.

Girl Scout Giving Scout Sign — A183

1966, May 26 Litho. *Perf. 13x12½*

947 A183 3s ultra & multi .35 .25
948 A183 6s emer & multi .35 .25
949 A183 20s brn & multi .50 .30
Nos. 947-949 (3) 1.20 .80

Philippine Girl Scouts, 25th anniversary.
For surcharge see No. 1019.

Pres. Marcos Taking Oath of Office
A184

1966, June 12 *Perf. 12½*

950 A184 6s bl & multi .35 .25
951 A184 20s emer & multi .50 .30
952 A184 30s yel & multi .60 .30
Nos. 950-952 (3) 1.45 .85

Inauguration of Pres. Ferdinand E. Marcos, 12/30/65.
For overprints & surcharge see #960-961, 1050.

Seal of Manila and Historical Scenes
A185

1966, June 24

953 A185 6s multi .40 .25
954 A185 30s multi .55 .30

Adoption of the new seal of Manila.
For surcharges see Nos. 1070, 1118, 1235.

Old and New Philippine National Bank Buildings
A186

Designs: 6s, Entrance to old bank building and 1p silver coin.

1966, July 22 Photo. *Perf. 14x13½*

955 A186 6s gold, ultra, sil & blk .35 .25
956 A186 10s multi .50 .25

50th anniv. of the Philippine Natl. Bank. See #C93. For surcharges see #1071, 1100, 1236.

Post Office, Annex Three — A187

1966, Oct. 1 Wmk. 233 *Perf. 14½*

957 A187 6s lt vio, yel & grn .35 .25
958 A187 10s rose cl, yel & grn .35 .25
959 A187 20s ultra, yel & grn .45 .30
Nos. 957-959 (3) 1.15 .80

60th anniversary of Postal Savings Bank.
For surcharges see Nos. 1104, 1112, 1189.

Nos. 950 and 952 Overprinted in Emerald or Black

Perf. 12½

1966, Oct. 24 Litho. Unwmk.

960 A184 6s multi (E) .40 .25
961 A184 30s multi .60 .30

Manila Summit Conference, Oct. 23-27.
No. 960 eixsts with overprint in black and double impression of blue on base stamp. Value, $35. No. 961 exists with overprint inverted. Value, $40. No. 961 exists imperf. with emerald overprint. Value, $60.

Nos. 915a-918a Overprinted

Wmk. 233

1967, Jan. 14 Photo. *Imperf.*

962 A173 6s lt bl, dk brn & gold .60 .40
963 A173 10s gold, dk brn & pink .60 .40
964 A173 20s gold, dk brn & yel .75 .50
965 A173 30s emer, dk brn & gold 1.00 .70
Nos. 962-965 (4) 2.95 2.00

Lions Intl., 50th anniv. The Lions emblem is in the lower left corner on the 6s, in the upper left corner on the 10s and in the upper right corner on the 30s.
No. 962 exist both perf and imperf with overprint (for No. 963) inverted. Values: $75 perf, $50 imperf.

"Succor" by Fernando Amorsolo
A188

Unwmk.

1967, Apr. 9 Litho. *Perf. 14*

966 A188 5s sepia & multi	.40	.25
967 A188 20s blue & multi	1.00	.25
968 A188 2p green & multi	2.10	.75
Nos. 966-968 (3)	3.50	1.25

25th anniversary of the Battle of Bataan.

Nos. 857A and 913 Surcharged

1967, Aug. Engr. *Perf. 13½*

969 A158 4s on 6s pck bl .40 .25

Wmk. 233

Photo. *Perf. 14½*

970 A172 5s on 6s multi .50 .25

Issue dates: 4s, Aug. 10; 5s, Aug. 7.

Gen. Douglas MacArthur and Paratroopers Landing on Corregidor A189

Unwmk.

1967, Aug. 31 Litho. *Perf. 14*

971 A189 6s multi	1.00	.30
972 A189 5p multi	9.00	3.00

25th anniversary, Battle of Corregidor.

Bureau of Posts, Manila, Jones Bridge over Pasig River A190

1967, Sept. 15 Litho. *Perf. 14x13½*

973 A190 4s multi & blk	.50	.25
974 A190 20s multi & red	.50	.25
975 A190 50s multi & vio	.70	.40
Nos. 973-975 (3)	1.70	.90

65th anniversary of the Bureau of Posts. For overprint see No. 1015.

Philippine Nativity Scene — A191

1967, Dec. 1 Photo. *Perf. 13½*

976 A191 10s multi	.60	.25
977 A191 40s multi	.85	.30

Christmas 1967.

Chinese Garden, Rizal Park, Presidents Marcos and Chiang Kai-shek A192

Presidents' heads & scenes in Chinese Garden, Rizal Park, Manila: 10s, Gate. 20s, Landing pier.

1967-68 Photo. *Perf. 13½*

978 A192 5s multi	.35	.25
979 A192 10s multi ('68)	.70	.25
980 A192 20s multi	1.20	.30
Nos. 978-980 (3)	2.25	.80

Sino-Philippine Friendship Year 1966-67. Issued: Nos. 978, 980, 12/30/67; No. 979, 3/12/68.

Makati Center Post Office, Mrs. Marcos and Rotary Emblem A193

1968, Jan. 9 Litho. *Perf. 14*

981 A193 10s bl & multi	.45	.25
982 A193 20s grn & multi	.55	.25
983 A193 40s multi	1.00	.40
Nos. 981-983 (3)	2.00	.90

1st anniv. of the Makati Center Post Office.

Nos. 882, 883C and B27 Surcharged

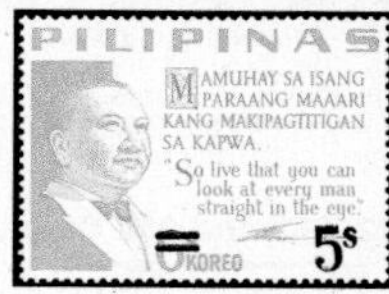

1968, Mar. 8

984 A161 5s on 6s grn & blk	.60	.25
a. Double overprint	15.00	
985 A161 5s on 6s lt red brn & blk	.60	.25
986 SP14 10s on 6s + 5s ultra & red	.80	.25
a. Double overprint	18.00	
Nos. 984-986 (3)	2.00	.75

The "1" in the surcharged value on No. 986 is serifed. For surcharge without serif on "1," see No. 1586.

Felipe G. Calderon, Barasoain Church and Malolos Constitution A194

1968, Apr. 4 Litho. *Perf. 14*

987 A194 10s lt ultra & multi	.45	.25
988 A194 40s grn & multi	.80	.30
989 A194 75s multi	1.50	.60
Nos. 987-989 (3)	2.75	1.15

Calderon (1868-1909), lawyer and author of the Malolos Constitution.

Earth and Transmission from Philippine Station to Satellite — A195

1968, Oct. 21 Photo. *Perf. 13½*

990 A195 10s blk & multi	.45	.25
991 A195 40s multi	.85	.30
992 A195 75s multi	2.00	.50
Nos. 990-992 (3)	3.30	1.05

Issued to commemorate the inauguration of the Philcomsat Station in Tany, Luzon, May 2, 1968.

Tobacco Industry and Tobacco Board's Emblem A196

1968, Nov. 15 Photo. *Perf. 13½*

993 A196 10s blk & multi	.35	.25
994 A196 40s bl & multi	.85	.50
995 A196 70s crim & multi	1.30	.90
Nos. 993-995 (3)	2.50	1.65

Philippine tobacco industry.

Kudyapi A197

Philippine Musical Instruments: 20s, Ludag (drum). 30s, Kulintangan. 50s, Subing (bamboo flute).

1968, Nov. 22 Photo. *Perf. 13½*

996 A197 10s multi	.50	.25
997 A197 20s multi	.60	.25
998 A197 30s multi	1.00	.30
999 A197 50s multi	1.40	.40
Nos. 996-999 (4)	3.50	1.20

Concordia College — A198

1968, Dec. 8 *Perf. 13x13½*

1000 A198 10s multi	.35	.25
1001 A198 20s multi	.50	.30
1002 A198 70s multi	.85	.35
Nos. 1000-1002 (3)	1.70	.90

Centenary of the Colegio de la Concordia, Manila, a Catholic women's school. Issued Dec. 8 (Sunday), but entered the mail Dec. 9.

Singing Children — A199

1968, Dec. 16 *Perf. 13½*

1003 A199 10s multi	.60	.25
1004 A199 40s multi	.70	.45
1005 A199 75s multi	1.50	.80
Nos. 1003-1005 (3)	2.80	1.50

Christmas 1968.

Animals — A200

1969, Jan. 8 Photo. *Perf. 13½*

1006 A200 2s Tarsier	.50	.25
1007 A200 10s Tamarau	.70	.25
1008 A200 20s Carabao	1.00	.30
1009 A200 75s Mouse deer	3.00	.90
Nos. 1006-1009 (4)	5.20	1.70

Opening of the hunting season.

Emilio Aguinaldo and Historical Building, Cavite A201

1969, Jan. 23 Litho. *Perf. 14*

1010 A201 10s yel & multi	.50	.25
1011 A201 40s bl & multi	1.00	.35
1012 A201 70s multi	1.50	.80
Nos. 1010-1012 (3)	3.00	1.40

Emilio Aguinaldo (1869-1964), commander of Filipino forces in rebellion against Spain.

Guard Turret, San Andres Bastion, Manila, and Rotary Emblem A202

1969, Jan. 29 Photo. *Perf. 12½*

1013 A202 10s ultra & multi	.50	.25
Nos. 1013,C96-C97 (3)	2.50	1.25

50th anniv. of the Manila Rotary Club.

Senator Claro M. Recto (1890-1960), Lawyer and Supreme Court Judge — A203

1969, Feb. 8 Engr. *Perf. 13*

1014 A203 10s bright rose lilac .50 .25

No. 973 Overprinted

1969, Feb. 14 Litho. *Perf. 14x13½*

1015 A190 4s multi & blk .60 .30

Philatelic Week, Nov. 24-30, 1968.

José Rizal College, Mandaluyong A204

1969, Feb. 19 Photo. *Perf. 13*

1016 A204 10s multicolored	.35	.25
1017 A204 40s multicolored	.55	.30
1018 A204 50s multicolored	1.00	.40
Nos. 1016-1018 (3)	1.90	.95

Founding of Rizal College, 50th anniv.

No. 948 Surcharged in Red

1969, May 10 Litho. *Perf. 13x12½*

1019 A183 5s on 6s multi .60 .25

A205

Map of Philippines, Red Crescent, Cross, Lion and Sun emblems.

1969, May 26 Photo. *Perf. 12½*

1020 A205 10s gray, ultra & red	.35	.25
1021 A205 40s lt ultra, dk bl & red	.55	.30
1022 A205 75s bister, brn & red	1.00	.45
Nos. 1020-1022 (3)	1.90	1.00

League of Red Cross Societies, 50th anniv.

A206

Pres. and Mrs. Marcos harvesting miracle rice.

1969, June 12 Photo. *Perf. 14*

1023 A206 10s multicolored	.50	.25
1024 A206 40s multicolored	.60	.30
1025 A206 75s multicolored	1.30	.45
Nos. 1023-1025 (3)	2.40	1.00

Introduction of IR8 (miracle) rice, produced by the International Rice Research Institute.

Holy Child of Leyte and Map of Leyte A207

1969, June 30 *Perf. 13½*

1026 A207 5s emerald & multi	.40	.25
1027 A207 10s crimson & multi	.50	.25

80th anniv. of the return of the image of the Holy Child of Leyte to Tacloban. See No. C98.

Philippine Development Bank — A208

1969, Sept. 12 Photo. *Perf. 13½*

1028 A208 10s dk bl, blk & grn .35 .25
1029 A208 40s rose car, blk & grn 1.00 .45
1030 A208 75s brown, blk & grn 1.65 .55
Nos. 1028-1030 (3) 3.00 1.25

Inauguration of the new building of the Philippine Development Bank in Makati, Rizal.

Common Birdwing — A209

Butterflies: 20s, Tailed jay. 30s, Red Helen. 40s, Birdwing.

1969, Sept. 15 Photo. *Perf. 13½*

1031 A209 10s multicolored .75 .25
1032 A209 20s multicolored 1.60 .30
1033 A209 30s multicolored 1.60 .40
1034 A209 40s multicolored 1.75 .50
Nos. 1031-1034 (4) 5.70 1.45

World's Children and UNICEF Emblem A210

1969, Oct. 6

1035 A210 10s blue & multi .35 .25
1036 A210 20s multicolored .40 .30
1037 A210 30s multicolored .50 .35
Nos. 1035-1037 (3) 1.25 .90

15th anniversary of Universal Children's Day.

Monument and Leyte Landing — A211

1969, Oct. 20 *Perf. 13½x14*

1038 A211 5s lt grn & multi .35 .25
1039 A211 10s yellow & multi .50 .25
1040 A211 40s pink & multi .75 .35
Nos. 1038-1040 (3) 1.60 .85

25th anniv. of the landing of the US forces under Gen. Douglas MacArthur on Leyte, Oct. 20, 1944.

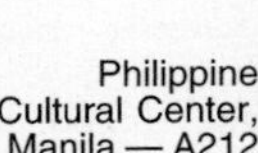

Philippine Cultural Center, Manila — A212

1969, Nov. 4 Photo. *Perf. 13½*

1041 A212 10s ultra .35 .25
1042 A212 30s brt rose lilac .65 .30

Cultural Center of the Philippines, containing theaters, a museum and libraries.

Nos. 889-892 Surcharged or Overprinted: "1969 PHILATELIC WEEK"

1969, Nov. 24 Photo. *Perf. 14*

1043 A164 5s multicolored .60 .30
1044 A164 5s on 6s multi .60 .30
1045 A164 10s multicolored .60 .30
1046 A164 10s on 20s multi .60 .30
a. Block of 4, #1043-1046 3.25 2.25

Philatelic Week, Nov. 23-29.

Melchora Aquino — A213

1969, Nov. 30 *Perf. 12½*

1047 A213 10s multicolored .35 .25
1048 A213 20s multicolored .35 .25
1049 A213 30s dk bl & multi .60 .30
Nos. 1047-1049 (3) 1.30 .80

Melchora Aquino (Tandang Sora; 1812-1919), the Grand Old Woman of the Revolution.

No. 950 Surcharged with New Value, 2 Bars and: "PASINAYA, IKA -2 PANUNUNGKULAN / PANGULONG FERDINAND E. MARCOS / DISYEMBRE 30, 1969"
Type I dash> Text has serifs. Type II dash> Text has no serifs.

1969, Dec. 30 Litho. *Perf. 12½*

1050 A184 5s on 6s multi .70 .25
a. Type II 1.50 .50
b. Double overprint 40.00
c. Double impression of blue 25.00

Inauguration of Pres. Marcos and Vice Pres. Fernando Lopez for 2nd term, 12/30.

Pouring Ladle and Iligan Steel Mills A214

1970, Jan. 20 Photo. *Perf. 13½*

1051 A214 10s ver & multi .50 .25
1052 A214 20s multicolored .80 .30
1053 A214 30s ultra & multi .80 .30
Nos. 1051-1053 (3) 2.10 .85

Iligan Integrated Steel Mills, Northern Mindanao, the first Philippine steel mills.

Nos. 857A, 904 and 906 Surcharged with New Value and Two Bars

1970, Apr. 30 As Before

1054 A158 4s on 6s peacock bl .60 .25
1055 A169 5s on 6s multi 1.00 .25
1056 A170 5s on 6s pur & gold 1.00 .25
a. Double overprint 25.00
Nos. 1054-1056 (3) 2.60 .75

New UPU Headquarters and Monument, Bern — A215

Perf. 13½

1970, May 20 Unwmk. Photo.

1057 A215 10s bl, dk bl & yel .35 .25
1058 A215 30s lt grn, dk bl & yel .60 .30

Opening of the new UPU Headquarters in Bern.

Emblem, Mayon Volcano and Filipina A216

1970, Sept. 6 Photo. *Perf. 13½x14*

1059 A216 10s brt blue & multi .35 .25
1060 A216 20s multicolored .40 .25
1061 A216 30s multicolored .60 .30
Nos. 1059-1061 (3) 1.35 .80

15th International Conference on Social Welfare, Manila, Sept. 6-12.

Crab, by Alexander Calder, and Map of Philippines A217

1970, Oct. 5 *Perf. 13x13½*

1062 A217 10s emerald & multi .35 .25
1063 A217 40s multicolored .50 .30
1064 A217 50s ultra & multi .80 .50
Nos. 1062-1064 (3) 1.65 1.05

Campaign against cancer.

Scaled Tridacna — A218

Sea Shells: 10s, Royal spiny oyster. 20s, Venus comb. 40s, Glory of the sea.

1970, Oct. 19 Photo. *Perf. 13½*

1065 A218 5s black & multi .70 .30
1066 A218 10s dk grn & multi 1.20 .30
1067 A218 20s multicolored 1.30 .40
1068 A218 40s dk blue & multi 2.30 .70
Nos. 1065-1068 (4) 5.50 1.70

Nos. 922, 953 and 955 Surcharged

Photogravure; Lithographed

1970, Oct. 26 *Perf. 13½, 12½*

1069 A175 4s on 6s multi 1.00 .25
1070 A185 4s on 6s multi 1.40 .25
1071 A186 4s on 6s multi 1.50 .25
Nos. 1069-1071 (3) 3.90 .75

On No. 1070, old denomination is obliterated by two bars.
One line surcharge on No. 1071.

Map of Philippines and FAPA Emblem — A219

1970, Nov. 16 Photo. *Perf. 13½*

1072 A219 10s dp org & multi .35 .25
1073 A219 50s lt violet & multi .90 .35

Opening of the 4th General Assembly of the Federation of Asian Pharmaceutical Assoc. (FAPA) & the 3rd Asian Cong. of Pharmaceutical Sciences.

Hundred Islands of Pangasinan, Peddler's Cart — A220

20s, Tree house in Pasonanca Park, Zamboanga City. 30s, Sugar industry, Negros Island, Mt. Kanlaon, Woman & Carabao statue, symbolizing agriculture. 2p, Miagao Church, Iloilo, & horse-drawn calesa.

1970, Nov. 12 *Perf. 12½x13½*

1074 A220 10s multicolored .35 .25
1075 A220 20s multicolored .65 .25
1076 A220 30s multicolored 1.20 .30
1077 A220 2p multicolored 3.50 1.00
Nos. 1074-1077 (4) 5.70 1.80

Tourist publicity. See Nos. 1086-1097.

No. 884 Surcharged: "UPU-AOPU / Regional Seminar / Nov. 23-Dec. 5, 1970 / TEN 10s"

1970, Nov. 22 Photo. *Perf. 13½x13*

1078 A162 10s on 6s multi .75 .50

Universal Postal Union and Asian-Oceanic Postal Union Regional Seminar, 11/23-12/5.

No. 915 Surcharged Vertically: "1970 PHILATELIC WEEK"

Perf. 14½x14

1970, Nov. 22 Wmk. 233

1079 A173 10s on 6s multi .60 .30

Philatelic Week, Nov. 22-28.

Exists imperf. Value, $60.

Pope Paul VI, Map of Far East and Australia A221

Perf. 13½x14

1970, Nov. 27 Photo. Unwmk.

1080 A221 10s ultra & multi .50 .25
1081 A221 30s multicolored .85 .30
Nos. 1080-1081,C99 (3) 2.75 .95

Visit of Pope Paul VI, Nov. 27-29, 1970.

Mariano Ponce — A222

1970, Dec. 30 Engr. *Perf. 14½*

1082 A222 10s rose carmine .45 .25

Mariano Ponce (1863-1918), editor and legislator. See #1136-1137. For surcharges & overprint see #1190, 1231, O70.

PATA Emblem A223

1971, Jan. 21 Photo. *Perf. 14½*

1083 A223 5s brt green & multi .40 .25
1084 A223 10s blue & multi .60 .25
1085 A223 70s brown & multi 1.20 .50
Nos. 1083-1085 (3) 2.20 1.00

Pacific Travel Association (PATA), 20th annual conference, Manila, Jan. 21-29.

Tourist Type of 1970

Designs: 10s, Filipina and Ang Nayong (7 village replicas around man-made lagoon). 20s, Woman and fisherman, Estancia. 30s, Pagsanjan Falls. 5p, Watch Tower, Punta Cruz, Boho.

Perf. 12½x13½

1971, Feb. 15 Photo.

1086 A220 10s multicolored .50 .25
1087 A220 20s multicolored .60 .30
1088 A220 30s multicolored 1.40 .40
1089 A220 5p multicolored 4.25 3.00
Nos. 1086-1089 (4) 6.75 3.95

1971, Apr. 19

Designs: 10s, Cultured pearl farm, Davao. 20s, Coral divers, Davao, Mindanao. 40s, Moslem Mosque, Zamboanga. 1p, Rice terraces, Banaue.

1090 A220 10s multicolored .50 .25
1091 A220 20s multicolored .60 .30
1092 A220 40s multicolored 1.40 .40
1093 A220 1p multicolored 3.00 1.00
Nos. 1090-1093 (4) 5.50 1.95

1971, May 3

10s, Spanish cannon, Zamboanga. 30s, Magellan's cross, Cebu City. 50s, Big Jar monument in Calamba, Laguna. 70s, Mayon Volcano, Legazpi city.

1094 A220 10s multicolored .50 .25
1095 A220 30s multicolored .60 .30
1096 A220 50s multicolored 1.50 .40
1097 A220 70s multicolored 1.70 .75
Nos. 1094-1097 (4) 4.30 1.70

Family and Emblem A224

1971, Mar. 21 Photo. *Perf. 13½*

1098 A224 20s lt grn & multi .35 .25
1099 A224 40s pink & multi .50 .30

Regional Conf. of the Intl. Planned Parenthood Federation for SE Asia & Oceania, Baguio City, Mar. 21-27.

No. 955 Surcharged

1971, June 10 Photo. *Perf. 14x13½*

1100 A186 5s on 6s multi .90 .25

Allegory of Law — A225

1971, June 15 Photo. *Perf. 13*

1101 A225 15s orange & multi .60 .30

60th anniversary of the University of the Philippines Law College. See No. C100.

Manila Anniversary Emblem — A226

1971, June 24

1102 A226 10s multicolored .50 .35

Founding of Manila, 400th anniv. See #C101.

Santo Tomas University, Arms of Schools of Medicine and Pharmacology A227

1971, July 8 Photo. *Perf. 13½*

1103 A227 5s yellow & multi .60 .35

Centenary of the founding of the Schools of Medicine and Surgery, and Pharmacology at the University of Santo Tomas, Manila. See No. C102.

No. 957 Surcharged

1971, July 11 Wmk. 233 *Perf. 14½*

1104 A187 5s on 6s multi .50 .25
a. Inverted overprint 12.00
b. Double overprint 20.00

World Congress of University Presidents, Manila.

Our Lady of Guia Appearing to Filipinos and Spanish Soldiers A228

1971, July 8 Photo. *Perf. 13½*

1105 A228 10s multi .35 .25
1106 A228 75s multi 1.45 .45

4th centenary of appearance of the statue of Our Lady of Guia, Ermita, Manila.

Bank Building, Plane, Car and Workers A229

1971, Sept. 14 *Perf. 12½*

1107 A229 10s blue & multi .35 .25
1108 A229 30s lt grn & multi .45 .25
1109 A229 1p multicolored 1.10 .45
Nos. 1107-1109 (3) 1.90 .95

1st Natl. City Bank in the Philippines, 70th anniv.

No. 944 Surcharged

Perf. 12x11

1971, Nov. 24 Engr. Unwmk.

1110 A182 4s on 6s blue .40 .25
1111 A182 5s on 6s blue .40 .25

No. 957 Surcharged

Wmk. 233

1971, Nov. 24 Photo. *Perf. 14½*

1112 A187 5s on 6s multi .65 .25

Philatelic Week, 1971.

Radar with Map of Far East and Oceania A230

1972, Feb. 29 Photo. *Perf. 14x14½*

1113 A230 5s org yel & multi .35 .25
1114 A230 40s red org & multi .65 .30

Electronics Conferences, Manila, 12/1-7/71.

Fathers Gomez, Burgos and Zamora — A231

1972, Apr. 3 *Perf. 13x12½*

1115 A231 5s gold & multi .50 .30
1116 A231 60s gold & multi 1.25 .50

Centenary of the deaths of Fathers Mariano Gomez, José Burgos and Jacinto Zamora, martyrs for Philippine independence from Spain.

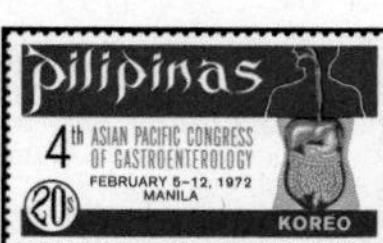

Digestive Tract — A232

1972, Apr. 11 Photo. *Perf. 12½x13*

1117 A232 20s ultra & multi .70 .25

4th Asian Pacific Congress of Gastroenterology, Manila, Feb. 5-12. See No. C103.

No. 953 Surcharged

1972, Apr. 20 *Perf. 12½*

1118 A185 5s on 6s multi 1.40 .25

No. O69 with Two Bars over "G." and "O."

1972, May 16 Engr. *Perf. 13½*

1119 A158 50s violet 1.40 .30

Nos. 883A, 909 and 929 Surcharged with New Value and 2 Bars

1972, May 29

1120 A161 10s on 6s dp cl & blk 1.40 .25
1121 A171 10s on 6s multi 1.40 .25
a. Inverted surcharge 20.00
1122 A177 10s on 6s multi 1.20 .25
Nos. 1120-1122 (3) 4.00 .75

During the production of No. 1121 some sheets of No. 911 were mixed with those of No. 909 and surcharged. Value for No. 911 surcharged 10s, $30 unused.

Independence Monument, Manila — A233

1972, May 31 Photo. *Perf. 13x12½*

1123 A233 5s brt blue & multi .35 .25
1124 A233 50s red & multi 1.00 .40
1125 A233 60s emerald & multi 1.40 .50
Nos. 1123-1125 (3) 2.75 1.15

Visit ASEAN countries (Association of South East Asian Nations).

"K," Skull and Crossbones A234

Development of Philippine Flag: No. 1126, 3 "K's" in a row ("K" stands for Katipunan). No. 1127, 3 "K's" as triangle. No. 1128, One "K." No. 1130, 3 "K's," sun over mountain on white triangle. No. 1131, Sun over 3 "K's." No. 1132, Tagalog "K" in sun. No. 1133, Sun with human face. No. 1134, Tricolor flag, forerunner of present flag. No. 1135, Present flag. Nos. 1126, 1128, 1130-1131, 1133, 1135 inscribed in Tagalog.

1972, June 12 Photo. *Perf. 13*

1126 A234 30s ultra & red 2.00 .45
1127 A234 30s ultra & red 2.00 .45
1128 A234 30s ultra & red 2.00 .45
1129 A234 30s ultra & blk 2.00 .45
1130 A234 30s ultra & red 2.00 .45
1131 A234 30s ultra & red 2.00 .45
1132 A234 30s ultra & red 2.00 .45
1133 A234 30s ultra & red 2.00 .45
1134 A234 30s ultra, red & blk 2.00 .45
1135 A234 30s ultra, yel & red 2.00 .45
a. Block of 10 25.00 10.00

Portrait Type of 1970

40s, Gen. Miguel Malvar. 1p, Julian Felipe.

1972 Engr. *Perf. 14*

1136 A222 40s rose red .60 .25
1137 A222 1p deep blue 1.40 .35

Honoring Gen. Miguel Malvar (1865-1911), revolutionary leader, and Julian Felipe (1861-1944), composer of Philippine national anthem.

Issue dates: 40s, July 10; 1p, June 26.

Parrotfish — A235

1972, Aug. 14 Photo. *Perf. 13*

1138 A235 5s shown .50 .25
1139 A235 10s Sunburst butterflyfish 1.25 .25
1140 A235 20s Moorish idol 1.60 .30
Nos. 1138-1140,C104 (4) 5.60 1.60

Tropical fish.

Development Bank of the Philippines — A236

1972, Sept. 12

1141 A236 10s gray blue & multi .30 .25
1142 A236 20s lilac & multi .40 .25
1143 A236 60s tan & multi .55 .35
Nos. 1141-1143 (3) 1.25 .85

Development Bank of the Philippines, 25th anniv.

Pope Paul VI — A237

1972, Sept. 26 Unwmk. *Perf. 14*

1144 A237 10s lt green & multi .60 .30
1145 A237 50s lt violet & multi 1.20 .40
Nos. 1144-1145,C105 (3) 3.20 1.20

First anniversary (in 1971) of the visit of Pope Paul VI to the Philippines, and for his 75th birthday.

Nos. 880, 899 and 925 Surcharged with New Value and 2 Bars

1972, Sept. 29 As Before

1146 A161 10s on 6s lil & blk 1.10 .25
a. Inverted overprint 20.00
1147 A167 10s on 6s multi 1.10 .25
a. Inverted overprint 20.00
1148 A176 10s on 6s multi .90 .25
a. Inverted overprint 15.00
Nos. 1146-1148 (3) 3.10 .75

Charon's Bark, by Resurrección Hidalgo — A238

Paintings: 10s, Rice Workers' Meal, by F. Amorsolo. 30s, "Spain and the Philippines," by Juan Luna, vert. 70s, Song of Maria Clara, by F. Amorsolo.

Perf. 14x13

1972, Oct. 16 Unwmk. Photo.

Size: 38x40mm

1149 A238 5s silver & multi .60 .25
1150 A238 10s silver & multi .60 .30

Size: 24x56mm

1151 A238 30s silver & multi 1.20 .45

Size: 38x40mm

1152 A238 70s silver & multi 1.60 .60
Nos. 1149-1152 (4) 4.00 1.60

25th anniversary of the organization of the Stamp and Philatelic Division.

Lamp, Nurse, Emblem A239

1972, Oct. 22 *Perf. 12½x13½*

1153 A239 5s violet & multi .35 .25
1154 A239 10s blue & multi .40 .25
1155 A239 70s orange & multi .75 .40
Nos. 1153-1155 (3) 1.50 .90

Philippine Nursing Association, 50th anniv.

Heart, Map of Philippines — A240

1972, Oct. 24 *Perf. 13*

1156 A240 5s pur, emer & red .35 .25
1157 A240 10s blue, emer & red .40 .25
1158 A240 30s emerald, bl & red .55 .35
Nos. 1156-1158 (3) 1.30 .85

"Your heart is your health," World Health Month.

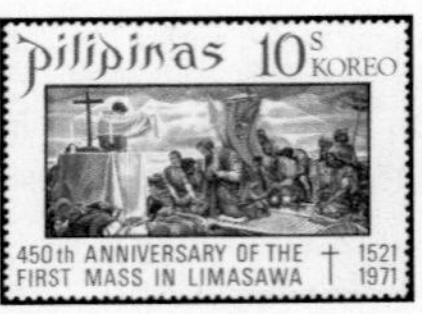

First Mass on Limasawa, by Carlos V. Francisco A241

1972, Oct. 31 *Perf. 14*

1159 A241 10s brown & multi .60 .30

450th anniversary of the first mass in the Philippines, celebrated by Father Valderama on Limasawa, Mar. 31, 1521. See No. C106.

Nos. 878, 882, 899 Surcharged: "ASIA PACIFIC SCOUT CONFERENCE NOV. 1972"

1972, Nov. 13 **As Before**

1160 A161 10s on 6s bl & blk .90 .30
1161 A161 10s on 6s grn & blk 1.25 .30
1162 A167 10s on 6s multi 1.25 .50
Nos. 1160-1162 (3) 3.40 1.10

Asia Pacific Scout Conference, Nov. 1972.

Torch, Olympic Emblems A242

Perf. 12½x13½

1972, Nov. 15 **Photo.**

1163 A242 5s blue & multi .40 .25
1164 A242 10s multicolored .60 .25
1165 A242 70s orange & multi 1.40 .50
Nos. 1163-1165 (3) 2.40 1.00

20th Olympic Games, Munich, 8/26-9/11.
For surcharges see Nos. 1297, 1758-1760.

Nos. 896 and 919 Surcharged with New Value, Two Bars and: "1972 PHILATELIC WEEK"

1972, Nov. 23 **Photo.** *Perf. 13½*

1166 A166 10s on 6s multi .75 .50
1167 A174 10s on 6s multi .75 .50

Philatelic Week 1972.

Manunggul Burial Jar, 890-710 B.C. — A243

#1169, Ngipet Duldug Cave ritual earthenware vessel, 155 B.C. #1170, Metal age chalice, 200-600 A.D. #1171, Earthenware vessel, 15th cent.

1972, Nov. 29

1168 A243 10s green & multi .60 .30
1169 A243 10s lilac & multi .60 .30
1170 A243 10s blue & multi .60 .30
1171 A243 10s yellow & multi .60 .30
Nos. 1168-1171 (4) 2.40 1.20

College of Pharmacy and Univ. of the Philippines Emblems A244

1972, Dec. 11 *Perf. 12½x13½*

1172 A244 5s lt vio & multi .40 .25
1173 A244 10s yel grn & multi .40 .25
1174 A244 30s ultra & multi .60 .35
Nos. 1172-1174 (3) 1.40 .85

60th anniversary of the College of Pharmacy of the University of the Philippines.

Christmas Lantern Makers, by Jorgé Pineda — A245

1972, Dec. 14 **Photo.** *Perf. 12½*

1175 A245 10s dk bl & multi .50 .25
1176 A245 30s brown & multi 1.00 .35
1177 A245 50s green & multi 1.75 .50
Nos. 1175-1177 (3) 3.25 1.10

Christmas 1972.

Red Cross Flags, Pres. Roxas and Mrs. Aurora Quezon — A246

1972, Dec. 21

1178 A246 5s ultra & multi .35 .25
1179 A246 20s multicolored .50 .25
1180 A246 30s brown & multi .60 .40
Nos. 1178-1180 (3) 1.45 .90

25th anniv. of the Philippine Red Cross.

Nos. 894 and 936 Surcharged with New Value and 2 Bars

1973, Jan. 22 **Photo.** *Perf. 14, 13*

1181 A165 10s on 6s multi .75 .25
a. Double overprint 20.00
1182 A180 10s on 6s multi .75 .25
a. Double overprint 20.00

San Luis University, Luzon A247

1973, Mar. 1 **Photo.** *Perf. 13½x14*

1183 A247 5s multicolored .40 .25
1184 A247 10s yellow & multi .45 .25
1185 A247 75s multicolored .75 .35
Nos. 1183-1185 (3) 1.60 .85

60th anniversary of San Luis University, Baguio City, Luzon.
For surcharge see No. 1305.

Jesus Villamor and Fighter Planes A248

1973, Apr. 9 **Photo.** *Perf. 13½x14*

1186 A248 10s multicolored .50 .25
1187 A248 2p multicolored 1.90 .80

Col. Jesus Villamor (1914-1971), World War II aviator who fought for liberation of the Philippines.
For surcharge see No. 1230.

Nos. 932, 957, O70 Surcharged with New Values and 2 Bars

1973, Apr. 23 **As Before**

1188 A178 5s on 6s multi 1.10 .80
1189 A187 5s on 6s multi 1.10 .25
a. Inverted overprint 20.00
1190 A222 15s on 10s rose car .80 .25
Nos. 1188-1190 (3) 3.00 1.30

Two additional bars through "G.O." on No. 1190.

ITI Emblem, Performance and Actor Vic Silayan A249

1973, May 15 **Photo.** *Perf. 13x12½*

1191 A249 5s blue & multi .35 .25
1192 A249 10s yel grn & multi .35 .25
1193 A249 50s orange & multi .70 .35
1194 A249 70s rose & multi 1.00 .45
Nos. 1191-1194 (4) 2.40 1.30

1st Third World Theater Festival, sponsored by the UNESCO affiliated International Theater Institute, Manila, Nov. 19-30, 1971.
For surcharge see No. 1229.

Josefa Llanes Escoda — A250

#1196, Gabriela Silang. No. 1197, Rafael Palma. 30s, Jose Rizal. 60s, Marcela Agoncillo. 90s, Teodoro R. Yangco. 1.10p, Dr. Pio Valenzuela. 1.20p, Gregoria de Jesus. #1204, Pedro A. Paterno. #1205, Teodora Alonso. 1.80p, Edilberto Evangelista. 5p, Fernando M. Guerrero.

1973-78 **Engr.** *Perf. 14½*

1195 A250 15s sepia .30 .25

Litho. *Perf. 12½*

1196 A250 15s violet ('74) .50 .25
b. Wmk. 372 5.00 1.50
1197 A273 15s emerald ('74) .40 .25
b. Wmk. 372 5.00 1.50
1198 A250 30s vio bl ('78) .40 .25
1199 A250 60s dl red brn 1.00 .40
1200 A273 90s brt bl ('74) 1.20 .40
1202 A273 1.10p brt bl ('74) 1.50 .45
b. Wmk. 372 5.00 3.00
1203 A250 1.20p dl red ('78) 1.20 .45
1204 A250 1.50p lil rose 2.50 1.50
1205 A273 1.50p brown ('74) 2.00 .40
b. Wmk. 372 8.50 2.50
1206 A250 1.80p green 3.50 2.00
1208 A250 5p blue 7.00 4.00
Nos. 1195-1208 (12) 21.50 10.60

1973-74 *Imperf.*

1196a A250 15s violet ('74) 1.25 *1.00*
1197a A273 15s emerald ('74) 1.25 *1.00*
1199a A250 60s dull red brown 3.50 2.00
1200a A273 90s bright blue ('74) 3.00 2.00
1202a A273 1.10p bright blue ('74) 4.00 3.00
1204a A250 1.50p lilac rose 5.00 3.50
1205a A273 1.50p brown ('74) 4.00 3.50
1206a A250 1.80p green 6.00 4.00
1208a A250 5p blue 13.00 6.00
Nos. 1196a-1208a (9) 41.00 26.00

Honoring: Escoda (1898-194?), leader of Girl Scouts and Federation of Women's Clubs. Silang (1731-63), "the Ilocana Joan of Arc". Palma (1874-1939), journalist, statesman, educator. Rizal (1861-96), natl. hero. Agoncillo (1859-1946), designer of 1st Philippine flag, 1898. Yangco (1861-1939), patriot and philanthropist. Valenzuela (1869-1956), physician and newspaperman.
Gregoria de Jesus, independence leader. Paterno (1857-1911), lawyer, writer, patriot. Alonso (1827-1911), mother of Rizal. Evangelista (1862-97), army engineer, patriot. Guerrero (1873-1929), journalist, political leader.
For overprint & surcharges see #1277, 1310, 1311, 1470, 1518, 1562..

No. 946 surcharged with New Value

1973, June 4 **Engr.** *Perf. 13½*

1209 A158 5s on 6s pck blue .75 .25

Anti-smuggling campaign.

No. 925 Surcharged

1973, June 4 **Wmk. 233**

1210 A176 5s on 6s multi .75 .25
a. Inverted overprint 20.00
b. Double overprint 20.00

10th anniv. of death of John F. Kennedy.

Pres. Marcos, Farm Family, Unfurling of Philippine Flag — A251

Perf. 12½x13½

1973, Sept. 24 **Photo.** **Unwmk.**

1211 A251 15s ultra & multi .50 .30
1212 A251 45s red & multi .80 .40
1213 A251 90s multi 1.50 .50
Nos. 1211-1213 (3) 2.80 1.20

75th anniversary of Philippine independence and 1st anniversary of proclamation of martial law.
First day covers exist dated Sept. 21, 1973.

Imelda Romualdez Marcos, First Lady of the Philippines — A252

1973, Oct. 31 **Photo.** *Perf. 13*

1214 A252 15s dl bl & multi .45 .30
1215 A252 50s multicolored .80 .50
1216 A252 60s lil & multi 1.00 .50
Nos. 1214-1216 (3) 2.25 1.30

Presidential Palace, Manila, Pres. and Mrs. Marcos A253

1973, Nov. 15 **Litho.** *Perf. 14*

1217 A253 15s rose & multi .45 .30
1218 A253 50s ultra & multi .90 .50
Nos. 1217-1218,C107 (3) 2.75 1.20

INTERPOL Emblem — A254

1973, Dec. 18 **Photo.** *Perf. 13*

1219 A254 15s ultra & multi .45 .25
1220 A254 65s lt grn & multi .75 .35

Intl. Criminal Police Organization, 50th anniv.

Cub and Boy Scouts — A255

15s, Various Scout activities; inscribed in Tagalog.

1973, Dec. 28 **Litho.** *Perf. 12½*

1221 A255 15s bister & emer .80 .40
a. Imperf, pair ('74) 4.00 3.00
1222 A255 65s bister & brt bl 1.50 .60
a. Imperf, pair ('74) 6.00 5.00

50th anniv. of Philippine Boy Scouts.
Nos. 1221a-1222a issued Feb. 4, although first day covers are dated Dec. 28, 1973.

Manila, Bank Emblem and Farmers A256

Designs: 60s, Old bank building. 1.50p, Modern bank building.

1974, Jan. 3 Photo. *Perf. 12½x13½*
1223 A256 15s silver & multi .35 .25
1224 A256 60s silver & multi .60 .30
1225 A256 1.50p silver & multi 1.50 .50
Nos. 1223-1225 (3) 2.45 1.05

Central Bank of the Philippines, 25th anniv.

UPU Emblem, Maria Clara Costume — A257

Filipino Costumes: 60s, Balintawak and UPU emblem. 80s, Malong costume and UPU emblem.

1974, Jan. 15 *Perf. 12½*
1226 A257 15s multicolored .35 .25
1227 A257 60s multicolored .85 .40
1228 A257 80s multicolored 1.20 .50
Nos. 1226-1228 (3) 2.40 1.15

Centenary of Universal Postal Union.

No. 1192 Surcharged in Red with New Value, 2 Bars and: "1973 / PHILATELIC WEEK"

1974, Feb. 4 Photo. *Perf. 13x12½*
1229 A249 15s on 10s multi 1.00 .30

Philatelic Week, 1973. First day covers exist dated Nov. 26, 1973.

Nos. 1186 and 1136 Overprinted and Surcharged

1974, Mar. 25 Photo. *Perf. 13½x14*
1230 A248 15s on 10s multi .90 .30

Engr. *Perf. 14*
1231 A222 45s on 40s rose red .90 .30

Lions Intl. of the Philippines, 25th anniv. The overprint on #1230 arranged to fit shape of stamp.

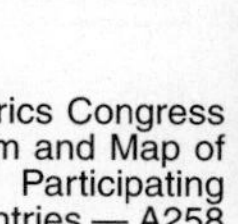

Pediatrics Congress Emblem and Map of Participating Countries — A258

1974, Apr. 30 Litho. *Perf. 12½*
1232 A258 30s brt bl & red .60 .25
a. Imperf, pair 3.00 2.50
1233 A258 1p dl grn & red 1.40 .50
a. Imperf, pair 5.50 4.50

Asian Congress of Pediatrics, Manila, Apr. 30-May 4.

Nos. 912, 954-955 Surcharged with New Value and Two Bars

1974, Aug. 1 As Before
1234 A172 5s on 3s multi .90 .30
1235 A185 5s on 6s multi 1.20 .30
1236 A186 5s on 6s multi 1.40 .30
Nos. 1234-1236 (3) 3.50 .90

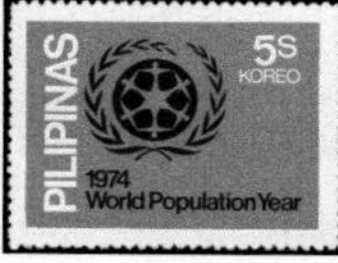
WPY Emblem — A259

1974, Aug. 15 Litho. *Perf. 12½*
1237 A259 5s org & bl blk .50 .25
a. Imperf, pair 2.00 1.50
1238 A259 2p lt grn & dk bl 2.50 .90
a. Imperf, pair 11.00 8.50
b. Wmk. 372 11.00 3.50

World Population Year, 1974.

Red Feather Community Chest Emblem — A260

Wmk. 372
1974, Sept. 5 Litho. *Perf. 12½*
1239 A260 15s brt bl & red .40 .25
1240 A260 40s emer & red .75 .35
1241 A260 45s red brn & red .80 .35
Nos. 1239-1241 (3) 1.95 .95

Philippine Community Chest, 25th anniv.

Imperf. Pairs
1239a A260 15s 4.00 3.50
1240a A260 40s 3.00 2.00
1241a A260 45s 3.00 2.00
Nos. 1239a-1241a (3) 10.00 7.50

Sultan Kudarat, Flag, Order and Map of Philippines A261

Perf. 13½x14
1975, Jan. 13 Photo. Unwmk.
1242 A261 15s multicolored .50 .25

Sultan Mohammad Dipatuan Kudarat, 16th-17th century ruler.

Mental Health Association Emblem — A262

Wmk. 372
1975, Jan. 20 Litho. *Perf. 12½*
1243 A262 45s emer & org .50 .30
a. Imperf, pair 2.50 2.00
1244 A262 1p emer & pur 1.00 .40
a. Imperf, pair 4.50 3.50

Philippine Mental Health Assoc., 25th anniv.

4-Leaf Clover — A263

1975, Feb. 14
1245 A263 15s vio bl & red .50 .25
a. Imperf, pair 3.00 2.00
1246 A263 50s emer & red 1.00 .40
a. Imperf, pair 5.50 4.50

Philippine Heart Center for Asia, inauguration.

Military Academy, Cadet and Emblem A264

Perf. 13½x14
1975, Feb. 17 Unwmk.
1247 A264 15s grn & multi .40 .30
1248 A264 45s plum & multi .80 .30

Philippine Military Academy, 70th anniv.

Helping the Disabled A265

Perf. 12½, Imperf.
1975, Mar. 17 Wmk. 372
1249 A265 Block of 10 8.50 *8.50*
a.-j. 45s grn, any single .60 .40

25th anniversary (in 1974) of Philippine Orthopedic Association.
For surcharge see No. 1635.
No. 1249 exists imperf. Value unused or used, $12.

Nos. B43, B50-B51 Surcharged with New Value and Two Bars

1975, Apr. 15 Unwmk.
1250 SP18 5s on 15s + 5s .60 *.25*
1251 SP16 60s on 70s + 5s 1.20 *.35*
1252 SP18 1p on 1.10p + 5s 1.50 *.60*
a. Double overprint 18.00
Nos. 1250-1252 (3) 3.30 1.20

"Grow and Conserve Forests" A266

1975, May 19 Litho. *Perf. 14½*
1253 45s "Grow" .45 .25
1254 45s "Conserve" .45 .25
a. A267 Pair, #1253-1254 1.00 .75

Forest conservation.

Jade Vine — A268

1975, June 9 Photo. *Perf. 14½*
1255 A268 15s multicolored .40 .25

Imelda R. Marcos, IWY Emblem — A269

Wmk. 372
1975, July 2 Litho. *Perf. 12½*
1256 A269 15s bl & blk .60 .25
a. Imperf, pair 3.00 2.50
1257 A269 80s pink, bl & grn .80 .35
a. Imperf, pair 7.00 5.00

International Women's Year 1975.
For surcharges see Nos. 1500, 1505.

Civil Service Emblem — A270

1975, Sept. 19 Litho. *Perf. 12½*
1258 A270 15s multicolored .55 .25
a. Imperf, pair 3.00 2.25
1259 A270 50s multicolored .75 .30
a. Imperf, pair 4.50 3.75

Dam and Emblem — A271

1975, Sept. 30
1260 A271 40s org & vio bl .70 .25
a. Imperf, pair 2.50 *2.00*
1261 A271 1.50p brt rose & vio bl 1.40 .40
a. Imperf, pair 6.00 5.00

For surcharges see Nos. 1517, 1520.

Manila Harbor, 1875 — A272

1975, Nov. 4 Unwmk. *Perf. 13x13½*
1262 A272 1.50p red & multi 1.80 .60

Hong Kong and Shanghai Banking Corporation, centenary of Philippines service.

Norberto Romualdez (1875-1941), Scholar and Legislator A273

Jose Rizal Monument, Luneta Park — A273a

Noted Filipinos: No. 1264, Rafael Palma (1874-1939), journalist, statesman, educator. No. 1265, Rajah Kalantiaw, chief of Panay, author of ethical-penal code (1443). 65s, Emilio Jacinto (1875-1899), patriot. No. 1269, Gen. Gregorio del Pilar (1875-1899), military hero. No. 1270, Lope K. Santos (1879-1963), grammarian, writer. 1.60p, Felipe Agoncillo (1859-1941), lawyer, cabinet member.

Wmk. 372
1975-81 Litho. *Perf. 12½*
1264 A273 30s brn ('77) .50 .25
1265 A273 30s dp rose ('78) .50 .25
1266 A273a 40s yel & blk ('81) .70 .30
1267 A273 60s violet 1.75 .35
a. Imperf, pair 6.00 4.00
1268 A273 65s lilac rose 1.50 .50
a. Imperf, pair 5.00 4.00
1269 A273 90s lilac rose 2.50 .75
a. Imperf, pair 6.00 4.50
1270 A273 90s grn ('78) *1.50* .40
1272 A273 1.60p blk ('76) 3.25 .60
Nos. 1264-1272 (8) 12.20 3.40

See #1195-1208. For overprint & surcharges see #1278, 1310, 1367, 1440, 1469, 1514, 1562, 1574, 1758-1760.

A274

1975, Nov. 22 Litho. *Perf. 12½*
1275 A274 60s multicolored .95 .50
1276 A274 1.50p multicolored 2.40 .60

1st landing of the Pan American World Airways China Clipper in the Philippines, 40th anniv.

Nos. 1199 and 1205 Overprinted

1975, Nov. 22 Unwmk.
1277 A250 60s dl red brn .70 .30
1278 A273 1.50p brown 1.80 .50

Airmail Exhibition, Nov. 22-Dec. 9.

APO Emblem — A275

1975, Nov. 24 Wmk. 372
1279 A275 5s ultra & multi .35 .25
a. Imperf, pair 2.00 1.50
1280 A275 1p bl & multi 1.00 .40
a. Imperf, pair 6.00 5.00

Amateur Philatelists' Org., 25th anniv.

For surcharge see No. 1338.

A276

Philippine Churches: 20s, San Agustin Church. 30s, Morong Church, horiz. 45s, Basilica of Taal, horiz. 60s, San Sebastian Church.

1975, Dec. 23 Litho. *Perf. 12½*

1281 A276 20s bluish grn .60 .25
1282 A276 30s yel org & blk .60 .25
a. Horiz. pair, imperf. vert. 35.00
1283 A276 45s rose, brn & blk .90 .35
1284 A276 60s yel, bis & blk 1.50 .45
Nos. 1281-1284 (4) 3.60 1.30

Holy Year 1975.

Imperf. Pairs

1281a A276 20s 2.50 2.00
1282a A276 30s 2.50 2.00
1283a A276 45s 4.00 3.50
1284a A276 60s 7.00 5.00
Nos. 1281a-1284a (4) 16.00 12.50

Conductor's Hands — A277

1976, Jan. 27

1285 A277 5s org & multi .45 .25
1286 A277 50s brt yel grn & multi .95 .35

Manila Symphony Orchestra, 50th anniv.

PAL Planes of 1946 and 1976 — A278

1976, Feb. 14

1287 A278 60s bl & multi 1.00 .50
1288 A278 1.50p red & multi 2.70 .70

Philippine Airlines, 30th anniversary.

National University — A279

1976, Mar. 30

1289 A279 45s bl, vio bl & yel .60 .25
1290 A279 60s lt bl, vio bl & pink 1.00 .30

National University, 75th anniversary.

Eye Exam — A280

1976, Apr. 7 Litho. *Perf. 12½*

1291 A280 15s multicolored .90 .40

World Health Day: "Foresight prevents blindness."

Book and Emblem — A281

1976, May 24 Unwmk.

1292 A281 1.50p grn & multi 1.75 .50

National Archives, 75th anniversary.

Santo Tomas University, Emblems A282

1976, June 7 Wmk. 372

1293 A282 15s yel & multi .45 .25
1294 A282 50s multicolored 1.00 .35

Colleges of Education and Science, Santo Tomas University, 50th anniversary.

Maryknoll College A283

Wmk. 372

1976, July 26 Litho. *Perf. 12½*

1295 A283 15s lt bl & multi .60 .25
1296 A283 1.50p bis & multi 1.40 .55

Maryknoll College, Quezon City, 50th anniv.

No. 1164 Surcharged in Dark Violet

Perf. 12½x13½

1976, July 30 Photo.

1297 A242 15s on 10s multi 1.00 *.50*

21st Olympic Games, Montreal, Canada, July 17-Aug. 1.

Police College, Manila A284

1976, Aug. 8 Litho. *Perf. 12½*

1298 A284 15s multicolored .50 .25
a. Imperf, pair 2.00 1.50
1299 A284 60s multicolored 1.00 .35
a. Imperf, pair 6.00 5.00

Philippine Constabulary, 75th anniversary. Imperfs. issued on Oct. 14 1976.

Surveyors A285

1976, Sept. 2 Wmk. 372

1300 A285 80s multicolored 2.00 .50

Bureau of Lands, 75th anniversary. No. 1300 exists imperf. Value for pair, $40.

Monetary Fund and World Bank Emblems — A286

1976, Oct. 4 Litho. *Perf. 12½*

1301 A286 60s multicolored .60 .40
a. Imperf. pair 50.00
1302 A286 1.50p multicolored 1.40 .60

Joint Annual Meeting of the Board of Governors of the International Monetary Fund and the World Bank, Manila, Oct. 4-8.

For surcharge see No. 1575.

Virgin of Antipollo — A287

1976, Nov. 26 *Perf. 12½*

1303 A287 30s multicolored .60 .40
1304 A287 90s multicolored 1.40 .60

Virgin of Antipolo, Our Lady of Peace and Good Voyage, 350th anniv. of arrival of statue in the Philippines and 50th anniv. of the canonical coronation.

No. 1184 Surcharged with New Value and 2 Bars and Overprinted: "1976 PHILATELIC WEEK"

Perf. 13½x14

1976, Nov. 26 Photo. Unwmk.

1305 A247 30s on 10s multi .80 .25

Philatelic Week 1976.

People Going to Church — A288

Wmk. 372

1976, Dec. 1 Litho. *Perf. 12½*

1306 A288 15s bl & multi .75 .40
1307 A288 30s bl & multi 1.50 .60

Christmas 1976.

Symbolic Diamond and Book — A289

1976, Dec. 13

1308 A289 30s grn & multi .50 .25
1309 A289 75s grn & multi .90 .40

Philippine Educational System, 75th anniv. Nos. 1308-1309 exist imperf. Value for pair, $40.

No. 1202 and 1208 Surcharged with New Value and 2 Bars

1977, Jan. 17 Unwmk.

1310 A273 1.20p on 1.10p brt bl 1.40 .50
1311 A250 3p on 5p bl 3.60 .80

Galicano Apacible — A290

Design: 30s, José Rizal.

1977 Litho. Wmk. 372 *Perf. 12½*

1313 A290 30s multicolored .40 .30
a. Horiz. pair, imperf. between 50.00
b. Horiz. pair, imperf. vertically 30.00
1318 A290 2.30p multicolored 2.00 .50

Dr. José Rizal (1861-1896) physician, poet and national hero (30s). Dr. Galicano Apacible (1864-1949), physician, statesman (2.30p).

Issue dates: 30s, Feb. 16; 2.30p, Jan. 24.

Emblem, Flags, Map of AOPU — A291

1977, Apr. 1 Wmk. 372

1322 A291 50s multicolored .60 .40
1323 A291 1.50p multicolored 1.80 .60

Asian-Oceanic Postal Union (AOPU), 15th anniv.

Cogwheels and Worker — A292

1977, Apr. 21 *Perf. 12½*

1324 A292 90s blk & multi .85 .30
1325 A292 2.30p blk & multi 2.00 .70

Asian Development Bank, 10th anniversary.

Farmer at Work and Receiving Money — A293

1977, May 14 Litho. Wmk. 372

1326 A293 30s org red & multi .60 .30

National Commission on Countryside Credit and Collection, campaign to strengthen the rural credit system.

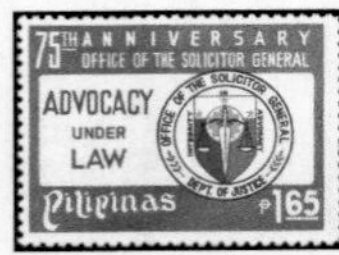

Solicitor General's Emblem — A294

1977, June 30 Litho. *Perf. 12½*

1327 A294 1.65p multicolored 1.75 .45

Office of the Solicitor General, 75th anniv.

For surcharges see Nos. 1483, 1519.

Conference Emblem — A295

1977, July 29 Litho. *Perf. 12½*

1328 A295 2.20p bl & multi 2.00 .50

8th World Conference of the World Peace through Law Center, Manila, Aug. 21-26.

For surcharge see No. 1576.

ASEAN Emblem — A296

1977, Aug. 8

1329 A296 1.50p grn & multi 2.25 .60
a. Horiz. pair, imperf. vertically 125.00

Association of South East Asian Nations (ASEAN), 10th anniversary.

For surcharge see No. 1559.

Cable-laying Ship, Map Showing Cable Route A297

1977, Aug. 26 **Litho.** ***Perf. 12½***
1330 A297 1.30p multicolored 1.50 .40

Inauguration of underwater telephone cable linking Okinawa, Luzon and Hong Kong.

President Marcos A298

1977, Sept. 11 **Wmk. 372**
1331 A298 30s multicolored .80 .50
1332 A298 2.30p multicolored 2.25 .70

Ferdinand E. Marcos, president of the Philippines, 60th birthday.

People Raising Flag — A299

1977, Sept. 21 **Litho.** ***Perf. 12½***
1333 A299 30s multicolored .60 .40
1334 A299 2.30p multicolored 1.90 .50

5th anniversary of "New Society."

Bishop Gregorio Aglipay — A300

1977, Oct. 1 **Litho.** ***Perf. 12½***
1335 A300 30s multicolored .50 .25
1336 A300 90s multicolored 1.70 .35

Philippine Independent Aglipayan Church, 75th anniversary.

Fokker F VIIa over World Map — A301

1977, Oct. 28 **Wmk. 372**
1337 A301 2.30p multicolored 2.50 .60

First scheduled Pan American airmail service, Havana to Key West, 50th anniversary.

No. 1280 Surcharged with New Value, 2 Bars and Overprinted in Red: "1977 / PHILATELIC / WEEK"

1977, Nov. 22 **Litho.** ***Perf. 12½***
1338 A275 90s on 1p multi 1.20 *.50*

Philatelic Week.

Children Celebrating and Star from Lantern — A302

1977, Dec. 1 **Unwmk.**
1339 A302 30s multicolored .70 .30
1340 A302 45s multicolored .80 .40

Christmas 1977.

Scouts and Map showing Jamboree Locations A303

1977, Dec. 27
1341 A303 30s multicolored .60 .30

National Boy Scout Jamboree, Tumauini, Isabela; Capitol Hills, Cebu City; Mariano Marcos, Davao, Dec. 27, 1977-Jan. 5, 1978.

Far Eastern University Arms — A304

1978, Jan. 26 **Litho.** **Wmk. 372**
1342 A304 30s gold & multi .60 .30

Far Eastern University, 50th anniversary.

Sipa — A305

Various positions of Sipa ball-game.

1978, Feb. 28 ***Perf. 12½***
1343 A305 5s bl & multi .40 .25
1344 A305 10s bl & multi .40 .25
1345 A305 40s bl & multi .50 .30
1346 A305 75s bl & multi 1.10 .40
a. Block, #1343-1346 2.75 1.75

No. 1346a has continuous design.

Arms of Meycauayan — A306

1978, Apr. 21 **Litho.** ***Perf. 12½***
1347 A306 1.05p multicolored 1.20 .30

Meycauayan, founded 1578-1579.
For surcharge see No. 1560.

Moro Vinta and UPU Emblem A307

2.50p, No. 1350b, Horse-drawn mail cart. No. 1350a, like 5p. No. 1350c, Steam locomotive. No. 1350d, Three-master.

1978, June 9 **Litho.** ***Perf. 13½***
1348 A307 2.50p multi 3.00 1.50
1349 A307 5p multi 4.00 2.00
a. Pair, #1348-1349 8.00 6.00

Souvenir Sheet

Perf. 12½x13

1350 Sheet of 4 22.50 18.00
a.-d. A307 7.50p, any single 4.50 4.00
e. Sheet, imperf 22.50 18.00

CAPEX International Philatelic Exhibition, Toronto, Ont., June 9-18. No. 1350 contains 36½x25mm stamps.
No. 1350 exists imperf. in changed colors.

Andres Bonifacio Monument, by Guillermo Tolentino A308

Wmk. 372

1978, July 10 **Litho.** ***Perf. 12½***
1351 A308 30s multicolored .60 .30
a. Imperf. pair 25.00

Rook, Knight and Globe — A309

1978, July 17
1352 A309 30s vio bl & red .70 .30
1353 A309 2p vio bl & red 2.50 .50

World Chess Championship, Anatoly Karpov and Viktor Korchnoi, Baguio City, 1978.

Miners — A310

1978, Aug. 12 **Litho.** ***Perf. 12½***
1354 A310 2.30p multicolored 2.00 .50

Benguet gold mining industry, 75th anniv.

Manuel Quezon and Quezon Memorial — A311

1978, Aug. 19
1355 A311 30s multicolored .50 .30
1356 A311 1p multicolored 1.80 .50

Manuel Quezon (1878-1944), first president of Commonwealth of the Philippines.

Law Association Emblem, Philippine Flag — A312

1978, Aug. 27 **Litho.** ***Perf. 12½***
1357 A312 2.30p multicolored 2.00 .50

58th Intl. Law Conf., Manila, 8/27-9/2.

Pres. Sergio Osmeña (1878-1961) — A313

1978, Sept. 8
1358 A313 30s multicolored .50 .30
1359 A313 1p multicolored 1.80 .50

For surcharge see No. 1501.

Map Showing Cable Route, Cablelaying Ship — A314

1978, Sept. 30
1360 A314 1.40p multicolored 1.80 .50

ASEAN Submarine Cable Network, Philippines-Singapore cable system, inauguration.

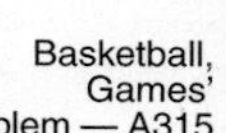

Basketball, Games' Emblem — A315

1978, Oct. 1
1361 A315 30s multicolored .60 *.30*
1362 A315 2.30p multicolored 2.40 .70

8th Men's World Basketball Championship, Manila, Oct. 1-15.

San Lazaro Hospital and Dr. Catalino Gavino — A316

1978, Oct. 13 **Litho.** ***Perf. 12½***
1363 A316 50s multicolored .75 .30
a. Vert. pair, imperf. horiz. 200.00
1364 A316 90s multicolored 1.50 .50

San Lazaro Hospital, 400th anniversary.
For surcharge see No. 1512.

Nurse Vaccinating Child — A317

1978, Oct. 24
1365 A317 30s multicolored .60 .30
1366 A317 1.50p multicolored 2.40 .80

Eradication of smallpox.

No. 1268 Surcharged

1978, Nov. 23
1367 A273 60s on 65s lil rose 1.00 .30

Philatelic Week.

"The Telephone Across Country and World" — A318

Wmk. 372

1978, Nov. 28 **Litho.** ***Perf. 12½***
1368 30s multicolored .60 .35
1369 2p multicolored 2.00 .55
a. A318 Pair, #1368-1369 3.00 1.80

Philippine Long Distance Telephone Company, 50th anniversary.

Traveling Family — A320

1978, Nov. 28

1370	A320	30s multicolored	.50	.25
1371	A320	1.35p multicolored	1.50	.75

Decade of Philippine children.
For surcharges see Nos. 1504, 1561.

Church and Arms of Agoo — A321

1978, Dec. 7 Litho. *Perf. 12½*

1372	A321	30s multicolored	.55	.25
1373	A321	45s multicolored	.60	.30

400th anniversary of the founding of Agoo.

Church and Arms of Balayan — A322

1978, Dec. 8

1374	A322	30s multicolored	.55	.30
1375	A322	90s multicolored	.95	.50

400th anniv. of the founding of Balayan.

Dr. Honoria Acosta Sison (1888-1970), 1st Philippine Woman Physician — A323

1978, Dec. 15

1376	A323	30s multicolored	.60	.30

Family, Houses, UN Emblem — A324

1978, Dec. 10 Litho. *Perf. 12½*

1377	A324	30s multicolored	.60	.30
1378	A324	3p multicolored	2.40	1.00

30th anniversary of Universal Declaration of Human Rights.

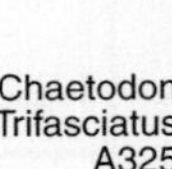

Chaetodon Trifasciatus A325

Fish: 1.20p, Balistoides niger. 2.20p, Rhinecanthus aculeatus. 2.30p, Chelmon rostratus. No. 1383, Chaetodon mertensi. No. 1384, Euxiphipops xanthometapon.

1978, Dec. 29 *Perf. 14*

1379	A325	30s multi	.50	.30
1380	A325	1.20p multi	1.30	.40
1381	A325	2.20p multi	2.00	.60
1382	A325	2.30p multi	2.00	.60
1383	A325	5p multi	4.00	1.40
1384	A325	5p multi	4.00	1.40
		Nos. 1379-1384 (6)	13.80	4.70

A total of 500,000 sets of Nos. 1379-1384 were CTO Dec. 29, 1978. Value for CTO set, $2.50.

Carlos P. Romulo, UN Emblem — A326

1979, Jan. 14 Litho. *Perf. 12½*

1385	A326	30s multi	.60	.30
1386	A326	2p multi	2.10	.80

Carlos P. Romulo (1899-1985), pres. of UN General Assembly and Security Council.

Rotary Emblem and "60" — A327

1979, Jan. 26 Wmk. 372

1387	A327	30s multi	.60	.30
1388	A327	2.30p multi	2.20	.80

Rotary Club of Manila, 60th anniversary.

Rosa Sevilla de Alvero — A328

1979, Mar. 4 Litho. *Perf. 12½*

1389	A328	30 rose	.45	.30

Rosa Sevilla de Alvero, educator and writer, birth centenary.
For surcharges see Nos. 1479-1482.

Oil Well and Map of Palawan — A329

Wmk. 372

1979, Mar. 21 Litho. *Perf. 12½*

1390	A329	30s multi	.60	.30
1391	A329	45s multi	.75	.30

First Philippine oil production, Nido Oil Reef Complex, Palawan.

Merrill's Fruit Doves — A330

Birds: 1.20p, Brown tit babbler. 2.20p, Mindoro imperial pigeons. 2.30p, Steere's pittas. No. 1396, Koch's and red-breasted pittas. No. 1397, Philippine eared nightjar.

Perf. 14x13½

1979, Apr. 16 Unwmk.

1392	A330	30s multi	*.60*	.30
1393	A330	1.20p multi	*1.40*	.50
1394	A330	2.20p multi	*3.00*	.75
1395	A330	2.30p multi	*3.00*	.75
1396	A330	5p multi	*11.00*	4.50
1397	A330	5p multi	*11.00*	2.50
		Nos. 1392-1397 (6)	*30.00*	9.30

A total of 500,000 sets of Nos. 1392-1397 were CTO April 16, 1979. Value for CTO set, $4.

Association Emblem and Reader — A331

Wmk. 372

1979, Apr. 30 Litho. *Perf. 12½*

1398	A331	30s multi	.45	.30
1399	A331	75s multi	1.00	.40
1400	A331	1p multi	1.40	.50
		Nos. 1398-1400 (3)	2.85	1.20

Association of Special Libraries of the Philippines, 25th anniversary.

UNCTAD Emblem — A332

Wmk. 372

1979, May 3 Litho. *Perf. 12½*

1401	A332	1.20p multi	1.20	.40
1402	A332	2.30p multi	2.30	.60

5th Session of UN Conference on Trade and Development, Manila, May 3-June 1.

Civet Cat — A333

Philippine Animals: 1.20p, Macaque. 2.20p, Wild boar. 2.30p, Dwarf leopard. No. 1407, Asiatic dwarf otter. No. 1408, Anteater.

1979, May 14 *Perf. 14*

1403	A333	30s multi	.50	.30
1404	A333	1.20p multi	1.30	.40
1405	A333	2.20p multi	2.00	.60
1406	A333	2.30p multi	2.00	.60
1407	A333	5p multi	4.00	1.50
1408	A333	5p multi	4.00	1.50
		Nos. 1403-1408 (6)	13.80	4.90

A total of 500,000 sets of Nos. 1403-1408 were CTO May 20, 1979. Value for CTO set, $2.50.

Dish Antenna — A334

1979, May 17 *Perf. 12½*

1409	A334	90s shown	1.75	.40
1410	A334	1.30p World map	1.25	.60

11th World Telecommunications Day, 5/17.

Mussaenda Donna Evangelina A335

Philippine Mussaendas: 1.20p, Dona Esperanza. 2.20p, Dona Hilaria. 2.30p, Dona Aurora. No. 1415, Gining Imelda. No. 1416, Dona Trining.

1979, June 11 Litho. *Perf. 14*

1411	A335	30s multi	.50	.30
1412	A335	1.20p multi	1.30	.40
1413	A335	2.20p multi	2.00	.60
1414	A335	2.30p multi	2.25	.60
1415	A335	5p multi	4.00	1.75
1416	A335	5p multi	4.00	1.75
		Nos. 1411-1416 (6)	14.05	5.40

A total of 500,000 sets of Nos. 1411-1416 were CTO June 15, 1979. Value for CTO set, $2.50.

Manila Cathedral, Coat of Arms — A336

1979, June 25 *Perf. 12½*

1417	A336	30s multi	.50	.30
1418	A336	75s multi	1.00	.40
1419	A336	90s multi	1.25	.50
		Nos. 1417-1419 (3)	2.75	1.20

Archdiocese of Manila, 400th anniversary.

Patrol Boat, Naval Arms — A337

1979, June 23

1420	A337	30s multi	.70	.30
1421	A337	45s multi	1.00	.40

Philippine Navy Day.

Man Breaking Chains, Broken Syringe — A338

1979, July 23 Litho. *Perf. 12½*

1422	A338	30s multi	.35	.25
1423	A338	90s multi	.95	.35
1424	A338	1.05p multi	1.40	.50
		Nos. 1422-1424 (3)	2.70	1.10

Fight drug abuse.
For surcharge see Nos. 1480, 1513.

Afghan Hound — A339

Designs: 90s, Striped tabbies. 1.20p, Dobermann pinscher. 2.20p, Siamese cats. 2.30p, German shepherd. 5p, Chinchilla cats.

1979, July 6 *Perf. 14*

1425	A339	30s multi	.50	.30
1426	A339	90s multi	1.20	.40
1427	A339	1.20p multi	1.30	.50
1428	A339	2.20p multi	2.00	.60
1429	A339	2.30p multi	2.00	.60
1430	A339	5p multi	4.50	1.50
		Nos. 1425-1430 (6)	11.50	3.90

A total of 500,000 sets of Nos. 1425-1430 were CTO July 30, 1979. Value for CTO set, $2.50.

Children Playing IYC Emblem — A340

Children playing and IYC emblem, diff.

1979, Aug. 31 Litho. *Perf. 12½*

1431	A340	15s multi	.45	.30
1432	A340	20s multi	.55	.30
1433	A340	25s multi	.55	.40
1434	A340	1.20p multi	1.25	.60
		Nos. 1431-1434 (4)	2.80	1.60

International Year of the Child.

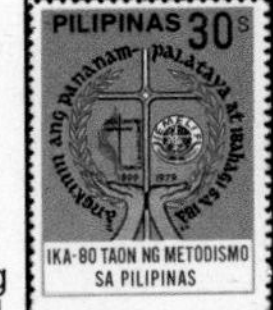

Hands Holding Emblem — A341

1979, Sept. 27 Litho. *Perf. 12½*

1435	A341	30s multi	.40	.25
1436	A341	1.35p multi	1.20	.50

Methodism in the Philippines, 80th anniv.

Emblem and Coins — A342

Wmk. 372

1979, Nov. 15 Litho. *Perf. 12½*

1437	A342	30s multi	.70	.50

Philippine Numismatic and Antiquarian Society, 50th anniversary.

Concorde over Manila and Paris — A343

Design: 2.20p, Concorde over Manila.

1979, Nov. 22

1438	A343	1.05p multi	2.00	.60
1439	A343	2.20p multi	4.00	1.00

Air France service to Manila, 25th anniversary.

No. 1272 Surcharged in Red

1979, Nov. 23

1440	A273	90s on 1.60 blk	1.20	.25

Philatelic Week. Surcharge similar to No. 1367.

Transport Association Emblem — A344

1979, Nov. 27

1441	A344	75s multi	1.00	.40
1442	A344	2.30p multi	2.50	1.00

International Air Transport Association, 35th annual general meeting, Manila.

Local Government Year — A345

1979, Dec. 14 Litho. *Perf. 12½*

1443	A345	30s multi	.30	.25
a.		A318 Horiz. pair, imperf. vert.	25.00	
1444	A345	45s multi	.45	.25

For surcharge, see No. 1481.

Mother and Children, Ornament — A346

1979, Dec. 17

1445	A346	30s shown	.75	.30
1446	A346	90s Stars	1.75	.40

Christmas. For surcharges see Nos. 1482, 1515.

Rheumatic Pain Spots and Congress Emblem — A347

Wmk. 372

1980, Jan. 20 Litho. *Perf. 12½*

1447	A347	30s multi	1.25	.75
1448	A347	90s multi	3.00	2.00

Southeast Asia and Pacific Area League Against Rheumatism, 4th Congress, Manila, Jan. 19-24.

Gen. Douglas MacArthur — A348

30s, MacArthur's birthplace (Little Rock, AR) & burial place (Norfolk, VA). 2.30p, MacArthur's cap, Sunglasses & pipe. 5p, MacArthur & troops wading ashore at Leyte, Oct. 20, 1944.

1980, Jan. 26 Wmk. 372 *Perf. 12½*

1449	A348	30s multi	.50	.30
1450	A348	75s multi	1.00	.50
1451	A348	2.30p multi	3.50	1.20
		Nos. 1449-1451 (3)	5.00	2.00

Souvenir Sheet

Imperf

1452	A348	5p multi	5.50	3.50

Gen. Douglas MacArthur (1880-1964).
No. 1449 exists imperf. Value for pair, $40.
For overprint see No. 2198.

Knights of Columbus of Philippines, 75th Anniversary — A349

1980, Feb. 14

1453	A349	30s multi	.45	.25
1454	A349	1.35p multi	1.25	.50

Philippine Military Academy, 75th Anniversary A350

Wmk. 372

1980, Feb. 17 Litho. *Perf. 12½*

1455	A350	30s multi	1.50	.60
1456	A350	1.20p multi	3.00	1.40

No. 1455-1456 exist imperf. Value for pair, $40.

Philippines Women's University, 75th Anniversary — A351

1980, Feb. 21

1457	A351	30s multi	.35	.25
1458	A351	1.05p multi	1.25	.40

A352

Disaster Relief — A352a

Rotary International, 75th Anniversary (Paintings by Carlos Botong Francisco): Nos. 1459 and 1460 each in continuous design.

1980, Feb. 23 *Perf. 12½*

1459	A352	Strip of 5	6.00	*6.00*
a.-e.		30s any single	.90	.60
1460	A352a	Strip of 5	16.00	12.00
a.-e.		2.30p any single	2.25	1.80

A353

Wmk. 372

1980, Mar. 28 Litho. *Perf. 12½*

1461	A353	30s multi	1.25	.50
1462	A353	1.30p multi	2.25	.30

6th centenary of Islam in Philippines.

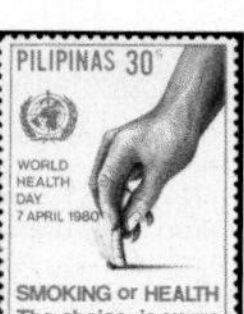

A354

Hand crushing cigarette, WHO emblem.

1980, Apr. 7

1463	A354	30s multi	1.00	*1.00*
1464	A354	75s multi	3.50	2.50

World Health Day (Apr. 7); anti-smoking campaign.

Philippine Girl Scouts, 40th Anniversary A355

Wmk. 372

1980, May 26 Litho. *Perf. 12½*

1465	A355	30s multi	.60	.30
1466	A355	2p multi	2.00	.70

Jeepney (Public Jeep) — A356

1980, June 24 Litho. *Perf. 12½*

1467	A356	30s Jeepney, diff.	.80	.30
1468	A356	1.20p shown	2.00	.55

For surcharge see No. 1503.

Nos. 1272, 1206 Surcharged in Red

Wmk. 372 (1.35p)

1980, Aug. 1 Litho. *Perf. 12½*

1469	A273	1.35p on 1.60p blk	1.80	.40
1470	A250	1.50p on 1.80p grn	2.20	.60
a.		Inverted overprint	25.00	
b.		Imperf. pair, overprint inverted	25.00	

Independence, 82nd Anniversary.

Association Emblem — A357

1980, Aug. 1 Wmk. 372

1471	A357	30s multi	.45	.30
1472	A357	2.30p multi	2.25	.60

International Association of Universities, 7th General Conference, Manila, Aug. 25-30.

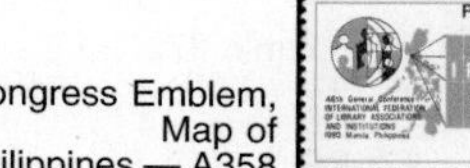

Congress Emblem, Map of Philippines — A358

Wmk. 372

1980, Aug. 18 Litho. *Perf. 12½*

1473	A358	30s lt grn & blk	.40	.35
1474	A358	75s lt bl & blk	.60	.45
1475	A358	2.30p sal & blk	2.25	.60
		Nos. 1473-1475 (3)	3.25	1.40

Intl. Federation of Library Associations and Institutions, 46th Congress, Manila, 8/18-23.

Kabataang Barangay (New Society), 5th Anniversary — A359

1980, Sept. 19 Litho. *Perf. 12½*

1476	A359	30s multi	.35	.25
1477	A359	40s multi	.50	.25
1478	A359	1p multi	1.20	.45
		Nos. 1476-1478 (3)	2.05	.95

Nos. 1389, 1422, 1443, 1445, 1327 Surcharged in Blue, Black or Red

1980 Litho. Wmk. 372 *Perf. 12½*

1479	A328	40s on 30s rose (Bl)	1.00	.40
1480	A338	40s on 30s multi	1.00	.25
1481	A345	40s on 30s multi	1.00	.30
1482	A346	40s on 30s multi (R)	2.00	.30
1483	A294	2p on 1.65p multi (R)	4.00	.70
		Nos. 1479-1483 (5)	9.00	1.95

Issue dates for Nos. 1479-1483: Nos. 1479, 1481, Sept. 26, 1980. No. 1480, Oct. 13, 1980; Nos. 1482, 1483, Oct. 14,1980.

Nos. 1479-1483 exist with overprints inverted. Value, from $35 each.

Catamaran, Conference Emblem — A360

1980, Sept. 27

1484	A360	30s multi	.50	.30
1485	A360	2.30p multi	2.25	.70

World Tourism Conf., Manila, Sept. 27.

Stamp Day — A361

1980, Oct. 9

1486	A361	40s multi	.60	.25
1487	A361	1p multi	.40	.50
1488	A361	2p multi	3.00	1.25
		Nos. 1486-1488 (3)	4.00	2.00

UN, 35th Anniv. — A362

Designs: 40s, UN Headquarters and Emblem, Flag of Philippines. 3.20p, UN and Philippine flags, UN headquarters.

1980, Oct. 20

1489	A362	40s multi	.50	.25
1490	A362	3.20p multi	3.50	.95

Murex Alabaster — A363

Designs: 60s, Bursa bubo. 1.20p, Homalocantha zamboi. 2p, Xenophora pallidula.

1980, Nov. 2

1491	A363	40s shown	1.20	.35
1492	A363	60s multi	.90	.35
1493	A363	1.20p multi	1.20	.65
1494	A363	2p multi	2.40	1.00
		Nos. 1491-1494 (4)	5.70	2.35

INTERPOL Emblem on Globe — A364

1980, Nov. 5 Litho. Wmk. 372

1495	A364	40s multi	.40	.25
1496	A364	1p multi	1.00	.40
1497	A364	3.20p multi	2.40	.75
		Nos. 1495-1497 (3)	3.80	1.40

49th General Assembly Session of INTERPOL (Intl. Police Organization), Manila, Nov. 13-21.

Central Philippine University, 75th Anniversary — A365

1980, Nov. 17 Unwmk.

1498	A365	40s multi	.85	.25
1499	A365	3.20p multi	3.00	1.00

No. 1257 Surcharged

Wmk. 372

1980, Nov. 21 Litho. *Perf. 12½*

1500	A269	1.20p on 80s multi	2.00	.45

Philatelic Week. Surcharge similar to No. 1367.

No. 1358 Surcharged

1980, Nov. 30
1501 A313 40s on 30s multi 1.70 .50

APO Philatelic Society, 30th anniversary.

Christmas Tree, Present and Candy Cane — A366

Perf. 12½
1980, Dec. 15 Litho. Unwmk.
1502 A366 40s multi .75 .35

Christmas 1980.

No. 1467 Surcharged

1981, Jan. 2
1503 A356 40c on 30s multi 1.25 .60

Nos. 1370, 1257 Surcharged in Red or Black

1981
1504 A320 10s on 30s (R) multi 1.00 .50
1505 A269 85s on 80s multi 3.00 1.50

Issue dates: 10s, Jan. 12; 85s, Jan. 2.

Heinrich Von Stephan, UPU Emblem — A367

1981, Jan. 30
1506 A367 3.20p multi 3.50 1.00

Heinrich von Stephan (1831-1897), founder of UPU, birth sesquicentennial.

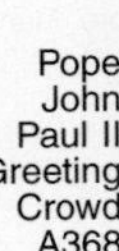

Pope John Paul II Greeting Crowd A368

Designs: 90s, Pope, signature, vert. 1.20p, Pope, cardinals, vert. 3p, Pope giving blessing, Vatican arms, Manila Cathedral. 7.50p, Pope, light on map of Philippines, vert.

Perf. 13½x14
1981, Feb. 17 Unwmk.
1507 A368 90s multi 1.00 .40
1508 A368 1.20p multi 1.50 .60
1509 A368 2.30p multi 2.50 1.20
1510 A368 3p multi 3.00 1.75
Nos. 1507-1510 (4) 8.00 3.95

Souvenir Sheet
Perf. 13¾x13¼
1511 A368 7.50p multi 8.00 *5.00*

Visit of Pope John Paul, Feb. 17-22.
Nos. 1507-1511 with year date "1980". were created but not issued. Value, $15 each, souvenir sheet $50,
For surcharge, see No. 3046.

Nos. 1364, 1423, 1268, 1446, 1261, 1206, 1327 Surcharged

1981 Litho. *Perf. 12½*
1512 A316 40s on 90s multi 1.50 .25
1513 A338 40s on 90s multi 1.50 .25
1514 A273 40s on 65s lil rose 1.40 .25
1515 A346 40s on 90s multi 2.00 .75
1517 A271 1p on 1.50p brt rose & vio bl 2.00 .60
1518 A250 1.20p on 1.80p grn 2.50 .70
1519 A294 1.20p on 1.65p multi 3.25 1.00
1520 A271 2p on 1.50p brt rose & vio bl 4.25 1.50
Nos. 1512-1520 (8) 18.40 5.30

A369

1981, Apr. 20 Wmk. 372
1521 A369 2p multi 2.00 .60
1522 A369 3.20p multi 3.00 .80

68th Spring Meeting of the Inter-Parliamentary Union, Manila, Apr. 20-25.

Unless otherwise stated, Nos. 1523-1580 are on granite paper.

A370

Wmk. 372
1981, May 22 Litho. *Perf. 12½*
1523 40s Bubble coral 1.00 .50
1524 40s Branching coral 1.00 .50
1525 40s Brain coral 1.00 .50
1526 40s Table coral 1.00 .50
a. A370 Block of 4, #1523-1526 6.00 3.50

Philippine Motor Assoc., 50th Anniv. — A371

Vintage cars.

1981, May 25
1527 40s Presidents car 1.00 .40
1528 40s 1930 1.00 .40
1529 40s 1937 1.00 .40
1530 40s shown 1.00 .40
a. A371 Block of 4, #1527-1530 6.00 3.00

Re-inauguration of Pres. Ferdinand E. Marcos — A372

Granite Paper
1531 A372 40s multi .80 .40
a. Wmk. 372 (II) ('83) 2.50 1.20

Souvenir Sheet
Imperf
1532 A372 5p multi 6.00 *5.00*
a. Wmk. 372 (II) ('84) 20.00 20.00
b. On glossy, fiberless paper 50.00 50.00

No. 1531 exists imperf. Value $1.50.
For overprint see No. 1753.
Nos. 1531-1532 exist with a surface varnish applied for use in presentation folders. Values, 7-8 times values for regular stamps.

St. Ignatius Loyola, Founder of Jesuit Order — A373

400th Anniv. of Jesuits in Philippines: No. 1534, Jose Rizal, Ateneo University. No. 1535, Father Federico Faura, Manila Observatory. No. 1536, Father Saturnino Urios, map of Philippines.

1981, July 31
1533 A373 40s multi .70 .30
1534 A373 40s multi .70 .30
1535 A373 40s multi .70 .30
1536 A373 40s multi .70 .30
a. Block of 4, #1533-1536 3.50 3.00

Souvenir Sheet
Imperf
1537 A373 2p multi 4.00 *3.50*

#1537 contains vignettes of #1533-1536.
For surcharge see No. 1737.

A374

Design: 40s, Isabelo de los Reyes (1867-1938), labor union founder. 1p, Gen. Gregorio del Pilar (1875-1899). No. 1540, Magsaysay. No. 1541, Francisco Dagohoy. No. 1543, Ambrosia R. Bautista, signer of Declaration of Independence, 1898, No. 1544, Juan Sumulong (1875-1942), statesman. 2.30p, Nicanor Abelardo (1893-1934), composer. 3.20p, Gen. Vicente Lim (1888-1945), first Philippine graduate of West Point.

Wmk. 372
1981-82 Litho. *Perf. 12½*
1538 A374 40s grnsh bl ('82) .50 .25
1539 A374 1p blk & red brn 1.40 .25
1540 A374 1.20p blk & lt red brn 1.60 .40
1541 A374 1.20p brown ('82) 2.00 .50
1543 A374 2p blk & red brn 2.00 .50
1544 A374 2p rose lil ('82) 2.25 .50
a. Wmk. 372 (II) 4.50 .70
1545 A374 2.30p lt red brn ('82) 2.50 .60
1546 A374 3.20p gray bl ('82) 3.00 .70
a. Wmk. 372 (II) 5.50 .90
Nos. 1538-1546 (8) 15.25 3.70

See Nos. 1672-1680, 1682-1683, 1685. For surcharges see Nos. 1668-1669.

A375

1981, Sept. 2 Granite Paper
1551 A375 40s multi .60 .30

Chief Justice Fred Ruiz Castro, 67th birth anniv.
No. 1551 exists on dull ordinary paper. Value, $10 unused, $5 used.

Intl. Year of the Disabled — A376

Wmk. 372
1981, Oct. 24 Litho. *Perf. 12½*
1552 A376 40s multi .60 .30
1553 A376 3.20p multi 3.40 .80

A376a

1981, Nov. 7 Granite Paper
1554 A376a 40s multi .50 .30
1555 A376a 2p multi 2.00 .70
1556 A376a 3.20p multi 3.00 .80
Nos. 1554-1556 (3) 5.50 1.80

24th Intl. Red Cross Conf., Manila, 11/7-14.
No. 1556 exists on glossy ordinary paper, issued Feb. 17, 1983. Value, $10 mint, $5 used.

Intramuros Gate, Manila — A377

1981, Nov. 13
1557 A377 40s black .70 .25

No. 1557 exists on dull ordinary paper, issued April 2, 1982. Value, $2 mint, 50¢ used.

Manila Park Zoo Concert Series, Nov. 20-30 — A378

1981, Nov. 20
1558 A378 40s multi .75 .30

No. 1558 exists on dull ordinary paper, issued April 26, 1982. Value, $10 mint, $6 used.

No. 1329 Overprinted "1981 Philatelic Week" and Surcharged
Wmk. 372
1981, Nov. 23 Litho. *Perf. 12½*
1559 A296 1.20p on 1.50p multi 3.00 1.00

Nos. 1205, 1347, 1371 Surcharged
1981, Nov. 25 Litho. *Perf. 12½*
1560 A306 40s on 1.05p multi 1.25 .50
1561 A320 40s on 1.35p multi 1.25 .50
1562 A273 1.20p on 1.50p brn 3.50 1.00
Nos. 1560-1562 (3) 6.00 2.00

11th Southeast Asian Games, Manila, Dec. 6-15 — A379

40s, Running. 1p, Bicycling. 2p, Pres. Marcos, Intl. Olympic Pres. Samaranch. 2.30p, Soccer. 2.80p, Shooting. 3.20p, Bowling.

1981, Dec. 3
1563 A379 40s multi .70 .30
1564 A379 1p multi 1.30 .40
1565 A379 2p multi 2.50 .50
1566 A379 2.30p multi 3.00 .60
1567 A379 2.80p multi 4.00 1.00
1568 A379 3.20p multi 4.50 1.20
Nos. 1563-1568 (6) 16.00 4.00

Manila Intl. Film Festival, Jan. 18-29 — A380

40s, Film Center. 2p, Golden trophy, vert. 3.20p, Trophy, diff., vert.

Wmk. 372
1982, Jan. 18 Litho. *Perf. 12½*
1569 A380 40s multicolored .60 .30
1570 A380 2p multicolored 2.50 .60
1571 A380 3.20p multicolored 3.50 1.10

No. 1570-1571 exist on dull ordinary paper. Value, $10 each mint, $5 each used.

Dull paper examples issued Aug. 3, 1982 (No. 1570), July 9, 1982 (No. 1571),

Nos. 1569-1571 (3) 6.60 2.00

Manila Metropolitan Waterworks and Sewerage System Centenary
A381

1982, Jan. 22

1572 A381 40s blue .50 .30
1573 A381 1.20p brown 1.90 .40

Nos. 1268, 1302, 1328 Surcharged

1981

1574 A273 1p on 65s lil rose 2.25 .60
1575 A286 1p on 1.50p multi 1.50 .40
1576 A295 3.20p on 2.20p multi 4.00 1.00
Nos. 1574-1576 (3) 7.75 2.00

Issue dates: No. 1574, Feb. 24; No. 1575, Feb. 10; No. 1576, March 19.

Scouting Year — A382

40s, Portrait. 2p, Scout giving salute.

1982, Feb. 22

1577 A382 40s multi .60 .30
a. Wmk. 372 (II) 20.00 15.00
1578 A382 2p multi 3.00 .75

Nos. 1577-1578 exist on dull ordinary paper. Issue dates: No. 1577, Jun. 8, 1982. Value, $1.25 mint, 75¢ used; No. 1578, Sept. 21, 1983. Value, $4.25 mint, $2.75 used.

25th Anniv. of Children's Museum and Library Foundation
A383

1982, Feb. 25

1579 A383 40s Mural .60 .30
a. Wmk. 372 (II) 1.50 .50
1580 A383 1.20p Children playing 1.60 .50
a. Wmk. 372 (II) 3.50 1.00

77th Anniv. of Philippine Military Academy — A384

Wmk. 372

1982, Mar. 25 Litho. ***Perf. 12½***

1581 A384 40s multi .60 .30
1582 A384 1p multi 1.40 .40

Nos. 1581 and 1582 exist on orindary paper. Value No. 1581, $1.50 mint, 50¢ used; No. 1582, $2.50 mint, 75¢ used.

40th Bataan Day — A385

40s, Soldier. 2p, "Reunion for Peace." 3.20p, Cannon, flag.

1982, Apr. 9

1583 A385 40s multi .60 .30
a. Wmk. 372 (II) 3.50 1.50
1584 A385 2p multi 2.00 .60

Souvenir Sheet
Imperf

1585 A385 3.20p multi 4.50 *3.00*

No. 1585 contains one 38x28mm stamp. No. 1585 comes on two different papers, the second being thicker with cream gum. Value: unused $7; used $5.

For surcharge see No. 2114.

No. B27 Surcharged

1982, Mar. 15 Photo. ***Perf. 13½***

1586 SP14 10s on 6 + 5s multi 1.50 .40

The "1" in the surcharged value of No. 1586 is unserifed. For similar surcharge with serifed "1," see No. 986.

A386

1982, Apr. 28 Litho. ***Perf. 12½***

1587 A386 1p rose pink 1.75 .35
a. Wmk. 372 (II) 5.50 .70

Aurora Aragon Quezon (1888-1949), former First Lady.

There are three types of No. 1587.

See Nos. 1684-1684A.

Man Holding Award — A387

1982, May 1

1588 A387 40s multi .60 .30
a. Wmk. 372 (II) 125.00 125.00
1589 A387 1.20p Award 1.80 .40
a. Wmk. 372 (II) 10.00 9.00

7th Towers Awards.

No. 1588a bottom inscription in brown instead of green.

See Nos. 1611B-1611C.

UN Conf. on Human Environment, 10th Anniv. — A388

1982, June 5

1590 A388 40s Turtle 1.20 .40
a. Wmk. 372 (II) 2.00 .50
1591 A388 3.20p Philippine eagle 5.00 1.00
a. Wmk. 372 (II) 8.00 2.50

75th Anniv. of Univ. of Philippines College of Medicine — A389

1982, June 10

1592 A389 40s multi .60 .30
a. Wmk. 372 (II) 1.25 .40
1593 A389 3.20p multi 2.90 .80
a. Wmk. 372 (II) 4.75 1.60

Natl. Livelihood Movement — A390

1982, June 12

1594 A390 40s multi .50 .25
a. Wmk. 372 (II) 1.50 .40

See #1681-1681A. For overprint see #1634.

Adamson Univ., 50th Anniv. — A391

1982, June 21

1595 A391 40s bl & multi .50 .25
a. Wmk. 372 (II) ('83) 25.00 25.00
1596 A391 1.20p lt vio & multi 1.50 .40

Social Security, 25th Anniv. — A392

1982, Sept. 1 ***Perf. 13½x13***

1597 A392 40s multi .60 .25
1598 A392 1.20p multi 1.40 .40

Pres. Marcos, 65th Birthday — A393

1982, Sept. 11 ***Perf. 13¼x13***

1599 A393 40s sil & multi .60 .25
a. Wmk. 372 (II) 1.50 .40
b. Perf. 12½ 20.00 2.00
c. As "b," Wmk. 372 (II) 1.00 .25
1600 A393 3.20p sil & multi 2.25 .90
a. Souv. sheet of 2, #1599-1600, imperf. 6.00 4.00
b. Perf. 12½ 3.00 1.00
c. Wmk. 372 (II) 4.00 1.00
d. As "a," Wmk. 372 (II) 25.00 25.00
e. As "b," Wmk. 372 (II) 15.00 12.00

For surcharge see No. 1666.

Perf. 13¼x13 was comb perforated; perf. 12½ was line perforated.

15th Anniv. of Assoc. of Southeast Asian Nations (ASEAN) — A394

1982, Sept. 22 Litho. ***Perf. 12½***

1601 A394 40s Flags .90 .30
c. Wmk. 372 (II) 2.00 .50

St. Teresa of Avila (1515-1582)
A395

1982, Oct. 15 ***Perf. 13x13½***

1602 A395 40s Text .50 .25
1603 A395 1.20p Map 1.00 .40
a. Perf. 12½ 3.50 2.50
b. As "a," Wmk. 372 (II) 4.50 1.75
1604 A395 2p like #1603 1.75 .60
a. Perf. 12½ 5.00 3.50
Nos. 1602-1604 (3) 3.25 1.25

A396

A396a

On Type I the shading on President Marcos is much darker as if he is under the shade of a tree. This was changed in Type II so that he appears under the sun. The new design plates are ½mm shorter than that of the original cutting off the bottom of the design. There are also numerous other slight differences.

Perf. 13x13½

1982, Oct. 21 Litho. Wmk. 372

1605 A396 40s Type I 3.75 1.50
1605A A396a 40s Type II 2.00 .50

10th Anniv. of Tenant Farmers' Emancipation Decree.

See No. 1654.

350th Anniv. of St. Isabel College — A397

1982, Oct. 22

1606 A397 40s multi .45 .25
1607 A397 1p multi 1.95 .40

Reading Campaign
A398

1982, Nov. 4

1608 A398 40s yel & multi .60 .30
a. Perf. 12½, Wmk. 372 (II) 2.50 .50
1609 A398 2.30p grn & multi 2.40 1.00
a. Wmk. 372 (II) 5.00 2.00

For surcharge see No. 1713.

42nd Skal Club World Congress, Manila, Nov. 7-12 — A399

1982, Nov. 7

1610 A399 40s Heads .60 .35
a. Perf. 12½, Wmk. 372 (II) 1.75 .75
1611 A399 2p Chief 3.30 .85
a. Perf. 12½, Wmk. 372 (II) 5.00 1.75

Man Holding Award — A399a

1982, Nov. ***Perf. 12½***

1611B A399a 40s multi 3.50 .75
1611C A399a 1.20p Award 6.50 2.75

Issue dates: No. 1611A, 11/24; No. 1611B, 11/8.

Nos. 1611B-1611C are actually the first printing of Nos. 1588-1589 containing the mispellling "Mangagawa" instead of "Manggagawa".

See Nos. 1588-1589.

25th Anniv. of Bayanihan Folk Arts Center — A400

Designs: Various folk dances.

1982, Nov. 10 Litho. ***Perf. 13x13½***

1612 A400 40s multi .60 .40
a. Perf. 12½, Wmk. 372 (II) 1.25 .35
1613 A400 2.80p multi 3.40 .80

TB Bacillus Centenary A401

1982, Dec. 7 **Wmk. 372**
1614 A401 40s multi .60 .30
1615 A401 2.80p multi 3.40 .90

Christmas 1982 — A402

1982, Dec. 10
1616 A402 40s multi 1.40 .40
1617 A402 1p multi 4.40 .60

Philatelic Week, Nov. 22-28 — A403

Perf. 13x13½
1983, Jan. 21 **Litho.** **Wmk. 372**
1618 A403 40s yel & multi .60 .25
a. Perf. 12½, Wmk. 372 (II) 1.00 .35
1619 A403 1p sil & multi 1.25 .35
a. Perf. 12½ 2.50 .50
b. As "a," Wmk. 372 (II) 3.00 1.00

For surcharge see No. 1667.
First-day covers dated 1982, Nov. 28.

Visit of Pres. Marcos to the US, Sept. — A404

1982, Dec. 18
1620 A404 40s multi .60 *.40*
1621 A404 3.20p multi 3.80 1.00
a. Souv. sheet of 2, #1620-1621 5.00 *4.00*

UN World Assembly on Aging, July 26-Aug. 6 — A405

1982, Dec. 24
1622 A405 1.20p Woman 1.30 .35
a. Wmk. 372 (II) 15.00 7.00
1623 A405 2p Man 2.70 .65

Senate Pres. Eulogio Rodriguez, Sr. (1883-1964) — A406

1983, Jan. 21
1624 A406 40s grn & multi .75 .35
a. Wmk. 372 (II) 1.00 .30
1625 A406 1.20p org & multi 1.25 .45
a. Perf. 12½ 4.75 1.75
b. As "a," Wmk. 372 (II) 1.75 .50

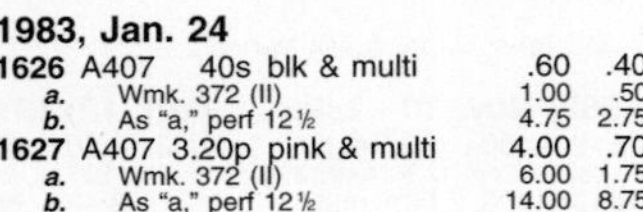
1983 Manila Intl. Film Festival, Jan. 24-Feb. 4 — A407

1983, Jan. 24
1626 A407 40s blk & multi .60 .40
a. Wmk. 372 (II) 1.00 .50
b. As "a," perf 12½ 4.75 2.75
1627 A407 3.20p pink & multi 4.00 .70
a. Wmk. 372 (II) 6.00 1.75
b. As "a," perf 12½ 14.00 8.75

Beatification of Lorenzo Ruiz (1981) — A408

Perf. 13x13½
1983, Feb. 18 **Litho.** **Wmk. 372**
1628 A408 40s multi .65 .35
a. Wmk. 372 (II) 1.50 .40
b. Perf 12½ 5.00 2.00
1629 A408 1.20p multi 1.75 .60
a. Wmk. 372 (II) 2.50 .60
b. Perf 12½ 8.50 5.00

400th Anniv. of Local Printing Press — A409

1983, Mar. 14
1630 A409 40s blk & grn .60 .30
a. Wmk. 372 (II) 1.50 .40

Safety at Sea — A410

1983, Mar. 17 ***Perf. 13½x13***
1631 A410 40s multi .60 .30
a. Wmk. 372 (II) 1.75 .40

25th anniv. of Inter-Governmental Maritime Consultation Org. Convention.

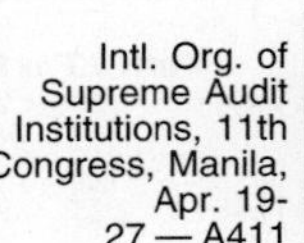

Intl. Org. of Supreme Audit Institutions, 11th Congress, Manila, Apr. 19-27 — A411

Perf. 13x13½
1983, Apr. 8 **Litho.** **Wmk. 372**
1632 A411 40s Symbols .50 .30
a. Wmk. 372 (II) 1.75 .75
1633 A411 2.80p Emblem 2.00 1.00
a. Souv. sheet of 2, 1632-1633, imperf. 5.00 *4.00*
b. Wmk. 372 (II) 5.00 1.75
c. As "a," Wmk. 372 (II) 15.00 12.00

No. 1633a comes on two papers: cream gum, normal watermark; white gum, watermark made up of smaller letters.

Type of 1982 Overprinted in Red: "7th BSP NATIONAL JAMBOREE 1983"

1983, Apr. 13 ***Perf. 12½***
1634 A390 40s multi 1.00 .35

Boy Scouts of Philippines jamboree.

No. 1249 Surcharged

1983, Apr. 15
1635 Block of 10 14.00 *12.00*
a.-j. A265 40s on 45s, any single .90 .45

A412

Perf. 13½x13
1983, May 9 **Litho.** **Wmk. 372**
1636 A412 40s multi .60 .30
b. Wmk. 372 (II) 1.75 .75

75th anniv. of Dental Assoc.

A413

Perf. 13½x13
1983, June 17 **Litho.** **Wmk. 372**
1637 A413 40s Statue .50 .30
a. Perf. 12½, Wmk. 372 (II) 3.50 1.50
1638 A413 1.20p Statue, diff., diamond 1.25 .60
a. Perf. 12½, Wmk. 372 (II) 4.50 2.00

75th anniv. of University of the Philippines.

Visit of Japanese Prime Minister Yasuhiro Nakasone, May 6-8 — A414

Perf. 13x13½
1983, June 20 **Litho.** **Wmk. 372**
1639 A414 40s multi .60 .30
a. Wmk. 372 (II) 6.00 5.00

25th Anniv. of Natl. Science and Technology Authority — A415

No. 1640, Animals, produce. No. 1641, Heart, food, pill. No. 1642, Factories, windmill, car. No. 1643, Chemicals, house, book.

1983, July 11
1640 A415 40s multicolored .60 *.40*
a. Perf. 12½, Wmk. 372 (II) 1.25 1.00
1641 A415 40s multicolored .60 *.40*
a. Perf. 12½, Wmk. 372 (II) 1.25 1.00
1642 A415 40s multicolored .60 *.40*
a. Perf. 12½, Wmk. 372 (II) 1.25 1.00
1643 A415 40s multicolored .60 *.40*
a. Perf. 12½, Wmk. 372 (II) 1.25 1.00
b. Block of 4, #1640-1643 3.50 *2.50*
b. Block of 4, #1640a-1643a 8.00 *6.00*

Science Week.

World Communications Year — A416

Wmk. 372 (II)
1983, Oct. 24 **Litho.** ***Perf. 12½***
1644 A416 3.20p multi 3.00 1.00

Philippine Postal System Bicentennial A417

1983, Oct. 31
1645 A417 40s multi .60 .30

Christmas — A418

Star of the East and Festival Scene in continuous design.

Wmk. 372 (I)
1983, Nov. 15 **Litho.** ***Perf. 12½***
1646 Strip of 5 5.50 4.00
a.-e. A418 40s single stamp 1.00 .40
f. Souvenir sheet 5.00 *4.00*
g. Strip of 5, Wmk. 372 (II) 10.00 7.00
h.-l. As "g," any single 1.25 1.00

Xavier University, 50th Anniv. — A419

Wmk. 372 (II)
1983, Dec. 1 **Litho.** ***Perf. 14***
1647 A419 40s multi .50 .30
a. Wmk. 372 (I) 1.50 .50
1648 A419 60s multi 1.25 .35
a. Wmk. 372 (I) 3.00 1.00

A420

1983, Dec. 8 **Litho.** ***Perf. 12½***
1649 A420 40s brt ultra & multi .50 .30
a. Wmk. 372 (I) 5.00 2.75
1650 A420 60s gold & multi 1.25 .40
a. Wmk. 372 (I) 4.25 2.50

Ministry of Labor and Employment, golden jubilee.

A421

1983, Dec. 7
1651 A421 40s multi .50 .40
1652 A421 60s multi 1.25 .40

50th anniv. of Women's Suffrage Movement.

Philatelic Week — A422

Stamp Collecting: a, Cutting. b, Sorting. c, Soaking. d, Affixing hinges. e, Mounting stamp.

1983, Dec. 20
1653 Strip of 5 *4.50* 3.50
a.-e. A422 50s any single .75 .50
f. Strip of 5, Wmk. 372 (I) 30.00 30.00
g.-k. As "f," any single 5.00 4.00

Emancipation Type of 1982

1983 **Litho.** ***Perf. 13***
Size: 32x22mm
1654 A396 40s multi 2.50 .30
a. Perf. 12½ 15.00 1.00

Philippine Cockatoo — A423

40s, Philippine Cockatoo, 2.30p, Guaiabero. 2.80p, Crimson-spotted racket-tailed parrots. 3.20p, Large-billed parrot. 3.60p, Tanygnathus sumatranus. 5p, Hanging parakeets.

1984, Jan. 9 **Unwmk.** ***Perf. 14***
1655 A423 40s multi .60 .30
1656 A423 2.30p multi *1.60* .60
1657 A423 2.80p multi *2.10* .80
1658 A423 3.20p multi *2.50* 1.00
1659 A423 3.60p multi *2.75* 1.00
1660 A423 5p multi *3.50* 1.50
Nos. 1655-1660 (6) *13.05* 5.20

There were 500,000 of each value created cto with Jan 9 1984, cancel in the center of each block of 4. These were sold at 15 percent of face value. Value for CTO set, $3.

Princess Tarhata Kiram — A424

Wmk. 372 (II)

1984, Jan. 16 *Perf. 13*

1661 A424 3p grn & red 2.25 .50
a. Perf. 12½ 7.00 2.00
b. As "a," Wmk. 372 (I) 5.00 1.25

Order of Virgin Mary, 300th Anniv. — A425

Perf. 13½x13

1984, Jan. 23 **Wmk. 372 (I)**

1662 A425 40s blk & multi .60 .30
a. Perf. 12½ 1.75 .70
1663 A425 60s red & multi 1.25 .50
a. Perf. 12½ 4.00 1.30

Dona Concha Felix de Calderon — A426

1984, Feb. 9 **Wmk. 372 (II)** ***Perf. 13***

1664 A426 60s blk & bl grn .60 *.30*
a. Perf. 12½ 2.00 .50
b. Wmk. 372 (I) 25.00 18.00
1665 A426 3.60p red & bl grn 2.00 .70
a. Perf. 12½ 4.00 1.00
b. As "a," Wmk. 372 (I) 5.00 1.75
c. Wmk. 372 (I) 25.00 18.00

Nos. 1546, 1599, 1618 Surcharged

1984, Feb. 20

1666 A393 60s on 40s (R) .50 .25
a. Perf. 12½ .50 .25
b. As "a," Wmk. 372 (I) 8.00 5.00
1667 A403 60s on 40s, Wmk. 372 (I) .70 .25
1668 A374 3.60p on 3.20p, perf. 12½ (R) 3.80 1.00
Nos. 1666-1668 (3) 5.00 1.50

No. 1685 Surcharged

1985, Oct. 21 **Litho.** ***Perf. 12½***

1669 A374 3.60p on 4.20p rose lil 6.00 3.00
a. Perf. 13 35.00 25.00

Portrait Type of 1981

Designs: No. 1672, Gen. Artemio Ricarte. No. 1673, Teodoro M. Kalaw. No. 1674, Pres. Carlos P. Garcia. No. 1675, Senator Quintin Paredes. No. 1676, Dr. Deogracias V. Villadolid (1896-1976), 1st director, Bureau of Fisheries. No. 1677, Santiago Fonacier (1885-1940), archbishop. No. 1678, 2p, Vicente Orestes Romualdez (1885-1970), lawyer. 3p, Francisco Dagohoy.

Types of 3p:
Type I — Medium size "PILIPINAS," large, heavy denomination.
Type II — Large "PILIPINAS," medium denomination.

Perf. 13, 12¾ (#1678, 2p), 12½x13 (3p)

1984-85 **Litho.**

1672 A374 60s blk & lt brn 1.50 .30
1673 A374 60s blk & pur 1.80 .30
1674 A374 60s black 1.80 .30
1675 A374 60s dull blue .70 .25
a. Perf. 12½ 1.75 .30
b. Wmk. 391 1.00 .25
c. As "a". Wmk. 391 3.50 .30
1676 A374 60s brn blk ('85) .85 .25
a. Perf. 12½ 1.75 .30
1677 A374 60s dk red ('85) .60 .25
a. Horiz. miniature sheet of 20 45.00 45.00
b. Vert. miniature sheet of 20 37.50 37.50
c. Wmk. 391 2.50 .40
1678 A374 60s cobalt blue ('85) .90 *.40*
a. Perf. 12¾ 1.80 1.00
1679 A374 2p brt rose ('85) 3.00 .50
a. Perf. 12¾ 1.80 1.00
1680 A374 3p pale brn, type I 6.00 .60
a. Perf. 12½ 12.00 1.20
1680A A374 3p pale brn, type II .90 .80
Nos. 1672-1680A (10) 18.05 3.95

Issued: #1672, 3/22; #1673, 3/31; #1674, 6/14; #1675, 9/12; #1676, 3/22; #1677, 5/21; #1678, 2p, 7/3; 3p, 9/7.
No. 1677 was normally issued in panes of 100.

Types of 1982

Types of 3.60p:
Type I — Thick Frame line, large "P," "360" with line under "60."
Type II — Medium Frame line, small "p," "3.60."

Perf. 12½ (#1684), 12¾x13, 13x12¾ (#1681, 1681A)
Wmk. 372 (II), 391 (#1684A)

1984-86

1681 A390 60s green & multi .35 .25
a. Perf. 12½ .50 .25
b. Wmk. 372 (I) 25.00 18.00
1681A A390 60s red & multi 1.00 .30
b. Perf. 12½ 4.00 .60
c. As "b," Wmk. 372 (I) 15.00 9.00
1682 A374 1.80p #1546 1.50 .45
a. Perf. 12½ 2.50 .50
1683 A374 2.40p #1545 1.60 .50
a. Perf. 12½ 1.75 .40
b. As "a," Wmk. 372 (I) 20.00 10.00
1684 A386 3.60p Quezon, type I 2.00 .40
b. Wmk. 372 (I) 35.00 22.50
1684A A386 3.60p As #1684, type II 4.00 .50
1685 A374 4.20p #1544 3.00 .75
Nos. 1681-1685 (7) 13.45 3.15

Issued: #1681A, 10/19; #1684A, 2/14/86; others 3/26.
Postal forgeries of No. 1684 exist perf. 11.

Ayala Corp. Sesquicentenary A427

Night Views of Manila.

1984, Apr. 25 **Litho.** ***Perf. 13x13½***

1686 A427 70s multi .65 .30
a. Perf. 12½ 1.75 .50
1687 A427 3.60p multi 2.75 .70

ESPANA '84 — A428

Designs: 2.50p, No. 1690d, Our Lady of the Most Holy Rosary with St. Dominic, by C. Francisco. 5p, No. 1690a, Spoliarium, by Juan Luna. No. 1690b, Blessed Virgin of Manila as Patroness of Voyages, Galleon showing map of Panama-Manila. No. 1690c. Illustrations from The Monkey and the Turtle, by Rizal (first children's book published in Philippines, 1885.)

1984, Apr. 27 **Unwmk.** ***Perf. 14***

1688 A428 2.50p multi 3.00 2.50
1689 A428 5p multi 8.00 5.00
a. Pair, #1688-1689 13.00 10.00

Souvenir Sheet

Perf. 14½x15, Imperf.

1690 Sheet of 4, #a.-d. 25.00 20.00
a.-d. A428 7.50p, any single 5.00 3.00
e. Sheet of 4, one value ovpt. "O.L. Lady" instead of "O.L. Holy" 300.00 300.00
f. Error single from No 1690e sheet 50.00 50.00

Surcharged in Black

Perf. 14½x15

1690A Sheet of 4, #a.-d. 200.00 200.00
a.-d. A428 7.20p on 7.50p, any single 22.00 20.00

Surcharged in Red

Imperf

1690B Sheet of 4, #a.-d. 200.00 200.00
a.-d. A428 7.20p on 7.50p, any single 22.00 20.00

Surcharged in Black

Imperf

1690C Sheet of 4, #a.-d. 250.00 250.00
a.-d. A428 7.20p on 7.50p, any single 60.00 60.00

Nos. 1690Aa-1690Ad and 1690Ba-1690Bd are each surcharged 7.20p and bear the following overprints: #1690Aa and #1690Ba, "10-5-84 NATIONAL MUSEUM WEEK" on #1690a; #1690Ab and #1690Bb, "8-3-84 PHILIPPINE-MEXICAN FRIENDSHIP 420th ANNIVERSARY" on #1690b; #1690Ac and #1690Bc, "7-17-84 NATIONAL CHILDREN'S BOOK DAY" on #1690c; #1690Ad and #1690Bd, "9-1-84 O.L. OF HOLY ROSARY PARISH 300TH YEAR" on #1690d. Nos. 1690Aa-1690Bd were released as single stamps on the dates shown in their respective overprints. A few intact sheets were sold after the release of the last of these stamps.

Maria Paz Mendoza Guazon — A429

1984, May 26 **Wmk. 372** ***Perf. 13***

1691 A429 60s brt blue & red 1.20 .30
1692 A429 65s brt blue, red & blk 1.50 .40

Butterflies A430

60s, Adolias amlana. 2.40p, Papilio daedalus. 3p, Prothoe frankii semperi. 3.60p, Troides magellanus. 4.20p, Yoma sabina vasuki. 5p, Chilasa idaeoides.

Unwmk.

1984, Aug. 2 **Litho.** ***Perf. 14***

1693 A430 60s multi .60 .40
1694 A430 2.40p multi *1.50* .80
1695 A430 3p multi *2.00* 1.00
1696 A430 3.60p multi *2.50* 1.20
1697 A430 4.20p multi *3.00* *1.50*
1698 A430 5p multi *4.00* *1.80*
Nos. 1693-1698 (6) *13.60* 6.70

There were 500,000 of each value created cto with Jul 5 1984 cancel in the center of each block of 4. These were sold at 15 percent face value.Value for CTO set, $3.50.

Summer Olympics, Los Angeles, 1984 — A431

Designs: 60s, Running (man). 2.40p, Boxing. 6p, Swimming. 7.20p, Windsurfing. 8.40p, Cycling. 20p, Running (woman).

Unwmk.

1984, Aug. 9 **Litho.** ***Perf. 14***

1699 A431 60s multi .60 *.50*
1700 A431 2.40p multi 1.40 .70
1701 A431 6p multi 3.00 1.80
1702 A431 7.20p multi 3.50 2.50
1703 A431 8.40p multi 4.00 2.50
1704 A431 20p multi 10.00 5.00
Nos. 1699-1704 (6) 22.50 13.00

Souvenir Sheet

1705 Sheet of 4 15.00 *15.00*
a.-d. A431 6p, any single 2.50 2.50

There were 500,000 of each value created cto with Aug 8 1984 cancel in the center of each block of 4. These were sold at15 percent face value. Used value, set of 6 cto, $4.
Nos. 1699-1705 were also issued imperf, with blue, instead of red, stars at sides. Value, set of 6 stamps $100, souvenir sheet $40.

Baguio City, 75th Anniv. — A432

Wmk. 372

1984, Aug. 24 **Litho.** ***Perf. 12½***

1706 A432 1.20p The Mansion 2.00 .60

Light Rail Transit — A433

1984, Sept. 10 ***Perf. 13x13½***

1707 A433 1.20p multi 2.00 .40

No. 1, Australia No. 59 and Koalas — A434

Perf. 14½x15

1984, Sept. 21 **Unwmk.**

1708 A434 3p multi 3.50 1.50
1709 A434 3.60p multi 4.50 2.00

Souvenir Sheet

1710 Sheet of 3 *20.00* *18.00*
a. A434 20p multi *6.00* *5.00*

AUSIPEX '84. No. 1710 exists imperf. Value, $25.

No. 1609 Surcharged with 2 Black Bars and Ovptd. "14-17 NOV. 84 / R.I. ASIA REGIONAL CONFERENCE"

Perf. 13x13½

1984, Nov. 11 **Wmk. 372** **Litho.**

1713 A398 1.20p on 2.30p multi 2.00 *.80*
a. Wmk. 372 (II) 2.00 .80

Philatelic Week — A435

1.20p, Gold medal. 3p, Winning stamp exhibit.

Wmk. 372 (II)

1984, Nov. 22 ***Perf. 13½x13***

1714 A435 1.20p multi .80 .50
1715 A435 3p multi 2.25 1.10
a. Pair, #1714-1715 4.00 3.00

AUSIPEX '84 and Mario Que, 1st Philippine exhibitor to win FIP Gold Award.
For overprints see Nos. 1737A and 1737B.

Ships — A436

60s, Caracao canoes. 1.20p, Chinese junk. 6p, Spanish galleon. 7.20p, Casco. 8.40p, Steamboat. 20p, Cruise liner.

Unwmk.

1984, Nov. 26 **Litho.** ***Perf. 14***

1718 A436 60s multi .50 .30
1719 A436 1.20p multi 1.00 .50
1720 A436 6p multi 2.25 1.30
1721 A436 7.20p multi 2.80 1.50
1722 A436 8.40p multi 3.00 1.90
1723 A436 20p multi 6.00 2.50
Nos. 1718-1723 (6) *15.55* 8.00

There were 500,000 of each value created cto with Oct 5 1984 cancel in the center of each block of 4. These were sold at 15 percentf face value. Value, set of 6 cto, $3.50.
For surcharge, see No. 3051.

Ateneo de Manila University, 125th Anniv. — A438

Wmk. 372 (II)

1984, Dec. 7 **Litho.** ***Perf. 13x13½***

1730 A438 60s ultra & gold .65 .30
1731 A438 1.20p dk ultra & sil 1.35 .40

A438a

60s, Manila-Dagupan, 1892. 1.20p, Light rail transit, 1984. 6p, Bicol Express, 1955. 7.20p, Tranvis (1905, electric street car). 8.40, Commuter train, 1984. 20p, Early street car pulled by horses, 1898.

Perf. 14x13¾

1984, Dec. 18				**Unwmk.**	
1731A	A438a	60s	multi	.50	.40
1731B	A438a	1.20p	multi	1.00	.50
1731C	A438a	6p	multi	3.00	1.20
1731D	A438a	7.20p	multi	4.00	1.50
1731E	A438a	8.40p	multi	3.50	1.50
1731F	A438a	20p	multi	7.50	2.50
	Nos. 1731A-1731F (6)			19.50	7.60

There were 500,000 of each value created cto with Dec 5 1984 cancel in the center of each block of 4. These were sold at15 percentf face value. Value, set of 6 cto, $3.50.

For surcharges see #1772-1773.

Christmas — A439

60s, Madonna and Child. 1.20p, Holy family.

Wmk. 372 (II)

1984, Dec. 8			***Perf. 13½x13***	
1732 A439	60s	multi	1.00	.40
1733 A439	1.20p	multi	2.50	1.00
a.	Pair, #1732-1733		4.00	2.50

Natl. Jaycees Awards, 25th anniv. — A440

Philippines Jaycees Commitment to Youth Development.

Abstract painting by Raoul G. Isidro.

1984, Dec. 19			
1734	Strip of 10	*30.00*	*30.00*
a.-e.	A440 60s any single	1.25	.80
f.-j.	A440 3p any single	3.75	2.25
k.	Strip of 10, Wmk. 372 (I)	125.00	125.00
l.-p.	A440 60s any single	5.00	4.00
q.-u.	A440 3p any single	15.00	12.50

Dried Tobacco Leaf and Plant — A441

1985, Jan. 14			***Perf. 13x13½***	
1735 A441	60s	multicolored	.80	.30
1736 A441	3p	multicolored	2.70	.80

Philippine-Virginia Tobacco Admin., 25th anniv.

No. 1537 Surcharged

1984, Nov. 28	**Litho.**	***Imperf.***	
1737 A373 3p on 2p multi		5.00	4.00

First printing had missing period ("p300"). Value $12.

First-day cancels are for Nov. 20.

Nos. 1714-1715 Overprinted "Philatelic Week 1984"

1.20p, Gold medal. 3p, Winning stamp exhibit.

1985, Jan. 25			***Perf. 13½x13***	
1737A A435	1.20p	multi	.80	.50
1737B A435	3p	multi	2.25	1.30
c.	Pair, #1737A-1737B		4.00	3.00

Natl. Research Council Emblem — A442

1985, Feb. 3	**Litho.**	***Perf. 13x13½***		
1738 A442	60s	bl, dk bl & blk	.35	.25
1739 A442	1.20p	org, dk bl & blk	1.00	.35

Pacific Science Assoc., 5th intl. congress, Manila, Feb. 3-7.

Medicinal Plants — A443

60s, Carmona retusa. 1.20p, Orthosiphon aristatus. 2.40p, Vitex negundo. 3p, Aloe barbadensis. 3.60p, Quisqualis indica. 4.20p, Blumea balsamifera.

Wmk. 372 (II)

1985, Mar. 15			***Perf. 13x13½***	
1740 A443	60s	multi	1.20	.40
a.	Perf. 12½		2.00	1.00
1741 A443	1.20p	multi	2.75	1.00
a.	Perf. 12½		3.50	1.00
1742 A443	2.40p	multi	4.00	2.00
a.	Perf. 12½		4.00	1.00
1743 A443	3p	multi	6.00	2.00
a.	Perf. 12½		4.50	1.50
1744 A443	3.60p	multi	5.00	2.25
a.	Perf. 12½		6.50	2.75
b.	Wmk. 372 (I)		80.00	80.00
c.	As "a," Wmk. 372 (I)		40.00	40.00
1745 A443	4.20p	multi	7.00	3.50
a.	Perf. 12½		7.00	3.00
	Nos. 1740-1745 (6)		25.95	11.15

INTELSAT, 20th Anniv. — A444

1985, Apr. 6			***Perf. 13x13½***	
1746 A444	60s	multicolored	.50	.30
1747 A444	3p	multicolored	2.50	.70

A444a

Philippine Horses: 60s, Pintos. 1.20p, Palomino. 6p, Bay. 7.20p, Brown. 8.40p, Gray. 20p, Chestnut.

#1747G: h, as 1.20p. i, as 7.20p. j, as 6p. k, as 20p.

Perf. 14x13¾

1984, Dec. 18				**Unwmk.**	
1747A	A444a	60s	multi	.50	.40
1747B	A444a	1.20p	multi	1.00	.50
1747C	A444a	6p	multi	2.00	1.20
1747D	A444a	7.20p	multi	3.00	1.50
1747E	A444a	8.40p	multi	3.50	1.80
1747F	A444a	20p	multi	7.00	2.80
	Nos. 1747A-1747F (6)			17.00	8.20

Souvenir Sheet of 4

1747G	A444a 8.40p h.-k.	15.00	*15.00*

There were 500,000 each of #1747A-1747F created cto with Apr 12 1985 cancel in the center of each block of 4. These were sold at 15 percentf face value. Value, set of 6 cto, $4.

Tax Research Institute, 25th Anniv. — A445

Perf. 13½x13

1985, Apr. 22		**Wmk. 372**	
1748 A445 60s multicolored		.70	.30

Intl. Rice Research Institute, 25th Anniv. — A446

1985, May 27			***Perf. 13x13½***	
1749 A446	60s	Planting	.50	.40
a.	Perf. 12½		6.50	3.00
1750 A446	3p	Paddies	2.50	.80

1st Spain-Philippines Peace Treaty, 420th Anniv. — A447

Designs: 1.20p, Blessed Infant of Cebu, statue, shrine and basilica. 3.60p, King Tupas of Cebu and Miguel Lopez de Legaspi signing treaty, 1565.

1985, June 4			***Perf. 12½***	
1751 A447	1.20p	multi	.80	.30
1752 A447	3.60p	multi	2.00	.70
a.	Pair, #1751-1752 + label		5.00	4.00

No. 1532 Ovptd. "10th Anniversary Philippines and People's Republic of China Diplomatic Relations 1975-1985"

1985, June 8		***Imperf.***	
1753 A372 5p multi		7.00	*5.00*

In the first printing, the apostrophe in *People's* was omitted and then added by hand. Value: $12 unused, $10 used. The apostrophe is included in later printings.

Arbor Week, June 9-15 — A448

1985, June 9			***Perf. 13½x13***	
1754 A448	1.20p	multi	1.50	.40
a.	Perf. 12½		75.00	75.00

Battle of Bessang Pass, 40th Anniv. — A449

1985, June 14			***Perf. 13x13½***	
1755 A449	1.20p	multi	1.50	.50
a.	Perf. 12½		12.50	3.50

No. 1755a issued 12/13.

Natl. Tuberculosis Soc., 75th Anniv. — A450

60s, Immunization, research. 1.20p, Charity seal.

1985, July 29				
1756 A450	60s	multi	.80	.40
1757 A450	1.20p	multi	1.20	.60
a.	Pair, #1756-1757		3.00	2.00

No. 1297 Surcharged with Bars, New Value and Scout Emblem in Gold, Ovptd. "GSP" and "45th Anniversary Girl Scout Charter" in Black

Perf. 12½x13½

1985, Aug. 19	**Unwmk.**	**Photo.**	
1758 A242 2.40p on 15s on 10s		2.00	1.00
1759 A242 4.20p on 15s on 10s		3.00	1.50
1760 A242 7.20p on 15s on 10s		5.00	2.50
Nos. 1758-1760 (3)		10.00	5.00

Virgin Mary Birth Bimillennium — A451

Statues and paintings.

Perf. 13½x13

1985, Sept. 8		**Wmk. 372**		**Litho.**	
1761 A451	1.20p	Fatima		1.20	.40
1762 A451	2.40p	Beaterio		1.80	.60
1763 A451	3p	Penafrancia		3.00	1.00
1764 A451	3.60p	Guadalupe		3.50	1.50
	Nos. 1761-1764 (4)			9.50	3.50

A small quantity of No. 1762 was issued with a large *2* in the denomination. The top of the *2* touches the frameline. Value, $10 mint, $4 used.

Intl. Youth Year — A452

Prize-winning children's drawings.

1985, Sept. 23			***Perf. 13x13½***	
1765 A452	2.40p	Agriculture	1.80	.50
1766 A452	3.60p	Education	2.75	.90

Girl and Rice Terraces — A453

1985, Sept. 26				
1767 A453	2.40p	multi	2.50	.75
a.	Perf. 12½		8.50	8.50

World Tourism Organization, 6th general assembly, Sofia, Bulgaria, Sept. 17-26.

Export Year — A454

1985, Oct. 8	***Perf. 13½x13***	
1768 A454 1.20p multi	1.50	.35

UN, 40th Anniv. — A455

1985, Oct. 24		
1769 A455 3.60p multi	3.50	.70

1st Transpacific Airmail Service, 50th Anniv. — A456

3p, China Clipper on water. 3.60p, China Clipper, map.

1985, Nov. 22			***Perf. 13x13½***	
1770 A456	3p	multi	2.75	1.00
1771 A456	3.60p	multi	3.25	1.00

Nos. 1731C-1731D Surcharged in Black

Perf. 14x13¾

1985, Nov. 24 **Unwmk.**
1772 A438a 60s on 6p 1.00 .50
1773 A438a 3p on 7.20p 5.00 1.50

No. 1773 is airmail.

Natl. Bible Week — A457

1985, Dec. 3 **Wmk. 372** ***Perf. 12½***
1774 A457 60s multicolored .50 .40
1775 A457 3p multicolored 2.50 1.00

Christmas 1985 — A458

1985, Dec. 8 ***Perf. 13x13½***
1776 A458 60s Panuluyan .80 .50
a. Perf. 12½ 5.00 3.50
1777 A458 3p Pagdalaw 3.75 1.20
a. Perf. 12½ 13.00 10.00

Scales of Justice — A459

1986, Jan. 12
1778 A459 60s lilac rose & blk .50 .30
1779 A459 3p brt grn, lil rose & blk 2.10 .80

University of the Philippines, College of Law, 75th anniv.
See No. 1838.

Flores de Heidelberg, by Jose Rizal — A460

Design: 60s, Noli Me Tangere.

1986 **Wmk. 391** **Litho.** ***Perf. 13***
1780 A460 60s violet .40 .25
a. Wmk. 372 (II) 20.00 20.00
1781 A460 1.20p bluish grn 1.50 .30
a. Wmk. 372 (II) 15.00 15.00
1782 A460 3.60p redsh brn 2.40 .45
Nos. 1780-1782 (3) 4.30 1.00

Issued: 60s, 1.20p, Feb. 21; 3.60p, July 10.
For surcharges see Nos. 1834, 1913.
Nos. 1780a-1781a were printed for presentation purposes. Remainders were sold over post office counters.

Philippine Airlines, 45th Anniv. — A461

Aircraft: No. 1783a, Douglas DC3, 1946. b, Douglas DC4 Skymaster, 1946. c, Douglas DC6, 1948. d, Vickers Viscount 784, 1957.
No. 1784a, Fokker Friendship F27 Mark 100, 1960. b, Douglas DC8 Series 50, 1962. c, Bac One Eleven Series 500, 1964. d, McDonnell Douglas DC10 Series 30, 1974.
No. 1785a, Beech Model 18, 1941. b, Boeing 747, 1980.

1986, Mar. 15
1783 A461 Block of 4 4.00 4.00
a.-d. 60s, any single .50 .30
e. Block of 4, Wmk. 372 (II) 80.00 80.00
f.-j. As "e," 60s, any single 16.00 16.00
1784 A461 Block of 4 8.00 8.00
a.-d. 2.40p, any single 1.00 1.00
e. Block of 4, Wmk. 372 (II) 100.00 100.00
f.-j. As "e," 2.40p, any single 20.00 20.00
1785 A461 Pair 5.50 5.50
a.-b. 3.60p, any single 2.25 1.50
c. Pair, Wmk. 372 (II) 50.00 50.00
d.-e. As "e," 3.60p, any single 10.00 10.00
Nos. 1783-1785 (3) 17.50 17.50

See No. 1842.

Bataan Oil Refining Corp., 25th Anniv. — A462

Perf. 13½x13, 13x13½

1986, Apr. 12 **Wmk. 372**
1786 A462 60s Refinery, vert. .50 .35
a. Wmk. 391 1.00 .50
1787 A462 3p shown 2.50 .85
a. Wmk. 391 4.00 2.00

EXPO '86, Vancouver A463

Perf. 13x13½

1986, May 2 **Wmk. 391**
1788 A463 60s multicolored .50 .35
a. Wmk. 372 (II) 30.00 30.00
1789 A463 3p multicolored 2.50 1.00
a. Wmk. 372 (II) 30.00 30.00

Asian Productivity Organization, 25th Anniv. — A464

1986, May 15
1790 A464 60s multicolored .50 .40
a. Wmk. 372 (II) 15.00 15.00
1791 A464 3p multicolored 2.50 2.00
a. Wmk. 372 (II) 15.00 15.00

Size: 30x22mm

1792 A464 3p pale brown 1.25 .50
Nos. 1790-1792 (3) 4.25 2.90

Issued: #1790-1791, 5/15; #1792, 7/10.

AMERIPEX '86 — A465

1986, May 22 ***Perf. 13½x13***
1793 A465 60s No. 241 .60 .35
a. Wmk. 372 (II) 7.00 5.00
1794 A465 3p No. 390 2.75 1.00
a. Wmk. 372 (II) 7.00 5.00

See No. 1835.

Election of Corazon Aquino, 7th Pres. — A466

Portrait of Aquino and: 60s, Salvador Laurel, vice-president, and hands in symbolic gestures of peace and freedom. 1.20p, Symbols of communication and transportation. 2.40p, Parade. 3p, Military. 7.20p, Vice-president, parade, horiz.

1986, May 25 **Wmk. 372**
1795 A466 60s multi .50 .30
a. Wmk. 389 .50 .60
1796 A466 1.20p multi .70 .35
a. Wmk. 389 .90 .70
1797 A466 2.40p multi 1.25 .40
a. Wmk. 389 1.60 .80
1798 A466 3p multi 1.50 .50
a. Wmk. 389 2.00 .90
Nos. 1795-1798 (4) 3.95 1.55

Souvenir Sheet

Imperf

1799 A466 7.20p multi 4.25 4.00
a. Wmk. 389 4.50 4.00

For surcharge see No. 1939.

De La Salle University, 75th Anniv. — A467

60s, Statue of St. John the Baptist de la Salle, Paco buildings, 1911, & university, 1986. 2.40p, St. Miguel Febres Cordero, buildings, 1911. 3p, St. Benilde, buildings, 1986. 7.20p, Founding fathers.

Perf. 13x13½

1986, June 16 **Wmk. 391**
1800 A467 60s grn, blk & pink .50 .30
1801 A467 2.40p grn, blk & bl 1.50 .50
1802 A467 3p grn, blk & yel 2.50 .75
Nos. 1800-1802 (3) 4.50 1.55

Souvenir Sheet

Imperf

1803 A467 7.20p grn & blk 6.00 5.00

For surcharge see No. 1940.

A468

Memorial to Benigno S. Aquino, Jr. (1932-83) — A469

3.60p, The Filipino is worth dying for, horiz. 10p, Hindi ka nag-iisa, horiz.

Perf. 13½x13, 13x13½

1986, Aug. 21 **Wmk. 389**
1804 A468 60s dl bluish grn .60 .30
1805 A469 2p shown 1.25 .40
1806 A469 3.60p multicolored 2.40 1.00
Nos. 1804-1806 (3) 4.25 1.70

Souvenir Sheet

Imperf

1807 A469 10p multicolored 5.00 4.00

See No. 1836. For surcharges see No. 1914 and 2706A.

Indigenous Orchids — A470

60s, Vanda sanderiana. 1.20p, Epigeneium lyonii. 2.40p, Paphiopedilum philippinense. 3p, Amesiella philippinensis.

1986, Aug. 28 ***Perf. 13½x13***
1808 A470 60s multi .50 .30
1809 A470 1.20p multi 2.00 .40
1810 A470 2.40p multi 3.50 .80
1811 A470 3p multi 3.50 1.50
Nos. 1808-1811 (4) 9.50 3.00

For surcharge see No. 1941.

Quiapo District, 400th Anniv. — A471

60s, Our Lord Jesus the Nazarene, statue, Quiapo church. 3.60p, Quiapo church, 1930, horiz.

Perf. 13½x13, 13x13½

1986, Aug. 29 **Wmk. 391**
1812 A471 60s pink, blk & lake .50 .30
1813 A471 3.60p pale grn, blk & dk ultra 3.50 .90

For surcharge see No. 1915.

General Hospital, 75th Anniv. — A472

1986, Sept. 1 ***Perf. 13½x13***
1814 A472 60s bl & multi .40 .30
1815 A472 3p grn & multi 2.00 .50

See No. 1841. For surcharge see No. 1888.

Halley's Comet — A473

60s, Comet, Earth. 2.40p, Comet, Earth, Moon.

Perf. 13x13½

1986, Sept. 25 **Wmk. 389**
1816 A473 60s multi .80 .30
1817 A473 2.40p multi 2.75 .50

For surcharge see No. 1942.

74th FDI World Dental Congress, Manila — A474

1986, Nov. 10 **Litho.** ***Perf. 13x13½***
1818 A474 60s Handshake .80 .30
1819 A474 3p Jeepney bus 5.00 2.00

See Nos. 1837, 1840.

Insects — A475

Intl. Peace Year — A476

Perf. 13x13½, 13½x13

1986, Nov. 21
1820 A475 60s Butterfly, beetles 1.00 .40
1821 A476 1p blue & blk 2.00 .60
1822 A475 3p Dragonflies 3.50 2.00
Nos. 1820-1822 (3) 6.50 3.00

Philately Week.

Manila YMCA, 75th Anniv. — A477

Perf. 13x13½

1986, Nov. 28 **Wmk. 391**
1823 A477 2p blue 1.25 .40
1824 A477 3.60p red 3.25 .60

See No. 1839, 1839A. For surcharge see No. 1916.

Philippine Normal College, 85th Anniv. — A478

Various arrangements of college crest and buildings, 1901-1986.

1986, Dec. 12 **Wmk. 389**
1825 A478 60s multi *1.00* .80
1826 A478 3.60p buff, ultra & gldn brn 3.25 1.00

For surcharge see No. 1917.

Christmas A479

No. 1827, Holy family. No. 1828, Mother and child, doves. No. 1829, Child touching mother's face. No. 1830, Adoration of the shepherds. No. 1831, Mother, child signaling peace. No. 1832, Holy family, lamb. No. 1833, Mother, child blessing food.

1986, Dec. 15 ***Perf. 13½x13, 13x13½***
1827 A479 60s multicolored *.50* .30
1828 A479 60s multicolored *.80* .30
1829 A479 60s multicolored *.80* .30
1830 A479 1p multicolored *1.00* .40
1831 A479 1p multicolored *1.00* .40
1832 A479 1p multicolored *1.00* .40
1833 A479 1p multicolored *1.00* .40
Nos. 1827-1833 (7) *6.10* 2.50

Nos. 1827-1829, vert.

No. 1780 Surcharged

Wmk. 391

1987, Jan. 6 **Litho.** ***Perf. 13***
1834 A460 1p on 60s vio 1.00 .25

Types of 1986

Designs: 75s, No. 390, AMERIPEX '86. 1p, Benigno S. Aquino, Jr. 3.25p, Handshake, 74th World Dental Congress. 3.50p, Scales of Justice. 4p, Manila YMCA emblem. 4.75p, Jeepney bus. 5p, General Hospital. 5.50p, Boeing 747, 1980.

Types of 4p
Type I — "4" is taller than "0's."
Type II — "4" is same height as "0's."

1987 **Litho.** ***Perf. 13***
Size: 22x31mm, 31x22mm
1835 A465 75s brt yel grn .75 .25
1836 A468 1p blue .75 .25
1837 A474 3.25p dull grn 2.00 .75
1838 A459 3.50p dark car 2.00 .40
1839 A477 4p blue, type I 3.00 .40
1839A A477 4p blue, type II 6.00 3.00
1840 A474 4.75p dl yel grn 3.00 .50
1841 A472 5p olive bister 3.00 .50
1842 A461 5.50p dk bl gray 3.00 .80
Nos. 1835-1842 (9) *23.50* 6.85

All No. 1839 dated "1-1-87."
Issued: #1839A, 12/17; others, 1/16.

Manila Hotel, 75th Anniv. — A480

Perf. 13x13½

1987, Jan. 30 **Wmk. 389**
1843 A480 1p Hotel, c. 1912 .70 .50
1844 A480 4p Hotel, 1987 2.80 1.00
1845 A480 4.75p Lobby 3.50 1.50
1846 A480 5.50p Foyer 5.00 2.00
Nos. 1843-1846 (4) 12.00 5.00

Intl. Eucharistic Congress, Manila, 50th Anniv. — A481

1987, Feb. 7 ***Perf. 13½x13, 13x13½***
1847 A481 75s Emblem, vert. .60 .50
1848 A481 1p shown 1.00 .50

Pres. Aquino Taking Oath — A482

Text — A483

1987, Mar. 4 ***Perf. 13½x13, 13x13½***
1849 A482 1p multi .60 .50
1850 A483 5.50p bl & deep bis 3.50 1.00

Ratification of the new constitution.
See No. 1905. For surcharge see No. 2005.

Lyceum College and Founder, Jose P. Laurel — A484

1987, May 7 **Litho.** ***Perf. 13x13½***
1851 A484 1p multi .80 .50
1852 A484 2p multi 2.00 1.00

Lyceum of the Philippines, 35th anniv.

Government Service Insurance System — A485

1p, Salary and policy loans. 1.25p, Disability, medicare. 2p, Retirement benefits. 3.50p, Life insurance.

1987, June 1 ***Perf. 13½x13***
1853 A485 1p multi .70 .50
1854 A485 1.25p multi 1.00 .60
1855 A485 2p multi 1.80 .80
1856 A485 3.50p multi 2.50 1.00
Nos. 1853-1856 (4) 6.00 2.90

Davao City, 50th Anniv. — A486

1p, Falconer, woman planting, city seal.

1987, Mar. 16 **Litho.** ***Perf. 13x13½***
1857 A486 1p multicolored 1.00 .50

Salvation Army in the Philippines, 50th Anniv. — A487

1987, June 5 **Photo.** ***Perf. 13½x13***
1858 A487 1p multi 1.40 .50

Natl. League of Women Voters, 50th Anniv. — A488

1987, July 15
1859 A488 1p pink & blue 1.00 .50

A489

#1861, Gen. Vicente Lukban (1860-1916). #1862, Wenceslao Q. Vinzons (1910-1942). #1863, Brig.-gen. Mateo M. Capinpin (1887-1958). #1864, Jesus Balmori (1882-1948).

Perf. 13x13½, 12½ (#1862)

1987 **Litho.** **Wmk. 391**
1861 A489 1p olive grn .60 .25
1862 A489 1p dull greenish blue .70 .25
a. Perf. 12¾ 5.00 1.25
1863 A489 1p dull red brn .70 .25
1864 A489 1p rose red & rose claret .70 .25
Nos. 1861-1864 (4) 2.70 1.00

Issued: #1861, 7/31; #1862, 9/9; #1863, 10/15; #1862a, 11/16; #1864, 12/17.

A490

Nuns (1862-1987), children, Crucifix, Sacred Heart.

Perf. 13½x13

1987, July 22 **Litho.** **Wmk. 389**
1881 A490 1p multi 1.20 .50

Daughters of Charity of St. Vincent de Paul in the Philippines, 125th anniv.

Map of Southeast Asia, Flags of ASEAN Members — A491

1987, Aug. 7 ***Perf. 13x13½***
1882 A491 1p multi 1.70 .60

ASEAN, 20th anniv.

Exports Campaign — A492

1987, Aug. 11 **Wmk. 391** ***Perf. 13***
1883 A492 1p shown .50 .25
1884 A492 2p Worker, gearwheel 1.00 .30

See No. 1904.

Canonization of Lorenzo Ruiz by Pope John Paul II, Oct. 18 — A493

First Filipino saint: 1p, Ruiz, stained glass window showing Crucifixion. 5.50p, Ruiz at prayer, execution in 1637.

Perf. 13½x13

1987, Oct. 10 **Litho.** **Wmk. 389**
1885 A493 1p multi 1.20 .60
1886 A493 5.50p multi 4.80 1.40

Size: 57x57mm

Imperf

1887 A493 8p like 5.50p 7.00 5.50
Nos. 1885-1887 (3) 13.00 7.50

No. 1887 has denomination at LL.

No. 1841 Surcharged

1987, Oct. 12 **Wmk. 391** ***Perf. 13***
1888 A472 4.75p on 5p olive bis 2.30 .70

Order of the Good Shepherd Sisters in Philippines, 65th Anniv. — A494

Perf. 13x13½

1987, Oct. 27 **Wmk. 389**
1889 A494 1p multi 1.80 .75

Natl. Boy Scout Movement, 50th Anniv. — A495

Founders: J. Vargas, M. Camus, J.E.H. Stevenot, A.N. Luz, V. Lim, C. Romulo and G.A. Daza.

1987, Oct. 28 **Litho.** ***Perf. 13x13½***
1890 A495 1p multi 2.00 1.00

Philippine Philatelic Club, 50th Anniv. — A496

1987, Nov. 7 ***Perf. 13x13½***
1891 A496 1p multi 2.00 .75

Order of the Dominicans in the Philippines, 400th Anniv. — A497

Designs: 1p, First missionaries shipwrecked, church and image of the Virgin, vert. 4.75p, J.A. Jeronimo Guerrero, Br., Diego de St. Maria and Letran Dominican College. 5.50p, Pope with Dominican representatives.

Perf. 13½x13, 13x13½

1987, Nov. 11
1892 A497 1p multi .60 .50
1893 A497 4.75p multi 2.40 .70
1894 A497 5.50p multi 3.50 1.50
Nos. 1892-1894 (3) 6.50 2.70

3rd ASEAN Summit Meeting, Dec. 14-15 — A498

1987, Dec. 5 ***Perf. 13x13½***
1895 A498 4p multicolored 3.00 1.25

Christmas 1987 — A499

No. 1896, Postal service. No. 1897, 5-Pointed stars. No. 1898, Procession, church. No. 1899, Gift exchange. No. 1900, Bamboo cannons. No. 1901, Pig, holiday foods. No. 1902, Traditional foods. No. 1903, Serving meal.

1987, Dec. 8 ***Perf. 13½x13***
1896 A499 1p multicolored .90 .50
1897 A499 1p multicolored .90 .50
1898 A499 4p multicolored 3.00 1.00
1899 A499 4.75p multicolored 3.00 1.00
1900 A499 5.50p multicolored 3.00 1.50
1901 A499 8p multicolored 5.00 2.00
1902 A499 9.50p multicolored 6.00 2.50
1903 A499 11p multicolored 7.00 3.00
Nos. 1896-1903 (8) 28.80 12.00

Exports Type of 1987

Design: Worker, gearwheel.

Wmk. 391

1987, Dec. 16 **Litho.** ***Perf. 13***
1904 A492 4.75p lt blue & blk 1.70 .40

Constitution Ratification Type of 1987

1987, Dec. 16 *Perf. 13*
Size: 22x31½mm

1905 A483 5.50p brt yel grn & fawn 2.00 .50

Grand Masonic Lodge of the Philippines, 75th Anniv. — A500

Perf. 13x13½

1987, Dec. 19 **Wmk. 389**

1906 A500 1p multi 2.50 .80
a. Wmk. 372 (II) 17.50 8.50

United Nations Projects — A501

Designs: a, Intl. Fund for Agricultural Development (IFAD). b, Transport and Communications Decade for Asia and the Pacific. c, Intl. Year of Shelter for the Homeless (IYSH). d, World Health Day, 1987.

1987, Dec. 22 **Litho.** *Perf. 13x13½*

1907 Strip of 4 + label *8.00* 6.00
a.-d. A501 1p, any single 1.50 1.25

Label pictures UN emblem. Exists imperf. Value $28.

7th Opening of Congress — A502

Designs: 1p, Official seals of the Senate and Quezon City House of Representatives, gavel, vert. 5.50p, Congress in session.

Perf. 13½x13, 13x13½

1988, Jan. 25 **Wmk. 389**

1908 A502 1p multi 1.00 .50
1909 A502 5.50p multi 4.00 1.25

St. John Bosco (1815-1888), Educator — A503

1988, Jan. 31 *Perf. 13x13½*

1910 A503 1p multi .80 .40
a. Wmk. 372 (II) 1.75 .75
1911 A503 5.50p multi 3.25 1.00
a. Wmk. 372 (II) 10.00 2.75

Buy Philippine Goods — A504

1988, Feb. 1 **Litho.** *Perf. 13½x13*

1912 A504 1p buff, ultra, blk & scar .90 .40
a. Wmk. 372 (II) 1.25 .50

Nos. 1782, 1806, 1813, 1824, 1826 Surcharged

Wmk. 389 (#1914, 1917), 391 (#1913, 1915, 1916)

Perf. 13 (#1782), 13x13½

1988, Feb. 14

1913 A460 3p on 3.60p redsh brn 2.50 .65
1914 A469 3p on 3.60p multi 3.00 .90
1915 A471 3p on 3.60p pale grn, blk & dark ultra 3.50 1.00
1916 A477 3p on 3.60p red 3.00 .65
1917 A478 3p on 3.60p buff, ultra & golden brn 4.00 1.25
Nos. 1913-1917 (5) 16.00 4.45

Use Zip Codes — A505

1988, Feb. 25 **Wmk. 391** *Perf. 13*

1918 A505 60s multi .35 .25
1919 A505 1p multi .55 .25

Insects That Prey on Other Insects — A506

1p, Vesbius purpureus. 5.50p, Campsomeris aurulenta.

1988, Mar. 11 *Perf. 13*

1920 A506 1p multi .60 .25
1921 A506 5.50p multi 3.50 .75

Solar Eclipse 1988 — A507

Perf. 13x13½

1988, Mar. 18 **Wmk. 389**

1922 A507 1p multi 1.00 .50
a. Wmk. 372 (II) 1.40 .45
1923 A507 5.50p multi 4.00 1.00
a. Wmk. 372 (II) 5.00 1.50

Toribio M. Teodoro (1887-1965), Shoe Manufacturer A508

Wmk. 391

1988, Apr. 27 **Litho.** *Perf. 13*

1924 A508 1p multicolored .50 .25
1925 A508 1.20p multicolored 1.00 .25

A509 A509a

College of the Holy Spirit, 75th anniv.: 1p, Emblem and motto "Truth in Love." 4p, Arnold Janssen, founder, and Sr. Edelwina, director 1920-1947.

Wmk. 372 (II)

1988, May 22 *Perf. 13½x13*

1926 A509 1p blk, mar & gold .50 .35
a. Miniature sheet of 15 17.50 17.50
1927 A509a 4p blk, ol grn & mar 2.25 1.00
a. Miniature sheet of 15 70.00 70.00

Nos. 1926-1927 were issued in sheets of 50.

A510

Wmk. 372 (II)

1988, June 4 **Litho.** *Perf. 13½x13*

1928 A510 4p dark ultra, brt blue & blk 3.00 .75
a. Miniature sheet of 15 100.00 100.00

Intl. Conf. of Newly Restored Democracies. No. 1928 was issued in sheets of 50. They were also issued in a miniature sheet of 15.

A511

Juan Luna and Felix Hidalgo.

1988, June 15 **Wmk. 391** *Perf. 13*

1929 A511 1p multi .40 .25
1930 A511 5.50p multi 2.20 .55

First Natl. Juan Luna and Felix Resurreccion Hidalgo Commemorative Exhibition, June 15-Aug. 15. Artists Luna and Hidalgo won medals at the 1884 Madrid Fine Arts Exhibition.

A512

Wmk. 372 (II)

1988, June 22 **Litho.** *Perf. 13½x13*

1931 A512 1p multi .50 .25
a. Miniature sheet of 15 17.50 17.50
1932 A512 5.50p multi 3.00 .75
a. Miniature sheet of 15 100.00 100.00

Natl. Irrigation Administration, 25th anniv. Nos. 1931-1932 were issued in sheets of 50. They were also issued in miniature sheets of 15.

Natl. Olympic Committee Emblem and Sporting Events — A513

Designs: 1p, Scuba diving, Siquijor Is. 1.20p, Big game fishing, Aparri, Cagayan Province. 4p, Yachting, Manila Central. 5.50p, Climbing Mt. Apo. 8p, Golf, Cebu, Cebu Is. 11p, Cycling through Marawi, Mindanao Is.

1988, July 11 *Perf. 13x13½*

1933 A513 1p multi .50 .35
1934 A513 1.20p multi .70 .45
1935 A513 4p multi 2.30 .70
1936 A513 5.50p multi 3.00 1.20
1937 A513 8p multi 4.00 1.75
1938 A513 11p multi 4.50 2.00
Nos. 1933-1938 (6) *15.00* 6.45

Exist imperf. 4p, 8p, 1p and 5.50p also exist in strips of 4 plus center label, perf and imperf, picturing torch and inscribed "Philippine Olympic Week, May 1-7, 1988."

Nos. 1797, 1801, 1810 and 1817 Surcharged with 2 Bars and New Value in Black or Gold (#1942)

1988, Aug. 1 **As Before**

1939 A466 1.90p on 2.40p #1797 2.00 .60
1940 A467 1.90p on 2.40p #1801 2.50 1.25
1941 A470 1.90p on 2.40p #1810 2.00 .60
1942 A473 1.90p on 2.40p #1817 2.50 .60
Nos. 1939-1942 (4) 9.00 3.05

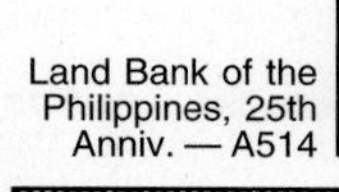

Land Bank of the Philippines, 25th Anniv. — A514

Philippine Intl. Commercial Bank, 50th Anniv. — A515

Wmk. 372 (II)

1988, Aug. 8 **Litho.** *Perf. 13x13½*

1943 A514 1p shown .50 .40
a. Miniature sheet of 6 10.00 10.00
1944 A515 1p shown .50 .40
a. Miniature sheet of 6 10.00 10.00
1945 A514 5.50p like No. 1943 3.00 .80
a. Miniature sheet of 6 35.00 35.00
1946 A515 5.50p like No. 1944 3.00 .80
a. Miniature sheet of 6 35.00 35.00
Nos. 1943-1946 (4) 7.00 2.40

Nos. 1943-1944 and 1945-1946 exist in se-tenant pairs from center rows of the sheet. Value, $2.50 and $12.50, respectively.

Joint uncut sheets of 12 with gutter in between the two miniature sheets of the same denomination exist. Nos. 1944a and 1945a, value, $25. Nos. 1946a and 1947a, value, $85.

Profile of Francisco Balagtas Baltasar (b. 1788), Tagalog Language Poet, Author — A516

Wmk. 391

1988, Aug. 8 **Litho.** *Perf. 13*

1947 A516 1p Facing right .35 .25
1948 A516 1p Facing left .35 .25
a. Pair, #1947-1948 1.25 1.00

Quezon Institute, 50th Anniv. — A517

Wmk. 372 (II)

1988, Aug. 18 **Litho.** *Perf. 13x13½*

1949 A517 1p multi .50 .25
a. Miniature sheet of 15 17.50 17.50
1950 A517 5.50p multi 3.50 .65
a. Minature sheet of 15 175.00 175.00

Philippine Tuberculosis Soc. Nos. 1949-1950 were printed in sheets of 50 and were also issued in minature sheets of 15.

Mushrooms — A518

1988, Sept. 13 **Wmk. 391** *Perf. 13*

1951 A518 60s Brown .40 .25
1952 A518 1p Rat's ear fungus .60 .25
1953 A518 2p Abalone 1.60 .50
1954 A518 4p Straw 2.20 .75
Nos. 1951-1954 (4) 4.80 1.75

1988 Summer Olympics, Seoul — A519

1p, Women's archery. 1.20p, Women's tennis. 4p, Boxing. 5.50p, Women's running. 8p, Swimming. 11p, Cycling.

Wmk. 372 (II)

1988, Sept. 19 *Perf. 13½x13*

1955 A519 1p multi .50 .45
1956 A519 1.20p multi .70 .50
1957 A519 4p multi 2.00 .85
1958 A519 5.50p multi 2.50 1.20
1959 A519 8p multi 3.50 2.00
1960 A519 11p multi 4.50 2.50
Nos. 1955-1960 (6) 13.70 7.50

Souvenir Sheet

Imperf

1961 Sheet of 4 15.00 12.00
a. A519 5.50p Weight lifting 3.25 2.75
b. A519 5.50p Basketball, horiz. 3.25 2.75
c. A519 5.50p Judo 3.25 2.75
d. A519 5.50p Shooting, horiz. 3.25 2.75

Nos. 1955-1960 exist imperf. Value $25.

Department of Justice, Cent. — A520

1988, Sept. 26 *Perf. 13x13½*
1962 A520 1p multi .70 .30
a. Miniature sheet of 6 10.00 10.00

No. 1962 was normally issued in sheets of 50 stamps.

Intl. Red Cross and Red Crescent Organizations, 125th Annivs. — A521

1988, Sept. 30 *Perf. 13½x13*
1963 A521 1p multi .50 .25
a. Miniature sheet of 6 10.00 10.00
1964 A521 5.50p multi 3.00 .75
a. Miniature sheet of 6 50.00 30.00

No. 1963-1964 were normally issued in sheets of 50.

Christian Children's Fund, 50th Anniv. — A522

1988, Oct. 6
1965 A522 1p multi .75 .30
a. Miniature sheet of 6 12.00 12.00

No. 1965 normally issued in sheets of 50.

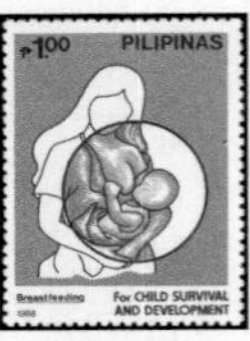

UN Campaigns — A523

Designs: a, Breast-feeding. b, Growth monitoring. c, Immunization. d, Oral rehydration. e, Oral rehydration therapy. f, Youth on crutches.

1988, Oct. 24 Litho. *Perf. 13½x13*
1966 Strip of 5 *4.00* 4.00
a.-e. A523 1p any single .60 .40
f. Miniature sheet of 15 25.00 25.00

Child Survival Campaign (Nos. 1966a-1966d); Decade for Disabled Persons (No. 1966e).

No. 1966 normally issued in sheets of 50.

Bacolod City Charter, 50th Anniv. — A524

1988, Oct. 19 Litho. *Perf. 13x13½*
1967 A524 1p multi .80 .35
a. Miniature sheet of 6 12.00 12.00

No. 1967 normally issued in sheets of 50.

UST Graduate School, 50th Anniv. — A525

1988, Dec. 20 Litho. *Perf. 13½x13*
1968 A525 1p multi .75 .30
a. Miniature sheet of 6 12.00 12.00

No. 1968 was normally issued in sheets of 50.

Dona Aurora Aragon Quezon (b. 1888) — A526

1988, Nov. 7 Wmk. 391 *Perf. 13*
1969 A526 1p multi .40 .25
1970 A526 5.50p multi 2.30 .40

Malate Church, 400th Anniv. A527

a, Church, 1776. b, Statue & anniv. emblem. c, Church, 1880. d, Church, 1988. Continuous design.

1988, Dec. 16 **Wmk. 391**
1971 A527 Block of 4 2.00 2.00
a.-d. 1p any single .40 .30

UN Declaration of Human Rights, 40th Anniv. — A528

No. 1973, Commission on human rights.

Wmk. 372 (II)

1988, Dec. 9 *Perf. 13½x13*
1972 A528 1p shown .65 .35
1973 A528 1p multicolored .65 .35
a. Miniature sheet of 12, 6 #1972 and 6 #1973 with gutter between 22.00 22.00
b. Pair, Nos. 1972-1973 from #1973a 5.00 5.00
c. Se-tenant pair from sheet of 50 2.50 2.50

Long Distance Telephone Company — A529

1p, Communications tower.

1988, Nov. 28
1974 A529 1p multi .70 .30
a. Miniature sheet of 6 9.00 9.00

No. 1974 normally issued in sheets of 50.

Philatelic Week, Nov. 24-30 A530

Emblem and: a, Post Office. b, Stamp counter. c, Framed stamp exhibits, four people. d, Exhibits, 8 people. Has a continuous design.

1988, Nov. 24 Wmk. 391 *Perf. 13*
1975 A530 Block of 4 4.00 3.00
a.-d. 1p any single .70 .50
e. As "a," dated "1938" (error) 8.00 6.50

Christmas — A531

Designs: 75s, Handshake, peave dove, vert. 1p, Children making ornaments. 2p, Boy carrying decoration. 3.50p, Tree, vert. 4.75p, Candle, vert. 5.50p, Man, star, heart.

1988, Dec. 2
1976 A531 75s multi .60 .30
1977 A531 1p multi .60 .25
1978 A531 2p multi 1.20 .35
1979 A531 3.50p multi 1.80 .50
1980 A531 4.75p multi 2.40 .60
1981 A531 5.50p multi 2.70 .70
Nos. 1976-1981 (6) 9.30 2.70

Gen. Santos City, 50th Anniv. — A532

Wmk. 372 (II)

1989, Feb, 27 Litho. *Perf. 13x13½*
1982 A532 1p multi .80 .30
a. Miniature sheet of 6 10.00 10.00

No. 1982 normally issued in sheets of 50.

Guerrilla Fighters A533

Emblem and: No. 1983, Miguel Z. Ver (1918-42). No. 1984, Eleuterio L. Adevoso (1922-75). Printed in continuous design.

1989, Feb. 18 **Wmk. 391**
1983 1p multi .50 .25
1984 1p multi .50 .25
a. A533 Pair, #1983-1984 1.50 .75

Oblates of Mary Immaculate, 50th Anniv. — A534

Wmk. 372 (II)

1989, Feb. 17 *Perf. 13½x13*
1985 A534 1p multicolored .60 .30
a. Miniature sheet of 6 14.00 14.00

No. 1985 normally issued in sheets of 50.

Fiesta Islands '89 — A535

No. 1986, Turumba. No. 1987, Pahiyas. No. 1988, Pagoda Sa Wawa. No. 1989, Masskara. No. 1990, Independence Day. No. 1990A, like #1995. No. 1991, Sinulog. No. 1992, Cagayan de Oro. No. 1993, Grand Canao. No. 1994, Lenten festival. No. 1995, Penafrancia. No. 1996, Fireworks. No. 1997, Iloilo Paraw regatta.

Perf. 13 (Nos. 1991, 1994, 1997), 13½x14

1989-90 Litho. Wmk. 391
1986 A535 60s multicolored .35 .25
1987 A535 75s multicolored .35 .25
1988 A535 1p multicolored .35 .25
1989 A535 1p multicolored .50 .25
1990 A535 3.50p multicolored 1.20 .35
1990A A535 4p multicolored 2.50 .40
1991 A535 4.75p multicolored 1.30 .35
1992 A535 4.75p multicolored 1.30 .35
1993 A535 4.75p multicolored 1.30 .35
1994 A535 5.50p multicolored 1.30 .50
1995 A535 5.50p multicolored 1.65 .55
1996 A535 5.50p multicolored 1.85 .60
1997 A535 6.25p multicolored 2.30 .90
Nos. 1986-1997 (13) 16.25 5.35

Issued: No. 1991, 1994, 6.25p, 3/1/89; 60s, 75s, 3.50p, 6/28/89; No. 1988, 1992, 1995, 9/1/89; No. 1989, 1993, 1996, 12/4/89; 4p, 8/6/90.

Great Filipinos — A536

Men and women: a, Don Tomas B. Mapua (1888-), educator. b, Camilo O. Osias (1889-), educator. c, Dr. Olivia D. Salamanca (1889-), physician. d, Dr. Francisco S. Santiago (1889-), composer. e, Leandro H. Fernandez (1889-), educator.

Wmk. 372 (II)

1989, May 18 Litho. *Perf. 14x13½*
1998 Strip of 5 4.00 3.00
a.-e. A536 1p any single .50 .30

See Nos. 2022, 2089, 2151, 2240, 2307, 2360, 2414, 2486, 2536.

26th World Congress of the Intl. Federation of Landscape Architects — A537

Designs: a, Adventure Pool. b, Paco Park. c, Beautification of Malacanang area streets. d, Erosion control at an upland farm.

1989, May 31 **Wmk. 391**
1999 A537 Block of 4 2.00 1.80
a.-d. 1p any single .40 .30

Printed in continuous design.

French Revolution, Bicent. — A538

1989, July 1 Wmk. 372 (II) *Perf. 14*
2000 A538 1p multicolored .50 .30
a. Miniature sheet of 6 10.00 10.00
2001 A538 5.50p multicolored 2.50 .60
a. Miniature sheet of 6 40.00 40.00

Nos. 2000-2001 normally issued in sheets of 50.

Supreme Court — A539

1989, June 11 **Wmk. 372 (II)**
2002 A539 1p multicolored .65 .30
a. Miniature sheet of 6 10.00 10.00

No. 2002 normally issued in sheets of 50.

Natl. Science and Technology Week — A540

No. 2003, GNP chart. No. 2004, Science High School emblem.

1989, July 14
2003 1p multicolored .40 .30
2004 1p multicolored .40 .30
a. A540 Pair, #2003-2004 1.00 .70
b. Miniature sheet of 6, #2003-2004 7.50 7.50

No. 2003-2004 normally issued in sheets of 50.

No. 1905 Surcharged

Wmk. 391

1989, Aug. 21 Litho. *Perf. 13*
2005 A483 4.75p on 5.50p 1.50 .40

Philippine Environment Month A542

No. 2006, Palawan peacock pheasant. No. 2007, Palawan bear cat.

Wmk. 391

1989, June 5 Litho. *Perf. 14*
2006 1p multicolored .80 .30
2007 1p multicolored .80 .30
a. A542 Pair, #2006-2007 2.50 1.50

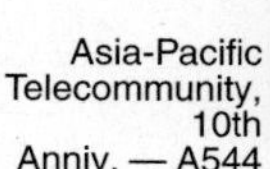

Asia-Pacific Telecommunity, 10th Anniv. — A544

Wmk. 372 (II)

1989, Oct. 30 Litho. *Perf. 14*
2008 A544 1p multicolored .75 .30
a. Miniature sheet of 6 10.00 10.00

No. 2008 normally issued in sheets of 50.

Dept. of Natl. Defense, 50th Anniv. — A545

1989, Oct. 23
2009 A545 1p multicolored .75 .30
a. Miniature sheet of 6 10.00 10.00

No. 2009 normally issued in sheets of 50.

Intl. Maritime Organization A546

1989, Nov. 13 *Perf. 14*
2010 A546 1p multicolored .80 .30
a. Miniature sheet of 6 12.00 12.00

No. 2010 normally issued in sheets of 50.

World Stamp Expo '89 — A546a

1989, Nov. 17 Litho. *Perf. 14*
2010A A546a 1p #1, Y1 .70 *.40*
d. Miniature sheet of 6 12.00 12.00
2010B A546a 4p #219, 398 3.00 *1.00*
e. Miniature sheet of 6 35.00 35.00
2010C A546a 5.50p #N1, 500 4.00 *1.50*
f. Miniature sheet of 6 65.00 65.00
Nos. 2010A-2010C (3) 7.70 *2.90*

Nos. 2010A-2010C withdrawn from sale week of release, but placed on sale again a few weeks later.

Nos. 2010A-2010C normally issued in sheets of 50.

Teaching Philately in the Classroom, Close-up of Youth Collectors — A547

1989, Nov. 20 *Perf. 14x13½*
2011 A547 1p shown .60 .30
2012 A547 1p Class, diff. .60 .30

Christmas — A548

60s, Annunciation. 75s, Visitation. 1p, Journey to Bethlehem. 2p, Search for the inn. 4p, Appearance of the star. 4.75p, Birth of Jesus Christ.

1989, Nov. 10 *Perf. 13½x14*
2013 A548 60s multi .40 .25
2014 A548 75s multi .60 .25
2015 A548 1p multi .60 .25
2016 A548 2p multi 1.20 .40
2017 A548 4p multi 2.00 .60
2018 A548 4.75p multi 2.50 1.00
Nos. 2013-2018 (6) 7.30 2.75

First-day covers are canceled Nov. 8.

11th World Cardiology Congress — A549

Wmk. 391

1990, Feb. 12 Photo. *Perf. 14*
2019 A549 5.50p black, dark red & deep blue 1.50 .40

Beer Production, Cent. — A550

1990, Apr. 16
2020 A550 1p multicolored .40 .30
2021 A550 5.50p multicolored 1.60 .50

Great Filipinos Type of 1989

Designs: a, Claro M. Recto (1890-1960), politician. b, Manuel H. Bernabe. c, Guillermo E. Tolentino. d, Elpidio R. Quirino (1890-1956), politician. e, Bienvenido Ma. Gonzalez.

Wmk. 372 (II)

1990, June 1 Litho. *Perf. 14x13½*
2022 Strip of 5, #a.-e. 4.00 3.00

1990 Census A551

Wmk. 391

1990, Apr. 30 Photo. *Perf. 14*

Color of Buildings

2023 1p light blue .50 .30
2024 1p peach .50 .30
a. A551 Pair, #2023-2024 1.25 1.00

Legion of Mary, 50th Anniv. — A552

1990, July 21 Photo. *Perf. 14*
2025 A552 1p multicolored .75 .30

Girl Scouts of the Philippines, 50th Anniv. — A553

1990, May 21
2026 A553 1p yellow & multi .50 .30
2027 A553 1.20p lt lilac & multi .60 .35

Asian Pacific Postal Training Center, 20th Anniv. — A554

Wmk. 391

1990, Sept. 10 Photo. *Perf. 14*
2028 A554 1p red & multi .50 .30
2029 A554 4p blue & multi 1.50 .50

Natl. Catechetical Year — A555

1990, Sept. 28
2030 A555 1p blk & multi .50 .30
2031 A555 3.50p grn & multi 1.30 .40

Intl. Literacy Year — A556

1990, Oct. 24 Photo. *Perf. 14*
2032 A556 1p blk, org & grn .50 .30
2033 A556 5.50p blk, yel & grn 2.00 .50

UN Development Program, 40th Anniv. — A557

1990, Oct. 24
2034 A557 1p yel & multi .50 .30
2035 A557 5.50p orange & multi 2.00 .50

Flowers — A558

1990 Photo. Wmk. 391 *Perf. 14*
2036 A558 1p Waling waling 1.20 .50
2037 A558 4p Sampaguita 2.50 .80

29th Orient and Southeast Asian Lions forum.

Issued: 1p, Oct. 3; 4p, Oct. 18.

A559

Christmas — A560

Drawings of the Christmas star: a, Yellow star, pink beading. b, Yellow star, white beading. c, Green, blue, yellow and orange star. d, Red star, white outlines.

1990, Dec. 3
2038 A559 Strip of 4 3.00 2.50
a.-d. 1p any single .60 .40
2039 A560 5.50p multicolored 4.00 1.50

Blind Safety Day — A561

1990, Dec. 7 Photo. *Perf. 14*
2040 A561 1p bl, blk & yel .75 .40

Publication of Rizal's "Philippines After 100 Years," Cent. — A562

1990, Dec.17
2041 A562 1p multicolored .75 .40

Philatelic Week — A563

Paintings: 1p, Family by F. Amorsolo. 4.75p, The Builders by V. Edades. 5.50p, Laughter by A. Magsaysay-Ho.

1990, Nov. 16
2042 A563 1p multicolored .50 .30
2043 A563 4.75p multi, vert. 1.50 .40
2044 A563 5.50p multi, vert. 1.75 .50
Nos. 2042-2044 (3) 3.75 1.20

A564

1991, Jan. 30
2045 A564 1p multicolored .60 .30

2nd Plenary Council of the Philippines.

A565

1991, Mar. 15 Litho. *Perf. 14*
2046 A565 1p multicolored .50 .30
2047 A565 5.50p multicolored 1.00 .50

Philippine Airlines, 50th anniv. No. 2047 is airmail.

Flowers — A566

Flowers: 1p, 2p, Plumeria. 4p, 6p, Ixora. 4.75p, 7p, Bougainvillea. 5.50p, 8p, Hibiscus.

1991 Photo. *Perf. 14x13½*

"1991" Below Design

2048 A566 60s Gardenia .35 .25
2049 A566 75s Allamanda *.35* .25
2050 A566 1p yellow *.40* .25
2051 A566 1p red *.40* .25
2052 A566 1p salmon *.40* .25
2053 A566 1p white *.40* .25
a. Block of 4, #2050-2053 *2.00* 2.00
2054 A566 1.20p Nerium *.70* .25
2055 A566 1.50p like #2048 *.85* .30
2056 A566 2p yellow *.90* .30
2057 A566 2p red *.90* .30
2058 A566 2p rose & yel *.90* .30
2059 A566 2p white *.90* .30
a. Block of 4, #2056-2059 *4.25* 4.25
2060 A566 3p like #2054 *1.40* .35
2061 A566 3.25p Cananga *1.50* .45
2062 A566 4p dull rose *1.50* .50
2063 A566 4p pale yellow *1.50* .50
2064 A566 4p orange yel *1.50* .50
2065 A566 4p scarlet *1.50* .50
a. Block of 4, #2062-2065 *9.00* 9.00
2066 A566 4.75p vermilion *2.00* .70
2067 A566 4.75p brt rose lil *2.00* .70
2068 A566 4.75p white *2.00* .70
2069 A566 4.75p lilac rose *2.00* .70
a. Block of 4, #2066-2069 *10.00* 10.00
2070 A566 5p Canna *3.00* .80
2071 A566 5p like #2061 *2.50* .80
2072 A566 5.50p red *2.00* .85
2073 A566 5.50p yellow *2.00* .85
2074 A566 5.50p white *2.00* .85
2075 A566 5.50p pink *2.00* .85
a. Block of 4, #2072-2075 *12.50* 12.50
2076 A566 6p dull rose *2.75* 1.00
2077 A566 6p pale yellow *2.75* 1.00

2078 A566 6p orange yel *2.75* 1.00
2079 A566 6p scarlet *2.75* 1.00
a. Block of 4, #2076-2079 *13.00* 13.00
2080 A566 7p vermilion *3.00* 1.10
2081 A566 7p brt rose lil *3.00* 1.10
2082 A566 7p white *3.00* 1.10
2083 A566 7p dp lil rose *3.00* 1.10
a. Block of 4, #2080-2083 *15.00* 15.00
2084 A566 8p red *3.50* 1.25
2085 A566 8p yellow *3.50* 1.25
2086 A566 8p white *3.50* 1.25
2087 A566 8p deep pink *3.50* 1.25
a. Block of 4, #2084-2087 *16.50* 16.50
2088 A566 10p like #2070 *5.00* *2.00*
Nos. 2048-2088 (41) *79.85* 29.25

Issued: Nos. 2053a, 2075a, 4/1/91. Nos. 2048, 2049, 2061, 4/11. Nos. 2054, 2065a, 2069a, 2070, 6/7. Nos. 2059a, 2079a, 2083a, 2087a, 12/1. Nos. 2055, 2060, 2071, 2088, 12/13.

1992-93 "1992" Below Design

2048a A566 60s Gardenia 1.50 .50
2050a A566 1p yellow *1.50* .50
2051a A566 1p red *1.50* .50
2052a A566 1p salmon *1.50* .50
2053c A566 1p white *1.50* .50
d. Block of 4, #2050a-2052a, 2053c *8.50* 8.50
2053B A566 1p like #2049 *.75* .35
2055a A566 1.50p like #2048 *4.00* .60
2056a A566 2p yellow *2.00* .45
2057a A566 2p red *2.00* .45
2058a A566 2p rose & yel *2.00* .45
2059b A566 2p white *2.00* .45
c. Block of 4, , #2056a-2058a, 2059b *11.50* 11.50
2060a A566 3p like #2054 *2.00* .80
2071a A566 5p like #2061 *20.00* 2.00
2076a A566 6p dull rose *5.00* 2.50
2077a A566 6p pale yellow *5.00* 2.50
2078a A566 6p orange yel *5.00* 2.50
2079b A566 6p scarlet *5.00* 2.50
c. Block of 4, #2076a-2078a, 2079b *40.00* 40.00
2080a A566 7p vermilion *8.50* 4.00
2081a A566 7p brt rose lil *8.50* 4.00
2082a A566 7p white *8.50* 4.00
2083b A566 7p dp lil rose *8.50* 4.00
c. Block of 4, #2080a-2082a, 2083b *50.00* 50.00
2084a A566 8p red *8.50* 4.00
2085a A566 8p yellow *8.50* 4.00
2086a A566 8p white *8.50* 4.00
2087b A566 8p deep pink *8.50* 4.00
c. Block of 4, #2084a-2086a, 2087b *50.00* 50.00
2088a A566 10p like #2070 *13.50* *3.00*
Nos. 2048a-2088a (26) *143.75* 53.05

Issued: 2059c, 1/24/92. 2053d, 2060a, 2/10. #2079c, 2/12. No. 2083c, 2/27. No. 2048a, 3/4. No. 2071a, 3/24. No. 2087c, 3/25. No. 2088a, 9/22. No. 2053B, 1/23/93.

No. 2053B, although issued in 1993, is inscribed "1992."

Great Filipinos Type of 1989

Designs: a, Jorge B. Vargas (1890-1980). b, Ricardo M. Paras (1891-1984). c, Jose P. Laurel (1891-1959), politician. d, Vicente Fabella (1891-1959). e, Maximo M. Kalaw (1891-1954).

1991, June 3 Litho. *Perf. 14x13½*
2089 A536 1p Strip of 5, #a.-e. 4.00 3.00

12th Asia-Pacific Boy Scout Jamboree A567

1p, Square knot. 4p, Sheepshank knot. 4.75p, Figure 8 knot.

1991, Apr. 22 *Perf. 14x13½*
2090 A567 1p multicolored .50 .30
2091 A567 4p multicolored 1.25 .40
2092 A567 4.75p multicolored 1.50 .50
a. Souv. sheet of 3, #2090-2092, imperf. 6.00 6.00
Nos. 2090-2092 (3) 3.25 1.20

No. 2092a sold for 16.50p and has simulated perfs.

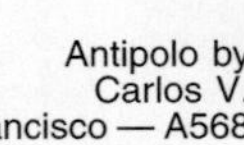

Antipolo by Carlos V. Francisco — A568

1991, June 23 Litho. *Perf. 14*
Granite Paper
2093 A568 1p multicolored .80 .30

Pithecophaga Jefferyi — A569

1p, Head. 4.75p, Perched on limb. 5.50p, In flight. 8p, Feeding young.

1991, July 31 Photo.
2094 A569 1p multi *1.00* .40
2095 A569 4.75p multi *2.50* .60
2096 A569 5.50p multi *3.50* 1.00
2097 A569 8p multi *5.00* 2.00
Nos. 2094-2097 (4) *12.00* 4.00

World Wildlife Fund.

Philippine Bar Association, Cent. — A570

Wmk. 391
1991, Aug. 20 Photo. *Perf. 14*
2098 A570 1p multicolored .60 .30

A571

1991, Aug. 29
2099 A571 1p multicolored .75 .30

Size: 82x88mm
Imperf
2100 A571 16p like #2099 8.00 6.00

Induction of Filipinos into USAFFE (US Armed Forces in the Far East), 50th Anniv. For overprint see No. 2193.

A572

Independence Movement, cent.: a, Basil at graveside. b, Simon carrying lantern. c, Father Florentino, treasure chest. d, Sister Juli with rosary.

1991, Sept. 18
2101 A572 1p Block of 4, #a.-d. 4.00 4.00

A573

Wmk. 391
1991, Oct. 15 Photo. *Perf. 14*
2102 A573 1p multicolored .65 .30

Size: 60x60mm
Imperf
2103 A573 16p multicolored 6.00 5.00

St. John of the Cross, 400th death anniv.

United Nations Agencies — A574

Designs: 1p, UNICEF, children. 4p, High Commissioner for Refugees, hands supporting boat people. 5.50p, Postal Administration, 40th anniv., UN #29, #C3.

1991, Oct. 24 *Perf. 14*
2104 A574 1p multicolored .35 .30
2105 A574 4p multicolored 1.00 .30
2106 A574 5.50p multicolored 1.50 .60
Nos. 2104-2106 (3) 2.85 1.20

Philatelic Week — A575

Paintings: 2p, Bayanihan by Carlos Francisco. 7p, Sari-sari Vendor by Mauro Malang Santos. 8p, Give Us This Day by Vicente Manansala.

1991, Nov. 20
2107 A575 2p multicolored .50 .30
2108 A575 7p multicolored 2.00 .50
2109 A575 8p multicolored 2.50 .70
Nos. 2107-2109 (3) 5.00 1.50

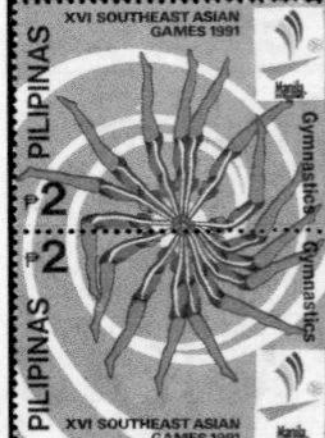

16th Southeast Asian Games, Manila — A576

#2110, Gymnastics, games emblem at UR. #2111, Gymnastics, games emblem at LR. #2112, Martial arts, games emblem at LL, vert. #2113, Martial arts, games emblem at LR, vert.

Wmk. 391
1991, Nov. 22 Photo. *Perf. 14*
2110 2p multicolored .40 .35
2111 2p multicolored .40 .35
a. A576 Pair, #2110-2111 1.50 1.00
2112 6p multicolored 1.00 .50
2113 6p multicolored 1.00 .50
a. A576 Pair, #2112-2113 3.00 2.00
b. Souv. sheet of 2, #2112-2113, imperf. 4.50 *3.50*
c. Souv. sheet of 4, #2110-2113 5.50 *4.75*
Nos. 2110-2113 (4) 2.80 1.70

No. 2113b has simulated perforations.

No. 1585 Surcharged in Red
Souvenir Sheet

1991, Nov. 27 Wmk. 372 *Imperf.*
2114 A385 4p on 3.20p 3.50 *3.50*

First Philippine Philatelic Convention.

Children's Christmas Paintings — A577

1991, Dec. 4 Wmk. 391 *Perf. 14*
2115 A577 2p shown .60 .30
2116 A577 6p Wrapped gift 2.00 .50
2117 A577 7p Santa, tree 2.40 .70
2118 A577 8p Tree, star 3.00 1.00
Nos. 2115-2118 (4) 8.00 2.50

Insignias of Military Groups Inducted into USAFFE A578

White background: No. 2119a, 1st Regular Div. b, 2nd Regular Div. c, 11th Div. d, 21st Div. e, 31st Div. f, 41st Div. g, 51st Div. h, 61st Div. i, 71st Div. j, 81st Div. k, 91st Div. l, 101st Div. m, Bataan Force. n, Philippine Div. o, Philippine Army Air Corps. p, Offshore Patrol.

Nos. 2120a-2120p, like #2119a-2119p with yellow background.

Perf. 14x13½
1991, Dec. 8 Photo. Wmk. 391
2119 A578 2p Block of 16, #a.-p. 16.50 *16.50*
2120 A578 2p Block of 16, #a.-p. 16.50 *16.50*
q. Block of 32, #2119-2120 *50.00* *50.00*

Induction of Filipinos into USAFFE, 50th anniv.

Nos. 2119-2120 were printed in sheets of 200 containing 5 #2120q plus five blocks of 8.

Basketball, Cent. — A579

Designs: 2p, PBA Games, vert. 6p, Map, player dribbling. 7p, Early players. 8p, Men shooting basketball, vert. 16p, Tip-off.

Wmk. 391
1991, Dec. 19 Litho. *Perf. 14*
2121 A579 2p multicolored .70 .30
2122 A579 6p multicolored 1.80 .50
2123 A579 7p multicolored 2.50 .80
2124 A579 8p multicolored 3.00 1.20
a. Souv. sheet of 4, #2121-2124 8.50 7.25
Nos. 2121-2124 (4) 8.00 2.80

Souvenir Sheet
Imperf
2125 A579 16p multicolored 6.50 6.50

No. 2125 has simulated perforations.

New Year 1992, Year of the Monkey — A580

Wmk. 391
1991, Dec. 27 Litho. *Perf. 14*
2126 A580 2p violet & multi *1.50* .40
2127 A580 6p green & multi *3.50* 1.00

See Nos. 2459a, 2460a.

Services and Products — A581

Wmk. 391
1992, Jan. 15 Litho. *Perf. 14*
2128 A581 2p Mailing center .50 .30
2129 A581 6p Housing project 1.25 .40
2130 A581 7p Livestock 1.75 .65
2131 A581 8p Handicraft 2.00 1.00
Nos. 2128-2131 (4) 5.50 2.35

Medicinal Plants — A582

2p, Curcuma longa. 6p, Centella asiatica. 7p, Cassia alata. 8p, Ervatamia pandacaqui.

Wmk. 391
1992, Feb. 7 Litho. *Perf. 14*
2132 A582 2p multi .80 .30
2133 A582 6p multi 1.60 .50
2134 A582 7p multi 2.00 .60
2135 A582 8p multi 2.80 .80
Nos. 2132-2135 (4) 7.20 2.20

Love — A583

"I Love You" in English on Nos. 2137a-2140a, in Filipino on Nos. 2137b-2140b with designs: No. 2137, Letters, map. No. 2138, Heart, doves. No. 2139, Bouquet of flowers. No. 2140, Map, Cupid with bow and arrow.

Wmk. 391

1992, Feb. 10 Photo. *Perf. 14*
2137 A583 2p Pair, #a.-b. 1.00 1.00
2138 A583 6p Pair, #a.-b. 3.00 3.00
2139 A583 7p Pair, #a.-b. 4.00 4.00
2140 A583 8p Pair, #a.-b. 8.50 8.50
Nos. 2137-2140 (4) 16.50 16.50

A584

Wmk. 391

1992, Apr. 12 Litho. *Perf. 14*
2141 A584 2p blue & multi .50 .30
2142 A584 8p red vio & multi 2.30 .60

Our Lady of Sorrows of Porta Vaga, 400th anniv.

A585

Expo '92, Seville: 2p, Man and woman celebrating. 8p, Philippine discovery scenes. 16p, Pavilion, horiz.

1992, Mar. 27
2143 A585 2p multicolored .50 .30
2144 A585 8p multicolored 2.30 .70

Souvenir Sheet
Imperf
2145 A585 16p multicolored 7.50 6.00

Department of Agriculture, 75th Anniv. — A586

a, Man planting seed. b, Fish trap. c, Pigs.

1992, May 4
2146 A586 2p Strip of 3, #a.-c. 2.40 2.00

Manila Jockey Club, 125th Anniv. — A588

Wmk. 391

1992, May 14 Litho. *Perf. 14*
2149 A588 2p multicolored 1.00 .40

Souvenir Sheet
Imperf
2150 A588 8p multicolored 4.00 *3.00*

No. 2150 has simulated perfs.

Great Filipinos Type of 1989

Designs: a, Pres. Manuel A. Roxas (1892-1948). b, Justice Natividad Almeda-Lopez (1892-1977). c, Justice Roman A. Ozaeta (b. 1892). d, Engracia Cruz-Reyes (1892-1975). e, Fernando Amorsolo (1892-1972).

Perf. 14x13½

1992, June 1 Wmk. 391
2151 A536 2p Strip of 5, #a.-e. 4.00 3.00

30th Chess Olympiad, Manila — A589

#2154: a, like #2152. b, like #2153.

1992, June 7 *Perf. 14*
2152 A589 2p No. 1352 .60 .30
2153 A589 6p No. B21 1.80 .50

Souvenir Sheet
Imperf
2154 A589 8p Sheet of 2, #a.-b. 6.00 *5.25*

No. 2154 has simulated perfs.

World War II, 50th Anniv. — A590

2p, Bataan, cross. 6p, Insignia of defenders of Bataan & Corregidor. 8p, Corregidor, Monument. #2158, Cross, map of Bataan. #2159, Monument, map of Corregidor.

Wmk. 391

1992, June 12 Photo. *Perf. 14*
2155 A590 2p multicolored .75 .40
2156 A590 6p multicolored 2.00 .60
2157 A590 8p multicolored 2.25 1.00

Size: 63x76mm, 76x63mm
Imperf
2158 A590 16p multicolored 6.50 5.00
2159 A590 16p multicolored 6.50 5.00
Nos. 2155-2159 (5) 18.00 12.00

Nos. 2158-2159 have simulated perforations.

President Corazon C. Aquino and President-Elect Fidel V. Ramos — A591

1992, June 30 *Perf. 14*
2160 A591 2p multicolored .75 .40

Anniversary of Democracy.

Jose Rizal's Exile to Dapitan, Cent. — A592

1992, June 17
2161 A592 2p Dapitan shrine 1.50 .50
2162 A592 2p Portrait, vert. 1.50 .50

ASEAN, 25th Anniv. — A593

Contemporary paintings: Nos. 2163, 2165, Spirit of ASEAN. Nos. 2164, 2166, ASEAN Sea.

Wmk. 391

1992, July 18 Litho. *Perf. 14*
2163 A593 2p multicolored .60 .30
2164 A593 2p multicolored .60 .30
2165 A593 6p multicolored 1.80 .70
2166 A593 6p multicolored 1.80 .70
Nos. 2163-2166 (4) 4.80 2.00

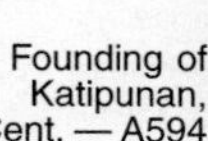

Founding of Katipunan, Cent. — A594

Details or entire paintings of revolutionaries, by Carlos "Botong" Francisco: No. 2167a, Preparing for battle, vert. No. 2167b, Attack leader (detail), vert. No. 2168a, Attack. No. 2168b, Signing papers.

Wmk. 391

1992, July 27 Photo. *Perf. 14*
2167 A594 2p Pair, #a.-b. 2.50 1.50
2168 A594 2p Pair, #a.-b. 2.50 1.50

Philippine League, Cent. — A595

Wmk. 391

1992, July 31 Photo. *Perf. 14*
2169 A595 2p multicolored 1.20 .75

1992 Summer Olympics, Barcelona A596

Wmk. 391

1992, Aug. 4 Litho. *Perf. 14*
2170 A596 2p Swimming .60 .40
2171 A596 7p Boxing 2.20 .60
2172 A596 8p Hurdling 2.50 .75
Nos. 2170-2172 (3) 5.30 1.75

Souvenir Sheet
Imperf
2172A A596 Sheet of 3, #2171-2172, 2172Ab 6.00 *6.00*
b. 1p like #2170 .65 .65

No. 2172A has simulated perforations.

Religious of the Assumption in Philippines, Cent. A597

Cathedral of San Sebastian, Cent. A597a

Wmk. 391

1992, Aug. 15 Photo. *Perf. 14*
2173 A597 2p multicolored .60 .30
2174 A597a 2p multicolored .60 .30

Founding of Nilad Masonic Lodge, Cent. — A598

Various Masonic symbols and: 6p, A. Luna. 8p, M.H. Del Pilar.

Wmk. 391

1992, Aug. 15 Photo. *Perf. 14*
2175 A598 2p green & black 1.50 1.00
2176 A598 6p yellow, black & brown 3.25 1.50
2177 A598 8p blue, black & violet 4.25 2.50
Nos. 2175-2177 (3) 9.00 5.00

Pres. Fidel V. Ramos Taking Oath of Office, June 30, 1992 — A599

1992, July 30
2178 A599 2p Ceremony, people .75 .30
2179 A599 8p Ceremony, flag 2.00 .70

Freshwater Aquarium Fish — A600

Designs: No. 2180a, Red-tailed guppy, b, Tiger lacetail guppy. c, Flamingo guppy. d, Neon tuxedo guppy. e, King cobra guppy.

No. 2181a, Black moor. b, Bubble eye. c, Pearl scale goldfish. d, Red cap. e, Lionhead goldfish.

No. 2182, Golden arowana.

No. 2183a, Delta topsail variatus. b, Orange spotted hi-fin platy. c, Red lyretail swordtail. d, Bleeding heart hi-fin platy.

No. 2184a, 6p, Green discus. b, 6p, Brown discus. c, 7p, Red discus. d, 7p, Blue discus.

1992, Sept. 9 *Perf. 14*
2180 A600 1.50p Strip of 5, #a.-e. 4.00 4.00
2181 A600 2p Strip of 5, #a.-e. 4.00 4.00

Imperf
Size: 65x45mm
2182 A600 8p multicolored 5.00 3.50

Souvenir Sheets of 4
Perf. 14
2183 A600 4p #a.-d. 6.00 *6.00*
2184 A600 6p, 7p #a.-d. 11.00 *11.00*

Nos. 2182 and 2184 were overprinted "PHILIPPINE STAMP EXHIBITION 1992 — TAIPEI" in margins. Most of this overprinted issue was sold to the dealer to co-sponsored the exhibit. Value, $6 and $12, respectively.

See Nos. 2253-2257.

Birthday Greetings — A601

1992, Sept 28 *Perf. 14*
2185 A601 2p Couple dancing .60 .30
2186 A601 6p like #2185 1.50 .50
2187 A601 7p Cake, balloons 1.50 .50
2188 A601 8p like #2187 2.00 .75
Nos. 2185-2188 (4) 5.60 2.05

Columbus' Discovery of America, 500th Anniv. — A602

Various fruits and vegetables.

1992, Oct. 14
2189 A602 2p multicolored .60 .30
2190 A602 6p multi, diff. 1.60 .50
2191 A602 8p multi, diff. 2.30 .60
Nos. 2189-2191 (3) 4.50 1.40

Intl. Conference on Nutrition, Rome — A603

1992, Oct. 27
2192 A603 2p multicolored .70 .30

No. 2100 Ovptd. in Blue "Second / National Philatelic Convention / Cebu, Philippines, Oct. 22-24, 1992"

Wmk. 391

1992, Oct. 15 Photo. *Imperf.*
2193 A571 16p multicolored 6.50 6.00

Christmas — A604

Various pictures of mother and child.

Wmk. 391

1992, Nov. 5	**Litho.**		***Perf. 14***
2194	A604 2p multicolored	.75	.40
2195	A604 6p multicolored	2.00	.60
2196	A604 7p multicolored	2.00	.80
2197	A604 8p multicolored	2.50	1.20
	Nos. 2194-2197 (4)	7.25	3.00

No. 1452 Ovptd. "INAUGURATION OF THE PHILIPPINE POSTAL MUSEUM / AND PHILATELIC LIBRARY, NOVEMBER 10, 1992" in Red

Wmk. 372

1992, Nov. 10	**Litho.**		***Imperf.***
	Souvenir Sheet		
2198	A348 5p multicolored	4.00	3.50

Fight Against Drug Abuse — A605

Wmk. 391

1992, Nov. 15	**Litho.**		***Perf. 14***
2199	A605 2p People, boat	.60	.30
2200	A605 8p People, boat, diff.	1.80	.60

A606

Paintings: 2p, Family, by Cesar Legaspi. 6p, Pounding Rice, by Nena Saguil. 7p, Fish Vendors, by Romeo V. Tabuena.

1992, Nov. 24			
2201	A606 2p multicolored	.60	.30
2202	A606 6p multicolored	1.60	.50
2203	A606 7p multicolored	1.80	.60
	Nos. 2201-2203 (3)	4.00	1.40

Philatelic Week.

Birds — A607

Designs: No. 2204a, Black shama. b, Philippine cockatoo. c, Sulu hornbill. d, Mindoro imperial pigeon. e, Blue-headed fantail.

No. 2205a, Philippine trogon, vert. b, Rufous hornbill, vert. c, White-bellied woodpecker, vert. d, Spotted wood kingfisher, vert.

No. 2206a, Brahminy kite. b, Philippine falconet. c, Pacific reef egret. d, Philippine mallard.

Wmk. 391

1992, Nov. 25	**Litho.**		***Perf. 14***
2204	A607 2p Strip of 5, #a.-e.	3.50	3.00
	Souvenir Sheets		
2205	A607 2p Sheet of 4, #a.-d.	4.00	*4.00*
2206	A607 2p Sheet of 4, #a.-d.	4.00	*4.00*

No. 2204 printed in sheets of 10 with designs in each row shifted one space to the right from the preceding row. Two rows in each sheet are tete-beche.

The 1st printing of this set was rejected. The unissued stamps do not have the frame around the birds. The denominations on the sheet stamps and the 2nd souvenir sheet are larger. On the 1st souvenir sheet they are smaller.

For overprint see No. 2405.

New Year 1993, Year of the Rooster — A608

2p, Native fighting cock. 6p, Legendary Maranao bird.

1992, Nov. 2			
2207	A608 2p multi	.60	.40
2208	A608 6p multi	2.00	.60
a.	Souvenir sheet of 2, #2207-2208 + 2 labels	3.50	*3.00*
b.	As "a," ovptd. in sheet margin	3.00	*2.50*

Nos. 2208a and 2208b exist imperf. Overprint on No. 2208b reads: "PHILIPPINE STAMP EXHIBIT / TAIPEI, DECEMBER 1-3, 1992" in English and Chinese.

Issued: Nos. 2207-2208, 2208a, 11/27; No. 2208b, 12/1.

See Nos. 2459b, 2460b.

Guerrilla Units of World War II A609

Units: a, Bulacan Military Area, Anderson's Command, Luzon Guerrilla Army Forces. b, Marking's Fil-American Guerrillas, Hunters ROTC Guerrillas, President Quezon's Own Guerrillas. c, 61st Division, 71st Division, Cebu Area Command. d, 48th Chinese Guerrilla Squadron, 101st Division, Vinzons Guerrillas.

1992, Dec. 7			
2209	A609 2p Block of 4, #a.-d.	4.00	3.50

National Symbols

Tree — A610　A610c Fish

Flower

A610a　A610b

Flag

A610d　A610e

Animal

A610f　A610g

Bird

A610h　A610i

Leaf

A610j　A610k

A610l　A610m Costume

Fruit

A610n　A610o

A610p House　A610q Various

A610r José Rizal　A610s National Dance

National Sport — A610t

Nos. 2210-2236 inscribed with year of issue unless noted otherwise

Wmk. 391, except #2212A, 2214, 2215, 2216A, 2218A, 2220, 2222 (Unwmk.)

Red (R) or Blue (B) "PILIPINAS" on bottom, except #2212 (Brown (Br) "PILIPINAS" on top)

1993-98	**Litho.**			***Perf. 14x13½***	
2210	A610	60s (R)		1.50	*.70*
2211	A610b	1p (R)		.50	.25
2211A	A610b	1p (R)		.35	.25
2212	A610a	1p (Br)		.35	.25
2212A	A610b	1p (B)		.35	.25
2213	A610c	1.50p (R)		.65	.25
a.	Dated "1995"			.40	.25
2214	A610c	1.50p (B)		.70	.25

Nos. 2212A and 2214 have blue security printing.

Issued: #2210, 6/12/93; #2211, 5/3/94; #2211A, 2/6/95; #2212, 4/29/93; #2212A, 2/12/96; #2213, 6/12/93; #2213a, 2/6/95; #2214, 2/13/96.

For surcharge see No. 2795.

Red "PILIPINAS" on bottom, except #2215a (Brown "PILIPINAS" on top)

Blue Security Printing

2215	2p Block of 14, #a.-n.	9.00	9.00
a.	A610d 2p multi	.40	.90
b.	A610r 2p multi	.40	.25
c.	A610p 2p multi	.40	.25
d.	A610m 2p multi	.40	.25
e.	A610s 2p multi	.40	.25
f.	A610t 2p multi	.40	.25
g.	A610i 2p multi	.40	.25
h.	A610e 2p multi	.40	.40
i.	A610f 2p multi	.40	.25
j.	A610b 2p multi	.40	.25
k.	A610 2p multi	.40	.25
l.	A610o 2p multi	.40	.25
m.	A610k 2p multi	.40	.25
n.	A610c 2p multi	.40	.25

Issued 11/2/95.

Red "PILIPINAS" on bottom, except #2216, 2217a (Brown "PILIPINAS" on top)

No Security Printing

2216	A610d 2p multi	.80	.25
2216A	A610e 2p multi	2.50	.30
2217	2p Block of 14, #a.-n.	9.00	9.00
a.	A610d 2p multi	.40	.90
b.	A610r 2p multi	.40	.25
c.	A610p 2p multi	.40	.25
d.	A610m 2p multi	.40	.25
e.	A610s 2p multi	.40	.25
f.	A610t 2p multi	.40	.25
g.	A610h 2p multi	.40	.25
h.	A610e 2p multi	.40	.40
i.	A610f 2p multi	.40	.25
j.	A610b 2p multi	.40	.25
k.	A610 2p multi	.40	.25
l.	A610o 2p multi	.40	.25
m.	A610k 2p multi	.40	.25
n.	A610c 2p multi	.40	.25

Issued: #2216, 4/29/93; #2216A (dated 1993), 2/10/94; #2217, 10/28/93.

#2217a is a later printing of #2216, in which the word "watawat" is much smaller. #2217h is a later printing of #2216A, in which the date is lowered near the middle of "PILIPINAS," rather than near the top of "PILIPINAS."

Red "PILIPINAS" on bottom

2218	A610f 3p multi	1.35	.35
a.	Dated "1994"	2.00	.35
b.	Dated "1995"	6.50	.35

Blue Security Printing at Top, Blue "PILIPINAS" on bottom

2218C	A610g 3p multi, dated "1996"	1.00	.35

"PILIPINAS" red: Nos. 2218, 2218a, 2218c. Blue security printing: Nos. 2218C, 2281d.

Issued: No. 2218, 6/12/93; No. 2218a, 4/19/94; No. 2218b, 2/1/95; No. 2218C, 3/1/96.

Blue "PILIPINAS" on bottom, except #2219n (Blue "PILIPINAS" on top)

Blue Security Printing

2219	4p Block of 14, #a.-n.	15.00	15.00
a.	A610d 4p multi	1.00	.30
b.	A610r 4p multi	1.00	.30
c.	A610p 4p multi	1.00	.30
d.	A610m 4p multi	1.00	.30
e.	A610s 4p multi	1.00	.30
f.	A610t 4p multi	1.00	.30
g.	A610i 4p multi	1.00	.30
h.	A610d 4p multi	1.00	.30
i.	A610f 4p multi	1.00	.30
j.	A610b 4p multi	1.00	.30
k.	A610 4p multi	1.00	.30
l.	A610o 4p multi	1.00	.30
m.	A610k 4p multi	1.00	.30
n.	A610c 4p multi	1.00	.30

Issued 1/8/96. Stamps are dated "1995."

Blue "PILIPINAS" on bottom, except #2220a (Blue "PILIPINAS" on top)

Blue Security Printing

2220	4p Block of 14, #a.-n.	17.00	17.00
a.	A610d 4p multi	1.00	.30
b.	A610r 4p multi	1.00	.30
c.	A610p 4p multi	1.00	.30
d.	A610m 4p multi	1.00	.30
e.	A610s 4p multi	1.00	.30
f.	A610t 4p multi	1.00	.30
g.	A610i 4p multi	1.00	.30
h.	A610e 4p multi	1.00	.30
i.	A610g 4p multi	1.00	.30
j.	A610b 4p multi	1.00	.30
k.	A610 4p multi	1.00	.30
l.	A610o 4p multi	1.00	.30
m.	A610k 4p multi	1.00	.30
n.	A610c 4p multi	1.00	.30

Issued 2/12/96.

Red "PILIPINAS" on bottom (R): #2221-2221b, 2223B, 2223c, 2224B, 2224c, 2226, 2226a, 2228-2228b. Blue "PILIPINAS" on bottom (B): #2222, 2223A, 2224A, 2227, 2229. Brown "PILIPINAS" on top (Br): #2223, 2224, 2225.

2221	A610h	5p (R)	2.00	.40
a.	Dated "1994"		2.40	.50
b.	Dated "1995"		2.20	.50
2222	A610i	5p (B)	1.70	.50
2223	A610j	6p (Br)	2.50	.40
2223A	A610k	6p (B)	2.50	1.00
2223B	A610k	6p (R)	2.50	.70
c.	Dated "1995"		2.50	.50
2224	A610l	7p (Br)	3.00	.40
2224A	A610m	7p (B)	3.00	.40
2224B	A610m	7p (R)	3.00	.80
c.	Dated "1995"		3.00	.80
2225	A610n	8p (Br)	3.50	.60
2226	A610o	8p (R)	7.50	1.00
a.	Dated "1995"		3.50	1.00
2227	A610o	8p (B)	3.50	1.00
2228	A610p	10p (R)	4.00	1.50
a.	Dated "1994"		4.50	1.50
b.	Dated "1995"		4.00	1.50
2229	A610p	10p (B)	4.00	1.50
	Nos. 2210-2229 (28)		102.75	63.65

Blue security printing: #2222, 2223A, 2224A, 2227, 2229.

Issued: #2221, 2228, 6/12/93; #2221a, 2228a, 4/19/94; #2221b, 2/1/95; #2222, 2/12/96; #2223, 2224, 2225, 4/29/93; #2223A, 11/21/96; #2223B, 12/1/94; #2223Bc, 2228b, 4/3/95; #2224A, 2227, 2229, 4/19/96; #2224Bc, 5/5/95; #2226, 10/4/93; #2226a, 3/14/95; #2224B, 7/6/94.

See Nos. 2463-2469A, 2544-2545.

Souvenir Sheets

Philippine Flag with National Symbols — A610u

Unwmk. ***Perf. 13½***

2231	A610u 1p, Sheet of 12, #a.-j.+2 labels		15.00	15.00
a.	A610e	1p multi	1.00	.80
b.	A610p	1p multi	1.00	.80
c.	A610m	1p multi	1.00	.80
d.	A610	1p multi	1.00	.80
e.	A610b	1p multi	1.00	.80
f.	A610o	1p multi	1.00	.80
g.	A610k	1p multi	1.00	.80
h.	A610c	1p multi	1.00	.80
i.	A610f	1p multi	1.00	.80
j.	A610h	1p multi	1.00	.80

No. 2231e does not have the blue security printing, present on No. 2212A.
Issued: 6/12/93.

Philippine Flag with National Landmarks — A610v

Designs: a, Aquinaldo Shrine; b, Rizal Shrine; c, Barasoian Shrine; d, Mabini Shrine.

2232	A610v 2p, 3p, #a.-d.		9.00	8.00
a.	A610q	2p multi	1.00	.80
b.	A610q	3p multi	1.00	.80
c.	A610q	2p multi	1.00	.80
d.	A610q	3p multi	1.00	.80

Issued 6/12/94.

1872 Cavite Mutiny A610w

Designs: a, Cavite Arsenal; b, La Fuerza de San Felipe-Cavite; c, Commemorative marker; d, Cristanto de Los Reyes y Mendoza.

2233	A610w 2p, 3p, Sheet of 4, #a.-d.		9.00	8.00
a.	A610q	2p multi	1.00	.80
b.	A610q	3p multi	1.00	.80
c.	A610q	2p multi	1.00	.80
d.	A610q	3p multi	1.00	.80

Issued 6/12/95.

1896 Philippine Revolution — A610x

Designs: a, Cry of Pudgadlawin; b, Battle of Pinaglabanan; c, Cry of Nueca Ecija; d, Battle of Binakayan.
Nos. 2234a-2234d have blue security printing.

2234	A610x 4p, Sheet of 4, #a.-d.		9.00	8.00
a.	A610q	4p multi	1.00	.80
b.	A610q	4p multi	1.00	.80
c.	A610q	4p multi	1.00	.80
d.	A610q	4p multi	1.00	.80

Issued 6/12/96.

Historical Events and Personages (1897) — A610y

Designs: a, Edilberto Evangelista; b, Vicente Alvarez; c, Francisco Del Castillo; d, Pantaleon Vallegas.
Nos. 2235a-2235d have blue security printing.

2235	A610y 4p, Sheet of 4, #a.-d.		9.00	8.00
a.	A610y	4p multi	1.00	.80
b.	A610q	4p multi	1.00	.80
c.	A610q	4p multi	1.00	.80
d.	A610q	4p multi	1.00	.80

Issued 6/12/97.

Historical Events of 1898 A610z

Designs: a, Tres de Abril Uprising in Cebu; b, Negros Uprising, 1898; c, Iligan Uprising, 1898; d, Philippine Centennial Logo, Kalayaan.
Nos. 2236a-2236d have blue security printing.

2236	A610z 4p, Sheet of 4, #a.-d.		9.00	8.00
a.	A610q	4p multi	1.00	.80
b.	A610q	4p multi	1.00	.80
c.	A610q	4p multi	1.00	.80
d.	A610q	4p multi	1.00	.80

Issued 6/12/98.

Butterflies A611

Designs: No. 2237a, Euploea mulciber. b, Cheritra orpheus. c, Delias henningia. d, Mycalesis ita. e, Delias diaphana.
No. 2238a, Papilio rumanzobia. b, Papilio palinurus. c, Trogonoptera trojana. d, Graphium agamemnon.
No. 2239, Papilio lowi, Valeria boebera, Delias themis.

Wmk. 391

1993, May 28 **Litho.** ***Perf. 14***

2237	A611	2p Strip of 5, #a.-e.	5.00	4.50

Souvenir Sheets

2238	A611	2p Sheet of 4, #a.-d.	5.50	5.00
e.		Ovptd. in sheet margin	6.00	6.00
2239	A611	10p multicolored	7.50	7.00
a.		Ovptd. in sheet margin	6.00	6.00
b.		Ovptd. in blue in sheet margin	*15.00*	12.50

Issue dates: Nos. 2237-2239, May 28. Nos. 2238e, 2239a, May 29. No. 2239b, July 1.
Nos. 2238a-2238d are vert. No. 2239 contains one 116x28mm stamp.
Overprint on Nos. 2238e, 2239a reads "INDOPEX '93 / INDONESIA PHILATELIC EXHIBITION 1993" and "6th ASIAN INTERNATIONAL PHILATELIC EXHIBITION / 29th MAY-4th JUNE 1993 SURABAYA-INDONESIA." Issued June 29.
Overprint on No. 2239b reads "Towards the Year 2000 / 46th PAF Anniversary 1 July 1993" and includes Philippine Air Force emblem and jet. Issued July 1.

Great Filipinos Type of 1989

Designs: a, Nicanor Abelardo, composer. b, Pilar Hidalgo-Lim, mathematician, educator. c, Manuel Viola Gallego, lawyer, educator. d, Maria Ylagan Orosa (1893-1943), pharmacist, health advocate. e, Eulogio B. Rodriguez, historian.

1993, June 10 ***Perf. 13½***

2240	A536	2p Strip of 5, #a.-e.	3.00	2.50

17th South East Asia Games, Singapore A612

No. 2241: a, Weight lifting, archery, fencing, shooting. b, Boxing, judo. c, Track, cycling, gymnastics, golf.
No. 2242: a, Table tennis, soccer, volleyball, badminton. b, Billiards, bowling. c, Swimming, water polo, yachting, diving.
No. 2243, Basketball, vert.

1993, June 18 ***Perf. 13***

2241	A612	2p Strip of 3, #a.-c.	2.00	2.00
2242	A612	6p Strip of 3, #a.-c.	5.00	5.00

Souvenir Sheet

2243	A612	10p multicolored	7.00	6.00

#2241a, 2241c, 2242a, 2242c are 80x30mm. No. 2243 contains one 30x40mm stamp. No. 2242a exists inscribed "June 13-20, 1993." Value, strips of 3, $22.

Orchids — A613

No. 2244: a, Spathoglottis chrysantha. b, Arachnis longicaulis. c, Phalaenopsis mariae. d, Coelogyne marmorata. e, Dendrobium sanderae.
No. 2245: a, Dendrobium serratilabium. b, Phalaenopsis equestris. c, Vanda merrillii. d, Vanda luzonica. e, Grammatophyllum martae.
No. 2246, Aerides quinquevulnera. No. 2247, Vanda lamellata.

1993, Aug. 14 **Unwmk.** ***Perf. 14***

2244	A613	2p Block of 5, #a.-e.	3.50	3.50
2245	A613	3p Block of 5, #a.-e.	4.75	4.75

Souvenir Sheets

2246	A613	8p multicolored	3.50	3.50
a.		With additional inscription	3.25	3.25

Imperf

2247	A613	8p multicolored	3.50	3.50
a.		With additional inscription	3.25	3.50

No. 2246 contains one 27x78mm stamp.
Nos. 2246a, 2247a inscribed in sheet margin with Taipei '93 emblem in blue and yellow. Additional black inscription in English and Chinese reads: "ASIAN INTERNATIONAL INVITATION STAMP EXHIBITION / TAIPEI '93."

Greetings — A614

"Thinking of You" in English on Nos. 2248a-2251a, in Filipino on Nos. 2248b-2251b with designs: 2p, Flowers, dog at window. 6p, Dog looking at alarm clock. 7p, Dog looking at calendar. 8p, Dog with slippers.

Wmk. 391

1993, Aug. 20 **Litho.** ***Perf. 14***

2248	A614	2p Pair, #a.-b.	1.50	1.00
2249	A614	6p Pair, #a.-b.	4.25	3.25
2250	A614	7p Pair, #a.-b.	4.25	3.25
2251	A614	8p Pair, #a.-b.	5.50	4.00
		Nos. 2248-2251 (4)	15.50	11.50

Natl. Coconut Week — A615

1993, Aug. 24

2252	A615	2p multicolored	.80	.35

Fish Type of 1992

No. 2253: a, Paradise fish. b, Pearl gourami. c, Red-tailed black shark. d, Tiger barb. e, Cardinal tetra.
No. 2254: a, Albino ryukin goldfish. b, Black oranda goldfish. c, Lionhead goldfish. d, Celestial-eye goldfish. e, Pompon goldfish.
No. 2255: a, Pearl-scale angelfish. b, Zebra angelfish. c, Marble angelfish. d, Black angelfish.
No. 2256: a, Neon betta. b, Libby betta. c, Split-tailed betta. d, Butterfly betta.
No. 2257, Albino oscar.

1993, Sep. 9 **Unwmk.** ***Perf. 14***

2253	A600	2p Strip of 5, #a.-e.	4.00	4.00
2254	A600	2p Strip of 5, #a.-e.	4.00	4.00

Souvenir Sheets

Perf. 14

2255	A600	2p Sheet of 4, #a.-d.	5.25	5.25
2256	A600	3p Sheet of 4, #a.-d.	5.25	5.25
e.		Ovptd. in margin	5.25	5.25

Imperf

Stamp Size: 70x45mm

2257	A600	6p multicolored	4.50	4.00
a.		Ovptd. in margin	4.50	4.00

Nos. 2256e, 2257a overprinted in black "QUEEN SIRIKIT NATIONAL CONVENTION CENTER / 1-10 OCTOBER 1993," "BANGKOK WORLD PHILATELIC EXHIBITION 1993" with Bangkok '93 show emblem in purple in margin.
Nos. 2255a-2255d are vert.
Issued: #2256e, 2257a, 9/20; others, 9/9.

A616

Wmk. 391

1993, Sept. 20 **Photo.** ***Perf. 14***

2258	A616	2p multicolored	.60	.30

Basic Petroleum and Minerals, Inc., 25th anniv.

16th World Law Conference, Manila — A617

6p, Globe on scales, gavel, flag, vert. 7p, Justice holding scales, courthouse. 8p, Fisherman, vert.

Unwmk.

1993, Sept. 30 **Litho.** ***Perf. 14***

2259	A617	2p multicolored	.40	.30
2260	A617	6p multicolored	1.30	.40
2261	A617	7p multicolored	1.50	.50
2262	A617	8p multicolored	1.80	.50
		Nos. 2259-2262 (4)	5.00	1.70

Our Lady of the Rosary of la Naval, 400th Anniv. — A618

1993, Oct. 18 **Wmk. 391**

2263	A618	2p multicolored	.60	.30

Intl. Year of Indigenous People — A619

People wearing traditional costumes.

1993, Oct. 24 **Unwmk.**

2264	A619	2p multicolored	.50	.30
2265	A619	6p multicolored	1.75	.40
2266	A619	7p multicolored	1.75	.50
2267	A619	8p multicolored	2.25	.60
		Nos. 2264-2267 (4)	6.25	1.80

Environmental Protection A620

Paintings: 2p, Trees. 6p, Marine life. 7p, Bird, trees. 8p, Man and nature.

1993, Nov. 22

2268 A620 2p multicolored .50 .30
2269 A620 6p multicolored 1.75 .40
2270 A620 7p multicolored 1.75 .50
2271 A620 8p multicolored 2.25 .60
Nos. 2268-2271 (4) 6.25 1.80

Philately Week.

A621

a, Lunar buggy. b, Floating power tiller.

Unwmk.

1993, Nov. 30 Litho. *Perf. 14*

2272 A621 2p Pair, #a.-b. 1.40 1.40

Filipino Inventors Society, Inc., 50th Anniv.

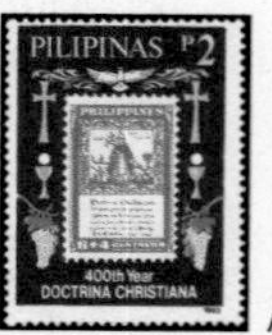

A622

1993, Nov. 30

2273 A622 2p multicolored .65 .30

Printing of Doctrina Christiana in Spanish and Tagalog, 400th anniv.

A623

Christmas: 2p, Nativity scene. 6p, Church, people. 7p, Water buffalo carrying fruits, vegetables, sea food. 8p, Christmas lantern, carolers.

1993, Dec. 1

2274 A623 2p multicolored .60 .40
2275 A623 6p multicolored 2.00 .50
2276 A623 7p multicolored 2.40 .70
2277 A623 8p multicolored 3.00 .80
Nos. 2274-2277 (4) 8.00 2.40

A624

Maps, Philippine guerrilla units of World War II: a, US Army Forces in the Philippines Northern Luzon. b, Bohol Area Command. c, Leyte Area Command. d, Palawan Special Battalion, Sulu Area Command.

1993, Dec. 10

2278 A624 2p Block or strip of 4, #a.-d. 4.00 4.00

Philippines 2000 — A625

Designs: 2p, Peace and Order. 6p, Transportation, communications. 7p, Infrastructure, industry. No. 2282, People empowerment. No. 2283, Transportation, communications, buildings, people.

Unwmk.

1993, Dec. 14 Litho. *Perf. 14*

2279 A625 2p multicolored .50 .35
2280 A625 6p multicolored 1.25 .45
2281 A625 7p multicolored 1.50 .50
2282 A625 8p multicolored 1.75 .60
Nos. 2279-2282 (4) 5.00 1.90

Souvenir Sheet

Imperf

Size: 110x85mm

2283 A625 8p multicolored 4.50 4.00

New Year 1994 (Year of the Dog) — A626

2p, Manigong bagong taon. 6p, Happy new year.

Unwmk.

1993, Dec. 15 Litho. *Perf. 14*

2284 A626 2p multi .50 .40
2285 A626 6p multi 2.00 .60
a. Souvenir sheet of 2, #2284-2285 + 2 labels 4.00 4.00

No. 2285a exists imperf. Same values. See Nos. 2459c, 2460c.

First ASEAN Scout Jamboree, Mt. Makiling — A627

2p, Flags of ASEAN countries, Boy Scout emblem. 6p, Flags, Boy Scout, emblem.

1993, Dec. 28

2286 A627 2p multicolored .50 .40
2287 A627 6p multicolored 1.50 .60
a. Souv. sheet of 2, #2286-2287 4.00 4.00

Rotary Club of Manila, 75th Anniv. — A628

Unwmk.

1994, Jan. 19 Litho. *Perf. 14*

2288 A628 2p multicolored .60 .30

17th Asian Pacific Dental Congress, Manila — A629

2p, Healthy teeth. 6p, Globe, flags, teeth.

1994, Feb. 3

2289 A629 2p multicolored .50 .30
2290 A629 6p multicolored 1.50 .50

Corals — A630

#2291: a, Acropora micropthalma. b, Seriatopora hystrix. c, Acropora latistella. d, Millepora tenella. e, Millepora tenella, up close. f, Pachyseris valenciennesi. g, Pavona decussata. h, Galaxea fascicularis. i, Acropora formosa. j, Acropora humilis.

#2292: a, Isis. b, Plexaura. c, Dendronepthya. d, Heteroxenia.

#2293: a, Xenia puertogalerae. b, Plexaura, diff. c, Dendrophyllia gracilis. d, Plerogyra sinuosa.

1994, Feb. 15 Litho. *Perf. 14*

2291 A630 2p Block of 10, #a.-j. 10.00 9.00

Souvenir Sheets

2292 A630 2p Sheet of 4, #a.-d. 5.75 5.75
2293 A630 3p Sheet of 4, #a.-d. 5.75 5.75
e. With added inscription 12.50 12.50

No. 2293e is inscribed in sheet margin "NAPHILCON '94 / 1ST NATIONAL / PHILATELIC CONGRESS / 21 FEBRUARY - 5 MARCH 1994 / PHILATELY 2000."

Issued: No. 2293e, 2/21.

Hong Kong '94 — A631

2p, Nos. 2126, 2207. 6p, Nos. 2284, 2285.

1994, Feb. 18

2294 A631 2p multicolored .40 .30
2295 A631 6p multicolored 1.40 .50
a. Souv. sheet of 2, #2294-2295, blue 3.00 3.00
b. As "a," green 3.00 3.00

Backgrounds differ on Nos. 2295a, 2295b.

A632

1994, Feb. 20

2296 A632 2p multicolored .60 .30

Philippine Military Academy Class of 1944, 50th Anniv.

A633

1994, Mar. 1

2297 A633 2p multicolored .60 .30

Federation of Filipino-Chinese Chambers of Commerce and Industry, 40th Anniv.

A634

"Congratulations" in English on Nos. 2298a-2301a, in Tagalog on Nos. 2298b-2301b with designs: No. 2298, Books, diploma, mortarboard. No. 2299, Baby carried by stork. No. 2300, Valentine bouquet with portraits in heart. No. 2301, Bouquet.

1994, Apr. 15

2298 A634 2p Pair, #a.-b. 1.25 1.25
2299 A634 2p Pair, #a.-b. 1.25 1.25
2300 A634 2p Pair, #a.-b. 1.25 1.25
2301 A634 2p Pair, #a.-b. 1.25 1.25
Nos. 2298-2301 (4) 5.00 5.00

A635

1994 Miss Universe Pageant, Manila: Nos. 2302a (2p), 2304a, Gloria Diaz, 1969 winner. No. 2302b (6p), Crown, Philippine jeepney. Nos. 2303a (2p), 2304b, Margie Moran, 1973 winner. No. 2303b (7p), Pageant participant, Kalesa horse-drawn cart.

1994, May 5 Litho. *Perf. 14*

2302 A635 Pair, #a.-b. 2.50 1.25
2303 A635 Pair, #a.-b. 2.50 1.50

Souvenir Sheet

2304 A635 8p Sheet of 2, #a.-b. 5.00 *4.00*

Great Filipinos Type of 1989

Designs: a, Antonio J. Molina, musician. b, Jose Yulo, politician. c, Josefa Jara-Martinez, social worker. d, Nicanor Reyes, Sr., accountant. e, Sabino B. Padilla, lawyer.

1994, June 10

2307 A536 2p Strip of 5, #a.-e. 2.50 2.50

Philippine Export Processing Zones — A637

No. 2308: a, Baguio City. b, Bataan. c, Mactan. d, Cavite.

No. 2309a, 7p, Map of Philippines, export products. b, 8p, Export products flowing around world map.

Unwmk.

1994, July 4 Litho. *Perf. 14*

2308 A637 2p Block of 4, #a.-d. 2.00 2.00
2309 A637 Pair, #a.-b. 3.50 3.50

Fight Illegal Recruitment Year — A638

1994, July 15

2310 A638 2p multicolored .60 .30

Wildlife A639

a, Palawan bearcat. b, Philippine tarsier. c, Scaly anteater. d, Palawan porcupine.

12p, Visayan spotted deer.

1994, Aug. 12 Litho. *Perf. 14*

2311 A639 6p Block of 4, #a.-d. 6.00 5.75

Souvenir Sheet

2312 A639 12p multicolored 7.00 7.00
a. Ovptd. in margin 7.00 7.00

No. 2312a overprinted in white, black and red in sheet margin with "SINGPEX '94 / 31 August-3 September 1994" and show emblem.

PHILAKOREA '94 — A640

Shells: a, Conus gloriamaris. b, Conus striatus. c, Conus geographus. d, Conus textile.

No. 2314a, Conus marmoreus. No. 2314b, Conus geographus, diff. No. 2315a, Conus striatus, diff. No. 2315b, Conus marmoreus, diff.

1994, Aug. 16

2313 A640 2p Block of 4, #a.-d. 4.00 3.50

Souvenir Sheets

2314 A640 6p Sheet of 2, #a.-b. 5.00 *4.50*
2315 A640 6p Sheet of 2, #a.-b. 5.00 *4.50*

Landings at Leyte Gulf, 50th Anniv. — A641

Designs: a, Pres. Sergio Osmena, Sr. b, Gen. MacArthur wading ashore. c, Dove of Peace. d, Carlos P. Romulo.

1994, Sept. 15

2316 A641 2p Block of 4, #a.-d. 3.50 2.50

See Nos. 2391a-2391d.

Intl. Anniversaries & Events — A642

Unwmk.

1994, Oct. 24 Litho. *Perf. 14*

2317 A642 2p Family .50 .30
2318 A642 6p Labor workers 1.25 .40
2319 A642 7p Feather, clouds 1.50 .50
Nos. 2317-2319 (3) 3.25 1.20

Intl. Year of the Family (#2317). ILO, 75th anniv. (#2318). ICAO, 50th anniv. (#2319).

Visit of US Pres. Bill Clinton — A643

1994, Nov. 12

2320 A643 2p green & multi .60 .35
2321 A643 8p blue & multi 2.40 .65

East Asean Business Convention, Davao — A644

1994, Nov. 15

2322 A644 2p violet & multi .40 .30
2323 A644 6p brown & multi 1.35 .50

Nos. 2322-2323 not issued without overprint "Nov. 15-20, 1994" and obliterator covering original date at lower left.

Philatelic Week — A645

Portraits by Philippine artists: 2p, Soteranna Puson Y Quintos de Ventenilla, by Dionisio de Castro. 6p, Quintina Castor de Sadie, by Simon Flores y de la Rosa. 7p, Artist's mother, by Felix Eduardo Resurreccion Hidalgo y Padilla. 8p, Una Bulaquena, by Juan Luna y Novicio.

12p, Cirilo and Severina Quiason Family, by Simon Flores y de la Rosa.

1994, Nov. 21

2324 A645 2p multicolored .50 .30
2325 A645 6p multicolored 1.00 .45
2326 A645 7p multicolored 1.25 .55
2327 A645 8p multicolored 1.50 .65
Nos. 2324-2327 (4) 4.25 1.95

Souvenir Sheet

2328 A645 12p multicolored 3.00 *3.00*

No. 2328 contains one 29x80mm stamp.

Christmas — A646

1994, Nov. 25

2329 A646 2p Wreath .60 .35
2330 A646 6p Angels 1.40 .65
2331 A646 7p Bells 2.00 .80
2332 A646 8p Basket 2.50 1.20
Nos. 2329-2332 (4) 6.50 3.00

ASEANPEX '94 — A647

#2333: a, Blue-naped parrot. b, Bleeding heart pigeon. c, Palawan peacock pheasant. d, Koch's pitta.

No. 2334, Philippine eagle, vert.

1994, Nov. 8

2333 A647 2p Block of 4, #a.-d. 6.00 4.50

Souvenir Sheet

2334 A647 12p multicolored 7.50 6.00

A648

Philippine Guerrilla Units in World War II — A649

No. 2335: a, Troops entering prison. b, Prisoners escaping.

Bombed building and — #2336: a, Emblem of East Central Luzon Guerrilla Area. b, Map, Mindoro Provincial Batallion, Marinduque Guerrilla Force. c, Map, Zambales Military District, Masbate Guerrilla Regiment. d, Map, Samar Area Command.

Unwmk.

1994, Dec. 8 Litho. *Perf. 14*

2335 A648 2p Pair, #a.-b. 1.25 1.00
2336 A649 2p Block of 4, #a.-d. 2.50 2.00

No. 2335 is a continuous design.
See Nos. 2392a-2392b.

New Year 1995 (Year of the Boar) — A650

1994, Dec. 5

2337 A650 2p shown .50 .35
2338 A650 6p Boy, girl pigs 2.00 .50
a. Souvenir sheet of 2, #2337-2338 + 2 labels 3.75 *3.75*

No. 2338 exists imperf. Value, unused $3.75.
See Nos. 2459d, 2460d.

Kalayaan, Cent. (in 1998) — A651

a, Flag, 1898. b, Philippine flag. c, Cent. emblem.

1994, Dec. 15

2339 A651 2p Strip of 3, #a.-c. 2.00 1.50

AIDS Awareness — A652

1994, Dec. 12

2340 A652 2p multicolored 1.20 .40

Visit of Pope John Paul II — A653

Pope John Paul II and: #2342, Papal arms, globe showing Philippines. 6p, Emblem, map of Asia. #2344, Children.

#2341, a, Archdiocese of Manila. b, Diocese of Cebu. c, Diocese of Caceres. d, Diocese of Nueva Segovia.

#2345, Pres. Fidel V. Ramos, Pope John Paul II.

1995, Jan. 2

2341 A653 2p Block of 4, #a.-d. 2.00 1.50
2342 A653 2p multicolored .50 .30
2343 A653 6p multicolored 1.00 .40
2344 A653 8p multicolored 1.50 .60
Nos. 2341-2344 (4) 5.00 2.80

Souvenir Sheet

2345 A653 8p multicolored 3.50 3.00
a. Overprinted in margin 3.50 3.00

Federation of Asian Bishops' Conferences (#2343). 10th World Youth Day (#2344).

Overprint in margin of No. 2345a reads "CHRISTYPEX '95 / JANUARY 4-16, 1995 / University of Santo Tomas, Manila / PHILIPPINE PHILATELIC FEDERATION."

Lingayen Gulf Landings, 50th Anniv. — A654

a, Map of Lingayen Gulf, ships, troops. b, Map, emblems of 6th, 37th, 40th, 43rd Divisions.

1995, Jan. 9

2346 A654 2p Pair, #a.-b. 1.40 1.00

No. 2346 is a continuous design.
See Nos. 2391e-2391f.

Liberation of Manila, 50th Anniv. — A655

Statue honoring victims and: 2p, 8p, Various destroyed buildings.

1995, Feb. 3

2347 A655 2p magenta & multi .60 .35
2348 A655 8p blue & multi 2.40 .65

See Nos. 2392m, 2392r.

Jose W. Diokno (1922-87), Politician — A656

1995, Feb. 26

2349 A656 2p multicolored .50 .30

Intl. School, Manila, 75th Anniv. — A657

8p, Globe, cut out figures.

Unwmk.

1995, Mar. 4 Litho. *Perf. 14*

2350 A657 2p shown .50 .30
2351 A657 8p multi 1.50 .50

Wildlife A658

No. 2352: a, Mousedeer. b, Tamaraw. c, Visayan warty pig. d, Palm civet.

No. 2353, vert: a, Flying lemur. b, Philippine deer.

1995, Mar. 20

2352 A658 2p Block of 4, #a.-d. 3.00 2.00

Souvenir Sheet

2353 A658 8p Sheet of 2, #a.-b. 4.50 3.25

Battles of World War II, 50th Anniv. — A659

Unit emblems and and maps showing: No. 2354, Battle of Nichols Airbase and Ft. Mckinley. No. 2355: a, Nasugbu landings. b, Tagaytay landings.

1995, Apr. 9

2354 A659 2p multicolored .75 .30
2355 A659 2p Pair, #a.-b. 1.50 1.25

See Nos. 2391g-2391h, 2392c.

Liberation of Baguio, 50th Anniv. — A660

1995, Apr. 27

2356 A660 2p multicolored .80 .30

See No. 2392d.

Liberation of Internment Camps, 50th Anniv. — A661

1995, May 28

2357 A661 2p UST .80 .30
2358 A661 2p Cabanatuan .80 .30
2359 A661 2p Los Banos .80 .30
Nos. 2357-2359 (3) 2.40 .90

See Nos. 2392e-2392g.

Great Filipinos Type of 1989

Persons born in 1895: a, Victorio C. Edades. b, Jovita Fuentes. c, Candido M. Africa. d, Asuncion Arriola-Perez. e, Eduardo A. Quisumbing.

Perf. 14x13½

1995, June 1 Litho. Unwmk.

2360 A536 2p Strip of 5, #a.-e. 3.00 2.75

Catholic Bishops' Conference of the Philippines, 50th Anniv. — A662

1995, July 22 *Perf. 14*

2361 A662 2p multicolored .60 .30

A663

1995, Aug. 2

2362 A663 2p multicolored .75 .40

Jaime N. Ferrer (1916-87),

A664

Jars — #2363: a, Manunggul. b, Non-anthropomorphic. c, Anthropomorphic. d, Leta-leta yawning jarlet.
12p, Double spouted and legged vessel, presentation tray.

1995, Aug. 4

2363 A664 2p Block of 4, #a.-d. 3.00 2.00

Souvenir Sheet

2364 A664 12p multi, no show emblem in margin 3.50 3.00
a. Show emblem in margin 3.50 3.00

Archaeological finds. No. 2364 contains one 80x30mm stamp.
No. 2364a has Jakarta '95 show emblem in margin. Issued 8/19/95.

ASEAN Environment Year 1995 — A665

Designs: Nos. 2365a, 2366a, Left hand holding turtle, wildlife scene. Nos. 2365b, 2366b, Right hand below fish, bird, wildlife scene.

1995, Aug. 10

2365 A665 2p Pair, #a.-b. 1.75 1.50

Souvenir Sheet

2366 A665 6p Sheet of 2, #a.-b. 7.00 6.00

Nos. 2365-2366 are each continuous designs.

Souvenir Sheet

Philippine Eagle, New Natl. Bird — A666

1995, Aug. 11

2367 A666 16p multicolored 8.00 7.00

Mercury Drug Co., 50th Anniv. — A667

1995, Aug. 15

2368 A667 2p multicolored .60 .30

Parish of St. Louis Bishop, 400th Anniv. — A668

1995, Aug. 18

2369 A668 2p multicolored .50 .30

Asian-Pacific Postal Training Center, 25th Anniv. — A669

Unwmk.

1995, Sept. 1 Litho. ***Perf. 14***

2370 A669 6p multicolored 1.20 .50

UN, 50th Anniv. A670

Filipinos serving in UN: No. 2371a, #2372, Carlos P. Romulo. b, Rafael M. Salas. c, Salvador P. Lopez. d, Jose D. Ingles.

1995, Sept. 25

2371 A670 2p Block of 4, #a.-d. 3.00 3.00
2371E A670 2p Cesar C. Bengson *125.00 125.00*
f. Block of 4, #2371b-2731d, 2371E *175.00*

Souvenir Sheet

2372 A670 16p multi 4.00 4.00

No. 2371E was issued with the wrong portrait and was withdrawn after two days.

FAO, 50th Anniv. — A671

1995, Sept. 25

2373 A671 8p multicolored 2.00 .65

A671a

Unwmk.

1995, Oct. 5 Litho. ***Perf. 14***

2373A A671a 2p multicolored .50 .30

Manila Overseas Press Club, 50th anniv.

Total Eclipse of the Sun — A672

1995, Oct. 24

2374 A672 2p multicolored 1.00 .35

Natl. Stamp Collecting Month — A673

Paintings: 2p, Two Igorot Women, by Victorio Edades. 6p, Serenade, by Carlos "Botong" Francisco. 7p, Tuba Drinkers, by Vincente Manansala. 8p, Genesis, by Hernando Ocampo.
12p, The Builders, by Edades.

1995, Nov. 6

2375 A673 2p multicolored .50 .30
2376 A673 6p multicolored 1.50 .50
2377 A673 7p multicolored 1.75 .75
2378 A673 8p multicolored 2.00 1.00
Nos. 2375-2378 (4) 5.75 2.55

Souvenir Sheet

2379 A673 12p multicolored 3.50 3.50

No. 2379 contains one 76x26mm stamp.

Christmas — A674

Musical instruments, Christmas carols.

1995, Nov. 22

2380 A674 2p Tambourine .60 .45
2381 A674 6p Maracas 2.00 .65
2382 A674 7p Guitar 2.00 .80
2383 A674 8p Drum 2.40 1.20
Nos. 2380-2383 (4) 7.00 3.10

Sycip Gorres Velayo & Co. Accounting Firm, 50th Anniv. — A675

1995, Nov. 27

2384 A675 2p Abacus .50 .30

Souvenir Sheet

Pres. Fidel V. Ramos Proclaiming November as Natl. Stamp Collecting Month — A676

1995, Nov. 29

2385 A676 8p multicolored 6.00 5.00

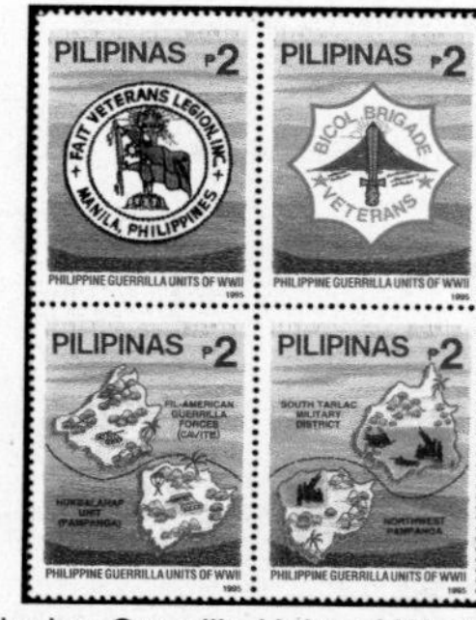

New Year 1996 (Year of the Rat) — A677

1995, Dec. 1

2386 A677 2p shown .50 .35
2387 A677 6p Outline of rat 1.50 .65
a. Souv. sheet, #2386-2387+2 labels 4.50 3.50
b. As "a," imperf 4.00 3.50

Printed in sheets of 20 stamps.
See Nos. 2459e, 2460e.

Philippine Guerrilla Units of World War II — A678

Designs: a, Emblem, FIL-American Irregular Troops (FAIT). b, Emblem, BICOL Brigade. c, Map, FIL-American Guerrilla Forces (Cavite), Hukbalahap Unit (Pampanga). d, Map, South Tarlac, Northwest Pampanga Military Districts.

1995, Dec. 8 Litho. ***Perf. 14***

2388 A678 2p Block of 4, #a.-d. 3.50 3.50

Significant Events of World War II, 50th Anniv. — A679

Designs: a, Map, liberation of Panay and Romblon, 61st Division. b, Map, Liberation of Cebu, Americal Division. c, Battle of Ipo Dam, 43rd Division, FIL-American Guerrillas. d, Map, Battle of Bessang Pass, 37th Division. e, Sculpture, surrender of Gen. Yamashita.

1995, Dec. 15

2389 A679 2p Strip of 5, #a.-e. 6.00 6.00

See Nos. 2392h-2392 l.

Revolutionary Heroes — A680

a, Jose P. Rizal (1861-96) b, Andres Bonifacio, (1863-97). c, Apolinario Mabini (1864-1903).

1995, Dec. 27

2390 A680 2p Set of 3, #a.-c. 3.00 2.00

World War II Types of 1994-95 and

Map of Philippines — A681

Color of Pilipinas and denomination: Nos. 2391a-2391d, like #2316, red. Nos. 2391e-2391f, like #2346, red. Nos. 2391g-2391h, like #2355, red. Nos. 2391i-2391l, map of Philippines with blue background showing sites of Allied landings.
No. 2392: a-b, like #2335, white. c, like #2354, red. d, like #2356, white. e, like #2358, white. f, like #2357, white. g, like #2359, white. h.-l., like #2389a-2389e, purple. m, like #2347, red. n.-q., map of Philippines with green background showing location of prison camps. r, like #2348, red.

Miniature Sheets

1995, Dec. 27 Litho. ***Perf. 14***

2391 A681 2p Sheet of 12, #a.-l. 9.00 8.00
2392 A681 2p Sheet of 18, #a.-r. 14.00 *12.00*

23rd Intl. Congress of Internal Medicine — A682

1996, Jan. 10 Litho. ***Perf. 14***

2393 A682 2p multicolored .60 .30

Sun Life Assurance Company of Canada in the Philippines, Cent. — A683

1996, Jan. 26

2394 A683 2p shown .50 .30
2395 A683 8p Sun over horizon 1.50 .60

Valentine's Day — A684

"I Love You" on Nos. 2396a-2399a, "Happy Valentine" on Nos. 2396b-2399b and: No. 2396, Pair of love birds. No. 2397, Cupid with bow and arrow. No. 2398, Box of chocolates. No. 2399, Bouquet of roses, butterfly.

1996, Feb. 9

2396 A684 2p Pair, #a.-b. 1.00 .75
2397 A684 6p Pair, #a.-b. 2.50 2.25
2398 A684 7p Pair, #a.-b. 3.25 2.50
2399 A684 8p Pair, #a.-b. 2.75 3.00
Nos. 2396-2399 (4) 9.50 8.50

St. Thomas University Hospital, 50th Anniv. — A685

1996, Mar. 5

2400 A685 2p multicolored .60 .30

Gregorio Araneta University Foundation, 50th Anniv. — A686

1996, Mar. 5

2401 A686 2p multicolored .60 .30

Fish — A687

No. 2402: a, Emperor fish. b, Mandarinfish. c, Regal angelfish. d, Clown triggerfish. e, Raccoon butterflyfish. g, Powder brown tang. h, Two-banded anemonefish. i, Moorish idol. j, Blue tang. k, Majestic angelfish.

No. 2403: a, like #2402d. b, like #2402k. c, like #2402c. d, like #2402h.

1996, Mar. 12

2402 A687 4p Strip of 5, #a.-e. 6.00 5.50
2402F A687 4p Strip of 5, #g.-k. 6.00 5.50

Miniature Sheet

2403 A687 4p Sheet of 4, #a.-d. 5.50 4.50
e. #2403 with new inscriptions 5.50 4.50

Souvenir Sheet

2404 A687 12p Lionfish 4.50 4.00
a. #2404 with new inscriptions 4.50 4.00

Nos. 2402, 2402F have blue compressed security printing at left, black denomination, white background, margin. Nos. 2403-2404 have blue background, violet denomination, continuous design.

ASEANPEX '96 (No. 2403-2404).

Nos. 2403e, 2404a inscribed in sheet margins with various INDONESIA '96 exhibition emblems. Issued: Nos. 2403e, 2404a, 3/21/96.

See Nos. 2410-2413.

No. 2206 Overprinted in Green

1996 Litho. Wmk. 391 ***Perf. 14***

2405 A607 2p Sheet of 4, #a.-d. 8.00 7.00

Ovpt. in sheet margin reads: "THE YOUNG PHILATELISTS' SOCIETY 10TH ANNIVERSARY".

Souvenir Sheet

Basketball — A688

1996, Apr. 14

2406 A688 10p multicolored 14.00 12.50

PALARONG/PAMBANSA '96.

Francisco B. Ortigas, Sr. — A689

1996, Apr. 30 **Unwmk.**

2407 A689 4p multicolored .75 .40

Discovery of Radioactivity, Cent. — A690

1996, Apr. 30

2408 A690 4p multicolored .60 .30

Congregation of Dominican Sisters of St. Catherine of Siena, 300th Anniv. — A691

1996, Apr. 30

2409 A691 4p multicolored .65 .30

Fish Type of 1996

No. 2410: a, Long-horned cowfish. b, Queen angelfish. c, Long-nosed butterflyfish. d, Yellow tang. e, Blue-faced angelfish.

No. 2411: a, Saddleback butterflyfish. b, Sailfin tang. c, Harlequin tuskfish. d, Clown wrasse. e, Spotted boxfish.

No. 2412: a, like #2410e. b, like #2410c. c, like #2410b. d, like #2411c.

No. 2413, vert: a, Purple firefish. b, Pacific seahorse. c, Red-faced batfish. d, Long-nosed hawksfish.

1996

2410 A687 4p Strip of 5, #a.-e. 6.00 5.50
2411 A687 4p Strip of 5, #a.-e. 6.00 5.50
2412 A687 4p Sheet of 4, #a.-d. 5.50 5.00
e. With added inscription 5.50 5.00
2413 A687 4p Sheet of 4, #a.-d. 5.50 5.00
e. With added inscription 5.50 5.00

Nos. 2412-2413 have white background. Nos. 2410-2411 have blue background.

ASEANPEX '96 (#2412-2413). Added inscription in sheet margin of #2412e, 2413e includes CHINA '96 emblem and "CHINA '96 - 9th Asian International Exhibition" in red.

Issued: #2410-2413, 5/10; #2412e, 2413e, 5/16.

Great Filipinos Type of 1989

Designs: a, Carlos P. Garcia (1896-1971), politician. b, Casimiro del Rosario (1896-1962), physicist. c, Geronima T. Pecson (1896-1989), politician. d, Cesar C. Bengson (1896-1992), lawyer. e, Jose Corazon de Jesus (1896-1932), writer.

Perf. 13½

1996, June 1 Litho. Unwmk.

2414 A536 4p Strip of 5, #a.-e. 4.00 3.75

ABS CBN (Broadcasting Network), 50th Anniv. — A692

8p, Rooster, world map.

1996, June 13 ***Perf. 14***

2415 A692 4p shown 1.00 .40
2416 A692 8p multicolored 2.50 .80

Manila, Convention City — A693

1996, June 24

2417 A693 4p multicolored .80 .30

Jose Cojuangco, Sr. (1896-1976), Businessman, Public Official — A694

1996, July 3

2418 A694 4p multicolored .80 .40

Philippine-American Friendship Day — A695

Symbols of Philippines, U.S.: 4p, Hats. 8p, National birds. 16p, Flags, vert.

1996, July 4

2419 A695 4p multicolored .80 .40
2420 A695 8p multicolored 2.25 .80

Souvenir Sheet

2421 A695 16p multicolored 3.50 3.50

See No. 2475.

Modern Olympic Games, Cent. — A696

4p, No. 2426a, Boxing. 6p, No. 2426b, Athletics. 7p, No. 2426c, Swimming. 8p, No. 2426d, Equestrian.

Unwmk.

1996, July 19 Litho. ***Perf. 14***

2422 A696 4p multicolored .80 .40
2423 A696 6p multicolored 1.25 .60
2424 A696 7p multicolored 1.75 .70
2425 A696 8p multicolored 1.90 .80
Nos. 2422-2425 (4) 5.70 2.50

Miniature Sheet

2426 A696 4p Sheet of 4, #a.-d. 4.50 4.00

Nos. 2422-2425 have colored background, blue security code at right, denominations at LR. Nos. 2426a-2426d have colored circles on white background, blue security code at top, and denominations at UR, UL, LR, LL, respectively.

University of the East, 50th Anniv. — A697

1996, Aug. 15

2427 A697 4p multicolored .80 .40

Orchids A698

No. 2428: a, Dendrobium anosmum. b, Phalaenopsis. equestris-alba. c, Aerides lawrenceae. d, Vanda javierii.

No. 2429: a, Renanthera philippinensis. b, Dendrobium schuetzei. c, Dendrobium taurinum. d, Vanda lamellata.

No. 2430: a, Coelogyne pandurata. b, Vanda merrilii. c, Cymbidium aliciae. d, Dendrobium topaziacum.

1996, Sept. 26

2428 A698 4p Block or strip of 4, #a.-d. 4.00 3.00
2429 A698 4p Block or strip of 4, #a.-d. 4.00 3.00

Miniature Sheet

2430 A698 4p Sheet of 4, #a.-d. 4.00 3.50

#2428-2429 were printed in sheets of 16 stamps.

ASEANPEX '96 (#2430). Complete sheets of Nos. 2428-2429 have ASEANPEX emblem in selvage.

6th Asia Pacific Intl. Trade Fair — A699

1996, Sept. 30

2431 A699 4p multicolored .80 .30

UNICEF, 50th Anniv. A700

Children in montage of scenes studying, working, playing — #2432: a, Blue & multi. b, Purple & multi. c, Green & multi. d, Red & multi.

16p, Four children, horiz.

1996, Oct. 9

2432 A700 4p Block of 4, #a.-d. 3.25 2.50

Souvenir Sheet

2433 A700 16p multicolored 3.50 3.00

TAIPEX '96 A701

Orchids: No. 2434: a, Fran's Fantasy "Alea." b, Malvarosa Green Goddess "Nani." c, Ports of Paradise "Emerald Isle." d, Mem. Conrada Perez "Nani."

No. 2435: a, Pokai tangerine "Lea." b, Mem. Roselyn Reisman "Diana." c, C. Moscombe x Toshi Aoki. d, Mem. Benigno Aquino "Flying Aces."

12p, Pamela Hetherington "Coronation," Living Gold "Erin Treasure," Eleanor Spicer "White Bouquet."

1996, Oct. 21 Litho. ***Perf. 14***

2434 A701 4p Block of 4, #a.-d. 3.50 2.50
2435 A701 4p Block of 4, #a.-d. 3.50 2.50

Souvenir Sheet

2436 A701 12p multicolored 4.50 3.50

Nos. 2434-2435 were issued in sheets of 16 stamps. No. 2436 contains one 80x30mm stamp.

1996 Asia-Pacific Economic Cooperation A702

Winning entries of stamp design competition: 4p, Sun behind mountains, airplane, skyscrapers, tower, ship, satellite dish, vert. 7p, Skyscrapers. 8p, Flags of nations beside path, globe, skyscrapers, sun, vert.

1996, Oct. 30

2437 A702 4p multicolored .80 .30
2438 A702 6p shown 1.25 .50
2439 A702 7p multicolored 1.35 .60
2440 A702 8p multicolored 1.50 .70
Nos. 2437-2440 (4) 4.90 2.10

Christmas A703

Designs: 4p, Philippine Nativity scene, vert. 6p, Midnight Mass. 7p, Carolers. 8p, Carolers with Carabao, vert.

1996, Nov. 5

2441 A703 4p multicolored .75 .40
2442 A703 6p multicolored 1.50 .60
2443 A703 7p multicolored 1.75 .80
2444 A703 8p multicolored 2.00 1.00
Nos. 2441-2444 (4) 6.00 2.80

Eugenio P. Perez (1896-1957), Politician — A704

1996, Nov. 11 Litho. *Perf. 14*

2445 A704 4p multicolored .80 .40

New Year 1997 (Year of the Ox) — A705

1996, Dec. 1

2446 A705 4p Carabao .75 .40
2447 A705 6p Tamaraw 1.25 .60
a. Souv. sheet, #2446-2447 + 2 labels 3.50 3.50

Printed in sheets of 20 stamps. No. 2447a exists imperf. Value, $3.50.

See Nos. 2459f, 2460f.

ASEANPEX '96, Intl. Philatelic Exhibition, Manila — A706

Jose P. Rizal (1861-96): No. 2448: a, At 14 years. b, At 18. c, At 25. d, At 31.

No. 2449: a, "Noli Me Tangere." b, Gomburza to whom Rizal dedicated "El Filbusterismo." c, Oyang Dapitana, by Rizal. d, Ricardo Camicero, by Rizal.

No. 2450, horiz: a, Rizal's house, Calamba. b, University of St. Tomas, Manila, 1611. c, Orient Hotel, Manila. d, Dapitan during Rizal's time.

No. 2451, horiz: a, Central University, Madrid. b, British Museum, London. c, Botanical Garden, Madrid. d, Heidelberg, Germany.

No. 2452, Rizal at 14, horiz. No. 2453, Rizal at 18, horiz. No. 2454, Rizal at 25, horiz. No. 2455, Rizal at 31, horiz.

1996

2448 A706 4p Block of 4, #a.-d. 3.50 3.00
2449 A706 4p Block of 4, #a.-d. 3.50 3.00
2450 A706 4p Block of 4, #a.-d. 3.50 3.00
2451 A706 4p Block of 4, #a.-d. 3.50 3.00

Souvenir Sheets

2452 A706 12p multicolored 3.00 2.50
2453 A706 12p multicolored 3.00 2.50
2454 A706 12p multicolored 3.00 2.50
2455 A706 12p multicolored 3.00 2.50

Issued: #2448, 2452, 12/14; #2449, 2453, 12/15; #2450, 2454, 12/16; #2451, 2455, 12/17. Nos. 2448-2451 were issued in sheets of 16 stamps.

Independence, Cent. (in 1998) — A707

Revolutionary heroes: a, Fr. Mariano C. Gomez (1799-1872). b, Fr. Jose A. Burgos (1837-72). c, Fr. Jacinto Zamora (1835-72).

1996, Dec. 20

2456 A707 4p Strip of 3, #a.-c. 3.00 2.00

Jose Rizal — A709

1996, Dec. 30 Litho. *Perf. 14*

2458 A709 4p multicolored .90 .45

New Year Types of 1991-96
Unwmk.

1997, Feb. 12 Litho. *Perf. 14*

2459 Sheet of 6 7.00 *7.00*
a. A580 4p like #2126 .90 .60
b. A608 4p like #2208 .90 .60
c. A626 4p like #2284 .90 .60
d. A650 4p like #2337 .90 .60
e. A677 4p like #2386 .90 .60
f. A705 4p like #2446 .90 .60
2460 Sheet of 6 12.00 *12.00*
a. A580 6p like #2127 1.50 .90
b. A608 6p like #2207 1.50 .90
c. A626 6p like #2285 1.50 .90
d. A650 6p like #2338 1.50 .90
e. A677 6p like #2387 1.50 .90
f. A705 6p like #2447 1.50 .90

Hong Kong '97.

Nos. 2459a-2459b, 2460a-2460b have white margins, color differences. Nos. 2459c-2459d, 2459f, 2460c-2460d, 2460f have color differences. Nos. 2459e, 2460e, do not have blue security printing, and have color differences.

Nos. 2459a-2459f, 2460a-2460f are all dated "1997."

Holy Rosary Seminary, Bicent. — A710

1997, Feb. 18

2461 A710 4p multicolored .65 .30

Philippine Army, Cent. — A711

1997, Feb. 18

2462 A711 4p multicolored .65 .30

Natl. Symbols Type of 1993-96 and

Gem — A711a

Blue "PILIPINAS" on bottom, except #2464 (Black)

1997 Litho. Unwmk. *Perf. 14x13½*

2463 A610b 1p like #2212A .40 .25
2463A A610b 2p like #2212A .80 .30
2463B A610g 3p like #2212A .60 .60
2464 A711a 4p multicolored .90 .35
2465 A610i 5p like #2222 1.00 .70
2465A A610i 5p like #2222 1.75 .70
2466 A610k 6p like #2223A 2.25 .70
2466A A610k 6p like #2223A 2.25 .75
2467 A610m 7p like #2224A 3.50 1.00
2467A A610m 7p like #2224A 3.50 1.00
2468 A610o 8p like #2227 3.50 1.25
2468A A610o 8p like #2227 3.50 1.25
2469 A610p 10p like #2229 4.50 1.50
2469A A610p 10p like #2229 4.50 1.50
Nos. 2463-2469A (14) 32.95 11.85

Nos. 2463, 2465, 2466, 2467, 2468 and 2469 do not have blue compressed security printing at top and are dated "1997."

Nos. 2463A-2464, 2465A, 2466A, 2467A, 2468A and 2469A have blue compressed security printing at top and are dated "1997."

Issued: #2463, 2469, 2/27/97; 2463A, 4/15; 2463B, 2466A, 4/18; #2465A, 4/29; #2464, 6/10; #2465, 2/26; #2466, 3/10; #2467, 3/7; #2467A, 5/8; #2468, 3/6; #2468A, 5/8; #2469A, 4/22.

Dept. of Finance, Cent. — A712

1997, Apr. 8 *Perf. 14*

2471 A712 4p multicolored .80 .30

Philippine Red Cross, 50th Anniv. — A713

1997, Apr. 8

2472 A713 4p multicolored .80 .40

Philamlife Insurance Co., 50th Anniv. — A714

1997, Apr. 8

2473 A714 4p multicolored .80 .30

J. Walter Thompson Advertising, 50th Anniv. in Philippines A715

1997, Apr. 18

2474 A715 4p multicolored .80 .30

Souvenir Sheet

Philippine-American Friendship Day, Republic Day, 50th Anniv. — A716

1997, May 29

2475 A716 16p multicolored 4.50 3.75

PACIFIC 97.

See No. 2421.

Wild Animals A717

World Wildlife Fund: No. 2476, Visayan spotted deer. No. 2477, Visayan spotted deer (doe & fawn). No. 2478, Visayan warty pig. No. 2479, Visayan warty pig (adult, young).

1997, July 24

2476 4p multicolored 1.00 .70
a. Sheet of 8 9.00 9.00
2477 4p multicolored 1.00 .70
a. Sheet of 8 9.00 9.00
2478 4p multicolored 1.00 .70
a. Sheet of 8 9.00 9.00
2479 4p multicolored 1.00 .70
a. Sheet of 8 9.00 9.00
b. A717 Block or strip of 4, #2476-2479 4.25 3.50
Set of 4 sheets, #2476a-2479a 34.00 34.00

No. 2479b was issued in sheets of 16 stamps.

ASEAN, 30th Anniv. A718

Founding signatories: No. 2480, Adam Malik, Indonesia, Tun Abdul Razak, Malaysia, Narciso Ramos, Philippines, S. Rajaratnam, Singapore, Thanat Khoman, Thailand. No. 2481, Natl. flags of founding signatories. No. 2482, Flags of current ASEAN countries. No. 2483, Flags of ASEAN countries surrounding globe.

1997, Aug. 7 *Perf. 14*

2480 4p multicolored 1.00 .50
2481 4p multicolored 1.00 .50
a. A718 Pair, #2480-2481 2.50 1.25
2482 6p multicolored 1.25 .60
2483 6p multicolored 1.25 .60
a. A718 Pair, #2482-2483 3.50 2.00
Nos. 2480-2483 (4) 4.50 2.20

World Scout Parliamentary Union, 2nd General Assembly — A719

1997, Aug. 17

2484 A719 4p multicolored 1.00 .40

Manuel L. Quezon University, 50th Anniv. — A720

1997, Aug. 19

2485 A720 4p multicolored .80 .30

Great Filipinos Type of 1989

Famous people: a, Justice Roberto Regala (1897-1979). b, Doroteo Espiritu, dental surgeon, inventor (b. 1897). c, Elisa R. Ochoa (1897-1978), nurse, tennis champion. d, Mariano Marcos (1897-1945), lawyer, educator. e, Jose F. Romero (1897-1978), editor.

Perf. 14x13½

1997, June 1 Litho. Unwmk.

2486 A536 4p Strip of 5, #a.-e. 4.00 3.00

Battle of Candon, 1898 — A721

4p, Don Federico Isabelo Abaya, revolutionary leader against Spanish. 6p, Soldier on horseback.

1997, Sept. 24 *Perf. 14*

2487 A721 4p multi, vert. .80 .35
2488 A721 6p multi 1.00 .60

St. Therese of Lisieux (1873-97) — A722

1997, Oct. 16

2489 A722 6p multicolored 1.00 .50

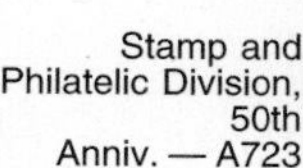

Stamp and Philatelic Division, 50th Anniv. — A723

Abstract art: 4p, Homage to the Heroes of Bessang Pass, by Hernando Ruiz Ocampo. 6p, Jardin III, by Fernando Zobel. 7p, Abstraction, by Nena Saguil, vert. 8p, House of Life, by Jose Joya, vert.

16p, Dimension of Fear, by Jose Joya.

1997, Oct. 16

2490 A723 4p multicolored .80 .35
2491 A723 6p multicolored 1.00 .45
2492 A723 7p multicolored 1.50 .60
2493 A723 8p multicolored 1.75 .80
Nos. 2490-2493 (4) 5.05 2.20

Souvenir Sheet

2494 A723 16p multicolored 5.25 5.00

No. 2494 contains one 80x30mm stamp.

Heinrich von Stephan (1831-97) — A724

1997, Oct. 24 Litho. *Perf. 14*

2495 A724 4p multicolored 1.00 .40

Asian and Pacific Decade of Disabled Persons — A725

1997, Oct. 24 Litho. *Perf. 14*

2496 A725 6p multicolored 1.00 .45

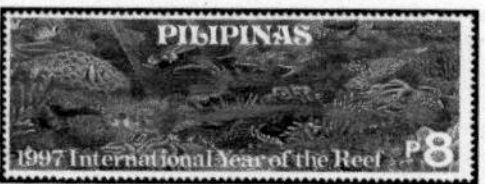

Intl. Year of the Reef A726

1997, Oct. 24 Litho. *Perf. 14*

2497 A726 8p multicolored 1.75 1.20

Souvenir Sheet

2498 A726 16p multicolored 4.50 4.00

No. 2498 is a continuous design printed in sheets of 10 stamps.

Natl. Stamp Collecting Month — A726a

Paintings: 4p, Dalagang Bukid, by Fernando Amorsolo, vert. 6p, Bagong Taon, by Arturo Luz, vert. 7p, Jeepneys, by Vincente Manansala. 8p, encounter of the Nuestra Sra. de Cavadonga and the Centurion, by Alfredo Carmelo.

16p, Pista sa Nayon, by Carlos Francisco.

1997, Nov. 4 Litho. *Perf. 14*

2498A A726a 4p multicolored .80 .40
2498B A726a 6p multicolored 1.00 .60
2498C A726a 7p multicolored 1.50 .70
2498D A726a 8p multicolored 1.75 .80
Nos. 2498A-2498D (4) 5.05 2.50

Souvenir Sheet

2498E A726a 16p multicolored 4.00 3.50

No. 2498E contains one 80x30mm stamp.

Christmas — A727

Various stained glass windows.

1997, Nov. 7

2499 A727 4p multicolored .80 .40
2500 A727 6p multicolored 1.20 .60
2501 A727 7p multicolored 1.50 .80
2502 A727 8p multicolored 2.00 1.20
Nos. 2499-2502 (4) 5.50 3.00

Independence, Cent. — A728

Various monuments to Andres Bonifacio (1863-97), revolutionary, founder of the Katipunan: a, red & multi. b, yellow & multi. c, blue & multi.

1997, Nov. 30

2503 A728 4p Strip of 3, #a.-c. 3.00 2.00

New Year 1998 (Year of the Tiger) — A729

1997, Dec. 1

2504 A729 4p shown .90 .40
2505 A729 6p Tigers, diff. 1.60 .60
a. Souvenir sheet, #2504-2505 + 2 labels 4.00 3.50

Printed in sheets of 20.
No. 2505a exists imperf. Value, $4.

Philippine Eagle — A730

1997, Dec. 5

2506 A730 20p Looking right 5.00 1.80
2507 A730 30p Looking forward 5.00 2.20
2508 A730 50p On cliff 10.00 3.50
Nos. 2506-2508 (3) 20.00 7.50

Game Cocks A731

No. 2509: a, Hatch grey. b, Spangled roundhead. c, Racey mug. d, Silver grey.

No. 2510, vert: a, Grey. b, Kelso. c, Bruner roundhead. d, Democrat.

No. 2511, Cock fight, vert. No. 2512, Cocks facing each other ready to fight.

1997, Dec. 18

2509 A731 4p Block of 4, #a.-d. 3.50 2.50
2510 A731 4p Block of 4, #a.-d. 3.50 2.50

Souvenir Sheets

2511 A731 12p multicolored 3.50 3.00
2512 A731 16p multicolored 4.50 4.00

Nos. 2509-2510 printed in sheets of 16. Initial delivery has excess untrimmed margins.

No. 2512 contains one 80x30mm stamp.

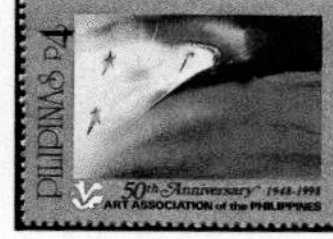

Art Association of the Philippines, 50th Anniv. — A732

Stylized designs: No. 2513, Colors of flag, sunburst. No. 2514, Association's initials, clenched fist holding artist's implements.

Unwmk.

1998, Feb. 14 Litho. *Perf. 14*

2513 A732 4p multicolored 1.00 .35
2514 A732 4p multicolored 1.00 .40
a. Pair, #2513-2514 2.50 1.50

Club Filipino Social Organization, Cent. — A733

1998, Feb. 25

2515 A733 4p multicolored .80 .30

Blessed Marie Eugenie (1817-98) — A734

1998, Feb. 25

2516 A734 4p multicolored .80 .30

Fulbright Educational Exchange Program in the Philippines, 50th Anniv. — A735

1998, Feb. 25

2517 A735 4p multicolored .80 .40

Heroes of the Revolution — A736

National flag and: 4p, Melchora Aquino (1812-1919). 11p, Andres Bonifacio (1863-97). 13p, Apolinario Mabini (1864-1903). 15p, Emilio Aguinaldo (1869-1964).

1998 Litho. Unwmk. *Perf. 13½*

Inscribed "1998"

2518 A736 4p multicolored .90 .25
2519 A736 11p multicolored 2.40 .50
a. Inscribed "1999" 3.00 .65
2520 A736 13p multicolored 3.00 .60
a. Inscribed "1999" 3.50 .70
2521 A736 15p multicolored 3.50 .75
a. Inscribed "1999" 4.50 1.00
Nos. 2518-2521 (4) 9.80 2.10

Issued: 4p, 3/3/98. 11p, 13p, 15p, 3/24/98.

See Nos. 2528, 2546-2550, 2578-2597, 2607.

Apo View Hotel, 50th Anniv. — A737

1998, Mar. 20 *Perf. 14*

2522 A737 4p multicolored 1.00 .35

Philippine Cultural High School, 75th Anniv. — A738

1998, May 5

2523 A738 4p multicolored .80 .40

Victorino Mapa High School, 75th Anniv. — A739

1998, May 5

2524 A739 4p multicolored .80 .30

Philippine Navy, Cent. — A740

1998, May 5

2525 A740 4p multicolored .80 .40

University of Baguio, 50th Anniv. — A741

1998, May 5

2526 A741 4p multicolored .80 .40

Philippine Maritime Institute, 50th Anniv. — A742

1998, May 5

2527 A742 4p multicolored .80 .40

Heroes of the Revolution Type of 1998

Design: Gen. Antonio Luna (1866-99).

Perf. 13½

1998, Apr. 30 Litho. Unwmk.

2528 A736 5p multicolored .90 .30

Expo '98, Lisbon — A743

4p, Boat on lake, vert. 15p, Vinta on water. 15p, Main lobby, Philippine Pavilion.

1998, May 22 *Perf. 14*

2529 A743 4p multicolored 1.00 .50
2530 A743 15p multicolored 3.00 1.50

Souvenir Sheet

2531 A743 15p multicolored 5.00 4.00

No. 2531 contains one 80x30mm stamp.

Clark Special Economic Zone — A744

1998, May 28

2532 A744 15p multicolored 3.50 2.50

Printed in sheets of 10 stamps.

Flowers A745

#2533: a, Artrabotrys hexapetalus. b, Hibiscus rosa-sinensis. c, Nerium oleander. d, Jasminum sambac.

#2534, vert: a, Gardenia jasminoides. b, Ixora coccinea. c, Erythrina indica. d, Abelmoschus moschatus.

#2535, Medinilla magnifica.

1998, May 29

2533 A745 4p Block of 4, #a.-d. 3.50 3.00
2534 A745 4p Block of 4, #a.-d. 3.50 3.00

Souvenir Sheet

2535 A745 15p multicolored 6.00 5.00

Nos. 2533-2534 were printed in sheets of 16. The initial delivery has untrimmed excess selvage.

Great Filipinos Type of 1989

Designs: a, Andres R. Soriano (1898-1964). b, Tomas Fonacier (1898-1991). c, Josefa L. Escoda (1898-1945). d, Lorenzo M. Tañada (1898-1992). e, Lazaro Francisco (1898-1980).

1998, June 1 *Perf. 14x13½*

2536 A536 4p Strip of 5, #a.-e. 3.50 3.00

Philippine Indepencence, Cent. — A746

No. 2537, Mexican flag, sailing ship. No. 2538, Woman holding Philippine flag, monument, sailing ship, map of Philippines. No. 2539, Spanish flag, Catholic Church, religious icon, Philippine flag.

1998, June 3 *Perf. 14*

2537 A746 15p multicolored 2.00 1.25
2538 A746 15p multicolored 2.00 1.25
2539 A746 15p multicolored 2.00 1.25
a. Strip of 3, #2537-2539 8.00 6.00
b. Souvenir sheet, #2537-2539 + 3 labels 8.00 7.00

Printed in sheets of 15.

See Mexico #2079-2080, Spain #2949. For overprint see #2629.

Philippine Independence, Cent. — A747

Patriots of the revolution: a, Melchora Aquino. b, Nazaria Lagos. c, Agueda Kahabagan.

Unwmk.

1998, June 9 **Litho.** *Perf. 14*

2540 A747 4p Strip of 3, #a.-c. 3.00 2.00

Pasig River Campaign for Waste Management A748

1998, June 19

2541 A748 4p multicolored .80 .30

Marine Mammals — A749

No. 2542: a, Bottlenose dolphin. b, Humpback whale. c, Fraser's dolphin. d, Melon-headed whale. e, Minke whale. f, Striped dolphin. g, Sperm whale. h, Pygmy killer whale. i, Cuvier's beaked whale. j, Killer whale. k, Bottlenose dolphin. l, Long-snouted pinner dolphin. m, Risso's dolphin. n, Finless porpoise. o, Pygmy sperm whale. p, Pantropical spotted dolphin. q, False killer whale. r, Blainville's beaked whale. s, Rough-toothed dolphin. t, Bryde's whale.

15p, Dugong.

1998, June 19

2542 A749 4p Sheet of 20, #a.-t. 20.00 20.00

Souvenir Sheet

2543 A749 15p multicolored 5.50 *5.00*

Nos. 2218a, 2218b, 2220 Ovptd. in Gold with Philippine Independence Centennial Emblem

1998 Litho. Unwmk. *Perf. 14x13½*

2544 A610f 3p multi, dated "1995" (#2218b) .70 .25
2544A A610f 3p multi, dated "1994" (#2218a) 75.00 75.00
2545 A610g 4p Block of 14, #a.-n. 15.00 15.00
a. A610d 4p multi .75 .40
b. A610r 4p multi .75 .40
c. A610p 4p multi .75 .40
d. A610m 4p multi .75 .40
e. A610s 4p multi .75 .40
f. A610t 4p multi .75 .40
g. A610i 4p multi .75 .40
h. A610e 4p multi .75 .40
i. A610g 4p multi .75 .40
j. A610b 4p multi .75 .40
k. A610 4p multi .75 .40
l. A610o 4p multi .75 .40
m. A610k 4p multi .75 .40
n. A610c 4p multi .75 .40

Issued: No. 2544, 7/7/98; 2545, 6/12/98.

No. 2544A, dated "1994," was overprinted in error.

Heroes of the Revolution Type of 1998

2p, Emilio Jacinto. 4p, Jose P. Rizal. 8p, Marcelo H. del Pilar. 10p, Gregorio del Pilar. 18p, Juan Luna.

1998 **Inscribed "1998"** *Perf. 13½*

2546 A736 2p multicolored .85 .25
2547 A736 4p multicolored 1.00 .30
2548 A736 8p multicolored 1.80 .45
a. Inscribed "1999" 2.40 .50
2549 A736 10p multicolored 2.50 .80
a. Inscribed "1999" 3.50 .80
2550 A736 18p multicolored 5.00 1.50
Nos. 2546-2550 (5) 11.15 3.30

Issued: 4p, 10p, 18p, 5/18/98. 2p, 8p, 7/20/98.

For surcharges, see Nos. 2879-2882.

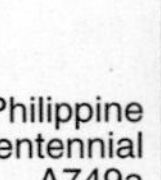

Philippine Centennial A749a

No. 2550A: b, Spoliarium, by Juan Luna. c, 1st display of Philippine flag, 1898. d, Execution of Jose Rizal, 1896. e, Andres Bonifacio. f, Church, Malolos.

1998, July *Perf. 14*

2550A Souv. booklet *35.00 35.00*
b. A749a 4p multicolored 1.00 *.80*
c. A749a 8p multicolored 2.00 *1.50*
d.-e. A749a 16p multicolored 3.00 *2.50*
f. A749a 20p multicolored 3.50 *2.75*

No. 2550A contains panes of 4 each of Nos. 2550Ab-2550Ac and one pane of 1 each of Nos. 2550Ad-2550Af. Sold for 150p.

For surcharges, see Nos. 2879-2882.

Philippine Coconut Industry, Cent. — A750

1998, Oct. 9 *Perf. 14*

2551 A750 4p multicolored 1.00 .60

Holy Spirit Adoration Sisters in Philippines, 75th Anniv. — A751

1998, Oct. 9

2552 A751 4p multicolored 1.25 .60

Universal Delclaration of Human Rights, 50th Anniv. — A752

1998, Oct. 24

2553 A752 4p multicolored 1.00 .60

Intl. Year of the Ocean A753

1998, Oct. 24

2554 A753 15p multicolored 3.50 2.50
a. Souvenir sheet, #2554 5.00 4.50

No. 2554a is a continuous design printed in sheets of 10.

A754

Philippine Postal Service, Cent. — #2555: a, Child placing envelope into mailbox, globe. b, Arms encircling globe, envelopes, Philippine flag as background. c, Airplane, globe, various stamps over building. d, Child holding up hands, natl. flag colors, envelopes.

15p, Child holding envelope as it crisscrosses globe.

1998, Nov. 4

2555 A754 6p Block of 4, #a.-d. 4.00 4.00

Souvenir Sheet

2556 A754 15p multicolored 4.50 4.50

No. 2555 was printed in sheets of 16. No. 2556 contains one 76x30mm stamp.

A755

Christmas: Various star lanterns.

1998, Nov. 5

2557 A755 6p multicolored 1.25 .50
2558 A755 11p multicolored 2.00 .80
2559 A755 13p multicolored 2.50 1.20
2560 A755 15p multicolored 2.75 1.50
Nos. 2557-2560 (4) 8.50 4.00

Pasko '98.

Souvenir Sheets

Philippines '98, Philippine Cent. Invitational Intl. Philatelic Exhibition — A756

Revolutionary scenes, stamps of revolutionary govt.: No. 2561, Soldiers celebrating, #Y1-Y2. No. 2562, Signing treaty, telegraph stamps. No. 2563, Waving flag from balcony, #YF1, "Recibos" (Offical receipt) stamps. No. 2564, Procession, #Y3, perf. and imperf. examples of #YP1. No. 2565, New government convening, "Trans de Ganades" (cattle transfer) stamp, Libertad essay.

1998

2561 A756 15p multicolored 5.50 4.50
2562 A756 15p multicolored 5.50 4.50
2563 A756 15p multicolored 5.50 4.50
2564 A756 15p multicolored 5.50 4.50
2565 A756 15p multicolored 5.50 4.50
Nos. 2561-2565 (5) 27.50 22.50

No. 2561 exists imperf. The first printing has varying amounts of black offset on the reverse. Value, $75. The second printing does not have the offset. Value, $12.50.

Nos. 2561-2565 were issued one each day from 11/5-11/9.

Pres. Joseph Ejercito Estrada — A757

1998, Nov. 10

2566 A757 6p Taking oath 1.00 .50
2567 A757 15p Giving speech 3.00 1.50

Shells A758

No. 2568: a, Mitra papalis. b, Vexillum citrinum. c, Vexillum rugosum. d, Volema carinifera.

No. 2569: a, Teramachia dalli. b, Nassarius vitiensis. c, Cymbiola imperialis. d, Cymbiola aulica.

No. 2570: a, Nassarius papillosus. b, Fasciolaria trapezium.

Unwmk.

1998, Nov. 6 **Litho.** *Perf. 14*

2568 A758 4p Block of 4, #a.-d. 4.00 3.50
2569 A758 4p Block of 4, #a.-d. 4.00 3.50

Souvenir Sheet

2570 A758 8p Sheet of 2, #a.-b. 6.50 5.00
c. Souvenir sheet, Type II 10.00 10.00

Cloud in sheet margin touches "s" of Shells on #2570. On #2570c, cloud does not touch "s" of Shells. Colors are dark on #2570c, lighter on #2570.

Nos. 2568-2569 were printed in sheets of 16.

Natl. Stamp Collecting Month — A759

Motion picture, director: 6p, "Dyesebel," Gerardo de Leon. 11p, "Ang Sawa Sa Lumang Simboryo," Gerardo de Leon. 13p, "Prinsipe Amante," Lamberto V. Avellana. No. 2574, "Anak Dalita," Lamberto V. Avellana.

No. 2575, "Siete Infantes de Lara," costume design by Carlos "Botong" Francisco.

1998, Nov. 25

2571 A759 6p black & blue 1.00 .40
2572 A759 11p black & brown 1.75 .70
2573 A759 13p black & lilac 2.25 .80
2574 A759 15p black & green 3.00 1.00
Nos. 2571-2574 (4) 8.00 2.90

Souvenir Sheet

2575 A759 15p black 3.50 3.25

No. 2575 contains one 26x76mm stamp.

Philippine Centennial — A759a

Pride, various women and: No. 2575A, Eagle (Resources). No. 2575B, Costume (Heritage). No. 2575C, Flag (Filipino People). No. 2575D, Artifacts with text (Literature). No. 2575E, Rice terraces (Engineering). No. 2575F, "Noli Me Tangere" (Citizenry).

Unwmk.

1998, Nov. 20 Litho. *Imperf.*

2575A A759a 15p multi 3.50 3.00
2575B A759a 15p multi 3.50 3.00
2575C A759a 15p multi 3.50 3.00
2575D A759a 15p multi 3.50 3.00
2575E A759a 15p multi 3.50 3.00
2575F A759a 15p multi 3.50 3.00
Nos. 2575A-2575F (6) 21.00 18.00

Nos. 2575A-2575F have simulated perforations.

New Year 1999 (Year of the Rabbit) — A760

1998, Dec. 1

2576 A760 4p shown .80 .40
2577 A760 11p Two rabbits 2.00 .80
a. Souvenir sheet, #2576-2577 4.00 4.00

Printed in sheets of 20. No. 2577a exists imperf. Value, $4.

Heroes of the Revolution Type of 1998

1998, Dec. 15 Litho. *Perf. 13½*

Booklet Stamps

Yellow Background

2578 A736 6p like #2518 1.20 .50
2579 A736 6p like #2519 1.20 .50
2580 A736 6p like #2520 1.20 .50
2581 A736 6p like #2521 1.20 .50
2582 A736 6p like #2528 1.20 .50
2583 A736 6p like #2547 1.20 .50
2584 A736 6p like #2549 1.20 .50
2585 A736 6p like #2550 1.20 .50
2586 A736 6p like #2546 1.20 .50
2587 A736 6p like #2548 1.20 .50
a. Booklet pane, #2578-2587 16.00 16.00
Complete booklet, #2587a 16.00 16.00

Green Background

2588 A736 15p like #2546 3.00 1.50
2589 A736 15p like #2518 3.00 1.50
2590 A736 15p like #2547 3.00 1.50
2591 A736 15p like #2528 3.00 1.50
2592 A736 15p like #2548 3.00 1.50
2593 A736 15p like #2549 3.00 1.50
2594 A736 15p like #2519 3.00 1.50
2595 A736 15p like #2520 3.00 1.50
2596 A736 15p like #2521 3.00 1.50
a. Booklet pane, 2c #2546, 8c #2548, 2 each 11c, 13c, #2519-2520, 6c #2583, #2596 24.00 24.00
Complete booklet, #2596a 24.00 24.00
2597 A736 15p like #2550 3.00 1.50
a. Booklet pane, #2588-2597 34.00 34.00
Complete booklet, #2597a 34.00 34.00

Nos. 2587a, 2596a, 2597a were made available to collectors unattached to the booklet cover.

Philippine Central Bank, 50th Anniv. — A761

1999, Jan. 3 Litho. *Perf. 14*

2598 A761 6p multicolored 1.00 .40

Philippine Centennial — A762

Designs: a, Centennial emblem. b, Proclamation of Independence. c, Malolos Congress. d, Nov. 5th uprising. e, Cry of Santa Barbara Iloilo. f, Victory over colonial forces. g, Flag raising, Butuan City. h, Ratification of Malolos Constitution. i, Philippine Republic formed. j, Barasoain Church.

1999, Jan. 11

2599 A762 6p Sheet of 10, #a.-j. 12.00 12.00

Scouting — A762a

Designs: No. 2599K, Girl Scout, boys planting tree. No. 2599L, Boy Scout, Girl Scout, flag, people representing various professions.

Perf. 13½

1999, Jan. 16 Litho. Unwmk.

2599K A762a 5p multicolored 2.50 .40
2599L A762a 5p multicolored 2.50 .40

Nos. 2599K-2599L are dated 1995, are inscribed "THRIFT STAMP," and were valid for postage due to stamp shortage.

Dept. of Transportation and Communications, Cent. — A763

Emblem and: a, Ship. b, Jet. c, Control tower. d, Satellite dish, bus.

15p, Philpost Headquarters, truck, motorcycle on globe.

1999, Jan. 20

2600 A763 6p Block of 4, #a.-d. 4.50 *4.00*

Souvenir Sheet

2601 A763 15p multicolored 4.00 *3.50*

No. 2600 was printed in sheets of 16. No. 2601 contains one 80x30mm stamp.

Filipino-American War, Cent. — A764

1999, Feb. 4

2602 A764 5p multicolored .85 .35

Philippine Military Academy, Cent. — A765

1999-2001 *Perf. 14*

2603 A765 5p multicolored 1.25 .50
a. Small "P" in denomination ('01) 2.50 1.75

"P" in denomination is 1¾mm tall on No. 2603, 1½mm tall on No. 2603a.

Issue dates: No. 2603, 2/4/99. No. 2063a, 2001.

Birds A766

#2604: a, Greater crested tern. b, Ruddy turnstone. c, Green-backed heron. d, Common tern.

#2605: a, Black-winged stilt. b, Asiatic dowitcher. c, Whimbrel. d, Reef heron.

#2606: a, Spotted greenshank. b, Tufted duck.

1999, Feb. 22 Litho. *Perf. 14*

2604 A766 5p Block of 4, #a.-d. 4.00 3.50
2605 A766 5p Block of 4, #a.-d. 4.00 3.50

Souvenir Sheets

2606 A766 8p Sheet of 2, #a.-b. 7.00 6.00
c. As #2606, diff. sheet margin, inscription 6.00 5.00

Issued: #2604-2606, 2/22; #2606c, 3/19.

Nos. 2604-2605 were printed in sheets of 16.

No. 2606c contains inscription, emblem for Australia '99 World Stamp Expo.

Heroes of the Revolution Type

Perf. 13½

1999, Mar. 12 Litho. Unwmk.

Pink Background

2607 A736 5p like #2547 .90 .30

Manila Lions Club, 50th Anniv. — A767

Design: Emblem, Francisco "Paquito" Ortigas, Jr., first president.

1999, Mar. 20 *Perf. 14*

2608 A767 5p multicolored 1.00 .40

Philippine Orthopedic Assoc., 50th Anniv. — A768

1999, Mar. 20

2609 A768 5p multicolored 1.00 .40

La Union Botanical Garden, San Fernando — A769

Designs: No. 2610, Entrance sign, birdhouse. No. 2611, Ticket booth at entrance.

1999, Mar. 20

2610 5p multicolored 1.00 .70
2611 5p multicolored 1.00 .70
a. A769 Pair, #2610-2611 2.50 2.00

Printed in panes of 20 (10 #2611a).

Frogs A770

#2612: a, Woodworth's frog. b, Giant Philippine frog. c, Gliding tree frog. d, Common forest frog.

#2613: a, Spiny tree frog. b, Truncate-toed chorus frog. c, Variable-backed frog.

1999, Apr. 5

2612 A770 5p Block of 4, #a.-d. 4.00 3.00

Sheet of 3

2613 A770 5p #a.-c. + label 6.50 6.00

No. 2612 was printed in sheets of 16.

Marine Life A771

No. 2614: a, Sea squirt. b, Banded sea snake. c, Manta ray. d, Painted rock lobster.

No. 2615: a, Sea grapes. b, Branching coral. c, Sea urchin.

1999, May 11 Litho. *Perf. 14*

2614 A771 5p Block of 4, #a.-d. 4.00 3.00

Sheet of 3

2615 A771 5p #a.-c. + label 8.00 7.50

No. 2614 printed in panes of 16.

Juan F. Nakpil, Architect, Birth Cent. — A772

1999, May 25

2616 A772 5p multicolored .80 .40

UPU, 125th Anniv. — A773

Designs: 5p, Globe, boy writing letter. 15p, Globe, girl looking at stamp collection.

1999, May 26 Litho. *Perf. 14*

2617 A773 5p multicolored 1.00 .40
2618 A773 15p multicolored 2.50 1.00

Philippines-Thailand Diplomatic Relations, 50th Anniv. — A774

Orchids: 5p, 11p, Euanthe sanderiana, cattleya Queen Sirikit.

1999, June 13 Litho. *Perf. 14*

2619 A774 5p multicolored 1.00 .50
2620 A774 11p multicolored 2.00 1.00

Order of flowers from top is reversed on 11p value.

Issued in sheets of 20 (10 of each denomination in two rows of 5, separated by a central gutter). Most sheets of 20 were cut in half through the central gutter.

See #2623-2624, 2640-2641, 2664-2666, 2719-2721, 2729-2731.

Masonic Charities for Crippled Children, Inc., 75th Anniv. — A775

1999, July 5

2621 A775 5p multicolored 1.25 .70

Production of Eberhard Faber "Mongol" Pencils, 150th Anniv. — A776

1999, July 5

2622 A776 5p multicolored .80 .40

Diplomatic Relations Type of 1999

Philippines-Korea diplomatic relations, 50th anniv., flowers: 5p, 11p, Jasminum sambac, hibiscus synacus.

1999, Aug. 9 **Litho.** ***Perf. 14***

2623 A774 5p multicolored 1.50 .60
2624 A774 11p multicolored 2.50 1.20

Order of flowers from top is reversed on 11p value.

issued in sheets of 20 (10 of each denomination in two rows of 5, separated by a central gutter). Most sheets of 20 were cut in half through the central gutter.

Community Chest, 50th Anniv. — A777

1999, Aug. 30

2625 A777 5p multicolored .80 .40

Philippine Bible Society, Cent. — A778

1999, Aug. 30

2626 A778 5p multicolored .80 .40

A779

1999, Sept. 3

2627 A779 5p multicolored .80 .40

St. Francis of Assisi Parish, Sariaya, 400th anniv.

National Anthem, Cent. — A780

1999, Sept. 3

2628 A780 5p multicolored 1.20 .50

No. 2539b Overprinted in Silver "25th ANNIVERSARY IPPS"

Souvenir Sheet

1999, Sept. 24 **Litho.** ***Perf. 14***

2629 A746 15p Sheet of 3, #a.-c., + 3 labels 8.00 6.00

Ovpt. in sheet margin has same inscription twice, "25th ANNIVERSARY INTERNATIONAL PHILIPPINE PHILATELIC SOCIETY 1974-99" and two society emblems.

Senate — A781

1999, Oct. 15

2630 A781 5p multicolored .80 .40

A782

1999, Oct. 20

2631 A782 5p multicolored .90 .45

New Building of Chiang Kai-shek College, Manila.

Issued in sheets of 10.

Tanza National Comprehensive High School, 50th Anniv. — A783

1999, Oct. 24

2632 A783 5p multicolored .80 .40

San Agustin Church, Paoay, World Heritage Site — A784

Intl. Year of Older Persons — A785

World Teachers' Day — A786

1999, Oct. 24

2633 A784 5p multicolored 1.00 .50
2634 A785 11p multicolored 2.00 1.00
2635 A786 15p multicolored 3.00 2.00
Nos. 2633-2635 (3) 6.00 3.50

United Nations Day.

Christmas — A787

1999, Oct. 27

Color of Angel's Gown

2636 A787 5p red violet 1.20 .40
2637 A787 11p yellow 2.40 .70
2638 A787 13p blue 3.00 1.20
2639 A787 15p green 3.50 1.80
a. Sheet of 4, #2636-2639 10.00 8.00
Nos. 2636-2639 (4) 10.10 4.10

Nos. 2636-2639 each issued in sheets of 10 stamps with two central labels.

Diplomatic Relations Type of 1999

Philippines-Canada diplomatic relations, 50th anniv., mammals: 5p, 15p, Tamaraw, polar bear.

1999, Nov. 15 ***Perf. 14***

2640 A774 5p multi 1.25 .75
2641 A774 15p multi 3.00 1.50

Order of mammals from top is reversed on 15p value.

Issued in sheets of 20 (10 of each denomination in two rows of 5, separated by a central gutter). Most sheets of 20 were cut in half through central gutter.

Renovation of Araneta Coliseum — A788

1999, Nov. 19 **Litho.**

2642 A788 5p multicolored 1.00 .40

A789

1999, Nov. 19 **Color of Sky**

2643 A789 5p dark blue 1.00 .50
2644 A789 11p blue green 2.50 .80

3rd ASEAN Informal Summit.

A790

Sculptures: No. 2645, Kristo, by Arturo Luz. 11p, Homage to Dodgie Laurel, by J. Elizalde Navarro. 13p, Hilojan, by Napoleon Abueva. No. 2648, Mother and Child, by Abueva.

No. 2649: a, 5p, Mother's Revenge, by José Rizal, horiz. b, 15p, El Ermitano, by Rizal, horiz.

1999, Nov. 29

2645 A790 5p multi 1.00 .25
2646 A790 11p multi 2.00 .50
2647 A790 13p multi 2.50 .60
2648 A790 15p multi 3.00 .80
Nos. 2645-2648 (4) 8.50 2.15

Souvenir Sheet

2649 A790 Sheet of 2, #a.-b. 6.00 5.00

Natl. Stamp Collecting Month.

New Year 2000 (Year of the Dragon) — A791

5p, Dragon in water. 11p, Dragon in sky.

1999, Dec. 1 ***Perf. 14***

2650 A791 5p multicolored 1.25 .70
2651 A791 11p multicolored 2.75 1.30
a. Sheet of 2, #2650-2651 3.50 3.00
b. As "a," imperf. 3.50 3.00

Nos. 2650-2651 were normally printed in sheets of 20.

Battle of Tirad Pass, Cent. — A792

1999, Dec. 2 ***Perf. 14***

2652 A792 5p multicolored .80 .40

Orchids A793

No. 2653: a, Paphiopedilum urbanianum. b, Phalaenopsis schilleriana. c, Dendrobium amethystoglossum. d, Paphiopedilum barbatum.

No. 2654, horiz.: a, Paphiopedilum haynaldianum. b, Phalaenopsis stuartiana. c, Trichoglottis brachiata. d, Ceratostylis rubra.

1999, Dec. 3 **Litho.**

2653 A793 5p Block of 4, #a.-d. 4.50 4.00

Souvenir Sheet

2654 A793 5p Sheet of 4, #a.-d. 5.50 5.00

No. 2653 was printed in sheets of 16.

Battle of San Mateo, Cent. — A794

1999, Dec. 19

2655 A794 5p multicolored .80 .40

People Power A795

People and: a, Tank. b, Tower. c, Crucifix.

1999, Dec. 31

2656 A795 5p Strip of 3, #a.-c. 3.50 3.00

Printed in sheets of 12.

Natl. Commission on the Role of Filipino Women — A796

2000, Jan. 7 **Litho.** ***Perf. 14***

2657 A796 5p multicolored .80 .40

Printed in sheets of 10.

Manila Bulletin, Cent. — A797

2000, Feb. 2 **Litho.** ***Perf. 14***

2658 A797 5p multicolored 1.00 .50
a. Year at LR 1.50 .60

Issued: No. 2658a, 6/7.

La Union Province, 150th Anniv. A798

Arms of province and: a, Sailboat, golfer. b, Tractor, worker, building. c, Building, flagpole. d, Airplane, ship, telephone tower, people on telephone, computer.

2000, Mar. 2
2659 A798 5p Block of 4, #a.-d. 3.00 2.50

Civil Service Commission, Cent. — A799

2000, Mar. 20
2660 A799 5p multicolored .80 .30

Millennium — A800

Designs: a, Golden Garuda of Palawan. b, First sunrise of the millennium, Pusan Point. c, Golden Tara of Agusan.

2000, Mar. 31
2661 A800 5p Strip of 3, #a.-c. 5.00 4.00

Printed in sheets of 12.

GMA Radio and Television Network, 50th Anniv. — A802

2000, Mar. 1 **Litho.** ***Perf. 14***
2662 A802 5p multicolored .80 .40

Philippine Presidents A803

No. 2662A: b, Manuel Roxas. c, Elpidio Quirino. No. 2663: a, Presidential seal. b, Joseph Ejercito Estrada. c, Fidel V. Ramos. d, Corazon C. Aquino. e, Ferdinand E. Marcos. f, Diosdado Macapagal. g, Carlos P. Garcia. h, Ramon Magsaysay. i, Elpidio Quirino. j, Manuel Roxas.

2000 ***Perf. 13½***
2662A A803 Pair 1.80 1.25
b.-c. 5p Any single .60 .30
2663 Block of 10 9.00 7.50
a.-j. A803 5p Any single .60 .35

Nos. 2662b-2662c have presidential seal but lack blue lines at bottom. No. 2663a has denomination at left. Nos. 2663b-2663j have small Presidential seal at bottom.

Issued: No. 2662A, 2/6. No. 2663, 3/16.

See Type A828 for stamps showing Presidential seal with colored background.

See Nos. 2672-2676, 2786.

Diplomatic Relations Type of 1999

5p, Sarimanok, Great Wall of China. 11p, Phoenix, Banaue rice terraces.

No. 2666: a, 5p, Great Wall, horiz. b, 11p, Rice terraces, horiz.

2000, May 8 ***Perf. 14***
2664-2665 A774 Set of 2 3.50 2.00

Souvenir Sheet

2666 A774 Sheet of 2, #a-b 4.50 3.50

Issued in sheets of 20 (10 of each denomination in two rows of 5, separated by a central gutter). Most sheets of 20 were cut in half through central gutter.

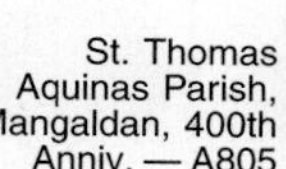

St. Thomas Aquinas Parish, Mangaldan, 400th Anniv. — A805

2000, June 1
2667 A805 5p multicolored .80 .45

Battle Centenaries A806

Battles in Philippine Insurrection: #2668, Mabitac. #2669, Paye, vert. #2670, Makahambus Hill, vert. #2671, Pulang Lupa.

2000, June 19
2668-2671 A806 5p Set of 4 3.25 1.60

Presidents Type of 2000 Redrawn

No. 2672: a, Presidential seal. b, Joseph Ejercito Estrada. c, Fidel V. Ramos. d, Corazon C. Aquino. e, Ferdinand E. Marcos. f, Diosdado Macapagal. g, Carlos P. Garcia. h, Ramon Magsaysay. i, Elpidio Quirino. j, Manuel Roxas.

No. 2673: a, Magsaysay. b, Garcia.
No. 2674: a, Macapagal. b, Marcos.
No. 2675: a, Aquino. b, Ramos.
No. 2676: a, Estrada. b, Presidential seal.

2000 **Litho.** ***Perf. 13½***

Blue Lines at Bottom

2672 Block of 10 *13.00 10.00*
a.-j. A803 5p Any single *1.00 .50*
2673 Pair *4.50 3.75*
a.-b. A803 10p Any single *1.75 .60*
2674 Pair *5.00 4.25*
a.-b. A803 11p Any single *2.00 .70*
2675 Pair *5.50 4.00*
a.-b. A803 13p Any single *2.25 .80*
2676 Pair *6.50 5.50*
a.-b. A803 15p Any single *2.75 1.00*
Nos. 2672-2676 (5) 34.50 27.50

Issued: No. 2672, 7/3; Nos. 2673-2674, 8/4. Nos. 2675-2676, 6/19.

No. 2672a has denomination at R, while No. 2663a has denomination at L. Nos. 2672b-2672j have no presidential seal, while Nos. 2662Ab-2662Ac, 2663b-2663j have seal.

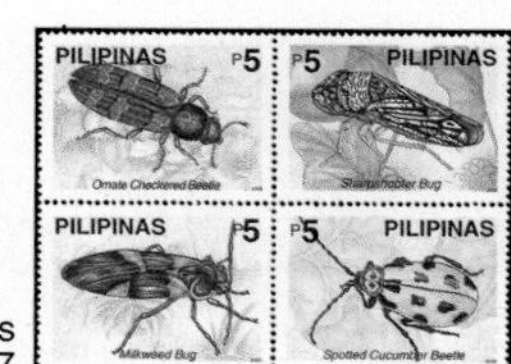

Insects A807

No. 2677: a, Ornate checkered beetle. b, Sharpshooter bug. c, Milkweed bug. d, Spotted cucumber beetle.

No. 2678: a, Green June beetle. b, Convergent ladybird. c, Eastern Hercules beetle. d, Harlequin cabbage bug.

2000, July 21 ***Perf. 14***
2677 A807 5p Block of 4, #a-d 4.00 3.00
e. Souevnir sheet, #2677 6.00 6.00
2678 A807 5p Block of 4, #a-d 4.00 3.50
e. Souevnir sheet, #2678 6.00 6.00

Nos. 2677-2678 were printed in sheets of 16.

Occupational Health Nurses Association, 50th Anniv. — A808

2000, Aug. 30
2679 A808 5p multicolored .85 .40

Diocese of Lucena, 50th Anniv. — A809

2000. Aug. 30
2680 A809 5p multicolored .80 .40

Millennium — A810

Boats: a, Balanghai. b, Vinta. c, Caracoa.

2000, Sept. 21
2681 A810 Horiz. strip of 3 3.50 3.00
a.-c. 5p Any single *.90 .60*

Printed in sheets of 12.

Equitable PCI Bank, 50th Anniv. — A811

2000, Sept. 26
2682 A811 5p multicolored .80 .40

Year of the Overseas Filipino Worker — A812

2000, Sept. 29 **Litho.**
2683 A812 5p multicolored .80 .50

2000 Olympics, Sydney — A813

No. 2684: a, Running. b, Archery. c, Shooting. d, Diving.

No. 2685, horiz.: a, Boxing. b, Equestrian. c, Rowing. d, Taekwondo.

2000, Sept. 30
2684 A813 5p Block of 4, #a-d 4.00 3.50

Souvenir Sheet

2685 A813 5p Sheet of 4, #a-d 6.00 5.00

No. 2684 was printed in sheets of 16.

Teresian Association in the Philippines, 50th Anniv. — A814

2000, Oct. 10
2686 A814 5p multicolored .80 .60
a. Miniature sheet of 20 30.00 30.00

No. 2686 normally issued in sheets of 50.

House of Representatives A815

2000, Oct. 15 ***Perf. 14***
2687 A815 5p multicolored .80 .45

Marine Corps, 50th Anniv. — A816

2000, Oct. 18
2688 A816 5p multicolored .80 .40

Souvenir Sheet

Postal Service, Cent. (in 1998) A817

2000, Nov. 6
2689 A817 15p multicolored 4.00 3.00

Clothing Exhibit at Metropolitan Museum of Manila — A818

No. 2690, 5p: a, Kalinga / Gaddang cotton loincloth. b, Portrait of Leticia Jimenez, by unknown artist.

No. 2691, 5p, horiz.: a, B'laan female upper garment. b, T'boli T'nalak abaca cloth.

No. 2692: a, 5p, Portrait of Teodora Devera Ygnacio, by Justiniano Asunción. b, 15p, Detail of Tawsug silk sash.

2000, Nov. 15 **Pairs, #a-b**
2690-2691 A818 Set of 2 4.00 3.00
#2690a-b, 2691a-b, any single .60 .40

Souvenir Sheet

2692 A818 Sheet of 2, #a-b 4.50 4.50

Nos. 2690-2691 were printed in sheets of 16.

Natl. Stamp Collecting Month — A819

Designs: 5p, Portrait of an Unkown Lady, by Juan Luna, vert. 11p, Nude, by José Joya. 13p, Lotus Odalisque, by Rodolfo Paras-Perez. No. 2696, 15p, Untitled Nude, by Fernando Amorsolo.

No. 2697, The Memorial, by Cesar Legaspi.

2000, Nov. 20 ***Perf. 14***
2693-2696 A819 Set of 4 8.00 4.50

Souvenir Sheet

2697 A819 15p multi 5.00 4.00

No. 2697 contains one 80x29 stamp and label.

Christmas — A820

Angels: No. 2698, 5p, In pink robe, with bouquet of flowers. No. 2699, 5p, As #2698, with Holy Year 2000 emblem and inscription. 11p, In green robe. 13p, In orange robe. 15p, In red robe, with garland of flowers.

2000, Nov. 22 **Litho.**
2698-2702 A820 Set of 5 7.50 4.00

Nos. 2698-2702 were printed in sheets of 12.

APO Philatelic Society, 50th Anniv. — A821

Emblem and stamps: No. 2703, 5p, #620 (yellow background). No. 2704, 5p, #639 (light blue background), horiz. No. 2705, 5p, #850 (dull green background). No. 2706, 5p, #B21 (pink background), horiz.

2000, Nov. 23
2703-2706 A821 Set of 4 8.50 5.00

Printed in sheets of 16 in blocks of 4, each of the four designs on each corner, creating a se-tenant block of 4 in the center of each of the two types of sheets of 16 (horiz. or vert).

No. 1806 Handstamp Surcharged in Red

Perf. 13x13½

2000, Nov. 24 Litho. Wmk.
2706A A469 5p on 3.60p multi 10.00 6.00

Nine varieties of the surcharge on No. 2706A exist.

New Year 2001 (Year of the Snake) — A822

Snakes with inscription in: 5p, Tagalog. 11p, English.

2000, Dec. 20 Unwmk. *Perf. 14*
2707-2708 A822 Set of 2 3.50 2.00
2708a Souvenir sheet, #2707-2708 + 2 labels 5.00 5.00

Nos. 2707-2708 were printed in sheets of 20.
No. 2708a exists imperf. Value, $5.

Millennium A823

No. 2709: a, Trade and progress. b, Education and knowledge. c, Communication and information.

2000, Dec. 28
2709 Horiz. strip of 3 4.00 3.00
a.-c. A823 5p Any single .80 .50

No. 2709 was printed in sheets of 12.

Bank of the Philippine Islands, 150th Anniv. — A824

2001, Jan. 30 Litho.
2710 A824 5p multicolored .80 .50
a. Miniature sheet of 20 25.00 25.00

No. 2710 was normally issued in sheets of 50.

Hong Kong 2001 Stamp Exhibition — A825

Designs: No. 2711a, 5p, No. 2712, 11p, Tamaraw. No. 2711b, 5p, No. 2713, 11p, Agila. No. 2711c, 5p, No. 2714, 11p, Tarsier. No. 2711d, 5p, No. 2715, 11p, Talisman Cove orchid. No. 2711e, 5p, No. 2716, 11p, Pawikan.

2001, Feb. 1
2711 Horiz. strip of 5 5.00 4.00
a.-e. A825 5p Any single .80 .50

Souvenir Sheets

2712-2716 A825 Set of 5 20.00 15.00
2713a Ovptd. in margin in red 6.50 5.00
2715a Ovptd. in margin in red 6.50 5.00

No. 2711 was printed in sheets of 25. Nos. 2712-2716 have show emblem on sheet margin instead of on stamp.

Issued: Nos. 2713a, 2715a, 6/30/01. Overprint in margin on Nos. 2713a, 2715a has Chinese inscriptions and English text "PHILIPPINE-CHINESE PHILATELIC SOCIETY / 1951 GOLDEN JUBILEE 2001."

Gen. Paciano Rizal (1851-1930) — A826

2001, Mar. 7 Litho. *Perf. 14*
2717 A826 5p multicolored 1.00 .50

San Beda College, Cent. — A827

2001, Mar. 9
2718 A827 5p multicolored .80 .40

Diplomatic Relations Type of 1999

Philippines-Vatican City diplomatic relations, 50th anniv., main altars at: 5p, St. Peter's Basilica, Vatican City. No. 2720, 15p, San Agustin Church, Manila.

No. 2721: a, Adam, from Creation of Adam, by Michelangelo. b, God, from Creation of Adam.

2001, Mar. 14
2719-2720 A774 Set of 2 4.00 3.00

Souvenir Sheet

2721 A774 15p Sheet of 2, #a-b 6.50 5.00

Nos. 2719-2720 issued in sheets of 20 (10 of each denomination in two rows of 5, separated by a central gutter). Most sheets of 20 were cut in half through central gutter.

Presidential Seal With Colored Background — A828

2001, Apr. 5 *Perf. 13¾*

Background Colors

2722 A828 5p yellow .50 .30
2723 A828 15p blue 1.75 .50

Stamps of the same denomination showing the Presidential seal with white backgrounds are listed as Nos. 2663a, 2672a and 2676b.

See Nos. 2746-2748. For surcharges, see Nos. 2834-2836. For overprints, see Nos. 2865-2866.

Tourist Spots — A829

No. 2724: a, El Nido, Palawan Province. b, Vigan House, Ilocos Sur Province. c, Boracay, Aklan Province. d, Chocolate Hills, Bohol Province.

15p, Banaue Rice Terraces, Ifugao Province.

2000, Apr. 14 *Perf. 14*
2724 Horiz. strip of 4 3.00 2.50
a.-d. A829 5p Any single .60 .40

Souvenir Sheet

2725 A829 15p multi 4.50 3.50

No. 2725 contains one 80x30mm stamp.
No. 2725 exists with washed-out colors and a larger year date. Value, $25.

Canonical Coronation of Our Lady of Manaoag, 75th Anniv. — A830

2001, Apr. 22
2726 A830 5p multicolored .75 .40

Pres. Gloria Macapagal-Arroyo A831

Pres. Macapagal-Arroyo: No. 2727, 5p, Waving. No. 2728, 5p, Taking oath of office.

2001, Apr. 29
2727-2728 A831 Set of 2 1.75 1.00

Diplomatic Relations Type of 1999

Philippines-Australia diplomatic relations, landmarks: 5p, Nos. 2730-2731, 13p, Sydney Opera House, Cultural Center of the Philippines. No. 2731 is horiz.

2001, May 21
2729-2730 A774 Set of 2 3.25 1.50

Souvenir Sheet

2731 A774 13p multi 4.50 3.50

Nos. 2729-2730 issued in sheets of 20 (10 of each denomination in two rows of 5, separated by a central gutter. Most sheets of 20 were cut in half through central gutter.
No. 2731 contains one 80x30mm stamp.

Supreme Court, Cent. — A832

2001, May 31
2732 A832 5p multicolored .80 .40

Silliman University, Dumaguete City, Cent. — A833

2001, June 1
2733 A833 5p multicolored .80 .40

Philippine Normal University, Cent. — A834

2001, June 1
2734 A834 5p multicolored .80 .40

Joaquin J. Ortega (1870-1943), First Civil Governor of La Union Province — A835

2001, July 12
2735 A835 5p multicolored .80 .50

Printed in panes of 20.

Eugenio Lopez (1901-75), Businessman — A836

2001, July 12
2736 A836 5p multicolored .80 .50

Printed in panes of 20.

Illustrations from Boxer Codex, c. 1590 — A837

No. 2737: a, Visayan couple. b, Tagalog couple. c, Moros of Luzon (multicolored frame). d, Moros of Luzon (blue frame).

No. 2738: a, Pintados (denomination at left). b, Pintados (denomination at right). c, Cagayan female. d, Zambal.

2001, Aug. 1
2737 A837 5p Block of 4, #a-d 3.00 2.50

Souvenir Sheet

2738 A837 5p Sheet of 4, #a-d 3.75 3.00
e. Sheet of 4, #a-d, with Phila Nippon '01 margin 4.00 3.00

No. 2737 was printed in sheets of 16.

Arrival of American Educators (Thomasites), Cent. — A838

Designs: 5p, Thomasite teachers, US transport ship Thomas. 15p, Philippine students.

2001, Aug. 23
2739-2740 A838 Set of 2 3.00 1.60

Technological University of the Philippines, Cent. — A839

2001, Aug. 20 Litho. *Perf. 14*
2741 A839 5p multicolored .80 .40

National Museum of the Philippines, Cent. — A840

2001, Sept. 3
2742 A840 5p multicolored .80 .40

Lands Management Bureau, Cent. — A841

2001, Sept. 17
2743 A841 5p multicolored .80 .40

Colegio de San Jose and San Jose Seminary, 400th Anniv. — A842

2001, Oct. 1

2744 A842 5p multicolored .80 .40

Makati City Financial District — A843

2001, Oct. 1

2745 A843 5p multicolored .70 .40

Presidential Seal With Colored Background Type of 2001

2001, Oct. 5 ***Perf. 13¾***

Background Colors

2746 A828 10p green 1.00 .35
2747 A828 11p pink 1.25 .40
2748 A828 13p gray 1.50 .45
Nos. 2746-2748 (3) 3.75 1.20

Musical Instruments — A844

No. 2749: a, Trumpet. b, Tuba. c, French horn. d, Trombone.

No. 2750, vert.: a, Bass drum. b, Clarinet, oboe. c, Xylophone. d, Sousaphone.

2001, Oct. 8 ***Perf. 14***

2749 A844 5p Block of 4, #a-d 3.00 2.50

Souvenir Sheet

2750 A844 5p Sheet of 4, #a-d 5.00 4.00

No. 2749 printed in panes of 16.

Malampaya Deep Water Gas Power Project — A845

Frame colors: 5p, Silver. 15p, Gold.

2001, Oct. 16

2751-2752 A845 Set of 2 4.00 2.00

Printed in panes of 20.

Intl. Volunteers Year — A846

2001, Oct. 24

2753 A846 5p multicolored 1.00 .50

Year of Dialogue Among Civilizations — A847

2001, Oct. 24

2754 A847 15p multicolored 2.25 .80

Christmas — A848

Designs: 5p, Herald Angels. 11p, Kumukutikutitap. 13p, Pasko ni Bitoy. 15p, Pasko na naman.

2001, Oct. 30

2755-2758 A848 Set of 4 6.50 3.50

Philippines — Switzerland Relations, 150th Anniv. — A849

Monument statues by Richard Kissling: 5p, William Tell. No. 2760, 15p, Jose P. Rizal.

No. 2761, 15p, Mayon Volcano, Philippines, and Matterhorn, Switzerland.

2001, Nov. 26

2759-2760 A849 Set of 2 3.75 2.00

Souvenir Sheet

2761 A849 15p multicolored 4.00 3.00

No. 2761 contains one 79x29mm stamp. Nos. 2759-2760 issued in sheets of 20 (10 of each denomination in two rows of 5, separated by a central gutter). Most sheets of 20 were cut in half through central gutter.

Drawings of Manila Inhabitants, c. 1840 — A850

Designs: 17p, Woman with hat, man with green pants. 21p, Woman with veil, man with brown pants. 22p, Man, woman at mortar and pestle.

2001, Dec. 1 ***Perf. 13¾***

Inscribed "2001"

2762 A850 17p multicolored 2.00 .60
a. Inscribed "2002" 2.50 .70
b. Inscribed "2003" 5.00 2.00
2763 A850 21p multicolored 3.00 1.00
a. Inscribed "2002" 3.50 1.50
2764 A850 22p multicolored 3.00 1.00
a. Inscribed "2002" 3.00 1.00
Nos. 2762-2764 (3) 8.00 2.60

See No. 2779.

Solicitor General, Cent. — A851

2001, Dec. 7 ***Perf. 14***

2765 A851 5p multicolored .80 .40

Natl. Stamp Collecting Month — A852

Art: 5p, PUJ, by Antonio Austria. 17p, Hesus Nazareno, by Angelito Antonio. 21p, Three Women with Basket, by Anita Magsaysay-Ho, vert. No. 2769, 22p, Church with Yellow Background, by Mauro "Malang" Santos, vert.

No. 2770, 22p, Komedya ng Pakil, by Danilo Dalena.

2001, Dec. 7 **Litho.**

2766-2769 A852 Set of 4 9.00 6.00

Souvenir Sheet

2770 A852 22p multicolored 4.50 3.50

No. 2770 contains one 79x29mm stamp.

New Year 2002 (Year of the Horse) — A853

Horse color: 5p, Red. 17p, White.

2001, Dec. 14 ***Perf. 14***

2771-2772 A853 Set of 2 4.00 2.50
2772a Souvenir sheet, #2771-2772, + 2 labels 6.00 5.00

Nos. 2771-2772 were printed in sheets of 20. No. 2772a exists imperf. Value $6.

Josemaria Escrivá (1902-75), Founder of Opus Dei — A854

2002, Jan. 9

2773 A854 5p multicolored .80 .50
a. Miniature sheet of 20 35.00 35.00

No. 2773 was normally issued in sheets of 50.

World Heritage Sites — A855

Vigan City sites: 5p, St. Paul's Metropolitan Cathedral. 22p, Calle Crisologo.

2002, Jan. 22

2774-2775 A855 Set of 2 5.00 3.50

Nos. 2774-2775 were printed in sheets of 14 stamps plus one central label.

Salvador Z. Araneta, Statesman, Birth Cent. — A856

2002, Jan. 31

2776 A856 5p multicolored .80 .40

Customs Service, Cent. — A857

2002, Feb. 1

2777 A857 5p multicolored 1.25 .60

Printed in sheets of 20, with "fade away" blue background, so each of the 20 stamps has a different blue background.

Valentine's Day — A858

No. 2778: a, Envelope. b, Man and woman. c, Cat and dog. d, Balloon.

2002, Feb. 8

2778 A858 5p Block of 4, #a-d 4.00 3.00

Printed in sheets of 16.

Drawings of Manila Inhabitants Type of 2001

2002, Mar. 1 **Litho.** ***Perf. 13¾***

Inscribed "2002"

2779 A850 5p Man, woman on horses .50 .25
a. Inscribed "2003" .30 .25

Baguio General Hospital and Medical Center, Cent. — A859

2002, Mar. 22 ***Perf. 14***

2780 A859 5p multicolored .75 .40

Beatification of Blessed Pedro Calungsod — A860

Designs: 5p, Calungsod with palm frond. 22p, Map of Guam, ship, Calungsod with cross.

2002, Apr. 2 ***Perf. 14***

2781 A860 5p multicolored 1.00 .50
a. Miniature sheet of 20 30.00 30.00

Size: 102x72mm

Imperf

2782 A860 22p multicolored 4.50 3.00

No. 2781 printed in sheets of 50 and miniature sheets of 20.

Negros Occidental High School, Cent. — A861

2002, Apr. 12 ***Perf. 14***

2783 A861 5p multicolored .75 .40

La Consolacion College, Manila, Cent. — A862

2002, Apr. 12

2784 A862 5p multicolored .75 .40

Vesak Day — A863

2002, May 26

2785 A863 5p multicolored 1.25 .70
a. Miniature sheet of 20 30.00 30.00

No. 2785 was normally issued in sheets of 50.

Presidents Type of 2000 Redrawn Without Years of Service

No. 2786: a, Gloria Macapagal-Arroyo. b, Joseph Ejercito Estrada. c, Fidel V. Ramos. d, Corazon C. Aquino. e, Ferdinand E. Marcos. f, Diosdado Macapagal. g, Carlos P. Garcia. h, Ramon Magsaysay. i, Elpidio Quirino. j, Manuel Roxas.

2002, June 12 ***Perf. 13½***

Without Presidential Seal

Blue Lines at Bottom

2786 Block of 10 8.00 *8.00*
a.-j. A803 5p Any single .60 .30

Cavite National High School, Cent. — A864

2002, June 19 ***Perf. 14***

2787 A864 5p multicolored .75 .40

Mangroves A865

Fish — A866

Fish — A867

Hands and Small Fish — A868

No. 2792: a, Monitors in boats at marine sanctuary. b, Mangrove reforestation. c, Monitors checking reefs. d, Seaweed farming.

Unwmk.

2002, June 24 Litho. *Perf. 14*

2788 A865 5p multicolored 1.20 .50
2789 A866 5p multicolored 1.20 .50
2790 A867 5p multicolored 1.20 .50
2791 A868 5p multicolored 1.20 .50
Nos. 2788-2791 (4) 4.80 2.00

Souvenir Sheet

2792 A865 5p Sheet of 4, #a-d 4.00 3.00

Coastal resources conservation.

Nos. 2788-2791 were printed in sheets of 20.

Iglesia Filipina Independiente, Cent. — A869

2002, July 4

2793 A869 5p multicolored .75 .40

Souvenir Sheet

Philakorea 2002 World Stamp Exhibition, Seoul — A870

No. 2794: a, 5p, Mangrove. b, 17p, Buddhist, temple and flower.

2002, Aug. 2 Unwmk.

2794 A870 Sheet of 2, #a-b 4.50 3.50

No. 2794 exists imperf. with changed background color. Value $10.

No. 2210 Surcharged

Method & Perf. as Before

2002, Aug. 15 Wmk. 391

2795 A610 3p on 60s multi .80 .40

Telecommunications Officials Meetings, Manila — A870a

2002, Aug. 22 Litho. *Perf. 14*

2795A A870a 5p multicolored .75 .40

Second Telecommunications Ministerial Meeting, Third ASEAN Telecommunications Senior Officials Meeting, Eighth ASEAN Telecommunications Regulators Council Meeting.

Marikina, Shoe Capital of the Philippines A871

Unwmk.

2002, Oct. 15 Litho. *Perf. 14*

2796 A871 5p multicolored .75 .40

Souvenir Sheet

Intl. Year of Mountains — A872

2002, Oct. 28

2797 A872 22p multicolored 3.00 2.50

Christmas — A873

Various holiday foods: 5p, 17p, 21p, 22p.

2002, Nov. 5

2798-2801 A873 Set of 4 9.00 5.00

Stamp Collecting Month — A874

Designs: 5p, Gerardo de Leon (1913-81), movie director. 17p, Francisca Reyes Aquino (1899-1983), founder of Philippine Folk Dance Society. 21p, Pablo S. Antonio (1901-75), architect. No. 2805, 22p, Jose Garcia Villa (1912-97), writer.

No. 2806, 22p, Honorata de la Rama (1902-91), singer and actress.

2002, Nov. 2 *Perf. 14*

2802-2805 A874 Set of 4 8.00 5.00

Size: 99x74mm

Imperf

2806 A874 22p multicolored 3.25 2.50

First Circumnavigation of the World, 480th Anniv. — A875

No. 2807 — Ship and: a, Antonio Pigafetta. b, Ferdinand Magellan. c, King Charles I of Spain. d, Sebastian Elcano.

22p, World Map and King Charles I of Spain.

2002 *Perf. 14*

2807 A875 5p Vert. strip of 4, #a-d 4.00 3.00

Size: 104x85mm

Imperf

2808 A875 22p multicolored 4.50 3.50

No. 2807 printed in sheets of 20.

Issued: No. 2807, 12/2; No. 2808, 2/10.

Fourth World Meeting of Families — A876

Designs: 5p, Sculpture of Holy Family. 11p, Family, crucifix, Holy Spirit.

2002, Nov. 23 *Perf. 14*

2809-2810 A876 Set of 2 2.50 1.00

New Year 2003 (Year of the Ram) — A877

Ram facing: 5p, Left. 17p, Right.

2002, Dec. 1

2811-2812 A877 Set of 2 4.00 2.50
a. Souvenir sheet, #2811-2812 + 2 labels 6.00 5.00

Nos. 2811-2812 were printed in sheets of 20.

No. 2812a exists imperf. Value, $6.

Lyceum of the Philippines, 50th Anniv. — A878

2002, Dec. 5 *Perf. 14*

2813 A878 5p multicolored .75 .40

Orchids A879

No. 2814: a, Luisia teretifolia. b, Dendrobium victoria-reginae, horiz. c, Gedorum densiflorum. d, Nervilia plicata, horiz.

22p, Grammatophyllum scriptum, horiz.

2002, Dec. 19 *Perf. 14*

2814 A879 5p Block of 4, #a-d 4.50 3.50

Souvenir Sheet

Imperf

2815 A879 22p multicolored 4.50 3.50

No. 2814 was printed in sheets of 16. No. 2815 contains one 69x40mm stamp.

No. 2814 was reprinted with a larger "2002" date. Value, block of 4, $11.

La Union National High School, Cent. — A880

2003, Jan. 22 *Perf. 14*

2816 A880 5p multicolored .75 .40

St. Luke's Medical Center, Cathedral Heights, Cent. — A881

2003, Jan. 23

2817 A881 5p multicolored .75 .40

Far Eastern University, 75th Anniv. — A882

2003, Jan. 28

2818 A882 5p multicolored .75 .40

Manila Electric Railroad and Light Company, Cent. — A883

2003, Jan. 31

2819 A883 5p multicolored .75 .40

St. Valentine's Day — A884

Mailman and: 5p, Heart-shaped strawberry. 17p, Hearts and mountains. 21p, Hearts and clouds. 22p, Butterflies and heart-shaped flowers.

2003, Feb. 11

2820-2823 A884 Set of 4 10.00 4.00

Nos. 2820-2823 were printed in sheets of 16.

Souvenir Sheets

Summer Institute of Linguistics, 50th Anniv. in Philippines — A885

No. 2824: a, 5p, Yakan weaving. b, 6p, Ifugao weaving. c, 5p, Kagayanen weaving. d, Bagobo Abaca weaving.
No. 2825, 11p: a, Ayta bow and arrows. b, Ibatan baskets. c, Palawano gong. d, Mindanao instruments.
No. 2826: a, 17p, Tboli cross-stitch. b, 5p, Aklanon Piña weaving. c, Kalinga weaving. d, Manobo beadwork.

2003, Feb. 28 **Litho.**

Sheets of 4, #a-d

2824-2826	A885	Set of 3	25.00	22.00

Intl. Decade of the World's Indigenous People.

Arrival of Japanese Workers for Construction of Kennon Road, Cent. — A886

2003, Feb. 20 ***Perf. 14***

2827	A886	5p multi	.75	.40

National Heroes — A887

Designs: No. 2828, 6p, Apolinario Mabini (1864-1903), independence advocate. No. 2829, 6p, Luciano San Miguel (1875-1903), military leader.

2003, May 13 **Litho.** ***Perf. 14***

2828-2829	A887	Set of 2	1.75	1.00

Orchids — A888

Designs (no flower names shown): 6p, Dendrobium uniflorum. 9p, Paphiopedilum urbanianum. 17p, Epigeneium lyonii. 21p, Thrixspermum subulatum.

2003, May 16 ***Perf. 14½, 13¾ (9p)***

2830	A888	6p multi	.70	.25
2831	A888	9p multi	1.00	.35
2832	A888	17p multi	2.25	.90
2833	A888	21p multi	2.50	1.00
		Nos. 2830-2833 (4)	6.45	2.50

See Nos. 2849-2853, 2904-2912 for stamps with flower names.

No. 2722 Surcharged in Black or Red

2003 ***Perf. 13¾***

2834	A828	1p on 5p multi	.70	.25
2835	A828	1p on 5p multi (R)	.60	.25
2836	A828	6p on 5p multi	.60	.25
		Nos. 2834-2836 (3)	1.90	.75

Issued: Nos. 2834-2835, 5/19; No. 2836, 6/4.

Philippine Medical Association, Cent. — A889

2003, May 21 ***Perf. 14***

2837	A889	6p multi	.75	.40

Rural Banking, 50th Anniv. — A890

2003, May 22

2838	A890	6p multi	.75	.40

Mountains — A891

No. 2839: a, Mt. Makiling. b, Mt. Kanlaon. c, Mt. Kitanglad. d, Mt. Mating-oy.
No. 2840: a, Mt. Iraya. b, Mt. Hibok-Hibok. c, Mt. Apo. d, Mt. Santo Tomas.

2003, June 16

2839	A891	6p Block of 4, #a-d	3.75	3.00

Souvenir Sheet

2840	A891	6p Sheet of 4, #a-d	5.00	4.00

No. 2839 was printed in sheets of 16.

Chinese Roots of José Rizal — A892

Designs: 6p, Rizal Monument, Rizal Park, Jinjiang, People's Republic of China, vert. 17p, Rizal and Pagoda, Jinjiang.

2003, June 19

2841-2842	A892	Set of 2	3.25	2.50

Waterfalls — A893

No. 2843: a, Maria Cristina Falls. b, Katibawasan Falls. c, Bagongbong Falls. d, Pagsanjan Falls.
No. 2844: a, Casiawan Falls. b, Pangi Falls. c, Tinago Falls. d, Kipot Twin Falls.

2003, June 27

2843	A893	6p Block of 4, #a-d	3.75	3.00

Souvenir Sheet

2844	A893	6p Sheet of 4, #a-d	5.00	4.00

No. 2843 was printed in sheets of 16.

Philippine — Spanish Friendship Day — A894

Designs: 6p, Poster for Madoura Exhibit, by Pablo Picasso. 22p, Flashback, by José T. Joya.

2003, June 30

2845-2846	A894	Set of 2	3.75	2.25

Philippines Chamber of Commerce, Cent. — A895

2003, July 15

2847	A895	6p multi	.75	.40

Benguet Corporation, Cent. — A896

2003, Aug. 12

2848	A896	6p multi	.75	.40

Orchid Type of 2003 With Plant Names and

A897

Designs: 6p, Dendrobium uniflorum. 9p, Paphiopedilum urbanianum. 10p, Kingidium philippinense. 17p, Epigeneium lyonii. 21p, Thrixspermum subulatum. 22p, Trichoglottis philippinensis. 30p, Mariposa. 50p, Sanggumay. 75p, Lady's slipper. 100p, Walingwaling.

2003-04 ***Perf. 14½***

2849	A888	6p multi	.65	.25
2849A	A888	9p multi	.95	.35
2850	A888	10p multi	1.00	.40
a.		With space between "P" and "10," dated 2004 ('04)	1.20	.50
2851	A888	17p multi	2.25	.70
a.		Base of "P" even with base of "17," dated 2004 ('04)	2.00	.75
2852	A888	21p multi	2.40	1.00
a.		Base of "P" even with base of "21," dated 2004 ('04)	2.25	1.00
2853	A888	22p multi	2.60	1.10
a.		Base of "P" even with base of "22," dated 2004, plant name 14mm long ('04)	2.50	1.00
b.		As "a," plant name 12½mm long ('04)	3.25	1.50

Perf. 14

2854	A897	30p multi	3.75	2.00
2855	A897	50p multi	6.00	3.50
2856	A897	75p multi	9.00	4.00
2857	A897	100p multi	12.00	5.50
		Nos. 2849-2857 (10)	40.60	18.80

Issued: 6p, 10p, 17p, 21p, 22p, 8/8; 30p, 100p, 8/21; 50p, 75p, 9/9. 9p, 11/4.
No. 2850a, 6/2/04; No. 2851a, 8/2/04; No. 2852a, 7/21/04; No. 2853a, 6/10/04. No, 2853b, 2004.
See Nos. 2904-2912.

Philippines — Mexico Diplomatic Relations, 50th Anniv. — A898

Designs: 5p, Our Lady of Guadalupe. No. 2859, 22p, Miraculous Image of the Black Nazarene.
No. 2860, 22p, Crowd around church.

2003, Apr. 23 ***Perf. 14***

2858-2859	A898	Set of 2	4.50	3.50

Souvenir Sheet

2860	A898	22p multi	4.50	4.00

Nos. 2858-2859 were issued in sheets of 20 (10 of each denomination in two rows of 5, separated by a central gutter). Most sheets of 20 were cut in half through central gutter.
No. 2860 contains one 80x30mm stamp.

Our Lady of Caysasay, 400th Anniv. — A899

2003, Sept. 8

2861	A899	6p multi	.75	.40

Cornelio T. Villareal, Sr., House Speaker, Birth Cent. — A900

2003, Sept. 11

2862	A900	6p multi	.75	.40

National Teachers College, 75th Anniv. — A901

2003, Sept. 15

2863	A901	6p multi	.75	.40

Sanctuary of San Antonio Parish, 50th Anniv. — A902

2003, Oct. 4 **Litho.**

2864	A902	6p multi	.75	.40

Nos. 2722-2723 Overprinted in Red

2003, Oct. 17 ***Perf. 13¾***

2865	A828	5p multi	.70	.30
2866	A828	15p multi	1.75	1.00

Souvenir Sheet

Intl. Year of Fresh Water A903

2003, Oct. 24 ***Perf. 14***

2867	A903	22p multi + label	3.00	2.50

Federation of Free Farmers, 50th Anniv. — A904

2003, Oct. 25

2868	A904	6p multi	.75	.40

Christmas — A905

Inscriptions: 6p, Mano po ninong ii. 17p, Himig at kulay ng Pasko, vert. 21p, Noche buena, vert. 22p, Karoling sa jeepney.

2003, Oct. 28

2869-2872 A905 Set of 4 9.00 6.00

National Stamp Collecting Month — A906

Cartoon art: 6p, Kenkoy, by Tony Velasquez, vert. 17p, Ikabod, by Nonoy Marcelo, vert. 21p, Sakay N'Moy, by Hugo C. Yonzon, Jr. No. 2876, 22p, Kalabong en Bosyo, by Larry Alcala.
No. 2877, 22p, Hugo, the Sidewalk Vendor, by Rodolfo Y. Ragodon.

2003, Nov. 1

2873-2876 A906 Set of 4 8.00 5.00

Souvenir Sheet

2877 A906 22p multi 4.00 3.00

No. 2877 contains one 80x30mm stamp.

Winning Children's Art in National Anti-Drug Stamp Design Contest — A907

No. 2878: a, Globe, child with broom, by Nicole Fernan L. Caminian. b, Children, "No Drugs" symbol, by Jairus Cabajar. c, Children painting over "Drug Addiction" picture, by Genevieve V. Lazarte. d, Child chopping tree with hatchet, by Martin F. Rivera.

2003, Nov. 3

2878 A907 6p Block of 4, #a-d 4.00 3.00

Nos. 2550Ab, 2550Ac, 2550Ad and 2550Ae Surcharged

2003, Nov. 11 ***Perf. 14***

2879 A749a 17p on 4p #2550Ab 3.00 1.75
2880 A749a 17p on 8p #2550Ac 3.00 1.75
2881 A749a 22p on 16p #2550Ad 4.00 2.50
2882 A749a 22p on 16p #2550Ae 4.00 2.50
Nos. 2879-2882 (4) 14.00 8.50

Nos. 2879-2882 were sold removed from the booklet the basic stamps were in.

Souvenir Sheet

First Philippine Stamps, 150th Anniv. — A908

2003, Nov. 14

2883 A908 22p Nos. 1, 2, 4 & 5, org to yellow background 3.00 2.50

Filipinas 2004 Stamp Exhibition, Mandaluyong City.
See Nos. 2891-2897.

Camera Club of the Philippines, 75th Anniv. — A909

2003, Dec. 1 **Litho.**

2884 A909 6p multi .75 .40

New Year 2004 (Year of the Monkey) — A910

Monkey: 6p, Perched on branch. 17p, Hanging from branch.

2003, Dec. 1

2885-2886 A910 Set of 2 4.00 2.50
2886a Souvenir sheet, #2885-2886 + 2 labels 5.50 4.50

Nos. 2885-2886 were printed in sheets of 20.
No. 2886a exists imperf. Value $5.50.

Succulent Plants — A911

No. 2887: a, Mammilaria spinosissima (yellow frame). b, Epithelantha bokei. c, Rebutia spinosissima. d, Turbinicarpus alonsoi.
No. 2888, horiz.: a, Aloe humilis. b, Euphorbia golisana. c, Gymnocalycium spinosissima. d, Mammilaria spinosissima (green frame).

2003, Dec. 5

2887 A911 6p Block of 4, #a-d 4.50 3.50

Souvenir Sheet

2888 A911 6p Sheet of 4, #a-d 5.00 4.00

No. 2887 was printed in sheets of 16 stamps.

Powered Flight, Cent. — A911a

No. 2888E — Do24TT: f, Green background. g, Yellow background.

2003, Dec. 17 **Litho.** ***Perf. 14***

2888E A911a 6p Horiz. pair, #f-g 1.75 1.40

Printed in sheets of 8.

Architecture — A912

No. 2889: a, Luneta Hotel. b, Hong Kong Shanghai Bank. c, El Hogar. d, Regina Building.
No. 2890, horiz.: a, Pangasinan Capitol. b, Metropolitan Theater. c, Philtrust. d, University of Manila.

2003, Dec. 22

2889 A912 6p Block of 4, #a-d 4.50 3.50

Souvenir Sheet

2890 A912 6p Sheet of 4, #a-d 5.00 4.00

No. 2889 was printed in sheets of 16 stamps.

First Philippine Stamps, 150th Anniv. Type of 2003

No. 2891 (36x26mm each): a, Blue to lilac background, #1. b, Orange to yellow background, #2. c, Light to dark green background, #4. d, Dark to light pink background, #5.
Nos. 2892-2897: Like #2883.

2003-04 **Litho.** ***Perf. 14***

2891 Horiz. strip of 4 4.50 3.50
a.-d. A908 6p Any single .85 .50

Souvenir Sheets

Background Colors

2892 A908 22p dk to lt rose 3.50 *3.00*
2893 A908 22p dk to lt blue 3.50 *3.00*
2894 A908 22p blue to lt grn 3.50 *3.00*
2895 A908 22p dk to lt pink 3.50 *3.00*
2896 A908 22p brn to yellow 3.50 *3.00*
2897 A908 22p white 3.50 *3.00*
a. With Postpex 2004 inscription added in red and black in sheet margin 4.00 *3.50*

Filipinas 2004 Stamp Exhibition, Mandaluyong City.
No. 2891 was printed in sheets of 16 stamps.
Issued: No. 2892, 12/15/03, No. 2893, 1/15/04; No. 2894, 1/30/04; No. 2895, 1/31/04; Nos. 2891, 2896, 2897, 2/1/04. No. 2897a, 4/19/04.
A sheet containing a block of four of perf. and imperf. examples of Nos. 2891a-2891d sold for 100p. Value, $20.

Arrival in Philippines of Sisters of St. Paul of Chartres, Cent. — A913

2004, Jan. 22 ***Perf. 14***

2898 A913 6p multi .75 .35

Polytechnic University of the Philippines, Cent. — A914

2004, Jan. 22

2899 A914 6p multi .75 .35

Tanduay Distillers, Inc., 150th Anniv. — A915

2004, Jan. 22

2900 A915 6p multi .75 .35

Grepalife Life Insurance Co., 50th Anniv. — A916

2004, Jan. 22

2901 A916 6p multi .75 .35

2003 State Visit of U.S. Pres. George W. Bush — A917

Flags of U.S. and Philippines, George W. Bush and: 6p, Crowd. 22p, Philippines Pres. Gloria Macapagal-Arroyo, Malacañang Palace.

2004, Feb. 23 **Litho.** ***Perf. 13x13½***

2902-2903 A917 Set of 2 3.00 2.00

Orchid Type of 2003 With Plant Names

Designs: 1p, Liparis latifolia. 2p, Cymbidium finlaysonianum. 3p, Phalaenopsis philippinensis. 4p, Phalaenopsis fasciata. 5p, Spathoglottis plicata.
No. 2909: a, Phalaenopsis fuscata. b, Phalaenopsis stuartiana. c, Renanthera monachia. d, Aerides quinquevulnera.
8p, Phalaenopsis schilleriana. 9p, Phalaenopsis pulchra. 20p, Phaius tankervilleae.
Two types of 1p and 5p:
I — Denomination and year date not touching edges of background color, digits of year date touching.
II — Denomination and year date touch edges of background color, digits of year date spaced.
Three types of 2p:
I — Plant name 13½mm long and 1mm from year date, denomination and year date not touching edges of background color.
II — Plant name 13½ mm long and 2mm from year date, denomination and year date touching edges of background color.
III — Plant name 14mm long and 1½mm from year date, denomination and year date touching edges of background color.

2004 **Litho.** ***Perf. 14½***

2904 A888 1p multi, type I .50 .25
a. Type II .60 .25
2905 A888 2p multi, type I .65 .30
a. Type II .40 .25
b. Type III 9.00 5.00
2906 A888 3p multi .45 .25
2907 A888 4p multi .50 .30
2908 A888 5p multi, type I .50 .25
a. Type II .90 .35
2909 Block of 4 3.50 1.75
a.-d. A888 6p Any single .75 .25
2910 A888 8p multi .80 .35
2911 A888 9p multi 1.00 .40
2912 A888 20p multi 2.25 .80
Nos. 2904-2912 (9) 10.15 4.65

Issued: Nos. 2904, 2908, 3/9; Nos. 2904a, 2905, 2905b, 2910, 4/1; Nos. 2905a, 2908a, 4/28; Nos. 2906, 2907, 2911, 2912, 6/11; No. 2909, 12/20.

Pfizer Pharmaceuticals, 50th Anniv. in Philippines — A918

2004, Apr. 30 ***Perf. 14***

2913 A918 6p multi .75 .35

Our Lady of Piat, 400th Anniv. — A919

2004, June 21

2914 A919 6p multi .75 .35
a. Miniature sheet of 8 15.00 15.00

Normally issued in sheets of 50.

Bonsai — A920

No. 2915, vert. — Orange to yellow background: a, Bantigue. b, Kamuning Binangonan with thick trunk, dark brown pot. c, Balete. d, Mulawin aso. e, Kamuning Binangonan with root-like trunk, dark brown pot. f, Logwood. g, Kamuning Binangonan, orange clay pot. h, Bantolinao.

No. 2916 — Purple to white background: a, Bantigue with thick trunk, brown pot. b, Chinese elm. c, Bantigue with two trunks, brown pot. d, Bantigue, white pot. e, Balete with many green leaves, black and brown pot. f, Balete with few green leaves, brown pot. g, Bantigue, light brown rectangular pot. h, Mansanita.

Nos. 2917a, 2918a, Lomonsito. Nos. 2917b, 2918b, Bougainvillea, pot on table. Nos. 2917c, 2918c, Bougainvillea, orange brown pot. Nos. 2917d, 2918d, Kalyos.

2004 ***Perf. 14***

2915 Block of 8 8.00 *6.50*
a.-h. A920 6p Any single .80 .50
2916 Block of 8 8.00 *6.50*
a.-h. A920 6p Any single .80 .50

Souvenir Sheets

Solid Blue Background

2917 Sheet of 4 5.00 4.00
a.-d. A920 6p Any single 1.00 .75

Blue to White Background

2918 Sheet of 4 5.00 4.00
a.-d. A920 6p Any single 1.00 .75

Nos. 2915-2916 were printed in sheets of 16.

Issued: Nos. 2915-2917, 7/27; No. 2918, 8/28. 2004 World Stamp Championship, Singapore (No. 2918).

2004 Summer Olympics, Athens — A921

Designs: 6p, Shooting. 17p, Taekwondo. 21p, Swimming. No. 2922, 22p, Archery.

No. 2923, 22p, Boxing.

2004, Aug. 13

2919-2922 A921 Set of 4 9.00 6.00

Souvenir Sheet

2923 A921 22p multi 3.50 2.75

Miguel Lopez de Legazpi (c. 1510-72), Founder of Manila — A922

2004, Aug. 20 **Litho.**

2924 A922 6p multi .75 .50

Admiral Tomas A. Cloma, Sr. (1904-96) A923

2004, Aug. 20

2925 A923 6p multi .75 .40

Animals of the Lunar New Year Cycle A924

Designs: Nos. 2926a, 2927a, Rat. Nos. 2926b, 2927b, Ox. Nos. 2926c, 2927c, Tiger. Nos. 2926d, 2927d, Rabbit. Nos. 2926e, 2927e, Dragon. Nos. 2926f, 2927f, Snake. Nos. 2926g, 2928a, Horse. Nos. 2926h, 2928b, Goat. Nos. 2926i, 2928c, Monkey. Nos. 2926j, 2928d, Cock. Nos. 2926k, 2928e, Dog. Nos. 2926l, 2928f, Pig.

2004, Sept. 9 ***Perf. 14***

English Inscriptions at Left

2926 A924 6p Sheet of 12, #a-l, + 3 labels 15.00 15.00

Chinese Inscriptions at Left

2927 A924 6p Sheet of 6, #a-f, + 6 labels 20.00 20.00
2928 A924 6p Sheet of 6, #a-f, + 6 labels 20.00 20.00

Manila Central University, Cent. — A925

2004, Sept. 21

2929 A925 6p multi .75 .35
a. Miniature sheet of 8 12.50 12.50

Christmas — A926

Various Christmas trees: 6p, 17p, 21p, 22p.

2004, Oct. 1

2930-2933 A926 Set of 4 10.00 7.00

Filipino-Chinese General Chamber of Commerce, Cent. — A927

No. 2934: a, Intramuros, Philippines. b, Great Wall of China.

2004, Oct. 12

2934 A927 6p Horiz. pair, #a-b 2.00 1.50
a. Miniature sheet of 8 12.50 12.50

Normally issued in sheets of 40.

Winning Designs in Rice Is Life National Stamp Design Contest A928

No. 2935, 6p: a, By Maria Enna T. Alegre. b, By Lady Fatima M. Velasco.

No. 2936, 6p: a, By Sean Y. Pajaron. b, By Ljian B. Delgado.

No. 2937, 6p: a, By Michael O. Villadolid. b, By Gary M. Manalo.

2004, Oct. 15 **Litho.**

Horiz. Pairs, #a-b

2935-2937 A928 Set of 3 6.00 5.00
2937c Miniature sheet, #2935a-2935b, 2936a-2936b, 2937a-2937b 9.00 9.00

Intl. Year of Rice.

Natl. Stamp Collecting Month — A929

Comic strip and comic book illustrations: No. 2938, 6p, Darna, by Nestor P. Redondo. No. 2939, 6p, Kulafu, by Francisco Reyes. No. 2940, 6p, El Vibora, by Federico C. Javinal, vert. No. 2941, 6p, Lapu-Lapu, by Francisco V. Coching, vert.

22p, Darna, by Mars Ravelo, vert

2004 ***Perf. 14***

2938-2941 A929 Set of 4 4.00 3.00

Souvenir Sheet

2942 A929 22p multi 4.50 3.50

No. 2942 contains one 30x80mm stamp.

San Agustin Church, Manila, 400th Anniv. A930

No. 2943: a, Denomination at left. b, Denomination at right.

2004, Nov. 13

2943 A930 6p Horiz. pair, #a-b 1.75 1.40
a. Miniature sheet of 8 12.50 12.50

Normally issued in sheets of 40.

New Year 2005 (Year of the Rooster) — A931

Designs: 6p, Rooster's head. 17p, Rooster.

2004, Dec. 1

2944-2945 A931 Set of 2 4.00 3.00
2945a Souvenir sheet, 2 each #2944-2945 8.00 8.00

Printed in sheets of 20 and in sheets of 10.

Worldwide Fund for Nature (WWF) — A932

Owls: No. 2946, 6p, Giant Scops owl. No. 2947, 6p, Philippine eagle owl. No. 2948, 6p, Negros Scops owl. No. 2949, 6p, West Visayan hawk owl.

2004, Dec. 22

2946-2949 A932 Set of 4 4.50 3.50
2949a Block of 4, #2946-2949 5.50 5.00
2949b Miniature sheet of 8 50.00 50.00

No. 2946-2949 were normally printed in sheets of 16.

Liceo de Cagayan University A933

2005, Feb. 5 **Litho.** ***Perf. 14***

2950 A933 6p multi .75 .40
a. Miniature sheet of 8 12.50 12.50

Normally printed in sheets of 50.

Seventh-Day Adventist Church in the Philippines, Cent. — A934

2005, Feb. 18

2951 A934 6p multi .75 .40
a. Miniature sheet of 8 12.50 12.50

Normally issued in sheets of 50.

Baguio Country Club, Cent. A935

No. 2952: a, Club in 1905. b, Club in 2005.

2005, Feb. 18

2952 A935 6p Horiz. pair, #a-b 2.00 1.75
a. Miniature sheet of 8 12.50 12.50

Normally issued in sheets of 40.

Butterflies — A936

Designs: 1p, Arisbe decolor stratos.

No. 2954: a, Parantica noeli. b, Chilasa osmana osmana. c, Graphium sandawanum joreli. d, Papilio xuthus benguetanus.

2005 **Litho.** ***Perf. 14½***

2953 A936 1p multi .50 .25
a. Butterfly redrawn with two antennae .50 .30
2954 Block of 4 11.00 8.00
a.-d. A936 22p Any single 2.25 1.50

Issued: 1p, 4/12; No. 2954, 3/3.

See Nos. 2978-2981.

Shells A937

No. 2955: a, Chicoreus saulii. b, Spondylus varians. c, Spondylus linquaefelis. d, Melo broderipii.

No. 2956: a, Chlamys senatoria. b, Siphonofusus vicdani. c, Epitonium scalare. d, Harpa harpa.

No. 2957: a, Siliquaria armata. b, Argonauta argo. c, Perotrochus vicdani. d, Corculum cardissa.

2005, Apr. 15 ***Perf. 14***

2955 A937 Block of 4 4.00 3.00
a.-d. 6p Any single .80 .65
2956 A937 Block of 4 4.00 3.00
a.-d. 6p Any single .80 .65

Souvenir Sheet

2957 A937 Sheet of 4 + 2 labels 7.50 7.50
a.-d. 6p Any single 1.60 1.20

Nos. 2955-2956 were normally issued in sheets of 16.

State Visit of Hu Jintao, Pres. of People's Republic of China — A938

Flags of Philippines and People's Republic of China, Philippines Pres. Gloria Macapagal-Arroyo and: 6p, Pres. Hu at right. 17p, Pres. Hu at left.

2005, Apr. 27

2958-2959 A938 Set of 2 4.00 2.50
2959a Souvenir sheet, #2958-2959 6.00 5.00

Architecture — A939

No. 2960: a, Ernesto de la Cruz Ancestral House. b, Limjoco Residence. c, Pelaez Ancestral House. d, Vergara House.

No. 2961: a, Gliceria Marella Villavicencio. b, Lasala-Guarin House. c, Claparols House. d, Ilagan Ancestral House.

2005, May 7

2960 A939 Block of 4 3.50 3.00
a.-d. 6p Any single .75 .65

Souvenir Sheet

2961 A939 Sheet of 4 5.00 4.00
a.-d. 6p Any single 1.00 .80

No. 2960 was printed in sheets of 16.

Central Philippine University, Cent. — A940

2005, May 13

2962	A940 6p multi	.75	.40
a.	Miniature sheet of 8	12.50	12.50

Normally issued in sheets of 50 stamps.

Rotary International, Cent. — A941

Denomination: 6p, At left, in blue. 22p, At right, in red.

2005, May 31

2963-2964	A941 Set of 2	5.00	4.00
2964a	Miniature sheet, 6 #2963, 2 #2964	16.00	16.00

San Bartolome Parish, 400th Anniv. — A942

2005, July 25 Litho. *Perf. 14*

2965	A942 6p multi	.75	.40

Senator Blas F. Ople (1927-2003) — A943

2005, July 28

2966	A943 6p multi	.75	.40

Shells A944

No. 2967, 6p: a, Chrysallis fischeri. b, Helicostyla bicolorata. c, Helicostyla dobiosa. d, Helicostyla portei.

No. 2968, 6p: a, Cochlostyla imperator. b, Helicostyla turbinoides. c, Helicostyla lignaria. d, Amphidromus dubius.

No. 2969, horiz.: a, Calocochlia depressa. b, Cochlostyla sarcinosa. c, Calocochlia schadenbergi. d, Helicostyla pulcherrina.

2005 Blocks of 4, #a-d *Perf. 14*

2967-2968	A944 Set of 2	10.00	8.00

Souvenir Sheets

2969	A944 6p Sheet of 4, #a-d, + 2 labels	6.00	5.00
2970	Sheet, #2969a, 2969b, 2970a, 2970b	6.00	5.00
a.	A944 2p Like #2969c	1.00	.75
b.	A944 3p Like #2969d	1.00	.75

Nos. 2967-2968 issued in sheets of 16.

Issued: Nos. 2967-2969, 8/8; No. 2970, 8/19. Upper left label on No. 2970 has Taipei 2005 Stamp Exhibition emblem, lower right label has "Greetings from the Philippines" inscription.

Intl. Year of the Eucharist — A945

Winning pictures in stamp design contest by: No. 2971, 6p, Carlos Vincent H. Ruiz. No. 2972, 6p, Rommer A. Fajardo. No. 2973, 6p, Telly Farolan-Somera. No. 2974, 6p, Allen A. Moran. No. 2975, 6p, Elouiza Athena Tentativa. No. 2976, 6p, Jianina Marishka C. Montealto.

2005, Sept. 8

2971-2976	A945 Set of 6	4.50	3.00
2976a	Souvenir sheet, #2971-2976, + 6 labels	8.00	*8.00*

No. 1887 Surcharged in Red

Souvenir Sheet

Wmk. 389

2005, Sept. 14 Litho. *Imperf.*

2977	A493 15p on 8p multi	2.50	2.00

Butterflies Type of 2005 and

A946

A947

Designs: 5p, Parantica danatti danatti.

No. 2979: a, Hebemoia glaucippe philippinensis. b, Moduza urdaneta aynii. c, Lexias satrapes hiwaga. d, Cheritra orpheus orpheus. e, Achillides chikae chikae. f, Arisbe ideaoides ideaoides. g, Dellas schoenigi hermeli. h, Achillides palinurus daedalus. i, Dellas levicki justini. j, Troides magellanus magellanus.

No. 2980: a, Idea electra electra. b, Charaxes bajula adoracion. c, Tanaecia calliphorus calliphorus. d, Trogonoptera trojana. e, Charaxes bajula adoracion, diff.

No. 2981: a, Cethosia biblis barangingi. b, Menalaides polytes ledebouria. c, Appias nero palawanica. d, Udara tyotaroi.

2005 Unwmk. *Perf. 14½*

2978	A946 5p multi	.60	.25
2979	Block of 10	10.00	9.00
a.-j.	A946 6p Any single	.65	.30
2980	Block of 4, #a-d	8.00	7.00
a.	A946 17p multi	1.60	1.00
b.	A946 17p multi	1.60	1.00
c.	A946 17p multi	1.60	1.00
d.	A946 17p multi	1.60	1.00
e.	A947 17p multi	25.00	25.00
f.	Block of 4, #2980a, 2980c, 2980d, 2980e	*60.00*	60.00
2981	Block of 4	9.00	8.00
a.-d.	A946 21p Any single	2.00	1.50
	Nos. 2978-2981 (4)	27.60	24.25

Issued: No. 2978, 11/22; No. 2979, 10/12; No. 2980, 12/9. No. 2981, 12/2.

Intl. Year of Sports and Physical Education — A948

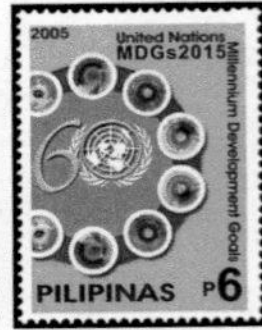

UN Millennium Development Goals — A949

No. 2982: a, Dove, open book, Philippines flag, basketball, emblem at LL. b, Torch, sports equipment, people with joined hands, dove flying to right, emblem at LR. c, Torch, sports equipment, people with joined hands, dove flying to left, emblem at LL.

2005, Oct. 19 *Perf. 14*

2982	A948 6p Horiz. pair, #a-b	2.00	1.50
c.	6p multi	.75	.50
d.	Horiz. pair, #2982a, 2982c	2.50	1.75
2983	A949 6p multi	1.00	*1.00*

Souvenir Sheet

2984	Sheet, #2982a, 2982b, 2984a	3.00	2.50
a.	A949 10p multi	1.00	.80
b.	Sheet, #2982a, 2982c, 2984a	4.00	3.50

United Nations, 60th anniv.

Bureau of Corrections, Cent. — A950

2005, Nov. 4

2985	A950 6p multi	.75	.40
a.	Miniature sheet of 8	12.50	12.50

Normally issued in sheets of 50.

Inauguration of Pres. Gloria Macapagal-Arroyo — A951

Pres. Macapagal-Arroyo: 6p, Taking oath. 22p, Giving inaugural speech.

2005, Nov. 9

2986-2987	A951 Set of 2	4.00	2.50

Christmas A952

Various department store window Christmas displays: 6p, 17p, 21p, 22p.

2005, Nov. 16

2988-2991	A952 Set of 4	9.00	6.50

23rd Southeast Asia Games, Philippines — A953

No. 2992: a, Boxing. b, Cycling. c, Wushu. d, Bowling. e, Badminton. f, Billiards. Eagle has black beak on all stamps.

No. 2993, horiz.: a, Track. b, Soccer. c, Taekwondo. d, Judo. e, Chess. f, Karate. g, Gymnastics. h, Pencaksilat. i, Dragon boat racing. j, Swimming.

No. 2994: a, Baseball. b, Shooting. c, Archery. d, Bowling (eagle with brown beak). e, Volleyball. f, Boxing (eagle with brown beak). g, Cycling (eagle with brown beak). h, Badminton (eagle with brown beak).

No. 2995: a, Archery. b, Shooting. c, Equestrian.

No. 2996, horiz.: a, Arnis. b, Chess. c, Dragon boat racing.

2005, Nov. 22 Red Frames

2992	Block of 6	7.50	6.50
a.-f.	A953 6p Any single	1.00	.75
2993	Sheet of 10 + 8 labels	20.00	20.00
a.-j.	A953 6p Any single	1.50	1.50
2994	Sheet of 10, #2992c, 2992f, 2994a-2994h, + 20 labels	20.00	20.00
a.-h.	A953 6p Any single	1.50	1.50

Blue Frames

2995	Sheet of 3	5.00	4.00
a.	A953 5p multi	1.20	.75
b.-c.	A953 6p Either single	1.20	.75
2996	Sheet of 3	5.00	4.00
a.	A953 5p multi	1.20	.75
b.-c.	A953 6p Either single	1.20	.75

No. 2992 was printed in sheets of 12 containing two blocks. Nos. 2993a-2993j lack perforations between the stamp and the adjacent labels that are the same size as the stamp. There are perforations between the stamps and labels on No. 2994. The labels to the right of the stamps could be personalized. Nos. 2993 and 2994 each sold for 99p with generic flag labels, and for 350p with personalized labels.

National Stamp Collecting Month — A954

Prints: No. 2997, 6p, Pinoy Worker Abr'd., by Ben Cab. No. 2998, 6p, Bulbs, by M. Parial. No. 2999, 6p, The Fourth Horseman, by Tequi. No. 3000, 6p, Breaking Ground, by R. Olazo. 22p, Form XV, by Brenda Fajardo, horiz.

2005, Nov. 28

2997-3000	A954 Set of 4	3.50	2.50

Souvenir Sheet

3001	A954 22p multi	4.00	3.00

No. 3001 contains one 80x30mm stamp.

New Year 2006 (Year of the Dog) — A955

Dog and inscription: a, 6p, "Manigong Bagong Taon." b, 17p, "Happy New Year."

2005, Dec. 1

3002-3003	A955 Set of 2	3.75	2.50
3003a	Souvenir sheet, 2 each #3002-3003	8.00	7.00

Nos. 2002-2003 were issued both in sheets of 20 and sheets of 10.

Third Asian Para Games — A956

Designs: 6p, Runner with amputated arm. 17p, Wheelchair racer.

2005, Dec. 6

3004-3005	A956 Set of 2	3.00	2.00

Pope John Paul II (1920-2005) — A957

Pope John Paul II, Vatican arms and text: 6p, "Mahal Namin Kayo!" 22p, "We Love You!"

2005, June 28 Litho. *Perf. 14*

3006-3007	A957 Set of 2	4.00	2.50
3006a	Miniature sheet of 6 + 6 labels	25.00	
3007a	Miniature sheet of 6 + 6 labels	25.00	

Nos. 3006-3007 normally issued in sheets of 50 stamps.

Lighthouses — A958

No. 3008: a, Cape Santiago Lighthouse, Calatagan. b, Bacagay Lighthouse, Liloan. c, Malabrigo Lighthouse, Lobo. d, Capones Lighthouse, San Antonio.

No. 3009: a, Tubbataha Lighthouse, Cagayancillo. b, Cape Bojeador Lighthouse, Burgos. c, Cape Bolinao Lighthouse, Bolinao. d, San Fernando Point Lighthouse, San Fernando.

2005, Dec. 22

3008 A958 6p Block of 4, #a-d 4.00 3.00

Souvenir Sheet

3009 A958 6p Sheet of 4, #a-d 5.00 4.00

No. 3008 printed in sheets of 16 stamps.

St. Scholastica's College, Manila, Cent. — A959

2006, Jan. 3

3010 A959 6p multi .70 .40
a. Miniature sheet of 8 12.50 12.50

Normally printed in sheets of 50 stamps.

Filipinos in Hawaii, Cent. — A960

Contest-winning designs: 6p, Filipinos in Hawaii, by Allen A. Moran. 22p, Filipinos and flags, by Crisanto S. Umali.

No. 3013: a, Like 6p. b, Like 22p.

2006, Jan. 5

3011-3012 A960 Set of 2 3.50 2.50

Souvenir Sheet

3013 A960 11p Sheet of 2, #a-b 5.00 4.00

Mary Johnston Hospital, Manila, Cent. A961

No. 3014: a, Hospital building and founder Rebecca Parish. b, Surgeons, hospital building.

2006, Jan. 20

3014 A961 6p Horiz. pair, #a-b 2.00 1.50
a. Miniature sheet of 8 14.50 14.50

Normally issued in sheet of 40 stamps.

Love A962

No. 3015 — Angel with: a, Letter. b, Flower.

2006, Feb. 8

3015 A962 7p Horiz. pair, #a-b 2.00 1.50

Jaime Cardinal Sin (1928-2005), Archbishop of Manila — A963

Sin and: 7p, Cathedral. 22p, Statue.

2006, Feb. 25

3016-3017 A963 Set of 2 3.00 2.00
3017a Souvenir sheet, 2 each #3016-3017 8.00 7.00

Marine Turtles — A964

No. 3018: a, Olive Ridley turtle. b, Hawksbill turtle. c, Loggerhead turtle. d, Leatherback turtle.

26p, Green turtle.

2006, Mar. 31

3018 A964 Horiz. strip of 4 4.50 3.50
a.-d. 7p Any single .75 .45

Souvenir Sheet

3019 A964 26p multi 5.00 4.00

No. 3018 normally issued in sheet of 16 stamps. No. 3019 contains one 80x30mm stamp.

Butterfly Type of 2005 and

Butterfly With Fully-colored Background A965

Butterfly With Blue Lines At Bottom A966

Butterfly With Partially-colored Background A967

Butterfly With Framed and Colored Background A968

Designs: 1p, Arisbe decolor stratos. 2p, Arhopala anthelus impar. 3p, Zophoessa dataensis nihrai. 4p, Liphyra brassolis justini. 5p, Parantica danatti danatti. 9p, Lexias satrapes amlana. 10p, Tanaecia aruna pallida. 30p, Appias nero domitia. 100p, Cepora aspasia olga.

Nos. 3030 and 3031: a, Hebemoia glaucippe philippensis. b, Moduza urdaneta aynii. c, Lexias satrapes hiwaga. d, Cheritra orpheus orpheus. e, Achillides chikae chikae. f, Arisbe ideaoiedes ideaoiedes. g, Delias schoenigi hermeli. h, Achillides palinurus daedalus. i, Delias levicki justini. j, Troides magellanus magellanus.

Nos. 3036 and 3037: a, Idea electra electra. b, Charaxes bajula adoracion. c, Tanaecia calliphorus calliphorus. d, Trogonoptera trojana.

Nos. 3038 and 3039: a, Cethosia biblis barangingi. b, Menalaides polytes ledebouria. c, Appias nero palawanica. d, Udara tyotaroi.

Nos. 3040 and 3041: a, Parantica noeli. b, Chilasa osmana osmana. c, Graphium sandawanum joreli. d, Papilio xuthus benguetanus.

Perf. 14½ (A936, A965), 13¾ (A966), 13x13¼ (A967), 14 (A968)

2006 **Inscribed "2006"**

3020 A965 1p multi .50 .25
3021 A966 1p multi .50 .25
a. Inscribed "2007" .50 .25
3022 A965 2p multi .50 .25
3023 A966 2p multi .50 .25
a. Inscribed "2007" .60 .25
3024 A936 3p multi .60 .25
3025 A966 3p multi .60 .30
a. Inscribed "2007" .70 .30
3026 A936 4p multi .70 .30
3027 A966 4p multi .70 .30
a. Inscribed "2007" .70 .30
3028 A965 5p multi .70 .30
3029 A966 5p multi .70 .30
a. Inscribed "2007" .70 .30
3030 Block of 10 8.00 7.50
a.-j. A965 7p Any single .70 .35
3031 Block of 10 9.00 8.00
a.-j. A966 7p Any single .75 .35
k. Block of 10, inscr. "2007" 11.00 10.00
l.-u. A966 7p Any single, inscr. "2007" .80 .35
3032 A936 9p multi 1.10 .40
3033 A966 9p multi 1.20 .40
a. Inscribed "2007" 1.20 .40
3034 A936 10p multi 1.20 .50
3035 A966 10p multi 1.20 .50
a. Inscribed "2007" 1.50 .50
3036 Block of 4 10.00 8.00
a.-d. A965 20p Any single 2.50 1.25
3037 Block of 4 11.00 9.00
a.-d. A966 20p Any single 2.40 1.60
e. Block of 4, inscr. "2007" 11.00 7.00
f.-i. A966 20p Any single, inscr. "2007" 2.40 1.60
3038 Block of 4 12.50 10.50
a.-d. A965 24p Any single 2.50 1.50
3039 Block of 4 12.50 10.50
a.-d. A966 24p Any single 3.00 1.50
e. Block of 4, inscr. "2007" 13.50 11.00
f.-i. A966 24p Any single, inscr. "2007" 3.00 1.50
3040 Block of 4 12.50 11.00
a.-d. A965 26p Any single 2.50 2.00
3041 Block of 4 12.50 11.00
a.-d. A966 26p Any single 3.00 2.00
e. Block of 4, inscr. "2007" 13.50 11.00
f.-i. A966 26p Any single, inscr. "2007" 3.00 2.00
3042 A967 30p multi 3.00 2.25
3043 A968 30p multi 3.75 2.50
3044 A967 100p multi 11.50 6.00
3045 A968 100p multi 12.00 6.00
Nos. 3020-3045 (26) 128.95 96.80

Issued: Nos. 3020, 3030, 4/28; Nos. 3021, 3029, 7/3; Nos. 3022, 3028, 5/10; No. 3023, 12/27; Nos. 3024, 3034, 11/10; Nos. 3025, 3027, 3033, 3035, 12/26; Nos. 3026, 3032, 9/9; No. 3031, 12/14; No. 3036, 6/7; Nos. 3037, 3039, 3041, 12/21; No. 3038, 6/15; No. 3040, 6/9; No. 3042, 9/18; Nos. 3043, 3045, 12/29; No. 3044, 9/26.

See Nos. 3101-3102.

No. 1511 Surcharged

2006, May 2 Litho. *Perf. 13¾x13¼*

3046 A368 26p on 7.50p #1511 4.00 3.00

Lighthouses — A969

No. 3047: a, Punta Bugui Lighthouse, Aroroy. b, Capul Island Lighthouse, Samar del Norte. c, Corregidor Island Lighthouse, Cavite. d, Pasig River Lighthouse, Manila.

No. 3048: a, Cabo Engaño Lighthouse, Santa Ana. b, Punta Cabra Lighthouse, Lubang. c, Cabo Melville Lighthouse, Balabac Island. d, Gintotolo Island Lighthouse, Balud.

2006, May 17 ***Perf. 14***

3047 A969 7p Block of 4, #a-d 4.50 3.50

Souvenir Sheet

3048 A969 7p Sheet of 4, #a-d 6.00 5.00

No. 3047 issued in sheets of 16 stamps.

Xavier School, Manila, 50th Anniv. A970

No. 3049: a, Emblems. b, School building. c, Paul Hsu Kuang-ch'i, Chinese Christian convert. d, St. Francis Xavier (1506-52).

2006, June 6

3049 A970 7p Block of 4, #a-d 4.00 4.00
a. Miniature sheet of 8 11.00 11.00

Normally issued in sheets of 16 stamps.

Air Materiel Wing Savings and Loan Association, Inc., 50th Anniv. — A971

No. 3050 — Emblem and: a, Soldier's family, piggy bank. b, Building.

2006, June 13

3050 A971 7p Horiz. pair, #a-b 1.75 1.50
a. Miniature sheet of 8 15.00 15.00

Normally issued in sheet of 40 stamps.

No. 1721 Surcharged in Blue Violet

2006, July 4 Litho. *Perf. 14*

3051 A436 26p on 7.20p multi 4.00 2.50

Knights of Columbus, 100th Anniv. in Philippines A972

2006, July 7

3052 A972 7p multi .75 .40
a. Miniature sheet of 8 12.50 12.50

Normally issued in sheets of 50.

Ortigas & Company, 75th Anniv. — A973

Anniversary emblem and: 7p, Map of Mandaloyon. 26p, Building.

2006, July 10

3053-3054 A973 Set of 2 4.50 2.50
3054a Souvenir sheet, 2 each #3053-3054 11.00 10.00

Ozamiz Cotta Military Fort, 250th Anniv. — A974

2006, July 16

3055 A974 7p multi .75 .40
a. Miniature sheet of 8 12.50 12.50

Normally issued in sheets of 50.

Friendship Between Philippines and Japan, 50th Anniv. — A975

José P. Rizal and: 7p, Mt. Fuji and cherry blossoms. 20p, Mt. Mayon and flowers.

2006, July 23

3056-3057 A975 Set of 2 4.00 2.50
3057a Miniature sheet of 8 12.50 12.50
3057b Souvenir sheet, 2 each #3056-3057 9.00 8.00

Nos. 3056-3057 issued in sheets of 20 (10 of each denomination in two rows of 5, separated by a central gutter). Most sheets of 20 were cut in half through the central gutter.

Roque B. Ablan, (1906-43) Politician, Military Hero — A976

2006, Aug. 9

3058 A976 7p multi .65 .40
a. Miniature sheet of 8 12.50 12.50

Normally printed in sheets of 50.

No. 1809 Surcharged in Gold

Perf. 13½x13

2006, Aug. 15 Litho. Wmk. 389

3059 A470 7p on 1.20p multi 1.25 .90

Chan-Cu Association, Cent. — A977

No. 3060: a, Centennial emblem. b, Figurine of Chan-Tze, Chinese scholar.

2006, Aug. 28 Unwmk. *Perf. 14*

3060 A977 7p Horiz. pair, #a-b 2.00 1.65
a. Miniature sheet of 8 10.00 10.00

Issued in sheets of 20 with 5 central labels.

Cats A978

No. 3061: a, Himalayan cat. b, Maine Coon cat. c, Red point Siamese cat. d, Persian cat.
No. 3062: a, Japanese bobtail cat. b, Ragdoll cat. c, Egyptian mau cat. d, Abyssinian cat.

2006, Sept. 29

3061 A978 7p Block of 4, #a-d 5.00 4.00

Souvenir Sheet

3062 A978 7p Sheet of 4, #a-d 5.00 4.00

No. 3061 printed in sheet of 16 stamps.

United Nations Month — A979

Text in: 7p, Tagalog and English. 26p, English.

2006, Oct. 19

3063-3064 A979 Set of 2 4.50 3.00

Issued in sheets of 20 with 5 central labels.

Philippines Postal Service, 108th Anniv. — A980

No. 3065: a, Ruins of Manila Post Office after Battle of Manila. b, Manila Central Post Office, 2006.

2006, Nov. 6 *Perf. 13¾*

3065 A980 Horiz. pair 2.50 2.00
a.-b. 7p Either single 1.00 .80

Printed in sheets of 10 stamps.

National Stamp Collecting Month — A981

Designs: No. 3066, 7p, Mother and child. No. 3067, 7p, Fish and fruit, horiz.. No. 3068, 7p, Oranges and grapes, horiz. No. 3069, 7p, Watermelon and coconut, horiz.
26p, Roses.

2006, Nov. 15

3066-3069 A981 Set of 4 4.00 3.00

Souvenir Sheet

3070 A981 26p multi 3.50 3.00

No. 3070 contains one 30x80mm stamp.

Ascent of Mt. Everest by Filipino Climbers A982

Designs: No. 3071, 7p, Climbers ascending mountain. No. 3072, 20p, No. 3074a, 10p, Climbers ascending mountain and Philippines flag. No. 3073, 26p, No. 3074b, 7p, Climbers at summit with flag.

2006, Nov. 23 *Perf. 13¾*

3071-3073 A982 Set of 3 7.00 5.50

Souvenir Sheet

3074 A982 Sheet of 3, #3071, 3074a, 3074b 3.00 2.50

Christmas A983

Stars and: 7p, Manila Cathedral. 20p, Paoay Church. 24p, Miagao Church. 26p, Barasoain Church.

Litho. with Hologram Affixed

2006 *Perf. 14*

3075-3078 A983 Set of 4 10.00 8.50

Issued: 7p, 20p, 12/15; 24p, 26p, 12/19.

New Year 2007 (Year of the Pig) — A984

Designs: 7p, Head of pig. 20p, Pig.

2006, Dec. 27 Litho.

3079-3080 A984 Set of 2 4.50 3.50
3080a Souvenir sheet, 2 each #3079-3080 9.00 8.00

Printed in sheets of 20 and in sheets of 10.

Fruit A985

No. 3081: a, Watermelons. b, Mangos. c, Custard apples. d, Pomelos.
No. 3082: a, Jackfruit. b, Lanzones. c, Coconuts. d, Bananas.

2006, Dec. 15

3081 A985 7p Block or strip of 4, #a-d 4.50 3.50

Souvenir Sheet

3082 A985 7p Sheet of 4, #a-d 5.50 5.00

Printed in sheets of 15 stamps.

Graciano Lopez Jaena (1856-96), Journalist — A986

2006, Dec. 18

3083 A986 7p multi .80 .40

Centro Escolar University, Cent. — A987

2007, Jan. 18 Litho. *Perf. 14*

3084 A987 7p multi .75 .40
a. Miniature sheet of 8 12.50 12.50

Normally issued in sheets of 50.

Philippine School of the Deaf, Cent. — A988

2007, Jan. 19

3085 A988 7p multi .75 .40

Rare Flowers A989

No. 3086: a, Medinilla magnifica. b, Strongylodon elmeri. c, Amyema incarnatiflora. d, Dillenia monantha. e, Xanthostemon fruticosus. f, Plumeria acuminata. g, Paphiopedilum adductum. h, Rafflesia manillana.
26p, Rafflesia manillana and man, horiz.

2007, Mar. 30

3086 A989 7p Sheet of 8, #a-h 8.00 *7.00*

Souvenir Sheet

3087 A989 26p multi 6.00 5.00

No. 3087 contains one 120x30mm stamp.

Manulife Philippines Insurance, Cent. — A990

2007, Apr. 26

3088 A990 7p multi 1.00 .60
a. Souvenir sheet of 4 12.50 12.50

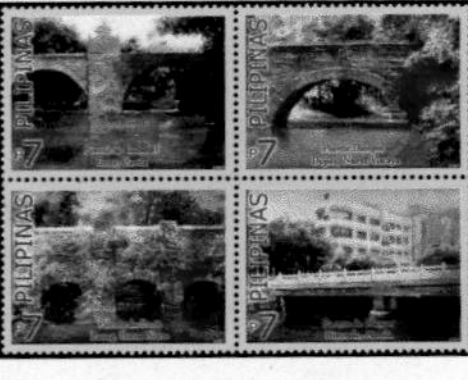

Colonial Era Bridges A991

No. 3089: a, Isabel II Bridge, Imus, Cavite. b, Dampol Bridge, Dupax, Nueva Viscaya. c, Barit Bridge, Laoad, Ilocos Norte. d, Blanco Bridge, Binondo, Manila.
No. 3090: a, Malagonlong Bridge, Tayabas, Quezon. b, Fort Santiago Bridge. c, Mahacao Bridge, Maragondon, Cavite. d, Busay Bridge, Guinobatan, Albay.

2007, May 16

3089 A991 7p Block of 4, #a-d 6.50 3.50

Souvenir Sheet

3090 A991 7p Sheet of 4, #a-d 5.00 4.00

No. 3089 printed in sheets of 16.

Diplomatic Relations Between Philippines and France, 60th Anniv. — A992

Symbols of France and Philippines including: 7p, Eiffel Tower. No. 3092, 26p, Castle.
No. 3093, 26p, Flags of France and Philippines, symbols of countries.

2007, June 26

3091-3092 A992 Set of 2 4.50 3.00

Souvenir Sheet

3093 A992 26p multi 4.50 3.50

No. 3093 contains one 30x80mm stamp.
Nos. 3091-3092 issued in sheets of 20 (10 of each denomination in two rows of 5, separated by a central gutter). Most sheets of 20 were cut in half through the central gutter.

Bureau of Fisheries and Aquatic Resources, 60th Anniv. — A993

No. 3094: a, Diana. b, Giant trevally. c, Skipjack tuna. d, Yellowfin tuna.
No. 3095: a, Cuttlefish. b, Bigfin reef squid and sacol (80x30mm).

2007, July 2

3094 A993 Horiz. strip of 4 5.00 4.00
a.-d. 7p Any single .80 .50

Souvenir Sheet

3095 Sheet of 2 6.00 5.00
a. A993 7p multi 1.25 .90
b. A993 20p multi 3.00 2.40

No. 3094 printed in sheets of 16 stamps.

Scouting, Cent. — A994

Designs: No. 3096, 7p, Scouting flag, hand giving scout sign. No. 3097, 7p, Scouting and Scouting Centenary emblems.

2007, Aug. 1

3096-3097 A994 Set of 2 2.25 1.50
3097a Souvenir sheet, 2 each #3096-3097 + label 5.00 5.00

A995

Ducks and Geese A996

No. 3098: a, Mallards. b, Green-winged teal. c, Tufted ducks. d, Cotton pygmy geese.
Nos. 3099 and 3100: a, Northern pintails. b, Common shelducks. c, Northern shovelers. d, Greater scaups.

2007, Aug. 3

3098 A995 7p Block of 4, #a-d 5.00 4.00

Souvenir Sheets

3099 A996 7p Sheet of 4, #a-d 6.00 6.00

With Bangkok 2007 Emblem Added to Stamps

3100 A996 7p Sheet of 4, #a-d 9.00 9.00

No. 3100 sold for 50p.
No. 3098 printed in sheets of 16 stamps.

Butterfly Type of 2006

Designs: 8p, Troidaes magellanus magellanus. 17p, Achillides palinurus daedalus.

2007, Aug. 7 ***Perf. 13¾x13½***

3101 A966 8p multi 1.20 .60
3102 A966 17p multi 2.25 .90

Association of South East Asian Nations (ASEAN), 40th Anniv. — A997

Designs: 7p, Malacañang Palace, Philippines.
No. 3104: a, Secretariat Building, Bandar Seri Begawan, Brunei. b, National Museum, Cambodia. c, Fatahillah Museum, Jakarta, Indonesia. d, Typical house, Laos. e, Malayan Railway Headquarters Building, Kuala Lumpur, Malaysia. f, Yangon Post Office, Myanmar (Burma). g, Malacañang Palace, Philippines. h, National Museum, Singapore. i, Vimanmek Mansion, Bangkok, Thailand. j, Presidential Palace, Hanoi, Viet Nam.
No. 3105, Malacañang Palace, Philippines (80x30mm).

2007, Aug. 8 ***Perf. 14***

3103 A997 7p multi .90 .60
3104 A997 20p Sheet of 10, #a-j 30.00 30.00

Souvenir Sheet

3105 A997 20p multi 3.00 2.50

See Brunei No. 607, Burma No. 370, Cambodia No. 2339, Indonesia Nos. 2120-2121, Laos Nos. 1717-1718, Malaysia No. 1170, Singapore No. 1265, Thailand No. 2315, and Viet Nam Nos. 3302-3311.

Pres. Ramon F. Magsaysay (1907-57) A998

2007, Aug. 31 **Litho.**

3106 A998 7p multi .80 .40

Social Security System, 50th Anniv. A999

Nos. 3107 and 3108 — Anniversary emblem and: a, Family and building. b, Pres. Ramon Magsaysay. c, Pres. Magsaysay signing Social Security Act of 1954. d, Building.

2007, Sept. 1 ***Perf. 14***

Stamps With White Margins

3107 A999 7p Block of 4, #a-d 4.50 3.50

Souvenir Sheet

Stamps With Gray Margins

3108 A999 7p Sheet of 4, #a-d 5.00 5.00

First Philippine Assembly, Cent. — A1000

Designs: No. 3109, 7p, People in front of Manila Opera House. No. 3110, 7p, Manila municipal building.

2007, Oct. 16

3109-3110 A1000 Set of 2 1.70 1.20

United Nations Month — A1001

Text in: 7p, Tagalog and English. 26p, English.

2007, Oct. 24

3111-3112 A1001 Set of 2 4.50 3.00

Nos. 3111-3112 were printed in a sheet of 20 stamps containing ten of each stamp separated by a central gutter of 5 different labels.

Paintings by Juan Luna (1857-99) — A1002

Designs: No. 3113, 7p, El Violinista. No. 3114, 7p, Indio Bravo. No. 3115, 7p, Old Man With a Pipe. No. 3116, 7p, La Bulakeña.
No. 3117a, Picnic in Normandy, horiz. (60x40mm).
No. 3118, horiz. — Parisian Life, with background color of: a, Light yellow and blue. b, Yellow orange and green. c, Yellow orange and red. d, Yellow orange and purple.

2007 ***Perf. 14***

3113-3116 A1002 Set of 4 4.00 3.00
3117 Sheet of 4, #3113-3115, 3117a 5.00 5.00
a. A1002 7p brown & multi, imperf. 1.20 1.00
3118 Sheet of 4 5.00 5.00
a. A1002 7p Imperf. (73x48mm) 1.25 1.00
b.-d. A1002 7p Any single 1.00 .80

Issued: Nos. 3113-3116, 10/24; No. 3117, 11/23; No. 3118, 12/21. No. 3116 was issued in sheets of 6.

Birds — A1003

Designs: 1p, Black-naped oriole. 2p, Asian fairy bluebird. 3p, Writhed hornbill. 4p, Crimson sunbird. 5p, Barn swallow. 8p, Hoopoe. 9p, Short-eared owl. 10p, Blue-winged pita. 50p, Head of Philippine eagle. 100p, Philippine eagle on tree branch.
No. 3124: a, Mindanao bleeding heart pigeon. b, Nicobar pigeon. c, Black-chinned fruit dove. d, Metallic pigeon. e, Pink-necked green pigeon. f, Amethyst brown dove. g, Gray imperial pigeon. h, Red turtle dove. i, Pied imperial pigeon. j, Spotted imperial pigeon.
No. 3128: a, Dwarf kingfisher. b, Blue-capped wood kingfisher. c, White-throated kingfisher. d, White-collared kingfisher.
No. 3129: a, Green-faced parrotfinch. b, Java sparrow. c, Yellow-breasted bunting. d, White-cheeked bullfinch.
No. 3130: a, Great-billed parrot. b, Philippine cockatoo. c, Blue-naped parrot. d, Blue-backed parrot.

2007 ***Perf. 13¾x13½***

Inscribed "2007"

3119 A1003 1p multi .50 .25
a. Inscribed "2008" .50 .25
b. Inscribed "2008A" .60 .25
c. Inscribed "2008B" .60 .25
3120 A1003 2p multi .50 .25
a. Inscribed "2008" .50 .25
b. Inscribed "2008A" .60 .30
c. Inscribed "2008B" .50 .25
3121 A1003 3p multi .65 .30
3122 A1003 4p multi .80 .35
a. Inscribed "2008" .75 .30
3123 A1003 5p multi .65 .25
a. Inscribed "2008" .80 .30
3124 Block of 10 12.00 12.00
a.-j. A1003 7p Any single .75 .30
k. Block of 10, inscr. "2008" 25.00 25.00
l.-u. A1003 7p Any single, inscr. "2008" 1.25 .65
3125 A1003 8p multi .80 .50
3126 A1003 9p multi 1.20 .50
3127 A1003 10p multi 1.75 .65
a. Inscribed "2008" 1.60 .45
b. Inscribed "2008A" 1.75 .60
3128 Block of 4 10.00 9.00
a.-d. A1003 20p Any single 1.75 1.20
3129 Block of 4 12.50 11.00
a.-d. A1003 24p Any single 2.40 1.25
3130 Block of 4 12.50 11.00
a.-d. A1003 26p Any single 2.60 1.50
e. Block of 4, inscr. "2008" 17.00 14.00
f.-i. A1003 26p Any single, inscr. "2008" 3.50 2.40
j. Block of 4, inscr. "2008A" 20.00 18.00
k.-n. A1003 26p Any single, inscr. "2008A" 2.75 1.75

Size: 30x40mm

Perf. 14

3131 A1003 50p multi 6.00 3.50
a. Inscribed "2008" 12.00 10.50
b. Inscribed "2008A" 6.00 4.50
3132 A1003 100p multi 12.50 7.00
a. Inscribed "2008" 45.00 40.00
b. Inscribed "2008A" 13.00 10.00
Nos. 3119-3132 (14) 72.35 56.55

Issued: 1p, 100p, 10/30; 2p, 20p, 11/15; 3p, 4p, 8p, 26p, 12/12; 5p, 50p, 11/5; 7p, 12/10; 9p, 10p, 24p, 12/19.
For stamps without blue lines at bottom, see No. 3151.

Manila Central Post Office, 1926 — A1004

No. 3133: a, Shown. b, Manila Central Post Office and architect Juan Marcos Arellano (80x30mm).

2007, Nov. 5 ***Perf. 14***

3133 Horiz. pair 4.50 3.50
a. A1004 7p multi .80 .60
b. A1004 20p multi 2.40 1.40

No. 3133 was printed in sheets of 10 stamps.

San Diego de Alcala Cathedral, Cumaca, 425th Anniv. — A1005

2007, Nov. 13 ***Perf. 13¾x13½***

3134 A1005 7p multi 1.20 .80
a. Miniature sheet of 5 7.50 7.50

Sacred Heart School, Cebu, 50th Anniv. A1006

No. 3135: a, School building and Philippines flag. b, School building and statue. c, Nun, school crest. d, Nun, school building.

2007, Nov. 16 ***Perf. 14***

Stamps With White Margins

3135 A1006 7p Block of 4, #a-d 4.00 3.00

Souvenir Sheet

3136 Sheet of 4, #3135a, 3135b, 3135d, 3136a 4.50 4.50
a. A1006 7p As #3135c, with greenish gray tint in margin at LL 1.00 .80

No. 3135 printed in sheets of 16 stamps.

Development Bank of the Philippines, 60th Anniv. — A1007

No. 3137: a, Ship emblem, blue background. b, Bank building, brown background. c, Bank building at left, dark green background. d, Bank building at right, olive green background.

2007, Nov. 26

3137 A1007 7p Block of 4, #a-d 4.00 3.00
e. Souvenir sheet, #3137a-3137d 4.50 4.50

No. 3137 printed in sheets of 16 stamps.

Christmas — A1008

Designs: 7p, Teddy bear. 20p, Toy train. 24p, Toy truck. 26p, Angel with candle decoration.

2007, Nov. 28

3138-3141 A1008 Set of 4 9.00 7.00

New Year 2008 (Year of the Rat) — A1009

Designs: 7p, Head of rat. 20p, Rat.

2007, Dec. 3

3142-3143 A1009 Set of 2 4.50 3.50
3143a Souvenir sheet, 2 each #3142-3143 10.00 10.00

Nos. 3142-3143 printed in sheets of 10 stamps.

World Vision in Philippines, 50th Anniv. — A1010

Designs: 7p, Pres. Ramon F. Magsaysay and World Vision founder, Rev. Bob Pierce. 20p, World Vision anniversary emblem, horiz.

2007, Dec. 5

3144-3145 A1010 Set of 2 5.00 3.00

No. 1810 Surcharged in Silver

Methods, Perfs and Watermark As Before

2007, Dec. 14

3146 A470 7p on 2.40p #1810 1.00 .70

Dominican School, Manila, 50th Anniv. — A1011

No. 3147: a, St. Dominic de Guzman. b, St. Dominic, school, emblem. c, Two emblems. d, School, emblem.

Unwmk.

2008, Feb. 1 **Litho.** ***Perf. 14***

3147 A1011 7p Block of 4, #a-d 4.00 3.00

Valentine's Day — A1012

No. 3148: a, Roses in heart. b, Cupid, hearts.

2008, Feb. 6

3148 A1012 7p Pair, #a-b		2.40	1.60
c. Sheet of 10, 5 each #3148a-3148b		14.00	14.00

No. 3148c sold for 100p.

Missionary Catechists of St. Therese of the Infant Jesus, 50th Anniv. — A1013

Designs: No. 3149, 7p, Emblem and nuns. No. 3150, 7p, 50th anniv. emblem, St. Therese of the Infant Jesus, Bishop Alfredo Obviar.

2008, Feb. 23

3149-3150 A1013 Set of 2	1.75	1.20
3150a Pair, #3149-3150	2.00	1.50
3150b Miniature sheet of 8, 4 each #3149-3150	12.50	12.50

No. 3149-3150 normally issued in sheets of 50.

Bird Type of 2007 Without Blue Lines at Bottom

Miniature Sheet

No. 3151: a, Mindanao bleeding heart pigeon. b, Nicobar pigeon. c, Black-chinned fruit dove. d, Metallic pigeon. e, Pink-necked green pigeon. f, Amethyst brown dove. g, Gray imperial pigeon. h, Red turtle dove. i, Pied imperial pigeon. j, Spotted imperial pigeon. k, Philippine eagle. l, Philippine cockatoo. m, Java sparrow. n, Blue-capped wood kingfisher.

2008, Mar. 7 ***Perf. 13¾x13½***

3151 A1003 7p Sheet of 14, #a-n, + label	18.00	18.00

2008 Taipei Intl. Stamp Exhibition. No. 3151 sold for 125p.

Rodents of Luzon Island A1014

No. 3152: a, Luzon furry-tailed rat. b, Cordillera striped earth rat. c, Cordillera forest mouse. d, Cordillera shrew mouse.

No. 3153: a, 7p, Northern giant cloud rat. b, 7p, Lesser dwarf cloud rat. c, 20p, Bushy-tailed cloud rat, vert. (40x70mm).

2008, Mar. 7 ***Perf. 14***

3152 A1014 7p Block of 4, #a-d	4.50	3.50

Souvenir Sheet

Perf. 14, Imperf. (20p)

3153 A1014 Sheet of 3, #a-c	5.00	4.00

Natl. Research Council, 75th Anniv. — A1015

2008, Mar. 12 ***Perf. 14***

3154 A1015 7p multi	.75	.40

Baguio Teachers Camp, Cent. A1016

No. 3155: a, Camp. b, Teachers, bridge.

2008, May 10

3155 A1016 7p Horiz. pair, #a-b	1.75	1.40

Bridges of the American Era — A1017

No. 3156: a, Gasan Bridge, Gasan, Marinduque. b, Hinigaran Bridge, Hinigaran, Negros Occidental. c, Wahig Bridge, Dagoboy, Bohol. d, Pan-ay Bridge, Pan-ay, Capiz.

No. 3157: a, Quezon Bridge, Quiapo, Manila. b, Governor Reynolds Bridge, Guinobatan, Albay. c, Mauca Railway Bridge, Ragay, Camarines Sur. d, Balucuan Bridge, Dao, Capiz.

Illustration reduced.

2008, May 16

3156 A1017 7p Block of 4, #a-d	4.50	3.50

Miniature Sheet

3157 A1017 7p Sheet of 4, #a-d	5.00	5.00

Issued in sheets of 16.

Miniature Sheet

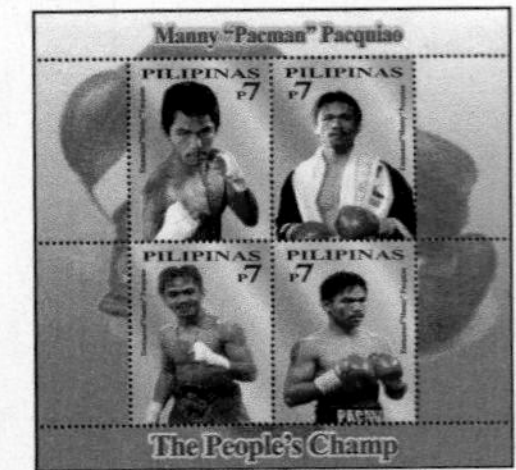

Manny Pacquiao, World Boxing Council Lightweight Champion — A1018

No. 3158 — Pacquiao: a, With hands taped. b, Wearing robe and gloves. c, Wearing championship belt. d, Wearing gloves.

2008, May 30

3158 A1018 7p Sheet of 4, #a-d	7.00	7.00

Dept. of Science and Technology, 50th Anniv. — A1019

Philippine Nuclear Research Institute, 50th Anniv. — A1020

2008, June 4

3159 A1019 7p multi	.75	.40
3160 A1020 7p multi	.75	.40

Liong Tek Go Family Association, Cent. — A1021

No. 3161: a, Association centenary emblem. b, Tai Bei Kong.

2008, June 11

3161 A1021 7p Pair, #a-b	1.50	1.50
a. Miniature sheet of 8	12.50	12.50

Normally printed in sheets of 20.

University of the Philippines, Cent. — A1022

Designs: Nos. 3162a, 3163c, 3164c, Emblem (with eagle). Nos. 3162b, 3163a, 3164a, Carillon. Nos. 3162c, 3163d, 3164d, Oblation sculpture. Nos. 3162d, 3163b, 3164b, Centenary emblem (with Oblation sculpture).

2008 ***Perf. 13¾x13½***

3162 A1022 7p Block of 4, #a-d	3.50	3.00

Stamp Size: 40x30mm

Perf. 14

3163 A1022 7p Block of 4, #a-d	5.00	4.50
e. Souvenir sheet, #3163a-3163d	5.00	5.00

Litho. With Foil Application

3164 A1022 7p Block of 4, #a-d	6.00	6.00
e. Souvenir sheet, #3164a-3164d	8.00	8.00

No. 3164 was printed in sheets containing four blocks that sold for 160p. No. 3164e sold for 50p.

Friar Andres de Urdaneta (c. 1608-1568), Navigator — A1023

2008, June 26 ***Perf. 14***

3165 A1023 7p multi	.80	.40

Philippine-Spanish Friendship Day.

Xavier University, Ateneo de Cagayan, 75th Anniv. — A1024

No. 3166: a, Immaculate Conception Chapel. b, Statue of St. Francis Xavier. c, Archbishop James T. G. Hayes. d, Science Center.

2008, June 26

3166 A1024 7p Block of 4, #a-d	3.25	3.00
a. Miniature sheet of 8	12.00	12.00

Normally issued in sheets of 40.

Ateneo de Davao University, 60th Anniv. — A1025

No. 3167: a, College building. b, High school building, statue. c, Grade school building, flags. d, Assumption (stained glass).

2008, July 31

3167 A1025 7p Block of 4, #a-d	3.50	3.00
e. Souvenir sheet, #3167a-3167d	5.00	5.00

2008 Summer Olympics, Beijing — A1026

Designs: 7p, Archery. 20p, Judo. 24p, Equestrian. 26p, Weight lifting.

2008, Aug. 11 **Litho.**

3168-3171 A1026 Set of 4	12.00	8.00

Se Jo Lim Family Association, Cent. — A1027

Designs: Nos. 3172a, 3173a, Pi Kan, Lim family ancestor. Nos. 3172b, 3173b, Senator Roselier T. Lim, Gen. Vicente P. Lim. Nos. 3172c, 3173c, Binondo Church, Chinese gate. Nos. 3172d, 3173d, Association centenary emblem, sun, stars and colors of Philippines flag.

2008, Aug. 22 ***Perf. 14***

3172 A1027 7p Block of 4, #a-d	3.50	3.00

Souvenir Sheet

Perf. 14 on 3 Sides

3173 A1027 7p Sheet of 4, #a-d, + 2 labels	4.50	4.50

Printed in sheets of 16 with large horizontal central label.

Philippine Bonsai Society, 35th Anniv. — A1028

No. 3174: a, Pemphis acidula (on short-legged table), red background. b, Ficus microcarpa. c, Serissa foetida. d, Pemphis acidula, violet background. e, Pemphis acidula, blue background. f, Triphasia trifolia. g, Pemphis acidula (on piece of wood), cerise background. h, Bougainville sp.

No. 3175, vert.: a, Murraya sp. b, Pemphis acidula, tan background. c, Pemphis acidula, gray blue background. d, Pemphis acidula, violet background. e, Pemphis acidula, blue background. f, Antidesma bunius. g, Maba buxifolia. h, Ficus concina.

No. 3176: a, Lagerstroemia indica. b, Pemphis acidula, yellow green background. c, Vitex sp. d, Ixora chinensis.

2008, Oct. 17 ***Perf. 14***

3174 Block of 8	9.00	9.00
a.-h. A1028 7p Any single	.80	.65
3175 Block of 8	9.00	9.00
a.-h. A1028 7p Any single	.80	.65

Souvenir Sheet

3176 Sheet of 4	5.00	5.00
a.-d. A1028 7p Any single	1.10	.50

Printed in sheets of 16.

Miniature Sheet

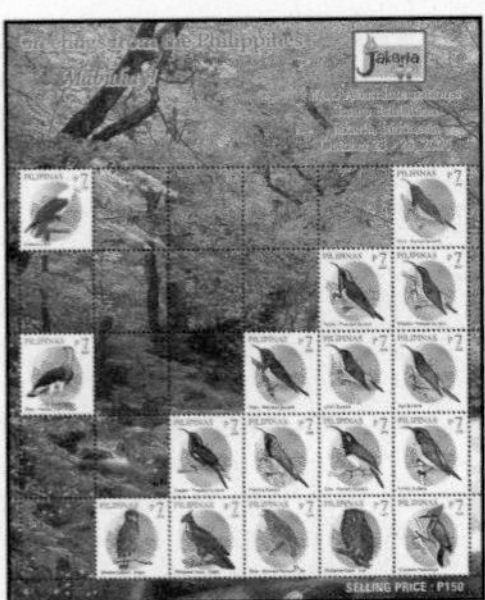

Jakarta 2008 Intl. Stamp Exhibition — A1029

No. 3177 — Birds: a, Brahminy kite. b, Olive-backed sunbird. c, Purple-throated sunbird. d, Metallic-winged sunbird. e, Gray-headed fish eagle. f, Plain-throated sunbird. g,

Lina's sunbird. h, Apo sunbird. i, Copper-throated sunbird. j, Flaming sunbird. k, Gray-hooded sunbird. l, Lovely sunbird. m, Crested serpent eagle. n, Philippine hawk eagle. o, Blue-crowned racquet-tail. p, Philippine eagle owl. q, Common flameback.

2008, Oct. 23 ***Perf. 13¾x13½***
3177 A1029 7p Sheet of 17, #a-q, + 13 labels 20.00 20.00

No. 3177 sold for 150p.

Visit of Ban Ki-moon, United Nations Secretary General — A1030

Ban Ki-moon and: 7p, UN emblem. 26p, Philippines President Gloria Macapagal-Arroyo.

2008, Oct. 29 ***Perf. 14***
3178-3179 A1030 Set of 2 3.50 2.50

Tourism A1031

No. 3180: a, Boracay Beach, Aklan. b, Intramuros, Manila. c, Banaue Rice Terraces, Mountain Province. d, Mayon Volcano, Bicol.
20p, Puerto Princesa Underground River, Palawan. 24p, Chocolate Hills, Bohol. 26p, Tubbataha Reef, Palawan.

2008, Nov. 3 ***Perf. 13½x13¾***
3180 Block of 4 4.00 3.00
a.-d. A1031 7p Any single .80 .65
3181 A1031 20p multi 2.25 1.50
3182 A1031 24p multi 3.00 1.75
3183 A1031 26p multi 3.25 1.75
Nos. 3180-3183 (4) 12.50 8.00

Philippine Postal Service, 110th anniv.

Christmas — A1032

Designs: 7p, Mother with brown hair, and child. 20p, Mother nursing child. 24p, Mother, child, dove. 26p, Mother with child in sling.
No. 3188: a, 7p, Madonna and Child. b, 26m, Mother with sleeping child.

2008, Nov. 10 ***Perf. 14***
3184-3187 A1032 Set of 4 10.00 7.50

Souvenir Sheet

3188 A1032 Sheet of 2, #a-b 5.00 4.00

Comic Book Superheroes of Carlo J. Caparas — A1033

No. 3189, 7p: a, Joaquin Bordado. b, Totoy Bato. c, Gagambino. d, Pieta.
No. 3190: a, 7p, Ang Panday (with hammer). b, 20p, Ang Panday (holding sword).

2008, Nov. 17
3189 A1033 7p Block of 4, #a-d 3.50 3.00

Souvenir Sheet

3190 A1033 Sheet of 2, #a-b 4.50 3.50

Natl. Stamp Collecting Month.

Senator Benigno S. Aquino, Jr. (1932-83) — A1034

No. 3191: a, 7p, Photograph. b, 26p, Drawing.

2008, Nov. 27
3191 A1034 Horiz. pair, #a-b 4.50 3.50

Fernando G. Bautista (1908-2002), Founder of University of Baguio — A1035

2008, Dec. 8
3192 A1035 7p multi .75 .40

New Year 2009 (Year of the Ox) — A1036

Designs: 7p, Ox head. 20p, Ox.

2008, Dec. 10
3193-3194 A1036 Set of 2 4.50 3.50
3194a Souvenir sheet of 4, 2 each #3193-3194 11.00 11.00

Printed in sheets of 10.

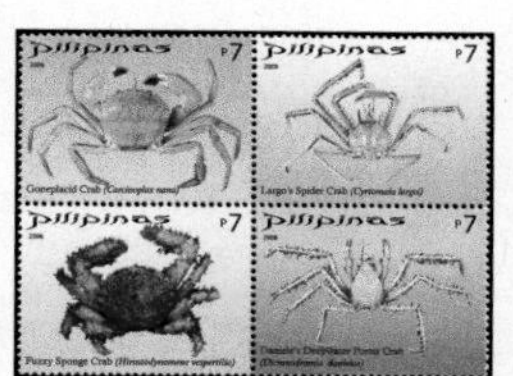

Crabs A1037

No. 3195: a, Goneplacid crab. b, Largo's spider crab. c, Fuzzy sponge crab. d, Daniele's deepwater porter crab.
No. 3196: a, Stimpson's intricate spider crab. b, Spider crab.

2008, Dec. 19
3195 A1037 7p Block of 4, #a-d 4.00 3.00

Souvenir Sheet

3196 A1037 20p Sheet of 2, #a-b, + 2 labels 6.00 6.00

No. 3196 sold for 50p.
Printed in sheets of 16.

Dr. Manuel Sarmiento Enverga (1909-81), Educator and Politician — A1038

2009, Jan. 1 **Litho.** ***Perf. 14***
3197 A1038 7p multi .75 .40

Love A1039

No. 3198: a, Roses and heart. b, Hearts and envelope.

2009, Feb. 2
3198 A1039 7p Pair, #a-b 1.75 1.20

Philippine Intl. Arts Festival — A1040

Emblem and: a, Painting. b, Theater masks and book of poetry. c, Cymbal and dancers. d, Theater and movie poster.

2009, Feb. 16
3199 A1040 7p Block of 4, #a-d 3.50 3.00

Diplomatic Relations Between Philippines and Republic of Korea, 60th Anniv. — A1041

No. 3200: a, Panagbenga Flower Festival, Philippines. b, Cow Play, Hangawi, Republic of Korea.

2009, Mar. 3
3200 A1041 7p Horiz. pair, #a-b 2.00 1.50

See Republic of Korea Nos. 2304-2305.
Printed in sheets of 10.

Birds — A1042

Designs: 1p, Mugimaki flycatcher. 2p, Narcissus flycatcher.3p, Mountain verditer-flycatcher. 4p, Blue rock thrush. 5p, Brown shrike. 8p, Apo myna. 9p, Crested serpent-eagle. 10p, Blue-crowned racquet-tail. 17p, Common flameback. 50p, Gray-headed fish-eagle. 100p, Philippine hawk-eagle.
No. 3206: a, Olive-backed sunbird. b, Metallic-winged sunbird. c, Plain-throated sunbird. d, Lina's sunbird. e, Purple-throated sunbird. f, Apo sunbird. g, Copper-throated sunbird. h, Flaming sunbird. i, Gray-hooded sunbird. j, Lovely sunbird.
No. 3211: a, Palawan flowerpecker. b, Fire-breasted flowerpecker. c, Cebu flowerpecker. d, Red-keeled flowerpecker.
No. 3212: a, Philippine tailorbird. b, Mountain tailorbird. c, Black-headed tailorbird. d, Ashy tailorbird.

2009 **Litho.** ***Perf. 13¾x13½***
3201 A1042 1p multi .50 .25
3202 A1042 2p multi .75 .30
3203 A1042 3p multi .50 .30
3204 A1042 4p multi .75 .30
3205 A1042 5p multi 1.50 .35
3206 Block of 10 35.00 *35.00*
a.-j. A1042 7p Any single 1.50 .70
3207 A1042 8p multi 1.00 .35
3208 A1042 9p multi 1.20 .90
3209 A1042 10p multi 1.50 .45
3210 A1042 17p multi 2.00 .85
3211 Block of 4 12.50 *10.00*
a.-d. A1042 20p Any single, dated "2009" 2.50 1.20
3212 Block of 4 15.00 *13.00*
a.-d. A1042 26p Any single, dated "2009" 3.00 1.75

Size: 30x40mm

Perf. 14

3213 A1042 50p multi 6.00 2.00
3214 A1042 100p multi 12.50 9.00
Nos. 3201-3214 (14) 90.70 73.05

Issued: 1p, 2p, No. 3206, 3/9; 3p, 4p, No. 3211, 6/2; 5p, 100p, 3/13; 8p, 9p, 10p, 17p, 50p, 3/23; No. 3212, 5/25.
See No. 3258.

2009-10 **Litho.** ***Perf. 13¾x13½***
3201a Dated "2009A" .50 .25
3201b Dated "2009B" .50 .25
3201c Dated "2009C" .60 .25
3202a Dated "2009A" .60 .25
3202b Dated "2009B" .60 .25
3202c Dated "2009C" .50 .25
3203a Dated "2009A" .60 .25
3203b Dated "2009B" .70 .30
3203c Dated "2009C" .70 .30
3204a Dated "2009A" .70 .30
3204b Dated "2009B" .90 .35
3204c Dated "2009C" .80 .30
3205a Dated "2009A" 1.00 .30
3205b Dated "2009B" .70 .30
3205c Dated "2009C" .70 .30
3206k Block of 10, #3206l-3206u, dated "2009A" 15.00 *15.00*
3206l-3206u Like Nos. 3206a-3206j, any single, dated "2009A" 1.20 .50
3207a Dated "2009A" 1.20 .40
3207b Dated "2009B" 1.00 .30
3207c Dated "2009C" 1.00 .35
3208a Dated "2009A" 1.50 .50
3208b Dated "2009B" 1.20 .35
3208c Dated "2009C" 1.50 .50
3208d Dated "2009D" 1.10 .50
3209a Dated "2009A" 1.25 .60
3209b Dated "2009B" 1.25 .60
3210a Dated "2009A" 2.50 1.00
3210b Dated "2009B" 3.00 1.50
3210c Dated "2009C" 2.25 1.20
3211e Block of 4, #3211f-3211i, dated "2009A" 10.00 8.00
3211f-3211i Like Nos. 3211a-3211d, any single, dated "2009A" 2.00 1.20
3212e Block of 4, #3212f-3212i, dated "2009A" 13.00 11.00
3212f-3212i Like Nos. 3212a-3212d, any single, dated "2009A" 2.50 1.25
3212j Block of 4, #3212k-3212n, dated "2009B" 13.00 13.00
3212k-3212n Like Nos. 3212a-3212d, any single, dated "2009B" 2.50 1.50

Size: 30x40mm

Perf. 14

3213a Dated "2009A" 8.00 4.00
3213b Dated "2009B" 6.00 3.50
3213c Dated "2009C" 8.00 5.50
3213d Dated "2009D" 6.00 3.50
3214a Dated "2009A" 16.00 10.00
3214b Dated "2009B" 13.00 8.00
3214c Dated "2009C" 18.00 12.00
3214d Dated "2009D" 13.00 7.00

Issued: No. 3206k, 5/13; No. 3205a, 5/25; Nos. 3201a, 3202a, 6/2; Nos. 3207a, 3208a, 3213a, 3214a, 6/8; Nos. 3201b, 3202b, 3205b, 8/6; No. 3208b, 8/10; Nos. 3203a, 3204a, 3210a, 8/13; Nos. 3207b, 3212e, 8/17; Nos. 3213b, 3214b, 9/1; Nos. 3209a, 3211e, 9/9; Nos. 3213c, 3214c, 11/24; No. 3201c, 12/11; Nos. 3209b, 3212j, 12/28; Nos. 3202c, 3204b, 3205c, 3210b, 1/11/10; Nos. 3203b, 3207c, 3208c, 1/12/10; Nos. 3213d, 3214d, 1/28/10; Nos. 3203c, 3204c, 3208d, 3210c, 2/5/10.

Minerals A1043

No. 3215: a, Quartz. b, Rhodochrosite. c, Malachite. d, Nickel.
No. 3216: a, Cinnabar. b, Native gold. c, Native copper. d, Magnetite.

2009, Mar. 25 ***Perf. 14***
3215 A1043 7p Block of 4, #a-d 4.00 3.00

Souvenir Sheet

3216 A1043 7p Sheet of 4, #a-d 5.00 5.00

Mothers Dionisia (1691-1732) and Cecilia Rosa Talangpaz (1693-1731), Founders of Augustinian Recollect Sisters — A1044

2009, Apr. 28
3217 A1044 7p multi .75 .40

Art Deco Theaters A1045

No. 3218: a, King's Theater. b, Capitol Theater. c, Joy Theater. d, Scala Theater.
No. 3219, horiz.: a, Life Theater. b, Times Theater. c, Bellevue Theater. d, Pines Theater.

2009, May 8
3218 A1045 7p Block of 4, #a-d 4.00 3.50

Souvenir Sheet

3219 A1045 7p Sheet of 4, #a-d 5.00 4.00

Rodolfo S. Cornejo (1909-91), Composer — A1046

2009, May 15
3220 A1046 7p multi .75 .30

Tourist Attractions in Taguig — A1047

No. 3221: a, City Hall. b, Global City. c, Santa Ana Church. d, Blue Mosque.

2009, June 5 **Litho.**
3221 A1047 7p Block of 4, #a-d 3.75 3.00

Diplomatic Relations Between Philippines and Thailand, 60th Anniv. — A1048

No. 3222 — Dances: a, Tinikling, Philippines. b, Ten Krathop Sark, Thailand.

2009, June 14 ***Perf. 14***
3222 A1048 7p Horiz. pair, #a-b 2.25 1.75

Printed in sheets of 10.
See Thailand No. 2429.

Ateneo de Manila University, 150th Anniv. — A1049

No. 3223: a, Sesquicentennial emblem. b, Blue eagle. c, St. Ignatius of Loyola. d, José Rizal.

2009, June 14
3223 A1049 7p Block of 4, #a-d 4.50 4.00
e. Souvenir sheet, #3223a-3223d, + 2 labels 16.00 16.00

No. 3223e sold for 40p.

Baler, 400th Anniv. A1050

No,. 3224: a, Old church. b, New church.

2009, June 30 **Litho.**
3224 A1050 7p Horiz. pair, #a-b 1.75 1.40

Che Yong Cua and Chua Family Association, Cent. — A1051

No. 3225: a, Chua Tiong. b, Chua Siok To.

2009, July 15 ***Perf. 14***
3225 A1051 7p Horiz. pair, #a-b 2.10 1.75

Souvenir Sheet

3226 A1051 Sheet of 4, #3225a-3225b, 3226a-3226b, + 2 labels 5.50 5.00
a. 7p Like #3225a, perf. 14 at left 1.25 1.00
b. 7p Like #3225b, perf. 14 at right 1.25 1.00

Printed in sheets of 12 stamps with 4 labels.
See Nos. 3239-3240.

Pheepoy, Mascot of Philippine Postal Corporation — A1052

2009, July 27 ***Perf. 13½x13¾***
3227 A1052 7p multi .75 .40

See Nos. 3255, 3260, 3335, and 3336.

Knights of Columbus in Philippines, 50th Anniv. — A1053

Color of denomination outline: 7p, Red. 9p, Dark blue.

2009, July 31 ***Perf. 14***
3228-3229 A1053 Set of 2 2.10 1.50

Agricultural Cooperation Agreement Between Philippines and Brunei — A1054

2009, Aug. 3
3230 A1054 7p multi .80 .50

Diplomatic Relations Between Philippines and Singapore, 40th Anniv. — A1055

No. 3231: a, Bamban Bridge, Philippines. b, Marcelo B. Fernan Bridge, Philippines. c, Cavenagh Bridge, Singapore. d, Henderson Waves and Alexandra Arch, Singapore.

2009, Aug. 29 **Litho.**
3231 A1055 7p Block of 4, #a-d 4.00 3.50
e. Souvenir sheet, #3231a-3231d 5.00 5.00

Printed in sheets of 16.
See Singapore Nos. 1398-1401.

Baguio, Cent. A1056

No. 3232 — Butterfly on posters and Baguio landmarks: a, Mansion House. b, Mines View Park. c, Baguio Cathedral. d, Kennon Road.

2009, Sept. 1 ***Perf. 13¾x13½***
3232 A1056 7p Horiz. strip of 4, #a-d 5.00 4.00
e. Souvenir sheet, #3232a-3232d 7.50 7.50

Pres. Corazon Aquino (1933-2009) — A1057

No. 3233: a, With raised arm, denomination at UL. b, Head and signature, denomination at UR.
No. 3234: a, With raised arm, denomination at UR. b, Head and signature, denomination at UL.

2009 **Litho.** ***Perf. 14***
3233 A1057 7p Horiz. pair, #a-b 4.50 4.00
3234 A1057 7p Horiz. pair, #a-b 2.50 1.75

Issued: No. 3233, 9/8; No. 3234, 9/18.

Intl. Year of Natural Fibers — A1058

No. 3235: a, Ananas comosus, clothing made from pineapple fibers. b, Musa textilis, bags and hats made from abaca fibers. c, Musa textilis, Philippines bank notes made from abaca fibers. d, Musa textilis, abaca rope.

2009, Sept. 10
3235 Horiz. strip of 4 3.50 3.00
a.-d. A1058 7p Any single .75 .65

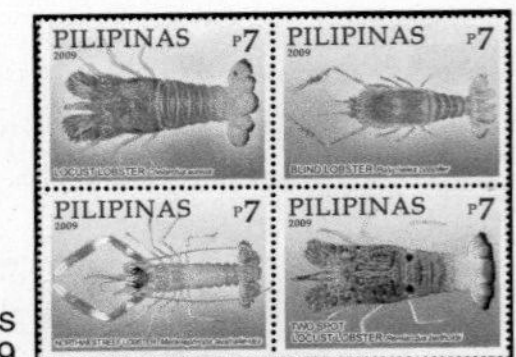

Lobsters A1059

No. 3236: a, Locust lobster. b, Blind lobster. c, Northwest Reef lobster. d, Two-spot locust lobster.
No. 3237: a, Neptune Reef lobster. b, Fan lobster. c, Blue-back locust lobster. d, Banded whip lobster.

2009, Sept. 30
3236 A1059 7p Block of 4, #a-d 4.50 3.50

Souvenir Sheet

3237 A1059 7p Sheet of 4, #a-d 5.00 5.00

Printed in sheets of 16.

Quezon City, 70th Anniv. A1060

No. 3238: a, Statue of Pres. Manuel L. Quezon, Philippines flag. b, City Hall. c, Araneta Center. d, Eastwood City.

2009, Oct. 12
3238 A1060 7p Block of 4, #a-d 4.00 3.00
e. Souvenir sheet, #3238a-3238d 4.50 4.50

Che Yong Cua and Chua Family Association, Cent. — A1061

No. 3239 — Philippines flag, emblem and: a, Cua Lo.

2009, Oct. 15 ***Perf. 14***
3239 A1061 7p Horiz. pair, #3225a, 3239a. 2.00 1.75

Souvenir Sheet

3240 A1061 Sheet of 4, #3225a, 3226a, 3239a, 3240a + 2 labels 5.00 5.00
a. 7p Like #3239a, perf. 14 at right 1.00 1.00

Printed in sheets of 16.

Alpha Phi Beta Fraternity of the University of the Philippines, 70th Anniv. — A1062

No. 3241 — Fraternity emblem and: a, 70th anniv. emblem. b, Quezon Hall Oblation. c, Malcolm Hall. d, Founding fathers of fraternity.

2009, Oct. 17 ***Perf. 14***
3241 A1062 7p Block of 4, #a-d 3.50 3.00

A1063

Children's Games and Activities — A1064

No. 3242: a, Tumbang preso. b, Luksong tinik. c, Holen (marbles). d, Sungka.
No. 3243: a, Taguan (hide-and seek) (30x40mm). b, Sipa (30x40mm). c, Saranggola (kite flying) (30x40mm). d, Bangkang papel (paper boat racing) (30x40mm). e, Paluan ng palayok (piñata) (48x38mm). f, Luksong lubid (rope jumping) (48x38mm).
Illustrations reduced.

2009, Nov. 9 ***Perf. 14***
3242 A1063 7p Block of 4, #a-d 4.50 4.00

Souvenir Sheet

Perf. 14, Imperf. (#3243e-3243f)

3243 A1064 7p Sheet of 6, #a-f 7.50 7.50

Natl. Stamp Collecting Month.
Printed in sheets of 16.

Christmas — A1065

No. 3244 — Lyrics from Christmas carol "Ang Pasko ay Sumapit" and: a, Four children caroling. b, Nativity. c, Magi on camels. d, Angels and baby Jesus. e, Christmas decorations.

2009, Nov. 18 *Perf. 14*
3244 Horiz. strip of 5 5.00 4.50
a.-e. A1065 7p Any single .85 .70

Cecilia Muñoz Palma (1913-2006), First Female Supreme Court Justice — A1066

2009, Nov. 22
3245 A1066 7p multi .75 .50

Diplomatic Relations Between the Philippines and India, 60th Anniv. — A1067

Endangered marine mammals: Nos. 3246a, 3247a, Whale shark. No. 3246b, Gangetic dolphin.

2009, Nov. 27 **Litho.**
3246 A1067 7p Horiz. pair, #a-b 2.50 2.00

Souvenir Sheet

3247 A1067 Sheet of 2, #3246b, 3247a + 2 labels 6.00 6.00
a. 20p multi 4.50 3.50

See India No. 2374.

New Year 2010 (Year of the Tiger) — A1068

Designs: 7p, Tiger's head. 20p, Tiger.

2009, Dec. 1 *Perf. 14*
3248-3249 A1068 Set of 2 4.50 4.00
3249a Souvenir sheet, 2 each #3248-3249 11.00 11.00

Printed in sheets of 10.

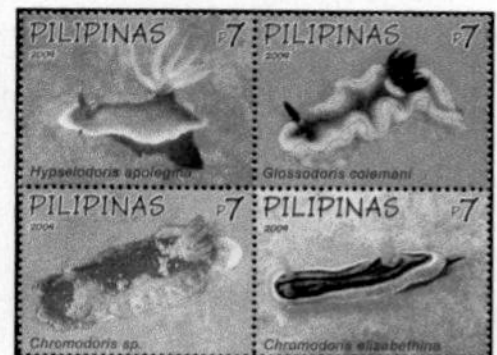

Nudibranchs — A1069

No. 3250: a, Hypselodoris apolegma. b, Glossodoris colemani. c, Chromodoris sp. d, Chromodoris elizabethina.

No. 3251: a, Jorunna funebris. b, Chromodoris lochi. c, Noumea alboannulata. d, Chromodoris hintuanesis. e, Risbechi tryoni. f, Chromodoris leopardus.

2009, Dec. 4
3250 A1069 7p Block of 4, #a-d 4.50 4.00

Souvenir Sheet

3251 A1069 7p Sheet of 6, #a-f, + 2 labels 7.50 7.50

Printed in sheets of 16.

Stamp Collage Depicting Daedalus — A1070

Designs: No. 3252, Entire collage.
No. 3253 — Quadrants of entire collage: a, UL. b, UR. c, LL. d, LR.

2009, Dec. 7
3252 A1070 7p multi .75 .50

Souvenir Sheet

3253 A1070 7p Sheet of 4, #a-d 4.50 4.50

Intl. Civil Aviation Organization, 65th anniv.

Return of Olongapo to the Philippines, 50th Anniv. — A1071

No. 3254 — Official seals of the Philippines and US and: a, Turnover ceremony. b, Parade of flags of the Philippines and US.

2009, Dec. 7 *Perf. 14*
3254 A1071 7p Horz. pair, #a-b 1.75 1.40

Pheepoy Delivering Mail — A1072

2009, Dec. 10 *Perf. 13½x13¾*
3255 A1072 7p multi .75 .40

See No. 3227, 3260, 3335-3336.

Philippine Charity Sweepstakes Office, 75th Anniv. — A1073

No. 3256 — 75th anniv. emblem and: a, Charity Sweepstakes Office Building, Presidents Manuel L. Quezon and Gloria Macapagal Arroyo. b, Building. c, Building and family. d, Building and employees.

2009, Dec. 18 *Perf. 14*
3256 A1073 7p Block of 4, #a-d 3.50 3.00
e. Souvenir sheet, #3256a-3256d 4.50 4.50

Potter From San Nicolas — A1074

2009, Dec. 21
3257 A1074 7p multi .75 .50

San Nicolas, Ilocos Norte Province, cent.

Birds Type of 2009

No. 3258: a, Philippine eagle owl. b, Luzon Scops owl. c, Philippine Scops owl. d, Spotted wood owl.

2010 **Litho.** *Perf. 13¾x13½*
3258 Block of 4 12.00 *9.50*
a.-d. A1042 24p Any single 3.00 1.50
e. Block of 4, #3258f-3258i, dated "2009A" 12.00 *10.00*
f.-i. Like #3258a-3258d, any single, dated "2009A" 2.50 1.50

Nos. 3258a-3258d are dated "2009." Issued: No. 3258, 1/11; No. 3258e, 2/8.

St. Valentine's Day — A1075

No. 3259 — Cupid: a, With bow and arrow. b, Blowing flower petals.

2010, Jan. 25 *Perf. 14*
3259 A1075 7p Horiz. pair, #a-b 1.75 1.50

Pheepoy on Motorcycle — A1076

2010, Feb. 12 *Perf. 13½x13¾*
3260 A1076 7p multi .75 .40

See No. 3227, 3255, 3335-3336.

Rotary International in the Philippines, 90th Anniv. — A1077

Nos. 3261 and 3262: a, Peace dove above people. b, Construction workers. c, Child receiving polio vaccine. d, Rizal Monument, map of the Philippines. No. 3262 has Rotary International emblem instead of "Service Above Self" slogan.

2010, Feb. 23 *Perf. 14*
3261 A1077 7p Block of 4, #a-d 4.50 4.00

Souvenir Sheet

Imperf

3262 A1077 7p Sheet of 4, #a-d 5.00 5.00

Beetles A1078

No. 3263: a, Agestra luconica. b, Glycyphana. c, Paraplectrone crassa. d, Astrea.

No. 3264: a, Agestra semperi. b, Heterorhina. c, Agestra antoinei. d, Clerota rodriguezi.

2010, Mar. 29 **Litho.** *Perf. 14*
3263 A1078 7p Block of 4, #a-d 4.50 4.00

Souvenir Sheet

3264 A1078 7p Sheet of 4, #a-d 5.00 5.00

Printed in sheets of 16.

Marine Life — A1079

Designs: No. 3265, Christmas tree worm. No. 3266, Yellow seahorse. No. 3267, Manta ray. No. 3268, Sea slug. No. 3269, Pencil urchin. No. 3270, Daisy coral. No. 3271, Magnificent sea anemone. No. 3272, Striped surgeonfish. No. 3273, Sundial. No. 3274, Blue linkia sea star. No. 3275, Sea hare. No. 3276, Giant clam. No. 3277, Green sea turtle. No. 3278, Sacoglossan sea slug. No. 3279, Lionfish. No. 3280, True clownfish. 8p, Harlequin shrimp. No. 3282, Coral beauty. No. 3283, Blue-ringed angelfish. No. 3284, Mandarinfish. No. 3285, Ribbon eel. 15p, Bowmouth guitarfish. No. 3287, Bigfin reef squid. No. 3288, Blue-spotted fantail stingray. No. 3289, Blue sea squirts. No. 3290, Scarlet-fringed flatworm. 24p, Branching anemone. 25p, Boxer crab. 26p, Spotted porcelain crab. 30p, Chambered nautilus. No. 3295, Red grouper. No. 3296, Giant moray eel. 40p, Textile cone. No. 3298, Marble sea star. No. 3299, Upside-down jellyfish. No. 3300, Bottlenose dolphin. No. 3301, Blue-ringed octopus.

2010-11 **Litho.** *Perf. 13½x13¾*

3265	A1079	1p multi	.65	.25
3266	A1079	1p multi	.75	.25
3267	A1079	1p multi	.90	.25
3268	A1079	2p multi	.70	.25
3269	A1079	2p multi	.90	.25
3270	A1079	3p multi	.90	.25
3271	A1079	3p multi	.90	.25
3272	A1079	3p multi	.90	.30
3273	A1079	4p multi	.90	.30
3274	A1079	4p multi	.90	.30
3275	A1079	5p multi	1.25	.30
3276	A1079	5p multi	1.25	.30
3277	A1079	5p multi	.90	.30
3278	A1079	5p multi	1.25	.35
3279	A1079	7p multi	.90	.25
3280	A1079	7p multi	.90	.30
3281	A1079	8p multi	.90	.30
3282	A1079	9p multi	1.75	.50
3283	A1079	9p multi	1.60	.35
3284	A1079	10p multi	1.60	.40
3285	A1079	10p multi	1.60	.40
3286	A1079	15p multi	2.25	.65
3287	A1079	17p multi	3.50	1.40
3288	A1079	17p multi	1.40	1.70
3289	A1079	20p multi	2.75	1.40
3290	A1079	20p multi	3.00	1.70
3291	A1079	24p multi	3.25	2.50
3292	A1079	25p multi	3.25	1.80
3293	A1079	26p multi	3.45	1.70
3294	A1079	30p multi	4.00	2.25
3295	A1079	35p multi	5.00	2.40
3296	A1079	35p multi	4.50	2.40
3297	A1079	40p multi	5.50	3.00

Size: 40x30mm

Perf. 14

3298	A1079	50p multi	8.00	4.75
3299	A1079	50p multi	11.00	3.65
3300	A1079	100p multi	14.00	7.25
3301	A1079	100p multi	14.00	7.25
		Nos. 3265-3301 (36)	110.25	51.90

Nos. 3275 and 3278 have the same vignette; No. 3275 has an incorrect inscription and No. 3278 has the corrected inscription.

Issued: Nos. 3265, 3284, 3293, 3/29; Nos. 3266, 3276, 3290, 6/15; Nos. 3267, 3277, 3297, 11/18; Nos. 3268, 3275, 4/16; Nos. 3269, 3295, 7/15; Nos. 3270, 3273, 3298, 5/17; Nos. 3271, 3274, 3299, 12/3; Nos. 3278, 3292, 12/22; Nos. 3279, 3300, 5/13; Nos. 3280, 3296, 12/17; Nos. 3281, 3289, 4/21; Nos. 3282, 3287, 3291, 5/21; Nos. 3283, 3288, 12/13; No. 3285, 11/8; Nos. 3286, 3294, 7/23; No. 3301, 12/1; No. 3272, 1/20/11.

See Nos. 3357-3368, 3389-3403, 3447-3450, 3471-3481.

Intl. Rice Research Institute, 50th Anniv. — A1080

No. 3302: a, 50th anniversary emblem. b, Buildings. c, Rice field, water, mountains. d, Rice plants.

2010, Apr. 14 *Perf. 14*
3302 A1080 7p Block of 4, #a-d 3.50 3.00
e. Souvenir sheet of 4 #3302a-3302d 4.50 4.50

Eraño G. Manalo (1925-2009), Executive Minister of Iglesia ni Cristo — A1081

Manalo, church and: No. 3303, Country name in brown, "2010" at left under "P." No. 3304, Like #3303, "2010" under denomination. No. 3305, Like #3303, country name in black. No. 3306, Like #3305, "2010" under denomination.

2010

3303 A1081 7p multi 2.75 1.60
3304 A1081 7p multi 2.00 1.25
3305 A1081 7p multi 1.25 .80
3306 A1081 7p multi 1.25 .80
Nos. 3303-3306 (4) 7.25 4.45

Issued: No. 3303, 4/23; No. 3304, 4/28; No. 3305, 5/11; No. 3306, 12/15.

Paintings by Vicente S. Manansala (1910-81) — A1082

Designs: No. 3307, 7p, Sabungero. No. 3308, 7p, Bayanihan, horiz. No. 3309, 7p, Fish Vendor, horiz. No. 3310, 7p, Nipa Hut, horiz. 20p, Planting of the First Cross, horiz. (80x30mm).

No. 3312: a, Rooster. b, Mamimintakasi. c, I Believe in God, horiz. d, Three Carabaos, horiz.

2010, May 20 ***Perf. 14***
3307-3311 A1082 Set of 5 6.50 5.00

Perf. 14, Imperf. (#3312c-3312d)

3312 A1082 7p Sheet of 4, #a-d 5.00 5.00

Nos. 3307-3310 were printed in sheets of 8.
No. 3311 was printed in sheets of 4.

Philippine Centennial Tree and Emblem of Municipality of Magallanes A1083

Tree at: 7p, Right. 9p, Left.

2010, May 28 ***Perf. 14***
3313-3314 A1083 Set of 2 2.00 1.50

Bukidnon State University, 86th Anniv. — A1084

No. 3315 — University emblem and: a, Main building and sign. b, Education building and flagpole.

2010, June 18
3315 A1084 7p Horiz. pair, #a-b 2.00 1.50

Veterans Federation of the Philippines, 50th Anniv. — A1085

No. 3316 — Soldiers and: a, Emblem at left. b, Emblem at right.

2010, June 18
3316 A1085 7p Horiz. pair, #a-b 2.00 1.50

Light Rail Transit Authority, 30th Anniv. A1086

Nos. 3317 and 3318: a, Train on curved bridge. b, Train, domed building at right. c, Train, pink and blue buildings. d, Cars on road below train.

2010, July 12 ***Perf. 14***
3317 A1086 7p Block of 4, #a-d 4.00 3.50

Souvenir Sheet

Imperf

3318 A1086 10p Sheet of 4, #a-d 6.00 6.00

Inauguration of Pres. Benigno S. Aquino III — A1087

Pres. Aquino: 7p, Taking oath. 40p, Giving inaugural speech, vert.

2010, July 26 ***Perf. 14***
3319-3320 A1087 Set of 2 5.00 4.00

Philippine Tuberculosis Society, Cent. — A1088

Society emblem and health care workers with inscription at bottom in: 7p, Tagalog. 9p, English.

26p, Emblem and 1935 Manuel L. Quezon birthday seal.

2010, July 29 ***Perf. 14***
3321-3322 A1088 Set of 2 2.00 1.60

Souvenir Sheet

3323 A1088 26p multi 5.00 5.00

No. 3323 contains one 120x30mm stamp.

Devotion to Our Lady of Peñafrancia, 300th Anniv. — A1089

No. 3324: a, Our Lady of Peñafrancia, red panel. b, Our Lady of Peñafrancia, green panel. c, Our Lady of Peñafrancia Shrine, blue panel. d, Our Lady of Peñafrancia Basilica, yellow panel.

20p, Our Lady of Peñafrancia Shrine, Naga City, horiz.

2010, Sept. 8 ***Perf. 14***
3324 A1089 7p Block of 4, #a-d 3.50 3.00

Souvenir Sheet

3325 A1089 28p multi 3.50 3.00

No. 3325 contains one 80x30mm stamp.

Dogs A1090

No. 3326: a, Chow chow. b, Bull terrier. c, Labrador retriever. d, Beagle.

No. 3327: a, American Eskimo dog. b, Black and tan coonhound. c, Afghan hound. d, Mastiff.

2010, Sept. 9 ***Perf. 14***
3326 A1090 7p Block of 4, #a-d 4.50 4.00

Souvenir Sheet

3327 A1090 7p Sheet of 4, #a-d 5.00 5.00

No. 3326 printed in sheets of 16.

Ozone Layer Protection — A1091

No. 3328: a, Hand over globe. b, Hands below globe.

2010, Sept. 16
3328 A1091 7p Horiz. pair, #a-b 1.75 1.50

Central Mindanao University, Cent. — A1092

No. 3329 — University emblem and: a, Administration Building and lamp poles. b, University building.

2010, Sept. 17
3329 A1092 7p Horiz. pair, #a-b 1.85 1.50

Pres. Diosdado Macapagal (1910-97) — A1093

2010, Sept. 28
3330 A1093 7p multi .80 .50

Day of the Galleon A1094

No. 3331 — Galleon and map of: a, Pacific Ocean, East Asia, Western North America. b, Atlantic Ocean, Eastern North America, Western Europe and West Africa.

40p, Like #3331b.

2010, Oct. 8
3331 A1094 7p Horiz. pair, #a-b 2.50 2.00
c. Souvenir sheet of 2, #3331a-3331b 3.00 3.00

Souvenir Sheet

3332 Sheet of 2, #3331a, 3332a 7.50 7.50
a. A1094 40p multi 5.00 5.00

Intl. Year of Biodiversity — A1095

No. 3333 — Children's art by: a, Krysten Alarice Tan. b. Justen Paul Tolentino.

2010, Oct. 26
3333 A1095 7p Horiz. pair, #a-b 2.50 2.00

Philippine Rice Research Institute, 25th Anniv. — A1096

No. 3334: a, Building. b, Plants in test tubes. c, Farmer in field. d, Farm workers and tractor.

2010, Nov. 5 **Litho.** ***Perf. 14***
3334 A1096 7p Block of 4, #a-d 3.50 3.00

Pheepoy Types of 2009-10 Redrawn and

Pheepoy in Mail Van — A1097

2010, Nov. 8 ***Perf. 13½x13¾***
3335 A1097 7p multi, "Pheepoy" 7mm wide .80 .40

Souvenir Sheet

3336 Sheet of 4 4.50 4.50
a. A1052 7p multi, "Pheepoy" 6mm wide, dated "2010" .80 .65
b. A1072 7p multi, dark blue sky, dated "2010" .80 .65
c. A1076 7p multi, "Pheepoy" at bottom center .80 .65
d. A1097 7p multi, "Pheepoy" 6mm wide .80 .65
e. Sheet of 4, #3336f-3336i, imperf. 4.50 4.50
f. As "a," imperf. .80 .65
g. As "b," imperf. .80 .65
h. As "c," imperf. .80 .65
i. As "d," imperf. .80 .65

See Nos. 3227, 3255, 3260.

A1098

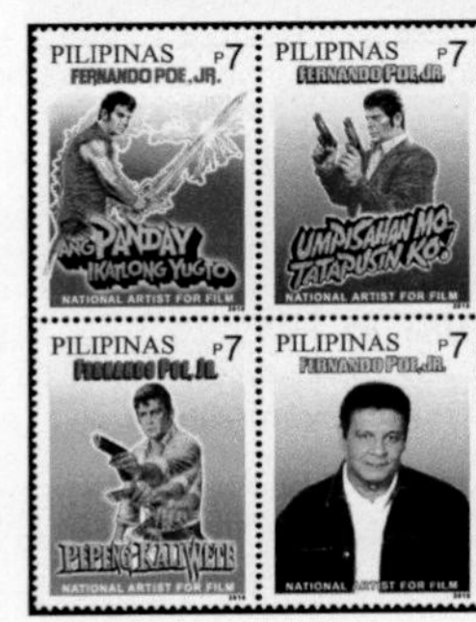

National Stamp Collecting Month — A1099

No. 3337: a, Levi Celerio (1910-2002), composer. b, Leonor Orosa Goquingco (1917-2005), dancer. c, Carlos L. Quirino (1910-99), historian. d, Nick Joaquin (1917-2004), writer.

No. 3338 — Fernando Poe, Jr. (1939-2004), actor: a, Scene from film *Ang Panday Ikatlong Yugto* (The Blacksmith, Part 3). b, Scene from film *Umpisahan Mo. . . Tatapusin Ko!* (You Start. . . I'll Finish). c, Scene from *Pepeng Kaliwete* (Pepe Lefty). d, Portrait.

2010 ***Perf. 14***
3337 A1098 7p Block of 4, #a-d 4.50 4.00
3338 A1099 7p Block of 4, #a-d 5.00 4.50
e. Souvenir sheet of 3, #3338a-3338c, + label 3.50 *3.50*

Issued: Nos. 3337, 3338e, 11/10; No. 3338, 11/25.

Nos. 3337 and 3338 printed in separate sheets of 16.

Inauguration of Vice-President Jejomar C. Binay — A1100

2010, Nov. 11 **Litho.** ***Perf. 14***
3339 A1100 7p multi .80 .50

Printed in sheets of 15.

Christmas — A1101

No. 3340: a, Holy Family in Filipino clothing, St. Peter's Basilica. b, Holy Family. c, Holy Family on jar. d, Adoration of the Shepherds.

2010, Nov. 23
3340 A1101 7p Block of 4, #a-d 5.00 4.50

Ateneo de Manila Class of 1960, 50th Anniv. A1102

No. 3341: a, Ateneo de Manila emblems, "Fabilioh!" b, Eagle, cross on steeple, bell. c, Man, boy, statue of Virgin Mary. d, Bell.

2010, Dec. 2
3341 A1102 7p Block of 4, #a-d 3.75 3.25

New Year 2011 (Year of the Rabbit) — A1103

Designs: 7p, Head of rabbit. 30p, Rabbit.

2010, Dec. 6
3342-3343 A1103 Set of 2 5.00 4.00
3343a Souvenir sheet of 4, 2 each #3342-3343 11.00 11.00

Printed in sheets of 10.

Senator Ambrosio B. Padilla (1910-90) — A1104

No. 3344 — Portrait of Padilla and: a, Padilla at microphone. b, Padilla playing basketball.

2010, Dec. 7
3344 A1104 7p Horiz. pair, #a-b 1.75 1.50

SyCip, Salazar, Hernandez & Gatmaitan Law Firm, 65th Anniv. — A1105

2010, Dec. 10
3345 A1105 7p multi .80 .50

Grace Christian College, Manila, 60th Anniv. A1106

No. 3346: a, Emblem and building. b, Emblem, "Grace at 60." c, Building, Chinese characters. d, Building, Chinese characters, founders Julia L. Tan, Dr. and Mrs. Edward Spahr.

2010, Dec. 16 ***Perf. 14***
3346 A1106 7p Block of 4, #a-d 4.00 3.50
e. Souvenir sheet of 4 #3346a-3346d 4.50 4.50
f. Block of 4, #3346g-3346j 5.00 4.50
g.-j. Like #3346a-3346d with "2010" date inside of frames, any single 1.00 .80
k. Souvenir sheet, #3346g-3346j 6.00 6.00

The "2010" year dates on Nos. 3346a-3346d and 3346e are below the frame lines at the lower right of each stamp. Issued: Nos. 3346f, 3346k, 5/10/11.

Valentine's Day — A1107

No. 3347 — Earth, hearts and Philippine Postal Corporation mascot Pheepoy: a, Carrying flowers. b, Driving postal van.

2011, Jan. 14 **Litho.** ***Perf. 14***
3347 A1107 7p Horiz. pair, #a-b 1.75 1.40

Kiwanis Club of Manila, 47th Anniv. — A1108

2011, Jan. 21
3348 A1108 7p multi .80 .35

University of Santo Tomas, Manila, 400th Anniv. — A1109

No. 3349: a, Main Building. b, Central Seminary. c, Arch of the Centuries. d, The foundation of the University of Santo Tomas by Archbishop Miguel de Benavides.

No. 3350, vert.: a, 7p, Statue of Archbishop Benavides. b, 30p, Quattro Mondial Monument.

2011, Jan. 25
3349 A1109 7p Block of 4, #a-d 4.00 3.50

Souvenir Sheet

3350 A1109 Sheet of 2, #a-b, + central label 6.00 5.00

Hoyas A1110

No. 3351: a, Mindoro hoya. b, Grandmother's wax plant. c, Summer hoya. d, Benito Tan's hoya.

No. 3352: a, Siar's hoya. b, Shooting star hoya. c, Imperial hoya. d, Buot's hoya.

2011, Mar. 8
3351 A1110 7p Block of 4, #a-d 4.50 4.00

Souvenir Sheet

3352 A1110 7p Sheet of 4, #a-d, + 2 labels 5.00 5.00

Printed in sheets of 16.

University of the Philippines College of Law, Cent. — A1111

No. 3353 — Building and emblem with: a, Scales. b, Lady Justice (centennial emblem).

2011, Apr. 11
3353 A1111 7p Horiz. pair, #a-b 1.75 1.40

Center for Agriculture and Rural Development Mutually Reinforcing Institutions, 25th Anniv. — A1112

2011, Apr. 25
3354 A1112 7p multi .80 .50

Department of Budget and Management, 75th Anniv. — A1113

2011, Apr. 25 ***Perf. 13½***
3355 A1113 7p multi .80 .50

Wenceslao Q. Vinzons (1910-42), Leader of Resistance Forces in World War II — A1114

2011, May 3 ***Perf. 14***
3356 A1114 7p multi .80 .50

Dated 2010.

Marine Life Type of 2010

Designs: 1p, Dendronephthya soft coral. 2p, Yellowstripe snapper. 4p, Branded vexillum. 5p, Sea apple. 7p, Spotted boxfish. 9p, Broad-club cuttlefish. 10p, Mushroom coral. 17p, Cowfish. 20p, Two-banded anemone fish. 30p, Lipstick tang. 40p, Yellow-backed damselfish. 100p, Pink tube sponge.

2011 ***Perf. 13½x13¾***

3357	A1079	1p multi	.65	.25
3358	A1079	2p multi	.75	.25
3359	A1079	4p multi	1.00	.35
3360	A1079	5p multi	1.00	.35
3361	A1079	7p multi	1.00	.50
3362	A1079	9p multi	1.50	.60
3363	A1079	10p multi	1.75	.70
3364	A1079	17p multi	2.50	1.40
3365	A1079	20p multi	2.75	1.40
3366	A1079	30p multi	5.00	2.40
3367	A1079	40p multi	6.50	3.00

Size: 40x30mm

Perf. 14

3368 A1079 100p multi 16.00 9.00
Nos. 3357-3368 (12) 40.40 20.20

Issued: 1p, 5p, 7p, 9p, 8/17; 2p, 20p, 30p, 40p, 5/5; 4p, 10p, 17p, 100p, 5/12.

Worldwide Fund for Nature (WWF) — A1115

Philippine crocodile: No. 3369, Hatchling and eggs (yellow and brown frame). No. 3370, Juvenile on log (olive green and yellow green frame). No. 3371, Adult on rock (blue green and blue frame). No. 3372, Adult with open mouth (orange and green frame).

2011, May 16 ***Perf. 14***
3369 A1115 7p multi 1.20 1.00
a. Miniature sheet of 8 12.50 12.50
3370 A1115 7p multi 1.20 1.00
a. Miniature sheet of 8 12.50 12.50
3371 A1115 7p multi 1.20 1.00
a. Miniature sheet of 8 12.50 12.50
3372 A1115 7p multi 1.20 1.00
a. Block of 4, #3369-3372 6.00 6.00
b. Miniature sheet of 8 12.50 12.50
Nos. 3369-3372 (4) 4.80 4.00

Nos. 3369-3372 were printed in sheets of 16 containing four of each stamp.

Arnis A1116

No. 3373 — Arnis fighters wearing: a, Protective gear. b, White robes.

2011, May 23
3373 A1116 7p Horiz. pair, #a-b 1.75 1.50
c. Sheet of 4, 2 each #a-b 4.50 4.50

Beatification of Pope John Paul II — A1117

No. 3374 — Pope John Paul II and: a, Grandstand, Rizal Park (denomination in green at UL). b, University of Santo Tomas (denomination in red at UR). c, Philippine International Convention Center (denomination in red at UL). d, Popemobile (denomination in green at UR).

40p, Pope with crucifix, vert.

2011, May 30
3374 A1117 7p Block of 4, #a-d 4.50 4.00

Souvenir Sheet

3375 A1117 40p multi + 2 labels 5.00 5.00

Printed in sheets of 16.

National Information and Communications Technology Month — A1118

No. 3376 — Inscriptions: a, Community eCenter. b, Creative content industries. c, Nationwide automated elections. d, Business process outsourcing.

2011, June 13
3376 A1118 7p Block of 4, #a-d 3.50 3.00

Security Bank Corporation, 60th Anniv. — A1119

No. 3377: a, Corporate Headquarters in 1951 and 2011. b, Company emblems.

2011, June 18
3377 A1119 10p Horiz. pair, #a-b 1.75 1.60

Goethe Institute in the Philippines, 50th Anniv. — A1120

No. 3378: a, José Rizal Statue, Wilhelmsfeld, Germany. b, Fountain from Wilhelmsfeld in Luneta Park. c, Residence of Rizal, Wilhelmsfeld. d, Anniversary emblem.

2011, June 19
3378 A1120 7p Block of 4, #a-d 4.00 3.50

A1121

A1122

José Rizal (1861-96), Patriot — A1123

No. 3379 — Rizal, anniversary emblem and: a, Dove, cover of *Noli Me Tangere*. b, Philippines flag elements.

No. 3380 — Annivesary emblem and Rizal in: a, Blue. b, Red.

No. 3381 — Philippines stamps depicting Rizal and monuments: a, 7p, #241, monument in Daet. b, 7p, #383, monument in Guinobatan. c, 7p, #461, monument in Santa Barbara. d, 7p, #497, monument in Biñan. e, 7p, #527, monument in Zamboanga. f, 12p, #813, monument in San Fernando. g, 13p, #857, monument in Lucban. h, 20p, #857A, monument in Romblon. i, 30p, #1313, monument in Jinjiang, China. j, 40p, #1198, monument in Illinois.

2011, June 19 ***Perf. 14***
3379 A1121 7p Horiz. pair, #a-b 2.25 1.60
3380 A1122 7p Horiz. pair, #a-b 2.25 1.60

Perf. 13¾

3381 A1123 Sheet of 10, #a-j 20.00 *20.00*

Yuchengco Group of Companies, Cent. — A1124

2011, July 20 ***Perf. 14***
3382 A1124 7p multi .80 .60

People Power Revolution, 25th Anniv. — A1125

No. 3383: a, Pres. Corazon C. Aquino (1933-2009), with collar visible, person with raised arm at LL, small helicopter at UL. b, Jaime Cardinal Sin (1928-2005), wearing biretta, helicopter at UR. c, Sin, without biretta, wearing black vestments, people with raised arms at left, helicopter at UL. d, Aquino, nun at LR.

No. 3384: a, Aquino, without collar visible, background like #3383a. b, Aquino, backgrond like #3383b. c, Aquino, background like #3383c. d, Sin, without biretta like #3383c, crowds in background. e, Sin, wearing white vestments, people carrying crucifix at right. f, Sin, wearing rosary around neck, crowds in background. g, Sin, wearing biretta like #3383b, religious statue at left.

2011, Aug. 1 **Litho.**
3383 A1125 7p Block of 4, #a-d 4.50 4.00
3384 A1125 7p Sheet of 8, #3383d, 3384a-3384g 11.00 11.00

Holy Cross of Davao College, 60th Anniv. A1126

No. 3385: a, Bajada Campus facade. b, Grade school and high school buildings. c, Palma Gil and Mabutas Halls. d, Babak and Camudmud Campuses.

2011, Aug. 15 ***Perf. 14***
3385 A1126 7p Block of 4, #a-d 3.50 3.00

Mother Francisca del Espiritu Santo de Fuentes (1647-1711), Founder of Dominican Sisters of St. Catherine of Siena — A1127

2011, Aug. 24
3386 A1127 7p multi .80 .60

Lizards A1128

No. 3387: a, Luzon giant forest skink. b, Luzon karst gecko. c, Southern Philippines bent-toed gecko. d, Luzon white-spotted forest skink.

No. 3388: a, Philippine forest dragon. b, Philippine spiny stream skink. c, Philippine sailfin lizard. d, Cordilleras slender skink.

2011, Aug. 30 ***Perf. 14***
3387 A1128 7p Block of 4, #a-d 4.50 4.00
3388 A1128 7p Sheet of 4, #a-d, + 2 labels 5.00 5.00

Printed in sheets of 16.

Marine Life Type of 2010 With Optical Code at Lower Right

Designs: 1p, Picasso triggerfish. 2p, Marmorated cone shell. 4p, Blue-faced angelfish. 5p, Copper-band butterflyfish. 7p, Murex shell. 9p, Polyclad flatworm. 10p, Triton trumpet shell. 13p, Valentine puffer. 17p, Polka-dot grouper. 20p, Bennett's feather star. 25p, Oriental sweetlips. 30p, Eibl's angelfish. 35p, Kunie's chromodoris. 40p, Royal empress angelfish. 100p, Regal tang.

2011		**Litho.**	***Perf. 14½***	
3389	A1079	1p multi	.65	.25
3390	A1079	2p multi	.75	.25
3391	A1079	4p multi	.75	.35
3392	A1079	5p multi	.90	.30
3393	A1079	7p multi	1.25	.30
3394	A1079	9p multi	1.60	.75
3395	A1079	10p multi	1.60	.60
3396	A1079	13p multi	2.25	1.75
3397	A1079	17p multi	2.25	1.75
3398	A1079	20p multi	4.25	1.75
3399	A1079	25p multi	4.25	2.40
3400	A1079	30p multi	5.75	3.00
3401	A1079	35p multi	6.50	3.50
3402	A1079	40p multi	6.50	3.50

Size: 40x30mm

Perf. 13x13½

3403 A1079 100p multi 21.00 15.00
Nos. 3389-3403 (15) 60.25 35.45

Issued: 1p, 2p, 5p, 10p, 20p, 30p, 10/17; 4p, 7p, 100p, 10/25; 9p, 25p, 35p, 11/4; 13p, 17p, 40p, 11/11.

Intl. Year of Forests A1129

No. 3404: a, Batlag Falls, Tanay. b, Tree, Pansol.

2011, Oct. 24 ***Perf. 13½x13***
3404 A1129 7p Horiz. pair, #a-b 1.75 1.50

Day of the Galleon — A1130

Nos. 3405 and 3406: a, Galleon at right, map of East Asia. b, Galleon at left, map of Central and North America. c, Galleon at center, map of Atlantic Ocean, Europe and Africa.

2011, Nov. 10 ***Perf. 13x13½***
3405 Horiz. strip of 3 3.50 3.00
a.-c. A1130 7p Any single 1.00 .75

Souvenir Sheet

Perf. 13x13½ on 2 or 3 Sides

3406 Sheet of 3 + label 3.50 3.50
a.-c. A1130 7p Any single 1.00 .80

Printed in sheets of 12. Adjacent stamps in No. 3406 are separated by simulated perforations.

Paintings by Hernando R. Ocampo (1911-78) — A1131

No. 3407: a, Homage to José Rizal. b, Break of Day. c, Summer in September. d, Mother and Child.

No. 3408, horiz.: a, Fiesta. b, Abstraction #15, 17. c, Kasaysayan ng Lahi. d, Abstraction #22, 26.

2011, Nov. 11 ***Perf. 13½x13***
3407 A1131 7p Block of 4, #a-d 4.50 4.00

Perf. 13x13½

3408 A1131 7p Sheet of 4, #a-d 5.00 5.00

Stamp Collecting Month.

National Bureau of Investigation, 75th Anniv. — A1132

No. 3409: a, Emblem of National Bureau of Investigation. b, Justice José Yulo and Pres. Manuel L. Quezon. c, Pres. Manuel A. Roxas signing bill, J. Pardo de Tavera, first director of National Bureau of Investigation. d, Fingerprint under magnifying glass, laptop computer, "Justice."

2011, Nov. 14 ***Perf. 13½x13***
3409 A1132 7p Block of 4, #a-d 3.50 3.00

Christmas — A1133

No. 3410: a, Bells. b, Poinsettias. c, Toys and gifts. d, Parol (Christmas star lantern).

2011, Nov. 26
3410 A1133 7p Block of 4, #a-d 4.00 3.50

New Year 2012 (Year of the Dragon) — A1134

Designs: 7p, Head of dragon. 30p, Dragon.

2011, Dec. 5 ***Perf. 13x13½***
3411-3412 A1134 Set of 2 7.50 6.00
3412a Sheet of 4, 2 each #3411-3412 30.00 30.00

Printed in sheets of 10.

See Nos. 3435-3436.

Office of the Solicitor General, 110th Anniv. — A1135

2011, Dec. 15 ***Perf. 13½x13***
3413 A1135 7p multi .70 .50

Frogs A1136

No. 3414: a, Philippine spiny cinnamon frog. b, Philippine pygmy forest frog. c, Philippine flat-headed frog. d, Luzon limestone forest frog.

No. 3415: a, Gliding tree frog. b, Northern Luzon tree-hole frog. c, Taylor's igorot frog. d, Mary Inger's wart frog.

2011, Dec. 15 ***Perf. 13x13½***
3414 A1136 7p Block of 4, #a-d 4.50 4.00
3415 A1136 7p Sheet of 4, #a-d + 2 labels 5.00 5.00

Printed in sheets of 16.

Lyceum of the Philippines University, 60th Anniv. — A1137

2012, Jan. 2 **Litho.** ***Perf. 12***
3416 A1137 7p multi .70 .40

Printed in sheets of 16.

Grand Lodge of Free and Accepted Masons of the Philippines, Cent. — A1138

No. 3417 — Centenary emblem and: a, Grand Lodge, Pres. Manuel L. Quezon. b, José Rizal, Marcelo H. del Pilar, Mariano Ponce, Plaridel Masonic Temple.

2012, Jan. 19
3417 A1138 7p Horiz. pair, #a-b 2.50 2.00

Diocese of Malolos, 50th Anniv. A1139

No. 3418 — Centenary emblem and: a, Virgin of the Immaculate Conception of Malolos. b, Immaculate Conception Cathedral and Basilica.
40p, Virgin of the Immaculate Conception of Malolos, vert.

2012, Jan. 25
3418 A1139 7p Horiz. pair, #a-b 1.75 1.50

Souvenir Sheet

3419 A1139 40p multi + 2 labels 5.00 4.00

Davao, 75th Anniv. A1140

No. 3420: a, Davao City Hall. b, Kadayawan Festival. c, Waling-waling orchids. d, Mt. Apo, Philippine eagle.

2012, Mar. 16 **Litho.** ***Perf. 14***
3420 A1140 7p Block of 4, #a-d 4.50 3.50

Ateneo de Zamboanga University, Cent. — A1141

No. 3421 — Centenary emblem and: a, Fort Pilar Shrine. b, Father William H. Kreutz, S.J. Campus. c, Ateneo Brebeuf Gymnasium. d, St. Ignatius of Loyola.

2012, Mar. 19
3421 A1141 7p Block of 4, #a-d 4.50 3.50
e. Souvenir sheet of 4, #3421a-3421d 4.50 4.50

St. Agnes Academy, Legazpi City, Cent. — A1142

No. 3422 — Centenary emblem and Main Building: a, Facade (denomination at UR). b, In ruins after World War II (denomination at UL). c, Facade, with flag at right (denomination at UR). d, Facade, flowers and flagpole in front (denomination at UL).

2012, Mar. 21
3422 A1142 7p Block of 4, #a-d 4.00 3.50

Maria Makiling, Mythical Forest Guardian — A1143

2012, Mar. 30 ***Perf. 13½x13¾***
3423 A1143 7p multi .70 .40

Asian-Pacific Postal Union, 50th Anniv. — A1144

Designs: 7p, Emblem and flags. 30p, Emblem, flags, Philippines #1323 (80x30mm).

2012, Apr. 1 ***Perf. 14***
3424-3425 A1144 Set of 2 4.00 3.00

Philippine Postal Corporation, 20th Anniv. — A1145

No. 3426: a, Pres. Corazon Aquino, Postal Service Act of 1992. b, Main Post Office, Manila.

2012, Apr. 10
3426 A1145 7p Horiz. pair, #a-b 1.75 1.40

Felipe Padilla de Leon (1912-92), Composer A1146

2012, May 1
3427 A1146 7p multi .70 .40

Churches — A1147

No. 3428: a, La Immaculada Concepcion Parish Church, Guiuan. b, San Joaquin Parish Church, San Joaquin. c, Nuestra Señora de la Porteria Parish Church, Daraga. d, San Isidro Labrador Parish Church, Lazi.
No. 3429: a, Santiago Apostol Parish Church, Betis. b, La Immaculada Concepcion Parish Church, Jasaan. c, Our Lady of Light Parish Church, Loon. d, San Gregorio Magno Parish Church, Majayjay.

2012, May 1
3428 A1147 7p Block of 4, #a-d 3.00 2.50

Souvenir Sheet

3429 A1147 7p Sheet of 4, #a-d 4.00 4.00

45th Annual Meeting of Asian Development Bank Board of Governors, Manila — A1148

2012, May 2 ***Perf. 14***
3430 A1148 7p multi .75 .50

Day of Valor, 70th Anniv. — A1149

Designs: 7p, Soldiers in Bataan Death March. 10p, Battery Hearn, Corregidor Island. 30p, Shrine of Valor, Mt. Samat, Bataan.

2012, May 6 **Litho.**
3431-3433 A1149 Set of 3 4.50 4.00

Government Service Insurance System, 75th Anniv. — A1150

No. 3434 — Emblem and: a, Head office in Solano, 1937 (25x22mm). b, Head office in Arroceros, 1957 (25x22mm). c, Financial Center, Pasay City (50x22mm).

2012, May 28 ***Perf. 13½x13¾***
3434 Horiz. strip of 3 6.00 5.00
a. A1150 7p multi .70 .50
b. A1150 9p multi .85 .60
c. A1150 40p multi 3.25 2.50

Year of the Dragon Type of 2011 Redrawn Without Line To Right of "Pilipinas" and Dated "2012"

Designs as before.

2012, June 8 ***Perf. 14***
3435-3436 A1134 Set of 2 6.00 5.00
3436a Souvenir sheet of 4, 2 each #3435-3436 11.00 11.00

Printed in sheets of 10.

Whitewater Rafters, Cagayan de Oro — A1151

2012, June 15
3437 A1151 9p multi .80 .80

Winning Design in Intl. Year of Forests Children's Art Contest — A1152

2012, June 18
3438 A1152 9p multi .80 .80

Bonifacio Monument, Caloocan A1153

2012, June 25
3439 A1153 7p multi .70 .50

Habagat, God of Winds — A1154

2012, June 28 ***Perf. 13½x13¾***
3440 A1154 7p multi .70 .40

2012 Summer Olympics, London — A1155

No. 3441: a, Athletics. b, Shooting. c, Swimming. d, Boxing.

2012, July 27 ***Perf. 14***
3441 A1155 7p Block of 4, #a-d 4.50 4.00

Printed in sheets of 16.

Metrobank, 50th Anniv. — A1156

No. 3442: a, Binondo Branch, 1962. b, Metrobank Plaza, Makati City, 1977. c, GT International Tower, Makati City, 2004. d, Metrobank Plaza, Shanghai, People's Republic of China, 2001.

2012, Aug. 25 **Litho.**
3442 A1156 7p Block of 4, #a-d 3.50 3.00

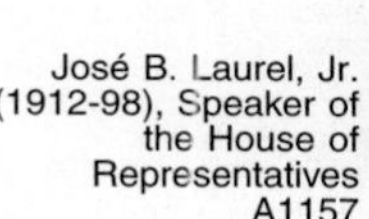

José B. Laurel, Jr. (1912-98), Speaker of the House of Representatives A1157

2012, Aug. 27 ***Perf. 14***
3443 A1157 9p multi .80 .50

Ramon O. Valera (1912-72), Fashion Designer A1158

2012, Aug. 31
3444 A1158 7p multi .70 .50

Amihan, Goddess of Monsoon Weather — A1159

2012, Sept. 28 ***Perf. 13½x13¾***
3445 A1159 7p multi .70 .40

Manila Hotel, Cent. A1160

No. 3446: a, Facade. b, Maynila Ballroom. c, MacArthur Suite. d, Grand Lobby.

2012, Oct. 5 ***Perf. 14***
3446 A1160 7p Block of 4, #a-d 3.00 2.50

Marine Life Type of 2010-11

Designs: 1p, Twin-spot wrasse. 5p, Pearl-scale butterflyfish. 40p, Tassle filefish. 100p, Koran angelfish.

2012 *Perf. 13½x13¾*

3447 A1079 1p multi .75 .25
3448 A1079 5p multi .75 .40
3449 A1079 40p multi 5.50 3.50

Size: 40x30mm

Perf. 14

3450 A1079 100p multi 13.00 6.50
Nos. 3447-3450 (4) 20.00 10.65

Issued: 1p, 5p, 40p, 10/18; 100p, 11/16.

Canonization of Blessed Pedro Calungsod (1654-72) A1161

2012, Oct. 21 *Perf. 14*

3451 A1161 9p multi .90 .60
a. Miniature sheet of 20 24.00 24.00

No. 3451 was originally printed in sheet of 40, which sold out within a week. The additional printing was in sheets of 20, released on Nov. 28.

Carlos "Botong" Francisco (1912-69), Painter — A1162

2012, Nov. 4

3452 A1162 7p multi .70 .40

Christmas — A1163

No. 3453: a, Nativity. b, People arriving at church for dawn mass.

2012, Nov. 20 **Litho.**

3453 A1163 10p Horiz. pair, #a-b 2.25 1.75

Printed in sheets of 16.

Bernardo Carpio, Mythical Cause of Earthquakes — A1164

2012, Nov. 28 *Perf. 13½x13¾*

3454 A1164 7p multi .70 .40

Lepanto Consolidated Mining Corporation, 75th Anniv. — A1165

No. 3455: a, Reforestation. b, Miners in mine entrance.

2012, Dec. 7 **Litho.** *Perf. 14*

3455 A1165 7p Horiz. pair, #a-b 1.75 1.40

New Year 2013 (Year of the Snake) — A1166

Designs: 10p, Head of snake. 30p, Coiled snake.

2012, Dec. 12 **Litho.** *Perf. 14*

3456-3457 A1166 Set of 2 7.00 5.00
3457a Souvenir sheet of 4, 2 each #3456-3457 12.50 12.50

Printed in sheets of 10.

Miniature Sheet

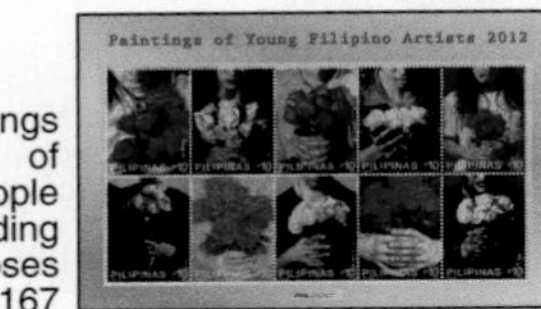

Paintings of People Holding Roses A1167

No. 3458 — Paintings by various artists numbered at LR: a, 1/10. b, 2/10. c, 3/10. d, 4/10. e, 5/10. f, 6/10. g, 7/10. h, 8/10. i, 9/10. j, 10/10.

2012, Dec. 14 *Perf. 14*

3458 A1167 10p Sheet of 10, #a-j 14.00 14.00

Valentine's Day — A1168

2013, Jan. 14 **Litho.** *Perf. 14*

3459 A1168 10p multi .90 .50

Far Eastern University Save the Tamaraw Project — A1169

Designs: No. 3460, 10p, Tamaraw. No. 3461, 10p, Tamerarw, vert.

2013, Jan. 25 **Litho.** *Perf. 14*

3460-3461 A1169 Set of 2 2.00 1.50

Printed in sheets of 16.

Lucio D. San Pedro (1913-2002), Composer A1170

2013, Feb. 11 **Litho.** *Perf. 14*

3462 A1170 10p multi .80 .50

Teresita "Mama Sita" Reyes (1917-98), Restauranteur A1171

2013, Feb. 11 **Litho.** *Perf. 14*

Stamp With Pink Shading at Top and Bottom

3463 A1171 10p multi .80 .50

Souvenir Sheet

Stamp with White Frame at Top and Bottom

3464 A1171 10p multi + 2 labels 3.50 3.50

No. 3464 was sold at 30p.

Pitcher Plants A1172

No. 3465: a, Nepenthes peltata. b, Nepenthes truncata. c, Nepenthes burkei. d, Nepenthes attenboroughii.

No. 3466: a, Nepenthes mindanaoensis. b, Nepenthes sibuyanensis. c, Nepenthes mira. d, Nepenthes mantalingajanensis.

2013, Mar. 13 **Litho.** *Perf. 14*

3465 A1172 10p Block of 4, #a-d 4.00 3.50

Souvenir Sheet

Imperf

3466 A1172 10p Block of 4, #a-d 5.00 5.00

No. 3466 has simulated perforations.

University of the Philippines Alumni Association, Cent. — A1173

No. 3467: a, Emblem and Oblation, purple panel. b, Emblem and Carillon Tower, blue panel. c, Emblem and Ang Bahay Ng Building, green panel. d, Emblem, orange panel.

2013, Apr. 2 **Litho.** *Perf. 14*

3467 A1173 10p Block of 4, #a-d 3.50 3.00

Diplomatic Relations Between Italy and the Philippines, 65th Annv. — A1174

No. 3468 — Flags of the Philippines and Italy and: a, Cinque Terre National Park, Italy. b, Banaue Rice Terraces, Philippines.

2013, Apr. 4 **Litho.** *Perf. 14*

3468 A1174 40p Pair, #a-b 8.00 7.00

Printed in sheets of 16.

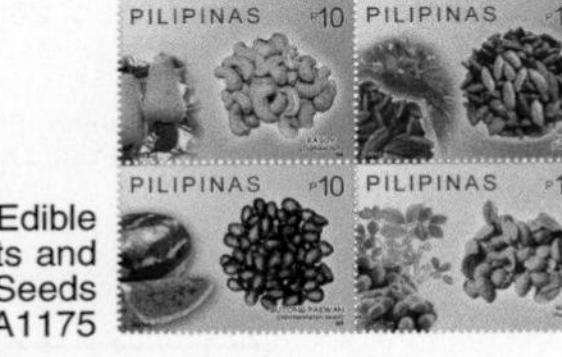

Edible Nuts and Seeds A1175

No. 3469: a, Cashews. b, Pili nuts. c, Watermelon seeds. d, Peanuts.
No. 3470: a, Sunflower seeds. b, Mung beans. c, Coffee beans. d, Squash seeds.

2013, Apr. 15 **Litho.** *Perf. 14*

3469 A1175 10p Block of 4, #a-d 4.00 3.50

Souvenir Sheet

3470 A1175 10p Sheet of 4, #a-d 4.00 4.00

Printed in sheets of 16.

Marine Life Type of 2010-11

Designs: 1p, Pinecone fish. 3p, Purple firefish. 5p, Pyjama cardinalfish. No. 3474, Long-nosed butterflyfish. No. 3475, Longnose filefish. 13p, Raccoon butterflyfish. 20p, Fire clown. 25p, Two-lined monocle bream. 30p, Green chromis. 40p, Common squirrelfish. 100p, Black-backed butterflyfish.

2013 **Litho.** *Perf. 13½x13¾*

3471 A1079 1p multi .65 .25
3472 A1079 3p multi .65 .25
3473 A1079 5p multi .80 .25
3474 A1079 10p multi 1.25 .60
3475 A1079 10p multi 1.25 .60
3476 A1079 13p multi 1.85 .80
3477 A1079 20p multi 2.60 1.20
3478 A1079 25p multi 3.25 1.50
3479 A1079 30p multi 4.00 1.75
3480 A1079 40p multi 5.00 2.40

Size: 40x30mm

Perf. 14

3481 A1079 100p multi 13.00 6.00
Nos. 3471-3481 (11) 34.30 15.60

Issued: 1p, 100p, 12/6; 3p, 5p, #3475, 13p, 12/10; #3474, 4/23; 20p, 40p, 12/13; 25p, 30p, 12/16.

Jesse M. Robredo (1958-2012), Interior Secretary — A1176

2013, May 27 **Litho.** *Perf. 14*

3482 A1176 10p multi .90 .50

Philpost Emblem and Manila Central Post Office A1177

Philpost Emblem A1178

2013, May 29 **Litho.** *Perf. 13½x13¼*

Denomination Color

3483 A1177 1p brown .50 .25
3484 A1177 7p blue gray .75 .30
3485 A1177 9p org brn 1.00 .35
3486 A1177 12p yel org 1.25 .60
3487 A1177 30p orange 3.50 1.50
3488 A1177 35p violet 4.00 1.75
3489 A1177 40p green 4.50 2.25
3490 A1177 45p lilac 6.00 2.40

Perf. 14

3491 A1178 100p dull vio brn 13.00 6.00
Nos. 3483-3491 (9) 34.50 15.40

See Nos. 3593-3594, 3789-3790.

Malacañan Palace, Manila, 150th Anniv. A1179

Perf. 13½x13¾

2013, June 11 **Litho.**

3492 A1179 10p multi 1.00 .60

Miniature Sheet

Marine Biodiversity — A1180

No. 3493: a, Lemon goby. b, Dragon wrasse. c, Three-spot angelfish. d, White-tailed damselfish. e, Orange sea perch. f, Spotted puffer. g, Lemonpeel angelfish. h, Electric blue damsel.

2013, Aug. 2 **Litho.** *Perf. 12*

3493 A1180 10p Sheet of 8, #a-h, + central label 11.00 11.00
i. As #3493, with Thailand 2013 World Stamp Exhibition emblem on center label 13.00 13.00

Nos. 3493 and 3493i each sold for 100p.

Shrimp A1181

No. 3494: a, Banded deep-sea spiny shrimp. b, Deep-sea shrimp. c, Huxley's scissor-foot shrimp. d, Deep-sea armored shrimp.

2013, Aug. 8 Litho. *Perf. 14*

3494 A1181 10p Block of 4, #a-d 4.50 4.00
e. Souvenir sheet of 4, #3494a-3494d 4.50 4.50

Printed in sheets of 16.

Mariano Ponce (1863-1918), Writer — A1182

2013, Sept. 5 Litho. *Perf. 14*

3495 A1182 10p multi 1.00 .60

Printed in sheets of 10.

Boysen Paints, 60th Anniv. A1183

No. 3496: a, Tree, logo for Knoxout Air Cleaning Paint. b, Boysen logo, eagle with paint can, house. c, Houses, anniversary emblem. d, Map of Philippines, logo for Nation Quality Paint.
40p, Eagle with paint can, horiz.

2013, Sept. 9 Litho. *Perf. 14*

3496 A1183 10p Block of 4, #a-d 5.00 4.50

Souvenir Sheet

3497 A1183 40p multi + 2 labels 6.00 6.00

No. 3497 contains one 80x30mm stamp.

Gerardo "Gerry" De León (1913-81), Film Actor and Director — A1184

2013, Sept. 12 Litho. *Perf. 14*

3498 A1184 10p multi 1.00 .50

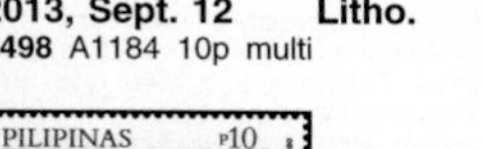

50th Fish Conservation Week — A1185

No. 3499 — Winning paintings of endangered species in Bureau of Fisheries and Aquatic Resources art contest: a, Green Sea Turtle with Giant Manta Ray and Hammerhead Sharks, by Jaylord G. Aligway. b, Tabios (dwarf pygmy goby), by Jon Carlos A. Tabios. c, Butanding (whale shark), by Bernardo V. Vergara, Jr.
40p, Tabios, by Tabios, diff.

2013, Oct. 14 Litho. *Perf. 14*

3499 Horiz. strip of 3 3.50 3.00
a.-c. A1185 10p Any single 1.00 .70

Souvenir Sheet

3500 A1185 40p multi + label 5.00 4.50

Motorized Tricycles — A1186

No. 3501 — Tricycle from: a, Cabadbaran. b, Puerto Princesa. c, Ozamiz City. d, Bukidnon.

2013, Nov. 13 Litho. *Perf. 14*

3501 A1186 10p Block of 4, #a-d 4.50 4.00
e. Souvenir sheet of 4, #3501a-3501d 5.00 5.00

Printed in sheets of 16.

Souvenir Sheet

Rodolfo "Dolphy" Vera Quizon (1928-2012), Comedian — A1187

Litho. With Foil Application

2013, Nov. 23 *Perf. 14*

3502 A1187 100p multi + label 13.00 13.00

A1188

Christmas — A1189

No. 3503 — Paintings by Filipino members of Association of Mouth and Foot Painting Artists: a, The Family, by Jovita Sasutona (1/4). b, The Nativity Star, by Sasutona (2/4). c, Christmas Lantern, by Amado Dulnuan (3/4). d, Christmas at the Lake, by Bernard Pesigan (4/4).
No. 3504: a, Fruit Stand, by Sasutona. b, Lantern Maker, by Sasutona. c, Season Delight, by Sasutona.

2013, Nov. 25 Litho. *Perf. 14*

3503 A1188 10p Block of 4, #a-d 5.00 4.50

Souvenir Sheet

3504 A1189 10p Sheet of 3, #a-c 4.50 4.00

Andrés Bonifacio (1863-97), Founder of Katipunan Revolutionary Movement — A1190

No. 3505 — Winning designs in art contest: a, Dangal at Kabayanihan, by Roderick C. Macutay (1/4). b, Bonifacio Monument, by Marrion Dabalos (2/4). c, Dangal at Kabayanihan, by John Mark Nathaniel Trancales (3/4). d, Bonifacio, the Great Plebeian, by Julius R. Satparam (4/4).
No. 3506 — 150th anniversary emblem and vignette of: a, 30p, #3505a. b, 35p, #3505b. c, 40p, #3505d. d, 45p, #3505c.

2013, Nov. 30 Litho. *Perf. 14*

3505 A1190 10p Block of 4, #a-d 4.50 4.00

Miniature Sheet

3506 A1190 Sheet of 4, #a-d 18.00 18.00

No. 3506 contains four 30x80mm stamps.

New Year 2014 (Year of the Horse) — A1191

Chinese characters and: 10p, Horse's head. 30p, Horse.

2013, Dec. 2 Litho. *Perf. 14*

3507-3508 A1191 Set of 2 4.50 4.00
3508a Souvenir sheet of 4, 2 each #3507-3508 11.00 11.00

Printed in sheets of 10.

Philippine Deposit Insurance Corporation, 50th Anniv. — A1192

2013, Dec. 5 Litho. *Perf. 14*

3509 A1192 10p multi 1.00 .60

National Parks Development Committee, 50th Anniv. — A1193

2013, Dec. 5 Litho. *Perf. 14*

3510 A1193 20p multi 2.25 1.50

Parts of the design are covered with ink that glows in the dark.

Diplomatic Relations Between Nigeria and the Philippines, 50th Anniv. — A1194

No. 3511 — Flags of Philippines and Nigeria and: a, 10p, Coat of arms of Nigeria, daisies. b, 45p, Coat of arms of the Philippines, sampaguita flowers.

2013, Dec. 20 Litho. *Perf. 14*

3511 A1194 Horiz. pair, #a-b 6.50 5.00

Printed in sheets of 10.
See Nigeria Nos. 853-854.

Saint Louis College, San Fernando, 50th Anniv. — A1195

2014, Jan. 20 Litho. *Perf. 14*

3512 A1195 10p multi 1.00 .60

Valentine's Day — A1196

2014, Jan. 27 Litho. *Perf. 14*

3513 A1196 10p multi 1.00 .60

Souvenir Sheet

New Year 2014 (Year of the Horse) A1197

No. 3514: a, 50p, Snake (40x30mm). b, 50p, Goat (40x30mm). c, 100p, Horse (50x40mm).

Perf. 13¼x13x13¼x13¼ (#3514a), 13¼x13¼x13¼x13 (#3514b), 13 (#3514c)

Litho., Litho. & Embossed With Foil Application (100p)

2014, Jan. 31

3514 A1197 Sheet of 3, #a-c 25.00 25.00

Selection of Megan Lynne Young as Miss World 2013 A1198

No. 3515 — Young with: a, 30p, Arms not visible. b, 40p, Arms visible.
No. 3516: a, Like #3515a. b, Like #3515b.

2014, Feb. 24 Litho. *Perf. 14*

3515 A1198 Horiz. pair, #a-b 8.50 7.50

Souvenir Sheet

Litho. & Embossed With Foil Application

3516 A1198 50p Sheet of 2, #a-b 14.00 14.00

No. 3515 printed in sheets of 8.

Main Post Office, Manila A1199

2014, Feb. 24 Litho. *Perf. 14*

3517 A1199 35p multi 8.00 8.00

No. 3517 was printed in sheets of six that sold for 250p. The right half of the stamp could be personalized. See Nos. 3703, 3763 and the footnotes below Nos. 3527 and 3550.

Alpha Phi Beta Fraternity at University of Philippines, 75th Anniv. — A1200

No. 3518: a, 75th anniv. emblem (1/4). b, 75th anniv. emblem, University of the Philippines emblem, statue (2/4). c, Statue, University building and emblem, fraternity members, 75th anniv. emblem (3/4). d, Silhouettes of statues, 75th anniv. emblem (4/4).

2014, Mar. 8 Litho. *Perf. 14*

3518 A1200 10p Block of 4, #a-d 5.00 4.00

Election of Pope Francis, 1st Anniv. — A1201

2014, Mar. 21 Litho. *Perf. 14*
3519 A1201 40p multi 5.00 3.00

Printed in sheets of 9.
See Vatican City Nos. 1553-1556.

Beach on Boracay Island A1202

2014, Mar. 28 Litho. *Perf. 14*
3520 A1202 15p multi *8.00 8.00*

No. 3520 was printed in sheets of six that sold for 250p. The right half of the stamp could be personalized.

Watchtowers — A1203

No. 3521 — Watchtower at: a, Luna, La Union Province. b, Panglao, Bohol Province. c, Oslob, Cebu Province. d, Narvacan, Ilocos Sur Province.

No. 3522, vert. — Watchtower at: a, Boljoon, Cebu Province. b, Bantay, Ilocos Sur Province. c, Samboan, Cebu Province. d, Tabaco, Albay Province.

Litho. & Silk-Screened

2014, Mar. 28 *Perf. 14*
3521 A1203 25p Block of 4, #a-d 12.00 12.00

Miniature Sheet

3522 A1203 25p Sheet of 4, #a-d 14.00 14.00

Central Luzon State University, 50th Anniv. — A1204

No. 3523 — 50th anniv. emblem and: a, Science and Technology Centrum. b, José Rizal.

2014, Apr. 4 Litho. *Perf. 14*
3523 A1204 10p Horiz. pair, #a-b 2.00 1.60

Souvenir Sheets

2014 Canonization of Popes — A1205

Designs: No. 3524, 200p, Pope John XXIII. No. 3525, 200p, Pope John Paul II.

Litho. & Embossed

2014, Apr. 27 *Perf.*
3524-3525 A1205 Set of 2 48.00 45.00

Philippine Charity Sweepstakes Office, 80th Anniv. — A1206

No. 3526: a, People at Lotto office (1/2). b, Family, sweepstakes office vehicle (2/2).

2014, Apr. 28 Litho. *Perf. 14*
3526 A1206 10p Horiz. pair, #a-b 2.00 1.60

Minister Felix Y. Manalo (1886-1963) and Iglesia ni Cristo Central Temple, Quezon City — A1207

2014, May 10 Litho. *Perf. 13½*
3527 A1207 10p multi 1.20 .80

Printed in sheets of 10.

Three miniature sheets of 6 were issued on July 27, 2014, for the Iglesia ni Cristo centennial. The right half of each stamp could be personalized. One sheet bore design No. A1207 on the left half of each stamp. The other two bore images of the Iglesia ni Cristo Central Office Complex and the Philippine Arena. These sheets were only sold through the Iglesia ni Cristo and were not sold through any post office.

Teresita "Mama Sita" Reyes (1917-98), Restauranteur — A1208

No. 3528 — Reyes, various foods, with background colors of: a, Orange (1/4). b, Lilac (2/4). c, Blue green (3/4). d, Orange and red (4/4).

2014, May 11 Litho. *Perf. 14*
3528 A1208 10p Block of 4, #a-d 4.50 4.00

San Bartolome Parish, 400th Anniv. — A1209

2014, May 17 Litho. *Perf. 14*
3529 A1209 20p multi 2.00 1.50

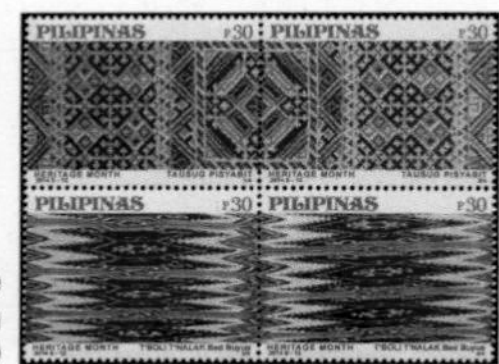

Heritage Month A1210

No. 1210 — Various textile designs numbered: a, (1/4). b, (2/4). c, (3/4). d, (4/4).
100p, Weaver.

Litho. & Silk-Screened

2014, May 30 *Perf. 14*
3530 A1210 30p Block of 4, #a-b 15.00 15.00

Souvenir Sheet

Perf. 13½x13¾

3531 A1210 100p multi 24.00 24.00

No. 3530 printed in sheets of 8.
No. 3531 contains one 50x35mm stamp.

Diplomatic Relations Between the Philippines and Germany, 60th Anniv. — A1211

No. 3532 — Flags of the Philippines and Germany and: a, 20p, Brandenburg Gate, Berlin. b, 40p, People Power Revolution Monument, Quezon City.

2014, June 25 Litho. *Perf. 14*
3532 A1211 Horiz. pair, #a-b 7.00 6.00

Printed in sheets of 10.

Aquatic Flowers A1212

No. 3533: a, Lotus. b, Amazon lily. c, Water lily. d, Water hyacinth.
40p, Marsh marigold, horiz.

2014, June 27 Litho. *Perf. 14*
3533 A1212 10p Block of 4, #a-d 4.50 4.00

Souvenir Sheet

3534 A1212 40p multi 5.50 5.00

No. 3533 printed in sheets of 8.

Kapatagan Municipal Building, Seal of Kapatagan, Cathedral Falls — A1213

2014, July 5 Litho. *Perf. 14*
3535 A1213 10p multi 1.00 .60

Kapatagan, Lanao del Norte Province, 65th anniv.

DZRH Radio Station, 75th Anniv. — A1214

2014, July 15 Litho. *Perf. 14*
3536 A1214 25p multi 2.50 1.50

Apolinario Mabini (1864-1903), Prime Minister — A1215

No. 3537 — 150th anniv. emblem and depiction of Mabini by: a, Pinky Ludovice. b, Kenneth V. Cantimbuhan. c, Julius R. Satparam.
40s, Mabini, by Dylan Ray A. Talon.

2014, July 23 Litho. *Perf. 14*
3537 Horiz. strip of 3 4.00 3.50
a.-c. A1215 10p Any single 1.00 .80

Souvenir Sheet

3538 A1215 40p multi + label 6.00 5.00

No. 3537 printed in sheets of 9.

ISO 9001: 2008 Certification of University of Mindanao — A1216

No. 3539: a, Bolton Campus. b, University emblem and check mark.

2014, July 27 Litho. *Perf. 14*
3539 A1216 10p Horiz. pair, #a-b 2.00 1.60

Paintings by Pres. Corazon C. Aquino (1933-2009) — A1217

No. 3540: a, Enchanting Blossoms. b, Overflowing with Good Wishes. c, Blooms of Unity. d, Fifth Painting.
100p, Rosary and Roses.

2014, Aug. 1 Litho. *Perf. 14*
3540 A1217 25p Block of 4, #a-d 12.00 10.00

Souvenir Sheet

Perf. 13½x13¾

3541 A1217 100p multi 14.00 12.00

Nos. 3540-3541 are impregnated with a rose scent. No. 3540 was printed in sheets of 8. No. 3541 contains one 50x35mm stamp.

Scouting in the Philippines, Cent. — A1218

No. 3542 — Centennial emblem and emblem of Philippines Scouting and: a, Boy Scout in Action Monument. b, Old and new Boy Scout National Headquarters.
30p, Emblems, Boy Scout in Action Monument, map of Philippines, vert.

2014, Aug. 30 Litho. *Perf. 14*
3542 A1218 10p Horiz. pair, #a-b 2.50 2.00

Souvenir Sheet

3543 A1218 30p multi 4.00 3.50

No. 3543 contains one 30x80mm stamp.

National Teachers' Month — A1219

2014, Sept. 5 Litho. *Perf. 14*
3544 A1219 10p multi 1.00 .60

University of San Carlos College of Engineering, 75th Anniv. — A1220

2014, Sept. 8 Litho. *Perf. 14*
3545 A1220 10p multi 1.00 .50

Waterfalls — A1221

No. 3546: a, Balagbag Falls. b, Merloquet Falls. c, Tinago Falls. d, Asik-asik Falls.
40p, Tinuy-an Falls.

Perf. 13½x13¾

2014, Sept. 22 Litho.

3546 A1221 10p Block of 4, #a-d 5.00 4.50

Souvenir Sheet

3547 A1221 40p multi 5.00 5.00

No. 3546 was printed in sheets of 16. No. 3547 contains one 100x35mm stamp.

National Family Week A1222

No. 3548 — Winning art in stamp design contest by: a, Leah Anne Rulloda. b, Maria Joannes R. Puno.

2014, Sept. 26 Litho. *Perf. 14*

3548 A1222 10p Horiz. pair, #a-b 2.00 1.60

Quezon City, 75th Anniv. A1223

No. 3549: a, Tandang Sora Shrine. b, Emilio Jacinto Shrine. c, North EDSA Shopping Mall. d, University of Philippines Ayala Techno Hub.
100p, Quezon Memorial Circle, horiz.

2014, Oct. 12 Litho. *Perf. 13¾x13½*

3549 A1223 10p Block of 4, #a-d 7.50 6.00

Litho. & Silk-Screened (Margin With Foil Application)

Souvenir Sheet

Perf. 13¾ Horiz.

3550 A1223 100p multi 14.00 14.00

No. 3549 was printed in sheets of 16.
No. 3550 contains one 86x50mm stamp.
A miniature sheet of 6 stamps showing a fountain on the left half, and being personalizable on the right of each stamp, was issued for the 75th anniversary of Quezon City. However, only 112 sheets were available at the post office. Each stamp has a face value of 10p. Sheets were sold for 250p.

Leyte Gulf Landing, 70th Anniv. — A1224

2014, Oct. 20 Litho. *Perf. 14*

3551 A1224 10p multi 1.20 .70

Christmas — A1225

No. 3552: a, Holy Family (1/4). b, Carolers (2/4). c, Respect for elders (3/4). d, Christmas Eve feast (4/4).

2014, Oct. 30 Litho. *Perf. 14*

3552 A1225 10p Block of 4, #a-d 5.00 4.50

Printed in sheets of 16.

Growing Plant — A1226

2014, Nov. 8 Litho. *Perf. 14*

3553 A1226 10p multi 1.00 .60

Philippine recovery after Typhoon Haiyan.

First Philippine Postage Stamps, 160th Anniv. — A1227

No. 3554 and 3555
Philippines #1-2, 4-5, with large illustration of: a, #1. b, #2. c, #4. d, #5.

Perf. 13½x13¾

2014, Nov. 10 Litho.

3554 A1227 10p Block of 4, #a-d 5.50 5.00

3555 A1227 20p Sheet of 4, #a-d 10.00 10.00

National Stamp Collecting Month.
Printed in sheets of 16.

Filipino-Chinese General Chamber of Commerce, 110th Anniv. — A1228

No. 3556: a, Traders, ship, abacuses (1/2). b, People with computer, city skyline, airplane (2/2).

2014, Nov. 19 Litho. *Perf. 14*

3556 A1228 10p Horiz. pair, #a-b 1.75 1.75

a. Miniature sheet of 8 12.00 12.00

Festival Masks and Facial Decorations — A1229

No. 3557: a, Moriones Festival mask. b, Higantes Festival mask. c, Pintados Festival face decoration.
100p, Masskara Festival mask, horiz.

2014, Nov. 22 Litho. *Perf. 14*

3557 Horiz. strip of 3 3.50 3.00

a.-c. A1229 10p Any single 1.00 .80

Litho. & Silk-Screened

Souvenir Sheet

3558 A1229 100p multi 12.00 12.00

No. 3557 was printed in sheets of 12.
No. 3558 contains one 80x30mm stamp.

New Year 2015 (Year of the Goat) — A1229a

Designs: 10p, Head of goat. 30p, Goat.

2014, Nov. 24 Litho. *Perf. 14*

3558A-3558B A1229a Set of 2 5.00 4.00

3558Bc Souvenir sheet of 4, 2 each #3558A-3558B 11.00 11.00

Printed in sheets of 10.

Claudio Teehankee (1918-89), Chief Justice — A1230

2014, Nov. 27 Litho. *Perf. 14*

3559 A1230 10p multi 1.00 .60

St. Paul University, Dumaguete City, 110th Anniv. — A1231

2014, Dec. 8 Litho. *Perf. 14*

3560 A1231 10p multi 1.00 .60

National Anti-Corruption Day — A1232

2014, Dec. 9 Litho. *Perf. 14*

3561 A1232 10p multi 1.00 .80

Shell Oil in the Philippines, Cent. — A1233

No. 3562: a. Shell Tabangao Refinery, 1960s (1/4). b, Shell Tabangao Refinery, 2014 (2/4). c, Shell retail station, 1930s (3/4). d, Shell retail station, 2014 (4/4).

Litho. With Foil Application

2014, Dec. 13 *Perf. 13½x13¼*

3562 A1233 25p Block of 4, #a-d 12.00 10.00

Printed in sheets of 8.

Severino Montano (1915-80), Playwright A1234

2015, Jan. 3 Litho. *Perf. 14*

3563 A1234 10p multi 1.00 .60

A1235

Visit of Pope Francis to the Philippines — A1236

No. 3564 — Winning art in Pope Francis stamp design contest by: a, Bryan Michael Bunag (1/4). b, Dave Arjay Tan (2/4). c, Salvador Banares, Jr. (3/4). d, Mark Leo Maac (4/4).
100p, Pope Francis.

2015 Litho. *Perf. 14*

3564 A1235 10p Block of 4, #a-d 5.00 4.50

Litho. & Embossed With Foil Application

Souvenir Sheet

Perf.

3565 A1236 200p multi 25.00 22.00

Issued: No. 3564, 1/8; No. 3565, 1/12.

St. Valentine's Day — A1237

No. 3566 — Hearts and: a, Cupid (1/4). b, Boy and girl (2/4). c, Bride and groom (3/4). d, Elderly couple (4/4).

2015, Jan. 14 Litho. *Perf. 14*

3566 Horiz. strip of 4 5.00 4.00

a.-d. A1237 10p Any single .80 .80

Printed in sheets of 16.

Open Doors Monument, Rishon LeZion, Israel, Flags of Philippines and Israel — A1238

2015, Jan. 27 Litho. *Perf. 14*

3567 A1238 35p multi 4.00 3.00

See Israel No. 2048.

Laua-an, Cent. — A1239

2015, Jan. 31 **Litho.** ***Perf. 14***
3568 A1239 10p multi 1.00 .80

Fruit — A1240

Designs: No. 3569, Bananas. No. 3570, Black plums. 3p, Mangos. No. 3572, Papayas. No. 3573, Aratiles fruit. No. 3574, Pineapples. No. 3575, Rose apples. 13p, Lanzones. No. 3577, Santols. No. 3578, Strawberries. 25p, Custard apples. No. 3580, Soursops. No. 3581, Ramboutaniers. No. 3582, Avocados. No. 3583, Jocotes. No. 3584, Cashew fruit. No. 3585, Johey oaks.

Perf. 13½, 12¾ (#3570, 3573, 3575, 3578, 3581, 3583, 3585)

2015 **Litho.**

3569	A1240	1p multi	.60	.25
3570	A1240	1p multi	.60	.25
3571	A1240	3p multi	.80	.25
3572	A1240	5p multi	1.00	.25
3573	A1240	5p multi	1.00	.25
3574	A1240	10p multi	1.25	.40
3575	A1240	10p multi	1.50	.40
3576	A1240	13p multi	1.50	.70
3577	A1240	20p multi	2.00	1.00
3578	A1240	20p multi	2.00	1.00
3579	A1240	25p multi	2.50	1.25
3580	A1240	30p multi	3.00	1.50
3581	A1240	30p multi	3.00	1.50
3582	A1240	40p multi	4.00	2.00
3583	A1240	40p multi	4.00	2.00

Size: 43x43mm

3584	A1240	100p multi	10.00	5.00
3585	A1240	100p multi	10.00	5.00
		Nos. 3569-3585 (17)	48.75	23.00

Issued: Nos. 3569, 3584, 3/12; Nos. 3570, 3585, 12/15; 3p, 13p, 25p, No. 3580, 2/10; Nos. 3572, 3577, 2/6; Nos. 3573, 3575, 3578, 12/10; Nos. 3574, 3582, 2/4; Nos. 3581, 3583, 12/11.

See Nos, 3651-3660, 3714-3718.

Salud S. Tesoro (1915-2000), Business Entrepreneur A1241

2015, Feb. 6 **Litho.** ***Perf. 13¾x13½***
3586 A1241 10p multi 1.00 .60

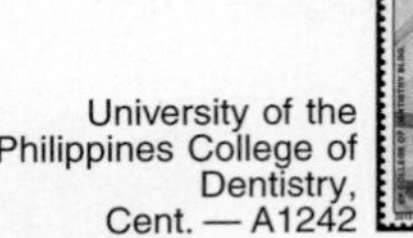

University of the Philippines College of Dentistry, Cent. — A1242

2015, Feb. 6 **Litho.** ***Perf. 14***
3587 A1242 10p multi 1.00 .50

University of Saint Louis, Baguio, 50th Anniv. — A1243

2015, Feb. 11 **Litho.** ***Perf. 14***
3588 A1243 10p multi 1.00 .50

Lamberto V. Avellana (1915-91), Film Director — A1244

2015, Feb. 12 **Litho.** ***Perf. 14***
3589 A1244 10p multi 1.00 .50

Philippine Health Insurance Corporation, 20th Anniv. — A1245

2015, Feb. 14 **Litho.** ***Perf. 14***
3590 A1245 10p multi 1.00 .50

Souvenir Sheet

New Year 2015 (Year of the Goat) A1246

No. 3514: a, 50p, Horse (40x30mm). b, 50p, Monkey (40x30mm). c, 100p, Goat (50x40mm).

Perf. 13¼x13x13¼x13¼ (#3591a), 13¼x13¼x13¼x13 (#3591b), 13 (#3591c)

Litho., Litho. & Embossed With Foil Application (100p)

2015, Feb. 19
3591 A1246 Sheet of 3, #a-c 38.00 38.00

Liceo de Cagayan University, Cagayan de Oro City, 60th Anniv. — A1247

2015, Feb. 24 **Litho.** ***Perf. 14***
3592 A1247 10p multi 1.00 .50

Philpost Type of 2013

Perf. 13½x13¼

2015, Mar. 20 **Litho.**

Denomination Color

3593 A1177 10p brown 1.00 .40
3594 A1177 15p gray olive 1.50 .60

Visit the Philippines Year — A1248

Perf. 13¾x13½

2015, Mar. 25 **Litho.**
3595 A1248 10p multi 1.00 .60

Dragonflies — A1249

No. 3596: a, Beautiful demoiselle. b, Small red damselfly. c, Golden-ringed dragonfly. d, Blue-tailed damselfly, e, White-legged damselfly. f, Emperor dragonfly. g, Club-tailed dragonfly. h, Ruddy darter. i, Halloween pennant. 40p, Broad-bodied chaser.

2015, Mar. 27 **Litho.** ***Perf. 14***
3596 A1249 10p Sheet of 9, #a-i 12.00 12.00

Souvenir Sheet

Perf. 13½x13¾

3597 A1249 40p multi + label 6.00 5.00

No. 3597 contains one 50x35mm stamp.

A1250

Discovery of Santo Niño Icon of Cebu, 450th Anniv. — A1251

2015, Apr. 20 **Litho.** ***Perf. 14***
3598 A1250 10p multi 1.00 .50

Souvenir Sheet

Litho. & Embossed, Sheet Margin Litho. & Embossed With Foil Application

Perf. 13¼

3599 A1251 200p gold & multi 28.00 28.00

Philippine Econonic Zone Authority, 20th Anniv. — A1252

2015, Apr. 20 **Litho.** ***Perf. 14***
3600 A1252 10p multi 1.00 .50

Souvenir Sheet

Litho. & Embossed With Foil Application

Perf.

3601 A1252 200p Emblem, diff. 22.00 22.00

No. 3601 contains one 38mm diameter stamp.

Emmanuel "Manny" Pacquiao, Boxer and Politician — A1253

2015, Apr. 20 **Litho.** ***Perf. 14***
3602 A1253 10p multi 1.50 .80

Souvenir Sheet

Perf. 13½x13¾

3603 A1253 40p Pacquiao, diff. 6.00 5.00

No. 3603 contains one 50x35mm stamp.

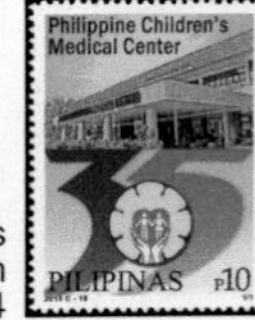

Philippine Children's Medical Center, 35th Anniv. — A1254

2015, Apr. 20 **Litho.** ***Perf. 14***
3604 A1254 10p multi 1.00 .50

Miniature Sheet

Mythical Creatures — A1255

No. 3605: a, Nuno sa Punso. b, Sirena. c, Si Malakas at Si Maganda. d, Diwata (Maria Sinukuan).

2015, Apr. 24 **Litho.** ***Perf. 14***
3605 A1255 10p Sheet of 4, #a-d 15.00 15.00

Taipei 2015 Intl. Stamp Exhibition. No. 3605 was sold for 150p at the date of issue.

City of San Pablo, 75th Anniv. of Chartering — A1256

No. 3606: a, Municipal Building. b, Sampaloc Lake.

2015, May 7 **Litho.** ***Perf. 14***
3606 A1256 10p Horiz. pair, #a-b 2.00 1.60

Hibiscus Varieties A1257

No. 3607 — Variety named: a, Goria. b, Nay Isa. c, Tandang Sora. d, Nazaria.

No. 3608 — Variety named: a, Emerita V. de Guzman. b, Helen L. Valmayor. c, Gelia T. Castillo. d, Dolores A. Ramirez.

2015, May 12 **Litho.** ***Perf. 14***
3607 A1257 10p Block of 4, #a-d 4.50 4.00
3608 A1257 10p Sheet of 4, #a-d, + 2 labels 5.00 5.00

Romblon State University, Cent. — A1258

2015, May 22 **Litho.** ***Perf. 14***
3609 A1258 10p multi 1.00 .50

Archdiocese of Jaro, 150th Anniv. — A1259

No. 3610: a, Jaro Cathedral. b, Nuestra Señora de la Candelaria icon.

2015, May 27 **Litho.** ***Perf. 14***
3610 A1259 10p Horiz. pair, #a-b 2.00 1.60

Bilateral Relations Between the Philippines and Finland, 60th Anniv. — A1260

No. 3611 — Flags of the Philippines and Finland and: a, 10p, Brown bear. b, 40p, Philippine tamaraw.

2015, June 3 Litho. *Perf. 14*
3611 A1260 Horiz. pair, #a-b 6.00 5.00

Ateneo de Naga University, Naga City, 75th Anniv. — A1261

No. 3612: a, Emblem. b, University building.

2015, June 5 Litho. *Perf. 14*
3612 A1261 10p Horiz. pair, #a-b 2.00 1.60

Diplomatic Relations Between Philippines and People's Republic of China, 40th Anniv. — A1262

2015, June 9 Litho. *Perf. 14*
3613 A1262 30p multi 3.50 2.50

Kites A1263

No. 3614 — Various kites numbered: a, 1/10. b, 2/10. c, 3/10. d, 4/10. e, 5/10. f, 6/10. g, 7/10. h, 8/10. i, 9/10. j, 10/10.
40p, Kites.

2015, June 23 Litho. *Perf. 14*
3614 A1263 10p Sheet of 10, #a-j 12.00 12.00

Souvenir Sheet
Perf. 13¾x13½

3615 A1263 40p multi 6.00 5.00

No. 3615 contains one 35x50mm stamp.

City of San Carlos, 55th Anniv. of Chartering — A1264

No. 3616: a, City Hall. b, Pinta Flores Festival.

2015, July 1 Litho. *Perf. 14*
3616 A1264 15p Horiz. pair, #a-b 3.00 2.40

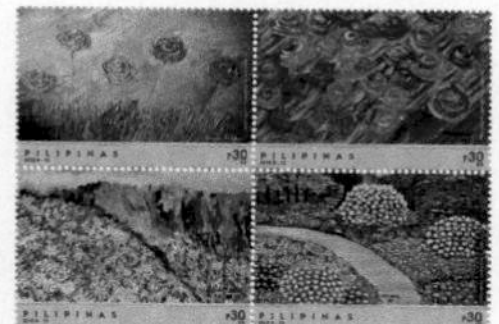

Paintings of Flowers by Pres. Corazon A. Aquino (1933-2009) — A1265

No. 3617: a, Harmony of Flowers (1/4). b, Blue and Green Sea of Flowers (2/4). c, Valley of Flowers (3/4). d, Flowers by Forest Hills (4/4).
120p, Pink Flowers in a Vase, vert.

2015, July 28 Litho. *Perf. 13½x13¾*
3617 A1265 30p Block of 4, #a-d 15.00 15.00

Souvenir Sheet
Perf. 13¾x13½

3618 A1265 120p multi + label 13.00 11.00

No. 3617 printed in sheets of 8.

Flags and Emblem of Association of Southeast Asian Nations — A1266

2015, Aug. 8 Litho. *Perf. 13¼*
3619 A1266 13p multi 1.50 1.20

See Brunei No. 656, Burma Nos. 417-418, Cambodia No. 2428, Indonesia No. 2428, Laos No. 1906, Malaysia No. 1562; Singapore No. 1742, Thailand No. 2875, Viet Nam No. 3529.

Teresita "Mama Sita" Reyes (1917-98), Restauranteur — A1267

No. 3620 — Reyes and: a, Fish, fruit and vegetables (2/3). b, Basket and blue swirls (3/3). c, Foods and stars (1/3).

Perf. 13¾x13½
2015, Aug. 24 Litho.
3620 A1267 10p Strip of 3, #a-c 3.00 2.50

Printed in sheets of 9.

Bureau of Immigration, 75th Anniv. A1268

2015, Sept. 4 Litho. *Perf. 13½x13¾*
3621 A1268 30p multi 3.00 2.50

Pres. Elpidio Quirino (1890-1956) A1269

2015, Sept. 5 Litho. *Perf. 13¾x13½*
3622 A1269 15p multi 1.50 .70

N. V. M. Gonzales (1915-99), Writer — A1270

2015, Sept. 8 Litho. *Perf. 14*
3623 A1270 10p multi 1.00 .60

Bandera Newspaper, 25th Anniv. — A1271

Perf. 13¾x13½
2015, Sept. 10 Litho.
3624 A1271 15p multi 1.50 .90

Manila Observatory, 150th Anniv. — A1272

2015, Sept. 25 Litho. *Perf. 14*
3625 A1272 15p multi 1.50 .90

General Miguel Malvar (1865-1911) A1273

2015, Sept. 27 Litho. *Perf. 14*
3626 A1273 10p multi 1.00 .60

San Miguel Brewery, 125th Anniv. A1274

No. 3627: a, Brewery building. b, 125th anniversary emblem.
40p, 125th anniversary emblem, vert.

2015, Sept. 29 Litho. *Perf. 14*
3627 A1274 15p Horiz. pair, #a-b 3.00 2.50

Souvenir Sheet
Perf. 13¾x13½

3628 A1274 40p multi 5.00 4.00

No. 3628 contains one 35x50mm stamp.

Western Union in the Philippines, 25th Anniv. — A1275

No. 3629 — Western Union emblem and: a, Various Filipinos. b, Text, "25 Years of Moving the Filipino for Better."

Perf. 13½x13¾
2015, Sept. 30 Litho.
3629 A1275 25p Horiz. pair, #a-b 5.00 4.00

Mahaguyog Festival — A1276

2015, Oct. 2 Litho. *Perf. 14*
3630 A1276 10p multi 1.00 .60

Manuel Conde (1915-85), Film Director — A1277

2015, Oct. 15 Litho. *Perf. 14*
3631 A1277 10p multi 1.00 .60

2015 Asian-Pacific Economic Cooperation Summit, Manila — A1278

Perf. 13¾x13½
2015, Nov. 10 Litho.
3632 A1278 30p multi 3.50 2.50

Miniature Sheet

National Stamp Collecting Month — A1279

No. 3633: a, Boy holding stamp. b, Boy holdind stamp album. c, Girl holding stamps. d, Man holding stamps and magnifying glass.

2015, Nov. 10 Litho. *Perf. 14*
Self-Adhesive
3633 A1279 15p Sheet of 4, #a-d 7.00 7.00

Miniature Sheet

Wildlife A1280

No. 3634: a, Vizaysa flowerpecker. b, Philippine sail-fin lizard. c, Philippine pangolin anteater. d, Freshwater purple crab.

2015, Nov. 11 Litho. *Perf. 14*
3634 A1280 15p Sheet of 4, #a-d 7.00 7.00

Christmas — A1281

No. 3635 -- Children's art depicting Christmas tree by: a, Kobie Trambulo (2/4). b, Vernice Prado (3/4). c, Lomi Capili (4/4). d, Javee Fua (1/4).
No. 3636 — Children's art depicting Christmas lanterns by: a, Cedric Chua. b, Julius Cabuang. c, Thridy Cabading.

2015, Nov. 25 Litho. *Perf. 14*
3635 A1281 10p Block or strip of 4, #a-d 9.00 8.00

Souvenir Sheet

3636 A1281 10p Sheet of 3, #a-c 4.00 3.00

Office of the Government Corporate Counsel, 80th Anniv. A1282

2015, Dec. 1 Litho. *Perf. 13½x13¾*
3637 A1282 10p multi 1.00 .60

New Year 2016 (Year of the Monkey) — A1283

Designs: 10p, Head of monkey. 30p, Monkey.

2015, Dec. 1 Litho. *Perf. 14*
3638-3639 A1283 Set of 2 5.00 4.00
3639a Souvenir sheet of 4, 2 each #3638-3639 11.00 11.00

Printed in sheets of 10.

Philippine Daily Inquirer Newspaper, 30th Anniv. — A1284

Litho. & Embossed With Foil Application

2015, Dec. 5 *Perf. 13¼*
3640 A1284 30p multi 3.50 3.00

51st Intl. Eucharistic Congress, Cebu City — A1285

Design: 15p, Emblem. 40p, Emblem and dove's wing.

2015, Dec. 8 **Litho.** *Perf. 14*
3641 A1285 15p multi 1.50 .80

Souvenir Sheet
Perf. 13¾x13½

3642 A1285 40p multi + label 4.50 3.50

No. 3642 contains one 35x50mm stamp.

Cagayan Economic Zone Authority, 20th Anniv. — A1286

2015, Dec. 18 **Litho.** *Perf. 14*
3643 A1286 15p multi 1.50 .80

Commission on Elections, 75th Anniv. — A1287

2015, Dec. 18 **Litho.** *Perf. 14*
3644 A1287 15p multi 1.50 .80

Liberty City Center, 70th Anniv. — A1288

2015, Dec. 21 **Litho.** *Perf. 14*
3645 A1288 15p multi 1.50 .80

Pacita Madrigal Gonzalez (1915-2008), Senator — A1289

2015, Dec. 22 **Litho.** *Perf. 14*
3646 A1289 15p multi 1.50 .80

Mabitac Church, 400th Anniv. — A1290

2016, Jan. 2 **Litho.** *Perf. 14*
3647 A1290 15p multi 1.50 .80

San Sebastian College, Manila, 75th Anniv. — A1291

2016, Jan. 20 **Litho.** *Perf. 14*
3648 A1291 15p multi 1.50 .80

Court of Appeals, 80th Anniv. — A1292

2016, Feb. 1 **Litho.** *Perf. 14*
3649 A1292 15p multi 1.50 .80

Senate, Cent. — A1293

2016, Feb. 1 **Litho.** *Perf. 14*
3650 A1293 15p multi 1.50 .80

Fruit Type of 2015

Designs: 1p, Egg fruit. 5p, Philippine wild raspberry. No. 3653, Tangerine orange. No. 3654, Grapes. 13p, Star fruit. 14p, Pomelo. 15p, Star apple. 17p, Calamansi. 35p, Sweet tamarind. 45p, Durian.

Perf. 13½, 12¾ (#3653, 3655, 3657, 3659)

2016			**Litho.**	
3651	A1240	1p multi	.50	.25
a.		Dated "2017"	.50	.25
3652	A1240	5p multi	.50	.25
a.		Dated "2017"	.50	.25
3653	A1240	12p multi	1.20	.50
3654	A1240	12p multi	1.20	.50
a.		Dated "2017"	1.20	.50
3655	A1240	13p multi	1.40	.70
3656	A1240	14p multi	1.60	.80
a.		Dated "2017"	1.40	.70
3657	A1240	15p multi	1.75	.80
3658	A1240	17p multi	1.75	.90
a.		Dated "2017"	1.25	1.00
3659	A1240	35p multi	4.00	1.75
3660	A1240	45p multi	5.00	2.40
a.		Dated "2017"	4.00	2.50
		Nos. 3651-3660 (10)	18.90	8.85

Issued: 1p, 5p, No. 3654, 17p, 6/23; No. 3653, 13p, 15p, 35p, 2/2; 14p, 12/8; 45p, 6/30. Nos. 3651a, 3652a, 3/14/17; No. 3654a, 3/29/17; Nos. 3656a, 3658a, 3/21/17; No. 3660a, 4/18/17.

St. Valentine's Day — A1294

2016, Feb. 5 **Litho.** *Perf. 13½*
3661 A1294 25p multi 2.50 2.00

Tagkawayan, 75th Anniv. — A1295

2016, Feb. 10 **Litho.** *Perf. 14*
3662 A1295 15p multi 1.50 .80

Leprosy Prevention and Control Week — A1296

2016, Feb. 15 **Litho.** *Perf. 14*
3663 A1296 15p multi 1.50 .80

Bago, 50th Anniv. — A1297

2016, Feb. 19 **Litho.** *Perf. 14*
3664 A1297 15p multi 1.50 .80

Pia Alonzo Wurtzbach, 2015 Miss Universe — A1298

Wurtzbach with background color of: 15p, Gray. 40p, Pink.

2016, Apr. 17 **Litho.** *Perf. 13½*
3665 A1298 15p multi 2.00 1.50

Souvenir Sheet
Litho. With Glitter Affixed

3666 A1298 40p multi 8.00 8.00

Festivals A1299

No. 3667: a, Sinulog Festival (1/4). b, Panagbenga Festival (2/4). c, Pahiyas Festival (3/4). d, Higantes Festival (4/4).

2016, Apr. 27 **Litho.** *Perf. 14*
3667 A1299 15p Horiz. strip of 4, #a-d 8.00 7.00

Printed in sheets of 16.

Heritage Month A1300

No. 3668 — Musical instruments: a, Kulintang. b, Kudyapi. c, Dabakan. d, Gangsa.
No. 3669 — Musical instruments: a, Kudlong. b, Libbit. c, Agung. d, Gabbang.

2016, May 5 **Litho.** *Perf. 14*
3668 A1300 15p Block of 4, #a-d 6.00 5.00
3669 A1300 15p Sheet of 4, #a-d 6.00 6.00

No. 3668 printed in sheets of 16.

A1301

2016, May 6 **Litho.** *Perf. 14*
3670 A1301 15p multi 1.50 .80

Intl. Organization for Standardization Certification of Office of the Regional Governor for Autonomous Region in Muslim Mindanao.

Tiaong, 325th Anniv. — A1302

2016, May 14 **Litho.** *Perf. 14*
3671 A1302 15p multi 1.50 .80

A1303

Philippine National Bank, Cent. — A1304

No. 3672 — Winning art in stamp design contest by: a, Kenneth Olivar. b, Jean Christian Tormes. c, Jerico Martinez. d, Michael Montanez.

100p, Ferdinand Magellan from 100-peso banknote.

2016, June 12 **Litho.** *Perf. 14*
3672 A1303 15p Block of 4, #a-d 7.00 6.00

Souvenir Sheet
Perf. 13½

3673 A1304 100p multi 12.00 12.00

Knights of Rizal, Cent. — A1305

2016, June 19 **Litho.** *Perf. 14*
3674 A1305 15p multi 2.00 1.00

Tagbilaran, 50th Anniv. — A1306

Designs: 15p, Tagbilaran City Hall. 100p, Saulog Festival.

2016, July 1 **Litho.** *Perf. 14*
3675 A1306 15p multi 1.50 1.00

Souvenir Sheet
Litho. With Foil Application

3676 A1306 100p multi 20.00 20.00

Inauguration of Pres. Rodrigo Roa Duterte A1307

Size of photograph of ceremony: 17p, 43x26mm. 55p, 49x23mm.

2016, Aug. 1 **Litho.** *Perf. 13½*
3677 A1307 17p multi 2.00 1.00

Souvenir Sheet

3678 A1307 55p multi 7.00 5.00

No. 3678 contains one 60x30mm stamp.

Lal-Lo, 435th Anniv. — A1308

2016, Aug. 4 **Litho.** *Perf. 14*
3679 A1308 15p multi 1.50 .80

2016 Summer Olympics, Rio de Janeiro — A1309

No. 3680: a, Taekwondo. b, Boxing. c, Equestrian dressage. d, Archery.
55p, Basketball.

2016, Aug. 9 Litho. *Perf. 14*
3680 A1309 12p Block of 4, #a-d 7.50 6.00

Souvenir Sheet
Perf. 13½

3681 A1309 55p multi + label 6.00 5.00

No. 3680 printed in sheets of 16.
No. 3681 contains one 35x50mm stamp.

Year of the Monkey Type of 2015
Miniature Sheet

No. 3682: a, Head of monkey. b, Monkey.

2016, Aug. 10 Litho. *Perf. 14*
3682 Sheet of 4, 2 each #3682a-3682b 12.50 12.50
a. A1283 12p multi 1.50 .70
b. A1283 45p multi 3.00 2.25

Thailand 2016 Intl. Stamp Exhibition, Bangkok.

National Teacher's Month — A1310

2016, Sept. 5 Litho. *Perf. 14*
3683 A1310 12p multi 1.20 .80

Orchids A1311

No. 3684: a, Mrs. Sander's dendrobium. b, Moth orchid (yellow background). c, Waling-waling. d, Dancing lady orchid.
No. 3685, horiz.: a, Deer antler moth orchid. b, Cattleya Hsiying rouge. c, Moth orchid (light blue background). d, Cattleya dark purple trichoglottis.

2016, Sept. 30 Litho. *Perf. 14*
3684 A1311 12p Block of 4, #a-d 5.00 4.00

Souvenir Sheet

3685 A1311 12p Sheet of 4, #a-d 6.00 6.00

No. 3684 printed in sheets of 16.
No. 3685a "Deer" is spelled incorrectly on stamp.

Philippine Airlines, 75th Anniv. — A1312

2016, Oct. 19 Litho. *Perf. 14*
3686 A1312 12p multi 1.20 .80

Philtrust Bank, Cent. — A1313

2016, Oct. 19 Litho. *Perf. 14*
3687 A1313 12p multi 1.20 .80

National Stamp Collecting Month A1314

No. 3688: a, Philippines #502. b, Philippines #501. c, Philippines #500.
55p, Philippines #500-502.

2016, Oct. 21 Litho. *Perf. 13½*
3688 Horiz. strip of 3 4.50 4.00
a.-c. A1314 12p Any single 1.20 1.00

Souvenir Sheet

3689 A1314 55p multi 6.50 6.00

No. 3688 printed in sheets of 9.
No. 3689 contains one 100x35mm stamp.

Souvenir Sheet

New Year 2016 (Year of the Monkey) A1315

No. 3690: a, 75p, Goat (40x30mm). b, 75p, Rooster (40x30mm). c, 100p, Monkey (50x40mm).

Perf. 13¼x13x13¼x13¼ (#3690a), 13¼x13¼x13¼x13 (#3690b), 13 (#3690c)
Litho., Sheet Margin Litho. & Embossed With Foil Application
2016, Oct. 21
3690 A1315 Sheet of 3, #a-c 28.00 28.00

2016 Philataipei World Stamp Exhibition, Taipei.

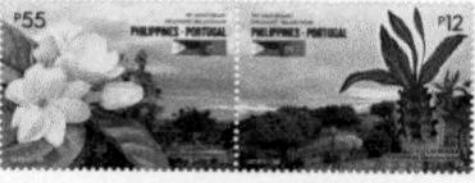

Diplomatic Relations Between Philippines and Portugal, 75th Anniv. — A1316

No. 3691 — Flags of Philippines and Portugal and: a, 12p, Lavender, national flower of Portugal. b, 55p, Sampaguita, national flower of Philippines.

2016, Oct. 24 Litho. *Perf. 14*
3691 A1316 Horiz. pair, #a-b 7.50 6.00

Printed in sheets of 8.
See Portugal Nos. 3855-3856.

Philippines Securities and Exchange Commission, 80th Anniv. — A1317

2016, Nov. 11 Litho. *Perf. 14*
3692 A1317 12p multi 1.20 .80

Dr. Sun Yat-sen (1866-1925), First President of the Republic of China — A1318

Designs: 18p, Drs. Sun Yat-sen and Mariano Ponce (1863-1918), Philippine physician and revolutionary hero.
45p, Drs. Sun Yat-sen and Ponce, diff.

2016, Nov. 12 Litho. *Perf. 14*
3693 A1318 18p multi 2.00 1.50

Souvenir Sheet
Perf. 13¾x13½

3694 A1318 45p multi + label 5.50 5.00

No. 3694 contains one 35x50mm stamp.

Christmas — A1319

No. 3695 — Star lantern with "Pasko" in: a, 12p, White on red panel. b, 12p, Red on white panel. c, 17p, White on green panel. d, 17p, Green on white panel.

2016, Nov. 25 Litho. *Perf. 14*
3695 A1319 Block of 4, #a-d 6.00 5.00

Printed in sheets of 16.

University of the Philippines College of Business Administration Alumni Association, Cent. — A1320

2016, Dec. 4 Litho. *Perf. 14*
3696 A1320 12p multi 1.20 .80

A1321

New Year 2017 (Year of the Rooster) A1322

No. 3697 — Rooster facing: a, 18p, Left. b, 45p, Right.

2016, Dec. 16 Litho. *Perf. 14*
3697 A1321 Horiz. pair, #a-b 7.50 6.00

Souvenir Sheet
Litho. & Embossed With Foil Application
Perf.

3698 A1322 200p multi 24.00 20.00

Printed in sheets of 16.

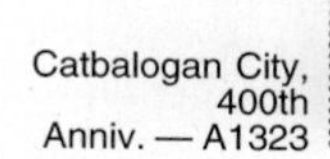

Catbalogan City, 400th Anniv. — A1323

2016, Dec. 20 Litho. *Perf. 14*
3699 A1323 18p multi 1.50 .80

Teresita "Mama Sita" Reyes (1917-98), Restauranteur A1324

2016, Dec. 20 Litho. *Perf. 14*
3700 A1324 18p multi 1.50 .80

10th-13th Century Items From Ayala Museum "Gold of Ancestors" Exhibition — A1325

No. 3701: a, Pectoral disc. b, Garuda-shaped ear ornaments. c, Ear ornaments. d, Kinnari.
No. 3702: a, Like #3701b. b, Like #3701c. c, Like #3701a. d, Like #3701d.

2016, Dec. 21 Litho. *Perf. 14*
3701 A1325 18p Block of 4, #a-d 8.00 7.00

Litho. & Embossed With Foil Application

3702 A1325 50p Sheet of 4, #a-d, + 2 labels 22.00 22.00

No. 3701 printed in sheets of 16.

Main Post Office, Manila Type of 2014

2016, Dec. 23 Litho. *Perf. 14*
3703 A1199 18p multi 10.00 10.00

No. 3703 was printed in sheets of six that sold for 250p. The right half of the stamp could be personalized.
Exists in a generic sheet of 6 with 6 different printed labels. Value, $80.

Association of Southeast Asian Nations, 50th Anniv. — A1326

2017, Jan. 15 Litho. *Perf. 14*
3704 A1326 12p multi 1.40 .80

In Nov. 2017, sheets of four 25p stamps of type A1326 were printed in limited quantities and sold only at the Philippine Postal Service booth at ASEANPEX in Pasay City. Customers wanting to purchase these sheets could do so only if they had purchased 500p worth of stamps at the booth. A sheet containing four stamps inscribed "S-27" was put on sale on Nov. 4, a sheet containing four stamps inscribed "S-32" was put on sale on Nov. 5, and another sheet of 4 stamps inscribed "S-33" was put on sale on Nov. 6.

Bustos, 100th Anniv. as Municipality A1327

2017, Jan. 15 Litho. *Perf. 14*
3705 A1327 12p multi 1.20 .60

Santa Rosa, 225th Anniv. — A1328

2017, Jan. 18 Litho. *Perf. 14*

3706	A1328	12p multi	1.20	.60

Miss Universe Pageant, Pasay A1329

No. 3707 — Crown and: a, Philippines #2304a. b, Philippines #2304b. c, Philippines #3665.

100p, Philippines #2304a, 2304b, 3655.

2017, Jan. 24 Litho. *Perf. 13¾*

3707		Horiz. strip of 3	10.00	8.00
a.	A1329	12p multi	1.20	.80
b.	A1329	17p multi	1.75	1.20
c.	A1329	55p multi	5.50	2.50

Souvenir Sheet

Perf. 13½

3708	A1329	100p multi	12.00	10.00

No. 3707 printed in sheets of 9.

No. 3708 contains one 60x30mm stamp.

Souvenir Sheet

Association of Southeast Asian Nations, 50th Anniv. — A1330

Litho. & Embossed With Foil Application

2017, Jan. 30 *Perf. 13¼*

3709	A1330	100p gold	12.00	10.00

National College of Business and Arts, 50th Anniv. — A1331

2017, Feb. 2 Litho. *Perf. 14*

3710	A1331	12p multi	1.20	.60

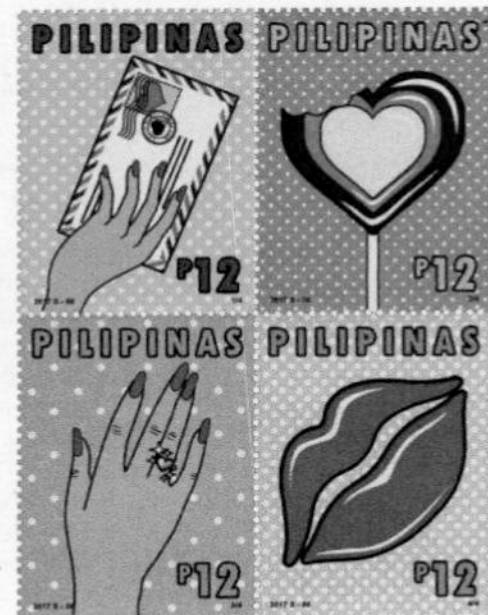

St. Valentine's Day — A1332

Designs: Nos. 3711a, 3712a, Hand holding letter. Nos. 3711b, 3712b, Heart-shaped lollipop. Nos. 3711c, 3712c, Ring on woman's hand. Nos. 3711d, 3712d, Lips.

2017, Feb. 6 Litho. *Perf. 14*

3711	A1332	12p Block of 4, #a-d	4.00	3.00
3712	A1332	17p Sheet of 4, #a-d, + 4 labels	25.00	25.00

No. 3711 printed in sheets of 8.

No. 3712 sold for 150p. Labels could be personalized. No. 3712 was also printed with generic labels showing Cupid, roses, heart-shaped balloons and champagne flutes.

Cosmos Masonic Lodge No. 8, Manila, Cent. — A1333

2017, Feb. 13 Litho. *Perf. 14*

3713	A1333	12p multi	1.50	1.00

Fruit Type of 2015 and

Dragon Fruit — A1334

Designs: 3p, Wild sweet sops. 23p, Bignays. 28p, Coconuts. 34p, Apples. 40p, Tamarinds.

2017 Litho. *Perf. 13½*

3714	A1199	3p multi	.50	.25
3715	A1199	23p multi	2.00	1.00
3716	A1199	28p multi	2.75	1.25
3717	A1199	34p multi	3.50	1.75
3718	A1199	40p multi	4.00	2.00

Perf. 14

3719	A1334	100p multi	10.00	5.00
		Nos. 3714-3719 (6)	22.75	11.25

Issued: 3p, 100p, 3/14; 23p, 28p, 3/29; 34p, 4/18; 40p, 3/21.

Lizards A1335

No. 3720: a, Luzon bicolored earth skink. b, Philippine false gecko. c, Gigante limestone gecko. d, Striped tree skink.

No. 3721: a, Emerald false gecko. b, Marbled agamid lizard. c, Spotted forest dragon. d, Mindanao water skink.

2017, Mar. 27 Litho. *Perf. 14*

3720	A1335	12p Block of 4, #a-d	5.00	4.00
3721	A1335	12p Sheet of 4, #a-d, + 2 labels	5.00	5.00

No. 3720 printed in sheets of 16.

Philippine Postal Corporation, 25th Anniv. — A1336

Phipost emblem and: 12p, Main Post Office, Manila. 55p, "25" and wreath.

2017, Apr. 3 Litho. *Perf. 14*

3722	A1336	12p multi	1.20	.60

Souvenir Sheet

Litho. With Foil Application

Perf.

3723	A1336	55p dk blue & sil	6.00	5.00

No. 3723 contains one 38mm diameter stamp.

Bataan Death March, 75th Anniv. A1337

2017, Apr. 9 Litho. *Perf. 14*

3724	A1337	17p multi	1.75	1.00

Silver Medalists at 2016 Summer Olympics, Rio de Janeiro — A1338

No. 3725: a, Anthony N. Villanueva, boxing. b, Mansueto B. Velasco, Jr., boxing. c, Hidilyn F. Diaz, weight lifting.

55p, Villanueva, Diaz and Velasco, horiz.

2017, Apr. 23 Litho. *Perf. 14*

3725		Horiz. strip of 3	4.00	3.00
a.-c.	A1338	12p Any single	1.00	.75

Souvenir Sheet

Perf. 13½

3726	A1338	55p multi	6.00	5.00

No. 3725 printed in sheets of 9. No. 3726 contains one 50x35mm stamp.

Sunsets A1339

No. 3727 — Sunset at: a, Ilocos Norte. b, Pangasinan. c, Batanes. d, Cebu.

No. 3728 — Sunset at: a, Manila. b, Camiguin. c, Zambales. d, Zamboanga.

2017, May 8 Litho. *Perf. 14*

3727	A1339	12p Block or horiz. strip of 4, #a-d	5.00	4.00

Litho. With Foil Application

3728	A1339	25p Sheet of 4, #a-d	10.00	10.00

National Heritage Month.

No. 3727 printed in sheets of 16.

Diocese of Butuan, 50th Anniv. — A1340

2017, May 10 Litho. *Perf. 14*

3729	A1340	12p multi	1.20	.60

Independence Day — A1341

No. 3730: a, Rizal Monument, Manila. b, Barasoain Church, Malolos. c, Emilio Aguinaldo Shrine, Kawit. d, Andres Bonifacio Monument, Caloocan.

Litho. With Foil Application

2017, June 12 *Perf. 14*

3730	A1341	12p Block of 4, #a-d	5.00	4.00

Printed in sheets of 16.

St. Stephen's High School, Luzon, Cent. — A1342

No. 3731: a, Building and praying hands, denomination at UR. b, Building, denomination at UL.

2017, June 22 Litho. *Perf. 14*

3731	A1342	12p Horiz. pair, #a-b	2.50	2.00

Printed in sheets of 8.

Diplomatic Relations Between Philippines and France, 70th Anniv. — A1343

No. 3732 — Unnamed painting by: a, 12p, French painter Jacques Villon (1875-1963). b, 55p, Philippine painter Macario Vitalis (1898-1989).

2017, June 26 Litho. *Perf. 14*

3732	A1343	Horiz. pair, #a-b	7.00	5.00

Printed in sheets of 8.

See France Nos. 5259-5260.

Davao del Norte Province, 50th Anniv. — A1344

2017, July 1 Litho. *Perf. 14*

3733	A1344	12p multi	1.20	.60

Jasminum Sambac (National Flower) — A1345

Litho. With Foil Application

2017, Aug. 8 *Perf. 14*

3734	A1345	12p multi	1.50	.80

Association of Southeast Asian Nations, 50th anniv.

Snakes A1346

No. 3735: a, Philippine forest cat snake. b, Luzon forest cat snake. c, Yellow-spotted Philippine pit viper. d, Red-tailed blind snake.

No. 3736: a, Philippine variable paradise snake. b, Eastern Visayas wolf snake. c, Zigzag-lined keelback. d, Philippine whip snake.

2017, Aug. 16 Litho. *Perf. 14*

3735	A1346	12p Block of 4, #a-d	5.00	4.00

Litho. With Foil Application

3736	A1346	25p Sheet of 4, #a-d	12.00	12.00

No. 3735 printed in sheets of 16.

National Teachers Month — A1347

2017, Sept. 5 Litho. *Perf. 14*

3737	A1347	12p multi	1.20	.80

Souvenir Sheet

New Year 2017 (Year of the Rooster) A1348

Litho., Sheet Margin Litho. With Foil Application

2017, Sept. 8 *Perf. 13¼*

3738	A1348	100p multi	12.00	12.00

2017 China International Collection Expo, Nanjing.

Pres. Ferdinand E. Marcos (1917-89) — A1349

2017, Sept. 11 Litho. Perf. 14
3739 A1349 12p multi 1.50 1.00

Miniature Sheet

Greetings — A1350

No. 3740 — Inscriptions: a, "Cheers!" b, "Best Wishes!" c, "Congrats!" d, "Thank you!"

2017, Oct. 9 Litho. Perf. 14
3740 A1350 17p Sheet of 4, #a-d, + 4 labels 15.00 15.00

No. 3740 sold for 150p, and was available with the generic labels shown or with labels that could be personalized.

Flowers A1351

No. 3741: a, Medinilla cordata. b, Begonia gutierrezii. c, Begonia cumingii. d, Hoya buotii.
No. 3742: a, Begonia oxysperma. b, Coelogyne candoonensis. c, Strongylodon macrobotrys. d, Plocoglottis lucbanensis.

2017, Oct. 16 Litho. Perf. 14
3741 A1351 12p Block of 4, #a-d 5.00 4.00

Souvenir Sheet

3742 A1351 12p Sheet of 4, #a-d, + 2 labels 5.00 5.00

No. 3741 printed in sheets of 16.

Jeepneys A1352

No. 3743: a, 1943 Willys Jeep. b, 1945 Transformed Jeep. c, Decorated jeepney. d, Modern jumbo Jeep.

2017, Nov. 4 Litho. Perf. 14
3743 Horiz. strip of 4 5.00 4.00
a.-d. A1352 12p Any single 1.00 .75

Miniature Sheet

National Flowers of Association of Southeast Asian Nations Members — A1353

No. 3744 — ASEANPEX emblem and: a, Sampauita (Philippines). b, Vanda "Miss Joaquim" (Singapore), Rumdul (Cambodia), Melati putih (Indonesia). c, Dok champa (Laos), Ratchaphruek (Thailand), Lotus (Viet Nam). d, Padauk (Myanmar), Simpor (Brunei). Hibiscus (Malaysia).

2017, Nov. 4 Litho. Perf. 14
3744 A1353 17p Sheet of 4, #a-d, + 4 labels 16.00 16.00

Association of Southeast Asian Nations, 50th anniv. No. 3744 sold for 150p, and was available with the generic labels shown or with labels that could be personalized.

Emblem of 2017 ASEANPEX, Pasay City — A1354

2017, Nov. 4 Litho. Perf. 14
3745 A1354 17p multi + label 4.00 4.00

No. 3745 was printed in sheets of 4 + 4 labels, which sold for 150p. The sheets were available with the generic label shown or with labels that could be personalized.

Souvenir Sheet

New Year 2017 (Year of the Rooster) A1355

No. 3746: a, 75p, Monkey (40x30mm). b, 75p, Dog (40x30mm). c, 100p, Rooster (50x40mm).

Perf. 13¼x13x13¼x13¼ (#3746a), 13¼x13¼x13¼x13 (#746b), 13 (#3746c)

Litho. & Embossed With Foil Application

2017, Nov. 5
3746 A1355 Sheet of 3, #a-c 28.00 28.00

2017 ASEANPEX, Pasay City.

Postal Transportation — A1356

No. 3747: a, Galleon. b, Bagadero on horse. c, Train. d, Postman with bicycle.
55p, Two Philpost vans.

2017, Nov. 6 Litho. Perf. 14
3747 A1356 12p Block of 4, #a-d 5.00 4.00

Souvenir Sheet

Perf. 13½x13¼

3748 A1356 55p multi 6.00 5.00

Philippine Postal Service, 250th anniv. No. 3748 contains one 60x30mm stamp.

Subic Bay Metropolitan Authority, 25th Anniv. — A1357

Designs: 12p, Family Monument. 100p, Subic Bay, 25th anniv. emblem, horiz.

2017, Nov. 24 Litho. Perf. 14
3749 A1357 12p multi 1.00 .60

Souvenir Sheet

Perf. 13½

3750 A1357 100p multi 10.00 8.00

No. 3750 contains one 50x35mm stamp.

Christmas — A1358

No. 3751 — Children's art by: a, Roselyn Mahipas. b, Juan Dimata. c, Estella Benavidez. d, Jan Aton.
55p, Children's art by Rhey de Ocampo, horiz.

2017, Nov. 29 Litho. Perf. 13¾
3751 A1358 12p Block or strip of 4, #a-d 5.00 5.00

Souvenir Sheet

Perf. 13½

3752 A1358 55p multi 6.00 5.00

No. 3751 printed in sheets of 16. No. 3752 contains one 50x35mm stamp.

A1359

New Year 2018 (Year of the Dog) A1360

No: 3753 — Dog, with background color of: a, 12p, Light blue. b, 45p, Pink.

2017, Dec. 1 Litho. Perf. 14
3753 A1359 Horiz. pair, #a-b 6.50 5.00

Souvenir Sheet

Litho. & Embossed With Foil Application

Perf.

3754 A1360 200p gold & red 20.00 20.00

No. 3753 printed in sheets of16.

A1361

Famous People — A1362

Designs: No. 3755, Nick Joaquin (1917-2004), writer. No. 3756, José Maceda (1917-2004), composer. No. 3757, Wilfrido Maria Guerrero (1911-95), playwright. No. 3758, Cesar Legaspi (1917-94), painter. No. 3759, Leonor Orosa Goquinco (1917-2005), dancer. No. 3760, Daisy Avellana (1917-2013), actress.

2017, Dec. 13 Litho. Perf. 14
3755 A1361 12p multi 1.20 .75
3756 A1362 12p multi 1.20 .75
3757 A1362 12p multi 1.20 .75
3758 A1362 12p multi 1.20 .75
3759 A1362 12p multi 1.20 .75
3760 A1362 12p multi 1.20 .75
Nos. 3755-3760 (6) 7.20 4.50

Apparition of the Virgin Mary at Fatima, Portugal, Cent. — A1363

No. 3761 — Inscription: a, The Apparition of Our Lady of Fatima. b, Our Lady of Fatima. c, The Miracle of the Sun. d, Lucia Dos Santos, Francisco Marto & Jacinta Marto.

2017, Dec. 14 Litho. Perf. 14
3761 A1363 12p Block of 4, #a-d 5.00 5.00

Printed in sheets of 8.

Teresita "Mama Sita" Reyes (1917-98), Restaurateur — A1364

2017, Dec. 22 Litho. Perf. 13½
3762 A1364 12p multi 1.00 .80

Main Post Office, Manila Type of 2014

2018, Jan. 29 Litho. Perf. 14
3763 A1199 17p multi *10.00 10.00*

No. 3763 was printed in sheets of six that sold for 250p. The right half of the stamp could be personalized. Some sheets were made available with generic images in the blank right half of the stamp. Value of sheet with generic images, $80.

Ilocos Sur Province, 200th Anniv. A1365

No. 3764: a, Bantay Bell Tower. b, Potter. c, Pinsal Falls. d, Bessang Pass.
No. 3765: a, Calle Crisologo. b, Santa Maria Church.

2018, Feb. 8 Litho. Perf. 13¾
3764 A1365 12p Block of 4, #a-d 4.00 3.00

Souvenir Sheet

Perf.

3765 A1365 75p Sheet of 2, #a-b 10.00 9.00

No. 3764 printed in sheets of 16.
No. 3765 sheet is in the shape of "200".

Miniature Sheet

Ilocos Sur Province, 200th Anniv. A1366

No. 3766: a, Bantay Bell Tower. b, Street in Vigan City at night. c, Pinsal Falls. d, Bessang Pass.

2018, Feb. 8 Litho. *Perf. 14*

3766 A1366 17p Sheet of 4, #a-d, + 4 labels 8.00 8.00

No. 3766 exists with blank labels that could be personalized and the printed labels shown, that could not be personalized, each of which sold for 150p.

Municipality of Mabini, Cent. — A1367

No. 3767: a, Centenary emblem. b, Underwater scene, Anilao Beach Resort.

2018, Feb. 10 Litho. *Perf. 14*

3767 A1367 12p Horiz. pair, #a-b 1.50 1.50

St. Valentine's Day — A1368

2018, Feb. 14 Litho. *Perf. 14*

3768 A1368 12p multi .75 .55

Dumaguete Cathedral Credit Cooperative, 50th Anniv. — A1369

2018, Feb. 17 Litho. *Perf. 14*

3769 A1369 12p multi .75 .55

La Castellana Municipality, Cent. — A1370

No. 3770 — Centenary emblem, municipality emblem and: a, Centennial Arch (denomination at UL). b, Municipal building (denomination at UR).

2018, Apr. 5 Litho. *Perf. 14*

3770 A1370 12p Horiz. pair, #a-b 1.50 1.50

Miniature Sheet

Sports A1371

No. 3771: a, Boxing. b, Gymnastics. c, Volleyball. d, Basketball.

2018, Apr. 16 Litho. *Perf. 14*

3771 A1371 17p Sheet of 4, #a-d, + 4 labels 9.00 9.00

No. 3771 sold for 150p. Generic labels are shown, but labels could be personalized.

Flowers — A1372

Designs: 1p, Jasminum sambac. 5p, Hibiscus sp. 12p, Kopsia fruticosa. 17p, Strelitzia reginae. 35p, Pseuderanthemum reticulatum.

2018 Litho. *Perf. 13½*

3772 A1372 1p multi .30 .25
3773 A1372 5p multi .30 .25
3774 A1372 12p multi .75 .55
3775 A1372 17p multi 1.00 .75
3776 A1372 35p multi 2.10 1.60
Nos. 3772-3776 (5) 4.45 3.40

Issued: 1p, 5p, 12p, 35p, 4/23; 17p, 10/9. See Nos. 3813-3818.

Colonial Era Churches — A1373

No. 3777: a, Santa Monica Church, Minalin. b, Santa Catalina de Alejandria Church, Tayum. c, San Matias Church, Tumauini. d, Santa Monica Church, Pan-ay.

No. 3778: a, San Carlos Borromeo Church, Mahatao. b, Santa Catalina de Alejandria Church, Luna. c, Nuestra Señora del Patrocinio de Maria Church, Boljoon. d, Nuestra Señora de la Asuncion Church, Santa Maria. e, Nuestra Señora de la Asuncion Church, Dauis. f, Santo Tomas de Villanueva Church, Miagao.

2018, May 2 Litho. *Perf. 14*

3777 A1373 12p Block or horiz. strip of 4, #a-d 3.00 3.00

Miniature Sheet

3778 A1373 12p Sheet of 6, #a-f 4.50 4.50

Heritage Month.
No. 3777 printed in sheets of 16.

Independence, 120th Anniv. — A1374

2018, June 12 Litho. *Perf. 14*

3779 A1374 12p multi .75 .55

Rotary Club of Manila, Cent. — A1375

Designs: 12p, Centenary emblem. 55p, Two different centenary emblems, horiz.

2018, July 19 Litho. *Perf. 14*

3780 A1375 12p multi .75 .55

Souvenir Sheet

Perf. 13½ Horiz.

3781 A1375 55p multi 5.00 3.50

No. 3781 contains one 85x50mm stamp.

Miniature Sheets

Presidential Automobiles — A1376

No. 3782, 12p: a, 1924 Packard Single-6 Touring car of Pres. Emilio Aguinaldo. b, 1937 Chrysler Airflow Custom Imperial CW of Pres. Manuel L Quezon. c, 1942 Packard Custom Super Eight 180 Limousine of Pres. Jose P. Laurel. d, 1953 Chrysler Crown Imperial Limousine of Pres. Elpidio Quirino. e, 1955 Cadillac Series 75-23 of Pres. Ramon Magsaysay.

No. 3783, 12p: a, 1980 Lincoln Continental Mark VI Signature Series Limousine of Pres. Ferdinand E. Marcos. b, Mercedes-Benz 500SEL of Pres. Corazon C. Aquino. c, Mercedes-Benz 500SEL Guard of Pres. Fidel V. Ramos. d, Mercedes-Benz S600 of Pres. Joseph Ejercito Estrada. e, Mercedes-Benz S600 Limousine V140 of Pres. Gloria Macapagal-Arroyo.

2018, Aug. 10 Litho. *Perf. 14*

Sheets of 5, #a-e

3782-3783 A1376 Set of 2 7.25 7.25

National Teacher's Month — A1377

2018, Aug. 30 Litho. *Perf. 14*

3784 A1377 12p multi .75 .55

Lucrecia R. Kasilag (1918-2008), Composer — A1378

2018, Aug. 31 Litho. *Perf. 14*

3785 A1378 12p multi .75 .55

Christmas — A1379

No. 3786: a, Boy with Puto Bumbong and fruit (1/4). b, Father and daughter with Roast pig and fruit (2/4). c, Mother and son with Pancit noodles and fruit (3/4). d, Girl with Queso de Bola and fruit (4/4).

2018, Oct. 31 Litho. *Perf. 14*

3786 Horiz. strip of 4 3.00 3.00
a.-d. A1379 12p Any single .75 .75

Printed in sheets of 16.

Lakes A1380

No. 3787: a, Lake Danum. b, Lake Balinsasayao. c, Mount Pinatubo Crater Lake. d, Gabawan Lake. e, Lake Apo. f, Lake Sebu.

No. 3788: a, 45p, Kabalin-An Lake. b, 55p, Lake Leonard.

2018 Litho. *Perf. 13½x13¾*

3787 A1380 12p Sheet of 6, #a-f 4.50 4.50

Souvenir Sheet

Litho. With Foil Application

3788 A1380 Sheet of 2, #a-b 6.00 6.00
c. As #3788, with Thailand 2018 World Stamp Exhibition emblem in sheet margin 6.00 6.00

Issued: Nos. 3787-3788, 11/5; No. 3788c, 11/28. No. 3788 contains two 75x35mm stamps.

Philpost Type of 2013

2018, Nov. 8 Litho. *Perf. 13½x13¼*

Denomination Color

3789 A1177 5p olive green .30 .25
3790 A1177 17p red violet .30 .25

Estancia Municipality, Cent. — A1381

No. 3791 — Centenary emblem and: a, Fishing village (denomination at UR). b, Fishing village, diff. (denomination at UL).

2018, Nov. 21 Litho. *Perf. 14*

3791 A1381 12p Horiz. pair, #a-b 1.50 1.50

A1382

New Year 2019 (Year of the Pig) A1383

No. 3792 — Pig with background color of: a, 12p, Blue green. b, 45p, Yellow green.

2018, Nov. 23 Litho. *Perf. 14*

3792 A1382 Horiz. pair, #a-b 3.50 3.50

Souvenir Sheet

Litho. & Embossed With Foil Application

Perf.

3793 A1383 200p gold & multi 12.00 12.00

No. 3792 printed in sheets of 8.

Souvenir Sheet

Diplomatic Relations Between Philippines and Croatia, 25th Anniv. — A1384

No. 3794: a, 12p, St. Michael's Fortress, Sibenik, Croatia. b, 55p, Fort Santiago, Intramuros, Philippines.

2018, Dec. 5 Litho. *Perf. 14*
3794 A1384 Sheet of 2, #a-b 4.00 4.00

See Croatia No. 1099.

Dagupan Doctors Villaflor Memorial Hospital, Dagupan City, 50th Anniv. — A1385

Litho. With Foil Application

2018, Dec. 7 ***Perf. 14***
3795 A1385 12p gold & multi .75 .55

Pangasinan Province Capital Builiding, Cent. — A1386

No. 3796 — Capital Building with: a, Dark brown background. b, Sky in background.

2018, Dec. 17 Litho. *Perf. 14*
3796 A1386 12p Horiz. pair, #a-b 1.50 1.50

General Santos City, 50th Anniv. A1387

No. 3797: a, General Santos City Tuna Festival. b, Fresh tuna. c, Statue of General Paulino A. Santos. d, General Santos Plaza.

2018, Dec. 10 Litho. *Perf. 14*
3797 A1387 12p Block or horiz. strip of 4, #a-d 3.00 3.00

Printed in sheets of 16.

University of the Visayas, Cent. — A1388

2019, Jan. 12 Litho. *Perf. 14*
3798 A1388 12p multi .75 .55

St. Valentine's Day — A1389

No. 3799: a, King of Hearts. b, Queen of Hearts.

2019, Feb. 1 Litho. *Perf. 14*
3799 A1389 12p Horiz. pair, #a-b 1.50 1.50

Printed in sheets of 8.

A1390

Catriona Gray, 2018 Miss Universe A1391

2019, Feb. 27 Litho. *Perf. 13¾*
3800 A1390 12p multi .75 .55

Souvenir Sheet

3801 A1391 55p multi 3.50 3.50

Manila Central Post Office A1392

2019, Mar. 22 Litho. *Perf. 14*
3802 A1392 17p multi + label — —

No. 3802 was printed in sheets of 4 + 4 labels that sold for 150p. Sheets were available with labels that could be personalized, which were first made available on Mar. 22, 2019, and with labels that had pre-printed images that could not be personalized, such as the label shown, which were produced in 2018 and later years.

No. 3802 exists dated "2022" and "2023" from sheets of 4 + 4 labels issued that year that sold for 150p. It is not known if th labels on these sheets could be personalized.

Compare with No. 3964.

A1393

Emilio Aguinaldo (1869-1964), First President of the Philippines — A1394

2019, Mar. 22 Litho. *Perf. 13¾*
3803 A1393 12p multi .75 .55

Souvenir Sheet

3804 A1394 55p multi 3.50 3.50

"100" and Map of Philippines — A1395

2019, Apr. 4 Litho. *Perf. 14*
3805 A1395 12p multi .75 .55

Tribute to Filipino centenarians. No. 3805 was printed in sheets of 40. Sheets containing four stamps and four labels were printed in limited quantities: 500 generic sheets with 4 blank labels printed, and 1,000 sheets with blank labels. The latter were given free to centenarians.

Claudio Teehankee (1918-89), Chief Justice — A1396

2019, Apr. 18 Litho. *Perf. 14*
3806 A1396 12p multi .75 .55

Francisco V. Coching (1919-98), Comic Book Illustrator A1397

2019, Apr. 19 Litho. *Perf. 14*
3807 A1397 12p multi .75 .55

Edith L. Tiempo (1919-2011), Writer — A1398

2019, Apr. 19 Litho. *Perf. 14*
3808 A1398 12p multi .75 .55

Women at Work A1399

No. 3809: a, Laguna rafters. b, Aurora hat weavers. c, Badjao mat weaver. d, Ilocos burnay potter. e, T'boli beadworker. f, Liliw coconut sap collector. g, Ifugao farmer. h, Tawi-Tawi seaweed farmer.

2019, May 9 Litho. *Perf. 14*
3809 A1399 12p Block of 8, #a-h 6.00 6.00

Heritage Month. Printed in sheets of 16.

Victorias Milling Company, Cent. — A1400

Centenary emblem and: 12p, Sugar mill. 55p, Sugar mill, diff.

2019, May 17 Litho. *Perf. 14*
3810 A1400 12p multi .75 .55

Souvenir Sheet

Perf. 14 Horiz.

3811 A1400 55p multi 3.50 3.50

No. 3811 contains one 85x50mm stamp.

Butterflies — A1401

No. 3812 — Flags of the Philippines and Singapore and: a, 12p, Common rose butterfly. b, 45p, Luzon lacewing butterfly.

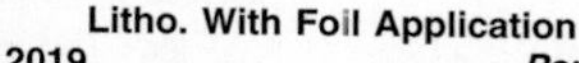

Litho. With Foil Application

2019 ***Perf. 14***
3812 A1401 Horiz. pair, #a-b 3.50 3.50
c. Sheet of 4, 2 each #3812a-3812b, with Singpex 2019 emblem added in sheet margin 7.00 7.00

Diplomatic relations between Philippines and Singapore, 50th anniv. Issued: No. 3812, 5/16; No. 3812c, 7/31. No. 3812 was printed in sheets containing two pairs. See Singapore Nos. 1969-1970.

Flowers Type of 2018

Designs: 14p, Rafflesia. 45p, Everlasting. 50p, Blue plumbago. 55p, Lobster claws. 60p, Lantana. 100p, Bougainvillea.

2019 Litho. *Perf. 13½*
3813 A1372 14p multi .85 .65
3814 A1372 45p multi 2.75 2.10
3815 A1372 50p multi 3.00 2.25
3816 A1372 55p multi 3.50 2.60
3817 A1372 60p multi 3.75 2.75

Size: 30x30mm

Perf. 13¼

3818 A1372 100p multi 6.00 4.50
Nos. 3813-3818 (6) 19.85 14.85

Issued: 14p, 45p, 8/28; 100p, 6/10; 50p, 55p, 60p, 9/21.

Souvenir Sheet

New Year 2019 (Year of the Pig) A1402

Litho., Sheet Margin Litho. With Foil Application

2019, June 11 ***Perf. 13½***
3819 A1402 100p gold & multi 6.00 6.00
a. As #3819, with China 2019 World Stamp Exhibition emblem added in sheet margin 6.00 6.00

Diplomatic Relations Between the Philippines and Thailand, 70th Anniv. — A1403

No. 3820 — Flags of the Philippines and Thailand and: a, 12p, Elephant. b, 45p, Carabao.

2019, June 14 Litho. *Perf. 14*
3820 A1403 Horiz. pair, #a-b 3.50 3.50

Printed in sheets of 8.
See Thailand No. 3062.

Souvenir Sheet

New Year 2018 (Year of the Dog) A1404

Litho., Sheet Margin Litho. With Foil Application

2019, July 11 ***Perf. 13½***
3821 A1404 100p gold & multi 6.00 6.00

National Electrification Administration, 50th Anniv. — A1405

2019, Aug. 6 Litho. *Perf. 14*
3822 A1405 12p multi .75 .55

Man and Woman Wearing Traditional Filipino Clothing — A1406

2019, Aug. 8 Litho. *Perf. 13¾*

3823 A1406 12p multi .75 .55

National Teacher's Month — A1407

No. 3824: a, Student's raised hand. b, Stylized teacher and student reading.

2019, Sept. 5 Litho. *Perf. 13¾*

3824 A1407 12p Horiz. pair, #a-b 1.50 1.50

Express Mail Service, 20th Anniv. — A1408

2019, Sept. 10 Litho. *Perf. 14*

3825 A1408 45p multi 2.75 2.10

Philippine Cinema, Cent. — A1409

José Nepomuceno (1893-1959), Film Director and Producer — A1410

2019, Sept. 12 Litho. *Perf. 14*

3826 A1409 12p multi .75 .55

Souvenir Sheet

Perf. 13¾

3827 A1410 55p multi 3.50 3.50

Cultural Center of the Philippines, Manila, 50th Anniv. — A1411

2019, Oct. 15 Litho. *Perf. 14*

3828 A1411 12p multi .75 .55

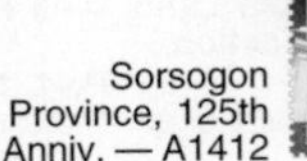
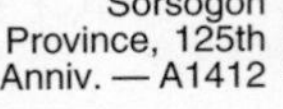

Sorsogon Province, 125th Anniv. — A1412

2019, Oct. 17 Litho. *Perf. 14*

3829 A1412 12p multi .75 .55

Leyte Gulf Landing, 75th Anniv. A1413

No. 3830: a, MacArthur's Landing, sculpture by Anastacio Caedo. b, Gen. Douglas MacArthur and others walking ashore at Leyte Gulf.

2019, Oct. 20 Litho. *Perf. 14*

3830 A1413 12p Horiz. pair, #a-b 1.50 1.10

St. Raphael, the Archangel Parish, Pili, 200th Anniv. — A1414

Designs: 12p, Church and text. 55p, Church.

2019, Oct. 24 Litho. *Perf. 14*

3831 A1414 12p multi .75 .55

Souvenir Sheet

Perf. 13¾

3832 A1414 55p multi 3.50 3.50

No. 3832 contains one 35x50mm stamp.

Pinoy Rock Music Stars — A1415

No. 3833: a, Rene Garcia (1953-2018). b, Rico J. Puno (1953-2018). c, Pepe Smith (1947-2019).

Litho., Sheet Margin Litho. With Foil Application

2019, Nov. 11 *Perf.*

3833 Souvenir sheet of 3 8.25 8.25

a.-c. A1415 45p Any single 2.75 2.10

Miniature Sheets

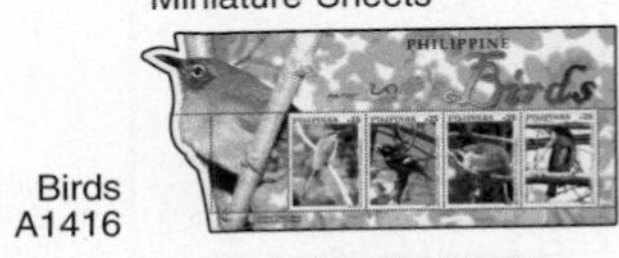

Birds A1416

Mushrooms — A1417

Rivers A1418

Shrimp A1419

No. 3834: a, Blue-tailed bee-eater. b, Visayan broadbill. c, Mountain white-eye. d, Fire-breasted flowerpecker.

No. 3835: a, Brittle gill fungus. b, Earthstar. c, Circular bracket fungus. d, Parasol mushrooms.

No. 3836: a, Bayabas River. b, Baroro River. c, Cantingas River. d, Enchanted River.

No. 3837: a, Brilliant red carid. b, Domino shrimp. c, Mino nylon shrimp. d, Rock shrimp. e, Narwal soldier shrimp.

2019, Nov. Litho. *Perf. 14*

3834 A1416 25p Sheet of 4, #a-d, + label 6.00 6.00

3835 A1417 25p Sheet of 4, #a-d, + 3 labels 6.00 6.00

3836 A1418 25p Sheet of 4, #a-d, + label 6.00 6.00

3837 A1419 25p Sheet of 5, #a-e 7.50 7.50

Nos. 3834-3837 (4) 25.50 25.50

Issued: 3834, 3836, 11/20; 3835, 3837, 11/21.

Christmas — A1420

No. 3838 — Choir members and: a, Lyrist. b, Guitarist. c, Piper, drummer and tambourine player. d, Maracas player.

2019, Nov. 25 Litho. *Perf. 14*

3838 A1420 12p Block of 4, #a-d 3.00 3.00

Printed in sheets of 16.

A1421

Southeast Asian Games, 30th Anniv. — A1422

No. 3839: a, Weight lifting. b, Badminton. c, Cycling. d, Billiards.

No. 3840: a, 12p, Clasped hands (30x30mm). b, 55p, Tennis player, handicapped runner, gymnast (60x30mm).

2019, Nov. 30 Litho. *Perf. 14*

3839 A1421 12p Block of 4, #a-d 3.00 3.00

Souvenir Sheet

Perf. 13¼

3840 A1422 Sheet of 2, #a-b 4.00 4.00

Printed in sheets of 8.

International Civil Aviation Organization, 75th Anniv. — A1423

Designs: 12p, Emblems of ICAO and Civil Aviation Authority of the Philippines, map of Asia, airplanes, control tower.

55p, Airplanes and emblem of the ICAO and Civil Aviation Authority of the Philippines, horiz.

2019, Dec. 7 Litho. *Perf. 14*

3841 A1423 12p multi .75 .55

Souvenir Sheet

Perf. 13¾

3842 A1423 55p multi 3.50 3.50

No. 3832 contains one 50x35mm stamp.

Commission on Higher Education, 25th Anniv. — A1424

2019, Dec. 9 Litho. *Perf. 14*

3843 A1424 12p multi .75 .55

A1425

New Year 2020 (Year of the Rat) A1426

No. 3844 — Rat with background color of: a, 12p, Lemon. b, 45p, Pink.

2019, Dec. 13 Litho. *Perf. 14*

3844 A1425 Horiz. pair, #a-b 2.75 2.10

Souvenir Sheet

Litho. & Embossed With Foil Application

Perf.

3845 A1426 200p gold & multi 12.00 12.00

Cebu Province, 450th Anniv. — A1427

2019, Dec. 16 Litho. *Perf. 14*

3846 A1427 12p multi .75 .55

Chartering of Mandaue City, 50th Anniv. — A1428

2019, Dec. 20 Litho. *Perf. 14*

3847 A1428 12p multi .75 .55

Miniature Sheet

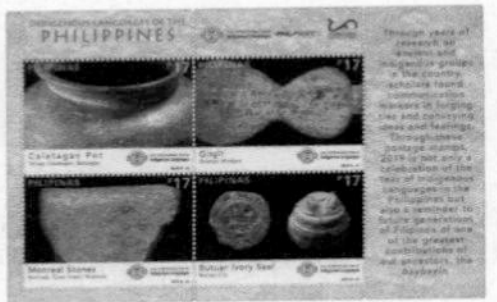

International Year of Indigenous Languages — A1429

No. 3848: a, Calatagan pot. b, Gitgit. c, Monreal stones. d, Butuan ivory seal.

2019, Dec. 23 Litho. *Perf. 13¾*

3848 A1429 17p Sheet of 4, #a-d 4.25 4.25

Municipality of Consolacion, Cent. — A1430

2020, Jan. 23 Litho. *Perf. 14*

3849 A1430 12p multi .75 .55

Valentine's Day — A1431

No. 3850 — Heart and inscription: a, Love Nature. b, Love for Country. c, Love Knows No Gender. d, Love Yourself.

2020, Feb. 6 Litho. *Perf. 14*
3850 A1431 12p Block of 4, #a-d 3.00 2.25

Battle of Manila, 75th Anniv. — A1432

2020, Feb. 15 Litho. *Perf. 14*
3851 A1432 12p multi .75 .55

A1433

Aboitiz & Company, Cent. — A1434

2020, Apr. 27 Litho. *Perf. 14*
3852 A1433 12p multi .75 .55

Souvenir Sheet
Perf.
3853 A1434 55p multi 3.50 3.50

A1435

Traditional Games — A1436

No. 3854: a, 12p, Jack-en-Poy (Rock, Paper, Scissors). b, 14p, Bahay-bahayan (Playing house). c, 15p, Luksong Tinik (Jumping over thorns). d, 17p, Trumpo (Top spinning).

No. 3855: a, 45p, Jolen and Piko (Marbles and Hopscotch). b, 55p, Tumband Preso and Saranggola (Knock Down the Prisoner and Kite Flying).

2020, May 2 Litho. *Perf. 14*
3854 A1435 Block of 4, #a-d 3.50 2.60

Souvenir Sheet
Perf. 13¾
3855 A1436 Sheet of 2, #a-b 6.00 6.00

A1437

Tribute to Workers During the COVID-19 Pandemic A1438

No. 3856 — Inscription: a, Nurses. b, Military personnel. c, Grocery personnel. d, Police officers. e, Doctors. f, Delivery personnel. g, Medical technicians. h, Chefs.

2020, July 13 Litho. *Perf. 13¾*
3856 A1437 12p Block of 8, #a-h 5.75 4.50

Souvenir Sheet
3857 A1438 55p multi 3.50 3.50

National Teachers' Month — A1439

No. 3858 — Inscription: a, 12p, I am good. b, 14p, I am a star. c, 15p, I am bright. d, 17p, I am brave.

2020, Sept. 4 Litho. *Perf. 14*
3858 A1439 Block of 4, #a-d 3.50 2.60

Camarines Norte Province, Cent. — A1440

2020, Sept. 14 Litho. *Perf. 14*
3859 A1440 12p multi .75 .55

Christmas — A1441

2020, Nov. 23 Litho. *Perf. 14*
3860 A1441 12p multi .75 .55

Salinta Monon (1920-2009), Textile Weaver — A1442

2020, Dec. 12 Litho. *Perf. 14*
3861 A1442 12p multi .75 .55

Shells — A1443

Designs: 1p, Hebrew cone. 5p, Black-striped or liver triton. 12p, Banded trochus snail. 14p, Asian moon scallop. 17p, Martini's tibia. 35p, Pontifical mitre. 45p, Yoka star turban. 100p, Fluted giant clam, horiz.

2020-21 Litho. *Perf. 13¾*

3862	A1443	1p multi	.25	.25
3863	A1443	5p multi	.30	.25
3864	A1443	12p multi	.75	.55
3865	A1443	14p multi	.85	.65
3866	A1443	17p multi	1.10	.85
3867	A1443	35p multi	2.10	1.10
3868	A1443	45p multi	2.75	2.10

Size: 40x30mm
Perf. 14

3869	A1443	100p multi	6.00	4.50
	Nos. 3862-3869 (8)		14.10	10.25

Issued: 1p, 5p, 12p, 35p, 12/21; 14p, 100p, 1/13/21; 17p, 45p, 1/6/21. 14p, 17p, 45p, 100p are dated 2020.

Souvenir Sheet

New Year 2020 (Year of the Rat) A1444

Litho., Sheet Margin Litho With Foil Application
2020, Dec. 28 *Perf. 13½*
3870 A1444 100p gold & multi 6.00 6.00

A1445

New Year 2021 (Year of the Ox) A1446

No. 3871: a, 12p, Ox in hay. b, 45p, Ox standing.

2020, Dec. 28 Litho. *Perf. 14*
3871 A1445 Horiz. pair #a-b 3.50 2.60

Souvenir Sheet
Litho. & Embossed With Foil Application
Perf.
3872 A1446 200p gold & multi 12.00 12.00

China Bank, Cent. (in 2020) A1447

No. 3873: a, Bank building, Binondo. b, Centennial emblem.

2021, Jan. 26 Litho. *Perf. 14*
3873 A1447 12p Horiz. pair, #a-b 1.50 1.10
Dated 2020.

Valentine's Day — A1448

2021, Feb. 10 Litho. *Perf. 14*
3874 A1448 12p multi .75 .60

A1449

A1450

A1451

A1452

A1453

A1454

A1455

A1456

A1457

A1458

A1459

A1460

1734 Map and Illustrations, by Pedro Murillo Velarde — A1461

2021, Mar. 16 **Litho.** ***Perf. 14x13¼***
3875

Del Carmen Municipality, Cent. — A1461a

2021, Mar. 19 **Litho.** ***Perf. 14***
3875N A1461a 12p multi .75 .60

Dated 2020. First day covers have 7/16/20 cancel, but stamps were not issued until 3/19/21.

Balasan Municipality, 125th Anniv. — A1461b

2021, Mar. 19 **Litho.** ***Perf. 14***
3875O A1461b 12p multi .75 .60

Dated 2020. First day covers have 7/10/20 cancel, but stamps were not issued until 3/19/21.

a.	A1449 12p multi	.75	.60
b.	A1450 12p multi	.75	.60
c.	A1451 12p multi	.75	.60
d.	A1452 14p multi	.85	.65
e.	A1453 14p multi	.85	.65
f.	A1454 14p multi	.85	.65
g.	A1455 17p multi	1.10	.85
h.	A1456 45p multi	2.75	2.10
i.	A1457 45p multi	2.75	2.10
j.	A1458 50p multi	3.00	2.25
k.	A1459 55p multi	3.25	2.50
l.	A1460 60p multi	3.75	3.00
m.	A1461 150p multi	9.00	6.75

Christianity in the Philippines, 500th Anniv. — A1462

No. 3876: a, Limasawa Island, site of first Easter Mass in the Philippines. b, Priest celebrating Mass.

2021, Mar. 22 **Litho.** ***Perf. 14***
3876 A1462 12p Horiz. pair, #a-b 1.50 1.50

Arrival of Santo Niño de Cebu Icon in the Philippines, 500th Anniv. — A1463

No. 3877: a, Santo Niño de Cebu icon. b, 500th anniversary emblem.

2021, Apr. 14 **Litho.** ***Perf. 14***
3877 A1463 12p Horiz. pair, #a-b 1.50 1.50

Printed in sheets of 10.

Liberty Shrine, Lapu-Lapu City — A1464

2021, Apr. 27 **Litho.** ***Perf. 14***
3878 A1464 12p multi .75 .60

Battle of Mactan and death of Ferdinand Magellan, 500th anniv. Printed in sheets of 10.

Boats A1465

No. 3879: a, Vinta. b, Casco. c, Boanga. d, Salisipan. e, Balangay. f, Paraw. g, Panco. h, Guilalo. i, Parao Mangayaw. j, Caracoa.
55p, Bancas Filipinas.

2021, May 18 **Litho.** ***Perf. 14***
3879 A1465 12p Sheet of 10, #a-j 7.25 7.25

Souvenir Sheet
Perf. 13½

3880 A1465 55p multi 6.75 6.75

No. 3880 contains one 50x35mm stamp.

1971 Constitutional Convention, 50th Anniv. — A1466

2021, June 1 **Litho.** ***Perf. 14***
3881 A1466 12p multi .75 .60

City of Manila, 450th Anniv. A1467

No. 3882: a, Jones Bridge. b, City Hall Clock Tower.

2021, Apr. 14 **Litho.** ***Perf. 14***
3882 A1467 12p Horiz. pair, #a-b 1.50 1.50

Two 17p stamps, depicting the Bonifacio Shrine and Scyphiphora flowers were printed in limited quantities in sheets of 4 stamps + 4 labels that could not be personalized that sold for 150p.

Diplomatic Relations Between the Philippines and the United States, 75th Anniv. — A1468

2021, July 4 **Litho.** ***Perf. 13½***
3883 A1468 12p multi .75 .60

Paulino Txanton Aboitiz, Hemp Trader, 150th Anniv. of Birth — A1469

Aboitiz and hemp rope coils at: 12p, Right. 55p, Left and right, horiz.

2021, July 27 **Litho.** ***Perf. 14***
3884 A1469 12p multi .75 .60

Souvenir Sheet
Perf. 13½

3885 A1469 55p multi 3.25 3.25

No. 3885 contains one 50x35mm stamp.

Pres. Benigno S. Aquino III (1960-2021) — A1470

2021, Aug. 2 **Litho.** ***Perf. 14***
3886 A1470 12p multi .75 .60

National Teachers' Month — A1471

2021, Sept. 6 **Litho.** ***Perf. 14***
3887 A1471 12p multi .75 .60

University of Bohol, 75th Anniv. — A1472

2021, Sept. 10 **Litho.** ***Perf. 14***
3888 A1472 12p multi .75 .60

Miniature Sheet

Campaign for COVID-19 Vaccination — A1473

No. 3889 — Hypodermic needle, map of Philippines and vaccinated: a, 12p, Man and woman (dark red panels). b, 12p, Man (blue panels). c, 14p, Man and woman (bister panels). d, 14p, Woman (brown orange panels). e, 15p, Man and woman (gray blue panels). f, 15p, Man, (violet panels). g, 17p, Woman (green panels). h, 17p, Man and woman (rose panels).

2021, Sept. 16 **Litho.** ***Perf. 13½***
3889 A1473 Sheet of 8, #a-h 7.00 7.00

Philippine Medalists at 2020 Summer Olympics — A1474

No. 3890: a, 12p, Hidilyn F. Diaz, weight lifting gold medalist. b, 14p, Nesthy A. Petecio, boxing silver medalist. c, 15p, Carlo C. Paalam, boxing silver medalist. d, 17p, Eumer D. S. Marcial, boxing bronze medalist.
55p, Diaz, Petecio, Paalam and Marcial.

2021, Sept. 18 **Litho.** ***Perf. 14***
3890 A1474 Block of 4, #a-d 3.50 3.50

Souvenir Sheet
Perf. 13¼

3891 A1474 55p multi 3.25 3.25

The 2020 Summer Olympics were postponed until 2021 because of the COVID-19 pandemic. No. 3891 contains one 30x60mm stamp. No. 3890 printed in sheets of 8.

Hidilyn F. Diaz, First Filipino Olympic Gold Medalist A1475

No. 3892 — Diaz: a, 12p, Preparing to lift weights (green circle). b, 12p, Lifting weights (blue circle). c, 12p, Wearing protective mask and gold medal, holding flowers (green circle). d, 14p, Lifting weights (black circle). e, 14p, Celebrating (red circle). f, 14p, Holding gold medal (black circle). g, 15p, Lifting weights (blue circle). h, 15p, Celebrating (blue circle). i, 17p, Lifting weights (red circle). g, Wearing protective mask and gold medal, holding flowers (red circle).
100p, Diaz lifting weights.

2021, Sept. 18 **Litho.** ***Perf. 14***
3892 A1475 Sheet of 10, #a-j 8.50 8.50

Souvenir Sheet
Litho., Sheet Margin Litho. With Foil Application
Perf.

3893 A1475 100p multi 12.00 12.00

No. 3893 contains one 38mm diameter stamp.

Grandparent's Day — A1476

2021, Sept. 27 **Litho.** ***Perf. 14***
3894 A1476 12p multi .75 .60

Robert Jaworski, Basketball Player — A1477

No. 3895 — Jaworski: a, Holding ball for free throw (stamp 1/8). b, Dribbling and pointing finger (stamp 2/8). c, Wearing Gordon's Gin uniform (stamp 3/8). d, Making layup shot (stamp 4/8). e, Holding basketball on palm (stamp 5/8). f, Running, holding basketball with both hands (stamp 6/8). g, Holding basketall in process of dribbling (stamp 7/8). h, Running, holding basketball with one hand (stamp 8/8).
60p, Jaworski dribbling basketball.

2021, Oct. 16 **Litho.** ***Perf. 13¾***
3895 A1477 17p Sheet of 8, #a-h 8.75 8.75

Souvenir Sheet

Perf. 13¼

3896 A1477 60p multi 3.75 3.75

No. 3896 contains one 30x60mm stamp.

World Reknowned Filipinos A1478

No. 3897: a, Efren "Bata" Reyes, world champion pool player (stamp 1/10). b, Josie Natori, fashion designer (stamp 2/10). c, Jordan Clarkson, professional basketball player (stamp 3/10). d, Lea Salonga, singer and actress (stamp 4/10). e, Diosdado "Dado" Banatao, computer engineer and entrepreneur (stamp 5/10). f, Monique Lhuillier, fashion designer (stamp 6/10). g, Kenneth Cobonpue, industrial designer (stamp 7/10). h, Mascot for Jollibee Restaurants (stamp 8/10). i, Eugene Torre, chess grandmaster (stamp 9/10). j, Rafael "Paeng" Nepomuceno, world champion bowler (stamp 10/10).

2021, Nov. 13 Litho. ***Perf. 13¾***

3897 Sheet of 10 10.00 10.00

a.-j. A1478 16p Any single 1.00 .75

St. La Salle Hall of De La Salle University, Manila, Cent. — A1479

2021, Nov. 22 Litho. ***Perf. 14***

3898 A1479 12p dp green .75 .60

Christmas — A1480

No. 3899 — Various people celebrating Christmas with inscription at bottom of: a, "Narito na, Pasko ng Pag-asa" (Here it is, the Christmas of Hope). b, "Sama-sama pa rin tayo ngayong Pasko" (We are still together this Christmas). c, "Taus-pusong pananalig sa Paskong puno ng Pag-ibig" (Whole-hearted faith in Christmas full of love). d, "Maniwala, magtiwala, Pasko ng Himala" (Trust, believe, Christmas of miracles).

2021, Dec. 3 Litho. ***Perf. 14***

3899 A1480 12p Block of 4, #a-d 3.00 3.00

City of Bislig, Cent. A1481

No. 3900 — Philippine eagle and: a, Centennial poster. b, Tinuy-an Falls. c, Kawa Kawa Hills. d, Karawasan Festival.

2021, Dec. 15 Litho. ***Perf. 14***

3900 A1481 12p Block of 4, #a-d 3.00 3.00

Printed in sheets of 8.

Famous People — A1482

No. 3901: a, Olivia "Bong" Coo, world champion bowler (stamp 1/10). b, Gloria Romero, actress (stamp 2/10). c, Ramon Fernandez, basketball player (stamp 3/10). d, Vilma Santos, actress and politician (stamp 4/10). e, Romulo Galicano, painter (stamp 5/10). f, Susan Roces (1941-2022), actress (stamp 6/10). g, Dr. Baldomero Olivera, chemist (stamp 7/10). h, Rosa Rosal, actress (stamp 8/10). i, Dr. Ernesto Ochoa Domingo, physician (stamp 9/10). j, Nora Aunor, actress (stamp 10/10).

2021, Dec. 28 Litho. ***Perf. 13¾***

3901 Sheet of 10 10.00 10.00

a.-j. A1482 16p Any single 1.00 .75

José Rizal (1861-96), National Hero — A1483

No. 3902 — Rizal: a, With hand over heart. b, Holding book. c, Writing. d, Being executed.

2021, Dec. 30 Litho. ***Perf. 14***

3902 A1483 12p Block of 4, #a-d 3.00 3.00

A1484

New Year 2022 (Year of the Tiger) A1485

No. 3903 — Tiger: a, 12p, Raising paw. b, 45p, Roaring.

2022, Jan. 31 Litho. ***Perf. 14***

3903 A1484 Horiz. pair, #a-b 3.50 3.50

Souvenir Sheet

Litho. & Embossed With Foil Application

Perf.

3904 A1485 200p gold & multi 12.00 12.00

Miniature Sheet

Valentine's Day — A1486

No. 3905 — Heart with inscription: a, "Titibok pa rin." (stamp 1/8) b, "Magmamahal pa rin." (stamp 2/8). c, "Lalaban pa rin." (stamp 3/8). d, "Nagmamalasakit pa rin." (stamp 4/8). e, "Nagmamahal pa rin." (stamp 5/8). f, "Titibok para rin sa bayan." (stamp 6/8). g, "Buo pa rin." (stamp 7/8). h, "Lumalaban pa rin." (stamp 8/8).

2022, Feb. 10 Litho. ***Perf. 13¾***

3905 A1486 12p Sheet of 8, #a-h 5.75 5.75

Yuka Saso, 2021 United States Women's Open Golf Champion — A1487

No. 3906 — Saso: a, 12p, Holding putter. b, 14p, Addressing ball. c, 15p, Finishing swing. d, 17p, Holding trophy.

2022, Feb. 22 Litho. ***Perf. 14***

3906 A1487 Block of 4, #a-d 3.50 3.50

Printed in sheets of 8.

Fall of Bataan, 80th Anniv. — A1488

2022, Apr. 9 Litho. ***Perf. 14***

3907 A1488 12p multi .75 .60

Map of Philippine Rise — A1489

2022, Apr. 25 Litho. ***Perf. 14***

3908 A1489 12p multi .75 .60

Territorial claim of Philippines government of Philippine Rise continental shelf, 10th anniv.

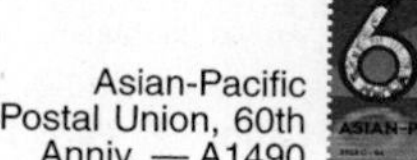

Asian-Pacific Postal Union, 60th Anniv. — A1490

2022, Apr. 28 Litho. ***Perf. 14***

3909 A1490 12p multi .75 .60

Miniature Sheets

A1491

National Heritage Month A1492

No. 3910 — Cartoons by Lauro "Larry" Alcala depicting: a, Batangas shellcraft makers (stamp 1/8). b, Cebu guitar makers (stamp 2/8). c, Bohol basket weavers (stamp 3/8). d, Bicol blacksmith (stamp 4/8). e, Bulacan mat weavers (stamp 5/8). f, Taal embroiderers (stamp 6/8). g, Ilocos potters (stamp 7/8). h, Iloilo rattan furniture makers (stamp 8/8).

No. 3911 — Details from "Cooking for a Fiesta" cartoon by Alcala, showing: a, House, tree, man with cart. b, People cooking food. c, House, men moving stove. d, House, horse cart, man chasing chickens.

2022, May 20 Litho. ***Perf. 14***

3910 A1491 12p Sheet of 8, #a-h 5.75 5.75

3911 A1492 17p Sheet of 4, #a-d 4.25 4.25

Miniature Sheet

Execution of Catholic Priests by Spanish Colonial Authorities, 150th Anniv. — A1493

No. 3912 — Inscriptions: a, "Kilusang Sekularisasyon." b, "Gomburza." c, "Pagmamalabis at Pag-aglahi." d, "1872 Pag-aaklas sa Kabite." e, "Paghatol, Pagbibintang." f, "Mga Taong nagmamahal sa 3 Pari." g, "Pebrero 17, 1872." h, "Pagsiklab ng Himagsikan."

2022, June 12 Litho. ***Perf. 14***

3912 A1493 12p Sheet of 8, #a-h 5.75 5.75

Independence Day.

Department of Finance, 125th Anniv. — A1494

2022, June 28 Litho. ***Perf. 14***

3913 A1494 12p multi .75 .60

Kidapawan City, 75th Anniv. — A1495

No. 3914: a, Lake Venado, Mount Apo Natural Park. b, Kidapawan Municipal Hall. c, Fruits at Fruit Festival. d, Paniki Falls, Eco-River Park.

2022, Aug. 18 Litho. ***Perf. 14***

3914 Block of 4 3.00 3.00

a.-d. A1495 12p Any single .75 .60

National Teacher's Month — A1496

2022, Oct. 5 Litho. ***Perf. 14***

3915 A1496 12p multi .75 .60

Ormoc City, 75th Anniv. — A1497

2022, Oct. 20 Litho. *Perf. 14*

3916 A1497 12p multi .75 .60

Holy Name University, Tagbilaran City, 75th Anniv. — A1498

No. 3917 — University crest and crest of Holy Name College, and: a, Green building. b, Brown building. c, Brown, green and yellow green buildings.

55p, Father Alphonse Lesage (1905-77), founder, vert.

2022, Nov. 1 Litho. *Perf. 14*

3917 Horiz. strip of 3 3.50 3.50
- *a.* A1498 16p multi 1.00 .75
- *b.* A1498 18p multi 1.10 .85
- *c.* A1498 21p multi 1.30 1.00

Souvenir Sheet

Perf. 13¾

3918 A1498 55p multi 3.50 3.50

No. 3918 contains one 35x50mm stamp.

Inauguration of Pres. Ferdinand Marcos, Jr. — A1499

Pres. Marcos: 12p, Taking oath. 55p, Behind microphones, vert.

2022, Nov. 17 Litho. *Perf. 14*

3919 A1499 12p multi .75 .60

Souvenir Sheet

Perf. 13¾

3920 A1499 55p multi 3.50 3.50

No. 3920 contains one 35x50mm stamp.

Inauguration of Vice President Sara Z. Duterte — A1500

Vice President Duterte: 12p, Taking oath. 55p, Behind microphones, vert.

2022, Nov. 17 Litho. *Perf. 14*

3921 A1500 12p multi .75 .60

Souvenir Sheet

Perf. 13¾

3922 A1500 55p multi 3.50 3.50

No. 3922 contains one 35x50mm stamp.

Pres. Fidel V. Ramos (1928-2022) — A1501

Pres. Ramos: 12p, Wearing military cap. 55p, Standing next to flag.

2022, Nov. 25 Litho. *Perf. 14*

3923 A1501 12p multi .75 .60

Souvenir Sheet

Perf. 13¾

3924 A1501 55p multi 3.50 3.50

National Stamp Collecting Month. No. 3924 contains one 35x50mm stamp.

Christmas — A1502

No. 3925 — People celebrating Christmas with stamps numbered: a, 1/4. b, 2/4. c, 3/4. d, 4/4.

2022, Dec. 7 Litho. *Perf. 13¾*

3925 A1502 12p Block of 4, #a-d 3.00 3.00

Philippines Delegation to Third United Nations Conference on the Law of the Sea, 1973 — A1503

2022, Dec. Litho. *Perf. 14*

3926 A1503 12p multi .75 .60

Third United Nations Conference on the Law of the Sea, 40th anniv.

St. Mary's Academy, Pasay City, Cent. — A1504

2023, Jan. 20 Litho. *Perf. 14*

3927 A1504 12p multi .75 .60

Dated 2022.

Miniature Sheet

First Circumnavigation of the Earth, 500th Anniv. (in 2021) — A1505

No. 3928 — Inscriptions: a, Humanity in Homonhon, 18 March 1521. b, Friendship with Rajah Calanao of Kipit, May 1521. c, Introduction of Christianity in Mazawa, 31 March 1521. d, Introduction of Christianity in Cebu, 14 April 1521. e, Crossing the Pacific, November 1520-March 1521. f, Ferdinand Magellan. g, Victoria, the Ship that First Circumnavigated the World. h, Battle of Mactan, 27 April 1521. i, Mutiny Against Magellan, April 1520. j, Emperor Charles Approves Magellan's Expedition, 22 March 1518. k, Return to Spain, 6 September 1521. l, Arrival in Maluku, 8 November 1521.

2023, Jan. 20 Litho. *Perf. 14*

3928 A1505 12p Sheet of 12, #a-l 8.75 8.75

Dated 2022. Compare with Type A1537.

A1506

New Year 2023 (Year of the Rabbit) A1507

No. 3929 — Rabbit: a, 12p, Facing left. b, 45p, Head.

2023, Jan. 20 Litho. *Perf. 14*

3929 A1506 Horiz. pair, #a-b 3.50 3.50

Souvenir Sheet

Litho. & Embossed With Foil Application

Perf.

3930 A1507 200p gold & multi 12.00 12.00

Dated 2022. No. 3929 printed in sheets of 8.

Development Bank of the Philippines, 75th Anniv. (in 2022) — A1508

No. 3931 — 75th anniversary emblem and: a, Bank building (1/4). b, Various development projects (2/4). c, Bank building, diff. (3/4). d, Bank building, diff. (4/4).

100p, Bank building, vert.

2023, Jan. 20 Litho. *Perf. 14*

3931 A1508 12p Block of 4, #a-d 3.00 3.00

Souvenir Sheet

Perf. 13¾

3932 A1508 100p multi 6.00 6.00

No. 3932 contains one 35x50mm stamp.

St. Valentine's Day — A1509

No. 3933 — Inscription: a, Pusong Nagmamahal (Loving heart) (1/4). b, Pusong para sa Iyo (Heart for you) (2/4). c, Itong Puso Ko (This is my heart) (3/4). d, Ikaw ang Puso Ko (You are my heart) (4/4).

2023, Feb. 10 Litho. *Perf. 14*

3933 A1509 16p Block of 4, #a-d 4.00 4.00

SEMI-POSTAL STAMPS

Catalogue values for unused stamps in this section are for Never Hinged items.

Republic

Epifanio de los Santos, Trinidad H. Pardo and Teodoro M. Kalaw — SP1

Doctrina Christiana, Cover Page — SP2

"Noli Me Tangere," Cover Page — SP3

Unwmk.

1949, Apr. 1 Engr. *Perf. 12*

B1	SP1	4c + 2c sepia	1.80	1.80
B2	SP2	6c + 4c violet	6.20	6.20
B3	SP3	18c + 7c blue	7.50	7.50
		Nos. B1-B3 (3)	15.50	15.50

The surtax was for restoration of war-damaged public libraries.

War Widow and Children SP4

Disabled Veteran SP5

1950, Nov. 30

B4	SP4	2c + 2c red	.50	.30
B5	SP5	4c + 4c violet	.70	.40

The surtax was for war widows and children and disabled veterans of World War II.

For surcharges see Nos. 648-649.

Mrs. Manuel L. Quezon — SP6

1952, Aug. 19 *Perf. 12*

B6	SP6	5c + 1c dp bl	.50	.30
B7	SP6	6c + 2c car rose	.70	.50

The surtax was used to encourage planting and care of fruit trees among Philippine children. For surcharge see No. 872.

Quezon Institute — SP7

1958, Aug. 19 Photo. *Perf. 13½*

Cross in Red

B8	SP7	5c + 5c grn	.30	.25
a.		Perf. 12	1.75	.90
B9	SP7	10c + 5c dp vio	.50	.30
a.		Perf. 12	7.50	1.75

These stamps were obligatory on all mail from Aug. 19-Sept. 30.

For surcharges see Nos. 849, B12-B13, B16.

The surtax on all semi-postals from Nos. B8-B9 onward was for the Philippine Tuberculosis Society unless otherwise stated.

Scout Cooking — SP8

1959 Engr. *Perf. 13*
Yellow Paper

B10 SP8 6c + 4c shown .60 *.60*
B11 SP8 25c + 5c Archery .80 *.80*
a. Nos. B10-B11 tête bêche, *white* 1.75 *1.75*
Nos. B10-B11,CB1-CB3 (5) 5.70 *4.90*

10th Boy Scout World Jamboree, Makiling National Park, July 17-26. The surtax was to finance the Jamboree.
For souvenir sheet see No. CB3a. For surcharges see Nos. 832-833, C111.

Nos. B8-B9 Surcharged in Red

1959 Photo. *Perf. 13½*
B12 SP7 3c + 5c on 5c + 5c .30 .25
a. "3 + 5" and bars omitted
b. Perf. 12 5.00 3.00
B13 SP7 6c + 5c on 10c + 5c .50 .25
a. Perf. 12 3.50 1.75

Bohol Sanatorium SP9

1959, Aug. 19 Engr. *Perf. 12*
Cross in Red
B14 SP9 6c + 5c yel grn .30 .25
B15 SP9 25c + 5c vio bl .60 .30

No. B8 Surcharged "Help Prevent TB" and New Value

1960, Aug. 19 Photo. *Perf. 13½*
B16 SP7 6c + 5c on 5c + 5c .50 .25

Roxas Memorial T.B. Pavilion — SP10

Perf. 11½
1961, Aug. 19 Unwmk. Photo.
B17 SP10 6c + 5c brn & red .50 .25

Emiliano J. Valdes T.B. Pavilion — SP11

1962, Aug. 19 Cross in Red
B18 SP11 6s + 5s dk vio .30 .25
B19 SP11 30s + 5s ultra .55 .25
B20 SP11 70s + 5s brt bl 1.05 .50
Nos. B18-B20 (3) 1.90 1.00

José Rizal Playing Chess — SP12

Design: 30s+5s, Rizal fencing.

1962, Dec. 30 Engr. *Perf. 13*
B21 SP12 6s + 4s grn & rose lil .65 *.65*
B22 SP12 30s + 5s brt bl & cl 1.25 *1.25*

Surtax for Rizal Foundation.
For surcharges see Nos. 942-943.

Map of Philippines and Cross — SP13

1963, Aug. 19 Unwmk. *Perf. 13*
B23 SP13 6s + 5s vio & red .30 .25
B24 SP13 10s + 5s grn & red .50 .25
B25 SP13 50s + 5s brn & red 1.00 .35
Nos. B23-B25 (3) 1.80 .85

Negros Oriental T.B. Pavilion SP14

1964, Aug. 19 Photo. *Perf. 13½*
Cross in Red
B26 SP14 5s + 5s brt pur .30 .25
B27 SP14 6s + 5s ultra .30 .25
B28 SP14 30s + 5s brown .55 .30
B29 SP14 70s + 5s green .95 .60
Nos. B26-B29 (4) 2.10 1.40

For surcharges see Nos. 986, 1586.

No. B27 Surcharged in Red with New Value and Two Bars

1965, Aug. 19 Cross in Red
B30 SP14 1s + 5s on 6s + 5s .50 .25
B31 SP14 3s + 5s on 6s + 5s .60 .25

Stork-billed Kingfisher — SP15

Birds: 5s+5s, Rufous hornbill. 10s+5s, Monkey-eating eagle. 30s+5s, Great-billed parrot.

1967, Aug. 19 Photo. *Perf. 13½*
B32 SP15 1s + 5s multi .40 .25
B33 SP15 5s + 5s multi .50 .30
B34 SP15 10s + 5s multi 1.25 .40
B35 SP15 30s + 5s multi 4.25 .95
Nos. B32-B35 (4) 6.40 1.90

1969, Aug. 15 Litho. *Perf. 13½*

Birds: 1s+5s, Three-toed woodpecker. 5s+5s, Philippine trogon. 10s+5s, Mt. Apo lorikeet. 40s+5s, Scarlet minivet.

B36 SP15 1s + 5s multi .50 .25
B37 SP15 5s + 5s multi .80 .25
B38 SP15 10s + 5s multi 1.50 .75
B39 SP15 40s + 5s multi 3.25 .85
Nos. B36-B39 (4) 6.05 2.10

Julia V. de Ortigas and Tuberculosis Society Building SP16

1970, Aug. 3 Photo. *Perf. 13½*
B40 SP16 1s + 5s multi .40 .25
B41 SP16 5s + 5s multi .40 .25
B42 SP16 30s + 5s multi 1.50 .60
B43 SP16 70s + 5s multi 2.50 .80
Nos. B40-B43 (4) 4.80 1.90

Mrs. Julia V. de Ortigas was president of the Philippine Tuberculosis Soc., 1932-69.
For surcharge see No. 1251.

Mabolo, Santol, Chico, Papaya SP17

Philippine Fruits: 10s+5s, Balimbing, atis, mangosteen, macupa, bananas. 40s+5s, Susong-kalabao, avocado, duhat, watermelon, guava, mango. 1p+5s, Lanzones, oranges, sirhuelas, pineapple.

1972, Aug. 1 Litho. *Perf. 13*
B44 SP17 1s + 5s multi .40 .25
B45 SP17 10s + 5s multi .50 .25
B46 SP17 40s + 5s multi 1.00 .45
B47 SP17 1p + 5s multi 3.00 .75
Nos. B44-B47 (4) 4.90 1.70

Nos. B45-B46 Surcharged with New Value and 2 Bars

1973, June 15
B48 SP17 15s + 5s on 10s + 5s .60 .25
B49 SP17 60s + 5s on 40s + 5s 1.90 .45

Dr. Basilio J. Valdes and Veterans Memorial Hospital SP18

1974, July 8 Litho. *Perf. 12½*
Cross in Red
B50 SP18 15s + 5s blue grn .50 .25
a. Imperf. 1.00 .70
B51 SP18 1.10p + 5s vio blue 2.00 1.00
a. Imperf. 5.00 3.00

Dr. Valdes (1892-1970) was president of Philippine Tuberculosis Society.
For surcharges see Nos. 1250, 1252.

AIR POST STAMPS

Madrid-Manila Flight Issue

Issued to commemorate the flight of Spanish aviators Gallarza and Loriga from Madrid to Manila.

Regular Issue of 1917-26 Overprinted in Red or Violet

Designs: Nos. C7-C8, Adm. William T. Sampson. No. C9, Adm. George Dewey.

1926, May 13 Unwmk. *Perf. 11*
C1 A40 2c green (R) 20.00 25.00
Never hinged 45.00
C2 A40 4c carmine (V) 30.00 35.00
Never hinged 55.00
a. Inverted overprint *2,600.* —
C3 A40 6c lilac (R) 60.00 90.00
Never hinged 125.00
C4 A40 8c org brn (V) 60.00 85.00
Never hinged 125.00
C5 A40 10c deep blue (R) 80.00 85.00
Never hinged 140.00
C6 A40 12c red org (V) 70.00 95.00
Never hinged 150.00
C7 A40 16c lt ol grn (V) *2,800.* *3,250.*
C8 A40 16c ol bister (R) *5,000.* *5,000.*
C9 A40 16c ol grn (V) 90.00 125.00
Never hinged 160.00
C10 A40 20c org ye (V) 90.00 125.00
Never hinged 160.00
C11 A40 26c blue grn (V) 90.00 125.00
Never hinged 160.00
C12 A40 30c gray (V) 90.00 125.00
Never hinged 160.00
C13 A41 2p vio brn (R) 500.00 600.00
Never hinged 1,100.
C14 A41 4p dk blue (R) 800.00 900.00
Never hinged 1,300.
C15 A41 10p dp grn (V) 1,000. 1,350.

Same Overprint on No. 269
Wmk. Single-lined PIPS (190)
Perf. 12
C16 A40 26c blue grn (V) *5,000.*

Same Overprint on No. 284
Perf. 10
C17 A41 1p pale violet (V) 300.00 250.00
Never hinged 450.00

London-Orient Flight Issue

Issued Nov. 9, 1928, to celebrate the arrival of a British squadron of hydroplanes.

Regular Issue of 1917-25 Overprinted in Red

1928, Nov. 9 *Perf. 11*
C18 A40 2c green 1.00 1.00
Never hinged 2.00
C19 A40 4c carmine 1.25 1.50
Never hinged 2.00
C20 A40 6c violet 5.00 3.00
Never hinged 10.00
C21 A40 8c orange brown 5.00 3.00
Never hinged 10.00
C22 A40 10c deep blue 5.00 3.00
Never hinged 10.00
C23 A40 12c red orange 8.00 4.00
Never hinged 12.00
C24 A40 16c ol grn (No. 303a) 8.00 4.00
Never hinged 12.00
C25 A40 20c orange yellow 8.00 4.00
Never hinged 12.00
C26 A40 26c blue green 20.00 8.00
Never hinged 35.00
C27 A40 30c gray 20.00 8.00
Never hinged 35.00

Same Overprint on No. 271
Wmk. Single-lined PIPS (190)
Perf. 12
C28 A41 1p pale violet 55.00 30.00
Never hinged 90.00
Nos. C18-C28 (11) 136.25 69.50
Set, never hinged 230.00

Von Gronau Issue

Commemorating the visit of Capt. Wolfgang von Gronau's airplane on its round-the-world flight.

Nos. 354-360 Overprinted

1932, Sept. 27 Unwmk. *Perf. 11*
C29 A43 2c yellow green .90 .60
Never hinged 1.40
C30 A44 4c rose carmine .90 .40
Never hinged 1.40
C31 A45 12c orange 1.25 .65
Never hinged 2.00
C32 A46 18c red orange 5.00 5.00
Never hinged 8.00
C33 A47 20c yellow 3.50 3.50
Never hinged 5.75
C34 A48 24c deep violet 3.50 4.00
Never hinged 5.75
C35 A49 32c olive brown 3.50 3.00
Never hinged 5.75
Nos. C29-C35 (7) 18.55 17.15
Set, never hinged 31.55

Rein Issue

Commemorating the flight from Madrid to Manila of the Spanish aviator Fernando Rein y Loring.

Regular Issue of 1917-25 Overprinted

1933, Apr. 11
C36 A40 2c green .75 .45
Never hinged 1.10
C37 A40 4c carmine .90 .45
Never hinged 1.40
C38 A40 6c deep violet 1.10 .80
Never hinged 1.75
C39 A40 8c orange brown 3.75 2.00
Never hinged 5.75
P# block of 10, Impt. 120.00
Never hinged 150.00
C40 A40 10c dark blue 3.75 2.25
Never hinged 5.75
P# block of 10, Impt. 120.00
Never hinged 150.00
C41 A40 12c orange 3.75 2.00
Never hinged 5.75
P# block of 10, Impt. 120.00
Never hinged 150.00
C42 A40 16c olive green 3.50 2.00
Never hinged 5.25
P# block of 6 160.00
Never hinged 200.00
C43 A40 20c yellow 3.75 2.00
Never hinged 5.75
P# block of 10, Impt. 160.00
Never hinged 200.00
C44 A40 26c green 3.75 2.75
Never hinged 5.75
a. 26c blue green 4.00 2.00
Never hinged 6.00
C45 A40 30c gray 4.00 3.00
Never hinged 6.00
Nos. C36-C45 (10) 29.00 17.70
Set, never hinged 44.25

No. 290a Overprinted

Printed by the Philippine Bureau.

1933, May 26
C46 A40 2c green .65 .40
Never hinged 1.00
P# block of 6 12.00
Never hinged 15.00

Regular Issue of 1932 Overprinted

C47 A44 4c rose carmine .30 .25
Never hinged .45
P# block of 6 16.00
Never hinged 20.00
C48 A45 12c orange .60 .25
Never hinged .90
P# block of 6 20.00
Never hinged 25.00
C49 A47 20c yellow .60 .25
Never hinged .90
P# block of 6 20.00
Never hinged 25.00
C50 A48 24c deep violet .65 .25
Never hinged 1.00
P# block of 6 24.00
Never hinged 30.00
C51 A49 32c olive brown .85 .35
Never hinged 1.40
Nos. C46-C51 (6) 3.65 1.75
Set, never hinged 5.65

Transpacific Issue

Issued to commemorate the China Clipper flight from Manila to San Francisco, Dec. 2-5, 1935.

Nos. 387, 392 Overprinted in Gold

1935, Dec. 2
C52 A57 10c rose carmine .40 .25
Never hinged .60
C53 A62 30c orange red .60 .35
Never hinged .90

Manila-Madrid Flight Issue

Issued to commemorate the Manila-Madrid flight by aviators Antonio Arnaiz and Juan Calvo.

Regular Issue of 1917-25 Surcharged in Various Colors

1936, Sept. 6
C54 A40 2c on 4c carmine (Bl) .25 .25
Never hinged .25
C55 A40 6c on 12c red org (V) .25 .25
Never hinged .30
C56 A40 16c on 26c blue grn (Bk) .25 .25
Never hinged .40
a. 16c on 26c green 2.00 .70
Never hinged 3.00
Nos. C54-C56 (3) .75 .75
Set, never hinged .95

Air Mail Exhibition Issue

Issued to commemorate the first Air Mail Exhibition, held Feb. 17-19, 1939.

Regular Issue of 1917-37 Surcharged in Black or Red

1939, Feb. 17
C57 A40 8c on 26c blue grn (Bk) 2.00 2.00
Never hinged 4.00
a. 8c on 26c green (Bk) 10.00 4.00
Never hinged 16.00
C58 A71 1p on 10p gray (R) 8.00 4.00
Never hinged 12.00

Moro Vinta and Clipper — AP1

1941, June 30
C59 AP1 8c carmine 2.00 .60
Never hinged 2.75
C60 AP1 20c ultramarine 3.00 .50
Never hinged 4.00
C61 AP1 60c blue green 3.00 1.00
Never hinged 4.00
C62 AP1 1p sepia .70 .50
Never hinged 1.00
Nos. C59-C62 (4) 8.70 2.60
Set, never hinged 11.75

For overprint see No. NO7. For surcharges see Nos. N10-N11, N35-N36.

No. C47 Hstmpd. in Violet

1944, Dec. 3
C63 A44 4c rose carmine *3,750. 2,750.*

Catalogue values for unused stamps in this section, from this point to the end of the section, are for Never Hinged items.

Republic

Manuel L. Quezon and Franklin D. Roosevelt — AP2

Unwmk.

1947, Aug. 19 Engr. *Perf. 12*
C64 AP2 6c dark green .75 .50
C65 AP2 40c red orange 1.75 1.25
C66 AP2 80c deep blue 6.50 3.25
Nos. C64-C66 (3) 9.00 5.00

FAO Type

1948, Feb. 23 Typo. *Perf. 12½*
C67 A89 40c dk car & pink 15.00 7.00

Junior Chamber Type

1950, Mar. 1 Engr. *Perf. 12*
C68 A96 30c deep orange 1.80 .50
C69 A96 50c carmine rose 3.00 .85

F. D. Roosevelt Type

Souvenir Sheet

1950, May 22 *Imperf.*
C70 A98 80c deep green 5.00 3.00

Lions Club Type

1950, June 2 *Perf. 12*
C71 A99 30c emerald 2.50 .55
C72 A99 50c ultra 3.00 .75
a. Souvenir sheet of 2, #C71-C72 6.50 5.00

Maria Clara Type

1952, Nov. 16 *Perf. 12½*
C73 A112 30c rose carmine 2.50 1.00

Exists imperf. Value, $25.

Postage Stamp Cent. Type

1954, Apr. 25 *Perf. 13*

1854 Stamp in Orange
C74 A119 10c dark brown 3.50 1.25
C75 A119 20c dark green 6.00 2.00
C76 A119 50c carmine 12.50 5.00
Nos. C74-C76 (3) 22.00 8.25

Rotary Intl. Type

1955, Feb. 23
C77 A123 50c blue green 3.00 1.25

Lt. José Gozar — AP10

20c, 50c, Lt. Gozar. 30c, 70c, Lt. Basa.

1955 Engr. *Perf. 13*
C78 AP10 20c deep violet 1.80 .30
C79 AP10 30c red 1.20 .30
C80 AP10 50c bluish green 1.20 .30
C81 AP10 70c blue 1.80 1.10
Nos. C78-C81 (4) 6.00 2.00

Lt. José Gozar and Lt. Cesar Fernando Basa, Filipino aviators in World War II.

Constitution Type of Regular Issue

1960, Feb. 8 Photo. *Perf. 12½x13½*
C82 A146 30c brt bl & silver 1.00 .35

Air Force Plane of 1935 and Saber Jet — AP11

1960, May 2 Engr. *Perf. 14x14½*
C83 AP11 10c carmine .50 .25
C84 AP11 20c ultra .75 .30

25th anniversary of Philippine Air Force.
For surcharge see No. 847.

Olympic Type of Regular Issue

30c, Sharpshooter. 70c, Woman swimmer.

1960, Nov. 30 Photo. *Perf. 13x13½*
C85 A150 30c orange & brn .75 .40
C86 A150 70c grnsh bl & vio brn 1.75 .80

Postal Conference Type

1961, Feb. 23 *Perf. 13½x13*
C87 A152 30c multicolored .80 .30

Freedom from Hunger Type

1963, Dec. 20 Photo.
C88 A168 30s lt grn & multi .50 .30
C89 A168 50s multicolored 1.00 .40

Land Reform Type

1964, Dec. 21 Wmk. 233 *Perf. 14½*
C90 A172 30s multicolored .70 .30

Mass Baptism by Father Andres de Urdaneta, Cebu
AP12

70s, World map showing route of the Cross from Spain to Mexico to Cebu, and two galleons.

Unwmk.

1965, Oct. 4 Photo. *Perf. 13*
C91 AP12 30s multicolored .85 .30
C92 AP12 70s multicolored 1.85 .70
a. Souvenir sheet of 4 7.50 6.00

400th anniv. of the Christianization of the Philippines. No. C92a contains four imperf. stamps similar to Nos. 934-935 and C91-C92 with simulated perforation.
For surcharge see No. C108.

Souvenir Sheet

Family and Progress Symbols AP13

1966, July 22 Photo. *Imperf.*
C93 AP13 70s multicolored 7.50 5.00

50th anniv. of the Philippine Natl. Bank. No. C93 contains one stamp with simulated perforation superimposed on a facsimile of a 50p banknote of 1916.

Eruption of Taal Volcano and Refugees AP14

1967, Oct. 1 Photo. *Perf. 13½x13*
C94 AP14 70s multicolored 1.20 .50

Eruption of Taal Volcano, Sept. 28, 1965.

Eruption of Taal Volcano — AP15

1968, Oct. 1 Litho. *Perf. 13½*
C95 AP15 70s multicolored 1.20 .55

Eruption of Taal Volcano, Sept. 28, 1965.

Rotary Type of 1969

1969, Jan. 29 Photo. *Perf. 12½*
C96 A202 40s green & multi .60 .30
C97 A202 75s red & multi 1.40 .70

Holy Child Type of Regular Issue

1969, June 30 Photo. *Perf. 13½*
C98 A207 40s ultra & multi 1.40 .30

Pope Type of Regular Issue

1970, Nov. 27 Photo. *Perf. 13½x14*
C99 A221 40s violet & multi 1.40 .40

Law College Type of Regular Issue

1971, June 15 *Perf. 13*
C100 A225 1p green & multi 1.40 .50

Manila Type of Regular Issue

1971, June 24
C101 A226 1p multi & blue 1.40 .80

Santo Tomas Type of Regular Issue

1971, July 8 Photo. *Perf. 13½*
C102 A227 2p lt blue & multi 1.50 .80

Congress Type of Regular Issue

1972, Apr. 11 Photo. *Perf. 13½x13*
C103 A232 40s green & multi 1.20 .30

Tropical Fish Type of Regular Issue

1972, Aug. 14 Photo. *Perf. 13*
C104 A235 50s Dusky angelfish 2.25 .80

Pope Paul VI Type of Regular Issue

1972, Sept. 26 Photo. *Perf. 14*
C105 A237 60s lt blue & multi 1.40 .50

First Mass Type of Regular Issue

1972, Oct. 31 Photo. *Perf. 14*
C106 A241 60s multicolored 1.20 .50

Presidential Palace Type of Regular Issue

1973, Nov. 15 Litho. *Perf. 14*
C107 A253 60s multicolored 1.40 .40

No. C92a Surcharged and Overprinted with US Bicentennial Emblems and: "U.S.A. BICENTENNIAL / 1776-1976" in Black or Red

Unwmk.

1976, Sept. 20 Photo. *Imperf.*
C108 Sheet of 4 (B) 4.00 4.00
a. A179 5s on 3s multi .50 .40
b. A179 5s on 6s multi .50 .40
c. AP12 15s on 30s multi .75 .50
d. AP12 50s on 70s multi 1.00 .70
C108A Sheet of 4 (R) 6.00 6.00

American Bicentennial. Nos. C108a-C108d are overprinted with Bicentennial emblem and 2 bars over old denomination. Inscription and 2 Bicentennial emblems overprinted in margin.

Souvenir Sheet

AMPHILEX '77, Intl. Stamp Exhibition — AP16

Netherlands No. 1 and Philippines No. 1 and Windmill

1977, May 26 Litho. *Perf. 14½*
C109 AP16 Sheet of 3 12.50 10.00
a. 7.50p multicolored 3.50 3.00

AMPHILEX '77, International Stamp Exhibition, Amsterdam, May 26-June 5.
Exists imperf. Value $20.

Souvenir Sheet

ESPAMER '77 — AP17

Philippines and Spain Nos. 1, Bull and Matador.

1977, Oct. 7 Litho. Perf. 12½x13

C110 AP17 Sheet of 3 12.50 10.00
a. 7.50p multicolored 3.50 3.00

ESPAMER '77 (Exposicion Filatelica de America y Europa), Barcelona, Spain, 10/7-13.

Exists imperf. Value $18.

Nos. B10 and CB3a Surcharged

1979, July 5 Engr. Perf. 13

C111 SP8 90s on 6c + 4c car, *yel* 2.50 *1.00*

Souvenir Sheet

White Paper

C112 Sheet of 5 7.50 6.00
a. SP8 50s on 6c + 4c carmine .90 .60
b. SP8 50s on 25c + 5c blue .90 .60
c. SP8 50s on 30c + 10c green .90 .60
d. SP8 50s on 70c + 20c red brown .90 .60
e. SP8 50s on 80c + 20c violet .90 .60

First Scout Philatelic Exhibition, Quezon City, July 4-14, commemorating 25th anniversary of First National Jamboree.

Surcharge on No. C111 includes "AIR-MAIL." Violet marginal inscriptions on No. C112 overprinted with heavy bars; new commemorative inscriptions and Scout emblem added.

AIR POST SEMI-POSTAL STAMPS

Catalogue values for unused stamps in this section are for Never Hinged items.

Type of Semi-Postal Issue, 1959

Designs: 30c+10c, Bicycling. 70c+20c, Scout with plane model. 80c+20c, Pres. Carlos P. Garcia and scout shaking hands.

Unwmk.

1959, July 17 Engr. Perf. 13

CB1 SP8 30c + 10c green 1.00 .75
CB2 SP8 70c + 20c red brown 1.50 1.25
CB3 SP8 80c + 20c violet 1.80 1.50
a. Souvenir sheet of 5 8.50 8.00
Nos. CB1-CB3 (3) 4.30 3.50

10th Boy Scout World Jamboree, Makiling Natl. Park, July 17-26. Surtax was for the Jamboree.

No. CB3a measures 171x89mm. and contains one each of Nos. CB1-CB3 and types of Nos. B10-B11 on white paper. Sold for 4p.

For surcharge see No. C112.

SPECIAL DELIVERY STAMPS

United States No. E5 Overprinted in Red

Wmk. Double-lined USPS (191)

1901, Oct. 15 Perf. 12

E1 SD3 10c dark blue 100. 80.
Never hinged 185.
a. Dots in curved frame above messenger (Pl. 882) *175. 160.*

Special Delivery Messenger SD2

Wmk. Double-lined PIPS (191PI)

1906, Sept. 8

E2 SD2 20c deep ultra 45.00 8.00
Never hinged 90.00
b. 20c pale ultramarine 35.00 8.00
Never hinged 70.00

See Nos. E3-E6. For overprints see Nos. E7-E10, EO1.

SPECIAL PRINTING

U.S. No. E6 Overprinted in Red

Wmk. Double-lined USPS (191)

1907

E2A SD4 10c ultramarine *3,250.*

Wmk. Single-lined PIPS (190PI)

1911, Apr.

E3 SD2 20c deep ultra 22.00 1.75
Never hinged 42.00

1916 Perf. 10

E4 SD2 20c deep ultra 175.00 150.00
Never hinged 275.00

1919 Unwmk. Perf. 11

E5 SD2 20c ultramarine .60 .25
Never hinged .90
a. 20c pale blue .75 .25
Never hinged 1.00
b. 20c dull violet .60 .25
Never hinged .90

Type of 1906 Issue

1925-31 Imperf.

E6 SD2 20c dull violet ('31) 27.50 *75.00*
Never hinged 40.00
a. 20c violet blue ('25) 50.00 —
Never hinged 80.00

Type of 1919 Overprinted in Black

1939, Apr. 27 Perf. 11

E7 SD2 20c blue violet .25 .25
Never hinged .40

Nos. E5b and E7, Hstmpd. in Violet

1944

E8 SD2 20c dull violet (On E5b) *1,400. 550.00*
On cover —
Block of 4 *6,000.*
E9 SD2 20c blue violet (On E7) *550.00 250.00*

Type SD2 Overprinted

1945, May 1

E10 SD2 20c blue violet .70 .55
Never hinged 1.10
a. "IC" close together 3.25 2.75
Never hinged 4.75

Catalogue values for unused stamps in this section, from this point to the end of the section, are for Never Hinged items.

Republic

Manila Post Office and Messenger — SD3

Unwmk.

1947, Dec. 22 Engr. Perf. 12

E11 SD3 20c rose lilac .70 .40

Post Office Building, Manila, and Hands with Letter — SD4

1962, Jan. 23 Perf. 13½x13

E12 SD4 20c lilac rose .80 .30

SPECIAL DELIVERY OFFICIAL STAMP

Type of 1906 Issue Overprinted

1931 Unwmk. Perf. 11

EO1 SD2 20c dull violet 3.00 *75.00*
Never hinged 4.50
P# block of 6 150.00
Never hinged 190.00
a. No period after "B" 50.00 *250.00*
Never hinged 75.00
b. Double overprint —

It is strongly recommended that expert opinion be acquired for Nos. EO1 and EO1a used.

POSTAGE DUE STAMPS

U.S. Nos. J38-J44 Overprinted in Black

Wmk. Double-lined USPS (191)

1899, Aug. 16 Perf. 12

J1 D2 1c deep claret 7.50 2.50
Never hinged 15.00
J2 D2 2c deep claret 7.50 2.50
Never hinged 15.00
J3 D2 5c deep claret 15.00 2.50
Never hinged 30.00
J4 D2 10c deep claret 19.00 5.50
Never hinged 37.50
J5 D2 50c deep claret 250.00 100.00
Never hinged 425.00

No. J1 was used to pay regular postage Sept. 5-19, 1902.

1901, Aug. 31

J6 D2 3c deep claret 17.50 7.00
Never hinged 35.00
J7 D2 30c deep claret 250.00 110.00
Never hinged 415.00
Nos. J1-J7 (7) 566.50 230.00
Set, never hinged 882.50

Post Office Clerk — D3

1928, Aug. 21 Unwmk. Perf. 11

J8 D3 4c brown red .25 .25
Never hinged .25
P# block of 6 14.00
Never hinged 17.50
J9 D3 6c brown red .30 .75
Never hinged .45
P# block of 6 14.00
Never hinged 17.50
J10 D3 8c brown red .25 .75
Never hinged .35
P# block of 6 14.00
Never hinged 17.50
J11 D3 10c brown red .30 .75
Never hinged .45
P# block of 6 14.00
Never hinged 17.50
J12 D3 12c brown red .25 .75
Never hinged .35
P# block of 6 14.00
Never hinged 17.50
J13 D3 16c brown red .30 .75
Never hinged .45
P# block of 6 14.00
Never hinged 17.50
J14 D3 20c brown red .30 .75
Never hinged .45
P# block of 6 14.00
Never hinged 17.50
Nos. J8-J14 (7) 1.95 4.75
Set, never hinged 2.75

No. J8 Surcharged in Blue

1937, July 29 Unwmk. Perf. 11

J15 D3 3c on 4c brown red .25 .25
Never hinged .35

See note after No. NJ1.

Nos. J8 to J14 Handstamped in Violet

1944, Dec. 3

J16 D3 4c brown red *150.00* —
J17 D3 6c brown red *100.00* —
J18 D3 8c brown red *110.00 350.00*
J19 D3 10c brown red *100.00* —
J20 D3 12c brown red *100.00* —
J21 D3 16c brown red *100.00* 350.00
a. Pair, one without ovpt. —
J22 D3 20c brown red *110.00* —
Nos. J16-J22 (7) *770.00*

Catalogue values for unused stamps in this section, from this point to the end of the section, are for Never Hinged items.

Republic

D4

Unwmk.

1947, Oct. 20 Engr. Perf. 12

J23 D4 3c rose carmine .40 .25
J24 D4 4c brt violet blue .70 .25
J25 D4 6c olive green 1.00 .40
J26 D4 10c orange 1.20 .50
Nos. J23-J26 (4) 3.30 1.40

OFFICIAL STAMPS

Official Handstamped Overprints

"Officers purchasing stamps for government business may, if they so desire, surcharge them with the letters O.B. either in writing with black ink or by rubber stamps but in such a manner as not to obliterate the stamp that postmasters will be unable to determine whether the stamps have been previously used." C.M. Cotterman, Director of Posts, December 26, 1905.

Beginning January 1, 1906, all branches of the Insular Government used postage stamps to prepay postage instead of franking them as before. Some officials used manuscript, some utilized the typewriting machines but by far the larger number provided themselves with rubber stamps. The majority of these read "O.B." but other forms were: "OFFICIAL BUSINESS" or "OFFICIAL MAIL" in two lines, with variations on many of these.

These "O.B." overprints are known on U.S. 1899-1901 stamps; on 1903-06 stamps in red and blue; on 1906 stamps in red, blue, black, yellow and green.

"O.B." overprints were also made on the centavo and peso stamps of the Philippines, per order of May 25, 1907.

Beginning in 1926 the Bureau of Posts issued press-printed official stamps, but many government offices continued to handstamp ordinary postage stamps "O.B." The press-printed "O.B." overprints are listed below.

During the Japanese occupation period 1942-45, the same system of handstamped official overprints prevailed, but the handstamp usually consisted of "K.P.", initials of the Tagalog words, "Kagamitang Pampamahalaan" (Official Business), and the two Japanese characters used in the printed overprint on Nos. NO1 to NO4.

Regular Issue of 1926 Ovptd. in Red

1926, Dec. 20 Unwmk. *Perf. 12*
O1 A42 2c green & black 3.00 1.00
Never hinged 4.50
O2 A42 4c car & blk 3.00 1.25
Never hinged 4.50
a. Vertical pair, imperf. between 550.00
O3 A42 18c lt brn & blk 8.00 4.00
Never hinged 12.00
O4 A42 20c org & blk 7.75 1.75
Never hinged 11.50
Nos. O1-O4 (4) 21.75 8.00
Set, never hinged 32.50

Opening of the Legislative Palace.

Regular Issue of 1917-26 Overprinted by the U.S. Bureau of Engraving and Printing

1931 *Perf. 11*
O5 A40 2c green .40 .25
Never hinged .65
P# block of 6 20.00
Never hinged 25.00
a. No period after "B" 17.50 17.50
Never hinged 27.50
b. No period after "O" 40.00 30.00
O6 A40 4c carmine .45 .25
Never hinged .70
P# block of 6 20.00
Never hinged 25.00
a. No period after "B" 40.00 20.00
Never hinged 60.00
O7 A40 6c deep violet .75 .25
Never hinged 1.25
P# block of 10, Impt. 40.00
Never hinged 50.00
O8 A40 8c yellow brown .75 .25
Never hinged 1.25
P# block of 6 32.00
Never hinged 40.00
P# block of 10, Impt. 40.00
Never hinged 50.00
O9 A40 10c deep blue 1.20 .25
Never hinged 1.90
P# block of 10, Impt. 32.00
Never hinged 40.00
O10 A40 12c red orange 2.00 .25
Never hinged 3.00
P# block of 6 65.00
Never hinged 80.00
P# block of 10, Impt. 80.00
Never hinged 95.00
a. No period after "B" 80.00 80.00
Never hinged 120.00
O11 A40 16c lt ol grn 1.00 .25
Never hinged 1.50
P# block of 6 24.00
Never hinged 30.00
a. 16c olive bister 2.00 .25
Never hinged 3.00
P# block of 6 20.00
Never hinged 25.00
O12 A40 20c orange yellow 1.25 .25
Never hinged 1.90
P# block of 10, Impt. 75.00
Never hinged 95.00
a. No period after "B" 80.00 80.00
Never hinged 120.00
O13 A40 26c green 2.00 1.00
Never hinged 3.25
P# block of 6 120.00
Never hinged 150.00
a. 26c blue green 2.50 1.50
Never hinged 4.00
P# block of 6 130.00
Never hinged 165.00
O14 A40 30c gray 2.00 .25
Never hinged 3.25
P# block of 10, Impt. 80.00
Never hinged 100.00
Nos. O5-O14 (10) 11.80 3.25
Set, never hinged 18.65

Many collectors prefer to collect the plate blocks of 6 of Nos. O5-O6, O8, O10-O11a and O14 as blocks of 10 so they fit aesthetically with the other plate blocks of 10 with imprints.

Overprinted on Nos. 383-392

1935
O15 A53 2c rose .25 .25
Never hinged .30
P# block of 6 4.75
Never hinged 6.00
a. No period after "B" 15.00 10.00
Never hinged 22.50
b. No period after "O" — —
O16 A54 4c yellow green .25 .25
Never hinged .30
P# block of 6 4.00
Never hinged 5.00
a. No period after "B" 15.00 *40.00*
Never hinged 22.50
O17 A55 6c dark brown .25 .25
Never hinged .40
P# block of 6 8.00
Never hinged 10.00
a. No period after "B" 35.00 35.00
Never hinged 52.50
O18 A56 8c violet .30 .25
Never hinged .45
P# block of 6 9.50
Never hinged 12.00
O19 A57 10c rose carmine .30 .25
Never hinged .45
P# block of 6 8.00
Never hinged 10.00
O20 A58 12c black .75 .25
Never hinged 1.10
P# block of 6 8.00
Never hinged 10.00
O21 A59 16c dark blue .55 .25
Never hinged .85
P# block of 6 8.00
Never hinged 10.00
O22 A60 20c light olive green .60 .25
Never hinged .90
P# block of 6 12.00
Never hinged 15.00
O23 A61 26c indigo .90 .25
Never hinged 1.50
P# block of 6 20.00
Never hinged 25.00
O24 A62 30c orange red .80 .25
Never hinged 1.20
P# block of 6 20.00
Never hinged 25.00
Nos. O15-O24 (10) 4.95 2.50
Set, never hinged 7.40

Nos. 411 and 418 with Additional Overprint in Black

1937-38
O25 A53 2c rose .25 .25
Never hinged .30
a. No period after "B" 25.00 25.00
Never hinged 45.00
b. Period after "B" raised (UL 4) 150.00
O26 A60 20c lt ol grn ('38) .70 .50
Never hinged 1.10
P# block of 6 20.00
Never hinged 25.00

Regular Issue of 1935 Overprinted In Black

a

b

1938-40
O27 A53(a) 2c rose .25 .25
Never hinged .30
P# block of 6 4.75
Never hinged 6.00
a. Hyphen omitted 10.00 10.00
Never hinged 15.00
b. No period after "B" 20.00 *30.00*
Never hinged 30.00
O28 A54(b) 4c yellow green .75 1.00
Never hinged 1.10
P# block of 6 24.00
Never hinged 30.00
O29 A55(a) 6c dark brown .30 .25
Never hinged .45
P# block of 6 12.00
Never hinged 15.00
O30 A56(b) 8c violet .75 .85
Never hinged 1.10
P# block of 6 9.50
Never hinged 12.00
O31 A57(b) 10c rose carmine .25 .25
Never hinged .30
P# block of 6 16.00
Never hinged 20.00
a. No period after "O" 50.00 40.00
Never hinged 75.00
O32 A58(b) 12c black .30 .25
Never hinged .45
P# block of 6 12.00
Never hinged 15.00
O33 A59(b) 16c dark blue .30 .25
Never hinged .45
P# block of 6 16.00
Never hinged 20.00
O34 A60(a) 20c lt ol grn ('40) .55 .85
Never hinged .85
P# block of 6 16.00
Never hinged 20.00
O35 A61(b) 26c indigo 1.50 *2.00*
Never hinged 2.25
P# block of 6 12.00
Never hinged 15.00
O36 A62(b) 30c orange red .75 .85
Never hinged 1.10
P# block of 6 16.00
Never hinged 20.00
Nos. O27-O36 (10) 5.70 6.80
Set, never hinged 8.25

No. 461 Overprinted in Black — c

1941, Apr. 14 *Perf. 11x10½*
O37 A75(c) 2c apple green .25 *.40*
Never hinged .30

Official Stamps Handstamped in Violet

1944 *Perf. 11, 11x10½*
O38 A53 2c rose (On O27) *375.00 200.00*
Never hinged *750.00*
O39 A75 2c apple grn (On O37) 15.00 *20.00*
Never hinged 20.00
O40 A54 4c yel grn (On O16) 45.00 *30.00*
Never hinged 80.00
O40A A55 6c dk brn (On O29) *8,000.* —
O41 A57 10c rose car (On O31) *500.00*
a. No period after "O" *4,000.*
O42 A60 20c lt ol grn (On O22) *8,000.*
O43 A60 20c lt ol grn (On O26) *1,750.*

No. 497 Overprinted Type "c" in Black

1946, June 19 *Perf. 11x10½*
O44 A76 2c sepia .25 .25
Never hinged .25
a. Vertical pair, bottom stamp without ovpt. —

Catalogue values for unused stamps in this section, from this point to the end of the section, are for Never Hinged items.

Republic

Nos. 504, 505 and 507 Overprinted in Black — d

1948, May Unwmk. *Perf. 12*
O50 A78 4c black brown .70 .25
a. Inverted overprint 25.00
b. Double overprint 25.00
O51 A79 10c red orange 1.20 .25
O52 A81 16c slate gray 4.00 .80
Nos. O50-O52 (3) 5.90 1.30

Issue dates: Nos. O50-O51, 5/1; No. O52, 5/28.

The overprint on No. O51 comes in two sizes: 13mm, applied in Manila, and 12½mm, applied in New York.

Nos. 527, 508 and 509 Overprinted in Black — e

Overprint Measures 14mm
O53 A91 2c bright green .70 .25

1949, July 4
O54 A82 20c red brown 1.75 .50

Overprint Measures 12mm

1949, Jan. 23
O55 A83 50c dull green 2.00 .60

No. 550 Overprinted Type "e" in Black

1950, Sep. 20

Overprint Measures 14mm
O56 A91 1c on 2c brt green .70 .25

Nos. 589, 592, 595 and 597 Overprinted in Black — f

1952-55

Overprint Measures 15mm
O57 A117 1c red brown ('53) .70 .25
O58 A117 5c crim rose .70 .25
O59 A117 10c ultra ('55) .70 .25
O60 A117 20c car lake ('55) 2.00 .40
Nos. O57-O60 (4) 4.10 1.15

No. 647 Overprinted — g

1959 Engr. *Perf. 12*
O61 A117 1c on 5c crim rose .50 .25

No. 813 Overprinted Type "f" Overprint measures 16½mm

1959
O62 A145 6c gray blue .60 .25

Nos. 856-861 Overprinted

h

j

k

1962-64 *Perf. 13½*
O63 A158(j) 5s car rose ('63) .70 .25
Perf. 13x12
O64 A158(h) 6s dk red brn .70 .25
Perf. 13½
O65 A158(k) 6s pck blue ('64) .70 .25
O66 A158(j) 10s brt purple ('63) .70 .25
O67 A158(j) 20s Prus blue ('63) .70 .25
O68 A158(j) 30s vermilion 1.20 .35
O69 A158(k) 50s violet ('63) 1.50 .45
Nos. O63-O69 (7) 6.20 2.05

"G.O." stands for "Gawaing Opisyal," Tagalog for "Official Business."

On 6s overprint "k" is 10mm wide.

On No. O69, overprint "k" is 16mm wide.

For overprint see No. 1119.

No. 1082 Overprinted

l

1970, Dec. 30 Engr. *Perf. 14*
O70 A222(l) 10s rose carmine .70 .25

NEWSPAPER STAMPS

N1

1886-89 Unwmk. Typo. *Perf. 14*
P1 N1 ⅛c yellow green .30 *7.50*
P2 N1 1m rose ('89) .30 *15.00*
P3 N1 2m blue ('89) .30 *15.00*
P4 N1 5m dk brown ('89) .30 *15.00*
Nos. P1-P4 (4) 1.20 *52.50*

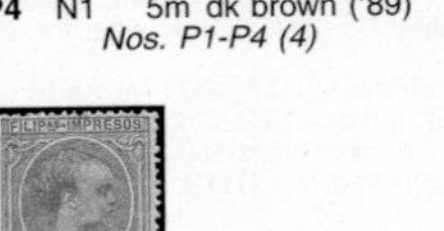

N2

1890-96
P5 N2 ⅛c dark violet .25 .25
P6 N2 ⅛c green ('92) 6.75 *10.00*
P7 N2 ⅛c org brn ('94) .25 .25
P8 N2 ⅛c dull blue ('96) .85 .60
P9 N2 1m dark violet .25 .25
P10 N2 1m green ('92) 2.25 *5.50*
P11 N2 1m olive gray ('94) .25 1.00
P12 N2 1m ultra ('96) .35 .25
P13 N2 2m dark violet .25 1.00
P14 N2 2m green ('92) 2.50 *13.00*
P15 N2 2m olive gray ('94) .25 *.45*

P16 N2 2m brown ('96) .30 .25
P17 N2 5m dark violet .25 *1.10*
P18 N2 5m green ('92) 250.00 75.00
P19 N2 5m olive gray ('94) .25 *.45*
P20 N2 5m dp blue grn ('96) 2.50 1.00
Nos. P5-P20 (16) 267.50 *110.35*

Imperfs. exist of Nos. P8, P9, P11, P12, P16, P17 and P20.

POSTAL TAX STAMPS

Mt. Pinatubo Fund — PT1

25c, Lahar flow. #RA2, Erupting volcano. #RA3, Animals after eruption. #RA4, Village after eruption. #RA5, People clearing ash.

Wmk. 391

1992, Nov. 16 Litho. *Perf. 13¾*

RA1 PT1 25c multi .60 .25
RA2 PT1 1p multi .90 .35
RA3 PT1 1p multi .90 .35
RA4 PT1 1p multi .90 .35
RA5 PT1 1p multi .90 .35
a. Block of 4, #RA2-RA5 4.50 2.00
Nos. RA1-RA5 (5) 4.20 1.65

Use of Nos. RA1-RA5 as postal tax stamps was suspended on 2/1/93. These stamps became valid for postage on 6/14/93.

OCCUPATION STAMPS

Issued Under Japanese Occupation

No. 461 Overprinted in Black

No. 438 Overprinted in Black

No. 439 Overprinted in Black

1942-43 Unwmk. *Perf. 11x10½, 11*

N1 A75 2c apple green .25 *1.00*
Never hinged .30
a. Pair, one without overprint —
N2 A58 12c black ('43) .25 *2.00*
Never hinged .40
P# block of 6 12.00
Never hinged 15.00
N3 A59 16c dark blue 5.00 3.75
Never hinged 7.50
P# block of 6 37.50
Never hinged 55.00
Nos. N1-N3 (3) 5.50 6.75
Set, never hinged 8.20

Nos. 435a, 435, 442, 443, and 423 Surcharged in Black

a

b

c

d

Type I

CENTAVOS
Type II

Two types of 50c surcharge
Type I: Center of "A" is a triangle.
Type II: Center of "A" is a pin hole.

1942-43 *Perf. 11*

N4 A55(a) 5(c) on 6c gold-en brown .25 *.75*
Never hinged .35
a. Top bar shorter and thinner .25 *1.00*
Never hinged .35
P# block of 6 50.00
Never hinged 60.00
b. 5(c) on 6c dark brown .25 *.85*
Never hinged .35
c. As "b," top bar shorter and thinner .25 *1.00*
Never hinged .35
d. Double surcharge, on cover —
N5 A62(b) 16(c) on 30c org red ('43) .25 *.60*
Never hinged .45
N6 A63(c) 50c on 1p red org & blk ('43) .75 *1.25*
Never hinged 1.10
P# block of 4, 2 P# 16.00
Never hinged 20.00
a. Double surcharge *300.00*
b. Type I surcharge 100.00 90.00
Never hinged 125.00
P# block of 4 500.00
Never hinged 600.00
N7 A65(d) 1p on 4p bl & blk ('43) 100.00 *150.00*
Never hinged 155.00
Nos. N4-N7 (4) 101.25 152.60
Set, never hinged 156.90

On Nos. N4 and N4b, the top bar measures 1½x22½mm. On Nos. N4a and N4c, the top bar measures 1x21mm and the "5" is smaller and thinner.

The used value for No. N7 is for postal cancellation. Used stamps exist with first day cancellations. They are worth somewhat less.

No. 384 Surcharged in Black

1942, May 18

N8 A54 2(c) on 4c yellow green 4.00 5.00
Never hinged 8.75

Issued to commemorate Japan's capture of Bataan and Corregidor. The American-Filipino forces finally surrendered May 7, 1942. No. N8 exists with "R" for "B" in BATAAN.

No. 384 Surcharged in Black

1942, Dec. 8

N9 A54 5(c) on 4c yellow green .50 *1.00*
Never hinged .75

1st anniversary of the "Greater East Asia War."

Nos. C59 and C62 Surcharged in Black

1943, Jan. 23

N10 AP1 2(c) on 8c carmine .25 *1.00*
Never hinged .35
P# block of 6 20.00
Never hinged 25.00
N11 AP1 5c on 1p sepia .50 *1.50*
Never hinged .75

1st anniv. of the Philippine Executive Commission.

Nipa Hut OS1

Rice Planting OS2

Mt. Mayon and Mt. Fuji OS3

Moro Vinta OS4

The "c" currency is indicated by four Japanese characters, "p" currency by two.

Engraved; Typographed (2c, 6c, 25c)

1943-44 Wmk. 257 *Perf. 13*

N12 OS1 1c dp orange .25 .40
Never hinged .30
Margin block of 6, inscription 2.40
Never hinged 3.00
N13 OS2 2c brt green .25 .40
Never hinged .30
Margin block of 6, inscription 2.40
Never hinged 3.00
N14 OS1 4c slate green .25 .40
Never hinged .30
Margin block of 6, inscription 2.40
Never hinged 3.00
N15 OS3 5c orange brown .25 .40
Never hinged .30
Margin block of 6, inscription 2.40
Never hinged 3.00
N16 OS2 6c red .25 .60
Never hinged .30
Margin block of 6, inscription 2.40
Never hinged 3.00
N17 OS3 10c blue green .25 .40
Never hinged .30
Margin block of 6, inscription 2.40
Never hinged 3.00
N18 OS4 12c steel blue 1.00 1.50
Never hinged 1.50
Margin block of 6, inscription 11.00
Never hinged 14.00
N19 OS4 16c dk brown .25 .40
Never hinged .30
Margin block of 6, inscription 2.40
Never hinged 3.00
N20 OS1 20c rose violet 1.25 1.75
Never hinged 1.90
Margin block of 6, inscription 15.00
Never hinged 19.00
N21 OS3 21c violet .25 .40
Never hinged .35
Margin block of 6, inscription 2.40
Never hinged 3.00
N22 OS2 25c pale brown .25 .40
Never hinged .35
Margin block of 6, inscription 2.40
Never hinged 3.00
N23 OS3 1p dp carmine .75 1.25
Never hinged 1.15
Margin block of 6, inscription 9.50
Never hinged 12.00
N24 OS4 2p dull violet 6.50 6.50
Never hinged 10.00
N25 OS4 5p dark olive 16.00 18.00
Never hinged 25.00
Nos. N12-N25 (14) 27.75 32.80
Set, never hinged 42.00

Issued: Nos. N13, N15, 4/1; Nos. N12, N14, N23, 6/7; Nos. N16-N19, 7/14; Nos. N20-N22, 8/16; No. N24, 9/16; No. N25, 4/1/44.

For surcharges see Nos. NB5-NB7.

OS5

1943, May 7 Photo. Unwmk.

N26 OS5 2c carmine red .25 *.75*
Never hinged .30
Margin block of 6, inscription 4.00
Never hinged 5.00
N27 OS5 5c bright green .25 *1.00*
Never hinged .35
Margin block of 6, inscription 6.50
Never hinged 8.00

1st anniversary of the fall of Bataan and Corregidor.

No. 440 Surcharged in Black

1943, June 20 Engr. *Perf. 11*

N28 A60 12(c) on 20c light olive green .25 *.75*
Never hinged .35
a. Double surcharge —

350th anniversary of the printing press in the Philippines. "Limbagan" is Tagalog for "printing press."

Rizal Monument, Filipina and Philippine Flag — OS6

1943, Oct. 14 Photo. *Perf. 12*

N29 OS6 5c light blue .25 *.90*
Never hinged .30
a. Imperf. .25 *.90*
N30 OS6 12c orange .25 *.90*
Never hinged .30
a. Imperf. .25 *.90*
N31 OS6 17c rose pink .25 *.90*
Never hinged .30
a. Imperf. .25 *.90*
Nos. N29-N31 (3) .75 *2.70*
Set, never hinged .90

"Independence of the Philippines." Japan granted "independence" Oct. 14, 1943, when the puppet republic was founded.

The imperforate stamps were issued without gum.

José Rizal OS7

Rev. José Burgos OS8

Apolinario Mabini — OS9

1944, Feb. 17 Litho.

N32 OS7 5c blue .25 *1.00*
Never hinged .30
a. Imperf. .25 *2.00*
Never hinged .35
N33 OS8 12c carmine .25 *1.00*
Never hinged .30
a. Imperf. .25 *2.00*
Never hinged .35
N34 OS9 17c deep orange .25 *1.00*
Never hinged .30
a. Imperf. .25 *2.00*
Never hinged .35
Nos. N32-N34 (3) .75 *3.00*
Set, never hinged .90

See No. NB8.

Nos. C60 and C61 Surcharged in Black

1944, May 7 *Perf. 11*

N35 AP1 5(c) on 20c ultra .50 1.00
Never hinged .75
P# block of 6 32.50
Never hinged 40.00
N36 AP1 12(c) on 60c blue green 1.75 1.75
Never hinged 2.50
P# block of 6 42.50
Never hinged 52.50

2nd anniversary of the fall of Bataan and Corregidor.

OS10

1945, Jan. 12 Litho. *Imperf.*
Without Gum

N37 OS10 5c dull violet brown .25 *.50*
Never hinged .30
N38 OS10 7c blue green .25 *.50*
Never hinged .30
N39 OS10 20c chalky blue .25 *.50*
Never hinged .30
Nos. N37-N39 (3) .75 1.50
Set, never hinged .90

Issued belatedly on Jan. 12, 1945, to commemorate the first anniversary of the puppet Philippine Republic, Oct. 14, 1944. "S" stands for "sentimos."

OCCUPATION SEMI-POSTAL STAMPS

Woman, Farming and Cannery — OSP1

Unwmk.
1942, Nov. 12 Litho. *Perf. 12*

NB1 OSP1 2c + 1c pale violet .25 *.60*
Never hinged .30
NB2 OSP1 5c + 1c brt grn .25 *1.00*
Never hinged .30
NB3 OSP1 16c + 2c orange 25.00 *32.50*
Never hinged 42.00
Nos. NB1-NB3 (3) 25.50 34.10
Set, never hinged 42.60

Issued to promote the campaign to produce and conserve food. The surtax aided the Red Cross.

Souvenir Sheet

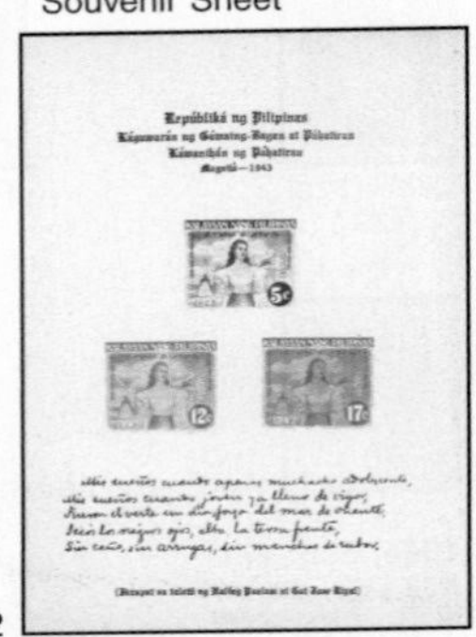
OSP2

1943, Oct. 14 Without Gum *Imperf.*
NB4 OSP2 Sheet of 3 60.00 *17.50*

"Independence of the Philippines."

No. NB4 contains one each of Nos. N29a-N31a. Marginal inscription is from Rizal's "Last Farewell." Sold for 2.50p.

The value of No. NB4 used is for a sheet from a first day cover. Commercially used sheets are extremely scarce and worth much more.

Nos. N18, N20 and N21 Surcharged in Black

1943, Dec. 8 Wmk. 257 *Perf. 13*

NB5 OS4 12c + 21c steel blue .25 *1.50*
Never hinged .30
Margin block of 6, inscription 4.00
Never hinged 5.00
NB6 OS1 20c + 36c rose violet .25 *1.50*
Never hinged .30
Margin block of 6, inscription 4.00
Never hinged 5.00
NB7 OS3 21c + 40c violet .25 *2.00*
Never hinged .30
Margin block of 6, inscription 4.75
Never hinged 6.00
Nos. NB5-NB7 (3) .75 5.00
Set, never hinged .90

The surtax was for the benefit of victims of a Luzon flood. "Baha" is Tagalog for "flood."

Souvenir Sheet

OSP3

Unwmk.
1944, Feb. 9 Litho. *Imperf.*
Without Gum

NB8 OSP3 Sheet of 3 6.50 3.50

No. NB8 contains 1 each of Nos. N32a-N34a.

Sheet sold for 1p, surtax going to a fund for the care of heroes' monuments.

The value for No. NB8 used is for a stamp from a first day cover. Commercially used examples are worth much more.

OCCUPATION POSTAGE DUE STAMP

No. J15 Overprinted in Blue

1942, Oct. 14 Unwmk. *Perf. 11*
NJ1 D3 3c on 4c brown red 25.00 *35.00*
Never hinged 37.50

On examples of No. J15, two lines were drawn in India ink with a ruling pen across "United States of America" by employees of the Short Paid Section of the Manila Post Office to make a provisional 3c postage due stamp which was used from Sept. 1, 1942 (when the letter rate was raised from 2c to 5c) until Oct. 14 when No. NJ1 went on sale. Value on cover, $175.

Bottom plate blocks of 6 of No. NJ1 are much scarcer than the right side plate blocks. Value $325 hinged, $450 never hinged.

OCCUPATION OFFICIAL STAMPS

Nos. 461, 413, 435, 435a and 442 Ovptd. or Srchd. in Black with Bars and

1943-44 Unwmk. *Perf. 11x10½, 11*

NO1 A75 2c apple green .25 *.75*
Never hinged .30
a. Double overprint 400.00
Never hinged 600.00
NO2 A55 5(c) on 6c dk brn (On No. 413) ('44) 40.00 *45.00*
Never hinged 55.00
NO3 A55 5(c) on 6c golden brn (On No. 435a) .25 *.90*
Never hinged .35
P# block of 6 14.00
Never hinged 17.50
a. Narrower spacing between bars .25 *.90*
Never hinged .35
b. 5(c) on 6c dark brown (On No. 435) .25 *.90*
Never hinged .35
c. As "b," narrower spacing between bars .25 *.90*
Never hinged .35
d. Double overprint —
NO4 A62 16(c) on 30c org red .30 *1.25*
Never hinged .45
P# block of 6 20.00
Never hinged 25.00
a. Wider spacing between bars .30 *1.25*
Never hinged .45
Nos. NO1-NO4 (4) 40.80 47.90
Set, never hinged 56.10

On Nos. NO3 and NO3b the bar deleting "United States of America" is 9¾ to 10mm above the bar deleting "Common." On Nos. NO3a and NO3c, the spacing is 8 to 8½mm.

On No. NO4, the center bar is 19mm long, 3½mm below the top bar and 6mm above the Japanese characters. On No. NO4a, the center bar is 20½mm long, 9mm below the top bar and 1mm above the Japanese characters.

"K.P." stands for Kagamitang Pampamahalaan, "Official Business" in Tagalog.

Nos. 435 & 435a Surcharged in Black

1944, Aug. 28 *Perf. 11*
NO5 A55 (5c) on 6c gldn brn .30 *.40*
Never hinged .45
P# block of 6 20.00
Never hinged 25.00
a. 5(c) on 6c dark brown .30 *.40*
Never hinged .45
P# block of 6 20.00
Never hinged 25.00

Nos. O34 and C62 Overprinted in Black

a

b

NO6 A60(a) 20c light olive green .40 *.50*
Never hinged .60
P# block of 6 12.00
Never hinged 15.00
NO7 AP1(b) 1p sepia .90 *1.00*
Never hinged 1.45
P# block of 6 20.00
Never hinged 25.00
Nos. NO5-NO7 (3) 1.60 1.90
Set, never hinged 2.05

FILIPINO REVOLUTIONARY GOVERNMENT

Following the defeat of the Spanish fleet by U.S. Commodore Dewey in Manila on May 1, 1898, which essentially ended the Spanish-American War in the Philippines, postal services were disrupted throughout the Philippines. Postal service was reestablished through U.S. Army military stations, beginning in June 1898 near Manila, continuing province by province until culminating at Zamboanga and other cities in the southern areas in late 1899.

Provisional stamps were prepared for use in the central part of the island of Luzon at Malolos in late 1898 under the leadership of General Emilio Aguinaldo, who had proclaimed the Philippine Republic on June 12, 1898. Later, other provisional stamps were prepared by local Filipino insurgents at Iloilo (Panay Island), Bohol, Cebu and Negros, and Spanish period stamps were overprinted and/or surcharged for use by postal officials at Zamboanga and La Union.

The most familiar of these provisionals were the "Aguinaldo" issues of the Filipino Revolutionary Government in central Luzon near Manila. The letters "KKK," the initials of the revolutionary society, "Kataas-taasang, Kagalang-galang Katipunan nang Mañga Anak nang Bayan," meaning "Sovereign Worshipful Association of the Sons of the Country," readily identify the Aguinaldo provisionals. Hostilities broke out between the Aguinaldo regime and the occupying American administration in February 1899, and the Filipino-American War continued until the American capture of Aguinaldo on March 23, 1901.

The Aguinaldo regular postage, registration, revenue, newspaper and telegraph stamps were in use in Luzon as early as November 10, 1898, and continued in use through early 1901. Although the postal regulations specified that these stamps be used for their inscribed purpose, they were commonly used interchangeably.

The Filipino Republic was instituted by Gen. Emilio Aguinaldo on June 23, 1899. At the same time he assumed the office of President. Aguinaldo dominated the greater part of the island of Luzon and some of the smaller islands until late in 1899. He was taken prisoner by United States troops on March 23, 1901.

The devices composing the National Arms, adopted by the Filipino Revolutionary Government, are emblems of the Katipunan political secret society or of Katipunan origin. The letters "K K K" on these stamps are the initials of this society whose complete name is "Kataas-taasang, Kagalang-galang Katipunan nang Mañga Anak nang Bayan," meaning "Sovereign Worshipful Association of the Sons of the Country."

The regular postage and telegraph stamps were in use on Luzon as early as Nov. 10, 1898. Owing to the fact that stamps for the different purposes were not always available together with a lack of proper instructions, any of the adhesives were permitted to be used in the place of the other. Hence telegraph and revenue stamps were accepted for postage and postage stamps for revenue or telegraph charges. In addition to the regular postal emission, there are a number of provisional stamps, issues of local governments of islands and towns.

POSTAGE ISSUES

A1

A2

Coat of Arms — A3

1898-99 Unwmk. *Perf. 11½*
Y1 A1 2c red 250.00 300.00
a. Double impression 325.00
Y2 A2 2c red .30 4.00
b. Double impression —
d. Horiz. pair, imperf. between —
e. Vert. pair, imperf. between 225.00
Y3 A3 2c red 150.00 *300.00*

Imperf pairs and pairs, imperf horizontally, have been created from No. Y2e.

REGISTRATION STAMP

RS1

YF1 RS1 8c green 5.00 *30.00*
a. Imperf., pair 400.00
b. Imperf. vertically, pair —

NEWSPAPER STAMP

N1

YP1	N1	1m black	2.00	*20.00*
a.		Imperf., pair	5.00	*20.00*

INDEX AND IDENTIFIER

All page numbers shown are those in this Volume 5A.

Postage stamps that do not have English words on them are shown in the Illustrated Identifier.

INDEX TO ADVERTISERS 2025 VOLUME 5A

2025
VOLUME 5A
DEALER DIRECTORY
YELLOW PAGE LISTINGS

This section of your Scott Catalogue contains advertisements to help you conveniently find what you need, when you need it...!

Appraisals

DR. ROBERT FRIEDMAN & SONS STAMP & COIN BUYING CENTER
2029 W. 75th St.
Woodridge, IL 60517
PH: 800-588-8100
FAX: 630-985-1588
stampcollections@drbobstamps.com
www.drbobfriedmanstamps.com

Asia

THE STAMP ACT
PO Box 1136
Belmont, CA 94002
PH: 650-703-2342
thestampact@sbcglobal.net

Auctions

DUTCH COUNTRY AUCTIONS
The Stamp Center
4115 Concord Pike
Wilmington, DE 19803
PH: 302-478-8740
FAX: 302-478-8779
auctions@dutchcountryauctions.com
www.dutchcountryauctions.com

British Commonwealth

ARON R. HALBERSTAM PHILATELISTS, LTD.
PO Box 150168
Van Brunt Station
Brooklyn, NY 11215-0168
PH: 718-788-3978
arh@arhstamps.com
www.arhstamps.com

ROY'S STAMPS
PO Box 28001
600 Ontario Street
St. Catharines, ON
CANADA L2N 7P8
Phone: 905-934-8377
Email: roystamp@cogeco.ca
www.roysstamps.com

THE STAMP ACT
PO Box 1136
Belmont, CA 94002
PH: 650-703-2342
thestampact@sbcglobal.net

Buying

DR. ROBERT FRIEDMAN & SONS STAMP & COIN BUYING CENTER
2029 W. 75th St.
Woodridge, IL 60517
PH: 800-588-8100
FAX: 630-985-1588
stampcollections@drbobstamps.com
www.drbobfriedmanstamps.com

Canada

ROY'S STAMPS
PO Box 28001
600 Ontario Street
St. Catharines, ON
CANADA L2N 7P8
Phone: 905-934-8377
Email: roystamp@cogeco.ca
www.roysstamps.com

Collections

DR. ROBERT FRIEDMAN & SONS STAMP & COIN BUYING CENTER
2029 W. 75th St.
Woodridge, IL 60517
PH: 800-588-8100
FAX: 630-985-1588
stampcollections@drbobstamps.com
www.drbobfriedmanstamps.com

Ducks

MICHAEL JAFFE
PO Box 61484
Vancouver, WA 98666
PH: 360-695-6161
PH: 800-782-6770
FAX: 360-695-1616
mjaffe@brookmanstamps.com
www.brookmanstamps.com

New Issues

DAVIDSON'S STAMP SERVICE
Personalized Service since 1970
PO Box 36355
Indianapolis, IN 46236-0355
PH: 317-826-2620
ed-davidson@earthlink.net
www.newstampissues.com

Stamp Stores

Delaware

DUTCH COUNTRY AUCTIONS
The Stamp Center
4115 Concord Pike
Wilmington, DE 19803
PH: 302-478-8740
FAX: 302-478-8779
auctions@dutchcountryauctions.com
www.dutchcountryauctions.com

Florida

DR. ROBERT FRIEDMAN & SONS STAMP & COIN BUYING CENTER
PH: 800-588-8100
FAX: 630-985-1588
stampcollections@drbobstamps.com
www.drbobfriedmanstamps.com

ROBERT M. SAZAMA
The Villages, FL 32163
PH: 931-561-7167
Email: bob@bobsazama.com
www.floridastampbuyer.com

Illinois

DR. ROBERT FRIEDMAN & SONS STAMP & COIN BUYING CENTER
2029 W. 75th St.
Woodridge, IL 60517
PH: 800-588-8100
FAX: 630-985-1588
stampcollections@drbobstamps.com
www.drbobfriedmanstamps.com

Indiana

KNIGHT STAMP & COIN CO.
237 Main St.
Hobart, IN 46342
PH: 219-942-4341
PH: 800-634-2646
knight@knightcoin.com
www.knightcoin.com

Stamp Stores

New Jersey

TRENTON STAMP & COIN
Thomas DeLuca
Store: Forest Glen Plaza
1800 Highway #33, Suite 103
Hamilton Square, NJ 08690
Mail: PO Box 8574
Trenton, NJ 08650
PH: 609-584-8100
FAX: 609-587-8664
TOMD4TSC@aol.com
www.trentonstampandcoin.com

Ohio

HILLTOP STAMP SERVICE
Richard A. Peterson
PO Box 626
Wooster, OH 44691
PH: 330-262-8907 (0)
PH: 330-201-1377 (C)
hilltop@bright.net
hilltopstamps@sssnet.com
www.hilltopstamps.com

Supplies

BROOKLYN GALLERY COIN & STAMP, INC.
8725 4th Ave.
Brooklyn, NY 11209
PH: 718-745-5701
FAX: 718-745-2775
info@brooklyngallery.com
www.brooklyngallery.com

Topicals - Columbus

MR. COLUMBUS
PO Box 1492
Fennville, MI 49408
PH: 269-543-4755
David@MrColumbus1492.com
www.MrColumbus1492.com

United States

ACS STAMP COMPANY
2914 W 135th Ave
Broomfield, Colorado 80020
303-841-8666
www.ACSStamp.com

BROOKMAN STAMP CO.
PO Box 90
Vancouver, WA 98666
PH: 360-695-1391
PH: 800-545-4871
FAX: 360-695-1616
info@brookmanstamps.com
www.brookmanstamps.com

U.S. Classics/Moderns

BARDO STAMPS
PO Box 7437
Buffalo Grove, IL 60089
PH: 847-634-2676
jfb7437@aol.com
www.bardostamps.com

U.S.-Collections Wanted

DUTCH COUNTRY AUCTIONS
The Stamp Center
4115 Concord Pike
Wilmington, DE 19803
PH: 302-478-8740
FAX: 302-478-8779
auctions@dutchcountryauctions.com
www.dutchcountryauctions.com

U.S.-Collections Wanted

DR. ROBERT FRIEDMAN & SONS STAMP & COIN BUYING CENTER
2029 W. 75th St.
Woodridge, IL 60517
PH: 800-588-8100
FAX: 630-985-1588
stampcollections@drbobstamps.com
www.drbobfriedmanstamps.com

Wanted - Worldwide Collections

DUTCH COUNTRY AUCTIONS
The Stamp Center
4115 Concord Pike
Wilmington, DE 19803
PH: 302-478-8740
FAX: 302-478-8779
auctions@dutchcountryauctions.com
www.dutchcountryauctions.com

Websites

ACS STAMP COMPANY
2914 W 135th Ave
Broomfield, Colorado 80020
303-841-8666
www.ACSStamp.com

Worldwide

GUILLERMO JALIL
Maipu 466, local 4
1006 Buenos Aires
Argentina
guillermo@jalilstamps.com
philatino@philatino.com
www.philatino.com (worldwide stamp auctions)
www.jalilstamps.com (direct sale, worldwide stamps)

Worldwide-Collections

DR. ROBERT FRIEDMAN & SONS STAMP & COIN BUYING CENTER
2029 W. 75th St.
Woodridge, IL 60517
PH: 800-588-8100
FAX: 630-985-1588
stampcollections@drbobstamps.com
www.drbobfriedmanstamps.com